2000IMI 消费行为与生活形态年鉴

北京·上海·广州·重庆·武汉·西安·沈阳

IMI（创研）市场信息研究所
北京广播学院广告学系
人民日报华泰投资管理有限公司
《国际广告》杂志社

下
卷

Y&D Marketing Service LTD.
北京华泰创研数据有限公司

北京广播学院出版社

目　　录

上　卷

第一篇　七城市基本情况与样本结构

第二篇 消费者分析

第三篇 消费者日常生活形态

第四篇 媒介分析

第五篇 食品

第六篇 饮料

下 卷

第七篇 烟酒

第八篇 洗涤日用品

第九篇　化妆品、卫生用品

第十篇 药品、营养保健品

第十一篇 家用电器、照相器材

第十二篇 电脑、通讯工具

第十三篇　住房、汽车、金融、保险

第十四篇 饮食、购物场所

Contents

Part I The General Market Conditions of the Seven Cities and Sample Compositions

Part II Consumer Analysis

Part III Consumers' Everyday Life

Part V Food

Part X Medicine and Health Care Products

Part XIII Housing, Car, Finance and Insurance

Part XIV Restaurant and Shopping Places

第七篇　烟酒
Part VII　Alcohol Products and Cigarette

- 啤酒　Beer
- 白酒　Hard Liquor
- 葡萄酒　Wine
- 香烟　Cigarette

5-13-2 广告态度指标/ Advertising Attitude Index

	人数 Number	广告淡漠指向 indifferent orientation	中间层 medium	信赖广告指向 loyal orientation
样本 Sample	54	14.8	66.7	18.5
天天喝 daily	5	0.0	40.0	60.0
一周 3 次或以上 3 times or over a week	14	7.1	85.7	7.1
一周 1~2 次 once or twice a week	35	20.0	62.9	17.1

5-13-3 饮食健康指标/ Foods & Drink Quality Index

	人数 Number	饮食"温饱"指向 "basic" orientation	中间层 medium	健康营养指向 health & nutrition orientation
样本 Sample	54	14.8	51.9	33.3
天天喝 daily	5	0.0	40.0	60.0
一周 3 次或以上 3 times or over a week	14	7.1	78.6	14.3
一周 1~2 次 once or twice a week	35	20.0	42.9	37.1

酒

中国是产酒大国，也是酒的消费大国。近年来，随着市场经济的发展和人们健康意识的提高，白酒一统天下的局面已不复存在。啤酒异军突起，在酒类产品市场上形成三足鼎立之势。全国酒业目前的现状是：白酒依然供过于求，年产 700～800 万吨，比前几年略有下降，但品种多了；啤酒去年总产量 1900 万吨位居世界第二，销量并不旺盛，但市场逐步向农村拓展；葡萄酒市场消费日渐成熟，问题是原料基地的发展远远落后于葡萄酒生产的发展；葡萄酒、啤酒每年都以 20%的幅度增长，啤酒市场基本形成了规模，但葡萄酒市场比较乱，国外企业进来得比较多；黄酒产量上升，市场拓展缓慢，仅在江、浙等地旺销。截至 1998 年底，我国酒类产品出口创汇 14691 万美元，比 1997 年降低 21.4%，实现贸易顺差为 7502 万美元，比 1997 年降低 39%。目前，酒类共有 11 个品牌被认定为驰名商标，其中白酒类 7 个：贵州茅台、五粮液、泸州老窖、杏花村、郎酒、剑南春、古井贡；啤酒类 2 个：青岛啤酒和燕京啤酒；葡萄酒类为张裕；黄酒类为古越龙山。

从 1998 年销售情况看，白酒行业出现了以规模化、集团化的大型企业集团为主垄断城市市场、以地域性白酒占据农村市场的格局。1998 年股份制啤酒企业已占 16%，这些企业发挥了经营机制灵活、适应市场能力强、增产增效较为显著的优势；同时，民族品牌啤酒发展势头较快，98 年全国 20 万吨以上的啤酒企业 18 个，其中外资合作企业只有 6 个。1998 年葡萄酒企业的经济效益普遍提高，王朝、张裕、长城三大葡萄酒企业的经济效益仍处于领先地位，大中型企业的高档葡萄酒生产发展较快，全汁酒产量比例逐步上升。

1999 年是建国 50 大庆，又逢澳门回归，国家把内需作为重要措施，市场形势有所改观，酒类行业也好过些。但由于酒类市场首先是白酒产大于销、供过于求的状况一时尚难改变，所以，当前白酒市场利润分配还不是很合理，不可能取消流通环节，但不很好发挥流通环节作用对经济发展不利，酒厂自行销售产品，抛开中间流通环节，造成人力资源、物力资源的浪费；另一方面，企业对流通中间环节不放心也是其中的原因。

啤酒

随着我国经济的快速发展和人民生活水平的不断改善，啤酒需求量趋旺，啤酒市场逐渐红火，直接推动了啤酒行业的迅速发展。1998 年，全国啤酒产量 1987.67 万吨，比 1997 年增加 99.2 万吨，增长 5.3%在消费品中，啤酒属于零售增长较多的产品，据全国 250 家大型商场的调查，啤酒销售量增长 54%，在消费品中占第 15 位（《99 中国经济年鉴》）。据中国酿酒协会啤酒分会对今年上半年的产销情况分析，1999 年我国啤酒工业产量比去年增长 9%以上，年产量可达 2200 万吨左右，从而将首次超过美国成为世界啤酒产量冠军。

目前，我国年产量在 5 万吨以上的啤酒生产企业有 104 家。其总产量占全国总产量的 70%左右，这表明我国啤酒工业已向规模化发展。1998 年，利税总额达 1 亿元以上的啤酒企业达 21 家，名列前茅的依次为燕京、青岛、蓝剑、珠江、蓝带、金威；利润达亿元以上的有 5 家，分别为燕京、青岛、金威、蓝带、珠江，其中广东省深圳金威啤酒有限公司摘取了 1998 年啤酒销售收入、吨酒利税、吨酒利润三项桂冠。1998 年，啤酒出口量和啤酒出口额比上年减少 22%，而啤酒进口量却增加 15%，进口额增加 50%，每千升啤酒进口价 657 美元，大大高于出口价 472 美元，使啤酒的出口创汇和进口额之比，从 97 年的 1：0.4 降为 1：0.8。

1998 年，燕京啤酒集团公司的产量突破 80 万吨，珠江、青岛啤酒集团的产量也超过 60 万吨，啤酒生产规模不断扩大。青岛啤酒是我国在世界范围内拥有最大的品牌，尤其是在美国这个啤酒生产第一大国已获得一席之地。仅 1999 年上半年，青岛啤酒的产量已达 44.6 万吨，比去年同期增长 59.5%，销售收入和利税同比均在 50%以上，其销售、产量和利税均首次跃居全国同行业之首。1998 全国 20 万吨以上的啤酒生产企业达 18 个，比 1997 年增加 5 个，合计产量占全国总产量的 31.3%，比 97 年提高 10.2 个百分点。一些大啤酒生产企业近年来相继组建集团公司，并收到较理想的效果。北京燕京啤酒、青岛啤酒和广东珠江啤酒组成集团公司后，其产量和利税均已稳居全国前三位。

我国啤酒工业在努力实现规模化、集约化经营发展的同时，通过技术创新，还致力于品种多样化，以迎接市场的挑战。目前，国内一些知名的啤酒集团公司除生产传统的产品外，各公司相继开发出新型啤酒产品，如淡色啤酒、清爽啤酒、黑啤酒、白啤酒、低糖低热量啤酒、无醇啤酒及保健啤酒等品种。技术创新不仅使我国啤酒家族添了新成员，而且适应了消费者和出口的需求。同时，啤酒品种增多、质量提高、成本降低，使这两年来国产啤酒在洋啤酒充斥市场、强手如林的竞争中站稳了脚根。国产啤酒目前在国内市场的占有率达 70%以上，显示了国产啤酒已受到了广大消费者的青睐，同时也说明我国啤酒工业开始走向世界。

白酒

我国现有白酒企业 3.7 万家，其中乡以上独立核算白酒企业约 4870 家，1998 年全国白酒产量约为 573.33 万吨，白酒行业工业总产值约为 350 亿元，利税近 130 亿元。据统计，年产量万吨以上的白酒企业有 61 家，其产量合计占全国白酒总量的 31.3%，其中年产 2 万吨以上企业的产量占总产量的 9.8%，1～2 万吨之间的企业产量占总产量的 21.5%，1 万吨以下的企业产量占总产量的 68.3%（《99 中国经济年鉴》）。

1999 年的白酒市场可谓是“物竞天择、适者生存”，也是众多商家无奈又孕育着希望的一年。有的厂家因积压成山、积重难返而丧失了经营白酒的信心；有的厂家在经历“广告酒”时代后凭借自身的品牌、实力，又欲一搏。业内人士发现市场需求不断萎缩，白酒价格一跌再跌，竞争环境日趋险恶，许多厂家发现自己的生存空间不断缩小。1999 年上半年白酒的销售形势走低，白酒产销对大多数企业来说已步入困境。

我国白酒产业呈现这种状况，其根本原因在于生产能力过剩、购买力相对萎缩、供大于求的矛盾未能彻底解决。此外国家的宏观产业政策及相关管理部门对白酒的生产有所限制，啤酒、果酒及洋酒对消费市场的挤占以及假酒对消费者的负面影响导致需求不旺。再者价格大战狼烟四起，有些名酒为了保住市场份额不惜低价销售，更有其他变相的压价措施。这些都带来了灾难性后果，不仅影响了竞争中的每一方，大大地消耗了各自的实力，更重要的是影响了各企业的效益增长使企业无法面对新一轮的竞争。

就目前白酒竞争的状况而言，全国白酒业正处在调整期，在调整的同时无序的竞争将被肢解，取而代之的是有序、理智化和战略营销的良性局面。其具体表现为实力与品牌的竞争、营销与策划的竞争，信息与网络的竞争。而品牌特别是名牌的竞争已成为白酒市场竞争的主要环节。各大企业越来越多的将文化内涵、文化营销巧妙地融合到公司的知名度和美誉度中去，同时，市场份额相对集中在国家名牌、地区名牌、地方名牌之中。知名品牌的知名度和美誉度以及内涵，决定了品牌的延伸与扩展的优势。

世纪之交的 1999 年，是中国白酒行业最困难的一年，无论是生产企业还是营销企业大多步履维艰、困难重重。1999 年，又是白酒行业充满希望的一年。人们不断寻找白酒产销中的谋略、趋向、新的需求和商机。中国酒类商业协会有关专家认为，面对 21 世纪，我国白酒企业当正确认识白酒过去和未来的发展大势，在未来市场的拓展中制订和把握科学而有效的营销战略：

1.白酒的销售应以当地市场为主，省外市场为辅，抓市场重在巩固阵地，树立企业形象，提高美誉度、知名度。

2.白酒的价格要注意定位。产品的价格定位一是要依据其成本加入合理利润；二是要遵从产品档次就高就低的原则。

3.掌握市场信息，调整产品结构。

4.白酒希望在农村。

5.酒厂要把工作重点放在市场上，“一分科技、三分管理、六分市场”。

6.走工商联手开拓市场之路。

7.合理调整工商利益分配，特别是经销商的利益，充分调动其主动性。这是白酒企业发展生产、提高效益的关键之举。

葡萄酒

1998 年，全国葡萄酒总产量约 23 万吨，比 1997 年的 18.55 万吨增长 18%左右。产量 1 万吨以上的企业有 4 家：张裕、长城、王朝、威龙。葡萄酒产量增幅较大的企业有：张裕增长近 90%，威龙增长 1 倍以上，仅次于张裕；长城和威龙在 98 年稳步增长，增幅在 5%～6%。1998 年干葡萄酒产量比 1997 年上升 50%，干红与干白比例由 97 年的 60：40 上升为 80：20。（《99 中国经济年鉴》）据轻工信息统计，98 年进口葡萄酒 49843 吨，比 97 年增长 25.6%，而出口量较小，仅为 4285 吨。

1999 年，葡萄酒大战打出落差：洋酒订单锐减，国产干红走红。洋酒之所以失利，主要有以下几个原因：

1．洋酒在质量方面失信于消费者。众多洋品牌只抢强占市场，大举进攻，致使上市产品质量参差不齐，不少洋葡萄酒都曾被消费者投诉。

2．洋酒的价格太高。一般每瓶都在上百元，甚至上千元，这在我国属于高消费，无法进入大众家庭。

3．“疯牛病”事件爆发后，以进口法国葡萄酒为代表的洋酒销售受到严重影响。因为法国一些传统小酒店，在酿酒的部分工序上仍沿用着传统手工操作方法，用牛血粉作净化剂就是其中之一。

与此同时，在“干红大战”中获胜的国内葡萄酿酒企业也并未因一时得势而沾沾自喜，而是时刻铭记洋酒失败的教训，继续在质量上狠下功夫，丝毫不敢懈怠。国家质量技术监督局今年 1 月 26 日公布的调查结果，国内 58 家企业的 70 种葡萄酒产品合格率为 90%，其中张裕的产品合格率为 100%，这使消费者饮之更放心了。

1999 年的中国葡萄酒业谁的质量过硬，谁的品牌更有影响力，谁就是最大的受益者。从质量上看，张裕、长城、王朝、通化等企业都具有一定的水平，其中以龙头老大张裕为突出，而作为中国葡萄酒的后生代，长城、王朝、通化也具备自己的质量特色。

据悉，有关部门已制定了葡萄酒生产发展规划，2000 年葡萄酒产量达到 50 万吨，2010 年达到 80 万吨。为保证葡萄酒行业的健康持续发展，国内葡萄酒企业应注意以下几点：

1．必须重视酿酒葡萄基地的建设，葡萄酒企业必须把原料基地作为第一车间，以建立稳固的优质原料基地。

2．要在短期内将葡萄酒变成大范围现实的需求，生产企业还要在引导消费、培育市场等方面下下大力气。

3．虽然开拓市场不在早晚，创立名牌不分先后，对于业内和即将进入葡萄酒业的企业来说，不但要有雄厚的资金实力、缜密的技术和良好的营销计划，更要有承担市场风险的心理准备。因为所有商家的杀手锏，几乎都是在同品质下的低价位销售。

Alcohol Products

China has been a big country in liquor producing and consuming. Recently, with the development of market economy and the stronger consciousness of health in the people, the dominance of spirit has passed away forever, and with the upbringing of beer, a tripartite balance of power has formed in the alcohol market. The current situation of China's liquor industry goes as: in spirit market, supply still exceeds demand, with a yearly output of 7-8 million tons, slightly declining from last year, while variety increases; beer was No.2 in the world with an output of 19 million tons last year, but the market demand was not big enough, and gradually penetrated into countryside. Wine market is improved day by day, except that the source of raw materials can't keep up with the production in the terms of development. Wine and beer have been growing at a rate of 20%. Beer market has come into large form. But wine market is not as reasonable as people think. There are many foreign-funded plants in China. There is also a rise in yellow rice or millet wine, whose market, however, is expanding slowly, only thrives in Jiansu and Zhejiang provinces. By the end of 1998, China's liquor export, cut off by 21.4% in comparison with 1997, had earned 146.91 million dollars and realized a favorable balance of 75.02 million dollars, which was also less than 1997 by 39%. For the moment, there are totally 11 brands in liquor market deemed as famous, among which 7 are in spirit class such as: Guizhou Moutai, Wuliangye, Luzhou Laojiao, Xinhuacun, Langjiu, Jiannancun and GuJingong; 2 beer as: TsingTao Beer and Yanjing Beer; one for wine: Zhangyu, and Guyuelongshan for yellow rice wine.

The sales condition of 1998 showed that the spirit industry had formed a pattern where standardized business blocs monopolized the urban markets while the local brands went for countryside. In 1998, joint-stock beer plants occupied 16% of the business, they took advantage of flexible operation, strong ability in catering to market and efficient in improving of output with quality. Besides, the native brand beer enjoyed a satisfying developing rate. For instance, among 18 big beer plants with output above 0.2 million tons in 1998, there were only 6 foreign-funded plants. In 1998, the wine industry also saw a general increase in the profit, with Dynasty, Zhangyu and GreatWall being the top three. High-grade wine by big plants is developing faster and the proportion of whole-juice wine is enlarged.

Beer

With the swift development of China's economy and the continuous improvement of people living standard, the demand for beer is stronger than before and its market thrives, which then naturally promote the beer industry. In 1998, the overall beer output was 19.8767 million tons, 992 thousand tons or 5.3% more than that in 1997. Among the consumer goods, beer was the one that enjoyed a higher rising rate in retail, which, according to the survey over 250 big department stores around the country, was 54%, ranked 15 the in the consumer goods ("*99 China Economy Yearbook*"). The China Wine-making Association Beer Branch analyzed the sales of the early half year, in 1999 our beer output has increased by over 9%, with yearly output of 22 million tons, which will make China for the first time surpass America and become the best one.

For the moment, there are 104 beer businesses with annual output over 50 thousand tons each. Their overall output accounts for 70% of the nation's whole output, which shows our beer industry is developing toward a large-scale pattern. In 98, there were 21 beer enterprises, which produced a gross, tax over 100 million yuan. The leading brands rank as: Yanjing, Tsingtao, Lanjian, Zhujiang, Blue Ribbon, Jinwei while there were 5 which earned profits over 100 million yuan, rank as: Yanjing, Tsingtao, Jingwei, Blue Ribbon and Zhujiang. Among them, Jingwei Beer Limited Company of Guandong Province did best in sales revenue, net profits and net taxes in 1998. In the same year, the export value and export valume have been reduced by 22% while import increased by 15% and import yuan 50%. Every kiloliter imported beer was priced as 657 dollars, far above the export price of 472 dollars. This made the ratio of export and import fall from 1:0.4 of 1997 to 1:0.8.

In 1998, the output of Yanjing Beer Corporation broke the record of 800 thousand tons, and Zhujiang and Tsingtao also produced 60 thousand tons. Beer industry scale expanded. Tsingtao beer is our biggest brand in the world, even holding one share in America, the No 1 beer making country. Merely in the first half of 1999, the output of Tsingtao beer reached 446 thousand tons, rising by 59.5% over the same term last year, with sales revenue and taxes rising by over 50%. For the first time, its sales output and taxes ranked No. 1 in the beer industry of China. In 1998, the beer enterprises with output over 200 thousand tons were 18, 5 more than 1997. Their overall output accounted for 31.3% in that of whole country, rising by 10.2% than 1997. Some large-scaled beer enterprises have been built or allied into group company, which has turned out a satisfying influence. For example, Beijing Yanjing Beer, Tsingtao beer and Guandon Zhujiang Beer merged into one group company. Its output and taxes definitely rank as the top three in the country.

Our country's beer industry is making efforts to realize a large-scale and tensified operation while going its own way to make products diversified through technological reform, so as to face the challenge from the market. Currently, besides traditional items, the well-known beer enterprises are going on developing new products like light beer, cool beer, black beer, white beer, low-sugar-and-calorie beer, mellow-free beer and diet beer. Technology reform not only add new members to our beer family but also cater to the needs of consumers, which, eked out with a higher quality, a lower cost, and helps the native beer brands find its standing place in the severe competition with the prevalence of foreign rivals. Now local beer products have enjoyed 70% market share. This means the local beer has been widely accepted by mass consumers and China's beer industry is beginning to enter the international market.

Hard Liquor

Now our country has 37 thousand spirit firms, among which the independent firms account for about 4870. In 1998, the spirit industry got a total output of about 5.7333 million tons, the industrial gross revenue of 35 billion yuan, and produced a tax of 13 billion yuan. According to statistics, there are 61 businesses with annual output over ten thousand tons, whose overall output account for 31.3% of the whole country. 9.8% of the overall output come from the enterprises with annual output over 20 thousand tons, 21.5% from the ones with output between 10 and 20 thousand tons while 68.3% from those with output under 10 thousand tons (*"99 China Economy Yearbook"*).

The spirit market in 1999 is typical of the principle "the fittest survive", which gives some firms hope while the others misfortune. Some firms even lost confidence in producing spirit due to the problem of overstocking and sluggish marketing, some wanted to return to market with its strength and brand after the "advertised liquor age". But some experts find the market .demand is still shrinking, the price of spirit declining and competition severe, so that many businesses can't find a place to survive. In the first half of 1999, spirit sales kept declining.

The problem appeared in spirit business roots in the contradiction between a shrinking demand and a overproduction. Besides, the government's macro economy policy and the relevant authorities keep a rein over the spirit production. At the same time other liquor like beer or foreign wine are snapping the market, with the negative influences from the shoddy liquor over the consumers. All these lead to the declining of demands for spirit. More importantly, the price fight is prevalent, some famous brands offer a low, even ridiculous prices to keep their market share, which, not only hurt every part joining in the competition, weaken everyone's strength, but also prohibit the profit promotion, then competition potential of the business.

As far as the current spirit competition is concerned, the whole industry is going on a readjust when the disorderliness in the competition would be stopped, replaced with a orderly, and strategic one. Firms will compete with each other in terms of strength and brand, marketing and planning, information and networks.

Brand competition will be the main efforts the firms pay. More and more large firms integrate culture and cultural marketing into their company names and prestige. At this time, markets are comparatively hold concentratedly by the famous national brands, regional brands and local brands. The fame, prestige and quality of the famous brands give the brands the advantage of expanding and developing.

1999, facing the overturn of the century, is a black year for China's spirit industry, both in production and sales. But it is also a hopeful year as people search for new strategies, trends, needs and opportunities in spirit marketing. Some experts in China Liquor Association believe that in 21st century, all the spirit business should have a clear idea of the past and future developing tendency, so as to gain a scientific and efficient marketing strategy in the future operation and sales:

1. The sales of spirit should focus within province and take out–of-province as a supplement. The most important thing in reaching the market is to consolidate the current market, to build the image and to promote the credit and fame.

2. Pay attention to the spirit's pricing positioning: one formula of pricing is to add an acceptable profit margin to the cost, another is to position it either as a high-class spirit or a low-class one.

3. Collect effective market information and adjust the product accordingly.

4. Countryside is the potential base for spirit.

5. Be market-oriented by dividing the efforts as "one-tenth on science and technology, three-tenths on management and six-tenths on marketing".

6. Take the way of associating industry with business in exploring the market.

7. Have a reasonable allocation of the profits, esp. that to the distributors whose initiative should thus be encouraged. This is a key for the development of production and improvement of the effectiveness.

Wine

In 1998, the overall output of wine was about 0.23 million tons, increasing by 18% over that of 185.5 thousand tons in 1997. There are four big enterprises with output over 10 thousand tons, which are Zhangyu, Greatwall, Dinasty, and Weilong. Among them the highest increasing rate belong to Zhangyu, almost 90%, followed by Weilong, over one time's rise than before. Greatwall and Weilong grew steadily in 1998 with a rise span of 5% to 6%. Also in 1998, dry wine saw a rise rate of 50%. The ratio between dry red wine to wine also increased from 60:40 of 97 to 80:20. (*"1999 China Economy Yearbook"*) According to the light industry statistics, the imported wine in 98 was 4.9843 thousand tons, 25.6% more than that of 97, while the exported amount only 4.285 thousand tons.

In 1999, a severe fight in wine businesses has resulted in the fact that the order for foreign wine has been cut down sharply and native wine gets upper hand. The reasons for the loss of the foreign businesses go as the following:

1. The quality of foreign wine doesn't live up to its claims. The foreign wine only cared for conquering the market and they rushed into China's market without careful planning. That caused an uneven quality standard. Many of them have once been complained by the consumers.

2. The price of foreign wine is too high. A bottle costs more than 100, even 1000 yuan. It is impossible for a common family to afford.

3. With the breaking out of " accident", the sales of foreign wine, esp. the imported French wine have been influenced a lot since some traditional French wineries still keep the traditional handwork operation during the

winery procedures, say, using bulls' blood powder as purification.

At the same time, the native wine enterprises, stick to improve the quality. According to the survey published by the National Quality&Technology Supervision Bureau on Jan.26th, the qualification rate of the 70 wine products produced by the 58 domestic enterprises is as high as 90%, Zhangyu even getting 100%.

In 1999's wine market, those quality ones come out influential and most benefited. In terms of quality, Zhangyu, Greatwall, Dynasty, Tonghua and the sort are satisfying. As the new comers, the other three brands enjoy their own features.

It has been known that the relevant authorities have made the development blueprint for the wine industry. The output is expected to reach 500thousand tons in 2000 and 800 thousand tons in 2010. To have a healthy and continuous development, several points should be paid special attention to:

1. Emphasis the construction of a stable base for wine grapes. Wine business should regard the raw materials base as the first workshop.

2. Trigger the wine demand within a short term. The enterprises should make great efforts to lead consumers and to build up the market.

3. It doesn't matter much who enters the market or builds brand earlier, but abundant funds, delicate technology, excellent marketing plan, along with a psychological preparation for market risk will be the key factors for both the existing enterprises and those intending to join in the industry. The last card for every marketer will be the lower price at the same quality.

1.啤酒 / Beer

● 北京 / Beijing

1-1 最近三个月饮用频率的比例/ Proportion of the Sample Consuming Beer in the Last Three Months

	人数 Number	百分比 Percent
天天喝 daily	95	9.4
一周 3 次或以上 3 times or over a week	127	12.6
一周 1~2 次 once or twice a week	185	18.4
一个月 2～3 次 2 or 3 times a month	154	15.3
一个月 1 次或以下 once a month or below	115	11.4
没喝过 never	331	32.9

n=1007

1-2 最常用品牌排名/ Ranking of the Most Frequently Used Brands

排名 Brand Ranking	品牌 Brands	人数 Number	百分比 Percent
1	燕京 Yanjing	613	90.7
2	五星 Five Star	20	3.0
3	北京 Beijing	10	1.5
4	青岛 Tsing Tao	7	1.0
5	百威 Budweiser	6	0.9

n=676

1-3 样本、男性各年龄层、女性各年龄层的常用品牌/ The Most Frequently Used Brands by the Whole Sample, Age and Gender Groups

	人数 Number	第一品牌及百分比 1st/ percent	第二品牌及百分比 2nd/ percent	第三品牌及百分比 3rd/ percent	第四品牌及百分比 4th/ percent
样本 Sample	**676**	**燕京 Yanjing(90.7)**	**五星 Five Star(3.0)**	**北京 Beijing(1.5)**	**青岛 Tsing Tao(1.0)**
男性 Male	**400**	**燕京 Yanjing(92.0)**	**五星 Five Star(3.0)**	**北京 Beijing(1.5)**	**青岛 Tsing Tao(0.8)**
16~24 岁 Age	72	燕京 Yanjing(83.3)	五星 Five Star(8.3)	北京 Beijing(2.8)	科罗娜 Corona(1.4) 喜力 Heineken(1.4)
25~34 岁 Age	125	燕京 Yanjing(94.4)	青岛 Tsing Tao(1.6)	百威 Budweiser(0.8) 科罗娜 Corona(0.8) 五星 Five Star(0.8) 雪津 Xuejin(0.8)	
35~44 岁 Age	115	燕京 Yanjing(97.4)	北京 Beijing(0.9) 青岛 Tsing Tao(0.9) 五星 Five Star(0.9)		
45~54 岁 Age	61	燕京 Yanjing(85.2)	五星 Five Star(6.6)	北京 Beijing(3.3) 燕山 Yanshan(3.3)	双合胜 Shuanghesheng(1.6)
55~60 岁 Age	27	燕京 Yanjing(96.3)	北京 Beijing(3.7)		
女性 Female	**276**	**燕京 Yanjing(88.8)**	**五星 Five Star(2.9)**	**百威 Budweiser(1.8)**	**青岛 Tsing Tao(1.4)** **北京 Beijing(1.4)**
16~24 岁 Age	38	燕京 Yanjing(76.3)	百威 Budweiser(7.9)	北京 Beijing(5.3)	虎牌 Tiger(2.6) 五星 Five Star(2.6) 喜力 Heineken(2.6) 双合胜 Shuanghesheng(2.6)
25~34 岁 Age	99	燕京 Yanjing(88.9)	五星 Five Star(3.0)	百威 Budweiser(2.0) 青岛 Tsing Tao(2.0)	北京 Beijing(1.0) 贝克 Beck's(1.0) 朝日/舒波乐 Asahi(1.0) 虎牌 Tiger(1.0)
35~44 岁 Age	73	燕京 Yanjing(90.4)	五星 Five Star(2.7)	北京 Beijing(1.4) 青岛 Tsing Tao(1.4) 喜力 Heineken(1.4) 双合胜 Shuanghesheng(1.4) 威力 Weile(1.4)	
45~54 岁 Age	45	燕京 Yanjing(93.3)	青岛 Tsing Tao(2.2) 五星 Five Star(2.2) 威乐 Weile(2.2)		
55~60 岁 Age	21	燕京 Yanjing(95.2)	五星 Five Star(4.8)		

1-4 理想品牌排名/ Ranking of the Ideal Brands

排名 Brand Ranking	品牌 Brands	人数 Number	百分比 Percent
1	燕京 Yanjing	750	74.2
2	青岛 Tsing Tao	44	4.4
3	五星 Five Star	30	3.0
4	北京 Beijing	20	2.0
5	百威 Budweiser	16	1.6
6	贝克 Beck's	8	0.8
7	蓝带 Blue Ribbon	7	0.7
7	喜力 Heineken	7	0.7
8	双合胜 Shuanghesheng	6	0.6
9	虎牌 Tiger	5	0.5

n=1011

1-5 样本、男性各年龄层、女性各年龄层最近三个月有无购买的比例/ Purchasing in the Last Three Months by the Whole Sample, Age and Gender Groups

	人数 Number	买过 yes	没买过 no
样本 Sample	1012	63.0	37.0
男性 Male	504	72.0	28.0
16~24 岁 Age	105	61.9	38.1
25~34 岁 Age	151	75.5	24.5
35~44 岁 Age	131	80.2	19.8
45~54 岁 Age	77	70.1	29.9
55~60 岁 Age	40	62.5	37.5
女性 Female	508	54.1	45.9
16~24 岁 Age	108	28.7	71.3
25~34 岁 Age	150	61.3	38.7
35~44 岁 Age	124	64.5	35.5
45~54 岁 Age	84	57.1	42.9
55~60 岁 Age	42	57.1	42.9

1-6 样本、男性各年龄层、女性各年龄层最近三个月的饮用频率/ Frequencies of Consuming Beer in the Last Three Months by the Whole Sample, Age and Gender Groups

	人数 Number	天天喝 daily	一周 3 次或以上 3 times or over a week	一周 1~2 次 once or twice a week	一个月 2~3 次 2 or 3 times a month	一个月 1 次或以下 once a month or below	没喝过 never
样本 Sample	1007	9.4	12.6	18.4	15.3	11.4	32.9
男性 Male	500	12.8	18.4	23.0	16.2	9.6	20.0
16~24 岁 Age	105	6.7	10.5	19.0	18.1	14.3	31.4
25~34 岁 Age	149	17.4	19.5	22.1	19.5	5.4	16.1
35~44 岁 Age	131	17.6	26.7	26.7	9.9	6.9	12.2
45~54 岁 Age	76	9.2	15.8	22.4	17.1	15.8	19.7
55~60 岁 Age	39	2.6	12.8	25.6	17.9	10.3	30.8
女性 Female	507	6.1	6.9	13.8	14.4	13.2	45.6
16~24 岁 Age	107	1.9	3.7	7.5	9.3	13.1	64.5
25~34 岁 Age	150	7.3	6.7	18.0	16.0	18.0	34.0
35~44 岁 Age	124	8.9	10.5	15.3	14.5	9.7	41.1
45~54 岁 Age	84	4.8	6.0	13.1	17.9	11.9	46.4
55~60 岁 Age	42	7.1	7.1	11.9	14.3	9.5	50.0

1-7 样本、男性各年龄层、女性各年龄层的品牌习惯/ Brand Habit in Consuming Beer by the Whole Sample, Age and Gender Groups

	人数 Number	基本固定饮用一个牌子 used in only one brand	比较固定地饮用两个或三个牌子 used in two or three brands	基本上不太固定牌子 no brand preference
样本 Sample	676	76.0	18.9	5.0
男性 Male	400	79.3	17.3	3.5
16~24 岁 Age	72	76.4	15.3	8.3
25~34 岁 Age	125	76.8	21.6	1.6
35~44 岁 Age	115	82.6	15.7	1.7
45~54 岁 Age	61	83.6	13.1	3.3
55~60 岁 Age	27	74.1	18.5	7.4
女性 Female	276	71.4	21.4	7.2
16~24 岁 Age	38	44.7	36.8	18.4
25~34 岁 Age	99	71.7	24.2	4.0
35~44 岁 Age	73	78.1	13.7	8.2
45~54 岁 Age	45	77.8	20.0	2.2
55~60 岁 Age	21	81.0	9.5	9.5

1-8 选择该类商品的考虑因素/ Ranking of the Considerations in Purchasing

注：本题为多选题，合计百分比超过 100%(Multiple answers）

排名 Ranking	考虑因素 Considerations	人次 Person-time	百分比 Percent
1	口味好 pleasant taste	392	58.0
2	有名的牌子 famous brand	261	38.6
3	价格适中 reasonable price	258	38.2
4	生产日期 date of producing	143	21.2
5	购买方便 easy to buy	119	17.6
6	只是由于习惯 out of habit	81	12.0
7	单位发的 offered by the working unit	38	5.6
8	生产地 place of production	36	5.3
9	广告影响 influence of advertising	30	4.4
10	别人送的 given by other people	21	3.1
11	朋友推荐 introduction of friends	9	1.3
11	有优惠条件 with preferential terms	9	1.3
12	其它 others	5	0.7
13	包装吸引人 appealing package	4	0.6
14	售货员介绍 introduced by the shop assistants	1	0.1

n=676

1-9 样本、男性各年龄层、女性各年龄层最常饮用的包装形式/ Types of Package of the Consumed Beer by the Whole Sample, Age and Gender Groups

	人数 Number	瓶装 bottle	听装 tin	散装扎啤 jar without package	其它 others
样本 Sample	672	77.5	21.4	0.7	0.3
男性 Male	398	79.1	19.8	0.8	0.3
16~24 岁 Age	70	81.4	17.1	1.4	0.0
25~34 岁 Age	125	81.6	16.8	0.8	0.8
35~44 岁 Age	115	83.5	16.5	0.0	0.0
45~54 岁 Age	61	70.5	29.5	0.0	0.0
55~60 岁 Age	27	63.0	33.3	3.7	0.0
女性 Female	274	75.2	23.7	0.7	0.4
16~24 岁 Age	37	59.5	40.5	0.0	0.0
25~34 岁 Age	99	75.8	22.2	2.0	0.0
35~44 岁 Age	73	79.5	20.5	0.0	0.0
45~54 岁 Age	45	71.1	26.7	0.0	2.2
55~60 岁 Age	20	95.0	5.0	0.0	0.0

1-10 样本、男性各年龄层、女性各年龄层最常饮用的口味/ The Taste of the Consumed Beer by the Whole Sample, Age and Gender Groups

	人数 Number	清爽型 fresh and cool	醇厚型 mellow	其它 others
样本 Sample	668	93.1	5.1	1.8
男性 Male	393	92.9	5.6	1.5
16~24 岁 Age	72	93.1	2.8	4.2
25~34 岁 Age	123	93.5	5.7	0.8
35~44 岁 Age	113	88.5	9.7	1.8
45~54 岁 Age	58	96.6	3.4	0.0
55~60 岁 Age	27	100.0	0.0	0.0
女性 Female	275	93.5	4.4	2.2
16~24 岁 Age	37	89.2	8.1	2.7
25~34 岁 Age	99	91.9	7.1	1.0
35~44 岁 Age	73	97.3	1.4	1.4
45~54 岁 Age	45	93.3	2.2	4.4
55~60 岁 Age	21	95.2	0.0	4.8

1-11 样本、男性各年龄层、女性各年龄层最常饮用的场合/ Settings of Consumption by the Whole Sample, Age and Gender Groups

注：本题为多选题，合计百分比超过 100%(Multiple answers）

	人数 Number	口渴时 when thirsty	平时吃饭喝 at dinner	宴席、聚会喝 at banquet	去酒吧喝 at bar	外出/旅游时 outing/traveling	其它 others
样本 Sample	674	6.1	63.1	51.5	4.6	3.6	1.5
男性 Male	399	5.5	64.9	50.6	5.8	3.5	1.8
16~24 岁 Age	72	9.7	48.6	63.9	8.3	4.2	1.4
25~34 岁 Age	124	4.0	62.9	52.4	8.9	1.6	0.8
35~44 岁 Age	115	3.5	73.9	44.3	4.3	6.1	0.9
45~54 岁 Age	61	8.2	67.2	45.9	1.6	1.6	3.3
55~60 岁 Age	27	3.7	74.1	44.4	0.0	3.7	7.4
女性 Female	275	6.9	60.4	52.7	2.9	3.6	1.1
16~24 岁 Age	38	2.6	60.5	50.0	13.2	2.6	0.0
25~34 岁 Age	99	7.1	58.6	47.5	3.0	5.1	1.0
35~44 岁 Age	73	9.6	57.5	64.4	0.0	5.5	2.7
45~54 岁 Age	45	4.4	64.4	46.7	0.0	0.0	0.0
55~60 岁 Age	20	10.0	70.0	55.0	0.0	0.0	0.0

1-12 重度消费者人口分布/ Demographics of the Heavy Consumers

	人数 Number	16-24 岁 Age	25-34 岁 Age	35-44 岁 Age	45-54 岁 Age	55-60 岁 Age
样本 Sample	407	12.8	33.4	33.4	13.8	6.6
男性 Male	271	14.0	32.5	34.3	13.3	5.9
天天喝 daily	64	10.9	40.6	35.9	10.9	1.6
一周 3 次或以上 3 times or over a week	92	12.0	31.5	38.0	13.0	5.4
一周 1~2 次 once or twice a week	115	17.4	28.7	30.4	14.8	8.7
女性 Female	136	10.3	35.3	31.6	14.7	8.1
天天喝 daily	31	6.5	35.5	35.5	12.9	9.7
一周 3 次或以上 3 times or over a week	35	11.4	28.6	37.1	14.3	8.6
一周 1~2 次 once or twice a week	70	11.4	38.6	27.1	15.7	7.1

1-13 不同消费者层的常用品牌/ The Most Frequently Used Brands by Market Segments

1-13-1 时尚流行指标/ Fads Popular Index

	人数 Number	第一品牌及百分比 1st/percent	第二品牌及百分比 2nd/percent	第三品牌及百分比 3rd/percent	第四品牌及百分比 4th/percent
样本 Sample	**666**	**燕京 Yanjing(90.5)**	**五星 Five Star(3.0)**	**北京 Beijing(1.5)**	**青岛 Tsing Tao(1.1)**
平实生活指向 simple living orientation	315	燕京 Yanjing(92.1)	五星 Five Star(3.5)	北京 Beijing(1.0) 青岛 Tsing Tao(1.0)	百威 Budweiser(0.6) 燕山 Yanshan(0.6)
时尚流行指向 fashion orientation	351	燕京 Yanjing(89.2)	五星 Five Star(2.6)	北京 Beijing(2.0)	百威 Budweiser(1.1) 青岛 Tsing Tao(1.1)

1-13-2 广告态度指标/ Advertising Attitude Index

	人数 Number	第一品牌及百分比 1st/percent	第二品牌及百分比 2nd/percent	第三品牌及百分比 3rd/percent	第四品牌及百分比 4th/percent
样本 Sample	**661**	**燕京 Yanjing(90.6)**	**五星 Five Star(3.0)**	**北京 Beijing(1.5)**	**青岛 Tsing Tao(1.1)**
广告淡漠指向 indifferent orientation	191	燕京 Yanjing(92.1)	五星 Five Star(2.6)	北京 Beijing(1.0) 喜力 Heineken(1.0)	百威 Budweiser(0.5) 贝克 Beck's(0.5) 虎牌 Tiger(0.5) 青岛 Tsing Tao(0.5)
中间层 medium	385	燕京 Yanjing(91.7)	五星 Five Star(3.1)	百威 Budweiser(1.3)	北京 Beijing(1.0)
信赖广告指向 loyal orientation	85	燕京 Yanjing(82.4)	北京 Beijing(4.7)	青岛 Tsing Tao(3.5) 五星 Five Star(3.5) 双合胜 Shuanghesheng(3.5)	朝日/舒波乐 Asahi(1.2) 燕山 Yanshan(1.2)

1-13-3 饮食健康指标/ Foods & Drink Quality Index

	人数 Number	第一品牌及百分比 1st/percent	第二品牌及百分比 2nd/percent	第三品牌及百分比 3rd/percent	第四品牌及百分比 4th/percent
样本 Sample	**671**	**燕京 Yanjing(90.9)**	**五星 Five Star(2.8)**	**北京 Beijing(1.5)**	**青岛 Tsing Tao(1.0)**
饮食"温饱"指向 "basic" orientation	191	燕京 Yanjing(92.7)	五星 Five Star(3.1)	北京 Beijing(1.0) 青岛 Tsing Tao(1.0)	百威 Budweiser(0.5) 贝克 Beck's(0.5) 虎牌 Tiger(0.5)
中间层 medium	326	燕京 Yanjing(91.4)	五星 Five Star(2.8)	北京 Beijing(1.5)	百威 Budweiser(0.9) 青岛 Tsing Tao(0.9) 喜力 Heineken(0.9)
健康营养指向 health & nutrition orientation	154	燕京 Yanjing(87.7)	五星 Five Star(2.6)	北京 Beijing(1.9) 双合胜 Shuanghesheng(1.9)	百威 Budweiser(1.3) 科罗娜 Corona(1.3) 青岛 Tsing Tao(1.3)

1-14 重度消费者的消费者层构成/ The Composition of the Heavy Consumers

1-14-1 时尚流行指标/ Fads Popular Index

	人数 Number	平实生活指向 simple living orientation	时尚流行指向 fashion orientation
样本 Sample	**400**	**42.8**	**57.3**
天天喝 daily	95	41.1	58.9
一周 3 次或以上 3 times or over a week	124	40.3	59.7
一周 1~2 次 once or twice a week	181	45.3	54.7

1-14-2 广告态度指标/ Advertising Attitude Index

	人数 Number	广告淡漠指向 indifferent orientation	中间层 medium	信赖广告指向 loyal orientation
样本 Sample	**397**	**30.2**	**56.4**	**13.4**
天天喝 daily	90	34.4	53.3	12.2
一周 3 次或以上 3 times or over a week	124	27.4	57.3	15.3
一周 1~2 次 once or twice a week	183	30.1	57.4	12.6

1-14-3 饮食健康指标/ Foods & Drink Quality Index

	人数 Number	饮食"温饱"指向 "basic" orientation	中间层 medium	健康营养指向 health & nutrition orientation
样本 Sample	406	27.6	49.3	23.2
天天喝 daily	95	30.5	45.3	24.2
一周 3 次或以上 3 times or over a week	127	27.6	50.4	22.0
一周 1~2 次 once or twice a week	184	26.1	50.5	23.4

● 上海 / Shanghai

1-1 最近三个月饮用频率的比例/ Proportion of the Sample Consuming Beer in the Last Three Months

	人数 Number	百分比 Percent
天天喝 daily	94	9.3
一周 3 次或以上 3 times or over a week	110	10.8
一周 1~2 次 once or twice a week	151	14.9
一个月 2～3 次 2 or 3 times a month	130	12.8
一个月 1 次或以下 once a month or below	103	10.2
没喝过 never	426	42.0

n=1014

1-2 最常用品牌排名/ Ranking of the Most Frequently Used Brands

排名 Brand Ranking	品牌 Brands	人数 Number	百分比 Percent
1	三得利 Suntory	315	53.6
2	力波 Reeb	112	19.0
3	百威 Budweiser	48	8.2
4	青岛 Tsing Tao	30	5.1
5	贝克 Beck's	23	3.9
6	光明 Guangming	19	3.2
7	上海 Shanghai	9	1.5
8	喜力 Heineken	7	1.2
9	嘉士伯 Carlsberg	5	0.9
10	虎牌 Tiger	3	0.5
10	莱克 Luck	3	0.5

n=588

1-3 样本、男性各年龄层、女性各年龄层的常用品牌/ The Most Frequently Used Brands by the Whole Sample, Age and Gender Groups

	人数 Number	第一品牌及百分比 1st/ percent	第二品牌及百分比 2nd/ percent	第三品牌及百分比 3rd/ percent
样本 Sample	588	**三得利 Suntory(53.6)**	**力波 Reeb(19.0)**	**百威 Budweiser(8.2)**
男性 Male	383	**三得利 Suntory(54.6)**	**力波 Reeb(19.1)**	**百威 Budweiser(8.4)**
16~24 岁 Age	62	三得利 Suntory(59.7)	百威 Budweiser(12.9)	力波 Reeb(11.3)
25~34 岁 Age	114	三得利 Suntory(51.8)	百威 Budweiser(13.2) 力波 Reeb(13.2)	贝克 Beck's(7.0)
35~44 岁 Age	113	三得利 Suntory(55.8)	力波 Reeb(25.7)	光明 Guangming(5.3)
45~54 岁 Age	69	三得利 Suntory(60.9)	力波 Reeb(15.9)	青岛 Tsing Tao(11.6)
55~60 岁 Age	25	力波 Reeb(44.0)	三得利 Suntory(32.0)	上海 Shanghai(8.0)
女性 Female	205	**三得利 Suntory(51.7)**	**力波 Reeb(19.0)**	**百威 Budweiser(7.8)**
16~24 岁 Age	22	三得利 Suntory(50.0)	力波 Reeb(18.2)	百威 Budweiser(13.6)
25~34 岁 Age	65	三得利 Suntory(55.4)	力波 Reeb(10.8)	百威 Budweiser(9.2)
35~44 岁 Age	61	三得利 Suntory(60.7)	力波 Reeb(16.4)	百威 Budweiser(6.6)
45~54 岁 Age	41	三得利 Suntory(39.0)	力波 Reeb(31.7)	百威 Budweiser(7.3)
55~60 岁 Age	16	三得利 Suntory(37.5)	力波 Reeb(31.3)	青岛 Tsing Tao(25.0)

1-4 理想品牌排名/ Ranking of the Ideal Brands

排名 Brand Ranking	品牌 Brands	人数 Number	百分比 Percent
1	三得利 Suntory	493	48.6
2	力波 Reeb	130	12.8
3	百威 Budweiser	96	9.5
4	贝克 Beck's	68	6.7
4	青岛 Tsing Tao	68	6.7
5	喜力 Heineken	32	3.2
6	光明 Guangming	19	1.9
7	虎牌 Tiger	17	1.7
8	嘉士伯 Carlsberg	10	1.0
9	上海 Shanghai	8	0.8
10	蓝带 Blue Ribbon	7	0.7
11	麒麟 Kirin	5	0.5
12	世好 Shihao	4	0.4
12	莱克 Luck	4	0.4
13	生力 San Miguel	3	0.3
13	朝日/舒波乐 Asahi	3	0.3
14	新东海(东海）Donghai	2	0.2

n=1014

1-5 样本、男性各年龄层、女性各年龄层最近三个月有无购买的比例/ Purchasing in the Last Three Months by the Whole Sample, Age and Gender Groups

	人数 Number	买过 yes	没买过 no
样本 Sample	1014	59.9	40.1
男性 Male	509	72.3	27.7
16~24 岁 Age	109	53.2	46.8
25~34 岁 Age	146	73.3	26.7
35~44 岁 Age	130	85.4	14.6
45~54 岁 Age	85	80.0	20.0
55~60 岁 Age	39	61.5	38.5
女性 Female	505	47.3	52.7
16~24 岁 Age	108	16.7	83.3
25~34 岁 Age	144	51.4	48.6
35~44 岁 Age	130	62.3	37.7
45~54 岁 Age	82	57.3	42.7
55~60 岁 Age	41	46.3	53.7

1-6 样本、男性各年龄层、女性各年龄层最近三个月的饮用频率/ Frequencies of Consuming Beer in the Last Three Months by the Whole Sample, Age and Gender Groups

	人数 Number	天天喝 daily	一周 3 次或以上 3 times or over a week	一周 1~2 次 once or twice a week	一个月 2~3 次 2 or 3 times a month	一个月 1 次或以下 once a month or below	没喝过 never
样本 Sample	1014	9.3	10.8	14.9	12.8	10.2	42.0
男性 Male	509	13.8	17.5	19.1	15.3	9.6	24.8
16~24 岁 Age	109	4.6	7.3	19.3	8.3	17.4	43.1
25~34 岁 Age	146	14.4	17.1	21.2	19.2	6.2	21.9
35~44 岁 Age	130	19.2	30.0	17.7	12.3	7.7	13.1
45~54 岁 Age	85	16.5	17.6	14.1	23.5	9.4	18.8
55~60 岁 Age	39	12.8	5.1	25.6	12.8	7.7	35.9
女性 Female	505	4.8	4.2	10.7	10.3	10.7	59.4
16~24 岁 Age	108	1.9	0.9	2.8	5.6	9.3	79.6
25~34 岁 Age	144	4.2	8.3	11.1	11.8	9.7	54.9
35~44 岁 Age	130	6.9	3.1	16.2	10.0	10.8	53.1
45~54 岁 Age	82	7.3	2.4	13.4	11.0	15.9	50.0
55~60 岁 Age	41	2.4	4.9	7.3	17.1	7.3	61.0

1-7 样本、男性各年龄层、女性各年龄层的品牌习惯/ Brand Habit in Consuming Beer by the Whole Sample, Age and Gender Groups

	人数 Number	基本固定饮用一个牌子 used in only one brand	比较固定地饮用两个或三个牌子 used in two or three brands	基本上不太固定牌子 no brand preference
样本 Sample	588	52.2	37.2	10.5
男性 Male	383	52.7	38.1	9.1
16~24 岁 Age	62	48.4	40.3	11.3
25~34 岁 Age	114	50.0	40.4	9.6
35~44 岁 Age	113	50.4	39.8	9.7
45~54 岁 Age	69	65.2	29.0	5.8
55~60 岁 Age	25	52.0	40.0	8.0
女性 Female	205	51.2	35.6	13.2
16~24 岁 Age	22	36.4	50.0	13.6
25~34 岁 Age	65	49.2	36.9	13.8
35~44 岁 Age	61	55.7	36.1	8.2
45~54 岁 Age	41	58.5	24.4	17.1
55~60 岁 Age	16	43.8	37.5	18.8

1-8 选择该类商品的考虑因素/ Ranking of the Considerations in Purchasing

注：本题为多选题，合计百分比超过 100%(Multiple answers）

排名 Ranking	考虑因素 Considerations	人次 Person-time	百分比 Percent
1	口味好 pleasant taste	369	62.9
2	价格适中 reasonable price	253	43.1
3	有名的牌子 famous brand	229	39.0
4	购买方便 easy to buy	104	17.7
5	生产日期 date of producing	82	14.0
6	广告影响 influence of advertising	81	13.8
7	只是由于习惯 out of habit	55	9.4
8	生产地 place of production	19	3.2
9	有优惠条件 with preferential terms	13	2.2
10	朋友推荐 introduction of friends	10	1.7
11	单位发的 offered by the working unit	8	1.4
12	别人送的 given by other people	6	1.0
12	包装吸引人 appealing package	6	1.0
13	售货员介绍 introduced by the shop assistants	3	0.5
13	其它 others	3	0.5

n=587

1-9 样本、男性各年龄层、女性各年龄层最常饮用的包装形式/ Types of Package of the Consumed Beer by the Whole Sample, Age and Gender Groups

	人数 Number	瓶装 bottle	听装 tin	散装扎啤 jar without package	其它 others
样本 Sample	588	91.7	8.2	0.2	0.0
男性 Male	383	92.4	7.6	0.0	0.0
16~24 岁 Age	62	82.3	17.7	0.0	0.0
25~34 岁 Age	114	92.1	7.9	0.0	0.0
35~44 岁 Age	113	97.3	2.7	0.0	0.0
45~54 岁 Age	69	91.3	8.7	0.0	0.0
55~60 岁 Age	25	100.0	0.0	0.0	0.0
女性 Female	205	90.2	9.3	0.5	0.0
16~24 岁 Age	22	77.3	22.7	0.0	0.0
25~34 岁 Age	65	93.8	6.2	0.0	0.0
35~44 岁 Age	61	90.2	9.8	0.0	0.0
45~54 岁 Age	41	92.7	4.9	2.4	0.0
55~60 岁 Age	16	87.5	12.5	0.0	0.0

1-10 样本、男性各年龄层、女性各年龄层最常饮用的口味/ The Taste of the Consumed Beer by the Whole Sample, Age and Gender Groups

	人数 Number	清爽型 fresh and cool	醇厚型 mellow	其它 others
样本 Sample	587	88.8	10.4	0.9
男性 Male	382	87.7	11.3	1.0
16~24 岁 Age	62	91.9	8.1	0.0
25~34 岁 Age	114	86.8	11.4	1.8
35~44 岁 Age	112	87.5	11.6	0.9
45~54 岁 Age	69	88.4	11.6	0.0
55~60 岁 Age	25	80.0	16.0	4.0
女性 Female	205	90.7	8.8	0.5
16~24 岁 Age	22	100.0	0.0	0.0
25~34 岁 Age	65	90.8	9.2	0.0
35~44 岁 Age	61	95.1	4.9	0.0
45~54 岁 Age	41	82.9	17.1	0.0
55~60 岁 Age	16	81.3	12.5	6.3

1-11 样本、男性各年龄层、女性各年龄层最常饮用的场合/ Settings of Consumption by the Whole Sample, Age and Gender Groups

注：本题为多选题，合计百分比超过 100%(Multiple answers)

	人数 Number	口渴时 when thirsty	平时吃饭喝 at dinner	宴席、聚会喝 at banquet	去酒吧喝 at bar	外出/旅游时 outing/ traveling	其它 others
样本 Sample	588	3.6	61.7	49.7	5.1	3.2	1.0
男性 Male	383	3.1	64.0	49.3	6.3	3.1	1.0
16~24 岁 Age	62	1.6	46.8	66.1	12.9	3.2	1.6
25~34 岁 Age	114	0.9	60.5	52.6	6.1	3.5	0.9
35~44 岁 Age	113	3.5	76.1	36.3	5.3	4.4	0.9
45~54 岁 Age	69	4.3	66.7	50.7	2.9	1.4	1.4
55~60 岁 Age	25	12.0	60.0	48.0	4.0	0.0	0.0
女性 Female	205	4.4	57.6	50.2	2.9	3.4	1.0
16~24 岁 Age	22	0.0	40.9	63.6	18.2	4.5	0.0
25~34 岁 Age	65	6.2	58.5	47.7	0.0	4.6	1.5
35~44 岁 Age	61	6.6	60.7	49.2	1.6	3.3	1.6
45~54 岁 Age	41	2.4	61.0	46.3	2.4	2.4	0.0
55~60 岁 Age	16	0.0	56.3	56.3	0.0	0.0	0.0

1-12 重度消费者人口分布/ Demographics of the Heavy Consumers

	人数 Number	16-24 岁 Age	25-34 岁 Age	35-44 岁 Age	45-54 岁 Age	55-60 岁 Age
样本 Sample	355	11.3	31.3	34.1	16.9	6.5
男性 Male	256	13.3	30.1	34.0	16.0	6.6
天天喝 daily	70	7.1	30.0	35.7	20.0	7.1
一周 3 次或以上 3 times or over a week	89	9.0	28.1	43.8	16.9	2.2
一周 1~2 次 once or twice a week	97	21.6	32.0	23.7	12.4	10.3
女性 Female	99	6.1	34.3	34.3	19.2	6.1
天天喝 daily	24	8.3	25.0	37.5	25.0	4.2
一周 3 次或以上 3 times or over a week	21	4.8	57.1	19.0	9.5	9.5
一周 1~2 次 once or twice a week	54	5.6	29.6	38.9	20.4	5.6

1-13 不同消费者层的常用品牌/ The Most Frequently Used Brands by Market Segments

1-13-1 时尚流行指标/ Fads Popular Index

	人数 Number	第一品牌及百分比 1st/percent	第二品牌及百分比 2nd/percent	第三品牌及百分比 3rd/percent
样本 Sample	**580**	**三得利 Suntory(54.0)**	**力波 Reeb(19.0)**	**百威 Budweiser(8.3)**
平实生活指向 simple living orientation	271	三得利 Suntory(54.6)	力波 Reeb(23.2)	百威 Budweiser(5.2) 青岛 Tsing Tao(5.2)
时尚流行指向 fashion orientation	309	三得利 Suntory(53.4)	力波 Reeb(15.2)	百威 Budweiser(11.0)

1-13-2 广告态度指标/ Advertising Attitude Index

	人数 Number	第一品牌及百分比 1st/percent	第二品牌及百分比 2nd/percent	第三品牌及百分比 3rd/percent
样本 Sample	**584**	**三得利 Suntory(53.6)**	**力波 Reeb(19.2)**	**百威 Budweiser(8.2)**
广告淡漠指向 indifferent orientation	135	三得利 Suntory(46.7)	力波 Reeb(23.0)	百威 Budweiser(9.6)
中间层 medium	376	三得利 Suntory(54.8)	力波 Reeb(18.9)	百威 Budweiser(7.2)
信赖广告指向 loyal orientation	73	三得利 Suntory(60.3)	力波 Reeb(13.7)	百威 Budweiser(11.0)

1-13-3 饮食健康指标/ Foods & Drink Quality Index

	人数 Number	第一品牌及百分比 1st/percent	第二品牌及百分比 2nd/percent	第三品牌及百分比 3rd/percent
样本 Sample	**584**	**三得利 Suntory(53.8)**	**力波 Reeb(18.7)**	**百威 Budweiser(8.2)**
饮食“温饱”指向 "basic" orientation	136	三得利 Suntory(51.5)	力波 Reeb(22.8)	百威 Budweiser(8.8)
中间层 medium	283	三得利 Suntory(51.6)	力波 Reeb(18.7)	百威 Budweiser(7.8)
健康营养指向 health & nutrition orientation	165	三得利 Suntory(59.4)	力波 Reeb(15.2)	百威 Budweiser(8.5)

1-14 重度消费者的消费者层构成/ The Composition of the Heavy Consumers

1-14-1 时尚流行指标/ Fads Popular Index

	人数 Number	平实生活指向 simple living orientation	时尚流行指向 fashion orientation
样本 Sample	**350**	**44.3**	**55.7**
天天喝 daily	92	44.6	55.4
一周 3 次或以上 3 times or over a week	110	44.5	55.5
一周 1~2 次 once or twice a week	148	43.9	56.1

1-14-2 广告态度指标/ Advertising Attitude Index

	人数 Number	广告淡漠指向 indifferent orientation	中间层 medium	信赖广告指向 loyal orientation
样本 Sample	**353**	**22.4**	**64.0**	**13.6**
天天喝 daily	94	22.3	61.7	16.0
一周 3 次或以上 3 times or over a week	109	17.4	72.5	10.1
一周 1~2 次 once or twice a week	150	26.0	59.3	14.7

1-14-3 饮食健康指标/ Foods & Drink Quality Index

	人数 Number	饮食“温饱”指向 "basic" orientation	中间层 medium	健康营养指向 health & nutrition orientation
样本 Sample	**353**	**23.8**	**46.5**	**29.7**
天天喝 daily	93	18.3	45.2	36.6
一周 3 次或以上 3 times or over a week	109	24.8	46.8	28.4
一周 1~2 次 once or twice a week	151	26.5	47.0	26.5

● 广州 / Guangzhou

1-1 最近三个月饮用频率的比例/ Proportion of the Sample Consuming Beer in the Last Three Months

	人数 Number	百分比 Percent
天天喝 daily	21	2.0
一周 3 次或以上 3 times or over a week	85	8.2
一周 1~2 次 once or twice a week	157	15.2
一个月 2～3 次 2 or 3 times a month	213	20.6
一个月 1 次或以下 once a month or below	146	14.1
没喝过 never	410	39.7

n=1032

1-2 最常用品牌排名/ Ranking of the Most Frequently Used Brands

排名 Brand Ranking	品牌 Brands	人数 Number	百分比 Percent
1	珠江 Zhujiang	322	51.8
2	生力 San Miguel	110	17.7
3	青岛 Tsing Tao	56	9.0
4	广氏 Guangshi	46	7.4
5	蓝带 Blue Ribbon	29	4.7
6	百威 Budweiser	21	3.4
7	喜力 Heineken	8	1.3
8	金威 Jinwei	5	0.8

n=622

1-3 样本、男性各年龄层、女性各年龄层的常用品牌/ The Most Frequently Used Brands by the Whole Sample, Age and Gender Groups

	人数 Number	第一品牌及百分比 1st/ percent	第二品牌及百分比 2nd/ percent	第三品牌及百分比 3rd/ percent	第四品牌及百分比 4th/ percent
样本 Sample	**622**	**珠江 Zhujiang(51.8)**	**生力 San Miguel(17.7)**	**青岛 Tsing Tao(9.0)**	**广氏 Guangshi(7.4)**
男性 Male	**375**	**珠江 Zhujiang(54.9)**	**生力 San Miguel(18.4)**	**青岛 Tsing Tao(9.1)**	**蓝带 Blue Ribbon(4.3)** **广氏 Guangshi(4.3)**
16~24 岁 Age	69	珠江 Zhujiang(47.8)	生力 San Miguel(20.3)	百威 Budweiser(10.1)	蓝带 Blue Ribbon(8.7)
25~34 岁 Age	118	珠江 Zhujiang(48.3)	生力 San Miguel(19.5)	青岛 Tsing Tao(11.0)	广氏 Guangshi(5.1)
35~44 岁 Age	102	珠江 Zhujiang(61.8)	生力 San Miguel(15.7)	青岛 Tsing Tao(7.8)	蓝带 Blue Ribbon(3.9)
45~54 岁 Age	54	珠江 Zhujiang(59.3)	生力 San Miguel(18.5)	青岛 Tsing Tao(14.8)	广氏 Guangshi(5.6)
55~60 岁 Age	32	珠江 Zhujiang(65.6)	生力 San Miguel(18.8)	青岛 Tsing Tao(9.4)	广氏 Guangshi(3.1)
女性 Female	**247**	**珠江 Zhujiang(47.0)**	**生力 San Miguel(16.6)**	**广氏 Guangshi(12.1)**	**青岛 Tsing Tao(8.9)**
16~24 岁 Age	42	珠江 Zhujiang(31.0)	生力 San Miguel(21.4)	百威 Budweiser(14.3)	广氏 Guangshi(11.9)
25~34 岁 Age	83	珠江 Zhujiang(41.0)	生力 San Miguel(18.1)	广氏 Guangshi(14.5)	青岛 Tsing Tao(13.3)
35~44 岁 Age	67	珠江 Zhujiang(55.2)	生力 San Miguel(14.9)	青岛 Tsing Tao(9.0)	广氏 Guangshi(7.5) 蓝带 Blue Ribbon(7.5)
45~54 岁 Age	44	珠江 Zhujiang(59.1)	广氏 Guangshi(13.6) 生力 San Miguel(13.6)	青岛 Tsing Tao(4.5)	蓝带 Blue Ribbon(2.3) 喜力 Heineken(2.3) 燕京 Yanjing(2.3) 喜乐 Xile(2.3)
55~60 岁 Age	11	珠江 Zhujiang(54.5)	广氏 Guangshi(18.2)	蓝带 Blue Ribbon(9.1) 青岛 Tsing Tao(9.1) 生力 San Miguel(9.1)	

1-4 理想品牌排名/ Ranking of the Ideal Brands

排名 Brand Ranking	品牌 Brands	人数 Number	百分比 Percent
1	珠江 Zhujiang	383	37.0
2	生力 San Miguel	202	19.5
3	青岛 Tsing Tao	106	10.3
4	蓝带 Blue Ribbon	57	5.5
5	广氏 Guangshi	44	4.3
6	百威 Budweiser	30	2.9
7	喜力 Heineken	26	2.5
8	金威 Jinwei	11	1.1

n=1034

1-5 样本、男性各年龄层、女性各年龄层最近三个月有无购买的比例/ Purchasing in the Last Three Months by the Whole Sample, Age and Gender Groups

	人数 Number	买过 yes	没买过 no
样本 Sample	1034	59.4	40.6
男性 Male	499	71.3	28.7
16~24 岁 Age	106	59.4	40.6
25~34 岁 Age	150	73.3	26.7
35~44 岁 Age	127	77.2	22.8
45~54 岁 Age	73	74.0	26.0
55~60 岁 Age	43	72.1	27.9
女性 Female	535	48.2	51.8
16~24 岁 Age	112	30.4	69.6
25~34 岁 Age	158	57.0	43.0
35~44 岁 Age	137	57.7	42.3
45~54 岁 Age	87	49.4	50.6
55~60 岁 Age	41	29.3	70.7

1-6 样本、男性各年龄层、女性各年龄层最近三个月的饮用频率/ Frequencies of Consuming Beer in the Last Three Months by the Whole Sample, Age and Gender Groups

	人数 Number	天天喝 daily	一周 3 次或以上 3 times or over a week	一周 1~2 次 once or twice a week	一个月 2～3 次 2 or 3 times a month	一个月 1 次或以下 once a month or below	没喝过 never
样本 Sample	1032	2.0	8.2	15.2	20.6	14.1	39.7
男性 Male	497	3.4	13.1	22.5	24.3	12.1	24.5
16~24 岁 Age	106	1.9	7.5	17.9	28.3	9.4	34.9
25~34 岁 Age	150	4.7	15.3	22.7	23.3	12.7	21.3
35~44 岁 Age	127	3.1	15.7	26.0	22.0	13.4	19.7
45~54 岁 Age	72	2.8	12.5	18.1	27.8	13.9	25.0
55~60 岁 Age	42	4.8	11.9	31.0	19.0	9.5	23.8
女性 Female	535	0.7	3.7	8.4	17.2	16.1	53.8
16~24 岁 Age	112	0.0	0.9	4.5	10.7	21.4	62.5
25~34 岁 Age	158	0.0	4.4	10.1	23.4	14.6	47.5
35~44 岁 Age	137	1.5	3.6	7.3	19.0	17.5	51.1
45~54 岁 Age	87	1.1	6.9	13.8	14.9	13.8	49.4
55~60 岁 Age	41	2.4	2.4	4.9	9.8	7.3	73.2

1-7 样本、男性各年龄层、女性各年龄层的品牌习惯/ Brand Habit in Consuming Beer by the Whole Sample, Age and Gender Groups

	人数 Number	基本固定饮用一个牌子 used in only one brand	比较固定地饮用两个或三个牌子 used in two or three brands	基本上不太固定牌子 no brand preference
样本 Sample	620	43.4	44.7	11.9
男性 Male	375	44.8	45.3	9.9
16~24 岁 Age	69	37.7	47.8	14.5
25~34 岁 Age	118	36.4	55.9	7.6
35~44 岁 Age	102	44.1	46.1	9.8
45~54 岁 Age	54	63.0	27.8	9.3
55~60 岁 Age	32	62.5	28.1	9.4
女性 Female	245	41.2	43.7	15.1
16~24 岁 Age	42	45.2	33.3	21.4
25~34 岁 Age	83	32.5	51.8	15.7
35~44 岁 Age	65	44.6	43.1	12.3
45~54 岁 Age	44	47.7	40.9	11.4
55~60 岁 Age	11	45.5	36.4	18.2

1-8 选择该类商品的考虑因素/ Ranking of the Considerations in Purchasing

注：本题为多选题，合计百分比超过 100%(Multiple answers）

排名 Ranking	考虑因素 Considerations	人次 Person-time	百分比 Percent
1	口味好 pleasant taste	365	59.0
2	价格适中 reasonable price	267	43.1
3	有名的牌子 famous brand	241	38.9
4	购买方便 easy to buy	131	21.2
5	生产日期 date of producing	90	14.5
6	只是由于习惯 out of habit	68	11.0
7	生产地 place of production	26	4.2
7	广告影响 influence of advertising	26	4.2
8	朋友推荐 introduction of friends	25	4.0
9	包装吸引人 appealing package	13	2.1
10	别人送的 given by other people	11	1.8
11	有优惠条件 with preferential terms	10	1.6
12	单位发的 offered by the working unit	7	1.1
13	售货员介绍 introduced by the shop assistants	4	0.6
13	其它 others	4	0.6

n=619

1-9 样本、男性各年龄层、女性各年龄层最常饮用的包装形式/ Types of Package of the Consumed Beer by the Whole Sample, Age and Gender Groups

	人数 Number	瓶装 bottle	听装 tin	散装扎啤 jar without package	其它 others
样本 Sample	621	88.4	8.5	1.6	1.4
男性 Male	374	89.8	8.0	1.3	0.8
16~24 岁 Age	69	81.2	11.6	5.8	1.4
25~34 岁 Age	118	88.1	11.0	0.8	0.0
35~44 岁 Age	101	96.0	3.0	0.0	1.0
45~54 岁 Age	54	94.4	5.6	0.0	0.0
55~60 岁 Age	32	87.5	9.4	0.0	3.1
女性 Female	247	86.2	9.3	2.0	2.4
16~24 岁 Age	42	81.0	11.9	2.4	4.8
25~34 岁 Age	83	84.3	12.0	2.4	1.2
35~44 岁 Age	67	92.5	6.0	0.0	1.5
45~54 岁 Age	44	86.4	9.1	2.3	2.3
55~60 岁 Age	11	81.8	0.0	9.1	9.1

1-10 样本、男性各年龄层、女性各年龄层最常饮用的口味/ The Taste of the Consumed Beer by the Whole Sample, Age and Gender Groups

	人数 Number	清爽型 fresh and cool	醇厚型 mellow	其它 others
样本 Sample	619	70.8	26.0	3.2
男性 Male	373	68.4	29.5	2.1
16~24 岁 Age	69	79.7	17.4	2.9
25~34 岁 Age	118	67.8	29.7	2.5
35~44 岁 Age	101	62.4	34.7	3.0
45~54 岁 Age	53	75.5	24.5	0.0
55~60 岁 Age	32	53.1	46.9	0.0
女性 Female	246	74.4	20.7	4.9
16~24 岁 Age	42	71.4	21.4	7.1
25~34 岁 Age	83	77.1	18.1	4.8
35~44 岁 Age	66	75.8	19.7	4.5
45~54 岁 Age	44	70.5	25.0	4.5
55~60 岁 Age	11	72.7	27.3	0.0

1-11 样本、男性各年龄层、女性各年龄层最常饮用的场合/ Settings of Consumption by the Whole Sample, Age and Gender Groups

注：本题为多选题，合计百分比超过 100%(Multiple answers)

	人数 Number	口渴时 when thirsty	平时吃饭喝 at dinner	宴席、聚会喝 at banquet	去酒吧喝 at bar	外出/旅游时 outing/traveling	其它 others
样本 Sample	619	10.8	34.7	63.2	18.1	2.4	0.8
男性 Male	374	11.2	34.5	63.9	19.0	2.9	0.5
16~24 岁 Age	69	5.8	23.2	73.9	27.5	7.2	1.4
25~34 岁 Age	118	16.1	28.8	64.4	29.7	0.8	0.8
35~44 岁 Age	102	8.8	41.2	58.8	13.7	2.9	0.0
45~54 岁 Age	53	9.4	37.7	67.9	1.9	3.8	0.0
55~60 岁 Age	32	15.6	53.1	50.0	6.3	0.0	0.0
女性 Female	245	10.2	35.1	62.0	16.7	1.6	1.2
16~24 岁 Age	42	7.1	23.8	69.0	31.0	2.4	0.0
25~34 岁 Age	83	13.3	33.7	63.9	19.3	2.4	0.0
35~44 岁 Age	65	7.7	36.9	67.7	12.3	1.5	0.0
45~54 岁 Age	44	9.1	45.5	47.7	6.8	0.0	6.8
55~60 岁 Age	11	18.2	36.4	45.5	9.1	0.0	0.0

1-12 重度消费者人口分布/ Demographics of the Heavy Consumers

	人数 Number	16-24 岁 Age	25-34 岁 Age	35-44 岁 Age	45-54 岁 Age	55-60 岁 Age
样本 Sample	263	13.3	33.1	28.1	16.3	9.1
男性 Male	194	14.9	33.0	29.4	12.4	10.3
天天喝 daily	17	11.8	41.2	23.5	11.8	11.8
一周 3 次或以上 3 times or over a week	65	12.3	35.4	30.8	13.8	7.7
一周 1~2 次 once or twice a week	112	17.0	30.4	29.5	11.6	11.6
女性 Female	69	8.7	33.3	24.6	27.5	5.8
天天喝 daily	4	0.0	0.0	50.0	25.0	25.0
一周 3 次或以上 3 times or over a week	20	5.0	35.0	25.0	30.0	5.0
一周 1~2 次 once or twice a week	45	11.1	35.6	22.2	26.7	4.4

1-13 不同消费者层的常用品牌/ The Most Frequently Used Brands by Market Segments

1-13-1 时尚流行指标/ Fads Popular Index

	人数 Number	第一品牌及百分比 1st/percent	第二品牌及百分比 2nd/percent	第三品牌及百分比 3rd/percent	第四品牌及百分比 4th/percent
样本 Sample	616	**珠江 Zhujiang(51.9)**	**生力 San Miguel(17.7)**	**青岛 Tsing Tao(8.8)**	**广氏 Guangshi(7.5)**
平实生活指向 simple living orientation	318	珠江 Zhujiang(56.3)	生力 San Miguel(16.0)	青岛 Tsing Tao(10.7)	广氏 Guangshi(8.2)
时尚流行指向 fashion orientation	298	珠江 Zhujiang(47.3)	生力 San Miguel(19.5)	青岛 Tsing Tao(6.7) 广氏 Guangshi(6.7)	蓝带 Blue Ribbon(6.4)

1-13-2 广告态度指标/ Advertising attitude Index

	人数 Number	第一品牌及百分比 1st/percent	第二品牌及百分比 2nd/percent	第三品牌及百分比 3rd/percent	第四品牌及百分比 4th/percent
样本 Sample	613	**珠江 Zhujiang(52.0)**	**生力 San Miguel(17.8)**	**青岛 Tsing Tao(8.8)**	**广氏 Guangshi(7.3)**
广告淡漠指向 indifferent orientation	201	珠江 Zhujiang(55.7)	生力 San Miguel(16.9)	青岛 Tsing Tao(10.0)	广氏 Guangshi(5.0) 蓝带 Blue Ribbon(5.0)
中间层 medium	358	珠江 Zhujiang(51.1)	生力 San Miguel(17.9)	广氏 Guangshi(8.9)	青岛 Tsing Tao(8.4)
信赖广告指向 loyal orientation	54	珠江 Zhujiang(44.4)	生力 San Miguel(20.4)	百威 Budweiser(9.3)	青岛 Tsing Tao(7.4)

1-13-3 饮食健康指标/ Foods & Drink Quality Index

	人数 Number	第一品牌及百分比 1st/percent	第二品牌及百分比 2nd/percent	第三品牌及百分比 3rd/percent	第四品牌及百分比 4th/percent
样本 Sample	**619**	**珠江 Zhujiang(51.5)**	**生力 San Miguel(17.8)**	**青岛 Tsing Tao(9.0)**	**广氏 Guangshi(7.4)**
饮食"温饱"指向 "basic" orientation	191	珠江 Zhujiang(55.0)	生力 San Miguel(15.2)	青岛 Tsing Tao(11.0)	广氏 Guangshi(9.9)
中间层 medium	327	珠江 Zhujiang(52.3)	生力 San Miguel(17.1)	青岛 Tsing Tao(8.0)	广氏 Guangshi(6.7)
健康营养指向 health & nutrition orientation	101	珠江 Zhujiang(42.6)	生力 San Miguel(24.8)	青岛 Tsing Tao(8.9)	百威 Budweiser(5.0) 广氏 Guangshi(5.0) 蓝带 Blue Ribbon(5.0)

1-14 重度消费者的消费者层构成/ The Composition of the Heavy Consumers

1-14-1 时尚流行指标/ Fads Popular Index

	人数 Number	平实生活指向 simple living orientation	时尚流行指向 fashion orientation
样本 Sample	**262**	**51.5**	**48.5**
天天喝 daily	21	52.4	47.6
一周 3 次或以上 3 times or over a week	85	54.1	45.9
一周 1~2 次 once or twice a week	156	50.0	50.0

1-14-2 广告态度指标/ Advertising Attitude Index

	人数 Number	广告淡漠指向 indifferent orientation	中间层 medium	信赖广告指向 loyal orientation
样本 Sample	**262**	**35.5**	**56.1**	**8.4**
天天喝 daily	21	38.1	47.6	14.3
一周 3 次或以上 3 times or over a week	85	34.1	52.9	12.9
一周 1~2 次 once or twice a week	156	35.9	59.0	5.1

1-14-3 饮食健康指标/ Foods & Drink Quality Index

	人数 Number	饮食"温饱"指向 "basic" orientation	中间层 medium	健康营养指向 health & nutrition orientation
样本 Sample	**262**	**34.0**	**50.4**	**15.6**
天天喝 daily	21	38.1	38.1	23.8
一周 3 次或以上 3 times or over a week	84	35.7	50.0	14.3
一周 1~2 次 once or twice a week	157	32.5	52.2	15.3

● 重庆 / Chongqing

1-1 最近三个月饮用频率的比例/ Proportion of the Sample Consuming Beer in the Last Three Months

	人数 Number	百分比 Percent
天天喝 daily	52	8.3
一周 3 次或以上 3 times or over per week	73	11.7
一周 1~2 次 once or twice a week	98	15.7
一个月 2~3 次 2 or 3 times a month	108	17.3
一个月 1 次或以下 once a month or below	75	12.0
没喝过 never	218	34.9

n=624

1-2 最常用品牌排名/ Ranking of the Most Frequently Used Brands

排名 Brand Ranking	品牌 Brands	人数 Number	百分比 Percent
1	山城 Shancheng	312	76.8
2	重庆 Chongqing	61	15.0
3	蓝剑 Lanjian	12	3.0
4	黄河 Huanghe	10	2.5
5	蓝带 Blue Ribbon	2	0.5

n=406

1-3 样本、男性各年龄层、女性各年龄层的常用品牌/ The Most Frequently Used Brands by the Whole Sample, Age and Gender Groups

	人数 Number	第一品牌及百分比 1st/ percent	第二品牌及百分比 2nd/ percent	第三品牌及百分比 3rd/ percent	第四品牌及百分比 4th/ percent
样本 Sample	406	**山城 Shancheng(76.8)**	**重庆 Chongqing(15.0)**	**蓝剑 Lanjian(3.0)**	**黄河 Huanghe(2.5)**
男性 Male	250	**山城 Shancheng(76.8)**	**重庆 Chongqing(15.6)**	**黄河 Huanghe(2.4)** **蓝剑 Lanjian(2.4)**	**行吟阁 Xingyinge(0.4)** **长城(0.4)** **宝鸡 Baoji(0.4)** **百威 Budweiser(0.4)** **喜力 Heineken(0.4)** **嘉士伯 Carlsberg(0.4)** **贝克 Beck's(0.4)**
16~24 岁 Age	44	山城 Shancheng(68.2)	重庆 Chongqing(13.6)	黄河 Huanghe(4.5) 蓝剑 Lanjian(4.5)	百威 Budweiser(2.3) 贝克 Beck's(2.3) 嘉士伯 Carlsberg(2.3) 喜力 Heineken(2.3)
25~34 岁 Age	80	山城 Shancheng(77.5)	重庆 Chongqing(12.5)	黄河 Huanghe(3.8) 蓝剑 Lanjian(3.8)	行吟阁 Xingyinge(1.3) 宝鸡 Baoji(1.3)
35~44 岁 Age	59	山城 Shancheng(78.0)	重庆 Chongqing(22.0)		
45~54 岁 Age	47	山城 Shancheng(85.1)	重庆 Chongqing(14.9)		
55~60 岁 Age	20	山城 Shancheng(70.0)	重庆 Chongqing(15.0)	黄河 Huanghe(5.0) 蓝剑 Lanjian(5.0) 长城(5.0)	
女性 Female	156	**山城 Shancheng(76.9)**	**重庆 Chongqing(14.1)**	**蓝剑 Lanjian(3.8)**	**黄河 Huanghe(2.6)**
16~24 岁 Age	29	山城 Shancheng(69.0)	蓝剑 Lanjian(10.3)	蓝带 Blue Ribbon(6.9) 重庆 Chongqing(6.9)	黄河 Huanghe(3.4)
25~34 岁 Age	53	山城 Shancheng(79.2)	重庆 Chongqing(15.1)	蓝剑 Lanjian(5.7)	
35~44 岁 Age	39	山城 Shancheng(82.1)	重庆 Chongqing(12.8)	黄河 Huanghe(5.1)	
45~54 岁 Age	28	山城 Shancheng(67.9)	重庆 Chongqing(25.0)	黄河 Huanghe(3.6) 云湖 Yunhu(3.6)	
55~60 岁 Age	7	山城 Shancheng(100.0)			

1-4 理想品牌排名/ Ranking of the Ideal Brands

排名 Brand Ranking	品牌 Brands	人数 Number	百分比 Percent
1	山城 Shancheng	428	68.6
2	重庆 Chongqing	88	14.1
3	蓝剑 Lanjian	26	4.2
4	青岛 Tsing Tao	17	2.7
5	蓝带 Blue Ribbon	15	2.4
6	黄河 Huanghe	13	2.1

n=624

1-5 样本、男性各年龄层、女性各年龄层最近三个月有无购买的比例/ Purchasing in the Last Three Months by the Whole Sample, Age and Gender Groups

	人数 Number	买过 yes	没买过 no
样本 Sample	622	69.0	31.0
男性 Male	312	79.5	20.5
16~24 岁 Age	63	68.3	31.7
25~34 岁 Age	93	86.0	14.0
35~44 岁 Age	75	78.7	21.3
45~54 岁 Age	54	85.2	14.8
55~60 岁 Age	27	74.1	25.9
女性 Female	310	58.4	41.6
16~24 岁 Age	64	45.3	54.7
25~34 岁 Age	90	71.1	28.9
35~44 岁 Age	73	57.5	42.5
45~54 岁 Age	60	60.0	40.0
55~60 岁 Age	23	43.5	56.5

1-6 样本、男性各年龄层、女性各年龄层最近三个月的饮用频率/ Frequencies of Consuming Beer in the Last Three Months by the Whole Sample, Age and Gender Groups

	人数 Number	天天喝 daily	一周 3 次或以上 3 times or over a week	一周 1~2 次 once or twice a week	一个月 2～3 次 2 or 3 times a month	一个月 1 次或以下 once a month or below	没喝过 never
样本 Sample	624	8.3	11.7	15.7	17.3	12.0	34.9
男性 Male	314	14.3	17.2	19.4	20.4	8.3	20.4
16~24 岁 Age	64	4.7	9.4	21.9	23.4	9.4	31.3
25~34 岁 Age	93	18.3	22.6	24.7	18.3	2.2	14.0
35~44 岁 Age	75	16.0	22.7	12.0	20.0	8.0	21.3
45~54 岁 Age	54	18.5	11.1	22.2	20.4	14.8	13.0
55~60 岁 Age	28	10.7	14.3	10.7	21.4	14.3	28.6
女性 Female	310	2.3	6.1	11.9	14.2	15.8	49.7
16~24 岁 Age	64	1.6	4.7	6.3	9.4	23.4	54.7
25~34 岁 Age	90	3.3	10.0	13.3	16.7	15.6	41.1
35~44 岁 Age	73	0.0	5.5	19.2	13.7	15.1	46.6
45~54 岁 Age	60	0.0	5.0	8.3	18.3	15.0	53.3
55~60 岁 Age	23	13.0	0.0	8.7	8.7	0.0	69.6

1-7 样本、男性各年龄层、女性各年龄层的品牌习惯/ Brand Habit in Consuming Beer by the Whole Sample, Age and Gender Groups

	人数 Number	基本固定饮用一个牌子 used in only one brand	比较固定地饮用两个或三个牌子 used in two or three brands	基本上不太固定牌子 no brand preference
样本 Sample	404	68.3	24.5	7.2
男性 Male	248	69.4	24.6	6.0
16~24 岁 Age	43	62.8	32.6	4.7
25~34 岁 Age	80	71.3	23.8	5.0
35~44 岁 Age	59	72.9	23.7	3.4
45~54 岁 Age	46	71.7	17.4	10.9
55~60 岁 Age	20	60.0	30.0	10.0
女性 Female	156	66.7	24.4	9.0
16~24 岁 Age	29	51.7	24.1	24.1
25~34 岁 Age	53	73.6	20.8	5.7
35~44 岁 Age	39	61.5	30.8	7.7
45~54 岁 Age	28	75.0	21.4	3.6
55~60 岁 Age	7	71.4	28.6	0.0

1-8 选择该类商品的考虑因素/ Ranking of the Considerations in Purchasing

排名 Ranking	考虑因素 Considerations	人次 Person-time	百分比 Percent
1	口味好 pleasant taste	229	56.8
2	价格适中 reasonable price	158	39.2
3	购买方便 easy to buy	102	25.3
4	有名的牌子 famous brand	101	25.1
5	只是由于习惯 out of habit	72	17.9
6	生产日期 date of producing	63	15.6
7	生产地 place of production	48	11.9
8	广告影响 influence of advertising	11	2.7
9	朋友推荐 introduction of friends	8	2.0
10	售货员介绍 introduced by the shop assistants	4	1.0
11	别人送的 given by other people	3	0.7
12	有优惠条件 with preferential terms	2	0.5
12	包装吸引人 appealing package	2	0.5
12	其它 others	2	0.5

n=403

1-9 样本、男性各年龄层、女性各年龄层最常饮用的包装形式/ Types of Package of the Consumed Beer by the Whole Sample, Age and Gender Groups

	人数 Number	瓶装 bottle	听装 tin	散装扎啤 jar without package	其它 others
样本 Sample	404	98.0	1.2	0.7	0.0
男性 Male	248	99.2	0.4	0.4	0.0
16~24 岁 Age	43	97.7	2.3	0.0	0.0
25~34 岁 Age	80	98.8	0.0	1.3	0.0
35~44 岁 Age	59	100.0	0.0	0.0	0.0
45~54 岁 Age	46	100.0	0.0	0.0	0.0
55~60 岁 Age	20	100.0	0.0	0.0	0.0
女性 Female	156	96.2	2.6	1.3	0.0
16~24 岁 Age	29	86.2	10.3	3.4	0.0
25~34 岁 Age	53	96.2	1.9	1.9	0.0
35~44 岁 Age	39	100.0	0.0	0.0	0.0
45~54 岁 Age	28	100.0	0.0	0.0	0.0
55~60 岁 Age	7	100.0	0.0	0.0	0.0

1-10 样本、男性各年龄层、女性各年龄层最常饮用的口味/ The Taste of the Consumed Beer by the Whole Sample, Age and Gender Groups

	人数 Number	清爽型 fresh and cool	醇厚型 mellow	其它 others
样本 Sample	401	78.1	20.7	1.2
男性 Male	246	74.4	24.0	1.6
16~24 岁 Age	43	67.4	25.6	7.0
25~34 岁 Age	80	70.0	28.8	1.3
35~44 岁 Age	58	82.8	17.2	0.0
45~54 岁 Age	45	80.0	20.0	0.0
55~60 岁 Age	20	70.0	30.0	0.0
女性 Female	155	83.9	15.5	0.6
16~24 岁 Age	29	89.7	10.3	0.0
25~34 岁 Age	52	82.7	17.3	0.0
35~44 岁 Age	39	82.1	17.9	0.0
45~54 岁 Age	28	82.1	14.3	3.6
55~60 岁 Age	7	85.7	14.3	0.0

1-11 样本、男性各年龄层、女性各年龄层最常饮用的场合/ Settings of Consumption by the Whole Sample, Age and Gender Groups

注：本题为多选题，合计百分比超过 100%(Multiple answers）

	人数 Number	口渴时 when thirsty	平时吃饭喝 at dinner	宴席、聚会喝 at banquet	去酒吧喝 at bar	外出/旅游时 outing/ traveling	其它 others
样本 Sample	404	4.7	53.7	57.4	5.4	3.2	0.7
男性 Male	248	6.5	56.5	54.0	4.8	3.6	1.2
16~24 岁 Age	43	9.3	34.9	62.8	16.3	7.0	0.0
25~34 岁 Age	80	6.3	56.3	56.3	6.3	3.8	1.3
35~44 岁 Age	59	3.4	66.1	49.2	0.0	5.1	1.7
45~54 岁 Age	47	6.4	61.7	43.9	0.0	0.0	2.1
55~60 岁 Age	19	10.5	63.2	52.6	0.0	0.0	0.0
女性 Female	156	1.9	49.4	62.8	6.4	2.6	0.0
16~24 岁 Age	29	0.0	37.9	58.6	20.7	3.4	0.0
25~34 岁 Age	53	3.8	52.8	60.4	7.5	3.8	0.0
35~44 岁 Age	39	2.6	46.2	66.7	0.0	0.0	0.0
45~54 岁 Age	28	0.0	53.6	67.9	0.0	3.6	0.0
55~60 岁 Age	7	0.0	71.4	57.1	0.0	0.0	0.0

1-12 重度消费者人口分布/ Demographics of the Heavy Consumers

	人数 Number	16-24 岁 Age	25-34 岁 Age	35-44 岁 Age	45-54 岁 Age	55-60 岁 Age
样本 Sample	223	13.9	38.1	25.1	16.1	6.7
男性 Male	160	14.4	38.1	23.8	17.5	6.3
天天喝 daily	45	6.7	37.8	26.7	22.2	6.7
一周 3 次或以上 3 times or over a week	54	11.1	38.9	31.5	11.1	7.4
一周 1~2 次 once or twice a week	61	23.0	37.7	14.8	19.7	4.9
女性 Female	63	12.7	38.1	28.6	12.7	7.9
天天喝 daily	7	14.3	42.9	0.0	0.0	42.9
一周 3 次或以上 3 times or over a week	19	15.8	47.4	21.1	15.8	0.0
一周 1~2 次 once or twice a week	37	10.8	32.4	37.8	13.5	5.4

1-13 不同消费者层的常用品牌/ The Most Frequently Used Brands by Market Segments

1-13-1 时尚流行指标/ Fads Popular Index

	人数 Number	第一品牌及百分比 1st/percent	第二品牌及百分比 2nd/percent	第三品牌及百分比 3rd/percent	第四品牌及百分比 4th/percent
样本 Sample	401	**山城 Shancheng(77.1)**	**重庆 Chongqing(15.2)**	**蓝剑 Lanjian(2.7)**	**黄河 Huanghe(2.5)**
平实生活指向 simple living orientation	236	山城 Shancheng(78.8)	重庆 Chongqing(14.8)	黄河 Huanghe(3.0)	蓝剑 Lanjian(1.7)
时尚流行指向 fashion orientation	165	山城 Shancheng(74.5)	重庆 Chongqing(15.8)	蓝剑 Lanjian(4.2)	黄河 Huanghe(1.8)

1-13-2 广告态度指标/ Advertising Attitude Index

	人数 Number	第一品牌及百分比 1st/percent	第二品牌及百分比 2nd/percent	第三品牌及百分比 3rd/percent	第四品牌及百分比 4th/percent
样本 Sample	403	**山城 Shancheng(77.2)**	**重庆 Chongqing(14.9)**	**蓝剑 Lanjian(2.7)**	**黄河 Huanghe(2.5)**
广告淡漠指向 indifferent orientation	114	山城 Shancheng(82.5)	重庆 Chongqing(11.4)	黄河 Huanghe(1.8)	百威 Budweiser(0.9) 蓝剑 Lanjian(0.9) 宝鸡 Baoji(0.9) 长城 Great Wall(0.9)
中间层 medium	233	山城 Shancheng(74.2)	重庆 Chongqing(17.6)	蓝剑 Lanjian(3.9)	黄河 Huanghe(2.1)
信赖广告指向 loyal orientation	56	山城 Shancheng(78.6)	重庆 Chongqing(10.7)	黄河 Huanghe(5.4)	嘉士伯 Carlsberg(1.8) 蓝剑 Lanjian(1.8) 云湖 Yunhu(1.8)

1-13-3 饮食健康指标/ Foods & Drink Quality Index

	人数 Number	第一品牌及百分比 1st/percent	第二品牌及百分比 2nd/percent	第三品牌及百分比 3rd/percent	第四品牌及百分比 4th/percent
样本 Sample	402	**山城 Shancheng(77.1)**	**重庆 Chongqing(14.9)**	**蓝剑 Lanjian(2.7)**	**黄河 Huanghe(2.5)**
饮食"温饱"指向 "basic" orientation	154	山城 Shancheng(72.7)	重庆 Chongqing(15.6)	黄河 Huanghe(4.5)	蓝剑 Lanjian(1.9)
中间层 medium	168	山城 Shancheng(79.8)	重庆 Chongqing(13.1)	蓝剑 Lanjian(3.6)	黄河 Huanghe(1.8)
健康营养指向 health & nutrition orientation	80	山城 Shancheng(80.0)	重庆 Chongqing(17.5)	蓝剑 Lanjian(2.5)	

1-14 重度消费者的消费者层构成/ The Composition of the Heavy Consumers

1-14-1 时尚流行指标/ Fads Popular Index

	人数 Number	平实生活指向 simple living orientation	时尚流行指向 fashion orientation
样本 Sample	220	62.3	37.7
天天喝 daily	50	68.0	32.0
一周 3 次或以上 3 times or over a week	73	61.6	38.4
一周 1~2 次 once or twice a week	97	59.8	40.2

1-14-2 广告态度指标/ Advertising Attitude Index

	人数 Number	广告淡漠指向 indifferent orientation	中间层 medium	信赖广告指向 loyal orientation
样本 Sample	221	31.7	55.2	13.1
天天喝 daily	51	33.3	49.0	17.6
一周 3 次或以上 3 times or over a week	72	30.6	56.9	12.5
一周 1~2 次 once or twice a week	98	31.6	57.1	11.2

1-14-3 饮食健康指标/ Foods & Drink Quality Index

	人数 Number	饮食"温饱"指向 "basic" orientation	中间层 medium	健康营养指向 health & nutrition orientation
样本 Sample	221	39.8	42.5	17.6
天天喝 daily	50	36.0	46.0	18.0
一周 3 次或以上 3 times or over a week	73	38.4	45.2	16.4
一周 1~2 次 once or twice a week	98	42.9	38.8	18.4

● 武汉 / Wuhan

1-1 最近三个月饮用频率的比例/ Proportion of the Sample Consuming Beer in the Last Three Months

	人数 Number	百分比 Percent
天天喝 daily	36	5.6
一周 3 次或以上 3 times or over a week	62	9.7
一周 1~2 次 once or twice a week	86	13.4
一个月 2~3 次 2 or 3 times a month	81	12.6
一个月 1 次或以下 once a month or below	74	11.5
没喝过 never	302	47.1

n=641

1-2 最常用品牌排名/ Ranking of the Most Frequently Used Brands

排名 Brand Ranking	品牌 Brands	人数 Number	百分比 Percent
1	行吟阁 Xingyinge	272	80.2
2	金龙泉 Kinglong	26	7.7
3	百威 Budweiser	21	6.2
4	蓝带 Blue Ribbon	5	1.5
5	青岛 Tsing Tao	4	1.2
6	喜力 Heineken	2	0.6
6	无花果 Wuhuaguo	2	0.6

n=339

1-3 样本、男性各年龄层、女性各年龄层的常用品牌/ The Most Frequently Used Brands by the Whole Sample, Age and Gender Groups

	人数 Number	第一品牌及百分比 1st/ percent	第二品牌及百分比 2nd/ percent	第三品牌及百分比 3rd/ percent
样本 Sample	339	**行吟阁 Xingyinge(80.2)**	**金龙泉 Kinglong(7.7)**	**百威 Budweiser(6.2)**
男性 Male	236	**行吟阁 Xingyinge(80.5)**	**金龙泉 Kinglong(8.5)**	**百威 Budweiser(4.7)**
16~24 岁 Age	49	行吟阁 Xingyinge(77.6)	金龙泉 Kinglong(10.2)	蓝带 Blue Ribbon(4.1)
25~34 岁 Age	73	行吟阁 Xingyinge(82.2)	金龙泉 Kinglong(8.2)	百威 Budweiser(4.1)
35~44 岁 Age	67	行吟阁 Xingyinge(86.6)	百威 Budweiser(6.0) 金龙泉 Kinglong(6.0)	无花果 Wuhuaguo(1.5)
45~54 岁 Age	37	行吟阁 Xingyinge(70.3)	百威 Budweiser(8.1) 金龙泉 Kinglong(8.1)	蓝带 Blue Ribbon(5.4)
55~60 岁 Age	10	行吟阁 Xingyinge(80.0)	金龙泉 Kinglong(20.0)	
女性 Female	103	**行吟阁 Xingyinge(79.6)**	**百威 Budweiser(9.7)**	**金龙泉 Kinglong(5.8)**
16~24 岁 Age	16	行吟阁 Xingyinge(68.8)	百威 Budweiser(25.0)	金龙泉 Kinglong(6.3)
25~34 岁 Age	39	行吟阁 Xingyinge(84.6)	百威 Budweiser(7.7)	金龙泉 Kinglong(2.6) 青岛 Tsing Tao(2.6) 生力 San Miguel(2.6)
35~44 岁 Age	23	行吟阁 Xingyinge(78.3)	百威 Budweiser(8.7) 金龙泉 Kinglong(8.7)	喜力 Heineken(4.3)
45~54 岁 Age	21	行吟阁 Xingyinge(76.2)	金龙泉 Kinglong(9.5)	百威 Budweiser(4.8) 蓝带 Blue Ribbon(4.8) 沱牌 Tuopai(4.8)
55~60 岁 Age	4	行吟阁 Xingyinge(100.0)		

1-4 理想品牌排名/ Ranking of the Ideal Brands

排名 Brand Ranking	品牌 Brands	人数 Number	百分比 Percent
1	行吟阁 Xingyinge	322	50.2
2	百威 Budweiser	95	14.8
3	金龙泉 Kinglong	34	5.3
4	青岛 Tsing Tao	29	4.5
5	蓝带 Blue Ribbon	18	2.8
6	贝克 Beck's	5	0.8
7	喜力 Heineken	4	0.6
8	嘉士伯 Carlsberg	2	0.3
8	东德 Dongde	2	0.3

n=642

1-5 样本、男性各年龄层、女性各年龄层最近三个月有无购买的比例/ Purchasing in the Last Three Months by the Whole Sample, Age and Gender Groups

	人数 Number	买过 yes	没买过 no
样本 Sample	641	57.7	42.3
男性 Male	311	72.3	27.7
16~24 岁 Age	65	67.7	32.3
25~34 岁 Age	89	82.0	18.0
35~44 岁 Age	80	81.3	18.8
45~54 岁 Age	52	67.3	32.7
55~60 岁 Age	25	32.0	68.0
女性 Female	330	43.9	56.1
16~24 岁 Age	69	29.0	71.0
25~34 岁 Age	96	53.1	46.9
35~44 岁 Age	77	48.1	51.9
45~54 岁 Age	62	48.4	51.6
55~60 岁 Age	26	26.9	73.1

1-6 样本、男性各年龄层、女性各年龄层最近三个月的饮用频率/ Frequencies of Consuming Beer in the Last Three Months by the Whole Sample, Age and Gender Groups

	人数 Number	天天喝 daily	一周 3 次或以上 3 times or over a week	一周 1~2 次 once or twice a week	一个月 2～3 次 2 or 3 times a month	一个月 1 次或以下 once a month or below	没喝过 never
样本 Sample	641	5.6	9.7	13.4	12.6	11.5	47.1
男性 Male	311	9.6	16.7	21.2	17.7	10.6	24.1
16~24 岁 Age	65	4.6	7.7	23.1	26.2	13.8	24.6
25~34 岁 Age	89	11.2	23.6	23.6	15.7	7.9	18.0
35~44 岁 Age	80	17.5	21.3	21.3	15.0	8.8	16.3
45~54 岁 Age	52	5.8	15.4	19.2	13.5	17.3	28.8
55~60 岁 Age	25	0.0	4.0	12.0	20.0	4.0	60.0
女性 Female	330	1.8	3.0	6.1	7.9	12.4	68.8
16~24 岁 Age	69	0.0	0.0	4.3	2.9	15.9	76.8
25~34 岁 Age	95	1.1	3.2	9.5	12.6	14.7	58.9
35~44 岁 Age	78	2.6	3.8	5.1	5.1	12.8	70.5
45~54 岁 Age	62	4.8	6.5	3.2	11.3	8.1	66.1
55~60 岁 Age	26	0.0	0.0	7.7	3.8	3.8	84.6

1-7 样本、男性各年龄层、女性各年龄层的品牌习惯/ Brand Habit in Consuming Beer by the Whole Sample, Age and Gender Groups

	人数 Number	基本固定饮用一个牌子 used in only one brand	比较固定地饮用两个或三个牌子 used in two or three brands	基本上不太固定牌子 no brand preference
样本 Sample	339	66.7	23.3	10.0
男性 Male	236	67.8	22.5	9.7
16~24 岁 Age	49	63.3	20.4	16.3
25~34 岁 Age	73	69.9	23.3	6.8
35~44 岁 Age	67	74.6	20.9	4.5
45~54 岁 Age	37	59.5	27.0	13.5
55~60 岁 Age	10	60.0	20.0	20.0
女性 Female	103	64.1	25.2	10.7
16~24 岁 Age	16	43.8	43.8	12.5
25~34 岁 Age	39	64.1	20.5	15.4
35~44 岁 Age	23	65.2	26.1	8.7
45~54 岁 Age	21	76.2	19.0	4.8
55~60 岁 Age	4	75.0	25.0	0.0

1-8 选择该类商品的考虑因素/ Ranking of the Considerations in Purchasing

注：本题为多选题，合计百分比超过 100%(Multiple answers）

排名 Ranking	考虑因素 Considerations	人次 Person-time	百分比 Percent
1	口味好 pleasant taste	175	51.8
2	价格适中 reasonable price	158	46.7
3	有名的牌子 famous brand	99	29.3
4	购买方便 easy to buy	92	27.2
5	生产日期 date of producing	70	20.7
6	只是由于习惯 out of habit	64	18.9
7	生产地 place of production	46	13.6
8	广告影响 influence of advertising	11	3.3
8	朋友推荐 introduction of friends	11	3.3
9	有优惠条件 with preferential terms	9	2.7
10	单位发的 offered by the working unit	5	1.5
10	别人送的 given by other people	5	1.5
10	其它 others	5	1.5
11	售货员介绍 introduced by the shop assistants	2	0.6
12	包装吸引人 appealing package	1	0.3

n=338

1-9 样本、男性各年龄层、女性各年龄层最常饮用的包装形式/ Types of Package of the Consumed Beer by the Whole Sample, Age and Gender Groups

	人数 Number	瓶装 bottle	听装 tin	散装扎啤 jar without package	其它 others
样本 Sample	339	93.5	6.2	0.0	0.3
男性 Male	236	95.3	4.7	0.0	0.0
16~24 岁 Age	49	95.9	4.1	0.0	0.0
25~34 岁 Age	73	97.3	2.7	0.0	0.0
35~44 岁 Age	67	97.0	3.0	0.0	0.0
45~54 岁 Age	37	86.5	13.5	0.0	0.0
55~60 岁 Age	10	100.0	0.0	0.0	0.0
女性 Female	103	89.3	9.7	0.0	1.0
16~24 岁 Age	16	81.3	18.8	0.0	0.0
25~34 岁 Age	39	94.9	5.1	0.0	0.0
35~44 岁 Age	23	95.7	4.3	0.0	0.0
45~54 岁 Age	21	76.2	19.0	0.0	4.8
55~60 岁 Age	4	100.0	0.0	0.0	0.0

1-10 样本、男性各年龄层、女性各年龄层最常饮用的口味/ The Taste of the Consumed Beer by the Whole Sample, Age and Gender Groups

	人数 Number	清爽型 fresh and cool	醇厚型 mellow	其它 others
样本 Sample	339	91.2	7.4	1.5
男性 Male	236	89.4	8.9	1.7
16~24 岁 Age	49	89.8	10.2	0.0
25~34 岁 Age	73	86.3	9.6	4.1
35~44 岁 Age	67	94.0	6.0	0.0
45~54 岁 Age	37	89.2	10.8	0.0
55~60 岁 Age	10	80.0	10.0	10.0
女性 Female	103	95.1	3.9	1.0
16~24 岁 Age	16	100.0	0.0	0.0
25~34 岁 Age	39	94.9	5.1	0.0
35~44 岁 Age	23	95.7	4.3	0.0
45~54 岁 Age	21	90.5	4.8	4.8
55~60 岁 Age	4	100.0	0.0	0.0

1-11 样本、男性各年龄层、女性各年龄层最常饮用的场合/ Settings of Consumption by the Whole Sample, Age and Gender Groups

注：本题为多选题，合计百分比超过 100%(Multiple answers)

	人数 Number	口渴时 when thirsty	平时吃饭喝 at dinner	宴席、聚会喝 at banquet	去酒吧喝 at bar	外出/旅游时 outing/ travelling	其它 others
样本 Sample	339	5.3	61.1	56.9	5.9	2.1	1.8
男性 Male	236	7.6	62.7	55.1	5.5	2.1	2.1
16~24 岁 Age	49	2.0	44.9	69.4	10.2	0.0	4.1
25~34 岁 Age	73	8.2	64.4	56.2	6.8	5.5	1.4
35~44 岁 Age	67	7.5	79.1	43.3	0.0	1.5	1.5
45~54 岁 Age	37	13.5	54.1	56.8	8.1	0.0	2.7
55~60 岁 Age	10	10.0	60.0	50.0	0.0	0.0	0.0
女性 Female	103	0.0	57.3	61.2	6.8	1.9	1.0
16~24 岁 Age	16	0.0	43.8	62.5	18.8	0.0	0.0
25~34 岁 Age	39	0.0	48.7	71.8	10.3	2.6	2.6
35~44 岁 Age	23	0.0	73.9	47.8	0.0	0.0	0.0
45~54 岁 Age	21	0.0	61.9	61.9	0.0	4.8	0.0
55~60 岁 Age	4	0.0	75.0	25.0	0.0	0.0	0.0

1-12 重度消费者人口分布/ Demographics of the Heavy Consumers

	人数 Number	16-24 岁 Age	25-34 岁 Age	35-44 岁 Age	45-54 岁 Age	55-60 岁 Age
样本 Sample	184	14.1	35.3	31.0	16.3	3.3
男性 Male	148	15.5	35.1	32.4	14.2	2.7
天天喝 daily	30	10.0	33.3	46.7	10.0	0.0
一周 3 次或以上 3 times or over a week	52	9.6	40.4	32.7	15.4	1.9
一周 1~2 次 once or twice a week	66	22.7	31.8	25.8	15.2	4.5
女性 Female	36	8.3	36.1	25.0	25.0	5.6
天天喝 daily	6	0.0	16.7	33.3	50.0	0.0
一周 3 次或以上 3 times or over a week	10	0.0	30.0	30.0	40.0	0.0
一周 1~2 次 once or twice a week	20	15.0	45.0	20.0	10.0	10.0

1-13 不同消费者层的常用品牌/ The Most Frequently Used Brands by Market Segments

1-13-1 时尚流行指标/ Fads Popular Index

	人数 Number	第一品牌及百分比 1st/percent	第二品牌及百分比 2nd/percent	第三品牌及百分比 3rd/percent
样本 Sample	331	行吟阁 Xingyinge(81.0)	金龙泉 Kinglong(6.9)	百威 Budweiser(6.3)
平实生活指向 simple living orientation	168	行吟阁 Xingyinge(81.5)	金龙泉 Kinglong(9.5)	百威 Budweiser(5.4)
时尚流行指向 fashion orientation	163	行吟阁 Xingyinge(80.4)	百威 Budweiser(7.4)	金龙泉 Kinglong(4.3)

1-13-2 广告态度指标/ Advertising Attitude Index

	人数 Number	第一品牌及百分比 1st/percent	第二品牌及百分比 2nd/percent	第三品牌及百分比 3rd/percent
样本 Sample	**333**	**行吟阁 Xingyinge(80.8)**	**金龙泉 Kinglong(6.9)**	**百威 Budweiser(6.3)**
广告淡漠指向 indifferent orientation	96	行吟阁 Xingyinge(80.2)	金龙泉 Kinglong(7.3)	百威 Budweiser(5.2)
中间层 medium	200	行吟阁 Xingyinge(82.5)	百威 Budweiser(6.5) 金龙泉 Kinglong(6.5)	蓝带 Blue Ribbon(1.0) 青岛 Tsing Tao(1.0) 喜力 Heineken(1.0)
信赖广告指向 loyal orientation	37	行吟阁 Xingyinge(73.0)	百威 Budweiser(8.1) 金龙泉 Kinglong(8.1)	蓝带 Blue Ribbon(2.7) 青岛 Tsing Tao(2.7) 东德 Dongde(2.7) 无花果 Wuhuaguo(2.7)

1-13-3 饮食健康指标/ Foods & Drink Quality Index

	人数 Number	第一品牌及百分比 1st/percent	第二品牌及百分比 2nd/percent	第三品牌及百分比 3rd/percent
样本 Sample	**333**	**行吟阁 Xingyinge(80.8)**	**金龙泉 Kinglong(7.2)**	**百威 Budweiser(6.3)**
饮食“温饱”指向 "basic" orientation	116	行吟阁 Xingyinge(79.3)	金龙泉 Kinglong(8.6)	百威 Budweiser(6.9)
中间层 medium	144	行吟阁 Xingyinge(81.9)	金龙泉 Kinglong(7.6)	百威 Budweiser(6.3)
健康营养指向 health & nutrition orientation	73	行吟阁 Xingyinge(80.8)	百威 Budweiser(5.5)	金龙泉 Kinglong(4.1)

1-14 重度消费者的消费者层构成/ The Composition of the Heavy Consumers

1-14-1 时尚流行指标/ Fads Popular Index

	人数 Number	平实生活指向 simple living orientation	时尚流行指向 fashion orientation
样本 Sample	179	48.0	52.0
天天喝 daily	36	47.2	52.8
一周 3 次或以上 3 times or over a week	59	52.5	47.5
一周 1~2 次 once or twice a week	84	45.2	54.8

1-14-2 广告态度指标/ Advertising Attitude Index

	人数 Number	广告淡漠指向 indifferent orientation	中间层 medium	信赖广告指向 loyal orientation
样本 Sample	181	28.2	60.8	11.0
天天喝 daily	36	38.9	55.6	5.6
一周 3 次或以上 3 times or over a week	60	30.0	61.7	8.3
一周 1~2 次 once or twice a week	85	22.4	62.4	15.3

1-14-3 饮食健康指标/ Foods & Drink Quality Index

	人数 Number	饮食“温饱”指向 "basic" orientation	中间层 medium	健康营养指向 health & nutrition orientation
样本 Sample	181	35.4	44.2	20.4
天天喝 daily	36	30.6	41.7	27.8
一周 3 次或以上 3 times or over a week	60	36.7	43.3	20.0
一周 1~2 次 once or twice a week	85	36.5	45.9	17.6

● 西安 / Xi'an

1-1 最近三个月饮用频率的比例/ Proportion of the Sample Consuming Beer in the Last Three Months

	人数 Number	百分比 Percent
天天喝 daily	36	6.0
一周 3 次或以上 3 times or over a week	75	12.5
一周 1~2 次 once or twice a week	106	17.7
一个月 2～3 次 2 or 3 times a month	108	18.0
一个月 1 次或以下 once a month or below	64	10.7
没喝过 never	211	35.2

n=600

1-2 最常用品牌排名/ Ranking of the Most Frequently Used Brands

排名 Brand Ranking	品牌 Brands	人数 Number	百分比 Percent
1	汉斯 Hans	244	62.7
2	宝鸡 Baoji	118	30.3
3	青岛 Tsing Tao	10	2.6
4	百威 Budweiser	4	1.0
5	生力 San Miguel	2	0.5

n=389

1-3 样本、男性各年龄层、女性各年龄层的常用品牌/ The Most Frequently Used Brands by the Whole Sample, Age and Gender Groups

	人数 Number	第一品牌及百分比 1st/ percent	第二品牌及百分比 2nd/ percent	第三品牌及百分比 3rd/ percent
样本 Sample	389	**汉斯 Hans(62.7)**	**宝鸡 Baoji(30.3)**	**青岛 Tsing Tao(2.6)**
男性 Male	244	**汉斯 Hans(61.5)**	**宝鸡 Baoji(30.3)**	**青岛 Tsing Tao(2.5)**
16~24 岁 Age	44	汉斯 Hans(61.4)	宝鸡 Baoji(25)	百威 Budweiser(2.3) 蓝带 Blue Ribbon(2.3) 青岛 Tsing Tao(2.3) 生力 San Miguel(2.3) 金龙王 Jinlongwang(2.3)
25~34 岁 Age	74	汉斯 Hans(70.3)	宝鸡 Baoji(25.7)	青岛 Tsing Tao(2.7)
35~44 岁 Age	71	汉斯 Hans(57.7)	宝鸡 Baoji(32.4)	青岛 Tsing Tao(4.2)
45~54 岁 Age	38	汉斯 Hans(57.9)	宝鸡 Baoji(36.8)	生力 San Miguel(2.6) 亚太啤酒 Yatai(2.6)
55~60 岁 Age	17	汉斯 Hans(47.1)	宝鸡 Baoji(41.2)	爵士 Vinho Tinto(5.9) 西安啤酒 Xi'an(5.9)
女性 Female	145	**汉斯 Hans(64.8)**	**宝鸡 Baoji(30.3)**	**青岛 Tsing Tao(2.8)**
16~24 岁 Age	24	汉斯 Hans(70.8)	宝鸡 Baoji(25.0)	青岛 Tsing Tao(4.2)
25~34 岁 Age	52	汉斯 Hans(69.2)	宝鸡 Baoji(23.1)	百威 Budweiser(1.9) 嘉士伯 Carlsberg(1.9) 青岛 Tsing Tao(1.9) 中德啤酒 Zhongde(1.9)
35~44 岁 Age	38	汉斯 Hans(63.2)	宝鸡 Baoji(34.2)	青岛 Tsing Tao(2.6)
45~54 岁 Age	17	宝鸡 Baoji(52.9)	汉斯 Hans(41.2)	青岛 Tsing Tao(5.9)
55~60 岁 Age	14	汉斯 Hans(71.4)	宝鸡 Baoji(28.6)	

1-4 理想品牌排名/ Ranking of the Ideal Brands

排名 Brand Ranking	品牌 Brands	人数 Number	百分比 Percent
1	汉斯 Hans	324	53.9
2	宝鸡 Baoji	168	28.0
3	青岛 Tsing Tao	42	7.0
4	百威 Budweiser	16	2.7
5	蓝带 Blue Ribbon	5	0.8
6	嘉士伯 Carlsberg	4	0.7
7	黄河 Huanghe	3	0.5

n=601

1-5 样本、男性各年龄层、女性各年龄层最近三个月有无购买的比例/ Purchasing in the Last Three Months by the Whole Sample, Age and Gender Groups

	人数 Number	买过 yes	没买过 no
样本 Sample	601	67.1	32.9
男性 Male	302	77.8	22.2
16~24 岁 Age	64	67.2	32.8
25~34 岁 Age	91	81.3	18.7
35~44 岁 Age	77	89.6	10.4
45~54 岁 Age	46	71.7	28.3
55~60 岁 Age	24	66.7	33.3
女性 Female	299	**56.2**	**43.8**
16~24 岁 Age	61	44.3	55.7
25~34 岁 Age	90	63.3	36.7
35~44 岁 Age	74	59.5	40.5
45~54 岁 Age	49	42.9	57.1
55~60 岁 Age	25	76.0	24.0

1-6 样本、男性各年龄层、女性各年龄层最近三个月的饮用频率/ Frequencies of Consuming Beer in the Last Three Months by the Whole Sample, Age and Gender Groups

	人数 Number	天天喝 daily	一周 3 次或以上 3 times or over a week	一周 1~2 次 once or twice a week	一个月 2~3 次 2 or 3 times a month	一个月 1 次或以下 once a month or below	没喝过 never
样本 Sample	600	6.0	12.5	17.7	18.0	10.7	35.2
男性 Male	301	9.0	19.3	23.9	21.6	7.3	18.9
16~24 岁 Age	64	9.4	14.1	15.5	23.4	6.3	31.3
25~34 岁 Age	90	12.2	21.1	23.3	16.7	8.9	17.8
35~44 岁 Age	77	6.5	31.2	29.9	18.2	6.5	7.8
45~54 岁 Age	46	10.9	8.7	23.9	32.6	6.5	17.4
55~60 岁 Age	24	0.0	8.3	29.2	25.0	8.3	29.2
女性 Female	299	3.0	5.7	11.4	14.4	14.0	51.5
16~24 岁 Age	61	1.6	1.6	4.9	13.1	18.0	60.7
25~34 岁 Age	90	5.6	3.3	16.7	15.6	16.7	42.2
35~44 岁 Age	74	4.1	9.5	10.8	16.2	10.8	48.6
45~54 岁 Age	49	0.0	4.1	10.2	14.3	6.1	65.3
55~60 岁 Age	25	0.0	16.0	12.0	8.0	20.0	44.0

1-7 样本、男性各年龄层、女性各年龄层的品牌习惯/ Brand Habit in Consuming Beer by the Whole Sample, Age and Gender Groups

	人数 Number	基本固定饮用一个牌子 used in only one brand	比较固定地饮用两个或三个牌子 used in two or three brands	基本上不太固定牌子 no brand preference
样本 Sample	389	55.3	37.0	7.7
男性 Male	244	53.7	39.3	7.0
16~24 岁 Age	44	47.7	45.5	6.8
25~34 岁 Age	74	56.8	37.8	5.4
35~44 岁 Age	71	57.7	36.6	5.6
45~54 岁 Age	38	42.1	47.4	10.5
55~60 岁 Age	17	64.7	23.5	11.8
女性 Female	145	57.9	33.1	9.0
16~24 岁 Age	24	54.2	33.3	12.5
25~34 岁 Age	52	55.8	34.6	9.6
35~44 岁 Age	38	52.6	42.1	5.3
45~54 岁 Age	17	88.2	11.8	0.0
55~60 岁 Age	14	50.0	28.6	21.4

1-8 选择该类商品的考虑因素/ Ranking of the Considerations in Purchasing

注：本题为多选题，合计百分比超过 100%(Multiple answers）

排名 Ranking	考虑因素 Considerations	人次 Person-time	百分比 Percent
1	口味好 pleasant taste	255	65.6
2	价格适中 reasonable price	126	32.4
2	有名的牌子 famous brand	126	32.4
3	生产日期 date of producing	71	18.3
4	购买方便 easy to buy	70	18.0
5	只是由于习惯 out of habit	51	13.1
6	生产地 place of production	27	6.9
7	朋友推荐 introduction of friends	22	5.7
8	广告影响 influence of advertising	17	4.4
9	包装吸引人 appealing package	7	1.8
10	单位发的 offered by the working unit	6	1.5
11	售货员介绍 introduced by the shop assistants	3	0.8
11	其它 others	3	0.8
12	有优惠条件 with preferential terms	2	0.5
12	别人送的 given by other people	2	0.5

n=389

1-9 样本、男性各年龄层、女性各年龄层最常饮用的包装形式/ Types of Package of the Consumed Beer by the Whole Sample, Age and Gender Groups

	人数 Number	瓶装 bottle	听装 tin	散装扎啤 jar without package
样本 Sample	388	95.9	3.1	1.0
男性 Male	243	95.5	2.9	1.6
16~24 岁 Age	43	88.4	9.3	2.3
25~34 岁 Age	74	97.3	2.7	0.0
35~44 岁 Age	71	95.8	1.4	2.8
45~54 岁 Age	38	100.0	0.0	0.0
55~60 岁 Age	17	94.1	0.0	5.9
女性 Female	145	96.6	3.4	0.0
16~24 岁 Age	24	95.8	4.2	0.0
25~34 岁 Age	52	94.2	5.8	0.0
35~44 岁 Age	38	97.4	2.6	0.0
45~54 岁 Age	17	100.0	0.0	0.0
55~60 岁 Age	14	100.0	0.0	0.0

1-10 样本、男性各年龄层、女性各年龄层最常饮用的口味/ The Taste of the Consumed Beer by the Whole Sample, Age and Gender Groups

	人数 Number	清爽型 fresh and cool	醇厚型 mellow	其它 others
样本 Sample	389	79.9	19.5	0.5
男性 Male	244	78.3	21.3	0.4
16~24 岁 Age	44	75.0	25.0	0.0
25~34 岁 Age	74	83.8	16.2	0.0
35~44 岁 Age	71	74.6	23.9	1.4
45~54 岁 Age	38	76.3	23.7	0.0
55~60 岁 Age	17	82.4	17.6	0.0
女性 Female	145	82.8	16.6	0.7
16~24 岁 Age	24	70.8	29.2	0.0
25~34 岁 Age	52	78.8	21.2	0.0
35~44 岁 Age	38	94.7	2.6	2.6
45~54 岁 Age	17	76.5	23.5	0.0
55~60 岁 Age	14	92.9	7.1	0.0

1-11 样本、男性各年龄层、女性各年龄层最常饮用的场合/ Settings of Consumption by the Whole Sample, Age and Gender Groups

注：本题为多选题，合计百分比超过 100%(Multiple answers)

	人数 Number	口渴时 when thirsty	平时吃饭喝 at dinner	宴席、聚会喝 at banquet	去酒吧喝 at bar	外出/旅游时 outing/traveling	其它 others
样本 Sample	389	8.0	52.4	55.3	5.1	5.9	0.3
男性 Male	244	7.4	56.1	52.9	5.3	6.6	0.0
16~24 岁 Age	44	9.1	45.5	45.5	13.6	6.8	0.0
25~34 岁 Age	74	9.5	50.0	56.8	5.4	4.1	0.0
35~44 岁 Age	71	4.2	67.6	50.7	4.2	9.9	0.0
45~54 岁 Age	38	10.5	60.5	50.0	0.0	7.9	0.0
55~60 岁 Age	17	0.0	52.9	70.6	0.0	0.0	0.0
女性 Female	145	9.0	46.2	59.3	4.8	4.8	0.7
16~24 岁 Age	24	12.5	16.7	75.0	12.5	4.2	4.2
25~34 岁 Age	52	7.7	50.0	55.8	5.8	5.8	0.0
35~44 岁 Age	38	10.5	50.0	63.2	2.6	5.3	0.0
45~54 岁 Age	17	11.8	58.8	35.3	0.0	0.0	0.0
55~60 岁 Age	14	0.0	57.1	64.3	0.0	7.1	0.0

1-12 重度消费者人口分布/ Demographics of the Heavy Consumers

	人数 Number	16-24 岁 Age	25-34 岁 Age	35-44 岁 Age	45-54 岁 Age	55-60 岁 Age
样本 Sample	217	13.8	34.1	32.3	12.4	7.4
男性 Male	157	15.9	32.5	33.[illegible]	12.7	5.7
天天喝 daily	27	22.2	40.7	18.5	18.5	0.0
一周 3 次或以上 3 times or over a week	58	15.5	32.8	41.4	6.9	3.4
一周 1~2 次 once or twice a week	72	13.9	29.2	31.9	15.3	9.7
女性 Female	60	8.3	38.3	30.0	11.7	11.7
天天喝 daily	9	11.1	55.6	33 3	0.0	0.0
一周 3 次或以上 3 times or over a week	17	5.9	17.6	41 2	11.8	23.5
一周 1~2 次 once or twice a week	34	8.8	44.1	23.5	14.7	8.8

1-13 不同消费者层的常用品牌/ The Most Frequently Used Brands by Market Segments

1-13-1 时尚流行指标/ Fads Popular Index

	人数 Number	第一品牌及百分比 1st/percent	第二品牌及百分比 2nd/percent	第三品牌及百分比 3rd/percent	第四品牌及百分比 4th/percent
样本 Sample	387	**汉斯 Hans(63.0)**	**宝鸡 Baoji(30.0)**	**青岛 Tsing Tao(2.6)**	**百威 Budweiser(1.0)**
平实生活指向 simple living orientation	219	汉斯 Hans(58.9)	宝鸡 Baoji(34.7)	青岛 Tsing Tao(1.4)	百威 Budweiser(0.9)
时尚流行指向 fashion orientation	168	汉斯 Hans(68.5)	宝鸡 Baoji(23.8)	青岛 Tsing Tao(4.2)	百威 Budweiser(1.2)

1-13-2 广告态度指标/ Advertising Attitude Index

	人数 Number	第一品牌及百分比 1st/percent	第二品牌及百分比 2nd/percent	第三品牌及百分比 3rd/percent	第四品牌及百分比 4th/percent
样本 Sample	386	**汉斯 Hans(62.4)**	**宝鸡 Baoji(30.6)**	**青岛 Tsing Tao(2.6)**	**百威 Budweiser(1.0)**
广告淡漠指向 indifferent orientation	115	汉斯 Hans(64.3)	宝鸡 Baoji(32.2)	青岛 Tsing Tao(2.6)	百威 Budweiser(0.9)
中间层 medium	224	汉斯 Hans(60.7)	宝鸡 Baoji(31.7)	青岛 Tsing Tao(1.8)	百威 Budweiser(0.9)
信赖广告指向 loyal orientation	47	汉斯 Hans(66.0)	宝鸡 Baoji(21.3)	青岛 Tsing Tao(6.4)	百威 Budweiser(2.1) 生力 San Miguel(2.1) 中德啤酒 Zhongde(2.1)

1-13-3 饮食健康指标/ Foods & Drink Quality Index

	人数 Number	第一品牌及百分比 1st/percent	第二品牌及百分比 2nd/percent	第三品牌及百分比 3rd/percent	第四品牌及百分比 4th/percent
样本 Sample	389	**汉斯 Hans(62.7)**	**宝鸡 Baoji(30.3)**	**青岛 Tsing Tao(2.6)**	**百威 Budweiser(1.0)**
饮食“温饱”指向 "basic" orientation	150	汉斯 Hans(56.7)	宝鸡 Baoji(36.0)	青岛 Tsing Tao(4.0)	百威 Budweiser(1.3)
中间层 medium	179	汉斯 Hans(67.6)	宝鸡 Baoji(26.8)	百威 Budweiser(1.1)	西安啤酒 Xi'an(0.6) 金龙王 Jinlongwang(0.6) 中德啤酒 Zhongde(0.6) 燕京 Yanjing(0.6) 生力 San Miguel(0.6) 青岛 Tsing Tao(0.6) 爵士 Vinho Tinto(0.6) 嘉士伯 Carlsberg(0.6)
健康营养指向 health & nutrition orientation	60	汉斯 Hans(63.3)	宝鸡 Baoji(26.7)	青岛 Tsing Tao(5.0)	蓝带 Blue Ribbon(1.7) 生力 San Miguel(1.7) 亚太啤酒 Yatai(1.7)

1-14 重度消费者的消费者层构成/ The Composition of the Heavy Consumers

1-14-1 时尚流行指标/ Fads Popular Index

	人数 Number	平实生活指向 simple living orientation	时尚流行指向 fashion orientation
样本 Sample	216	56.0	44.0
天天喝 daily	36	58.3	41.7
一周 3 次或以上 3 times or over a week	74	47.3	52.7
一周 1~2 次 once or twice a week	106	61.3	38.7

1-14-2 广告态度指标/ Advertising Attitude Index

	人数 Number	广告淡漠指向 indifferent orientation	中间层 medium	信赖广告指向 loyal orientation
样本 Sample	215	29.3	54.0	16.7
天天喝 daily	36	25.0	58.3	16.7
一周 3 次或以上 3 times or over a week	74	28.4	52.7	18.9
一周 1~2 次 once or twice a week	105	31.4	53.3	15.2

1-14-3 饮食健康指标/ Foods & Drink Quality Index

	人数 Number	饮食"温饱"指向 "basic" orientation	中间层 medium	健康营养指向 health & nutrition orientation
样本 Sample	217	39.2	42.9	18.0
天天喝 daily	36	44.4	33.3	22.2
一周 3 次或以上 3 times or over a week	75	30.7	50.7	18.7
一周 1~2 次 once or twice a week	106	43.4	40.6	16.0

● 沈阳 / Shenyang

1-1 最近三个月饮用频率的比例/ Proportion of the Sample Consuming Beer in the Last Three Months

	人数 Number	百分比 Percent
天天喝 daily	54	9.0
一周 3 次或以上 3 times or over a week	81	13.5
一周 1~2 次 once or twice a week	120	20.0
一个月 2～3 次 2 or 3 times a month	94	15.6
一个月 1 次或以下 once a month or below	58	9.7
没喝过 never	194	32.3

n=601

1-2 最常用品牌排名/ Ranking of the Most Frequently Used Brands

排名 Brand Ranking	品牌 Brands	人数 Number	百分比 Percent
1	(沈阳) 雪花(鲜啤) SNOW	259	63.6
2	沈阳(黄牌，绿牌) SHENYANG	116	28.5
3	蓝带 Blue Ribbon	6	1.5
3	青岛 Tsing Tao	6	1.5
4	虎牌 Tiger	4	1.0
5	百威 Budweiser	3	0.7
6	嘉士伯 Carlsberg	2	0.5

n=407

1-3 样本、男性各年龄层、女性各年龄层的常用品牌/ The Most Frequently Used Brands by the Whole Sample, Age and Gender Groups

	人数 Number	第一品牌及百分比 1st/ percent	第二品牌及百分比 2nd/ percent	第三品牌及百分比 3rd/ percent
样本 Sample	407	**(沈阳）雪花(鲜啤）SNOW(63.6)**	**沈阳(黄牌，绿牌）SHENYANG(28.5)**	**蓝带 Blue Ribbon(1.5)** **青岛 Tsing Tao(1.5)**
男性 Male	251	**(沈阳）雪花(鲜啤）SNOW(61.0)**	**沈阳(黄牌，绿牌）SHENYANG(32.7)**	**百威 Budweiser(1.2)** **青岛 Tsing Tao(1.2)**
16~24 岁 Age	36	(沈阳）雪花(鲜啤）SNOW(69.4)	沈阳(黄牌，绿牌）SHENYANG(25.0)	嘉士伯 Carlsberg(2.8) 蓝带 Blue Ribbon(2.8)
25~34 岁 Age	80	(沈阳）雪花(鲜啤）SNOW(68.8)	沈阳(黄牌，绿牌）SHENYANG(26.3)	百威 Budweiser(1.3) 虎牌 Tiger(1.3) 蓝带 Blue Ribbon(1.3) 生力 San Miguel(1.3)
35~44 岁 Age	71	(沈阳）雪花(鲜啤）SNOW(47.9)	沈阳(黄牌，绿牌）SHENYANG(45.1)	百威 Budweiser(1.4) 虎牌 Tiger(1.4) 青岛 Tsing Tao(1.4) 哈尔滨 Ha'erbin(1.4)
45~54 岁 Age	43	(沈阳）雪花(鲜啤）SNOW(55.8)	沈阳(黄牌，绿牌）SHENYANG(34.9)	百威 Budweiser(2.3) 青岛 Tsing Tao(2.3) 梅河 Meihe(2.3) 墨尼 Meni(2.3)
55~60 岁 Age	21	(沈阳）雪花(鲜啤）SNOW(71.4)	沈阳(黄牌，绿牌）SHENYANG(23.8)	青岛 Tsing Tao(4.8)
女性 Female	156	**(沈阳）雪花(鲜啤）SNOW(67.9)**	**沈阳(黄牌，绿牌）SHENYANG(21.8)**	**蓝带 Blue Ribbon(2.6)**
16~24 岁 Age	18	(沈阳）雪花(鲜啤）SNOW(66.7)	朝日/舒波乐 Asahi(5.6) 虎牌 Tiger(5.6) 蓝带 Blue Ribbon(5.6) 青岛 Tsing Tao(5.6) 威乐 Weile(5.6) 沈阳(黄牌，绿牌）SHENYANG(5.6)	
25~34 岁 Age	51	(沈阳）雪花(鲜啤）SNOW(66.7)	沈阳(黄牌，绿牌）SHENYANG(25.5)	虎牌 Tiger(2.0) 青岛 Tsing Tao(2.0) 五星 Five Star(2.0)
35~44 岁 Age	48	(沈阳）雪花(鲜啤）SNOW(64.6)	沈阳(黄牌，绿牌）SHENYANG(27.1)	嘉士伯 Carlsberg(2.1) 蓝带 Blue Ribbon(2.1) 青岛 Tsing Tao(2.1) 红带王 Hongdaiwang(2.1)
45~54 岁 Age	29	(沈阳）雪花(鲜啤）SNOW(72.4)	沈阳(黄牌，绿牌）SHENYANG(20.7)	蓝带 Blue Ribbon(3.4)
55~60 岁 Age	10	(沈阳）雪花(鲜啤）SNOW(80.0)	蓝带 Blue Ribbon(10.0) 沈阳(黄牌，绿牌）SHENYANG(10.0)	

1-4 理想品牌排名/ Ranking of the Ideal Brands

排名 Brand Ranking	品牌 Brands	人数 Number	百分比 Percent
1	(沈阳）雪花(鲜啤）SNOW	353	58.7
2	沈阳(黄牌，绿牌）SHENYANG	122	20.3
3	青岛 Tsing Tao	28	4.7
4	百威 Budweiser	19	3.2
5	蓝带 Blue Ribbon	15	2.5
6	虎牌 Tiger	7	1.2
7	贝克 Beck's	6	1.0
7	喜力 Heineken	6	1.0
8	梅河 Meihe	5	0.8
9	嘉士伯 Carlsberg	4	0.7
10	生力 San Miguel	3	0.5

n=601

1-5 样本、男性各年龄层、女性各年龄层最近三个月有无购买的比例/ Purchasing in the Last Three Months by the Whole Sample, Age and Gender Groups

	人数 Number	买过 yes	没买过 no
样本 Sample	601	76.4	23.6
男性 Male	299	83.6	16.4
16~24 岁 Age	64	59.4	40.6
25~34 岁 Age	89	89.9	10.1
35~44 岁 Age	76	90.8	9.2
45~54 岁 Age	46	93.5	6.5
55~60 岁 Age	24	83.3	16.7
女性 Female	302	69.2	30.8
16~24 岁 Age	64	53.1	46.9
25~34 岁 Age	90	80.0	20.0
35~44 岁 Age	76	78.9	21.1
45~54 岁 Age	48	60.4	39.6
55~60 岁 Age	24	58.3	41.7

1-6 样本、男性各年龄层、女性各年龄层最近三个月的饮用频率/ Frequencies of Consuming Beer in the Last Three Months by the Whole Sample, Age and Gender Groups

	人数 Number	天天喝 daily	一周 3 次或以上 3 times or over a week	一周 1~2 次 once or twice a week	一个月 2~3 次 2 or 3 times a month	一个月 1 次或以下 once a month or below	没喝过 never
样本 Sample	601	9.0	13.5	20.0	15.6	9.7	32.3
男性 Male	299	14.0	21.7	24.4	14.7	9.0	16.1
16~24 岁 Age	64	3.1	10.9	15.6	15.6	10.9	43.8
25~34 岁 Age	89	21.3	24.7	21.3	16.9	5.6	10.1
35~44 岁 Age	76	14.5	30.3	25.0	17.1	6.6	6.6
45~54 岁 Age	46	19.6	21.7	30.4	13.0	8.7	6.5
55~60 岁 Age	24	4.2	12.5	45.8	0.0	25.0	12.5
女性 Female	302	4.0	5.3	15.6	16.6	10.3	48.3
16~24 岁 Age	64	0.0	3.1	9.4	7.8	7.8	71.9
25~34 岁 Age	90	5.6	4.4	22.2	17.8	6.7	43.3
35~44 岁 Age	76	3.9	10.5	11.8	25.0	11.8	36.8
45~54 岁 Age	48	4.2	4.2	18.8	16.7	16.7	39.6
55~60 岁 Age	24	8.3	0.0	12.5	8.3	12.5	58.3

1-7 样本、男性各年龄层、女性各年龄层的品牌习惯/ Brand Habit in Consuming Beer by the Whole Sample, Age and Gender Groups

	人数 Number	基本固定饮用一个牌子 used in only one brand	比较固定地饮用两个或三个牌子 used in two or three brands	基本上不太固定牌子 no brand preference
样本 Sample	406	66.7	25.6	7.6
男性 Male	250	67.6	26.0	6.4
16~24 岁 Age	36	58.3	30.6	11.1
25~34 岁 Age	79	65.8	25.3	8.9
35~44 岁 Age	71	74.6	19.7	5.6
45~54 岁 Age	43	60.5	37.2	2.3
55~60 岁 Age	21	81.0	19.0	0.0
女性 Female	156	65.4	25.0	9.6
16~24 岁 Age	18	50.0	33.3	16.7
25~34 岁 Age	51	66.7	25.5	7.8
35~44 岁 Age	48	68.8	20.8	10.4
45~54 岁 Age	29	69.0	20.7	10.3
55~60 岁 Age	10	60.0	40.0	0.0

1-8 选择该类商品的考虑因素/ Ranking of the Considerations in Purchasing

注：本题为多选题，合计百分比超过 100%(Multiple answers）

排名 Ranking	考虑因素 Considerations	人次 Person-time	百分比 Percent
1	口味好 pleasant taste	253	62.3
2	价格适中 reasonable price	164	40.4
3	有名的牌子 famous brand	127	31.3
4	生产日期 date of producing	105	25.9
5	购买方便 easy to buy	89	21.9
6	只是由于习惯 out of habit	56	13.8
7	生产地 place of production	49	12.1
8	广告影响 influence of advertising	11	2.7
9	朋友推荐 introduction of friends	10	2.5
10	单位发的 offered by the working unit	6	1.5
10	包装吸引人 appealing package	6	1.5
11	售货员介绍 introduced by the shop assistants	3	0.7
12	其它 others	2	0.5
13	有优惠条件 with preferential terms	1	0.2
13	别人送的 given by other people	1	0.2

n=406

1-9 样本、男性各年龄层、女性各年龄层最常饮用的包装形式/ Types of Package of the Consumed Beer by the Whole Sample, Age and Gender Groups

	人数 Number	瓶装 bottle	听装 tin	散装扎啤 jar without package	其它 others
样本 Sample	406	94.1	5.7	0.2	0.0
男性 Male	250	96.0	4.0	0.0	0.0
16~24 岁 Age	36	97.2	2.8	0.0	0.0
25~34 岁 Age	80	92.5	7.5	0.0	0.0
35~44 岁 Age	71	98.6	1.4	0.0	0.0
45~54 岁 Age	43	95.3	4.7	0.0	0.0
55~60 岁 Age	20	100.0	0.0	0.0	0.0
女性 Female	156	91.0	8.3	0.6	0.0
16~24 岁 Age	18	77.8	22.2	0.0	0.0
25~34 岁 Age	51	94.1	5.9	0.0	0.0
35~44 岁 Age	48	91.7	6.3	2.1	0.0
45~54 岁 Age	29	93.1	6.9	0.0	0.0
55~60 岁 Age	10	90.0	10.0	0.0	0.0

1-10 样本、男性各年龄层、女性各年龄层最常饮用的口味/ The Taste of the Consumed Beer by the Whole Sample, Age and Gender Groups

	人数 Number	清爽型 fresh and cool	醇厚型 mellow	其它 others
样本 Sample	407	79.9	20.1	0.0
男性 Male	251	78.1	21.9	0.0
16~24 岁 Age	36	88.9	11.1	0.0
25~34 岁 Age	80	73.8	26.3	0.0
35~44 岁 Age	71	81.7	18.3	0.0
45~54 岁 Age	43	76.7	23.3	0.0
55~60 岁 Age	21	66.7	33.3	0.0
女性 Female	156	82.7	17.3	0.0
16~24 岁 Age	18	88.9	11.1	0.0
25~34 岁 Age	51	82.4	17.6	0.0
35~44 岁 Age	48	77.1	22.9	0.0
45~54 岁 Age	29	82.8	17.2	0.0
55~60 岁 Age	10	100.0	0.0	0.0

1-11 样本、男性各年龄层、女性各年龄层最常饮用的场合/ Settings of Consumption by the Whole Sample, Age and Gender Groups

注：本题为多选题，合计百分比超过 100%(Multiple answers）

	人数 Number	口渴时 when thirsty	平时吃饭喝 at dinner	宴席、聚会喝 at banquet	去酒吧喝 at bar	外出/旅游时 outing/ traveling	其它 others
样本 Sample	407	6.1	59.0	56.3	2.2	5.7	0.2
男性 Male	251	4.0	62.2	57.8	2.0	5.2	0.4
16~24 岁 Age	36	8.3	36.1	83.3	0.0	5.6	0.0
25~34 岁 Age	80	2.5	66.3	58.8	5.0	3.8	0.0
35~44 岁 Age	71	5.6	67.6	53.5	1.4	4.2	0.0
45~54 岁 Age	43	2.3	69.8	41.9	0.0	9.3	0.0
55~60 岁 Age	21	0.0	57.1	57.1	0.0	4.8	4.8
女性 Female	156	9.6	53.8	53.8	2.6	6.4	0.0
16~24 岁 Age	18	16.7	27.8	66.7	5.6	16.7	0.0
25~34 岁 Age	51	5.9	58.8	52.9	3.9	5.9	0.0
35~44 岁 Age	48	10.4	52.1	56.3	2.1	8.3	0.0
45~54 岁 Age	29	10.3	55.2	51.7	0.0	0.0	0.0
55~60 岁 Age	10	10.0	80.0	30.0	0.0	0.0	0.0

1-12 重度消费者人口分布/ Demographics of the Heavy Consumers

	人数 Number	16-24 岁 Age	25-34 岁 Age	35-44 岁 Age	45-54 岁 Age	55-60 岁 Age
样本 Sample	255	10.6	34.9	28.6	18.0	7.8
男性 Male	180	10.6	33.3	29.4	18.3	8.3
天天喝 daily	42	4.8	45.2	26.2	21.4	2.4
一周 3 次或以上 3 times or over a week	65	10.8	33.8	35.4	15.4	4.6
一周 1~2 次 once or twice a week	73	13.7	26.0	26.0	19.2	15.1
女性 Female	75	10.7	38.7	26.7	17.3	6.7
天天喝 daily	12	0.0	41.7	25.0	16.7	16.7
一周 3 次或以上 3 times or over a week	16	12.5	25.0	50.0	12.5	0.0
一周 1~2 次 once or twice a week	47	12.8	42.6	19.1	19.1	6.4

1-13 不同消费者层的常用品牌/ The Most Frequently Used Brands by Market Segments

1-13-1 时尚流行指标/ Fads Popular Index

	人数 Number	第一品牌及百分比 1st/ percent	第二品牌及百分比 2nd/ percent	第三品牌及百分比 3rd/ percent
样本 Sample	407	**（沈阳）雪花(鲜啤）SNOW(63.6)**	**沈阳(黄牌，绿牌） SHENYANG(28.5)**	**蓝带 Blue Ribbon(1.5)** **青岛 Tsing Tao(1.5)**
平实生活指向 simple living orientation	204	（沈阳）雪花(鲜啤）SNOW(58.8)	沈阳(黄牌，绿牌） SHENYANG(33.8)	青岛 Tsing Tao(2.0)
时尚流行指向 fashion orientation	203	（沈阳）雪花(鲜啤）SNOW(68.5)	沈阳(黄牌，绿牌） SHENYANG(23.2)	蓝带 Blue Ribbon(2.0)

1-13-2 广告态度指标/ Advertising Attitude Index

	人数 Number	第一品牌及百分比 1st/ percent	第二品牌及百分比 2nd/ percent	第三品牌及百分比 3rd/ percent
样本 Sample	407	**（沈阳）雪花(鲜啤）SNOW(63.6)**	**沈阳(黄牌，绿牌） SHENYANG(28.5)**	**蓝带 Blue Ribbon(1.5)** **青岛 Tsing Tao(1.5)**
广告淡漠指向 indifferent orientation	109	（沈阳）雪花(鲜啤）SNOW(56.0)	沈阳(黄牌，绿牌） SHENYANG(34.9)	蓝带 Blue Ribbon(2.8)
中间层 medium	243	（沈阳）雪花(鲜啤）SNOW(67.5)	沈阳(黄牌，绿牌） SHENYANG(25.5)	虎牌 Tiger(1.6)
信赖广告指向 loyal orientation	55	（沈阳）雪花(鲜啤）SNOW(61.8)	沈阳(黄牌，绿牌） SHENYANG(29.1)	百威 Budweiser(1.8) 嘉士伯 Carlsberg(1.8) 青岛 Tsing Tao(1.8) 墨尼 Meni(1.8) 红带王 Hongdaiwang(1.8)

1-13-3 饮食健康指标/ Foods & Drink Quality Index

	人数 Number	第一品牌及百分比 1st/ percent	第二品牌及百分比 2nd/ percent	第三品牌及百分比 3rd/ percent
样本 Sample	**407**	**(沈阳）雪花(鲜啤）SNOW(63.6)**	**沈阳(黄牌，绿牌）SHENYANG(28.5)**	**蓝带 Blue Ribbon(1.5)** **青岛 Tsing Tao(1.5)**
饮食“温饱”指向 "basic" orientation	135	(沈阳）雪花(鲜啤）SNOW(60.7)	沈阳(黄牌，绿牌）SHENYANG(33.3)	蓝带 Blue Ribbon(1.5)
中间层 medium	176	(沈阳）雪花(鲜啤）SNOW(65.3)	沈阳(黄牌，绿牌）SHENYANG(24.4)	青岛 Tsing Tao(3.4)
健康营养指向 health & nutrition orientation	96	(沈阳）雪花(鲜啤）SNOW(64.6)	沈阳(黄牌，绿牌）SHENYANG(29.2)	百威 Budweiser(1.0) 蓝带 Blue Ribbon(1.0) 五星 Five Star(1.0) 威乐 Weile(1.0) 红带王 Hongdaiwang(1.0)

1-14 重度消费者的消费者层构成/ The Composition of the Heavy Consumers

1-14-1 时尚流行指标/ Fads Popular Index

	人数 Number	平实生活指向 simple living orientation	时尚流行指向 fashion orientation
样本 Sample	**255**	**49.8**	**50.2**
天天喝 daily	54	46.3	53.7
一周 3 次或以上 3 times or over a week	81	53.1	46.9
一周 1~2 次 once or twice a week	120	49.2	50.8

1-14-2 广告态度指标/ Advertising Attitude Index

	人数 Number	广告淡漠指向 indifferent orientation	中间层 medium	信赖广告指向 loyal orientation
样本 Sample	**255**	**27.1**	**58.4**	**14.5**
天天喝 daily	54	31.5	55.6	13.0
一周 3 次或以上 3 times or over a week	81	29.6	51.9	18.5
一周 1~2 次 once or twice a week	120	23.3	64.2	12.5

1-14-3 饮食健康指标/ Foods & Drink Quality Index

	人数 Number	饮食“温饱”指向 "basic" orientation	中间层 medium	健康营养指向 health & nutrition orientation
样本 Sample	**255**	**31.0**	**47.1**	**22.0**
天天喝 daily	54	37.0	44.4	18.5
一周 3 次或以上 3 times or over a week	81	28.4	49.4	22.2
一周 1~2 次 once or twice a week	120	30.0	46.7	23.3

2.白酒 / Hard Liquor

● 北京 / Beijing

2-1 最近三个月饮用频率的比例/ Proportion of the Sample Consuming Hard Liquor in the Last Three Months

	人数 Number	百分比 Percent
天天喝 daily	72	7.2
一周 3 次或以上 3 times or over a week	59	5.9
一周 1~2 次 once or twice a week	87	8.7
一个月 2～3 次 2 or 3 times a month	67	6.7
一个月 1 次 once a month	38	3.8
两个月 1 次 once two months	12	1.2
三个月 1 次或以下 once three months or below	31	3.1
没有喝 never	636	63.5

n=1002

2-2 最常用品牌排名/ Ranking of the Most Frequently Used Brands

排名 Brand Ranking	品牌 Brand	人数 Number	百分比 Percent
1	红星二锅头 Hong Xing Er Guo Tou	172	47.5
2	京酒 Jingjiu	68	18.8
3	红星御酒 Hong Xing Yu Jiu	21	5.8
4	华灯牌北京醇 Huadeng Beijingchun	13	3.6
5	北京二锅头 Bei Jing Er Guo Tou	12	3.3
6	贵州醇 Guizhouchun	7	1.9
7	京都二锅头 Jingdu Er Guo Tou	6	1.7
8	茅台 Moutai	4	1.1
8	五粮液 Wuliangye	4	1.1

n=362

2-3 样本、男性各年龄层、女性各年龄层的常用品牌/ The Most Frequently Used Brands by the Whole Sample, Age and Gender Groups

	人数 Number	第一品牌及百分比 1st/ percent	第二品牌及百分比 2nd/ percent	第三品牌及百分比 3rd/ percent
样本 Sample	362	**红星二锅头 Hong Xing Er Guo Tou(47.5)**	**京酒 Jingjiu(18.8)**	**红星御酒 Hong Xing Yu Jiu(5.8)**
男性 Male	251	**红星二锅头 Hong Xing Er Guo Tou(48.6)**	**京酒 Jingjiu(19.9)**	**红星御酒 Hong Xing Yu Jiu(4.8)**
16~24 岁 Age	24	红星二锅头 Hong Xing Er Guo Tou(54.2)	京酒 Jingjiu(16.7)	红星御酒 Hong Xing Yu Jiu(8.3) 茅台 Moutai(8.3)
25~34 岁 Age	78	红星二锅头 Hong Xing Er Guo Tou(47.4)	京酒 Jingjiu(24.4)	红星御酒 Hong Xing Yu Jiu(7.7)
35~44 岁 Age	89	红星二锅头 Hong Xing Er Guo Tou(49.4)	京酒 Jingjiu(19.1)	北京二锅头 Bei Jing Er Guo Tou(5.6) 贵州醇 Guizhouchun(5.6)
45~54 岁 Age	42	红星二锅头 Hong Xing Er Guo Tou(47.6)	京酒 Jingjiu(23.8)	华灯牌北京醇 Huadeng Beijingchun(2.4) 红星御酒 Hong Xing Yu Jiu(2.4) 牛栏山二锅头 Niulanshan(2.4) 北京二锅头 Bei Jing Er Guo Tou(2.4) 贵州醇 Guizhouchun(2.4) 京都二锅头 Jingdu Er Guo Tou (2.4) 金鑫二锅头 Jin Xin Er Guo Tou(2.4)
55~60 岁 Age	18	红星二锅头 Hong Xing Er Guo Tou(44.4)	华灯牌北京醇 Huadeng Beijingchun(16.7) 北京二锅头 Bei Jing Er Guo Tou(16.7)	红星御酒 Hong Xing Yu Jiu(5.6) 尖庄 Jianzhuang(5.6) 京都二锅头 Jingdu Er Guo Tou(5.6)
女性 Female	111	**红星二锅头 Hong Xing Er Guo Tou(45.0)**	**京酒 Jingjiu(16.2)**	**红星御酒 Hong Xing Yu Jiu(8.1)**
16~24 岁 Age	3	红星二锅头 Hong Xing Er Guo Tou(33.3) 京酒 Jingjiu(33.3)		
25~34 岁 Age	39	红星二锅头 Hong Xing Er Guo Tou(35.9)	京酒 Jingjiu(17.9)	红星御酒 Hong Xing Yu Jiu(7.7)
35~44 岁 Age	38	红星二锅头 Hong Xing Er Guo Tou(42.1)	京酒 Jingjiu(21.1)	红星御酒 Hong Xing Yu Jiu(13.2)
45~54 岁 Age	22	红星二锅头 Hong Xing Er Guo Tou(59.1)	京酒 Jingjiu(9.1)	红星御酒 Hong Xing Yu Jiu(4.5) 孔府家酒 Confucius Family Liquor(4.5) 华都 Huadu(4.5)
55~60 岁 Age	9	红星二锅头 Hong Xing Er Guo Tou(66.7)	华灯牌北京醇 Huadeng Beijingchun(22.2)	

2-4 理想品牌排名/ Ranking of the Ideal Brands

排名 Brand Ranking	品牌 Brand	人数 Number	百分比 Percent
1	红星二锅头 Hong Xing Er Guo Tou	221	21.9
2	茅台 Moutai	111	11.0
3	京酒 Jingjiu	71	7.0
4	五粮液 Wuliangye	56	5.5
5	红星御酒 Hong Xing Yu Jiu	33	3.3
6	华灯牌北京醇 Huadeng Beijingchun	33	3.3
7	北京二锅头 Bei Jing Er Guo Tou	21	2.1

n=1011

2-5 样本、男性各年龄层、女性各年龄层最近三个月有无购买的比例/ Purchasing in the Last Three Months by the Whole Sample, Age and Gender Groups

	人数 Number	买过 yes	没买过 no
样本 Sample	1011	40.9	59.1
男性 Male	503	46.7	53.3
16~24 岁 Age	105	25.7	74.3
25~34 岁 Age	151	46.4	53.6
35~44 岁 Age	130	60.0	40.0
45~54 岁 Age	77	54.5	45.5
55~60 岁 Age	40	45.0	55.0
女性 Female	508	35.2	64.8
16~24 岁 Age	108	17.6	82.4
25~34 岁 Age	150	31.3	68.7
35~44 岁 Age	124	47.6	52.4
45~54 岁 Age	84	42.9	57.1
55~60 岁 Age	42	42.9	57.1

2-6 样本、男性各年龄层、女性各年龄层最近三个月是否拿白酒送过礼/ To Offer Hard Liquor as Gift in the Last Three Months by the Whole Sample, Age and Gender Groups

	人数 Number	送过 yes	没送过 no
样本 Sample	998	17.5	82.5
男性 Male	497	18.7	81.3
16~24 岁 Age	104	9.6	90.4
25~34 岁 Age	151	17.9	82.1
35~44 岁 Age	126	19.0	81.0
45~54 岁 Age	77	31.2	68.8
55~60 岁 Age	39	20.5	79.5
女性 Female	501	16.4	83.6
16~24 岁 Age	106	14.2	85.8
25~34 岁 Age	147	12.9	87.1
35~44 岁 Age	123	22.8	77.2
45~54 岁 Age	83	18.1	81.9
55~60 岁 Age	42	11.9	88.1

2-7 样本、男性各年龄层、女性各年龄层最近三个月的饮用频率/ Frequencies of Consuming Hard Liquor in the Last Three Months by the Whole Sample, Age and Gender Groups

	人数 Number	天天喝 daily	一周 3 次或以上 3 times or over a week	一周 1~2 次 once or twice a week	一个月 2~3 次 2 or 3 times a month	一个月 1 次 once a month	两个月 1 次 once two months	三个月 1 次或以下 once three months or below	没有喝 never
样本 Sample	1002	7.2	5.9	8.7	6.7	3.8	1.2	3.1	63.5
男性 Male	500	11.4	9.2	13.2	8.4	4.6	1.2	2.6	49.4
16~24 岁 Age	103	1.0	3.9	5.8	2.9	2.9	2.9	3.9	76.7
25~34 岁 Age	150	10.0	10.7	11.3	10.7	6.7	0.7	2.7	47.3
35~44 岁 Age	131	16.8	13.0	20.6	10.7	4.6	1.5	1.5	31.3
45~54 岁 Age	77	16.9	6.5	15.6	6.5	5.2	0.0	3.9	45.5
55~60 岁 Age	39	15.4	10.3	10.3	10.3	0.0	0.0	0.0	53.8
女性 Female	502	3.0	2.6	4.2	5.0	3.0	1.2	3.6	77.5
16~24 岁 Age	106	0.9	0.9	0.0	0.0	0.0	0.0	0.9	97.2
25~34 岁 Age	147	3.4	2.7	6.1	4.1	4.8	0.0	6.1	72.8
35~44 岁 Age	123	3.3	4.9	5.7	6.5	4.9	4.1	2.4	68.3
45~54 岁 Age	84	3.6	1.2	2.4	11.9	2.4	1.2	3.6	73.8
55~60 岁 Age	42	4.8	2.4	7.1	2.4	0.0	0.0	4.8	78.6

2-8 样本、男性各年龄层、女性各年龄层的品牌习惯/ Brand Habit in Consuming Hard Liquor by the Whole Sample, Age and Gender Groups

	人数 Number	基本固定饮用一个牌子 used in only one brand	比较固定地饮用两个或三个牌子 used in two or three brands	基本上不太固定牌子 no brand preference
样本 Sample	364	63.5	23.9	12.6
男性 Male	253	62.8	22.9	14.2
16~24 岁 Age	24	50.0	37.5	12.5
25~34 岁 Age	79	64.6	21.5	13.9
35~44 岁 Age	90	60.0	21.1	18.9
45~54 岁 Age	42	78.6	14.3	7.1
55~60 岁 Age	18	50.0	38.9	11.1
女性 Female	111	64.9	26.1	9.0
16~24 岁 Age	3	100.0	0.0	0.0
25~34 岁 Age	39	56.4	28.2	15.4
35~44 岁 Age	38	63.2	34.2	2.6
45~54 岁 Age	22	68.2	22.7	9.1
55~60 岁 Age	9	88.9	0.0	11.1

2-9 选择该类商品的考虑因素/ Ranking of the Considerations in Purchasing

注：本题为多选题，合计百分比超过 100%(Multiple answers)

排名 Ranking	考虑因素 Considerations	人次 Person-time	百分比 Percent
1	口味好 pleasant taste	218	60.1
2	价格适中 reasonable price	160	44.1
3	有名的牌子 famous brand	124	34.2
4	只是由于习惯 out of habit	56	15.4
5	购买方便 easy to buy	53	14.6
6	生产日期 date of producing	42	11.6
7	朋友推荐 introduction of friends	21	5.8
8	别人送的 given by other people	20	5.5
9	广告影响 influence of advertising	13	3.6
10	其它 others	10	2.8
11	有优惠条件 with preferential terms	6	1.7
12	包装吸引人 appealing package	5	1.4
13	售货员介绍 introduced by the shop assistants	3	0.8

n=363

2-10 样本、男性各年龄层、女性各年龄层最常饮用的度数/ Degree of the Consumed Hard Liquor by the Whole Sample, Age and Gender Groups

	人数 Number	55 度以上 55^0 or over	39—55 度 39^0--55^0	38 度及以下 38^0 or below	其它 others
样本 Sample	360	42.8	28.9	28.3	0.0
男性 Male	249	42.6	30.1	27.3	0.0
16~24 岁 Age	23	34.8	39.1	26.1	0.0
25~34 岁 Age	79	36.7	30.4	32.9	0.0
35~44 岁 Age	87	46.0	28.7	25.3	0.0
45~54 岁 Age	42	50.0	21.4	28.6	0.0
55~60 岁 Age	18	44.4	44.4	11.1	0.0
女性 Female	111	43.2	26.1	30.6	0.0
16~24 岁 Age	3	66.7	0.0	33.3	0.0
25~34 岁 Age	39	38.5	35.9	25.6	0.0
35~44 岁 Age	38	44.7	15.8	39.5	0.0
45~54 岁 Age	22	50.0	22.7	27.3	0.0
55~60 岁 Age	9	33.3	44.4	22.2	0.0

2-11 样本、男性各年龄层、女性各年龄层最常饮用的场合/ Settings of Consumption by the Whole Sample, Age and Gender Groups

注：本题为多选题，合计百分比超过 100%(Multiple answers）

	人数 Number	请客 entertain guests	节假日团聚 get-together on holiday	日常饮用 drink daily	服药 drink with medicine	做菜 cooking meal	其它 others
样本 Sample	**363**	**29.5**	**37.5**	**57.3**	**1.9**	**9.6**	**1.7**
男性 Male	**252**	**29.4**	**36.9**	**61.5**	**2.4**	**4.8**	**1.2**
16~24 岁 Age	24	50.0	41.7	41.7	4.2	4.2	0.0
25~34 岁 Age	79	35.4	34.2	54.4	1.3	6.3	1.3
35~44 岁 Age	89	21.3	39.3	67.4	2.2	3.4	1.1
45~54 岁 Age	42	28.6	35.7	66.7	2.4	7.1	2.4
55~60 岁 Age	18	16.7	33.3	77.8	5.6	0.0	0.0
女性 Female	**111**	**29.7**	**38.7**	**47.7**	**0.9**	**20.7**	**2.7**
16~24 岁 Age	3	33.3	66.7	66.7	0.0	33.3	0.0
25~34 岁 Age	39	28.2	35.9	48.7	0.0	15.4	5.1
35~44 岁 Age	38	36.8	44.7	44.7	2.6	21.1	2.6
45~54 岁 Age	22	27.3	36.4	45.5	0.0	22.7	0.0
55~60 岁 Age	9	11.1	22.2	55.6	0.0	33.3	0.0

2-12 重度消费者人口分布/ Demographics of the Heavy Consumers

	人数 Number	16-24 岁 Age	25-34 岁 Age	35-44 岁 Age	45-54 岁 Age	55-60 岁 Age
样本 Sample	**218**	**6.0**	**30.3**	**38.1**	**16.5**	**9.2**
男性 Male	**169**	**6.5**	**28.4**	**39.1**	**17.8**	**8.3**
天天喝 daily	57	1.8	26.3	38.6	22.8	10.5
一周 3 次或以上 3 times or over a week	46	8.7	34.8	37.0	10.9	8.7
一周 1~2 次 once or twice a week	66	9.1	25.8	40.9	18.2	6.1
女性 Female	**49**	**4.1**	**36.7**	**34.7**	**12.2**	**12.2**
天天喝 daily	15	6.7	33.3	26.7	20.0	13.3
一周 3 次或以上 3 times or over a week	13	7.7	30.8	46.2	7.7	7.7
一周 1~2 次 once or twice a week	21	0.0	42.9	33.3	9.5	14.3

2-13 不同消费者层的常用品牌/ The Most Frequently Used Brands by Market Segments

2-13-1 时尚流行指标/ Fads Popular Index

	人数 Number	第一品牌及百分比 1st/percent	第二品牌及百分比 2nd/percent	第三品牌及百分比 3rd/percent	第四品牌及百分比 4th/percent
样本 Sample	**357**	**红星二锅头 Hong Xing Er Guo Tou(47.6)**	**京酒 Jingjiu(18.8)**	**红星御酒 Hong Xing Yu Jiu(5.9)**	**华灯牌北京醇 Huadeng Beijingchun(3.6)**
平实生活指向 simple living orientation	179	红星二锅头 Hong Xing Er Guo Tou(47.5)	京酒 Jingjiu(19.6)	红星御酒 Hong Xing Yu Jiu(5.6)	华灯牌北京醇 Huadeng Beijingchun(3.9)
时尚流行指向 fashion orientation	178	红星二锅头 Hong Xing Er Guo Tou(47.8)	京酒 Jingjiu(18.0)	红星御酒 Hong Xing Yu Jiu(6.2)	华灯牌北京醇 Huadeng Beijingchun(3.4) 北京二锅头 Bei Jing Er Guo Tou(3.4)

2-13-2 广告态度指标/ Advertising Attitude Index

	人数 Number	第一品牌及百分比 1st/percent	第二品牌及百分比 2nd/percent	第三品牌及百分比 3rd/percent	第四品牌及百分比 4th/percent
样本 Sample	**355**	**红星二锅头 Hong Xing Er Guo Tou(47.0)**	**京酒 Jingjiu(18.6)**	**红星御酒 Hong Xing Yu Jiu(5.9)**	**华灯牌北京醇 Huadeng Beijingchun(3.7)**
广告淡漠指向 indifferent orientation	105	红星二锅头 Hong Xing Er Guo Tou(55.2)	京酒 Jingjiu(17.1)	华灯牌北京醇 Huadeng Beijingchun(3.8)	红星御酒 Hong Xing Yu Jiu(2.9) 北京二锅头 Bei Jing Er Guo Tou(2.9)
中间层 medium	206	红星二锅头 Hong Xing Er Guo Tou(45.1)	京酒 Jingjiu(18.9)	红星御酒 Hong Xing Yu Jiu(6.3)	北京二锅头 Bei Jing Er Guo Tou(4.4)
信赖广告指向 loyal orientation	44	红星二锅头 Hong Xing Er Guo Tou(36.4)	京酒 Jingjiu(20.5)	红星御酒 Hong Xing Yu Jiu(11.4)	华灯牌北京醇 Huadeng Beijingchun(9.1)

2-13-3 饮食健康指标/ Foods & Drink Quality Index

	人数 Number	第一品牌及百分比 1st/percent	第二品牌及百分比 2nd/percent	第三品牌及百分比 3rd/percent	第四品牌及百分比 4th/percent
样本 Sample	359	**红星二锅头 Hong Xing Er Guo Tou(47.4)**	**京酒 Jingjiu(18.9)**	**红星御酒 Hong Xing Yu Jiu(5.6)**	**华灯牌北京醇 Huadeng Beijingchun(3.6)**
饮食"温饱"指向 "basic" orientation	120	红星二锅头 Hong Xing Er Guo Tou(49.2)	京酒 Jingjiu(18.3)	红星御酒 Hong Xing Yu Jiu(4.2) 华灯牌北京醇 Huadeng Beijingchun(4.2)	北京二锅头 Bei Jing Er Guo Tou(3.3)
中间层 medium	157	红星二锅头 Hong Xing Er Guo Tou(45.2)	京酒 Jingjiu(21.7)	红星御酒 Hong Xing Yu Jiu(7.6)	北京二锅头 Bei Jing Er Guo Tou(5.1)
健康营养指向 health & nutrition orientation	82	红星二锅头 Hong Xing Er Guo Tou(48.8)	京酒 Jingjiu(14.6)	华灯牌北京醇 Huadeng Beijingchun(6.1)	红星御酒 Hong Xing Yu Jiu(3.7) 茅台 Moutai(3.7) 贵州醇 Guizhouchun(3.7) 京都二锅头 Jingdu Er Guo Tou(3.7)

2-14 重度消费者的消费者层构成/ The Composition of the Heavy Consumers

2-14-1 时尚流行指标/ Fads Popular Index

	人数 Number	平实生活指向 simple living orientation	时尚流行指向 fashion orientation
样本 Sample	**216**	**52.3**	**47.7**
天天喝 daily	72	56.9	43.1
一周 3 次或以上 3 times or over a week	59	42.4	57.6
一周 1~2 次 once or twice a week	85	55.3	44.7

2-14-2 广告态度指标/ Advertising Attitude Index

	人数 Number	广告淡漠指向 indifferent orientation	中间层 medium	信赖广告指向 loyal orientation
样本 Sample	**213**	**32.4**	**56.3**	**11.3**
天天喝 daily	69	40.6	49.3	10.1
一周 3 次或以上 3 times or over a week	57	22.8	63.2	14.0
一周 1~2 次 once or twice a week	87	32.2	57.5	10.3

2-14-3 饮食健康指标/ Foods & Drink Quality Index

	人数 Number	饮食"温饱"指向 "basic" orientation	中间层 medium	健康营养指向 health & nutrition orientation
样本 Sample	**217**	**35.0**	**43.3**	**21.7**
天天喝 daily	72	41.7	40.3	18.1
一周 3 次或以上 3 times or over a week	59	25.4	45.8	28.8
一周 1~2 次 once or twice a week	86	36.0	44.2	19.8

● 上海 / Shanghai

2-1 最近三个月饮用频率的比例/ Proportion of the Sample Consuming Hard Liquor in the Last Three Months

	人数 Number	百分比 Percent
天天喝 daily	29	2.9
一周 3 次或以上 3 times or over a week	15	1.5
一周 1~2 次 once or twice a week	35	3.5
一个月 2～3 次 2 or 3 times a month	42	4.2
一个月 1 次 once a month	25	2.5
两个月 1 次 once two months	14	1.4
三个月 1 次或以下 once three months or below	32	3.2
没有喝 never	816	81.0

n=1008

2-2 最常用品牌排名/ Ranking of the Most Frequently Used Brands

排名 Brand Ranking	品牌 Brands	人数 Number	百分比 Percent
1	双沟大曲 Shuang Gou Da Qu	42	22.1
2	孔府家酒 Confucius Family Liquor	26	13.7
3	尖庄 Jianzhuang	19	10.0
4	泸州老窖 Lu Zhou Lao Jiao	17	8.9
5	五粮液 Wuliangye	16	8.4
6	洋河大曲 Yang He Da Qu	10	5.3
7	剑南春 Jiannanchun	9	4.7
8	孔府酒 Kong Fu	5	2.6
8	孔府宴酒 Kong Fu Yan Jiu	5	2.6
9	四特酒 Sitejiu	4	2.1
10	古井贡酒 Gu Jing Gong Jiu	3	1.6
10	五粮春 Wuliangchun	3	1.6

n=190

2-3 样本、男性各年龄层、女性各年龄层的常用品牌/ The Most Frequently Used Brands by the Whole Sample, Age and Gender Groups

	人数 Number	第一品牌及百分比 1st/ percent	第二品牌及百分比 2nd/ percent	第三品牌及百分比 3rd/ percent
样本 Sample	**190**	**双沟大曲 Shuang Gou Da Qu(22.1)**	**孔府家酒 Confucius Family Liquor(13.7)**	**尖庄 Jianzhuang(10.0)**
男性 Male	**144**	**双沟大曲 Shuang Gou Da Qu(23.6)**	**孔府家酒 Confucius Family Liquor(11.8)**	**泸州老窖 Lu Zhou Lao Jiao(10.4)**
16~24 岁 Age	17	孔府家酒 Confucius Family Liquor(23.5) 双沟大曲 Shuang Gou Da Qu(23.5)	尖庄 Jianzhuang(11.8) 五粮液 Wuliangye(11.8)	剑南春 Jiannanchun(5.9) 泸州老窖 Lu Zhou Lao Jiao(5.9) 洋河大曲 Yang He Da Qu(5.9) 竹叶青 Zhuyeqing(5.9) 红星 Hongxing (5.9)
25~34 岁 Age	40	双沟大曲 Shuang Gou Da Qu(20.0)	泸州老窖 Lu Zhou Lao Jiao(17.5)	尖庄 Jianzhuang(10.0) 孔府家酒 Confucius Family Liquor(10.0) 五粮液 Wuliangye(10.0)
35~44 岁 Age	41	双沟大曲 Shuang Gou Da Qu(31.7)	孔府家酒 Confucius Family Liquor(12.2)	洋河大曲 Yang He Da Qu(7.3) 五粮液 Wuliangye(7.3)
45~54 岁 Age	32	双沟大曲 Shuang Gou Da Qu(21.9)	尖庄 Jianzhuang(12.5)	孔府家酒 Confucius Family Liquor(9.4) 泸州老窖 Lu Zhou Lao Jiao(9.4) 五粮液 Wuliangye(9.4)
55~60 岁 Age	14	泸州老窖 Lu Zhou Lao Jiao(14.3) 双沟大曲 Shuang Gou Da Qu(14.3) 洋河大曲 Yang He Da Qu(14.3)	孔府酒(7.1) Kong Fu 剡溪大曲 Shan Xi Da Qu(7.1) 习水 Xisui(7.1) 一滴香 Yi Di Xiang(7.1) 古井贡酒 Gu Jing Gong Jiu(7.1) 孔府宴酒 Kong Fu Yan Jiu(7.1) 孔府家酒 Confucius Family Liquor(7.1) 尖庄 Jianzhuang(7.1)	
女性 Female	**46**	**孔府家酒 Confucius Family Liquor(19.6)**	**双沟大曲 Shuang Gou Da Qu(17.4)**	**尖庄 Jianzhuang(13.0)**
16~24 岁 Age	6	双沟大曲 Shuang Gou Da Qu(50.0)	孔府家酒 Confucius Family Liquor(33.3)	尖庄 Jianzhuang(16.7)
25~34 岁 Age	19	双沟大曲 Shuang Gou Da Qu(15.8)	孔府家酒 Confucius Family Liquor(10.5) 孔府宴酒 Kong Fu Yan Jiu(10.5)	五粮春 Wuliangchun(5.3) 青稞 Qingke(5.3) 洋河大曲 Yang He Da Qu(5.3) 西凤酒 Xifengjiu(5.3) 五粮液 Wuliangye(5.3) 泸州老窖 Lu Zhou Lao Jiao(5.3) 郎酒 Langjiu(5.3) 京酒 Jingjiu(5.3) 剑南春 Jiannanchun(5.3) 尖庄 Jianzhuang(5.3)
35~44 岁 Age	13	尖庄 Jianzhuang(23.1) 孔府家酒 Confucius Family Liquor(23.1)	双沟大由 Shuang Gou DaQu(15.4) 五粮液 Wuliangye(15.4)	剑南春 Jiannanchun(7.7) 泸州老窖 Lu Zhou Lao Jiao(7.7) 茅台 Moutai(7.7)
45~54 岁 Age	6	孔府家酒 Confucius Family Liquor(33.3)	汾酒 Fenjiu(16.7) 尖庄 Jianzhuang(16.7) 剑南春 Jiannanchun(16.7) 熊猫大由 Xiong Mao Da Qu(16.7)	
55~60 岁 Age	2	五粮液 Wuliangye(50.0) 一滴香 Yidixiang(50.0)		

2-4 理想品牌排名/ Ranking of the Ideal Brands

排名 Brand Ranking	品牌 Brands	人数 Number	百分比 Percent
1	五粮液 Wuliangye	247	24.4
2	茅台 Moutai	139	13.7
3	双沟大曲 Shuang Gou Da Qu	60	5.9
4	孔府家酒 Confucius Family Liquor	59	5.8
5	剑南春 Jiannanchun	45	4.4
6	尖庄 Jianzhuang	31	3.1
7	洋河大曲 Yang He Da Qu	28	2.8
8	泸州老窖 Lu Zhou Lao Jiao	19	1.9
9	汾酒 Fenjiu	15	1.5
10	熊猫大曲 Xiong Mao Da Qu	13	1.3
11	孔府宴酒 Kong Fu Yan Jiu	10	1.0

n=1014

2-5 样本、男性各年龄层、女性各年龄层最近三个月有无购买的比例/ Purchasing in the Last Three Months by the Whole Sample, Age and Gender Groups

	人数 Number	买过 yes	没买过 no
样本 Sample	1014	23.3	76.7
男性 Male	509	28.9	71.1
16~24 岁 Age	109	17.4	82.6
25~34 岁 Age	146	28.1	71.9
35~44 岁 Age	130	33.1	66.9
45~54 岁 Age	85	34.1	65.9
55~60 岁 Age	39	38.5	61.5
女性 Female	505	17.6	82.4
16~24 岁 Age	108	10.2	89.8
25~34 岁 Age	144	21.5	78.5
35~44 岁 Age	130	23.1	76.9
45~54 岁 Age	82	8.5	91.5
55~60 岁 Age	41	24.4	75.6

2-6 样本、男性各年龄层、女性各年龄层最近三个月是否拿白酒送过礼/ To Offer Hard Liquor as Gift in the Last Three Months by the Whole Sample, Age and Gender Groups

	人数 Number	送过 yes	没送过 no
样本 Sample	1011	9.2	90.8
男性 Male	509	11.8	88.2
16~24 岁 Age	109	10.1	89.9
25~34 岁 Age	146	13.0	87.0
35~44 岁 Age	130	13.8	86.2
45~54 岁 Age	85	8.2	91.8
55~60 岁 Age	39	12.8	87.2
女性 Female	502	6.6	93.4
16~24 岁 Age	108	4.6	95.4
25~34 岁 Age	142	8.5	91.5
35~44 岁 Age	130	6.2	93.8
45~54 岁 Age	82	4.9	95.1
55~60 岁 Age	40	10.0	90.0

2-7 样本、男性各年龄层、女性各年龄层最近三个月的饮用频率/ Frequencies of Consuming Hard Liquor in the Last Three Months by the Whole Sample, Age and Gender Groups

	人数 Number	天天喝 daily	一周3次或以上 3 times or over a week	一周1~2次 once or twice a week	一个月2~3次 2 or 3 times a month	一个月1次 once a month	两个月1次 once two months	三个月1次或以下 once three months or below	没有喝 never
样本 Sample	1008	2.9	1.5	3.5	4.2	2.5	1.4	3.2	81.0
男性 Male	508	4.9	2.8	5.1	6.5	4.1	1.8	3.3	71.5
16~24 岁 Age	108	1.9	0.9	1.9	6.5	2.8	0.9	0.9	84.3
25~34 岁 Age	146	4.8	0.7	4.8	5.5	3.4	2.7	6.2	71.9
35~44 岁 Age	130	5.4	5.4	5.4	6.9	4.6	3.1	0.8	68.5
45~54 岁 Age	85	7.1	5.9	8.2	4.7	5.9	0.0	5.9	62.4
55~60 岁 Age	39	7.7	0.0	7.7	12.8	5.1	0.0	2.6	64.1
女性 Female	500	0.8	0.2	1.8	1.8	0.8	1.0	3.0	90.6
16~24 岁 Age	107	0.0	0.0	0.0	0.9	0.0	0.0	4.7	94.4
25~34 岁 Age	141	1.4	0.7	3.5	2.8	0.7	0.7	3.5	86.5
35~44 岁 Age	129	0.8	0.0	2.3	3.1	1.6	1.6	0.8	89.9
45~54 岁 Age	82	1.2	0.0	1.2	0.0	1.2	1.2	2.4	92.7
55~60 岁 Age	41	0.0	0.0	0.0	0.0	0.0	2.4	4.9	92.7

2-8 样本、男性各年龄层、女性各年龄层的品牌习惯/ Brand Habit in Consuming Hard Liquor by the Whole Sample, Age and Gender Groups

	人数 Number	基本固定饮用一个牌子 used in only one brand	比较固定地饮用两个或三个牌子 used in two or three brands	基本上不太固定牌子 no brand preference
样本 Sample	192	45.8	35.9	18.2
男性 Male	145	49.7	33.1	17.2
16~24 岁 Age	17	41.2	47.1	11.8
25~34 岁 Age	41	51.2	31.7	17.1
35~44 岁 Age	41	56.1	22.0	22.0
45~54 岁 Age	32	53.1	34.4	12.5
55~60 岁 Age	14	28.6	50.0	21.4
女性 Female	47	34.0	44.7	21.3
16~24 岁 Age	6	16.7	50.0	33.3
25~34 岁 Age	19	31.6	52.6	15.8
35~44 岁 Age	13	46.2	38.5	15.4
45~54 岁 Age	6	50.0	33.3	16.7
55~60 岁 Age	3	0.0	33.3	66.7

2-9 选择该类商品的考虑因素/ Ranking of the Considerations in Purchasing

注：本题为多选题，合计百分比超过 100%(Multiple answers)

排名 Ranking	考虑因素 Considerations	人次 Person-time	百分比 Percent
1	口味好 pleasant taste	108	56.3
2	价格适中 reasonable price	88	45.8
3	有名的牌子 famous brand	67	34.9
4	只是由于习惯 out of habit	25	13.0
5	购买方便 easy to buy	20	10.4
6	生产日期 date of producing	17	8.9
7	别人送的 given by other people	13	6.8
8	广告影响 influence of advertising	9	4.7
9	朋友推荐 introduction of friends	7	3.6
10	其它 others	4	2.1
11	包装吸引人 appealing package	3	1.6
12	有优惠条件 with preferential terms	2	1.0
13	售货员介绍 introduced by the shop assistants	1	0.5

n=192

2-10 样本、男性各年龄层、女性各年龄层最常饮用的度数/ Degree of the Consumed Hard Liquor by the Whole Sample, Age and Gender Groups

	人数 Number	55 度以上 55° or over	39—55 度 39—55°	38 度及以下 38° or below	其它 others
样本 Sample	192	9.9	55.2	34.9	0.0
男性 Male	145	10.3	60.7	29.0	0.0
16~24 岁 Age	17	11.8	52.9	35.3	0.0
25~34 岁 Age	41	9.8	58.5	31.7	0.0
35~44 岁 Age	41	9.8	61.0	29.3	0.0
45~54 岁 Age	32	12.5	65.6	21.9	0.0
55~60 岁 Age	14	7.1	64.3	28.6	0.0
女性 Female	47	8.5	38.3	53.2	0.0
16~24 岁 Age	6	0.0	16.7	83.3	0.0
25~34 岁 Age	19	5.3	47.4	47.4	0.0
35~44 岁 Age	13	15.4	38.5	46.2	0.0
45~54 岁 Age	6	16.7	33.3	50.0	0.0
55~60 岁 Age	3	0.0	33.3	66.7	0.0

2-11 样本、男性各年龄层、女性各年龄层最常饮用的场合/ Settings of Consumption by the Whole Sample, Age and Gender Groups

注：本题为多选题，合计百分比超过 100%(Multiple answers)

	人数 Number	请客 entertain guests	节假日团聚 get-together on holiday	日常饮用 drink daily	服药 drink with medicine	做菜 cooking meal	其它 others
样本 Sample	192	36.5	30.7	46.9	1.6	9.9	1.6
男性 Male	145	35.2	26.2	51.0	1.4	9.0	1.4
16~24 岁 Age	17	70.6	41.2	23.5	0.0	0.0	0.0
25~34 岁 Age	41	34.1	22.0	53.7	0.0	7.3	2.4
35~44 岁 Age	41	22.0	22.0	63.4	0.0	17.1	0.0
45~54 岁 Age	32	46.9	28.1	37.5	0.0	9.4	3.1
55~60 岁 Age	14	7.1	28.6	71.4	14.3	0.0	0.0
女性 Female	47	40.4	44.7	34.0	2.1	12.8	2.1
16~24 岁 Age	6	16.7	33.3	33.3	16.7	16.7	16.7
25~34 岁 Age	19	36.8	26.3	57.9	0.0	10.5	0.0
35~44 岁 Age	13	61.5	69.2	15.4	0.0	0.0	0.0
45~54 岁 Age	6	33.3	50.0	16.7	0.0	33.3	0.0
55~60 岁 Age	3	33.3	66.7	0.0	0.0	33.3	0.0

2-12 重度消费者人口分布/ Demographics of the Heavy Consumers

	人数 Number	16-24 岁 Age	25-34 岁 Age	35-44 岁 Age	45-54 岁 Age	55-60 岁 Age
样本 Sample	79	6.3	29.1	31.6	25.3	7.6
男性 Male	65	7.7	23.1	32.3	27.7	9.2
天天喝 daily	25	8.0	28.0	28.0	24.0	12.0
一周 3 次或以上 3 times or over a week	14	7.1	7.1	50.0	35.7	0.0
一周 1~2 次 once or twice a week	26	7.7	26.9	26.9	26.9	11.5
女性 Female	14	0.0	57.1	28.6	14.3	0.0
天天喝 daily	4	0.0	50.0	25.0	25.0	0.0
一周 3 次或以上 3 times or over a week	1	0.0	100.0	0.0	0.0	0.0
一周 1~2 次 once or twice a week	9	0.0	55.6	33.3	11.1	0.0

2-13 不同消费者层的常用品牌/ The Most Frequently Used Brands by Market Segments

2-13-1 时尚流行指标/ Fads Popular Index

	人数 Number	第一品牌及百分比 1st/percent	第二品牌及百分比 2nd/percent	第三品牌及百分比 3rd/percent
样本 Sample	186	**双沟大曲 Shuang Gou Da Qu(22.0)**	**孔府家酒 Confucius Family Liquor(13.4)**	**尖庄 Jianzhuang(9.7)**
平实生活指向 simple living orientation	88	双沟大曲 Shuang Gou Da Qu(26.1)	孔府家酒 Confucius Family Liquor(13.6)	尖庄 Jianzhuang(9.1)
时尚流行指向 fashion orientation	98	双沟大曲 Shuang Gou Da Qu(18.4)	孔府家酒 Confucius Family Liquor(13.3)	五粮液 Wuliangye(12.2)

2-13-2 广告态度指标/ Advertising Attitude Index

	人数 Number	第一品牌及百分比 1st/percent	第二品牌及百分比 2nd/percent	第三品牌及百分比 3rd/percent
样本 Sample	188	**双沟大曲 Shuang Gou Da Qu(22.3)**	**孔府家酒 Confucius Family Liquor(13.3)**	**尖庄 Jianzhuang(9.6)**
广告淡漠指向 indifferent orientation	43	孔府家酒 Confucius Family Liquor(16.3) 双沟大曲 Shuang Gou Da Qu(16.3)	洋河大曲 Yang He Da Qu(11.6)	剑南春 Jiannanchun(9.3)
中间层 medium	120	双沟大曲 Shuang Gou Da Qu(28.3)	尖庄 Jianzhuang(10.8) 泸州老窖 Lu Zhou Lao Jiao(10.8)	孔府家酒 Confucius Family Liquor(9.2)
信赖广告指向 loyal orientation	25	孔府家酒 Confucius Family Liquor(28.0)	五粮液 Wuliangye(16.0)	红星二锅头 Hong Xing Er Guo Tou(8.0) 尖庄 Jianzhuang(8.0) 洋河大曲 Yang He Da Qu(8.0)

2-13-3 饮食健康指标/ Foods & Drink Quality Index

	人数 Number	第一品牌及百分比 1st/percent	第二品牌及百分比 2nd/percent	第三品牌及百分比 3rd/percent
样本 Sample	188	**双沟大曲 Shuang Gou Da Qu(22.3)**	**孔府家酒 Confucius Family Liquor(13.3)**	**尖庄 Jianzhuang(10.1)**
饮食"温饱"指向 "basic" orientation	50	孔府家酒 Confucius Family Liquor(24.0)	双沟大曲 Shuang Gou Da Qu(14.0)	尖庄 Jianzhuang(12.0)
中间层 medium	93	双沟大曲 Shuang Gou Da Qu(31.2)	尖庄 Jianzhuang(10.8)	泸州老窖 Lu Zhou Lao Jiao(8.6)
健康营养指向 health & nutrition orientation	45	孔府家酒 Confucius Family Liquor(13.3) 双沟大曲 Shuang Gou Da Qu(13.3) 五粮液 Wuliangye(13.3)	泸州老窖 Lu Zhou Lao Jiao(8.9)	尖庄 Jianzhuang(6.7) 剑南春 Jiannanchun(6.7) 孔府宴酒 Kong Fu Yan Jiu(6.7)

2-14 重度消费者的消费者层构成/ The Composition of the Heavy Consumers

2-14-1 时尚流行指标/ Fads Popular Index

	人数 Number	平实生活指向 simple living orientation	时尚流行指向 fashion orientation
样本 Sample	76	48.7	51.3
天天喝 daily	26	61.5	38.5
一周 3 次或以上 3 times or over a week	15	53.3	46.7
一周 1~2 次 once or twice a week	35	37.1	62.9

2-14-2 广告态度指标/ Advertising Attitude Index

	人数 Number	广告淡漠指向 indifferent orientation	中间层 medium	信赖广告指向 loyal orientation
样本 Sample	77	29.9	58.4	11.7
天天喝 daily	28	35.7	53.6	10.7
一周 3 次或以上 3 times or over a week	15	40.0	53.3	6.7
一周 1~2 次 once or twice a week	34	20.6	64.7	14.7

2-14-3 饮食健康指标/ Foods & Drink Quality Index

	人数 Number	饮食"温饱"指向 "basic" orientation	中间层 medium	健康营养指向 health & nutrition orientation
样本 Sample	79	27.8	53.2	19.0
天天喝 daily	29	27.6	58.6	13.8
一周 3 次或以上 3 times or over a week	15	40.0	33.3	26.7
一周 1~2 次 once or twice a week	35	22.9	57.1	20.0

● 广州 / Guangzhou

2-1 最近三个月饮用频率的比例/ Proportion of the Sample Consuming Hard Liquor in the Last Three Months

	人数 Number	百分比 Percent
天天喝 daily	15	1.5
一周 3 次或以上 3 times or over a week	14	1.4
一周 1~2 次 once or twice a week	69	6.7
一个月 2～3 次 2 or 3 times a month	65	6.3
一个月 1 次 once a month	39	3.8
两个月 1 次 once two months	21	2.0
三个月 1 次或以下 once three months or below	36	3.5
没有喝 never	771	74.9

n=1030

2-2 最常用品牌排名/ Ranking of the Most Frequently Used Brands

排名 Brand Ranking	品牌 Brand	人数 Number	百分比 Percent
1	远航牌 Yuanhang	80	31.0
2	石湾米酒 Shiwan	30	11.6
3	九江 Jiujiang	19	7.4
4	贵州醇 Guizhouchun	15	5.8
5	古绵醇 Gumianchun	14	5.4
6	广东米酒 Guang Dong Mi Jiu	12	4.7
7	五粮液 Wuliangye	10	3.9
8	剑南春 Jiannanchun	7	2.7
9	泸州老窖 Lu Zhou Lao Jiao	5	1.9

n=258

2-3 样本、男性各年龄层、女性各年龄层的常用品牌/ The Most Frequently Used Brands by the Whole Sample, Age and Gender Groups

	人数 Number	第一品牌及百分比 1st/ percent	第二品牌及百分比 2nd/ percent	第三品牌及百分比 3rd/ percent
样本 Sample	258	**远航牌 Yuanhang(31.0)**	**石湾米酒 Shiwan(11.6)**	**九江 Jiujiang(7.4)**
男性 Male	163	**远航牌 Yuanhang(34.4)**	**石湾米酒 Shiwan(11.7)**	**贵州醇 Guizhouchun(6.7)**
16~24 岁 Age	19	远航牌 Yuanhang(31.6)	石湾米酒 Shiwan(10.5) 贵州醇 Guizhouchun(10.5)	古绵醇 Gumianchun(5.3) 石湾特酿 Shiwan(5.3) 皖酒王 Wanjiuwang(5.3) 皇朝 Huangchao(5.3) 茅台 Moutai(5.3) 孔府家酒 Confucius Family Liquor(5.3) 尖庄 Jianzhuang(5.3) 广东米酒 Guang Dong Mi Jiu(5.3)
25~34 岁 Age	49	远航牌 Yuanhang(36.7)	贵州醇 Guizhouchun(10.2)	石湾米酒 Shiwan(8.2)
35~44 岁 Age	48	远航牌 Yuanhang(35.4)	九江 Jiujiang(12.5)	石湾米酒 Shiwan(10.4)
45~54 岁 Age	27	远航牌 Yuanhang(37.0)	石湾米酒 Shiwan(14.8)	贵州醇 Guizhouchun(7.4) 广东米酒 Guang Dong Mi Jiu(7.4) 剑南春 Jiannanchun(7.4)
55~60 岁 Age	20	远航牌 Yuanhang(25.0)	石湾米酒 Shiwan(20.0)	剑南春 Jiannanchun(10.0) 贵州醇 Guizhouchun(10.0)
女性 Female	95	**远航牌 Yuanhang(25.3)**	**石湾米酒 Shiwan(11.6)**	**九江 Jiujiang(10.5)**
16~24 岁 Age	11	九江 Jiujiang(27.3)	古绵醇(18.2)	绵竹大曲 Mian Zhu Da Qu(9.1) 石湾米酒 Shiwan(9.1) 远航牌 Yuanhang(9.1) 盛古川酒 Shengguchuan(9.1) 大佬酒 Dalao(9.1) 珠江桥 Zhujiang(9.1)
25~34 岁 Age	27	远航牌 Yuanhang(18.5)	广东米酒 Guang Dong Mi Jiu(11.1) 贵州醇 Guizhouchun(11.1)	九江 Jiujiang(7.4) 石湾米酒 Shiwan(7.4) 五粮液 Wuliangye(7.4)
35~44 岁 Age	28	远航牌 Yuanhang(28.6)	石湾米酒 Shiwan(17.9)	广东米酒 Guang Dong Mi Jiu(7.1) 九江 Jiujiang(7.1) 五粮液 Wuliangye(7.1) 古绵醇 Gumianchun(7.1)
45~54 岁 Age	24	远航牌 Yuanhang(33.3)	九江 Jiujiang(12.5)	古绵醇 Gumianchun(8.3) 石湾米酒 Shiwan(8.3)
55~60 岁 Age	5	远航牌 Yuanhang(40.0)	石湾米酒 Shiwan(20.0) 贵州醇 Guizhouchun(20.0) 小糊涂仙 Tipsy Spirit(20.0)	

2-4 理想品牌排名/ Ranking of the Ideal Brands

排名 Brand Ranking	品牌 Brand	人数 Number	百分比 Percent
1	远航牌 Yuanhang	143	13.8
2	茅台 Moutai	83	8.0
3	九江 Jiujiang	55	5.3
4	五粮液 Wuliangye	53	5.1
5	石湾米酒 Shiwan	52	5.0
6	贵州醇 Guizhouchun	45	4.4
7	古绵醇 Gumianchun	25	2.4
8	剑南春 Jiannanchun	21	2.0
8	广东米酒 Guang Dong Mi Jiu	21	2.0

n=1034

2-5 样本、男性各年龄层、女性各年龄层最近三个月有无购买的比例/ Purchasing in the Last Three Months by the Whole Sample, Age and Gender Groups

	人数 Number	买过 yes	没买过 no
样本 Sample	1034	29.9	70.1
男性 Male	499	32.3	67.7
16~24 岁 Age	106	20.8	79.2
25~34 岁 Age	150	30.7	69.3
35~44 岁 Age	127	39.4	60.6
45~54 岁 Age	73	35.6	64.4
55~60 岁 Age	43	39.5	60.5
女性 Female	535	27.7	72.3
16~24 岁 Age	112	13.4	86.6
25~34 岁 Age	158	29.1	70.9
35~44 岁 Age	137	32.1	67.9
45~54 岁 Age	87	35.6	64.4
55~60 岁 Age	41	29.3	70.7

2-6 样本、男性各年龄层、女性各年龄层最近三个月是否拿白酒送过礼/ To Offer Hard Liquor as Gift in the Last Three Months by the Whole Sample, Age and Gender Groups

	人数 Number	送过 yes	没送过 no
样本 Sample	1029	8.0	92.0
男性 Male	496	7.7	92.3
16~24 岁 Age	106	4.7	95.3
25~34 岁 Age	149	14.1	85.9
35~44 岁 Age	126	4.8	95.2
45~54 岁 Age	72	4.2	95.8
55~60 岁 Age	43	7.0	93.0
女性 Female	533	8.3	91.7
16~24 岁 Age	111	3.6	96.4
25~34 岁 Age	158	8.9	91.1
35~44 岁 Age	136	8.1	91.9
45~54 岁 Age	87	12.6	87.4
55~60 岁 Age	41	9.8	90.2

2-7 样本、男性各年龄层、女性各年龄层最近三个月的饮用频率/ Frequencies of Consuming Hard Liquor in the Last Three Months by the Whole Sample, Age and Gender Groups

	人数 Number	天天喝 daily	一周3次或以上 3 times or over a week	一周1~2次 once or twice a week	一个月2~3次 2 or 3 times a month	一个月1次 once a month	两个月1次 once two months	三个月1次或以下 once three months or below	没有喝 never
样本 Sample	1030	1.5	1.4	6.7	6.3	3.8	2.0	3.5	74.9
男性 Male	498	1.8	2.2	10.0	8.2	5.6	2.0	3.0	67.1
16~24 岁 Age	106	0.0	0.0	3.8	3.8	6.6	0.9	2.8	82.1
25~34 岁 Age	150	1.3	0.7	9.3	8.7	7.3	2.0	4.0	66.7
35~44 岁 Age	127	1.6	3.9	12.6	9.4	5.5	2.4	2.4	62.2
45~54 岁 Age	73	2.7	2.7	9.6	12.3	2.7	4.1	2.7	63.0
55~60 岁 Age	42	7.1	7.1	21.4	7.1	2.4	0.0	2.4	52.4
女性 Female	532	1.1	0.6	3.6	4.5	2.1	2.1	3.9	82.1
16~24 岁 Age	112	0.0	0.0	3.6	0.9	1.8	0.0	3.6	90.2
25~34 岁 Age	156	0.0	0.0	3.2	5.1	1.9	2.6	4.5	82.7
35~44 岁 Age	137	2.2	0.0	2.2	6.6	1.5	2.9	5.1	79.6
45~54 岁 Age	86	1.2	1.2	7.0	7.0	4.7	3.5	3.5	72.1
55~60 岁 Age	41	4.9	4.9	2.4	0.0	0.0	0.0	0.0	87.8

2-8 样本、男性各年龄层、女性各年龄层的品牌习惯/ Brand Habit in Consuming Hard Liquor by the Whole Sample, Age and Gender Groups

	人数 Number	基本固定饮用一个牌子 used in only one brand	比较固定地饮用两个或三个牌子 used in two or three brands	基本上不太固定牌子 no brand preference
样本 Sample	**258**	**39.5**	**35.7**	**24.8**
男性 Male	**163**	**39.3**	**34.4**	**26.4**
16~24 岁 Age	19	47.4	31.6	21.1
25~34 岁 Age	50	32.0	30.0	38.0
35~44 岁 Age	47	38.3	42.6	19.1
45~54 岁 Age	27	40.7	29.6	29.6
55~60 岁 Age	20	50.0	35.0	15.0
女性 Female	**95**	**40.0**	**37.9**	**22.1**
16~24 岁 Age	11	9.1	54.5	36.4
25~34 岁 Age	27	33.3	40.7	25.9
35~44 岁 Age	28	53.6	32.1	14.3
45~54 岁 Age	24	41.7	41.7	16.7
55~60 岁 Age	5	60.0	0.0	40.0

2-9 选择该类商品的考虑因素/ Ranking of the Considerations in Purchasing

注：本题为多选题，合计百分比超过 100%(Multiple answers）

排名 Ranking	考虑因素 Considerations	人次 Person-time	百分比 Percent
1	口味好 pleasant taste	121	46.7
2	价格适中 reasonable price	102	39.4
3	有名的牌子 famous brand	95	36.7
4	购买方便 easy to buy	45	17.4
5	只是由于习惯 out of habit	41	15.8
6	朋友推荐 introduction of friends	24	9.3
6	生产日期 date of producing	24	9.3
7	广告影响 influence of advertising	11	4.2
8	别人送的 given by other people	10	3.9
9	包装吸引人 appealing package	8	3.1
10	其它 others	7	2.7
11	有优惠条件 with preferential terms	5	1.9
12	售货员介绍 introduced by the shop assistants	2	0.8

n=259

2-10 样本、男性各年龄层、女性各年龄层最常饮用的度数/ Degree of the Consumed Hard Liquor by the Whole Sample, Age and Gender Groups

	人数 Number	55 度以上 55^0 or over	39—55 度 39^0--55^0	38 度及以下 38^0 or below	其它 others
样本 Sample	**259**	**5.0**	**29.3**	**64.1**	**1.5**
男性 Male	**164**	**4.9**	**31.7**	**62.2**	**1.2**
16~24 岁 Age	19	5.3	36.8	57.9	0.0
25~34 岁 Age	50	6.0	30.0	62.0	2.0
35~44 岁 Age	48	8.3	25.0	66.7	0.0
45~54 岁 Age	27	0.0	37.0	63.0	0.0
55~60 岁 Age	20	0.0	40.0	55.0	5.0
女性 Female	**95**	**5.3**	**25.3**	**67.4**	**2.1**
16~24 岁 Age	11	9.1	9.1	81.8	0.0
25~34 岁 Age	27	3.7	33.3	59.3	3.7
35~44 岁 Age	28	0.0	32.1	67.9	0.0
45~54 岁 Age	24	8.3	20.8	66.7	4.2
55~60 岁 Age	5	20.0	0.0	80.0	0.0

2-11 样本、男性各年龄层、女性各年龄层最常饮用的场合/ Settings of Consumption by the Whole Sample, Age and Gender Groups

注：本题为多选题，合计百分比超过 100%(Multiple answers）

	人数 Number	请客 entertain guests	节假日团聚 get-together on holiday	日常饮用 drink daily	服药 drink with medicine	做菜 cooking meal	其它 others
样本 Sample	258	32.2	41.1	37.2	0.4	20.9	1.2
男性 Male	164	34.1	43.3	39.6	0.6	14.6	1.2
16~24 岁 Age	19	52.6	36.8	15.8	0.0	26.3	5.3
25~34 岁 Age	50	28.0	42.0	40.0	0.0	10.0	2.0
35~44 岁 Age	48	35.4	41.7	45.8	0.0	12.5	0.0
45~54 岁 Age	27	44.4	59.3	22.2	0.0	18.5	0.0
55~60 岁 Age	20	15.0	35.0	70.0	5.0	15.0	0.0
女性 Female	94	28.7	37.2	33.0	0.0	31.9	1.1
16~24 岁 Age	11	27.3	45.5	27.3	0.0	36.4	0.0
25~34 岁 Age	27	33.3	51.9	25.9	0.0	14.8	3.7
35~44 岁 Age	27	29.6	29.6	22.2	0.0	40.7	0.0
45~54 岁 Age	24	25.0	33.3	45.8	0.0	41.7	0.0
55~60 岁 Age	5	20.0	0.0	80.0	0.0	20.0	0.0

2-12 重度消费者人口分布/ Demographics of the Heavy Consumers

	人数 Number	16-24 岁 Age	25-34 岁 Age	35-44 岁 Age	45-54 岁 Age	55-60 岁 Age
样本 Sample	98	8.2	22.4	29.6	19.4	20.4
男性 Male	70	5.7	24.3	32.9	15.7	21.4
天天喝 daily	9	0.0	22.2	22.2	22.2	33.3
一周 3 次或以上 3 times or over a week	11	0.0	9.1	45.5	18.2	27.3
一周 1~2 次 once or twice a week	50	8.0	28.0	32.0	14.0	18.0
女性 Female	28	14.3	17.9	21.4	28.6	17.9
天天喝 daily	6	0.0	0.0	50.0	16.7	33.3
一周 3 次或以上 3 times or over a week	3	0.0	0.0	0.0	33.3	66.7
一周 1~2 次 once or twice a week	19	21.1	26.3	15.8	31.6	5.3

2-13 不同消费者层的常用品牌/ The Most Frequently Used Brands by Market Segments

2-13-1 时尚流行指标/ Fads Popular Index

	人数 Number	第一品牌及百分比 1st/percent	第二品牌及百分比 2nd/percent	第三品牌及百分比 3rd/percent
样本 Sample	256	远航牌 Yuanhang(30.9)	石湾米酒 Shiwan(11.7)	九江 Jiujiang(7.0)
平实生活指向 simple living orientation	138	远航牌 Yuanhang(30.4)	石湾米酒 Shiwan(12.3)	九江 Jiujiang(7.2)
时尚流行指向 fashion orientation	118	远航牌 Yuanhang(31.4)	石湾米酒 Shiwan(11.0)	九江 Jiujiang(6.8)

2-13-2 广告态度指标/ Advertising attitude Index

	人数 Number	第一品牌及百分比 1st/percent	第二品牌及百分比 2nd/percent	第三品牌及百分比 3rd/percent
样本 Sample	253	远航牌 Yuanhang(31.6)	石湾米酒 Shiwan(11.5)	九江 Jiujiang(7.1)
广告淡漠指向 indifferent orientation	90	远航牌 Yuanhang(27.8)	九江 Jiujiang(7.8) 石湾米酒 Shiwan(7.8)	古绵醇 Gumianchun(6.7)
中间层 medium	140	远航牌 Yuanhang(33.6)	石湾米酒 Shiwan(14.3)	九江 Jiujiang(7.1)
信赖广告指向 loyal orientation	23	远航牌 Yuanhang(34.8)	贵州醇 Guizhouchun(13.0)	石湾米酒 Shiwan(8.7)

2-13-3 饮食健康指标/ Foods & Drink Quality Index

	人数 Number	第一品牌及百分比 1st/percent	第二品牌及百分比 2nd/percent	第三品牌及百分比 3rd/percent
样本 Sample	256	远航牌 Yuanhang(30.9)	石湾米酒 Shiwan(11.3)	九江 Jiujiang(7.4)
饮食“温饱”指向 "basic" orientation	83	远航牌 Yuanhang(33.7)	石湾米酒 Shiwan(14.5)	贵州醇 Guizhouchun(7.2) 古绵醇 Gumianchun(7.2)
中间层 medium	127	远航牌 Yuanhang(28.3)	九江 Jiujiang(9.4)	石湾米酒 Shiwan(7.9)
健康营养指向 health & nutrition orientation	46	远航牌 Yuanhang(32.6)	石湾米酒 Shiwan(15.2)	五粮液 Wuliangye(6.5) 贵州醇 Guizhouchun(6.5)

2-14 重度消费者的消费者层构成/ The Composition of the Heavy Consumers

2-14-1 时尚流行指标/ Fads Popular Index

	人数 Number	平实生活指向 simple living orientation	时尚流行指向 fashion orientation
样本 Sample	97	61.9	38.1
天天喝 daily	15	73.3	26.7
一周 3 次或以上 3 times or over a week	14	78.6	21.4
一周 1~2 次 once or twice a week	68	55.9	44.1

2-14-2 广告态度指标/ Advertising Attitude Index

	人数 Number	广告淡漠指向 indifferent orientation	中间层 medium	信赖广告指向 loyal orientation
样本 Sample	97	42.3	48.5	9.3
天天喝 daily	14	64.3	21.4	14.3
一周 3 次或以上 3 times or over a week	14	50.0	50.0	0.0
一周 1~2 次 once or twice a week	69	36.2	53.6	10.1

2-14-3 饮食健康指标/ Foods & Drink Quality Index

	人数 Number	饮食“温饱”指向 "basic" orientation	中间层 medium	健康营养指向 health & nutrition orientation
样本 Sample	96	36.5	52.1	11.5
天天喝 daily	15	46.7	46.7	6.7
一周 3 次或以上 3 times or over a week	13	53.8	46.2	0.0
一周 1~2 次 once or twice a week	68	30.9	54.4	14.7

● 重庆 / Chongqing

2-1 最近三个月饮用频率的比例/ Proportion of the Sample Consuming Hard Liquor in the Last Three Months

	人数 Number	百分比 Percent
天天喝 daily	39	6.3
一周 3 次或以上 3 times or over a week	32	5.2
一周 1~2 次 once or twice a week	50	8.1
一个月 2～3 次 2 or 3 times a month	36	5.8
一个月 1 次 once a month	18	2.9
两个月 1 次 once two months	15	2.4
三个月 1 次或以下 once three months or below	23	3.7
没有喝 never	405	65.5

n=618

2-2 最常用品牌排名/ Ranking of the Most Frequently Used Brands

排名 Brand Ranking	品牌 Brand	人数 Number	百分比 Percent
1	几江 Jijiang	61	28.6
2	全兴大曲 Quan Xing Da Qu	40	18.8
3	石松 Shisong	39	18.3
4	鸭溪窖 Yaxijiao	11	5.2
4	江津 Jiangjin	11	5.2
5	五粮液 Wuliangye	9	4.2
6	泸州老窖 Lu Zhou Lao Jiao	8	3.8
7	五粮春 Wuliangchun	3	1.4
7	剑南春 Jiannanchun	3	1.4
7	尖庄 Jianzhuang	3	1.4

n=213

2-3 样本、男性各年龄层、女性各年龄层的常用品牌/ The Most Frequently Used Brands by the Whole Sample, Age and Gender Groups

	人数 Number	第一品牌及百分比 1st/ percent	第二品牌及百分比 2nd/ percent	第三品牌及百分比 3rd/ percent
样本 Sample	213	**几江 Jijiang(28.6)**	**全兴大曲 Quan Xing Da Qu(18.8)**	**石松 Shisong(18.3)**
男性 Male	154	**几江 Jijiang(24.7)**	**全兴大曲 Quan Xing Da Qu(20.8)**	**石松 Shisong(20.1)**
16~24 岁 Age	16	全兴大曲 Quan Xing Da Qu(37.5)	几江 Jijiang(25.0)	五粮液 Wuliangye(12.5)
25~34 岁 Age	52	全兴大曲 Quan Xing Da Qu(26.9)	几江 Jijiang(21.2)	石松 Shisong(17.3)
35~44 岁 Age	39	几江 Jijiang(41.0)	石松 Shisong(28.2)	全兴大曲 Quan Xing Da Qu(12.8)
45~54 岁 Age	29	全兴大曲 Quan Xing Da Qu(17.2) 石松 Shisong(17.2) 几江 Jijiang(17.2)	江津 Jiangjin(13.8)	鸭溪窖 Yaxijiao(6.9)
55~60 岁 Age	18	石松 Shisong(27.8)	江津 Jiangjin(11.1) 几江 Jijiang(11.1) 全兴大曲 Quan Xing Da Qu(11.1)	鸭溪窖 Yaxijiao(5.6) 五粮液 Wuliangye(5.6) 泸州老窖 Lu Zhou Lao Jiao(5.6) 孔府家酒 Confucius Family Liquor(5.6) 剑南春 Jiannanchun(5.6)
女性 Female	59	**几江 Jijiang(39.0)**	**石松 Shisong(13.6)** **全兴大曲 Quan Xing Da Qu(13.6)**	**泸州老窖 Lu Zhou Lao Jiao(6.8)**
16~24 岁 Age	1	阳城 Yangcheng(100.0)		
25~34 岁 Age	20	几江 Jijiang(40.0)	全兴大曲 Quan Xing Da Qu(15.0)	鸭溪窖 Yaxijiao(10.0)
35~44 岁 Age	18	几江 Jijiang(33.3)	全兴大曲 Quan Xing Da Qu(22.2)	泸州老窖 Lu Zhou Lao Jiao(11.1) 石松 Shisong(11.1)
45~54 岁 Age	16	几江 Jijiang(43.8)	石松 Shisong(25.0)	泸州老窖 Lu Zhou Lao Jiao(6.3) 绵竹大曲 Mian Zhu Da Qu(6.3) 全兴大曲 Quan Xing Da Qu(6.3) 五粮液 Wuliangye(6.3) 平坝窖酒 Ping Ba Jiao Jiu(6.3)
55~60 岁 Age	4	几江 Jijiang(50.0)	五粮液 Wuliangye(25.0) 石松 Shisong(25.0)	

2-4 理想品牌排名/ Ranking of the Ideal Brands

排名 Brand Ranking	品牌 Brands	人数 Number	百分比 Percent
1	几江 Jijiang	148	23.7
2	五粮液 Wuliangye	112	17.9
3	全兴大曲 Quan Xing Da Qu	72	11.5
4	茅台 Moutai	55	8.8
5	石松 Shisong	41	6.6
6	江津 Jiangjin	28	4.5
7	泸州老窖 Lu Zhou Lao Jiao	22	3.5
8	尖庄 Jianzhuang	9	1.4
8	鸭溪窖 Yaxijiao	9	1.4
9	小绵曲 Xiaomianqu	5	0.8
10	五粮春 Wuliangchun	4	0.6
10	剑南春 Jiannanchun	4	0.6

n=624

2-5 样本、男性各年龄层、女性各年龄层最近三个月有无购买的比例/ Purchasing in the Last Three Months by the Whole Sample, Age and Gender Groups

	人数 Number	买过 yes	没买过 no
样本 Sample	624	44.2	55.8
男性 Male	314	49.7	50.3
16~24 岁 Age	64	32.8	67.2
25~34 岁 Age	93	53.8	46.2
35~44 岁 Age	75	50.7	49.3
45~54 岁 Age	54	53.7	46.3
55~60 岁 Age	28	64.3	35.7
女性 Female	310	38.7	61.3
16~24 岁 Age	64	21.9	78.1
25~34 岁 Age	90	44.4	55.6
35~44 岁 Age	73	38.4	61.6
45~54 岁 Age	60	48.3	51.7
55~60 岁 Age	23	39.1	60.9

2-6 样本、男性各年龄层、女性各年龄层最近三个月是否拿白酒送过礼/ To Offer Hard Liquor as Gift in the Last Three Months by the Whole Sample, Age and Gender Groups

	人数 Number	送过 yes	没送过 no
样本 Sample	620	11.9	88.1
男性 Male	312	11.9	88.1
16~24 岁 Age	63	12.7	87.3
25~34 岁 Age	93	12.9	87.1
35~44 岁 Age	75	10.7	89.3
45~54 岁 Age	53	11.3	88.7
55~60 岁 Age	28	10.7	89.3
女性 Female	308	12.0	88.0
16~24 岁 Age	63	4.8	95.2
25~34 岁 Age	90	18.9	81.1
35~44 岁 Age	72	8.3	91.7
45~54 岁 Age	60	15.0	85.0
55~60 岁 Age	23	8.7	91.3

2-7 样本、男性各年龄层、女性各年龄层最近三个月的饮用频率/ Frequencies of Consuming Hard Liquor in the Last Three Months by the Whole Sample, Age and Gender Groups

	人数 Number	天天喝 daily	一周3次或以上 3 times or over a week	一周1~2次 once or twice a week	一个月2~3次 2 or 3 times a month	一个月1次 once a month	两个月1次 once two months	三个月1次或以下 once three months or below	没有喝 never
样本 Sample	618	6.3	5.2	8.1	5.8	2.9	2.4	3.7	65.5
男性 Male	311	10.6	8.7	10.0	9.0	4.2	3.9	3.2	50.5
16~24 岁 Age	64	3.1	1.6	4.7	4.7	1.6	3.1	6.3	75.0
25~34 岁 Age	93	7.5	14.0	9.7	11.8	7.5	3.2	2.2	44.1
35~44 岁 Age	72	13.9	6.9	19.4	6.9	4.2	2.8	0.0	45.8
45~54 岁 Age	54	16.7	13.0	3.7	11.1	1.9	5.6	1.9	46.3
55~60 岁 Age	28	17.9	3.6	10.7	10.7	3.6	7.1	10.7	35.7
女性 Female	307	2.0	1.6	6.2	2.6	1.6	1.0	4.2	80.8
16~24 岁 Age	64	0.0	0.0	1.6	0.0	0.0	0.0	0.0	98.4
25~34 岁 Age	89	2.2	4.5	5.6	4.5	1.1	1.1	3.4	77.5
35~44 岁 Age	71	4.2	0.0	11.3	1.4	0.0	2.8	5.6	74.6
45~54 岁 Age	60	0.0	1.7	6.7	5.0	6.7	0.0	6.7	73.3
55~60 岁 Age	23	4.3	0.0	4.3	0.0	0.0	0.0	8.7	82.6

2-8 样本、男性各年龄层、女性各年龄层的品牌习惯/ Brand Habit in Consuming Hard Liquor by the Whole Sample, Age and Gender Groups

	人数 Number	基本固定饮用一个牌子 used in only one brand	比较固定地饮用两个或三个牌子 used in two or three brands	基本上不太固定牌子 no brand preference
样本 Sample	213	53.5	27.2	19.2
男性 Male	154	53.2	27.9	18.8
16~24 岁 Age	16	43.8	25.0	31.3
25~34 岁 Age	52	40.4	28.8	30.8
35~44 岁 Age	39	64.1	25.6	10.3
45~54 岁 Age	29	58.6	34.5	6.9
55~60 岁 Age	18	66.7	22.2	11.1
女性 Female	59	54.2	25.4	20.3
16~24 岁 Age	1	100.0	0.0	0.0
25~34 岁 Age	20	30.0	40.0	30.0
35~44 岁 Age	18	66.7	22.2	11.1
45~54 岁 Age	16	62.5	18.8	18.8
55~60 岁 Age	4	75.0	0.0	25.0

2-9 选择该类商品的考虑因素/ Ranking of the Considerations in Purchasing

注：本题为多选题，合计百分比超过 100%(Multiple answers)

排名 Ranking	考虑因素 Considerations	人次 Person-time	百分比 Percent
1	口味好 pleasant taste	124	58.2
2	价格适中 reasonable price	95	44.6
3	有名的牌子 famous brand	45	21.1
4	购买方便 easy to buy	38	17.8
5	只是由于习惯 out of habit	36	16.9
6	生产日期 date of producing	22	10.3
7	朋友推荐 introduction of friends	13	6.1
8	别人送的 given by other people	6	2.8
8	广告影响 influence of advertising	6	2.8
9	其它 others	3	1.4
10	有优惠条件 with preferential terms	2	0.9

n=213

2-10 样本、男性各年龄层、女性各年龄层最常饮用的度数/ Degree of the Consumed Hard Liquor by the Whole Sample, Age and Gender Groups

	人数 Number	55 度以上 55° or over	39—55 度 39°—55°	38 度及以下 38° or below	其它 others
样本 Sample	212	44.3	44.8	10.8	0.0
男性 Male	153	46.4	44.4	9.2	0.0
16~24 岁 Age	16	37.5	56.3	6.3	0.0
25~34 岁 Age	52	34.6	51.9	13.5	0.0
35~44 岁 Age	39	51.3	38.5	10.3	0.0
45~54 岁 Age	28	53.6	42.9	3.6	0.0
55~60 岁 Age	18	66.7	27.8	5.6	0.0
女性 Female	59	39.0	45.8	15.3	0.0
16~24 岁 Age	1	0.0	0.0	100.0	0.0
25~34 岁 Age	20	25.0	55.0	20.0	0.0
35~44 岁 Age	18	38.9	50.0	11.1	0.0
45~54 岁 Age	16	62.5	25.0	12.5	0.0
55~60 岁 Age	4	25.0	75.0	0.0	0.0

2-11 样本、男性各年龄层、女性各年龄层最常饮用的场合/ Settings of Consumption by the Whole Sample, Age and Gender Groups

注：本题为多选题，合计百分比超过 100%(Multiple answers）

	人数 Number	请客 entertain guests	节假日团聚 get-together on holiday	日常饮用 drink daily	服药 drink with medicine	做菜 cooking meal	其它 others
样本 Sample	213	35.7	32.9	47.9	4.7	13.1	0.9
男性 Male	154	35.1	33.1	49.4	3.2	10.4	1.3
16~24 岁 Age	16	50.0	50.0	31.3	0.0	12.5	0.0
25~34 岁 Age	52	42.3	36.5	42.3	0.0	5.8	3.8
35~44 岁 Age	39	23.1	20.5	64.1	5.1	15.4	0.0
45~54 岁 Age	29	24.1	41.4	55.2	3.4	10.3	0.0
55~60 岁 Age	18	44.4	22.2	44.4	11.1	11.1	0.0
女性 Female	59	37.3	32.2	44.1	8.5	20.3	0.0
16~24 岁 Age	1	0.0	0.0	100.0	0.0	0.0	0.0
25~34 岁 Age	20	45.0	45.0	35.0	0.0	15.0	0.0
35~44 岁 Age	18	44.4	22.2	61.1	0.0	16.7	0.0
45~54 岁 Age	16	25.0	37.5	37.5	18.8	37.5	0.0
55~60 岁 Age	4	25.0	0.0	25.0	50.0	0.0	0.0

2-12 重度消费者人口分布/ Demographics of the Heavy Consumers

	人数 Number	16-24 岁 Age	25-34 岁 Age	35-44 岁 Age	45-54 岁 Age	55-60 岁 Age
样本 Sample	121	5.8	33.1	33.1	19.0	9.1
男性 Male	91	6.6	31.9	31.9	19.8	9.9
天天喝 daily	33	6.1	21.2	30.3	27.3	15.2
一周 3 次或以上 3 times or over a week	27	3.7	48.1	18.5	25.9	3.7
一周 1~2 次 once or twice a week	31	9.7	29.0	45.2	6.5	9.7
女性 Female	30	3.3	36.7	36.7	16.7	6.7
天天喝 daily	6	0.0	33.3	50.0	0.0	16.7
一周 3 次或以上 3 times or over a week	5	0.0	80.0	0.0	20.0	0.0
一周 1~2 次 once or twice a week	19	5.3	26.3	42.1	21.1	5.3

2-13 不同消费者层的常用品牌/ The Most Frequently Used Brands by Market Segments

2-13-1 时尚流行指标/ Fads Popular Index

	人数 Number	第一品牌及百分比 1st/percent	第二品牌及百分比 2nd/percent	第三品牌及百分比 3rd/percent	第四品牌及百分比 4th/percent	第五品牌及百分比 5th/percent
样本 Sample	210	**几江 Jijiang(29.0)**	**全兴大曲 Quan Xing Da Qu(19.0)**	**石松 Shisong(18.6)**	**江津 Jiangjin(5.2) 鸭溪窖 Yaxijiao(5.2)**	**五粮液 Wuliangye(4.3)**
平实生活指向 simple living orientation	131	几江 Jijiang(31.3)	石松 Shisong(22.1)	全兴大曲 Quan Xing Da Qu (13.0)	江津 Jiangjin(5.3)	泸州老窖 Lu Zhou Lao Jiao (4.6) 鸭溪窖 Yaxijiao(4.6)
时尚流行指向 fashion orientation	79	全兴大曲 Quan Xing Da Qu (29.1)	几江 Jijiang(25.3)	石松 Shisong(12.7)	五粮液 Wuliangye(6.3) 鸭溪窖 Yaxijiao(6.3)	江津 Jiangjin(5.1)

2-13-2 广告态度指标/ Advertising Attitude Index

	人数 Number	第一品牌及百分比 1st/percent	第二品牌及百分比 2nd/percent	第三品牌及百分比 3rd/percent	第四品牌及百分比 4th/percent	第五品牌及百分比 5th/percent
样本 Sample	211	**几江 Jijiang(28.4)**	**全兴大曲 Quan Xing Da Qu(19.0)**	**石松 Shisong(18.5)**	**鸭溪窖 Yaxijiao(5.2) 江津 Jiangjin(5.2)**	**五粮液 Wuliangye(4.3)**
广告淡漠指向 indifferent orientation	75	几江 Jijiang(26.7)	石松 Shisong(24.0)	全兴大曲 Quan Xing Da Qu (17.3)	江津 Jiangjin(8.0)	鸭溪窖 Yaxijiao(6.7)
中间层 medium	112	几江 Jijiang(28.6)	全兴大曲 Quan Xing Da Qu (18.8)	石松 Shisong(17.0)	五粮液 Wuliangye(7.1)	泸州老窖 Lu Zhou Lao Jiao (4.5) 鸭溪窖 Yaxijiao(4.5)
信赖广告指向 loyal orientation	24	几江 Jijiang(33.3)	全兴大曲 Quan Xing Da Qu (25.0)	江津 Jiangjin(12.5)	石松 Shisong(8.3)	泸州老窖 Lu Zhou Lao Jiao (4.2) 沱牌大曲 Tuo Pai Da Qu (4.2) 五粮液 Wuliangye(4.2) 鸭溪窖 Yaxijiao(4.2) 泸州二曲 Lu Zhou Er Qu (4.2)

2-13-3 饮食健康指标/ Foods & Drink Quality Index

	人数 Number	第一品牌及百分比 1st/percent	第二品牌及百分比 2nd/percent	第三品牌及百分比 3rd/percent	第四品牌及百分比 4th/percent	第五品牌及百分比 5th/percent
样本 Sample	210	**几江 Jijiang(29.0)**	**全兴大曲 Quan Xing Da Qu(19.0)**	**石松 Shisong(18.1)**	**鸭溪窖 Yaxijiao(5.2) 江津 Jiangjin(5.2)**	**五粮液 Wuliangye(4.3)**
饮食"温饱"指向 "basic" orientation	91	几江 Jijiang(31.9)	全兴大曲 Quan Xing Da Qu (20.9)	石松 Shisong(19.8)	江津 Jiangjin(4.4)	泸州老窖 Lu Zhou Lao Jiao (3.3) 五粮春 Wuliangchun(3.3) 五粮液 Wuliangye(3.3)
中间层 medium	85	几江 Jijiang(28.2)	全兴大曲 Quan Xing Da Qu (20.0)	石松 Shisong(16.5)	五粮液 Wuliangye(7.1)	鸭溪窖 Yaxijiao(5.9)
健康营养指向 health & nutrition orientation	34	几江 Jijiang(23.5)	石松 Shisong(17.6)	全兴大曲 Quan Xing Da Qu (11.8) 鸭溪窖 Yaxijiao(11.8)	江津 Jiangjin(8.8)	剑南春 Jiannanchun(5.9)

2-14 重度消费者的消费者层构成/ The Composition of the Heavy Consumers

2-14-1 时尚流行指标/ Fads Popular Index

	人数 Number	平实生活指向 simple living orientation	时尚流行指向 fashion orientation
样本 Sample	119	68.9	31.1
天天喝 daily	38	65.8	34.2
一周 3 次或以上 3 times or over a week	32	68.8	31.3
一周 1~2 次 once or twice a week	49	71.4	28.6

2-14-2 广告态度指标/ Advertising Attitude Index

	人数 Number	广告淡漠指向 indifferent orientation	中间层 medium	信赖广告指向 loyal orientation
样本 Sample	119	38.7	52.9	8.4
天天喝 daily	38	52.6	42.1	5.3
一周 3 次或以上 3 times or over a week	31	32.3	58.1	9.7
一周 1~2 次 once or twice a week	50	32.0	58.0	10.0

2-14-3 饮食健康指标/ Foods & Drink Quality Index

	人数 Number	饮食"温饱"指向 "basic" orientation	中间层 medium	健康营养指向 health & nutrition orientation
样本 Sample	119	40.3	42.9	16.8
天天喝 daily	38	39.5	42.1	18.4
一周 3 次或以上 3 times or over a week	31	54.8	22.6	22.6
一周 1~2 次 once or twice a week	50	32.0	56.0	12.0

● 武汉 / Wuhan

2-1 最近三个月饮用频率的比例/ Proportion of the Sample Consuming Hard Liquor in the Last Three Months

	人数 Number	百分比 Percent
天天喝 daily	52	8.2
一周 3 次或以上 3 times or over a week	27	4.3
一周 1~2 次 once or twice a week	29	4.6
一个月 2～3 次 2 or 3 times a month	37	5.8
一个月 1 次 once a month	13	2.1
两个月 1 次 once two months	11	1.7
三个月 1 次或以下 once three months or below	21	3.3
没有喝 never	444	70.0

n=634

2-2 最常用品牌排名/ Ranking of the Most Frequently Used Brands

排名 Brand Ranking	品牌 Brands	人数 Number	百分比 Percent
1	沱牌大曲 Tuo Pai Da Qu	70	36.8
2	枝江大曲 Zhi Jiang Da Qu	51	26.8
3	黄鹤楼 Huanghelou	17	8.9
4	白云边 Baiyunbian	8	4.2
5	稻花香 Daohuaxiang	7	3.7
6	红星二锅头 Hong Xing Er Guo Tou	5	2.6
7	五粮液 Wuliangye	3	1.6
8	西陵大曲 Xi Ling Da Qu	2	1.1
8	贵州醇 Guizhouchun	2	1.1

n=190

2-3 样本、男性各年龄层、女性各年龄层的常用品牌/ The Most Frequently Used Brands by the Whole Sample, Age and Gender Groups

	人数 Number	第一品牌及百分比 1st/ percent	第二品牌及百分比 2nd/ percent	第三品牌及百分比 3rd/ percent
样本 Sample	190	**沱牌大曲 Tuo Pai Da Qu(36.8)**	**枝江大曲 Zhi Jiang Da Qu (26.8)**	**黄鹤楼 Huanghelou(8.9)**
男性 Male	155	**沱牌大曲 Tuo Pai Da Qu(36.8)**	**枝江大曲 Zhi Jiang Da Qu (27.7)**	**黄鹤楼 Huanghelou(8.4)**
16~24 岁 Age	14	枝江大曲 Zhi Jiang Da Qu (28.6)	沱牌大曲 Tuo Pai Da Qu(21.4)	稻花香 Daohuaxiang(14.3)
25~34 岁 Age	50	沱牌大曲 Tuo Pai Da Qu(40.0)	枝江大曲 Zhi Jiang Da Qu (30.0)	白云边 Baiyunbian(4.0) 红星二锅头 Hong Xing Er Guo Tou(4.0) 黄鹤楼 Huanghelou(4.0) 稻花香 Daohuaxiang(4.0)
35~44 岁 Age	51	沱牌大曲 Tuo Pai Da Qu(37.3)	枝江大曲 Zhi Jiang Da Qu (27.5)	黄鹤楼 Huanghelou(11.8)
45~54 岁 Age	31	沱牌大曲 Tuo Pai Da Qu(35.5)	枝江大曲 Zhi Jiang Da Qu (29.0)	黄鹤楼 Huanghelou(16.1)
55~60 岁 Age	9	沱牌大曲 Tuo Pai Da Qu(44.4)	红星二锅头 Hong Xing Er Guo Tou(11.1) 五粮春 Wuliangchun(11.1) 枝江大曲 Zhi Jiang Da Qu (11.1) 白云边 Baiyunbian(11.1)	
女性 Female	35	**沱牌大曲 Tuo Pai Da Qu(37.1)**	**枝江大曲 Zhi Jiang Da Qu (22.9)**	**黄鹤楼 Huanghelou(11.4)**
16~24 岁 Age	1	白云边 Baiyunbian(100.0)		
25~34 岁 Age	10	沱牌大曲 Tuo Pai Da Qu(40.0) 枝江大曲 Zhi Jiang Da Qu (40.0)	黄鹤楼 Huanghelou(10.0) 五粮液 Wuliangye(10.0)	
35~44 岁 Age	9	沱牌大曲 Tuo Pai Da Qu(55.6)	枝江大曲 Zhi Jiang Da Qu (22.2)	白云边 Baiyunbian(11.1)
45~54 岁 Age	11	沱牌大曲 Tuo Pai Da Qu(36.4)	黄鹤楼 Huanghelou(9.1) 赊店老酒 She Dian Lao Jiu(9.1) 枝江大曲 Zhi Jiang Da Qu (9.1) 白云边 Baiyunbian(9.1) 贵州醇 Guizhouchun(9.1)	
55~60 岁 Age	4	黄鹤楼 Huanghelou(50.0)	枝江大曲 Zhi Jiang Da Qu (25.0) 西陵大曲 Xi Ling Da Qu(25.0)	

2-4 理想品牌排名/ Ranking of the Ideal Brands

排名 Brand Ranking	品牌 Brands	人数 Number	百分比 Percent
1	茅台 Moutai	85	13.2
2	枝江大曲 Zhi Jiang Da Qu	74	11.5
3	沱牌大曲 Tuo Pai Da Qu	71	11.1
4	五粮液 Wuliangye	63	9.8
5	黄鹤楼 Huanghelou	22	3.4
6	稻花香 Daohuaxiang	12	1.9
7	剑南春 Jiannanchun	11	1.7
8	白云边 Baiyunbian	10	1.6
9	郎酒 Langjiu	9	1.4
10	金六福 Jinliufu	7	1.1
11	全兴大曲 Quan Xing Da Qu	6	0.9

n=642

2-5 样本、男性各年龄层、女性各年龄层最近三个月有无购买的比例/ Purchasing in the Last Three Months by the Whole Sample, Age and Gender Groups

	人数 Number	买过 yes	没买过 no
样本 Sample	640	42.3	57.7
男性 Male	311	50.8	49.2
16~24 岁 Age	65	24.6	75.4
25~34 岁 Age	89	56.2	43.8
35~44 岁 Age	80	67.5	32.5
45~54 岁 Age	52	53.8	46.2
55~60 岁 Age	25	40.0	60.0
女性 Female	329	34.3	65.7
16~24 岁 Age	69	15.9	84.1
25~34 岁 Age	95	41.1	58.9
35~44 岁 Age	77	41.6	58.4
45~54 岁 Age	62	40.3	59.7
55~60 岁 Age	26	23.1	76.9

2-6 样本、男性各年龄层、女性各年龄层最近三个月是否拿白酒送过礼/ To Offer Hard Liquor as Gift in the Last Three Months by the Whole Sample, Age and Gender Groups

	人数 Number	送过 yes	没送过 no
样本 Sample	638	21.3	78.7
男性 Male	308	21.4	78.6
16~24 岁 Age	64	10.9	89.1
25~34 岁 Age	88	27.3	72.7
35~44 岁 Age	80	26.3	73.8
45~54 岁 Age	52	11.5	88.5
55~60 岁 Age	24	33.3	66.7
女性 Female	330	21.2	78.8
16~24 岁 Age	69	11.6	88.4
25~34 岁 Age	96	22.9	77.1
35~44 岁 Age	78	25.6	74.4
45~54 岁 Age	61	27.9	72.1
55~60 岁 Age	26	11.5	88.5

2-7 样本、男性各年龄层、女性各年龄层最近三个月的饮用频率/ Frequencies of Consuming Hard Liquor in the Last Three Months by the Whole Sample, Age and Gender Groups

	人数 Number	天天喝 daily	一周3次或以上 3 times or over a week	一周1~2次 once or twice a week	一个月2~3次 2 or 3 times a month	一个月1次 once a month	两个月1次 once two months	三个月1次或以下 once three months or below	没有喝 never
样本 Sample	634	8.2	4.3	4.6	5.8	2.1	1.7	3.3	70.0
男性 Male	310	15.5	7.7	5.2	11.0	2.9	3.2	4.5	50.0
16~24 岁 Age	64	3.1	1.6	1.6	6.3	1.6	4.7	3.1	78.1
25~34 岁 Age	89	12.4	5.6	9.0	15.7	4.5	1.1	7.9	43.8
35~44 岁 Age	80	21.3	16.3	3.8	12.5	1.3	5.0	3.8	36.3
45~54 岁 Age	52	25.0	7.7	5.8	11.5	3.8	1.9	3.8	40.4
55~60 岁 Age	25	20.0	4.0	4.0	0.0	4.0	4.0	0.0	64.0
女性 Female	324	1.2	0.9	4.0	0.9	1.2	0.3	2.2	89.2
16~24 岁 Age	66	0.0	0.0	0.0	0.0	0.0	1.5	0.0	98.5
25~34 岁 Age	95	0.0	0.0	4.2	2.1	3.2	0.0	1.1	89.5
35~44 岁 Age	76	2.6	1.3	1.3	1.3	1.3	0.0	3.9	88.2
45~54 岁 Age	61	1.6	1.6	9.8	0.0	0.0	0.0	4.9	82.0
55~60 岁 Age	26	3.8	3.8	7.7	0.0	0.0	0.0	0.0	84.6

2-8 样本、男性各年龄层、女性各年龄层的品牌习惯/ Brand Habit in Consuming Hard Liquor by the Whole Sample, Age and Gender Groups

	人数 Number	基本固定饮用一个牌子 used in only one brand	比较固定地饮用两个或三个牌子 used in two or three brands	基本上不太固定牌子 no brand preference
样本 Sample	190	43.2	32.1	24.7
男性 Male	155	43.2	32.9	23.9
16~24 岁 Age	14	42.9	21.4	35.7
25~34 岁 Age	50	38.0	40.0	22.0
35~44 岁 Age	51	58.8	33.3	7.8
45~54 岁 Age	31	29.0	25.8	45.2
55~60 岁 Age	9	33.3	33.3	33.3
女性 Female	35	42.9	28.6	28.6
16~24 岁 Age	1	0.0	100.0	0.0
25~34 岁 Age	10	40.0	30.0	30.0
35~44 岁 Age	9	33.3	33.3	33.3
45~54 岁 Age	11	54.5	18.2	27.3
55~60 岁 Age	4	50.0	25.0	25.0

2-9 选择该类商品的考虑因素/ Ranking of the Considerations in Purchasing

注：本题为多选题，合计百分比超过 100%(Multiple answers）

排名 Ranking	考虑因素 Considerations	人次 Person-time	百分比 Percent
1	价格适中 reasonable price	130	68.4
2	口味好 pleasant taste	96	50.5
3	有名的牌子 famous brand	45	23.7
4	购买方便 easy to buy	40	21.1
5	只是由于习惯 out of habit	30	15.8
6	广告影响 influence of advertising	16	8.4
7	别人送的 given by other people	15	7.9
8	生产日期 date of producing	13	6.8
9	朋友推荐 introduction of friends	12	6.3
10	包装吸引人 appealing package	7	3.7
11	其它 others	5	2.6
12	售货员介绍 introduced by the shop assistants	3	1.6
12	有优惠条件 with preferential terms	3	1.6

n=190

2-10 样本、男性各年龄层、女性各年龄层最常饮用的度数/ Degree of the Consumed Hard Liquor by the Whole Sample, Age and Gender Groups

	人数 Number	55 度以上 55° or over	39—55 度 39°--55°	38 度及以下 38° or below	其它 others
样本 Sample	190	7.9	70.0	21.6	0.5
男性 Male	155	8.4	69.7	21.3	0.6
16~24 岁 Age	14	7.1	64.3	28.6	0.0
25~34 岁 Age	50	6.0	70.0	22.0	2.0
35~44 岁 Age	51	9.8	68.6	21.6	0.0
45~54 岁 Age	31	9.7	67.7	22.6	0.0
55~60 岁 Age	9	11.1	88.9	0.0	0.0
女性 Female	35	5.7	71.4	22.9	0.0
16~24 岁 Age	1	0.0	100.0	0.0	0.0
25~34 岁 Age	10	10.0	90.0	0.0	0.0
35~44 岁 Age	9	11.1	66.7	22.2	0.0
45~54 岁 Age	11	0.0	63.6	36.4	0.0
55~60 岁 Age	4	0.0	50.0	50.0	0.0

2-11 样本、男性各年龄层、女性各年龄层最常饮用的场合/ Settings of Consumption by the Whole Sample, Age and Gender Groups

注：本题为多选题，合计百分比超过100%(Multiple answers）

	人数 Number	请客 entertain guests	节假日团聚 get-together on holiday	日常饮用 drink daily	服药 drink with medicine	做菜 cooking meal	其它 others
样本 Sample	188	44.1	28.7	53.2	2.1	8.0	2.1
男性 Male	153	45.8	26.8	54.9	0.7	7.2	1.3
16~24 岁 Age	14	64.3	21.4	28.6	0.0	0.0	0.0
25~34 岁 Age	50	54.0	36.0	44.0	0.0	6.0	4.0
35~44 岁 Age	51	39.2	17.6	70.6	0.0	7.8	0.0
45~54 岁 Age	29	41.4	27.6	55.2	3.4	13.8	0.0
55~60 岁 Age	9	22.2	33.3	66.7	0.0	0.0	0.0
女性 Female	35	37.1	37.1	45.7	8.6	11.4	5.7
16~24 岁 Age	1	0.0	100.0	0.0	0.0	0.0	0.0
25~34 岁 Age	10	50.0	60.0	20.0	0.0	10.0	20.0
35~44 岁 Age	9	22.2	33.3	44.4	11.1	22.2	0.0
45~54 岁 Age	11	45.5	18.2	63.6	9.1	9.1	0.0
55~60 岁 Age	4	25.0	25.0	75.0	25.0	0.0	0.0

2-12 重度消费者人口分布/ Demographics of the Heavy Consumers

	人数 Number	16-24 岁 Age	25-34 岁 Age	35-44 岁 Age	45-54 岁 Age	55-60 岁 Age
样本 Sample	108	3.7	25.9	34.3	25.9	10.2
男性 Male	88	4.5	27.3	37.5	22.7	8.0
天天喝 daily	48	4.2	22.9	35.4	27.1	10.4
一周 3 次或以上 3 times or over a week	24	4.2	20.8	54.2	16.7	4.2
一周 1~2 次 once or twice a week	16	6.3	50.0	18.8	18.8	6.3
女性 Female	20	0.0	20.0	20.0	40.0	20.0
天天喝 daily	4	0.0	0.0	50.0	25.0	25.0
一周 3 次或以上 3 times or over a week	3	0.0	0.0	33.3	33.3	33.3
一周 1~2 次 once or twice a week	13	0.0	30.8	7.7	46.2	15.4

2-13 不同消费者层的常用品牌/ The Most Frequently Used Brands by Market Segments

2-13-1 时尚流行指标/ Fads Popular Index

	人数 Number	第一品牌及百分比 1st/percent	第二品牌及百分比 2nd/percent	第三品牌及百分比 3rd/percent
样本 Sample	185	**沱牌大曲 Tuo Pai Da Qu(36.8)**	**枝江大曲 Zhi Jiang Da Qu (27.0)**	**黄鹤楼 Huanghelou(9.2)**
平实生活指向 simple living orientation	105	沱牌大曲 Tuo Pai Da Qu(36.2)	枝江大曲 Zhi Jiang Da Qu (24.8)	黄鹤楼 Huanghelou(11.4)
时尚流行指向 fashion orientation	80	沱牌大曲 Tuo Pai Da Qu(37.5)	枝江大曲 Zhi Jiang Da Qu (30.0)	黄鹤楼 Huanghelou(6.3) 稻花香 Daohuaxiang(6.3)

2-13-2 广告态度指标/ Advertising Attitude Index

	人数 Number	第一品牌及百分比 1st/percent	第二品牌及百分比 2nd/percent	第三品牌及百分比 3rd/percent
样本 Sample	**187**	**沱牌大曲 Tuo Pai Da Qu(36.9)**	**枝江大曲 Zhi Jiang Da Qu (27.3)**	**黄鹤楼 Huanghelou(9.1)**
广告淡漠指向 indifferent orientation	62	沱牌大曲 Tuo Pai Da Qu(40.3)	枝江大曲 Zhi Jiang Da Qu (24.2)	黄鹤楼 Huanghelou(12.9)
中间层 medium	106	沱牌大曲 Tuo Pai Da Qu(36.8)	枝江大曲 Zhi Jiang Da Qu (24.5)	黄鹤楼 Huanghelou(6.6)
信赖广告指向 loyal orientation	19	枝江大曲 Zhi Jiang Da Qu (52.6)	沱牌大曲 Tuo Pai Da Qu(26.3)	黄鹤楼 Huanghelou(10.5)

2-13-3 饮食健康指标/ Foods & Drink Quality Index

	人数 Number	第一品牌及百分比 1st/percent	第二品牌及百分比 2nd/percent	第三品牌及百分比 3rd/percent
样本 Sample	**188**	**沱牌大曲 Tuo Pai Da Qu(37.2)**	**枝江大曲 Zhi Jiang Da Qu (27.1)**	**黄鹤楼 Huanghelou(9.0)**
饮食"温饱"指向 "basic" orientation	70	沱牌大曲 Tuo Pai Da Qu(35.7)	枝江大曲 Zhi Jiang Da Qu (17.1)	黄鹤楼 Huanghelou(15.7)
中间层 medium	86	沱牌大曲 Tuo Pai Da Qu(38.4)	枝江大曲 Zhi Jiang Da Qu (32.6)	白云边 Baiyunbian(4.7) 黄鹤楼 Huanghelou(4.7)
健康营养指向 health & nutrition orientation	32	沱牌大曲 Tuo Pai Da Qu(37.5)	枝江大曲 Zhi Jiang Da Qu (34.4)	黄鹤楼 Huanghelou(6.3) 稻花香 Daohuaxiang(6.3)

2-14 重度消费者的消费者层构成/ The Composition of the Heavy Consumers

2-14-1 时尚流行指标/ Fads Popular Index

	人数 Number	平实生活指向 simple living orientation	时尚流行指向 fashion orientation
样本 Sample	**104**	**56.7**	**43.3**
天天喝 daily	51	74.5	25.5
一周 3 次或以上 3 times or over a week	25	40.0	60.0
一周 1~2 次 once or twice a week	28	39.3	60.7

2-14-2 广告态度指标/ Advertising Attitude Index

	人数 Number	广告淡漠指向 indifferent orientation	中间层 medium	信赖广告指向 loyal orientation
样本 Sample	**106**	**37.7**	**53.8**	**8.5**
天天喝 daily	51	47.1	51.0	2.0
一周 3 次或以上 3 times or over a week	27	29.6	59.3	11.1
一周 1~2 次 once or twice a week	28	28.6	53.6	17.9

2-14-3 饮食健康指标/ Foods & Drink Quality Index

	人数 Number	饮食"温饱"指向 "basic" orientation	中间层 medium	健康营养指向 health & nutrition orientation
样本 Sample	**106**	**40.6**	**40.6**	**18.9**
天天喝 daily	51	39.2	47.1	13.7
一周 3 次或以上 3 times or over a week	27	55.6	22.2	22.2
一周 1~2 次 once or twice a week	28	28.6	46.4	25.0

● 西安 / Xi'an

2-1 最近三个月饮用频率的比例/ Proportion of the Sample Consuming Hard Liquor in the Last Three Months

	人数 Number	百分比 Percent
天天喝 daily	21	3.5
一周 3 次或以上 3 times or over a week	24	4.0
一周 1~2 次 once or twice a week	57	9.5
一个月 2～3 次 2 or 3 times a month	54	9.0
一个月 1 次 once a month	29	4.8
两个月 1 次 once two months	20	3.3
三个月 1 次或以下 once three months or below	27	4.5
没有喝 never	366	61.2

n=598

2-2 最常用品牌排名/ Ranking of the Most Frequently Used Brands

排名 Brand Ranking	品牌 Brands	人数 Number	百分比 Percent
1	西凤酒 Xifengjiu	52	22.4
2	伊利特曲 Yi Li Te Qu	38	16.4
3	全兴大曲 Quan Xing Da Qu	20	8.6
4	绵竹大曲 Mian Zhu Da Qu	19	8.2
5	秦川 Qinchuan	15	6.5
6	太白 Taibai	9	3.9
7	五粮液 Wuliangye	8	3.4
7	泸州老窖 Lu Zhou Lao Jiao	8	3.4
8	城古特曲 Cheng Gu Te Qu	7	3.0
9	尖庄 Jianzhuang	6	2.6
10	红星二锅头 Hong Xing Er Guo Tou	5	2.2

n=232

2-3 样本、男性各年龄层、女性各年龄层的常用品牌/ The Most Frequently Used Brands by the Whole Sample, Age and Gender Groups

	人数 Number	第一品牌及百分比 1st/ percent	第二品牌及百分比 2nd/ percent	第三品牌及百分比 3rd/ percent
样本 Sample	232	**西凤酒 Xifengjiu(22.4)**	**伊利特曲 Yi Li Te Qu(16.4)**	**全兴大曲 Quan Xing Da Qu(8.6)**
男性 Male	162	**西凤酒 Xifengjiu(20.4)**	**伊利特曲 Yi Li Te Qu(18.5)**	**全兴大曲 Quan Xing Da Qu(9.3)**
16~24 岁 Age	20	全兴大曲 Quan Xing Da Qu(15.0) 西凤酒 Xifengjiu(15.0)	伊利特曲 Yi Li Te Qu(10.0)	湘泉 Xiangquan(5.0) 小糊涂仙 Tipsy Spirit(5.0) 城古特曲 Cheng Gu Te Qu(5.0) 秦川 Qinchuan(5.0) 北京二锅头 Bei Jing Er Guo Tou(5.0) 金鑫二锅头 Jin Xin Er Guo Tou(5.0) 沱牌大曲 Tuo Pai Da Qu(5.0) 剑南春 Jiannanchun(5.0) 红星二锅头 Hong Xing Er Guo Tou(5.0)
25~34 岁 Age	52	伊利特曲 Yi Li Te Qu(28.8)	全兴大曲 Quan Xing Da Qu(15.4)	西凤酒 Xifengjiu(11.5)
35~44 岁 Age	55	西凤酒 Xifengjiu(23.6)	伊利特曲 Yi Li Te Qu(16.4)	绵竹大曲 Mian Zhu Da Qu(10.9)
45~54 岁 Age	25	西凤酒 Xifengjiu(24.0)	绵竹大曲 Mian Zhu Da Qu(16.0)	伊利特曲 Yi Li Te Qu(12.0)
55~60 岁 Age	10	西凤酒 Xifengjiu(50.0)	绵竹大曲 Mian Zhu Da Qu(20.0)	尖庄 Jianzhuang(10.0) 泸州老窖 Lu Zhou Lao Jiao(10.0) 伊利特曲 Yi Li Te Qu(10.0)
女性 Female	70	**西凤酒 Xifengjiu(27.1)**	**伊利特曲 Yi Li Te Qu(11.4)**	**绵竹大曲 Mian Zhu Da Qu(7.1)** **全兴大曲 Quan Xing Da Qu(7.1)**
16~24 岁 Age	6	全兴大曲 Quan Xing Da Qu(33.3)	泸州老窖 Lu Zhou Lao Jiao(16.7) 西凤酒 Xifengjiu(16.7) 太白 Taibai(16.7) 伊利特曲 Yi Li Te Qu(16.7)	
25~34 岁 Age	20	西凤酒 Xifengjiu(30.0)	伊利特曲 Yi Li Te Qu(20.0)	秦池 Qinchi(15.0)
35~44 岁 Age	22	绵竹大曲 Mian Zhu Da Qu(22.7)	西凤酒 Xifengjiu(18.2)	
45~54 岁 Age	14	西凤酒 Xifengjiu(35.7)	汾酒 Fenjiu(7.1) 全兴大曲 Quan Xing Da Qu(7.1) 沱牌大曲 Tuo Pai Da Qu(7.1) 五粮液 Wuliangye(7.1) 北京二锅头 Bei Jing Er Guo Tou(7.1) 伊利特曲 Yi Li Te Qu(7.1) 秦川 Qinchuan(7.1) 城古特曲 Cheng Gu Te Qu(7.1)	
55~60 岁 Age	8	西凤酒 Xifengjiu(37.5)	扳倒井 Bandaojing(12.5) 沱牌大曲 Tuo Pai Da Qu(12.5) 五粮液 Wuliangye(12.5) 秦川 Qinchuan(12.5) 城古特曲 Cheng Gu Te Qu(12.5)	

2-4 理想品牌排名/ Ranking of the Ideal Brands

排名 Brand Ranking	品牌 Brands	人数 Number	百分比 Percent
1	西凤酒 Xifengjiu	122	20.3
2	茅台 Moutai	95	15.8
3	五粮液 Wuliangye	75	12.5
4	伊利特曲 Yi Li Te Qu	42	7.0
5	全兴大曲 Quan Xing Da Qu	21	3.5
6	太白 Taibai	15	2.5
7	绵竹大曲 Mian Zhu Da Qu	11	1.8
7	泸州老窖 Lu Zhou Lao Jiao	11	1.8
7	尖庄 Jianzhuang	11	1.8
7	秦川 Qinchuan	11	1.8
8	剑南春 Jiannanchun	8	1.3
9	汾酒 Fenjiu	7	1.2
10	孔府家酒 Confucius Family Liquor	5	0.8

n=601

2-5 样本、男性各年龄层、女性各年龄层最近三个月有无购买的比例/ Purchasing in the Last Three Months by the Whole Sample, Age and Gender Groups

	人数 Number	买过 yes	没买过 no
样本 Sample	**601**	**41.3**	**58.7**
男性 Male	**302**	**50.0**	**50.0**
16~24 岁 Age	64	35.9	64.1
25~34 岁 Age	91	52.7	47.3
35~44 岁 Age	77	63.6	36.4
45~54 岁 Age	46	45.7	54.3
55~60 岁 Age	24	41.7	58.3
女性 Female	**299**	**32.4**	**67.6**
16~24 岁 Age	61	23.0	77.0
25~34 岁 Age	90	26.7	73.3
35~44 岁 Age	74	45.9	54.1
45~54 岁 Age	49	30.6	69.4
55~60 岁 Age	25	40.0	60.0

2-6 样本、男性各年龄层、女性各年龄层最近三个月是否拿白酒送过礼/ To Offer Hard Liquor as Gift in the Last Three Months by the Whole Sample, Age and Gender Groups

	人数 Number	送过 yes	没送过 no
样本 Sample	**593**	**15.5**	**84.5**
男性 Male	**299**	**19.1**	**80.9**
16~24 岁 Age	63	12.7	87.3
25~34 岁 Age	91	25.3	74.7
35~44 岁 Age	75	25.3	74.7
45~54 岁 Age	46	8.7	91.3
55~60 岁 Age	24	12.5	87.5
女性 Female	**294**	**11.9**	**88.1**
16~24 岁 Age	60	6.7	93.3
25~34 岁 Age	88	14.8	85.2
35~44 岁 Age	74	16.2	83.8
45~54 岁 Age	48	6.3	93.8
55~60 岁 Age	24	12.5	87.5

2-7 样本、男性各年龄层、女性各年龄层最近三个月的饮用频率/ Frequencies of Consuming Hard Liquor in the Last Three Months by the Whole Sample, Age and Gender Groups

	人数 Number	天天喝 daily	一周3次或以上 3 times or over a week	一周1~2次 once or twice a week	一个月2~3次 2 or 3 times a month	一个月1次 once a month	两个月1次 once two months	三个月1次或以下 once three months or below	没有喝 never
样本 Sample	598	3.5	4.0	9.5	9.0	4.8	3.3	4.5	61.2
男性 Male	301	5.3	7.0	14.0	13.6	7.0	2.7	4.3	46.2
16~24 岁 Age	64	1.6	4.7	6.3	4.7	6.3	1.6	6.3	68.8
25~34 岁 Age	91	2.2	6.6	9.9	22.0	8.8	2.2	5.5	42.9
35~44 岁 Age	77	9.1	9.1	24.7	10.4	10.4	3.9	3.9	28.6
45~54 岁 Age	45	8.9	8.9	15.6	17.8	0.0	4.4	0.0	44.4
55~60 岁 Age	24	8.3	4.2	12.5	8.3	4.2	0.0	4.2	58.3
女性 Female	297	1.7	1.0	5.1	4.4	2.7	4.0	4.7	76.4
16~24 岁 Age	60	0.0	0.0	1.7	1.7	3.3	0.0	3.3	90.0
25~34 岁 Age	90	2.2	1.1	4.4	3.3	1.1	5.6	4.4	77.8
35~44 岁 Age	74	2.7	1.4	10.8	5.4	1.4	4.1	4.1	70.3
45~54 岁 Age	48	0.0	2.1	2.1	4.2	8.3	4.2	8.3	70.8
55~60 岁 Age	25	4.0	0.0	4.0	12.0	0.0	8.0	4.0	68.0

2-8 样本、男性各年龄层、女性各年龄层的品牌习惯/ Brand Habit in Consuming Hard Liquor by the Whole Sample, Age and Gender Groups

	人数 Number	基本固定饮用一个牌子 used in only one brand	比较固定地饮用两个或三个牌 used in two or three brands	基本上不太固定牌子 no brand preference
样本 Sample	231	39.0	33.8	27.3
男性 Male	162	42.6	32.1	25.3
16~24 岁 Age	20	45.0	30.0	25.0
25~34 岁 Age	52	32.7	50.0	17.3
35~44 岁 Age	55	45.5	23.5	30.9
45~54 岁 Age	25	52.0	16.0	32.0
55~60 岁 Age	10	50.0	30.0	20.0
女性 Female	69	30.4	37.7	31.9
16~24 岁 Age	6	0.0	66.7	33.3
25~34 岁 Age	20	30.0	35.0	35.0
35~44 岁 Age	22	31.8	40.9	27.3
45~54 岁 Age	13	46.2	38.5	15.4
55~60 岁 Age	8	25.0	12.5	62.5

2-9 选择该类商品的考虑因素/ Ranking of the Considerations in Purchasing

注：本题为多选题，合计百分比超过100%(Multiple answers）

排名 Ranking	考虑因素 Considerations	人次 Person-time	百分比 Percent
1	口味好 pleasant taste	127	55.0
2	价格适中 reasonable price	105	45.5
3	有名的牌子 famous brand	66	28.6
4	只是由于习惯 out of habit	35	15.2
5	购买方便 easy to buy	33	14.3
6	生产日期 date of producing	24	10.4
7	别人送的 given by other people	17	7.4
8	朋友推荐 introduction of friends	15	6.5
9	广告影响 influence of advertising	10	4.3
10	包装吸引人 appealing package	5	2.2
11	有优惠条件 with preferential terms	4	1.7
12	售货员介绍 introduced by the shop assistants	2	0.9
13	其它 others	1	0.4

n=231

2-10 样本、男性各年龄层、女性各年龄层最常饮用的度数/ Degree of the Consumed Hard Liquor by the Whole Sample, Age and Gender Groups

	人数 Number	55 度以上 55° or over	39—55 度 39° --55°	38 度及以下 38° or below	其它 others
样本 Sample	231	19.5	66.2	13.9	0.4
男性 Male	162	21.0	64.2	14.8	0.0
16~24 岁 Age	20	15.0	80.0	5.0	0.0
25~34 岁 Age	52	23.1	57.7	19.2	0.0
35~44 岁 Age	55	25.5	56.4	18.2	0.0
45~54 岁 Age	25	16.0	72.0	12.0	0.0
55~60 岁 Age	10	10.0	90.0	0.0	0.0
女性 Female	69	15.9	71.0	11.6	1.4
16~24 岁 Age	6	0.0	100.0	0.0	0.0
25~34 岁 Age	20	10.0	70.0	20.0	0.0
35~44 岁 Age	22	27.3	59.1	9.1	4.5
45~54 岁 Age	13	0.0	92.3	7.7	0.0
55~60 岁 Age	8	37.5	50.0	12.5	0.0

2-11 样本、男性各年龄层、女性各年龄层最常饮用的场合/ Settings of Consumption by the Whole Sample, Age and Gender Groups

注：本题为多选题，合计百分比超过 100%(Multiple answers)

	人数 Number	请客 entertain guests	节假日团聚 get-together on holiday	日常饮用 drink daily	服药 drink with medicine	做菜 cooking meal	其它 others
样本 Sample	230	38.3	44.3	40.4	2.2	12.2	2.2
男性 Male	161	37.9	44.7	43.5	2.5	5.6	2.5
16~24 岁 Age	20	15.0	55.0	35.0	0.0	10.0	0.0
25~34 岁 Age	52	50.0	48.1	26.9	3.8	5.8	1.9
35~44 岁 Age	54	33.3	40.7	53.7	1.9	1.9	5.6
45~54 岁 Age	25	36.0	36.0	56.0	4.0	12.0	0.0
55~60 岁 Age	10	50.0	50.0	60.0	0.0	0.0	0.0
女性 Female	69	39.1	43.5	33.3	1.4	27.5	1.4
16~24 岁 Age	6	83.3	33.3	33.3	0.0	33.3	0.0
25~34 岁 Age	20	35.0	35.0	15.0	0.0	35.0	5.0
35~44 岁 Age	22	36.4	50.0	45.5	4.5	31.8	0.0
45~54 岁 Age	13	23.1	46.2	38.5	0.0	23.1	0.0
55~60 岁 Age	8	50.0	50.0	37.5	0.0	0.0	0.0

2-12 重度消费者人口分布/ Demographics of the Heavy Consumers

	人数 Number	16-24 岁 Age	25-34 岁 Age	35-44 岁 Age	45-54 岁 Age	55-60 岁 Age
样本 Sample	102	8.8	23.5	43.1	16.7	7.8
男性 Male	79	10.1	21.5	41.8	19.0	7.6
天天喝 daily	16	6.3	12.5	43.8	25.0	12.5
一周 3 次或以上 3 times or over a week	21	14.3	28.6	33.3	19.0	4.8
一周 1~2 次 once or twice a week	42	9.5	21.4	45.2	16.7	7.1
女性 Female	23	4.3	30.4	47.8	8.7	8.7
天天喝 daily	5	0.0	40.0	40.0	0.0	20.0
一周 3 次或以上 3 times or over a week	3	0.0	33.3	33.3	33.3	0.0
一周 1~2 次 once or twice a week	15	6.7	26.7	53.3	6.7	6.7

2-13 不同消费者层的常用品牌/ The Most Frequently Used Brands by Market Segments

2-13-1 时尚流行指标/ Fads Popular Index

	人数 Number	第一品牌及百分比 1st/percent	第二品牌及百分比 2nd/percent	第三品牌及百分比 3rd/percent	第四品牌及百分比 4th/percent
样本 Sample	231	**西凤酒 Xifengjiu(22.1)**	**伊利特曲 Yi Li Te Qu(16.5)**	**全兴大曲 Quan Xing Da Qu(8.7)**	**绵竹大曲 Mian Zhu Da Qu(8.2)**
平实生活指向 simple living orientation	138	西凤酒 Xifengjiu(21.0)	伊利特曲 Yi Li Te Qu(16.7)	绵竹大曲 Mian Zhu Da Qu(10.1) 全兴大曲 Quan Xing Da Qu(10.1)	秦川 Qinchuan(7.2)
时尚流行指向 fashion orientation	93	西凤酒 Xifengjiu(23.7)	伊利特曲 Yi Li Te Qu(16.1)	全兴大曲 Quan Xing Da Qu(6.5) 泸州老窖 Lu Zhou Lao Jiao(6.5)	秦川 Qinchuan(5.4) 绵竹大曲 Mian Zhu Da Qu(5.4)

2-13-2 广告态度指标/ Advertising Attitude Index

	人数 Number	第一品牌及百分比 1st/percent	第二品牌及百分比 2nd/percent	第三品牌及百分比 3rd/percent	第四品牌及百分比 4th/percent
样本 Sample	228	**西凤酒 Xifengjiu(21.9)**	**伊利特曲 Yi Li Te Qu(16.2)**	**全兴大曲 Quan Xing Da Qu(8.8)**	**绵竹大曲 Mian Zhu Da Qu(8.3)**
广告淡漠指向 indifferent orientation	75	西凤酒 Xifengjiu(29.3)	伊利特曲 Yi Li Te Qu(17.3)	全兴大曲 Quan Xing Da Qu(12.0)	绵竹大曲 Mian Zhu Da Qu(8.0)
中间层 medium	127	西凤酒 Xifengjiu(17.3)	伊利特曲 Yi Li Te Qu(15.0)	绵竹大曲 Mian Zhu Da Qu(8.7)	全兴大曲 Quan Xing Da Qu(7.9)
信赖广告指向 loyal orientation	26	西凤酒 Xifengjiu(23.1)	伊利特曲 Yi Li Te Qu(19.2)	秦川 Qinchuan(11.5)	绵竹大曲 Mian Zhu Da Qu(7.7) 宁城老窖 Ning Cheng Lao Jiao (7.7)

2-13-3 饮食健康指标/ Foods & Drink Quality Index

	人数 Number	第一品牌及百分比 1st/percent	第二品牌及百分比 2nd/percent	第三品牌及百分比 3rd/percent	第四品牌及百分比 4th/percent
样本 Sample	232	**西凤酒 Xifengjiu(22.4)**	**伊利特曲 Yi Li Te Qu(16.4)**	**全兴大曲 Quan Xing Da Qu(8.6)**	**绵竹大曲 Mian Zhu Da Qu(8.2)**
饮食“温饱”指向 "basic" orientation	95	西凤酒 Xifengjiu(21.1)	伊利特曲 Yi Li Te Qu(11.6)	绵竹大曲 Mian Zhu Da Qu(10.5)	全兴大曲 Quan Xing Da Qu(9.5)
中间层 medium	95	伊利特曲 Yi Li Te Qu(22.1)	西凤酒 Xifengjiu(20.0)	全兴大曲 Quan Xing Da Qu(9.5)	秦川 Qinchuan(7.4)
健康营养指向 health & nutrition orientation	42	西凤酒 Xifengjiu(31.0)	伊利特曲 Yi Li Te Qu(14.3)	绵竹大曲 Mian Zhu Da Qu(9.5)	五粮液 Wuliangye(7.1)

2-14 重度消费者的消费者层构成/ The Composition of the Heavy Consumers

2-14-1 时尚流行指标/ Fads Popular Index

	人数 Number	平实生活指向 simple living orientation	时尚流行指向 fashion orientation
样本 Sample	102	60.8	39.2
天天喝 daily	21	61.9	38.1
一周 3 次或以上 3 times or over a week	24	58.3	41.7
一周 1~2 次 once or twice a week	57	61.4	38.6

2-14-2 广告态度指标/ Advertising Attitude Index

	人数 Number	广告淡漠指向 indifferent orientation	中间层 medium	信赖广告指向 loyal orientation
样本 Sample	100	33.0	53.0	14.0
天天喝 daily	21	28.6	57.1	14.3
一周 3 次或以上 3 times or over a week	24	29.2	54.2	16.7
一周 1~2 次 once or twice a week	55	36.4	50.9	12.7

2-14-3 饮食健康指标/ Foods & Drink Quality Index

	人数 Number	饮食"温饱"指向 "basic" orientation	中间层 medium	健康营养指向 health & nutrition orientation
样本 Sample	102	40.2	42.2	17.6
天天喝 daily	21	47.6	33.3	19.0
一周 3 次或以上 3 times or over a week	24	41.7	45.8	12.5
一周 1~2 次 once or twice a week	57	36.8	43.9	19.3

● 沈阳 / Shenyang

2-1 最近三个月饮用频率的比例/ Proportion of the Sample Consuming Hard Liquor in the Last Three Months

	人数 Number	百分比 Percent
天天喝 daily	50	8.4
一周 3 次或以上 3 times or over a week	29	4.8
一周 1~2 次 once or twice a week	50	8.4
一个月 2～3 次 2 or 3 times a month	31	5.2
一个月 1 次 once a month	20	3.3
两个月 1 次 once two months	7	1.2
三个月 1 次或以下 once three months or below	15	2.5
没有喝 never	396	66.2

n=598

2-2 最常用品牌排名/ Ranking of the Most Frequently Used Brands

排名 Brand Ranking	品牌 Brands	人数 Number	百分比 Percent
1	老龙口 Laolongkou	63	31.8
2	高粱王 Gaoliangwang	13	6.6
3	北大仓 Beidacang	9	4.5
4	沱牌大曲 Tuo Pai Da Qu	8	4.0
4	古井贡酒 Gu Jing Gong Jiu	8	4.0
4	大高粱 Dagaoliang	8	4.0
4	钓鱼台 Diaoyutai	8	4.0
5	三九龙滨(999 龙滨) San Jiu Long Bin	6	3.0
6	小金斗 Xiaojindou	5	2.5
6	尖庄 Jianzhuang	5	2.5

n=198

2-3 样本、男性各年龄层、女性各年龄层的常用品牌/ The Most Frequently Used Brands by the Whole Sample, Age and Gender Groups

	人数 Number	第一品牌及百分比 1st/ percent	第二品牌及百分比 2nd/ percent	第三品牌及百分比 3rd/ percent
样本 Sample	198	**老龙口 Laolongkou(31.8)**	**高粱王 Gaoliangwang(6.6)**	**北大仓 Beidacang(4.5)**
男性 Male	154	**老龙口 Laolongkou(33.8)**	**高粱王 Gaoliangwang(7.1)**	**钓鱼台 Diaoyutai(4.5)** **沱牌大曲 Tuo Pai Da Qu(4.5)**
16~24 岁 Age	14	老龙口 Laolongkou(28.6)	钓鱼台 Diaoyutai(14.3)	古井贡酒 Gu Jing Gong Jiu(7.1) 沱牌大曲 Tuo Pai Da Qu(7.1) 高梁白 Gaoliangbai(7.1) 三九龙滨(999 龙滨) San Jiu Long Bin(7.1) 大高粱 Dagaoliang(7.1) 剑波春 Jianbochun(7.1) 酒霸王 Jiubawang(7.1)
25~34 岁 Age	53	老龙口 Laolongkou(45.3)	高粱王 Gaoliangwang(13.2)	钓鱼台 Diaoyutai(5.7)
35~44 岁 Age	44	老龙口 Laolongkou(34.1)	北大仓 Beidacang(6.8) 沱牌大曲 Tuo Pai Da Qu(6.8) 小金斗 Xiaojindou(6.8)	北京二锅头 Bei Jing Er Guo Tou(4.5) 高粱王 Gaoliangwang(4.5)
45~54 岁 Age	28	老龙口 Laolongkou(21.4)	尖庄 Jianzhuang(10.7)	沱牌大曲 Tuo Pai Da Qu(7.1)
55~60 岁 Age	15	老龙口 Laolongkou(20.0)	古井贡酒 Gu Jing Gong Jiu(6.7) 尖庄 Jianzhuang(6.7) 双沟大曲 Shuang Gou Da Qu(6.7) 北大仓 Beidacang(6.7) 古井醇 Gujingchun(6.7) 高粱王 Gaoliangwang(6.7) 钓鱼台 Diaoyutai(6.7) 大高粱 Dagaoliang(6.7) 沈阳陈酿 Shen Yang Chen Niang(6.7) 金州曲酒 Jin Zhou Qu Jiu(6.7)	
女性 Female	44	**老龙口 Laolongkou(25.0)**	**北大仓 Beidacang(6.8)** **大高粱 Dagaoliang(6.8)**	**古井贡酒 Gu Jing Gong Jiu(4.5)** **小金斗 Xiaojindou(4.5)** **高粱王 Gaoliangwang(4.5)**
16~24 岁 Age	2	剑南春 Jiannanchun(50.0) 三九龙滨(999 龙滨) San Jiu Long Bin(50.0)		
25~34 岁 Age	13	老龙口 Laolongkou(30.8)	高粱王 Gaoliangwang(15.4)	北大仓 Beidacang(7.7) 钓鱼台 Diaoyutai(7.7) 大高粱 Dagaoliang(7.7) 新民 Xinmin(7.7)
35~44 岁 Age	14	老龙口 Laolongkou(21.4)	北大仓 Beidacang(14.3)	洋河大曲 Yang He Da Qu(7.1) 老白干 Laobaigan(7.1) 鹤乡王 Hexiangwang(7.1) 高丽 Gaoliwang(7.1) 大高粱 Dagaoliang(7.1) 蒙古王 Mengguwang(7.1) 板桥 Banqiao(7.1)
45~54 岁 Age	7	老龙口 Laolongkou(42.9)	沱牌大曲 Tuo Pai Da Qu(14.3)	
55~60 岁 Age	8	古井贡酒 Gu Jing Gong Jiu(25.0) 小金斗 Xiaojindou(25.0)	老龙口 Laolongkou(12.5) 大高粱 Dagaoliang(12.5)	

2-4 理想品牌排名/ Ranking of the Ideal Brands

排名 Brand Ranking	品牌 Brands	人数 Number	百分比 Percent
1	老龙口 Laolongkou	122	20.3
2	茅台 Moutai	110	18.3
3	五粮液 Wuliangye	67	11.1
4	古井贡酒 Gu Jing Gong Jiu	19	3.2
5	剑南春 Jiannanchun	15	2.5
6	高粱王 Gaoliangwang	14	2.3
7	北大仓 Beidacang	13	2.2
8	沱牌大曲 Tuo Pai Da Qu	12	2.0
9	汾酒 Fenjiu	11	1.8

n=601

2-5 样本、男性各年龄层、女性各年龄层最近三个月有无购买的比例/ Purchasing in the Last Three Months by the Whole Sample, Age and Gender Groups

	人数 Number	买过 yes	没买过 no
样本 Sample	601	42.6	57.4
男性 Male	299	52.8	47.2
16~24 岁 Age	64	34.4	65.6
25~34 岁 Age	89	60.7	39.3
35~44 岁 Age	76	55.3	44.7
45~54 岁 Age	46	54.3	45.7
55~60 岁 Age	24	62.5	37.5
女性 Female	302	32.5	67.5
16~24 岁 Age	64	20.3	79.7
25~34 岁 Age	90	37.8	62.2
35~44 岁 Age	76	31.6	68.4
45~54 岁 Age	48	31.3	68.8
55~60 岁 Age	24	50.0	50.0

2-6 样本、男性各年龄层、女性各年龄层最近三个月是否拿白酒送过礼/ To Offer Hard Liquor as Gift in the Last Three Months by the Whole Sample, Age and Gender Groups

	人数 Number	送过 yes	没送过 no
样本 Sample	601	7.2	92.8
男性 Male	299	8.4	91.6
16~24 岁 Age	64	3.1	96.9
25~34 岁 Age	89	14.6	85.4
35~44 岁 Age	76	3.9	96.1
45~54 岁 Age	46	10.9	89.1
55~60 岁 Age	24	8.3	91.7
女性 Female	302	6.0	94.0
16~24 岁 Age	64	1.6	98.4
25~34 岁 Age	90	12.2	87.8
35~44 岁 Age	76	3.9	96.1
45~54 岁 Age	48	2.1	97.9
55~60 岁 Age	24	8.3	91.7

2-7 样本、男性各年龄层、女性各年龄层最近三个月的饮用频率/ Frequencies of Consuming Hard Liquor in the Last Three Months by the Whole Sample, Age and Gender Groups

	人数 Number	天天喝 daily	一周 3 次或以上 3 times or over a week	一周 1~2 次 once or twice a week	一个月 2~3 次 2 or 3 times a month	一个月 1 次 once a month	两个月 1 次 once two months	三个月 1 次或以下 once three months or below	没有喝 never
样本 Sample	598	8.4	4.8	8.4	5.2	3.3	1.2	2.5	66.2
男性 Male	297	13.8	8.8	13.8	7.1	5.7	1.3	2.0	47.5
16~24 岁 Age	62	3.2	3.2	6.5	1.6	3.2	3.2	1.6	77.4
25~34 岁 Age	89	7.9	7.9	22.5	10.1	6.7	0.0	4.5	40.4
35~44 岁 Age	76	21.1	7.9	13.2	9.2	7.9	0.0	1.3	39.5
45~54 岁 Age	46	23.9	15.2	13.0	2.2	2.2	4.3	0.0	39.1
55~60 岁 Age	24	20.8	16.7	4.2	12.5	8.3	0.0	0.0	37.5
女性 Female	301	3.0	1.0	3.0	3.3	1.0	1.0	3.0	84.7
16~24 岁 Age	64	0.0	0.0	1.6	1.6	0.0	0.0	1.6	95.3
25~34 岁 Age	90	2.2	0.0	2.2	4.4	2.2	1.1	2.2	85.6
35~44 岁 Age	76	2.6	2.6	5.3	3.9	0.0	1.3	3.9	80.3
45~54 岁 Age	47	4.3	2.1	2.1	4.3	2.1	0.0	0.0	85.1
55~60 岁 Age	24	12.5	0.0	4.2	0.0	0.0	4.2	12.5	66.7

2-8 样本、男性各年龄层、女性各年龄层的品牌习惯/ Brand Habit in Consuming Hard Liquor by the Whole Sample, Age and Gender Groups

	人数 Number	基本固定饮用一个牌子 used in only one brand	比较固定地饮用两个或三个牌子 used in two or three brands	基本上不太固定牌子 no brand preference
样本 Sample	199	46.2	23.1	30.7
男性 Male	154	45.5	24.7	29.9
16~24 岁 Age	14	42.9	14.3	42.9
25~34 岁 Age	53	41.5	28.3	30.2
35~44 岁 Age	44	45.5	25.0	29.5
45~54 岁 Age	28	50.0	21.4	28.6
55~60 岁 Age	15	53.3	26.7	20.0
女性 Female	45	48.9	17.8	33.3
16~24 岁 Age	3	33.3	33.3	33.3
25~34 岁 Age	13	38.5	23.1	38.5
35~44 岁 Age	14	42.9	14.3	42.9
45~54 岁 Age	7	71.4	14.3	14.3
55~60 岁 Age	8	62.5	12.5	25.0

2-9 选择该类商品的考虑因素/ Ranking of the Considerations in Purchasing

注：本题为多选题，合计百分比超过 100%(Multiple answers）

排名 Ranking	考虑因素 Considerations	人次 Person-time	百分比 Percent
1	口味好 pleasant taste	124	62.3
2	价格适中 reasonable price	93	46.7
3	购买方便 easy to buy	43	21.6
4	有名的牌子 famous brand	38	19.1
5	只是由于习惯 out of habit	25	12.6
6	生产日期 date of producing	24	12.1
7	朋友推荐 introduction of friends	12	6.0
8	别人送的 given by other people	7	3.5
9	其它 others	5	2.5
10	广告影响 influence of advertising	4	2.0
10	有优惠条件 with preferential terms	4	2.0
11	售货员介绍 introduced by the shop assistants	3	1.5
12	包装吸引人 appealing package	2	1.0

n=199

2-10 样本、男性各年龄层、女性各年龄层最常饮用的度数/ Degree of the Consumed Hard Liquor by the Whole Sample, Age and Gender Groups

	人数 Number	55 度以上 55° or over	39—55 度 39°--55°	38 度及以下 38° or below	其它 others
样本 Sample	197	13.2	52.8	34.0	0.0
男性 Male	153	12.4	55.6	32.0	0.0
16~24 岁 Age	14	0.0	71.4	28.6	0.0
25~34 岁 Age	52	9.6	44.2	46.2	0.0
35~44 岁 Age	44	13.6	65.9	20.5	0.0
45~54 岁 Age	28	25.0	53.6	21.4	0.0
55~60 岁 Age	15	6.7	53.3	40.0	0.0
女性 Female	44	15.9	43.2	40.9	0.0
16~24 岁 Age	3	33.3	0.0	66.7	0.0
25~34 岁 Age	13	15.4	30.8	53.8	0.0
35~44 岁 Age	14	7.1	57.1	35.7	0.0
45~54 岁 Age	7	42.9	57.1	0.0	0.0
55~60 岁 Age	7	0.0	42.9	57.1	0.0

2-11 样本、男性各年龄层、女性各年龄层最常饮用的场合/ Settings of Consumption by the Whole Sample, Age and Gender Groups

注：本题为多选题，合计百分比超过 100%(Multiple answers）

	人数 Number	请客 entertain guests	节假日团聚 get-together on holiday	日常饮用 drink daily	服药 drink with medicine	做菜 cooking meal	其它 others
样本 Sample	199	21.6	39.7	64.3	4.5	4.5	0.0
男性 Male	154	18.8	39.0	66.2	3.2	4.5	0.0
16~24 岁 Age	14	21.4	42.9	42.9	7.1	0.0	0.0
25~34 岁 Age	53	24.5	39.6	58.5	5.7	5.7	0.0
35~44 岁 Age	44	20.5	43.2	70.5	0.0	9.1	0.0
45~54 岁 Age	28	7.1	25.0	78.6	0.0	0.0	0.0
55~60 岁 Age	15	13.3	46.7	80.0	6.7	0.0	0.0
女性 Female	45	31.1	42.2	57.8	8.9	4.4	0.0
16~24 岁 Age	3	100.0	100.0	0.0	0.0	0.0	0.0
25~34 岁 Age	13	38.5	38.5	61.5	7.7	7.7	0.0
35~44 岁 Age	14	28.6	50.0	57.1	7.1	0.0	0.0
45~54 岁 Age	7	14.3	28.6	85.7	14.3	14.3	0.0
55~60 岁 Age	8	12.5	25.0	50.0	12.5	0.0	0.0

2-12 重度消费者人口分布/ Demographics of the Heavy Consumers

	人数 Number	16-24 岁 Age	25-34 岁 Age	35-44 岁 Age	45-54 岁 Age	55-60 岁 Age
样本 Sample	129	7.0	29.5	31.0	21.7	10.9
男性 Male	108	7.4	31.5	29.6	22.2	9.3
天天喝 daily	41	4.9	17.1	39.0	26.8	12.2
一周 3 次或以上 3 times or over a week	26	7.7	26.9	23.1	26.9	15.4
一周 1~2 次 once or twice a week	41	9.8	48.8	24.4	14.6	2.4
女性 Female	21	4.8	19.0	38.1	19.0	19.0
天天喝 daily	9	0.0	22.2	22.2	22.2	33.3
一周 3 次或以上 3 times or over a week	3	0.0	0.0	66.7	33.3	0.0
一周 1~2 次 once or twice a week	9	11.1	22.2	44.4	11.1	11.1

2-13 不同消费者层的常用品牌/ The Most Frequently Used Brands by Market Segments

2-13-1 时尚流行指标/ Fads Popular Index

	人数 Number	第一品牌及百分比 1st/ percent	第二品牌及百分比 2nd/ percent	第三品牌及百分比 3rd/ percent
样本 Sample	198	老龙口 Laolongkou(31.8)	高粱王 Gaoliangwang(6.6)	北大仓 Beidacang(4.5)
平实生活指向 simple living orientation	110	老龙口 Laolongkou(30.0)	高粱王 Gaoliangwang(6.4)	古井贡酒 Gu Jing Gong Jiu(5.5) 三九龙滨(999 龙滨）San Jiu Long Bing(5.5)
时尚流行指向 fashion orientation	88	老龙口 Laolongkou(34.1)	高粱王 Gaoliangwang(6.8)	沱牌大曲 Tuo Pai Da Qu(5.7)

2-13-2 广告态度指标/ Advertising Attitude Index

	人数 Number	第一品牌及百分比 1st/ percent	第二品牌及百分比 2nd/ percent	第三品牌及百分比 3rd/ percent
样本 Sample	198	老龙口 Laolongkou(31.8)	高粱王 Gaoliangwang(6.6)	北大仓 Beidacang(4.5)
广告淡漠指向 indifferent orientation	56	老龙口 Laolongkou(35.7)	钓鱼台 Diaoyutai(8.9)	三九龙滨(999 龙滨）San Jiu Long Bin (5.4) 古井贡酒 Gu Jing Gong Jiu(5.4)
中间层 medium	115	老龙口 Laolongkou(30.4)	高粱王 Gaoliangwang(10.4)	大高粱 Dagaoliang(6.1)
信赖广告指向 loyal orientation	27	老龙口 Laolongkou(29.6)	小金斗 Xiaojindou(11.1)	沱牌大曲 Tuo Pai Da Qu(7.4) 北大仓 Beidacang(7.4) 尖庄 Jianzhuang(7.4)

2-13-3 饮食健康指标/ Foods & Drink Quality Index

	人数 Number	第一品牌及百分比 1st/ percent	第二品牌及百分比 2nd/ percent	第三品牌及百分比 3rd/ percent
样本 Sample	198	**老龙口 Laolongkou(31.8)**	**高粱王 Gaoliangwang (6.6)**	**北大仓 Beidacang(4.5)**
饮食“温饱”指向 "basic" orientation	72	老龙口 Laolongkou(31.9)	北大仓 Beidacang(6.9)	高粱王 Gaoliangwang (5.6) 沱牌大曲 Tuo Pai Da Qu(5.6) 钓鱼台 Diaoyutai(5.6)
中间层 medium	85	老龙口 Laolongkou (32.9)	三九龙滨(999 龙滨）San Jiu Long Bin (5.9) 高粱王 Gaoliangwang (5.9)	钓鱼台 Diaoyutai (4.7) 古井贡酒 Gu Jing Gong Jiu(4.7) 沱牌大曲 Tuo Pai Da Qu(4.7)
健康营养指向 health & nutrition orientation	41	老龙口 Laolongkou (29.3)	高粱王 Gaoliangwang (9.8)	大高粱 Dagaoliang(4.9) 尖庄 Jianzhuang(4.9) 北大仓 Beidacang(4.9)

2-14 重度消费者的消费者层构成/ The Composition of the Heavy Consumers

2-14-1 时尚流行指标/ Fads Popular Index

	人数 Number	平实生活指向 simple living orientation	时尚流行指向 fashion orientation
样本 Sample	129	57.4	42.6
天天喝 daily	50	64.0	36.0
一周 3 次或以上 3 times or over a week	29	58.6	41.4
一周 1~2 次 once or twice a week	50	50.0	50.0

2-14-2 广告态度指标/ Advertising Attitude Index

	人数 Number	广告淡漠指向 indifferent orientation	中间层 medium	信赖广告指向 loyal orientation
样本 Sample	129	30.2	52.7	17.1
天天喝 daily	50	40.0	44.0	16.0
一周 3 次或以上 3 times or over a week	29	17.2	48.3	34.5
一周 1~2 次 once or twice a week	50	28.0	64.0	8.0

2-14-3 饮食健康指标/ Foods & Drink Quality Index

	人数 Number	饮食“温饱”指向 "basic" orientation	中间层 medium	健康营养指向 health & nutrition orientation
样本 Sample	129	38.0	42.6	19.4
天天喝 daily	50	38.0	46.0	16.0
一周 3 次或以上 3 times or over a week	29	44.8	31.0	24.1
一周 1~2 次 once or twice a week	50	34.0	46.0	20.0

3.葡萄酒 / Wine

● 北京 / Beijing

3-1 最近三个月饮用频率的比例/ Proportion of the Sample Consuming Wine in the Last Three Months

	人数 Number	百分比 Percent
天天喝 daily	13	1.3
一周 3 次或以上 3 times or over a week	26	2.6
一周 1~2 次 once or twice a week	68	6.8
一个月 2～3 次 2 or 3 times a month	120	12.0
一个月 1 次 once a month	73	7.3
两个月 1 次 once two months	37	3.7
三个月 1 次或以下 once three months or below	76	7.6
没有喝 never	589	58.8

n=1002

3-2 最常用品牌排名/ Ranking of the Most Frequently Used Brands

排名 Brand Ranking	品牌 Brands	人数 Number	百分比 Percent
1	长城 Great Wall	129	31.5
2	中国红葡萄酒 China Red Wine	110	26.9
3	张裕 Zhangyu	35	8.6
4	丰收 Fengshou	18	4.4
5	千禧 Qianxi	14	3.4
6	桂花陈 Guihua Chen	13	3.2
7	通化 Tonghua	10	2.4
7	王朝 Dynasty	10	2.4
7	夜光杯 Cumnous Cup	10	2.4
8	北京 Beijing	6	1.5
9	威龙 Weilon	4	1.0

n=409

3-3 样本、男性各年龄层、女性各年龄层的常用品牌/ The Most Frequently Used Brands by the Whole Sample, Age and Gender Groups

	人数 Number	第一品牌及百分比 1st/ percent	第二品牌及百分比 2nd/ percent	第三品牌及百分比 3rd/ percent
样本 Sample	409	**长城 Great Wall(31.5)**	**中国红葡萄酒 China Red Wine(26.9)**	**张裕 Zhangyu(8.6)**
男性 Male	204	**长城 Great Wall(37.3)**	**中国红葡萄酒 China Red Wine(24.5)**	**张裕 Zhangyu(7.8)**
16~24 岁 Age	28	长城 Great Wall(39.3)	中国红葡萄酒 China Red Wine(14.3)	张裕 Zhangyu(10.7)
25~34 岁 Age	65	长城 Great Wall(49.2)	中国红葡萄酒 China Red Wine(16.9)	桂花陈 Guihua Chen(6.2) 张裕 Zhangyu(6.2)
35~44 岁 Age	57	长城 Great Wall(31.6)	中国红葡萄酒 China Red Wine(26.3)	张裕 Zhangyu(8.8)
45~54 岁 Age	29	中国红葡萄酒 China Red Wine(34.5)	长城 Great Wall(27.6)	张裕 Zhangyu(10.3)
55~60 岁 Age	25	中国红葡萄酒 China Red Wine(40.0)	长城 Great Wall(28.0)	丰收 Fengshou(4.0) 千禧 Qianxi(4.0) 王朝 Dynasty(4.0) 威龙 Weilon(4.0) 张裕 Zhangyu(4.0) 桂花陈 Guihua Chen(4.0) 北京 Beijing(4.0)
女性 Female	205	**中国红葡萄酒 China Red Wine(29.3)**	**长城 Great Wall(25.9)**	**张裕 Zhangyu(9.3)**
16~24 岁 Age	33	长城 Great Wall(48.5)	丰收 Fengshou(9.1) 张裕 Zhangyu(9.1) 中国红葡萄酒 China Red Wine(9.1)	千禧 Qianxi(6.1) 通化 Tonghua(6.1)
25~34 岁 Age	61	长城 Great Wall(34.4)	中国红葡萄酒 China Red Wine(21.3)	张裕 Zhangyu(9.8)
35~44 岁 Age	53	中国红葡萄酒 China Red Wine(45.3)	长城 Great Wall(17.0)	张裕 Zhangyu(5.7) 丰收 Fengshou(5.7)
45~54 岁 Age	44	中国红葡萄酒 China Red Wine(31.8)	长城 Great Wall(13.6) 张裕 Zhangyu(13.6)	丰收 Fengshou(9.1)
55~60 岁 Age	14	中国红葡萄酒 China Red Wine(42.9)	千禧 Qianxi(14.3)	丰收 Fengshou(7.1) 张裕 Zhangyu(7.1) 天然红 Tianranhong(7.1) 长城 Great Wall(7.1) 北京 Beijing(7.1) 烟台顺风 Yantai Shunfeng(7.1)

3-4 理想品牌排名/ Ranking of the Ideal Brands

排名 Brand Ranking	品牌 Brands	人数 Number	百分比 Percent
1	长城 Great Wall	238	23.5
2	中国红葡萄酒 China Red Wine	158	15.6
3	张裕 Zhangyu	61	6.0
4	王朝 Dynasty	25	2.5
5	夜光杯 Cumnous Cup	22	2.2
6	千禧 Qianxi	20	2.0
7	丰收 Fengshou	19	1.9
8	桂花陈 Guihua Chen	16	1.6
9	通化 Tonghua	13	1.3
10	野力 Yely	10	1.0
11	北京 Beijing	9	0.9

n=1012

3-5 样本、男性各年龄层、女性各年龄层最近三个月有无购买的比例/ Purchasing in the Last Three Months by the Whole Sample, Age and Gender Groups

	人数 Number	买过 yes	没买过 no
样本 Sample	1011	35.9	64.1
男性 Male	504	35.3	64.7
16~24 岁 Age	105	22.9	77.1
25~34 岁 Age	151	37.7	62.3
35~44 岁 Age	131	38.9	61.1
45~54 岁 Age	77	28.6	71.4
55~60 岁 Age	40	60.0	40.0
女性 Female	507	36.5	63.5
16~24 岁 Age	108	30.6	69.4
25~34 岁 Age	149	36.2	63.8
35~44 岁 Age	124	37.1	62.9
45~54 岁 Age	84	44.0	56.0
55~60 岁 Age	42	35.7	64.3

3-6 样本、男性各年龄层、女性各年龄层最近三个月是否拿葡萄酒送过礼/ To Offer Wine as Gift in the Last Three Months by the Whole Sample, Age and Gender Groups

	人数 Number	送过 yes	没送过 no
样本 Sample	998	9.9	90.1
男性 Male	497	9.3	90.7
16~24 岁 Age	104	2.9	97.1
25~34 岁 Age	148	8.8	91.2
35~44 岁 Age	129	11.6	88.4
45~54 岁 Age	76	11.8	88.2
55~60 岁 Age	40	15.0	85.0
女性 Female	501	10.6	89.4
16~24 岁 Age	106	8.5	91.5
25~34 岁 Age	147	8.2	91.8
35~44 岁 Age	123	13.8	86.2
45~54 岁 Age	83	13.3	86.7
55~60 岁 Age	42	9.5	90.5

3-7 样本、男性各年龄层、女性各年龄层最近三个月的饮用频率/ Frequencies of Consuming Wine in the Last Three Months by the Whole Sample, Age and Gender Groups

	人数 Number	天天喝 daily	一周 3 次或以上 3 times or over a week	一周 1~2 次 once or twice a week	一个月 2~3 次 2 or 3 times a month	一个月 1 次 once a month	两个月 1 次 once two months	三个月 1 次或以下 once three months or below	没有喝 never
样本 Sample	1002	1.3	2.6	6.8	12.0	7.3	3.7	7.6	58.8
男性 Male	498	1.0	2.6	6.4	12.7	8.0	3.6	7.0	58.6
16~24 岁 Age	104	1.0	1.0	3.8	5.8	3.8	3.8	7.7	73.1
25~34 岁 Age	149	0.0	3.4	6.0	16.1	6.0	4.7	7.4	56.4
35~44 岁 Age	129	0.8	1.6	7.8	14.0	10.1	4.7	7.0	54.3
45~54 岁 Age	76	0.0	3.9	5.3	11.8	10.5	1.3	5.3	61.8
55~60 岁 Age	40	7.5	5.0	12.5	15.0	15.0	0.0	7.5	37.5
女性 Female	504	1.6	2.6	7.1	11.3	6.5	3.8	8.1	58.9
16~24 岁 Age	107	0.0	2.8	1.9	5.6	7.5	3.7	10.3	68.2
25~34 岁 Age	149	1.3	2.0	8.1	12.8	5.4	4.0	7.4	59.1
35~44 岁 Age	123	0.8	1.6	8.1	14.6	8.9	3.3	5.7	56.9
45~54 岁 Age	83	3.6	4.8	8.4	14.5	6.0	4.8	10.8	47.0
55~60 岁 Age	42	4.8	2.4	11.9	4.8	2.4	2.4	7.1	64.3

3-8 样本、男性各年龄层、女性各年龄层的品牌习惯/ Brand Habit in Consuming Wine by the Whole Sample, Age and Gender Groups

	人数 Number	基本固定饮用一个牌子 used in only one brand	比较固定地饮用两个或三个牌子 used in two or three brands	基本上不太固定牌子 no brand preference
样本 Sample	410	43.4	34.9	21.7
男性 Male	206	39.3	35.9	24.8
16~24 岁 Age	28	25.0	39.3	35.7
25~34 岁 Age	65	38.5	43.1	18.5
35~44 岁 Age	59	39.0	30.5	30.5
45~54 岁 Age	29	41.4	37.9	20.7
55~60 岁 Age	25	56.0	24.0	20.0
女性 Female	204	47.5	33.8	18.6
16~24 岁 Age	32	37.5	34.4	28.1
25~34 岁 Age	61	50.8	29.5	19.7
35~44 岁 Age	53	49.1	35.8	15.1
45~54 岁 Age	43	48.8	39.5	11.6
55~60 岁 Age	15	46.7	26.7	26.7

3-9 选择该类商品的考虑因素/ Ranking of the Considerations in Purchasing

注：本题为多选题，合计百分比超过 100%(Multiple answers）

排名 Ranking	考虑因素 Considerations	人次 Person-time	百分比 Percent
1	口味好 pleasant taste	251	61.1
2	有名的牌子 famous brand	151	36.7
3	价格适中 reasonable price	138	33.6
4	生产日期 date of producing	52	12.7
5	只是由于习惯 out of habit	51	12.4
6	别人送的 given by other people	38	9.2
7	购买方便 easy to buy	36	8.8
8	朋友推荐 introduction of friends	27	6.6
9	广告影响 influence of advertising	24	5.8
10	其它 others	11	2.7
11	包装吸引人 appealing package	10	2.4
12	有优惠条件 with preferential terms	9	2.2
13	售货员介绍 introduced by the shop assistants	5	1.2

n=411

3-10 样本、男性各年龄层、女性各年龄层最常饮用的种类/ Kinds of the Consumed Wine by the Whole Sample, Age and Gender Groups

	人数 Number	干红 dry red	干白 dry white	甜型 sweet	其他 others
样本 Sample	410	57.3	11.7	30.0	1.0
男性 Male	205	57.1	16.6	26.3	0.0
16~24 岁 Age	28	67.9	17.9	14.3	0.0
25~34 岁 Age	65	69.2	12.3	18.5	0.0
35~44 岁 Age	59	45.8	20.3	33.9	0.0
45~54 岁 Age	29	34.5	24.1	41.4	0.0
55~60 岁 Age	24	66.7	8.3	25.0	0.0
女性 Female	205	57.6	6.8	33.7	2.0
16~24 岁 Age	32	56.3	15.6	28.1	0.0
25~34 岁 Age	61	65.6	4.9	24.6	4.9
35~44 岁 Age	53	43.4	7.5	49.1	0.0
45~54 岁 Age	44	70.5	4.5	22.7	2.3
55~60 岁 Age	15	40.0	0.0	60.0	0.0

3-11 样本、男性各年龄层、女性各年龄层最常饮用场合/ Settings of Consumption by the Whole Sample, Age and Gender Groups

注：本题为多选题，合计百分比超过 100%(Multiple answers）

	人数 Number	请客 entertain guests	节假日团聚 get-together on holiday	日常饮用 drink daily	睡觉前喝 before sleeping	做菜 cooking meal	其它 others
样本 Sample	409	33.5	57.0	36.2	4.2	0.7	2.4
男性 Male	205	32.7	59.5	34.1	3.4	0.5	2.0
16~24 岁 Age	28	35.7	75.0	21.4	0.0	0.0	0.0
25~34 岁 Age	64	34.4	57.8	34.4	6.3	1.6	1.6
35~44 岁 Age	59	40.7	66.1	30.5	3.4	0.0	1.7
45~54 岁 Age	29	17.2	55.2	37.9	3.4	0.0	3.4
55~60 岁 Age	25	24.0	36.0	52.0	0.0	0.0	4.0
女性 Female	204	34.3	54.4	38.2	4.9	1.0	2.9
16~24 岁 Age	32	28.1	56.3	34.4	0.0	0.0	6.3
25~34 岁 Age	60	38.3	51.7	33.3	3.3	0.0	6.7
35~44 岁 Age	53	35.8	54.7	47.2	5.7	1.9	0.0
45~54 岁 Age	44	36.4	54.5	34.1	11.4	0.0	0.0
55~60 岁 Age	15	20.0	60.0	46.7	0.0	6.7	0.0

3-12 重度消费者人口分布/ Demographics of the Heavy Consumers

	人数 Number	16-24 岁 Age	25-34 岁 Age	35-44 岁 Age	45-54 岁 Age	55-60 岁 Age
样本 Sample	107	10.3	29.0	24.3	19.6	16.8
男性 Male	50	12.0	28.0	26.0	14.0	20.0
天天喝 daily	5	20.0	0.0	20.0	0.0	60.0
一周 3 次或以上 3 times or over a week	13	7.7	38.5	15.4	23.1	15.4
一周 1~2 次 once or twice a week	32	12.5	28.1	31.3	12.5	15.6
女性 Female	57	8.8	29.8	22.8	24.6	14.0
天天喝 daily	8	0.0	25.0	12.5	37.5	25.0
一周 3 次或以上 3 times or over a week	13	23.1	23.1	15.4	30.8	7.7
一周 1~2 次 once or twice a week	36	5.6	33.3	27.8	19.4	13.9

3-13 不同消费者层的常用品牌/ The Most Frequently Used Brands by Market Segments

3-13-1 时尚流行指标/ Fads Popular Index

	人数 Number	第一品牌及百分比 1st/percent	第二品牌及百分比 2nd/percent	第三品牌及百分比 3rd/percent	第四品牌及百分比 4th/percent
样本 Sample	405	**长城 Great Wall(31.9)**	**中国红葡萄酒 China Red Wine(26.4)**	**张裕 Zhangyu(8.6)**	**丰收 Fengshou(4.4)**
平实生活指向 simple living orientation	184	长城 Great Wall(30.4)	中国红葡萄酒 China Red Wine(28.3)	张裕 Zhangyu(9.2)	丰收 Fengshou(4.3)
时尚流行指向 fashion orientation	221	长城 Great Wall(33.0)	中国红葡萄酒 China Red Wine(24.9)	张裕 Zhangyu(8.1)	丰收 Fengshou(4.5) 千禧 Qianxi(4.5)

3-13-2 广告态度指标/ Advertising Attitude Index

	人数 Number	第一品牌及百分比 1st/percent	第二品牌及百分比 2nd/percent	第三品牌及百分比 3rd/percent	第四品牌及百分比 4th/percent
样本 Sample	399	**长城 Great Wall(31.6)**	**中国红葡萄酒 China Red Wine(26.8)**	**张裕 Zhangyu(8.8)**	**丰收 Fengshou(4.5)**
广告淡漠指向 indifferent orientation	112	中国红葡萄酒 China Red Wine(26.8)	长城 Great Wall(25.0)	张裕 Zhangyu(11.6)	丰收 Fengshou(5.4) 桂花陈 GuihuachenF(5.4)
中间层 medium	239	长城 Great Wall(32.6)	中国红葡萄酒 China Red Wine(26.4)	张裕 Zhangyu(8.4)	丰收 Fengshou(4.2)
信赖广告指向 loyal orientation	48	长城 Great Wall(41.7)	中国红葡萄酒 China Red Wine(29.2)	丰收 Fengshou(4.2) 千禧 Qianxi(4.2) 张裕 Zhangyu(4.2)	贝丽塔 Beilita(2.1) 龙威 Longwei(2.1) 桂花陈 Guihuachen(2.1) 中华 Zhonghua(2.1) 夜光杯 Cumnous Cup(2.1) 太阳 Taillan(2.1)

3-13-3 饮食健康指标/ Foods & Drink Quality Index

	人数 Number	第一品牌及百分比 1st/percent	第二品牌及百分比 2nd/percent	第三品牌及百分比 3rd/percent	第四品牌及百分比 4th/percent
样本 Sample	404	**长城 Great Wall(31.2)**	**中国红葡萄酒 China Red Wine(27.0)**	**张裕 Zhangyu(8.7)**	**丰收 Fengshou(4.5)**
饮食“温饱”指向 "basic" orientation	101	长城 Great Wall(34.7)	中国红葡萄酒 China Red Wine(22.8)	张裕 Zhangyu(8.9)	千禧 Qianxi(5.0)
中间层 medium	186	长城 Great Wall(31.7)	中国红葡萄酒 China Red Wine(23.7)	张裕 Zhangyu(10.2)	夜光杯 Cumnous Cup(3.8) 丰收 Fengshou(3.8) 桂花陈 Guihuachen(3.8) 千禧 Qianxi(3.8)
健康营养指向 health & nutrition orientation	117	中国红葡萄酒 China Red Wine(35.9)	长城 Great Wall(27.4)	丰收 Fengshou(6.0) 张裕 Zhangyu(6.0)	王朝 Dynasty(4.3)

3-14 重度消费者的消费者层构成/ The Composition of the Heavy Consumers

3-14-1 时尚流行指标/ Fads Popular Index

	人数 Number	平实生活指向 simple living orientation	时尚流行指向 fashion orientation
样本 Sample	107	42.1	57.9
天天喝 daily	13	61.5	38.5
一周 3 次或以上 3 times or over a week	26	38.5	61.5
一周 1~2 次 once or twice a week	68	39.7	60.3

3-14-2 广告态度指标/ Advertising Attitude Index

	人数 Number	广告淡漠指向 indifferent orientation	中间层 medium	信赖广告指向 loyal orientation
样本 Sample	106	25.5	57.5	17.0
天天喝 daily	13	30.8	46.2	23.1
一周 3 次或以上 3 times or over a week	26	30.8	61.5	7.7
一周 1~2 次 once or twice a week	67	22.4	58.2	19.4

3-14-3 饮食健康指标/ Foods & Drink Quality Index

	人数 Number	饮食“温饱”指向 "basic" orientation	中间层 medium	健康营养指向 health & nutrition orientation
样本 Sample	106	18.9	46.2	34.9
天天喝 daily	13	7.7	53.8	38.5
一周 3 次或以上 3 times or over a week	26	19.2	46.2	34.6
一周 1~2 次 once or twice a week	67	20.9	44.8	34.3

● 上海 / Shanghai

3-1 最近三个月饮用频率的比例/ Proportion of the Sample Consuming Wine in the Last Three Months

	人数 Number	百分比 Percent
天天喝 daily	5	0.5
一周 3 次或以上 3 times or over a week	9	0.9
一周 1~2 次 once or twice a week	32	3.2
一个月 2~3 次 2 or 3 times a month	49	4.9
一个月 1 次 once a month	42	4.2
两个月 1 次 once two months	35	3.5
三个月 1 次或以下 once three months or below	65	6.4
没有喝 never	771	76.5

n=1008

3-2 最常用品牌排名/ Ranking of the Most Frequently Used Brands

排名 Brand Ranking	品牌 Brands	人数 Number	百分比 Percent
1	张裕 Zhangyu	74	31.2
2	王朝 Dynasty	59	24.9
3	长城 Great Wall	17	7.2
4	野力 Yely	16	6.8
5	皇轩 Imperial Court	11	4.6
6	通化 Tonghua	8	3.4
7	皇城干 Huangchenggan	7	3.0
8	皇朝 Huangchao	4	1.7

n=237

3-3 样本、男性各年龄层、女性各年龄层的常用品牌/ The Most Frequently Used Brands by the Whole Sample, Age and Gender Groups

	人数 Number	第一品牌及百分比 1st/ percent	第二品牌及百分比 2nd/ percent	第三品牌及百分比 3rd/ percent
样本 Sample	237	**张裕 Zhangyu(31.2)**	**王朝 Dynasty(24.9)**	**长城 Great Wall(7.2)**
男性 Male	142	**张裕 Zhangyu(27.5)**	**王朝 Dynasty(24.6)**	**野力 Yely(6.3)** **长城 Great Wall(6.3)**
16~24 岁 Age	18	张裕 Zhangyu(27.8)	王朝 Dynasty(22.2)	皇轩 Imperial Court(11.1)
25~34 岁 Age	43	王朝 Dynasty(23.3) 张裕 Zhangyu(23.3)	长城 Great Wall(11.6)	皇轩 Imperial Court(9.3)
35~44 岁 Age	41	王朝 Dynasty(29.3)	张裕 Zhangyu(22.0)	通化 Tonghua(9.8) 野力 Yely(9.8)
45~54 岁 Age	29	张裕 Zhangyu(41.4)	王朝 Dynasty(20.7)	青岛 Tsing Tao(6.9) 野力 Yely(6.9)
55~60 岁 Age	11	王朝 Dynasty(27.3) 张裕 Zhangyu(27.3)	长白山 Changbaishan(9.1) 皇城干 Huangchenggan(9.1) 长城 Great Wall(9.1) 西班牙干红 Spanish Dry(9.1) 烟台 Yantai(9.1)	
女性 Female	95	**张裕 Zhangyu(36.8)**	**王朝 Dynasty(25.3)**	**长城 Great Wall(8.4)**
16~24 岁 Age	16	王朝 Dynasty(50.0)	张裕 Zhangyu(37.5)	皇轩 Imperial Court(6.3)
25~34 岁 Age	31	王朝 Dynasty(32.3)	张裕 Zhangyu(25.8)	野力 Yely(9.7)
35~44 岁 Age	28	张裕 Zhangyu(39.3)	长城 Great Wall(17.9)	王朝 Dynasty(10.7)
45~54 岁 Age	11	张裕 Zhangyu(54.5)	王朝 Dynasty(18.2) 野力 Yely(18.2)	
55~60 岁 Age	9	张裕 Zhangyu(44.4)	长城 Great Wall(22.2)	皇轩 Imperial Court(11.1) 王朝 Dynasty(11.1)

3-4 理想品牌排名/ Ranking of the Ideal Brands

排名 Brand Ranking	品牌 Brands	人数 Number	百分比 Percent
1	王朝 Dynasty	234	23.1
2	张裕 Zhangyu	223	22.0
3	野力 Yely	84	8.3
4	长城 Great Wall	48	4.7
5	皇朝 Huangchao	27	2.7
6	皇轩 Imperial Court	22	2.2
7	皇城干 Huangchenggan	18	1.8
8	通化 Tonghua	17	1.7
9	李华 Lihua	8	0.8

n=1014

3-5 样本、男性各年龄层、女性各年龄层最近三个月有无购买的比例/ Purchasing in the Last Three Months by the Whole Sample, Age and Gender Groups

	人数 Number	买过 yes	没买过 no
样本 Sample	1014	21.9	78.1
男性 Male	509	23.6	76.4
16~24 岁 Age	109	9.2	90.8
25~34 岁 Age	146	24.7	75.3
35~44 岁 Age	130	25.4	74.6
45~54 岁 Age	85	35.3	64.7
55~60 岁 Age	39	28.2	71.8
女性 Female	505	20.2	79.8
16~24 岁 Age	108	15.7	84.3
25~34 岁 Age	144	22.9	77.1
35~44 岁 Age	130	25.4	74.6
45~54 岁 Age	82	12.2	87.8
55~60 岁 Age	41	22.0	78.0

3-6 样本、男性各年龄层、女性各年龄层最近三个月是否拿葡萄酒送过礼/ To Offer Wine as Gift in the Last Three Months by the Whole Sample, Age and Gender Groups

	人数 Number	送过 yes	没送过 no
样本 Sample	1012	7.8	92.2
男性 Male	507	8.9	91.1
16~24 岁 Age	109	5.5	94.5
25~34 岁 Age	144	7.6	92.4
35~44 岁 Age	130	12.3	87.7
45~54 岁 Age	85	10.6	89.4
55~60 岁 Age	39	7.7	92.3
女性 Female	505	6.7	93.3
16~24 岁 Age	108	6.5	93.5
25~34 岁 Age	144	7.6	92.4
35~44 岁 Age	130	6.2	93.8
45~54 岁 Age	82	6.1	93.9
55~60 岁 Age	41	7.3	92.7

3-7 样本、男性各年龄层、女性各年龄层最近三个月的饮用频率/ Frequencies of Consuming Wine in the Last Three Months by the Whole Sample, Age and Gender Groups

	人数 Number	天天喝 daily	一周 3 次或以上 3 times or over a week	一周 1~2 次 once or twice a week	一个月 2~3 次 2 or 3 times a month	一个月 1 次 once a month	两个月 1 次 once two months	三个月 1 次或以下 once three months or below	没有喝 never
样本 Sample	1008	0.5	0.9	3.2	4.9	4.2	3.5	6.4	76.5
男性 Male	507	0.8	1.2	4.1	6.3	5.1	4.5	5.9	72.0
16~24 岁 Age	108	0.0	0.9	0.0	3.7	4.6	2.8	4.6	83.3
25~34 岁 Age	145	0.0	2.1	3.4	8.3	2.8	5.5	7.6	70.3
35~44 岁 Age	130	2.3	1.5	6.2	4.6	6.9	4.6	5.4	68.5
45~54 岁 Age	85	0.0	0.0	5.9	5.9	9.4	5.9	7.1	65.9
55~60 岁 Age	39	2.6	0.0	7.7	12.8	0.0	2.6	2.6	71.8
女性 Female	501	0.2	0.6	2.2	3.4	3.2	2.4	7.0	81.0
16~24 岁 Age	107	0.0	0.0	0.9	4.7	0.9	2.8	5.6	85.0
25~34 岁 Age	142	0.0	0.7	3.5	4.2	3.5	2.8	7.0	78.2
35~44 岁 Age	129	0.0	1.6	2.3	3.9	5.4	2.3	6.2	78.3
45~54 岁 Age	82	1.2	0.0	1.2	1.2	2.4	0.0	7.3	86.6
55~60 岁 Age	41	0.0	0.0	2.4	0.0	2.4	4.9	12.2	78.0

3-8 样本、男性各年龄层、女性各年龄层的品牌习惯/ Brand Habit in Consuming Wine by the Whole Sample, Age and Gender Groups

	人数 Number	基本固定饮用一个牌子 used in only one brand	比较固定地饮用两个或三个牌子 used in two or three brands	基本上不太固定牌子 no brand preference
样本 Sample	237	44.7	33.3	21.9
男性 Male	142	43.0	33.8	23.2
16~24 岁 Age	18	33.3	38.9	27.8
25~34 岁 Age	43	44.2	37.2	18.6
35~44 岁 Age	41	51.2	19.5	29.3
45~54 岁 Age	29	34.5	51.7	13.8
55~60 岁 Age	11	45.5	18.2	36.4
女性 Female	95	47.4	32.6	20.0
16~24 岁 Age	16	25.0	43.8	31.3
25~34 岁 Age	31	51.6	35.5	12.9
35~44 岁 Age	28	57.1	21.4	21.4
45~54 岁 Age	11	54.5	27.3	18.2
55~60 岁 Age	9	33.3	44.4	22.2

3-9 选择该类商品的考虑因素/ Ranking of the Considerations in Purchasing

注：本题为多选题，合计百分比超过 100%(Multiple answers)

排名 Ranking	考虑因素 Considerations	人次 Person-time	百分比 Percent
1	口味好 pleasant taste	155	65.7
2	有名的牌子 famous brand	103	43.6
3	价格适中 reasonable price	81	34.3
4	购买方便 easy to buy	23	9.7
4	生产日期 date of producing	23	9.7
5	广告影响 influence of advertising	17	7.2
5	朋友推荐 introduction of friends	17	7.2
6	只是由于习惯 out of habit	12	5.1
7	别人送的 given by other people	11	4.7
8	有优惠条件 with preferential terms	6	2.5
9	其它 others	4	1.7
10	包装吸引人 appealing package	3	1.3
10	售货员介绍 introduced by the shop assistants	3	1.3

n=236

3-10 样本、男性各年龄层、女性各年龄层最常饮用的种类/ Kinds of the Consumed Wine by the Whole Sample, Age and Gender Groups

	人数 Number	干红 dry red	干白 dry white	甜型 sweet	其他 others
样本 Sample	236	73.3	10.2	16.1	0.4
男性 Male	141	75.9	10.6	13.5	0.0
16~24 岁 Age	18	94.4	5.6	0.0	0.0
25~34 岁 Age	43	76.7	7.0	16.3	0.0
35~44 岁 Age	41	70.7	14.6	14.6	0.0
45~54 岁 Age	28	75.0	10.7	14.3	0.0
55~60 岁 Age	11	63.6	18.2	18.2	0.0
女性 Female	95	69.5	9.5	20.0	1.1
16~24 岁 Age	16	75.0	6.3	18.8	0.0
25~34 岁 Age	31	67.7	6.5	25.8	0.0
35~44 岁 Age	28	67.9	14.3	17.9	0.0
45~54 岁 Age	11	72.7	9.1	9.1	9.1
55~60 岁 Age	9	66.7	11.1	22.2	0.0

3-11 样本、男性各年龄层、女性各年龄层最常饮用场合/ Settings of Consumption by the Whole Sample, Age and Gender Groups

注：本题为多选题，合计百分比超过 100%(Multiple answers)

	人数 Number	请客 entertain guests	节假日团聚 get-together on holiday	日常饮用 drink daily	睡觉前喝 before sleeping	做菜 cooking meal	其它 others
样本 Sample	236	42.8	55.5	22.0	1.7	1.7	1.7
男性 Male	142	43.7	51.4	26.8	2.1	0.7	2.1
16~24 岁 Age	18	55.6	66.7	11.1	5.6	0.0	0.0
25~34 岁 Age	43	34.9	58.1	16.3	0.0	0.0	4.7
35~44 岁 Age	41	41.5	51.2	34.1	2.4	0.0	2.4
45~54 岁 Age	29	51.7	41.4	31.0	0.0	3.4	0.0
55~60 岁 Age	11	45.5	27.3	54.5	9.1	0.0	0.0
女性 Female	94	41.5	61.7	14.9	1.1	3.2	1.1
16~24 岁 Age	16	43.8	68.8	0.0	0.0	6.3	0.0
25~34 岁 Age	31	45.2	58.1	12.9	0.0	0.0	3.2
35~44 岁 Age	27	44.4	63.0	22.2	3.7	3.7	0.0
45~54 岁 Age	11	27.3	63.6	18.2	0.0	0.0	0.0
55~60 岁 Age	9	33.3	55.6	22.2	0.0	11.1	0.0

3-12 重度消费者人口分布/ Demographics of the Heavy Consumers

	人数 Number	16-24 岁 Age	25-34 岁 Age	35-44 岁 Age	45-54 岁 Age	55-60 岁 Age
样本 Sample	46	4.3	30.4	39.1	15.2	10.9
男性 Male	31	3.2	25.8	41.9	16.1	12.9
天天喝 daily	4	0.0	0.0	75.0	0.0	25.0
一周 3 次或以上 3 times or over a week	6	16.7	50.0	33.3	0.0	0.0
一周 1~2 次 once or twice a week	21	0.0	23.8	38.[illegible]	23.8	14.3
女性 Female	15	6.7	40.0	33.3	13.3	6.7
天天喝 daily	1	0.0	0.0	0.0	100.0	0.0
一周 3 次或以上 3 times or over a week	3	0.0	33.3	66.7	0.0	0.0
一周 1~2 次 once or twice a week	11	9.1	45.5	27.3	9.1	9.1

3-13 不同消费者层的常用品牌/ The Most Frequently Used Brands by Market Segments

3-13-1 时尚流行指标/ Fads Popular Index

	人数 Number	第一品牌及百分比 1st/percent	第二品牌及百分比 2nd/percent	第三品牌及百分比 3rd/percent
样本 Sample	234	**张裕 Zhangyu(31.2)**	**王朝 Dynasty(24.4)**	**长城 Great Wall(7.3)**
平实生活指向 simple living orientation	109	张裕 Zhangyu(34.9)	王朝 Dynasty(19.3)	长城 Great Wall(9.2)
时尚流行指向 fashion orientation	125	王朝 Dynasty(28.8)	张裕 Zhangyu(28.0)	野力 Yely(8.0)

3-13-2 广告态度指标/ Advertising Attitude Index

	人数 Number	第一品牌及百分比 1st/percent	第二品牌及百分比 2nd/percent	第三品牌及百分比 3rd/percent
样本 Sample	236	**张裕 Zhangyu(30.9)**	**王朝 Dynasty(25.0)**	**长城 Great Wall(7.2)**
广告淡漠指向 indifferent orientation	65	王朝 Dynasty(26.2) 张裕 Zhangyu(26.2)	皇轩 Imperial Court(7.7)	长城 Great Wall(4.6) 野力 Yely(4.6)
中间层 medium	139	张裕 Zhangyu(33.1)	王朝 Dynasty(24.5)	长城 Great Wall(7.9)
信赖广告指向 loyal orientation	32	张裕 Zhangyu(31.3)	王朝 Dynasty(25.0)	野力 Yely(12.5)

3-13-3 饮食健康指标/ Foods & Drink Quality Index

	人数 Number	第一品牌及百分比 1st/percent	第二品牌及百分比 2nd/percent	第三品牌及百分比 3rd/percent
样本 Sample	235	张裕 Zhangyu(31.1)	王朝 Dynasty(25.1)	长城 Great Wall(7.2)
饮食"温饱"指向 "basic" orientation	43	王朝 Dynasty(31.3) 张裕 Zhangyu(31.3)	野力 Yely(8.3)	皇朝 Huangchao(4.2) 皇轩 Imperial Court(4.2) 通化 Tonghua(4.2)
中间层 medium	108	张裕 Zhangyu(28.7)	王朝 Dynasty(22.2)	长城 Great Wall(9.3)
健康营养指向 health & nutrition orientation	79	张裕 Zhangyu(34.2)	王朝 Dynasty(25.3)	长城 Great Wall(7.6)

3-14 重度消费者的消费者层构成/ The Composition of the Heavy Consumers

3-14-1 时尚流行指标/ Fads Popular Index

	人数 Number	平实生活指向 simple living orientation	时尚流行指向 fashion orientation
样本 Sample	46	63.0	37.0
天天喝 daily	5	80.0	20.0
一周 3 次或以上 3 times or over a week	9	44.4	55.6
一周 1~2 次 once or twice a week	32	65.6	34.4

3-14-2 广告态度指标/ Advertising Attitude Index

	人数 Number	广告淡漠指向 indifferent orientation	中间层 medium	信赖广告指向 loyal orientation
样本 Sample	46	41.3	52.2	6.5
天天喝 daily	5	80.0	20.0	0.0
一周 3 次或以上 3 times or over a week	9	33.3	66.7	0.0
一周 1~2 次 once or twice a week	32	37.5	53.1	9.4

3-14-3 饮食健康指标/ Foods & Drink Quality Index

	人数 Number	饮食"温饱"指向 "basic" orientation	中间层 medium	健康营养指向 health & nutrition orientation
样本 Sample	46	23.9	43.5	32.6
天天喝 daily	5	40.0	20.0	40.0
一周 3 次或以上 3 times or over a week	9	11.1	66.7	22.2
一周 1~2 次 once or twice a week	32	25.0	40.6	34.4

● 广州 / Guangzhou

3-1 最近三个月饮用频率的比例/ Proportion of the Sample Consuming Wine in the Last Three Months

	人数 Number	百分比 Percent
天天喝 daily	4	0.4
一周 3 次或以上 3 times or over a week	2	0.2
一周 1~2 次 once or twice a week	10	1.0
一个月 2～3 次 2 or 3 times a month	31	3.0
一个月 1 次 once a month	36	3.5
两个月 1 次 once two months	28	2.7
三个月 1 次或以下 once three months or below	49	4.8
没有喝 never	860	84.3

n=1020

3-2 最常用品牌排名/ Ranking of the Most Frequently Used Brands

排名 Brand Ranking	品牌 Brands	人数 Number	百分比 Percent
1	长城 Great Wall	77	48.4
2	张裕 Zhangyu	24	15.1
3	丰收 Fengshou	4	2.5
4	威龙 Weilon	3	1.9
4	野力 Yely	3	1.9
5	武当干红 Wudang	2	1.3
5	珍珠红 Pearl	2	1.3
5	王朝 Dynasty	2	1.3
5	中华 Zhonghua	2	1.3
5	中国红葡萄酒 China Red Wine	2	1.3
5	红玫瑰 Red Rose	2	1.3

n=159

3-3 样本、男性各年龄层、女性各年龄层的常用品牌/ The Most Frequently Used Brands by the Whole Sample, Age and Gender Groups

	人数 Number	第一品牌及百分比 1st/ percent	第二品牌及百分比 2nd/ percent	第三品牌及百分比 3rd/ percent
样本 Sample	159	**长城 Great Wall(48.4)**	**张裕 Zhangyu(15.1)**	**丰收 Fengshou(2.5)**
男性 Male	84	**长城 Great Wall(51.2)**	**张裕 Zhangyu(19.0)**	**红玫瑰 Red Rose (2.4)** **野力 Yely(2.4)** **中华 Zhonghua(2.4)**
16~24 岁 Age	14	长城 Great Wall(42.9)	张裕 Zhangyu(21.4)	皇朝 Huangchao(7.1) 华夏 Huaxia(7.1)
25~34 岁 Age	38	长城 Great Wall(60.5)	张裕 Zhangyu(10.5)	野力 Yely(5.3)
35~44 岁 Age	15	张裕 Zhangyu(40.0)	长城 Great Wall(33.3)	红玫瑰 Red Rose (13.3)
45~54 岁 Age	12	长城 Great Wall(58.3)	张裕 Zhangyu(8.3) 中华 Zhonghua(8.3) 法国波尔多 Bordeaux(8.3)	
55~60 岁 Age	5	张裕 Zhangyu(40.0) 长城 Great Wall(40.0)	密丝嘉 Muscat(20.0)	
女性 Female	75	**长城 Great Wall(45.3)**	**张裕 Zhangyu(10.7)**	**丰收 Fengshou(4.0)** **威龙 Weilon(4.0)**
16~24 岁 Age	12	长城 Great Wall(41.7)	王朝 Dynasty(8.3) 威龙 Weilon(8.3) 张裕 Zhangyu(8.3)	
25~34 岁 Age	23	长城 Great Wall(56.5)	张裕 Zhangyu(8.7)	Chatean St.Jean(4.3) 威龙 Weilon(4.3) 烟台 100 Yantai 100(4.3) 武当干红 Wudang(4.3) 珍珠红 Pearl (4.3) BAIRRADA(4.3) Johney walker(4.3)
35~44 岁 Age	20	长城 Great Wall(55.0)	张裕 Zhangyu(10.0)	丰收 Fengshou(5.0) 威龙 Weilon(5.0) 野力 Yely(5.0) 法国干红 France(5.0) 荷里活 Hollywood(5.0)
45~54 岁 Age	19	长城 Great Wall(21.1)	张裕 Zhangyu(15.8)	丰收 Fengshou(10.5)
55~60 岁 Age	1	长城 Great Wall(100.0)		

3-4 理想品牌排名/ Ranking of the Ideal Brands

排名 Brand Ranking	品牌 Brands	人数 Number	百分比 Percent
1	长城 Great Wall	165	16.0
2	张裕 Zhangyu	66	6.4
3	野力 Yely	10	1.0
4	皇朝 Huangchao	9	0.9
5	珍珠红 Pearl	6	0.6
5	丰收 Fengshou	6	0.6
6	王朝 Dynasty	5	0.5
6	中国红葡萄酒 China Red Wine	5	0.5

n=1034

3-5 样本、男性各年龄层、女性各年龄层最近三个月有无购买的比例/ Purchasing in the Last Three Months by the Whole Sample, Age and Gender Groups

	人数 Number	买过 yes	没买过 no
样本 Sample	1034	13.2	86.8
男性 Male	499	13.6	86.4
16~24 岁 Age	106	11.3	88.7
25~34 岁 Age	150	18.7	81.3
35~44 岁 Age	127	9.4	90.6
45~54 岁 Age	73	16.4	83.6
55~60 岁 Age	43	9.3	90.7
女性 Female	535	12.7	87.3
16~24 岁 Age	112	7.1	92.9
25~34 岁 Age	158	13.9	86.1
35~44 岁 Age	137	14.6	85.4
45~54 岁 Age	87	17.2	82.8
55~60 岁 Age	41	7.3	92.7

3-6 样本、男性各年龄层、女性各年龄层最近三个月是否拿葡萄酒送过礼/ To Offer Wine as Gift in the Last Three Months by the Whole Sample, Age and Gender Groups

	人数 Number	送过 yes	没送过 no
样本 Sample	1030	4.0	96.0
男性 Male	498	5.0	95.0
16~24 岁 Age	106	3.8	96.2
25~34 岁 Age	150	8.7	91.3
35~44 岁 Age	126	4.0	96.0
45~54 岁 Age	73	1.4	98.6
55~60 岁 Age	43	4.7	95.3
女性 Female	532	3.0	97.0
16~24 岁 Age	112	0.0	100.0
25~34 岁 Age	157	3.8	96.2
35~44 岁 Age	136	3.7	96.3
45~54 岁 Age	86	4.7	95.3
55~60 岁 Age	41	2.4	97.6

3-7 样本、男性各年龄层、女性各年龄层最近三个月的饮用频率/ Frequencies of Consuming Wine in the Last Three Months by the Whole Sample, Age and Gender Groups

	人数 Number	天天喝 daily	一周 3 次或以上 3 times or over aweek	一周 1~2 次 once or twice a week	一个月 2～3 次 2 or 3 times a month	一个月 1 次 once a month	两个月 1 次 once two months	三个月 1 次或以下 once three months or below	没有喝 never
样本 Sample	1020	0.4	0.2	1.0	3.0	3.5	2.7	4.8	84.3
男性 Male	492	0.4	0.2	1.4	3,9	3.9	3.3	4.3	82.7
16~24 岁 Age	104	0.0	1.0	1.0	2.9	1.0	1.9	5.8	86.5
25~34 岁 Age	149	0.0	0.0	1.3	4.0	6.7	6.7	7.4	73.8
35~44 岁 Age	125	0.8	0.0	0.8	2.4	4.0	0.8	3.2	88.0
45~54 岁 Age	71	0.0	0.0	2.8	8.5	4.2	1.4	0.0	83.1
55~60 岁 Age	43	2.3	0.0	2.3	2.3	0.0	4.7	0.0	88.4
女性 Female	528	0.4	0.2	0.6	2.3	3.2	2.3	5.3	85.8
16~24 岁 Age	110	0.9	0.0	0.0	1.8	1.8	2.7	3.6	89.1
25~34 岁 Age	155	0.0	0.0	1.3	3.2	1.9	1.9	6.5	85.2
35~44 岁 Age	137	0.0	0.0	0.0	1.5	4.4	2.2	6.6	85.4
45~54 岁 Age	86	1.2	1.2	1.2	3.5	7.0	2.3	5.8	77,9
55~60 岁 Age	40	0.0	0.0	0.0	0.0	0.0	2.5	0.0	97.5

3-8 样本、男性各年龄层、女性各年龄层的品牌习惯/ Brand Habit in Consuming Wine by the Whole Sample, Age and Gender Groups

	人数 Number	基本固定饮用一个牌子 used in only one brand	比较固定地饮用两个或三个牌子 used in two or three brands	基本上不太固定牌子 no brand preference
样本 Sample	160	37.5	28.8	33.8
男性 Male	85	38.8	30.6	30.6
16~24 岁 Age	14	42.9	28.6	28.6
25~34 岁 Age	39	35.9	33.3	30.8
35~44 岁 Age	15	26.7	46.7	26.7
45~54 岁 Age	12	41.7	16.7	41.7
55~60 岁 Age	5	80.0	0.0	20.0
女性 Female	75	36.0	26.7	37.3
16~24 岁 Age	12	50.0	8.3	41.7
25~34 岁 Age	23	26.1	34.8	39.1
35~44 岁 Age	20	40.0	35.0	25.0
45~54 岁 Age	19	31.6	21.1	47.4
55~60 岁 Age	1	100.0	0.0	0.0

3-9 选择该类商品的考虑因素/ Ranking of the Considerations in Purchasing

注：本题为多选题，合计百分比超过 100%(Multiple answers）

排名 Ranking	考虑因素 Considerations	人次 Person-time	百分比 Percent
1	口味好 pleasant taste	86	53.8
2	有名的牌子 famous brand	60	37.5
3	价格适中 reasonable price	51	31.9
4	别人送的 given by other people	22	13.8
5	生产日期 date of producing	21	13.1
6	朋友推荐 introduction of friends	20	12.5
7	购买方便 easy to buy	19	11.9
8	包装吸引人 appealing package	10	6.3
9	广告影响 influence of advertising	7	4.4
9	有优惠条件 with preferential terms	7	4.4
10	只是由于习惯 out of habit	6	3.8
11	售货员介绍 introduced by the shop assistants	4	2.5
12	其它 others	2	1.3

n=160

3-10 样本、男性各年龄层、女性各年龄层最常饮用的种类/ Kinds of the Consumed Wine by the Whole Sample, Age and Gender Groups

	人数 Number	干红 dry red	干白 dry white	甜型 sweet	其他 others
样本 Sample	160	58.1	6.3	33.1	2.5
男性 Male	85	63.5	11.8	23.5	1.2
16~24 岁 Age	14	71.4	7.1	21.4	0.0
25~34 岁 Age	39	59.0	17.9	23.1	0.0
35~44 岁 Age	15	46.7	6.7	46.7	0.0
45~54 岁 Age	12	91.7	0.0	8.3	0.0
55~60 岁 Age	5	60.0	20.0	0.0	20.0
女性 Female	75	52.0	0.0	44.0	4.0
16~24 岁 Age	12	41.7	0.0	41.7	16.7
25~34 岁 Age	23	56.5	0.0	43.5	0.0
35~44 岁 Age	20	50.0	0.0	50.0	0.0
45~54 岁 Age	19	52.6	0.0	42.1	5.3
55~60 岁 Age	1	100.0	0.0	0.0	0.0

3-11 样本、男性各年龄层、女性各年龄层最常饮用场合/ Settings of Consumption by the Whole Sample, Age and Gender Groups

注：本题为多选题，合计百分比超过 100%(Multiple answers）

	人数 Number	请客 entertain guests	节假日团聚 get-together on holiday	日常饮用 drink daily	睡觉前喝 before sleeping	做菜 cooking meal	其它 others
样本 Sample	160	43.1	56.9	21.3	1.9	2.5	3.1
男性 Male	85	49.4	54.1	20.0	1.2	2.4	1.2
16~24 岁 Age	14	71.4	57.1	21.4	0.0	0.0	0.0
25~34 岁 Age	39	43.6	59.0	12.8	0.0	2.6	2.6
35~44 岁 Age	15	26.7	46.7	26.7	6.7	6.7	0.0
45~54 岁 Age	12	58.3	41.7	33.3	0.0	0.0	0.0
55~60 岁 Age	5	80.0	60.0	20.0	0.0	0.0	0.0
女性 Female	75	36.0	60.0	22.7	2.7	2.7	5.3
16~24 岁 Age	12	16.7	75.0	25.0	0.0	8.3	8.3
25~34 岁 Age	23	60.9	43.5	26.1	0.0	0.0	8.7
35~44 岁 Age	20	35.0	75.0	10.0	0.0	0.0	0.0
45~54 岁 Age	19	15.8	57.9	31.6	10.5	5.3	5.3
55~60 岁 Age	1	100.0	0.0	0.0	0.0	0.0	0.0

3-12 重度消费者人口分布/ Demographics of the Heavy Consumers

	人数 Number	16-24 岁 Age	25-34 岁 Age	35-44 岁 Age	45-54 岁 Age	55-60 岁 Age
样本 Sample	16	18.8	25.0	12.5	31.3	12.5
男性 Male	10	20.0	20.0	20.0	20.0	20.0
天天喝 daily	2	0.0	0.0	50.0	0.0	50.0
一周 3 次或以上 3 times or over a week	1	100.0	0.0	0.0	0.0	0.0
一周 1~2 次 once or twice a week	7	14.3	28.6	14.3	28.6	14.3
女性 Female	6	16.7	33.3	0.0	50.0	0.0
天天喝 daily	2	50.0	0.0	0.0	50.0	0.0
一周 3 次或以上 3 times or over a week	1	0.0	0.0	0.0	100.0	0.0
一周 1~2 次 once or twice a week	3	0.0	66.7	0.0	33.3	0.0

3-13 不同消费者层的常用品牌/ The Most Frequently Used Brands by Market Segments

3-13-1 时尚流行指标/ Fads Popular Index

	人数 Number	第一品牌及百分比 1st/percent	第二品牌及百分比 2nd/percent	第三品牌及百分比 3rd/percent
样本 Sample	157	**长城 Great Wall(49.0)**	**张裕 Zhangyu(15.3)**	**丰收 Fengshou(2.5)**
平实生活指向 simple living orientation	79	长城 Great Wall(44.3)	张裕 Zhangyu(11.4)	丰收 Fengshou(2.5) 红玫瑰 Red Rose(2.5) 王朝 Dynasty(2.5) 珍珠红 Pearl(2.5) 中华 Zhonghua(2.5)
时尚流行指向 fashion orientation	78	长城 Great Wall(53.8)	张裕 Zhangyu(19.2)	丰收 Fengshou(2.6) 野力 Yely(2.6)

3-13-2 广告态度指标/ Advertising Attitude Index

	人数 Number	第一品牌及百分比 1st/percent	第二品牌及百分比 2nd/percent	第三品牌及百分比 3rd/percent
样本 Sample	154	**长城 Great Wall(48.1)**	**张裕 Zhangyu(15.6)**	**丰收 Fengshou(2.6)**
广告淡漠指向 indifferent orientation	52	长城 Great Wall(48.1)	张裕 Zhangyu(7.7)	丰收 Fengshou(3.8) 威龙 Weilon(3.8) 野力 Yely(3.8)
中间层 medium	85	长城 Great Wall(45.9)	张裕 Zhangyu(21.2)	丰收 Fengshou(2.4) 珍珠红 Pearl(2.4)
信赖广告指向 loyal orientation	17	长城 Great Wall(58.8)	张裕 Zhangyu(11.8)	中国红葡萄酒 China Red Wine(5.9) BAIRRADA(5.9) 荷里活 Hollywood(5.9)

3-13-3 饮食健康指标/ Foods & Drink Quality Index

	人数 Number	第一品牌及百分比 1st/percent	第二品牌及百分比 2nd/percent	第三品牌及百分比 3rd/percent
样本 Sample	158	**长城 Great Wall(48.7)**	**张裕 Zhangyu(15.2)**	**丰收 Fengshou(2.5)**
饮食“温饱”指向 "basic" orientation	27	长城 Great Wall(37.0)	张裕 Zhangyu(18.5)	王朝 Dynasty(3.7) 野力 Yely(3.7) 民权 Minquan(3.7) 七城 Qicheng(3.7) 武当干红 Wudang (3.7) 红玫瑰 Red Rose(3.7) 密丝嘉 Misijia(3.7)
中间层 medium	92	长城 Great Wall(51.1)	张裕 Zhangyu(13.0)	
健康营养指向 health & nutrition orientation	39	长城 Great Wall(51.3)	张裕 Zhangyu(17.9)	法国佐丹红葡萄酒 France Zuodan(2.6) BAIRRADA(2.6) 武当干红 Wudang(2.6) 桂花陈 Guihuachen(2.6) 法国波尔多 Bordeaux(2.6) 中华 Zhonghua(2.6) 丰收 Fengshou(2.6) 登喜门 Don Simon(2.6)

3-14 重度消费者的消费者层构成/ The Composition of the Heavy Consumers

3-14-1 时尚流行指标/ Fads Popular Index

	人数 Number	平实生活指向 simple living orientation	时尚流行指向 fashion orientation
样本 Sample	16	62.5	37.5
天天喝 daily	4	75.0	25.0
一周 3 次或以上 3 times or over a week	2	0.0	100.0
一周 1~2 次 once or twice a week	10	70.0	30.0

3-14-2 广告态度指标/ Advertising Attitude Index

	人数 Number	广告淡漠指向 indifferent orientation	中间层 medium	信赖广告指向 loyal orientation
样本 Sample	16	37.5	56.3	6.3
天天喝 daily	4	50.0	50.0	0.0
一周 3 次或以上 3 times or over a week	2	50.0	50.0	0.0
一周 1~2 次 once or twice a week	10	30.0	60.0	10.0

3-14-3 饮食健康指标/ Foods & Drink Quality Index

	人数 Number	饮食“温饱”指向 "basic" orientation	中间层 medium	健康营养指向 health & nutrition orientation
样本 Sample	16	25.0	43.8	31.3
天天喝 daily	4	25.0	50.0	25.0
一周 3 次或以上 3 times or over a week	2	50.0	0.0	50.0
一周 1~2 次 once or twice a week	10	20.0	50 0	30.0

● 重庆 / Chongqing

3-1 最近三个月饮用频率的比例/ Proportion of the Sample Consuming Wine in the Last Three Months

	人数 Number	百分比 Percent
天天喝 daily	4	0.6
一周 3 次或以上 3 times or over a week	5	0.8
一周 1~2 次 once or twice a week	12	1.9
一个月 2～3 次 2 or 3 times a month	27	4.4
一个月 1 次 once a month	51	8.3
两个月 1 次 once two months	27	4.4
三个月 1 次或以下 once three months or below	52	8.4
没有喝 never	440	71.2

n=618

3-2 最常用品牌排名/ Ranking of the Most Frequently Used Brands

排名 Brand Ranking	品牌 Brands	人数 Number	百分比 Percent
1	长城 Great Wall	98	55.1
2	张裕 Zhangyu	35	19.7
3	通化 Tonghua	23	12.9
4	王朝 Dynasty	5	2.8
5	长白山 Changbaishan	3	1.7
6	法国波尔多 Bordeaux	2	1.1

n=178

3-3 样本、男性各年龄层、女性各年龄层的常用品牌/ The Most Frequently Used Brands by the Whole Sample, Age and Gender Groups

	人数 Number	第一品牌及百分比 1st/ percent	第二品牌及百分比 2nd/ percent	第三品牌及百分比 3rd/ percent
样本 Sample	178	**长城 Great Wall(55.1)**	**张裕 Zhangyu(19.7)**	**通化 Tonghua(12.9)**
男性 Male	100	**长城 Great Wall(62.0)**	**张裕 Zhangyu(18.0)**	**通化 Tonghua(9.0)**
16~24 岁 Age	18	长城 Great Wall(66.7)	张裕 Zhangyu(22.2)	通化 Tonghua(5.6)
25~34 岁 Age	34	长城 Great Wall(70.6)	张裕 Zhangyu(14.7)	通化 Tonghua(2.9) 王朝 Dynasty(2.9) 中华 Zhonghua(2.9) 法国波尔多 Bordeaux(2.9) 狮王 Lion King(2.9)
35~44 岁 Age	25	长城 Great Wall(64.0)	通化 Tonghua(12.0) 张裕 Zhangyu(12.0)	王朝 Dynasty(8.0)
45~54 岁 Age	15	长城 Great Wall(46.7)	张裕 Zhangyu(20.0)	通化 Tonghua(13.3)
55~60 岁 Age	8	张裕 Zhangyu(37.5) 长城 Great Wall(37.5)	通化 Tonghua(25.0)	
女性 Female	78	**长城 Great Wall(46.2)**	**张裕 Zhangyu(21.8)**	**通化 Tonghua(17.9)**
16~24 岁 Age	21	长城 Great Wall(61.9)	张裕 Zhangyu(23.8)	通化 Tonghua(4.8) 法国波尔多 Bordeaux(4.8)
25~34 岁 Age	26	长城 Great Wall(53.8)	张裕 Zhangyu(19.2)	通化 Tonghua(11.5)
35~44 岁 Age	16	张裕 Zhangyu(31.3) 长城 Great Wall(31.3)	通化 Tonghua(18.8)	王朝 Dynasty(6.3) 长白山 Changbaishan(6.3)
45~54 岁 Age	12	通化 Tonghua(41.7)	长城 Great Wall(33.3)	楼兰 Loulan(8.3) 张裕 Zhangyu(8.3) 长白山 Changbaishan(8.3)
55~60 岁 Age	3	通化 Tonghua(66.7)	张裕 Zhangyu(33.3)	

3-4 理想品牌排名/ Ranking of the Ideal Brands

排名 Brand Ranking	品牌 Brands	人数 Number	百分比 Percent
1	长城 Great Wall	228	36.5
2	张裕 Zhangyu	117	18.8
3	通化 Tonghua	49	7.9
4	王朝 Dynasty	9	1.4
5	长白山 Changbaishan	4	0.6
6	白洋河牌天然红葡萄酒 Baiyanghe	3	0.5

n=624

3-5 样本、男性各年龄层、女性各年龄层最近三个月有无购买的比例/ Purchasing in the Last Three Months by the Whole Sample, Age and Gender Groups

	人数 Number	买过 yes	没买过 no
样本 Sample	624	30.3	69.7
男性 Male	314	31.2	68.8
16~24 岁 Age	64	23.4	76.6
25~34 岁 Age	93	38.7	61.3
35~44 岁 Age	75	30.7	69.3
45~54 岁 Age	54	29.6	70.4
55~60 岁 Age	28	28.6	71.4
女性 Female	310	29.4	70.6
16~24 岁 Age	64	32.8	67.2
25~34 岁 Age	90	38.9	61.1
35~44 岁 Age	73	23.3	76.7
45~54 岁 Age	60	21.7	78.3
55~60 岁 Age	23	21.7	78.3

3-6 样本、男性各年龄层、女性各年龄层最近三个月是否拿葡萄酒送过礼/ To Offer Wine as Gift in the Last Three Months by the Whole Sample, Age and Gender Groups

	人数 Number	送过 yes	没送过 no
样本 Sample	617	6.5	93.5
男性 Male	311	6.8	93.2
16~24 岁 Age	63	4.8	95.2
25~34 岁 Age	93	8.6	91.4
35~44 岁 Age	73	9.6	90.4
45~54 岁 Age	54	5.6	94.4
55~60 岁 Age	28	0.0	100.0
女性 Female	306	6.2	93.8
16~24 岁 Age	62	4.8	95.2
25~34 岁 Age	90	12.2	87.8
35~44 岁 Age	72	4.2	95.8
45~54 岁 Age	59	3.4	96.6
55~60 岁 Age	23	0.0	100.0

3-7 样本、男性各年龄层、女性各年龄层最近三个月的饮用频率/ Frequencies of Consuming Wine in the Last Three Months by the Whole Sample, Age and Gender Groups

	人数 Number	天天喝 daily	一周 3 次或以上 3 times or over a week	一周 1~2 次 once or twice a week	一个月 2~3 次 2 or 3 times a month	一个月 1 次 once a month	两个月 1 次 once two months	三个月 1 次或以下 once three months or below	没有喝 never
样本 Sample	618	0.6	0.8	1.9	4.4	8.3	4.4	8.4	71.2
男性 Male	310	1.0	1.0	2.6	5.8	10.3	4.2	7.4	67.7
16~24 岁 Age	64	1.6	1.6	0.0	4.7	4.7	4.7	10.9	71.9
25~34 岁 Age	93	1.1	1.1	3.2	9.7	14.0	3.2	4.3	63.4
35~44 岁 Age	72	0.0	1.4	4.2	4.2	12.5	4.2	8.3	65.3
45~54 岁 Age	53	0.0	0.0	1.9	3.8	11.3	3.8	7.5	71.7
55~60 岁 Age	28	3.6	0.0	3.6	3.6	3.6	7.1	7.1	71.4
女性 Female	308	0.3	0.6	1.3	2.9	6.2	4.5	9.4	74.7
16~24 岁 Age	64	0.0	0.0	0.0	3.1	6.3	6.3	17.2	67.2
25~34 岁 Age	90	0.0	1.1	1.1	3.3	7.8	3.3	12.2	71.1
35~44 岁 Age	72	0.0	1.4	1.4	5.6	2.8	5.6	5.6	77.8
45~54 岁 Age	59	1.7	0.0	1.7	0.0	8.5	3.4	5.1	79.7
55~60 岁 Age	23	0.0	0.0	4.3	0.0	4.3	4.3	0.0	87.0

3-8 样本、男性各年龄层、女性各年龄层的品牌习惯/ Brand Habit in Consuming Wine by the Whole Sample, Age and Gender Groups

	人数 Number	基本固定饮用一个牌子 used in only one brand	比较固定地饮用两个或三个牌子 used in two or three brands	基本上不太固定牌子 no brand preference
样本 Sample	176	54.5	28.4	17.0
男性 Male	99	57.6	22.2	20.2
16~24 岁 Age	18	72.2	16.7	11.1
25~34 岁 Age	34	55.9	32.4	11.8
35~44 岁 Age	24	50.0	8.3	41.7
45~54 岁 Age	15	53.3	26.7	20.0
55~60 岁 Age	8	62.5	25.0	12.5
女性 Female	77	50.6	36.4	13.0
16~24 岁 Age	21	61.9	28.6	9.5
25~34 岁 Age	26	30.8	46.2	23.1
35~44 岁 Age	16	62.5	31.3	6.3
45~54 岁 Age	11	54.5	45.5	0.0
55~60 岁 Age	3	66.7	0.0	33.3

3-9 选择该类商品的考虑因素/ Ranking of the Considerations in Purchasing

注：本题为多选题，合计百分比超过 100%(Multiple answers）

排名 Ranking	考虑因素 Considerations	人次 Person-time	百分比 Percent
1	口味好 pleasant taste	134	75.3
2	有名的牌子 famous brand	71	39.9
3	价格适中 reasonable price	51	28.7
4	购买方便 easy to buy	22	12.4
4	生产日期 date of producing	22	12.4
5	只是由于习惯 out of habit	15	8.4
6	广告影响 influence of advertising	13	7.3
7	朋友推荐 introduction of friends	9	5.1
8	包装吸引人 appealing package	6	3.4
9	别人送的 given by other people	3	1.7
10	售货员介绍 introduced by the shop assistants	2	1.1
11	有优惠条件 with preferential terms	1	0.6

n=178

3-10 样本、男性各年龄层、女性各年龄层最常饮用的种类/ Kinds of the Consumed Wine by the Whole Sample, Age and Gender Groups

	人数 Number	干红 dry red	干白 dry white	甜型 sweet	其他 others
样本 Sample	178	62.4	19.7	18.0	0.0
男性 Male	100	63.0	23.0	14.0	0.0
16~24 岁 Age	18	55.6	33.3	11.1	0.0
25~34 岁 Age	34	58.8	29.4	11.8	0.0
35~44 岁 Age	25	72.0	16.0	12.0	0.0
45~54 岁 Age	15	53.3	20.0	26.7	0.0
55~60 岁 Age	8	87.5	0.0	12.5	0.0
女性 Female	78	61.5	15.4	23.1	0.0
16~24 岁 Age	21	81.0	14.3	4.8	0.0
25~34 岁 Age	26	61.5	15.4	23.1	0.0
35~44 岁 Age	16	62.5	12.5	25.0	0.0
45~54 岁 Age	12	41.7	25.0	33.3	0.0
55~60 岁 Age	3	0.0	0.0	100.0	0.0

3-11 样本、男性各年龄层、女性各年龄层最常饮用场合/ Settings of Consumption by the Whole Sample, Age and Gender Groups

注：本题为多选题，合计百分比超过 100%(Multiple answers）

	人数 Number	请客 entertain guests	节假日团聚 get together on holiday	日常饮用 drink daily	睡觉前喝 before sleeping	做菜 cooking meal	其它 others
样本 Sample	178	56.2	61.2	15.2	0.6	1.1	3.4
男性 Male	100	61.0	54.0	18.0	0.0	0.0	2.0
16~24 岁 Age	18	61.1	55.6	16.7	0.0	0.0	0.0
25~34 岁 Age	34	52.9	61.8	17.6	0.0	0.0	2.9
35~44 岁 Age	25	72.0	44.0	24.0	0.0	0.0	0.0
45~54 岁 Age	15	66.7	46.7	13.3	0.0	0.0	6.7
55~60 岁 Age	8	50.0	62.5	12.5	0.0	0.0	0.0
女性 Female	78	50.0	70.5	11.5	1.3	2.6	5.1
16~24 岁 Age	21	38.1	81.0	0.0	0.0	0.0	19.0
25~34 岁 Age	26	65.4	69.2	7.7	3.8	7.7	0.0
35~44 岁 Age	16	43.8	75.0	12.5	0.0	0.0	0.0
45~54 岁 Age	12	58.3	50.0	25.0	0.0	0.0	0.0
55~60 岁 Age	3	0.0	66.7	66.7	0.0	0.0	0.0

3-12 重度消费者人口分布/ Demographics of the Heavy Consumers

	人数 Number	16-24 岁 Age	25-34 岁 Age	35-44 岁 Age	45-54 岁 Age	55-60 岁 Age
样本 Sample	21	9.5	33.3	28.6	14.3	14.3
男性 Male	14	14.3	35.7	28.6	7.1	14.3
天天喝 daily	3	33.3	33.3	0.0	0.0	33.3
一周 3 次或以上 3 times or over a week	3	33.3	33.3	33.3	0.0	0.0
一周 1~2 次 once or twice a week	8	0.0	37.5	37.5	12.5	12.5
女性 Female	7	0.0	28.6	28.6	28.6	14.3
天天喝 daily	1	0.0	0.0	0.0	100.0	0.0
一周 3 次或以上 3 times or over a week	2	0.0	50.0	50.0	0.0	0.0
一周 1~2 次 once or twice a week	4	0.0	25.0	25.0	25.0	25.0

3-13 不同消费者层的常用品牌/ The Most Frequently Used Brands by Market Segments

3-13-1 时尚流行指标/ Fads Popular Index

	人数 Number	第一品牌及百分比 1st/percent	第二品牌及百分比 2nd/percent	第三品牌及百分比 3rd/percent
样本 Sample	173	**长城 Great Wall(55.5)**	**张裕 Zhangyu(19.1)**	**通化 Tonghua(13.3)**
平实生活指向 simple living orientation	91	长城 Great Wall(56.0)	张裕 Zhangyu(20.9)	通化 Tonghua(15.4)
时尚流行指向 fashion orientation	82	长城 Great Wall(54.9)	张裕 Zhangyu(17.1)	通化 Tonghua(11.0)

3-13-2 广告态度指标/ Advertising Attitude Index

	人数 Number	第一品牌及百分比 1st/percent	第二品牌及百分比 2nd/percent	第三品牌及百分比 3rd/percent
样本 Sample	176	**长城 Great Wall(55.7)**	**张裕 Zhangyu(19.3)**	**通化 Tonghua(13.1)**
广告淡漠指向 indifferent orientation	46	长城 Great Wall(58.7)	张裕 Zhangyu(19.6)	通化 Tonghua(13.0)
中间层 medium	110	长城 Great Wall(54.5)	张裕 Zhangyu(19.1)	通化 Tonghua(13.6)
信赖广告指向 loyal orientation	20	长城 Great Wall(55.0)	张裕 Zhangyu(20.0)	通化 Tonghua(10.0)

3-13-3 饮食健康指标/ Foods & Drink Quality Index

	人数 Number	第一品牌及百分比 1st/percent	第二品牌及百分比 2nd/percent	第三品牌及百分比 3rd/percent
样本 Sample	175	**长城 Great Wall(54.9)**	**张裕 Zhangyu(19.4)**	**通化 Tonghua(13.1)**
饮食"温饱"指向 "basic" orientation	55	长城 Great Wall(52.7)	张裕 Zhangyu(18.2)	通化 Tonghua(16.4)
中间层 medium	79	长城 Great Wall(59.5)	张裕 Zhangyu(21.5)	通化 Tonghua(8.9)
健康营养指向 health & nutrition orientation	41	长城 Great Wall(48.8)	通化 Tonghua(17.1) 张裕 Zhangyu(17.1)	王朝 Dynasty(4.9)

3-14 重度消费者的消费者层构成/ The Composition of the Heavy Consumers

3-14-1 时尚流行指标/ Fads Popular Index

	人数 Number	平实生活指向 simple living orientation	时尚流行指向 fashion orientation
样本 Sample	20	55.0	45.0
天天喝 daily	3	66.7	33.3
一周 3 次或以上 3 times or over a week	5	60.0	40.0
一周 1~2 次 once or twice a week	12	50.0	50.0

3-14-2 广告态度指标/ Advertising Attitude Index

	人数 Number	广告淡漠指向 indifferent orientation	中间层 medium	信赖广告指向 loyal orientation
样本 Sample	20	20.0	80.0	0.0
天天喝 daily	3	33.3	66.7	0.0
一周 3 次或以上 3 times or over a week	5	40.0	60.0	0.0
一周 1~2 次 once or twice a week	12	8.3	91.7	0.0

3-14-3 饮食健康指标/ Foods & Drink Quality Index

	人数 Number	饮食"温饱"指向 "basic" orientation	中间层 medium	健康营养指向 health & nutrition orientation
样本 Sample	20	15.0	45.0	40.0
天天喝 daily	3	0.0	33.3	66.7
一周 3 次或以上 3 times or over a week	5	40.0	20.0	40.0
一周 1~2 次 once or twice a week	12	8.3	58.3	33.3

● 武汉 / Wuhan

3-1 最近三个月饮用频率的比例/ Proportion of the Sample Consuming Wine in the Last Three Months

	人数 Number	百分比 Percent
天天喝 daily	1	0.2
一周 3 次或以上 3 times or over a week	3	0.5
一周 1~2 次 once or twice a week	5	0.8
一个月 2～3 次 2 or 3 times a month	20	3.1
一个月 1 次 once a month	10	1.6
两个月 1 次 once two months	14	2.2
三个月 1 次或以下 once three months or below	36	5.7
没有喝 never	547	86.0

n=636

3-2 最常用品牌排名/ Ranking of the Most Frequently Used Brands

排名 Brand Ranking	品牌 Brands	人数 Number	百分比 Percent
1	张裕 Zhangyu	27	30.3
2	王朝 Dynasty	21	23.6
3	长白山 Changbaishan	7	7.9
4	威龙 Weilon	6	6.7
5	长城 Great Wall	5	5.6
6	通化 Tonghua	2	2.2
6	天津干红 Tianjin	2	2.2

n=89

3-3 样本、男性各年龄层、女性各年龄层的常用品牌/ The Most Frequently Used Brands by the Whole Sample, Age and Gender Groups

	人数 Number	第一品牌及百分比 1st/ percent	第二品牌及百分比 2nd/ percent	第三品牌及百分比 3rd/ percent
样本 Sample	89	**张裕 Zhangyu(30.3)**	**王朝 Dynasty(23.6)**	**长白山 Changbaishan(7.9)**
男性 Male	56	**张裕 Zhangyu(25.0)** **王朝 Dynasty(25.0)**	**长白山 Changbaishan(10.7)**	**威龙 Weilon(8.9)**
16~24 岁 Age	13	王朝 Dynasty(38.5)	威龙 Weilon(15.4)	野力 Yely(7.7) 张裕 Zhangyu(7.7) 长城 Great Wall(7.7)
25~34 岁 Age	17	张裕 Zhangyu(35.3)	王朝 Dynasty(23.5)	长白山 Changbaishan(17.6)
35~44 岁 Age	8	张裕 Zhangyu(50.0)	王朝 Dynasty(37.5)	
45~54 岁 Age	11	王朝 Dynasty(18.2) 长白山 Changbaishan(18.2)	青岛 Tsing Tao(9.1) 通化 Tonghua(9.1) 张裕 Zhangyu(9.1) 长城 Great Wall(9.1) 秦池 Qinchi9.1)	
55~60 岁 Age	7	威龙 Weilon(28.6) 张裕 Zhangyu(28.6)	长白山 Changbaishan(14.3) 古井双喜 Gu Jing Shuang Xi(14.3)	
女性 Female	33	**张裕 Zhangyu(39.4)**	**王朝 Dynasty(21.2)**	**天津干红 Tianjin(6.1)**
16~24 岁 Age	7	王朝 Dynasty(28.6) 张裕 Zhangyu(28.6)	天津干红 Tianjin(14.3) 武当 Wudang(14.3)	
25~34 岁 Age	9	王朝 Dynasty(44.4)	张裕 Zhangyu(22.2)	通化 Tonghua(11.1)
35~44 岁 Age	8	张裕 Zhangyu(50.0)	王朝 Dynasty(12.5) 威龙 Weilon(12.5) 长白山 Changbaishan(12.5) 天津干红 Tianjin(12.5)	
45~54 岁 Age	8	张裕 Zhangyu(50.0)	威王 Weiwang(12.5) 长城 Great Wall(12.5)	
55~60 岁 Age	1	张裕 Zhangyu(100.0)		

3-4 理想品牌排名/ Ranking of the Ideal Brands

排名 Brand Ranking	品牌 Brands	人数 Number	百分比 Percent
1	张裕 Zhangyu	95	14.8
2	王朝 Dynasty	60	9.4
3	长城 Great Wall	30	4.7
4	长白山 Changbaishan	15	2.3
5	威龙 Weilon	4	0.6
6	法国干红 France	2	0.3
6	野力 Yely	2	0.3
6	天津干红 Tianjin	2	0.3

n=641

3-5 样本、男性各年龄层、女性各年龄层最近三个月有无购买的比例/ Purchasing in the Last Three Months by the Whole Sample, Age and Gender Groups

	人数 Number	买过 yes	没买过 no
样本 Sample	641	**13.9**	**86.1**
男性 Male	310	**16.1**	**83.9**
16~24 岁 Age	65	12.3	87.7
25~34 岁 Age	89	15.7	84.3
35~44 岁 Age	80	13.8	86.3
45~54 岁 Age	51	19.6	80.4
55~60 岁 Age	25	28.0	72.0
女性 Female	331	**11.8**	**88.2**
16~24 岁 Age	69	11.6	88.4
25~34 岁 Age	96	9.4	90.6
35~44 岁 Age	78	10.3	89.7
45~54 岁 Age	62	19.4	80.6
55~60 岁 Age	26	7.7	92.3

3-6 样本、男性各年龄层、女性各年龄层最近三个月是否拿葡萄酒送过礼/ To Offer Wine as Gift in the Last Three Months by the Whole Sample, Age and Gender Groups

	人数 Number	送过 yes	没送过 no
样本 Sample	642	6.2	93.8
男性 Male	311	6.1	93.9
16~24 岁 Age	65	4.6	95.4
25~34 岁 Age	89	10.1	89.9
35~44 岁 Age	80	6.3	93.8
45~54 岁 Age	52	0.0	100.0
55~60 岁 Age	25	8.0	92.0
女性 Female	331	6.3	93.7
16~24 岁 Age	69	4.3	95.7
25~34 岁 Age	96	3.1	96.9
35~44 岁 Age	78	6.4	93.6
45~54 岁 Age	62	12.9	87.1
55~60 岁 Age	26	7.7	92.3

3-7 样本、男性各年龄层、女性各年龄层最近三个月的饮用频率/ Frequencies of Consuming Wine in the Last Three Months by the Whole Sample, Age and Gender Groups

	人数 Number	天天喝 daily	一周3次或以上 3 times or over a week	一周1~2次 once or twice a week	一个月2~3次 2 or 3 times a month	一个月1次 once a month	两个月1次 once two months	三个月1次或以下 once three months or below	没有喝 never
样本 Sample	636	0.2	0.5	0.8	3.1	1.6	2.2	5.7	86.0
男性 Male	306	0.0	1.0	1.0	4.9	1.3	2.6	7.5	81.7
16~24 岁 Age	62	0.0	1.6	1.6	1.6	0.0	4.8	11.3	79.0
25~34 岁 Age	87	0.0	1.1	2.3	4.6	2.3	1.1	8.0	80.5
35~44 岁 Age	80	0.0	0.0	0.0	3.8	1.3	1.3	3.8	90.0
45~54 岁 Age	52	0.0	0.0	0.0	5.8	1.9	3.8	9.6	78.8
55~60 岁 Age	25	0.0	4.0	0.0	16.0	0.0	4.0	4.0	72.0
女性 Female	330	0.3	0.0	0.6	1.5	1.8	1.8	3.9	90.0
16~24 岁 Age	69	0.0	0.0	0.0	0.0	0.0	4.3	5.8	89.9
25~34 岁 Age	96	0.0	0.0	1.0	3.1	2.1	1.0	2.1	90.6
35~44 岁 Age	77	1.3	0.0	1.3	0.0	2.6	1.3	3.9	89.6
45~54 岁 Age	62	0.0	0.0	0.0	3.2	3.2	1.6	4.8	87.1
55~60 岁 Age	26	0.0	0.0	0.0	0.0	0.0	0.0	3.8	96.2

3-8 样本、男性各年龄层、女性各年龄层的品牌习惯/ Brand Habit in Consuming Wine by the Whole Sample, Age and Gender Groups

	人数 Number	基本固定饮用一个牌子 used in only one brand	比较固定地饮用两个或三个牌子 used in two or three brands	基本上不太固定牌子 no brand preference
样本 Sample	89	32.6	32.6	34.8
男性 Male	56	35.7	32.1	32.1
16~24 岁 Age	13	30.8	23.1	46.2
25~34 岁 Age	17	47.1	41.2	11.8
35~44 岁 Age	8	37.5	37.5	25.0
45~54 岁 Age	11	27.3	27.3	45.5
55~60 岁 Age	7	28.6	28.6	42.9
女性 Female	33	27.3	33.3	39.4
16~24 岁 Age	7	0.0	42.9	57.1
25~34 岁 Age	9	22.2	55.6	22.2
35~44 岁 Age	8	25.0	25.0	50.0
45~54 岁 Age	8	50.0	12.5	37.5
55~60 岁 Age	1	100.0	0.0	0.0

3-9 选择该类商品的考虑因素/ Ranking of the Considerations in Purchasing

注：本题为多选题，合计百分比超过 100%(Multiple answers）

排名 Ranking	考虑因素 Considerations	人次 Person-time	百分比 Percent
1	口味好 pleasant taste	58	65.2
2	有名的牌子 famous brand	43	48.3
3	价格适中 reasonable price	34	38.2
4	生产日期 date of producing	16	18.0
5	广告影响 influence of advertising	10	11.2
6	购买方便 easy to buy	7	7.9
7	包装吸引人 appealing package	6	6.7
7	朋友推荐 introduction of friends	6	6.7
8	只是由于习惯 out of habit	5	5.6
9	别人送的 given by other people	4	4.5
10	其它 others	2	2.2
11	售货员介绍 introduced by the shop assistants	1	1.1

n=89

3-10 样本、男性各年龄层、女性各年龄层最常饮用的种类/ Kinds of the Consumed Wine by the Whole Sample, Age and Gender Groups

	人数 Number	干红 dry red	干白 dry white	甜型 sweet	其他 others
样本 Sample	**89**	**69.7**	**9.0**	**20.2**	**1.1**
男性 Male	**56**	**73.2**	**10.7**	**14.3**	**1.8**
16~24 岁 Age	13	84.6	7.7	7.7	0.0
25~34 岁 Age	17	70.6	17.6	5.9	5.9
35~44 岁 Age	8	75.0	12.5	12.5	0.0
45~54 岁 Age	11	63.6	9.1	27.3	0.0
55~60 岁 Age	7	71.4	0.0	28.6	0.0
女性 Female	**33**	**63.6**	**6.1**	**30.3**	**0.0**
16~24 岁 Age	7	85.7	0.0	14.3	0.0
25~34 岁 Age	9	77.8	11.1	11.1	0.0
35~44 岁 Age	8	50.0	12.5	37.5	0.0
45~54 岁 Age	8	50.0	0.0	50.0	0.0
55~60 岁 Age	1	0.0	0.0	100.0	0.0

3-11 样本、男性各年龄层、女性各年龄层最常饮用场合/ Settings of Consumption by the Whole Sample, Age and Gender Groups

注：本题为多选题，合计百分比超过 100%(Multiple answers）

	人数 Number	请客 entertain guests	节假日团聚 get-together on holiday	日常饮用 drink daily	睡觉前喝 before sleeping	做菜 cooking meal	其它 others
样本 Sample	**89**	**50.6**	**61.8**	**19.1**	**1.1**	**2.2**	**2.2**
男性 Male	**56**	**53.6**	**67.9**	**14.3**	**1.8**	**1.8**	**3.6**
16~24 岁 Age	13	61.5	53.8	15.4	0.0	0.0	7.7
25~34 岁 Age	17	52.9	70.6	17.6	5.9	5.9	5.9
35~44 岁 Age	8	75.0	75.0	12.5	0.0	0.0	0.0
45~54 岁 Age	11	36.4	63.6	9.1	0.0	0.0	0.0
55~60 岁 Age	7	42.9	85.7	14.3	0.0	0.0	0.0
女性 Female	**33**	**45.5**	**51.5**	**27.3**	**0.0**	**3.0**	**0.0**
16~24 岁 Age	7	57.1	42.9	14.3	0.0	0.0	0.0
25~34 岁 Age	9	33.3	44.4	44.4	0.0	0.0	0.0
35~44 岁 Age	8	50.0	50.0	25.0	0.0	0.0	0.0
45~54 岁 Age	8	37.5	62.5	25.0	0.0	12.5	0.0
55~60 岁 Age	1	100.0	100.0	0.0	0.0	0.0	0.0

3-12 重度消费者人口分布/ Demographics of the Heavy Consumers

	人数 Number	16-24 岁 Age	25-34 岁 Age	35-44 岁 Age	45-54 岁 Age	55-60 岁 Age
样本 Sample	9	22.2	44.4	22.2	0.0	11.1
男性 Male	6	33.3	50.0	0.0	0.0	16.7
天天喝 daily	0	0.0	0.0	0.0	0.0	0.0
一周 3 次或以上 3 times or over a week	3	33.3	33.3	0.0	0.0	33.3
一周 1~2 次 once or twice a week	3	33.3	66.7	0.0	0.0	0.0
女性 Female	3	0.0	33.3	66.7	0.0	0.0
天天喝 daily	1	0.0	0.0	100.0	0.0	0.0
一周 3 次或以上 3 times or over a week	0	0.0	0.0	0.0	0.0	0.0
一周 1~2 次 once or twice a week	2	0.0	50.0	50.0	0.0	0.0

3-13 不同消费者层的常用品牌/ The Most Frequently Used Brands by Market Segments

3-13-1 时尚流行指标/ Fads Popular Index

	人数 Number	第一品牌及百分比 1st/percent	第二品牌及百分比 2nd/percent	第三品牌及百分比 3rd/percent	第四品牌及百分比 4th/percent
样本 Sample	89	**张裕 Zhangyu(30.3)**	**王朝 Dynasty(23.6)**	**长白山 Changbaishan(7.9)**	**威龙 Weilon(6.7)**
平实生活指向 simple living orientation	48	张裕 Zhangyu(35.4)	王朝 Dynasty(18.8)	长白山 Changbaishan(12.5)	威龙 Weilon(8.3)
时尚流行指向 fashion orientation	41	王朝 Dynasty(29.3)	张裕 Zhangyu(24.4)	长城 Great Wall(7.3)	威龙 Weilon(4.9)

3-13-2 广告态度指标/ Advertising Attitude Index

	人数 Number	第一品牌及百分比 1st/percent	第二品牌及百分比 2nd/percent	第三品牌及百分比 3rd/percent	第四品牌及百分比 4th/percent
样本 Sample	89	**张裕 Zhangyu(30.3)**	**王朝 Dynasty(23.6)**	**长白山 Changbaishan(7.9)**	**威龙 Weilon(6.7)**
广告淡漠指向 indifferent orientation	24	张裕 Zhangyu(29.2)	王朝 Dynasty(16.7)	威龙 Weilon(12.5) 长白山 Changbaishan(12.5)	通化 Tonghua(4.2) 野力 Yely(4.2) 天津干红 Tianjin(4.2)
中间层 medium	51	张裕 Zhangyu(27.5)	王朝 Dynasty(25.5)	长白山 Changbaishan(7.8) 长城 Great Wall(7.8)	
信赖广告指向 loyal orientation	14	张裕 Zhangyu(42.9)	王朝 Dynasty(28.6)	通化 Tonghua(7.1) 威龙 Weilon(7.1) 长城 Great Wall(7.1)	

3-13-3 饮食健康指标/ Foods & Drink Quality Index

	人数 Number	第一品牌及百分比 1st/percent	第二品牌及百分比 2nd/percent	第三品牌及百分比 3rd/percent	第四品牌及百分比 4th/percent
样本 Sample	89	**张裕 Zhangyu(30.3)**	**王朝 Dynasty(23.6)**	**长白山 Changbaishan(7.9)**	**威龙 Weilon(6.7)**
饮食"温饱"指向 "basic" orientation	26	王朝 Dynasty(23.1) 张裕 Zhangyu(23.1)	威龙 Weilon(15.4)	长白山 Changbaishan(11.5)	通化 Tonghua(3.8) 野力 Yely(3.8) 威王 Weiwang(3.8) 天津干红 Tianjin(3.8) 长城 Great Wall(3.8)
中间层 medium	45	张裕 Zhangyu(33.3)	王朝 Dynasty(31.1)	长白山 Changbaishan(4.4)	
健康营养指向 health & nutrition orientation	18	张裕 Zhangyu(33.3)	长城 Great Wall(16.7)	长白山 Changbaishan(11.1)	王朝 Dynasty(5.6) 威龙 Weilon(5.6) 古井双喜 Gu Jing Shuang Xi(5.6) 秦池 Qinchi(5.6)

3-14 重度消费者的消费者层构成/ The Composition of the Heavy Consumers

3-14-1 时尚流行指标/ Fads Popular Index

	人数 Number	平实生活指向 simple living orientation	时尚流行指向 fashion orientation
样本 Sample	9	55.6	44.4
天天喝 daily	1	100.0	0.0
一周 3 次或以上 3 times or over a week	3	66.7	33.3
一周 1~2 次 once or twice a week	5	40.0	60.0

3-14-2 广告态度指标/ Advertising Attitude Index

	人数 Number	广告淡漠指向 indifferent orientation	中间层 medium	信赖广告指向 loyal orientation
样本 Sample	9	55.6	33.3	11.1
天天喝 daily	1	100.0	0.0	0.0
一周 3 次或以上 3 times or over a week	3	66.7	33.3	0.0
一周 1~2 次 once or twice a week	5	40.0	40.0	20.0

3-14-3 饮食健康指标/ Foods & Drink Quality Index

	人数 Number	饮食"温饱"指向 "basic" orientation	中间层 medium	健康营养指向 health & nutrition orientation
样本 Sample	9	44.4	33.3	22.2
天天喝 daily	1	0.0	100.0	0.0
一周 3 次或以上 3 times or over a week	3	100.0	0.0	0.0
一周 1~2 次 once or twice a week	5	20.0	40.0	40.0

● 西安 / Xi'an

3-1 最近三个月饮用频率的比例/ Proportion of the Sample Consuming Wine in the Last Three Months

	人数 Number	百分比 Percent
天天喝 daily	0	0.0
一周 3 次或以上 3 times or over a week	11	1.8
一周 1~2 次 once or twice a week	24	4.0
一个月 2～3 次 2 or 3 times a month	50	8.4
一个月 1 次 once a month	34	5.7
两个月 1 次 once two months	29	4.9
三个月 1 次或以下 once three months or below	40	6.7
没有喝 never	407	68.4

n=595

3-2 最常用品牌排名/ Ranking of the Most Frequently Used Brands

排名 Brand Ranking	品牌 Brands	人数 Number	百分比 Percent
1	张裕 Changyu	88	46.8
2	长城 Great Wall	60	31.9
3	丹凤 Danfeng	17	9.0
4	天韵 Tianyun	5	2.7
5	皇轩 Imperial Court	2	1.1
5	王朝 Dynasty	2	1.1
5	西夏 Xixia	2	1.1

n=188

3-3 样本、男性各年龄层、女性各年龄层的常用品牌/ The Most Frequently Used Brands by the Whole Sample, Age and Gender Groups

	人数 Number	第一品牌及百分比 1st/ percent	第二品牌及百分比 2nd/ percent	第三品牌及百分比 3rd/ percent
样本 Sample	188	**张裕 Changyu(46.8)**	**长城 Great Wall(31.9)**	**丹凤 Danfeng(9.0)**
男性 Male	99	**张裕 Changyu(45.5)**	**长城 Great Wall(34.3)**	**丹凤 Danfeng(10.1)**
16~24 岁 Age	16	张裕 Changyu(37.5) 长城 Great Wall(37.5)	丹凤 Danfeng(18.8)	皇轩 Imperial Court(6.3)
25~34 岁 Age	34	长城 Great Wall(44.1)	张裕 Changyu(41.2)	皇轩 Imperial Court(2.9) 民权 Minquan(2.9) 丹凤 Danfeng(2.9) 西夏 Xixia(2.9) 烟台 Yantai(2.9)
35~44 岁 Age	28	张裕 Changyu(42.9)	长城 Great Wall(28.6)	丹凤 Danfeng(14.3)
45~54 岁 Age	12	张裕 Changyu(58.3)	长城 Great Wall(25.0)	王朝 Dynasty(8.3) 丹凤 Danfeng(8.3)
55~60 岁 Age	9	张裕 Changyu(66.7)	长城 Great Wall(22.2)	丹凤 Danfeng(11.1)
女性 Female	89	**张裕 Changyu(48.3)**	**长城 Great Wall(29.2)**	**丹凤 Danfeng(7.9)**
16~24 岁 Age	17	张裕 Changyu(52.9)	长城 Great Wall(41.2)	天韵 Tianyun(5.9)
25~34 岁 Age	27	长城 Great Wall(44.4)	张裕 Changyu(37.0)	天韵 Tianyun(7.4)
35~44 岁 Age	22	张裕 Changyu(50.0)	长城 Great Wall(18.2)	丹凤 Danfeng(13.6)
45~54 岁 Age	14	张裕 Changyu(64.3)	丹凤 Danfeng(14.3) 长城 Great Wall(14.3)	天韵 Tianyun(7.1)
55~60 岁 Age	9	张裕 Changyu(44.4)	丹凤 Danfeng(11.1) 西夏 Xixia(11.1) 天韵 Tianyun(11.1) 长城 Great Wall(11.1) 万达(11.1)	

3-4 理想品牌排名/ Ranking of the Ideal Brands

排名 Brand Ranking	品牌 Brands	人数 Number	百分比 Percent
1	张裕 Changyu	226	37.6
2	长城 Great Wall	161	26.8
3	丹凤 Danfeng	28	4.7
4	王朝 Dynasty	8	1.3
5	天韵 Tianyun	4	0.7
6	皇轩 Imperial Court	3	0.5
6	西夏 Xixia	3	0.5

n=601

3-5 样本、男性各年龄层、女性各年龄层最近三个月有无购买的比例/ Purchasing in the Last Three Months by the Whole Sample, Age and Gender Groups

	人数 Number	买过 yes	没买过 no
样本 Sample	600	29.5	70.5
男性 Male	301	30.6	69.4
16~24 岁 Age	64	21.9	78.1
25~34 岁 Age	91	39.6	60.4
35~44 岁 Age	76	28.9	71.1
45~54 岁 Age	46	21.7	78.3
55~60 岁 Age	24	41.7	58.3
女性 Female	299	28.4	71.6
16~24 岁 Age	61	27.9	72.1
25~34 岁 Age	90	24.4	75.6
35~44 岁 Age	74	32.4	67.6
45~54 岁 Age	49	30.6	69.4
55~60 岁 Age	25	28.0	72.0

3-6 样本、男性各年龄层、女性各年龄层最近三个月是否拿葡萄酒送过礼/ To Offer Wine as Gift in the Last Three Months by the Whole Sample, Age and Gender Groups

	人数 Number	送过 yes	没送过 no
样本 Sample	601	8.2	91.8
男性 Male	302	7.9	92.1
16~24 岁 Age	64	6.3	93.8
25~34 岁 Age	91	8.8	91.2
35~44 岁 Age	77	9.1	90.9
45~54 岁 Age	46	6.5	93.5
55~60 岁 Age	24	8.3	91.7
女性 Female	299	8.4	91.6
16~24 岁 Age	61	6.6	93.4
25~34 岁 Age	90	7.8	92.2
35~44 岁 Age	74	14.9	85.1
45~54 岁 Age	49	4.1	95.9
55~60 岁 Age	25	4.0	96.0

3-7 样本、男性各年龄层、女性各年龄层最近三个月的饮用频率/ Frequencies of Consuming Wine in the Last Three Months by the Whole Sample, Age and Gender Groups

	人数 Number	天天喝 daily	一周 3 次或以上 3 times or over a week	一周 1~2 次 once or twice a week	一个月 2～3 次 2 or 3 times a month	一个月 1 次 once a month	两个月 1 次 once two months	三个月 1 次或以下 once three months or below	没有喝 never
样本 Sample	595	0.0	1.8	4.0	8.4	5.7	4.9	6.7	68.4
男性 Male	297	0.0	2.7	4.4	10.4	7.1	3.4	5.4	66.7
16~24 岁 Age	64	0.0	0.0	0.0	12.5	3.1	4.7	4.7	75.0
25~34 岁 Age	88	0.0	2.3	6.8	11.4	9.1	2.3	6.8	61.4
35~44 岁 Age	76	0.0	3.9	2.6	11.8	5.3	3.9	9.2	63.2
45~54 岁 Age	45	0.0	2.2	8.9	6.7	6.7	2.2	0.0	73.3
55~60 岁 Age	24	0.0	8.3	4.2	4.2	16.7	4.2	0.0	62.5
女性 Female	298	0.0	1.0	3.7	6.4	4.4	6.4	8.1	70.1
16~24 岁 Age	61	0.0	0.0	1.6	6.6	3.3	4.9	11.5	72.1
25~34 岁 Age	90	0.0	0.0	4.4	7.8	3.3	6.7	7.8	70.0
35~44 岁 Age	74	0.0	1.4	6.8	4.1	4.1	8.1	5.4	70.3
45~54 岁 Age	48	0.0	2.1	2.1	8.3	8.3	4.2	4.2	70.8
55~60 岁 Age	25	0.0	4.0	0.0	4.0	4.0	8.0	16.0	64.0

3-8 样本、男性各年龄层、女性各年龄层的品牌习惯/ Brand Habit in Consuming Wine by the Whole Sample, Age and Gender Groups

	人数 Number	基本固定饮用一个牌子 used in only one brand	比较固定地饮用两个或三个牌子 used in two or three brands	基本上不太固定牌子 no brand preference
样本 Sample	188	43.6	31.9	24.5
男性 Male	99	43.4	35.4	21.2
16~24 岁 Age	16	43.8	37.5	18.8
25~34 岁 Age	34	52.9	32.4	14.7
35~44 岁 Age	28	39.3	32.1	28.6
45~54 岁 Age	12	50.0	25.0	25.0
55~60 岁 Age	9	11.1	66.7	22.2
女性 Female	89	43.8	28.1	28.1
16~24 岁 Age	17	47.1	23.5	29.4
25~34 岁 Age	27	37.0	25.9	37.0
35~44 岁 Age	22	40.9	45.5	13.6
45~54 岁 Age	14	64.3	7.1	28.6
55~60 岁 Age	9	33.3	33.3	33.3

3-9 选择该类商品的考虑因素/ Ranking of the Considerations in Purchasing

注：本题为多选题，合计百分比超过 100%(Multiple answers）

排名 Ranking	考虑因素 Considerations	人次 Person-time	百分比 Percent
1	口味好 pleasant taste	115	61.2
2	有名的牌子 famous brand	70	37.2
3	价格适中 reasonable price	66	35.1
4	生产日期 date of producing	20	10.6
5	购买方便 easy to buy	19	10.1
5	朋友推荐 introduction of friends	19	10.1
6	只是由于习惯 out of habit	14	7.4
7	别人送的 given by other people	12	6.4
8	广告影响 influence of advertising	11	5.9
8	包装吸引人 appealing package	11	5.9
9	有优惠条件 with preferential terms	4	2.1
10	售货员介绍 introduced by the shop assistants	3	1.6
11	其它 others	2	1.1

n=188

3-10 样本、男性各年龄层、女性各年龄层最常饮用的种类/ Kinds of the Consumed Wine by the Whole Sample, Age and Gender Groups

	人数 Number	干红 dry red	干白 dry white	甜型 sweet	其他 others
样本 Sample	187	69.5	14.4	15.5	0.5
男性 Male	98	66.3	18.4	15.3	0.0
16~24 岁 Age	16	81.3	6.3	12.5	0.0
25~34 岁 Age	34	64.7	26.5	8.8	0.0
35~44 岁 Age	28	57.1	21.4	21.4	0.0
45~54 岁 Age	11	81.8	9.1	9.1	0.0
55~60 岁 Age	9	55.6	11.1	33.3	0.0
女性 Female	89	73.0	10.1	15.7	1.1
16~24 岁 Age	17	76.5	5.9	11.8	5.9
25~34 岁 Age	27	77.8	7.4	14.8	0.0
35~44 岁 Age	22	68.2	13.6	18.2	0.0
45~54 岁 Age	14	71.4	14.3	14.3	0.0
55~60 岁 Age	9	66.7	11.1	22.2	0.0

3-11 样本、男性各年龄层、女性各年龄层最常饮用场合/ Settings of Consumption by the Whole Sample, Age and Gender Groups

注：本题为多选题，合计百分比超过 100%(Multiple answers）

	人数 Number	请客 entertain guests	节假日团聚 get-together on holiday	日常饮用 drink daily	睡觉前喝 before sleeping	做菜 cooking meal	其它 others
样本 Sample	188	35.1	66.0	26.1	1.6	2.7	0.5
男性 Male	99	32.3	59.6	30.3	2.0	2.0	1.0
16~24 岁 Age	16	31.3	50.0	31.3	6.3	0.0	0.0
25~34 岁 Age	34	29.4	64.7	20.6	0.0	5.9	0.0
35~44 岁 Age	28	39.3	57.1	39.3	0.0	0.0	0.0
45~54 岁 Age	12	41.7	50.0	33.3	0.0	0.0	8.3
55~60 岁 Age	9	11.1	77.8	33.3	11.1	0.0	0.0
女性 Female	89	38.2	73.0	21.3	1.1	3.4	0.0
16~24 岁 Age	17	29.4	88.2	5.9	0.0	0.0	0.0
25~34 岁 Age	27	40.7	77.8	14.8	0.0	0.0	0.0
35~44 岁 Age	22	40.9	50.0	40.9	0.0	13.6	0.0
45~54 岁 Age	14	21.4	64.3	28.6	7.1	0.0	0.0
55~60 岁 Age	9	66.7	100.0	11.1	0.0	0.0	0.0

3-12 重度消费者人口分布/ Demographics of the Heavy Consumers

	人数 Number	16-24 岁 Age	25-34 岁 Age	35-44 岁 Age	45-54 岁 Age	55-60 岁 Age
样本 Sample	35	2.9	34.3	31.4	20.0	11.4
男性 Male	21	0.0	38.1	23.8	23.8	14.3
天天喝 daily	0	0.0	0.0	0.0	0.0	0.0
一周 3 次或以上 3 times or over a week	8	0.0	25.0	37.5	12.5	25.0
一周 1~2 次 once or twice a week	13	0.0	46.2	15.4	30.8	7.7
女性 Female	14	7.1	28.6	42.9	14.3	7.1
天天喝 daily	0	0.0	0.0	0.0	0.0	0.0
一周 3 次或以上 3 times or over a week	3	0.0	0.0	33.3	33.3	33.3
一周 1~2 次 once or twice a week	11	9.1	36.4	45.5	9.1	0.0

3-13 不同消费者层的常用品牌/ The Most Frequently Used Brands by Market Segments

3-13-1 时尚流行指标/ Fads Popular Index

	人数 Number	第一品牌及百分比 1st/percent	第二品牌及百分比 2nd/percent	第三品牌及百分比 3rd/percent
样本 Sample	188	**张裕 Changyu(46.8)**	**长城 Great Wall(31.9)**	**丹凤 Danfeng(9.0)**
平实生活指向 simple living orientation	109	张裕 Changyu(45.0)	长城 Great Wall(33.9)	丹凤 Danfeng(9.2)
时尚流行指向 fashion orientation	79	张裕 Changyu(49.4)	长城 Great Wall(29.1)	丹凤 Danfeng(8.9)

3-13-2 广告态度指标/ Advertising Attitude Index

	人数 Number	第一品牌及百分比 1st/percent	第二品牌及百分比 2nd/percent	第三品牌及百分比 3rd/percent
样本 Sample	186	**张裕 Changyu(46.8)**	**长城 Great Wall(32.3)**	**丹凤 Danfeng(8.6)**
广告淡漠指向 indifferent orientation	55	长城 Great Wall(41.8)	张裕 Changyu(38.2)	丹凤 Danfeng(9.1)
中间层 medium	102	张裕 Changyu(49.0)	长城 Great Wall(31.4)	丹凤 Danfeng(8.8)
信赖广告指向 loyal orientation	29	张裕 Changyu(55.2)	长城 Great Wall(17.2)	天韵 Tianyun(10.3)

3-13-3 饮食健康指标/ Foods & Drink Quality Index

	人数 Number	第一品牌及百分比 1st/percent	第二品牌及百分比 2nd/percent	第三品牌及百分比 3rd/percent
样本 Sample	188	**张裕 Changyu(46.8)**	**长城 Great Wall(31.9)**	**丹凤 Danfeng(9.0)**
饮食“温饱”指向 "basic" orientation	70	张裕 Changyu(42.9)	长城 Great Wall(35.7)	丹凤 Danfeng(8.6)
中间层 medium	82	张裕 Changyu(46.3)	长城 Great Wall(32.9)	丹凤 Danfeng(7.3)
健康营养指向 health & nutrition orientation	36	张裕 Changyu(55.6)	长城 Great Wall(22.2)	丹凤 Danfeng(13.9)

3-14 重度消费者的消费者层构成/ The Composition of the Heavy Consumers

3-14-1 时尚流行指标/ Fads Popular Index

	人数 Number	平实生活指向 simple living orientation	时尚流行指向 fashion orientation
样本 Sample	35	54.3	45.7
天天喝 daily	0	0.0	0.0
一周 3 次或以上 3 times or over a week	11	54.5	45.5
一周 1~2 次 once or twice a week	24	54.2	45.8

3-14-2 广告态度指标/ Advertising Attitude Index

	人数 Number	广告淡漠指向 indifferent orientation	中间层 medium	信赖广告指向 loyal orientation
样本 Sample	35	31.4	40.0	28.6
天天喝 daily	0	0.0	0.0	0.0
一周 3 次或以上 3 times or over a week	11	36.4	45.5	18.2
一周 1~2 次 once or twice a week	24	29.2	37.5	33.3

3-14-3 饮食健康指标/ Foods & Drink Quality Index

	人数 Number	饮食"温饱"指向 "basic" orientation	中间层 medium	健康营养指向 health & nutrition orientation
样本 Sample	35	25.7	45.7	28.6
天天喝 daily	0	0.0	0.0	0.0
一周 3 次或以上 3 times or over a week	11	27.3	63.6	9.1
一周 1~2 次 once or twice a week	24	25.0	37.5	37.5

● 沈阳 / Shenyang

3-1 最近三个月饮用频率的比例/ Proportion of the Sample Consuming Wine in the Last Three Months

	人数 Number	百分比 Percent
天天喝 daily	3	0.5
一周 3 次或以上 3 times or over a week	3	0.5
一周 1~2 次 once or twice a week	17	2.8
一个月 2～3 次 2 or 3 times a month	37	6.2
一个月 1 次 once a month	29	4.8
两个月 1 次 once two months	33	5.5
三个月 1 次或以下 once three months or below	54	9.0
没有喝 never	422	70.6

n=598

3-2 最常用品牌排名/ Ranking of the Most Frequently Used Brands

排名 Brand Ranking	品牌 Brands	人数 Number	百分比 Percent
1	通化 Tonghua	71	40.3
2	长城 Great Wall	44	25.0
3	张裕 Changyu	10	5.7
4	野山 Yeshan	6	3.4
5	奥马 AoMa	5	2.8
6	天池 Tianchi	4	2.3

n=176

3-3 样本、男性各年龄层、女性各年龄层的常用品牌/ The Most Frequently Used Brands by the Whole Sample, Age and Gender Groups

	人数 Number	第一品牌及百分比 1st/ percent	第二品牌及百分比 2nd/ percent	第三品牌及百分比 3rd/ percent
样本 Sample	176	**通化 Tonghua(40.3)**	**长城 Great Wall(25.0)**	**张裕 Changyu(5.7)**
男性 Male	97	**通化 Tonghua(42.3)**	**长城 Great Wall(26.8)**	**张裕 Changyu(4.1)**
16~24 岁 Age	17	长城 Great Wall(58.8)	通化 Tonghua(41.2)	
25~34 岁 Age	37	通化 Tonghua(40.5)	长城 Great Wall(21.6)	天池 Tianchi(5.4) 奥马 AoMa(5.4)
35~44 岁 Age	26	通化 Tonghua(53.8)	长城 Great Wall(15.4)	张裕 Changyu(7.7) 长白山 Changbaishan(7.7)
45~54 岁 Age	12	通化 Tonghua(33.3)	长城 Great Wall(16.7)	张裕 Changyu(8.3) 野山 Yeshan(8.3) 烟台 Yantai(8.3) 奥马 AoMa(8.3) 千山 Qianshan(8.3) 吉林农大 Ji Lin Nong Da(8.3)
55~60 岁 Age	5	长城 Great Wall(40.0)	通化 Tonghua(20.0) 长白山 Changbaishan(20.0) 吉林红 Jilinhong(20.0)	
女性 Female	79	**通化 Tonghua(38.0)**	**长城 Great Wall(22.8)**	**张裕 Changyu(7.6)**
16~24 岁 Age	15	通化 Tonghua(26.7) 长城 Great Wall(26.7)	张裕 Changyu(6.7) 野山 Yeshan(6.7) 天池 Tianchi(6.7) 奥马 AoMa(6.7) 玫瑰红 Meiguihong(6.7) 巴黎之春 Paris' Spring(6.7) 野葡萄汁葡萄酒 (原汁野生葡萄酒) Ye Pu Tao Zhi Pu Tao Jiu(6.7)	
25~34 岁 Age	25	通化 Tonghua(32.0)	长城 Great Wall(20.0)	张裕 Changyu(8.0) 野山 Yeshan(8.0)
35~44 岁 Age	22	通化 Tonghua(36.4)	长城 Great Wall(22.7)	张裕 Changyu(13.6)
45~54 岁 Age	10	通化 Tonghua(50.0)	长城 Great Wall(30.0)	威王 Weiwang(10.0)
55~60 岁 Age	7	通化 Tonghua(71.4)	长城 Great Wall(14.3) 野原汁 Ye Yuan Zhi(14.3)	

3-4 理想品牌排名/ Ranking of the Ideal Brands

排名 Brand Ranking	品牌 Brands	人数 Number	百分比 Percent
1	通化 Tonghua	182	30.3
2	长城 Great Wall	109	18.1
3	张裕 Changyu	39	6.5
4	奥马 AoMa	12	2.0
5	野山 Yeshan	10	1.7
6	长白山 Changbaishan	9	1.5
7	万达 Wanda	7	1.2
8	天池 Tianchi	6	1.0
9	野葡萄汁葡萄酒(原汁野生葡萄酒) Ye Pu Tao Zhi Pu Tao Jiu	5	0.8
10	威王 Weiwang	4	0.7

n=601

3-5 样本、男性各年龄层、女性各年龄层最近三个月有无购买的比例/ Purchasing in the Last Three Months by the Whole Sample, Age and Gender Groups

	人数 Number	买过 yes	没买过 no
样本 Sample	601	26.1	73.9
男性 Male	299	25.8	74.2
16~24 岁 Age	64	18.8	81.3
25~34 岁 Age	89	36.0	64.0
35~44 岁 Age	76	26.3	73.7
45~54 岁 Age	46	19.6	80.4
55~60 岁 Age	24	16.7	83.3
女性 Female	302	26.5	73.5
16~24 岁 Age	64	25.0	75.0
25~34 岁 Age	90	31.1	68.9
35~44 岁 Age	76	27.6	72.4
45~54 岁 Age	48	16.7	83.3
55~60 岁 Age	24	29.2	70.8

3-6 样本、男性各年龄层、女性各年龄层最近三个月是否拿葡萄酒送过礼/ To Offer Wine as Gift in the Last Three Months by the Whole Sample, Age and Gender Groups

	人数 Number	送过 yes	没送过 no
样本 Sample	600	4.0	96.0
男性 Male	298	3.0	97.0
16~24 岁 Age	64	0.0	100.0
25~34 岁 Age	89	4.5	95.5
35~44 岁 Age	75	4.0	96.0
45~54 岁 Age	46	2.2	97.8
55~60 岁 Age	24	4.2	95.8
女性 Female	302	5.0	95.0
16~24 岁 Age	64	4.7	95.3
25~34 岁 Age	90	7.8	92.2
35~44 岁 Age	76	3.9	96.1
45~54 岁 Age	48	2.1	97.9
55~60 岁 Age	24	4.2	95.8

3-7 样本、男性各年龄层、女性各年龄层最近三个月的饮用频率/ Frequencies of Consuming Wine in the Last Three Months by the Whole Sample, Age and Gender Groups

	人数 Number	天天喝 daily	一周 3 次或以上 3 times or over a week	一周 1~2 次 once or twice a week	一个月 2~3 次 2 or 3 times a month	一个月 1 次 once a month	两个月 1 次 once two months	三个月 1 次或以下 once three months or below	没有喝 never
样本 Sample	598	0.5	0.5	2.8	6.2	4.8	5.5	9.0	70.6
男性 Male	297	0.7	1.0	2.7	6.7	4.7	7.4	9.4	67.3
16~24 岁 Age	64	0.0	0.0	3.1	3.1	4.7	4.7	10.9	73.4
25~34 岁 Age	89	2.2	0.0	4.5	10.1	4.5	10.1	10.1	58.4
35~44 岁 Age	75	0.0	2.7	1.3	6.7	5.3	9.3	9.3	65.3
45~54 岁 Age	45	0.0	0.0	2.2	8.9	4.4	6.7	4.4	73.3
55~60 岁 Age	24	0.0	4.2	0.0	0.0	4.2	0.0	12.5	79.2
女性 Female	301	0.3	0.0	3.0	5.6	5.0	3.7	8.6	73.8
16~24 岁 Age	64	0.0	0.0	3.1	6.3	6.3	1.6	6.3	76.6
25~34 岁 Age	90	1.1	0.0	1.1	6.7	6.7	1.1	11.1	72.2
35~44 岁 Age	76	0.0	0.0	5.3	3.9	5.3	7.9	6.6	71.1
45~54 岁 Age	47	0.0	0.0	2.1	6.4	2.1	0.0	10.6	78.7
55~60 岁 Age	24	0.0	0.0	4.2	4.2	0.0	12.5	8.3	70.8

3-8 样本、男性各年龄层、女性各年龄层的品牌习惯/ Brand Habit in Consuming Wine by the Whole Sample, Age and Gender Groups

	人数 Number	基本固定饮用一个牌子 used in only one brand	比较固定地饮用两个或三个牌子 used in two or three brands	基本上不太固定牌子 no brand preference
样本 Sample	176	44.9	29.5	25.6
男性 Male	97	48.5	25.8	25.8
16~24 岁 Age	17	41.2	17.6	41.2
25~34 岁 Age	37	45.9	35.1	18.9
35~44 岁 Age	26	53.8	23.1	23.1
45~54 岁 Age	12	50.0	8.3	41.7
55~60 岁 Age	5	60.0	40.0	0.0
女性 Female	79	40.5	34.2	25.3
16~24 岁 Age	15	20.0	40.0	40.0
25~34 岁 Age	25	48.0	40.0	12.0
35~44 岁 Age	22	31.8	31.8	36.4
45~54 岁 Age	10	70.0	20.0	10.0
55~60 岁 Age	7	42.9	28.6	28.6

3-9 选择该类商品的考虑因素/ Ranking of the Considerations in Purchasing

注：本题为多选题，合计百分比超过100%(Multiple answers）

排名 Ranking	考虑因素 Considerations	人次 Person-time	百分比 Percent
1	口味好 pleasant taste	133	76.4
2	价格适中 reasonable price	73	42.0
3	有名的牌子 famous brand	51	29.3
4	生产日期 date of producing	40	23.0
5	购买方便 easy to buy	19	10.9
6	只是由于习惯 out of habit	12	6.9
7	朋友推荐 introduction of friends	11	6.3
8	别人送的 given by other people	9	5.2
9	广告影响 influence of advertising	6	3.4
10	包装吸引人 appealing package	5	2.9
11	有优惠条件 with preferential terms	1	0.6
11	其它 others	1	0.6

n=174

3-10 样本、男性各年龄层、女性各年龄层最常饮用的种类/ Kinds of the Consumed Wine by the Whole Sample, Age and Gender Groups

	人数 Number	干红 dry red	干白 dry white	甜型 sweet	其他 others
样本 Sample	176	52.8	9.7	36.9	0.6
男性 Male	97	53.6	8.2	38.1	0.0
16~24 岁 Age	17	58.8	5.9	35.3	0.0
25~34 岁 Age	37	48.6	8.1	43.2	0.0
35~44 岁 Age	26	53.8	11.5	34.6	0.0
45~54 岁 Age	12	66.7	0.0	33.3	0.0
55~60 岁 Age	5	40.0	20.0	40.0	0.0
女性 Female	79	51.9	11.4	35.4	1.3
16~24 岁 Age	15	66.7	6.7	26.7	0.0
25~34 岁 Age	25	52.0	8.0	36.0	4.0
35~44 岁 Age	22	54.5	9.1	36.4	0.0
45~54 岁 Age	10	40.0	30.0	30.0	0.0
55~60 岁 Age	7	28.6	14.3	57.1	0.0

3-11 样本、男性各年龄层、女性各年龄层最常饮用场合/ Settings of Consumption by the Whole Sample, Age and Gender Groups

注：本题为多选题，合计百分比超过 100%(Multiple answers)

	人数 Number	请客 entertain guests	节假日团聚 get-together on holiday	日常饮用 drink daily	睡觉前喝 before sleeping	做菜 cooking meal	其它 others
样本 Sample	176	30.7	69.3	26.7	0.6	2.3	0.6
男性 Male	97	29.9	66.0	32.0	0.0	1.0	0.0
16~24 岁 Age	17	11.8	82.4	17.6	0.0	0.0	0.0
25~34 岁 Age	37	35.1	56.8	35.1	0.0	0.0	0.0
35~44 岁 Age	26	38.5	65.4	38.5	0.0	3.8	0.0
45~54 岁 Age	12	16.7	58.3	33.3	0.0	0.0	0.0
55~60 岁 Age	5	40.0	100.0	20.0	0.0	0.0	0.0
女性 Female	79	31.6	73.4	20.3	1.3	3.8	1.3
16~24 岁 Age	15	46.7	66.7	26.7	0.0	0.0	0.0
25~34 岁 Age	25	28.0	68.0	24.0	4.0	4.0	0.0
35~44 岁 Age	22	31.8	77.3	13.6	0.0	4.5	4.5
45~54 岁 Age	10	40.0	80.0	20.0	0.0	10.0	0.0
55~60 岁 Age	7	0.0	85.7	14.3	0.0	0.0	0.0

3-12 重度消费者人口分布/ Demographics of the Heavy Consumers

	人数 Number	16-24 岁 Age	25-34 岁 Age	35-44 岁 Age	45-54 岁 Age	55-60 岁 Age
样本 Sample	23	17.4	34.8	30.4	8.7	8.7
男性 Male	13	15.4	46.2	23.1	7.7	7.7
天天喝 daily	2	0.0	100.0	0.0	0.0	0.0
一周 3 次或以上 3 times or over a week	3	0.0	0.0	66.7	0.0	33.3
一周 1~2 次 once or twice a week	8	25.0	50.0	12.5	12.5	0.0
女性 Female	10	20.0	20.0	40.0	10.0	10.0
天天喝 daily	1	0.0	100.0	0.0	0.0	0.0
一周 3 次或以上 3 times or over a week	0	0.0	0.0	0.0	0.0	0.0
一周 1~2 次 once or twice a week	9	22.2	11.1	44.4	11.1	11.1

3-13 不同消费者层的常用品牌/ The Most Frequently Used Brands by Market Segments

3-13-1 时尚流行指标/ Fads Popular Index

	人数 Number	第一品牌及百分比 1st/ percent	第二品牌及百分比 2nd/ percent	第三品牌及百分比 3rd/ percent
样本 Sample	176	**通化 Tonghua(40.3)**	**长城 Great Wall(25.0)**	**张裕 Changyu(5.7)**
平实生活指向 simple living orientation	77	通化 Tonghua(41.6)	长城 Great Wall(18.2)	张裕 Changyu(6.5)
时尚流行指向 fashion orientation	99	通化 Tonghua(39.4)	长城 Great Wall(30.3)	张裕 Changyu(5.1)

3-13-2 广告态度指标/ Advertising Attitude Index

	人数 Number	第一品牌及百分比 1st/ percent	第二品牌及百分比 2nd/ percent	第三品牌及百分比 3rd/ percent
样本 Sample	176	**通化 Tonghua(40.3)**	**长城 Great Wall(25.0)**	**张裕 Changyu(5.7)**
广告淡漠指向 indifferent orientation	48	通化 Tonghua(37.5)	长城 Great Wall(27.1)	张裕 Changyu(4.2) 天池 Tianchi(4.2)
中间层 medium	105	通化 Tonghua(44.8)	长城 Great Wall(22.9)	张裕 Changyu(5.7)
信赖广告指向 loyal orientation	23	长城 Great Wall(30.4)	通化 Tonghua(26.1)	张裕 Changyu(8.7) 长白山 Changbaishan(8.7)

3-13-3 饮食健康指标/ Foods & Drink Quality Index

	人数 Number	第一品牌及百分比 1st/ percent	第二品牌及百分比 2nd/ percent	第三品牌及百分比 3rd/ percent
样本 Sample	176	**通化 Tonghua(40.3)**	**长城 Great Wall(25.0)**	**张裕 Changyu(5.7)**
饮食"温饱"指向 "basic" orientation	45	通化 Tonghua(46.7)	长城 Great Wall(22.2)	张裕 Changyu(6.7)
中间层 medium	89	通化 Tonghua(33.7)	长城 Great Wall(29.2)	张裕 Changyu(4.5) 野山 Yeshan(4.5 天池 Tianchi(4.5)
健康营养指向 health & nutrition orientation	42	通化 Tonghua(47.6)	长城 Great Wall(19.0)	张裕 Changyu(7.1)

3-14 重度消费者的消费者层构成/ The Composition of the Heavy Consumers

3-14-1 时尚流行指标/ Fads Popular Index

	人数 Number	平实生活指向 simple living orientation	时尚流行指向 fashion orientation
样本 Sample	23	34.8	65.2
天天喝 daily	3	33.3	66.7
一周 3 次或以上 3 times or over a week	3	66.7	33.3
一周 1~2 次 once or twice a week	17	29.4	70.6

3-14-2 广告态度指标/ Advertising Attitude Index

	人数 Number	广告淡漠指向 indifferent orientation	中间层 medium	信赖广告指向 loyal orientation
样本 Sample	23	17.4	73.9	8.7
天天喝 daily	3	0.0	66.7	33.3
一周 3 次或以上 3 times or over a week	3	33.3	66.7	0.0
一周 1~2 次 once or twice a week	17	17.6	76.5	5.9

3-14-3 饮食健康指标/ Foods & Drink Quality Index

	人数 Number	饮食"温饱"指向 "basic" orientation	中间层 medium	健康营养指向 health & nutrition orientation
样本 Sample	23	34.8	56.5	8.7
天天喝 daily	3	0.0	100.0	0.0
一周 3 次或以上 3 times or over a week	3	33.3	66.7	0.0
一周 1~2 次 once or twice a week	17	41.2	47.1	11.8

4.香烟 / Cigarette

● 北京 / Beijing

4-1 是否抽烟的比例/ Proportion of the Smoking in the Last Three Months

	人数 Number	百分比 Percent
是 yes	330	33.1
否 no	667	66.9

n=997

4-2 最常用品牌排名/ Ranking of the Most Used Brands

排名 Brand Ranking	品牌 Brands	人数 Number	百分比 Percent
1	希尔顿 Hilton	46	14.0
1	中南海 Lights	46	14.0
2	都宝 Derby	36	11.0
3	红塔山 Hongtashan	19	5.8
4	红河 Honghe	16	4.9
5	万宝路 Marlboro	15	4.6
6	555	14	4.3
7	金桥 Jinqiao	13	4.0
8	云烟 Yunyan	9	2.7
9	威龙 Weilong	8	2.4
9	红梅 Hongmei	8	2.4
10	石林 Stone Forest	7	2.1

n=328

4-3 样本、男性各年龄层、女性各年龄层的常用品牌/ The Most Frequently Used Brands by the Whole Sample, Age and Gender Groups

	人数 Number	第一品牌及百分比 1st/ percent	第二品牌及百分比 2nd/ percent	第三品牌及百分比 3rd/ percent	第四品牌及百分比 4th/ percent
样本 Sample	328	**希尔顿 Hilton(14.0)** **中南海 Lights(14.0)**	**都宝 Derby(11.0)**	**红塔山 Hongtashan (5.8)**	**红河 Honghe(4.9)**
男性 Male	291	**中南海 Lights(13.7)**	**希尔顿 Hilton(13.1)**	**都宝 Derby(11.7)**	**红河 Honghe(5.2)** **红塔山 Hongtashan (5.2)**
16~24 岁 Age	37	中南海 Lights(37.8)	希尔顿 Hilton(10.8)	都宝 Derby(8.1) 红河 Honghe(8.1)	金桥 Jinqiao(5.4) 沙龙 Salem(5.4)
25~34 岁 Age	95	中南海 Lights(12.6) 希尔顿 Hilton(12.6)	都宝 Derby(8.4)	红塔山 Hongtashan (6.3) 红河 Honghe(6.3)	万宝路 Marlboro(5.3)
35~44 岁 Age	91	希尔顿 Hilton(15.4)	都宝 Derby(13.2)	中南海 Lights(8.8)	555(7.7)
45~54 岁 Age	49	都宝 Derby(18.4)	希尔顿 Hilton(14.3)	中南海 Lights(10.2)	红塔山 Hongtashan (6.1)
55~60 岁 Age	19	红塔山 Hongtashan (10.5) 威龙 Weilong(10.5) 石林 Stone Forest(10.5) 555(10.5) 都宝 Derby(10.5)	黄果树 Huang Guoshu(5.3) 骆驼 Camel(5.3) 万宝路 Marlboro(5.3) 希尔顿 Hilton(5.3) 中南海 Lights(5.3) 龙泉 Longquan(5.3) 北京 Beijing(5.3) 以礼河 Yilihe(5.3) 凤牌 Feng(5.3)		
女性 Female	37	**希尔顿 Hilton(21.6)**	**中南海 Lights(16.2)**	**红塔山 Hongtashan (10.8)**	**希尔 Hill(8.1)**
16~24 岁 Age	2	哈德门 Ha Demen(50.0) 希尔顿 Hilton(50.0)			
25~34 岁 Age	14	希尔顿 Hilton(21.4) 中南海 Lights(21.4)	都宝 Derby(7.1) 红河 Honghe(7.1) 红梅 Hongmei(7.1) 红山茶 Hongshancha(7.1) 红塔山 Hongtashan (7.1) 万宝路 Marlboro(7.1) 中美 Zhongmei(7.1) 双叶 Shuangye(7.1)		
35~44 岁 Age	14	红塔山 Hongtashan (21.4) 中南海 Lights(21.4)	希尔顿 Hilton(14.3) 希尔 Hill(14.3)	柔和七星 Mild Seven(7.1) 圣罗兰 Yves Saint Laurent(7.1) 万宝路 Marlboro(7.1) 绿丹兰 Lvdanlan(7.1)	
45~54 岁 Age	3	都宝 Derby(33.3) 希尔顿 Hilton(33.3) 希尔 Hill(33.3)			
55~60 岁 Age	4	金健 jinjian(25.0) 希尔顿 Hilton(25.0) 画苑 Huayuan(25.0) 嘉得乐 Jiadele(25.0)			

4-4 理想品牌排名/ Ranking of the Ideal Brands

排名 Brand Ranking	品牌 Brands	人数 Number	百分比 Percent
1	555	108	10.7
2	红塔山 Hongtashan	104	10.3
3	万宝路 Marlboro	86	8.5
4	希尔顿 Hilton	66	6.5
5	中南海 Lights	52	5.1
6	中华 Zhonghua	48	4.7
7	云烟 Yunyan	24	2.4
8	都宝 Derby	22	2.2
9	红河 Honghe	21	2.1

n=1012

4-5 样本、男性各年龄层、女性各年龄层最近三个月有无购买的比例/ Purchasing in the Last Three Months by the Whole Sample, Age and Gender Groups

	人数 Number	买过 yes	没买过 no
样本 Sample	1012	40.5	59.5
男性 Male	504	58.5	41.5
16~24 岁 Age	105	34.3	65.7
25~34 岁 Age	151	62.9	37.1
35~44 岁 Age	131	74.0	26.0
45~54 岁 Age	77	64.9	35.1
55~60 岁 Age	40	42.5	57.5
女性 Female	508	22.6	77.4
16~24 岁 Age	108	14.8	85.2
25~34 岁 Age	150	24.0	76.0
35~44 岁 Age	124	27.4	72.6
45~54 岁 Age	84	19.0	81.0
55~60 岁 Age	42	31.0	69.0

4-6 样本、男性各年龄层、女性各年龄层最近三个月是否拿香烟送过礼/ To Offer Cigarette as Gift in the Last Three Months by the Whole Sample, Age and Gender Groups

	人数 Number	送过 yes	没送过 no
样本 Sample	993	12.2	87.8
男性 Male	492	14.0	86.0
16~24 岁 Age	104	8.7	91.3
25~34 岁 Age	148	14.9	85.1
35~44 岁 Age	128	15.6	84.4
45~54 岁 Age	74	16.2	83.8
55~60 岁 Age	38	15.8	84.2
女性 Female	501	10.4	89.6
16~24 岁 Age	105	5.7	94.3
25~34 岁 Age	148	6.8	93.2
35~44 岁 Age	124	18.5	81.5
45~54 岁 Age	82	12.2	87.8
55~60 岁 Age	42	7.1	92.9

4-7 样本、男性各年龄层、女性各年龄层是否抽烟的比例/ Smoking or Not by the Whole Sample, Age and Gender Groups

	人数 Number	是 yes	否 no
样本 Sample	997	33.1	66.9
男性 Male	502	58.4	41.6
16~24 岁 Age	105	35.2	64.8
25~34 岁 Age	150	64.7	35.3
35~44 岁 Age	131	69.5	30.5
45~54 岁 Age	76	64.5	35.5
55~60 岁 Age	40	47.5	52.5
女性 Female	495	7.5	92.5
16~24 岁 Age	106	1.9	98.1
25~34 岁 Age	146	9.6	90.4
35~44 岁 Age	121	11.6	88.4
45~54 岁 Age	82	3.7	96.3
55~60 岁 Age	40	10.0	90.0

4-8 样本、男性各年龄层、女性各年龄层的品牌习惯/ Brand Habit in Consuming Cigarette by the Whole Sample, Age and Gender Groups

	人数 Number	基本固定用一个牌子 used in only one brand	比较固定地用两个或三个牌子 used in two or three brands	基本上不太固定牌子 no brand preference
样本 Sample	330	64.5	27.6	7.9
男性 Male	293	62.5	30.0	7.5
16~24 岁 Age	37	43.2	45.9	10.8
25~34 岁 Age	97	68.0	24.7	7.2
35~44 岁 Age	91	63.7	31.9	4.4
45~54 岁 Age	49	65.3	30.6	4.1
55~60 岁 Age	19	57.9	15.8	26.3
女性 Female	37	81.1	8.1	10.8
16~24 岁 Age	2	100.0	0.0	0.0
25~34 岁 Age	14	78.6	14.3	7.1
35~44 岁 Age	14	78.6	7.1	14.3
45~54 岁 Age	3	66.7	0.0	33.3
55~60 岁 Age	4	100.0	0.0	0.0

4-9 选择该类商品的考虑因素/ Ranking of the Considerations in Purchasing

注：本题为多选题，合计百分比超过 100%(Multiple answers）

排名 Ranking	考虑因素 considerations	人次 Person-time	百分比 Percent
1	口味好 pleasant taste	186	56.4
2	价格适中 reasonable price	166	50.3
3	只是由于习惯 out of habit	95	28.8
4	有名的牌子 famous brand	66	20.0
5	购买方便 easy to buy	37	11.2
6	生产日期 date of producing	19	5.8
7	朋友推荐 introduction of friends	15	4.5
8	别人送的 given by other people	11	3.3
9	包装吸引人 appealing package	3	0.9
9	其它 others	3	0.9
10	广告影响 influence of advertising	2	0.6
11	有优惠条件 with preferential terms	1	0.3
11	售货员介绍 introduced by the shop assistants	1	0.3

n=330

4-10 样本、男性各年龄层、女性各年龄层抽烟的口味偏好/ Taste of the Consumed Cigarette by the Whole Sample, Age and Gender Groups

	人数 Number	混合型 combination type	烤烟型 flue-cured type	雪茄口味 cigar	其它 others
样本 Sample	326	62.0	36.2	0.9	0.9
男性 Male	290	60.0	38.3	1.0	0.7
16~24 岁 Age	37	64.9	35.1	0.0	0.0
25~34 岁 Age	96	56.3	41.7	1.0	1.0
35~44 岁 Age	90	60.0	38.9	0.0	1.1
45~54 岁 Age	49	65.3	32.7	2.0	0.0
55~60 岁 Age	18	55.6	38.9	5.6	0.0
女性 Female	36	77.8	19.4	0.0	2.8
16~24 岁 Age	2	100.0	0.0	0.0	0.0
25~34 岁 Age	14	78.6	21.4	0.0	0.0
35~44 岁 Age	13	69.2	30.8	0.0	0.0
45~54 岁 Age	3	66.7	0.0	0.0	33.3
55~60 岁 Age	4	100.0	0.0	0.0	0.0

4-11 样本、男性各年龄层、女性各年龄层一天抽烟的数量/ Number of Smoking a Day by the Whole Sample, Age and Gender Groups

	人数 Number	2 包以上 2 boxes or over	1～2 包 1 or 2 boxes	1 包左右 about a box	半包左右 about half a box	一天两三支或以下 2 or 3 cigarettes or below	没有抽 never
样本 Sample	329	1.5	6.7	36.5	42.2	11.6	1.5
男性 Male	293	1.4	6.1	38.2	43.0	10.6	0.7
16~24 岁 Age	37	0.0	2.7	29.7	48.6	16.2	2.7
25~34 岁 Age	97	1.0	7.2	38.1	42.3	11.3	0.0
35~44 岁 Age	91	3.3	8.8	38.5	40.7	8.8	0.0
45~54 岁 Age	49	0.0	4.1	36.7	49.0	8.2	2.0
55~60 岁 Age	19	0.0	0.0	57.9	31.6	10.5	0.0
女性 Female	36	2.8	11.1	22.2	36.1	19.4	8.3
16~24 岁 Age	2	0.0	100.0	0.0	0.0	0.0	0.0
25~34 岁 Age	13	0.0	15.4	30.8	38.5	7.7	7.7
35~44 岁 Age	14	7.1	0.0	21.4	35.7	28.6	7.1
45~54 岁 Age	3	0.0	0.0	0.0	33.3	33.3	33.3
55~60 岁 Age	4	0.0	0.0	25.0	50.0	25.0	0.0

4-12 样本、男性各年龄层、女性各年龄层抽烟的包装形式/ Types of Package of the Consumed Cigarette by the Whole Sample, Age and Gender Groups

	人数 Number	软盒装 soft box	硬盒装 hard box
样本 Sample	328	45.7	54.3
男性 Male	292	46.9	53.1
16~24 岁 Age	37	27.0	73.0
25~34 岁 Age	97	44.3	55.7
35~44 岁 Age	90	53.3	46.7
45~54 岁 Age	49	53.1	46.9
55~60 岁 Age	19	52.6	47.4
女性 Female	36	36.1	63.9
16~24 岁 Age	2	0.0	100.0
25~34 岁 Age	14	42.9	57.1
35~44 岁 Age	14	14.3	85.7
45~54 岁 Age	2	100.0	0.0
55~60 岁 Age	4	75.0	25.0

4-13 重度消费者人口分布/ Demographics of the Heavy Consumers

	人数 Number	16-24 岁 Age	25-34 岁 Age	35-44 岁 Age	45-54 岁 Age	55-60 岁 Age
样本 Sample	286	11.2	33.9	32.2	15.7	7.0
男性 Male	260	11.5	33.1	31.9	16.9	6.5
一天 2 包以上 2 boxes or over a day	4	0.0	25.0	75.0	0.0	0.0
一天 1～2 包 1 or 2 boxes a day	18	5.6	38.9	44.4	11.1	0.0
一天 1 包左右 about a box a day	112	9.8	33.0	31.3	16.1	9.8
一天半包左右 about half a box a day	126	14.3	32.5	29.4	19.0	4.8
女性 Female	26	7.7	42.3	34.6	3.8	11.5
一天 2 包以上 2 boxes or over a day	1	0.0	0.0	100.0	0.0	0.0
一天 1～2 包 1 or 2 boxes a day	4	50.0	50.0	0.0	0.0	0.0
一天 1 包左右 about a box a day	8	0.0	50.0	37.5	0.0	12.5
一天半包左右 about half a box a day	13	0.0	38.5	38.5	7.7	15.4

4-14 不同消费者层的常用品牌/ The Most Frequently Used Brands by Market Segments

4-14-1 时尚流行指标/ Fads Popular Index

	人数 Number	第一品牌及百分比 1st/percent	第二品牌及百分比 2nd/percent	第三品牌及百分比 3rd/percent	第四品牌及百分比 4th/percent
样本 Sample	324	**中南海 Lights(14.2)**	**希尔顿 Hilton(13.6)**	**都宝 Derby(10.8)**	**红塔山 Hongtashan (5.9)**
平实生活指向 simple living orientation	176	都宝 Derby(14.8) 希尔顿 Hilton(14.8)	中南海 Lights(10.2)	红塔山 Hongtashan (4.5) 红河 Honghe(4.5)	万宝路 Marlboro(4.0) 555(4.0)
时尚流行指向 fashion orientation	148	中南海 Lights(18.9)	希尔顿 Hilton(12.2)	红塔山 Hongtashan (7.4)	都宝 Derby(6.1)

4-14-2 广告态度指标/ Advertising Attitude Index

	人数 Number	第一品牌及百分比 1st/percent	第二品牌及百分比 2nd/percent	第三品牌及百分比 3rd/percent	第四品牌及百分比 4th/percent
样本 Sample	321	**中南海 Lights(14.3)**	**希尔顿 Hilton(14.0)**	**都宝 Derby(10.9)**	**红塔山 Hongtashan (5.9)**
广告淡漠指向 indifferent orientation	104	希尔顿 Hilton(16.3)	中南海 Lights(14.4)	都宝 Derby(11.5)	金桥 Jinqiao(5.8)
中间层 medium	176	中南海 Lights(14.2)	希尔顿 Hilton(11.9)	都宝 Derby(10.8)	红塔山 Hongtashan (6.8)
信赖广告指向 loyal orientation	41	希尔顿 Hilton(17.1)	中南海 Lights(14.6)	都宝 Derby(9.8)	红塔山 Hongtashan (7.3) 555(7.3)

4-14-3 饮食健康指标/ Foods & Drink Quality Index

	人数 Number	第一品牌及百分比 1st/percent	第二品牌及百分比 2nd/percent	第三品牌及百分比 3rd/percent	第四品牌及百分比 4th/percent
样本 Sample	326	**希尔顿 Hilton(14.1)**	**中南海 Lights(13.8)**	**都宝 Derby(11.0)**	**红塔山 Hongtashan (5.8)**
饮食“温饱”指向 "basic" orientation	124	希尔顿 Hilton(17.7)	中南海 Lights(13.7)	都宝 Derby(8.9)	万宝路 Marlboro(5.6)
中间层 medium	149	都宝 Derby(14.1)	中南海 Lights(13.4)	希尔顿 Hilton(12.8)	红塔山 Hongtashan (7.4)
健康营养指向 health & nutrition orientation	53	中南海 Lights(15.1)	红塔山 Hongtashan (9.4) 希尔顿 Hilton(9.4)	都宝 Derby(7.5) 红河 Honghe(7.5)	北京 Beijing(3.8) 希尔 Hill(3.8) 威龙 Weilong(3.8) 嘉得乐 Jiadele(3.8) 金桥 Jinqiao(3.8) 555(3.8) 石林 Stone Forest(3.8)

4-15 重度消费者的消费者层构成/ The Composition of the Heavy Consumers

4-15-1 时尚流行指标/ Fads Popular Index

	人数 Number	平实生活指向 simple living orientation	时尚流行指向 fashion orientation
样本 Sample	282	54.6	45.4
一天 2 包以上 2 boxes or over a day	5	40.0	60.0
一天 1～2 包 1 or 2 boxes a day	21	42.9	57.1
一天 1 包左右 about a box a day	119	57.1	42.9
一天半包左右 about half a box a day	137	54.7	45.3

4-15-2 广告态度指标/ Advertising Attitude Index

	人数 Number	广告淡漠指向 indifferent orientation	中间层 medium	信赖广告指向 loyal orientation
样本 Sample	279	33.0	53.8	13.3
一天 2 包以上 2 boxes or over a day	5	20.0	40.0	40.0
一天 1～2 包 1 or 2 boxes a day	22	45.5	45.5	9.1
一天 1 包左右 about a box a day	116	27.6	57.8	14.7
一天半包左右 about half a box a day	136	36.0	52.2	11.8

4-15-3 饮食健康指标/ Foods & Drink Quality Index

	人数 Number	饮食"温饱"指向 "basic" orientation	中间层 medium	健康营养指向 health & nutrition orientation
样本 Sample	285	40.0	44.2	15.8
一天2包以上 2 boxes or over a day	5	60.0	20.0	20.0
一天1~2包 1 or 2 boxes a day	22	63.6	22.7	13.6
一天1包左右 about a box a day	119	39.5	47.1	13.4
一天半包左右 half a box a day	139	36.0	46.0	18.0

● 上海 / Shanghai

4-1 是否抽烟的比例/ Proportion of the Smoking in the Last Three Months

	人数 Number	百分比 Percent
是 yes	370	36.6
否 no	641	63.4

n=1011

4-2 最常用品牌排名/ Ranking of the Most Used Brands

排名 Brand Ranking	品牌 Brands	人数 Number	百分比 Percent
1	红双喜 Double Happiness	149	40.4
2	牡丹 Peony	85	23.0
3	555	57	15.4
4	双喜 Shuangxi	19	5.1
5	红塔山 Hongtashan	12	3.3
6	柔和七星 Mild Seven	10	2.7
7	大前门 Daqianmen	7	1.9
8	上海 Shanghai	5	1.4
9	阿诗玛 Ashima	4	1.1
9	中华 Zhonghua	4	1.1
10	万宝路 Marlboro	2	0.5
10	云烟 Yunyan	2	0.5

n=369

4-3 样本、男性各年龄层、女性各年龄层的常用品牌/ The Most Frequently Used Brands by the Whole Sample, Age and Gender Groups

	人数 Number	第一品牌及百分比 1st/ percent	第二品牌及百分比 2nd/ percent	第三品牌及百分比 3rd/ percent
样本 Sample	369	**红双喜 Double Happiness(40.4)**	**牡丹 Peony(23.0)**	**555(15.4)**
男性 Male	322	**红双喜 Double Happiness(41.3)**	**牡丹 Peony(23.3)**	**555(14.0)**
16~24 岁 Age	31	红双喜 Double Happiness(58.1)	柔和七星(12.9)	555(6.5) 双喜 Shuangxi(6.5)
25~34 岁 Age	98	红双喜 Double Happiness(43.9)	555(21.4)	牡丹 Peony(13.3)
35~44 岁 Age	106	红双喜 Double Happiness(43.4)	牡丹 Peony(30.2)	555(10.4)
45~54 岁 Age	68	红双喜 Double Happiness(33.8)	牡丹 Peony(27.9)	555(14.7)
55~60 岁 Age	19	牡丹 Peony(52.6)	红双喜 Double Happiness(15.8)	555(5.3) 大前门 Daqianmen(5.3) 红山茶 Hongshancha(5.3) 云烟 Yunyan(5.3) 双喜 Shuangxi(5.3) 飞马 Feima(5.3)
女性 Female	47	**红双喜 Double Happiness(34.0)**	**555(25.5)**	**牡丹 Peony(21.3)**
16~24 岁 Age	6	555(33.3)	红塔山 Hongtashan (16.7) 牡丹 Peony(16.7) 双喜 Shuangxi(16.7) Luxman(16.7)	
25~34 岁 Age	14	555(35.7)	牡丹 Peony(21.4)	红双喜 Double Happiness(14.3)
35~44 岁 Age	17	红双喜 Double Happiness(41.2)	555(29.4)	牡丹 Peony(23.5)
45~54 岁 Age	8	红双喜 Double Happiness(62.5)	牡丹 Peony(25.0)	双喜 Shuangxi(12.5)
55~60 岁 Age	2	红双喜 Double Happiness(100.0)		

4-4 理想品牌排名/ Ranking of the Ideal Brands

排名 Brand Ranking	品牌 Brands	人数 Number	百分比 Percent
1	中华 Zhonghua	311	30.7
2	红双喜 Double Happiness	232	22.9
3	555	146	14.4
4	牡丹 Peony	74	7.3
5	红塔山 Hongtashan	48	4.7
6	双喜 Shuangxi	33	3.3
7	万宝路 Marlboro	23	2.3
8	柔和七星 Mild Seven	19	1.9
9	熊猫 Xiongmao	8	0.8
10	玉溪 Yuxi	7	0.7

n=1014

4-5 样本、男性各年龄层、女性各年龄层最近三个月有无购买的比例/ Purchasing in the Last Three Months by the Whole Sample, Age and Gender Groups

	人数 Number	买过 yes	没买过 no
样本 Sample	1014	43.9	56.1
男性 Male	509	61.9	38.1
16~24 岁 Age	109	27.5	72.5
25~34 岁 Age	146	64.4	35.6
35~44 岁 Age	130	78.5	21.5
45~54 岁 Age	85	80.0	20.0
55~60 岁 Age	39	53.8	46.2
女性 Female	505	25.7	74.3
16~24 岁 Age	108	19.4	80.6
25~34 岁 Age	144	28.5	71.5
35~44 岁 Age	130	30.0	70.0
45~54 岁 Age	82	24.4	75.6
55~60 岁 Age	41	22.0	78.0

4-6 样本、男性各年龄层、女性各年龄层最近三个月是否拿香烟送过礼/ To Offer Cigarette as Gift in the Last Three Months by the Whole Sample, Age and Gender Groups

	人数 Number	送过 yes	没送过 no
样本 Sample	1012	14.0	86.0
男性 Male	508	15.6	84.4
16~24 岁 Age	109	9.2	90.8
25~34 岁 Age	146	20.5	79.5
35~44 岁 Age	130	14.6	85.4
45~54 岁 Age	85	17.6	82.4
55~60 岁 Age	38	13.2	86.8
女性 Female	504	12.5	87.5
16~24 岁 Age	108	11.1	88.9
25~34 岁 Age	143	14.0	86.0
35~44 岁 Age	130	13.1	86.9
45~54 岁 Age	82	12.2	87.8
55~60 岁 Age	41	9.8	90.2

4-7 样本、男性各年龄层、女性各年龄层是否抽烟的比例/ Smoking or Not by the Whole Sample, Age and Gender Groups

	人数 Number	是 yes	否 no
样本 Sample	1011	36.6	63.4
男性 Male	508	63.4	36.6
16~24 岁 Age	109	28.4	71.6
25~34 岁 Age	146	67.1	32.9
35~44 岁 Age	129	82.2	17.8
45~54 岁 Age	85	80.0	20.0
55~60 岁 Age	39	48.7	51.3
女性 Female	503	9.5	90.5
16~24 岁 Age	107	5.6	94.4
25~34 岁 Age	144	9.7	90.3
35~44 岁 Age	129	13.2	86.8
45~54 岁 Age	82	11.0	89.0
55~60 岁 Age	41	4.9	95.1

4-8 样本、男性各年龄层、女性各年龄层的品牌习惯/ Brand Habit in Consuming Cigarette by the Whole Sample, Age and Gender Groups

	人数 Number	基本固定用一个牌子 used in only one brand	比较固定地用两个或三个牌子 used in two or three brands	基本上不太固定牌子 no brand preference
样本 Sample	368	72.0	24.7	3.3
男性 Male	321	72.0	24.9	3.1
16~24 岁 Age	31	58.1	35.5	6.5
25~34 岁 Age	98	69.4	27.6	3.1
35~44 岁 Age	105	76.2	21.9	1.9
45~54 岁 Age	68	77.9	19.1	2.9
55~60 岁 Age	19	63.2	31.6	5.3
女性 Female	47	72.3	23.4	4.3
16~24 岁 Age	6	16.7	66.7	16.7
25~34 岁 Age	14	78.6	21.4	0.0
35~44 岁 Age	17	82.4	17.6	0.0
45~54 岁 Age	8	100.0	0.0	0.0
55~60 岁 Age	2	0.0	50.0	50.0

4-9 选择该类商品的考虑因素/ Ranking of the Considerations in Purchasing

注：本题为多选题，合计百分比超过 100%(Multiple answers）

排名 Ranking	考虑因素 considerations	人次 Person-time	百分比 Percent
1	价格适中 reasonable price	189	51.2
2	口味好 pleasant taste	158	42.8
3	有名的牌子 famous brand	124	33.6
4	只是由于习惯 out of habit	113	30.6
5	购买方便 easy to buy	50	13.6
6	生产日期 date of producing	20	5.4
7	有优惠条件 with preferential terms	10	2.7
8	别人送的 given by other people	8	2.2
9	广告影响 influence of advertising	6	1.6
9	包装吸引人 appealing package	6	1.6
10	朋友推荐 introduction of friends	5	1.4
10	其它 others	5	1.4

n=369

4-10 样本、男性各年龄层、女性各年龄层抽烟的口味偏好/ Taste of the Consumed Cigarette by the Whole Sample, Age and Gender Groups

	人数 Number	混合型 combination type	烤烟型 flue-cured type	雪茄口味 cigar	其它 others
样本 Sample	367	31.3	66.2	0.3	2.2
男性 Male	322	29.8	68.0	0.0	2.2
16~24 岁 Age	31	29.0	71.0	0.0	0.0
25~34 岁 Age	98	35.7	61.2	0.0	3.1
35~44 岁 Age	106	27.4	69.8	0.0	2.8
45~54 岁 Age	68	30.9	67.6	0.0	1.5
55~60 岁 Age	19	10.5	89.5	0.0	0.0
女性 Female	45	42.2	53.3	2.2	2.2
16~24 岁 Age	6	66.7	33.3	0.0	0.0
25~34 岁 Age	13	38.5	46.2	7.7	7.7
35~44 岁 Age	17	41.2	58.8	0.0	0.0
45~54 岁 Age	8	37.5	62.5	0.0	0.0
55~60 岁 Age	1	0.0	100.0	0.0	0.0

4-11 样本、男性各年龄层、女性各年龄层一天抽烟的数量/ Number of Smoking a Day by the Whole Sample, Age and Gender Groups

	人数 Number	2 包以上 2 boxes or over	1~2 包 1 or 2 boxes	1 包左右 about a box	半包左右 about half a box	一天两三支或以下 2 or 3 cigarettes or below	没有抽 never
样本 Sample	369	2.2	9.8	47.7	27.9	12.2	0.3
男性 Male	322	2.2	9.9	48.8	28.3	10.6	0.3
16~24 岁 Age	31	0.0	0.0	32.3	38.7	29.0	0.0
25~34 岁 Age	98	2.0	9.2	45.9	28.6	13.3	1.0
35~44 岁 Age	106	2.8	10.4	51.9	28.3	6.6	0.0
45~54 岁 Age	68	2.9	13.2	55.9	22.1	5.9	0.0
55~60 岁 Age	19	0.0	15.8	47.4	31.6	5.3	0.0
女性 Female	47	2.1	8.5	40.4	25.5	23.4	0.0
16~24 岁 Age	6	0.0	16.7	33.3	33.3	16.7	0.0
25~34 岁 Age	14	0.0	7.1	42.9	21.4	28.6	0.0
35~44 岁 Age	17	0.0	11.8	35.3	29.4	23.5	0.0
45~54 岁 Age	8	12.5	0.0	62.5	12.5	12.5	0.0
55~60 岁 Age	2	0.0	0.0	0.0	50.0	50.0	0.0

4-12 样本、男性各年龄层、女性各年龄层抽烟的包装形式/ Types of Package of the Consumed Cigarette by the Whole Sample, Age and Gender Groups

	人数 Number	软盒装 soft box	硬盒装 hard box
样本 Sample	368	19.0	81.0
男性 Male	321	19.3	80.7
16~24 岁 Age	31	3.2	96.8
25~34 岁 Age	98	16.3	83.7
35~44 岁 Age	105	21.0	79.0
45~54 岁 Age	68	25.0	75.0
55~60 岁 Age	19	31.6	68.4
女性 Female	47	17.0	83.0
16~24 岁 Age	6	33.3	66.7
25~34 岁 Age	14	14.3	85.7
35~44 岁 Age	17	5.9	94.1
45~54 岁 Age	8	37.5	62.5
55~60 岁 Age	2	0.0	100.0

4-13 重度消费者人口分布/ Demographics of the Heavy Consumers

	人数 Number	16-24 岁 Age	25-34 岁 Age	35-44 岁 Age	45-54 岁 Age	55-60 岁 Age
样本 Sample	323	8.4	29.1	34.7	22.0	5.9
男性 Male	287	7.7	29.3	34.5	22.3	6.3
2 包以上 2 boxes or over	7	0.0	28.6	42.9	28.6	0.0
1～2 包 1 or 2 boxes	32	0.0	28.1	34.4	28.1	9.4
1 包左右 about a box	157	6.4	28.7	35.0	24.2	5.7
半包左右 about half a box	91	13.2	30.8	33.0	16.5	6.6
女性 Female	36	13.9	27.8	36.1	19.4	2.8
2 包以上 2 boxes or over	1	0.0	0.0	0.0	100.0	0.0
1～2 包 1 or 2 boxes	4	25.0	25.0	50.0	0.0	0.0
1 包左右 about a box	19	10.5	31.6	31.6	26.3	0.0
半包左右 about half a box	12	16.7	25.0	41.7	8.3	8.3

4-14 不同消费者层的常用品牌/ The Most Frequently Used Brands by Market Segments

4-14-1 时尚流行指标/ Fads Popular Index

	人数 Number	第一品牌及百分比 1st/percent	第二品牌及百分比 2nd/percent	第三品牌及百分比 3rd/percent
样本 Sample	363	**红双喜 Double Happiness(40.5)**	**牡丹 Peony(22.6)**	**555(15.7)**
平实生活指向 simple living orientation	171	红双喜 Double Happiness(41.5)	牡丹 Peony(31.0)	555(9.4)
时尚流行指向 fashion orientation	192	红双喜 Double Happiness(39.6)	555(21.4)	牡丹 Peony(15.1)

4-14-2 广告态度指标/ Advertising Attitude Index

	人数 Number	第一品牌及百分比 1st/percent	第二品牌及百分比 2nd/percent	第三品牌及百分比 3rd/percent
样本 Sample	364	**红双喜 Double Happiness(40.7)**	**牡丹 Peony(22.8)**	**555(15.4)**
广告淡漠指向 indifferent orientation	92	红双喜 Double Happiness(44.6)	牡丹 Peony(19.6)	555(15.2)
中间层 medium	224	红双喜 Double Happiness(39.7)	牡丹 Peony(24.6)	555(16.1)
信赖广告指向 loyal orientation	48	红双喜 Double Happiness(37.5)	牡丹 Peony(20.8)	555(12.5)

4-14-3 饮食健康指标/ Foods & Drink Quality Index

	人数 Number	第一品牌及百分比 1st/percent	第二品牌及百分比 2nd/percent	第三品牌及百分比 3rd/percent
样本 Sample	366	**红双喜 Double Happiness(40.7)**	**牡丹 Peony(23.0)**	**555(15.3)**
饮食"温饱"指向 "basic" orientation	95	红双喜 Double Happiness(48.4)	牡丹 Peony(25.3)	555(7.4)
中间层 medium	174	红双喜 Double Happiness(37.9)	牡丹 Peony(26.4)	555(14.9)
健康营养指向 health & nutrition orientation	97	红双喜 Double Happiness(38.1)	555(23.7)	牡丹 Peony(14.4)

4-15 重度消费者的消费者层构成/ The Composition of the Heavy Consumers

4-15-1 时尚流行指标/ Fads Popular Index

	人数 Number	平实生活指向 simple living orientation	时尚流行指向 fashion orientation
样本 Sample	317	49.2	50.8
一天 2 包以上 2 boxes or over a day	8	62.5	37.5
一天 1～2 包 1 or 2 boxes a day	35	51.4	48.6
一天 1 包左右 about a box a day	171	45.6	54.4
一天半包左右 bout half a box a day	103	53.4	46.6

4-15-2 广告态度指标/ Advertising Attitude Index

	人数 Number	广告淡漠指向 indifferent orientation	中间层 medium	信赖广告指向 loyal orientation
样本 Sample	**319**	**25.7**	**61.4**	**12.9**
一天 2 包以上 2 boxes or over a day	8	37.5	37.5	25.0
一天 1～2 包 1 or 2 boxes a day	35	31.4	48.6	20.0
一天 1 包左右 about a box a day	175	22.9	63.4	13.7
一天半包左右 about half a box a day	101	27.7	64.4	7.9

4-15-3 饮食健康指标/ Foods & Drink Quality Index

	人数 Number	饮食"温饱"指向 "basic" orientation	中间层 medium	健康营养指向 health & nutrition orientation
样本 Sample	**321**	**27.7**	**47.0**	**25.2**
一天 2 包以上 2 boxes or over a day	8	50.0	37.5	12.5
一天 1～2 包 1 or 2 boxes a day	36	16.7	66.7	16.7
一天 1 包左右 about a box a day	174	27.6	45.4	27.0
一天半包左右 half a box a day	103	30.1	43.7	26.2

● 广州 / Guangzhou

4-1 是否抽烟的比例/ Proportion of the Smoking in the Last Three Months

	人数 Number	百分比 Percent
是 yes	294	28.6
否 no	734	71.4

n=1028

4-2 最常用品牌排名/ Ranking of the Most Used Brands

排名 Brand Ranking	品牌 Brands	人数 Number	百分比 Percent
1	双喜 Shuangxi	81	27.6
2	椰树 Coconut Palm	43	14.7
3	红双喜 Double Happiness	37	12.6
4	555	23	7.8
5	万宝路 Marlboro	16	5.5
6	羊城 Yangcheng	13	4.4
7	红塔山 Hongtashan	11	3.8
8	总督 Viceroy	7	2.4
8	白沙 Baisha	7	2.4
9	云烟 Yunyan	6	2.0

n=293

4-3 样本、男性各年龄层、女性各年龄层的常用品牌/ The Most Frequently Used Brands by the Whole Sample, Age and Gender Groups

	人数 Number	第一品牌及百分比 1st/ percent	第二品牌及百分比 2nd/ percent	第三品牌及百分比 3rd/ percent
样本 Sample	**293**	**双喜 Shuangxi(27.6)**	**椰树 Coconut Palm(14.7)**	**红双喜 Double Happiness(12.6)**
男性 Male	**247**	**双喜 Shuangxi(26.3)**	**椰树 Coconut Palm(15.0)**	**红双喜 Double Happiness(13.4)**
16~24 岁 Age	23	双喜 Shuangxi(26.1)	柔和七星 Mild Seven(13.0) 555(13.0)	红双喜 Double Happiness(8.7) 椰树 Coconut Palm(8.7)
25~34 岁 Age	74	双喜 Shuangxi(24.3)	红双喜 Double Happiness(13.5)	椰树 Coconut Palm(12.2)
35~44 岁 Age	80	双喜 Shuangxi(25.0)	椰树 Coconut Palm(18.8)	红双喜 Double Happiness(11.3)
45~54 岁 Age	47	双喜 Shuangxi(36.2)	红双喜 Double Happiness(19.1)	椰树 Coconut Palm(17.0)
55~60 岁 Age	23	双喜 Shuangxi(17.4) 羊城 Yangcheng(17.4)	椰树 Coconut Palm(13.0) 红双喜 Double Happiness(13.0)	金双喜(8.7)
女性 Female	**46**	**双喜 Shuangxi(34.8)**	**椰树 Coconut Palm(13.0)**	**红双喜 Double Happiness(8.7)** **羊城 Yangcheng(8.7)**
16~24 岁 Age	7	双喜 Shuangxi(42.9)	宏声 Hongsheng(14.3) 红双喜 Double Happiness(14.3) 万宝路 Marlboro(14.3) 椰树 Coconut Palm(14.3)	
25~34 岁 Age	8	双喜 Shuangxi(37.5)	沙龙 Salem(25.0)	555(12.5) 白沙 Baisha(12.5) 圣罗兰 Yves Saint Laurent(12.5)
35~44 岁 Age	17	双喜 Shuangxi(41.2)	椰树 Coconut Palm(17.6)	555(5.9) 云烟 Yunyan(5.9) 红双喜 Double Happiness(5.9) 柔和七星 Mild Seven (5.9) 万宝路 Marlboro(5.9) 羊城 Yangcheng(5.9) 卡碧 Kabi(5.9)
45~54 岁 Age	10	红双喜 Double Happiness(20.0) 羊城 Yangcheng(20.0) 双喜 Shuangxi(20.0)	555(10.0) 健牌 Kent(10.0) 椰树 Coconut Palm(10.0) 丰城(10.0)	
55~60 岁 Age	4	万宝路 Marlboro(25.0) 羊城 Yangcheng(25.0) 椰树 Coconut Palm(25.0) 双喜 Shuangxi(25.0)		

4-4 理想品牌排名/ Ranking of the Ideal Brands

排名 Brand Ranking	品牌 Brands	人数 Number	百分比 Percent
1	555	169	16.3
2	双喜 Shuangxi	124	12.0
3	万宝路 Marlboro	94	9.1
4	红塔山 Hongtashan	65	6.3
4	红双喜 Double Happiness	65	6.3
5	中华 Zhonghua	35	3.4
6	椰树 Coconut Palm	33	3.2

n=1034

4-5 样本、男性各年龄层、女性各年龄层最近三个月有无购买的比例/ Purchasing in the Last Three Months by the Whole Sample, Age and Gender Groups

	人数 Number	买过 yes	没买过 no
样本 Sample	**1033**	**37.2**	**62.8**
男性 Male	**498**	**50.0**	**50.0**
16~24 岁 Age	106	25.5	74.5
25~34 岁 Age	150	52.0	48.0
35~44 岁 Age	126	61.9	38.1
45~54 岁 Age	73	60.3	39.7
55~60 岁 Age	43	51.2	48.8
女性 Female	**535**	**25.2**	**74.8**
16~24 岁 Age	112	17.0	83.0
25~34 岁 Age	158	24.7	75.3
35~44 岁 Age	137	29.9	70.1
45~54 岁 Age	87	29.9	70.1
55~60 岁 Age	41	24.4	75.6

4-6 样本、男性各年龄层、女性各年龄层最近三个月是否拿香烟送过礼/ To Offer Cigarette as Gift in the Last Three Months by the Whole Sample, Age and Gender Groups

	人数 Number	送过 yes	没送过 no
样本 Sample	1030	9.5	90.5
男性 Male	497	11.3	88.7
16~24 岁 Age	106	6.6	93.4
25~34 岁 Age	149	16.8	83.2
35~44 岁 Age	126	11.1	88.9
45~54 岁 Age	73	8.2	91.8
55~60 岁 Age	43	9.3	90.7
女性 Female	533	7.9	92.1
16~24 岁 Age	112	7.1	92.9
25~34 岁 Age	156	9.0	91.0
35~44 岁 Age	137	8.0	92.0
45~54 岁 Age	87	8.0	92.0
55~60 岁 Age	41	4.9	95.1

4-7 样本、男性各年龄层、女性各年龄层是否抽烟的比例/ Smoking or Not by the Whole Sample, Age and Gender Groups

	人数 Number	是 yes	否 no
样本 Sample	1028	28.6	71.4
男性 Male	497	49.7	50.3
16~24 岁 Age	105	21.9	78.1
25~34 岁 Age	150	49.3	50.7
35~44 岁 Age	127	63.0	37.0
45~54 岁 Age	72	65.3	34.7
55~60 岁 Age	43	53.5	46.5
女性 Female	531	8.9	91.1
16~24 岁 Age	112	7.1	92.9
25~34 岁 Age	155	5.2	94.8
35~44 岁 Age	137	12.4	87.6
45~54 岁 Age	87	11.5	88.5
55~60 岁 Age	40	10.0	90.0

4-8 样本、男性各年龄层、女性各年龄层的品牌习惯/ Brand Habit in Consuming Cigarette by the Whole Sample, Age and Gender Groups

	人数 Number	基本固定用一个牌子 used in only one brand	比较固定地用两个或三个牌子 used in two or three brands	基本上不太固定牌子 no brand preference
样本 Sample	292	63.4	31.2	5.5
男性 Male	247	60.3	33.6	6.1
16~24 岁 Age	23	65.2	30.4	4.3
25~34 岁 Age	74	55.4	40.5	4.1
35~44 岁 Age	80	60.0	31.3	8.8
45~54 岁 Age	47	61.7	31.9	6.4
55~60 岁 Age	23	69.6	26.1	4.3
女性 Female	45	80.0	17.8	2.2
16~24 岁 Age	6	66.7	16.7	16.7
25~34 岁 Age	8	62.5	37.5	0.0
35~44 岁 Age	17	94.1	5.9	0.0
45~54 岁 Age	10	80.0	20.0	0.0
55~60 岁 Age	4	75.0	25.0	0.0

4-9 选择该类商品的考虑因素/ Ranking of the Considerations in Purchasing

注：本题为多选题，合计百分比超过 100%(Multiple answers）

排名 Ranking	考虑因素 considerations	人次 Person-time	百分比 Percent
1	口味好 pleasant taste	152	51.9
2	价格适中 reasonable price	146	49.8
3	只是由于习惯 out of habit	87	29.7
4	有名的牌子 famous brand	76	25.9
5	购买方便 easy to buy	53	18.1
6	生产日期 date of producing	16	5.5
7	有优惠条件 with preferential terms	7	2.4
8	朋友推荐 introduction of friends	5	1.7
9	别人送的 given by other people	4	1.4
10	包装吸引人 appealing package	3	1.0
10	售货员介绍 introduced by the shop assistants	3	1.0
11	广告影响 influence of advertising	2	0.7

n=293

4-10 样本、男性各年龄层、女性各年龄层抽烟的口味偏好/ Taste of the Consumed Cigarette by the Whole Sample, Age and Gender Groups

	人数 Number	混合型 combination type	烤烟型 flue-cured type	雪茄口味 cigar	其它 others
样本 Sample	288	28.8	66.3	2.1	2.8
男性 Male	242	29.8	65.7	2.5	2.1
16~24 岁 Age	23	26.1	60.9	8.7	4.3
25~34 岁 Age	72	23.6	73.6	1.4	1.4
35~44 岁 Age	79	38.0	58.2	2.5	1.3
45~54 岁 Age	46	21.7	73.9	2.2	2.2
55~60 岁 Age	22	40.9	54.5	0.0	4.5
女性 Female	46	23.9	69.6	0.0	6.5
16~24 岁 Age	7	0.0	100.0	0.0	0.0
25~34 岁 Age	8	37.5	50.0	0.0	12.5
35~44 岁 Age	17	17.6	70.6	0.0	11.8
45~54 岁 Age	10	40.0	60.0	0.0	0.0
55~60 岁 Age	4	25.0	75.0	0.0	0.0

4-11 样本、男性各年龄层、女性各年龄层一天抽烟的数量/ Number of Smoking a Day by the Whole Sample, Age and Gender Groups

	人数 Number	2 包以上 2 boxes or over	1~2 包 1 or 2 boxes	1 包左右 about a box	半包左右 about half a box	一天两三支或以下 2 or 3 cigarettes or below	没有抽 never
样本 Sample	293	1.7	14.0	37.5	28.0	17.7	1.0
男性 Male	247	2.0	14.6	40.9	25.5	16.6	0.4
16~24 岁 Age	23	8.7	8.7	21.7	34.8	21.7	4.3
25~34 岁 Age	74	0.0	18.9	35.1	23.0	23.0	0.0
35~44 岁 Age	80	1.3	15.0	47.5	27.5	8.8	0.0
45~54 岁 Age	47	2.1	10.6	53.2	21.3	12.8	0.0
55~60 岁 Age	23	4.3	13.0	30.4	26.1	26.1	0.0
女性 Female	46	0.0	10.9	19.6	41.3	23.9	4.3
16~24 岁 Age	7	0.0	28.6	0.0	57.1	14.3	0.0
25~34 岁 Age	8	0.0	0.0	25.0	12.5	62.5	0.0
35~44 岁 Age	17	0.0	11.8	23.5	41.2	11.8	11.8
45~54 岁 Age	10	0.0	0.0	30.0	50.0	20.0	0.0
55~60 岁 Age	4	0.0	25.0	0.0	50.0	25.0	0.0

4-12 样本、男性各年龄层、女性各年龄层抽烟的包装形式/ Types of Package of the Consumed Cigarette by the Whole Sample, Age and Gender Groups

	人数 Number	软盒装 soft box	硬盒装 hard box
样本 Sample	292	53.1	46.9
男性 Male	247	51.4	48.6
16~24 岁 Age	23	47.8	52.2
25~34 岁 Age	74	45.9	54.1
35~44 岁 Age	80	51.3	48.8
45~54 岁 Age	47	57.4	42.6
55~60 岁 Age	23	60.9	39.1
女性 Female	45	62.2	37.8
16~24 岁 Age	7	42.9	57.1
25~34 岁 Age	8	25.0	75.0
35~44 岁 Age	17	82.4	17.6
45~54 岁 Age	9	66.7	33.3
55~60 岁 Age	4	75.0	25.0

4-13 重度消费者人口分布/ Demographics of the Heavy Consumers

	人数 Number	16-24 岁 Age	25-34 岁 Age	35-44 岁 Age	45-54 岁 Age	55-60 岁 Age
样本 Sample	238	9.7	25.2	36.1	20.6	8.4
男性 Male	205	8.3	27.8	35.6	20.0	8.3
一天 2 包以上 2 boxes or over a day	5	40.0	0.0	20.0	20.0	20.0
一天 1~2 包 1 or 2 boxes a day	36	5.6	38.9	33.3	13.9	8.3
一天 1 包左右 about a box a day	101	5.0	25.7	37.6	24.8	6.9
一天半包左右 about half a box a day	63	12.7	27.0	34.9	15.9	9.5
女性 Female	33	18.2	9.1	39.4	24.2	9.1
一天 2 包以上 2 boxes or over a day	0	0	0	0	0	0
一天 1~2 包 1 or 2 boxes a day	5	40.0	0.0	40.0	0.0	20.0
一天 1 包左右 about a box a day	9	0.0	22.2	44.4	33.3	0.0
一天半包左右 about half a box a day	19	21.1	5.3	36.8	26.3	10.5

4-14 不同消费者层的常用品牌/ The Most Frequently Used Brands by Market Segments

4-14-1 时尚流行指标/ Fads Popular Index

	人数 Number	第一品牌及百分比 1st/percent	第二品牌及百分比 2nd/percent	第三品牌及百分比 3rd/percent	第四品牌及百分比 4th/percent
样本 Sample	291	**双喜 Shuangxi(27.8)**	**椰树 Coconut Palm(14.4)**	**红双喜 Double Happiness(12.4)**	**555(7.9)**
平实生活指向 simple living orientation	154	双喜 Shuangxi(32.5)	椰树 Coconut Palm(14.3)	红双喜 Double Happiness(11.7)	555(8.4)
时尚流行指向 fashion orientation	137	双喜 Shuangxi(22.6)	椰树 Coconut Palm(14.6)	红双喜 Double Happiness(13.1)	万宝路 Marlboro(8.0)

4-14-2 广告态度指标/ Advertising attitude Index

	人数 Number	第一品牌及百分比 1st/percent	第二品牌及百分比 2nd/percent	第三品牌及百分比 3rd/percent	第四品牌及百分比 4th/percent
样本 Sample	**289**	**双喜 Shuangxi(27.7)**	**椰树 Coconut Palm(14.9)**	**红双喜 Double Happiness(12.5)**	**555(8.0)**
广告淡漠指向 indifferent orientation	100	双喜 Shuangxi(31.0)	椰树 Coconut Palm(12.0)	555(9.0)	红双喜 Double Happiness(8.0)
中间层 medium	163	双喜 Shuangxi(25.2)	椰树 Coconut Palm(16.6)	红双喜 Double Happiness(14.7)	555(7.4)
信赖广告指向 loyal orientation	26	双喜 Shuangxi(30.8)	椰树 Coconut Palm(15.4) 红双喜 Double Happiness(15.4)	555(7.7)	总督 Viceroy(3.8) 中华 Zhonghua(3.8) 沙龙 Salem(3.8) 羊城 Yangcheng(3.8) 万宝路 Marlboro(3.8) 白沙 Baisha(3.8)

4-14-3 饮食健康指标/ Foods & Drink Quality Index

	人数 Number	第一品牌及百分比 1st/percent	第二品牌及百分比 2nd/percent	第三品牌及百分比 3rd/percent	第四品牌及百分比 4th/percent
样本 Sample	**291**	**双喜 Shuangxi(27.5)**	**椰树 Coconut Palm(14.8)**	**红双喜 Double Happiness(12.7)**	**555(7.9)**
饮食"温饱"指向 "basic" orientation	93	双喜 Shuangxi(24.7)	椰树 Coconut Palm(16.1)	红双喜 Double Happiness(15.1)	555(7.5)
中间层 medium	158	双喜 Shuangxi(27.2)	椰树 Coconut Palm(13.9)	红双喜 Double Happiness(12.0)	555(8.9)
健康营养指向 health & nutrition orientation	40	双喜 Shuangxi(35.0)	羊城 Yangcheng(15.0) 椰树 Coconut Palm(15.0)	红双喜 Double Happiness(10.0)	555(5.0)

4-15 重度消费者的消费者层构成/ The Composition of the Heavy Consumers

4-15-1 时尚流行指标/ Fads Popular Index

	人数 Number	平实生活指向 simple living orientation	时尚流行指向 fashion orientation
样本 Sample	**236**	**53.0**	**47.0**
一天2包以上 2 boxes or over a day	5	60.0	40.0
一天1～2包 1 or 2 boxes a day	40	45.0	55.0
一天1包左右 about a box a day	109	55.0	45.0
一天半包左右 about half a box a day	82	53.7	46.3

4-15-2 广告态度指标/ Advertising Attitude Index

	人数 Number	广告淡漠指向 indifferent orientation	中间层 medium	信赖广告指向 loyal orientation
样本 Sample	**234**	**33.3**	**57.7**	**9.0**
一天2包以上 2 boxes or over a day	5	60.0	40.0	0.0
一天1～2包 1 or 2 boxes a day	41	24.4	61.0	14.6
一天1包左右 about a box a day	108	34.3	57.4	8.3
一天半包左右 about half a box a day	80	35.0	57.5	7.5

4-15-3 饮食健康指标/ Foods & Drink Quality Index

	人数 Number	饮食"温饱"指向 "basic" orientation	中间层 medium	健康营养指向 health & nutrition orientation
样本 Sample	**236**	**30.9**	**55.5**	**13.6**
一天2包以上 2 boxes or over a day	5	60.0	20.0	20.0
一天1～2包 1 or 2 boxes a day	41	24.4	65.9	9.8
一天1包左右 about a box a day	109	32.1	50.5	17.4
一天半包左右 about half a box a day	81	30.9	59.3	9.9

● 重庆 / Chongqing

4-1 是否抽烟的比例/ Proportion of the Smoking in the Last Three Months

	人数 Number	百分比 Percent
是 yes	230	37.1
否 no	390	62.9

n=620

4-2 最常用品牌排名/ Ranking of the Most Used Brands

排名 Brand Ranking	品牌 Brands	人数 Number	百分比 Percent
1	山城 Shancheng	53	23.2
2	宏声 Hongsheng	49	21.5
3	红塔山 Hongtashan	37	16.2
4	红梅 Hongmei	24	10.5
5	红山茶 Hongshancha	14	6.1
6	红山城 Hongshancheng	11	4.8
7	阿诗玛 Ashima	6	2.6
7	龙凤呈祥 LongFeng ChengXiang	6	2.6
8	555	5	2.2
8	红河 Honghe	5	2.2
9	云烟 Yunyan	3	1.3
9	宏馨 Hongxin	3	1.3

n=228

4-3 样本、男性各年龄层、女性各年龄层的常用品牌/ The Most Frequently Used Brands by the Whole Sample, Age and Gender Groups

	人数 Number	第一品牌及百分比 1st/ percent	第二品牌及百分比 2nd/ percent	第三品牌及百分比 3rd/ percent	第四品牌及百分比 4th/ percent
样本 Sample	228	**山城 Shancheng(23.2)**	**宏声 Hongsheng(21.5)**	**红塔山 Hongtashan (16.2)**	**红梅 Hongmei(10.5)**
男性 Male	203	**山城 Shancheng(24.1)**	**宏声 Hongsheng(23.2)**	**红塔山 Hongtashan (16.3)**	**红梅 Hongmei(9.9)**
16~24 岁 Age	24	红梅 Hongmei(25.0)	红山茶 Hongshancha(16.7)	红塔山 Hongtashan (12.5)	山城 Shancheng(8.3) 宏声 Hongsheng(8.3)
25~34 岁 Age	67	宏声 Hongsheng(23.9)	山城 Shancheng(22.4) 红塔山 Hongtashan (22.4)	红山茶 Hongshancha(6.0) 红梅 Hongmei(6.0)	阿诗玛 Ashima(4.5)
35~44 岁 Age	57	宏声 Hongsheng(31.6)	山城 Shancheng(22.8)	红塔山 Hongtashan (12.3)	红梅 Hongmei(7.0) 红山城 Hongshancheng (7.0)
45~54 岁 Age	39	山城 Shancheng(33.3)	宏声 Hongsheng(17.9)	红塔山 Hongtashan (15.4)	红梅 Hongmei(12.8)
55~60 岁 Age	16	山城 Shancheng(37.5)	宏声 Hongsheng(25.0)	红塔山 Hongtashan (12.5)	红梅 Hongmei(6.3) 杪椤 Miaoluo(6.3) 玉溪 Yuxi(6.3) 宝牌 Baopai(6.3)
女性 Female	25	**红塔山 Hongtashan (16.0)** **山城 Shancheng(16.0)** **红梅 Hongmei(16.0)**	**红山茶 Hongshancha (12.0)**	**龙凤呈祥 LongFeng ChengXiang(8.0)** **555(8.0)** **宏声 Hongsheng(8.0)**	**云烟 Yunyan(4.0)** **宏馨 Hongxin(4.0)** **茶花 CameUia(4.0)** **红山城 Hongshancheng(4.0)**
16~24 岁 Age	4	红塔山 Hongtashan (50.0)	555(25.0) 红山茶 Hongshancha(25.0)		
25~34 岁 Age	12	山城 Shancheng(25.0)	红梅 Hongmei(16.7)	555(8.3) 茶花 CameUia(8.3) 宏声 Hongsheng(8.3) 红塔山 Hongtashan (8.3) 云烟 Yunyan(8.3) 龙凤呈祥 LongFeng ChengXiang (8.3) 红山城 Hongshancheng(8.3)	
35~44 岁 Age	4	红山茶 Hongshancha(25.0) 山城 Shancheng(25.0) 宏馨 Hongxin(25.0) 龙凤呈祥 LongFeng ChengXiang (25.0)			
45~54 岁 Age	3	红梅 Hongmei(66.7)	红塔山 Hongtashan (33.3)		
55~60 岁 Age	2	宏声 Hongsheng(50.0) 红山茶 Hongshancha(50.0)			

4-4 理想品牌排名/ Ranking of the Ideal Brands

排名 Brand Ranking	品牌 Brands	人数 Number	百分比 Percent
1	红塔山 Hongtashan	244	39.1
2	山城 Shancheng	64	10.3
3	中华 Zhonghua	49	7.9
4	宏声 Hongsheng	37	5.9
5	555	26	4.2
6	阿诗玛 Ashima	21	3.4
6	红梅 Hongmei	21	3.4
7	玉溪 Yuxi	17	2.7
8	红山城 Hongshancheng	13	2.1
9	娇子 Pride	8	1.3
9	云烟 Yunyan	8	1.3
10	龙凤呈祥 LongFeng ChengXiang	7	1.1
10	红山茶 Hongshancha	7	1.1
10	万宝路 Marlboro	7	1.1

n=624

4-5 样本、男性各年龄层、女性各年龄层最近三个月有无购买的比例/ Purchasing in the Last Three Months by the Whole Sample, Age and Gender Groups

	人数 Number	买过 yes	没买过 no
样本 Sample	624	50.3	49.7
男性 Male	314	68.8	31.2
16~24 岁 Age	64	48.4	51.6
25~34 岁 Age	93	71.0	29.0
35~44 岁 Age	75	81.3	18.7
45~54 岁 Age	54	77.8	22.2
55~60 岁 Age	28	57.1	42.9
女性 Female	310	31.6	68.4
16~24 岁 Age	64	28.1	71.9
25~34 岁 Age	90	42.2	57.8
35~44 岁 Age	73	24.7	75.3
45~54 岁 Age	60	31.7	68.3
55~60 岁 Age	23	21.7	78.3

4-6 样本、男性各年龄层、女性各年龄层最近三个月是否拿香烟送过礼/ To Offer Cigarette as Gift in the Last Three Months by the Whole Sample, Age and Gender Groups

	人数 Number	送过 yes	没送过 no
样本 Sample	619	9.4	90.6
男性 Male	312	9.0	91.0
16~24 岁 Age	64	10.9	89.1
25~34 岁 Age	93	7.5	92.5
35~44 岁 Age	73	15.1	84.9
45~54 岁 Age	54	5.6	94.4
55~60 岁 Age	28	0.0	100.0
女性 Female	307	9.8	90.2
16~24 岁 Age	64	7.8	92.2
25~34 岁 Age	88	19.3	80.7
35~44 岁 Age	73	5.5	94.5
45~54 岁 Age	59	6.8	93.2
55~60 岁 Age	23	0.0	100.0

4-7 样本、男性各年龄层、女性各年龄层是否抽烟的比例/ Smoking or Not by the Whole Sample, Age and Gender Groups

	人数 Number	是 yes	否 no
样本 Sample	**620**	**37.1**	**62.9**
男性 Male	**314**	**65.0**	**35.0**
16~24 岁 Age	64	37.5	62.5
25~34 岁 Age	93	72.0	28.0
35~44 岁 Age	75	77.3	22.7
45~54 岁 Age	54	72.2	27.8
55~60 岁 Age	28	57.1	42.9
女性 Female	**306**	**8.5**	**91.5**
16~24 岁 Age	63	6.3	93.7
25~34 岁 Age	90	14.4	85.6
35~44 岁 Age	71	5.6	94.4
45~54 岁 Age	60	5.0	95.0
55~60 岁 Age	22	9.1	90.9

4-8 样本、男性各年龄层、女性各年龄层的品牌习惯/ Brand Habit in Consuming Cigarette by the Whole Sample, Age and Gender Groups

	人数 Number	基本固定用一个牌子 used in only one brand	比较固定地用两个或三个牌子 used in two or three brands	基本上不太固定牌子 no brand preference
样本 Sample	**227**	**53.7**	**38.3**	**7.9**
男性 Male	**202**	**55.9**	**37.6**	**6.4**
16~24 岁 Age	24	58.3	37.5	4.2
25~34 岁 Age	67	49.3	40.3	10.4
35~44 岁 Age	56	60.7	37.5	1.8
45~54 岁 Age	39	51.3	38.5	10.3
55~60 岁 Age	16	75.0	25.0	0.0
女性 Female	**25**	**36.0**	**44.0**	**20.0**
16~24 岁 Age	4	50.0	50.0	0.0
25~34 岁 Age	12	41.7	25.0	33.3
35~44 岁 Age	4	25.0	75.0	0.0
45~54 岁 Age	3	0.0	100.0	0.0
55~60 岁 Age	2	50.0	0.0	50.0

4-9 选择该类商品的考虑因素/ Ranking of the Considerations in Purchasing

注：本题为多选题，合计百分比可能超过 100%（Multiple answers）

排名 Ranking	考虑因素 considerations	人次 Person-time	百分比 Percent
1	价格适中 reasonable price	125	54.8
2	口味好 pleasant taste	107	46.9
3	只是由于习惯 out of habit	59	25.9
4	有名的牌子 famous brand	50	21.9
5	购买方便 easy to buy	36	15.8
6	生产日期 date of producing	9	3.9
7	朋友推荐 introduction of friends	7	3.1
8	广告影响 influence of advertising	3	1.3
9	有优惠条件 with preferential terms	2	0.9
9	其它 others	2	0.9
10	售货员介绍 introduced by the shop assistants	1	0.4
10	别人送的 given by other people	1	0.4
10	包装吸引人 appealing package	1	0.4

n=228

4-10 样本、男性各年龄层、女性各年龄层抽烟的口味偏好/ Taste of the Consumed Cigarette by the Whole Sample, Age and Gender Groups

	人数 Number	混合型 combination type	烤烟型 flue-cured type	雪茄口味 cigar	其它 others
样本 Sample	226	13.3	86.3	0.4	0.0
男性 Male	202	12.9	87.1	0.0	0.0
16~24 岁 Age	24	16.7	83.3	0.0	0.0
25~34 岁 Age	67	10.4	89.6	0.0	0.0
35~44 岁 Age	57	14.0	86.0	0.0	0.0
45~54 岁 Age	38	15.8	84.2	0.0	0.0
55~60 岁 Age	16	6.3	93.8	0.0	0.0
女性 Female	24	16.7	79.2	4.2	0.0
16~24 岁 Age	4	0.0	100.0	0.0	0.0
25~34 岁 Age	12	25.0	66.7	8.3	0.0
35~44 岁 Age	3	33.3	66.7	0.0	0.0
45~54 岁 Age	3	0.0	100.0	0.0	0.0
55~60 岁 Age	2	0.0	100.0	0.0	0.0

4-11 样本、男性各年龄层、女性各年龄层一天抽烟的数量/ Number of Smoking a Day by the Whole Sample, Age and Gender Groups

	人数 Number	2 包以上 2 boxes or over	1~2 包 1 or 2 boxes	1 包左右 about a box	半包左右 about half a box	一天两三支或以下 2 or 3 cigarettes or below	没有抽 never
样本 Sample	228	2.6	11.4	41.2	32.9	11.0	0.9
男性 Male	203	3.0	11.8	43.8	32.0	8.9	0.5
16~24 岁 Age	24	0.0	0.0	33.3	33.3	33.3	0.0
25~34 岁 Age	67	3.0	13.4	38.8	35.8	9.0	0.0
35~44 岁 Age	57	3.5	12.3	50.9	31.6	0.0	1.8
45~54 岁 Age	39	5.1	12.8	46.2	33.3	2.6	0.0
55~60 岁 Age	16	0.0	18.8	50.0	12.5	18.8	0.0
女性 Female	25	0.0	8.0	20.0	40.0	28.0	4.0
16~24 岁 Age	4	0.0	0.0	0.0	25.0	50.0	25.0
25~34 岁 Age	12	0.0	0.0	25.0	50.0	25.0	0.0
35~44 岁 Age	4	0.0	25.0	25.0	25.0	25.0	0.0
45~54 岁 Age	3	0.0	33.3	33.3	0.0	33.3	0.0
55~60 岁 Age	2	0.0	0.0	0.0	100.0	0.0	0.0

4-12 样本、男性各年龄层、女性各年龄层抽烟的包装形式/ Types of Package of the Consumed Cigarette by the Whole Sample, Age and Gender Groups

	人数 Number	软盒装 soft box	硬盒装 hard box
样本 Sample	228	35.1	64.9
男性 Male	203	34.5	65.5
16~24 岁 Age	24	25.0	75.0
25~34 岁 Age	67	32.8	67.2
35~44 岁 Age	57	24.6	75.4
45~54 岁 Age	39	46.2	53.8
55~60 岁 Age	16	62.5	37.5
女性 Female	25	40.0	60.0
16~24 岁 Age	4	25.0	75.0
25~34 岁 Age	12	33.3	66.7
35~44 岁 Age	4	50.0	50.0
45~54 岁 Age	3	66.7	33.3
55~60 岁 Age	2	50.0	50.0

4-13 重度消费者人口分布/ Demographics of the Heavy Consumers

	人数 Number	16-24 岁 Age	25-34 岁 Age	35-44 岁 Age	45-54 岁 Age	55-60 岁 Age
样本 Sample	201	8.5	34.8	29.4	19.9	7.5
男性 Male	184	8.7	33.2	30.4	20.7	7.1
一天 2 包以上 2 boxes or over a day	6	0.0	33.3	33.3	33.3	0.0
一天 1～2 包 1 or 2 boxes a day	24	0.0	37.5	29.2	20.8	12.5
一天 1 包左右 about a box a day	89	9.0	29.2	32.6	20.2	9.0
一天半包左右 about half a box a day	65	12.3	36.9	27.7	20.0	3.1
女性 Female	17	5.9	52.9	17.6	11.8	11.8
一天 2 包以上 2 boxes or over a day	0	0	0	0	0	0
一天 1～2 包 1 or 2 boxes a day	2	0.0	0.0	50.0	50.0	0.0
一天 1 包左右 about a box a day	5	0.0	60.0	20.0	20.0	0.0
一天半包左右 about half a box a day	10	10.0	60.0	10.0	0.0	20.0

4-14 不同消费者层的常用品牌/ The Most Frequently Used Brands by Market Segments

4-14-1 时尚流行指标/ Fads Popular Index

	人数 Number	第一品牌及百分比 1st/percent	第二品牌及百分比 2nd/percent	第三品牌及百分比 3rd/percent	第四品牌及百分比 4th/percent	第五品牌及百分比 5th/percent
样本 Sample	227	**山城 Shancheng(23.3)**	**宏声 Hongsheng(21.6)**	**红塔山 Hongtashan (15.9)**	**红梅 Hongmei(10.6)**	**红山茶 Hongshancha (6.2)**
平实生活指向 simple living orientation	146	山城 Shancheng(30.1)	宏声 Hongsheng(24.7)	红塔山 Hongtashan (13.7)	红梅 Hongmei(9.6)	红山城 Hongshancheng (4.8)
时尚流行指向 fashion orientation	81	红塔山 Hongtashan (19.8)	宏声 Hongsheng(16.0)	红梅 Hongmei(12.3) 红山茶 Hongshancha (12.3)	山城 Shancheng(11.1)	红山城 Hongshancheng (4.9) 龙凤呈祥 LongFeng ChengXiang (4.9) 555(4.9)

4-14-2 广告态度指标/ Advertising Attitude Index

	人数 Number	第一品牌及百分比 1st/percent	第二品牌及百分比 2nd/percent	第三品牌及百分比 3rd/percent	第四品牌及百分比 4th/percent	第五品牌及百分比 5th/percent
样本 Sample	226	**山城 Shancheng(23.5)**	**宏声 Hongsheng(21.2)**	**红塔山 Hongtashan (15.9)**	**红梅 Hongmei(10.6)**	**红山茶 Hongshancha (6.2)**
广告淡漠指向 indifferent orientation	79	宏声 Hongsheng(29.1) 山城 Shancheng(29.1)	红梅 Hongmei(8.9)	红塔山 Hongtashan (6.3) 红山茶 Hongshancha(6.3)	龙凤呈祥 LongFeng ChengXiang (3.8) 阿诗玛 Ashima(3.8)	宏馨 Hongxin(2.5) 红山城 Hongshancheng (2.5)
中间层 medium	124	山城 Shancheng(21.0)	红塔山 Hongtashan (19.4)	宏声 Hongsheng(16.1)	红梅 Hongmei(12.9)	红山城 Hongshancheng (7.3) 红山茶 Hongshancha(7.3)
信赖广告指向 loyal orientation	23	红塔山 Hongtashan (30.4)	宏声 Hongsheng(21.7)	山城 Shancheng(17.4)	阿诗玛 Ashima(8.7)	555(4.3) 大前门 Daqianmen(4.3) 红梅 Hongmei(4.3) 红岩 Hongyan(4.3) 龙凤呈祥 LongFeng ChengXiang (4.3)

4-14-3 饮食健康指标/ Foods & Drink Quality Index

	人数 Number	第一品牌及百分比 1st/percent	第二品牌及百分比 2nd/percent	第三品牌及百分比 3rd/percent	第四品牌及百分比 4th/percent	第五品牌及百分比 5th/percent
样本 Sample	226	**山城 Shancheng(23.5)**	**宏声 Hongsheng(21.7)**	**红塔山 Hongtashan (15.9)**	**红梅 Hongmei(10.6)**	**红山茶 Hongshancha (6.2)**
饮食"温饱"指向 "basic" orientation	106	山城 Shancheng(27.4)	宏声 Hongsheng(25.5)	红塔山 Hongtashan (14.2)	红梅 Hongmei(9.4)	红山茶 Hongshancha(4.7)
中间层 medium	89	山城 Shancheng(20.2)	红塔山 Hongtashan (18.0)	宏声 Hongsheng(16.9)	红梅 Hongmei(10.1)	红山城 Hongshancheng (6.7)
健康营养指向 health & nutrition orientation	31	宏声 Hongsheng(22.6)	山城 Shancheng(19.4)	红梅 Hongmei(16.1) 红塔山 Hongtashan (16.1)	红山茶 Hongshancha (12.9)	555(3.2) 宏馨 Hongxin(3.2) 龙凤呈祥 LongFeng ChengXiang (3.2) 红山城 Hongshancheng (3.2)

4-15 重度消费者的消费者层构成/ The Composition of the Heavy Consumers

4-15-1 时尚流行指标/ Fads Popular Index

	人数 Number	平实生活指向 simple living orientation	时尚流行指向 fashion orientation
样本 Sample	200	**66.5**	**33.5**
一天 2 包以上 2 boxes or over a day	6	83.3	16.7
一天 1～2 包 1 or 2 boxes a day	26	76.9	23.1
一天 1 包左右 about a box a day	93	68.8	31.2
一天半包左右 about half a box a day	75	58.7	41.3

4-15-2 广告态度指标/ Advertising Attitude Index

	人数 Number	广告淡漠指向 indifferent orientation	中间层 medium	信赖广告指向 loyal orientation
样本 Sample	199	**35.2**	**53.8**	**11.1**
一天 2 包以上 2 boxes or over a day	6	83.3	16.7	0.0
一天 1～2 包 1 or 2 boxes a day	26	50.0	34.6	15.4
一天 1 包左右 about a box a day	93	34.4	54.3	10.8
一天半包左右 about half a box a day	74	27.0	62.2	10.8

4-15-3 饮食健康指标/ Foods & Drink Quality Index

	人数 Number	饮食"温饱"指向 "basic" orientation	中间层 medium	健康营养指向 health & nutrition orientation
样本 Sample	199	**47.2**	**39.2**	**13.6**
一天 2 包以上 2 boxes or over a day	6	50.0	33.3	16.7
一天 1～2 包 1 or 2 boxes a day	26	69.2	23.1	7.7
一天 1 包左右 about a box a day	93	43.0	40.9	16.1
一天半包左右 half a box a day	74	44.6	43.2	12.2

● 武汉 / Wuhan

4-1 是否抽烟的比例/ Proportion of the Smoking in the Last Three Months

	人数 Number	百分比 Percent
是 yes	203	31.8
否 no	435	68.2

n=638

4-2 最常用品牌排名/ Ranking of the Most Used Brands

排名 Brand Ranking	品牌 Brands	人数 Number	百分比 Percent
1	红金龙 Hongjinlong	57	28.1
2	长城 Great Wall	36	17.7
3	阿诗玛 Ashima	24	11.8
4	红塔山 Hongtashan	15	7.4
5	555	11	5.4
5	红河 Honghe	11	5.4
6	红双喜 Double Happiness	7	3.4
7	云烟 Yunyan	6	3.0
8	白金龙 Baijinlong	5	2.5
8	红梅 Hongmei	5	2.5

n=203

4-3 样本、男性各年龄层、女性各年龄层的常用品牌/ The Most Frequently Used Brands by the Whole Sample, Age and Gender Groups

	人数 Number	第一品牌及百分比 1st/ percent	第二品牌及百分比 2nd/ percent	第三品牌及百分比 3rd/ percent
样本 Sample	203	**红金龙 Hongjinlong(28.1)**	**长城 Great Wall(17.7)**	**阿诗玛 Ashima(11.8)**
男性 Male	189	**红金龙 Hongjinlong(27.5)**	**长城 Great Wall(18.0)**	**阿诗玛 Ashima(11.1)**
16~24 岁 Age	26	阿诗玛 Ashima(19.2) 红塔山 Hongtashan (19.2)	红金龙 Hongjinlong(15.4)	红梅 Hongmei(11.5)
25~34 岁 Age	57	红金龙 Hongjinlong(29.8)	阿诗玛 Ashima(15.8)	长城 Great Wall(10.5)
35~44 岁 Age	57	红金龙 Hongjinlong(28.1)	长城 Great Wall(26.3)	555(7.0) 阿诗玛 Ashima(7.0) 红塔山 Hongtashan (7.0)
45~54 岁 Age	35	红金龙 Hongjinlong(34.3)	长城 Great Wall(20.0)	阿诗玛 Ashima(8.6)
55~60 岁 Age	14	长城 Great Wall(42.9)	红金龙 Hongjinlong(21.4)	红双喜 Double Happiness(14.3)
女性 Female	14	**红金龙 Hongjinlong(35.7)**	**阿诗玛 Ashima(21.4)**	**长城 Great Wall(14.3)** **红双喜 Double Happiness(14.3)**
16~24 岁 Age	1	红金龙 Hongjinlong(100.0)		
25~34 岁 Age	4	红金龙 Hongjinlong(50.0)	555(25.0) 阿诗玛 Ashima(25.0)	
35~44 岁 Age	3	阿诗玛 Ashima(66.7)	红双喜 Double Happiness(33.3)	
45~54 岁 Age	5	长城 Great Wall(40.0)	红金龙 Hongjinlong(20.0) 红双喜 Double Happiness(20.0) 永光 Yongguang(20.0)	
55~60 岁 Age	1	红金龙 Hongjinlong(100.0)		

4-4 理想品牌排名/ Ranking of the Ideal Brands

排名 Brand Ranking	品牌 Brands	人数 Number	百分比 Percent
1	红塔山 Hongtashan	95	14.8
2	红金龙 Hongjinlong	94	14.6
3	阿诗玛 Ashima	45	7.0
4	中华 Zhonghua	40	6.2
5	555	29	4.5
6	玉溪 Yuxi	25	3.9
6	长城 Great Wall	25	3.9
7	黄鹤楼 Huanghelou	24	3.7

n=642

4-5 样本、男性各年龄层、女性各年龄层最近三个月有无购买的比例/ Purchasing in the Last Three Months by the Whole Sample, Age and Gender Groups

	人数 Number	买过 yes	没买过 no
样本 Sample	641	46.3	53.7
男性 Male	311	66.9	33.1
16~24 岁 Age	65	44.6	55.4
25~34 岁 Age	89	71.9	28.1
35~44 岁 Age	80	81.3	18.8
45~54 岁 Age	52	69.2	30.8
55~60 岁 Age	25	56.0	44.0
女性 Female	330	27.0	73.0
16~24 岁 Age	69	13.0	87.0
25~34 岁 Age	96	32.3	67.7
35~44 岁 Age	78	28.2	71.8
45~54 岁 Age	61	37.7	62.3
55~60 岁 Age	26	15.4	84.6

4-6 样本、男性各年龄层、女性各年龄层最近三个月是否拿香烟送过礼/ To Offer Cigarette as Gift in the Last Three Months by the Whole Sample, Age and Gender Groups

	人数 Number	送过 yes	没送过 no
样本 Sample	641	15.8	84.2
男性 Male	311	16.1	83.9
16~24 岁 Age	65	12.3	87.7
25~34 岁 Age	89	22.5	77.5
35~44 岁 Age	80	13.8	86.3
45~54 岁 Age	52	9.6	90.4
55~60 岁 Age	25	24.0	76.0
女性 Female	330	15.5	84.5
16~24 岁 Age	69	10.1	89.9
25~34 岁 Age	96	20.8	79.2
35~44 岁 Age	78	14.1	85.9
45~54 岁 Age	61	18.0	82.0
55~60 岁 Age	26	7.7	92.3

4-7 样本、男性各年龄层、女性各年龄层是否抽烟的比例/ Smoking or Not by the Whole Sample, Age and Gender Groups

	人数 Number	是 yes	否 no
样本 Sample	638	31.8	68.2
男性 Male	310	61.0	39.0
16~24 岁 Age	65	40.0	60.0
25~34 岁 Age	89	64.0	36.0
35~44 岁 Age	79	72.2	27.8
45~54 岁 Age	52	67.3	32.7
55~60 岁 Age	25	56.0	44.0
女性 Female	328	4.3	95.7
16~24 岁 Age	69	1.4	98.6
25~34 岁 Age	96	4.2	95.8
35~44 岁 Age	77	3.9	96.1
45~54 岁 Age	60	8.3	91.7
55~60 岁 Age	26	3.8	96.2

4-8 样本、男性各年龄层、女性各年龄层的品牌习惯/ Brand Habit in Consuming Cigarette by the Whole Sample, Age and Gender Groups

	人数 Number	基本固定用一个牌子 used in only one brand	比较固定地用两个或三个牌子 used in two or three brands	基本上不太固定牌子 no brand preference
样本 Sample	203	54.7	35.5	9.9
男性 Male	189	55.0	35.4	9.5
16~24 岁 Age	26	42.3	42.3	15.4
25~34 岁 Age	57	47.4	40.4	12.3
35~44 岁 Age	57	54.4	35.1	10.5
45~54 岁 Age	35	68.6	28.6	2.9
55~60 岁 Age	14	78.6	21.4	0.0
女性 Female	14	50.0	35.7	14.3
16~24 岁 Age	1	100.0	0.0	0.0
25~34 岁 Age	4	75.0	25.0	0.0
35~44 岁 Age	3	0.0	100.0	0.0
45~54 岁 Age	5	60.0	20.0	20.0
55~60 岁 Age	1	0.0	0.0	100.0

4-9 选择该类商品的考虑因素/ Ranking of the Considerations in Purchasing

注：本题为多选题，合计百分比超过 100%(Multiple answers）

排名 Ranking	考虑因素 considerations	人次 Person-time	百分比 Percent
1	价格适中 reasonable price	122	60.1
2	口味好 pleasant taste	111	54.7
3	只是由于习惯 out of habit	56	27.6
4	有名的牌子 famous brand	55	27.1
5	购买方便 easy to buy	36	17.7
6	生产日期 date of producing	9	4.4
7	包装吸引人 appealing package	8	3.9
8	有优惠条件 with preferential terms	7	3.4
9	别人送的 given by other people	6	3.0
10	广告影响 influence of advertising	4	2.0
10	朋友推荐 introduction of friends	4	2.0
11	其它 others	2	1.0
12	售货员介绍 introduced by the shop assistants	1	0.5

n=203

4-10 样本、男性各年龄层、女性各年龄层抽烟的口味偏好/ Taste of the Consumed Cigarette by the Whole Sample, Age and Gender Groups

	人数 Number	混合型 combination type	烤烟型 flue-cured type	雪茄口味 cigar	其它 others
样本 Sample	203	16.7	82.3	0.0	1.0
男性 Male	189	16.9	82.0	0.0	1.1
16~24 岁 Age	26	0.0	92.3	0.0	7.7
25~34 岁 Age	57	15.8	84.2	0.0	0.0
35~44 岁 Age	57	22.8	77.2	0.0	0.0
45~54 岁 Age	35	14.3	85.7	0.0	0.0
55~60 岁 Age	14	35.7	64.3	0.0	0.0
女性 Female	14	14.3	85.7	0.0	0.0
16~24 岁 Age	1	0.0	100.0	0.0	0.0
25~34 岁 Age	4	0.0	100.0	0.0	0.0
35~44 岁 Age	3	33.3	66.7	0.0	0.0
45~54 岁 Age	5	20.0	80.0	0.0	0.0
55~60 岁 Age	1	0.0	100.0	0.0	0.0

4-11 样本、男性各年龄层、女性各年龄层一天抽烟的数量/ Number of Smoking a Day by the Whole Sample, Age and Gender Groups

	人数 Number	2 包以上 2 boxes or over	1~2 包 1 or 2 boxes	1 包左右 about a box	半包左右 about half a box	一天两三支或以下 2 or 3 cigarettes or below	没有抽 never
样本 Sample	203	2.5	10.8	41.9	30.0	14.3	0.5
男性 Male	189	2.6	11.6	42.3	30.2	12.7	0.5
16~24 岁 Age	26	0.0	0.0	19.2	46.2	30.8	3.8
25~34 岁 Age	57	0.0	10.5	36.8	36.8	15.8	0.0
35~44 岁 Age	57	0.0	12.3	57.9	28.1	1.8	0.0
45~54 岁 Age	35	11.4	14.3	45.7	14.3	14.3	0.0
55~60 岁 Age	14	7.1	28.6	35.7	21.4	7.1	0.0
女性 Female	14	0.0	0.0	35.7	28.6	35.7	0.0
16~24 岁 Age	1	0.0	0.0	0.0	100.0	0.0	0.0
25~34 岁 Age	4	0.0	0.0	75.0	0.0	25.0	0.0
35~44 岁 Age	3	0.0	0.0	33.3	0.0	66.7	0.0
45~54 岁 Age	5	0.0	0.0	20.0	40.0	40.0	0.0
55~60 岁 Age	1	0.0	0.0	0.0	100.0	0.0	0.0

4-12 样本、男性各年龄层、女性各年龄层抽烟的包装形式/ Types of Package of the Consumed Cigarette by the Whole Sample, Age and Gender Groups

	人数 Number	软盒装 soft box	硬盒装 hard box
样本 Sample	203	20.2	79.8
男性 Male	189	20.6	79.4
16~24 岁 Age	26	15.4	84.6
25~34 岁 Age	57	8.8	91.2
35~44 岁 Age	57	24.6	75.4
45~54 岁 Age	35	31.4	68.6
55~60 岁 Age	14	35.7	64.3
女性 Female	14	14.3	85.7
16~24 岁 Age	1	0.0	100.0
25~34 岁 Age	4	0.0	100.0
35~44 岁 Age	3	33.3	66.7
45~54 岁 Age	5	20.0	80.0
55~60 岁 Age	1	0.0	100.0

4-13 重度消费者人口分布/ Demographics of the Heavy Consumers

	人数 Number	16-24 岁 Age	25-34 岁 Age	35-44 岁 Age	45-54 岁 Age	55-60 岁 Age
样本 Sample	173	10.4	29.5	32.9	19.1	8.1
男性 Male	164	10.4	29.3	34.1	18.3	7.9
一天 2 包以上 2 boxes or over a day	5	0.0	0.0	0.0	80.0	20.0
一天 1～2 包 1 or 2 boxes a day	22	0.0	27.3	31.8	22.7	18.2
一天 1 包左右 about a box a day	80	6.3	26.3	41.3	20.0	6.3
一天半包左右 about half a box a day	57	21.1	36.8	28.1	8.8	5.3
女性 Female	9	11.1	33.3	11.1	33.3	11.1
一天 2 包以上 2 boxes or over a day	0	0.0	0.0	0.0	0.0	0.0
一天 1～2 包 1 or 2 boxes a day	0	0.0	0.0	0.0	0.0	0.0
一天 1 包左右 about a box a day	5	0.0	60.0	20.0	20.0	0.0
一天半包左右 about half a box a day	4	25.0	0.0	0.0	50.0	25.0

4-14 不同消费者层的常用品牌/ The Most Frequently Used Brands by Market Segments

4-14-1 时尚流行指标/ Fads Popular Index

	人数 Number	第一品牌及百分比 1st/percent	第二品牌及百分比 2nd/percent	第三品牌及百分比 3rd/percent	第四品牌及百分比 4th/percent
样本 Sample	199	**红金龙 Hongjinlong(28.1)**	**长城 Great Wall(17.1)**	**阿诗玛 Ashima(11.6)**	**红塔山 Hongtashan (7.5)**
平实生活指向 simple living orientation	107	红金龙 Hongjinlong(27.1)	长城 Great Wall(24.3)	阿诗玛 Ashima(9.3)	红河 Honghe(7.5)
时尚流行指向 fashion orientation	92	红金龙 Hongjinlong(29.3)	阿诗玛 Ashima(14.1)	红塔山 Hongtashan (9.8)	长城 Great Wall(8.7)

4-14-2 广告态度指标/ Advertising Attitude Index

	人数 Number	第一品牌及百分比 1st/percent	第二品牌及百分比 2nd/percent	第三品牌及百分比 3rd/percent	第四品牌及百分比 4th/percent
样本 Sample	201	**红金龙 Hongjinlong(27.9)**	**长城 Great Wall(17.4)**	**阿诗玛 Ashima(11.9)**	**红塔山 Hongtashan (7.5)**
广告淡漠指向 indifferent orientation	69	红金龙 Hongjinlong(26.1)	长城 Great Wall(21.7)	阿诗玛 Ashima(11.6)	红塔山 Hongtashan (7.2)
中间层 medium	114	红金龙 Hongjinlong(27.2)	长城 Great Wall(14.9)	阿诗玛 Ashima(12.3)	555(7.9)
信赖广告指向 loyal orientation	18	红金龙 Hongjinlong(38.9)	长城 Great Wall(16.7)	阿诗玛 Ashima(11.1) 红塔山 Hongtashan (11.1)	白金龙 Baijinlong(5.6) 红河 Honghe(5.6) 柔和七星 Mild Seven(5.6) 黄鹤楼 Huanghelou(5.6)

4-14-3 饮食健康指标/ Foods & Drink Quality Index

	人数 Number	第一品牌及百分比 1st/percent	第二品牌及百分比 2nd/percent	第三品牌及百分比 3rd/percent	第四品牌及百分比 4th/percent
样本 Sample	200	红金龙 Hongjinlong(27.5)	长城 Great Wall(17.5)	阿诗玛 Ashima(12.0)	红塔山 Hongtashan (7.5)
饮食"温饱"指向 "basic" orientation	78	红金龙 Hongjinlong(29.5)	长城 Great Wall(17.9)	阿诗玛 Ashima(10.3)	红河 Honghe(7.7) 红塔山 Hongtashan (7.7)
中间层 medium	91	红金龙 Hongjinlong(26.4)	长城 Great Wall(15.4)	阿诗玛 Ashima(14.3)	555(8.8)
健康营养指向 health & nutrition orientation	31	红金龙 Hongjinlong(25.8)	长城 Great Wall(22.6)	阿诗玛 Ashima(9.7) 红塔山 Hongtashan (9.7)	红梅 Hongmei(6.5) 红双喜 Double Happiness(6.5)

4-15 重度消费者的消费者层构成/ The Composition of the Heavy Consumers

4-15-1 时尚流行指标/ Fads Popular Index

	人数 Number	平实生活指向 simple living orientation	时尚流行指向 fashion orientation
样本 Sample	169	52.7	47.3
一天 2 包以上 2 boxes or over a day	5	60.0	40.0
一天 1～2 包 1 or 2 boxes a day	21	76.2	23.8
一天 1 包左右 about a box a day	84	51.2	48.8
一天半包左右 about half a box a day	59	45.8	54.2

4-15-2 广告态度指标/ Advertising Attitude Index

	人数 Number	广告淡漠指向 indifferent orientation	中间层 medium	信赖广告指向 loyal orientation
样本 Sample	171	35.1	55.6	9.4
一天 2 包以上 2 boxes or over a day	5	60.0	40.0	0.0
一天 1～2 包 1 or 2 boxes a day	21	33.3	66.7	0.0
一天 1 包左右 about a box a day	85	37.6	49.4	12.9
一天半包左右 about half a box a day	60	30.0	61.7	8.3

4-15-3 饮食健康指标/ Foods & Drink Quality Index

	人数 Number	饮食"温饱"指向 "basic" orientation	中间层 medium	健康营养指向 health & nutrition orientation
样本 Sample	170	39.4	42.4	18.2
一天 2 包以上 2 boxes or over a day	5	40.0	40.0	20.0
一天 1～2 包 1 or 2 boxes a day	21	28.6	57.1	14.3
一天 1 包左右 about a box a day	84	39.3	39.3	21.4
一天半包左右 half a box a day	60	43.3	41.7	15.0

● 西安 / Xi'an

4-1 是否抽烟的比例/ Proportion of the Smoking in the Last Three Months

	人数 Number	百分比 Percent
是 yes	233	38.9
否 no	366	61.1

n=599

4-2 最常用品牌排名/ Ranking of the Most Used Brands

排名 Brand Ranking	品牌 Brands	人数 Number	百分比 Percent
1	白沙 Baisha	82	35.3
2	长沙 Changsha	22	9.5
3	金丝猴 Jinsihou	16	6.9
4	石林 Stone Forest	15	6.5
5	希尔顿 Hilton	14	6.0
6	555	13	5.6
7	红山茶 Hongshancha	11	4.7
8	猴王 Houwang	8	3.4
9	好猫 Haomao	7	3.0
10	红河 Honghe	6	2.6

n=232

4-3 样本、男性各年龄层、女性各年龄层的常用品牌/ The Most Frequently Used Brands by the Whole Sample, Age and Gender Groups

	人数 Number	第一品牌及百分比 1st/ percent	第二品牌及百分比 2nd/ percent	第三品牌及百分比 3rd/ percent
样本 Sample	232	**白沙 Baisha(35.3)**	**长沙 Changsha(9.5)**	**金丝猴 Jinsihou(6.9)**
男性 Male	202	**白沙 Baisha(34.7)**	**长沙 Changsha(8.9)**	**金丝猴 Jinsihou(6.9)** **石林 Stone Forest(6.9)**
16~24 岁 Age	27	白沙 Baisha(44.4)	555(11.1)	长沙 Changsha(7.4) 猴王 Houwang(7.4)
25~34 岁 Age	69	白沙 Baisha(31.9)	石林 Stone Forest(14.5)	希尔顿 Hilton(10.1)
35~44 岁 Age	59	白沙 Baisha(28.8)	长沙 Changsha(16.9)	555(8.5)
45~54 岁 Age	34	白沙 Baisha(44.1)	金丝猴 Jinsihou(8.8)	长沙 Changsha(5.9) 红山茶 Hongshancha(5.9) 祝尔康 Zek(5.9) 沙河 Shahe(5.9) 石林 Stone Forest(5.9)
55~60 岁 Age	13	白沙 Baisha(30.8) 金丝猴 Jinsihou(30.8)	金白沙 Jinbaisha(15.4)	红塔山 Hongtashan (7.7) 祝尔康 Zek(7.7) 巴山雪茄 Ba Shan Xue Jia(7.7)
女性 Female	30	**白沙 Baisha(40.0)**	**长沙 Changsha(13.3)**	**红山茶 Hongshancha(10.0)**
16~24 岁 Age	2	555(50.0) 希尔顿 Hilton(50.0)		
25~34 岁 Age	17	白沙 Baisha(47.1)	好猫 Haomao(11.8) 红山茶 Hongshancha(11.8) 长沙 Changsha(11.8)	555(5.9) 希尔顿 Hilton(5.9) 总督 Viceroy(5.9)
35~44 岁 Age	7	白沙 Baisha(28.6)	红山茶 Hongshancha(14.3) 金丝猴 Jinsihou(14.3) 石林 Stone Forest(14.3) 红云 Hongyun(14.3) 长沙 Changsha(14.3)	
45~54 岁 Age	3	白沙 Baisha(66.7)	长沙 Changsha(33.3)	
55~60 岁 Age	1	金丝猴 Jinsihou(100.0)		

4-4 理想品牌排名/ Ranking of the Ideal Brands

排名 Brand Ranking	品牌 Brands	人数 Number	百分比 Percent
1	白沙 Baisha	142	23.6
2	555	55	9.2
3	中华 Zhonghua	44	7.3
4	好猫 Haomao	38	6.3
4	红塔山 Hongtashan	38	6.3
5	长沙 Changsha	20	3.3
6	金白沙 Jinbaisha	18	3.0
7	金丝猴 Jinsihou	17	2.8
8	希尔顿 Hilton	16	2.7
8	猴王 Houwang	16	2.7
9	石林 Stone Forest	14	2.3
10	云烟 Yunyan	13	2.2
10	红河 Honghe	13	2.2
10	红山茶 Hongshancha	13	2.2

n=601

4-5 样本、男性各年龄层、女性各年龄层最近三个月有无购买的比例/ Purchasing in the Last Three Months by the Whole Sample, Age and Gender Groups

	人数 Number	买过 yes	没买过 no
样本 Sample	600	51.7	48.3
男性 Male	302	66.9	33.1
16~24 岁 Age	64	42.2	57.8
25~34 岁 Age	91	75.8	24.2
35~44 岁 Age	77	76.6	23.4
45~54 岁 Age	46	73.9	26.1
55~60 岁 Age	24	54.2	45.8
女性 Female	298	36.2	63.8
16~24 岁 Age	61	34.4	65.6
25~34 岁 Age	90	44.4	55.6
35~44 岁 Age	73	34.2	65.8
45~54 岁 Age	49	28.6	71.4
55~60 岁 Age	25	32.0	68.0

4-6 样本、男性各年龄层、女性各年龄层最近三个月是否拿香烟送过礼/ To Offer Cigarette as Gift in the Last Three Months by the Whole Sample, Age and Gender Groups

	人数 Number	送过 yes	没送过 no
样本 Sample	599	13.2	86.8
男性 Male	301	14.3	85.7
16~24 岁 Age	64	12.5	87.5
25~34 岁 Age	90	17.8	82.2
35~44 岁 Age	77	16.9	83.1
45~54 岁 Age	46	8.7	91.3
55~60 岁 Age	24	8.3	91.7
女性 Female	298	12.1	87.9
16~24 岁 Age	61	11.5	88.5
25~34 岁 Age	90	16.7	83.3
35~44 岁 Age	73	8.2	91.8
45~54 岁 Age	49	10.2	89.8
55~60 岁 Age	25	12.0	88.0

4-7 样本、男性各年龄层、女性各年龄层是否抽烟的比例/ Smoking or Not by the Whole Sample, Age and Gender Groups

	人数 Number	是 yes	否 no
样本 Sample	599	38.9	61.1
男性 Male	301	67.1	32.9
16~24 岁 Age	64	42.2	57.8
25~34 岁 Age	91	75.8	24.2
35~44 岁 Age	77	76.6	23.4
45~54 岁 Age	45	75.6	24.4
55~60 岁 Age	24	54.2	45.8
女性 Female	298	10.4	89.6
16~24 岁 Age	61	3.3	96.7
25~34 岁 Age	90	20.0	80.0
35~44 岁 Age	73	9.6	90.4
45~54 岁 Age	49	6.1	93.9
55~60 岁 Age	25	4.0	96.0

4-8 样本、男性各年龄层、女性各年龄层的品牌习惯/ Brand Habit in Consuming Cigarette by the Whole Sample, Age and Gender Groups

	人数 Number	基本固定用一个牌子 used in only one brand	比较固定地用两个或三个牌子 used in two or three brands	基本上不太固定牌子 no brand preference
样本 Sample	**232**	**58.6**	**35.8**	**5.6**
男性 Male	**202**	**58.4**	**35.1**	**6.4**
16~24 岁 Age	27	44.4	44.4	11.1
25~34 岁 Age	69	53.6	42.0	4.3
35~44 岁 Age	59	67.8	27.1	5.1
45~54 岁 Age	34	67.6	26.5	5.9
55~60 岁 Age	13	46.2	38.5	15.4
女性 Female	**30**	**60.0**	**40.0**	**0.0**
16~24 岁 Age	2	50.0	50.0	0.0
25~34 岁 Age	17	70.6	29.4	0.0
35~44 岁 Age	7	42.9	57.1	0.0
45~54 岁 Age	3	33.3	66.7	0.0
55~60 岁 Age	1	100.0	0.0	0.0

4-9 选择该类商品的考虑因素/ Ranking of the Considerations in Purchasing

注：本题为多选题，合计百分比超过 100%(Multiple answers)

排名 Ranking	考虑因素 Considerations	人次 Person-time	百分比 Percent
1	口味好 pleasant taste	115	49.6
2	价格适中 reasonable price	112	48.3
3	只是由于习惯 out of habit	61	26.3
4	有名的牌子 famous brand	49	21.1
5	购买方便 easy to buy	29	12.5
6	生产日期 date of producing	15	6.5
7	包装吸引人 appealing package	8	3.4
8	别人送的 given by other people	6	2.6
9	广告影响 influence of advertising	4	1.7
9	朋友推荐 introduction of friends	4	1.7
10	有优惠条件 with preferential terms	3	1.3
11	其它 others	1	0.4

n=232

4-10 样本、男性各年龄层、女性各年龄层抽烟的口味偏好/ Taste of the Consumed Cigarette by the Whole Sample, Age and Gender Groups

	人数 Number	混合型 combination type	烤烟型 flue-cured type	雪茄口味 cigar	其它 others
样本 Sample	**232**	**20.3**	**76.7**	**2.2**	**0.9**
男性 Male	**202**	**21.8**	**74.8**	**2.5**	**1.0**
16~24 岁 Age	27	7.4	85.2	7.4	0.0
25~34 岁 Age	69	26.1	71.0	1.4	1.4
35~44 岁 Age	59	23.7	72.9	1.7	1.7
45~54 岁 Age	34	23.5	76.5	0.0	0.0
55~60 岁 Age	13	15.4	76.9	7.7	0.0
女性 Female	**30**	**10.0**	**90.0**	**0.0**	**0.0**
16~24 岁 Age	2	50.0	50.0	0.0	0.0
25~34 岁 Age	17	11.8	88.2	0.0	0.0
35~44 岁 Age	7	0.0	100.0	0.0	0.0
45~54 岁 Age	3	0.0	100.0	0.0	0.0
55~60 岁 Age	1	0.0	100.0	0.0	0.0

4-11 样本、男性各年龄层、女性各年龄层一天抽烟的数量/ Number of Smoking a Day by the Whole Sample, Age and Gender Groups

	人数 Number	2 包以上 over 2 boxes	1~2 包 1 or 2 boxes	1 包左右 about a box	半包左右 about half a box	一天两三支或以下 2 or 3 cigarettes or below	没有抽 never
样本 Sample	232	2.2	11.6	42.2	24.1	18.5	1.3
男性 Male	202	2.5	11.4	45.5	26.2	13.9	0.5
16~24 岁 Age	27	3.7	14.8	40.7	18.5	22.2	0.0
25~34 岁 Age	69	0.0	10.1	49.3	29.0	10.1	1.4
35~44 岁 Age	59	5.1	15.3	45.8	18.6	15.3	0.0
45~54 岁 Age	34	2.9	5.9	44.1	41.2	5.9	0.0
55~60 岁 Age	13	0.0	7.7	38.5	23.1	30.8	0.0
女性 Female	30	0.0	13.3	20.0	10.0	50.0	6.7
16~24 岁 Age	2	0.0	0.0	50.0	0.0	50.0	0.0
25~34 岁 Age	17	0.0	11.8	17.6	11.8	58.8	0.0
35~44 岁 Age	7	0.0	28.6	14.3	14.3	14.3	28.6
45~54 岁 Age	3	0.0	0.0	0.0	0.0	100.0	0.0
55~60 岁 Age	1	0.0	0.0	100.0	0.0	0.0	0.0

4-12 样本、男性各年龄层、女性各年龄层抽烟的包装形式/ Types of Package of the Consumed Cigarette by the Whole Sample, Age and Gender Groups

	人数 Number	软盒装 soft box	硬盒装 hard box
样本 Sample	232	35.8	64.2
男性 Male	202	37.1	62.9
16~24 岁 Age	27	37.0	63.0
25~34 岁 Age	69	20.3	79.7
35~44 岁 Age	59	37.3	62.7
45~54 岁 Age	34	61.8	38.2
55~60 岁 Age	13	61.5	38.5
女性 Female	30	26.7	73.3
16~24 岁 Age	2	0.0	100.0
25~34 岁 Age	17	17.6	82.4
35~44 岁 Age	7	42.9	57.1
45~54 岁 Age	3	33.3	66.7
55~60 岁 Age	1	100.0	0.0

4-13 重度消费者人口分布/ Demographics of the Heavy Consumers

	人数 Number	16-24 岁 Age	25-34 岁 Age	35-44 岁 Age	45-54 岁 Age	55-60 岁 Age
样本 Sample	186	11.8	36.6	29.0	17.2	5.4
男性 Male	173	12.1	35.3	28.9	18.5	5.2
一天 2 包以上 over 2 boxes a day	5	20.0	0.0	60.0	20.0	0.0
一天 1~2 包 1 or 2 boxes a day	23	17.4	30.4	39.1	8.7	4.3
一天 1 包左右 about a box a day	92	12.0	37.0	29.3	16.3	5.4
一天半包左右 about half a box a day	53	9.4	37.7	20.8	26.4	5.7
女性 Female	13	7.7	53.8	30.8	0.0	7.7
一天 2 包以上 over 2 boxes a day	0	0.0	0.0	0.0	0.0	0.0
一天 1~2 包 1 or 2 boxes a day	4	0.0	50.0	50.0	0.0	0.0
一天 1 包左右 about a box a day	6	16.7	50.0	16.7	0.0	16.7
一天半包左右 about half a box a day	3	0.0	66.7	33.3	0.0	0.0

4-14 不同消费者层的常用品牌/ The Most Frequently Used Brands by Market Segments

4-14-1 时尚流行指标/ Fads Popular Index

	人数 Number	第一品牌及百分比 1st/percent	第二品牌及百分比 2nd/percent	第三品牌及百分比 3rd/percent	第四品牌及百分比 4th/percent
样本 Sample	232	**白沙 Baisha(35.3)**	**长沙 Changsha(9.5)**	**金丝猴 Jinsihou(6.9)**	**石林 Stone Forest(6.5)**
平实生活指向 simple living orientation	138	白沙 Baisha(32.6)	金丝猴 Jinsihou(10.9)	长沙 Changsha(10.1)	石林 Stone Forest(7.2)
时尚流行指向 fashion orientation	94	白沙 Baisha(39.4)	555(11.7)	长沙 Changsha(8.5)	希尔顿 Hilton(7.4)

4-14-2 广告态度指标/ Advertising Attitude Index

	人数 Number	第一品牌及百分比 1st/percent	第二品牌及百分比 2nd/percent	第三品牌及百分比 3rd/percent	第四品牌及百分比 4th/percent
样本 Sample	230	**白沙 Baisha(35.7)**	**长沙 Changsha(9.1)**	**金丝猴 Jinsihou(7.0)**	**石林 Stone Forest(6.5)**
广告淡漠指向 indifferent orientation	81	白沙 Baisha(40.7)	金丝猴 Jinsihou(7.4)	长沙 Changsha(6.2) 红河 Honghe(6.2) 石林 Stone Forest(6.2)	希尔顿 Hilton(4.9) 555(4.9)
中间层 medium	119	白沙 Baisha(32.8)	长沙 Changsha(10.1)	金丝猴 Jinsihou(7.6) 石林 Stone Forest(7.6)	555(6.7)
信赖广告指向 loyal orientation	30	白沙 Baisha(33.3)	红山茶 Hongshancha(13.3) 希尔顿 Hilton(13.3) 长沙 Changsha(13.3)	芙蓉 Furong(6.7) 云烟 Yunyan(6.7)	555(3.3) 猴王 Houwang(3.3) 金丝猴 Jinsihou(3.3) 石林 Stone Forest(3.3)

4-14-3 饮食健康指标/ Foods & Drink Quality Index

	人数 Number	第一品牌及百分比 1st/percent	第二品牌及百分比 2nd/percent	第三品牌及百分比 3rd/percent	第四品牌及百分比 4th/percent
样本 Sample	232	**白沙 Baisha(35.3)**	**长沙 Changsha(9.5)**	**金丝猴 Jinsihou(6.9)**	**石林 Stone Forest(6.5)**
饮食"温饱"指向 "basic" orientation	103	白沙 Baisha(34.0)	长沙 Changsha(10.7) 金丝猴 Jinsihou(10.7)	希尔顿 Hilton(7.8)	红山茶 Hongshancha(5.8)
中间层 medium	94	白沙 Baisha(42.6)	石林 Stone Forest(10.6)	长沙 Changsha(9.6)	555(6.4)
健康营养指向 health & nutrition orientation	35	白沙 Baisha(20.0)	555(14.3)	好猫 Haomao(11.4) 红山茶 Hongshancha(11.4)	长沙 Changsha(5.7) 红塔山 Hongtashan (5.7)

4-15 重度消费者的消费者层构成/ The Composition of the Heavy Consumers

4-15-1 时尚流行指标/ Fads Popular Index

	人数 Number	平实生活指向 simple living orientation	时尚流行指向 fashion orientation
样本 Sample	186	60.2	39.8
一天 2 包以上 over 2 boxes a day	5	40.0	60.0
一天 1～2 包 1 or 2 boxes a day	27	63.0	37.0
一天 1 包左右 about a box a day	98	58.2	41.8
一天半包左右 about half a box a day	56	64.3	35.7

4-15-2 广告态度指标/ Advertising Attitude Index

	人数 Number	广告淡漠指向 indifferent orientation	中间层 medium	信赖广告指向 loyal orientation
样本 Sample	184	36.4	50.5	13.0
一天 2 包以上 over 2 boxes a day	5	40.0	40.0	20.0
一天 1～2 包 1 or 2 boxes a day	26	42.3	46.2	11.5
一天 1 包左右 about a box a day	97	36.1	50.5	13.4
一天半包左右 about half a box a day	56	33.9	53.6	12.5

4-15-3 饮食健康指标/ Foods & Drink Quality Index

	人数 Number	饮食"温饱"指向 "basic" orientation	中间层 medium	健康营养指向 health & nutrition orientation
样本 Sample	186	43.5	40.9	15.6
一天 2 包以上 over 2 boxes a day	5	80.0	0.0	20.0
一天 1～2 包 1 or 2 boxes a day	27	33.3	55.6	11.1
一天 1 包左右 about a boxes a day	98	42.9	41.8	15.3
一天半包左右 about half a box a day	56	46.4	35.7	17.9

● 沈阳 / Shenyang

4-1 是否抽烟的比例/ Proportion of the Smoking in the Last Three Months

	人数 Number	百分比 Percent
是 yes	205	34.2
否 no	395	65.8

n=600

4-2 最常用品牌排名/ Ranking of the Most Used Brands

排名 Brand Ranking	品牌 Brands	人数 Number	百分比 Percent
1	石林 Stone Forest	41	20.4
2	三塔 Santa	28	13.9
3	吉庆 Jiqing	25	12.4
4	大生产(生产）Dashengchan	10	5.0
5	云烟 Yunyan	9	4.5
6	画苑 Huayuan	8	4.0
7	红山茶 Hongshancha	7	3.5
8	醒宝 Xingbao	6	3.0
9	云雾山 Yunwushan	5	2.5
9	特美思 Temeisi	5	2.5
9	黄果树 Huang Guoshu	5	2.5
10	阿波罗 Apollo	4	2.0
10	红河 Honghe	4	2.0
10	红塔山 Hongtashan	4	2.0

n=201

4-3 样本、男性各年龄层、女性各年龄层的常用品牌/ The Most Frequently Used Brands by the Whole Sample, Age and Gender Groups

	人数 Number	第一品牌及百分比 1st/ percent	第二品牌及百分比 2nd/ percent	第三品牌及百分比 3rd/ percent
样本 Sample	201	**石林 Stone Forest(20.4)**	**三塔 Santa(13.9)**	**吉庆 Jiqing(12.4)**
男性 Male	172	**石林 Stone Forest(17.4)**	**三塔 Santa(14.5)**	**吉庆 Jiqing(13.4)**
16~24 岁 Age	15	石林 Stone Forest(26.7)	三塔 Santa(13.3) 云烟 Yunyan(13.3)	红河 Honghe(6.7) 红山茶 Hongshancha(6.7) 黄山 Huangshan(6.7) 希尔顿 Hilton(6.7) 吉庆 Jiqing(6.7) 一品梅 Yipinmei(6.7) 白云 Baiyun(6.7)
25~34 岁 Age	60	石林 Stone Forest(21.7)	三塔 Santa(20.0)	吉庆 Jiqing(15.0)
35~44 岁 Age	52	三塔 Santa(15.4)	吉庆 Jiqing(13.5)	石林 Stone Forest(11.5) 画苑 Huayuan(11.5)
45~54 岁 Age	29	石林 Stone Forest(20.7)	吉庆 Jiqing(13.8)	黄果树 Huang Guoshu(6.9) 云雾山 Yunwushan(6.9)
55~60 岁 Age	16	大生产(生产）Dashengchan(12.5) 三塔 Santa(12.5) 吉庆 Jiqing(12.5)	画苑 Huayuan(6.3) 白猫 Baimao(6.3) 阿波罗 Apollo(6.3) 广州 Guangzhou(6.3) 茶花 CameUia(6.3) 云烟 Yunyan(6.3) 石林 Stone Forest(6 3) 黄果树 Huang Guoshu(6.3) 红塔山 Hongtashan (6.3) 大前门 Daqianmen(6.3)	
女性 Female	29	**石林 Stone Forest(37.9)**	**大生产(生产）Dashengchan(10.3)** **三塔 Santa(10.3)**	**吉庆 Jiqing(6.9)** **醒宝 Xingbao(6.9)** **红山茶 Hongshancha(6.9)**
16~24 岁 Age	0			
25~34 岁 Age	8	红山茶 Hongshancha(25.0) 三塔 Santa(25.0)	红河 Honghe(12.5) 石林 Stone Forest(12.5) 云雾山 Yunwushan(12.5) 醒宝 Xingbao(12.5)	
35~44 岁 Age	12	石林 Stone Forest(50.0)	吉庆 Jiqing(16.7)	三塔 Santa(8.3) 红云 Hongyun(8.3) 特美思 Temeisi(8.3) 古田 Gutian(8.3)
45~54 岁 Age	2	石林 Stone Forest(100.0)		
55~60 岁 Age	7	大生产(生产）Dashengchan(42.9)	石林 Stone Forest(28.6)	红杏 Hongxing(14.3) 醒宝 Xingbao(14.3)

4-4 理想品牌排名/ Ranking of the Ideal Brands

排名 Brand Ranking	品牌 Brands	人数 Number	百分比 Percent
1	中华 Zhonghua	95	15.8
2	石林 Stone Forest	87	14.5
3	555	51	8.5
4	七匹狼 SEPTWOLVES	42	7.0
5	红塔山 Hongtashan	41	6.8
6	黄山 Huangshan	38	6.3
7	三塔 Santa	27	4.5
8	吉庆 Jiqing	21	3.5
9	云烟 Yunyan	19	3.2
10	红山茶 Hongshancha	14	2.3
11	大生产(生产）Dashengchan	13	2.2

n=601

4-5 样本、男性各年龄层、女性各年龄层最近三个月有无购买的比例/ Purchasing in the Last Three Months by the Whole Sample, Age and Gender Groups

	人数 Number	买过 yes	没买过 no
样本 Sample	601	48.1	51.9
男性 Male	299	61.2	38.8
16~24 岁 Age	64	31.3	68.8
25~34 岁 Age	89	74.2	25.8
35~44 岁 Age	76	67.1	32.9
45~54 岁 Age	46	67.4	32.6
55~60 岁 Age	24	62.5	37.5
女性 Female	302	35.1	64.9
16~24 岁 Age	64	21.9	78.1
25~34 岁 Age	90	38.9	61.1
35~44 岁 Age	76	44.7	55.3
45~54 岁 Age	48	29.2	70.8
55~60 岁 Age	24	37.5	62.5

4-6 样本、男性各年龄层、女性各年龄层最近三个月是否拿香烟送过礼/ To Offer Cigarette as Gift in the Last Three Months by the Whole Sample, Age and Gender Groups

	人数 Number	送过 yes	没送过 no
样本 Sample	600	7.2	92.8
男性 Male	298	7.0	93.0
16~24 岁 Age	64	3.1	96.9
25~34 岁 Age	88	10.2	89.8
35~44 岁 Age	76	6.6	93.4
45~54 岁 Age	46	8.7	91.3
55~60 岁 Age	24	4.2	95.8
女性 Female	302	7.3	92.7
16~24 岁 Age	64	3.1	96.9
25~34 岁 Age	90	13.3	86.7
35~44 岁 Age	76	7.9	92.1
45~54 岁 Age	48	2.1	97.9
55~60 岁 Age	24	4.2	95.8

4-7 样本、男性各年龄层、女性各年龄层是否抽烟的比例/ Smoking or Not by the Whole Sample, Age and Gender Groups

	人数 Number	是 yes	否 no
样本 Sample	600	34.2	65.8
男性 Male	299	58.2	41.8
16~24 岁 Age	64	23.4	76.6
25~34 岁 Age	89	67.4	32.6
35~44 岁 Age	76	69.7	30.3
45~54 岁 Age	46	65.2	34.8
55~60 岁 Age	24	66.7	33.3
女性 Female	301	10.3	89.7
16~24 岁 Age	64	0.0	100.0
25~34 岁 Age	90	8.9	91.1
35~44 岁 Age	76	18.4	81.6
45~54 岁 Age	47	4.3	95.7
55~60 岁 Age	24	29.2	70.8

4-8 样本、男性各年龄层、女性各年龄层的品牌习惯/ Brand Habit in Consuming Cigarette by the Whole Sample, Age and Gender Groups

	人数 Number	基本固定用一个牌子 used in only one brand	比较固定地用两个或三个牌子 used in two or three brands	基本上不太固定牌子 no brand preference
样本 Sample	**203**	**63.1**	**26.6**	**10.3**
男性 Male	**173**	**63.6**	**26.6**	**9.8**
16~24 岁 Age	15	53.3	26.7	20.0
25~34 岁 Age	59	55.9	37.3	6.8
35~44 岁 Age	53	73.6	15.1	11.3
45~54 岁 Age	30	70.0	23.3	6.7
55~60 岁 Age	16	56.3	31.3	12.5
女性 Female	**30**	**60.0**	**26.7**	**13.3**
16~24 岁 Age	0	0.0	0.0	0.0
25~34 岁 Age	8	37.5	50.0	12.5
35~44 岁 Age	13	69.2	15.4	15.4
45~54 岁 Age	2	0.0	50.0	50.0
55~60 岁 Age	7	85.7	14.3	0.0

4-9 选择该类商品的考虑因素/ Ranking of the Considerations in Purchasing

注：本题为多选题，合计百分比超过 100%(Multiple answers）

排名 Ranking	考虑因素 considerations	人次 Person-time	百分比 Percent
1	价格适中 reasonable price	115	56.4
2	口味好 pleasant taste	114	55.9
3	只是由于习惯 out of habit	66	32.4
4	购买方便 easy to buy	37	18.1
5	有名的牌子 famous brand	28	13.7
6	生产日期 date of producing	11	5.4
7	别人送的 given by other people	5	2.5
8	有优惠条件 with preferential terms	4	2.0
9	朋友推荐 introduction of friends	3	1.5
10	广告影响 influence of advertising	1	0.5
10	包装吸引人 appealing package	1	0.5
10	其它 others	1	0.5

n=204

4-10 样本、男性各年龄层、女性各年龄层抽烟的口味偏好/ Taste of the Consumed Cigarette by the Whole Sample, Age and Gender Groups

	人数 Number	混合型 combination type	烤烟型 flue-cured type	雪茄口味 cigar	其它 others
样本 Sample	**204**	**27.5**	**71.6**	**1.0**	**0.0**
男性 Male	**174**	**25.3**	**73.6**	**1.1**	**0.0**
16~24 岁 Age	15	13.3	86.7	0.0	0.0
25~34 岁 Age	60	23.3	75.0	1.7	0.0
35~44 岁 Age	53	34.0	66.0	0.0	0.0
45~54 岁 Age	30	13.3	83.3	3.3	0.0
55~60 岁 Age	16	37.5	62.5	0.0	0.0
女性 Female	**30**	**40.0**	**60.0**	**0.0**	**0.0**
16~24 岁 Age	0	0.0	0.0	0.0	0.0
25~34 岁 Age	8	25.0	75.0	0.0	0.0
35~44 岁 Age	13	46.2	53.8	0.0	0.0
45~54 岁 Age	2	0.0	100.0	0.0	0.0
55~60 岁 Age	7	57.1	42.9	0.0	0.0

4-11 样本、男性各年龄层、女性各年龄层一天抽烟的数量/ Number of Smoking a Day by the Whole Sample, Age and Gender Groups

	人数 Number	2 包以上 2 boxes or over	1~2 包 1 or 2 boxes	1 包左右 about a box	半包左右 about half a box	一天两三支或以下 2 or 3 cigarettes or below	没有抽 never
样本 Sample	204	2.5	8.8	38.2	35.3	15.2	0.0
男性 Male	174	1.7	8.6	40.8	36.2	12.6	0.0
16~24 岁 Age	15	0.0	0.0	26.7	60.0	13.3	0.0
25~34 岁 Age	60	0.0	6.7	45.0	31.7	16.7	0.0
35~44 岁 Age	53	3.8	3.8	39.6	39.6	13.2	0.0
45~54 岁 Age	30	3.3	23.3	36.7	26.7	10.0	0.0
55~60 岁 Age	16	0.0	12.5	50.0	37.5	0.0	0.0
女性 Female	30	6.7	10.0	23.3	30.0	30.0	0.0
16~24 岁 Age	0	0.0	0.0	0.0	0.0	0.0	0.0
25~34 岁 Age	8	0.0	0.0	12.5	37.5	50.0	0.0
35~44 岁 Age	13	15.4	15.4	23.1	30.8	15.4	0.0
45~54 岁 Age	2	0.0	0.0	0.0	100.0	0.0	0.0
55~60 岁 Age	7	0.0	14.3	42.9	0.0	42.9	0.0

4-12 样本、男性各年龄层、女性各年龄层抽烟的包装形式/ Types of Package of the Consumed Cigarette by the Whole Sample, Age and Gender Groups

	人数 Number	软盒装 soft box	硬盒装 hard box
样本 Sample	203	52.2	47.8
男性 Male	173	53.8	46.2
16~24 岁 Age	15	26.7	73.3
25~34 岁 Age	59	44.1	55.9
35~44 岁 Age	53	60.4	39.6
45~54 岁 Age	30	70.0	30.0
55~60 岁 Age	16	62.5	37.5
女性 Female	30	43.3	56.7
16~24 岁 Age	0	0	0
25~34 岁 Age	8	25.0	75.0
35~44 岁 Age	13	30.8	69.2
45~54 岁 Age	2	50.0	50.0
55~60 岁 Age	7	85.7	14.3

4-13 重度消费者人口分布/ Demographics of the Heavy Consumers

	人数 Number	16-24 岁 Age	25-34 岁 Age	35-44 岁 Age	45-54 岁 Age	55-60 岁 Age
样本 Sample	173	7.5	31.2	32.9	16.8	11.6
男性 Male	152	8.6	32.9	30.3	17.8	10.5
一天 2 包以上 2 boxes or over a day	3	0.0	0.0	66.7	33.3	0.0
一天 1~2 包 1 or 2 boxes a day	15	0.0	26.7	13.3	46.7	13.3
一天 1 包左右 about a box a day	71	5.6	38.0	29.6	15.5	11.3
一天半包左右 about half a box a day	63	14.3	30.2	33.3	12.7	9.5
女性 Female	21	0.0	19.0	52.4	9.5	19.0
一天 2 包以上 2 boxes or over a day	2	0.0	0.0	100.0	0.0	0.0
一天 1~2 包 1 or 2 boxes a day	3	0.0	0.0	66.7	0.0	33.3
一天 1 包左右 about a box a day	7	0.0	14.3	42.9	0.0	42.9
一天半包左右 about half a box a day	9	0.0	33.3	44.4	22.2	0.0

4-14 不同消费者层的常用品牌/ The Most Frequently Used Brands by Market Segments

4-14-1 时尚流行指标/ Fads Popular Index

	人数 Number	第一品牌及百分比 1st/ percent	第二品牌及百分比 2nd/ percent	第三品牌及百分比 3rd/ percent
样本 Sample	201	**石林 Stone Forest(20.4)**	**三塔 Santa(13.9)**	**吉庆 Jiqing(12.4)**
平实生活指向 simple living orientation	102	石林 Stone Forest(19.6)	吉庆 Jiqing(12.7)	三塔 Santa(11.8)
时尚流行指向 fashion orientation	99	石林 Stone Forest(21.2)	三塔 Santa(16.2)	吉庆 Jiqing(12.1)

4-14-2 广告态度指标/ Advertising Attitude Index

	人数 Number	第一品牌及百分比 1st/ percent	第二品牌及百分比 2nd/ percent	第三品牌及百分比 3rd/ percent
样本 Sample	201	**石林 Stone Forest(20.4)**	**三塔 Santa(13.9)**	**吉庆 Jiqing(12.4)**
广告淡漠指向 indifferent orientation	64	石林 Stone Forest(18.8)	三塔 Santa(15.6)	吉庆 Jiqing(10.9)
中间层 medium	108	石林 Stone Forest(22.2)	吉庆 Jiqing(13.9)	三塔 Santa(13.0)
信赖广告指向 loyal orientation	29	石林 Stone Forest(17.2)	三塔 Santa(13.8) 云烟 Yunyan(13.8)	吉庆 Jiqing(10.3)

4-14-3 饮食健康指标/ Foods & Drink Quality Index

	人数 Number	第一品牌及百分比 1st/ percent	第二品牌及百分比 2nd/ percent	第三品牌及百分比 3rd/ percent
样本 Sample	201	**石林 Stone Forest(20.4)**	**三塔 Santa(13.9)**	**吉庆 Jiqing(12.4)**
饮食"温饱"指向 "basic" orientation	82	石林 Stone Forest(17.1)	三塔 Santa(13.4) 吉庆 Jiqing (13.4)	云雾山 Yunwushan(4.9) 大生产(生产) Dashengchan(4.9) 黄果树 Huang Guoshu(4.9)
中间层 medium	78	石林 Stone Forest(19.2)	三塔 Santa(15.4)	吉庆 Jiqing(14.1)
健康营养指向 health & nutrition orientation	41	石林 Stone Forest(29.3)	三塔 Santa(12.2)	吉庆 Jiqing(7.3) 画苑 Huayuan(7.3) 醒宝 Xingbao(7.3)

4-15 重度消费者的消费者层构成/ The Composition of the Heavy Consumers

4-15-1 时尚流行指标/ Fads Popular Index

	人数 Number	平实生活指向 simple living orientation	时尚流行指向 fashion orientation
样本 Sample	173	54.3	45.7
一天 2 包以上 2 boxes or over a day	5	60.0	40.0
一天 1～2 包 1 or 2 boxes a day	18	55.6	44.4
一天 1 包左右 about a box a day	78	52.6	47.4
一天半包左右 about half a box a day	72	55.6	44.4

4-15-2 广告态度指标/ Advertising Attitude Index

	人数 Number	广告淡漠指向 indifferent orientation	中间层 medium	信赖广告指向 loyal orientation
样本 Sample	173	34.7	52.0	13.3
一天 2 包以上 2 boxes or over a day	5	20.0	80.0	0.0
一天 1～2 包 1 or 2 boxes a day	18	33.3	50.0	16.7
一天 1 包左右 about a box a day	78	30.8	52.6	16.7
一天半包左右 about half a box a day	72	40.3	50.0	9.7

4-15-3 饮食健康指标/ Foods & Drink Quality Index

	人数 Number	饮食“温饱”指向 "basic" orientation	中间层 medium	健康营养指向 health & nutrition orientation
样本 Sample	173	41.6	40.5	17.9
一天 2 包以上 2 boxes or over a day	5	20.0	60.0	20.0
一天 1～2 包 1 or 2 boxes a day	18	27.8	50.0	22.2
一天 1 包左右 about a box a day	78	39.7	41.0	19.2
一天半包左右 half a box a day	72	48.6	36.1	15.3

第八篇　洗涤日用品
Part VIII　Household Necessities

- 牙膏　Toothpaste
- 洗发水　Shampoo
- 香皂　Perfumed Soap
- 沐浴液　Bath Shampoo
- 洗衣粉　Washing Powder
- 洗涤灵/洗涤精　Liquid Detergent
- 洗面乳　Facial Cleaner
- 脸部润肤霜　Skin-care Products

洗涤日用品

中国日用品市场是一个充满活力的大市场，其销售额已从 1982 年的 2 亿元发展到现在的 253 亿元，预计到 2010 年，我国日用品消费可达 800 亿元，如此之大的市场空间引得许多国际知名企业纷纷抢滩中国。美国宝洁、庄臣、安利、露华浓，英国联合利华，德国汉高，日本资生堂、花王等，都在中国投资办厂。目前，三资企业总数已达 450 家，占全部日用品生产厂总数的 15%。

跨国企业的大举进入，使日用品行业的产品结构发生变化，品种、花色、质量等都较以前有大幅提高，推动和促进了国内日用品行业的发展，同时，也使得行业竞争加剧，并显现出民族品牌日用品的明显差距。目前中国日用品市场基本上是独资企业和外来品牌唱主角，民族品牌阵地正在缩小，日用品消费正在向名优品牌集中。今年 1—8 月份，全国牙膏前十个品牌占据 90%的市场份额，洗护用品前十个品牌占据 80%的市场，香皂前十个品牌的市场占有总和接近 80%，即使集中程度最低的美容护肤品和清洁洗涤剂，前十个品牌也控制了三分之二的市场份额。

1998 年中国主要城市居民消费品调查日用品品牌市场占有率（单位：%）

排位比例 / 产品种类	第一位		第二位		第三位	
	品牌名称	所占比例	品牌名称	所占比例	品牌名称	所占比例
牙膏	高露洁	20.5	佳洁士	15.2	中华	11.3
香皂	舒肤佳	38.5	力士	31.1	夏士莲	6.1
洗衣粉	奥妙	14.9	汰渍	14.5	白猫	12.9
洗发水/护发素	飘柔	27.3	海飞丝	9.9	潘婷	9.7
沐浴露	力士	17.9	六神	14.3	舒肤佳	13.0
家用清洁剂	白猫	34.6	安利	10.9	高富力	6.6
妇女卫生巾	护舒宝	32.2	安尔乐	11.9	舒而美	8.3
化妆品	羽西	9.2	C.D.	8.8	美宝莲	6.8
护肤/润肤品	玉兰油	16.1	大宝	7.2	资生堂	6.8

（资料来源：《中国消费者报》99.1.1）

独资企业和外来品牌抢占中国市场的成功，为民族企业提供了十分有益的经验。这些经验主要是：

——强劲的广告宣传攻势。三资企业每开发创造出一个新品牌，都不惜巨资大做电视广告，在消费者中树立良好形象。

——成功的营销策略。许多三资企业配备专门营销人员，充分了解市场，开展多种形式促销活动用以扩大影响力。

——三资企业日用品品种多、花色全，能适应不同消费层次需要，符合个性消费需求。

——精致美观、高雅华贵的外形设计，讲究外观包装，个性鲜明。

——国外品牌重视市场信息收集、反馈和研究，注重科技投入。

以上外资企业成功的经验，正是目前民族企业在跨入市场经济的过程中所急需改进和建设的重点。

牙膏

世界上第一支管装牙膏诞生于 1893 年。在 29 年之后即 1922 年，我国生产出第一支管装牙膏。70 余年来，我国的各类型保健牙膏得到了极为迅速的发展，中国牙膏行业在产量、功能、品种等方面均居世界前列。1998 年全国牙膏产量为 28.07 亿支，比 1997 年的 27.17 亿支增长 3.31%；销售收入完成 45.91 亿元，比 1997 年的 40.24 亿元增长 14.09%；实现利税 6.15 亿元，比 1997 年的 5.44 亿元增长 13.05%：其中实现利润 3.05 亿元，比 1997 年的 2.85 亿元增长 7.02%。

全国牙膏行业 1998 年出口量为 1.83 万吨，比 1997 年增长 41.91%，创汇额为 3468 万美元，比 1997 年增长 42.36%。

全国目前有牙膏生产企业 40 余家，其中“三资”企业 5 家，牙膏原材料生产企业 12 家（含合资企业 2 家），牙膏设备制造厂 2 家。民族工业及所拥有的民族品牌是中国牙膏行业的主力军。1998 年，柳州两面针股份有限公司产量达 3.9 亿余支；上海牙膏厂产量达 1 亿多支；中华牌牙膏产量达 6 亿支；广州美晨股份有限公司产量达 2.25 亿支；天津蓝天集团有限责任公司产量达 1.76 亿支；安徽芳草日化股份有限公司产量达 9550 万支；广西梧州奥奇丽集团股份有限公司产量达 6100 万支；江西草珊瑚企业（集团）公司产量达 5437 万支；杭州牙膏厂产量达 4548 万支。上述几家企业的牙膏产量超过 20 亿支，占全国总产量的 75%左右。

中国牙膏市场在当前和将来的巨大潜力已将国际跨国公司吸引进来。美国 P&G 公司推出佳洁士（Crest）牙膏，美国 C-P 公司推出高露洁（Colgate）牙膏，英国联合利华公司推出洁诺（Signal）牙膏，韩国 LG 公司及黑人牙膏等在中国牙膏市场上也取得了一席之地。国际公司加盟中国牙膏市场的竞争，带来了先进的技术和设备、先进的管理、先进的科学配方，这无疑会对中国牙膏工业的发展起到促进作用。

按照我国 2000 年口腔卫生保健的预期目标规定，到 2000 年我国人民的刷牙率城市达 85%，农村达到 50%。按全国城市刷牙人数每人每年平均消费 5 支牙膏、农村刷牙人数每人每年平均消费 3 支牙膏计算，到本世纪末，全国牙膏销量将达 30.5 亿支，销售额将达到 50 亿元；2005 年牙膏产量将达到 40 亿支，销售额将达到 70 亿元；2010 年产量将达到 60 亿支，销售额将达到 100 亿元。这是一个充满商机和挑战的市场。企业必须在生产中提高科技含量，在经营中提高管理力度，在销售中提高营销水平，全面包装自己的产品，才可能使自身发展壮大。

洗发水

洗发水在取代香皂成为人们专用的洗发用品之后所显示出的巨大商机，令国内外的生产厂家及商家获得极大的发展空间。市场上的品牌和产量都大幅增加，市场竞争也格外激烈。

目前市场上的洗发水以独资和合资企业的品牌占主导地位，其中合资为主的国产品牌近年来在质量、功能、包装、营销手段等方面的水平迅速提高，对进口品牌产生强烈冲击，使其市场份额从 1997 年的 14%下降为 1998 年的 12%。而国产品牌仅有奥妮一家挤进前十名（见表）。

1999 年 6 月份全国洗发护发品牌市场占有率表 (单位：%)

品牌名称	飘柔	海飞丝	潘婷	舒蕾	夏士莲	沙宣	力士	奥妮	伊卡璐	诗芬
市场占有率	23.9%	14.4%	12.2%	10.1%	9.4%	5.9%	3.6%	2.4%	1.9%	1.5%

（资料来源：中华全国商业信息中心）

奥妮公司成功的关键，就在于把重心放在了市场和科研两个关节点上。公司已拥有世界先进水平的市场营销理念，正是有了这个基础，奥妮的产品定位理念才得以实践，才创出了全国知名的“奥妮”品牌，这是国内企业发展的重要借鉴经验。

市场的激烈竞争带来了品牌大战，也促使洗发水种类在不断更新。从六、七十年代的以清洁头发为最终目的的洗发水到配套出现的护发素，再到为便利使用而推出的二合一、三合一甚至四合一洗护发用品，不断完善着洗发水市场。目前，一些产品，如潘婷、伊卡璐中，出现了洗护发产品再度分离的趋势。专业人士认为，功能的专门化和单一化更利于头发的护理和保养。所谓“分久必合，合久必分”，现代的护发理念似乎正在顺应着“古老”的天意而自然发展。

香皂

在洗涤用品市场上，也许香皂的市场份额争夺是最激烈的。香皂的价格不高，因此其竞争并不表现在价格上，而是包含了功能、香型、份量、包装、广告等综合因素。如“力士”以迷人的芳香、美容、护肤、适应性广而深受各地消费者的喜爱；“舒肤佳”则以天然的清香、杀菌除臭等优点，凭借强大的广告攻势，受到不同地区消费者的欢迎。在北京、上海、天津、广州、深圳等大中城市，同样125克的重量，国外品牌的售价一般在4元以上，而国产的香皂大多不到3元，然而国产香皂的低价态势并未受到消费者的垂青。

由于国外品牌的香皂占据市场的主导地位，直接导致了香皂售价较国产品牌高的结果。随着国外品牌香皂的主导地位的日益凸现，全国消费者也习以为常，其价格高并未影响销售，反而演变成一个优势的既定态势。与此相适应，大量无知名度、低知名度企业生产的香皂已被淘汰出局。

据业内人士分析，由于香皂不是功能性很强的日用消费品，品牌的影响几乎是决定性的。既然国外品牌及合资品牌占据了绝对优势，国产品牌要重新夺回本土市场，是非常困难的。

随着生活质量的提升，香皂消费已经由季节性消费转向常年消费，由青年人扩展到中老年人，由洁肤型转向护肤美容、营养疗效型。这种消费走向将给厂家带来新的挑战和发展契机，关键是看谁能抓住市场动态，并在生产技术和经营理念上领先一步。

沐浴液

沐浴液以液体皂的形式出现，使用方便，效果舒适清爽。广大消费者对这类产品怀有浓厚的兴趣。随着人们生活水平的提高，各种品牌的沐浴液在日益取代延续了几十年的香皂。

据专家解释，常见的沐浴液有三种类型：一是表面为活性剂型，主要由具有洗涤作用的表面活性剂复配而成，温和光滑。二是皂基型，基于制皂的原理改性而成，泡沫丰富，易于清洗；三是表面活性剂型和皂基型复配型，取二者之优点，泡沫丰富，易于清洗，洗后皮肤清爽滋润。目前市场上后两类沐浴液较多，因而也给人不同以往的舒适感觉。

国内外的各大日化厂家结合市场信息和消费特点，争先恐后地推出了新产品，如广州宝洁公司的舒肤佳、联合利华的力士、丽花丝宝的舒蕾、花王的碧柔、强生的强生 Baby、高露洁公司的棕榄、上海家化的六神等数十种品牌。如今，沐浴液已风行一时。使用者的范围也从青年人扩展到中老年人。

在对市场使用者的调查中，综合评价最佳的是肤安，家庭拥有率最高、用后留存气味最佳的是六神，洁肤效果评价最佳的是伊卡璐、肤安，倾倒方便性评价最佳的是强生，功能多样性评价最佳的是舒肤佳（资料来源：《消费指南》99 年 8 月，第 63 页）。虽然沐浴液取代香皂是现代生活洗浴的一大趋势，但由于沐浴液的价格稍高于香皂，同时人们生活习惯的转变也并非一日之功，所以沐浴液市场需要逐渐培养。企业在研发产品的同时，也应注意培养消费者的使用习惯。

洗衣粉

近几年来，洗衣机拥有量的不断上升，带动了洗衣粉市场销售量的上升。在我国的一个三口之家，洗衣粉的年耗用量在 5 公斤至 6.5 公斤之间。尽管当前仍有部分消费者使用肥皂洗涤，但从大城市的趋势来看，功能单一的肥皂正逐渐被多功能的洗衣粉所取代。国内巨大的市场需求使得各类洗衣粉生产商的生产经营都非常活跃，竞争也日趋激烈。

我国洗衣粉的市场竞争，主要集中在上海白猫集团（白猫、佳美）、广州宝洁 P&G（碧浪、汰渍）、联合利华（奥妙）、德国汉高（宝莹）之间展开。在激烈的市场竞争中，各大公司各有其制胜的法宝：白猫在 1958 年进入市场以来，一度成为优质与实惠的代名词，其低廉的价格至今仍受中年家庭主妇的喜爱；联合利华利用其强大的广告优势及丰富的产品线，给消费者的视觉、听觉以极大的冲击；广州宝洁公司则在第三代碧浪洗衣粉上推陈出新，利用目前唯一拥有的全球专利，生产出去油污因子洗衣粉，其去油污能力是普通洗衣粉的 2 至 3 倍。由此可见，各大公司在价格、促销、技术上各有动作，以期进一步占领市场。

在目前的洗衣粉市场上，国产品牌如白猫、佳美、活力 28、熊猫、佳佳，合资品牌如奥妙、宝莹、汰渍、碧浪等都占主导地位，它们不仅拥有较高的知名度，而且消费者对这些产品的曾用率和再用率均比较高。白猫、奥妙、汰渍、碧浪洗衣粉以各自不同的优点占据了全国洗衣粉市场的大半份额，形成了洗衣粉市场的第一集团。同时，由于地方品牌的亲和力等因素，区域性品牌亦有一席之地，如天津加酶的市场知名度在天津、石家庄地区占 95%以上。市场占有率超过 50%；南京加佳、郑州熊猫的名气最大；在西安、武汉、成都等地是活力 28 一统天下，占有率超过 70%。

纵观洗衣粉市场，消费正由过去的通用型、丰泡型向专用型、低泡型发展，对浓缩型洗衣粉需求增长较快。目前，城市以中高价洗衣粉销售为主，而低价洗衣粉的市场仍在农村。

洗洁精

洗洁精进入中国普通家庭只是近十几年的事。在短短的时间里，洗洁精已成为不可或缺的家庭必用品，得到极大的普及。国内每年洗洁精的消费量在 30—40 万吨之间，仅北京市场占有率很高的金鱼洗涤灵年产量就有 2 万吨。目前，市场上的洗洁精的品牌多达几十种，产品也有普通型、浓缩型、杀菌型之分，还有机洗、手洗之别。在市场占有率中居前列的几个品牌是白猫、金鱼、开米、波尔、得其利是、巧手等。

在国产品牌中，上海白猫、北京金鱼叫得最响。上海白猫有限公司是目前我国洗涤剂市场中份额最大的国企，洗洁精的市场占有率达 50%以上。金鱼洗涤灵由于价格适中、好用、质量稳定而在北京市场中雄居霸主地位，市场占有率达 80%。

洗洁精作为家庭常用品，与人们的生活健康息息相关，因此消费者在选购此类产品时比较谨慎，主要考虑以下几个因素：一是洁净效果，消费者注重洁净效果，如果产品名不符实，以后就不会再去购买这种产品了；二是价格水平，如果效果相差不多，大多数消费者倾向于买便宜的，但也有一些人是买贵不买贱，只要效果好，贵点也照样买；三是使用便捷，产品必须符合消费者使用方便、快捷的要求，如果使用麻烦、费事，消费者则不愿购买；四是品牌，品牌只有在质量好、价格适中的前提条件下，才会被消费者所接受；五是香型，消费者在香型上具有特有的偏好，如北京市消费者偏好柠檬香和果香；六是包装，色彩新颖、形状别致、包装精美的产品也是激发消费者购买欲的一个必要条件。

现阶段，许多洗洁精生产厂家在保证产品除油、去垢能力的同时，也在增添消除农药残留、杀菌等辅助功能。专业人士认为，消费者对具有杀菌效果的洗洁精的需求在不断增长，这也是洗洁精产品发展的一种趋势。

Household Necessities

The market for household items in China is energetic and its total sales has risen from 0.2 billion RMB in the year of 1982 to 25.3 billion RMB nowadays. It is estimated that the total sales of household items in China can come up to 80 billion RMB. Such a potential market attracts numerous enterprises with international fame to China. Many companies have invested in China, such as P&G, Johnson, Amway, Revion from America, Unilever from England, Hencel from Germany, Shiselod and Kao from Japan. The number of joint ventures in China has come to 450, accounting for 15% of the total number of manufacturers in this trade.

The entrance of the transnational corporations makes changes in the product mix. The great variety of designs and patterns of products with better quality are welcomed and have promoted domestic development of the industry of household items whereas the deficiency of the products of the national brands becomes apparent in the keen competition. It is from abroad or produced by the foreign-invested companies that play the most important role in the present household items market and the market of the local brands are shrinking. Products of quality and fame have become the choice of most consumers. In the period from January to August of this year, the first 10 brands of toothpaste share 90%of the total market, the first 10 brands for body and facial wash and shampoo share 80% of the market, and the first 10 brands of scented soaps share almost 80% market. Even least concentratedly distributed products and detergents market, the first 10 brands hold 2/3 of the total market.

The data listed here are about percentage of market shares of the most commonly used brands according to the research on urban citizens in major Chinese cities in the year of 1998:

Rank / Category	First		Second		Third	
	Brand	%	Brand	%	Brand	%
Toothpaste	Cologate	20.5	Crest	15.2	Zhonghua	11.3
Soap	Safeguard	38.5	Lux	31.1	Hazline	6.1
Washing Powder	Omo	14.9	Tide	14.5	White Cat	12.9
Shampoo	Rejoice	27.3	Head & Shoulders	9.9	Pantene	9.7
Bath Shampoo	Lux	17.9	Liushen	14.3	Safeguard	13.0
Detergent	White Cat	34.6	Amway	10.9	Gaofuli	6.6
Napkin	Whisper	32.2	An'erla	11.9	Comfort & Beauty	8.3
Cosmetics	Yue-sai	9.2	C. D.	8.8	Maybelline	6.8
Skin Cream &Lotion	Oil of Olay	16.1	Dabao	7.2	Shisedo	6.8

(Sources: China Consumers Newspaper, Jan.1.99)

The success of the international and foreign brands provides Chinese local companies with some useful experiences:

---Powerful advertising campaign. Every new brand exploited by the joint or foreign ventures are heavily advertised on TV to set up good image among consumers. 50%to 69% of the consumers accepted such brands as Safeguard, Lux and Hazeline through media advertising.

---Sound marketing strategies help marketers succeed. There are professional personel to deal with marketing. They study and analyses the market, the consumers and develop various kinds of promotion events to push their products to consumers.

----The joint ventures and foreign can provide products of various patterns to meet different needs of consumers and to fit in with customization.

----The products are characterized by the highly delicate shape, refined package design and distinctive personality.

----Special attention is focused on collecting marketing information, feedback and on technical investment, e.g. O'Learel Corporation(America) uses 3% of its sales revenue to research and develop cosmetics and dermatology.

The above-mentioned experiences are the most important things. Chinese local enterprises need market-oriented economy.

Toothpaste

The first toothpaste in the world was invented in 1893 and 29 years later, that is, in the year of 1922, China had its own first toothpaste. Great development in kinds of health-care toothpaste has been made from then on and China's toothpaste business is among the world top ones in terms of quality, function and pattern.

The total output of toothpaste in China is 2.807 billions in 1998, 3.31% more than that of 1997; the total sales revenue comes to 4.591 billion RMB, 14.09 % more than that of 1997, and produced tax 0.615 billion RMB, 13.05% more than that of 1997, the total profit is 0.305 billion RMB, 7.02% more than that of 1997.

In 1998 the amount of toothpaste export was 18300 tons, 41.91%more than that of 1997 and had earned 34680 thousand dollars through export, 42.36% more than that of 1997.

There are at present more than 40 toothpaste enterprises among which 5 are joint or foreign ventures, 12 suppliers provide raw materials and 2 toothpaste equipment manufacturers.

The main force in toothpaste business is Chinese local enterprises. In 1998, LiangMianzhen Cop. Ltd. in Liuzhou produced 0.39 billion tubes of toothpaste and Shanghai Toothpaste Factory produced more than 0.1 billion, Zhonghua produced 0.6 billion, Guangzhou Meichen Cop. Ltd. produced 0.225 billion, Blue Sky Cop. Ltd. 0.176 billion, Anhui Fangcao 95.5 million, Guangxi Aoqi 61 million, Jiangxi Caoshanhu 54.37 million, and Hangzhou Toothpaste Factory produced 45.48 million tubes. The toothpaste factories mentioned above produced more than 2 billion tubes of toothpaste, holding 75% share of the total toothpaste output of China.

The great potential of Chinese toothpaste market has attracted many transnational companies to China. Many foreign brands, such as Crest introduced by P&G, Colgate by C-P (America), Signal by Unilever(England), Blackman by LG Cop (Korea), have got a share of the market. The participation of these companies in the competition brought the advanced techniques, equipments, advanced managing methods and scientific formula into China. Undoubtedly, that will encourage the development of Chinese toothpaste business.

According to China's anticipated objectives of hygiene in 2000, 85% of the Chinese urban citizens, 50% of the rural citizens will be toothpaste users. Suppose every urban toothpaste user consumes 5 tubes and rural user consumes 3 tubes per year, the total sales of toothpaste may come to 3.05 billion tubes and earn 5 billion RMB by the end of this century. By the year of 2005, the toothpaste output can come to 4 billion tubes, producing 7 billion RMB and the toothpaste output of 2010 can come to 6 billion tubes, producing 10 billion RMB. The toothpaste market is full of opportunities and challenges. The toothpaste producers must improve their technology, reinforce their management, improve their marketing strategies and package their products all the ways. By doing so, Chinese toothpaste producers can make themselves stronger in the competition.

Shampoo

Shampoo's replacement of toilet soap provides both Chinese and foreign manufacturers and dealers with many commercial chances Both the number of brands and the amount of output of Shampoo have been increased to a great degree and the competition has become extremely keener.

The brands of the foreign-invested or joint ventures take the leading in current market and the shampoo of Chinese brands, mainly produced by joint ventures has been greatly developed in the terms of quality, function, package and marketing tactics. The imported shampoo is set back under such a circumstance and shares only 12% of the total sale in 1998, 2% less than that of the previous year. Olive is the only Chinese local brand which is listed in the top ten in competition.

Share of shampoo Brands (nation-wide (June, 1999))

Brand	Rejoice	Head & Shoulders	Pantene	Slek	Hazeline	Sassoon	Lux	Olive	Clairol	Sifone
Market Share %	23.9	14.4	12.2	10.1	9.4	5.9	3.6	2.4	1.9	1.5

(Sources: National Commercial Information Center of China)

The success of Olive lies in its emphasis on marketing and research. The sophisticated marketing philosophy of Olive enables it to carry out its product positioning idea and crear the national famous brand Olive. It is a piece of important experience from which other Chinese enterprises can learn from.

The keen competition among different brands advocates the innovation of shampoo. The hair-washing shampoo in 1960s and 1970s has given its way to the series of shampoo with hair treatment, shampoo with combined functions, such as 2 in 1, 3 in 1 and even 4 in 1 Shampoo. But some companies now tend to separate the functions of hair-washing and hair-treatment, for example Pantine and , Clairol. Experts say that the shampoo with specialized function is more helpful for hair. Such a trend is in agreement with the old saying "division and unity can transform to each other".

Perfumed Soap

In the detergent market, the competition for soap sales might be the keenest. Due to the low price of soap, its competition doesn't lie in price, but in factors such as function, fragrance, net weight, package and advertising. Lux is widely accepted because of its fascinating fragrance, its beauty element and skin-care and wide-range of usage, on the other hand, Safeguard is welcomed because of its refreshing fragrance, anti-bacteria functions backed up with powerful advertising campaign. The prices for the soaps of 125 grams with foreign brands are normally more than 4 RMB and most of the soaps, equal in weight with local brands are sold no more than 3 RMB. But the lower price doesn't attract the consumers in the large-and-medium-sized cities such as Beijing, Shanghai, Tianjin, Guangzhou and Shenzhen.

The foreign-brand soap dominants the market and this directly results in the higher prices of them. Most consumers have become accustomed to that the high price has become a token of superiority of these soaps. In such circumstances the soap produced by Chinese local companies with no or little fame have been eliminated.

According to the analysis of the experts of this business, since soap is a household item containing little functions, therefore the brand can be a decisive factor in competition. Since now the foreign soaps have taken an upper hand it's rather difficult for Chinese local companies to take back the local market.

With the improvement of living standards, consumption has shifted from seasonal to year-round, from youth only to people at various age, from skin cleaning to skin-care and nutritious remedy. Such a change provides the enterprises with new opportunities and challenges. Those who catch up with the trends and make improvement in techniques and management can win higher itself in competition.

Bath Shampoo

The liquid body wash makes it more convenient to use than the traditional soaps and has aroused the consumers' interest. With the improvement of living conditions, body wash is now taking the place of the scented soap, which has been used for years.

There are 3 kinds of common body wash. The first kind is named activation style. One of its major ingredients is the surface-active agent which feels soft and smooth. But if it is not properly mixed, it will make the user feel that he/she doesn't clean himself/herself completely. The second kind is soap-based style. It makes use of the principles of producing scented soaps but changes the nature, and makes it rich in foam and easy to wash off. The third kind is actually the combined style of the above two and is characterized by the advantages of both the first and second kinds. It is rich in foam, easy to wash off and refreshing to feel. The body wash sold in the stores generally are classified into the 2nd and 3rd styles.

The major Chinese and foreign chemicals factories bring forth new products after analyzing the marketing information and consumers characteristics. There are kinds of brands such as Safeguard by P&G, Lux by Unilever, Slek by C-bon, Biore by Kao Corp., Johnson's Baby Wash by Johnson & Johnson, Palmotive by Coglate, Lioushen by Shanghai Household Chemicals, etc. Nowadays, body wash has become so fashionable that it has been accepted by the youth, as well as the middle or old aged.

According to the research on body wash, the most highly appraised is Fu'an, with the highest degree of ownership. Liushen's fragrance lasts longest; Clairol and Fu'an clean best; Johnson is easiest to pour out and Safeguard has most functions. (Sources: Consumers Guide, Aug, 99, P63)

Although body wash is showing a tendency to replace soaps, the change of people's consuming habits will still take time and effort since body wash is more expensive than soap. In this case, the body wash market has to be built gradually. Enterprises' attention should be paid not only to develop new products but also to build the consumer's habits.

Washing Powder

Accelerated by high ownership of washing machines, the sale of washing powder has been highly raised in recent years. The annual consumption of washing powder in a family of 3 is from 5 kg to 6.5kg. Although some consumers use soaps to wash, the multi-functional washing powder is taking place of the single-functional soaps in many big cities. The immense need motivates both the producers as well as the sellers. And competition becomes severe.

The competition mainly taken place among White Cat Group in Shanghai (White Cat, Jiamei), P&G in Guangzhou (Ariel,Tide), Unilever Corp from England (Omo) and Hencel from Germany(Persil), and each has its uniqueness to try to get the upper hand over others. For example, White Cat, first produced in 1958, once the symbol of quality and benefit, is still welcomed by middle-aged housewives, due to its low price Unilever Corp. impacts the consumers with great advertising campaign and great diversity of produced lines. P&G Corp introduces new items on the basis of old pattern of Ariel. Each company tries different means in terms of price, promotion and technology in hope to get a bigger share of the total sale.

At present, some Chinese brands such as White Cat, Jiamei, Power28, Panda, Jiajia and some joint venture brands such as OMO, Persil, Tide and Ariel take the leading places. These brands are well-known and widely used. White Cat, OMO, Tide and Ariel hold occupy more than half of the market through their own unique characteristics and different advantages:they have formed the most important group in washing powder market. Meanwhile, some regional brands are also welcomed because they are dear to local consumers. For instance, the awareness of Tianjin Jiajia accounts for more than 95% share of voice in Tianjin and Shijiazhuang market, and more than 50% of the actual market. Jiajia is the most famous washing powder in Nanjing and Panda in Zhengzhou. More than 70% of the consumers prefer Power 28 in Xi'an, Wuhan, Chengdu and some neighboring regions.

In short, consumers prefer low foamed or specialty washing powder instead of the ordinary, rich-foamed washing powder. The need for condensed washing powder is increasing. At present, the high-and-medium price washing powder are mainly sold in urban areas, low-price washing powder are mainly sold in rural areas.

Liquid Detergent

The use of detergent in Chinese common families is about a dozen of years. Soon it has been popularized and become one of the daily necessities. The annual consumption of liquid detergent is 300 to 400 thousand tons and the annual output of Golden fish, popular in Beijing, is about 20 thousand tons. At present, there are dozens of brands, including ordinary, densed or anti-bacteria styles and detergent both for machine washing and hand washing are also available. The brands hold the first places in market are White Cat, Golden Fish, Kami, Boer(波尔),Tugaris and Dosia,etc.

White Cat, Golden Fish are the two most famous Chinese brands. Shanghai White Cat Corp. Ltd. is a state-owned enterprise which holds more than 50% of the total detergent sale. Golden Fish is dominant in Beijing, 80% share of the total market because of its reasonable price, convenient use and stable quality.

Careful consideration is necessary before choose a certain brand since detergent, being a daily necessity, is greatly related with health. There are several elements which should be taken into consideration. First, cleaning effect. Consumers mind the cleaning effect much and they will not try it again if they find advertising falls short of the reality. Second, the price. Most of the consumers prefer the cheap ones if there is no obvious difference in cleaning effect between the cheap ones and expensive ones. But some consumers care little about price. They may buy at higher price only if the effects meets their requirement. Third, convenience for use. The products must be convenient and easy to use since no one tend to take troubles. Forth, brand. A brand can only be accepted when it is good in quality and moderate in price. Fifth, flavor of fragrance. Different consumers prefer different flavor of fragrance, e.g. the consumers in Beijing normally like lemon or fruit fragrance. Sixth, package. The varied color, original shape and beautiful package can also arouse the consumer's desire to buy.

Nowadays many enterprises add some supplementary functions such as anti-bacteria and anti-pesticide residue to the original functions of getting rid of dirt and grease. It is maintained by the experts that the increasing need for anti-bacteria detergent is a new trend for the development of detergent.

1.牙膏 / Toothpaste

● 北京 / Beijing

1-1 最常用品牌排名/ Ranking of the Most Frequently Used Brands

排名 Brand Ranking	品牌 Brands	人数 Number	百分比 Percent
1	高露洁 Colgate	363	36.0
2	佳洁士 Crest	132	13.1
3	中华 Zhonghua	114	11.3
4	洁诺 Signal	85	8.4
5	两面针 Liangmianzhen	69	6.9
6	蓝天六必治 Blue Sky LBZ	64	6.4
7	黑妹 Heimei	59	5.9
8	洁银 Jieyin	43	4.3
9	冷酸灵 Lengsuanling	13	1.3

n=1007

1-2 样本、男性各年龄层、女性各年龄层的常用品牌/ The Most Frequently Used Brands by the Whole Sample, Age and Gender Groups

	人数 Number	第一品牌及百分比 1st/ percent	第二品牌及百分比 2nd/ percent	第三品牌及百分比 3rd/ percent	第四品牌及百分比 4th/ percent
样本 Sample	**1007**	**高露洁 Colgate(36.0)**	**佳洁士 Crest(13.1)**	**中华 Zhonghua(11.3)**	**洁诺 Signal(8.4)**
男性 Male	**499**	**高露洁 Colgate(34.7)**	**中华 Zhonghua(14.2)**	**佳洁士 Crest(12.8)**	**洁诺 Signal(8.0)**
16~24 岁 Age	105	高露洁 Colgate(37.1)	佳洁士 Crest(18.1)	中华 Zhonghua(14.3)	两面针 Liangmianzhen(10.5)
25~34 岁 Age	151	高露洁 Colgate(43.7)	中华 Zhonghua(13.2)	佳洁士 Crest(9.3)	黑妹 Heimei(7.3) 洁诺 Signal(7.3)
35~44 岁 Age	127	高露洁 Colgate(31.5)	佳洁士 Crest(14.2)	中华 Zhonghua(11.8)	洁诺 Signal(10.2)
45~54 岁 Age	76	高露洁 Colgate(25.0)	中华 Zhonghua(17.1)	佳洁士 Crest(14.5)	蓝天六必治 Blue Sky LBZ(11.8)
55~60 岁 Age	40	高露洁 Colgate(22.5)	中华 Zhonghua(20.0)	蓝天六必治 Blue Sky LBZ(10.0)	洁诺 Signal(7.5)
女性 Female	**508**	**高露洁 Colgate(37.4)**	**佳洁士 Crest(13.4)**	**洁诺 Signal(8.9)**	**中华 Zhonghua(8.5)**
16~24 岁 Age	108	高露洁 Colgate(51.9)	佳洁士 Crest(14.8)	洁诺 Signal(12.0)	蓝天六必治 Blue Sky LBZ(4.6)
25~34 岁 Age	150	高露洁 Colgate(40.0)	佳洁士 Crest(15.3)	洁诺 Signal(8.7)	两面针 Liangmianzhen(7.3) 黑妹 Heimei(7.3)
35~44 岁 Age	124	高露洁 Colgate(28.2)	佳洁士 Crest(16.9)	中华 Zhonghua(11.3)	蓝天六必治 Blue Sky LBZ(10.5)
45~54 岁 Age	84	高露洁 Colgate(29.8)	中华 Zhonghua(13.1)	洁诺 Signal(9.5)	蓝天六必治 Blue Sky LBZ(8.3)
55~60 岁 Age	42	高露洁 Colgate(33.3)	蓝天六必治 Blue Sky LBZ(14.3)	洁银 Jieyin(11.9)	中华 Zhonghua(9.5)

1-3 正在使用的品牌排名/ Ranking of the Brands Used Now

排名 Brand Ranking	品牌 Brands	人数 Number	百分比 Percent
1	高露洁 Colgate	338	33.5
2	佳洁士 Crest	150	14.9
3	中华 Zhonghua	96	9.5
3	洁诺 Signal	96	9.5
4	两面针 Liangmianzhen	73	7.2
5	黑妹 Heimei	64	6.3
6	蓝天六必治 Blue Sky LBZ	60	5.9
7	洁银 Jieyin	48	4.8
8	三笑 Sanxiao	14	1.4
8	冷酸灵 Lengsuanling	14	1.4
9	黑人 Darlie	12	1.2
10	安利 Amway	10	1.0

n=1010

1-4 品牌转换习惯/ Brand Habit in Consuming Toothpaste

	人数 Number	第一次使用该品牌 first use this brand	上一次也是这个牌子 used it last time	上一次不是这个牌子 not used it last time
样本 Sample	1009	7.4	70.9	21.7
高露洁 Colgate	338	3.6	80.5	16.0
佳洁士 Crest	149	8.7	73.2	18.1
中华 Zhonghua	96	8.3	69.8	21.9
洁诺 Signal	96	6.3	67.7	26.0
两面针 Liangmianzhen	73	4.1	61.6	34.2
黑妹 Heimei	64	4.7	60.9	34.4
蓝天六必治 Blue Sky LBZ	60	5.0	70.0	25.0
洁银 Jieyin	48	6.3	79.2	14.6
三笑 Sanxiao	14	78.6	7.1	14.3
冷酸灵 Lengsuanling	14	0.0	57.1	42.9
黑人 Darlie	12	8.3	50.0	41.7
安利 Amway	10	0.0	50.0	50.0
倍瑞傲 Perioe	7	57.1	14.3	28.6

1-5 下一次打算使用的品牌排名/ Ranking of the Brands to be Used Next Time

排名 Brand Ranking	品牌 Brands	人数 Number	百分比 Percent
1	高露洁 Colgate	329	32.6
2	佳洁士 Crest	179	17.7
3	洁诺 Signal	116	11.5
4	中华 Zhonghua	89	8.8
5	两面针 Liangmianzhen	56	5.6
6	洁银 Jieyin	51	5.1
7	蓝天六必治 Blue Sky LBZ	47	4.7
8	黑妹 Heimei	44	4.4

n=1009

1-6 样本、男性各年龄层、女性各年龄层是否是主要购买者/ Purchasers in the Household by the Whole Sample, Age and Gender Groups

	人数 Number	是 yes	不是 no
样本 Sample	1010	61.0	39.0
男性 Male	502	44.0	56.0
16~24 岁 Age	105	31.4	68.6
25~34 岁 Age	151	43.0	57.0
35~44 岁 Age	130	48.5	51.5
45~54 岁 Age	76	48.7	51.3
55~60 岁 Age	40	57.5	42.5
女性 Female	508	77.8	22.2
16~24 岁 Age	108	42.6	57.4
25~34 岁 Age	150	82.7	17.3
35~44 岁 Age	124	90.3	9.7
45~54 岁 Age	84	91.7	8.3
55~60 岁 Age	42	85.7	14.3

1-7 样本、男性各年龄层、女性各年龄层的使用方式/ Ways of Using the Products by the Whole Sample, Age and Gender Groups

	人数 Number	个人专用 personal use	家人共用 all family members share
样本 Sample	1011	26.0	74.0
男性 Male	503	27.2	72.8
16~24 岁 Age	105	35.2	64.8
25~34 岁 Age	151	24.5	75.5
35~44 岁 Age	130	26.2	73.8
45~54 岁 Age	77	28.6	71.4
55~60 岁 Age	40	17.5	82.5
女性 Female	508	24.8	75.2
16~24 岁 Age	108	31.5	68.5
25~34 岁 Age	150	20.0	80.0
35~44 岁 Age	124	21.8	78.2
45~54 岁 Age	84	29.8	70.2
55~60 岁 Age	42	23.8	76.2

1-8 样本、男性各年龄层、女性各年龄层的使用频率/ Frequencies of the Consumed Toothpaste by the Whole Sample, Age and Gender Groups

	人数 Number	一天4次或以上 4 times or over a day	一天3次 3 times a day	一天2次 twice a day	一天1次 once a day	一天1次以下 once a day below
样本 Sample	1009	1.0	8.7	74.6	15.0	0.7
男性 Male	501	0.8	8.0	71.1	18.8	1.4
16~24 岁 Age	104	1.0	9.6	73.1	16.3	0.0
25~34 岁 Age	151	0.7	9.3	71.5	16.6	2.0
35~44 岁 Age	131	0.8	3.8	68.7	24.4	2.3
45~54 岁 Age	76	1.3	7.9	75.0	15.8	0.0
55~60 岁 Age	39	0.0	12.8	64.1	20.5	2.6
女性 Female	508	1.2	9.4	78.1	11.2	0.0
16~24 岁 Age	108	0.9	9.3	75.9	13.9	0.0
25~34 岁 Age	150	2.0	7.3	83.3	7.3	0.0
35~44 岁 Age	124	0.0	9.7	82.3	8.1	0.0
45~54 岁 Age	84	0.0	13.1	70.2	16.7	0.0
55~60 岁 Age	42	4.8	9.5	69.0	16.7	0.0

1-9 选择该类商品的考虑因素/ Ranking of the Considerations in Purchasing

注：本题为多选题，合计百分比超过 100%（Multiple answers）

排名 Ranking	考虑因素 Considerations	人次 Person-time	百分比 Percent
1	产品功用 product function	457	45.3
2	有名的牌子 famous brand	443	43.9
3	价格适中 reasonable price	418	41.4
4	广告影响 influence of advertising	247	24.5
5	购买方便 easy to buy	169	16.7
6	单位发的 offered by the working unit	68	6.7
7	别人推荐 introduced by other people	46	4.6
8	有优惠条件 with preferential terms	39	3.9
9	其它 others	32	3.2
10	包装吸引人 appealing package	23	2.3

n=1009

1-10 对产品功能的侧重方面/ Ranking of the Considerations about the Function of this Kind of Product

注：本题为多选题，合计百分比超过 100%（Multiple answers）

排名 Ranking	侧重方面 Items	人次 Person-time	百分比 Percent
1	含氟 with fluoride	494	49.1
2	含钙 with calcium	388	38.5
3	有中药成分 containing Chinese herb	247	24.5
4	有薄荷味 mint	216	21.4
5	有水果味 fruit fragrance	200	19.9
6	是塑料软管包装 plastic soft packing	180	17.9
7	膏体的颜色 color	139	13.8
8	其他 others	60	6.0
9	含盐 with saline	14	1.4

n=1007

1-11 重度消费者的人口分布/ Demographics of the Heavy Consumers

	人数 Number	16-24 岁 Age	25-34 岁 Age	35-44 岁 Age	45-54 岁 Age	55-60 岁 Age
样本 Sample	851	21.2	30.8	24.7	15.7	7.6
男性 Male	400	21.8	30.8	24.0	16.0	7.5
一天 4 次或以上 4 times or over a day	4	25.0	25.0	25.0	25.0	0.0
一天 3 次 3 times a day	40	25.0	35.0	12.5	15.0	12.5
一天 2 次 twice a day	356	21.3	30.3	25.3	16.0	7.0
女性 Female	451	20.6	30.8	25.3	15.5	7.8
一天 4 次或以上 4 times or over a day	6	16.7	50.0	0.0	0.0	33.3
一天 3 次 3 times a day	48	20.8	22.9	25.0	22.9	8.3
一天 2 次 twice a day	397	20.7	31.5	25.7	14.9	7.3

1-12 不同消费者层的常用品牌/ The Most Frequently Used Brands by Market Segments

1-12-1 时尚流行指标/ Fads Popular Index

	人数 Number	第一品牌及百分比 1st / percent	第二品牌及百分比 2nd / percent	第三品牌及百分比 3rd / percent	第四品牌及百分比 4th / percent
样本 Sample	**993**	**高露洁 Colgate(36.2)**	**佳洁士 Crest(13.2)**	**中华 Zhonghua(11.4)**	**洁诺 Signal(8.5)**
平实生活指向 simple living orientation	489	高露洁 Colgate(32.1)	佳洁士 Crest(13.1)	中华 Zhonghua(12.7)	两面针 Liangmianzhen(7.6)
时尚流行指向 fashion orientation	504	高露洁 Colgate(40.1)	佳洁士 Crest(13.3)	中华 Zhonghua(10.1)	洁诺 Signal(9.9)

1-12-2 广告态度指标/ Advertising Attitude Index

	人数 Number	第一品牌及百分比 1st / percent	第二品牌及百分比 2nd / percent	第三品牌及百分比 3rd / percent	第四品牌及百分比 4th / percent
样本 Sample	**990**	**高露洁 Colgate(36.3)**	**佳洁士 Crest(13.0)**	**中华 Zhonghua(11.2)**	**洁诺 Signal(8.2)**
广告淡漠指向 indifferent orientation	286	高露洁 Colgate(31.8)	中华 Zhonghua(12.9)	佳洁士 Crest(11.9)	蓝天六必治 Blue Sky LBZ(9.4)
中间层 medium	571	高露洁 Colgate(37.8)	佳洁士 Crest(13.5)	中华 Zhonghua(10.3)	洁诺 Signal(8.4)
信赖广告指向 loyal orientation	133	高露洁 Colgate(39.1)	佳洁士 Crest(13.5)	中华 Zhonghua(11.3)	洁诺 Signal(8.3)

1-13 重度消费者的消费层构成/ The Composition of the Heavy Consumers

1-13-1 时尚流行指标/ Fads Popular Index

	人数 Number	平实生活指向 simple living orientation	时尚流行指向 fashion orientation
样本 Sample	**839**	**46.6**	**53.4**
一天 4 次或以上 4 times or over a day	10	40.0	60.0
一天 3 次 3 times a day	86	40.7	59.3
一天 2 次 twice a day	743	47.4	52.6

1-13-2 广告态度指标/ Advertising Attitude Index

	人数 Number	广告淡漠指向 indifferent orientation	中间层 medium	信赖广告指向 loyal orientation
样本 Sample	**833**	**27.9**	**58.7**	**13.4**
一天 4 次或以上 4 times or over a day	10	10.0	50.0	40.0
一天 3 次 3 times a day	87	32.2	56.3	11.5
一天 2 次 twice a day	736	27.6	59.1	13.3

● 上海 / Shanghai

1-1 最常用品牌排名/ Ranking of the Most Frequently Used Brands

排名 Brand Ranking	品牌 Brands	人数 Number	百分比 Percent
1	高露洁 Colgate	251	24.8
2	上海 Shanghai	234	23.1
3	洁诺 Signal	178	17.6
4	中华 Zhonghua	130	12.8
5	美加净 Maxmam	80	7.9
6	佳洁士 Crest	36	3.6
7	白玉 Baiyu	24	2.4
8	黑人 Darlie	19	1.9
9	洁银 Jieyin	18	1.8
10	黑妹 Heimei	8	0.8
11	两面针 Liangmianzhen	7	0.7

n=1012

1-2 样本、男性各年龄层、女性各年龄层的常用品牌/ The Most Frequently Used Brands by the Whole Sample, Age and Gender Groups

	人数 Number	第一品牌及百分比 1st/ percent	第二品牌及百分比 2nd/ percent	第三品牌及百分比 3rd/ percent
样本 Sample	1012	**高露洁 Colgate(24.8)**	**上海 Shanghai(23.1)**	**洁诺 Signal(17.6)**
男性 Male	508	**上海 Shanghai(23.6)**	**高露洁 Colgate(23.4)**	**中华 Zhonghua(15.9)**
16~24 岁 Age	109	高露洁 Colgate(31.2)	上海 Shanghai(18.3)	中华 Zhonghua(15.6) 洁诺 Signal(15.6)
25~34 岁 Age	146	高露洁 Colgate(31.5)	洁诺 Signal(18.5)	上海 Shanghai(15.8)
35~44 岁 Age	130	上海 Shanghai(28.5)	中华 Zhonghua(18.5)	高露洁 Colgate(15.4)
45~54 岁 Age	85	上海 Shanghai(28.2)	中华 Zhonghua(16.5)	高露洁 Colgate(15.3)
55~60 岁 Age	38	上海 Shanghai(42.1)	中华 Zhonghua(18.4)	高露洁 Colgate(15.8)
女性 Female	504	**高露洁 Colgate(26.2)**	**上海 Shanghai(22.6)**	**洁诺 Signal(20.6)**
16~24 岁 Age	108	高露洁 Colgate(33.3)	洁诺 Signal(29.6)	上海 Shanghai(11.1)
25~34 岁 Age	143	高露洁 Colgate(30.8)	上海 Shanghai(21.7)	洁诺 Signal(19.6)
35~44 岁 Age	130	高露洁 Colgate(26.2)	上海 Shanghai(24.6)	洁诺 Signal(18.5)
45~54 岁 Age	82	上海 Shanghai(29.3)	洁诺 Signal(20.7)	高露洁 Colgate(12.2) 美加净 Maxmam(12.2)
55~60 岁 Age	41	上海 Shanghai(36.6)	高露洁 Colgate(19.5)	美加净 Maxmam(9.8) 中华 Zhonghua(9.8)

1-3 正在使用的品牌排名/ Ranking of the Brands Used Now

排名 Brand Ranking	品牌 Brands	人数 Number	百分比 Percent
1	高露洁 Colgate	262	25.8
2	上海 Shanghai	209	20.6
3	洁诺 Signal	172	17.0
4	中华 Zhonghua	132	13.0
5	美加净 Maxmam	65	6.4
6	佳洁士 Crest	51	5.0
7	黑人 Darlie	32	3.2
8	白玉 Baiyu	27	2.7
9	洁银 Jieyin	24	2.4

n=1014

1-4 品牌转换习惯/ Brand Habit in Consuming Toothpaste

	人数 Number	第一次使用该品牌 first use this brand	上一次也是这个牌子 used it last time	上一次不是这个牌子 not used it last time
样本 Sample	1012	**4.2**	**76.6**	**19.2**
高露洁 Colgate	261	1.1	82.4	16.5
上海 Shanghai	209	2.9	82.8	14.4
洁诺 Signal	172	2.9	77.3	19.8
中华 Zhonghua	132	4.5	75.0	20.5
美加净 Maxmam	65	3.1	73.8	23.1
佳洁士 Crest	51	11.8	66.7	21.6
黑人 Darlie	32	6.3	68.8	25.0
白玉 Baiyu	27	7.4	59.3	33.3
洁银 Jieyin	24	8.3	70.8	20.8

1-5 下一次打算使用的品牌排名/ Ranking of the Brands to be Used Next Time

排名 Brand Ranking	品牌 Brands	人数 Number	百分比 Percent
1	高露洁 Colgate	260	25.6
2	洁诺 Signal	188	18.5
3	上海 Shanghai	171	16.9
4	中华 Zhonghua	113	11.1
5	佳洁士 Crest	73	7.2
6	美加净 Maxmam	62	6.1
7	黑人 Darlie	41	4.0
8	白玉 Baiyu	26	2.6
9	洁银 Jieyin	20	2.0
10	黑妹 Heimei	11	1.1

n=1014

1-6 样本、男性各年龄层、女性各年龄层是否是主要购买者/ Purchasers in the Household by the Whole Sample, Age and Gender Groups

	人数 Number	是 yes	不是 no
样本 Sample	1012	64.8	35.2
男性 Male	508	51.2	48.8
16~24 岁 Age	108	38.0	62.0
25~34 岁 Age	146	48.6	51.4
35~44 岁 Age	130	53.8	46.2
45~54 岁 Age	85	64.7	35.3
55~60 岁 Age	39	59.0	41.0
女性 Female	504	78.6	21.4
16~24 岁 Age	108	42.6	57.4
25~34 岁 Age	143	78.3	21.7
35~44 岁 Age	130	94.6	5.4
45~54 岁 Age	82	95.1	4.9
55~60 岁 Age	41	90.2	9.8

1-7 样本、男性各年龄层、女性各年龄层的使用方式/ Ways of Using the Products by the Whole Sample, Age and Gender Groups

	人数 Number	个人专用 personal use	家人共用 all family members share
样本 Sample	1013	13.1	86.9
男性 Male	509	14.3	85.7
16~24 岁 Age	109	23.9	76.1
25~34 岁 Age	146	13.7	86.3
35~44 岁 Age	130	10.0	90.0
45~54 岁 Age	85	11.8	88.2
55~60 岁 Age	39	10.3	89.7
女性 Female	504	11.9	88.1
16~24 岁 Age	108	21.3	78.7
25~34 岁 Age	143	13.3	86.7
35~44 岁 Age	130	8.5	91.5
45~54 岁 Age	82	4.9	95.1
55~60 岁 Age	41	7.3	92.7

1-8 样本、男性各年龄层、女性各年龄层的使用频率/ Frequencies of the Consumed Toothpaste by the Whole Sample, Age and Gender Groups

	人数 Number	一天 4 次或以上 4 times or over a day	一天 3 次 3 times a day	一天 2 次 twice a day	一天 1 次 once a day	一天 1 次以下 once a day below
样本 Sample	1012	2.5	5.1	76.2	16.2	0.0
男性 Male	509	2.8	6.1	72.3	18.9	0.0
16~24 岁 Age	109	2.8	11.9	69.7	15.6	0.0
25~34 岁 Age	146	1.4	2.7	78.8	17.1	0.0
35~44 岁 Age	130	3.1	4.6	69.2	23.1	0.0
45~54 岁 Age	85	0.0	7.1	69.4	23.5	0.0
55~60 岁 Age	39	12.8	5.1	71.8	10.3	0.0
女性 Female	503	2.2	4.2	80.1	13.5	0.0
16~24 岁 Age	108	2.8	6.5	72.2	18.5	0.0
25~34 岁 Age	143	4.2	3.5	80.4	11.9	0.0
35~44 岁 Age	130	1.5	2.3	82.3	13.8	0.0
45~54 岁 Age	81	0.0	7.4	84.0	8.6	0.0
55~60 岁 Age	41	0.0	0.0	85.4	14.6	0.0

1-9 选择该类商品的考虑因素/ Ranking of the Considerations in Purchasing

注：本题为多选题，合计百分比超过 100%（Multiple answers）

排名 Ranking	考虑因素 Considerations	人次 Person-time	百分比 Percent
1	价格适中 reasonable price	500	49.4
2	产品功用 product function	442	43.6
3	有名的牌子 famous brand	402	39.7
4	购买方便 easy to buy	252	24.9
5	广告影响 influence of advertising	187	18.5
6	有优惠条件 with preferential terms	69	6.8
7	别人推荐 introduced by other people	51	5.0
8	包装吸引人 appealing package	31	3.1
9	其它 others	26	2.6
10	单位发的 offered by the working unit	21	2.1

n=1013

1-10 对产品功能的侧重方面/ Ranking of the Considerations about the Function of this Kind of Product

注：本题为多选题，合计百分比超过 100%（Multiple answers）

排名 Ranking	侧重方面 Items	人次 Person-time	百分比 Percent
1	含氟 with fluoride	449	44.3
2	含钙 with calcium	353	34.8
3	有薄荷味 mint	303	29.9
4	有中药成分 containing Chinese herb	250	24.7
5	是塑料软管包装 plastic soft packing	213	21.0
6	膏体的颜色 color	125	12.3
7	有水果味 fruit fragrance	117	11.5
8	其他 others	35	3.5
9	含盐 with saline	13	1.3

n=1013

1-11 重度消费者的人口分布/ Demographics of the Heavy Consumers

	人数 Number	16-24 岁 Age	25-34 岁 Age	35-44 岁 Age	45-54 岁 Age	55-60 岁 Age
样本 Sample	848	21.2	29.1	25.0	16.4	8.3
男性 Male	413	22.3	29.3	24.2	15.7	8.5
一天 4 次或以上 4 times or over a day	14	21.4	14.3	28.6	0.0	35.7
一天 3 次 3 times a day	31	41.9	12.9	19.4	19.4	6.5
一天 2 次 twice a day	368	20.7	31.3	24.5	16.0	7.6
女性 Female	435	20.2	29.0	25.7	17.0	8.0
一天 4 次或以上 4 times or over a day	11	27.3	54.5	18.2	0.0	0.0
一天 3 次 3 times a day	21	33.3	23.8	14.3	28.6	0.0
一天 2 次 twice a day	403	19.4	28.5	26.6	16.9	8.7

1-12 不同消费者层的常用品牌/ The Most Frequently Used Brands by Market Segments

1-12-1 时尚流行指标/ Fads Popular Index

	人数 Number	第一品牌及百分比 1st / percent	第二品牌及百分比 2nd / percent	第三品牌及百分比 3rd / percent	第四品牌及百分比 4th / percent
样本 Sample	1003	**高露洁 Colgate（24.8）**	**上海 Shanghai（23.1）**	**洁诺 Signal（17.6）**	**中华 Zhonghua（12.9）**
平实生活指向 simple living orientation	471	上海 Shanghai（27.4）	高露洁 Colgate（20.8）	洁诺 Signal（16.1）	中华 Zhonghua（14.0）
时尚流行指向 fashion orientation	532	高露洁 Colgate（28.4）	上海 Shanghai（19.4）	洁诺 Signal（19.0）	中华 Zhonghua（11.8）

1-12-2 广告态度指标/ Advertising Attitude Index

	人数 Number	第一品牌及百分比 1st / percent	第二品牌及百分比 2nd / percent	第三品牌及百分比 3rd / percent	第四品牌及百分比 4th / percent
样本 Sample	1000	**高露洁 Colgate（25.0）**	**上海 Shanghai（23.3）**	**洁诺 Signal（17.5）**	**中华 Zhonghua（12.4）**
广告淡漠指向 indifferent orientation	255	上海 Shanghai（27.5）	高露洁 Colgate（23.5）	洁诺 Signal（16.5）	中华 Zhonghua（9.8） 美加净 Maxmam（9.8）
中间层 medium	610	高露洁 Colgate（25.9）	上海 Shanghai（22.3）	洁诺 Signal（17.4）	中华 Zhonghua（13.0）
信赖广告指向 loyal orientation	135	高露洁 Colgate（23.7）	上海 Shanghai（20.0） 洁诺 Signal（20.0）	中华 Zhonghua（14.8）	佳洁士 Crest（6.7）

1-13 重度消费者的消费层构成/ The Composition of the Heavy Consumers

1-13-1 时尚流行指标/ Fads Popular Index

	人数 Number	平实生活指向 simple living orientation	时尚流行指向 fashion orientation
样本 Sample	839	47.2	52.8
一天 4 次或以上 4 times or over a day	24	50.0	50.0
一天 3 次 3 times a day	52	38.5	61.5
一天 2 次 twice a day	763	47.7	52.3

1-13-2 广告态度指标/ Advertising Attitude Index

	人数 Number	广告淡漠指向 indifferent orientation	中间层 medium	信赖广告指向 loyal orientation
样本 Sample	839	25.4	61 3	13.3
一天 4 次或以上 4 times or over a day	24	33.3	62.5	4.2
一天 3 次 3 times a day	52	23.1	51.9	25.0
一天 2 次 twice a day	763	25.3	61.9	12.8

● 广州 / Guangzhou

1-1 最常用品牌排名/ Ranking of the Most Frequently Used Brands

排名 Brand Ranking	品牌 Brands	人数 Number	百分比 Percent
1	高露洁 Colgate	326	31.6
2	洁银 Jieyin	169	16.4
3	黑妹 Heimei	158	15.3
4	黑人 Darlie	138	13.4
5	佳洁士 Crest	82	8.0
6	洁诺 Signal	31	3.0
7	中华 Zhonghua	23	2.2

n=1031

1-2 样本、男性各年龄层、女性各年龄层的常用品牌/ The Most Frequently Used Brands by the Whole Sample, Age and Gender Groups

	人数 Number	第一品牌及百分比 1st/ percent	第二品牌及百分比 2nd/ percent	第三品牌及百分比 3rd/ percent	第四品牌及百分比 4th/ percent
样本 Sample	1031	**高露洁 Colgate(31.6)**	**洁银 Jieyin(16.4)**	**黑妹 Heimei(15.3)**	**黑人 Darlie(13.4)**
男性 Male	499	**高露洁 Colgate(33.1)**	**黑妹 Heimei(18.0)**	**洁银 Jieyin(16.0)**	**黑人 Darlie(12.6)**
16~24 岁 Age	106	高露洁 Colgate(46.2)	黑妹 Heimei(15.1)	黑人 Darlie(10.4) 佳洁士 Crest(10.4)	洁银 Jieyin(4.7)
25~34 岁 Age	150	高露洁 Colgate(32.7)	黑妹 Heimei(20.0)	洁银 Jieyin(14.7)	黑人 Darlie(14.0)
35~44 岁 Age	127	高露洁 Colgate(29.9)	洁银 Jieyin(22.0)	黑妹 Heimei(15.0)	黑人 Darlie(14.2)
45~54 岁 Age	73	高露洁 Colgate(26.0)	洁银 Jieyin(20.5)	黑妹 Heimei(17.8)	佳洁士 Crest(12.3)
55~60 岁 Age	43	黑妹 Heimei(27.9)	高露洁 Colgate(23.3) 洁银 Jieyin(23.3)	黑人 Darlie(16.3)	佳洁士 Crest(2.3) 洁诺 Signal(2.3) 中华 Zhonghua(2.3) 立白 Libai(2.3)
女性 Female	532	**高露洁 Colgate(30.3)**	**洁银 Jieyin(16.7)**	**黑人 Darlie(14.1)**	**黑妹 Heimei(12.8)**
16~24 岁 Age	112	高露洁 Colgate(41.1)	黑人 Darlie(17.9)	黑妹 Heimei(12.5)	洁银 Jieyin(8.0)
25~34 岁 Age	157	高露洁 Colgate(26.1)	黑人 Darlie(17.8)	洁银 Jieyin(15.9)	黑妹 Heimei(15.3)
35~44 岁 Age	137	高露洁 Colgate(29.9)	洁银 Jieyin(16.8)	佳洁士 Crest(13.1)	黑妹 Heimei(11.7)
45~54 岁 Age	85	高露洁 Colgate(28.2)	洁银 Jieyin(22.4)	黑妹 Heimei(15.3)	黑人 Darlie(10.6)
55~60 岁 Age	41	洁银 Jieyin(31.7)	高露洁 Colgate(22.0)	黑人 Darlie(9.8) 佳洁士 Crest(9.8)	中华 Zhonghua(4.9) 洁诺 Signal(4.9)

1-3 正在使用的品牌排名/ Ranking of the Brands Used Now

排名 Brand Ranking	品牌 Brands	人数 Number	百分比 Percent
1	高露洁 Colgate	309	29.9
2	洁银 Jieyin	174	16.8
3	黑妹 Heimei	160	15.5
4	黑人 Darlie	139	13.5
5	佳洁士 Crest	100	9.7
6	洁诺 Signal	34	3.3
7	中华 Zhonghua	22	2.1
8	两面针 Liangmianzhen	15	1.5
9	LG 竹盐 Bamboo Salt	11	1.1

n=1033

1-4 品牌转换习惯/ Brand Habit in Consuming Toothpaste

	人数 Number	第一次使用该品牌 first use this brand	上一次也是这个牌子 used it last time	上一次不是这个牌子 not used it last time
样本 Sample	1029	6.4	68.1	25.5
高露洁 Colgate	307	4.2	76.9	18.9
洁银 Jieyin	174	4.6	70.7	24.7
黑妹 Heimei	158	2.5	65.8	31.6
黑人 Darlie	139	4.3	68.3	27.3
佳洁士 Crest	100	10.0	61.0	29.0
洁诺 Signal	34	17.6	61.8	20.6
中华 Zhonghua	22	18.2	54.5	27.3
两面针 Liangmianzhen	15	13.3	40.0	46.7
LG 竹盐 Bamboo Salt	11	18.2	18.2	63.6

1-5 下一次打算使用的品牌排名/ Ranking of the Brands to be Used Next Time

排名 Brand Ranking	品牌 Brands	人数 Number	百分比 Percent
1	高露洁 Colgate	316	30.6
2	黑人 Darlie	146	14.1
3	洁银 Jieyin	132	12.8
4	佳洁士 Crest	123	11.9
5	黑妹 Heimei	121	11.7
6	中华 Zhonghua	26	2.5
7	洁诺 Signal	23	2.2
8	LG 竹盐 Bamboo Salt	18	1.7

n=1034

1-6 样本、男性各年龄层、女性各年龄层是否是主要购买者/ Purchasers in the Household by the Whole Sample, Age and Gender Groups

	人数 Number	是 yes	不是 no
样本 Sample	1032	62.1	37.9
男性 Male	498	46.2	53.8
16~24 岁 Age	106	35.8	64.2
25~34 岁 Age	150	47.3	52.7
35~44 岁 Age	126	50.8	49.2
45~54 岁 Age	73	43.8	56.2
55~60 岁 Age	43	58.1	41.9
女性 Female	534	77.0	23.0
16~24 岁 Age	112	37.5	62.5
25~34 岁 Age	158	82.9	17.1
35~44 岁 Age	136	90.4	9.6
45~54 岁 Age	87	92.0	8.0
55~60 岁 Age	41	85.4	14.6

1-7 样本、男性各年龄层、女性各年龄层的使用方式/ Ways of Using the Products by the Whole Sample, Age and Gender Groups

	人数 Number	个人专用 personal use	家人共用 all family members share
样本 Sample	1033	21.8	78.2
男性 Male	499	23.4	76.6
16~24 岁 Age	106	34.9	65.1
25~34 岁 Age	150	25.3	74.7
35~44 岁 Age	127	14.2	85.8
45~54 岁 Age	73	17.8	82.2
55~60 岁 Age	43	25.6	74.4
女性 Female	534	20.2	79.8
16~24 岁 Age	112	24.1	75.9
25~34 岁 Age	158	15.8	84.2
35~44 岁 Age	136	20.6	79.4
45~54 岁 Age	87	16.1	83.9
55~60 岁 Age	41	34.1	65.9

1-8 样本、男性各年龄层、女性各年龄层的使用频率/ Frequencies of the Consumed Toothpaste by the Whole Sample, Age and Gender Groups

	人数 Number	一天 4 次或以上 4 times or over a day	一天 3 次 3 times a day	一天 2 次 twice a day	一天 1 次 once a day	一天 1 次以下 once a day below
样本 Sample	1032	2.1	10.1	73.1	14.3	0.4
男性 Male	498	2.4	9.4	68.9	18.7	0.6
16~24 岁 Age	106	0.9	12.3	61.3	24.5	0.9
25~34 岁 Age	150	2.0	8.7	72.0	17.3	0.0
35~44 岁 Age	126	3.2	7.9	69.0	19.0	0.8
45~54 岁 Age	73	1.4	8.2	79.5	11.0	0.0
55~60 岁 Age	43	7.0	11.6	58.1	20.9	2.3
女性 Female	534	1.9	10.7	77.0	10.3	0.2
16~24 岁 Age	111	0.9	12.6	82.0	3.6	0.9
25~34 岁 Age	158	1.9	8.2	79.7	10.1	0.0
35~44 岁 Age	137	1.5	15.3	73.7	9.5	0.0
45~54 岁 Age	87	3.4	8.0	69.0	19.5	0.0
55~60 岁 Age	41	2.4	4.9	80.5	12.2	0.0

1-9 选择该类商品的考虑因素/ Ranking of the Considerations in Purchasing

注：本题为多选题，合计百分比超过 100%（Multiple answers）

排名 Ranking	考虑因素 Considerations	人次 Person-time	百分比 Percent
1	产品功用 product function	502	48.6
2	价格适中 reasonable price	463	44.9
3	有名的牌子 famous brand	446	43.2
4	购买方便 easy to buy	256	24.8
5	广告影响 influence of advertising	168	16.3
6	有优惠条件 with preferential terms	62	6.0
7	别人推荐 introduced by other people	36	3.5
8	包装吸引人 appealing package	27	2.6
9	其它 others	19	1.8
10	单位发的 offered by the working unit	14	1.4

n=1032

1-10 对产品功能的侧重方面/ Ranking of the Considerations about the Function of this Kind of Product

注：本题为多选题，合计百分比超过 100%（Multiple answers）

排名 Ranking	侧重方面 Items	人次 Person-time	百分比 Percent
1	含氟 with fluoride	462	44.9
2	有薄荷味 mint	359	34.9
3	含钙 with calcium	271	26.3
4	有中药成分 containing Chinese herb	255	24.8
5	是塑料软管包装 plastic soft packing	186	18.1
6	膏体的颜色 color	148	14.4
7	有水果味 fruit fragrance	100	9.7
8	其他 others	49	4.8
9	含盐 with saline	47	4.6

n=1030

1-11 重度消费者的人口分布/ Demographics of the Heavy Consumers

	人数 Number	16-24 岁 Age	25-34 岁 Age	35-44 岁 Age	45-54 岁 Age	55-60 岁 Age
样本 Sample	880	21.0	30.2	25.6	15.3	7.8
男性 Male	402	19.7	30.8	25.1	16.2	8.2
一天 4 次或以上 4 times or over a day	12	8.3	25.0	33.3	8.3	25.0
一天 3 次 3 times a day	47	27.7	27.7	21.3	12.8	10.6
一天 2 次 twice a day	343	19.0	31.5	25.4	16.9	7.3
女性 Female	478	22.2	29.7	25.9	14.6	7.5
一天 4 次或以上 4 times or over a day	10	10.0	30.0	20.0	30.0	10.0
一天 3 次 3 times a day	57	24.6	22.8	36.8	12.3	3.5
一天 2 次 twice a day	411	22.1	30.7	24.6	14.6	8.0

1-12 不同消费者层的常用品牌/ The Most Frequently Used Brands by Market Segments

1-12-1 时尚流行指标/ Fads Popular Index

	人数 Number	第一品牌及百分比 1st / percent	第二品牌及百分比 2nd / percent	第三品牌及百分比 3rd / percent	第四品牌及百分比 4th / percent
样本 Sample	1019	**高露洁 Colgate(31.6)**	**洁银 Jieyin(16.3)**	**黑妹 Heimei(15.4)**	**黑人 Darlie(13.4)**
平实生活指向 simple living orientation	517	高露洁 Colgate(26.7)	洁银 Jieyin(19.5)	黑妹 Heimei(16.2)	黑人 Darlie(13.3)
时尚流行指向 fashion orientation	502	高露洁 Colgate(36.7)	黑妹 Heimei(14.5)	黑人 Darlie(13.5)	洁银 Jieyin(12.9)

1-12-2 广告态度指标/ Advertising Attitude Index

	人数 Number	第一品牌及百分比 1st / percent	第二品牌及百分比 2nd / percent	第三品牌及百分比 3rd / percent	第四品牌及百分比 4th / percent
样本 Sample	1019	**高露洁 Colgate(31.6)**	**洁银 Jieyin(16.4)**	**黑妹 Heimei(15.4)**	**黑人 Darlie(13.2)**
广告淡漠指向 indifferent orientation	332	高露洁 Colgate(30.1)	洁银 Jieyin(17.8)	黑妹 Heimei(16.6)	黑人 Darlie(12.3)
中间层 medium	592	高露洁 Colgate(33.1)	洁银 Jieyin(16.0)	黑人 Darlie(14.0)	黑妹 Heimei(13.9)
信赖广告指向 loyal orientation	95	高露洁 Colgate(27.4)	黑妹 Heimei(21.1)	洁银 Jieyin(13.7)	佳洁士 Crest(12.6)

1-13 重度消费者的消费层构成/ The Composition of the Heavy Consumers

1-13-1 时尚流行指标/ Fads Popular Index

	人数 Number	平实生活指向 simple living orientation	时尚流行指向 fashion orientation
样本 Sample	871	50.5	49.5
一天 4 次或以上 4 times or over a day	22	50.0	50.0
一天 3 次 3 times a day	103	38.8	61.2
一天 2 次 twice a day	746	52.1	47.9

1-13-2 广告态度指标/ Advertising Attitude Index

	人数 Number	广告淡漠指向 indifferent orientation	中间层 medium	信赖广告指向 loyal orientation
样本 Sample	870	32.9	58.2	9.0
一天 4 次或以上 4 times or over a day	22	31.8	68.2	0.0
一天 3 次 3 times a day	102	28.4	61.8	9.8
一天 2 次 twice a day	746	33.5	57.4	9.1

重庆 / Chongqing

1-1 最常用品牌排名/ Ranking of the Most Frequently Used Brands

排名 Brand Ranking	品牌 Brands	人数 Number	百分比 Percent
1	冷酸灵 Lengsuanling	292	46.8
2	高露洁 Colgate	66	10.6
3	佳洁士 Crest	57	9.1
4	中华 Zhonghua	47	7.5
5	两面针 Liangmianzhen	43	6.9
6	四新 Sixin	24	3.8
7	洁诺 Signal	16	2.6
8	黑妹 Heimei	15	2.4
9	黑人 Darlie	11	1.8
10	洁银 Jieyin	8	1.3

n=624

1-2 样本、男性各年龄层、女性各年龄层的常用品牌/ The Most Frequently Used Brands by the Whole Sample, Age and Gender Groups

	人数 Number	第一品牌及百分比 1st/ percent	第二品牌及百分比 2nd/ percent	第三品牌及百分比 3rd/ percent	第四品牌及百分比 4th/ percent
样本 Sample	624	**冷酸灵 Lengsuanling(46.8)**	**高露洁 Colgate(10.6)**	**佳洁士 Crest(9.1)**	**中华 Zhonghua(7.5)**
男性 Male	314	**冷酸灵 Lengsuanling(46.2)**	**高露洁 Colgate(9.6)**	**中华 Zhonghua(8.3)**	**佳洁士 Crest(7.3)**
16~24 岁 Age	64	冷酸灵 Lengsuanling(29.7)	高露洁 Colgate(18.8)	佳洁士 Crest(12.5)	中华 Zhonghua(9.4)
25~34 岁 Age	93	冷酸灵 Lengsuanling(46.2)	高露洁 Colgate(12.9)	中华 Zhonghua(7.5) 佳洁士 Crest(7.5)	黑妹 Heimei(4.3) 四新 Sixin(4.3) 洁诺 Signal(4.3) 两面针 Liangmianzhen(4.3)
35~44 岁 Age	75	冷酸灵 Lengsuanling(52.0)	两面针 Liangmianzhen(10.7)	中华 Zhonghua(9.3)	四新 Sixin(5.3) 佳洁士 Crest(5.3)
45~54 岁 Age	54	冷酸灵 Lengsuanling(53.7)	两面针 Liangmianzhen(11.1)	高露洁 Colgate(7.4) 四新 Sixin(7.4)	
55~60 岁 Age	28	冷酸灵 Lengsuanling(53.6)	中华 Zhonghua(14.3)	佳洁士 Crest(10.7)	四新 Sixin(7.1)
女性 Female	310	**冷酸灵 Lengsuanling(47.4)**	**高露洁 Colgate(11.6)**	**佳洁士 Crest(11.0)**	**中华 Zhonghua(6.8) 两面针 Liangmianzhen(6.8)**
16~24 岁 Age	64	冷酸灵 Lengsuanling(40.6)	佳洁士 Crest(21.9)	高露洁 Colgate(14.1)	洁诺 Signal(6.3) 两面针 Liangmianzhen(6.3)
25~34 岁 Age	90	冷酸灵 Lengsuanling(44.4)	高露洁 Colgate(14.4)	佳洁士 Crest(13.3)	两面针 Liangmianzhen(6.7)
35~44 岁 Age	73	冷酸灵 Lengsuanling(47.9)	高露洁 Colgate(15.1)	中华 Zhonghua(8.2) 两面针 Liangmianzhen(8.2)	四新 Sixin(4.1) 佳洁士 Crest(4.1)
45~54 岁 Age	60	冷酸灵 Lengsuanling(53.3)	中华 Zhonghua(13.3)	佳洁士 Crest(6.7)	两面针 Liangmianzhen(5.0) 高露洁 Colgate(5.0)
55~60 岁 Age	23	冷酸灵 Lengsuanling(60.9)	中华 Zhonghua(13.0)	两面针 Liangmianzhen(8.7)	黑妹 Heimei(4.3) 佳洁士 Crest(4.3) 洁诺 Signal(4.3) 蓝天六必治 Blue Sky LBZ(4.3)

1-3 正在使用的品牌排名/ Ranking of the Brands Used Now

排名 Brand Ranking	品牌 Brands	人数 Number	百分比 Percent
1	冷酸灵 Lengsuanling	273	43.8
2	高露洁 Colgate	69	11.1
3	两面针 Liangmianzhen	55	8.8
4	佳洁士 Crest	53	8.5
5	中华 Zhonghua	45	7.2
6	四新 Sixin	24	3.8
7	洁诺 Signal	20	3.2
8	三笑 San Xiao	19	3.0
9	黑妹 Heimei	17	2.7
10	黑人 Darlie	15	2.4

n=624

1-4 品牌转换习惯/ Brand Habit in Consuming Toothpaste

	人数 Number	第一次使用该品牌 first use this brand	上一次也是这个牌子 used it last time	上一次不是这个牌子 not used it last time
样本 Sample	622	3.7	70.9	25.4
冷酸灵 Lengsuanling	272	1.5	82.0	16.5
高露洁 Colgate	68	1.5	79.4	19.1
两面针 Liangmianzhen	55	1.8	50.9	47.3
佳洁士 Crest	53	1.9	69.8	28.3
中华 Zhonghua	45	6.7	46.7	46.7
四新 Sixin	24	0.0	83.3	16.7
洁诺 Signal	20	20.0	55.0	25.0
三笑 Sanxiao	19	5.3	42.1	52.6
黑妹 Heimei	17	0.0	64.7	35.3
黑人 Darlie	15	13.3	60.0	26.7
蓝天六必治 Blue Sky LBZ	11	9.1	36.4	54.5

1-5 下一次打算使用的品牌排名/ Ranking of the Brands to be Used Next Time

排名 Brand Ranking	品牌 Brands	人数 Number	百分比 Percent
1	冷酸灵 Lengsuanling	218	34.9
2	高露洁 Colgate	84	13.5
3	佳洁士 Crest	75	12.0
4	两面针 Liangmianzhen	59	9.5
5	中华 Zhonghua	49	7.9
6	洁诺 Signal	26	4.2
6	黑妹 Heimei	26	4.2
7	四新 Sixin	24	3.8
8	蓝天六必治 Blue Sky LBZ	14	2.2
9	黑人 Darlie	8	1.3
10	洁银 Jieyin	7	1.1

n=624

1-6 样本、男性各年龄层、女性各年龄层是否是主要购买者/ Purchasers in the Household by the Whole Sample, Age and Gender Groups

	人数 Number	是 yes	不是 no
样本 Sample	624	62.0	38.0
男性 Male	314	45.5	54.5
16~24 岁 Age	64	29.7	70.3
25~34 岁 Age	93	49.5	50.5
35~44 岁 Age	75	49.3	50.7
45~54 岁 Age	54	48.1	51.9
55~60 岁 Age	28	53.6	46.4
女性 Female	310	78.7	21.3
16~24 岁 Age	64	53.1	46.9
25~34 岁 Age	90	78.9	21.1
35~44 岁 Age	73	93.2	6.8
45~54 岁 Age	60	86.7	13.3
55~60 岁 Age	23	82.6	17.4

1-7 样本、男性各年龄层、女性各年龄层的使用方式/ Ways of Using the Products by the Whole Sample, Age and Gender Groups

	人数 Number	个人专用 personal use	家人共用 all family members share
样本 Sample	**624**	**8.7**	**91.3**
男性 Male	**314**	**10.5**	**89.5**
16~24 岁 Age	64	18.8	81.3
25~34 岁 Age	93	12.9	87.1
35~44 岁 Age	75	9.3	90.7
45~54 岁 Age	54	1.9	98.1
55~60 岁 Age	28	3.6	96.4
女性 Female	**310**	**6.8**	**93.2**
16~24 岁 Age	64	14.1	85.9
25~34 岁 Age	90	4.4	95.6
35~44 岁 Age	73	5.5	94.5
45~54 岁 Age	60	5.0	95.0
55~60 岁 Age	23	4.3	95.7

1-8 样本、男性各年龄层、女性各年龄层的使用频率/ Frequencies of the Consumed Toothpaste by the Whole Sample, Age and Gender Groups

	人数 Number	4 次或以上一天 4 times or over a day	3 次一天 3 times a day	2 次一天 twice a day	1 次一天 once a day	1 次以下一天 once a day below
样本 Sample	**624**	**2.6**	**8.2**	**70.2**	**18.3**	**0.8**
男性 Male	**314**	**3.5**	**8.0**	**65.6**	**21.7**	**1.3**
16~24 岁 Age	64	6.3	4.7	76.6	12.5	0.0
25~34 岁 Age	93	1.1	12.9	65.6	19.4	1.1
35~44 岁 Age	75	2.7	8.0	52.0	33.3	4.0
45~54 岁 Age	54	3.7	5.6	70.4	20.4	0.0
55~60 岁 Age	28	7.1	3.6	67.9	21.4	0.0
女性 Female	**310**	**1.6**	**8.4**	**74.8**	**14.8**	**0.3**
16~24 岁 Age	64	0.0	12.5	71.9	14.1	1.6
25~34 岁 Age	90	3.3	8.9	75.6	12.2	0.0
35~44 岁 Age	73	2.7	8.2	79.5	9.6	0.0
45~54 岁 Age	60	0.0	6.7	73.3	20.0	0.0
55~60 岁 Age	23	0.0	0.0	69.6	30.4	0.0

1-9 选择该类商品的考虑因素/ Ranking of the Considerations in Purchasing

注：本题为多选题，合计百分比超过 100%（Multiple answers）

排名 Ranking	考虑因素 Considerations	人次 Person-time	百分比 Percent
1	价格适中 reasonable price	340	54.5
2	产品功用 product function	282	45.2
3	有名的牌子 famous brand	176	28.2
4	购买方便 easy to buy	138	22.1
5	广告影响 influence of advertising	122	19.6
6	有优惠条件 with preferential terms	29	4.6
7	别人推荐 introduced by other people	24	3.8
8	其它 others	16	2.6
9	单位发的 offered by the working unit	15	2.4
10	包装吸引人 appealing package	13	2.1

n=624

1-10 对产品功能的侧重方面/ Ranking of the Considerations about the Function of this Kind of Product

注：本题为多选题，合计百分比超过 100%（Multiple answers）

排名 Ranking	侧重方面 Items	人次 Person-time	百分比 Percent
1	含氟 with fluoride	227	36.6
2	有水果味 fruit fragrance	175	28.2
3	有中药成分 containing Chinese herb	164	26.4
4	有薄荷味 mint	148	23.8
5	含钙 with calcium	143	23.0
6	膏体的颜色 color	91	14.7
7	是塑料软管包装 plastic soft packing	60	9.7
8	其他 others	32	5.2
9	含盐 with saline	2	0.3

n=621

1-11 重度消费者的人口分布/ Demographics of the Heavy Consumers

	人数 Number	16-24 岁 Age	25-34 岁 Age	35-44 岁 Age	45-54 岁 Age	55-60 岁 Age
样本 Sample	**505**	**21.8**	**30.3**	**22.4**	**18.0**	**7.5**
男性 Male	**242**	**23.1**	**30.6**	**19.4**	**17.8**	**9.1**
一天 4 次或以上 4 times or over a day	11	36.4	9.1	18.2	18.2	18.2
一天 3 次 3 times a day	25	12.0	48.0	24.0	12.0	4.0
一天 2 次 twice a day	206	23.8	29.6	18.9	18.4	9.2
女性 Female	**263**	**20.5**	**30.0**	**25.1**	**18.3**	**6.1**
一天 4 次或以上 4 times or over a day	5	0.0	60.0	40.0	0.0	0.0
一天 3 次 3 times a day	26	30.8	30.8	23.1	15.4	0.0
一天 2 次 twice a day	232	19.8	29.3	25.0	19.0	6.9

1-12 不同消费者层的常用品牌/ The Most Frequently Used Brands by Market Segments

1-12-1 时尚流行指标/ Fads Popular Index

	人数 Number	第一品牌及百分比 1st / percent	第二品牌及百分比 2nd / percent	第三品牌及百分比 3rd / percent	第四品牌及百分比 4th / percent
样本 Sample	**616**	**冷酸灵 Lengsuanling(47.2)**	**高露洁 Colgate(10.4)**	**佳洁士 Crest(9.1)**	**中华 Zhonghua(7.5)**
平实生活指向 simple living orientation	369	冷酸灵 Lengsuanling(52.3)	中华 Zhonghua(8.1)	两面针 Liangmianzhen(7.9)	高露洁 Colgate(7.6)
时尚流行指向 fashion orientation	247	冷酸灵 Lengsuanling(39.7)	佳洁士 Crest(15.0)	高露洁 Colgate(14.6)	中华 Zhonghua(6.5)

1-12-2 广告态度指标/ Advertising Attitude Index

	人数 Number	第一品牌及百分比 1st / percent	第二品牌及百分比 2nd / percent	第三品牌及百分比 3rd / percent	第四品牌及百分比 4th / percent
样本 Sample	**618**	**冷酸灵 Lengsuanling(46.8)**	**高露洁 Colgate(10.7)**	**佳洁士 Crest(9.1)**	**中华 Zhonghua(7.4)**
广告淡漠指向 indifferent orientation	167	冷酸灵 Lengsuanling(53.9)	高露洁 Colgate(9.0)	中华 Zhonghua(7.8)	两面针 Liangmianzhen(6.6)
中间层 medium	367	冷酸灵 Lengsuanling(44.4)	高露洁 Colgate(11.4)	佳洁士 Crest(10.9)	两面针 Liangmianzhen(7.6) 中华 Zhonghua(7.6)
信赖广告指向 loyal orientation	84	冷酸灵 Lengsuanling(42.9)	高露洁 Colgate(10.7)	佳洁士 Crest(9.5)	四新 Sixin(7.1)

1-13 重度消费者的消费层构成/ The Composition of the Heavy Consumers

1-13-1 时尚流行指标/ Fads Popular Index

	人数 Number	平实生活指向 simple living orientation	时尚流行指向 fashion orientation
样本 Sample	**498**	**58.0**	**42.0**
一天 4 次或以上 4 times or over a day	15	53.3	46.7
一天 3 次 3 times a day	50	58.0	42.0
一天 2 次 twice a day	433	58.2	41.8

1-13-2 广告态度指标/ Advertising Attitude Index

	人数 Number	广告淡漠指向 indifferent orientation	中间层 medium	信赖广告指向 loyal orientation
样本 Sample	**499**	**25.5**	**61.1**	**13.4**
一天 4 次或以上 4 times or over a day	15	13.3	66.7	20.0
一天 3 次 3 times a day	50	22.0	66.0	12.0
一天 2 次 twice a day	434	26.3	60.4	13.4

● 武汉 / Wuhan

1-1 最常用品牌排名/ Ranking of the Most Frequently Used Brands

排名 Brand Ranking	品牌 Brands	人数 Number	百分比 Percent
1	两面针 Liangmianzhen	151	23.5
2	高露洁 Colgate	108	16.8
3	冷酸灵 Lengsuanling	78	12.1
4	佳洁士 Crest	74	11.5
4	中华 Zhonghua	74	11.5
5	洁诺 Signal	52	8.1
6	黑妹 Heimei	32	5.0
7	蓝天六必治 Blue Sky LBZ	17	2.6
8	三笑 Sanxiao	9	1.4

n=642

1-2 样本、男性各年龄层、女性各年龄层的常用品牌/ The Most Frequently Used Brands by the Whole Sample, Age and Gender Groups

	人数 Number	第一品牌及百分比 1st/ percent	第二品牌及百分比 2nd/ percent	第三品牌及百分比 3rd/ percent	第四品牌及百分比 4th/ percent
样本 Sample	642	**两面针 Liangmianzhen(23.5)**	**高露洁 Colgate(16.8)**	**冷酸灵 Lengsuanling(12.1)**	**佳洁士 Crest(11.5) 中华 Zhonghua(11.5)**
男性 Male	311	**两面针 Liangmianzhen(23.8)**	**高露洁 Colgate(17.4)**	**中华 Zhonghua(13.8)**	**冷酸灵 Lengsuanling(12.5)**
16~24 岁 Age	65	两面针 Liangmianzhen(23.1)	高露洁 Colgate(20.0)	中华 Zhonghua(15.4)	佳洁士 Crest(12.3)
25~34 岁 Age	89	两面针 Liangmianzhen(20.2) 高露洁 Colgate(20.2)	冷酸灵 Lengsuanling(14.6)	中华 Zhonghua(12.4)	洁诺 Signal(11.2)
35~44 岁 Age	80	两面针 Liangmianzhen(25.0)	高露洁 Colgate(21.3)	中华 Zhonghua(12.5) 佳洁士 Crest(12.5)	冷酸灵 Lengsuanling(11.3)
45~54 岁 Age	52	两面针 Liangmianzhen(26.9)	中华 Zhonghua(17.3)	冷酸灵 Lengsuanling(11.5)	高露洁 Colgate(9.6) 佳洁士 Crest(9.6)
55~60 岁 Age	25	冷酸灵 Lengsuanling(32.0)	两面针 Liangmianzhen(28.0)	蓝天六必治 Blue Sky LBZ(12.0) 中华 Zhonghua(12.0)	黑妹 Heimei(8.0)
女性 Female	331	**两面针 Liangmianzhen(23.3)**	**高露洁 Colgate(16.3)**	**佳洁士 Crest(13.0)**	**冷酸灵 Lengsuanling(11.8)**
16~24 岁 Age	69	高露洁 Colgate(20.3) 佳洁士 Crest(20.3)	两面针 Liangmianzhen(17.4)	黑妹 Heimei(10.1)	洁诺 Signal(8.7) 中华 Zhonghua(8.7)
25~34 岁 Age	96	两面针 Liangmianzhen(19.8)	高露洁 Colgate(18.8)	洁诺 Signal(13.5)	冷酸灵 Lengsuanling(11.5) 中华 Zhonghua(11.5)
35~44 岁 Age	78	两面针 Liangmianzhen(28.2)	佳洁士 Crest(16.7)	高露洁 Colgate(14.1) 冷酸灵 Lengsuanling(14.1)	洁诺 Signal(5.1)
45~54 岁 Age	62	两面针 Liangmianzhen(27.4)	高露洁 Colgate(16.1) 冷酸灵 Lengsuanling(16.1)	佳洁士 Crest(12.9)	中华 Zhonghua(11.3)
55~60 岁 Age	26	两面针 Liangmianzhen(26.9)	中华 Zhonghua(19.2)	洁诺 Signal(11.5) 蓝天六必治 Blue Sky LBZ(11.5) 冷酸灵 Lengsuanling(11.5)	芳草 Fangcao(7.7)

1-3 正在使用的品牌排名/ Ranking of the Brands Used Now

排名 Brand Ranking	品牌 Brands	人数 Number	百分比 Percent
1	两面针 Liangmianzhen	117	18.2
2	高露洁 Colgate	116	18.1
3	佳洁士 Crest	85	13.2
4	中华 Zhonghua	75	11.7
5	冷酸灵 Lengsuanling	71	11.1
6	洁诺 Signal	58	9.0
7	黑妹 Heimei	38	5.9
8	蓝天六必治 Blue Sky LBZ	27	4.2
9	三笑 Sanxiao	12	1.9
10	黑人 Darlie	8	1.2

n=642

1-4 品牌转换习惯/ Brand Habit in Consuming Toothpaste

	人数 Number	第一次使用该品牌 first use this brand	上一次也是这个牌子 used it last time	上一次不是这个牌子 not used it last time
样本 Sample	641	5.3	60.5	34.2
两面针 Liangmianzhen	117	3.4	66.7	29.9
高露洁 Colgate	116	5.2	64.7	30.2
佳洁士 Crest	85	4.7	64.7	30.6
中华 Zhonghua	75	5.3	64.0	30.7
冷酸灵 Lengsuanling	71	2.8	62.0	35.2
洁诺 Signal	58	1.7	65.5	32.8
黑妹 Heimei	38	10.5	42.1	47.4
蓝天六必治 Blue Sky LBZ	27	11.1	29.6	59.3
三笑 Sanxiao	12	25.0	50.0	25.0
黑人 Darlie	8	12.5	50.0	37.5

1-5 下一次打算使用的品牌排名/ Ranking of the Brands to be Used Next Time

排名 Brand Ranking	品牌 Brands	人数 Number	百分比 Percent
1	高露洁 Colgate	116	18.1
2	佳洁士 Crest	104	16.2
3	两面针 Liangmianzhen	94	14.6
4	中华 Zhonghua	71	11.1
4	洁诺 Signal	71	11.1
5	冷酸灵 Lengsuanling	66	10.3
6	黑妹 Heimei	33	5.1
7	蓝天六必治 Blue Sky LBZ	15	2.3
8	芳草 Fangcao	10	1.6
9	三笑 Sanxiao	9	1.4

n=642

1-6 样本、男性各年龄层、女性各年龄层是否是主要购买者/ Purchasers in the Household by the Whole Sample, Age and Gender Groups

	人数 Number	是 yes	不是 no
样本 Sample	642	57.9	42.1
男性 Male	311	41.5	58.5
16~24 岁 Age	65	21.5	78.5
25~34 岁 Age	89	38.2	61.8
35~44 岁 Age	80	42.5	57.5
45~54 岁 Age	52	57.7	42.3
55~60 岁 Age	25	68.0	32.0
女性 Female	331	73.4	26.6
16~24 岁 Age	69	29.0	71.0
25~34 岁 Age	96	74.0	26.0
35~44 岁 Age	78	93.6	6.4
45~54 岁 Age	62	93.5	6.5
55~60 岁 Age	26	80.8	19.2

1-7 样本、男性各年龄层、女性各年龄层的使用方式/ Ways of Using the Products by the Whole Sample, Age and Gender Groups

	人数 Number	个人专用 personal use	家人共用 all family members share
样本 Sample	642	9.0	91.0
男性 Male	311	9.0	91.0
16~24 岁 Age	65	16.9	83.1
25~34 岁 Age	89	11.2	88.8
35~44 岁 Age	80	3.8	96.3
45~54 岁 Age	52	5.8	94.2
55~60 岁 Age	25	4.0	96.0
女性 Female	331	9.1	90.9
16~24 岁 Age	69	17.4	82.6
25~34 岁 Age	96	5.2	94.8
35~44 岁 Age	78	3.8	96.2
45~54 岁 Age	62	3.2	96.8
55~60 岁 Age	26	30.8	69.2

1-8 样本、男性各年龄层、女性各年龄层的使用频率/ Frequencies of the Consumed Toothpaste by the Whole Sample, Age and Gender Groups

	人数 Number	一天 4 次或以上 4 times or over a day	一天 3 次 3 times a day	一天 2 次 twice a day	一天 1 次 once a day	一天 1 次以下 once a day below
样本 Sample	642	2.0	6.9	66.4	24.3	0.5
男性 Male	311	1.9	7.1	62.4	28.3	0.3
16~24 岁 Age	65	3.1	10.8	63.1	23.1	0.0
25~34 岁 Age	89	1.1	4.5	69.7	23.6	1.1
35~44 岁 Age	80	2.5	11.3	55.0	31.3	0.0
45~54 岁 Age	52	0.0	3.8	55.8	40.4	0.0
55~60 岁 Age	25	4.0	0.0	72.0	24.0	0.0
女性 Female	331	2.1	6.6	70.1	20.5	0.6
16~24 岁 Age	69	2.9	5.8	72.5	18.8	0.0
25~34 岁 Age	96	1.0	5.2	76.0	16.7	1.0
35~44 岁 Age	78	1.3	5.1	66.7	26.9	0.0
45~54 岁 Age	62	3.2	9.7	66.1	19.4	1.6
55~60 岁 Age	26	3.8	11.5	61.5	23.1	0.0

1-9 选择该类商品的考虑因素/ Ranking of the Considerations in Purchasing

注：本题为多选题，合计百分比超过 100%（Multiple answers）

排名 Ranking	考虑因素 Considerations	人次 Person-time	百分比 Percent
1	产品功用 product function	343	53.4
2	价格适中 reasonable price	339	52.8
3	有名的牌子 famous brand	224	34.9
4	广告影响 influence of advertising	163	25.4
5	购买方便 easy to buy	141	22.0
6	有优惠条件 with preferential terms	40	6.2
7	其它 others	36	5.6
8	别人推荐 introduced by other people	31	4.8
9	包装吸引人 appealing package	17	2.6
10	单位发的 offered by the working unit	12	1.9

n=642

1-10 对产品功能的侧重方面/ Ranking of the Considerations about the Function of this Kind of Product

注：本题为多选题，合计百分比超过 100%（Multiple answers）

排名 Ranking	侧重方面 Items	人次 Person-time	百分比 Percent
1	含氟 with fluoride	301	47.0
2	有中药成分 containing Chinese herb	208	32.4
3	含钙 with calcium	180	28.1
4	有薄荷味 mint	176	27.5
5	有水果味 fruit fragrance	155	24.2
6	是塑料软管包装 plastic soft packing	127	19.8
7	膏体的颜色 color	104	16.2
8	其他 others	37	5.8
9	含盐 with saline	7	1.1

n=641

1-11 重度消费者的人口分布/ Demographics of the Heavy Consumers

	人数 Number	16-24 岁 Age	25-34 岁 Age	35-44 岁 Age	45-54 岁 Age	55-60 岁 Age
样本 Sample	483	21.9	30.2	23.2	16.6	8.1
男性 Male	222	22.5	30.2	24.8	14.0	8.6
一天 4 次或以上 4 times or over a day	6	33.3	16.7	33.3	0.0	16.7
一天 3 次 3 times a day	22	31.8	18.2	40.9	9.1	0.0
一天 2 次 twice a day	194	21.1	32.0	22.7	14.9	9.3
女性 Female	261	21.5	30.3	21.8	18.8	7.7
一天 4 次或以上 4 times or over a day	7	28.6	14.3	14.3	28.6	14.3
一天 3 次 3 times a day	22	18.2	22.7	18.2	27.3	13.6
一天 2 次 twice a day	232	21.6	31.5	22.4	17.7	6.9

1-12 不同消费者层的常用品牌/ The Most Frequently Used Brands by Market Segments

1-12-1 时尚流行指标/ Fads Popular Index

	人数 Number	第一品牌及百分比 1st / percent	第二品牌及百分比 2nd / percent	第三品牌及百分比 3rd / percent	第四品牌及百分比 4th / percent
样本 Sample	**632**	**两面针 Liangmianzhen(23.6)**	**高露洁 Colgate(16.9)**	**冷酸灵 Lengsuanling(12.2)**	**中华 Zhonghua(11.7)**
平实生活指向 simple living orientation	330	两面针 Liangmianzhen(27.0)	高露洁 Colgate(14.5)	中华 Zhonghua(13.6)	冷酸灵 Lengsuanling(11.5)
时尚流行指向 fashion orientation	302	两面针 Liangmianzhen(19.9)	高露洁 Colgate(19.5)	冷酸灵 Lengsuanling(12.9)	佳洁士 Crest(12.6)

1-12-2 广告态度指标/ Advertising Attitude Index

	人数 Number	第一品牌及百分比 1st / percent	第二品牌及百分比 2nd / percent	第三品牌及百分比 3rd / percent	第四品牌及百分比 4th / percent
样本 Sample	**634**	**两面针 Liangmianzhen(23.7)**	**高露洁 Colgate(16.9)**	**冷酸灵 Lengsuanling(12.1)**	**中华 Zhonghua(11.7)**
广告淡漠指向 indifferent orientation	188	两面针 Liangmianzhen(31.4)	冷酸灵 Lengsuanling(14.4)	高露洁 Colgate(11.7)	佳洁士 Crest(10.6) 中华 Zhonghua(10.6)
中间层 medium	373	两面针 Liangmianzhen(20.4)	高露洁 Colgate(19.6)	冷酸灵 Lengsuanling(11.8)	中华 Zhonghua(11.3)
信赖广告指向 loyal orientation	73	两面针 Liangmianzhen(20.5)	中华 Zhonghua(16.4) 高露洁 Colgate(16.4)	佳洁士 Crest(15.1)	冷酸灵 Lengsuanling(8.2)

1-13 重度消费者的消费层构成/ The Composition of the Heavy Consumers

1-13-1 时尚流行指标/ Fads Popular Index

	人数 Number	平实生活指向 simple living orientation	时尚流行指向 fashion orientation
样本 Sample	**473**	**49.0**	**51.0**
一天 4 次或以上 4 times or over a day	13	61.5	38.5
一天 3 次 3 times a day	44	56.8	43.2
一天 2 次 twice a day	416	47.8	52.2

1-13-2 广告态度指标/ Advertising Attitude Index

	人数 Number	广告淡漠指向 indifferent orientation	中间层 medium	信赖广告指向 loyal orientation
样本 Sample	**475**	**28.8**	**60.2**	**10.9**
一天 4 次或以上 4 times or over a day	13	46.2	30.8	23.1
一天 3 次 3 times a day	44	47.7	43.2	9.1
一天 2 次 twice a day	418	26.3	62.9	10.8

● 西安 / Xi'an

1-1 最常用品牌排名/ Ranking of the Most Frequently Used Brands

排名 Brand Ranking	品牌 Brands	人数 Number	百分比 Percent
1	中华 Zhonghua	212	35.3
2	高露洁 Colgate	89	14.8
3	两面针 Liangmianzhen	55	9.2
4	佳洁士 Crest	50	8.3
5	冷酸灵 Lengsuanling	45	7.5
6	洁诺 Signal	44	7.3
7	黑妹 Heimei	42	7.0
8	蓝天六必治 Blue Sky LBZ	19	3.2
9	一口净 Yikoujing	15	2.5

n=601

1-2 样本、男性各年龄层、女性各年龄层的常用品牌/ The Most Frequently Used Brands by the Whole Sample, Age and Gender Groups

	人数 Number	第一品牌及百分比 1st/ percent	第二品牌及百分比 2nd/ percent	第三品牌及百分比 3rd/ percent	第四品牌及百分比 4th/ percent
样本 Sample	601	**中华 Zhonghua(35.3)**	**高露洁 Colgate(14.8)**	**两面针 Liangmianzhen(9.2)**	**佳洁士 Crest(8.3)**
男性 Male	302	**中华 Zhonghua(38.7)**	**高露洁 Colgate(13.2)**	**佳洁士 Crest(8.6)**	**两面针 Liangmianzhen(7.9)**
16~24 岁 Age	64	中华 Zhonghua(39.1)	高露洁 Colgate(14.1)	洁诺 Signal(10.9)	冷酸灵 Lengsuanling(7.8)
25~34 岁 Age	91	中华 Zhonghua(34.1)	高露洁 Colgate(16.5)	两面针 Liangmianzhen(11.0)	佳洁士 Crest(9.9)
35~44 岁 Age	77	中华 Zhonghua(36.4)	高露洁 Colgate(13.0)	佳洁士 Crest(10.4)	黑妹 Heimei(9.1)
45~54 岁 Age	46	中华 Zhonghua(41.3)	两面针 Liangmianzhen(10.9)	高露洁 Colgate(8.7) 佳洁士 Crest(8.7) 冷酸灵 Lengsuanling(8.7)	黑妹 Heimei(6.5)
55~60 岁 Age	24	中华 Zhonghua(58.3)	高露洁 Colgate(8.3)	佳洁士 Crest(4.2) 洁诺 Signal(4.2) 冷酸灵 Lengsuanling(4.2) 两面针 Liangmianzhen(4.2) 三笑 Sanxiao(4.2) 田七 Tianqi(4.2) 一口净 Yikoujing(4.2)	
女性 Female	299	**中华 Zhonghua(31.8)**	**高露洁 Colgate(16.4)**	**两面针 Liangmianzhen(10.4)**	**冷酸灵 Lengsuanling(8.4)** **黑妹 Heimei(8.4)**
16~24 岁 Age	61	中华 Zhonghua(37.7)	高露洁 Colgate(18.0)	黑妹 Heimei(9.8)	两面针 Liangmianzhen(6.6) 洁诺 Signal(6.6) 冷酸灵 Lengsuanling(6.6)
25~34 岁 Age	90	中华 Zhonghua(32.2)	高露洁 Colgate(21.1)	佳洁士 Crest(10.0)	洁诺 Signal(8.9)
35~44 岁 Age	74	中华 Zhonghua(18.9)	两面针 Liangmianzhen(13.5) 佳洁士 Crest(13.5)	黑妹 Heimei(12.2)	高露洁 Colgate(10.8)
45~54 岁 Age	49	中华 Zhonghua(42.9)	高露洁 Colgate(16.3)	两面针 Liangmianzhen(12.2)	洁诺 Signal(10.2)
55~60 岁 Age	25	中华 Zhonghua(32.0)	两面针 Liangmianzhen(16.0)	高露洁 Colgate(12.0) 冷酸灵 Lengsuanling(12.0)	黑妹 Heimei(8.0) 洁诺 Signal(8.0) 洁银 Jieyin(8.0)

1-3 正在使用的品牌排名/ Ranking of the Brands Used Now

排名 Brand Ranking	品牌 Brands	人数 Number	百分比 Percent
1	中华 Zhonghua	182	30.3
2	高露洁 Colgate	77	12.8
3	佳洁士 Crest	68	11.3
4	两面针 Liangmianzhen	56	9.3
5	冷酸灵 Lengsuanling	48	8.0
6	洁诺 Signal	46	7.7
7	黑妹 Heimei	42	7.0
8	蓝天六必治 Blue Sky LBZ	26	4.3
9	一口净 Yikoujing	17	2.8
10	洁银 Jieyin	6	1.0

n=601

1-4 品牌转换习惯/ Brand Habit in Consuming Toothpaste

	人数 Number	第一次使用该品牌 first use this brand	上一次也是这个牌子 used it last time	上一次不是这个牌子 not used it last time
样本 Sample	601	5.2	69.6	25.3
中华 Zhonghua	182	1.6	77.5	20.9
高露洁 Colgate	77	6.5	75.3	18.2
佳洁士 Crest	68	10.3	69.1	20.6
两面针 Liangmianzhen	56	0.0	67.9	32.1
冷酸灵 Lengsuanling	48	8.3	68.8	22.9
洁诺 Signal	46	2.2	71.7	26.1
黑妹 Heimei	42	4.8	57.1	38.1
蓝天六必治 Blue Sky LBZ	26	15.4	57.7	26.9
一口净 Yikoujing	17	5.9	64.7	29.4
洁银 Jieyin	6	16.7	33.3	50.0

1-5 下一次打算使用的品牌排名/ Ranking of the Brands to be Used Next Time

排名 Brand Ranking	品牌 Brands	人数 Number	百分比 Percent
1	中华 Zhonghua	179	29.8
2	佳洁士 Crest	98	16.3
3	高露洁 Colgate	81	13.5
4	洁诺 Signal	54	9.0
5	两面针 Liangmianzhen	42	7.0
6	黑妹 Heimei	38	6.3
7	冷酸灵 Lengsuanling	34	5.7
8	蓝天六必治 Blue Sky LBZ	23	3.8
9	一口净 Yikoujing	11	1.8
10	黑人 Darlie	7	1.2

n=601

1-6 样本、男性各年龄层、女性各年龄层是否是主要购买者/ Purchasers in the Household by the Whole Sample, Age and Gender Groups

	人数 Number	是 yes	不是 no
样本 Sample	600	66.7	33.3
男性 Male	301	47.8	52.2
16~24 岁 Age	64	32.8	67.2
25~34 岁 Age	90	52.2	47.8
35~44 岁 Age	77	57.1	42.9
45~54 岁 Age	46	41.3	58.7
55~60 岁 Age	24	54.2	45.8
女性 Female	299	85.6	14.4
16~24 岁 Age	61	60.7	39.3
25~34 岁 Age	90	87.8	12.2
35~44 岁 Age	74	93.2	6.8
45~54 岁 Age	49	95.9	4.1
55~60 岁 Age	25	96.0	4.0

1-7 样本、男性各年龄层、女性各年龄层的使用方式/ Ways of Using the Products by the Whole Sample, Age and Gender Groups

	人数 Number	个人专用 personal use	家人共用 all family members share
样本 Sample	601	15.0	85.0
男性 Male	302	12.9	87.1
16~24 岁 Age	64	18.8	81.3
25~34 岁 Age	91	13.2	86.8
35~44 岁 Age	77	7.8	92.2
45~54 岁 Age	46	15.2	84.8
55~60 岁 Age	24	8.3	91.7
女性 Female	299	17.1	82.9
16~24 岁 Age	61	24.6	75.4
25~34 岁 Age	90	17.8	82.2
35~44 岁 Age	74	18.9	81.1
45~54 岁 Age	49	8.2	91.8
55~60 岁 Age	25	8.0	92.0

1-8 样本、男性各年龄层、女性各年龄层的使用频率/ Frequencies of the Consumed Toothpaste by the Whole Sample, Age and Gender Groups

	人数 Number	一天 4 次或以上 4 times or over a day	一天 3 次 3 times a day	一天 2 次 twice a day	一天 1 次 once a day	一天 1 次以下 once a day below
样本 Sample	601	2.5	6.2	71.9	19.1	0.3
男性 Male	302	2.0	4.6	68.9	23.8	0.7
16~24 岁 Age	64	1.6	1.6	78.1	18.8	0.0
25~34 岁 Age	91	1.1	5.5	73.5	19.8	0.0
35~44 岁 Age	77	2.6	6.5	58.4	32.5	0.0
45~54 岁 Age	46	2.2	4.3	60.9	28.3	4.3
55~60 岁 Age	24	4.2	4.2	75.0	16.7	0.0
女性 Female	299	3.0	7.7	74.9	14.4	0.0
16~24 岁 Age	61	4.9	6.6	83.6	4.9	0.0
25~34 岁 Age	90	2.2	6.7	77.8	13.3	0.0
35~44 岁 Age	74	5.4	10.8	68.9	14.9	0.0
45~54 岁 Age	49	0.0	8.2	67.3	24.5	0.0
55~60 岁 Age	25	0.0	4.0	76.0	20.0	0.0

1-9 选择该类商品的考虑因素/ Ranking of the Considerations in Purchasing

注：本题为多选题，合计百分比超过 100%（Multiple answers）

排名 Ranking	考虑因素 Considerations	人次 Person-time	百分比 Percent
1	价格适中 reasonable price	303	50.4
2	产品功用 product function	262	43.6
3	有名的牌子 famous brand	202	33.6
4	购买方便 easy to buy	134	22.3
5	广告影响 influence of advertising	99	16.5
6	别人推荐 introduced by other people	43	7.2
7	包装吸引人 appealing package	24	4.0
8	有优惠条件 with preferential terms	18	3.0
9	其它 others	12	2.0
10	单位发的 offered by the working unit	8	1.3

n=601

1-10 对产品功能的侧重方面/ Ranking of the Considerations about the Function of this Kind of Product

注：本题为多选题，合计百分比超过 100%（Multiple answers）

排名 Ranking	侧重方面 Items	人次 Person-time	百分比 Percent
1	含氟 with fluoride	243	40.5
2	含钙 with calcium	182	30.3
3	有水果味 fruit fragrance	174	29.0
4	有中药成分 containing Chinese herb	163	27.2
5	有薄荷味 mint	114	19.0
6	是塑料软管包装 plastic soft packing	86	14.3
7	膏体的颜色 color	62	10.3
8	其他 others	20	3.3
9	含盐 with saline	5	0.8

n=600

1-11 重度消费者的人口分布/ Demographics of the Heavy Consumers

	人数 Number	16-24 岁 Age	25-34 岁 Age	35-44 岁 Age	45-54 岁 Age	55-60 岁 Age
样本 Sample	484	22.7	31.2	23.8	14.0	8.3
男性 Male	228	22.8	32.0	22.8	13.6	8.8
一天 4 次或以上 4 times or over a day	6	16.7	16.7	33.3	16.7	16.7
一天 3 次 3 times a day	14	7.1	35.7	35.7	14.3	7.1
一天 2 次 twice a day	208	24.0	32.2	21.6	13.5	8.7
女性 Female	256	22.7	30.5	24.6	14.5	7.8
一天 4 次或以上 4 times or over a day	9	33.3	22.2	44.4	0.0	0.0
一天 3 次 3 times a day	23	17.4	26.1	34.8	17.4	4.3
一天 2 次 twice a day	224	22.8	31.3	22.8	14.7	8.5

1-12 不同消费者层的常用品牌/ The Most Frequently Used Brands by Market Segments

1-12-1 时尚流行指标/ Fads Popular Index

	人数 Number	第一品牌及百分比 1st / percent	第二品牌及百分比 2nd / percent	第三品牌及百分比 3rd / percent	第四品牌及百分比 4th / percent
样本 Sample	**599**	**中华 Zhonghua(35.2)**	**高露洁 Colgate(14.9)**	**两面针 Liangmianzhen(9.2)**	**佳洁士 Crest(8.3)**
平实生活指向 simple living orientation	341	中华 Zhonghua(39.0)	高露洁 Colgate(14.7)	两面针 Liangmianzhen(11.1)	黑妹 Heimei(7.0)
时尚流行指向 fashion orientation	258	中华 Zhonghua(30.2)	高露洁 Colgate(15.1)	佳洁士 Crest(12.0)	洁诺 Signal(10.9)

1-12-2 广告态度指标/ Advertising Attitude Index

	人数 Number	第一品牌及百分比 1st / percent	第二品牌及百分比 2nd / percent	第三品牌及百分比 3rd / percent	第四品牌及百分比 4th / percent
样本 Sample	**597**	**中华 Zhonghua(35.2)**	**高露洁 Colgate(14.9)**	**两面针 Liangmianzhen(9.2)**	**佳洁士 Crest(8.4)**
广告淡漠指向 indifferent orientation	184	中华 Zhonghua(37.5)	高露洁 Colgate(13.6)	两面针 Liangmianzhen(11.4)	冷酸灵 Lengsuanling(7.6)
中间层 medium	334	中华 Zhonghua(34.4)	高露洁 Colgate(15.3)	两面针 Liangmianzhen(8.7)	佳洁士 Crest(8.4) 洁诺 Signal(8.4)
信赖广告指向 loyal orientation	79	中华 Zhonghua(32.9)	高露洁 Colgate(16.5)	佳洁士 Crest(11.4)	黑妹 Heimei(8.9)

1-13 重度消费者的消费层构成/ The Composition of the Heavy Consumers

1-13-1 时尚流行指标/ Fads Popular Index

	人数 Number	平实生活指向 simple living orientation	时尚流行指向 fashion orientation
样本 Sample	**483**	**54.2**	**45.8**
一天 4 次或以上 4 times or over a day	15	40.0	60.0
一天 3 次 3 times a day	37	45.9	54.1
一天 2 次 twice a day	431	55.5	44.5

1-13-2 广告态度指标/ Advertising Attitude Index

	人数 Number	广告淡漠指向 indifferent orientation	中间层 medium	信赖广告指向 loyal orientation
样本 Sample	**480**	**31.0**	**55.6**	**13.3**
一天 4 次或以上 4 times or over a day	15	26.7	66.7	6.7
一天 3 次 3 times a day	37	37.8	51.4	10.8
一天 2 次 twice a day	428	30.6	55.6	13.8

● 沈阳 / Shenyang

1-1 最常用品牌排名/ Ranking of the Most Frequently Used Brands

排名 Brand Ranking	品牌 Brands	人数 Number	百分比 Percent
1	中华 Zhonghua	171	28.5
2	康齿灵 Kangchiling	107	17.8
3	佳洁士 Crest	88	14.7
4	高露洁 Colgate	72	12.0
5	洁诺 Signal	56	9.3
6	冷酸灵 Lengsuanling	29	4.8
7	黑妹 Heimei	20	3.3
8	蓝天六必治 Blue Sky LBZ	14	2.3
9	两面针 Liangmianzhen	13	2.2
10	三笑 Sanxiao	6	1.0

n=600

1-2 样本、男性各年龄层、女性各年龄层的常用品牌/ The Most Frequently Used Brands by the Whole Sample, Age and Gender Groups

	人数 Number	第一品牌及百分比 1st/ percent	第二品牌及百分比 2nd/ percent	第三品牌及百分比 3rd/ percent	第四品牌及百分比 4th/ percent
样本 Sample	600	**中华 Zhonghua(28.5)**	**康齿灵 Kangchiling(17.8)**	**佳洁士 Crest(14.7)**	**高露洁 Colgate(12.0)**
男性 Male	298	**中华 Zhonghua(30.5)**	**康齿灵 Kangchiling(17.8)**	**佳洁士 Crest(15.4)**	**高露洁 Colgate(11.4)**
16~24 岁 Age	64	中华 Zhonghua(26.6)	佳洁士 Crest(23.4)	高露洁 Colgate(12.5) 康齿灵 Kangchiling(12.5)	洁诺 Signal(9.4)
25~34 岁 Age	89	中华 Zhonghua(28.1)	佳洁士 Crest(18.0)	高露洁 Colgate(14.6)	洁诺 Signal(12.4)
35~44 岁 Age	76	中华 Zhonghua(35.5)	康齿灵 Kangchiling(25.0)	佳洁士 Crest(10.5)	高露洁 Colgate(9.2)
45~54 岁 Age	46	中华 Zhonghua(34.8)	康齿灵 Kangchiling(17.4)	高露洁 Colgate(10.9) 佳洁士 Crest(10.9)	冷酸灵 Lengsuanling(6.5)
55~60 岁 Age	23	康齿灵 Kangchiling(39.1)	中华 Zhonghua(26.1)	佳洁士 Crest(8.7) 洁诺 Signal(8.7) 冷酸灵 Lengsuanling(8.7)	高露洁 Colgate(4.3) 上海 Shanghai(4.3)
女性 Female	302	**中华 Zhonghua(26.5)**	**康齿灵 Kangchiling(17.9)**	**佳洁士 Crest(13.9)**	**高露洁 Colgate(12.6)**
16~24 岁 Age	64	佳洁士 Crest(18.8)	中华 Zhonghua(15.6) 洁诺 Signal(15.6)	高露洁 Colgate(14.1)	康齿灵 Kangchiling(10.9)
25~34 岁 Age	90	中华 Zhonghua(27.8)	康齿灵 Kangchiling(16.7) 高露洁 Colgate(15.7)	佳洁士 Crest(11.1)	洁诺 Signal(10.0)
35~44 岁 Age	76	中华 Zhonghua(32.9)	高露洁 Colgate(17.1)	佳洁士 Crest(14.5) 康齿灵 Kangchiling(14.5)	洁诺 Signal(6.6)
45~54 岁 Age	48	康齿灵 Kangchiling(27.1) 中华 Zhonghua(27.1)	佳洁士 Crest(14.6)	洁诺 Signal(10.4)	冷酸灵 Lengsuanling(6.3)
55~60 岁 Age	24	康齿灵 Kangchiling(33.3)	中华 Zhonghua(29.2)	洁诺 Signal(16.7)	佳洁士 Crest(8.3)

1-3 正在使用的品牌排名/ Ranking of the Brands Used Now

排名 Brand Ranking	品牌 Brands	人数 Number	百分比 Percent
1	中华 Zhonghua	147	24.5
2	康齿灵 Kangchiling	91	15.2
3	佳洁士 Crest	89	14.8
4	高露洁 Colgate	79	13.2
5	洁诺 Signal	55	9.2
6	冷酸灵 Lengsuanling	37	6.2
7	黑妹 Heimei	17	2.8
8	倍瑞傲 Perioe	16	2.7
8	两面针 Liangmianzhen	16	2.7
9	蓝天六必治 Blue Sky LBZ	13	2.2
10	三笑 Sanxiao	6	1.0

n=600

1-4 品牌转换习惯/ Brand Habit in Consuming Toothpaste

	人数 Number	第一次使用该品牌 first use this brand	上一次也是这个牌子 used it last time	上一次不是这个牌子 not used it last time
样本 Sample	**599**	**9.5**	**66.6**	**23.9**
中华 Zhonghua	146	2.1	71.9	26.0
康齿灵 Kangchiling	91	4.4	73.6	22.0
佳洁士 Crest	89	4.5	76.4	19.1
高露洁 Colgate	79	10.1	69.6	20.3
洁诺 Signal	55	10.9	63.6	25.5
冷酸灵 Lengsuanling	37	8.1	54.1	37.8
黑妹 Heimei	17	11.8	64.7	23.5
倍瑞傲 Perioe	16	56.3	18.8	25.0
两面针 Liangmianzhen	16	18.8	50.0	31.3
蓝天六必治 Blue Sky LBZ	13	23.1	53.8	23.1

1-5 下一次打算使用的品牌排名/ Ranking of the Brands to be Used Next Time

排名 Brand Ranking	品牌 Brands	人数 Number	百分比 Percent
1	中华 Zhonghua	135	22.5
2	佳洁士 Crest	114	19.0
3	康齿灵 Kangchiling	87	14.5
4	高露洁 Colgate	68	11.3
5	洁诺 Signal	66	11.0
6	冷酸灵 Lengsuanling	29	4.8
7	黑妹 Heimei	21	3.5
8	两面针 Liangmianzhen	19	3.2
9	蓝天六必治 Blue Sky LBZ	14	2.3
10	倍瑞傲 Perioe	13	2.2

n=600

1-6 样本、男性各年龄层、女性各年龄层是否是主要购买者/ Purchasers in the Household by the Whole Sample, Age and Gender Groups

	人数 Number	是 yes	不是 no
样本 Sample	600	62.5	37.5
男性 Male	298	43.0	57.0
16~24 岁 Age	64	35.9	64.1
25~34 岁 Age	89	48.3	51.7
35~44 岁 Age	76	39.5	60.5
45~54 岁 Age	45	46.7	53.3
55~60 岁 Age	24	45.8	54.2
女性 Female	302	81.8	18.2
16~24 岁 Age	64	51.6	48.4
25~34 岁 Age	90	91.1	8.9
35~44 岁 Age	76	93.4	6.6
45~54 岁 Age	48	79.2	20.8
55~60 岁 Age	24	95.8	4.2

1-7 样本、男性各年龄层、女性各年龄层的使用方式/ Ways of Using the Products by the Whole Sample, Age and Gender Groups

	人数 Number	个人专用 personal use	家人共用 all family members share
样本 Sample	600	18.0	82.0
男性 Male	298	19.8	80.2
16~24 岁 Age	64	32.8	67.2
25~34 岁 Age	89	16.9	83.1
35~44 岁 Age	76	18.4	81.6
45~54 岁 Age	46	17.4	82.6
55~60 岁 Age	23	4.3	95.7
女性 Female	302	16.2	83.8
16~24 岁 Age	64	35.9	64.1
25~34 岁 Age	90	7.8	92.2
35~44 岁 Age	76	14.5	85.5
45~54 岁 Age	48	6.3	93.8
55~60 岁 Age	24	20.8	79.2

1-8 样本、男性各年龄层、女性各年龄层的使用频率/ Frequencies of the Consumed Toothpaste by the Whole Sample, Age and Gender Groups

	人数 Number	一天 4 次或以上 4 times or over a day	一天 3 次 3 times a day	一天 2 次 twice a day	一天 1 次 once a day	一天 1 次以下 once a day below
样本 Sample	599	2.5	6.5	69.6	20.9	0.5
男性 Male	298	2.3	6.0	64.1	27.2	0.3
16~24 岁 Age	64	3.1	10.9	64.1	21.9	0.0
25~34 岁 Age	89	3.4	3.4	67.4	25.8	0.0
35~44 岁 Age	76	2.6	5.3	59.2	32.9	0.0
45~54 岁 Age	46	0.0	6.5	71.7	19.6	2.2
55~60 岁 Age	23	0.0	4.3	52.2	43.5	0.0
女性 Female	301	2.7	7.0	75.1	14.6	0.7
16~24 岁 Age	63	1.6	7.9	71.4	17.5	1.6
25~34 岁 Age	90	7.8	3.3	73.3	15.6	0.0
35~44 岁 Age	76	0.0	11.8	76.3	11.8	0.0
45~54 岁 Age	48	0.0	4.2	79.2	14.6	2.1
55~60 岁 Age	24	0.0	8.3	79.2	12.5	0.0

1-9 选择该类商品的考虑因素/ Ranking of the Considerations in Purchasing

注：本题为多选题，合计百分比超过 100%（Multiple answers）

排名 Ranking	考虑因素 Considerations	人次 Person-time	百分比 Percent
1	价格适中 reasonable price	297	49.6
2	产品功用 product function	287	47.9
3	有名的牌子 famous brand	210	35.1
4	广告影响 influence of advertising	139	23.2
5	购买方便 easy to buy	124	20.7
6	别人推荐 introduced by other people	43	7.2
7	有优惠条件 with preferential terms	29	4.8
8	包装吸引人 appealing package	20	3.3
9	其它 others	14	2.3
10	单位发的 offered by the working unit	4	0.7

n=599

1-10 对产品功能的侧重方面/ Ranking of the Considerations about the Function of this Kind of Product

注：本题为多选题，合计百分比超过 100%（Multiple answers）

排名 Ranking	侧重方面 Items	人次 Person-time	百分比 Percent
1	含钙 with calcium	225	37.8
2	含氟 with fluoride	204	34.2
3	有中药成分 containing Chinese herb	162	27.2
4	有水果味 fruit fragrance	150	25.2
5	有薄荷味 mint	136	22.8
6	是塑料软管包装 plastic soft packing	111	18.6
7	膏体的颜色 color	85	14.3
8	其他 others	14	2.3
9	含盐 with saline	11	1.8

n=596

1-11 重度消费者的人口分布/ Demographics of the Heavy Consumers

	人数 Number	16-24 岁 Age	25-34 岁 Age	35-44 岁 Age	45-54 岁 Age	55-60 岁 Age
样本 Sample	471	21.4	30.1	25.1	16.1	7.2
男性 Male	216	23.1	30.6	23.6	16.7	6.0
一天 4 次或以上 4 times or over a day	7	28.6	42.9	28.6	0.0	0.0
一天 3 次 3 times a day	18	38.9	16.7	22.2	16.7	5.6
一天 2 次 twice a day	191	21.5	31.4	23.6	17.3	6.3
女性 Female	255	20.0	29.8	26.3	15.7	8.2
一天 4 次或以上 4 times or over a day	8	12.5	87.5	0.0	0.0	0.0
一天 3 次 3 times a day	21	23.8	14.3	42.9	9.5	9.5
一天 2 次 twice a day	226	19.9	29.2	25.7	16.8	8.4

1-12 不同消费者层的常用品牌/ The Most Frequently Used Brands by Market Segments

1-12-1 时尚流行指标/ Fads Popular Index

	人数 Number	第一品牌及百分比 1st/ percent	第二品牌及百分比 2nd/ percent	第三品牌及百分比 3rd/ percent	第四品牌及百分比 4th/ percent
样本 Sample	600	**中华 Zhonghua(28.5)**	**康齿灵 Kangchiling(17.8)**	**佳洁士 Crest(14.7)**	**高露洁 Colgate(12.0)**
平实生活指向 simple living orientation	291	中华 Zhonghua(28.5)	康齿灵 Kangchiling(23.0)	佳洁士 Crest(11.3)	高露洁 Colgate(8.9)
时尚流行指向 fashion orientation	309	中华 Zhonghua(28.5)	佳洁士 Crest(17.8)	高露洁 Colgate(14.9)	康齿灵 Kangchiling(12.9)

1-12-2 广告态度指标/ Advertising Attitude Index

	人数 Number	第一品牌及百分比 1st/ percent	第二品牌及百分比 2nd/ percent	第三品牌及百分比 3rd/ percent	第四品牌及百分比 4th/ percent
样本 Sample	600	**中华 Zhonghua(28.5)**	**康齿灵 Kangchiling(17.8)**	**佳洁士 Crest(14.7)**	**高露洁 Colgate(12.0)**
广告淡漠指向 indifferent orientation	172	中华 Zhonghua(30.2)	康齿灵 Kangchiling(21.5)	佳洁士 Crest(14.5)	洁诺 Signal(9.3)
中间层 medium	353	中华 Zhonghua(27.2)	康齿灵 Kangchiling(15.9)	佳洁士 Crest(14.4)	高露洁 Colgate(13.0)
信赖广告指向 loyal orientation	75	中华 Zhonghua(30.7)	康齿灵 Kangchiling (18.7)	高露洁 Colgate(17.3)	佳洁士 Crest(16.0)

1-13 重度消费者的消费层构成/ The Composition of the Heavy Consumers

1-13-1 时尚流行指标/ Fads Popular Index

	人数 Number	平实生活指向 simple living orientation	时尚流行指向 fashion orientation
样本 Sample	471	46.3	53.7
一天 4 次或以上 4 times or over a day	15	20.0	80.0
一天 3 次 3 times a day	39	56.4	43.6
一天 2 次 twice a day	417	46.3	53.7

1-13-2 广告态度指标/ Advertising Attitude Index

	人数 Number	广告淡漠指向 indifferent orientation	中间层 medium	信赖广告指向 loyal orientation
样本 Sample	471	27.0	60.1	13.0
一天 4 次或以上 4 times or over a day	15	0.0	93.3	6.7
一天 3 次 3 times a day	39	30.8	59.0	10.3
一天 2 次 twice a day	417	27.6	59.0	13.4

2.洗发水 / Shampoo

● 北京 / Beijing

2-1 最常用品牌排名/ Ranking of the Most Frequently Used Brands

排名 Brand Ranking	品牌 Brands	人数 Number	百分比 Percent
1	飘柔 Rejoice	389	38.7
2	力士 Lux	100	10.0
3	沙宣 Vidal Sassoon	92	9.2
4	海飞丝 Head&Shoulder	88	8.8
5	潘婷 Pentene	56	5.6
6	夏士莲 Hazeline	41	4.1
7	诗芬 Sifone	26	2.6
8	蜂花 Bee&Flower	22	2.2
9	威娜宝 Wella	17	1.7
10	伊卡璐 Clairol	13	1.3
10	奥妮 Olive	13	1.3
11	奥妮首乌 SW Olive	12	1.2
11	舒蕾 Slek	12	1.2

n=1005

2-2 样本、男性各年龄层、女性各年龄层的常用品牌/ The Most Frequently Used Brands by the Whole Sample, Age and Gender Groups

	人数 Number	第一品牌及百分比 1st/ percent	第二品牌及百分比 2nd/ percent	第三品牌及百分比 3rd/ percent	第四品牌及百分比 4th/ percent
样本 Sample	1005	**飘柔 Rejoice(38.7)**	**力士 Lux(10.0)**	**沙宣 Vidal Sassoon(9.2)**	**海飞丝 Head &Shoulder(8.8)**
男性 Male	497	**飘柔 Rejoice(41.4)**	**海飞丝 Head&Shoulder(11.1)**	**力士 Lux(9.1)**	**沙宣 Vidal Sassoon(8.2)**
16~24 岁 Age	104	飘柔 Rejoice(41.3)	沙宣 Vidal Sassoon(15.4)	力士 Lux(7.7) 海飞丝 Head&Shoulder(7.7)	诗芬 Sifone(5.8)
25~34 岁 Age	151	飘柔 Rejoice(45.7)	海飞丝 Head&Shoulder(10.6)	力士 Lux(9.3)	沙宣 Vidal Sassoon(7.3)
35~44 岁 Age	128	飘柔 Rejoice(35.2)	海飞丝 Head&Shoulder(15.6)	力士 Lux(9.4)	沙宣 Vidal Sassoon(7.8)
45~54 岁 Age	76	飘柔 Rejoice(38.2)	海飞丝 Head&Shoulder(10.5) 力士 Lux(10.5)	潘婷 Pentene(3.9) 沙宣 Vidal Sassoon(3.9)	诗芬 Sifone(2.6) 花香 Huaxiang(2.6) 太阳神 Apollo(2.6) 夏士莲 Hazeline(2.6)
55~60 岁 Age	38	飘柔 Rejoice(52.6)	海飞丝 Head&Shoulder(7.9) 力士 Lux(7.9)	夏士莲 Hazeline(5.3) 首乌 Shouwu(5.3) 潘婷 Pentene(5.3)	花王 Kao(2.6) 伊卡璐 Clairol(2.6) 沙宣 Vidal Sassoon(2.6) 可蒙 Kemeng(2.6) 奥妮皂角 ZJ Olive(2.6)
女性 Female	508	**飘柔 Rejoice(36.0)**	**力士 Lux(10.8)**	**沙宣 Vidal Sassoon(10.0)**	**海飞丝 Head&Shoulder(6.5)**
16~24 岁 Age	108	飘柔 Rejoice(37.0)	沙宣 Vidal Sassoon(13.0)	夏士莲 Hazeline(10.2)	力士 Lux(9.3)
25~34 岁 Age	150	飘柔 Rejoice(38.7)	力士 Lux(13.3)	潘婷 Pentene(8.7)	沙宣 Vidal Sassoon(8.0)
35~44 岁 Age	124	飘柔 Rejoice(26.6)	力士 Lux(15.3)	沙宣 Vidal Sassoon(12.1)	海飞丝 Head&Shoulder(9.7)
45~54 岁 Age	84	飘柔 Rejoice(42.9)	沙宣 Vidal Sassoon(9.5)	潘婷 Pentene(6.0)	力士 Lux(4.8)
55~60 岁 Age	42	飘柔 Rejoice(38.1)	蜂花 Bee&Flower(9.5)	潘婷 Pentene(4.8) 夏士莲 Hazeline(4.8) 沙宣 Vidal Sassoon(4.8) 奥妮首乌 SW Olive(4.8) 力士 Lux(4.8) 海飞丝 Head&Shoulder(4.8)	华姿 Huazi(2.4) 诗芬 Sifone(2.4) 舒蕾 Slek(2.4) 奥妮皂角 ZJ Olive(2.4) 花香 Huaxiang(2.4) 奥妮 Olive(2.4) 绞股蓝 AOQILI(2000 型)(2.4)

2-3 正在使用的品牌排名/ Ranking of the Brands Used Now

排名 Brand Ranking	品牌 Brands	人数 Number	百分比 Percent
1	飘柔 Rejoice	275	27.3
2	沙宣 Vidal Sassoon	130	12.9
3	力士 Lux	93	9.2
4	海飞丝 Head&Shoulder	79	7.9
5	夏士莲 Hazeline	71	7.1
6	潘婷 Pentene	58	5.8
7	诗芬 Sifone	35	3.5
8	伊卡璐 Clairol	26	2.6
9	舒蕾 Slek	25	2.5
10	奥妮百年润发 Olive100	21	2.1
11	蜂花 Bee&Flower	19	1.9
11	威娜宝 Wella	19	1.9
12	奥妮 Olive	18	1.8
13	奥妮首乌 SW Olive	16	1.6

n=1006

2-4 品牌转换习惯/ Brand Habit in Consuming Shampoo

	人数 Number	第一次使用该品牌 first use this brand	上一次也是这个牌子 used it last time	上一次不是这个牌子 not used it last time
样本 Sample	998	10.1	70.2	19.6
飘柔 Rejoice	273	2.6	86.4	11.0
沙宣 Vidal Sassoon	129	12.4	65.9	21.7
力士 Lux	93	3.2	71.0	25.8
海飞丝 Head&Shoulder	79	2.5	74.7	22.8
夏士莲 Hazeline	71	12.7	62.0	25.4
潘婷 Pentene	58	5.2	74.1	20.7
诗芬 Sifone	35	17.1	57.1	25.7
伊卡璐 Clairol	26	34.6	53.8	11.5
舒蕾 Slek	24	37.5	41.7	20.8
奥妮百年润发 Olive100	21	14.3	52.4	33.3
蜂花 Bee&Flower	19	0.0	89.5	10.5
威娜宝 Wella	19	5.3	73.7	21.1
奥妮 Olive	17	29.4	58.8	11.8
奥妮首乌 SW Olive	16	6.3	50.0	43.8

2-5 下一次打算使用的品牌排名/ Ranking of the Brands to be Used Next Time

排名 Brand Ranking	品牌 Brands	人数 Number	百分比 Percent
1	飘柔 Rejoice	299	29.8
2	沙宣 Vidal Sassoon	133	13.3
3	力士 Lux	97	9.7
4	海飞丝 Head &Shoulder	86	8.6
5	夏士莲 Hazeline	55	5.5
5	潘婷 Pentene	55	5.5
6	伊卡璐 Clairol	36	3.6
7	诗芬 Sifone	23	2.3
8	蜂花 Bee & Flower	20	2.0
9	威娜宝 Wella	17	1.7
10	舒蕾 Slek	15	1.5

n=1003

2-6 样本、男性各年龄层、女性各年龄层是否是主要购买者/ Purchasers in the Household by the Whole Sample, Age and Gender Groups

	人数 Number	是 yes	不是 no
样本 Sample	1006	59.0	41.0
男性 Male	499	42.3	57.7
16~24 岁 Age	105	36.2	63.8
25~34 岁 Age	151	49.7	50.3
35~44 岁 Age	129	46.5	53.5
45~54 岁 Age	76	30.3	69.7
55~60 岁 Age	38	39.5	60.5
女性 Female	507	75.5	24.5
16~24 岁 Age	108	44.4	55.6
25~34 岁 Age	150	82.0	18.0
35~44 岁 Age	123	89.4	10.6
45~54 岁 Age	84	82.1	17.9
55~60 岁 Age	42	78.6	21.4

2-7 样本、男性各年龄层、女性各年龄层的使用方式/ Ways of Using the Products by the Whole Sample, Age and Gender Groups

	人数 Number	个人专用 personal use	家人共用 all family members share
样本 Sample	1004	24.9	75.1
男性 Male	498	24.3	75.7
16~24 岁 Age	103	31.1	68.9
25~34 岁 Age	151	23.2	76.8
35~44 岁 Age	130	23.8	76.2
45~54 岁 Age	76	21.1	78.9
55~60 岁 Age	38	18.4	81.6
女性 Female	506	25.5	74.5
16~24 岁 Age	107	36.4	63.6
25~34 岁 Age	150	26.7	73.3
35~44 岁 Age	123	20.3	79.7
45~54 岁 Age	84	22.6	77.4
55~60 岁 Age	42	14.3	85.7

2-8 样本、男性各年龄层、女性各年龄层的使用频率/ Frequencies of the Consumed Shampoo by the Whole Sample, Age and Gender Groups

	人数 Number	天天用 daily	两三天用 1 次 once 2 or 3 days	一周 1~2 次 once or twice a week	半个月 1 次或以下 once half a month or below
样本 Sample	1002	10.5	50.0	38.5	1.0
男性 Male	495	13.3	50.9	34.1	1.6
16~24 岁 Age	104	13.5	59.6	26.9	0.0
25~34 岁 Age	151	16.6	53.0	27.8	2.6
35~44 岁 Age	129	13.2	52.7	33.3	0.8
45~54 岁 Age	74	10.8	44.6	43.2	1.4
55~60 岁 Age	37	5.4	24.3	64.9	5.4
女性 Female	507	7.7	49.1	42.8	0.4
16~24 岁 Age	108	9.3	62.0	28.7	0.0
25~34 岁 Age	149	8.1	52.3	39.6	0.0
35~44 岁 Age	124	6.5	45.2	48.4	0.0
45~54 岁 Age	84	6.0	42.9	51.2	0.0
55~60 岁 Age	42	9.5	28.6	57.1	4.8

2-9 选择该类商品的考虑因素/ Ranking of the Considerations in Purchasing

注：本题为多选题，合计百分比超过 100%（Multiple answers）

排名 Ranking	考虑因素 Considerations	人次 Person-time	百分比 Percent
1	产品功用 product function	468	46.8
2	有名的牌子 famous brand	453	45.3
3	价格适中 reasonable price	322	32.2
4	广告影响 influence of advertising	243	24.3
5	单位发的 offered by the working unit	138	13.8
6	购买方便 easy to buy	131	13.1
7	别人推荐 introduced by other people	60	6.0
8	有优惠条件 with preferential terms	42	4.2
9	其它 others	25	2.5
10	包装吸引人 appealing package	21	2.1

n=1000

2-10 对产品功能的侧重方面/ Ranking of the Considerations about the Function of this Kind of Product

注：本题为多选题，合计百分比超过 100%（Multiple answers）

排名 Ranking	侧重方面 Items	人次 Person-time	百分比 Percent
1	去头屑 dandruff control	485	48.6
2	气味好 pleasant smell	391	39.2
3	柔顺营养 soft & nutritious	377	37.8
4	洗护合一 2 in 1	319	32.0
5	焗油功能 containing hair conditioning ingredient	116	11.6
6	多效功能 many performance	91	9.1
7	去痒 itch-easing	85	8.5
8	是天然制品 natural product	84	8.4
9	防止脱发 anti-baldness	83	8.3
10	某种发质专用 special to a certain type	61	6.1
11	防止分岔 anti-split	31	3.1
12	洗护分开 separate use	24	2.4
13	染发功能 dyeing	17	1.7
14	其他 others	12	1.2
15	含果酸 containing tartaric acid	8	0.8

n=998

2-11 重度消费者的人口分布/ Demographics of the Heavy Consumers

	人数 Number	16-24 岁 Age	25-34 岁 Age	35-44 岁 Age	45-54 岁 Age	55-60 岁 Age
样本 Sample	606	25.2	32.2	24.6	13.5	4.5
男性 Male	318	23.9	33.0	26.7	12.9	3.5
天天用 daily	66	21.2	37.9	25.8	12.1	3.0
两三天用 1 次 once 2 or 3 days	252	24.6	31.7	27.0	13.1	3.6
女性 Female	288	26.7	31.3	22.2	14.2	5.6
天天用 daily	39	25.6	30.8	20.5	12.8	10.3
两三天用 1 次 once 2 or 3 days	249	26.9	31.3	22.5	14.5	4.8

2-12 不同消费者层的常用品牌/ The Most Frequently Used Brands by Market Segments

2-12-1 时尚流行指标/ Fads Popular Index

	人数 Number	第一品牌及百分比 1st / percent	第二品牌及百分比 2nd / percent	第三品牌及百分比 3rd / percent	第四品牌及百分比 4th / percent
样本 Sample	991	**飘柔 Rejoice(38.5)**	**力士 Lux(9.8)**	**沙宣 Vidal Sassoon(9.3)**	**海飞丝 Head&Shoulder(8.9)**
平实生活指向 simple living orientation	484	飘柔 Rejoice(41.5)	力士 Lux(10.1)	海飞丝 Head&Shoulder(9.1)	沙宣 Vidal Sassoon(6.4)
时尚流行指向 fashion orientation	507	飘柔 Rejoice(35.7)	沙宣 Vidal Sassoon(12.0)	力士 Lux(9.5)	海飞丝 Head&Shoulder(8.7)

2-12-2 广告态度指标/ Advertising Attitude Index

	人数 Number	第一品牌及百分比 1st / percent	第二品牌及百分比 2nd / percent	第三品牌及百分比 3rd / percent	第四品牌及百分比 4th / percent
样本 Sample	987	**飘柔 Rejoice(38.6)**	**力士 Lux(10.0)**	**沙宣 Vidal Sassoon(9.0)**	**海飞丝 Head&Shoulder(8.7)**
广告淡漠指向 indifferent orientation	285	飘柔 Rejoice(38.2)	沙宣 Vidal Sassoon(11.2)	力士 Lux(7.4) 海飞丝 Head&Shoulder(7.4)	潘婷 Pentene(5.3)
中间层 medium	570	飘柔 Rejoice(38.9)	力士 Lux(10.5)	海飞丝 Head&Shoulder(9.5)	沙宣 Vidal Sassoon(8.4)
信赖广告指向 loyal orientation	132	飘柔 Rejoice(37.9)	力士 Lux(13.6)	潘婷 Pentene(9.1)	海飞丝 Head&Shoulder(8.3)

2-13 重度消费者的消费层构成/ The Composition of the Heavy Consumers

2-13-1 时尚流行指标/ Fads Popular Index

	人数 Number	平实生活指向 simple living orientation	时尚流行指向 fashion orientation
样本 Sample	599	44.9	55.1
天天用 daily	102	46.1	53.9
两三天用 1 次 once 2 or 3 days	497	44.7	55.3

2-13-2 广告态度指标/ Advertising Attitude Index

	人数 Number	广告淡漠指向 indifferent orientation	中间层 medium	信赖广告指向 loyal orientation
样本 Sample	594	27.3	58.2	14.5
天天用 daily	101	33.7	51.5	14.9
两三天用 1 次 once 2 or 3 days	493	26.0	59.6	14.4

● 上海 / Shanghai

2-1 最常用品牌排名/ Ranking of the Most Frequently Used Brands

排名 Brand Ranking	品牌 Brands	人数 Number	百分比 Percent
1	飘柔 Rejoice	369	37.6
2	力士 Lux	133	13.6
3	沙宣 Vidal Sassoon	74	7.5
4	潘婷 Pentene	58	5.9
4	夏士莲 Hazeline	58	5.9
5	伊卡璐 Clairol	47	4.8
5	海飞丝 Head&Shoulder	47	4.8
6	诗芬 Sifcne	40	4.1
7	舒蕾 Slek	18	1.8
8	海鸥 Seagull	16	1.6

n=981

2-2 样本、男性各年龄层、女性各年龄层的常用品牌/ The Most Frequently Used Brands by the Whole Sample, Age and Gender Groups

	人数 Number	第一品牌及百分比 1st/ percent	第二品牌及百分比 2nd/ percent	第三品牌及百分比 3rd/ percent	第四品牌及百分比 4th/ percent
样本 Sample	**981**	**飘柔 Rejoice(37.6)**	**力士 Lux(13.6)**	**沙宣 Vidal Sassoon(7.5)**	**潘婷 Pentene(5.9)** **夏士莲 Hazeline(5.9)**
男性 Male	**480**	**飘柔 Rejoice(39.6)**	**力士 Lux(12.9)**	**沙宣 Vidal Sassoon(6.9)**	**潘婷 Pentene(6.3)**
16~24 岁 Age	109	飘柔 Rejoice(41.3)	力士 Lux(10.1)	沙宣 Vidal Sassoon(9.2)	伊卡璐 Clairol(8.3)
25~34 岁 Age	142	飘柔 Rejoice(35.9)	力士 Lux(16.9)	海飞丝 Head&Shoulder(7.0)	伊卡璐 Clairol(6.3)
35~44 岁 Age	117	飘柔 Rejoice(41.0)	力士 Lux(13.7)	海飞丝 Head&Shoulder(8.5)	沙宣 Vidal Sassoon(7.7)
45~54 岁 Age	78	飘柔 Rejoice(44.9)	潘婷 Pentene(10.3)	夏士莲 Hazeline(7.7)	力士 Lux(6.4)
55~60 岁 Age	34	飘柔 Rejoice(32.4)	力士 Lux(17.6)	资生堂 Shiseido(5.9) 诗芬 Sifone(5.9) 沙宣 Vidal Sassoon(5.9) 花王飞逸 Feather(5.9) 潘婷 Pentene(5.9) 海飞丝 Head&Shoulder(5.9)	飘洒 Halsa(2.9) 可蒙 Kemeng(2.9) 海鸥 Seagull(2.9) 舒蕾 Slek(2.9) 蜂花 Bee&Flower(2.9)
女性 Female	**501**	**飘柔 Rejoice(35.7)**	**力士 Lux(14.2)**	**沙宣 Vidal Sassoon(8.2)**	**夏士莲 Hazeline(6.8)**
16~24 岁 Age	108	飘柔 Rejoice(25.9)	沙宣 Vidal Sassoon(20.4)	力士 Lux(14.8)	潘婷 Pentene(9.3) 伊卡璐 Clairol(9.3)
25~34 岁 Age	143	飘柔 Rejoice(35.0)	力士 Lux(14.0)	沙宣 Vidal Sassoon(8.4)	诗芬 Sifone(6.3)
35~44 岁 Age	127	飘柔 Rejoice(36.2)	力士 Lux(18.9)	夏士莲 Hazeline(8.7)	海飞丝 Head&Shoulder(5.5) 潘婷 Pentene(5.5) 诗芬 Sifone(5.5)
45~54 岁 Age	82	飘柔 Rejoice(37.8)	力士 Lux(12.2)	夏士莲 Hazeline(8.5)	海飞丝 Head&Shoulder(7.3)
55~60 岁 Age	41	飘柔 Rejoice(58.5)	诗芬 Sifone(7.3)	海鸥 Seagull(4.9) 潘婷 Pentene(4.9) 伊卡璐 Clairol(4.9)	舒蕾 Slek(2.4) 好发质 Haofazhi(2.4) 百爱神 Bai'ai Shen (2.4) 蜂花 Bee&Flower(2.4) 施美 Shimei(2.4) 沙宣 Vidal Sassoon(2.4) 力士 Lux(2.4) 洁雅 JR(2.4)

2-3 正在使用的品牌排名/ Ranking of the Brands Used Now

排名 Brand Ranking	品牌 Brands	人数 Number	百分比 Percent
1	飘柔 Rejoice	293	29.8
2	力士 Lux	128	13.0
3	夏士莲 Hazeline	91	9.3
4	沙宣 Vidal Sassoon	76	7.7
5	舒蕾 Slek	50	5.1
6	伊卡璐 Clairol	48	4.9
7	海飞丝 Head&Shoulder	45	4.6
8	潘婷 Pentene	43	4.4
9	诗芬 Sifone	38	3.9
10	花王蓝蓓丝 Labienus	24	2.4

n=982

2-4 品牌转换习惯/ Brand Habit in Consuming Shampoo

	人数 Number	第一次使用该品牌 first use this brand	上一次也是这个牌子 used it last time	上一次不是这个牌子 not used it last time
样本 Sample	**979**	**9.4**	**68.3**	**22.3**
飘柔 Rejoice	293	3.8	82.3	14.0
力士 Lux	128	3.1	71.9	25.0
夏士莲 Hazeline	91	13.2	59.3	27.5
沙宣 Vidal Sassoon	76	11.8	57.9	30.3
舒蕾 Slek	49	28.6	38.8	32.7
伊卡璐 Clairol	48	2.1	66.7	31.3
海飞丝 Head&Shoulder	45	4.4	66.7	28.9
潘婷 Pentene	43	4.7	74.4	20.9
诗芬 Sifone	38	5.3	68.4	26.3
花王蓝蓓丝 Labienus	24	25.0	45.8	29.2

2-5 下一次打算使用的品牌排名/ Ranking of the Brands to be Used Next Time

排名 Brand Ranking	品牌 Brands	人数 Number	百分比 Percent
1	飘柔 Rejoice	308	31.3
2	力士 Lux	121	12.3
3	沙宣 Vidal Sassoon	92	9.3
4	潘婷 Pentene	66	6.7
5	海飞丝 Head&Shoulder	65	6.6
6	夏士莲 Hazeline	62	6.3
7	伊卡璐 Clairol	55	5.6
8	舒蕾 Slek	40	4.1
9	诗芬 Sifone	31	3.2
10	花王蓝蓓丝 Labienus	17	1.7
11	资生堂 Shiseido	14	1.4
12	飘洒 Halsa	12	1.2

n=984

2-6 样本、男性各年龄层、女性各年龄层是否是主要购买者/ Purchasers in the Household by the Whole Sample, Age and Gender Groups

	人数 Number	是 yes	不是 no
样本 Sample	**1013**	**67.2**	**32.8**
男性 Male	**509**	**49.3**	**50.7**
16~24 岁 Age	109	54.1	45.9
25~34 岁 Age	146	56.8	43.2
35~44 岁 Age	130	45.4	54.6
45~54 岁 Age	85	42.4	57.6
55~60 岁 Age	39	35.9	64.1
女性 Female	**504**	**85.3**	**14.7**
16~24 岁 Age	108	63.0	37.0
25~34 岁 Age	143	93.0	7.0
35~44 岁 Age	130	96.9	3.1
45~54 岁 Age	82	86.6	13.4
55~60 岁 Age	41	78.0	22.0

2-7 样本、男性各年龄层、女性各年龄层的使用方式/ Ways of Using the Products by the Whole Sample, Age and Gender Groups

	人数 Number	个人专用 personal use	家人共用 all family members share
样本 Sample	**983**	**25.9**	**74.1**
男性 Male	**484**	**25.2**	**74.8**
16~24 岁 Age	109	39.4	60.6
25~34 岁 Age	143	28.0	72.0
35~44 岁 Age	117	18.8	81.2
45~54 岁 Age	79	13.9	86.1
55~60 岁 Age	36	16.7	83.3
女性 Female	**499**	**26.7**	**73.3**
16~24 岁 Age	108	38.9	61.1
25~34 岁 Age	141	36.9	63.1
35~44 岁 Age	127	18.9	81.1
45~54 岁 Age	82	14.6	85.4
55~60 岁 Age	41	7.3	92.7

2-8 样本、男性各年龄层、女性各年龄层的使用频率/ Frequencies of the Consumed Shampoo by the Whole Sample, Age and Gender Groups

	人数 Number	天天用 daily	两三天用 1 次 once 2 or 3 days	一周 1~2 次 once or twice a week	半个月 1 次或以下 once half a month or below
样本 Sample	980	7.3	43.5	48.3	0.9
男性 Male	480	11.9	44.6	42.5	1.0
16~24 岁 Age	109	11.9	50.5	37.6	0.0
25~34 岁 Age	142	14.1	45.8	40.1	0.0
35~44 岁 Age	117	12.8	44.4	41.0	1.7
45~54 岁 Age	78	9.0	42.3	46.2	2.6
55~60 岁 Age	34	5.9	26.5	64.7	2.9
女性 Female	500	3.0	42.4	53.8	0.8
16~24 岁 Age	108	3.7	48.1	48.1	0.0
25~34 岁 Age	142	2.1	48.6	48.6	0.7
35~44 岁 Age	127	3.1	44.9	52.0	0.0
45~54 岁 Age	82	4.9	29.3	63.4	2.4
55~60 岁 Age	41	0.0	24.4	73.2	2.4

2-9 选择该类商品的考虑因素/ Ranking of the Considerations in Purchasing

注：本题为多选题，合计百分比超过 100%（Multiple answers）

排名 Ranking	考虑因素 Considerations	人次 Person-time	百分比 Percent
1	产品功用 product function	454	46.2
2	有名的牌子 famous brand	409	41.6
3	价格适中 reasonable price	325	33.1
4	广告影响 influence of advertising	290	29.5
5	购买方便 easy to buy	186	18.9
6	别人推荐 introduced by other people	79	8.0
7	有优惠条件 with preferential terms	55	5.6
8	包装吸引人 appealing package	45	4.6
9	单位发的 offered by the working unit	40	4.1
10	其它 others	20	2.0

n=982

2-10 对产品功能的侧重方面/ Ranking of the Considerations about the Function of this Kind of Product

注：本题为多选题，合计百分比超过 100%（Multiple answers）

排名 Ranking	侧重方面 Items	人次 Person-time	百分比 Percent
1	去头屑 dandruff control	591	60.2
2	气味好 pleasant smell	434	44.2
3	柔顺营养 soft & nutritious	353	35.9
4	洗护合一 2 in 1	279	28.4
5	去痒 itch-easing	94	9.6
6	多效功能 many performance	92	9.4
7	焗油功能 containing hair conditioning ingredient	85	8.7
8	某种发质专用 special to a certain type	81	8.2
9	防止脱发 anti-baldness	68	6.9
10	是天然制品 natural product	58	5.9
11	防止分岔 anti-split	26	2.6
12	洗护分开 separate use	19	1.9
13	含果酸 containing tartaric acid	17	1.7
13	染发功能 dyeing	17	1.7
14	其他 others	4	0.4

n=982

2-11 重度消费者的人口分布/ Demographics of the Heavy Consumers

	人数 Number	16-24 岁 Age	25-34 岁 Age	35-44 岁 Age	45-54 岁 Age	55-60 岁 Age
样本 Sample	498	24.9	31.5	25.7	13.7	4.2
男性 Male	271	25.1	31.4	24.7	14.8	4.1
天天用 daily	57	22.8	35.1	26.3	12.3	3.5
两三天用 1 次 once 2 or 3 days	214	25.7	30.4	24.3	15.4	4.2
女性 Female	227	24.7	31.7	26.9	12.3	4.4
天天用 daily	15	26.7	20.0	26.7	26.7	0.0
两三天用 1 次 once 2 or 3 days	212	24.5	32.5	26.9	11.3	4.7

2-12 不同消费者层的常用品牌/ The Most Frequently Used Brands by Market Segments

2-12-1 时尚流行指标/ Fads Popular Index

	人数 Number	第一品牌及百分比 1st / percent	第二品牌及百分比 2nd / percent	第三品牌及百分比 3rd / percent	第四品牌及百分比 4th / percent
样本 Sample	**972**	**飘柔 Rejoice（37.7）**	**力士 Lux（13.5）**	**沙宣 Vidal Sassoon（7.6）**	**夏士莲 Hazeline（6.0）**
平实生活指向 simple living orientation	451	飘柔 Rejoice（40.4）	力士 Lux（13.5）	海飞丝 Head&Shoulder（6.4）	夏士莲 Hazeline（6.0）
时尚流行指向 fashion orientation	521	飘柔 Rejoice（35.3）	力士 Lux（13.4）	沙宣 Vidal Sassoon（9.2）	潘婷 Pentene（6.1）

2-12-2 广告态度指标/ Advertising Attitude Index

	人数 Number	第一品牌及百分比 1st / percent	第二品牌及百分比 2nd / percent	第三品牌及百分比 3rd / percent	第四品牌及百分比 4th / percent
样本 Sample	**970**	**飘柔 Rejoice（37.7）**	**力士 Lux（13.5）**	**沙宣 Vidal Sassoon（7.5）**	**潘婷 Pentene（6.0） 夏士莲 Hazeline（6.0）**
广告淡漠指向 indifferent orientation	244	飘柔 Rejoice（38.5）	力士 Lux（13.1）	夏士莲 Hazeline（6.1） 潘婷 Pentene（6.1） 诗芬 Sifone（6.1）	沙宣 Vidal Sassoon（5.7） 伊卡璐 Clairol（5.7）
中间层 medium	592	飘柔 Rejoice（38.3）	力士 Lux（13.0）	沙宣 Vidal Sassoon（8.4）	夏士莲 Hazeline（5.6） 海飞丝 Head&Shoulder（5.6）
信赖广告指向 loyal orientation	134	飘柔 Rejoice（33.6）	力士 Lux（16.4）	潘婷 Pentene（8.2）	夏士莲 Hazeline（7.5）

2-13 重度消费者的消费层构成/ The Composition of the Heavy Consumers

2-13-1 时尚流行指标/ Fads Popular Index

	人数 Number	平实生活指向 simple living orientation	时尚流行指向 fashion orientation
样本 Sample	**493**	**40.2**	**59.8**
天天用 daily	72	33.3	66.7
两三天用 1 次 once 2 or 3 days	421	41.3	58.7

2-13-2 广告态度指标/ Advertising Attitude Index

	人数 Number	广告淡漠指向 indifferent orientation	中间层 medium	信赖广告指向 loyal orientation
样本 Sample	**490**	**22.0**	**62.9**	**15.1**
天天用 daily	69	18.8	62.3	18.8
两三天用 1 次 once 2 or 3 days	421	22.6	62.9	14.5

● 广州 / Guangzhou

2-1 最常用品牌排名/ Ranking of the Most Frequently Used Brands

排名 Brand Ranking	品牌 Brands	人数 Number	百分比 Percent
1	飘柔 Rejoice	380	36.9
2	棕榄美之选 Palmotive Optima	90	8.7
3	沙宣 Vidal Sassoon	73	7.1
4	潘婷 Pentene	69	6.7
5	海飞丝 Head&Shoulder	55	5.3
6	花王 Kao	42	4.1
7	诗芬 Sifone	35	3.4
8	奥妮首乌 SW Olive	30	2.9
9	夏士莲 Hazeline	27	2.6
10	力士 Lux	24	2.3

n=1031

2-2 样本、男性各年龄层、女性各年龄层的常用品牌/ The Most Frequently Used Brands by the Whole Sample, Age and Gender Groups

	人数 Number	第一品牌及百分比 1st/ percent	第二品牌及百分比 2nd/ percent	第三品牌及百分比 3rd/ percent
样本 Sample	**1031**	**飘柔 Rejoice(36.9)**	**棕榄美之选 Palmotive Optima(8.7)**	**沙宣 Vidal Sassoon(7.1)**
男性 Male	**498**	**飘柔 Rejoice(38.4)**	**棕榄美之选 Palmotive Optima(8.6)**	**海飞丝 Head&Shoulder(6.2)**
16~24 岁 Age	106	飘柔 Rejoice(36.8)	沙宣 Vidal Sassoon(8.5)	棕榄美之选 Palmotive Optima(7.5) 潘婷 Pentene(7.5)
25~34 岁 Age	150	飘柔 Rejoice(38.0)	棕榄美之选 Palmotive Optima(9.3)	海飞丝 Head&Shoulder(8.7) 潘婷 Pentene(8.7)
35~44 岁 Age	127	飘柔 Rejoice(33.9)	棕榄美之选 Palmotive Optima(11.8)	花王 Kao(8.7)
45~54 岁 Age	73	飘柔 Rejoice(45.2)	棕榄美之选 Palmotive Optima(8.2)	花王 Kao(6.8) 诗芬 Sifone(6.8)
55~60 岁 Age	42	飘柔 Rejoice(45.2)	奥妮首乌 SW Olive(7.1) 海飞丝 Head&Shoulder(7.1) 沙宣 Vidal Sassoon(7.1)	诗芬 Sifone(4.8) 夏士莲 Hazeline(4.8)
女性 Female	**533**	**飘柔 Rejoice(35.5)**	**棕榄美之选 Palmotive Optima(8.8)**	**沙宣 Vidal Sassoon(8.4)**
16~24 岁 Age	112	飘柔 Rejoice(23.2)	沙宣 Vidal Sassoon(17.0)	潘婷 Pentene(9.8)
25~34 岁 Age	158	飘柔 Rejoice(40.5)	棕榄美之选 Palmotive Optima(10.8)	海飞丝 Head&Shoulder(7.0)
35~44 岁 Age	136	飘柔 Rejoice(31.6)	潘婷 Pentene(10.3)	沙宣 Vidal Sassoon(9.6)
45~54 岁 Age	86	飘柔 Rejoice(41.9)	棕榄美之选 Palmotive Optima(9.3)	奥妮首乌 SW Olive(5.8) 沙宣 Vidal Sassoon(5.8)
55~60 岁 Age	41	飘柔 Rejoice(48.8)	潘婷 Pentene(7.3)	奥妮百年润发 Olive100(4.9) 沙宣 Vidal Sassoon(4.9)

2-3 正在使用的品牌排名/ Ranking of the Brands Used Now

排名 Brand Ranking	品牌 Brands	人数 Number	百分比 Percent
1	飘柔 Rejoice	306	29.7
2	棕榄美之选 Palmotive Optima	88	8.5
3	沙宣 Vidal Sassoon	79	7.7
4	海飞丝 Head&Shoulder	59	5.7
4	潘婷 Pentene	59	5.7
5	花王 Kao	49	4.8
6	夏士莲 Hazeline	40	3.9
7	诗芬 Sifone	34	3.3
7	力士 Lux	34	3.3
8	奥妮首乌 SW Olive	26	2.5
9	伊卡璐 Clairol	24	2.3
10	无限美 Wuxianmei	23	2.2
10	奥妮 Olive	23	2.2

n=1030

2-4 品牌转换习惯/ Brand Habit in Consuming Shampoo

	人数 Number	第一次使用该品牌 first use this brand	上一次也是这个牌子 used it last time	上一次不是这个牌子 not used it last time
样本 Sample	**1025**	**9.3**	**64.2**	**26.5**
飘柔 Rejoice	306	2.9	73.5	23.5
棕榄美之选 Palmotive Optima	87	9.2	66.7	24.1
沙宣 Vidal Sassoon	78	9.0	65.4	25.6
海飞丝 Head&Shoulder	59	1.7	64.4	33.9
潘婷 Pentene	59	1.7	72.9	25.4
花王 Kao	49	0.0	71.4	28.6
夏士莲 Hazeline	40	17.5	45.0	37.5
诗芬 Sifone	34	5.9	61.8	32.4
力士 Lux	34	8.8	52.9	38.2
奥妮首乌 SW Olive	26	11.5	69.2	19.2

2-5 下一次打算使用的品牌排名/ Ranking of the Brands to be Used Next Time

排名 Brand Ranking	品牌 Brands	人数 Number	百分比 Percent
1	飘柔 Rejoice	311	30.1
2	沙宣 Vidal Sassoon	87	8.4
3	棕榄美之选 Palmotive Optima	67	6.5
4	潘婷 Pentene	62	6.0
5	海飞丝 Head&Shoulder	54	5.2
6	夏士莲 Hazeline	44	4.3
7	诗芬 Sifone	42	4.1
8	花王 Kao	38	3.7
9	力士 Lux	30	2.9
10	奥妮 Olive	27	2.6

n=1032

2-6 样本、男性各年龄层、女性各年龄层是否是主要购买者/ Purchasers in the Household by the Whole Sample, Age and Gender Groups

	人数 Number	是 yes	不是 no
样本 Sample	1031	63.2	36.8
男性 Male	497	46.3	53.7
16~24 岁 Age	106	36.8	63.2
25~34 岁 Age	149	52.3	47.7
35~44 岁 Age	126	50.8	49.2
45~54 岁 Age	73	37.0	63.0
55~60 岁 Age	43	51.2	48.8
女性 Female	534	79.0	21.0
16~24 岁 Age	112	50.0	50.0
25~34 岁 Age	158	85.4	14.6
35~44 岁 Age	136	91.9	8.1
45~54 岁 Age	87	86.2	13.8
55~60 岁 Age	41	75.6	24.4

2-7 样本、男性各年龄层、女性各年龄层的使用方式/ Ways of Using the Products by the Whole Sample, Age and Gender Groups

	人数 Number	个人专用 personal use	家人共用 all family members share
样本 Sample	1030	18.3	81.7
男性 Male	496	17.7	82.3
16~24 岁 Age	106	31.1	68.9
25~34 岁 Age	148	23.0	77.0
35~44 岁 Age	127	6.3	93.7
45~54 岁 Age	73	9.6	90.4
55~60 岁 Age	42	14.3	85.7
女性 Female	534	18.7	81.3
16~24 岁 Age	112	29.5	70.5
25~34 岁 Age	158	13.3	86.7
35~44 岁 Age	136	21.3	78.7
45~54 岁 Age	87	12.6	87.4
55~60 岁 Age	41	14.6	85.4

2-8 样本、男性各年龄层、女性各年龄层的使用频率/ Frequencies of the Consumed Shampoo by the Whole Sample, Age and Gender Groups

	人数 Number	天天用 daily	两三天用 1 次 once 2 or 3 days	一周 1~2 次 once or twice a week	半个月 1 次或以下 once half a month or below
样本 Sample	1030	22.0	51.6	25.8	0.6
男性 Male	497	32.4	49.9	17.3	0.4
16~24 岁 Age	106	50.0	41.5	8.5	0.0
25~34 岁 Age	150	32.0	56.7	10.7	0.7
35~44 岁 Age	126	23.8	49.2	26.2	0.8
45~54 岁 Age	73	27.4	50.7	21.9	0.0
55~60 岁 Age	42	23.8	47.6	28.6	0.0
女性 Female	533	12.4	53.1	33.8	0.8
16~24 岁 Age	112	12.5	64.3	23.2	0.0
25~34 岁 Age	158	8.9	57.6	33.5	0.0
35~44 岁 Age	135	15.6	46.7	37.0	0.7
45~54 岁 Age	87	16.1	46.0	35.6	2.3
55~60 岁 Age	41	7.3	41.5	48.8	2.4

2-9 选择该类商品的考虑因素/ Ranking of the Considerations in Purchasing

注：本题为多选题，合计百分比超过 100%（Multiple answers）

排名 Ranking	考虑因素 Considerations	人次 Person-time	百分比 Percent
1	产品功用 product function	517	50.2
2	有名的牌子 famous brand	481	46.7
3	价格适中 reasonable price	368	35.7
4	广告影响 influence of advertising	228	22.1
5	购买方便 easy to buy	187	18.2
6	别人推荐 introduced by other people	87	8.4
7	包装吸引人 appealing package	49	4.8
8	有优惠条件 with preferential terms	41	4.0
9	单位发的 offered by the working unit	27	2.6
10	其它 others	21	2.0

n=1030

2-10 对产品功能的侧重方面/ Ranking of the Considerations about the Function of this Kind of Product

注：本题为多选题，合计百分比超过 100%（Multiple answers）

排名 Ranking	侧重方面 Items	人次 Person-time	百分比 Percent
1	去头屑 dandruff control	537	52.3
2	柔顺营养 soft & nutritious	411	40.0
3	气味好 pleasant smell	358	34.9
4	洗护合一 2 in 1	288	28.0
5	焗油功能 containing hair conditioning ingredient	132	12.9
6	防止脱发 anti-baldness	129	12.6
7	多效功能 many performance	126	12.3
8	去痒 itch-easing	116	11.3
9	是天然制品 natural product	62	6.0
10	某种发质专用 special to a certain type	43	4.2
11	染发功能 dyeing	21	2.0
12	防止分岔 anti-split	19	1.9
13	含果酸 containing tartaric acid	13	1.3
14	洗护分开 separate use	10	1.0
15	其他 others	9	0.9

n=1027

2-11 重度消费者的人口分布/ Demographics of the Heavy Consumers

	人数 Number	16-24 岁 Age	25-34 岁 Age	35-44 岁 Age	45-54 岁 Age	55-60 岁 Age
样本 Sample	758	24.1	31.4	23.2	14.6	6.6
男性 Male	409	23.7	32.5	22.5	13.9	7.3
天天用 daily	161	32.9	29.8	18.6	12.4	6.2
两三天用 1 次 once 2 or 3 days	248	17.7	34.3	25.0	14.9	8.1
女性 Female	349	24.6	30.1	24.1	15.5	5.7
天天用 daily	66	21.2	21.2	31.8	21.2	4.5
两三天用 1 次 once 2 or 3 days	283	25.4	32.2	22.3	14.1	6.0

2-12 不同消费者层的常用品牌/ The Most Frequently Used Brands by Market Segments

2-12-1 时尚流行指标/ Fads Popular Index

	人数 Number	第一品牌及百分比 1st / percent	第二品牌及百分比 2nd / percent	第三品牌及百分比 3rd / percent	第四品牌及百分比 4th / percent
样本 Sample	1019	**飘柔 Rejoice(36.6)**	**棕榄美之选 Palmotive Optima(8.6)**	**沙宣 Vidal Sassoon(7.2)**	**潘婷 Pentene(6.8)**
平实生活指向 simple living orientation	515	飘柔 Rejoice(39.0)	棕榄美之选 Palmotive Optima(8.3)	海飞丝 Head&Shoulder(6.4)	潘婷 Pentene(5.8)
时尚流行指向 fashion orientation	504	飘柔 Rejoice(34.1)	棕榄美之选 Palmotive Optima(8.9)	沙宣 Vidal Sassoon(8.7)	潘婷 Pentene(7.7)

2-12-2 广告态度指标/ Advertising Attitude Index

	人数 Number	第一品牌及百分比 1st / percent	第二品牌及百分比 2nd / percent	第三品牌及百分比 3rd / percent	第四品牌及百分比 4th / percent
样本 Sample	1019	**飘柔 Rejoice(36.8)**	**棕榄美之选 Palmotive Optima(8.8)**	**沙宣 Vidal Sassoon(7.2)**	**潘婷 Pentene(6.8)**
广告淡漠指向 indifferent orientation	333	飘柔 Rejoice(35.4)	棕榄美之选 Palmotive Optima(9.0)	沙宣 Vidal Sassoon(6.6)	海飞丝 Head&Shoulder(5.7)
中间层 medium	591	飘柔 Rejoice(37.7)	棕榄美之选 Palmotive Optima(9.5)	沙宣 Vidal Sassoon(7.6)	潘婷 Pentene(7.3)
信赖广告指向 loyal orientation	95	飘柔 Rejoice(35.8)	潘婷 Pentene(9.5)	沙宣 Vidal Sassoon(6.3)	奥妮首乌 SW Olive(5.3) 伊卡璐 Clairol(5.3)

2-13 重度消费者的消费层构成/ The Composition of the Heavy Consumers

2-13-1 时尚流行指标/ Fads Popular Index

	人数 Number	平实生活指向 simple living orientation	时尚流行指向 fashion orientation
样本 Sample	751	46.9	53.1
天天用 daily	225	42.7	57.3
两三天用 1 次 once 2or 3 days	526	48.7	51.3

2-13-2 广告态度指标/ Advertising Attitude Index

	人数 Number	广告淡漠指向 indifferent orientation	中间层 medium	信赖广告指向 loyal orientation
样本 Sample	749	32.8	57.1	10.0
天天用 daily	225	33.8	56.0	10.2
两三天用 1 次 once 2or 3 days	524	32.4	57.6	9.9

● 重庆 / Chongqing

2-1 最常用品牌排名/ Ranking of the Most Frequently Used Brands

排名 Brand Ranking	品牌 Brands	人数 Number	百分比 Percent
1	飘柔 Rejoice	181	29.4
2	海飞丝 Head&Shoulder	96	15.6
3	力士 Lux	52	8.5
4	潘婷 Pentene	43	7.0
5	夏士莲 Hazeline	41	6.7
6	沙宣 Vidal Sassoon	33	5.4
7	奥妮 Olive	25	4.1
8	奥妮皂角 ZJ Olive	20	3.3
9	舒蕾 Slek	19	3.1
10	奥妮百年润发 Olive100	16	2.6
11	奥妮首乌 SW Olive	14	2.3

n=615

2-2 样本、男性各年龄层、女性各年龄层的常用品牌/ The Most Frequently Used Brands by the Whole Sample, Age and Gender Groups

	人数 Number	第一品牌及百分比 1st/ percent	第二品牌及百分比 2nd/ percent	第三品牌及百分比 3rd/ percent	第四品牌及百分比 4th/ percent
样本 Sample	615	**飘柔 Rejoice(29.4)**	**海飞丝 Head&Shoulder(15.6)**	**力士 Lux(8.5)**	**潘婷 Pentene(7.0)**
男性 Male	306	**飘柔 Rejoice(28.8)**	**海飞丝 Head&Shoulder(17.3)**	**力士 Lux(8.2)**	**潘婷 Pentene(6.9)**
16~24 岁 Age	64	飘柔 Rejoice(25.0)	海飞丝 Head&Shoulder(17.2)	舒蕾 Slek(7.8) 力士 Lux(7.8) 潘婷 Pentene(7.8)	沙宣 Vidal Sassoon(6.3)
25~34 岁 Age	92	飘柔 Rejoice(23.9)	海飞丝 Head&Shoulder(21.7)	力士 Lux(10.9)	潘婷 Pentene(8.7)
35~44 岁 Age	71	飘柔 Rejoice(42.3)	海飞丝 Head&Shoulder(15.5)	夏士莲 Hazeline(11.3)	奥妮 Olive(5.6)
45~54 岁 Age	51	飘柔 Rejoice(25.5)	力士 Lux(11.8)	奥妮 Olive(9.8) 海飞丝 Head&Shoulder(9.8)	沙宣 Vidal Sassoon(7.8) 潘婷 Pentene(7.8)
55~60 岁 Age	28	飘柔 Rejoice(25.0)	海飞丝 Head&Shoulder(21.4)	力士 Lux(10.7)	奥妮 Olive(7.1) 奥妮皂角 ZJ Olive(7.1)
女性 Female	309	**飘柔 Rejoice(30.1)**	**海飞丝 Head&Shoulder(13.9)**	**力士 Lux(8.7)**	**潘婷 Pentene(7.1)**
16~24 岁 Age	64	飘柔 Rejoice(26.6)	海飞丝 Head&Shoulder(17.2)	力士 Lux(14.1)	沙宣 Vidal Sassoon(10.9)
25~34 岁 Age	90	飘柔 Rejoice(32.2)	海飞丝 Head&Shoulder(8.9) 潘婷 Pentene(8.9)	夏士莲 Hazeline(6.7)	沙宣 Vidal Sassoon(5.6)
35~44 岁 Age	73	飘柔 Rejoice(27.4)	海飞丝 Head&Shoulder(13.7)	力士 Lux(9.6)	夏士莲 Hazeline(8.2) 潘婷 Pentene(8.2)
45~54 岁 Age	60	飘柔 Rejoice(30.0)	海飞丝 Head&Shoulder(15.0)	奥妮皂角 ZJ Olive(11.7) 力士 Lux(11.7)	潘婷 Pentene(6.7)
55~60 岁 Age	22	飘柔 Rejoice(40.9)	海飞丝 Head&Shoulder(22.7)	奥妮百年润发 Olive100(9.1) 夏士莲 Hazeline(9.1)	生态美 Natural Balance(4.5) 奥妮皂角 ZJ Olive(4.5) 潘婷 Pentene(4.5) 沙宣 Vidal Sassoon(4.5)

2-3 正在使用的品牌排名/ Ranking of the Brands Used Now

排名 Brand Ranking	品牌 Brands	人数 Number	百分比 Percent
1	飘柔 Rejoice	141	22.9
2	海飞丝 Head&Shoulder	91	14.8
3	夏士莲 Hazeline	51	8.3
4	力士 Lux	47	7.6
5	沙宣 Vidal Sassoon	46	7.5
6	潘婷 Pentene	33	5.4
7	奥妮 Olive	32	5.2
8	奥妮皂角 ZJ Olive	25	4.1
8	舒蕾 Slek	25	4.1
9	奥妮首乌 SW Olive	15	2.4
10	奥妮百年润发 Olive100	13	2.1

n=615

2-4 品牌转换习惯/ Brand Habit in Consuming Shampoo

	人数 Number	第一次使用该品牌 first use this brand	上一次也是这个牌子 used it last time	上一次不是这个牌子 not used it last time
样本 Sample	**602**	**8.0**	**65.6**	**26.4**
飘柔 Rejoice	140	2.1	77.1	20.7
海飞丝 Head&Shoulder	90	3.3	72.2	24.4
夏士莲 Hazeline	50	8.0	62.0	30.0
力士 Lux	45	8.9	53.3	37.8
沙宣 Vidal Sassoon	46	13.0	52.2	34.8
潘婷 Pentene	32	6.3	68.8	25.0
奥妮 Olive	31	9.7	67.7	22.6
奥妮皂角 ZJ Olive	25	0.0	76.0	24.0
舒蕾 Slek	24	25.0	50.0	25.0
奥妮首乌 SW Olive	15	13.3	73.3	13.3
奥妮百年润发 Olive100	12	8.3	83.3	8.3

2-5 下一次打算使用的品牌排名/ Ranking of the Brands to be Used Next Time

排名 Brand Ranking	品牌 Brands	人数 Number	百分比 Percent
1	飘柔 Rejoice	157	25.5
2	海飞丝 Head&Shoulder	91	14.8
3	力士 Lux	48	7.8
4	沙宣 Vidal Sassoon	44	7.1
5	潘婷 Pentene	42	6.8
6	夏士莲 Hazeline	36	5.8
7	奥妮 Olive	24	3.9
8	舒蕾 Slek	22	3.6
9	奥妮百年润发 Olive100	20	3.2
9	奥妮皂角 ZJ Olive	20	3.2
10	奥妮首乌 SW Olive	15	2.4

n=616

2-6 样本、 男性各年龄层、 女性各年龄层是否是主要购买者/ Purchasers in the Household by the Whole Sample, Age and Gender Groups

	人数 Number	是 yes	不是 no
样本 Sample	**623**	**63.4**	**36.6**
男性 Male	**313**	**42.5**	**57.5**
16~24 岁 Age	64	43.8	56.3
25~34 岁 Age	92	45.7	54.3
35~44 岁 Age	75	41.3	58.7
45~54 岁 Age	54	40.7	59.3
55~60 岁 Age	28	35.7	64.3
女性 Female	**310**	**84.5**	**15.5**
16~24 岁 Age	64	71.9	28.1
25~34 岁 Age	90	91.1	8.9
35~44 岁 Age	73	94.5	5.5
45~54 岁 Age	60	83.3	16.7
55~60 岁 Age	23	65.2	34.8

2-7 样本、男性各年龄层、女性各年龄层的使用方式/ Ways of Using the Products by the Whole Sample, Age and Gender Groups

	人数 Number	个人专用 personal use	家人共用 all family members share
样本 Sample	**614**	**11.7**	**88.3**
男性 Male	**305**	**11.5**	**88.5**
16~24 岁 Age	64	20.3	79.7
25~34 岁 Age	91	15.4	84.6
35~44 岁 Age	71	5.6	94.4
45~54 岁 Age	52	5.8	94.2
55~60 岁 Age	27	3.7	96.3
女性 Female	**309**	**12.0**	**88.0**
16~24 岁 Age	64	20.3	79.7
25~34 岁 Age	90	13.3	86.7
35~44 岁 Age	73	6.8	93.2
45~54 岁 Age	60	10.0	90.0
55~60 岁 Age	22	4.5	95.5

2-8 样本、男性各年龄层、女性各年龄层的使用频率/ Frequencies of the Consumed Shampoo by the Whole Sample, Age and Gender Groups

	人数 Number	天天用 use daily	两三天用 1 次 once 2 or 3 days	一周 1~2 次 once or twice a week	半个月 1 次或以下 once half a month or below
样本 Sample	610	4.4	50.2	44.8	0.7
男性 Male	302	6.6	52.6	39.4	1.3
16~24 岁 Age	64	6.3	65.6	28.1	0.0
25~34 岁 Age	91	8.8	50.5	40.7	0.0
35~44 岁 Age	69	2.9	58.0	37.7	1.4
45~54 岁 Age	50	8.0	42.0	48.0	2.0
55~60 岁 Age	28	7.1	35.7	50.0	7.1
女性 Female	308	2.3	47.7	50.0	0.0
16~24 岁 Age	64	1.6	59.4	39.1	0.0
25~34 岁 Age	90	2.2	52.2	45.6	0.0
35~44 岁 Age	73	2.7	46.6	50.7	0.0
45~54 岁 Age	59	3.4	35.6	61.0	0.0
55~60 岁 Age	22	0.0	31.8	68.2	0.0

2-9 选择该类商品的考虑因素/ Ranking of the Considerations in Purchasing

注：本题为多选题，合计百分比超过 100%（Multiple answers）

排名 Ranking	考虑因素 Considerations	人次 Person-time	百分比 Percent
1	产品功用 product function	311	51.5
2	价格适中 reasonable price	245	40.6
3	有名的牌子 famous brand	236	39.1
4	广告影响 influence of advertising	177	29.3
5	购买方便 easy to buy	78	12.9
6	别人推荐 introduced by other people	32	5.3
7	有优惠条件 with preferential terms	28	4.6
8	包装吸引人 appealing package	16	2.6
9	单位发的 offered by the working unit	14	2.3
10	其它 others	9	1.5

n=604

2-10 对产品功能的侧重方面/ Ranking of the Considerations about the Function of this Kind of Product

注：本题为多选题，合计百分比超过 100%（Multiple answers）

排名 Ranking	侧重方面 Items	人次 Person-time	百分比 Percent
1	去头屑 dandruff control	389	64.2
2	气味好 pleasant smell	222	36.6
3	柔顺营养 soft & nutritious	206	34.0
4	去痒 itch-easing	139	22.9
5	洗护合一 2 in 1	89	14.7
6	防止脱发 anti-baldness	62	10.2
7	多效功能 many performance	59	9.7
8	是天然制品 natural product	51	8.4
9	焗油功能 containing hair conditioning ingredient	42	6.9
10	某种发质专用 special to a certain type	24	4.0
11	其他 others	9	1.5
12	防止分岔 anti-split	6	1.0
12	染发功能 dyeing	6	1.0
13	含果酸 containing tartaric acid	5	0.8
14	洗护分开 separate use	3	0.5

n=606

2-11 重度消费者的人口分布/ Demographics of the Heavy Consumers

	人数 Number	16-24 岁 Age	25-34 岁 Age	35-44 岁 Age	45-54 岁 Age	55-60 岁 Age
样本 Sample	333	25.5	30.9	23.4	14.4	5.7
男性 Male	179	25.7	30.2	23.5	14.0	6.7
天天用 daily	20	20.0	40.0	10.0	20.0	10.0
两三天用 1 次 once 2 or 3 days	159	26.4	28.9	25.2	13.2	6.3
女性 Female	154	25.3	31.8	23.4	14.9	4.5
天天用 daily	7	14.3	28.6	28.6	28.6	0.0
两三天用 1 次 once 2 or 3 days	147	25.9	32.0	23.1	14.3	4.8

2-12 不同消费者层的常用品牌/ The Most Frequently Used Brands by Market Segments

2-12-1 时尚流行指标/ Fads Popular Index

	人数 Number	第一品牌及百分比 1st / percent	第二品牌及百分比 2nd / percent	第三品牌及百分比 3rd / percent	第四品牌及百分比 4th / percent
样本 Sample	**607**	**飘柔 Rejoice(29.7)**	**海飞丝 Head&Shoulder(15.7)**	**力士 Lux(8.6)**	**潘婷 Pentene(6.9)**
平实生活指向 simple living orientation	361	飘柔 Rejoice(32.1)	海飞丝 Head&Shoulder(16.1)	力士 Lux(7.5)	夏士莲 Hazeline(6.1)
时尚流行指向 fashion orientation	246	飘柔 Rejoice(26.0)	海飞丝 Head&Shoulder(15.0)	力士 Lux(10.2)	沙宣 Vidal Sassoon(8.9) 潘婷 Pentene(8.9)

2-12-2 广告态度指标/ Advertising Attitude Index

	人数 Number	第一品牌及百分比 1st / percent	第二品牌及百分比 2nd / percent	第三品牌及百分比 3rd / percent	第四品牌及百分比 4th / percent
样本 Sample	**609**	**飘柔 Rejoice(29.2)**	**海飞丝 Head&Shoulder(15.6)**	**力士 Lux(8.5)**	**潘婷 Pentene(7.1)**
广告淡漠指向 indifferent orientation	162	飘柔 Rejoice(24.7)	海飞丝 Head&Shoulder(13.6)	力士 Lux(11.1)	沙宣 Vidal Sassoon(7.4)
中间层 medium	366	飘柔 Rejoice(30.9)	海飞丝 Head&Shoulder(15.8)	力士 Lux(8.2)	夏士莲 Hazeline(7.4) 潘婷 Pentene(7.4)
信赖广告指向 loyal orientation	81	飘柔 Rejoice(30.9)	海飞丝 Head&Shoulder(18.5)	潘婷 Pentene(11.1)	沙宣 Vidal Sassoon(7.4)

2-13 重度消费者的消费层构成/ The Composition of the Heavy Consumers

2-13-1 时尚流行指标/ Fads Popular Index

	人数 Number	平实生活指向 simple living orientation	时尚流行指向 fashion orientation
样本 Sample	**328**	**52.4**	**47.6**
天天用 daily	26	57.7	42.3
两三天用 1 次 once 2or 3 days	302	52.0	48.0

2-13-2 广告态度指标/ Advertising Attitude Index

	人数 Number	广告淡漠指向 indifferent orientation	中间层 medium	信赖广告指向 loyal orientation
样本 Sample	**330**	**27.0**	**61.5**	**11.5**
天天用 daily	26	11.5	30.8	7.7
两三天用 1 次 once 2or 3 days	304	28.3	59.9	11.8

● 武汉 / Wuhan

2-1 最常用品牌排名/ Ranking of the Most Frequently Used Brands

排名 Brand Ranking	品牌 Brands	人数 Number	百分比 Percent
1	飘柔 Rejoice	163	27.2
2	舒蕾 Slek	73	12.2
3	潘婷 Pentene	70	11.7
4	海飞丝 Head&Shoulder	68	11.4
5	夏士莲 Hazeline	32	5.3
6	沙宣 Vidal Sassoon	30	5.0
6	力士 Lux	30	5.0
7	诗芬 Sifone	14	2.3
8	奥妮首乌 SW Olive	12	2.0
9	花王飞逸 Feather	11	1.8

n=599

2-2 样本、男性各年龄层、女性各年龄层的常用品牌/ The Most Frequently Used Brands by the Whole Sample, Age and Gender Groups

	人数 Number	第一品牌及百分比 1st/ percent	第二品牌及百分比 2nd/ percent	第三品牌及百分比 3rd/ percent	第四品牌及百分比 4th/ percent
样本 Sample	599	**飘柔 Rejoice(27.2)**	**舒蕾 Slek(12.2)**	**潘婷 Pentene(11.7)**	**海飞丝 Head&Shoulder(11.4)**
男性 Male	274	**飘柔 Rejoice(30.3)**	**海飞丝 Head&Shoulder(14.2)**	**潘婷 Pentene(13.5)**	**舒蕾 Slek(8.4)**
16~24 岁 Age	65	飘柔 Rejoice(30.8)	海飞丝 Head&Shoulder(18.5)	舒蕾 Slek(10.8) 潘婷 Pentene(10.8)	夏士莲 Hazeline(9.2)
25~34 岁 Age	85	飘柔 Rejoice(30.6)	潘婷 Pentene(17.6)	海飞丝 Head&Shoulder(15.3)	舒蕾 Slek(7.1)
35~44 岁 Age	67	飘柔 Rejoice(29.9)	海飞丝 Head&Shoulder(14.9)	舒蕾 Slek(11.9)	潘婷 Pentene(9.0)
45~54 岁 Age	43	飘柔 Rejoice(25.6)	潘婷 Pentene(20.9)	海飞丝 Head&Shoulder(9.3)	沙宣 Vidal Sassoon(7.0) 夏士莲 Hazeline(7.0)
55~60 岁 Age	14	飘柔 Rejoice(42.9)	奥妮首乌 SW Olive(7.1) 奥妮皂角 ZJ Olive(7.1) 蜂花 Bee&Flower(7.1) 力士 Lux(7.1) 夏士莲 Hazeline(7.1) 美波 Meibo(7.1) 花霸 Huaba(7.1)		
女性 Female	325	**飘柔 Rejoice(24.6)**	**舒蕾 Slek(15.4)**	**潘婷 Pentene(10.2)**	**海飞丝 Head&Shoulder(8.9)**
16~24 岁 Age	69	飘柔 Rejoice(33.3)	舒蕾 Slek(14.5)	力士 Lux(10.1)	潘婷 Pentene(8.7)
25~34 岁 Age	95	舒蕾 Slek(22.1)	飘柔 Rejoice(18.9)	潘婷 Pentene(10.5)	海飞丝 Head&Shoulder(9.5)
35~44 岁 Age	78	飘柔 Rejoice(26.9)	舒蕾 Slek(16.7)	力士 Lux(10.3)	夏士莲 Hazeline(7.7) 海飞丝 Head&Shoulder(7.7)
45~54 岁 Age	62	飘柔 Rejoice(19.4)	潘婷 Pentene(17.7)	海飞丝 Head&Shoulder(12.9)	舒蕾 Slek(9.7)
55~60 岁 Age	21	飘柔 Rejoice(28.6)	潘婷 Pentene(9.5)	威娜宝 Wella(4.8) 奥妮 Olive(4.8) 美波 Meibo(4.8) 夏士莲 Hazeline(4.8) 海飞丝 Head&Shoulder(4.8) 发嘉丽 Eastan(4.8) 奥妮首乌 SW Olive(4.8) 奥妮百年润发 Olive100(4.8)	

2-3 正在使用的品牌排名/ Ranking of the Brands Used Now

排名 Brand Ranking	品牌 Brands	人数 Number	百分比 Percent
1	飘柔 Rejoice	115	19.2
2	海飞丝 Head&Shoulder	68	11.4
3	舒蕾 Slek	67	11.2
4	夏士莲 Hazeline	54	9.0
5	沙宣 Vidal Sassoon	52	8.7
5	潘婷 Pentene	52	8.7
6	力士 Lux	32	5.3
7	诗芬 Sifone	20	3.3
8	花王飞逸 Feather	15	2.5
9	奥妮首乌 SW Olive	12	2.0
9	花王 Kao	12	2.0

n=599

2-4 品牌转换习惯/ Brand Habit in Consuming Shampoo

	人数 Number	第一次使用该品牌 first use this brand	上一次也是这个牌子 used it last time	上一次不是这个牌子 not used it last time
样本 Sample	594	12.0	58.8	29.3
飘柔 Rejoice	115	6.1	80.0	13.9
海飞丝 Head&Shoulder	68	4.4	60.3	35.3
舒蕾 Slek	66	7.6	63.6	28.8
夏士莲 Hazeline	53	18.9	41.5	39.6
沙宣 Vidal Sassoon	51	23.5	52.9	23.5
潘婷 Pentene	51	11.8	66.7	21.6
力士 Lux	32	6.3	56.3	37.5
诗芬 Sifone	20	0.0	50.0	50.0
花王飞逸 Feather	15	6.7	46.7	46.7
奥妮首乌 SW Olive	12	0.0	33.3	66.7
花王 Kao	12	16.7	58 3	25.0

2-5 下一次打算使用的品牌排名/ Ranking of the Brands to be Used Next Time

排名 Brand Ranking	品牌 Brands	人数 Number	百分比 Percent
1	飘柔 Rejoice	125	20.9
2	海飞丝 Head&Shoulder	79	13.2
3	沙宣 Vidal Sassoon	63	10.5
4	舒蕾 Slek	62	10.4
4	潘婷 Pentene	62	10.4
5	夏士莲 Hazeline	42	7.0
6	力士 Lux	41	6.8
7	奥妮首乌 SW Olive	13	2.2
8	花王 Kao	11	1.8
8	诗芬 Sifone	11	1.8
9	伊卡璐 Clairol	10	1.7

n=599

2-6 样本、男性各年龄层、女性各年龄层是否是主要购买者/ Purchasers in the Household by the Whole Sample, Age and Gender Groups

	人数 Number	是 yes	不是 no
样本 Sample	637	56.4	43.6
男性 Male	309	33.7	66.3
16~24 岁 Age	65	36.9	63.1
25~34 岁 Age	88	39.8	60.2
35~44 岁 Age	80	30.0	70.0
45~54 岁 Age	52	34.6	65.4
55~60 岁 Age	24	12.5	87.5
女性 Female	328	77.7	22.3
16~24 岁 Age	69	55.1	44.9
25~34 岁 Age	96	82.3	17.7
35~44 岁 Age	78	93.6	6.4
45~54 岁 Age	60	86.7	13.3
55~60 岁 Age	25	52.0	48.0

2-7 样本、男性各年龄层、女性各年龄层的使用方式/ Ways of Using the Products by the Whole Sample, Age and Gender Groups

	人数 Number	个人专用 personal use	家人共用 all family members share
样本 Sample	603	15.6	84.4
男性 Male	279	14.0	86.0
16~24 岁 Age	65	26.2	73.8
25~34 岁 Age	85	14.1	85.9
35~44 岁 Age	70	10.0	90.0
45~54 岁 Age	44	4.5	95.5
55~60 岁 Age	15	6.7	93.3
女性 Female	324	17.0	83.0
16~24 岁 Age	69	23.2	76.8
25~34 岁 Age	95	20.0	80.0
35~44 岁 Age	77	7.8	92.2
45~54 岁 Age	62	12.9	87.1
55~60 岁 Age	21	28.6	71.4

2-8 样本、男性各年龄层、女性各年龄层的使用频率/ Frequencies of the Consumed Shampoo by the Whole Sample, Age and Gender Groups

	人数 Number	天天用 use daily	两三天用 1 次 once 2 or 3 days	一周 1~2 次 once or twice a week	半个月 1 次或以下 once half a month or below
样本 Sample	**600**	**6.2**	**49.5**	**42.7**	**1.7**
男性 Male	**275**	**9.1**	**51.6**	**36.7**	**2.5**
16~24 岁 Age	65	12.3	58.5	27.7	1.5
25~34 岁 Age	85	10.6	47.1	41.2	1.2
35~44 岁 Age	68	10.3	54.4	33.8	1.5
45~54 岁 Age	43	0.0	53.5	41.9	4.7
55~60 岁 Age	14	7.1	28.6	50.0	14.3
女性 Female	**325**	**3.7**	**47.7**	**47.7**	**0.9**
16~24 岁 Age	69	1.4	59.4	39.1	0.0
25~34 岁 Age	95	5.3	47.4	46.3	1.1
35~44 岁 Age	78	3.8	44.9	50.0	1.3
45~54 岁 Age	62	3.2	45.2	51.6	0.0
55~60 岁 Age	21	4.8	28.6	61.9	4.8

2-9 选择该类商品的考虑因素/ Ranking of the Considerations in Purchasing

注：本题为多选题，合计百分比超过 100%（Multiple answers）

排名 Ranking	考虑因素 Considerations	人次 Person-time	百分比 Percent
1	产品功用 product function	311	51.8
2	有名的牌子 famous brand	260	43.3
3	价格适中 reasonable price	250	41.7
4	广告影响 influence of advertising	172	28.7
5	购买方便 easy to buy	92	15.3
6	别人推荐 introduced by other people	51	8.5
7	有优惠条件 with preferential terms	37	6.2
8	单位发的 offered by the working unit	36	6.0
9	包装吸引人 appealing package	28	4.7
10	其它 others	23	3.8

n=600

2-10 对产品功能的侧重方面/ Ranking of the Considerations about the Function of this Kind of Product

注：本题为多选题，合计百分比超过 100%（Multiple answers）

排名 Ranking	侧重方面 Items	人次 Person-time	百分比 Percent
1	去头屑 dandruff control	344	57.5
2	气味好 pleasant smell	269	45.0
3	柔顺营养 soft & nutritious	212	35.5
4	洗护合一 2 in 1	155	25.9
5	去痒 itch-easing	96	16.1
6	防止脱发 anti-baldness	72	12.0
7	焗油功能 containing hair conditioning ingredient	60	10.0
8	多效功能 many performance	55	9.2
9	是天然制品 natural product	41	6.9
10	某种发质专用 special to a certain type	31	5.2
11	防止分岔 anti-split	18	3.0
12	洗护分开 separate use	16	2.7
13	其他 others	10	1.7
14	含果酸 containing tartaric acid	8	1.3
15	染发功能 dyeing	6	1.0

n=598

2-11 重度消费者的人口分布/ Demographics of the Heavy Consumers

	人数 Number	16-24 岁 Age	25-34 岁 Age	35-44 岁 Age	45-54 岁 Age	55-60 岁 Age
样本 Sample	**334**	**26.3**	**29.6**	**24.6**	**15.9**	**3.6**
男性 Male	**167**	**27.5**	**29.3**	**26.3**	**13.8**	**3.0**
天天用 daily	25	32.0	36.0	28.0	0.0	4.0
两三天用 1 次 once 2 or 3 days	142	26.8	28.2	26.1	16.2	2.8
女性 Female	**167**	**25.1**	**29.9**	**22.8**	**18.0**	**4.2**
天天用 daily	12	8.3	41.7	25.0	16.7	8.3
两三天用 1 次 once 2 or 3 days	155	26.5	29.0	22.6	18.1	3.9

2-12 不同消费者层的常用品牌/ The Most Frequently Used Brands by Market Segments

2-12-1 时尚流行指标/ Fads Popular Index

	人数 Number	第一品牌及百分比 1st / percent	第二品牌及百分比 2nd / percent	第三品牌及百分比 3rd / percent	第四品牌及百分比 4th / percent
样本 Sample	589	**飘柔 Rejoice(27.2)**	**舒蕾 Slek(12.4)**	**海飞丝 Head&Shoulder(11.5)** **潘婷 Pentene(11.5)**	**夏士莲 Hazeline(5.3)**
平实生活指向 simple living orientation	296	飘柔 Rejoice(27.4)	潘婷 Pentene(12.8)	海飞丝 Head&Shoulder(12.5)	舒蕾 Slek(8.1)
时尚流行指向 fashion orientation	293	飘柔 Rejoice(27.0)	舒蕾 Slek(16.7)	海飞丝 Head&Shoulder(10.6)	潘婷 Pentene(10.2)

2-12-2 广告态度指标/ Advertising Attitude Index

	人数 Number	第一品牌及百分比 1st / percent	第二品牌及百分比 2nd / percent	第三品牌及百分比 3rd / percent	第四品牌及百分比 4th / percent
样本 Sample	591	**飘柔 Rejoice(27.2)**	**舒蕾 Slek(12.4)**	**潘婷 Pentene(11.7)**	**海飞丝 Head&Shoulder(11.5)**
广告淡漠指向 indifferent orientation	165	飘柔 Rejoice(27.3)	海飞丝 Head&Shoulder(13.3)	舒蕾 Slek(10.3)	潘婷 Pentene(9.7)
中间层 medium	356	飘柔 Rejoice(26.7)	舒蕾 Slek(12.9)	潘婷 Pentene(11.5)	海飞丝 Head&Shoulder(11.2)
信赖广告指向 loyal orientation	70	飘柔 Rejoice(30.0)	潘婷 Pentene(17.1)	舒蕾 Slek(14.3)	海飞丝 Head&Shoulder(8.6)

2-13 重度消费者的消费层构成/ The Composition of the Heavy Consumers

2-13-1 时尚流行指标/ Fads Popular Index

	人数 Number	平实生活指向 simple living orientation	时尚流行指向 fashion orientation
样本 Sample	329	43.8	56.2
天天用 daily	35	42.9	57.1
两三天用 1 次 once 2or 3 days	294	43.9	56.1

2-13-2 广告态度指标/ Advertising Attitude Index

	人数 Number	广告淡漠指向 indifferent orientation	中间层 medium	信赖广告指向 loyal orientation
样本 Sample	330	24.8	61.2	13.9
天天用 daily	36	19.4	61.1	19.4
两三天用 1 次 once 2or 3 days	294	25.5	61.2	13.3

● 西安 / Xi'an

2-1 最常用品牌排名/ Ranking of the Most Frequently Used Brands

排名 Brand Ranking	品牌 Brands	人数 Number	百分比 Percent
1	飘柔 Rejoice	132	22.3
2	海飞丝 Head&Shoulder	104	17.5
3	力士 Lux	82	13.8
4	潘婷 Pentene	51	8.6
5	夏士莲 Hazeline	43	7.3
6	蜂花 Bee&Flower	30	5.1
7	沙宣 Vidal Sassoon	24	4.0
8	海鸥 Seagull	22	3.7
9	舒蕾 Slek	13	2.2
10	奥妮 Olive	8	1.3

n=593

2-2 样本、男性各年龄层、女性各年龄层的常用品牌/ The Most Frequently Used Brands by the Whole Sample, Age and Gender Groups

	人数 Number	第一品牌及百分比 1st/ percent	第二品牌及百分比 2nd/ percent	第三品牌及百分比 3rd/ percent	第四品牌及百分比 4th/ percent
样本 Sample	**593**	**飘柔 Rejoice(22.3)**	**海飞丝 Head&Shoulder(17.5)**	**力士 Lux(13.8)**	**潘婷 Pentene(8.6)**
男性 Male	**295**	**飘柔 Rejoice(22.0)**	**海飞丝 Head&Shoulder(18.0)**	**力士 Lux(12.9)**	**夏士莲 Hazeline(7.1) 潘婷 Pentene(7.1)**
16~24 岁 Age	64	海飞丝 Head&Shoulder(26.6)	飘柔 Rejoice(23.4)	力士 Lux(9.4)	潘婷 Pentene(6.3) 沙宣 Vidal Sassoon(6.3)
25~34 岁 Age	89	飘柔 Rejoice(25.8)	力士 Lux(18.0)	海飞丝 Head&Shoulder(15.7)	潘婷 Pentene(7.9)
35~44 岁 Age	75	飘柔 Rejoice(21.3)	海飞丝 Head&Shoulder(17.3)	力士 Lux(10.7)	夏士莲 Hazeline(9.3)
45~54 岁 Age	44	力士 Lux(18.2) 飘柔 Rejoice(18.2)	夏士莲 Hazeline(13.6)	海飞丝 Head&Shoulder(11.4)	潘婷 Pentene(9.1)
55~60 岁 Age	23	海飞丝 Head&Shoulder(17.4)	潘婷 Pentene(13.0) 飘柔 Rejoice(13.0)	首乌 Shouwu(8.7) 海鸥 Seagull(8.7) 蜂花 Bee&Flower(8.7)	沙宣 Vidal Sassoon(4.3) 舒蕾 Slek(4.3) 浪奴 Launo(4.3) 一叶兰 Yiyelan(4.3) 奥妮 Olive(4.3)
女性 Female	**298**	**飘柔 Rejoice(22.5)**	**海飞丝 Head&Shoulder(17.1)**	**力士 Lux(14.8)**	**潘婷 Pentene(10.1)**
16~24 岁 Age	61	海飞丝 Head&Shoulder(23.0) 飘柔 Rejoice(23.0)	夏士莲 Hazeline(14.8)	力士 Lux(13.1)	舒蕾 Slek(6.6)
25~34 岁 Age	90	飘柔 Rejoice(23.3)	海飞丝 Head&Shoulder(16.7)	力士 Lux(15.6) 潘婷 Pentene(15.6)	夏士莲 Hazeline(6.7)
35~44 岁 Age	74	飘柔 Rejoice(17.6) 力士 Lux(17.6)	蜂花 Bee&Flower(13.5)	海飞丝 Head&Shoulder(10.8)	潘婷 Pentene(9.5)
45~54 岁 Age	48	飘柔 Rejoice(27.1)	海飞丝 Head&Shoulder(16.7)	力士 Lux(14.6)	蜂花 Bee&Flower(8.3) 沙宣 Vidal Sassoon(8.3)
55~60 岁 Age	25	海飞丝 Head&Shoulder(24.0) 飘柔 Rejoice(24.0)	海鸥 Seagull(12.0) 潘婷 Pentene(12.0)	力士 Lux(8.0)	安利 Amway(4.0) 蜂花 Bee&Flower(4.0) 沙宣 Vidal Sassoon(4.0) 诗芬 Sifone(4.0) 一叶兰 Yiyelan(4.0)

2-3 正在使用的品牌排名/ Ranking of the Brands Used Now

排名 Brand Ranking	品牌 Brands	人数 Number	百分比 Percent
1	飘柔 Rejoice	95	16.0
2	海飞丝 Head&Shoulder	91	15.3
3	力士 Lux	70	11.8
4	夏士莲 Hazeline	66	11.1
5	潘婷 Pentene	41	6.9
6	沙宣 Vidal Sassoon	32	5.4
7	舒蕾 Slek	26	4.4
7	蜂花 Bee&Flower	26	4.4
8	海鸥 Seagull	22	3.7
9	好迪 Haodi	14	2.4
10	莹朴 Yingpu	12	2.0

n=593

2-4 品牌转换习惯/ Brand Habit in Consuming Shampoo

	人数 Number	第一次使用该品牌 first use this brand	上一次也是这个牌子 used it last time	上一次不是这个牌子 not used it last time
样本 Sample	**592**	**9.3**	**66.0**	**24.7**
飘柔 Rejoice	95	5.3	77.9	16.8
海飞丝 Head&Shoulder	91	4.4	78.0	17.6
力士 Lux	70	0.0	74.3	25.7
夏士莲 Hazeline	66	13.6	53.0	33.3
潘婷 Pentene	41	7.3	65.9	26.8
沙宣 Vidal Sassoon	32	12.5	59.4	28.1
舒蕾 Slek	26	26.9	50.0	23.1
蜂花 Bee&Flower	26	0.0	92.3	7.7
海鸥 Seagull	22	18.2	77.3	4.5
好迪 Haodi	14	0.0	64.3	35.7
莹朴 Yingpu	12	8.3	50.0	41.7

2-5 下一次打算使用的品牌排名/ Ranking of the Brands to be Used Next Time

排名 Brand Ranking	品牌 Brands	人数 Number	百分比 Percent
1	飘柔 Rejoice	99	16.7
2	海飞丝 Head&Shoulder	91	15.3
3	力士 Lux	81	13.7
4	夏士莲 Hazeline	52	8.8
5	沙宣 Vidal Sassoon	47	7.9
6	潘婷 Pentene	43	7.3
7	蜂花 Bee&Flower	26	4.4
8	舒蕾 Slek	18	3.0
8	海鸥 Seagull	18	3.0
9	莹朴 Yingpu	11	1.9
10	奥妮百年润发 Olive 100	9	1.5

n=593

2-6 样本、男性各年龄层、女性各年龄层是否是主要购买者/ Purchasers in the Household by the Whole Sample, Age and Gender Groups

	人数 Number	是 yes	不是 no
样本 Sample	**601**	**62.7**	**37.3**
男性 Male	**302**	**39.1**	**60.9**
16~24 岁 Age	64	35.9	64.1
25~34 岁 Age	91	45.1	54.9
35~44 岁 Age	77	49.4	50.6
45~54 岁 Age	46	21.7	78.3
55~60 岁 Age	24	25.0	75.0
女性 Female	**299**	**86.6**	**13.4**
16~24 岁 Age	61	68.9	31.1
25~34 岁 Age	90	91.1	8.9
35~44 岁 Age	74	91.9	8.1
45~54 岁 Age	49	91.8	8.2
55~60 岁 Age	25	88.0	12.0

2-7 样本、男性各年龄层、女性各年龄层的使用方式/ Ways of Using the Products by the Whole Sample, Age and Gender Groups

	人数 Number	个人专用 personal use	家人共用 all family members share
样本 Sample	**595**	**15.6**	**84.4**
男性 Male	**297**	**14.1**	**85.9**
16~24 岁 Age	64	23.4	76.6
25~34 岁 Age	89	13.5	86.5
35~44 岁 Age	76	13.2	86.8
45~54 岁 Age	45	6.7	93.3
55~60 岁 Age	23	8.7	91.3
女性 Female	**298**	**17.1**	**82.9**
16~24 岁 Age	61	18.0	82.0
25~34 岁 Age	90	23.3	76.7
35~44 岁 Age	74	14.9	85.1
45~54 岁 Age	48	8.3	91.7
55~60 岁 Age	25	16.0	84.0

2-8 样本、男性各年龄层、女性各年龄层的使用频率/ Frequencies of the Consumed Shampoo by the Whole Sample, Age and Gender Groups

	人数 Number	天天用 daily	两三天用 1 次 once 2 or 3 days	一周 1~2 次 once or twice a week	半个月 1 次或以下 once half a month or below
样本 Sample	593	2.0	35.6	61.2	1.2
男性 Male	295	2.4	35.3	60.7	1.7
16~24 岁 Age	64	4.7	43.8	51.6	0.0
25~34 岁 Age	89	1.1	38.2	59.6	1.1
35~44 岁 Age	75	2.7	29.3	65.3	2.7
45~54 岁 Age	44	2.3	29.5	63.6	4.5
55~60 岁 Age	23	0.0	30.4	69.6	0.0
女性 Female	298	1.7	35.9	61.7	0.7
16~24 岁 Age	61	0.0	47.5	52.5	0.0
25~34 岁 Age	90	2.2	35.6	61.1	1.1
35~44 岁 Age	74	2.7	40.5	56.8	0.0
45~54 岁 Age	48	2.1	25.0	72.9	0.0
55~60 岁 Age	25	0.0	16.0	80.0	4.0

2-9 选择该类商品的考虑因素/ Ranking of the Considerations in Purchasing

注：本题为多选题，合计百分比超过 100%（Multiple answers）

排名 Ranking	考虑因素 Considerations	人次 Person-time	百分比 Percent
1	产品功用 product function	270	45.5
2	有名的牌子 famous brand	226	38.1
3	价格适中 reasonable price	212	35.8
4	广告影响 influence of advertising	149	25.1
5	购买方便 easy to buy	86	14.5
6	别人推荐 introduced by other people	65	11.0
7	单位发的 offered by the working unit	28	4.7
8	包装吸引人 appealing package	20	3.4
9	其它 others	19	3.2
10	有优惠条件 with preferential terms	14	2.4

n=593

2-10 对产品功能的侧重方面/ Ranking of the Considerations about the Function of this Kind of Product

注：本题为多选题，合计百分比超过 100%（Multiple answers）

排名 Ranking	侧重方面 Items	人次 Person-time	百分比 Percent
1	去头屑 dandruff control	349	58.9
2	气味好 pleasant smell	256	43.2
3	柔顺营养 soft & nutritious	217	36.6
4	洗护合一 2 in 1	114	19.2
5	去痒 itch-easing	69	11.6
6	防止脱发 anti-baldness	67	11.3
7	焗油功能 containing hair conditioning ingredient	59	9.9
8	多效功能 many performance	51	8.6
9	是天然制品 natural product	41	6.9
10	某种发质专用 special to a certain type	29	4.9
11	洗护分开 separate use	13	2.2
12	染发功能 dyeing	9	1.5
13	防止分岔 anti-split	5	0.8
13	其他 others	5	0.8
14	含果酸 containing tartaric acid	4	0.7

n=593

2-11 重度消费者的人口分布/ Demographics of the Heavy Consumers

	人数 Number	16-24 岁 Age	25-34 岁 Age	35-44 岁 Age	45-54 岁 Age	55-60 岁 Age
样本 Sample	223	26.9	30.9	25.1	12.1	4.9
男性 Male	111	27.9	31.5	21.6	12.6	6.3
天天用 daily	7	42.9	14.3	28.6	14.3	0.0
两三天用 1 次 once 2 or 3 days	104	26.9	32.7	21.2	12.5	6.7
女性 Female	112	25.9	30.4	28.6	11.6	3.6
天天用 daily	5	0.0	40.0	40.0	20.0	0.0
两三天用 1 次 once 2 or 3 days	107	27.1	29.9	28.0	11.2	3.7

2-12 不同消费者层的常用品牌/ The Most Frequently Used Brands by Market Segments

2-12-1 时尚流行指标/ Fads Popular Index

	人数 Number	第一品牌及百分比 1st / percent	第二品牌及百分比 2nd / percent	第三品牌及百分比 3rd / percent	第四品牌及百分比 4th / percent
样本 Sample	591	**飘柔 Rejoice(22.3)**	**海飞丝 Head&Shoulder(17.4)**	**力士 Lux(13.9)**	**潘婷 Pentene(8.6)**
平实生活指向 simple living orientation	335	飘柔 Rejoice(20.3)	力士 Lux(15.5)	海飞丝 Head&Shoulder(14.3)	潘婷 Pentene(8.4)
时尚流行指向 fashion orientation	256	飘柔 Rejoice(25.0)	海飞丝 Head&Shoulder(21.5)	力士 Lux(11.7)	潘婷 Pentene(9.0)

2-12-2 广告态度指标/ Advertising Attitude Index

	人数 Number	第一品牌及百分比 1st / percent	第二品牌及百分比 2nd / percent	第三品牌及百分比 3rd / percent	第四品牌及百分比 4th / percent
样本 Sample	589	**飘柔 Rejoice(22.1)**	**海飞丝 Head&Shoulder(17.7)**	**力士 Lux(13.9)**	**潘婷 Pentene(8.5)**
广告淡漠指向 indifferent orientation	183	飘柔 Rejoice(20.8)	力士 Lux(19.1)	海飞丝 Head&Shoulder(14.2)	潘婷 Pentene(8.7)
中间层 medium	328	飘柔 Rejoice(24.1)	海飞丝 Head&Shoulder(18.6)	力士 Lux(11.0)	潘婷 Pentene(8.8)
信赖广告指向 loyal orientation	78	海飞丝 Head&Shoulder(21.8)	飘柔 Rejoice(16.7)	力士 Lux(14.1)	潘婷 Pentene(6.4)

2-13 重度消费者的消费层构成/ The Composition of the Heavy Consumers

2-13-1 时尚流行指标/ Fads Popular Index

	人数 Number	平实生活指向 simple living orientation	时尚流行指向 fashion orientation
样本 Sample	222	45.5	54.5
天天用 daily	12	41.7	58.3
两三天用 1 次 once 2 or 3 days	210	45 7	54.3

2-13-2 广告态度指标/ Advertising Attitude Index

	人数 Number	广告淡漠指向 indifferent orientation	中间层 medium	信赖广告指向 loyal orientation
样本 Sample	222	27.9	53.6	18.5
天天用 daily	12	33.3	41.7	25.0
两三天用 1 次 once 2 or 3 days	210	27.6	54.3	18.1

● 沈阳 / Shenyang

2-1 最常用品牌排名/ Ranking of the Most Frequently Used Brands

排名 Brand Ranking	品牌 Brands	人数 Number	百分比 Percent
1	飘柔 Rejoice	172	29.3
2	海飞丝 Head&Shoulder	135	23.0
3	潘婷 Pentene	43	7.3
4	夏士莲 Hazeline	42	7.2
5	海鸥 Seagull	37	6.3
6	沙宣 Vidal Sassoon	28	4.8
7	舒蕾 Slek	24	4.1
8	力士 Lux	19	3.2
9	脱普 Top	13	2.2
10	诗芬 Sifone	7	1.2
10	奥妮 Olive	7	1.2

n=587

2-2 样本、男性各年龄层、女性各年龄层的常用品牌/ The Most Frequently Used Brands by the Whole Sample, Age and Gender Groups

	人数 Number	第一品牌及百分比 1st/ percent	第二品牌及百分比 2nd/ percent	第三品牌及百分比 3rd/ percent	第四品牌及百分比 4th/ percent
样本 Sample	587	**飘柔 Rejoice(29.3)**	**海飞丝 Head&Shoulder(23.0)**	**潘婷 Pentene(7.3)**	**夏士莲 Hazeline(7.2)**
男性 Male	287	**飘柔 Rejoice(30.3)**	**海飞丝 Head&Shoulder(26.5)**	**海鸥 Seagull(7.0)**	**潘婷 Pentene(6.3)**
16~24 岁 Age	64	飘柔 Rejoice(29.7)	海飞丝 Head&Shoulder(28.1)	沙宣 Vidal Sassoon(9.4)	海鸥 Seagull(4.7) 潘婷 Pentene(4.7) 舒蕾 Slek(4.7)
25~34 岁 Age	87	飘柔 Rejoice(29.9)	海飞丝 Head&Shoulder(23.0)	潘婷 Pentene(9.2)	沙宣 Vidal Sassoon(5.7) 舒蕾 Slek(5.7) 夏士莲 Hazeline(5.7)
35~44 岁 Age	74	海飞丝 Head&Shoulder(32.4)	飘柔 Rejoice(31.1)	海鸥 Seagull(8.1)	潘婷 Pentene(5.4)
45~54 岁 Age	43	飘柔 Rejoice(34.9)	海飞丝 Head&Shoulder(27.9)	海鸥 Seagull(7.0) 潘婷 Pentene(7.0)	夏士莲 Hazeline(4.7) 沙宣 Vidal Sassoon(4.7)
55~60 岁 Age	19	海鸥 Seagull(31.6)	飘柔 Rejoice(21.1)	海飞丝 Head&Shoulder(10.5) 夏士莲 Hazeline(10.5)	蜂花 Bee&Flower(5.3) 力士 Lux(5.3) 俏丽 Qiaoli(5.3) 奥妮 Olive(5.3) 海浪 Hailang(5.3)
女性 Female	300	**飘柔 Rejoice(28.3)**	**海飞丝 Head&Shoulder(19.7)**	**夏士莲 Hazeline(9.7)**	**潘婷 Pentene(8.3)**
16~24 岁 Age	64	飘柔 Rejoice(25.0)	海飞丝 Head&Shoulder(21.9)	夏士莲 Hazeline(17.2)	舒蕾 Slek(6.3) 潘婷 Pentene(6.3) 力士 Lux(6.3)
25~34 岁 Age	90	飘柔 Rejoice(34.4)	海飞丝 Head&Shoulder(20.0)	夏士莲 Hazeline(6.7) 力士 Lux(6.7) 潘婷 Pentene(6.7)	沙宣 Vidal Sassoon(5.6) 舒蕾 Slek(5.6)
35~44 岁 Age	76	飘柔 Rejoice(30.3)	海飞丝 Head&Shoulder(19.7)	潘婷 Pentene(11.8)	夏士莲 Hazeline(9.2)
45~54 岁 Age	48	飘柔 Rejoice(22.9)	海飞丝 Head&Shoulder(16.7) 海鸥 Seagull(16.7)	夏士莲 Hazeline(10.4)	潘婷 Pentene(8.3)
55~60 岁 Age	22	海飞丝 Head&Shoulder(18.2) 海鸥 Seagull(18.2) 飘柔 Rejoice(18.2)	潘婷 Pentene(9.1)	芦荟 Luhui(4.5) 派丽 Paili(4.5) 海浪 Hailang(4.5) 梦丽西施 Menglixishi(4.5) 奥妮百年润发 Olive100(4.5) 脱普 Top(4.5) 舒蕾 Slek(4.5) 蜂花 Bee&Flower(4.5)	

2-3 正在使用的品牌排名/ Ranking of the Brands Used Now

排名 Brand Ranking	品牌 Brands	人数 Number	百分比 Percent
1	飘柔 Rejoice	138	23.5
2	海飞丝 Head&Shoulder	116	19.8
3	夏士莲 Hazeline	56	9.5
4	潘婷 Pentene	45	7.7
5	舒蕾 Slek	36	6.1
6	海鸥 Seagull	27	4.6
7	沙宣 Vidal Sassoon	26	4.4
8	力士 Lux	22	3.7
9	脱普 Top	14	2.4
10	诗芬 Sifone	10	1.7

n=587

2-4 品牌转换习惯/ Brand Habit in Consuming Shampoo

	人数 Number	第一次使用该品牌 first use this brand	上一次也是这个牌子 used it last time	上一次不是这个牌子 not used it last time
样本 Sample	586	11.9	67.7	20.3
飘柔 Rejoice	138	5.8	76.8	17.4
海飞丝 Head&Shoulder	116	6.9	75.9	17.2
夏士莲 Hazeline	56	14.3	66.1	19.6
潘婷 Pentene	45	11.1	64.4	24.4
舒蕾 Slek	36	25.0	61.1	13.9
海鸥 Seagull	27	3.7	92.6	3.7
沙宣 Vidal Sassoon	26	11.5	73.[illegible]	15.4
力士 Lux	22	9.1	50.0	40.9
脱普 Top	14	7.1	50.0	42.9
诗芬 Sifone	10	10.0	50.0	40.0

2-5 下一次打算使用的品牌排名/ Ranking of the Brands to be Used Next Time

排名 Brand Ranking	品牌 Brands	人数 Number	百分比 Percent
1	飘柔 Rejoice	138	23.5
2	海飞丝 Head&Shoulder	128	21.8
3	潘婷 Pentene	53	9.0
4	夏士莲 Hazeline	47	8.0
5	舒蕾 Slek	38	6.5
5	沙宣 Vidal Sassoon	38	6.5
6	海鸥 Seagull	27	4.6
7	力士 Lux	25	4.3
8	脱普 Top	12	2.0

n=587

2-6 样本、 男性各年龄层、 女性各年龄层是否是主要购买者/ Purchasers in the Household by the Whole Sample, Age and Gender Groups

	人数 Number	是 yes	不是 no
样本 Sample	600	61.8	38.2
男性 Male	298	39.3	60.7
16~24 岁 Age	64	45.3	54.7
25~34 岁 Age	89	44.9	55.1
35~44 岁 Age	76	31.6	68.4
45~54 岁 Age	45	33.3	66.7
55~60 岁 Age	24	37.5	62.5
女性 Female	302	84.1	15.9
16~24 岁 Age	64	65.6	34.4
25~34 岁 Age	90	94.4	5.6
35~44 岁 Age	76	96.1	3.9
45~54 岁 Age	48	77.1	22.9
55~60 岁 Age	24	70.8	29.2

2-7 样本、男性各年龄层、女性各年龄层的使用方式/ Ways of Using the Products by the Whole Sample, Age and Gender Groups

	人数 Number	个人专用 personal use	家人共用 all family members share
样本 Sample	587	15.5	84.5
男性 Male	287	17.4	82.6
16~24 岁 Age	64	25.0	75.0
25~34 岁 Age	87	18.4	81.6
35~44 岁 Age	74	16.2	83.8
45~54 岁 Age	43	11.6	88.4
55~60 岁 Age	19	5.3	94.7
女性 Female	300	13.7	86.3
16~24 岁 Age	64	29.7	70.3
25~34 岁 Age	90	8.9	91.1
35~44 岁 Age	76	9.2	90.8
45~54 岁 Age	48	4.2	95.8
55~60 岁 Age	22	22.7	77.3

2-8 样本、男性各年龄层、女性各年龄层的使用频率/ Frequencies of the Consumed Shampoo by the Whole Sample, Age and Gender Groups

	人数 Number	天天用 daily	两三天用 1 次 once 2 or 3 days	一周 1~2 次 once or twice a week	半个月 1 次或以下 once half a month or below
样本 Sample	587	1.9	33.9	63.7	0.5
男性 Male	287	3.1	35.9	59.9	1.0
16~24 岁 Age	64	3.1	42.2	53.1	1.6
25~34 岁 Age	87	6.9	34.5	58.6	0.0
35~44 岁 Age	74	1.4	33.8	62.2	2.7
45~54 岁 Age	43	0.0	41.9	58.1	0.0
55~60 岁 Age	19	0.0	15.8	84.2	0.0
女性 Female	300	0.7	32.0	67.3	0.0
16~24 岁 Age	64	1.6	48.4	50.0	0.0
25~34 岁 Age	90	0.0	26.7	73.3	0.0
35~44 岁 Age	76	1.3	30.3	68.4	0.0
45~54 岁 Age	48	0.0	31.3	68.8	0.0
55~60 岁 Age	22	0.0	13.6	86.4	0.0

2-9 选择该类商品的考虑因素/ Ranking of the Considerations in Purchasing

注：本题为多选题，合计百分比超过 100%（Multiple answers）

排名 Ranking	考虑因素 Considerations	人次 Person-time	百分比 Percent
1	产品功用 product function	291	49.7
2	价格适中 reasonable price	249	42.5
3	有名的牌子 famous brand	247	42.2
4	广告影响 influence of advertising	153	26.1
5	购买方便 easy to buy	101	17.2
6	别人推荐 introduced by other people	62	10.6
7	有优惠条件 with preferential terms	24	4.1
8	包装吸引人 appealing package	12	2.0
9	单位发的 offered by the working unit	6	1.0
10	其它 others	4	0.7

n=586

2-10 对产品功能的侧重方面/ Ranking of the Considerations about the Function of this Kind of Product

注：本题为多选题，合计百分比超过 100%（Multiple answers）

排名 Ranking	侧重方面 Items	人次 Person-time	百分比 Percent
1	去头屑 dandruff control	401	68.7
2	气味好 pleasant smell	258	44.2
3	柔顺营养 soft & nutritious	189	32.4
4	洗护合一 2 in 1	116	19.9
5	去痒 itch-easing	78	13.4
6	焗油功能 containing hair conditioning ingredient	61	10.4
7	防止脱发 anti-baldness	59	10.1
8	多效功能 many performance	44	7.5
9	某种发质专用 special to a certain type	29	5.0
10	是天然制品 natural product	26	4.5
11	染发功能 dyeing	10	1.7
12	防止分岔 anti-splitend	9	1.5
13	洗护分开 separate use	7	1.2
14	含果酸 containing tartaric acid	3	0.5
15	其他 others	2	0.3

n=584

2-11 重度消费者的人口分布/ Demographics of the Heavy Consumers

	人数 Number	16-24 岁 Age	25-34 岁 Age	35-44 岁 Age	45-54 岁 Age	55-60 岁 Age
样本 Sample	210	29.0	28.6	23.8	15.7	2.9
男性 Male	112	25.9	32.1	23.2	16.1	2.7
天天用 daily	9	22.2	66.7	11.1	0.0	0.0
两三天用 1 次 once 2 or 3 days	103	26.2	29.1	24.3	17.5	2.9
女性 Female	98	32.7	24.5	24.5	15.3	3.1
天天用 daily	2	50.0	0.0	50.0	0.0	0.0
两三天用 1 次 once 2 or 3 days	96	32.3	25.0	24.0	15.6	3.1

2-12 不同消费者层的常用品牌/ The Most Frequently Used Brands by Market Segments

2-12-1 时尚流行指标/ Fads Popular Index

	人数 Number	第一品牌及百分比 1st/ percent	第二品牌及百分比 2nd/ percent	第三品牌及百分比 3rd/ percent	第四品牌及百分比 4th/ percent
样本 Sample	**587**	**飘柔 Rejoice(29.3)**	**海飞丝 Head&Shoulder(23.0)**	**潘婷 Pentene(7.3)**	**夏士莲 Hazeline(7.2)**
平实生活指向 simple living orientation	279	飘柔 Rejoice(26.5)	海飞丝 Head&Shoulder(25.4)	海鸥 Seagull(9.7)	潘婷 Pentene(7.5)
时尚流行指向 fashion orientation	308	飘柔 Rejoice(31.8)	海飞丝 Head&Shoulder(20.8)	夏士莲 Hazeline(9.1)	潘婷 Pentene(7.1) 沙宣 Vidal Sassoon(7.1)

2-12-2 广告态度指标/ Advertising Attitude Index

	人数 Number	第一品牌及百分比 1st/ percent	第二品牌及百分比 2nd/ percent	第三品牌及百分比 3rd/ percent	第四品牌及百分比 4th/ percent
样本 Sample	**587**	**飘柔 Rejoice(29.3)**	**海飞丝 Head&Shoulder(23.0)**	**潘婷 Pentene(7.3)**	**夏士莲 Hazeline(7.2)**
广告淡漠指向 indifferent orientation	168	飘柔 Rejoice(30.4)	海飞丝 Head&Shoulder(20.8)	潘婷 Pentene(7.7)	海鸥 Seagull(7.1)
中间层 medium	346	飘柔 Rejoice(28.6)	海飞丝 Head&Shoulder(23.4)	潘婷 Pentene(7.2)	夏士莲 Hazeline(6.9)
信赖广告指向 loyal orientation	73	飘柔 Rejoice(30.1)	海飞丝 Head&Shoulder(26.0)	夏士莲 Hazeline(9.6)	潘婷 Pentene(6.8)

2-13 重度消费者的消费层构成/ The Composition of the Heavy Consumers

2-13-1 时尚流行指标/ Fads Popular Index

	人数 Number	平实生活指向 simple living orientation	时尚流行指向 fashion orientation
样本 Sample	**210**	**42.9**	**57.1**
天天用 daily	11	54.5	45.5
两三天用 1 次 once 2 or 3 days	199	42.2	57.8

2-13-2 广告态度指标/ Advertising Attitude Index

	人数 Number	广告淡漠指向 indifferent orientation	中间层 medium	信赖广告指向 loyal orientation
样本 Sample	**210**	**27.1**	**56.7**	**16.2**
天天用 daily	11	18.2	63.6	18.2
两三天用 1 次 once 2 or 3 days	199	27.6	56.3	16.1

3.香皂 / Perfumed Soap

● 北京 / Beijing

3-1 最常用品牌排名/ Ranking of the Most Frequently Used Brands

排名 Brand Ranking	品牌 Brands	人数 Number	百分比 Percent
1	舒肤佳 Safeguard	529	52.4
2	力士 Lux	296	29.3
3	夏士莲 Hazeline	51	5.0
4	花 Fa	22	2.2
5	梦幻 Mely	21	2.1
7	三笑 Sanxiao	11	1.1
8	安利 Amway	6	0.6
9	纳爱斯 Nice	5	0.5
10	六神 Liushen	4	0.4

n=1010

3-2 样本、男性各年龄层、女性各年龄层的常用品牌/ The Most Frequently Used Brands by the Whole Sample, Age and Gender Groups

	人数 Number	第一品牌及百分比 1st/ percent	第二品牌及百分比 2nd/ percent	第三品牌及百分比 3rd/ percent	第四品牌及百分比 4th/ percent
样本 Sample	1010	**舒肤佳 Safeguard(52.4)**	**力士 Lux(29.3)**	**夏士莲 Hazeline(5.0)**	**花 Fa(2.2)**
男性 Male	503	**舒肤佳 Safeguard(51.5)**	**力士 Lux(33.2)**	**夏士莲 Hazeline(4.0)**	
16~24 岁 Age	105	舒肤佳 Safeguard(61.9)	力士 Lux(22.9)	夏士莲 Hazeline(6.7)	
25~34 岁 Age	151	舒肤佳 Safeguard(47.0)	力士 Lux(36.4)	梦幻 Mely(3.3)	夏士莲 Hazeline(2.6)
35~44 岁 Age	131	舒肤佳 Safeguard(48.9)	力士 Lux(37.4)	夏士莲 Hazeline(5.3)	
45~54 岁 Age	77	舒肤佳 Safeguard(50.6)	力士 Lux(35.1)	梦幻 Mely(2.6)	三笑 Sanxiao(1.3) 夏士莲 Hazeline(1.3) 纳爱斯 Nice(1.3) 加信氏 Cussons(1.3) 花 Fa(1.3)
55~60 岁 Age	39	舒肤佳 Safeguard(51.3)	力士 Lux(30.8)	梦幻 Mely(5.1)	花 Fa(2.6) 夏士莲 Hazeline(2.6) 白玉 Baiyu(2.6)
女性 Female	507	**舒肤佳 Safeguard(53.3)**	**力士 Lux(25.4)**	**夏士莲 Hazeline(6.1)**	**花 Fa(3.4)**
16~24 岁 Age	108	舒肤佳 Safeguard(46.3)	力士 Lux(26.9)	夏士莲 Hazeline(10.2)	花 Fa(6.5)
25~34 岁 Age	150	舒肤佳 Safeguard(55.3)	力士 Lux(26.7)	夏士莲 Hazeline(3.3)	花 Fa(2.7)
35~44 岁 Age	124	舒肤佳 Safeguard(54.8)	力士 Lux(23.4)	夏士莲 Hazeline(6.5)	花 Fa(4.0)
45~54 岁 Age	84	舒肤佳 Safeguard(56.0)	力士 Lux(25.0)	夏士莲 Hazeline(6.0)	三笑 Sanxiao(3.6)
55~60 岁 Age	41	舒肤佳 Safeguard(53.7)	力士 Lux(24.4)	梦幻 Mely(7.3)	夏士莲 Hazeline(4.9)

3-3 正在使用的品牌排名/ Ranking of the Brands Used Now

排名 Brand Ranking	品牌 Brands	人数 Number	百分比 Percent
1	舒肤佳 Safeguard	496	49.2
2	力士 Lux	270	26.8
3	夏士莲 Hazeline	68	6.7
4	花 Fa	28	2.8
4	梦幻 Mely	28	2.8
5	三笑 Sanxiao	14	1.4
6	安利 Amway	7	0.7
7	玉兰油 Oil of Olay	6	0.6
7	强生 Johnson&Johnson	6	0.6

n=1008

3-4 品牌转换习惯/ Brand Habit in Consuming Perfumed Soap

	人数 Number	第一次使用该品牌 first use this brand	上一次也是这个牌子 used it last time	上一次不是这个牌子 not used it last time
样本 Sample	1000	3.7	82.9	13.4
舒肤佳 Safeguard	492	2.0	89.2	8.7
力士 Lux	270	2.2	81.9	15.9
夏士莲 Hazeline	68	7.4	73.5	19.1
花 Fa	28	7.1	71.4	21.4
梦幻 Mely	28	10.7	71.4	17.9
三笑 Sanxiao	14	21.4	64.3	14.3
安利 Amway	7	0.0	71.4	28.6
玉兰油 Oil of Olay	5	20.0	60.0	20.0
强生 Johnson&Johnson	6	0.0	83.3	16.7

3-5 下一次打算使用的品牌排名/ Ranking of the Brands to be Used Next Time

排名 Brand Ranking	品牌 Brands	人数 Number	百分比 Percent
1	舒肤佳 Safeguard	483	47.9
2	力士 Lux	277	27.5
3	夏士莲 Hazeline	68	6.7
5	梦幻 Mely	21	2.1
6	花 Fa	20	2.0
8	三笑 Sanxiao	10	1.0
9	皇宝 Huangbao	8	0.8
10	佳洁士 Crest	7	0.7
11	安利 Amway	6	0.6
11	玉兰油 Oil of Olay	6	0.6
12	索芙特 Sofito	5	0.5

n=1008

3-6 样本、男性各年龄层、女性各年龄层是否是主要购买者/ Purchasers in the Household by the Whole Sample, Age and Gender Groups

	人数 Number	是 yes	不是 no
样本 Sample	1007	56.4	43.6
男性 Male	501	41.7	58.3
16~24 岁 Age	105	31.4	68.6
25~34 岁 Age	150	44.0	56.0
35~44 岁 Age	130	47.7	52.3
45~54 岁 Age	77	37.7	62.3
55~60 岁 Age	39	48.7	51.3
女性 Female	506	70.9	29.1
16~24 岁 Age	107	36.4	63.6
25~34 岁 Age	149	75.8	24.2
35~44 岁 Age	124	83.9	16.1
45~54 岁 Age	84	79.8	20.2
55~60 岁 Age	42	85.7	14.3

3-7 样本、男性各年龄层、女性各年龄层的使用方式/ Ways of Using the Products by the Whole Sample, Age and Gender Groups

	人数 Number	个人专用 personal use	家人共用 all family members share
样本 Sample	1005	16.6	83.4
男性 Male	500	18.4	81.6
16~24 岁 Age	104	29.8	70.2
25~34 岁 Age	149	16.1	83.9
35~44 岁 Age	131	17.6	82.4
45~54 岁 Age	77	13.0	87.0
55~60 岁 Age	39	10.3	89.7
女性 Female	505	14.9	85.1
16~24 岁 Age	107	22.4	77.6
25~34 岁 Age	149	14.1	85.9
35~44 岁 Age	124	11.3	88.7
45~54 岁 Age	84	11.9	88.1
55~60 岁 Age	41	14.6	85.4

3-8 样本、男性各年龄层、女性各年龄层的使用频率/ Frequencies of the Consumed Perfumed Soap by the Whole Sample, Age and Gender Groups

	人数 Number	一天 3 次或以上 3 times or over a day	一天 1~2 次 once or twice a day	两三天用 1 次 once 2 or 3 days	一周 1~2 次 once or twice a week	半个月 1 次或以下 once half a month or below
样本 Sample	1007	61.1	35.1	1.6	1.9	0.4
男性 Male	502	55.2	40.6	1.6	2.4	0.2
16~24 岁 Age	105	58.1	38.1	1.9	1.9	0.0
25~34 岁 Age	151	53.0	40.4	0.7	5.3	0.7
35~44 岁 Age	131	59.5	38.9	0.8	0.8	0.0
45~54 岁 Age	76	50.0	44.7	3.9	1.3	0.0
55~60 岁 Age	39	51.3	46.2	2.6	0.0	0.0
女性 Female	505	66.9	29.5	1.6	1.4	0.6
16~24 岁 Age	108	76.9	21.3	0.9	0.9	0.0
25~34 岁 Age	148	71.6	26.4	0.7	0.0	1.4
35~44 岁 Age	124	66.9	26.6	2.4	3.2	0.8
45~54 岁 Age	84	51.2	44.0	2.4	2.4	0.0
55~60 岁 Age	41	56.1	41.5	2.4	0.0	0.0

3-9 选择该类商品的考虑因素/ Ranking of the Considerations in Purchasing

注：本题为多选题，合计百分比超过 100%（Multiple answers）

排名 Ranking	考虑因素 Considerations	人次 Person-time	百分比 Percent
1	有名的牌子 famous brand	457	45.7
2	产品功用 product function	417	41.7
3	价格适中 reasonable price	379	37.9
4	广告影响 influence of advertising	219	21.9
5	单位发的 offered by the working unit	159	15.9
6	购买方便 easy to buy	140	14.0
7	有优惠条件 with preferential terms	36	3.6
8	包装吸引人 appealing package	28	2.8
9	别人推荐 introduced by other people	24	2.4
10	其它 others	19	1.9

n=1001

3-10 对产品功能的侧重方面/ Ranking of the Considerations about the Function of this Kind of Product

注：本题为多选题，合计百分比超过 100%（Multiple answers）

排名 Ranking	侧重方面 Items	人次 Person-time	百分比 Percent
1	气味好 pleasant smell	661	65.8
2	能杀菌 bacteria-killing ability	435	43.3
3	不刺激皮肤 harmless to my skin	317	31.6
4	洗净力强 wash more cleanly	255	25.4
5	适合自己肤质 suitable to my skin	206	20.5
6	泡沫多 rich foam	135	13.4
7	洗后不紧绷 without causing tightness	89	8.9
8	有美容功能 beautifying effect	51	5.1
9	有药用功能 medicine-like effect	28	2.8
10	其他 others	9	0.9

n=1004

3-11 重度消费者的人口分布/ Demographics of the Heavy Consumers

	人数 Number	16-24 岁 Age	25-34 岁 Age	35-44 岁 Age	45-54 岁 Age	55-60 岁 Age
样本 Sample	968	21.4	29.5	25.3	15.7	8.1
男性 Male	481	21.0	29.3	26.8	15.0	7.9
一天 3 次或以上 3 times or over a day	277	22.0	28.9	28.2	13.7	7.2
一天 1～2 次 once or twice a day	204	19.6	29.9	25.0	16.7	8.8
女性 Female	487	21.8	29.8	23.8	16.4	8.2
一天 3 次或以上 3 times or over a day	338	24.6	31.4	24.6	12.7	6.8
一天 1～2 次 once or twice a day	149	15.4	26.2	22.1	24.8	11.4

3-12 不同消费者层的常用品牌/ The Most Frequently Used Brands by Market Segments

3-12-1 时尚流行指标/ Fads Popular Index

	人数 Number	第一品牌及百分比 1st / percent	第二品牌及百分比 2nd / percent	第三品牌及百分比 3rd / percent
样本 Sample	996	**舒肤佳 Safeguard(52.5)**	**力士 Lux(29.1)**	**夏士莲 Hazeline(5.1)**
平实生活指向 simple living orientation	489	舒肤佳 Safeguard(56.4)	力士 Lux(27.8)	夏士莲 Hazeline(3.7)
时尚流行指向 fashion orientation	507	舒肤佳 Safeguard(48.7)	力士 Lux(30.4)	夏士莲 Hazeline(6.5)

3-12-2 广告态度指标/ Advertising Attitude Index

	人数 Number	第一品牌及百分比 1st / percent	第二品牌及百分比 2nd / percent	第三品牌及百分比 3rd / percent
样本 Sample	992	**舒肤佳 Safeguard(52.3)**	**力士 Lux(29.2)**	**夏士莲 Hazeline(5.0)**
广告淡漠指向 indifferent orientation	288	舒肤佳 Safeguard(49.7)	力士 Lux(33.7)	夏士莲 Hazeline(4.2)
中间层 medium	571	舒肤佳 Safeguard(52.9)	力士 Lux(28.2)	夏士莲 Hazeline(5.3)
信赖广告指向 loyal orientation	133	舒肤佳 Safeguard(55.6)	力士 Lux(24.1)	夏士莲 Hazeline(6.0)

3-13 重度消费者的消费层构成/ The Composition of the Heavy Consumers

3-13-1 时尚流行指标/ Fads Popular Index

	人数 Number	平实生活指向 simple living orientation	时尚流行指向 fashion orientation
样本 Sample	954	49.0	51.0
一天 3 次或以上 3 times or over a day	607	46.3	53.7
一天 1～2 次 once or twice a day	347	53.6	46.4

3-13-2 广告态度指标/ Advertising Attitude Index

	人数 Number	广告淡漠指向 indifferent orientation	中间层 medium	信赖广告指向 loyal orientation
样本 Sample	951	28.9	57.3	13.8
一天 3 次或以上 3 times or over a day	603	29.5	55.4	15.1
一天 1～2 次 once or twice a day	348	27.9	60.6	11.5

● 上海 / Shanghai

3-1 最常用品牌排名/ Ranking of the Most Frequently Used Brands

排名 Brand Ranking	品牌 Brands	人数 Number	百分比 Percent
1	力士 Lux	457	45.2
2	舒肤佳 Safeguard	276	27.3
3	夏士莲 Hazeline	103	10.2
4	白丽 Baili	69	6.8
5	裕华 Yuhua	18	1.8
6	上海药皂/硫磺香皂 Shanghai	9	0.9
7	多芬 Dove	6	0.6
8	花王 Kao	5	0.5

n=1011

3-2 样本、男性各年龄层、女性各年龄层的常用品牌/ The Most Frequently Used Brands by the Whole Sample, Age and Gender Groups

	人数 Number	第一品牌及百分比 1st/ percent	第二品牌及百分比 2nd/ percent	第三品牌及百分比 3rd/ percent
样本 Sample	1011	**力士 Lux(45.2)**	**舒肤佳 Safeguard(27.3)**	**夏士莲 Hazeline(10.2)**
男性 Male	506	**力士 Lux(46.8)**	**舒肤佳 Safeguard(26.5)**	**夏士莲 Hazeline(8.9)**
16~24 岁 Age	109	力士 Lux(43.1)	舒肤佳 Safeguard(28.4)	夏士莲 Hazeline(9.2)
25~34 岁 Age	146	力士 Lux(49.3)	舒肤佳 Safeguard(31.5)	夏士莲 Hazeline(9.6)
35~44 岁 Age	130	力士 Lux(49.2)	舒肤佳 Safeguard(18.5)	白丽 Baili(8.5) 夏士莲 Hazeline(8.5)
45~54 岁 Age	83	力士 Lux(41.0)	舒肤佳 Safeguard(32.5)	白丽 Baili(10.8)
55~60 岁 Age	38	力士 Lux(52.6)	舒肤佳 Safeguard(15.8)	白丽 Baili(7.9) 夏士莲 Hazeline(7.9)
女性 Female	505	**力士 Lux(43.6)**	**舒肤佳 Safeguard(28.1)**	**夏士莲 Hazeline(11.5)**
16~24 岁 Age	108	力士 Lux(42.6)	舒肤佳 Safeguard(31.5)	夏士莲 Hazeline(11.1)
25~34 岁 Age	144	力士 Lux(41.0)	舒肤佳 Safeguard(33.3)	夏士莲 Hazeline(9.0)
35~44 岁 Age	130	力士 Lux(48.5)	舒肤佳 Safeguard(23.8)	夏士莲 Hazeline(13.8)
45~54 岁 Age	82	力士 Lux(40.2)	舒肤佳 Safeguard(25.6)	夏士莲 Hazeline(14.6)
55~60 岁 Age	41	力士 Lux(46.3)	舒肤佳 Safeguard(19.5)	白丽 Baili(14.6)

3-3 正在使用的品牌排名/ Ranking of the Brands Used Now

排名 Brand Ranking	品牌 Brands	人数 Number	百分比 Percent
1	力士 Lux	448	44.3
2	舒肤佳 Safeguard	259	25.6
3	夏士莲 Hazeline	120	11.9
4	白丽 Baili	72	7.1
5	裕华 Yuhua	16	1.6
6	妮维雅 Nivea	11	1.1
7	花王 Kao	8	0.8
8	美加净 Maxam	7	0.7
9	花 Fa	6	0.6
10	多芬 Dove	5	0.5
10	六神 Liushen	5	0.5
11	上海药皂/硫磺香皂 Shanghai	4	0.4
11	三笑 Sanxiao	4	0.4
12	纳爱斯 Nice	3	0.3

n=1011

3-4 品牌转换习惯/ Brand Habit in Consuming Perfumed Soap

	人数 Number	第一次使用该品牌 first use this brand	上一次也是这个牌子 used it last time	上一次不是这个牌子 not used it last time
样本 Sample	1010	3.6	81.0	15.4
力士 Lux	448	2.2	84.6	13.2
舒肤佳 Safeguard	259	2.3	86.9	10.8
夏士莲 Hazeline	120	4.2	69.2	26.7
白丽 Baili	72	6.9	73.6	19.4
裕华 Yuhua	16	6.3	75.0	18.8
妮维雅 Nivea	11	18.2	36.4	45.5
花王 Kao	8	12.5	75.0	12.5
美加净 Maxam	7	0.0	57.1	42.9
花 Fa	6	0.0	100.0	0.0
多芬 Dove	5	0.0	80.0	20.0
六神 Liushen	5	0.0	40.0	60.0

3-5 下一次打算使用的品牌排名/ Ranking of the Brands to be Used Next Time

排名 Brand Ranking	品牌 Brands	人数 Number	百分比 Percent
1	力士 Lux	428	42.3
2	舒肤佳 Safeguard	287	28.4
3	夏士莲 Hazeline	124	12.3
4	白丽 Baili	56	5.5
5	裕华 Yuhua	11	1.1
6	妮维雅 Nivea	8	0.8
6	花 Fa	8	0.8
7	多芬 Dove	7	0.7
7	上海药皂/硫磺香皂 Shanghai	7	0.7
8	三笑 Sanxiao	4	0.4
8	六神 Liushen	4	0.4
8	美加净 Maxam	4	0.4
8	花王 Kao	4	0.4

n=1011

3-6 样本、 男性各年龄层、 女性各年龄层是否是主要购买者/ Purchasers in the Household by the Whole Sample, Age and Gender Groups

	人数 Number	是 yes	不是 no
样本 Sample	1013	63.3	36.7
男性 Male	509	50.3	49.7
16~24 岁 Age	109	38.5	61.5
25~34 岁 Age	146	51.4	48.6
35~44 岁 Age	130	54.6	45.4
45~54 岁 Age	85	54.1	45.9
55~60 岁 Age	39	56.4	43.6
女性 Female	504	76.4	23.6
16~24 岁 Age	108	38.9	61.1
25~34 岁 Age	143	78.3	21.7
35~44 岁 Age	130	93.1	6.9
45~54 岁 Age	82	90.2	9.8
55~60 岁 Age	41	87.8	12.2

3-7 样本、男性各年龄层、女性各年龄层的使用方式/ Ways of Using the Products by the Whole Sample, Age and Gender Groups

	人数 Number	个人专用 personal use	家人共用 all family members share
样本 Sample	1011	17.2	82.8
男性 Male	507	20.9	79.1
16~24 岁 Age	109	25.7	74.3
25~34 岁 Age	146	22.6	77.4
35~44 岁 Age	130	25.4	74.6
45~54 岁 Age	83	8.4	91.6
55~60 岁 Age	39	12.8	87.2
女性 Female	504	13.5	86.5
16~24 岁 Age	108	21.3	78.7
25~34 岁 Age	143	18.2	81.8
35~44 岁 Age	130	9.2	90.8
45~54 岁 Age	82	6.1	93.9
55~60 岁 Age	41	4.9	95.1

3-8 样本、男性各年龄层、女性各年龄层的使用频率/ Frequencies of the Consumed Perfumed Soap by the Whole Sample, Age and Gender Groups

	人数 Number	一天 3 次或以上 3 times or over a day	一天 1~2 次 once or twice a day	两三天用 1 次 once 2 or 3 days	一周 1~2 次 once or twice a week	半个月 1 次或以下 once half a month or below
样本 Sample	1008	27.9	58.2	8.2	5.6	0.1
男性 Male	504	26.6	59.5	8.3	5.6	0.0
16~24 岁 Age	108	26.9	53.7	9.3	10.2	0.0
25~34 岁 Age	145	36.6	52.4	6.9	4.1	0.0
35~44 岁 Age	130	15.4	70.8	9.2	4.6	0.0
45~54 岁 Age	83	24.1	65.1	7.2	3.6	0.0
55~60 岁 Age	38	31.6	52.6	10.5	5.3	0.0
女性 Female	504	29.2	56.9	8.1	5.6	0.2
16~24 岁 Age	108	29.6	54.6	4.6	10.2	0.9
25~34 岁 Age	143	34.3	54.5	6.3	4.9	0.0
35~44 岁 Age	130	21.5	66.2	8.5	3.8	0.0
45~54 岁 Age	82	31.7	51.2	13.4	3.7	0.0
55~60 岁 Age	41	29.3	53.7	12.2	4.9	0.0

3-9 选择该类商品的考虑因素/ Ranking of the Considerations in Purchasing

注：本题为多选题，合计百分比超过 100%（Multiple answers）

排名 Ranking	考虑因素 Considerations	人次 Person-time	百分比 Percent
1	价格适中 reasonable price	461	45.6
2	有名的牌子 famous brand	458	45.3
3	产品功用 product function	357	35.3
4	购买方便 easy to buy	240	23.8
5	广告影响 influence of advertising	212	21.0
6	单位发的 offered by the working unit	85	8.4
7	包装吸引人 appealing package	48	4.8
8	有优惠条件 with preferential terms	43	4.3
9	别人推荐 introduced by other people	37	3.7
10	其它 others	17	1.7

n=1010

3-10 对产品功能的侧重方面/ Ranking of the Considerations about the Function of this Kind of Product

注：本题为多选题，合计百分比超过 100%（Multiple answers）

排名 Ranking	侧重方面 Items	人次 Person-time	百分比 Percent
1	气味好 pleasant smell	663	65.7
2	不刺激皮肤 harmless to my skin	368	36.5
3	能杀菌 bacteria-killing ability	319	31.6
4	洗净力强 wash more cleanly	260	25.8
5	适合自己肤质 suitable to my skin	213	21.1
6	泡沫多 rich foam	148	14.7
7	洗后不紧绷 without causing tightness	128	12.7
8	有美容功能 beautifying effect	73	7.2
9	有药用功能 medicine-like effect	26	2.6
10	其他 others	7	0.7

n=1009

3-11 重度消费者的人口分布/ Demographics of the Heavy Consumers

	人数 Number	16-24 岁 Age	25-34 岁 Age	35-44 岁 Age	45-54 岁 Age	55-60 岁 Age
样本 Sample	868	20.5	29.5	26.0	16.4	7.6
男性 Male	434	20.0	29.7	25.8	17.1	7.4
一天 3 次或以上 3 times or over a day	134	21.6	39.6	14.9	14.9	9.0
一天 1~2 次 once or twice a day	300	19.3	25.3	30.7	18.0	6.7
女性 Female	434	21.0	29.3	26.3	15.7	7.8
一天 3 次或以上 3 times or over a day	147	21.8	33.3	19.0	17.7	8.2
一天 1~2 次 once or twice a day	287	20.6	27.2	30.0	14.6	7.7

3-12 不同消费者层的常用品牌/ The Most Frequently Used Brands by Market Segments

3-12-1 时尚流行指标/ Fads Popular Index

	人数 Number	第一品牌及百分比 1st / percent	第二品牌及百分比 2nd / percent	第三品牌及百分比 3rd / percent	第四品牌及百分比 4th / percent
样本 Sample	1002	**力士 Lux(45.2)**	**舒肤佳 Safeguard(27.3)**	**夏士莲 Hazeline(10.3)**	**白丽 Baili(6.8)**
平实生活指向 simple living orientation	468	力士 Lux(43.6)	舒肤佳 Safeguard(25.9)	夏士莲 Hazeline(9.8)	白丽 Baili(9.0)
时尚流行指向 fashion orientation	534	力士 Lux(46.6)	舒肤佳 Safeguard(28.7)	夏士莲 Hazeline(10.7)	白丽 Baili(4.9)

3-12-2 广告态度指标/ Advertising Attitude Index

	人数 Number	第一品牌及百分比 1st / percent	第二品牌及百分比 2nd / percent	第三品牌及百分比 3rd / percent	第四品牌及百分比 4th / percent
样本 Sample	999	**力士 Lux(45.1)**	**舒肤佳 Safeguard(27.2)**	**夏士莲 Hazeline(10.3)**	**白丽 Baili(6.9)**
广告淡漠指向 indifferent orientation	256	力士 Lux(44.1)	舒肤佳 Safeguard(28.5)	夏士莲 Hazeline(9.0)	白丽 Baili(7.4)
中间层 medium	608	力士 Lux(46.5)	舒肤佳 Safeguard(27.1)	夏士莲 Hazeline(10.0)	白丽 Baili(6.7)
信赖广告指向 loyal orientation	135	力士 Lux(40.7)	舒肤佳 Safeguard(25.2)	夏士莲 Hazeline(14.1)	白丽 Baili(6.7)

3-13 重度消费者的消费层构成/ The Composition of the Heavy Consumers

3-13-1 时尚流行指标/ Fads Popular Index

	人数 Number	平实生活指向 simple living orientation	时尚流行指向 fashion orientation
样本 Sample	859	45.3	54.7
一天 3 次或以上 3 times or over a day	278	44.2	55.8
一天 1～2 次 once or twice a day	581	45.8	54.2

3-13-2 广告态度指标/ Advertising Attitude Index

	人数 Number	广告淡漠指向 indifferent orientation	中间层 medium	信赖广告指向 loyal orientation
样本 Sample	857	25.1	60.7	14.2
一天 3 次或以上 3 times or over a day	277	22.4	62.5	15.2
一天 1～2 次 once or twice a day	580	26.4	59.8	13.8

● 广州 / Guangzhou

3-1 最常用品牌排名/ Ranking of the Most Frequently Used Brands

排名 Brand Ranking	品牌 Brands	人数 Number	百分比 Percent
1	舒肤佳 Safeguard	422	44.8
2	力士 Lux	258	27.4
3	夏士莲 Hazeline	49	5.2
4	花王 Kao	26	2.8
5	棕榄 Palmotive	15	1.6
5	加信氏 Cussons	15	1.6
5	天丽 Tianli	15	1.6
6	爵士 Zest	14	1.5
7	滴露 Dettol	12	1.3
7	浪奇 Langqi	12	1.3
8	皇室 Imperal	9	1.0

n=943

3-2 样本、男性各年龄层、女性各年龄层的常用品牌/ The Most Frequently Used Brands by the Whole Sample, Age and Gender Groups

	人数 Number	第一品牌及百分比 1st/ percent	第二品牌及百分比 2nd/ percent	第三品牌及百分比 3rd/ percent
样本 Sample	**943**	**舒肤佳 Safeguard(44.8)**	**力士 Lux(27.4)**	**夏士莲 Hazeline(5.2)**
男性 Male	**457**	**舒肤佳 Safeguard(44.6)**	**力士 Lux(31.7)**	**夏士莲 Hazeline(5.0)**
16~24 岁 Age	96	舒肤佳 Safeguard(47.9)	力士 Lux(24.0)	爵士 Zest(5.2)
25~34 岁 Age	138	舒肤佳 Safeguard(46.4)	力士 Lux(33.3)	夏士莲 Hazeline(6.5)
35~44 岁 Age	116	舒肤佳 Safeguard(44.0)	力士 Lux(33.6)	夏士莲 Hazeline(4.3)
45~54 岁 Age	71	力士 Lux(39.4)	舒肤佳 Safeguard(36.6)	夏士莲 Hazeline(5.6)
55~60 岁 Age	36	舒肤佳 Safeguard(47.2)	力士 Lux(25.0)	夏士莲 Hazeline(8.3)
女性 Female	**486**	**舒肤佳 Safeguard(44.9)**	**力士 Lux(23.3)**	**夏士莲 Hazeline(5.3)**
16~24 岁 Age	100	舒肤佳 Safeguard(55.0)	力士 Lux(17.0)	花王 Kao(3.0) 夏士莲 Hazeline(3.0)
25~34 岁 Age	144	舒肤佳 Safeguard(38.2)	力士 Lux(28.5)	夏士莲 Hazeline(7.6)
35~44 岁 Age	126	舒肤佳 Safeguard(39.7)	力士 Lux(28.6)	夏士莲 Hazeline(4.8)
45~54 岁 Age	81	舒肤佳 Safeguard(49.4)	力士 Lux(17.3)	夏士莲 Hazeline(4.9)
55~60 岁 Age	35	舒肤佳 Safeguard(51.4)	力士 Lux(14.3)	天丽 Tianli(8.6)

3-3 正在使用的品牌排名/ Ranking of the Brands Used Now

排名 Brand Ranking	品牌 Brands	人数 Number	百分比 Percent
1	舒肤佳 Safeguard	408	43.3
2	力士 Lux	253	26.8
3	夏士莲 Hazeline	55	5.8
4	花王 Kao	25	2.7
5	加信氏 Cussons	20	2.1
6	天丽 Tianli	18	1.9
7	棕榄 Palmotive	14	1.5
8	浪奇 Langqi	12	1.3
8	爵士 Zest	12	1.3
9	皇室 Imperal	10	1.1

n=943

3-4 品牌转换习惯/ Brand Habit in Consuming Perfumed Soap

	人数 Number	第一次使用该品牌 first use this brand	上一次也是这个牌子 used it last time	上一次不是这个牌子 not used it last time
样本 Sample	**937**	**4.8**	**75.9**	**19.3**
舒肤佳 Safeguard	407	3.7	82.1	14.3
力士 Lux	252	3.6	77.8	18.7
夏士莲 Hazeline	54	5.6	68.5	25.9
花王 Kao	25	8.0	72.0	20.0
加信氏 Cussons	19	0.0	73.7	26.3
天丽 Tianli	18	11.1	72.2	16.7
棕榄 Palmotive	14	0.0	71.4	28.6
浪奇 Langqi	12	0.0	83.3	16.7
爵士 Zest	12	16.7	58.3	25.0

3-5 下一次打算使用的品牌排名/ Ranking of the Brands to be Used Next Time

排名 Brand Ranking	品牌 Brands	人数 Number	百分比 Percent
1	舒肤佳 Safeguard	383	40.6
2	力士 Lux	258	27.3
3	夏士莲 Hazeline	63	6.7
4	花王 Kao	27	2.9
5	加信氏 Cussons	17	1.8
6	爵士 Zest	13	1.4
7	滴露 Dettol	11	1.2
7	天丽 Tianli	11	1.2
7	多芬 Dove	11	1.2
8	浪奇 Langqi	10	1.1
8	皇室 Imperal	10	1.1

n=944

3-6 样本、男性各年龄层、女性各年龄层是否是主要购买者/ Purchasers in the Household by the Whole Sample, Age and Gender Groups

	人数 Number	是 yes	不是 no
样本 Sample	1015	53.9	46.1
男性 Male	491	40.7	59.3
16~24 岁 Age	105	27.6	72.4
25~34 岁 Age	146	43.8	56.2
35~44 岁 Age	125	44.8	55.2
45~54 岁 Age	72	40.3	59.7
55~60 岁 Age	43	51.2	48.8
女性 Female	524	66.2	33.8
16~24 岁 Age	109	31.2	68.8
25~34 岁 Age	157	70.7	29.3
35~44 岁 Age	134	78.4	21.6
45~54 岁 Age	84	81.0	19.0
55~60 岁 Age	40	72.5	27.5

3-7 样本、男性各年龄层、女性各年龄层的使用方式/ Ways of Using the Products by the Whole Sample, Age and Gender Groups

	人数 Number	个人专用 personal use	家人共用 all family members share
样本 Sample	941	28.3	71.7
男性 Male	455	29.5	70.5
16~24 岁 Age	96	36.5	63.5
25~34 岁 Age	136	36.8	63.2
35~44 岁 Age	116	23.3	76.7
45~54 岁 Age	71	18.3	81.7
55~60 岁 Age	36	25.0	75.0
女性 Female	486	27.2	72.8
16~24 岁 Age	101	42.6	57.4
25~34 岁 Age	144	24.3	75.7
35~44 岁 Age	125	21.6	78.4
45~54 岁 Age	81	21.0	79.0
55~60 岁 Age	35	28.6	71.4

3-8 样本、男性各年龄层、女性各年龄层的使用频率/ Frequencies of the Consumed Perfumed Soap by the Whole Sample, Age and Gender Groups

	人数 Number	一天 3 次或以上 3 times or over a day	一天 1~2 次 once or twice a day	两三天用 1 次 once 2 or 3 day	一周 1~2 次 once or twice a week	半个月 1 次或以下 once half a month or below
样本 Sample	939	11.9	74.5	6.9	4.2	2.4
男性 Male	456	9.9	79.2	5.9	3.3	1.8
16~24 岁 Age	96	10.4	78.1	5.2	5.2	1.0
25~34 岁 Age	138	13.0	76.8	4.3	3.6	2.2
35~44 岁 Age	115	5.2	80.0	9.6	4.3	0.9
45~54 岁 Age	71	8.5	84.5	2.8	0.0	4.2
55~60 岁 Age	36	13.9	77.8	8.3	0.0	0.0
女性 Female	483	13.9	70.2	7.9	5.0	3.1
16~24 岁 Age	99	13.1	69.7	7.1	6.1	4.0
25~34 岁 Age	143	14.0	69.2	9.1	5.6	2.1
35~44 岁 Age	125	14.4	65.6	9.6	5.6	4.8
45~54 岁 Age	81	13.6	77.8	3.7	2.5	2.5
55~60 岁 Age	35	14.3	74.3	8.6	2.9	0.0

3-9 选择该类商品的考虑因素/ Ranking of the Considerations in Purchasing

注：本题为多选题，合计百分比超过 100%（Multiple answers）

排名 Ranking	考虑因素 Considerations	人次 Person-time	百分比 Percent
1	价格适中 reasonable price	451	48.0
2	产品功用 product function	398	42.4
3	有名的牌子 famous brand	395	42.1
4	购买方便 easy to buy	188	20.0
5	广告影响 influence of advertising	165	17.6
6	包装吸引人 appealing package	53	5.6
7	别人推荐 introduced by other people	39	4.2
8	有优惠条件 with preferential terms	35	3.7
9	单位发的 offered by the working unit	24	2.6
9	其它 others	24	2.6

n=939

3-10 对产品功能的侧重方面/ Ranking of the Considerations about the Function of this Kind of Product

注：本题为多选题，合计百分比超过 100%（Multiple answers）

排名 Ranking	侧重方面 Items	人次 Person-time	百分比 Percent
1	气味好 pleasant smell	507	54.0
2	能杀菌 bacteria-killing ability	403	42.9
3	洗净力强 wash more cleanly	269	28.6
4	不刺激皮肤 harmless to my skin	256	27.3
5	适合自己肤质 suitable to my skin	230	24.5
6	泡沫多 rich foam	120	12.8
7	洗后不紧绷 without causing tightness	96	10.2
8	有美容功能 beautifying effect	35	3.7
9	有药用功能 medicine-like effect	28	3.0
10	其他 others	7	0.7

n=939

3-11 重度消费者的人口分布/ Demographics of the Heavy Consumers

	人数 Number	16-24 岁 Age	25-34 岁 Age	35-44 岁 Age	45-54 岁 Age	55-60 岁 Age
样本 Sample	812	20.6	29.9	24.4	17.2	7.9
男性 Male	406	20.9	30.5	24.1	16.3	8.1
一天 3 次或以上 3 times or over a day	45	22.2	40.0	13.3	13.3	11.1
一天 1～2 次 once or twice a day	361	20.8	29.4	25.5	16.6	7.8
女性 Female	406	20.2	29.3	24.6	18.2	7.6
一天 3 次或以上 3 times or over a day	67	19.4	29.9	26.9	16.4	7.5
一天 1～2 次 once or twice a day	339	20.4	29.2	24.2	18.6	7.7

3-12 不同消费者层的常用品牌/ The Most Frequently Used Brands by Market Segments

3-12-1 时尚流行指标/ Fads Popular Index

	人数 Number	第一品牌及百分比 1st / percent	第二品牌及百分比 2nd / percent	第三品牌及百分比 3rd / percent
样本 Sample	933	**舒肤佳 Safeguard(44.7)**	**力士 Lux(27.3)**	**夏士莲 Hazeline(5.1)**
平实生活指向 simple living orientation	475	舒肤佳 Safeguard(46.5)	力士 Lux(26.5)	夏士莲 Hazeline(4.6)
时尚流行指向 fashion orientation	458	舒肤佳 Safeguard(42.8)	力士 Lux(28.2)	夏士莲 Hazeline(5.7)

3-12-2 广告态度指标/ Advertising Attitude Index

	人数 Number	第一品牌及百分比 1st / percent	第二品牌及百分比 2nd / percent	第三品牌及百分比 3rd / percent
样本 Sample	932	**舒肤佳 Safeguard(44.7)**	**力士 Lux(27.4)**	**夏士莲 Hazeline(5.2)**
广告淡漠指向 indifferent orientation	306	舒肤佳 Safeguard(40.8)	力士 Lux(27.1)	夏士莲 Hazeline(5.6)
中间层 medium	540	舒肤佳 Safeguard(46.3)	力士 Lux(27.4)	夏士莲 Hazeline(4.4)
信赖广告指向 loyal orientation	86	舒肤佳 Safeguard(48.8)	力士 Lux(27.9)	夏士莲 Hazeline(8.1)

3-13 重度消费者的消费层构成/ The Composition of the Heavy Consumers

3-13-1 时尚流行指标/ Fads Popular Index

	人数 Number	平实生活指向 simple living orientation	时尚流行指向 fashion orientation
样本 Sample	802	51.7	48.3
一天 3 次或以上 3 times or over a day	110	47.3	52.7
一天 1～2 次 once or twice a day	692	52.5	47.5

3-13-2 广告态度指标/ Advertising Attitude Index

	人数 Number	广告淡漠指向 indifferent orientation	中间层 medium	信赖广告指向 loyal orientation
样本 Sample	802	33.4	57.9	8.7
一天 3 次或以上 3 times or over a day	110	24.5	70.0	5.5
一天 1～2 次 once or twice a day	692	34.8	55.9	9.2

● 重庆 / Chongqing

3-1 最常用品牌排名/ Ranking of the Most Frequently Used Brands

排名 Brand Ranking	品牌 Brands	人数 Number	百分比 Percent
1	舒肤佳 Safeguard	272	43.8
2	力士 Lux	160	25.8
3	蜀秀 Shuxiu	83	13.4
4	夏士莲 Hazeline	53	8.5
5	三笑 Sanxiao	15	2.4

n=621

3-2 样本、男性各年龄层、女性各年龄层的常用品牌/ The Most Frequently Used Brands by the Whole Sample, Age and Gender Groups

	人数 Number	第一品牌及百分比 1st/ percent	第二品牌及百分比 2nd/ percent	第三品牌及百分比 3rd/ percent	第四品牌及百分比 4th/ percent
样本 Sample	621	**舒肤佳 Safeguard(43.8)**	**力士 Lux(25.8)**	**蜀秀 Shuxiu(13.4)**	**夏士莲 Hazeline(8.5)**
男性 Male	313	**舒肤佳 Safeguard(38.7)**	**力士 Lux(28.8)**	**蜀秀 Shuxiu(14.7)**	**夏士莲 Hazeline(9.3)**
16~24 岁 Age	64	舒肤佳 Safeguard(35.9)	力士 Lux(31.3)	夏士莲 Hazeline(9.4) 蜀秀 Shuxiu(9.4)	三笑 Sanxiao(4.7)
25~34 岁 Age	93	舒肤佳 Safeguard(43.0)	力士 Lux(31.2)	夏士莲 Hazeline(11.8)	蜀秀 Shuxiu(8.6)
35~44 岁 Age	75	舒肤佳 Safeguard(32.0)	力士 Lux(26.7)	蜀秀 Shuxiu(22.7)	夏士莲 Hazeline(8.0)
45~54 岁 Age	53	舒肤佳 Safeguard(37.7)	力士 Lux(34.0)	蜀秀 Shuxiu(15.1)	夏士莲 Hazeline(5.7)
55~60 岁 Age	28	舒肤佳 Safeguard(50.0)	蜀秀 Shuxiu(25.0)	力士 Lux(10.7) 夏士莲 Hazeline(10.7)	
女性 Female	308	**舒肤佳 Safeguard(49.0)**	**力士 Lux(22.7)**	**蜀秀 Shuxiu(12.0)**	**夏士莲 Hazeline(7.8)**
16~24 岁 Age	64	舒肤佳 Safeguard(54.7)	力士 Lux(21.9)	夏士莲 Hazeline(6.3)	六神 Liushen(3.1) 三笑 Sanxiao(3.1)
25~34 岁 Age	89	舒肤佳 Safeguard(52.8)	力士 Lux(18.0)	蜀秀 Shuxiu(12.4)	三笑 Sanxiao(4.5) 夏士莲 Hazeline(4.5)
35~44 岁 Age	73	舒肤佳 Safeguard(47.9)	力士 Lux(28.8)	夏士莲 Hazeline(13.7)	蜀秀 Shuxiu(8.2)
45~54 岁 Age	59	舒肤佳 Safeguard(42.4)	力士 Lux(25.4)	蜀秀 Shuxiu(23.7)	夏士莲 Hazeline(6.8)
55~60 岁 Age	23	舒肤佳 Safeguard(39.1)	蜀秀 Shuxiu(21.7)	力士 Lux(17.4)	夏士莲 Hazeline(8.7)

3-3 正在使用的品牌排名/ Ranking of the Brand Used Now

排名 Brand Ranking	品牌 Brands	人数 Number	百分比 Percent
1	舒肤佳 Safeguard	270	43.4
2	力士 Lux	152	24.4
3	蜀秀 Shuxiu	74	11.9
4	夏士莲 Hazeline	58	9.3
5	三笑 Sanxiao	23	3.7
6	两面针 Liangmianzhen	4	0.6

n=622

3-4 品牌转换习惯/ Brand Habit in Consuming Perfumed Soap

	人数 Number	第一次使用该品牌 first use this brand	上一次也是这个牌子 used it last time	上一次不是这个牌子 not used it last time
样本 Sample	615	4.7	75.8	19.5
舒肤佳 Safeguard	268	4.1	83.6	12.3
力士 Lux	150	2.0	75.3	22.7
蜀秀 Shuxiu	73	6.8	75.3	17.8
夏士莲 Hazeline	58	3.4	63.8	32.8
三笑 Sanxiao	23	8.7	47.8	43.5

3-5 下一次打算使用的品牌排名/ Ranking of the Brands to be Used Next Time

排名 Brand Ranking	品牌 Brands	人数 Number	百分比 Percent
1	舒肤佳 Safeguard	267	42.9
2	力士 Lux	179	28.8
3	蜀秀 Shuxiu	70	11.3
4	夏士莲 Hazeline	56	9.0
5	三笑 Sanxiao	10	1.6

n=622

3-6 样本、男性各年龄层、女性各年龄层是否是主要购买者/ Purchasers in the Household by the Whole Sample, Age and Gender Groups

	人数 Number	是 yes	不是 no
样本 Sample	620	60.8	39.2
男性 Male	311	44.1	55.9
16~24 岁 Age	64	32.8	67.2
25~34 岁 Age	93	45.2	54.8
35~44 岁 Age	75	45.3	54.7
45~54 岁 Age	51	49.0	51.0
55~60 岁 Age	28	53.6	46.4
女性 Female	309	77.7	22.3
16~24 岁 Age	64	54.7	45.3
25~34 岁 Age	90	82.2	17.8
35~44 岁 Age	73	87.7	12.3
45~54 岁 Age	60	83.3	16.7
55~60 岁 Age	22	77.3	22.7

3-7 样本、男性各年龄层、女性各年龄层的使用方式/ Ways of Using the Products by the Whole Sample, Age and Gender Groups

	人数 Number	个人专用 personal use	家人共用 all family members share
样本 Sample	621	10.1	89.9
男性 Male	313	12.5	87.5
16~24 岁 Age	64	20.3	79.7
25~34 岁 Age	93	12.9	87.1
35~44 岁 Age	75	13.3	86.7
45~54 岁 Age	53	5.7	94.3
55~60 岁 Age	28	3.6	96.4
女性 Female	308	7.8	92.2
16~24 岁 Age	64	15.6	84.4
25~34 岁 Age	89	10.1	89.9
35~44 岁 Age	73	5.5	94.5
45~54 岁 Age	59	1.7	98.3
55~60 岁 Age	23	0.0	100.0

3-8 样本、男性各年龄层、女性各年龄层的使用频率/ Frequencies of the Consumed Perfumed Soap by the Whole Sample, Age and Gender Groups

	人数 Number	一天 3 次或以上 3 times or over a day	一天 1~2 次 once or twice a day	两三天用 1 次 once 2 or 3 days	一周 1~2 次 once or twice a week	半个月 1 次或以下 once half a month or below
样本 Sample	620	13.4	58.9	18.5	8.5	0.6
男性 Male	312	15.1	57.1	19.9	7.7	0.3
16~24 岁 Age	64	9.4	50.0	31.3	9.4	0.0
25~34 岁 Age	93	17.2	58.1	20.4	4.3	0.0
35~44 岁 Age	74	13.5	62.2	16.2	8.1	0.0
45~54 岁 Age	53	18.9	52.8	15.1	13.2	0.0
55~60 岁 Age	28	17.9	64.3	10.7	3.6	3.6
女性 Female	308	11.7	60.7	17.2	9.4	1.0
16~24 岁 Age	64	17.2	54.7	14.1	12.5	1.6
25~34 岁 Age	90	15.6	56.7	18.9	7.8	1.1
35~44 岁 Age	73	8.2	68.5	16.4	6.8	0.0
45~54 岁 Age	58	5.2	65.5	17.2	10.3	1.7
55~60 岁 Age	23	8.7	56.5	21.7	13.0	0.0

3-9 选择该类商品的考虑因素/ Ranking of the Considerations in Purchasing

注：本题为多选题，合计百分比超过 100%（Multiple answers）

排名 Ranking	考虑因素 Considerations	人次 Person-time	百分比 Percent
1	价格适中 reasonable price	290	46.9
2	产品功用 product function	252	40.8
3	有名的牌子 famous brand	238	38.5
4	广告影响 influence of advertising	138	22.3
5	购买方便 easy to buy	106	17.2
6	单位发的 offered by the working unit	46	7.4
7	别人推荐 introduced by other people	22	3.6
8	包装吸引人 appealing package	16	2.6
9	有优惠条件 with preferential terms	14	2.3
10	其它 others	10	1.6

n=618

3-10 对产品功能的侧重方面/ Ranking of the Considerations about the Function of this Kind of Product

注：本题为多选题，合计百分比超过 100%（Multiple answers）

排名 Ranking	侧重方面 Items	人次 Person-time	百分比 Percent
1	气味好 pleasant smell	413	66.7
2	能杀菌 bacteria-killing ability	219	35.4
3	不刺激皮肤 harmless to my skin	189	30.5
4	适合自己肤质 suitable to my skin	151	24.4
5	洗净力强 wash more cleanly	146	23.6
6	泡沫多 rich foam	77	12.4
7	洗后不紧绷 without causing tightness	66	10.7
8	有美容功能 beautifying effect	31	5.0
9	有药用功能 medicine-like effect	20	3.2
10	其他 others	4	0.6

n=619

3-11 重度消费者的人口分布/ Demographics of the Heavy Consumers

	人数 Number	16-24 岁 Age	25-34 岁 Age	35-44 岁 Age	45-54 岁 Age	55-60 岁 Age
样本 Sample	448	18.8	30.1	25.0	17.6	8.5
男性 Male	225	16.9	31.1	24.9	16.9	10.2
一天 3 次或以上 3 times or over a day	47	12.8	34.0	21.3	21.3	10.6
一天 1~2 次 once or twice a day	178	18.0	30.3	25.8	15.7	10.1
女性 Female	223	20.6	29.1	25.1	18.4	6.7
一天 3 次或以上 3 times or over a day	36	30.6	38.9	16.7	8.3	5.6
一天 1~2 次 once or twice a day	187	18.7	27.3	26.7	20.3	7.0

3-12 不同消费者层的常用品牌/ The Most Frequently Used Brands by Market Segments

3-12-1 时尚流行指标/ Fads Popular Index

	人数 Number	第一品牌及百分比 1st / percent	第二品牌及百分比 2nd / percent	第三品牌及百分比 3rd / percent	第四品牌及百分比 4th / percent
样本 Sample	613	**舒肤佳 Safeguard(43.7)**	**力士 Lux(25.9)**	**蜀秀 Shuxiu(13.5)**	**夏士莲 Hazeline(8.3)**
平实生活指向 simple living orientation	366	舒肤佳 Safeguard(42.9)	力士 Lux(24.9)	蜀秀 Shuxiu(16.7)	夏士莲 Hazeline(6.3)
时尚流行指向 fashion orientation	247	舒肤佳 Safeguard(44.9)	力士 Lux(27.5)	夏士莲 Hazeline(11.3)	蜀秀 Shuxiu(8.9)

3-12-2 广告态度指标/ Advertising Attitude Index

	人数 Number	第一品牌及百分比 1st / percent	第二品牌及百分比 2nd / percent	第三品牌及百分比 3rd / percent	第四品牌及百分比 4th / percent
样本 Sample	615	**舒肤佳 Safeguard(44.1)**	**力士 Lux(25.7)**	**蜀秀 Shuxiu(13.5)**	**夏士莲 Hazeline(8.5)**
广告淡漠指向 indifferent orientation	167	舒肤佳 Safeguard(42.5)	力士 Lux(29.3)	蜀秀 Shuxiu(11.4)	夏士莲 Hazeline(9.6)
中间层 medium	365	舒肤佳 Safeguard(42.2)	力士 Lux(26.8)	蜀秀 Shuxiu(14.0)	夏士莲 Hazeline(8.5)
信赖广告指向 loyal orientation	83	舒肤佳 Safeguard(55.4)	蜀秀 Shuxiu(15.7)	力士 Lux(13.3)	夏士莲 Hazeline(6.0)

3-13 重度消费者的消费层构成/ The Composition of the Heavy Consumers

3-13-1 时尚流行指标/ Fads Popular Index

	人数 Number	平实生活指向 simple living orientation	时尚流行指向 fashion orientation
样本 Sample	443	58.2	41.8
一天 3 次或以上 3 times or over a day	82	54.9	45.1
一天 1～2 次 once or twice a day	361	59.0	41.0

3-13-2 广告态度指标/ Advertising Attitude Index

	人数 Number	广告淡漠指向 indifferent orientation	中间层 medium	信赖广告指向 loyal orientation
样本 Sample	444	25.2	59.0	15.8
一天 3 次或以上 3 times or over a day	82	29.3	61.0	9.8
一天 1～2 次 once or twice a day	362	24.3	58.6	17.1

● 武汉 / Wuhan

3-1 最常用品牌排名/ Ranking of the Most Frequently Used Brands

排名 Brand Ranking	品牌 Brands	人数 Number	百分比 Percent
1	舒肤佳 Safeguard	262	40.9
2	力士 Lux	161	25.1
3	夏士莲 Hazeline	60	9.4
4	梦幻 Mely	47	7.3
5	三笑 Sanxiao	37	5.8
6	青龙 Dragon	8	1.2
7	佳洁士 Crest	5	0.8
8	花王 Kao	4	0.6

n=641

3-2 样本、男性各年龄层、女性各年龄层的常用品牌/ The Most Frequently Used Brands by the Whole Sample, Age and Gender Groups

	人数 Number	第一品牌及百分比 1st/ percent	第二品牌及百分比 2nd/ percent	第三品牌及百分比 3rd/ percent	第四品牌及百分比 4th/ percent
样本 Sample	641	**舒肤佳 Safeguard(40.9)**	**力士 Lux(25.1)**	**夏士莲 Hazeline(9.4)**	**梦幻 Mely(7.3)**
男性 Male	311	**舒肤佳 Safeguard(42.1)**	**力士 Lux(24.8)**	**夏士莲 Hazeline(8.4)**	**梦幻 Mely(6.8)**
16~24 岁 Age	65	舒肤佳 Safeguard(38.5)	力士 Lux(35.4)	夏士莲 Hazeline(13.8)	梦幻 Mely(4.6)
25~34 岁 Age	89	舒肤佳 Safeguard(49.4)	力士 Lux(22.5)	三笑 Sanxiao(7.9)	夏士莲 Hazeline(5.6)
35~44 岁 Age	80	舒肤佳 Safeguard(40.0)	力士 Lux(18.8)	梦幻 Mely(13.8)	夏士莲 Hazeline(6.3) 三笑 Sanxiao(6.3)
45~54 岁 Age	52	舒肤佳 Safeguard(40.4)	力士 Lux(28.8)	夏士莲 Hazeline(9.6)	梦幻 Mely(5.8)
55~60 岁 Age	25	舒肤佳 Safeguard(36.0)	力士 Lux(16.0)	梦幻 Mely(8.0) 三笑 Sanxiao(8.0) 夏士莲 Hazeline(8.0)	青龙 Dragon(4.0) 茉莉 Moli(4.0) 碧绿 Bilv(4.0)
女性 Female	330	**舒肤佳 Safeguard(39.7)**	**力士 Lux(25.5)**	**夏士莲 Hazeline(10.3)**	**梦幻 Mely(7.9)**
16~24 岁 Age	68	舒肤佳 Safeguard(44.1)	力士 Lux(30.9)	夏士莲 Hazeline(7.4)	梦幻 Mely(5.9) 三笑 Sanxiao(5.9)
25~34 岁 Age	96	舒肤佳 Safeguard(41.7)	力士 Lux(26.0)	夏士莲 Hazeline(11.5)	梦幻 Mely(7.3)
35~44 岁 Age	78	舒肤佳 Safeguard(37.2)	力士 Lux(25.6)	夏士莲 Hazeline(9.0)	三笑 Sanxiao(7.7)
45~54 岁 Age	62	舒肤佳 Safeguard(41.9)	力士 Lux(17.7)	夏士莲 Hazeline(12.9)	梦幻 Mely(11.3)
55~60 岁 Age	26	力士 Lux(26.9)	舒肤佳 Safeguard(23.1)	梦幻 Mely(11.5) 夏士莲 Hazeline(11.5)	三笑 Sanxiao(7.7)

3-3 正在使用的品牌排名/ Ranking of the Brands Used Now

排名 Brand Ranking	品牌 Brands	人数 Number	百分比 Percent
1	舒肤佳 Safeguard	242	37.8
2	力士 Lux	171	26.7
3	夏士莲 Hazeline	67	10.5
4	三笑 Sanxiao	43	6.7
5	梦幻 Mely	41	6.4
6	青龙 Dragon	8	1.2
7	玉兰油 Oil of Olay	6	0.9
7	上海药皂/硫磺香皂 Shanghai	6	0.9
8	花王 Kao	4	0.6
8	佳洁士 Crest	4	0.6
8	强生 Johnson&Johnson	4	0.6

n=641

3-4 品牌转换习惯/ Brand Habit in Consuming Perfumed Soap

	人数 Number	第一次使用该品牌 first use this brand	上一次也是这个牌子 used it last time	上一次不是这个牌子 not used it last time
样本 Sample	640	4.7	76.1	19.2
舒肤佳 Safeguard	241	4.1	79.3	16.6
力士 Lux	171	4.1	74.3	21.6
夏士莲 Hazeline	67	6.0	68.7	25.4
三笑 Sanxiao	43	9.3	74.4	16.3
梦幻 Mely	41	2.4	87.8	9.8
青龙 Dragon	8	0.0	75.0	25.0
玉兰油 Oil of Olay	6	0.0	66.7	33.3
上海药皂/硫磺香皂 Shanghai	6	0.0	33.3	66.7

3-5 下一次打算使用的品牌排名/ Ranking of the Brands to be Used Next Time

排名 Brand Ranking	品牌 Brands	人数 Number	百分比 Percent
1	舒肤佳 Safeguard	266	41.5
2	力士 Lux	139	21.7
3	夏士莲 Hazeline	69	10.8
4	梦幻 Mely	36	5.6
5	三笑 Sanxiao	33	5.1
6	玉兰油 Oil of Olay	12	1.9
7	青龙 Dragon	8	1.2
8	佳洁士 Crest	7	1.1
9	花王 Kao	5	0.8

n=641

3-6 样本、男性各年龄层、女性各年龄层是否是主要购买者/ Purchasers in the Household by the Whole Sample, Age and Gender Groups

	人数 Number	是 yes	不是 no
样本 Sample	641	54.9	45.1
男性 Male	311	37.3	62.7
16~24 岁 Age	65	15.4	84.6
25~34 岁 Age	89	36.0	64.0
35~44 岁 Age	80	42.5	57.5
45~54 岁 Age	52	50.0	50.0
55~60 岁 Age	25	56.0	44.0
女性 Female	330	71.5	28.5
16~24 岁 Age	69	33.3	66.7
25~34 岁 Age	96	75.0	25.0
35~44 岁 Age	78	84.6	15.4
45~54 岁 Age	61	93.4	6.6
55~60 岁 Age	26	69.2	30.8

3-7 样本、男性各年龄层、女性各年龄层的使用方式/ Ways of Using the Products by the Whole Sample, Age and Gender Groups

	人数 Number	个人专用 personal use	家人共用 all family members share
样本 Sample	639	9.7	90.3
男性 Male	311	10.3	89.7
16~24 岁 Age	65	16.9	83.1
25~34 岁 Age	89	12.4	87.6
35~44 岁 Age	80	8.8	91.3
45~54 岁 Age	52	1.9	98.1
55~60 岁 Age	25	8.0	92.0
女性 Female	328	9.1	90.9
16~24 岁 Age	67	13.4	86.6
25~34 岁 Age	96	10.4	89.6
35~44 岁 Age	78	3.8	96.2
45~54 岁 Age	61	4.9	95.1
55~60 岁 Age	26	19.2	80.8

3-8 样本、男性各年龄层、女性各年龄层的使用频率/ Frequencies of the Consumed Perfumed Soap by the Whole Sample, Age and Gender Groups

	人数 Number	一天 3 次或以上 3 times or over a day	一天 1~2 次 once or twice a day	两三天用 1 次 once 2 or 3 days	一周 1~2 次 once or twice a week	半个月 1 次或以下 once half a month or below
样本 Sample	641	25.9	60.5	8.0	4.8	0.8
男性 Male	311	25.1	60.8	8.7	4.8	0.6
16~24 岁 Age	65	24.6	56.9	12.3	6.2	0.0
25~34 岁 Age	89	29.2	57.3	7.9	4.5	1.1
35~44 岁 Age	80	20.0	70.0	5.0	3.8	1.3
45~54 岁 Age	52	23.1	57.7	13.5	5.8	0.0
55~60 岁 Age	25	32.0	60.0	4.0	4.0	0.0
女性 Female	330	26.7	60.3	7.3	4.8	0.9
16~24 岁 Age	68	29.4	52.9	11.8	5.9	0.0
25~34 岁 Age	96	31.3	61.5	5.2	2.1	0.0
35~44 岁 Age	78	25.6	56.4	12.8	3.8	1.3
45~54 岁 Age	62	19.4	67.7	1.6	9.7	1.6
55~60 岁 Age	26	23.1	69.2	0.0	3.8	3.8

3-9 选择该类商品的考虑因素/ Ranking of the Considerations in Purchasing

注：本题为多选题，合计百分比超过 100%（Multiple answers）

排名 Ranking	考虑因素 Considerations	人次 Person-time	百分比 Percent
1	价格适中 reasonable price	324	50.5
2	产品功用 product function	274	42.7
3	有名的牌子 famous brand	251	39.2
4	广告影响 influence of advertising	152	23.7
5	购买方便 easy to buy	131	20.4
6	单位发的 offered by the working unit	62	9.7
7	包装吸引人 appealing package	36	5.6
8	其它 others	33	5.1
9	有优惠条件 with preferential terms	32	5.0
10	别人推荐 introduced by other people	29	4.5

n=641

3-10 对产品功能的侧重方面/ Ranking of the Consideration about the Function of this Kind of Product

注：本题为多选题，合计百分比超过 100%（Multiple answers）

排名 Ranking	侧重方面 Items	人次 Person-time	百分比 Percent
1	气味好 pleasant smell	448	70.0
2	不刺激皮肤 harmless to my skin	242	37.8
2	能杀菌 bacteria-killing ability	242	37.8
3	洗净力强 wash more cleanly	192	30.0
4	适合自己肤质 suitable to my skin	126	19.7
5	泡沫多 rich foam	83	13.0
6	洗后不紧绷 without causing tightness	70	10.9
7	有美容功能 beautifying effect	43	6.7
8	有药用功能 medicine-like effect	24	3.8
9	其他 others	13	2.0

n=640

3-11 重度消费者的人口分布/ Demographics of the Heavy Consumers

	人数 Number	16-24 岁 Age	25-34 岁 Age	35-44 岁 Age	45-54 岁 Age	55-60 岁 Age
样本 Sample	554	19.7	30.0	24.5	17.3	8.5
男性 Male	267	19.9	28.8	27.0	15.7	8.6
一天 3 次或以上 3 times or over a day	78	20.5	33.3	20.5	15.4	10.3
一天 1～2 次 once or twice a day	189	19.6	27.0	29.6	15.9	7.9
女性 Female	287	19.5	31.0	22.3	18.8	8.4
一天 3 次或以上 3 times or over a day	88	22.7	34.1	22.7	13.6	6.8
一天 1～2 次 once or twice a day	199	18.1	29.6	22.1	21.1	9.0

3-12 不同消费者层的常用品牌/ The Most Frequently Used Brands by Market Segments

3-12-1 时尚流行指标/ Fads Popular Index

	人数 Number	第一品牌及百分比 1st / percent	第二品牌及百分比 2nd / percent	第三品牌及百分比 3rd / percent	第四品牌及百分比 4th / percent
样本 Sample	631	**舒肤佳 Safeguard(41.0)**	**力士 Lux(25.2)**	**夏士莲 Hazeline(9.4)**	**梦幻 Mely(7.4)**
平实生活指向 simple living orientation	330	舒肤佳 Safeguard(39.7)	力士 Lux(25.2)	夏士莲 Hazeline(8.8)	梦幻 Mely(8.2)
时尚流行指向 fashion orientation	301	舒肤佳 Safeguard(42.5)	力士 Lux(25.2)	夏士莲 Hazeline(10.0)	梦幻 Mely(6.6)

3-12-2 广告态度指标/ Advertising Attitude Index

	人数 Number	第一品牌及百分比 1st / percent	第二品牌及百分比 2nd / percent	第三品牌及百分比 3rd / percent	第四品牌及百分比 4th / percent
样本 Sample	633	**舒肤佳 Safeguard(41.1)**	**力士 Lux(25.1)**	**夏士莲 Hazeline(9.3)**	**梦幻 Mely(7.4)**
广告淡漠指向 indifferent orientation	188	舒肤佳 Safeguard(34.6)	力士 Lux(28.2)	夏士莲 Hazeline(13.3)	梦幻 Mely(8.0)
中间层 medium	372	舒肤佳 Safeguard(43.8)	力士 Lux(23.4)	夏士莲 Hazeline(7.8)	梦幻 Mely(6.7)
信赖广告指向 loyal orientation	73	舒肤佳 Safeguard(43.8)	力士 Lux(26.0)	梦幻 Mely(9.6)	夏士莲 Hazeline(6.8)

3-13 重度消费者的消费层构成/ The Composition of the Heavy Consumers

3-13-1 时尚流行指标/ Fads Popular Index

	人数 Number	平实生活指向 simple living orientation	时尚流行指向 fashion orientation
样本 Sample	545	51.4	48.6
一天 3 次或以上 3 times or over a day	163	43.6	56.4
一天 1～2 次 once or twice a day	382	54.7	45.3

3-13-2 广告态度指标/ Advertising Attitude Index

	人数 Number	广告淡漠指向 indifferent orientation	中间层 medium	信赖广告指向 loyal orientation
样本 Sample	547	29.1	58.3	12.6
一天 3 次或以上 3 times or over a day	163	28.2	59.5	12.3
一天 1～2 次 once or twice a day	384	29.4	57.8	12.8

● 西安 / Xi'an

3-1 最常用品牌排名/ Ranking of the Most Frequently Used Brands

排名 Brand Ranking	品牌 Brands	人数 Number	百分比 Percent
1	舒肤佳 Safeguard	250	41.7
2	力士 Lux	235	39.2
3	三笑 Sanxiao	30	5.0
4	夏士莲 Hazeline	24	4.0
5	纳爱斯 Nice	12	2.0
6	两面针 Liangmianzhen	6	1.0
7	花 Fa	5	0.8
7	中华皂 Zhonghuazao	5	0.8

n=599

3-2 样本、男性各年龄层、女性各年龄层的常用品牌/ The Most Frequently Used Brands by the Whole Sample, Age and Gender Groups

	人数 Number	第一品牌及百分比 1st/ percent	第二品牌及百分比 2nd/ percent	第三品牌及百分比 3rd/ percent	第四品牌及百分比 4th/ percent
样本 Sample	599	**舒肤佳 Safeguard(41.7)**	**力士 Lux(39.2)**	**三笑 Sanxiao(5.0)**	**夏士莲 Hazeline(4.0)**
男性 Male	301	**力士 Lux(41.9)**	**舒肤佳 Safeguard(40.5)**	**夏士莲 Hazeline(5.0)**	**三笑 Sanxiao(4.7)**
16~24 岁 Age	64	力士 Lux(40.6)	舒肤佳 Safeguard(39.1)	三笑 Sanxiao(7.8)	夏士莲 Hazeline(6.3)
25~34 岁 Age	91	力士 Lux(48.4)	舒肤佳 Safeguard(37.4)	纳爱斯 Nice(4.4)	夏士莲 Hazeline(2.2)
35~44 岁 Age	77	力士 Lux(41.6)	舒肤佳 Safeguard(40.3)	三笑 Sanxiao(10.4)	夏士莲 Hazeline(2.6) 中华皂 Zhonghuazao(2.6)
45~54 岁 Age	45	舒肤佳 Safeguard(42.2)	力士 Lux(37.8)	夏士莲 Hazeline(11.1)	美加净 Maxam(2.2) 纳爱斯 Nice(2.2) 强生 Johnson&Johnson(2.2)
55~60 岁 Age	24	舒肤佳 Safeguard(54.2)	力士 Lux(29.2)	夏士莲 Hazeline(8.3)	中华皂 Zhonghuazao(4.2)
女性 Female	298	**舒肤佳 Safeguard(43.0)**	**力士 Lux(36.6)**	**三笑 Sanxiao(5.4)**	**夏士莲 Hazeline(3.0)**
16~24 岁 Age	60	力士 Lux(38.3) 舒肤佳 Safeguard(38.3)	三笑 Sanxiao(8.3)	纳爱斯 Nice(5.0)	夏士莲 Hazeline(3.3)
25~34 岁 Age	90	力士 Lux(43.3)	舒肤佳 Safeguard(37.8)	三笑 Sanxiao(5.6)	夏士莲 Hazeline(3.3)
35~44 岁 Age	74	舒肤佳 Safeguard(51.4)	力士 Lux(32.4)	三笑 Sanxiao(4.1)	
45~54 岁 Age	49	舒肤佳 Safeguard(44.9)	力士 Lux(34.7)	夏士莲 Hazeline(6.1)	三笑 Sanxiao(4.1)
55~60 岁 Age	25	舒肤佳 Safeguard(44.0)	力士 Lux(24.0)	海鸥 Seagull(4.0) 六神 Liushen(4.0) 三笑 Sanxiao(4.0) 双喜 Shuangxi(4.0)	

3-3 正在使用的品牌排名/ Ranking of the Brands Used Now

排名 Brand Ranking	品牌 Brands	人数 Number	百分比 Percent
1	舒肤佳 Safeguard	250	41.7
2	力士 Lux	210	35.1
3	夏士莲 Hazeline	42	7.0
4	三笑 Sanxiao	32	5.3
5	纳爱斯 Nice	12	2.0
6	花 Fa	5	0.8
7	六神 Liushen	4	0.7
7	强生 Johnson&Johnson	4	0.7

n=599

3-4 品牌转换习惯/ Brand Habit in Consuming Perfumed Soap

	人数 Number	第一次使用该品牌 first use this brand	上一次也是这个牌子 used it last time	上一次不是这个牌子 not used it last time
样本 Sample	599	4.7	78.8	16.5
舒肤佳 Safeguard	250	3.2	85.6	11.2
力士 Lux	210	4.3	79.5	16.2
夏士莲 Hazeline	42	11.9	54.8	33.3
三笑 Sanxiao	32	0.0	71.9	28.1
纳爱斯 Nice	12	0.0	75.0	25.0
花 Fa	5	0.0	100.0	0.0

3-5 下一次打算使用的品牌排名/ Ranking of the Brands to be Used Next Time

排名 Brand Ranking	品牌 Brands	人数 Number	百分比 Percent
1	舒肤佳 Safeguard	246	41.1
2	力士 Lux	214	35.7
3	夏士莲 Hazeline	42	7.0
4	三笑 Sanxiao	28	4.7
5	纳爱斯 Nice	11	1.8
6	六神 Liushen	6	1.0
7	强生 Johnson&Johnson	5	0.8
8	花 Fa	4	0.7
8	中华皂 Zhonghuazao	4	0.7

n=599

3-6 样本、男性各年龄层、女性各年龄层是否是主要购买者/ Purchasers in the Household by the Whole Sample, Age and Gender Groups

	人数 Number	是 yes	不是 no
样本 Sample	600	62.3	37.7
男性 Male	302	42.1	57.9
16~24 岁 Age	64	32.8	67.2
25~34 岁 Age	91	51.6	48.4
35~44 岁 Age	77	49.4	50.6
45~54 岁 Age	46	26.1	73.9
55~60 岁 Age	24	37.5	62.5
女性 Female	298	82.9	17.1
16~24 岁 Age	61	62.3	37.7
25~34 岁 Age	90	85.6	14.4
35~44 岁 Age	73	89.0	11.0
45~54 岁 Age	49	91.8	8.2
55~60 岁 Age	25	88.0	12.0

3-7 样本、男性各年龄层、女性各年龄层的使用方式/ Ways of Using the Products by the Whole Sample, Age and Gender Groups

	人数 Number	个人专用 personal use	家人共用 all family members share
样本 Sample	596	9.1	90.9
男性 Male	300	9.0	91.0
16~24 岁 Age	64	17.2	82.8
25~34 岁 Age	91	7.7	92.3
35~44 岁 Age	77	6.5	93.5
45~54 岁 Age	44	6.8	93.2
55~60 岁 Age	24	4.2	95.8
女性 Female	296	9.1	90.9
16~24 岁 Age	60	13.3	86.7
25~34 岁 Age	90	12.2	87.8
35~44 岁 Age	72	6.9	93.1
45~54 岁 Age	49	2.0	98.0
55~60 岁 Age	25	8.0	92.0

3-8 样本、男性各年龄层、女性各年龄层的使用频率/ Frequencies of the Consumed Perfumed Soap by the Whole Sample, Age and Gender Groups

	人数 Number	一天 3 次或以上 3 times or over a day	一天 1~2 次 once or twice a day	两三天用 1 次 once 2 or 3 day	一周 1~2 次 once or twice a week	半个月 1 次或以下 once half a month or below
样本 Sample	599	31.9	55.3	6.0	6.3	0.5
男性 Male	301	28.2	59.1	6.6	6.0	0.0
16~24 岁 Age	64	39.1	50.0	3.1	7.8	0.0
25~34 岁 Age	91	25.3	61.5	8.8	4.4	0.0
35~44 岁 Age	77	24.7	58.4	10.4	6.5	0.0
45~54 岁 Age	45	26.7	64.4	4.4	4.4	0.0
55~60 岁 Age	24	25.0	66.7	0.0	8.3	0.0
女性 Female	298	35.6	51.3	5.4	6.7	1.0
16~24 岁 Age	60	43.3	43.3	5.0	8.3	0.0
25~34 岁 Age	90	37.8	51.1	6.7	4.4	0.0
35~44 岁 Age	74	33.8	50.0	5.4	8.1	2.7
45~54 岁 Age	49	32.7	57.1	4.1	4.1	2.0
55~60 岁 Age	25	20.0	64.0	4.0	12.0	0.0

3-9 选择该类商品的考虑因素/ Ranking of the Considerations in Purchasing

注：本题为多选题，合计百分比超过 100%（Multiple answers）

排名 Ranking	考虑因素 Considerations	人次 Person-time	百分比 Percent
1	有名的牌子 famous brand	247	41.3
2	价格适中 reasonable price	233	39.0
3	产品功用 product function	225	37.6
4	广告影响 influence of advertising	140	23.4
5	购买方便 easy to buy	120	20.1
6	别人推荐 introduced by other people	40	6.7
7	单位发的 offered by the working unit	26	4.3
8	包装吸引人 appealing package	25	4.2
9	有优惠条件 with preferential terms	15	2.5
10	其它 others	12	2.0

n=598

3-10 对产品功能的侧重方面/ Ranking of the Considerations about the Function of this Kind of Product

注：本题为多选题，合计百分比超过 100%（Multiple answers）

排名 Ranking	侧重方面 Items	人次 Person-time	百分比 Percent
1	气味好 pleasant smell	380	63.4
2	能杀菌 bacteria-killing ability	226	37.7
3	洗净力强 wash more cleanly	196	32.7
4	不刺激皮肤 harmless to my skin	175	29.2
5	适合自己肤质 suitable to my skin	120	20.0
6	泡沫多 rich foam	62	10.4
7	洗后不紧绷 without causing tightness	58	9.7
8	有美容功能 beautifying effect	32	5.3
9	有药用功能 medicine-like effect	14	2.3
10	其他 others	3	0.5

n=599

3-11 重度消费者的人口分布/ Demographics of the Heavy Consumers

	人数 Number	16-24 岁 Age	25-34 岁 Age	35-44 岁 Age	45-54 岁 Age	55-60 岁 Age
样本 Sample	522	20.9	30.5	24.1	16.3	8.2
男性 Male	263	21.7	30.0	24.3	15.6	8.4
一天 3 次或以上 3 times or over a day	85	29.4	27.1	22.4	14.1	7.1
一天 1～2 次 once or twice a day	178	18.0	31.5	25.3	16.3	9.0
女性 Female	259	20.1	30.9	23.9	17.0	8.1
一天 3 次或以上 3 times or over a day	106	24.5	32.1	23.5	15.1	4.7
一天 1～2 次 once or twice a day	153	17.0	30.1	24.2	18.3	10.5

3-12 不同消费者层的常用品牌/ The Most Frequently Used Brands by Market Segments

3-12-1 时尚流行指标/ Fads Popular Index

	人数 Number	第一品牌及百分比 1st / percent	第二品牌及百分比 2nd / percent	第三品牌及百分比 3rd / percent	第四品牌及百分比 4th / percent
样本 Sample	597	**舒肤佳 Safeguard(41.5)**	**力士 Lux(39.4)**	**三笑 Sanxiao(5.0)**	**夏士莲 Hazeline(4.0)**
平实生活指向 simple living orientation	339	舒肤佳 Safeguard(42.2)	力士 Lux(38.6)	三笑 Sanxiao(6.5)	夏士莲 Hazeline(3.8)
时尚流行指向 fashion orientation	258	舒肤佳 Safeguard(40.7)	力士 Lux(40.3)	夏士莲 Hazeline(4.3)	三笑 Sanxiao(3.1)

3-12-2 广告态度指标/ Advertising Attitude Index

	人数 Number	第一品牌及百分比 1st / percent	第二品牌及百分比 2nd / percent	第三品牌及百分比 3rd / percent	第四品牌及百分比 4th / percent
样本 Sample	595	**舒肤佳 Safeguard(41.7)**	**力士 Lux(39.2)**	**三笑 Sanxiao(5.0)**	**夏士莲 Hazeline(4.0)**
广告淡漠指向 indifferent orientation	183	力士 Lux(41.5)	舒肤佳 Safeguard(39.9)	三笑 Sanxiao(4.4)	纳爱斯 Nice(2.7) 夏士莲 Hazeline(2.7)
中间层 medium	334	舒肤佳 Safeguard(43.7)	力士 Lux(36.8)	三笑 Sanxiao(5.1)	夏士莲 Hazeline(4.5)
信赖广告指向 loyal orientation	78	力士 Lux(43.6)	舒肤佳 Safeguard(37.2)	三笑 Sanxiao(6.4)	夏士莲 Hazeline(5.1)

3-13 重度消费者的消费层构成/ The Composition of the Heavy Consumers

3-13-1 时尚流行指标/ Fads Popular Index

	人数 Number	平实生活指向 simple living orientation	时尚流行指向 fashion orientation
样本 Sample	520	54.8	45.2
一天 3 次或以上 3 times or over a day	190	50.0	50.0
一天 1～2 次 once or twice a day	330	57.6	42.4

3-13-2 广告态度指标/ Advertising Attitude Index

	人数 Number	广告淡漠指向 indifferent orientation	中间层 medium	信赖广告指向 loyal orientation
样本 Sample	520	29.4	57.5	13.1
一天 3 次或以上 3 times or over a day	191	27.2	62.8	9.9
一天 1～2 次 once or twice a day	329	30.7	54.4	14.9

● 沈阳 / Shenyang

3-1 最常用品牌排名/ Ranking of the Most Frequently Used Brands

排名 Brand Ranking	品牌 Brands	人数 Number	百分比 Percent
1	舒肤佳 Safeguard	249	41.6
2	力士 Lux	229	38.3
3	夏士莲 Hazeline	33	5.5
4	三笑 Sanxiao	21	3.5
5	纳爱斯 Nice	7	1.2

n=598

3-2 样本、男性各年龄层、女性各年龄层的常用品牌/ The Most Frequently Used Brands by the Whole Sample, Age and Gender Groups

	人数 Number	第一品牌及百分比 1st/ percent	第二品牌及百分比 2nd/ percent	第三品牌及百分比 3rd/ percent
样本 Sample	**598**	**舒肤佳 Safeguard(41.6)**	**力士 Lux(38.3)**	**夏士莲 Hazeline(5.5)**
男性 Male	**296**	**力士 Lux(41.9)** **舒肤佳 Safeguard(41.9)**	**夏士莲 Hazeline(4.4)**	**三笑 Sanxiao(2.7)**
16~24 岁 Age	63	舒肤佳 Safeguard(50.8)	力士 Lux(39.7)	三笑 Sanxiao(1.6) 上海药皂/硫磺香皂 Shanghai(1.6) 夏士莲 Hazeline(1.6) 飞天 Feitian(1.6)
25~34 岁 Age	88	舒肤佳 Safeguard(46.6)	力士 Lux(40.9)	纳爱斯 Nice(2.3) 三笑 Sanxiao(2.3) 夏士莲 Hazeline(2.3) 芦荟 Luhui(2.3)
35~44 岁 Age	75	力士 Lux(42.7)	舒肤佳 Safeguard(33.3)	三笑 Sanxiao(6.7) 夏士莲 Hazeline(6.7)
45~54 岁 Age	46	力士 Lux(43.5)	舒肤佳 Safeguard(39.1)	夏士莲 Hazeline(8.7)
55~60 岁 Age	24	力士 Lux(45.8)	舒肤佳 Safeguard(33.3)	LG(4.2) 纳爱斯 Nice(4.2) 上海檀香皂 Shanghai Wood Soap(4.2) 夏士莲 Hazeline(4.2)
女性 Female	**302**	**舒肤佳 Safeguard(41.4)**	**力士 Lux(34.8)**	**夏士莲 Hazeline(6.6)**
16~24 岁 Age	64	舒肤佳 Safeguard(46.9)	力士 Lux(31.3)	夏士莲 Hazeline(7.8)
25~34 岁 Age	90	舒肤佳 Safeguard(43.3)	力士 Lux(36.7)	三笑 Sanxiao(5.6) 夏士莲 Hazeline(5.6)
35~44 岁 Age	76	舒肤佳 Safeguard(39.5)	力士 Lux(28.9)	三笑 Sanxiao(6.6)
45~54 岁 Age	48	力士 Lux(39.6) 舒肤佳 Safeguard(39.6)	夏士莲 Hazeline(12.5)	两面针 Liangmianzhen(2.1) 纳爱斯 Nice(2.1) 玛丽莲 Malilian(2.1) 飞天 Feitian(2.1)
55~60 岁 Age	24	力士 Lux(45.8)	舒肤佳 Safeguard(29.2)	三笑 Sanxiao(8.3)

3-3 正在使用的品牌排名/ Ranking of the Brands Used Now

排名 Brand Ranking	品牌 Brands	人数 Number	百分比 Percent
1	舒肤佳 Safeguard	237	39.6
2	力士 Lux	216	36.1
3	夏士莲 Hazeline	38	6.4
4	三笑 Sanxiao	25	4.2
5	芦荟 Luhui	9	1.5
6	纳爱斯 Nice	5	0.8

n=598

3-4 品牌转换习惯/ Brand Habit in Consuming Perfumed Soap

	人数 Number	第一次使用该品牌 first use this brand	上一次也是这个牌子 used it last time	上一次不是这个牌子 not used it last time
样本 Sample	**596**	**7.2**	**78.7**	**14.1**
舒肤佳 Safeguard	237	3.8	82.3	13.9
力士 Lux	214	3.3	83.6	13.1
夏士莲 Hazeline	38	18.4	63.2	18.4
三笑 Sanxiao	25	8.0	80.0	12.0

3-5 下一次打算使用的品牌排名/ Ranking of the Brands to be Used Next Time

排名 Brand Ranking	品牌 Brands	人数 Number	百分比 Percent
1	舒肤佳 Safeguard	240	40.2
2	力士 Lux	213	35.7
3	夏士莲 Hazeline	42	7.0
4	三笑 Sanxiao	24	4.0
5	芦荟 Luhui	7	1.2
5	纳爱斯 Nice	7	1.2

n=597

3-6 样本、男性各年龄层、女性各年龄层是否是主要购买者/ Purchasers in the Household by the Whole Sample, Age and Gender Groups

	人数 Number	是 yes	不是 no
样本 Sample	601	59.4	40.6
男性 Male	299	35.1	64.9
16~24 岁 Age	64	28.1	71.9
25~34 岁 Age	89	40.4	59.6
35~44 岁 Age	76	34.2	65.8
45~54 岁 Age	46	32.6	67.4
55~60 岁 Age	24	41.7	58.3
女性 Female	302	83.4	16.6
16~24 岁 Age	64	64.1	35.9
25~34 岁 Age	90	92.2	7.8
35~44 岁 Age	76	93.4	6.6
45~54 岁 Age	48	79.2	20.8
55~60 岁 Age	24	79.2	20.8

3-7 样本、男性各年龄层、女性各年龄层的使用方式/ Ways of Using the Products by the Whole Sample, Age and Gender Groups

	人数 Number	个人专用 personal use	家人共用 all family members share
样本 Sample	599	9.8	90.2
男性 Male	297	12.5	87.5
16~24 岁 Age	63	20.6	79.4
25~34 岁 Age	88	10.2	89.8
35~44 岁 Age	76	13.2	86.8
45~54 岁 Age	46	8.7	91.3
55~60 岁 Age	24	4.2	95.8
女性 Female	302	7.3	92.7
16~24 岁 Age	64	21.9	78.1
25~34 岁 Age	90	2.2	97.8
35~44 岁 Age	76	3.9	96.1
45~54 岁 Age	48	2.1	97.9
55~60 岁 Age	24	8.3	91.7

3-8 样本、男性各年龄层、女性各年龄层的使用频率/ Frequencies of the Consumed Perfumed Soap by the Whole Sample, Age and Gender Groups

	人数 Number	一天 3 次或以上 3 times or over a day	一天 1~2 次 once or twice a day	两三天用 1 次 once 2 or 3 day	一周 1~2 次 once or twice a week	半个月 1 次或以下 once half a month or below
样本 Sample	598	44.5	53.0	1.7	0.8	0.0
男性 Male	296	39.9	58.8	1.0	0.3	0.0
16~24 岁 Age	63	52.4	46.0	0.0	1.6	0.0
25~34 岁 Age	88	43.2	54.5	2.3	0.0	0.0
35~44 岁 Age	75	36.0	62.7	1.3	0.0	0.0
45~54 岁 Age	46	32.6	67.4	0.0	0.0	0.0
55~60 岁 Age	24	20.8	79.2	0.0	0.0	0.0
女性 Female	302	49.0	47.4	2.3	1.3	0.0
16~24 岁 Age	64	54.7	39.1	3.1	3.1	0.0
25~34 岁 Age	90	52.2	45.6	1.1	1.1	0.0
35~44 岁 Age	76	43.4	52.6	2.6	1.3	0.0
45~54 岁 Age	48	54.2	45.8	0.0	0.0	0.0
55~60 岁 Age	24	29.2	62.5	8.3	0.0	0.0

3-9 选择该类商品的考虑因素/ Ranking of the Considerations in Purchasing

注：本题为多选题，合计百分比超过 100%（Multiple answers）

排名 Ranking	考虑因素 Considerations	人次 Person-time	百分比 Percent
1	价格适中 reasonable price	320	53.7
2	产品功用 product function	251	42.1
3	有名的牌子 famous brand	233	39.1
4	购买方便 easy to buy	140	23.5
5	广告影响 influence of advertising	106	17.8
6	别人推荐 introduced by other people	46	7.7
7	有优惠条件 with preferential terms	24	4.0
8	包装吸引人 appealing package	20	3.4
9	单位发的 offered by the working unit	12	2.0
10	其它 others	7	1.2

n=596

3-10 对产品功能的侧重方面/ Ranking of the Considerations about the Function of this Kind of Product

注：本题为多选题，合计百分比超过 100%（Multiple answers）

排名 Ranking	侧重方面 Items	人次 Person-time	百分比 Percent
1	气味好 pleasant smell	404	67.6
2	洗净力强 wash more cleanly	210	35.1
3	不刺激皮肤 harmless to my skin	207	34.6
4	能杀菌 bacteria-killing ability	194	32.4
5	适合自己肤质 suitable to my skin	137	22.9
6	泡沫多 rich foam	71	11.9
7	洗后不紧绷 without causing tightness	58	9.7
8	有美容功能 beautifying effect	40	6.7
9	有药用功能 medicine-like effect	11	1.8
10	其他 others	5	0.8

n=598

3-11 重度消费者的人口分布/ Demographics of the Heavy Consumers

	人数 Number	16-24 岁 Age	25-34 岁 Age	35-44 岁 Age	45-54 岁 Age	55-60 岁 Age
样本 Sample	583	20.9	29.8	25.2	16.1	7.9
男性 Male	292	21.2	29.5	25.3	15.8	8.2
一天 3 次或以上 3 times or over a day	118	28.0	32.2	22.9	12.7	4.2
一天 1～2 次 once or twice a day	174	16.7	27.6	27.0	17.8	10.9
女性 Female	291	20.6	30.2	25.1	16.5	7.6
一天 3 次或以上 3 times or over a day	148	23.6	31.8	22.3	17.6	4.7
一天 1～2 次 once or twice a day	143	17.5	28.7	28.0	15.4	10.5

3-12 不同消费者层的常用品牌/ The Most Frequently Used Brands by Market Segments

3-12-1 时尚流行指标/ Fads Popular Index

	人数 Number	第一品牌及百分比 1st/ percent	第二品牌及百分比 2nd/ percent	第三品牌及百分比 3rd/ percent	第四品牌及百分比 4th/ percent
样本 Sample	598	**舒肤佳 Safeguard(41.6)**	**力士 Lux(38.3)**	**夏士莲 Hazeline(5.5)**	**三笑 Sanxiao(3.5)**
平实生活指向 simple living orientation	289	舒肤佳 Safeguard(42.6)	力士 Lux(37.0)	夏士莲 Hazeline(4.5)	三笑 Sanxiao(3.8)
时尚流行指向 fashion orientation	309	舒肤佳 Safeguard(40.8)	力士 Lux(39.5)	夏士莲 Hazeline(6.5)	三笑 Sanxiao(3.2)

3-12-2 广告态度指标/ Advertising Attitude Index

	人数 Number	第一品牌及百分比 1st/ percent	第二品牌及百分比 2nd/ percent	第三品牌及百分比 3rd/ percent	第四品牌及百分比 4th/ percent
样本 Sample	598	**舒肤佳 Safeguard(41.6)**	**力士 Lux(38.3)**	**夏士莲 Hazeline(5.5)**	**三笑 Sanxiao(3.5)**
广告淡漠指向 indifferent orientation	170	舒肤佳 Safeguard(40.6)	力士 Lux(38.8)	三笑 Sanxiao(5.9)	夏士莲 Hazeline(5.3)
中间层 medium	353	舒肤佳 Safeguard(43.3)	力士 Lux(37.1)	夏士莲 Hazeline(4.0)	三笑 Sanxiao(2.5)
信赖广告指向 loyal orientation	75	力士 Lux(42.7)	舒肤佳 Safeguard(36.0)	夏士莲 Hazeline(13.3)	三笑 Sanxiao(2.7)

3-13 重度消费者的消费层构成/ The Composition of the Heavy Consumers

3-13-1 时尚流行指标/ Fads Popular Index

	人数 Number	平实生活指向 simple living orientation	时尚流行指向 fashion orientation
样本 Sample	**583**	**47.7**	**52.3**
一天 3 次或以上 3 times or over a day	266	48.5	51.5
一天 1～2 次 once or twice a day	317	47.0	53.0

3-13-2 广告态度指标/ Advertising Attitude Index

	人数 Number	广告淡漠指向 indifferent orientation	中间层 medium	信赖广告指向 loyal orientation
样本 Sample	**583**	**28.5**	**59.2**	**12.3**
一天 3 次或以上 3 times or over a day	266	25.9	64.7	9.4
一天 1～2 次 once or twice a day	317	30.6	54.6	14.8

4.沐浴液 / Bath Shampoo

● 北京 / Beijing

4-1 使用方式的比例/ Ways of Using Bath Shampoo

	人数 Number	百分比 Percent
个人专用 personal use	142	14.0
与家人共用 all family members share	423	41.8
不用 never use	446	44.1

n=1011

4-2 最常用品牌排名/ Ranking of the Most Frequently Used Brands

排名 Brand Ranking	品牌 Brands	人数 Number	百分比 Percent
1	力士 Lux	135	24.2
2	舒肤佳 Safeguard	107	19.1
3	六神 Liushen	94	16.8
4	花王碧柔 Biore	23	4.1
5	玉兰油 Oil of Olay	21	3.8
6	花 Fa	20	3.6
8	爽爽 Shuangshuang	17	3.0
9	安利 Amway	11	2.0
10	芦荟 Luhui	10	1.8
10	肤安 Fu'an	10	1.8
11	夏士莲 Hazeline	7	1.3
11	伊卡璐 Clairol	7	1.3

n=559

4-3 样本、男性各年龄层、女性各年龄层的常用品牌/ The Most Frequently Used Brands by the Whole Sample, Age and Gender Groups

	人数 Number	第一品牌及百分比 1st/ percent	第二品牌及百分比 2nd/ percent	第三品牌及百分比 3rd/ percent	第四品牌及百分比 4th/ percent
样本 Sample	559	**力士 Lux(24.2)**	**舒肤佳 Safeguard(19.1)**	**六神 Liushen(16.8)**	**花王碧柔 Biore(4.1)**
男性 Male	220	**力士 Lux(23.6)**	**舒肤佳 Safeguard(20.0)**	**六神 Liushen(15.0)**	
16~24 岁 Age	52	舒肤佳 Safeguard(26.9)	六神 Liushen(21.2)	力士 Lux(17.3)	
25~34 岁 Age	60	力士 Lux(26.7)	舒肤佳 Safeguard(20.0)	六神 Liushen(15.0)	花王碧柔 Biore(8.3)
35~44 岁 Age	53	力士 Lux(28.3)	舒肤佳 Safeguard(15.1)	六神 Liushen(9.4)	花王碧柔 Biore(7.5)
45~54 岁 Age	37	力士 Lux(21.6)	六神 Liushen(16.2)	舒肤佳 Safeguard(13.5)	爽爽 Shuangshuang(8.1) 玉兰油 Oil of Olay(8.1) 花 Fa(8.1)
55~60 岁 Age	18	舒肤佳 Safeguard(27.8)	力士 Lux(22.2)	六神 Liushen(11.1)	金威 Kingway(5.6) 玉兰油 Oil of Olay(5.6) 爽爽 Shuangshuang(5.6) 美加净 Maxam(5.6) 桃丽丝 Doris(5.6) 洁露 Jielu(5.6)
女性 Female	339	**力士 Lux(24.5)**	**舒肤佳 Safeguard(18.6)**	**六神 Liushen(18.0)**	**花 Fa(4.1)**
16~24 岁 Age	73	舒肤佳 Safeguard(28.8)	力士 Lux(19.2)	六神 Liushen(12.3)	玉兰油 Oil of Olay(6.8) 花 Fa(6.8)
25~34 岁 Age	117	力士 Lux(25.6)	六神 Liushen(21.4)	舒肤佳 Safeguard(17.9)	花 Fa(4.3)
35~44 岁 Age	82	力士 Lux(29.3)	六神 Liushen(14.6) 舒肤佳 Safeguard(14.6)	肤安 Fu'an(6.1) 爽爽 Shuangshuang(6.1)	花 Fa(3.7) 花王碧柔 Biore(3.7) 玉兰油 Oil of Olay(3.7) 大宝 Dabao(3.7)
45~54 岁 Age	48	力士 Lux(22.9)	六神 Liushen(18.8)	舒肤佳 Safeguard(16.7)	花王碧柔 Biore(6.3)
55~60 岁 Age	19	六神 Liushen(31.6)	力士 Lux(21.1)	花王碧柔 Biore(15.8)	花 Fa(5.3) 舒肤佳 Safeguard(5.3) 爽爽 Shuangshuang(5.3) 芦荟 Luhui(5.3) 迪莉斯 Dilisi(5.3)

4-4 正在使用的品牌排名/ Ranking of the Brands Used Now

排名 Brand Ranking	品牌 Brands	人数 Number	百分比 Percent
1	力士 Lux	126	22.6
2	六神 Liushen	96	17.2
3	舒肤佳 Safeguard	89	16.0
4	花 Fa	27	4.8
5	花王碧柔 Biore	25	4.5
6	玉兰油 Oil of Olay	20	3.6
7	爽爽 Shuangshuang	14	2.5
8	芦荟 Luhui	12	2.2
9	肤安 Fu'an	11	2.0
9	安利 Amway	11	2.0
10	夏士莲 Hazeline	9	1.6

n=557

4-5 品牌转换习惯/ Brand Habit in Consuming Bath Shampoo

	人数 Number	第一次使用该品牌 first use this brand	上一次也是这个牌子 used it last time	上一次不是这个牌子 not used it last time
样本 Sample	547	16.3	68.0	15.7
力士 Lux	124	8.9	75.8	15.3
六神 Liushen	95	15.8	70.5	13.7
舒肤佳 Safeguard	87	9.2	79.3	11.5
花 Fa	27	40.7	48.1	11.1
花王碧柔 Biore	24	29.2	66.7	4.2
玉兰油 Oil of Olay	20	20.0	65.0	15.0
爽爽 Shuangshuang	14	0.0	100.0	0.0
芦荟 Luhui	12	41.7	50.0	8.3
肤安 Fu'an	11	9.1	81.8	9.1
安利 Amway	11	18.2	72.7	9.1

4-6 下一次打算使用的品牌排名/ Ranking of the Brands to be Used Next Time

排名 Brand Ranking	品牌 Brands	人数 Number	百分比 Percent
1	力士 Lux	143	25.6
2	舒肤佳 Safeguard	113	20.3
3	六神 Liushen	71	12.7
4	玉兰油 Oil of Olay	24	4.3
5	花王碧柔 Biore	19	3.4
6	花 Fa	17	3.0
7	夏士莲 Hazeline	14	2.5
8	安利 Amway	11	2.0
9	爽爽 Shuangshuang	10	1.8
9	肤安 Fu'an	10	1.8

n=558

4-7 样本、 男性各年龄层、 女性各年龄层是否是主要购买者/ Purchasers in the Household by the Whole Sample, Age and Gender Groups

	人数 Number	是 yes	不是 no
样本 Sample	1008	35.1	64.9
男性 Male	502	16.3	83.7
16~24 岁 Age	105	16.2	83.8
25~34 岁 Age	151	15.9	84.1
35~44 岁 Age	130	16.2	83.8
45~54 岁 Age	77	16.9	83.1
55~60 岁 Age	39	17.9	82.1
女性 Female	506	53.8	46.2
16~24 岁 Age	103	29.6	70.4
25~34 岁 Age	150	68.7	31.3
35~44 岁 Age	123	57.7	42.3
45~54 岁 Age	84	56.0	44.0
55~60 岁 Age	41	46.3	53.7

4-8 样本、男性各年龄层、女性各年龄层的使用方式/ Ways of Using Bath Shampoo by the Whole Sample, Age and Gender Groups

	人数 Number	是个人专用 personal use	与家人共用 all family members share	不用 never use
样本 Sample	1011	14.0	41.8	44.1
男性 Male	503	8.2	36.2	55.7
16~24 岁 Age	104	12.5	37.5	50.0
25~34 岁 Age	151	9.3	30.5	60.3
35~44 岁 Age	131	3.8	38.2	58.0
45~54 岁 Age	77	7.8	41.6	50.6
55~60 岁 Age	40	7.5	37.5	55.0
女性 Female	508	19.9	47.4	32.7
16~24 岁 Age	108	23.1	44.4	32.4
25~34 岁 Age	150	30.0	48.7	21.3
35~44 岁 Age	124	14.5	51.6	33.9
45~54 岁 Age	84	9.5	48.8	41.7
55~60 岁 Age	42	11.9	35.7	52.4

4-9 样本、男性各年龄层、女性各年龄层的使用频率/ Frequencies of the Consumed Bath Shampoo by the Whole Sample, Age and Gender Groups

	人数 Number	天天用 daily	两三天用 1 次 once 2 or 3 days	一周 1~2 次 once or twice a week	半个月 1 次或以下 once half a month or below
样本 Sample	555	13.7	40.5	41.8	4.0
男性 Male	217	9.2	43.3	43.8	3.7
16~24 岁 Age	50	12.0	44.0	40.0	4.0
25~34 岁 Age	60	10.0	60.0	26.7	3.3
35~44 岁 Age	52	7.7	36.5	51.9	3.8
45~54 岁 Age	37	5.4	35.1	54.1	5.4
55~60 岁 Age	18	11.1	22.2	66.7	0.0
女性 Female	338	16.6	38.8	40.5	4.1
16~24 岁 Age	73	11.0	49.3	37.0	2.7
25~34 岁 Age	117	19.7	41.0	33.3	6.0
35~44 岁 Age	82	22.0	36.6	37.8	3.7
45~54 岁 Age	47	10.6	27.7	59.6	2.1
55~60 岁 Age	19	10.5	21.1	63.2	5.3

4-10 选择该类商品的考虑因素/ Ranking of the Considerations in Purchasing

注：本题为多选题，合计百分比超过 100%（Multiple answers）

排名 Ranking	考虑因素 Considerations	人次 Person-time	百分比 Percent
1	产品功用 product function	236	42.8
2	有名的牌子 famous brand	210	38.0
3	价格适中 reasonable price	192	34.8
4	单位发的 offered by the working unit	106	19.2
5	广告影响 influence of advertising	102	18.5
6	购买方便 easy to buy	76	13.8
7	别人推荐 introduced by other people	39	7.1
8	有优惠条件 with preferential terms	24	4.3
9	其它 others	12	2.2
10	包装吸引人 appealing package	11	2.0

n=552

4-11 对产品功能的侧重方面/ Ranking of the Considerations about the Function of this Kind of Product

注：本题为多选题，合计百分比超过 100%（Multiple answers）

排名 Ranking	侧重方面 Items	人次 Person-time	百分比 Percent
1	气味好 pleasant smell	363	65.9
2	滋润效果 nourishing effect	238	43.2
3	能杀菌 bacteria-killing ability	160	29.0
4	清洁力强 powerful cleaning	158	28.7
5	易于冲洗 easy to clean	137	24.9
6	止痒 itch-easing	107	19.4
7	有特殊功能 special function	32	5.8
8	其他 others	9	1.6

n=551

4-12 重度消费者的人口分布/ Demographics of the Heavy Consumers

	人数 Number	16-24 岁 Age	25-34 岁 Age	35-44 岁 Age	45-54 岁 Age	55-60 岁 Age
样本 Sample	301	23.9	37.5	23.6	11.0	4.0
男性 Male	114	24.6	36.8	20.2	13.2	5.3
天天用 daily	20	30.0	30.0	20.0	10.0	10.0
两三天用 1 次 once 2 or 3 days	94	23.4	38.3	20.2	13.8	4.3
女性 Female	187	23.5	38.0	25.7	9.6	3.2
天天用 daily	56	14.3	41.1	32.1	8.9	3.6
两三天用 1 次 once 2 or 3 days	131	27.5	36.6	22.9	9.9	3.1

4-13 不同消费者层的常用品牌/ The Most Frequently Used Brands by Market Segments

4-13-1 时尚流行指标/ Fads Popular Index

	人数 Number	第一品牌及百分比 1st / percent	第二品牌及百分比 2nd / percent	第三品牌及百分比 3rd / percent	第四品牌及百分比 4th / percent
样本 Sample	552	**力士 Lux(24.3)**	**舒肤佳 Safeguard(19.4)**	**六神 Liushen(16.5)**	**花王碧柔 Biore(4.2)**
平实生活指向 simple living orientation	235	力士 Lux(21.3)	舒肤佳 Safeguard(19.1)	六神 Liushen(18.3)	爽爽 Shuangshuang(4.7)
时尚流行指向 fashion orientation	317	力士 Lux(26.5)	舒肤佳 Safeguard(19.6)	六神 Liushen(15.1)	玉兰油 Oil of Olay(4.7)

4-13-2 广告态度指标/ Advertising Attitude Index

	人数 Number	第一品牌及百分比 1st / percent	第二品牌及百分比 2nd / percent	第三品牌及百分比 3rd / percent	第四品牌及百分比 4th / percent
样本 Sample	546	**力士 Lux(24.0)**	**舒肤佳 Safeguard(18.9)**	**六神 Liushen(17.2)**	**花王碧柔 Biore(4.2)**
广告淡漠指向 indifferent orientation	135	力士 Lux(25.2)	六神 Liushen(16.3)	舒肤佳 Safeguard(14.1)	花王碧柔 Biore(5.9)
中间层 medium	329	力士 Lux(21.9)	舒肤佳 Safeguard(20.1)	六神 Liushen(19.1)	花 Fa(4.0)
信赖广告指向 loyal orientation	82	力士 Lux(30.5)	舒肤佳 Safeguard(22.0)	六神 Liushen(11.0)	花王碧柔 Biore (4.9)

4-14 重度消费者的消费层构成/ The Composition of the Heavy Consumers

4-14-1 时尚流行指标/ Fads Popular Index

	人数 Number	平实生活指向 simple living orientation	时尚流行指向 fashion orientation
样本 Sample	299	38.8	61.2
天天用 daily	76	36.8	63.2
两三天用 1 次 once 2 or 3 days	223	39.5	60.5

4-14-2 广告态度指标/ Advertising Attitude Index

	人数 Number	广告淡漠指向 indifferent orientation	中间层 medium	信赖广告指向 loyal orientation
样本 Sample	293	25.6	57.7	16.7
天天用 daily	72	22.2	61.1	16.7
两三天用 1 次 once 2 or 3 days	22[illegible]	26.7	56.6	16.7

● 上海 / Shanghai

4-1 使用方式的比例/ Ways of Using Bath Shampoo

	人数 Number	百分比 Percent
个人专用 personal use	120	11.8
与家人共用 all family members share	295	29.1
不用 never use	599	59.1

n=1014

4-2 最常用品牌排名/ Ranking of the Most Frequently Used Brands

排名 Brand Ranking	品牌 Brands	人数 Number	百分比 Percent
1	力士 Lux	130	31.3
2	六神 Liushen	125	30.1
3	舒肤佳 Safeguard	38	9.2
4	强生 Johnson&Johnson	30	7.2
5	花王碧柔 Biore	13	3.1
6	安利 Amway	9	2.2
7	夏士莲 Hazeline	6	1.4
7	花 Fa	6	1.4
8	澎澎 Pengpeng	5	1.2
8	资生堂 Shiseido	5	1.2
9	雅蜜 Yami	4	1.0

n=415

4-3 样本、男性各年龄层、女性各年龄层的常用品牌/ The Most Frequently Used Brands by the Whole Sample, Age and Gender Groups

	人数 Number	第一品牌及百分比 1st/ percent	第二品牌及百分比 2nd/ percent	第三品牌及百分比 3rd/ percent
样本 Sample	**415**	**力士 Lux(31.3)**	**六神 Liushen(30.1)**	**舒肤佳 Safeguard(9.2)**
男性 Male	**165**	**力士 Lux(35.2)**	**六神 Liushen(30.9)**	**舒肤佳 Safeguard(10.3)**
16~24 岁 Age	39	六神 Liushen(46.2)	力士 Lux(35.9)	舒肤佳 Safeguard(12.8)
25~34 岁 Age	44	力士 Lux(45.5)	六神 Liushen(20.5)	强生 Johnson&Johnson(6.8)
35~44 岁 Age	44	力士 Lux(27.3)	六神 Liushen(25.0)	舒肤佳 Safeguard(13.6)
45~54 岁 Age	27	力士 Lux(40.7)	六神 Liushen(29.6)	舒肤佳 Safeguard(11.1)
55~60 岁 Age	11	六神 Liushen(45.5)	花王碧柔 Biore(9.1) 力士 Lux(9.1) 屈臣氏 Watson's(9.1) 舒肤佳 Safeguard(9.1) 资生堂 Shiseido(9.1) 丝华路 Sihualu(9.1)	
女性 Female	**250**	**六神 Liushen(29.6)**	**力士 Lux(28.8)**	**强生 Johnson&Johnson(9.2)**
16~24 岁 Age	58	力士 Lux(43.1)	六神 Liushen(20.7)	强生 Johnson&Johnson(12.1)
25~34 岁 Age	87	力士 Lux(28.7) 六神 Liushen(28.7)	舒肤佳 Safeguard(9.2) 强生 Johnson&Johnson(9.2)	花王碧柔 Biore(4.6)
35~44 岁 Age	60	六神 Liushen(33.3)	力士 Lux(26.7)	强生 Johnson&Johnson(10.0)
45~54 岁 Age	31	六神 Liushen(32.3)	力士 Lux(12.9) 舒肤佳 Safeguard(12.9)	花王碧柔 Biore(6.5) 樱雪 Enaer(6.5)
55~60 岁 Age	14	六神 Liushen(50.0)	力士 Lux(14.3)	强生 Johnson&Johnson(7.1) 夏士莲 Hazeline(7.1) 雅蜜 Yami(7.1) 澎澎 Pengpeng(7.1) 桂花 Guihua(7.1)

4-4 正在使用的品牌排名/ Ranking of the Brands Used Now

排名 Brand Ranking	品牌 Brands	人数 Number	百分比 Percent
1	六神 Liushen	116	28.0
2	力士 Lux	112	27.0
3	舒肤佳 Safeguard	38	9.2
4	强生 Johnson&Johnson	32	7.7
5	澎澎 Pengpeng	16	3.9
6	花王碧柔 Biore	12	2.9
7	安利 Amway	8	1.9
8	伊卡璐 Clairol	7	1.7
8	夏士莲 Hazeline	7	1.7
9	资生堂 Shiseido	6	1.4
9	花 Fa	6	1.4

n=415

4-5 品牌转换习惯/ Brand Habit in Consuming Bath Shampoo

	人数 Number	第一次使用该品牌 first use this brand	上一次也是这个牌子 used it last time	上一次不是这个牌子 not used it last time
样本 Sample	415	11.3	74.7	14.0
六神 Liushen	116	8.6	80.2	11.2
力士 Lux	112	5.4	83.0	11.6
舒肤佳 Safeguard	38	2.6	81.6	15.8
强生 Johnson&Johnson	32	9.4	75.0	15.6
澎澎 Pengpeng	16	56.3	25.0	18.8
花王碧柔 Biore	12	8.3	83.3	8.3
安利 Amway	8	0.0	87.5	12.5
伊卡璐 Clairol	7	0.0	57.1	42.9
夏士莲 Hazeline	7	0.0	85.7	14.3

4-6 下一次打算使用的品牌排名/ Ranking of the Brands to be Used Next Time

排名 Brand Ranking	品牌 Brands	人数 Number	百分比 Percent
1	力士 Lux	119	28.7
2	六神 Liushen	114	27.5
3	舒肤佳 Safeguard	33	8.0
4	强生 Johnson&Johnson	28	6.7
5	澎澎 Pengpeng	17	4.1
6	花王碧柔 Biore	16	3.9
7	资生堂 Shiseido	11	2.7
8	夏士莲 Hazeline	8	1.9
9	多芬 Dove	6	1.4
9	伊卡璐 Clairol	6	1.4
10	安利 Amway	5	1.2
10	花王 Kao	5	1.2
10	花 Fa	5	1.2

n=415

4-7 样本、男性各年龄层、女性各年龄层是否是主要购买者/ Purchasers in the Household by the Whole Sample, Age and Gender Groups

	人数 Number	是 yes	不是 no
样本 Sample	1014	31.6	68.4
男性 Male	509	16.3	83.7
16~24 岁 Age	109	14.7	85.3
25~34 岁 Age	146	18.5	81.5
35~44 岁 Age	130	14.6	85.4
45~54 岁 Age	85	17.6	82.4
55~60 岁 Age	39	15.4	84.6
女性 Female	505	46.9	53.1
16~24 岁 Age	108	35.2	64.8
25~34 岁 Age	144	58.3	41.7
35~44 岁 Age	130	51.5	48.5
45~54 岁 Age	82	40.2	59.8
55~60 岁 Age	41	36.6	63.4

4-8 样本、男性各年龄层、女性各年龄层的使用方式/ Ways of Using Bath Shampoo by the Whole Sample, Age and Gender Groups

	人数 Number	是个人专用 personal use	与家人共用 all family members share	不用 never use
样本 Sample	1014	11.8	29.1	59.1
男性 Male	509	6.9	25.5	67.6
16~24 岁 Age	109	11.9	23.9	64.2
25~34 岁 Age	146	11.6	18.5	69.9
35~44 岁 Age	130	3.1	30.8	66.2
45~54 岁 Age	85	1.2	30.6	68.2
55~60 岁 Age	39	0.0	28.2	71.8
女性 Female	505	16.8	32.7	50.5
16~24 岁 Age	108	28.7	25.0	46.3
25~34 岁 Age	144	28.5	31.9	39.6
35~44 岁 Age	130	6.9	39.2	53.8
45~54 岁 Age	82	3.7	34.1	62.2
55~60 岁 Age	41	2.4	31.7	65.9

4-9 样本、男性各年龄层、女性各年龄层的使用频率/ Frequencies of the Consumed Bath Shampoo by the Whole Sample, Age and Gender Groups

	人数 Number	天天用 daily	两三天用 1 次 once 2 or 3 days	一周 1~2 次 once or twice a week	半个月 1 次或以下 once half a month or below
样本 Sample	413	22.8	44.8	29.1	3.4
男性 Male	164	23.2	45.7	27.4	3.7
16~24 岁 Age	39	12.8	51.3	33.3	2.6
25~34 岁 Age	44	18.2	47.7	29.5	4.5
35~44 岁 Age	43	23.3	51.2	20.9	4.7
45~54 岁 Age	27	48.1	25.9	25.9	0.0
55~60 岁 Age	11	18.2	45.5	27.3	9.1
女性 Female	249	22.5	44.2	30.1	3.2
16~24 岁 Age	58	13.8	58.6	24.1	3.4
25~34 岁 Age	87	20.7	40.2	33.3	5.7
35~44 岁 Age	60	25.0	45.0	28.3	1.7
45~54 岁 Age	31	41.9	29.0	29.0	0.0
55~60 岁 Age	13	15.4	38.5	46.2	0.0

4-10 选择该类商品的考虑因素/ Ranking of the Considerations in Purchasing

注：本题为多选题，合计百分比超过 100%（Multiple answers）

排名 Ranking	考虑因素 Considerations	人次 Person-time	百分比 Percent
1	有名的牌子 famous brand	176	42.4
2	产品功用 product function	170	41.0
3	价格适中 reasonable price	147	35.4
4	广告影响 influence of advertising	96	23.1
5	购买方便 easy to buy	67	16.1
6	单位发的 offered by the working unit	41	9.9
7	别人推荐 introduced by other people	40	9.6
8	有优惠条件 with preferential terms	18	4.3
9	包装吸引人 appealing package	14	3.4
10	其它 others	6	1.4

n=415

4-11 对产品功能的侧重方面/ Ranking of the Considerations about the Function of this Kind of Product

注：本题为多选题，合计百分比超过 100%（Multiple answers）

排名 Ranking	侧重方面 Items	人次 Person-time	百分比 Percent
1	气味好 pleasant smell	263	63.5
2	滋润效果 nourishing effect	179	43.2
3	能杀菌 bacteria-killing ability	129	31.2
4	易于冲洗 easy to clean	120	29.0
5	清洁力强 powerful cleaning	105	25.4
6	止痒 itch-easing	83	20.0
7	有特殊功能 special function	21	5.1
8	其他 others	9	2.2

n=414

4-12 重度消费者的人口分布/ Demographics of the Heavy Consumers

	人数 Number	16-24 岁 Age	25-34 岁 Age	35-44 岁 Age	45-54 岁 Age	55-60 岁 Age
样本 Sample	279	24.0	29.4	26.5	15.1	5.0
男性 Male	113	22.1	25.7	28.3	17.7	6.2
天天用 daily	38	13.2	21.1	26.3	34.2	5.3
两三天用 1 次 once 2 or 3 days	75	26.7	28.0	29.3	9.3	6.7
女性 Female	166	25.3	31.9	25.3	13.3	4.2
天天用 daily	56	14.3	32.1	26.8	23.2	3.6
两三天用 1 次 once 2 or 3 days	110	30.9	31.8	24.5	8.2	4.5

4-13 不同消费者层的常用品牌/ The Most Frequently Used Brands by Market Segments

4-13-1 时尚流行指标/ Fads Popular Index

	人数 Number	第一品牌及百分比 1st / percent	第二品牌及百分比 2nd / percent	第三品牌及百分比 3rd / percent	第四品牌及百分比 4th / percent
样本 Sample	412	**力士 Lux（31.6)**	**六神 Liushen（29.9)**	**舒肤佳 Safeguard（9.0)**	**强生 Johnson&Johnson（7.3)**
平实生活指向 simple living orientation	159	六神 Liushen（39.6)	力士 Lux（22.6)	舒肤佳 Safeguard（10.7)	强生 Johnson&Johnson（4.4)
时尚流行指向 fashion orientation	253	力士 Lux（37.2)	六神 Liushen（23.7)	强生 Johnson&Johnson（9.1)	舒肤佳 Safeguard（7.9)

4-13-2 广告态度指标/ Advertising Attitude Index

	人数 Number	第一品牌及百分比 1st / percent	第二品牌及百分比 2nd / percent	第三品牌及百分比 3rd / percent	第四品牌及百分比 4th / percent
样本 Sample	410	**力士 Lux（31.5)**	**六神 Liushen（30.0)**	**舒肤佳 Safeguard（9.0)**	**强生 Johnson&Johnson（7.3)**
广告淡漠指向 indifferent orientation	96	六神 Liushen（40.6)	力士 Lux（16.7)	强生 Johnson&Johnson（9.4)	舒肤佳 Safeguard（5.2)
中间层 medium	244	力士 Lux（38.5)	六神 Liushen（27.0)	舒肤佳 Safeguard（8.6)	强生 Johnson&Johnson（7.0)
信赖广告指向 loyal orientation	70	力士 Lux（27.1)	六神 Liushen（25.7)	舒肤佳 Safeguard（15.7)	强生 Johnson&Johnson（5.7)

4-14 重度消费者的消费层构成/ The Composition of the Heavy Consumers

4-14-1 时尚流行指标/ Fads Popular Index

	人数 Number	平实生活指向 simple living orientation	时尚流行指向 fashion orientation
样本 Sample	276	35.5	64.5
天天用 daily	93	31.2	68.8
两三天用1次 once 2or 3 days	183	37.7	62.3

4-14-2 广告态度指标/ Advertising Attitude Index

	人数 Number	广告淡漠指向 indifferent orientation	中间层 medium	信赖广告指向 loyal orientation
样本 Sample	275	21.5	59.3	19.3
天天用 daily	94	25.5	54.3	20.2
两三天用1次 once 2or 3 days	181	19.3	61.9	18.8

● 广州 / Guangzhou

4-1 使用方式的比例/ Ways of Using Bath Shampoo

	人数 Number	百分比 Percent
个人专用 personal use	128	12.4
与家人共用 all family members share	597	57.7
不用 never use	309	29.9

n=1034

4-2 最常用品牌排名/ Ranking of the Most Frequently Used Brands

排名 Brand Ranking	品牌 Brands	人数 Number	百分比 Percent
1	肤安 Fuan	76	10.5
2	强生 Johnson&Johnson	74	10.2
3	澳雪 Aoxue	73	10.1
4	力士 Lux	51	7.1
4	花世界 Venic	51	7.1
5	舒肤佳 Safeguard	49	6.8
6	樱雪 Enaer	29	4.0
7	花王 Kao	26	3.6
7	金威 Kingway	26	3.6
8	六神 Liushen	20	2.8
9	多芬 Dove	19	2.6
10	花王碧柔 Biore	16	2.2

n=723

4-3 样本、男性各年龄层、女性各年龄层的常用品牌/ The Most Frequently Used Brands by the Whole Sample, Age and Gender Groups

	人数 Number	第一品牌及百分比 1st/ percent	第二品牌及百分比 2nd/ percent	第三品牌及百分比 3rd/ percent
样本 Sample	723	**肤安 Fuan(10.5)**	**强生 Johnson&Johnson(10.2)**	**澳雪 Aoxue(10.1)**
男性 Male	307	**肤安 Fuan(13.0)**	**澳雪 Aoxue(11.7)**	**力士 Lux(10.7)**
16~24 岁 Age	75	肤安 Fuan(17.3)	舒肤佳 Safeguard(12.0)	力士 Lux(9.3)
25~34 岁 Age	93	澳雪 Aoxue(12.9) 力士 Lux(12.9) 舒肤佳 Safeguard(12.9)	肤安 Fuan(9.7)	花世界 Venic(7.5)
35~44 岁 Age	81	澳雪 Aoxue(14.8)	力士 Lux(11.1) 强生 Johnson&Johnson(11.1)	花世界 Venic(9.9)
45~54 岁 Age	38	肤安 Fuan(23.7)	舒肤佳 Safeguard(10.5)	澳雪 Aoxue(7.9)
55~60 岁 Age	20	澳雪 Aoxue(25.0)	力士 Lux(15.0) 花世界 Venic(15.0)	肤安 Fuan(10.0) 六神 Liushen(10.0)
女性 Female	416	**强生 Johnson&Johnson(13.2)**	**澳雪 Aoxue(8.9)**	**肤安 Fuan(8.7)**
16~24 岁 Age	95	强生 Johnson&Johnson(26.3)	澳雪 Aoxue(11.6)	樱雪 Enaer(7.4)
25~34 岁 Age	125	强生 Johnson&Johnson(11.2)	花世界 Venic(8.8)	肤安 Fuan(8.0)
35~44 岁 Age	117	肤安 Fuan(9.4)	澳雪 Aoxue(8.5)	强生 Johnson&Johnson(7.7)
45~54 岁 Age	56	澳雪 Aoxue(12.5)	肤安 Fuan(10.7)	强生 Johnson&Johnson(7.1) 舒肤佳 Safeguard(7.1) 花王 Kao(7.1)
55~60 岁 Age	23	肤安 Fuan(13.0) 强生 Johnson&Johnson(13.0)	六神 Liushen(8.7) 花世界 Venic(8.7) 舒肤佳 Safeguard(8.7) 金威 Kingway(8.7)	卡妮 Kanei(4.3) 沐歌 Skin's Song(4.3) 健康 Jiankang(4.3) 樱雪 Enaer(4.3) 花王碧柔 Biore(4.3) 澳雪 Aoxue(4.3) 花王 Kao(4.3)

4-4 正在使用的品牌排名/ Ranking of the Brands Used Now

排名 Brand Ranking	品牌 Brands	人数 Number	百分比 Percent
1	澳雪 Aoxue	93	12.8
2	强生 Johnson&Johnson	69	9.5
3	肤安 Fuan	68	9.4
4	花世界 Venic	58	8.0
5	舒肤佳 Safeguard	46	6.3
6	力士 Lux	44	6.1
7	樱雪 Enaer	29	4.0
8	花王 Kao	28	3.9
9	金威 Kingway	23	3.2
10	艳宝 Yanbao	19	2.6
10	多芬 Dove	19	2.6

n=725

4-5 品牌转换习惯/ Brand Habit in Consuming Bath Shampoo

	人数 Number	第一次使用该品牌 first use this brand	上一次也是这个牌子 used it last time	上一次不是这个牌子 not used it last time
样本 Sample	723	16.9	62.4	20.7
澳雪 Aoxue	93	16.1	57.0	26.9
强生 Johnson&Johnson	69	5.8	78.3	15.9
肤安 Fuan	68	10.3	61.8	27.9
花世界 Venic	58	15.5	62.1	22.4
舒肤佳 Safeguard	46	8.7	78.3	13.0
力士 Lux	44	11.4	70.5	18.2
樱雪 Enaer	29	31.0	55.2	13.8
花王 Kao	28	14.3	71.4	14.3
金威 Kingway	23	34.8	52.2	13.0

4-6 下一次打算使用的品牌排名/ Ranking of the Brands to be Used Next Time

排名 Brand Ranking	品牌 Brands	人数 Number	百分比 Percent
1	强生 Johnson&Johnson	69	9.5
2	肤安 Fuan	68	9.4
3	澳雪 Aoxue	67	9.3
4	花世界 Venic	59	8.1
5	力士 Lux	58	8.0
6	舒肤佳 Safeguard	46	6.4
7	樱雪 Enaer	29	4.0
8	花王 Kao	28	3.9
9	多芬 Dove	25	3.5
10	艾诗 Enchanteur	17	2.3

n=724

4-7 样本、男性各年龄层、女性各年龄层是否是主要购买者/ Purchasers in the Household by the Whole Sample, Age and Gender Groups

	人数 Number	是 yes	不是 no
样本 Sample	**1033**	**48.1**	**51.9**
男性 Male	**498**	**31.7**	**68.3**
16~24 岁 Age	106	25.5	74.5
25~34 岁 Age	150	31.3	68.7
35~44 岁 Age	127	38.6	61.4
45~54 岁 Age	73	27.4	72.6
55~60 岁 Age	42	35.7	64.3
女性 Female	**535**	**63.4**	**36.6**
16~24 岁 Age	112	42.9	57.1
25~34 岁 Age	158	70.3	29.7
35~44 岁 Age	137	78.8	21.2
45~54 岁 Age	87	57.5	42.5
55~60 岁 Age	41	53.7	46.3

4-8 样本、男性各年龄层、女性各年龄层的使用方式/ Ways of Using Bath Shampoo by the Whole Sample, Age and Gender Groups

	人数 Number	是个人专用 personal use	与家人共用 all family members share	不用 never use
样本 Sample	**1034**	**12.4**	**57.7**	**29.9**
男性 Male	**499**	**9.2**	**52.3**	**38.5**
16~24 岁 Age	106	12.3	58.5	29.2
25~34 岁 Age	150	13.3	48.7	38.0
35~44 岁 Age	127	3.9	59.8	36.2
45~54 岁 Age	73	6.8	45.2	47.9
55~60 岁 Age	43	7.0	39.5	53.5
女性 Female	**535**	**15.3**	**62.8**	**21.9**
16~24 岁 Age	112	25.9	58.9	15.2
25~34 岁 Age	158	13.9	65.8	20.3
35~44 岁 Age	137	11.7	73.7	14.6
45~54 岁 Age	87	13.8	51.7	34.5
55~60 岁 Age	41	7.3	48.8	43.9

4-9 样本、男性各年龄层、女性各年龄层的使用频率/ Frequencies of the Consumed Bath Shampoo by the Whole Sample, Age and Gender Groups

	人数 Number	天天用 daily	两三天用 1 次 once 2 or 3 days	一周 1~2 次 once or twice a week	半个月 1 次或以下 once half a month or below
样本 Sample	723	85.5	9.8	3.9	0.8
男性 Male	306	84.3	11.4	3.3	1.0
16~24 岁 Age	74	83.8	12.2	2.7	1.4
25~34 岁 Age	93	83.9	11.8	2.2	2.2
35~44 岁 Age	81	81.5	12.3	6.2	0.0
45~54 岁 Age	38	89.5	7.9	2.6	0.0
55~60 岁 Age	20	90.0	10.0	0.0	0.0
女性 Female	417	86.3	8.6	4.3	0.7
16~24 岁 Age	95	87.4	8.4	4.2	0.0
25~34 岁 Age	126	86.5	9.5	4.0	0.0
35~44 岁 Age	116	86.2	9.5	4.3	0.0
45~54 岁 Age	57	82.5	7.0	5.3	5.3
55~60 岁 Age	23	91.3	4.3	4.3	0.0

4-10 选择该类商品的考虑因素/ Ranking of the Considerations in Purchasing

注：本题为多选题，合计百分比超过 100%（Multiple answers）

排名 Ranking	考虑因素 Considerations	人次 Person-time	百分比 Percent
1	产品功用 product function	331	45.8
2	价格适中 reasonable price	328	45.4
3	有名的牌子 famous brand	266	36.8
4	购买方便 easy to buy	147	20.3
5	广告影响 influence of advertising	127	17.6
6	别人推荐 introduced by other people	70	9.7
7	有优惠条件 with preferential terms	58	8.0
8	包装吸引人 appealing package	46	6.4
9	单位发的 offered by the working unit	17	2.4
10	其它 others	13	1.8

n=723

4-11 对产品功能的侧重方面/ Ranking of the Considerations about the Function of this Kind of Product

注：本题为多选题，合计百分比超过 100%（Multiple answers）

排名 Ranking	侧重方面 Items	人次 Person-time	百分比 Percent
1	气味好 pleasant smell	457	63.3
2	滋润效果 nourishing effect	339	47.0
3	能杀菌 bacteria-killing ability	226	31.3
4	清洁力强 powerful cleaning	194	26.9
5	止痒 itch-easing	186	25.8
6	易于冲洗 easy to clean	155	21.5
7	有特殊功能 special function	29	4.0
8	其他 others	4	0.6

n=722

4-12 重度消费者的人口分布/ Demographics of the Heavy Consumers

	人数 Number	16-24 岁 Age	25-34 岁 Age	35-44 岁 Age	45-54 岁 Age	55-60 岁 Age
样本 Sample	689	23.5	30.5	27.1	12.8	6.1
男性 Male	293	24.2	30.4	25.9	12.6	6.8
天天用 daily	258	24.0	30.2	25.6	13.2	7.0
两三天用 1 次 once 2 or 3 days	35	25.7	31.4	28.6	8.6	5.7
女性 Female	396	23.0	30.6	28.0	12.9	5.6
天天用 daily	360	23.1	30.3	27.8	13.1	5.8
两三天用 1 次 once 2 or 3 days	36	22.2	33.3	30.6	11.1	2.8

4-13 不同消费者层的常用品牌/ The Most Frequently Used Brands by Market Segments

4-13-1 时尚流行指标/ Fads Popular Index

	人数 Number	第一品牌及百分比 1st / percent	第二品牌及百分比 2nd / percent	第三品牌及百分比 3rd / percent	第四品牌及百分比 4th / percent
样本 Sample	716	**肤安 Fuan(10.6)**	**强生 Johnson&Johnson(10.3)**	**澳雪 Aoxue(10.2)**	**花世界 Venic(7.1)**
平实生活指向 simple living orientation	345	肤安 Fuan(9.9)	澳雪 Aoxue(9.6)	强生 Johnson&Johnson(9.3)	花世界 Venic(8.1)
时尚流行指向 fashion orientation	371	肤安 Fuan(11.3) 强生 Johnson&Johnson(11.3)	澳雪 Aoxue(10.8)	力士 Lux(7.3)	舒肤佳 Safeguard(6.5)

4-13-2 广告态度指标/ Advertising Attitude Index

	人数 Number	第一品牌及百分比 1st / percent	第二品牌及百分比 2nd / percent	第三品牌及百分比 3rd / percent	第四品牌及百分比 4th / percent
样本 Sample	712	**肤安 Fuan(10.4)**	**强生 Johnson&Johnson(10.1)**	**澳雪 Aoxue(10.0)**	**花世界 Venic(7.2)** **力士 Lux(7.2)**
广告淡漠指向 indifferent orientation	224	肤安 Fuan(11.2)	强生 Johnson&Johnson(9.8)	澳雪 Aoxue(8.9)	力士 Lux(8.5)
中间层 medium	415	澳雪 Aoxue(10.1)	肤安 Fuan(9.6)	强生 Johnson&Johnson(8.9)	舒肤佳 Safeguard(8.0)
信赖广告指向 loyal orientation	73	强生 Johnson&Johnson(17.8)	澳雪 Aoxue(12.3) 肤安 Fuan(12.3)	花世界 Venic(9.6) 舒肤佳 Safeguard(9.6)	六神 Liushen(5.5) 力士 Lux(5.5)

4-14 重度消费者的消费层构成/ The Composition of the Heavy Consumers

4-14-1 时尚流行指标/ Fads Popular Index

	人数 Number	平实生活指向 simple living orientation	时尚流行指向 fashion orientation
样本 Sample	**683**	**47.6**	**52.4**
天天用 daily	612	46.7	53.3
两三天用 1 次 once 2 or 3 days	71	54.9	45.1

4-14-2 广告态度指标/ Advertising Attitude Index

	人数 Number	广告淡漠指向 indifferent orientation	中间层 medium	信赖广告指向 loyal orientation
样本 Sample	**678**	**31.6**	**58.1**	**10.3**
天天用 daily	607	31.5	58.3	10.2
两三天用 1 次 once 2 or 3 days	71	32.4	56.3	11.3

● 重庆 / Chongqing

4-1 使用方式的比例/ Ways of Using Bath Shampoo

	人数 Number	百分比 Percent
个人专用 personal use	31	5.0
与家人共用 all family members share	85	13.6
不用 never use	507	81.4

n=623

4-2 最常用品牌排名/ Ranking of the Most Frequently Used Brands

排名 Brand Ranking	品牌 Brands	人数 Number	百分比 Percent
1	力士 Lux	27	23.3
1	舒肤佳 Safeguard	27	23.3
2	六神 Liushen	19	16.4
3	强生 Johnson&Johnson	4	3.4
3	夏士莲 Hazeline	4	3.4
4	屈臣氏 Watson's	3	2.6
5	雅芳 Avon	2	1.7
5	蜀秀 Shuxiu	2	1.7

n=116

4-3 样本、男性各年龄层、女性各年龄层的常用品牌/ The Most Frequently Used Brands by the Whole Sample, Age and Gender Groups

	人数 Number	第一品牌及百分比 1st/ percent	第二品牌及百分比 2nd/ percent	第三品牌及百分比 3rd/ percent
样本 Sample	116	**力士 Lux(23.3)** **舒肤佳 Safeguard(23.3)**	**六神 Liushen(16.4)**	**强生 Johnson&Johnson(3.4)** **夏士莲 Hazeline(3.4)**
男性 Male	43	**力士 Lux(27.9)**	**舒肤佳 Safeguard(23.3)**	**六神 Liushen(11.6)**
16~24 岁 Age	5	力士 Lux(60.0)	舒肤佳 Safeguard(20.0) 夏士莲 Hazeline(20.0)	
25~34 岁 Age	16	舒肤佳 Safeguard(37.5)	力士 Lux(18.8)	六神 Liushen(12.5)
35~44 岁 Age	8	舒肤佳 Safeguard(37.5)	力士 Lux(25.0) 六神 Liushen(25.0)	
45~54 岁 Age	8	力士 Lux(25.0)	卡妮 Kanei(12.5) 六神 Liushen(12.5) 天葆丽 Tianbaoli(12.5) 美丝维 E 香浴 Meisiwei E(12.5)	
55~60 岁 Age	6	力士 Lux(33.3)	强生 Johnson&Johnson(16.7) 屈臣氏 Watson's(16.7) 雨水 Yushui(16.7) 蜀秀 Shuxiu(16.7)	
女性 Female	73	**舒肤佳 Safeguard(23.3)**	**力士 Lux(20.5)**	**六神 Liushen(19.2)**
16~24 岁 Age	21	舒肤佳 Safeguard(33.3)	力士 Lux(14.3)	六神 Liushen(9.5) 雅芳 Avon(9.5)
25~34 岁 Age	31	六神 Liushen(29.0)	力士 Lux(19.4) 舒肤佳 Safeguard(19.4)	强生 Johnson&Johnson(9.7)
35~44 岁 Age	11	舒肤佳 Safeguard(36.4)	六神 Liushen(18.2)	力士 Lux(9.1) 夏士莲 Hazeline(9.1) 雅蜜 Yami(9.1) 桃花雨 Taohuayu(9.1)
45~54 岁 Age	9	力士 Lux(44.4)	六神 Liushen(11.1) 夏士莲 Hazeline(11.1) 阿迪达斯 adidas(11.1) 桑瑞 Sangrui(11.1)	
55~60 岁 Age	1	力士 Lux(100.0)		

4-4 正在使用的品牌排名/ Ranking of the Brands Used Now

排名 Brand Ranking	品牌 Brands	人数 Number	百分比 Percent
1	力士 Lux	30	25.9
2	舒肤佳 Safeguard	24	20.7
3	六神 Liushen	18	15.5
4	强生 Johnson&Johnson	4	3.4
5	屈臣氏 Watson's	3	2.6
5	夏士莲 Hazeline	3	2.6

n=116

4-5 品牌转换习惯/ Brand Habit in Consuming Bath Shampoo

	人数 Number	第一次使用该品牌 first use this brand	上一次也是这个牌子 used it last time	上一次不是这个牌子 not used it last time
样本 Sample	116	**19.0**	**65.5**	**15.5**
力士 Lux	30	23.3	53.3	23.3
舒肤佳 Safeguard	24	0.0	83.3	16.7
六神 Liushen	18	11.1	72.2	16.7
强生 Johnson&Johnson	4	0.0	100.0	0.0
屈臣氏 Watson's	3	0.0	66.7	33.3
夏士莲 Hazeline	3	33.3	66.7	0.0

4-6 下一次打算使用的品牌排名/ Ranking of the Brands to be Used Next Time

排名 Brand Ranking	品牌 Brands	人数 Number	百分比 Percent
1	力士 Lux	27	23.3
2	舒肤佳 Safeguard	25	21.6
3	六神 Liushen	13	11.2
4	强生 Johnson&Johnson	5	4.3
5	夏士莲 Hazeline	3	2.6
5	屈臣氏 Watson's	3	2.6
5	花王碧柔 Biore	3	2.6

n=116

4-7 样本、 男性各年龄层、 女性各年龄层是否是主要购买者/ Purchasers in the Household by the Whole Sample, Age and Gender Groups

	人数 Number	是 yes	不是 no
样本 Sample	623	16.5	83.5
男性 Male	314	8.6	91.4
16~24 岁 Age	64	4.7	95.3
25~34 岁 Age	93	10.8	89.2
35~44 岁 Age	75	5.3	94.7
45~54 岁 Age	54	9.3	90.7
55~60 岁 Age	28	17.9	82.1
女性 Female	309	24.6	75.4
16~24 岁 Age	64	21.9	78.1
25~34 岁 Age	90	40.0	60.0
35~44 岁 Age	73	19.2	80.8
45~54 岁 Age	59	16.9	83.1
55~60 岁 Age	23	8.7	91.3

4-8 样本、男性各年龄层、女性各年龄层的使用方式/ Ways of Using Bath Shampoo by the Whole Sample, Age and Gender Groups

	人数 Number	是个人专用 personal use	与家人共用 all family members share	不用 never use
样本 Sample	623	5.0	13.6	81.4
男性 Male	314	1.9	11.8	86.3
16~24 岁 Age	64	0.0	7.8	92.2
25~34 岁 Age	93	2.2	15.1	82.8
35~44 岁 Age	75	0.0	10.7	89.3
45~54 岁 Age	54	5.6	9.3	85.2
55~60 岁 Age	28	3.6	17.9	78.6
女性 Female	309	8.1	15.5	76.4
16~24 岁 Age	64	15.6	17.2	67.2
25~34 岁 Age	90	13.3	21.1	65.6
35~44 岁 Age	73	2.7	12.3	84.9
45~54 岁 Age	59	1.7	13.6	84.7
55~60 岁 Age	23	0.0	4.3	95.7

4-9 样本、男性各年龄层、女性各年龄层的使用频率/ Frequencies of the Consumed Bath Shampoo by the Whole Sample, Age and Gender Groups

	人数 Number	天天用 daily	两三天用 1 次 once 2 or 3 days	一周 1~2 次 once or twice a week	半个月 1 次或以下 once half a month or below
样本 Sample	115	20.0	45.2	32.2	2.6
男性 Male	43	14.0	46.5	32.6	7.0
16~24 岁 Age	5	20.0	60.0	0.0	20.0
25~34 岁 Age	16	12.5	56.3	31.3	0.0
35~44 岁 Age	8	12.5	37.5	50.0	0.0
45~54 岁 Age	8	12.5	25.0	37.5	25.0
55~60 岁 Age	6	16.7	50.0	33.3	0.0
女性 Female	72	23.6	44.4	31.9	0.0
16~24 岁 Age	21	23.8	52.4	23.8	0.0
25~34 岁 Age	31	32.3	32.3	35.5	0.0
35~44 岁 Age	11	0.0	54.5	45.5	0.0
45~54 岁 Age	8	25.0	50.0	25.0	0.0
55~60 岁 Age	1	0.0	100.0	0.0	0.0

4-10 选择该类商品的考虑因素/ Ranking of the Considerations in Purchasing

注：本题为多选题，合计百分比超过 100%（Multiple answers）

排名 Ranking	考虑因素 Considerations	人次 Person-time	百分比 Percent
1	产品功用 product function	44	37.9
2	有名的牌子 famous brand	40	34.5
2	价格适中 reasonable price	40	34.5
3	广告影响 influence of advertising	31	26.7
4	别人推荐 introduced by other people	14	12.1
5	购买方便 easy to buy	12	10.3
6	有优惠条件 with preferential terms	10	8.6
7	包装吸引人 appealing package	8	6.9
8	单位发的 offered by the working unit	4	3.4
9	其它 others	2	1.7

n=116

4-11 对产品功能的侧重方面/ Ranking of the Considerations about the Function of this Kind of Product

注：本题为多选题，合计百分比超过 100%（Multiple answers）

排名 Ranking	侧重方面 Items	人次 Person-time	百分比 Percent
1	气味好 pleasant smell	64	55.2
2	滋润效果 nourishing effect	43	37.1
3	清洁力强 powerful cleaning	40	34.5
4	能杀菌 bacteria-killing ability	37	31.9
5	止痒 itch-easing	30	25.9
6	易于冲洗 easy to clean	25	21.6
7	有特殊功能 special function	6	5.2
8	其他 others	1	0.9

n=116

4-12 重度消费者的人口分布/ Demographics of the Heavy Consumers

	人数 Number	16-24 岁 Age	25-34 岁 Age	35-44 岁 Age	45-54 岁 Age	55-60 岁 Age
样本 Sample	75	26.7	41.3	13.3	12.0	6.7
男性 Male	26	15.4	42.3	15.4	11.5	15.4
天天用 daily	6	16.7	33.3	16.7	16.7	16.7
两三天用 1 次 once 2 or 3 days	20	15.0	45.0	15.0	10.0	15.0
女性 Female	49	32.7	40.8	12.2	12.2	2.0
天天用 daily	17	29.4	58.8	0.0	11.8	0.0
两三天用 1 次 once 2 or 3 days	32	34.4	31.3	18.8	12.5	3.1

4-13 不同消费者层的常用品牌/ The Most Frequently Used Brands by Market Segments

4-13-1 时尚流行指标/ Fads Popular Index

	人数 Number	第一品牌及百分比 1st / percent	第二品牌及百分比 2nd / percent	第三品牌及百分比 3rd / percent
样本 Sample	114	**舒肤佳 Safeguard(23.7)**	**力士 Lux(22.8)**	**六神 Liushen(16.7)**
平实生活指向 simple living orientation	40	舒肤佳 Safeguard(25.0)	六神 Liushen(17.5)	力士 Lux(15.0)
时尚流行指向 fashion orientation	74	力士 Lux(27.0)	舒肤佳 Safeguard(23.0)	六神 Liushen(16.2)

4-13-2 广告态度指标/ Advertising Attitude Index

	人数 Number	第一品牌及百分比 1st / percent	第二品牌及百分比 2nd / percent	第三品牌及百分比 3rd / percent
样本 Sample	114	**力士 Lux(23.7)** **舒肤佳 Safeguard(23.7)**	**六神 Liushen(16.7)**	**强生 Johnson&Johnson(3.5)** **夏士莲 Hazeline(3.5)**
广告淡漠指向 indifferent orientation	18	力士 Lux(22.2) 舒肤佳 Safeguard(22.2)	六神 Liushen(16.7)	安利 Amway(5.6) 强生 Johnson&Johnson(5.6) 夏士莲 Hazeline(5.6) 雅蜜 Yami(5.6) 花世界 Venic(5.6) 桃花雨 Taohuayu(5.6)
中间层 medium	74	力士 Lux(23.0)	舒肤佳 Safeguard(20.3)	六神 Liushen(14.9)
信赖广告指向 loyal orientation	22	舒肤佳 Safeguard(36.4)	力士 Lux(27.3)	六神 Liushen(22.7)

4-14 重度消费者的消费层构成/ The Composition of the Heavy Consumers

4-14-1 时尚流行指标/ Fads Popular Index

	人数 Number	平实生活指向 simple living orientation	时尚流行指向 fashion orientation
样本 Sample	73	24.7	75.3
天天用 daily	22	22.7	77.3
两三天用 1 次 once 2or 3 days	51	25.5	74.5

4-14-2 广告态度指标/ Advertising Attitude Index

	人数 Number	广告淡漠指向 indifferent orientation	中间层 medium	信赖广告指向 loyal orientation
样本 Sample	74	13.5	66.2	20.3
天天用 daily	22	9.1	72.7	18.2
两三天用 1 次 once 2or 3 days	52	15.4	63.5	21.2

● 武汉 / Wuhan

4-1 使用方式的比例/ Ways of Using Bath Shampoo

	人数 Number	百分比 Percent
个人专用 personal use	37	5.8
与家人共用 all family members share	127	19.8
不用 never use	477	74.4

n=641

4-2 最常用品牌排名/ Ranking of the Most Frequently Used Brands

排名 Brand Ranking	品牌 Brands	人数 Number	百分比 Percent
1	舒肤佳 Safeguard	31	19.6
2	六神 Liushen	29	18.4
3	玉兰油 Oil of Olay	19	12.0
3	力士 Lux	19	12.0
4	强生 Johnson&Johnson	10	6.3
5	舒蕾 Slek	6	3.8
6	花王碧柔 Biore	5	3.2
7	安利 Amway	4	2.5
8	夏士莲 Hazeline	3	1.9

n=158

4-3 样本、男性各年龄层、女性各年龄层的常用品牌/ The Most Frequently Used Brands by the Whole Sample, Age and Gender Groups

	人数 Number	第一品牌及百分比 1st/ percent	第二品牌及百分比 2nd/ percent	第三品牌及百分比 3rd/ percent
样本 Sample	158	**舒肤佳 Safeguard(19.6)**	**六神 Liushen(18.4)**	**玉兰油 Oil of Olay(12.0)** **力士 Lux(12.0)**
男性 Male	61	**舒肤佳 Safeguard(26.2)**	**六神 Liushen(21.3)**	**力士 Lux(8.2)**
16~24 岁 Age	13	舒肤佳 Safeguard(30.8)	花王碧柔 Biore(15.4) 力士 Lux(15.4) 玉兰油 Oil of Olay(15.4)	安利 Amway(7.7) 六神 Liushen(7.7) 夏士莲 Hazeline(7.7)
25~34 岁 Age	21	六神 Liushen(28.6)	舒肤佳 Safeguard(19.0)	安利 Amway(9.5) 玉兰油 Oil of Olay(9.5)
35~44 岁 Age	11	六神 Liushen(27.3) 舒肤佳 Safeguard(27.3)	强生 Johnson&Johnson(9.1) 舒蕾 Slek(9.1) 诗乐仕 Shileshi(9.1) 彩迪 Caidi(9.1)	
45~54 岁 Age	13	舒肤佳 Safeguard(38.5)	六神 Liushen(23.1)	力士 Lux(15.4)
55~60 岁 Age	3	兰幽草 Lanyoucao(33.3) 孩儿面 Haiermian(33.3)		
女性 Female	97	**六神 Liushen(16.5)**	**玉兰油 Oil of Olay(15.5)** **舒肤佳 Safeguard(15.5)**	**力士 Lux(14.4)**
16~24 岁 Age	25	六神 Liushen(20.0) 舒肤佳 Safeguard(20.0)	玉兰油 Oil of Olay(12.0)	强生 Johnson&Johnson(8.0)
25~34 岁 Age	40	力士 Lux(20.0) 舒肤佳 Safeguard(20.0) 玉兰油 Oil of Olay(20.0)	六神 Liushen(10.0) 强生 Johnson&Johnson(10.0)	鳄鱼宝宝 Croco baby(2.5) 花王碧柔 Biore(2.5) 洁莱雅 Jielaiya(2.5) 多芬 Dove(2.5) 沐歌 Skin's Song(2.5) 滴露 Dettol(2.5) 夏士莲 Hazeline(2.5) 安利 Amway(2.5)
35~44 岁 Age	18	力士 Lux(16.7) 六神 Liushen(16.7)	舒蕾 Slek(11.1) 玉兰油 Oil of Olay(11.1) 花王碧柔 Biore(11.1)	舒肤佳 Safeguard(5.6) 索芙特木瓜 Softto(5.6) 强生 Johnson&Johnson(5.6) 海飞丝 Head&Shoulder(5.6) 蓝月亮 Lanyuelang(5.6)
45~54 岁 Age	12	六神 Liushen(25.0)	力士 Lux(16.7) 玉兰油 Oil of Olay(16.7)	强生 Johnson&Johnson(8.3) 舒肤佳 Safeguard(8.3) 舒蕾 Slek(8.3) 蜂花 Bee&Flower(8.3)
55~60 岁 Age	2	六神 Liushen(50.0) 强生 Johnson&Johnson(50.0)		

4-4 正在使用的品牌排名/ Ranking of the Brands Used Now

排名 Brand Ranking	品牌 Brands	人数 Number	百分比 Percent
1	六神 Liushen	29	18.1
2	力士 Lux	20	12.5
3	玉兰油 Oil of Olay	19	11.9
4	舒肤佳 Safeguard	18	11.3
5	花王碧柔 Biore	11	6.9
6	强生 Johnson&Johnson	8	5.0
7	舒蕾 Slek	6	3.8
8	安利 Amway	5	3.1
9	鳄鱼宝宝 Croco baby	4	2.5
10	夏士莲 Hazeline	3	1.9

n=160

4-5 品牌转换习惯/ Brand Habit in Consuming Bath Shampoo

	人数 Number	第一次使用该品牌 first use this brand	上一次也是这个牌子 used it last time	上一次不是这个牌子 not used it last time
样本 Sample	159	25.2	56.0	18.9
六神 Liushen	28	28.6	53.6	17.9
力士 Lux	20	30.0	55.0	15.0
玉兰油 Oil of Olay	19	21.1	52.6	26.3
舒肤佳 Safeguard	18	16.7	72.2	11.1
花王碧柔 Biore	11	27.3	27.3	45.5
强生 Johnson&Johnson	8	25.0	75.0	0.0
舒蕾 Slek	6	0.0	100.0	0.0
安利 Amway	5	20.0	80.0	0.0
鳄鱼宝宝 Croco Baby	4	25.0	50.0	25.0
夏士莲 Hazeline	3	33.3	66.7	0.0

4-6 下一次打算使用的品牌排名/ Ranking of the Brands to be Used Next Time

排名 Brand Ranking	品牌 Brands	人数 Number	百分比 Percent
1	玉兰油 Oil of Olay	29	18.1
2	舒肤佳 Safeguard	24	15.0
3	力士 Lux	21	13.1
4	六神 Liushen	19	11.9
5	强生 Johnson&Johnson	8	5.0
6	安利 Amway	6	3.8
6	舒蕾 Slek	6	3.8
7	花王碧柔 Biore	5	3.1
8	夏士莲 Hazeline	3	1.9
8	花 Fa	3	1.9

n=160

4-7 样本、男性各年龄层、女性各年龄层是否是主要购买者/ Purchasers in the Household by the Whole Sample, Age and Gender Groups

	人数 Number	是 yes	不是 no
样本 Sample	641	22.5	77.5
男性 Male	311	9.3	90.7
16~24 岁 Age	65	7.7	92.3
25~34 岁 Age	89	12.4	87.6
35~44 岁 Age	80	7.5	92.5
45~54 岁 Age	52	9.6	90.4
55~60 岁 Age	25	8.0	92.0
女性 Female	330	34.8	65.2
16~24 岁 Age	69	23.2	76.8
25~34 岁 Age	96	40.6	59.4
35~44 岁 Age	78	44.9	55.1
45~54 岁 Age	61	36.1	63.9
55~60 岁 Age	26	11.5	88.5

4-8 样本、男性各年龄层、女性各年龄层的使用方式/ Ways of Using Bath Shampoo by the Whole Sample, Age and Gender Groups

	人数 Number	是个人专用 personal use	与家人共用 all family members share	不用 never use
样本 Sample	641	5.8	19.8	74.4
男性 Male	311	4.8	15.8	79.4
16~24 岁 Age	65	6.2	13.8	80.0
25~34 岁 Age	89	7.9	16.9	75.3
35~44 岁 Age	80	3.8	12.5	83.8
45~54 岁 Age	52	1.9	23.1	75.0
55~60 岁 Age	25	0.0	12.0	88.0
女性 Female	330	6.7	23.6	69.7
16~24 岁 Age	68	8.8	29.4	61.8
25~34 岁 Age	96	11.5	30.2	58.3
35~44 岁 Age	78	2.6	20.5	76.9
45~54 岁 Age	62	4.8	17.7	77.4
55~60 岁 Age	26	0.0	7.7	92.3

4-9 样本、男性各年龄层、女性各年龄层的使用频率/ Frequencies of the Consumed Bath Shampoo by the Whole Sample, Age and Gender Groups

	人数 Number	天天用 daily	两三天用 1 次 once 2 or 3 days	一周 1~2 次 once or twice a week	半个月 1 次或以下 once half a month or below
样本 Sample	160	25.0	28.8	43.8	2.5
男性 Male	61	24.6	31.1	42.6	1.6
16~24 岁 Age	13	30.8	30.8	38.5	0.0
25~34 岁 Age	21	38.1	23.8	38.1	0.0
35~44 岁 Age	11	18.2	45.5	27.3	9.1
45~54 岁 Age	13	7.7	23.1	69.2	0.0
55~60 岁 Age	3	0.0	66.7	33.3	0.0
女性 Female	99	25.3	27.3	44.4	3.0
16~24 岁 Age	26	19.2	30.8	46.2	3.8
25~34 岁 Age	40	32.5	25.0	40.0	2.5
35~44 岁 Age	18	27.8	16.7	55.6	0.0
45~54 岁 Age	13	15.4	38.5	38.5	7.7
55~60 岁 Age	2	0.0	50.0	50.0	0.0

4-10 选择该类商品的考虑因素/ Ranking of the Considerations in Purchasing

注：本题为多选题，合计百分比超过 100%（Multiple answers）

排名 Ranking	考虑因素 Considerations	人次 Person-time	百分比 Percent
1	产品功用 product function	83	51.6
2	价格适中 reasonable price	68	42.2
3	有名的牌子 famous brand	62	38.5
4	广告影响 influence of advertising	43	26.7
5	单位发的 offered by the working unit	22	13.7
6	购买方便 easy to buy	18	11.2
7	别人推荐 introduced by other people	16	9.9
8	有优惠条件 with preferential terms	12	7.5
9	包装吸引人 appealing package	8	5.0
10	其它 others	5	3.1

n=161

4-11 对产品功能的侧重方面/ Ranking of the Considerations about the Function of this Kind of Product

注：本题为多选题，合计百分比超过 100%（Multiple answers）

排名 Ranking	侧重方面 Items	人次 Person-time	百分比 Percent
1	气味好 pleasant smell	110	68.8
2	滋润效果 nourishing effect	82	51.2
3	能杀菌 bacteria-killing ability	67	41.9
4	清洁力强 powerful cleaning	51	31.9
5	止痒 itch-easing	33	20.6
6	易于冲洗 easy to clean	27	16.9
7	有特殊功能 special function	16	10.0
8	其他 others	1	0.6

n=160

4-12 重度消费者的人口分布/ Demographics of the Heavy Consumers

	人数 Number	16-24 岁 Age	25-34 岁 Age	35-44 岁 Age	45-54 岁 Age	55-60 岁 Age
样本 Sample	86	24.4	41.9	17.4	12.8	3.5
男性 Male	34	23.5	38.2	20.6	11.8	5.9
天天用 daily	15	26.7	53.3	13.3	6.7	0.0
两三天用 1 次 once 2 or 3 days	19	21.1	26.3	26.3	15.8	10.5
女性 Female	52	25.0	44.2	15.4	13.5	1.9
天天用 daily	25	20.0	52.0	20.0	8.0	0.0
两三天用 1 次 once 2 or 3 days	27	29.6	37.0	11.1	18.5	3.7

4-13 不同消费者层的常用品牌/ The Most Frequently Used Brands by Market Segments

4-13-1 时尚流行指标/ Fads Popular Index

	人数 Number	第一品牌及百分比 1st / percent	第二品牌及百分比 2nd / percent	第三品牌及百分比 3rd / percent	第四品牌及百分比 4th / percent
样本 Sample	156	**舒肤佳 Safeguard(19.9)**	**六神 Liushen(18.6)**	**玉兰油 Oil of Olay(12.2) 力士 Lux(12.2)**	**强生 Johnson&Johnson(5.8)**
平实生活指向 simple living orientation	60	六神 Liushen(23.3)	舒肤佳 Safeguard(21.7)	玉兰油 Oil of Olay(11.7)	力士 Lux(8.3)
时尚流行指向 fashion orientation	96	舒肤佳 Safeguard(18.8)	六神 Liushen(15.6)	力士 Lux(14.6)	玉兰油 Oil of Olay(12.5)

4-13-2 广告态度指标/ Advertising Attitude Index

	人数 Number	第一品牌及百分比 1st / percent	第二品牌及百分比 2nd / percent	第三品牌及百分比 3rd / percent	第四品牌及百分比 4th / percent
样本 Sample	156	**舒肤佳 Safeguard(19.9)**	**六神 Liushen(18.6)**	**玉兰油 Oil of Olay(12.2) 力士 Lux(12.2)**	**强生 Johnson&Johnson(5.8)**
广告淡漠指向 indifferent orientation	37	六神 Liushen(21.6)	玉兰油 Oil of Olay(18.9)	力士 Lux(10.8) 舒肤佳 Safeguard(10.8)	花王碧柔 Biore(5.4)
中间层 medium	102	舒肤佳 Safeguard(23.5)	六神 Liushen(18.6)	力士 Lux(12.7)	玉兰油 Oil of Olay(9.8)
信赖广告指向 loyal orientation	17	舒肤佳 Safeguard(17.6)	力士 Lux(11.8) 六神 Liushen(11.8) 强生 Johnson&Johnson(11.8) 舒蕾 Slek(11.8) 玉兰油 Oil of Olay(11.8)	多芬 Dove(5.9) 沐歌 Skin's Song(5.9) 夏士莲 Hazeline(5.9) 蓝月亮 Lanyuelang(5.9)	

4-14 重度消费者的消费层构成/ The Composition of the Heavy Consumers

4-14-1 时尚流行指标/ Fads Popular Index

	人数 Number	平实生活指向 simple living orientation	时尚流行指向 fashion orientation
样本 Sample	85	27.1	72.9
天天用 daily	40	27.5	72.5
两三天用 1 次 once 2 or 3 days	45	26.7	73.3

4-14-2 广告态度指标/ Advertising Attitude Index

	人数 Number	广告淡漠指向 indifferent orientation	中间层 medium	信赖广告指向 loyal orientation
样本 Sample	85	27.1	61.2	11.8
天天用 daily	40	25.0	60.0	15.0
两三天用 1 次 once 2 or 3 days	45	28.9	62.2	8.9

● 西安 / Xi'an

4-1 使用方式的比例/ Ways of Using Bath Shampoo

	人数 Number	百分比 Percent
个人专用 personal use	38	6.3
与家人共用 all family members share	188	31.3
不用 never use	375	62.4

n=601

4-2 最常用品牌排名/ Ranking of the Most Frequently Used Brands

排名 Brand Ranking	品牌 Brands	人数 Number	百分比 Percent
1	六神 Liushen	63	27.9
2	舒肤佳 Safeguard	33	14.6
3	力士 Lux	30	13.3
4	安利 Amway	7	3.1
4	夏士莲 Hazeline	7	3.1
4	强生 Johnson&Johnson	7	3.1
5	莹朴 Ying Pu	6	2.7
6	舒蕾 Slek	5	2.2
7	花 Fa	4	1.8
7	浪奴 Launo	4	1.8

n=226

4-3 样本、男性各年龄层、女性各年龄层的常用品牌/ The Most Frequently Used Brands by the Whole Sample, Age and Gender Groups

	人数 Number	第一品牌及百分比 1st/ percent	第二品牌及百分比 2nd/ percent	第三品牌及百分比 3rd/ percent
样本 Sample	226	**六神 Liushen(27.9)**	**舒肤佳 Safeguard(14.6)**	**力士 Lux(13.3)**
男性 Male	102	**六神 Liushen(28.4)**	**力士 Lux(14.7)**	**舒肤佳 Safeguard(13.7)**
16~24 岁 Age	20	六神 Liushen(35.0)	力士 Lux(15.0)	舒肤佳 Safeguard(10.0)
25~34 岁 Age	31	力士 Lux(19.4) 六神 Liushen(19.4)	舒肤佳 Safeguard(12.9)	强生 Johnson&Johnson(9.7)
35~44 岁 Age	32	六神 Liushen(28.1)	力士 Lux(15.6) 舒肤佳 Safeguard(15.6)	开米 Kami(6.3)
45~54 岁 Age	13	六神 Liushen(38.5)	舒肤佳 Safeguard(15.4)	安利 Amway(7.7) 美浴液 Meiyuye(7.7) 雅邦 Yabang(7.7)
55~60 岁 Age	6	六神 Liushen(33.3)	爱蕾丝 Repos(16.7) 力士 Lux(16.7) 舒肤佳 Safeguard(16.7) 莹朴 Ying Pu(16.7)	
女性 Female	124	**六神 Liushen(27.4)**	**舒肤佳 Safeguard(15.3)**	**力士 Lux(12.1)**
16~24 岁 Age	26	六神 Liushen(23.1) 舒肤佳 Safeguard(23.1)	力士 Lux(11.5)	花王碧柔 Biore(7.7)
25~34 岁 Age	48	六神 Liushen(22.9)	力士 Lux(14.6) 舒肤佳 Safeguard(14.6)	安利 Amway(6.3) 金威 Kingway(6.3) 舒蕾 Slek(6.3)
35~44 岁 Age	25	舒肤佳 Safeguard(20.0)	六神 Liushen(16.0)	力士 Lux(12.0)
45~54 岁 Age	20	六神 Liushen(55.0)	力士 Lux(10.0)	花 Fa(5.0) 浪奴 Launo(5.0) 舒肤佳 Safeguard(5.0) 莹朴 Ying Pu(5.0) 安乐 Anle(5.0) 爱德利 Aideli(5.0)
55~60 岁 Age	5	六神 Liushen(40.0)	安利 Amway(20.0) 莹朴 Ying Pu(20.0) 蜂花 Bee&Flower(20.0)	

4-4 正在使用的品牌排名/ Ranking of the Brands Used Now

排名 Brand Ranking	品牌 Brands	人数 Number	百分比 Percent
1	六神 Liushen	59	26.1
2	力士 Lux	31	13.7
3	舒肤佳 Safeguard	30	13.3
4	强生 Johnson&Johnson	11	4.9
5	夏士莲 Hazeline	8	3.5
6	安利 Amway	7	3.1
7	浪奴 Launo	6	2.7
8	维奥 VO	5	2.2
8	莹朴 Ying Pu	5	2.2
9	花 Fa	4	1.8
9	花王碧柔 Biore	4	1.8
9	舒蕾 Slek	4	1.8

n=226

4-5 品牌转换习惯/ Brand Habit in Consuming Bath Shampoo

	人数 Number	第一次使用该品牌 first use this brand	上一次也是这个牌子 used it last time	上一次不是这个牌子 not used it last time
样本 Sample	225	18.2	70.7	11.1
六神 Liushen	59	15.3	78.0	6.8
力士 Lux	31	9.7	67.7	22.6
舒肤佳 Safeguard	30	10.0	80.0	10.0
强生 Johnson&Johnson	11	18.2	72.7	9.1
夏士莲 Hazeline	8	0.0	75.0	25.0
安利 Amway	7	14.3	85.7	0.0
浪奴 Launo	6	50.0	50.0	0.0
维奥 VO	5	20.0	60.0	20.0
莹朴 Ying Pu	5	40.0	60.0	0.0

4-6 下一次打算使用的品牌排名/ Ranking of the Brands to be Used Next Time

排名 Brand Ranking	品牌 Brands	人数 Number	百分比 Percent
1	六神 Liushen	56	24.8
2	力士 Lux	39	17.3
3	舒肤佳 Safeguard	37	16.4
4	强生 Johnson&Johnson	10	4.4
5	夏士莲 Hazeline	6	2.7
6	花王碧柔 Biore	5	2.2
7	莹朴 Ying Pu	4	1.8
7	金威 Kingway	4	1.8
7	安利 Amway	4	1.8

n=226

4-7 样本、男性各年龄层、女性各年龄层是否是主要购买者/ Purchasers in the Household by the Whole Sample, Age and Gender Groups

	人数 Number	是 yes	不是 no
样本 Sample	**601**	**29.0**	**71.0**
男性 Male	**302**	**18.5**	**81.5**
16~24 岁 Age	64	17.2	82.8
25~34 岁 Age	91	23.1	76.9
35~44 岁 Age	77	20.8	79.2
45~54 岁 Age	46	8.7	91.3
55~60 岁 Age	24	16.7	83.3
女性 Female	**299**	**39.5**	**60.5**
16~24 岁 Age	61	31.1	68.9
25~34 岁 Age	90	50.0	50.0
35~44 岁 Age	74	40.5	59.5
45~54 岁 Age	49	36.7	63.3
55~60 岁 Age	25	24.0	76.0

4-8 样本、男性各年龄层、女性各年龄层的使用方式/ Ways of Using Bath Shampoo by the Whole Sample, Age and Gender Groups

	人数 Number	是个人专用 personal use	与家人共用 all family members share	不用 never use
样本 Sample	**601**	**6.3**	**31.3**	**62.4**
男性 Male	**302**	**4.3**	**29.5**	**66.2**
16~24 岁 Age	64	6.3	25.0	68.8
25~34 岁 Age	91	3.3	30.8	65.9
35~44 岁 Age	77	5.2	36.4	58.4
45~54 岁 Age	46	4.3	23.9	71.7
55~60 岁 Age	24	0.0	25.0	75.0
女性 Female	**299**	**8.4**	**33.1**	**58.5**
16~24 岁 Age	61	13.1	29.5	57.4
25~34 岁 Age	90	11.1	42.2	46.7
35~44 岁 Age	74	8.1	25.7	66.2
45~54 岁 Age	49	0.0	40.8	59.2
55~60 岁 Age	25	4.0	16.0	80.0

4-9 样本、男性各年龄层、女性各年龄层的使用频率/ Frequencies of the Consumed Bath Shampoo by the Whole Sample, Age and Gender Groups

	人数 Number	天天用 daily	两三天用 1 次 once 2 or 3 days	一周 1~2 次 once or twice a week	半个月 1 次或以下 once half a month or below
样本 Sample	225	3.6	24.9	65.3	6.2
男性 Male	102	2.0	20.6	69.6	7.8
16~24 岁 Age	20	10.0	20.0	65.0	5.0
25~34 岁 Age	31	0.0	29.0	58.1	12.9
35~44 岁 Age	32	0.0	15.6	81.3	3.1
45~54 岁 Age	13	0.0	23.1	61.5	15.4
55~60 岁 Age	6	0.0	0.0	100.0	0.0
女性 Female	123	4.9	28.5	61.8	4.9
16~24 岁 Age	26	3.8	38.5	57.7	0.0
25~34 岁 Age	48	4.2	31.3	58.3	6.3
35~44 岁 Age	25	8.0	20.0	68.0	4.0
45~54 岁 Age	19	5.3	21.1	63.2	10.5
55~60 岁 Age	5	0.0	20.0	80.0	0.0

4-10 选择该类商品的考虑因素/ Ranking of the Considerations in Purchasing

注：本题为多选题，合计百分比超过 100%（Multiple answers）

排名 Ranking	考虑因素 Considerations	人次 Person-time	百分比 Percent
1	产品功用 product function	98	43.6
2	价格适中 reasonable price	82	36.4
3	有名的牌子 famous brand	80	35.6
4	别人推荐 introduced by other people	42	18.7
5	购买方便 easy to buy	33	14.7
6	广告影响 influence of advertising	31	13.8
7	单位发的 offered by the working unit	16	7.1
8	有优惠条件 with preferential terms	8	3.6
9	包装吸引人 appealing package	7	3.1
10	其它 others	2	0.9

n=225

4-11 对产品功能的侧重方面/ Ranking of the Considerations about the Function of this Kind of Product

注：本题为多选题，合计百分比超过 100%（Multiple answers）

排名 Ranking	侧重方面 Items	人次 Person-time	百分比 Percent
1	气味好 pleasant smell	127	56.4
2	滋润效果 nourishing effect	92	40.9
3	能杀菌 bacteria-killing ability	89	39.6
4	清洁力强 powerful cleaning	60	26.7
5	止痒 itch-easing	52	23.1
6	易于冲洗 easy to clean	41	18.2
7	有特殊功能 special function	11	4.9
8	其他 others	4	1.8

n=225

4-12 重度消费者的人口分布/ Demographics of the Heavy Consumers

	人数 Number	16-24 岁 Age	25-34 岁 Age	35-44 岁 Age	45-54 岁 Age	55-60 岁 Age
样本 Sample	64	26.6	40.6	18.8	12.5	1.6
男性 Male	23	26.1	39.1	21.7	13.0	0.0
天天用 daily	2	100.0	0.0	0.0	0.0	0.0
两三天用 1 次 once 2 or 3 days	21	19.0	42.9	23.8	14.3	0.0
女性 Female	41	26.8	41.5	17.1	12.2	2.4
天天用 daily	6	16.7	33.3	33.3	16.7	0.0
两三天用 1 次 once 2 or 3 days	35	28.6	42.9	14.3	11.4	2.9

4-13 不同消费者层的常用品牌/ The Most Frequently Used Brands by Market Segments

4-13-1 时尚流行指标/ Fads Popular Index

	人数 Number	第一品牌及百分比 1st / percent	第二品牌及百分比 2nd / percent	第三品牌及百分比 3rd / percent
样本 Sample	226	**六神 Liushen(27.9)**	**舒肤佳 Safeguard(14.6)**	**力士 Lux(13.3)**
平实生活指向 simple living orientation	107	六神 Liushen(30.8)	舒肤佳 Safeguard(14.0)	力士 Lux(13.1)
时尚流行指向 fashion orientation	119	六神 Liushen(25.2)	舒肤佳 Safeguard(15.1)	力士 Lux(13.4)

4-13-2 广告态度指标/ Advertising Attitude Index

	人数 Number	第一品牌及百分比 1st / percent	第二品牌及百分比 2nd / percent	第三品牌及百分比 3rd / percent
样本 Sample	225	**六神 Liushen(28.0)**	**舒肤佳 Safeguard(14.2)**	**力士 Lux(13.3)**
广告淡漠指向 indifferent orientation	61	六神 Liushen(31.1)	舒肤佳 Safeguard(18.0)	力士 Lux(16.4)
中间层 medium	137	六神 Liushen(26.3)	舒肤佳 Safeguard(13.9)	力士 Lux(11.7)
信赖广告指向 loyal orientation	27	六神 Liushen(29.6)	力士 Lux(14.8)	舒肤佳 Safeguard(7.4) 夏士莲 Hazeline(7.4) 玉兰油 Oil of Olay(7.4)

4-14 重度消费者的消费层构成/ The Composition of the Heavy Consumers

4-14-1 时尚流行指标/ Fads Popular Index

	人数 Number	平实生活指向 simple living orientation	时尚流行指向 fashion orientation
样本 Sample	64	42.2	57.8
天天用 daily	8	37.5	62.5
两三天用 1 次 once 2 or 3 days	56	42.9	57.1

4-14-2 广告态度指标/ Advertising Attitude Index

	人数 Number	广告淡漠指向 indifferent orientation	中间层 medium	信赖广告指向 loyal orientation
样本 Sample	64	20.3	60.9	18.8
天天用 daily	8	12.5	75.0	12.5
两三天用 1 次 once 2 or 3 days	56	21.4	58.9	19.6

● 沈阳 / Shenyang

4-1 使用方式的比例/ Ways of Using Bath Shampoo

	人数 Number	百分比 Percent
个人专用 personal use	39	6.5
与家人共用 all family members share	121	20.2
不用 never use	440	73.3

n=600

4-2 最常用品牌排名/ Ranking of the Most Frequently Used Brands

排名 Brand Ranking	品牌 Brands	人数 Number	百分比 Percent
1	舒肤佳 Safeguard	34	21.4
2	力士 Lux	31	19.5
3	六神 Liushen	20	12.6
4	安利 Amway	9	5.7
5	芦荟 Luhui	6	3.8
5	强生 Johnson&Johnson	6	3.8

n=159

4-3 样本、男性各年龄层、女性各年龄层的常用品牌/ The Most Frequently Used Brands by the Whole Sample, Age and Gender Groups

	人数 Number	第一品牌及百分比 1st/ percent	第二品牌及百分比 2nd/ percent	第三品牌及百分比 3rd/ percent
样本 Sample	159	**舒肤佳 Safeguard(21.4)**	**力士 Lux(19.5)**	**六神 Liushen(12.6)**
男性 Male	49	**力士 Lux(22.4)**	**舒肤佳 Safeguard(18.4)**	**六神 Liushen(16.3)**
16~24 岁 Age	6	力士 Lux(33.3)	舒肤佳 Safeguard(16.7) 完美 Wanmei(16.7) 芦荟 Luhui(16.7) 牛奶 Milk(16.7)	
25~34 岁 Age	19	力士 Lux(31.6)	六神 Liushen(26.3)	舒肤佳 Safeguard(21.1)
35~44 岁 Age	15	舒肤佳 Safeguard(26.7)	完美 Wanmei(6.7) 大象 Daxiang(6.7) 三立 Sanli(6.7) 无限极 Wujixian(6.7) 芦荟 Luhui(6.7) 夏士莲 Hazeline(6.7) 六神 Liushen(6.7) 力士 Lux(6.7) 卡妮 Kanei(6.7) 安利 Amway(6.7)	
45~54 岁 Age	8	安利 Amway(25.0) 力士 Lux(25.0)	六神 Liushen(12.5) 黛丽 Daili(12.5) 艾浓 Ainong(12.5) 妙馨 Miaoxin(12.5)	
55~60 岁 Age	1	六神 Liushen(100.0)		
女性 Female	110	**舒肤佳 Safeguard(22.7)**	**力士 Lux(18.2)**	**六神 Liushen(10.9)**
16~24 岁 Age	35	力士 Lux(20.0)	舒肤佳 Safeguard(17.1)	六神 Liushen(11.4)
25~34 岁 Age	32	力士 Lux(25.0)	舒肤佳 Safeguard(21.9)	强生 Johnson&Johnson(9.4)
35~44 岁 Age	23	舒肤佳 Safeguard(26.1)	力士 Lux(17.4)	六神 Liushen(8.7)
45~54 岁 Age	15	六神 Liushen(26.7) 舒肤佳 Safeguard(26.7)	力士 Lux(6.7) 舒蕾 Slek(6.7) 玉兰油 Oil of Olay(6.7) 牛奶 Milk(6.7) 花王 Kao(6.7) 香海 Xianghai(6.7) 永大 Yongda(6.7)	
55~60 岁 Age	5	舒肤佳 Safeguard(40.0)	雪柠 Since(20.0) 芦荟 Luhui(20.0) 仙妮 Xianni(20.0)	

4-4 正在使用的品牌排名/ Ranking of the Brands Used Now

排名 Brand Ranking	品牌 Brands	人数 Number	百分比 Percent
1	舒肤佳 Safeguard	33	20.8
2	力士 Lux	28	17.6
3	六神 Liushen	20	12.6
4	安利 Amway	10	6.3
5	强生 Johnson&Johnson	7	4.4
6	芦荟 Luhui	5	3.1
7	卡妮 Kanei	4	2.5

n=159

4-5 品牌转换习惯/ Brand Habit in Consuming Bath Shampoo

	人数 Number	第一次使用该品牌 first use this brand	上一次也是这个牌子 used it last time	上一次不是这个牌子 not used it last time
样本 Sample	158	13.3	76.6	10.1
舒肤佳 Safeguard	33	3.0	90.9	6.1
力士 Lux	28	3.6	85.7	10.7
六神 Liushen	20	10.0	80.0	10.0
安利 Amway	10	20.0	70.0	10.0

4-6 下一次打算使用的品牌排名/ Ranking of the Brands to be Used Next Time

排名 Brand Ranking	品牌 Brands	人数 Number	百分比 Percent
1	舒肤佳 Safeguard	33	20.8
2	力士 Lux	32	20.1
3	六神 Liushen	22	13.8
4	安利 Amway	10	6.3
5	强生 Johnson&Johnson	7	4.4
6	芦荟 Luhui	4	2.5
6	玉兰油 Oil of Olay	4	2.5

n=159

4-7 样本、男性各年龄层、女性各年龄层是否是主要购买者/ Purchasers in the Household by the Whole Sample, Age and Gender Groups

	人数 Number	是 yes	不是 no
样本 Sample	600	21.5	78.5
男性 Male	298	9.1	90.9
16~24 岁 Age	63	6.3	93.7
25~34 岁 Age	89	14.6	85.4
35~44 岁 Age	76	9.2	90.8
45~54 岁 Age	46	4.3	95.7
55~60 岁 Age	24	4.2	95.8
女性 Female	302	33.8	66.2
16~24 岁 Age	64	40.6	59.4
25~34 岁 Age	90	35.6	64.4
35~44 岁 Age	76	34.2	65.8
45~54 岁 Age	48	22.9	77.1
55~60 岁 Age	24	29.2	70.8

4-8 样本、男性各年龄层、女性各年龄层的使用方式/ Ways of Using Bath Shampoo by the Whole Sample, Age and Gender Groups

	人数 Number	是个人专用 personal use	与家人共用 all family members share	不用 never use
样本 Sample	600	6.5	20.2	73.3
男性 Male	299	4.3	12.0	83.6
16~24 岁 Age	64	4.7	4.7	90.6
25~34 岁 Age	89	6.7	14.6	78.7
35~44 岁 Age	76	3.9	15.8	80.3
45~54 岁 Age	46	2.2	15.2	82.6
55~60 岁 Age	24	0.0	4.2	95.8
女性 Female	301	8.6	28.2	63.1
16~24 岁 Age	64	20.3	34.4	45.3
25~34 岁 Age	90	8.9	26.7	64.4
35~44 岁 Age	75	2.7	28.0	69.3
45~54 岁 Age	48	4.2	27.1	68.8
55~60 岁 Age	24	4.2	20.8	75.0

4-9 样本、男性各年龄层、女性各年龄层的使用频率/ Frequencies of the Consumed Bath Shampoo by the Whole Sample, Age and Gender Groups

	人数 Number	天天用 daily	两三天用 1 次 once 2 or 3 days	一周 1~2 次 once or twice a week	半个月 1 次或以下 once half a month or below
样本 Sample	160	5.6	20.6	68.8	5.0
男性 Male	49	10.2	18.4	65.3	6.1
16~24 岁 Age	6	16.7	33.3	33.3	16.7
25~34 岁 Age	19	5.3	26.3	68.4	0.0
35~44 岁 Age	15	20.0	6.7	66.7	6.7
45~54 岁 Age	8	0.0	12.5	75.0	12.5
55~60 岁 Age	1	0.0	0.0	100.0	0.0
女性 Female	111	3.6	21.6	70.3	4.5
16~24 岁 Age	35	2.9	25.7	65.7	5.7
25~34 岁 Age	32	6.3	21.9	68.8	3.1
35~44 岁 Age	23	0.0	21.7	78.3	0.0
45~54 岁 Age	15	6.7	20.0	60.0	13.3
55~60 岁 Age	6	0.0	0.0	100.0	0.0

4-10 选择该类商品的考虑因素/ Ranking of the Considerations in Purchasing

注：本题为多选题，合计百分比超过 100%（Multiple answers）

排名 Ranking	考虑因素 Considerations	人次 Person-time	百分比 Percent
1	产品功用 product function	85	53.1
2	价格适中 reasonable price	67	41.9
3	有名的牌子 famous brand	54	33.8
4	购买方便 easy to buy	32	20.0
5	别人推荐 introduced by other people	23	14.4
6	广告影响 influence of advertising	21	13.1
7	有优惠条件 with preferential terms	8	5.0
8	单位发的 offered by the working unit	5	3.1
9	包装吸引人 appealing package	3	1.9
10	其它 others	2	1.3

n=160

4-11 对产品功能的侧重方面/ Ranking of the Considerations about the Function of this Kind of Product

注：本题为多选题，合计百分比超过 100%（Multiple answers）

排名 Ranking	侧重方面 Items	人次 Person-time	百分比 Percent
1	气味好 pleasant smell	108	67.9
2	滋润效果 nourishing effect	61	38.4
3	能杀菌 bacteria-killing ability	58	36.5
4	清洁力强 powerful cleaning	48	30.2
5	止痒 itch-easing	40	25.2
6	易于冲洗 easy to clean	22	13.8
7	有特殊功能 special function	11	6.9

n=159

4-12 重度消费者的人口分布/ Demographics of the Heavy Consumers

	人数 Number	16-24 岁 Age	25-34 岁 Age	35-44 岁 Age	45-54 岁 Age	55-60 岁 Age
样本 Sample	42	31.0	35.7	21.4	11.9	0.0
男性 Male	14	21.4	42.9	28.6	7.1	0.0
天天用 daily	5	20.0	20.0	60.0	0.0	0.0
两三天用 1 次 once 2 or 3 days	9	22.2	55.6	11.1	11.1	0.0
女性 Female	28	35.7	32.1	17.9	14.3	0.0
天天用 daily	4	25.0	50.0	0.0	25.0	0.0
两三天用 1 次 once 2 or 3 days	24	37.5	29.2	20.8	12.5	0.0

4-13 不同消费者层的常用品牌/ The Most Frequently Used Brands by Market Segments

4-13-1 时尚流行指标/ Fads Popular Index

	人数 Number	第一品牌及百分比 1st/ percent	第二品牌及百分比 2nd/ percent	第三品牌及百分比 3rd/ percent
样本 Sample	159	**舒肤佳 Safeguard(21.4)**	**力士 Lux(19.5)**	**六神 Liushen(12.6)**
平实生活指向 simple living orientation	62	力士 Lux(27.4)	舒肤佳 Safeguard(19.4)	六神 Liushen(14.5)
时尚流行指向 fashion orientation	97	舒肤佳 Safeguard(22.7)	力士 Lux(14.4)	六神 Liushen(11.3)

4-13-2 广告态度指标/ Advertising Attitude Index

	人数 Number	第一品牌及百分比 1st/ percent	第二品牌及百分比 2nd/ percent	第三品牌及百分比 3rd/ percent
样本 Sample	159	**舒肤佳 Safeguard(21.4)**	**力士 Lux(19.5)**	**六神 Liushen(12.6)**
广告淡漠指向 indifferent orientation	47	力士 Lux(19.1)	六神 Liushen(14.9) 舒肤佳 Safeguard(14.9)	卡妮 Kanei(6.4)
中间层 medium	93	舒肤佳 Safeguard(24.7)	力士 Lux(21.5)	六神 Liushen(11.8)
信赖广告指向 loyal orientation	19	安利 Amway(21.1) 舒肤佳 Safeguard(21.1)	力士 Lux(10.5) 六神 Liushen(10.5)	雅蜜 Yami(5.3) 黛丽丝 Dailisi(5.3) 花王 Kao(5.3) 强生 Johnson&Johnson(5.3) 夏士莲 Hazeline(5.3) 洁莱雅 Jielaiya(5.3) 花王碧柔 Biore(5.3)

4-14 重度消费者的消费层构成/ The Composition of the Heavy Consumers

4-14-1 时尚流行指标/ Fads Popular Index

	人数 Number	平实生活指向 simple living orientation	时尚流行指向 fashion orientation
样本 Sample	42	40.5	59.5
天天用 daily	9	66.7	33.3
两三天用 1 次 once 2 or 3 days	33	33.3	66.7

4-14-2 广告态度指标/ Advertising Attitude Index

	人数 Number	广告淡漠指向 indifferent orientation	中间层 medium	信赖广告指向 loyal orientation
样本 Sample	42	21.4	61.9	16.7
天天用 daily	9	33.3	44.4	22.2
两三天用 1 次 once 2 or 3 days	33	18.2	66.7	15.2

5.洗衣粉 / Washing Powder

● 北京 / Beijing

5-1 最常用品牌排名/ Ranking of the Most Frequently Used Brands

排名 Brand Ranking	品牌 Brands	人数 Number	百分比 Percent
1	碧浪 Ariel	267	26.5
2	活力 28 Power28	205	20.3
3	奥妙 OMO	143	14.2
4	巧手 Dosia	104	10.3
5	熊猫 Panda	83	8.2
6	白猫 White Cat	71	7.0
7	汰渍 Tide	23	2.3
8	奇强 Qiqiang	22	2.2
9	宝莹 Persil	20	2.0
10	洛娃 Reward	8	0.8
10	雕牌 Diao	8	0.8
10	威白 Wipp	8	0.8

n=1008

5-2 样本、男性各年龄层、女性各年龄层的常用品牌/ The Most Frequently Used Brands by the Whole Sample, Age and Gender Groups

	人数 Number	第一品牌及百分比 1st/ percent	第二品牌及百分比 2nd/ percent	第三品牌及百分比 3rd/ percent	第四品牌及百分比 4th/ percent
样本 Sample	1008	**碧浪 Ariel(26.5)**	**活力 28 Power28(20.3)**	**奥妙 OMO(14.2)**	**巧手 Dosia(10.3)**
男性 Male	502	**碧浪 Ariel(27.9)**	**活力 28 Power28(21.3)**	**奥妙 OMO(12.0)**	**巧手 Dosia(9.4)**
16~24 岁 Age	104	碧浪 Ariel(37.5)	活力 28 Power28(18.3)	熊猫 Panda(12.5)	奥妙 OMO(8.7)
25~34 岁 Age	151	碧浪 Ariel(33.8)	奥妙 OMO(13.9)	活力 28 Power28(13.2)	熊猫 Panda(9.3) 巧手 Dosia(9.3)
35~44 岁 Age	131	活力 28 Power28(22.1) 碧浪 Ariel(22.1)	巧手 Dosia(16.0)	奥妙 OMO(13.0)	白猫 White Cat(6.9)
45~54 岁 Age	76	活力 28 Power28(32.9)	碧浪 Ariel(19.7)	白猫 White Cat(10.5)	奥妙 OMO(9.2)
55~60 岁 Age	40	活力 28 Power28(35.0)	熊猫 Panda(17.5)	奥妙 OMO(15.0) 碧浪 Ariel(15.0)	巧手 Dosia(10.0)
女性 Female	506	**碧浪 Ariel(25.1)**	**活力 28 Power28(19.4)**	**奥妙 OMO(16.4)**	**巧手 Dosia(11.3)**
16~24 岁 Age	108	碧浪 Ariel(26.9)	奥妙 OMO(23.1)	活力 28 Power28(13.0)	熊猫 Panda(11.1)
25~34 岁 Age	148	碧浪 Ariel(23.0)	奥妙 OMO(14.9)	活力 28 Power28(14.2) 巧手 Dosia(14.2)	白猫 White Cat(9.5)
35~44 岁 Age	124	碧浪 Ariel(30.6)	活力 28 Power28(25.8)	奥妙 OMO(15.3)	巧手 Dosia(11.3)
45~54 岁 Age	84	活力 28 Power28(23.8)	碧浪 Ariel(21.4)	奥妙 OMO(14.3)	熊猫 Panda(11.9)
55~60 岁 Age	42	活力 28 Power28(26.2)	碧浪 Ariel(19.0)	熊猫 Panda(11.9) 奥妙 OMO(11.9)	奇强 Qiqiang(9.5) 巧手 Dosia(9.5)

5-3 正在使用的品牌排名/ Ranking of the Brands Used Now

排名 Brand Ranking	品牌 Brands	人数 Number	百分比 Percent
1	碧浪 Ariel	251	24.9
2	活力 28 Power28	207	20.5
3	奥妙 OMO	136	13.5
4	巧手 Dosia	112	11.1
5	白猫 White Cat	73	7.2
6	熊猫 Panda	66	6.5
7	奇强 Qiqiang	26	2.6
8	宝莹 Persil	25	2.5
9	汰渍 Tide	24	2.4

n=1008

5-4 品牌转换习惯/ Brand Habit in Consuming Laundry Detergent

	人数 Number	第一次使用该品牌 first use this brand	上一次也是这个牌子 used it last time	上一次不是这个牌子 not used it last time
样本 Sample	996	5.4	77.0	17.6
碧浪 Ariel	250	5.2	81.6	13.2
活力 28 Power28	206	2.4	80.1	17.5
奥妙 OMO	135	1.5	82.2	16.3
巧手 Dosia	111	9.0	77.5	13.5
白猫 White Cat	72	6.9	72.2	20.8
熊猫 Panda	64	1.6	76.6	21.9
奇强 Qiqiang	25	8.0	68.0	24.0
宝莹 Persil	25	12.0	64.0	24.0
汰渍 Tide	24	0.0	66.7	33.3

5-5 下一次打算使用的品牌排名/ Ranking of the Brands to be Used Next Time

排名 Brand Ranking	品牌 Brands	人数 Number	百分比 Percent
1	碧浪 Ariel	296	29.7
2	活力 28 Power28	181	18.2
3	奥妙 OMO	140	14.1
4	巧手 Dosia	100	10.0
5	白猫 White Cat	56	5.6
6	熊猫 Panda	51	5.1
7	汰渍 Tide	35	3.5
8	奇强 Qiqiang	18	1.8
9	宝莹 Persil	17	1.7
10	洛娃 Reward	14	1.4

n=996

5-6 样本、男性各年龄层、女性各年龄层是否是主要购买者/ Purchasers in the Household by the Whole Sample, Age and Gender Groups

	人数 Number	是 yes	不是 no
样本 Sample	1010	48.0	52.0
男性 Male	502	33.9	66.1
16~24 岁 Age	105	18.1	81.9
25~34 岁 Age	151	36.4	63.6
35~44 岁 Age	129	40.3	59.7
45~54 岁 Age	77	35.1	64.9
55~60 岁 Age	40	42.5	57.5
女性 Female	508	62.0	38.0
16~24 岁 Age	108	18.5	81.5
25~34 岁 Age	150	66.7	33.3
35~44 岁 Age	124	77.4	22.6
45~54 岁 Age	84	77.4	22.6
55~60 岁 Age	42	81.0	19.0

5-7 样本、男性各年龄层、女性各年龄层的使用方式/ Ways of Using the Products by the Whole Sample, Age and Gender Groups

	人数 Number	个人专用 personal use	家人共用 all family members share
样本 Sample	1009	4.0	96.0
男性 Male	502	5.0	95.0
16~24 岁 Age	104	6.7	93.3
25~34 岁 Age	151	4.0	96.0
35~44 岁 Age	131	5.3	94.7
45~54 岁 Age	76	1.3	98.7
55~60 岁 Age	40	10.0	90.0
女性 Female	507	3.0	97.0
16~24 岁 Age	108	1.9	98.1
25~34 岁 Age	149	2.7	97.3
35~44 岁 Age	124	1.6	98.4
45~54 岁 Age	84	4.8	95.2
55~60 岁 Age	42	7.1	92.9

5-8 样本、男性各年龄层、女性各年龄层的使用频率/ Frequencies of the Consumed Laundry Detergent by the Whole Sample, Age and Gender Groups

	人数 Number	一天 2 次或以上 twice a day or over	一天 1 次 once a day	两三天用 1 次 once 2 or 3 days	一周 1~2 次 once or twice a week	半个月 1 次或以下 once half a month or below
样本 Sample	997	2.8	9.9	35.6	49.0	2.6
男性 Male	497	3.0	8.5	33.8	51.3	3.4
16~24 岁 Age	101	5.9	5.9	33.7	51.5	3.0
25~34 岁 Age	149	3.4	8.7	32.9	50.3	4.7
35~44 岁 Age	131	0.8	10.7	33.6	51.1	3.8
45~54 岁 Age	76	1.3	6.6	36.8	53.9	1.3
55~60 岁 Age	40	5.0	10.0	32.5	50.0	2.5
女性 Female	500	2.6	11.4	37.4	46.8	1.8
16~24 岁 Age	105	0.0	9.5	27.6	59.0	3.8
25~34 岁 Age	146	2.1	13.0	40.4	43.2	1.4
35~44 岁 Age	124	3.2	12.1	41.9	41.9	0.8
45~54 岁 Age	83	4.8	7.2	37.3	49.4	1.2
55~60 岁 Age	42	4.8	16.7	38.1	38.1	2.4

5-9 选择该类商品的考虑因素/ Ranking of the Considerations in Purchasing

注：本题为多选题，合计百分比超过 100%（Multiple answers）

排名 Ranking	考虑因素 Considerations	人次 Person-time	百分比 Percent
1	价格适中 reasonable price	470	47.2
2	产品功用 product function	389	39.1
3	有名的牌子 famous brand	333	33.4
4	单位发的 offered by the working unit	228	22.9
5	广告影响 influence of advertising	184	18.5
6	购买方便 easy to buy	148	14.9
7	有优惠条件 with preferential terms	58	5.8
8	别人推荐 introduced by other people	31	3.1
9	其它 others	16	1.6
10	包装吸引人 appealing package	14	1.4

n=996

5-10 对产品功能的侧重方面/ Ranking of the Considerations about the Function of this Kind of Product

注：本题为多选题，合计百分比超过 100%（Multiple answers）

排名 Ranking	侧重方面 Items	人次 Person-time	百分比 Percent
1	去污力强 powerful cleaning	786	79.2
2	味道清香 fresh smell	408	41.1
3	不伤手 harmless to hand	176	17.7
4	容易冲洗 easy to clean	175	17.6
5	容易溶解 easy to solve	173	17.4
6	不损害衣物 harmless to clothes	156	15.7
7	是浓缩型 condensed	87	8.8
8	是加酶型 with enzyme	68	6.9
9	无磷/低磷 non-phosphorus/low-phosphorus	61	6.1
10	有护色功能 color protect	34	3.4
11	含特殊配方 special formula	21	2.1
12	其他 others	13	1.3

n=992

5-11 家中其他洗衣用品的比例/ Proportion of the Other Products Used for Laundry in the Household

注：本题为多选题，合计百分比超过 100%（Multiple answers）

	人次 Person-time	百分比 Percent
肥皂 soap	718	72.2
皂粉 soap powder	39	3.9
洗衣剂 detergent	208	20.9
洗衣膏 laundry paste	15	1.5
衣领净 collar cleaner	782	78.7
漂白剂 bleacher	84	8.5
丝麻专用 specified for silk lines	201	20.2
衣物柔顺剂 fabric softener	562	56.5
其他 others	6	0.6
以上都不用 none of above	33	3.3

n=994

5-12 重度消费者的人口分布/ Demographics of the Heavy Consumers

	人数 Number	16-24 岁 Age	25-34 岁 Age	35-44 岁 Age	45-54 岁 Age	55-60 岁 Age
样本	482	17.6	30.7	27.0	15.6	9.1
男性 Male	225	20.4	29.8	26.2	15.1	8.4
一天 2 次或以上 twice a day or over	15	40.0	33.3	6.7	6.7	13.3
一天 1 次 once a day	42	14.3	31.0	33.3	11.9	9.5
两三天用 1 次 once 2 or 3 days	168	20.2	29.2	26.2	16.7	7.7
女性 Female	257	15.2	31.5	27.6	16.0	9.7
一天 2 次或以上 twice a day or over	13	0.0	23.1	30.8	30.8	15.4
一天 1 次 once a day	57	17.5	33.3	26.3	10.5	12.3
两三天用 1 次 once 2 or 3 days	187	15.5	31.6	27.8	16.6	8.6

5-13 不同消费者层的常用品牌/ The Most Frequently Used Brands by Market Segments

5-13-1 时尚流行指标/ Fads Popular Index

	人数 Number	第一品牌及百分比 1st / percent	第二品牌及百分比 2nd / percent	第三品牌及百分比 3rd / percent	第四品牌及百分比 4th / percent
样本 Sample	994	碧浪 Ariel(26.8)	活力 28 Power28(20.3)	奥妙 OMO(14.3)	巧手 Dosia(10.2)
平实生活指向 simple living orientation	488	碧浪 Ariel(24.2)	活力 28 Power28(20.3)	奥妙 OMO(12.5)	巧手 Dosia(11.7)
时尚流行指向 fashion orientation	506	碧浪 Ariel(29.2)	活力 28 Power28(20.4)	奥妙 OMO(16.0)	巧手 Dosia(8.7)

5-13-2 广告态度指标/ Advertising Attitude Index

	人数 Number	第一品牌及百分比 1st / percent	第二品牌及百分比 2nd / percent	第三品牌及百分比 3rd / percent	第四品牌及百分比 4th / percent
样本 Sample	990	碧浪 Ariel(26.0)	活力 28 Power28(20.6)	奥妙 OMO(14.1)	巧手 Dosia(10.3)
广告淡漠指向 indifferent orientation	289	碧浪 Ariel(23.2)	活力 28 Power28(19.7)	奥妙 OMO(10.7)	巧手 Dosia(10.0) 熊猫 Panda(10.0)
中间层 medium	568	碧浪 Ariel(26.8)	活力 28 Power28(20.8)	奥妙 OMO(16.0)	巧手 Dosia(10.2)
信赖广告指向 loyal orientation	133	碧浪 Ariel(28.6)	活力 28 Power28(21.8)	奥妙 OMO(13.5)	巧手 Dosia(11.3)

5-14 重度消费者的消费层构成/ The Composition of the Heavy Consumers

5-14-1 时尚流行指标/ Fads Popular Index

	人数 Number	平实生活指向 simple living orientation	时尚流行指向 fashion orientation
样本 Sample	474	46.4	53.6
一天 2 次或以上 twice a day or over	27	44.4	55.6
一天 1 次 once a day	98	40.8	59.2
两三天用 1 次 once 2 or 3 days	349	48.1	51.9

5-14-2 广告态度指标/ Advertising Attitude Index

	人数 Number	广告淡漠指向 indifferent orientation	中间层 medium	信赖广告指向 loyal orientation
样本 Sample	470	26.4	58.5	15.1
一天 2 次或以上 twice a day or over	28	21.4	64.3	14.3
一天 1 次 once a day	92	15.2	67.4	17.4
两三天用 1 次 once 2 or 3 days	350	29.7	55.7	14.6

● 上海 / Shanghai

5-1 最常用品牌排名/ Ranking of the Most Frequently Used Brands

排名 Brand Ranking	品牌 Brands	人数 Number	百分比 Percent
1	佳美 Jiamei	316	31.3
2	奥妙 OMO	301	29.8
3	白猫 White Cat	245	24.3
4	碧浪 Ariel	35	3.5
5	巧手 Dosia	25	2.5
6	美加净 Maxam	18	1.8
7	裕华 Yuhua	14	1.4
8	洁霸 Attack	13	1.3
9	汰渍 Tide	12	1.2
10	奇强 Qiqiang	7	0.7
11	扇牌 Fan	6	0.6
12	雕牌 Diao	4	0.4
13	宝莹 Persil	2	0.2

n=1009

5-2 样本、男性各年龄层、女性各年龄层的常用品牌/ The Most Frequently Used Brands by the Whole Sample, Age and Gender Groups

	人数 Number	第一品牌及百分比 1st/ percent	第二品牌及百分比 2nd/ percent	第三品牌及百分比 3rd/ percent
样本 Sample	1009	**佳美 Jiamei(31.3)**	**奥妙 OMO(29.8)**	**白猫 White Cat(24.3)**
男性 Male	506	**佳美 Jiamei(31.2)**	**奥妙 OMO(28.9)**	**白猫 White Cat(25.9)**
16~24 岁 Age	109	佳美 Jiamei(33.9)	奥妙 OMO(33.0)	白猫 White Cat(17.4)
25~34 岁 Age	144	奥妙 OMO(36.1)	白猫 White Cat(25.7)	佳美 Jiamei(23.6)
35~44 岁 Age	129	佳美 Jiamei(31.8)	白猫 White Cat(26.4)	奥妙 OMO(24.8)
45~54 岁 Age	85	佳美 Jiamei(36.5)	白猫 White Cat(35.3)	奥妙 OMO(21.2)
55~60 岁 Age	39	佳美 Jiamei(38.5)	白猫 White Cat(28.2)	奥妙 OMO(20.5)
女性 Female	503	**佳美 Jiamei(31.4)**	**奥妙 OMO(30.8)**	**白猫 White Cat(22.7)**
16~24 岁 Age	107	奥妙 OMO(39.3)	佳美 Jiamei(24.3)	白猫 White Cat(21.5)
25~34 岁 Age	144	奥妙 OMO(31.3)	白猫 White Cat(23.6)	佳美 Jiamei(22.9)
35~44 岁 Age	130	佳美 Jiamei(38.5)	奥妙 OMO(30.0)	白猫 White Cat(21.5)
45~54 岁 Age	81	佳美 Jiamei(44.4)	奥妙 OMO(24.7)	白猫 White Cat(19.8)
55~60 岁 Age	41	白猫 White Cat(31.7) 佳美 Jiamei(31.7)	奥妙 OMO(22.0)	碧浪 Ariel(4.9) 巧手 Dosia(4.9)

5-3 正在使用的品牌排名/ Ranking of the Brands Used Now

排名 Brand Ranking	品牌 Brands	人数 Number	百分比 Percent
1	奥妙 OMO	301	29.8
2	佳美 Jiamei	292	28.9
3	白猫 White Cat	223	22.1
4	碧浪 Ariel	44	4.4
5	巧手 Dosia	43	4.3
6	洁霸 Attack	21	2.1
7	美加净 Maxam	18	1.8
8	汰渍 Tide	13	1.3
9	奇强 Qiqiang	12	1.2
10	裕华 Yuhua	11	1.1

n=1010

5-4 品牌转换习惯/ Brand Habit in Consuming Laundry Detergent

	人数 Number	第一次使用该品牌 first use this brand	上一次也是这个牌子 used it last time	上一次不是这个牌子 not used it last time
样本 Sample	1008	6.3	82.5	11.1
奥妙 OMO	301	5.0	86.7	8.3
佳美 Jiamei	292	2.7	89.7	7.5
白猫 White Cat	222	2.7	83.8	13.5
碧浪 Ariel	44	11.4	70.5	18.2
巧手 Dosia	43	18.6	51.2	30.2
洁霸 Attack	21	42.9	52.4	4.8
美加净 Maxam	18	5.6	77.8	16.7
汰渍 Tide	13	15.4	61.5	23.1
奇强 Qiqiang	12	16.7	66.7	16.7
裕华 Yuhua	11	0.0	90.9	9.1

5-5 下一次打算使用的品牌排名/ Ranking of the Brands to be Used Next Time

排名 Brand Ranking	品牌 Brands	人数 Number	百分比 Percent
1	奥妙 OMO	331	32.8
2	佳美 Jiamei	245	24.3
3	白猫 White Cat	206	20.4
4	碧浪 Ariel	68	6.7
5	巧手 Dosia	37	3.7
6	洁霸 Attack	25	2.5
7	汰渍 Tide	16	1.6
7	美加净 Maxam	16	1.6
8	奇强 Qiqiang	13	1.3
9	裕华 Yuhua	9	0.9
10	扇牌 Fan	6	0.6

n=1009

5-6 样本、男性各年龄层、女性各年龄层是否是主要购买者/ Purchasers in the Household by the Whole Sample, Age and Gender Groups

	人数 Number	是 yes	不是 no
样本 Sample	1014	55.7	44.3
男性 Male	509	40.9	59.1
16~24 岁 Age	109	24.8	75.2
25~34 岁 Age	146	34.9	65.1
35~44 岁 Age	130	44.6	55.4
45~54 岁 Age	85	57.6	42.4
55~60 岁 Age	39	59.0	41.0
女性 Female	505	70.7	29.3
16~24 岁 Age	108	23.1	76.9
25~34 岁 Age	144	70.1	29.9
35~44 岁 Age	130	92.3	7.7
45~54 岁 Age	82	90.2	9.8
55~60 岁 Age	41	90.2	9.8

5-7 样本、男性各年龄层、女性各年龄层的使用方式/ Ways of Using the Products by the Whole Sample, Age and Gender Groups

	人数 Number	个人专用 personal use	家人共用 all family members share
样本 Sample	1009	4.5	95.5
男性 Male	507	5.5	94.5
16~24 岁 Age	109	5.5	94.5
25~34 岁 Age	145	6.2	93.8
35~44 岁 Age	129	7.0	93.0
45~54 岁 Age	85	1.2	98.8
55~60 岁 Age	39	7.7	92.3
女性 Female	502	3.4	96.6
16~24 岁 Age	106	2.8	97.2
25~34 岁 Age	144	3.5	96.5
35~44 岁 Age	130	3.1	96.9
45~54 岁 Age	81	3.7	96.3
55~60 岁 Age	41	4.9	95.1

5-8 样本、男性各年龄层、女性各年龄层的使用频率/ Frequencies of the Consumed Laundry Detergent by the Whole Sample, Age and Gender Groups

	人数 Number	一天 2 次或以上 twice a day or over	一天 1 次 once a day	两三天用 1 次 once 2 or 3 days	一周 1~2 次 once or twice a week	半个月 1 次或以下 once half a month or below
样本 Sample	1004	3.9	35.5	32.4	25.8	2.5
男性 Male	505	3.4	32.9	33.9	26.3	3.6
16~24 岁 Age	109	1.8	20.2	33.9	38.5	5.5
25~34 岁 Age	145	3.4	30.3	41.4	22.1	2.8
35~44 岁 Age	127	3.1	35.4	30.7	27.6	3.1
45~54 岁 Age	85	4.7	45.9	30.6	15.3	3.5
55~60 岁 Age	39	5.1	41.0	23.1	28.2	2.6
女性 Female	499	4.4	38.1	30.9	25.3	1.4
16~24 岁 Age	106	4.7	27.4	32.1	32.1	3.8
25~34 岁 Age	142	4.2	38.7	32.4	23.9	0.7
35~44 岁 Age	129	3.9	39.5	36.4	18.6	1.6
45~54 岁 Age	81	4.9	43.2	22.2	29.6	0.0
55~60 岁 Age	41	4.9	48.8	22.0	24.4	0.0

5-9 选择该类商品的考虑因素/ Ranking of the Considerations in Purchasing

注：本题为多选题，合计百分比超过 100%（Multiple answers）

排名 Ranking	考虑因素 Considerations	人次 Person-time	百分比 Percent
1	价格适中 reasonable price	592	58.6
2	产品功用 product function	440	43.6
3	有名的牌子 famous brand	354	35.0
4	购买方便 easy to buy	241	23.9
5	广告影响 influence of advertising	174	17.2
6	有优惠条件 with preferential terms	68	6.7
7	单位发的 offered by the working unit	53	5.2
8	别人推荐 introduced by other people	42	4.2
9	包装吸引人 appealing package	21	2.1
10	其它 others	9	0.9

n=1010

5-10 对产品功能的侧重方面/ Ranking of the Considerations about the Function of this Kind of Product

注：本题为多选题，合计百分比超过 100%（Multiple answers）

排名 Ranking	侧重方面 Items	人次 Person-time	百分比 Percent
1	去污力强 powerful cleaning	798	79.4
2	味道清香 fresh smell	315	31.3
3	不伤手 harmless to hand	293	29.2
4	容易溶解 easy to solve	227	22.6
5	容易冲洗 easy to clean	215	21.4
6	不损害衣物 harmless to clothes	167	16.6
7	是加酶型 with enzyme	114	11.3
8	是浓缩型 condensed	58	5.8
9	有护色功能 color protect	51	5.1
10	无磷/低磷 non-phosphorus/low-phosphorus	27	2.7
11	含特殊配方 special formula	17	1.7
12	其他 others	4	0.4

n=1005

5-11 家中其他洗衣用品的比例/ Proportion of the Other Products Used for Laundry in the Household

注：本题为多选题，合计百分比超过 100%（Multiple answers）

	人次 Person-time	百分比 Percent
肥皂 soap	812	80.7
皂粉 soap powder	223	22.2
洗衣剂 detergent	98	9.7
洗衣膏 laundry paste	11	1.1
衣领净 collar cleaner	266	26.4
漂白剂 bleacher	68	6.8
丝麻专用 specified for silk lines	161	16.0
衣物柔顺剂 fabric softener	409	40.7
其他 others	8	0.8
以上都不用 none of above	63	6.3

n=1006

5-12 重度消费者的人口分布/ Demographics of the Heavy Consumers

	人数 Number	16-24 岁 Age	25-34 岁 Age	35-44 岁 Age	45-54 岁 Age	55-60 岁 Age
样本	**720**	**17.9**	**30.0**	**26.5**	**17.5**	**8.1**
男性 Male	**354**	**17.2**	**30.8**	**24.9**	**19.5**	**7.6**
一天 2 次或以上 twice a day or over	17	11.8	29.4	23.5	23.5	11.8
一天 1 次 once a day	166	13.3	26.5	27.1	23.5	9.6
两三天用 1 次 once 2 or 3 days	171	21.6	35.1	22.8	15.2	5.3
女性 Female	**366**	**18.6**	**29.2**	**28.1**	**15.6**	**8.5**
一天 2 次或以上 twice a day or over	22	22.7	27.3	22.7	18.2	9.1
一天 1 次 once a day	190	15.3	28.9	26 8	18.4	10.5
两三天用 1 次 once 2 or 3 days	154	22.1	29.9	30 5	11.7	5.8

5-13 不同消费者层的常用品牌/ The Most Frequently Used Brands by Market Segments

5-13-1 时尚流行指标/ Fads Popular Index

	人数 Number	第一品牌及百分比 1st / percent	第二品牌及百分比 2nd / percent	第三品牌及百分比 3rd / percent
样本 Sample	**1001**	**佳美 Jiamei（31.1）**	**奥妙 OMO（29.9）**	**白猫 White Cat（24.5）**
平实生活指向 simple living orientation	470	佳美 Jiamei（37.7）	奥妙 OMO（26.6）	白猫 White Cat（24.9）
时尚流行指向 fashion orientation	531	奥妙 OMO（32.8）	佳美 Jiamei（25.2）	白猫 White Cat（24.1）

5-13-2 广告态度指标/ Advertising Attitude Index

	人数 Number	第一品牌及百分比 1st / percent	第二品牌及百分比 2nd / percent	第三品牌及百分比 3rd / percent
样本 Sample	**997**	**佳美 Jiamei（31.5）**	**奥妙 OMO（29.9）**	**白猫 White Cat（24.1）**
广告淡漠指向 indifferent orientation	255	佳美 Jiamei（34.5）	奥妙 OMO（27.1）	白猫 White Cat（24.3）
中间层 medium	609	佳美 Jiamei（30.9）	奥妙 OMO（29.9）	白猫 White Cat（24.5）
信赖广告指向 loyal orientation	133	奥妙 OMO（35.3）	佳美 Jiamei（28.6）	白猫 White Cat（21.8）

5-14 重度消费者的消费层构成/ The Composition of the Heavy Consumers

5-14-1 时尚流行指标/ Fads Popular Index

	人数 Number	平实生活指向 simple living orientation	时尚流行指向 fashion orientation
样本 Sample	**713**	**46.7**	**53.3**
一天 2 次或以上 twice a day or over	38	44.7	55.3
一天 1 次 once a day	352	49.7	50.3
两三天用 1 次 once 2 or 3 days	323	43.7	56.3

5-14-2 广告态度指标/ Advertising Attitude Index

	人数 Number	广告淡漠指向 indifferent orientation	中间层 medium	信赖广告指向 loyal orientation
样本 Sample	**715**	**23.9**	**62.9**	**13.1**
一天 2 次或以上 twice a day or over	38	26.3	68.4	5.3
一天 1 次 once a day	354	24.6	60.5	15.0
两三天用 1 次 once 2 or 3 days	323	22.9	65.0	12.1

● 广州 / Guangzhou

5-1 最常用品牌排名/ Ranking of the Most Frequently Used Brands

排名 Brand Ranking	品牌 Brands	人数 Number	百分比 Percent
1	高富力 Gaofuli	381	36.9
2	碧浪 Ariel	170	16.5
3	立白 Libai	130	12.6
4	汰渍 Tide	92	8.9
5	奥妙 OMO	78	7.6
6	白猫 White Cat	60	5.8
7	浪奇 Langqi	30	2.9
8	洁霸 Attack	20	1.9

n=1032

5-2 样本、男性各年龄层、女性各年龄层的常用品牌/ The Most Frequently Used Brands by the Whole Sample, Age and Gender Groups

	人数 Number	第一品牌及百分比 1st/ percent	第二品牌及百分比 2nd/ percent	第三品牌及百分比 3rd/ percent	第四品牌及百分比 4th/ percent
样本 Sample	**1032**	**高富力 Gaofuli(36.9)**	**碧浪 Ariel(16.5)**	**立白 Libai(12.6)**	**汰渍 Tide(8.9)**
男性 Male	**497**	**高富力 Gaofuli(38.2)**	**碧浪 Ariel(16.1)**	**立白 Libai(11.5)**	**汰渍 Tide(8.5)**
16~24 岁 Age	106	高富力 Gaofuli(36.8)	碧浪 Ariel(18.9)	汰渍 Tide(13.2)	立白 Libai(11.3)
25~34 岁 Age	148	高富力 Gaofuli(37.8)	碧浪 Ariel(16.9)	立白 Libai(12.2)	汰渍 Tide(8.8)
35~44 岁 Age	127	高富力 Gaofuli(37.0)	碧浪 Ariel(15.0)	立白 Libai(12.6)	白猫 White Cat(10.2)
45~54 岁 Age	73	高富力 Gaofuli(41.1)	碧浪 Ariel(16.4)	立白 Libai(11.0)	奥妙 OMO(8.2)
55~60 岁 Age	43	高富力 Gaofuli(41.9)	白猫 White Cat(9.3) 碧浪 Ariel(9.3)	立白 Libai(7.0)	奥妙 OMO(4.7)
女性 Female	**535**	**高富力 Gaofuli(35.7)**	**碧浪 Ariel(16.8)**	**立白 Libai(13.6)**	**汰渍 Tide(9.3)**
16~24 岁 Age	112	高富力 Gaofuli(31.3)	碧浪 Ariel(23.2)	立白 Libai(13.4)	奥妙 OMO(8.0) 汰渍 Tide(8.0)
25~34 岁 Age	158	高富力 Gaofuli(32.3)	碧浪 Ariel(19.0)	立白 Libai(13.3)	汰渍 Tide(11.4)
35~44 岁 Age	137	高富力 Gaofuli(38.7)	碧浪 Ariel(13.9)	立白 Libai(11.7)	奥妙 OMO(10.9)
45~54 岁 Age	87	高富力 Gaofuli(42.5)	立白 Libai(13.8)	奥妙 OMO(11.5)	汰渍 Tide(9.2) 碧浪 Ariel(9.2)
55~60 岁 Age	41	高富力 Gaofuli(36.6)	立白 Libai(22.0)	碧浪 Ariel(17.1)	白猫 White Cat(7.3) 汰渍 Tide(7.3)

5-3 正在使用的品牌排名/ Ranking of the Brands Used Now

排名 Brand Ranking	品牌 Brands	人数 Number	百分比 Percent
1	高富力 Gaofuli	346	33.6
2	碧浪 Ariel	176	17.1
3	立白 Libai	143	13.9
4	汰渍 Tide	104	10.1
5	奥妙 OMO	75	7.3
6	白猫 White Cat	65	6.3
7	浪奇 Langqi	29	2.8
8	洁霸 Attack	26	2.5

n=1031

5-4 品牌转换习惯/ Brand Habit in Consuming Laundry Detergent

	人数 Number	第一次使用该品牌 first use this brand	上一次也是这个牌子 used it last time	上一次不是这个牌子 not used it last time
样本 Sample	1026	4.7	82.1	13.3
高富力 Gaofuli	345	2.3	90.7	7.0
碧浪 Ariel	175	1.1	81.7	17.1
立白 Libai	142	4.9	77.5	17.6
汰渍 Tide	104	9.6	73.1	17.3
奥妙 OMO	75	2.7	89.3	8.0
白猫 White Cat	65	4.6	76.9	18.5
浪奇 Langqi	28	7.1	78.6	14.3
洁霸 Attack	26	3.8	73.1	23.1

5-5 下一次打算使用的品牌排名/ Ranking of the Brands to be Used Next Time

排名 Brand Ranking	品牌 Brands	人数 Number	百分比 Percent
1	高富力 Gaofuli	278	27.0
2	碧浪 Ariel	210	20.4
3	立白 Libai	136	13.2
4	汰渍 Tide	107	10.4
5	奥妙 OMO	88	8.6
6	白猫 White Cat	55	5.3
8	洁霸 Attack	27	2.6
9	浪奇 Langqi	25	2.4

n=1029

5-6 样本、男性各年龄层、女性各年龄层是否是主要购买者/ Purchasers in the Household by the Whole Sample, Age and Gender Groups

	人数 Number	是 yes	不是 no
样本 Sample	1033	55.9	44.1
男性 Male	499	38.1	61.9
16~24 岁 Age	106	22.6	77.4
25~34 岁 Age	150	34.0	66.0
35~44 岁 Age	127	47.2	52.8
45~54 岁 Age	73	42.5	57.5
55~60 岁 Age	43	55.8	44.2
女性 Female	534	72.5	27.5
16~24 岁 Age	112	29.5	70.5
25~34 岁 Age	158	74.1	25.9
35~44 岁 Age	136	89.7	10.3
45~54 岁 Age	87	89.7	10.3
55~60 岁 Age	41	90.2	9.8

5-7 样本、男性各年龄层、女性各年龄层的使用方式/ Ways of Using the Products by the Whole Sample, Age and Gender Groups

	人数 Number	个人专用 personal use	家人共用 all family members share
样本 Sample	1033	4.1	95.9
男性 Male	498	4.6	95.4
16~24 岁 Age	106	7.5	92.5
25~34 岁 Age	149	7.4	92.6
35~44 岁 Age	127	1.6	98.4
45~54 岁 Age	73	0.0	100.0
55~60 岁 Age	43	4.7	95.3
女性 Female	535	3.6	96.4
16~24 岁 Age	112	3.6	96.4
25~34 岁 Age	158	3.2	96.8
35~44 岁 Age	137	4.4	95.6
45~54 岁 Age	87	3.4	96.6
55~60 岁 Age	41	2.4	97.6

5-8 样本、男性各年龄层、女性各年龄层的使用频率/ Frequencies of the Consumed Laundry Detergent by the Whole Sample, Age and Gender Groups

	人数 Number	一天 2 次或以上 twice a day or over	一天 1 次 once a day	两三天用 1 次 once 2 or 3 days	一周 1~2 次 once or twice a week	半个月 1 次或以下 once half a month or below
样本 Sample	1031	13.9	70.1	10.7	4.5	0.9
男性 Male	496	10.9	71.0	10.5	5.8	1.8
16~24 岁 Age	106	9.4	69.8	13.2	4.7	2.8
25~34 岁 Age	147	11.6	66.7	12.9	6.8	2.0
35~44 岁 Age	127	15.0	74.0	6.3	3.9	0.8
45~54 岁 Age	73	6.8	74.0	11.0	5.5	2.7
55~60 岁 Age	43	7.0	74.4	7.0	11.6	0.0
女性 Female	535	16.6	69.3	10.8	3.2	0.0
16~24 岁 Age	112	20.5	66.1	11.6	1.8	0.0
25~34 岁 Age	158	14.6	67.1	14.6	3.8	0.0
35~44 岁 Age	137	16.8	73.7	5.8	3.6	0.0
45~54 岁 Age	87	16.1	70.1	11.5	2.3	0.0
55~60 岁 Age	41	14.6	70.7	9.8	4.9	0.0

5-9 选择该类商品的考虑因素/ Ranking of the Considerations in Purchasing

注：本题为多选题，合计百分比超过 100%（Multiple answers）

排名 Ranking	考虑因素 Considerations	人次 Person-time	百分比 Percent
1	价格适中 reasonable price	576	56.0
2	产品功用 product function	430	41.8
3	有名的牌子 famous brand	347	33.7
4	购买方便 easy to buy	241	23.4
5	广告影响 influence of advertising	150	14.6
6	单位发的 offered by the working unit	82	8.0
7	有优惠条件 with preferential terms	66	6.4
8	包装吸引人 appealing package	45	4.4
9	别人推荐 introduced by other people	38	3.7
10	其它 others	16	1.6

n=1029

5-10 对产品功能的侧重方面/ Ranking of the Considerations about the Function of this Kind of Product

注：本题为多选题，合计百分比超过 100%（Multiple answers）

排名 Ranking	侧重方面 Items	人次 Person-time	百分比 Percent
1	去污力强 powerful cleaning	838	81.8
2	味道清香 fresh smell	399	38.9
3	容易冲洗 easy to clean	233	22.7
4	不损害衣物 harmless to clothes	187	18.2
5	容易溶解 easy to solve	161	15.7
6	不伤手 harmless to hand	151	14.7
7	是浓缩型 condensed	111	10.8
8	有护色功能 color protect	42	4.1
9	是加酶型 with enzyme	21	2.0
9	含特殊配方 special formula	21	2.0
10	无磷/低磷 non-phosphorus/low-phosphorus	19	1.9
11	其他 others	11	1.1

n=1025

5-11 家中其他洗衣用品的比例/ Proportion of the Other Products Used for Laundry in the Household

注：本题为多选题，合计百分比超过 100%（Multiple answers）

	人次 Person-time	百分比 Percent
肥皂 soap	347	34.5
皂粉 soap powder	91	9.0
洗衣剂 detergent	112	11.1
洗衣膏 laundry paste	19	1.9
衣领净 collar cleaner	325	32.3
漂白剂 bleacher	286	28.4
丝麻专用 specified for silk lines	27	2.7
衣物柔顺剂 fabric softener	335	33.3
其他 others	8	0.8
以上都不用 none of above	212	21.1

n=1007

5-12 重度消费者的人口分布/ Demographics of the Heavy Consumers

	人数 Number	16-24 岁 Age	25-34 岁 Age	35-44 岁 Age	45-54 岁 Age	55-60 岁 Age
样本 Sample	976	21.3	29.3	25.9	15.6	7.9
男性 Male	458	21.4	29.3	26.4	14.6	8.3
一天 2 次或以上 twice a day or over	54	18.5	31.5	35.2	9.3	5.6
一天 1 次 once a day	352	21.0	27.8	26.7	15.3	9.1
两三天用 1 次 once 2 or 3 days	52	26.9	36.5	15.4	15.4	5.8
女性 Female	518	21.2	29.3	25.5	16.4	7.5
一天 2 次或以上 twice a day or over	89	25.8	25.8	25.8	15.7	6.7
一天 1 次 once a day	371	19.9	28.6	27.2	16.4	7.8
两三天用 1 次 once 2 or 3 days	58	22.4	39.7	13.8	17.2	6.9

5-13 不同消费者层的常用品牌/ The Most Frequently Used Brands by Market Segments

5-13-1 时尚流行指标/ Fads Popular Index

	人数 Number	第一品牌及百分比 1st / percent	第二品牌及百分比 2nd / percent	第三品牌及百分比 3rd / percent	第四品牌及百分比 4th / percent
样本 Sample	1020	**高富力 Gaofuli(36.8)**	**碧浪 Ariel(16.5)**	**立白 Libai(12.5)**	**汰渍 Tide(9.0)**
平实生活指向 simple living orientation	517	高富力 Gaofuli(40.0)	碧浪 Ariel(14.1)	立白 Libai(13.2)	汰渍 Tide(9.5)
时尚流行指向 fashion orientation	503	高富力 Gaofuli(33.4)	碧浪 Ariel(18.9)	立白 Libai(11.7)	汰渍 Tide(8.5)

5-13-2 广告态度指标/ Advertising Attitude Index

	人数 Number	第一品牌及百分比 1st / percent	第二品牌及百分比 2nd / percent	第三品牌及百分比 3rd / percent	第四品牌及百分比 4th / percent
样本 Sample	1020	**高富力 Gaofuli(37.1)**	**碧浪 Ariel(16.5)**	**立白 Libai(12.6)**	**汰渍 Tide(8.9)**
广告淡漠指向 indifferent orientation	334	高富力 Gaofuli(38.3)	碧浪 Ariel(15.9)	立白 Libai(11.7)	汰渍 Tide(10.5)
中间层 medium	591	高富力 Gaofuli(36.9)	碧浪 Ariel(16.2)	立白 Libai(13.2)	汰渍 Tide(8.3)
信赖广告指向 loyal orientation	95	高富力 Gaofuli(33.7)	碧浪 Ariel(20.0)	立白 Libai(12.6)	奥妙 OMO(8.4)

5-14 重度消费者的消费层构成/ The Composition of the Heavy Consumers

5-14-1 时尚流行指标/ Fads Popular Index

	人数 Number	平实生活指向 simple living orientation	时尚流行指向 fashion orientation
样本 Sample	965	50.2	49.8
一天 2 次或以上 twice a day or over	141	44.0	56.0
一天 1 次 once a day	715	51.7	48.3
两三天用 1 次 once 2 or 3 days	109	47.7	52.3

5-14-2 广告态度指标/ Advertising Attitude Index

	人数 Number	广告淡漠指向 indifferent orientation	中间层 medium	信赖广告指向 loyal orientation
样本 Sample	964	31.8	58.7	9.4
一天 2 次或以上 twice a day or over	141	28.4	62.4	9.2
一天 1 次 once a day	714	34.2	56.2	9.7
两三天用 1 次 once 2 or 3 days	109	21.1	70.6	8.3

● 重庆 / Chongqing

5-1 最常用品牌排名/ Ranking of the Most Frequently Used Brands

排名 Brand Ranking	品牌 Brands	人数 Number	百分比 Percent
1	汰渍 Tide	147	23.6
2	白猫 White Cat	103	16.6
3	碧浪 Ariel	99	15.9
4	奥妙 OMO	90	14.5
5	蜀秀 Shuxiu	53	8.5
6	活力 28 Power28	24	3.9
7	立白 Libai	15	2.4
8	鹅牌 Epai	12	1.9
8	巧手 Dosia	12	1.9
8	黑猫 Heimao	12	1.9
9	奇强 Qiqiang	10	1.6
10	雕牌 Diao	9	1.4
11	威白 Wipp	8	1.3

n=622

5-2 样本、男性各年龄层、女性各年龄层的常用品牌/ The Most Frequently Used Brands by the Whole Sample, Age and Gender Groups

	人数 Number	第一品牌及百分比 1st/ percent	第二品牌及百分比 2nd/ percent	第三品牌及百分比 3rd/ percent	第四品牌及百分比 4th/ percent
样本 Sample	622	**汰渍 Tide(23.6)**	**白猫 White Cat(16.6)**	**碧浪 Ariel(15.9)**	**奥妙 OMO(14.5)**
男性 Male	312	**汰渍 Tide(25.6)**	**白猫 White Cat(17.6)**	**奥妙 OMO(15.1)**	**碧浪 Ariel(13.1)**
16~24 岁 Age	64	汰渍 Tide(21.9)	碧浪 Ariel(17.2)	白猫 White Cat(14.1)	奥妙 OMO(12.5)
25~34 岁 Age	92	汰渍 Tide(28.3)	奥妙 OMO(16.3)	白猫 White Cat(15.2)	碧浪 Ariel(12.0)
35~44 岁 Age	74	汰渍 Tide(25.7)	奥妙 OMO(17.6) 白猫 White Cat(17.6)	碧浪 Ariel(12.2)	蜀秀 Shuxiu(8.1)
45~54 岁 Age	54	汰渍 Tide(25.9)	白猫 White Cat(22.2)	奥妙 OMO(13.0) 碧浪 Ariel(13.0) 蜀秀 Shuxiu(13.0)	活力 28 Power28(5.6)
55~60 岁 Age	28	白猫 White Cat(25.0) 汰渍 Tide(25.0)	奥妙 OMO(14.3)	碧浪 Ariel(10.7) 蜀秀 Shuxiu(10.7)	立白 Libai(7.1) 威白 Wipp(7.1)
女性 Female	310	**汰渍 Tide(21.6)**	**碧浪 Ariel(18.7)**	**白猫 White Cat(15.5)**	**奥妙 OMO(13.9)**
16~24 岁 Age	64	碧浪 Ariel(26.6)	汰渍 Tide(18.8)	奥妙 OMO(12.5)	白猫 White Cat(10.9)
25~34 岁 Age	90	汰渍 Tide(27.8)	碧浪 Ariel(18.9)	白猫 White Cat(14.4)	奥妙 OMO(13.3)
35~44 岁 Age	73	汰渍 Tide(23.3)	碧浪 Ariel(16.4)	白猫 White Cat(15.1)	蜀秀 Shuxiu(9.6)
45~54 岁 Age	60	奥妙 OMO(25.0)	白猫 White Cat(16.7 汰渍 Tide(16.7)	碧浪 Ariel(15.0)	蜀秀 Shuxiu(6.7)
55~60 岁 Age	23	白猫 White Cat(30.4)	碧浪 Ariel(13.0) 汰渍 Tide(13.0)	奥妙 OMO(8.7) 活力 28 Power28(8.7) 黑猫 Heimao(8.7)	立白 Libai(4.3) 蜀秀 Shuxiu(4.3)

5-3 正在使用的品牌排名/ Ranking of the Brands Used Now

排名 Brand Ranking	品牌 Brands	人数 Number	百分比 Percent
1	汰渍 Tide	148	23.8
2	碧浪 Ariel	105	16.9
3	白猫 White Cat	100	16.1
4	奥妙 OMO	89	14.3
5	蜀秀 Shuxiu	48	7.7
6	活力 28 Power28	25	4.0
7	立白 Libai	19	3.1
8	巧手 Dosia	16	2.6
9	黑猫 Heimao	12	1.9
10	奇强 Qiqiang	11	1.8
11	雕牌 Diao	8	1.3
12	威白 Wipp	7	1.1
12	鹅牌 Epai	7	1.1

n=622

5-4 品牌转换习惯/ Brand Habit in Consuming Laundry Detergent

	人数 Number	第一次使用该品牌 first use this brand	上一次也是这个牌子 used it last time	上一次不是这个牌子 not used it last time
样本 Sample	619	5.5	72.4	22.1
汰渍 Tide	148	2.0	76.4	21.6
碧浪 Ariel	105	6.7	66.7	26.7
白猫 White Cat	99	6.1	71.7	22.2
奥妙 OMO	87	3.4	80.5	16.1
蜀秀 Shuxiu	48	2.1	81.3	16.7
活力 28 Power28	25	12.0	72.0	16.0
立白 Libai	19	10.5	63.2	26.3
巧手 Dosia	16	0.0	68.8	31.3
黑猫 Heimao	12	8.3	91.7	0.0
奇强 Qiqiang	11	18.2	63.6	18.2

5-5 下一次打算使用的品牌排名/ Ranking of the Brands to be Used Next Time

排名 Brand Ranking	品牌 Brands	人数 Number	百分比 Percent
1	汰渍 Tide	148	23.9
2	碧浪 Ariel	115	18.5
3	白猫 White Cat	96	15.5
4	奥妙 OMO	93	15.0
5	蜀秀 Shuxiu	39	6.3
6	活力 28 Power28	24	3.9
7	巧手 Dosia	15	2.4
8	立白 Libai	14	2.3
9	黑猫 Heimao	12	1.9
10	雕牌 Diao	9	1.5
10	奇强 Qiqiang	9	1.5
11	威白 Wipp	7	1.1

n=620

5-6 样本、男性各年龄层、女性各年龄层是否是主要购买者/ Purchasers in the Household by the Whole Sample, Age and Gender Groups

	人数 Number	是 yes	不是 no
样本 Sample	624	54.8	45.2
男性 Male	314	37.9	62.1
16~24 岁 Age	64	20.3	79.7
25~34 岁 Age	93	41.9	58.1
35~44 岁 Age	75	44.0	56.0
45~54 岁 Age	54	37.0	63.0
55~60 岁 Age	28	50.0	50.0
女性 Female	310	71.9	28.1
16~24 岁 Age	64	35.9	64.1
25~34 岁 Age	90	76.7	23.3
35~44 岁 Age	73	87.7	12.3
45~54 岁 Age	60	80.0	20.0
55~60 岁 Age	23	82.6	17.4

5-7 样本、男性各年龄层、女性各年龄层的使用方式/ Ways of Using the Products by the Whole Sample, Age and Gender Groups

	人数 Number	个人专用 personal use	家人共用 all family members share
样本 Sample	622	2.6	97.4
男性 Male	312	3.2	96.8
16~24 岁 Age	64	3.1	96.9
25~34 岁 Age	92	5.4	94.6
35~44 岁 Age	74	4.1	95.9
45~54 岁 Age	54	0.0	100.0
55~60 岁 Age	28	0.0	100.0
女性 Female	310	1.9	98.1
16~24 岁 Age	64	4.7	95.3
25~34 岁 Age	90	0.0	100.0
35~44 岁 Age	73	2.7	97.3
45~54 岁 Age	60	1.7	98.3
55~60 岁 Age	23	0.0	100.0

5-8 样本、男性各年龄层、女性各年龄层的使用频率/ Frequencies of the Consumed Laundry Detergent by the Whole Sample, Age and Gender Groups

	人数 Number	一天 2 次或以上 twice a day over	一天 1 次 once a day	两三天用 1 次 once 2 or 3 days	一周 1~2 次 once or twice a week	半个月 1 次或以下 once half a month or below
样本 Sample	619	3.9	21.2	41.8	29.2	3.9
男性 Male	310	4.8	19.0	37.7	32.3	6.1
16~24 岁 Age	64	1.6	10.9	40.6	32.8	14.1
25~34 岁 Age	92	6.5	14.1	38.0	35.9	5.4
35~44 岁 Age	73	4.1	26.0	37.0	28.8	4.1
45~54 岁 Age	53	5.7	30.2	32.1	30.2	1.9
55~60 岁 Age	28	7.1	14.3	42.9	32.1	3.6
女性 Female	309	2.9	23.3	46.0	26.2	1.6
16~24 岁 Age	64	0.0	20.3	40.6	34.4	4.7
25~34 岁 Age	90	2.2	27.8	52.2	17.8	0.0
35~44 岁 Age	73	5.5	19.2	42.5	31.5	1.4
45~54 岁 Age	60	1.7	23.3	43.3	30.0	1.7
55~60 岁 Age	22	9.1	27.3	54.5	9.1	0.0

5-9 选择该类商品的考虑因素/ Ranking of the Considerations in Purchasing

注：本题为多选题，合计百分比超过 100%（Multiple answers）

排名 Ranking	考虑因素 Considerations	人次 Person-time	百分比 Percent
1	价格适中 reasonable price	326	52.7
2	产品功用 product function	272	43.9
3	有名的牌子 famous brand	172	27.8
4	广告影响 influence of advertising	134	21.6
5	购买方便 easy to buy	105	17.0
6	单位发的 offered by the working unit	66	10.7
7	有优惠条件 with preferential terms	22	3.6
8	别人推荐 introduced by other people	21	3.4
9	包装吸引人 appealing package	16	2.6
10	其它 others	10	1.6

n=619

5-10 对产品功能的侧重方面/ Ranking of the Considerations about the Function of this Kind of Product

注：本题为多选题，合计百分比超过 100%（Multiple answers）

排名 Ranking	侧重方面 Items	人次 Person-time	百分比 Percent
1	去污力强 powerful cleaning	522	84.5
2	味道清香 fresh smell	271	43.9
3	容易冲洗 easy to clean	106	17.2
4	不伤手 harmless to hand	102	16.5
5	不损害衣物 harmless to clothes	96	15.5
6	容易溶解 easy to solve	89	14.4
7	是加酶型 with enzyme	44	7.1
8	是浓缩型 condensed	35	5.7
9	含特殊配方 special formula	15	2.4
10	有护色功能 color protect	14	2.3
11	无磷/低磷 non-phosphorus/low-phosphorus	10	1.6
12	其他 others	9	1.5

n=618

5-11 家中其他洗衣用品的比例/ Proportion of the Other Products Used for Laundry in the Household

注：本题为多选题，合计百分比超过 100%（Multiple answers）

	人次 Person-time	百分比 Percent
肥皂 soap	550	89.6
皂粉 soap powder	61	9.9
洗衣剂 detergent	50	8.1
洗衣膏 laundry paste	30	4.9
衣领净 collar cleaner	86	14.0
漂白剂 bleacher	18	2.9
丝麻专用 specified for silk lines	23	3.7
衣物柔顺剂 fabric softener	36	5.9
其他 others	7	1.1
以上都不用 none of above	43	7.0

n=614

5-12 重度消费者的人口分布/ Demographics of the Heavy Consumers

	人数 Number	15-24 岁 Age	25-34 岁 Age	35-44 岁 Age	45-54 岁 Age	55-60 岁 Age
样本 Sample	414	17.6	30.9	23.7	18.6	9.2
男性 Male	191	17.8	28.3	25.7	18.8	9.4
一天 2 次或以上 twice or over a day	15	6.7	40.0	20.0	20.0	13.3
一天 1 次 once a day	59	11.9	22.0	32.2	27.1	6.8
两三天用 1 次 once 2 or 3 days	117	22.2	29.9	23.7	14.5	10.3
女性 Female	223	17.5	33.2	22.0	18.4	9.0
一天 2 次或以上 twice or over a day	9	0.0	22.2	44.4	11.1	22.2
一天 1 次 once a day	72	18.1	34.7	19.4	19.4	8.3
两三天用 1 次 once 2 or 3 days	142	18.3	33.1	21.8	18.3	8.5

5-13 不同消费者层的常用品牌/ The Most Frequently Used Brands by Market Segments

5-13-1 时尚流行指标/ Fads Popular Index

	人数 Number	第一品牌及百分比 1st / percent	第二品牌及百分比 2nd / percent	第三品牌及百分比 3rd / percent	第四品牌及百分比 4th / percent
样本 Sample	614	**汰渍 Tide(23.6)**	**白猫 White Cat(16.1) 碧浪 Ariel(16.1)**	**奥妙 OMO(14.5)**	**蜀秀 Shuxiu(8.6)**
平实生活指向 simple living orientation	367	汰渍 Tide(23.2)	白猫 White Cat(15.6)	奥妙 OMO(15.3)	碧浪 Ariel(13.6)
时尚流行指向 fashion orientation	247	汰渍 Tide(24.3)	碧浪 Ariel(19.8)	白猫 White Cat(15.4)	奥妙 OMO(13.4)

5-13-2 广告态度指标/ Advertising Attitude Index

	人数 Number	第一品牌及百分比 1st / percent	第二品牌及百分比 2nd / percent	第三品牌及百分比 3rd / percent	第四品牌及百分比 4th / percent
样本 Sample	616	**汰渍 Tide(23.7)**	**白猫 White Cat(16.6)**	**碧浪 Ariel(16.1)**	**奥妙 OMO(14.6)**
广告淡漠指向 indifferent orientation	165	汰渍 Tide(22.4)	奥妙 OMO(18.8)	白猫 White Cat(16.4)	碧浪 Ariel(14.5)
中间层 medium	367	汰渍 Tide(22.3)	白猫 White Cat(16.3)	碧浪 Ariel(15.8)	奥妙 OMO(13.6)
信赖广告指向 loyal orientation	84	汰渍 Tide(32.1)	碧浪 Ariel(20.2)	白猫 White Cat(17.9)	奥妙 OMO(10.7)

5-14 重度消费者的消费层构成/ The Composition of the Heavy Consumers

5-14-1 时尚流行指标/ Fads Popular Index

	人数 Number	平实生活指向 simple living orientation	时尚流行指向 fashion orientation
样本 Sample	408	58.6	41.4
一天 2 次或以上 twice a day or over	22	59.1	40.9
一天 1 次 once a day	131	58.0	42.0
两三天用 1 次 once 2 or 3 days	255	58.8	41.2

5-14-2 广告态度指标/ Advertising Attitude Index

	人数 Number	广告淡漠指向 indifferent orientation	中间层 medium	信赖广告指向 loyal orientation
样本 Sample	410	25.4	59.3	15.4
一天 2 次或以上 twice a day or over	23	21.7	56.5	21.7
一天 1 次 once a day	131	19.8	61.1	19.1
两三天用 1 次 once 2 or 3 days	256	28.5	58.6	12.9

● 武汉 / Wuhan

5-1 最常用品牌排名/ Ranking of the Most Frequently Used Brands

排名 Brand Ranking	品牌 Brands	人数 Number	百分比 Percent
1	活力 28 Power28	158	24.8
2	汰渍 Tide	91	14.3
3	奥妙 OMO	70	11.0
4	一枝花 A flower	67	10.5
5	白猫 White Cat	46	7.2
6	洗丽 Xili	43	6.8
7	威白 Wipp	33	5.2
8	巧手 Dosia	26	4.1
9	波尔 Boer	22	3.5
10	碧浪 Ariel	16	2.5

n=636

5-2 样本、男性各年龄层、女性各年龄层的常用品牌/ The Most Frequently Used Brands by the Whole Sample, Age and Gender Groups

	人数 Number	第一品牌及百分比 1st/ percent	第二品牌及百分比 2nd/ percent	第三品牌及百分比 3rd/ percent
样本 Sample	**636**	**活力 28 Power28(24.8)**	**汰渍 Tide(14.3)**	**奥妙 OMO(11.0)**
男性 Male	**307**	**活力 28 Power28(23.8)**	**汰渍 Tide(16.6)**	**一枝花 A flower(12.4)**
16~24 岁 Age	63	汰渍 Tide(28.6)	活力 28 Power28(17.5)	奥妙 OMO(9.5)
25~34 岁 Age	88	活力 28 Power28(23.9)	汰渍 Tide(15.9)	一枝花 A flower(14.8)
35~44 岁 Age	79	活力 28 Power28(24.1)	一枝花 A flower(11.4) 洗丽 Xili(11.4)	汰渍 Tide(10.1)
45~54 岁 Age	52	活力 28 Power28(25.0)	汰渍 Tide(17.3)	一枝花 A flower(15.4)
55~60 岁 Age	25	活力 28 Power28(36.0)	奥妙 OMO(12.0) 一枝花 A flower(12.0)	汰渍 Tide(8.0)
女性 Female	**329**	**活力 28 Power28(25.8)**	**奥妙 OMO(12.5)**	**汰渍 Tide(12.2)**
16~24 岁 Age	68	汰渍 Tide(23.5)	奥妙 OMO(20.6)	活力 28 Power28(13.2)
25~34 岁 Age	95	活力 28 Power28(20.0)	奥妙 OMO(13.7)	白猫 White Cat(11.6) 汰渍 Tide(11.6)
35~44 岁 Age	78	活力 28 Power28(33.3)	汰渍 Tide(10.3)	一枝花 A flower(9.0)
45~54 岁 Age	62	活力 28 Power28(33.9)	洗丽 Xili(14.5)	奥妙 OMO(11.3)
55~60 岁 Age	26	活力 28 Power28(38.5)	一枝花 A flower(11.5)	白猫 White Cat(7.7) 汰渍 Tide(7.7)

5-3 正在使用的品牌排名/ Ranking of the Brands Used Now

排名 Brand Ranking	品牌 Brands	人数 Number	百分比 Percent
1	活力 28 Power28	156	24.5
2	汰渍 Tide	89	14.0
3	一枝花 A flower	64	10.1
4	奥妙 OMO	60	9.4
5	白猫 White Cat	41	6.4
6	巧手 Dosia	37	5.8
6	洗丽 Xili	37	5.8
7	威白 Wipp	32	5.0
8	波尔 Boer	29	4.6
9	碧浪 Ariel	21	3.3

n=636

5-4 品牌转换习惯/ Brand Habit in Consuming Laundry Detergent

	人数 Number	第一次使用该品牌 first use this brand	上一次也是这个牌子 used it last time	上一次不是这个牌子 not used it last time
样本 Sample	**635**	**5.8**	**75.1**	**19.1**
活力 28 Power28	156	3.8	78.2	17.9
汰渍 Tide	89	2.2	79.8	18.0
一枝花 A flower	64	3.1	84.4	12.5
奥妙 OMO	60	6.7	71.7	21.7
白猫 White Cat	41	4.9	70.7	24.4
巧手 Dosia	37	8.1	56.8	35.1
洗丽 Xili	37	10.8	83.8	5.4
威白 Wipp	32	0.0	84.4	15.6
波尔 Boer	29	6.9	72.4	20.7
碧浪 Ariel	21	9.5	61.9	28.6

5-5 下一次打算使用的品牌排名/ Ranking of the Brands to be Used Next Time

排名 Brand Ranking	品牌 Brands	人数 Number	百分比 Percent
1	活力 28 Power28	138	21.7
2	汰渍 Tide	89	14.0
3	奥妙 OMO	82	12.9
4	一枝花 A flower	55	8.6
5	碧浪 Ariel	41	6.4
6	洗丽 Xili	38	6.0
7	白猫 White Cat	32	5.0
8	威白 Wipp	30	4.7
9	巧手 Dosia	27	4.2
10	波尔 Boer	21	3.3

n=636

5-6 样本、男性各年龄层、女性各年龄层是否是主要购买者/ Purchasers in the Household by the Whole Sample, Age and Gender Groups

	人数 Number	是 yes	不是 no
样本 Sample	641	52.7	47.3
男性 Male	311	36.3	63.7
16~24 岁 Age	65	10.8	89.2
25~34 岁 Age	89	31.5	68.5
35~44 岁 Age	80	43.8	56.3
45~54 岁 Age	52	53.8	46.2
55~60 岁 Age	25	60.0	40.0
女性 Female	330	68.2	31.8
16~24 岁 Age	69	15.9	84.1
25~34 岁 Age	96	67.7	32.3
35~44 岁 Age	77	93.5	6.5
45~54 岁 Age	62	93.5	6.5
55~60 岁 Age	26	73.1	26.9

5-7 样本、男性各年龄层、女性各年龄层的使用方式/ Ways of Using the Products by the Whole Sample, Age and Gender Groups

	人数 Number	个人专用 personal use	家人共用 all family members share
样本 Sample	635	2.8	97.2
男性 Male	307	3.6	96.4
16~24 岁 Age	63	6.3	93.7
25~34 岁 Age	88	3.4	96.6
35~44 岁 Age	79	1.3	98.7
45~54 岁 Age	52	1.9	98.1
55~60 岁 Age	25	8.0	92.0
女性 Female	328	2.1	97.9
16~24 岁 Age	68	2.9	97.1
25~34 岁 Age	95	1.1	98.9
35~44 岁 Age	78	0.0	100.0
45~54 岁 Age	62	1.6	98.4
55~60 岁 Age	25	12.0	88.0

5-8 样本、男性各年龄层、女性各年龄层的使用频率/ Frequencies of the Consumed Laundry Detergent by the Whole Sample, Age and Gender Groups

	人数 Number	一天 2 次或以上 twice a day or over	一天 1 次 once a day	两三天用 1 次 once 2 or 3 days	一周 1~2 次 once or twice a week	半个月 1 次或以下 once half a month or below
样本 Sample	633	6.8	39.5	32.7	17.9	3.2
男性 Male	307	5.5	38.8	32.9	18.6	4.2
16~24 岁 Age	63	1.6	27.0	44.4	19.0	7.9
25~34 岁 Age	88	8.0	34.1	33.0	21.6	3.4
35~44 岁 Age	79	6.3	45.6	29.1	16.5	2.5
45~54 岁 Age	52	3.8	42.3	28.8	19.2	5.8
55~60 岁 Age	25	8.0	56.0	24.0	12.0	0.0
女性 Female	326	8.0	40.2	32.5	17.2	2.1
16~24 岁 Age	68	10.3	30.9	39.7	16.2	2.9
25~34 岁 Age	93	9.7	45.2	25.8	19.4	0.0
35~44 岁 Age	78	5.1	38.5	30.8	23.1	2.6
45~54 岁 Age	62	8.1	43.5	37.1	8.1	3.2
55~60 岁 Age	25	4.0	44.0	32.0	16.0	4.0

5-9 选择该类商品的考虑因素/ Ranking of the Considerations in Purchasing

注：本题为多选题，合计百分比超过 100%（Multiple answers）

排名 Ranking	考虑因素 Considerations	人次 Person-time	百分比 Percent
1	价格适中 reasonable price	383	60.4
2	产品功用 product function	294	46.4
3	有名的牌子 famous brand	187	29.5
4	购买方便 easy to buy	142	22.4
5	广告影响 influence of advertising	106	16.7
6	单位发的 offered by the working unit	79	12.5
7	有优惠条件 with preferential terms	53	8.4
8	别人推荐 introduced by other people	35	5.5
9	包装吸引人 appealing package	24	3.8
10	其它 others	18	2.8

n=634

5-10 对产品功能的侧重方面/ Ranking of the Considerations about the Function of this Kind of Product

注：本题为多选题，合计百分比超过 100%（Multiple answers）

排名 Ranking	侧重方面 Items	人次 Person-time	百分比 Percent
1	去污力强 powerful cleaning	550	86.8
2	味道清香 fresh smell	288	45.4
3	不伤手 harmless to hand	144	22.7
4	容易冲洗 easy to clean	132	20.8
5	不损害衣物 harmless to clothes	110	17.4
6	容易溶解 easy to solve	105	16.6
7	是浓缩型 condensed	73	11.5
8	是加酶型 with enzyme	40	6.3
9	无磷/低磷 non-phosphorus/low-phosphorus	19	3.0
10	有护色功能 color protect	18	2.8
11	其他 others	9	1.4
12	含特殊配方 special formula	8	1.3

n=634

5-11 家中其他洗衣用品的比例/ Proportion of the Other Products Used for Laundry in the Household

注：本题为多选题，合计百分比超过 100%（Multiple answers）

	人次 Person-time	百分比 Percent
肥皂 soap	509	80.2
皂粉 soap powder	41	6.5
洗衣剂 detergent	74	11.7
洗衣膏 laundry paste	7	1.1
衣领净 collar cleaner	235	37.0
漂白剂 bleacher	27	4.3
丝麻专用 specified for silk lines	83	13.1
衣物柔顺剂 fabric softener	57	9.0
其他 others	7	1.1
以上都不用 none of above	56	8.8

n=635

5-12 重度消费者的人口分布/ Demographics of the Heavy Consumers

	人数 Number	16-24 岁 Age	25-34 岁 Age	35-44 岁 Age	45-54 岁 Age	55-60 岁 Age
样本	500	20.2	28.2	24.4	18.8	8.4
男性 Male	237	19.4	27.8	27.0	16.5	9.3
一天 2 次或以上 twice a day or over	17	5.9	41.2	29.4	11.8	11.8
一天 1 次 once a day	119	14.3	25.2	30.3	18.5	11.8
两三天用 1 次 once 2 or 3 days	101	27.7	28.7	22.3	14.9	5.9
女性 Female	263	20.9	28.5	22.1	20.9	7.6
一天 2 次或以上 twice a day or over	26	26.9	34.6	15.4	19.2	3.8
一天 1 次 once a day	131	16.0	32.1	22.9	20.6	8.4
两三天用 1 次 once 2 or 3 days	106	25.5	22.6	22.6	21.7	7.5

5-13 不同消费者层的常用品牌/ The Most Frequently Used Brands by Market Segments

5-13-1 时尚流行指标/ Fads Popular Index

	人数 Number	第一品牌及百分比 1st / percent	第二品牌及百分比 2nd / percent	第三品牌及百分比 3rd / percent	第四品牌及百分比 4th / percent
样本 Sample	626	**活力 28 Power28(24.9)**	**汰渍 Tide(14.1)**	**奥妙 OMO(11.2)**	**一枝花 A flower(10.4)**
平实生活指向 simple living orientation	328	活力 28 Power28(25.0)	汰渍 Tide(12.5)	一枝花 A flower(11.9)	奥妙 OMO(8.8)
时尚流行指向 fashion orientation	298	活力 28 Power28(24.8)	汰渍 Tide(15.8)	奥妙 OMO(13.8)	一枝花 A flower(8.7)

5-13-2 广告态度指标/ Advertising Attitude Index

	人数 Number	第一品牌及百分比 1st / percent	第二品牌及百分比 2nd / percent	第三品牌及百分比 3rd / percent	第四品牌及百分比 4th / percent
样本 Sample	628	**活力 28 Power28(25.0)**	**汰渍 Tide(14.2)**	**奥妙 OMO(11.1)**	**一枝花 A flower(10.4)**
广告淡漠指向 indifferent orientation	186	活力 28 Power28(29.0)	一枝花 A flower(11.3)	白猫 White Cat(9.7)	洗丽 Xili(9.1)
中间层 medium	369	活力 28 Power28(24.1)	汰渍 Tide(15.7)	奥妙 OMO(12.5)	一枝花 A flower(10.6)
信赖广告指向 loyal orientation	73	汰渍 Tide(20.5)	活力 28 Power28(19.2)	奥妙 OMO(16.4)	波尔 Boer(8.2)

5-14 重度消费者的消费层构成/ The Composition of the Heavy Consumers

5-14-1 时尚流行指标/ Fads Popular Index

	人数 Number	平实生活指向 simple living orientation	时尚流行指向 fashion orientation
样本 Sample	492	51.6	48.4
一天 2 次或以上 twice a day or over	43	37.2	62.8
一天 1 次 once a day	246	50.8	49.2
两三天用 1 次 once 2 or 3 days	203	55.7	44.3

5-14-2 广告态度指标/ Advertising Attitude Index

	人数 Number	广告淡漠指向 indifferent orientation	中间层 medium	信赖广告指向 loyal orientation
样本 Sample	494	28.9	58.3	12.8
一天 2 次或以上 twice a day or over	43	27.9	60.5	11.6
一天 1 次 once a day	247	34.0	56.7	9.3
两三天用 1 次 once 2 or 3 days	204	23.0	59.8	17.2

● 西安 / Xi'an

5-1 最常用品牌排名/ Ranking of the Most Frequently Used Brands

排名 Brand Ranking	品牌 Brands	人数 Number	百分比 Percent
1	汰渍 Tide	173	28.8
2	奇强 Qiqiang	135	22.5
3	活力 28 Power28	106	17.7
4	奥妙 OMO	58	9.7
5	雕牌 Diao	19	3.2
6	中华 Zhonghua	17	2.8
7	碧浪 Ariel	15	2.5
7	山丹丹 Shandandan	15	2.5
8	白猫 White Cat	11	1.8

n=600

5-2 样本、男性各年龄层、女性各年龄层的常用品牌/ The Most Frequently Used Brands by the Whole Sample, Age and Gender Groups

	人数 Number	第一品牌及百分比 1st/ percent	第二品牌及百分比 2nd/ percent	第三品牌及百分比 3rd/ percent	第四品牌及百分比 4th/ percent
样本 Sample	600	**汰渍 Tide(28.8)**	**奇强 Qiqiang(22.5)**	**活力 28 Power28(17.7)**	**奥妙 OMO(9.7)**
男性 Male	301	**汰渍 Tide(29.2)**	**奇强 Qiqiang(21.6)**	**活力 28 Power28(18.3)**	**奥妙 OMO(9.0)**
16~24 岁 Age	64	奇强 Qiqiang(31.3)	汰渍 Tide(29.7)	奥妙 OMO(12.5)	活力 28 Power28(9.4)
25~34 岁 Age	90	汰渍 Tide(31.1)	活力 28 Power28(20.0)	奇强 Qiqiang(18.9)	奥妙 OMO(11.1)
35~44 岁 Age	77	汰渍 Tide(29.9)	活力 28 Power28(22.1)	奇强 Qiqiang(19.5)	奥妙 OMO(5.2)
45~54 岁 Age	46	汰渍 Tide(28.3)	活力 28 Power28(23.9)	奇强 Qiqiang(15.2)	奥妙 OMO(6.5)
55~60 岁 Age	24	奇强 Qiqiang(25.0)	汰渍 Tide(20.8)	活力 28 Power28(12.5)	奥妙 OMO(8.3) 白猫 White Cat(8.3) 中华 Zhonghua(8.3)
女性 Female	299	**汰渍 Tide(28.4)**	**奇强 Qiqiang(23.4)**	**活力 28 Power28(17.1)**	**奥妙 OMO(10.4)**
16~24 岁 Age	61	汰渍 Tide(29.5)	活力 28 Power28(18.0)	奇强 Qiqiang(14.8)	奥妙 OMO(8.2)
25~34 岁 Age	90	奇强 Qiqiang(27.8)	汰渍 Tide(25.6)	活力 28 Power28(14.4)	奥妙 OMO(11.1)
35~44 岁 Age	74	汰渍 Tide(29.7)	奇强 Qiqiang(20.3)	活力 28 Power28(18.9)	奥妙 OMO(12.2)
45~54 岁 Age	49	汰渍 Tide(32.7)	奇强 Qiqiang(24.5)	活力 28 Power28(20.4)	奥妙 OMO(10.2)
55~60 岁 Age	25	奇强 Qiqiang(36.0)	汰渍 Tide(24.0)	活力 28 Power28(12.0)	奥妙 OMO(8.0) 中华 Zhonghua(8.0)

5-3 正在使用的品牌排名/ Ranking of the Brands Used Now

排名 Brand Ranking	品牌 Brands	人数 Number	百分比 Percent
1	汰渍 Tide	170	28.3
2	奇强 Qiqiang	138	23.0
3	活力 28 Power28	98	16.3
4	奥妙 OMO	58	9.7
5	雕牌 Diao	24	4.0
6	中华 Zhonghua	17	2.8
7	碧浪 Ariel	16	2.7
8	白猫 White Cat	14	2.3
9	山丹丹 Shandandan	10	1.7

n=600

5-4 品牌转换习惯/ Brand Habit in Consuming Laundry Detergent

	人数 Number	第一次使用该品牌 first use this brand	上一次也是这个牌子 used it last time	上一次不是这个牌子 not used it last time
样本 Sample	599	5.3	78.1	16.5
汰渍 Tide	170	2.4	79.4	18.2
奇强 Qiqiang	138	3.6	84.1	12.3
活力 28 Power28	98	3.1	84.7	12.2
奥妙 OMO	58	1.7	79.3	19.0
雕牌 Diao	24	12.5	62.5	25.0
中华 Zhonghua	17	5.9	76.5	17.6
碧浪 Ariel	16	31.3	43.8	25.0
白猫 White Cat	14	0.0	71.4	28.6
山丹丹 Shandandan	10	30.0	60.0	10.0

5-5 下一次打算使用的品牌排名/ Ranking of the Brands to be Used Next Time

排名 Brand Ranking	品牌 Brands	人数 Number	百分比 Percent
1	汰渍 Tide	241	40.3
2	奇强 Qiqiang	90	15.1
3	活力 28 Power28	83	13.9
4	奥妙 OMO	49	8.2
5	碧浪 Ariel	27	4.5
6	雕牌 Diao	24	4.0
7	中华 Zhonghua	11	1.8
8	白猫 White Cat	10	1.7
9	山丹丹 Shandandan	8	1.3
10	立白 Libai	6	1.0

n=598

5-6 样本、男性各年龄层、女性各年龄层是否是主要购买者/ Purchasers in the Household by the Whole Sample, Age and Gender Groups

	人数 Number	是 yes	不是 no
样本 Sample	601	57.6	42.4
男性 Male	302	35.8	64.2
16~24 岁 Age	64	25.0	75.0
25~34 岁 Age	91	39.6	60.4
35~44 岁 Age	77	41.6	58.4
45~54 岁 Age	46	28.3	71.7
55~60 岁 Age	24	45.8	54.2
女性 Female	299	79.6	20.4
16~24 岁 Age	61	45.9	54.1
25~34 岁 Age	90	84.4	15.6
35~44 岁 Age	74	90.5	9.5
45~54 岁 Age	49	91.8	8.2
55~60 岁 Age	25	88.0	12.0

5-7 样本、男性各年龄层、女性各年龄层的使用方式/ Ways of Using the Products by the Whole Sample, Age and Gender Groups

	人数 Number	个人专用 personal use	家人共用 all family members share
样本 Sample	601	3.8	96.2
男性 Male	302	4.6	95.4
16~24 岁 Age	64	7.8	92.2
25~34 岁 Age	91	4.4	95.6
35~44 岁 Age	77	2.6	97.4
45~54 岁 Age	46	2.2	97.8
55~60 岁 Age	24	8.3	91.7
女性 Female	299	3.0	97.0
16~24 岁 Age	61	3.3	96.7
25~34 岁 Age	90	4.4	95.6
35~44 岁 Age	74	2.7	97.3
45~54 岁 Age	49	0.0	100.0
55~60 岁 Age	25	4.0	96.0

5-8 样本、男性各年龄层、女性各年龄层的使用频率/ Frequencies of the Consumed Laundry Detergent by the Whole Sample, Age and Gender Groups

	人数 Number	一天 2 次或以上 twice a day or more	一天 1 次 once a day	两三天用 1 次 once 2 or 3 days	一周 1~2 次 once or twice a week	半个月 1 次或以下 once half a month or below
样本 Sample	599	2.7	9.5	40.2	42.1	5.5
男性 Male	300	2.0	9.7	37.3	43.7	7.3
16~24 岁 Age	63	0.0	14.3	30.2	44.4	11.1
25~34 岁 Age	90	2.2	7.8	40.0	44.4	5.6
35~44 岁 Age	77	2.6	9.1	45.5	35.1	7.8
45~54 岁 Age	46	2.2	6.5	37.0	47.8	6.5
55~60 岁 Age	24	4.2	12.5	20.8	58.3	4.2
女性 Female	299	3.3	9.4	43.1	40.5	3.7
16~24 岁 Age	61	1.6	8.2	37.7	47.5	4.9
25~34 岁 Age	90	3.3	11.1	37.8	42.2	5.6
35~44 岁 Age	74	2.7	6.8	48.6	41.9	0.0
45~54 岁 Age	49	4.1	14.3	49.0	30.6	2.0
55~60 岁 Age	25	8.0	4.0	48.0	32.0	8.0

5-9 选择该类商品的考虑因素/ Ranking of the Considerations in Purchasing

注：本题为多选题，合计百分比超过 100%（Multiple answers）

排名 Ranking	考虑因素 Considerations	人次 Person-time	百分比 Percent
1	价格适中 reasonable price	281	46.9
2	产品功用 product function	258	43.1
3	有名的牌子 famous brand	176	29.4
4	购买方便 easy to buy	140	23.4
5	广告影响 influence of advertising	113	18.9
6	单位发的 offered by the working unit	56	9.3
7	有优惠条件 with preferential terms	40	6.7
8	别人推荐 introduced by other people	29	4.8
9	包装吸引人 appealing package	20	3.3
10	其它 others	8	1.3

n=599

5-10 对产品功能的侧重方面/ Ranking of the Considerations about the Function of this Kind of Product

注：本题为多选题，合计百分比超过 100%（Multiple answers）

排名 Ranking	侧重方面 Items	人次 Person-time	百分比 Percent
1	去污力强 powerful cleaning	482	80.6
2	味道清香 fresh smell	246	41.1
3	容易冲洗 easy to clean	122	20.4
4	不伤手 harmless to hand	105	17.6
5	容易溶解 easy to solve	94	15.7
6	不损害衣物 harmless to clothes	83	13.9
7	是加酶型 with enzyme	52	8.7
8	是浓缩型 condensed	47	7.9
9	无磷/低磷 non-phosphorus/low-phosphorus	20	3.3
10	有护色功能 color protect	14	2.3
11	含特殊配方 special formula	5	0.8
12	其他 others	3	0.5

n=598

5-11 家中其他洗衣用品的比例/ Proportion of the Other Products Used for Laundry in the Household

注：本题为多选题，合计百分比超过 100%（Multiple answers）

	人次 Person-time	百分比 Percent
肥皂 soap	530	88.5
皂粉 soap powder	16	2.7
洗衣剂 detergent	78	13.0
洗衣膏 laundry paste	9	1.5
衣领净 collar cleaner	116	19.4
漂白剂 bleacher	26	4.3
丝麻专用 specified for silk lines	66	11.0
衣物柔顺剂 fabric softener	164	27.4
其他 others	3	0.5
以上都不用 none of above	28	4.7

n=599

5-12 重度消费者的人口分布/ Demographics of the Heavy Consumers

	人数 Number	16-24 岁 Age	25-34 岁 Age	35-44 岁 Age	45-54 岁 Age	55-60 岁 Age
样本 Sample	314	18.2	29.3	27.7	17.2	7.6
男性 Male	147	19.0	30.6	29.9	14.3	6.1
一天 2 次或以上 twice a day or over	6	0.0	33.3	33.3	16.7	16.7
一天 1 次 once a day	29	31.0	24.1	24.1	10.3	10.3
两三天用 1 次 once 2 or 3 days	112	17.0	32.1	31.3	15.2	4.5
女性 Female	167	17.4	28.1	25.7	19.8	9.0
一天 2 次或以上 twice a day or over	10	10.0	30.0	20.0	20.0	20.0
一天 1 次 once a day	28	17.9	35.7	17.9	25.0	3.6
两三天用 1 次 once 2 or 3 days	129	17.8	26.4	27.9	18.6	9.3

5-13 不同消费者层的常用品牌/ The Most Frequently Used Brands by Market Segments

5-13-1 时尚流行指标/ Fads Popular Index

	人数 Number	第一品牌及百分比 1st / percent	第二品牌及百分比 2nd / percent	第三品牌及百分比 3rd / percent	第四品牌及百分比 4th / percent
样本 Sample	598	**汰渍 Tide(28.8)**	**奇强 Qiqiang(22.6)**	**活力 28 Power28(17.7)**	**奥妙 OMO(9.7)**
平实生活指向 simple living orientation	340	奇强 Qiqiang(25.9)	汰渍 Tide(25.0)	活力 28 Power28(18.8)	奥妙 OMO(7.9)
时尚流行指向 fashion orientation	258	汰渍 Tide(33.7)	奇强 Qiqiang(18.2)	活力 28 Power28(16.3)	奥妙 OMO(12.0)

5-13-2 广告态度指标/ Advertising Attitude Index

	人数 Number	第一品牌及百分比 1st / percent	第二品牌及百分比 2nd / percent	第三品牌及百分比 3rd / percent	第四品牌及百分比 4th / percent
样本 Sample	596	**汰渍 Tide(28.7)**	**奇强 Qiqiang(22.5)**	**活力 28 Power28(17.6)**	**奥妙 OMO(9.7)**
广告淡漠指向 indifferent orientation	184	奇强 Qiqiang(25.0)	汰渍 Tide(23.4)	活力 28 Power28(19.0)	奥妙 OMO(10.3)
中间层 medium	334	汰渍 Tide(31.1)	奇强 Qiqiang(23.7)	活力 28 Power28(15.3)	奥妙 OMO(10.2)
信赖广告指向 loyal orientation	78	汰渍 Tide(30.8)	活力 28 Power28(24.4)	奇强 Qiqiang(11.5)	奥妙 OMO(6.4)

5-14 重度消费者的消费层构成/ The Composition of the Heavy Consumers

5-14-1 时尚流行指标/ Fads Popular Index

	人数 Number	平实生活指向 simple living orientation	时尚流行指向 fashion orientation
样本 Sample	312	56.1	43.9
一天 2 次或以上 twice a day or over	16	50.0	50.0
一天 1 次 once a day	56	50.0	50.0
两三天用 1 次 once 2 or 3 days	240	57.9	42.1

5-14-2 广告态度指标/ Advertising Attitude Index

	人数 Number	广告淡漠指向 indifferent orientation	中间层 medium	信赖广告指向 loyal orientation
样本 Sample	312	32.1	54.2	13.8
一天 2 次或以上 twice a day or over	16	50.0	37.5	12.5
一天 1 次 once a day	57	31.6	56.1	12.3
两三天用 1 次 once 2 or 3 days	239	31.0	54.8	14.2

● 沈阳 / Shenyang

5-1 最常用品牌排名/ Ranking of the Most Frequently Used Brands

排名 Brand Ranking	品牌 Brands	人数 Number	百分比 Percent
1	三威 Sanwei	172	29.1
2	碧浪 Ariel	111	18.8
3	巧手 Dosia	56	9.5
4	汰渍 Tide	53	9.0
5	8 分钟 8 Fenzhong	33	5.6
5	白猫 White Cat	33	5.6
6	奥妙 OMO	32	5.4
7	威白 Wipp	20	3.4
8	天天 Tiantian	18	3.0
9	雕牌 Diao	16	2.7
10	奇强 Qiqiang	12	2.0

n=592

5-2 样本、男性各年龄层、女性各年龄层的常用品牌/ The Most Frequently Used Brands by the Whole Sample, Age and Gender Groups

	人数 Number	第一品牌及百分比 1st/ percent	第二品牌及百分比 2nd/ percent	第三品牌及百分比 3rd/ percent
样本 Sample	592	**三威 Sanwei(29.1)**	**碧浪 Ariel(18.8)**	**巧手 Dosia(9.5)**
男性 Male	291	**三威 Sanwei(27.8)**	**碧浪 Ariel(20.3)**	**巧手 Dosia(9.3)**
16~24 岁 Age	61	碧浪 Ariel(24.6)	三威 Sanwei(23.0)	汰渍 Tide(13.1)
25~34 岁 Age	87	三威 Sanwei(26.4)	碧浪 Ariel(16.1)	巧手 Dosia(10.3)
35~44 岁 Age	74	三威 Sanwei(28.4)	碧浪 Ariel(23.0)	巧手 Dosia(10.8)
45~54 岁 Age	46	三威 Sanwei(28.3)	碧浪 Ariel(21.7)	8 分钟 8 Fenzhong(13.0)
55~60 岁 Age	23	三威 Sanwei(43.5)	白猫 White Cat(17.4) 巧手 Dosia(17.4)	碧浪 Ariel(13.0)
女性 Female	301	**三威 Sanwei(30.2)**	**碧浪 Ariel(17.3)**	**巧手 Dosia(9.6)**
16~24 岁 Age	63	三威 Sanwei(25.4)	碧浪 Ariel(22.2)	巧手 Dosia(14.3)
25~34 岁 Age	90	三威 Sanwei(28.9)	碧浪 Ariel(14.4)	汰渍 Tide(10.0) 奥妙 OMO(10.0)
35~44 岁 Age	76	三威 Sanwei(28.9)	碧浪 Ariel(18.4)	巧手 Dosia(11.8) 汰渍 Tide(11.8)
45~54 岁 Age	48	三威 Sanwei(35.4)	碧浪 Ariel(16.7)	奥妙 OMO(10.4)
55~60 岁 Age	24	三威 Sanwei(41.7)	碧浪 Ariel(12.5) 白猫 White Cat(12.5)	天鹅 Tian'e(4.2) 雪燕 Xueyan(4.2) 丽人 Liren(4.2) 天天 Tiantian(4.2) 8 分钟 8 Fenzhong(4.2) 天津 Tianjin(4.2) 汰渍 Tide(4.2) 巧手 Dosia(4.2)

5-3 正在使用的品牌排名/ Ranking of the Brands Used Now

排名 Brand Ranking	品牌 Brands	人数 Number	百分比 Percent
1	三威 Sanwei	139	23.5
2	碧浪 Ariel	122	20.6
3	巧手 Dosia	74	12.5
4	汰渍 Tide	45	7.6
5	白猫 White Cat	38	6.4
6	8 分钟 8 Fenzhong	37	6.3
7	奥妙 OMO	27	4.6
8	威白 Wipp	23	3.9
9	奇强 Qiqiang	19	3.2
10	雕牌 Diao	16	2.7
11	天天 Tiantian	13	2.2

n=592

5-4 品牌转换习惯/ Brand Habit in Consuming Laundry Detergent

	人数 Number	第一次使用该品牌 first use this brand	上一次也是这个牌子 used it last time	上一次不是这个牌子 not used it last time
样本 Sample	591	6.6	77.8	15.6
三威 Sanwei	139	4.3	87.8	7.9
碧浪 Ariel	122	8.2	79.5	12.3
巧手 Dosia	73	13.7	58.9	27.4
汰渍 Tide	45	2.2	86.7	11.1
白猫 White Cat	38	7.9	76.3	15.8
8 分钟 8 Fenzhong	37	2.7	81.1	16.2
奥妙 OMO	27	0.0	88.9	11.1
威白 Wipp	23	8.7	65.2	26.1
奇强 Qiqiang	19	10.5	57.9	31.6
雕牌 Diao	16	0.0	81.3	18.8
天天 Tiantian	13	0.0	100.0	0.0

5-5 下一次打算使用的品牌排名/ Ranking of the Brands to be Used Next Time

排名 Brand Ranking	品牌 Brands	人数 Number	百分比 Percent
1	碧浪 Ariel	145	24.5
2	三威 Sanwei	136	23.0
3	巧手 Dosia	63	10.6
4	汰渍 Tide	47	7.9
5	奥妙 OMO	38	6.4
6	白猫 White Cat	31	5.2
7	8 分钟 8 Fenzhong	29	4.9
8	雕牌 Diao	17	2.9
9	奇强 Qiqiang	16	2.7
10	天天 Tiantian	15	2.5
10	威白 Wipp	15	2.5
11	活力 28 Power28	10	1.7

n=592

5-6 样本、男性各年龄层、女性各年龄层是否是主要购买者/ Purchasers in the Household by the Whole Sample, Age and Gender Groups

	人数 Number	是 yes	不是 no
样本 Sample	601	53.6	46.4
男性 Male	299	27.4	72.6
16~24 岁 Age	64	20.3	79.7
25~34 岁 Age	89	28.1	71.9
35~44 岁 Age	76	28.9	71.1
45~54 岁 Age	46	30.4	69.6
55~60 岁 Age	24	33.3	66.7
女性 Female	302	79.5	20.5
16~24 岁 Age	64	40.6	59.4
25~34 岁 Age	90	86.7	13.3
35~44 岁 Age	76	93.4	6.6
45~54 岁 Age	48	87.5	12.5
55~60 岁 Age	24	95.8	4.2

5-7 样本、男性各年龄层、女性各年龄层的使用方式/ Ways of Using the Products by the Whole Sample, Age and Gender Groups

	人数 Number	个人专用 personal use	家人共用 all family members share
样本 Sample	593	2.2	97.8
男性 Male	292	1.7	98.3
16~24 岁 Age	62	0.0	100.0
25~34 岁 Age	87	1.1	98.9
35~44 岁 Age	74	4.1	95.9
45~54 岁 Age	46	2.2	97.8
55~60 岁 Age	23	0.0	100.0
女性 Female	301	2.7	97.3
16~24 岁 Age	63	3.2	96.8
25~34 岁 Age	90	2.2	97.8
35~44 岁 Age	76	2.6	97.4
45~54 岁 Age	48	2.1	97.9
55~60 岁 Age	24	4.2	95.8

5-8 样本、男性各年龄层、女性各年龄层的使用频率/ Frequencies of the Consumed Laundry Detergent by the Whole Sample, Age and Gender Groups

	人数 Number	一天 2 次或以上 twice a day or more	一天 1 次 once a day	两三天用 1 次 once 2 or 3 days	一周 1~2 次 once or twice a week	半个月 1 次或以下 once half a month or below
样本 Sample	591	4.4	12.0	37.9	39.6	6.1
男性 Male	290	2.4	10.3	37.2	42.8	7.2
16~24 岁 Age	61	3.3	4.9	32.8	44.3	14.8
25~34 岁 Age	87	4.6	16.1	39.1	34.5	5.7
35~44 岁 Age	73	0.0	12.3	34.2	45.2	8.2
45~54 岁 Age	46	2.2	0.0	45.7	52.2	0.0
55~60 岁 Age	23	0.0	17.4	34.8	43.5	4.3
女性 Female	301	6.3	13.6	38.5	36.5	5.0
16~24 岁 Age	63	6.3	20.6	31.7	34.9	6.3
25~34 岁 Age	90	6.7	10.0	37.8	40.0	5.6
35~44 岁 Age	76	5.3	18.4	39.5	34.2	2.6
45~54 岁 Age	48	6.3	8.3	43.8	33.3	8.3
55~60 岁 Age	24	8.3	4.2	45.8	41.7	0.0

5-9 选择该类商品的考虑因素/ Ranking of the Considerations in Purchasing

注：本题为多选题，合计百分比超过 100%（Multiple answers）

排名 Ranking	考虑因素 Considerations	人次 Person-time	百分比 Percent
1	价格适中 reasonable price	335	56.7
2	产品功用 product function	281	47.5
3	有名的牌子 famous brand	199	33.7
4	购买方便 easy to buy	139	23.5
5	广告影响 influence of advertising	109	18.4
6	别人推荐 introduced by other people	36	6.1
7	有优惠条件 with preferential terms	26	4.4
8	单位发的 offered by the working unit	14	2.4
9	包装吸引人 appealing package	13	2.2
10	其它 others	3	0.5

n=591

5-10 对产品功能的侧重方面/ Ranking of the Considerations about the Function of this Kind of Product

注：本题为多选题，合计百分比超过 100%（Multiple answers）

排名 Ranking	侧重方面 Items	人次 Person-time	百分比 Percent
1	去污力强 powerful cleaning	495	83.8
2	味道清香 fresh smell	269	45.5
3	不伤手 harmless to hand	116	19.6
4	容易溶解 easy to solve	110	18.6
5	容易冲洗 easy to clean	103	17.4
6	不损害衣物 harmless to clothes	79	13.4
7	是加酶型 with enzyme	57	9.6
8	是浓缩型 condensed	53	9.0
9	有护色功能 color protect	18	3.0
10	无磷/低磷 non-phosphorus/low-phosphorus	17	2.9
11	含特殊配方 special formula	13	2.2
12	其他 others	4	0.7

n=591

5-11 家中其他洗衣用品的比例/ Proportion of the Other Products Used for Laundry in the Household

注：本题为多选题，合计百分比超过 100%（Multiple answers）

	人次 Person-time	百分比 Percent
肥皂 soap	482	81.4
皂粉 soap powder	24	4.1
洗衣剂 detergent	52	8.8
洗衣膏 laundry paste	41	6.9
衣领净 collar cleaner	67	11.3
漂白剂 bleacher	46	7.8
丝麻专用 specified for silk lines	22	3.7
衣物柔顺剂 fabric softener	53	9.0
其他 others	18	3.0
以上都不用 none of above	54	9.1

n=592

5-12 重度消费者的人口分布/ Demographics of the Heavy Consumers

	人数 Number	16-24 岁 Age	25-34 岁 Age	35-44 岁 Age	45-54 岁 Age	55-60 岁 Age
样本 Sample	321	19.3	31.5	25.5	15.6	8.1
男性 Male	145	17.2	35.9	23.4	15.2	8.3
一天 2 次或以上 twice a day or over	7	28.6	57.1	0.0	14.3	0.0
一天 1 次 once a day	30	10.0	46.7	30.0	0.0	13.3
两三天用 1 次 once 2 or 3 days	108	18.5	31.5	23.1	19.4	7.4
女性 Female	176	21.0	27.8	27.3	15.9	8.0
一天 2 次或以上 twice a day or over	19	21.1	31.6	21.1	15.8	10.5
一天 1 次 once a day	41	31.7	22.0	34.1	9.8	2.4
两三天用 1 次 once 2 or 3 days	116	17.2	29.3	25.9	18.1	9.5

5-13 不同消费者层的常用品牌/ The Most Frequently Used Brands by Market Segments

5-13-1 时尚流行指标/ Fads Popular Index

	人数 Number	第一品牌及百分比 1st / percent	第二品牌及百分比 2nd/ percent	第三品牌及百分比 3rd/ percent	第四品牌及百分比 4th/ percent
样本 Sample	592	**三威 Sanwei(29.1)**	**碧浪 Ariel(18.8)**	**巧手 Dosia(9.5)**	**汰渍 Tide(9.0)**
平实生活指向 simple living orientation	288	三威 Sanwei(30.6)	碧浪 Ariel(18.8)	巧手 Dosia(9.0)	8 分钟 8 Fenzhong(7.6) 汰渍 Tide(7.6)
时尚流行指向 fashion orientation	304	三威 Sanwei(27.6)	碧浪 Ariel(18.8)	汰渍 Tide(10.2)	巧手 Dosia(9.9)

5-13-2 广告态度指标/ Advertising Attitude Index

	人数 Number	第一品牌及百分比 1st/ percent	第二品牌及百分比 2nd/ percent	第三品牌及百分比 3rd/ percent	第四品牌及百分比 4th/ percent
样本 Sample	592	**三威 Sanwei(29.1)**	**碧浪 Ariel(18.8)**	**巧手 Dosia(9.5)**	**汰渍 Tide(9.0)**
广告淡漠指向 indifferent orientation	170	三威 Sanwei(29.4)	碧浪 Ariel(15.3)	汰渍 Tide(11.8)	巧手 Dosia(11.2)
中间层 medium	347	三威 Sanwei(31.1)	碧浪 Ariel(19.6)	巧手 Dosia(9.8)	汰渍 Tide(6.9)
信赖广告指向 loyal orientation	75	碧浪 Ariel(22.7)	三威 Sanwei(18.7)	汰渍 Tide(12.0)	奥妙 OMO(9.3) 8 分钟 8 Fenzhong(9.3)

5-14 重度消费者的消费层构成/ The Composition of the Heavy Consumers

5-14-1 时尚流行指标/ Fads Popular Index

	人数 Number	平实生活指向 simple living orientation	时尚流行指向 fashion orientation
样本 Sample	321	48.0	52.0
一天 2 次或以上 twice a day or over	26	42.3	57.7
一天 1 次 once a day	71	45.1	54.9
两三天用 1 次 once 2 or 3 days	224	49.6	50.4

5-14-2 广告态度指标/ Advertising Attitude Index

	人数 Number	广告淡漠指向 indifferent orientation	中间层 medium	信赖广告指向 loyal orientation
样本 Sample	321	26.8	61.7	11.5
一天 2 次或以上 twice a day or over	26	30.8	65.4	3.8
一天 1 次 once a day	71	29.6	56.3	14.1
两三天用 1 次 once 2 or 3 days	224	25.4	62.9	11.6

6.洗涤灵/洗洁精 / Liquid Detergent

● 北京 / Beijing

6-1 是否使用的比例/ Proportion of the Sample Consuming Liquid Detergent in the Last Three Months

	人数 Number	百分比 Percent
用 yes	958	94.8
不用 no	53	5.2

n=1011

6-2 最常用品牌排名/ Ranking of the Most Frequently Used Brands

排名 Brand Ranking	品牌 Brands	人数 Number	百分比 Percent
1	金鱼 Gold Fish	819	85.6
2	白猫 White Cat	72	7.5
3	安利 Amway	15	1.6
4	巧手 Dosia	10	1.0
5	靓靓 Liangliang	8	0.8

n=957

6-3 样本、男性各年龄层、女性各年龄层的常用品牌/ The Most Frequently Used Brands by the Whole Sample, Age and Gender Groups

	人数 Number	第一品牌及百分比 1st/ percent	第二品牌及百分比 2nd/ percent	第三品牌及百分比 3rd/ percent
样本 Sample	957	**金鱼 Gold Fish(85.6)**	**白猫 White Cat(7.5)**	**安利 Amway(1.6)**
男性 Male	459	**金鱼 Gold Fish(87.4)**	**白猫 White Cat(7.0)**	**安利 Amway(1.1)**
16~24 岁 Age	89	金鱼 Gold Fish(93.3)	白猫 White Cat(3.4)	安利 Amway(2.2)
25~34 岁 Age	139	金鱼 Gold Fish(91.4)	白猫 White Cat(5.0)	安利 Amway(0.7) 菜籽 Caizi(0.7) 雕牌 Diao(0.7) 开米 Kami(0.7) 巧手 Dosia(0.7)
35~44 岁 Age	124	金鱼 Gold Fish(79.0)	白猫 White Cat(11.3)	安利 Amway(1.6) 巧手 Dosia(1.6)
45~54 岁 Age	71	金鱼 Gold Fish(83.1)	白猫 White Cat(9.9)	洁宝 Job(1.4) 靓靓 Liangliang(1.4)
55~60 岁 Age	36	金鱼 Gold Fish(94.4)	白猫 White Cat(2.8)	
女性 Female	498	**金鱼 Gold Fish(83.9)**	**白猫 White Cat(8.0)**	**安利 Amway(2.0)**
16~24 岁 Age	105	金鱼 Gold Fish(93.3)	巧手 Dosia(2.9)	安利 Amway(1.0) 白猫 White Cat(1.0) 妈咪 Mami(1.0)
25~34 岁 Age	147	金鱼 Gold Fish(81.0)	白猫 White Cat(10.2)	安利 Amway(3.4)
35~44 岁 Age	122	金鱼 Gold Fish(80.3)	白猫 White Cat(9.0)	安利 Amway(2.5)
45~54 岁 Age	82	金鱼 Gold Fish(80.5)	白猫 White Cat(11.0)	安利 Amway(1.2) 菜籽 Caizi(1.2) 洁芙 Jif(1.2) 靓靓 Liangliang(1.2) 开米 Kami(1.2) 碟新 Diexin(1.2) 得其利是 Tugaris(1.2)
55~60 岁 Age	42	金鱼 Gold Fish(88.1)	白猫 White Cat(9.5)	巧手 Dosia(2.4)

6-4 正在使用的品牌排名/ Ranking of the Brands Used Now

排名 Brand Ranking	品牌 Brands	人数 Number	百分比 Percent
1	金鱼 Gold Fish	742	77.5
2	白猫 White Cat	83	8.7
3	巧手 Dosia	23	2.4
3	靓靓 Liangliang	23	2.4
4	安利 Amway	21	2.2
5	狮王妈妈柠檬 Mama Lemon	11	1.1
6	得其利是 Tugaris	7	0.7
7	阿香 Axiang	4	0.4

n=957

6-5 品牌转换习惯/ Brand Habit in Consuming Liquid Detergent

	人数 Number	第一次使用该品牌 first use this brand	上一次也是这个牌子 used it last time	上一次不是这个牌子 not used it last time
样本 Sample	954	4.8	89.3	5.9
金鱼 Gold Fish	740	1.9	95.4	2.7
白猫 White Cat	82	4.9	81.7	13.4
巧手 Dosia	23	26.1	56.5	17.4
靓靓 Liangliang	23	26.1	56.5	17.4
安利 Amway	21	14.3	76.2	9.5
狮王妈妈柠檬 Mama Lemon	11	18.2	54.5	27.3
得其利是 Tugaris	7	42.9	28.6	28.6
阿香 Axiang	4	25.0	25.0	50.0
奇强 Qiqiang	3	33.3	33.3	33.3
洛娃 Reward	3	33.3	66.7	0.0
疏果 Shuguo	3	0.0	0.0	100.0
雕牌 Diao	3	33.3	66.7	0.0

6-6 下一次打算使用的品牌排名/ Ranking of the Brands to be Used Next Time

排名 Brand Ranking	品牌 Brands	人数 Number	百分比 Percent
1	金鱼 Gold Fish	711	74.5
2	白猫 White Cat	107	11.2
3	安利 Amway	24	2.5
4	巧手 Dosia	23	2.4
5	靓靓 Liangliang	20	2.1
6	狮王妈妈柠檬 Mama Lemon	11	1.2

n=955

6-7 样本、 男性各年龄层、 女性各年龄层是否是主要购买者/ Purchasers in the Household by the Whole Sample, Age and Gender Groups

	人数 Number	是 yes	不是 no
样本 Sample	1011	52.3	47.7
男性 Male	503	37.4	62.6
16~24 岁 Age	105	18.1	81.9
25~34 岁 Age	151	44.4	55.6
35~44 岁 Age	130	45.4	54.6
45~54 岁 Age	77	39.0	61.0
55~60 岁 Age	40	32.5	67.5
女性 Female	508	67.1	32.9
16~24 岁 Age	108	18.5	81.5
25~34 岁 Age	150	70.0	30.0
35~44 岁 Age	124	85.5	14.5
45~54 岁 Age	84	88.1	11.9
55~60 岁 Age	42	85.7	14.3

6-8 样本、男性各年龄层、女性各年龄层是否使用/ Whether to Use Liquid Detergent by the Whole Sample, Age and Gender Groups

	人数 Number	用 yes	不用 no
样本 Sample	1011	94.8	5.2
男性 Male	503	91.5	8.5
16~24 岁 Age	104	85.6	14.4
25~34 岁 Age	151	92.7	7.3
35~44 岁 Age	131	94.7	5.3
45~54 岁 Age	77	92.2	7.8
55~60 岁 Age	40	90.0	10.0
女性 Female	508	98.0	2.0
16~24 岁 Age	108	97.2	2.8
25~34 岁 Age	150	98.0	2.0
35~44 岁 Age	124	98.4	1.6
45~54 岁 Age	84	97.6	2.4
55~60 岁 Age	42	100.0	0.0

6-9 样本、男性各年龄层、女性各年龄层的使用频率/ Frequencies of the Consumed Liquid Detergent by the Whole Sample, Age and Gender Groups

	人数 Number	一天 3 次或以上 3 times or over a day	一天 1~2 次 once or twice a day	两三天用 1 次 once 2 or 3 days	一周 1~2 次 once or twice a week	半个月 1 次或以下 once half a month or below
样本 Sample	955	46.5	49.2	2.3	1.5	0.5
男性 Male	457	45.7	49.9	2.4	2.0	0.0
16~24 岁 Age	88	39.8	56.8	2.3	1.1	0.0
25~34 岁 Age	138	44.2	47.8	4.3	3.6	0.0
35~44 岁 Age	124	40.3	56.5	1.6	1.6	0.0
45~54 岁 Age	71	56.3	40.8	1.4	1.4	0.0
55~60 岁 Age	36	63.9	36.1	0.0	0.0	0.0
女性 Female	498	47.2	48.6	2.2	1.0	1.0
16~24 岁 Age	105	43.8	51.4	2.9	1.0	1.0
25~34 岁 Age	147	48.3	46.3	3.4	1.4	0.7
35~44 岁 Age	122	50.0	46.7	0.8	1.6	0.8
45~54 岁 Age	82	42.7	54.9	2.4	0.0	0.0
55~60 岁 Age	42	52.4	42.9	0.0	0.0	4.8

6-10 选择该类商品的考虑因素/ Ranking of the Considerations in Purchasing

注：本题为多选题，合计百分比超过 100%（Multiple answers）

排名 Ranking	考虑因素 Considerations	人次 Person-time	百分比 Percent
1	价格适中 reasonable price	528	55.4
2	产品功用 product function	398	41.8
3	有名的牌子 famous brand	357	37.5
4	购买方便 easy to buy	240	25.2
5	单位发的 offered by the working unit	123	12.9
6	广告影响 influence of advertising	76	8.0
7	有优惠条件 with preferential terms	31	3.3
8	别人推荐 introduced by other people	25	2.6
9	其它 others	16	1.7
10	包装吸引人 appealing package	9	0.9

n=953

6-11 对产品功能的侧重方面/ Ranking of the Considerations about the Function of this Kind of Product

注：本题为多选题，合计百分比超过 100%（Multiple answers）

排名 Ranking	侧重方面 Items	人次 Person-time	百分比 Percent
1	洗涤力强 powerful cleaning	706	73.9
2	无毒性可洗水果 can be directly used to wash fruit	426	44.6
3	味道清香 fresh smell	335	35.1
4	不伤手 harmless to hand	301	31.5
5	不污染环境 without pollution	116	12.1
6	其他 others	14	1.5

n=955

6-12 重度消费者的人口分布/ Demographics of the Heavy Consumers

	人数 Number	16-24 岁 Age	25-34 岁 Age	35-44 岁 Age	45-54 岁 Age	55-60 岁 Age
样本 Sample	914	20.2	29.1	26.0	16.3	8.3
男性 Male	437	19.5	29.1	27.5	15.8	8.2
一天 3 次或以上 3 times or over a day	209	16.7	29.2	23.9	19.1	11.0
一天 1~2 次 once or twice a day	228	21.9	28.9	30.7	12.7	5.7
女性 Female	477	21.0	29.1	24.7	16.8	8.4
一天 3 次或以上 3 times or over a day	235	19.6	30.2	26.0	14.9	9.4
一天 1~2 次 once or twice a day	242	22.3	28.1	23.6	18.6	7.4

6-13 不同消费者层的常用品牌/ The Most Frequently Used Brands by Market Segments

6-13-1 时尚流行指标/ Fads Popular Index

	人数 Number	第一品牌及百分比 1st / percent	第二品牌及百分比 2nd / percent	第三品牌及百分比 3rd / percent
样本 Sample	943	**金鱼 Gold Fish(85.6)**	**白猫 White Cat(7.4)**	**安利 Amway(1.6)**
平实生活指向 simple living orientation	461	金鱼 Gold Fish(85.2)	白猫 White Cat(6.7)	安利 Amway(1.3) 巧手 Dosia(1.3)
时尚流行指向 fashion orientation	482	金鱼 Gold Fish(85.9)	白猫 White Cat(8.1)	安利 Amway(1.9)

6-13-2 广告态度指标/ Advertising Attitude Index

	人数 Number	第一品牌及百分比 1st / percent	第二品牌及百分比 2nd / percent	第三品牌及百分比 3rd / percent
样本 Sample	939	**金鱼 Gold Fish(85.5)**	**白猫 White Cat(7.7)**	**安利 Amway(1.5)**
广告淡漠指向 indifferent orientation	270	金鱼 Gold Fish(83.3)	白猫 White Cat(8.1)	安利 Amway(1.5) 巧手 Dosia(1.5)
中间层 medium	543	金鱼 Gold Fish(86.7)	白猫 White Cat(7.2)	安利 Amway(1.5)
信赖广告指向 loyal orientation	126	金鱼 Gold Fish(84.9)	白猫 White Cat(8.7)	安利 Amway(1.6)

6-14 重度消费者的消费层构成/ The Composition of the Heavy Consumers

6-14-1 时尚流行指标/ Fads Popular Index

	人数 Number	平实生活指向 simple living orientation	时尚流行指向 fashion orientation
样本 Sample	900	49.1	50.9
一天 3 次或以上 3 times or over a day	436	47.9	52.1
一天 1~2 次 once or twice a day	464	50.2	49.8

6-14-2 广告态度指标/ Advertising Attitude Index

	人数 Number	广告淡漠指向 indifferent orientation	中间层 medium	信赖广告指向 loyal orientation
样本 Sample	897	29.0	57.9	13.2
一天 3 次或以上 3 times or over a day	435	28.5	57.5	14.0
一天 1~2 次 once or twice a day	462	29.4	58.2	12.3

● 上海 / Shanghai

6-1 是否使用的比例/ Proportion of the Sample Consuming Liquid Detergent in the Last Three Months

	人数 Number	百分比 Percent
用 yes	829	81.8
不用 no	184	18.2

n=1013

6-2 最常用品牌排名/ Ranking of the Most Frequently Used Brands

排名 Brand Ranking	品牌 Brands	人数 Number	百分比 Percent
1	白猫 White Cat	772	93.1
2	巧手 Dosia	14	1.7
3	安利 Amway	10	1.2
3	狮王妈妈柠檬 Mama Lemon	10	1.2
4	雕牌 Diao	3	0.4
5	碟新 Diexin	2	0.2

n=829

6-3 样本、男性各年龄层、女性各年龄层的常用品牌/ The Most Frequently Used Brands by the Whole Sample, Age and Gender Groups

	人数 Number	第一品牌及百分比 1st / percent	第二品牌及百分比 2nd / percent	第三品牌及百分比 3rd / percent
样本 Sample	**829**	**白猫 White Cat(93.1)**	**巧手 Dosia (1.7)**	**安利 Amway(1.2)** **狮王妈妈柠檬 Mama Lemon(1.2)**
男性 Male	**384**	**白猫 White Cat(93.2)**	**巧手 Dosia (1.6)**	**狮王妈妈柠檬 Mama Lemon(1.3)**
16~24 岁 Age	71	白猫 White Cat(93.0)	安利 Amway(1.4) 高富力 Gaofuli(1.4) 巧手 Dosia (1.4) 狮王妈妈柠檬 Mama Lemon(1.4) 双鲸 Shuangjing(1.4)	
25~34 岁 Age	105	白猫 White Cat(91.4)	巧手 Dosia (3.8)	狮王妈妈柠檬 Mama Lemon(1.9)
35~44 岁 Age	105	白猫 White Cat(95.2)	安利 Amway(1.0) 雕牌 Diao(1.0) 巧手 Dosia (1.0) 碟新 Diexin(1.0) 丝宝 c'bons(1.0)	
45~54 岁 Age	70	白猫 White Cat(91.4)	狮王妈妈柠檬 Mama Lemon(2.9)	安利 Amway(1.4) 碟新 Diexin(1.4) 联华 Lianhua(1.4)
55~60 岁 Age	33	白猫 White Cat(97.0)	清亮 Qingliang(3.0)	
女性 Female	**445**	**白猫 White Cat(93.0)**	**巧手 Dosia (1.8)**	**安利 Amway(1.6)**
16~24 岁 Age	78	白猫 White Cat(92.3)	安利 Amway(2.6)	巧手 Dosia (1.3) 狮王妈妈柠檬 Mama Lemon(1.3) 威猛先生 Mr. Muscle(1.3) 奇强 Qiqiang(1.3)
25~34 岁 Age	133	白猫 White Cat(91.7)	巧手 Dosia (2.3) 狮王妈妈柠檬 Mama Lemon(2.3)	安利 Amway(0.8) 雕牌 Diao(0.8) 妈咪 Mamee(0.8) 澳尔 Aor(0.8)
35~44 岁 Age	118	白猫 White Cat(91.5)	安利 Amway(2.5) 巧手 Dosia (2.5)	雕牌 Diao(0.8) 佳美 Jiamei(0.8) 力士洁尔亮 Li Shi Jie Er Liang(0.8) 狮王妈妈柠檬 Mama Lemon(0.8)
45~54 岁 Age	77	白猫 White Cat(97.4)	灵巧 Lingqiao(1.3)	
55~60 岁 Age	39	白猫 White Cat(94.9)	安利 Amway(2.6) 巧手 Dosia (2.6)	

6-4 正在使用的品牌排名/ Ranking of the Brands Used Now

排名 Brand Ranking	品牌 Brands	人数 Number	百分比 Percent
1	白猫 White Cat	747	90.1
2	巧手 Dosia	26	3.1
3	狮王妈妈柠檬 Mama Lemon	15	1.8
4	安利 Amway	11	1.3
5	雕牌 Diao	7	0.8

n=829

6-5 品牌转换习惯/ Brand Habit in Consuming Liquid Detergent

	人数 Number	第一次使用该品牌 first use this brand	上一次也是这个牌子 used it last time	上一次不是这个牌子 not used it last time
样本 Sample	**827**	**4.1**	**92.6**	**3.3**
白猫 White Cat	747	2.9	95.2	1.9
巧手 Dosia	26	15.4	61.5	23.1
狮王妈妈柠檬 Mama Lemon	15	13.3	66.7	20.0
安利 Amway	11	9.1	72.7	18.2
雕牌 Diao	6	33.3	50.0	16.7

6-6 下一次打算使用的品牌排名/ Ranking of the Brands to be Used Next Time

排名 Brand Ranking	品牌 Brands	人数 Number	百分比 Percent
1	白猫 White Cat	726	87.6
2	巧手 Dosia	32	3.9
3	狮王妈妈柠檬 Mama Lemon	25	3.0
4	安利 Amway	12	1.4
5	雕牌 Diao	4	0.5

n=829

6-7 样本、 男性各年龄层、 女性各年龄层是否是主要购买者/ Purchasers in the Household by the Whole Sample, Age and Gender Groups

	人数 Number	是 yes	不是 no
样本 Sample	1014	50.3	49.7
男性 Male	509	35.4	64.6
16~24 岁 Age	109	18.3	81.7
25~34 岁 Age	146	28.8	71.2
35~44 岁 Age	130	40.0	60.0
45~54 岁 Age	85	57.6	42.4
55~60 岁 Age	39	43.6	56.4
女性 Female	505	65.3	34.7
16~24 岁 Age	108	20.4	79.6
25~34 岁 Age	144	63.2	36.8
35~44 岁 Age	130	84.6	15.4
45~54 岁 Age	82	86.6	13.4
55~60 岁 Age	41	87.8	12.2

6-8 样本、男性各年龄层、女性各年龄层是否使用/ Whether to Use Liquid Detergent by the Whole Sample, Age and Gender Groups

	人数 Number	用 yes	不用 no
样本 Sample	1013	81.8	18.2
男性 Male	509	75.4	24.6
16~24 岁 Age	109	65.1	34.9
25~34 岁 Age	146	71.9	28.1
35~44 岁 Age	130	80.8	19.2
45~54 岁 Age	85	82.4	17.6
55~60 岁 Age	39	84.6	15.4
女性 Female	504	88.3	11.7
16~24 岁 Age	107	72.9	27.1
25~34 岁 Age	144	92.4	7.6
35~44 岁 Age	130	90.8	9.2
45~54 岁 Age	82	93.9	6.1
55~60 岁 Age	41	95.1	4.9

6-9 样本、男性各年龄层、女性各年龄层的使用频率/ Frequencies of the Consumed Liquid Detergent by the Whole Sample, Age and Gender Groups

	人数 Number	一天 3 次或以上 3 times or over a day	一天 1~2 次 once or twice a day	两三天用 1 次 once 2 or 3 days	一周 1~2 次 once or twice a week	半个月 1 次或以下 once half a month or below
样本 Sample	829	23.3	68.3	4.6	2.7	1.2
男性 Male	384	21.6	68.8	4.7	3.4	1.6
16~24 岁 Age	71	23.9	59.2	5.6	9.9	1.4
25~34 岁 Age	105	23.8	66.7	3.8	2.9	2.9
35~44 岁 Age	105	19.0	70.5	6.7	1.9	1.9
45~54 岁 Age	70	20.0	75.7	2.9	1.4	0.0
55~60 岁 Age	33	21.2	75.8	3.0	0.0	0.0
女性 Female	445	24.7	67.9	4.5	2.0	0.9
16~24 岁 Age	78	20.5	67.9	6.4	3.8	1.3
25~34 岁 Age	133	24.1	69.2	5.3	0.0	1.5
35~44 岁 Age	113	26.3	66.9	4.2	2.5	0.0
45~54 岁 Age	77	24.7	71.4	2.6	0.0	1.3
55~60 岁 Age	39	30.8	59.0	2.6	7.7	0.0

6-10 选择该类商品的考虑因素/ Ranking of the Considerations in Purchasing

注：本题为多选题，合计百分比超过 100%（Multiple answers）

排名 Ranking	考虑因素 Considerations	人次 Person-time	百分比 Percent
1	价格适中 reasonable price	543	65.5
2	产品功用 product function	331	39.9
3	有名的牌子 famous brand	326	39.3
4	购买方便 easy to buy	250	30.2
5	广告影响 influence of advertising	69	8.3
6	有优惠条件 with preferential terms	41	4.9
7	单位发的 offered by the working unit	32	3.9
8	别人推荐 introduced by other people	24	2.9
9	包装吸引人 appealing package	16	1.9
10	其它 others	13	1.6

n=829

6-11 对产品功能的侧重方面/ Ranking of the Considerations about the Function of this Kind of Product

注：本题为多选题，合计百分比超过 100%（Multiple answers）

排名 Ranking	侧重方面 Items	人次 Person-time	百分比 Percent
1	洗涤力强 powerful cleaning	605	73.1
2	味道清香 fresh smell	413	49.9
3	不伤手 harmless to hand	392	47.3
4	无毒性可洗水果 can be directly used to wash fruit	252	30.4
5	不污染环境 without pollution	53	6.4
6	其他 others	6	0.7

n=828

6-12 重度消费者的人口分布/ Demographics of the Heavy Consumers

	人数 Number	16-24 岁 Age	25-34 岁 Age	35-44 岁 Age	45-54 岁 Age	55-60 岁 Age
样本 Sample	**759**	**16.9**	**28.9**	**26.9**	**18.6**	**8.8**
男性 Male	**347**	**17.0**	**27.4**	**27.1**	**19.3**	**9.2**
一天 3 次或以上 3 times or over a day	83	20.5	30.1	24.1	16.9	8.4
一天 1~2 次 once or twice a day	264	15.9	26.5	28.0	20.1	9.5
女性 Female	**412**	**16.7**	**30.1**	**26.7**	**18.0**	**8.5**
一天 3 次或以上 3 times or over a day	110	14.5	29.1	28.2	17.3	10.9
一天 1 次左右 about once a day	302	17.5	30.5	26.2	18.2	7.6

6-13 不同消费者层的常用品牌/ The Most Frequently Used Brands by Market Segments

6-13-1 时尚流行指标/ Fads Popular Index

	人数 Number	第一品牌及百分比 1st / percent	第二品牌及百分比 2nd / percent	第三品牌及百分比 3rd / percent
样本 Sample	821	**白猫 White Cat(93.1)**	**巧手 Dosia (1.7)**	**安利 Amway(1.2)** **狮王妈妈柠檬 Mama Lemon(1.2)**
平实生活指向 simple living orientation	396	白猫 White Cat(94.7)	巧手 Dosia (1.0) 狮王妈妈柠檬 Mama Lemon(1.0)	安利 Amway(0.8)
时尚流行指向 fashion orientation	425	白猫 White Cat(91.5)	巧手 Dosia (2.4)	安利 Amway(1.6)

6-13-2 广告态度指标/ Advertising Attitude Index

	人数 Number	第一品牌及百分比 1st / percent	第二品牌及百分比 2nd / percent	第三品牌及百分比 3rd / percent
样本 Sample	820	**白猫 White Cat(93.2)**	**巧手 Dosia (1.6)**	**安利 Amway(1.2)** **狮王妈妈柠檬 Mama Lemon(1.2)**
广告淡漠指向 indifferent orientation	212	白猫 White Cat(92.9)	巧手 Dosia (2.4)	狮王妈妈柠檬 Mama Lemon(1.9)
中间层 medium	500	白猫 White Cat(93.0)	安利 Amway(1.8)	巧手 Dosia (1.2)
信赖广告指向 loyal orientation	108	白猫 White Cat(94.4)	巧手 Dosia(1.9) 狮王妈妈柠檬 Mama Lemon(1.9)	高富力 Gaofuli(0.9) 碟新 Diexin(0.9)

6-14 重度消费者的消费层构成/ The Composition of the Heavy Consumers

6-14-1 时尚流行指标/ Fads Popular Index

	人数 Number	平实生活指向 simple living orientation	时尚流行指向 fashion orientation
样本 Sample	751	48.9	51.1
一天 3 次或以上 3 times or over a day	191	46.6	53.4
一天 1~2 次 once or twice a day	560	49.6	50.4

6-14-2 广告态度指标/ Advertising Attitude Index

	人数 Number	广告淡漠指向 indifferent orientation	中间层 medium	信赖广告指向 loyal orientation
样本 Sample	751	25.6	61.3	13.2
一天 3 次或以上 3 times or over a day	192	22.9	62.5	14.6
一天 1~2 次 once or twice a day	559	26.5	60.3	12.7

● 广州 / Guangzhou

6-1 是否使用的比例/ Proportion of the Sample Consuming Liquid Detergent in the Last Three Months

	人数 Number	百分比 Percent
用 yes	879	85.0
不用 no	155	15.0

n=1034

6-2 最常用品牌排名/ Ranking of the Most Frequently Used Brands

排名 Brand Ranking	品牌 Brands	人数 Number	百分比 Percent
1	高富力 Gaofuli	619	70.4
2	立白 Libai	54	6.1
3	浪奇 Langqi	28	3.2
4	白猫 White Cat	22	2.5
5	劳工 Labour	20	2.3
6	安利 Amway	10	1.1
7	保洁 Mori	8	0.9
7	天丽 TianLi	8	0.9

n=879

6-3 样本、男性各年龄层、女性各年龄层的常用品牌/ The Most Frequently Used Brands by the Whole Sample, Age and Gender Groups

	人数 Number	第一品牌及百分比 1st / percent	第二品牌及百分比 2nd / percent	第三品牌及百分比 3rd / percent
样本 Sample	879	**高富力 Gaofuli(70.4)**	**立白 Libai(6.1)**	**浪奇 Langqi(3.2)**
男性 Male	404	**高富力 Gaofuli(68.8)**	**立白 Libai(6.9)**	**浪奇 Langqi(3.5)**
16~24 岁 Age	74	高富力 Gaofuli(66.2)	立白 Libai(5.4)	白猫 White Cat(2.7) 劳工 Labour(2.7)
25~34 岁 Age	117	高富力 Gaofuli(71.8)	立白 Libai(6.8) 浪奇 Langqi(6.8)	保洁 Mori(1.7) 劳工 Labour(1.7) 白猫 White Cat(1.7)
35~44 岁 Age	116	高富力 Gaofuli(66.4)	立白 Libai(9.5)	劳工 Labour(2.6) 天丽 TianLi(2.6) 浪奇 Langqi(2.6)
45~54 岁 Age	61	高富力 Gaofuli(72.1)	立白 Libai(4.9)	浪奇 Langqi(3.3)
55~60 岁 Age	36	高富力 Gaofuli(66.7)	白猫 White Cat(8.3)	立白 Libai(5.6)
女性 Female	475	**高富力 Gaofuli(71.8)**	**立白 Libai(5.5)**	**白猫 White Cat(2.9)** **浪奇 Langqi(2.9)**
16~24 岁 Age	92	高富力 Gaofuli(75.0)	立白 Libai(10.9)	斧头 Axe(2.2) 白猫 White Cat(2.2)
25~34 岁 Age	141	高富力 Gaofuli(67.4)	立白 Libai(6.4)	安利 Amway(3.5) 劳工 Labour(3.5)
35~44 岁 Age	125	高富力 Gaofuli(72.8)	白猫 White Cat(4.0)	劳工 Labour(3.2) 立白 Libai(3.2)
45~54 岁 Age	79	高富力 Gaofuli(68.4)	浪奇 Langqi(8.9)	白猫 White Cat(5.1)
55~60 岁 Age	38	高富力 Gaofuli(84.2)	立白 Libai(5.3)	浪奇 Langqi(2.6) 金宝 Jinbao(2.6)

6-4 正在使用的品牌排名/ Ranking of the Brands Used Now

排名 Brand Ranking	品牌 Brands	人数 Number	百分比 Percent
1	高富力 Gaofuli	600	68.3
2	立白 Libai	60	6.8
3	浪奇 Langqi	28	3.2
4	白猫 White Cat	20	2.3
4	劳工 Labour	20	2.3
5	安利 Amway	15	1.7
6	保洁 Mori	10	1.1
7	天丽 TianLi	8	0.9
8	斧头 Axe	7	0.8

n=879

6-5 品牌转换习惯/ Brand Habit in Consuming Liquid Detergent

	人数 Number	第一次使用该品牌 first use this brand	上一次也是这个牌子 used it last time	上一次不是这个牌子 not used it last time
样本 Sample	876	4.1	88.1	7.8
高富力 Gaofuli	598	1.8	91.6	6.5
立白 Libai	60	6.7	85.0	8.3
浪奇 Langqi	28	0.0	92.9	7.1
白猫 White Cat	20	10.0	85.0	5.0
劳工 Labour	20	10.0	75.0	15.0
安利 Amway	15	6.7	73.3	20.0
保洁 Mori	10	30.0	60.0	10.0

6-6 下一次打算使用的品牌排名/ Ranking of the Brands to be Used Next Time

排名 Brand Ranking	品牌 Brands	人数 Number	百分比 Percent
1	高富力 Gaofuli	564	64.2
2	立白 Libai	75	8.5
3	浪奇 Langqi	25	2.8
4	白猫 White Cat	22	2.5
5	劳工 Labour	18	2.0
6	安利 Amway	17	1.9
7	斧头 Axe	14	1.6
8	保洁 Mori	10	1.1

n=879

6-7 样本、男性各年龄层、女性各年龄层是否是主要购买者/ Purchasers in the Household by the Whole Sample, Age and Gender Groups

	人数 Number	是 yes	不是 no
样本 Sample	1033	50.2	49.8
男性 Male	499	32.3	67.7
16~24 岁 Age	106	14.2	85.8
25~34 岁 Age	150	28.7	71.3
35~44 岁 Age	127	43.3	56.7
45~54 岁 Age	73	34.2	65.8
55~60 岁 Age	43	53.5	46.5
女性 Female	534	67.0	33.0
16~24 岁 Age	112	25.0	75.0
25~34 岁 Age	158	74.1	25.9
35~44 岁 Age	136	82.4	17.6
45~54 岁 Age	87	77.0	23.0
55~60 岁 Age	41	82.9	17.1

6-8 样本、男性各年龄层、女性各年龄层是否使用/ Whether to Use Liquid Detergent by the Whole Sample, Age and Gender Groups

	人数 Number	用 yes	不用 no
样本 Sample	1034	85.0	15.0
男性 Male	499	81.0	19.0
16~24 岁 Age	106	69.8	30.2
25~34 岁 Age	150	78.0	22.0
35~44 岁 Age	127	91.3	8.7
45~54 岁 Age	73	83.6	16.4
55~60 岁 Age	43	83.7	16.3
女性 Female	535	88.8	11.2
16~24 岁 Age	112	82.1	17.9
25~34 岁 Age	158	89.2	10.8
35~44 岁 Age	137	91.2	8.8
45~54 岁 Age	87	90.8	9.2
55~60 岁 Age	41	92.7	7.3

6-9 样本、男性各年龄层、女性各年龄层的使用频率/ Frequencies of the Consumed Liquid Detergent by the Whole Sample, Age and Gender Groups

	人数 Number	一天 3 次或以上 3 times or over a day	一天 1~2 次 once or twice a day	两三天用 1 次 once 2 or 3 days	一周 1~2 次 once or twice a week	半个月 1 次或以下 once half a month or below
样本 Sample	879	25.3	65.2	5.2	3.1	1.3
男性 Male	404	20.8	67.8	5.2	4.5	1.7
16~24 岁 Age	74	17.6	71.6	4.1	5.4	1.4
25~34 岁 Age	117	23.9	62.4	6.0	4.3	3.4
35~44 岁 Age	116	19.8	69.8	6.9	3.4	0.0
45~54 岁 Age	61	18.0	73.8	3.3	1.6	3.3
55~60 岁 Age	36	25.0	61.1	2.8	11.1	0.0
女性 Female	475	29.1	62.9	5.3	1.9	0.8
16~24 岁 Age	92	32.6	58.7	5.4	2.2	1.1
25~34 岁 Age	141	32.6	58.2	6.4	2.1	0.7
35~44 岁 Age	125	28.0	64.8	5.6	0.0	1.6
45~54 岁 Age	79	19.0	72.2	3.8	5.1	0.0
55~60 岁 Age	38	31.6	65.8	2.6	0.0	0.0

6-10 选择该类商品的考虑因素/ Ranking of the Considerations in Purchasing

注：本题为多选题，合计百分比超过 100%（Multiple answers）

排名 Ranking	考虑因素 Considerations	人次 Person-time	百分比 Percent
1	价格适中 reasonable price	513	58.4
2	产品功用 product function	373	42.4
3	有名的牌子 famous brand	280	31.9
4	购买方便 easy to buy	260	29.6
5	广告影响 influence of advertising	70	8.0
6	有优惠条件 with preferential terms	64	7.3
7	别人推荐 introduced by other people	41	4.7
8	单位发的 offered by the working unit	29	3.3
9	包装吸引人 appealing package	26	3.0
10	其它 others	10	1.1

n=879

6-11 对产品功能的侧重方面/ Ranking of the Considerations about the Function of this Kind of Product

注：本题为多选题，合计百分比超过 100%（Multiple answers）

排名 Ranking	侧重方面 Items	人次 Person-time	百分比 Percent
1	洗涤力强 powerful cleaning	642	73.1
2	味道清香 fresh smell	444	50.6
3	不伤手 harmless to hand	369	42.0
4	无毒性可洗水果 can be directly used to wash fruit	204	23.2
5	不污染环境 without pollution	46	5.2
6	其他 others	6	0.7

n=878

6-12 重度消费者的人口分布/ Demographics of the Heavy Consumers

	人数 Number	16-24 岁 Age	25-34 岁 Age	35-44 岁 Age	45-54 岁 Age	55-60 岁 Age
样本 Sample	795	18.9	28.8	27.7	16.1	8.6
男性 Male	358	18.4	28.2	29.1	15.6	8.7
一天 3 次或以上 3 times or over a day	84	15.5	33.3	27.4	13.1	10.7
一天 1~2 次 once or twice a day	274	19.3	26.6	29.6	16.4	8.0
女性 Female	437	19.2	29.3	26.5	16.5	8.5
一天 3 次或以上 3 times or over a day	138	21.7	33.3	25.4	10.9	8.7
一天 1~2 次 once or twice a day	299	18.1	27.4	27.1	19.1	8.4

6-13 不同消费者层的常用品牌/ The Most Frequently Used Brands by Market Segments

6-13-1 时尚流行指标/ Fads Popular Index

	人数 Number	第一品牌及百分比 1st / percent	第二品牌及百分比 2nd / percent	第三品牌及百分比 3rd / percent
样本 Sample	869	**高富力 Gaofuli(70.3)**	**立白 Libai(6.1)**	**浪奇 Langqi(3.2)**
平实生活指向 simple living orientation	454	高富力 Gaofuli(70.5)	立白 Libai(5.3)	浪奇 Langqi(3.5)
时尚流行指向 fashion orientation	415	高富力 Gaofuli(70.1)	立白 Libai(7.0)	劳工 Labour(3.1)

6-13-2 广告态度指标/ Advertising Attitude Index

	人数 Number	第一品牌及百分比 1st / percent	第二品牌及百分比 2nd / percent	第三品牌及百分比 3rd / percent
样本 Sample	867	**高富力 Gaofuli(70.5)**	**立白 Libai(6.2)**	**浪奇 Langqi(3.1)**
广告淡漠指向 indifferent orientation	290	高富力 Gaofuli(67.9)	立白 Libai(7.6)	白猫 White Cat(4.1)
中间层 medium	493	高富力 Gaofuli(70.4)	立白 Libai(5.9)	浪奇 Langqi(3.2)
信赖广告指向 loyal orientation	84	高富力 Gaofuli(79.8)	立白 Libai(3.6)	保洁 Mori(2.4) 劳工 Labour(2.4)

6-14 重度消费者的消费层构成/ The Composition of the Heavy Consumers

6-14-1 时尚流行指标/ Fads Popular Index

	人数 Number	平实生活指向 simple living orientation	时尚流行指向 fashion orientation
样本 Sample	786	52.8	47.2
一天 3 次或以上 3 times or over a day	219	48.9	51.1
一天 1~2 次 once or twice a day	567	54.3	45.7

6-14-2 广告态度指标/ Advertising Attitude Index

	人数 Number	广告淡漠指向 indifferent orientation	中间层 medium	信赖广告指向 loyal orientation
样本 Sample	785	33.1	57.5	9.4
一天 3 次或以上 3 times or over a day	217	27.6	64.5	7.8
一天 1~2 次 once or twice a day	568	35.2	54.8	10.0

● 重庆 / Chongqing

6-1 是否使用的比例/ Proportion of the Sample Consuming Liquid Detergent in the Last Three Months

	人数 Number	百分比 Percent
用 yes	386	61.9
不用 no	238	38.1

n=624

6-2 最常用品牌排名/ Ranking of the Most Frequently Used Brands

排名 Brand Ranking	品牌 Brands	人数 Number	百分比 Percent
1	白猫 White Cat	135	35.0
2	蜀秀 Shuxiu	120	31.1
3	洁牌 Jiepai	50	13.0
4	雕牌 Diao	6	1.6
5	黑猫 Heimao	4	1.0
5	洁尔芬 Jierfen	4	1.0
6	立白 Libai	3	0.8

n=386

6-3 样本、男性各年龄层、女性各年龄层的常用品牌/ The Most Frequently Used Brands by the Whole Sample, Age and Gender Groups

	人数 Number	第一品牌及百分比 1st/ percent	第二品牌及百分比 2nd/ percent	第三品牌及百分比 3rd/ percent
样本 Sample	386	**白猫 White Cat(35.0)**	**蜀秀 Shuxiu(31.1)**	**洁牌 Jiepai(13.0)**
男性 Male	188	**白猫 White Cat(33.0)** **蜀秀 Shuxiu(33.0)**	**洁牌 Jiepai(16.0)**	**雕牌 Diao(1.6)**
16~24 岁 Age	34	白猫 White Cat(44.1)	蜀秀 Shuxiu(26.5)	洁牌 Jiepai(8.8)
25~34 岁 Age	52	白猫 White Cat(36.5)	蜀秀 Shuxiu(32.7)	洁牌 Jiepai(13.5)
35~44 岁 Age	48	白猫 White Cat(33.3)	蜀秀 Shuxiu(27.1)	洁牌 Jiepai(18.8)
45~54 岁 Age	36	蜀秀 Shuxiu(41.7)	洁牌 Jiepai(22.2)	白猫 White Cat(19.4)
55~60 岁 Age	18	蜀秀 Shuxiu(44.4)	白猫 White Cat(27.8)	洁牌 Jiepai(16.7)
女性 Female	198	**白猫 White Cat(36.9)**	**蜀秀 Shuxiu(29.3)**	**洁牌 Jiepai(10.1)**
16~24 岁 Age	39	白猫 White Cat(56.4)	蜀秀 Shuxiu(23.1)	洁牌 Jiepai(2.6) 立白 Libai(2.6)
25~34 岁 Age	58	白猫 White Cat(39.7)	蜀秀 Shuxiu(25.9)	洁牌 Jiepai(5.2)
35~44 岁 Age	44	蜀秀 Shuxiu(34.1)	洁牌 Jiepai(20.5)	白猫 White Cat(15.9)
45~54 岁 Age	40	白猫 White Cat(40.0)	蜀秀 Shuxiu(32.5)	洁牌 Jiepai(15.0)
55~60 岁 Age	17	蜀秀 Shuxiu(35.3)	白猫 White Cat(29.4)	倍洁 Beijie(5.9) 洁牌 Jiepai(5.9) 立白 Libai(5.9) 黑猫 Heimao(5.9) 洁尔芬 Jierfen(5.9)

6-4 正在使用的品牌排名/ Ranking of the Brand Used Now

排名 Brand Ranking	品牌 Brands	人数 Number	百分比 Percent
1	白猫 White Cat	136	35.2
2	蜀秀 Shuxiu	119	30.8
3	洁牌 Jiepai	46	11.9
4	雕牌 Diao	5	1.3
5	洁尔芬 Jierfen	4	1.0
5	黑猫 Heimao	4	1.0

n=386

6-5 品牌转换习惯/ Brand Habit in Consuming Liquid Detergent

	人数 Number	第一次使用该品牌 first use this brand	上一次也是这个牌子 used it last time	上一次不是这个牌子 not used it last time
样本 Sample	382	4.7	88.2	7.1
白猫 White Cat	136	3.7	87.5	8.8
蜀秀 Shuxiu	117	2.6	90.6	6.8
洁牌 Jiepai	46	2.2	95.7	2.2
雕牌 Diao	5	20.0	60.0	20.0
洁尔芬 Jierfen	4	0.0	100.0	0.0
黑猫 Heimao	4	0.0	75.0	25.0

6-6 下一次打算使用的品牌排名/ Ranking of the Brands to be Used Next Time

排名 Brand Ranking	品牌 Brands	人数 Number	百分比 Percent
1	白猫 White Cat	157	40.7
2	蜀秀 Shuxiu	109	28.2
3	洁牌 Jiepai	42	10.9
4	雕牌 Diao	7	1.8
5	黑猫 Heimao	4	1.0
6	洁尔芬 Jierfen	3	0.8

n=386

6-7 样本、男性各年龄层、女性各年龄层是否是主要购买者/ Purchasers in the Household by the Whole Sample, Age and Gender Groups

	人数 Number	是 yes	不是 no
样本 Sample	624	35.9	64.1
男性 Male	314	21.0	79.0
16~24 岁 Age	64	7.8	92.2
25~34 岁 Age	93	26.9	73.1
35~44 岁 Age	75	26.7	73.3
45~54 岁 Age	54	16.7	83.3
55~60 岁 Age	28	25.0	75.0
女性 Female	310	51.0	49.0
16~24 岁 Age	64	23.4	76.6
25~34 岁 Age	90	53.3	46.7
35~44 岁 Age	73	58.9	41.1
45~54 岁 Age	60	63.3	36.7
55~60 岁 Age	23	60.9	39.1

6-8 样本、男性各年龄层、女性各年龄层是否使用/ Whether to Use Liquid Detergent by the Whole Sample, Age and Gerber Groups

	人数 Number	用 yes	不用 no
样本 Sample	624	61.9	38.1
男性 Male	314	59.9	40.1
16~24 岁 Age	64	53.1	46.9
25~34 岁 Age	93	55.9	44.1
35~44 岁 Age	75	64.0	36.0
45~54 岁 Age	54	66.7	33.3
55~60 岁 Age	28	64.3	35.7
女性 Female	310	63.9	36.1
16~24 岁 Age	64	60.9	39.1
25~34 岁 Age	90	64.4	35.6
35~44 岁 Age	73	60.3	39.7
45~54 岁 Age	60	66.7	33.3
55~60 岁 Age	23	73.9	26.1

6-9 样本、男性各年龄层、女性各年龄层的使用频率/ Frequencies of the Consumed Liquid Detergent by the Whole Sample, Age and Gender Groups

	人数 Number	一天 3 次或以上 3 times or over a day	一天 1~2 次 once or twice a day	两三天用 1 次 once 2 or 3 days	一周 1~2 次 once or twice a week	半个月 1 次或以下 once half a month or below
样本 Sample	385	33.8	53.2	4.7	4.7	3.6
男性 Male	188	36.2	52.7	4.8	4.3	2.1
16~24 岁 Age	34	29.4	58.8	0.0	8.8	2.9
25~34 岁 Age	52	38.5	53.8	1.9	1.9	3.8
35~44 岁 Age	48	39.6	47.9	10.4	2.1	0.0
45~54 岁 Age	36	25.0	58.3	8.3	8.3	0.0
55~60 岁 Age	18	55.6	38.9	0.0	0.0	5.6
女性 Female	197	31.5	53.8	4.6	5.1	5.1
16~24 岁 Age	39	25.6	51.3	5.1	7.7	10.3
25~34 岁 Age	57	31.6	57.9	5.3	5.3	0.0
35~44 岁 Age	44	18.2	63.6	6.8	2.3	9.1
45~54 岁 Age	40	50.0	37.5	2.5	5.0	5.0
55~60 岁 Age	17	35.3	58.8	0.0	5.9	0.0

6-10 选择该类商品的考虑因素/ Ranking of the Considerations in Purchasing

注：本题为多选题，合计百分比超过 100%（Multiple answers）

排名 Ranking	考虑因素 Considerations	人次 Person-time	百分比 Percent
1	价格适中 reasonable price	236	61.3
2	产品功用 product function	151	39.2
3	购买方便 easy to buy	95	24.7
4	有名的牌子 famous brand	61	15.8
5	广告影响 influence of advertising	41	10.6
6	单位发的 offered by the working unit	19	4.9
7	别人推荐 introduced by other people	15	3.9
8	其它 others	9	2.3
9	有优惠条件 with preferential terms	7	1.8
10	包装吸引人 appealing package	2	0.5

n=385

6-11 对产品功能的侧重方面/ Ranking of the Considerations about the Function of this Kind of Product

注：本题为多选题，合计百分比超过 100%（Multiple answers）

排名 Ranking	侧重方面 Items	人次 Person-time	百分比 Percent
1	洗涤力强 powerful cleaning	306	79.3
2	味道清香 fresh smell	153	39.6
3	无毒性可洗水果 can be directly used to wash fruit	126	32.6
4	不伤手 harmless to hand	94	24.4
5	不污染环境 without pollution	23	6.0
6	其他 others	5	1.3

n=386

6-12 重度消费者的人口分布/ Demographics of the Heavy Consumers

	人数 Number	16-24 岁 Age	25-34 岁 Age	35-44 岁 Age	45-54 岁 Age	55-60 岁 Age
样本 Sample	335	17.9	29.6	23.3	19.4	9.9
男性 Male	167	18.0	28.7	25 1	18.0	10.2
一天 3 次或以上 3 times or over a day	68	14.7	29.4	27 9	13.2	14.7
一天 1~2 次 once or twice a day	99	20.2	28.3	23.2	21.2	7.1
女性 Female	168	17.9	30.4	21.4	20.8	9.5
一天 3 次或以上 3 times or over a day	62	16.1	29.0	12.9	32.3	9.7
一天 1~2 次 once or twice a day	106	18.9	31.1	26.4	14.2	9.4

6-13 不同消费者层的常用品牌/ The Most Frequently Used Brands by Market Segments

6-13-1 时尚流行指标/ Fads Popular Index

	人数 Number	第一品牌及百分比 1st / percent	第二品牌及百分比 2nd / percent	第三品牌及百分比 3rd / percent
样本 Sample	381	**白猫 White Cat(34.4)**	**蜀秀 Shuxiu(31.2)**	**洁牌 Jiepai(13.1)**
平实生活指向 simple living orientation	219	蜀秀 Shuxiu(36.5)	白猫 White Cat(31.1)	洁牌 Jiepai(11.0)
时尚流行指向 fashion orientation	162	白猫 White Cat(38.9)	蜀秀 Shuxiu(24.1)	洁牌 Jiepai(16.0)

6-13-2 广告态度指标/ Advertising Attitude Index

	人数 Number	第一品牌及百分比 1st / percent	第二品牌及百分比 2nd / percent	第三品牌及百分比 3rd / percent
样本 Sample	382	**白猫 White Cat(35.1)**	**蜀秀 Shuxiu(31.2)**	**洁牌 Jiepai(12.8)**
广告淡漠指向 indifferent orientation	100	白猫 White Cat(35.0)	蜀秀 Shuxiu(29.0)	洁牌 Jiepai(15.0)
中间层 medium	229	白猫 White Cat(34.9)	蜀秀 Shuxiu(31.9)	洁牌 Jiepai(12.2)
信赖广告指向 loyal orientation	53	白猫 White Cat(35.8)	蜀秀 Shuxiu(32.1)	洁牌 Jiepai(11.3)

6-14 重度消费者的消费层构成/ The Composition of the Heavy Consumers

6-14-1 时尚流行指标/ Fads Popular Index

	人数 Number	平实生活指向 simple living orientation	时尚流行指向 fashion orientation
样本 Sample	333	59.5	40.5
一天 3 次或以上 3 times or over a day	129	61.2	38.8
一天 1~2 次 once or twice a day	204	58.3	41.7

6-14-2 广告态度指标/ Advertising Attitude Index

	人数 Number	广告淡漠指向 indifferent orientation	中间层 medium	信赖广告指向 loyal orientation
样本 Sample	331	26.0	60.1	13.9
一天 3 次或以上 3 times or over a day	128	26.6	57.8	15.6
一天 1~2 次 once or twice a day	203	25.6	61.6	12.8

● 武汉 / Wuhan

6-1 是否使用的比例/ Proportion of the Sample Consuming Liquid Detergent in the Last Three Months

	人数 Number	百分比 Percent
用 yes	460	71.8
不用 no	181	28.2

n=641

6-2 最常用品牌排名/ Ranking of the Most Frequently Used Brands

排名 Brand Ranking	品牌 Brands	人数 Number	百分比 Percent
1	白猫 White Cat	333	72.4
2	一枝花 A flower	50	10.9
3	波尔 Boer	8	1.7
4	安利 Amway	7	1.5
4	巧手 Dosia	7	1.5
5	雕牌 Diao	4	0.9
5	传化 Chuanhua	4	0.9
6	活力 28 Power 28	3	0.7
6	青龙 Qinglong	3	0.7

n=460

6-3 样本、男性各年龄层、女性各年龄层的常用品牌/ The Most Frequently Used Brands by the Whole Sample, Age and Gender Groups

	人数 Number	第一品牌及百分比 1st/ percent	第二品牌及百分比 2nd/ percent	第三品牌及百分比 3rd/ percent
样本 Sample	460	**白猫 White Cat(72.4)**	**一枝花 A flower(10.9)**	**波尔 Boer(1.7)**
男性 Male	199	**白猫 White Cat(70.4)**	**一枝花 A flower(11.6)**	**波尔 Boer(2.0)**
16~24 岁 Age	35	白猫 White Cat(85.7)	巧手 Dosia(2.9) 一枝花 A flower(2.9) 青龙 Qinglong(2.9) 洁亮 Jieliang(2.9)	
25~34 岁 Age	57	白猫 White Cat(63.2)	一枝花 A flower(17.5)	安利 Amway(3.5) 波尔 Boer(3.5)
35~44 岁 Age	57	白猫 White Cat(77.2)	一枝花 A flower(5.3)	雕牌 Diao(3.5)
45~54 岁 Age	34	白猫 White Cat(61.8)	一枝花 A flower(14.7)	波尔 Boer(2.9) 巧手 Dosia(2.9) 碟新 Diexin(2.9) 洗源 Xiyuan(2.9) 高洁 Gaojie(2.9) 雪莱 Xuelai(2.9) 奥奇丽 Aoqili(2.9)
55~60 岁 Age	16	白猫 White Cat(56.3)	一枝花 A flower(25.0)	绿伞 Evergreen(6.3)
女性 Female	261	**白猫 White Cat(73.9)**	**一枝花 A flower(10.3)**	**安利 Amway(1.5)** **波尔 Boer(1.5)** **巧手 Dosia(1.5)**
16~24 岁 Age	48	白猫 White Cat(83.3)	巧手 Dosia(6.3) 一枝花 A flower(6.3)	雕牌 Diao(2.1)
25~34 岁 Age	83	白猫 White Cat(75.9)	一枝花 A flower(10.8)	安利 Amway(3.6)
35~44 岁 Age	58	白猫 White Cat(69.0)	一枝花 A flower(10.3)	波尔 Boer(3.4) 青龙 Qinglong(3.4)
45~54 岁 Age	53	白猫 White Cat(73.6)	一枝花 A flower(11.3)	安利 Amway(1.9) 波尔 Boer(1.9) 传化 Chuanhua(1.9)
55~60 岁 Age	19	白猫 White Cat(57.9)	一枝花 A flower(15.8)	波尔 Boer(5.3) 武钢产 Wugang(5.3)

6-4 正在使用的品牌排名/ Ranking of the Brand Used Now

排名 Brand Ranking	品牌 Brands	人数 Number	百分比 Percent
1	白猫 White Cat	304	66.1
2	一枝花 A flower	55	12.0
3	雕牌 Diao	14	3.0
4	巧手 Dosia	12	2.6
5	波尔 Boer	10	2.2
6	安利 Amway	7	1.5
7	传化 Chuanhua	6	1.3
8	立净 Lijing	4	0.9

n=460

6-5 品牌转换习惯/ Brand Habit in Consuming Liquid Detergent

	人数 Number	第一次使用该品牌 first use this brand	上一次也是这个牌子 used it last time	上一次不是这个牌子 not used it last time
样本 Sample	459	6.5	84.1	9.4
白猫 White Cat	304	2.6	89.8	7.6
一枝花 A flower	55	7.3	83.6	9.1
雕牌 Diao	14	35.7	42.9	21.4
巧手 Dosia	12	25.0	33.3	41.7
波尔 Boer	9	11.1	55.6	33.3
安利 Amway	7	14.3	85.7	0.0
传化 Chuanhua	6	16.7	66.7	16.7
立净 Lijing	4	50.0	50.0	0.0

6-6 下一次打算使用的品牌排名/ Ranking of the Brands to be Used Next Time

排名 Brand Ranking	品牌 Brands	人数 Number	百分比 Percent
1	白猫 White Cat	302	65.7
2	一枝花 A flower	49	10.7
3	巧手 Dosia	14	3.0
4	雕牌 Diao	13	2.8
5	波尔 Boer	12	2.6
6	安利 Amway	8	1.7
7	传化 Chuanhua	5	1.1
8	青龙 Qinglong	3	0.7

n=460

6-7 样本、男性各年龄层、女性各年龄层是否是主要购买者/ Purchasers in the Household by the Whole Sample, Age and Gender Groups

	人数 Number	是 yes	不是 no
样本 Sample	640	40.9	59.1
男性 Male	311	24.8	75.2
16~24 岁 Age	65	6.2	93.8
25~34 岁 Age	89	24.7	75.3
35~44 岁 Age	80	27.5	72.5
45~54 岁 Age	52	36.5	63.5
55~60 岁 Age	25	40.0	60.0
女性 Female	329	56.2	43.8
16~24 岁 Age	69	13.0	87.0
25~34 岁 Age	96	59.4	40.6
35~44 岁 Age	77	74.0	26.0
45~54 岁 Age	61	82.0	18.0
55~60 岁 Age	26	46.2	53.8

6-8 样本、男性各年龄层、女性各年龄层是否使用该类商品/ Whether to Use Liquid Detergent by the Whole Sample, Age and Gender Groups

	人数 Number	用 yes	不用 no
样本 Sample	641	71.8	28.2
男性 Male	311	64.0	36.0
16~24 岁 Age	65	53.8	46.2
25~34 岁 Age	89	64.0	36.0
35~44 岁 Age	80	71.3	28.8
45~54 岁 Age	52	65.4	34.6
55~60 岁 Age	25	64.0	36.0
女性 Female	330	79.1	20.9
16~24 岁 Age	69	69.6	30.4
25~34 岁 Age	96	86.5	13.5
35~44 岁 Age	77	75.3	24.7
45~54 岁 Age	62	85.5	14.5
55~60 岁 Age	26	73.1	26.9

6-9 样本、男性各年龄层、女性各年龄层的使用频率/ Frequencies of the Consumed Liquid Detergent by the Whole Sample, Age and Gender Groups

	人数 Number	一天 3 次或以上 3 times or over a day	一天 1~2 次 once or twice a day	两三天用 1 次 once 2 or 3 days	一周 1~2 次 once or twice a week	半个月 1 次或以下 once half a month or below
样本 Sample	458	16.6	64.8	10.3	5.9	2.4
男性 Male	198	19.2	61.1	10.6	6.6	2.5
16~24 岁 Age	35	14.3	65.7	11.4	8.6	0.0
25~34 岁 Age	57	24.6	59.6	8.8	5.3	1.8
35~44 岁 Age	57	15.8	63.2	10.5	8.8	1.8
45~54 岁 Age	33	15.2	66.7	6.1	6.1	6.1
55~60 岁 Age	16	31.3	37.5	25.0	0.0	6.3
女性 Female	260	14.6	67.7	10.0	5.4	2.3
16~24 岁 Age	48	16.7	68.8	10.4	0.0	4.2
25~34 岁 Age	82	12.2	65.9	11.0	9.8	1.2
35~44 岁 Age	58	13.8	69.0	6.9	5.2	5.2
45~54 岁 Age	53	15.1	64.2	15.1	5.7	0.0
55~60 岁 Age	19	21.1	78.9	0.0	0.0	0.0

6-10 选择该类商品的考虑因素/ Ranking of the Considerations in Purchasing

注：本题为多选题，合计百分比超过 100%（Multiple answers）

排名 Ranking	考虑因素 Considerations	人次 Person-time	百分比 Percent
1	价格适中 reasonable price	278	60.4
2	产品功用 product function	203	44.1
3	有名的牌子 famous brand	157	34.1
4	购买方便 easy to buy	120	26.1
5	广告影响 influence of advertising	59	12.8
6	单位发的 offered by the working unit	49	10.7
7	别人推荐 introduced by other people	21	4.6
8	有优惠条件 with preferential terms	19	4.1
9	其它 others	15	3.3
10	包装吸引人 appealing package	3	0.7

n=460

6-11 对产品功能的侧重方面/ Ranking of the Considerations about the Function of this Kind of Product

注：本题为多选题，合计百分比超过 100%（Multiple answers）

排名 Ranking	侧重方面 Items	人次 Person-time	百分比 Percent
1	洗涤力强 powerful cleaning	347	75.6
2	味道清香 fresh smell	252	54.9
3	不伤手 harmless to hand	173	37.7
4	无毒性可洗水果 can be directly used to wash fruit	161	35.1
5	不污染环境 without pollution	57	12.4
6	其他 others	4	0.9

n=459

6-12 重度消费者的人口分布/ Demographics of the Heavy Consumers

	人数 Number	16-24 岁 Age	25-34 岁 Age	35-44 岁 Age	45-54 岁 Age	55-60 岁 Age
样本 Sample	373	18.5	30.0	24.9	18.5	8.0
男性 Male	159	17.6	30.2	28.3	17.0	6.9
一天 3 次或以上 3 times or over a day	38	13.2	36.8	23.7	13.2	13.2
一天 1~2 次 once or twice a day	121	19.0	28.1	29.3	18.2	5.0
女性 Female	214	19.2	29.9	22.4	19.6	8.9
一天 3 次或以上 3 times or over a day	38	21.1	26.3	21.1	21.1	10.5
一天 1~2 次 once or twice a day	176	18.8	30.7	22.7	19.3	8.5

6-13 不同消费者层的常用品牌/ The Most Frequently Used Brands by Market Segments

6-13-1 时尚流行指标/ Fads Popular Index

	人数 Number	第一品牌及百分比 1st / percent	第二品牌及百分比 2nd / percent	第三品牌及百分比 3rd / percent
样本 Sample	454	**白猫 White Cat(72.5)**	**一枝花 A flower(11.0)**	**安利 Amway(1.5)** **波尔 Boer(1.5)** **巧手 Dosia(1.5)**
平实生活指向 simple living orientation	238	白猫 White Cat(70.6)	一枝花 A flower(11.8)	波尔 Boer(2.5)
时尚流行指向 fashion orientation	216	白猫 White Cat(74.5)	一枝花 A flower(10.2)	巧手 Dosia(2.3)

6-13-2 广告态度指标/ Advertising Attitude Index

	人数 Number	第一品牌及百分比 1st / percent	第二品牌及百分比 2nd / percent	第三品牌及百分比 3rd / percent
样本 Sample	455	**白猫 White Cat(72.5)**	**一枝花 A flower(11.0)**	**安利 Amway(1.5)** **波尔 Boer(1.5)** **巧手 Dosia(1.5)**
广告淡漠指向 indifferent orientation	133	白猫 White Cat(66.2)	一枝花 A flower(12.0)	
中间层 medium	264	白猫 White Cat(73.5)	一枝花 A flower(11.4)	安利 Amway(2.3)
信赖广告指向 loyal orientation	58	白猫 White Cat(82.8)	一枝花 A flower(6.9)	青龙 Qinglong(3.4)

6-14 重度消费者的消费层构成/ The Composition of the Heavy Consumers

6-14-1 时尚流行指标/ Fads Popular Index

	人数 Number	平实生活指向 simple living orientation	时尚流行指向 fashion orientation
样本 Sample	368	51.9	48.1
一天 3 次或以上 3 times or over a day	75	53.3	46.7
一天 1~2 次 once or twice a day	293	51.5	48.5

6-14-2 广告态度指标/ Advertising Attitude Index

	人数 Number	广告淡漠指向 indifferent orientation	中间层 medium	信赖广告指向 loyal orientation
样本 Sample	368	27.2	60.6	12.2
一天 3 次或以上 3 times or over a day	75	29.3	54.7	16.0
一天 1~2 次 once or twice a day	293	26.6	62.1	11.3

● 西安 / Xi'an

6-1 是否使用的比例/ Proportion of the Sample Consuming Liquid Detergent in the Last Three Months

	人数 Number	百分比 Percent
用 yes	494	82.3
不用 no	106	17.7

n=600

6-2 最常用品牌排名/ Ranking of the Most Frequently Used Brands

排名 Brand Ranking	品牌 Brands	人数 Number	百分比 Percent
1	白猫 White Cat	449	90.9
2	雕牌 Diao	13	2.6
3	活力 28 Power 28	4	0.8
4	奇强 Qiqiang	3	0.6
4	开米 Kami	3	0.6
5	安利 Amway	2	0.4
5	金鱼 Gold Fish	2	0.4
5	中华 Zhonghua	2	0.4

n=494

6-3 样本、男性各年龄层、女性各年龄层的常用品牌/ The Most Frequently Used Brands by the Whole Sample, Age and Gender Groups

	人数 Number	第一品牌及百分比 1st/ percent	第二品牌及百分比 2nd/ percent	第三品牌及百分比 3rd/ percent
样本 Sample	494	**白猫 White Cat(90.9)**	**雕牌 Diao(2.6)**	**活力 28 Power 28(0.8)**
男性 Male	242	**白猫 White Cat(88.4)**	**雕牌 Diao(4.1)**	**奇强 Qiqiang(0.8)**
16~24 岁 Age	46	白猫 White Cat(84.8)	雕牌 Diao(8.7)	波尔 Boer(2.2) 中华 Zhonghua(2.2) 天狮 Tianshi(2.2)
25~34 岁 Age	69	白猫 White Cat(89.9)	雕牌 Diao(5.8)	金鱼 Gold Fish(1.4) 奇强 Qiqiang(1.4) 熊猫 Panda(1.4)
35~44 岁 Age	66	白猫 White Cat(83.3)	巧手 Dosia(1.5) 洁翔 Jiexiang(1.5) 加佳 Gige(1.5) 奇强 Qiqiang(1.5) 开米 Kami(1.5) 立白 Libai(1.5) 活力 28 Power 28(1.5) 雕牌 Diao(1.5) 安利 Amway(1.5)	
45~54 岁 Age	40	白猫 White Cat(95.0)	雕牌 Diao(2.5) 洁宝 Job(2.5)	
55~60 岁 Age	21	白猫 White Cat(95.2)		
女性 Female	252	**白猫 White Cat(93.3)**	**雕牌 Diao(1.2)** **活力 28 Power 28(1.2)**	**开米 Kami(0.8)**
16~24 岁 Age	47	白猫 White Cat(93.6)	雕牌 Diao(4.3)	开米 Kami(2.1)
25~34 岁 Age	80	白猫 White Cat(95.0)	高富力 Gaofuli(1.3) 活力 28 Power 28(1.3) 靓靓 Liangliang(1.3) 晨逸 Morning Fresh(1.3)	
35~44 岁 Age	60	白猫 White Cat(93.3)	达尔美 Da'ermei(1.7) 开米 Kami(1.7) 中华 Zhonghua(1.7) 奇强 Qiqiang(1.7)	
45~54 岁 Age	44	白猫 White Cat(90.9)	活力 28 Power 28(4.5)	金鱼 Gold Fish(2.3) 亲亲 Qinqin(2.3)
55~60 岁 Age	21	白猫 White Cat(90.5)	安利 Amway(4.8) 雕牌 Diao(4.8)	

6-4 正在使用的品牌排名/ Ranking of the Brands Used Now

排名 Brand Ranking	品牌 Brands	人数 Number	百分比 Percent
1	白猫 White Cat	435	88.1
2	雕牌 Diao	21	4.3
3	奇强 Qiqiang	5	1.0
3	开米 Kami	5	1.0
4	活力 28 Power 28	3	0.6
4	安利 Amway	3	0.6
5	波尔 Boer	2	0.4
5	中华 Zhonghua	2	0.4

N=494

6-5 品牌转换习惯/ Brand Habit in Consuming Liquid Detergent

	人数 Number	第一次使用该品牌 first use this brand	上一次也是这个牌子 used it last time	上一次不是这个牌子 not used it last time
样本 Sample	493	2.2	93.7	4.1
白猫 White Cat	434	1.4	97.0	1.6
雕牌 Diao	21	9.5	57.1	33.3
开米 Kami	5	20.0	40.0	40.0
奇强 Qiqiang	5	0.0	80.0	20.0

6-6 下一次打算使用的品牌排名/ Ranking of the Brands to be Used Next Time

排名 Brand Ranking	品牌 Brands	人数 Number	百分比 Percent
1	白猫 White Cat	426	86.2
2	雕牌 Diao	24	4.9
3	奇强 Qiqiang	9	1.8
4	立白 Libai	5	1.0
5	中华 Zhonghua	3	0.6
5	开米 Kami	3	0.6
6	安利 Amway	2	0.4
6	波尔 Boer	2	0.4
6	达尔美 Da'ermei	2	0.4
6	活力 28 Power 28	2	0.4

n=494

6-7 样本、男性各年龄层、女性各年龄层是否是主要购买者/ Purchasers in the Household by the Whole Sample, Age and Gender Groups

	人数 Number	是 yes	不是 no
样本 Sample	600	51.2	48.8
男性 Male	301	33.6	66.4
16~24 岁 Age	64	17.2	82.8
25~34 岁 Age	91	36.3	63.7
35~44 岁 Age	77	45.5	54.5
45~54 岁 Age	46	28.3	71.7
55~60 岁 Age	23	39.1	60.9
女性 Female	299	68.9	31.1
16~24 岁 Age	61	42.6	57.4
25~34 岁 Age	90	73.3	26.7
35~44 岁 Age	74	77.0	23.0
45~54 岁 Age	49	79.6	20.4
55~60 岁 Age	25	72.0	28.0

6-8 样本、男性各年龄层、女性各年龄层是否使用/ Whether to Use Liquid Detergent by the Whole Sample, Age and Gender Groups

	人数 Number	用 yes	不用 no
样本 Sample	600	82.3	17.7
男性 Male	301	80.4	19.6
16~24 岁 Age	64	71.9	28.1
25~34 岁 Age	91	75.8	24.2
35~44 岁 Age	77	85.7	14.3
45~54 岁 Age	46	87.0	13.0
55~60 岁 Age	23	91.3	8.7
女性 Female	299	84.3	15.7
16~24 岁 Age	61	77.0	23.0
25~34 岁 Age	90	88.9	11.1
35~44 岁 Age	74	81.1	18.9
45~54 岁 Age	49	89.8	10.2
55~60 岁 Age	25	84.0	16.0

6-9 样本、男性各年龄层、女性各年龄层的使用频率/ Frequencies of the Consumed Liquid Detergent by the Whole Sample, Age and Gender Groups

	人数 Number	一天 3 次或以上 3 times or over a day	一天 1~2 次 once or twice a day	两三天用 1 次 once 2 or 3 days	一周 1~2 次 once or twice a week	半个月 1 次或以下 once half a month or below
样本 Sample	494	25.3	60.9	7.3	4.9	1.6
男性 Male	242	19.8	63.6	7.9	6.2	2.5
16~24 岁 Age	46	19.6	63.0	8.7	6.5	2.2
25~34 岁 Age	69	27.5	62.3	4.3	2.9	2.9
35~44 岁 Age	66	15.2	63.6	12.1	6.1	3.0
45~54 岁 Age	40	15.0	70.0	5.0	7.5	2.5
55~60 岁 Age	21	19.0	57.1	9.5	14.3	0.0
女性 Female	252	30.6	58.3	6.7	3.6	0.8
16~24 岁 Age	47	31.9	57.4	8.5	2.1	0.0
25~34 岁 Age	80	33.8	55.0	7.5	3.8	0.0
35~44 岁 Age	60	25.0	58.3	10.0	3.3	3.3
45~54 岁 Age	44	27.3	70.5	0.0	2.3	0.0
55~60 岁 Age	21	38.1	47.6	4.8	9.5	0.0

6-10 选择该类商品的考虑因素/ Ranking of the Considerations in Purchasing

注：本题为多选题，合计百分比超过 100%（Multiple answers）

排名 Ranking	考虑因素 Considerations	人次 Person-time	百分比 Percent
1	价格适中 reasonable price	251	50.9
2	产品功用 product function	206	41.8
3	有名的牌子 famous brand	197	40.0
4	购买方便 easy to buy	109	22.1
5	广告影响 influence of advertising	47	9.5
6	别人推荐 introduced by other people	23	4.7
7	单位发的 offered by the working unit	17	3.4
8	有优惠条件 with preferential terms	15	3.0
9	包装吸引人 appealing package	8	1.6
10	其它 others	5	1.0

n=493

6-11 对产品功能的侧重方面/ Ranking of the Considerations about the Function of this Kind of Product

注：本题为多选题，合计百分比超过 100%（Multiple answers）

排名 Ranking	侧重方面 Items	人次 Person-time	百分比 Percent
1	洗涤力强 powerful cleaning	331	67.1
2	味道清香 fresh smell	248	50.3
3	无毒性可洗水果 can be directly used to wash fruit	186	37.7
4	不伤手 harmless to hand	177	35.9
5	不污染环境 without pollution	43	8.7
6	其他 others	4	0.8

n=493

6-12 重度消费者的人口分布/ Demographics of the Heavy Consumers

	人数 Number	16-24 岁 Age	25-34 岁 Age	35-44 岁 Age	45-54 岁 Age	55-60 岁 Age
样本 Sample	426	18.8	31.2	23.9	18.1	8.0
男性 Male	202	18.8	30.7	25.7	16.8	7.9
一天 3 次或以上 3 times or over a day	48	18.8	39.6	20.8	12.5	8.3
一天 1~2 次 once or twice a day	154	18.8	27.9	27.3	18.2	7.8
女性 Female	224	18.8	31.7	22.3	19.2	8.0
一天 3 次或以上 3 times or over a day	77	19.5	35.1	19.5	15.6	10.4
一天 1~2 次 once or twice a day	147	18.4	29.9	23.8	21.1	6.8

6-13 不同消费者层的常用品牌/ The Most Frequently Used Brands by Market Segments

6-13-1 时尚流行指标/ Fads Popular Index

	人数 Number	第一品牌及百分比 1st / percent	第二品牌及百分比 2nd / percent	第三品牌及百分比 3rd / percent
样本 Sample	493	**白猫 White Cat(90.9)**	**雕牌 Diao(2.6)**	**活力 28 Power 28(0.8)**
平实生活指向 simple living orientation	287	白猫 White Cat(90.9)	雕牌 Diao(3.1)	奇强 Qiqiang(1.0)
时尚流行指向 fashion orientation	206	白猫 White Cat(90.8)	雕牌 Diao(1.9)	开米 Kami(1.0) 活力 28 Power 28(1.0) 金鱼 Gold Fish(1.0)

6-13-2 广告态度指标/ Advertising Attitude Index

	人数 Number	第一品牌及百分比 1st / percent	第二品牌及百分比 2nd / percent	第三品牌及百分比 3rd / percent
样本 Sample	490	**白猫 White Cat(90.8)**	**雕牌 Diao(2.7)**	**活力 28 Power 28(0.8)**
广告淡漠指向 indifferent orientation	154	白猫 White Cat(89.0)	雕牌 Diao(4.5)	开米 Kami(1.3)
中间层 medium	279	白猫 White Cat(90.7)	雕牌 Diao(2.2)	活力 28 Power 28(1.1) 奇强 Qiqiang(1.1)
信赖广告指向 loyal orientation	57	白猫 White Cat(96.5)	安利 Amway(1.8) 开米 Kami(1.8)	

6-14 重度消费者的消费层构成/ The Composition of the Heavy Consumers

6-14-1 时尚流行指标/ Fads Popular Index

	人数 Number	平实生活指向 simple living orientation	时尚流行指向 fashion orientation
样本 Sample	425	56.9	43.1
一天 3 次或以上 3 times or over a day	124	57.3	42.7
一天 1~2 次 once or twice a day	301	56.8	43.2

6-14-2 广告态度指标/ Advertising Attitude Index

	人数 Number	广告淡漠指向 indifferent orientation	中间层 medium	信赖广告指向 loyal orientation
样本 Sample	423	29.6	57.9	12.5
一天 3 次或以上 3 times or over a day	124	24.2	67.7	8.1
一天 1~2 次 once or twice a day	299	31.8	53.8	14.4

● 沈阳 / Shenyang

6-1 是否使用的比例/ Proportion of the Sample Consuming Liquid Detergent in the Last Three Months

	人数 Number	百分比 Percent
用 yes	466	77.5
不用 no	135	22.5

n=601

6-2 最常用品牌排名/ Ranking of the Most Frequently Used Brands

排名 Brand Ranking	品牌 Brands	人数 Number	百分比 Percent
1	白猫 White Cat	385	82.8
2	雕牌 Diao	33	7.1
3	巧手 Dosia	25	5.4
4	金鱼 Gold Fish	7	1.5
5	安利 Amway	3	0.6

n=465

6-3 样本、男性各年龄层、女性各年龄层的常用品牌/ The Most Frequently Used Brands by the Whole Sample, Age and Gender Groups

	人数 Number	第一品牌及百分比 1st/ percent	第二品牌及百分比 2nd/ percent	第三品牌及百分比 3rd/ percent
样本 Sample	**465**	**白猫 White Cat(82.8)**	**雕牌 Diao(7.1)**	**巧手 Dosia(5.4)**
男性 Male	**201**	**白猫 White Cat(78.1)**	**雕牌 Diao(8.5)**	**巧手 Dosia(5.0)**
16~24 岁 Age	37	白猫 White Cat(86.5)	雕牌 Diao(8.1)	金鱼 Gold Fish(2.7) 巧手 Dosia(2.7)
25~34 岁 Age	66	白猫 White Cat(74.2)	雕牌 Diao(7.6) 金鱼 Gold Fish(7.6)	巧手 Dosia(4.5)
35~44 岁 Age	49	白猫 White Cat(77.6)	雕牌 Diao(12.2)	巧手 Dosia(8.2)
45~54 岁 Age	29	白猫 White Cat(75.9)	雕牌 Diao(10.3)	巧手 Dosia(6.9)
55~60 岁 Age	20	白猫 White Cat(80.0)	金鱼 Gold Fish(5.0) 雅娜 Yana(5.0)	
女性 Female	**264**	**白猫 White Cat(86.4)**	**雕牌 Diao(6.1)**	**巧手 Dosia(5.7)**
16~24 岁 Age	53	白猫 White Cat(83.0)	巧手 Dosia(9.4)	雕牌 Diao(5.7)
25~34 岁 Age	79	白猫 White Cat(82.3)	雕牌 Diao(8.9)	巧手 Dosia(6.3)
35~44 岁 Age	65	白猫 White Cat(87.7)	巧手 Dosia(6.2)	雕牌 Diao(4.6)
45~54 岁 Age	44	白猫 White Cat(95.5)	雕牌 Diao(2.3)	
55~60 岁 Age	23	白猫 White Cat(87.0)	雕牌 Diao(8.7)	巧手 Dosia(4.3)

6-4 正在使用的品牌排名/ Ranking of the Brands Used Now

排名 Brand Ranking	品牌 Brands	人数 Number	百分比 Percent
1	白猫 White Cat	346	74.4
2	雕牌 Diao	50	10.8
3	巧手 Dosia	32	6.9
4	安利 Amway	8	1.7
5	金鱼 Gold Fish	6	1.3

n=465

6-5 品牌转换习惯/ Brand Habit in Consuming Liquid Detergent

	人数 Number	第一次使用该品牌 first use this brand	上一次也是这个牌子 used it last time	上一次不是这个牌子 not used it last time
样本 Sample	**464**	**5.0**	**86.0**	**9.1**
白猫 White Cat	345	2.3	92.8	4.9
雕牌 Diao	50	8.0	76.0	16.0
巧手 Dosia	32	6.3	75.0	18.8
安利 Amway	8	50.0	25.0	25.0
金鱼 Gold Fish	6	0.0	50.0	50.0

6-6 下一次打算使用的品牌排名/ Ranking of the Brands to be Used Next Time

排名 Brand Ranking	品牌 Brands	人数 Number	百分比 Percent
1	白猫 White Cat	348	74.7
2	雕牌 Diao	49	10.5
3	巧手 Dosia	37	7.9
4	安利 Amway	9	1.9
4	金鱼 Gold Fish	9	1.9
5	三威 Sanwei	3	0.6

n=466

6-7 样本、男性各年龄层、女性各年龄层是否是主要购买者/ Purchasers in the Household by the Whole Sample, Age and Gender Groups

	人数 Number	是 yes	不是 no
样本 Sample	601	47.1	52.9
男性 Male	299	20.1	79.9
16~24 岁 Age	64	15.6	84.4
25~34 岁 Age	89	27.0	73.0
35~44 岁 Age	76	17.1	82.9
45~54 岁 Age	46	13.0	87.0
55~60 岁 Age	24	29.2	70.8
女性 Female	302	73.8	26.2
16~24 岁 Age	64	43.8	56.3
25~34 岁 Age	90	76.7	23.3
35~44 岁 Age	76	82.9	17.1
45~54 岁 Age	48	85.4	14.6
55~60 岁 Age	24	91.7	8.3

6-8 样本、男性各年龄层、女性各年龄层是否使用该类商品/ Whether to Use Liquid Detergent by the Whole Sample, Age and Gender Groups

	人数 Number	用 yes	不用 no
样本 Sample	601	77.5	22.5
男性 Male	299	67.6	32.4
16~24 岁 Age	64	57.8	42.2
25~34 岁 Age	89	75.3	24.7
35~44 岁 Age	76	64.5	35.5
45~54 岁 Age	46	63.0	37.0
55~60 岁 Age	24	83.3	16.7
女性 Female	302	87.4	12.6
16~24 岁 Age	64	82.8	17.2
25~34 岁 Age	90	87.8	12.2
35~44 岁 Age	76	85.5	14.5
45~54 岁 Age	48	91.7	8.3
55~60 岁 Age	24	95.8	4.2

6-9 样本、男性各年龄层、女性各年龄层的使用频率/ Frequencies of the Consumed Liquid Detergent by the Whole Sample, Age and Gender Groups

	人数 Number	一天 3 次或以上 3 times or over a day	一天 1~2 次 once or twice a day	两三天用 1 次 once 2 or 3 days	一周 1~2 次 once or twice a week	半个月 1 次或以下 once half a month or below
样本 Sample	465	38.7	52.9	5.6	2.4	0.4
男性 Male	201	32.8	57.7	6.5	2.0	1.0
16~24 岁 Age	37	32.4	54.1	10.8	2.7	0.0
25~34 岁 Age	66	36.4	56.1	3.0	3.0	1.5
35~44 岁 Age	49	26.5	63.3	8.2	2.0	0.0
45~54 岁 Age	29	31.0	58.6	10.3	0.0	0.0
55~60 岁 Age	20	40.0	55.0	0.0	0.0	5.0
女性 Female	264	43.2	49.2	4.9	2.7	0.0
16~24 岁 Age	53	39.6	52.8	0.0	7.5	0.0
25~34 岁 Age	79	51.9	43.0	5.1	0.0	0.0
35~44 岁 Age	65	40.0	49.2	10.8	0.0	0.0
45~54 岁 Age	44	34.1	59.1	0.0	6.8	0.0
55~60 岁 Age	23	47.8	43.5	8.7	0.0	0.0

6-10 选择该类商品的考虑因素/ Ranking of the Considerations in Purchasing

注：本题为多选题，合计百分比超过 100%（Multiple answers）

排名 Ranking	考虑因素 Considerations	人次 Person-time	百分比 Percent
1	价格适中 reasonable price	270	58.2
2	产品功用 product function	219	47.2
3	有名的牌子 famous brand	153	33.0
4	购买方便 easy to buy	128	27.6
5	广告影响 influence of advertising	64	13.8
6	别人推荐 introduced by other people	26	5.6
7	有优惠条件 with preferential terms	12	2.6
8	包装吸引人 appealing package	7	1.5
9	单位发的 offered by the working unit	5	1.1
10	其它 others	4	0.9

n=464

6-11 对产品功能的侧重方面/ Ranking of the Considerations about the Function of this Kind of Product

注：本题为多选题，合计百分比超过 100%（Multiple answers）

排名 Ranking	侧重方面 Items	人次 Person-time	百分比 Percent
1	洗涤力强 powerful cleaning	342	73.9
2	味道清香 fresh smell	236	51.0
3	无毒性可洗水果 can be directly used to wash fruit	186	40.2
4	不伤手 harmless to hand	140	30.2
5	不污染环境 without pollution	34	7.3
6	其他 others	2	0.4

n=463

6-12 重度消费者的人口分布/ Demographics of the Heavy Consumers

	人数 Number	16-24 岁 Age	25-34 岁 Age	35-44 岁 Age	45-54 岁 Age	55-60 岁 Age
样本 Sample	426	19.0	31.9	23.9	15.7	9.4
男性 Male	182	17.6	33.5	24.2	14.3	10.4
一天 3 次或以上 3 times or over a day	66	18.2	36.4	19.7	13.6	12.1
一天 1~2 次 once or twice a day	116	17.2	31.9	26.7	14.7	9.5
女性 Female	244	20.1	30.7	23.8	16.8	8.6
一天 3 次或以上 3 times or over a day	114	18.4	36.0	22.8	13.2	9.6
一天 1~2 次 once or twice a day	130	21.5	26.2	24.6	20.0	7.7

6-13 不同消费者层的常用品牌/ The Most Frequently Used Brands by Market Segments

6-13-1 时尚流行指标/ Fads Popular Index

	人数 Number	第一品牌及百分比 1st/ percent	第二品牌及百分比 2nd/ percent	第三品牌及百分比 3rd/ percent
样本 Sample	465	**白猫 White Cat(82.8)**	**雕牌 Diao(7.1)**	**巧手 Dosia(5.4)**
平实生活指向 simple living orientation	226	白猫 White Cat(84.5)	雕牌 Diao(5.8)	巧手 Dosia(4.4)
时尚流行指向 fashion orientation	239	白猫 White Cat(81.2)	雕牌 Diao(8.4)	巧手 Dosia(6.3)

6-13-2 广告态度指标/ Advertising Attitude Index

	人数 Number	第一品牌及百分比 1st/ percent	第二品牌及百分比 2nd/ percent	第三品牌及百分比 3rd/ percent
样本 Sample	465	**白猫 White Cat(82.8)**	**雕牌 Diao(7.1)**	**巧手 Dosia(5.4)**
广告淡漠指向 indifferent orientation	130	白猫 White Cat(83.1)	雕牌 Diao(5.4)	巧手 Dosia(4.6)
中间层 medium	280	白猫 White Cat(83.6)	雕牌 Diao(6.4)	巧手 Dosia(5.7)
信赖广告指向 loyal orientation	55	白猫 White Cat(78.2)	雕牌 Diao(14.5)	巧手 Dosia(5.5)

6-14 重度消费者的消费层构成/ The Composition of the Heavy Consumers

6-14-1 时尚流行指标/ Fads Popular Index

	人数 Number	平实生活指向 simple living orientation	时尚流行指向 fashion orientation
样本 Sample	426	48.4	51.6
一天 3 次或以上 3 times or over a day	180	48.9	51.1
一天 1~2 次 once or twice a day	246	48.0	52.0

6-14-2 广告态度指标/ Advertising Attitude Index

	人数 Number	广告淡漠指向 indifferent orientation	中间层 medium	信赖广告指向 loyal orientation
样本 Sample	426	27.0	60.6	12.4
一天 3 次或以上 3 times or over a day	180	27.8	61.1	11.1
一天 1~2 次 once or twice a day	246	26.4	60.2	13.4

7.洗面乳 / Facial Cleaner

● 北京 / Beijing

7-1 最近三个月使用频率的比例/ Proportion of the Sample Consuming Facial Cleaner in the Last Three Months

	人数 Number	百分比 Percent
一天 3 次或以上 3 times or over a day	37	3.7
一天 1~2 次 once or twice a day	305	30.7
两三天用 1 次 once 2 or 3 days	30	3.0
一周 1~2 次 once or twice a week	23	2.3
半个月 1 次或以下 once half a month or below	16	1.6
没用过 never use	584	58.7

n=995

7-2 最常用品牌排名/ Ranking of the Most Frequently Used Brands

排名 Brand Ranking	品牌 Brands	人数 Number	百分比 Percent
1	花王碧柔 Biore	72	17.6
2	大宝 Dabao	43	10.5
3	小护士 Mininurse	28	6.9
4	可伶可俐 Clean & Clear	22	5.4
5	旁氏 Pond's	17	4.2
6	资生堂 Shiseido	15	3.7
7	安安 An'an	13	3.2
8	芦荟 Luhui	12	2.9
9	欧珀莱 Aupres	11	2.7
9	高丝 Kose	11	2.7
10	东洋之花 Sakula	10	2.5
10	玉兰油 Oil of Olay	10	2.5
11	力士 Lux	9	2.2

n=408

7-3 样本、男性各年龄层、女性各年龄层的常用品牌/ The Most Frequently Used Brands by the Whole Sample, Age and Gender Groups

	人数 Number	第一品牌及百分比 1st/ percent	第二品牌及百分比 2nd/ percent	第三品牌及百分比 3rd/ percent	第四品牌及百分比 4th/ percent
样本 Sample	408	**花王碧柔 Biore(17.6)**	**大宝 Dabao(10.5)**	**小护士 Mininurse(6.9)**	**可伶可俐 Clean & Clear(5.4)**
男性 Male	71	**花王碧柔 Biore(19.7)**	**大宝 Dabao(18.3)**	**可伶可俐 Clean & Clear(7.0)**	**安安 An'an(4.2)** **东洋之花 Sakula (4.2)** **资生堂 Shiseido (4.2)**
16~24 岁 Age	25	花王碧柔 Biore(16.0) 大宝 Dabao(16.0)	可伶可俐 Clean & Clear(12.0)	力士 Lux(8.0) 安安 An'an(8.0)	肤美灵 Fumeiling(4.0) 东洋之花 Sakula(4.0) 姗拉娜 Samsara(4.0) 夏士莲 Hazeline(4.0) 小护士 Mininurse(4.0) 比夫 Bifu(4.0) 莉威娜 Liweina(4.0)
25~34 岁 Age	27	花王碧柔 Biore(25.9)	大宝 Dabao(22.2)	东洋之花 Sakula(7.4) 资生堂 Shiseido(7.4)	小护士 Mininurse(3.7) 比夫 Bifu(3.7) 可伶可俐 Clean & Clear(3.7) 欧珀莱 Aupres(3.7) 少女之春 Shao Nv Zhi Chun(3.7) 洁莱雅 Jielaiya(3.7) 高丝 Kose(3.7) 肤美灵 Fumeiling(3.7) 法兰西施 Miss de France(3.7)
35~44 岁 Age	11	大宝 Dabao(18.2) 花王碧柔 Biore(18.2)	安安 An'an(9.1) 欧珀莱 Aupres(9.1) 可伶可俐 Clean & Clear(9.1) 精华素保湿洗面乳 Jinghuasu(9.1)		
45~54 岁 Age	7	大宝 Dabao(14.3) 花王碧柔 Biore(14.3) 资生堂 Shiseido(14.3) 倩雪 Qianxue(14.3) 艾圣 Aisheng(14.3)			
55~60 岁 Age	1	水果之源 Shui Guo Zhi Yuan(100.0)			
女性 Female	337	**花王碧柔 Biore(17.2)**	**大宝 Dabao(8.9)**	**小护士 Mininurse(7.7)**	**可伶可俐 Clean & Clear(5.0)** **旁氏 Pond's(5.0)**
16~24 岁 Age	89	花王碧柔 Biore(20.2)	可伶可俐 Clean & Clear(15.7)	小护士 Mininurse(9.0)	玉兰油 Oil of Olay(6.7)
25~34 岁 Age	119	花王碧柔 Biore(17.6)	大宝 Dabao(7.6) 旁氏 Pond's(7.6)	小护士 Mininurse(6.7) 资生堂 Shiseido(6.7)	安安 An'an(4.2) 欧珀莱 Aupres(4.2) 芦荟 Luhui (4.2)
35~44 岁 Age	81	花王碧柔 Biore(16.0)	大宝 Dabao(12.3)	小护士 Mininurse(8.6)	安安 An'an(4.9) 高丝 Kose(4.9)
45~54 岁 Age	41	花王碧柔 Biore(12.2)	大宝 Dabao(9.8)	小护士 Mininurse(7.3)	玉兰油 Oil of Olay(4.9) 欧珀莱 Aupres(4.9) 自然美 Natural Beauty(4.9) 高丝 Kose(4.9) 旁氏 Pond's(4.9)
55~60 岁 Age	7	大宝 Dabao(42.9)	花王碧柔 Biore(14.3) 嘉娜宝 Kanebo(14.3) 洁莱雅 Jielaiya(14.3) 欧莱雅 L'oreal(14.3)		

7-4 正在使用的品牌排名/ Ranking of the Brands Used Now

排名 Brand Ranking	品牌 Brands	人数 Number	百分比 Percent
1	花王碧柔 Biore	63	15.4
2	大宝 Dabao	38	9.3
3	小护士 Mininurse	28	6.8
4	可伶可俐 Clean & Clear	25	6.1
5	东洋之花 Sakula	18	4.4
6	资生堂 Shiseico	17	4.2
7	玉兰油 Oil of Olay	16	3.9
8	芦荟 Luhui	15	3.7
9	欧珀莱 Aupres	14	3.4
10	安安 An'an	12	2.9
11	索夫特 Softto	10	2.4

n=409

7-5 品牌转换习惯/ Brand Habit in Consuming Facial Cleaner

	人数 Number	第一次使用该品牌 first use this brand	上一次也是这个牌子 used it last time	上一次不是这个牌子 not used it last time
样本 Sample	**409**	**24.0**	**61.1**	**14.9**
花王碧柔 Biore	63	9.5	71.4	19.0
大宝 Dabao	38	10.5	81.6	7.9
小护士 Mininurse	28	21.4	71.4	7.1
可伶可俐 Clean & Clear	25	32.0	56.0	12.0
东洋之花 Sakula	18	33.3	55.6	11.1
资生堂 Shiseido	17	35.3	58.8	5.9
玉兰油 Oil of Olay	16	25.0	62.5	12.5
芦荟 Luhui	15	66.7	26.7	6.7
欧珀莱 Aupres	14	21.4	50.0	28.6
安安 An'an	12	16.7	75.0	8.3
索芙特 Softto	10	30.0	50.0	20.0

7-6 下一次打算使用的品牌排名/ Ranking of the Brands to be Used Next Time

排名 Brand Ranking	品牌 Brands	人数 Number	百分比 Percent
1	花王碧柔 Biore	71	17.4
2	大宝 Dabao	41	10.0
3	小护士 Mininurse	24	5.9
4	可伶可俐 Clean & Clear	23	5.6
5	玉兰油 Oil of Olay	20	4.9
6	资生堂 Shiseido	18	4.4
7	芦荟 Luhui	15	3.7
7	旁氏 Pond's	15	3.7
8	东洋之花 Sakula	13	3.2
9	力士 Lux	10	2.4
9	欧珀莱 Aupres	10	2.4
9	高丝 Kose	10	2.4
10	安安 An'an	9	2.2

n=409

7-7 样本、男性各年龄层、女性各年龄层的使用频率/ Frequencies of the Consumed Facial Cleaner by the Whole Sample, Age and Gender Groups

	人数 Number	一天3次或以上 3 times or over a day	一天1~2次 once or twice a day	两三天用1次 once 2 or 3 days	一周1~2次 once or twice a week	半个月1次或以下 once half a month or below	没用过 never use
样本 Sample	**995**	**3.7**	**30.7**	**3.0**	**2.3**	**1.6**	**58.7**
男性 Male	**488**	**0.6**	**9.6**	**2.0**	**1.4**	**1.2**	**85.0**
16~24 岁 Age	98	0.0	17.3	4.1	4.1	1.0	73.5
25~34 岁 Age	150	2.0	11.3	2.7	1.3	1.3	81.3
35~44 岁 Age	125	0.0	6.4	1.6	0.0	0.8	91.2
45~54 岁 Age	76	0.0	5.3	0.0	1.3	2.6	90.8
55~60 岁 Age	39	0.0	2.6	0.0	0.0	0.0	97.4
女性 Female	**507**	**6.7**	**50.9**	**3.9**	**3.2**	**2.0**	**33.3**
16~24 岁 Age	108	11.1	63.9	0.9	4.6	1.9	17.6
25~34 岁 Age	149	6.7	64.4	4.7	3.4	0.7	20.1
35~44 岁 Age	124	6.5	42.7	7.3	4.0	4.8	34.7
45~54 岁 Age	84	4.8	41.7	1.2	1.2	1.2	50.0
55~60 岁 Age	42	0.0	11.9	4.8	0.0	0.0	83.3

7-8 选择该类商品的考虑因素/ Ranking of the Considerations in Purchasing

注：本题为多选题，合计百分比超过 100%（Multiple answers）

排名 Ranking	考虑因素 Considerations	人次 Person-time	百分比 Percent
1	产品功用 product function	236	57.8
2	价格适中 reasonable price	158	38.7
3	有名的牌子 famous brand	145	35.5
4	别人推荐 introduced by other people	77	18.9
5	广告影响 influence of advertising	76	18.6
6	购买方便 easy to buy	48	11.8
7	有优惠条件 with preferential terms	18	4.4
8	包装吸引人 appealing package	11	2.7
9	其它 others	9	2.2
10	单位发的 offered by the working unit	8	2.0

n=408

7-9 对产品功能的侧重方面/ Ranking of the Considerations about the Function of this Kind of Product

注：本题为多选题，合计百分比超过 100%（Multiple answers）

排名 Ranking	侧重方面 Items	人次 Person-time	百分比 Percent
1	适合自己的肤质 suitable to my skin	183	44.6
2	洗后不紧绷 soft & elastic after bath	164	40.0
3	洁净力强 powerful cleaning	146	35.6
4	含滋润成分 containing nourishing ingredient	135	32.9
5	气味好 pleasant smell	114	27.8
6	泡沫多 rich foam	80	19.5
7	含爽肤成分 containing skin cleaning ingredient	55	13.4
8	含磨砂颗粒 with granites	28	6.8
8	含果酸成分 containing tartaric acid	28	6.8
9	其他 others	4	1.0

n=410

7-10 重度消费者的人口分布/ Demographics of the Heavy Consumers

	人数 Number	16-24 岁 Age	25-34 岁 Age	35-44 岁 Age	45-54 岁 Age	55-60 岁 Age
样本 Sample	342	28.7	36.8	20.2	12.6	1.8
男性 Male	50	34.0	40.0	16.0	8.0	2.0
一天 3 次或以上 3 times or over a day	3	0.0	100.0	0.0	0.0	0.0
一天 1~2 次 once or twice a day	47	36.2	36.2	17.0	8.5	2.1
女性 Female	292	27.7	36.3	20.9	13.4	1.7
一天 3 次或以上 3 times or over a day	34	35.3	29.4	23.5	11.8	0.0
一天 1~2 次 once or twice a day	258	26.7	37.2	20.5	13.6	1.9

7-11 不同消费者层的常用品牌/ The Most Frequently Used Brands by Market Segments

7-11-1 时尚流行指标/ Fads Popular Index

	人数 Number	第一品牌及百分比 1st / percent	第二品牌及百分比 2nd / percent	第三品牌及百分比 3rd / percent	第四品牌及百分比 4th / percent
样本 Sample	402	**花王碧柔 Biore(17.4)**	**大宝 Dabao(10.7)**	**小护士 Mininurse(6.7)**	**可伶可俐 Clean & Clear(5.2)**
平实生活指向 simple living orientation	144	花王碧柔 Biore(18.8)	大宝 Dabao(11.8)	小护士 Mininurse(7.6)	旁氏 Pond's(5.6)
时尚流行指向 fashion orientation	258	花王碧柔 Biore(16.7)	大宝 Dabao(10.1)	可伶可俐 Clean & Clear(6.6)	小护士 Mininurse(6.2)

7-11-2 广告态度指标/ Advertising Attitude Index

	人数 Number	第一品牌及百分比 1st / percent	第二品牌及百分比 2nd / percent	第三品牌及百分比 3rd / percent	第四品牌及百分比 4th / percent
样本 Sample	397	**花王碧柔 Biore(17.4)**	**大宝 Dabao(10.6)**	**小护士 Mininurse(6.5)**	**可伶可俐 Clean & Clear(5.3)**
广告淡漠指向 indifferent orientation	88	花王碧柔 Biore(22.7)	大宝 Dabao(9.1)	可伶可俐 Clean & Clear(6.8)	玉兰油 Oil of Olay(5.7)
中间层 medium	246	花王碧柔 Biore(16.7)	大宝 Dabao(11.0)	小护士 Mininurse(6.5)	旁氏 Pond's(4.9)
信赖广告指向 loyal orientation	63	花王碧柔 Biore(12.7)	大宝 Dabao(11.1) 可伶可俐 Clean & Clear(11.1)	小护士 Mininurse(9.5)	旁氏 Pond's(6.3)

7-12 重度消费者的消费层构成/ The Composition of the Heavy Consumers

7-12-1 时尚流行指标/ Fads Popular Index

	人数 Number	平实生活指向 simple living orientation	时尚流行指向 fashion orientation
样本 Sample	338	34.6	65.4
一天 3 次或以上 3 times or over a day	37	29.7	70.3
一天 1~2 次 once or twice a day	301	35.2	64.8

7-12-2 广告态度指标/ Advertising Attitude Index

	人数 Number	广告淡漠指向 indifferent orientation	中间层 medium	信赖广告指向 loyal orientation
样本 Sample	331	21.8	62.2	16.0
一天 3 次或以上 3 times or over a day	35	17.1	71.4	11.4
一天 1~2 次 once or twice a day	296	22.3	61.1	16.6

● 上海 / Shanghai

7-1 最近三个月使用频率的比例/ Proportion of the Sample Consuming Facial Cleaner in the Last Three Months

	人数 Number	百分比 Percent
一天 3 次或以上 3 times or over a day	12	1.2
一天 1~2 次 once or twice a day	322	32.5
两三天用 1 次 once 2 or 3 days	62	6.3
一周 1~2 次 once or twice a week	43	4.3
半个月 1 次或以下 once half a month or below	16	1.6
没用过 never use	536	54.1

n=991

7-2 最常用品牌排名/ Ranking of the Most Frequently Used Brands

排名 Brand Ranking	品牌 Brands	人数 Number	百分比 Percent
1	花王碧柔 Biore	154	33.8
2	旁氏 Pond's	45	9.9
3	可伶可俐 Clean & Clear	29	6.4
4	信芬 Synform	17	3.7
4	小护士 Mininurse	17	3.7
5	东洋之花 Sakula	16	3.5
6	力士 Lux	15	3.3
6	洁莱雅 Jielaiya	15	3.3
7	资生堂 Shiseido	9	2.0
8	玉兰油 Oil of Olay	7	1.5
8	少女之春 Shao Nv Zhi Chun	7	1.5
9	美加净 Maxam	6	1.3
9	妮维雅 Nivea	6	1.3
10	夏士莲 Hazeline	5	1.1
10	隆力奇 Longliqi	5	1.1
10	奥 C	5	1.1

n=455

7-3 样本、男性各年龄层、女性各年龄层的常用品牌/ The Most Frequently Used Brands by the Whole Sample, Age and Gender Groups

	人数 Number	第一品牌及百分比 1st/ percent	第二品牌及百分比 2nd/ percent	第三品牌及百分比 3rd/ percent
样本 Sample	455	**花王碧柔 Biore(33.8)**	**旁氏 Pond's(9.9)**	**可伶可俐 Clean & Clear(6.4)**
男性 Male	131	**花王碧柔 Biore(43.5)**	**旁氏 Pond's(9.2)**	**力士 Lux(4.6)**
16~24 岁 Age	36	花王碧柔 Biore(52.8)	力士 Lux(8.3)	可伶可俐 Clean & Clear(5.6)
25~34 岁 Age	49	花王碧柔 Biore(40.8)	旁氏 Pond's(12.2)	东洋之花 Sakula(6.1) 信芬 Synform(6.1)
35~44 岁 Age	26	花王碧柔 Biore(34.6)	旁氏 Pond's(15.4)	洁莱雅 Jielaiya(7.7) 力士 Lux(7.7)
45~54 岁 Age	15	花王碧柔 Biore(40.0)	旁氏 Pond's(13.3)	大宝 Dabao(6.7) 高丝 Kose(6.7) 洁莱雅 Jielaiya(6.7) 美加净 Maxam(6.7) 玉兰油 Oil of Olay(6.7)
55~60 岁 Age	5	花王碧柔 Biore(60.0)	信芬 Synform(20.0) 资生堂 Shiseido(20.0)	
女性 Female	324	**花王碧柔 Biore(29.9)**	**旁氏 Pond's(10.2)**	**可伶可俐 Clean & Clear(8.0)**
16~24 岁 Age	90	花王碧柔 Biore(34.4)	旁氏 Pond's(15.6) 可伶可俐 Clean & Clear(15.6)	信芬 Synform(6.7)
25~34 岁 Age	109	花王碧柔 Biore(33.9)	旁氏 Pond's(8.3)	小护士 Mininurse(5.5)
35~44 岁 Age	82	花王碧柔 Biore(19.5)	旁氏 Pond's(9.8)	小护士 Mininurse(7.3)
45~54 岁 Age	35	花王碧柔 Biore(31.4)	东洋之花 Sakula(5.7) 洁莱雅 Jielaiya(5.7) 力士 Lux(5.7) 可伶可俐 Clean & Clear(5.7)	信芬 Synform(2.9) SK-II(2.9) 奥 C(2.9) 芦荟 Luhui(2.9) 雅倩 Arche(2.9) 隆力奇 Longliqi(2.9) 小护士 Mininurse(2.9) 索芙特 Softto(2.9) 少女之春 Shao Nv Zhi Chun(2.9) 旁氏 Pond's(2.9) 妮维雅 Nivea(2.9) 法兰西施 Miss de France(2.9) 安安 An'an(2.9)
55~60 岁 Age	8	花王碧柔 Biore(25.0)	大宝 Dabao(12.5) 美加净 Maxam(12.5) 旁氏 Pond's(12.5) 芦荟 Luhui(12.5) 可伶可俐 Clean & Clear(12.5) 梦婷 Mengting(12.5)	

7-4 正在使用的品牌排名/ Ranking of the Brands Used Now

排名 Brand Ranking	品牌 Brands	人数 Number	百分比 Percent
1	花王碧柔 Biore	122	26.8
2	旁氏 Pond's	39	8.6
3	可伶可俐 Clean & Clear	30	6.6
4	东洋之花 Sakula	23	5.1
5	信芬 Synform	20	4.4
6	小护士 Mininurse	18	4.0
7	力士 Lux	14	3.1
8	洁莱雅 Jielaiya	13	2.9
9	资生堂 Shiseido	10	2.2
10	玉兰油 Oil of Olay	9	2.0
11	夏士莲 Hazeline	8	1.8
12	美加净 Maxam	7	1.5
13	奥 C	6	1.3

7-5 品牌转换习惯/ Brand Habit in Consuming Facial Cleaner

	人数 Number	第一次使用该品牌 first use this brand	上一次也是这个牌子 used it last time	上一次不是这个牌子 not used it last time
样本 Sample	**455**	**16.9**	**72.3**	**10.8**
花王碧柔 Biore	122	9.0	83.6	7.4
旁氏 Pond's	39	2.6	84.6	12.8
可伶可俐 Clean&Clear	30	13.3	80.0	6.7
东洋之花 Sakula	23	21.7	60.9	17.4
信芬 Synform	20	30.0	50.0	20.0
小护士 Mininurse	18	5.6	88.9	5.6
力士 Lux	14	0.0	92.9	7.1
洁莱雅 Jielaiya	13	23.1	69.2	7.7
资生堂 Shiseido	10	30.0	60.0	10.0
玉兰油 Oil of Olay	9	33.3	66.7	0.0

7-6 下一次打算使用的品牌排名/ Ranking of the Brands to be Used Next Time

排名 Brand Ranking	品牌 Brands	人数 Number	百分比 Percent
1	花王碧柔 Biore	143	31.4
2	旁氏 Pond's	48	10.5
3	可伶可俐 Clean & Clear	26	5.7
4	小护士 Mininurse	22	4.8
5	玉兰油 Oil of Olay	19	4.2
6	力士 Lux	16	3.5
7	东洋之花 Sakula	14	3.1
8	资生堂 Shiseido	13	2.9
9	洁莱雅 Jielaiya	8	1.8
9	信芬 Synform	8	1.8
10	美加净 Maxam	7	1.5
10	夏士莲 Hazeline	7	1.5

n=455

7-7 样本、男性各年龄层、女性各年龄层的使用频率/ Frequencies of the Consumed Facial Cleaner by the Whole Sample, Age and Gender Groups

	人数 Number	一天 3 次或以上 3 times or over a day	一天 1~2 次 once or twice a day	两三天用 1 次 once 2 or 3 days	一周 1~2 次 once or twice a week	半个月 1 次或以下 once half a month or below	没用过 never use
样本 Sample	**991**	**1.2**	**32.5**	**6.3**	**4.3**	**1.6**	**54.1**
男性 Male	**491**	**0.6**	**14.7**	**5.7**	**4.3**	**1.4**	**73.3**
16~24 岁 Age	107	1.9	21.5	7.5	2.8	0.0	66.4
25~34 岁 Age	142	0.0	19.0	6.3	6.3	2.8	65.5
35~44 岁 Age	129	0.8	8.5	3.9	6.2	0.8	79.8
45~54 岁 Age	79	0.0	8.9	6.3	1.3	2.5	81.0
55~60 岁 Age	34	0.0	11.8	2.9	0.0	0.0	85.3
女性 Female	**500**	**1.8**	**50.0**	**6.8**	**4.4**	**1.8**	**35.2**
16~24 岁 Age	107	2.8	68.2	8.4	2.8	1.9	15.9
25~34 岁 Age	143	2.1	60.1	7.7	4.2	2.1	23.8
35~44 岁 Age	129	2.3	45.0	8.5	5.4	2.3	36.4
45~54 岁 Age	81	0.0	34.6	3.7	4.9	0.0	56.8
55~60 岁 Age	40	0.0	12.5	0.0	5.0	2.5	80.0

7-8 选择该类商品的考虑因素/ Ranking of the Considerations in Purchasing

注：本题为多选题，合计百分比超过 100%（Multiple answers）

排名 Ranking	考虑因素 Considerations	人次 Person-time	百分比 Percent
1	产品功用 product function	217	47.7
2	价格适中 reasonable price	177	38.9
3	有名的牌子 famous brand	161	35.4
4	广告影响 influence of advertising	119	26.2
5	别人推荐 introduced by other people	74	16.3
6	购买方便 easy to buy	72	15.8
7	包装吸引人 appealing package	23	5.1
8	有优惠条件 with preferential terms	20	4.4
9	单位发的 offered by the working unit	11	2.4
9	其它 others	11	2.4

n=455

7-9 对产品功能的侧重方面/ Ranking of the Considerations about the Function of this Kind of Product

注：本题为多选题，合计百分比超过 100%（Multiple answers）

排名 Ranking	侧重方面 Items	人次 Person-time	百分比 Percent
1	洗后不紧绷 soft & elastic after bath	216	47.5
2	洁净力强 powerful cleaning	152	33.4
3	气味好 pleasant smell	151	33.2
4	适合自己的肤质 suitable to my skin	150	33.0
5	泡沫多 rich foam	127	27.9
6	含爽肤成分 containing skin cleaning ingredient	77	16.9
7	含滋润成分 containing nourishing ingredient	71	15.6
8	含磨砂颗粒 with granites	40	8.8
9	含果酸成分 containing tartaric acid	18	4.0
10	其他 others	4	0.9

n=455

7-10 重度消费者的人口分布/ Demographics of the Heavy Consumers

	人数 Number	16-24 岁 Age	25-34 岁 Age	35-44 岁 Age	45-54 岁 Age	55-60 岁 Age
样本 Sample	334	30.2	34.7	21.9	10.5	2.7
男性 Male	75	33.3	36.0	16.0	9.3	5.3
一天 3 次或以上 3 times or over a day	3	66.7	0.0	33.3	0.0	0.0
一天 1~2 次 once or twice a day	72	31.9	37.5	15.3	9.7	5.6
女性 Female	259	29.3	34.4	23.6	10.8	1.9
一天 3 次或以上 3 times or over a day	9	33.3	33.3	33.3	0.0	0.0
一天 1~2 次 once or twice a day	250	29.2	34.4	23.2	11.2	2.0

7-11 不同消费者层的常用品牌/ The Most Frequently Used Brands by Market Segments

7-11-1 时尚流行指标/ Fads Popular Index

	人数 Number	第一品牌及百分比 1st / percent	第二品牌及百分比 2nd / percent	第三品牌及百分比 3rd / percent	第四品牌及百分比 4th / percent
样本 Sample	451	**花王碧柔 Biore(33.5)**	**旁氏 Pond's(10.0)**	**可伶可俐 Clean & Clear(6.4)**	**小护士 Mininurse(3.8)** **信芬 Synform(3.8)**
平实生活指向 simple living orientation	154	花王碧柔 Biore(30.5)	旁氏 Pond's(8.4)	可伶可俐 Clean & Clear(5.2) 信芬 Synform(5.2)	小护士 Mininurse(3.9) 洁莱雅 Jielaiya(3.9) 东洋之花 Sakula(3.9)
时尚流行指向 fashion orientation	297	花王碧柔 Biore(35.0)	旁氏 Pond's(10.8)	可伶可俐 Clean & Clear(7.1)	力士 Lux(4.0)

7-11-2 广告态度指标/ Advertising Attitude Index

	人数 Number	第一品牌及百分比 1st / percent	第二品牌及百分比 2nd / percent	第三品牌及百分比 3rd / percent	第四品牌及百分比 4th / percent
样本 Sample	452	**花王碧柔 Biore(33.6)**	**旁氏 Pond's(10.0)**	**可伶可俐 Clean & Clear(6.4)**	**小护士 Mininurse(3.8)** **信芬 Synform(3.8)**
广告淡漠指向 indifferent orientation	100	花王碧柔 Biore(20.0)	可伶可俐 Clean & Clear(13.0)	旁氏 Pond's(12.0)	小护士 Mininurse(7.0)
中间层 medium	273	花王碧柔 Biore(36.3)	旁氏 Pond's(10.3)	可伶可俐 Clean & Clear(5.1)	东洋之花 Sakula(4.4)
信赖广告指向 loyal orientation	79	花王碧柔 Biore(41.8)	旁氏 Pond's(6.3) 小护士 Mininurse(6.3) 信芬 Synform(6.3)	洁莱雅 Jielaiya(5.1)	

7-12 重度消费者的消费层构成/ The Composition of the Heavy Consumers

7-12-1 时尚流行指标/ Fads Popular Index

	人数 Number	平实生活指向 simple living orientation	时尚流行指向 fashion orientation
样本 Sample	330	33.3	66.7
一天 3 次或以上 3 times or over a day	12	41.7	58.3
一天 1~2 次 once or twice a day	318	33.0	67.0

7-12-2 广告态度指标/ Advertising Attitude Index

	人数 Number	广告淡漠指向 indifferent orientation	中间层 medium	信赖广告指向 loyal orientation
样本 Sample	331	22.7	59.2	18.1
一天 3 次或以上 3 times or over a day	12	50.0	41.7	8.3
一天 1~2 次 once or twice a day	319	21.6	59.9	18.5

● 广州 / Guangzhou

7-1 最近三个月使用频率的比例/ Proportion of the Sample Consuming Facial Cleaner in the Last Three Months

	人数 Number	百分比 Percent
一天 3 次或以上 3 times or over a day	19	1.9
一天 1~2 次 once or twice a day	312	31.2
两三天用 1 次 once 2 or 3 days	66	6.6
一周 1~2 次 once or twice a week	43	4.3
半个月 1 次或以下 once half a month or below	15	1.5
没用过 never use	546	54.5

n=1001

7-2 最常用品牌排名/ Ranking of the Most Frequently Used Brands

排名 Brand Ranking	品牌 Brands	人数 Number	百分比 Percent
1	花王碧柔 Biore	121	26.7
2	安安 An'an	31	6.8
3	小护士 Mininurse	27	6.0
4	旁氏 Pond's	25	5.5
5	可伶可俐 Clean&Clear	21	4.6
6	索芙特 Softto	17	3.8
7	玉兰油 Oil of Olay	13	2.9
8	夏士莲 Hazeline	11	2.4
9	雅芳 Avon	10	2.2
9	茵子 Yinzi	10	2.2
10	肤安 Fu'an	9	2.0

n=453

7-3 样本、男性各年龄层、女性各年龄层的常用品牌/ The Most Frequently Used Brands by the Whole Sample, Age and Gender Groups

	人数 Number	第一品牌及百分比 1st/ percent	第二品牌及百分比 2nd/ percent	第三品牌及百分比 3rd/ percent
样本 Sample	**453**	**花王碧柔 Biore(26.7)**	**安安 An'an(6.8)**	**小护士 Mininurse(6.0)**
男性 Male	**116**	**花王碧柔 Biore(35.3)**	**安安 An'an(5.2)**	**旁氏 Pond's(4.3)**
16~24 岁 Age	31	花王碧柔 Biore(38.7)	玉兰油 Oil of Olay(6.5) 洁柔 Jierou(6.5) 可伶可俐 Clean & Clear(6.5)	梦丝冠尔 Meng Si Guan Er(3.2) 花世界 Huashijie(3.2) 安婷 Anting(3.2) 净白 Jingbai(3.2) 飞扬草 Feiyangcao(3.2) 维伊 Weiyi(3.2) 绿柔 Lvrou(3.2) 维倩 Weiqian(3.2) 艳宝 Yanbao(3.2) 隆力奇 Longliqi(3.2) 小护士 Mininurse(3.2) 力士 Lux(3.2)
25~34 岁 Age	41	花王碧柔 Biore(34.1)	夏士莲 Hazeline(7.3)	安安 An'an(4.9) 力士 Lux(4.9) 旁氏 Pond's(4.9) 茵子 Yinzi (4.9)
35~44 岁 Age	24	花王碧柔 Biore(37.5)	七日香 Qirixiang(8.3) 安安 An'an(8.3)	
45~54 岁 Age	15	花王碧柔 Biore(26.7)	安安 An'an(13.3) 旁氏 Pond's(13.3)	大宝 Dabao(6.7) 姗拉娜 Samsara(6.7) 诗留美屋 Shi Liu Mei Wu(6.7) 小护士 Mininurse(6.7) 雅芳 Avon(6.7) 隆力奇 Longliqi(6.7) 采诗 Caishi(6.7)
55~60 岁 Age	5	花王碧柔 Biore(40.0)	肤安 Fu'an(20.0) 艳宝 Yanbao(20.0)	
女性 Female	**337**	**花王碧柔 Biore(23.7)**	**安安 An'an(7.4)**	**小护士 Mininurse(7.1)**
16~24 岁 Age	96	花王碧柔 Biore(33.3)	可伶可俐 Clean & Clear(11.5)	小护士 Mininurse(5.2)
25~34 岁 Age	116	花王碧柔 Biore(19.8)	安安 An'an(11.2)	小护士 Mininurse(10.3)
35~44 岁 Age	81	花王碧柔 Biore(18.5)	旁氏 Pond's(8.6)	安安 An'an(6.2)
45~54 岁 Age	36	花王碧柔 Biore(25.0)	安安 An'an(11.1)	小护士 Mininurse(8.3) 可伶可俐 Clean & Clear(8.3)
55~60 岁 Age	8	肤安 Fu'an(25.0)	花王碧柔 Biore(12.5) 旁氏 Pond's(12.5) 索芙特 Softto(12.5) 小护士 Mininurse(12.5)	

7-4 正在使用的品牌排名/ Ranking of the Brands Used Now

排名 Brand Ranking	品牌 Brands	人数 Number	百分比 Percent
1	花王碧柔 Biore	101	22.2
2	安安 An'an	27	5.9
3	小护士 Mininurse	26	5.7
4	可伶可俐 Clean&Clear	22	4.8
4	玉兰油 Oil of Olay	22	4.8
5	旁氏 Pond's	19	4.2
5	索芙特 Softto	19	4.2
6	夏士莲 Hazeline	11	2.4
7	茵子 Yinzi	9	2.0
8	美媛春 Meiyuanchun	8	1.8
8	雅芳 Avon	8	1.8
8	采诗 Caishi	8	1.8

n=454

7-5 品牌转换习惯/ Brand Habit in Consuming Facial Cleaner

	人数 Number	第一次使用该品牌 first use this brand	上一次也是这个牌子 used it last time	上一次不是这个牌子 not used it last time
样本 Sample	**449**	**16.3**	**63.0**	**20.7**
花王碧柔 Biore	101	12.9	72.3	14.9
小护士 Mininurse	26	11.5	80.8	7.7
安安 An'an	25	4.0	88.0	8.0
可伶可俐 Clean&Clear	22	22.7	63.6	13.6
玉兰油 Oil of Olay	22	22.7	54.5	22.7
旁氏 Pond's	19	5.3	63.2	31.6
索芙特 Softto	19	15.8	68.4	15.8
夏士莲 Hazeline	11	18.2	54.5	27.3

7-6 下一次打算使用的品牌排名/ Ranking of the Brands to be Used Next Time

排名 Brand Ranking	品牌 Brands	人数 Number	百分比 Percent
1	花王碧柔 Biore	105	23.1
2	玉兰油 Oil of Olay	35	7.7
3	小护士 Mininurse	27	5.9
4	旁氏 Pond's	25	5.5
5	可伶可俐 Clean&Clear	23	5.1
6	安安 An'an	18	4.0
7	索芙特 Softto	14	3.1
8	雅芳 Avon	11	2.4

n=454

7-7 样本、男性各年龄层、女性各年龄层的使用频率/ Frequencies of the Consumed Facial Cleaner by the Whole Sample, Age and Gender Groups

	人数 Number	一天 3 次或以上 3 times or over a day	一天 1~2 次 once or twice a day	两三天用 1 次 once 2 or 3 days	一周 1~2 次 once or twice a week	半个月 1 次或以下 once half a month or below	没用过 never use
样本 Sample	**1001**	**1.9**	**31.2**	**6.6**	**4.3**	**1.5**	**54.5**
男性 Male	**480**	**0.8**	**13.5**	**4.4**	**3.5**	**2.1**	**75.6**
16~24 岁 Age	104	1.9	18.3	5.8	2.9	1.0	70.2
25~34 岁 Age	146	0.7	15.1	6.2	4.8	1.4	71.9
35~44 岁 Age	121	0.8	8.3	3.3	3.3	5.0	79.3
45~54 岁 Age	69	0.0	15.9	1.4	4.3	0.0	78.3
55~60 岁 Age	40	0.0	7.5	2.5	0.0	2.5	87.5
女性 Female	**521**	**2.9**	**47.4**	**8.6**	**5.0**	**1.0**	**35.1**
16~24 岁 Age	109	8.3	64.2	11.0	2.8	1.8	11.9
25~34 岁 Age	156	1.9	57.1	8.3	7.1	0.0	25.6
35~44 岁 Age	132	2.3	42.4	9.8	5.3	1.5	38.6
45~54 岁 Age	84	0.0	32.1	8.3	2.4	0.0	57.1
55~60 岁 Age	40	0.0	12.5	0.0	7.5	2.5	77.5

7-8 选择该类商品的考虑因素/ Ranking of the Considerations in Purchasing

注：本题为多选题，合计百分比超过 100%（Multiple answers）

排名 Ranking	考虑因素 Considerations	人次 Person-time	百分比 Percent
1	产品功用 product function	238	52.4
2	价格适中 reasonable price	182	40.1
3	有名的牌子 famous brand	168	37.0
4	广告影响 influence of advertising	99	21.8
5	别人推荐 introduced by other people	79	17.4
6	购买方便 easy to buy	73	16.1
7	有优惠条件 with preferential terms	24	5.3
8	包装吸引人 appealing package	17	3.7
9	单位发的 offered by the working unit	5	1.1
9	其它 others	5	1.1

n=454

7-9 对产品功能的侧重方面/ Ranking of the Considerations about the Function of this Kind of Product

注：本题为多选题，合计百分比超过 100%（Multiple answers）

排名 Ranking	侧重方面 Items	人次 Person-time	百分比 Percent
1	适合自己的肤质 suitable to my skin	180	39.8
2	洗后不紧绷 soft & elastic after bath	172	38.1
3	洁净力强 powerful cleaning	161	35.6
4	气味好 pleasant smell	140	31.0
5	含滋润成分 containing nourishing ingredient	138	30.5
6	泡沫多 rich foam	73	16.2
7	含爽肤成分 containing skin cleaning ingredient	68	15.0
8	含果酸成分 containing tartaric acid	35	7.7
9	含磨砂颗粒 with granites	34	7.5
10	其他 others	8	1.8

n=452

7-10 重度消费者的人口分布/ Demographics of the Heavy Consumers

	人数 Number	16-24 岁 Age	25-34 岁 Age	35-44 岁 Age	45-54 岁 Age	55-60 岁 Age
样本 Sample	**331**	**30.2**	**34.7**	**21.1**	**11.5**	**2.4**
男性 Male	**69**	**30.4**	**33.3**	**15.9**	**15.9**	**4.3**
一天 3 次或以上 3 times or over a day	4	50.0	25.0	25.0	0.0	0.0
一天 1~2 次 once or twice a day	65	29.2	33.8	15.4	16.9	4.6
女性 Female	**262**	**30.2**	**35.1**	**22.5**	**10.3**	**1.9**
一天 3 次或以上 3 times or over a day	15	60.0	20.0	20.0	0.0	0.0
一天 1~2 次 once or twice a day	247	28.3	36.0	22.7	10.9	2.0

7-11 不同消费者层的常用品牌/ The Most Frequently Used Brands by Market Segments

7-11-1 时尚流行指标/ Fads Popular Index

	人数 Number	第一品牌及百分比 1st / percent	第二品牌及百分比 2nd / percent	第三品牌及百分比 3rd / percent	第四品牌及百分比 4th / percent
样本 Sample	**447**	**花王碧柔 Biore(27.1)**	**安安 An'an(6.9)**	**小护士 Mininurse(5.8)**	**旁氏 Pond's(5.1)**
平实生活指向 simple living orientation	178	花王碧柔 Biore(25.3)	安安 An'an(8.4)	旁氏 Pond's(5.6)	小护士 Mininurse(5.1)
时尚流行指向 fashion orientation	269	花王碧柔 Biore(28.3)	小护士 Mininurse(6.3)	安安 An'an(5.9)	可伶可俐 Clean & Clear(5.6)

7-11-2 广告态度指标/ Advertising Attitude Index

	人数 Number	第一品牌及百分比 1st / percent	第二品牌及百分比 2nd / percent	第三品牌及百分比 3rd / percent	第四品牌及百分比 4th / percent
样本 Sample	**449**	**花王碧柔 Biore(26.7)**	**安安 An'an(6.7)**	**小护士 Mininurse(6.0)**	**旁氏 Pond's(5.1)**
广告淡漠指向 indifferent orientation	118	花王碧柔 Biore(24.6)	安安 An'an(9.3)	旁氏 Pond's(6.8)	小护士 Mininurse(5.1)
中间层 medium	289	花王碧柔 Biore(28.0)	小护士 Mininurse(6.2)	可伶可俐 Clean & Clear(5.9)	安安 An'an(5.2)
信赖广告指向 loyal orientation	42	花王碧柔 Biore(23.8)	安安 An'an(9.5)	可伶可俐 Clean & Clear(7.1) 小护士 Mininurse(7.1)	思丽宝 Silibao(4.8) 索芙特 Softto(4.8) 茵子 Yinzi(4.8)

7-12 重度消费者的消费层构成/ The Composition of the Heavy Consumers

7-12-1 时尚流行指标/ Fads Popular Index

	人数 Number	平实生活指向 simple living orientation	时尚流行指向 fashion orientation
样本 Sample	**328**	**38.4**	**61.6**
一天 3 次或以上 3 times or over a day	19	15.8	84.2
一天 1~2 次 once or twice a day	309	39.8	60.2

7-12-2 广告态度指标/ Advertising Attitude Index

	人数 Number	广告淡漠指向 indifferent orientation	中间层 medium	信赖广告指向 loyal orientation
样本 Sample	**328**	**25.6**	**64.9**	**9.5**
一天 3 次或以上 3 times or over a day	19	21.1	68.4	10.5
一天 1~2 次 once or twice a day	309	25.9	64.7	9.4

● 重庆 / Chongqing

7-1 最近三个月使用频率的比例/ Proportion of the Sample Consuming Facial Cleaner in the Last Three Months

	人数 Number	百分比 Percent
一天 3 次或以上 3 times or over a day	5	0.8
一天 1~2 次 once or twice a day	138	22.1
两三天用 1 次 once 2 or 3 days	30	4.8
一周 1~2 次 once or twice a week	16	2.6
半个月 1 次或以下 once half a month or below	5	0.8
没用过 never use	430	68.9

n=624

7-2 最常用品牌排名/ Ranking of the Most Frequently Used Brands

排名 Brand Ranking	品牌 Brands	人数 Number	百分比 Percent
1	花王碧柔 Biore	20	10.3
2	小护士 Mininurse	18	9.3
3	大宝 Dabao	17	8.8
4	玉兰油 Oil of Olay	11	5.7
5	丁家宜 Dingjiayi	10	5.2
6	旁氏 Pond's	9	4.6
6	芦荟 Luhui	9	4.6
6	可伶可俐 Clean & Clear	9	4.6
9	奥 C	5	2.6
9	洁莱雅 Jielaiya	5	2.6
10	夏士莲 Hazeline	4	2.1

n=194

7-3 样本、男性各年龄层、女性各年龄层的常用品牌/ The Most Frequently Used Brands by the Whole Sample, Age and Gender Groups

	人数 Number	第一品牌及百分比 1st/ percent	第二品牌及百分比 2nd/ percent	第三品牌及百分比 3rd/ percent
样本 Sample	194	**花王碧柔 Biore(10.3)**	**小护士 Mininurse(9.3)**	**大宝 Dabao(8.8)**
男性 Male	43	**芦荟 Luhui(14.0)**	**小护士 Mininurse(11.6)**	**大宝 Dabao(9.3)** **花王碧柔 Biore(9.3)**
16~24 岁 Age	10	花王碧柔 Biore(20.0)	艾琳 Irlene(10.0) 大宝 Dabao(10.0) 东洋之花 Sakula(10.0) 小护士 Mininurse(10.0) 丁家宜 Dingjiayi(10.0) 可伶可俐 Clean & Clear(10.0) 莎士比亚 Shakespeare(10.0) 喜得白 Xidebai(10.0)	
25~34 岁 Age	18	大宝 Dabao(16.7) 小护士 Mininurse(16.7)	芦荟 Luhui(11.1)	情丝青瓜 QingSi QingGua(5.6) 绮梦 Qimeng(5.6) 奥 C (5.6) 可伶可俐 Clean & Clear(5.6) 玉兰油 Oil of Olay(5.6) 夏士莲 Hazeline(5.6) 力士 Lux(5.6) 花王碧柔 Biore(5.6)
35~44 岁 Age	9	芦荟 Luhui(33.3)	夏士莲 Hazeline(11.1) 小护士 Mininurse(11.1) 雅娜 Yana(11.1) 丁家宜 Dingjiayi(11.1) 柔美 Roumei(11.1) 可伶可俐 Clean & Clear(11.1)	
45~54 岁 Age	4	宝思妮 Intouch(25.0) 花王碧柔 Biore(25.0) 芦荟 Luhui(25.0) 奥 C (25.0)		
55~60 岁 Age	2	洁莱雅 Jielaiya(50.0) 力士 Lux(50.0)		
女性 Female	151	**花王碧柔 Biore(10.6)**	**小护士 Mininurse(8.6)** **大宝 Dabao(8.6)**	**玉兰油 Oil of Olay(6.6)**
16~24 岁 Age	50	花王碧柔 Biore(22.0)	大宝 Dabao(12.0)	可伶可俐 Clean & Clear(8.0)
25~34 岁 Age	53	旁氏 Pond's(11.3)	玉兰油 Oil of Olay(9.4) 小护士 Mininurse(9.4)	花王碧柔 Biore(7.5)
35~44 岁 Age	26	大宝 Dabao(15.4)	丁家宜 Dingjiayi(11.5)	小护士 Mininurse(7.7) 艾琳 Irlene(7.7)
45~54 岁 Age	21	小护士 Mininurse(19.0)	旁氏 Pond's(9.5) 奥 C (9.5)	雅倩 Arche(4.8) 绿荟 Lvhui(4.8) 蕾迪奥 Leidiao(4.8) 王妃 Queen(4.8) 芦荟 Luhui(4.8) 雨水 Yushui(4.8) 玉兰油 Oil of Olay(4.8) 羽西 Yue-sai(4.8) 少女之春 Shao Nv Zhi Chun(4.8) 兰贵人 Lan Guiren(4.8) 洁莱雅 Jielaiya(4.8)
55~60 岁 Age	1	霞飞 Xiafei(100.0)		

7-4 正在使用的品牌排名/ Ranking of the Brands Used Now

排名 Brand Ranking	品牌 Brands	人数 Number	百分比 Percent
1	小护士 Mininurse	19	9.8
2	大宝 Dabao	16	8.2
3	花王碧柔 Biore	15	7.7
4	玉兰油 Oil of Olay	14	7.2
5	可伶可俐 Clean & Clear	13	6.7
6	芦荟 Luhui	10	5.2
7	丁家宜 Dingjiayi	8	4.1
8	旁氏 Pond's	6	3.1
8	奥 C	6	3.1
9	雅倩 Arche	4	2.1
9	洁莱雅 Jielaiya	4	2.1
10	丽花丝宝 Laifa-C'bons	3	1.5
10	雨水 Yushui	3	1.5
10	力士 Lux	3	1.5

n=194

7-5 品牌转换习惯/ Brand Habit in Consuming Facial Cleaner

	人数 Number	第一次使用该品牌 first use this brand	上一次也是这个牌子 used it last time	上一次不是这个牌子 not used it last time
样本 Sample	194	26.3	58.8	14.9
小护士 Mininurse	19	42.1	47.4	10.5
大宝 Dabao	16	18.8	68.8	12.5
花王碧柔 Biore	15	0.0	100.0	0.0
玉兰油 Oil of Olay	14	35.7	57.1	7.1
可伶可俐 Clean & Clear	13	23.1	53.8	23.1
芦荟 Luhui	10	30.0	60.0	10.0
丁家宜 Dingjiayi	8	25.0	75.0	0.0
旁氏 Pond's	6	0.0	83.3	16.7
奥 C	6	50.0	50.0	0.0
雅倩 Arche	4	25.0	50.0	25.0
洁莱雅 Jielaiya	4	0.0	100.0	0.0

7-6 下一次打算使用的品牌排名/ Ranking of the Brands to be Used Next Time

排名 Brand Ranking	品牌 Brands	人数 Number	百分比 Percent
1	花王碧柔 Biore	18	9.3
1	玉兰油 Oil of Olay	18	9.3
2	大宝 Dabao	17	8.8
3	小护士 Mininurse	16	8.2
4	丁家宜 Dingjiayi	11	5.7
5	旁氏 Pond's	10	5.2
6	芦荟 Luhui	8	4.1
7	奥 C	6	3.1
8	洁莱雅 Jielaiya	5	2.6
9	可伶可俐 Clean & Clear	4	2.1

n=194

7-7 样本、男性各年龄层、女性各年龄层的使用频率/ Frequencies of the Consumed Facial Cleaner by the Whole Sample, Age and Gender Groups

	人数 Number	一天 3 次或以上 3 times or over a day	一天 1~2 次 once or twice a day	两三天用 1 次 once 2 or 3 days	一周 1~2 次 once or twice a week	半个月 1 次或以下 once half a month or below	没用过 never use
样本 Sample	624	0.8	22.1	4.8	2.6	0.8	68.9
男性 Male	314	0.3	8.0	3.8	1.3	0.3	86.3
16~24 岁 Age	64	1.6	12.5	1.6	0.0	0.0	84.4
25~34 岁 Age	93	0.0	7.5	8.6	2.2	1.1	80.6
35~44 岁 Age	75	0.0	6.7	2.7	2.7	0.0	88.0
45~54 岁 Age	54	0.0	5.6	1.9	0.0	0.0	92.6
55~60 岁 Age	28	0.0	7.1	0.0	0.0	0.0	92.9
女性 Female	310	1.3	36.5	5.8	3.9	1.3	51.3
16~24 岁 Age	64	3.1	57.8	7.8	6.3	3.1	21.9
25~34 岁 Age	90	1.1	50.0	6.7	1.1	0.0	41.1
35~44 岁 Age	73	0.0	26.0	2.7	5.5	1.4	64.4
45~54 岁 Age	60	1.7	18.3	8.3	5.0	1.7	65.0
55~60 岁 Age	23	0.0	4.3	0.0	0.0	0.0	95.7

7-8 选择该类商品的考虑因素/ Ranking of the Considerations in Purchasing

注：本题为多选题，合计百分比超过 100%（Multiple answers）

排名 Ranking	考虑因素 Considerations	人次 Person-time	百分比 Percent
1	产品功用 product function	92	47.7
2	价格适中 reasonable price	64	33.2
3	有名的牌子 famous brand	53	27.5
4	别人推荐 introduced by other people	52	26.9
5	广告影响 influence of advertising	51	26.4
6	购买方便 easy to buy	19	9.8
7	包装吸引人 appealing package	7	3.6
8	有优惠条件 with preferential terms	5	2.6
9	单位发的 offered by the working unit	3	1.6
10	其它 others	2	1.0

n=193

7-9 对产品功能的侧重方面/ Ranking of the Considerations about the Function of this Kind of Product

注：本题为多选题，合计百分比超过 100%（Multiple answers）

排名 Ranking	侧重方面 Items	人次 Person-time	百分比 Percent
1	洗后不紧绷 soft & elastic after bath	76	39.2
2	气味好 pleasant smell	75	38.7
3	适合自己的肤质 suitable to my skin	74	38.1
4	含滋润成分 containing nourishing ingredient	58	29.9
5	洁净力强 powerful cleaning	55	28.4
6	泡沫多 rich foam	34	17.5
7	含爽肤成分 containing skin cleaning ingredient	31	16.0
8	含果酸成分 containing tartaric acid	16	8.2
9	含磨砂颗粒 with granites	10	5.2
10	其他 others	4	2.1

n=194

7-10 重度消费者的人口分布/ Demographics of the Heavy Consumers

	人数 Number	16-24 岁 Age	25-34 岁 Age	35-44 岁 Age	45-54 岁 Age	55-60 岁 Age
样本 Sample	143	33.6	37.1	16.8	10.5	2.1
男性 Male	26	34.6	26.9	19.2	11.5	7.7
一天 3 次或以上 3 times or over a day	1	100.0	0.0	0.0	0.0	0.0
一天 1~2 次 once or twice a day	25	32.0	28.0	20.0	12.0	8.0
女性 Female	117	33.3	39.3	16.2	10.3	0.9
一天 3 次或以上 3 times or over a day	4	50.0	25.0	0.0	25.0	0.0
一天 1~2 次 once or twice a day	113	32.7	39.8	16.8	9.7	0.9

7-11 不同消费者层的常用品牌/ The Most Frequently Used Brands by Market Segments

7-11-1 时尚流行指标/ Fads Popular Index

	人数 Number	第一品牌及百分比 1st / percent	第二品牌及百分比 2nd / percent	第三品牌及百分比 3rd / percent
样本 Sample	192	**花王碧柔 Biore(9.9)**	**小护士 Mininurse(9.4)**	**大宝 Dabao(8.9)**
平实生活指向 simple living orientation	76	小护士 Mininurse(9.2)	花王碧柔 Biore(7.9)	可伶可俐 Clean & Clear(6.6) 大宝 Dabao(6.6) 玉兰油 Oil of Olay(6.6)
时尚流行指向 fashion orientation	116	花王碧柔 Biore(11.2)	大宝 Dabao(10.3)	小护士 Mininurse(9.5)

7-11-2 广告态度指标/ Advertising Attitude Index

	人数 Number	第一品牌及百分比 1st / percent	第二品牌及百分比 2nd / percent	第三品牌及百分比 3rd / percent
样本 Sample	193	**花王碧柔 Biore(10.4)**	**小护士 Mininurse(9.3)**	**大宝 Dabao(8.8)**
广告淡漠指向 indifferent orientation	37	大宝 Dabao(13.5)	花王碧柔 Biore(8.1) 旁氏 Pond's(8.1)	夏士莲 Hazeline(5.4) 可伶可俐 Clean & Clear(5.4) 玉兰油 Oil of Olay(5.4) 小护士 Mininurse(5.4)
中间层 medium	125	花王碧柔 Biore(11.2)	小护士 Mininurse(8.8)	玉兰油 Oil of Olay(7.2) 大宝 Dabao(7.2)
信赖广告指向 loyal orientation	31	小护士 Mininurse(16.1)	大宝 Dabao(9.7) 花王碧柔 Biore(9.7) 可伶可俐 Clean & Clear(9.7)	芦荟 Luhui(6.5)

7-12 重度消费者的消费层构成/ The Composition of the Heavy Consumers

7-12-1 时尚流行指标/ Fads Popular Index

	人数 Number	平实生活指向 simple living orientation	时尚流行指向 fashion orientation
样本 Sample	141	**34.0**	**66.0**
一天 3 次或以上 3 times or over a day	5	40.0	60.0
一天 1~2 次 once or twice a day	136	33.8	66.2

7-12-2 广告态度指标/ Advertising Attitude Index

	人数 Number	广告淡漠指向 indifferent orientation	中间层 medium	信赖广告指向 loyal orientation
样本 Sample	142	**19.0**	**64.1**	**16.9**
一天 3 次或以上 3 times or over a day	5	40.0	60.0	0.0
一天 1~2 次 once or twice a day	137	18.2	64.2	17.5

● 武汉 / Wuhan

7-1 最近三个月使用频率的比例/ Proportion of the Sample Consuming Facial Cleaner in the Last Three Months

	人数 Number	百分比 Percent
一天 3 次或以上 3 times or over a day	9	1.4
一天 1~2 次 once or twice a day	163	25.5
两三天用 1 次 once 2 or 3 days	26	4.1
一周 1~2 次 once or twice a week	19	3.0
半个月 1 次或以下 once half a month or below	9	1.4
没用过 never use	414	64.7

n=640

7-2 最常用品牌排名/ Ranking of the Most Frequently Used Brands

排名 Brand Ranking	品牌 Brands	人数 Number	百分比 Percent
1	丁家宜 Dingjiayi	33	14.7
2	花王碧柔 Biore	28	12.5
3	旁氏 Pond's	18	8.0
4	大宝 Dabao	10	4.5
5	玉兰油 Oil of Olay	9	4.0
6	可伶可俐 Clean & Clear	8	3.6
7	丽花丝宝 Laifa-C'bons	7	3.1
7	小护士 Mininurse	7	3.1
7	东洋之花 Sakula	7	3.1

n=224

7-3 样本、男性各年龄层、女性各年龄层的常用品牌/ The Most Frequently Used Brands by the Whole Sample, Age and Gender Groups

	人数 Number	第一品牌及百分比 1st/ percent	第二品牌及百分比 2nd/ percent	第三品牌及百分比 3rd/ percent
样本 Sample	224	**丁家宜 Dingjiayi(14.7)**	**花王碧柔 Biore(12.5)**	**旁氏 Pond's(8.0)**
男性 Male	39	**花王碧柔 Biore(15.4)** **丁家宜 Dingjiayi(15.4)**	**大宝 Dabao(7.7)**	**小护士 Mininurse(5.1)** **伊婷 Yiting(5.1)**
16~24 岁 Age	18	丁家宜 Dingjiayi(22.2)	大宝 Dabao(11.1) 花王碧柔 Biore(11.1)	伊婷 Yiting(5.6) 邦氏 Bangshi(5.6) 采诗 Caishi(5.6) 柔娜 Rouna(5.6) 小护士 Mininurse(5.6) 索芙特 Softto(5.6) 少女之春 Shao Nu Zhi Chun(5.6) 东洋之花 Sakula(5.6)
25~34 岁 Age	15	花王碧柔 Biore(20.0)	资生堂 Shiseido(6.7) 伊婷 Yiting(6.7) 可伶可俐 Clean & Clear(6.7) 丁家宜 Dingjiayi(6.7) 芦荟 Luhui(6.7) 雅倩 Arche(6.7) 安安 An'an(6.7) 小护士 Mininurse(6.7) 旁氏 Pond's(6.7) 丽花丝宝 Laifa-C'bons(6.7) 大宝 Dabao(6.7) 安利 Amway(6.7)	
35~44 岁 Age	5	艾琳 Irlene(20.0) 花王碧柔 Biore(20.0) 丁家宜 Dingjiayi(20.0) 舒蕾(20.0) AIKI(20.0)		
45~54 岁 Age	1			
55~60 岁 Age	0			
女性 Female	185	**丁家宜 Dingjiayi(14.6)**	**花王碧柔 Biore(11.9)**	**旁氏 Pond's(9.2)**
16~24 岁 Age	60	花王碧柔 Biore(11.7)	可伶可俐 Clean & Clear(10.0) 丁家宜 Dingjiayi(10.0)	旁氏 Pond's(8.3)
25~34 岁 Age	59	丁家宜 Dingjiayi(22.0)	花王碧柔 Biore(11.9)	玉兰油 Oil of Olay(8.5) 旁氏 Pond's(8.5)
35~44 岁 Age	36	花王碧柔 Biore(13.9) 旁氏 Pond's(13.9)	少女之春 Shao Nu Zhi Chun(8.3) 丁家宜 Dingjiayi(8.3)	玉兰油 Oil of Olay(5.6)
45~54 岁 Age	28	丁家宜 Dingjiayi(17.9)	花王碧柔 Biore(10.7)	艾琳 Irlene(7.1) 旁氏 Pond's(7.1)
55~60 岁 Age	2	雅芳 Avon(50.0)		

7-4 正在使用的品牌排名/ Ranking of the Brands Used Now

排名 Brand Ranking	品牌 Brands	人数 Number	百分比 Percent
1	丁家宜 Dingjiayi	33	14.8
2	花王碧柔 Biore	21	9.4
3	可伶可俐 Clean & Clear	15	6.7
4	大宝 Dabao	11	4.9
4	旁氏 Pond's	11	4.9
4	玉兰油 Oil of Olay	11	4.9
5	东洋之花 Sakula	10	4.5
6	丽花丝宝 Laifa-C'bons	9	4.0
7	小护士 Mininurse	8	3.6
8	雅倩 Arche	7	3.1
9	雅芳 Avon	6	2.7

n=223

7-5 品牌转换习惯/ Brand Habit in Consuming Facial Cleaner

	人数 Number	第一次使用该品牌 first use this brand	上一次也是这个牌子 used it last time	上一次不是这个牌子 not used it last time
样本 Sample	223	18.8	59.2	22.0
丁家宜 Dingjiayi	33	12.1	72.7	15.2
花王碧柔 Biore	21	14.3	76.2	9.5
可伶可俐 Clean & Clear	15	26.7	6.7	66.7
大宝 Dabao	11	27.3	63.6	9.1
旁氏 Pond's	11	9.1	63.6	27.3
玉兰油 Oil of Olay	11	9.1	81.8	9.1
东洋之花 Sakula	10	20.0	30.0	50.0
丽花丝宝 Laifa-C'bons	9	22.2	44.4	33.3
小护士 Mininurse	8	25.0	37.5	37.5
雅倩 Arche	7	28.6	57.1	14.3

7-6 下一次打算使用的品牌排名/ Ranking of the Brands to be Used Next Time

排名 Brand Ranking	品牌 Brands	人数 Number	百分比 Percent
1	丁家宜 Dingjiayi	31	14.1
2	玉兰油 Oil of Olay	21	9.5
3	旁氏 Pond's	20	9.1
4	花王碧柔 Biore	18	8.2
5	小护士 Mininurse	13	5.9
6	大宝 Dabao	9	4.1
7	可伶可俐 Clean & Clear	8	3.6
8	东洋之花 Sakula	7	3.2
9	雅倩 Arche	6	2.7

n=220

7-7 样本、男性各年龄层、女性各年龄层的使用频率/ Frequencies of the Consumed Facial Cleaner by the Whole Sample, Age and Gender Groups

	人数 Number	一天 3 次或以上 3 times or over a day	一天 1~2 次 once or twice a day	两三天用 1 次 once 2 or 3 days	一周 1~2 次 once or twice a week	半个月 1 次或以下 once half a month or below	没用过 never use
样本 Sample	640	1.4	25.5	4.1	3.0	1.4	64.7
男性 Male	309	0.0	7.4	1.9	1.6	1.9	87.1
16~24 岁 Age	65	0.0	16.9	4.6	4.6	1.5	72.3
25~34 岁 Age	88	0.0	9.1	3.4	2.3	3.4	81.8
35~44 岁 Age	80	0.0	3.8	0.0	0.0	2.5	93.8
45~54 岁 Age	51	0.0	2.0	0.0	0.0	0.0	98.0
55~60 岁 Age	25	0.0	0.0	0.0	0.0	0.0	100.0
女性 Female	331	2.7	42.3	6.0	4.2	0.9	43.8
16~24 岁 Age	69	5.8	69.6	4.3	5.8	1.4	13.0
25~34 岁 Age	96	1.0	45.8	8.3	5.2	1.0	38.5
35~44 岁 Age	78	2.6	35.9	5.1	2.6	1.3	52.6
45~54 岁 Age	62	3.2	32.3	4.8	4.8	0.0	54.8
55~60 岁 Age	26	0.0	0.0	7.7	0.0	0.0	92.3

7-8 选择该类商品的考虑因素/ Ranking of the Considerations in Purchasing

注：本题为多选题，合计百分比超过 100%（Multiple answers）

排名 Ranking	考虑因素 Considerations	人次 Person-time	百分比 Percent
1	产品功用 product function	129	57.3
2	价格适中 reasonable price	106	47.1
3	有名的牌子 famous brand	94	41.8
4	广告影响 influence of advertising	49	21.8
5	别人推荐 introduced by other people	46	20.4
6	有优惠条件 with preferential terms	19	8.4
7	购买方便 easy to buy	16	7.1
8	单位发的 offered by the working unit	8	3.6
9	包装吸引人 appealing package	7	3.1
10	其它 others	6	2.7

n=225

7-9 对产品功能的侧重方面/ Ranking of the Considerations about the Function of this Kind of Product

注：本题为多选题，合计百分比超过 100%（Multiple answers）

排名 Ranking	侧重方面 Items	人次 Person-time	百分比 Percent
1	洗后不紧绷 soft & elastic after bath	100	44.4
2	适合自己的肤质 suitable to my skin	97	43.1
3	气味好 pleasant smell	90	40.0
4	洁净力强 powerful cleaning	76	33.8
5	含滋润成分 containing nourishing ingredient	71	31.6
6	泡沫多 rich foam	39	17.3
7	含爽肤成分 containing skin cleaning ingredient	28	12.4
8	含果酸成分 containing tartaric acid	22	9.8
9	含磨砂颗粒 with granites	17	7.6
10	其他 others	4	1.8

n=225

7-10 重度消费者的人口分布/ Demographics of the Heavy Consumers

	人数 Number	16-24 岁 Age	25-34 岁 Age	35-44 岁 Age	45-54 岁 Age	55-60 岁 Age
样本 Sample	172	36.6	30.8	19.2	13.4	0.0
男性 Male	23	47.8	34.8	13.0	4.3	0.0
一天 3 次或以上 3 times or over a day	0	0.0	0.0	0.0	0.0	0.0
一天 1~2 次 once or twice a day	23	47.8	34.8	13.0	4.3	0.0
女性 Female	149	34.9	30.2	20.1	14.8	0.0
一天 3 次或以上 3 times or over a day	9	44.4	11.1	22.2	22.2	0.0
一天 1~2 次 once or twice a day	140	34.3	31.4	20.0	14.3	0.0

7-11 不同消费者层的常用品牌/ The Most Frequently Used Brands by Market Segments

7-11-1 时尚流行指标/ Fads Popular Index

	人数 Number	第一品牌及百分比 1st / percent	第二品牌及百分比 2nd / percent	第三品牌及百分比 3rd / percent
样本 Sample	218	**丁家宜 Dingjiayi(15.1)**	**花王碧柔 Biore(11.9)**	**旁氏 Pond's(8.3)**
平实生活指向 simple living orientation	76	丁家宜 Dingjiayi(14.5)	旁氏 Pond's(11.8)	花王碧柔 Biore(10.5)
时尚流行指向 fashion orientation	142	丁家宜 Dingjiayi(15.5)	花王碧柔 Biore(12.7)	旁氏 Pond's(6.3)

7-11-2 广告态度指标/ Advertising Attitude Index

	人数 Number	第一品牌及百分比 1st / percent	第二品牌及百分比 2nd / percent	第三品牌及百分比 3rd / percent
样本 Sample	218	**丁家宜 Dingjiayi(15.1)**	**花王碧柔 Biore(11.9)**	**旁氏 Pond's(8.3)**
广告淡漠指向 indifferent orientation	52	丁家宜 Dingjiayi(17.3)	花王碧柔 Biore(15.4)	大宝 Dabao(7.7) 旁氏 Pond's(7.7)
中间层 medium	129	丁家宜 Dingjiayi(14.0)	旁氏 Pond's(10.1)	花王碧柔 Biore(7.8)
信赖广告指向 loyal orientation	37	花王碧柔 Biore(21.6)	丁家宜 Dingjiayi(16.2)	丽花丝宝 Laifa-C'bons(8.1)

7-12 重度消费者的消费层构成/ The Composition of the Heavy Consumers

7-12-1 时尚流行指标/ Fads Popular Index

	人数 Number	平实生活指向 simple living orientation	时尚流行指向 fashion orientation
样本 Sample	166	31.3	68.7
一天 3 次或以上 3 times or over a day	9	22.2	77.8
一天 1~2 次 once or twice a day	157	31.8	68.2

7-12-2 广告态度指标/ Advertising Attitude Index

	人数 Number	广告淡漠指向 indifferent orientation	中间层 medium	信赖广告指向 loyal orientation
样本 Sample	166	20.5	62.0	17.5
一天 3 次或以上 3 times or over a day	9	22.2	44.4	33.3
一天 1~2 次 once or twice a day	157	20.4	63.1	16.6

● 西安 / Xi'an

7-1 最近三个月使用频率的比例/ Proportion of the Sample Consuming Facial Cleaner in the Last Three Months

	人数 Number	百分比 Percent
一天 3 次或以上 3 times or over a day	15	2.5
一天 1~2 次 once or twice a day	202	33.7
两三天用 1 次 once 2 or 3 days	26	4.3
一周 1~2 次 once or twice a week	12	2.0
半个月 1 次或以下 once half a month or below	6	1.0
没用过 never use	339	56.5

n=600

7-2 最常用品牌排名/ Ranking of the Most Frequently Used Brands

排名 Brand Ranking	品牌 Brands	人数 Number	百分比 Percent
1	丁家宜 Dingjiayi	35	13.5
2	旁氏 Pond's	27	10.4
3	花王碧柔 Biore	24	9.2
4	大宝 Dabao	22	8.5
5	小护士 Mininurse	14	5.4
6	雅倩 Arche	13	5.0
6	洁莱雅 Jielaiya	13	5.0
7	玉兰油 Oil of Olay	11	4.2
8	信芬 Synform	9	3.5
9	逸芙雪 Yifuxue	8	3.1

n=260

7-3 样本、男性各年龄层、女性各年龄层的常用品牌/ The Most Frequently Used Brands by the Whole Sample, Age and Gender Groups

	人数 Number	第一品牌及百分比 1st/ percent	第二品牌及百分比 2nd/ percent	第三品牌及百分比 3rd/ percent
样本 Sample	260	**丁家宜 Dingjiayi(13.5)**	**旁氏 Pond's(10.4)**	**花王碧柔 Biore(9.2)**
男性 Male	62	**大宝 Dabao(12.9)**	**花王碧柔 Biore(11.3)**	**丁家宜 Dingjiayi(8.1)** **旁氏 Pond's(8.1)**
16~24 岁 Age	20	大宝 Dabao(25.0)	花王碧柔 Biore(20.0)	丹芭碧 Tobaby(10.0) 可伶可俐 Clean & Clear(10.0)
25~34 岁 Age	20	丁家宜 Dingjiayi(10.0) 大宝 Dabao(10.0) 花王碧柔 Biore(10.0) 旁氏 Pond's(10.0) 小护士 Mininurse(10.0) 玉兰油 Oil of Olay(10.0)	雅妆 Yazhuang(5.0) 高夫 G.lf(5.0) 柔婷 Routing(5.0) 欧珀莱 Aupres(5.0) 资生堂 Shiseido(5.0)	
35~44 岁 Age	18	信芬 Synform(16.7)	莹扑 Yingpu(11.1) 旁氏 Pond's(11.1)	雪 Beauty Snow(5.6) 雅婷 Yating(5.6) 丁家宜 Dingjiayi(5.6) 玉兰油 Oil of Olay(5.6) 雅芳 Avon(5.6) 大宝 Dabao(5.6) 小护士 Mininurse(5.6) 兰丹 Landen(5.6) 花王碧柔 Biore(5.6) 高丝 Kose(5.6) 东洋之花 Sakula(5.6)
45~54 岁 Age	3	洁莱雅 Jielaiya(33.3) 资生堂 Shiseido(33.3) 丁家宜 Dingjiayi(33.3)		
55~60 岁 Age	1	信芬 Synform(100.0)		
女性 Female	198	**丁家宜 Dingjiayi(15.2)**	**旁氏 Pond's(11.1)**	**花王碧柔 Biore(8.6)**
16~24 岁 Age	51	花王碧柔 Biore(15.7)	丁家宜 Dingjiayi(13.7)	大宝 Dabao(7.8) 雅倩 Arche(7.8) 旁氏 Pond's(7.8)
25~34 岁 Age	76	丁家宜 Dingjiayi(13.2)	旁氏 Pond's(10.5)	雅倩 Arche(7.9) 逸芙雪 Yifuxue(7.9)
35~44 岁 Age	46	丁家宜 Dingjiayi(21.7)	旁氏 Pond's(13.0)	大宝 Dabao(8.7) 洁莱雅 Jielaiya(8.7) 小护士 Mininurse(8.7)
45~54 岁 Age	21	丁家宜 Dingjiayi(14.3) 洁莱雅 Jielaiya(14.3) 旁氏 Pond's(14.3)	花王碧柔 Biore(9.5) 美加净 Maxam(9.5)	凯琳 Kilin(4.8) 可伶可俐 Clean & Clear(4.8) 雅嘉 Aikai(4.8) 大宝 Dabao(4.8) 雅倩 Arche(4.8) 夏士莲 Hazeline(4.8) 丽花丝宝 Laifa-C'bons(4.8) 力士 Lux(4.8)
55~60 岁 Age	4	东洋之花 Sakula(25.0) 花王碧柔 Biore(25.0) 旁氏 Pond's(25.0) 劳伦特·克丽斯汀 Cristin(25.0)		

7-4 正在使用的品牌排名/ Ranking of the Brands Used Now

排名 Brand Ranking	品牌 Brands	人数 Number	百分比 Percent
1	丁家宜 Dingjiayi	31	11.9
2	旁氏 Pond's	25	9.6
3	大宝 Dabao	23	8.8
4	花王碧柔 Biore	16	6.1
4	信芬 Synform	16	6.1
5	玉兰油 Oil of Olay	13	5.0
5	雅倩 Arche	13	5.0
5	小护士 Mininurse	13	5.0
6	洁莱雅 Jielaiya	12	4.6
7	逸芙雪 Yifuxue	8	3.1

n=261

7-5 品牌转换习惯/ Brand Habit in Consuming Facial Cleaner

	人数 Number	第一次使用该品牌 first use this brand	上一次也是这个牌子 used it last time	上一次不是这个牌子 not used it last time
样本 Sample	261	20.3	63.6	16.1
丁家宜 Dingjiayi	31	35.5	51.6	12.9
旁氏 Pond's	25	8.0	80.0	12.0
大宝 Dabao	23	13.0	78.3	8.7
花王碧柔 Biore	16	6.3	81.3	12.5
信芬 Synform	16	37.5	43.8	18.8
玉兰油 Oil of Olay	13	7.7	53.8	38.5
雅倩 Arche	13	7.7	84.6	7.7
小护士 Mininurse	13	30.8	53.8	15.4
洁莱雅 Jielaiya	12	16.7	66.7	16.7

7-6 下一次打算使用的品牌排名/ Ranking of the Brands to be Used Next Time

排名 Brand Ranking	品牌 Brands	人数 Number	百分比 Percent
1	丁家宜 Dingjiayi	35	13.4
2	旁氏 Pond's	24	9.2
3	花王碧柔 Biore	22	8.4
4	大宝 Dabao	19	7.3
5	小护士 Mininurse	15	5.7
6	玉兰油 Oil of Olay	14	5.4
6	雅倩 Arche	14	5.4
7	洁莱雅 Jielaiya	12	4.6
8	逸芙雪 Yifuxue	10	3.8
9	信芬 Synform	9	3.4

n=261

7-7 样本、男性各年龄层、女性各年龄层的使用频率/ Frequencies of the Consumed Facial Cleaner by the Whole Sample, Age and Gender Groups

	人数 Number	一天 3 次或以上 3 times or over a day	一天 1~2 次 once or twice a day	两三天用 1 次 once 2 or 3 days	一周 1~2 次 once or twice a week	半个月 1 次或以下 once half a month or below	没用过 never use
样本 Sample	600	2.5	33.7	4.3	2.0	1.0	56.5
男性 Male	301	1.0	13.6	3.3	1.0	1.7	79.4
16~24 岁 Age	64	0.0	25.0	3.1	0.0	3.1	68.8
25~34 岁 Age	91	2.2	12.1	3.3	2.2	2.2	78.0
35~44 岁 Age	77	0.0	15.6	5.2	1.3	1.3	76.6
45~54 岁 Age	46	2.2	4.3	0.0	0.0	0.0	93.5
55~60 岁 Age	23	0.0	0.0	4.3	0.0	0.0	95.7
女性 Female	299	4.0	53.8	5.4	3.0	0.3	33.4
16~24 岁 Age	61	8.2	72.1	1.6	1.6	1.6	14.8
25~34 岁 Age	90	4.4	64.4	8.9	6.7	0.0	15.6
35~44 岁 Age	74	1.4	54.1	4.1	2.7	0.0	37.8
45~54 岁 Age	49	2.0	36.7	4.1	0.0	0.0	57.1
55~60 岁 Age	25	4.0	4.0	8.0	0.0	0.0	84.0

7-8 选择该类商品的考虑因素/ Ranking of the Considerations in Purchasing

注：本题为多选题，合计百分比超过 100%（Multiple answers）

排名 Ranking	考虑因素 Considerations	人次 Person-time	百分比 Percent
1	产品功用 product function	121	46.4
2	价格适中 reasonable price	91	34.9
3	有名的牌子 famous brand	90	34.5
4	广告影响 influence of advertising	62	23.8
5	别人推荐 introduced by other people	51	19.5
6	购买方便 easy to buy	36	13.8
7	有优惠条件 with preferential terms	11	4.2
8	包装吸引人 appealing package	10	3.8
9	单位发的 offered by the working unit	4	1.5
9	其它 others	4	1.5

n=261

7-9 对产品功能的侧重方面/ Ranking of the Considerations about the Function of this Kind of Product

注：本题为多选题，合计百分比超过 100%（Multiple answers）

排名 Ranking	侧重方面 Items	人次 Person-time	百分比 Percent
1	适合自己的肤质 suitable to my skin	106	40.6
2	气味好 pleasant smell	99	37.9
3	洗后不紧绷 soft & elastic after bath	88	33.7
4	洁净力强 powerful cleaning	81	31.0
5	含滋润成分 containing nourishing ingredient	71	27.2
6	泡沫多 rich foam	50	19.2
7	含爽肤成分 containing skin cleaning ingredient	33	12.6
8	含果酸成分 containing tartaric acid	28	10.7
9	含磨砂颗粒 with granites	14	5.4
10	其他 others	1	0.4

n=261

7-10 重度消费者的人口分布/ Demographics of the Heavy Consumers

	人数 Number	16-24 岁 Age	25-34 岁 Age	35-44 岁 Age	45-54 岁 Age	55-60 岁 Age
样本 Sample	217	30.0	34.6	24.4	10.1	0.9
男性 Male	44	36.4	29.5	27.3	6.8	0.0
一天 3 次或以上 3 times or over a day	3	0.0	66.7	0.0	33.3	0.0
一天 1~2 次 once or twice a day	41	39.0	26.8	29.3	4.9	0.0
女性 Female	173	28.3	35.8	23.7	11.0	1.2
一天 3 次或以上 3 times or over a day	12	41.7	33.3	8.3	8.3	8.3
一天 1~2 次 once or twice a day	161	27.3	36.0	24.8	11.2	0.6

7-11 不同消费者层的常用品牌/ The Most Frequently Used Brands by Market Segments

7-11-1 时尚流行指标/ Fads Popular Index

	人数 Number	第一品牌及百分比 1st / percent	第二品牌及百分比 2nd / percent	第三品牌及百分比 3rd / percent	第四品牌及百分比 4th / percent
样本 Sample	260	**丁家宜 Dingjiayi(13.5)**	**旁氏 Pond's(10.4)**	**花王碧柔 Biore(9.2)**	**大宝 Dabao(8.5)**
平实生活指向 simple living orientation	110	丁家宜 Dingjiayi(11.8)	旁氏 Pond's(10.0)	大宝 Dabao(9.1) 花王碧柔 Biore(9.1)	雅倩 Arche(7.3) 洁莱雅 Jielaiya(7.3)
时尚流行指向 fashion orientation	150	丁家宜 Dingjiayi(14.7)	旁氏 Pond's(10.7)	花王碧柔 Biore(9.3)	大宝 Dabao(8.0)

7-11-2 广告态度指标/ Advertising Attitude Index

	人数 Number	第一品牌及百分比 1st / percent	第二品牌及百分比 2nd / percent	第三品牌及百分比 3rd / percent	第四品牌及百分比 4th / percent
样本 Sample	259	**丁家宜 Dingjiayi(13.5)**	**旁氏 Pond's(10.4)**	**花王碧柔 Biore(9.3)**	**大宝 Dabao(8.5)**
广告淡漠指向 indifferent orientation	70	丁家宜 Dingjiayi(15.7)	旁氏 Pond's(10.0)	花王碧柔 Biore(8.6)	雅倩 Arche(7.1) 大宝 Dabao(7.1)
中间层 medium	154	丁家宜 Dingjiayi(12.3)	大宝 Dabao(10.4)	花王碧柔 Biore(9.7)	旁氏 Pond's(8.4)
信赖广告指向 loyal orientation	35	旁氏 Pond's(20.0)	丁家宜 Dingjiayi(14.3)	花王碧柔 Biore(8.6) 雅倩 Arche(8.6)	洁莱雅 Jielaiya(5.7) 力士 Lux(5.7)

7-12 重度消费者的消费层构成/ The Composition of the Heavy Consumers

7-12-1 时尚流行指标/ Fads Popular Index

	人数 Number	平实生活指向 simple living orientation	时尚流行指向 fashion orientation
样本 Sample	217	41.0	59.0
一天 3 次或以上 3 times or over a day	15	20.0	80.0
一天 1~2 次 once or twice a day	202	42.6	57.4

7-12-2 广告态度指标/ Advertising Attitude Index

	人数 Number	广告淡漠指向 indifferent orientation	中间层 medium	信赖广告指向 loyal orientation
样本 Sample	**216**	**25.9**	**60.6**	**13.4**
一天 3 次或以上 3 times or over a day	14	21.4	64.3	14.3
一天 1~2 次 once or twice a day	202	26.2	60.4	13.4

● 沈阳 / Shenyang

7-1 最近三个月使用频率的比例/ Proportion of the Sample Consuming Facial Cleaner in the Last Three Months

	人数 Number	百分比 Percent
一天 3 次或以上 3 times or over a day	5	0.8
一天 1~2 次 once or twice a day	141	23.6
两三天用 1 次 once 2 or 3 days	14	2.3
一周 1~2 次 once or twice a week	10	1.7
半个月 1 次或以下 once half a month or below	7	1.2
没用过 never use	421	70.4

n=598

7-2 最常用品牌排名/ Ranking of the Most Frequently Used Brands

排名 Brand Ranking	品牌 Brands	人数 Number	百分比 Percent
1	芦荟 Luhui	17	9.6
2	花王碧柔 Biore	13	7.3
2	玉兰油 Oil of Olay	13	7.3
3	安安 An'an	11	6.2
4	小护士 Mininurse	10	5.6
5	高丝 Kose	7	4.0
6	大宝 Dabao	6	3.4
6	可伶可俐 Clean & Clear	6	3.4
7	旁氏 Pond's	5	2.8
8	欧珀莱 Aupres	4	2.3
8	信芬 Synform	4	2.3

n=177

7-3 样本、男性各年龄层、女性各年龄层的常用品牌/ The Most Frequently Used Brands by the Whole Sample, Age and Gender Groups

	人数 Number	第一品牌及百分比 1st/ percent	第二品牌及百分比 2nd/ percent	第三品牌及百分比 3rd/ percent
样本 Sample	177	**芦荟 Luhui(9.6)**	**花王碧柔 Biore(7.3)** **玉兰油 Oil of Olay(7.3)**	**安安 An'an(6.2)**
男性 Male	27	**安安 An'an(7.4)** **花王碧柔 Biore(7.4)** **小护士 Mininurse(7.4)** **芦荟 Luhui(7.4)**	**郑明明 Cheng Mingming(3.7)** **白雪 Baixue(3.7)** **樱花 Yinghua(3.7)** **露美 Lumei(3.7)** **米雪 Mixue(3.7)** **信芬 Synform(3.7)** **奥 C (3.7)** **可伶可俐 Clean & Clear(3.7)** **玉兰油 Oil of Olay(3.7)** **伊思丽 Eesli(3.7)** **夏士莲 Hazeline(3.7)** **旁氏 Pond's(3.7)** **美加净 Maxam(3.7)** **力士 Lux(3.7)** **兰贵人 Lan Guiren(3.7)** **大宝 Dabao(3.7)**	
16~24 岁 Age	10	安安 An'an(10.0) 兰贵人 Lan Guiren(10.0) 力士 Lux(10.0) 郑明明 Cheng Mingming(10.0) 芦荟 Luhui(10.0) 奥 C (10.0) 信芬 Synform(10.0) 樱花 Yinghua(10.0) 白雪 Baixue(10.0)		
25~34 岁 Age	8	花王碧柔 Biore(25.0)	大宝 Dabao(12.5) 夏士莲 Hazeline(12.5) 玉兰油 Oil of Olay(12.5) 芦荟 Luhui(12.5) 可伶可俐 Clean & Clear(12.5) 米雪 Mixue(12.5)	
35~44 岁 Age	7	小护士 Mininurse(28.6)	安安 An'an(14.3) 美加净 Maxam(14.3) 旁氏 Pond's(14.3) 露美 Lumei(14.3)	
45~54 岁 Age	2	伊思丽 Eesli(50.0)		
55~60 岁 Age	0			
女性 Female	150	**芦荟 Luhui(10.0)**	**玉兰油 Oil of Olay(8.0)**	**花王碧柔 Biore(7.3)**
16~24 岁 Age	48	玉兰油 Oil of Olay(12.5)	芦荟 Luhui(8.3) 花王碧柔 Biore(8.3) 安安 An'an(8.3)	可伶可俐 Clean & Clear(6.3)
25~34 岁 Age	52	芦荟 Luhui(17.3)	高丝 Kose(9.6)	花王碧柔 Biore(7.7) 小护士 Mininurse(7.7)
35~44 岁 Age	35	安安 An'an(11.4)	花王碧柔 Biore(8.6)	大宝 Dabao(5.7) 小护士 Mininurse(5.7) 玉兰油 Oil of Olay(5.7) 艾依 Ainong(5.7) 丁家宜 Dingjiayi(5.7)
45~54 岁 Age	12	芦荟 Luhui(16.7)	可伶可俐 Clean & Clear(8.3) 黄菊 Huangju(8.3) 鲜奶嫩 Xiannainen(8.3) 法诺雅 Fanuoya(8.3) 南珠王 Nanzhuwang(8.3) 安安 An'an(8.3) 雅娜 Yana(8.3) 旁氏 Pond's(8.3) 莉奥兰 Lyolan(8.3)	
55~60 岁 Age	3	玉兰油 Oil of Olay(33.3) 欧珀莱 Aupres(33.3) 脱普 Top(33.3)		

7-4 正在使用的品牌排名/ Ranking of the Brands Used Now

排名 Brand Ranking	品牌 Brands	人数 Number	百分比 Percent
1	玉兰油 Oil of Olay	16	9.0
2	芦荟 Luhui	14	7.9
3	花王碧柔 Biore	12	6.8
4	安安 An'an	10	5.6
5	小护士 Mininurse	9	5.1
6	高丝 Kose	7	4.0
6	可伶可俐 Clean & Clear	7	4.0
7	信芬 Synform	6	3.4
8	旁氏 Pond's	5	2.8
9	丁家宜 Dingjiayi	4	2.3
9	欧珀莱 Aupres	4	2.3
9	大宝 Dabao	4	2.3
10	郑明明 Cheng Mingming	3	1.7
10	索芙特 Softto	3	1.7
10	艾依 Ainong	3	1.7

n=177

7-5 品牌转换习惯/ Brand Habit in Consuming Facial Cleaner

	人数 Number	第一次使用该品牌 first use this brand	上一次也是这个牌子 used it last time	上一次不是这个牌子 not used it last time
样本 Sample	177	18.1	69.5	12.4
玉兰油 Oil of Olay	16	6.3	81.3	12.5
芦荟 Luhui	14	21.4	71.4	7.1
花王碧柔 Biore	12	0.0	91.7	8.3
安安 An'an	10	20.0	70.0	10.0
小护士 Mininurse	9	44.4	55.6	0.0
高丝 Kose	7	14.3	85.7	0.0
可伶可俐 Clean & Clear	7	0.0	71.4	28.6

7-6 下一次打算使用的品牌排名/ Ranking of the Brands to be Used Next Time

排名 Brand Ranking	品牌 Brands	人数 Number	百分比 Percent
1	玉兰油 Oil of Olay	23	13.0
2	芦荟 Luhui	13	7.3
3	花王碧柔 Biore	12	6.8
4	安安 An'an	9	5.1
5	小护士 Mininurse	8	4.5
5	高丝 Kose	8	4.5
6	旁氏 Pond's	6	3.4
6	丁家宜 Dingjiayi	6	3.4
7	信芬 Synform	4	2.3
7	可伶可俐 Clean & Clear	4	2.3
7	大宝 Dabao	4	2.3
7	安利 Amway	4	2.3
8	羽西 Yue-sai	3	1.7
8	欧珀莱 Aupres	3	1.7
8	郑明明 Cheng Mingming	3	1.7

n=177

7-7 样本、男性各年龄层、女性各年龄层的使用频率/ Frequencies of the Consumed Facial Cleaner by the Whole Sample, Age and Gender Groups

	人数 Number	一天 3 次或以上 3 times or over a day	一天 1~2 次 once or twice a day	两三天用 1 次 once 2 or 3 days	一周 1~2 次 once or twice a week	半个月 1 次或以下 once half a month or below	没用过 never use
样本 Sample	598	0.8	23.6	2.3	1.7	1.2	70.4
男性 Male	296	0.3	7.1	1.7	0.0	0.0	90.9
16~24 岁 Age	62	0.0	11.3	4.8	0.0	0.0	83.9
25~34 岁 Age	89	0.0	9.0	0.0	0.0	0.0	91.0
35~44 岁 Age	75	1.3	6.7	1.3	0.0	0.0	90.7
45~54 岁 Age	46	0.0	2.2	2.2	0.0	0.0	95.7
55~60 岁 Age	24	0.0	0.0	0.0	0.0	0.0	100.0
女性 Female	302	1.3	39.7	3.0	3.3	2.3	50.3
16~24 岁 Age	64	3.1	59.4	4.7	6.3	1.6	25.0
25~34 岁 Age	90	0.0	45.6	2.2	5.6	4.4	42.2
35~44 岁 Age	76	2.6	38.2	3.9	0.0	1.3	53.9
45~54 岁 Age	48	0.0	18.8	2.1	2.1	2.1	75.0
55~60 岁 Age	24	0.0	12.5	0.0	0.0	0.0	87.5

7-8 选择该类商品的考虑因素/ Ranking of the Considerations in Purchasing

注：本题为多选题，合计百分比超过 100%（Multiple answers）

排名 Ranking	考虑因素 Considerations	人次 Person-time	百分比 Percent
1	产品功用 product function	94	53.1
2	价格适中 reasonable price	80	45.2
3	有名的牌子 famous brand	59	33.3
4	别人推荐 introduced by other people	46	26.0
5	广告影响 influence of advertising	27	15.3
6	购买方便 easy to buy	25	14.1
7	有优惠条件 with preferential terms	9	5.1
8	包装吸引人 appealing package	4	2.3
8	其它 others	4	2.3
9	单位发的 offered by the working unit	2	1.1

n=177

7-9 对产品功能的侧重方面/ Ranking of the Considerations about the Function of this Kind of Product

注：本题为多选题，合计百分比超过 100%（Multiple answers）

排名 Ranking	侧重方面 Items	人次 Person-time	百分比 Percent
1	适合自己的肤质 suitable to my skin	75	42.4
2	气味好 pleasant smell	67	37.9
3	洁净力强 powerful cleaning	62	35.0
3	洗后不紧绷 soft & elastic after bath	62	35.0
4	含滋润成分 containing nourishing ingredient	56	31.6
5	泡沫多 rich foam	33	18.6
6	含磨砂颗粒 with granites	16	9.0
6	含爽肤成分 containing skin cleaning ingredient	16	9.0
7	含果酸成分 containing tartaric acid	12	6.8
8	其他 others	3	1.7

n=177

7-10 重度消费者的人口分布/ Demographics of the Heavy Consumers

	人数 Number	16-24 岁 Age	25-34 岁 Age	35-44 岁 Age	45-54 岁 Age	55-60 岁 Age
样本 Sample	146	32.2	33.6	25.3	6.8	2.1
男性 Male	22	31.8	36.4	27.3	4.5	0.0
一天 3 次或以上 3 times or over a day	1	0.0	0.0	100.0	0.0	0.0
一天 1~2 次 once or twice a day	21	33.3	38.1	23.8	4.8	0.0
女性 Female	124	32.3	33.1	25.0	7.3	2.4
一天 3 次或以上 3 times or over a day	4	50.0	0.0	50.0	0.0	0.0
一天 1~2 次 once or twice a day	120	31.7	34.2	24.2	7.5	2.5

7-11 不同消费者层的常用品牌/ The Most Frequently Used Brands by Market Segments

7-11-1 时尚流行指标/ Fads Popular Index

	人数 Number	第一品牌及百分比 1st/ percent	第二品牌及百分比 2nd/ percent	第三品牌及百分比 3rd/ percent
样本 Sample	177	**芦荟 Luhui(9.6)**	**花王碧柔 Biore(7.3)** **玉兰油 Oil of Olay(7.3)**	**安安 An'an(6.2)**
平实生活指向 simple living orientation	64	芦荟 Luhui(12.5)	安安 An'an(9.4)	花王碧柔 Biore(7.8)
时尚流行指向 fashion orientation	113	玉兰油 Oil of Olay(8.8)	芦荟 Luhui(8.0)	花王碧柔 Biore(7.1)

7-11-2 广告态度指标/ Advertising Attitude Index

	人数 Number	第一品牌及百分比 1st/ percent	第二品牌及百分比 2nd/ percent	第三品牌及百分比 3rd/ percent
样本 Sample	177	**芦荟 Luhui(9.6)**	**花王碧柔 Biore(7.3)** **玉兰油 Oil of Olay(7.3)**	**安安 An'an(6.2)**
广告淡漠指向 indifferent orientation	41	安安 An'an(9.8) 芦荟 Luhui(9.8)	花王碧柔 Biore(7.3) 小护士 Mininurse(7.3)	高丝 Kose(4.9) 可伶可俐 Clean & Clear(4.9) 玉兰油 Oil of Olay(4.9)
中间层 medium	113	花王碧柔 Biore(8.8)	玉兰油 Oil of Olay(6.2) 小护士 Mininurse(6.2)	大宝 Dabao(5.3) 芦荟 Luhui(5.3)
信赖广告指向 loyal orientation	23	芦荟 Luhui(30.4)	玉兰油 Oil of Olay(17.4)	安安 An'an(8.7) 高丝 Kose(8.7)

7-12 重度消费者的消费层构成/ The Composition of the Heavy Consumers

7-12-1 时尚流行指标/ Fads Popular Index

	人数 Number	平实生活指向 simple living orientation	时尚流行指向 fashion orientation
样本 Sample	146	31.5	68.5
一天 3 次或以上 3 times or over a day	5	20.0	80.0
一天 1~2 次 once or twice a day	141	31.9	68.1

7-12-2 广告态度指标/ Advertising Attitude Index

	人数 Number	广告淡漠指向 indifferent orientation	中间层 medium	信赖广告指向 loyal orientation
样本 Sample	146	23.3	63.0	13.7
一天 3 次或以上 3 times or over a day	5	20.0	20.0	60.0
一天 1~2 次 once or twice a day	141	23.4	64.5	12.1

8.脸部润肤霜 / Skin-care Products

● 北京 / Beijing

8-1 最近三个月使用频次的比例/ Proportion of the Sample Consuming Skin-care Products in the Last Three Months

	人数 Number	百分比 Percent
一天 3 次或以上 3 times or over a day	65	6.5
一天 1~2 次 once or twice a day	511	51.5
两三天用 1 次 once 2 or 3 days	15	1.5
一周 1~2 次 once or twice a week	10	1.0
半个月 1 次或以下 once half a month or below	4	0.4
没用过 never use	388	39.1

n=993

8-2 最常用品牌排名/ Ranking of the Most Frequently Used Brands

排名 Brand Ranking	品牌 Brands	人数 Number	百分比 Percent
1	大宝 Dabao	194	32.2
2	玉兰油 Oil of Olay	56	9.3
3	旁氏 Pond's	29	4.8
4	小护士 Mininurse	26	4.3
4	郁美净 Yumeijing	26	4.3
5	高丝 Kose	17	2.8
5	欧珀莱 Aupres	17	2.8
6	东洋之花 Sakula	15	2.5
7	旁士凡士林 Vaseline	12	2.0
8	强生 Johnson&Johnson	11	1.8
9	宝贝 Baby	10	1.7
10	兰贵人 Languiren	9	1.5
10	花 Fa	9	1.5
11	资生堂 Shiseido	8	1.3

n=602

8-3 样本、男性各年龄层、女性各年龄层的常用品牌/ The Most Frequently Used Brands by the Whole Sample, Age and Gender Groups

	人数 Number	第一品牌及百分比 1st / percent	第二品牌及百分比 2nd / percent	第三品牌及百分比 3rd / percent
样本 Sample	602	**大宝 Dabao(32.2)**	**玉兰油 Oil of Olay(9.3)**	**旁氏 Pond's(4.8)**
男性 Male	175	**大宝 Dabao(55.4)**	**郁美净 Yumeijing(3.4)** **旁氏凡士林 Vaseline(3.4)**	**玉兰油 Oil of Olay(2.9)**
16~24 岁 Age	32	大宝 Dabao(50.0)	旁氏凡士林 Vaseline(6.3) 夏士莲 Hazeline(6.3)	柔迪 Roudi(3.1) 奥 C (3.1) 碧柔 Biore(3.1) 雅密 Yami(3.1) 安利 Amway(3.1) 郁美净 Yumeijing(3.1) 玉兰油 Oil of Olay(3.1) 倩碧 Clinique(3.1) 妮维雅 Nivea(3.1) 可伶可俐 Clean & Clear(3.1)
25~34 岁 Age	62	大宝 Dabao(66.1)	东洋之花 Sakula(3.2) 旁氏凡士林 Vaseline(3.2) 强生 Johnson&Johnson(3.2)	欧珀莱 Aupres(1.6) 蓝色 Blue(1.6) 美加净 Maxam(1.6) 资生堂 Shiseido(1.6) 郁美净 Yumeijing(1.6) 玉兰油 Oil of Olay(1.6) 珊拉娜 Samsara(1.6) 妮维雅 Nivea(1.6) 可伶可俐 Clean & Clear(1.6) 花 Fa(1.6) 高天 G.L.F.(1.6) 凤凰 Phoenix(1.6) 丹芭碧 Tobaby(1.6) 宝贝 Baby(1.6)
35~44 岁 Age	50	大宝 Dabao(54.0)	宝贝 Baby(4.0) 旁氏凡士林 Vaseline(4.0) 欧珀莱 Aupres(4.0) 旁氏 Pond's(4.0) 玉兰油 Oil of Olay(4.0) 郁美净 Yumeijing(4.0) 男士 Nanshi(4.0)	美加净 Maxam(2.0) 小护士 Mininurse(2.0) 夏士莲 Hazeline(2.0) 奥琪 Aoqi(2.0)
45~54 岁 Age	19	大宝 Dabao(31.6)	友谊 Youyi(15.8)	郁美净 Yumeijing(10.5)
55~60 岁 Age	12	大宝 Dabao(58.3)	强生 Johnson&Johnson(8.3) 友谊 Youyi(8.3)	
女性 Female	427	**大宝 Dabao(22.7)**	**玉兰油 Oil of Olay(11.9)**	**旁氏 Pond's(6.1)**
16~24 岁 Age	93	大宝 Dabao(20.4)	玉兰油 Oil of Olay(19.4)	小护士 Mininurse(12.9)
25~34 岁 Age	137	大宝 Dabao(15.3)	玉兰油 Oil of Olay(10.2)	旁氏 Pond's(8.8)
35~44 岁 Age	103	大宝 Dabao(20.4)	玉兰油 Oil of Olay(8.7)	旁氏 Pond's(5.8) 兰贵人 Languiren(5.8)
45~54 岁 Age	69	大宝 Dabao(34.8)	玉兰油 Oil of Olay(13.0)	郁美净 Yumeijing(5.8) 旁氏 Pond's(5.8)
55~60 岁 Age	25	大宝 Dabao(48.0)	郁美净 Yumeijing(8.0) 旁氏 Pond's(8.0)	仙姿 Xianzi(4.0) 嘉娜宝 Kanebo(4.0) 协和硅霜 Xiehe(4.0) 宝贝 Baby(4.0) 玉兰油 Oil of Olay(4.0) 友谊 Youyi(4.0) 凤凰 Phoenix(4.0) 旁氏凡士林 Vaseline(4.0)

8-4 正在使用的品牌排名/ Ranking of the Brands Used Now

排名 Brand Ranking	品牌 Brands	人数 Number	百分比 Percent
1	大宝 Dabao	181	30.1
2	玉兰油 Oil of Olay	61	10.1
3	郁美净 Yumeijing	26	4.3
4	小护士 Mininurse	22	3.7
5	欧珀莱 Aupres	19	3.2
5	旁氏 Pond's	19	3.2
6	东洋之花 Sakula	16	2.7
7	旁士凡士林 Vaseline	14	2.3
7	高丝 Kose	14	2.3
8	花 Fa	10	1.7
8	可伶可俐 Clean & Clear	10	1.7
8	宝贝 Baby	10	1.7
8	资生堂 Shiseido	10	1.7

n=602

8-5 品牌转换习惯/ Brand Habit in Consuming Skin-care Products

	人数 Number	第一次使用该品牌 first use this brand	上一次也是这个牌子 used it last time	上一次不是这个牌子 not used it last time
样本 Sample	599	13.5	74.3	12.2
大宝 Dabao	181	4.4	88.4	7.2
玉兰油 Oil of Olay	60	6.7	81.7	11.7
郁美净 Yumeijing	24	4.2	83.3	12.5
小护士 Mininurse	22	0.0	81.8	18.2
欧珀莱 Aupres	19	10.5	73.7	15.8
旁氏 Pond's	19	10.5	78.9	10.5
东洋之花 Sakula	16	43.8	37.5	18.8
旁士凡士林 Vaseline	14	7.1	85.7	7.1
高丝 Kose	14	14.3	64.3	21.4
花 Fa	10	20.0	80.0	0.0
可伶可俐 Clean & Clear	10	20.0	30.0	50.0
宝贝 Baby	10	0.0	90.0	10.0
资生堂 Shiseido	10	10.0	80.0	10.0

8-6 下一次打算使用的品牌排名/ Ranking of the Brands to be Used Next Time

排名 Brand Ranking	品牌 Brands	人数 Number	百分比 Percent
1	大宝 Dabao	168	27.9
2	玉兰油 Oil of Olay	70	11.6
3	旁氏 Pond's	27	4.5
4	小护士 Mininurse	23	3.8
5	郁美净 Yumeijing	22	3.7
6	欧珀莱 Aupres	19	3.2
7	东洋之花 Sakula	14	2.3
7	高丝 Kose	14	2.3
8	旁士凡士林 Vaseline	12	2.0
9	资生堂 Shiseido	10	1.7
9	兰贵人 Languiren	10	1.7

n=602

8-7 样本、男性各年龄层、女性各年龄层的使用频率/ Frequencies of the Consumed Skin-care Products by the Whole Sample, Age and Gender Groups

	人数 Number	一天 3 次或以上 3 times or over a day	一天 1~2 次 once or twice a day	两三天用 1 次 once 2 or 3 days	一周 1~2 次 once or twice a week	半个月 1 次或以下 once half a month or below	没用过 never use
样本 Sample	993	6.5	51.5	1.5	1.0	0.4	39.1
男性 Male	487	2.3	29.8	2.5	1.4	0.2	63.9
16~24 岁 Age	97	1.0	23.7	7.2	2.1	0.0	66.0
25~34 岁 Age	149	5.4	34.9	0.0	1.3	0.0	58.4
35~44 岁 Age	126	0.0	34.9	2.4	1.6	0.8	60.3
45~54 岁 Age	76	0.0	21.1	2.6	1.3	0.0	75.0
55~60 岁 Age	39	5.1	25.6	0.0	0.0	0.0	69.2
女性 Female	506	10.7	72.3	0.6	0.6	0.6	15.2
16~24 岁 Age	108	14.8	67.6	2.8	1.9	0.9	12.0
25~34 岁 Age	148	7.4	84.5	0.0	0.0	0.7	7.4
35~44 岁 Age	124	15.3	66.1	0.0	0.8	0.8	16.9
45~54 岁 Age	84	7.1	75.0	0.0	0.0	0.0	17.9
55~60 岁 Age	42	4.8	54.8	0.0	0.0	0.0	40.5

8-8 选择该类商品的考虑因素/ Ranking of the Considerations in Purchasing

注：本题为多选题，合计百分比超过 100%（Multiple answers）

排名 Ranking	考虑因素 Considerations	人次 Person-time	百分比 Percent
1	产品功用 product function	317	52.8
2	价格适中 reasonable price	256	42.7
3	有名的牌子 famous brand	234	39.0
4	广告影响 influence of advertising	107	17.8
5	别人推荐 introduced by other people	92	15.3
6	购买方便 easy to buy	71	11.8
7	有优惠条件 with preferential terms	25	4.2
8	包装吸引人 appealing package	13	2.2
9	其它 others	10	1.7
10	单位发的 offered by the working unit	6	1.0

n=600

8-9 对产品功能的侧重方面/ Ranking of the Considerations about the Function of this Kind of Product

注：本题为多选题，合计百分比超过 100%（Multiple answers）

排名 Ranking	侧重方面 Items	人次 Person-time	百分比 Percent
1	容易吸收 easy to dissolve	247	41.1
2	不油腻 not oil	235	39.1
3	适合自己的肤质 suitable to my skin	221	36.8
4	气味好 pleasant smell	197	32.8
5	保湿功能 keeping moisture	194	32.3
6	美白功能 beauty & white	87	14.5
7	防皱功能 wrinkle-preventing	61	10.1
8	纯天然制品 natural product	41	6.8
9	防晒功能 anti-UV	33	5.5
10	除痘功能 pimple-easing	22	3.7
11	药用功能 medicine-like effect	12	2.0
12	其他 others	5	0.8

n=601

8-10 重度消费者的人口分布/ Demographics of the Heavy Consumers

	人数 Number	16-24 岁 Age	25-34 岁 Age	35-44 岁 Age	45-54 岁 Age	55-60 岁 Age
样本 Sample	576	19.6	34.0	25.2	14.8	6.4
男性 Male	156	15.4	38.5	28.2	10.3	7.7
一天 3 次或以上 3 times or over a day	11	9.1	72.7	0.0	0.0	18.2
一天 1~2 次 once or twice a day	145	15.9	35.9	30.3	11.0	6.9
女性 Female	420	21.2	32.4	24.0	16.4	6.0
一天 3 次或以上 3 times or over a day	54	29.6	20.4	35.2	11.1	3.7
一天 1~2 次 once or twice a day	366	19.9	34.2	22.4	17.2	6.3

8-11 不同消费者层的常用品牌/ The Most Frequently Used Brands by Market Segments

8-11-1 时尚流行指标/ Fads Popular Index

	人数 Number	第一品牌及百分比 1st / percent	第二品牌及百分比 2nd / percent	第三品牌及百分比 3rd / percent	第四品牌及百分比 4th / percent
样本 Sample	594	**大宝 Dabao(32.2)**	**玉兰油 Oil of Olay(9.3)**	**旁氏 Pond's(4.9)**	**小护士 Mininurse(4.4)** **郁美净 Yumeijing(4.4)**
平实生活指向 simple living orientation	260	大宝 Dabao(41.5)	玉兰油 Oil of Olay(8.1)	旁氏 Pond's(5.0) 郁美净 Yumeijing(5.0)	花 Fa(2.3) 小护士 Mininurse(2.3)
时尚流行指向 fashion orientation	334	大宝 Dabao(24.9)	玉兰油 Oil of Olay(10.2)	小护士 Mininurse(6.0)	旁氏 Pond's(4.8)

8-11-2 广告态度指标/ Advertising Attitude Index

	人数 Number	第一品牌及百分比 1st / percent	第二品牌及百分比 2nd / percent	第三品牌及百分比 3rd / percent	第四品牌及百分比 4th / percent
样本 Sample	589	**大宝 Dabao(32.1)**	**玉兰油 Oil of Olay(9.3)**	**旁氏 Pond's(4.9)**	**小护士 Mininurse(4.4)**
广告淡漠指向 indifferent orientation	148	大宝 Dabao(37.2)	玉兰油 Oil of Olay(7.4)	郁美净 Yumeijing(4.1)	旁氏 Pond's(3.4) 东洋之花 Sakula(3.4)
中间层 medium	358	大宝 Dabao(31.3)	玉兰油 Oil of Olay(9.8)	旁氏 Pond's(4.7) 小护士 Mininurse(4.7)	郁美净 Yumeijing(3.9)
信赖广告指向 loyal orientation	83	大宝 Dabao(26.5)	玉兰油 Oil of Olay(10.8)	旁氏 Pond's(8.4) 小护士 Mininurse(8.4)	郁美净 Yumeijing(6.0)

8-12 重度消费者的消费层构成/ The Composition of the Heavy Consumers

8-12-1 时尚流行指标/ Fads Popular Index

	人数 Number	平实生活指向 simple living orientation	时尚流行指向 fashion orientation
样本 Sample	569	42.9	57.1
一天 3 次或以上 3 times or over a day	65	33.8	66.2
一天 1~2 次 once or twice a day	504	44.0	56.0

8-12-2 广告态度指标/ Advertising Attitude Index

	人数 Number	广告淡漠指向 indifferent orientation	中间层 medium	信赖广告指向 loyal orientation
样本 Sample	563	24.7	61.6	13.7
一天 3 次或以上 3 times or over a day	63	22.2	65.1	12.7
一天 1~2 次 once or twice a day	500	25.0	61.2	13.8

● 上海 / Shanghai

8-1 最近三个月使用频次的比例/ Proportion of the Sample Consuming Skin-care Products in the Last Three Months

	人数 Number	百分比 Percent
一天 3 次或以上 3 times or over a day	48	4.9
一天 1~2 次 once or twice a day	461	46.8
两三天用 1 次 once 2 or 3 days	15	1.5
一周 1~2 次 once or twice a week	8	0.8
半个月 1 次或以下 once half a month or below	5	0.5
没用过 never use	447	45.4

n=984

8-2 最常用品牌排名/ Ranking of the Most Frequently Used Brands

排名 Brand Ranking	品牌 Brands	人数 Number	百分比 Percent
1	旁氏 Pond's	73	13.6
2	玉兰油 Oil of Olay	60	11.2
3	美加净 Maxam	42	7.8
4	凡士林 Vaseline	37	6.9
4	夏士莲 Hazeline	37	6.9
5	强生 Johnson&Johnson	34	6.3
6	妮维雅 Nivea	26	4.9
7	大宝 Dabao	25	4.7
8	小护士 Mininurse	24	4.5
9	舒欣 Softsense	18	3.4
10	可蒙 Kemeng	10	1.9
10	可伶可俐 Clean & Clear	10	1.9

n=536

8-3 样本、男性各年龄层、女性各年龄层的常用品牌/ The Most Frequently Used Brands by the Whole Sample, Age and Gender Groups

	人数 Number	第一品牌及百分比 1st / percent	第二品牌及百分比 2nd / percent	第三品牌及百分比 3rd / percent
样本 Sample	536	**旁氏 Pond's(13.6)**	**玉兰油 Oil of Olay(11.2)**	**美加净 Maxam(7.8)**
男性 Male	153	**旁氏 Pond's(15.0)**	**大宝 Dabao(11.1)** **凡士林 Vaseline(11.1)**	**美加净 Maxam(7.2)** **妮维雅 Nivea(7.2)**
16~24 岁 Age	32	大宝 Dabao(18.8)	凡士林 Vaseline(15.6) 旁氏 Pond's(15.6)	可伶可俐 Clean & Clear(6.3) 妮维雅 Nivea(6.3) 牡丹雪花膏 Mudan(6.3) 夏士莲 Hazeline(6.3)
25~34 岁 Age	55	旁氏 Pond's(12.7)	强生 Johnson&Johnson(10.9)	大宝 Dabao(9.1) 凡士林 Vaseline(9.1) 妮维雅 Nivea(9.1) 玉兰油 Oil of Olay(9.1)
35~44 岁 Age	32	旁氏 Pond's(18.8)	大宝 Dabao(12.5) 凡士林 Vaseline(12.5) 夏士莲 Hazeline(12.5)	美加净 Maxam(6.3)
45~54 岁 Age	24	美加净 Maxam(20.8)	旁氏 Pond's(16.7)	妮维雅 Nivea(12.5)
55~60 岁 Age	10	百雀灵 Baiqueling(10.0) 大宝 Dabao(10.0) 凡士林 Vaseline(10.0) 可蒙 Kemeng(10.0) 旁氏 Pond's(10.0) 倩碧 Clinique(10.0) 强生 Johnson&Johnson(10.0) 永芳 Yinfong(10.0) 雅密 Yami(10.0) 美加净 Maxam(10.0)		
女性 Female	383	**玉兰油 Oil of Olay(13.3)**	**旁氏 Pond's(13.1)**	**美加净 Maxam(8.1)**
16~24 岁 Age	91	强生 Johnson&Johnson(13.2)	玉兰油 Oil of Olay(11.0)	旁氏 Pond's(9.9)
25~34 岁 Age	122	旁氏 Pond's(13.9)	玉兰油 Oil of Olay(13.1)	夏士莲 Hazeline(8.2)
35~44 岁 Age	92	旁氏 Pond's(16.3)	玉兰油 Oil of Olay(14.1)	美加净 Maxam(10.9)
45~54 岁 Age	51	玉兰油 Oil of Olay(19.6)	旁氏 Pond's(11.8)	凡士林 Vaseline(7.8) 妮维雅 Nivea(7.8) 夏士莲 Hazeline(7.8)
55~60 岁 Age	27	美加净 Maxam(14.8)	旁氏 Pond's(11.1)	玉兰油 Oil of Olay(7.4) 凡士林 Vaseline(7.4) 凤凰 Phoenix(7.4) 强生 Johnson&Johnson(7.4) 小护士 Mininurse(7.4)

8-4 正在使用的品牌排名/ Ranking of the Brands Used Now

排名 Brand Ranking	品牌 Brands	人数 Number	百分比 Percent
1	旁氏 Pond's	67	12.5
2	玉兰油 Oil of Olay	55	10.3
3	夏士莲 Hazeline	39	7.3
4	美加净 Maxam	37	6.9
5	凡士林 Vaseline	35	6.5
6	强生 Johnson&Johnson	32	6.0
7	妮维雅 Nivea	29	5.4
8	小护士 Mininurse	26	4.9
9	大宝 Dabao	22	4.1
10	舒欣 Softsense	19	3.5
11	东洋之花 Sakula	13	2.4
12	可伶可俐 Clean & Clear	11	2.1

n=536

8-5 品牌转换习惯/ Brand Habit in Consuming Skin-care Products

	人数 Number	第一次使用该品牌 first use this brand	上一次也是这个牌子 used it last time	上一次不是这个牌子 not used it last time
样本 Sample	**534**	**12.2**	**75.1**	**12.7**
旁氏 Pond's	67	9.0	70.1	20.9
玉兰油 Oil of Olay	55	9.1	78.2	12.7
夏士莲 Hazeline	39	12.8	71.8	15.4
美加净 Maxam	37	13.5	81.1	5.4
凡士林 Vaseline	34	5.9	88.2	5.9
强生 Johnson&Johnson	31	12.9	83.9	3.2
妮维雅 Nivea	29	6.9	82.8	10.3
小护士 Mininurse	26	26.9	53.8	19.2
大宝 Dabao	22	22.7	68.2	9.1
舒欣 Softsense	19	0.0	84.2	15.8
东洋之花 Sakula	13	30.8	69.2	0.0

8-6 下一次打算使用的品牌排名/ Ranking of the Brands to be Used Next Time

排名 Brand Ranking	品牌 Brands	人数 Number	百分比 Percent
1	旁氏 Pond's	77	14.4
2	玉兰油 Oil of Olay	70	13.1
3	美加净 Maxam	35	6.5
4	夏士莲 Hazeline	34	6.3
5	凡士林 Vaseline	32	6.0
6	强生 Johnson&Johnson	31	5.8
7	大宝 Dabao	27	5.0
8	小护士 Mininurse	26	4.9
9	妮维雅 Nivea	23	4.3
10	东洋之花 Sakula	12	2.2
10	资生堂 Shiseido	12	2.2
11	清妃 Chinf	11	2.1
11	舒欣 Softsense	11	2.1

n=536

8-7 样本、男性各年龄层、女性各年龄层的使用频率/ Frequencies of the Consumed Skin-care Products by the Whole Sample, Age and Gender Groups

	人数 Number	一天 3 次或以上 3 times or over a day	一天 1~2 次 once or twice a day	两三天用 1 次 once 2 or 3 days	一周 1~2 次 once or twice a week	半个月 1 次或以下 once half a month or below	没用过 never use
样本 Sample	**984**	**4.9**	**46.8**	**1.5**	**0.8**	**0.5**	**45.4**
男性 Male	**485**	**2.5**	**26.2**	**1.2**	**1.2**	**0.4**	**68.5**
16~24 岁 Age	105	1.0	25.7	1.0	2.9	0.0	69.5
25~34 岁 Age	140	5.0	30.0	2.1	1.4	0.7	60.7
35~44 岁 Age	128	1.6	21.9	0.8	0.8	0.0	75.0
45~54 岁 Age	79	2.5	25.3	1.3	0.0	1.3	69.6
55~60 岁 Age	33	0.0	30.3	0.0	0.0	0.0	69.7
女性 Female	**499**	**7.2**	**66.9**	**1.8**	**0.4**	**0.6**	**23.0**
16~24 岁 Age	107	9.3	69.2	4.7	0.0	1.9	15.0
25~34 岁 Age	143	7.7	76.2	0.7	0.0	0.7	14.7
35~44 岁 Age	129	6.2	62.0	2.3	1.6	0.0	27.9
45~54 岁 Age	81	6.2	56.8	0.0	0.0	0.0	37.0
55~60 岁 Age	39	5.1	64.1	0.0	0.0	0.0	30.8

8-8 选择该类商品的考虑因素/ Ranking of the Considerations in Purchasing

注：本题为多选题，合计百分比超过 100%（Multiple answers）

排名 Ranking	考虑因素 Considerations	人次 Person-time	百分比 Percent
1	产品功用 product function	249	46.5
2	有名的牌子 famous brand	218	40.7
3	价格适中 reasonable price	204	38.1
4	广告影响 influence of advertising	105	19.6
5	购买方便 easy to buy	86	16.1
6	别人推荐 introduced by other people	61	11.4
7	单位发的 offered by the working unit	23	4.3
8	有优惠条件 with preferential terms	22	4.1
9	包装吸引人 appealing package	17	3.2
10	其它 others	10	1.9

n=535

8-9 对产品功能的侧重方面/ Ranking of the Considerations about the Function of this Kind of Product

注：本题为多选题，合计百分比超过 100%（Multiple answers）

排名 Ranking	侧重方面 Items	人次 Person-time	百分比 Percent
1	容易吸收 easy to dissolve	216	40.4
2	不油腻 not oil	204	38.2
3	适合自己的肤质 suitable to my skin	183	34.3
4	气味好 pleasant smell	180	33.7
5	保湿功能 keeping moisture	132	24.7
6	美白功能 beauty & white	99	18.5
7	防皱功能 wrinkle-preventing	43	8.1
8	纯天然制品 natural product	34	6.4
9	防晒功能 anti-UV	28	5.2
10	除痘功能 pimple-easing	18	3.4
11	药用功能 medicine-like effect	9	1.7
12	其他 others	4	0.7

n=534

8-10 重度消费者的人口分布/ Demographics of the Heavy Consumers

	人数 Number	16-24 岁 Age	25-34 岁 Age	35-44 岁 Age	45-54 岁 Age	55-60 岁 Age
样本 Sample	509	22.0	33.2	23.2	14.3	7.3
男性 Male	139	20.1	35.3	21.5	15.8	7.2
一天 3 次或以上 3 times or over a day	12	8.3	58.3	16.7	16.7	0.0
一天 1~2 次 once or twice a day	127	21.3	33.1	22.0	15.7	7.9
女性 Female	370	22.7	32.4	23 8	13.8	7.3
一天 3 次或以上 3 times or over a day	36	27.8	30.6	22 2	13.9	5.6
一天 1~2 次 once or twice a day	334	22.2	32.6	24.0	13.8	7.5

8-11 不同消费者层的常用品牌/ The Most Frequently Used Brands by Market Segments

8-11-1 时尚流行指标/ Fads Popular Index

	人数 Number	第一品牌及百分比 1st / percent	第二品牌及百分比 2nd / percent	第三品牌及百分比 3rd / percent
样本 Sample	532	**旁氏 Pond's(13.7)**	**玉兰油 Oil of Olay(11.3)**	**美加净 Maxam(7.7)**
平实生活指向 simple living orientation	216	旁氏 Pond's(15.7)	凡士林 Vaseline(11.6)	玉兰油 Oil of Olay(10.6)
时尚流行指向 fashion orientation	316	旁氏 Pond's(12.3)	玉兰油 Oil of Olay(11.7)	美加净 Maxam(7.9)

8-11-2 广告态度指标/ Advertising Attitude Index

	人数 Number	第一品牌及百分比 1st / percent	第二品牌及百分比 2nd / percent	第三品牌及百分比 3rd / percent
样本 Sample	532	**旁氏 Pond's(13.5)**	**玉兰油 Oil of Olay(11.1)**	**美加净 Maxam(7.7)**
广告淡漠指向 indifferent orientation	123	旁氏 Pond's(11.4) 凡士林 Vaseline(11.4)	强生 Johnson&Johnson(10.6)	妮维雅 Nivea(8.1)
中间层 medium	327	旁氏 Pond's(14.4)	玉兰油 Oil of Olay(11.9)	美加净 Maxam(8.0)
信赖广告指向 loyal orientation	82	玉兰油 Oil of Olay(18.3)	旁氏 Pond's(13.4)	小护士 Mininurse(9.8)

8-12 重度消费者的消费层构成/ The Composition of the Heavy Consumers

8-12-1 时尚流行指标/ Fads Popular Index

	人数 Number	平实生活指向 simple living orientation	时尚流行指向 fashion orientation
样本 Sample	505	41.0	59.0
一天 3 次或以上 3 times or over a day	48	35.4	64.6
一天 1~2 次 once or twice a day	457	41.6	58.4

8-12-2 广告态度指标/ Advertising Attitude Index

	人数 Number	广告淡漠指向 indifferent orientation	中间层 medium	信赖广告指向 loyal orientation
样本 Sample	505	23.0	61.4	15.6
一天 3 次或以上 3 times or over a day	48	22.9	54.2	22.9
一天 1~2 次 once or twice a day	457	23.0	62.1	14.9

● 广州 / Guangzhou

8-1 最近三个月使用频次的比例/ Proportion of the Sample Consuming Skin-care Products in the Last Three Months

	人数 Number	百分比 Percent
一天 3 次或以上 3 times or over a day	53	5.3
一天 1~2 次 once or twice a day	370	37.3
两三天用 1 次 once 2 or 3 days	44	4.4
一周 1~2 次 once or twice a week	17	1.7
半个月 1 次或以下 once half a month or below	12	1.2
没用过 never use	496	50.0

n=992

8-2 最常用品牌排名/ Ranking of the Most Frequently Used Brands

排名 Brand Ranking	品牌 Brands	人数 Number	百分比 Percent
1	玉兰油 Oil of Olay	116	23.4
2	七日香 Qirixiang	53	10.7
3	强生 Johnson&Johnson	48	9.7
4	旁氏 Pond's	39	7.9
5	夏士莲 Hazeline	27	5.4
6	小护士 Mininurse	18	3.6
7	雅芳 Avon	15	3.0
8	碧柔歌婷 Qualite	12	2.4
8	美加净 Maxam	12	2.4
9	永芳 Yinfong	8	1.6
9	人参雪花膏 Renshen	8	1.6
10	凡士林 Vaseline	7	1.4

n=496

8-3 样本、男性各年龄层、女性各年龄层的常用品牌/ The Most Frequently Used Brands by the Whole Sample, Age and Gender Groups

	人数 Number	第一品牌及百分比 1st / percent	第二品牌及百分比 2nd / percent	第三品牌及百分比 3rd / percent
样本 Sample	496	**玉兰油 Oil of Olay(23.4)**	**七日香 Qirixiang(10.7)**	**强生 Johnson&Johnson(9.7)**
男性 Male	118	**玉兰油 Oil of Olay(23.7)**	**七日香 Qirixiang(14.4)**	**强生 Johnson&Johnson(8.5)**
16~24 岁 Age	14	强生 Johnson&Johnson(21.4) 玉兰油 Oil of Olay(21.4)	大宝 Dabao(7.1) 可伶可俐 Clean & Clear(7.1) 夏士莲 Hazeline(7.1) 小护士 Mininurse(7.1) 美加净 Maxam(7.1) JOHISON(7.1)	
25~34 岁 Age	38	玉兰油 Oil of Olay(31.6)	旁氏 Pond's(13.2)	七日香 Qirixiang(5.3) 强生 Johnson&Johnson(5.3) 夏士莲 Hazeline(5.3) 永芳 Yinfong(5.3)
35~44 岁 Age	38	玉兰油 Oil of Olay(23.7)	七日香 Qirixiang(18.4)	强生 Johnson&Johnson(10.5)
45~54 岁 Age	20	玉兰油 Oil of Olay(20.0)	旁氏 Pond's(15.0) 七日香 Qirixiang(15.0)	永芳 Yinfong(10.0) 人参雪花膏 Renshen(10.0)
55~60 岁 Age	8	七日香 Qirixiang(62.5)	碧柔歌婷 Qualite(12.5) 旁氏 Pond's(12.5) 绿之韵 Lvzhiyun(12.5)	
女性 Female	378	**玉兰油 Oil of Olay(23.3)**	**强生 Johnson&Johnson(10.1)**	**七日香 Qirixiang(9.5)**
16~24 岁 Age	94	玉兰油 Oil of Olay(24.5)	强生 Johnson&Johnson(16.0)	七日香 Qirixiang(7.4)
25~34 岁 Age	123	玉兰油 Oil of Olay(29.3)	旁氏 Pond's(8.1)	强生 Johnson&Johnson(6.5)
35~44 岁 Age	98	玉兰油 Oil of Olay(18.4)	强生 Johnson&Johnson(13.3) 七日香 Qirixiang(13.3)	旁氏 Pond's(9.2)
45~54 岁 Age	48	七日香 Qirixiang(20.8)	玉兰油 Oil of Olay(16.7)	旁氏 Pond's(8.3)
55~60 岁 Age	15	夏士莲 Hazeline(26.7)	七日香 Qirixiang(20.0) 玉兰油 Oil of Olay(20.0)	花 Fa(6.7) 旁氏 Pond's(6.7) 强生 Johnson&Johnson(6.7) 雅芳 Avon(6.7) 雅密 Yami(6.7)

8-4 正在使用的品牌排名/ Ranking of the Brands Used Now

排名 Brand Ranking	品牌 Brands	人数 Number	百分比 Percent
1	玉兰油 Oil of Olay	119	24.0
2	七日香 Qirixiang	48	9.7
3	强生 Johnson&Johnson	46	9.3
4	旁氏 Pond's	36	7.3
5	夏士莲 Hazeline	27	5.4
6	小护士 Mininurse	20	4.0
7	雅芳 Avon	14	2.8
8	美加净 Maxam	12	2.4
9	碧柔歌婷 Qualite	10	2.0
9	永芳 Yinfong	10	2.0
10	凡士林 Vaseline	9	1.8

n=496

8-5 品牌转换习惯/ Brand Habit in Consuming Skin-care Products

	人数 Number	第一次使用该品牌 first use this brand	上一次也是这个牌子 used it last time	上一次不是这个牌子 not used it last time
样本 Sample	492	11.2	73.0	15.9
玉兰油 Oil of Olay	118	7.6	72.9	19.5
七日香 Qirixiang	48	6.3	87.5	6.3
强生 Johnson&Johnson	46	8.7	76.1	15.2
旁氏 Pond's	35	2.9	77.1	20.0
夏士莲 Hazeline	27	3.7	77.8	18.5
小护士 Mininurse	20	15.0	70.0	15.0
雅芳 Avon	14	28.6	64.3	7.1
美加净 Maxam	12	8.3	75.0	16.7
碧柔歌婷 Qualite	10	10.0	80.0	10.0
永芳 Yinfong	10	0.0	80.0	20.0

8-6 下一次打算使用的品牌排名/ Ranking of the Brands to be Used Next Time

排名 Brand Ranking	品牌 Brands	人数 Number	百分比 Percent
1	玉兰油 Oil of Olay	130	26.3
2	七日香 Qirixiang	43	8.7
3	强生 Johnson&Johnson	39	7.9
4	旁氏 Pond's	32	6.5
5	夏士莲 Hazeline	26	5.3
6	小护士 Mininurse	23	4.6
7	碧柔歌婷 Qualite	15	3.0
8	美加净 Maxam	11	2.2

n=495

8-7 样本、男性各年龄层、女性各年龄层的使用频率/ Frequencies of the Consumed Skin-care Products by the Whole Sample, Age and Gender Groups

	人数 Number	一天 3 次或以上 3 times or over a day	一天 1~2 次 once or twice a day	两三天用 1 次 once 2 or 3 days	一周 1~2 次 once or twice a week	半个月 1 次或以下 once half a month or below	没用过 never use
样本 Sample	992	5.3	37.3	4.4	1.7	1.2	50.0
男性 Male	478	1.9	14.2	4.4	2.1	2.1	75.3
16~24 岁 Age	103	1.0	5.8	2.9	1.9	1.9	86.4
25~34 岁 Age	145	1.4	13.8	4.8	2.8	3.4	73.8
35~44 岁 Age	121	3.3	19.0	5.0	2.5	1.7	68.6
45~54 岁 Age	69	1.4	18.8	5.8	1.4	1.4	71.0
55~60 岁 Age	40	2.5	15.0	2.5	0.0	0.0	80.0
女性 Female	514	8.6	58.8	4.5	1.4	0.4	26.5
16~24 岁 Age	107	15.0	68.2	3.7	0.9	0.0	12.1
25~34 岁 Age	155	9.7	63.2	4.5	1.9	0.0	20.6
35~44 岁 Age	129	4.7	62.8	7.0	0.8	0.8	24.0
45~54 岁 Age	83	4.8	47.0	3.6	2.4	0.0	42.2
55~60 岁 Age	40	7.5	27.5	0.0	0.0	2.5	62.5

8-8 选择该类商品的考虑因素/ Ranking of the Considerations in Purchasing

注：本题为多选题，合计百分比超过 100%（Multiple answers）

排名 Ranking	考虑因素 Considerations	人次 Person-time	百分比 Percent
1	产品功用 product function	261	52.7
2	有名的牌子 famous brand	226	45.7
3	价格适中 reasonable price	193	39.0
4	广告影响 influence of advertising	83	16.8
5	别人推荐 introduced by other people	75	15.2
6	购买方便 easy to buy	59	11.9
7	有优惠条件 with preferential terms	22	4.4
8	包装吸引人 appealing package	15	3.0
9	其它 others	10	2.0
10	单位发的 offered by the working unit	9	1.8

n=495

8-9 对产品功能的侧重方面/ Ranking of the Considerations about the Function of this Kind of Product

注：本题为多选题，合计百分比超过 100%（Multiple answers）

排名 Ranking	侧重方面 Items	人次 Person-time	百分比 Percent
1	气味好 pleasant smell	175	35.5
2	适合自己的肤质 suitable to my skin	171	34.7
3	不油腻 not oil	167	33.9
4	容易吸收 easy to dissolve	165	33.5
5	保湿功能 keeping moisture	144	29.2
6	美白功能 beauty & white	128	26.0
7	防皱功能 wrinkle-preventing	70	14.2
8	纯天然制品 natural product	29	5.9
9	除痘功能 pimple-easing	28	5.7
10	防晒功能 anti-UV	27	5.5
11	药用功能 medicine-like effect	13	2.6
12	其他 others	3	0.6

n=493

8-10 重度消费者的人口分布/ Demographics of the Heavy Consumers

	人数 Number	16-24 岁 Age	25-34 岁 Age	35-44 岁 Age	45-54 岁 Age	55-60 岁 Age
样本 Sample	423	22.7	31.9	27.0	13.5	5.0
男性 Male	77	9.1	28.6	35.1	18.2	9.1
一天 3 次或以上 3 times or over a day	9	11.1	22.2	44.4	11.1	11.1
一天 1~2 次 once or twice a day	68	8.8	29.4	33.8	19.1	8.8
女性 Female	346	25.7	32.7	25.1	12.4	4.0
一天 3 次或以上 3 times or over a day	44	36.4	34.1	13.6	9.1	6.8
一天 1~2 次 once or twice a day	302	24.2	32.5	26.8	12.9	3.6

8-11 不同消费者层的常用品牌/ The Most Frequently Used Brands by Market Segments

8-11-1 时尚流行指标/ Fads Popular Index

	人数 Number	第一品牌及百分比 1st/ percent	第二品牌及百分比 2nd/ percent	第三品牌及百分比 3rd/ percent	第四品牌及百分比 4th/ percent
样本 Sample	489	玉兰油 Oil of Olay(23.5)	七日香 Qirixiang(10.6)	强生 Johnson&Johnson(9.6)	旁氏 Pond's(8.0)
平实生活指向 simple living orientation	212	玉兰油 Oil of Olay(20.8)	七日香 Qirixiang(17.9)	强生 Johnson&Johnson(7.5)	夏士莲 Hazeline(6.6)
时尚流行指向 fashion orientation	277	玉兰油 Oil of Olay(25.6)	强生 Johnson&Johnson(11.2)	旁氏 Pond's(9.7)	七日香 Qirixiang(5.1)

8-11-2 广告态度指标/ Advertising Attitude Index

	人数 Number	第一品牌及百分比 1st / percent	第二品牌及百分比 2nd / percent	第三品牌及百分比 3rd / percent	第四品牌及百分比 4th / percent
样本 Sample	489	玉兰油 Oil of Olay(23.3)	七日香 Qirixiang(10.8)	强生 Johnson&Johnson(9.8)	旁氏 Pond's(7.8)
广告淡漠指向 indifferent orientation	135	玉兰油 Oil of Olay(19.3)	强生 Johnson&Johnson(9.6) 七日香 Qirixiang(9.6)	旁氏 Pond's(4.4) 雅芳 Avon(4.4) 夏士莲 Hazeline(4.4)	美加净 Maxam(3.7)
中间层 medium	307	玉兰油 Oil of Olay(24.8)	七日香 Qirixiang(12.1)	强生 Johnson&Johnson(10.7)	旁氏 Pond's(9.1)
信赖广告指向 loyal orientation	47	玉兰油 Oil of Olay(25.5)	小护士 Mininurse(8.5) 旁氏 Pond's(8.5)	七日香 Qirixiang(6.4)	夏士莲 Hazeline(4.3) 雅芳 Avon(4.3) 强生 Johnson&Johnson(4.3) 碧柔歌婷 Qualite (4.3)

8-12 重度消费者的消费层构成/ The Composition of the Heavy Consumers

8-12-1 时尚流行指标/ Fads Popular Index

	人数 Number	平实生活指向 simple living orientation	时尚流行指向 fashion orientation
样本 Sample	417	43.2	56.8
一天 3 次或以上 3 times or over a day	53	34.0	66.0
一天 1~2 次 once or twice a day	364	44.5	55.5

8-12-2 广告态度指标/ Advertising Attitude Index

	人数 Number	广告淡漠指向 indifferent orientation	中间层 medium	信赖广告指向 loyal orientation
样本 Sample	417	27.1	63.5	9.4
一天 3 次或以上 3 times or over a day	52	32.7	53.8	13.5
一天 1~2 次 once or twice a day	365	26.3	64.9	8.8

● 重庆 / Chongqing

8-1 最近三个月使用频次的比例/ Proportion of the Sample Consuming Skin-care Products in the Last Three Months

	人数 Number	百分比 Percent
一天 3 次或以上 3 times or over a day	7	1.1
一天 1~2 次 once or twice a day	198	31.9
两三天用 1 次 once 2 or 3 days	15	2.4
一周 1~2 次 once or twice a week	5	0.8
半个月 1 次或以下 once half a month or below	4	0.6
没用过 never use	392	63.1

n=621

8-2 最常用品牌排名/ Ranking of the Most Frequently Used Brands

排名 Brand Ranking	品牌 Brands	人数 Number	百分比 Percent
1	大宝 Dabao	41	17.9
2	玉兰油 Oil of Olay	35	15.3
3	郁美净 Yumeijing	24	10.5
4	小护士 Mininurse	14	6.1
5	夏士莲 Hazeline	12	5.2
6	旁氏 Pond's	11	4.8
7	美加净 Maxam	7	3.1
8	雅倩 Arche	6	2.6
8	雅芳 Avon	6	2.6
9	宝宝霜 Baobaoshuang	5	2.2
10	春娟 Chunjuan	4	1.7
10	蝴蝶柠檬霜 Hu Die Ning Meng Shuang	4	1.7

n=229

8-3 样本、男性各年龄层、女性各年龄层的常用品牌/ The Most Frequently Used Brands by the Whole Sample, Age and Gender Groups

	人数 Number	第一品牌及百分比 1st/ percent	第二品牌及百分比 2nd/ percent	第三品牌及百分比 3rd/ percent
样本 Sample	**229**	**大宝 Dabao(17.9)**	**玉兰油 Oil of Olay(15.3)**	**郁美净 Yumeijing(10.5)**
男性 Male	**37**	**大宝 Dabao(40.5)**	**郁美净 Yumeijing(13.5)**	**玉兰油 Oil of Olay(8.1)**
16~24 岁 Age	8	大宝 Dabao(37.5)	玉兰油 Oil of Olay(25.0) 郁美净 Yumeijing(25.0)	小护士 Mininurse(12.5)
25~34 岁 Age	11	大宝 Dabao(45.5)	郁美净 Yumeijing(18.2)	旁氏 Pond's(9.1) 夏士莲 Hazeline(9.1) 雅霜 Yashuang(9.1)
35~44 岁 Age	8	大宝 Dabao(50.0)	雅芳 Avon(12.5) 玉兰油 Oil of Olay(12.5) 郁美净 Yumeijing(12.5) 蝴蝶柠檬霜 Hu Die Ning Meng Shuang(12.5)	
45~54 岁 Age	7	百雀灵 Baiqueling(14.3) 大宝 Dabao(14.3) 丹芭碧 Tobaby(14.3) 夏士莲 Hazeline(14.3) 春娟 Chunjian(14.3) 宝宝霜 Baobaoshuang(14.3) 邦氏 Bangshi(14.3)		
55~60 岁 Age	3	大宝 Dabao(66.7)	东洋之花 Sakula(33.3)	
女性 Female	**192**	**玉兰油 Oil of Olay(16.7)**	**大宝 Dabao(13.5)**	**郁美净 Yumeijing(9.9)**
16~24 岁 Age	49	玉兰油 Oil of Olay(20.4)	夏士莲 Hazeline(12.2)	小护士 Mininurse(10.2)
25~34 岁 Age	60	玉兰油 Oil of Olay(21.7)	大宝 Dabao(11.7)	夏士莲 Hazeline(6.7) 郁美净 Yumeijing(6.7)
35~44 岁 Age	42	玉兰油 Oil of Olay(21.4)	大宝 Dabao(16.7)	郁美净 Yumeijing(7.1)
45~54 岁 Age	36	郁美净 Yumeijing(19.4) 大宝 Dabao(19.4)	美加净 Maxam(11.1) 小护士 Mininurse(11.1)	旁氏 Pond's(5.6) 雅倩 Arche(5.6)
55~60 岁 Age	5	大宝 Dabao(20.0) 旁氏 Pond's(20.0) 郁美净 Yumeijing(20.0) 宝宝霜 Baobaoshuang (20.0)		

8-4 正在使用的品牌排名/ Ranking of the Brand Used Now

排名 Brand Ranking	品牌 Brands	人数 Number	百分比 Percent
1	大宝 Dabao	37	16.2
2	玉兰油 Oil of Olay	36	15.8
3	郁美净 Yumeijing	23	10.1
4	小护士 Mininurse	16	7.0
5	旁氏 Pond's	12	5.3
6	美加净 Maxam	7	3.1
7	夏士莲 Hazeline	6	2.6
8	宝宝霜 Baobaoshuang	5	2.2
8	蝴蝶柠檬霜 Hu Die Ning Meng Shuang	5	2.2
8	雅芳 Avon	5	2.2

n=228

8-5 品牌转换习惯/ Brand Habit in Consuming Skin-care Products

	人数 Number	第一次使用该品牌 first use this brand	上一次也是这个牌子 used it last time	上一次不是这个牌子 not used it last time
样本 Sample	226	16.8	70.8	12.4
大宝 Dabao	37	8.1	81.1	10.8
玉兰油 Oil of Olay	35	17.1	71.4	11.4
郁美净 Yumeijing	23	4.3	87.0	8.7
小护士 Mininurse	16	18.8	75.0	6.3
旁氏 Pond's	12	25.0	75.0	0.0
美加净 Maxam	7	0.0	85.7	14.3
夏士莲 Hazeline	6	0.0	83.3	16.7
蝴蝶柠檬霜 Hu Die Ning Meng Shuang	5	0.0	80.0	20.0
宝宝霜 Baobaoshuang	5	0.0	100.0	0.0
雅倩 Arche	5	20.0	60.0	20.0
雅芳 Avon	5	0.0	100.0	0.0

8-6 下一次打算使用的品牌排名/ Ranking of the Brands to be Used Next Time

排名 Brand Ranking	品牌 Brands	人数 Number	百分比 Percent
1	玉兰油 Oil of Olay	52	22.7
2	大宝 Dabao	37	16.2
3	郁美净 Yumeijing	21	9.2
4	旁氏 Pond's	16	7.0
5	小护士 Mininurse	11	4.8
6	夏士莲 Hazeline	8	3.5
6	美加净 Maxam	8	3.5
7	丁家宜 Dingjiayi	6	2.6
7	雅芳 Avon	6	2.6
8	雅倩 Arche	5	2.2

n=229

8-7 样本、男性各年龄层、女性各年龄层的使用频率/ Frequencies of the Consumed Skin-care Products by the Whole Sample, Age and Gender Groups

	人数 Number	一天3次或以上 3 times or over a day	一天1~2次 once or twice a day	两三天用1次 once 2 or 3 days	一周1~2次 once or twice a week	半个月1次或以下 once half a month or below	没用过 never use
样本 Sample	621	1.1	31.9	2.4	0.8	0.6	63.1
男性 Male	312	0.3	8.3	1.0	1.6	0.6	88.1
16~24 岁 Age	63	0.0	9.5	1.6	1.6	0.0	87.3
25~34 岁 Age	93	0.0	7.5	1.1	2.2	1.1	88.2
35~44 岁 Age	74	0.0	9.5	0.0	0.0	1.4	89.2
45~54 岁 Age	54	1.9	7.4	1.9	1.9	0.0	87.0
55~60 岁 Age	28	0.0	7.1	0.0	3.6	0.0	89.3
女性 Female	309	1.9	55.7	3.9	0.0	0.6	37.9
16~24 岁 Age	64	6.3	64.1	6.3	0.0	0.0	23.4
25~34 岁 Age	89	0.0	65.2	1.1	0.0	1.1	32.6
35~44 岁 Age	73	1.4	53.4	2.7	0.0	0.0	42.5
45~54 岁 Age	60	1.7	50.0	6.7	0.0	1.7	40.0
55~60 岁 Age	23	0.0	17.4	4.3	0.0	0.0	78.3

8-8 选择该类商品的考虑因素/ Ranking of the Considerations in Purchasing

注：本题为多选题，合计百分比超过 100%（Multiple answers）

排名 Ranking	考虑因素 Considerations	人次 Person-time	百分比 Percent
1	产品功用 product function	123	54.2
2	价格适中 reasonable price	89	39.2
3	有名的牌子 famous brand	76	33.5
4	广告影响 influence of advertising	57	25.1
5	别人推荐 introduced by other people	36	15.9
6	购买方便 easy to buy	16	7.0
7	有优惠条件 with preferential terms	9	4.0
8	包装吸引人 appealing package	6	2.6
9	其它 others	2	0.9
10	单位发的 offered by the working unit	1	0.4

n=227

8-9 对产品功能的侧重方面/ Ranking of the Considerations about the Function of this Kind of Product

注：本题为多选题，合计百分比超过 100%（Multiple answers）

排名 Ranking	侧重方面 Items	人次 Person-time	百分比 Percent
1	气味好 pleasant smell	102	44.5
2	适合自己的肤质 suitable to my skin	91	39.7
3	保湿功能 keeping moisture	67	29.3
4	容易吸收 easy to dissolve	64	27.9
5	美白功能 beauty & white	63	27.5
6	不油腻 not oil	54	23.6
7	防皱功能 wrinkle-preventing	36	15.7
8	纯天然制品 natural product	16	7.0
9	防晒功能 anti-UV	13	5.7
10	除痘功能 pimple-easing	6	2.6
11	药用功能 medicine-like effect	3	1.3
12	其他 others	2	0.9

n=229

8-10 重度消费者的人口分布/ Demographics of the Heavy Consumers

	人数 Number	16-24 岁 Age	25-34 岁 Age	35-44 岁 Age	45-54 岁 Age	55-60 岁 Age
样本 Sample	205	24.9	31.7	22.9	17.6	2.9
男性 Male	27	22.2	25.9	25.9	18.5	7.4
一天 3 次或以上 3 times or over a day	1	0.0	0.0	0.0	100.0	0.0
一天 1~2 次 once or twice a day	26	23.1	26.9	26.9	15.4	7.7
女性 Female	178	25.3	32.6	22.5	17.4	2.2
一天 3 次或以上 3 times or over a day	6	66.7	0.0	16.7	16.7	0.0
一天 1~2 次 once or twice a day	172	23.8	33.7	22.7	17.4	2.3

8-11 不同消费者层的常用品牌/ The Most Frequently Used Brands by Market Segments

8-11-1 时尚流行指标/ Fads Popular Index

	人数 Number	第一品牌及百分比 1st / percent	第二品牌及百分比 2nd / percent	第三品牌及百分比 3rd / percent	第四品牌及百分比 4th / percent
样本 Sample	227	**大宝 Dabao(17.6)**	**玉兰油 Oil of Olay(15.4)**	**郁美净 Yumeijing(10.6)**	**小护士 Mininurse(6.2)**
平实生活指向 simple living orientation	102	大宝 Dabao(22.5)	玉兰油 Oil of Olay(12.7)	郁美净 Yumeijing(11.8)	小护士 Mininurse(5.9)
时尚流行指向 fashion orientation	125	玉兰油 Oil of Olay(17.6)	大宝 Dabao(13.6)	郁美净 Yumeijing(9.6)	夏士莲 Hazeline(7.2)

8-11-2 广告态度指标/ Advertising Attitude Index

	人数 Number	第一品牌及百分比 1st/ percent	第二品牌及百分比 2nd/ percent	第三品牌及百分比 3rd/ percent	第四品牌及百分比 4th/ percent
样本 Sample	226	**大宝 Dabao(17.7)**	**玉兰油 Oil of Olay(15.0)**	**郁美净 Yumeijing(10.6)**	**小护士 Mininurse(6.2)**
广告淡漠指向 indifferent orientation	45	大宝 Dabao(22.2)	玉兰油 Oil of Olay(13.3)	郁美净 Yumeijing(11.1)	旁氏 Pond's(6.7)
中间层 medium	151	大宝 Dabao(15.9) 玉兰油 Oil of Olay(15.9)	郁美净 Yumeijing(11.3)	夏士莲 Hazeline(6.0)	小护士 Mininurse(5.3)
信赖广告指向 loyal orientation	30	大宝 Dabao(20.0)	玉兰油 Oil of Olay(13.3) 小护士 Mininurse(13.3)	雅倩 Arche(6.7) 郁美净 Yumeijing(6.7) 夏士莲 Hazeline(6.7)	妍芙阑 Yanfulan(3.3) 春娟 Chunjuan(3.3) 雅诗兰黛 Esteelauder(3.3) 雅芳 Avon(3.3) 强生 Johnson&Johnson(3.3) 旁氏 Pond's(3.3) 绿丹兰 Ludanlan(3.3) 蕾迪雅 Ladian(3.3) 丁家宜 Dingjiayi(3.3)

8-12 重度消费者的消费层构成/ The Composition of the Heavy Consumers

8-12-1 时尚流行指标/ Fads Popular Index

	人数 Number	平实生活指向 simple living orientation	时尚流行指向 fashion orientation
样本 Sample	204	**43.6**	**56.4**
一天 3 次或以上 3 times or over a day	7	28.6	71.4
一天 1~2 次 once or twice a day	197	44.2	55.8

8-12-2 广告态度指标/ Advertising Attitude Index

	人数 Number	广告淡漠指向 indifferent orientation	中间层 medium	信赖广告指向 loyal orientation
样本 Sample	203	**17.7**	**69.0**	**13.3**
一天 3 次或以上 3 times or over a day	7	14.3	71.4	14.3
一天 1~2 次 once or twice a day	196	17.9	68.9	13.3

● 武汉 / Wuhan

8-1 最近三个月使用频次的比例/ Proportion of the Sample Consuming Skin-care Products in the Last Three Months

	人数 Number	百分比 Percent
一天 3 次或以上 3 times or over a day	16	2.5
一天 1~2 次 once or twice a day	286	45.0
两三天用 1 次 once 2 or 3 days	12	1.9
一周 1~2 次 once or twice a week	1	0.2
半个月 1 次或以下 once half a month or below	2	0.3
没用过 never use	318	50.1

n=635

8-2 最常用品牌排名/ Ranking of the Most Frequently Used Brands

排名 Brand Ranking	品牌 Brands	人数 Number	百分比 Percent
1	玉兰油 Oil of Olay	54	17.2
2	大宝 Dabao	35	11.1
3	旁氏 Pond's	17	5.4
4	东洋之花 Sakula	15	4.8
5	可蒙 Kemeng	14	4.5
6	丽花丝宝 Laifa-C'bons	12	3.8
6	雅霜 Yashuang	12	3.8
6	雅倩 Arche	12	3.8
7	小护士 Mininurse	11	3.5
8	夏士莲 Hazeline	10	3.2

n=314

8-3 样本、男性各年龄层、女性各年龄层的常用品牌/ The Most Frequently Used Brands by the Whole Sample, Age and Gender Groups

	人数 Number	第一品牌及百分比 1st/ percent	第二品牌及百分比 2nd/ percent	第三品牌及百分比 3rd/ percent
样本 Sample	314	**玉兰油 Oil of Olay(17.2)**	**大宝 Dabao(11.1)**	**旁氏 Pond's(5.4)**
男性 Male	63	**大宝 Dabao(23.8)**	**东洋之花 Sakula(9.5)**	**玉兰油 Oil of Olay(7.9)**
16~24 岁 Age	20	大宝 Dabao(30.0)	东洋之花 Sakula(15.0) 可蒙 Kemeng(15.0)	夏士莲 Hazeline(5.0) 雅霜 Yashuang(5.0) 玉兰油 Oil of Olay(5.0) 雅倩 Arche(5.0) 少女之春 Shao Nv Zhi Chun(5.0) 旁氏凡士林 Vaseline(5.0) 百雀灵 Baiqueling(5.0)
25~34 岁 Age	19	大宝 Dabao(26.3)	玉兰油 Oil of Olay(15.8)	霞飞 Xiafei(5.3) 夏士莲 Hazeline(5.3) 小护士 Mininurse(5.3) 雅倩 Arche(5.3) 东洋之花 Sakula(5.3) 郁美净 Yumeijing(5.3) 男士 Nanshi(5.3) 雅霜 Yashuang(5.3) 雪馥 Xuefu(5.3) 美加净 Maxam(5.3)
35~44 岁 Age	9	百雀灵 Baiqueling(11.1) 丁家宜 Dingjiayi(11.1) 丽花丝宝 Laifa-C'bons (11.1) 夏士莲 Hazeline(11.1) 小护士 Mininurse(11.1) 玉兰油 Oil of Olay(11.1) 维生素 E 霜 VE cream(11.1) 美加净 Maxam(11.1) 得资 Dezi(11.1)		
45~54 岁 Age	9	维生素 E 霜 VE cream(22.2)	百雀灵(11.1) 大宝 Dabao(11.1) 雅芳 Avon(11.1) 永芳 Yinfong(11.1) 马牌 Mapai(11.1) 润宝 Runbao(11.1) 丝洋参乳液 Siyangshen(11.1)	
55~60 岁 Age	6	大宝 Dabao(50.0)	东洋之花 Sakula(33.3)	男士 Nanshi(16.7)
女性 Female	251	**玉兰油 Oil of Olay(19.5)**	**大宝 Dabao(8.0)**	**旁氏 Pond's(6.8)**
16~24 岁 Age	57	玉兰油 Oil of Olay(22.8)	大宝 Dabao(14.0)	小护士 Mininurse(8.8)
25~34 岁 Age	84	玉兰油 Oil of Olay(22.6)	东洋之花 Sakula(7.1) 可蒙 Kemeng(7.1) 旁氏 Pond's(7.1)	丽花丝宝 Laifa-C'bons(6.0)
35~44 岁 Age	57	玉兰油 Oil of Olay(17.5)	大宝 Dabao(8.8)	雅倩 Arche(7.0)
45~54 岁 Age	42	大宝 Dabao(11.9) 玉兰油 Oil of Olay(11.9)	旁氏 Pond's(9.5)	丽花丝宝 Laifa-C'bons(4.8) 郁美净 Yumeijing(4.8) 永芳 Yinfong(4.8) 雅倩 Arche(4.8) 可蒙 Kemeng(4.8) 丁家宜 Dingjiayi(4.8)
55~60 岁 Age	11	雅霜 Yashuang(36.4)	玉兰油 Oil of Olay(18.2) 亨得利 Hengdeli(18.2)	旁氏 Pond's(9.1) 永芳 Yinfong(9.1) 美加净 Maxam(9.1)

8-4 正在使用的品牌排名/ Ranking of the Brands Used Now

排名 Brand Ranking	品牌 Brands	人数 Number	百分比 Percent
1	玉兰油 Oil of Olay	54	17.3
2	大宝 Dabao	33	10.5
3	可蒙 Kemeng	20	6.4
4	东洋之花 Sakula	15	4.8
4	小护士 Mininurse	15	4.8
5	雅倩 Arche	13	4.2
5	丽花丝宝 Laifa-C'bons	13	4.2
6	旁氏 Pond's	12	3.8
7	雅霜 Yashuang	11	3.5

n=313

8-5 品牌转换习惯/ Brand Habit in Consuming Skin-care Products

	人数 Number	第一次使用该品牌 first use this brand	上一次也是这个牌子 used it last time	上一次不是这个牌子 not used it last time
样本 Sample	312	14.1	67.0	18.9
玉兰油 Oil of Olay	54	18.5	66.7	14.8
大宝 Dabao	33	12.1	75.8	12.1
可蒙 Kemeng	19	0.0	68.4	31.6
东洋之花 Sakula	15	6.7	46.7	46.7
小护士 Mininurse	15	40.0	40.0	20.0
雅倩 Arche	13	15.4	69.2	15.4
丽花丝宝 Laifa-C'bons	13	15.4	76.9	7.7
旁氏 Pond's	12	8.3	83.3	8.3
雅霜 Yashuang	11	0.0	100.0	0.0

8-6 下一次打算使用的品牌排名/ Ranking of the Brands to be Used Next Time

排名 Brand Ranking	品牌 Brands	人数 Number	百分比 Percent
1	玉兰油 Oil of Olay	65	20.8
2	大宝 Dabao	35	11.2
3	旁氏 Pond's	18	5.8
4	可蒙 Kemeng	14	4.5
5	雅倩 Arche	12	3.8
5	东洋之花 Sakula	12	3.8
5	雅霜 Yashuang	12	3.8
6	丽花丝宝 Laifa-C'bons	11	3.5
7	美加净 Maxam	9	2.9
7	夏士莲 Hazeline	9	2.9

n=313

8-7 样本、男性各年龄层、女性各年龄层的使用频率/ Frequencies of the Consumed Skin-care Products by the Whole Sample, Age and Gender Groups

	人数 Number	一天 3 次或以上 3 times or over a day	一天 1~2 次 once or twice a day	两三天用 1 次 once 2 or 3 days	一周 1~2 次 once or twice a week	半个月 1 次或以下 once half a month or below	没用过 never use
样本 Sample	635	2.5	45.0	1.9	0.2	0.3	50.1
男性 Male	305	0.3	17.7	3.0	0.0	0.3	78.7
16~24 岁 Age	65	1.5	24.6	4.6	0.0	1.5	67.7
25~34 岁 Age	87	0.0	20.7	2.3	0.0	0.0	77.0
35~44 岁 Age	78	0.0	9.0	2.6	0.0	0.0	88.5
45~54 岁 Age	50	0.0	16.0	2.0	0.0	0.0	82.0
55~60 岁 Age	25	0.0	20.0	4.0	0.0	0.0	76.0
女性 Female	330	4.5	70.3	0.9	0.3	0.3	23.6
16~24 岁 Age	69	7.2	73.9	0.0	1.4	0.0	17.4
25~34 岁 Age	96	5.2	79.2	2.1	0.0	1.0	12.5
35~44 岁 Age	78	3.8	69.2	0.0	0.0	0.0	26.9
45~54 岁 Age	61	3.3	67.2	0.0	0.0	0.0	29.5
55~60 岁 Age	26	0.0	38.5	3.8	0.0	0.0	57.7

8-8 选择该类商品的考虑因素/ Ranking of the Considerations in Purchasing

注：本题为多选题，合计百分比超过 100%（Multiple answers）

排名 Ranking	考虑因素 Considerations	人次 Person-time	百分比 Percent
1	产品功用 product function	166	52.5
2	价格适中 reasonable price	152	48.1
3	有名的牌子 famous brand	117	37.0
4	广告影响 influence of advertising	61	19.3
5	别人推荐 introduced by other people	54	17.1
6	购买方便 easy to buy	41	13.0
7	单位发的 offered by the working unit	22	7.0
8	有优惠条件 with preferential terms	16	5.1
8	其它 others	16	5.1
9	包装吸引人 appealing package	12	3.8

n=316

8-9 对产品功能的侧重方面/ Ranking of the Considerations about the Function of this Kind of Product

注：本题为多选题，合计百分比超过 100%（Multiple answers）

排名 Ranking	侧重方面 Items	人次 Person-time	百分比 Percent
1	气味好 pleasant smell	149	47.0
2	适合自己的肤质 suitable to my skin	128	40.4
3	容易吸收 easy to dissolve	123	38.8
4	不油腻 not oily	97	30.6
5	保湿功能 keeping moisture	87	27.4
6	美白功能 beauty & white	68	21.5
7	纯天然制品 natural product	34	10.7
8	防皱功能 wrinkle-preventing	32	10.1
9	防晒功能 anti-UV	15	4.7
10	除痘功能 pimple-easing	11	3.5
11	药用功能 medicine-like effect	7	2.2
12	其他 others	6	1.9

n=317

8-10 重度消费者的人口分布/ Demographics of the Heavy Consumers

	人数 Number	16-24 岁 Age	25-34 岁 Age	35-44 岁 Age	45-54 岁 Age	55-60 岁 Age
样本 Sample	302	24.2	32.8	21.2	16.9	5.0
男性 Male	55	30.9	32.7	12.7	14.5	9.1
一天 3 次或以上 3 times or over a day	1	100.0	0.0	0.0	0.0	0.0
一天 1~2 次 once or twice a day	54	29.6	33.3	13.0	14.8	9.3
女性 Female	247	22.7	32.8	23.1	17.4	4.0
一天 3 次或以上 3 times or over a day	15	33.3	33.3	20.0	13.3	0.0
一天 1~2 次 once or twice a day	232	22.0	32.8	23.3	17.7	4.3

8-11 不同消费者层的常用品牌/ The Most Frequently Used Brands by Market Segments

8-11-1 时尚流行指标/ Fads Popular Index

	人数 Number	第一品牌及百分比 1st/ percent	第二品牌及百分比 2nd/ percent	第三品牌及百分比 3rd/ percent
样本 Sample	309	**玉兰油 Oil of Olay(17.2)**	**大宝 Dabao(10.7)**	**旁氏 Pond's(5.2)**
平实生活指向 simple living orientation	136	玉兰油 Oil of Olay(14.7)	大宝 Dabao(11.0)	雅霜 Yashuang(6.6) 旁氏 Pond's(6.6) 可蒙 Kemeng(6.6)
时尚流行指向 fashion orientation	173	玉兰油 Oil of Olay(19.1)	大宝 Dabao(10.4)	东洋之花 Sakula(4.6) 郁美净 Yumeijing(4.6)

8-11-2 广告态度指标/ Advertising Attitude Index

	人数 Number	第一品牌及百分比 1st/ percent	第二品牌及百分比 2nd/ percent	第三品牌及百分比 3rd/ percent
样本 Sample	309	**玉兰油 Oil of Olay(17.2)**	**大宝 Dabao(10.7)**	**旁氏 Pond's(5.2)**
广告淡漠指向 indifferent orientation	74	玉兰油 Oil of Olay(20.3)	大宝 Dabao(13.5)	美加净 Maxam(6.8)
中间层 medium	192	玉兰油 Oil of Olay(16.1)	大宝 Dabao(10.4)	旁氏 Pond's(6.3)
信赖广告指向 loyal orientation	43	玉兰油 Oil of Olay(16.3)	东洋之花 Sakula(9.3) 雅倩 Arche(9.3)	大宝 Dabao(7.0) 丽花丝宝 Laifa-C'bons(7.0)

8-12 重度消费者的消费层构成/ The Composition of the Heavy Consumers

8-12-1 时尚流行指标/ Fads Popular Index

	人数 Number	平实生活指向 simple living orientation	时尚流行指向 fashion orientation
样本 Sample	298	44.3	55.7
一天 3 次或以上 3 times or over a day	16	43.8	56.3
一天 1~2 次 once or twice a day	282	44.3	55.7

8-12-2 广告态度指标/ Advertising Attitude Index

	人数 Number	广告淡漠指向 indifferent orientation	中间层 medium	信赖广告指向 loyal orientation
样本 Sample	**298**	**23.8**	**62.1**	**14.1**
一天 3 次或以上 3 times or over a day	16	25.0	50.0	25.0
一天 1~2 次 once or twice a day	282	23.8	62.8	13.5

● 西安 / Xi'an

8-1 最近三个月使用频次的比例/ Proportion of the Sample Consuming Skin-care Products in the Last Three Months

	人数 Number	百分比 Percent
一天 3 次或以上 3 times or over a day	26	4.3
一天 1~2 次 once or twice a day	319	53.3
两三天用 1 次 once 2 or 3 days	12	2.0
一周 1~2 次 once or twice a week	4	0.7
半个月 1 次或以下 once half a month or below	0	0.0
没用过 never use	237	39.6

n=598

8-2 最常用品牌排名/ Ranking of the Most Frequently Used Brands

排名 Brand Ranking	品牌 Brands	人数 Number	百分比 Percent
1	大宝 Dabao	94	26.0
2	玉兰油 Oil of Olay	33	9.1
3	旁氏 Pond's	23	6.4
4	美加净 Maxam	22	6.1
5	小护士 Mininurse	14	3.9
5	丁家宜 Dingjiayi	14	3.9
6	可蒙 Kemeng	12	3.3
7	郁美净 Yumeijing	8	2.2
7	雅倩 Arche	8	2.2
8	丹芭碧 Tobaby	7	1.9
8	东洋之花 Sakula	7	1.9

n=361

8-3 样本、男性各年龄层、女性各年龄层的常用品牌/ The Most Frequently Used Brands by the Whole Sample, Age and Gender Groups

	人数 Number	第一品牌及百分比 1st/ percent	第二品牌及百分比 2nd/ percent	第三品牌及百分比 3rd/ percent
样本 Sample	361	**大宝 Dabao(26.0)**	**玉兰油 Oil of Olay(9.1)**	**旁氏 Pond's(6.4)**
男性 Male	115	**大宝 Dabao(47.0)**	**玉兰油 Oil of Olay(5.2)** **美加净 Maxam(5.2)** **旁氏 Pond's(5.2)**	**可蒙 Kemeng(4.3)**
16~24 岁 Age	25	大宝 Dabao(52.0)	旁氏 Pond's(12.0)	可伶可俐 Clean & Clear(8.0)
25~34 岁 Age	35	大宝 Dabao(51.4)	玉兰油 Oil of Olay(14.3)	小护士 Mininurse(5.7)
35~44 岁 Age	32	大宝 Dabao(40.6)	东洋之花 Sakula(6.3) 美加净 Maxam(6.3) 可蒙 Kemeng(6.3) 小护士 Mininurse(6.3)	玉兰油 Oil of Olay(3.1) 爱之梦 Aizhimeng(3.1) 圣梦 Shengmeng(3.1) 雪馥 Xuefu(3.1) 旁氏 Pond's(3.1) 史泰龙 Shitailong(3.1) 卡洛琳 Kaluolin(3.1) 凤凰 Phoenix(3.1) 丁家宜 Dingjiayi(3.1)
45~54 岁 Age	16	大宝 Dabao(50.0)	丁家宜 Dingjiayi(6.3) 可蒙 Kemeng(6.3) 旁氏 Pond's(6.3) 霞飞 Xiafei(6.3) 郁美净 Yumeijing(6.3) 资生堂 Shiseido(6.3) 美加净 Maxam(6.3) 嘉娜宝 Kanebo(6.3)	
55~60 岁 Age	7	大宝 Dabao(28.6) 美加净 Maxam(28.6)	丹芭碧 Tobaby(14.3) 凡士林 Vaseline(14.3) 可蒙 Kemeng(14.3)	
女性 Female	246	**大宝 Dabao(16.3)**	**玉兰油 Oil of Olay(11.0)**	**旁氏 Pond's(6.9)**
16~24 岁 Age	54	大宝 Dabao(18.5)	玉兰油 Oil of Olay(9.3)	丹芭碧 Tobaby(7.4) 美加净 Maxam(7.4) 雅倩 Arche(7.4) 小护士 Mininurse(7.4)
25~34 岁 Age	80	玉兰油 Oil of Olay(20.0)	大宝 Dabao(15.0)	美加净 Maxam(7.5) 旁氏 Pond's(7.5)
35~44 岁 Age	58	大宝 Dabao(19.0)	旁氏 Pond's(10.3)	小护士 Mininurse(6.9) 丁家宜 Dingjiayi(6.9)
45~54 岁 Age	40	大宝 Dabao(12.5)	美加净 Maxam(10.0) 玉兰油 Oil of Olay(10.0)	旁氏 Pond's(7.5)
55~60 岁 Age	14	大宝 Dabao(14.3) 可蒙 Kemeng(14.3) 郁美净 Yumeijing(14.3)	蓓蕾 Beilei(7.1) 玉兰油 Oil of Olay(7.1) 柔婷 Routing(7.1) 丁家宜 Dingjiayi(7.1)	

8-4 正在使用的品牌排名/ Ranking of the Brands Used Now

排名 Brand Ranking	品牌 Brands	人数 Number	百分比 Percent
1	大宝 Dabao	90	24.9
2	玉兰油 Oil of Olay	34	9.4
3	旁氏 Pond's	23	6.4
3	美加净 Maxam	23	6.4
4	可蒙 Kemeng	14	3.9
5	丁家宜 Dingjiayi	12	3.3
6	小护士 Mininurse	10	2.8
7	郁美净 Yumeijing	7	1.9
8	雅倩 Arche	6	1.7
8	资生堂 Shiseido	6	1.7
8	夏士莲 Hazeline	6	1.7
8	丹芭碧 Tobaby	6	1.7

n=361

8-5 品牌转换习惯/ Brand Habit in Consuming Skin-care Products

	人数 Number	第一次使用该品牌 first use this brand	上一次也是这个牌子 used it last time	上一次不是这个牌子 not used it last time
样本 Sample	361	11.9	74.2	13.9
大宝 Dabao	90	3.3	87.8	8.9
玉兰油 Oil of Olay	34	8.8	73.5	17.6
美加净 Maxam	23	13.0	69.6	17.4
旁氏 Pond's	23	4.3	87.0	8.7
丁家宜 Dingjiayi	12	8.3	58.3	33.3
可蒙 Kemeng	14	7.1	78.5	14.3
小护士 Mininurse	10	10.0	60.0	30.0
郁美净 Yumeijing	7	0.0	57.1	42.9
资生堂 Shiseido	6	33.3	66.7	0.0
夏士莲 Hazeline	6	33.3	50.0	16.7
丹芭碧 Tobaby	6	0.0	83.3	16.7

8-6 下一次打算使用的品牌排名/ Ranking of the Brands to be Used Next Time

排名 Brand Ranking	品牌 Brands	人数 Number	百分比 Percent
1	大宝 Dabao	88	24.4
2	玉兰油 Oil of Olay	46	12.7
3	旁氏 Pond's	22	6.1
4	美加净 Maxam	19	5.3
5	丁家宜 Dingjiayi	13	3.6
6	小护士 Mininurse	11	3.0
7	可蒙 Kemeng	10	2.8
8	雅倩 Arche	9	2.5
8	凤凰 Phoenix	9	2.5

n=361

8-7 样本、男性各年龄层、女性各年龄层的使用频率/ Frequencies of the Consumed Skin-care Products by the Whole Sample, Age and Gender Groups

	人数 Number	一天3次或以上 3 times or over a day	一天1~2次 once or twice a day	两三天用1次 once 2 or 3 days	一周1~2次 once or twice a week	半个月1次或以下 once half a month or below	没用过 never use
样本 Sample	598	4.3	53.3	2.0	0.7	0.0	39.6
男性 Male	299	1.7	33.4	2.3	1.0	0.0	61.5
16~24 岁 Age	64	1.6	31.3	3.1	3.1	0.0	60.9
25~34 岁 Age	90	2.2	33.3	3.3	0.0	0.0	61.1
35~44 岁 Age	77	1.3	37.7	1.3	1.3	0.0	58.4
45~54 岁 Age	45	2.2	31.1	2.2	0.0	0.0	64.4
55~60 岁 Age	23	0.0	30.4	0.0	0.0	0.0	69.6
女性 Female	299	7.0	73.2	1.7	0.3	0.0	17.7
16~24 岁 Age	61	9.8	73.8	3.3	1.6	0.0	11.5
25~34 岁 Age	90	8.9	77.8	2.2	0.0	0.0	11.1
35~44 岁 Age	74	8.1	70.3	0.0	0.0	0.0	21.6
45~54 岁 Age	49	2.0	77.6	2.0	0.0	0.0	18.4
55~60 岁 Age	25	0.0	56.0	0.0	0.0	0.0	44.0

8-8 选择该类商品的考虑因素/ Ranking of the Considerations in Purchasing

注：本题为多选题，合计百分比超过 100%（Multiple answers）

排名 Ranking	考虑因素 Considerations	人次 Person-time	百分比 Percent
1	价格适中 reasonable price	165	45.7
2	产品功用 product function	164	45.4
3	有名的牌子 famous brand	105	29.1
4	广告影响 influence of advertising	70	19.4
5	别人推荐 introduced by other people	60	16.6
6	购买方便 easy to buy	37	10.2
7	有优惠条件 with preferential terms	12	3.3
8	包装吸引人 appealing package	10	2.8
9	单位发的 offered by the working unit	8	2.2
10	其它 others	4	1.1

n=361

8-9 对产品功能的侧重方面/ Ranking of the Considerations about the Function of this Kind of Product

注：本题为多选题，合计百分比超过 100%（Multiple answers）

排名 Ranking	侧重方面 Items	人次 Person-time	百分比 Percent
1	容易吸收 easy to dissolve	130	36.0
2	保湿功能 keeping moisture	125	34.6
3	适合自己的肤质 suitable to my skin	123	34.1
4	气味好 pleasant smell	114	31.6
5	不油腻 not oil	110	30.5
6	美白功能 beauty & white	63	17.5
7	防皱功能 wrinkle-preventing	42	11.6
8	纯天然制品 natural product	22	6.1
9	防晒功能 anti-UV	14	3.9
10	除痘功能 pimple-easing	11	3.0
11	药用功能 medicine-like effect	4	1.1
12	其他 others	3	0.8

n=361

8-10 重度消费者的人口分布/ Demographics of the Heavy Consumers

	人数 Number	16-24 岁 Age	25-34 岁 Age	35-44 岁 Age	45-54 岁 Age	55-60 岁 Age
样本 Sample	345	20.9	31.9	25.5	15.7	6.1
男性 Male	105	20.0	30.5	28.6	14.3	6.7
一天 3 次或以上 3 times or over a day	5	20.0	40.0	20.0	20.0	0.0
一天 1~2 次 once or twice a day	100	20.0	30.0	29.0	14.0	7.0
女性 Female	240	21.3	32.5	24.2	16.3	5.8
一天 3 次或以上 3 times or over a day	21	28.6	38.1	28.6	4.8	0.0
一天 1~2 次 once or twice a day	219	20.5	32.0	23.7	17.4	6.4

8-11 不同消费者层的常用品牌/ The Most Frequently Used Brands by Market Segments

8-11-1 时尚流行指标/ Fads Popular Index

	人数 Number	第一品牌及百分比 1st/ percent	第二品牌及百分比 2nd/ percent	第三品牌及百分比 3rd/ percent	第四品牌及百分比 4th/ percent
样本 Sample	360	**大宝 Dabao(26.1)**	**玉兰油 Oil of Olay(9.2)**	**旁氏 Pond's(6.4)**	**美加净 Maxam(6.1)**
平实生活指向 simple living orientation	178	大宝 Dabao(27.0)	玉兰油 Oil of Olay(8.4)	美加净 Maxam(7.9)	旁氏 Pond's(5.1) 可蒙 Kemeng(5.1)
时尚流行指向 fashion orientation	182	大宝 Dabao(25.3)	玉兰油 Oil of Olay(9.9)	旁氏 Pond's(7.7)	丁家宜 Dingjiayi(5.5)

8-11-2 广告态度指标/ Advertising Attitude Index

	人数 Number	第一品牌及百分比 1st/ percent	第二品牌及百分比 2nd/ percent	第三品牌及百分比 3rd/ percent	第四品牌及百分比 4th/ percent
样本 Sample	359	**大宝 Dabao(26.2)**	**玉兰油 Oil of Olay(9.2)**	**旁氏 Pond's(6.4)**	**美加净 Maxam(6.1)**
广告淡漠指向 indifferent orientation	99	大宝 Dabao(22.2)	玉兰油 Oil of Olay(11.1)	美加净 Maxam(10.1)	旁氏 Pond's(6.1)
中间层 medium	207	大宝 Dabao(29.0)	旁氏 Pond's(7.2)	玉兰油 Oil of Olay(6.8)	美加净 Maxam(5.3)
信赖广告指向 loyal orientation	53	大宝 Dabao(22.6)	玉兰油 Oil of Olay(15.1)	劳动护肤霜 Labor(3.8) 旁氏 Pond's(3.8) 花 Fa(3.8) 雅倩 Arche(3.8) 丁家宜 Dingjiayi(3.8) 丹芭碧 Tobaby(3.8)	采诗 Caishi(1.9) 美加净 Maxam(1.9) 劳士果酸 Laoshi(1.9) 圣梦 Shengmeng(1.9) 蓓蕾 Beilei(1.9) 夏士莲 Hazeline(1.9) 雨水 Yushui(1.9) 雅芳 Avon(1.9) 小护士 Mininurse(1.9) 丽花丝宝 Laifa-C'bons(1.9) 可蒙 Kemeng(1.9) 可伶可俐 Clean & Clear(1.9) 卡洛琳 Kaluolin(1.9) 凡士林 Vaseline(1.9) 东洋之花 Sakula(1.9) 芭蕾 Ballet

8-12 重度消费者的消费层构成/ The Composition of the Heavy Consumers

8-12-1 时尚流行指标/ Fads Popular Index

	人数 Number	平实生活指向 simple living orientation	时尚流行指向 fashion orientation
样本 Sample	344	49.1	50.9
一天 3 次或以上 3 times or over a day	26	46.2	53.8
一天 1~2 次 once or twice a day	318	49.4	50.6

8-12-2 广告态度指标/ Advertising Attitude Index

	人数 Number	广告淡漠指向 indifferent orientation	中间层 medium	信赖广告指向 loyal orientation
样本 Sample	343	27.1	59.2	13.7
一天 3 次或以上 3 times or over a day	25	12.0	72.0	16.0
一天 1~2 次 once or twice a day	318	28.3	58.2	13.5

● 沈阳 / Shenyang

8-1 最近三个月使用频次的比例/ Proportion of the Sample Consuming Skin-care Products in the Last Three Months

	人数 Number	百分比 Percent
一天 3 次或以上 3 times or over a day	11	1.8
一天 1~2 次 once or twice a day	295	49.5
两三天用 1 次 once 2 or 3 days	10	1.7
一周 1~2 次 once or twice a week	2	0.3
半个月 1 次或以下 once half a month or below	1	0.2
没用过 never use	277	46.5

n=596

8-2 最常用品牌排名/ Ranking of the Most Frequently Used Brands

排名 Brand Ranking	品牌 Brands	人数 Number	百分比 Percent
1	大宝 Dabao	70	21.9
2	玉兰油 Oil of Olay	33	10.3
3	高丝 Kose	19	6.0
4	友谊 Youyi	17	5.3
4	旁氏 Pond's	17	5.3
5	小护士 Mininurse	15	4.7

n=319

8-3 样本、男性各年龄层、女性各年龄层的常用品牌/ The Most Frequently Used Brands by the Whole Sample, Age and Gender Groups

	人数 Number	第一品牌及百分比 1st/ percent	第二品牌及百分比 2nd/ percent	第三品牌及百分比 3rd/ percent
样本 Sample	319	**大宝 Dabao(21.9)**	**玉兰油 Oil of Olay(10.3)**	**高丝 Kose(6.0)**
男性 Male	85	**大宝 Dabao(50.6)**	**友谊 Youyi(5.9)**	**旁氏 Pond's(3.5)**
16~24 岁 Age	16	大宝 Dabao(68.8)	芦荟 Luhui(12.5)	男士 Nanshi(6.3) 影后 Yinghou(6.3) 玛丽艳娜 Maliyana(6.3)
25~34 岁 Age	31	大宝 Dabao(64.5)	小护士 Mininurse(3.2) 雅派 Yapai(3.2) 韩国银杏 Hanguo Yingxing(3.2) WENDY(3.2) 玉兰油 Oil of Olay(3.2) 安利 Amway(3.2) 强生 Johnson&Johnson(3.2) 旁氏 Pond's(3.2) 妮维雅 Nivea(3.2) 高丝 Kose(3.2) 东洋之花 Sakula(3.2)	
35~44 岁 Age	18	大宝 Dabao(22.2)	友谊 Youyi(16.7)	旁氏 Pond's(11.1)
45~54 岁 Age	16	大宝 Dabao(37.5)	丽花丝宝 Laifa-C'bons(12.5) 友谊 Youyi(12.5)	艾侬 Ainong(6.3) 凤凰 Phoenix(6.3) 仙妮雷德 Xiannileide(6.3) 小护士 Mininurse(6.3) 世纪丽人 Shijiliren(6.3) 杏仁蜜 Xingrenmi(6.3)
55~60 岁 Age	4	大宝 Dabao(50.0)	高丝 Kose(25.0) 上海杏仁露 Shanghai(25.0)	
女性 Female	234	**玉兰油 Oil of Olay(13.7)**	**大宝 Dabao(11.5)**	**高丝 Kose(7.3)**
16~24 岁 Age	53	玉兰油 Oil of Olay(18.9)	安安 An'an(9.4)	大宝 Dabao(7.5) 强生 Johnson&Johnson(7.5)
25~34 岁 Age	75	高丝 Kose(13.3) 玉兰油 Oil of Olay(13.3)	大宝 Dabao(8.0)	小护士 Mininurse(6.7)
35~44 岁 Age	59	玉兰油 Oil of Olay(15.3)	大宝 Dabao(13.6)	旁氏 Pond's(8.5) 小护士 Mininurse(8.5)
45~54 岁 Age	34	友谊 Youyi(17.6)	大宝 Dabao(14.7)	旁氏 Pond's(11.8)
55~60 岁 Age	13	大宝 Dabao(30.8)	友谊 Youyi(23.1)	丹芭碧 Tobaby(7.7) 丽花丝宝 Laifa-C'bons(7.7) 妮维雅 Nivea(7.7) 欧莱雅 L'oreal(7.7) 旁氏 Pond's(7.7) PLAGENTA(7.7)

8-4 正在使用的品牌排名/ Ranking of the Brands Used Now

排名 Brand Ranking	品牌 Brands	人数 Number	百分比 Percent
1	大宝 Dabao	66	20.7
2	玉兰油 Oil of Olay	29	9.1
3	高丝 Kose	18	5.6
4	小护士 Mininurse	17	5.3
5	友谊 Youyi	16	5.0
5	旁氏 Pond's	16	5.0
6	强生 Johnson&Johnson	10	3.1
7	芦荟 Luhui	9	2.8
8	丽花丝宝 Laifa-C'bons	6	1.9
8	碧柔歌婷 Qualite	6	1.9
8	兰贵人 Lan Guiren	6	1.9
9	安利 Amway	5	1.6
9	安安 An'an	5	1.6
9	郑明明 Cheng Mingming	5	1.6
10	羽西 Yue-sai	4	1.3
10	妮维雅 Nivea	4	1.3
10	欧珀莱 Aupres	4	1.3
10	雅倩 Arche	4	1.3

n=319

8-5 品牌转换习惯/ Brand Habit in Consuming Skin-care Products

	人数 Number	第一次使用该品牌 first use this brand	上一次也是这个牌子 used it last time	上一次不是这个牌子 not used it last time
样本 Sample	319	10.3	80.3	9.4
大宝 Dabao	66	6.1	90.9	3.0
玉兰油 Oil of Olay	29	6.9	89.7	3.4
高丝 Kose	18	5.6	94.4	0.0
小护士 Mininurse	17	23.5	70.6	5.9
友谊 Youyi	16	0.0	100.0	0.0
旁氏 Pond's	16	12.5	68.8	18.8
强生 Johnson&Johnson	10	10.0	70.0	20.0

8-6 下一次打算使用的品牌排名/ Ranking of the Brands to be Used Next Time

排名 Brand Ranking	品牌 Brands	人数 Number	百分比 Percent
1	大宝 Dabao	61	19.1
2	玉兰油 Oil of Olay	38	11.9
3	旁氏 Pond's	18	5.6
4	友谊 Youyi	16	5.0
5	高丝 Kose	15	4.7
6	小护士 Mininurse	14	4.4
7	兰贵人 Lan Guiren	9	2.8
8	雅倩 Arche	7	2.2
8	强生 Johnson&Johnson	7	2.2
9	丽花丝宝 Balance	6	1.9
9	芦荟 Luhui	6	1.9
9	碧柔歌婷 Qualite	6	1.9
9	羽西 Yue-sai	6	1.9
10	安安 An'an	5	1.6
10	郑明明 Cheng Mingming	5	1.6
10	欧珀莱 Aupres	5	1.6

n=319

8-7 样本、男性各年龄层、女性各年龄层的使用频率/ Frequencies of the Consumed Skin-care Products by the Whole Sample, Age and Gender Groups

	人数 Number	一天 3 次或以上 3 times or over a day	一天 1~2 次 once or twice a day	两三天用 1 次 once 2 or 3 days	一周 1~2 次 once or twice a week	半个月 1 次或以下 once half a month or below	没用过 never use
样本 Sample	596	1.8	49.5	1.7	0.3	0.2	46.5
男性 Male	294	1.4	24.8	2.4	0.3	0.0	71.1
16~24 岁 Age	62	3.2	22.6	0.0	0.0	0.0	74.2
25~34 岁 Age	83	1.1	29.5	4.5	0.0	0.0	64.8
35~44 岁 Age	74	0.0	24.3	0.0	0.0	0.0	75.7
45~54 岁 Age	46	0.0	28.3	4.3	2.2	0.0	65.2
55~60 岁 Age	24	4.2	8.3	4.2	0.0	0.0	83.3
女性 Female	302	2.3	73.5	1.0	0.3	0.3	22.5
16~24 岁 Age	64	3.1	79.7	0.0	0.0	0.0	17.2
25~34 岁 Age	90	3.3	80.0	0.0	0.0	0.0	16.7
35~44 岁 Age	76	2.6	72.4	1.3	1.3	0.0	22.4
45~54 岁 Age	48	0.0	66.7	2.1	0.0	2.1	29.2
55~60 岁 Age	24	0.0	50.0	4.2	0.0	0.0	45.8

8-8 选择该类商品的考虑因素/ Ranking of the Considerations in Purchasing

注：本题为多选题，合计百分比超过 100%（Multiple answers）

排名 Ranking	考虑因素 Considerations	人次 Person-time	百分比 Percent
1	产品功用 product function	153	48.1
2	价格适中 reasonable price	151	47.5
3	有名的牌子 famous brand	118	37.1
4	别人推荐 introduced by other people	61	19.2
5	广告影响 influence of advertising	53	16.7
6	购买方便 easy to buy	43	13.5
7	包装吸引人 appealing package	10	3.1
8	有优惠条件 with preferential terms	9	2.8
9	其它 others	8	2.5

n=318

8-9 对产品功能的侧重方面/ Ranking of the Considerations about the Function of this Kind of Product

注：本题为多选题，合计百分比超过 100%（Multiple answers）

排名 Ranking	侧重方面 Items	人次 Person-time	百分比 Percent
1	适合自己的肤质 suitable to my skin	125	39.2
2	容易吸收 easy to dissolve	117	36.7
3	保湿功能 keeping moisture	109	34.2
4	气味好 pleasant smell	97	30.4
5	不油腻 not oily	82	25.7
6	美白功能 beauty & white	63	19.7
7	防皱功能 wrinkle-preventing	40	12.5
8	防晒功能 anti-UV	22	6.9
9	纯天然制品 natural product	19	6.0
10	除痘功能 pimple-easing	8	2.5
11	药用功能 medicine-like effect	4	1.3
12	其他 others	3	0.9

n=319

8-10 重度消费者的人口分布/ Demographics of the Heavy Consumers

	人数 Number	16-24 岁 Age	25-34 岁 Age	35-44 岁 Age	45-54 岁 Age	55-60 岁 Age
样本 Sample	306	22.5	33.3	24.5	14.7	4.9
男性 Male	77	20.8	35.1	23.4	16.9	3.9
一天 3 次或以上 3 times or over a day	4	50.0	25.0	0.0	0.0	25.0
一天 1~2 次 once or twice a day	73	19.2	35.6	24.7	17.8	2.7
女性 Female	229	23.1	32.8	24.9	14.0	5.2
一天 3 次或以上 3 times or over a day	7	28.6	42.9	28.6	0.0	0.0
一天 1~2 次 once or twice a day	222	23.0	32.4	24.8	14.4	5.4

8-11 不同消费者层的常用品牌/ The Most Frequently Used Brands by Market Segments

8-11-1 时尚流行指标/ Fads Popular Index

	人数 Number	第一品牌及百分比 1st/ percent	第二品牌及百分比 2nd/ percent	第三品牌及百分比 3rd/ percent	第四品牌及百分比 4th/ percent
样本 Sample	319	**大宝 Dabao(21.9)**	**玉兰油 Oil of Olay(10.3)**	**高丝 Kose(6.0)**	**友谊 Youyi(5.3)** **旁氏 Pond's(5.3)**
平实生活指向 simple living orientation	141	大宝 Dabao(27.0)	友谊 Youyi(9.9)	玉兰油 Oil of Olay(6.4)	高丝 Kose(5.7)
时尚流行指向 fashion orientation	178	大宝 Dabao(18.0)	玉兰油 Oil of Olay(13.5)	高丝 Kose(6.2)	旁氏 Pond's(5.6) 小护士 Mininurse(5.6)

8-11-2 广告态度指标/ Advertising Attitude Index

	人数 Number	第一品牌及百分比 1st/ percent	第二品牌及百分比 2nd/ percent	第三品牌及百分比 3rd/ percent	第四品牌及百分比 4th/ percent
样本 Sample	319	**大宝 Dabao(21.9)**	**玉兰油 Oil of Olay(10.3)**	**高丝 Kose(6.0)**	**友谊 Youyi(5.3)** **旁氏 Pond's(5.3)**
广告淡漠指向 indifferent orientation	71	大宝 Dabao(25.4)	友谊 Youyi(8.5)	玉兰油 Oil of Olay(7.0)	芦荟 Luhui(5.6)
中间层 medium	206	大宝 Dabao(18.9)	玉兰油 Oil of Olay(11.7)	高丝 Kose(6.3)	旁氏 Pond's(5.8)
信赖广告指向 loyal orientation	42	大宝 Dabao(31.0)	玉兰油 Oil of Olay(9.5)	高丝 Kose(7.1) 安安 An'an(7.1)	妮维雅 Nivea(4.8) 旁氏 Pond's(4.8) 小护士 Mininurse(4.8) 友谊 Youyi(4.8)

8-12 重度消费者的消费层构成/ The Composition of the Heavy Consumers

8-12-1 时尚流行指标/ Fads Popular Index

	人数 Number	平实生活指向 simple living orientation	时尚流行指向 fashion orientation
样本 Sample	306	43.8	56.2
一天 3 次或以上 3 times or over a day	11	45.5	54.5
一天 1~2 次 once or twice a day	295	43.7	56.3

8-12-2 广告态度指标/ Advertising Attitude Index

	人数 Number	广告淡漠指向 indifferent orientation	中间层 medium	信赖广告指向 loyal orientation
样本 Sample	306	21.9	65.0	13.1
一天 3 次或以上 3 times or over a day	11	9.1	72.7	18.2
一天 1~2 次 once or twice a day	295	22.4	64.7	12.9

第九篇　化妆品、卫生用品
Part IX　Cosmetics & Napkins

- 化妆水　Cosmetic Water
- 粉底　Pre-makeup
- 口红　Lipstick
- 卫生巾　Napkins

化妆品、卫生用品

化妆品

20 年前，中国化妆品工业基础十分薄弱，全国不足 200 家化妆品企业，绝大多数企业属手工作坊式生产，更无专业的生产设备及良好的生产环境，品种只有香粉、雪花膏、花露水及蛤蜊油等有限的几种。1978 年，开放政策为我国化妆品工业带来了新的生机和冲击，化妆品企业犹如雨后春笋，数量迅速增加，到 1997 年底，全国已领取化妆品生产许可证的企业多达 3514 余家，其中国有企业 317 家，占全行业的 12.3%；集体企业 1110 家，占 44%；私营企业 258 家，占 10.2%；“三资”企业 539 家，占 21.4%；其它经济结构约占 12%。

1982 年，北京日用化学四厂成为第一家与美国爱芳公司技术合作生产护肤产品的化妆品企业。紧接着，天津第一日用化学厂与德国威娜公司合资成立了我国第一家化妆品合资企业——天津丽明化妆品合营工业公司，生产香波及护发素，从此逐步打开了化妆品领域引进外资的大门。国际上一些著名的化妆品公司看好我国这个巨大化妆品消费市场，纷纷于 80 年代末、90 年代初先后来我国投资，建立起合资或独资企业。如美国的 P&G 公司、雅芳公司、安利公司、庄臣公司、玫琳凯公司、露华浓公司；法国的欧莱雅公司、克丽丝汀·迪奥公司；英国的联合利华公司；德国的威娜公司、汉高公司、妮维雅公司；日本的资生堂株式会社、奇士美株式会社；韩国的 LG 公司、露姿公司；瑞士的芬莎公司等，东南亚和香港、台湾地区的化妆品公司也先后来我国进行合资、合作，对我国化妆品工业的发展起到推波助澜的促进作用，加快了化妆品工业的发展步伐，缩短了同国际化妆品发展的差距。全国现有年销售额 1 亿元以上的化妆品企业 50 余家，其中年销售额 5 亿元以上的化妆品企业有 8 家，即广州宝洁有限公司、安利（中国）日用品有限公司、上海家化有限公司、重庆奥妮化妆品有限公司、北京三露厂、上海联合利华公司、广州雅芳公司、上海日用化学（集团）公司。

目前我国人均年消费化妆品为 20 元（约 2.5 美元），而发达国家人均年消费化妆品约 35 美元至 70 美元。我国广大农村及边远地区尚未普及使用化妆品。随着我国人民生活水平的不断提高，消费结构也发生了变化。据 1997 年秋季（天津）全国首届化妆洗涤商品交易会上的消息，目前的化妆品消费结构为：护肤品 35%，发用品 28%，美容类 29%，香水类 8%。护肤品仍是主流、美容品发展迅速，人们的消费意识趋向成熟和转向多样化的品牌，城乡消费差异还依然明显，高档名牌化妆品如进口化妆品、美容品主要消费者还是大中城市的高薪消费群。农村市场低档品已有相当比例，仍有增长的势头。广大消费者青睐中、低档化妆品。

化妆品作为日耗品，将会有广阔的市场及巨大的发展潜力，在相当长的一段时期内化妆品的生产和销售将保持稳步增长的趋势。

在今后发展中，化妆品仍将以清洁类及护肤类为主流产品，迎合一定时期内的广大消费者的需求。防晒化妆品、中草药化妆品是 21 世纪国内外重视和发展的主要种类。开发高保湿、延缓衰老、防皱和抗皱等化妆品也是发展护肤品的主题。

随着人们生活水平的提高，美容、美发业发展很快，美容院正在蓬勃兴起，美容院用的美容美发产品在不断扩大，这也是化妆品行业一个新兴的重要市场。从美容、美发类产品来看，以多品种、多色彩、使用方便、安全、自然为发展方向。在化妆品工业的发展中，随着产品的细分化，儿童用护肤品、男士用化妆品、老年人用妆化品也将得到发展。化妆品行业 2000 年计划工业生产总值 300 亿元，出口创汇 1.5 亿美元。2010 年化妆品计划工业生产总值为 800 亿元，出口创汇 5 亿美元。

卫生巾

随着经济的发展和人们在思想文化观念以及消费习惯上的变化，中国的卫生用品市场异军突起，市场消费潜力得到了空前的提升。1985—1998 年间，中国妇女卫生巾的消费量从 10 亿片增长到 275 亿片，卫生巾市场渗透率也从 1985 年的 2%增长到现在的 44.7%。截止到 1998 年底，我国的卫生巾生产厂家已达 1000 多家。

目前我国卫生巾产品可分为 3 类：

1．护翼卫生巾，属中高档产品，售价较高。这类产品在我国的生产始于 90 年代初期，目前主要集中在家庭收入较高的城市及沿海地区销售；

2．直条卫生巾产品，与护翼卫生巾相比，售价普遍较低，1997 年直条卫生巾产品的产量约占中国卫生巾总产量的 79%；

3．护垫，在中国自 1992 年开始生产，消费者主要是家庭收入较高及个人卫生意识较强的城市消费者。1998 年护垫的总产量约占中国卫生巾总产量的 1%。

中国卫生巾的大部分市场有几个主要品牌占据，它们是安尔乐、安乐、护舒宝、舒而美、高洁丝、娇爽、乐而雅、苏菲、维达、舒婷、佳期等。恒安集团是目前中国最大的卫生巾制造商，市场占有率为 40%。我国是世界上人口最多的国家，1998 年全国年龄介于 15—49 岁的妇女人数占我国总人口的 28%，而卫生巾是妇女生活中的的消费必需品，因此，中国的卫生巾市场具有很大的潜力，将成为世界上最大的卫生巾市场之一。

Cosmetics & Toilet

Cosmetics

20 years ago, the cosmetic industry in China lacked qualified technical personnel and advanced machines. There were less than 200 companies, and among them most were manual workshops without any professional production facilities or qualified production environment. The products were simply facial powder, cream, toilet water and vaseline. The open-up policy of 1978 provided Chinese cosmetic industry with energy and chance. Numerous new cosmetic factories were set up. By the end of 1997, the number of cosmetic enterprises with authorized licenses had come to more than 3514, among which 317 were state-owned, accounting for 12.3% of the whole business, 1110 were collective, 44% of the whole business, 258 were private, 10.2%, 539 were joint, 21.4% and some were of other economic structure, accounting for 12% of the whole business.

The 4th Household Chemicals Factory in Beijing was the first one cooperating with American Avon in technology to produce skin cream in 1982. Later, the 1st Household Chemicals in Tianjin and German Wella Corp. set up the first cosmetic joint venture in China to produce shampoo and hair treatment. From then on foreign companies rush to China to invest in cosmetic industry. Many famous international cosmetic companies of the world were attracted by China's potential market and came to set up joint ventures or foreign-funded companies in succession in the late 1980s and the early 1990s. For example, P&G, Avon, Amway, Johnson & Johnson. Marykay, Revlon from America, L'oreal, Christine.Dior.from France, Unilever from England, Wella, Hencel, Nivea from Germany, Shiseido, Kissme from Japan, L.G., Luzi from Korea. Vanessa from Sweden. Meanwhile some cosmetic companies of southeast Asia, Hongkong and Taiwan came to China to cooperate with Chinese local enterprises and have accelerated the growth of Chinese cosmetic and shortened the distance with the international cosmetic industry.

There are more than 50 cosmetic enterprises with sales over 100 million RMB and 8 enterprises over 500 million RMB: They are Guangzhou P&G, Amway Chemicals. Ltd. (China), Shanghai Jiahua Ltd.. Chongqing Olive Cosmetic Corp. Ltd., Beijing Sanlu, Shanghai Unilever Ltd., Guangzhou Avon Corp., Shanghai Household Chemicals Group. At present Chinese people consumes average 20 RMB (about $2.5) on cosmetics per year whereas the consumer in the developed countries spends 35-70 dollars. Cosmetics are not yet popular among the people in the rural areas. And also as the living condition improves, people's consuming structure changes. According to the information issued by Chinese First Cosmetic and Detergent Products Trade Fair in 1997, the present cosmetic consuming structure goes in this way: skin cream, 35%, shampoo and hair treatment, 28%, cosmetics, 29% and perfume, 8%. It seems that skin creams are still the dominant one and cosmetics are accepted by more and more people. People have more sophisticated idea of consumption and prefer brands with a wide-range of diversity. Meanwhile, the difference in cosmetic consumption between urban and rural areas is still obvious and the consumers with higher income in big cities prefer the first-class brands e.g the imported ones. In the rural areas, the consumers prefer low-grade brands. But still there is great potential. Both the middle-grade brands and low-grade brands may take greater sharest in the market.

Being a household item, cosmetics is facing a broad and potential market, thus the cosmetic production and sale will keep increasing in future.

The major products will be skin cleaners and skin-care item in order to meet the need of most of the consumers. Suntan cream and herbal cosmetics will be emphasized by both Chinese and foreign companies in 21st century. The developing of cosmetics with hydro, debility-resistant and anti-wrinkle formulas will be the major subjects.

The improvement of living condition leads to the growth of cosmetology. The vigorous springing up of the beauty saloon has formed another important market for cosmetics produces. Cosmetic products will have much more diversity of styles and colors, the convenience and safety. As the cosmetics market segments gradually, skin-care item for children, cosmetics for men and the olds will also grow.

The anticipated gross production will be 30 billion RMB, earning 150 million dollars through export The anticipated gross production will be 80 billion RMB, earning 500 million dolllars.

Napkin

With the development of economy and changes in culture and habits of consuming, personal hygiene products suddenly come into the market. The potential of the market is explored in a manner never occurred before. From 1985 to 1988, the amount of sanitary napkin consumed has greatly increased from 1billion pieces to 27.5 billion pieces. 44.7% of the napkin market is penetrated compared with 2% of 1985. There were more than 1000 sanitary napkins marketers by the end of 1998.There are 3 kinds of sanitary napkin currently:

1. Sanitary napkin with wings. It is goods of medium and top-classes at higher prices. It first appeared in the early 1990s and is now mainly sold in the urban and coastal areas where the average family income is comparatively high.

2. Sanitary napkin without wings. Compared with the above, it is normally cheaper and in 1997 hold 79% share of the total sanitary napkin output.

3. Hygiene pad. It was first produced in 1992 and is mainly accepted by the consumers with higher income and stronger sense of personal health. In 1998, its output accounts for 1% of the total sanitary napkin output.

The sanitary napkin market is dominated by several major brands: Anerle, Anle, Whisper, Comfort&Beauty, Cotex, Carefree, Le'erya, Soft, Vida, Shuting and Jiaqi. Heng'an Group, whose products occupy 40% of the total sale, is the largest producer of sanitary napkin in China.

China has the largest population in the world. In the year of 1998, 28% of the whole population is woman at the age of 15 to 49, sanitary napkins as woman's necessary consumer goods, the market of sanitary napkins will have great potential in China.

1.化妆水 / Cosmetics Water

● 北京 / Beijing

1-1 最近三个月使用频次的比例/ Proportion of the Sample Consuming Cosmetics Water in the Last Three Months

	人数 Number	百分比 Percent
天天用 daily	96	19.0
两三天用 1 次 once 2 or 3 days	22	4.4
一周 1～2 次 once or twice a week	15	3.0
半个月一次 once half a month	4	0.8
一个月 1 次或以下 once a month or below	8	1.6
没用过 never use	360	71.3

n=505

1-2 最常用品牌排名/ Ranking of the Most Frequently Used Brands

排名 Brand Ranking	品牌 Brands	人数 Number	百分比 Percent
1	欧珀莱 Aupres	20	13.8
2	高丝 Kose	17	11.7
3	资生堂 Shiseido	11	7.6
4	大宝.高丽雅娜.阿特皮雅 Dabao Coreana Artpla	8	5.5
5	强生可伶可俐 Clean&Clear	7	4.8
6	雅芳 Avon	4	2.8
7	花王碧柔 Biore	3	2.1
7	东洋之花 Sakula	3	2.1
7	郑明明 Cheng Mingming	3	2.1
7	羽西 Yue-sai	3	2.1
7	柔婷 Routing	3	2.1
7	安利 Amway	3	2.1
7	迪奥 CD	3	2.1

n=145

1-3 样本、女性各年龄层的常用品牌/ The Most Frequently Used Brands by the Female Sample and Age Groups

	人数 Number	第一品牌及百分比 1st/ percent	第二品牌及百分比 2nd/ percent	第三品牌及百分比 3rd/ percent
女性 Female	145	**欧珀莱 Aupres(13.8)**	**高丝 Kose(11.7)**	**资生堂 Shiseido(7.6)**
16~24 岁 Age	26	强生可伶可俐 Clean&Clear(23.1)	法兰西施 Miss de France(7.7) 高丝 Kose(7.7) 资生堂 Shiseido(7.7)	郑明明 Cheng Mingming(3.8) 岑凯伦 Cenkailun(3.8) 美宝莲 Maybelline(3.8) 丹芭碧 To Baby(3.8) 蜜施华 Mishihua(3.8) 柔婷 Routing(3.8) 雅芳 Avon(3.8) 姗拉娜 SamSara(3.8) 欧珀莱 Aupres(3.8) 玫琳凯 Mary kay(3.8) 爱心 Aixin(3.8)
25~34 岁 Age	66	欧珀莱 Aupres(16.7)	高丝 Kose(15.2)	资生堂 Shiseido(10.6)
35~44 岁 Age	35	欧珀莱 Aupres(17.1)	高丝 Kose(11.4)	大宝.高丽雅娜.阿特皮雅 Dabao Coreana Artpla(8.6)
45~54 岁 Age	15	自然美 Natural Beauty(13.3)	羽西 Yue-sai(6.7) 芬莎 Fensha(6.7) 海宝 Haibao(6.7) 玉兰油 Oil of Olay(6.7) 东洋之花 Sakula(6.7) 资生堂 Shiseido(6.7) 安利 Amway(6.7) 柔婷 Routing(6.7) 欧珀莱 Aupres(6.7) 丽花丝宝 Laifa-C'bons(6.7) 高丝 Kose(6.7) 迪奥 CD(6.7) 大宝.高丽雅娜.阿特支雅 Dabao Coreana Artpla(6.7)	
55~60 岁 Age	3	大宝.高丽雅娜.阿特皮雅 Dabao Coreana Artpla(33.3) 欧珀莱 Aupres(33.3) 诗芙侬 Shifunong(33.3)		

1-4 正在使用的品牌排名/ Ranking of the Brands Used Now

排名 Brand Ranking	品牌 Brands	人数 Number	百分比 Percent
1	欧珀莱 Aupres	21	14.5
2	高丝 Kose	15	10.3
3	资生堂 Shiseido	12	8.3
4	大宝.高丽雅娜.阿特皮雅 Dabao Coreana Artpla	7	4.8
5	强生可伶可俐 Clean&Clear	6	4.1
6	雅芳 Avon	5	3.4
7	安利 Amway	4	2.8
7	柔婷 Routing	4	2.8

n=145

1-5 品牌转换习惯/ Brand Habit in Consuming Cosmetics Water

	人数 Number	第一次使用该品牌 first use this brand	上一次也是这个牌子 used it last time	上一次不是这个牌子 not used it last time
女性 Female	143	21.0	65.0	14.0
欧珀莱 Aupres	21	14.3	71.4	14.3
高丝 Kose	15	20.0	73.3	6.7
资生堂 Shiseido	12	16.7	66.7	16.7
大宝.高丽雅娜.阿特皮雅 Dabao Coreana Artpla	7	0.0	71.4	28.6
强生可伶可俐 Clean&Clear	6	33.3	66.7	0.0
雅芳 Avon	5	0.0	80.0	20.0
安利 Amway	4	75.0	25.0	0.0
柔婷 Routing	4	50.0	25.0	25.0

1-6 下一次打算使用的品牌排名/ Ranking of the Brands to be Used Next Time

排名 Brand Ranking	品牌 Brands	人数 Number	百分比 Percent
1	欧珀莱 Aupres	23	16.0
2	资生堂 Shiseido	14	9.7
3	高丝 Kose	13	9.0
4	大宝.高丽雅娜.阿特皮雅 Dabao Coreana Artpla	7	4.9
4	强生可伶可俐 Clean&Clear	7	4.9
5	雅芳 Avon	5	3.5
6	柔婷 Routing	4	2.8

n=144

1-7 样本、女性各年龄层的使用频率/ Frequencies of the Consumed Cosmetics Water by the Female Sample and Age Groups

	人数 Number	天天用 daily	两三天用 1 次 once 2 or 3 days	一周 1～2 次 once or twice a week	半个月一次 once half a month	一个月 1 次或以下 once a month or below	没用过 never use
女性 Female	505	19.0	4.4	3.0	0.8	1.6	71.3
16~24 岁 Age	108	17.6	2.8	0.9	1.9	0.9	75.9
25~34 岁 Age	149	24.8	8.1	6.7	1.3	3.4	55.7
35~44 岁 Age	123	22.0	4.1	1.6	0.0	0.8	71.5
45~54 岁 Age	84	11.9	2.4	2.4	0.0	1.2	82.1
55~60 岁 Age	41	7.3	0.0	0.0	0.0	0.0	92.7

1-8 选择该类商品的考虑因素/ Ranking of the Considerations in Purchasing

注：本题为多选题，合计百分比超过 100%（Multiple answers）

排名 Ranking	考虑因素 Considerations	人次 Person-time	百分比 Percent
1	产品功用 product function	85	59.4
2	有名的牌子 famous brand	59	41.3
3	价格适中 reasonable price	40	28.0
4	别人推荐 introduced by other people	35	24.5
5	广告影响 influence of advertising	11	7.7
6	购买方便 easy to buy	8	5.6
7	包装吸引人 appealing package	4	2.8
7	有优惠条件 with preferential terms	4	2.8
8	其它 others	3	2.1

n=143

1-9 对产品功能的侧重方面/ Ranking of the Considerations about the Function of this Kind of Product

注：本题为多选题，合计百分比超过 100%（Multiple answers）

排名 Ranking	侧重方面 Items	人次 Person-time	百分比 Percent
1	保湿功能 keeping moisture	96	66.7
2	易于吸收 easy to dissolve	56	38.9
3	收缩毛孔 pore contracting	53	36.8
4	平衡功能 balancing	27	18.8
5	不含香料 containing no perfume	24	16.7
6	隔离功能 protecting effect	12	8.3
7	其他 others	4	2.8

n=144

1-10 重度消费者的人口分布/ Demographics of the Heavy Consumers

	人数 Number	16-24 岁 Age	25-34 岁 Age	35-44 岁 Age	45-54 岁 Age	55-60 岁 Age
女性 Female	118	18.6	41.5	27.1	10.2	2.5
天天用 daily	96	19.8	38.5	28.1	10.4	3.1
两三天用 1 次 once 2 or 3 days	22	13.6	54.5	22.7	9.1	0.0

1-11 不同消费者层的常用品牌/ The Most Frequently Used Brands by Market Segments

1-11-1 时尚流行指标/ Fads Popular Index

	人数 Number	第一品牌及百分比 1st/ percent	第二品牌及百分比 2nd/ percent	第三品牌及百分比 3rd/ percent
女性 Female	143	**欧珀莱 Aupres(13.3)**	**高丝 Kose(11.9)**	**资生堂 Shiseido(7.7)**
平实生活指向 simple living orientation	37	高丝 Kose(16.2)	大宝.高丽雅娜.阿特皮雅 Dabao Coreana Artpla(8.1) 欧珀莱 Aupres(8.1) 资生堂 Shiseido(8.1)	爱心 Aixin(5.4) 强生可伶可俐 Clean&Clear(5.4)
时尚流行指向 fashion orientation	106	欧珀莱 Aupres(15.1)	高丝 Kose(10.4)	资生堂 Shiseido(7.5)

1-11-2 广告态度指标/ Advertising Attitude Index

	人数 Number	第一品牌及百分比 1st/ percent	第二品牌及百分比 2nd/ percent	第三品牌及百分比 3rd/ percent
女性 Female	141	**欧珀莱 Aupres(14.2)**	**高丝 Kose(12.1)**	**资生堂 Shiseido(7.1)**
广告淡漠指向 indifferent orientation	28	欧珀莱 Aupres(21.4)	高丝 Kose(14.3)	资生堂 Shiseido(10.7)
中间层 medium	93	高丝 Kose(12.9) 欧珀莱 Aupres(12.9)	资生堂 Shiseido(7.5)	强生可伶可俐 Clean&Clear(5.4)
信赖广告指向 loyal orientation	20	大宝.高丽雅娜.阿特皮雅 Dabao Coreana Artpla(15.0)	欧珀莱 Aupres(10.0)	诗芙侬 Shifunong(5.0) 欧琳凯 Oulinkai(5.0) CYTACT(5.0) 花蕊 Huarui(5.0) 倩黛 Qiandai(5.0) 旁氏 Pond's(5.0) 东洋之花 Sakula(5.0) 安利 Amway(5.0) 姗拉娜 SamSara(5.0) 欧莱雅 L'oreal(5.0) 玫琳凯 Mary kay(5.0) 丽花丝宝 Laifa-C'bons(5.0) 兰寇 Lancome(5.0) 花王碧柔 Biore(5.0) 高丝 Kose(5.0)

1-12 重度消费者的消费层构成/ The Composition of the Heavy Consumers

1-12-1 时尚流行指标/ Fads Popular Index

	人数 Number	平实生活指向 simple living orientation	时尚流行指向 fashion orientation
女性 Female	116	22.4	77.6
天天用 daily	94	21.3	78.7
两三天用 1 次 once 2 or 3 days	22	27.3	72.7

1-12-2 广告态度指标/ Advertising Attitude Index

	人数 Number	广告淡漠指向 indifferent orientation	中间层 medium	信赖广告指向 loyal orientation
女性 Female	114	17.5	71.9	10.5
天天用 daily	93	18.3	69.9	11.8
两三天用 1 次 once 2 or 3 days	21	14.3	81.0	4.8

● 上海 / Shanghai

1-1 最近三个月使用频次的比例/ Proportion of the Sample Consuming Cosmetics Water in the Last Three Months

	人数 Number	百分比 Percent
天天用 daily	81	16.4
两三天用 1 次 once 2 or 3 days	15	3.0
一周 1~2 次 once or twice a week	16	3.2
半个月一次 once half a month	6	1.2
一个月 1 次或以下 once a month or below	2	0.4
没用过 never use	373	75.7

n=493

1-2 最常用品牌排名/ Ranking of the Most Frequently Used Brands

排名 Brand Ranking	品牌 Brands	人数 Number	百分比 Percent
1	强生可伶可俐 Clean&Clear	14	11.7
2	资生堂 Shiseido	13	10.8
3	妮维雅 Nivea	10	8.3
4	羽西 Yue-sai	8	6.7
4	郑明明 Cheng Mingming	8	6.7
5	法兰西施 Miss de France	5	4.2
6	ZA	4	3.3
7	清妃 Chinf	3	2.5
7	欧珀莱 Aupres	3	2.5
7	美宝莲 Maybelline	3	2.5
7	自然美 Natural Beauty	3	2.5
7	大宝.高丽雅娜.阿特皮雅 Dabao Coreana Artpla	3	2.5

n=120

1-3 样本、女性各年龄层的常用品牌/ The Most Frequently Used Brands by the Female Sample and Age Groups

	人数 Number	第一品牌及百分比 1st/ percent	第二品牌及百分比 2nd/ percent	第三品牌及百分比 3rd/ percent
女性 Female	120	**强生可伶可俐 Clean&Clear(11.7)**	**资生堂 Shiseido(10.8)**	**妮维雅 Nivea(8.3)**
16~24 岁 Age	35	资生堂 Shiseido(22.9)	强生可伶可俐 Clean&Clear(17.1)	妮维雅 Nivea(8.6)
25~34 岁 Age	51	妮维雅 Nivea(11.8)	郑明明 Cheng Mingming(9.8) 强生可伶可俐 Clean&Clear(9.8)	羽西 Yue-sai(7.8) 资生堂 Shiseido(7.8)
35~44 岁 Age	24	强生可伶可俐 Clean&Clear(8.3) 郑明明 Cheng Mingming(8.3) 羽西 Yue-sai(8.3)	倩碧 Clinique(4.2) 花 FA(4.2) 诗丽雅 Ginvere(4.2) 雅诗兰黛 Estee Lauder(4.2) 法兰西施 Miss de France(4.2) 大宝.高丽雅娜.阿特皮雅 Dabao Coreana Artpla(4.2) 资生堂 Shiseido(4.2) 绿世界 Green World(4.2) 旁氏 Pond's(4.2) 小护士 Mininurse(4.2) 凤凰 Phoenix(4.2) 芬兰馨 Fenlanxin(4.2) 绵羊油 Mianyangyou(4.2) 凡士林 Vaseline(4.2) 美宝莲 Maybelline(4.2) 八天 Batian(4.2)	
45~54 岁 Age	7	法兰西施 Miss de France(28.6)	高丝 Kose(14.3) 花王碧柔 Biore(14.3) 妮维雅 Nivea(14.3) 倩碧 Clinique(14.3) 郑明明 Cheng Mingming(14.3)	
55~60 岁 Age	3	强生可伶可俐 Clean&Clear(33.3) 诗芙侬 Shifunong(33.3) 尤雅 Youya(33.3)		

1-4 正在使用的品牌排名/ Ranking of the Brands Used Now

排名 Brand Ranking	品牌 Brands	人数 Number	百分比 Percent
1	强生可伶可俐 Clean&Clear	16	13.3
2	资生堂 Shiseido	12	10.0
3	妮维雅 Nivea	10	8.3
4	郑明明 Cheng Mingming	8	6.7
4	羽西 Yue-sai	8	6.7
5	法兰西施 Miss de France	5	4.2
6	欧珀莱 Aupres	4	3.3
7	美宝莲 Maybelline	3	2.5
7	自然美 Natural Beauty	3	2.5
7	清妃 Chinf	3	2.5
7	倩碧 Clinique	3	2.5
7	旁氏 Pond's	3	2.5
7	伊丽特 Yilite	3	2.5
7	ZA	3	2.5
7	大宝.高丽雅娜.阿特皮雅 Dabao Coreana Artpla	3	2.5

n=120

1-5 品牌转换习惯/ Brand Habit in Consuming Cosmetics Water

	人数 Number	第一次使用该品牌 first use this brand	上一次也是这个牌子 used it last time	上一次不是这个牌子 not used it last time
女性 Female	120	20.8	73.3	5.8
强生可伶可俐 Clean&Clear	16	18.8	81.3	0.0
资生堂 Shiseido	12	16.7	83.3	0.0
妮维雅 Nivea	10	30.0	70.0	0.0
郑明明 Cheng Mingming	8	12.5	87.5	0.0
羽西 Yue-sai	8	25.0	75.0	0.0
法兰西施 Miss de France	5	0.0	80.0	20.0
欧珀莱 Aupres	4	50.0	50.0	0.0

1-6 下一次打算使用的品牌排名/ Ranking of the Brands to be Used Next Time

排名 Brand Ranking	品牌 Brands	人数 Number	百分比 Percent
1	资生堂 Shiseido	18	15.0
2	强生可伶可俐 Clean&Clear	10	8.3
3	妮维雅 Nivea	9	7.5
4	羽西 Yue-sai	7	5.8
5	郑明明 Cheng Mingming	5	4.2
5	法兰西施 Miss de France	5	4.2
6	欧珀莱 Aupres	4	3.3
6	倩碧 Clinique	4	3.3
6	ZA	4	3.3
7	旁氏 Pond's	3	2.5
7	清妃 Chinf	3	2.5
7	自然美 Natural Beauty	3	2.5
7	玫琳凯 Mary Kay	3	2.5
7	花 FA	3	2.5
7	美宝莲 Maybelline	3	2.5
7	大宝.高丽雅娜.阿特皮雅 Dabao Coreana Artpla	3	2.5

n=120

1-7 样本、女性各年龄层的使用频率/ Frequencies of the Consumed Cosmetics Water by the Female Sample and Age Groups

	人数 Number	天天用 daily	两三天用 1 次 once 2 or 3 days	一周 1～2 次 once or twice a week	半个月一次 once half a month	一个月 1 次或以下 once a month or below	没用过 never use
女性 Female	493	16.4	3.0	3.2	1.2	0.4	75.7
16~24 岁 Age	103	19.4	4.9	6.8	1.9	1.0	66.0
25~34 岁 Age	141	24.1	4.3	4.3	2.8	0.7	63.8
35~44 岁 Age	128	14.8	2.3	1.6	0.0	0.0	81.3
45~54 岁 Age	81	7.4	1.2	0.0	0.0	0.0	91.4
55~60 岁 Age	40	5.0	0.0	2.5	0.0	0.0	92.5

1-8 选择该类商品的考虑因素/ Ranking of the Considerations in Purchasing

注：本题为多选题，合计百分比超过 100%（Multiple answers）

排名 Ranking	考虑因素 Considerations	人次 Person-time	百分比 Percent
1	产品功用 product function	55	45.8
2	有名的牌子 famous brand	52	43.3
3	价格适中 reasonable price	40	33.3
4	别人推荐 introduced by other people	22	18.3
5	广告影响 influence of advertising	17	14.2
6	购买方便 easy to buy	15	12.5
7	有优惠条件 with preferential terms	7	5.8
8	包装吸引人 appealing package	2	1.7
8	其它 others	2	1.7

n=120

1-9 对产品功能的侧重方面/ Ranking of the Considerations about the Function of this Kind of Product

注：本题为多选题，合计百分比超过 100%（Multiple answers）

排名 Ranking	侧重方面 Items	人次 Person-time	百分比 Percent
1	保湿功能 keeping moisture	65	54.2
2	收缩毛孔 pore contracting	55	45.8
3	易于吸收 easy to dissolve	44	36.7
4	平衡功能 balancing	32	26.7
5	不含香料 containing no perfume	17	14.2
6	隔离功能 protecting effect	8	6.7
7	其他 others	2	1.7

n=120

1-10 重度消费者的人口分布/ Demographics of the Heavy Consumers

	人数 Number	16-24 岁 Age	25-34 岁 Age	35-44 岁 Age	45-54 岁 Age	55-60 岁 Age
女性 Female	96	26.0	41.7	22.9	7.3	2.1
天天用 daily	81	24.7	42.0	23.5	7.4	2.5
两三天用 1 次 once 2 or 3 days	15	33.3	40.0	20.0	6.7	0.0

1-11 不同消费者层的常用品牌/ The Most Frequently Used Brands by Market Segments

1-11-1 时尚流行指标/ Fads Popular Index

	人数 Number	第一品牌及百分比 1st/ percent	第二品牌及百分比 2nd/ percent	第三品牌及百分比 3rd/ percent
女性 Female	119	**强生可伶可俐 Clean&Clear（11.8)**	**资生堂 Shiseido（10.9)**	**妮维雅 Nivea（8.4)**
平实生活指向 simple living orientation	23	郑明明 Cheng Mingming（13.0) 强生可伶可俐 Clean&Clear（13.0)	大宝.高丽雅娜.阿特皮雅 Dabao Coreana Artpla（8.7)	赵小蝶 Zhaoxiaodie（4.3) ZA（4.3) 美宝莲 Maybelline（4.3) 夏士莲 Hazeline（4.3) 旁氏 Pond's（4.3) 东洋之花 Sakula（4.3) 资生堂 Shiseido（4.3) 羽西 Yuesai（4.3) 诗芙侬 Shifunong（4.3) 清妃 Chinf（4.3) 欧珀莱 Aupres（4.3) 妮维雅 Nivea（4.3) 高丝 Kose（4.3) 法兰西施 Miss de France（4.3)
时尚流行指向 fashion orientation	96	资生堂 Shiseido（12.5)	强生可伶可俐 Clean&Clear（11.5)	妮维雅 Nivea（9.4)

1-11-2 广告态度指标/ Advertising Attitude Index

	人数 Number	第一品牌及百分比 1st/ percent	第二品牌及百分比 2nd/ percent	第三品牌及百分比 3rd/ percent
女性 Female	119	**强生可伶可俐 Clean&Clear（11.8）**	**资生堂 Shiseido（10.9）**	**妮维雅 Nivea（8.4）**
广告淡漠指向 indifferent orientation	22	郑明明 Cheng Mingming（18.2）	强生可伶可俐 Clear&Clear（13.6）	资生堂 Shiseido（9.1） ZA（9.1）
中间层 medium	76	强生可伶可俐 Clean&Clear（11.8）	资生堂 Shiseido（10.5）	妮维雅 Nivea（7.9）
信赖广告指向 loyal orientation	21	资生堂 Shiseido（14.3） 妮维雅 Nivea（14.3）	强生可伶可俐 Clean&Clear（9.5） 雅芳 Avon（9.5） 羽西 Yue-sai（9.5）	ZA（4.8） 凡士林 Vaseline（4.8） 夏士莲 Hazeline（4.8） 小护士 Mininurse（4.8） 法兰西施 Miss de France（4.8） 郑明明 Cheng Mingming（4.8） 圣罗兰 Yves Saint Laurent（4.8） 清妃 Chinf（4.8） 花 FA（4.8）

1-12 重度消费者的消费层构成/ The Composition of the Heavy Consumers

1-12-1 时尚流行指标/ Fads Popular Index

	人数 Number	平实生活指向 simple living orientation	时尚流行指向 fashion orientation
女性 Female	**96**	**20.8**	**79.2**
天天用 daily	81	23.5	76.5
两三天用 1 次 once 2 or 3 days	15	6.7	93.3

1-12-2 广告态度指标/ Advertising Attitude Index

	人数 Number	广告淡漠指向 indifferent orientation	中间层 medium	信赖广告指向 loyal orientation
女性 Female	**96**	**20.8**	**61.5**	**17.7**
天天用 daily	81	17.3	64.2	18.5
两三天用 1 次 once 2 or 3 days	15	40.0	46.7	13.3

● 广州 / Guangzhou

1-1 最近三个月使用频次的比例/ Proportion of the Sample Consuming Cosmetics Water in the Last Three Months

	人数 Number	百分比 Percent
天天用 daily	80	15.5
两三天用 1 次 once 2 or 3 days	22	4.3
一周 1～2 次 once or twice a week	20	3.9
半个月一次 once half a month	7	1.4
一个月 1 次或以下 once a month or below	8	1.6
没用过 never use	378	73.4

n=515

1-2 最常用品牌排名/ Ranking of the Most Frequently Used Brands

排名 Brand Ranking	品牌 Brands	人数 Number	百分比 Percent
1	强生可伶可俐 Clean&Clear	23	16.8
2	花王碧柔 Biore	12	8.8
2	雅芳 Avon	12	8.8
3	资生堂 Shiseido	6	4.4
4	旁氏 Pond's	5	3.6
5	羽西 Yue-sai	4	2.9
5	花 Fa	4	2.9
5	采诗 Caishi	4	2.9
5	玉兰油 Oil of Olay	4	2.9
5	绿之韵 Lvzhiyun	4	2.9

n=137

1-3 样本、女性各年龄层的常用品牌/ The Most Frequently Used Brands by the Female Sample and Age Groups

	人数 Number	第一品牌及百分比 1st/ percent	第二品牌及百分比 2nd/ percent	第三品牌及百分比 3rd/ percent
女性 Female	137	强生可伶可俐 Clean&Clear(16.8)	花王碧柔 Biore(8.8) 雅芳 Avon(8.8)	资生堂 Shiseido(4.4)
16~24 岁 Age	42	强生可伶可俐 Clean&Clear(33.3)	花王碧柔 Biore(16.7)	高丝 Kose(4.8) 米一夜 Miyiye(4.8) 树一派 Shuyipai(4.8)
25~34 岁 Age	54	雅芳 Avon(13.0)	资生堂 Shiseido(9.3)	强生可伶可俐 Clean&Clear(7.4)
35~44 岁 Age	30	强生可伶可俐 Clean&Clear(13.3)	雅芳 Avon(10.0)	花王碧柔 Biore(6.7) 旁氏 Pond's(6.7) 朵而 Duoer(6.7)
45~54 岁 Age	10	艾琳 Irlene(20.0)	诗芙侬 Shifunong(10.0) 雅芳 Avon(10.0) 羽西 Yue-sai(10.0) 旁氏 Pond's(10.0) 美加净 Maxam(10.0) 绿之韵 Lvzhiyun(10.0)	
55~60 岁 Age	1	强生可伶可俐 Clean&Clear(100.0)		

1-4 正在使用的品牌排名/ Ranking of the Brands Used Now

排名 Brand Ranking	品牌 Brands	人数 Number	百分比 Percent
1	强生可伶可俐 Clean&Clear	21	15.3
2	雅芳 Avon	13	9.5
3	花王碧柔 Biore	12	8.8
4	资生堂 Shiseido	6	4.4
5	艾琳 Irlene	4	2.9
5	旁氏 Pond's	4	2.9
5	羽西 Yue-sai	4	2.9
5	绿之韵 Lvzhiyun	4	2.9
5	玉兰油 Oil of Olay	4	2.9
5	花 Fa	4	2.9

n=137

1-5 品牌转换习惯/ Brand Habit in Consuming Cosmetics Water

	人数 Number	第一次使用该品牌 first use this brand	上一次也是这个牌子 used it last time	上一次不是这个牌子 not used it last time
女性 Female	135	23.0	62.2	14.8
强生可伶可俐 Clean&Clear	21	19.0	66.7	14.3
雅芳 Avon	13	15.4	76.9	7.7
花王碧柔 Biore	12	16.7	75.0	8.3

1-6 下一次打算使用的品牌排名/ Ranking of the Brands to be Used Next Time

排名 Brand Ranking	品牌 Brands	人数 Number	百分比 Percent
1	强生可伶可俐 Clean&Clear	18	13.1
2	雅芳 Avon	13	9.5
3	花王碧柔 Biore	11	8.0
4	资生堂 Shiseido	7	5.1
5	旁氏 Pond's	6	4.4
6	玉兰油 Oil of Olay	5	3.6
7	绿之韵 Lvzhiyun	4	2.9
7	采诗 Caishi	4	2.9
7	艾琳 Irlene	4	2.9

n=137

1-7 样本、女性各年龄层的使用频率/ Frequencies of the Consumed Cosmetics Water by the Female Sample and Age Groups

	人数 Number	天天用 daily	两三天用 1 次 once 2 or 3 days	一周 1~2 次 once or twice a week	半个月一次 once half a month	一个月 1 次或以下 once a month or below	没用过 never use
女性 Female	515	15.5	4.3	3.9	1.4	1.6	73.4
16~24 岁 Age	112	25.0	6.3	2.7	2.7	0.9	62.5
25~34 岁 Age	155	19.4	7.1	5.8	1.3	1.3	65.2
35~44 岁 Age	129	11.6	3.1	5.4	0.8	2.3	76.7
45~54 岁 Age	81	7.4	0.0	1.2	1.2	2.5	87.7
55~60 岁 Age	38	2.6	0.0	0.0	0.0	0.0	97.4

1-8 选择该类商品的考虑因素/ Ranking of the Considerations in Purchasing

注：本题为多选题，合计百分比超过 100%（Multiple answers）

排名 Ranking	考虑因素 Considerations	人次 Person-time	百分比 Percent
1	产品功用 product function	70	51.1
2	有名的牌子 famous brand	53	38.7
3	价格适中 reasonable price	48	35.0
4	别人推荐 introduced by other people	38	27.7
5	广告影响 influence of advertising	23	16.8
6	购买方便 easy to buy	17	12.4
7	有优惠条件 with preferential terms	8	5.8
8	包装吸引人 appealing package	6	4.4
9	其它 others	1	0.7

n=137

1-9 对产品功能的侧重方面/ Ranking of the Considerations about the Function of this Kind of Product

注：本题为多选题，合计百分比超过 100%（Multiple answers）

排名 Ranking	侧重方面 Items	人次 Person-time	百分比 Percent
1	收缩毛孔 pore contracting	90	65.7
2	保湿功能 keeping moisture	82	59.9
3	易于吸收 easy to dissolve	40	29.2
4	平衡功能 balancing	36	26.3
5	不含香料 containing no perfume	21	15.3
6	隔离功能 protecting effect	9	6.6
7	其他 others	2	1.5

n=137

1-10 重度消费者的人口分布/ Demographics of the Heavy Consumers

	人数 Number	16-24 岁 Age	25-34 岁 Age	35-44 岁 Age	45-54 岁 Age	55-60 岁 Age
女性 Female	102	34.3	40.2	18.6	5.9	1.0
天天用 daily	80	35.0	37.5	13.8	7.5	1.3
两三天用 1 次 once 2 or 3 days	22	31.8	50.0	18.2	0.0	0.0

1-11 不同消费者层的常用品牌/ The Most Frequently Used Brands by Market Segments

1-11-1 时尚流行指标/ Fads Popular Index

	人数 Number	第一品牌及百分比 1st/ percent	第二品牌及百分比 2nd/ percent	第三品牌及百分比 3rd/ percent
女性 Female	134	强生可伶可俐 Clean&Clear(16.4)	花王碧柔 Biore(9.0) 雅芳 Avon(9.0)	资生堂 Shiseido(4.5)
平实生活指向 simple living orientation	40	花王碧柔 Biore(12.5)	强生可伶可俐 Clean&Clear(10.0)	雅芳 Avon(7.5)
时尚流行指向 fashion orientation	94	强生可伶可俐 Clean&Clear(19.1)	雅芳 Avon(9.6)	花王碧柔 Biore(7.4)

1-11-2 广告态度指标/ Advertising Attitude Index

	人数 Number	第一品牌及百分比 1st/ percent	第二品牌及百分比 2nd/ percent	第三品牌及百分比 3rd/ percent
女性 Female	**133**	**强生可伶可俐 Clean&Clear(16.5)**	**花王碧柔 Biore(9.0)**	**雅芳 Avon(8.3)**
广告淡漠指向 indifferent orientation	33	花王碧柔 Biore(9.1) 强生可伶可俐 Clean&Clear(9.1)	露洁 Lujie(6.1) 雅芳 Avon(6.1) 旁氏 Pond's(6.1)	柔美 Roumei(3.0) BB 油 Bbyou(3.0) 朵而 Duoer(3.0) 树一派 Shuyipai(3.0) 金阑 Jinlan(3.0) 采诗 Caishi(3.0) 美宝王齿 Mei Bao Wang Chi(3.0) 浪奇 Langqi(3.0) 克丽提 Keliti(3.0) 丁家宜 Dingjiayi(3.0) 绿之韵 Lvzhiyun(3.0) 丹芭碧 Tobaby(3.0) 莎莉 Shali(3.0) 艾琳 Irlene(3.0) 小护士 Mininurse(3.0) 羽西 Yue-sai(3.0) 唯美嘉露 Miss Carol(3.0) 诗芙侬 Shifunong(3.0) 花 Fa(3.0)
中间层 medium	89	强生可伶可俐 Clean&Clear(18.0)	雅芳 Avon(9.0)	花王碧柔 Biore(7.9)
信赖广告指向 loyal orientation	11	强生可伶可俐 Clean&Clear(27.3)	花王碧柔 Biore(18.2)	安利 Amway(9.1) 花 Fa(9.1) 雅芳 Avon(9.1) 资生堂 Shiseido(9.1) 树一派 Shuyipai(9.1) LG(9.1)

1-12 重度消费者的消费层构成/ The Composition of the Heavy Consumers

1-12-1 时尚流行指标/ Fads Popular Index

	人数 Number	平实生活指向 simple living orientation	时尚流行指向 fashion orientation
女性 Female	**101**	**25.7**	**74.3**
天天用 daily	79	21.5	78.5
两三天用 1 次 once 2 or 3 days	22	40.9	59.1

1-12-2 广告态度指标/ Advertising Attitude Index

	人数 Number	广告淡漠指向 indifferent orientation	中间层 medium	信赖广告指向 loyal orientation
女性 Female	**99**	**23.2**	**67.7**	**9.1**
天天用 daily	79	22.8	68.4	8.9
两三天用 1 次 once 2 or 3 days	20	25.0	65.0	10.0

● 重庆 / Chongqing

1-1 最近三个月使用频次的比例/ Proportion of the Sample Consuming Cosmetics Water in the Last Three Months

	人数 Number	百分比 Percent
天天用 daily	27	8.8
两三天用 1 次 once 2 or 3 days	1	0.3
一周 1～2 次 once or twice a week	6	2.0
半个月一次 once half a month	3	1.0
一个月 1 次或以下 once a month or below	0	0.0
没用过 never use	270	87.9

n=307

1-2 最常用品牌排名/ Ranking of the Most Frequently Used Brands

排名 Brand Ranking	品牌 Brands	人数 Number	百分比 Percent
1	蕾迪雅 Ladiera	2	5.4
1	夏士莲 Hazeline	2	5.4
1	玉兰油 Oil of Olay	2	5.4
1	资生堂 Shiseido	2	5.4
1	芦荟 Luhui	2	5.4
1	强生可伶可俐 Clean&Clear	2	5.4
1	欧珀莱 Aupres	2	5.4
1	蝶妆 Debon LG	2	5.4

n=37

1-3 样本、女性各年龄层的常用品牌/ The Most Frequently Used Brands by the Female Sample and Age Groups

	人数 Number	第一品牌及百分比 1st/ percent	第二品牌及百分比 2nd/ percent
女性 Female	37	**蕾迪雅 Ladiera(5.4)** **夏士莲 Hazeline(5.4)** **玉兰油 Oil of Olay(5.4)** **资生堂 Shiseido(5.4)** **芦荟 Luhui(5.4)** **强生可伶可俐 Clean&Clear(5.4)** **欧珀莱 Aupres(5.4)** **蝶妆 Debon LG(5.4)**	**比肤 Bifu(2.7)** **谭氏红堂草 TanShiHongTangCao (2.7)** **安尚秀 Anshangxiu(2.7)** **白美诗 Baimeishi(2.7)** **LG(2.7)** **妍芙阑 Yanfulan(2.7)** **绿之韵 Lvzhiyun(2.7)** **雅倩 Arche(2.7)** **小护士 Mininurse(2.7)** **雨水 Yushui(2.7)** **丹芭碧 Tobaby(2.7)** **羽西 Yue-sai(2.7)** **依贝佳 Ebeca(2.7)** **雅芳 Avon(2.7)** **柔婷 Routing(2.7)** **清妃 Chinf(2.7)** **花王碧柔 Biore(2.7)**
16~24 岁 Age	13	欧珀莱 Aupres(15.4) 强生可伶可俐 Clean&Clear(15.4)	蕾迪雅 Ladiera(7.7) LG(7.7) 谭氏红堂草 TanShiHongTangCao (7.7) 雅倩 Arche(7.7) 蝶妆 Debon LG(7.7) 夏士莲 Hazeline(7.7) 资生堂 Shiseido(7.7) 羽西 Yue-sai(7.7) 花王碧柔 Biore(7.7)
25~34 岁 Age	14	丹芭碧 Tobaby(7.1) 比肤 Bifu(7.1) 安尚秀 Anshangxiu(7.1) 白美诗 Baimeishi(7.1) 芦荟 Luhui(7.1) 雨水 Yushui(7.1) 小护士 Mininurse(7.1) 雅芳 Avon(7.1) 柔婷 Routing(7.1) 清妃 Chinf(7.1) 蝶妆 Debon LG(7.1)	
35~44 岁 Age	5	资生堂 Shiseido(20.0) 玉兰油 Oil of Olay(20.0) 芦荟 Luhui(20.0) 妍芙阑 Yanfulan(20.0)	
45~54 岁 Age	5	依贝佳 Ebeca(20.0) 玉兰油 Oil of Olay(20.0) 夏士莲 Hazeline(20.0) 蕾迪雅 Ladiera(20.0) 绿之韵 Lvzhiyun(20.0)	
55~60 岁 Age	0		

1-4 正在使用的品牌排名/ Ranking of the Brands Used Now

排名 Brand Ranking	品牌 Brands	人数 Number	百分比 Percent
1	高丝 Kose	2	5.4
1	蕾迪雅 Ladiera	2	5.4
1	欧珀莱 Aupres	2	5.4
1	强生可伶可俐 Clean&Clear	2	5.4
1	玉兰油 Oil of Olay	2	5.4
1	夏士莲 Hazeline	2	5.4
1	绿之韵 Lvzhiyun	2	5.4

n=37

1-5 品牌转换习惯/ Brand Habit in Consuming Cosmetics Water

	人数 Number	第一次使用该品牌 first use this brand	上一次也是这个牌子 used it last time	上一次不是这个牌子 not used it last time
女性 Female	37	27.0	54.1	18.9
高丝 Kose	2	50.0	0.0	50.0
蕾迪雅 Ladiera	2	0.0	100.0	0.0
欧珀莱 Aupres	2	0.0	100.0	0.0
强生可伶可俐 Clean&Clear	2	0.0	0.0	100.0
玉兰油 Oil of Olay	2	0.0	100.0	0.0
夏士莲 Hazeline	2	0.0	100.0	0.0
绿之韵 Lvzhiyun	2	100.0	0.0	0.0

1-6 下一次打算使用的品牌排名/ Ranking of the Brands to be Used Next Time

排名 Brand Ranking	品牌 Brands	人数 Number	百分比 Percent
1	欧珀莱 Aupres	2	5.4
1	资生堂 Shiseido	2	5.4
1	蕾迪雅 Ladiera	2	5.4
1	夏士莲 Hazeline	2	5.4

n=37

1-7 样本、女性各年龄层的使用频率/ Frequencies of the Consumed Cosmetics Water by the Female Sample and Age Groups

	人数 Number	天天用 daily	两三天用 1 次 once 2 or 3 days	一周 1～2 次 once or twice a week	半个月一次 once half a month	一个月 1 次或以下 once a month or below	没用过 never use
女性 Female	307	8.8	0.3	2.0	1.0	0.0	87.9
16~24 岁 Age	64	10.9	1.6	6.3	1.6	0.0	79.7
25~34 岁 Age	88	12.5	0.0	1.1	2.3	0.0	84.1
35~44 岁 Age	72	5.6	0.0	1.4	0.0	0.0	93.1
45~54 岁 Age	60	8.3	0.0	0.0	0.0	0.0	91.7
55~60 岁 Age	23	0.0	0.0	0.0	0.0	0.0	100.0

1-8 选择该类商品的考虑因素/ Ranking of the Considerations in Purchasing

注：本题为多选题，合计百分比超过 100%（Multiple answers）

排名 Ranking	考虑因素 Considerations	人次 Person-time	百分比 Percent
1	别人推荐 introduced by other people	14	37.8
2	产品功用 product function	12	32.4
3	广告影响 influence of advertising	9	24.3
4	价格适中 reasonable price	8	21.6
5	有名的牌子 famous brand	7	18.9
6	购买方便 easy to buy	6	16.2
6	有优惠条件 with preferential terms	6	16.2
7	包装吸引人 appealing package	2	5.4
8	其它 others	1	2.7

n=37

1-9 对产品功能的侧重方面/ Ranking of the Considerations about the Function of this Kind of Product

注：本题为多选题，合计百分比超过 100%（Multiple answers）

排名 Ranking	侧重方面 Items	人次 Person-time	百分比 Percent
1	保湿功能 keeping moisture	20	55.6
2	收缩毛孔 pore contracting	16	44.4
3	易于吸收 easy to dissolve	12	33.3
4	平衡功能 balancing	11	30.6
5	不含香料 containing no perfume	4	11.1
6	隔离功能 protecting effect	3	8.3

n=36

1-10 重度消费者的人口分布/ Demographics of the Heavy Consumers

	人数 Number	16-24 岁 Age	25-34 岁 Age	35-44 岁 Age	45-54 岁 Age	55-60 岁 Age
女性 Female	28	28.6	39.3	14.3	17.9	0.0
天天用 daily	27	25.9	40.7	14.8	18.5	0.0
两三天用 1 次 once 2 or 3 days	1	100.0	0.0	0.0	0.0	0.0

1-11 不同消费者层的常用品牌/ The Most Frequently Used Brands by Market Segments

1-11-1 时尚流行指标/ Fads Popular Index

	人数 Number	第一品牌及百分比 1st/ percent	第二品牌及百分比 2nd/ percent
女性 Female	37	**蕾迪雅 Ladiera(5.4)** **夏士莲 Hazeline(5.4)** **玉兰油 Oil of Olay(5.4)** **资生堂 Shiseido(5.4)** **芦荟 Luhui(5.4)** **强生可伶可俐 Clean&Clear(5.4)** **欧珀莱 Aupres(5.4)** **蝶妆 Debon LG(5.4)**	**比肤 Bifu(2.7)** **谭氏红堂草 TanShiHongTangCao(2.7)** **安尚秀 Anshangxiu(2.7)** **白美诗 Baimeishi(2.7)** **LG(2.7)** **妍芙阑 Yanfulan(2.7)** **绿之韵 Lvzhiyun(2.7)** **雅倩 Arche(2.7)** **小护士 Mininurse(2.7)** **雨水 Yushui(2.7)** **丹芭碧 Tobaby(2.7)** **羽西 Yue-sai(2.7)** **依贝佳 Ebeca(2.7)** **雅芳 Avon(2.7)** **柔婷 Routing(2.7)** **清妃 Chinf(2.7)** **花王碧柔 Biore(2.7)**
平实生活指向 simple living orientation	10	花王碧柔 Biore(10.0) 欧珀莱 Aupres(10.0) 柔婷 Routing(10.0) 资生堂 Shiseido(10.0) 丹芭碧 Tobaby (10.0) 夏士莲 Hazeline(10.0) 妍芙阑 Yanfulan(10.0) 安尚秀 Anshangxiu(10.0)	
时尚流行指向 fashion orientation	27	蝶妆 Debon LG(7.4) 强生可伶可俐 Clean&Clear(7.4) 蕾迪雅 Ladiera(7.4) 玉兰油 Oil of Olay(7.4) 芦荟 Luhui(7.4)	夏士莲 Hazeline(3.7) LG(3.7) 比肤 Bifu(3.7) 谭氏红堂草 TanShiHongTangCao (3.7) 雅倩 Arche(3.7) 白美诗 Baimeishi(3.7) 绿之韵 Lvzhiyun(3.7) 雨水 Yushui(3.7) 小护士 Mininurse(3.7) 资生堂 Shiseido(3.7) 羽西 Yue-sai(3.7) 依贝佳 Ebeca(3.7) 雅芳 Avon(3.7) 清妃 Chinf(3.7) 欧珀莱 Aupres(3.7)

1-11-2 广告态度指标/ Advertising Attitude Index

	人数 Number	第一品牌及百分比 1st/ percent	第二品牌及百分比 2nd/ percent
女性 Female	37	**蕾迪雅 Ladiera(5.4)** **夏士莲 Hazeline(5.4)** **玉兰油 Oil of Olay(5.4)** **资生堂 Shiseido(5.4)** **芦荟 Luhui(5.4)** **强生可伶可俐 Clean&Clear(5.4)** **欧珀莱 Aupres(5.4)** **蝶妆 Debon LG(5.4)**	**比肤 Bifu(2.7)** **谭氏红堂草 TanShiHongTangCao (2.7)** **安尚秀 Anshangxiu(2.7)** **白美诗 Baimeishi(2.7)** **LG(2.7)** **妍芙阑 Yanfulan(2.7)** **绿之韵 Lvzhiyun(2.7)** **雅倩 Arche(2.7)** **小护士 Mininurse(2.7)** **雨水 Yushui(2.7)** **丹芭碧 Tobaby(2.7)** **羽西 Yue-sai(2.7)** **依贝佳 Ebeca(2.7)** **雅芳 Avon(2.7)** **柔婷 Routing(2.7)** **清妃 Chinf(2.7)** **花王碧柔 Biore(2.7)**
广告淡漠指向 indifferent orientation	9	资生堂 Shiseido(22.2)	欧珀莱 Aupres(11.1) 依贝佳 Ebeca(11.1) 玉兰油 Oil of Olay(11.1) 丹芭碧 Tobaby (11.1) 雨水 Yushui(11.1) 夏士莲 Hazeline(11.1) 绿之韵 Lvzhiyun(11.1)
中间层 medium	23	强生可伶可俐 Clean&Clear(8.7)	夏士莲 Hazeline(4.3) LG(4.3) 比肤 Bifu(4.3) 谭氏红堂草 TanShiHongTangCao (4.3) 雅倩 Arche(4.3) 安尚秀 Anshangxiu(4.3) 蕾迪雅 Ladiera(4.3) 芦荟 Luhui(4.3) 羽西 Yue-sai(4.3) 小护士 Mininurse(4.3) 玉兰油 Oil of Olay(4.3) 雅芳 Avon(4.3) 柔婷 Routing(4.3) 清妃 Chinf(4.3) 欧珀莱 Aupres(4.3) 花王碧柔 Biore(4.3) 蝶妆 Debon LG(4.3)
信赖广告指向 loyal orientation	5	蝶妆 Debon LG(20.0) 芦荟 Luhui(20.0) 蕾迪雅 Ladiera(20.0) 妍芙阑 Yanfulan(20.0) 白美诗 Baimeishi(20.0)	

1-12 重度消费者的消费层构成/ The Composition of the Heavy Consumers

1-12-1 时尚流行指标/ Fads Popular Index

	人数 Number	平实生活指向 simple living orientation	时尚流行指向 fashion orientation
女性 Female	28	**28.6**	**71.4**
天天用 daily	27	25.9	74.1
两三天用 1 次 once 2 or 3 days	1	100.0	0.0

1-12-2 广告态度指标/ Advertising Attitude Index

	人数 Number	广告淡漠指向 indifferent orientation	中间层 medium	信赖广告指向 loyal orientation
女性 Female	28	**28.6**	**57.1**	**14.3**
天天用 daily	27	29.6	55.6	14.8
两三天用 1 次 once 2 or 3 days	1	0.0	100.0	0.0

● 武汉 / Wuhan

1-1 最近三个月使用频次的比例/ Proportion of the Sample Consuming Cosmetics Water in the Last Three Months

	人数 Number	百分比 Percent
天天用 daily	25	7.6
两三天用 1 次 once 2 or 3 days	8	2.4
一周 1～2 次 once or twice a week	7	2.1
半个月一次 once half a month	2	0.6
一个月 1 次或以下 once a month or below	1	0.3
没用过 never use	284	86.9

n=327

1-2 最常用品牌排名/ Ranking of the Most Frequently Used Brands

排名 Brand Ranking	品牌 Brands	人数 Number	百分比 Percent
1	强生可伶可俐 Clean&Clear	5	11.6
2	欧珀莱 Aupres	3	7.0
2	雅芳 Avon	3	7.0
3	花王碧柔 Biore	2	4.7
3	丽花丝宝 Laifa-C'bons	2	4.7
3	欧莱雅 L'oreal	2	4.7
3	羽西 Yue-sai	2	4.7

n=43

1-3 样本、女性各年龄层的常用品牌/ The Most Frequently Used Brands by the Female Sample and Age Groups

	人数 Number	第一品牌及百分比 1st/ percent	第二品牌及百分比 2nd/ percent	第三品牌及百分比 3rd/ percent
女性 Female	43	**强生可伶可俐 Clean&Clear(11.6)**	**欧珀莱 Aupres(7.0)** **雅芳 Avon(7.0)**	**花王碧柔 Biore(4.7)** **丽花丝宝 Laifa-C'bons(4.7)** **欧莱雅 L'oreal(4.7)** **羽西 Yue-sai(4.7)**
16~24 岁 Age	15	强生可伶可俐 Clean&Clear(20.0)	雅倩 Arche(6.7) 天使 Tianshi(6.7) 奥岚雪 Aolanxue(6.7) 丝丽人 Siliren(6.7) 美宝莲 Maybelline(6.7) 永芳 Yinfong(6.7) 高丝 Kose(6.7) 羽西 Yue-sai(6.7) 雅芳 Avon(6.7) 欧莱雅 L'oreal(6.7) 欧珀莱 Aupres(6.7) 花王碧柔 Biore(6.7)	
25~34 岁 Age	22	丽花丝宝 Laifa-C'bons(9.1) 欧珀莱 Aupres(9.1)	小护士 Mininurse(4.5) 雪柔 Xuerou(4.5) 宝丽 Baoli(4.5) 丝莉雅 Siliya(4.5) 蕾迪雅 Ladiera(4.5) 兰贵人 Languiren(4.5) 宝拉 Baola(4.5) 莎莉 Shali(4.5) 美加净 Maxam(4.5) 旁氏 Pond's(4.5) 资生堂 Shiseido(4.5) 羽西 Yue-sai(4.5) 雅芳 Avon(4.5) 圣罗兰 Yves Saint Laurent(4.5) 强生可伶可俐 Clean&Clear(4.5) 欧莱雅 L'oreal(4.5) 丽妃 Lifei(4.5)	
35~44 岁 Age	1			
45~54 岁 Age	4	高姿 Gogi(25.0) 花王碧柔 Biore(25.0) 强生可伶可俐 Clean&Clear(25.0) 施百丽 Shibaili(25.0)		
55~60 岁 Age	1	雅芳 Avon(100.0)		

1-4 正在使用的品牌排名/ Ranking of the Brand Used Now

排名 Brand Ranking	品牌 Brands	人数 Number	百分比 Percent
1	强生可伶可俐 Clean&Clear	6	14.0
2	雅芳 Avon	3	7.0
3	欧珀莱 Aupres	2	4.7
3	欧莱雅 L'oreal	2	4.7
3	羽西 Yue-sai	2	4.7

n=43

1-5 品牌转换习惯/ Brand Habit in Consuming Cosmetics Water

	人数 Number	第一次使用该品牌 first use this brand	上一次也是这个牌子 used it last time	上一次不是这个牌子 not used it last time
女性 Female	43	25.6	65.1	9.3
强生可伶可俐 Clean&Clear	6	50.0	33.3	16.7
雅芳 Avon	3	33.3	66.7	0.0
欧珀莱 Aupres	2	0.0	100.0	0.0
欧莱雅 L'oreal	2	50.0	50.0	0.0
羽西 Yue-sai	2	0.0	100.0	0.0

1-6 下一次打算使用的品牌排名/ Ranking of the Brands to be Used Next Time

排名 Brand Ranking	品牌 Brands	人数 Number	百分比 Percent
1	雅芳 Avon	4	9.3
1	强生可伶可俐 Clean&Clear	4	9.3
2	羽西 Yue-sai	3	7.0
2	丽花丝宝 Laifa-C'bons	3	7.0
3	欧珀莱 Aupres	2	4.7
3	旁氏 Pond's	2	4.7
3	宝拉 Baola	2	4.7
3	花王碧柔 Biore	2	4.7
3	高丝 Kose	2	4.7

n=43

1-7 样本、女性各年龄层的使用频率/ Frequencies of the Consumed Cosmetics Water by the Female Sample and Age Groups

	人数 Number	天天用 daily	两三天用 1 次 once 2 or 3 days	一周 1~2 次 once or twice a week	半个月一次 once half a month	一个月 1 次或以下 once a month or below	没用过 never use
女性 Female	327	7.6	2.4	2.1	0.6	0.3	86.9
16~24 岁 Age	69	11.6	4.3	4.3	1.4	0.0	78.3
25~34 岁 Age	95	15.8	4.2	2.1	0.0	1.1	76.8
35~44 岁 Age	78	0.0	1.3	0.0	0.0	0.0	98.7
45~54 岁 Age	60	3.3	0.0	1.7	1.7	0.0	93.3
55~60 岁 Age	25	0.0	0.0	4.0	0.0	0.0	96.0

1-8 选择该类商品的考虑因素/ Ranking of the Considerations in Purchasing

注：本题为多选题，合计百分比超过 100%（Multiple answers）

排名 Ranking	考虑因素 Considerations	人次 Person-time	百分比 Percent
1	产品功用 product function	22	51.2
2	有名的牌子 famous brand	16	37.2
3	价格适中 reasonable price	13	30.2
4	别人推荐 introduced by other people	10	23.3
5	广告影响 influence of advertising	5	11.6
6	有优惠条件 with preferential terms	4	9.3
7	包装吸引人 appealing package	3	7.0
7	购买方便 easy to buy	3	7.0

n=43

1-9 对产品功能的侧重方面/ Ranking of the Considerations about the Function of this Kind of Product

注：本题为多选题，合计百分比超过 100%（Multiple answers）

排名 Ranking	侧重方面 Items	人次 Person-time	百分比 Percent
1	收缩毛孔 pore contracting	30	69.8
2	保湿功能 keeping moisture	24	55.8
3	易于吸收 easy to dissolve	18	41.9
4	平衡功能 balancing	10	23.3
5	不含香料 containing no perfume	7	16.3
6	隔离功能 protecting effect	4	9.3
7	其他 others	1	2.3

n=43

1-10 重度消费者的人口分布/ Demographics of the Heavy Consumers

	人数 Number	16-24 岁 Age	25-34 岁 Age	35-44 岁 Age	45-54 岁 Age	55-60 岁 Age
女性 Female	33	33.3	57.6	3.0	6.1	0.0
天天用 daily	25	32.0	60.0	0.0	8.0	0.0
两三天用 1 次 once 2 or 3 days	8	37.5	50.0	12.5	0.0	0.0

1-11 不同消费者层的常用品牌/ The Most Frequently Used Brands by Market Segments

1-11-1 时尚流行指标/ Fads Popular Index

	人数 Number	第一品牌及百分比 1st/ percent	第二品牌及百分比 2nd/ percent	第三品牌及百分比 3rd/ percent
女性 Female	43	**强生可伶可俐 Clean&Clear(11.6)**	**欧珀莱 Aupres(7.0)** **雅芳 Avon(7.0)**	**花王碧柔 Biore(4.7)** **丽花丝宝 Laifa-C'bons(4.7)** **欧莱雅 L'oreal(4.7)** **羽西 Yue-sai(4.7)**
平实生活指向 simple living orientation	9	花王碧柔 Biore(11.1) 丽花丝宝 Laifa-C'bons(11.1) 强生可伶可俐 Clean&Clear(11.1) 雅芳 Avon(11.1) 旁氏 Pond's(11.1) 雅倩 Arche(11.1) 丝莉雅 Siliya(11.1) 奥岚雪 Aulanxue(11.1)		
时尚流行指向 fashion orientation	34	强生可伶可俐 Clean&Clear(11.8)	欧珀莱 Aupres(8.8)	欧莱雅 L'oreal(5.9) 雅芳 Avon(5.9) 羽西 Yue-sai(5.9)

1-11-2 广告态度指标/ Advertising Attitude Index

	人数 Number	第一品牌及百分比 1st/ percent	第二品牌及百分比 2nd/ percent	第三品牌及百分比 3rd/ percent
女性 Female	43	**强生可伶可俐 Clean&Clear(11.6)**	**欧珀莱 Aupres(7.0)** **雅芳 Avon(7.0)**	**花王碧柔 Biore(4.7)** **丽花丝宝 Laifa-C'bons(4.7)** **欧莱雅 L'oreal(4.7)** **羽西 Yue-sai(4.7)**
广告淡漠指向 indifferent orientation	8	强生可伶可俐 Clean&Clear(25.0)	花王碧柔 Biore(12.5) 羽西 Yue-sai(12.5) 旁氏 Pond's(12.5) 美宝莲 Maybelline(12.5) 丝莉雅 Siliya(12.5) 宝丽 Baoli(12.5)	
中间层 medium	27	强生可伶可俐 Clean&Clear(11.1) 雅芳 Avon(11.1)	丽花丝宝 Laifa-C'bons(7.4) 欧珀莱 Aupres(7.4)	宝拉 Baola(3.7) 天使 Tianshi(3.7) 施百丽 Shibaili(3.7) 奥岚雪 Aulanxue(3.7) 丝丽人 Siliren(3.7) 雪柔 Xuerou(3.7) 永芳 Yinfong(3.7) 羽西 Yue-sai(3.7) 美加净 Maxam(3.7) 小护士 Mininurse(3.7) 雅倩 Arche(3.7) 圣罗兰 Yves Saint Laurent(3.7) 欧莱雅 L'oreal(3.7) 花王碧柔 Biore(3.7) 高丝 Kose(3.7)
信赖广告指向 loyal orientation	8	高姿 Gogi(12.5) 丽妃 Lifei(12.5) 欧珀莱 Aupres(12.5) 欧莱雅 L'oreal(12.5) 资生堂 Shiseido(12.5) 莎莉 Shali(12.5) 兰贵人 Languiren(12.5) 蕾迪雅 Ladiera (12.5)		

1-12 重度消费者的消费层构成/ The Composition of the Heavy Consumers

1-12-1 时尚流行指标/ Fads Popular Index

	人数 Number	平实生活指向 simple living orientation	时尚流行指向 fashion orientation
女性 Female	33	18.2	81.8
天天用 daily	25	12.0	88.0
两三天用 1 次 once 2 or 3 days	8	37.5	62.5

1-12-2 广告态度指标/ Advertising Attitude Index

	人数 Number	广告淡漠指向 indifferent orientation	中间层 medium	信赖广告指向 loyal orientation
女性 Female	33	18.2	63.6	18.2
天天用 daily	25	16.0	60.0	24.0
两三天用 1 次 once 2 or 3 days	8	25.0	75.0	0.0

● 西安 / Xi'an

1-1 最近三个月使用频次的比例/ Proportion of the Sample Consuming Cosmetics Water in the Last Three Months

	人数 Number	百分比 Percent
天天用 daily	24	8.1
两三天用 1 次 once 2 or 3 days	6	2.0
一周 1～2 次 once or twice a week	7	2.4
半个月一次 once half a month	1	0.3
一个月 1 次或以下 once a month or below	0	0.0
没用过 never use	258	87.2

n=296

1-2 最常用品牌排名/ Ranking of the Most Frequently Used Brands

排名 Brand Ranking	品牌 Brands	人数 Number	百分比 Percent
1	旁氏 Pond's	5	13.5
2	雅芳 Avon	4	10.8
2	资生堂 Shiseido	4	10.8
3	丁家宜 Dingjiayi	3	8.1
3	羽西 Yue-sai	3	8.1
4	伊思丽 Eesli	2	5.4

n=37

1-3 样本、女性各年龄层的常用品牌/ The Most Frequently Used Brands by the Female Sample and Age Groups

	人数 Number	第一品牌及百分比 1st/ percent	第二品牌及百分比 2nd/ percent	第三品牌及百分比 3rd/ percent
女性 Female	**37**	**旁氏 Pond's(13.5)**	**雅芳 Avon(10.8) 资生堂 Shiseido(10.8)**	**丁家宜 Dingjiayi(8.1) 羽西 Yue-sai(8.1)**
16~24 岁 Age	4	诗芙侬 Shifunong(25.0) 雅芳 Avon(25.0) 旁氏 Pond's(25.0) 逸芙雪 Yifuxue(25.0)		
25~34 岁 Age	22	资生堂 Shiseido(18.2)	羽西 Yue-sai(13.6) 雅芳 Avon(13.6)	圣梦 Shengmeng(4.5) 美宝莲 Maybelline(4.5) 美加净 Maxam(4.5) 旁氏 Pond's(4.5) 东洋之花 Sakula(4.5) 大宝.高丽雅娜.阿特皮雅 Dabao Coreana Artpla (4.5) 伊思丽 Eesli(4.5) 姗拉娜 SamSara(4.5) 强生可伶可俐 Clean&Clear(4.5) 欧莱雅 L'oreal(4.5) 欧珀莱 Aupres(4.5) 迪奥 CD(4.5)
35~44 岁 Age	6	丁家宜 Dingjiayi(33.3)	伊思丽 Eesli(16.7) 旁氏 Pond's(16.7) 雅倩 Arche(16.7) 艾琳 Irlene(16.7)	
45~54 岁 Age	3	旁氏 Pond's(66.7)	小护士 Mininurse(33.3)	
55~60 岁 Age	2	柔婷 Routing(50.0) 丁家宜 Dingjiayi(50.0)		

1-4 正在使用的品牌排名/ Ranking of the Brands Used Now

排名 Brand Ranking	品牌 Brands	人数 Number	百分比 Percent
1	旁氏 Pond's	5	13.5
2	资生堂 Shiseido	4	10.8
2	雅芳 Avon	4	10.8
3	丁家宜 Dingjiayi	3	8.1
3	羽西 Yue-sai	3	8.1
4	雅倩 Arche	2	5.4
4	伊思丽 Eesli	2	5.4

n=37

1-5 品牌转换习惯/ Brand Habit in Consuming Cosmetics Water

	人数 Number	第一次使用该品牌 first use this brand	上一次也是这个牌子 used it last time	上一次不是这个牌子 not used it last time
女性 Female	37	10.8	75.7	13.5
旁氏 Pond's	5	20.0	20.0	60.0
资生堂 Shiseido	4	25.0	75.0	0.0
雅芳 Avon	4	0.0	100.0	0.0
丁家宜 Dingjiayi	3	0.0	66.7	33.3
羽西 Yue-sai	3	0.0	100.0	0.0
雅倩 Arche	2	0.0	50.0	50.0
伊思丽 Eesli	2	0.0	100.0	0.0

1-6 下一次打算使用的品牌排名/ Ranking of the Brands to be Used Next Time

排名 Brand Ranking	品牌 Brands	人数 Number	百分比 Percent
1	雅芳 Avon	4	10.8
1	丁家宜 Dingjiayi	4	10.8
1	资生堂 Shiseido	4	10.8
1	羽西 Yue-sai	4	10.8
2	旁氏 Pond's	2	5.4
2	伊思丽 Eesli	2	5.4

n=37

1-7 样本、女性各年龄层的使用频率/ Frequencies of the Consumed Cosmetics Water by the Female Sample and Age Groups

	人数 Number	天天用 daily	两三天用 1 次 once 2 or 3 days	一周 1～2 次 once or twice a week	半个月一次 once half a month	一个月 1 次或以下 once a month or below	没用过 never use
女性 Female	296	8.1	2.0	2.4	0.3	0.0	87.2
16~24 岁 Age	60	1.7	1.7	3.3	0.0	0.0	93.3
25~34 岁 Age	89	16.9	4.5	2.2	1.1	0.0	75.3
35~44 岁 Age	73	8.2	1.4	0.0	0.0	0.0	90.4
45~54 岁 Age	49	4.1	0.0	2.0	0.0	0.0	93.9
55~60 岁 Age	25	0.0	0.0	8.0	0.0	0.0	92.0

1-8 选择该类商品的考虑因素/ Ranking of the Considerations in Purchasing

注：本题为多选题，合计百分比超过 100%（Multiple answers）

排名 Ranking	考虑因素 Considerations	人次 Person-time	百分比 Percent
1	有名的牌子 famous brand	18	48.6
2	价格适中 reasonable price	14	37.8
3	产品功用 product function	11	29.7
4	别人推荐 introduced by other people	10	27.0
5	广告影响 influence of advertising	6	16.2
6	购买方便 easy to buy	5	13.5
7	有优惠条件 with preferential terms	4	10.8

n=37

1-9 对产品功能的侧重方面/ Ranking of the Considerations about the Function of this Kind of Product

注：本题为多选题，合计百分比超过 100%（Multiple answers）

排名 Ranking	侧重方面 Items	人次 Person-time	百分比 Percent
1	保湿功能 keeping moisture	22	59.5
2	收缩毛孔 pore contracting	17	45.9
3	易于吸收 easy to dissolve	15	40.5
4	平衡功能 balancing	11	29.7
5	不含香料 containing no perfume	8	21.6
6	隔离功能 protecting effect	3	8.1

n=37

1-10 重度消费者的人口分布/ Demographics of the Heavy Consumers

	人数 Number	16-24 岁 Age	25-34 岁 Age	35-44 岁 Age	45-54 岁 Age	55-60 岁 Age
女性 Female	30	6.7	63.3	23.3	6.7	0.0
天天用 daily	24	4.2	62.5	25.0	8.3	0.0
两三天用 1 次 once 2 or 3 days	6	16.7	66.7	16.7	0.0	0.0

1-11 不同消费者层的常用品牌/ The Most Frequently Used Brands by Market Segments

1-11-1 时尚流行指标/ Fads Popular Index

	人数 Number	第一品牌及百分比 1st/ percent	第二品牌及百分比 2nd/ percent	第三品牌及百分比 3rd/ percent
女性 Female	36	**旁氏 Pond's(13.9)**	**雅芳 Avon(11.1)** **资生堂 Shiseido(11.1)**	**丁家宜 Dingjiayi(8.3)** **羽西 Yue-sai(8.3)**
平实生活指向 simple living orientation	10	伊思丽 Eesli(20.0) 旁氏 Pond's(20.0)	诗芙侬 Shifunong(10.0) 雅芳 Avon(10.0) 资生堂 Shiseido(10.0) 小护士 Mininurse(10.0) 丁家宜 Dingjiayi(10.0) 圣梦 Shengmeng(10.0)	
时尚流行指向 fashion orientation	26	旁氏 Pond's(11.5) 雅芳 Avon(11.5) 羽西 Yue-sai(11.5) 资生堂 Shiseido(11.5)	丁家宜 Dingjiayi(7.7)	东洋之花 Sakula(3.8) 逸芙雪 Yifuxue(3.8) 美宝莲 Maybelline(3.8) 美加净 Maxam(3.8) 艾琳 Irlene(3.8) 大宝.高丽雅娜.阿特皮雅 Dabao Coreana Artpla(3.8) 姗拉娜 Samsara(3.8) 柔婷 Routing(3.8) 强生可伶可俐 Clean&Clear(3.8) 欧莱雅 L'oreal(3.8) 欧珀莱 Aupres(3.8) 迪奥 CD(3.8)

1-11-2 广告态度指标/ Advertising Attitude Index

	人数 Number	第一品牌及百分比 1st/ percent	第二品牌及百分比 2nd/ percent	第三品牌及百分比 3rd/ percent
女性 Female	37	**旁氏 Pond's(13.5)**	**雅芳 Avon(10.8)** **资生堂 Shiseido(10.8)**	**丁家宜 Dingjiayi(8.1)** **羽西 Yue-sai(8.1)**
广告淡漠指向 indifferent orientation	11	旁氏 Pond's(18.2)	迪奥 CD(9.1) 欧珀莱 Aupres(9.1) 柔婷 Routing(9.1) 诗芙侬 Shifunong(9.1) 伊思丽 Eesli(9.1) 艾琳 Irlene(9.1) 美加净 Maxam(9.1) 丁家宜 Dingjiayi(9.1) 逸芙雪 Yifuxue(9.1) 丁家宜 Dingjiayi(9.1)	
中间层 medium	22	雅芳 Avon(13.6) 羽西 Yue-sai(13.6) 资生堂 Shiseido(13.6)		旁氏 Pond's(4.5) 圣梦 Shengmeng(4.5) 美宝莲 Maybelline(4.5) 小护士 Mininurse(4.5) 雅倩 Arche(4.5) 大宝.高丽雅娜.阿特皮雅 Dabao Coreana Artpla (4.5) 东洋之花 Sakula(4.5) 伊思丽 Eesli(4.5) 姗拉娜 Samsara(4.5) 强生可伶可俐 Clean&Clear(4.5) 欧莱雅 L'oreal(4.5)
信赖广告指向 loyal orientation	4	旁氏 Pond's(50.0)	雅芳 Avon(25.0) 资生堂 Shiseido(25.0)	

1-12 重度消费者的消费层构成/ The Composition of the Heavy Consumers

1-12-1 时尚流行指标/ Fads Popular Index

	人数 Number	平实生活指向 simple living orientation	时尚流行指向 fashion orientation
女性 Female	29	27.6	72.4
天天用 daily	23	30.4	69.6
两三天用 1 次 once 2 or 3 days	6	16.7	83.3

1-12-2 广告态度指标/ Advertising Attitude Index

	人数 Number	广告淡漠指向 indifferent orientation	中间层 medium	信赖广告指向 loyal orientation
女性 Female	30	30.0	66.7	3.3
天天用 daily	24	29.2	66.7	4.2
两三天用 1 次 once 2 or 3 days	6	33.3	66.7	0.0

● 沈阳 / Shenyang

1-1 最近三个月使用频次的比例/ Proportion of the Sample Consuming Cosmetics Water in the Last Three Months

	人数 Number	百分比 Percent
天天用 daily	46	15.2
两三天用 1 次 once 2 or 3 days	11	3.6
一周 1～2 次 once or twice a week	4	1.3
半个月一次 once half a month	1	0.3
一个月 1 次或以下 once a month or below	3	1.0
没用过 never use	237	78.5

n=302

1-2 最常用品牌排名/ Ranking of the Most Frequently Used Brands

排名 Brand Ranking	品牌 Brands	人数 Number	百分比 Percent
1	高丝 Kose	11	17.2
2	强生可伶可俐 Clean&Clear	5	7.8
3	欧珀莱 Aupres	4	6.3
4	芦荟 Luhui	3	4.7
4	小护士 Mininurse	3	4.7
4	玉兰油 Oil of Olay	3	4.7
4	资生堂 Shiseido	3	4.7
4	郑明明 Cheng Mingming	3	4.7
4	爱茉莉兰芝 Lanelge	3	4.7
4	安利 Amway	3	4.7
5	安安 An'an	2	3.1
5	大宝.高丽雅娜.阿特皮雅 Dabao Coreana Artpla	2	3.1
5	雪丽肤 Xuelifu	2	3.1

n=64

1-3 样本、女性各年龄层的常用品牌/ The Most Frequently Used Brands by the Female Sample and Age Groups

	人数 Number	第一品牌及百分比 1st/ percent	第二品牌及百分比 2nd/ percent	第三品牌及百分比 3rd/ percent
女性 Female	64	**高丝 Kose(17.2)**	**强生可伶可俐 Clean&Clear(7.8)**	**欧珀莱 Aupres(6.3)**
16~24 岁 Age	17	强生可伶可俐 Clean&Clear(17.6)	安利 Amway(11.8) 玉兰油 Oil of Olay(11.8)	水晶 Shuijing(5.9) 露美 Lumei(5.9) 安安 An'an(5.9) 情丝 Qingsi(5.9) 芦荟 Luhui(5.9) 爱茉莉兰芝 Lanelge(5.9) 郑明明 Cheng Mingming(5.9) 羽西 Yue-sai(5.9) 高丝 Kose(5.9) 蝶妆 Debon LG(5.9)
25~34 岁 Age	25	高丝 Kose(24.0)	欧珀莱 Aupres(8.0) 小护士 Mininurse(8.0) 雪丽肤 Xuelifu(8.0) 资生堂 Shiseido(8.0)	旁氏 Pond's(4.0) 安利 Amway(4.0) 柔加 Roujia(4.0) 芦荟 Luhui(4.0) 玉兰油 Oil of Olay(4.0) 雅芳 Avon(4.0) 郑明明 Cheng Mingming(4.0) 诗芙侬 Shifunong(4.0) 柔婷 Routing(4.0) 强生可伶可俐 Clean&Clear(4.0) 高姿 Gogi(4.0)
35~44 岁 Age	16	高丝 Kose(18.8)	爱茉莉兰芝 Lanelge(12.5)	小护士 Mininurse(6.3) 夏绿帝 Xialvdi(6.3) ESTEE LAUDER(6.3) 梦正 Mengzheng(6.3) 芦荟 Luhui(6.3) 郑明明 Cheng Mingming(6.3) 资生堂 Shiseido(6.3) 强生可伶可俐 Clean&Clear(6.3) 欧莱雅 L'oreal(6.3) 欧珀莱 Aupres(6.3) 碧妮 Peony(6.3)
45~54 岁 Age	5	大宝.高丽雅娜.阿特皮雅 Dabao Coreana Artpla(40.0)	高丝 Kose(20.0) 依莎美尔 Yishamei'er(20.0) 安安 An'an(20.0)	
55~60 岁 Age	1	欧珀莱 Aupres(100.0)		

1-4 正在使用的品牌排名/ Ranking of the Brands Used Now

排名 Brand Ranking	品牌 Brands	人数 Number	百分比 Percent
1	高丝 Kose	10	16.1
2	玉兰油 Oil of Olay	5	8.1
2	强生可伶可俐 Clean&Clear	5	8.1
3	欧珀莱 Aupres	4	6.5
3	爱茉莉兰芝 Lanelge	4	6.5
4	资生堂 Shiseido	3	4.8
4	安利 Amway	3	4.8
5	雪丽肤 Xuelifu	2	3.2
5	大宝.高丽雅娜.阿特皮雅 Dabao Coreana Artpla	2	3.2
5	郑明明 Cheng Mingming	2	3.2
5	小护士 Mininurse	2	3.2
5	高姿 Gogi	2	3.2
5	芦荟 Luhui	2	3.2

n=62

1-5 品牌转换习惯/ Brand Habit in Consuming Cosmetics Water

	人数 Number	第一次使用该品牌 first use this brand	上一次也是这个牌子 used it last time	上一次不是这个牌子 not used it last time
女性 Female	62	14.5	77.4	8.1
高丝 Kose	10	10.0	90.0	0.0
玉兰油 Oil of Olay	5	40.0	60.0	0.0
强生可伶可俐 Clean&Clear	5	0.0	100.0	0.0
欧珀莱 Aupres	4	0.0	100.0	0.0
爱茉莉兰芝 Lanelge	4	0.0	100.0	0.0
资生堂 Shiseido	3	33.3	66.7	0.0
安利 Amway	3	0.0	66.7	33.3

1-6 下一次打算使用的品牌排名/ Ranking of the Brands to be Used Next Time

排名 Brand Ranking	品牌 Brands	人数 Number	百分比 Percent
1	高丝 Kose	9	14.3
2	玉兰油 Oil of Olay	7	11.1
3	安利 Amway	4	6.3
3	欧珀莱 Aupres	4	6.3
3	强生可伶可俐 Clean&Clear	4	6.3
4	羽西 Yue-sai	3	4.8
4	爱茉莉兰芝 Lanelge	3	4.8
4	资生堂 Shiseido	3	4.8
5	雪丽肤 Xuelifu	2	3.2
5	小护士 Mininurse	2	3.2
5	郑明明 Cheng Mingming	2	3.2
5	芦荟 Luhui	2	3.2

n=63

1-7 样本、女性各年龄层的使用频率/ Frequencies of the Consumed Cosmetics Water by the Female Sample and Age Groups

	人数 Number	天天用 daily	两三天用 1 次 once 2 or 3 days	一周 1~2 次 once or twice a week	半个月一次 once half a month	一个月 1 次或以下 once a month or below	没用过 never use
女性 Female	302	15.2	3.6	1.3	0.3	1.0	78.5
16~24 岁 Age	64	21.9	4.7	0.0	0.0	0.0	73.4
25~34 岁 Age	90	17.8	6.7	3.3	0.0	0.0	72.2
35~44 岁 Age	76	13.2	2.6	1.3	1.3	3.9	77.6
45~54 岁 Age	48	10.4	0.0	0.0	0.0	0.0	89.6
55~60 岁 Age	24	4.2	0.0	0.0	0.0	0.0	95.8

1-8 选择该类商品的考虑因素/ Ranking of the Considerations in Purchasing

注：本题为多选题，合计百分比超过 100%（Multiple answers）

排名 Ranking	考虑因素 Considerations	人次 Person-time	百分比 Percent
1	有名的牌子 famous brand	30	46.2
2	价格适中 reasonable price	22	33.8
2	产品功用 product function	22	33.8
3	别人推荐 introduced by other people	19	29.2
4	广告影响 influence of advertising	11	16.9
5	购买方便 easy to buy	7	10.8
6	有优惠条件 with preferential terms	4	6.2
7	包装吸引人 appealing package	3	4.6
8	其它 others	2	3.1

n=65

1-9 对产品功能的侧重方面/ Ranking of the Considerations about the Function of this Kind of Product

注：本题为多选题，合计百分比超过 100%（Multiple answers）

排名 Ranking	侧重方面 Items	人次 Person-time	百分比 Percent
1	保湿功能 keeping moisture	38	58.5
2	易于吸收 easy to dissolve	31	47.7
3	收缩毛孔 pore contracting	30	46.2
4	平衡功能 balancing	10	15.4
4	不含香料 containing no perfume	10	15.4
5	隔离功能 protecting effect	7	10.8
6	其他 others	2	3.1

n=65

1-10 重度消费者的人口分布/ Demographics of the Heavy Consumers

	人数 Number	16-24 岁 Age	25-34 岁 Age	35-44 岁 Age	45-54 岁 Age	55-60 岁 Age
女性 Female	57	29.8	38.6	21.1	8.8	1.8
天天用 daily	46	30.4	34.8	21.7	10.9	2.2
两三天用 1 次 once 2 or 3 days	11	27.3	54.5	18.2	0.0	0.0

1-11 不同消费者层的常用品牌/ The Most Frequently Used Brands by Market Segments

1-11-1 时尚流行指标/ Fads Popular Index

	人数 Number	第一品牌及百分比 1st/ percent	第二品牌及百分比 2nd/ percent	第三品牌及百分比 3rd/ percent
女性 Female	64	**高丝 Kose(17.2)**	**强生可伶可俐 Clean&Clear(7.8)**	**欧珀莱 Aupres(6.3)**
平实生活指向 simple living orientation	9	高丝 Kose(22.2) 芦荟 Luhui(22.2)	大宝.高丽雅娜.阿特皮雅 Dabao Coreana Artpla(11.1) 欧珀莱 Aupres(11.1) 郑明明 Cheng Mingming(11.1) 资生堂 Shiseido(11.1) 雪丽肤 Xulifu(11.1)	
时尚流行指向 fashion orientation	55	高丝 Kose(16.4)	强生可伶可俐 Clean&Clear(9.1)	安利 Amway(5.5) 小护士 Mininurse(5.5) 玉兰油 Oil of Olay(5.5) 欧珀莱 Aupres(5.5) 爱莱莉兰芝 Lanelge(5.5)

1-11-2 广告态度指标/ Advertising Attitude Index

	人数 Number	第一品牌及百分比 1st/ percent	第二品牌及百分比 2nd/ percent	第三品牌及百分比 3rd/ percent
女性 Female	64	**高丝 Kose(17.2)**	**强生可伶可俐 Clean&Clear(7.8)**	**欧珀莱 Aupres(6.3)**
广告淡漠指向 indifferent orientation	14	芦荟 Luhui(14.3) 高丝 Kose(14.3) 小护士 Mininurse(14.3)	资生堂 Shiseido(7.1) 雪丽肤 Xulifu(7.1) 旁氏 Pond's(7.1) 爱莱莉兰芝 Lanelge(7.1) 强生可伶可俐 Clean&Clear(7.1) 欧珀莱 Aupres(7.1) 蝶妆 Debon LG(7.1) 大宝.高丽雅娜.阿特皮雅 Dabao Coreana Artpla(7.1)	
中间层 medium	36	高丝 Kose(13.9)	强生可伶可俐 Clean&Clear(11.1)	欧珀莱 Aupres(8.3) 郑明明 Cheng Mingming(8.3) 玉兰油 Oil of Olay(8.3)
信赖广告指向 loyal orientation	14	高丝 Kose(28.6)	雪丽肤 Xulifu(7.1) 露美 Lumei(7.1) 夏绿帝 Xialvdi(7.1) 梦正 Mengzheng(7.1) 安安 An'an(7.1) 安利 Amway(7.1) 柔加 Roujia(7.1) 资生堂 Shiseido(7.1) 柔婷 Routing(7.1) 欧莱雅 L'oreal(7.1)	

1-12 重度消费者的消费层构成/ The Composition of the Heavy Consumers

1-12-1 时尚流行指标/ Fads Popular Index

	人数 Number	平实生活指向 simple living orientation	时尚流行指向 fashion orientation
女性 Female	57	15.8	84.2
天天用 daily	46	15.2	84.8
两三天用 1 次 once 2 or 3 days	11	18.2	81.8

1-12-2 广告态度指标/ Advertising Attitude Index

	人数 Number	广告淡漠指向 indifferent orientation	中间层 medium	信赖广告指向 loyal orientation
女性 Female	57	22.8	54.4	22.8
天天用 daily	46	23.9	52.2	23.9
两三天用 1 次 once 2 or 3 days	11	18.2	63.6	18.2

2.粉底 / Pre-makeup

● 北京 / Beijing

2-1 最近三个月使用频次的比例/ Proportion of the Sample Consuming Pre-makeup in the Last Three Months

	人数 Number	百分比 Percent
天天用 daily	49	9.7
两三天用 1 次 once 2 or 3 days	32	6.3
一周 1～2 次 once or twice a week	27	5.3
半个月 1 次 once half a month	8	1.6
一个月 1 次或以下 once a month or below	19	3.8
没用过 never use	370	73.3

n=505

2-2 最常用品牌排名/ Ranking of the Most Frequently Used Brands

排名 Brand Ranking	品牌 Brands	人数 Number	百分比 Percent
1	高丝 Kose	17	12.7
2	欧珀莱 Aupres	15	11.2
3	华姿 Huazi	8	6.0
4	资生堂 Shiseido	7	5.2
4	郑明明 Cheng Mingming	7	5.2
4	羽西 Yue-sai	7	5.2
4	大宝.高丽雅娜.阿特皮雅 Dabao Coreana Artpla	7	5.2
5	雅芳 Avon	6	4.5
6	迪奥 CD	5	3.7

n=134

2-3 样本、女性各年龄层的常用品牌/ The Most Frequently Used Brands by the Female Sample and Age Groups

	人数 Number	第一品牌及百分比 1st/ percent	第二品牌及百分比 2nd/ percent	第三品牌及百分比 3rd/ percent
女性 Female	134	**高丝 Kose(12.7)**	**欧珀莱 Aupres(11.2)**	**华姿 Huazi(6.0)**
16~24 岁 Age	25	高丝 Kose(16.0)	欧珀莱 Aupres(12.0)	紫罗兰 Ziluolan(8.0) 雅芳 Avon(8.0) 资生堂 Shiseido(8.0)
25~34 岁 Age	54	高丝 Kose(16.7)	资生堂 Shiseido(9.3) 迪奥 CD(9.3) 欧珀莱 Aupres(9.3)	华姿 Huazi(5.6)
35~44 岁 Age	35	大宝.高丽雅娜.阿特皮雅 Dabao Coreana Artpla(14.3)	欧珀莱 Aupres(11.4)	华姿 Huazi(8.6)
45~54 岁 Age	18	羽西 Yue-sai(16.7) 欧珀莱 Aupres(16.7)	高丝 Kose(11.1) 郑明明 Cheng Mingming(11.1)	安利 Amway(5.6) 玉兰油 Oil of Olay(5.6) 大宝.高丽雅娜.阿特皮雅 Dabao Coreana Artpla(5.6) 雅芳 Avon(5.6) 丽妃 Lifei(5.6) 华姿 Huazi(5.6) 东洋之花 Sakula(5.6)
55~60 岁 Age	2	华姿 Huazi(50.0)		

2-4 正在使用的品牌排名/ Ranking of the Brands Used Now

排名 Brand Ranking	品牌 Brands	人数 Number	百分比 Percent
1	高丝 Kose	16	11.9
2	欧珀莱 Aupres	13	9.7
3	资生堂 Shiseido	7	5.2
3	雅芳 Avon	7	5.2
4	大宝.高丽雅娜.阿特皮雅 Dabao Coreana Artpla	6	4.5
4	迪奥 CD	6	4.5
4	华姿 Huazi	6	4.5
4	羽西 Yue-sai	6	4.5
5	郑明明 Cheng Mingming	5	3.7

n=134

2-5 品牌转换习惯/ Brand Habit in Consuming Pre-makeup

	人数 Number	第一次使用该品牌 first use this brand	上一次也是这个牌子 used it last time	上一次不是这个牌子 not used it last time
女性 Female	133	25.6	62.4	12.0
高丝 Kose	16	6.3	93.8	0.0
欧珀莱 Aupres	13	0.0	100.0	0.0
资生堂 Shiseido	7	14.3	85.7	0.0
雅芳 Avon	7	0.0	71.4	28.6
大宝.高丽雅娜.阿特皮雅 Dabao Coreana Artpla	6	16.7	50.0	33.3
迪奥 CD	6	0.0	66.7	33.3
华姿 Huazi	5	60.0	40.0	0.0
羽西 Yue-sai	6	33.3	66.7	0.0
郑明明 Cheng Mingming	5	60.0	40.0	0.0

2-6 下一次打算使用的品牌排名/ Ranking of the Brands to be Used Next Time

排名 Brand Ranking	品牌 Brands	人数 Number	百分比 Percent
1	高丝 Kose	15	11.2
2	欧珀莱 Aupres	13	9.7
3	资生堂 Shiseido	9	6.7
4	华姿 Huazi	7	5.2
4	大宝.高丽雅娜.阿特皮雅 Dabao Coreana Artpla	7	5.2
5	玉兰油 Oil of Olay	5	3.7
5	羽西 Yue-sai	5	3.7
5	雅芳 Avon	5	3.7
5	迪奥 CD	5	3.7
6	美宝莲 Maybelline	4	3.0
6	郑明明 Cheng Mingming	4	3.0

n=134

2-7 样本、女性各年龄层的使用频率/ Frequencies of the Consumed Pre-makeup by the Female Sample and Age Groups

	人数 Number	天天用 daily	两三天用 1 次 once 2 or 3 days	一周 1~2 次 once or twice a week	半个月 1 次 once half a month	一个月 1 次或以下 once a month or below	没用过 never use
女性 Female	505	9.7	6.3	5.3	1.6	3.8	73.3
16~24 岁 Age	107	7.5	5.6	3.7	1.9	4.7	76.6
25~34 岁 Age	149	11.4	5.4	10.7	2.0	7.4	63.1
35~44 岁 Age	124	12.1	11.3	1.6	1.6	1.6	71.8
45~54 岁 Age	84	9.5	4.8	4.8	1.2	1.2	78.6
55~60 岁 Age	41	2.4	0.0	2.4	0.0	0.0	95.1

2-8 选择该类商品的考虑因素/ Ranking of the Considerations in Purchasing

注：本题为多选题，合计百分比超过 100%（Multiple answers）

排名 Ranking	考虑因素 Considerations	人次 Person-time	百分比 Percent
1	产品功用 product function	75	56.0
2	有名的牌子 famous brand	57	42.5
3	价格适中 reasonable price	44	32.8
4	别人推荐 introduced by other people	28	20.9
5	有优惠条件 with preferential terms	12	9.0
6	包装吸引人 appealing package	10	7.5
7	广告影响 influence of advertising	7	5.2
8	购买方便 easy to buy	6	4.5
9	其它 others	2	1.5

n=134

2-9 对产品功能的侧重方面/ Ranking of the Considerations about the Function of this Kind of Product

注：本题为多选题，合计百分比超过 100%（Multiple answers）

排名 Ranking	侧重方面 Items	人次 Person-time	百分比 Percent
1	调整肤色 color	85	63.4
2	光滑细腻 smooth and fine	62	46.3
3	遮盖功能 covering function	42	31.3
4	着色稳定 color stability	32	23.9
5	防晒功能 anti-UV	28	20.9
6	不含香料 containing no perfume	14	10.4

n=134

2-10 重度消费者的人口分布/ Demographics of the Heavy Consumers

	人数 Number	16-24 岁 Age	25-34 岁 Age	35-44 岁 Age	45-54 岁 Age	55-60 岁 Age
女性 Female	81	17.3	30.9	35.8	14.8	1.2
天天用 daily	49	16.3	34.7	30.6	16.3	2.0
两三天用 1 次 once 2 or 3 days	32	18.8	25.0	43.8	12.5	0.0

2-11 不同消费者层的常用品牌/ The Most Frequently Used Brands by Market Segments

2-11-1 时尚流行指标/ Fads Popular Index

	人数 Number	第一品牌及百分比 1st/ percent	第二品牌及百分比 2nd/ percent	第三品牌及百分比 3rd/ percent
女性 Female	132	**高丝 Kose(12.9)**	**欧珀莱 Aupres(11.4)**	**华姿 Huazi(6.1)**
平实生活指向 simple living orientation	36	大宝.高丽雅娜.阿特皮雅 Dabao Coreana Artpla(11.1)	郑明明 Cheng Mingming(8.3) 迪奥 CD(8.3) 高丝 Kose(8.3) 华姿 Huazi(8.3) 羽西 Yue-sai(8.3)	欧珀莱 Aupres(5.6)
时尚流行指向 fashion orientation	96	高丝 Kose(14.6)	欧珀莱 Aupres(13.5)	资生堂 Shiseido(6.3)

2-11-2 广告态度指标/ Advertising Attitude Index

	人数 Number	第一品牌及百分比 1st/ percent	第二品牌及百分比 2nd/ percent	第三品牌及百分比 3rd/ percent
女性 Female	129	**高丝 Kose(13.2)**	**欧珀莱 Aupres(10.9)**	**华姿 Huazi(5.4)** **郑明明 Cheng Mingming(5.4)** **羽西 Yue-sai(5.4)** **大宝.高丽雅娜.阿特皮雅 Dabao Coreana Artpla(5.4)**
广告淡漠指向 indifferent orientation	30	欧珀莱 Aupres(16.7)	高丝 Kose(10.0) 华姿 Huazi(10.0)	郑明明 Cheng Mingming(6.7) 雅芳 Avon(6.7) 羽西 Yue-sai(6.7)
中间层 medium	70	高丝 Kose(17.1)	大宝.高丽雅娜.阿特皮雅 Dabao Coreana Artpla(10.0)	欧珀莱 Aupres(8.6)
信赖广告指向 loyal orientation	29	欧珀莱 Aupres(10.3) 资生堂 Shiseido(10.3)	高丝 Kose(6.9) 华姿 Huazi(6.9)	天姿 Tianzi(3.4) 伊思汉 Yisihan(3.4) 香海 Xianghai(3.4) 姗拉娜 SamSara(3.4) 四星 Sixing(3.4) 小护士 Mininurse(3.4) 爱诺 Ainuo(3.4) 雅倩 Arche(3.4) 郑明明 Cheng Mingming(3.4) 雅黛 Ador(3.4) 欧莱雅 L'oreal(3.4) 东洋之花 Sakula(3.4) 迪奥 CD(3.4) 碧妮 Peony(3.4) 艾迪丝 Aidieces(3.4)

2-12 重度消费者的消费层构成/ The Composition of the Heavy Consumers

2-12-1 时尚流行指标/ Fads Popular Index

	人数 Number	平实生活指向 simple living orientation	时尚流行指向 fashion orientation
女性 Female	80	25.0	75.0
天天用 daily	49	32.7	67.3
两三天用 1 次 once 2 or 3 days	31	12.9	87.1

2-12-2 广告态度指标/ Advertising Attitude Index

	人数 Number	广告淡漠指向 indifferent orientation	中间层 medium	信赖广告指向 loyal orientation
女性 Female	77	23.4	51.9	24.7
天天用 daily	47	19.1	57.4	23.4
两三天用 1 次 once 2 or 3 days	30	30.0	43.3	26.7

● 上海 / Shanghai

2-1 最近三个月使用频次的比例/ Proportion of the Sample Consuming Pre-makeup in the Last Three Months

	人数 Number	百分比 Percent
天天用 daily	44	8.9
两三天用 1 次 once 2 or 3 days	23	4.7
一周 1～2 次 about once or twice a week	22	4.5
半个月 1 次 once half a month	13	2.6
一个月 1 次或以下 once a month or below	17	3.5
没用过 never use	373	75.8

n=492

2-2 最常用品牌排名/ Ranking of the Most Frequently Used Brands

排名 Brand Ranking	品牌 Brands	人数 Number	百分比 Percent
1	羽西 Yue-sai	14	11.8
2	ZA	13	10.9
3	郑明明 Cheng Mingming	11	9.2
4	资生堂 Shiseido	7	5.9
5	美宝莲 Maybelline	6	5.0
6	宝璐丝 Paolarlus	5	4.2
6	迪奥 CD	5	4.2
6	雅芳 Avon	5	4.2
6	高丝 Kose	5	4.2

n=119

2-3 样本、女性各年龄层的常用品牌/ The Most Frequently Used Brands by the Female Sample and Age Groups

	人数 Number	第一品牌及百分比 1st/ percent	第二品牌及百分比 2nd/ percent	第三品牌及百分比 3rd/ percent
女性 Female	119	**羽西 Yue-sai(11.8)**	**ZA(10.9)**	**郑明明 Cheng Mingming(9.2)**
16~24 岁 Age	35	ZA(20.0)	羽西 Yue-sai(14.3)	郑明明 Cheng Mingming(8.6)
25~34 岁 Age	51	羽西 Yue-sai(13.7)	ZA(11.8)	郑明明 Cheng Mingming(9.8)
35~44 岁 Age	27	郑明明 Cheng Mingming(7.4) 玫琳凯 Mary Kay(7.4) 美宝莲 Maybelline(7.4) 旁氏 Pond's(7.4) 资生堂 Shiseido(7.4) 羽西 Yue-sai(7.4)	东方之宝 Dong Fang Zhi Bao(3.7) 香海 Xianghai(3.7) 芳芳 Fangfang(3.7) 永芳 Yinfong(3.7) 玉兰油 Oil of Olay(3.7) 雅芳 Avon(3.7) 雅艾芬迪 Latan taiao(3.7) 美加净 Maxam(3.7) 丽妃 Lifei(3.7) 高丝 Kose(3.7) 凤凰 Phoenix(3.7) 宝璐丝 Paolarlus(3.7)	
45~54 岁 Age	4	丽妃 Lifei(50.0)	郑明明 Cheng Mingming(25.0) 资生堂 Shiseido(25.0)	
55~60 岁 Age	2	迪奥 CD(50.0) 丽花丝宝 Laifa-C'bons(50.0)		

2-4 正在使用的品牌排名/ Ranking of the Brands Used Now

排名 Brand Ranking	品牌 Brands	人数 Number	百分比 Percent
1	ZA	13	10.9
1	郑明明 Cheng Mingming	13	10.9
1	羽西 Yue-sai	13	10.9
2	资生堂 Shiseido	7	5.9
3	玫琳凯 Mary Kay	5	4.2
3	宝璐丝 Paolarlus	5	4.2
3	迪奥 CD	5	4.2
3	美宝莲 Maybelline	5	4.2
4	高丝 Kose	4	3.4
4	雅芳 Avon	4	3.4
5	清妃 Chinf	3	2.5
5	欧珀莱 Aupres	3	2.5
5	雅艾芬迪 Latan Taiao	3	2.5
5	丽妃 Lifei	3	2.5
5	旁氏 Pond's	3	2.5

n=119

2-5 品牌转换习惯/ Brand Habit in Consuming Pre-makeup

	人数 Number	第一次使用该品牌 first use this brand	上一次也是这个牌子 used it last time	上一次不是这个牌子 not used it last time
女性 Female	119	**21.0**	**72.3**	**6.7**
ZA	13	7.7	84.6	7.7
郑明明 Cheng Mingming	13	15.4	76.9	7.7
羽西 Yue-sai	13	7.7	76.9	15.4
资生堂 Shiseido	7	0.0	100.0	0.0
玫琳凯 Mary Kay	5	40.0	60.0	0.0
宝璐丝 Paolarlus	5	0.0	100.0	0.0
迪奥 CD	5	20.0	80.0	0.0
美宝莲 Maybelline	5	60.0	40.0	0.0
高丝 Kose	4	25.0	50.0	25.0
雅芳 Avon	4	0.0	100.0	0.0

2-6 下一次打算使用的品牌排名/ Ranking of the Brands to be Used Next Time

排名 Brand Ranking	品牌 Brands	人数 Number	百分比 Percent
1	羽西 Yue-sai	15	12.6
2	ZA	12	10.1
3	资生堂 Shiseido	10	8.4
4	郑明明 Cheng Mingming	9	7.6
5	美宝莲 Maybelline	6	5.0
5	迪奥 CD	6	5.0
6	宝璐丝 Paolarlus	5	4.2
6	高丝 Kose	5	4.2
7	倩碧 Clinique	4	3.4

n=119

2-7 样本、女性各年龄层的使用频率/ Frequencies of the Consumed Pre-makeup by the Female Sample and Age Groups

	人数 Number	天天用 daily	两三天用 1 次 once 2 or 3 days	一周 1~2 次 once or twice a week	半个月 1 次 once half a month	一个月 1 次或以下 once a month or below	没用过 never use
女性 Female	**492**	**8.9**	**4.7**	**4.5**	**2.6**	**3.5**	**75.8**
16~24 岁 Age	103	14.6	5.8	5.8	2.9	4.9	66.0
25~34 岁 Age	142	13.4	6.3	5.6	4.2	6.3	64.1
35~44 岁 Age	128	7.0	4.7	5.5	2.3	1.6	78.9
45~54 岁 Age	79	1.3	2.5	0.0	0.0	1.3	94.9
55~60 岁 Age	40	0.0	0.0	2.5	2.5	0.0	95.0

2-8 选择该类商品的考虑因素/ Ranking of the Considerations in Purchasing

注：本题为多选题，合计百分比超过 100%（Multiple answers）

排名 Ranking	考虑因素 Considerations	人次 Person-time	百分比 Percent
1	有名的牌子 famous brand	51	43.2
2	价格适中 reasonable price	50	42.4
3	产品功用 product function	40	33.9
4	别人推荐 introduced by other people	26	22.0
5	广告影响 influence of advertising	15	12.7
6	购买方便 easy to buy	11	9.3
7	有优惠条件 with preferential terms	6	5.1
8	包装吸引人 appealing package	4	3.4
9	其它 others	3	2.5

n=118

2-9 对产品功能的侧重方面/ Ranking of the Considerations about the Function of this Kind of Product

注：本题为多选题，合计百分比超过 100%（Multiple answers）

排名 Ranking	侧重方面 Items	人次 Person-time	百分比 Percent
1	调整肤色 color	78	66.1
2	光滑细腻 smooth and fine	63	53.4
3	着色稳定 color stability	29	24.6
3	遮盖功能 covering function	29	24.6
4	防晒功能 anti-UV	19	16.1
5	不含香料 containing no perfume	18	15.3
6	其他 others	3	2.5

n=118

2-10 重度消费者的人口分布/ Demographics of the Heavy Consumers

	人数 Number	16-24 岁 Age	25-34 岁 Age	35-44 岁 Age	45-54 岁 Age	55-60 岁 Age
女性 Female	**67**	**31.3**	**41.8**	**22.4**	**4.5**	**0.0**
天天用 daily	44	34.1	43.2	20.5	2.3	0.0
两三天用 1 次 once 2 or 3 days	23	26.1	39.1	26.1	8.7	0.0

2-11 不同消费者层的常用品牌/ The Most Frequently Used Brands by Market Segments

2-11-1 时尚流行指标/ Fads Popular Index

	人数 Number	第一品牌及百分比 1st/ percent	第二品牌及百分比 2nd/ percent	第三品牌及百分比 3rd/ percent	第四品牌及百分比 4th/ percent
女性 Female	117	**羽西 Yue-sai（11.1）** **ZA（11.1）**	**郑明明 Cheng Mingming（9.4)**	**资生堂 Shiseido（6.0）**	**美宝莲 Maybelline（5.1）**
平实生活指向 simple living orientation	23	玫琳凯 Mary Kay（13.0）	高姿 Gogi（8.7）	东洋之花 Sakula（4.3） 凤凰 Phoenix（4.3） 高丝 Kose（4.3） 丽妃 Lifei（4.3） 丽花丝宝 Laifa-C'bons（4.3） 宝璐丝 Paolarlus（4.3） 美宝莲 Maybelline（4.3） 清妃 Chinf（4.3） 雅艾芬迪 Latan Taiao（4.3） 雅芳 Avon（4.3） 郑明明 Cheng Mingming（4.3） 资生堂 Shiseido（4.3） ZA（4.3） 贝加斯 Beijiasi（4.3） 东方之宝 Dongfangzhibao（4.3）	
时尚流行指向 fashion orientation	94	羽西 Yue-sai（13.8）	ZA（12.8）	郑明明 Cheng Mingming（10.6）	资生堂 Shiseido（6.4）

2-11-2 广告态度指标/ Advertising Attitude Index

	人数 Number	第一品牌及百分比 1st/ percent	第二品牌及百分比 2nd/ percent	第三品牌及百分比 3rd/ percent	第四品牌及百分比 4th/ percent
女性 Female	118	**羽西 Yue-sai（11.0）** **ZA（11.0）**	**郑明明 Cheng Mingming（9.3）**	**资生堂 Shiseido（5.9）**	**美宝莲 Maybelline（5.1）**
广告淡漠指向 indifferent orientation	27	美宝莲 Maybelline（7.4） 资生堂 Shiseido（7.4） 郑明明 Cheng Mingming（7.4） 羽西 Yue-sai（7.4） 雅芳 Avon（7.4）	美加净 Maxam（3.7） 摩蕾娜 Marait（3.7） 欧珀莱 Aupres（3.7） 清妃 Chinf（3.7） 丽妃 Lifei（3.7） 凤凰 Phoenix（3.7） 迪奥 CD（3.7） 艾琳 Irlene（3.7） 玉兰油 Oil of Olay（3.7） 永芳 Yinfong（3.7） ZA（3.7） 贝加斯 Beijiashi（3.7） 东方之宝 Dongfangzhinbao（3.7） 美伊娜多 Meiyinaduo（3.7）		
中间层 medium	66	ZA（15.2）	郑明明 Cheng Mingming（9.1）	资生堂 Shiseido（7.6） 羽西 Yue-sai（7.6） 高丝 Kose（7.6）	宝璐丝 Paolarlus（6.1）
信赖广告指向 loyal orientation	25	羽西 Yue-sai（24.0）	郑明明 Cheng Mingming（12.0） 美宝莲 Maybelline（12.0）	ZA（8.0） 雅芳 Avon（8.0）	旁氏 Pond's（4.0） 自然美 Natural Beauty（4.0） 雅艾芬迪 Latan taiao（4.0） 伊丽莎白·雅顿 ElizabethArden（4.0） 玫琳凯 Mary Kay（4.0） 丽妃 Lifei（4.0） 迪奥 CD（4.0） 宝璐丝 Paolarlus（4.0）

2-12 重度消费者的消费层构成/ The Composition of the Heavy Consumers

2-12-1 时尚流行指标/ Fads Popular Index

	人数 Number	平实生活指向 simple living orientation	时尚流行指向 fashion orientation
女性 Female	67	13.4	86.6
天天用 daily	44	15.9	84.1
两三天用 1 次 once 2 or 3 days	23	8.7	91.3

2-12-2 广告态度指标/ Advertising Attitude Index

	人数 Number	广告淡漠指向 indifferent orientation	中间层 medium	信赖广告指向 loyal orientation
女性 Female	67	22.4	52.2	25.4
天天用 daily	44	13.6	61.4	25.0
两三天用 1 次 once 2 or 3 days	23	39.1	34.8	26.1

● 广州 / Guangzhou

2-1 最近三个月使用频次的比例/ Proportion of the Sample Consuming Pre-makeup in the Last Three Months

	人数 Number	百分比 Percent
天天用 daily	14	2.7
两三天用 1 次 once 2 or 3 days	11	2.1
一周 1～2 次 once or twice a week	14	2.7
半个月 1 次 once half a month	16	3.1
一个月 1 次或以下 once a month or below	24	4.7
没用过 never use	434	84.6

n=513

2-2 最常用品牌排名/ Ranking of the Most Frequently Used Brands

排名 Brand Ranking	品牌 Brands	人数 Number	百分比 Percent
1	雅芳 Avon	13	16.5
2	美宝莲 Maybelline	9	11.4
3	永芳 Yinfong	6	7.6
4	蜜丝佛陀 Maxfactor	5	6.3
5	迪奥 CD	4	5.1
5	旁氏 Pond's	4	5.1

n=79

2-3 样本、女性各年龄层的常用品牌/ The Most Frequently Used Brands by the Female Sample and Age Groups

	人数 Number	第一品牌及百分比 1st/ percent	第二品牌及百分比 2nd/ percent	第三品牌及百分比 3rd/ percent
女性 Female	79	**雅芳 Avon(16.5)**	**美宝莲 Maybelline(11.4)**	**永芳 Yinfong(7.6)**
16~24 岁 Age	21	花王碧柔歌婷 Qualite(14.3)	迪奥 CD(9.5) 雅芳 Avon(9.5)	资生堂 Shiseido(4.8) Syuania(4.8) Temptation(4.8) Nuskin(4.8) 佳琳 Jialin(4.8) 永芳 Yinfong(4.8) 生态美 Ecological beauty(4.8) 郑明明 Cheng Mingming(4.8) 蜜丝佛陀 Maxfactor(4.8) 美宝莲 Maybelline(4.8) 高丝 Kose(4.8) 柏姿 Payot(4.8)
25~34 岁 Age	32	雅芳 Avon(25.0)	美宝莲 Maybelline(15.6)	永芳 Yinfong(6.3) 露华浓 Revlon(6.3) 蜜丝佛陀 Maxfactor(6.3) 资生堂 Shiseido(6.3)
35~44 岁 Age	20	一枝花 Yizhihua(10.0) 美宝莲 Maybelline(10.0) 玉兰油 Oil of Olay(10.0) 旁氏 Pond's(10.0) 雅芳 Avon(10.0)	自然美 Natural Beauty(5.0) 姬顺 Jishun(5.0) 永芳 Yinfong(5.0) 羽西 Yue-sai(5.0) 欧莱雅 L'oreal(5.0) 蜜丝佛陀 Maxfactor(5.0) 美人鱼 Meirenyu(5.0) 迪奥 CD(5.0) 柏姿 Payot(5.0)	
45~54 岁 Age	6	永芳 Yinfong(33.3)	美宝莲 Maybelline(16.7) 蜜丝佛陀 Maxfactor(16.7) 雅芳 Avon(16.7) 旁氏 Pond's(16.7)	
55~60 岁 Age	0			

2-4 正在使用的品牌排名/ Ranking of the Brands Used Now

排名 Brand Ranking	品牌 Brands	人数 Number	百分比 Percent
1	雅芳 Avon	12	15.2
2	美宝莲 Maybelline	8	10.1
3	蜜丝佛陀 Maxfactor	7	8.9
4	永芳 Yinfong	4	5.1
4	旁氏 Pond's	4	5.1
5	资生堂 Shiseido	3	3.8
5	花王碧柔歌婷 Quallrte	3	3.8
5	露华浓 Revlon	3	3.8
5	美人鱼 Meirenyu	3	3.8
5	玉兰油 Oil of Olay	3	3.8

n=79

2-5 品牌转换习惯/ Brand Habit in Consuming Pre-makeup

	人数 Number	第一次使用该品牌 first use this brand	上一次也是这个牌子 used it last time	上一次不是这个牌子 not used it last time
女性 Female	**77**	**18.2**	**70.1**	**11.7**
雅芳 Avon	11	0.0	90.9	9.1
美宝莲 Maybelline	7	0.0	100.0	0.0
蜜丝佛陀 Maxfactor	7	14.3	71.4	14.3
永芳 Yinfong	4	25.0	50.0	25.0
旁氏 Pond's	4	25.0	50.0	25.0
资生堂 Shiseido	3	0.0	66.7	33.3
花王碧柔歌婷 Quslite	3	0.0	66.7	33.3
露华浓 Revlon	3	0.0	100.0	0.0
美人鱼 Meirenyu	3	66.7	33.3	0.0

2-6 下一次打算使用的品牌排名/ Ranking of the Brands to be Used Next Time

排名 Brand Ranking	品牌 Brands	人数 Number	百分比 Percent
1	雅芳 Avon	10	12.8
2	蜜丝佛陀 Maxfactor	9	11.5
3	露华浓 Revlon	6	7.7
3	资生堂 Shiseido	6	7.7
4	旁氏 Pond's	4	5.1
5	美宝莲 Maybelline	3	3.8
5	玉兰油 Oil of Olay	3	3.8
5	永芳 Yinfong	3	3.8
5	迪奥 CD	3	3.8

n=78

2-7 样本、女性各年龄层的使用频率/ Frequencies of the Consumed Pre-makeup by the Female Sample and Age Groups

	人数 Number	天天用 daily	两三天用 1 次 once 2 or 3 days	一周 1~2 次 once or twice a week	半个月 1 次 once half a month	一个月 1 次或以下 once a month or below	没用过 never use
女性 Female	**513**	**2.7**	**2.1**	**2.7**	**3.1**	**4.7**	**84.6**
16~24 岁 Age	112	4.5	0.9	5.4	1.8	6.3	81.3
25~34 岁 Age	154	1.3	4.5	1.9	7.8	5.2	79.2
35~44 岁 Age	129	3.1	2.3	2.3	0.8	7.0	84.5
45~54 岁 Age	81	3.7	0.0	2.5	1.2	0.0	92.6
55~60 岁 Age	37	0.0	0.0	0.0	0.0	0.0	100.0

2-8 选择该类商品的考虑因素/ Ranking of the Considerations in Purchasing

注：本题为多选题，合计百分比超过 100%（Multiple answers）

排名 Ranking	考虑因素 Considerations	人次 Person-time	百分比 Percent
1	有名的牌子 famous brand	42	53.8
2	产品功用 product function	32	41.0
3	价格适中 reasonable price	20	25.6
4	别人推荐 introduced by other people	16	20.5
5	广告影响 influence of advertising	14	17.9
6	包装吸引人 appealing package	6	7.7
6	购买方便 easy to buy	6	7.7
7	有优惠条件 with preferential terms	3	3.8
8	其它 others	1	1.3

n=78

2-9 对产品功能的侧重方面/ Ranking of the Considerations about the Function of this Kind of Product

注：本题为多选题，合计百分比超过 100%（Multiple answers）

排名 Ranking	侧重方面 Items	人次 Person-time	百分比 Percent
1	调整肤色 color	50	63.3
2	光滑细腻 smooth and fine	35	44.3
3	遮盖功能 covering function	28	35.4
4	防晒功能 anti-UV	22	27.8
5	着色稳定 color stability	17	21.5
6	不含香料 containing no perfume	11	13.9
7	其他 others	1	1.3

n=79

2-10 重度消费者的人口分布/ Demographics of the Heavy Consumers

	人数 Number	16-24 岁 Age	25-34 岁 Age	35-44 岁 Age	45-54 岁 Age	55-60 岁 Age
女性 Female	25	24.0	36.0	28.0	12.0	0.0
天天用 daily	14	35.7	14.3	28.6	21.4	0.0
两三天用 1 次 once 2 or 3 days	11	9.1	63.6	27.3	0.0	0.0

2-11 不同消费者层的常用品牌/ The Most Frequently Used Brands by Market Segments

2-11-1 时尚流行指标/ Fads Popular Index

	人数 Number	第一品牌及百分比 1st/ percent	第二品牌及百分比 2nd/ percent	第三品牌及百分比 3rd/ percent
女性 Female	78	**雅芳 Avon(16.7)**	**美宝莲 Maybelline(10.3)**	**永芳 Yinfong(7.7)**
平实生活指向 simple living orientation	22	雅芳 Avon(22.7)	美宝莲 Maybelline(13.6)	旁氏 Pond's(9.1) 美人鱼 Meirenyu(9.1) 蜜丝佛陀 Maxfactor(9.1)
时尚流行指向 fashion orientation	56	雅芳 Avon(14.3)	永芳 Yinfong(10.7)	美宝莲 Maybelline(8.9)

2-11-2 广告态度指标/ Advertising Attitude Index

	人数 Number	第一品牌及百分比 1st/ percent	第二品牌及百分比 2nd/ percent	第三品牌及百分比 3rd/ percent
女性 Female	76	**雅芳 Avon(14.5)**	**美宝莲 Maybelline(11.8)**	**永芳 Yinfong(7.9)**
广告淡漠指向 indifferent orientation	15	雅芳 Avon(26.7)	旁氏 Pond's(13.3)	Temptation(6.7) 纯晶 Chunjing(6.7) 佳琳 Jialin(6.7) 玉兰油 Oil of Olay(6.7) 自然美 Natural Beauty(6.7) 蜜丝佛陀 Maxfactor(6.7) 美人鱼 Meirenyu(6.7) 花王碧柔歌婷 Qualite(6.7)
中间层 medium	52	雅芳 Avon(11.5) 美宝莲 Maybelline(11.5)	永芳 Yinfong(9.6)	蜜丝佛陀 Maxfactor(7.7)
信赖广告指向 loyal orientation	9	美宝莲 Maybelline(33.3)	高丝 Kose(11.1) 雅芳 Avon(11.1) 资生堂 Shiseido(11.1) 永芳 Yinfong(11.1) 雨水 Yushui(11.1) 一枝花 Yizhihua(11.1)	

2-12 重度消费者的消费层构成/ The Composition of the Heavy Consumers

2-12-1 时尚流行指标/ Fads Popular Index

	人数 Number	平实生活指向 simple living orientation	时尚流行指向 fashion orientation
女性 Female	24	29.2	70.8
天天用 daily	13	30.8	69.2
两三天用 1 次 once 2 or 3 days	11	27.3	72.7

2-12-2 广告态度指标/ Advertising Attitude Index

	人数 Number	广告淡漠指向 indifferent orientation	中间层 medium	信赖广告指向 loyal orientation
女性 Female	24	8.3	79.2	12.5
天天用 daily	14	7.1	85.7	7.1
两三天用 1 次 once 2 or 3 days	10	10.0	70.0	20.0

● 重庆 / Chongqing

2-1 最近三个月使用频次的比例/ Proportion of the Sample Consuming Pre-makeup in the Last Three Months

	人数 Number	百分比 Percent
天天用 daily	21	6.8
两三天用 1 次 once 2 or 3 days	7	2.3
一周 1～2 次 about once or twice a week	7	2.3
半个月 1 次 once half a month	3	1.0
一个月 1 次或以下 once a month or below	4	1.3
没用过 never use	268	86.5

n=310

2-2 最常用品牌排名/ Ranking of the Most Frequently Used Brands

排名 Brand Ranking	品牌 Brands	人数 Number	百分比 Percent
1	雅芳 Avon	4	9.5
2	高丝 Kose	3	7.1
2	羽西 Yue-sai	3	7.1
2	雅倩 Arche	3	7.1
2	美人鱼 Meirenyu	3	7.1
2	蝶妆 Debon LG	3	7.1
3	芬宝 Fenbao	2	4.8
3	丹桂 Dangui	2	4.8
3	兰贵人 Lan Guiren	2	4.8
3	欧珀莱 Aupres	2	4.8

n=42

2-3 样本、女性各年龄层的常用品牌/ The Most Frequently Used Brands by the Female Sample and Age Groups

	人数 Number	第一品牌及百分比 1st/ percent	第二品牌及百分比 2nd/ percent	第三品牌及百分比 3rd/ percent
女性 Female	42	**雅芳 Avon(9.5)**	**高丝 Kose(7.1) 羽西 Yue-sai(7.1) 雅倩 Arche(7.1) 美人鱼 Meirenyu(7.1) 蝶妆 Debon LG(7.1)**	**芬宝 Fenbao(4.8) 丹桂 Dangui(4.8) 兰贵人 Lan Guiren(4.8) 欧珀莱 Aupres(4.8)**
16~24 岁 Age	6	蝶妆 Debon LG(16.7) 蕾迪雅 Ladiera（Maxis）(16.7) 美人鱼 Meirenyu(16.7) 雅芳 Avon(16.7) 雅倩 Arche(16.7)		
25~34 岁 Age	22	雅芳 Avon(13.6)	高丝 Kose(9.1) 羽西 Yue-sai(9.1) 欧珀莱 Aupres(9.1)	兰贵人 Lan Guiren(4.5) 美人鱼 Meirenyu(4.5) 蝶妆 Debon LG(4.5) 艾丽碧丝 Elegbacae(4.5) 芬宝 Fenbao(4.5) 夏士莲 Hazeline(4.5) 保美雅 Baomeiya(4.5) AD(4.5) 洁雅 Jieya(4.5) 丹桂 Dangui(4.5)
35~44 岁 Age	9	艾迪丝 Aidieces(11.1) 蝶妆 Debon LG(11.1) 高丝 Kose(11.1) 美人鱼 Meirenyu(11.1) 雅倩 Arche(11.1) 羽西 Yue-sai(11.1) 雅婷 Yating(11.1) 丹桂 Dangui(11.1)		
45~54 岁 Age	5	兰贵人 Lan Guiren(20.0) 雅倩 Arche(20.0) 依贝佳 Ebeca (20.0) 芬宝 Fenbao(20.0) 伍昱 Wuyu(20.0)		
55~60 岁 Age	0			

2-4 正在使用的品牌排名/ Ranking of the Brands Used Now

排名 Brand Ranking	品牌 Brands	人数 Number	百分比 Percent
1	雅芳 Avon	4	9.5
2	高丝 Kose	3	7.1
2	雅倩 Arche	3	7.1
3	欧珀莱 Aupres	2	4.8
3	丹桂 Dangui	2	4.8
3	芬宝 Fenbao	2	4.8
3	羽西 Yue-sai	2	4.8
3	依贝佳 Ebeca	2	4.8
3	美人鱼 Meirenyu	2	4.8
3	兰贵人 Lan Guiren	2	4.8
3	蝶妆 Debon LG	2	4.8

n=42

2-5 品牌转换习惯/ Brand Habit in Consuming Pre-makeup

	人数 Number	第一次使用该品牌 first use this brand	上一次也是这个牌子 used it last time	上一次不是这个牌子 not used it last time
女性 Female	42	19.0	71.4	9.5
雅芳 Avon	4	25.0	50.0	25.0
高丝 Kose	3	33.3	66.7	0.0
雅倩 Arche	3	0.0	100.0	0.0
欧珀莱 Aupres	2	0.0	100.0	0.0
丹桂 Dangui	2	0.0	100.0	0.0
芬宝 Fenbao	2	0.0	100.0	0.0
羽西 Yue-sai	2	50.0	50.0	0.0
依贝佳 Ebeca	2	50.0	0.0	50.0
美人鱼 Meirenyu	2	0.0	100.0	0.0
兰贵人 Lan Guiren	2	50.0	50.0	0.0
蝶妆 Debon LG	2	0.0	100.0	0.0

2-6 下一次打算使用的品牌排名/ Ranking of the Brands to be Used Next Time

排名 Brand Ranking	品牌 Brands	人数 Number	百分比 Percent
1	雅倩 Arche	4	9.5
2	羽西 Yue-sai	3	7.1
2	高丝 Kose	3	7.1
2	兰贵人 Lan Guiren	3	7.1
3	美人鱼 Meirenyu	2	4.8
3	欧珀莱 Aupres	2	4.8
3	雅芳 Avon	2	4.8

n=42

2-7 样本、女性各年龄层的使用频率/ Frequencies of the Consumed Pre-makeup by the Female Sample and Age Groups

	人数 Number	天天用 daily	两三天用 1 次 once 2 or 3 days	一周 1~2 次 once or twice a week	半个月 1 次 once half a month	一个月 1 次或以下 once a month or below	没用过 never use
女性 Female	310	6.8	2.3	2.3	1.0	1.3	86.5
16~24 岁 Age	64	3.1	0.0	3.1	3.1	0.0	90.6
25~34 岁 Age	90	15.6	2.2	5.6	0.0	1.1	75.6
35~44 岁 Age	73	5.5	4.1	0.0	0.0	2.7	87.7
45~54 岁 Age	60	1.7	3.3	0.0	1.7	1.7	91.7
55~60 岁 Age	23	0.0	0.0	0.0	0.0	0.0	100.0

2-8 选择该类商品的考虑因素/ Ranking of the Considerations in Purchasing

注：本题为多选题，合计百分比超过 100%（Multiple answers）

排名 Ranking	考虑因素 Considerations	人次 Person-time	百分比 Percent
1	产品功用 product function	17	40.5
2	有名的牌子 famous brand	15	35.7
3	价格适中 reasonable price	14	33.3
3	别人推荐 introduced by other people	14	33.3
4	广告影响 influence of advertising	7	16.7
5	购买方便 easy to buy	3	7.1
6	包装吸引人 appealing package	2	4.8
7	有优惠条件 with preferential terms	1	2.4
7	其它 others	1	2.4

n=42

2-9 对产品功能的侧重方面/ Ranking of the Considerations about the Function of this Kind of Product

注：本题为多选题，合计百分比超过 100%（Multiple answers）

排名 Ranking	侧重方面 Items	人次 Person-time	百分比 Percent
1	调整肤色 color	28	66.7
2	光滑细腻 smooth and fine	19	45.2
3	遮盖功能 covering function	9	21.4
4	防晒功能 anti-UV	7	16.7
5	着色稳定 color stability	4	9.5
6	不含香料 containing no perfume	3	7.1
7	其他 others	2	4.8

n=42

2-10 重度消费者的人口分布/ Demographics of the Heavy Consumers

	人数 Number	16-24 岁 Age	25-34 岁 Age	35-44 岁 Age	45-54 岁 Age	55-60 岁 Age
女性 Female	28	7.1	57.1	25.0	10.7	0.0
天天用 daily	21	9.5	66.7	19.0	4.8	0.0
两三天用 1 次 once 2 or 3 days	7	0.0	28.6	42.9	28.6	0.0

2-11 不同消费者层的常用品牌/ The Most Frequently Used Brands by Market Segments

2-11-1 时尚流行指标/ Fads Popular Index

	人数 Number	第一品牌及百分比 1st/ percent	第二品牌及百分比 2nd/ percent	第三品牌及百分比 3rd/ percent
女性 Female	42	**雅芳 Avon(9.5)**	**高丝 Kose(7.1)** **羽西 Yue-sai(7.1)** **雅倩 Arche(7.1)** **美人鱼 Meirenyu(7.1)** **蝶妆 Debon LG(7.1)**	**芬宝 Fenbao(4.8)** **丹桂 Dangui(4.8)** **兰贵人 Lan Guiren(4.8)** **欧珀莱 Aupres(4.8)**
平实生活指向 simple living orientation	9	艾迪丝 Aidieces(11.1) 艾丽碧丝 Elegbacae(11.1) 蝶妆 Debon LG(11.1) 兰贵人 Lan Guiren(11.1) 雅芳 Avon(11.1) 雅倩 Arche(11.1) 保美雅 Baomeiya(11.1) 丹桂 Dangui(11.1)		
时尚流行指向 fashion orientation	33	高丝 Kose(9.1) 美人鱼 Meirenyu(9.1) 雅芳 Avon(9.1) 羽西 Yue-sai(9.1)	蝶妆 Debon LG(6.1) 欧珀莱 Aupres(6.1) 雅倩 Arche(6.1) 芬宝 Fenbao(6.1)	雅婷 Yating(3.0) 丹桂 Dangui(3.0) 洁雅 Jieya(3.0) 伍昱 Wuyu(3.0) AD(3.0) 依贝佳 Ebeca (3.0) 夏士莲 Hazeline(3.0) 蕾迪雅 Ladiera（Maxis）(3.0) 兰贵人 Lan Guiren(3.0)

2-11-2 广告态度指标/ Advertising Attitude Index

	人数 Number	第一品牌及百分比 1st/ percent	第二品牌及百分比 2nd/ percent	第三品牌及百分比 3rd/ percent
女性 Female	41	**雅芳 Avon(9.8)**	**高丝 Kose(7.3)** **羽西 Yue-sai(7.3)** **雅倩 Arche(7.3)** **美人鱼 Meirenyu(7.3)** **蝶妆 Debon LG(7.3)**	**欧珀莱 Aupres(4.9)** **芬宝 Fenbao(4.9)** **丹桂 Dangui(4.9)**
广告淡漠指向 indifferent orientation	6	艾丽碧丝 Elegbacae(16.7) 蝶妆 Debon LG(16.7) 雅倩 Arche(16.7) 依贝佳 Ebeca (16.7) 羽西 Yue-sai(16.7)		
中间层 medium	28	雅芳 Avon(14.3)	欧珀莱 Aupres(7.1) 丹桂 Dangui(7.1) 雅倩 Arche(7.1) 高丝 Kose(7.1)	兰贵人 Lan Guiren(3.6) 蕾迪雅 Ladiera（Maxis）(3.6) 美人鱼 Meirenyu(3.6) 蝶妆 Debon LG(3.6) 艾迪丝 Aidieces(3.6) 羽西 Yue-sai(3.6) 芬宝 Fenbao(3.6) 夏士莲 Hazeline(3.6) 保美雅 Baomeiya(3.6) AD(3.6) 伍昱 Wuyu(3.6) 洁雅 Jieya(3.6)
信赖广告指向 loyal orientation	7	美人鱼 Meirenyu(28.6)	蝶妆 Debon LG(14.3) 高丝 Kose(14.3) 羽西 Yue-sai(14.3) 芬宝 Fenbao(14.3) 雅婷 Yating(14.3)	

2-12 重度消费者的消费层构成/ The Composition of the Heavy Consumers

2-12-1 时尚流行指标/ Fads Popular Index

	人数 Number	平实生活指向 simple living orientation	时尚流行指向 fashion orientation
女性 Female	28	21.4	78.6
天天用 daily	21	19.0	81.0
两三天用 1 次 once 2 or 3 days	7	28.6	71.4

2-12-2 广告态度指标/ Advertising Attitude Index

	人数 Number	广告淡漠指向 indifferent orientation	中间层 medium	信赖广告指向 loyal orientation
女性 Female	28	14.3	75.0	10.7
天天用 daily	21	9.5	76.2	14.3
两三天用 1 次 once 2 or 3 days	7	28.6	71.4	0.0

● 武汉 / Wuhan

2-1 最近三个月使用频次的比例/ Proportion of the Sample Consuming Pre-makeup in the Last Three Months

	人数 Number	百分比 Percent
天天用 daily	18	5.5
两三天用 1 次 once 2 or 3 days	13	4.0
一周 1～2 次 about once or twice a week	17	5.2
半个月 1 次 once half a month	10	3.0
一个月 1 次或以下 once a month or below	5	1.5
没用过 never use	266	80.9

n=329

2-2 最常用品牌排名/ Ranking of the Most Frequently Used Brands

排名 Brand Ranking	品牌 Brands	人数 Number	百分比 Percent
1	丽妃 Lifei	7	11.1
2	丽花丝宝 Laifa-C'bons	6	9.5
3	欧珀莱 Aupres	5	7.9
3	雅芳 Avon	5	7.9
4	美人鱼 Meirenyu	4	6.3
5	佳美 Jiamei	3	4.8
6	郑明明 Cheng Mingming	2	3.2
6	丁家宜 Dingjiayi	2	3.2
6	清妃 Chinf	2	3.2

n=63

2-3 样本、女性各年龄层的常用品牌/ The Most Frequently Used Brands by the Female Sample and Age Groups

	人数 Number	第一品牌及百分比 1st/ percent	第二品牌及百分比 2nd/ percent	第三品牌及百分比 3rd/ percent
女性 Female	**63**	**丽妃 Lifei(11.1)**	**丽花丝宝 Laifa-C'bons(9.5)**	**欧珀莱 Aupres(7.9)** **雅芳 Avon(7.9)**
16~24 岁 Age	20	雅芳 Avon(15.0)	郑明明 Cheng Mingming(10.0) 欧珀莱 Aupres(10.0)	赛雅 Saiya (5.0) 佳美 Jiamei (5.0) 丁家宜 Dingjiayi(5.0) 旁氏 Pond's(5.0) 羽西 Yue-sai(5.0) 清妃 Chinf(5.0) 茜素丝 Sans Soucis(5.0) 欧莱雅 L'oreal(5.0) 美宝莲 Maybelline(5.0) 丽花丝宝 Laifa-C'bons(5.0) 丽妃 Lifei(5.0) 高丝 Kose(5.0)
25~34 岁 Age	30	丽妃 Lifei(16.7)	美人鱼 Meirenyu(10.0) 欧珀莱 Aupres(10.0)	丽花丝宝 Laifa-C'bons(6.7) 佳美 Jiamei(6.7)
35~44 岁 Age	10	丽花丝宝 Laifa-C'bons(20.0)	丽妃 Lifei(10.0) 美人鱼 Meirenyu(10.0) 雅芳 Avon(10.0) 依贝佳 Ebeca (10.0) 丁家宜 Dingjiayi(10.0) 芳宝 Fangbao(10.0) 纯晶 Chunjing(10.0) 思娇 Sijiao(10.0)	
45~54 岁 Age	3	丽花丝宝 Laifa-C'bons(33.3) 伊思丽 Eesli(33.3)		
55~60 岁 Age	0			

2-4 正在使用的品牌排名/ Ranking of the Brands Used Now

排名 Brand Ranking	品牌 Brands	人数 Number	百分比 Percent
1	丽妃 Lifei	7	11.1
2	丽花丝宝 Laifa-C'bons	6	9.5
2	美人鱼 Meirenyu	6	9.5
3	欧珀莱 Aupres	5	7.9
4	雅芳 Avon	3	4.8
4	美宝莲 Maybelline	3	4.8
5	羽西 Yue-sai	2	3.2
5	纯晶 Chunjing	2	3.2
5	丁家宜 Dingjiayi	2	3.2
5	佳美 Jiamei	2	3.2

n=63

2-5 品牌转换习惯/ Brand Habit in Consuming Pre-makeup

	人数 Number	第一次使用该品牌 first use this brand	上一次也是这个牌子 used it last time	上一次不是这个牌子 not used it last time
女性 Female	63	12.7	65.1	22.2
丽妃 Lifei	7	0.0	71.4	28.6
丽花丝宝 Laifa-C'bons	6	0.0	66.7	33.3
美人鱼 Meirenyu	6	16.7	50.0	33.3
欧珀莱 Aupres	5	0.0	80.0	20.0
雅芳 Avon	3	0.0	100.0	0.0
美宝莲 Maybelline	3	0.0	33.3	66.7
羽西 Yue-sai	2	0.0	50.0	50.0
纯晶 Chunjing	2	50.0	50.0	0.0
丁家宜 Dingjiayi	2	0.0	50.0	50.0
佳美 Jiamei	2	0.0	100.0	0.0

2-6 下一次打算使用的品牌排名/ Ranking of the Brands to be Used Next Time

排名 Brand Ranking	品牌 Brands	人数 Number	百分比 Percent
1	丽妃 Lifei	5	8.1
2	雅芳 Avon	4	6.5
2	丽花丝宝 Laifa-C'bons	4	6.5
2	美宝莲 Maybelline	4	6.5
2	羽西 Yue-sai	4	6.5
2	欧珀莱 Aupres	4	6.5
3	美人鱼 Meirenyu	3	4.8

n=62

2-7 样本、女性各年龄层的使用频率/ Frequencies of the Consumed Pre-makeup by the Female Sample and Age Groups

	人数 Number	天天用 daily	两三天用 1 次 once 2 or 3 days	一周 1~2 次 once or twice a week	半个月 1 次 once half a month	一个月 1 次或以下 once a month or below	没用过 never use
女性 Female	329	5.5	4.0	5.2	3.0	1.5	80.9
16~24 岁 Age	69	2.9	2.9	13.0	8.7	1.4	71.0
25~34 岁 Age	95	10.5	8.4	4.2	4.2	4.2	68.4
35~44 岁 Age	78	5.1	3.8	3.8	0.0	0.0	87.2
45~54 岁 Age	61	3.3	0.0	1.6	0.0	0.0	95.1
55~60 岁 Age	26	0.0	0.0	0.0	0.0	0.0	100.0

2-8 选择该类商品的考虑因素/ Ranking of the Considerations in Purchasing

注：本题为多选题，合计百分比超过 100%（Multiple answers）

排名 Ranking	考虑因素 Considerations	人次 Person-time	百分比 Percent
1	产品功用 product function	29	46.0
2	价格适中 reasonable price	28	44.4
3	有名的牌子 famous brand	22	34.9
4	别人推荐 introduced by other people	19	30.2
5	广告影响 influence of advertising	10	15.9
6	有优惠条件 with preferential terms	7	11.1
7	购买方便 easy to buy	6	9.5
8	包装吸引人 appealing package	2	3.2
8	其它 others	2	3.2

n=63

2-9 对产品功能的侧重方面/ Ranking of the Considerations about the Function of this Kind of Product

注：本题为多选题，合计百分比超过 100%（Multiple answers）

排名 Ranking	侧重方面 Items	人次 Person-time	百分比 Percent
1	调整肤色 color	42	66.7
2	光滑细腻 smooth and fine	34	54.0
3	遮盖功能 covering function	23	36.5
4	防晒功能 anti-UV	12	19.0
5	着色稳定 color stability	10	15.9
5	不含香料 containing no perfume	10	15.9
6	其他 others	2	3.2

n=63

2-10 重度消费者的人口分布/ Demographics of the Heavy Consumers

	人数 Number	16-24 岁 Age	25-34 岁 Age	35-44 岁 Age	45-54 岁 Age	55-60 岁 Age
女性 Female	31	12.9	58.1	22.6	6.5	0.0
天天用 daily	18	11.1	55.6	22.2	11.1	0.0
两三天用 1 次 once 2 or 3 days	13	15.4	61.5	23.1	0.0	0.0

2-11 不同消费者层的常用品牌/ The Most Frequently Used Brands by Market Segments

2-11-1 时尚流行指标/ Fads Popular Index

	人数 Number	第一品牌及百分比 1st/ percent	第二品牌及百分比 2nd/ percent	第三品牌及百分比 3rd/ percent
女性 Female	63	**丽妃 Lifei(11.1)**	**丽花丝宝 Laifa-C'bons(9.5)**	**欧珀莱 Aupres(7.9)** **雅芳 Avon(7.9)**
平实生活指向 simple living orientation	16	丽妃 Lifei(18.8)	丽花丝宝 Laifa-C'bons(12.5)	郑明明 Cheng Mingming(6.3) 赛雅 Saiya(6.3) 芳宝 Fangbao(6.3) 丁家宜 Dingjiayi(6.3) 绿丹兰 Lvdanlan(6.3) 雅嘉 Aikai(6.3) 伊思丽 Eesli(6.3) 雅芳 Avon(6.3) 清妃 Chinf(6.3) 欧珀莱 Aupres(6.3) 欧莱雅 L'oreal(6.3)
时尚流行指向 fashion orientation	47	丽妃 Lifei(8.5) 丽花丝宝 Laifa-C'bons(8.5) 美人鱼 Meirenyu(8.5) 欧珀莱 Aupres(8.5) 雅芳 Avon(8.5)	佳美 Jiamei(6.4)	沙莉 Shali(2.1) 紫罗兰 Ziluolan(2.1) OCTARD(2.1) 丁家宜 Dingjiayi(2.1) 玉兰油 Oil of Olay(2.1) 纯晶 Chunjing(2.1) 大花 Dahua(2.1) 海咸 Haixian(2.1) 思娇 Sijiao(2.1) 得资 Dezi(2.1) 旁氏 Pond's(2.1) 郑明明 Cheng Mingming(2.1) 羽西 Yue-sai(2.1) 依贝佳 Ebeca (2.1) 雅倩 Arche(2.1) 生态美 Ecological beauty(2.1) 清妃 Chinf(2.1) 茜素丝 Sans Soucis(2.1) 美宝莲 Maybelline(2.1) 兰贵人 Lan Guiren（2.1）

2-11-2 广告态度指标/ Advertising Attitude Index

	人数 Number	第一品牌及百分比 1st/ percent	第二品牌及百分比 2nd/ percent	第三品牌及百分比 3rd/ percent
女性 Female	**63**	**丽妃 Lifei(11.1)**	**丽花丝宝 Laifa-C'bons(9.5)**	**欧珀莱 Aupres(7.9)** **雅芳 Avon(7.9)**
广告淡漠指向 indifferent orientation	14	丁家宜 Dingjiayi(14.3) 丽妃 Lifei(14.3)	大花 Dahua(7.1) 纯晶 Chunjing(7.1) 芳宝 Fangbao(7.1) 佳美 Jiamei(7.1) 雅倩 Arche(7.1) 玉兰油 Oil of Olay(7.1) 雅芳 Avon(7.1) 生态美 Ecological beauty(7.1) 美人鱼 Meirenyu(7.1) 丽花丝宝 Laifa-C'bons(7.1)	
中间层 medium	39	丽妃 Lifei(12.8) 欧珀莱 Aupres(12.8)	丽花丝宝 Laifa-C'bons(10.3) 雅芳 Avon(10.3)	美人鱼 Meirenyu(5.1) 佳美 Jiamei(5.1) 清妃 Chinf(5.1) 郑明明 Cheng Mingming(5.1)
信赖广告指向 loyal orientation	10	丽花丝宝 Laifa-C'bons(10.0) 美宝莲 Maybelline(10.0) 美人鱼 Meirenyu(10.0) 雅嘉 Aikai(10.0) 依贝佳 Ebeca (10.0) 沙莉 Shali(10.0) OCTARD(10.0) 海咸 Haixian(10.0)		

2-12 重度消费者的消费层构成/ The Composition of the Heavy Consumers

2-12-1 时尚流行指标/ Fads Popular Index

	人数 Number	平实生活指向 simple living orientation	时尚流行指向 fashion orientation
女性 Female	31	25.8	74.2
天天用 daily	18	22.2	77.8
两三天用 1 次 once 2 or 3 days	13	30.8	69.2

2-12-2 广告态度指标/ Advertising Attitude Index

	人数 Number	广告淡漠指向 indifferent orientation	中间层 medium	信赖广告指向 loyal orientation
女性 Female	31	22.6	51.6	25.8
天天用 daily	18	16.7	61.1	22.2
两三天用 1 次 once 2 or 3 days	13	30.8	38.5	30.8

● 西安 / Xi'an

2-1 最近三个月使用频次的比例/ Proportion of the Sample Consuming Pre-makeup in the Last Three Months

	人数 Number	百分比 Percent
天天用 daily	15	5.0
两三天用 1 次 once 2 or 3 days	6	2.0
一周 1～2 次 about once or twice a week	10	3.4
半个月 1 次 once half a month	6	2.0
一个月 1 次或以下 once a month or below	3	1.0
没用过 never use	258	86.6

n=298

2-2 最常用品牌排名/ Ranking of the Most Frequently Used Brands

排名 Brand Ranking	品牌 Brands	人数 Number	百分比 Percent
1	美宝莲 Maybelline	5	12.5
1	羽西 Yue-sai	5	12.5
2	美人鱼 Meirenyu	4	10.0
2	雅芳 Avon	4	10.0
3	雅倩 Arche	2	5.0
3	圣梦 Shengmeng	2	5.0
3	资生堂 Shiseido	2	5.0
3	清妃 Chinf	2	5.0

n=40

2-3 样本、女性各年龄层的常用品牌/ The Most Frequently Used Brands by the Female Sample and Age Groups

	人数 Number	第一品牌及百分比 1st/ percent	第二品牌及百分比 2nd/ percent	第三品牌及百分比 3rd/ percent
女性 Female	40	美宝莲 Maybelline(12.5) 羽西 Yue-sai(12.5)	美人鱼 Meirenyu(10.0) 雅芳 Avon(10.0)	雅倩 Arche(5.0) 圣梦 Shengmeng(5.0) 资生堂 Shiseido(5.0) 清妃 Chinf(5.0)
16~24 岁 Age	4	美宝莲 Maybelline(25.0) 雅芳 Avon(25.0) 羽西 Yue-sai(25.0) 资生堂 Shiseido(25.0)		
25~34 岁 Age	23	美宝莲 Maybelline(13.0)	雅倩 Arche(8.7) 美人鱼 Meirenyu(8.7) 圣梦 Shengmeng(8.7) 雅芳 Avon(8.7) 羽西 Yue-sai(8.7)	柔婷 Routing(4.3) 玉兰油 Oil of Olay(4.3) 资生堂 Shiseido(4.3) 清妃 Chinf(4.3) 雅嘉 Aikai(4.3) 欧莱雅 L'oreal(4.3) 美加净 Maxam(4.3) 高丝 Kose(4.3) 迪奥 CD(4.3)
35~44 岁 Age	11	美人鱼 Meirenyu(18.2) 羽西 Yue-sai(18.2)	东洋之花 Sakula(9.1) 凤凰 Phoenix(9.1) 美宝莲 Maybelline(9.1) 奇士美 Kissme(9.1) 清妃 Chinf(9.1) 雅芳 Avon(9.1) 永芳 Yinfong(9.1)	
45~54 岁 Age	2	旁氏 Pond's(50.0) 深丽 Shenli(50.0)		
55~60 岁 Age	0			

2-4 正在使用的品牌排名/ Ranking of the Brands Used Now

排名 Brand Ranking	品牌 Brands	人数 Number	百分比 Percent
1	美宝莲 Maybelline	6	15.0
2	雅芳 Avon	4	10.0
2	羽西 Yue-sai	4	10.0
3	雅倩 Arche	2	5.0
3	圣梦 Shengmeng	2	5.0
3	美人鱼 Meirenyu	2	5.0
3	清妃 Chinf	2	5.0
3	资生堂 Shiseido	2	5.0

n=40

2-5 品牌转换习惯/ Brand Habit in Consuming Pre-makeup

	人数 Number	第一次使用该品牌 first use this brand	上一次也是这个牌子 used it last time	上一次不是这个牌子 not used it last time
女性 Female	40	22.5	70.0	7.5
美宝莲 Maybelline	6	16.7	83.3	0.0
雅芳 Avon	4	25.0	75.0	0.0
羽西 Yue-sai	4	25.0	50.0	25.0
雅倩 Arche	2	0.0	100.0	0.0
圣梦 Shengmeng	2	0.0	100.0	0.0
美人鱼 Meirenyu	2	50.0	50.0	0.0
清妃 Chinf	2	50.0	0.0	50.0
资生堂 Shiseido	2	50.0	50.0	0.0

2-6 下一次打算使用的品牌排名/ Ranking of the Brands to be Used Next Time

排名 Brand Ranking	品牌 Brands	人数 Number	百分比 Percent
1	羽西 Yue-sai	7	17.5
2	美宝莲 Maybelline	3	7.5
3	圣梦 Shengmeng	2	5.0
3	资生堂 Shiseido	2	5.0
3	雅倩 Arche	2	5.0
3	雅芳 Avon	2	5.0
3	清妃 Chinf	2	5.0
3	艾迪丝 Aidieces	2	5.0

n=40

2-7 样本、女性各年龄层的使用频率/ Frequencies of the Consumed Pre-makeup by the Female Sample and Age Groups

	人数 Number	天天用 daily	两三天用 1 次 once 2 or 3 days	一周 1~2 次 once or twice a week	半个月 1 次 once half a month	一个月 1 次或以下 once a month or below	没用过 never use
女性 Female	298	5.0	2.0	3.4	2.0	1.0	86.6
16~24 岁 Age	60	3.3	0.0	1.7	1.7	0.0	93.3
25~34 岁 Age	90	8.9	5.6	4.4	4.4	2.2	74.4
35~44 岁 Age	74	5.4	1.4	5.4	1.4	1.4	85.1
45~54 岁 Age	49	2.0	0.0	2.0	0.0	0.0	95.9
55~60 岁 Age	25	0.0	0.0	0.0	0.0	0.0	100.0

2-8 选择该类商品的考虑因素/ Ranking of the Considerations in Purchasing

注：本题为多选题，合计百分比超过 100%（Multiple answers）

排名 Ranking	考虑因素 Considerations	人次 Person-time	百分比 Percent
1	有名的牌子 famous brand	14	35.0
1	产品功用 product function	14	35.0
2	别人推荐 introduced by other people	11	27.5
3	价格适中 reasonable price	10	25.0
4	广告影响 influence of advertising	5	12.5
5	购买方便 easy to buy	4	10.0
6	包装吸引人 appealing package	2	5.0
6	有优惠条件 with preferential terms	2	5.0

n=40

2-9 对产品功能的侧重方面/ Ranking of the Considerations about the Function of this Kind of Product

注：本题为多选题，合计百分比超过 100%（Multiple answers）

排名 Ranking	侧重方面 Items	人次 Person-time	百分比 Percent
1	调整肤色 color	23	57.5
1	光滑细腻 smooth and fine	23	57.5
2	遮盖功能 covering function	13	32.5
3	着色稳定 color stability	10	25.0
4	防晒功能 anti-UV	4	10.0
5	不含香料 containing no perfume	2	5.0
6	其他 others	1	2.5

n=40

2-10 重度消费者的人口分布/ Demographics of the Heavy Consumers

	人数 Number	16-24 岁 Age	25-34 岁 Age	35-44 岁 Age	45-54 岁 Age	55-60 岁 Age
女性 Female	21	9.5	61.9	23.8	4.8	0.0
天天用 daily	15	13.3	53.3	26.7	6.7	0.0
两三天用 1 次 once 2 or 3 days	6	0.0	83.3	16.7	0.0	0.0

2-11 不同消费者层的常用品牌/ The Most Frequently Used Brands by Market Segments

2-11-1 时尚流行指标/ Fads Popular Index

	人数 Number	第一品牌及百分比 1st/ percent	第二品牌及百分比 2nd/ percent	第三品牌及百分比 3rd/ percent
女性 Female	40	**美宝莲 Maybelline(12.5)** **羽西 Yue-sai(12.5)**	**美人鱼 Meirenyu(10.0)** **雅芳 Avon(10.0)**	**雅倩 Arche(5.0)** **圣梦 Shengmeng(5.0)** **资生堂 Shiseido(5.0)** **清妃 Chinf(5.0)**
平实生活指向 simple living orientation	11	美宝莲 Maybelline(18.2) 美人鱼 Meirenyu(18.2)	美加净 Maxam(9.1) 奇士美 Kissme(9.1) 清妃 Chinf(9.1) 羽西 Yue-sai(9.1) 资生堂 Shiseido(9.1) 玉兰油 Oil of Olay(9.1) 圣梦 Shengmeng(9.1)	
时尚流行指向 fashion orientation	29	雅芳 Avon(13.8) 羽西 Yue-sai(13.8)	美宝莲 Maybelline(10.3)	雅倩 Arche(6.9) 美人鱼 Meirenyu(6.9)

2-11-2 广告态度指标/ Advertising Attitude Index

	人数 Number	第一品牌及百分比 1st/ percent	第二品牌及百分比 2nd/ percent	第三品牌及百分比 3rd/ percent
女性 Female	40	**美宝莲 Maybelline(12.5)** **羽西 Yue-sai(12.5)**	**美人鱼 Meirenyu(10.0)** **雅芳 Avon(10.0)**	**雅倩 Arche(5.0)** **圣梦 Shengmeng(5.0)** **资生堂 Shiseido(5.0)** **清妃 Chinf(5.0)**
广告淡漠指向 indifferent orientation	9	美人鱼 Meirenyu(33.3)	迪奥 CD(11.1) 凤凰 Phoenix(11.1) 美宝莲 Maybelline(11.1) 羽西 Yue-sai(11.1) 永芳 Yinfong(11.1) 柔婷 Routing(11.1)	
中间层 medium	28	美宝莲 Maybelline(14.3) 雅芳 Avon(14.3)	羽西 Yue-sai(10.7)	雅倩 Arche(7.1) 圣梦 Shengmeng(7.1) 资生堂 Shiseido(7.1) 清妃 Chinf(7.1)
信赖广告指向 loyal orientation	3	东洋之花 Sakula(33.3) 羽西 Yue-sai(33.3) 玉兰油 Oil of Olay(33.3)		

2-12 重度消费者的消费层构成/ The Composition of the Heavy Consumers

2-12-1 时尚流行指标/ Fads Popular Index

	人数 Number	平实生活指向 simple living orientation	时尚流行指向 fashion orientation
女性 Female	21	23.8	76.2
天天用 daily	15	20.0	80.0
两三天用 1 次 once 2 or 3 days	6	33.3	66.7

2-12-2 广告态度指标/ Advertising Attitude Index

	人数 Number	广告淡漠指向 indifferent orientation	中间层 medium	信赖广告指向 loyal orientation
女性 Female	21	19.0	71.4	9.5
天天用 daily	15	20.0	73.3	6.7
两三天用 1 次 once 2 or 3 days	6	16.7	66.7	16.7

● 沈阳 / Shenyang

2-1 最近三个月使用频次的比例/ Proportion of the Sample Consuming Pre-makeup in the Last Three Months

	人数 Number	百分比 Percent
天天用 daily	73	24.2
两三天用 1 次 once 2 or 3 days	7	2.3
一周 1～2 次 about once or twice a week	5	1.7
半个月 1 次 once half a month	3	1.0
一个月 1 次或以下 once a month or below	2	0.7
没用过 never use	212	70.2

n=302

2-2 最常用品牌排名/ Ranking of the Most Frequently Used Brands

排名 Brand Ranking	品牌 Brands	人数 Number	百分比 Percent
1	高丝 Kose	16	17.8
2	雅芳 Avon	5	5.6
2	欧珀莱 Aupres	5	5.6
3	诗芙侬 Shifunong	4	4.4
4	爱茉莉 Amore	3	3.3
4	羽西 Yue-sai	3	3.3
4	雅佳 Aikai	3	3.3
4	小护士 Mininurse	3	3.3

n=90

2-3 样本、女性各年龄层的常用品牌/ The Most Frequently Used Brands by the Female Sample and Age Groups

	人数 Number	第一品牌及百分比 1st/ percent	第二品牌及百分比 2nd/ percent	第三品牌及百分比 3rd/ percent
女性 Female	90	**高丝 Kose(17.8)**	**雅芳 Avon(5.6)** **欧珀莱 Aupres(5.6)**	**诗芙侬 Shifunong(4.4)**
16~24 岁 Age	21	小护士 Mininurse(14.3)	雅芳 Avon(9.5) 郑明明 Cheng Mingming(9.5) 丽花丝宝 Laifa-C'bons(9.5)	沙宣 Vidal Sassoon(4.8) 格兰蒙 GLM(4.8) 卡汀娜 CARDINA A'oe(4.8) 资生堂 Shiseido(4.8) 欧莱雅 L'oreal(4.8) 兰贵人 Lan Guiren(4.8) 东洋之花 Sakula(4.8) 碧妮 Peony(4.8) 奥琪 Aoqi(4.8) 爱茉莉 Amore(4.8) 艾迪丝 Aidieces(4.8)
25~34 岁 Age	40	高丝 Kose(22.5)	欧珀莱 Aupres(10.0)	雅芳 Avon(7.5) 雅佳 Aikai(7.5)
35~44 岁 Age	22	高丝 Kose(13.6)	爱茉莉 Amore(9.1) 大宝.高丽雅娜.阿特皮雅 Dabao Coreana Artpla(9.1) 诗芙侬 Shifunong(9.1)	MAMONDE(4.5) 影后 Yinghou(4.5) 丝充郎 Sichonglang(4.5) Cotty(4.5) 芦荟保湿蜜 Luhui(4.5) 柏香 Baixiang(4.5) 艾迪丝 Aidieces(4.5) 旁氏 Pond's(4.5) 羽西 Yue-sai(4.5) 奇士美 Kissme(4.5) 美宝莲 Maybelline(4.5) 东洋之花 Sakula(4.5) 碧妮 Peony(4.5)
45~54 岁 Age	6	高丝 Kose(66.7)	美人鱼 Meirenyu(16.7) 碧芬兰 Bifenlan(16.7)	
55~60 岁 Age	1	欧珀莱 Aupres(100.0)		

2-4 正在使用的品牌排名/ Ranking of the Brands Used Now

排名 Brand Ranking	品牌 Brands	人数 Number	百分比 Percent
1	高丝 Kose	16	17.8
2	欧珀莱 Aupres	5	5.6
3	雅芳 Avon	4	4.4
3	诗芙侬 Shifunong	4	4.4
4	小护士 Mininurse	3	3.3
4	玉兰油 Oil of Olay	3	3.3
4	爱茉莉 Amore	3	3.3
4	羽西 Yue-sai	3	3.3
4	雅佳 Aikai	3	3.3

n=90

2-5 品牌转换习惯/ Brand Habit in Consuming Pre-makeup

	人数 Number	第一次使用该品牌 first use this brand	上一次也是这个牌子 used it last time	上一次不是这个牌子 not used it last time
女性 Female	90	13.3	80.0	6.7
高丝 Kose	16	0.0	93.8	6.3
欧珀莱 Aupres	5	0.0	100.0	0.0
雅芳 Avon	4	0.0	100.0	0.0
诗芙侬 Shifunong	4	25.0	75.0	0.0
小护士 Mininurse	3	66.7	33.3	0.0
玉兰油 Oil of Olay	3	33.3	0.0	66.7
爱茉莉 Amore	3	0.0	100.0	0.0
羽西 Yue-sai	3	0.0	100.0	0.0
雅佳 Aikai	3	33.3	33.3	33.3

2-6 下一次打算使用的品牌排名/ Ranking of the Brands to be Used Next Time

排名 Brand Ranking	品牌 Brands	人数 Number	百分比 Percent
1	高丝 Kose	14	15.6
2	欧珀莱 Aupres	6	6.7
3	羽西 Yue-sai	5	5.6
4	玉兰油 Oil of Olay	4	4.4
4	爱茉莉 Amore	4	4.4
5	资生堂 Shiseido	3	3.3
5	郑明明 Cheng Mingming	3	3.3
5	雅芳 Avon	3	3.3
5	诗芙侬 Shifunong	3	3.3

n=90

2-7 样本、女性各年龄层的使用频率/ Frequencies of the Consumed Pre-makeup by the Female Sample and Age Groups

	人数 Number	天天用 daily	两三天用 1 次 once 2 or 3 days	一周 1~2 次 once or twice a week	半个月 1 次 once half a month	一个月 1 次或以下 once a month or below	没用过 never use
女性 Female	302	24.2	2.3	1.7	1.0	0.7	70.2
16~24 岁 Age	64	29.7	1.6	1.6	0.0	0.0	67.2
25~34 岁 Age	90	33.3	4.4	4.4	2.2	0.0	55.6
35~44 岁 Age	76	25.0	1.3	0.0	1.3	1.3	71.1
45~54 岁 Age	48	8.3	2.1	0.0	0.0	2.1	87.5
55~60 岁 Age	24	4.2	0.0	0.0	0.0	0.0	95.8

2-8 选择该类商品的考虑因素/ Ranking of the Considerations in Purchasing

注：本题为多选题，合计百分比超过 100%（Multiple answers）

排名 Ranking	考虑因素 Considerations	人次 Person-time	百分比 Percent
1	有名的牌子 famous brand	39	43.3
2	产品功用 product function	37	41.1
3	价格适中 reasonable price	34	37.8
4	别人推荐 introduced by other people	28	31.1
5	购买方便 easy to buy	13	14.4
6	广告影响 influence of advertising	9	10.0
7	有优惠条件 with preferential terms	6	6.7
8	其它 others	2	2.2

n=90

2-9 对产品功能的侧重方面/ Ranking of the Considerations about the Function of this Kind of Product

注：本题为多选题，合计百分比超过 100%（Multiple answers）

排名 Ranking	侧重方面 Items	人次 Person-time	百分比 Percent
1	调整肤色 color	54	60.0
2	光滑细腻 smooth and fine	53	58.9
3	遮盖功能 covering function	24	26.7
4	着色稳定 color stability	19	21.1
5	防晒功能 anti-UV	13	14.4
6	不含香料 containing no perfume	9	10.0

n=90

2-10 重度消费者的人口分布/ Demographics of the Heavy Consumers

	人数 Number	16-24 岁 Age	25-34 岁 Age	35-44 岁 Age	45-54 岁 Age	55-60 岁 Age
女性 Female	80	25.0	42.5	25.0	6.3	1.3
天天用 daily	73	26.0	41.1	26.0	5.5	1.4
两三天用 1 次 once 2 or 3 days	7	14.3	57.1	14.3	14.3	0.0

2-11 不同消费者层的常用品牌/ The Most Frequently Used Brands by Market Segments

2-11-1 时尚流行指标/ Fads Popular Index

	人数 Number	第一品牌及百分比 1st/ percent	第二品牌及百分比 2nd/ percent	第三品牌及百分比 3rd/ percent
女性 Female	90	高丝 Kose(17.8)	雅芳 Avon(5.6) 欧珀莱 Aupres(5.6)	诗芙侬 Shifunong(4.4)
平实生活指向 simple living orientation	27	高丝 Kose(14.8)	诗芙侬 Shifunong(11.1)	雅芳 Avon(7.4)
时尚流行指向 fashion orientation	63	高丝 Kose(19.0)	欧珀莱 Aupres(6.3)	羽西 Yue-sai(4.8) 雅芳 Avon(4.8)

2-11-2 广告态度指标/ Advertising Attitude Index

	人数 Number	第一品牌及百分比 1st/ percent	第二品牌及百分比 2nd/ percent	第三品牌及百分比 3rd/ percent
女性 Female	90	**高丝 Kose(17.8)**	**雅芳 Avon(5.6)** **欧珀莱 Aupres(5.6)**	**诗芙侬 Shifunong(4.4)**
广告淡漠指向 indifferent orientation	14	雅芳 Avon(14.3) 高丝 Kose(14.3)	格兰蒙 Gelanyi(7.1) 芦荟保湿蜜 Luhui(7.1) 玉兰油 Oil of Olay(7.1) 雅嘉 Aikai(7.1) 欧珀莱 Aupres(7.1) 欧莱雅 L'oreal(7.1) 爱茉莉 Amore(7.1) 艾迪丝 Aidieces(7.1)	
中间层 medium	61	高丝 Kose(16.4)	欧珀莱 Aupres(6.6)	小护士 Mininurse(4.9) 羽西 Yue-sai(4.9) 雅芳 Avon(4.9) 诗芙侬 Shifunong(4.9)
信赖广告指向 loyal orientation	15	高丝 Kose(26.7)	美宝莲 Maybelline(13.3)	郑明明 Cheng Mingming(6.7) 沙宣 Vidal Sassoon (6.7) 雪丽肤 Xuelifu(6.7) 玉兰油 Oil of Olay(6.7) 诗芙侬 Shifunong(6.7) 奇士美 Kissme(6.7) 奥琪 Aoqi(6.7) 艾迪丝 Aidieces(6.7)

2-12 重度消费者的消费层构成/ The Composition of the Heavy Consumers

2-12-1 时尚流行指标/ Fads Popular Index

	人数 Number	平实生活指向 simple living orientation	时尚流行指向 fashion orientation
女性 Female	80	30.0	70.0
天天用 daily	73	27.4	72.6
两三天用 1 次 once 2 or 3 days	7	57.1	42.9

2-12-2 广告态度指标/ Advertising Attitude Index

	人数 Number	广告淡漠指向 indifferent orientation	中间层 medium	信赖广告指向 loyal orientation
女性 Female	80	17.5	65.0	17.5
天天用 daily	73	17.8	65.8	16.4
两三天用 1 次 once 2 or 3 days	7	14.3	57.1	28.6

3.口红 / Lipstick

● 北京 / Beijing

3-1 最近三个月使用频次的比例/ Proportion of the Sample Consuming Lipstick in the Last Three Months

	人数 Number	百分比 Percent
天天用 daily	163	32.2
两三天用 1 次 once 2 or 3 days	46	9.1
一周 1～2 次 once or twice a week	40	7.9
半个月 1 次 once half a month	15	3.0
一个月 1 次或以下 once a month or below	18	3.6
没用过 never use	224	44.3

n=506

3-2 最常用品牌排名/ Ranking of the Most Frequently Used Brands

注：本题为多选题，合计百分比超过 100%（Multiple answers）

排名 Brand Ranking	品牌 Brands	人次 Person-time	百分比 Percent
1	美宝莲 Maybelline	74	26.8
2	羽西 Yue-sai	52	18.8
3	迪奥 CD	22	8.0
4	奇士美 Kissme	19	6.9
5	欧珀莱 Aupres	14	5.1
5	雅芳 Avon	14	5.1
6	华姿 Huazi	11	4.0
7	资生堂 Shiseido	9	3.3
8	欧莱雅 L'Oreal	7	2.5
8	露华浓 Revlon	7	2.5
9	郑明明 Cheng Mingming	5	1.8
9	高丝 Kose	5	1.8

n=276

3-3 样本、女性各年龄层的常用品牌/ The Most Frequently Used Brands by the Female Sample and Age Groups

注：本题为多选题，合计百分比超过 100%（Multiple answers）

	人数 Number	第一品牌及百分比 1st/ percent	第二品牌及百分比 2nd/ percent	第三品牌及百分比 3rd/ percent	第四品牌及百分比 4th/ percent
女性 Female	276	**美宝莲 Maybelline(26.8)**	**羽西 Yue-sai(18.8)**	**迪奥 CD(8.0)**	**奇士美 Kissme(6.9)**
16~24 岁 Age	45	美宝莲 Maybelline(51.1)	羽西 Yue-sai(17.8)	露华浓 Revlon(8.9)	雅芳 Avon(6.7)
25~34 岁 Age	114	美宝莲 Maybelline(27.2)	羽西 Yue-sai(14.0) 迪奥 CD(14.0)	奇士美 Kissme(9.6)	欧珀莱 Aupres(7.9)
35~44 岁 Age	82	羽西 Yue-sai(22.0)	美宝莲 Maybelline(18.3)	奇士美 Kissme(7.3) 华姿 Huazi(7.3)	雅芳 Avon(4.9)
45~54 岁 Age	33	羽西 Yue-sai(30.3)	美宝莲 Maybelline(15.2)	迪奥 CD(9.1) 华姿 Huazi(9.1)	欧珀莱 Aupres(6.1)
55~60 岁 Age	2	绿世界 Greenworld(50.0)			

3-4 正在使用的品牌排名/ Ranking of the Brands Used Now

注：本题为多选题，合计百分比超过 100%（Multiple answers）

排名 Brand Ranking	品牌 Brands	人次 Person-time	百分比 Percent
1	美宝莲 Maybelline	67	24.4
2	羽西 Yue-sai	39	14.2
3	迪奥 CD	21	7.6
4	奇士美 Kissme	18	6.5
5	雅芳 Avon	14	5.1
6	欧珀莱 Aupres	10	3.6
7	华姿 Huazi	9	3.3
8	资生堂 Shiseido	8	2.9
9	欧莱雅 L'Oreal	7	2.5

n=275

3-5 品牌转换习惯/ Brand Habit in Consuming Lipstick

	人数 Number	第一次使用该品牌 first use this brand	上一次也是这个牌子 used it last time	上一次不是这个牌子 not used it last time
女性 Female	270	22.2	62.6	15.2
美宝莲 Maybelline	65	18.5	73.8	7.7
羽西 Yue-sai	39	10.3	79.5	10.3
迪奥 CD	21	19.0	81.0	0.0
奇士美 Kissme	18	11.1	83.3	5.6
雅芳 Avon	14	14.3	42.9	42.9
欧珀莱 Aupres	10	40.0	60.0	0.0
华姿 Huazi	8	62.5	37.5	0.0
资生堂 Shiseido	8	12.5	87.5	0.0
欧莱雅 L'Oreal	6	50.0	16.7	33.3
郑明明 Cheng Mingming	4	25.0	75.0	0.0
高丝 Kose	5	20.0	80.0	0.0

3-6 下一次打算使用的品牌排名/ Ranking of the Brands to be Used Next Time

排名 Brand Ranking	品牌 Brands	人数 Number	百分比 Percent
1	美宝莲 Maybelline	67	24.1
2	羽西 Yue-sai	38	13.7
3	迪奥 CD	22	7.9
4	欧珀莱 Aupres	14	5.0
5	奇士美 Kissme	11	4.0
6	资生堂 Shiseido	8	2.9
7	华姿 Huazi	7	2.5
8	雅芳 Avon	6	2.2
9	高丝 Kose	5	1.8
10	倩碧 Clinique	4	1.4
11	莲娜丽姿 Nina ricci	3	1.1
11	欧莱雅 L'Oreal	3	1.1
11	露华浓 Revlon	3	1.1
11	郑明明 Cheng Mingming	3	1.1
11	宝璐丝 Paolarlus	3	1.1

n=278

3-7 样本、女性各年龄层的使用频率/ Frequencies of the Consumed Lipstick by the Female Sample and Age Groups

	人数 Number	天天用 daily	两三天用 1 次 once 2 or 3 days	一周 1~2 次 once or twice a week	半个月 1 次 once half a month	一个月 1 次或以下 once a month or below	没用过 never use
女性 Female	506	32.2	9.1	7.9	3.0	3.6	44.3
16~24 岁 Age	108	18.5	6.5	11.1	3.7	1.9	58.3
25~34 岁 Age	149	51.7	11.4	6.7	4.7	2.7	22.8
35~44 岁 Age	124	41.1	11.3	10.5	1.6	4.0	31.5
45~54 岁 Age	84	16.7	9.5	6.0	2.4	4.8	60.7
55~60 岁 Age	41	2.4	0.0	0.0	0.0	7.3	90.2

3-8 选择该类商品的考虑因素/ Ranking of Considerations in Purchasing

注：本题为多选题，合计百分比超过 100%（Multiple answers）

排名 Ranking	考虑因素 Considerations	人次 Person-time	百分比 Percent
1	有名的牌子 famous brand	118	42.8
2	价格适中 reasonable price	100	36.2
3	产品功用 product function	97	35.1
4	别人推荐 introduced by other people	69	25.0
5	广告影响 influence of advertising	23	8.3
5	购买方便 easy to buy	23	8.3
6	包装吸引人 appealing package	11	4.0
6	有优惠条件 with preferential terms	11	4.0
7	其它 others	10	3.6

n=276

3-9 对产品功能的侧重方面/ Ranking of Considerations about the Function of this Kind of Product

注：本题为多选题，合计百分比超过 100%（Multiple answers）

排名 Ranking	侧重方面 Items	人次 Person-time	百分比 Percent
1	颜色 color	211	75.6
2	滋润 containing nourishing ingredient	145	52.0
3	不易脱色 color stability	98	35.1
4	光泽 glossing	53	19.0
5	不含香料 containing no perfume	43	15.4
6	不油腻 not oily	41	14.7
7	有银光 with fluorescent ingredient	8	2.9
8	其他 others	3	1.1

n=279

3-10 重度消费者的人口分布/ Demographics of the Heavy Consumers

	人数 Number	16-24 岁 Age	25-34 岁 Age	35-44 岁 Age	45-54 岁 Age	55-60 岁 Age
女性 Female	209	12.9	45.0	31.1	10.5	0.5
天天用 daily	163	12.3	47.2	31.3	8.6	0.6
两三天用 1 次 once 2 or 3 days	46	15.2	37.0	30.4	17.4	0.0

3-11 不同消费者层的常用品牌/ The Most Frequently Used Brands by Market Segments

3-11-1 时尚流行指标/ Fads Popular Index

注：本题为多选题，合计百分比超过 100%（Multiple answers）

	人数 Number	第一品牌及百分比 1st/ percent	第二品牌及百分比 2nd/ percent	第三品牌及百分比 3rd/ percent	第四品牌及百分比 4th/ percent
女性 Female	272	美宝莲 Maybelline(26.8)	羽西 Yue-sai(18.8)	迪奥 CD(8.1)	奇士美 Kissme(7.0)
平实生活指向 simple living orientation	90	美宝莲 Maybelline(25.6)	羽西 Yue-sai(21.1)	奇士美 Kissme(11.1)	迪奥 CD(7.8)
时尚流行指向 fashion orientation	182	美宝莲 Maybelline(27.5)	羽西 Yue-sai(17.6)	迪奥 CD(8.2)	欧珀莱 Aupres(5.5)

3-11-2 广告态度指标/ Advertising Attitude Index

注：本题为多选题，合计百分比超过 100%（Multiple answers）

	人数 Number	第一品牌及百分比 1st/ percent	第二品牌及百分比 2nd/ percent	第三品牌及百分比 3rd/ percent	第四品牌及百分比 4th/ percent
女性 Female	269	美宝莲 Maybelline(26.4)	羽西 Yue-sai(19.3)	迪奥 CD(8.2)	奇士美 Kissme(6.3)
广告淡漠指向 indifferent orientation	56	美宝莲 Maybelline(37.5)	羽西 Yue-sai(21.4)	迪奥 CD(7.1)	雅芳 Avon(5.4) 华姿 Huazi(5.4)
中间层 medium	169	美宝莲 Maybelline(24.3)	羽西 Yue-sai(19.5)	迪奥 CD(8.9)	奇士美 Kissme(7.7)
信赖广告指向 loyal orientation	44	美宝莲 Maybelline(20.5)	羽西 Yue-sai(15.9)	欧珀莱 Aupres(9.1)	资生堂 Shiseido(6.8) 奇士美 Kissme(6.8) 迪奥 CD(6.8)

3-12 重度消费者的消费层构成/ The Composition of the Heavy Consumers

3-12-1 时尚流行指标/ Fads Popular Index

	人数 Number	平实生活指向 simple living orientation	时尚流行指向 fashion orientation
女性 Female	206	28.6	71.4
天天用 daily	161	24.2	75.8
两三天用 1 次 once 2 or 3 days	45	44.4	55.6

3-12-2 广告态度指标/ Advertising Attitude Index

	人数 Number	广告淡漠指向 indifferent orientation	中间层 medium	信赖广告指向 loyal orientation
女性 Female	204	19.6	62.7	17.6
天天用 daily	159	19.5	64.8	15.7
两三天用 1 次 once 2 or 3 days	45	20.0	55.6	24.4

● 上海 / Shanghai

3-1 最近三个月使用频次的比例/ Proportion of the Sample Consuming Lipstick in the Last Three Months

	人数 Number	百分比 Percent
天天用 daily	131	26.5
两三天用 1 次 once 2 or 3 days	39	7.9
一周 1～2 次 once or twice a week	46	9.3
半个月 1 次 once half a month	23	4.6
一个月 1 次或以下 once a month or below	22	4.4
没用过 never use	234	47.3

n=495

3-2 最常用品牌排名/ Ranking of the Most Frequently Used Brands

注：本题为多选题，合计百分比超过 100%（Multiple answers）

排名 Brand Ranking	品牌 Brands	人次 Person-time	百分比 Percent
1	美宝莲 Maybelline	85	32.6
2	迪奥 CD	32	12.3
2	羽西 Yue-sai	32	12.3
3	郑明明 Cheng Mingming	17	6.5
4	清妃 Chinf	14	5.4
5	资生堂 Shiseido	9	3.4
6	丽妃 Lifei	8	3.1
6	Red earth (Esprit)	8	3.1
7	伊思丽 Eesli	7	2.7
7	ZA	7	2.7
7	玫琳凯 Mary Kay	7	2.7
8	露华浓 Revlon	6	2.3
9	法兰西施 Miss de France	5	1.9
9	兰蔻 Lancom	5	1.9
10	宝璐丝 Paolarlus	4	1.5
10	欧莱雅 L'Oreal	4	1.5

n=261

3-3 样本、女性各年龄层的常用品牌/ The Most Frequently Used Brands by the Female Sample and Age Groups

注：本题为多选题，合计百分比超过 100%（Multiple answers）

	人数 Number	第一品牌及百分比 1st/ percent	第二品牌及百分比 2nd/ percent	第三品牌及百分比 3rd/ percent
女性 Female	261	**美宝莲 Maybelline(32.6)**	**迪奥 CD(12.3)** **羽西 Yue-sai(12.3)**	**郑明明 Cheng Mingming(6.5)**
16~24 岁 Age	58	美宝莲 Maybelline(58.6)	迪奥 CD(17.2)	露华浓 Revlon(6.9) Red earth (Esprit)(6.9) 羽西 Yue-sai(6.9)
25~34 岁 Age	107	美宝莲 Maybelline(25.2)	羽西 Yue-sai(16.8)	迪奥 CD(13.1)
35~44 岁 Age	71	美宝莲 Maybelline(29.6)	郑明明 Cheng Mingming(11.3)	迪奥 CD(8.5)
45~54 岁 Age	17	羽西 Yue-sai(29.4)	迪奥 CD(11.8) 郑明明 Cheng Mingming(11.8) 美宝莲 Maybelline(11.8) 倩碧 Clinique(11.8)	夏奈儿 Chanel(5.9) 得姿 Dezi(5.9) 丽妃 Lifei(5.9) 高丝 Kose(5.9)
55~60 岁 Age	8	Red earth (Esprit)(12.5) 高丝 Kose(12.5) 美宝莲 Maybelline(12.5) 清妃 Chinf(12.5) 郑明明 Cheng Mingming(12.5) 资生堂 Shiseido(12.5) 明星 Mingxing(12.5) 露美 Lumei(12.5) 伊思丹 Yisidan(12.5)		

3-4 正在使用的品牌排名/ Ranking of the Brands Used Now

注：本题为多选题，合计百分比超过 100%（Multiple answers）

排名 Brand Ranking	品牌 Brands	人次 Person-time	百分比 Percent
1	美宝莲 Maybelline	75	28.7
2	羽西 Yue-sai	31	11.9
3	迪奥 CD	26	10.0
4	郑明明 Cheng Mingming	15	5.7
5	清妃 Chinf	14	5.4
6	Red earth (Esprit)	10	3.8
7	ZA	9	3.4
8	伊思丽 Eesli	8	3.1
8	资生堂 Shiseido	8	3.1
9	玫琳凯 Mary Kay	7	2.7
9	露华浓 Revlon	7	2.7
10	丽妃 Lifei	6	2.3
11	兰蔻 Lancom	5	1.9
11	法兰西施 Miss de France	5	1.9
12	欧莱雅 L'Oreal	4	1.5
13	倩碧 Clinique	3	1.1
13	宝璐丝 Paolarlus	3	1.1

n=261

3-5 品牌转换习惯/ Brand Habit in Consuming Lipstick

	人数 Number	第一次使用该品牌 first use this brand	上一次也是这个牌子 used it last time	上一次不是这个牌子 not used it last time
女性 Female	257	15.2	72.8	12.1
美宝莲 Maybelline	75	13.3	72.0	14.7
羽西 Yue-sai	31	9.7	77.4	12.9
迪奥 CD	25	8.0	88.0	4.0
郑明明 Cheng Mingming	15	13.3	66.7	20.0
清妃 Chinf	14	7.1	71.4	21.4
Red earth (Esprit)	10	40.0	60.0	0.0
ZA	9	11.1	77.8	11.1
伊思丽 Eesli	8	25.0	75.0	0.0
资生堂 Shiseido	8	12.5	75.0	12.5

3-6 下一次打算使用的品牌排名/ Ranking of the Brands to be Used Next Time

排名 Brand Ranking	品牌 Brands	人数 Number	百分比 Percent
1	美宝莲 Maybelline	59	22.6
2	羽西 Yue-sai	30	11.5
3	迪奥 CD	29	11.1
4	郑明明 Cheng Mingming	11	4.2
5	资生堂 Shiseido	10	3.8
6	清妃 Chinf	9	3.4
7	Red earth (Esprit)	8	3.1
8	倩碧 Clinique	6	2.3
8	ZA	6	2.3
8	伊思丽 Eesli	6	2.3
9	兰蔻 Lancom	5	1.9
9	丽妃 Lifei	5	1.9
9	法兰西施 Miss de France	5	1.9
10	欧莱雅 L'Oreal	4	1.5
10	玫琳凯 Mary Kay	4	1.5
10	雅艾芬迪 Latan taiao	4	1.5
10	宝璐丝 Paolarlus	4	1.5
11	夏奈儿 Chanel	3	1.1
11	露华浓 Revlon	3	1.1

n=261

3-7 样本、女性各年龄层的使用频率/ Frequencies of the Consumed Lipstick by the Female Sample and Age Groups

	人数 Number	天天用 daily	两三天用 1 次 once 2 or 3 days	一周 1~2 次 once or twice a week	半个月 1 次 once half a month	一个月 1 次或以下 once a month or below	没用过 never use
女性 Female	495	26.5	7.9	9.3	4.6	4.4	47.3
16~24 岁 Age	105	26.7	7.6	9.5	4.8	6.7	44.8
25~34 岁 Age	143	37.1	10.5	11.9	10.5	4.9	25.2
35~44 岁 Age	128	30.5	7.8	10.9	1.6	4.7	44.5
45~54 岁 Age	79	11.4	3.8	5.1	1.3	0.0	78.5
55~60 岁 Age	40	5.0	7.5	2.5	0.0	5.0	80.0

3-8 选择该类商品的考虑因素/ Ranking of the Considerations in Purchasing

注：本题为多选题，合计百分比超过 100%（Multiple answers）

排名 Ranking	考虑因素 Considerations	人次 Person-time	百分比 Percent
1	有名的牌子 famous brand	137	52.9
2	价格适中 reasonable price	89	34.4
3	产品功用 product function	71	27.4
4	别人推荐 introduced by other people	54	20.8
5	广告影响 influence of advertising	52	20.1
6	购买方便 easy to buy	31	12.0
7	有优惠条件 with preferential terms	16	6.2
8	包装吸引人 appealing package	12	4.6
9	其它 others	7	2.7

n=259

3-9 对产品功能的侧重方面/ Ranking of the Considerations about the Function of This Kind of Product

注：本题为多选题，合计百分比超过 100%（Multiple answers）

排名 Ranking	侧重方面 Items	人次 Person-time	百分比 Percent
1	颜色 color	180	69.0
2	滋润 containing nourishing ingredient	135	51.7
3	不易脱色 color stability	97	37.2
4	光泽 glossing	91	34.9
5	不油腻 not oily	33	12.6
6	不含香料 containing no perfume	30	11.5
7	有银光 with fluorescent ingredient	7	2.7
8	其他 others	1	0.4

n=261

3-10 重度消费者的人口分布/ Demographics of the Heavy Consumers

	人数 Number	16-24 岁 Age	25-34 岁 Age	35-44 岁 Age	45-54 岁 Age	55-60 岁 Age
女性 Female	170	21.2	40.0	28.8	7.1	2.9
天天用 daily	131	21.4	40.5	29.8	6.9	1.5
两三天用 1 次 once 2 or 3 days	39	20.5	38.5	25.6	7.7	7.7

3-11 不同消费者层的常用品牌/ The Most Frequently Used Brands by Market Segments

3-11-1 时尚流行指标/ Fads Popular Index

注：本题为多选题，合计百分比超过 100%（Multiple answers）

	人数 Number	第一品牌及百分比 1st/ percent	第二品牌及百分比 2nd/ percent	第三品牌及百分比 3rd/ percent
女性 Female	259	**美宝莲 Maybelline（32.4）**	**羽西 Yue-sai（12.4）**	**迪奥 CD（12.0）**
平实生活指向 simple living orientation	71	美宝莲 Maybelline（23.9）	清妃 Chinf（11.3） 迪奥 CD（11.3） 羽西 Yue-sai（11.3）	郑明明 Cheng Mingming（7.0）
时尚流行指向 fashion orientation	188	美宝莲 Maybelline（35.6）	羽西 Yue-sai（12.8）	迪奥 CD（12.2）

3-11-2 广告态度指标/ Advertising Attitude Index

注：本题为多选题，合计百分比超过 100%（Multiple answers）

	人数 Number	第一品牌及百分比 1st/ percent	第二品牌及百分比 2nd/ percent	第三品牌及百分比 3rd/ percent
女性 Female	258	**美宝莲 Maybelline（32.2）**	**迪奥 CD（12.4）** **羽西 Yue-sai（12.4）**	**郑明明 Cheng Mingming（6.6）**
广告淡漠指向 indifferent orientation	55	美宝莲 Maybelline（21.8）	羽西 Yue-sai（16.4）	郑明明 Cheng Mingming（9.1）
中间层 medium	160	美宝莲 Maybelline（34.4）	迪奥 CD（13.1）	羽西 Yue-sai（10.6）
信赖广告指向 loyal orientation	43	美宝莲 Maybelline（37.2）	迪奥 CD（16.3）	羽西 Yue-sai（14.0）

3-12 重度消费者的消费层构成/ The Composition of the Heavy Consumers

3-12-1 时尚流行指标/ Fads Popular Index

	人数 Number	平实生活指向 simple living orientation	时尚流行指向 fashion orientation
女性 Female	169	21.9	78.1
天天用 daily	130	18.5	81.5
两三天用 1 次 once 2 or 3 days	39	33.3	66.7

3-12-2 广告态度指标/ Advertising Attitude Index

	人数 Number	广告淡漠指向 indifferent orientation	中间层 medium	信赖广告指向 loyal orientation
女性 Female	169	20.1	61.5	18.3
天天用 daily	130	16.2	66.2	17.7
两三天用 1 次 once 2 or 3 days	39	33.3	46.2	20.5

● 广州 / Guangzhou

3-1 最近三个月使用频次的比例/ Proportion of the Sample Consuming Lipstick in the Last Three Months

	人数 Number	百分比 Percent
天天用 daily	82	16.0
两三天用 1 次 once 2 or 3 days	36	7.0
一周 1～2 次 once or twice a week	42	8.2
半个月 1 次 once half a month	15	2.9
一个月 1 次或以下 once a month or below	23	4.5
没用过 never use	313	61.3

n=511

3-2 最常用品牌排名/ Ranking of the Most Frequently Used Brands

注：本题为多选题，合计百分比超过 100%（Multiple answers）

排名 Brand Ranking	品牌 Brands	人次 Person-time	百分比 Percent
1	美宝莲 Maybelline	63	32.0
2	雅芳 Avon	40	20.3
3	露华浓 Revlon	13	6.6
3	羽西 Yue-sai	13	6.6
4	艾琳 Irlene	8	4.1
5	资生堂 Shiseido	6	3.0
6	欧莱雅 L'Oreal	5	2.5

n=197

3-3 样本、女性各年龄层的常用品牌/ The Most Frequently Used Brands by the Female Sample and Age Groups

注：本题为多选题，合计百分比超过 100%（Multiple answers）

	人数 Number	第一品牌及百分比 1st/ percent	第二品牌及百分比 2nd/ percent	第三品牌及百分比 3rd/ percent
女性 Female	197	美宝莲 Maybelline(32.0)	雅芳 Avon(20.3)	露华浓 Revlon(6.6) 羽西 Yue-sai(6.6)
16~24 岁 Age	42	美宝莲 Maybelline(45.2)	雅芳 Avon(14.3)	欧莱雅 L'Oreal(4.8)
25~34 岁 Age	94	美宝莲 Maybelline(27.7)	雅芳 Avon(23.4)	露华浓 Revlon(10.6)
35~44 岁 Age	48	美宝莲 Maybelline(29.2)	雅芳 Avon(18.8)	羽西 Yue-sai(10.4)
45~54 岁 Age	12	美宝莲 Maybelline(25.0) 雅芳 Avon(25.0)	羽西 Yue-sai(16.7)	资生堂 Shiseido(8.3) 旁氏 Pond's(8.3) GOLDEN RAZSIN(8.3)
55~60 岁 Age	1	美宝莲 Maybelline(100.0)		

3-4 正在使用的品牌排名/ Ranking of the Brands Used Now

注：本题为多选题，合计百分比超过 100%（Multiple answers）

排名 Brand Ranking	品牌 Brands	人次 Person-time	百分比 Percent
1	美宝莲 Maybelline	60	30.5
2	雅芳 Avon	37	18.8
3	羽西 Yue-sai	12	6.1
3	露华浓 Revlon	12	6.1
4	资生堂 Shiseido	8	4.1
5	艾琳 Irlene	7	3.6

n=197

3-5 品牌转换习惯/ Brand Habit in Consuming Lipstick

	人数 Number	第一次使用该品牌 first use this brand	上一次也是这个牌子 used it last time	上一次不是这个牌子 not used it last time
女性 Female	194	15.5	67.5	17.0
美宝莲 Maybelline	58	13.8	72.4	13.8
雅芳 Avon	37	13.5	75.7	10.8
羽西 Yue-sai	12	33.3	50.0	16.7
露华浓 Revlon	12	16.7	75.0	8.3
资生堂 Shiseido	8	25.0	37.5	37.5
艾琳 Irlene	7	28.6	57.1	14.3
欧莱雅 L'Oreal	4	25.0	75.0	0.0
蜜丝佛陀 Maxfactor	4	0.0	75.0	25.0

3-6 下一次打算使用的品牌排名/ Ranking of the Brands to be Used Next Time

排名 Brand Ranking	品牌 Brands	人数 Number	百分比 Percent
1	美宝莲 Maybelline	57	28.9
2	雅芳 Avon	31	15.7
3	露华浓 Revlon	11	5.6
4	羽西 Yue-sai	10	5.1
5	欧莱雅 L'Oreal	8	4.1
6	艾琳 Irlene	7	3.6
6	资生堂 Shiseido	7	3.6

n=197

3-7 样本、女性各年龄层的使用频率/ Frequencies of the Consumed Lipstick by the Female Sample and Age Groups

	人数 Number	天天用 daily	两三天用 1 次 once 2 or 3 days	一周 1~2 次 once or twice a week	半个月 1 次 once half a month	一个月 1 次或以下 once a month or below	没用过 never use
女性 Female	511	16.0	7.0	8.2	2.9	4.5	61.3
16~24 岁 Age	111	13.5	6.3	10.8	2.7	4.5	62.2
25~34 岁 Age	154	25.3	13.0	13.0	4.5	5.8	38.3
35~44 岁 Age	128	19.5	4.7	4.7	3.1	5.5	62.5
45~54 岁 Age	81	3.7	3.7	3.7	1.2	2.5	85.2
55~60 岁 Age	37	0.0	0.0	2.7	0.0	0.0	97.3

3-8 选择该类商品的考虑因素/ Ranking of the Considerations in Purchasing

注：本题为多选题，合计百分比超过 100%（Multiple answers）

排名 Ranking	考虑因素 Considerations	人次 Person-time	百分比 Percent
1	有名的牌子 famous brand	99	50.5
2	价格适中 reasonable price	71	36.2
3	产品功用 product function	63	32.1
4	别人推荐 introduced by other people	48	24.5
5	广告影响 influence of advertising	26	13.3
6	包装吸引人 appealing package	22	11.2
7	购买方便 easy to buy	16	8.2
8	有优惠条件 with preferential terms	14	7.1
9	其它 others	2	1.0

n=196

3-9 对产品功能的侧重方面/ Ranking of the Considerations about the Function of This Kind of Product

注：本题为多选题，合计百分比超过 100%（Multiple answers）

排名 Ranking	侧重方面 Items	人次 Person-time	百分比 Percent
1	颜色 color	138	69.7
2	滋润 containing nourishing ingredient	112	56.6
3	光泽 glossing	63	31.8
4	不易脱色 color stability	59	29.8
5	不油腻 not oily	22	11.1
6	不含香料 containing no perfume	19	9.6
7	有银光 with fluorescent ingredient	10	5.1
8	其他 others	4	2.0

n=198

3-10 重度消费者的人口分布/ Demographics of the Heavy Consumers

	人数 Number	16-24 岁 Age	25-34 岁 Age	35-44 岁 Age	45-54 岁 Age	55-60 岁 Age
女性 Female	118	18.6	50.0	26.3	5.1	0.0
天天用 daily	82	18.3	47.6	30.5	3.7	0.0
两三天用 1 次 once 2 or 3 days	36	19.4	55.6	16.7	8.3	0.0

3-11 不同消费者层的常用品牌/ The Most Frequently Used Brands by Market Segments

3-11-1 时尚流行指标/ Fads Popular Index

注：本题为多选题，合计百分比超过 100%（Multiple answers）

	人数 Number	第一品牌及百分比 1st/ percent	第二品牌及百分比 2nd/ percent	第三品牌及百分比 3rd/ percent
女性 Female	194	**美宝莲 Maybelline(31.4)**	**雅芳 Avon(20.1)**	**露华浓 Revlon(6.7)** **羽西 Yue-sai(6.7)**
平实生活指向 simple living orientation	61	美宝莲 Maybelline(27.9)	雅芳 Avon(18.0)	露华浓 Revlon(6.6) 羽西 Yue-sai(6.6) 艾琳 Irlene(6.6)
时尚流行指向 fashion orientation	133	美宝莲 Maybelline(33.1)	雅芳 Avon(21.1)	露华浓 Revlon(6.8) 羽西 Yue-sai(6.8)

3-11-2 广告态度指标/ Advertising Attitude Index

注：本题为多选题，合计百分比超过 100%（Multiple answers）

	人数 Number	第一品牌及百分比 1st/ percent	第二品牌及百分比 2nd/ percent	第三品牌及百分比 3rd/ percent
女性 Female	193	**美宝莲 Maybelline(32.1)**	**雅芳 Avon(20.2)**	**露华浓 Revlon(6.7)** **羽西 Yue-sai(6.7)**
广告淡漠指向 indifferent orientation	42	美宝莲 Maybelline(28.6)	雅芳 Avon(19.0)	资生堂 Shiseido(7.1)
中间层 medium	132	美宝莲 Maybelline(34.1)	雅芳 Avon(18.9)	羽西 Yue-sai(7.6)
信赖广告指向 loyal orientation	19	雅芳 Avon(31.6)	美宝莲 Maybelline(26.3)	露华浓 Revlon(10.5) 芭莎 Basha(10.5) 曼秀雷敦 Mentholatum(10.5)

3-12 重度消费者的消费层构成/ The Composition of the Heavy Consumers

3-12-1 时尚流行指标/ Fads Popular Index

	人数 Number	平实生活指向 simple living orientation	时尚流行指向 fashion orientation
女性 Female	115	28.7	71.3
天天用 daily	79	27.8	72.2
两三天用 1 次 once 2 or 3 days	36	30.6	69.4

3-12-2 广告态度指标/ Advertising Attitude Index

	人数 Number	广告淡漠指向 indifferent orientation	中间层 medium	信赖广告指向 loyal orientation
女性 Female	114	18.4	70.2	11.4
天天用 daily	80	20.0	68.8	11.3
两三天用 1 次 once 2 or 3 days	34	14.7	73.5	11.8

● 重庆 / Chongqing

3-1 最近三个月使用频次的比例/ Proportion of the Sample Consuming Lipstick in the Last Three Months

	人数 Number	百分比 Percent
天天用 daily	55	17.9
两三天用 1 次 once 2 or 3 days	23	7.5
一周 1～2 次 once or twice a week	22	7.1
半个月 1 次 once half a month	4	1.3
一个月 1 次或以下 once a month or below	10	3.2
没用过 never use	194	63.0

n=308

3-2 最常用品牌排名/ Ranking of the Most Frequently Used Brands

注：本题为多选题，合计百分比超过 100%（Multiple answers）

排名 Brand Ranking	品牌 Brands	人次 Person-time	百分比 Percent
1	美宝莲 Maybelline	34	29.8
2	羽西 Yue-sai	14	12.3
3	雅芳 Avon	11	9.6
4	丹桂 Dangui	7	6.1
5	迪奥 CD	5	4.4
6	艾琳 Irlene	4	3.5
6	欧莱雅 L'Oreal	4	3.5
6	天娜 Tiav Nuo	4	3.5

n=114

3-3 样本、女性各年龄层的常用品牌/ The Most Frequently Used Brands by the Female Sample and Age Groups

注：本题为多选题，合计百分比超过 100%（Multiple answers）

	人数 Number	第一品牌及百分比 1st/ percent	第二品牌及百分比 2nd/ percent	第三品牌及百分比 3rd/ percent	第四品牌及百分比 4th/ percent
女性 Female	114	**美宝莲 Maybelline(29.8)**	**羽西 Yue-sai(12.3)**	**雅芳 Avon(9.6)**	**丹桂 Dangui(6.1)**
16~24 岁 Age	24	美宝莲 Maybelline(37.5)	雅芳 Avon(25.0)	羽西 Yue-sai(12.5)	露华浓 Revlon(8.3) 资生堂 Shiseido(8.3) 丹妮 Danni(8.3)
25~34 岁 Age	50	美宝莲 Maybelline(34.0)	羽西 Yue-sai(16.0)	欧莱雅 L'Oreal(6.0) 艾琳 Irlene(6.0) 雅芳 Avon(6.0) 迪奥 CD(6.0)	
35~44 岁 Age	22	美宝莲 Maybelline(18.2)	丹桂 Dangui(13.6)	天娜 Tiav Nuo(9.1) 雅芳 Avon(9.1)	羽西 Yue-sai(4.5) 恒芳 Hengfang(4.5) 碧丹 Bidan(4.5) 丽花丝宝 Laifa-c'bons(4.5) 蕾迪雅 Ladiera(4.5) 迪奥 CD(4.5)
45~54 岁 Age	18	美宝莲 Maybelline(22.2)	丹桂 Dangui(16.7)	羽西 Yue-sai(11.1)	迪奥 CD(5.6) 艾琳 Irlene(5.6) 雅嘉 Aikai(5.6) 依贝佳 Ebeca(5.6) 郑明明 Cheng Mingming(5.6) 绿丹兰 Lvdanlan(5.6) 沙氏雪芙 ShaShi XueFu(5.6)
55~60 岁 Age	0				

3-4 正在使用的品牌排名/ Ranking of the Brand Used Now

注：本题为多选题，合计百分比超过 100%（Multiple answers）

排名 Brand Ranking	品牌 Brands	人次 Person-time	百分比 Percent
1	美宝莲 Maybelline	30	26.3
2	羽西 Yue-sai	15	13.2
3	雅芳 Avon	10	8.8
4	丹桂 Dangui	7	6.1
5	迪奥 CD	6	5.3
6	艾琳 Irlene	5	4.4
7	依贝佳 Ebeca	3	2.6
8	天娜 Tiav Nuo	2	1.8
8	丹妮 Danni	2	1.8
8	欧莱雅 L'Oreal	2	1.8
8	碧丹 Bidan	2	1.8
8	露华浓 Revlon	2	1.8
8	丽花丝宝 Laifa-c'bons	2	1.8

n=114

3-5 品牌转换习惯/ Brand Habit in Consuming Lipstick

	人数 Number	第一次使用该品牌 first use this brand	上一次也是这个牌子 used it last time	上一次不是这个牌子 not used it last time
女性 Female	108	20.4	58.3	21.3
美宝莲 Maybelline	29	13.8	69.0	17.2
羽西 Yue-sai	15	20.0	73.3	6.7
雅芳 Avon	10	30.0	60.0	10.0
丹桂 Dangui	7	14.3	71.4	14.3
迪奥 CD	5	20.0	20.0	60.0
艾琳 Irlene	4	50.0	50.0	0.0
依贝佳 Ebeca	3	0.0	0.0	100.0
天娜 Tiav Nuo	2	0.0	50.0	50.0
丹妮 Danni	2	0.0	100.0	0.0
欧莱雅 L'Oreal	2	0.0	0.0	100.0
露华浓 Revlon	2	0.0	50.0	50.0
丽花丝宝 Laifa-c'bons	2	0.0	50.0	50.0
碧丹 Bidan	1	0.0	100.0	0.0

3-6 下一次打算使用的品牌排名/ Ranking of the Brands to be Used Next Time

排名 Brand Ranking	品牌 Brands	人数 Number	百分比 Percent
1	美宝莲 Maybelline	35	30.7
2	羽西 Yue-sai	11	9.6
3	雅芳 Avon	8	7.0
4	迪奥 CD	6	5.3
4	欧莱雅 L'Oreal	6	5.3
5	丹桂 Dangui	5	4.4
6	依贝佳 Ebeca	3	2.6
6	丹妮 Danni	3	2.6

n=114

3-7 样本、女性各年龄层的使用频率/ Frequencies of the Consumed Lipstick by the Female Sample and Age Groups

	人数 Number	天天用 daily	两三天用 1 次 once 2 or 3 days	一周 1~2 次 once or twice a week	半个月 1 次 once half a month	一个月 1 次或以下 once a month or below	没用过 never use
女性 Female	308	17.9	7.5	7.1	1.3	3.2	63.0
16~24 岁 Age	63	14.3	6.3	11.1	1.6	4.8	61.9
25~34 岁 Age	90	28.9	10.0	11.1	2.2	3.3	44.4
35~44 岁 Age	72	16.7	8.3	2.8	1.4	1.4	69.4
45~54 岁 Age	60	13.3	6.7	5.0	0.0	5.0	70.0
55~60 岁 Age	23	0.0	0.0	0.0	0.0	0.0	100.0

3-8 选择该类商品的考虑因素/ Ranking of the Considerations in Purchasing

注：本题为多选题，合计百分比超过 100%（Multiple answers）

排名 Ranking	考虑因素 Considerations	人次 Person-time	百分比 Percent
1	价格适中 reasonable price	47	42.3
2	有名的牌子 famous brand	45	40.5
3	产品功用 product function	27	24.3
4	别人推荐 introduced by other people	24	21.6
5	广告影响 influence of advertising	20	18.0
6	购买方便 easy to buy	10	9.0
6	有优惠条件 with preferential terms	10	9.0
7	包装吸引人 appealing package	3	2.7

n=111

3-9 对产品功能的侧重方面/ Ranking of the Considerations about the Function of This Kind of Product

注：本题为多选题，合计百分比超过 100%（Multiple answers）

排名 Ranking	侧重方面 Items	人次 Person-time	百分比 Percent
1	颜色 color	81	71.7
2	滋润 containing nourishing ingredient	62	54.9
3	不易脱色 color stability	51	45.1
4	光泽 glossing	26	23.0
5	不油腻 not oily	13	11.5
6	不含香料 containing no perfume	11	9.7

n=113

3-10 重度消费者的人口分布/ Demographics of the Heavy Consumers

	人数 Number	16-24 岁 Age	25-34 岁 Age	35-44 岁 Age	45-54 岁 Age	55-60 岁 Age
女性 Female	78	16.7	44.9	23.1	15.4	0.0
天天用 daily	55	16.4	47.3	21.8	14.5	0.0
两三天用 1 次 once 2 or 3 days	23	17.4	39.1	26.1	17.4	0.0

3-11 不同消费者层的常用品牌/ The Most Frequently Used Brands by Market Segments

3-11-1 时尚流行指标/ Fads Popular Index

注：本题为多选题，合计百分比超过 100%（Multiple answers）

	人数 Number	第一品牌及百分比 1st/ percent	第二品牌及百分比 2nd/ percent	第三品牌及百分比 3rd/ percent
女性 Female	113	**美宝莲 Maybelline(29.2)**	**羽西 Yue-sai(12.4)**	**雅芳 Avon(9.7)**
平实生活指向 simple living orientation	40	美宝莲 Maybelline(17.5)	羽西 Yue-sai(12.5)	艾琳 Irlene(10.0) 丹桂 Dangui(10.0) 迪奥 CD(10.0)
时尚流行指向 fashion orientation	73	美宝莲 Maybelline(35.6)	羽西 Yue-sai(12.3)	雅芳 Avon(11.0)

3-11-2 广告态度指标/ Advertising Attitude Index

注：本题为多选题，合计百分比超过 100%（Multiple answers）

	人数 Number	第一品牌及百分比 1st/ percent	第二品牌及百分比 2nd/ percent	第三品牌及百分比 3rd/ percent
女性 Female	112	**美宝莲 Maybelline(30.4)**	**羽西 Yue-sai(12.5)**	**雅芳 Avon(9.8)**
广告淡漠指向 indifferent orientation	21	美宝莲 Maybelline(38.1)	羽西 Yue-sai(19.0)	丹桂 Dangui(9.5) 依贝佳 Ebeca(9.5)
中间层 medium	75	美宝莲 Maybelline(29.3)	雅芳 Avon(10.7)	羽西 Yue-sai(8.0)
信赖广告指向 loyal orientation	16	美宝莲 Maybelline(25.0) 羽西 Yue-sai(25.0)	雅芳 Avon(18.8)	艾琳 Irlene(6.3) 丹桂 Dangui(6.3) 欧珀莱 Aupres(6.3) 绿丹兰 Lvdanlan(6.3)

3-12 重度消费者的消费层构成/ The Composition of the Heavy Consumers

3-12-1 时尚流行指标/ Fads Popular Index

	人数 Number	平实生活指向 simple living orientation	时尚流行指向 fashion orientation
女性 Female	78	32.1	67.9
天天用 daily	55	27.3	72.7
两三天用 1 次 once 2 or 3 days	23	43.5	56.5

3-12-2 广告态度指标/ Advertising Attitude Index

	人数 Number	广告淡漠指向 indifferent orientation	中间层 medium	信赖广告指向 loyal orientation
女性 Female	78	16.7	66.7	16.7
天天用 daily	55	14.5	69.1	16.4
两三天用 1 次 once 2 or 3 days	23	21.7	60.9	17.4

● 武汉 / Wuhan

3-1 最近三个月使用频次的比例/ Proportion of the Sample Consuming Lipstick in the Last Three Months

	人数 Number	百分比 Percent
天天用 daily	75	22.8
两三天用 1 次 once 2 or 3 days	30	9.1
一周 1～2 次 once or twice a week	23	7.0
半个月 1 次 once half a month	9	2.7
一个月 1 次或以下 once a month or below	15	4.6
没用过 never use	177	53.8

n=329

3-2 最常用品牌排名/ Ranking of the Most Frequently Used Brands

注：本题为多选题，合计百分比超过 100%（Multiple answers）

排名 Brand Ranking	品牌 Brands	人次 Person-time	百分比 Percent
1	美宝莲 Maybelline	50	32.9
2	雅芳 Avon	28	18.4
3	羽西 Yue-sai	18	11.8
4	丽花丝宝 Laifa-c'bons	12	7.9
5	丽妃 Lifei	8	5.3
6	欧莱雅 L'Oreal	6	3.9
7	奇士美 Kissme	4	2.6
8	欧珀莱 Aupres	2	1.3
8	得姿 Dezi	2	1.3

n=152

3-3 样本、女性各年龄层的常用品牌/ The Most Frequently Used Brands by the Female Sample and Age Groups

注：本题为多选题，合计百分比超过 100%（Multiple answers）

	人数 Number	第一品牌及百分比 1st/ percent	第二品牌及百分比 2nd/ percent	第三品牌及百分比 3rd/ percent	第四品牌及百分比 4th/ percent
女性 Female	152	**美宝莲 Maybelline(32.9)**	**雅芳 Avon(18.4)**	**羽西 Yue-sai(11.8)**	**丽花丝宝 Laifa-c'bons(7.9)**
16~24 岁 Age	36	美宝莲 Maybelline(38.9)	雅芳 Avon(27.8)	羽西 Yue-sai(16.7)	丽花丝宝 Laifa-c'bons(8.3)
25~34 岁 Age	72	美宝莲 Maybelline(36.1)	雅芳 Avon(13.9)	羽西 Yue-sai(12.5)	丽妃 Lifei(8.3)
35~44 岁 Age	32	美宝莲 Maybelline(25.0)	丽花丝宝 Laifa-c'bons(12.5) 雅芳 Avon(12.5)	羽西 Yue-sai(9.4)	祖儿 Zu'er(3.1) 黛安娜 Diana(3.1) ROSE(3.1) AMOUR(3.1) 伊思丽 Eesli(3.1) 爱诺 Ainuo(3.1) 爱倩 Aiqian(3.1) 欧莱雅 L'Oreal(3.1) 丽妃 Lifei(3.1)
45~54 岁 Age	11	雅芳 Avon(27.3)	丽花丝宝 Laifa-c'bons(18.2) 美宝莲 Maybelline(18.2)	奇士美 Kissme(9.1) 得姿 Dezi(9.1) 雪儿 Xue'er(9.1) Bidan(9.1)	
55~60 岁 Age	1	雅芳 Avon(100.0)			

3-4 正在使用的品牌排名/ Ranking of the Brands Used Now

注：本题为多选题，合计百分比超过 100%（Multiple answers）

排名 Brand Ranking	品牌 Brands	人次 Person-time	百分比 Percent
1	美宝莲 Maybelline	48	32.0
2	雅芳 Avon	24	16.0
3	羽西 Yue-sai	13	8.7
4	丽花丝宝 Laifa-c'bons	10	6.7
5	丽妃 Lifei	8	5.3
6	欧莱雅 L'Oreal	5	3.3
7	欧珀莱 Aupres	3	2.0

n=150

3-5 品牌转换习惯/ Brand Habit in Consuming Lipstick

	人数 Number	第一次使用该品牌 first use this brand	上一次也是这个牌子 used it last time	上一次不是这个牌子 not used it last time
女性 Female	149	16.1	67.1	16.8
美宝莲 Maybelline	48	10.4	77.1	12.5
雅芳 Avon	24	20.8	70.8	8.3
羽西 Yue-sai	13	7.7	69.2	23.1
丽花丝宝 Laifa-c'bons	10	0.0	90.0	10.0
丽妃 Lifei	8	12.5	62.5	25.0
欧莱雅 L'Oreal	5	0.0	100.0	0.0
欧珀莱 Aupres	3	0.0	66.7	33.3

3-6 下一次打算使用的品牌排名/ Ranking of the Brands to be Used Next Time

排名 Brand Ranking	品牌 Brands	人数 Number	百分比 Percent
1	美宝莲 Maybelline	51	33.8
2	雅芳 Avon	16	10.6
3	羽西 Yue-sai	13	8.6
4	欧莱雅 L'Oreal	11	7.3
5	丽花丝宝 Laifa-s'bons	7	4.6
6	丽妃 Lifei	5	3.3
7	欧珀莱 Aupres	2	1.3

n=151

3-7 样本、女性各年龄层的使用频率/ Frequencies of the Consumed Lipstick by the Female Sample and Age Groups

	人数 Number	天天用 daily	两三天用 1 次 once 2 or 3 days	一周 1~2 次 once or twice a week	半个月 1 次 once half a month	一个月 1 次或以下 once a month or below	没用过 never use
女性 Female	**329**	**22.8**	**9.1**	**7.0**	**2.7**	**4.6**	**53.8**
16~24 岁 Age	69	21.7	11.6	8.7	2.9	7.2	47.8
25~34 岁 Age	95	36.8	17.9	9.5	4.2	7.4	24.2
35~44 岁 Age	78	23.1	5.1	7.7	2.6	2.6	59.0
45~54 岁 Age	61	9.8	1.6	3.3	1.6	1.6	82.0
55~60 岁 Age	26	3.8	0.0	0.0	0.0	0.0	96.2

3-8 选择该类商品的考虑因素/ Ranking of the Considerations in Purchasing

注：本题为多选题，合计百分比超过 100%（Multiple answers）

排名 Ranking	考虑因素 Considerations	人次 Person-time	百分比 Percent
1	有名的牌子 famous brand	62	41.1
2	价格适中 reasonable price	59	39.1
2	产品功用 product function	59	39.1
3	别人推荐 introduced by other people	41	27.2
4	广告影响 influence of advertising	22	14.6
5	购买方便 easy to buy	18	11.9
5	有优惠条件 with preferential terms	18	11.9
6	包装吸引人 appealing package	8	5.3
7	其它 others	3	2.0

n=151

3-9 对产品功能的侧重方面/ Ranking of the Considerations about the Function of This Kind of Product

注：本题为多选题，合计百分比超过 100%（Multiple answers）

排名 Ranking	侧重方面 Items	人次 Person-time	百分比 Percent
1	颜色 color	114	75.5
2	滋润 containing nourishing ingredient	80	53.0
3	不易脱色 color stability	64	42.4
4	光泽 glossing	46	30.5
5	不含香料 containing no perfume	26	17.2
6	不油腻 not oily	16	10.6
7	有银光 with fluorescent ingredient	5	3.3
8	其他 others	1	0.7

n=151

3-10 重度消费者的人口分布/ Demographics of the Heavy Consumers

	人数 Number	16-24 岁 Age	25-34 岁 Age	35-44 岁 Age	45-54 岁 Age	55-60 岁 Age
女性 Female	105	21.9	49.5	21.0	6.7	1.0
天天用 daily	75	20.0	46.7	24.0	8.0	1.3
两三天用 1 次 once 2 or 3 days	30	26.7	56.7	13.3	3.3	0.0

3-11 不同消费者层的常用品牌/ The Most Frequently Used Brands by Market Segments

3-11-1 时尚流行指标/ Fads Popular Index

注：本题为多选题，合计百分比超过 100%（Multiple answers）

	人数 Number	第一品牌及百分比 1st/ percent	第二品牌及百分比 2nd/ percent	第三品牌及百分比 3rd/ percent
女性 Female	150	**美宝莲 Maybelline(32.7)**	**雅芳 Avon(18.0)**	**羽西 Yue-sai(12.0)**
平实生活指向 simple living orientation	50	美宝莲 Maybelline(22.0)	雅芳 Avon(20.0)	羽西 Yue-sai(10.0)
时尚流行指向 fashion orientation	100	美宝莲 Maybelline(38.0)	雅芳 Avon(17.0)	羽西 Yue-sai(13.0)

3-11-2 广告态度指标/ Advertising Attitude Index

注：本题为多选题，合计百分比超过 100%（Multiple answers）

	人数 Number	第一品牌及百分比 1st/ percent	第二品牌及百分比 2nd/ percent	第三品牌及百分比 3rd/ percent
女性 Female	150	**美宝莲 Maybelline(32.7)**	**雅芳 Avon(18.0)**	**羽西 Yue-sai(12.0)**
广告淡漠指向 indifferent orientation	32	美宝莲 Maybelline(43.8)	雅芳 Avon(12.5)	羽西 Yue-sai(9.4)
中间层 medium	93	美宝莲 Maybelline(29.0)	雅芳 Avon(22.6)	羽西 Yue-sai(12.9)
信赖广告指向 loyal orientation	25	美宝莲 Maybelline(32.0)	丽妃 Lifei(12.0) 羽西 Yue-sai(12.0)	丽花丝宝 Laifa-c'bons(8.0) 雅芳 Avon(8.0)

3-12 重度消费者的消费层构成/ The Composition of the Heavy Consumers

3-12-1 时尚流行指标/ Fads Popular Index

	人数 Number	平实生活指向 simple living orientation	时尚流行指向 fashion orientation
女性 Female	104	**31.7**	**68.3**
天天用 daily	74	29.7	70.3
两三天用 1 次 once 2 or 3 days	30	36.7	63.3

3-12-2 广告态度指标/ Advertising Attitude Index

	人数 Number	广告淡漠指向 indifferent orientation	中间层 medium	信赖广告指向 loyal orientation
女性 Female	104	**20.2**	**59.6**	**20.2**
天天用 daily	74	21.6	59.5	18.9
两三天用 1 次 once 2 or 3 days	30	16.7	60.0	23.3

● 西安 / Xi'an

3-1 最近三个月使用频次的比例/ Proportion of the Sample Consuming Lipstick in the Last Three Months

	人数 Number	百分比 Percent
天天用 daily	75	25.2
两三天用 1 次 once 2 or 3 days	27	9.1
一周 1～2 次 once or twice a week	20	6.7
半个月 1 次 once half a month	6	2.0
一个月 1 次或以下 once a month or below	7	2.3
没用过 never use	163	54.7

n=298

3-2 最常用品牌排名/ Ranking of the Most Frequently Used Brands

注：本题为多选题，合计百分比超过 100%（Multiple answers）

排名 Brand Ranking	品牌 Brands	人次 Person-time	百分比 Percent
1	美宝莲 Maybelline	37	27.4
2	雅芳 Avon	22	16.3
3	奇士美 Kissme	15	11.1
4	柔婷 Routing	6	4.4
5	灰姑娘 Huiguniang	5	3.7
5	清妃 Chinf	5	3.7
5	羽西 Yue-sai	5	3.7
6	迪奥 CD	3	2.2
6	碧丹 Bidan	3	2.2
6	天娜 Tiav Nuo	3	2.2

n=135

3-3 样本、女性各年龄层的常用品牌/ The Most Frequently Used Brands by the Female Sample and Age Groups

注：本题为多选题，合计百分比超过 100%（Multiple answers）

	人数 Number	第一品牌及百分比 1st/ percent	第二品牌及百分比 2nd/ percent	第三品牌及百分比 3rd/ percent
女性 Female	135	**美宝莲 Maybelline(27.4)**	**雅芳 Avon(16.3)**	**奇士美 Kissme(11.1)**
16~24 岁 Age	24	美宝莲 Maybelline(33.3)	雅芳 Avon(20.8)	灰姑娘 Huiguniang(8.3)
25~34 岁 Age	60	美宝莲 Maybelline(36.7)	雅芳 Avon(20.0)	奇士美 Kissme(15.0)
35~44 岁 Age	39	美宝莲 Maybelline(12.8)	奇士美 Kissme(10.3) 雅芳 Avon(10.3)	柔婷 Routing(7.7) 碧丹 Bidan(7.7)
45~54 岁 Age	9	美宝莲 Maybelline(22.2)	奇士美 Kissme(11.1) 清妃 Chinf(11.1) 天娜 Tiav Nuo(11.1) 伊思汉 Yisihan(11.1)	
55~60 岁 Age	3	柔婷 Routing(33.3) 雅芳 Avon(33.3) 羽西 Yue-sai(33.3)		

3-4 正在使用的品牌排名/ Ranking of the Brands Used Now

注：本题为多选题，合计百分比超过 100%（Multiple answers）

排名 Brand Ranking	品牌 Brands	人次 Person-time	百分比 Percent
1	美宝莲 Maybelline	32	23.7
2	雅芳 Avon	22	16.3
3	奇士美 Kissme	11	8.1
4	羽西 Yue-sai	10	7.4
5	柔婷 Routing	6	4.4
6	灰姑娘 Huiguniang	5	3.7
7	清妃 Chinf	4	3.0

n=135

3-5 品牌转换习惯/ Brand Habit in Consuming Lipstick

	人数 Number	第一次使用该品牌 first use this brand	上一次也是这个牌子 used it last time	上一次不是这个牌子 not used it last time
女性 Female	134	18.7	61.2	20.1
雅芳 Avon	22	13.6	63.6	22.7
奇士美 Kissme	11	27.3	63.6	9.1
羽西 Yue-sai	10	30.0	50.0	20.0
柔婷 Routing	6	33.3	66.7	0.0
灰姑娘 Huiguniang	5	0.0	80.0	20.0
清妃 Chinf	4	0.0	50.0	50.0

3-6 下一次打算使用的品牌排名/ Ranking of the Brands to be Used Next Time

注：本题为多选题，合计百分比超过 100%（Multiple answers）

排名 Brand Ranking	品牌 Brands	人数 Number	百分比 Percent
1	美宝莲 Maybelline	42	31.1
2	雅芳 Avon	21	15.6
3	羽西 Yue-sai	12	8.9
4	奇士美 Kissme	9	6.7
5	灰姑娘 Huiguniang	4	3.0
5	柔婷 Routing	4	3.0

n=135

3-7 样本、女性各年龄层的使用频率/ Frequencies of the Consumed Lipstick by the Female Sample and Age Groups

	人数 Number	天天用 daily	两三天用 1 次 once 2 or 3 days	一周 1~2 次 once or twice a week	半个月 1 次 once half a month	一个月 1 次或下 once a month or below	没用过 never use
女性 Female	298	25.2	9.1	6.7	2.0	2.3	54.7
16~24 岁 Age	60	21.7	10.0	5.0	1.7	1.7	60.0
25~34 岁 Age	90	36.7	13.3	11.1	3.3	2.2	33.3
35~44 岁 Age	74	27.0	12.2	6.8	2.7	4.1	47.3
45~54 岁 Age	49	14.3	0.0	4.1	0.0	0.0	81.6
55~60 岁 Age	25	8.0	0.0	0.0	0.0	4.0	88.0

3-8 选择该类商品的考虑因素/ Ranking of the Considerations in Purchasing

注：本题为多选题，合计百分比超过 100%（Multiple answers）

排名 Ranking	考虑因素 Considerations	人次 Person-time	百分比 Percent
1	价格适中 reasonable price	49	36.3
2	有名的牌子 famous brand	45	33.3
3	产品功用 product function	44	32.6
4	别人推荐 introduced by other people	40	29.6
5	购买方便 easy to buy	17	12.6
6	包装吸引人 appealing package	12	8.9
6	广告影响 influence of advertising	12	8.9
7	有优惠条件 with preferential terms	11	8.1
8	其它 others	5	3.7

n=135

3-9 对产品功能的侧重方面/ Ranking of the Considerations about the Function of This Kind of Product

注：本题为多选题，合计百分比超过 100%（Multiple answers）

排名 Ranking	侧重方面 Items	人次 Person-time	百分比 Percent
1	颜色 color	90	66.7
2	滋润 containing nourishing ingredient	66	48.9
3	不易脱色 color stability	50	37.0
4	光泽 glossing	35	25.9
5	不油腻 not oily	16	11.9
6	不含香料 containing no perfume	15	11.1
7	有银光 with fluorescent ingredient	6	4.4
8	其他 others	2	1.5

n=135

3-10 重度消费者的人口分布/ Demographics of the Heavy Consumers

	人数 Number	16-24 岁 Age	25-34 岁 Age	35-44 岁 Age	45-54 岁 Age	55-60 岁 Age
女性 Female	102	18.6	44.1	28.4	6.9	2.0
天天用 daily	75	17.3	44.0	26.7	9.3	2.7
两三天用 1 次 once 2 or 3 days	27	22.2	44.4	33.3	0.0	0.0

3-11 不同消费者层的常用品牌/ The Most Frequently Used Brands by Market Segments

3-11-1 时尚流行指标/ Fads Popular Index

注：本题为多选题，合计百分比超过 100%（Multiple answers）

	人数 Number	第一品牌及百分比 1st/ percent	第二品牌及百分比 2nd/ percent	第三品牌及百分比 3rd/ percent
女性 Female	135	美宝莲 Maybelline(27.4)	雅芳 Avon(16.3)	奇士美 Kissme(11.1)
平实生活指向 simple living orientation	50	雅芳 Avon(20.0)	美宝莲 Maybelline(18.0)	奇士美 Kissme(12.0)
时尚流行指向 fashion orientation	85	美宝莲 Maybelline(32.9)	雅芳 Avon(14.1)	奇士美 Kissme(10.6)

3-11-2 广告态度指标/ Advertising Attitude Index

注：本题为多选题，合计百分比超过 100%（Multiple answers）

	人数 Number	第一品牌及百分比 1st/ percent	第二品牌及百分比 2nd/ percent	第三品牌及百分比 3rd/ percent
女性 Female	134	美宝莲 Maybelline(27.6)	雅芳 Avon(16.4)	奇士美 Kissme(11.2)
广告淡漠指向 indifferent orientation	37	美宝莲 Maybelline(24.3)	雅芳 Avon(18.9)	羽西 Yue-sai(5.4) 奇士美 Kissme(5.4) 柔婷 Routing(5.4)
中间层 medium	80	美宝莲 Maybelline(35.0)	雅芳 Avon(12.5)	奇士美 Kissme(11.3)
信赖广告指向 loyal orientation	17	雅芳 Avon(29.4)	奇士美 Kissme(23.5)	迪奥 CD(5.9) 清妃 Chinf(5.9) 柔婷 Routing(5.9) 雅达 Yada(5.9) 祖儿 Zuer(5.9) 好女孩 Good Girl(5.9)

3-12 重度消费者的消费层构成/ The Composition of the Heavy Consumers

3-12-1 时尚流行指标/ Fads Popular Index

	人数 Number	平实生活指向 simple living orientation	时尚流行指向 fashion orientation
女性 Female	102	36.3	63.7
天天用 daily	75	37.3	62.7
两三天用 1 次 once 2 or 3 days	27	33.3	66.7

3-12-2 广告态度指标/ Advertising Attitude Index

	人数 Number	广告淡漠指向 indifferent orientation	中间层 medium	信赖广告指向 loyal orientation
女性 Female	102	24.5	63.7	11.8
天天用 daily	75	24.0	65.3	10.7
两三天用 1 次 once 2 or 3 days	27	25.9	59.3	14.8

● 沈阳 / Shenyang

3-1 最近三个月使用频次的比例/ Proportion of the Sample Consuming Lipstick in the Last Three Months

	人数 Number	百分比 Percent
天天用 daily	122	40.4
两三天用 1 次 once 2 or 3 days	20	6.6
一周 1～2 次 once or twice a week	12	4.0
半个月 1 次 once half a month	6	2.0
一个月 1 次或以下 once a month or below	5	1.7
没用过 never use	137	45.4

n=302

3-2 最常用品牌排名/ Ranking of the Most Frequently Used Brands

注：本题为多选题，合计百分比超过 100%（Multiple answers）

排名 Brand Ranking	品牌 Brands	人次 Person-time	百分比 Percent
1	奇士美 Kissme	40	24.2
2	美宝莲 Maybelline	25	15.2
3	雅达 Yada	15	9.1
4	羽西 Yue-sai	11	6.7
5	雅芳 Avon	7	4.2
6	郑明明 Cheng Mingming	6	3.6
7	亨达 Hengda	4	2.4
7	丹菲.可丽斯 Danfei.Kelisi	4	2.4
8	高丝 Kose	3	1.8
8	爱茉莉 Amore	3	1.8
8	欧珀莱 Aupres	3	1.8

n=165

3-3 样本、女性各年龄层的常用品牌/ The Most Frequently Used Brands by the Female Sample and Age Groups

注：本题为多选题，合计百分比超过 100%（Multiple answers）

	人数 Number	第一品牌及百分比 1st/ percent	第二品牌及百分比 2nd/ percent	第三品牌及百分比 3rd/ percent
女性 Female	165	**奇士美 Kissme(24.2)**	**美宝莲 Maybelline(15.2)**	**雅达 Yada(9.1)**
16~24 岁 Age	31	美宝莲 Maybelline(22.6)	奇士美 Kissme(9.7) 郑明明 Cheng Mingming(9.7)	丹菲.可丽斯 Danfei.Kelisi(6.5) 雅达 Yada(6.5) 羽西 Yue-sai(6.5)
25~34 岁 Age	69	奇士美 Kissme(30.4)	美宝莲 Maybelline(15.9)	雅达 Yada(14.5)
35~44 岁 Age	52	奇士美 Kissme(25.0)	美宝莲 Maybelline(11.5)	羽西 Yue-sai(7.7)
45~54 岁 Age	12	奇士美 Kissme(25.0)	雅达 Yada(16.7)	美宝莲 Maybelline(8.3) 天娜 Tiav Nuo(8.3) 植树秀 Shu uemura(8.3) 丰采 Fengcai(8.3) 万紫千红 Wan Zi Qian Hong(8.3) INDIGO(8.3)
55~60 岁 Age	1	迪奥 CD(100.0)		

3-4 正在使用的品牌排名/ Ranking of the Brands Used Now

注：本题为多选题，合计百分比超过 100%（Multiple answers）

排名 Brand Ranking	品牌 Brands	人次 Person-time	百分比 Percent
1	奇士美 Kissme	35	21.2
2	美宝莲 Maybelline	24	14.5
3	雅达 Yada	11	6.7
4	羽西 Yue-sai	10	6.1
5	雅芳 Avon	7	4.2
6	蕾琪 Leiqi	4	2.4
6	亨达 Hengda	4	2.4
6	郑明明 Cheng Mingming	4	2.4
6	丹菲.可丽斯 Danfei.Kelisi	4	2.4
7	高丝 Kose	3	1.8
7	欧珀莱 Aupres	3	1.8
7	植树秀 Shu uemura	3	1.8

n=165

3-5 品牌转换习惯/ Brand Habit in Consuming Lipstick

	人数 Number	第一次使用该品牌 first use this brand	上一次也是这个牌子 used it last time	上一次不是这个牌子 not used it last time
女性 Female	**165**	**15.8**	**67.9**	**16.4**
奇士美 Kissme	35	8.6	85.7	5.7
美宝莲 Maybelline	24	29.2	62.5	8.3
雅达 Yada	11	0.0	72.7	27.3
羽西 Yue-sai	10	20.0	70.0	10.0
雅芳 Avon	7	0.0	85.7	14.3
蕾琪 Leiqi	4	25.0	75.0	0.0
亨达 Hengda	4	0.0	100.0	0.0
郑明明 Cheng Mingming	4	0.0	75.0	25.0
丹菲.可丽斯 Danfei.Kelisi	4	0.0	100.0	0.0

3-6 下一次打算使用的品牌排名/ Ranking of the Brands to be Used Next Time

排名 Brand Ranking	品牌 Brands	人数 Number	百分比 Percent
1	奇士美 Kissme	36	21.8
2	美宝莲 Maybelline	32	19.4
3	羽西 Yue-sai	11	6.7
4	雅达 Yada	9	5.5
5	郑明明 Cheng Mingming	6	3.6
6	高丝 Kose	4	2.4
6	雅芳 Avon	4	2.4
7	欧珀莱 Aupres	3	1.8

n=165

3-7 样本、女性各年龄层的使用频率/ Frequencies of the Consumed Lipstick by the Female Sample and Age Groups

	人数 Number	天天用 daily	两三天用 1 次 once 2 or 3 days	一周 1~2 次 once or twice a week	半个月 1 次 once half a month	一个月 1 次或以下 once a month or below	没用过 never use
女性 Female	**302**	**40.4**	**6.6**	**4.0**	**2.0**	**1.7**	**45.4**
16~24 岁 Age	64	35.9	3.1	3.1	4.7	1.6	51.6
25~34 岁 Age	90	55.6	10.0	6.7	3.3	1.1	23.3
35~44 岁 Age	76	55.3	6.6	3.9	0.0	2.6	31.6
45~54 岁 Age	48	12.5	8.3	2.1	0.0	2.1	75.0
55~60 岁 Age	24	4.2	0.0	0.0	0.0	0.0	95.8

3-8 选择该类商品的考虑因素/ Ranking of the Considerations in Purchasing

注：本题为多选题，合计百分比超过 100%（Multiple answers）

排名 Ranking	考虑因素 Considerations	人次 Person-time	百分比 Percent
1	价格适中 reasonable price	76	46.1
2	有名的牌子 famous brand	54	32.7
3	别人推荐 introduced by other people	44	26.7
4	产品功用 product function	39	23.6
5	购买方便 easy to buy	37	22.4
6	广告影响 influence of advertising	20	12.1
7	有优惠条件 with preferential terms	11	6.7
8	其它 others	4	2.4
9	包装吸引人 appealing package	3	1.8

n=165

3-9 对产品功能的侧重方面/ Ranking of the Considerations about the Function of This Kind of Product

注：本题为多选题，合计百分比超过 100%（Multiple answers）

排名 Ranking	侧重方面 Items	人次 Person-time	百分比 Percent
1	颜色 color	121	73.8
2	滋润 containing nourishing ingredient	63	38.4
2	不易脱色 color stability	63	38.4
3	光泽 glossing	46	28.0
4	不油腻 not oily	23	14.0
5	不含香料 containing no perfume	22	13.4
6	有银光 with fluorescent ingredient	3	1.8

n=164

3-10 重度消费者的人口分布/ Demographics of the Heavy Consumers

	人数 Number	16-24 岁 Age	25-34 岁 Age	35-44 岁 Age	45-54 岁 Age	55-60 岁 Age
女性 Female	142	17.6	41.5	33.1	7.0	0.7
天天用 daily	122	18.9	41.0	34.4	4.9	0.8
两三天用 1 次 once 2 or 3 days	20	10.0	45.0	25.0	20.0	0.0

3-11 不同消费者层的常用品牌/ The Most Frequently Used Brands by Market Segments

3-11-1 时尚流行指标/ Fads Popular Index

注：本题为多选题，合计百分比可能超过 100%（Multiple answers）

	人数 Number	第一品牌及百分比 1st/ percent	第二品牌及百分比 2nd/ percent	第三品牌及百分比 3rd/ percent
女性 Female	165	**奇士美 Kissme(24.2)**	**美宝莲 Maybelline(15.2)**	**雅达 Yada(9.1)**
平实生活指向 simple living orientation	50	奇士美 Kissme(22.0)	美宝莲 Maybelline(14.0)	雅达 Yada(12.0)
时尚流行指向 fashion orientation	115	奇士美 Kissme(25.2)	美宝莲 Maybelline(15.7)	雅达 Yada(7.8)

3-11-2 广告态度指标/ Advertising Attitude Index

注：本题为多选题，合计百分比可能超过 100%（Multiple answers）

	人数 Number	第一品牌及百分比 1st/ percent	第二品牌及百分比 2nd/ percent	第三品牌及百分比 3rd/ percent
女性 Female	165	**奇士美 Kissme(24.2)**	**美宝莲 Maybelline(15.2)**	**雅达 Yada(9.1)**
广告淡漠指向 indifferent orientation	29	美宝莲 Maybelline(24.1)	奇士美 Kissme(17.2)	雅芳 Avon(10.3) 雅达 Yada(10.3)
中间层 medium	115	奇士美 Kissme(25.2)	美宝莲 Maybelline(14.8)	雅达 Yada(7.8)
信赖广告指向 loyal orientation	21	奇士美 Kissme(28.6)	雅达 Yaca(14.3)	高丝 Kose(9.5) 郑明明 Cheng Mingming(9.5) 羽西 Yue-sai(9.5)

3-12 重度消费者的消费层构成/ The Composition of the Heavy Consumers

3-12-1 时尚流行指标/ Fads Popular Index

	人数 Number	平实生活指向 simple living orientation	时尚流行指向 fashion orientation
女性 Female	142	28.9	71.1
天天用 daily	122	29.5	70.5
两三天用 1 次 once 2 or 3 days	20	25.0	75.0

3-12-2 广告态度指标/ Advertising Attitude Index

	人数 Number	广告淡漠指向 indifferent orientation	中间层 medium	信赖广告指向 loyal orientation
女性 Female	142	17.6	68.3	14.1
天天用 daily	122	17.2	70.5	12.3
两三天用 1 次 once 2 or 3 days	20	20.0	55.0	25.0

4.卫生巾 / Napkins

● 北京 / Beijing

4-1 最近一次使用量的比例/ Proportion of the Sample Consuming Napkins Last Time

	人数 Number	百分比 Percent
30 片以上 over 30 pieces	24	4.8
21-30 片 21-30 pieces	75	14.9
11-20 片 11-20 pieces	200	39.8
10 片及以下 10 pieces or below	121	24.1
没有用 not use	82	16.3

n=502

4-2 最常用品牌排名/ Ranking of the Most Frequently Used Brands

排名 Brand Ranking	品牌 Brands	人数 Number	百分比 Percent
1	护舒宝 Whisper	99	23.7
2	舒而美 Comfort & Beauty	94	22.5
3	娇爽 Carefree	54	12.9
4	苏菲 Sofy	41	9.8
5	高洁丝 Kotex	36	8.6
6	安尔乐 An'erle	19	4.5
7	一片云 Soft Cloud	17	4.1
8	佳期 Godcare	9	2.2
9	依依 Yi Yi	8	1.9

n=418

4-3 样本、女性各年龄层的常用品牌/ The Most Frequently Used Brands by the Female Sample and Age Groups

	人数 Number	第一品牌及百分比 1st/ percent	第二品牌及百分比 2nd/ percent	第三品牌及百分比 3rd/ percent	第四品牌及百分比 4th/ percent
女性 Female	418	**护舒宝 Whisper(23.7)**	**舒而美 Comfort & Beauty (22.5)**	**娇爽 Carefree(12.9)**	**苏菲 Sofy(9.8)**
16~24 岁 Age	107	护舒宝 Whisper(29.9)	娇爽 Carefree(14.0)	高洁丝 Kotex(13.1) 苏菲 Sofy(13.1)	舒而美 Comfort & Beauty (8.4)
25~34 岁 Age	142	护舒宝 Whisper(33.1)	舒而美 Comfort & Beauty (20.4)	娇爽 Carefree(15.5)	高洁丝 Kotex(9.2)
35~44 岁 Age	121	舒而美 Comfort & Beauty (28.9)	娇爽 Carefree(13.2)	护舒宝 Whisper(11.6)	苏菲 Sofy(10.7)
45~54 岁 Age	48	舒而美 Comfort & Beauty (43.8)	安尔乐 An'erle(14.6)	护舒宝 Whisper(12.5)	苏菲 Sofy(6.3)
55~60 岁 Age	0				

4-4 正在使用的品牌排名/ Ranking of the Brands Used Now

排名 Brand Ranking	品牌 Brands	人数 Number	百分比 Percent
1	护舒宝 Whisper	90	21.6
2	舒而美 Comfort & Beauty	88	21.1
3	娇爽 Carefree	56	13.4
4	苏菲 Sofy	49	11.8
5	高洁丝 Kotex	38	9.1
6	安尔乐 An'erle	18	4.3
7	一片云 Soft Cloud	15	3.6
8	依依 Yi Yi	12	2.9
9	佳期 Godcare	11	2.6
9	特日欣 Terixin	11	2.6
10	安乐 Anle	6	1.4
10	乐而雅 Laurier	6	1.4

n=417

4-5 品牌转换习惯/ Brand Habit in Consuming Napkins

	人数 Number	第一次使用该品牌 first use this brand	上一次也是这个牌子 used it last time	上一次不是这个牌子 not used it last time
女性 Female	416	4.6	85.1	10.3
护舒宝 Whisper	90	2.2	88.9	8.9
舒而美 Comfort & Beauty	88	3.4	88.6	8.0
娇爽 Carefree	55	1.8	92.7	5.5
苏菲 Sofy	49	4.1	81.6	14.3
高洁丝 Kotex	38	5.3	81.6	13.2
安尔乐 An'erle	18	0.0	77.8	22.2
一片云 Soft Cloud	15	0.0	80.0	20.0
依依 Yi Yi	12	0.0	91.7	8.3
佳期 Godcare	11	36.4	54.5	9.1
特日欣 Terixin	11	0.0	90.9	9.1

4-6 下一次打算使用的品牌排名/ Ranking of the Brands to be Used Next Time

排名 Brand Ranking	品牌 Brands	人数 Number	百分比 Percent
1	护舒宝 Whisper	107	25.5
2	舒而美 Comfort & Beauty	74	17.7
3	苏菲 Sofy	55	13.1
3	娇爽 Carefree	55	13.1
4	高洁丝 Kotex	41	9.8
5	安尔乐 An'erle	17	4.1
6	佳期 Godcare	10	2.4
7	依依 Yi Yi	8	1.9
8	一片云 Soft Cloud	7	1.7

n=419

4-7 样本、女性各年龄层最近一次的使用量/ Pieces of the Consumed Napkins Last Time by the Female Sample and Age Groups

	人数 Number	30 片以上 over 30 pieces	21-30 片 21-30 pieces	11-20 片 11-20 pieces	10 片及以下 10 pieces or below	没有用 not use
女性 Female	502	4.8	14.9	39.8	24.1	16.3
16~24 岁 Age	107	5.6	22.4	45.8	26.2	0.0
25~34 岁 Age	149	5.4	17.4	49.0	24.8	3.4
35~44 岁 Age	121	5.0	17.4	45.5	32.2	0.0
45~54 岁 Age	84	4.8	4.8	27.4	20.2	42.9
55~60 岁 Age	41	0.0	0.0	0.0	0.0	100.0

4-8 选择该类商品的考虑因素/ Ranking of the Considerations in Purchasing

注：本题为多选题，合计百分比超过 100%（Multiple answers）

排名 Ranking	考虑因素 Considerations	人次 Person-time	百分比 Percent
1	价格适中 reasonable price	210	50.1
2	使用经验 using experiences	195	46.5
3	产品功用 product function	134	32.0
4	有名的牌子 famous brand	125	29.8
5	购买方便 easy to buy	59	14.1
6	广告影响 influence of advertising	48	11.5
7	有优惠条件 with preferential terms	41	9.8
8	别人推荐 introduced by other people	20	4.8
9	其它 others	10	2.4
10	包装吸引人 appealing package	6	1.4

n=419

4-9 对产品功能的侧重方面/ Ranking of the Considerations about the Function of this Kind of Product

注：本题为多选题，合计百分比超过 100%（Multiple answers）

排名 Ranking	侧重方面 Items	人次 Person-time	百分比 Percent
1	吸水性强 high water-absorbility	262	62.8
2	触感舒适 comfortable to touch	216	51.8
2	有护翼 wing or not	216	51.8
3	透气性强 with good ventilation	155	37.2
4	有隔离网面 mesh	64	15.3
5	粘帖牢固 safety	53	12.7
6	有凹槽 with notch	43	10.3
7	其他 others	3	0.7

n=417

4-10 样本、女性各年龄层白天最常使用的类型/ Types of the Consumed Napkins in the Daytime by the Female Sample and Age Groups

	人数 Number	普通型 regular	普通加长型 XL regular	普通护翼型 regular wings	加长护翼型 XL wings	丝薄型 ultra slim	其他 others
女性 Female	409	36.2	7.1	38.4	6.1	12.2	0.0
16~24 岁 Age	102	23.5	7.8	44.1	7.8	16.7	0.0
25~34 岁 Age	141	29.8	5.7	45.4	5.0	14.2	0.0
35~44 岁 Age	119	51.3	6.7	26.1	5.9	10.1	0.0
45~54 岁 Age	47	44.7	10.6	36.2	6.4	2.1	0.0
55~60 岁 Age	0	0.0	0.0	0.0	0.0	0.0	0.0

4-11 样本、女性各年龄层夜间最常使用的类型/ Types of the Consumed Napkins at Night by the Female Sample and Age Groups

	人数 Number	普通型 regular	普通加长型 XL regular	普通护翼型 regular wings	加长护翼型 XL wings	丝薄型 ultra slim	其他 others
女性 Female	408	10.8	10.3	13.2	59.6	5.1	1.0
16~24 岁 Age	103	3.9	5.8	9.7	73.8	4.9	1.9
25~34 岁 Age	138	6.5	8.0	13.0	67.4	3.6	1.4
35~44 岁 Age	120	16.7	15.0	15.8	44.2	8.3	0.0
45~54 岁 Age	47	23.4	14.9	14.9	44.7	2.1	0.0
55~60 岁 Age	0	0.0	0.0	0.0	0.0	0.0	0.0

4-12 样本、女性各年龄层使用其他卫生用品的比例/ Proportion of the Female Consumed Others

注：本题为多选题，合计百分比超过 100%（Multiple answers）

	人次 Person-time	卫生棉条 cotton pads	卫生护垫 panty shields	以上都不用 none of above	其他 others
女性 Female	473	9.1	63.0	33.8	1.1
16~24 岁 Age	107	1.9	83.2	15.9	0.9
25~34 岁 Age	148	12.2	68.9	28.4	0.0
35~44 岁 Age	120	13.3	65.8	30.8	2.5
45~54 岁 Age	71	7.0	38.0	56.3	1.4
55~60 岁 Age	27	7.4	3.7	88.9	0.0

4-13 重度消费者的人口分布/ Demographics of the Heavy Consumers

	人数 Number	16-24 岁 Age	25-34 岁 Age	35-44 岁 Age	45-54 岁 Age	55-60 岁 Age
女性 Female	299	26.4	35.8	27.4	10.4	0.0
30 片以上 over 30 pieces	24	25.0	33.3	25.0	16.7	0.0
21-30 片 21-30 pieces	75	32.0	34.7	28.0	5.3	0.0
11-20 片 11-20 pieces	200	24.5	36.5	27.5	11.5	0.0

4-14 不同消费者层的常用品牌/ The Most Frequently Used Brands by Market Segments

4-14-1 时尚流行指标/ Fads Popular Index

	人数 Number	第一品牌及百分比 1st/ percent	第二品牌及百分比 2nd/ percent	第三品牌及百分比 3rd/ percent	第四品牌及百分比 4th/ percent
女性 Female	411	护舒宝 Whisper(23.6)	舒而美 Comfort & Beauty(22.9)	娇爽 Carefree(12.9)	苏菲 Sofy(9.7)
平实生活指向 simple living orientation	165	舒而美 Comfort & Beauty(25.5)	护舒宝 Whisper(23.6)	安尔乐 An'erle(9.1)	苏菲 Sofy(8.5) 娇爽 Carefree(8.5)
时尚流行指向 fashion orientation	246	护舒宝 Whisper(23.6)	舒而美 Comfort & Beauty(21.1)	娇爽 Carefree(15.9)	苏菲 Sofy(10.6)

4-14-2 广告态度指标/ Advertising Attitude Index

	人数 Number	第一品牌及百分比 1st/ percent	第二品牌及百分比 2nd/ percent	第三品牌及百分比 3rd/ percent	第四品牌及百分比 4th/ percent
女性 Female	407	护舒宝 Whisper(24.1)	舒而美 Comfort & Beauty(22.1)	娇爽 Carefree(13.0)	苏菲 Sofy(9.3)
广告淡漠指向 indifferent orientation	91	护舒宝 Whisper(24.2)	舒而美 Comfort & Beauty(20.9)	娇爽 Carefree(12.1)	高洁丝 Kotex(11.0)
中间层 medium	245	护舒宝 Whisper(23.3)	舒而美 Comfort & Beauty(20.8)	娇爽 Carefree(14.7)	苏菲 Sofy(11.0)
信赖广告指向 loyal orientation	71	舒而美 Comfort & Beauty(28.2)	护舒宝 Whisper(26.8)	苏菲 Sofy(9.9)	一片云 Soft Cloud(8.5) 娇爽 Carefree(8.5)

4-15 重度消费者的消费层构成/ The Composition of the Heavy Consumers

4-15-1 时尚流行指标/ Fads Popular Index

	人数 Number	平实生活指向 simple living orientation	时尚流行指向 fashion orientation
女性 Female	**294**	**39.8**	**60.2**
30 片以上 over 30 pieces	23	26.1	73.9
21-30 片 21-30 pieces	75	34.7	65.3
11-20 片 11-20 pieces	196	43.4	56.6

4-15-2 广告态度指标/ Advertising Attitude Index

	人数 Number	广告淡漠指向 indifferent orientation	中间层 medium	信赖广告指向 loyal orientation
女性 Female	**293**	**20.8**	**61.8**	**17.4**
30 片以上 over 30 pieces	24	16.7	62.5	20.8
21-30 片 21-30 pieces	74	23.0	63.5	13.5
11-20 片 11-20 pieces	195	20.5	61.0	18.5

● 上海 / Shanghai

4-1 最近一次使用量的比例/ Proportion of the Sample Consuming Napkins Last Time

	人数 Number	百分比 Percent
30 片以上 over 30 pieces	19	3.8
21-30 片 21-30 pieces	64	12.8
11-20 片 11-20 pieces	222	44.4
10 片及以下 10 pieces or below	127	25.4
没有用 not use	68	13.6

n=500

4-2 最常用品牌排名/ Ranking of the Most Frequently Used Brands

排名 Brand Ranking	品牌 Brands	人数 Number	百分比 Percent
1	护舒宝 Whisper	138	31.9
2	苏菲 Sofy	97	22.5
3	娇爽 Carefree	82	19.0
4	唯尔福 Welcare	39	9.0
5	安尔乐 An'erle	14	3.2
6	安乐 Anle	13	3.0
7	乐而雅 Laurier	12	2.8
8	佳期 Godcare	9	2.1
8	柔柔 Soft	9	2.1
9	兰花棉 Hactie	4	0.9
10	娇柔 Jiaorou	3	0.7

n=432

4-3 样本、女性各年龄层的常用品牌/ The Most Frequently Used Brands by the Female Sample and Age Groups

	人数 Number	第一品牌及百分比 1st/ percent	第二品牌及百分比 2nd/ percent	第三品牌及百分比 3rd/ percent
女性 Female	**432**	**护舒宝 Whisper(31.9)**	**苏菲 Sofy(22.5)**	**娇爽 Carefree(19.0)**
16~24 岁 Age	105	护舒宝 Whisper(36.2)	娇爽 Carefree(24.8)	苏菲 Sofy(21.0)
25~34 岁 Age	140	护舒宝 Whisper(31.4)	娇爽 Carefree(23.6)	苏菲 Sofy(21.4)
35~44 岁 Age	124	护舒宝 Whisper(33.1)	苏菲 Sofy(26.6)	唯尔福 Welcare(10.5) 娇爽 Carefree(10.5)
45~54 岁 Age	61	护舒宝 Whisper(23.0)	苏菲 Sofy(18.0)	娇爽 Carefree(16.4) 唯尔福 Welcare(16.4)
55~60 岁 Age	2	护舒宝 Whisper(50.0) 苏菲 Sofy(50.0)		

4-4 正在使用的品牌排名/ Ranking of the Brands Used Now

排名 Brand Ranking	品牌 Brands	人数 Number	百分比 Percent
1	护舒宝 Whisper	129	29.9
2	苏菲 Sofy	100	23.1
3	娇爽 Carefree	78	18.1
4	唯尔福 Welcare	38	8.8
5	乐而雅 Laurier	16	3.7
6	安尔乐 An'erle	13	3.0
6	佳期 Godcare	13	3.0
7	安乐 Anle	11	2.5
8	柔柔 Soft	8	1.9

n=432

4-5 品牌转换习惯/ Brand Habit in Consuming Napkins

	人数 Number	第一次使用该品牌 first use this brand	上一次也是这个牌子 used it last time	上一次不是这个牌子 not used it last time
女性 Female	430	4.4	87.7	7.9
护舒宝 Whisper	128	2.3	93.0	4.7
苏菲 Sofy	100	4.0	88.0	8.0
娇爽 Carefree	78	2.6	91.0	6.4
唯尔福 Welcare	38	7.9	86.8	5.3
乐而雅 Laurier	16	12.5	81.3	6.3

4-6 下一次打算使用的品牌排名/ Ranking of the Brands to be Used Next Time

排名 Brand Ranking	品牌 Brands	人数 Number	百分比 Percent
1	护舒宝 Whisper	145	33.6
2	苏菲 Sofy	101	23.4
3	娇爽 Carefree	89	20.6
4	唯尔福 Welcare	28	6.5
5	乐而雅 Laurier	14	3.2
6	安尔乐 An'erle	12	2.8
7	安乐 Anle	10	2.3
8	佳期 Godcare	7	1.6
8	柔柔 Soft	7	1.6

n=431

4-7 样本、女性各年龄层的最近一次的使用量/ Pieces of the Consumed Napkins Last Time by the Female Sample and Age Groups

	人数 Number	30 片以上 over 30 pieces	21-30 片 21-30 pieces	11-20 片 11-20 pieces	10 片及以下 10 pieces or below	没有用 not use
女性 Female	500	3.8	12.8	44.4	25.4	13.6
16~24 岁 Age	106	1.9	21.7	48.1	27.4	0.9
25~34 岁 Age	144	3.5	14.6	53.5	25.7	2.8
35~44 岁 Age	129	3.9	10.9	51.2	30.2	3.9
45~54 岁 Age	81	7.4	7.4	34.6	25.9	24.7
55~60 岁 Age	40	2.5	0.0	0.0	2.5	95.0

4-8 选择该类商品的考虑因素/ Ranking of the Considerations in Purchasing

注：本题为多选题，合计百分比超过 100%（Multiple answers）

排名 Ranking	考虑因素 Considerations	人次 Person-time	百分比 Percent
1	使用经验 using experiences	186	43.4
2	价格适中 reasonable price	182	42.4
3	产品功用 product function	147	34.3
4	有名的牌子 famous brand	136	31.7
5	购买方便 easy to buy	75	17.5
6	广告影响 influence of advertising	57	13.3
7	有优惠条件 with preferential terms	36	8.4
8	其它 others	19	4.4
9	别人推荐 introduced by other people	18	4.2
10	包装吸引人 appealing package	12	2.8

n=429

4-9 对产品功能的侧重方面/ Ranking of the Considerations about the Function of this Kind of Product

注：本题为多选题，合计百分比超过 100%（Multiple answers）

排名 Ranking	侧重方面 Items	人次 Person-time	百分比 Percent
1	吸水性强 high water-absorbility	305	70.8
2	有护翼 wing or not	203	47.1
3	触感舒适 comfortable to touch	193	44.8
4	透气性强 with good ventilation	177	41.1
5	有凹槽 with notch	59	13.7
6	有隔离网面 mesh	56	13.0
7	粘帖牢固 safety	48	11.1
8	其他 others	9	2.1

n=431

4-10 样本、女性各年龄层白天最常使用的类型/ Types of the Consumed Napkins in the Daytime by the Female Sample and Age Groups

	人数 Number	普通型 regular	普通加长型 XL regular	普通护翼型 regular wings	加长护翼型 XL wings	丝薄型 ultra slim	其他 others
女性 Female	430	41.9	7.0	35.1	3.0	12.8	0.2
16~24 岁 Age	105	27.6	3.8	41.0	1.9	24.8	1.0
25~34 岁 Age	139	36.0	5.8	43.2	4.3	10.8	0.0
35~44 岁 Age	124	54.8	8.1	26.6	2.4	8.1	0.0
45~54 岁 Age	60	55.0	13.3	21.7	3.3	6.7	0.0
55~60 岁 Age	2	0.0	0.0	100.0	0.0	0.0	0.0

4-11 样本、女性各年龄层夜间最常使用的类型/ Types of the Consumed Napkins at Night by the Female Sample and Age Groups

	人数 Number	普通型 regular	普通加长型 XL regular	普通护翼型 regular wings	加长护翼型 XL wings	丝薄型 ultra slim	其他 others
女性 Female	430	12.1	12.1	12.3	59.5	3.7	0.2
16~24 岁 Age	105	4.8	6.7	13.3	66.7	8.6	0.0
25~34 岁 Age	140	5.0	10.7	10.0	72.9	1.4	0.0
35~44 岁 Age	124	17.7	18.5	13.7	46.8	3.2	0.0
45~54 岁 Age	59	30.5	11.9	13.6	40.7	1.7	1.7
55~60 岁 Age	2	0.0	0.0	0.0	100.0	0.0	0.0

4-12 样本、女性各年龄层使用其他卫生用品的比例/ Proportion of the Female Consuming Others

注：本题为多选题，合计百分比超过 100%（Multiple answers）

	人次 Person-time	卫生棉条 cotton pads	卫生护垫 panty shields	以上都不用 none of above	其他 others
女性 Female	489	10.4	53.2	39.7	1.2
16~24 岁 Age	106	9.4	74.5	22.6	0.9
25~34 岁 Age	144	16.0	65.3	23.6	0.7
35~44 岁 Age	128	12.5	47.7	41.4	1.6
45~54 岁 Age	79	1.3	30.4	67.1	2.5
55~60 岁 Age	32	3.1	6.3	93.8	0.0

4-13 重度消费者的人口分布/ Demographics of the Heavy Consumers

	人数 Number	16-24 岁 Age	25-34 岁 Age	35-44 岁 Age	45-54 岁 Age	55-60 岁 Age
女性 Female	305	24.9	33.8	27.9	13.1	0.3
30 片以上 over 30 pieces	19	10.5	26.3	26.3	31.6	5.3
21-30 片 21-30 pieces	64	35.9	32.8	21.9	9.4	0.0
11-20 片 11-20 pieces	222	23.0	34.7	29.7	12.6	0.0

4-14 不同消费者层的常用品牌/ The Most Frequently Used Brands by Market Segments

4-14-1 时尚流行指标/ Fads Popular Index

	人数 Number	第一品牌及百分比 1st/ percent	第二品牌及百分比 2nd/ percent	第三品牌及百分比 3rd/ percent
女性 Female	429	护舒宝 Whisper（32.2）	苏菲 Sofy（22.4）	娇爽 Carefree（18.9）
平实生活指向 simple living orientation	175	护舒宝 Whisper（25.1）	唯尔福 Welcare（17.7）	苏菲 Sofy（17.1）
时尚流行指向 fashion orientation	254	护舒宝 Whisper（37.0）	苏菲 Sofy（26.0）	娇爽 Carefree（20.5）

4-14-2 广告态度指标/ Advertising Attitude Index

	人数 Number	第一品牌及百分比 1st/ percent	第二品牌及百分比 2nd/ percent	第三品牌及百分比 3rd/ percent
女性 Female	429	**护舒宝 Whisper（31.9）**	**苏菲 Sofy（22.4）**	**娇爽 Carefree（18.9）**
广告淡漠指向 indifferent orientation	101	护舒宝 Whisper（32.7）	苏菲 Sofy（19.8）	娇爽 Carefree（13.9）
中间层 medium	260	护舒宝 Whisper（31.9）	娇爽 Carefree（21.5）	苏菲 Sofy（20.4）
信赖广告指向 loyal orientation	68	苏菲 Sofy（33.8）	护舒宝 Whisper（30.9）	娇爽 Carefree（16.2）

4-15 重度消费者的消费层构成/ The Composition of the Heavy Consumers

4-15-1 时尚流行指标/ Fads Popular Index

	人数 Number	平实生活指向 simple living orientation	时尚流行指向 fashion orientation
女性 Female	302	36.4	63.6
30 片以上 over 30 pieces	19	26.3	73.7
21-30 片 21-30 pieces	63	42.9	57.1
11-20 片 11-20 pieces	220	35.5	64.5

4-15-2 广告态度指标/ Advertising Attitude Index

	人数 Number	广告淡漠指向 indifferent orientation	中间层 medium	信赖广告指向 loyal orientation
女性 Female	303	22.1	60.7	17.2
30 片以上 over 30 pieces	19	21.1	52.6	26.3
21-30 片 21-30 pieces	64	20.3	62.5	17.2
11-20 片 11-20 pieces	220	22.7	60.9	16.4

● 广州 / Guangzhou

4-1 最近一次使用量的比例/ Proportion of the Sample Consuming Napkins Last Time

	人数 Number	百分比 Percent
30 片以上 over 30 pieces	22	4.2
21-30 片 21-30 pieces	80	15.3
11-20 片 11-20 pieces	240	45.9
10 片及以下 10 pieces or below	117	22.4
没有用 not use	64	12.2

n=523

4-2 最常用品牌排名/ Ranking of the Most Frequently Used Brands

排名 Brand Ranking	品牌 Brands	人数 Number	百分比 Percent
1	护舒宝 Whisper	187	40.8
2	娇爽 Carefree	60	13.1
3	安尔乐 An'erle	42	9.2
4	苏菲 Sofy	34	7.4
4	乐而雅 Laurier	34	7.4
5	安乐 Anle	28	6.1
6	妇康 Fukang	25	5.5

n=458

4-3 样本、女性各年龄层的常用品牌/ The Most Frequently Used Brands by the Female Sample and Age Groups

	人数 Number	第一品牌及百分比 1st/ percent	第二品牌及百分比 2nd/ percent	第三品牌及百分比 3rd/ percent	第四品牌及百分比 4th/ percent
女性 Female	458	**护舒宝 Whisper(40.8)**	**娇爽 Carefree(13.1)**	**安尔乐 An'erle(9.2)**	**苏菲 Sofy(7.4)** **乐而雅 Laurier(7.4)**
16~24 岁 Age	107	护舒宝 Whisper(42.1)	苏菲 Sofy(14.0)	娇爽 Carefree(12.1) 乐而雅 Laurier(12.1)	安尔乐 An'erle(8.4)
25~34 岁 Age	155	护舒宝 Whisper(41.9)	娇爽 Carefree(15.5)	安尔乐 An'erle(12.3)	妇康 Fukang(5.8)
35~44 岁 Age	131	护舒宝 Whisper(39.7)	娇爽 Carefree(10.7)	安乐 Anle(9.9)	乐而雅 Laurier(8.4)
45~54 岁 Age	61	护舒宝 Whisper(41.0)	娇爽 Carefree(13.1)	安乐 Anle(11.5)	安尔乐 An'erle(9.8) 妇康 Fukang(9.8)
55~60 岁 Age	4	安乐 Anle(25.0) 乐芙爽 Love Some(25.0) 娇爽 Carefree(25.0) 苏菲 Sofy(25.0)			

4-4 正在使用的品牌排名/ Ranking of the Brands Used Now

排名 Brand Ranking	品牌 Brands	人数 Number	百分比 Percent
1	护舒宝 Whisper	172	37.7
2	苏菲 Sofy	55	12.1
3	娇爽 Carefree	52	11.4
4	安尔乐 An'erle	45	9.9
5	乐而雅 Laurier	33	7.2
6	安乐 Anle	26	5.7
7	妇康 Fukang	25	5.5

n=456

4-5 品牌转换习惯/ Brand Habit in Consuming Napkins

	人数 Number	第一次使用该品牌 first use this brand	上一次也是这个牌子 used it last time	上一次不是这个牌子 not used it last time
女性 Female	456	8.3	82.2	9.4
护舒宝 Whisper	172	3.5	85.5	11.0
苏菲 Sofy	55	25.5	67.3	7.3
娇爽 Carefree	52	3.8	88.5	7.7
安尔乐 An'erle	45	6.7	82.2	11.1
乐而雅 Laurier	33	3.0	90.9	6.1
安乐 Anle	26	11.5	80.8	7.7
妇康 Fukang	25	4.0	84.0	12.0

4-6 下一次打算使用的品牌排名/ Ranking of the Brands to be Used Next Time

排名 Brand Ranking	品牌 Brands	人数 Number	百分比 Percent
1	护舒宝 Whisper	172	37.5
2	苏菲 Sofy	62	13.5
3	娇爽 Carefree	51	11.1
4	安尔乐 An'erle	33	7.2
5	乐而雅 Laurier	30	6.5
6	妇康 Fukang	23	5.0
7	安乐 Anle	22	4.8

n=459

4-7 样本、女性各年龄层最近一次的使用量/ Pieces of the Consumed Napkins Last time by the Female Sample and Age Groups

	人数 Number	30 片以上 over 30 pieces	21-30 片 21-30 pieces	11-20 片 11-20 pieces	10 片及以下 10 pieces or below	没有用 not use
女性 Female	523	4.2	15.3	45.9	22.4	12.2
16~24 岁 Age	110	6.4	21.8	47.3	21.8	2.7
25~34 岁 Age	157	3.2	18.5	54.8	22.9	0.6
35~44 岁 Age	134	5.2	17.9	52.2	22.4	2.2
45~54 岁 Age	85	3.5	3.5	35.3	29.4	28.2
55~60 岁 Age	37	0.0	0.0	5.4	5.4	89.2

4-8 选择该类商品的考虑因素/ Ranking of the Considerations in Purchasing

注：本题为多选题，合计百分比超过 100%（Multiple answers）

排名 Ranking	考虑因素 Considerations	人次 Person-time	百分比 Percent
1	使用经验 using experiences	212	46.4
2	价格适中 reasonable price	206	45.1
3	有名的牌子 famous brand	163	35.7
4	产品功用 product function	162	35.4
5	购买方便 easy to buy	84	18.4
6	广告影响 influence of advertising	52	11.4
7	有优惠条件 with preferential terms	30	6.6
8	别人推荐 introduced by other people	25	5.5
9	包装吸引人 appealing package	18	3.9
10	其它 others	5	1.1

n=457

4-9 对产品功能的侧重方面/ Ranking of the Considerations about the Function of this Kind of Product

注：本题为多选题，合计百分比超过 100%（Multiple answers）

排名 Ranking	侧重方面 Items	人次 Person-time	百分比 Percent
1	吸水性强 high water-absorbability	334	73.4
2	有护翼 wing or not	260	57.1
3	触感舒适 comfortable to touch	219	48.1
4	透气性强 with good ventilation	171	37.6
5	有隔离网面 mesh	52	11.4
6	粘帖牢固 safety	41	9.0
7	有凹槽 with notch	39	8.6
8	其他 others	3	0.7

n=455

4-10 样本、女性各年龄层白天最常使用的类型/ Types of the Consumed Napkins in the Daytime by the Female Sample and Age Groups

	人数 Number	普通型 regular	普通加长型 XL regular	普通护翼型 regular wings	加长护翼型 XL wings	丝薄型 ultra slim	其他 others
女性 Female	454	26.7	7.9	40.7	5.5	18.9	0.2
16~24 岁 Age	107	18.7	5.6	45.8	4.7	24.3	0.9
25~34 岁 Age	154	24.0	7.1	46.1	6.5	16.2	0.0
35~44 岁 Age	128	29.7	9.4	35.2	5.5	20.3	0.0
45~54 岁 Age	61	39.3	11.5	31.1	4.9	13.1	0.0
55~60 岁 Age	4	50.0	0.0	25.0	0.0	25.0	0.0

4-11 样本、女性各年龄层夜间最常使用的类型/ Types of the Consumed Napkins at Night by the Female Sample and Age Groups

	人数 Number	普通型 regular	普通加长型 XL regular	普通护翼型 regular wings	加长护翼型 XL wings	丝薄型 ultra slim	其他 others
女性 Female	455	7.7	8.6	13.0	65.9	4.2	0.7
16~24 岁 Age	107	1.9	8.4	7.5	73.8	6.5	1.9
25~34 岁 Age	154	7.1	6.5	9.7	73.4	2.6	0.6
35~44 岁 Age	129	6.2	9.3	17.8	62.8	3.9	0.0
45~54 岁 Age	61	21.3	13.1	19.7	41.0	4.9	0.0
55~60 岁 Age	4	25.0	0.0	25.0	50.0	0.0	0.0

4-12 样本、女性各年龄层使用其他卫生用品的比例/ Proportion of the Female Consumed Others

注：本题为多选题，合计百分比超过 100%（Multiple answers）

	人次 Person-time	卫生棉条 cotton pads	卫生护垫 panty shields	以上都不用 none of above	其他 others
女性 Female	510	5.5	52.0	44.5	0.6
16~24 岁 Age	111	4.5	59.5	37.8	0.9
25~34 岁 Age	156	5.8	61.5	34.6	0.6
35~44 岁 Age	135	5.2	54.8	42.2	0.0
45~54 岁 Age	78	6.4	37.2	59.0	1.3
55~60 岁 Age	30	6.7	0.0	93.3	0.0

4-13 重度消费者的人口分布/ Demographics of the Heavy Consumers

	人数 Number	16-24 岁 Age	25-34 岁 Age	35-44 岁 Age	45-54 岁 Age	55-60 岁 Age
女性 Female	342	24.3	35.1	29.5	10.5	0.6
30 片以上 over 30 pieces	22	31.8	22.7	31.8	13.6	0.0
21-30 片 21-30 pieces	80	30.0	36.3	30.0	3.8	0.0
11-20 片 11-20 pieces	240	21.7	35.8	29.2	12.5	0.8

4-14 不同消费者层的常用品牌/ The Most Frequently Used Brands by Market Segments

4-14-1 时尚流行指标/ Fads Popular Index

	人数 Number	第一品牌及百分比 1st/ percent	第二品牌及百分比 2nd/ percent	第三品牌及百分比 3rd/ percent	第四品牌及百分比 4th/ percent
女性 Female	452	护舒宝 Whisper(40.5)	娇爽 Carefree(13.3)	安尔乐 An'erle(9.1)	苏菲 Sofy(7.5) 乐而雅 Laurier(7.5)
平实生活指向 simple living orientation	190	护舒宝 Whisper(41.1)	娇爽 Carefree(12.6)	安尔乐 An'erle(8.4) 妇康 Fukang(8.4)	安乐 Anle(7.4) 乐而雅 Laurier(7.4)
时尚流行指向 fashion orientation	262	护舒宝 Whisper(40.1)	娇爽 Carefree(13.7)	安尔乐 An'erle(9.5)	苏菲 Sofy(9.2)

4-14-2 广告态度指标/ Advertising Attitude Index

	人数 Number	第一品牌及百分比 1st/ percent	第二品牌及百分比 2nd/ percent	第三品牌及百分比 3rd/ percent	第四品牌及百分比 4th/ percent
女性 Female	**452**	**护舒宝 Whisper(40.7)**	**娇爽 Carefree(13.1)**	**安尔乐 An'erle(9.3)**	**乐而雅 Laurier(7.5)**
广告淡漠指向 indifferent orientation	125	护舒宝 Whisper(39.2)	娇爽 Carefree(16.0)	安尔乐 An'erle(8.0) 苏菲 Sofy(8.0)	安乐 Anle(6.4)
中间层 medium	282	护舒宝 Whisper(40.8)	娇爽 Carefree(12.8)	乐而雅 Laurier(8.5)	安尔乐 An'erle(8.2)
信赖广告指向 loyal orientation	45	护舒宝 Whisper(44.4)	安尔乐 An'erle(20.0)	乐而雅 Laurier(11.1)	苏菲 Sofy(8.9)

4-15 重度消费者的消费层构成/ The Composition of the Heavy Consumers

4-15-1 时尚流行指标/ Fads Popular Index

	人数 Number	平实生活指向 simple living orientation	时尚流行指向 fashion orientation
女性 Female	**337**	**41.2**	**58.8**
30 片以上 over 30 pieces	22	31.8	68.2
21-30 片 21-30 pieces	80	37.5	62.5
11-20 片 11-20 pieces	235	43.4	56.6

4-15-2 广告态度指标/ Advertising Attitude Index

	人数 Number	广告淡漠指向 indifferent orientation	中间层 medium	信赖广告指向 loyal orientation
女性 Female	**339**	**27.4**	**62.2**	**10.3**
30 片以上 over 30 pieces	22	9.1	77.3	13.6
21-30 片 21-30 pieces	80	18.8	68.8	12.5
11-20 片 11-20 pieces	237	32.1	58.5	9.3

● 重庆 / Chongqing

4-1 最近一次使用量的比例/ Proportion of the Sample Consuming Napkins Last Time

	人数 Number	百分比 Percent
30 片以上 over 30 pieces	1	0.3
21-30 片 21-30 pieces	11	3.6
11-20 片 11-20 pieces	112	36.2
10 片及以下 10 pieces or below	127	41.1
没有用 not use	58	18.8

n=309

4-2 最常用品牌排名/ Ranking of the Most Frequently Used Brands

排名 Brand Ranking	品牌 Brands	人数 Number	百分比 Percent
1	舒而美 Comfort & Beauty	107	43.0
2	护舒宝 Whisper	76	30.5
3	安尔乐 An'erle	13	5.2
4	高洁丝 Kotex	11	4.4
5	舒婷 Shuting	6	2.4
6	娇爽 Carefree	4	1.6
6	美洁 Meijie	4	1.6
6	安乐 Anle	4	1.6
7	洁婷 Ludu eaze	3	1.2

n=249

4-3 样本、女性各年龄层的常用品牌/ The Most Frequently Used Brands by the Female Sample and Age Groups

	人数 Number	第一品牌及百分比 1st/ percent	第二品牌及百分比 2nd/ percent	第三品牌及百分比 3rd/ percent	第四品牌及百分比 4th/ percent
女性 Female	249	**舒而美 Comfort & Beauty(43.0)**	**护舒宝 Whisper(30.5)**	**安尔乐 An'erle(5.2)**	**高洁丝 Kotex(4.4)**
16~24 岁 Age	61	护舒宝 Whisper(47.5)	舒而美 Comfort & Beauty(26.2)	高洁丝 Kotex(6.6)	芬兰馨 Fenlanxin(3.3) 美洁 Meijie(3.3) 娇爽 Carefree(3.3)
25~34 岁 Age	88	舒而美 Comfort & Beauty(44.3)	护舒宝 Whisper(30.7)	安尔乐 An'erle(6.8)	高洁丝 Kotex(4.5)
35~44 岁 Age	72	舒而美 Comfort & Beauty(51.4)	护舒宝 Whisper(18.1)	安尔乐 An'erle(8.3)	舒婷 Shuting(4.2)
45~54 岁 Age	28	舒而美 Comfort & Beauty(53.6)	护舒宝 Whisper(25.0)	妮丝爽 Nisishuang(7.1) 舒婷 Shuting(7.1)	高洁丝 Kotex(3.6) 乐芙爽 Love Some(3.6)
55~60 岁 Age	0				

4-4 正在使用的品牌排名/ Ranking of the Brands Used Now

排名 Brand Ranking	品牌 Brands	人数 Number	百分比 Percent
1	舒而美 Comfort & Beauty	99	39.4
2	护舒宝 Whisper	72	28.7
3	高洁丝 Kotex	15	6.0
4	安尔乐 An'erle	13	5.2
5	洁婷 Ludu caze	9	3.6
6	舒婷 Shuting	6	2.4
7	美洁 Meijie	5	2.0
8	娇爽 Carefree	4	1.6
8	乐芙爽 Love Some	4	1.6

n=251

4-5 品牌转换习惯/ Brand Habit in Consuming Napkins

	人数 Number	第一次使用该品牌 first use this brand	上一次也是这个牌子 used it last time	上一次不是这个牌子 not used it last time
女性 Female	250	8.4	80.4	11.2
舒而美 Comfort & Beauty	99	4.0	91.9	4.0
护舒宝 Whisper	71	2.8	85.9	11.3
高洁丝 Kotex	15	20.0	66.7	13.3
安尔乐 An'erle	13	7.7	61.5	30.8
洁婷 Ludu caze	9	33.3	44.4	22.2

4-6 下一次打算使用的品牌排名/ Ranking of the Brands to be Used Next Time

排名 Brand Ranking	品牌 Brands	人数 Number	百分比 Percent
1	舒而美 Comfort & Beauty	93	37.1
2	护舒宝 Whisper	86	34.3
3	高洁丝 Kotex	15	6.0
4	安尔乐 An'erle	10	4.0
5	娇爽 Carefree	7	2.8
5	舒婷 Shuting	7	2.8
6	洁婷 Ludu caze	6	2.4
7	美洁 Meijie	3	1.2
7	芬兰馨 Fenlanxin	3	1.2
8	舒美 Shumei	2	0.8
8	乐芙爽 Love Some	2	0.8

n=251

4-7 样本、女性各年龄层最近一次的使用量/ Pieces of the Consumed Napkins Last Time by the Female Sample and Age Groups

	人数 Number	30 片以上 over 30 pieces	21-30 片 21-30 pieces	11-20 片 11-20 pieces	10 片及以下 10 pieces or below	没有用 not use
女性 Female	309	0.3	3.6	36.2	41.1	18.8
16~24 岁 Age	64	0.0	6.3	51.6	39.1	3.1
25~34 岁 Age	89	1.1	3.4	46.1	49.4	0.0
35~44 岁 Age	73	0.0	4.1	34.2	60.3	1.4
45~54 岁 Age	60	0.0	1.7	21.7	23.3	53.3
55~60 岁 Age	23	0.0	0.0	0.0	0.0	100.0

4-8 选择该类商品的考虑因素/ Ranking of the Considerations in Purchasing

注：本题为多选题，合计百分比超过 100%（Multiple answers）

排名 Ranking	考虑因素 Considerations	人次 Person-time	百分比 Percent
1	价格适中 reasonable price	123	49.0
2	使用经验 using experiences	114	45.4
3	产品功用 product function	83	33.1
4	有名的牌子 famous brand	59	23.5
5	购买方便 easy to buy	42	16.7
6	广告影响 influence of advertising	28	11.2
7	有优惠条件 with preferential terms	15	6.0
7	别人推荐 introduced by other people	15	6.0
8	包装吸引人 appealing package	4	1.6
9	其它 others	1	0.4

n=251

4-9 对产品功能的侧重方面/ Ranking of the Considerations about the Function of this Kind of Product

注：本题为多选题，合计百分比超过 100%（Multiple answers）

排名 Ranking	侧重方面 Items	人次 Person-time	百分比 Percent
1	吸水性强 high water-absorbility	194	77.6
2	有护翼 wing or not	108	43.2
3	触感舒适 comfortable to touch	107	42.8
4	透气性强 with good ventilation	78	31.2
5	粘帖牢固 safety	34	13.6
6	有隔离网面 mesh	24	9.6
7	有凹槽 with notch	22	8.8
8	其他 others	4	1.6

n=250

4-10 样本、女性各年龄层白天最常使用的类型/ Types of the Consumed Napkins in the Daytime by the Female Sample and Age Groups

	人数 Number	普通型 regular	普通加长型 XL regular	普通护翼型 regular wings	加长护翼型 XL wings	丝薄型 ultra slim	其他 others
女性 Female	247	38.1	6.9	38.9	4.5	11.3	0.4
16~24 岁 Age	61	18.0	8.2	41.0	8.2	23.0	1.6
25~34 岁 Age	89	29.2	9.0	50.6	5.6	5.6	0.0
35~44 岁 Age	69	56.5	5.8	26.1	1.4	10.1	0.0
45~54 岁 Age	28	64.3	0.0	28.6	0.0	7.1	0.0
55~60 岁 Age	0	0.0	0.0	0.0	0.0	0.0	0.0

4-11 样本、女性各年龄层夜间最常使用的类型/ Types of the Consumed Napkins at Night by the Female Sample and Age Groups

	人数 Number	普通型 regular	普通加长型 XL regular	普通护翼型 regular wings	加长护翼型 XL wings	丝薄型 ultra slim	其他 others
女性 Female	246	10.2	12.2	24.4	45.9	6.9	0.4
16~24 岁 Age	62	1.6	6.5	19.4	62.9	9.7	0.0
25~34 岁 Age	88	11.4	9.1	21.6	50.0	8.0	0.0
35~44 岁 Age	68	13.2	20.6	32.4	27.9	5.9	0.0
45~54 岁 Age	28	17.9	14.3	25.0	39.3	0.0	3.6
55~60 岁 Age	0	0.0	0.0	0.0	0.0	0.0	0.0

4-12 样本、女性各年龄层使用其他卫生用品的比例/ Proportion of the Female Consuming Others

注：本题为多选题，合计百分比超过 100%（Multiple answers）

	人次 Persontime	卫生棉条 cotton pads	卫生护垫 panty shields	以上都不用 none of above	其他 others
女性 Female	293	6.5	39.9	56.0	0.7
16~24 岁 Age	63	3.2	65.1	33.3	1.6
25~34 岁 Age	88	10.2	48.9	46.6	0.0
35~44 岁 Age	73	6.8	28.8	64.4	1.4
45~54 岁 Age	54	3.7	22.2	75.9	0.0
55~60 岁 Age	15	6.7	0.0	93.3	0.0

4-13 重度消费者的人口分布/ Demographics of the Heavy Consumers

	人数 Number	16-24 岁 Age	25-34 岁 Age	35-44 岁 Age	45-54 岁 Age	55-60 岁 Age
女性 Female	124	29.8	36.3	22.6	11.3	0.0
30 片以上 over 30 pieces	1	0.0	100.0	0.0	0.0	0.0
21-30 片 21-30 pieces	11	36.4	27.3	27.3	9.1	0.0
11-20 片 11-20 pieces	112	29.5	36.6	22.3	11.6	0.0

4-14 不同消费者层的常用品牌/ The Most Frequently Used Brands by Market Segments

4-14-1 时尚流行指标/ Fads Popular Index

	人数 Number	第一品牌及百分比 1st/ percent	第二品牌及百分比 2nd/ percent	第三品牌及百分比 3rd/ percent	第四品牌及百分比 4th/ percent
女性 Female	246	舒而美 Comfort&Beauty(43.1)	护舒宝 Whisper(30.1)	安尔乐 An'erle(5.3)	高洁丝 Kotex(4.5)
平实生活指向 simple living orientation	123	舒而美 Comfort & Beauty(52.0)	护舒宝 Whisper(26.8)	高洁丝 Kotex(4.1) 安尔乐 An'erle(4.1)	舒婷 Shuting(2.4)
时尚流行指向 fashion orientation	123	舒而美 Comfort & Beauty(34.1)	护舒宝 Whisper(33.3)	安尔乐 An'erle(6.5)	高洁丝 Kotex(4.9)

4-14-2 广告态度指标/ Advertising Attitude Index

	人数 Number	第一品牌及百分比 1st/ percent	第二品牌及百分比 2nd/ percent	第三品牌及百分比 3rd/ percent	第四品牌及百分比 4th/ percent
女性 Female	245	舒而美 Comfort&Beauty(42.9)	护舒宝 Whisper(31.0)	安尔乐 An'erle(4.5) 高洁丝 Kotex(4.5)	舒婷 Shuting(2.4)
广告淡漠指向 indifferent orientation	50	舒而美 Comfort & Beauty(40.0)	护舒宝 Whisper(30.0)	高洁丝 Kotex(6.0)	乐芙爽 Love Some(4.0) 美洁 Meijie(4.0) 安乐 Anle(4.0)
中间层 medium	159	舒而美 Comfort & Beauty(44.7)	护舒宝 Whisper(31.4)	高洁丝 Kotex(4.4)	安尔乐 An'erle(3.8)
信赖广告指向 loyal orientation	36	舒而美 Comfort & Beauty(38.9)	护舒宝 Whisper(30.6)	安尔乐 An'erle(11.1)	舒婷 Shuting(5.6)

4-15 重度消费者的消费层构成/ The Composition of the Heavy Consumers

4-15-1 时尚流行指标/ Fads Popular Index

	人数 Number	平实生活指向 simple living orientation	时尚流行指向 fashion orientation
女性 Female	122	47.5	52.5
30 片以上 over 30 pieces	1	0.0	100.0
21-30 片 21-30 pieces	11	45.5	54.5
11-20 片 11-20 pieces	110	48.2	51.8

4-15-2 广告态度指标/ Advertising Attitude Index

	人数 Number	广告淡漠指向 indifferent orientation	中间层 medium	信赖广告指向 loyal orientation
女性 Female	121	21.5	62.8	15.7
30 片以上 over 30 pieces	1	0.0	100.0	0.0
21-30 片 21-30 pieces	11	36.4	36.4	27.3
11-20 片 11-20 pieces	109	20.2	65.1	14.7

● 武汉 / Wuhan

4-1 最近一次使用量的比例/ Proportion of the Sample Consuming Napkins Last Time

	人数 Number	百分比 Percent
30 片以上 over 30 pieces	16	4.9
21-30 片 21-30 pieces	43	13.1
11-20 片 11-20 pieces	138	42.1
10 片及以下 10 pieces or below	67	20.4
没有用 not use	64	19.5

n=328

4-2 最常用品牌排名/ Ranking of the Most Frequently Used Brands

排名 Brand Ranking	品牌 Brands	人数 Number	百分比 Percent
1	洁婷 Ludu caze	54	20.5
2	安乐 Anle	42	16.0
3	娇爽 Carefree	40	15.2
4	护舒宝 Whisper	38	14.4
5	安尔乐 An'erle	30	11.4
6	娇丽 Jiaoli	14	5.3
7	舒而美 Comfort & Beauty	10	3.8
8	佳期 Godcare	5	1.9
9	苏菲 Sofy	4	1.5
10	柔爱 Rou'ai	3	1.1

n=263

4-3 样本、女性各年龄层的常用品牌/ The Most Frequently Used Brands by the Female Sample and Age Groups

	人数 Number	第一品牌及百分比 1st/ percent	第二品牌及百分比 2nd/ percent	第三品牌及百分比 3rd/ percent	第四品牌及百分比 4th/ percent
女性 Female	**263**	**洁婷 Ludu caze(20.5)**	**安乐 Anle(16.0)**	**娇爽 Carefree(15.2)**	**护舒宝 Whisper(14.4)**
16~24 岁 Age	69	洁婷 Ludu caze(23.2)	娇爽 Carefree(20.3)	护舒宝 Whisper(17.4)	安尔乐 An'erle(14.5)
25~34 岁 Age	91	洁婷 Ludu caze(20.9)	安乐 Anle(18.7)	娇爽 Carefree(14.3) 护舒宝 Whisper(14.3)	娇丽 Jiaoli(6.6) 安尔乐 An'erle(6.6)
35~44 岁 Age	73	洁婷 Ludu caze(20.5)	安乐 Anle(19.2)	娇爽 Carefree(15.1)	安尔乐 An'erle(13.7)
45~54 岁 Age	30	安乐 Anle(16.7) 护舒宝 Whisper(16.7)	洁婷 Ludu caze(13.3) 安尔乐 An'erle(13.3) 娇丽 Jiaoli(13.3)	娇爽 Carefree(6.7)	新感觉 Xinganjue(3.3) 永芳 Yinfong(3.3) 福而康 Fuerkang(3.3) 舒而美 Comfort & Beauty(3.3) 柔爱 Rou'ai(3.3) 苏菲 Sofy(3.3)
55~60 岁 Age	0				

4-4 正在使用的品牌排名/ Ranking of the Brands Used Now

排名 Brand Ranking	品牌 Brands	人数 Number	百分比 Percent
1	洁婷 Ludu caze	59	22.3
2	娇爽 Carefree	38	14.4
3	安乐 Anle	33	12.5
4	护舒宝 Whisper	31	11.7
5	安尔乐 An'erle	26	9.8
6	娇丽 Jiaoli	16	6.1
7	舒而美 Comfort & Beauty	12	4.5
8	佳期 Godcare	8	3.0
9	苏菲 Sofy	7	2.7

n=264

4-5 品牌转换习惯/ Brand Habit in Consuming Napkins

	人数 Number	第一次使用该品牌 first use this brand	上一次也是这个牌子 used it last time	上一次不是这个牌子 not used it last time
女性 Female	264	8.0	76 1	15.9
洁婷 Ludu caze	59	8.5	71 2	20.3
娇爽 Carefree	38	5.3	73.7	21.1
安乐 Anle	33	0.0	97.0	3.0
护舒宝 Whisper	31	6.5	71.0	22.6
安尔乐 An'erle	26	7.7	80.8	11.5
娇丽 Jiaoli	16	6.3	93.8	0.0
舒而美 Comfort & Beauty	12	0.0	75.0	25.0
佳期 Godcare	8	0.0	75.0	25.0
苏菲 Sofy	7	0.0	85.7	14.3

4-6 下一次打算使用的品牌排名/ Ranking of the Brands to be Used Next Time

排名 Brand Ranking	品牌 Brands	人数 Number	百分比 Percent
1	护舒宝 Whisper	46	17.5
2	娇爽 Carefree	40	15.2
3	洁婷 Ludu caze	39	14.8
4	安乐 Anle	29	11.0
5	安尔乐 An'erle	28	10.6
6	娇丽 Jiaoli	14	5.3
7	苏菲 Sofy	12	4.6
8	舒而美 Comfort & Beauty	10	3.8
9	佳期 Godcare	5	1.9

n=263

4-7 样本、女性各年龄层最近一次的使用量/ Pieces of the Consumed Napkins Last Time by the Female Sample and Age Groups

	人数 Number	30 片以上 30 pieces or above	21-30 片 21-30 pieces	11-20 片 11-20 pieces	10 片及以下 10 pieces or below	没有用 not use
女性 Female	328	4.9	13.1	42.1	20.4	19.5
16~24 岁 Age	69	13.0	18.8	53.6	14.5	0.0
25~34 岁 Age	94	6.4	13.8	56.4	20.2	3.2
35~44 岁 Age	78	0.0	15.4	43.6	34.6	6.4
45~54 岁 Age	61	1.6	8.2	23.0	18.0	49.2
55~60 岁 Age	26	0.0	0.0	0.0	0.0	100.0

4-8 选择该类商品的考虑因素/ Ranking of the Considerations in Purchasing

注：本题为多选题，合计百分比超过 100%（Multiple answers）

排名 Ranking	考虑因素 Considerations	人次 Person-time	百分比 Percent
1	价格适中 reasonable price	149	56.7
2	使用经验 using experiences	103	39.2
2	产品功用 product function	103	39.2
3	有名的牌子 famous brand	69	26.2
4	购买方便 easy to buy	43	16.3
5	广告影响 influence of advertising	37	14.1
6	有优惠条件 with preferential terms	28	10.6
7	别人推荐 introduced by other people	23	8.7
8	其它 others	9	3.4
9	包装吸引人 appealing package	5	1.9

n=263

4-9 对产品功能的侧重方面/ Ranking of the Considerations about the Function of this Kind of Product

注：本题为多选题，合计百分比超过 100%（Multiple answers）

排名 Ranking	侧重方面 Items	人次 Person-time	百分比 Percent
1	吸水性强 high water-absorbility	189	72.1
2	触感舒适 comfortable to touch	139	53.1
3	有护翼 wing or not	121	46.2
4	透气性强 with good ventilation	92	35.1
5	粘帖牢固 safety	39	14.9
6	有凹槽 with notch	33	12.6
7	有隔离网面 mesh	32	12.2
8	其他 others	5	1.9

n=262

4-10 样本、女性各年龄层白天最常使用的类型/ Types of the Consumed Napkins in the Daytime by the Female Sample and Age Groups

	人数 Number	普通型 regular	普通加长型 XL regular	普通护翼型 regular wings	加长护翼型 XL wings	丝薄型 ultra slim	其他 others
女性 Female	262	45.0	11.1	29.0	5.0	9.5	0.4
16~24 岁 Age	69	33.3	5.8	40.6	4.3	14.5	1.4
25~34 岁 Age	90	44.4	14.4	24.4	5.6	11.1	0.0
35~44 岁 Age	72	50.0	12.5	29.2	5.6	2.8	0.0
45~54 岁 Age	31	61.3	9.7	16.1	3.2	9.7	0.0
55~60 岁 Age	0	0.0	0.0	0.0	0.0	0.0	0.0

4-11 样本、女性各年龄层夜间最常使用的类型/ Types of the Consumed Napkins at Night by the Female Sample and Age Groups

	人数 Number	普通型 regular	普通加长型 XL regular	普通护翼型 regular wings	加长护翼型 XL wings	丝薄型 ultra slim	其他 others
女性 Female	261	14.6	6.9	14.2	61.7	2.3	0.4
16~24 岁 Age	69	7.2	5.8	11.6	73.9	1.4	0.0
25~34 岁 Age	89	10.1	3.4	20.2	61.8	4.5	0.0
35~44 岁 Age	72	22.2	9.7	12.5	54.2	0.0	1.4
45~54 岁 Age	31	25.8	12.9	6.5	51.6	3.2	0.0
55~60 岁 Age	0	0.0	0.0	0.0	0.0	0.0	0.0

4-12 样本、女性各年龄层使用其他卫生用品的比例/ Proportion of the Female Consuming Others

注：本题为多选题，合计百分比超过 100%（Multiple answers）

	人次 Person-time	卫生棉条 cotton pads	卫生护垫 panty shields	以上都不用 none of above	其他 others
女性 Female	323	4.0	39.9	54.5	3.4
16~24 岁 Age	68	2.9	67.6	30.9	1.5
25~34 岁 Age	94	4.3	53.2	45.7	1.1
35~44 岁 Age	78	6.4	25.6	61.5	6.4
45~54 岁 Age	58	3.4	22.4	70.7	3.4
55~60 岁 Age	25	0.0	0.0	92.0	8.0

4-13 重度消费者的人口分布/ Demographics of the Heavy Consumers

	人数 Number	16-24 岁 Age	25-34 岁 Age	35-44 岁 Age	45-54 岁 Age	55-60 岁 Age
女性 Female	197	29.9	36.5	23.4	10.2	0.0
30 片以上 over 30 pieces	16	56.3	37.5	0.0	6.3	0.0
21-30 片 21-30 pieces	43	30.2	30.2	27.9	11.6	0.0
11-20 片 11-20 pieces	138	26.8	38.4	24.6	10.1	0.0

4-14 不同消费者层的常用品牌/ The Most Frequently Used Brands by Market Segments

4-14-1 时尚流行指标/ Fads Popular Index

	人数 Number	第一品牌及百分比 1st/ percent	第二品牌及百分比 2nd/ percent	第三品牌及百分比 3rd/ percent	第四品牌及百分比 4th/ percent
女性 Female	260	**洁婷 Ludu caze(20.4)**	**安乐 Anle(16.2)**	**娇爽 Carefree(15.4)**	**护舒宝 Whisper(14.2)**
平实生活指向 simple living orientation	112	安乐 Anle(17.9)	娇爽 Carefree(16.1)	洁婷 Ludu caze(15.2)	安尔乐 An'erle(14.3)
时尚流行指向 fashion orientation	148	洁婷 Ludu caze(24.3)	护舒宝 Whisper(16.2)	安乐 Anle(14.9) 娇爽 Carefree(14.9)	安尔乐 An'erle(9.5)

4-14-2 广告态度指标/ Advertising Attitude Index

	人数 Number	第一品牌及百分比 1st/ percent	第二品牌及百分比 2nd/ percent	第三品牌及百分比 3rd/ percent	第四品牌及百分比 4th/ percent
女性 Female	260	**洁婷 Ludu caze(20.4)**	**安乐 Anle(16.2)**	**娇爽 Carefree(15.4)**	**护舒宝 Whisper(14.2)**
广告淡漠指向 indifferent orientation	66	安乐 Anle(21.2)	洁婷 Ludu caze(18.2)	护舒宝 Whisper(16.7)	娇爽 Carefree(10.6)
中间层 medium	158	洁婷 Ludu caze(20.9)	娇爽 Carefree(17.7)	安乐 Anle(14.6)	安尔乐 An'erle(13.3) 护舒宝 Whisper(13.3)
信赖广告指向 loyal orientation	36	洁婷 Ludu caze(22.2)	娇爽 Carefree(13.9) 安乐 Anle(13.9) 护舒宝 Whisper(13.9)	安尔乐 An'erle(11.1)	舒而美 Comfort & Beauty(5.6)

4-15 重度消费者的消费层构成/ The Composition of the Heavy Consumers

4-15-1 时尚流行指标/ Fads Popular Index

	人数 Number	平实生活指向 simple living orientation	时尚流行指向 fashion orientation
女性 Female	195	41.5	58.5
30 片以上 over 30 pieces	16	50.0	50.0
21-30 片 21-30 pieces	42	40.5	59.5
11-20 片 11-20 pieces	137	40.9	59.1

4-15-2 广告态度指标/ Advertising Attitude Index

	人数 Number	广告淡漠指向 indifferent orientation	中间层 medium	信赖广告指向 loyal orientation
女性 Female	195	23.6	63.1	13.3
30 片以上 over 30 pieces	16	18.8	68.8	12.5
21-30 片 21-30 pieces	42	28.6	61.9	9.5
11-20 片 11-20 pieces	137	22.6	62.8	14.6

● 西安 / Xi'an

4-1 最近一次使用量的比例/ Proportion of the Sample Consuming Napkins Last Time

	人数 Number	百分比 Percent
30 片以上 over 30 pieces	3	1.0
21-30 片 21-30 pieces	32	10.7
11-20 片 11-20 pieces	123	41.3
10 片及以下 10 pieces or below	90	30.2
没有用 not use	50	16.8

n=298

4-2 最常用品牌排名/ Ranking of the Most Frequently Used Brands

排名 Brand Ranking	品牌 Brands	人数 Number	百分比 Percent
1	护舒宝 Whisper	64	26.0
2	特日欣 Terixin	59	24.0
3	安尔乐 An'erle	37	15.0
4	舒而美 Comfort & Beauty	36	14.6
5	魔妮 Moni	22	8.9
6	安乐 Anle	9	3.7
7	娇爽 Carefree	3	1.2

n=246

4-3 样本、女性各年龄层的常用品牌/ The Most Frequently Used Brands by the Female Sample and Age Groups

	人数 Number	第一品牌及百分比 1st/ percent	第二品牌及百分比 2nd/ percent	第三品牌及百分比 3rd/ percent
女性 Female	**246**	**护舒宝 Whisper(26.0)**	**特日欣 Terixin(24.0)**	**安尔乐 An'erle(15.0)**
16~24 岁 Age	**58**	**护舒宝 Whisper(25.9)**	**特日欣 Terixin(22.4)**	**舒而美 Comfort & Beauty(19.0)**
25~34 岁 Age	88	护舒宝 Whisper(30.7)	安尔乐 An'erle(20.5)	特日欣 Terixin(19.3)
35~44 岁 Age	73	特日欣 Terixin(27.4)	护舒宝 Whisper(23.3)	安尔乐 An'erle(12.3) 舒而美 Comfort & Beauty(12.3) 魔妮 Moni(12.3)
45~54 岁 Age	24	特日欣 Terixin(33.3)	护舒宝 Whisper(20.8) 舒而美 Comfort & Beauty(20.8)	魔妮 Moni(12.5)
55~60 岁 Age	3	安尔乐 An'erle(33.3) 特日欣 Terixin(33.3) 特舒佳 Teshujia(33.3)		

4-4 正在使用的品牌排名/ Ranking of the Brands Used Now

排名 Brand Ranking	品牌 Brands	人数 Number	百分比 Percent
1	护舒宝 Whisper	68	27.5
2	特日欣 Terixin	54	21.9
3	安尔乐 An'erle	44	17.8
4	舒而美 Comfort & Beauty	27	10.9
5	魔妮 Moni	19	7.7
6	安乐 Anle	7	2.8
7	洁婷 Ludu caze	4	1.6
8	美洁 Meijie	3	1.2

n=247

4-5 品牌转换习惯/ Brand Habit in Consuming Napkins

	人数 Number	第一次使用该品牌 first use this brand	上一次也是这个牌子 used it last time	上一次不是这个牌子 not used it last time
女性 Female	**247**	6.5	82.2	11.3
护舒宝 Whisper	68	2.9	86.8	10.3
特日欣 Terixin	54	1.9	85.2	13.0
安尔乐 An'erle	44	4.5	90.9	4.5
舒而美 Comfort & Beauty	27	3.7	88.9	7.4
魔妮 Moni	19	5.3	78.9	15.8
安乐 Anle	7	0.0	71.4	28.6
洁婷 Ludu caze	4	50.0	25.0	25.0
美洁 Meijie	3	33.3	66.7	0.0

4-6 下一次打算使用的品牌排名/ Ranking of the Brands to be Used Next Time

排名 Brand Ranking	品牌 Brands	人数 Number	百分比 Percent
1	护舒宝 Whisper	82	33.1
2	特日欣 Terixin	50	20.2
3	安尔乐 An'erle	46	18.5
4	舒而美 Comfort & Beauty	26	10.5
5	魔妮 Moni	14	5.6
6	安乐 Anle	6	2.4
7	娇爽 Carefree	4	1.6

n=248

4-7 样本、女性各年龄层的最近一次的使用量/ Pieces of the Consumed Napkins Last Time by the Female Sample and Age Groups

	人数 Number	30 片以上 over 30 pieces	21-30 片 21-30 pieces	11-20 片 11-20 pieces	10 片及以下 10 pieces or below	没有用 not use
女性 Female	298	1.0	10.7	41.3	30.2	16.8
16~24 岁 Age	60	0.0	6.7	51.7	38.3	3.3
25~34 岁 Age	90	2.2	20.0	44.4	31.1	2.2
35~44 岁 Age	74	0.0	9.5	52.7	37.8	0.0
45~54 岁 Age	49	2.0	4.1	22.4	22.4	49.0
55~60 岁 Age	25	0.0	4.0	8.0	0.0	88.0

4-8 选择该类商品的考虑因素/ Ranking of the Considerations in Purchasing

注：本题为多选题，合计百分比超过 100%（Multiple answers）

排名 Ranking	考虑因素 Considerations	人次 Person-time	百分比 Percent
1	价格适中 reasonable price	145	58.5
2	使用经验 using experiences	106	42.7
3	产品功用 product function	68	27.4
4	有名的牌子 famous brand	65	26.2
5	购买方便 easy to buy	44	17.7
6	广告影响 influence of advertising	27	10.9
6	别人推荐 introduced by other people	27	10.9
7	有优惠条件 with preferential terms	15	6.0
8	包装吸引人 appealing package	6	2.4
9	其它 others	3	1.2

n=248

4-9 对产品功能的侧重方面/ Ranking of the Considerations about the Function of this Kind of Product

注：本题为多选题，合计百分比超过 100%（Multiple answers）

排名 Ranking	侧重方面 Items	人次 Person-time	百分比 Percent
1	吸水性强 high water-absorbility	166	66.9
2	触感舒适 comfortable to touch	129	52.0
3	有护翼 wing or not	93	37.5
4	透气性强 with good ventilation	84	33.9
5	粘帖牢固 safety	30	12.1
6	有凹槽 with notch	28	11.3
7	有隔离网面 mesh	27	10.9
8	其他 others	4	1.6

n=248

4-10 样本、女性各年龄层白天最常使用的类型/ Types of the Consumed Napkins in the Daytime by the Female Sample and Age Groups

	人数 Number	普通型 regular	普通加长型 XL regular	普通护翼型 regular wings	加长护翼型 XL wings	丝薄型 ultra slim	其他 others
女性 Female	245	48.2	10.6	28.2	5.3	7.8	0.0
16~24 岁 Age	55	36.4	12.7	41.8	1.8	7.3	0.0
25~34 岁 Age	88	38.6	4.5	35.2	6.8	14.8	0.0
35~44 岁 Age	74	62.2	16.2	12.2	8.1	1.4	0.0
45~54 岁 Age	25	64.0	12.0	20.0	0.0	4.0	0.0
55~60 岁 Age	3	66.7	0.0	33.3	0.0	0.0	0.0

4-11 样本、女性各年龄层夜间最常使用的类型/ Types of the Consumed Napkins at Night by the Female Sample and Age Groups

	人数 Number	普通型 regular	普通加长型 XL regular	普通护翼型 regular wings	加长护翼型 XL wings	丝薄型 ultra slim	其他 others
女性 Female	248	7.3	20.6	16.9	53.2	2.0	0.0
16~24 岁 Age	58	3.4	10.3	31.0	53.4	1.7	0.0
25~34 岁 Age	88	2.3	19.3	13.6	61.4	3.4	0.0
35~44 岁 Age	74	13.5	25.7	10.8	50.0	0.0	0.0
45~54 岁 Age	25	12.0	36.0	12.0	36.0	4.0	0.0
55~60 岁 Age	3	33.3	0.0	33.3	33.3	0.0	0.0

4-12 样本、女性各年龄层使用其他卫生用品的比例/ Proportion of the Female Consumed Others

注：本题为多选题，合计百分比超过 100%（Multiple answers）

	人数 Number	卫生棉条 cotton pads	卫生护垫 panty shields	以上都不用 none of above	其他 others
女性 Female	290	4.1	53.8	43.4	0.7
16~24 岁 Age	60	0.0	73.3	26.7	0.0
25~34 岁 Age	90	7.8	63.3	33.3	0.0
35~44 岁 Age	74	4.1	55.4	39.2	2.7
45~54 岁 Age	45	2.2	26.7	71.1	0.0
55~60 岁 Age	21	4.8	9.5	90.5	0.0

4-13 重度消费者的人口分布/ Demographics of the Heavy Consumers

	人数 Number	16-24 岁 Age	25-34 岁 Age	35-44 岁 Age	45-54 岁 Age	55-60 岁 Age
女性 Female	158	22.2	38.0	29.1	8.9	1.9
30 片以上 over 30 pieces	3	0.0	66.7	0.0	33.3	0.0
21-30 片 21-30 pieces	32	12.5	56.3	21.9	6.3	3.1
11-20 片 11-20 pieces	123	25.2	32.5	31.7	8.9	1.6

4-14 不同消费者层的常用品牌/ The Most Frequently Used Brands by Market Segments

4-14-1 时尚流行指标/ Fads Popular Index

	人数 Number	第一品牌及百分比 1st/ percent	第二品牌及百分比 2nd/ percent	第三品牌及百分比 3rd/ percent	第四品牌及百分比 4th/ percent
女性 Female	244	**护舒宝 Whisper(26.2)**	**特日欣 Terixin(24.2)**	**安尔乐 An'erle(15.2)**	**舒而美 Comfort &Beauty(14.8)**
平实生活指向 simple living orientation	118	特日欣 Terixin(28.8)	安尔乐 An'erle(17.8) 护舒宝 Whisper(17.8) 舒而美 Comfort &Beauty (17.8)	魔妮 Moni(7.6)	安乐 Anle(4.2)
时尚流行指向 fashion orientation	126	护舒宝 Whisper(34.1)	特日欣 Terixin(19.8)	安尔乐 An'erle(12.7)	舒而美 Comfort &Beauty(11.9)

4-14-2 广告态度指标/ Advertising Attitude Index

	人数 Number	第一品牌及百分比 1st/ percent	第二品牌及百分比 2nd/ percent	第三品牌及百分比 3rd/ percent	第四品牌及百分比 4th/ percent
女性 Female	244	**护舒宝 Whisper(26.2)**	**特日欣 Terixin(24.2)**	**安尔乐 An'erle(15.2)**	**舒而美 Comfort & Beauty(14.3)**
广告淡漠指向 indifferent orientation	73	特日欣 Terixin(32.9)	护舒宝 Whisper(19.2)	安尔乐 An'erle(13.7)	舒而美 Comfort &Beauty(12.3)
中间层 medium	136	护舒宝 Whisper(30.1)	安尔乐 An'erle(18.4)	特日欣 Terixin(16.9)	舒而美 Comfort &Beauty(16.2)
信赖广告指向 loyal orientation	35	特日欣 Terixin(34.3)	护舒宝 Whisper(25.7)	舒而美 Comfort &Beauty(11.4) 魔妮 Moni(11.4)	安尔乐 An'erle(5.7) 娇爽 Carefree(5.7)

4-15 重度消费者的消费层构成/ The Composition of the Heavy Consumers

4-15-1 时尚流行指标/ Fads Popular Index

	人数 Number	平实生活指向 simple living orientation	时尚流行指向 fashion orientation
女性 Female	157	45.2	54.8
30 片以上 over 30 pieces	3	0.0	100.0
21-30 片 21-30 pieces	32	40.6	59.4
11-20 片 11-20 pieces	122	47.5	52.5

4-15-2 广告态度指标/ Advertising Attitude Index

	人数 Number	广告淡漠指向 indifferent orientation	中间层 medium	信赖广告指向 loyal orientation
女性 Female	157	30.6	56.1	13.4
30 片以上 over 30 pieces	3	0.0	66.7	33.3
21-30 片 21-30 pieces	32	34.4	59.4	6.3
11-20 片 11-20 pieces	122	30.3	54.9	14.8

● 沈阳 / Shenyang

4-1 最近一次使用量的比例/ Proportion of the Sample Consuming Napkins Last Time

	人数 Number	百分比 Percent
30 片以上 over 30 pieces	14	4.6
21-30 片 21-30 pieces	20	6.6
11-20 片 11-20 pieces	122	40.4
10 片及以下 10 pieces or below	95	31.5
没有用 not use	51	16.9

n=302

4-2 最常用品牌排名/ Ranking of the Most Frequently Used Brands

排名 Brand Ranking	品牌 Brands	人数 Number	百分比 Percent
1	柔柔 Soft	78	31.2
2	护舒宝 Whisper	68	27.2
3	舒而美 Comfort & Beauty	28	11.2
4	娇爽 Carefree	11	4.4
4	安尔乐 An'erle	11	4.4
5	苏菲 Sofy	8	3.2
6	柔而美 Rou'ermei	6	2.4
6	洁婷 Ludu caze	6	2.4

n=250

4-3 样本、女性各年龄层的常用品牌/ The Most Frequently Used Brands by the Female Sample and Age Groups

	人数 Number	第一品牌及百分比 1st/ percent	第二品牌及百分比 2nd/ percent	第三品牌及百分比 3rd/ percent
女性 Female	250	柔柔 Soft(31.2)	护舒宝 Whisper(27.2)	舒而美 Comfort & Beauty(11.2)
16~24 岁 Age	64	护舒宝 Whisper(31.3)	柔柔 Soft(21.9)	娇爽 Carefree(6.3) 舒而美 Comfort & Beauty(6.3)
25~34 岁 Age	86	柔柔 Soft(31.4)	护舒宝 Whisper(29.1)	舒而美 Comfort & Beauty(10.5)
35~44 岁 Age	75	柔柔 Soft(40.0)	护舒宝 Whisper(25.3)	舒而美 Comfort & Beauty(17.3)
45~54 岁 Age	25	柔柔 Soft(28.0)	护舒宝 Whisper(16.0) 安尔乐 An'erle(15.0)	舒而美 Comfort & Beauty(8.0) 小护士 Mininurse(8.0)
55~60 岁 Age	0			

4-4 正在使用的品牌排名/ Ranking of the Brands Used Now

排名 Brand Ranking	品牌 Brands	人数 Number	百分比 Percent
1	柔柔 Soft	68	27.1
2	护舒宝 Whisper	66	26.3
3	舒而美 Comfort & Beauty	24	9.6
4	娇爽 Carefree	14	5.6
5	安尔乐 An'erle	13	5.2
6	苏菲 Sofy	11	4.4
7	洁婷 Ludu caze	9	3.6
8	柔而美 Rou'ermei	6	2.4
9	安乐 Anle	4	1.6
9	高洁丝 Kotex	4	1.6
10	佳期 Godcare	3	1.2

n=251

4-5 品牌转换习惯/ Brand Habit in Consuming Napkins

	人数 Number	第一次使用该品牌 first use this brand	上一次也是这个牌子 used it last time	上一次不是这个牌子 not used it last time
女性 Female	251	7.6	79.7	12.7
柔柔 Soft	68	4.4	91.2	4.4
护舒宝 Whisper	66	6.1	84.8	9.1
舒而美 Comfort & Beauty	24	0.0	95.8	4.2
娇爽 Carefree	14	14.3	78.6	7.1
安尔乐 An'erle	13	7.7	61.5	30.8
苏菲 Sofy	11	9.1	72.7	18.2

4-6 下一次打算使用的品牌排名/ Ranking of the Brands to be Used Next Time

排名 Brand Ranking	品牌 Brands	人数 Number	百分比 Percent
1	护舒宝 Whisper	89	35.5
2	柔柔 Soft	61	24.3
3	舒而美 Comfort & Beauty	19	7.6
4	娇爽 Carefree	14	5.6
5	苏菲 Sofy	10	4.0
6	安尔乐 An'erle	9	3.6
6	洁婷 Ludu caze	9	3.6
7	安乐 Anle	6	2.4
8	柔而美 Rou'ermei	4	1.6

n=251

4-7 样本、女性各年龄层最近一次的使用量/ Pieces of the Consumed Napkins Last Time by the Female Sample and Age Groups

	人数 Number	30 片以上 over 30 pieces	21-30 片 21-30 pieces	11-20 片 11-20 pieces	10 片及以下 10 pieces or below	没有用 not use
女性 Female	302	4.6	6.6	40.4	31.5	16.9
16~24 岁 Age	64	7.8	9.4	59.4	23.4	0.0
25~34 岁 Age	90	4.4	8.9	44.4	37.8	4.4
35~44 岁 Age	76	5.3	5.3	39.5	48.7	1.3
45~54 岁 Age	48	2.1	4.2	29.2	18.8	45.8
55~60 岁 Age	24	0.0	0.0	0.0	0.0	100.0

4-8 选择该类商品的考虑因素/ Ranking of the Considerations in Purchasing

注：本题为多选题，合计百分比超过 100%（Multiple answers）

排名 Ranking	考虑因素 Considerations	人次 Person-time	百分比 Percent
1	价格适中 reasonable price	132	52.8
2	使用经验 using experiences	105	42.0
3	产品功用 product function	79	31.6
4	有名的牌子 famous brand	71	28.4
5	购买方便 easy to buy	47	18.8
6	广告影响 influence of advertising	29	11.6
7	别人推荐 introduced by other people	21	8.4
8	有优惠条件 with preferential terms	13	5.2
9	包装吸引人 appealing package	4	1.6
10	其它 others	2	0.8

n=250

4-9 对产品功能的侧重方面/ Ranking of the Considerations about the Function of this Kind of Product

注：本题为多选题，合计百分比超过 100%（Multiple answers）

排名 Ranking	侧重方面 Items	人次 Person-time	百分比 Percent
1	吸水性强 high water-absorbility	176	70.4
2	触感舒适 comfortable to touch	116	46.4
3	透气性强 with good ventilation	95	38.0
4	有护翼 wing or not	92	36.8
5	粘帖牢固 safety	36	14.4
6	有隔离网面 mesh	34	13.6
7	有凹槽 with notch	14	5.6
8	其他 others	1	0.4

n=250

4-10 样本、女性各年龄层白天最常使用的类型/ Types of the Consumed Napkins in the Daytime by the Female Sample and Age Groups

	人数 Number	普通型 regular	普通加长型 XL regular	普通护翼型 regular wings	加长护翼型 XL wings	丝薄型 ultra slim	其他 others
女性 Female	251	43.8	15.1	27.9	4.8	8.4	0.0
16~24 岁 Age	64	26.6	14.1	32.8	4.7	21.9	0.0
25~34 岁 Age	86	45.3	10.5	33.7	4.7	5.8	0.0
35~44 岁 Age	75	49.3	21.3	21.3	5.3	2.7	0.0
45~54 岁 Age	26	65.4	15.4	15.4	3.8	0.0	0.0
55~60 岁 Age	0	0.0	0.0	0.0	0.0	0.0	0.0

4-11 样本、女性各年龄层夜间最常使用的类型/ Types of the Consumed Napkins at Night by the Female Sample and Age Groups

	人数 Number	普通型 regular	普通加长型 XL regular	普通护翼型 regular wings	加长护翼型 XL wings	丝薄型 ultra slim	其他 others
女性 Female	251	16.3	16.7	16.3	47.8	2.8	0.0
16~24 岁 Age	64	4.7	12.5	10.9	65.6	6.3	0.0
25~34 岁 Age	86	12.8	16.3	18.6	50.0	2.3	0.0
35~44 岁 Age	75	21.3	18.7	20.0	38.7	1.3	0.0
45~54 岁 Age	26	42.3	23.1	11.5	23.1	0.0	0.0
55~60 岁 Age	0	0.0	0.0	0.0	0.0	0.0	0.0

4-12 样本、女性各年龄层使用其他卫生用品的比例/ Proportion of the Female Consuming Others

注：本题为多选题，合计百分比超过 100%（Multiple answers）

	人次 Person-time	卫生棉条 cotton pads	卫生护垫 panty shields	以上都不用 none of above	其他 others
女性 Female	276	7.6	44.9	50.0	1.8
16~24 岁 Age	64	4.7	60.9	35.9	0.0
25~34 岁 Age	88	9.1	45.5	50.0	1.1
35~44 岁 Age	76	9.2	39.5	52.6	3.9
45~54 岁 Age	39	5.1	38.5	59.0	2.6
55~60 岁 Age	9	11.1	0.0	88.9	0.0

4-13 重度消费者的人口分布/ Demographics of the Heavy Consumers

	人数 Number	16-24 岁 Age	25-34 岁 Age	35-44 岁 Age	45-54 岁 Age	55-60 岁 Age
女性 Female	156	31.4	33.3	24.4	10.9	0.0
30 片以上 over 30 pieces	14	35.7	28.6	28.6	7.1	0.0
21-30 片 21-30 pieces	20	30.0	40.0	20.0	10.0	0.0
11-20 片 11-20 pieces	122	31.1	32.8	24 6	11.5	0.0

4-14 不同消费者层的常用品牌/ The Most Frequently Used Brands by Market Segments

4-14-1 时尚流行指标/ Fads Popular Index

	人数 Number	第一品牌及百分比 1st/ percent	第二品牌及百分比 2nd/ percent	第三品牌及百分比 3rd/ percent
女性 Female	250	柔柔 Soft(31.2)	护舒宝 Whisper(27.2)	舒而美 Comfort & Beauty(11.2)
平实生活指向 simple living orientation	94	柔柔 Soft(30.9)	护舒宝 Whisper(19.1)	舒而美 Comfort & Beauty(16.0)
时尚流行指向 fashion orientation	156	护舒宝 Whisper(32.1)	柔柔 Soft(31.4)	舒而美 Comfort & Beauty(8.3)

4-14-2 广告态度指标/ Advertising Attitude Index

	人数 Number	第一品牌及百分比 1st/ percent	第二品牌及百分比 2nd/ percent	第三品牌及百分比 3rd/ percent
女性 Female	250	柔柔 Soft(31.2)	护舒宝 Whisper(27.2)	舒而美 Comfort & Beauty(11.2)
广告淡漠指向 indifferent orientation	57	柔柔 Soft(28.1)	护舒宝 Whisper(26.3)	舒而美 Comfort & Beauty(15.8)
中间层 medium	168	柔柔 Soft(33.3)	护舒宝 Whisper(25.0)	舒而美 Comfort & Beauty(10.1)
信赖广告指向 loyal orientation	25	护舒宝 Whisper(44.0)	柔柔 Soft(24.0)	娇爽 Carefree(12.0)

4-15 重度消费者的消费层构成/ The Composition of the Heavy Consumers

4-15-1 时尚流行指标/ Fads Popular Index

	人数 Number	平实生活指向 simple living orientation	时尚流行指向 fashion orientation
女性 Female	156	35.3	64.7
30 片以上 over 30 pieces	14	7.1	92.9
21-30 片 21-30 pieces	20	40.0	60.0
11-20 片 11-20 pieces	122	37.7	62.3

4-15-2 广告态度指标/ Advertising Attitude Index

	人数 Number	广告淡漠指向 indifferent orientation	中间层 medium	信赖广告指向 loyal orientation
女性 Female	156	25.6	66.0	8.3
30 片以上 over 30 pieces	14	7.1	78.6	14.3
21-30 片 21-30 pieces	20	25.0	65.0	10.0
11-20 片 11-20 pieces	122	27.9	64.8	7.4

第十篇　药品、营养保健品
Part X　Medicine and Health Care Products

- 感冒药　Cold Medicine
- 润喉药　Sore Throat Remedies
- 肠胃药　Digestive System Medicine
- 营养保健品　Health Care Products

药品、营养保健品

中国医药产业在1978年到1998年的发展中，取得了长足的进步。即使在遇到前所未有的困难的1998年，中国医药工业的总产值依然达到1630亿元，较1997年增长14%；商业销售总额1080亿元，增长8.1%。1999年，医药工业总产值完成858.2亿元，比上年同期增长16.9%，其中化学药品类完成产值654.61亿元，同比增长17.61%。工业增加值完成225.2亿元，同比增长19%，其中，化学原料药品产量比上年同期增长24%，中成药总产量增长9.3%。上半年，医药工业销售产值完成610亿元，比上年同期增长15%，产销率为91%，较上年同期下降1.8个百分点，主要是受药品价格普遍下调的影响。化学类工业销售产值完成427.31亿元，同比增长12.84%，产销率为91.41%。全国医药商业企业上半年完成销售额539.5亿元，比上年同期增长3..3%．实现利润1.56亿元，比上年同期增长63.3%。

目前国内医药生产企业达6391家，可以生产西药、化学原料药24大类，1350多种，总量36万吨，居世界第二位。1999上市公司中期报表显示，总资产规模大于15亿元的7家医药上市公司为：丽珠集团、白云、东北药、太极集团、哈医药、鲁抗医药和华北制药。目前中国已有制药合资企业1790家，但真正与跨国企业合资的企业不过20—30家。在合资企业中，1998年销售排名前15位的医药公司有西安杨森，排名第6，销售18.67亿；天津史克公司，排名第8，销售11.7亿元；上海施贵宝公司，排名第12，销售8.2亿元。

医药市场包括四大类商品——药品、医疗器械、化学试剂、玻璃仪器。

1999年上半年医药市场呈现以下特点：

1．社会需求平稳增长，幅度趋缓。

首先，人口的自然增长和人口老龄化社会的形成是医药市场消费需求平稳增长的基本因素。再者，医疗卫生事业的快速发展，人们对健康投资的增加均在一定程度上促进了医药市场的消费。1998年我国净增人口1991万人，按人均购药额5368元计算，新增药品销售支出达10亿元。但同时，整个社会配套改革政策的逐步到位，社会消费需求增速减缓，医药消费需求呈现出增幅趋缓的态势。主要是目前各方面的改革措施使居民未来支出预期增大，居民收入增长在较长一段时期较大幅度落后于GDP的增长，使居民即期消费倾向减弱，消费行为更加谨慎。此外，改革力度的加大、下岗、新增就业人员的压力均形成了消费需求不旺的动因，在某种程度上制约了医药消费的增长。

2．药品类所占比重持续上升，依然成为支撑医药市场稳定增长的决定性因素。

3．医药零售市场仍呈现持续快速发展态势。

医药零售以其周转快、无拖欠、经营灵活、可适应不同层次消费需求等特点，保持了快速发展的态势。城镇职工基本医疗保险制度改革，药品分类管理制度的建立，将为其提供较大的发展空间。

4．农村市场潜力巨大，营销策略仍需探索。

5．地区经济增长水平差距的扩大，使药品消费市场的发展出现不平衡。

销售额居前五位的地区依次为广东、江苏、浙江、山东、上海，这五省市药品销售额合计达161.40亿元，占全国药品类总销售额的45.77%，显示出经济发达地区的总体消费水平高于内陆和边远地区。

医药市场存在的问题有：

1．医药企业数量多，规模小，低水平重复建设。

2．医药工业与世界先进水平相比存在较大差距。

产品结构还不适应医药产业发展和临床需要。制剂剂型和品种单调，多数重大原料药品工业生产技术水平不高、装备落后、劳动生产率低。中药材质量控制方法和手段落后，质量不稳定，饮片和中成药制剂工艺相对落后。医疗器械产品质量差，性能不稳定，产品水平低，市场竞争力弱。

3．药价扭曲。

医药市场供大于求，但互相竞争的结果是药品价格越抬越高。从药品生产情况看，制药企业在生产能力严重过剩的情况下，进行恶性竞争；从药品流通领域看，国营药品批发主渠道功能萎缩，医药流通环节过多，导致管理费用上升，层层加价；从医院方面看，存在不严格遵守医疗治疗规范，以"多用药、用贵药"的手段追求药品加成收入等问题。医药市场中的新药多数是进口药或合资产品。我国自行生产的药品以老药为主，为数不多的新药大多是仿制品。新药开发能力弱，科技含量底，企业规模小，新药研究缺少强大的资金支持，同时，新药开发亦受到知识产权制度的限制。

4．1999 年上半年全国医药经济运行总体态势基本正常，但是当前有效需求不足的矛盾仍然比较突出。

5．我国医药市场已成为国际大药业公司的竞争之地，并呈现出专利封锁、限制开发、专利垄断市场的竞争趋势。

近年来，国外药业在中国申请医药专利数不断上升，增长幅度超过医药发明的增长率。1994 年国外药业公司在我国申请医药发明专利数占总申请量的 35.5%。1998 年所占比重高达 85%。

目前看来，影响我国医药市场因素如下：

1．国务院决定，自 1999 年在全国范围内进行城镇医疗保险制度改革，与此同时，已实行 40 多年的公费医疗和劳保医疗制度将自动取消。新的医疗保险制度为医药市场的拓展提供了空间，医药市场需求仍将持续稳步增长。医疗保险人群范围的扩大，使社会医疗总需求不会萎缩，因此整个医药市场将保持平稳增长。

2．国家基本药物及基本医疗保险药物目录的推行，对医药企业产品生产经营结构的调整将产生重大影响。

3．药品分类管理制度的建立，使药品零售业有较大的空间。随着医改推行，医院实行医药分开核算，患者持方外购和非处方购药的比例将会有较大增加。

4．医疗卫生机构的改革与医药流通体制的改革息息相关。目前医疗机构改革涉及医药流通领域如下 3 个方面，一是卫生服务体系的结构性调整，加强社区服务，扩大农村医疗；二是医疗机构的分类管理；三是控制医药费用过快增长的各项措施，理顺医疗机构补偿机制的改革等。

5．国家经贸委将有效遏制医药市场的盲目竞争。

6．国有医药企业战略性的调整与改组力度将加大。

进入 90 年代以来，我国研究开发新药的步伐明显加快，现开发的药物已逐步由化学药物向中药、植物药、生化药、海洋药、天然药及新型药物制剂扩展。据资料统计，1990 年我国化学制剂药仅开发了 162 个新品种，至 1995 年增加 577 个品种，年递增率为 29%。在个新品种中，各大类药物所占的比重分别是：抗感染类药物 22.2%，各科用药 17%，中药 16%，生物制品和生化药 8.6%，神经系统用药 7.7%，其它类药物 5.7%，心血管系统用药、消化系统用药、呼吸系统用药和抗肿瘤药物共占 4%－4.8%。从具体品种来看，新药审批的热点品种主要是氧氟沙星、环丙沙星、氟罗沙星、干扰素、法莫替丁、半诺环素、二磷酸果糖、氟康唑、优维显、氢溴酸右美沙芬、曲马多、注射用重组人白介素－α、双氯芬酸、欧派克、氨苯伪麻、红霉素衍生物等。

国家经贸委根据总量控制、结构调整的原则，最近发布了医药工业 1999－2001 年的投资重点。其重点是：发展临床需要的新型、运用新产品，实行 GMP 改造，提高医药产品质量，引进先进技术与装备，提高老产品的技术经济指标，降低成本，增加竞争能力。

（数据来源：《中国医药报》《医药经济报》《中国高新技术导报》）

感冒药

感冒作为一种多发性疾病，市场对其需求量极大。据统计，我国每年约有 75%的人至少患一次感冒，也就是说每年有近十亿人至少需用一次感冒药物，按每次平均用药 15—20 元推算，则意味着治疗感冒的药物每年至少有 150—200 亿元的市场空间，这还没有把重复患感冒的患者考虑在内。

由于感冒的病因较为复杂，医药生产企业研制生产了品种繁多的感冒治疗药物。目前市场上销售的就有50多种，加上同药异名和各种剂型的不同，总共有100多种。西药中的感冒治疗药物，主要有抗病毒药物、解热镇痛药、抗过敏药、解热消炎与抗病毒合剂型几种；另外干扰素治疗流感效果也不错，但由于价格太高，还难以大面积使用；中药中的感冒治疗药物则以清热解毒的方剂为主，如板蓝根、葛根、贯众等。大多数感冒药是生产厂家针对感冒病症的特点研制生产的，所以一般效果都较好。传统治疗感冒的用药，医生多选择抗病毒药物和解热镇痛药物。随着医疗技术的进步，人们发现由解热镇痛药物与抗病毒药物组成的复方制剂，对治疗感冒更具有针对性，疗效更好。例如目前率先在国内推广并已广泛使用的“快克”这一品牌，就是在这一新思路上先人一步、开创市场的。

市场上较为常见的品牌包括：百服宁、康泰克、康必得、快克、白加黑、丽珠感乐、泰诺、999感冒灵、康得、感康、迪嘉、联邦伤风素、力克舒、速效感冒胶囊、可立克、泰瑞宁、复方感冒灵、复方扑热息痛、必得痛、安乃近、索灭痛、阿斯匹林、安佳热、一滴清、泡腾、氨酚待因等。由于感冒治疗药物市场巨大，各大医药生产企业竞相投产治疗感冒的产品，尤其是一批中外合资企业，以全新的品牌形象、大规模的广告投入、有力的促销手段、新颖的包装设计，迅速抢占了中国感冒药品市场的制高点，建立了牢固的品牌优势，这反映了现代的经营观念，即由产品营销转向品牌营销。感冒治疗药品是我国医药产品中品牌营销最为成功的范例，它不仅把医药产品的竞争引向了一个更高的层次，也带来了医药生产企业经营观念上的创新。目前，中国感冒药市场已由康泰克、康必得、白加黑、999感冒灵四大品牌主导，它们共占据了七成以上的份额。上海强生制药有限公司的泰诺、中美施贵宝制药有限公司的百服咛以及吉林江城制药有限公司的感康则是后起之秀。

感冒药市场亦存在诸多问题，主要集中在这几个方面：

1．是感冒治疗药品的价格太高，不少药品已经超出了许多患者的可承受能力。

2．品牌过多过滥，加之不适当的宣传误导，使医生和患者无所适从，造成了感冒药品市场的混乱。有些治疗感冒的药品，配方基本没有什么改变，只是起了一个时髦的新名称，就大幅度提高价格推向市场，搅乱了感冒治疗药品的市场秩序，对医生和患者产生了很大的误导作用。。对此，除了要求生产企业加强自律外，更重要的是需要医药管理、技术监督部门加强对药品生产企业的宏观管理，用法律的手段来规范药品市场的竞争行为。

3．打击假冒伪劣药品也是目前广大消费者特别关心的问题。药品作为一种商品，它所对应的是比较特殊的消费者，所以近年来国家以及有关职能部门陆续制定了有关法律、法规对药品的生产和流通予以严格的要求和保障，同时也不断向产品质量、科技含量、用户服务等诸方面向医药生产企业方面提出越来越高、越来越精益求精的要求。然而，目前我国还没能杜绝假冒伪劣药品对消费者的危害，为了保护消费者的合法权益，全社会都在呼吁药品生产企业要将为消费者（患者）负责的观念贯彻始终，加强与消费者的沟通。

（数据来源：www.chinainfobank.com）

营养保健品

随着国家药品监督管理局停止审批“药健字”保健品政策的出台，当前混乱的食用保健品市场有望趋于规范。

目前，市场上食用保健品有药管局审批的“药健字”和由卫生部审批的“食健字”两种审批格式，于是形成保健食品与保健药品共存的混乱局面。今年起药管局已不再审批新的“药健字”保健品，此举对规范食用保健品的审批将起到推动作用。

据统计，中国食用保健品生产企业已由80年代不到100家，增加到现在的3000多家，因生产厂家骤增、管理混乱而形成了品牌杂乱，产品市场寿命短，配方、工艺、剂型、商品和企业形象雷同等无序竞争的局面。一些小企业因经费短缺、人才匮乏及在主观认识等方面受局限，对新产品的研制开发缺乏热情；行业布局散、乱，难以形成拳头产品和龙头企业。

脑力劳动者、亚健康状态人群、老龄人口对保健品的需求是食用保健品行业繁荣发展的基础。按照购买力水平等因素，中国人均年收入在 2 至 3 万元时，才会对食用保健品有稳定的需求。因此，预计到下世纪初，中国将形成成熟的食用保健品消费市场。

根据中国食用保健品行业的现状及未来发展趋势，相关企业应采取措施，以加快扭转行业混乱、无序竞争的局面：

1. 用资本运营的形式来改造食用保健品行业，鼓励有实力的大企业进行垄断扩张，优势企业可采用挂靠并联、引资入股、整体出售、科技入股、品牌作价等多种形式，以较低的价格获得弱势企业的资本和经营权，盘活存量资本，取得协同效益。

2. 加大科技投入，缩短新产品的研制周期。据调查，目前国内 41%的食用保健品生产企业投资额在 100 万元以下。由于规模有限，很多企业科研经费短缺，设备差，工艺落后，缺乏后备产品。食用保健品虽然是高附加值产品，企业也不能够只重视短期效益，而对长远发展缺乏规划。

3. 树立健康投资观念，培育成熟的食用保健品消费市场。据专家介绍，食用保健品不是一种必需品，它仅仅是在人的肌体无病时的一种对未来健康的投资，而不是目前为数不少的消费者理解的肌体有病后的补救。把保健品当作药是中国特色的保健品概念，既与中国药食同源的饮食养生传统习惯有关，也是夸大食用保健品功能给消费者带来的认识误区。

4. 加强对国际市场的重视程度。流传几千年的中医理论，药食同源的传统饮食养生文化，使中国食用保健品的发展有着得天独厚的优势。业内人士建议：应组织科技含量高、质量过硬的食用保健品生产企业组团，到国外宣传、推广、交流，树立中国保健品的国际形象，努力占领国际市场。日前，香港特区政府已建议当地的中小型药商积极发展较容易打进国际市场的营养补充品及健康食品，并鼓励其申请总额高达 50 亿港元的创新及科技基金。

随着中国食用保健品规范的审批办法出台，促进行业自律、产业合理布局的全国性会员制组织的形成，产品科技含量的不断增加，在今后较长的一段时间内，对于不断创新、具备一定规模且善于市场经营的企业来说，市场依然充满生机。

保健食品

自一九九六年六月《保健食品管理办法》颁布实施以来，卫生部已陆续给 1683 种产品颁发了保健食品批准文号。据悉，卫生部近日将给 90 余种保健食品颁布文号，就是说，我国市场上将有 1700 多种合法保健食品存在。为对于保健食品现状有一个比较全面的了解，卫生部食品卫生监督检验所对 1528 种保健食品进行了统计分析

在 1528 种保健食品中,国产保健食品有 1383 种，进口保健食品有 145 种，产地集中于广东、北京、山东、江苏、上海、天津，这六个省市的产品共 764 种，占了全部国产保健食品的 55.24%；进口产品中美国产品最多，占全部进口食品的半数左右。在产品中，具有免疫功能的保健食品共 602 种，其次是具有抗疲劳功能的保健食品和具有调节血脂的保健食品。在已批准的产品中，除卫生部已认可的二十四种保健功能外，还有抗氧化、改善微循环、阻断 N－亚硝基化合物合成、升高白细胞、改善骨质疏松、防龋护齿六种功能，还有美容功能中的丰乳等。

在 1528 种产品中，近 3/4 的产品只有一种保健功能，1/5 弱的产品具有两种功能，95 种产品具有三种以上的保健功能，有四种产品具有五种功能。营养素补充剂也占了相当大的比例，共计 131 种，其中国产 100 种，进口 31 种。补钙的产品最多、其次是补充各种维生素的产品，补充微量元素及矿物质的产品中，补铁产品最多，共 14 种。

进口营养素补充剂中补充维生素的产品最多，占全部维生素类产品的 50%。现有产品主要是胶囊、口服液、片剂，冲剂和酒也比较多，这些剂型的产品就占了近 70%；具有一般食品形态的产品，如糖、罐头、醋、

饼干、蜜饯有一定的比例，约 5%。

保健食品被认为是“21 世纪的食品”，随着亚健康人群的增加和人口日益老龄化，保健市场潜力巨大，诸如能防治心脑血管病、癌症、动脉硬化、糖尿病、肝硬化、骨质疏松、贫血等病的保健食品将广受青睐，同时具有益智、延衰老、促进生长发育、壮阳功能的保健食品，也将会成为 21 世纪世界保健市场的畅销货。

保健药品

1987 年我国颁布的《保健药品管理办法》规定，一些具有保健作用的中药，可按照三类新药的要求研究、申报，并由各地药政主管部门审批后成为保健药品。保健药品从药品角度看，只能起到辅助治疗效果，并不能代替药物疗效；从食品角度看，保健药品更多的表现为对身体滋补保健作用。

保健药品在我国的特殊身份，不仅与国际上的通行药品分类管理模式不一致，同时也造成了市场管理中的诸多问题。1996 年，国务院办公发布文件，要求各地停止审批保健药品，保护消费者利益。1999 年，药品监督部门清理整顿市场，逐步取消已上市的 3000 多种保健药品。将分三种情况处理：属药品范围的，按新药审批的办法进行申报注册；不属于药品范围的，取消其药品批准文号，可以按保健食品的有关管理办法进行注册；一些起保健作用的中草药，在实行药品分类管理后，可以划归为非处方药的范围，但必须经过重新申请、审批。我国保健药品实行分类管理后，无论对保健食品、处方药、非处方药市场都将起到规范化作用，从而促进各个市场的健康发展。对保健药品实行分类管理符合国际潮流，从而为我国原有的保健药品走向国际市场铺平道路。（数据来源：www.chinainfobank.com）

Medicines

China's medical industry has made great development during the period between 1978 and 1998. In these 20 years, its annual increase was 18%, higher than that of any other industries and even higher than the world's average annual increase. In 1998, the year with unprecedented difficulties, the total output value of China's medical industry still made 163 billion RMB, a 14% increase from 1997. The gross revenue of commercial sales reached 108 billion RMB with an increase of 8.1%. In 1999, the total output value of medical industry was 85.82 billion RMB, an increase of 16.9% compared with the same period of last year, among which chemical medicines had an output value of 65.461 billion RMB, a 17.6% increase. The increment of the industry was 22.52 billion RMB, an increase of 19% compared with the same period of last year, among which the production of chemical material medicines has increased 24% and readily made herbal medicines increased 9.3%. In the first half of year, the medical industry realized an output value of 61 billion RMB. Compared with the same period of last year, the increase was 15%, with a 91% rate of return which decreased by 1.8% from last year's same period. The decrease of rate of return was due to the general cut-down of medicine prices. Among this, chemical medicines had a sales revenue of 42.731 billion RMB, an increase of 12.84% from last year's same period, and a 91.41% rate of return. Also during the first half of this year, enterprises undertaking medical business in China realized sales revenue of 53.95 billion RMB, an increase of 3.3% compared with last year's same period, and net sales of 0.156 billion RMB, an increase of 63.3%. When compare industrial with business enterprises, it is clear that in both increases of quantity and quality, industrial enterprises did better than business enterprises. Although business enterprises have made progress, on the whole, it's in the disadvantageous side.

At present, China has 6391 medical manufacturers that produce chemical medicines and medicines material of 24 categories, including 1,350 classes with a total volume of 360 thousand tons. The quantity of output ranks the second in the world. In mid-1999, the report on all the listed companies showed that 7 medical companies have their total assets of more than 1.5 billion RMB: LiZhu Group, White Cloud, Northeast Medicine, TaiJi Group, Ha'er Bin Medicine, Shandong Medical. Corp, and North China Medical. Although China has now 1,790 joint medical ventures, less than 20 or 30 are actually operating with transnational corporations. Among those transnational joint ventures, the 15 companies with the highest ranks in 1998 are Xi'an Yang sen, Ranking 6 and having sales of 1.867 billion RMB; Tianjin TSKF, ranking 8 with sales of 1.17 billion RMB; Shanghai Squibb, ranking 12 with sales of 820 million RMB.

The medical products can be classified into four major categories--medicines, medical facilities, chemical reagents and class instruments. The market of medical products of the first half of 1999 saw the following points:

1. The social demand for medical products were increasing steadily but the increase was slowing down.

First of all, the steady increase of demand for medical products is based on the basic factors of increase of population and aging of society. Secondly, with the fast development of medical and health care undertaking, people begin to spend more in health care. This, in turn, stimulates the consumption of medical products. In 1998, China's population increased by 19.91 million. Assuming one person purchase 5,368 yuan's worth of medicine, the additional expenditures on medicines would come up to 1 billion yuan. But at the same time, with the carrying out of the welfare policies in the whole society, the demand for medicine decreased and resulted in a slower speed in the demand for medicines. Because the current reform practices from all walks of life make people's prospective expenses go up. While people's income increases more slowly than GDP in the long run. As a result, the tendency of immediate consumption goes down. People become more careful in buying things. Besides, the increasing efforts of the reform policies, the increasing number of workless people and the new comers in the labor-force market have formed great pressure which discouraged people's desire to buy. That in some sense hinders the increase of medical consumption.

2. Medicines continue to enlarge its share in medical products and are the key factor of supporting the steady increase in the medical market.

3. The medical retail market still shows a trend to develop fast.

Medicine retail has advantages like quick turnover, no delay, flexible to sell and easy to meet the needs of different consumers. That's why it keeps the fast pace of development. What's more, the reform of basic medical insurance system for employees, and the establishment of the management system for medicine classification will create more shares for retail business.

4. The enormous potential in the rural market makes it necessary to look for new marketing strategies.

5. The enlarging gap between in economic growth between different areas increase makes the development of medicine market out of balance.

The five regions with the highest medicine sales are (in the order of ranks): Guangdong, Jiangsu, Zhejiang, Shandong, and Shanghai. The gross revenue of these five provinces from nedicine sales is 16.14 billion yuans, holding 45.77% of the country's total sales. This demonstrates that the average consumption level in the developed areas is higher than that in inner-land areas and remote areas.

The problems now existing in the medicine are as follows:

1. There are too many small-sized medical enterprises and they were set up repeatedly at low levels. Both the categories and the types of finished medicines are not various.

2. There is a large gap between our medical industry and the world's level.

The structure of products can not meet the demand of this industry and the clinics. The technology used in the production of many important raw materials is backward. There are no advanced facilities and the productivity is slow. The quality control tools and techniques of herbal medicines are out-of-date and thus the quality is not steady. The techniques of making pills and instant herbal medicines are comparatively backward. The medical instruments are poor in quality and unsteady in performance, the products don't have quality good enough to meet the market competition.

3. The price is twisted.

There is more supply than need in the medicine market. However, the competition leads to higher prices. On one hand, the producers compete unfriendly in the case of over production. on the other hand, there are too many stages in the distribution system, thus the management charge increases and in turn leads to higher medicine prices. Besides, the hospitals don't follow the rules of professional treatment but focus on the markup through selling more medicines and selling more expensive medicines.

4. Most new medicines in the market are imported or produced by joint ventures. Our home made medicines are mainly traditional. The few of the new ones are generally imitative. We lack the ability to develop new medicines. We need hi-tech products, large scaled enterprises and strong financial support for research. And at the same time, the development of new medicines is limited by the copyright system.

5. In the first half of 1999, the overall operation of Chinese medical industry is under control. But the problem of stimulating enough effective demand remains unsolved.

6. International medical corporations have made China's medical market a place of competition and the competition is leading us under a state of patent blockade, development restrains and patent monopoly.

In recent years, many foreign companies have applied for patent medicine in China. The increase rate is higher than that of medical inventions. Take 1994 for example, the cases of patent applied for by foreign accounts for 35.5% of the total number of cases. And in 1998, the percentage is as high as 85%.

It seems that China's medical market is affected by the following factors:

1. The State Council has decided that starting with 1999, a reform of medical insurance system will be conducted in all the cities and towns throughout the country. At the same time, the free medical service system and labor protection medical system in use for all these 40 years shall be automatically terminated. The new medical insurance system will extend the developing space for the medical market, and the market demand shall increase steadily. The enlargement of the group taking medical insurance make it certain that the society's whole demand for medical service will not decrease and the medical market as a whole will maintain a steady increase.

2. The introduction of the national catalogues for basic medicines and basic insurance medicines will have a great effect on the reorganization of the production and marketing cf medicine.

3. The establishment of management system for medicine classification makes more room for the development of medicine retail business. As the reform in the medicine and related medical fields goes on, hospitals begin to separate the accounts of treatment and medicines. Thus the cases of buying out of hospitals with prescriptions or buying non-prescribed medicines will largely increase.

4. The reform of medical institutions and the reform of medical distribution system can not do without each other. Presently the three aspects of distribution system affected by the medical institution reform are: the restructuring of public health service system, the enforcing of community service and the expanding of medical service to rural areas; the management system for medicine classification and the various means to control the overgrowth of medical expenses and to successfully carry out the reform of compensation system in medical institutions.

5. The State Business Council has decided to effectively control the blind competition in medical market.

6. The efforts on strategic reform and reorganization of state-owned medical enterprises will be greater.

Coming to 1990s, China's research and development of new medicines are speeding up. The newly developed medicines include herbal medicines, plant medicines, bio-chemical medicines, ocean medicines, natural medicines and new forms of drug as compared with the previous chemical medicines. According to statistics, in 1990, we had only 162 kinds of newly developed medicines while by 1995, we had 577 kinds more of them. The annual increase was 29%.

Of the 577 kinds of new medicines, 22.2% were anti-infection, 17% were used to kill other diseases, 16% were herbal medicines, 8.6% were bio-medicine and bio-chemical medicines, 7.7% were for treatment of nervous system, 5.7% were used for treatment of other parts of the body, and 4%-4.8% were for heart and blood system, digestion system, respiratory system and for dealing with tumors. Based on this information, we can see that the most popular elements used in the authorized medicines are: Ofloxacin、Ciprofloxacin、Interferon、Famotidine、Biphosphate fructose、Fluconazok、Ultravist、Tramadol、Human recombinated interleucin α 、Diclofenac、Erythromycin devivative etc.

The State Business Council, based on their principals of volume control and reconstruction, has recently issued a guideline for investment points during 1999-2001. The main idea is that develop new and practical medicines for clinical needs; reform the GMP, enhance the quality of medical products; introduce advanced technology and equipment; promote the tech-and-economic index of the products; cut down costs and try to be more competitive. (Sources: *China Medicine Paper, Medical Economy Paper, China's Hi-Tech Guide)*

Medicines for cold

Cold is a very common disease and so there is a great demand for cold medicines. Statistics shows that every year in China, 75% of people are attacked by cold. That means every year, about 1 billion people in China need cold medicine. Supposing people spend 15~20 yuans on cold medicine each time when they get a cold, they may spend 1.5~2 billion yuans on cold medicine. And the above figure doesn't include the repeated cases of catching cold by one person.

Such a big market would naturally lead to the competition among pharmacists. As the cause of cold is quite complicated, a large variety of cold medicines have been developed and produced. Now there are over 50 kinds sold. But if we take the same medicine with different names or different format as different kinds, the figure will go over 100. The cold medicines of Western style are mainly anti-virus, painkillers, anti-allergy, anti-phlogistic and combined anti-virus medicines. Besides that, interferon is also a good choice for treating cold. But because of its high price, it is difficult to get widely accepted. Chinese traditional cold herbs are mainly used to relieve internal heat and fever. Some examples of the herbs are Banlangen etc. Since most cold medicines are produced with the aim to eliminate symptoms of cold, they have proved successful. Traditionally, the medicines used by doctors can only kill one of virus, fever, and pains. Only one of them now, with the development of medical technology, people have made combined medicines to kill fever, pains and virus at the same time, which are more effective and thus more popular. For instance, the newly introduced brand "Quick" entered the market with this creative idea and was rewarded a fairly good popularity.

The medicines commonly used in the market are: Bufferin, Contac, Fufang An'fenpuxinpian, Quick, White & Black, Tylenol Cold, 999, Gankang, Su Xiao Shang Feng Jiao Nang, Aspirin, and so on. Since the market of cold medicines is very promising, many large pharmacies take part in the competition of producing cold medicines. One distinct fact is that some joint ventures have taken the superiority of the market through fresh brand image, overwhelming advertising, powerful sales promotion and fascinating packages. Their success gives us a totally new idea of marketing: The brand marketing of cold medicines in China is one of the most successful examples. It not only advances the level of the competition of cold medicines, but also brings a new concept of marketing into the pharmaceutical industry. Currently, the four leading brands of cold medicines are Contac, Fufang An'fenpuxinpian, White & Black, 999. They hold at least 70% of the market. Tylenol by Johnson & Johnson, the Bufferin by Sino-US Squibb Ltd. and Gankang by Jiangcheng phatmacy, Ltd, Jilin are some of the new successful brands.

Despite all this, there are a lot of problems existing in the market. They can be summed as the following:

First, the price of cold medicines is too high for consumers to afford.

Second, the overflow of products and brands, plus the misleading advertising put the market in a mess. Doctors and patients are just confused and bewildered. Some cold medicines are given a new name and then pushed into the market at a high price, the formula remains actually the same. This really misleads both the doctors and the patients. This kind of money-oriented deed has damaged the market. To get rid of it, pharmacies should regulate themselves and what's more important, medical administrative organization and technology inspection departments should exert more control over macro-management of pharmacies, and control the competition.

Third, fake and inferior medicines are also a big concern of consumers. As a special kind of goods, its consumers are quite special. To protect the consumers, the state and some related departments have issued some laws and regulations to control the production and distribution of medical products in recent years. And the criteria set for pharmacies are higher and higher and more specific in terms of quality, technology and service, etc. By far, however, fake and inferior medicines haven't been swept out of China's market. They are still threatening consumers' rights. In order to protect the brand image and consumers' right, the whole society is appealing for the consistent effort from the pharmacies to protect consumers' (mostly patients') rights and to communicate with consumers.

(Sources: www.chinainfobank.com)

Health Care Products

After the introduction of policy to stop issuing No bearing "H and D"("H" stands for Health and "D" stands for Drug) to health care food, the National Medicine Supervision Administration decided to regulate the health food market which is in somewhat a mess.

At present, there are two types of authorization for the health food market. They are the " No bearing D&H" by Drug Administration and the 'No bearing F&H" By the ministry of Public Health. Thus the authorized health food and drug put the market of health products in a mess. Starting from this year, Medicine Administration has stopped authorizing any "No bearing D&H." This move greatly helps the standardization of the authorization systems of health food.

According to statistics, China's health food manufacturers have increased from 100 in 1980s to over 3,000 now. However, because of the sharp increase of manufacturers and the mismanagement, there come clusters of brands, imitation in formulas, techniques, forms, images and short life of products. The whole situation is characterized by unorganized competition. Because of the shortage of fund and talents, some small manufacturers are not keen on researching and developing new products. The industrial layout was so out of order that it's difficult to establish quality products and leading enterprises.

The demand for health products by intellectuals, sub-healthy people and the olds forms the basis of the booming of health food industry. Considering the buying power, the stable need for health food will be realized only when China's average annual income per person reaches 20-30 thousand RMB. Therefore, it is estimated that by the beginning of next century, China will has a mature market for health food.

Knowing the present state and trend of the development of China's health food industry, those enterprises involved should take measures to eliminate the disorderliness and unorganized competition in this industry.

1. Reform the industry of health food through capital operation, and encourage the qualified large enterprises to expand. Promising enterprises may use different tools as alliance, incorporation, package sales, technology equitifying, brand equitifying, so that they can realize a competitive price to gain the less privileged enterprises' capital and also the right to operate, liquidate assets, capital and realize the synergistic effect.

2. Increase the investment of technology and shorten the developing term of new products. According to the

research, at present, 41% of health food manufacturers in China only have an investment of up to 1 million RMB. Due to the limited scale, many enterprises are short of research fund, facilities, advanced techniques and supporting products. Though health food is a kind of product with high-added value, enterprises can not give up their long term plans for development while putting emphasis on the short term benefits.

3. Establish the concept of health investment and build a mature market of health food. According to specialists, health food is not a necessity. It's only a kind of investment made when people are not suffering from physical illnesses to ensure healthy in the future. It in no way should be a kind of make-up measure after disease occurs. However, many Chinese people take health food as drug, because Chinese people have long believed that medicines and food actually came from the same sources. That will somehow mislead consumers to be too much dependent on the health food.

4. Attach more importance to the international market. The thousands of history behind the Chinese medical theories, the traditional concept that medicine and food come from the same sources have granted the market of Chinese health food exclusive advantages. Professional in this industry suggest that: manufacturers, with hi-tech and quality products should be introduced to foreign countries to advertise, promote, communicate and finally build the image of Chinese health food in the world's market. And find a place in the international market. The other day, HKSAR suggested the local medium and small-sized pharmaceutical companies actively develop the nourishing food and tonics which can more easily find their way to the international market, and encouraged them to apply for innovation and technology funds as high as 5 billion HK dollars.

With the issuance of standardized authorization of Chinese health food, the set-up of national organizations to improve self-regulation and reasonable allocation. Chinese health food contains more science technology. In the long term, the market will show an optimistic prospect for those enterprises who make continuous effort in innovation, who run at proper sizes and manages the market skillfully.

Health food

Since the issuance and enforcement of the Guidelines of Health Food Administration in June, 1996, the Ministry of Public has granted the health food authorization number to 1683 products. It is said that the ministry is going to grant the health food authorization number to more than 90 products soon. That is to say, there are about 1,700 legal health food in the home market. In order to have a comprehensive understanding of the present state of the health food, the food hygienic supervision and inspection center of the ministry has made a statistic analysis based on 1,528 kinds of health food.

Among these 1,528 products, 1,383 kinds are home made, and 145 kinds imported. The places of origin concentrate on Guangdong, Beijing, Shandong, Jiangsu, Shanghai, and Tianjin. Which produced 764 kinds of products, accounting for 55.24% of the homemade health food. Those from the United States cover the largest part of the imported health food, accounting for 50%. Among all these foods, 602 products can help improve the immune system and the second largest group is made up of those that can relieve fatigue and adjust blood fat. Besides the 24 health protection functions approved by the ministry of Public Health, the protective functions also include six others such as anti-oxidation, improving micro-circulation, preventing the formation of synthetic N-nitrite chemicals, increasing the number of white cells in blood, fighting against osteoporosis and preventing teeth decay. What's more, these products have beautifying functions like enlarging breasts.

Among the 1,528 products, nearly 3/4 have only one function each, 1/5 have two functions each, 95 products have more than three functions, and 4 products have five functions. The 131 kinds of nourishment take a large share of health food with 100 homemade and 31 imported kinds. The largest group is Calcium supplementary products and the second largest is Vitamin supplementary. There are also some products to supplement micronutrient element and minerals. For example, 14 kinds are iron supplementary.

Most imported nourishment supplementary are vitamin supplementary, accounting for 50% of vitamin products. The forms of these products are mainly capsules, orally liquid, pills, instant powder and liquors, accounting for 70% altogether. On the other hand, the products with the forms of common food such as sugar, cans, vinegar, biscuits and preserved fruits constitute 5%.

Health food is considered "food of 21st century". With the increasing of sub-healthy people and the aging of population, health food market is very promising. The well-welcomed health food will be those preventing brain and blood vessels diseases, cancers, arteriosclerosis, diabetes mellitus, cirrhosis, osteoporosis and anemia etc. And those good to brain, youth keeping, growth and masculinity will also be commonly welcomed in 21st century.

Health Medicine

The Guideline of Medicine Administration issued in 1987 requires that some health protection herbal medicines may go into research and apply for production license medicines. If authorized by the local medical administration department, they can only be regarded as health medicines. From the perspective of medical effect, health medicines can only help in treatment, but by no means should they replace medicines. From the perspective of food, health medicines provide us with nourishment.

Health medicines have a special status in China. That is not only inconsistent with the current international pattern of management model of classification, but also leads to some problems in the market. In 1996, the State Council issued a guideline requiring that the authorization of health medicine must be stopped throughout the country in order to protect the consumer's rights. In 1999, departments of medicine supervision began to reorder the market and thus dropped 3,000 health medicines in the market. In the future, the health medicines will be classified into 3 categories: those classified as medicines will report and register as newly developed medicines; those classified as non-medicine products be deprived of the authorization number for medicines but can register as health food; those health protection herbs (which are non-medicine products) can be classified as non-prescribe medicines, but only after apply for the authorization and register again.

Ever since the management of health food by classification, the market of health food, both prescriptions and non-prescription will be in good order and therefore will speed up the healthy development of all the fields. It meets the international trend to adopt management by classification, and the change will pave the way for our country's health products to enter the international market.

(Sources: www.chinainfobank.com)

1.感冒药 / Cold Medicine

● 北京 / Beijing

1-1 最近一年内有无服用的比例/ Whether having Taken Cold Medicines Last Year

	人数 Number	百分比 Percent
吃过 yes	814	80.5
没吃过 no	197	19.5

n=1011

1-2 最常用品牌或品种排名/ Ranking of the Most Frequently Used Brands or Kinds

注：在药品品牌调查中，消费者经常出现将药品的名称与品牌名称混淆的现象，特此声明。/ In our research on medicines, we find consumers often confused the names and the brands.

排名 Brand Ranking	品牌或品种 Brands or Kinds	人数 Number	百分比 Percent
1	同仁堂 Tongrentang	213	26.4
2	康泰克 Contac	141	17.5
3	感冒通 Ganmaotong	102	12.6
4	感冒冲剂 Ganmao Chongji	25	3.1
5	重感灵 Zhong Gan Ling	23	2.9
6	快克 Quick	22	2.7
6	百服宁 Bufferin	22	2.7
7	强力维 C 银翘 Qiang Li VC	17	2.1
8	盖天力白加黑片 White&Black	16	2.0
8	感冒清热胶囊 Ganmao Qingre Jiaonang	16	2.0
9	板兰根 Banlangen	15	1.9
10	泰诺 Tylenol Cold	13	1.6

n=807

1-3 样本、男性各年龄层、女性各年龄层的常用品牌或品种/ The Most Frequently Used Brands or Kinds by the Whole Sample, Age and Gender Groups

注：在药品品牌调查中，消费者经常出现将药品的名称与品牌名称混淆的现象，特此声明。/ In our research on medicines, we find consumers often confused the names and the brands.

	人数 Number	第一品牌及百分比 1st/ percent	第二品牌及百分比 2nd/ percent	第三品牌及百分比 3rd/ percent
样本 Sample	807	**同仁堂 Tongrentang(26.4)**	**康泰克 Contac(17.5)**	**感冒通 Ganmaotong(12.6)**
男性 Male	380	**同仁堂 Tongrentang(23.9)**	**康泰克 Contac(20.3)**	**感冒通 Ganmaotong(15.0)**
16~24 岁 Age	83	康泰克 Contac(22.9)	感冒通 Ganmaotong(15.7)	同仁堂 Tongrentang(14.5)
25~34 岁 Age	113	同仁堂 Tongrentang(24.8)	康泰克 Contac(23.0)	感冒通 Ganmaotong(16.8)
35~44 岁 Age	93	同仁堂 Tongrentang(23.7)	康泰克 Contac(16.1)	感冒通 Ganmaotong(14.0)
45~54 岁 Age	58	同仁堂 Tongrentang(25.9)	康泰克 Contac(24.1)	感冒通 Ganmaotong(13.8)
55~60 岁 Age	33	同仁堂 Tongrentang(42.4)	感冒通 Ganmaotong(12.1)	康泰克 Contac(9.1) 感冒清热胶囊 Ganmao Qingre Jiaonang(9.1)
女性 Female	427	**同仁堂 Tongrentang(28.6)**	**康泰克 Contac(15.0)**	**感冒通 Ganmaotong(10.5)**
16~24 岁 Age	93	康泰克 Contac(22.6)	同仁堂 Tongrentang(21.5)	感冒通 Ganmaotong(17.2)
25~34 岁 Age	122	同仁堂 Tongrentang(32.0)	康泰克 Contac(12.3)	感冒通 Ganmaotong(7.4)
35~44 岁 Age	109	同仁堂 Tongrentang(28.4)	康泰克 Contac(13.8)	感冒通 Ganmaotong(10.1)
45~54 岁 Age	71	同仁堂 Tongrentang(33.8)	康泰克 Contac(16.9)	重感灵 Zhong Gan Ling(4.2) 感冒清热胶囊 Ganmao Qingre Jiaonang (4.2) 感冒冲剂 Ganmao Chongji(4.2) 快克 Quick(4.2)
55~60 岁 Age	32	同仁堂 Tongrentang(25.0)	感冒通 Ganmaotong(21.9)	百服宁 Bufferin(6.3) 双吉 Shuangji(6.3)

1-4 理想品牌或品种排名/ Ranking of the Ideal Brands or Kinds

注：在药品品牌调查中，消费者经常出现将药品的名称与品牌名称混淆的现象，特此声明。/ In our research on medicines, we find consumers often confused the names and the brands.

排名 Brand Ranking	品牌或品种 Brands or Kinds	人数 Number	百分比 Percent
1	康泰克 Contac	235	23.3
2	同仁堂 Tongrentang	190	18.8
3	感冒通 Ganmaotong	68	6.7
4	感冒冲剂 Gan Mao Chong Ji	32	3.2
5	百服宁 Bufferin	29	2.9
6	泰诺 Tylenol Cold	24	2.4
6	板兰根 Ban Lan Gen	24	2.4
7	快克 Quick	23	2.3
8	重感灵 Zhong Gan Ling	19	1.9
9	盖天力白加黑片 White&Black	18	1.8
10	强力维 C 银翘 Qiang Li VC	15	1.5

n=1009

1-5 样本、男性各年龄层、女性各年龄层的品牌习惯/ Brand Habit in Consuming Cold Medicines by the Whole Sample, Age and Gender Groups

	人数 Number	基本固定用一个牌子 used in only one brand	比较固定地用两个或三个牌子 used in two or three brands	基本上不太固定牌子 no brand preference
样本 Sample	**813**	**32.2**	**41.2**	**26.6**
男性 Male	**386**	**33.7**	**38.6**	**27.7**
16~24 岁 Age	84	32.1	44.0	23.8
25~34 岁 Age	114	33.3	46.5	20.2
35~44 岁 Age	96	34.4	29.2	36.5
45~54 岁 Age	59	39.0	33.9	27.1
55~60 岁 Age	33	27.3	33.3	39.4
女性 Female	**427**	**30.9**	**43.5**	**25.5**
16~24 岁 Age	93	30.1	52.7	17.2
25~34 岁 Age	122	28.7	45.1	26.2
35~44 岁 Age	109	31.2	37.6	31.2
45~54 岁 Age	71	28.2	47.9	23.9
55~60 岁 Age	32	46.9	21.9	31.3

1-6 易患感冒的季节/ Which Season to Prone to Catch Cold

注：本题为多选题，合计百分比超过100%（Multiple answers）

	人次 Person-time	百分比 Percent
冬春之交 between winter & spring	238	29.6
春天 spring	63	7.8
春末夏初 late spring & early summer	28	3.5
夏天 summer	17	2.1
夏秋之交 between summer & autumn	72	9.0
秋天 autumn	79	9.8
入冬之际 early winter	326	40.5
冬天 winter	99	12.3
不确定 not sure	189	23.5

n=804

1-7 样本、男性各年龄层、女性各年龄层最近一年内有无服用的比例/ Whether having Taken Cold Medicines Last Year by the Whole Sample, Age and Gender Groups

	人数 Number	吃过 yes	没吃过 no
样本 Sample	1011	80.5	19.5
男性 Male	503	76.7	23.3
16~24 岁 Age	105	80.0	20.0
25~34 岁 Age	151	75.5	24.5
35~44 岁 Age	131	73.3	26.7
45~54 岁 Age	76	77.6	22.4
55~60 岁 Age	40	82.5	17.5
女性 Female	508	84.3	15.7
16~24 岁 Age	108	86.1	13.9
25~34 岁 Age	150	82.0	18.0
35~44 岁 Age	124	87.9	12.1
45~54 岁 Age	84	84.5	15.5
55~60 岁 Age	42	76.2	23.8

1-8 选择该类商品的考虑因素/ Ranking of Considerations in Purchasing

注：本题为多选题，合计百分比超过 100%（Multiple answers）

排名 Ranking	考虑因素 Considerations	人次 Person-time	百分比 Percent
1	见效快 immediate effect	459	57.1
2	医生推荐 recommended by doctors	385	47.9
3	服用方式简便 simple to take	194	24.1
4	有名的牌子 famous brand	141	17.5
5	不嗜睡 not feeling sleepy	103	12.8
6	价格适中 reasonable price	98	12.2
7	购买方便 easy to buy	46	5.7
8	广告影响 influence of advertising	45	5.6
9	亲友介绍 introduced by relatives & friends	38	4.7
10	其他 others	17	2.1

n=804

1-9 样本、男性各年龄层、女性各年龄层最常服用的种类/ Types of Cold Medicine Consumed by the Whole Sample, Age and Gender Groups

	人数 Number	片剂 pill	冲剂 granular formulation	胶囊 capsule	药粉 powder	糖浆 syrup	药丸 bolus	其他 others
样本 Sample	786	33.7	35.4	28.4	0.6	0.8	0.6	0.5
男性 Male	370	35.9	34.9	27.0	0.5	0.3	0.5	0.8
16~24 岁 Age	83	49.4	22.9	24.1	0.0	0.0	1.2	2.4
25~34 岁 Age	109	36.7	29.4	32.1	1.8	0.0	0.0	0.0
35~44 岁 Age	92	32.6	37.0	29.3	0.0	1.1	0.0	0.0
45~54 岁 Age	54	25.9	50.0	22.2	0.0	0.0	1.9	0.0
55~60 岁 Age	32	25.0	53.1	18.8	0.0	0.0	0.0	3.1
女性 Female	416	31.7	35.8	29.6	0.7	1.2	0.7	0.2
16~24 岁 Age	93	41.9	23.7	31.2	1.1	1.1	1.1	0.0
25~34 岁 Age	120	30.8	41.7	24.2	0.8	0.0	1.7	0.8
35~44 岁 Age	107	33.6	32.7	29.9	0.9	2.8	0.0	0.0
45~54 岁 Age	66	13.6	43.9	40.9	0.0	1.5	0.0	0.0
55~60 岁 Age	30	36.7	43.3	20.0	0.0	0.0	0.0	0.0

1-10 样本、男性各年龄层、女性各年龄层最常服用的场合/ Settings of Consumption by the Whole Sample, Age and Gender Groups

注：本题为多选题，合计百分比超过 100%（Multiple answers）

	人数 Number	有感冒的前兆 having signs of cold	轻度感冒症状 light cold symptom	严重感冒症状 severe cold symptom	其他 others
样本 Sample	805	25.8	58.6	15.4	0.1
男性 Male	382	25.4	58.9	15.4	0.3
16~24 岁 Age	83	16.9	60.2	21.7	1.2
25~34 岁 Age	114	31.6	53.5	14.9	0.0
35~44 岁 Age	94	23.4	62.8	13.8	0.0
45~54 岁 Age	58	31.0	53.4	15.5	0.0
55~60 岁 Age	33	21.2	72.7	6.1	0.0
女性 Female	423	26.2	58.4	15.4	0.0
16~24 岁 Age	93	19.4	60.2	20.4	0.0
25~34 岁 Age	121	28.9	53.7	17.4	0.0
35~44 岁 Age	107	30.8	57.0	12.1	0.0
45~54 岁 Age	70	25.7	62.9	11.4	0.0
55~60 岁 Age	32	21.9	65.6	12.5	0.0

1-11 样本、男性各年龄层、女性各年龄层购买感冒药的场所/ Location of Buying Cold Medicine by the Whole Sample, Age and Gender Groups

注：本题为多选题，合计百分比超过 100%（Multiple answers）

	人数 Number	药店 drug store	医院/诊所 hospital	商场 department store/ shopping center
样本 Sample	811	38.6	74.6	1.2
男性 Male	385	39.2	70.9	1.8
16~24 岁 Age	84	51.2	60.7	3.6
25~34 岁 Age	114	43.0	68.4	1.8
35~44 岁 Age	96	33.3	76.0	1.0
45~54 岁 Age	58	31.0	77.6	1.7
55~60 岁 Age	33	27.3	78.8	0.0
女性 Female	426	38.0	77.9	0.7
16~24 岁 Age	93	43.0	72.0	1.1
25~34 岁 Age	121	47.9	66.9	0.8
35~44 岁 Age	109	32.1	87.2	0.9
45~54 岁 Age	71	31.0	85.9	0.0
55~60 岁 Age	32	21.9	87.5	0.0

1-12 家中是否有备用感冒药的习惯/ The Habit of Keeping Cold Medicine at Home

	人数 Number	百分比 Percent
有 yes	902	89.9
没有 no	101	10.1

n=1003

1-13 公费/自费医疗的比例/ Proportion of the Free Medical Service

	人数 Number	百分比 Percent
公费医疗 free medical service	636	64.6
自费医疗 own expense	349	35.4

n=985

1-14 不同消费者层的常用品牌/ The Most Frequently Used Brands by Market Segments

1-14-1 时尚流行指标/ Fads Popular Index

注：在药品品牌调查中，消费者经常出现将药品的名称与品牌名称混淆的现象，特此声明。/ In our research on medicines, we find consumers often confused the names and the brands.

	人数 Number	第一品牌及百分比 1st / percent	第二品牌及百分比 2nd / percent	第三品牌及百分比 3rd / percent
样本 Sample	797	**同仁堂 Tongrentang(26.6)**	**康泰克 Contac(17.3)**	**感冒通 Ganmaotong(12.5)**
平实生活指向 simple living orientation	382	同仁堂 Tongrentang(30.1)	康泰克 Contac(13.9)	感冒通 Ganmaotong(13.4)
时尚流行指向 fashion orientation	415	同仁堂 Tongrentang(23.4)	康泰克 Contac(20.5)	感冒通 Ganmaotong(11.8)

1-14-2 广告态度指标/ Advertising Attitude Index

注：在药品品牌调查中，消费者经常出现将药品的名称与品牌名称混淆的现象，特此声明。/ In our research on medicines, we find consumers often confused the names and the brands.

	人数 Number	第一品牌及百分比 1st / percent	第二品牌及百分比 2nd / percent	第三品牌及百分比 3rd / percent
样本 Sample	790	**同仁堂 Tongrentang(26.7)**	**康泰克 Contac(17.7)**	**感冒通 Ganmaotong(12.5)**
广告淡漠指向 indifferent orientation	224	同仁堂 Tongrentang(25.0)	康泰克 Contac(19.2)	感冒通 Ganmaotong(16.5)
中间层 medium	459	同仁堂 Tongrentang(29.0)	康泰克 Contac(16.6)	感冒通 Ganmaotong(10.7)
信赖广告指向 loyal orientation	107	同仁堂 Tongrentang(20.6)	康泰克 Contac(19.6)	感冒通 Ganmaotong(12.1)

1-14-3 饮食健康指标/ Foods & Drink Quality Index

注：在药品品牌调查中，消费者经常出现将药品的名称与品牌名称混淆的现象，特此声明。/ In our research on medicines, we find consumers often confused the names and the brands.

	人数 Number	第一品牌及百分比 1st / percent	第二品牌及百分比 2nd / percent	第三品牌及百分比 3rd / percent
样本 Sample	802	**同仁堂 Tongrentang(26.4)**	**康泰克 Contac(17.6)**	**感冒通 Ganmaotong(12.7)**
饮食“温饱”指向 "basic" orientation	220	同仁堂 Tongrentang(24.1)	康泰克 Contac(18.6)	感冒通 Ganmaotong(17.3)
中间层 medium	381	同仁堂 Tongrentang(27.6)	康泰克 Contac(18.1)	感冒通 Ganmaotong(11.8)
健康营养指向 health & nutrition orientation	201	同仁堂 Tongrentang(26.9)	康泰克 Contac(15.4)	感冒通 Ganmaotong(9.5)

● 上海 / Shanghai

1-1 最近一年内有无服用的比例/ Whether having Taken Cold Medicines Last Year

	人数 Number	百分比 Percent
吃过 yes	822	81.1
没吃过 no	192	18.9

n=1014

1-2 最常用品牌或品种排名/ Ranking of the Most Frequently Used Brands or Kinds

注：在药品品牌调查中，消费者经常出现将药品的名称与品牌名称混淆的现象，特此声明。/ In our research on medicines, we find consumers often confused the names and the brands.

排名 Brand Ranking	品牌或品种 Brands or Kinds	人数 Number	百分比 Percent
1	康泰克 Contac	253	30.9
2	克感敏 Keganmin	123	15.0
3	百服宁 Bufferin	78	9.5
4	泰诺 Tylenol Cold	72	8.8
5	天平牌 Tianping	40	4.9
6	上药 Shang Hai Zhi Yao	35	4.3
6	感冒通 Ganmaotong	35	4.3
7	福牌 Fupai	13	1.6
8	美优感冒通 Mei You Gan Mao Tong	10	1.2
9	宇宙 Yuzhou	9	1.1
9	康得 Contac	9	1.1
10	日夜百服宁 Bufferin Gold	8	1.0
10	白加黑 White&Black	8	1.0
10	明兴 Ming Xing	8	1.0
11	帕尔克 Pa'erke	7	0.9
11	头孢拉丁胶囊 Cefradine Capsules	7	0.9
12	板兰根 Banlangen	6	0.7
12	感冒冲剂 Gan Mao Chong Ji	6	0.7
13	正柴胡饮 Zheng Chai Hu Yin	5	0.6
13	强力维 C 银翘 Qiang Li VC	5	0.6
13	速效伤风胶囊 Su Xiao Shang Feng Jiao Nang	5	0.6
14	头孢氨苄胶囊 Tou Bao An Ka Jiao Nang	4	0.5
15	急支糖浆 Acute Bronchitis Syrup	3	0.4
15	黄浦感冒冲剂 Huang Pu Gan Mao Chong Ji	3	0.4
15	长城 Great Wall	3	0.4

n=820

1-3 样本、男性各年龄层、女性各年龄层的常用品牌或品种/ The Most Frequently Used Brands or Kinds by the Whole Sample, Age and Gender Groups

注：在药品品牌调查中，消费者经常出现将药品的名称与品牌名称混淆的现象，特此声明。/ In our research on medicines, we find consumers often confused the names and the brands.

	人数 Number	第一品牌及百分比 1st/ percent	第二品牌及百分比 2nd/ percent	第三品牌及百分比 3rd/ percent
样本 Sample	820	**康泰克 Contac(30.9)**	**克感敏 Keganmin(15.0)**	**百服宁 Bufferin(9.5)**
男性 Male	414	**康泰克 Contac(32.4)**	**克感敏 Keganmin(14.3)**	**百服宁 Bufferin(10.1)**
16~24 岁 Age	87	康泰克 Contac(44.8)	克感敏 Keganmin(11.5)	百服宁 Bufferin(10.3)
25~34 岁 Age	112	康泰克 Contac(34.8)	克感敏 Keganmin(16.1)	百服宁 Bufferin(14.3)
35~44 岁 Age	113	康泰克 Contac(29.2)	克感敏 Keganmin(15.0)	泰诺 Tylenol Cold(8.0)
45~54 岁 Age	69	康泰克 Contac(23.2)	克感敏 Keganmin(14.5)	泰诺 Tylenol Cold(11.6)
55~60 岁 Age	33	康泰克 Contac(21.2)	克感敏 Keganmin(12.1)	百服宁 Bufferin(9.1) 上药 Shang Hai Zhi Yao (9.1) 速效伤风胶囊 Su Xiao Shang Feng Jiao Nang(9.1)
女性 Female	406	**康泰克 Contac(29.3)**	**克感敏 Keganmin(15.8)**	**泰诺 Tylenol Cold(9.9)**
16~24 岁 Age	86	康泰克 Contac(37.2)	泰诺 Tylenol Cold(12.8)	克感敏 Keganmin(11.6) 百服宁 Bufferin(11.6)
25~34 岁 Age	120	康泰克 Contac(31.7)	泰诺 Tylenol Cold(17.5)	克感敏 Keganmin(15.0)
35~44 岁 Age	107	康泰克 Contac(25.2)	克感敏 Keganmin(21.5)	百服宁 Bufferin(9.3)
45~54 岁 Age	62	康泰克 Contac(22.6)	克感敏 Keganmin(16.1)	百服宁 Bufferin(9.7)
55~60 岁 Age	31	康泰克 Contac(25.8)	天平牌 Tianping (22.6)	上药 Shang Hai Zhi Yao (16.1)

1-4 理想品牌或品种排名/ Ranking of the Ideal Brands or Kinds

注：在药品品牌调查中，消费者经常出现将药品的名称与品牌名称混淆的现象，特此声明。/ In our research on medicines, we find consumers often confused the names and the brands.

排名 Brand Ranking	品牌或品种 Brands or Kinds	人数 Number	百分比 Percent
1	康泰克 Contac	398	39.3
2	泰诺 Tylenol Cold	123	12.1
3	百服宁 Bufferin	112	11.0
4	克感敏 Keganmin	95	9.4
5	上药 Shang Hai Zhi Yao	32	3.2
6	感冒通 Ganmaotong	30	3.0
7	天平牌 Tianping	28	2.8
8	白加黑片 White&Black	17	1.7
9	福牌 Fupai	11	1.1
9	日夜百服宁 Bufferin Gold	11	1.1
10	美优感冒通 Mei You Gan Mao Tong	9	0.9
10	明兴 Ming Xing	9	0.9
11	宇宙 Yuzhou	8	0.8
11	康得 Contac	8	0.8
12	感冒冲剂 Gan Mao Chong Ji	6	0.6
13	正柴胡饮 Zheng Chai Hu Yin	5	0.5
13	帕尔克 Pa'erke	5	0.5
13	板兰根 Banlangen	5	0.5
13	强力维 C 银翘 Qiang Li VC	5	0.5
14	速效伤风胶囊 Su Xiao Shang Feng Jiao Nang	4	0.4

n=1014

1-5 样本、男性各年龄层、女性各年龄层的品牌习惯/ Brand Habit in Consuming Cold Medicines by the Whole Sample, Age and Gender Groups

	人数 Number	基本固定用一个牌子 used in only one brand	比较固定地用两个或三个牌子 used in two or three brands	基本上不太固定牌子 no brand preference
样本 Sample	822	39.4	40.5	20.1
男性 Male	415	38.6	38.1	23.4
16~24 岁 Age	87	39.1	40.2	20.7
25~34 岁 Age	113	38.1	39.8	22.1
35~44 岁 Age	113	36.3	39.8	23.9
45~54 岁 Age	69	39.1	33.3	27.5
55~60 岁 Age	33	45.5	30.3	24.2
女性 Female	407	40.3	43.0	16.7
16~24 岁 Age	87	44.8	35.6	19.5
25~34 岁 Age	120	40.0	46.7	13.3
35~44 岁 Age	107	41.1	40.2	18.7
45~54 岁 Age	62	37.1	45.2	17.7
55~60 岁 Age	31	32.3	54.8	12.9

1-6 易患感冒的季节/ Which Season to Prone to Catch Cold

注：本题为多选题，合计百分比超过 100%（Multiple answers）

	人次 Person-time	百分比 Percent
冬春之交 between winter & spring	243	29.7
春天 spring	51	6.2
春末夏初 late spring & early summer	40	4.9
夏天 summer	15	1.8
夏秋之交 between summer & autumn	124	15.2
秋天 autumn	109	13.3
入冬之际 early winter	275	33.7
冬天 winter	65	8.0
不确定 not sure	188	23.0

n=817

1-7 样本、男性各年龄层、女性各年龄层最近一年内有无服用的比例/ Whether having Taken Cold Medicines Last Year by the Whole Sample, Age and Gender Groups

	人数 Number	吃过 yes	没吃过 no
样本 Sample	1014	81.1	18.9
男性 Male	509	81.5	18.5
16~24 岁 Age	109	79.8	20.2
25~34 岁 Age	146	77.4	22.6
35~44 岁 Age	130	86.9	13.1
45~54 岁 Age	85	81.2	18.8
55~60 岁 Age	39	84.6	15.4
女性 Female	505	80.6	19.4
16~24 岁 Age	108	80.6	19.4
25~34 岁 Age	144	83.3	16.7
35~44 岁 Age	130	82.3	17.7
45~54 岁 Age	82	75.6	24.4
55~60 岁 Age	41	75.6	24.4

1-8 选择该类商品的考虑因素/ Ranking of the Considerations in Purchasing

注：本题为多选题，合计百分比超过 100%（Multiple answers）

排名 Ranking	考虑因素 Considerations	人次 Person-time	百分比 Percent
1	医生推荐 recommended by doctors	402	49.0
2	见效快 immediate effect	398	48.5
3	服用方式简便 simple to take	160	19.5
4	有名的牌子 famous brand	152	18.5
5	价格适中 reasonable price	108	13.2
6	不嗜睡 not feeling sleepy	105	12.8
7	广告影响 influence of advertising	84	10.2
8	购买方便 easy to buy	78	9.5
9	亲友介绍 introduced by relatives & friends	38	4.6
10	其他 others	14	1.7

n=820

1-9 样本、男性各年龄层、女性各年龄层最常服用的种类/ Types of Cold Medicine Consumed by the Whole Sample, Age and Gender Groups

	人数 Number	片剂 pill	冲剂 granular formulation	胶囊 capsule	药粉 powder	糖浆 syrup	药丸 bolus	其他 others
样本 Sample	815	50.2	4.5	37.7	0.4	0.9	6.4	0.0
男性 Male	411	48.2	4.9	39.9	0.5	0.5	6.1	0.0
16~24 岁 Age	85	54.1	2.4	40.0	0.0	0.0	3.5	0.0
25~34 岁 Age	113	43.4	7.1	44.2	0.0	0.0	5.3	0.0
35~44 岁 Age	113	47.8	4.4	37.2	1.8	0.9	8.0	0.0
45~54 岁 Age	69	50.7	2.9	39.1	0.0	0.0	7.2	0.0
55~60 岁 Age	31	45.2	9.7	35.5	0.0	3.2	6.5	0.0
女性 Female	404	52.2	4.2	35.4	0.2	1.2	6.7	0.0
16~24 岁 Age	85	44.7	3.5	41.2	0.0	2.4	8.2	0.0
25~34 岁 Age	120	50.0	5.0	35.8	0.8	0.8	7.5	0.0
35~44 岁 Age	106	51.9	1.9	39.6	0.0	1.9	4.7	0.0
45~54 岁 Age	62	61.3	6.5	24.2	0.0	0.0	8.1	0.0
55~60 岁 Age	31	64.5	6.5	25.8	0.0	0.0	3.2	0.0

1-10 样本、男性各年龄层、女性各年龄层最常服用的场合/ Settings of Consumption by the Whole Sample, Age and Gender Groups

注：本题为多选题，合计百分比超过 100%（Multiple answers）

	人数 Number	有感冒的前兆 having signs of cold	轻度感冒症状 light cold symptom	严重感冒症状 severe cold symptom	其他 others
样本 Sample	822	20.3	60.1	19.2	0.4
男性 Male	415	19.0	60.0	20.2	0.7
16~24 岁 Age	87	19.5	56.3	24.1	0.0
25~34 岁 Age	113	20.4	56.6	22.1	0.9
35~44 岁 Age	113	20.4	59.3	19.5	0.9
45~54 岁 Age	69	13.0	66.7	20.3	0.0
55~60 岁 Age	33	21.2	69.7	6.1	3.0
女性 Female	407	21.6	60.2	18.2	0.0
16~24 岁 Age	87	13.8	59.8	26.4	0.0
25~34 岁 Age	120	28.3	52.5	19.2	0.0
35~44 岁 Age	107	20.6	64.5	15.0	0.0
45~54 岁 Age	62	19.4	67.7	12.9	0.0
55~60 岁 Age	31	25.8	61.3	12.9	0.0

1-11 样本、男性各年龄层、女性各年龄层购买感冒药的场所/ Location of Buying Cold Medicine by the Whole Sample, Age and Gender Groups

注：本题为多选题，合计百分比超过 100%（Multiple answers）

	人数 Number	药店 drug store	医院/诊所 hospital	商场 department store/ shopping center
样本 Sample	820	44.9	64.6	2.6
男性 Male	414	43.5	63.8	2.9
16~24 岁 Age	87	62.1	46.0	2.3
25~34 岁 Age	113	49.6	61.9	1.8
35~44 岁 Age	112	34.8	72.3	2.7
45~54 岁 Age	69	27.5	68.1	7.2
55~60 岁 Age	33	36.4	78.3	0.0
女性 Female	406	46.3	65.5	2.2
16~24 岁 Age	87	59.8	49.4	2.3
25~34 岁 Age	119	49.6	60.5	3.4
35~44 岁 Age	107	41.1	72.0	2.8
45~54 岁 Age	62	32.3	79.0	0.0
55~60 岁 Age	31	41.9	80.6	0.0

1-12 家中是否有备有感冒药的习惯/ The Habit of keeping Cold Medicine at Home

	人数 Number	百分比 Percent
有 yes	902	89.0
没有 no	111	11.0

n=1013

1-13 公费/自费医疗的比例/ Proportion of the Free Medical Service

	人数 Number	百分比 Percent
公费医疗 free medical service	689	69.5
自费医疗 own expense	302	30.5

n=991

1-14 不同消费者层的常用品牌/ The Most Frequently Used Brands by Market Segments

1-14-1 时尚流行指标/ Fads Popular Index

注：在药品品牌调查中，消费者经常出现将药品的名称与品牌名称混淆的现象，特此声明。/ In our research on medicines, we find consumers often confused the names and the brands.

	人数 Number	第一品牌及百分比 1st / percent	第二品牌及百分比 2nd / percent	第三品牌及百分比 3rd / percent	第四品牌及百分比 4th / percent
样本 Sample	812	**康泰克 Contac(30.9)**	**克感敏 Keganmin(15.1)**	**百服宁 Bufferin(9.2)**	**泰诺 Tylenol Cold(8.9)**
平实生活指向 simple living orientation	372	康泰克 Contac(29.6)	克感敏 Keganmin(14.2)	百服宁 Bufferin(8.6)	上药 Shang Hai Zhi Yao (7.0)
时尚流行指向 fashion orientation	440	康泰克 Contac(32.0)	克感敏 Keganmin(15.9)	泰诺 Tylenol Cold(11.8)	百服宁 Bufferin(9.8)

1-14-2 广告态度指标/ Advertising Attitude Index

注：在药品品牌调查中，消费者经常出现将药品的名称与品牌名称混淆的现象，特此声明。/ In our research on medicines, we find consumers often confused the names and the brands.

	人数 Number	第一品牌及百分比 1st / percent	第二品牌及百分比 2nd / percent	第三品牌及百分比 3rd / percent	第四品牌及百分比 4th / percent
样本 Sample	810	**康泰克 Contac(30.6)**	**克感敏 Keganmin(14.9)**	**百服宁 Bufferin(9.5)**	**泰诺 Tylenol Cold(8.9)**
广告淡漠指向 indifferent orientation	199	康泰克 Contac(31.7)	克感敏 Keganmin(16.6)	百服宁 Bufferin(8.5)	泰诺 Tylenol Cold(7.0)
中间层 medium	502	康泰克 Contac(31.3)	克感敏 Keganmin(13.9)	百服宁 Bufferin(9.2)	泰诺 Tylenol Cold(8.6)
信赖广告指向 loyal orientation	109	康泰克 Contac(25.7)	克感敏 Keganmin(16.5)	泰诺 Tylenol Cold(13.8)	百服宁 Bufferin(12.8)

1-14-3 饮食健康指标/ Foods & Drink Quality Index

注：在药品品牌调查中，消费者经常出现将药品的名称与品牌名称混淆的现象，特此声明。/ In our research on medicines, we find consumers often confused the names and the brands.

	人数 Number	第一品牌及百分比 1st / percent	第二品牌及百分比 2nd / percent	第三品牌及百分比 3rd / percent	第四品牌及百分比 4th / percent
样本 Sample	817	**康泰克 Contac(30.7)**	**克感敏 Keganmin(15.1)**	**百服宁 Bufferin(9.5)**	**泰诺 Tylenol Cold(8.7)**
饮食“温饱”指向 "basic" orientation	179	康泰克 Contac(31.3)	克感敏 Keganmin(14.0)	天平牌 Tianping(7.8) 百服宁 Bufferin(7.8)	泰诺 Tylenol Cold(5.6)
中间层 medium	409	康泰克 Contac(29.3)	克感敏 Keganmin(15.4)	百服宁 Bufferin(11.2)	泰诺 Tylenol Cold(7.6)
健康营养指向 health & nutrition orientation	229	康泰克 Contac(32.8)	克感敏 Keganmin(15.3)	泰诺 Tylenol Cold(13.1)	百服宁 Bufferin(7.9)

● 广州 / Guangzhou

1-1 最近一年内有无服用的比例/ Whether having Taken Cold Medicines Last Year

	人数 Number	百分比 Percent
吃过 yes	840	81.2
没吃过 no	194	18.8

n=1034

1-2 最常用品牌或品种排名/ Ranking of the Most Frequently Used Brands or Kinds

注：在药品品牌调查中，消费者经常出现将药品的名称与品牌名称混淆的现象，特此声明。/ In our research on medicines, we find consumers often confused the names and the brands.

排名 Brand Ranking	品牌或品种 Brands or Kinds	人数 Number	百分比 Percent
1	明兴 Ming Xing	254	30.2
2	康泰克 Contac	159	18.9
3	禾穗 Hesui	55	6.5
4	强力维 C 银翘 Qiang Li VC	54	6.4
5	百服宁 Bufferin	43	5.1
6	泰诺 Tylenol Cold	39	4.6
7	幸福伤风素 Coltalin	37	4.4

n=840

1-3 样本、男性各年龄层、女性各年龄层的常用品牌或品种/ The Most Frequently Used Brands or Kinds by the Whole Sample, Age and Gender Groups

注：在药品品牌调查中，消费者经常出现将药品的名称与品牌名称混淆的现象，特此声明。/ In our research on medicines, we find consumers often confused the names and the brands.

	人数 Number	第一品牌及百分比 1st/ percent	第二品牌及百分比 2nd/ percent	第三品牌及百分比 3rd/ percent	第四品牌及百分比 4th/ percent
样本 Sample	840	**明兴 Ming Xing(30.2)**	**康泰克 Contac(18.9)**	**禾穗 Hesui(6.5)**	**强力维 C 银翘 Qiang Li VC(6.4)**
男性 Male	409	**明兴 Ming Xing(29.3)**	**康泰克 Contac(20.5)**	**禾穗 Hesui(6.6)**	**幸福伤风素 Coltalin(5.4)**
16~24 岁 Age	76	明兴 Ming Xing(22.4) 康泰克 Contac(22.4)	泰诺 Tylenol Cold(9.2)	幸福伤风素 Coltalin(6.6)	圣济感冒片 Shengji (5.3) 百服宁 Bufferin(5.3)
25~34 岁 Age	122	明兴 Ming Xing(34.4)	康泰克 Contac(19.7)	幸福伤风素 Coltalin(9.0)	禾穗 Hesui(7.4)
35~44 岁 Age	107	明兴 Ming Xing(29.0)	康泰克 Contac(23.4)	泰诺 Tylenol Cold(7.5)	禾穗 Hesui(6.5)
45~54 岁 Age	65	明兴 Ming Xing(29.2)	康泰克 Contac(18.5)	禾穗 Hesui(9.2)	百服宁 Bufferin(7.7)
55~60 岁 Age	39	明兴 Ming Xing(28.2)	康泰克 Contac(15.4)	强力维 C 银翘 Qiang Li VC(10.3)	禾穗 Hesui(7.7)
女性 Female	431	**明兴 Ming Xing(31.1)**	**康泰克 Contac(17.4)**	**强力维 C 银翘 Qiang Li VC(7.7)**	**禾穗 Hesui(6.5)**
16~24 岁 Age	86	明兴 Ming Xing(37.2)	康泰克 Contac(16.3)	强力维 C 银翘 Qiang Li VC(7.0) 百服宁 Bufferin(7.0)	幸福伤风素 Coltalin(4.7)
25~34 岁 Age	127	明兴 Ming Xing(31.5)	康泰克 Contac(15.0)	禾穗 Hesui(8.7)	强力维 C 银翘 Qiang Li VC(7.9)
35~44 岁 Age	115	明兴 Ming Xing(27.8)	康泰克 Contac(22.6)	泰诺 Tylenol Cold(7.0) 禾穗 Hesui(7.0)	强力维 C 银翘 Qiang Li VC(5.2) 百服宁 Bufferin(5.2)
45~54 岁 Age	72	明兴 Ming Xing(29.2)	康泰克 Contac(15.3)	强力维 C 银翘 Qiang Li VC(12.5)	禾穗 Hesui(5.6)
55~60 岁 Age	31	明兴 Ming Xing(29.0)	康泰克 Contac(16.1)	禾穗 Hesui(9.7)	百服宁 Bufferin(6.5) 强力维 C 银翘 Qiang Li VC(6.5) 泰诺 Tylenol Cold(6.5)

1-4 理想品牌或品种排名/ Ranking of the Ideal Brands or Kinds

注：在药品品牌调查中，消费者经常出现将药品的名称与品牌名称混淆的现象，特此声明。/ In our research on medicines, we find consumers often confused the names and the brands.

排名 Brand Ranking	品牌或品种 Brands or Kinds	人数 Number	百分比 Percent
1	明兴 Ming Xing	233	22.5
2	康泰克 Contac	204	19.7
3	泰诺 Tylenol Cold	72	7.0
4	幸福伤风素 Coltalin	71	6.9
5	百服宁 Bufferin	56	5.4
6	强力维 C 银翘 Qiang Li VC	52	5.0
7	禾穗 Hesui	51	4.9

n=1034

1-5 样本、男性各年龄层、女性各年龄层的品牌习惯/ Brand Habit in Consuming Cold Medicines by the Whole Sample, Age and Gender Groups

	人数 Number	基本固定用一个牌子 used in only one brand	比较固定地用两个或三个牌子 used in two or three brands	基本上不太固定牌子 no brand preference
样本 Sample	839	32.4	44.5	23.1
男性 Male	409	33.3	44.3	22.5
16~24 岁 Age	76	36.8	48.7	14.5
25~34 岁 Age	122	30.3	45.9	23.8
35~44 岁 Age	107	35.5	39.3	25.2
45~54 岁 Age	65	29.2	47.7	23.1
55~60 岁 Age	39	35.9	38.5	25.6
女性 Female	430	31.6	44.7	23.7
16~24 岁 Age	86	25.6	55.8	18.6
25~34 岁 Age	127	29.1	45.7	25.2
35~44 岁 Age	115	33.9	43.5	22.6
45~54 岁 Age	71	38.0	38.0	23.9
55~60 岁 Age	31	35.5	29.0	35.5

1-6 易患感冒的季节/ Which Season to Prone to Catch Cold

注：本题为多选题，合计百分比超过 100%（Multiple answers）

	人次 Person-time	百分比 Percent
冬春之交 between winter & spring	118	14.1
春天 spring	42	5.0
春末夏初 late spring & early summer	86	10.3
夏天 summer	29	3.5
夏秋之交 between summer & autumn	106	12.7
秋天 autumn	63	7.5
入冬之际 early winter	193	23.1
冬天 winter	44	5.3
不确定 not sure	358	42.9

n=835

1-7 样本、男性各年龄层、女性各年龄层最近一年内有无服用的比例/ Whether having Taken Cold Medicines Last Year by the Whole Sample, Age and Gender Groups

	人数 Number	吃过 yes	没吃过 no
样本 Sample	1034	81.2	18.8
男性 Male	499	82.0	18.0
16~24 岁 Age	106	71.7	28.3
25~34 岁 Age	150	81.3	18.7
35~44 岁 Age	127	84.3	15.7
45~54 岁 Age	73	89.0	11.0
55~60 岁 Age	43	90.7	9.3
女性 Female	535	80.6	19.4
16~24 岁 Age	112	76.8	23.2
25~34 岁 Age	158	80.4	19.6
35~44 岁 Age	137	83.9	16.1
45~54 岁 Age	87	82.8	17.2
55~60 岁 Age	41	75.6	24.4

1-8 选择该类商品的考虑因素/ Ranking of the Considerations in Purchasing

注：本题为多选题，合计百分比超过 100%（Multiple answers）

排名 Ranking	考虑因素 Considerations	人次 Person-time	百分比 Percent
1	见效快 immediate effect	512	61.0
2	医生推荐 recommended by doctors	286	34.1
3	价格适中 reasonable price	165	19.7
4	有名的牌子 famous brand	149	17.8
5	服用方式简便 simple to take	137	16.3
6	不嗜睡 not feeling sleepy	131	15.6
7	购买方便 easy to buy	101	12.0
8	广告影响 influence of advertising	69	8.2
9	亲友介绍 introduced by relatives & friends	57	6.8
10	其他 others	7	0.8

n=839

1-9 样本、男性各年龄层、女性各年龄层最常服用的种类/ Ranking of the Types of Cold Medicine Consumed by the Whole Sample, Age and Gender Groups

	人数 Number	片剂 pill	冲剂 granular formulation	胶囊 capsule	药粉 powder	糖浆 syrup	药丸 bolus	其他 others
样本 Sample	**821**	**53.8**	**1.1**	**30.5**	**0.4**	**0.1**	**13.6**	**0.5**
男性 Male	**402**	**54.2**	**0.7**	**33.1**	**0.2**	**0.0**	**11.2**	**0.5**
16~24 岁 Age	74	54.1	0.0	32.4	1.4	0.0	12.2	0.0
25~34 岁 Age	121	52.1	0.8	37.2	0.0	0.0	9.1	0.8
35~44 岁 Age	105	54.3	0.0	33.3	0.0	0.0	12.4	0.0
45~54 岁 Age	64	51.6	0.0	31.3	0.0	0.0	15.6	1.6
55~60 岁 Age	38	65.8	5.3	23.7	0.0	0.0	5.3	0.0
女性 Female	**419**	**53.5**	**1.4**	**27.9**	**0.5**	**0.2**	**16.0**	**0.5**
16~24 岁 Age	82	50.0	2.4	29.3	0.0	0.0	18.3	0.0
25~34 岁 Age	123	61.0	1.6	24.4	0.8	0.8	11.4	0.0
35~44 岁 Age	114	53.5	0.9	27.2	0.0	0.0	18.4	0.0
45~54 岁 Age	69	53.6	0.0	30.4	1.4	0.0	13.0	1.4
55~60 岁 Age	31	32.3	3.2	35.5	0.0	0.0	25.8	3.2

1-10 样本、男性各年龄层、女性各年龄层最常服用的场合/ Settings of Consumption by the Whole Sample, Age and Gender Groups

	人数 Number	有感冒的前兆 having signs of cold	轻度感冒症状 light cold symptom	严重感冒症状 severe cold symptom	其他 others
样本 Sample	**838**	**27.3**	**57.0**	**15.6**	**0.0**
男性 Male	**409**	**24.2**	**60.1**	**15.6**	**0.0**
16~24 岁 Age	76	27.6	60.5	11.8	0.0
25~34 岁 Age	122	19.7	59.8	20.5	0.0
35~44 岁 Age	107	26.2	61.7	12.1	0.0
45~54 岁 Age	65	20.0	60.0	20.0	0.0
55~60 岁 Age	39	33.3	56.4	10.3	0.0
女性 Female	**429**	**30.3**	**54.1**	**15.6**	**0.0**
16~24 岁 Age	86	26.7	57.0	16.3	0.0
25~34 岁 Age	126	31.0	51.6	17.5	0.0
35~44 岁 Age	115	29.6	53.0	17.4	0.0
45~54 岁 Age	71	26.8	60.6	12.7	0.0
55~60 岁 Age	31	48.4	45.2	6.5	0.0

1-11 样本、男性各年龄层、女性各年龄层购买感冒药的场所/ Location of Buying Cold Medicine by the Whole Sample, Age and Gender Groups

注：本题为多选题，合计百分比超过 100%（Multiple answers）

	人数 Number	药店 drug store	医院/诊所 hospital	商场 department store/ shopping center
样本 Sample	**836**	**63.8**	**44.5**	**4.8**
男性 Male	**407**	**62.2**	**44.7**	**4.9**
16~24 岁 Age	75	62.7	45.3	1.3
25~34 岁 Age	122	63.1	44.3	8.2
35~44 岁 Age	107	60.7	42.1	4.7
45~54 岁 Age	64	64.1	45.3	6.3
55~60 岁 Age	39	59.0	51.3	0.0
女性 Female	**429**	**65.3**	**44.3**	**4.7**
16~24 岁 Age	85	70.6	34.1	9.4
25~34 岁 Age	127	67.7	39.4	4.7
35~44 岁 Age	115	68.7	44.3	3.5
45~54 岁 Age	71	56.3	57.7	1.4
55~60 岁 Age	31	48.4	61.3	3.2

1-12 家中是否有备用感冒药的习惯/ The Habit of Keeping Cold Medicine at Home

	人数 Number	百分比 Percent
有 yes	876	84.9
没有 no	156	15.1

n=1032

1-13 公费/自费医疗的比例/ Proportion of the Free Medical Service

	人数 Number	百分比 Percent
公费医疗 free medical service	423	40.9
自费医疗 own expense	610	59.1

n=1033

1-14 不同消费者层的常用品牌/ The Most Frequently Used Brands by Market Segments

1-14-1 时尚流行指标/ Fads Popular Index

注：在药品品牌调查中，消费者经常出现将药品的名称与品牌名称混淆的现象，特此声明。/ In our research on medicines, we find consumers often confused the names and the brands.

	人数 Number	第一品牌及百分比 1st / percent	第二品牌及百分比 2nd / percent	第三品牌及百分比 3rd / percent	第四品牌及百分比 4th / percent
样本 Sample	832	**明兴 Ming Xing(30.3)**	**康泰克 Contac(18.9)**	**强力维 C 银翘 Qiang Li VC(6.5)** **禾穗 Hesui(6.5)**	**百服宁 Bufferin(5.0)**
平实生活指向 simple living orientation	429	明兴 Ming Xing(29.8)	康泰克 Contac(18.4)	禾穗 Hesui(8.2)	强力维 C 银翘 Qiang Li VC(5.8)
时尚流行指向 fashion orientation	403	明兴 Ming Xing(30.8)	康泰克 Contac(19.4)	强力维 C 银翘 Qiang Li VC(7.2)	泰诺 Tylenol Cold(6.0)

1-14-2 广告态度指标/ Advertising Attitude Index

注：在药品品牌调查中，消费者经常出现将药品的名称与品牌名称混淆的现象，特此声明。/ In our research on medicines, we find consumers often confused the names and the brands.

	人数 Number	第一品牌及百分比 1st / percent	第二品牌及百分比 2nd / percent	第三品牌及百分比 3rd / percent	第四品牌及百分比 4th / percent
样本 Sample	831	**明兴 Ming Xing(30.6)**	**康泰克 Contac(18.8)**	**禾穗 Hesui(6.6)**	**强力维 C 银翘 Qiang Li VC(6.3)**
广告淡漠指向 indifferent orientation	266	明兴 Ming Xing(28.2)	康泰克 Contac(19.5)	禾穗 Hesui(7.1)	强力维 C 银翘 Qiang Li VC(6.0)
中间层 medium	495	明兴 Ming Xing(32.7)	康泰克 Contac(18.0)	强力维 C 银翘 Qiang Li VC(7.1)	禾穗 Hesui(5.7)
信赖广告指向 loyal orientation	70	明兴 Ming Xing(24.3)	康泰克 Contac(21.4)	禾穗 Hesui(11.4)	泰诺 Tylenol Cold(7.1) 百服宁 Bufferin(7.1)

1-14-3 饮食健康指标/ Foods & Drink Quality Index

注：在药品品牌调查中，消费者经常出现将药品的名称与品牌名称混淆的现象，特此声明。/ In our research on medicines, we find consumers often confused the names and the brands.

	人数 Number	第一品牌及百分比 1st / percent	第二品牌及百分比 2nd / percent	第三品牌及百分比 3rd / percent	第四品牌及百分比 4th / percent
样本 Sample	835	**明兴 Ming Xing(30.3)**	**康泰克 Contac(19.0)**	**禾穗 Hesui(6.6)**	**强力维 C 银翘 Qiang Li VC(6.5)**
饮食"温饱"指向 "basic" orientation	245	明兴 Ming Xing(27.8)	康泰克 Contac(20.0)	禾穗 Hesui(6.1)	强力维 C 银翘 Qiang Li VC(5.7)
中间层 medium	446	明兴 Ming Xing(31.8)	康泰克 Contac(18.4)	强力维 C 银翘 Qiang Li VC(6.5)	禾穗 Hesui(5.8)
健康营养指向 health & nutrition orientation	144	明兴 Ming Xing(29.9)	康泰克 Contac(19.4)	禾穗 Hesui(9.7)	强力维 C 银翘 Qiang Li VC(7.6)

● 重庆 / Chongqing

1-1 最近一年内有无服用的比例/ Whether having Taken Cold Medicines Last Year

	人数 Number	百分比 Percent
吃过 yes	511	81.9
没吃过 no	113	18.1

n=624

1-2 最常用品牌或品种排名/ Ranking of the Most Frequently Used Brands or Kinds

注：在药品品牌调查中，消费者经常出现将药品的名称与品牌名称混淆的现象，特此声明。/ In our research on medicines, we find consumers often confused the names and the brands.

排名 Brand Ranking	品牌或品种 Brands or Kinds	人数 Number	百分比 Percent
1	康泰克 Contac	109	21.3
2	感冒通 Ganmaotong	78	15.3
3	感康 Gankang	37	7.2
4	感冒清 Ganmaoqing	36	7.0
5	速效感冒胶囊 Su Xiao Gan Mao Jiao Nang	19	3.7
6	强力维 C 银翘 Qiang Li VC	18	3.5
7	散利痛 Sanlitong	16	3.1
8	感诺 Gannuo	13	2.5
8	重感灵 Zhong Gan Ling	13	2.5
9	泰诺 Tylenol Cold	10	2.0
9	白加黑 White&Black	10	2.0
10	三九 999	9	1.8

N=511

1-3 样本、男性各年龄层、女性各年龄层的常用品牌或品种/ The Most Frequently Used Brands or Kinds by the Whole Sample, Age and Gender Groups

注：在药品品牌调查中，消费者经常出现将药品的名称与品牌名称混淆的现象，特此声明。/ In our research on medicines, we find consumers often confused the names and the brands.

	人数 Number	第一品牌及百分比 1st/ percent	第二品牌及百分比 2nd/ percent	第三品牌及百分比 3rd/ percent
样本 Sample	511	**康泰克 Contac(21.3)**	**感冒通 Ganmaotong(15.3)**	**感康 Gankang(7.2)**
男性 Male	256	**康泰克 Contac(22.7)**	**感冒通 Ganmaotong(16.0)**	**感康 Gankang(7.4)**
16~24 岁 Age	55	康泰克 Contac(20.0)	感冒通 Ganmaotong(14.5)	感康 Gankang(10.9)
25~34 岁 Age	72	康泰克 Contac(25.0)	感康 Gankang(11.1)	感冒通 Ganmaotong(9.7)
35~44 岁 Age	60	感冒通 Ganmaotong(23.3)	康泰克 Contac(20.0)	三九 999(5.0) 感冒清 Ganmaoqing(5.0) 新宜感冒通 Xinyi(5.0)
45~54 岁 Age	44	康泰克 Contac(27.3)	感冒通 Ganmaotong(20.5)	速效感冒胶囊 Su Xiao Gan Mao Jiao Nang(11.4)
55~60 岁 Age	25	康泰克 Contac(20.0)	感冒通 Ganmaotong(12.0)	速效感冒胶囊 Su Xiao Gan Mao Jiao Nang(8.0) 快克 Quick(8.0) 感冒清 Ganmaoqing(8.0) 感康 Gankang(8.0)
女性 Female	255	**康泰克 Contac(20.0)**	**感冒通 Ganmaotong(14.5)**	**感冒清 Ganmaoqing(8.6)**
16~24 岁 Age	53	康泰克 Contac(22.6)	感康 Gankang(13.2)	感冒通 Ganmaotong(11.3)
25~34 岁 Age	67	康泰克 Contac(26.9)	感冒通 Ganmaotong(14.9)	感康 Gankang(6.0) 感冒清 Ganmaoqing(6.0) 散利痛 Sanlitong(6.0)
35~44 岁 Age	61	康泰克 Contac(16.4)	感冒通 Ganmaotong(14.8)	感康 Gankang(9.8) 感冒清 Ganmaoqing(9.8)
45~54 岁 Age	53	康泰克 Contac(18.9)	感冒通 Ganmaotong(15.1)	感冒清 Ganmaoqing(9.4)
55~60 岁 Age	21	感冒通 Ganmaotong(19.0) 感冒清 Ganmaoqing(19.0)	阿莫西林 A Me Xi Lin(4.8) 强力维 C 银翘 Qiang Li VC(4.8) 重生牌速效 Chongsheng(4.8) 板兰根 Ban Lan Gen(4.8) 速效感冒胶囊 Su Xiao Gan Mao Jiao Nang(4.8) 白云山 Bai Yun Shan(4.8) 银翘解毒片 Yinqiao(4.8) 重感灵 Zhong Gan Ling(4.8) 泰诺 Tylenol Cold(4.8) 速效伤风胶囊 Su Xiao Shang Feng Jiao Nang(4.8) 扑感敏 Puganmin(4.8) 克感敏 Keganmin(4.8) 康泰克 Contac(4.8)	

1-4 理想品牌或品种排名/ Ranking of the Ideal Brands or Kinds

注：在药品品牌调查中，消费者经常出现将药品的名称与品牌名称混淆的现象，特此声明。/ In our research on medicines, we find consumers often confused the names and the brands.

排名 Brand Ranking	品牌或品种 Brands or Kinds	人数 Number	百分比 Percent
1	康泰克 Contac	169	27.1
2	感康 Gankang	61	9.8
3	感冒通 Ganmaotong	60	9.6
4	感冒清 Ganmaoqing	31	5.0
5	散利痛 Sanlitong	22	3.5
6	泰诺 Tylenol Cold	20	3.2
7	速效感冒胶囊 Su Xiao Gan Mao Jiao Nang	17	2.7
8	白加黑片 White&Black	14	2.2
9	强力维 C 银翘 Qiang Li VC	13	2.1
9	三九 999	13	2.1
9	重感灵 Zhong Gan Ling	13	2.1
10	感诺 Gannuo	11	1.8

n=624

1-5 样本、男性各年龄层、女性各年龄层的品牌习惯/ Brand Habit in Consuming Cold Medicines by the Whole Sample, Age and Gender Groups

	人数 Number	基本固定用一个牌子 used in only one brand	比较固定地用两个或三个牌子 used in two or three brands	基本上不太固定牌子 no brand preference
样本 Sample	510	29.4	33.5	37.1
男性 Male	255	28.6	34.9	36.5
16~24 岁 Age	55	40.0	38.2	21.8
25~34 岁 Age	72	29.2	44.4	26.4
35~44 岁 Age	59	22.0	25.4	52.5
45~54 岁 Age	44	25.0	34.1	40.9
55~60 岁 Age	25	24.0	24.0	52.0
女性 Female	255	30.2	32.2	37.6
16~24 岁 Age	53	35.8	30.2	34.0
25~34 岁 Age	67	22.4	38.8	38.8
35~44 岁 Age	61	39.3	19.7	41.0
45~54 岁 Age	53	17.0	39.6	43.4
55~60 岁 Age	21	47.6	33.3	19.0

1-6 易患感冒的季节/ Which Season to Prone to Catch Cold

注：本题为多选题，合计百分比超过 100%（Multiple answers）

	人次 Person-time	百分比 Percent
冬春之交 between winter & spring	113	22.2
春天 spring	49	9.6
春末夏初 late spring & early summer	38	7.5
夏天 summer	11	2.2
夏秋之交 between summer & autumn	78	15.4
秋天 autumn	58	11.4
入冬之际 early winter	127	25.0
冬天 winter	68	13.4
不确定 not sure	148	29.1

n=508

1-7 样本、男性各年龄层、女性各年龄层最近一年内有无服用的比例/ Whether having Taken Cold Medicines Last Year by the Whole Sample, Age and Gender Groups

	人数 Number	吃过 yes	没吃过 no
样本 Sample	**624**	**81.9**	**18.1**
男性 Male	**314**	**81.5**	**18.5**
16~24 岁 Age	64	85.9	14.1
25~34 岁 Age	93	77.4	22.6
35~44 岁 Age	75	80.0	20.0
45~54 岁 Age	54	81.5	18.5
55~60 岁 Age	28	89.3	10.7
女性 Female	**310**	**82.3**	**17.7**
16~24 岁 Age	64	82.8	17.2
25~34 岁 Age	90	74.4	25.6
35~44 岁 Age	73	83.6	16.4
45~54 岁 Age	60	88.3	11.7
55~60 岁 Age	23	91.3	8.7

1-8 选择该类商品的考虑因素/ Ranking of the Considerations in Purchasing

注：本题为多选题，合计百分比超过 100%（Multiple answers）

排名 Ranking	考虑因素 Considerations	人次 Person-time	百分比 Percent
1	见效快 immediate effect	325	64.2
2	医生推荐 recommended by doctors	156	30.8
3	价格适中 reasonable price	128	25.3
4	服用方式简便 simple to take	80	15.8
5	购买方便 easy to buy	63	12.5
6	有名的牌子 famous brand	53	10.5
7	广告影响 influence of advertising	45	8.9
8	不嗜睡 not feeling sleepy	42	8.3
9	亲友介绍 introduced by relatives & friends	29	5.7
10	其他 others	6	1.2

n=506

1-9 样本、男性各年龄层、女性各年龄层最常服用的种类/ Types of Cold Medicine Consumed by the Whole Sample, Age and Gender Groups

	人数 Number	片剂 pill	冲剂 granular formulation	胶囊 capsule	药粉 powder	糖浆 syrup	药丸 bolus	其他 others
样本 Sample	**497**	**46.7**	**5.6**	**35.4**	**0.8**	**0.4**	**10.7**	**0.4**
男性 Male	**248**	**44.4**	**4.4**	**36.3**	**1.2**	**0.8**	**12.5**	**0.4**
16~24 岁 Age	55	36.4	1.8	36.4	0.0	1.8	23.6	0.0
25~34 岁 Age	69	46.4	2.9	37.7	1.4	1.4	10.1	0.0
35~44 岁 Age	58	46.6	8.6	32.8	1.7	0.0	10.3	0.0
45~54 岁 Age	42	47.6	2.4	40.5	0.0	0.0	9.5	0.0
55~60 岁 Age	24	45.8	8.3	33.3	4.2	0.0	4.2	4.2
女性 Female	**249**	**49.0**	**6.8**	**34.5**	**0.4**	**0.0**	**8.8**	**0.4**
16~24 岁 Age	52	50.0	1.9	40.4	0.0	0.0	7.7	0.0
25~34 岁 Age	66	53.0	3.0	31.8	1.5	0.0	10.6	0.0
35~44 岁 Age	58	48.3	12.1	32.8	0.0	0.0	5.2	1.7
45~54 岁 Age	52	48.1	9.6	34.6	0.0	0.0	7.7	0.0
55~60 岁 Age	21	38.1	9.5	33.3	0.0	0.0	19.0	0.0

1-10 样本、男性各年龄层、女性各年龄层最常服用的场合/ Settings of Consumption by the Whole Sample, Age and Gender Groups

	人数 Number	有感冒的前兆 having signs of cold	轻度感冒症状 light cold symptom	严重感冒症状 severe cold symptom	其他 others
样本 Sample	**511**	**18.4**	**59.5**	**22.1**	**0.0**
男性 Male	**256**	**16.8**	**59.0**	**24.2**	**0.0**
16~24 岁 Age	55	16.4	60.0	23.6	0.0
25~34 岁 Age	72	12.5	62.5	25.0	0.0
35~44 岁 Age	60	21.7	45.0	33.3	0.0
45~54 岁 Age	44	11.4	70.5	18.2	0.0
55~60 岁 Age	25	28.0	60.0	12.0	0.0
女性 Female	**255**	**20.0**	**60.0**	**20.0**	**0.0**
16~24 岁 Age	53	7.5	69.8	22.6	0.0
25~34 岁 Age	67	17.9	62.7	19.4	0.0
35~44 岁 Age	61	19.7	62.3	18.0	0.0
45~54 岁 Age	53	24.5	50.9	24.5	0.0
55~60 岁 Age	21	47.6	42.9	9.5	0.0

1-11 样本、男性各年龄层、女性各年龄层购买感冒药的场所/ Location of Buying Cold Medicine by the Whole Sample, Age and Gender Groups

注：本题为多选题，合计百分比可能超过 100%（Multiple answers）

	人数 Number	药店 drug store	医院/诊所 hospital	商场 department store/ shopping center
样本 Sample	**510**	**71.6**	**42.4**	**2.9**
男性 Male	**256**	**70.7**	**42.6**	**3.9**
16~24 岁 Age	55	63.6	41.8	5.5
25~34 岁 Age	72	70.8	40.3	1.4
35~44 岁 Age	60	76.7	36.7	5.0
45~54 岁 Age	44	75.0	47.7	4.5
55~60 岁 Age	25	64.0	56.0	4.0
女性 Female	**254**	**72.4**	**42.1**	**2.0**
16~24 岁 Age	53	66.0	43.4	5.7
25~34 岁 Age	67	76.1	43.3	1.5
35~44 岁 Age	61	72.1	45.9	0.0
45~54 岁 Age	53	71.7	37.7	1.9
55~60 岁 Age	20	80.0	35.0	0.0

1-12 家中是否有备用感冒药的习惯/ The Habit of keeping Cold Medicine at Home

	人数 Number	百分比 Percent
有 yes	508	81.4
没有 no	116	18.6

n=624

1-13 公费/自费医疗的比例/ Proportion of the Free Medical Service

	人数 Number	百分比 Percent
公费医疗 free medical service	180	29.2
自费医疗 own expense	437	70.8

n=617

1-14 不同消费者层的常用品牌/ The Most Frequently Used Brands by Market Segments

1-14-1 时尚流行指标/ Fads Popular Index

注：在药品品牌调查中，消费者经常出现将药品的名称与品牌名称混淆的现象，特此声明。/ In our research on medicines, we find consumers often confused the names and the brands.

	人数 Number	第一品牌及百分比 1st / percent	第二品牌及百分比 2nd / percent	第三品牌及百分比 3rd / percent
样本 Sample	**504**	**康泰克 Contac(21.6)**	**感冒通 Ganmaotong(15.1)**	**感康 Gankang(7.1)** **感冒清 Ganmaoqing(7.1)**
平实生活指向 simple living orientation	297	康泰克 Contac(20.2)	感冒通 Ganmaotong(18.2)	感冒清 Ganmaoqing(7.4)
时尚流行指向 fashion orientation	207	康泰克 Contac(23.7)	感康 Gankang(11.6)	感冒通 Ganmaotong(10.6)

1-14-2 广告态度指标/ Advertising Attitude Index

注：在药品品牌调查中，消费者经常出现将药品的名称与品牌名称混淆的现象，特此声明。/ In our research on medicines, we find consumers often confused the names and the brands.

	人数 Number	第一品牌及百分比 1st / percent	第二品牌及百分比 2nd / percent	第三品牌及百分比 3rd / percent
样本 Sample	509	**康泰克 Contac(21.4)**	**感冒通 Ganmaotong(15.1)**	**感康 Gankang(7.3)**
广告淡漠指向 indifferent orientation	141	感冒通 Ganmaotong(20.6)	康泰克 Contac(17.7)	感冒清 Ganmaoqing(9.2)
中间层 medium	301	康泰克 Contac(22.3)	感冒通 Ganmaotong(12.6)	感冒清 Ganmaoqing(7.3)
信赖广告指向 loyal orientation	67	康泰克 Contac(25.4)	感冒通 Ganmaotong(14.9)	感康 Gankang(9.0)

1-14-3 饮食健康指标/ Foods & Drink Quality Index

注：在药品品牌调查中，消费者经常出现将药品的名称与品牌名称混淆的现象，特此声明。/ In our research on medicines, we find consumers often confused the names and the brands.

	人数 Number	第一品牌及百分比 1st / percent	第二品牌及百分比 2nd / percent	第三品牌及百分比 3rd / percent
样本 Sample	507	**康泰克 Contac(21.3)**	**感冒通 Ganmaotong(15.4)**	**感康 Gankang(7.3)**
饮食"温饱"指向 "basic" orientation	191	感冒通 Ganmaotong(18.3) 康泰克 Contac(18.3)	感冒清 Ganmaoqing(7.9)	散利痛 Sanlitong(3.7)
中间层 medium	213	康泰克 Contac(23.0)	感冒通 Ganmaotong(14.1)	感康 Gankang(9.4)
健康营养指向 health & nutrition orientation	103	康泰克 Contac(23.3)	感冒通 Ganmaotong(12.6)	感康 Gankang(10.7)

● 武汉 / Wuhan

1-1 最近一年内有无服用的比例/ Whether having Taken Cold Medicines Last Year

	人数 Number	百分比 Percent
吃过 yes	536	83.5
没吃过 no	106	16.5

n=642

1-2 最常用品牌或品种排名/ Ranking of the Most Frequently Used Brands or Kinds

注：在药品品牌调查中，消费者经常出现将药品的名称与品牌名称混淆的现象，特此声明。/ In our research on medicines, we find consumers often confused the names and the brands.

排名 Brand Ranking	品牌或品种 Brands or Kinds	人数 Number	百分比 Percent
1	中联强效片 Zhong Lian Qiang Xiao Pian	103	19.2
2	康泰克 Contac	95	17.7
3	感冒通 Ganmaotong	43	8.0
4	强力维 C 银翘 Qiang Li VC	34	6.3
5	快克 Quick	24	4.5
6	感康 Gankang	23	4.3
7	感冒清 Ganmaoqing	22	4.1
8	速效伤风胶囊 Su Xiao Shang Feng Jiao Nang	21	3.9
9	三九 999	17	3.2
10	白加黑片 White&Black	14	2.6

n=536

1-3 样本、男性各年龄层、女性各年龄层的常用品牌或品种/ The Most Frequently Used Brands or Kinds by the Whole Sample, Age and Gender Groups

注：在药品品牌调查中，消费者经常出现将药品的名称与品牌名称混淆的现象，特此声明。/ In our research on medicines, we find consumers often confused the names and the brands.

	人数 Number	第一品牌及百分比 1st/ percent	第二品牌及百分比 2nd/ percent	第三品牌及百分比 3rd/ percent
样本 Sample	536	**中联强效片 Zhong Lian Qiang Xiao Pian(19.2)**	**康泰克 Contac(17.7)**	**感冒通 Ganmaotong(8.0)**
男性 Male	259	**康泰克 Contac(18.1)** **中联强效片 Zhong Lian Qiang Xiao Pian(18.1)**	**强力维 C 银翘 Qiang Li VC(8.1)**	**感冒通 Ganmaotong(7.7)**
16~24 岁 Age	52	中联强效片 Zhong Lian Qiang Xiao Pian(21.2)	康泰克 Contac(19.2)	感康 Gankang(7.7)
25~34 岁 Age	76	康泰克 Contac(19.7)	中联强效片 Zhong Lian Qiang Xiao Pian(10.5)	感冒通 Ganmaotong(9.2) 强力维 C 银翘 Qiang Li VC(9.2)
35~44 岁 Age	68	中联强效片 Zhong Lian Qiang Xiao Pian(17.6)	康泰克 Contac(14 7)	强力维 C 银翘 Qiang Li VC(7.4)
45~54 岁 Age	44	康泰克 Contac(22.7) 中联强效片 Zhong Lian Qiang Xiao Pian(22.7)	感冒通 Ganmaotong(11.4) 强力维 C 银翘 Qiang Li VC(11.4)	感冒清 Ganmaoqing(6.8)
55~60 岁 Age	19	中联强效片 Zhong Lian Qiang Xiao Pian(31.6)	康泰克 Contac(10.5) 速效伤风胶囊 Su Xiao Shang Feng Jiao Nang(10.5) 强力维 C 银翘 Qiang Li VC(10.5)	速效感冒片 Su Xiao Gan Mao Pian(5.3) 感冒通 Ganmaotong(5.3) 阿莫仙 Amoxian(5.3) 白云山 Bai Yun Shan(5.3) 民康 Minkang(5.3) 健民 Jianmin(5.3) 银翘解毒片 Yinqiao(5.3)
女性 Female	277	**中联强效片 Zhong Lian Qiang Xiao Pian(20.2)**	**康泰克 Contac(17.3)**	**感冒通 Ganmaotong(8.3)**
16~24 岁 Age	59	康泰克 Contac(28.8)	中联强效片 Zhong Lian Qiang Xiao Pian(16.9)	感冒通 Ganmaotong(10.2)
25~34 岁 Age	77	康泰克 Contac(19.5)	中联强效片 Zhong Lian Qiang Xiao Pian(9.1) 感冒通 Ganmaotong(9.1) 感康 Gankang(9.1)	三九 999(7.8) 强力维 C 银翘 Qiang Li VC(7.8)
35~44 岁 Age	67	中联强效片 Zhong Lian Qiang Xiao Pian(26.9)	康泰克 Contac(13.4)	速效伤风胶囊 Su Xiao Shang Feng Jiao Nang(9.0)
45~54 岁 Age	51	中联强效片 Zhong Lian Qiang Xiao Pian(29.4)	康泰克 Contac(11.8)	感冒通 Ganmaotong(9.8)
55~60 岁 Age	23	中联强效片 Zhong Lian Qiang Xiao Pian(26.1)	感冒清 Ganmaoqing(13.0)	速效感冒胶囊 Su Xiao Gan Mao Jiao Nang(8.7) 感冒通 Ganmaotong(8.7)

1-4 理想品牌或品种排名/ Ranking of the Ideal Brands or Kinds

注：在药品品牌调查中，消费者经常出现将药品的名称与品牌名称混淆的现象，特此声明。/ In our research on medicines, we find consumers often confused the names and the brands.

排名 Brand Ranking	品牌或品种 Brands or Kinds	人数 Number	百分比 Percent
1	康泰克 Contac	144	22.5
2	中联强效片 Zhong Lian Qiang Xiao Pian	106	16.5
3	感康 Gankang	34	5.3
4	感冒通 Ganmaotong	31	4.8
5	强力维 C 银翘 Qiang Li VC	30	4.7
6	白加黑片 White&Black	27	4.2
7	快克 Quick	21	3.3
7	泰诺 Tylenol Cold	21	3.3
8	感冒清 Ganmaoqing	19	3.0
9	速效伤风胶囊 Su Xiao Shang Feng Jiao Nang	17	2.7
9	三九 999	17	2.7

n=641

1-5 样本、男性各年龄层、女性各年龄层的品牌习惯/ Brand Habit in Consuming Cold Medicines by the Whole Sample, Age and Gender Groups

	人数 Number	基本固定用一个牌子 used in only one brand	比较固定地用两个或三个牌子 used in two or three brands	基本上不太固定牌子 no brand preference
样本 Sample	536	34.7	35.6	29.7
男性 Male	259	34.0	34.0	32.0
16~24 岁 Age	52	38.5	32.7	28.8
25~34 岁 Age	76	23.7	42.1	34.2
35~44 岁 Age	68	38.2	30.9	30.9
45~54 岁 Age	44	31.8	34.1	34.1
55~60 岁 Age	19	52.6	15.8	31.6
女性 Female	277	35.4	37.2	27.4
16~24 岁 Age	59	20.3	49.2	30.5
25~34 岁 Age	77	39.0	40.3	20.8
35~44 岁 Age	67	41.8	28.4	29.9
45~54 岁 Age	51	39.2	37.3	23.5
55~60 岁 Age	23	34.8	21.7	43.5

1-6 易患感冒的季节/ Which Season to Prone to Catch Cold

注：本题为多选题，合计百分比超过 100%（Multiple answers）

	人次 Person-time	百分比 Percent
冬春之交 between winter & spring	123	23.1
春天 spring	77	14.4
春末夏初 late spring & early summer	36	6.8
夏天 summer	21	3.9
夏秋之交 between summer & autumn	91	17.1
秋天 autumn	108	20.3
入冬之际 early winter	107	20.1
冬天 winter	27	5.1
不确定 not sure	149	28.0

n=533

1-7 样本、 男性各年龄层、 女性各年龄层最近一年内有无服用的比例/ Whether having Taken Cold Medicines Last Year by the Whole Sample, Age and Gender Groups

	人数 Number	吃过 yes	没吃过 no
样本 Sample	642	83.5	16.5
男性 Male	311	83.3	16.7
16~24 岁 Age	65	80.0	20.0
25~34 岁 Age	89	85.4	14.6
35~44 岁 Age	80	85.0	15.0
45~54 岁 Age	52	84.6	15.4
55~60 岁 Age	25	76.0	24.0
女性 Female	331	83.7	16.3
16~24 岁 Age	69	85.5	14.5
25~34 岁 Age	96	80.2	19.8
35~44 岁 Age	78	85.9	14.1
45~54 岁 Age	62	82.3	17.7
55~60 岁 Age	26	88.5	11.5

1-8 选择该类商品的考虑因素/ Ranking of the Considerations in Purchasing

注：本题为多选题，合计百分比超过 100%（Multiple answers）

排名 Ranking	考虑因素 Considerations	人次 Person-time	百分比 Percent
1	见效快 immediate effect	318	59.3
2	医生推荐 recommended by doctors	212	39.6
3	价格适中 reasonable price	124	23.1
4	服用方式简便 simple to take	108	20.1
5	不嗜睡 not feeling sleepy	85	15.9
6	有名的牌子 famous brand	82	15.3
7	广告影响 influence of advertising	49	9.1
7	购买方便 easy to buy	49	9.1
8	亲友介绍 introduced by relatives & friends	41	7.6
9	其他 others	9	1.7

n=536

1-9 样本、 男性各年龄层、 女性各年龄层最常服用的种类/ Types of Cold Medicine Consumed by the Whole Sample, Age and Gender Groups

	人数 Number	片剂 pill	冲剂 granular formulation	胶囊 capsule	药粉 powder	糖浆 syrup	药丸 bolus	其他 others
样本 Sample	528	43.8	2.7	47.7	0.0	0.0	5.9	0.0
男性 Male	253	43.9	2.0	47.4	0.0	0.0	6.7	0.0
16~24 岁 Age	51	45.1	2.0	47.1	0.0	0.0	5.9	0.0
25~34 岁 Age	75	41.3	4.0	46.7	0.0	0.0	8.0	0.0
35~44 岁 Age	68	36.8	1.5	55.9	0.0	0.0	5.9	0.0
45~54 岁 Age	40	55.0	0.0	37.5	0.0	0.0	7.5	0.0
55~60 岁 Age	19	52.6	0.0	42.1	0.0	0.0	5.3	0.0
女性 Female	275	43.6	3.3	48.0	0.0	0.0	5.1	0.0
16~24 岁 Age	59	40.7	3.4	45.8	0.0	0.0	10.2	0.0
25~34 岁 Age	77	44.2	6.5	46.8	0.0	0.0	2.6	0.0
35~44 岁 Age	67	41.8	1.5	50.7	0.0	0.0	6.0	0.0
45~54 岁 Age	49	51.0	0.0	46.9	0.0	0.0	2.0	0.0
55~60 岁 Age	23	39.1	4.3	52.2	0.0	0.0	4.3	0.0

1-10 样本、男性各年龄层、女性各年龄层最常服用的场合/ Settings of Consumption by the Whole Sample, Age and Gender Groups

	人数 Number	有感冒的前兆 having signs of cold	轻度感冒症状 light cold symptom	严重感冒症状 severe cold symptom	其他 others
样本 Sample	532	22.6	56.6	20.5	0.4
男性 Male	257	21.8	58.8	19.1	0.4
16~24 岁 Age	52	11.5	59.6	28.8	0.0
25~34 岁 Age	76	19.7	55.3	23.7	1.3
35~44 岁 Age	68	29.4	58.8	11.8	0.0
45~54 岁 Age	42	21.4	64.3	14.3	0.0
55~60 岁 Age	19	31.6	57.9	10.5	0.0
女性 Female	275	23.3	54.5	21.8	0.4
16~24 岁 Age	59	25.4	54.2	20.3	0.0
25~34 岁 Age	77	14.3	63.6	22.1	0.0
35~44 岁 Age	65	26.2	52.3	20.0	1.5
45~54 岁 Age	51	29.4	51.0	19.6	0.0
55~60 岁 Age	23	26.1	39.1	34.8	0.0

1-11 样本、男性各年龄层、女性各年龄层购买感冒药的场所/ Location of Buying Cold Medicine by the Whole Sample, Age and Gender Groups

注：本题为多选题，合计百分比超过 100%（Multiple answers）

	人数 Number	药店 drug store	医院/诊所 hospital	商场 department store/ shopping center
样本 Sample	535	56.1	56.8	2.4
男性 Male	258	58.1	53.5	2.7
16~24 岁 Age	51	52.9	54.9	2.0
25~34 岁 Age	76	68.4	44.7	5.3
35~44 岁 Age	68	69.1	45.6	2.9
45~54 岁 Age	44	36.4	75.0	0.0
55~60 岁 Age	19	42.1	63.2	0.0
女性 Female	277	54.2	59.9	2.2
16~24 岁 Age	59	59.3	55.9	1.7
25~34 岁 Age	77	61.0	50.6	5.2
35~44 岁 Age	67	58.2	64.2	0.0
45~54 岁 Age	51	39.2	68.6	2.0
55~60 岁 Age	23	39.1	69.6	0.0

1-12 家中是否有备用感冒药的习惯/ The Habit of Keeping Cold Medicine at Home

	人数 Number	百分比 Percent
有 yes	524	81.6
没有 no	118	18.4

n=642

1-13 公费/自费医疗的比例/ Proportion of the Free Medical Service

	人数 Number	百分比 Percent
公费医疗 free medical service	264	41.5
自费医疗 own expense	372	58.5

n=636

1-14 不同消费者层的常用品牌/ The Most Frequently Used Brands by Market Segments

1-14-1 时尚流行指标/ Fads Popular Index

注：在药品品牌调查中，消费者经常出现将药品的名称与品牌名称混淆的现象，特此声明。/ In our research on medicines, we find consumers often confused the names and the brands.

	人数 Number	第一品牌及百分比 1st / percent	第二品牌及百分比 2nd / percent	第三品牌及百分比 3rd / percent	第四品牌及百分比 4th / percent
样本 Sample	530	**中联强效片 Zhong Lian Qiang Xiao Pian(19.4)**	**康泰克 Contac(17.5)**	**感冒通 Ganmaotong(7.9)**	**强力维 C 银翘 Qiang Li VC(6.4)**
平实生活指向 simple living orientation	282	中联强效片 Zhong Lian Qiang Xiao Pian(19.5)	康泰克 Contac(17.4)	感冒通 Ganmaotong(8.2)	强力维 C 银翘 Qiang Li VC(7.8)
时尚流行指向 fashion orientation	248	中联强效片 Zhong Lian Qiang Xiao Pian(19.4)	康泰克 Contac(17.7)	感冒通 Ganmaotong(7.7)	感康 Gankang(6.9)

1-14-2 广告态度指标/ Advertising Attitude Index

注：在药品品牌调查中，消费者经常出现将药品的名称与品牌名称混淆的现象，特此声明。/ In our research on medicines, we find consumers often confused the names and the brands.

	人数 Number	第一品牌及百分比 1st / percent	第二品牌及百分比 2nd / percent	第三品牌及百分比 3rd / percent	第四品牌及百分比 4th / percent
样本 Sample	531	**中联强效片 Zhong Lian Qiang Xiao Pian(19.4)**	**康泰克 Contac(17.5)**	**感冒通 Ganmaotong(7.9)**	**强力维 C 银翘 Qiang Li VC(6.4)**
广告淡漠指向 indifferent orientation	154	中联强效片 Zhong Lian Qiang Xiao Pian(20.8)	康泰克 Contac(14.9)	感冒通 Ganmaotong(11.0)	强力维 C 银翘 Qiang Li VC(7.1)
中间层 medium	315	康泰克 Contac(18.7)	中联强效片 Zhong Lian Qiang Xiao Pian(18.4)	感冒通 Ganmaotong(7.9)	强力维 C 银翘 Qiang Li VC(5.4)
信赖广告指向 loyal orientation	62	中联强效片 Zhong Lian Qiang Xiao Pian(21.0)	康泰克 Contac(17.7)	强力维 C 银翘 Qiang Li VC(9.7)	快克 Quick(8.1)

1-14-3 饮食健康指标/ Foods & Drink Quality Index

注：在药品品牌调查中，消费者经常出现将药品的名称与品牌名称混淆的现象，特此声明。/ In our research on medicines, we find consumers often confused the names and the brands.

	人数 Number	第一品牌及百分比 1st / percent	第二品牌及百分比 2nd / percent	第三品牌及百分比 3rd / percent	第四品牌及百分比 4th / percent
样本 Sample	529	**中联强效片 Zhong Lian Qiang Xiao Pian(19.5)**	**康泰克 Contac(17.4)**	**感冒通 Ganmaotong(7.9)**	**强力维 C 银翘 Qiang Li VC(6.4)**
饮食“温饱”指向 "basic" orientation	187	康泰克 Contac(20.9)	中联强效片 Zhong Lian Qiang Xiao Pian(16.6)	感康 Gankang(7.5) 强力维 C 银翘 Qiang Li VC(7.5)	感冒通 Ganmaotong(6.4)
中间层 medium	236	中联强效片 Zhong Lian Qiang Xiao Pian(19.9)	康泰克 Contac(16.9)	感冒通 Ganmaotong(8.9)	强力维 C 银翘 Qiang Li VC(7.2)
健康营养指向 health & nutrition orientation	106	中联强效片 Zhong Lian Qiang Xiao Pian(23.6)	康泰克 Contac(12.3)	感冒通 Ganmaotong(8.5)	三九 999(6.6)

● 西安 / Xi'an

1-1 最近一年内有无服用的比例/ Whether having Taken Cold Medicines Last Year

	人数 Number	百分比 Percent
吃过 yes	532	88.5
没吃过 no	69	11.5

n=601

1-2 最常用品牌或品种排名/ Ranking of the Most Frequently Used Brands or Kinds

注：在药品品牌调查中，消费者经常出现将药品的名称与品牌名称混淆的现象，特此声明。/ In our research on medicines, we find consumers often confused the names and the brands.

排名 Brand Ranking	品牌或品种 Brands or Kinds	人数 Number	百分比 Percent
1	强力维 C 银翘 Qiang Li VC	81	15.2
2	康泰克 Contac	73	13.7
3	速效感冒胶囊 Su Xiao Gan Mao Jiao Nang	59	11.1
4	感冒通 Ganmaotong	53	10.0
5	康必得 Fufang An'fenpuxinpian	46	8.6
6	速效伤风胶囊 Su Xiao Shang Feng Jiao Nang	45	8.5
7	白加黑片 White & Black	17	3.2
8	三九 999	13	2.4
9	感冒清 Ganmaoqing	11	2.1
10	抗病毒冲剂 Kang Bing Du Chong Ji	10	1.9

n=532

1-3 样本、男性各年龄层、女性各年龄层的常用品牌或品种/ The Most Frequently Used Brands or Kinds by the Whole Sample, Age and Gender Groups

注：在药品品牌调查中，消费者经常出现将药品的名称与品牌名称混淆的现象，特此声明。/ In our research on medicines, we find consumers often confused the names and the brands.

	人数 Number	第一品牌及百分比 1st/ percent	第二品牌及百分比 2nd/ percent	第三品牌及百分比 3rd/ percent
样本 Sample	532	**强力维 C 银翘 Qiang Li VC(15.2)**	**康泰克 Contac(13.7)**	**速效感冒胶囊 Su Xiao Gan Mao Jiao Nang (11.1)**
男性 Male	260	**强力维 C 银翘 Qiang Li VC(15.4)** **康泰克 Contac(15.4)**	**速效感冒胶囊 Su Xiao Gan Mao JiaNang(10.0)**	**速效伤风胶囊 Su Xiao Shang Feng Jiao Nang (8.8)**
16~24 岁 Age	49	康泰克 Contac(24.5)	康必得 Fufang An'fenpuxinpian(14.3)	感冒通 Ganmaotong(10.2) 强力维 C 银翘 QianLiVC(10.2)
25~34 岁 Age	75	强力维 C 银翘 Qiang Li VC(18.7)	康泰克 Contac(16.0)	感冒通 Ganmaotong(10.7)
35~44 岁 Age	69	强力维 C 银翘 Qiang Li VC(14.5)	速效伤风胶囊 Su Xiao Shang Feng Jiao Nang (11.6) 速效感冒胶囊 Su Xiao Gan Mao Jiao Nang(11.6)	康必得 Fufang An'fenpuxinpian(7.2) 康泰克 Contac(7.2)
45~54 岁 Age	43	康泰克 Contac(16.3) 强力维 C 银翘 Qiang Li VC(16.3)	康必得 Fufang An'fenpuxinpian(11.6) 速效感冒胶囊 Su Xiao Gan Mao Jiao Nang(11.6)	速效伤风胶囊 Su Xiao Shang Feng Jiao Nang (9.3)
55~60 岁 Age	24	感冒通 Ganmaotong(16.7) 康泰克 Contac(16.7) 强力维 C 银翘 Qiang Li VC(16.7)	速效伤风胶囊 Su Xiao Shang Feng Jiao Nang (12.5) 速效感冒胶囊 Su Xiao Gan Mao Jiao Nang(12.5)	感冒清 Ganmaoqing(8.3)
女性 Female	272	**强力维 C 银翘 Qiang Li VC(15.1)**	**速效感冒胶囊 Su Xiao Gan Mao Jiao Nang (12.1)** **康泰克 Contac(12.1)**	**感冒通 Ganmaotong(11.8)**
16~24 岁 Age	54	康泰克 Contac(22.2)	康必得 Fufang An'fenpuxinpian(13.0)	速效感冒胶囊 Su Xiao Gan Mao Jiao Nang(11.1) 强力维 C 银翘 Qiang Li VC(11.1)
25~34 岁 Age	86	强力维 C 银翘 Qiang Li VC(12.8) 感冒通 Ganmaotong(12.8) 康泰克 Contac(12.8)	速效感冒胶囊 Su Xiao Gan Mao Jiao Nang(9.3)	速效伤风胶囊 Su Xiao Shang Feng Jiao Nang (7.0) 康必得 Fufang An'fenpuxinpian(7.0)
35~44 岁 Age	68	强力维 C 银翘 Qiang Li VC(20.6)	感冒通 Ganmaotong(13.2) 速效感冒胶囊 Su Xiao Gan Mao Jiao Nang(13.2)	速效伤风胶囊 Su Xiao Shang Feng Jiao Nang (10.3)
45~54 岁 Age	41	速效感冒胶囊 Su Xiao Gan Mao Jiao Nang(19.5)	强力维 C 银翘 Qiang Li VC(14.6)	感冒通 Ganmaotong(9.8)
55~60 岁 Age	23	康必得 Fufang An'fenpuxinpian(17.4) 速效伤风胶囊 Su Xiao Shang Feng Jiao Nang (17.4) 强力维 C 银翘 Qiang Li VC(17.4)	感冒通 Ganmaotong(13.0)	康泰克 Contac(8.7) 速效感冒胶囊 Su Xiao Gan Mao Jiao Nang(8.7)

1-4 理想品牌或品种排名/ Ranking of the Ideal Brands or Kinds

注：在药品品牌调查中，消费者经常出现将药品的名称与品牌名称混淆的现象，特此声明。/ In our research on medicines, we find consumers often confused the names and the brands.

排名 Brand Ranking	品牌或品种 Brands or Kinds	人数 Number	百分比 Percent
1	康泰克 Contac	130	21.6
2	强力维 C 银翘 Qiang Li VC	70	11.6
3	康必得 Fufang An'fenpuxinpian	49	8.2
4	速效伤风胶囊 Su Xiao Shang Feng Jiao Nang	41	6.8
5	速效感冒胶囊 Su Xiao Gan Mao Jiao Nang	39	6.5
6	感冒通 Ganmaotong	36	6.0
7	白加黑片 White & Black	35	5.8
8	泰诺 Tylenol Cold	18	3.0
9	三九 999	15	2.5
10	快克 Quick	13	2.2

n=601

1-5 样本、男性各年龄层、女性各年龄层的品牌习惯/ Brand Habit in Consuming Cold Medicines by the Whole Sample, Age and Gender Groups

	人数 Number	基本固定用一个牌子 used in only one brand	比较固定地用两个或三个牌子 used in two or three brands	基本上不太固定牌子 no brand preference
样本 Sample	**532**	**39.3**	**39.8**	**20.9**
男性 Male	**260**	**38.5**	**40.4**	**21.2**
16~24 岁 Age	49	28.6	53.1	18.4
25~34 岁 Age	75	42.7	33.3	24.0
35~44 岁 Age	69	39.1	36.2	24.6
45~54 岁 Age	43	41.9	39.5	18.6
55~60 岁 Age	24	37.5	50.0	12.5
女性 Female	**272**	**40.1**	**39.3**	**20.6**
16~24 岁 Age	54	50.0	33.3	16.7
25~34 岁 Age	86	44.2	32.6	23.3
35~44 岁 Age	68	32.4	47.1	20.6
45~54 岁 Age	41	34.1	41.5	24.4
55~60 岁 Age	23	34.8	52.2	13.0

1-6 易患感冒的季节/ Which Season to Prone to Catch Cold

注：本题为多选题，合计百分比超过 100%（Multiple answers）

	人次 Person-time	百分比 Percent
冬春之交 between winter & spring	127	24.0
春天 spring	27	5.1
春末夏初 late spring & early summer	18	3.4
夏天 summer	10	1.9
夏秋之交 between summer & autumn	59	11.1
秋天 autumn	90	17.0
入冬之际 early winter	214	40.4
冬天 winter	65	12.3
不确定 not sure	112	21.1

n=530

1-7 样本、男性各年龄层、女性各年龄层最近一年内有无服用的比例/ Whether having Taken Cold Medicines Last Year by the Whole Sample, Age and Gender Groups

	人数 Number	吃过 yes	没吃过 no
样本 Sample	601	88.5	11.5
男性 Male	302	86.1	13.9
16~24 岁 Age	64	76.6	23.4
25~34 岁 Age	91	82.4	17.6
35~44 岁 Age	77	89.6	10.4
45~54 岁 Age	46	93.5	6.5
55~60 岁 Age	24	100.0	0.0
女性 Female	299	91.0	9.0
16~24 岁 Age	61	88.5	11.5
25~34 岁 Age	90	95.6	4.4
35~44 岁 Age	74	91.9	8.1
45~54 岁 Age	49	83.7	16.3
55~60 岁 Age	25	92.0	8.0

1-8 选择该类商品的考虑因素/ Ranking of the Considerations in Purchasing

注：本题为多选题，合计百分比超过 100%（Multiple answers）

排名 Ranking	考虑因素 Considerations	人次 Person-time	百分比 Percent
1	见效快 immediate effect	305	57.4
2	医生推荐 recommended by doctors	192	36.2
3	价格适中 reasonable price	123	23.2
4	服用方式简便 simple to take	88	16.6
5	购买方便 easy to buy	77	14.5
6	有名的牌子 famous brand	65	12.2
7	广告影响 influence of advertising	45	8.5
8	不嗜睡 not feeling sleepy	34	6.4
9	亲友介绍 introduced by relatives & friends	32	6.0
10	其他 others	10	1.9

n=531

1-9 样本、男性各年龄层、女性各年龄层最常服用的种类/ Types of Cold Medicine Consumed by the Whole Sample, Age and Gender Groups

	人数 Number	片剂 pill	冲剂 granular formulation	胶囊 capsule	药粉 powder	糖浆 syrup	药丸 bolus
样本 Sample	527	46.9	6.8	43.8	0.2	0.2	2.1
男性 Male	257	48.2	5.4	44.7	0.4	0.4	0.8
16~24 岁 Age	48	50.0	2.1	45.8	0.0	2.1	0.0
25~34 岁 Age	74	44.6	6.8	45.9	0.0	0.0	2.7
35~44 岁 Age	69	46.4	7.2	44.9	1.4	0.0	0.0
45~54 岁 Age	43	58.1	4.7	37.2	0.0	0.0	0.0
55~60 岁 Age	23	43.5	4.3	52.2	0.0	0.0	0.0
女性 Female	270	45.6	8.1	43.0	0.0	0.0	3.3
16~24 岁 Age	54	50.0	11.1	38.9	0.0	0.0	0.0
25~34 岁 Age	84	41.7	7.1	45.2	0.0	0.0	6.0
35~44 岁 Age	68	47.1	10.3	38.2	0.0	0.0	4.4
45~54 岁 Age	41	46.3	4.9	46.3	0.0	0.0	2.4
55~60 岁 Age	23	43.5	4.3	52.2	0.0	0.0	0.0

1-10 样本、男性各年龄层、女性各年龄层最常服用的场合/ Settings of Consumption by the Whole Sample, Age and Gender Groups

	人数 Number	有感冒的前兆 having signs of cold	轻度感冒症状 light cold symptom	严重感冒症状 severe cold symptom
样本 Sample	531	18.6	61.0	20.3
男性 Male	259	20.8	57.5	21.6
16~24 岁 Age	49	14.3	67.3	18.4
25~34 岁 Age	75	16.0	54.7	29.3
35~44 岁 Age	69	20.3	60.9	18.8
45~54 岁 Age	43	30.2	48.8	20.9
55~60 岁 Age	23	34.8	52.2	13.0
女性 Female	272	16.5	64.3	19.1
16~24 岁 Age	54	14.8	66.7	18.5
25~34 岁 Age	86	16.3	62.8	20.9
35~44 岁 Age	68	13.2	67.6	19.1
45~54 岁 Age	41	19.5	63.4	17.1
55~60 岁 Age	23	26.1	56.5	17.4

1-11 样本、男性各年龄层、女性各年龄层购买感冒药的场所/ Location of Buying Cold Medicine by the Whole Sample, Age and Gender Groups

注：本题为多选题，合计百分比超过 100%（Multiple answers）

	人数 Number	药店 drug store	医院/诊所 hospital	商场 department store/ shopping center
样本 Sample	532	60.2	53.4	1.1
男性 Male	260	58.1	55.4	0.4
16~24 岁 Age	49	57.1	51.0	0.0
25~34 岁 Age	75	64.0	50.7	1.3
35~44 岁 Age	69	60.9	56.5	0.0
45~54 岁 Age	43	58.1	55.8	0.0
55~60 岁 Age	24	33.3	75.0	0.0
女性 Female	272	62.1	51.5	1.8
16~24 岁 Age	54	74.1	33.3	3.7
25~34 岁 Age	86	66.3	50.0	0.0
35~44 岁 Age	68	58.8	54.4	2.9
45~54 岁 Age	41	48.8	65.9	0.0
55~60 岁 Age	23	52.2	65.2	4.3

1-12 家中是否有备用感冒药的习惯/ The Habit of Keeping Cold Medicine at Home

	人数 Number	百分比 Percent
有 yes	535	89.2
没有 no	65	10.8

n=600

1-13 公费/自费医疗的比例/ Proportion of the Free Medical Service

	人数 Number	百分比 Percent
公费医疗 free medical service	263	44.1
自费医疗 own expense	333	55.9

n=596

1-14 不同消费者层的常用品牌或品种/ The Most Frequently Used Brands or Kinds by Market Segments

1-14-1 时尚流行指标/ Fads Popular Index

注：在药品品牌调查中，消费者经常出现将药品的名称与品牌名称混淆的现象，特此声明。/ In our research on medicines, we find consumers often confused the names and the brands.

	人数 Number	第一品牌及百分比 1st / percent	第二品牌及百分比 2nd / percent	第三品牌及百分比 3rd / percent	第四品牌及百分比 4th / percent
样本 Sample	530	**强力维 C 银翘 Qiang Li VC(15.3)**	**康泰克 Contac(13.6)**	**速效感冒胶囊 Su Xiao Gan Mao Jiao Nang(10.9)**	**感冒通 Ganmaotong(10.0)**
平实生活指向 simple living orientation	299	强力维 C 银翘 Qiang Li VC(17.4)	速效感冒胶囊 Su Xiao Gan Mao Jiao Nang(12.7)	康泰克 Contac(11.0)	康必得 Fufang An'fenpuxinpian (10.0)
时尚流行指向 fashion orientation	231	康泰克 Contac(16.9)	强力维 C 银翘 Qiang Li VC(12.6)	感冒通 Ganmaotong(10.4)	速效感冒胶囊 Su Xiao Gan Mao Jiao Nang (8.7)

1-14-2 广告态度指标/ Advertising Attitude Index

注：在药品品牌调查中，消费者经常出现将药品的名称与品牌名称混淆的现象，特此声明。/ In our research on medicines, we find consumers often confused the names and the brands.

	人数 Number	第一品牌及百分比 1st / percent	第二品牌及百分比 2nd / percent	第三品牌及百分比 3rd / percent	第四品牌及百分比 4th / percent
样本 Sample	530	**强力维 C 银翘 Qiang Li VC(15.3)**	**康泰克 Contac(13.8)**	**速效感冒胶囊 Su Xiao Gan Mao Jiao Nang(11.1)**	**感冒通 Ganmaotong(10.0)**
广告淡漠指向 indifferent orientation	166	强力维 C 银翘 Qiang Li VC(16.3)	感冒通 Ganmaotong(13.3)	康泰克 Contac(12.0)	康必得 Fufang An'fenpuxinpian (11.4)
中间层 medium	294	强力维 C 银翘 Qiang Li VC(14.3)	康泰克 Contac(13.3)	速效感冒胶囊 Su Xiao Gan Mao Jiao Nang(10.9)	速效伤风胶囊 Su Xiao Shang Feng Jiao Nang(9.2)
信赖广告指向 loyal orientation	70	康泰克 Contac(20.0)	强力维 C 银翘 Qiang Li VC(17.1)	速效感冒胶囊 Su Xiao Gan Mao Jiao Nang(15.7)	速效伤风胶囊 Su Xiao Shang Feng Jiao Nang(10.0)

1-14-3 饮食健康指标/ Foods & Drink Quality Index

注：在药品品牌调查中，消费者经常出现将药品的名称与品牌名称混淆的现象，特此声明。/ In our research on medicines, we find consumers often confused the names and the brands.

	人数 Number	第一品牌及百分比 1st / percent	第二品牌及百分比 2nd / percent	第三品牌及百分比 3rd / percent	第四品牌及百分比 4th / percent
样本 Sample	532	**强力维 C 银翘 Qiang Li VC(15.2)**	**康泰克 Contac(13.7)**	**速效感冒胶囊 Su Xiao Gan Mao Jiao Nang(11.1)**	**感冒通 Ganmaotong(10.0)**
饮食“温饱”指向 "basic" orientation	200	强力维 C 银翘 Qiang Li VC(15.5)	速效感冒胶囊 Su Xiao Gan Mao Jiao Nang(13.5)	康泰克 Contac(12.0)	感冒通 Ganmaotong(11.0)
中间层 medium	243	强力维 C 银翘 Qiang Li VC(16.0)	康泰克 Contac(12.8)	速效感冒胶囊 Su Xiao Gan Mao Jiao Nang(10.3)	康必得 Fufang An'fenpuxinpian (9.9)
健康营养指向 health & nutrition orientation	89	康泰克 Contac(20.2)	强力维 C 银翘 Qiang Li VC(12.4) 感冒通 Ganmaotong (12.4)	速效伤风胶囊 Su Xiao Shang Feng Jiao Nang(11.2)	速效感冒胶囊 Su Xiao Gan Mao Jiao Nang(7.9)

● 沈阳 / Shenyang

1-1 最近一年内有无服用的比例/ Whether having Taken Cold Medicines Last Year

	人数 Number	百分比 Percent
吃过 yes	496	82.5
没吃过 no	105	17.5

n=601

1-2 最常用品牌或品种排名/ Ranking of the Most Frequently Used Brands or Kinds

注：在药品品牌调查中，消费者经常出现将药品的名称与品牌名称混淆的现象，特此声明。/ In cur research on medicines, we find consumers often confused the names and the brands.

排名 Brand Ranking	品牌或品种 Brands or Kinds	人数 Number	百分比 Percent
1	感冒通 Ganmaotong	117	23.6
2	康泰克 Contac	77	15.5
3	扑热息痛 Pu Re Xi Tong	63	12.7
4	感康 Gankang	45	9.1
5	速效伤风胶囊 Su Xiao Shang Feng Jiao Nang	26	5.2
5	速效感冒胶囊 Su Xiao Gan Mao Jiao Nang	26	5.2
6	速效感冒片 Su Xiao Gan Mao Pian	12	2.4
7	强力维 C 银翘 Qiang Li VC	11	2.2
8	白加黑 White & Black	10	2.0
9	严迪 Yandi	9	1.8
9	快克 Quick	9	1.8
10	病毒灵(三九制药)San Jiu Bing Du Ling	7	1.4

n=496

1-3 样本、男性各年龄层、女性各年龄层的常用品牌或品种/ The Most Frequently Used Brands or Kinds by the Whole Sample, Age and Gender Groups

注：在药品品牌调查中，消费者经常出现将药品的名称与品牌名称混淆的现象，特此声明。/ In our research on medicines, we find consumers often confused the names and the brands.

	人数 Number	第一品牌及百分比 1st/ percent	第二品牌及百分比 2nd/ percent	第三品牌及百分比 3rd/ percent
样本 Sample	496	**感冒通 Ganmaotong(23.6)**	**康泰克 Contac(15.5)**	**扑热息痛 Pu Re Xi Tong(12.7)**
男性 Male	240	**感冒通 Ganmaotong(25.0)**	**康泰克 Contac(15.4)**	**扑热息痛 Pu Re Xi Tong(12.9)**
16~24 岁 Age	56	感冒通 Ganmaotong(30.4)	康泰克 Contac(17.9)	感康 Gankang(12.5)
25~34 岁 Age	69	感冒通 Ganmaotong(26.1)	康泰克 Contac(15.9)	扑热息痛 Pu Re Xi Tong(11.6)
35~44 岁 Age	61	感冒通 Ganmaotong(23.0)	扑热息痛 Pu Re Xi Tong(14.8)	康泰克 Contac(13.1)
45~54 岁 Age	35	感冒通 Ganmaotong(22.9)	感康 Gankang(20.0)	扑热息痛 Pu Re Xi Tong(14.3)
55~60 岁 Age	19	扑热息痛 Pu Re Xi Tong(26.3)	康泰克 Contac(21.1)	感冒通 Ganmaotong(15.8) 速效感冒胶囊 Su Xiao Gan Mao Jiao Nang(15.8)
女性 Female	256	**感冒通 Ganmaotong(22.3)**	**康泰克 Contac(15.6)**	**扑热息痛 Pu Re Xi Tong(12.5)**
16~24 岁 Age	52	康泰克 Contac(23.1)	感冒通 Ganmaotong(21.2)	白加黑 White&Black(7.7)
25~34 岁 Age	74	感冒通 Ganmaotong(21.6)	康泰克 Contac(14.9)	感康 Gankang(9.5)
35~44 岁 Age	68	感冒通 Ganmaotong(22.1)	扑热息痛 Pu Re Xi Tong(17.6)	康泰克 Contac(14.7)
45~54 岁 Age	41	感冒通 Ganmaotong(26.8)	扑热息痛 Pu Re Xi Tong(22.0)	康泰克 Contac(12.2)
55~60 岁 Age	21	感冒通 Ganmaotong(19.0)	扑热息痛 Pu Re Xi Tong(14.3)	康泰克 Contac(9.5) 速效伤风胶囊 Su Xiao Shang Feng Jiao Nang(9.5) 速效感冒胶囊 Su Xiao Gan Mao Jiao Nang(9.5) 病毒灵(三九制药) San Jiu Bing Du Ling(9.5)

1-4 理想品牌或品种排名/ Ranking of the Ideal Brands or Kinds

注：在药品品牌调查中，消费者经常出现将药品的名称与品牌名称混淆的现象，特此声明。/ In our research on medicines, we find consumers often confused the names and the brands.

排名 Brand Ranking	品牌或品种 Brands or Kinds	人数 Number	百分比 Percent
1	康泰克 Contac	136	22.7
2	感冒通 Ganmaotong	107	17.8
3	感康 Gankang	65	10.8
4	扑热息痛 Pu Re Xi Tong	51	8.5
5	速效感冒胶囊 Su Xiao Gan Mao Jiao Nang	30	5.0
6	速效伤风胶囊 Su Xiao Shang Feng Jiao Nang	28	4.7
7	白加黑 White & Black	20	3.3
8	强力维 C 银翘 Qiang Li VC	14	2.3
9	快克 Quick	12	2.0
10	严迪 Yandi	11	1.8
11	病毒灵(三九制药)San Jiu Bing Du Ling	10	1.7
11	速效感冒片 Su Xiao Gan Mao Pian	10	1.7
12	利君沙 Lijunsha	8	1.3
13	康必得 Fufang An'fenpuxinpian	6	1.0
14	阿莫西林 Amexilin	5	0.8

n=600

1-5 样本、男性各年龄层、女性各年龄层的品牌习惯/ Brand Habit in Consuming Cold Medicines by the Whole Sample, Age and Gender Groups

	人数 Number	基本固定用一个牌子 used in only one brand	比较固定地用两个或三个牌子 used in two or three brands	基本上不太固定牌子 no brand preference
样本 Sample	495	38.8	37.8	23.4
男性 Male	240	35.8	39.2	25.0
16~24 岁 Age	56	42.9	41.1	16.1
25~34 岁 Age	69	27.5	43.5	29.0
35~44 岁 Age	61	34.4	36.1	29.5
45~54 岁 Age	35	31.4	37.1	31.4
55~60 岁 Age	19	57.9	31.6	10.5
女性 Female	255	41.6	36.5	22.0
16~24 岁 Age	52	36.5	32.7	30.8
25~34 岁 Age	73	28.8	47.9	23.3
35~44 岁 Age	68	44.1	27.9	27.9
45~54 岁 Age	41	56.1	34.1	9.8
55~60 岁 Age	21	61.9	38.1	0.0

1-6 易患感冒的季节/ Which Season to Prone to Catch Cold

注：本题为多选题，合计百分比超过 100%（Multiple answers）

	人次 Person-time	百分比 Percent
冬春之交 between winter & spring	138	27.9
春天 spring	45	9.1
春末夏初 late spring & early summer	18	3.6
夏天 summer	11	2.2
夏秋之交 between summer & autumn	34	6.9
秋天 autumn	60	12.1
入冬之际 early winter	172	34.8
冬天 winter	59	11.9
不确定 not sure	135	27.3

n=494

1-7 样本、男性各年龄层、女性各年龄层最近一年内有无服用的比例/ Whether having Taken Cold Medicines Last Year by the Whole Sample, Age and Gender Groups

	人数 Number	吃过 yes	没吃过 no
样本 Sample	601	82.5	17.5
男性 Male	299	80.3	19.7
16~24 岁 Age	64	87.5	12.5
25~34 岁 Age	89	77.5	22.5
35~44 岁 Age	76	80.3	19.7
45~54 岁 Age	46	76.1	23.9
55~60 岁 Age	24	79.2	20.8
女性 Female	302	84.8	15.2
16~24 岁 Age	64	81.3	18.8
25~34 岁 Age	90	82.2	17.8
35~44 岁 Age	76	89.5	10.5
45~54 岁 Age	48	85.4	14.6
55~60 岁 Age	24	87.5	12.5

1-8 选择该类商品的考虑因素/ Ranking of the Considerations in Purchasing

注：本题为多选题，合计百分比超过 100%（Multiple answers）

排名 Ranking	考虑因素 Considerations	人次 Person-time	百分比 Percent
1	见效快 immediate effect	314	63.3
2	价格适中 reasonable price	155	31.3
3	医生推荐 recommended by doctors	127	25.6
4	服用方式简便 simple to take	99	20.0
5	有名的牌子 famous brand	83	16.7
6	购买方便 easy to buy	78	15.7
7	广告影响 influence of advertising	38	7.7
8	亲友介绍 introduced by relatives & friends	30	6.0
9	不嗜睡 not feeling sleepy	29	5.8
10	其他 others	2	0.4

n=496

1-9 样本、男性各年龄层、女性各年龄层最常服用的种类/ Types of Cold Medicine Consumed by the Whole Sample, Age and Gender Groups

	人数 Number	片剂 pill	冲剂 granular formulation	胶囊 capsule	药粉 powder	糖浆 syrup	药丸 bolus	其他 others
样本 Sample	490	66.1	1.4	30.6	0.4	0.2	1.0	0.2
男性 Male	238	66.8	1.3	30.3	0.4	0.0	1.3	0.0
16~24 岁 Age	56	64.3	0.0	30.4	1.8	0.0	3.6	0.0
25~34 岁 Age	67	65.7	1.5	32.8	0.0	0.0	0.0	0.0
35~44 岁 Age	61	68.9	1.6	29.5	0.0	0.0	0.0	0.0
45~54 岁 Age	35	68.6	2.9	28.6	0.0	0.0	0.0	0.0
55~60 岁 Age	19	68.4	0.0	26.3	0.0	0.0	5.3	0.0
女性 Female	252	65.5	1.6	31.0	0.4	0.4	0.8	0.4
16~24 岁 Age	50	60.0	0.0	38.0	0.0	0.0	2.0	0.0
25~34 岁 Age	73	60.3	1.4	35.6	1.4	0.0	1.4	0.0
35~44 岁 Age	68	70.6	2.9	23.5	0.0	1.5	0.0	1.5
45~54 岁 Age	41	68.3	2.4	29.3	0.0	0.0	0.0	0.0
55~60 岁 Age	20	75.0	0.0	25.0	0.0	0.0	0.0	0.0

1-10 样本、男性各年龄层、女性各年龄层最常服用的场合/ Settings of Consumption by the Whole Sample, Age and Gender Groups

	人数 Number	有感冒的前兆 having signs of cold	轻度感冒症状 light cold symptom	严重感冒症状 severe cold symptom	其他 others
样本 Sample	495	20.4	62.4	17.2	0.0
男性 Male	239	17.6	66.5	15.9	0.0
16~24 岁 Age	55	23.6	67.3	9.1	0.0
25~34 岁 Age	69	13.0	66.7	20.3	0.0
35~44 岁 Age	61	13.1	70.5	16.4	0.0
45~54 岁 Age	35	22.9	57.1	20.0	0.0
55~60 岁 Age	19	21.1	68.4	10.5	0.0
女性 Female	256	23.0	58.6	18.4	0.0
16~24 岁 Age	52	17.3	67.3	15.4	0.0
25~34 岁 Age	74	21.6	54.1	24.3	0.0
35~44 岁 Age	68	23.5	58.8	17.6	0.0
45~54 岁 Age	41	22.0	58.5	19.5	0.0
55~60 岁 Age	21	42.9	52.4	4.8	0.0

1-11 样本、男性各年龄层、女性各年龄层购买感冒药的场所/ Location of Buying Cold Medicine by the Whole Sample, Age and Gender Groups

注：本题为多选题，合计百分比超过 100%（Multiple answers）

	人数 Number	药店 drug store	医院/诊所 hospital	商场 department store/ shopping center
样本 Sample	496	76.8	37.1	0.8
男性 Male	240	75.8	35.8	0.8
16~24 岁 Age	56	83.9	30.4	0.0
25~34 岁 Age	69	79.7	27.5	2.9
35~44 岁 Age	61	75.4	39.3	0.0
45~54 岁 Age	35	65.7	42.9	0.0
55~60 岁 Age	19	57.9	57.9	0.0
女性 Female	256	77.7	38.3	0.8
16~24 岁 Age	52	75.0	38.5	1.9
25~34 岁 Age	74	82.4	32.4	0.0
35~44 岁 Age	68	75.0	45.6	1.5
45~54 岁 Age	41	80.5	36.6	0.0
55~60 岁 Age	21	71.4	38.1	0.0

1-12 家中是否有备用感冒药的习惯/ The Habit of Keeping Cold Medicine at Home

	人数 Number	百分比 Percent
有 yes	521	86.8
没有 no	79	13.2

n=600

1-13 公费/自费医疗的比例/ Proportion of the Free Medical Service

	人数 Number	百分比 Percent
公费医疗 free medical service	160	26.7
自费医疗 own expense	439	73.3

n=599

1-14 不同消费者层的常用品牌或品种/ The Most Frequently Used Brands or Kinds by Market Segments

1-14-1 时尚流行指标/ Fads Popular Index

注：在药品品牌调查中，消费者经常出现将药品的名称与品牌名称混淆的现象，特此声明。/ In our research on medicines, we find consumers often confused the names and the brands.

	人数 Number	第一品牌及百分比 1st/ percent	第二品牌及百分比 2nd/ percent	第三品牌及百分比 3rd/ percent	第四品牌及百分比 4th/ percent
样本 Sample	496	**感冒通 Ganmaotong(23.6)**	**康泰克 Contac(15.5)**	**扑热息痛 Pu Re Xi Tong(12.7)**	**感康 Gankang(9.1)**
平实生活指向 simple living orientation	239	感冒通 Ganmaotong(27.2)	扑热息痛 Pu Re Xi Tong(15.9)	康泰克 Contac(11.7)	感康 Gankang(7.1)
时尚流行指向 fashion orientation	257	感冒通 Ganmaotong(20.2)	康泰克 Contac(19.1)	感康 Gankang(10.9)	扑热息痛 Pu Re Xi Tong(9.7)

1-14-2 广告态度指标/ Advertising Attitude Index

注：在药品品牌调查中，消费者经常出现将药品的名称与品牌名称混淆的现象，特此声明。/ In our research on medicines, we find consumers often confused the names and the brands.

	人数 Number	第一品牌及百分比 1st/ percent	第二品牌及百分比 2nd/ percent	第三品牌及百分比 3rd/ percent	第四品牌及百分比 4th/ percent
样本 Sample	496	**感冒通 Ganmaotong(23.6)**	**康泰克 Contac(15.5)**	**扑热息痛 Pu Re Xi Tong(12.7)**	**感康 Gankang(9.1)**
广告淡漠指向 indifferent orientation	139	感冒通 Ganmaotong(24.5)	康泰克 Contac(13.7)	扑热息痛 Pu Re Xi Tong (11.5)	感康 Gankang(10.1)
中间层 medium	297	感冒通 Ganmaotong(22.2)	康泰克 Contac(15.5)	扑热息痛 Pu Re Xi Tong (12.5)	感康 Gankang(9.1)
信赖广告指向 loyal orientation	60	感冒通 Ganmaotong(28.3)	康泰克 Contac(20.0)	扑热息痛 Pu Re Xi Tong (16.7)	感康 Gankang(6.7)

1-14-3 饮食健康指标/ Foods & Drink Quality Index

注：在药品品牌调查中，消费者经常出现将药品的名称与品牌名称混淆的现象，特此声明。/ In our research on medicines, we find consumers often confused the names and the brands.

	人数 Number	第一品牌及百分比 1st/ percent	第二品牌及百分比 2nd/ percent	第三品牌及百分比 3rd/ percent	第四品牌及百分比 4th/ percent
样本 Sample	496	**感冒通 Ganmaotong(23.6)**	**康泰克 Contac(15.5)**	**扑热息痛 Pu Re Xi Tong(12.7)**	**感康 Gankang(9.1)**
饮食"温饱"指向 "basic" orientation	154	感冒通 Ganmaotong(26.6)	扑热息痛 Pu Re Xi Tong (18.2)	康泰克 Contac(13.0)	感康 Gankang(6.5) 速效伤风胶囊 Su Xiao Shang Feng Jiao Nang(6.5)
中间层 medium	218	感冒通 Ganmaotong(20.6)	康泰克 Contac(18.3)	感康 Gankang(11.0)	扑热息痛 Pu Re Xi Tong (10.1)
健康营养指向 health & nutrition orientation	124	感冒通 Ganmaotong(25.0)	康泰克 Contac(13.7)	扑热息痛 Pu Re Xi Tong(10.5)	感康 Gankang(8.9)

2.润喉药 / Sore throat Remedies

● 北京 / Beijing

2-1 最近一年内有无服用的比例/ Whether having Taken Sore Throat Remedies Last Year

	人数 Number	百分比 Percent
吃过 yes	525	51.9
没吃过 no	487	48.1

n=1012

2-2 最常用品牌或品种排名/ Ranking of the Most Frequently Used Brands or Kinds

注：在药品品牌调查中，消费者经常出现将药品的名称与品牌名称混淆的现象，特此声明。/ In our research on medicines, we find consumers often confused the names and the brands.

排名 Brand Ranking	品牌或品种 Brands or Kinds	人数 Number	百分比 Percent
1	三金西瓜霜 Sanjin	145	27.7
2	江中草珊瑚 Jiangzhong	117	22.4
3	广西金嗓子喉宝 Golden Throat	102	19.5
4	华素片 Tabellae Cydiodini	41	7.8
5	咽之爽 Yanzhishuang	32	6.1
6	金果含片 Jin Guo Han Pian	15	2.9
7	健民咽喉片 Jianmin	14	2.7
8	四季润喉片 Siji	10	1.9

n=523

2-3 样本、男性各年龄层、女性各年龄层的常用品牌或品种/ The Most Frequently Used Brands or Kinds by the Whole Sample, Age and Gender Groups

注：在药品品牌调查中，消费者经常出现将药品的名称与品牌名称混淆的现象，特此声明。/ In our research on medicines, we find consumers often confused the names and the brands.

	人数 Number	第一品牌及百分比 1st/ percent	第二品牌及百分比 2nd/ percent	第三品牌及百分比 3rd/ percent
样本 Sample	523	**三金西瓜霜 Sanjin(27.7)**	**江中草珊瑚 Jiangzhong(22.4)**	**广西金嗓子喉宝 Golden Throat(19.5)**
男性 Male	238	**三金西瓜霜 Sanjin(26.9)**	**江中草珊瑚 Jiangzhong(23.5)**	**广西金嗓子喉宝 Golden Throat(21.8)**
16~24 岁 Age	57	三金西瓜霜 Sanjin(31.6)	江中草珊瑚 Jiangzhong(26.3)	广西金嗓子喉宝 Golden Throat(24.6)
25~34 岁 Age	73	广西金嗓子喉宝 Golden Throat(26.0)	三金西瓜霜 Sanjin(24.7)	江中草珊瑚 Jiangzhong(21.9)
35~44 岁 Age	63	三金西瓜霜 Sanjin(25.4)	广西金嗓子喉宝 Golden Throat(20.6) 江中草珊瑚 Jiangzhong(20.6)	华素片 Tabellae Cydiodini(7.9)
45~54 岁 Age	28	江中草珊瑚 Jiangzhong(32.1)	三金西瓜霜 Sanjin(28.6)	广西金嗓子喉宝 Golden Throat(14.3)
55~60 岁 Age	17	三金西瓜霜 Sanjin(23.5)	江中草珊瑚 Jiangzhong(17.6)	广西金嗓子喉宝 Golden Throat(11.8) 华素片 Tabellae Cydiodini(11.8)
女性 Female	285	**三金西瓜霜 Sanjin(28.4)**	**江中草珊瑚 Jiangzhong(21.4)**	**广西金嗓子喉宝 Golden Throat(17.5)**
16~24 岁 Age	68	三金西瓜霜 Sanjin(27.9)	江中草珊瑚 Jiangzhong(25.0)	广西金嗓子喉宝 Golden Throat(19.1)
25~34 岁 Age	83	三金西瓜霜 Sanjin(31.3)	广西金嗓子喉宝 Golden Throat(20.5)	江中草珊瑚 Jiangzhong(18.1)
35~44 岁 Age	74	三金西瓜霜 Sanjin(31.1)	江中草珊瑚 Jiangzhong(16.2)	广西金嗓子喉宝 Golden Throat(14.9)
45~54 岁 Age	43	三金西瓜霜 Sanjin(30.2)	江中草珊瑚 Jiangzhong(27.9)	广西金嗓子喉宝 Golden Throat(14.0)
55~60 岁 Age	17	江中草珊瑚 Jiangzhong(29.4)	广西金嗓子喉宝 Golden Throat(17.6) 华素片 Tabellae Cydiodini(17.6)	金果含片 Jin Guo Han Pian(11.8)

2-4 理想品牌或品种排名/ Ranking of the Ideal Brands or Kinds

注：在药品品牌调查中，消费者经常出现将药品的名称与品牌名称混淆的现象，特此声明。/ In our research on medicines, we find consumers often confused the names and the brands.

排名 Brand Ranking	品牌或品种 Brands or Kinds	人数 Number	百分比 Percent
1	广西金嗓子喉宝 Golden Throat	202	20.0
2	三金西瓜霜 Sanjin	180	17.8
3	江中草珊瑚 Jiangzhong	171	16.9
4	华素片 Tabellae Cydiodini	57	5.6
5	咽之爽 Yanzhishuang	54	5.4
6	健民咽喉片 Jianmin	14	1.4
7	金果含片 Jin Guo Han Pian	13	1.3
8	四季润喉片 Siji	7	0.7

n=1009

2-5 样本、男性各年龄层、女性各年龄层的品牌习惯/ Brand Habit in Consuming Sore Throat Remedies by the Whole Sample, Age and Gender Groups

	人数 Number	基本固定用一个牌子 used in only one brand	比较固定地用两个或三个牌子 used in two or three brands	基本上不太固定牌子 no brand preference
样本 Sample	**525**	**44.6**	**36.8**	**18.7**
男性 Male	**240**	**47.1**	**33.8**	**19.2**
16~24 岁 Age	57	50.9	31.6	17.5
25~34 岁 Age	73	45.2	41.1	13.7
35~44 岁 Age	64	51.6	26.6	21.9
45~54 岁 Age	28	39.3	32.1	28.6
55~60 岁 Age	18	38.9	38.9	22.2
女性 Female	**285**	**42.5**	**39.3**	**18.2**
16~24 岁 Age	68	41.2	44.1	14.7
25~34 岁 Age	83	47.0	37.3	15.7
35~44 岁 Age	74	37.8	43.2	18.9
45~54 岁 Age	43	41.9	34.9	23.3
55~60 岁 Age	17	47.1	23.5	29.4

2-6 样本、男性各年龄层、女性各年龄层最近一年内有无服用的比例/ Whether having Taken Sore Throat Remedies Last Year by the Whole Sample, Age and Gender Groups

	人数 Number	吃过 yes	没吃过 no
样本 Sample	**1012**	**51.9**	**48.1**
男性 Male	**504**	**47.6**	**52.4**
16~24 岁 Age	105	54.3	45.7
25~34 岁 Age	151	48.3	51.7
35~44 岁 Age	131	48.9	51.1
45~54 岁 Age	77	36.4	63.6
55~60 岁 Age	40	45.0	55.0
女性 Female	**508**	**56.1**	**43.9**
16~24 岁 Age	108	63.0	37.0
25~34 岁 Age	150	55.3	44.7
35~44 岁 Age	124	59.7	40.3
45~54 岁 Age	84	51.2	48.8
55~60 岁 Age	42	40.5	59.5

2-7 选择该类商品的考虑因素/ Ranking of the Considerations in Purchasing

注：本题为多选题，合计百分比超过 100%（Multiple answers）

排名 Ranking	考虑因素 Considerations	人次 Person-time	百分比 Percent
1	见效快 immediate effect	247	47.5
2	医生推荐 recommended by doctors	231	44.4
3	无副作用 no side-effects	126	24.2
4	有名的牌子 famous brand	117	22.5
5	服用方式简便 simple to take	115	22.1
6	价格适中 reasonable price	56	10.8
7	广告影响 influence of advertising	47	9.0
8	购买方便 easy to buy	37	7.1
9	亲友介绍 introduced by relatives & friends	35	6.7
10	其他 others	5	1.0

n=520

2-8 样本、男性各年龄层、女性各年龄层最常服用的种类/ Types of Sore Throat Remedies Consumed by the Whole Sample, Age and Gender Groups

	人数 Number	片剂 pill	冲剂 granular formulation	糖浆 syrup	药粉 powder	膏状 paste-type	药丸 bolus	其他 others
样本 Sample	523	95.4	0.6	0.8	0.8	0.2	1.7	0.6
男性 Male	240	96.3	0.0	1.3	0.8	0.4	1.3	0.0
16~24 岁 Age	57	96.5	0.0	3.5	0.0	0.0	0.0	0.0
25~34 岁 Age	73	97.3	0.0	1.4	1.4	0.0	0.0	0.0
35~44 岁 Age	64	95.3	0.0	0.0	1.6	0.0	3.1	0.0
45~54 岁 Age	28	96.4	0.0	0.0	0.0	3.6	0.0	0.0
55~60 岁 Age	18	94.4	0.0	0.0	0.0	0.0	5.6	0.0
女性 Female	283	94.7	1.1	0.4	0.7	0.0	2.1	1.1
16~24 岁 Age	68	91.2	0.0	1.5	1.5	0.0	2.9	2.9
25~34 岁 Age	83	96.4	0.0	0.0	0.0	0.0	2.4	1.2
35~44 岁 Age	73	94.5	2.7	0.0	1.4	0.0	1.4	0.0
45~54 岁 Age	43	97.7	2.3	0.0	0.0	0.0	0.0	0.0
55~60 岁 Age	16	93.8	0.0	0.0	0.0	0.0	6.3	0.0

2-9 样本、男性各年龄层、女性各年龄层最常服用的场合/ Settings of Consumption by the Whole Sample, Age and Gender Groups

注：本题为多选题，合计百分比超过 100%（Multiple answers）

	人数 Number	喉咙发炎时 throat inflammation	喉咙轻度不适时 sore throat	长时间讲话后 long time speaking	抽烟后 after smoking	配药使用 taken with other medicine	其他 others
样本 Sample	523	49.1	65.0	8.6	3.3	1.1	0.8
男性 Male	239	46.9	63.2	8.4	6.7	2.1	0.8
16~24 岁 Age	57	49.1	57.9	15.8	7.0	1.8	0.0
25~34 岁 Age	73	50.7	61.6	5.5	4.1	1.4	1.4
35~44 岁 Age	63	42.9	68.3	6.3	9.5	3.2	1.6
45~54 岁 Age	28	39.3	75.0	7.1	7.1	3.6	0.0
55~60 岁 Age	18	50.0	50.0	5.6	5.6	0.0	0.0
女性 Female	284	51.1	66.5	8.8	0.4	0.4	0.7
16~24 岁 Age	68	41.2	69.1	11.8	0.0	0.0	1.5
25~34 岁 Age	83	48.2	71.1	7.2	1.2	0.0	0.0
35~44 岁 Age	73	57.5	63.0	8.2	0.0	1.4	1.4
45~54 岁 Age	43	58.1	58.1	9.3	0.0	0.0	0.0
55~60 岁 Age	17	58.8	70.6	5.9	0.0	0.0	0.0

2-10 样本、男性各年龄层、女性各年龄层购买润候药的场所/ Location of Buying Sore Throat Remedies by the Whole Sample, Age and Gender Groups

注：本题为多选题，合计百分比超过 100%（Multiple answers）

	人数 Number	药店 drug store	医院/诊所 hospital	商场 department store/ shopping center
样本 Sample	521	46.3	62.4	2.9
男性 Male	238	45.8	61.8	2.9
16~24 岁 Age	57	52.6	50.9	8.8
25~34 岁 Age	71	52.1	57.7	2.8
35~44 岁 Age	64	45.3	64.1	0.0
45~54 岁 Age	28	32.1	75.0	0.0
55~60 岁 Age	18	22.2	83.3	0.0
女性 Female	283	46.6	62.9	2.8
16~24 岁 Age	68	63.2	45.6	5.9
25~34 岁 Age	83	57.8	51.8	2.4
35~44 岁 Age	72	33.3	77.8	1.4
45~54 岁 Age	43	32.6	76.7	2.3
55~60 岁 Age	17	17.6	88.2	0.0

2-11 家中是否有备用润喉药的习惯/ The Habit of Keeping Sore Throat Remedies at Home

	人数 Number	百分比 Percent
有 yes	646	65.3
没有 no	343	34.7

n=989

2-12 公费/自费医疗的比例/ Proportion of the Free Medical Service

	人数 Number	百分比 Percent
公费医疗 free medical service	636	64.6
自费医疗 at my own expense	349	35.4

n=985

2-13 不同消费者层的常用品牌/ The Most Frequently Used Brands by Market Segments

2-13-1 时尚流行指标/ Fads Popular Index

注：在药品品牌调查中，消费者经常出现将药品的名称与品牌名称混淆的现象，特此声明。/ In our research on medicines, we find consumers often confused the names and the brands.

	人数 Number	第一品牌及百分比 1st / percent	第二品牌及百分比 2nd / percent	第三品牌及百分比 3rd / percent	第四品牌及百分比 4th / percent
样本 Sample	517	**三金西瓜霜 Sanjin(27.9)**	**江中草珊瑚 Jiangzhong(22.2)**	**广西金嗓子喉宝 Golden Throat(19.1)**	**华素片 Tabellae Cydiodini(7.9)**
平实生活指向 simple living orientation	243	江中草珊瑚 Jiangzhong(28.4)	三金西瓜霜 Sanjin(24.3)	广西金嗓子喉宝 Golden Throat(18.5)	华素片 Tabellae Cydiodini(7.8)
时尚流行指向 fashion orientation	274	三金西瓜霜 Sanjin(31.0)	广西金嗓子喉宝 Golden Throat(19.7)	江中草珊瑚 Jiangzhong(16.8)	华素片 Tabellae Cydiodini(8.0)

2-13-2 广告态度指标/ Advertising Attitude Index

注：在药品品牌调查中，消费者经常出现将药品的名称与品牌名称混淆的现象，特此声明。/ In our research on medicines, we find consumers often confused the names and the brands.

	人数 Number	第一品牌及百分比 1st / percent	第二品牌及百分比 2nd / percent	第三品牌及百分比 3rd / percent	第四品牌及百分比 4th / percent
样本 Sample	510	**三金西瓜霜 Sanjin(27.6)**	**江中草珊瑚 Jiangzhong(22.5)**	**广西金嗓子喉宝 Golden Throat(19.8)**	**华素片 Tabellae Cydiodini(7.6)**
广告淡漠指向 indifferent orientation	135	江中草珊瑚 Jiangzhong(27.4)	三金西瓜霜 Sanjin(22.2)	广西金嗓子喉宝 Golden Throat(20.0)	华素片 Tabellae Cydiodini(8.9)
中间层 medium	298	三金西瓜霜 Sanjin(29.2)	广西金嗓子喉宝 Golden Throat(21.8)	江中草珊瑚 Jiangzhong(19.8)	华素片 Tabellae Cydiodini(7.4)
信赖广告指向 loyal orientation	77	三金西瓜霜 Sanjin(31.2)	江中草珊瑚 Jiangzhong(24.7)	广西金嗓子喉宝 Golden Throat(11.7)	咽之爽 Yanzhishuang(10.4)

2-13-3 饮食健康指标/ Foods & Drink Quality Index

注：在药品品牌调查中，消费者经常出现将药品的名称与品牌名称混淆的现象，特此声明。/ In our research on medicines, we find consumers often confused the names and the brands.

	人数 Number	第一品牌及百分比 1st / percent	第二品牌及百分比 2nd / percent	第三品牌及百分比 3rd / percent	第四品牌及百分比 4th / percent
样本 Sample	520	**三金西瓜霜 Sanjin(27.7)**	**江中草珊瑚 Jiangzhong(22.3)**	**广西金嗓子喉宝 Golden Throat(19.6)**	**华素片 Tabellae Cydiodini(7.9)**
饮食"温饱"指向 "basic" orientation	141	三金西瓜霜 Sanjin(30.5)	江中草珊瑚 Jiangzhong(26.2)	广西金嗓子喉宝 Golden Throat(16.3)	咽之爽 Yanzhishuang(6.4) 华素片 Tabellae Cydiodini(6.4)
中间层 medium	245	三金西瓜霜 Sanjin(26.1)	江中草珊瑚 Jiangzhong(23.3)	广西金嗓子喉宝 Golden Throat(20.4)	华素片 Tabellae Cydiodini(7.8)
健康营养指向 health & nutrition orientation	134	三金西瓜霜 Sanjin(27.6)	广西金嗓子喉宝 Golden Throat(21.6)	江中草珊瑚 Jiangzhong(16.4)	华素片 Tabellae Cydiodini(9.7)

● 上海 / Shanghai

2-1 最近一年内有无服用的比例/ Whether having Taken Sore Throat Remedies Last Year

	人数 Number	百分比 Percent
吃过 yes	389	38.4
没吃过 no	625	61.6

n=1014

2-2 最常用品牌或品种排名/ Ranking of the Most Frequently Used Brands or Kinds

注：在药品品牌调查中，消费者经常出现将药品的名称与品牌名称混淆的现象，特此声明。/ In our research on medicines, we find consumers often confused the names and the brands.

排名 Brand Ranking	品牌或品种 Brands or Kinds	人数 Number	百分比 Percent
1	三金西瓜霜 Sanjin	136	35.1
2	江中草珊瑚 Jiangzhong	66	17.1
3	广西金嗓子喉宝 Golden Throat	64	16.5
4	四季润喉片 Siji	45	11.6
5	荷氏 Heshi	12	3.1
6	信可舒 Xin Ke Shu	11	2.8
7	桉叶糖 An Ye Tang	3	0.8
7	胖大海 Pang Da Hai	3	0.8
7	渔夫之宝 Fisherman's Friend	3	0.8

n=387

2-3 样本、男性各年龄层、女性各年龄层的常用品牌或品种/ The Most Frequently Used Brands or Kinds by the Whole Sample, Age and Gender Groups

注：在药品品牌调查中，消费者经常出现将药品的名称与品牌名称混淆的现象，特此声明。/ In our research on medicines, we find consumers often confused the names and the brands.

	人数 Number	第一品牌及百分比 1st/ percent	第二品牌及百分比 2nd/ percent	第三品牌及百分比 3rd/ percent
样本 Sample	**387**	**三金西瓜霜 Sanjin(35.1)**	**江中草珊瑚 Jiangzhong(17.1)**	**广西金嗓子喉宝 Golden Throat(16.5)**
男性 Male	**177**	**三金西瓜霜 Sanjin(35.6)**	**江中草珊瑚 Jiangzhong(17.5)**	**广西金嗓子喉宝 Golden Throat(15.8)**
16~24 岁 Age	34	三金西瓜霜 Sanjin(29.4)	广西金嗓子喉宝 Golden Throat(23.5)	江中草珊瑚 Jiangzhong(20.6)
25~34 岁 Age	51	三金西瓜霜 Sanjin(31.4)	广西金嗓子喉宝 Golden Throat(23.5)	江中草珊瑚 Jiangzhong(17.6)
35~44 岁 Age	54	三金西瓜霜 Sanjin(29.6)	江中草珊瑚 Jiangzhong(18.5)	广西金嗓子喉宝 Golden Throat(13.0) 四季润喉片 Siji(13.0)
45~54 岁 Age	28	三金西瓜霜 Sanjin(50.0)	四季润喉片 Siji(25.0)	江中草珊瑚 Jiangzhong(17.9)
55~60 岁 Age	10	三金西瓜霜 Sanjin(70.0)	度米芬含片 Du Mi Fen Han Pian(10.0) 四季润喉片 Siji(10.0) 桉叶糖 An Ye Tang (10.0)	
女性 Female	**210**	**三金西瓜霜 Sanjin(34.8)**	**广西金嗓子喉宝 Golden Throat(17.1)**	**江中草珊瑚 Jiangzhong(16.7)**
16~24 岁 Age	43	三金西瓜霜 Sanjin(25.6)	江中草珊瑚 Jiangzhong(23.3)	广西金嗓子喉宝 Golden Throat(20.9)
25~34 岁 Age	69	三金西瓜霜 Sanjin(33.3)	广西金嗓子喉宝 Golden Throat(18.8)	四季润喉片 Siji(15.9) 江中草珊瑚 Jiangzhong(15.9)
35~44 岁 Age	52	三金西瓜霜 Sanjin(44.2)	广西金嗓子喉宝 Golden Throat(13.5)	四季润喉片 Siji(11.5) 江中草珊瑚 Jiangzhong(11.5)
45~54 岁 Age	25	三金西瓜霜 Sanjin(32.0)	江中草珊瑚 Jiangzhong(24.0)	广西金嗓子喉宝 Golden Throat(20.0)
55~60 岁 Age	21	三金西瓜霜 Sanjin(38.1)	信可舒 Xin Ke Shu (14.3)	广西金嗓子喉宝 Golden Throat(9.5) 四季润喉片 Siji(9.5) 江中草珊瑚 Jiangzhong(9.5)

2-4 理想品牌或品种排名/ Ranking of the Ideal Brands or Kinds

注：在药品品牌调查中，消费者经常出现将药品的名称与品牌名称混淆的现象，特此声明。/ In our research on medicines, we find consumers often confused the names and the brands.

排名 Brand Ranking	品牌或品种 Brands or Kinds	人数 Number	百分比 Percent
1	三金西瓜霜 Sanjin	250	24.7
2	江中草珊瑚 Jiangzhong	170	16.8
3	广西金嗓子喉宝 Golden Throat	150	14.8
4	四季润喉片 Siji	93	9.2
5	荷氏 Heshi	15	1.5
6	信可舒 Xin Ke Shu	13	1.3
7	桉叶糖 An Ye Tang	5	0.5
7	胖大海 Pang Da Hai	5	0.5
8	凉可润 Liang Ke Run	4	0.4
8	华素片 Tabellae Cydiodini	4	0.4
8	渔夫之宝 Fisherman's Friend	4	0.4
9	健民咽喉片 Jianmin	3	0.3
9	信谊牌银黄含片 Xin Yi Pai Yin Huang Han Pian	3	0.3

n=1014

2-5 样本、男性各年龄层、女性各年龄层的品牌习惯/ Brand Habit in Consuming Sore Throat Remedies by the Whole Sample, Age and Gender Groups

	人数 Number	基本固定用一个牌子 used in only one brand	比较固定地用两个或三个牌子 used in two or three brands	基本上不太固定牌子 no brand preference
样本 Sample	389	49.6	28.5	21.9
男性 Male	179	48.6	28.5	22.9
16~24 岁 Age	34	50.0	26.5	23.5
25~34 岁 Age	52	46.2	34.6	19.2
35~44 岁 Age	55	43.6	27.3	29.1
45~54 岁 Age	28	53.6	28.6	17.9
55~60 岁 Age	10	70.0	10.0	20.0
女性 Female	210	50.5	28.6	21.0
16~24 岁 Age	43	55.8	18.6	25.6
25~34 岁 Age	69	43.5	37.7	18.8
35~44 岁 Age	52	46.2	25.0	28.8
45~54 岁 Age	25	72.0	20.0	8.0
55~60 岁 Age	21	47.6	38.1	14.3

2-6 样本、男性各年龄层、女性各年龄层最近一年内有无服用的比例/ Whether having Taken Sore Throat Remedies Last Year by the Whole Sample, Age and Gender Groups

	人数 Number	吃过 yes	没吃过 no
样本 Sample	1014	38.4	61.6
男性 Male	509	35.2	64.8
16~24 岁 Age	109	31.2	68.8
25~34 岁 Age	146	35.6	64.4
35~44 岁 Age	130	42.3	57.7
45~54 岁 Age	85	32.9	67.1
55~60 岁 Age	39	25.6	74.4
女性 Female	505	41.6	58.4
16~24 岁 Age	108	39.8	60.2
25~34 岁 Age	144	47.9	52.1
35~44 岁 Age	130	40.0	60.0
45~54 岁 Age	82	30.5	69.5
55~60 岁 Age	41	51.2	48.8

2-7 选择该类商品的考虑因素/ Ranking of the Considerations in Purchasing

注：本题为多选题，合计百分比超过 100%（Multiple answers）

排名 Ranking	考虑因素 Considerations	人次 Person-time	百分比 Percent
1	医生推荐 recommended by doctors	157	40.4
2	见效快 immediate effect	140	36.0
3	无副作用 no side-effects	92	23.7
4	价格适中 reasonable price	80	20.6
5	有名的牌子 famous brand	79	20.3
6	服用方式简便 simple to take	68	17.5
7	购买方便 easy to buy	48	12.3
8	广告影响 influence of advertising	42	10.8
9	亲友介绍 introduced by relatives & friends	31	8.0
10	其他 others	2	0.5

n=389

2-8 样本、男性各年龄层、女性各年龄层最常服用的种类/ Types of Sore Throat Remedies Consumed by the Whole Sample, Age and Gender Groups

	人数 Number	片剂 pill	冲剂 granular formulation	糖浆 syrup	药粉 powder	膏状 paste-type	药丸 bolus	其他 others
样本 Sample	386	80.8	0.8	2.3	2.1	0.8	9.3	3.9
男性 Male	176	78.4	1.7	4.0	1.7	1.1	8.0	5.1
16~24 岁 Age	34	79.4	0.0	0.0	0.0	0.0	8.8	11.8
25~34 岁 Age	51	70.6	0.0	3.9	2.0	3.9	13.7	5.9
35~44 岁 Age	53	79.2	5.7	5.7	1.9	0.0	3.8	3.8
45~54 岁 Age	28	89.3	0.0	3.6	0.0	0.0	7.1	0.0
55~60 岁 Age	10	80.0	0.0	10.0	10.0	0.0	0.0	0.0
女性 Female	210	82.9	0.0	1.0	2.4	0.5	10.5	2.9
16~24 岁 Age	43	69.8	0.0	2.3	4.7	0.0	18.6	4.7
25~34 岁 Age	69	87.0	0.0	0.0	0.0	1.4	10.1	1.4
35~44 岁 Age	52	82.7	0.0	1.9	1.9	0.0	11.5	1.9
45~54 岁 Age	25	88.0	0.0	0.0	8.0	0.0	4.0	0.0
55~60 岁 Age	21	90.5	0.0	0.0	0.0	0.0	0.0	9.5

2-9 样本、男性各年龄层、女性各年龄层最常服用的场合/ Settings of Consumption by the Whole Sample, Age and Gender Groups

注：本题为多选题，合计百分比超过 100%（Multiple answers）

	人数 Number	喉咙发炎时 throat inflammation	喉咙轻度不适时 sore throat	长时间讲话后 long time speaking	抽烟后 after smoking	配药使用 taken with other medicine	其他 others
样本 Sample	389	44.2	60.7	8.7	5.7	3.6	0.5
男性 Male	179	36.9	62.0	8.4	11.2	4.5	0.6
16~24 岁 Age	34	29.4	58.8	14.7	14.7	2.9	2.9
25~34 岁 Age	52	32.7	65.4	11.5	13.5	3.8	0.0
35~44 岁 Age	55	41.8	61.8	3.6	10.9	3.6	0.0
45~54 岁 Age	28	42.9	53.6	7.1	7.1	10.7	0.0
55~60 岁 Age	10	40.0	80.0	0.0	0.0	0.0	0.0
女性 Female	210	50.5	59.5	9.0	1.0	2.9	0.5
16~24 岁 Age	43	39.5	65.1	11.6	0.0	2.3	0.0
25~34 岁 Age	69	44.9	63.8	7.2	1.4	2.9	1.4
35~44 岁 Age	52	65.4	46.2	9.6	1.9	5.8	0.0
45~54 岁 Age	25	52.0	60.0	4.0	0.0	0.0	0.0
55~60 岁 Age	21	52.4	66.7	14.3	0.0	0.0	0.0

2-10 样本、男性各年龄层、女性各年龄层购买润候药的场所/ Location of Buying Sore Throat Remedies by the Whole Sample, Age and Gender Groups

注：本题为多选题，合计百分比超过 100%（Multiple answers）

	人数 Number	药店 drug store	医院/诊所 hospital	商场 department store/ shopping center
样本 Sample	387	41.1	47.0	21.4
男性 Male	178	40.4	43.3	26.4
16~24 岁 Age	34	47.1	20.6	38.2
25~34 岁 Age	51	39.2	37.3	39.2
35~44 岁 Age	55	36.4	50.9	18.2
45~54 岁 Age	28	46.4	60.7	7.1
55~60 岁 Age	10	30.0	60.0	20.0
女性 Female	209	41.6	50.2	17.2
16~24 岁 Age	43	48.8	30.2	23.3
25~34 岁 Age	68	35.3	50.0	22.1
35~44 岁 Age	52	40.4	57.7	19.2
45~54 岁 Age	25	52.0	52.0	4.0
55~60 岁 Age	21	38.1	71.4	0.0

2-11 家中是否有备有润喉药的习惯/ The Habit of Keeping Sore Throat Remedies at Home

	人数 Number	百分比 Percent
有 yes	429	42.7
没有 no	576	57.3

n=1005

2-12 公费/自费医疗的比例/ Proportion of the Free Medical Service

	人数 Number	百分比 Percent
公费医疗 free medical service	689	69.5
自费医疗 at my own expense	302	30.5

n=991

2-13 不同消费者层的常用品牌/ The Most Frequently Used Brands by Market Segments

2-13-1 时尚流行指标/ Fads Popular Index

注：在药品品牌调查中，消费者经常出现将药品的名称与品牌名称混淆的现象，特此声明。/ In our research on medicines, we find consumers often confused the names and the brands.

	人数 Number	第一品牌及百分比 1st / percent	第二品牌及百分比 2nd / percent	第三品牌及百分比 3rd / percent
样本 Sample	385	**三金西瓜霜 Sanjin（35.3）**	**广西金嗓子喉宝 Golden Throat（16.6）** **江中草珊瑚 Jiangzhong（16.6）**	**四季润喉片 Siji（11.7）**
平实生活指向 simple living orientation	169	三金西瓜霜 Sanjin（37.3）	江中草珊瑚 Jiangzhong（16.6）	广西金嗓子喉宝 Golden Throat（15.4）
时尚流行指向 fashion orientation	216	三金西瓜霜 Sanjin（33.8）	广西金嗓子喉宝 Golden Throat（17.6）	江中草珊瑚 Jiangzhong（16.7）

2-13-2 广告态度指标/ Advertising Attitude Index

注：在药品品牌调查中，消费者经常出现将药品的名称与品牌名称混淆的现象，特此声明。/ In our research on medicines, we find consumers often confused the names and the brands.

	人数 Number	第一品牌及百分比 1st / percent	第二品牌及百分比 2nd / percent	第三品牌及百分比 3rd / percent
样本 Sample	383	**三金西瓜霜 Sanjin（35.2）**	**广西金嗓子喉宝 Golden Throat（16.7）** **江中草珊瑚 Jiangzhong（16.7）**	**四季润喉片 Siji（11.7）**
广告淡漠指向 indifferent orientation	95	三金西瓜霜 Sanjin（36.8）	江中草珊瑚 Jiangzhong（16.8）	广西金嗓子喉宝 Golden Throat（14.7）
中间层 medium	234	三金西瓜霜 Sanjin（35.9）	广西金嗓子喉宝 Golden Throat（16.2） 江中草珊瑚 Jiangzhong（16.2）	四季润喉片 Siji（12.4）
信赖广告指向 loyal orientation	54	三金西瓜霜 Sanjin（29.6）	广西金嗓子喉宝 Golden Throat（22.2）	江中草珊瑚 Jiangzhong（18.5）

2-13-3 饮食健康指标/ Foods & Drink Quality Index

注：在药品品牌调查中，消费者经常出现将药品的名称与品牌名称混淆的现象，特此声明。/ In our research on medicines, we find consumers often confused the names and the brands.

	人数 Number	第一品牌及百分比 1st / percent	第二品牌及百分比 2nd / percent	第三品牌及百分比 3rd / percent
样本 Sample	385	**三金西瓜霜 Sanjin（35.1）**	**江中草珊瑚 Jiangzhong（16.9）**	**广西金嗓子喉宝 Golden Throat（16.6）**
饮食"温饱"指向 "basic" orientation	70	三金西瓜霜 Sanjin（37.1）	广西金嗓子喉宝 Golden Throat（21.4）	江中草珊瑚 Jiangzhong（17.1）
中间层 medium	201	三金西瓜霜 Sanjin（37.8）	江中草珊瑚 Jiangzhong（16.9）	四季润喉片 Siji（12.9）
健康营养指向 health & nutrition orientation	114	三金西瓜霜 Sanjin（28.9）	广西金嗓子喉宝 Golden Throat（24.6）	江中草珊瑚 Jiangzhong（16.7）

● 广州 / Guangzhou

2-1 最近一年内有无服用的比例/ Whether having Taken Sore Throat Remedies Last Year

	人数 Number	百分比 Percent
吃过 yes	465	45.0
没吃过 no	569	55.0

n=1034

2-2 最常用品牌或品种排名/ Ranking of the Most Frequently Used Brands or Kinds

注：在药品品牌调查中，消费者经常出现将药品的名称与品牌名称混淆的现象，特此声明。/ In our research on medicines, we find consumers often confused the names and the brands.

排名 Brand Ranking	品牌或品种 Brands or Kinds	人数 Number	百分比 Percent
1	三金西瓜霜 Sanjin	187	40.2
2	广西金嗓子喉宝 Golden Throat	146	31.4
3	潘高寿 PGS	21	4.5
4	陈李济喉疾灵 Chenliji	15	3.2
5	健民咽喉片 Jianmin	12	2.6
5	江中草珊瑚 Jiangzhong	12	2.6

n=465

2-3 样本、男性各年龄层、女性各年龄层的常用品牌或品种/ The Most Frequently Used Brands or Kinds by the Whole Sample, Age and Gender Groups

注：在药品品牌调查中，消费者经常出现将药品的名称与品牌名称混淆的现象，特此声明。/ In cur researca on medicines, we find consumers often confused the names and the brands.

	人数 Number	第一品牌及百分比 1st/ percent	第二品牌及百分比 2nd/ percent	第三品牌及百分比 3rd/ percent
样本 Sample	465	**三金西瓜霜 Sanjin(40.2)**	**广西金嗓子喉宝 Golden Throat(31.4)**	**潘高寿 PGS(4.5)**
男性 Male	210	**三金西瓜霜 Sanjin(39.5)**	**广西金嗓子喉宝 Golden Throat(32.9)**	**潘高寿 PGS(4.8)**
16~24 岁 Age	47	广西金嗓子喉宝 Golden Throat(34.0)	三金西瓜霜 Sanjin(27.7)	潘高寿 PGS(8.5)
25~34 岁 Age	61	三金西瓜霜 Sanjin(39.3)	广西金嗓子喉宝 Golden Throat(32.8)	健民咽喉片 Jianmin(4.9) 咽之爽 Yhanzhishuang(4.9)
35~44 岁 Age	47	三金西瓜霜 Sanjin(40.4)	广西金嗓子喉宝 Golden Throat(38.3)	江中草珊瑚 Jiangzhong(4.3) 潘高寿 PGS(4.3)
45~54 岁 Age	37	广西金嗓子喉宝 Golden Throat(35.1) 三金西瓜霜 Sanjin(35.1)	使立消 Streplis(5.4) 潘高寿 PGS(5.4)	华素片 Tabellae Cydiodini(2.7) 健民咽喉片 Jianmin(2.7) 喉宝 Houbao(2.7) 利口乐 Likoule(2.7) 利咽清 Liyanqing(2.7) 陈李济喉疾灵 Chenliji(2.7) 荷氏 Heshi(2.7)
55~60 岁 Age	18	三金西瓜霜 Sanjin(77.8)	广西金嗓子喉宝 Golden Throat(11.1)	陈李济喉疾灵 Chenliji(5.6)
女性 Female	255	**三金西瓜霜 Sanjin(40.8)**	**广西金嗓子喉宝 Golden Throat(30.2)**	**潘高寿 PGS(4.3)**
16~24 岁 Age	66	三金西瓜霜 Sanjin(33.3)	广西金嗓子喉宝 Golden Throat(31.3)	咽之爽(4.5) 潘高寿 PGS(4.5) 陈济李喉疾灵(4.5)
25~34 岁 Age	73	三金西瓜霜 Sanjin(45.2)	广西金嗓子喉宝 Golden Throat(30 1)	潘高寿 PGS(6.8)
35~44 岁 Age	59	三金西瓜霜 Sanjin(37.3)	广西金嗓子喉宝 Golden Throat(32.2)	江中草珊瑚 Jiangzhong(6.8)
45~54 岁 Age	45	三金西瓜霜 Sanjin(42.2)	广西金嗓子喉宝 Golden Throat(28.9)	健民咽喉片 Jianmin(6.7)
55~60 岁 Age	12	三金西瓜霜 Sanjin(66.7)	广西金嗓子喉宝 Golden Throat(16.7)	健民咽喉片 Jianmin(8.3) 健宝牌清凉润喉片 Jianbao(8.3)

2-4 理想品牌或品种排名/ Ranking of the Ideal Brands or Kinds

注：在药品品牌调查中，消费者经常出现将药品的名称与品牌名称混淆的现象，特此声明。/ In our research on medicines, we find consumers often confused the names and the brands.

排名 Brand Ranking	品牌或品种 Brands or Kinds	人数 Number	百分比 Percent
1	广西金嗓子喉宝 Golden Throat	244	23.6
2	三金西瓜霜 Sanjin	234	22.6
3	潘高寿 PGS	34	3.3
4	陈李济喉疾灵 Chenliji	18	1.7
5	使立消 Streplis	16	1.5
5	江中草珊瑚 Jiangzhong	16	1.5
6	健民咽喉片 Jianmin	15	1.5

n=1034

2-5 样本、男性各年龄层、女性各年龄层的品牌习惯/ Brand Habit in Consuming Sore Throat Remedies by the Whole Sample, Age and Gender Groups

	人数 Number	基本固定用一个牌子 used in only one brand	比较固定地用两个或三个牌子 used in two or three brands	基本上不太固定牌子 no brand preference
样本 Sample	465	39.8	39.6	20.6
男性 Male	210	45.2	33.3	21.4
16~24 岁 Age	47	57.4	25.5	17.0
25~34 岁 Age	61	37.7	37.7	24.6
35~44 岁 Age	47	40.4	40.4	19.1
45~54 岁 Age	37	35.1	32.4	32.4
55~60 岁 Age	18	72.2	22.2	5.6
女性 Female	255	35.3	44.7	20.0
16~24 岁 Age	66	36.4	40.9	22.7
25~34 岁 Age	73	23.3	56.2	20.5
35~44 岁 Age	59	39.0	42.4	18.6
45~54 岁 Age	45	48.9	35.6	15.6
55~60 岁 Age	12	33.3	41.7	25.0

2-6 样本、男性各年龄层、女性各年龄层最近一年内有无服用的比例/ Whether having Taken Sore Throat Remedies Last Year by the Whole Sample, Age and Gender Groups

	人数 Number	吃过 yes	没吃过 no
样本 Sample	1034	45.0	55.0
男性 Male	499	42.1	57.9
16~24 岁 Age	106	44.3	55.7
25~34 岁 Age	150	40.7	59.3
35~44 岁 Age	127	37.0	63.0
45~54 岁 Age	73	50.7	49.3
55~60 岁 Age	43	41.9	58.1
女性 Female	535	47.7	52.3
16~24 岁 Age	112	58.9	41.1
25~34 岁 Age	158	46.2	53.8
35~44 岁 Age	137	43.1	56.9
45~54 岁 Age	87	51.7	48.3
55~60 岁 Age	41	29.3	70.7

2-7 选择该类商品的考虑因素/ Ranking of the Considerations in Purchasing

注：本题为多选题，合计百分比超过 100%（Multiple answers）

排名 Ranking	考虑因素 Considerations	人次 Person-time	百分比 Percent
1	见效快 immediate effect	223	48.1
2	医生推荐 recommended by doctors	136	29.3
3	无副作用 no side-effects	121	26.1
4	价格适中 reasonable price	112	24.1
5	有名的牌子 famous brand	107	23.1
6	服用方式简便 simple to take	83	17.9
7	购买方便 easy to buy	55	11.9
8	广告影响 influence of advertising	54	11.6
9	亲友介绍 introduced by relatives & friends	49	10.6
10	其他 others	6	1.3

n=464

2-8 样本、男性各年龄层、女性各年龄层最常服用的种类/ Types of Sore Throat Remedies Consumed by the Whole Sample, Age and Gender Groups

	人数 Number	片剂 pill	冲剂 granular formulation	糖浆 syrup	药粉 powder	膏状 paste-type	药丸 bolus	其他 others
样本 Sample	459	77.8	1.1	2.6	0.9	1.7	12.9	3.1
男性 Male	208	77.9	1.4	2.4	0.5	1.4	13.5	2.9
16~24 岁 Age	47	63.8	0.0	4.3	0.0	0.0	29.8	2.1
25~34 岁 Age	60	85.0	1.7	0.0	1.7	3.3	8.3	0.0
35~44 岁 Age	47	80.9	0.0	4.3	0.0	2.1	10.6	2.1
45~54 岁 Age	37	78.4	2.7	2.7	0.0	0.0	8.1	8.1
55~60 岁 Age	17	82.4	5.9	0.0	0.0	0.0	5.9	5.9
女性 Female	251	77.7	0.8	2.8	1.2	2.0	12.4	3.2
16~24 岁 Age	63	66.7	0.0	4.8	1.6	1.6	22.2	3.2
25~34 岁 Age	73	80.8	1.4	1.4	2.7	1.4	8.2	4.1
35~44 岁 Age	59	78.0	0.0	3.4	0.0	1.7	13.6	3.4
45~54 岁 Age	45	84.4	0.0	2.2	0.0	4.4	6.7	2.2
55~60 岁 Age	11	90.9	9.1	0.0	0.0	0.0	0.0	0.0

2-9 样本、男性各年龄层、女性各年龄层最常服用的场合/ Settings of Consumption by the Whole Sample, Age and Gender Groups

注：本题为多选题，合计百分比超过 100%（Multiple answers）

	人数 Number	喉咙发炎时 throat inflammation	喉咙轻度不适时 sore throat	长时间讲话后 long time speaking	抽烟后 after smoking	配药使用 taken with other medicine	其他 others
样本 Sample	460	44.6	68.7	9.8	4.8	1.1	1.1
男性 Male	208	42.8	69.7	8 7	9.1	0.5	1.0
16~24 岁 Age	47	46.8	72.3	14.9	4.3	0.0	0.0
25~34 岁 Age	61	36.1	73.8	4.9	8.2	1.6	0.0
35~44 岁 Age	46	52.2	67.4	6.5	10.9	0.0	0.0
45~54 岁 Age	37	35.1	70.3	8.1	10.8	0.0	5.4
55~60 岁 Age	17	47.1	52.9	11.8	17.6	0.0	0.0
女性 Female	252	46.0	67.9	10.7	1.2	1.6	1.2
16~24 岁 Age	65	46.2	64.6	15.4	1.5	3.1	1.5
25~34 岁 Age	72	51.4	62.5	8.3	0.0	2.8	1.4
35~44 岁 Age	59	50.8	72.9	5.1	0.0	0.0	0.0
45~54 岁 Age	44	34.1	68.2	15.9	4.5	0.0	2.3
55~60 岁 Age	12	33.3	91.7	8.3	0.0	0.0	0.0

2-10 样本、男性各年龄层、女性各年龄层购买润候药的场所/ Location of Buying Sore Throat Remedies by the Whole Sample, Age and Gender Groups

注：本题为多选题，合计百分比超过 100%（Multiple answers）

	人数 Number	药店 drug store	医院/诊所 hospital	商场 department store/ shopping center
样本 Sample	465	60.6	31.2	17.6
男性 Male	210	61.4	28.1	17.6
16~24 岁 Age	47	57.4	25.5	25.5
25~34 岁 Age	61	70.5	26.2	13.1
35~44 岁 Age	47	53.2	36.2	10.6
45~54 岁 Age	37	56.8	29.7	24.3
55~60 岁 Age	18	72.2	16.7	16.7
女性 Female	255	60.0	33.7	17.6
16~24 岁 Age	66	59.1	18.2	30.3
25~34 岁 Age	73	58.9	38.4	13.7
35~44 岁 Age	59	67.8	33.9	11.9
45~54 岁 Age	45	55.6	44.4	17.8
55~60 岁 Age	12	50.0	50.0	0.0

2-11 家中是否有备用润喉药的习惯/ The Habit of Keeping Sore Throat Remedies at Home

	人数 Number	百分比 Percent
有 yes	424	41.4
没有 no	600	58.6

n=1024

2-12 公费/自费医疗的比例/ Proportion of the Free Medical Service

	人数 Number	百分比 Percent
公费医疗 free medical service	423	40.9
自费医疗 at my own expense	610	59.1

n=1033

2-13 不同消费者层的常用品牌/ The Most Frequently Used Brands by Market Segments

2-13-1 时尚流行指标/ Fads Popular Index

注：在药品品牌调查中，消费者经常出现将药品的名称与品牌名称混淆的现象，特此声明。/ In our research on medicines, we find consumers often confused the names and the brands.

	人数 Number	第一品牌及百分比 1st / percent	第二品牌及百分比 2nd / percent	第三品牌及百分比 3rd / percent
样本 Sample	458	**三金西瓜霜 Sanjin(40.4)**	**广西金嗓子喉宝 Golden Throat(31.2)**	**潘高寿 PGS(4.6)**
平实生活指向 simple living orientation	223	三金西瓜霜 Sanjin(46.2)	广西金嗓子喉宝 Golden Throat(26.0)	潘高寿 PGS(4.5)
时尚流行指向 fashion orientation	235	广西金嗓子喉宝 Golden Throat(36.2)	三金西瓜霜 Sanjin(34.9)	潘高寿 PGS(4.7)

2-13-2 广告态度指标/ Advertising Attitude Index

注：在药品品牌调查中，消费者经常出现将药品的名称与品牌名称混淆的现象，特此声明。/ In our research on medicines, we find consumers often confused the names and the brands.

	人数 Number	第一品牌及百分比 1st / percent	第二品牌及百分比 2nd / percent	第三品牌及百分比 3rd / percent
样本 Sample	457	**三金西瓜霜 Sanjin(40.3)**	**广西金嗓子喉宝 Golden Throat(31.3)**	**潘高寿 PGS(4.6)**
广告淡漠指向 indifferent orientation	132	三金西瓜霜 Sanjin(37.1)	广西金嗓子喉宝 Golden Throat(33.3)	陈李济喉疾灵 Chenliji(4.5)
中间层 medium	269	三金西瓜霜 Sanjin(42.0)	广西金嗓子喉宝 Golden Throat(31.6)	潘高寿 PGS(4.5)
信赖广告指向 loyal orientation	56	三金西瓜霜 Sanjin(39.3)	广西金嗓子喉宝 Golden Throat(25.0)	潘高寿 PGS(7.1)

2-13-3 饮食健康指标/ Foods & Drink Quality Index

注：在药品品牌调查中，消费者经常出现将药品的名称与品牌名称混淆的现象，特此声明。/ In our research on medicines, we find consumers often confused the names and the brands.

	人数 Number	第一品牌及百分比 1st / percent	第二品牌及百分比 2nd / percent	第三品牌及百分比 3rd / percent
样本 Sample	463	**三金西瓜霜 Sanjin(40.2)**	**广西金嗓子喉宝 Golden Throat(31.5)**	**潘高寿 PGS(4.3)**
饮食“温饱”指向 "basic" orientation	116	三金西瓜霜 Sanjin(37.9)	广西金嗓子喉宝 Golden Throat(32.8)	陈李济喉疾灵 Chenliji(4.3)
中间层 medium	245	三金西瓜霜 Sanjin(43.3)	广西金嗓子喉宝 Golden Throat(30.2)	潘高寿 PGS(5.7)
健康营养指向 health & nutrition orientation	102	三金西瓜霜 Sanjin(35.3)	广西金嗓子喉宝 Golden Throat(33.3)	陈李济喉疾灵 Chenliji(4.9)

● 重庆 / Chongqing

2-1 最近一年内有无服用的比例/ Whether having Taken Sore Throat Remedies Last Year

	人数 Number	百分比 Percent
吃过 yes	342	54.8
没吃过 no	282	45.2

n=624

2-2 最常用品牌或品种排名/ Ranking of the Most Frequently Used Brands or Kinds

注：在药品品牌调查中，消费者经常出现将药品的名称与品牌名称混淆的现象，特此声明。/ In our research on medicines, we find consumers often confused the names and the brands.

排名 Brand Ranking	品牌或品种 Brands or Kinds	人数 Number	百分比 Percent
1	三金西瓜霜 Sanjin	130	38.0
2	广西金嗓子喉宝 Golden Throat	101	29.5
3	江中草珊瑚 Jiangzhong	74	21.6
4	咽立爽 Yanlishuang	9	2.6
5	健民咽喉片 Jianmin	7	2.0
6	熊胆舒喉片 Xiong Dan Shu Hou Pian	6	1.8

N=342

2-3 样本、男性各年龄层、女性各年龄层的常用品牌或品种/ The Most Frequently Used Brands or Kinds by the Whole Sample, Age and Gender Groups

注：在药品品牌调查中，消费者经常出现将药品的名称与品牌名称混淆的现象，特此声明。/ In our research on medicines, we find consumers often confused the names and the brands.

	人数 Number	第一品牌及百分比 1st/ percent	第二品牌及百分比 2nd/ percent	第三品牌及百分比 3rd/ percent
样本 Sample	342	**三金西瓜霜 Sanjin(38.0)**	**广西金嗓子喉宝 Golden Throat(29.5)**	**江中草珊瑚 Jiangzhong(21.6)**
男性 Male	167	**三金西瓜霜 Sanjin(38.3)**	**广西金嗓子喉宝 Golden Throat(30.5)**	**江中草珊瑚 Jiangzhong(18.6)**
16~24 岁 Age	35	三金西瓜霜 Sanjin(51.4)	广西金嗓子喉宝 Golden Throat(20.0)	江中草珊瑚 Jiangzhong(14.3)
25~34 岁 Age	50	广西金嗓子喉宝 Golden Throat(40.0)	三金西瓜霜 Sanjin(38.0)	江中草珊瑚 Jiangzhong(12.0)
35~44 岁 Age	40	三金西瓜霜 Sanjin(47.5)	广西金嗓子喉宝 Golden Throat(32.5)	江中草珊瑚 Jiangzhong(15.0)
45~54 岁 Age	27	广西金嗓子喉宝 Golden Throat(37.0)	江中草珊瑚 Jiangzhong(33.3)	三金西瓜霜 Sanjin(14.8)
55~60 岁 Age	15	江中草珊瑚 Jiangzhong(33.3)	三金西瓜霜 Sanjin(26.7)	健民咽喉片 Jianmin(20.0)
女性 Female	175	**三金西瓜霜 Sanjin(37.7)**	**广西金嗓子喉宝 Golden Throat(28.6)**	**江中草珊瑚 Jiangzhong(24.6)**
16~24 岁 Age	37	广西金嗓子喉宝 Golden Throat(32.4) 三金西瓜霜 Sanjin(32.4)	江中草珊瑚 Jiangzhong(29.7)	咽立爽 Yanlishuang(2.7)
25~34 岁 Age	50	三金西瓜霜 Sanjin(42.0)	江中草珊瑚 Jiangzhong(32.0)	广西金嗓子喉宝 Golden Throat(18.0)
35~44 岁 Age	40	三金西瓜霜 Sanjin(37.5)	广西金嗓子喉宝 Golden Throat(27.5)	江中草珊瑚 Jiangzhong(22.5)
45~54 岁 Age	37	广西金嗓子喉宝 Golden Throat(45.9)	三金西瓜霜 Sanjin(29.7)	江中草珊瑚 Jiangzhong(13.5)
55~60 岁 Age	11	三金西瓜霜 Sanjin(63.6)	江中草珊瑚 Jiangzhong(18.2)	广西金嗓子喉宝 Golden Throat(9.1) 黄河药 Huanghe(9.1)

2-4 理想品牌或品种排名/ Ranking of the Ideal Brands or Kinds

注：在药品品牌调查中，消费者经常出现将药品的名称与品牌名称混淆的现象，特此声明。/ In our research on medicines, we find consumers often confused the names and the brands.

排名 Brand Ranking	品牌或品种 Brands or Kinds	人数 Number	百分比 Percent
1	三金西瓜霜 Sanjin	198	31.7
2	广西金嗓子喉宝 Golden Throat	182	29.2
3	江中草珊瑚 Jiangzhong	111	17.8
4	咽立爽 Yanlishuang	12	1.9
5	熊胆舒喉片 Xiong Dan Shu Hou Pian	9	1.4
5	健民咽喉片 Jianmin	9	1.4

N=624

2-5 样本、男性各年龄层、女性各年龄层的品牌习惯/ Brand Habit in Consuming Sore Throat Remedies by the Whole Sample, Age and Gender Groups

	人数 Number	基本固定用一个牌子 used in only one brand	比较固定地用两个或三个牌子 used in two or three brands	基本上不太固定牌子 no brand preference
样本 Sample	341	48.4	33.7	17.9
男性 Male	167	50.9	28.1	21.0
16~24 岁 Age	35	68.6	14.3	17.1
25~34 岁 Age	50	46.0	36.0	18.0
35~44 岁 Age	40	47.5	22.5	30.0
45~54 岁 Age	27	44.4	37.0	18.5
55~60 岁 Age	15	46.7	33.3	20.0
女性 Female	174	46.0	39.1	14.9
16~24 岁 Age	37	45.9	40.5	13.5
25~34 岁 Age	50	44.0	42.0	14.0
35~44 岁 Age	40	45.0	40.0	15.0
45~54 岁 Age	36	44.4	38.9	16.7
55~60 岁 Age	11	63.6	18.2	18.2

2-6 样本、男性各年龄层、女性各年龄层最近一年内有无服用的比例/ Whether having Taken Sore Throat Remedies Last Year by the Whole Sample, Age and Gender Groups

	人数 Number	吃过 yes	没吃过 no
样本 Sample	624	54.8	45.2
男性 Male	314	53.2	46.8
16~24 岁 Age	64	54.7	45.3
25~34 岁 Age	93	53.8	46.2
35~44 岁 Age	75	53.3	46.7
45~54 岁 Age	54	50.0	50.0
55~60 岁 Age	28	53.6	46.4
女性 Female	310	56.5	43.5
16~24 岁 Age	64	57.8	42.2
25~34 岁 Age	90	55.6	44.4
35~44 岁 Age	73	54.8	45.2
45~54 岁 Age	60	61.7	38.3
55~60 岁 Age	23	47.8	52.2

2-7 选择该类商品的考虑因素/ Ranking of the Considerations in Purchasing

注：本题为多选题，合计百分比超过 100%（Multiple answers）

排名 Ranking	考虑因素 Considerations	人次 Person-time	百分比 Percent
1	见效快 immediate effect	184	54.0
2	医生推荐 recommended by doctors	78	22.9
3	价格适中 reasonable price	75	22.0
4	无副作用 no side-effects	74	21.7
5	有名的牌子 famous brand	70	20.5
5	服用方式简便 simple to take	70	20.5
6	广告影响 influence of advertising	57	16.7
7	购买方便 easy to buy	34	10.0
8	亲友介绍 introduced by relatives & friends	19	5.6
9	其他 others	3	0.9

n=341

2-8 样本、男性各年龄层、女性各年龄层最常服用的种类/ Types of Sore Throat Remedies Consumed by the Whole Sample, Age and Gender Groups

	人数 Number	片剂 pill	冲剂 granular formulation	糖浆 syrup	药粉 powder	膏状 paste-type	药丸 bolus	其他 others
样本 Sample	338	86.1	0.0	0.3	0.6	0.3	12.1	0.6
男性 Male	165	88.5	0.0	0.6	0.6	0.0	10.3	0.0
16~24 岁 Age	35	71.4	0.0	0.0	2.9	0.0	25.7	0.0
25~34 岁 Age	49	100.0	0.0	0.0	0.0	0.0	0.0	0.0
35~44 岁 Age	39	92.3	0.0	0.0	0.0	0.0	7.7	0.0
45~54 岁 Age	27	77.8	0.0	3.7	0.0	0.0	18.5	0.0
55~60 岁 Age	15	100.0	0.0	0.0	0.0	0.0	0.0	0.0
女性 Female	173	83.8	0.0	0.0	0.6	0.6	13.9	1.2
16~24 岁 Age	36	83.3	0.0	0.0	0.0	0.0	13.9	2.8
25~34 岁 Age	49	91.8	0.0	0.0	0.0	0.0	8.2	0.0
35~44 岁 Age	40	80.0	0.0	0.0	0.0	2.5	15.0	2.5
45~54 岁 Age	37	81.1	0.0	0.0	2.7	0.0	16.2	0.0
55~60 岁 Age	11	72.7	0.0	0.0	0.0	0.0	27.3	0.0

2-9 样本、男性各年龄层、女性各年龄层最常服用的场合/ Settings of Consumption by the Whole Sample, Age and Gender Groups

注：本题为多选题，合计百分比超过 100%（Multiple answers）

	人数 Number	喉咙发炎时 throat inflammation	喉咙轻度不适时 sore throat	长时间讲话后 long time speaking	抽烟后 after smoking	配药使用 taken with other medicine	其他 others
样本 Sample	340	56.5	53.5	10.3	5.3	1.8	0.9
男性 Male	167	55.7	53.3	7.2	9.6	1.2	1.2
16~24 岁 Age	35	45.7	60.0	14.3	2.9	0.0	0.0
25~34 岁 Age	50	66.0	44.0	6.0	14.0	2.0	2.0
35~44 岁 Age	40	60.0	57.5	2.5	7.5	0.0	0.0
45~54 岁 Age	27	48.1	48.1	7.4	11.1	3.7	3.7
55~60 岁 Age	15	46.7	66.7	6.7	13.3	0.0	0.0
女性 Female	173	57.2	53.8	13.3	1.2	2.3	0.6
16~24 岁 Age	37	37.8	62.2	29.7	0.0	0.0	0.0
25~34 岁 Age	49	65.3	46.9	12.2	4.1	4.1	0.0
35~44 岁 Age	40	60.0	42.5	7.5	0.0	2.5	2.5
45~54 岁 Age	36	63.9	63.9	8.3	0.0	0.0	0.0
55~60 岁 Age	11	54.5	63.6	0.0	0.0	9.1	0.0

2-10 样本、男性各年龄层、女性各年龄层购买润候药的场所/ Location of Buying Sore Throat Remedies by the Whole Sample, Age and Gender Groups

注：本题为多选题，合计百分比超过 100%（Multiple answers）

	人数 Number	药店 drug store	医院/诊所 hospital	商场 department store/ shopping center
样本 Sample	341	76.8	32.3	4.4
男性 Male	166	76.5	30.1	6.6
16~24 岁 Age	35	71.4	22.9	8.6
25~34 岁 Age	49	73.5	28.6	6.1
35~44 岁 Age	40	82.5	27.5	5.0
45~54 岁 Age	27	85.2	40.7	3.7
55~60 岁 Age	15	66.7	40.0	13.3
女性 Female	175	77.1	34.3	2.3
16~24 岁 Age	37	78.4	32.4	2.7
25~34 岁 Age	50	74.0	32.0	2.0
35~44 岁 Age	40	75.0	40.0	0.0
45~54 岁 Age	37	81.1	32.4	5.4
55~60 岁 Age	11	81.8	36.4	0.0

2-11 家中是否有备用润喉药的习惯/ The Habit of Keeping Sore Throat Remedies at Home

	人数 Number	百分比 Percent
有 yes	319	51.5
没有 no	301	48.5

n=620

2-12 公费/自费医疗的比例/ Proportion of the Free Medical Service

	人数 Number	百分比 Percent
公费医疗 free medical service	180	29.2
自费医疗 at my own expense	437	70.8

n=617

2-13 不同消费者层的常用品牌/ The Most Frequently Used Brands by Market Segments

2-13-1 时尚流行指标/ Fads Popular Index

注：在药品品牌调查中，消费者经常出现将药品的名称与品牌名称混淆的现象，特此声明。/ In our research on medicines, we find consumers often confused the names and the brands.

	人数 Number	第一品牌及百分比 1st/ percent	第二品牌及百分比 2nd/ percent	第三品牌及百分比 3rd/ percent
样本 Sample	337	**三金西瓜霜 Sanjin(38.0)**	**广西金嗓子喉宝 Golden Throat(29.4)**	**江中草珊瑚 Jiangzhong(21.7)**
平实生活指向 simple living orientation	184	三金西瓜霜 Sanjin(40.2)	广西金嗓子喉宝 Golden Throat(27.2)	江中草珊瑚 Jiangzhong(21.2)
时尚流行指向 fashion orientation	153	三金西瓜霜 Sanjin(35.3)	广西金嗓子喉宝 Golden Throat(32.0)	江中草珊瑚 Jiangzhong(22.2)

2-13-2 广告态度指标/ Advertising Attitude Index

注：在药品品牌调查中，消费者经常出现将药品的名称与品牌名称混淆的现象，特此声明。/ In our research on medicines, we find consumers often confused the names and the brands.

	人数 Number	第一品牌及百分比 1st/ percent	第二品牌及百分比 2nd/ percent	第三品牌及百分比 3rd/ percent
样本 Sample	339	**三金西瓜霜 Sanjin(38.3)**	**广西金嗓子喉宝 Golden Throat(29.5)**	**江中草珊瑚 Jiangzhong(21.2)**
广告淡漠指向 indifferent orientation	86	三金西瓜霜 Sanjin(38.4)	广西金嗓子喉宝 Golden Throat(25.6)	江中草珊瑚 Jiangzhong(22.1)
中间层 medium	210	三金西瓜霜 Sanjin(39.5)	广西金嗓子喉宝 Golden Throat(30.0)	江中草珊瑚 Jiangzhong(21.4)
信赖广告指向 loyal orientation	43	广西金嗓子喉宝 Golden Throat(34.9)	三金西瓜霜 Sanjin(32.6)	江中草珊瑚 Jiangzhong(18.6)

2-13-3 饮食健康指标/ Foods & Drink Quality Index

注：在药品品牌调查中，消费者经常出现将药品的名称与品牌名称混淆的现象，特此声明。/ In our research on medicines, we find consumers often confused the names and the brands.

	人数 Number	第一品牌及百分比 1st/ percent	第二品牌及百分比 2nd/ percent	第三品牌及百分比 3rd/ percent
样本 Sample	338	**三金西瓜霜 Sanjin(38.5)**	**广西金嗓子喉宝 Golden Throat(29.3)**	**江中草珊瑚 Jiangzhong(21.6)**
饮食“温饱”指向 "basic" orientation	116	三金西瓜霜 Sanjin(37.1)	广西金嗓子喉宝 Golden Throat(32.8)	江中草珊瑚 Jiangzhong(19.0)
中间层 medium	141	三金西瓜霜 Sanjin(43.3)	广西金嗓子喉宝 Golden Throat(24.8)	江中草珊瑚 Jiangzhong(24.1)
健康营养指向 health & nutrition orientation	81	广西金嗓子喉宝 Golden Throat(32.1) 三金西瓜霜 Sanjin(32.1)	江中草珊瑚 Jiangzhong(21.0)	咽立爽 Yanlishuang(7.4)

● 武汉 / Wuhan

2-1 最近一年内有无服用的比例/ Whether having Taken Sore Throat Remedies Last Year

	人数 Number	百分比 Percent
吃过 yes	338	52.7
没吃过 no	303	47.3

n=641

2-2 最常用品牌或品种排名/ Ranking of the Most Frequently Used Brands or Kinds

注：在药品品牌调查中，消费者经常出现将药品的名称与品牌名称混淆的现象，特此声明。/ In our research on medicines, we find consumers often confused the names and the brands.

排名 Brand Ranking	品牌或品种 Brands or Kinds	人数 Number	百分比 Percent
1	健民咽喉片 Jianmin	103	30.5
2	三金西瓜霜 Sanjin	82	24.3
3	广西金嗓子喉宝 Golden Throat	80	23.7
4	江中草珊瑚 Jiangzhong	43	12.7
5	四季润喉片 Siji	8	2.4
6	华素片 Tabellae Cydiodini	4	1.2
7	蜜炼枇杷膏 Mi Lian Pi Pa Gao	2	0.6

n=338

2-3 样本、男性各年龄层、女性各年龄层的常用品牌或品种/ The Most Frequently Used Brands or Kinds by the Whole Sample, Age and Gender Groups

注：在药品品牌调查中，消费者经常出现将药品的名称与品牌名称混淆的现象，特此声明。/ In our research on medicines, we find consumers often confused the names and the brands.

	人数 Number	第一品牌及百分比 1st/ percent	第二品牌及百分比 2nd/ percent	第三品牌及百分比 3rd/ percent	第四品牌及百分比 4th/ percent
样本 Sample	338	**健民咽喉片 Jianmin(30.5)**	**三金西瓜霜 Sanjin(24.3)**	**广西金嗓子喉宝 Golden Throat(23.7)**	**江中草珊瑚 Jiangzhong(12.7)**
男性 Male	171	**健民咽喉片 Jianmin(35.1)**	**三金西瓜霜 Sanjin(24.0)**	**广西金嗓子喉宝 Golden Throat(21.6)**	**江中草珊瑚 Jiangzhong(10.5)**
16~24 岁 Age	37	广西金嗓子喉宝 Golden Throat(32.4)	健民咽喉片 Jianmin(24.3) 三金西瓜霜 Sanjin(24.3)	江中草珊瑚 Jiangzhong(13.5)	四季润喉片 Siji(2.7)
25~34 岁 Age	52	健民咽喉片 Jianmin(36.5)	三金西瓜霜 Sanjin(28.8)	江中草珊瑚 Jiangzhong(15.4)	广西金嗓子喉宝 Golden Throat(11.5)
35~44 岁 Age	45	健民咽喉片 Jianmin(42.2)	广西金嗓子喉宝 Golden Throat(26.7)	三金西瓜霜 Sanjin(20.0)	江中草珊瑚 Jiangzhong(6.7)
45~54 岁 Age	26	广西金嗓子喉宝 Golden Throat(26.9) 健民咽喉片 Jianmin(26.9)	三金西瓜霜 Sanjin(15.4)	江中草珊瑚 Jiangzhong(7.7)	四季润喉片 Siji(3.8) 咽特佳 Yantejia(3.8) 华素片 Tabellae Cydiodini(3.8) 蜜炼枇杷膏 Mi Lian Pi Pa Gao(3.8)
55~60 岁 Age	11	健民咽喉片 Jianmin(54.5)	三金西瓜霜 Sanjin(36.4)	蜜炼枇杷膏 Mi Lian Pi Pa Gao(9.1)	
女性 Female	167	**广西金嗓子喉宝 Golden Throat(25.7)** **健民咽喉片 Jianmin(25.7)**	**三金西瓜霜 Sanjin(24.6)**	**江中草珊瑚 Jiangzhong(15.0)**	**四季润喉片 Siji(1.8)** **华素片 Tabellae Cydiodini(1.8)**
16~24 岁 Age	36	广西金嗓子喉宝 Golden Throat(44.4)	三金西瓜霜 Sanjin(25.0)	健民咽喉片 Jianmin(16.7)	江中草珊瑚 Jiangzhong(11.1)
25~34 岁 Age	54	三金西瓜霜 Sanjin(33.3)	广西金嗓子喉宝 Golden Throat(27.8)	健民咽喉片 Jianmin(18.5)	江中草珊瑚 Jiangzhong(11.1)
35~44 岁 Age	33	健民咽喉片 Jianmin(36.4)	三金西瓜霜 Sanjin(21.2)	广西金嗓子喉宝 Golden Throat(18.2)	江中草珊瑚 Jiangzhong(9.1)
45~54 岁 Age	32	健民咽喉片 Jianmin(31.3)	江中草珊瑚 Jiangzhong(25.0)	广西金嗓子喉宝 Golden Throat(15.6) 三金西瓜霜 Sanjin(15.6)	四季润喉片 Siji(6.3)
55~60 岁 Age	12	健民咽喉片 Jianmin(41.7)	江中草珊瑚 Jiangzhong(33.3)	三金西瓜霜 Sanjin(16.7)	广西金嗓子喉宝 Golden Throat(8.3)

2-4 理想品牌或品种排名/ Ranking of the Ideal Brands or Kinds

注：在药品品牌调查中，消费者经常出现将药品的名称与品牌名称混淆的现象，特此声明。/ In our research on medicines, we find consumers often confused the names and the brands.

排名 Brand Ranking	品牌或品种 Brands or Kinds	人数 Number	百分比 Percent
1	健民咽喉片 Jianmin	170	26.5
2	广西金嗓子喉宝 Golden Throat	122	19.0
3	三金西瓜霜 Sanjin	114	17.8
4	江中草珊瑚 Jiangzhong	56	8.7
5	四季润喉片 Siji	8	1.2
6	华素片 Tabellae Cydiodini	4	0.6

n=641

2-5 样本、男性各年龄层、女性各年龄层的品牌习惯/ Brand Habit in Consuming Sore Throat Remedies by the Whole Sample, Age and Gender Groups

	人数 Number	基本固定用一个牌子 used in only one brand	比较固定地用两个或三个牌子 used in two or three brands	基本上不太固定牌子 no brand preference
样本 Sample	338	42.9	35.5	21.6
男性 Male	171	48.5	35.1	16.4
16~24 岁 Age	37	56.8	32.4	10.8
25~34 岁 Age	52	44.2	42.3	13.5
35~44 岁 Age	45	48.9	31.1	20.0
45~54 岁 Age	26	42.3	34.6	23.1
55~60 岁 Age	11	54.5	27.3	18.2
女性 Female	167	37.1	35.9	26.9
16~24 岁 Age	36	25.0	41.7	33.3
25~34 岁 Age	54	35.2	38.9	25.9
35~44 岁 Age	33	42.4	36.4	21.2
45~54 岁 Age	32	40.6	31.3	28.1
55~60 岁 Age	12	58.3	16.7	25.0

2-6 样本、 男性各年龄层、 女性各年龄层最近一年内有无服用的比例/ Whether having Taken Sore Throat Remedies Last Year by the Whole Sample, Age and Gender Groups

	人数 Number	吃过 yes	没吃过 no
样本 Sample	641	52.7	47.3
男性 Male	311	55.0	45.0
16~24 岁 Age	65	56.9	43.1
25~34 岁 Age	89	58.4	41.6
35~44 岁 Age	80	56.3	43.8
45~54 岁 Age	52	50.0	50.0
55~60 岁 Age	25	44.0	56.0
女性 Female	330	50.6	49.4
16~24 岁 Age	69	52.2	47.8
25~34 岁 Age	95	56.8	43.2
35~44 岁 Age	78	42.3	57.7
45~54 岁 Age	62	51.6	48.4
55~60 岁 Age	26	46.2	53.8

2-7 选择该类商品的考虑因素/ Ranking of the Considerations in Purchasing

注：本题为多选题，合计百分比超过 100%（Multiple answers）

排名 Ranking	考虑因素 Considerations	人次 Person-time	百分比 Percent
1	见效快 immediate effect	196	58.0
2	医生推荐 recommended by doctors	114	33.7
3	有名的牌子 famous brand	81	24.0
4	价格适中 reasonable price	77	22.8
5	无副作用 no side-effects	75	22.2
6	服用方式简便 simple to take	69	20.4
7	广告影响 influence of advertising	39	11.5
8	购买方便 easy to buy	31	9.2
9	亲友介绍 introduced by relatives & friends	27	8.0
10	其他 others	7	2.1

n=338

2-8 样本、男性各年龄层、女性各年龄层最常服用的种类/ Types of Sore Throat Remedies Consumed by the Whole Sample, Age and Gender Groups

	人数 Number	片剂 pill	冲剂 granular formulation	糖浆 syrup	药粉 powder	膏状 paste-type	药丸 bolus	其他 others
样本 Sample	335	88.1	0.9	0.6	0.6	0.6	8.7	0.6
男性 Male	170	89.4	0.6	0.6	0.6	1.2	7.6	0.0
16~24 岁 Age	37	86.5	0.0	0.0	0.0	0.0	13.5	0.0
25~34 岁 Age	52	90.4	0.0	0.0	0.0	0.0	9.6	0.0
35~44 岁 Age	45	95.6	2.2	0.0	0.0	2.2	0.0	0.0
45~54 岁 Age	25	80.0	0.0	4.0	4.0	0.0	12.0	0.0
55~60 岁 Age	11	90.9	0.0	0.0	0.0	9.1	0.0	0.0
女性 Female	165	86.7	1.2	0.6	0.6	0.0	9.7	1.2
16~24 岁 Age	36	80.6	0.0	2.8	2.8	0.0	11.1	2.8
25~34 岁 Age	53	90.6	0.0	0.0	0.0	0.0	7.5	1.9
35~44 岁 Age	32	90.6	3.1	0.0	0.0	0.0	6.3	0.0
45~54 岁 Age	32	78.1	3.1	0.0	0.0	0.0	18.8	0.0
55~60 岁 Age	12	100.0	0.0	0.0	0.0	0.0	0.0	0.0

2-9 样本、男性各年龄层、女性各年龄层最常服用的场合/ Settings of Consumption by the Whole Sample, Age and Gender Groups

注：本题为多选题，合计百分比超过 100%（Multiple answers）

	人数 Number	喉咙发炎时 throat inflammation	喉咙轻度不适时 sore throat	长时间讲话后 long time speaking	抽烟后 after smoking	配药使用 taken with other medicine	其他 others
样本 Sample	336	54.5	56.5	9.5	6.5	2.7	1.2
男性 Male	171	54.4	56.7	7.6	12.3	1.8	1.8
16~24 岁 Age	37	45.9	70.3	2.7	10.8	0.0	0.0
25~34 岁 Age	52	50.0	57.7	13.5	11.5	3.8	1.9
35~44 岁 Age	45	48.9	55.6	11.1	13.3	2.2	2.2
45~54 岁 Age	26	80.8	38.5	0.0	19.2	0.0	0.0
55~60 岁 Age	11	63.6	54.5	0.0	0.0	0.0	9.1
女性 Female	165	54.5	56.4	11.5	0.6	3.6	0.6
16~24 岁 Age	36	44.4	63.9	13.9	0.0	2.8	0.0
25~34 岁 Age	53	47.2	60.4	7.5	1.9	1.9	1.9
35~44 岁 Age	32	62.5	46.9	18.8	0.0	3.1	0.0
45~54 岁 Age	32	65.6	40.6	12.5	0.0	6.3	0.0
55~60 岁 Age	12	66.7	83.3	0.0	0.0	8.3	0.0

2-10 样本、男性各年龄层、女性各年龄层购买润候药的场所/ Location of Buying Sore Throat Remedies by the Whole Sample, Age and Gender Groups

注：本题为多选题，合计百分比超过 100%（Multiple answers）

	人数 Number	药店 drug store	医院/诊所 hospital	商场 department store/ shopping center
样本 Sample	338	58.6	49.4	3.3
男性 Male	171	64.3	46.2	2.3
16~24 岁 Age	37	56.8	45.9	2.7
25~34 岁 Age	52	67.3	53.8	1.9
35~44 岁 Age	45	80.0	28.9	4.4
45~54 岁 Age	26	50.0	53.8	0.0
55~60 岁 Age	11	45.5	63.6	0.0
女性 Female	167	52.7	52.7	4.2
16~24 岁 Age	36	55.6	47.2	11.1
25~34 岁 Age	54	66.7	35.2	3.7
35~44 岁 Age	33	54.5	63.6	0.0
45~54 岁 Age	32	37.5	62.5	3.1
55~60 岁 Age	12	16.7	91.7	0.0

2-11 家中是否有备用润喉药的习惯/ The Habit of Keeping Sore Throat Remedies at Home

	人数 Number	百分比 Percent
有 yes	319	49.9
没有 no	320	50.1

n=639

2-12 公费/自费医疗的比例/ Proportion of the Free Medical Service

	人数 Number	百分比 Percent
公费医疗 free medical service	264	41.5
自费医疗 at my own expense	372	58.5

n=636

2-13 不同消费者层的常用品牌/ The Most Frequently Used Brands by Market Segments

2-13-1 时尚流行指标/ Fads Popular Index

注：在药品品牌调查中，消费者经常出现将药品的名称与品牌名称混淆的现象，特此声明。/ In our research on medicines, we find consumers often confused the names and the brands.

	人数 Number	第一品牌及百分比 1st / percent	第二品牌及百分比 2nd / percent	第三品牌及百分比 3rd / percent	第四品牌及百分比 4th / percent
样本 Sample	334	**健民咽喉片 Jianmin(30.2)**	**三金西瓜霜 Sanjin(24.3)**	**广西金嗓子喉宝 Golden Throat(24.0)**	**江中草珊瑚 Jiangzhong(12.6)**
平实生活指向 simple living orientation	167	健民咽喉片 Jianmin(36.5)	三金西瓜霜 Sanjin(22.8)	广西金嗓子喉宝 Golden Throat(16.2)	江中草珊瑚 Jiangzhong(15.0)
时尚流行指向 fashion orientation	167	广西金嗓子喉宝 Golden Throat(31.7)	三金西瓜霜 Sanjin(25.7)	健民咽喉片 Jianmin(24.0)	江中草珊瑚 Jiangzhong(10.2)

2-13-2 广告态度指标/ Advertising Attitude Index

注：在药品品牌调查中，消费者经常出现将药品的名称与品牌名称混淆的现象，特此声明。/ In our research on medicines, we find consumers often confused the names and the brands.

	人数 Number	第一品牌及百分比 1st / percent	第二品牌及百分比 2nd / percent	第三品牌及百分比 3rd / percent	第四品牌及百分比 4th / percent
样本 Sample	335	**健民咽喉片 Jianmin(30.4)**	**三金西瓜霜 Sanjin(24.2)**	**广西金嗓子喉宝 Golden Throat(23.9)**	**江中草珊瑚 Jiangzhong(12.5)**
广告淡漠指向 indifferent orientation	93	健民咽喉片 Jianmin(30.1)	广西金嗓子喉宝 Golden Throat(20.4) 三金西瓜霜 Sanjin(20.4)	江中草珊瑚 Jiangzhong(18.3)	四季润喉片 Siji(2.2)
中间层 medium	205	健民咽喉片 Jianmin(30.2)	广西金嗓子喉宝 Golden Throat(26.8)	三金西瓜霜 Sanjin(24.9)	江中草珊瑚 Jiangzhong(10.2)
信赖广告指向 loyal orientation	37	健民咽喉片 Jianmin(32.4)	三金西瓜霜 Sanjin(29.7)	广西金嗓子喉宝 Golden Throat(16.2)	江中草珊瑚 Jiangzhong(10.8)

2-13-3 饮食健康指标/ Foods & Drink Quality Index

注：在药品品牌调查中，消费者经常出现将药品的名称与品牌名称混淆的现象，特此声明。/ In our research on medicines, we find consumers often confused the names and the brands.

	人数 Number	第一品牌及百分比 1st / percent	第二品牌及百分比 2nd / percent	第三品牌及百分比 3rd / percent	第四品牌及百分比 4th / percent
样本 Sample	334	**健民咽喉片 Jianmin(30.2)**	**三金西瓜霜 Sanjin(24.3)**	**广西金嗓子喉宝 Golden Throat(23.7)**	**江中草珊瑚 Jiangzhong(12.9)**
饮食“温饱”指向 "basic" orientation	107	健民咽喉片 Jianmin(34.6)	三金西瓜霜 Sanjin(24.3)	广西金嗓子喉宝 Golden Throat(22.4)	江中草珊瑚 Jiangzhong(8.4)
中间层 medium	162	健民咽喉片 Jianmin(30.9)	三金西瓜霜 Sanjin(22.8)	广西金嗓子喉宝 Golden Throat(21.6)	江中草珊瑚 Jiangzhong(17.3)
健康营养指向 health & nutrition orientation	65	广西金嗓子喉宝 Golden Throat(30.8)	三金西瓜霜 Sanjin(27.7)	健民咽喉片 Jianmin(21.5)	江中草珊瑚 Jiangzhong(9.2)

● 西安 / Xi'an

2-1 最近一年内有无服用的比例/ Whether having Taken Sore Throat Remedies Last Year

	人数 Number	百分比 Percent
吃过 yes	349	58.1
没吃过 no	252	41.9

n=601

2-2 最常用品牌或品种排名/ Ranking of the Most Frequently Used Brands or Kinds

注：在药品品牌调查中，消费者经常出现将药品的名称与品牌名称混淆的现象，特此声明。/ In our research on medicines, we find consumers often confused the names and the brands.

排名 Brand Ranking	品牌或品种 Brands or Kinds	人数 Number	百分比 Percent
1	广西金嗓子喉宝 Golden Throat	139	39.3
2	三金西瓜霜 Sanjin	106	30.4
3	江中草珊瑚 Jiangzhong	74	21.2
4	健民咽喉片 Jianmin	7	2.0
5	四季润喉片 Siji	4	1.1
6	金嗓灵 Jinhouling	3	0.9
6	金龙牌痰咳净 Jin Long Pai Tan Ke Jing	3	0.9

n=349

2-3 样本、男性各年龄层、女性各年龄层的常用品牌或品种/ The Most Frequently Used Brands or Kinds by the Whole Sample, Age and Gender Groups

注：在药品品牌调查中，消费者经常出现将药品的名称与品牌名称混淆的现象，特此声明。/ In our research on medicines, we find consumers often confused the names and the brands.

	人数 Number	第一品牌及百分比 1st/ percent	第二品牌及百分比 2nd/ percent	第三品牌及百分比 3rd/ percent
样本 Sample	349	**广西金嗓子喉宝 Golden Throat(39.8)**	**三金西瓜霜 Sanjin(30.4)**	**江中草珊瑚 Jiangzhong(21.2)**
男性 Male	177	**广西金嗓子喉宝 Golden Throat(36.7)**	**三金西瓜霜 Sanjin(33.3)**	**江中草珊瑚 Jiangzhong(22.0)**
16~24 岁 Age	40	三金西瓜霜 Sanjin(47.5)	广西金嗓子喉宝 Golden Throat(35.0)	江中草珊瑚 Jiangzhong(17.5)
25~34 岁 Age	52	广西金嗓子喉宝 Golden Throat(36.4)	三金西瓜霜 Sanjin(30.8)	江中草珊瑚 Jiangzhong(25.0)
35~44 岁 Age	46	广西金嗓子喉宝 Golden Throat(39.1)	三金西瓜霜 Sanjin(30.4)	江中草珊瑚 Jiangzhong(21.7)
45~54 岁 Age	25	广西金嗓子喉宝 Golden Throat(40.0)	三金西瓜霜 Sanjin(28.0)	江中草珊瑚 Jiangzhong(20.0)
55~60 岁 Age	14	广西金嗓子喉宝 Golden Throat(35.7)	江中草珊瑚 Jiangzhong(28.6)	三金西瓜霜 Sanjin(21.4)
女性 Female	172	**广西金嗓子喉宝 Golden Throat(43.0)**	**三金西瓜霜 Sanjin(27.3)**	**江中草珊瑚 Jiangzhong(20.3)**
16~24 岁 Age	34	广西金嗓子喉宝 Golden Throat(52.9)	三金西瓜霜 Sanjin(32.4)	江中草珊瑚 Jiangzhong(14.7)
25~34 岁 Age	52	广西金嗓子喉宝 Golden Throat(38.5)	江中草珊瑚 Jiangzhong(25.0)	三金西瓜霜 Sanjin(23.1)
35~44 岁 Age	45	广西金嗓子喉宝 Golden Throat(46.7)	三金西瓜霜 Sanjin(22.2)	江中草珊瑚 Jiangzhong(13.3)
45~54 岁 Age	26	广西金嗓子喉宝 Golden Throat(46.2)	江中草珊瑚 Jiangzhong(30.8)	三金西瓜霜 Sanjin(19.2)
55~60 岁 Age	15	三金西瓜霜 Sanjin(60.0)	广西金嗓子喉宝 Golden Throat(20.0) 江中草珊瑚 Jiangzhong(20.0)	

2-4 理想品牌或品种排名/ Ranking of the Ideal Brands or Kinds

注：在药品品牌调查中，消费者经常出现将药品的名称与品牌名称混淆的现象，特此声明。/ In our research on medicines, we find consumers often confused the names and the brands.

排名 Brand Ranking	品牌或品种 Brands or Kinds	人数 Number	百分比 Percent
1	广西金嗓子喉宝 Golden Throat	225	37.4
2	三金西瓜霜 Sanjin	169	28.1
3	江中草珊瑚 Jiangzhong	107	17.8
5	健民咽喉片 Jianmin	17	2.8
7	金嗓灵 Jinhouling	4	0.7
8	四季润喉片 Siji	3	0.5
8	金龙牌痰咳净 Jin Long Pai Tan Ke Jing	3	0.5
9	复方甘草合剂 Fu Fang Gan Cao He Ji	2	0.3

n=601

2-5 样本、男性各年龄层、女性各年龄层的品牌习惯/ Brand Habit in Consuming Sore Throat Remedies by the Whole Sample, Age and Gender Groups

	人数 Number	基本固定用一个牌子 used in only one brand	比较固定地用两个或三个牌子 used in two or three brands	基本上不太固定牌子 no brand preference
样本 Sample	349	50.7	33.2	16.0
男性 Male	177	48.0	37.9	14.1
16~24 岁 Age	40	37.5	52.5	10.0
25~34 岁 Age	52	51.9	34.6	13.5
35~44 岁 Age	46	58.7	26.1	15.2
45~54 岁 Age	25	48.0	28.0	24.0
55~60 岁 Age	14	28.6	64.3	7.1
女性 Female	172	53.5	28.5	18.0
16~24 岁 Age	34	55.9	26.5	17.6
25~34 岁 Age	52	57.7	21.2	21.2
35~44 岁 Age	45	57.8	24.4	17.8
45~54 岁 Age	26	38.5	38.5	23.1
55~60 岁 Age	15	46.7	53.3	0.0

2-6 样本、男性各年龄层、女性各年龄层最近一年内有无服用的比例/ Whether having Taken Sore Throat Remedies Last Year by the Whole Sample, Age and Gender Groups

	人数 Number	吃过 yes	没吃过 no
样本 Sample	601	58.1	41.9
男性 Male	302	58.6	41.4
16~24 岁 Age	64	62.5	37.5
25~34 岁 Age	91	57.1	42.9
35~44 岁 Age	77	59.7	40.3
45~54 岁 Age	46	54.3	45.7
55~60 岁 Age	24	58.3	41.7
女性 Female	299	57.5	42.5
16~24 岁 Age	61	55.7	44.3
25~34 岁 Age	90	57.8	42.2
35~44 岁 Age	74	60.8	39.2
45~54 岁 Age	49	53.1	46.9
55~60 岁 Age	25	60.0	40.0

2-7 选择该类商品的考虑因素/ Ranking of the Considerations in Purchasing

注：本题为多选题，合计百分比超过 100%（Multiple answers）

排名 Ranking	考虑因素 Considerations	人次 Person-time	百分比 Percent
1	见效快 immediate effect	173	49.6
2	医生推荐 recommended by doctors	116	33.2
3	有名的牌子 famous brand	79	22.6
4	价格适中 reasonable price	64	18.3
5	无副作用 no side-effects	58	16.6
6	广告影响 influence of advertising	50	14.3
6	服用方式简便 simple to take	50	14.3
7	购买方便 easy to buy	39	11.2
8	亲友介绍 introduced by relatives & friends	25	7.2
9	其他 others	1	0.3

n=349

2-8 样本、男性各年龄层、女性各年龄层最常服用的种类/ Types of Sore Throat Remedies Consumed by the Whole Sample, Age and Gender Groups

	人数 Number	片剂 pill	冲剂 granular formulation	糖浆 syrup	药粉 powder	膏状 paste-type	药丸 bolus	其他 others
样本 Sample	347	91.1	1.7	1.2	1.7	0.0	3.7	0.6
男性 Male	175	90.9	1.7	1.1	2.9	0.0	2.9	0.6
16~24 岁 Age	39	92.3	2.6	0.0	2.6	0.0	0.0	2.6
25~34 岁 Age	51	86.3	3.9	3.9	3.9	0.0	2.0	0.0
35~44 岁 Age	46	95.7	0.0	0.0	2.2	0.0	2.2	0.0
45~54 岁 Age	25	88.0	0.0	0.0	0.0	0.0	12.0	0.0
55~60 岁 Age	14	92.9	0.0	0.0	7.1	0.0	0.0	0.0
女性 Female	172	91.3	1.7	1.2	0.6	0.0	4.7	0.6
16~24 岁 Age	34	91.2	2.9	0.0	2.9	0.0	2.9	0.0
25~34 岁 Age	52	94.2	1.9	0.0	0.0	0.0	3.8	0.0
35~44 岁 Age	45	91.1	2.2	2.2	0.0	0.0	4.4	0.0
45~54 岁 Age	26	88.5	0.0	3.8	0.0	0.0	7.7	0.0
55~60 岁 Age	15	86.7	0.0	0.0	0.0	0.0	6.7	6.7

2-9 样本、男性各年龄层、女性各年龄层最常服用的场合/ Settings of Consumption by the Whole Sample, Age and Gender Groups

注：本题为多选题，合计百分比超过 100%（Multiple answers）

	人数 Number	喉咙发炎时 throat inflammation	喉咙轻度不适时 sore throat	长时间讲话后 long time speaking	抽烟后 after smoking	配药使用 taken with other medicine	其他 others
样本 Sample	348	47.4	59.8	6.6	6.0	1.4	0.6
男性 Male	176	46.0	58.5	6.3	10.8	1.7	0.0
16~24 岁 Age	40	35.0	65.0	15.0	2.5	0.0	0.0
25~34 岁 Age	52	53.8	48.1	0.0	15.4	3.8	0.0
35~44 岁 Age	46	45.7	60.9	8.7	6.5	2.2	0.0
45~54 岁 Age	25	40.0	64.0	0.0	24.0	0.0	0.0
55~60 岁 Age	13	61.5	61.5	7.7	7.7	0.0	0.0
女性 Female	172	48.8	61.0	7.0	1.2	1.2	1.2
16~24 岁 Age	34	50.0	50.0	20.6	2.9	0.0	0.0
25~34 岁 Age	52	48.1	63.5	1.9	0.0	1.9	1.9
35~44 岁 Age	45	46.7	57.8	6.7	0.0	0.0	2.2
45~54 岁 Age	26	50.0	76.9	0.0	3.8	0.0	0.0
55~60 岁 Age	15	53.3	60.0	6.7	0.0	6.7	0.0

2-10 样本、男性各年龄层、女性各年龄层购买润候药的场所/ Location of Buying Sore Throat Remedies by the Whole Sample, Age and Gender Groups

注：本题为多选题，合计百分比超过 100%（Multiple answers）

	人数 Number	药店 drug store	医院/诊所 hospital	商场 department store/ shopping center
样本 Sample	349	64.8	43.3	2.0
男性 Male	177	66.1	41.2	1.1
16~24 岁 Age	40	65.0	37.5	2.5
25~34 岁 Age	52	75.0	30.8	1.9
35~44 岁 Age	46	73.9	43.5	0.0
45~54 岁 Age	25	52.0	52.0	0.0
55~60 岁 Age	14	35.7	64.3	0.0
女性 Female	172	63.4	45.3	2.9
16~24 岁 Age	34	70.6	32.4	5.9
25~34 岁 Age	52	65.4	48.1	1.9
35~44 岁 Age	45	62.2	46.7	4.4
45~54 岁 Age	26	57.7	50.0	0.0
55~60 岁 Age	15	53.3	53.3	0.0

2-11 家中是否有备用润喉药的习惯/ The Habit of Keeping Sore Throat Remedies at Home

	人数 Number	百分比 Percent
有 yes	340	56.6
没有 no	261	43.4

n=601

2-12 公费/自费医疗的比例/ Proportion of the Free Medical Service

	人数 Number	百分比 Percent
公费医疗 free medical service	263	44.1
自费医疗 at my own expense	333	55.9

n=596

2-13 不同消费者层的常用品牌或品种/ The Most Frequently Used Brands or Kinds by Market Segments

2-13-1 时尚流行指标/ Fads Popular Index

注：在药品品牌调查中，消费者经常出现将药品的名称与品牌名称混淆的现象，特此声明。/ In our research on medicines, we find consumers often confused the names and the brands.

	人数 Number	第一品牌及百分比 1st / percent	第二品牌及百分比 2nd / percent	第三品牌及百分比 3rd / percent	第四品牌及百分比 4th / percent
样本 Sample	349	**广西金嗓子喉宝 Golden Throat(39.3)**	**三金西瓜霜 Sanjin(30.4)**	**江中草珊瑚 Jiangzhong(21.2)**	**健民咽喉片 Jianmin(2.0)**
平实生活指向 simple living orientation	188	广西金嗓子喉宝 Golden Throat(41.5)	三金西瓜霜 Sanjin(29.3)	江中草珊瑚 Jiangzhong(20.2)	健民咽喉片 Jianmin(2.7)
时尚流行指向 fashion orientation	161	广西金嗓子喉宝 Golden Throat(36.6)	三金西瓜霜 Sanjin(31.7)	江中草珊瑚 Jiangzhong(22.4)	金龙牌痰咳净 Jin Long Pai Tan Ke Jing(1.2) 四季润喉片 Siji(1.2) 健民咽喉片 Jianmin(1.2)

2-13-2 广告态度指标/ Advertising Attitude Index

注：在药品品牌调查中，消费者经常出现将药品的名称与品牌名称混淆的现象，特此声明。/ In our research on medicines, we find consumers often confused the names and the brands.

	人数 Number	第一品牌及百分比 1st / percent	第二品牌及百分比 2nd / percent	第三品牌及百分比 3rd / percent	第四品牌及百分比 4th / percent
样本 Sample	346	**广西金嗓子喉宝 Golden Throat(39.6)**	**三金西瓜霜 Sanjin(30.3)**	**江中草珊瑚 Jiangzhong(20.8)**	**健民咽喉片 Jianmin(2.0)**
广告淡漠指向 indifferent orientation	99	广西金嗓子喉宝 Golden Throat(39.4)	三金西瓜霜 Sanjin(33.3)	江中草珊瑚 Jiangzhong(20.2)	健民咽喉片 Jianmin(2.0)
中间层 medium	196	广西金嗓子喉宝 Golden Throat(41.3)	三金西瓜霜 Sanjin(27.0)	江中草珊瑚 Jiangzhong(22.4)	健民咽喉片 Jianmin(2.0)
信赖广告指向 loyal orientation	51	三金西瓜霜 Sanjin(37.3)	广西金嗓子喉宝 Golden Throat(33.3)	江中草珊瑚 Jiangzhong(15.7)	四季润喉片 Siji(3.9) 金龙牌痰咳净 Jin Long Pai Tan Ke Jing(3.9)

2-13-3 饮食健康指标/ Foods & Drink Quality Index

注：在药品品牌调查中，消费者经常出现将药品的名称与品牌名称混淆的现象，特此声明。/ In our research on medicines, we find consumers often confused the names and the brands.

	人数 Number	第一品牌及百分比 1st / percent	第二品牌及百分比 2nd / percent	第三品牌及百分比 3rd / percent	第四品牌及百分比 4th / percent
样本 Sample	349	**广西金嗓子喉宝 Golden Throat(39.3)**	**三金西瓜霜 Sanjin(30.4)**	**江中草珊瑚 Jiangzhong(21.2)**	**健民咽喉片 Jianmin(2.0)**
饮食“温饱”指向 "basic" orientation	132	广西金嗓子喉宝 Golden Throat(39.4)	三金西瓜霜 Sanjin(34.1)	江中草珊瑚 Jiangzhong(18.9)	健民咽喉片 Jianmin(1.5) 四季润喉片 Siji(1.5) 金嗓灵 Jinhouling(1.5)
中间层 medium	154	广西金嗓子喉宝 Golden Throat(40.9)	三金西瓜霜 Sanjin(27.3)	江中草珊瑚 Jiangzhong(20.1)	健民咽喉片 Jianmin(2.6)
健康营养指向 health & nutrition orientation	63	广西金嗓子喉宝 Golden Throat(34.9)	三金西瓜霜 Sanjin(30.2)	江中草珊瑚 Jiangzhong(28.6)	健民咽喉片 Jianmin(1.6) 乐普美心 Lepumeixin(1.6) 金龙牌痰咳净 Jin Long Pai Tan Ke Jing(1.6)

沈阳 / Shenyang

2-1 最近一年内有无服用的比例/ Whether having Taken Sore Throat Remedies Last Year

	人数 Number	百分比 Percent
吃过 yes	292	48.6
没吃过 no	309	51.4

n=601

2-2 最常用品牌或品种排名/ Ranking of the Most Frequently Used Brands or Kinds

注：在药品品牌调查中，消费者经常出现将药品的名称与品牌名称混淆的现象，特此声明。/ In our research on medicines, we find consumers often confused the names and the brands.

排名 Brand Ranking	品牌或品种 Brands or Kinds	人数 Number	百分比 Percent
1	广西金嗓子喉宝 Golden Throat	111	38.0
2	江中草珊瑚 Jiangzhong	82	28.1
3	三金西瓜霜 Sanjin	37	12.7
4	四季润喉片 Siji	14	4.8
5	咽之爽 Yan Zhi Shuang	9	3.1
6	六神丸 Liushenwan	7	2.4

n=292

2-3 样本、男性各年龄层、女性各年龄层的常用品牌或品种/ The Most Frequently Used Brands or Kinds by the Whole Sample, Age and Gender Groups

注：在药品品牌调查中，消费者经常出现将药品的名称与品牌名称混淆的现象，特此声明。/ In our research on medicines, we find consumers often confused the names and the brands.

	人数 Number	第一品牌及百分比 1st/ percent	第二品牌及百分比 2nd/ percent	第三品牌及百分比 3rd/ percent
样本 Sample	292	**广西金嗓子喉宝 Golden Throat(38.0)**	**江中草珊瑚 Jiangzhong(28.1)**	**三金西瓜霜 Sanjin(12.7)**
男性 Male	140	**广西金嗓子喉宝 Golden Throat(39.3)**	**江中草珊瑚 Jiangzhong(27.1)**	**三金西瓜霜 Sanjin(10.7)**
25~34 岁 Age	39	广西金嗓子喉宝 Golden Throat(38.5)	江中草珊瑚 Jiangzhong(33.3)	三金西瓜霜 Sanjin(12.8)
35~44 岁 Age	37	广西金嗓子喉宝 Golden Throat(40.5)	江中草珊瑚 Jiangzhong(24.3)	四季润喉片 Siji(10.8)
45~54 岁 Age	20	广西金嗓子喉宝 Golden Throat(30.0) 江中草珊瑚 Jiangzhong(30.0)	三金西瓜霜 Sanjin(15.0)	咽之爽 Yan Zhi Shuang(5.0) 甘草片 Gan Cao Pian(5.0) 桂林消喉片 Gui Lin Xiao Hou Pian(5.0) 五叶清火片 Wu Ye Qing Huo Pian(5.0)
55~60 岁 Age	9	三金西瓜霜 Sanjin(33.3)	六神丸 Liushenwan(22.2)	广西金嗓子喉宝 Golden Throat(11.1) 四季润喉片 Siji(11.1) 咽之爽 Yan Zhi Shuang(11.1) 江中草珊瑚 Jiangzhong(11.1)
女性 Female	152	**广西金嗓子喉宝 Golden Throat(36.8)**	**江中草珊瑚 Jiangzhong(28.9)**	**三金西瓜霜 Sanjin(14.5)**
16~24 岁 Age	37	广西金嗓子喉宝 Golden Throat(40.5)	江中草珊瑚 Jiangzhong(29.7)	三金西瓜霜 Sanjin(18.9)
25~34 岁 Age	40	广西金嗓子喉宝 Golden Throat(42.5)	江中草珊瑚 Jiangzhong(32.5)	三金西瓜霜 Sanjin(10.0)
35~44 岁 Age	45	广西金嗓子喉宝 Golden Throat(31.1)	江中草珊瑚 Jiangzhong(22.2)	三金西瓜霜 Sanjin(17.8)
45~54 岁 Age	19	广西金嗓子喉宝 Golden Throat(36.8)	江中草珊瑚 Jiangzhong(31.6)	三金西瓜霜 Sanjin(15.8)
55~60 岁 Age	11	江中草珊瑚 Jiangzhong(36.4)	广西金嗓子喉宝 Golden Throat(27.3) 四季润喉片 Siji(27.3)	健民咽喉片 Jianmin(9.1)

2-4 理想品牌或品种排名/ Ranking of the Ideal Brands or Kinds

注：在药品品牌调查中，消费者经常出现将药品的名称与品牌名称混淆的现象，特此声明。/ In our research on medicines, we find consumers often confused the names and the brands.

排名 Brand Ranking	品牌或品种 Brands or Kinds	人数 Number	百分比 Percent
1	广西金嗓子喉宝 Golden Throat	231	38.5
2	江中草珊瑚 Jiangzhong	145	24.2
3	三金西瓜霜 Sanjin	81	13.5
4	咽之爽 Yan Zhi Shuang	19	3.2
5	四季润喉片 Siji	12	2.0
6	六神丸 Liushenwan	10	1.7
7	喉痛灵 Houtongling	2	0.3
8	甘草片 Gan Cao Pian	2	0.3

n=600

2-5 样本、男性各年龄层、女性各年龄层的品牌习惯/ Brand Habit in Consuming Sore Throat Remedies by the Whole Sample, Age and Gender Groups

	人数 Number	基本固定用一个牌子 used in only one brand	比较固定地用两个或三个牌子 used in two or three brands	基本上不太固定牌子 no brand preference
样本 Sample	292	59.2	24.7	16.1
男性 Male	140	64.3	22.1	13.6
16~24 岁 Age	35	57.1	34.3	8.6
25~34 岁 Age	39	74.4	17.9	7.7
35~44 岁 Age	37	62.2	10.8	27.0
45~54 岁 Age	20	55.0	30.0	15.0
55~60 岁 Age	9	77.8	22.2	0.0
女性 Female	152	54.6	27.0	18.4
16~24 岁 Age	37	62.2	24.3	13.5
25~34 岁 Age	40	55.0	27.5	17.5
35~44 岁 Age	45	48.9	28.9	22.2
45~54 岁 Age	19	47.4	26.3	26.3
55~60 岁 Age	11	63.6	27.3	9.1

2-6 样本、男性各年龄层、女性各年龄层最近一年内有无服用的比例/ Whether having Taken Sore Throat Remedies Last Year by the Whole Sample, Age and Gender Groups

	人数 Number	吃过 yes	没吃过 no
样本 Sample	601	48.6	51.4
男性 Male	299	46.8	53.2
16~24 岁 Age	64	54.7	45.3
25~34 岁 Age	89	43.8	56.2
35~44 岁 Age	76	48.7	51.3
45~54 岁 Age	46	43.5	56.5
55~60 岁 Age	24	37.5	62.5
女性 Female	302	50.3	49.7
16~24 岁 Age	64	57.8	42.2
25~34 岁 Age	90	44.4	55.6
35~44 岁 Age	76	59.2	40.8
45~54 岁 Age	48	39.6	60.4
55~60 岁 Age	24	45.8	54.2

2-7 选择该类商品的考虑因素/ Ranking of the Considerations in Purchasing

注：本题为多选题，合计百分比超过 100%（Multiple answers）

排名 Ranking	考虑因素 Considerations	人次 Person-time	百分比 Percent
1	见效快 immediate effect	174	59.6
2	价格适中 reasonable price	80	27.4
3	有名的牌子 famous brand	77	26.4
4	无副作用 no side-effects	64	21.9
5	广告影响 influence of advertising	62	21.2
6	医生推荐 recommended by doctors	59	20.2
7	服用方式简便 simple to take	43	14.7
8	购买方便 easy to buy	31	10.6
9	亲友介绍 introduced by relatives & friends	17	5.8
10	其他 others	1	0.3

n=292

2-8 样本、男性各年龄层、女性各年龄层最常服用的种类/ Types of Sore Throat Remedies Consumed by the Whole Sample, Age and Gender Groups

	人数 Number	片剂 pill	冲剂 granular formulation	糖浆 syrup	药粉 powder	膏状 paste-type	药丸 bolus	其他 others
样本 Sample	290	89.3	0.7	1.0	2.4	0.0	5.9	0.7
男性 Male	139	89.9	0.7	0.7	2.2	0.0	5.0	1.4
16~24 岁 Age	34	88.2	0.0	2.9	0.0	0.0	8.8	0.0
25~34 岁 Age	39	92.3	2.6	0.0	0.0	0.0	2.6	2.6
35~44 岁 Age	37	91.9	0.0	0.0	2.7	0.0	5.4	0.0
45~54 岁 Age	20	100.0	0.0	0.0	0.0	0.0	0.0	0.0
55~60 岁 Age	9	55.6	0.0	0.0	22.2	0.0	11.1	11.1
女性 Female	151	88.7	0.7	1.3	2.6	0.0	6.6	0.0
16~24 岁 Age	36	91.7	0.0	0.0	5.6	0.0	2.8	0.0
25~34 岁 Age	40	85.0	0.0	5.0	2.5	0.0	7.5	0.0
35~44 岁 Age	45	93.3	0.0	0.0	0.0	0.0	6.7	0.0
45~54 岁 Age	19	84.2	0.0	0.0	5.3	0.0	10.5	0.0
55~60 岁 Age	11	81.8	9.1	0.0	0.0	0.0	9.1	0.0

2-9 样本、男性各年龄层、女性各年龄层最常服用的场合/ Settings of Consumption by the Whole Sample, Age and Gender Groups

注：本题为多选题，合计百分比超过 100%（Multiple answers）

	人数 Number	喉咙发炎时 throat inflammation	喉咙轻度不适时 sore throat	长时间讲话后 long time speaking	抽烟后 after smoking	配药使用 taken with other medicine	其他 others
样本 Sample	291	53.3	59.5	7.6	4.1	0.3	0.0
男性 Male	140	55.0	55.7	4.3	6.4	0.7	0.0
16~24 岁 Age	35	60.0	65.7	5.7	2.9	0.0	0.0
25~34 岁 Age	39	51.3	51.3	5.1	10.3	2.6	0.0
35~44 岁 Age	37	45.9	56.8	0.0	8.1	0.0	0.0
45~54 岁 Age	20	65.0	55.0	10.0	5.0	0.0	0.0
55~60 岁 Age	9	66.7	33.3	0.0	0.0	0.0	0.0
女性 Female	151	51.7	62.9	10.6	2.0	0.0	0.0
16~24 岁 Age	37	37.8	75.7	15.2	0.0	0.0	0.0
25~34 岁 Age	40	52.5	60.0	10.0	2.5	0.0	0.0
35~44 岁 Age	44	54.5	56.8	11.4	4.5	0.0	0.0
45~54 岁 Age	19	63.2	52.6	5.3	0.0	0.0	0.0
55~60 岁 Age	11	63.6	72.7	0.0	0.0	0.0	0.0

2-10 样本、男性各年龄层、女性各年龄层购买润候药的场所/ Location of Buying Sore Throat Remedies by the Whole Sample, Age and Gender Groups

注：本题为多选题，合计百分比超过 100%（Multiple answers）

	人数 Number	药店 drug store	医院/诊所 hospital	商场 department store/ shopping center
样本 Sample	292	80.8	28.4	0.3
男性 Male	140	81.4	27.1	0.7
16~24 岁 Age	35	94.3	20.0	0.0
25~34 岁 Age	39	76.9	25.6	2.6
35~44 岁 Age	37	81.1	29.7	0.0
45~54 岁 Age	20	80.0	30.0	0.0
55~60 岁 Age	9	55.6	44.4	0.0
女性 Female	152	80.3	29.6	0.0
16~24 岁 Age	37	83.8	29.7	0.0
25~34 岁 Age	40	85.0	30.0	0.0
35~44 岁 Age	45	77.8	28.9	0.0
45~54 岁 Age	19	84.2	21.1	0.0
55~60 岁 Age	11	54.5	45.5	0.0

2-11 家中是否有备用润喉药的习惯/ The Habit of Keeping Sore Throat Remedies at Home

	人数 Number	百分比 Percent
有 yes	305	51.1
没有 no	292	48.9

n=597

2-12 公费/自费医疗的比例/ Proportion of the Free Medical Service

	人数 Number	百分比 Percent
公费医疗 free medical service	160	26.7
自费医疗 at my own expense	439	73.3

n=599

2-13 不同消费者层的常用品牌或品种/ The Most Frequently Used Brands or Kinds by Market Segments

2-13-1 时尚流行指标/ Fads Popular Index

注：在药品品牌调查中，消费者经常出现将药品的名称与品牌名称混淆的现象，特此声明。/ In our research on medicines, we find consumers often confused the names and the brands.

	人数 Number	第一品牌及百分比 1st/ percent	第二品牌及百分比 2nd/ percent	第三品牌及百分比 3rd/ percent
样本 Sample	292	**广西金嗓子喉宝 Golden Throat(38.0)**	**江中草珊瑚 Jiangzhong(28.1)**	**三金西瓜霜 Sanjin(12.7)**
平实生活指向 simple living orientation	136	广西金嗓子喉宝 Golden Throat(36.0)	江中草珊瑚 Jiangzhong(24.3)	三金西瓜霜 Sanjin(14.0)
时尚流行指向 fashion orientation	156	广西金嗓子喉宝 Golden Throat(39.7)	江中草珊瑚 Jiangzhong(31.4)	三金西瓜霜 Sanjin(11.5)

2-13-2 广告态度指标/ Advertising Attitude Index

注：在药品品牌调查中，消费者经常出现将药品的名称与品牌名称混淆的现象，特此声明。/ In our research on medicines, we find consumers often confused the names and the brands.

	人数 Number	第一品牌及百分比 1st/ percent	第二品牌及百分比 2nd/ percent	第三品牌及百分比 3rd/ percent
样本 Sample	292	**广西金嗓子喉宝 Golden Throat(38.0)**	**江中草珊瑚 Jiangzhong(28.1)**	**三金西瓜霜 Sanjin(12.7)**
广告淡漠指向 indifferent orientation	85	广西金嗓子喉宝 Golden Throat(42.4)	江中草珊瑚 Jiangzhong(21.2)	三金西瓜霜 Sanjin(11.8)
中间层 medium	169	广西金嗓子喉宝 Golden Throat(36.7)	江中草珊瑚 Jiangzhong(27.8)	三金西瓜霜 Sanjin(14.2)
信赖广告指向 loyal orientation	38	江中草珊瑚 Jiangzhong(44.7)	广西金嗓子喉宝 Golden Throat(34.2)	三金西瓜霜 Sanjin(7.9)

2-13-3 饮食健康指标/ Foods & Drink Quality Index

注：在药品品牌调查中，消费者经常出现将药品的名称与品牌名称混淆的现象，特此声明。/ In our research on medicines, we find consumers often confused the names and the brands.

	人数 Number	第一品牌及百分比 1st/ percent	第二品牌及百分比 2nd/ percent	第三品牌及百分比 3rd/ percent
样本 Sample	292	**广西金嗓子喉宝 Golden Throat(38.0)**	**江中草珊瑚 Jiangzhong(28.1)**	**三金西瓜霜 Sanjin(12.7)**
饮食“温饱”指向 "basic" orientation	93	广西金嗓子喉宝 Golden Throat(35.5)	江中草珊瑚 Jiangzhong(26.9)	三金西瓜霜 Sanjin(14.0)
中间层 medium	125	广西金嗓子喉宝 Golden Throat(38.4)	江中草珊瑚 Jiangzhong(28.0)	三金西瓜霜 Sanjin(11.2)
健康营养指向 health & nutrition orientation	74	广西金嗓子喉宝 Golden Throat(40.5)	江中草珊瑚 Jiangzhong(29.7)	三金西瓜霜 Sanjin(13.5)

3.肠胃药 / Digestive System Medicine

● 北京 / Beijing

3-1 最近一年内有无服用的比例/ Whether having Taken Digestive System Medicines Last Year

	人数 Number	百分比 Percent
吃过 yes	402	39.7
没吃过 no	510	60.3

n=1012

3-2 最常用品牌或品种排名/ Ranking of the Most Frequently Used Brands or Kinds

注：在药品品牌调查中，消费者经常出现将药品的名称与品牌名称混淆的现象，特此声明。/ In our research on medicines, we find consumers often confused the names and the brands.

排名 Brand Ranking	品牌或品种 Brands or Kinds	人数 Number	百分比 Percent
1	吗叮啉 Tabeliae Domperidoni Gastrokinetic	62	15.6
2	黄连素 Bering Hydrochloride Tablets	48	12.1
3	三九胃泰 999	42	10.6
4	胃得乐 Dele	27	6.8
5	氟哌酸 Norfloxacin Capsules	14	3.5
5	气滞胃疼冲剂 Qi Zhi Wei Teng Chong Ji	14	3.5
6	胃舒平 Compound Aluminium Hydroxide Tablets	12	3.0
7	胃速乐 Weisule	11	2.8
8	胃苏冲剂 Weisu	10	2.5
9	丽珠得乐 LZ	9	2.3
10	泻立停 Xieliting	8	2.0
10	香砂养胃片 Xiangsha Yangwei	8	2.0

n=398

3-3 样本、男性各年龄层、女性各年龄层的常用品牌或品种/ The Most Frequently Used Brands or Kinds by the Whole Sample, Age and Gender Groups

注：在药品品牌调查中，消费者经常出现将药品的名称与品牌名称混淆的现象，特此声明。/ In our research on medicines, we find consumers often confused the names and the brands.

	人数 Number	第一品牌及百分比 1st/ percent	第二品牌及百分比 2nd/ percent	第三品牌及百分比 3rd/ percent
样本 Sample	398	**吗叮啉 Tabeliae Domperidoni Gastrokinetic(15.6)**	**黄连素 Bering Hydrochloride Tablets(12.1)**	**三九胃泰 999(10.6)**
男性 Male	180	**黄连素 Bering Hydrochloride Tablets(15.0)**	**吗叮啉 Tabeliae Domperidoni Gastrokinetic(13.9)**	**三九胃泰 999(10.6)**
16~24 岁 Age	35	三九胃泰 999(22.9)	吗叮啉 Tabeliae Domperidoni Gastrokinetic(17.1)	泻立停 Xieliting(8.6)
25~34 岁 Age	50	黄连素 Bering Hydrochloride Tablets(16.0)	吗叮啉 Tabeliae Domperidoni Gastrokinetic(12.0) 三九胃泰 999(12.0)	胃得乐 Dele(6.0)
35~44 岁 Age	50	吗叮啉 Tabeliae Domperidoni Gastrokinetic(16.0)	黄连素 Bering Hydrochloride Tablets(8.0) 胃得乐 Dele(8.0)	氟哌酸 Norfloxacin Capsules(6.0) 三九胃泰 999(6.0)
45~54 岁 Age	28	黄连素 Bering Hydrochloride Tablets(28.6)	吗叮啉 Tabeliae Domperidoni Gastrokinetic(14.3)	痢特灵 Liteling(10.7)
55~60 岁 Age	17	黄连素 Bering Hydrochloride Tablets(29.4)	氟哌酸 Norfloxacin Capsules(11.8)	史克肠虫清 Sika Changchongqing(5.9) 胃泰美 Weitaimei(5.9) 胃速乐 Weisule(5.9) 胃得乐 Dele(5.9) 三九胃泰 999(5.9) 吗叮啉 Tabeliae Domperidoni Gastrokinetic(5.9) 法莫替丁 Famotidine(5.9)
女性 Female	218	**吗叮啉 Tabeliae Domperidoni Gastrokinetic(17.0)**	**三九胃泰 999(10.6)**	**黄连素 Bering Hydrochloride Tablets(9.6)**
16~24 岁 Age	49	吗叮啉 Tabeliae Domperidoni Gastrokinetic(28.6)	三九胃泰 999(16.3)	胃舒平 Compound Aluminium Hydroxide Tablets(6.1)
25~34 岁 Age	51	三九胃泰 999(13.7)	黄连素 Bering Hydrochloride Tablets(11.8) 气滞胃疼冲剂 Qi Zhi Wei Teng Chong Ji(11.8),	吗叮啉 Tabeliae Domperidoni Gastrokinetic(9.8)
35~44 岁 Age	61	吗叮啉 Tabeliae Domperidoni Gastrokinetic(18.0)	胃得乐 Dele(11.5)	三九胃泰 999(9.8)
45~54 岁 Age	38	吗叮啉 Tabeliae Domperidoni Gastrokinetic(18.4)	黄连素 Bering Hydrochloride Tablets(15.8)	胃得乐 Dele(13.2)
55~60 岁 Age	19	黄连素 Bering Hydrochloride Tablets(10.5) 气滞胃疼冲剂 Qi Zhi Wei Teng Chong Ji(10.5) 胃得乐 Dele(10.5)	昂立一号 Only One(5.3) 吉他霉素片 Jita Meisu(5.3) 先锋 Cefradine(5.3) 枫蓼 Fengliao(5.3) 胃气止胃片 Weiqi Zhiweipian(5.3) 胃速乐 Weisule(5.3) 香砂养胃片 Xiang Sha Yang Wei Pian(5.3) 温胃舒 Wenweishu(5.3) 胃舒平 Compound Aluminium Hydroxide Tablets(5.3) 三九胃泰 999(5.3)	

3-4 理想品牌或品种排名/ Ranking of the Ideal Brands or Kinds

注：在药品品牌调查中，消费者经常出现将药品的名称与品牌名称混淆的现象，特此声明。/ In our research on medicines, we find consumers often confused the names and the brands.

排名 Brand Ranking	品牌或品种 Brands or Kinds	人数 Number	百分比 Percent
1	吗叮啉 Tabeliae Domperidoni Gastrokinetic	122	12.1
2	三九胃泰 999	105	10.4
3	黄连素 Bering Hydrochloride Tablets	63	6.3
4	胃得乐 Dele	40	4.0
5	胃速乐 Weisule	16	1.6
6	气滞胃疼冲剂 Qi Zhi Wei Teng Chong Ji	15	1.5
6	泻立停 Xieliting	15	1.5
7	胃舒平 Compound Aluminium Hydroxide Tablets	14	1.4
7	氟哌酸 Norfloxacin Capsules	14	1.4

n=1007

3-5 样本、男性各年龄层、女性各年龄层的品牌习惯/ Brand Habit in Consuming Digestive System Medicines by the Whole Sample, Age and Gender Groups

	人数 Number	基本固定用一个牌子 used in only one brand	比较固定地用两个或三个牌子 used in two or three brands	基本上不太固定牌子 no brand preference
样本 Sample	397	41.1	34.5	24.4
男性 Male	177	40.1	33.3	26.6
16~24 岁 Age	34	52.9	23.5	23.5
25~34 岁 Age	50	42.0	30.0	28.0
35~44 岁 Age	49	34.7	34.7	30.6
45~54 岁 Age	28	35.7	50.0	14.3
55~60 岁 Age	16	31.3	31.3	37.5
女性 Female	220	41.8	35.5	22.7
16~24 岁 Age	50	42.0	48.0	10.0
25~34 岁 Age	52	42.3	26.9	30.8
35~44 岁 Age	61	37.7	34.4	27.9
45~54 岁 Age	38	47.4	36.8	15.8
55~60 岁 Age	19	42.1	26.3	31.6

3-6 样本、男性各年龄层、女性各年龄层最近一年内有无服用的比例/ Whether having Taken Digestive System Medicines Last Year by the Whole Sample, Age and Gender Groups

	人数 Number	吃过 yes	没吃过 no
样本 Sample	1012	39.7	60.3
男性 Male	504	35.7	64.3
16~24 岁 Age	105	33.3	66.7
25~34 岁 Age	151	33.1	66.9
35~44 岁 Age	131	38.2	61.8
45~54 岁 Age	77	36.4	63.6
55~60 岁 Age	40	42.5	57.5
女性 Female	503	43.7	56.3
16~24 岁 Age	108	46.3	53.7
25~34 岁 Age	150	35.3	64.7
35~44 岁 Age	124	49.2	50.8
45~54 岁 Age	84	45.2	54.8
55~60 岁 Age	42	47.6	52.4

3-7 选择该类商品的考虑因素/ Ranking of the Considerations in Purchasing

注：本题为多选题，合计百分比超过 100%（Multiple answers）

排名 Ranking	考虑因素 Considerations	人次 Person-time	百分比 Percent
1	见效快 immediate effect	236	59.1
2	医生推荐 recommended by doctors	211	52.9
3	无副作用 no side-effects	113	28.3
4	服用方式简便 simple to take	54	13.5
5	有名的牌子 famous brand	47	11.8
6	价格适中 reasonable price	43	10.8
7	亲友介绍 introduced by relatives & friends	28	7.0
8	购买方便 easy to buy	18	4.5
9	广告影响 influence of advertising	17	4.3
10	其他 others	4	1.0

n=399

3-8 样本、男性各年龄层、女性各年龄层最常服用的种类/ Types of Digestive System Medicines Consumed by the Whole Sample, Age and Gender Groups

	人数 Number	片剂 pill	冲剂 granular formulation	胶囊 capsule	药粉 powder	糖浆 syrup	药丸 bolus	其他 others
样本 Sample	396	63.9	17.2	11.6	1.8	0.0	5.3	0.3
男性 Male	178	65.7	12.9	12.9	1.7	0.0	6.7	0.0
16~24 岁 Age	35	60.0	17.1	14.3	0.0	0.0	8.6	0.0
25~34 岁 Age	50	62.0	16.0	14.0	2.0	0.0	6.0	0.0
35~44 岁 Age	49	63.3	14.3	16.3	2.0	0.0	4.1	0.0
45~54 岁 Age	28	75.0	7.1	3.6	3.6	0.0	10.7	0.0
55~60 岁 Age	16	81.3	0.0	12.5	0.0	0.0	6.3	0.0
女性 Female	218	62.4	20.6	10.6	1.8	0.0	4.1	0.5
16~24 岁 Age	50	60.0	22.0	10.0	4.0	0.0	4.0	0.0
25~34 岁 Age	51	60.8	25.5	9.8	2.0	0.0	2.0	0.0
35~44 岁 Age	60	66.7	15.0	10.0	1.7	0.0	5.0	1.7
45~54 岁 Age	37	67.6	13.5	16.2	0.0	0.0	2.7	0.0
55~60 岁 Age	20	50.0	35.0	5.0	0.0	0.0	10.0	0.0

3-9 样本、男性各年龄层、女性各年龄层最常服用的场合/ Settings of Consumption by the Whole Sample, Age and Gender Groups

注：本题为多选题，合计百分比超过 100%（Multiple answers）

	人数 Number	胃痛时 stomach-ache	胃酸时 sour stomach	胃胀气时 bloated	消化不良时 dyslexia	吃太饱时 overeaten	腹泻时 diarrhea	没胃口时 when not want to eat	配药使用 taken with other medicine	其他 others
样本 Sample	393	48.6	12.7	17.3	25.2	2.5	26.5	1.0	0.8	1.3
男性 Male	177	41.2	14.7	15.8	24.3	2.3	32.2	1.7	1.1	1.1
16~24 岁 Age	34	52.9	8.8	14.7	23.5	2.9	29.4	2.9	2.9	0.0
25~34 岁 Age	48	37.5	10.4	14.6	27.1	0.0	31.3	0.0	2.1	2.1
35~44 岁 Age	50	42.0	22.0	22.0	18.0	6.0	28.0	2.0	0.0	0.0
45~54 岁 Age	28	42.9	10.7	10.7	39.3	0.0	35.7	3.6	0.0	3.6
55~60 岁 Age	17	23.5	23.5	11.8	11.8	0.0	47.1	0.0	0.0	0.0
女性 Female	216	54.6	11.1	18.5	25.9	2.8	21.8	0.5	0.5	1.4
16~24 岁 Age	50	60.0	8.0	8.0	30.0	6.0	18.0	2.0	2.0	0.0
25~34 岁 Age	50	60.0	8.0	16.0	28.0	4.0	24.0	0.0	0.0	2.0
35~44 岁 Age	59	59.3	15.3	25.4	16.9	0.0	20.3	0.0	0.0	3.4
45~54 岁 Age	37	35.1	16.2	29.7	18.9	2.7	35.1	0.0	0.0	0.0
55~60 岁 Age	20	50.0	5.0	10.0	50.0	0.0	5.0	0.0	0.0	0.0

3-10 样本、男性各年龄层、女性各年龄层购买肠胃药的场所/ Location of Buying Digestive System Medicines by the Whole Sample, Age and Gender Groups

注：本题为多选题，合计百分比超过 100%（Multiple answers）

	人数 Number	药店 drug store	医院/诊所 hospital	商场 department store/ shopping center
样本 Sample	401	36.9	73.8	1.2
男性 Male	180	41.7	67.8	1.7
16~24 岁 Age	35	54.3	57.1	5.7
25~34 岁 Age	50	48.0	66.0	0.0
35~44 岁 Age	50	48.0	64.0	0.0
45~54 岁 Age	28	17.9	78.6	3.6
55~60 岁 Age	17	17.6	88.2	0.0
女性 Female	221	33.0	78.7	0.9
16~24 岁 Age	50	40.0	68.0	2.0
25~34 岁 Age	52	36.5	71.2	0.0
35~44 岁 Age	61	27.9	86.9	0.0
45~54 岁 Age	38	28.9	86.8	2.6
55~60 岁 Age	20	30.0	85.0	0.0

3-11 家中是否有备用肠胃药的习惯/ The Habit of Keeping Digestive System Medicines at Home

	人数 Number	百分比 Percent
有 yes	697	70.2
没有 no	296	29.8

n=993

3-12 公费/自费医疗的比例/ Proportion of the Free Medical Service

	人数 Number	百分比 Percent
公费医疗 free medical service	636	64.6
自费医疗 own expense	349	35.4

n=985

3-13 不同消费者层的常用品牌/ The Most Frequently Used Brands by Market Segments

3-13-1 时尚流行指标/ Fads Popular Index

注：在药品品牌调查中，消费者经常出现将药品的名称与品牌名称混淆的现象，特此声明。/ In our research on medicines, we find consumers often confused the names and the brands.

	人数 Number	第一品牌及百分比 1st / percent	第二品牌及百分比 2nd / percent	第三品牌及百分比 3rd / percent
样本 Sample	391	**吗叮啉 Tabeliae Domperidoni Gastrokinetic(15.9)**	**黄连素 Bering Hydrochloride Tablets(12.0)**	**三九胃泰 999(10.2)**
平实生活指向 simple living orientation	184	黄连素 Bering Hydrochloride Tablets(13.6)	吗叮啉 Tabeliae Domperidoni Gastrokinetic(12.0)	三九胃泰 999(9.2)
时尚流行指向 fashion orientation	207	吗叮啉 Tabeliae Domperidoni Gastrokinetic(19.3)	三九胃泰 999(11.1)	黄连素 Bering Hydrochloride Tablets(10.6)

3-13-2 广告态度指标/ Advertising Attitude Index

注：在药品品牌调查中，消费者经常出现将药品的名称与品牌名称混淆的现象，特此声明。/ In our research on medicines, we find consumers often confused the names and the brands.

	人数 Number	第一品牌及百分比 1st / percent	第二品牌及百分比 2nd / percent	第三品牌及百分比 3rd / percent
样本 Sample	389	**吗叮啉 Tabeliae Domperidoni Gastrokinetic(15.7)**	**黄连素 Bering Hydrochloride Tablets(12.3)**	**三九胃泰 999(10.8)**
广告淡漠指向 indifferent orientation	120	黄连素 Bering Hydrochloride Tablets(14.2) 吗叮啉 Tabeliae Domperidoni Gastrokinetic(14.2)	胃得乐 Dele(8.3) 三九胃泰 999(8.3)	气滞胃疼冲剂 Qi Zhi Wei Teng Chong Ji(5.0)
中间层 medium	221	吗叮啉 Tabeliae Domperidoni Gastrokinetic(15.4)	黄连素 Bering Hydrochloride Tablets(11.3)	三九胃泰 999(10.9)
信赖广告指向 loyal orientation	48	吗叮啉 Tabeliae Domperidoni Gastrokinetic(20.8)	三九胃泰 999(16.7)	黄连素 Bering Hydrochloride Tablets(12.5)

3-13-3 饮食健康指标/ Foods & Drink Quality Index

注：在药品品牌调查中，消费者经常出现将药品的名称与品牌名称混淆的现象，特此声明。/ In our research on medicines, we find consumers often confused the names and the brands.

	人数 Number	第一品牌及百分比 1st / percent	第二品牌及百分比 2nd / percent	第三品牌及百分比 3rd / percent
样本 Sample	396	**吗叮啉 Tabeliae Domperidoni Gastrokinetic(15.7)**	**黄连素 Bering Hydrochloride Tablets(12.1)**	**三九胃泰 999(10.6)**
饮食“温饱”指向 "basic" orientation	96	吗叮啉 Tabeliae Domperidoni Gastrokinetic(16.7)	黄连素 Bering Hydrochloride Tablets(14.6)	三九胃泰 999(13.5)
中间层 medium	187	吗叮啉 Tabeliae Domperidoni Gastrokinetic(13.4)	黄连素 Bering Hydrochloride Tablets(12.3)	三九胃泰 999(8.0)
健康营养指向 health & nutrition orientation	113	吗叮啉 Tabeliae Domperidoni Gastrokinetic(18.6)	三九胃泰 999(12.4)	黄连素 Bering Hydrochloride Tablets(9.7)

● 上海 / Shanghai

3-1 最近一年内有无服用的比例/ Whether having Taken Digestive System Medicines Last Year

	人数 Number	百分比 Percent
吃过 yes	291	28.7
没吃过 no	723	71.3

n=1014

3-2 最常用品牌或品种排名/ Ranking of the Most Frequently Used Brands or Kinds

排名 Brand Ranking	品牌或品种 Brands or Kinds	人数 Number	百分比 Percent
1	吗叮啉 Tabeliae Domperidoni Gastrokinetic	119	41.0
2	三九胃泰 999	23	7.9
3	黄连素 Bering Hydrochloride Tablets	14	4.8
4	喉菇菌片 Hou Gu Jun Pian	11	3.8
4	胃舒平 Compound Aluminium Hydroxide Tablets	11	3.8
5	雷尼替丁 Lei Ni Ti Ding	8	2.8
6	养胃冲剂 Yang Wei Chong Ji	7	2.4
6	泰胃美 Tagamat	7	2.4
7	易蒙停 Lapsulae Loperanidi Hydrocaloridi	6	2.1
8	上海利生汇利黄莲素 Shang Hai Li Sheng	5	1.7

n=290

3-3 样本、男性各年龄层、女性各年龄层的常用品牌或品种/ The Most Frequently Used Brands or Kinds by the Whole Sample, Age and Gender Groups

	人数 Number	第一品牌及百分比 1st/ percent	第二品牌及百分比 2nd/ percent	第三品牌及百分比 3rd/ percent
样本 Sample	290	**吗叮啉 Tabeliae Domperidoni Gastrokinetic(41.0)**	**三九胃泰 999(7.9)**	**黄连素 Bering Hydrochloride Tablets(4.8)**
男性 Male	139	**吗叮啉 Tabeliae Domperidoni Gastrokinetic(37.4)**	**三九胃泰 999(7.2)**	**胃舒平 Compound Aluminum Hydroxide Tablets(5.0)**
16~24 岁 Age	15	吗叮啉 Tabeliae Domperidoni Gastrokinetic(66.7)	黄连素 Bering Hydrochloride Tablets(6.7) 诺氟沙星 Norfloxacin(6.7) 养胃冲剂 Yang Wei Chong Ji (6.7) 神箭健胃愈肠片 Shen Jian Jian Wei Yu Chuang Pian (6.7)	
25~34 岁 Age	33	吗叮啉 Tabeliae Domperidoni Gastrokinetic(45.5)	三九胃泰 999(9.1)	泰胃美 Tagamat(6.1) 胃舒平 Compound Aluminium Hydroxide Tablets(6.1) 雷尼替丁 Lei Ni Ti Ding(6.1) 养胃冲剂 Yang Wei Chong Ji (6.1)
35~44 岁 Age	40	吗叮啉 Tabeliae Domperidoni Gastrokinetic(30.0)	黄连素 Bering Hydrochloride Tablets(10.0) 三九胃泰 999(10.0) 胃舒平 Compound Aluminium Hydroxide Tablets(10.0)	泰胃美 Tagamat(5.0)
45~54 岁 Age	29	吗叮啉 Tabeliae Domperidoni Gastrokinetic(31.0)	天平牌 Tianping(6.9) 雷尼替丁 Lei Ni Ti Ding(6.9) 诺氟沙星 Norfloxacin(6.9) 三九胃泰 999(6.9)	宇宙健胃愈肠片 Yu Zhou Jian Wei Yu Chan Pian(3.4) 养胃冲剂 Yang Wei Chong Ji (3.4) 易蒙停 Lapsulae Loperanidi Hydrocaloridi(3.4) 胃舒平 Compound Aluminium Hydroxide Tablets(3.4) 泰胃美 Tagamat(3.4)
55~60 岁 Age	22	吗叮啉 Tabeliae Domperidoni Gastrokinetic(27.3)	培菲康 Pei Fei Kang(9.1) 雷尼替丁 Lei Ni Ti Ding(9.1)	胃复春 Wei Fu Chun (4.5) 胃苏冲剂 Wei Su Chong Ji(4.5) 易蒙停 Lapsulae Loperanidi Hydrocaloridi(4.5) 斯达舒 Si Da Shu(4.5) 三九胃泰 999(4.5) 黄连素 Bering Hydrochloride Tablets(4.5)
女性 Female	151	**吗叮啉 Tabeliae Domperidoni Gastrokinetic(44.4)**	**三九胃泰 999(8.6)**	**喉菇菌片 Hou Gu Jun Pian (6.0)**
16~24 岁 Age	26	吗叮啉 Tabeliae Domperidoni Gastrokinetic(42.3)	胃舒宁 Wei Shu Ling(7.7) 三九胃泰 999(7.7) 胃舒平 Compound Aluminium Hydroxide Tablets(7.7) 易蒙停 Lapsulae Loperanidi Hydrocaloridi(7.7)	果导片 Guo Dao Pian(3.8) 养胃冲剂 Yang Wei Chong Ji (3.8) 多酶片 Duo Mei Pian (3.8) 喉菇菌片 Hou Gu Jun Pian (3.8) 克痢痧 Ke Li Sha(3.8) 泰胃美 Tagamat(3.8)
25~34 岁 Age	39	吗叮啉 Tabeliae Domperidoni Gastrokinetic(53.8)	三九胃泰 999(12.8)	喇叭牌 Laba(5.1)
35~44 岁 Age	41	吗叮啉 Tabeliae Domperidoni Gastrokinetic(53.7)	黄连素 Bering Hydrochloride Tablets(9.8)	三九胃泰 999(4.9) 喉菇菌片 Hou Gu Jun Pian (4.9)
45~54 岁 Age	25	吗叮啉 Tabeliae Domperidoni Gastrokinetic(24.0)	喉菇菌片 Hou Gu Jun Pian (16.0)	三九胃泰 999(12.0)
55~60 岁 Age	20	吗叮啉 Tabeliae Domperidoni Gastrokinetic(35.0)	黄连素 Bering Hydrochloride Tablets(10.0)	胃美素 Wei Mei Su(5.0) 胡庆余堂 Hu Qing Yu Tang(5.0) 喇叭牌 Laba (5.0) 痢特灵 Liteling(5.0) 三九胃泰 999(5.0)

3-4 理想品牌或品种排名/ Ranking of the Ideal Brands or Kinds

排名 Brand Ranking	品牌或品种 Brands or Kinds	人数 Number	百分比 Percent
1	吗叮啉 Tabeliae Domperidoni Gastrokinetic	422	41.7
2	三九胃泰 999	125	12.4
3	黄连素 Bering Hydrochloride Tablets	30	3.0
4	胃舒平 Compound Aluminium Hydroxide Tablets	26	2.6
5	喉菇菌片 Hou Gu Jun Pian	15	1.5
5	泰胃美 Tagamat	15	1.5
6	雷尼替丁 Lei Ni Ti Ding	11	1.1
6	易蒙停 Lapsulae Loperanidi Hydrocaloridi	11	1.1
7	天平牌 Tianping	6	0.6
7	上海利生汇利黄莲素 Shang Hai Li Sheng	6	0.6
8	多酶片 Duo Mei Pian	5	0.5
8	胃达美 Weidamei	5	0.5
8	养胃冲剂 Yang Wei Chong Ji	5	0.5
9	胃仙 U Vikon-U	4	0.4
9	喇叭牌 Laba	4	0.4
9	万象法莫替丁 Wanxiang	4	0.4
9	诺氟沙星 Norfloxacin	4	0.4

n=1011

3-5 样本、男性各年龄层、女性各年龄层的品牌习惯/ Brand Habit in Consuming Digestive System Medicines by the Whole Sample, Age and Gender Groups

	人数 Number	基本固定用一个牌子 used in only one brand	比较固定地用两个或三个牌子 used in two or three brands	基本上不太固定牌子 no brand preference
样本 Sample	290	54.8	29.7	15.5
男性 Male	138	53.6	28.3	18.1
16~24 岁 Age	14	57.1	35.7	7.1
25~34 岁 Age	33	48.5	30.3	21.2
35~44 岁 Age	40	57.5	22.5	20.0
45~54 岁 Age	29	58.6	24.1	17.2
55~60 岁 Age	22	45.5	36.4	18.2
女性 Female	152	55.9	30.9	13.2
16~24 岁 Age	26	61.5	19.2	19.2
25~34 岁 Age	39	64.1	28.2	7.7
35~44 岁 Age	41	56.1	26.8	17.1
45~54 岁 Age	25	52.0	36.0	12.0
55~60 岁 Age	21	38.1	52.4	9.5

3-6 样本、男性各年龄层、女性各年龄层最近一年内有无服用的比例/ Whether having Taken Digestive System Medicines Last Year by the Whole Sample, Age and Gender Groups

	人数 Number	吃过 yes	没吃过 no
样本 Sample	1014	28.7	71.3
男性 Male	509	27.3	72.7
16~24 岁 Age	109	13.8	86.2
25~34 岁 Age	146	22.6	77.4
35~44 岁 Age	130	30.8	69.2
45~54 岁 Age	85	34.1	65.9
55~60 岁 Age	39	56.4	43.6
女性 Female	505	30.1	69.9
16~24 岁 Age	108	24.1	75.9
25~34 岁 Age	144	27.1	72.9
35~44 岁 Age	130	31.5	68.5
45~54 岁 Age	82	30.5	69.5
55~60 岁 Age	41	51.2	48.8

3-7 选择该类商品的考虑因素/ Ranking of the Considerations in Purchasing

注：本题为多选题，合计百分比超过 100%（Multiple answers）

排名 Ranking	考虑因素 Considerations	人次 Person-time	百分比 Percent
1	医生推荐 recommended by doctors	171	58.8
2	见效快 immediate effect	123	42.3
3	无副作用 no side-effects	47	16.2
4	有名的牌子 famous brand	41	14.1
5	服用方式简便 simple to take	34	11.7
6	价格适中 reasonable price	29	10.0
7	广告影响 influence of advertising	22	7.6
8	购买方便 easy to buy	14	4.8
9	亲友介绍 introduced by relatives & friends	11	3.8
10	其他 others	3	1.0

n=291

3-8 样本、男性各年龄层、女性各年龄层最常服用的种类/ Types of Digestive System Medicines Consumed by the Whole Sample, Age and Gender Groups

	人数 Number	片剂 pill	冲剂 granular formulation	胶囊 capsule	药粉 powder	糖浆 syrup	药丸 bolus	其他 others
样本 Sample	291	61.9	8.2	17.5	1.4	0.7	8.9	1.4
男性 Male	139	59.7	10.1	23.0	1.4	0.7	5.0	0.0
16~24 岁 Age	15	66.7	0.0	20.0	6.7	0.0	6.7	0.0
25~34 岁 Age	33	42.4	15.2	30.3	3.0	0.0	9.1	0.0
35~44 岁 Age	40	70.0	5.0	17.5	0.0	0.0	7.5	0.0
45~54 岁 Age	29	72.4	6.9	20.7	0.0	0.0	0.0	0.0
55~60 岁 Age	22	45.5	22.7	27.3	0.0	4.5	0.0	0.0
女性 Female	152	63.8	6.6	12.5	1.3	0.7	12.5	2.6
16~24 岁 Age	26	53.8	11.5	11.5	3.3	0.0	19.2	0.0
25~34 岁 Age	39	48.7	10.3	20.5	0.0	0.0	20.5	0.0
35~44 岁 Age	41	65.9	2.4	14.6	0.0	0.0	12.2	4.9
45~54 岁 Age	25	72.0	8.0	8.0	4.0	4.0	4.0	0.0
55~60 岁 Age	21	90.5	0.0	0.0	0.0	0.0	0.0	9.5

3-9 样本、男性各年龄层、女性各年龄层最常服用的场合/ Settings of Consumption by the Whole Sample, Age and Gender Groups

注：本题为多选题，合计百分比超过 100%（Multiple answers）

	人数 Number	胃痛时 stomach-ache	胃酸时 sour stomach	胃胀气时 bloated	消化不良时 dyslexia	吃太饱时 overeaten	腹泻时 diarrhea	没胃口时 when not want to eat	配药使用 taken with other medicine	其他 others
样本 Sample	289	41.9	13.1	25.6	28.0	3.5	17.6	1.4	3.1	2.4
男性 Male	137	43.8	13.9	24.1	22.6	2.2	19.7	2.2	2.9	2.2
16~24 岁 Age	15	53.3	6.7	26.7	33.3	6.7	13.3	0.0	6.7	0.0
25~34 岁 Age	33	42.4	21.2	21.2	30.3	0.0	18.2	3.0	3.0	0.0
35~44 岁 Age	39	51.3	17.9	28.2	23.1	0.0	12.8	0.0	0.0	2.6
45~54 岁 Age	29	41.4	10.3	27.6	13.8	0.0	24.1	3.4	3.4	0.0
55~60 岁 Age	21	28.6	4.8	14.3	14.3	9.5	33.3	4.8	4.8	9.5
女性 Female	152	40.1	12.5	27.0	32.9	4.6	15.8	0.7	3.3	2.6
16~24 岁 Age	26	57.7	15.4	3.8	34.6	3.8	19.2	0.0	3.8	3.8
25~34 岁 Age	39	23.1	7.7	43.6	43.6	5.1	10.3	2.6	0.0	0.0
35~44 岁 Age	41	51.2	7.3	29.3	26.8	9.8	12.2	0.0	7.3	0.0
45~54 岁 Age	25	24.0	16.0	20.0	28.0	0.0	24.0	0.0	0.0	4.0
55~60 岁 Age	21	47.6	23.8	28.6	28.6	0.0	19.0	0.0	4.8	9.5

3-10 样本、男性各年龄层、女性各年龄层购买肠胃药的场所/ Location of Buying Digestive System Medicines by the Whole Sample, Age and Gender Groups

注：本题为多选题，合计百分比超过 100%（Multiple answers）

	人数 Number	药店 drug store	医院/诊所 hospital	商场 department store/ shopping center
样本 Sample	290	39.0	71.4	1.4
男性 Male	139	38.8	70.5	1.4
16~24 岁 Age	15	53.3	66.7	0.0
25~34 岁 Age	33	45.5	60.6	0.0
35~44 岁 Age	40	35.0	70.0	2.5
45~54 岁 Age	29	31.0	75.9	3.4
55~60 岁 Age	22	36.4	81.8	0.0
女性 Female	151	39.1	72.2	1.3
16~24 岁 Age	26	65.4	53.8	3.8
25~34 岁 Age	38	36.8	63.2	2.6
35~44 岁 Age	41	39.0	73.2	0.0
45~54 岁 Age	25	24.0	88.0	0.0
55~60 岁 Age	21	28.6	90.5	0.0

3-11 家中是否有备有肠胃药的习惯/ The Habit of Keeping Digestive System Medicines at Home

	人数 Number	百分比 Percent
有 yes	527	52.5
没有 no	476	47.5

n=1003

3-12 公费/自费医疗的比例/ Proportion of the Free Medical Service

	人数 Number	百分比 Percent
公费医疗 free medical service	689	69.5
自费医疗 own expense	302	30.5

n=991

3-13 不同消费者层的常用品牌/ The Most Frequently Used Brands by Market Segments

3-13-1 时尚流行指标/ Fads Popular Index

注：在药品品牌调查中，消费者经常出现将药品的名称与品牌名称混淆的现象，特此声明。/ In our research on medicines, we find consumers often confused the names and the brands.

	人数 Number	第一品牌及百分比 1st / percent	第二品牌及百分比 2nd / percent	第三品牌及百分比 3rd / percent
样本 Sample	288	吗叮咻 Tabeliae Domperidoni Gastrokinetic（41.0)	三九胃泰 999（8.0)	黄连素 Bering Hydrochloride Tablets（4.9)
平实生活指向 simple living orientation	151	吗叮咻 Tabeliae Domperidoni Gastrokinetic（32.5)	黄连素 Bering Hydrochloride Tablets（6.6) 三九胃泰 999（6.6)	胃舒平 Compound Aluminium Hydroxide Tablets（6.0)
时尚流行指向 fashion orientation	137	吗叮咻 Tabeliae Domperidoni Gastrokinetic（50.4)	三九胃泰 999（9.5)	易蒙停 Lapsulae Loperanidi Hydrocaloridi（2.9) 喉菇菌片 Hougujunpian （2.9) 黄连素 Bering Hydrochloride Tablets（2.9) 雷尼替丁 Lei Ni Ti Ding（2.9)

3-13-2 广告态度指标/ Advertising Attitude Index

注：在药品品牌调查中，消费者经常出现将药品的名称与品牌名称混淆的现象，特此声明。/ In cur research on medicines, we find consumers often confused the names and the brands.

	人数 Number	第一品牌及百分比 1st / percent	第二品牌及百分比 2nd / percent	第三品牌及百分比 3rd / percent
样本 Sample	290	**吗叮啉 Tabeliae Domperidoni Gastrokinetic（41.0）**	**三九胃泰 999（7.9）**	**黄连素 Bering Hydrochloride Tablets（4.8）**
广告淡漠指向 indifferent orientation	90	吗叮啉 Tabeliae Domperidoni Gastrokinetic（38.9）	喉菇菌片 Hougujunpian （4.4）	黄连素 Bering Hydrochloride Tablets（3.3） 雷尼替丁 Lei Ni TiDing（3.3） 诺氟沙星 Norfloxacin（3.3） 胃舒平 Compound Aluminium Hydroxide Tablets（3.3） 养胃冲剂 Yangweichongji （3.3）
中间层 medium	173	吗叮啉 Tabeliae Domperidoni Gastrokinetic（39.9）	三九胃泰 999（11.6）	黄连素 Bering Hydrochloride Tablets（5.8）
信赖广告指向 loyal orientation	27	吗叮啉 Tabeliae Domperidoni Gastrokinetic（55.6）	喉菇菌片 Hougujunpian （7.4） 喇叭牌 Laba（7.4） 上海利生汇利黄莲素 Shang Hai Li Sheng（7.4）	黄连素 Bering Hydrochloride Tablets（3.7） 雷尼替丁 Lei Ni Ti Ding（3.7） 三九胃泰 999（3.7） 易蒙停 Lapsulae Loperanidi Hydrocaloridi（3.7） 果导片 Guo Dao Pian（3.7）

3-13-3 饮食健康指标/ Foods & Drink Quality Index

注：在药品品牌调查中，消费者经常出现将药品的名称与品牌名称混淆的现象，特此声明。/ In our research on medicines, we find consumers often confused the names and the brands.

	人数 Number	第一品牌及百分比 1st / percent	第二品牌及百分比 2nd / percent	第三品牌及百分比 3rd / percent
样本 Sample	287	**吗叮啉 Tabeliae Domperidoni Gastrokinetic（40.8）**	**三九胃泰 999（7.7）**	**黄连素 Bering Hydrochloride Tablets（4.9）**
饮食“温饱”指向 "basic" orientation	65	吗叮啉 Tabeliae Domperidoni Gastrokinetic（41.5）	三九胃泰 999（7.7） 黄连素 Bering Hydrochloride Tablets（7.7） 胃舒平 Compound Aluminium Hydroxide Tablets（7.7）	上海利生汇利黄莲素 Shang Hai Li Sheng（4.6） 易蒙停 Lapsulae Loperanidi Hydrocaloridi（4.6）
中间层 medium	135	吗叮啉 Tabeliae Domperidoni Gastrokinetic（35.6）	三九胃泰 999（6.7）	黄连素 Bering Hydrochloride Tablets（5.2）
健康营养指向 health & nutrition orientation	87	吗叮啉 Tabeliae Domperidoni Gastrokinetic（48.3）	三九胃泰 999（9.2）	喉菇菌片 Hougujunpian （6.9）

● 广州 / Guangzhou

3-1 最近一年内有无服用的比例/ Whether having Taken Digestive System Medicines Last Year

	人数 Number	百分比 Percent
吃过 yes	376	36.4
没吃过 no	658	63.6

n=1034

3-2 最常用品牌或品种排名/ Ranking of the Most Frequently Used Brands or Kinds

注：在药品品牌调查中，消费者经常出现将药品的名称与品牌名称混淆的现象，特此声明。/ In our research on medicines, we find consumers often confused the names and the brands.

排名 Brand Ranking	品牌或品种 Brands or Kinds	人数 Number	百分比 Percent
1	腹可安 Fukean	62	16.5
2	胃仙 U Vikon-U	36	9.6
3	三九胃泰 999	28	7.5
4	何济公 Hejigong	22	5.9
4	陈李济保济丸 Chenliji	22	5.9
4	喇叭牌 Laba	22	5.9
4	吗叮啉 Tabeliae Domperidoni Gastrokinetic	22	5.9
5	华天宝 Huatianbao	19	5.1
5	胃乃安 Weinai'an	19	5.1
6	胃康 U Vikon-U	10	2.7

n=375

3-3 样本、男性各年龄层、女性各年龄层的常用品牌或品种/ The Most Frequently Used Brands or Kinds by the Whole Sample, Age and Gender Groups

注：在药品品牌调查中，消费者经常出现将药品的名称与品牌名称混淆的现象，特此声明。/ In our research on medicines, we find consumers often confused the names and the brands.

	人数 Number	第一品牌及百分比 1st/ percent	第二品牌及百分比 2nd/ percent	第三品牌及百分比 3rd/ percent
样本 Sample	375	**腹可安 Fukean(16.5)**	**胃仙 U Vikon-U(9.6)**	**三九胃泰 999(7.5)**
男性 Male	183	**腹可安 Fukean(18.0)**	**胃仙 U Vikon-U(9.8)**	**喇叭牌 Laba(8.2)**
16~24 岁 Age	23	腹可安 Fukean(26.1)	胃仙 U Vikon-U(21.7)	吗叮啉 Tabeliae Domperidoni Gastrokinetic(8.7) 三九胃泰 999(8.7) 保济丸 Baojiwan(8.7)
25~34 岁 Age	56	胃仙 U Vikon-U(16.1)	腹可安 Fukean(14.3)	三九胃泰 999(10.7)
35~44 岁 Age	54	腹可安 Fukean(25.9)	喇叭牌 Laba(11.1)	陈李济保济丸 Chenliji(7.4)
45~54 岁 Age	35	腹可安 Fukean(14.3)	陈李济保济丸 Chenliji(11.4)	胃康 U Vikon-U(8.6)
55~60 岁 Age	15	三九胃泰 999(20.0)	雷尼替丁 Lei Ni Ti Ding(13.3) 丽珠得乐 LZ(13.3)	喇叭牌 Laba(6.7) 康宁黄连素 Kangning(6.7) 何济公 Hejigong(6.7) 陈李济保济丸 Chenliji(6.7) 氟哌酸 Norfloxacin Capsules(6.7) 胃友 Weiyou(6.7) 吗叮啉 Tabeliae Domperidoni Gastrokinetic(6.7)
女性 Female	192	**腹可安 Fukean(15.1)**	**胃仙 U Vikon-U(9.4)**	**三九胃泰 999(7.8)** **吗叮啉 Tabeliae Domperidoni Gastrokinetic(7.8)**
16~24 岁 Age	31	胃乃安 Weinai'an(12.9) 腹可安 Fukean(12.9)	华天宝 Huatianbao(9.7) 喇叭牌 Laba(9.7)	吗叮啉 Tabeliae Domperidoni Gastrokinetic(6.5) 胃仙 U Vikon-U(6.5)
25~34 岁 Age	52	腹可安 Fukean(17.3)	胃仙 U Vikon-U(13.5)	何济公 Hejigong(11.5)
35~44 岁 Age	51	腹可安 Fukean(13.7)	胃仙 U Vikon-U(11.8) 胃乃安 Weinai'an(11.8)	三九胃泰 999(7.8) 何济公 Hejigong(7.8)
45~54 岁 Age	43	三九胃泰 999(14.0) 腹可安 Fukean(14.0)	华天宝 Huatianbao(11.6)	吗叮啉 Tabeliae Domperidoni Gastrokinetic(7.0) 陈李济保济丸 Chenliji(7.0)
55~60 岁 Age	15	腹可安 Fukean(20.0) 吗叮啉 Tabeliae Domperidoni Gastrokinetic(20.0)	西安神龙 Xi'an Shenlong(6.7) 钓鱼牌 Dianyu(6.7) 园田牌保济丸 Yuantian(6.7) 速治灵 Suzhiling(6.7) 黄连素 Bering Hydrochloride Tablets(6.7) 胃仙 U Vikon-U(6.7) 胃舒平 Compound Aluminium Hydroxide Tablets(6.7) 胃得乐 Dele(6.7) 三九胃泰 999(6.7)	

3-4 理想品牌或品种排名/ Ranking of the Ideal Brands or Kinds

注：在药品品牌调查中，消费者经常出现将药品的名称与品牌名称混淆的现象，特此声明。/ In our research on medicines, we find consumers often confused the names and the brands.

排名 Brand Ranking	品牌或品种 Brands or Kinds	人数 Number	百分比 Percent
2	胃仙 U Vikon-U	92	8.9
3	腹可安 Fukean	85	8.2
4	三九胃泰 999	78	7.5
5	陈李济保济丸 Chenliji	46	4.4
5	吗叮啉 Tabeliae Domperidoni Gastrokinetic	46	4.4
6	喇叭牌 Laba	45	4.4

n=1034

3-5 样本、男性各年龄层、女性各年龄层的品牌习惯/ Brand Habit in Consuming Digestive System Medicines by the Whole Sample, Age and Gender Groups

	人数 Number	基本固定用一个牌子 used in only one brand	比较固定地用两个或三个牌子 used in two or three brands	基本上不太固定牌子 no brand preference
样本 Sample	373	51.2	30.8	18.0
男性 Male	181	59.7	26.5	13.8
16~24 岁 Age	22	63.6	31.8	4.5
25~34 岁 Age	55	52.7	32.7	14.5
35~44 岁 Age	54	55.6	25.9	18.5
45~54 岁 Age	35	68.6	17.1	14.3
55~60 岁 Age	15	73.3	20.0	6.7
女性 Female	192	43.2	34.9	21.9
16~24 岁 Age	30	33.3	50.0	16.7
25~34 岁 Age	52	40.4	38.5	21.2
35~44 岁 Age	51	45.1	29.4	25.5
45~54 岁 Age	44	50.0	31.8	18.2
55~60 岁 Age	15	46.7	20.0	33.3

3-6 样本、男性各年龄层、女性各年龄层最近一年内有无服用的比例/ Whether having Taken Digestive System Medicines Last Year by the Whole Sample, Age and Gender Groups

	人数 Number	吃过 yes	没吃过 no
样本 Sample	1034	36.4	63.6
男性 Male	499	36.7	63.3
16~24 岁 Age	106	21.7	78.3
25~34 岁 Age	150	37.3	62.7
35~44 岁 Age	127	42.5	57.5
45~54 岁 Age	73	47.9	52.1
55~60 岁 Age	43	34.9	65.1
女性 Female	535	36.1	63.9
16~24 岁 Age	112	27.7	72.3
25~34 岁 Age	158	32.9	67.1
35~44 岁 Age	137	37.2	62.8
45~54 岁 Age	87	50.6	49.4
55~60 岁 Age	41	36.6	63.4

3-7 选择该类商品的考虑因素/ Ranking of the Considerations in Purchasing

注：本题为多选题，合计百分比超过 100%（Multiple answers）

排名 Ranking	考虑因素 Considerations	人次 Person-time	百分比 Percent
1	见效快 immediate effect	206	54.8
2	医生推荐 recommended by doctors	150	39.9
3	无副作用 no side-effects	99	26.3
4	有名的牌子 famous brand	78	20.7
5	价格适中 reasonable price	70	18.6
6	服用方式简便 simple to take	53	14.1
7	购买方便 easy to buy	41	10.9
8	亲友介绍 introduced by relatives & friends	34	9.0
9	广告影响 influence of advertising	18	4.8
10	其他 others	3	0.8

n=376

3-8 样本、男性各年龄层、女性各年龄层最常服用的种类/ Types of Digestive System Medicines Consumed by the Whole Sample, Age and Gender Groups

	人数 Number	片剂 pill	冲剂 granular formulation	胶囊 capsule	药粉 powder	糖浆 syrup	药丸 bolus	其他 others
样本 Sample	373	44.0	3.2	10.7	0.8	0.3	40.5	0.5
男性 Male	181	40.3	4.4	13.3	0.6	0.6	40.3	0.6
16~24 岁 Age	23	47.8	8.7	8.7	0.0	4.3	30.4	0.0
25~34 岁 Age	54	40.7	5.6	9.3	0.0	0.0	44.4	0.0
35~44 岁 Age	54	40.7	1.9	13.0	1.9	0.0	42.6	0.0
45~54 岁 Age	35	37.1	0.0	17.1	0.0	0.0	42.9	2.9
55~60 岁 Age	15	33.3	13.3	26.7	0.0	0.0	26.7	0.0
女性 Female	192	47.4	2.1	8.3	1.0	0.0	40.6	0.5
16~24 岁 Age	31	29.0	0.0	12.9	6.5	0.0	51.6	0.0
25~34 岁 Age	52	48.1	0.0	7.7	0.0	0.0	44.2	0.0
35~44 岁 Age	50	54.0	2.0	12.0	0.0	0.0	32.0	0.0
45~54 岁 Age	44	52.3	2.3	2.3	0.0	0.0	40.9	2.3
55~60 岁 Age	15	46.7	13.3	6.7	0.0	0.0	33.3	0.0

3-9 样本、男性各年龄层、女性各年龄层最常服用的场合/ Settings of Consumption by the Whole Sample, Age and Gender Groups

注：本题为多选题，合计百分比超过 100%（Multiple answers）

	人数 Number	胃痛时 stomach-ache	胃酸时 sour stomach	胃胀气时 bloated	消化不良时 dyslexia	吃太饱时 overeaten	腹泻时 diarrhea	没胃口时 when not want to eat	配药使用 taken with other medicine	其他 others
样本 Sample	370	40.0	3.5	17.6	42.4	2.7	32.2	0.8	1.4	0.5
男性 Male	182	35.7	4.4	11.5	50.0	2.7	34.1	0.5	1.6	0.5
16~24 岁 Age	23	52.2	0.0	17.4	39.1	0.0	39.1	0.0	0.0	0.0
25~34 岁 Age	56	32.1	3.6	8.9	48.2	3.6	41.1	0.0	3.6	0.0
35~44 岁 Age	53	34.0	5.7	11.3	49.1	5.7	37.7	1.9	0.0	0.0
45~54 岁 Age	35	34.3	5.7	8.6	54.3	0.0	22.9	0.0	2.9	2.9
55~60 岁 Age	15	33.3	6.7	20.0	66.7	0.0	13.3	0.0	0.0	0.0
女性 Female	188	44.1	2.7	23.4	35.1	2.7	30.3	1.1	1.1	0.5
16~24 岁 Age	31	48.4	3.2	9.7	35.5	0.0	29.0	0.0	3.2	3.2
25~34 岁 Age	51	37.3	5.9	23.5	45.1	3.9	29.4	0.0	0.0	0.0
35~44 岁 Age	49	51.0	2.0	30.6	30.6	0.0	28.6	0.0	2.0	0.0
45~54 岁 Age	42	40.5	0.0	31.0	21.4	7.1	38.1	0.0	0.0	0.0
55~60 岁 Age	15	46.7	0.0	6.7	53.3	0.0	20.0	13.3	0.0	0.0

3-10 样本、男性各年龄层、女性各年龄层购买肠胃药的场所/ Location of Buying Digestive System Medicines by the Whole Sample, Age and Gender Groups

注：本题为多选题，合计百分比超过 100%（Multiple answers）

	人数 Number	药店 drug store	医院/诊所 hospital	商场 department store/ shopping center
样本 Sample	376	59.6	47.3	4.0
男性 Male	183	60.1	45.4	4.9
16~24 岁 Age	23	73.9	43.5	0.0
25~34 岁 Age	56	64.3	37.5	5.4
35~44 岁 Age	54	55.6	48.1	3.7
45~54 岁 Age	35	60.0	48.6	8.6
55~60 岁 Age	15	40.0	60.0	6.7
女性 Female	193	59.1	49.2	3.1
16~24 岁 Age	31	61.3	38.7	6.5
25~34 岁 Age	52	61.5	48.1	3.8
35~44 岁 Age	51	60.8	47.1	2.0
45~54 岁 Age	44	54.5	61.4	0.0
55~60 岁 Age	15	53.3	46.7	6.7

3-11 家中是否有备用肠胃药的习惯/ The Habit of Keeping Digestive System Medicines at Home

	人数 Number	百分比 Percent
有 yes	543	53.1
没有 no	480	46.9

n=1023

3-12 公费/自费医疗的比例/ Proportion of the Free Medical Service

	人数 Number	百分比 Percent
公费医疗 free medical service	423	40.9
自费医疗 own expense	610	59.1

n=1033

3-13 不同消费者层的常用品牌/ The Most Frequently Used Brands by Market Segments

3-13-1 时尚流行指标/ Fads Popular Index

注：在药品品牌调查中，消费者经常出现将药品的名称与品牌名称混淆的现象，特此声明。/ In our research on medicines, we find consumers often confused the names and the brands.

	人数 Number	第一品牌及百分比 1st / percent	第二品牌及百分比 2nd / percent	第三品牌及百分比 3rd / percent
样本 Sample	**371**	**腹可安 Fukean(16.2)**	**胃仙 U Vikon-U(9.7)**	**三九胃泰 999(7.5)**
平实生活指向 simple living orientation	190	腹可安 Fukean(16.8)	吗叮啉 Tabeliae Domperidoni Gastrokinetic(7.4) 三九胃泰 999(7.4)	胃仙 U Vikon-U(6.8)
时尚流行指向 fashion orientation	181	腹可安 Fukean(15.5)	胃仙 U Vikon-U(12.7)	何济公 Hejigong(9.4)

3-13-2 广告态度指标/ Advertising Attitude Index

注：在药品品牌调查中，消费者经常出现将药品的名称与品牌名称混淆的现象，特此声明。/ In our research on medicines, we find consumers often confused the names and the brands.

	人数 Number	第一品牌及百分比 1st / percent	第二品牌及百分比 2nd / percent	第三品牌及百分比 3rd / percent
样本 Sample	**368**	**腹可安 Fukean(16.6)**	**胃仙 U Vikon-U(9.5)**	**三九胃泰 999(7.6)**
广告淡漠指向 indifferent orientation	120	腹可安 Fukean(16.7)	陈李济保济丸 Chenliji(10.8)	三九胃泰 999(9.2)
中间层 medium	216	腹可安 Fukean(17.1)	胃仙 U Vikon-U(10.6)	三九胃泰 999(6.9)
信赖广告指向 loyal orientation	32	华天宝 Huatianbao(15.6)	胃仙 U Vikon-U(12.5) 腹可安 Fukean(12.5)	三九胃泰 999(6.3) 胃乃安 Weinaian(6.3)

3-13-3 饮食健康指标/ Foods & Drink Quality Index

注：在药品品牌调查中，消费者经常出现将药品的名称与品牌名称混淆的现象，特此声明。/ In our research on medicines, we find consumers often confused the names and the brands.

	人数 Number	第一品牌及百分比 1st / percent	第二品牌及百分比 2nd / percent	第三品牌及百分比 3rd / percent
样本 Sample	**372**	**腹可安 Fukean(16.4)**	**胃仙 U Vikon-U(9.7)**	**三九胃泰 999(7.5)**
饮食"温饱"指向 "basic" orientation	99	腹可安 Fukean(19.2)	陈李济保济丸 Chenliji(9.1)	胃仙 U Vikon-U(8.1)
中间层 medium	200	腹可安 Fukean(15.5)	胃仙 U Vikon-U(10.0)	吗叮啉 Tabeliae Domperidoni Gastrokinetic(8.0)
健康营养指向 health & nutrition orientation	75	腹可安 Fukean(15.1)	胃乃安 Weinaian(11.0) 胃仙 U Vikon-U(11.0) 华天宝 Huatianbao(11.0)	三九胃泰 999(9.6)

● 重庆 / Chongqing

3-1 最近一年内有无服用的比例/ Whether having Taken Digestive System Medicines Last Year

	人数 Number	百分比 Percent
吃过 yes	196	31.4
没吃过 no	428	68.6

n=624

3-2 最常用品牌或品种排名/ Ranking of the Most Frequently Used Brands or Kinds

注：在药品品牌调查中，消费者经常出现将药品的名称与品牌名称混淆的现象，特此声明。/ In our research on medicines, we find consumers often confused the names and the brands.

排名 Brand Ranking	品牌或品种 Brands or Kinds	人数 Number	百分比 Percent
1	三九胃泰 999	34	17.4
2	诺氟沙星 Norfloxacin	31	15.9
3	吗叮啉 Tabeliae Domperidoni Gastrokinetic	19	9.7
4	氟哌酸 Norfloxacin Capsules	10	5.1
4	胃舒平 Compound Aluminium Hydroxide Tablets	10	5.1
5	藿香正气水 Huo Xiang Zheng Qi Shui	6	3.1
5	快胃片 Kuaiweipian	6	3.1
6	泻立停 Xieliting	5	2.6
6	胃仙 U Vikon-U	5	2.6
7	痢特灵 Liteling	4	2.1
7	江中健胃消食片 Jiangzhong	4	2.1
7	黄连素 Bering Hydrochloride Tablets	4	2.1
8	雷尼替丁 Lei Ni Ti Ding	3	1.5

n=195

3-3 样本、男性各年龄层、女性各年龄层的常用品牌或品种/ The Most Frequently Used Brands or Kinds by the Whole Sample, Age and Gender Groups

注：在药品品牌调查中，消费者经常出现将药品的名称与品牌名称混淆的现象，特此声明。/ In our research on medicines, we find consumers often confused the names and the brands.

	人数 Number	第一品牌及百分比 1st/ percent	第二品牌及百分比 2nd/ percent	第三品牌及百分比 3rd/ percent
样本 Sample	195	**三九胃泰 999(17.4)**	**诺氟沙星 Norfloxacin(15.9)**	**吗叮啉 Tabeliae Domperidoni Gastrokinetic(9.7)**
男性 Male	98	**三九胃泰 999(21.4)**	**诺氟沙星 Norfloxacin(14.3)**	**氟哌酸 Norfloxacin Capsules(8.2)** **吗叮啉 Tabeliae Domperidoni Gastrokinetic(8.2)**
16~24 岁 Age	17	诺氟沙星 Norfloxacin(41.2)	吗叮啉 Tabeliae Domperidoni Gastrokinetic(11.8)	氟哌酸 Norfloxacin Capsules(5.9) 雷尼替丁 Lei Ni Ti Ding(5.9) 三九胃泰 999(5.9) 胃舒平 Compound Aluminium Hydroxide Tablets(5.9) 江中健胃消食片 Jiangzhong(5.9)
25~34 岁 Age	25	三九胃泰 999(32.0)	氟哌酸 Norfloxacin Capsules(12.0)	吗叮啉 Tabeliae Domperidoni Gastrokinetic(8.0) 诺氟沙星 Norfloxacin(8.0)
35~44 岁 Age	22	氟哌酸 Norfloxacin Capsules(18.2)	快胃片 Kuaiweipian(9.1) 吗叮啉 Tabeliae Domperidoni Gastrokinetic(9.1) 胃舒平 Compound Aluminium Hydroxide Tablets(9.1)	胃仙 U Vikon-U(4.5) 梅峰牌胃得安 MeiFeng Weidean(4.5) 西米提丁 Xi Mi Ti Ding(4.5) 痢特灵 Liteling(4.5) 诺氟沙星 Norfloxacin(4.5) 三九胃泰 999(4.5) 黄连素 Bering Hydrochloride Tablets(4.5)
45~54 岁 Age	19	三九胃泰 999(31.6)	诺氟沙星 Norfloxacin(15.8)	胃舒平 Compound Aluminium Hydroxide Tablets(10.5)
55~60 岁 Age	15	三九胃泰 999(33.3)	肠胃康 Changweikang(6.7) 快胃片 Kuaiweipian(6.7) 吗叮啉 Tabeliae Domperidoni Gastrokinetic(6.7) 诺氟沙星 Norfloxacin(6.7) 胃舒平 Compound Aluminium Hydroxide Tablets(6.7) 乳酶生 Rumeisheng(6.7) 盐酸雷尼替丁 Yan Suan Lei Ni Ti Ding(6.7) 弗兰西林 Fu Lan Xi Lin(6.7)	

续前表 continued

	人数 Number	第一品牌及百分比 1st/ percent	第二品牌及百分比 2nd/ percent	第三品牌及百分比 3rd/ percent
女性 Female	97	**诺氟沙星 Norfloxacin(17.5)**	**三九胃泰 999(13.4)**	**吗叮啉 Tabeliae Domperidoni Gastrokinetic(11.3)**
16~24 岁 Age	15	吗叮啉 Tabeliae Domperidoni Gastrokinetic(20.0)	诺氟沙星 Norfloxacin(13.3) 三九胃泰 999(13.3)	丽珠得乐 LZ(6.7) 胃舒平 Compound Aluminium HydroxideTablets(6.7) 泻立停 Xieliting(6.7) 肠康 Changkang(6.7) 菲伯瑞黄腾素片 Fei Bo Rui Huang Teng Su Pian(6.7)
25~34 岁 Age	21	吗叮啉 Tabeliae Domperidoni Gastrokinetic(14.3) 三九胃泰 999(14.3)	江中健胃消食片 Jiangzhong(4.8) 吉林辉南养胃宁 Ji Lin Hui Nan Yang Wei Ning(4.8) 结肠炎丸 Jie Chang Yan Wan(4.8) 肠炎宁 Changyanning(4.8) 胃得安 Weidean(4.8) 肠康 Changkang(4.8) 利君沙 Lijunsha(4.8) 藿香正气水 Huo Xiang Zheng Qi Shui(4.8) 泻立停 Xieliting(4.8) 胃仙 U Vikon-U(4.8) 诺氟沙星 Norfloxacin(4.8) 快胃片 Kuaiweipian(4.8)	
35~44 岁 Age	23	诺氟沙星 Norfloxacin(21.7)	吗叮啉 Tabeliae Domperidoni Gastrokinetic(13.0) 三九胃泰 999(13.0)	胃仙 U Vikon-U(8.7) 雷尼替丁 Lei Ni Ti Ding(8.7) 快胃片 Kuaiweipian(8.7)
45~54 岁 Age	28	诺氟沙星 Norfloxacin(28.6)	三九胃泰 999(14.3)	黄连素 Bering Hydrochloride Tablets(7.1) 吗叮啉 Tabeliae Domperidoni Gastrokinetic(7.1) 胃舒平 Compound Aluminium Hydroxide Tablets(7.1) 香砂养胃片 Xiang Sha Yang Wei Pian(7.1) 藿香正气水 Huo Xiang Zheng Qi Shui(7.1)
55~60 岁 Age	10	藿香正气水 Huo Xiang Zheng Qi Shui(30.0)	氟哌酸 Norfloxacin Capsules(10.0) 诺氟沙星 Norfloxacin(10.0) 三九胃泰 999(10.0) 痢特灵 Liteling(10.0) 江中健胃消食片 Jiangzhong(10.0) 步天胆万通 Bu Tian Dan Wan Tong(10.0)	

3-4 理想品牌或品种排名/ Ranking of the Ideal Brands or Kinds

注：在药品品牌调查中，消费者经常出现将药品的名称与品牌名称混淆的现象，特此声明。/ In our research on medicines, we find consumers often confused the names and the brands.

排名 Brand Ranking	品牌或品种 Brands or Kinds	人数 Number	百分比 Percent
1	三九胃泰 999	123	19.7
2	吗叮啉 Tabeliae Domperidoni Gastrokinetic	59	9.5
3	诺氟沙星 Norfloxacin	51	8.2
4	胃舒平 Compound Aluminium Hydroxide Tablets	19	3.0
5	藿香正气水 Huo Xiang Zheng Qi Shui	17	2.7
6	泻立停 Xieliting	16	2.6
7	氟哌酸 Norfloxacin Capsules	14	2.2
8	快胃片 Kuaiweipian	10	1.6
9	痢特灵 Liteling	8	1.3
9	昂立一号 Only One	8	1.3
10	胃仙 U Vikon-U	6	1.0

n=624

3-5 样本、男性各年龄层、女性各年龄层的品牌习惯/ Brand Habit in Consuming Digestive System Medicines by the Whole Sample, Age and Gender Groups

	人数 Number	基本固定用一个牌子 used in only one brand	比较固定地用两个或三个牌子 used in two or three brands	基本上不太固定牌子 no brand preference
样本 Sample	195	41.5	25.1	33.3
男性 Male	97	38.1	23.7	38.1
16~24 岁 Age	17	52.9	23.5	23.5
25~34 岁 Age	25	36.0	16.0	48.0
35~44 岁 Age	22	36.4	18.2	45.5
45~54 岁 Age	18	33.3	33.3	33.3
55~60 岁 Age	15	33.3	33.3	33.3
女性 Female	98	44.9	26.5	28.6
16~24 岁 Age	15	46.7	33.3	20.0
25~34 岁 Age	22	50.0	13.6	36.4
35~44 岁 Age	23	30.4	30.4	39.1
45~54 岁 Age	28	57.1	25.0	17.9
55~60 岁 Age	10	30.0	40.0	30.0

3-6 样本、男性各年龄层、女性各年龄层最近一年内有无服用的比例/ Whether having Taken Digestive System Medicines Last Year by the Whole Sample, Age and Gender Groups

	人数 Number	吃过 yes	没吃过 no
样本 Sample	624	31.4	68.6
男性 Male	314	31.2	68.8
16~24 岁 Age	64	26.6	73.4
25~34 岁 Age	93	26.9	73.1
35~44 岁 Age	75	29.3	70.7
45~54 岁 Age	54	35.2	64.8
55~60 岁 Age	28	53.6	46.4
女性 Female	310	31.6	68.4
16~24 岁 Age	64	23.4	76.6
25~34 岁 Age	90	24.4	75.6
35~44 岁 Age	73	31.5	68.5
45~54 岁 Age	60	46.7	53.3
55~60 岁 Age	23	43.5	56.5

3-7 选择该类商品的考虑因素/ Ranking of the Considerations in Purchasing

注：本题为多选题，合计百分比超过 100%（Multiple answers）

排名 Ranking	考虑因素 Considerations	人次 Person-time	百分比 Percent
1	见效快 immediate effect	120	61.5
2	医生推荐 recommended by doctors	81	41.5
3	无副作用 no side-effects	39	20.0
4	价格适中 reasonable price	28	14.4
5	有名的牌子 famous brand	22	11.3
6	服用方式简便 simple to take	17	8.7
7	亲友介绍 introduced by relatives & friends	14	7.2
8	广告影响 influence of advertising	9	4.6
8	购买方便 easy to buy	9	4.6
9	其他 others	2	1.0

n=195

3-8 样本、男性各年龄层、女性各年龄层最常服用的种类/ Types of Digestive System Medicines Consumed by the Whole Sample, Age and Gender Groups

	人数 Number	片剂 pill	冲剂 granular formulation	胶囊 capsule	药粉 powder	糖浆 syrup	药丸 bolus	其他 others
样本 Sample	192	39.1	14.1	34.4	0.0	3.6	6.8	2.1
男性 Male	97	36.1	20.6	33.0	0.0	3.1	5.2	2.1
16~24 岁 Age	17	5.9	11.8	82.4	0.0	0.0	0.0	0.0
25~34 岁 Age	25	28.0	36.0	24.0	0.0	4.0	8.0	0.0
35~44 岁 Age	21	71.4	0.0	23.8	0.0	0.0	4.8	0.0
45~54 岁 Age	19	36.8	15.8	26.3	0.0	10.5	10.5	0.0
55~60 岁 Age	15	33.3	40.0	13.3	0.0	0.0	0.0	13.3
女性 Female	95	42.1	7.4	35.8	0.0	4.2	8.4	2.1
16~24 岁 Age	14	50.0	7.1	35.7	0.0	0.0	7.1	0.0
25~34 岁 Age	22	45.5	4.5	36.4	0.0	4.5	9.1	0.0
35~44 岁 Age	22	36.4	9.1	36.4	0.0	0.0	13.6	4.5
45~54 岁 Age	27	44.4	7.4	37.0	0.0	3.7	7.4	0.0
55~60 岁 Age	10	30.0	10.0	30.0	0.0	20.0	0.0	10.0

3-9 样本、男性各年龄层、女性各年龄层最常服用的场合/ Settings of Consumption by the Whole Sample, Age and Gender Groups

注：本题为多选题，合计百分比超过 100%（Multiple answers）

	人数 Number	胃痛时 stomach-ache	胃酸时 sour stomach	胃胀气时 bloated	消化不良时 dyslexia	吃太饱时 over-eaten	腹泻时 diarrhea	没胃口时 when not want to eat	配药使用 taken with other medicine	其他 others
样本 Sample	192	39.1	4.7	18.8	25.0	2.1	37.5	1.6	3.6	1.0
男性 Male	96	40.6	6.3	17.7	26.0	1.0	36.5	1.0	2.1	2.1
16~24 岁 Age	17	35.3	5.9	5.9	52.9	0.0	35.3	0.0	0.0	0.0
25~34 岁 Age	25	28.0	8.0	28.0	24.0	0.0	40.0	0.0	0.0	4.0
35~44 岁 Age	21	42.9	4.8	19.0	19.0	0.0	42.9	4.8	4.8	0.0
45~54 岁 Age	18	55.6	0.0	16.7	11.1	0.0	33.3	0.0	0.0	0.0
55~60 岁 Age	15	46.7	13.3	13.3	26.7	6.7	26.7	0.0	6.7	6.7
女性 Female	96	37.5	3.1	19.8	24.0	3.1	38.5	2.1	5.2	0.0
16~24 岁 Age	15	26.7	0.0	26.7	33.3	6.7	33.3	0.0	6.7	0.0
25~34 岁 Age	22	45.5	9.1	22.7	27.3	4.5	27.3	0.0	4.5	0.0
35~44 岁 Age	22	50.0	0.0	22.7	27.3	4.5	36.4	0.0	0.0	0.0
45~54 岁 Age	27	29.6	3.7	11.1	7.4	0.0	55.6	7.4	7.4	0.0
55~60 岁 Age	10	30.0	0.0	20.0	40.0	0.0	30.0	0.0	10.0	0.0

3-10 样本、男性各年龄层、女性各年龄层购买肠胃药的场所/ Location of Buying Digestive System Medicines by the Whole Sample, Age and Gender Groups

注：本题为多选题，合计百分比超过 100%（Multiple answers）

	人数 Number	药店 drug store	医院/诊所 hospital	商场 department store/ shopping center
样本 Sample	195	68.2	46.7	2.6
男性 Male	97	69.1	49.5	2.1
16~24 岁 Age	17	64.7	47.1	0.0
25~34 岁 Age	25	68.0	52.0	0.0
35~44 岁 Age	22	68.2	45.5	4.5
45~54 岁 Age	18	77.8	44.4	0.0
55~60 岁 Age	15	66.7	60.0	6.7
女性 Female	98	67.3	43.9	3.1
16~24 岁 Age	15	53.3	53.3	13.3
25~34 岁 Age	22	59.1	54.5	4.5
35~44 岁 Age	23	78.3	39.1	0.0
45~54 岁 Age	28	67.9	39.3	0.0
55~60 岁 Age	10	80.0	30.0	0.0

3-11 家中是否有备用肠胃药的习惯/ The Habit of Keeping Digestive System Medicines at Home

	人数 Number	百分比 Percent
有 yes	265	42.7
没有 no	355	57.3

n=620

3-12 公费/自费医疗的比例/ Proportion of the Free Medical Service

	人数 Number	百分比 Percent
公费医疗 free medical service	180	29.2
自费医疗 own expense	437	70.8

n=617

3-13 不同消费者层的常用品牌/ The Most Frequently Used Brands by Market Segments

3-13-1 时尚流行指标/ Fads Popular Index

注：在药品品牌调查中，消费者经常出现将药品的名称与品牌名称混淆的现象，特此声明。/ In our research on medicines, we find consumers often confused the names and the brands.

	人数 Number	第一品牌及百分比 1st/ percent	第二品牌及百分比 2nd/ percent	第三品牌及百分比 3rd/ percent
样本 Sample	193	**三九胃泰 999(17.1)**	**诺氟沙星 Norfloxacin(16.1)**	**吗叮啉 Tabeliae Domperidoni Gastrokinetic(9.8)**
平实生活指向 simple living orientation	118	诺氟沙星 Norfloxacin(17.8)	三九胃泰 999(16.9)	吗叮啉 Tabeliae Domperidoni Gastrokinetic(10.2)
时尚流行指向 fashion orientation	75	三九胃泰 999(17.3)	诺氟沙星 Norfloxacin(13.3)	吗叮啉 Tabeliae Domperidoni Gastrokinetic(9.3)

3-13-2 广告态度指标/ Advertising Attitude Index

注：在药品品牌调查中，消费者经常出现将药品的名称与品牌名称混淆的现象，特此声明。/ In our research on medicines, we find consumers often confused the names and the brands.

	人数 Number	第一品牌及百分比 1st / percent	第二品牌及百分比 2nd / percent	第三品牌及百分比 3rd / percent
样本 Sample	193	**三九胃泰 999(17.1)**	**诺氟沙星 Norfloxacin(15.5)**	**吗叮啉 Tabeliae Domperidoni Gastrokinetic(9.8)**
广告淡漠指向 indifferent orientation	51	诺氟沙星 Norfloxacin(9.8) 胃舒平 Compound Aluminium Hydroxide Tablets(9.8) 三九胃泰 999(9.8)	氟哌酸 Norfloxacin Capsules(7.8)	藿香正气水 Huo Xiang Zheng Qi Shui(5.9)
中间层 medium	118	诺氟沙星 Norfloxacin(18.6)	三九胃泰 999(17.8)	吗叮啉 Tabeliae Domperidoni Gastrokinetic(11.9)
信赖广告指向 loyal orientation	24	三九胃泰 999(29.2)	吗叮啉 Tabeliae Domperidoni Gastrokinetic(12.5) 诺氟沙星 Norfloxacin(12.5)	龙门 Longmen(8.3)

3-13-3 饮食健康指标/ Foods & Drink Quality Index

注：在药品品牌调查中，消费者经常出现将药品的名称与品牌名称混淆的现象，特此声明。/ In our research on medicines, we find consumers often confused the names and the brands.

	人数 Number	第一品牌及百分比 1st/ percent	第二品牌及百分比 2nd/ percent	第三品牌及百分比 3rd/ percent
样本 Sample	192	**三九胃泰 999(17.2)**	**诺氟沙星 Norfloxacin(16.1)**	**吗叮啉 Tabeliae Domperidoni Gastrokinetic(9.9)**
饮食“温饱”指向 "basic" orientation	63	诺氟沙星 Norfloxacin(17.5)	三九胃泰 999(14.3)	吗叮啉 Tabeliae Domperidoni Gastrokinetic(11.1)
中间层 medium	90	三九胃泰 999(16.7)	诺氟沙星 Norfloxacin(15.6)	吗叮啉 Tabeliae Domperidoni Gastrokinetic(11.1)
健康营养指向 health & nutrition orientation	39	三九胃泰 999(23.1)	诺氟沙星 Norfloxacin(15.4)	黄连素 Bering Hydrochloride Tablets(5.1) 吗叮啉 Tabeliae Domperidoni Gastrokinetic(5.1) 胃仙U Vikon-U(5.1)

● 武汉 / Wuhan

3-1 最近一年内有无服用的比例/ Whether having Taken Digestive System Medicines Last Year

	人数 Number	百分比 Percent
吃过 yes	172	26.9
没吃过 no	468	73.1

n=640

3-2 最常用品牌或品种排名/ Ranking of the Most Frequently Used Brands or Kinds

注：在药品品牌调查中，消费者经常出现将药品的名称与品牌名称混淆的现象，特此声明。/ In our research on medicines, we find consumers often confused the names and the brands.

排名 Brand Ranking	品牌或品种 Brands or Kinds	人数 Number	百分比 Percent
1	三九胃泰 999	32	18.7
2	吗叮啉 Tabeliae Domperidoni Gastrokinetic	21	12.3
3	黄连素 Bering Hydrochloride Tablets	13	7.6
4	泻立停 Xieliting	9	5.3
5	雷尼替丁 Lei Ni Ti Ding	8	4.7
6	诺氟沙星 Norfloxacin	7	4.1
7	胃得乐 Dele	6	3.5
8	藿香正气丸 Huo Xiang Zheng Qi Wan	5	2.9
8	乐得胃 LDW	5	2.9
9	丽珠得乐 LZ	4	2.3
9	江中健胃消食片 Jiangzhong	4	2.3

n=171

3-3 样本、男性各年龄层、女性各年龄层的常用品牌或品种/ The Most Frequently Used Brands or Kinds by the Whole Sample, Age and Gender Groups

注：在药品品牌调查中，消费者经常出现将药品的名称与品牌名称混淆的现象，特此声明。/ In our research on medicines, we find consumers often confused the names and the brands.

	人数 Number	第一品牌及百分比 1st/ percent	第二品牌及百分比 2nd/ percent	第三品牌及百分比 3rd/ percent
样本 Sample	171	**三九胃泰 999(18.7)**	**吗叮啉 Tabeliae Domperidoni Gastrokinetic(12.3)**	**黄连素 Bering Hydrochloride Tablets(7.6)**
男性 Male	72	**三九胃泰 999(13.9)** **吗叮啉 Tabeliae Domperidoni Gastrokinetic(13.9)**	**泻立停 Xieliting(8.3)**	**雷尼替丁 Lei Ni Ti Ding(6.9)** **乐得胃 LDW(6.9)**
16~24 岁 Age	8	吗叮啉 Tabeliae Domperidoni Gastrokinetic(50.0)	三九胃泰 999(12.5) 胃乐 Weile(12.5) 藿香正气丸 Huo Xiang Zheng Qi Wan(12.5)	
25~34 岁 Age	26	泻立停 Xieliting(19.2)	吗叮啉 Tabeliae Domperidoni Gastrokinetic(15.4) 三九胃泰 999(15.4)	雷尼替丁 Lei Ni Ti Ding(7.7) 丽珠得乐 LZ(7.7)
35~44 岁 Age	17	诺氟沙星 Norfloxacin(17.6) 三九胃泰 999(17.6)	乐得胃 LDW(11.8)	胃仙 U Vikon-U(5.9) 胃痛安 Weitong'an(5.9) 盐酸雷尼替丁 Yan Suan Lei Ni Ti Ding(5.9) 泰胃美 Tagamat(5.9) 吗叮啉 Tabeliae Domperidoni Gastrokinetic(5.9) 丽珠得乐 LZ(5.9) 雷尼替丁 Lei Ni Ti Ding(5.9)
45~54 岁 Age	14	黄连素 Bering Hydrochloride Tablets(14.3) 三九胃泰 999(14.3) 痢特灵 Liteling(14.3)	泻立停 Xieliting(7.1) 江中健胃消食片 Jiangzhong(7.1) 易善力 Yishanli(7.1) 肠胃康 Changweikang(7.1) 胃得乐 Dele(7.1) 吗叮啉 Tabeliae Domperidoni Gastrokinetic(7.1) 雷尼替丁 Lei Ni Ti Ding(7.1) 乐得胃 LDW(7.1)	
55~60 岁 Age	7	陈香露百露 Chen Xiang Lu Bai Lu(14.3) 乐得胃 LDW(14.3) 雷尼替丁 Lei Ni Ti Ding(14.3) 斯达舒 Sidashu(14.3) 胃得乐 Dele(14.3) 胃友 Weiyou(14.3)		

续前表 continued

	人数 Number	第一品牌及百分比 1st/ percent	第二品牌及百分比 2nd/ percent	第三品牌及百分比 3rd/ percent
女性 Female	**99**	**三九胃泰 999(22.2)**	**吗叮啉 Tabeliae Domperidoni Gastrokinetic(11.1)** **黄连素 Bering Hydrochloride Tablets(11.1)**	**藿香正气丸 Huo Xiang Zheng Qi Wan(4.0)** **诺氟沙星 Norfloxacin(4.0)**
16~24 岁 Age	16	三九胃泰 999(31.3)	吗叮啉 Tabeliae Domperidoni Gastrokinetic(18.8)	黄连素 Bering Hydrochloride Tablets(12.5)
25~34 岁 Age	25	三九胃泰 999(20.0)	黄连素 Bering Hydrochloride Tablets(16.0)	吗叮啉 Tabeliae Domperidoni Gastrokinetic(12.0)
35~44 岁 Age	22	三九胃泰 999(31.8)	藿香正气丸 Huo Xiang Zheng Qi Wan(4.5) 江中健胃消食片 Jiangzhong(4.5) 午时茶 Wu Shi Cha (4.5) 胃仙 U Vikon-U(4.5) 易善力 Yishanli(4.5) 斯达舒 Sidashu(4.5) 诺氟沙星 Norfloxacin(4.5) 吗叮啉 Tabeliae Domperidoni Gastrokinetic(4.5) 雷尼替丁 Lei Ni Ti Ding(4.5) 黄连素 Bering Hydrochloride Tablets(4.5)	
45~54 岁 Age	27	三九胃泰 999(18.5)	吗叮啉 Tabeliae Domperidoni Gastrokinetic(14.8)	黄连素 Bering Hydrochloride Tablets(11.1) 藿香正气丸 Huo Xiang Zheng Qi Wan(11.1) 诺氟沙星 Norfloxacin(11.1)
55~60 岁 Age	9	胃得乐 Dele(22.2)	黄连素 Bering Hydrochloride Tablets(11.1) 雷尼替丁 Lei Ni Ti Ding(11.1) 胃仙 U Vikon-U(11.1) 胃乐 Weile(11.1) 肠菌理 Changjunli(11.1) 养胃冲剂 Yang Wei Chong Ji(11.1) 白雪山 Baixueshan(11.1)	

3-4 理想品牌或品种排名/ Ranking of the Ideal Brands or Kinds

注：在药品品牌调查中，消费者经常出现将药品的名称与品牌名称混淆的现象，特此声明。/ In our research on medicines, we find consumers often confused the names and the brands.

排名 Brand Ranking	品牌或品种 Brands or Kinds	人数 Number	百分比 Percent
1	三九胃泰 999	78	12.2
2	吗叮啉 Tabeliae Domperidoni Gastrokinetic	52	8.1
3	泻立停 Xieliting	15	2.3
4	黄连素 Bering Hydrochloride Tablets	13	2.0
5	胃得乐 Dele	9	1.4
6	乐得胃 LDW	7	1.1
6	诺氟沙星 Norfloxacin	7	1.1
7	雷尼替丁 Lei Ni Ti Ding	6	0.9
7	丽珠得乐 LZ	6	0.9
7	胃仙 U Vikon-U	6	0.9

n=640

3-5 样本、男性各年龄层、女性各年龄层的品牌习惯/ Brand Habit in Consuming Digestive System Medicines by the Whole Sample, Age and Gender Groups

	人数 Number	基本固定用一个牌子 used in only one brand	比较固定地用两个或三个牌子 used in two or three brands	基本上不太固定牌子 no brand preference
样本 Sample	172	47.7	31.4	20.9
男性 Male	72	47.2	34.7	18.1
16~24 岁 Age	8	75.0	12.5	12.5
25~34 岁 Age	26	46.2	38.5	15.4
35~44 岁 Age	17	52.9	29.4	17.6
45~54 岁 Age	14	35.7	42.9	21.4
55~60 岁 Age	7	28.6	42.9	28.6
女性 Female	100	48.0	29.0	23.0
16~24 岁 Age	16	37.5	37.5	25.0
25~34 岁 Age	25	40.0	40.0	20.0
35~44 岁 Age	22	59.1	18.2	22.7
45~54 岁 Age	28	50.0	21.4	28.6
55~60 岁 Age	9	55.6	33.3	11.1

3-6 样本、男性各年龄层、女性各年龄层最近一年内有无服用的比例/ Whether having Taken Digestive System Medicines Last Year by the Whole Sample, Age and Gender Groups

	人数 Number	吃过 yes	没吃过 no
样本 Sample	640	26.9	73.1
男性 Male	310	23.2	76.8
16~24 岁 Age	65	12.3	87.7
25~34 岁 Age	88	29.5	70.5
35~44 岁 Age	80	21.3	78.8
45~54 岁 Age	52	26.9	73.1
55~60 岁 Age	25	28.0	72.0
女性 Female	330	30.3	69.7
16~24 岁 Age	69	23.2	76.8
25~34 岁 Age	95	26.3	73.7
35~44 岁 Age	78	28.2	71.8
45~54 岁 Age	62	45.2	54.8
55~60 岁 Age	26	34.6	65.4

3-7 选择该类商品的考虑因素/ Ranking of the Considerations in Purchasing

注：本题为多选题，合计百分比超过 100%（Multiple answers）

排名 Ranking	考虑因素 Considerations	人次 Person-time	百分比 Percent
1	见效快 immediate effect	103	60.2
2	医生推荐 recommended by doctors	85	49.7
3	无副作用 no side-effects	44	25.7
4	服用方式简便 simple to take	24	14.0
5	有名的牌子 famous brand	22	12.9
6	价格适中 reasonable price	21	12.3
7	亲友介绍 introduced by relatives & friends	17	9.9
8	广告影响 influence of advertising	8	4.7
9	购买方便 easy to buy	7	4.1
10	其他 others	5	2.9

n=171

3-8 样本、男性各年龄层、女性各年龄层最常服用的种类/ Types of Digestive System Medicines Consumed by the Whole Sample, Age and Gender Groups

	人数 Number	片剂 pill	冲剂 granular formulation	胶囊 capsule	药粉 powder	糖浆 syrup	药丸 bolus	其他 others
样本 Sample	168	54.2	13.1	19.6	1.2	0.0	11.9	0.0
男性 Male	70	57.1	7.1	22.9	2.9	0.0	10.0	0.0
16~24 岁 Age	8	50.0	0.0	25.0	0.0	0.0	25.0	0.0
25~34 岁 Age	26	65.4	7.7	15.4	3.8	0.0	7.7	0.0
35~44 岁 Age	15	46.7	6.7	46.7	0.0	0.0	0.0	0.0
45~54 岁 Age	14	50.0	14.3	7.1	7.1	0.0	21.4	0.0
55~60 岁 Age	7	71.4	0.0	28.6	0.0	0.0	0.0	0.0
女性 Female	98	52.0	17.3	17.3	0.0	0.0	13.3	0.0
16~24 岁 Age	16	56.3	25.0	18.8	0.0	0.0	0.0	0.0
25~34 岁 Age	24	58.3	8.3	12.5	0.0	0.0	20.8	0.0
35~44 岁 Age	22	54.5	18.2	18.2	0.0	0.0	9.1	0.0
45~54 岁 Age	27	40.7	18.5	25.9	0.0	0.0	14.8	0.0
55~60 岁 Age	9	55.6	22.2	0.0	0.0	0.0	22.2	0.0

3-9 样本、男性各年龄层、女性各年龄层最常服用的场合/ Settings of Consumption by the Whole Sample, Age and Gender Groups

注：本题为多选题，合计百分比超过 100%（Multiple answers）

	人数 Number	胃痛时 stomach-ache	胃酸时 sour stomach	胃胀气时 bloated	消化不良时 dyslexia	吃太饱时 overeaten	腹泻时 diarrhea	没胃口时 when not want to eat	配药使用 taken with other medicine	其他 others
样本 Sample	169	40.8	5.9	15.4	32.5	1.8	30.8	1.2	2.4	0.6
男性 Male	70	47.1	4.3	11.4	28.6	2.9	30.0	0.0	1.4	1.4
16~24 岁 Age	8	37.5	0.0	12.5	62.5	12.5	12.5	0.0	0.0	0.0
25~34 岁 Age	26	46.2	0.0	3.8	30.8	0.0	42.3	0.0	0.0	3.8
35~44 岁 Age	15	46.7	6.7	6.7	20.0	6.7	20.0	0.0	6.7	0.0
45~54 岁 Age	14	42.9	14.3	21.4	21.4	0.0	35.7	0.0	0.0	0.0
55~60 岁 Age	7	71.4	0.0	28.6	14.3	0.0	14.3	0.0	0.0	0.0
女性 Female	99	36.4	7.1	18.2	35.4	1.0	31.3	2.0	3.0	0.0
16~24 岁 Age	16	25.0	6.3	18.8	43.8	0.0	25.0	6.3	0.0	0.0
25~34 岁 Age	25	40.0	8.0	12.0	40.0	0.0	36.0	0.0	8.0	0.0
35~44 岁 Age	22	40.9	9.1	9.1	50.0	4.5	18.2	0.0	0.0	0.0
45~54 岁 Age	28	32.1	7.1	35.7	21.4	0.0	39.3	3.6	3.6	0.0
55~60 岁 Age	8	50.0	0.0	0.0	12.5	0.0	37.5	0.0	0.0	0.0

3-10 样本、男性各年龄层、女性各年龄层购买肠胃药的场所/ Location of Buying Digestive System Medicines by the Whole Sample, Age and Gender Groups

注：本题为多选题，合计百分比超过 100%（Multiple answers）

	人数 Number	药店 drug store	医院/诊所 hospital	商场 department store/ shopping center
样本 Sample	172	45.3	69.8	0.0
男性 Male	72	52.8	68.1	0.0
16~24 岁 Age	8	62.5	62.5	0.0
25~34 岁 Age	26	53.8	61.5	0.0
35~44 岁 Age	17	47.1	82.4	0.0
45~54 岁 Age	14	50.0	64.3	0.0
55~60 岁 Age	7	57.1	71.4	0.0
女性 Female	100	40.0	71.0	0.0
16~24 岁 Age	16	56.3	62.5	0.0
25~34 岁 Age	25	36.0	68.0	0.0
35~44 岁 Age	22	36.4	77.3	0.0
45~54 岁 Age	28	39.3	75.0	0.0
55~60 岁 Age	9	33.3	66.7	0.0

3-11 家中是否有备用肠胃药的习惯/ The Habit of Keeping Digestive System Medicines at Home

	人数 Number	百分比 Percent
有 yes	278	43.6
没有 no	359	56.4

n=637

3-12 公费/自费医疗的比例/ Proportion of the Free Medical Service

	人数 Number	百分比 Percent
公费医疗 free medical service	264	41.5
自费医疗 own expense	372	58.5

n=636

3-13 不同消费者层的常用品牌/ The Most Frequently Used Brands by Market Segments

3-13-1 时尚流行指标/ Fads Popular Index

注：在药品品牌调查中，消费者经常出现将药品的名称与品牌名称混淆的现象，特此声明。/ In our research on medicines, we find consumers often confused the names and the brands.

	人数 Number	第一品牌及百分比 1st / percent	第二品牌及百分比 2nd / percent	第三品牌及百分比 3rd / percent
样本 Sample	170	**三九胃泰 999(18.8)**	**吗叮啉 Tabeliae Domperidoni Gastrokinetic(12.4)**	**黄连素 Bering Hydrochloride Tablets(7.6)**
平实生活指向 simple living orientation	85	三九胃泰 999(20.0)	黄连素 Bering Hydrochloride Tablets(11.8)	吗叮啉 Tabeliae Domperidoni Gastrokinetic(10.6)
时尚流行指向 fashion orientation	85	三九胃泰 999(17.6)	吗叮啉 Tabeliae Domperidoni Gastrokinetic(14.1)	泻立停 Xieliting(7.1)

3-13-2 广告态度指标/ Advertising Attitude Index

注：在药品品牌调查中，消费者经常出现将药品的名称与品牌名称混淆的现象，特此声明。/ In our research on medicines, we find consumers often confused the names and the brands.

	人数 Number	第一品牌及百分比 1st / percent	第二品牌及百分比 2nd / percent	第三品牌及百分比 3rd / percent
样本 Sample	170	**三九胃泰 999(18.8)**	**吗叮啉 Tabeliae Domperidoni Gastrokinetic(12.4)**	**黄连素 Bering Hydrochloride Tablets(7.6)**
广告淡漠指向 indifferent orientation	43	三九胃泰 999(16.3)	吗叮啉 Tabeliae Domperidoni Gastrokinetic(11.6)	易善力 Yishanli(7.0) 黄连素 Bering Hydrochloride Tablets(7.0)
中间层 medium	110	三九胃泰 999(20.0)	吗叮啉 Tabeliae Domperidoni Gastrokinetic(11.8)	黄连素 Bering Hydrochloride Tablets(8.2)
信赖广告指向 loyal orientation	17	吗叮啉 Tabeliae Domperidoni Gastrokinetic(17.6) 三九胃泰 999(17.6) 泻立停 Xieliting(17.6)	痢特灵 Liteling(5.9) 保和片 Baohepian(5.9) 江中健胃消食片 Jiangzhong(5.9) 盐酸雷尼替丁(5.9) 肠胃康 Changweikang(5.9) 雷尼替丁 Lei Ni Ti Ding(5.9) 乐得胃 LDW(5.9) 黄连素 Bering Hydrochloride Tablets(5.9)	

3-13-3 饮食健康指标/ Foods & Drink Quality Index

注：在药品品牌调查中，消费者经常出现将药品的名称与品牌名称混淆的现象，特此声明。/ In our research on medicines, we find consumers often confused the names and the brands.

	人数 Number	第一品牌及百分比 1st / percent	第二品牌及百分比 2nd / percent	第三品牌及百分比 3rd / percent
样本 Sample	169	**三九胃泰 999(18.9)**	**吗叮啉 Tabeliae Domperidoni Gastrokinetic(12.4)**	**黄连素 Bering Hydrochloride Tablets(7.7)**
饮食"温饱"指向 "basic" orientation	51	吗叮啉 Tabeliae Domperidoni Gastrokinetic(15.7) 三九胃泰 999(15.7)	黄连素 Bering Hydrochloride Tablets(7.8)	乐得胃 LDW(5.9) 诺氟沙星 Norfloxacin(5.9)
中间层 medium	85	三九胃泰 999(18.8)	吗叮啉 Tabeliae Domperidoni Gastrokinetic(11.8)	黄连素 Bering Hydrochloride Tablets(8.2)
健康营养指向 health & nutrition orientation	33	三九胃泰 999(24.2)	雷尼替丁 Lei Ni Ti Ding(9.1) 吗叮啉 Tabeliae Domperidoni Gastrokinetic(9.1)	黄连素 Bering Hydrochloride Tablets(6.1) 藿香正气丸 Huo Xiang Zheng Qi Wan(6.1) 斯达舒 Sidashu(6.1)

● 西安 / Xi'an

3-1 最近一年内有无服用的比例/ Whether having Taken Digestive System Medicines Last Year

	人数 Number	百分比 Percent
吃过 yes	254	42.3
没吃过 no	347	57.7

n=601

3-2 最常用品牌或品种排名/ Ranking of the Most Frequently Used Brands or Kinds

注：在药品品牌调查中，消费者经常出现将药品的名称与品牌名称混淆的现象，特此声明。/ In our research on medicines, we find consumers often confused the names and the brands.

排名 Brand Ranking	品牌或品种 Brands or Kinds	人数 Number	百分比 Percent
1	吗叮啉 Tabeliae Domperidoni Gastrokinetic	64	25.3
2	氟哌酸 Norfloxacin Capsules	39	15.4
3	三九胃泰 999	36	14.2
4	黄连素 Bering Hydrochloride Tablets	7	2.8
5	温胃舒 Wenweishu	6	2.4
5	胃友 Weiyou	6	2.4
5	快胃片 Kuaiweipian	6	2.4
6	胃必治 Bisuc	5	2.0
7	利君沙 Lijunsha	4	1.6

n=253

3-3 样本、男性各年龄层、女性各年龄层的常用品牌或品种/ The Most Frequently Used Brands or Kinds by the Whole Sample, Age and Gender Groups

	人数 Number	第一品牌及百分比 1st/ percent	第二品牌及百分比 2nd/ percent	第三品牌及百分比 3rd/ percent
样本 Sample	253	**吗叮啉 Tabeliae Domperidoni Gastrokinetic(25.3)**	**氟哌酸 Norfloxacin Capsules(15.4)**	**三九胃泰 999(14.2)**
男性 Male	121	**吗叮啉 Tabeliae Domperidoni Gastrokinetic(20.7)**	**氟哌酸 Norfloxacin Capsules(17.4)**	**三九胃泰 999(14.9)**
16~24 岁 Age	18	吗叮啉 Tabeliae Domperidoni Gastrokinetic(33.3)	氟哌酸 Norfloxacin Capsules(11.1) 三九胃泰 999(11.1)	温胃舒 Wenweishu(5.6) 芦荟胶囊 Lu Hui Jiao Nang(5.6) 胃泰 Weitai(5.6) 果胶铋 Bismuth Pectin(5.6) 胃得乐 Dele(5.6) 胃必治 Bisuc(5.6) 黄连素 Bering Hydrochloride Tablets(5.6)
25~34 岁 Age	35	氟哌酸 Norfloxacin Capsules(22.9)	吗叮啉 Tabeliae Domperidoni Gastrokinetic(17.1) 三九胃泰 999(17.1)	黄连素 Bering Hydrochloride Tablets(5.7) 胃友 Weiyou(5.7)
35~44 岁 Age	35	氟哌酸 Norfloxacin Capsules(22.9)	吗叮啉 Tabeliae Domperidoni Gastrokinetic(20.0)	三九胃泰 999(17.1)
45~54 岁 Age	23	吗叮啉 Tabeliae Domperidoni Gastrokinetic(17.4)	三九胃泰 999(8.7)	西米提丁 Xi Mi Ti Ding(4.3) 宝炉兰州佛慈 Bao Lu Lan Zhou Fo Ci(4.3) 健脾丸 Jianpiwan(4.3) 香沙养胃丸 Xiang Sha Yang Wei Wan(4.3) 霍香正气水 Huo Xiang Zheng Qi Shui(4.3) 保济丸 Baojiwan(4.3) 胃复安 Weifuan(4.3) 氟哌酸 Norfloxacin Capsules(4.3) 痢特灵 Liteling(4.3) 泻立停 Xieliting(4.3) 胃友 Weiyou(4.3) 胃苏冲剂 Wei Su Chong Ji(4.3) 胃舒平 Compound Aluminium Hydroxide Tablets(4.3) 快胃片 Kuaiweipian(4.3) 黄连素 Bering Hydrochloride Tablets(4.3)
55~60 岁 Age	10	氟哌酸 Norfloxacin Capsules(20.0) 吗叮啉 Tabeliae Domperidoni Gastrokinetic(20.0) 三九胃泰 999(20.0)	黄连素 Bering Hydrochloride Tablets (10.0) 快胃片 Kuaiweipian(10.0) 胃得乐 Dele(10.0) 胃友 Weiyou(10.0)	
女性 Female	132	**吗叮啉 Tabeliae Domperidoni Gastrokinetic(29.5)**	**氟哌酸 Norfloxacin Capsules(13.6)** **三九胃泰 999(13.6)**	
16~24 岁 Age	22	吗叮啉 Tabeliae Domperidoni Gastrokinetic(54.5)	氟哌酸 Norfloxacin Capsules(13.6)	三九胃泰 999(9.1)
25~34 岁 Age	40	吗叮啉 Tabeliae Domperidoni Gastrokinetic(35.0)	三九胃泰 999(20.0)	氟哌酸 Norfloxacin Capsules(12.5)
35~44 岁 Age	33	吗叮啉 Tabeliae Domperidoni Gastrokinetic(27.3)		氟哌酸 Norfloxacin Capsules(9.1) 三九胃泰 999(9.1)
45~54 岁 Age	26	氟哌酸 Norfloxacin Capsules(19.2)	吗叮啉 Tabeliae Domperidoni Gastrokinetic(15.4) 三九胃泰 999(15.4)	利君沙 Lijunsha(7.7) 诺氟沙星 Norfloxacin (7.7)
55~60 岁 Age	11	氟哌酸 Norfloxacin Capsules(18.2) 丽珠得乐 LZ(18.2) 酵母片 Xiaomupian(18.2)	三九胃泰 999(9.1) 香砂养胃片 Xiang Sha Yang Wei Pian(9.1) 胃得宁 Weidening(9.1) 健脾丸 Jianweiwan(9.1) 霍香正气丸 Huo Xiang Zheng Qi Wan(9.1)	

3-4 理想品牌或品种排名/ Ranking of the Ideal Brands or Kinds

注：在药品品牌调查中，消费者经常出现将药品的名称与品牌名称混淆的现象，特此声明。/ In our research on medicines, we find consumers often confused the names and the brands.

排名 Brand Ranking	品牌或品种 Brands or Kinds	人数 Number	百分比 Percent
1	吗叮啉 Tabeliae Domperidoni Gastrokinetic	127	21.2
2	三九胃泰 999	108	18.0
3	氟哌酸 Norfloxacin Capsules	52	8.7
4	胃友 Weiyou	12	2.0
4	胃必治 Bisuc	12	2.0
5	胃舒平 Compound Aluminium Hydroxide Tablets	9	1.5
5	泻立停 Xieliting	9	1.5
6	快胃片 Kuaiweipian	6	1.0
6	黄连素 Bering Hydrochloride Tablets	6	1.0
7	利君沙 Lijunsha	5	0.8
7	丽珠得乐 LZ	5	0.8
8	诺氟沙星 Norfloxacin	4	0.7
8	昂立一号 Only One	4	0.7

n=599

3-5 样本、男性各年龄层、女性各年龄层的品牌习惯/ Brand Habit in Consuming Digestive System Medicines by the Whole Sample, Age and Gender Groups

	人数 Number	基本固定用一个牌子 used in only one brand	比较固定地用两个或三个牌子 used in two or three brands	基本上不太固定牌子 no brand preference
样本 Sample	252	51.2	28.6	20.2
男性 Male	121	49.6	28.9	21.5
16~24 岁 Age	18	61.1	22.2	16.7
25~34 岁 Age	35	40.0	34.3	25.7
35~44 岁 Age	35	51.4	31.4	17.1
45~54 岁 Age	23	43.5	26.1	30.4
55~60 岁 Age	10	70.0	20.0	10.0
女性 Female	131	52.7	28.2	19.1
16~24 岁 Age	22	68.2	22.7	9.1
25~34 岁 Age	41	53.7	22.0	24.4
35~44 岁 Age	31	48.4	32.3	19.4
45~54 岁 Age	26	38.5	38.5	23.1
55~60 岁 Age	11	63.6	27.3	9.1

3-6 样本、男性各年龄层、女性各年龄层最近一年内有无服用的比例/ Whether having Taken Digestive System Medicines Last Year by the Whole Sample, Age and Gender Groups

	人数 Number	吃过 yes	没吃过 no
样本 Sample	601	42.3	57.7
男性 Male	302	40.1	59.9
16~24 岁 Age	64	28.1	71.9
25~34 岁 Age	91	38.5	61.5
35~44 岁 Age	77	45.5	54.5
45~54 岁 Age	46	50.0	50.0
55~60 岁 Age	24	41.7	58.3
女性 Female	299	44.5	55.5
16~24 岁 Age	61	36.1	63.9
25~34 岁 Age	90	45.6	54.4
35~44 岁 Age	74	44.6	55.4
45~54 岁 Age	49	53.1	46.9
55~60 岁 Age	25	44.0	56.0

3-7 选择该类商品的考虑因素/ Ranking of the Considerations in Purchasing

注：本题为多选题，合计百分比超过 100%（Multiple answers）

排名 Ranking	考虑因素 Considerations	人次 Person-time	百分比 Percent
1	见效快 immediate effect	158	62.2
2	医生推荐 recommended by doctors	119	46.9
3	无副作用 no side-effects	44	17.3
4	有名的牌子 famous brand	38	15.0
5	价格适中 reasonable price	36	14.2
6	亲友介绍 introduced by relatives & friends	19	7.5
6	服用方式简便 simple to take	19	7.5
7	广告影响 influence of advertising	15	5.9
8	购买方便 easy to buy	10	3.9
9	其他 others	3	1.2

n=254

3-8 样本、男性各年龄层、女性各年龄层最常服用的种类/ Types of Digestive System Medicines Consumed by the Whole Sample, Age and Gender Groups

	人数 Number	片剂 pill	冲剂 granular formulation	胶囊 capsule	药粉 powder	糖浆 syrup	药丸 bolus	其他 others
样本 Sample	253	51.0	15.4	24.9	0.8	0.4	6.3	1.2
男性 Male	121	48.8	18.2	27.3	0.3	0.8	4.1	0.0
16~24 岁 Age	18	50.0	11.1	33.3	5.6	0.0	0.0	0.0
25~34 岁 Age	35	40.0	25.7	31.4	0.0	0.0	2.9	0.0
35~44 岁 Age	35	42.9	17.1	34.3	0 0	2.9	2.9	0.0
45~54 岁 Age	23	65.2	13.0	8.7	0.0	0.0	13.0	0.0
55~60 岁 Age	10	60.0	20.0	20.0	0.0	0.0	0.0	0.0
女性 Female	132	53.0	12.9	22.7	0.8	0.0	8.3	2.3
16~24 岁 Age	22	72.7	4.5	22.7	0.0	0.0	0.0	0.0
25~34 岁 Age	41	53.7	17.1	19.5	0.0	0.0	4.9	4.9
35~44 岁 Age	33	54.5	9.1	18.2	0.0	0.0	15.2	3.0
45~54 岁 Age	25	48.0	20.0	28.0	0.0	0.0	4.0	0.0
55~60 岁 Age	11	18.2	9.1	36.4	9.1	0.0	27.3	0.0

3-9 样本、男性各年龄层、女性各年龄层最常服用的场合/ Settings of Consumption by the Whole Sample, Age and Gender Groups

注：本题为多选题，合计百分比超过 100%（Multiple answers）

	人数 Number	胃痛时 stomach-ache	胃酸时 sour stomach	胃胀气时 bloated	消化不良时 dyslexia	吃太饱时 overeaten	腹泻时 diarrhea	没胃口时 when not want to eat	配药使用 taken with other medicine	其他 others
样本 Sample	251	40.2	12.7	15.9	26.3	3.2	28.3	2.8	1.6	1.6
男性 Male	118	34.7	11.9	19.5	26 3	2.5	31.4	1.7	0.8	1.7
16~24 岁 Age	18	38.9	0.0	22.2	16.7	0.0	27.8	5.6	5.6	0.0
25~34 岁 Age	34	26.5	17.6	11.8	26.5	0.0	44.1	0.0	0.0	0.0
35~44 岁 Age	34	35.3	11.8	20.6	29.4	8.8	26.5	2.9	0.0	2.9
45~54 岁 Age	22	27.3	13.6	27.3	40.9	0.0	27.3	0.0	0.0	4.5
55~60 岁 Age	10	70.0	10.0	20.0	0.0	0.0	20.0	0.0	0.0	0.0
女性 Female	133	45.1	13.5	12.8	26.3	3.8	25.6	3.8	2.3	1.5
16~24 岁 Age	22	45.5	9.1	13.6	22.7	4.5	22.7	0.0	0.0	4.5
25~34 岁 Age	41	51.2	12.2	9.8	36.6	4.9	19.5	2.4	0.0	0.0
35~44 岁 Age	33	51.5	15.2	18.2	15.2	3.0	18.2	3.0	3.0	3.0
45~54 岁 Age	26	26.9	15.4	15.4	23.1	0.0	38.5	7.7	7.7	0.0
55~60 岁 Age	11	45.5	18.2	0.0	36.4	9.1	45.5	9.1	0.0	0.0

3-10 样本、男性各年龄层、女性各年龄层购买肠胃药的场所/ Location of Buying Digestive System Medicines by the Whole Sample, Age and Gender Groups

注：本题为多选题，合计百分比超过 100%（Multiple answers）

	人数 Number	药店 drug store	医院/诊所 hospital	商场 department store/ shopping center
样本 Sample	253	57.3	53.4	2.0
男性 Male	121	57.9	52.1	0.8
16~24 岁 Age	18	66.7	38.9	0.0
25~34 岁 Age	35	51.4	51.4	0.0
35~44 岁 Age	35	71.4	42.9	2.9
45~54 岁 Age	23	47.8	65.2	0.0
55~60 岁 Age	10	40.0	80.0	0.0
女性 Female	132	56.8	54.5	3.0
16~24 岁 Age	22	68.2	45.5	0.0
25~34 岁 Age	41	53.7	56.1	2.4
35~44 岁 Age	32	56.3	53.1	6.3
45~54 岁 Age	26	57.7	53.8	0.0
55~60 岁 Age	11	45.5	72.7	9.1

3-11 家中是否有备用肠胃药的习惯/ The Habit of Keeping Digestive System Medicines at Home

	人数 Number	百分比 Percent
有 yes	326	54.5
没有 no	272	45.5

n=598

3-12 公费/自费医疗的比例/ Proportion of the Free Medical Service

	人数 Number	百分比 Percent
公费医疗 free medical service	263	44.1
自费医疗 own expense	333	55.9

n=596

3-13 不同消费者层的常用品牌或品种/ The Most Frequently Used Brands or Kinds by Market Segments

3-13-1 时尚流行指标/ Fads Popular Index

注：在药品品牌调查中，消费者经常出现将药品的名称与品牌名称混淆的现象，特此声明。/ In our research on medicines, we find consumers often confused the names and the brands.

	人数 Number	第一品牌及百分比 1st / percent	第二品牌及百分比 2nd / percent	第三品牌及百分比 3rd / percent
样本 Sample	253	**吗叮啉 Tabeliae Domperidoni Gastrokinetic (25.3)**	**氟哌酸 Norfloxacin Capsules(15.4)**	**三九胃泰 999(14.2)**
平实生活指向 simple living orientation	149	吗叮啉 Tabeliae Domperidoni Gastrokinetic(22.8)	氟哌酸 Norfloxacin Capsules(17.4) 三九胃泰 999(17.4)	胃必治 Bisuc(2.7)
时尚流行指向 fashion orientation	104	吗叮啉 Tabeliae Domperidoni Gastrokinetic(28.8)	氟哌酸 Norfloxacin Capsules(12.5)	三九胃泰 999(9.6)

3-13-2 广告态度指标/ Advertising Attitude Index

注：在药品品牌调查中，消费者经常出现将药品的名称与品牌名称混淆的现象，特此声明。/ In our research on medicines, we find consumers often confused the names and the brands.

	人数 Number	第一品牌及百分比 1st / percent	第二品牌及百分比 2nd / percent	第三品牌及百分比 3rd / percent
样本 Sample	251	**吗叮啉 Tabeliae Domperidoni Gastrokinetic(25.5)**	**氟哌酸 Norfloxacin Capsules(15.5)**	**三九胃泰 999(14.3)**
广告淡漠指向 indifferent orientation	74	吗叮啉 Tabeliae Domperidoni Gastrokinetic(24.3)	三九胃泰 999(18.9)	氟哌酸 Norfloxacin Capsules(16.2)
中间层 medium	147	吗叮啉 Tabeliae Domperidoni Gastrokinetic(24.5)	氟哌酸 Norfloxacin Capsules(16.3)	三九胃泰 999(11.6)
信赖广告指向 loyal orientation	30	吗叮啉 Tabeliae Domperidoni Gastrokinetic(33.3)	三九胃泰 999(16.7)	氟哌酸 Norfloxacin Capsules(10.0)

3-13-3 饮食健康指标/ Foods & Drink Quality Index

注：在药品品牌调查中，消费者经常出现将药品的名称与品牌名称混淆的现象，特此声明。/ In our research on medicines, we find consumers often confused the names and the brands.

	人数 Number	第一品牌及百分比 1st / percent	第二品牌及百分比 2nd / percent	第三品牌及百分比 3rd / percent
样本 Sample	253	**吗叮啉 Tabeliae Domperidoni Gastrokinetic(25.3)**	**氟哌酸 Norfloxacin Capsules(15.4)**	**三九胃泰 999(14.2)**
饮食"温饱"指向 "basic" orientation	88	氟哌酸 Norfloxacin Capsules(19.3)	吗叮啉 Tabeliae Domperidoni Gastrokinetic(17.0)	三九胃泰 999(15.9)
中间层 medium	120	吗叮啉 Tabeliae Domperidoni Gastrokinetic(25.8)	三九胃泰 999(15.8)	氟哌酸 Norfloxacin Capsules(15.0)
健康营养指向 health & nutrition orientation	45	吗叮啉 Tabeliae Domperidoni Gastrokinetic(40.0)	氟哌酸 Norfloxacin Capsules(8.9)	三九胃泰 999(6.7)

● 沈阳 / Shenyang

3-1 最近一年内有无服用的比例/ Whether having Taken Digestive System Medicines Last Year

	人数 Number	百分比 Percent
吃过 yes	231	38.5
没吃过 no	369	61.5

n=600

3-2 最常用品牌或品种排名/ Ranking of the Most Frequently Used Brands or Kinds

注：在药品品牌调查中，消费者经常出现将药品的名称与品牌名称混淆的现象，特此声明。/ In our research on medicines, we find consumers often confused the names and the brands.

排名 Brand Ranking	品牌或品种 Brands or Kinds	人数 Number	百分比 Percent
1	胃必治 Bisuc	37	16.2
2	三九胃泰 999	23	10.0
3	黄连素 Bering Hydrochloride Tablets	22	9.6
4	170 胃片 Weipian	18	7.9
5	痢特灵 Liteling	11	4.8
6	磷素钙 Linsugai	10	4.4
6	氟哌酸 Norfloxacin Capsules	10	4.4
7	整肠生 Zhengchangsheng	9	3.9
8	吗叮啉 Tabeliae Domperidoni Gastrokinetic	8	3.5
9	胃舒平 Compound Aluminium Hydroxide Tablets	7	3.1
9	气滞胃疼冲剂 Qi Zhi Wei Teng Chong Ji	7	3.1
10	肝胃去病片 Gan Wei Qu Bing Pian	6	2.6

n=229

3-3 样本、男性各年龄层、女性各年龄层的常用品牌或品种/ The Most Frequently Used Brands or Kinds by the Whole Sample, Age and Gender Groups

注：在药品品牌调查中，消费者经常出现将药品的名称与品牌名称混淆的现象，特此声明。/ In our research on medicines, we find consumers often confused the names and the brands.

	人数 Number	第一品牌及百分比 1st/ percent	第二品牌及百分比 2nd/ percent	第三品牌及百分比 3rd/ percent
样本 Sample	229	**胃必治 Bisuc(16.2)**	**三九胃泰 999(10.0)**	**黄连素 Bering Hydrochloride Tablets(9.6)**
男性 Male	110	**胃必治 Bisuc(11.8)**	**黄连素 Bering Hydrochloride Tablets(10.9)**	**三九胃泰 999(10.0)**
16~24 岁 Age	20	痢特灵 Liteling(15.0) 胃必治 Bisuc(15.0)	三九胃泰 999(10.0) 170 胃片 Weipian(10.0) 多酶片 Duomeipian(10.0)	气滞胃疼冲剂 Qi Zhi Wei Teng Chong Ji(5.0) 吗叮啉 Tabeliae Domperidoni Gastrokinetic(5.0) 胃舒平 Compound Aluminium Hydroxide Tablets(5.0) 泻立停 Xieliting(5.0) 黄连素 Bering Hydrochloride Tablets(5.0) 吡哌酸片 Bi Pai Suan Pian(5.0) 氟哌酸 Norfloxacin Capsules(5.0)
25~34 岁 Age	33	氟哌酸 Norfloxacin Capsules(15.2) 胃必治 Bisuc(15.2)	黄连素 Bering Hydrochloride Tablets(9.1)	痢特灵 Liteling(6.1) 三九胃泰 999(6.1) 整肠生 Zhengchangsheng(6.1)
35~44 岁 Age	29	三九胃泰 999(17.2) 黄连素 Bering Hydrochloride Tablets(17.2)	磷素钙 Linsugai(13.8)	胃必治 Bisuc(10.3) 170 胃片 Weipian(10.3)
45~54 岁 Age	19	黄连素 Bering Hydrochloride Tablets(15.8)	170 胃片 Weipian(10.5) 胃必治 Bisuc(10.5)	整肠生 Zhengchangsheng(5.3) 肠炎宁 Changyanning(5.3) 痢特灵 Liteling(5.3) 泻立停 Xieliting(5.3) 泰胃美 Tagamat(5.3) 三九胃泰 999(5.3) 吗叮啉 Tabeliae Domperidoni Gastrokinetic(5.3) 雷尼替丁 Lei Ni Ti Ding(5.3) 氟哌酸 Norfloxacin Capsules(5.3)
55~60 岁 Age	9	胃舒平 Compound Aluminium Hydroxide Tablets(22.2)	吗叮啉 Tabeliae Domperidoni Gastrokinetic(11.1) 三九胃泰 999(11.1) 斯达舒 Sidashu(11.1) 雷尼替丁 Lei Ni Ti Ding(11.1) 果导片 Guodaopian(11.1) 170 胃片 Weipian(11.1) 磷素钙 Linsugai(11.1)	
女性 Female	119	**胃必治 Bisuc(20.2)**	**三九胃泰 999(10.1)**	**黄连素 Bering Hydrochloride Tablets(8.4)**
16~24 岁 Age	27	胃必治 Bisuc(18.5)	三九胃泰 999(14.8)	江中健胃消食片 Jiangzhong(7.4) 整肠生 Zhengchangsheng(7.4) 肠胃康 Changweikang(7.4) 快胃片 Kuaiweipian(7.4)
25~34 岁 Age	28	胃必治 Bisuc(17.9)	三九胃泰 999(10.7) 黄连素 Bering HydrochlorideTablets(10.7)	痢特灵 Liteling(7.1) 肠胃康 Changweikang(7.1) 肠炎灵 Changyanling(7.1)
35~44 岁 Age	30	胃必治 Bisuc(20.0)	三九胃泰 999(16.7)	胃得乐 Dele(10.0) 170 胃片 Weipian(10.0)
45~54 岁 Age	21	胃必治 Bisuc(23.8)	黄连素 Bering Hydrochloride Tablets(19.0)	气滞胃疼冲剂 Qi Zhi Wei Teng Chong Ji(9.5) 170 胃片 Weipian(9.5)
55~60 岁 Age	13	胃必治 Bisuc(23.1)	胃舒平 Compound Aluminium Hydroxide Tablets(15.4)	氟哌酸 Norfloxacin Capsules(7.7) 黄连素 Bering Hydrochloride Tablets(7.7) 气滞胃疼冲剂 Qi Zhi Wei Teng Chong Ji(7.7) 整肠生 Zhengchangsheng(7.7) 170 胃片 Weipian(7.7)

3-4 理想品牌或品种排名/ Ranking of the Ideal Brands or Kinds

注：在药品品牌调查中，消费者经常出现将药品的名称与品牌名称混淆的现象，特此声明。/ In our research on medicines, we find consumers often confused the names and the brands.

排名 Brand Ranking	品牌或品种 Brands or Kinds	人数 Number	百分比 Percent
1	三九胃泰 999	102	17.0
2	胃必治 Bisuc	85	14.2
3	整肠生 Zhenghcangsheng	31	5.2
3	吗叮啉 Tabeliae Domperidoni Gastrokinetic	31	5.2
4	170 胃片 Weipian	24	4.0
5	黄连素 Bering Hydrochloride Tablets	22	3.7
6	痢特灵 Liteling	18	3.0
7	泻立停 Xieliting	16	2.7
7	磷素钙 Linsugai	16	2.7
8	氟哌酸 Norfloxacin Capsules	13	2.2
9	气滞胃疼冲剂 Qi Zhi Wei Teng Chong Ji	10	1.7

n=600

3-5 样本、男性各年龄层、女性各年龄层的品牌习惯/ Brand Habit in Consuming Digestive System Medicines by the Whole Sample, Age and Gender Groups

	人数 Number	基本固定用一个牌子 used in only one brand	比较固定地用两个或三个牌子 used in two or three brands	基本上不太固定牌子 no brand preference
样本 Sample	231	47.2	29.0	23.8
男性 Male	112	56.3	21.4	22.3
16~24 岁 Age	20	55.0	25.0	20.0
25~34 岁 Age	33	69.7	6.1	24.2
35~44 岁 Age	31	41.9	35.5	22.6
45~54 岁 Age	19	52.6	26.3	21.1
55~60 岁 Age	9	66.7	11.1	22.2
女性 Female	119	38.7	36.1	25.2
16~24 岁 Age	27	33.3	37.0	29.6
25~34 岁 Age	28	28.6	42.9	28.6
35~44 岁 Age	30	26.7	43.3	30.0
45~54 岁 Age	21	71.4	19.0	9.5
55~60 岁 Age	13	46.2	30.8	23.1

3-6 样本、男性各年龄层、女性各年龄层最近一年内有无服用的比例/ Whether having Taken Digestive System Medicines Last Year by the Whole Sample, Age and Gender Groups

	人数 Number	吃过 yes	没吃过 no
样本 Sample	600	38.5	61.5
男性 Male	299	37.5	62.5
16~24 岁 Age	64	31.3	68.8
25~34 岁 Age	89	37.1	62.9
35~44 岁 Age	76	40.8	59.2
45~54 岁 Age	46	41.3	58.7
55~60 岁 Age	24	37.5	62.5
女性 Female	301	39.5	60.5
16~24 岁 Age	64	42.2	57.8
25~34 岁 Age	89	31.5	68.5
35~44 岁 Age	76	39.5	60.5
45~54 岁 Age	48	43.8	56.3
55~60 岁 Age	24	54.2	45.8

3-7 选择该类商品的考虑因素/ Ranking of the Considerations in Purchasing

注：本题为多选题，合计百分比超过 100%（Multiple answers）

排名 Ranking	考虑因素 Considerations	人次 Person-time	百分比 Percent
1	见效快 immediate effect	150	64.9
2	医生推荐 recommended by doctors	74	32.0
3	无副作用 no side-effects	60	26.0
4	价格适中 reasonable price	51	22.1
5	有名的牌子 famous brand	28	12.1
5	服用方式简便 simple to take	28	12.1
6	购买方便 easy to buy	18	7.8
7	亲友介绍 introduced by relatives & friends	17	7.4
8	广告影响 influence of advertising	12	5.2
9	其他 others	2	0.9

n=231

3-8 样本、男性各年龄层、女性各年龄层最常服用的种类/ Types of Digestive System Medicines Consumed by the Whole Sample, Age and Gender Groups

	人数 Number	片剂 pill	冲剂 granular formulation	胶囊 capsule	药粉 powder	糖浆 syrup	药丸 bolus	其他 others
样本 Sample	226	72.1	12.4	14.6	0.0	0.0	0.4	0.4
男性 Male	110	72.7	10.9	16.4	0.0	0.0	0.0	0.0
16~24 岁 Age	19	78.9	15.8	5.3	0.0	0.0	0.0	0.0
25~34 岁 Age	33	72.7	3.0	24.2	0.0	0.0	0.0	0.0
35~44 岁 Age	30	70.0	10.0	20.0	0.0	0.0	0.0	0.0
45~54 岁 Age	19	68.4	21.1	10.5	0.0	0.0	0.0	0.0
55~60 岁 Age	9	77.8	11.1	11.1	0.0	0.0	0.0	0.0
女性 Female	116	71.6	13.8	12.9	0.0	0.0	0.9	0.9
16~24 岁 Age	26	76.9	15.4	3.8	0.0	0.0	3.8	0.0
25~34 岁 Age	28	64.3	17.9	17.9	0.0	0.0	0.0	0.0
35~44 岁 Age	30	66.7	13.3	20.0	0.0	0.0	0.0	0.0
45~54 岁 Age	21	81.0	14.3	4.8	0.0	0.0	0.0	0.0
55~60 岁 Age	11	72.7	0.0	18.2	0.0	0.0	0.0	9.1

3-9 样本、男性各年龄层、女性各年龄层最常服用的场合/ Settings of Consumption by the Whole Sample, Age and Gender Groups

注：本题为多选题，合计百分比超过 100%（Multiple answers）

	人数 Number	胃痛时 stomach-ache	胃酸时 sour stomach	胃胀气时 bloated	消化不良时 dyslexia	吃太饱时 overeaten	腹泻时 diarrhea	没胃口时 when not want to eat	配药使用 taken with other medicine	其他 others
样本 Sample	229	50.7	10.9	8.3	17.5	1.3	32.3	1.3	0.4	1.3
男性 Male	111	44.1	12.6	7.2	18.9	1.8	39.6	1.8	0.0	0.9
16~24 岁 Age	20	45.0	15.0	5.0	20.0	5.0	50.0	0.0	0.0	0.0
25~34 岁 Age	33	48.5	6.1	12.1	9.1	0.0	36.4	3.0	0.0	3.0
35~44 岁 Age	30	43.3	16.7	0.0	16.7	3.3	40.0	3.3	0.0	0.0
45~54 岁 Age	19	47.4	5.3	10.5	26.3	0.0	36.8	0.0	0.0	0.0
55~60 岁 Age	9	22.2	33.3	11.1	44.4	0.0	33.3	0.0	0.0	0.0
女性 Female	118	56.8	9.3	9.3	16.1	0.8	25.4	0.8	0.8	1.7
16~24 岁 Age	27	74.1	7.4	11.1	14.8	0.0	11.1	0.0	0.0	0.0
25~34 岁 Age	28	42.9	10.7	3.6	14.3	0.0	35.7	3.6	3.6	0.0
35~44 岁 Age	30	56.7	10.0	6.7	10.0	3.3	30.0	0.0	0.0	3.3
45~54 岁 Age	21	52.4	14.3	9.5	19.0	0.0	23.8	0.0	0.0	4.8
55~60 岁 Age	12	58.3	0.0	25.0	33.3	0.0	25.0	0.0	0.0	0.0

3-10 样本、男性各年龄层、女性各年龄层购买肠胃药的场所/ Location of Buying Digestive System Medicines by the Whole Sample, Age and Gender Groups

注：本题为多选题，合计百分比超过 100%（Multiple answers）

	人数 Number	药店 drug store	医院/诊所 hospital	商场 department store/ shopping center
样本 Sample	231	72.7	39.4	0.0
男性 Male	112	77.7	35.7	0.0
16~24 岁 Age	20	80.0	40.0	0.0
25~34 岁 Age	33	81.8	24.2	0.0
35~44 岁 Age	31	71.0	41.9	0.0
45~54 岁 Age	19	73.7	36.8	0.0
55~60 岁 Age	9	88.9	44.4	0.0
女性 Female	119	68.1	42.9	0.0
16~24 岁 Age	27	66.7	44.4	0.0
25~34 岁 Age	28	67.9	39.3	0.0
35~44 岁 Age	30	70.0	43.3	0.0
45~54 岁 Age	21	71.4	47.6	0.0
55~60 岁 Age	13	61.5	38.5	0.0

3-11 家中是否有备用肠胃药的习惯/ The Habit of Keeping Digestive System Medicines at Home

	人数 Number	百分比 Percent
有 yes	340	56.7
没有 no	260	43.3

n=600

3-12 公费/自费医疗的比例/ Proportion of the Free Medical Service

	人数 Number	百分比 Percent
公费医疗 free medical service	160	26.7
自费医疗 own expense	439	73.3

n=599

3-13 不同消费者层的常用品牌或品种/ The Most Frequently Used Brands or Kinds by Market Segments

3-13-1 时尚流行指标/ Fads Popular Index

注：在药品品牌调查中，消费者经常出现将药品的名称与品牌名称混淆的现象，特此声明。/ In our research on medicines, we find consumers often confused the names and the brands.

	人数 Number	第一品牌及百分比 1st/ percent	第二品牌及百分比 2nd/ percent	第三品牌及百分比 3rd/ percent
样本 Sample	229	**胃必治 Bisuc(16.2)**	**三九胃泰 999(10.0)**	**黄连素 Bering Hydrochloride Tablets(9.6)**
平实生活指向 simple living orientation	107	胃必治 Bisuc(15.0)	三九胃泰 999(13.1)	170 胃片 Weipian(8.4)
时尚流行指向 fashion orientation	122	胃必治 Bisuc(17.2)	黄连素 Bering Hydrochloride Tablets(11.5)	三九胃泰 999(7.4) 170 胃片 Weipian(7.4)

3-13-2 广告态度指标/ Advertising Attitude Index

注：在药品品牌调查中，消费者经常出现将药品的名称与品牌名称混淆的现象，特此声明。/ In our research on medicines, we find consumers often confused the names and the brands.

	人数 Number	第一品牌及百分比 1st/ percent	第二品牌及百分比 2nd/ percent	第三品牌及百分比 3rd/ percent
样本 Sample	229	**胃必治 Bisuc(16.2)**	**三九胃泰 999(10.0)**	**黄连素 Bering Hydrochloride Tablets(9.6)**
广告淡漠指向 indifferent orientation	67	胃必治 Bisuc(11.9)	氟哌酸 Norfloxacin Capsules(9.0) 170 胃片 Weipian(9.0)	三九胃泰 999(7.5)
中间层 medium	135	胃必治 Bisuc(14.8)	三九胃泰 999(12.6)	黄连素 Bering Hydrochloride Tablets(10.4)
信赖广告指向 loyal orientation	27	胃必治 Bisuc(33.3)	黄连素 Bering Hydrochloride Tablets(14.8)	痢特灵 Liteling(11.1)

3-13-3 饮食健康指标/ Foods & Drink Quality Index

注：在药品品牌调查中，消费者经常出现将药品的名称与品牌名称混淆的现象，特此声明。/ In our research on medicines, we find consumers often confused the names and the brands.

	人数 Number	第一品牌及百分比 1st/ percent	第二品牌及百分比 2nd/ percent	第三品牌及百分比 3rd/ percent
样本 Sample	229	**胃必治 Bisuc(16.2)**	**三九胃泰 999(10.0)**	**黄连素 Bering Hydrochloride Tablets(9.6)**
饮食“温饱”指向 "basic" orientation	73	胃必治 Bisuc(12.3)	三九胃泰 999(11.0)	170 胃片 Weipian(6.8) 氟哌酸 Norfloxacin Capsules(6.8) 黄连素 Bering Hydrochloride Tablets(6.8)
中间层 medium	103	胃必治 Bisuc(16.5)	黄连素 Bering Hydrochloride Tablets(12.6)	170 胃片 Weipian(8.7) 三九胃泰 999(8.7)
健康营养指向 health & nutrition orientation	53	胃必治 Bisuc(20.8)	三九胃泰 999(11.3)	黄连素 Bering Hydrochloride Tablets(7.5) 170 胃片 Weipian(7.5)

4.营养保健品 / Health Care Products

● 北京 / Beijing

4-1 最近一年内有无服用的比例/ Whether having Taken Healthy Care Products Last Year

	人数 Number	百分比 Percent
吃过 yes	268	28.0
没吃过 no	690	72.0

n=958

4-2 最常用品牌或品种排名/ Ranking of the Most Frequently Used Brands or Kinds

注：在药品品牌调查中，消费者经常出现将药品的名称与品牌名称混淆的现象，特此声明。/ In our research on medicines, we find consumers often confused the names and the brands.

排名 Brand Ranking	品牌或品种 Brands or Kinds	人数 Number	百分比 Percent
1	金施尔康 Gold Theragran	17	6.4
2	阿拉斯加鱼油 Alaska Deep Sea Fish Oil	16	6.0
2	昂立一号 Only One	16	6.0
3	盘龙云排毒养颜胶囊 Capsule For Waste Discharging And Youth Ke	14	5.2
4	太太口服液 Taita	10	3.7
4	巨能钙 Junen	10	3.7
5	红太阳彼阳牦牛骨髓壮骨粉 BeYoung	8	3.0
6	钙尔奇 D 片 Gai'erqi D	7	2.6
6	忘不了三 A 脑营养胶丸 Memory Enhancer-3A	7	2.6
6	赛鲨力补氧较囊 Sai Sha Li Oxygen Supply Capsule	7	2.6
7	北京蜂王浆 Beijing Royal Jelly	6	2.2

n=267

4-3 样本、男性各年龄层、女性各年龄层的常用品牌或品种/ The Most Frequently Used Brands or Kinds by the Whole Sample, Age and Gender Groups

注：在药品品牌调查中，消费者经常出现将药品的名称与品牌名称混淆的现象，特此声明。/ In our research on medicines, we find consumers often confused the names and the brands.

	人数 Number	第一品牌及百分比 1st/ percent	第二品牌及百分比 2nd/ percent	第三品牌及百分比 3rd/ percent
样本 Sample	267	**金施尔康 Gold Theragran(6.4)**	**阿拉斯加鱼油 Alaska Deep Sea Fish Oil(6.0) 昂立一号 Only One(6.0)**	**盘龙云排毒养颜胶囊 Capsule For Waste Discharging And Youth Keeping(5.2)**
男性 Male	103	**阿拉斯加鱼油 Alaska Deep Sea Fish Oil(7.8) 昂立一号 Only One(7.8)**	**赛鲨力补氧胶囊 Sai Sha LI Oxygen Supply Capsule(4.9)**	**北京蜂王浆 Beijing Royal Jelly(3.9) 金施尔康 Gold Theragran(3.9)**
16~24 岁 Age	19	赛鲨力补氧胶囊 Sai Sha Li Oxygen Supply Capsule(21.1)	忘不了三 A 脑营养胶丸 Memory Enhancer-3A(10.5) 善存片（小儿善存）Shancun(10.5) 多灵多鱼脑筋 Dolindo(10.5)	盘龙云排毒养颜胶囊 Capsule For Waste Discharging And Youth Keeping(5.3) 巨能钙 Juneng(5.3) 钙尔奇 D 片 Gai'erqi D(5.3) 威士雅骨髓壮骨粉 Weishiya(5.3) 维格尔营养套餐 Vigor(5.3) 维生素 EC(5.3) 人参蜂王浆 Renshen(5.3) 双鹤 Shuanghe(5.3) 东方巨星速溶珍珠粉 Dong Fang Ju Xing(5.3)
25~34 岁 Age	24	金施尔康 Gold Theragran(12.5) 施贵宝 Squibb(12.5)	昂立一号 Only One(8.3)	绿 A Green-A (4.2) 善品生 Shanpinsheng(4.2) 总统 President(4.2) 鹰牌 Eagle's (4.2) 昂泰多帮 Ang Tai Duo Bang(4.2) 司各脱 Scott(4.2) 肾宝口服液 Shenbao(4.2) 荣发养颜宝 Rong Fa Yang Yan Bao(4.2) 金蓝鲨 Jinlansha(4.2) 喜悦洋参含片 Hi-Yeah(4.2) 忘不了三 A 脑营养胶丸 Memory Enhancer-3A(4.2) 太太口服液 Taita(4.2) 红桃 K RHK(4.2) 阿拉斯加鱼油 Alaska Deep Sea Fish Oil(4.2)
35~44 岁 Age	29	昂立一号 Only One(10.3)	蜂王浆 Fengwangjiang(6.9) 阿拉斯加鱼油 Alaska Deep Sea Fish Oil(6.9) 北京蜂王浆 Beijing Royal Jelly(6.9) 东阿阿胶浆 Dong'e(6.9) 金日牌美国洋参丸 Golden Sun(6.9)	华旗参片 Huaqi(3.4) 金日心源素 Jin Ri Xin Yuan Su(3.4) 盖中盖 Gaizhonggai(3.4) 花旗参 Huaqishen(3.4) 西洋参 Xiyangshen(3.4) 隆力奇蛇粉 Longliqi(3.4) 中华鳖精 Zhong Hua Bie Jing(3.4) 一通茶 Yitongcha(3.4) 巨能钙 Juneng(3.4) 钙尔奇 D 片 Gai'erqi D(3.4) 朵而 Duoer(3.4) 多灵多鱼脑筋 Dolindo(3.4) 敖东安神补脑液 Aodong(3.4)
45~54 岁 Age	14	昂立一号 Only One(14.3)	仙牌灵芝茶 Xian(7.1) 总统 President(7.1) 鱼肝油 Yuganyou(7.1) 金施尔康 Gold Theragran(7.1) 鹰牌 Eagle's (7.1) 卵磷脂（保健卵磷脂）Luanlinzhi(7.1) 天赐康黑加仑 Tiancikang(7.1) 赛鲨力补氧胶囊 Sai Sha Li Oxygen Supply Capsule(7.1) 阿拉斯加鱼油 Alaska Deep Sea Fish Oil(7.1)	
55~60 岁 Age	17	阿拉斯加鱼油 Alaska Deep Sea Fish Oil(23.5)	红太阳彼阳牦牛骨髓壮骨粉 Be Yong(17.6)	北京蜂王浆 Beijing Royal Jelly(11.8)

续前表 continued

	人数 Number	第一品牌及百分比 1st/ percent	第二品牌及百分比 2nd/ percent	第三品牌及百分比 3rd/ percent
女性 Female	164	**盘龙云排毒养颜胶囊 Capsule For Waste Discharging And Youth Keeping(7.9) 金施尔康 Gold Theragran(7.9)**	**太太口服液 Taita(5.5)**	**阿拉斯加鱼油 Alaska Deep Sea Fish Oil(4.9) 昂立一号 Only One(4.9) 巨能钙 Juneng(4.9)**
16~24 岁 Age	32	金施尔康 Gold Theragran(15.6)	忘不了三 A 脑营养胶丸 Memory Enhancer-3A(12.5)	昂立一号 Only One(6.3) 巨能钙 Juneng(6.3) 脑轻松 Brain Stranger Capsule(6.3) 太阳神 Apollo(6.3)
25~34 岁 Age	40	金施尔康 Gold Theragran(12.5)	盘龙云排毒养颜胶囊 Capsule For Waste Discharging And Youth Keeping(10.0)	太太口服液 Taita(7.5)
35~44 岁 Age	43	盘龙云排毒养颜胶囊 Capsule For Waste Discharging And Youth Keeping(11.6)	昂立一号 Cnly One(7.0) 太太口服液 Taita(7.0)	金施尔康 Gold Theragran(4.7) 鹰牌 Eagle's (4.7) 美国 T.T.牌天然卵磷脂 T.T(4.7) 双鹤 Shuanghe(4.7) 阿拉斯加鱼油 Alaska Deep Sea Fish Oil(4.7) 巨能钙 Juneng(4.7)
45~54 岁 Age	34	巨能钙 Juneng(11.8)	盘龙云排毒养颜胶囊 Capsule For Waste Discharging And Youth Keeping(8.8) 太太口服液 Taita(8 8)	阿拉斯加鱼油 Alaska Deep Sea Fish Oil(5.9) 朵而 Duoer(5.9) 红太阳彼阳牦牛骨髓壮骨粉 Be Yong(5.9)
55~60 岁 Age	15	阿拉斯加鱼油 Alaska Deep Sea Fish Oil(20.0) 红太阳彼阳牦牛骨髓壮骨粉 Be Yong(20.0)	中华鳖精 Zhong Hua Bie Jing(6.7) 金蜂王 Jinfengwang(6.7) 力思丁 Lisiding(6.7) 仙妮雷德 Xian Ni Lei De(6.7) 生命源 Shengmingyuan(6.7) 钙尔奇 D 片 Gai'erqi(6.7) 昂立一号 Only One(6.7)	

4-4 理想品牌或品种排名/ Ranking of the Ideal Brands or Kinds

注：在药品品牌调查中，消费者经常出现将药品的名称与品牌名称混淆的现象，特此声明。/ In our research on medicines, we find consumers often confused the names and the brands.

排名 Brand Ranking	品牌或品种 Brands or Kinds	人数 Number	百分比 Percent
1	太太口服液 Taita	42	4.2
2	昂立一号 Cnly One	40	4.0
3	朵而 Duoer	22	2.2
4	金施尔康 Gold Theragran	19	1.9
5	阿拉斯加鱼油 Alaska Deep Sea Fish Oil	18	1.8
6	红太阳彼阳牦牛骨髓壮骨粉 Be Young	17	1.7
7	盘龙云排毒养颜胶囊 Capsule For Waste Discharging And Youth Ke	16	1.6
8	忘不了三 A 脑营养胶丸 Memory Enhancer-3A	13	1.3
9	北京蜂王浆 Beijing Royal Jelly	11	1.1
10	三株口服液 3 Strain	10	1.0

n=1009

4-5 样本、男性各年龄层、女性各年龄层最近一年内有无购买的比例/ Proportion of Purchasing in the Last Year by the Whole Sample, Age and Gender Groups

	人数 Number	买过 yes	没买过 no
样本 Sample	1012	26.6	73.4
男性 Male	504	20.4	79.6
16~24 岁 Age	105	19.0	81.0
25~34 岁 Age	151	16.6	83.4
35~44 岁 Age	131	19.8	80.2
45~54 岁 Age	77	23.4	76.6
55~60 岁 Age	40	35.0	65.0
女性 Female	508	32.7	67.3
16~24 岁 Age	108	26.9	73.1
25~34 岁 Age	150	32.0	68.0
35~44 岁 Age	124	35.5	64.5
45~54 岁 Age	84	39.3	60.7
55~60 岁 Age	42	28.6	71.4

4-6 样本、男性各年龄层、女性各年龄层的品牌习惯/ Brand Habit in Consuming Healthy Care Products by the Whole Sample, Age and Gender Groups

	人数 Number	事先已决定品牌，买不到就到别家去买 have set brand in mind if can't buy in one shop then go to another	事先已决定品牌，买不到就换其他品牌 have set brand in mind change to another brand if can't buy	事先未决定品牌，当场才决定某一品牌 buy it depend on the situation
样本 Sample	262	69.1	7.6	23.3
男性 Male	97	64.9	7.2	27.8
16~24 岁 Age	19	78.9	10.5	10.5
25~34 岁 Age	24	58.3	12.5	29.2
35~44 岁 Age	25	72.0	8.0	20.0
45~54 岁 Age	16	50.0	0.0	50.0
55~60 岁 Age	13	61.5	0.0	38.5
女性 Female	165	71.5	7.9	20.6
16~24 岁 Age	29	58.6	17.2	24.1
25~34 岁 Age	48	68.8	6.3	25.0
35~44 岁 Age	44	77.3	2.3	20.5
45~54 岁 Age	32	75.0	9.4	15.6
55~60 岁 Age	12	83.3	8.3	8.3

4-7 样本、男性各年龄层、女性各年龄层最近一年内有无拿营养保健品送过礼/ Whether to Offer Healthy Care Products as Gift Last Year by the Whole Sample, Age and Gender Groups

	人数 Number	送过 yes	没送过 no
样本 Sample	966	12.9	87.1
男性 Male	479	12.5	87.5
16~24 岁 Age	99	10.1	89.9
25~34 岁 Age	148	16.2	83.8
35~44 岁 Age	123	12.2	87.8
45~54 岁 Age	71	8.5	91.5
55~60 岁 Age	38	13.2	86.8
女性 Female	487	13.3	86.7
16~24 岁 Age	107	9.3	90.7
25~34 岁 Age	143	14.0	86.0
35~44 岁 Age	117	14.5	85.5
45~54 岁 Age	80	17.5	82.5
55~60 岁 Age	40	10.0	90.0

4-8 样本、男性各年龄层、女性各年龄层最近一年内有无服用的比例/ Whether having Taken Health Care Products Last Year by the Whole Sample, Age and Gender Groups

	人数 Number	吃过 yes	没吃过 no
样本 Sample	958	28.0	72.0
男性 Male	478	21.8	78.2
16~24 岁 Age	98	19.4	80.6
25~34 岁 Age	144	16.7	83.3
35~44 岁 Age	124	24.2	75.8
45~54 岁 Age	72	19.4	80.6
55~60 岁 Age	40	42.5	57.5
女性 Female	480	34.2	65.8
16~24 岁 Age	106	30.2	69.8
25~34 岁 Age	143	28.0	72.0
35~44 岁 Age	116	37.1	62.9
45~54 岁 Age	78	43.6	56.4
55~60 岁 Age	37	40.5	59.5

4-9 该类商品的来源/ Where Got the Products

注：本题为多选题，合计百分比超过 100%（Multiple answers）

	人次 Person-time	百分比 Percent
药店 drug store	108	40.9
医院/诊所 hospital	15	5.7
商场 department store	76	28.8
超市 supermarket	70	26.5
别人送的 given by others	48	18.2
其他 others	6	2.3

n=264

4-10 选择该类商品的考虑因素/ Ranking of the Considerations in Purchasing

注：本题为多选题，合计百分比超过 100%（Multiple answers）

排名 Ranking	考虑因素 Considerations	人次 Person-time	百分比 Percent
1	功能 function	157	58.8
2	无副作用 no side-effects	66	24.7
3	有名的牌子 famous brand	65	24.3
4	亲友介绍 introduced by relatives & friends	59	22.1
5	服用方式简便 simple to take	57	21.3
6	广告影响 influence of advertising	45	16.9
7	价格适中 reasonable price	40	15.0
8	购买方便 easy to buy	13	4.9
9	其他 others	6	2.2

n=267

4-11 样本、男性各年龄层、女性各年龄层最常服用的种类/ Types of Healthy Care Products Consumed by the Whole Sample, Age and Gender Groups

	人数 Number	美容/养颜的 maintaining	提神醒脑的 refreshing	调节人体器官功能的 adjusting the performance of human organs	补血的 enriching the blood	其他 others
样本 Sample	253	15.0	13.8	62.1	3.6	5.5
男性 Male	99	6.1	20.2	66.7	2.0	5.1
16~24 岁 Age	18	0.0	38.9	50.0	0.0	11.1
25~34 岁 Age	24	12.5	12.5	62.5	4.2	8.3
35~44 岁 Age	27	11.1	25.9	59.3	3.7	0.0
45~54 岁 Age	14	0.0	14.3	85.7	0.0	0.0
55~60 岁 Age	16	0.0	6.3	87.5	0.0	6.3
女性 Female	154	20.8	9.7	59.1	4.5	5.8
16~24 岁 Age	31	9.7	32.3	41.9	3.2	12.9
25~34 岁 Age	34	35.3	8.8	44.1	2.9	8.8
35~44 岁 Age	41	36.6	2.4	58.5	2.4	0.0
45~54 岁 Age	33	6.1	3.0	75.8	9.1	6.1
55~60 岁 Age	15	0.0	0.0	93.3	6.7	0.0

4-12 样本、男性各年龄层、女性各年龄层最常服用的包装形式/ Types of Package of Healthy Care Products Consumed by the Whole Sample, Age and Gender Groups

	人数 Number	片剂 pill	冲剂 granular formulation	口服液 oral liquid	胶囊 capsule	药粉 powder	膏状 paste-type	药丸 bolus	其他 others
样本 Sample	265	23.0	10.2	23.8	35.1	3.0	1.9	1.9	1.1
男性 Male	102	21.6	9.8	25.5	35.3	2.0	2.0	2.9	1.0
16~24 岁 Age	19	31.6	0.0	10.5	47.4	0.0	0.0	10.5	0.0
25~34 岁 Age	24	37.5	4.2	29.2	25.0	0.0	4.2	0.0	0.0
35~44 岁 Age	28	14.3	7.1	35.7	35.7	0.0	3.6	3.6	0.0
45~54 岁 Age	14	21.4	14.3	21.4	35.7	0.0	0.0	0.0	7.1
55~60 岁 Age	17	0.0	29.4	23.5	35.3	11.8	0.0	0.0	0.0
女性 Female	163	23.9	10.4	22.7	35.0	3.7	1.8	1.2	1.2
16~24 岁 Age	32	31.3	9.4	18.8	40.6	0.0	0.0	0.0	0.0
25~34 岁 Age	39	28.2	2.6	30.8	25.6	5.1	2.6	5.1	0.0
35~44 岁 Age	43	18.6	14.0	20.9	34.9	7.0	2.3	0.0	2.3
45~54 岁 Age	34	26.5	11.8	23.5	38.2	0.0	0.0	0.0	0.0
55~60 岁 Age	15	6.7	20.0	13.3	40.0	6.7	6.7	0.0	6.7

4-13 样本、男性各年龄层、女性各年龄层最常服用的场合/ Settings of Consumption by the Whole Sample, Age and Gender Groups

	人数 Number	长期服用 long-time habit	疲劳时 tired	考试前后 before or after exam	睡觉前 before sleep	病愈后 post-illness	其他 others
样本 Sample	261	42.5	19.9	8.0	13.8	4.6	11.1
男性 Male	102	39.2	27.5	8.8	11.8	2.9	9.8
16~24 岁 Age	18	44.4	0.0	38.9	11.1	0.0	5.6
25~34 岁 Age	24	37.5	41.7	4.2	8.3	4.2	4.2
35~44 岁 Age	29	31.0	31.0	3.4	13.8	3.4	17.2
45~54 岁 Age	14	35.7	42.9	0.0	14.3	0.0	7.1
55~60 岁 Age	17	52.9	17.6	0.0	11.8	5.9	11.8
女性 Female	159	44.7	15.1	7.5	15.1	5.7	11.9
16~24 岁 Age	31	45.2	6.5	29.0	6.5	0.0	12.9
25~34 岁 Age	39	38.5	20.5	5.1	15.4	2.6	17.9
35~44 岁 Age	42	47.6	11.9	2.4	16.7	11.9	9.5
45~54 岁 Age	32	43.8	18.8	0.0	18.8	9.4	9.4
55~60 岁 Age	15	53.3	20.0	0.0	20.0	0.0	6.7

4-14 不同消费者层的常用品牌/ The Most Frequently Used Brands by Market Segments

4-14-1 时尚流行指标/ Fads Popular Index

注：在药品品牌调查中，消费者经常出现将药品的名称与品牌名称混淆的现象，特此声明。/ In our research on medicines, we find consumers often confused the names and the brands.

	人数 Number	第一品牌及百分比 1st / percent	第二品牌及百分比 2nd / percent	第三品牌及百分比 3rd / percent
样本 Sample	265	**金施尔康 Gold Theragran(6.0)** **阿拉斯加鱼油 Alaska Deep Sea Fish Oil(6.0)** **昂立一号 Only One(6.0)**	**盘龙云排毒养颜胶囊 Capsule For Waste Discharging And Youth Keeping(5.3)**	**太太口服液 Taita(3.8)** **巨能钙 Juneng(3.8)**
平实生活指向 simple living orientation	100	阿拉斯加鱼油 Alaska Deep Sea Fish Oil(8.0)	昂立一号 Only One(7.0)	金施尔康 Gold Theragran(5.0) 钙尔奇 D 片 Gai'erqi D(5.0) 盘龙云排毒养颜胶囊 Capsule For Waste Discharging And Youth Keeping(5.0)
时尚流行指向 fashion orientation	165	金施尔康 Gold Theragran(6.7)	昂立一号 Only One(5.5) 太太口服液 Taita(5.5) 盘龙云排毒养颜胶囊 Capsule For Waste Discharging And Youth Keeping(5.5)	阿拉斯加鱼油 Alaska Deep Sea Fish Oil(4.8)

4-14-2 广告态度指标/ Advertising Attitude Index

注：在药品品牌调查中，消费者经常出现将药品的名称与品牌名称混淆的现象，特此声明。/ In our research on medicines, we find consumers often confused the names and the brands.

	人数 Number	第一品牌及百分比 1st / percent	第二品牌及百分比 2nd / percent	第三品牌及百分比 3rd / percent
样本 Sample	263	**金施尔康 Gold Theragran(6.5)**	**阿拉斯加鱼油 Alaska Deep Sea Fish Oil(6.1) 昂立一号 Only One(6.1)**	**盘龙云排毒养颜胶囊 Capsule For Waste Discharging And Youth Keeping(5.3)**
广告淡漠指向 indifferent orientation	68	昂立一号 Only One(10.3)	盘龙云排毒养颜胶囊 Capsule For Waste Discharging And Youth Keeping(7.4) 金施尔康 Gold Theragran(7.4)	阿拉斯加鱼油 Alaska Deep Sea Fish Oil(4.4)
中间层 medium	154	阿拉斯加鱼油 Alaska Deep Sea Fish Oil(7.8)	金施尔康 Gold Theragran(7.1)	昂立一号 Only One(5.2)
信赖广告指向 loyal orientation	41	红太阳彼阳牦牛骨髓壮骨粉 BeYoung(9.8) 巨能钙 Juneng(9.8)	太太口服液 Taita(7.3)	盘龙云排毒养颜胶囊 Capsule For Waste Discharging And Youth Keeping(4.9) 朵而 Duoer(4.9)

4-14-3 饮食健康指标/ Foods & Drink Quality Index

注：在药品品牌调查中，消费者经常出现将药品的名称与品牌名称混淆的现象，特此声明。/ In our research on medicines, we find consumers often confused the names and the brands.

	人数 Number	第一品牌及百分比 1st / percent	第二品牌及百分比 2nd / percent	第三品牌及百分比 3rd / percent
样本 Sample	266	**金施尔康 Gold Theragran(6.4)**	**阿拉斯加鱼油 Alaska Deep Sea Fish Oil(6.0) 昂立一号 Only One(6.0)**	**盘龙云排毒养颜胶囊 Capsule For Waste Discharging And Youth Keeping(5.3)**
饮食"温饱"指向 "basic" orientation	39	昂立一号 Only One(12.8)		盘龙云排毒养颜胶囊 Capsule For Waste Discharging And Youth Keeping(7.7) 赛鲨力补氧胶囊 Saishali(7.7)
中间层 medium	119	阿拉斯加鱼油 Alaska Deep Sea Fish Oil(8.4)	昂立一号 Only One(6.7)	盘龙云排毒养颜胶囊 Capsule For Waste Discharging And Youth Keeping(5.9) 金施尔康 Gold Theragran(5.9)
健康营养指向 health & nutrition orientation	108	金施尔康 Gold Theragran(7.4)	巨能钙 Juneng(6.5)	红太阳彼阳牦牛骨髓壮骨粉 Be Young(5.6)

● 上海 / Shanghai

4-1 最近一年内有无服用的比例/ Whether having Taken Healthy Care Products Last Year

	人数 Number	百分比 Percent
吃过 yes	452	45.0
没吃过 no	552	55.0

n=1004

4-2 最常用品牌或品种排名/ Ranking of the Most Frequently Used Brands or Kinds

注：在药品品牌调查中，消费者经常出现将药品的名称与品牌名称混淆的现象，特此声明。/ In our research on medicines, we find consumers often confused the names and the brands.

排名 Brand Ranking	品牌或品种 Brands or Kinds	人数 Number	百分比 Percent
1	昂立一号 Only One	82	18.3
2	万基牌 Wanjipai	47	10.5
3	金日牌美国洋参丸 Golden Sun	28	6.2
4	施贵宝 Squibb	26	5.8
5	神象 Shenxiang	25	5.6
6	康富来洋参 Hongfulel	21	4.7
6	鹰牌 Eagle's	21	4.7
7	高博特盐水瓶 Cobtt	17	3.8
8	盘龙云排毒养颜胶囊 Capsule For Waste Discharging And Youth Ke	14	3.1
9	朵而 Duoer	12	2.7
10	太太口服液 Taita	10	2.2
10	脑白金 Naobaijin	10	2.2
10	恒寿堂 Henshoutang	10	2.2
11	上药牌珍珠粉 Shangyaopai	7	1.6
11	阿拉斯加鱼油 Alaska Deep Sea Fish Oil	7	1.6

n=449

4-3 样本、男性各年龄层、女性各年龄层的常用品牌或品种/ The Most Frequently Used Brands or Kinds by the Whole Sample, Age and Gender Groups

	人数 Number	第一品牌及百分比 1st/ percent	第二品牌及百分比 2nd/ percent	第三品牌及百分比 3rd/ percent
样本 Sample	449	**昂立一号 Only One(18.3)**	**万基牌 Wanjipai(10.5)**	**金日牌美国洋参丸 Golden Sun(6.2)**
男性 Male	210	**昂立一号 Only One(24.8)**	**万基牌 Wanjipai(10.0)**	**鹰牌 Eagle's (8.6)**
16~24 岁 Age	23	康富来洋参 Hongfulel(13.0) 万基牌 Wanjipai(13.0)	施贵宝 Squibb(8.7) 昂立一号 Only One(8.7) 脑白金 Naobaijin(8.7)	HYPER(4.3) 恒寿堂 Henshoudang(4.3) 脑轻松 Brain Stranger Capsule(4.3) 鹰牌 Eagle's (4.3) 绿 A Green-A(4.3) 金日牌美国洋参丸 Golden Sun(4.3) 丁维葡萄糖口服液 Dingwei(4.3) 安利 Amway(4.3) 隆力奇蛇粉 Longliqi(4.3) 阿拉斯加鱼油 Alaska Deep Sea Fish Oil(4.3)
25~34 岁 Age	63	昂立一号 Only One(27.0)	鹰牌 Eagle's (11.1)	康富来洋参 Hongfulel(9.5) 金日牌美国洋参丸 Golden Sun(9.5)
35~44 岁 Age	55	昂立一号 Only One(25.5)	万基牌 Wanjipai(12.7) 鹰牌 Eagle's (12.7)	高博特盐水瓶 Cobtt(7.3)
45~54 岁 Age	46	昂立一号 Only One(32.6)	万基牌 Wanjipai(13.0)	金日牌美国洋参丸 Golden Sun(8.7)
55~60 岁 Age	23	金日牌美国洋参丸 Golden Sun(17.4) 昂立一号 Only One(17.4)	神象 Shenxiang(13.0)	高博特盐水瓶 Cobtt(8.7) 施贵宝 Squibb(8.7)
女性 Female	239	**昂立一号 Only One(12.6)**	**万基牌 Wanjipai(10.9)**	**神象 Shenxiang (7.5)**
16~24 岁 Age	32	万基牌 Wanjipai(15.6)	恒寿堂 Henshoudang(9.4) 施贵宝 Squibb(9.4)	康富来洋参 Hongfulel(6.3) 盘龙云排毒养颜胶囊 Capsule For Waste Discharging And Youth Keeping(6.3)
25~34 岁 Age	64	昂立一号 Only One(15.6)	万基牌 Wanjipai(10.9)	太太口服液 Taita(9.4)
35~44 岁 Age	74	昂立一号 Only One(13.5)	万基牌 Wanjipai(10.8)	神象 Shenxiang (8.1)
45~54 岁 Age	44	昂立一号 Only One(13.6)	神象 Shenxiang (9.1)	金日牌美国洋参丸 Golden Sun(6.8) 万基牌 Wanjipai(6.8) 施贵宝 Squibb(6.8)
55~60 岁 Age	25	神象 Shenxiang (20.0)	施贵宝 Squibb(16.0)	昂立一号 Only One(12.0) 万基牌 Wanjipai(12.0)

4-4 理想品牌或品种排名/ Ranking of the Ideal Brands or Kinds

注：在药品品牌调查中，消费者经常出现将药品的名称与品牌名称混淆的现象，特此声明。/ In our research on medicines, we find consumers often confused the names and the brands.

排名 Brand Ranking	品牌或品种 Brands or Kinds	人数 Number	百分比 Percent
1	昂立一号 Only One	238	23.5
2	万基牌 Wanjipai	109	10.8
3	鹰牌 Eagle's	54	5.3
4	金日牌美国洋参丸 Golden Sun	53	5.2
5	脑白金 Naobaijin	52	5.1
6	康富来洋参 Hongfulel	49	4.8
7	神象 Shenxiang	38	3.8
8	施贵宝 Squibb	30	3.0
9	朵而 Duoer	29	2.9
10	高博特盐水瓶 Cobtt	28	2.8

n=1012

4-5 样本、男性各年龄层、女性各年龄层最近一年内有无购买的比例/ Proportion of Purchasing in the Last Year by the Whole Sample, Age and Gender Groups

	人数 Number	买过 yes	没买过 no
样本 Sample	1014	47.3	52.7
男性 Male	509	44.6	55.4
16~24 岁 Age	109	22.0	78.0
25~34 岁 Age	146	47.3	52.7
35~44 岁 Age	130	50.0	50.0
45~54 岁 Age	85	54.1	45.9
55~60 岁 Age	39	59.0	41.0
女性 Female	505	50.1	49.9
16~24 岁 Age	108	30.6	69.4
25~34 岁 Age	144	49.3	50.7
35~44 岁 Age	130	60.8	39.2
45~54 岁 Age	82	57.3	42.7
55~60 岁 Age	41	56.1	43.9

4-6 样本、男性各年龄层、女性各年龄层的品牌习惯/ Brand Habit in Consuming Healthy Care Products by the Whole Sample, Age and Gender Groups

	人数 Number	事先已决定品牌，买不到就到别家去买 have set brand in mind if can't buy in one shop then go to another	事先已决定品牌，买不到就换其他品牌 have set brand in mind change to another brand if can't buy	事先未决定品牌，当场才决定某一品牌 buy it depend on the situation
样本 Sample	478	56.9	21.1	22.0
男性 Male	225	52.9	22.2	24.9
16~24 岁 Age	23	60.9	8.7	30.4
25~34 岁 Age	69	56.5	24.6	18.8
35~44 岁 Age	64	45.3	25.0	29.7
45~54 岁 Age	46	56.5	21.7	21.7
55~60 岁 Age	23	47.8	21.7	30.4
女性 Female	253	60.5	20.2	19.4
16~24 岁 Age	33	60.6	21.2	18.2
25~34 岁 Age	71	59.2	15.5	25.4
35~44 岁 Age	79	59.5	22.8	17.7
45~54 岁 Age	47	68.1	14.9	17.0
55~60 岁 Age	23	52.2	34.8	13.0

4-7 样本、男性各年龄层、女性各年龄层最近一年内有无拿营养保健品送过礼/ Whether to Offer Healthy Care Products as Gift Last Year by the Whole Sample, Age and Gender Groups

	人数 Number	送过 yes	没送过 no
样本 Sample	**1002**	**29.8**	**70.2**
男性 Male	**504**	**26.2**	**73.8**
16~24 岁 Age	108	13.0	87.0
25~34 岁 Age	144	31.9	68.1
35~44 岁 Age	130	26.9	73.1
45~54 岁 Age	85	29.4	70.6
55~60 岁 Age	37	32.4	67.6
女性 Female	**498**	**33.5**	**66.5**
16~24 岁 Age	108	23.1	76.9
25~34 岁 Age	138	32.6	67.4
35~44 岁 Age	130	37.7	62.3
45~54 岁 Age	82	41.5	58.5
55~60 岁 Age	40	35.0	65.0

4-8 样本、男性各年龄层、女性各年龄层最近一年内有无服用的比例/ Whether having Taken Health Care Products Last Year by the Whole Sample, Age and Gender Groups

	人数 Number	吃过 yes	没吃过 no
样本 Sample	**1004**	**45.0**	**55.0**
男性 Male	**506**	**41.7**	**58.3**
16~24 岁 Age	108	21.3	78.7
25~34 岁 Age	145	44.1	55.9
35~44 岁 Age	129	42.6	57.4
45~54 岁 Age	85	54.1	45.9
55~60 岁 Age	39	59.0	41.0
女性 Female	**498**	**48.4**	**51.6**
16~24 岁 Age	108	29.6	70.4
25~34 岁 Age	138	46.4	53.6
35~44 岁 Age	129	57.4	42.6
45~54 岁 Age	82	54.9	45.1
55~60 岁 Age	41	63.4	36.6

4-9 该类商品的来源/ Where Got the Products

注：本题为多选题，合计百分比超过 100%（Multiple answers）

	人次 Person-time	百分比 Percent
药店 drug store	159	35.6
医院/诊所 hospital	7	1.6
商场 department store	76	17.0
超市 supermarket	212	47.4
别人送的 given by others	94	21.0
其他 others	3	0.7

n=447

4-10 选择该类商品的考虑因素/ Ranking of the Considerations in Purchasing

注：本题为多选题，合计百分比超过 100%（Multiple answers）

排名 Ranking	考虑因素 Considerations	人次 Person-time	百分比 Percent
1	功能 function	227	50.6
2	有名的牌子 famous brand	162	36.1
3	服用方式简便 simple to take	106	23.6
4	亲友介绍 introduced by relatives & friends	94	20.9
5	广告影响 influence of advertising	91	20.3
6	价格适中 reasonable price	87	19.4
7	无副作用 no side-effects	84	18.7
8	购买方便 easy to buy	54	12.0
9	其他 others	7	1.6

n=449

4-11 样本、男性各年龄层、女性各年龄层最常服用的种类/ Types of Healthy Care Products Consumed by the Whole Sample, Age and Gender Groups

	人数 Number	美容/养颜的 maintaining	提神醒脑的 refreshing	调节人体器官功能的 adjusting the performance of human organs	补血的 enriching the blood	其他 others
样本 Sample	438	11.6	17.4	65.3	1.8	3.9
男性 Male	205	2.4	19.0	73.7	1.0	3.9
16~24 岁 Age	21	0.0	47.6	42.9	4.8	4.8
25~34 岁 Age	63	3.2	19.0	71.4	0.0	6.3
35~44 岁 Age	54	1.9	16.7	79.6	1.9	0.0
45~54 岁 Age	45	2.2	8.9	84.4	0.0	4.4
55~60 岁 Age	22	4.5	18.2	72.7	0.0	4.5
女性 Female	233	19.7	15.9	57.9	2.6	3.9
16~24 岁 Age	31	22.6	29.0	45.2	3.2	0.0
25~34 岁 Age	61	32.8	16.4	44.3	3.3	3.3
35~44 岁 Age	72	18.1	20.8	59.7	1.4	0.0
45~54 岁 Age	43	11.6	0.0	69.8	4.7	14.0
55~60 岁 Age	26	3.8	11.5	80.8	0.0	3.8

4-12 样本、男性各年龄层、女性各年龄层最常服用的包装形式/ Types of Package of Healthy Care Products Consumed by the Whole Sample, Age and Gender Groups

	人数 Number	片剂 pill	冲剂 granular formulation	口服液 oral liquid	胶囊 capsule	药粉 powder	膏状 paste-toe	药丸 bolus	其他 others
样本 Sample	447	22.1	2.5	22.4	40.5	1.8	0.4	6.0	4.3
男性 Male	209	20.1	1.9	23.0	43.1	0.0	0.5	8.1	3.3
16~24 岁 Age	23	30.4	4.3	0.0	52.2	0.0	0.0	8.7	4.3
25~34 岁 Age	62	11.3	0.0	25.8	50.0	0.0	0.0	11.3	1.6
35~44 岁 Age	55	20.0	3.6	32.7	34.5	0.0	0.0	7.3	1.8
45~54 岁 Age	46	21.7	2.2	17.4	45.7	0.0	0.0	6.5	6.5
55~60 岁 Age	23	30.4	0.0	26.1	30.4	0.0	4.3	4.3	4.3
女性 Female	238	23.9	2.9	21.8	38.2	3.4	0.4	4.2	5.0
16~24 岁 Age	32	31.3	0.0	9.4	43.8	3.1	0.0	12.5	0.0
25~34 岁 Age	63	17.5	4.8	28.6	39.7	4.8	1.6	1.6	1.6
35~44 岁 Age	74	21.6	4.1	20.3	40.5	2.7	0.0	4.1	6.8
45~54 岁 Age	43	27.9	2.3	23.3	39.5	2.3	0.0	0.0	4.7
55~60 岁 Age	26	30.8	0.0	23.1	19.2	3.8	0.0	7.7	15.4

4-13 样本、男性各年龄层、女性各年龄层最常服用的场合/ Settings of Consumption by the Whole Sample, Age and Gender Groups

	人数 Number	长期服用 long-time habit	疲劳时 tired	考试前后 before or after exam	睡觉前 before sleep	病愈后 post-illness	其他 others
样本 Sample	447	43.4	31.5	3.1	13.0	2.9	6.0
男性 Male	208	43.3	36.1	2.4	12.0	1.9	4.3
16~24 岁 Age	22	27.3	40.9	22.7	9.1	0.0	0.0
25~34 岁 Age	62	37.1	43.5	0.0	14.5	0.0	4.8
35~44 岁 Age	55	45.5	36.4	0.0	9.1	3.6	5.5
45~54 岁 Age	46	47.8	32.6	0.0	13.0	4.3	2.2
55~60 岁 Age	23	60.9	17.4	0.0	13.0	0.0	8.7
女性 Female	239	43.5	27.6	3.8	13.8	3.8	7.5
16~24 岁 Age	32	34.4	15.6	18.8	21.9	6.3	3.1
25~34 岁 Age	63	47.6	27.0	4.8	9.5	3.2	7.9
35~44 岁 Age	74	37.8	36.5	0.0	18.9	1.4	5.4
45~54 岁 Age	44	45.5	29.5	0.0	13.6	4.5	6.8
55~60 岁 Age	26	57.7	15.4	0.0	0.0	7.7	19.2

4-14 不同消费者层的常用品牌/ The Most Frequently Used Brands by Market Segments

4-14-1 时尚流行指标/ Fads Popular Index

注：在药品品牌调查中，消费者经常出现将药品的名称与品牌名称混淆的现象，特此声明。/ In our research on medicines, we find consumers often confused the names and the brands.

	人数 Number	第一品牌及百分比 1st / percent	第二品牌及百分比 2nd / percent	第三品牌及百分比 3rd / percent
样本 Sample	445	昂立一号 Only One **(18.4)**	**万基牌 Wanjipai(10.6)**	**金日牌美国洋参丸 Golden Sun(6.1)**
平实生活指向 simple living orientation	208	昂立一号 Only One (18.8)	万基牌 Wanjipai(8.2)	金日牌美国洋参丸 Golden Sun(7.2) 神象 Shenxiang(7.2)
时尚流行指向 fashion orientation	237	昂立一号 Only One (18.1)	万基牌 Wanjipai(12.7)	施贵宝 Squibb(6.8)

4-14-2 广告态度指标/ Advertising Attitude Index

注：在药品品牌调查中，消费者经常出现将药品的名称与品牌名称混淆的现象，特此声明。/ In our research on medicines, we find consumers often confused the names and the brands.

	人数 Number	第一品牌及百分比 1st / percent	第二品牌及百分比 2nd / percent	第三品牌及百分比 3rd / percent
样本 Sample	445	昂立一号 Only One **(18.0)**	**万基牌 Wanjipai(10.6)**	**金日牌美国洋参丸 Golden Sun(6.3)**
广告淡漠指向 indifferent orientation	113	昂立一号 Only One (23.0)	神象 Shengxiang(6.2) 万基牌 Wanjipai(6.2)	高博特盐水瓶 Cobtt(4.4) 施贵宝 Squibb(4.4) 康富来洋参 Hongfulel(4.4) 金日牌美国洋参丸 Golden Sun(4.4)
中间层 medium	267	昂立一号 Only One (18.0)	万基牌 Wanjipai(11.2)	金日牌美国洋参丸 Golden Sun(7.5)
信赖广告指向 loyal orientation	65	万基牌 Wanjipai(15.4)	昂立一号 Only One (9.2) 朵而 Duoer(9.2) 康富来洋参 Hongfulel(9.2) 施贵宝 Squibb(9.2)	脑白金 Naobaijin(4.6) 鹰牌 Eagle's (4.6) 金日牌美国洋参丸 Golden Sun(4.6)

4-14-3 饮食健康指标/ Foods & Drink Quality Index

注：在药品品牌调查中，消费者经常出现将药品的名称与品牌名称混淆的现象，特此声明。/ In our research on medicines, we find consumers often confused the names and the brands.

	人数 Number	第一品牌及百分比 1st / percent	第二品牌及百分比 2nd / percent	第三品牌及百分比 3rd / percent
样本 Sample	447	昂立一号 Only One **(18.3)**	**万基牌 Wanjipai(10.5)**	**金日牌美国洋参丸 Golden Sun(6.3)**
饮食"温饱"指向 "basic" orientation	66	万基牌 Wanjipai(13.6)	鹰牌 Eagle's (9.1)	昂立一号 Only One (7.6) 施贵宝 Squibb(7.6)
中间层 medium	210	昂立一号 Only One (20.5)	万基牌 Wanjipai(10.0)	金日牌美国洋参丸 Golden Sun(7.6)
健康营养指向 health & nutrition orientation	171	昂立一号 Only One (19.9)	万基牌 Wanjipai(9.9)	施贵宝 Squibb(6.4) 神象 Shenxiang(6.4)

● 广州 / Guangzhou

4-1 最近一年内有无服用的比例/ Whether having Taken Healthy Care Products Last Year

	人数 Number	百分比 Percent
吃过 yes	206	20.4
没吃过 no	806	79.6

n=1012

4-2 最常用品牌或品种排名/ Ranking of the Most Frequently Used Brands or Kinds

注：在药品品牌调查中，消费者经常出现将药品的名称与品牌名称混淆的现象，特此声明。/ In our research on medicines, we find consumers often confused the names and the brands.

排名 Brand Ranking	品牌或品种 Brands or Kinds	人数 Number	百分比 Percent
1	白兰氏系列 Brand's	23	11.2
2	太阳神 Apollo	22	10.7
3	太太口服液 Taita	19	9.3
4	美媛春口服液 Meiyuanchun	9	4.4
5	自然饮 Ziranyin	8	3.9
6	红桃 K RHK	7	3.4
6	宝生园（宝生园蜂王浆）Baoshengyuan	7	3.4
7	施贵宝 Squibb	6	2.9
8	鹰牌 Eagle's	5	2.4
8	康富来洋参 Hongfulel	5	2.4

n=205

4-3 样本、男性各年龄层、女性各年龄层的常用品牌或品种/ The Most Frequently Used Brands or Kinds by the Whole Sample, Age and Gender Groups

注：在药品品牌调查中，消费者经常出现将药品的名称与品牌名称混淆的现象，特此声明。/ In our research on medicines, we find consumers often confused the names and the brands.

	人数 Number	第一品牌及百分比 1st/ percent	第二品牌及百分比 2nd/ percent	第三品牌及百分比 3rd/ percent
样本 Sample	205	**白兰氏系列 Brand's(11.2)**	**太阳神 Apollo(10.7)**	**太太口服液 Taita(9.3)**
男性 Male	70	**太阳神 Apollo(17.1)** **白兰氏系列 Brand's(17.1)**	**宝生园（宝生园蜂王浆）Baoshengyuan(5.7)** **鹰牌 Eagle's (5.7)**	
16~24 岁 Age	13	白兰氏系列 Brand's(23.1)	太阳神 Apollo(15.4) 宝生园 Baoshengyuan(15.4)	善存片 Centnm(7.7) 金施尔康 Gold Theragran(7.7) 山姆士 SAM'S(7.7)
25~34 岁 Age	26	太阳神 Apollo(23.1)	白兰氏系列 Brand's(15.4)	鹰牌 Eagle's (11.5)
35~44 岁 Age	16	太阳神 Apollo(25.0)	隆力奇蛇粉(12.5) 白兰氏系列 Brand's(12.5)	自然饮 Ziranyin(6.3) 宝生园 Baoshengyuan(6.3) 施贵宝 Squibb(6.3) 海天螺旋藻 Haitian(6.3) 东燕牌 Dongyan(6.3)
45~54 岁 Age	10	白兰氏系列 Brand's(30.0)	阿拉斯加鱼油 Alaska Deep Sea Fish Oil(10.0) 同仁堂 Tongrentang(10.0) 鹰牌 Eagle's (10.0) 海百福 Haibaifu(10.0)	
55~60 岁 Age	5	敖东安神补脑 Aodong(20.0) 园芝牌蜂王浆(20.0) 宝生园 Baoshengyuan(20.0) 梅雁螺旋藻 Meiyan(20.0) 康泰丝深海鱼油 Kangtaisi(20.0)		
女性 Female	135	**太太口服液 Taita(13.3)**	**白兰氏系列 Brand's(8.1)**	**太阳神 Apollo(7.4)**
16~24 岁 Age	31	美媛春口服液 Meiyuanchun(16.1)	白兰氏系列 Brand's(9.7) 太太口服液 Taita(9.7) 自然饮 Ziranyin(9.7)	朵而 Duoer(6.5) 红桃 K RHK(6.5)
25~34 岁 Age	43	太太口服液 Taita(16.3)	白兰氏系列 Brand's(11.6)	太阳神 Apollo(9.3)
35~44 岁 Age	27	太阳神 Apollo(14.8)	太太口服液 Taita(11.1)	白兰氏系列 Brand's(7.4) 维特健 Weitejian(7.4)
45~54 岁 Age	25	太太口服液 Taita(20.0)	阿拉斯加鱼油 Alaska Deep Sea Fish Oil(8.0) 红桃 K RHK(8.0) 海天螺旋藻 Haitian(8.0) 施贵宝 Squibb(8.0)	白兰氏系列 Brand's(4.0) AMWAY(4.0) 嘉美洋参冲剂 JIamei(4.0) 金芦荟 Jinluhui(4.0) 东阿阿胶浆 E-jiao(4.0) 绿 A (4.0) 太阳神 Apollo(4.0) 康麦斯 K-Max(4.0)
55~60 岁 Age	9	自然饮 Ziranyin(22.2)	红桃 K RHK(11.1) 绿 A (11.1) 华天宝 Huantianbao(11.1) 金芦荟 Jinluhui(11.1)	

4-4 理想品牌或品种排名/ Ranking of the Ideal Brands or Kinds

注：在药品品牌调查中，消费者经常出现将药品的名称与品牌名称混淆的现象，特此声明。/ In our research on medicines, we find consumers often confused the names and the brands.

排名 Brand Ranking	品牌或品种 Brands or Kinds	人数 Number	百分比 Percent
1	太阳神 Apollo	86	8.3
2	太太口服液 Taita	70	6.8
3	白兰氏系列 Brand's	42	4.1
4	红桃 K RHK	27	2.6
5	美媛春口服液 Meiyuanchun	15	1.5
5	康富来洋参 Hongfulel	15	1.5
5	鹰牌 Eagle's	15	1.5
6	自然饮 Ziranyin	13	1.3
7	施贵宝 Squibb	11	1.1

n=1034

4-5 样本、男性各年龄层、女性各年龄层最近一年内有无购买的比例/ Proportion of Purchasing in the Last Year by the Whole Sample, Age and Gender Groups

	人数 Number	买过 yes	没买过 no
样本 Sample	1034	20.0	80.0
男性 Male	499	14.0	86.0
16~24 岁 Age	106	12.3	87.7
25~34 岁 Age	150	16.7	83.3
35~44 岁 Age	127	15.7	84.3
45~54 岁 Age	73	11.0	89.0
55~60 岁 Age	43	9.3	90.7
女性 Female	535	25.6	74.4
16~24 岁 Age	112	24.1	75.9
25~34 岁 Age	158	29.1	70.9
35~44 岁 Age	137	22.6	77.4
45~54 岁 Age	87	31.0	69.0
55~60 岁 Age	41	14.6	85.4

4-6 样本、男性各年龄层、女性各年龄层的品牌习惯/ Brand Habit in Consuming Healthy Care Products by the Whole Sample, Age and Gender Groups

	人数 Number	事先已决定品牌，买不到就到别家去买 have set brand in mind if can't buy in one shop then go to another	事先已决定品牌，买不到就换其他品牌 have set brand in mind change to another brand if can't buy	事先未决定品牌，当场才决定某一品牌 buy it depend on the situation
样本 Sample	204	59.3	15.7	25.0
男性 Male	69	56.5	15.9	27.5
16~24 岁 Age	13	69.2	15.4	15.4
25~34 岁 Age	24	37.5	20.8	41.7
35~44 岁 Age	20	65.0	15.0	20.0
45~54 岁 Age	8	62.5	12.5	25.0
55~60 岁 Age	4	75.0	0.0	25.0
女性 Female	135	60.7	15.6	23.7
16~24 岁 Age	27	59.3	14.8	25.9
25~34 岁 Age	45	51.1	17.8	31.1
35~44 岁 Age	30	73.3	10.0	16.7
45~54 岁 Age	27	70.4	18.5	11.1
55~60 岁 Age	6	33.3	16.7	50.0

4-7 样本、男性各年龄层、女性各年龄层最近一年内有无拿营养保健品送过礼/ Whether to Offer Healthy Care Medicines as Gift Last Year by the Whole Sample, Age and Gender Groups

	人数 Number	送过 yes	没送过 no
样本 Sample	1020	5.2	94.8
男性 Male	492	4.9	95.1
16~24 岁 Age	104	3.8	96.2
25~34 岁 Age	149	6.7	93.3
35~44 岁 Age	125	4.0	96.0
45~54 岁 Age	72	4.2	95.8
55~60 岁 Age	42	4.8	95.2
女性 Female	528	5.5	94.5
16~24 岁 Age	111	6.3	93.7
25~34 岁 Age	157	5.7	94.3
35~44 岁 Age	136	2.9	97.1
45~54 岁 Age	83	8.4	91.6
55~60 岁 Age	41	4.9	95.1

4-8 样本、男性各年龄层、女性各年龄层最近一年内有无服用的比例/ Whether having Taken Health Care Products Last Year by the Whole Sample, Age and Gender Groups

	人数 Number	吃过 yes	没吃过 no
样本 Sample	1012	20.4	79.6
男性 Male	491	14.3	85.7
16~24 岁 Age	104	12.5	87.5
25~34 岁 Age	148	17.6	82.4
35~44 岁 Age	126	12.7	87.3
45~54 岁 Age	71	14.1	85.9
55~60 岁 Age	42	11.9	88.1
女性 Female	521	26.1	73.9
16~24 岁 Age	109	28.4	71.6
25~34 岁 Age	158	27.2	72.8
35~44 岁 Age	132	21.2	78.8
45~54 岁 Age	83	30.1	69.9
55~60 岁 Age	39	23.1	76.9

4-9 该类商品的来源/ Where Got the Products

注：本题为多选题，合计百分比超过 100%（Multiple answers）

	人次 Person-time	百分比 Percent
药店 drug store	94	45.9
医院/诊所 hospital	25	12.2
商场 department store	61	29.8
超市 supermarket	27	13.2
别人送的 given by others	32	15.6
其他 others	9	4.4

n=205

4-10 选择该类商品的考虑因素/ Ranking of the Considerations in Purchasing

注：本题为多选题，合计百分比超过 100%（Multiple answers）

排名 Ranking	考虑因素 Considerations	人次 Person-time	百分比 Percent
1	功能 function	111	53.9
2	有名的牌子 famous brand	63	30.6
3	无副作用 no side-effects	51	24.8
4	亲友介绍 introduced by relatives & friends	44	21.4
5	广告影响 influence of advertising	43	20.9
6	服用方式简便 simple to take	41	19.9
7	价格适中 reasonable price	34	16.5
8	购买方便 easy to buy	17	8.3
9	其他 others	2	1.0

n=206

4-11 样本、男性各年龄层、女性各年龄层最常服用的种类/ Types of Healthy Care Products Consumed by the Whole Sample, Age and Gender Groups

	人数 Number	美容/养颜的 maintaining	提神醒脑的 refreshing	调节人体器官功能的 adjusting the performance of human organs	补血的 enriching the blood	其他 others
样本 Sample	191	13.1	18.8	48.7	16.8	2.6
男性 Male	65	7.7	30.8	53.8	6.2	1.5
16~24 岁 Age	12	0.0	33.3	50.0	8.3	8.3
25~34 岁 Age	24	8.3	37.5	45.8	8.3	0.0
35~44 岁 Age	15	13.3	13.3	73.3	0.0	0.0
45~54 岁 Age	9	11.1	55.6	33.3	0.0	0.0
55~60 岁 Age	5	0.0	0.0	80.0	20.0	0.0
女性 Female	126	15.9	12.7	46.0	22.2	3.2
16~24 岁 Age	29	10.3	24.1	41.4	24.1	0.0
25~34 岁 Age	39	20.5	7.7	41.0	25.6	5.1
35~44 岁 Age	26	23.1	11.5	38.5	26.9	0.0
45~54 岁 Age	23	13.0	8.7	60.9	13.0	4.3
55~60 岁 Age	9	0.0	11.1	66.7	11.1	11.1

4-12 样本、男性各年龄层、女性各年龄层最常服用的包装形式/ Types of Package of Healthy Care Products Consumed by the Whole Sample, Age and Gender Groups

	人数 Number	片剂 pill	冲剂 granular formulation	口服液 oral liquid	胶囊 capsule	药粉 powder	膏状 paste-type	药丸 bolus	其他 others
样本 Sample	205	8.3	7.3	56.6	12.7	2.4	2.9	6.3	3.4
男性 Male	69	10.1	7.2	52.2	13.0	2.9	2.9	5.8	5.8
16~24 岁 Age	13	7.7	0.0	38.5	7.7	0.0	15.4	30.8	0.0
25~34 岁 Age	26	11.5	7.7	65.4	11.5	0.0	0.0	0.0	3.8
35~44 岁 Age	15	6.7	13.3	40.0	13.3	6.7	0.0	0.0	20.0
45~54 岁 Age	10	10.0	10.0	50.0	20.0	10.0	0.0	0.0	0.0
55~60 岁 Age	5	20.0	0.0	60.0	20.0	0.0	0.0	0.0	0.0
女性 Female	136	7.4	7.4	58.8	12.5	2.2	2.9	6.6	2.2
16~24 岁 Age	31	3.2	3.2	61.3	12.9	3.2	0.0	9.7	6.5
25~34 岁 Age	43	7.0	4.7	65.1	9.3	4.7	7.0	2.3	0.0
35~44 岁 Age	28	7.1	10.7	46.4	17.9	0.0	3.6	10.7	3.6
45~54 岁 Age	25	12.0	12.0	52.0	16.0	0.0	0.0	8.0	0.0
55~60 岁 Age	9	11.1	11.1	77.8	0.0	0.0	0.0	0.0	0.0

4-13 样本、男性各年龄层、女性各年龄层最常服用的场合/ Settings of Consumption by the Whole Sample, Age and Gender Groups

	人数 Number	长期服用 long-time habit	疲劳时 tired	考试前后 before or after exam	睡觉前 before sleep	病愈后 post-illness	其他 others
样本 Sample	203	21.2	36.0	6.9	21.2	9.4	5.4
男性 Male	69	21.7	42.0	7.2	17.4	4.3	7.2
16~24 岁 Age	13	30.8	15.4	30.8	15.4	0.0	7.7
25~34 岁 Age	25	0.0	72.0	0.0	12.0	8.0	8.0
35~44 岁 Age	16	50.0	12.5	0.0	25.0	0.0	12.5
45~54 岁 Age	10	10.0	50.0	10.0	20.0	10.0	0.0
55~60 岁 Age	5	40.0	40.0	0.0	20.0	0.0	0.0
女性 Female	134	20.9	32.8	6.7	23.1	11.9	4.5
16~24 岁 Age	31	22.6	32.3	19.4	12.9	6.5	6.5
25~34 岁 Age	43	16.3	44.2	2.3	20.9	11.6	4.7
35~44 岁 Age	28	17.9	28.6	3.6	25.0	25.0	0.0
45~54 岁 Age	23	30.4	26.1	4.3	30.4	8.7	0.0
55~60 岁 Age	9	22.2	11.1	0.0	44.4	0.0	22.2

4-14 不同消费者层的常用品牌/ The Most Frequently Used Brands by Market Segments

4-14-1 时尚流行指标/ Fads Popular Index

注：在药品品牌调查中，消费者经常出现将药品的名称与品牌名称混淆的现象，特此声明。/ In our research on medicines, we find consumers often confused the names and the brands.

	人数 Number	第一品牌及百分比 1st / percent	第二品牌及百分比 2nd / percent	第三品牌及百分比 3rd / percent
样本 Sample	202	**白兰氏系列 Brand's(11.4)**	**太阳神 Apollo(10.9)**	**太太口服液 Taita(9.4)**
平实生活指向 simple living orientation	91	白兰氏系列 Brand's(12.1)	太阳神 Apollo(9.9)	红桃 K RHK(6.6) 自然饮 Ziranyen(6.6)
时尚流行指向 fashion orientation	111	太太口服液 Taita(14.4)	太阳神 Apollo(11.7)	白兰氏系列 Brand's(10.8)

4-14-2 广告态度指标/ Advertising Attitude Index

注：在药品品牌调查中，消费者经常出现将药品的名称与品牌名称混淆的现象，特此声明。/ In our research on medicines, we find consumers often confused the names and the brands.

	人数 Number	第一品牌及百分比 1st / percent	第二品牌及百分比 2nd / percent	第三品牌及百分比 3rd / percent
样本 Sample	201	**白兰氏系列 Brand's(11.4)**	**太阳神 Apollo(10.9)**	**太太口服液 Taita(9.5)**
广告淡漠指向 indifferent orientation	60	太阳神 Apollo(15.0)	白兰氏系列 Brand's(13.3)	太太口服液 Taita(5.0) 鹰牌 Eagle's (5.0) 红桃 K RHK(5.0) 宝生园 Baoshengyuan(5.0)
中间层 medium	118	太太口服液 Taita(10.2) 白兰氏系列 Brand's(10.2)	太阳神 Apollo(9.3)	美媛春口服液 Meiyuanchun(5.1)
信赖广告指向 loyal orientation	23	太太口服液 Taita(17.4)	白兰氏系列 Brand's(13.0)	太阳神 Apollo(8.7) 自然饮 Ziranyen (8.7)

4-14-3 饮食健康指标/ Foods & Drink Quality Index

注：在药品品牌调查中，消费者经常出现将药品的名称与品牌名称混淆的现象，特此声明。/ In our research on medicines, we find consumers often confused the names and the brands.

	人数 Number	第一品牌及百分比 1st / percent	第二品牌及百分比 2nd / percent	第三品牌及百分比 3rd / percent
样本 Sample	203	**白兰氏系列 Brand's(11.3)**	**太阳神 Apollo(10.8)**	**太太口服液 Taita(9.4)**
饮食“温饱”指向 "basic" orientation	29	白兰氏系列 Brand's(17.2)	太太口服液 Taita(10.3) 太阳神 Apollo(10.3)	鹰牌 Eagle's (6.9) 红桃 K RHK(6.9)
中间层 medium	112	太阳神 Apollo(13.4)	太太口服液 Taita(8.9)	白兰氏系列 Brand's(8.0)
健康营养指向 health & nutrition orientation	62	白兰氏系列 Brand's(14.5)	太太口服液 Taita(9.7)	太阳神 Apollo(6.5)

● 重庆 / Chongqing

4-1 最近一年内有无服用的比例/ Whether having Taken Healthy Care Products Last Year

	人数 Number	百分比 Percent
吃过 yes	84	13.8
没吃过 no	525	86.2

n=609

4-2 最常用品牌或品种排名/ Ranking of the Most Frequently Used Brands or Kinds

注：在药品品牌调查中，消费者经常出现将药品的名称与品牌名称混淆的现象，特此声明。/ In our research on medicines, we find consumers often confused the names and the brands.

排名 Brand Ranking	品牌或品种 Brands or Kinds	人数 Number	百分比 Percent
1	太太口服液 Taita	10	12.2
2	红太阳彼阳牦牛骨髓壮骨粉 Be Young	6	7.3
3	红桃 K RHK	5	6.1
4	万基牌 Wanjipai	3	3.7
4	复方阿胶浆 Fu Fang E Jiao Jiang	3	3.7
4	雪莲虫草 Xue Lian Chong Cao	3	3.7
4	三勒浆 Sanlejiang	3	3.7

n=82

4-3 样本、男性各年龄层、女性各年龄层的常用品牌或品种/ The Most Frequently Used Brands or Kinds by the Whole Sample, Age and Gender Groups

	人数 Number	第一品牌及百分比 1st/ percent	第二品牌及百分比 2nd/ percent	第三品牌及百分比 3rd/ percent
样本 Sample	82	**太太口服液 Taita(12.2)**	**红太阳彼阳牦牛骨髓壮骨粉 Be Young(7.3)**	**红桃 K RHK(6.1)**
男性 Male	40	**红太阳彼阳牦牛骨髓壮骨粉 Be Young(10.0)**	**雪莲虫草 Xue Lian Chong Cao (7.5)**	**巨能钙 Juneng(5.0)** **太阳神 Apollo(5.0)** **蜂王浆 Fengwangjiang (5.0)** **三勒浆 Sanlejiang (5.0)**
16~24 岁 Age	9	三勒浆 Sanlejiang(22.2)	巨能钙 Juneng(11.1) 雪莲虫草 Xue Lian Chong Cao (11.1) 太阳神 Apollo(11.1) 洋参含片 Yang Shen Han Pian(11.1) 三精 Sanjing(11.1) 金施尔康 Gold Theragran (11.1)	
25~34 岁 Age	10	复方阿胶浆 Fu Fang E Jiao Jiang(10.0) 红太阳彼阳牦牛骨髓壮骨粉 Be Young (10.0) 红桃 K RHK(10.0) 太太口服液 Taita(10.0) 喜悦洋参含片 Hi-Yeah(10.0) 雪莲虫草 Xue Lian Chong Cao (10.0) 太阳神 Apollo(10.0) 紫云英蜂蜜 Zi Yun Ying Feng Mi(10.0)		
35~44 岁 Age	7	红太阳彼阳牦牛骨髓壮骨粉 Be Young (14.3) 美国花旗参 President(14.3) 御苁蓉 Yucongrong(14.3) 西洋参 Xiyangshen(14.3) 雪莲虫草 Xue Lian Chong Cao (14.3) 金日牌 Golden Sun(14.3) 鹰牌 Eagle's (14.3)		
45~54 岁 Age	10	红太阳彼阳牦牛骨髓壮骨粉 Be Young (20.0) 蜂王浆 Fengwangjiang (20.0)	巨能钙 Juneng(10.0) 万基牌 Wanjipai(10.0) 宝参片 Baoshenpian(10.0)	
55~60 岁 Age	4	阿拉斯加鱼油 Alaska Deep Sea Fish Oil(25.0) 广汉人参蜂王浆 Guang Han Ren Shen Feng Wang Jiang(25.0) 补肾益寿胶囊 Bu Shen Yi Shou Jiao Nang(25.0) 美国鱼油 Mei Guo Yu You(25.0)		

续前表 continued

	人数 Number	第一品牌及百分比 1st/ percent	第二品牌及百分比 2nd/ percent	第三品牌及百分比 3rd/ percent
女性 Female	**42**	**太太口服液 Taita(21.4)**	**红桃 K RHK(9.5)**	**蜂乳 Fengru (4.8) 复方阿胶浆 Fu Fang E Jiao Jiang (4.8) 红太阳彼阳牦牛骨髓壮骨粉 Be Young (4.8) 三株口服液 3 Strain(4.8) 人参蜂王浆 Ren Shen Feng Wang Jiang (4.8) 柔依 Rouyi (4.8) 万基牌 Wanjipai(4.8)**
16~24 岁 Age	9	柔依 Rouyi (22.2)	红桃 K RHK(11.1) 三株口服液 3 Strain(11.1) 人参蜂王浆 Ren Shen Feng Wang Jiang (11.1) 佳加钙 Jiajiagai(11.1) 三勒浆 Sanlejiang (11.1) 葡萄糖酸钙 Pu Tao Tang Suan Gai(11.1) 鱼肝油 Yuganyou(11.1)	
25~34 岁 Age	13	太太口服液 Taita(46.2)	红桃 K RHK(7.7) 美媛春口服液 Mei Yuan Chun Kou Fu Ye(7.7) 田田珍珠口服液 Tiantian Pearl Oral Liquid(7.7) 蜂乳 Fengru(7.7) 万基牌 Wanjipai(7.7) 宫宝 Gongbao(7.7) 雀巢冰糖燕窝(7.7)	
35~44 岁 Age	5	红桃 K RHK(40.0)	太太口服液 Taita(20.0) 枕中健 Zhenzhpngjian(20.0) 寿延春蜂王浆 Shouyanchun(20.0)	
45~54 岁 Age	12	复方阿胶浆 Fu Fang E Jiao Jiang (16.7) 太太口服液 Taita(16.7)	红太阳彼阳牦牛骨髓壮骨粉 Be Young (8.3) 盘龙云排毒养颜胶囊 Capsule For Waste Discharging And Youth Keeping(8.3) 三株口服液 3 Strain(8.3) 天狮营养高钙素 TSGC(8.3) 人参蜂王浆 Ren Shen Feng Wang Jiang (8.3) 西洋参 Xiyabgshen(8.3) 蜂乳 Fengru (8.3) 万基牌 Wanjipai(8.3)	
55~60 岁 Age	3	昂立一号 Only One(33.3) 钙尔奇 D 片 Gaierqi(33.3) 红太阳彼阳牦牛骨髓壮骨粉 Be Young (33.3)		

4-4 理想品牌或品种排名/ Ranking of the Ideal Brands or Kinds

注：在药品品牌调查中，消费者经常出现将药品的名称与品牌名称混淆的现象，特此声明。/ In our research on medicines, we find consumers often confused the names and the brands.

排名 Brand Ranking	品牌或品种 Brands or Kinds	人数 Number	百分比 Percent
1	太太口服液 Taita	93	14.9
2	红桃 K RHK	38	6.1
3	红太阳彼阳牦牛骨髓壮骨粉 Be Young	25	4.0
4	太阳神 Apollo	13	2.1
5	万基牌 Wanjipai	11	1.8
6	柔依 Rouyi	9	1.4
6	三勒浆 Sanlejiang	9	1.4
7	三株口服液 3 Strain	8	1.3
8	昂立一号 Only one	7	1.1

n=623

4-5 样本、男性各年龄层、女性各年龄层最近一年内有无购买的比例/ Proportion of Purchasing in the Last Year by the Whole Sample, Age and Gender Groups

	人数 Number	买过 yes	没买过 no
样本 Sample	623	14.8	85.2
男性 Male	313	13.7	86.3
16~24 岁 Age	63	12.7	87.3
25~34 岁 Age	93	8.6	91.4
35~44 岁 Age	75	12.0	88.0
45~54 岁 Age	54	24.1	75.9
55~60 岁 Age	28	17.9	82.1
女性 Female	310	15.8	84.2
16~24 岁 Age	64	17.2	82.8
25~34 岁 Age	90	20.0	80.0
35~44 岁 Age	73	9.6	90.4
45~54 岁 Age	60	16.7	83.3
55~60 岁 Age	23	13.0	87.0

4-6 样本、男性各年龄层、女性各年龄层的品牌习惯/ Brand Habit in Consuming Healthy Care Products by the Whole Sample, Age and Gender Groups

	人数 Number	事先已决定品牌，买不到就到别家去买 have set brand in mind if can't buy in one shop then go to another	事先已决定品牌，买不到就换其他品牌 have set brand in mind change to another brand if can't buy	事先未决定品牌，当场才决定某一品牌 buy it depend on the situation
样本 Sample	90	58.9	8.9	32.2
男性 Male	42	61.9	9.5	28.6
16~24 岁 Age	8	75.0	0.0	25.0
25~34 岁 Age	8	75.0	0.0	25.0
35~44 岁 Age	9	66.7	11.1	22.2
45~54 岁 Age	12	50.0	25.0	25.0
55~60 岁 Age	5	40.0	0.0	60.0
女性 Female	48	56.3	8.3	35.4
16~24 岁 Age	11	63.6	0.0	36.4
25~34 岁 Age	18	44.4	11.1	44.4
35~44 岁 Age	6	66.7	0.0	33.3
45~54 岁 Age	10	70.0	0.0	30.0
55~60 岁 Age	3	33.3	66.7	0.0

4-7 样本、男性各年龄层、女性各年龄层最近一年内有无拿营养保健品送过礼/ Whether to Offer Healthy Care Products as Gift Last Year by the Whole Sample, Age and Gender Groups

	人数 Number	送过 yes	没送过 no
样本 Sample	606	5.6	94.4
男性 Male	308	5.5	94.5
16~24 岁 Age	62	6.5	93.5
25~34 岁 Age	91	7.7	92.3
35~44 岁 Age	74	5.4	94.6
45~54 岁 Age	53	1.9	98.1
55~60 岁 Age	28	3.6	96.4
女性 Female	298	5.7	94.3
16~24 岁 Age	62	6.5	93.5
25~34 岁 Age	88	4.5	95.5
35~44 岁 Age	70	7.1	92.9
45~54 岁 Age	55	7.3	92.7
55~60 岁 Age	23	0.0	100.0

4-8 样本、男性各年龄层、女性各年龄层最近一年内有无服用的比例/ Whether having Taken Health Care Products Last Year by the Whole Sample, Age and Gender Groups

	人数 Number	吃过 yes	没吃过 no
样本 Sample	609	13.8	86.2
男性 Male	307	13.4	86.6
16~24 岁 Age	62	14.5	85.5
25~34 岁 Age	93	10.8	89.2
35~44 岁 Age	72	9.7	90.3
45~54 岁 Age	53	18.9	81.1
55~60 岁 Age	27	18.5	81.5
女性 Female	302	14.2	85.8
16~24 岁 Age	62	14.5	85.5
25~34 岁 Age	88	15.9	84.1
35~44 岁 Age	71	7.0	93.0
45~54 岁 Age	59	20.3	79.7
55~60 岁 Age	22	13.6	86.4

4-9 该类商品的来源/ Where Got the Products

注：本题为多选题，合计百分比超过 100%（Multiple answers）

	人次 Person-time	百分比 Percent
药店 drug store	52	62.7
医院/诊所 hospital	11	13.3
商场 department store	21	25.3
超市 supermarket	9	10.8
别人送的 given by others	11	13.3
其他 others	1	1.2

n=83

4-10 选择该类商品的考虑因素/ Ranking of the Considerations in Purchasing

注：本题为多选题，合计百分比超过 100%（Multiple answers）

排名 Ranking	考虑因素 Considerations	人次 Person-time	百分比 Percent
1	功能 function	41	50.0
2	价格适中 reasonable price	23	28.0
3	广告影响 influence of advertising	21	25.6
4	无副作用 no side-effects	19	23.2
5	有名的牌子 famous brand	16	19.5
6	服用方式简便 simple to take	15	18.3
7	亲友介绍 introduced by relatives & friends	12	14.6
8	购买方便 easy to buy	9	11.0
9	其他 others	1	1.2

n=82

4-11 样本、男性各年龄层、女性各年龄层最常服用的种类/ Types of Healthy Care Products Consumed by the Whole Sample, Age and Gender Groups

	人数 Number	美容/养颜的 maintaining	提神醒脑的 refreshing	调节人体器官功能的 adjusting the performance of human organs	补血的 enriching the blood	其他 others
样本 Sample	76	10.5	17.1	48.7	15.8	7.9
男性 Male	40	5.0	25.0	57.5	7.5	5.0
16~24 岁 Age	9	0.0	33.3	55.6	11.1	0.0
25~34 岁 Age	10	10.0	30.0	40.0	10.0	10.0
35~44 岁 Age	7	0.0	42.9	57.1	0.0	0.0
45~54 岁 Age	9	11.1	11.1	55.6	11.1	11.1
55~60 岁 Age	5	0.0	0.0	100.0	0.0	0.0
女性 Female	36	16.7	8.3	38.9	25.0	11.1
16~24 岁 Age	9	11.1	11.1	44.4	11.1	22.2
25~34 岁 Age	10	40.0	0.0	30.0	30.0	0.0
35~44 岁 Age	4	0.0	25.0	25.0	50.0	0.0
45~54 岁 Age	11	9.1	9.1	36.4	27.3	18.2
55~60 岁 Age	2	0.0	0.0	100.0	0.0	0.0

4-12 样本、男性各年龄层、女性各年龄层最常服用的包装形式/ Types of Package of Healthy Care Products Consumed by the Whole Sample, Age and Gender Groups

	人数 Number	片剂 pill	冲剂 granular formulation	口服液 oral liquid	胶囊 capsule	药粉 powder	膏状 paste-type	药丸 bolus	其他 others
样本 Sample	80	11.3	11.3	56.3	6.3	5.0	3.8	3.8	2.5
男性 Male	37	18.9	13.5	45.9	5.4	8.1	2.7	2.7	2.7
16~24 岁 Age	9	11.1	22.2	55.6	0.0	0.0	0.0	11.1	0.0
25~34 岁 Age	10	10.0	10.0	60.0	0.0	0.0	10.0	0.0	10.0
35~44 岁 Age	6	50.0	0.0	33.3	0.0	16.7	0.0	0.0	0.0
45~54 岁 Age	7	28.6	14.3	28.6	0.0	28.6	0.0	0.0	0.0
55~60 岁 Age	5	0.0	20.0	40.0	40.0	0.0	0.0	0.0	0.0
女性 Female	43	4.7	9.3	65.1	7.0	2.3	4.7	4.7	2.3
16~24 岁 Age	9	0.0	11.1	66.7	11.1	0.0	0.0	11.1	0.0
25~34 岁 Age	14	7.1	7.1	78.6	0.0	0.0	0.0	0.0	7.1
35~44 岁 Age	5	0.0	20.0	60.0	0.0	0.0	20.0	0.0	0.0
45~54 岁 Age	12	0.0	8.3	50.0	16.7	8.3	8.3	8.3	0.0
55~60 岁 Age	3	33.3	0.0	66.7	0.0	0.0	0.0	0.0	0.0

4-13 样本、男性各年龄层、女性各年龄层最常服用的场合/ Settings of Consumption by the Whole Sample, Age and Gender Groups

	人数 Number	长期服用 long-time habit	疲劳时 tired	考试前后 before or after exam	睡觉前 before sleep	病愈后 post-illness	其他 others
样本 Sample	82	29.3	25.6	8.5	15.9	7.3	13.4
男性 Male	39	30.8	28.2	12.8	10.3	5.1	12.8
16~24 岁 Age	9	0.0	33.3	55.6	0.0	0.0	11.1
25~34 岁 Age	10	20.0	40.0	0.0	0.0	20.0	20.0
35~44 岁 Age	7	42.9	28.6	0.0	28.6	0.0	0.0
45~54 岁 Age	8	50.0	25.0	0.0	12.5	0.0	12.5
55~60 岁 Age	5	60.0	0.0	0.0	20.0	0.0	20.0
女性 Female	43	27.9	23.3	4.7	20.9	9.3	14.0
16~24 岁 Age	9	44.4	22.2	22.2	11.1	0.0	0.0
25~34 岁 Age	14	21.4	28.6	0.0	28.6	7.1	14.3
35~44 岁 Age	5	20.0	40.0	0.0	20.0	0.0	20.0
45~54 岁 Age	12	25.0	8.3	0.0	25.0	25.0	16.7
55~60 岁 Age	3	33.3	33.3	0.0	0.0	0.0	33.3

4-14 不同消费者层的常用品牌/ The Most Frequently Used Brands by Market Segments

4-14-1 时尚流行指标/ Fads Popular Index

注：在药品品牌调查中，消费者经常出现将药品的名称与品牌名称混淆的现象，特此声明。/ In our research on medicines, we find consumers often confused the names and the brands.

	人数 Number	第一品牌及百分比 1st / percent	第二品牌及百分比 2nd / percent	第三品牌及百分比 3rd / percent
样本 Sample	82	太太口服液 Taita(12.2)	红太阳彼阳牦牛骨髓壮骨粉 Be Young(7.3)	红桃 K RHK(6.1)
平实生活指向 simple living orientation	36	红太阳彼阳牦牛骨髓壮骨粉 Be Young(11.1)	太太口服液 Taita(8.3) 三勒浆 Sanlejiang(8.3)	复方阿胶浆 Fu Fang E Jiao Jiang(5.6) 红桃 K RHK(5.6) 蜂王浆 Fengwangjiang(5.6) 雪莲虫草 Xue Lian Chong Cao(5.6)
时尚流行指向 fashion orientation	46	太太口服液 Taita(15.2)	红桃 K RHK(6.5)	三株口服液 3 Strain(4.3) 柔依 Rouyi(4.3) 人参蜂王浆 Ren Shen Feng Wang Jiang(4.3) 万基牌 Wanjipai(4.3) 巨能钙 Juneng(4.3) 红太阳彼阳牦牛骨髓壮骨粉 Be Young(4.3)

4-14-2 广告态度指标/ Advertising Attitude Index

注：在药品品牌调查中，消费者经常出现将药品的名称与品牌名称混淆的现象，特此声明。/ In our research on medicines, we find consumers often confused the names and the brands.

	人数 Number	第一品牌及百分比 1st / percent	第二品牌及百分比 2nd / percent	第三品牌及百分比 3rd / percent
样本 Sample	82	太太口服液 Taita(12.2)	红太阳彼阳牦牛骨髓壮骨粉 Be Young(7.3)	红桃 K RHK(6.1)
广告淡漠指向 indifferent orientation	22	红太阳彼阳牦牛骨髓壮骨粉 Be Young(13.6) 红桃 K RHK(13.6) 太太口服液 Taita(13.6)	三勒浆 Sanlejiang(4.5) 紫云英蜂蜜 Zi Yun Ying Feng Mi(4.5) 雀巢冰糖燕窝 Que Chao Bing Tang Yan Wo(4.5) 美国鱼油 Mei Guo Yu You(4.5) 补肾益寿胶囊 Bu Shen Yi Shou Jiao Nang(4.5) 洋参含片 Yang Shen Han Pian(4.5) 御苁蓉 Yucongrong(4.5) 喜悦洋参含片 Hi-Yeah(4.5) 三株口服液 3 Strain(4.5) 巨能钙 Juneng(4.5) 钙尔奇 D 片 Gaierqi(4.5) 复方阿胶浆 Fu Fang E Jiao Jiang(4.5)	
中间层 medium	49	太太口服液 Taita(8.2)	万基牌 Wanjipai(6.1) 雪莲虫草 Xue Lian Chong Cao(6.1)	柔依 Rouyi(4.1) 蜂王浆 Fengwangjiang(4.1) 人参蜂王浆 Ren Shen Feng Wang Jiang(4.1) 三勒浆 Sanlejiang(4.1) 红桃 K RHK(4.1) 红太阳彼阳牦牛骨髓壮骨粉 Be Young(4.1)
信赖广告指向 loyal orientation	11	太太口服液 Taita(27.3)	昂立一号 Only One(9.1) 复方阿胶浆 Fu Fang E Jiao Jiang(9.1) 红太阳彼阳牦牛骨髓壮骨粉 Be Young(9.1) 巨能钙 Juneng(9.1) 天狮营养高钙素 TSGC(9.1) 西洋参 Xiyangshen(9.1) 蜂乳 Fengru(9.1) 太阳神 Apollo(9.1)	

4-14-3 饮食健康指标/ Foods & Drink Quality Index

注：在药品品牌调查中，消费者经常出现将药品的名称与品牌名称混淆的现象，特此声明。/ In our research on medicines, we find consumers often confused the names and the brands.

	人数 Number	第一品牌及百分比 1st / percent	第二品牌及百分比 2nd / percent	第三品牌及百分比 3rd / percent
样本 Sample	82	太太口服液 Taita(12.2)	红太阳彼阳牦牛骨髓壮骨粉 Be Young(7.3)	红桃 K RHK(6.1)
饮食"温饱"指向 "basic" orientation	16	红太阳彼阳牦牛骨髓壮骨粉 Be Young (18.8)	复方阿胶浆 Fu Fang E Jiao Jiang(12.5)	鹰牌 Eagle's (6.3) 雀巢冰糖燕窝 Que Chao Bing Tang Yan Wo(6.3) 宝参片 Baoshenpian(6.3) 金施尔康 Gold Theragran(6.3) 三精 Sanjing(6.3) 广汉人参蜂王浆 Guang Han Ren Shen Feng Wang Jiang(6.3) 西洋参 Xiyangshen(6.3) 蜂王浆 Fengwangjiang(6.3) 太太口服液 Taita(6.3) 盘龙云排毒养颜胶囊 Capsule For Waste Discharging And Youth Keeping(6.3)
中间层 medium	43	太太口服液 Taita(20.9)	红桃 K RHK(11.6)	三勒浆 Sanlejiang(7.0) 雪莲虫草 Xue Lian Chong Cao(7.0)
健康营养指向 health & nutrition orientation	23	万基牌 Wanjipai(8.7) 巨能钙 Juneng(8.7)	美国鱼油 Mei Guo Yu You(4.3) 鱼肝油 Yuganyou(4.3) 葡萄糖酸钙 Pu Tao Tang Suan Gai(4.3) 寿延春蜂王浆 Shouyanchun(4.3) 枕中健 Zhenzhongjian(4.3) 柔依 Rouyi(4.3) 蜂王浆 Fengwangjiang(4.3) 蜂乳 Fengru(4.3) 西洋参 Xiyangshen(4.3) 人参蜂王浆 Ren Shen Feng Wang Jiang(4.3) 三株口服液 3 Strain(4.3) 红太阳彼阳牦牛骨髓壮骨粉 Be Young(4.3) 钙尔奇 D 片 Gaierqi(4.3) 昂立一号 Only One(4.3)	

● 武汉 / Wuhan

4-1 最近一年内有无服用的比例/ Whether having Taken Healthy Care Products Last Year

	人数 Number	百分比 Percent
吃过 yes	81	13.0
没吃过 no	544	87.0

n=625

4-2 最常用品牌或品种排名/ Ranking of the Most Frequently Used Brands or Kinds

注：在药品品牌调查中，消费者经常出现将药品的名称与品牌名称混淆的现象，特此声明。/ In our research on medicines, we find consumers often confused the names and the brands.

排名 Brand Ranking	品牌或品种 Brands or Kinds	人数 Number	百分比 Percent
1	红桃 K RHK	20	25.3
2	田田珍珠口服液 Tiantian Pearl Oral Liquid	9	11.4
3	西洋参 Xiyangshen	5	6.3
4	太太口服液 Taita	4	5.1
5	巨能钙 Junen	3	3.8
6	施贵宝 Squibb	2	2.5
6	太阳神 Apollo	2	2.5

n=79

4-3 样本、男性各年龄层、女性各年龄层的常用品牌或品种/ The Most Frequently Used Brands or Kinds by the Whole Sample, Age and Gender Groups

注：在药品品牌调查中，消费者经常出现将药品的名称与品牌名称混淆的现象，特此声明。/ In our research on medicines, we find consumers often confused the names and the brands.

	人数 Number	第一品牌及百分比 1st/ percent	第二品牌及百分比 2nd/ percent	第三品牌及百分比 3rd/ percent
样本 Sample	79	**红桃 K RHK(25.3)**	**田田珍珠口服液 Tiantian Pearl Oral Liquid(11.4)**	**西洋参 Xiyangshen(6.3)**
男性 Male	34	**红桃 K RHK(23.5)**	**西洋参 Xiyangshen(14.7)**	**红太阳彼阳牦牛骨髓壮骨粉 Be young(5.9) 花旗参 Huaqishen(5.9)**
16~24 岁 Age	8	红桃 K RHK(37.5)	西洋参 Xiyangshen(25.0)	巨能钙 Juneng(12.5) 施贵宝 Squibb(12.5) 万基牌 Wanjipai(12.5)
25~34 岁 Age	11	太阳神 Apollo(9.1) 花旗参 Huaqishen(9.1) 东阿阿胶浆 E-jiao(9.1) 花旗西洋参冲剂 Hua Qi Xi Yang Shen Chong Ji(9.1) 肾宝口服液 Shenbao(9.1) 西洋参 Xiyangshen(9.1) 三株口服液 3 Strain(9.1) 红桃 K RHK(9.1) 阿拉斯加鱼油 Alaska Deep Sea Fish Oil(9.1)		
35~44 岁 Age	7	红桃 K RHK(42.9)	花旗参 Huaqishen(14.3) 海狗油 Haigouyou(14.3) 金施尔康 Gold Theragran(14.3)	
45~54 岁 Age	4	西洋参 Xiyangshen(50.0)	红太阳彼阳牦牛骨髓壮骨粉 Be young(25.0)	
55~60 岁 Age	4		红太阳彼阳牦牛骨髓壮骨粉 Be young(25.0) 红桃 K RHK(25.0)	
女性 Female	45	**红桃 K RHK(26.7)**	**田田珍珠口服液 Tiantian Pearl Oral Liquid(20.0)**	**太太口服液 Taita(8.9)**
16~24 岁 Age	8	红桃 K RHK(25.0) 田田珍珠口服液 Tiantian Pearl Oral Liquid(25.0)	巨能钙 Juneng(12.5) 一洲洋参丸 Yat Chau(12.5) 三精 Sanjing(12.5) 蜂宝活性珍珠粉 Feng Bao Huo Xing Zhen Zhu Fen(12.5)	
25~34 岁 Age	16	田田珍珠口服液 Tiantian Pearl Oral Liquid(31.3)	红桃 K RHK(25.0)	巨能钙 Juneng(6.3) 太阳神 Apollo(6.3) 金日牌美国洋参丸 Golden Sun(6.3) 健民健脾生血颗粒 Jianmin(6.3) 氨基酸口服液(6.3) 羽西珍珠粉 Yue-sai(6.3)
35~44 岁 Age	9	红桃 K RHK(33.3)	太太口服液 Taita(22.2)	田七花粉口服液 Tianqi(11.1) 田田珍珠口服液 Tiantian Pearl Oral Liquid(11.1) 施贵宝 Squibb(11.1)
45~54 岁 Age	11	红桃 K RHK(27.3)	太太口服液 Taita(18.2)	隆力奇蛇粉 Longliqi(9.1) 田田珍珠口服液 Tiantian Pearl Oral Liquid(9.1) 茶春蜂王浆 Chachun(9.1) 施百健螺旋藻 Shibaijian(9.1)
55~60 岁 Age	1			

4-4 理想品牌或品种排名/ Ranking of the Ideal Brands or Kinds

注：在药品品牌调查中，消费者经常出现将药品的名称与品牌名称混淆的现象，特此声明。/ In our research on medicines, we find consumers often confused the names and the brands.

排名 Brand Ranking	品牌或品种 Brands or Kinds	人数 Number	百分比 Percent
1	红桃 K RHK	88	13.8
2	田田珍珠口服液 Tiantian Pearl Oral Liquid	24	3.8
3	太太口服液 Taita	19	3.0
4	太阳神 Apollo	9	1.4
5	三株口服液 3 Strain	8	1.3
6	施贵宝 Squibb	5	0.8
7	金日牌美国洋参丸 Golden Sun	4	0.6
8	巨能钙 Junen	3	0.5
8	西洋参	3	0.5

n=639

4-5 样本、 男性各年龄层、 女性各年龄层最近一年内有无购买的比例/ Proportion of Purchasing in the Last Year by the Whole Sample, Age and Gender Groups

	人数 Number	买过 yes	没买过 no
样本 Sample	641	13.6	86.4
男性 Male	311	11.6	88.4
16~24 岁 Age	65	12.3	87.7
25~34 岁 Age	89	15.7	84.3
35~44 岁 Age	80	11.3	88.8
45~54 岁 Age	52	5.8	94.2
55~60 岁 Age	25	8.0	92.0
女性 Female	330	15.5	84.5
16~24 岁 Age	69	7.2	92.8
25~34 岁 Age	95	23.2	76.8
35~44 岁 Age	78	12.8	87.2
45~54 岁 Age	62	22.6	77.4
55~60 岁 Age	26	0.0	100.0

4-6 样本、男性各年龄层、女性各年龄层的品牌习惯/ Brand Habit in Consuming Healthy Care Products by the Whole Sample, Age and Gender Groups

	人数 Number	事先已决定品牌，买不到就到别家去买 have set brand in mind if can't buy in one shop then go to another	事先已决定品牌，买不到就换其他品牌 have set brand in mind change to another brand if can't buy	事先未决定品牌，当场才决定某一品牌 buy it depend on the situation
样本 Sample	85	55.3	12.9	31.8
男性 Male	35	51.4	20.0	28.6
16~24 岁 Age	7	28.6	42.9	28.6
25~34 岁 Age	14	71.4	7.1	21.4
35~44 岁 Age	9	33.3	22.2	44.4
45~54 岁 Age	3	33.3	33.3	33.3
55~60 岁 Age	2	100.0	0.0	0.0
女性 Female	50	58.0	8.0	34.0
16~24 岁 Age	5	60.0	0.0	40.0
25~34 岁 Age	21	61.9	0.0	38.1
35~44 岁 Age	10	60.0	20.0	20.0
45~54 岁 Age	14	50.0	14.3	35.7
55~60 岁 Age	0	0	0	0

4-7 样本、 男性各年龄层、 女性各年龄层最近一年内有无拿营养保健品送过礼/ Whether to Offer Healthy Care Products as Gift Last Year by the Whole Sample, Age and Gender Groups

	人数 Number	送过 yes	没送过 no
样本 Sample	634	8.0	92.0
男性 Male	308	7.5	92.5
16~24 岁 Age	64	4.7	95.3
25~34 岁 Age	89	12.4	87.6
35~44 岁 Age	79	3.8	96.2
45~54 岁 Age	51	5.9	94.1
55~60 岁 Age	25	12.0	88.0
女性 Female	326	8.6	91.4
16~24 岁 Age	69	1.4	98.6
25~34 岁 Age	95	20.0	80.0
35~44 岁 Age	77	2.6	97.4
45~54 岁 Age	60	10.0	90.0
55~60 岁 Age	25	0.0	100.0

4-8 样本、 男性各年龄层、 女性各年龄层最近一年内有无服用的比例/ Whether having Taken Health Care Products Last Year by the Whole Sample, Age and Gender Groups

	人数 Number	吃过 yes	没吃过 no
样本 Sample	625	13.0	87.0
男性 Male	304	11.2	88.8
16~24 岁 Age	65	12.3	87.7
25~34 岁 Age	89	12.4	87.6
35~44 岁 Age	80	8.8	91.3
45~54 岁 Age	46	8.7	91.3
55~60 岁 Age	24	16.7	83.3
女性 Female	321	14.6	85.4
16~24 岁 Age	68	11.8	88.2
25~34 岁 Age	94	17.0	83.0
35~44 岁 Age	75	13.3	86.7
45~54 岁 Age	58	20.7	79.3
55~60 岁 Age	26	3.8	96.2

4-9 该类商品的来源/ Where Got the Products

注：本题为多选题，合计百分比超过 100%（Multiple answers）

	人次 Person-time	百分比 Percent
药店 drug store	45	56.3
医院/诊所 hospital	6	7.5
商场 department store	13	16.3
超市 supermarket	11	13.8
别人送的 given by others	18	22.5
其他 others	6	7.5

n=80

4-10 选择该类商品的考虑因素/ Ranking of the Considerations in Purchasing

注：本题为多选题，合计百分比超过 100%（Multiple answers）

排名 Ranking	考虑因素 Considerations	人次 Person-time	百分比 Percent
1	功能 function	48	61.5
2	有名的牌子 famous brand	20	25.6
3	广告影响 influence of advertising	17	21.8
3	亲友介绍 introduced by relatives & friends	17	21.8
3	服用方式简便 simple to take	17	21.8
4	价格适中 reasonable price	16	20.5
4	无副作用 no side-effects	16	20.5
5	其他 others	5	6.4
6	购买方便 easy to buy	3	3.8

n=78

4-11 样本、男性各年龄层、女性各年龄层最常服用的种类/ Types of Healthy Care Products Consumed by the Whole Sample, Age and Gender Groups

	人数 Number	美容/养颜的 maintaining	提神醒脑的 refreshing	调节人体器官功能的 adjusting the performance of human organs	补血的 enriching the blood	其他 others
样本 Sample	77	15.6	9.1	33.8	28.6	13.0
男性 Male	33	0.0	15.2	45.5	27.3	12.1
16~24 岁 Age	8	0.0	25.0	25.0	37.5	12.5
25~34 岁 Age	11	0.0	9.1	63.6	18.2	9.1
35~44 岁 Age	6	0.0	16.7	33.3	33.3	16.7
45~54 岁 Age	4	0.0	0.0	75.0	0.0	25.0
55~60 岁 Age	4	0.0	25.0	25.0	50.0	0.0
女性 Female	44	27.3	4.5	25.0	29.5	13.6
16~24 岁 Age	8	37.5	12.5	0.0	37.5	12.5
25~34 岁 Age	15	20.0	6.7	40.0	26.7	6.7
35~44 岁 Age	9	33.3	0.0	22.2	33.3	11.1
45~54 岁 Age	11	27.3	0.0	27.3	27.3	18.2
55~60 岁 Age	1	0.0	0.0	0.0	0.0	100.0

4-12 样本、男性各年龄层、女性各年龄层最常服用的包装形式/ Types of Package of Healthy Care Products Consumed by the Whole Sample, Age and Gender Groups

	人数 Number	片剂 pill	冲剂 granular formulation	口服液 oral liquid	胶囊 capsule	药粉 powder	膏状 paste-tyoe	药丸 bolus	其他 others
样本 Sample	78	17.9	12.8	56.4	6.4	3.8	1.3	0.0	1.3
男性 Male	34	26.5	11.8	47.1	8.8	2.9	0.0	0.0	2.9
16~24 岁 Age	8	37.5	0.0	50.0	12.5	0.0	0.0	0.0	0.0
25~34 岁 Age	11	18.2	9.1	63.6	9.1	0.0	0.0	0.0	0.0
35~44 岁 Age	7	28.6	14.3	42.9	14.3	0.0	0.0	0.0	0.0
45~54 岁 Age	4	50.0	25.0	25.0	0.0	0.0	0.0	0.0	0.0
55~60 岁 Age	4	0.0	25.0	25.0	0.0	25.0	0.0	0.0	25.0
女性 Female	44	11.4	13.6	63.6	4.5	4.5	2.3	0.0	0.0
16~24 岁 Age	8	25.0	0.0	62.5	0.0	12.5	0.0	0.0	0.0
25~34 岁 Age	15	6.7	13.3	60.0	6.7	6.7	6.7	0.0	0.0
35~44 岁 Age	9	11.1	11.1	77.8	0.0	0.0	0.0	0.0	0.0
45~54 岁 Age	11	9.1	18.2	63.6	9.1	0.0	0.0	0.0	0.0
55~60 岁 Age	1	0.0	100.0	0.0	0.0	0.0	0.0	0.0	0.0

4-13 样本、男性各年龄层、女性各年龄层最常服用的场合/ Settings of Consumption by the Whole Sample, Age and Gender Groups

	人数 Number	长期服用 long-time habit	疲劳时 tired	考试前后 before or after exam	睡觉前 before sleep	病愈后 post-illness	其他 others
样本 Sample	79	19.0	31.6	3.8	29.1	11.4	5.1
男性 Male	34	20.6	35.3	2.9	32.4	2.9	5.9
16~24 岁 Age	8	12.5	25.0	12.5	37.5	12.5	0.0
25~34 岁 Age	11	36.4	36.4	0.0	27.3	0.0	0.0
35~44 岁 Age	7	28.6	28.6	0.0	28.6	0.0	14.3
45~54 岁 Age	4	0.0	75.0	0.0	25.0	0.0	0.0
55~60 岁 Age	4	0.0	25.0	0.0	50.0	0.0	25.0
女性 Female	45	17.8	28.9	4.4	26.7	17.8	4.4
16~24 岁 Age	8	12.5	37.5	12.5	37.5	0.0	0.0
25~34 岁 Age	15	20.0	46.7	0.0	6.7	20.0	6.7
35~44 岁 Age	9	22.2	0.0	0.0	33.3	33.3	11.1
45~54 岁 Age	12	16.7	25.0	8.3	33.3	16.7	0.0
55~60 岁 Age	1	0.0	0.0	0.0	100.0	0.0	0.0

4-14 不同消费者层的常用品牌/ The Most Frequently Used Brands by Market Segments

4-14-1 时尚流行指标/ Fads Popular Index

注：在药品品牌调查中，消费者经常出现将药品的名称与品牌名称混淆的现象，特此声明。/ In our research on medicines, we find consumers often confused the names and the brands.

	人数 Number	第一品牌及百分比 1st / percent	第二品牌及百分比 2nd / percent	第三品牌及百分比 3rd / percent
样本 Sample	**79**	**红桃 K RHK(25.3)**	**田田珍珠口服液 Tiantian Pearl Oral Liquid(11.4)**	**西洋参 Xiyangshen(6.3)**
平实生活指向 simple living orientation	37	红桃 K RHK(21.6)	田田珍珠口服液 Tiantian Pearl Oral Liquid(8.1)	西洋参 Xiyangshen(5.4) 太阳神 Apollo(5.4) 巨能钙 Juneng(5.4)
时尚流行指向 fashion orientation	42	红桃 K RHK(28.6)	田田珍珠口服液 Tiantian Pearl Oral Liquid(14.3)	太太口服液 Taita(7.1) 西洋参 Xiyangshen(7.1)

4-14-2 广告态度指标/ Advertising Attitude Index

注：在药品品牌调查中，消费者经常出现将药品的名称与品牌名称混淆的现象，特此声明。/ In our research on medicines, we find consumers often confused the names and the brands.

	人数 Number	第一品牌及百分比 1st / percent	第二品牌及百分比 2nd / percent	第三品牌及百分比 3rd / percent
样本 Sample	**79**	**红桃 K RHK(25.3)**	**田田珍珠口服液 Tiantian Pearl Oral Liquid(11.4)**	**西洋参 Xiyangshen(6.3)**
广告淡漠指向 indifferent orientation	17	红桃 K RHK(35.3)	红太阳彼阳牦牛骨髓壮骨粉 Be young(5.9) 隆力奇蛇粉 Longliqi(5.9) 太太口服液 Taita(5.9) 太阳神 Apollo(5.9) 花旗参 Huaqishen(5.9) 健民健脾生血颗粒 Jianmin(5.9)	
中间层 medium	54	红桃 K RHK(22.2)	田田珍珠口服液 Tiantian Pearl Oral Liquid(16.7)	太太口服液 Taita(3.7) 西洋参 Xiyangshen(3.7) 施贵宝 Squibb(3.7) 巨能钙 Juneng(3.7)
信赖广告指向 loyal orientation	8	西洋参 Xiyangshen(37.5)	红桃 K RHK(25.0)	巨能钙 Juneng(12.5) 太太口服液 Taita(12.5)

4-14-3 饮食健康指标/ Foods & Drink Quality Index

注：在药品品牌调查中，消费者经常出现将药品的名称与品牌名称混淆的现象，特此声明。/ In our research on medicines, we find consumers often confused the names and the brands.

	人数 Number	第一品牌及百分比 1st / percent	第二品牌及百分比 2nd / percent	第三品牌及百分比 3rd / percent
样本 Sample	**78**	**红桃 K RHK(25.6)**	**田田珍珠口服液 Tiantian Pearl Oral Liquid(11.5)**	**太太口服液 Taita(5.1) 西洋参 Xiyangshen(5.1)**
饮食“温饱”指向 "basic" orientation	15	红桃 K RHK(33.3)	田田珍珠口服液 Tiantian Pearl Oral Liquid(13.3)	隆力奇蛇粉(6.7) 西洋参 Xiyangshen(6.7) 施贵宝 Squibb(6.7) 花旗参 Huaqishen(6.7) 三精 Sanjing(6.7)
中间层 medium	34	红桃 K RHK(32.4)	田田珍珠口服液 Tiantian Pearl Oral Liquid(5.9) 西洋参 Xiyangshen(5.9) 太阳神 Apollo(5.9) 巨能钙 Juneng(5.9) 红太阳彼阳牦牛骨髓壮骨粉 Be young(5.9)	
健康营养指向 health & nutrition orientation	29	田田珍珠口服液 Tiantian Pearl Oral Liquid(17.2)	红桃 K RHK(13.8) 太太口服液 Taita(13.8)	金日牌美国洋参 Golden Sun(3.4) 施百健螺旋藻 Shibaijian(3.4) 羽西珍珠粉 Yue-sai(3.4) 氨基酸口服液 An Ji Suan Kou Fu Ye(3.4) 施贵宝 Squibb(3.4) 东阿阿胶浆 E-jiao(3.4) 西洋参 Xiyangshen(3.4) 田七花粉口服液 Tianqi(3.4) 三株口服液 3 Strain(3.4) 巨能钙 Juneng(3.4)

● 西安 / Xi'an

4-1 最近一年内有无服用的比例/ Whether having Taken Healthy Care Products Last Year

	人数 Number	百分比 Percent
吃过 yes	98	16.4
没吃过 no	501	83.6

n=599

4-2 最常用品牌或品种排名/ Ranking of the Most Frequently Used Brands or Kinds

注：在药品品牌调查中，消费者经常出现将药品的名称与品牌名称混淆的现象，特此声明。/ In our research on medicines, we find consumers often confused the names and the brands.

排名 Brand Ranking	品牌或品种 Brands or Kinds	人数 Number	百分比 Percent
1	太太口服液 Taita	13	13.5
2	红桃 K RHK	8	8.3
3	荣发养颜宝 Rong Fa Yang Yan Bao	4	4.2
4	葡萄糖酸钙 Pu Tao Tang Suan Gai	3	3.1
4	汇仁肾宝 Hui Ren Shen Bao	3	3.1
4	太阳神 Apollo	3	3.1
4	佳加钙 Jiajiagai	3	3.1
4	西洋参 Xiyangshen	3	3.1
4	敖东安神补脑液 Aodong	3	3.1
4	昂立一号 Only one	3	3.1

n=96

4-3 样本、男性各年龄层、女性各年龄层的常用品牌或品种/ The Most Frequently Used Brands or Kinds by the Whole Sample, Age and Gender Groups

注：在药品品牌调查中，消费者经常出现将药品的名称与品牌名称混淆的现象，特此声明。/ In our research on medicines, we find consumers often confused the names and the brands.

	人数 Number	第一品牌及百分比 1st/ percent	第二品牌及百分比 2nd/ percent	第三品牌及百分比 3rd/ percent
样本 Sample	96	**太太口服液 Taita(13.5)**	**红桃 K RHK(8.3)**	**荣发养颜宝 Rong Fa Yang Yan Bao(4.2)**
男性 Male	45	**红桃 K RHK(11.1)**	**太阳神 Apollo(6.7)**	**敖东安神补脑液 Aodong(4.4)** **金维他 Jinweita(4.4)** **三株口服液 3 Strain(4.4)** **花旗参 Huaqishen(4.4)** **汇仁肾宝 Hui Ren Shen Bao(4.4)** **脑白金 Naobaijin(4.4)** **佳加钙 Jiajiagai(4.4)**
16~24 岁 Age	8	红桃 K RHK(12.5) 天狮营养高钙素 TSGC(12.5) 佳加钙 Jiajiagai(12.5) 爱德天维 Aidetianwei(12.5) 金维他 Jinweita(12.5) 金日牌 Golden Sun(12.5) 盖中盖 Gaizhonggai(12.5)		
25~34 岁 Age	13	红桃 K RHK(15.4) 太阳神 Apollo(15.4)	花旗参 Huaqishen(7.7) 螺旋藻 Luoxuanzao(7.7) 舒仲花粉 Shuzhonghuafen(7.7) 汇仁肾宝 Hui Ren Shen Bao(7.7) 昂立一号 Only One(7.7) 金维他 Jinweita(7.7) 洋参冲剂 Yang Shen Chong Ji(7.7) 盘龙云排毒养颜胶囊 Capsule For Waste Discharging And Youth Keeping(7.7) 敖东安神补脑液 Aodong(7.7)	
35~44 岁 Age	16	红桃 K RHK(12.5)	花旗参 Huaqishen(6.3) 鲨鱼甘油 Sha Yu Gan You(6.3) 汇仁肾宝 Hui Ren Shen Bao(6.3) 脑白金 Naobaijin(6.3) 西洋参 Xiyangshen(6.3) 花旗西洋参冲剂 Huaqi(6.3) 太阳神 Apollo(6.3) 佳加钙 Jiajiagai(6.3) 三株口服液 3 Strain(6.3)	
45~54 岁 Age	5	喜悦洋参含片 Hi-Yeah(20.0) 脑黄金 Naohuangjin(20.0) 洋参丸 Yangshenwan(20.0) 脑白金 Naobaijin(20.0) 海藻素 Haizaosu(20.0)		
55~60 岁 Age	3	敖东安神补脑液 Aodong(33.3) 三株口服液 3 Strain(33.3) 维生素 EC(33.3)		

续前表 continued

	人数 Number	第一品牌及百分比 1st/ percent	第二品牌及百分比 2nd/ percent	第三品牌及百分比 3rd/ percent
女性 Female	**51**	**太太口服液 Taita(25.5)**	**荣发养颜宝 Rong Fa Yang Yan Bao(7.8)**	**红桃 K RHK(5.9) 葡萄糖酸钙 Pu Tao Tang Suan Gai(5.9)**
16~24 岁 Age	6	葡萄糖酸钙 Pu Tao Tang Suan Gai(33.3)	佳加钙 Jiajiagai(16.7) 脑黄金 Naohuangjin(16.7) 盖中盖 Gaizhonggai(16.7) 气血和摩美得胶囊 Qi Xue He Mo Mei De Jiao Nang (16.7)	
25~34 岁 Age	20	太太口服液 Taita(35.0)	荣发养颜宝 Rong Fa Yang Yan Bao(15.0)	红桃 K RHK(10.0)
35~44 岁 Age	9	太太口服液 Taita(22.2)	阿拉斯加鱼油 Alaska Deep Sea Fish Oil(11.1) 昂立一号 Only One(11.1) 敖东安神补脑液 Aodong(11.1) 巨能钙 Junen(11.1) 荣发养颜宝 Rong Fa Yang Yan Bao(11.1) 风行牌蜂皇浆 Feng Xing Pai Feng Huang Jiang (11.1) 养血安神口服液 Yang Xue An Shen Kou Fu Ye (11.1)	
45~54 岁 Age	9	太太口服液 Taita(44.4)	西洋参 Yangshen(22.2)	昂立一号 Only One(11.1) 红太阳彼阳牦牛骨髓壮骨粉 Be Yong(11.1) 红桃 K RHK(11.1)
55~60 岁 Age	7	阿胶补血膏 E-jiao(14.3) 天赐康黑加仑 Tian Ci Kuang(14.3) 人参蜂王浆 Ren Shen Feng Wang Jiang(14.3) 吉尾斯酒 Ji Wei Si Jiu(14.3) 花旗洋参丸 Huaqi(14.3) 三精 Sanjin(14.3) 攀达康 Pandakang(14.3)		

4-4 理想品牌或品种排名/ Ranking of the Ideal Brands or Kinds

注：在药品品牌调查中，消费者经常出现将药品的名称与品牌名称混淆的现象，特此声明。/ In our research on medicines, we find consumers often confused the names and the brands.

排名 Brand Ranking	品牌或品种 Brands or Kinds	人数 Number	百分比 Percent
1	红桃 K RHK	34	5.7
2	太太口服液 Taita	30	5.0
3	昂立一号 Only one	19	3.2
4	太阳神 Apollo	12	2.0
5	三宝双喜 San Bao Shuang Xi	11	1.8
6	阿拉斯加鱼油 Alaska Deep Sea Fish Oil	8	1.3
7	人参蜂王浆 Ren Shen Feng Wang Jiang	7	1.2
7	荣发养颜宝 Rong Fa Yang Yan Bao	7	1.2

n=599

4-5 样本、男性各年龄层、女性各年龄层最近一年内有无购买的比例/ Proportion of Purchasing in the Last Year by the Whole Sample, Age and Gender Groups

	人数 Number	买过 yes	没买过 no
样本 Sample	601	17.8	82.2
男性 Male	302	15.6	84.4
16~24 岁 Age	64	7.8	92.2
25~34 岁 Age	91	18.7	81.3
35~44 岁 Age	77	19.5	80.5
45~54 岁 Age	46	15.2	84.8
55~60 岁 Age	24	12.5	87.5
女性 Female	299	20.1	79.9
16~24 岁 Age	61	11.5	88.5
25~34 岁 Age	90	27.8	72.2
35~44 岁 Age	74	17.6	82.4
45~54 岁 Age	49	16.3	83.7
55~60 岁 Age	25	28.0	72.0

4-6 样本、男性各年龄层、女性各年龄层的品牌习惯/ Brand Habit in Consuming Healthy Care Products by the Whole Sample, Age and Gender Groups

	人数 Number	事先已决定品牌，买不到就到别家买 have set brand in mind if can't buy in one shop then go to another	事先已决定品牌，买不到就换其品牌 have set brand in mind change to another brand if can't buy	事先未决定品牌，当场才决定某一品牌 buy it depend on the situation
样本 Sample	104	55.8	21.2	23.1
男性 Male	46	58.7	13.0	28.3
16~24 岁 Age	5	60.0	20.0	20.0
25~34 岁 Age	16	62.5	6.3	31.3
35~44 岁 Age	15	53.3	20.0	26.7
45~54 岁 Age	7	57.1	14.3	28.6
55~60 岁 Age	3	66.7	0.0	33.3
女性 Female	58	53.4	27.6	19.0
16~24 岁 Age	7	28.6	28.6	42.9
25~34 岁 Age	24	50.0	29.2	20.8
35~44 岁 Age	13	61.5	23.1	15.4
45~54 岁 Age	7	71.4	14.3	14.3
55~60 岁 Age	7	57.1	42.9	0.0

4-7 样本、男性各年龄层、女性各年龄层最近一年内有无拿营养保健品送过礼/ Whether to Offer Healthy Care Products as Gift Last Year by the Whole Sample, Age and Gender Groups

	人数 Number	送过 yes	没送过 no
样本 Sample	598	5.4	94.6
男性 Male	302	5.3	94.7
16~24 岁 Age	64	4.7	95.3
25~34 岁 Age	91	8.8	91.2
35~44 岁 Age	77	3.9	96.1
45~54 岁 Age	46	0.0	100.0
55~60 岁 Age	24	8.3	91.7
女性 Female	296	5.4	94.6
16~24 岁 Age	60	3.3	96.7
25~34 岁 Age	90	8.9	91.1
35~44 岁 Age	73	2.7	97.3
45~54 岁 Age	49	6.1	93.9
55~60 岁 Age	24	4.2	95.8

4-8 样本、男性各年龄层、女性各年龄层最近一年内有无服用的比例/ Whether having Taken Health Care Products Last Year by the Whole Sample, Age and Gender Groups

	人数 Number	吃过 yes	没吃过 no
样本 Sample	599	16.4	83.6
男性 Male	302	14.9	85.1
16~24 岁 Age	64	12.5	87.5
25~34 岁 Age	91	14.3	85.7
35~44 岁 Age	77	20.8	79.2
45~54 岁 Age	46	10.9	89.1
55~60 岁 Age	24	12.5	87.5
女性 Female	297	17.8	82.2
16~24 岁 Age	60	10.0	90.0
25~34 岁 Age	90	24.4	75.6
35~44 岁 Age	74	12.2	87.8
45~54 岁 Age	49	18.4	81.6
55~60 岁 Age	24	29.2	70.8

4-9 该类商品的来源/ Where Got the Products

注：本题为多选题，合计百分比超过 100%（Multiple answers）

	人次 Person-time	百分比 Percent
药店 drug store	60	61.9
医院/诊所 hospital	18	18.6
商场 department store	12	12.4
超市 supermarket	6	6.2
别人送的 given by others	11	11.3
其他 others	1	1.0

n=97

4-10 选择该类商品的考虑因素/ Ranking the Considerations in Purchasing

注：本题为多选题，合计百分比超过 100%（Multiple answers）

排名 Ranking	考虑因素 Considerations	人次 Person-time	百分比 Percent
1	功能 function	49	50.5
2	有名的牌子 famous brand	22	22.7
2	广告影响 influence of advertising	22	22.7
2	亲友介绍 introduced by relatives & friends	22	22.7
3	服用方式简便 simple to take	18	18.6
4	价格适中 reasonable price	16	16.5
4	无副作用 no side-effects	16	16.5
5	购买方便 easy to buy	4	4.1
6	其他 others	3	3.1

n=97

4-11 样本、男性各年龄层、女性各年龄层最常服用的种类/ Types of Healthy Care Products Consumed by the Whole Sample, Age and Gender Groups

	人数 Number	美容/养颜的 maintaining	提神醒脑的 refreshing	调节人体器官功能的 adjusting the performance of human organs	补血的 enriching the blood	其他 others
样本 Sample	92	16.3	18.5	48.9	12.0	4.3
男性 Male	45	6.7	24.4	53.3	11.1	4.4
16~24 岁 Age	8	12.5	12.5	50.0	12.5	12.5
25~34 岁 Age	13	7.7	38.5	38.5	15.4	0.0
35~44 岁 Age	16	6.3	18.8	62.5	12.5	0.0
45~54 岁 Age	5	0.0	20.0	60.0	0.0	20.0
55~60 岁 Age	3	0.0	33.3	66.7	0.0	0.0
女性 Female	47	25.5	12.8	44.7	12.8	4.3
16~24 岁 Age	6	0.0	16.7	33.3	33.3	16.7
25~34 岁 Age	19	47.4	5.3	36.8	10.5	0.0
35~44 岁 Age	9	33.3	22.2	44.4	0.0	0.0
45~54 岁 Age	7	0.0	14.3	71.4	14.3	0.0
55~60 岁 Age	6	0.0	16.7	50.0	16.7	16.7

4-12 样本、男性各年龄层、女性各年龄层最常服用的包装形式/ Types of Package of Healthy Care Products Consumed by the Whole Sample, Age and Gender Groups

	人数 Number	片剂 pill	冲剂 granular formulation	口服液 oral liquid	胶囊 capsule	药粉 powder	膏状 paste-type	药丸 bolus	其他 others
样本 Sample	95	13.7	5.3	56.8	17.9	1.1	1.1	3.2	1.1
男性 Male	43	23.3	7.0	51.2	14.0	2.3	0.0	2.3	0.0
16~24 岁 Age	7	14.3	0.0	57.1	28.6	0.0	0.0	0.0	0.0
25~34 岁 Age	13	15.4	7.7	53.8	7.7	7.7	0.0	7.7	0.0
35~44 岁 Age	16	18.8	12.5	56.3	12.5	0.0	0.0	0.0	0.0
45~54 岁 Age	4	75.0	0.0	0.0	25.0	0.0	0.0	0.0	0.0
55~60 岁 Age	3	33.3	0.0	66.7	0.0	0.0	0.0	0.0	0.0
女性 Female	52	5.8	3.8	61.5	21.2	0.0	1.9	3.8	1.9
16~24 岁 Age	6	16.7	0.0	50.0	33.3	0.0	0.0	0.0	0.0
25~34 岁 Age	21	0.0	4.8	61.9	28.6	0.0	0.0	4.8	0.0
35~44 岁 Age	9	11.1	0.0	66.7	11.1	0.0	11.1	0.0	0.0
45~54 岁 Age	9	11.1	11.1	77.8	0.0	0.0	0.0	0.0	0.0
55~60 岁 Age	7	0.0	0.0	42.9	28.6	0.0	0.0	14.3	14.3

4-13 样本、男性各年龄层、女性各年龄层最常服用的场合/ Settings of Consumption by the Whole Sample, Age and Gender Groups

	人数 Number	长期服用 long-time habit	疲劳时 tired	考试前后 before or after exam	睡觉前 before sleep	病愈后 post-illness	其他 others
样本 Sample	97	32.0	25.8	3.1	18.6	12.4	8.2
男性 Male	45	31.1	35.6	6.7	15.6	6.7	4.4
16~24 岁 Age	8	25.0	37.5	12.5	12.5	12.5	0.0
25~34 岁 Age	13	15.4	46.2	7.7	7.7	7.7	15.4
35~44 岁 Age	16	37.5	31.3	6.3	18.8	6.3	0.0
45~54 岁 Age	5	40.0	40.0	0.0	20.0	0.0	0.0
55~60 岁 Age	3	66.7	0.0	0.0	33.3	0.0	0.0
女性 Female	52	32.7	17.3	0.0	21.2	17.3	11.5
16~24 岁 Age	6	66.7	0.0	0.0	16.7	16.7	0.0
25~34 岁 Age	21	23.8	28.6	0.0	19.0	19.0	9.5
35~44 岁 Age	9	22.2	11.1	0.0	33.3	0.0	33.3
45~54 岁 Age	9	33.3	11.1	0.0	22.2	22.2	11.1
55~60 岁 Age	7	42.9	14.3	0.0	14.3	28.6	0.0

4-14 不同消费者层的常用品牌或品种/ The Most Frequently Used Brands or Kinds by Market Segments

4-14-1 时尚流行指标/ Fads Popular Index

注：在药品品牌调查中，消费者经常出现将药品的名称与品牌名称混淆的现象，特此声明。/ In our research on medicines, we find consumers often confused the names and the brands.

	人数 Number	第一品牌及百分比 1st / percent	第二品牌及百分比 2nd / percent	第三品牌及百分比 3rd / percent
样本 Sample	**96**	**太太口服液 Taita(13.5)**	**红桃 K RHK(8.3)**	**荣发养颜宝 Rong Fa Yang Yan Bao(4.2)**
平实生活指向 simple living orientation	51	太太口服液 Taita(15.7)	红桃 K RHK(5.9) 汇仁肾宝 Hui Ren Shen Bao(5.9)	三精 Sanjin(2.0) 金维他 Jinweita(2.0) 风行牌蜂皇浆 Feng Xing Pai Feng Huang Jiang(2.0) 花旗参 Huaqishen(2.0) 盖中盖 Gaizhonggai(2.0) 太阳神 Apollo(2.0) 气血和摩美得胶囊 Qi Xue He Mo Mei De Jiao Nang(2.0) 养血安神口服液 Yang Xue An Shen Kou Fu Ye(2.0) 舒仲花粉 Shu Zhong Hua Fen (2.0) 攀达康 Pandakang(2.0) 海藻素 Haizaosu(2.0) 螺旋藻 Luoxuanzao(2.0) 珍珠粉 Zhenzhufen(2.0) 脑黄金 Naohuangjin(2.0) 爱德天维 Aidetianwei(2.0) 西洋参 Xiyangshen(2.0) 佳加钙 Jiajiagai(2.0) 荣发养颜宝 Rong Fa Yang Yan Bao(2.0) 吉尾斯 Jiweisi (2.0)
时尚流行指向 fashion orientation	45	红桃 K RHK(11.1) 太太口服液 Taita(11.1)	荣发养颜宝 Rong Fa Yang Yan Bao(6.7) 葡萄糖酸钙 Pu Tao Tang Suan Gai(6.7)	太阳神 Apollo(4.4) 西洋参 Xiyangshen(4.4) 佳加钙 Jiajiagai(4.4) 盘龙云排毒养颜胶囊 Capsule For Waste Discharging And Youth Keeping(4.4) 昂立一号 Only One(4.4)

4-14-2 广告态度指标/ Advertising Attitude Index

注：在药品品牌调查中，消费者经常出现将药品的名称与品牌名称混淆的现象，特此声明。/ In our research on medicines, we find consumers often confused the names and the brands.

	人数 Number	第一品牌及百分比 1st / percent	第二品牌及百分比 2nd / percent	第三品牌及百分比 3rd / percent
样本 Sample	95	**太太口服液 Taita(13.7)**	**红桃 K RHK(8.4)**	**荣发养颜宝 Rong Fa Yang Yan Bao(4.2)**
广告淡漠指向 indifferent orientation	23	太太口服液 Taita(13.0)	红桃 K RHK(8.7)	太阳神 Apollo(4.3) 攀达康 Weidakang(4.3) 养血安神口服液 Yang Xue An Shen Kou Fu Ye(4.3) 葡萄糖酸钙 Pu Tao Tang Suan Gai(4.3) 三精 Sanjin(4.3) 脑白金 Naobaijin(4.3) 盖中盖 Gaizhonggai(4.3) 风行牌蜂皇浆 Feng Xing Pai Feng Huang Jiang(4.3) 金维他 Jinweita(4.3) 昂立一号 Only One(4.3) 爱德天维 Aidetianwei(4.3) 珍珠粉 Zhenzhufen(4.3) 佳加钙 Jiajiagai(4.3) 荣发养颜宝 Rong Fa Yang Yan Bao(4.3) 人参蜂王浆 Ren Shen Feng Wang Jiang(4.3) 三株口服液 3 Strain(4.3)
中间层 medium	54	太太口服液 Taita(13.0)	红桃 K RHK(11.1)	荣发养颜宝 Rong Fa Yang Yan Bao(5.6)
信赖广告指向 loyal orientation	18	太太口服液 Taita(16.7)	西洋参 Xiyangshen(5.6) 海藻素 Haizaosu(5.6) 葡萄糖酸钙 Pu Tao Tang Suan Gai(5.6) 汇仁肾宝 Hui Ren Shen Bao(5.6) 盖中盖 Gaizhonggai(5.6) 太阳神 Apollo(5.6) 天赐康黑加仑 Tiancikang(5.6) 佳加钙 Jiajiagai(5.6) 维生素 EC(5.5) 三株口服液 3 Strain(5.6) 昂立一号 Only One(5.6) 阿胶补血膏 E-jiao(5.6)	

4-14-3 饮食健康指标/ Foods & Drink Quality Index

注：在药品品牌调查中，消费者经常出现将药品的名称与品牌名称混淆的现象，特此声明。/ In our research on medicines, we find consumers often confused the names and the brands.

	人数 Number	第一品牌及百分比 1st / percent	第二品牌及百分比 2nd / percent	第三品牌及百分比 3rd / percent
样本 Sample	96	**太太口服液 Taita(13.5)**	**红桃 K RHK(8.3)**	**荣发养颜宝 Rong Fa Yang Yan Bao(4.2)**
饮食"温饱"指向 "basic" orientation	10	太太口服液 Taita(30.0)	红桃 K RHK(20.0)	脑黄金 Naohuangjin(10.0) 螺旋藻 Luoxuanzao(10.0)
中间层 medium	53	太太口服液 Taita(11.3)	红桃 K RHK(9.4)	西洋参 Xiyangshen(5.7) 汇仁肾宝 Hui Ren Shen Bao(5.7)
健康营养指向 health & nutrition orientation	33	太太口服液 Taita(12.1)	佳加钙 Jiajiagai(6.1) 昂立一号 Only One(6.1) 葡萄糖酸钙 Pu Tao Tang Suan Gai(6.1) 太阳神 Apollo(6.1) 人参蜂王浆 Ren Shen Feng Wang Jiang(6.1) 荣发养颜宝 Rong Fa Yang Yan Bao(6.1)	

● 沈阳 / Shenyang

4-1 最近一年内有无服用的比例/ Whether having Taken Healthy Care Products Last Year

	人数 Number	百分比 Percent
吃过 yes	73	12.3
没吃过 no	519	87.7

n=592

4-2 最常用品牌或品种排名/ Ranking of the Most Frequently Used Brands or Kinds

注：在药品品牌调查中，消费者经常出现将药品的名称与品牌名称混淆的现象，特此声明。/ In our research on medicines, we find consumers often confused the names and the brands.

排名 Brand Ranking	品牌或品种 Brands or Kinds	人数 Number	百分比 Percent
1	红太阳彼阳牦牛骨髓壮骨粉 Be young	7	9.9
1	盖中盖 Gaizhonggai	7	9.9
2	脑白金 Naobaijin	5	7.0
3	忘不了三 A 脑营养胶丸 Memory Enhancer-3A	3	4.2
3	无限极 Wuxianji	3	4.2
4	阿拉斯加鱼油 Alaska Deep Sea Fish Oil	2	2.8
4	钙尔奇 D 片 Caltrate	2	2.8
4	美肤冲剂 Mei Fu Chong Ji	2	2.8
4	西洋参 Xiyangshen	2	2.8
4	太阳神 Apollo	2	2.8

n=71

4-3 样本、男性各年龄层、女性各年龄层的常用品牌或品种/ The Most Frequently Used Brands or Kinds by the Whole Sample, Age and Gender Groups

注：在药品品牌调查中，消费者经常出现将药品的名称与品牌名称混淆的现象，特此声明。/ In our research on medicines, we find consumers often confused the names and the brands.

	人数 Number	第一品牌及百分比 1st/ percent	第二品牌及百分比 2nd/ percent	第三品牌及百分比 3rd/ percent
样本 Sample	71	**红太阳彼阳牦牛骨髓壮骨粉 Be young(9.9)** **盖中盖 Gaizhonggai(9.9)**	**脑白金 Naobaijin(7.0)**	**忘不了三 A 脑营养胶丸 Memory Enhancer-3A(4.2)** **无限极 Wuxianji(4.2)**
男性 Male	28	**脑白金 Naobaijin(14.3)**	**盖中盖 Gaizhonggai(10.7)**	**红太阳彼阳牦牛骨髓壮骨粉 Be young(7.1)**
16~24 岁 Age	5	太阳神 Apollo(20.0) 葡萄糖酸钙 Pu Tao Tang Suan Gai(20.0) 京祥 Jingxiang(20.0) 完美餐 Wanmeican(20.0) 北京天然保健品 Beijing(20.0)		
25~34 岁 Age	6	红太阳彼阳牦牛骨髓壮骨粉 Be young(16.7) 黄花精 Huanghuajing(16.7) 盖中盖 Gaizhonggai(16.7) 脑白金 Naobaijin(16.7) 汇仁肾宝 Hui Ren Shen Bao(16.7) 力克 Like(16.7)		
35~44 岁 Age	5	钙尔奇 D 片 Caltrate(20.0) 人参蜂王浆 Ren Shen Feng Wang Jiang(20.0) 沈阳飞龙 Shen Yang Fei Long(20.0) 红牛 Hongniu(20.0) 超微钙 Chaoweigai(20.0)		
45~54 岁 Age	7	脑白金 Naobaijin(42.9)	红太阳彼阳牦牛骨髓壮骨粉 Be young(4.3) 大天力 Datianli(14.3) 西洋参 Xiyangshen(14.3) 盖中盖 Gaizhonggai(14.3)	
55~60 岁 Age	5	阿拉斯加鱼油 Alaska Deep Sea Fish Oil(20.0) 威士雅骨髓壮骨粉 Weishiya(20.0) 盖中盖 Gaizhonggai(20.0) 冰糖花旗参 Bing Tang Hua Qi Shen(20.0) 洋参桂圆 Yang Shen Gui Yuan(20.0)		

续前表 continued

	人数 Number	第一品牌及百分比 1st/ percent	第二品牌及百分比 2nd/ percent	第三品牌及百分比 3rd/ percent
女性 Female	43	**红太阳彼阳牦牛骨髓壮骨粉 Be young(11.6)**	**盖中盖 Gaizhonggai(9.3)**	**无限极 Wuxianji(7.0)** **忘不了三 A 脑营养胶丸 Memory Enhancer-3A(7.0)**
16~24 岁 Age	11	忘不了三 A 脑营养胶丸 Memory Enhancer-3A(18.2) 盖中盖 Gaizhonggai(18.2)	无限极 Wuxianji(9.1) 金施尔康 Gold Theragran(9.1) 珍珠钙 Zhenzhugai(9.1) 美肤冲剂 Mei Fu Chong Ji(9.1) 先尖 Xianjian(9.1) 冰糖燕窝 Bing Tang Yan Wo(9.1) 胃宝 Weibao(9.1)	
25~34 岁 Age	6	敖东安神补脑液 Aodong(16.7) 富元洋参含片 Fu Yuan(16.7) 红太阳彼阳牦牛骨髓壮骨粉 Be young(16.7) 美肤冲剂 Mei Fu Chong Ji(16.7) 白领减肥茶 Bailing(16.7) 依莎贝尔 Yishabei'er(16.7)		
35~44 岁 Age	11	美国 T.T.牌天然卵磷脂(9.1) 30 天美丽 30Tian Mei Li(9.1) 脑白金 Naobaijin(9.1) 盖中盖 Gaizhonggai(9.1) 东阿阿胶浆 E-jiao(9.1) 朵而 Duoer(9.1) 太阳神 Apollo(9.1) 螺旋藻 Luoxuanzao(9.1) 忘不了三 A 脑营养胶丸 Memory Enhancer-3A(9.1) 红桃 K RHK(9.1) 钙尔奇 D 片 Caltrate(9.1)		
45~54 岁 Age	11	红太阳彼阳牦牛骨髓壮骨粉 Be young(27.3)	阿拉斯加鱼油 Alaska Deep Sea Fish Oil(9.1) 海健壮骨粉 Haijian(9.1) 盖中盖 Gaihzhonggai(9.1) 大豆卵磷脂 Da Dou Luan Lin Zhi(9.1) 维丁钙片 Weidinggai(9.1) 首乌精 Shouwujing(9.1) 康元螺旋藻 Kangyuan(9.1)	
55~60 岁 Age	4	无限极 Wuxianji(50.0)	红太阳彼阳牦牛骨髓壮骨粉 Be young(25.0) 西洋参 Xiyangshen(25.0)	

4-4 理想品牌或品种排名/ Ranking of the Ideal Brands or Kinds

注：在药品品牌调查中，消费者经常出现将药品的名称与品牌名称混淆的现象，特此声明。/ In our research on medicines, we find consumers often confused the names and the brands.

排名 Brand Ranking	品牌或品种 Brands or Kinds	人数 Number	百分比 Percent
1	红太阳彼阳牦牛骨髓壮骨粉 Be young	114	19.0
2	盖中盖 Gaizhonggai	25	4.2
2	忘不了三 A 脑营养胶丸 Memory Enhancer-3A	25	4.2
3	太阳神 Apollo	20	3.3
4	朵而 Duoer	15	2.5
5	脑白金 Naobaijin	11	1.8
6	太太口服液 Taita	10	1.7
7	大天力 Datianli	8	1.3
8	三株口服液 3 Strain	6	1.0
8	昂立一号 Only One	6	1.0
9	无限极 Wuxianji	5	0.8
9	红桃 K RHK	5	0.8

n=600

4-5 样本、男性各年龄层、女性各年龄层最近一年内有无购买的比例/ Proportion of Purchasing in the Last Year by the Whole Sample, Age and Gender Groups

	人数 Number	买过 yes	没买过 no
样本 Sample	600	12.8	87.2
男性 Male	299	10.0	90.0
16~24 岁 Age	64	9.4	90.6
25~34 岁 Age	89	10.1	89.9
35~44 岁 Age	76	9.2	90.8
45~54 岁 Age	46	8.7	91.3
55~60 岁 Age	24	16.7	83.3
女性 Female	301	15.6	84.4
16~24 岁 Age	64	21.9	78.1
25~34 岁 Age	89	10.1	89.9
35~44 岁 Age	76	13.2	86.8
45~54 岁 Age	48	22.9	77.1
55~60 岁 Age	24	12.5	87.5

4-6 样本、男性各年龄层、女性各年龄层的品牌习惯/ Brand Habit in Consuming Healthy Care Products by the Whole Sample, Age and Gender Groups

	人数 Number	事先已决定品牌，买不到就到别家去买 have set brand in mind if can't buy in one shop then go to another	事先已决定品牌，买不到就换其他品牌 have set brand in mind change to another brand if can't buy	事先未决定品牌，当场才决定某一品牌 buy it depend on the situation
样本 Sample	76	69.7	6.6	23.7
男性 Male	29	65.5	0.0	34.5
16~24 岁 Age	6	83.3	0.0	16.7
25~34 岁 Age	9	55.6	0.0	44.4
35~44 岁 Age	6	83.3	0.0	16.7
45~54 岁 Age	4	75.0	0.0	25.0
55~60 岁 Age	4	25.0	0.0	75.0
女性 Female	47	72.3	10.6	17.0
16~24 岁 Age	14	78.6	7.1	14.3
25~34 岁 Age	9	55.6	33.3	11.1
35~44 岁 Age	10	80.0	10.0	10.0
45~54 岁 Age	11	72.7	0.0	27.3
55~60 岁 Age	3	66.7	0.0	33.3

4-7 样本、男性各年龄层、女性各年龄层最近一年内有无拿营养保健品送过礼/ Whether to Offer Healthy Care Products as Gift Last Year by the Whole Sample, Age and Gender Groups

	人数 Number	送过 yes	没送过 no
样本 Sample	598	4.2	95.8
男性 Male	298	4.0	96.0
16~24 岁 Age	64	3.1	96.9
25~34 岁 Age	88	8.0	92.0
35~44 岁 Age	76	2.6	97.4
45~54 岁 Age	46	0.0	100.0
55~60 岁 Age	24	4.2	95.8
女性 Female	300	4.3	95.7
16~24 岁 Age	64	6.3	93.8
25~34 岁 Age	89	5.6	94.4
35~44 岁 Age	75	1.3	98.7
45~54 岁 Age	48	4.2	95.8
55~60 岁 Age	24	4.2	95.8

4-8 样本、男性各年龄层、女性各年龄层最近一年内有无服用的比例/ Whether having Taken Health Care Products Last Year by the Whole Sample, Age and Gender Groups

	人数 Number	吃过 yes	没吃过 no
样本 Sample	592	12.3	87.7
男性 Male	296	9.5	90.5
16~24 岁 Age	63	7.9	92.1
25~34 岁 Age	88	6.8	93.2
35~44 岁 Age	75	6.7	93.3
45~54 岁 Age	46	15.2	84.8
55~60 岁 Age	24	20.8	79.2
女性 Female	296	15.2	84.8
16~24 岁 Age	63	19.0	81.0
25~34 岁 Age	89	7.9	92.1
35~44 岁 Age	74	14.9	85.1
45~54 岁 Age	47	23.4	76.6
55~60 岁 Age	23	17.4	82.6

4-9 该类商品的来源/ Where Got the Products

注：本题为多选题，合计百分比超过 100%（Multiple answers）

	人次 Person-time	百分比 Percent
药店 drug store	38	52.8
医院/诊所 hospital	7	9.7
商场 department store	5	6.9
超市 supermarket	10	13.9
别人送的 given by others	22	30.6
其他 others	1	1.4

n=72

4-10 选择该类商品的考虑因素/ Ranking of the Considerations in Purchasing

注：本题为多选题，合计百分比超过 100%（Multiple answers）

排名 Ranking	考虑因素 Considerations	人次 Person-time	百分比 Percent
1	功能 function	38	52.8
2	亲友介绍 introduced by relatives & friends	21	29.2
3	有名的牌子 famous brand	19	26.4
3	无副作用 no side-effects	19	26.4
4	广告影响 influence of advertising	17	23.6
5	价格适中 reasonable price	11	15.3
6	服用方式简便 simple to take	8	11.1
7	购买方便 easy to buy	5	6.9
8	其他 others	2	2.8

n=72

4-11 样本、男性各年龄层、女性各年龄层最常服用的种类/ Types of Healthy Care Products Consumed by the Whole Sample, Age and Gender Groups

	人数 Number	美容/养颜的 maintaining	提神醒脑的 refreshing	调节人体器官功能的 adjusting the performance of human organs	补血的 enriching the blood	其他 others
样本 Sample	71	12.7	18.3	45.1	11.3	12.7
男性 Male	27	0.0	18.5	63.0	7.4	11.1
16~24 岁 Age	5	0.0	20.0	60.0	0.0	20.0
25~34 岁 Age	6	0.0	16.7	66.7	0.0	16.7
35~44 岁 Age	5	0.0	20.0	60.0	0.0	20.0
45~54 岁 Age	7	0.0	28.6	57.1	14.3	0.0
55~60 岁 Age	4	0.0	0.0	75.0	25.0	0.0
女性 Female	44	20.5	18.2	34.1	13.6	13.6
16~24 岁 Age	12	33.3	41.7	8.3	8.3	8.3
25~34 岁 Age	6	33.3	0.0	50.0	0.0	16.7
35~44 岁 Age	11	18.2	27.3	27.3	27.3	0.0
45~54 岁 Age	11	0.0	0.0	54.5	9.1	36.4
55~60 岁 Age	4	25.0	0.0	50.0	25.0	0.0

4-12 样本、男性各年龄层、女性各年龄层最常服用的包装形式/ Types of Package of Healthy Care Products Consumed by the Whole Sample, Age and Gender Groups

	人数 Number	片剂 pill	冲剂 granular formulation	口服液 oral liquid	胶囊 capsule	药粉 powder	膏状 paste-type	药丸 bolus	其他 others
样本 Sample	72	23.6	23.6	30.6	15.3	4.2	0.0	1.4	1.4
男性 Male	28	21.4	14.3	32.1	21.4	10.7	0.0	0.0	0.0
16~24 岁 Age	5	20.0	0.0	20.0	40.0	20.0	0.0	0.0	0.0
25~34 岁 Age	6	33.3	16.7	50.0	0.0	0.0	0.0	0.0	0.0
35~44 岁 Age	5	20.0	20.0	40.0	20.0	0.0	0.0	0.0	0.0
45~54 岁 Age	7	14.3	14.3	28.6	28.6	14.3	0.0	0.0	0.0
55~60 岁 Age	5	20.0	20.0	20.0	20.0	20.0	0.0	0.0	0.0
女性 Female	44	25.0	29.5	29.5	11.4	0.0	0.0	2.3	2.3
16~24 岁 Age	12	33.3	25.0	25.0	16.7	0.0	0.0	0.0	0.0
25~34 岁 Age	6	0.0	83.3	16.7	0.0	0.0	0.0	0.0	0.0
35~44 岁 Age	11	27.3	0.0	54.5	18.2	0.0	0.0	0.0	0.0
45~54 岁 Age	11	36.4	45.5	0.0	9.1	0.0	0.0	9.1	0.0
55~60 岁 Age	4	0.0	0.0	75.0	0.0	0.0	0.0	0.0	25.0

4-13 样本、男性各年龄层、女性各年龄层最常服用的场合/ Settings of Consumption by the Whole Sample, Age and Gender Groups

	人数 Number	长期服用 long-time habit	疲劳时 tired	考试前后 before or after exam	睡觉前 before sleep	病愈后 post-illness	其他 others
样本 Sample	72	30.6	19.4	5.6	30.6	8.3	5.6
男性 Male	28	32.1	28.6	3.6	17.9	10.7	7.1
16~24 岁 Age	5	60.0	0.0	0.0	20.0	20.0	0.0
25~34 岁 Age	6	33.3	33.3	16.7	0.0	0.0	16.7
35~44 岁 Age	5	20.0	20.0	0.0	40.0	20.0	0.0
45~54 岁 Age	7	28.6	42.9	0.0	28.6	0.0	0.0
55~60 岁 Age	5	20.0	40.0	0.0	0.0	20.0	20.0
女性 Female	44	29.5	13.6	6.8	38.6	6.8	4.5
16~24 岁 Age	12	41.7	0.0	16.7	41.7	0.0	0.0
25~34 岁 Age	6	33.3	16.7	0.0	50.0	0.0	0.0
35~44 岁 Age	11	9.1	18.2	9.1	45.5	18.2	0.0
45~54 岁 Age	11	27.3	18.2	0.0	27.3	9.1	18.2
55~60 岁 Age	4	50.0	25.0	0.0	25.0	0.0	0.0

4-14 不同消费者层的常用品牌或品种/ The Most Frequently Used Brands or Kinds by Market Segments

4-14-1 时尚流行指标/ Fads Popular Index

注：在药品品牌调查中，消费者经常出现将药品的名称与品牌名称混淆的现象，特此声明。/ In our research on medicines, we find consumers often confused the names and the brands.

	人数 Number	第一品牌及百分比 1st/ percent	第二品牌及百分比 2nd/ percent	第三品牌及百分比 3rd/ percent
样本 Sample	71	红太阳彼阳牦牛骨髓壮骨粉 Be young(9.9) 盖中盖 Gaizhonggai(9.9)	脑白金 Naobaijin(7.0)	忘不了三 A 脑营养胶丸 Memory Enhancer-3A(4.2) 无限极 Wuxianji(4.2)
平实生活指向 simple living orientation	29	脑白金 Naobaijin(13.8) 盖中盖 Gaizhonggai(13.8)	钙尔奇 D 片 Caltrate(6.9)	首乌精 Shouwujing(3.4) 维丁钙片 Weidinggai(3.4) 大豆卵磷脂 Da Dou Luan Lin Zhi(3.4) 汇仁肾宝 Hui Ren Shen Bao(3.4) 阿拉斯加鱼油 Alaska Deep Sea Fish Oil(3.4) 西洋参 Xiyangshen(3.4) 大天力 Datianli(3.4) 螺旋藻 Luoxuanzao(3.4) 红太阳彼阳牦牛骨髓壮骨粉 Be young(3.4) 富元洋参含片 Fu Yuan(3.4) 敖东安神补脑液 Aodon
时尚流行指向 fashion orientation	42	红太阳彼阳牦牛骨髓壮骨粉 Be young(14.3)	盖中盖 Gaizhonggai(7.1) 忘不了三 A 脑营养胶丸 Memory Enhancer-3A(7.1) 无限极 Wuxianji(7.1)	太阳神 Apollo(4.8) 美肤冲剂 Mei Fu Chong Ji(4.8)

4-14-2 广告态度指标/ Advertising Attitude Index

注：在药品品牌调查中，消费者经常出现将药品的名称与品牌名称混淆的现象，特此声明。/ In our research on medicines, we find consumers often confused the names and the brands.

	人数 Number	第一品牌及百分比 1st/ percent	第二品牌及百分比 2nd/ percent	第三品牌及百分比 3rd/ percent
样本 Sample	71	**红太阳彼阳牦牛骨髓壮骨粉 Be young(9.9)** **盖中盖 Gaizhonggai(9.9)**	**脑白金 Naobaijin(7.0)**	**忘不了三 A 脑营养胶丸 Memory Enhancer-3A(4.2)** **无限极 Wuxianji(4.2)**
广告淡漠指向 indifferent orientation	18	盖中盖 Gaizhonggai(11.1) 美肤冲剂 Mei Fu Chong Ji(11.1) 脑白金 Naobaijin(11.1) 阿拉斯加鱼油 Alaska Deep Sea Fish Oil(11.1)	大天力 Datianli(5.6) 西洋参 Xiyangshen(5.6) 威士雅骨髓壮骨粉 Weishiya(5.6) 忘不了三 A 脑营养胶丸 Memory Enhancer-3A(5.6) 大豆卵磷脂 Da Dou Luan Lin Zhi(5.6) 红太阳彼阳牦牛骨髓壮骨粉 Be young(5.6) 完美餐 Wanmeican(5.6) 先尖 Xianjian(5.6) 北京天然保健品 Beijing(5.6) 胃宝 Weibao(5.6)	
中间层 medium	41	红太阳彼阳牦牛骨髓壮骨粉 Be young(9.8) 盖中盖 Gaizhonggai(9.8)	无限极 Wuxianji(4.9) 钙尔奇 D 片 Caltrate(4.9) 太阳神 Apollo(4.9)	力克 Like(2.4) 脑白金 Naobaijin(2.4) 金施尔康 Gold Theragran(2.4) 汇仁肾宝 Hui Ren Shen Bao(2.4) 葡萄糖酸钙 Pu Tao Tang Suan Gai(2.4) 维丁钙片 Weidinggai(2.4) 京祥 Jingxiang(2.4) 超微钙 Chaoweigai(2.4) 首乌精 Shouwujing(2.4) 冰糖花旗参 Bing Tang Hua Qi Shen(2.4) 洋参桂圆 Yang Shen Gui Yuan(2.4) 冰糖燕窝 Bing Tang Yan Wo(2.4) 白领减肥茶 Bailing(2.4) 东阿阿胶浆 E-jiao(2.4) 美国 T.T.牌天然卵磷脂(2.4) 黄花精 Huanghuajing(2.4) 西洋参 Xiyangshen(2.4) 海健壮骨粉 Haijian(2.4) 人参蜂王浆 Ren Shen Feng Wang Jiang(2.4)
信赖广告指向 loyal orientation	12	红太阳彼阳牦牛骨髓壮骨粉 Be young(16.7) 脑白金 Naobaijin(16.7)	忘不了三 A 脑营养胶丸 Memory Enhancer-3A(8.3) 沈阳飞龙 Shen Yang Fei Long(8.3) 无限极 Wuxianji(8.3) 盖中盖 Gaizhonggai(8.3) 珍珠钙 Zhenzhugai(8.3) 康元螺旋藻 Kangyuan(8.3) 依莎贝尔 Yishabei'er(8.3) 30 天美丽 30Tian Meili(8.3)	

4-14-3 饮食健康指标/ Foods & Drink Quality Index

注：在药品品牌调查中，消费者经常出现将药品的名称与品牌名称混淆的现象，特此声明。/ In our research on medicines, we find consumers often confused the names and the brands.

	人数 Number	第一品牌及百分比 1st/ percent	第二品牌及百分比 2nd/ percent	第三品牌及百分比 3rd/ percent
样本 Sample	71	**红太阳彼阳牦牛骨髓壮骨粉 Be young(9.9)** **盖中盖 Gaizhonggai(9.9)**	**脑白金 Naobaijin(7.0)**	**忘不了三 A 脑营养胶丸 Memory Enhancer-3A(4.2)** **无限极 Wuxianji(4.2)**
饮食"温饱"指向 "basic" orientation	12	脑白金 Naobaijin(16.7)	胃宝 Weibao(8.3) 美肤冲剂 Mei Fu Chong Ji(8.3) 力克 Like(8.3) 汇仁肾宝 Hui Ren Shen Bao(8.3) 钙尔奇 D 片 Caltrate(8.3) 黄花精 Huanghuajing(8.3) 太阳神 Apollo(8.3) 海健壮骨粉 Haijian(8.3) 威士雅骨髓壮骨粉 Weishiya(8.3) 红太阳彼阳牦牛骨髓壮骨粉 Be young(8.3)	
中间层 medium	33	红太阳彼阳牦牛骨髓壮骨粉 Be young(9.1) 盖中盖 Gaihzhonggai(9.1)	阿拉斯加鱼油 Alaska Deep Sea Fish Oil(6.1) 无限极 Wuxianji(6.1) 脑白金 Naobaijin(6.1)	美肤冲剂 Mei Fu Chong Ji(3.0) 依莎贝尔 Yishabei'er(3.0) 白领减肥茶 Bailing(3.0) 冰糖燕窝 Bing Tang Yan Wo(3.0) 北京天然保健品 Beijing(3.0) 先尖 Xianjian(3.0) 洋参桂圆 Yang Shen Gui Yuan(3.0) 冰糖花旗参 Bing Tang Hua Qi Shen(3.0) 首乌精 Shouwujing(3.0) 维丁钙片 Weidinggai(3.0) 超微钙 Chaoweigai(3.0) 珍珠钙 Zhenzhugai(3.0) 东阿阿胶浆 E-jiao(3.0) 太阳神 Apollo(3.0) 螺旋藻 Luoxuanzao(3.0) 忘不了三 A 脑营养胶丸 Memory Enhancer-3A(3.0) 红桃 K RHK(3.0) 富元洋参含片 Fu Yuan(3.0) 敖东安 Aodong'an(3.0)
健康营养指向 health & nutrition orientation	26	盖中盖 Gaizhonggai(15.4)	红太阳彼阳牦牛骨髓壮骨粉 Be young(11.5)	忘不了三 A 脑营养胶丸 Memory Enhancer-3A(7.7) 西洋参 Xiyangshen(7.7)

第十一篇　家用电器、照相器材
Part XI　Home Electronic Products, Photographic Equipment

- 彩色电视机　Color TV
- 电冰箱　Refrigerator
- 微波炉　Microwave Oven
- 洗衣机　Washing Machine
- 空调机　Air-conditioner
- 录放像机　VTR
- 音响　Hi-Fi Stereo
- 影碟机　VCD / DVD / SVCD Player
- 照相机　Camera
- 胶卷　Film

家用电器、照相器材

家电产业是我国建国后的新兴产业，改革开放为其插上了翅膀。20 年来我国家电产业不断超越自我，逐渐成长为轻工支柱产业，我国现已成为跻身世界家电生产和消费的大国行列。据中国家电行业协会统计，1980 年我国家电工业总产值仅 8.6 亿元，1998 年超过 1300 亿元。1980 年我国冰箱、洗衣机产量分别只有 4.9 万和 24 万台，空调器主要依赖进口和散件组装，微波炉生产则一片空白。1998 年，我国冰箱、洗衣机、空调器、微波炉的产量分别达到 1014 万、1207 万、850 万和 650 万台。

经过长期探索和实践，我国家电工业已形成比较完善的科研、开发、生产、检测和营销体系，造就了一大批优秀企业家和工程技术人员。特别是海尔、科龙、春兰、小天鹅等企业的发展模式和管理经验已成为各行各业广泛借鉴的财富。目前，全行业拥有两个国家级产品质量检测中心，8 个国家级企业开发中心，在许多领域具备了跟踪国际最新技术动态并结合中国国情自主创新的能力，从而确立了中国作为世界家电生产大国的地位。

分析我国家电产业近两年的发展主要表现出以下特点：

1、家电出口量大幅增加。

随着技术的成熟，过去两年我国家电出口快速增长。1998 年已达 35.1 亿美元，中国家电产品进入 180 多个国家和地区，出口额超过 1000 万美元的国家和地区已达 35 个，其中对美、日、德、英、法的出口额均逾 1 亿美元。出口量以 1998 年为例，微波炉、空调器、电冰箱的出口量分别达 324 万台、119 万台和 165 万台。

2、企业对家电市场充满信心。

近年来亚洲经济危机影响到国内家电市场，但从宏观经济政策上来说，中央一直在下决心以更大的力度启动需求，国内实施积极的财政政策，尤其是国家规定自 1998 年 7 月 1 日起提高高档家电电器增值税的出口退税率，由原来的 9%提高到 11%，并且从今年 7 月 1 日起，国家再次提高部分商品的出口退税率，这在一定程度上可以降低家电企业的负担和成本。

3、新需求成为家用电器市场平稳运行的重要动力。

在 80 年代家电消费热潮中购买家电的家庭大多数将在近几年内实现更新换代，这是由消费者消费周期规律和家电产品寿命周期决定的。据有关部门统计，全国大约有 70%至 82%的家庭的家用电器进入更新换代期，包括约 300 万台洗衣机、250 万台冰箱和 300 万台电视机。

4、开拓农村市场已成为广大家电企业的共识。

国家下大力度改善农村消费环境，加强水、电、路、通讯和广播电视等基础设施建设，将为种种家用电器进入农村居民家庭创造基本条件。国家于 1998 年投资进行的大规模城乡电网改造工程已初具规模和成效，在东南沿海部分专区已经实现了同网同价，这为农民使用洗衣机、冰箱等家电创造了良好的条件。目前，我国农村家电普及率很低，正处于消费成长期。据国家统计局一项消费意向调查显示，接近四成的农村居民家庭今年准备购买彩电、冰箱、洗衣机等家用电器。据有关专家测算，农村居民主要家用电器百户保有率增加一个百分点，就会产生 150 亿元的需求，仅洗衣机一项就是 150 万台的销量，农村市场的开拓空间是非常大的。

5、房地产市场的启动，为家电市场带来新的生机。

近年来，全国房地产市场持续呈现良好态势，在市场销售方面，1999 年一季度商品房销售面积和销售额分别比去年同期增长 24%和 25%。房地产市场的启动，为家电市场的繁荣助了一臂之力。据《信息时报》报道，1999 年 7 月末城乡居民储蓄存款余额达到 59148 亿元，增幅比上月下降了近 2 个百分点，这是 1993 年以来居民储蓄首次出现负增长。居民储蓄的减少必然会使消费投资力度加大，这使家电企业面临新的生机。

6、全国半数以上的消费者认为当前是购买耐用消费品的良好时机，蕴含着很大的消费潜力。

消费者认为目前购买耐用消费品适时是有原因的。首先，6 月份第七次降息使得部分消费者对存款有了新的价值判断，即期消费的心理增强；其次，连续 20 个月的物价走低，不少商品的零售价格已经逼近成本，很难再降价，消费者有了看准机会购物划算的心态；第三，股市近期的火爆，不仅使广大的股民终于解了套，而且还鼓舞了消费者的消费信心。

彩电

我国第一台黑白电视机诞生于 1958 年的天津，它拉开了中国电视机生产的序幕。从黑白到彩色，由模拟到数字，显示器由球面到平面，以至掌握大屏幕等离子背投、立体、高清晰度等技术，步子越走越快。特别是近两年对于业内人士来说可谓是翻天覆地。

1、技术发展迅速，需求变化快。

中国的彩电工业已进入成熟期。根据产品寿命周期理论，处于成熟期产品销售量的增长会缓慢下来，销售点利润趋薄，市场竞争异常激烈。生产厂家为了实现利润目标，以改良的手段刺激消费者的习惯，形成新的消费需求。于是今年 100HZ 电视、纯平彩电成为市场的销售热点。电视从模拟走向数字化更是彩电工业发展的必然。

2、彩电展开价格战。

1999 年普通机型电视集体大降价，接着是“超平”机，最后连高贵的“纯平”机也开始掉价。降价的战火可谓级级升温。目前，海信 29 英寸“纯平”定价为 4980 元，几乎与 29 英寸主流“超平”机同日而语。长虹、康佳等厂家也坦言中底档的“纯平”价格已在 3500 元至 5500 元之间。北京松下彩管厂日前发出消息：最先进的第三代 29 英寸纯平彩管将于今年 11 月大批量投入市场。这意味着，纯平彩管必须进口的局面将被打破，目前 220 美元/只的彩管成本将还可再降。据此，行内人士预测：29 英寸纯平彩电在 2000 年前后定会跌破 4000 元大关。

3、品牌效应更加集中。

多年来的激烈竞争使中国的彩电市场已经呈现主导品牌垄断市场的趋势，销售不断向市场知名度高的品牌集中，而非名牌电视的市场份额则趋于萎缩。据调查，1998 年市场占有率位于前 10 名的品牌占据了 80%以上的市场份额。

4、市场需求多样化。

随着居民收入的不断增长，人们的消费需求呈现从温饱向小康型过度，向高品质、新产品、新功能转移的特点。

5、销售方式多样化。

随着我们流通体制的改革和彩电市场供求关系的变化，过去以大商场零售为主的彩电销售方式已经发生了深刻的变化，出现了市场零售、厂家直销、专卖店等多种方式并驾齐驱的局面。

21 世纪信息产业将是全球经济的重大发展方向，互联网将成为沟通各行业的枢纽，也将是各行业未来的新的经济增长点所在。因此，从模拟数字到全数字，从多媒体到全媒体，相关的液晶显示、等离子显示、数字技术等都是彩电厂家们所要考虑和所要做的。

电冰箱

目前, 我国电冰箱市场已进入平稳增长时期, 据有关业内人士估计, 1999 年我国城乡电冰箱总需求达到 1300 万台, 其中城镇需求量约为 950 万台, 农村需求量约为 350 万台, 分别比上一年增长 11.8%和 16.7%。

统计结果显示，我国电冰箱市场在 80 年代经历了一个快速发展时期，进入 90 年代后，发展速度趋缓，尤其是近一两年来，受整体消费市场不景气影响，电冰箱市场扩容极为缓慢。1998 年，我国共生产电冰箱 1014.94 万台，仅比 1997 年增长 1.5%，生产企业存在不同程度的设备闲置及生产能力空放现象，企业经营状况下滑。那么，近一两年的电冰箱市场有哪些特点呢？

其一是城镇市场需求量将保持相当规模，农村市场需求量将加快增长速度。据有关部门调查，到 1998 年，我国城镇每百户居民拥有电冰箱 81.89 台，已接近饱和；但城镇居民中的电冰箱由于使用年限的原因，大约有

1/5 的家庭需要更新或增购，因此，城镇市场仍能保持相当规模；而农村居民每百户只拥有 9.3 台，相当于城镇居民 80 年代中期的水平。农村居民由于生活水平的提高，电冰箱的需求量仍在增加，1998 年百户电冰箱购卖量为 2.5 台，约为 300 万台左右，但还远未达到城镇居民的饱和程度，因此，农村市场潜力巨大。

其二是农村市场增长速度将快于城镇，但城镇仍是需求主体。据中国家电协会估算，在今年电冰箱每百户需求量中，城镇为 10 台，农村为 3 台，也就是说城镇需求量为 950 万台左右，比上一年增长 11.8%；农村约为 350 万台，比上一年增长 16.7%。预计 2000 年，电冰箱市场将延续去年和今年的发展趋势，全社会总需求量将达到 1500 万台，其中城镇需求量约为 1080 万台，农村需求量约为 420 万台，市场前景较为乐观。

目前，我国城镇电冰箱市场已结束了快速扩容时期，呈平稳增长的态势，这是市场调节的必然结果。目前，广大消费者更关心的是，电冰箱产品的质量、功能、款式以及售后服务等问题。这里需要强调的是：国产电冰箱在质量上不逊于国外同类产品，在价格上低于国外同类产品，在售后服务上优于外国同类产品。市场调查结果显示，目前广大消费者已对国产电冰箱产品有了信任感和认同感，绝大多数的家庭中拥有的是海尔、美菱、新飞等国产知名品牌，买进口产品已不多见。因此，国内电冰箱企业应把握时机，注重产品质量，以功能和款式的不断更新，使自身在激烈的竞争中，立于不败之地。

21 世纪国际冰箱市场呈现多元化发展趋势，如美国冰箱向着大型化、对开门方向发展；日本冰箱注重多门多温区、电脑智能化；而欧洲冰箱则向简洁化和与厨房家具一体化发展；而适应中国市场需要的电冰箱应该是节能、环保、智能和多元。消费者在选购买冰箱时，有以下要素会考虑：如是否省电，为使用者今后省钱；是否低噪声和无氟，有利于环保和身体健康；是否具有自动调节温度和抗菌等多种功能，能尽量保持食品的营养价值和新鲜；等等。目前市场上不少进口和国产的电冰箱均推出了高质量、高技术含量的新款冰箱。如海尔电冰箱先后推出了能延长食品保鲜期和较好保持食品营养状况的"冰温王"，有自动制冰、冷藏和独立控温的变频智能冰箱"天王"，以及比普通冰箱节电 60%左右并有抗菌功能的"抗菌节能王"等新品种。而最新推出的海尔"金王子"冰箱，首次在我国冰箱行业把数字节能和智能模糊控制技术在家用冰箱上成功应用，具有国际一流水准。

微波炉

近年来，国内微波炉市场十分火爆。微波炉被世界誉为现代化厨房革命的标志产品，给人们生活质量提高带来许多益处。微波炉以其环保、健康、省时、省力、方便、卫生、安全的特点以及多种烹调方式迅速走入寻常百姓的家庭，受到消费者的青睐，销售直线上升，成为白色家电中的宠儿。

1995 年全国微波炉产销规模不过百万台，1996 年增幅高达 200%，至 1999 年国内龙头企业格兰仕产销规模计划 600 万台，其中一半左右出口，年底将形成 1200 万台的生产基地。可见微波炉市场属新兴市场，前景广阔。众多微波炉企业在 1996 年上马，使生产能力短期呈严重过剩态势，导致这几年微波炉市场竞争十分剧烈，行业平均价格直线下滑，1998 年已有二十几家退出市场，1999 年也有许多企业停止生产，虽然市场上还在销售，这主要是在消化社会库存。1998 年龙头企业战略重心转至海外，国内微波炉出口量剧增。在剧烈的市场竞争过程中，进口货的市场越来越小，进口量迅速萎缩，主要是进口货关税高、价格贵、服务不如国内企业，市场竞争力明显下降。取而代之的是在国内设厂的三资品牌，由于龙头企业格兰仕采取引进最先进的技术管理，而且其规模和专业水平已处在世界领先水平，导致进口品牌的优势完全丧失，国产明显优于进口的差异化已形成。

中国 3 亿多个家庭，大中城市百户微波炉拥有率仅为 10%左右，与发达国家 90%的水平相差甚远，尤其是农村市场尚处在空白状态，市场潜力巨大。微波炉市场目前主要集中在沿海发达地区和大中城市，上海的百户拥有率已超过 70%，接近发达国家的水平，沿海发达的省会城市市场增量仍不弱。

随着卖方市场转变为买方市场，人们的消费心理日益成熟，从盲目崇洋转变为崇质量、崇服务、崇性能价格比，以致强势品牌的消费呈高度集中态势。格兰仕日均产量 16 万台，1998 年年产量 450 万台，占全国总产量的 70%左右，对国内微波生产市场形成高度垄断。中国商业联合会提供的数据表明，1998 年百家大型商场按微波零售量排序的结果是，格兰仕市场占有率高达 61.22%。处于绝对优势。LG 微波炉以 11.82%的份额位居第二，其它品牌相对较小。目前市场不景气，收入预期小于支出预期，市场出现通货紧缩，但是前几年几千元一台微波炉现变成几百元一台，价格便宜了几倍，功能、性能、质量、服务都更优越。特别是医疗费预期支出上升，厨房油烟又是公认严重的致癌物质，微波炉安全、干净、卫生、健康、消毒等优点，又可作为人们健康生活的投资，加上厂家迅猛提高生产力水平，降低成本，向市场不断提供货真价实质优价廉的产品，使市场仍然十分旺盛活跃。

从生产方面看，尽管生产厂家多，但强弱势对比日趋悬殊，因此行业生产集中度日趋上升，强势企业的市场地位日趋稳固，竞争形势呈日趋稳定态势。市场第二层面至市场的下层，随着竞争的投入不同，排序可能仍有变化调整，而市场的第一层面格兰仕已占了一大半市场，而且其实力和各项比较优势十分突出，与其它层面差距十分悬殊，因此从市场竞争角度分析，市场竞争格局不会有明显变化。有关专家指出，目前国内微波炉价格水平已至最低谷，所以今后回升将成为市场的主旋律。淡季 5、6、7 月低一些，8、9 月进入外销和内销旺季，价格的上扬和企业的市场促销力度下降已成定局。

综合考虑各方面的因素，城市仍将是市场需求的主体，农村处于导入期阶段，上海、北京为较高饱有量地区，增幅趋缓，内陆省份呈快速增长势头，微波炉形成由东向西，由南朝北，从沿海地区向内陆地区逐步推进的格局。

洗衣机

家电行业在经历了第一次快速增长期和 80 年代末的暂时性低迷后，经过近年的高速发展，目前已基本步入成熟期，市场已基本饱和。在此大环境下，洗衣机行业正经历着强弱分化的巨大变革。

1998 年我国洗衣机全行业的产量为 1172 万台，比上一年下降 5.47%，首次出现全行业整体下降，整个行业经过十几年的增长调整后，已步入调整期。虽然全行业出现大滑波，但由荣事达、小天鹅、海尔组成的第一集团的势头却丝毫未减。荣事达以 204 万台的产量继续蝉联产销量第一的桂冠，多次连续排名行业第一；小天鹅在全自动洗衣机上连创佳绩，产量同比上一年也有大幅度的增长；海尔则由波轮机做到滚筒机，全面出击市场，当年也有所增长。在洗衣机行业的 43 个品牌中，荣事达、海尔、小天鹅三家的产量占全行业总产量的 60%以上，与上年同比增长 9.81%，三家的市场占有率超过 70%。事实表明，整个市场份额逐步向少数强势品牌集中。但值得注意的是，一部分涉足洗衣机行业的新军正在磨拳擦掌。美菱、春兰、TCL 等家电企业携巨大的品牌优势参与到洗衣机行业的竞争中。

业内的第一集团在技术上具有强大的优势，产品也各有各的特点。

小天鹅和海尔的小小系列洗衣机弥补了以前洗衣机市场没有 2.5 公斤以下小型洗衣机的历史；海尔在大瀑布水流式洗衣机和荣事达的分洗健康型全自动洗衣机，在打健康牌；荣事达潜心研制出的世界首台仿生搓洗式洗衣机首批产品在短期内即销售一空；在整个洗衣机行业的发展中，从半自动到全自动、从机械式到模糊控制式、从塑料内桶到抗菌不锈钢内桶，每一次的技术革命都是由第一集团率先完成的。
除了技术之争外各企业又展开了服务大战以提高品牌竞争力。

在售后服务上，强势品牌也尽出高招，出奇制胜。荣事达有闻名遐迩的“红地毯”售后服务，以“三大纪律，八项注意”为核心内容的“红地毯”一经推出，无形中提升了荣事达的品牌形象，增强了品牌的亲和效应；海尔的星级服务承诺让海尔的用户真正享受到上帝的待遇。可以拉近一批消费者；小天鹅也有自己的“一二三四五”式的售后服务。三家各自的营销网络更是遍布全国各地，基本上每个城市都有今后服务的场所为消费者及时提供服务。而弱势品牌由于营销网络不健全，在售后服务上远远跟不上消费者的需要。

可以预见，洗衣机行业在新一轮的淘汰竞争期内，强势品牌的企业将会通过兼并、合资、合作等方式不断将弱势企业淘汰出局，市场的品牌集中度将继续加大。

空调机

我国空调行业经过十几年的发展，从最开始的引进、消化、吸收，到后来的合资、独立创新，发展速度之快前所未有。目前我国制冷设备制造业在国际市场上已占有 12%以上的销售份额，成为国际商用空调器的生产大国。中国空调器行业发展现状呈现出如下特征：

1、年产量迅猛增长。

中国空调器生产的发展可以用“飞速”来形容。1981 年全国产量仅 1.28 万台，1990 年也就 24 万台，上年则达到 152 万台。目前我国具有一定规模的空调企业约 500 多家，产量从 1988 年的 24 万台猛增到去年的 850 万台，年工业产值平均增长率高达 20%。

2、制造商走规模发展之路。

1992 年以前，空调器的生产一直没有进入规模经济。从 1992 年开始有了质的飞跃。同时也有了 92、93、94 年的空调大战。1995 年后，生产开始出现集中，有十大生产制造商年产量超过 10 万台，占总产量的 70%左右。到 1998 年，空调器生产更趋集中在排名前 4 的企业，这标志着中国空调器行业的市场结构已逐渐优化。

3、制造水平提高、品种增多。

中国空调器制造商大多购买了美国、意大利、日本等国家的制造设备来生产，自动生产线已经多达百余条。由于空调器的制造技术规格均引自国外，尤其是日本。所以产品规模品种也由当初单一的窗式单冷发展到如今冷暖窗式、分体式、柜式和一拖二、三、四等机型。产品技术基本与国际先进技术接轨，产品出口逐年增长。主要的生产制造商还纷纷通过 ISO9000 质量体系国际认证，及其他欧美质量标准的认证，使这些制造商更具出口的优势。

而市场需求状况又如何呢？

中国空调器普及过程与中国国民经济发展密切相关。随着人民生活水平的提高，空调器自 1990 年以来已成为城乡居民的消费热点，空调拥有率也逐年呈上升走势。但到 1995 年中国城镇家庭的空调普及率仅为 8.09%。远远低于发达国家 80%以上的普及率。1997 年北京、上海、广州、深圳普及率已达 42.8%，深圳最高达 74%。预测到 2010 年，全国普及率达到 27%。特别是近两年更呈现出明显的市场销售特点：

1、 销售期高度集中。

据统计，1999 年 7 月份空调零售量占 1—7 月份总零售量的 44.9%，占总零售量的 84.8%，市场销售高度集中。

2、 分离式为市场主流，知名品牌受欢迎。

近年来，分离式空调仍是消费者的首选，7 月份分离式空调器的零售量为 84.8%。名牌在空调市场中的主导作用越来越明显，海尔、LG、科龙、春兰、上海三菱电机等知名品牌占据了大部分市场空间，它们的市场占有率高达 63%。

3、市场潜力巨大。

1995 年，经过“空调大战”之后，生产开始出现集中，竞争的结果是强者更强。市场上空调器品牌的知名度与其产品质量、服务、款式等因素密切相关。基本上可以说现在中国的空调器销售市场是买方市场。

尽管空调器行业竞争如此激烈，形势严峻。但中国的市场潜力是勿庸置疑的。改革开放 20 年来，中国的经济经历了一个快速发展的阶段，城乡居民的生活水平迅速提高。随着居住环境的改善及国家对电力市场的进一步放开，空调器的需求也逐年增加，市场旺盛。预计到 2010 年，全国 8000 万户城镇家庭，空调普及率将达 27%，期间平均年增长率将保持在 10%左右。

另一方面，由于国际市场一体化的发展走势，使空调行业中的佼佼者将目光放及世界市场。中国空调器的制造能力在 1000 万台以上，增加出口量也是势在必行的。

音响

随着人们音乐欣赏水平的不断提高, 以及现代家庭影院的日渐兴起, 音响组合系统已陆续进入普通家庭, 成为人们欣赏音乐或组建家庭影院的重要音响设备。

目前常见的家用音响器材可分为两类：组合音响和发烧音响。组合音响的全部组件（CD 机、功放、音箱等）都是由同一厂家设计生产并成套出售。普通消费者购买组合音响会很方便，可以像购买其他家电产品那样，买回来就用，无须考虑配套问题。由于工厂配套而成的组合音响格局单调，缺乏变化，很难满足所有人的需求。发烧音响则与此不同，它的器材不是成套出售，而是单件出售。消费者可以按照个人的需求，用不同厂家的产品组成自己的音响系统，使它具有风格和个性。

根据目前流行的音响风格来看,大致可分为英国声、美国声、德国声等几个流派。英国声的特点是柔和细腻，不过分强调动态表现能力，其特点是"以音乐为源，以音乐为本"，超凡脱俗。如英国雅伦（Aren）音响，工艺精湛，音色精确完美，体现尊贵典雅的英伦风范。而美国音响如飞达（Fider）音响，特点是音场适应性强，容易达到比较理想的声音效果。，独特的高音设计可减低对高音单元的烧毁，安全性高既有丰满结实的低音又能提供明亮甜美的人声。就德国声而言，德国人以精密严谨称世，德国声强调高解析能力和精确地表现原作，如德国宝笙（Prosound）音响，外观高雅华丽，低频动态凌厉，中频饱满丰润，高频清澈见底，整个音响表现力精确，完美。

从品牌和价格方面来看，目前流行的音响品牌五花八门，价格也是高低不同。如产地为日本的松下音响，产地为马来西亚的索尼音响，产地为新加坡的松下五碟 VCD 组合和北京产的飞利浦音响等。款式也是林林总总，有单碟，三碟，五碟等等，价格方面进口音响比国产更高一点。

1999 年，是我国音响产业发展史上最关键的一年。一方面近年来国产音响从外观到音质均有提高，性能价格比普遍超过进口品牌，加之音响厂家潜心开发新品，以期激活市场，因此市场上精品纷呈，另一方面市场上假冒浮夸和低价劣质音响器材泛滥，影响了国产音响声誉和前途；同时，"入关"在即，国产音响将面临洋品牌新的挑战。

照相机

照相机市场充斥国外品牌，国产相机与之竞争的品牌只有凤凰和海鸥，还有中外合资的甘光牌相机。据国内贸易部全国工商市场信息网提供的资料表明：在全国大型商场照相机的销量排序中，进口相机的销量占了绝对优势。其中销量居前十位的分别是：理光（25.8%）、佳能（16.4%）、美能达（14.1%）、三星（9.3%）、奥林巴斯（7.9%）、汤姆（6.6%）、海鸥（5.8%）、甘光（5.7%）、凤凰（4.3%）、企诺（4.0%）。从统计数据中不难看出：除海鸥、甘光、凤凰是国产品牌外，其余 7 种相机全部是外国品牌，而 7 种外国品牌当中仅日本就占了 5 种。据中华全国商业信息中心统计数据，照相机畅销品牌市场占有率 (1999 年 6 月份) 如下：

畅销品牌名称	市场占有率	畅销品牌名称	市场占有率
奥林巴斯	18.6%	理光	13.1%
佳能	10.8%	美能达	10.6%
凤凰	8.8%	三星	7.3%
奇能	3.4%	海鸥	4.5%
拍得丽	3.3%	柯尼卡	3.0%
其它	16.8%		

据《中国仪器仪表》报道，1999 年上半年中国仪器仪表工业生产运行概况统计，1999 年上半年照相机产、销、存累计完成情况如下：

产品生产量　　708.96 (万架)

产品销售量　　719.30 (万架)
产品库存量　　50.39 (万架)

我国照相机市场，是世界上最大的也是最后的照相消费市场，全世界每销出九架照相机，至少有1架是在我国市场销售的。即使如此，我国相机市场家庭持有量还不到14%。目前我国照相机普及率为城市每百户有30架，农村不足三架。

近年来随着光电技术的进步，立体静态影像撷取设备已不再只限于传统光学式照相机，传统摄影技术已渐渐朝电子化和数字化发展。数码相机由于具有立即显像、通讯传输、记忆体可重复作用、直接与电脑连接等特性与功能，目前已风行全世界。数码相机是1996年下半年才开始进入国内市场的，最先进入的品牌是柯达和卡西欧。从1997年下半年开始，奥林巴斯、索尼、三洋、富士、爱普生、佳能、飞利浦、松下等品牌同时进入中国市场。1996年，海鸥开始与复旦大学和台湾厂商联合研制数码相机；次年9月，海鸥数码相机被列入上海市跨世纪高新技术产品项目；1998年8月，全球首家配备了全中文界面的ＤＣ—３３数码相机投产；今年4月下旬，面向国内市场的100万像素数码相机已经投入市场；6月，海鸥建成全球日产量最大的轻便型数码相机生产线，日产数码相机700台。数码相机市场呈现以下特点：

1、数码相机产品发生很大变化，150万—200万像素的相机成为主流产品，相机更加小巧和多功能化，竞争从渠道竞争、价格竞争逐渐扩大到了产品竞争。

2、价格下降，使其应用领域不断拓宽。

3、中国数码相机虽经两年多的发展，但仍处于导入期，产品销量有限。

4、数码相机代理体系比较混乱，各代理的销量不大，价格的恶性竞争又导致代理无利润，在产品保修和服务方面都留下隐患。

5、水货使市场价格混乱，导致消费者无所适从。

虽然数码相机市场亟需规范，但通过这两年的市场发展，可以看出数码相机的方便性、实用性正为人们所接受，一个新兴市场正不断扩大。

胶卷

中国是胶卷消费的新兴市场，扩张速度为每年10%—15%（世界平均增速为5%）。据《中国经营报》报道，胶卷市场规模初步估算达30多亿人民币，目前中国每人每年消费彩卷0.07个，大大低于美国36个，日本27个的水平。中国胶卷市场潜力巨大。

现在世界范围能研制和生产彩卷的只有美国、日本、德国和中国。我国胶卷市场已经跨入名副其实的“品牌时代”。一般认可的全球六大品牌，柯达、富士、爱克发、柯尼卡、伊尔福、乐凯，均在中国胶卷市场占有一席之地，其中尤以柯达、富士、乐凯三个品牌为主。目前在中国市场上，柯达、富士已占据了主导地位，爱克发为避其锋芒，把目标定在内地及中小城市。民族品牌只有乐凯一家，国内其他感光材料企业，均与外商合资。国家为保护民族感光材料行业的发展，计划投资8亿资本金扶持乐凯集团。据《科技日报》报道，乐凯胶片1998年实现主营收入38607万元，同比增长9.4％，实现净利润7019万元，同比增长32.28％。乐凯胶片各产品产量均占全国总产量的80％以上，市场主要集中于西北、华北、东北“三北”地区。

据《中国消费者报》报道，1998年中国主要城市居民消费品调查胶卷品牌市场占有率如下：

第一名　柯达　　47.9%
第二名　富士　　40.4%
第三名　乐凯　　8.1%

据《中国化工报》报道，中国乐凯胶片集团1999年1－6月份的成绩显示：集团公司销售额比去年同期增长76％，主导产品彩色胶卷的市场占有率达25％，销售量比去年同期增长26％，销售额比去年同期增长150％，利税总额实现8930万元，比去年同期增长234％。

感光行业发展的趋势是数字化，即由化学成像变成数字成像，传统的照相、冲洗过程将变成采用数字照相机拍摄、计算机处理图像和打印机输出的过程。信息记录材料也将由传统的胶卷、相纸变成磁盘、光盘、打印纸等。由于成本及配套设施等方面的原因，即使在发达国家，传统感光材料仍将在 10 年内继续占据主导地位，在我国传统感光材料还会有更长的发展时间。

Household Electrical Appliances

Household electrical appliances (HEA) is a new industry after the setting-up of P.R. China , which has been carried on by leaps and jumps with the reform and open policy. For the 20 years, this industry has been improving itself so that it is now the pillar in light industry. Now our country is ranked one of the big country in electrical household appliances' consuming and production.

According to the statistics of China HEA trade union, the general output of the industry was only 860 million yuan in 1980 while that of 1998 was over 130 billion yuan. In 1980, the output of refrigerator and washing machine were separately 49 thousand and 240 thousand, with air-conditioner mainly depended on importing and spare-parts-assembled, and the production of microwave oven was in a zero. In 1998, the outputs of refrigerator, washing machine, air conditioner and microwave oven end up individually 10.14 million, 12.07 million, 8.5 million and 6.5 million.

With a long-term probing and practice, the HEA in our country has been run in a relatively developed system of R&D, production, inspection and marketing. It also gave birth to a lot of excellent entrepreneurs and technicians in this field. Haier, Kelong, Chunlan, Little Swan and other national brands are good examples, whose development stereotypes and management lessons have become an essence for all businesses. For the moment, the industry has owned two nation-grade products inspection centers, 8 nation-grade business development centers, which have the ability of catching up the world's edged technology and of self-reforming in terms of China's practical condition in a lot of ways. All these have helped to lay the base for China's being a production superpower in HEA.

The features shown in the development of HEA in China can be concluded as the following:

1. A big rise in the volume of export.

With the improvement of technology, the HEA's export in China has been rising rapidly in the past two years. In 1998, it reached 3.51 billion dollars and entered over 180 countries' overseas market, among which there were 35 countries and areas whose export volume was over 10 million dollars. And America, Japan, Germany, Britain and France have the import volume of Chinese HEA products over 100 million dollars each. Take the 1998 for example, the export volume for microwave oven, air-conditioner and refrigerator are separately 3.24 million, 1.19 million and 1.65 million.

2. The enterprises have a strong confidence over HEA market.

In spite of the negative influence from Asia Economy Crisis, the macro economy policy for the HEA is encouraging in that the central government is doing efforts to trigger the civil demands by implementing positive budget policy. For example, the government regulated that since July 1st, 1998, the high-grade HEA products' VAT would be improved from the former 9% to 11%, and since July 1st, 1999, a second improvement has been carried on the export drawback rate over some merchandises, which, has reduced the pressure and cost of HEA businesses to some degree.

3. New demands have been the important impetus for the stable operation of the HEA market.

Most families who bought electrical household appliances in the 1980's will realize an up-grading of them these years, which is decided by the principle in consuming cycle and the product life cycle of the HEA. According to the statistics from relative authorities, about 70% or 82% of the families in the country have entered the regeneration period, which encompassed about 3 million washing machines, 2.5 million refrigerators and 3 million televisions.

4. It has been a common sense for HEA enterprises to develop the rural market.

The country is making efforts in improving the consuming environment in countryside by strengthening basic facilities' construction of water, electricity, road, communication, radio and television, so to produce a basic condition for the entering of HEA to the countryside families. The large-scale town & country electricity network reformation project carried on by the government has taken its initial form and influence. And the fact of an equal price to equal net has been realized in the coastal areas in Southeast China, which lays a good case for the farmers' consumption of washing machines and refrigerators. The penetration of HEA in rural areas is still very low for the moment, just in the growth term. According to a survey of consuming intention carried by National Statistics Bureau, about four tenths rural families incline to buy HEA such as color TV, refrigerator and washing machine. According to some experts, with a rise of 1% in the main HEA's average occupancy rate for 100 rural families, a demand for 15 billion yuan will turn up, i.e. a sale volume of 1.5 million will go for washing machines. In this sense, the development possibility in countryside is strong.

5. The running of the real estate market also adds new hope for the HEA.

Recently, the real estate market has been keeping a satisfying posture. In this marketing, a rise of 24% and 25% have been separately going for the sales of houses' areas and volume in the first season this year. The great state of real estate market has given a push for the prosperity of HEA market. According to the reports of "Information Times", the deposit balance for the town & country inhabitants ended up 5914.8 billion yuan at the end of July in 1999, with the rising range decreased 2% than last month, which was the first time a declining appeared in the inhabitants' deposit since 1993. The descending of deposit, by turn, will definitely trigger consuming, while producing opportunity for HEA enterprise.

6. Over half consumers in China take current moment as a great timing for purchasing durable consumer goods, which indicate a big potential in consuming.

It is reasonable for consumers to hold such thought. First, the seventh interest-cut in June has ingrained in some consumers a new value-measure over the deposit and a stronger sense of immediate consuming. Second, the continuous depression for 20 months in price has caused the retail price of a lot of merchandises more close to the cost, which makes it impossible for the further price cut. So consumers take it as the greatest timing for purchasing. Third, the resent exuberance in the stock market not only made many stockholders free their stock from harness but also encouraged the confidence of consumers.

The competition focus in HEA of 21 century will be energy-economical, intellectual, graceful shaped, multi-functional and individualized.

Color TV

The first black and white TV was born in Tianjin in 1958, which opened the page of TV production in China. From black and white to color TV, from simulation to digital, from the screen's spherical surface to plane one, till the technology of big screen, rear-projecting, three-dimensional effect, high clarity and so on, the TV industry in China is developing by leaps and jumps. Especially in these two years, many insiders have experienced an earth-shaking change.

1. The technology develops quickly with a highly changeable demand.

The color TV industry in China has entered in mature period. According to the Product Life Cycle theory, the sales volume for such industry will slow down with thinner profit and more severe competition. To making more profits, producers tend to reform consumer's habits to form a new consuming need. That's the reason why the 100HZ TV and pure-plane color TV have become the hot selling points in this year's market. It is definitely necessary that color TV will step from simulation to digitalization.

2. Price fight in color TV industry.

In 1999, common style TVs are going on a general price cut-down, and then the same happened to "super-plane" ones, even then to the high-grade "pure-plane". The price-cut is accelerating continuously. For the moment, 29 inches "pure-plane" TV of Hisense is priced as 4980 yuan, almost as same as the main-stream TV set---29 inches "hyper-plane". Changhong and Konka are also declared that the middle or lower grade "pure-plane" TV have been priced between 3.5 thousand and 5.5 thousand yuan. Beijing Panasonic Color Kinescope Factory recently announced that the most edged third generation of 29 inches pure-plane color kinescope will be put into market largely in December this year. This means the fact that pure-plane color kinescope were all imported has been past forever and the cost of 220 dollars for each color kinescope will be cut down again. In terms of this, insiders estimate that 29 inches pure-plane color TV will break through the bottom line of 4000 yuan in 2000.

3. More concentration of brand effect.

The trends that some leading brands has dominated the color TV market in China is appearing after years' severe competition. With sales concentrating on brands that have a higher awareness, the other ones' market share is shrinking. According to the market survey, the former 10 leading brands in 98 market have owned over 80% market shares.

4. Various market demands.

With the continuous rise in the inhabitants' income, people's demands are proceeding from simply having enough food and clothing to leading a relatively comfortable life, with an emphasis on high quality, new products and new function.

5. Changes in Sales manners.

With the reform in distribution system and the change in supply & demand of color TV, the sales way of color TV has changed a lot: in past the big department store is the main way of selling, but now it has experienced a deep reform with market retail sales, producers' direct sales and special agent coexisting.

The information industry in 21 century will be the trend of global economy, and internet will become the key of communicating in all industries and fields, which is also the center where the future development of all industries lie. So, it is necessary for all color TV producers to take into consideration and make efforts in research of all the advanced technology, which including simulating digital and whole digital, multi media and whole media, the relative liquid crystal display, plasma display and digital technology and so on.

Refrigerator

For the moment, the refrigerator market in China has entered a stable development period. Expected by the insiders, the general demand of city and country for refrigerators in 1999 will be 13 million, with urban 9.5 million and rural 3.5 million, separately rising 11.8% and 16.7% than last year.

The statistics data shown in 1980's, the refrigerator market in China had gone through a flying development. But in 1990's, the developing speed has slowed down, esp. these two years when the expanding of the market is quite discouraging due to the influence from the general consuming market's gloomy state. In 1998, the total output of refrigerators reduced to 10.1494 million, only 1.5% more than 1997. The phenomenon of idle machines and waste of productive force exist to some degree in many refrigerate producers, leading to a decline in their business. Then, what are the features of the refrigerator market in these two years?

Firstly, the urban demand will keep strong while rural need will be paced up. According to the survey from relative authority, by 98, the occupancy of refrigerators per 100 households in city is 81.89, nearly being saturated. But for the reason of refrigerators' life span, about one fifth households need a regeneration or another purchasing, so that a satisfying size can still be kept in urban areas. In comparison, the occupancy per 100 households in countryside is only 9.3, equal to the standard of urban people in middle 1980's. With the improvement in the living standard of rural inhabitants, the need for refrigerators will be increased, and, in terms of the purchasing volume of 2.5 per 100 rural households in1998, will reach about 3 million in whole. This, whereas, is far not saturated, which is why the potential for rural market will be huge.

And then, the developing speed of rural market will be faster than urban areas, but the former will still be the focus. According to the estimation from China Electrical Household Appliances Union, the demand for refrigerators per 100 families this year will be separately 10 for urban areas and 3 for rural, and the general demand of urban areas will be 9.5 million, 11.8% more than last year while rural about 3.5 million, rising by 16.7%. It is estimated that in 2000, the refrigerator market will keep the developing trends of the former two years, with the social demand of 15 million, among which urban demand is 10.8 million and rural 4.2 million. This, anyway, is optimistic for the future.

Currently, our urban refrigerator market has ended the fast expanding period, staying on a balanced ascending, which is a natural result of market adjusting. Now the consumers are more concerned about the products' quality, function, shape and after-sale service. One thing needed to be addressed is: domestic products are nothing worse than foreign rivals, while cheaper in price and more excellent in after-sale service. Market survey indicates that at the moment, most consumers have developed trust in the domestic products. For example, most families owned the branded products of Haier, Meilin, Freshtech and so on. It has been rare to purchase foreign products. That's why national refrigerator producers should grasp the opportunity to emphasize a high quality, a reformed function and shape, so to make themselves prior in the severe competition.

In 21 century, international refrigerator market is also turning versatile. As the examples, American refrigerators are tending to be large-size and a mutual-opening door, Japan is prefer multi door with multi temperature section and computerized intellectual, while Europe is aiming plainness and kitchen appliances assembly. The products adapted to China market, however, will be energy saving, environmental-protective, intellectual and plural. In making the choices, consumers will consider the following factors as whether it's electricity-economical and then money-saving in the future; whether it's free from noises and fluorine as possible as it is; whether it's environmental-protective or healthy; whether it has the functions of auto-adjust in temperature and anti-bacterium so to keep the most possible nutrition value and freshness of the food; and etc.. For the moment, quite a few brands in the market have put forward high quality and high technological new style refrigerators. For example, Haier has come up with the "Freezer King" which can postpone the freshness preserve span and satisfyingly keep the nutrition of the food. And it also has the frequency-changeable high intellectual "Tianwang" which has the features of auto ice-making, freezing and independent temperature-control, and the "King in Anti-bacteria and energy-economical" that saves electricity 60% more than common ones and enjoys the function of anti-bacteria. Esp. the new Haier's "Gold Prince" refrigerator, for the first time successfully apply the digital energy-saving technology and the intellectual mixing-up control skill in household refrigerators in China, owning the first-class level in the world.

Microwave Oven

For the past years, the domestic Microwave Oven (MWO) market has been vigorous. MWO has been stamped as a signal for the modernized kitchen revolution in the world, bringing great convenience to people by being environmental-protective, healthy, energy and time economical, convenient, hygiene and safe, so that it has been a necessity for the common family. Preferred by consumers, MWO gets a sharp rise in sales volume.

In 1995, the production and sales volume of MWO was only million, rising by 200% in 1996. Glanz, the MWO leading company, aims the production of 6 million this year, half of which will be exported, and also plans to build a production base with an output of 12 million at the end of the year. Just as we can see, being a new industry, MWO has a bright future. But in 1996, too many MWO businesses got into run so that the production turn out overdone for the moment, leading to a severe competition in the market and a sharp decline in the field's average price. Over 20 enterprises had been drawn out of the market by the year 1998. Even in 1999, quite a few enterprises stopped production, though the sale of the stored products was still going on in the market. Last year, some important enterprises turned their business focus toward international market, causing a great rise in the MWO export. During the throat-cutting market competition, the volume of the imported MWO is becoming more limited gradually, mainly due to a high customs duty, high price with the imported product, and dissatisfying with after-sale service and other reasons. Instead, the joint venture's, Glanze, has taken up the most advanced technology management so that its size and grade are ranked top in the world. In such case, the imported brand lost advantage totally and a gap between it with national ones has formed.

Among over 300 million families in China, occupancy rate of MWO per 100 households in cities is only 10%, far away from the 90% of the developed countries. Especially the rural market is still in the vacancy with a large market potential.

MWO market currently focused in the coastal developed areas and cities, with Shanghai's occupancy rate of over 70%, which is near the developed countries' standard. Now the market potential in capital cities of coastal developed provinces is still powerful.

With the market turning from seller-oriented to buyer-oriented, people's consuming psyche are mature in that the worship for the foreign products has been replaced with the worship for quality, service, function and price, making the consuming of important brands stay highly assembled.

The daily output of Glanz reaches 160 thousand, while annual one in 1998 was 4.5 million, occupying about 70% in the country's general output, forming a monopoly in the domestic market. The data shown by China Business Union illustrate, in the rank of retail sales of MWO in 100 big-scale departments in 1998, the market share of Glanz is as high as 61.22% with an overpowering triumph. LG. was second with 11.82%, and the other brands were very limited in market. Currently, the market is still experiencing depression, expected revenue is lower than the expected spending with a shrink in price. The price of a micro wave is currently as several hundred yuan in stead of one thousand formerly, with a better function, feature, quality and service against the cut price. Besides, in consideration of the rising expected payment of medical care and a common realization of the cancer-triggering feature of kitchen's soot, MWO, safe, clean, healthy and poison killing, more and more becomes an investment toward a healthy life. If the MWO producers continue to improve the productivity and reduce the cost, providing the economical, high quality products, the vigor for MWO market will keep on vibrant.

In the terms of production, a gap between the strong and the weak will being enlarged in spite of the large number of enterprises. So, the concentrating degree of industry will ascend in that the up-handed enterprises are even stronger in market share with a more stable competition posture.

With the difference in the competition input, the rank among the second market layer and lower one will have some changes. But the top layer, with Glance dominates the majority of market and stands out in a lot of ways, has a great gap to the other layers. For all these, analyzed in terms of market competition, this market situation will remain unchangeable generally. Some experts point out that a future rise in price will be the main tune since it has been in the lowest point now. The months of May, June and July will be slack season while August and September are the golden time for the domestic or international sales. And it has been set that the price will keep on going up while the force of promotion is reduced.

In consideration of all factors, it is expected that the domestic demand for MWO in 1999 will be 5.5 or 6 million, making China surmount Japan to be second biggest market, only inferior to America. City will still be the demand focus and country stays on introduction period. In Beijing and Shanghai which are approaching saturation point, the rise scope for MWO consuming will be limited, but the inland provinces will see a quick increase so that a pattern of MWO proceeding from east to west, from south to north and from coastal areas to inland ones.

Washing Machine

After the first flying development and the momentary depression the end of 80's, the industry of HEA, with the fast improvement of these years, has generally entered the mature period with saturation in market. In such situation, washing machine industry is going on a huge reform causing a division of the strong and the weak.

The total output of washing machine industry in 1998 is of 11.72 million, 5.47% less than last year, with the first general decline in the whole field. Now the whole industry has entered the regulation period after more than ten years' adjusting and improvement. In spite of the discouraging state, the first group represented by "Rongshida", "Little Swan" and "Haier" has been keeping a vigorous posture. Rongshida continues being top one with a sales volume of 2.04 million; Little Swan got an excellent presentation in the sales of complete automatic washing machine; Haier also sees a rise with a complete market promotion by turning to cylinder washing from wave rotation. Among 43 brands of the washing machine industry, Rongshida, Haier and Little Swan have all together enjoy over 60% of the general output of the whole industry, 9.81% more than last year, and a market occupancy over 70%. Facts show that the market is more and more concentrating to few powerful brands.

But it needs to be addressed that some newcomers in the industry are making great efforts. Meilin, Chunlan and TCL are involving themselves in the competition with their huge brand advantages.

The first group in the industry has gained preponderance with personalized products.

The small size series products of Little Swan and Haier have made up the vacancy of small sized washing machines with weight under 2.5 kilogram in the market. Haier's waterfall-current washing machine and Rongshida's separated-washing hygiene style automatic products are emphasizing the healthy sense; While Rongshida's "Human-simulating scrubbing style" washing machine, the first in the world, is out of shelf shortly after its entering the market. During the whole industry's development, every technology reform has been started by the first group, such as the regeneration from half-automatic to complete automation, from mechanical style to mixing-up control style, from plastic inner tub to anti-bacteria and anti-must steel one.

Besides technology competition, all enterprises are putting up the service fight to improve the brand competitive force.

In the after-sale service, up-handed brands are making every effort to gain the superiority. Rongshida's well-known "Red carpet" after-sale service, centering on "Three Principles and Eight Attentions", has contributed much to its brand image, addressing its sense of homely. Haier's promise in star-service has made the consumers really enjoy being Gods, snapping their purchasing. Little Swan also swears with the future so called "One, Two, Three, Four, Five" service. The marketing networks belonging to these three brands are located all round the country where almost every city has their after-sale service agent to provide the prompt help to consumers. In stead, the lower-handed brands are far from the consumers' needs in after-sale service with an undeveloped marketing network.

In this term, we can estimate that in the new competition and screening period, up-handed brands will keep on drawing off the other brands by annexing, joint venture and cooperation, so that a higher assembly of the brands in the market will appear.

Air-conditioner

Through more than 10 years, our air-conditioner industry has been developing with an unimaginable speed, improving from the early times' introduction, digest and accept to the later period's joint-venture, independent creation. Currently, our country's refrigeration equipment producing industry has enjoyed over 12% sales allot in the international market, making China the superpower in the producing of international commercial air-conditioner.

The development of the industry shows the following features:

1. Annual output increased sharply.

The development in the air-conditioner production can be concluded as "flying". In 1981, the country's output was only 128 thousand, in comparison to 240 thousand in 1990 and 1.52 million in 1998. For the moment, our country has about 500 air-conditioner producing enterprises of certain scale, whose output in 1998 were 8.5 million, against 240 thousand in 1988, realizing an adding of 20% in annual average industrial revenue.

2. The producers are taking the way of large-scale production.

Before 1992, the production of air-conditioner was not in the channel of large-scale economy. Since 1992, an earth shaking flying happened, and then the price fight of the next three years also broke out. In 1995, the production began to be centralized, with ten big producers whose individual annual output were over 100 thousand, and in-all output occupied about 70% in the whole. As far as 1998, the air-conditioner production was more focused in the four leading companies, which marked a graduate improvement in the market structure of the industry.

3. Production skill increased, with the variety of products being enlarged.

China's air-conditioner producers are majority purchasing the machinery from America, Italy and Japan, owning more than 100 automatic production lines. Since the production technology and standards are mainly introduced from abroad, esp. Japan, the products' variety has been presently greatly enlarged: ranging from cooling & heating window type, split type, packaged type to the split type of one main engine with two, or three, or four splits, which is different from the only window type of cooling in past times. With the production technology channeled into the international one, the export is going up gradually. The main producers have even been registered by the ISO9000 quality system and by the other European & American quality standards, which also bring them some advantages to their export business.

Then what about the market demands?

The popularity procedure of air-conditioner in China is at the same pace with the whole national's social-economy development. With the improvement for the living standard, air-conditioner has become the urban and rural people's consuming hot point since 1990, shown by the continuous increase of the air-conditioner possession rate every year. But by 1995, China's urban families air-conditioner popularity was only 8.09%, far lower than the 80% of developed countries. In 1997, Beijing, Shanghai, Guangzhou, and Shengzhen have owned a popularity of 42.8%, with Shengzhen top at 74%. It's expected that by 2010, the air-conditioner popularity in China will be 27%. And these two years also have shown this possibility in market sales:

1. Centralization of the sales period.

According to the statistics, the air-conditioner retail sales volume in July of 1999 occupies 44.9% of the whole retail sales from January to July, displaying a high centralization of the market sales.

2. The split type is the main stream in the air-conditioner market and the famous brands are always preferred.

These years, split type air-conditioner is still the best choice for consumers. In July, such kind of air-conditioners got retail sales occupied 84.8% of all. The leading effects of famous brands have become more and more important, for example, Haier, LG, Kelong, Chunlan and Mistubishi in Shanghai dominated most of the market, whose market share are as high as 63%.

3. Market potential.

In 1995, after the air-conditioner fight, the production began to be centralized. The result of competition led to a result of the strong being stronger. The awareness of brands is close in connection with the products' quality, service and style. Basically, the air-conditioner market in China is a buyer-oriented market.

Although the competition in the industry is so severe and hard, the market potential in China is indubitably great. Through 20 years' reform and open, China's economy has experienced a flying development period and a sharp increase in the urban and rural people's living standard. As the living environment is improved and the further open of the electricity market by government, the need for air-conditioner is stronger yearly, making the market more vigorous. By the year of 2010, for the 80 million urban households in China, the air-conditioner's popularity will reach 27%, with an average annual rising rate of 10%.

On the other hand, influenced by the integration trend of international market, it is natural for the top brands in air-conditioner industry put their sight on the world's market. The productivity of air-conditioners in China is over 10 millions, leaving the adding of export volume necessary.

Hi-Fi Stereo

With an improvement of the peoples' music appreciation level, and the prosperity of the modern family museum, Hi-Fi stereo system has gradually got into the ordinary family as important equipment for people to appreciate music and build family museum.

Presently, ordinary stereo system can be commonly sorted as two types: componnent stereo system and Hi-Fi stereo. All components of combination (CD player, projector and sounder and ext.) are all produced and sold in set by the same producer. It's convenient for the common consumers to buy stereo component for they can be used shortly after being bought, just like the other electrical household appliances, with no troubling about management of the set. But the componnent stereo system, being set by factory, seeming much monotonous, can't meet all people. While Hi-Fi stereo is different in that its spare parts are sold individually so that the consumer can arrange his or her own stereo set with parts from different producers at personal will.

The current popular stereo styles can be sorted as: British, American and German schools. The British features gentle and sensitive, not emphasizing dynamic display. It is a super grace in "taking music as origin, as foundation". For example, Aren by Britain is delicate in aircraft, faithful and perfect in sound effects, showing a dignified British style. But Fider by America features at a strong adaptation to the site and simplicity in reaching a satisfying sound effect. Its special high-pitch design can reduce the burning of high-tone cells, with a high security, a forceful low-tone and clean or sweet human sound. As far as German's Prosound is concerned, it has a splendid outlook, a sharply dynamic low audio frequency, a vibrant medium frequency and clean high one, forming a perfect and faithful sound expression.

In terms of brands and price, the current popular stereo brands are versatile, with price different, such as the Panasonic from Japan, Sony from Malaysia, Panasonic's five-disk VCD set from Singapore and Philips from Beijing. The style is also changeable, ranging from single-disk, three-disk and five-disk. In price, imported stereos are higher than national ones.

The year of 1999 is one of the most important years in the history of China stereo industry. On one hand, national products recently have got improvement from outlook to sound effect, and a higher rate of feature against price than that of imported rivals. Besides, the stereo producers involve themselves in developing new products to trigger the market, which causes a series of elite products in the market. But on the other hand, some shoddy or counterfeited stereo equipment are soaring in the market, which influenced the credit standing and future of the national stereo equipment. Meanwhile, with the entry to "WTO" around the corner, national stereos are facing new challenge from the foreign rivals.

Camera

Camera market is flooded with foreign brands, only rivaled by the national brands of Phoenix and Seagull, also the joint-ventured Brand of Gan'guan. According to the reference from the industry & business market information network of China by the Ministry of Domestic Trade, imported cameras enjoy the superiority in the sales volume rank of camera in large-scaled department stores. The former ten are listed as Rico (25.8%), Canon (16.4%), Minolta (14.1%), Samsung (9.3%), Olympus (7.9%), Tom (6.6%), Seagull (5.8%), Gan'guang (5.7%), Phoenix (4.3%) and Chino (4.0%). It's obvious that except national brands of Seagull, Gan'guang and Phoenix, the other seven are all foreign products. While merely Japan has got 5 in these 7 ones. Reported by the statistics of China National Business Information Center, the welcomed camera brands separately enjoy the market shares (June in 1999) as the following:

Brand	Market Share
Olympus	18.6%
Ricoh	13.1%
Canon	10.8%
Minolta	10.6%
Phoenix	8.8%
Samsung	7.3%
Chino	3.4%
Pairdre	3.3%
Konica	3.0%
The others	16.8%

Reported by the statistics in production operation of China instruments and meters industry in the early half year of 99, which originated from "China Instruments and Meters", this camera production in this period's, sales and store is concluded as:

The products' output	7.0896 million sets
The sales volume	7.193 million
The stored products volume	503.9 thousand

The camera market of China is the biggest and last camera consuming market in the world. Among every 9 sold camera in the world there is at least one to China market. In spite of this, the household possessing rate of it in China is less than 14%. Currently, the popularity of camera is 30 sets per 100 households in cities, less than 3 sets in rural area.

Recently, with the progress of photoelectricity technology, three-dimensional static picture-taking equipment have not been limited to traditional optical cameras while the traditional photographing technology has been gradually turning electronic and digital.

Digital camera, which is featured with the functions of instant developing, communication transfer, memory organ's repetition usage and the ability in connection with PC directly, is making its way in the whole world. It entered China market in the latter half-year of 1996, leaded by Kodak and Casio. Since the latter half-year of 1997, Olympus, Sony, Sanyo, Fuji, Epson, Canon, Philips and Panasonic had taken their entry to China market. In 1996, Seagull began the cooperation research in digital camera with Fudan University and Taiwan producers. In September of the next year, Seagull digital camera was listed as the over-century high-technology product in Shanghai. In August of 1998, the world's first DC-33 digital cameral with all-Chinese screen ran into production. In the late of April of this year, the one-million-photoelement digital camera appealing to domestic market began to face the consumers. In June, Seagull built the simple typed digital cameral production line with the biggest daily output in the world, with daily output of 700. The digital camera market is featured as:

1. There is a big change in the products, and 1.5 million-2 million pix camera has become the main stream product, with a mini outlook and various functions. The competition expands from channel and price one to product itself.

2. The cut in the price makes a wider application field.

3. Though more than 2 years' development, the digital camera in China is still stay in the introduction period with a limited sales volume.

4. The agents system is a little messy in that agents' sales volumes are not satisfying, the vicious price competition make agents non-profited, which leave potential problems in products' maintenance and service.

5. The smuggled products make the market price messy, bewildering the consumers.

Though the digital camera market still need to be standardized, after two years' development, its convenience and practical sense are being acceptable by the people, which can make a newly prosperous market enlargen.

Film

China is a new market for film consuming, with an expansion speed of 10%-15% every year (average speed for the whole world market is 5%). According to "China Business", the estimated size of film market was about 3 billion yuan. The number of film consumed by Chinese per capita is about 0.07, far lower than that of America at 36 and Japan at 27, which indicates a huge potential for the China's film market.

The countries in the world that have the ability to research and produce color film are America, Japan, Germany and China only. Our film market has entered the namely "Brand age". The well-known global brands of Kodak, Fuji, Agfa, Konica, Elf and Lucky, have all shared a role in the China film market, esp. with Kodak, Fuji and Lucky important. Currently in Chinese market, Kodak and Fuji have led a major role while Agfa tries to avoid their direct rival by turning the focus on inland cities and the middle or small ones. The only national brand is Lucky. The other sensitive materials producers are all joint venture with foreigners. To protect the development in the national sensitive materials industry, the government plans to invest 800 million yuan to support Lucky Corporation. According to "Science & Technology Daily", Lucky film will gain a general revenue of 386.07 million yuan in 1998, rising by 9.4%, realizing a net profit of 70.19 million yuan, rising by 32.28%. The output of every product by Lucky all occupies 80% of the relative national output, with markets focused in North-west, North China and North-east areas.

According to "China Consumers", the market share of film brands ranked in the survey of urban inhabitants' consumer goods 1998 is as the following:

First Kodak, 47.9%

Second Fuji, 40.4%

Third Lucky, 8.1%

The "China Chemical Industry" reported that the sales records of Lucky during January to June in 1999 suggested: the sales revenue rose by 76% than last year. The market share of Lucky's leading product reached 25%, with sales volume enlarged by 26% and the sales revenue 150% more than last year, so that the general profits got 89.3 million yuan, up 234%.

The trend of sensitive materials industry is digital, that is, changing from chemical developing to digital developing, in which traditional photographing and developing procedure will turn to the one of digital photographing, computer processing and printing by printer. The information-recording material will also develop into disc, CD and typing-paper from former film and printing paper. For the sake of cost and set equipment, even in developed countries, the traditional sensitive materials will still play a leading role in the future 10 years, even longer in China.

1.彩色电视机 / Color TV

● 北京 / Beijing

1-1 彩色电视机拥有比例/ Proportion of Color TV Owners in the Sample

	人数 Number	百分比 Percent
有 yes	1000	98.8
没有 no	12	1.2

n=1012

1-2 彩色电视机的拥有量/ Number of Color TV Owned Per Household

	人数 Number	百分比 Percent
1 台 1 set	546	55.2
2 台 2 sets	386	39.0
3 台 3 sets	50	5.1
4 台及以上 4 sets or over	8	0.8

n=990

1-3 理想品牌排名/ Ranking of the Ideal Brands

排名 Brand Ranking	品牌 Brands	人数 Number	百分比 Percent
1	索尼 Sony	180	17.8
2	松下/乐声 Panasonic	158	15.6
3	康佳 Konka	106	10.5
4	长虹 Changhong	95	9.4
5	东芝 Toshiba	89	8.8
6	王牌 TCL	75	7.4
7	牡丹 Peony	57	5.6
8	海尔 Haier	43	4.3
9	日立 Hitachi	30	3.0
10	飞利浦 Philips	19	1.9
11	高士达/乐金 LG	18	1.8
12	海信 Hisense	16	1.6
13	三星 Samsung	13	1.3
14	创维 Skyworth-RGB	11	1.1

n=1011

1-4 对家中现有彩色电视机(最近购买的一台)的五个方面的描述/ About the Color TV Most Recently Purchased

1-4-1 家中现有彩色电视机的品牌排名/ Ranking of the Currently Owned Color TV Brands

排名 Brand Ranking	品牌 Brands	人数 Number	百分比 Percent
1	牡丹 Peony	164	16.4
2	长虹 Changhong	105	10.5
3	松下/乐声 Panasonic	104	10.4
4	王牌 TCL	81	8.1
5	康佳 Konka	76	7.6
6	东芝 Toshiba	72	7.2
7	索尼 Sony	58	5.8
8	日立 Hitachi	40	4.0
9	海信 Hisense	27	2.7
10	飞利浦 Philips	26	2.6
10	海尔 Haier	26	2.6
11	昆仑 Kunlun	24	2.4
12	创维 Skyworth-RGB	23	2.3

n=999

1-4-2 该彩色电视机的购买时间/ The Time of Purchasing of the Currently Owned Color TV

	人数 Number	百分比 Percent
1985 年或以前 1985 or before	52	5.2
1986～1990 年	162	16.3
1991 年	33	3.3
1992 年	28	2.8
1993 年	40	4.0
1994 年	53	5.3
1995 年	66	6.7
1996 年	90	9.1
1997 年	127	12.8
1998 年	162	16.3
1999 年	178	18.0

n=991

1-4-3 该彩色电视机的价格/ The Price of the Currently Owned Color TV

	人数 Number	百分比 Percent
2000 元或以下 2000 yuan or below	178	17.9
2001～4000 元 yuan	474	47.7
4001～6000 元 yuan	140	14.1
6001～8000 元 yuan	81	8.2
8001～10000 元 yuan	41	4.1
10001～12000 元 yuan	26	2.6
12001～14000 元 yuan	6	0.6
14001～16000 元 yuan	2	0.2
16001～18000 元 yuan	1	0.1
18001～20000 元 yuan	3	0.3
20000 元以上 over 20000 yuan	9	0.9
完全不知道 don't know	32	3.2

n=993

1-4-4 该彩色电视机的尺寸/ The Screen Size of the Currently Owned Color TV

	人数 Number	百分比 Percent
14 英寸 inches	14	1.4
16 英寸 inches	2	0.2
18 英寸 inches	64	6.5
20 英寸 inches	74	7.5
21 英寸 inches	254	25.8
22 英寸 inches	10	1.0
24 英寸 inches	8	0.8
25 英寸 inches	196	19.9
27 英寸 inches	3	0.3
28 英寸 inches	10	1.0
29 英寸 inches	328	33.3
31 英寸 inches	0	0.0
32 英寸 inches	1	0.1
33 英寸 inches	0	0.0
34 英寸 inches	12	1.2
34 英寸以上 over 34 inches	2	0.2
其他 others	6	0.6

n=984

1-4-5 该彩色电视机的类型/ The Type of the Currently Owned Color TV

	人数 Number	百分比 Percent
普通屏幕 traditional screen	387	38.9
平面直角 plane screen	475	47.7
超平 super plane screen	102	10.2
纯平 pure plane screen	29	2.9
其他 others	3	0.3

n=996

1-5 选择不同品牌的彩色电视机的考虑因素/ Considerations in Choosing from Different Brands

注：本题为多选题，合计百分比超过 100%（Multiple answers）

	人数 Number	品牌形象 brand image	外型 outlook	价格 price	功能齐备 all-function	图象清晰度 clarity	图象色彩 color	音响效果 sound effect	售后服务 follow-up service	其他 others
样本 Sample	988	45.6	16.9	39.1	27.7	34.8	17.2	11.3	17.5	3.9
牡丹 Peony	162	43.2	13.6	50.6	24.7	24.7	13.6	4.3	19.8	5.6
长虹 Changhong	105	57.1	8.6	50.5	24.8	31.4	10.5	8.6	31.4	1.0
松下/乐声 Panasonic	104	54.8	17.3	26.9	29.8	39.4	21.2	15.4	5.8	3.8
王牌 TCL	81	50.6	17.3	53.1	18.5	34.6	11.1	12.3	25.9	0.0
康佳 Konka	76	44.7	17.1	43.4	30.3	28.9	10.5	6.6	34.2	7.9
东芝 Toshiba	71	54.9	26.8	18.3	28.2	45.1	29.6	18.3	4.2	4.2
索尼 Sony	58	65.5	22.4	12.1	31.0	48.3	31.0	17.2	5.2	3.4
日立 Hitachi	37	45.9	2.7	13.5	43.2	48.6	27.0	10.8	5.4	5.4
海信 Hisense	25	28.0	4.0	64.0	23.0	40.0	24.0	8.0	32.0	0.0
飞利浦 Philips	26	57.7	11.5	7.7	30.8	46.2	19.2	34.6	3.8	7.7
海尔 Haier	26	38.5	26.9	34.6	19.2	30.8	15.4	19.2	50.0	0.0
昆仑 Kunlun	23	39.1	8.7	52.2	30.4	13.0	8.7	4.3	17.4	4.3
创维 Skyworth-RGB	23	39.1	17.4	60.9	21.7	43.5	13.0	13.0	13.0	0.0
三星 Samsung	18	16.7	33.3	11.1	50.0	44.4	22.2	27.8	16.7	0.0
夏普/声宝 Sharp	15	33.3	20.0	20.0	40.0	46.7	20.0	6.7	0.0	0.0

1-6 彩色电视机未来一年购买打算/ Plan for Future Purchasing of a Color TV

1-6-1 有无购买打算/ Whether Planning to Purchase Next Year

	人数 Number	百分比 Percent
是 yes	160	15.8
否 no	851	84.2

n=1011

1-6-2 打算购买的品牌排名/ Ranking of the Brands of the Planned Purchase Next Year

排名 Brand Ranking	品牌 Brands	人数 Number	百分比 Percent
1	康佳 Konka	28	17.6
2	长虹 Changhong	21	13.2
3	索尼 Sony	18	11.3
4	王牌 TCL	14	8.8
5	海尔 Haier	12	7.5
7	牡丹 Peony	9	5.7
7	东芝 Toshiba	9	5.7
9	松下/乐声 Panasonic	7	4.4

n=159

1-6-3 打算购买的尺寸/ The Screen Size of the Planned Purchase Next Year

	人数 Number	百分比 Percent
14 英寸 inches	3	1.9
16 英寸 inches	1	0.6
18 英寸 inches	4	2.6
20 英寸 inches	2	1.3
21 英寸 inches	10	6.5
22 英寸 inches	1	0.6
24 英寸 inches	2	1.3
25 英寸 inches	32	20.8
27 英寸 inches	2	1.3
28 英寸 inches	2	1.3
29 英寸 inches	70	45.5
31 英寸 inches	2	1.3
32 英寸 inches	1	0.6
33 英寸 inches	1	0.6
34 英寸 inches	15	9.7
34 英寸以上 over 34 inches	6	3.9
其他 others	0	0.0

n=154

1-6-4 打算购买的价格/ The Price of the Planned Purchase Next Year

	人数 Number	百分比 Percent
2000 元或以下 2000 yuan or below	16	10.4
2001～4000 元 yuan	76	49.4
4001～6000 元 yuan	30	19.5
6001～8000 元 yuan	12	7.8
8001～10000 元 yuan	6	3.9
10001～12000 元 yuan	3	1.9
12001～14000 元 yuan	3	1.9
14001～16000 元 yuan	0	0.0
16001～18000 元 yuan	1	0.6
18001～20000 元 yuan	1	0.6
20000 元以上 over 20000 yuan	5	3.2
完全不知道 don't know	1	0.6

n=154

1-7 选购彩色电视机时不同角色的人口特征/ Demographics of the Different Roles in Purchasing a Color TV

注：不同角色可以多选（Multiple answers）

	人数 Number	16-24 岁 Age	25-34 岁 Age	35-44 岁 Age	45-54 岁 Age	55-60 岁 Age
样本 Sample	919	20.2	30.0	25.4	16.6	7.7
男性 Male	461	20.4	29.9	26.2	16.1	7.4
提议者 advocate	93	23.7	28.0	24.7	18.3	5.4
影响者 influence	55	23.6	34.5	20.0	18.2	3.6
决定者 decider	226	9.7	27.4	32.3	20.4	10.2
使用者 user	340	23.2	30.0	24.1	15.9	6.8
女性 Female	458	20.1	30.1	24.5	17.2	8.1
提议者 advocate	113	19.5	26.5	27.4	15.0	11.5
影响者 influence	56	19.6	28.6	21.4	19.6	10.7
决定者 decider	128	7.0	34.4	32.0	18.0	8.6
使用者 user	363	22.6	28.7	24.8	16.5	7.4

1-8 不同消费者层的家中目前拥有品牌/ Brands of Color TV Owned in Household by Market Segments

1-8-1 时尚流行指标/ Fads Popular Index

	人数 Number	第一品牌及百分比 1st/ percent	第二品牌及百分比 2nd/ percent	第三品牌及百分比 3rd/ percent	第四品牌及百分比 4th/ percent
样本 Sample	986	牡丹 Peony(16.5)	长虹 Changhong(10.4)	松下/乐声 Panasonic(10.2)	王牌 TCL(8.2)
平实生活指向 simple living orientation	481	牡丹 Peony(18.7)	松下/乐声 Panasonic(10.8) 长虹 Changhong(10.8)	王牌 TCL(8.5)	东芝 Toshiba(7.1)
时尚流行指向 fashion orientation	505	牡丹 Peony(14.5)	长虹 Changhong(10.1)	松下/乐声 Panasonic(9.7)	康佳 Konka(9.1)

1-8-2 广告态度指标/ Advertising Attitude Index

	人数 Number	第一品牌及百分比 1st/ percent	第二品牌及百分比 2nd/ percent	第三品牌及百分比 3rd/ percent	第四品牌及百分比 4th/ percent
样本 Sample	981	牡丹 Peony(16.1)	长虹 Changhong(10.6)	松下/乐声 Panasonic(10.5)	王牌 TCL(8.0)
广告淡漠指向 indifferent orientation	286	牡丹 Peony(15.4)	松下/乐声 Panasonic(12.9)	长虹 Changhong(10.5)	康佳 Konka(7.7) 东芝 Toshiba(7.7)
中间层 medium	564	牡丹 Peony(16.8)	长虹 Changhong(10.5)	王牌 TCL(8.3)	松下/乐声 Panasonic(8.2)
信赖广告指向 loyal orientation	131	松下/乐声 Panasonic(15.3)	牡丹 Peony(14.5)	长虹 Changhong(11.5)	康佳 Konka(8.4)

1-8-3 价格态度指标/ Price Attitude Index

	人数	第一品牌及百分比 1st/ percent	第二品牌及百分比 2nd/ percent	第三品牌及百分比 3rd/ percent	第四品牌及百分比 4th/ percent
样本 Sample	989	牡丹 Peony(16.5)	长虹 Changhong(10.5)	松下/乐声 Panasonic(10.4)	王牌 TCL(8.1)
价格无关心指向 indifferent orientation	202	牡丹 Peony(11.9)	长虹 Changhong(9.4) 松下/乐声 Panasonic(9.4) 康佳 Konka(9.4)	东芝 Toshiba(8.9)	王牌 TCL(8.4) 索尼 Sony(8.4)
中间层 medium	493	牡丹 Peony(15.4)	松下/乐声 Panasonic(12.0)	长虹 Changhong(10.8)	王牌 TCL(8.9)
价格重视指向 careful orientation	294	牡丹 Peony(21.4)	长虹 Changhong(10.9)	松下/乐声 Panasonic(8.5)	东芝 Toshiba(7.5)

1-9 不同消费者层选择彩色电视机时的考虑因素/ Considerations in Choosing from Different Brands by Market Segments

1-9-1 时尚流行指标/ Fads Popular Index

注：本题为多选题，合计百分比超过 100%（Multiple answers）

	人数 Number	品牌形象 brand image	外型 outlook	价格 price	功能齐备 all-function	图象清晰度 clarity	图象色彩 color	音响效果 sound effect	售后服务 follow-up service	其他 others
样本 Sample	976	45.6	16.9	39.3	27.7	34.8	17.0	11.2	17.6	4.0
平实生活指向 simple living orientation	478	44.8	13.6	40.8	25.1	38.3	17.4	12.3	15.7	4.2
时尚流行指向 fashion orientation	498	46.4	20.1	38.0	30.1	31.5	16.7	10.0	19.5	3.8

1-9-2 广告态度指标/ Advertising Attitude Index

注：本题为多选题，合计百分比超过 100%（Multiple answers）

	人数 Number	品牌形象 brand image	外型 outlook	价格 price	功能齐备 all-function	图象清晰度 clarity	图象色彩 color	音响效果 sound effect	售后服务 follow-up service	其他 others
样本 Sample	971	45.7	16.8	39.3	27.9	34.7	16.7	11.3	17.5	4.0
广告淡漠指向 indifferent orientation	283	42.8	13.1	41.3	31.8	30.7	15.2	11.3	20.8	3.9
中间层 medium	558	47.3	17.6	37.5	25.8	37.3	17.9	11.8	16.3	4.1
信赖广告指向 loyal orientation	130	45.4	21.5	43.1	28.5	32.3	14.6	9.2	15.4	3.8

1-9-3 价格态度指标/ Price Attitude Index

注：本题为多选题，合计百分比超过 100%（Multiple answers）

	人数 Number	品牌形象 brand image	外型 outlook	价格 price	功能齐备 all-function	图象清晰度 clarity	图象色彩 color	音响效果 sound effect	售后服务 follow-up service	其他 others
样本 Sample	979	45.6	17.0	39.3	27.9	35.0	17.2	11.3	17.5	4.0
价格无关心指向 indifferent orientation	198	47.5	16.7	31.8	25.8	37.9	16.2	15.2	21.7	4.5
中间层 medium	489	46.4	16.4	38.9	29.7	32.3	19.0	11.0	16.6	3.7
价格重视指向 careful orientation	292	42.8	18.2	45.2	26.4	37.7	14.7	9.2	16.1	4.1

● 上海 / Shanghai

1-1 彩色电视机拥有比例/ Proportion of Color TV Owners in the Sample

	人数 Number	百分比 Percent
有 yes	1000	98.6
没有 no	14	1.4

n=1014

1-2 彩色电视机的拥有量/ Number of Color TV Owned Per Household

	人数 Number	百分比 Percent
1 台 1 set	634	63.8
2 台 2 sets	323	32.5
3 台 3 sets	34	3.4
4 台及以上 4 sets or over	3	0.3

n=994

1-3 理想品牌排名/ Ranking of the Ideal Brands

排名 Brand Ranking	品牌 Brands	人数 Number	百分比 Percent
1	索尼 Sony	282	27.8
2	金星 Golden Star	193	19.1
3	松下/乐声 Panasonic	191	18.9
4	长虹 Changhong	90	8.9
5	东芝 Toshiba	47	4.6
6	飞利浦 Philips	40	3.9
7	日立 Hitachi	36	3.6
8	夏普/声宝 Sharp	28	2.8
9	王牌 TCL	18	1.8

n=1013

1-4 对家中现有彩色电视机(最近购买的一台)的五个方面的描述/ About the Color TV Most Recently Purchased

1-4-1 家中现有彩色电视机的品牌排名/ Ranking of the Currently Owned Color TV Brands

排名 Brand Ranking	品牌 Brands	人数 Number	百分比 Percent
1	金星 Golden Star	303	30.4
2	松下/乐声 Panasonic	145	14.5
3	索尼 Sony	92	9.2
4	长虹 Changhong	76	7.6
5	东芝 Toshiba	52	5.2
6	上海 Shanghai	44	4.4
7	飞利浦 Philips	42	4.2
8	日立 Hitachi	32	3.2
9	夏普/声宝 Sharp	27	2.7
10	飞跃 Feiyue	22	2.2

n=998

1-4-2 该彩色电视机的购买时间/ The Time of Purchasing of the Currently Owned Color TV

	人数 Number	百分比 Percent
1985 年或以前 1985 or before	23	2.3
1986～1990 年	162	16.2
1991 年	49	4.9
1992 年	27	2.7
1993 年	49	4.9
1994 年	65	6.5
1995 年	65	6.5
1996 年	103	10.3
1997 年	171	17.1
1998 年	161	16.1
1999 年	123	12.3

n=998

1-4-3 该彩色电视机的价格/ The Price of the Currently Owned Color TV

	人数 Number	百分比 Percent
2000 元或以下 2000 yuan or below	188	18.8
2001～4000 元 yuan	421	42.1
4001～6000 元 yuan	209	20.9
6001～8000 元 yuan	89	8.9
8001～10000 元 yuan	37	3.7
10001～12000 元 yuan	20	2.0
12001～14000 元 yuan	8	0.8
14001～16000 元 yuan	1	0.1
16001～18000 元 yuan	1	0.1
18001～20000 元 yuan	4	0.4
20000 元以上 over 20000 yuan	9	0.9
完全不知道 don't know	12	1.2

n=999

1-4-4 该彩色电视机的尺寸/ The Screen Size of the Currently Owned Color TV

	人数 Number	百分比 Percent
14 英寸 inches	27	2.7
16 英寸 inches	2	0.2
18 英寸 inches	100	10.1
20 英寸 inches	31	3.1
21 英寸 inches	268	27.1
22 英寸 inches	16	1.6
24 英寸 inches	13	1.3
25 英寸 inches	214	21.7
27 英寸 inches	1	0.1
28 英寸 inches	7	0.7
29 英寸 inches	280	28.3
31 英寸 inches	4	0.4
32 英寸 inches	2	0.2
33 英寸 inches	4	0.4
34 英寸 inches	13	1.3
34 英寸以上 over 34 inches	1	0.1
其他 others	5	0.5

n=988

1-4-5 该彩色电视机的类型/ The Type of the Currently Owned Color TV

	人数 Number	百分比 Percent
普通屏幕 traditional screen	384	38.5
平面直角 plane screen	529	53.1
超平 super plane screen	63	6.3
纯平 pure plane screen	14	1.4
其他 others	7	0.7

n=997

1-5 选择不同品牌的彩色电视机的考虑因素/ Ranking of the Considerations in Choosing from Different Brands

注：本题为多选题，合计百分比超过 100%（Multiple answers）

	人数 Number	品牌形象 brand image	外型 outlook	价格 price	功能齐备 all-function	图象清晰度 clarity	图象色彩 color	音响效果 sound effect	售后服务 follow-up service	其他 others
样本 Sample	**995**	**47.4**	**14.9**	**38.1**	**26.7**	**38.4**	**22.5**	**12.6**	**17.4**	**3.2**
金星 Golden Star	302	49.0	10.9	48.3	19.9	30.5	15.9	7.0	26.8	3.0
松下/乐声 Panasonic	145	50.3	12.4	20.0	35.2	48.3	33.1	18.6	12.4	2.1
索尼 Sony	92	59.8	10.9	17.4	34.8	46.7	27.2	19.6	10.9	0.0
长虹 Changhong	76	48.7	21.1	56.6	26.3	31.6	15.8	14.5	19.7	1.3
东芝 Toshiba	52	50.0	21.2	15.4	28.8	48.1	34.6	11.5	11.5	3.8
上海 Shanghai	44	43.2	11.4	52.3	13.6	34.1	13.6	6.8	6.8	9.1
飞利浦 Philips	42	54.8	31.0	33.3	38.1	31.0	28.6	16.7	9.5	0.0
日立 Hitachi	32	56.3	18.8	25.0	34.4	53.1	25.0	15.6	9.4	0.0
夏普/声宝 Sharp	27	48.1	14.8	18.5	40.7	48.1	11.1	11.1	14.8	3.7
飞跃 Feiyue	22	54.5	18.2	54.5	13.6	13.6	18.2	9.1	22.7	4.5
王牌 TCL	21	28.6	23.8	47.6	28.6	52.4	23.8	28.6	28.6	0.0

1-6 彩色电视机未来一年购买打算/ Plan for Future Purchasing of a Color TV

1-6-1 有无购买打算/ Whether Planning to Purchase Next Year

	人数 Number	百分比 Percent
是 yes	130	12.8
否 no	884	87.2

n=1014

1-6-2 打算购买的品牌排名/ The Brand of the Planned Purchase Next Year

排名 Brand Ranking	品牌 Brands	人数 Number	百分比 Percent
1	索尼 Sony	32	24.8
1	金星 Golden Star	32	24.8
2	松下/乐声 Panasonic	18	14.0
3	长虹 Changhong	9	7.0
4	东芝 Toshiba	8	6.2
5	飞利浦 Philips	7	5.4
6	王牌 TCL	4	3.1
7	日立 Hitachi	2	1.6
7	康佳 Konka	2	1.6
7	高士达/乐金 LG	2	1.6

n=129

1-6-3 打算购买的尺寸/ The Screen Size of the Planned Purchase Next Year

	人数 Number	百分比 Percent
14 英寸 inches	1	0.8
16 英寸 inches	0	0.0
18 英寸 inches	1	0.8
20 英寸 inches	1	0.8
21 英寸 inches	4	3.1
22 英寸 inches	1	0.8
24 英寸 inches	0	0.0
25 英寸 inches	17	13.3
27 英寸 inches	3	2.3
28 英寸 inches	1	0.8
29 英寸 inches	70	54.7
31 英寸 inches	1	0.8
32 英寸 inches	1	0.8
33 英寸 inches	2	1.6
34 英寸 inches	18	14.1
34 英寸以上 over 34 inches	7	5.5
其他 others	0	0.0

n=128

1-6-4 打算购买的价格/ The Price of the Planned Purchase Next Year

	人数 Number	百分比 Percent
2000 元或以下 2000 yuan or below	6	4.7
2001～4000 元 yuan	39	30.5
4001～6000 元 yuan	31	24.2
6001～8000 元 yuan	20	15.6
8001～10000 元 yuan	13	10.2
10001～12000 元 yuan	8	6.3
12001～14000 元 yuan	2	1.6
14001～16000 元 yuan	2	1.6
16001～18000 元 yuan	3	2.3
18001～20000 元 yuan	2	1.6
20000 元以上 20000 over yuan	0	0.0
完全不知道 don't know	2	1.6

n=128

1-7 选购彩色电视机时不同角色的人口特征/ The Demographics of Different Roles in Purchasing a Color TV

注：不同角色可以多选（Multiple answers）

	人数 Number	16-24 岁 Age	25-34 岁 Age	35-44 岁 Age	45-54 岁 Age	55-60 岁 Age
样本 Sample	916	20.6	28.6	25.5	16.8	7.4
男性 Male	458	21.0	27.5	26.9	17.2	7.4
提议者 advocate	94	27.7	24.5	21.3	20.2	6.4
影响者 influence	60	21.7	25.0	20.0	21.7	11.7
决定者 decider	198	6.1	29.3	35.9	20.7	8.1
使用者 user	263	28.9	24.3	24.3	16.0	6.5
女性 Female	458	20.3	29.7	26.2	16.4	7.4
提议者 advocate	91	24.2	25.3	24.2	18.7	7.7
影响者 influence	71	16.9	26.8	29.6	18.3	8.5
决定者 decider	150	10.7	30.7	35.3	18.0	5.3
使用者 user	308	22.7	28.9	26.9	13.6	7.8

1-8 不同消费者层的家中目前拥有品牌/ Brands of Color TV Owned in Household by Market Segments

1-8-1 时尚流行指标/ Fads Popular Index

	人数 Number	第一品牌及百分比 1st/ percent	第二品牌及百分比 2nd/ percent	第三品牌及百分比 3rd/ percent	第四品牌及百分比 4th/ percent
样本 Sample	989	**金星 Golden Star(30.3)**	**松下/乐声 Panasonic(14.7)**	**索尼 Sony(9.2)**	**长虹 Changhong(7.6)**
平实生活指向 simple living orientation	461	金星 Golden Star(34.9)	松下/乐声 Panasonic(14.3)	长虹 Changhong(8.5)	索尼 Sony(8.2)
时尚流行指向 fashion orientation	528	金星 Golden Star(26.3)	松下/乐声 Panasonic(15.0)	索尼 Sony(10.0)	东芝 Toshiba(7.4)

1-8-2 广告态度指标/ Advertising attitude Index

	人数 Number	第一品牌及百分比 1st/ percent	第二品牌及百分比 2nd/ percent	第三品牌及百分比 3rd/ percent	第四品牌及百分比 4th/ percent
样本 Sample	986	**金星 Golden Star(30.1)**	**松下/乐声 Panasonic(14.5)**	**索尼 Sony(9.1)**	**长虹 Changhong(7.7)**
广告淡漠指向 indifferent orientation	250	金星 Golden Star(33.6)	松下/乐声 Panasonic(9.6) 长虹 Changhong(9.6)	索尼 Sony(7.2)	上海 Shanghai(6.0)
中间层 medium	503	金星 Golden Star(30.0)	松下/乐声 Panasonic(15.8)	索尼 Sony(9.3)	长虹 Changhong(7.5)
信赖广告指向 loyal orientation	133	金星 Golden Star(24.1)	松下/乐声 Panasonic(18.0)	索尼 Sony(12.0)	东芝 Toshiba(6.8)

1-8-3 价格态度指标/ Price Attitude Index

	人数 Number	第一品牌及百分比 1st/ percent	第二品牌及百分比 2nd/ percent	第三品牌及百分比 3rd/ percent	第四品牌及百分比 4th/ percent
样本 Sample	996	**金星 Golden Star（30.3）**	**松下/乐声 Panasonic（14.6）**	**索尼 Sony（9.2）**	**长虹 Changhong（7.5）**
价格无关心指向 indifferent orientation	148	金星 Golden Star（30.4）	松下/乐声 Panasonic（13.5）	索尼 Sony（10.8）	长虹 Changhong（7.4）
中间层 medium	517	金星 Golden Star（30.4）	松下/乐声 Panasonic（15.7）	索尼 Sony（9.7）	长虹 Changhong（7.2）
价格重视指向 careful orientation	331	金星 Golden Star（30.2）	松下/乐声 Panasonic（13.3）	长虹 Changhong（8.2）	索尼 Sony（7.9）

1-9 不同消费者层选择彩色电视机时的考虑因素/ Considerations in Choosing from Different Brands by Market Segments

1-9-1 时尚流行指标/ Fads Popular Index

注：本题为多选题，合计百分比超过 100%（Multiple answers）

	人数 Number	品牌形象 brand image	外型 outlook	价格 price	功能齐备 all-function	图象清晰度 clarity	图象色彩 color	音响效果 sound effect	售后服务 follow-up service	其他 others
样本 Sample	988	47.5	14.9	38.4	26.8	38.4	22.5	12.4	17.3	3.2
平实生活指向 simple living orientation	460	47.8	13.5	42.6	24.6	37.2	22.0	9.6	16.3	4.3
时尚流行指向 fashion orientation	528	47.2	16.1	34.7	28.8	39.4	22.9	15.0	18.2	2.3

1-9-2 广告态度指标/ Advertising Attitude Index

注：本题为多选题，合计百分比超过 100%（Multiple answers）

	人数 Number	品牌形象 brand image	外型 outlook	价格 price	功能齐备 all-function	图象清晰度 clarity	图象色彩 color	音响效果 sound effect	售后服务 follow-up service	其他 others
样本 Sample	985	47.2	14.6	37.9	26.6	38.8	22.7	12.5	17.2	3.2
广告淡漠指向 indifferent orientation	250	42.4	14.8	38.0	22.8	35.6	23.2	12.8	17.6	4.0
中间层 medium	602	46.8	13.0	38.5	27.6	41.0	21.9	12.1	17.8	3.3
信赖广告指向 loyal orientation	133	57.9	21.8	34.6	29.3	34.6	25.6	13.5	13.5	1.5

1-9-3 价格态度指标/ Price Attitude Index

注：本题为多选题，合计百分比超过 100%（Multiple answers）

	人数 Number	品牌形象 brand image	外型 outlook	价格 price	功能齐备 all-function	图象清晰度 clarity	图象色彩 color	音响效果 sound effect	售后服务 follow-up service	其他 others
样本 Sample	995	47.5	14.9	38.1	26.7	38.4	22.3	12.6	17.3	3.2
价格无关心指向 indifferent orientation	149	51.0	16.8	26.8	20.8	34.2	22.1	14.1	17.4	4.0
中间层 medium	517	46.6	15.3	40.0	28.6	37.9	21.3	11.8	18.6	2.7
价格重视指向 careful orientation	329	47.4	13.4	40.1	26.4	41.0	24.0	13.1	15.2	3.6

● 广州 / Guangzhou

1-1 彩色电视机拥有比例/ Proportion of Color TV Owners in the Sample

	人数 Number	百分比 Percent
有 yes	1022	98.8
没有 no	12	1.2

n=1034

1-2 彩色电视机的拥有量/ Number of Color TV Owned Per Household

	人数 Number	百分比 Percent
1 台 1 set	668	66.0
2 台 2 sets	296	29.2
3 台 3 sets	45	4.4
4 台及以上 4 sets or over	3	0.3

n=1012

1-3 理想品牌排名/ Ranking of the Ideal Brands

排名 Brand Ranking	品牌 Brands	人数 Number	百分比 Percent
1	松下/乐声 Panasonic	315	30.5
2	索尼 Sony	267	25.8
3	康佳 Konka	85	8.2
4	王牌 TCL	65	6.3
5	东芝 Toshiba	58	5.6
6	长虹 Changhong	51	4.9
7	日立 Hitachi	47	4.5
8	创维 Skyworth-RGB	31	3.0
9	飞利浦 Philips	26	2.5
10	乐华 Rowa	19	1.8

n=1034

1-4 对家中现有彩色电视机(最近购买的一台)的五个方面的描述/ About the Color TV Most Recently Purchased

1-4-1 家中现有彩色电视机的品牌排名/ Ranking of the Currently Owned Color TV Brands

排名 Brand Ranking	品牌 Brands	人数 Number	百分比 Percent
1	松下/乐声 Panasonic	301	29.5
2	索尼 Sony	130	12.7
3	康佳 Konka	97	9.5
4	东芝 Toshiba	71	6.9
5	日立 Hitachi	68	6.7
6	王牌 TCL	66	6.5
7	创维 Skyworth-RGB	57	5.6
8	长虹 Changhong	48	4.7
9	乐华 Rowa	41	4.0
10	声宝 Sharp	21	2.1

n=1022

1-4-2 该彩色电视机的购买时间/ The Time of Purchasing of the Currently Owned Color TV

	人数 Number	百分比 Percent
1985 年或以前 1985 or before	21	2.1
1986～1990 年	119	11.8
1991 年	43	4.3
1992 年	54	5.4
1993 年	56	5.6
1994 年	97	9.6
1995 年	114	11.3
1996 年	122	12.1
1997 年	150	14.9
1998 年	142	14.1
1999 年	90	8.9

n=1008

1-4-3 该彩色电视机的价格/ The Price of the Currently Owned Color TV

	人数 Number	百分比 Percent
2000 元或以下 2000 yuan or below	135	13.3
2001～4000 元 yuan	407	40.0
4001～6000 元 yuan	210	20.6
6001～8000 元 yuan	80	7.9
8001～10000 元 yuan	54	5.3
10001～12000 元 yuan	33	3.2
12001～14000 元 yuan	21	2.1
14001～16000 元 yuan	5	0.5
16001～18000 元 yuan	3	0.3
18001～20000 元 yuan	1	0.1
20000 元以上 over 20000 yuan	5	0.5
完全不知道 don't know	64	6.3

n=1018

1-4-4 该彩色电视机的尺寸/ The Screen Size of the Currently Owned Color TV

	人数 Number	百分比 Percent
14 英寸 inches	13	1.3
16 英寸 inches	4	0.4
18 英寸 inches	58	5.8
20 英寸 inches	36	3.6
21 英寸 inches	287	28.6
22 英寸 inches	10	1.0
24 英寸 inches	18	1.8
25 英寸 inches	239	23.8
27 英寸 inches	10	1.0
28 英寸 inches	18	1.8
29 英寸 inches	278	27.7
31 英寸 inches	5	0.5
32 英寸 inches	4	0.4
33 英寸 inches	5	0.5
34 英寸 inches	14	1.4
34 英寸以上 over 34 inches	5	0.5
其他 others	1	0.1

n=1005

1-4-5 该彩色电视机的类型/ The Type of the Currently Owned Color TV

	人数 Number	百分比 Percent
普通屏幕 traditional screen	506	49.9
平面直角 plane screen	452	44.5
超平 super plane screen	45	4.4
纯平 pure plane screen	11	1.1
其他 others	1	0.1

n=1015

1-5 选择不同品牌的彩色电视机的考虑因素/ Considerations in Choosing from Different Brands

注：本题为多选题，合计百分比超过 100%（Multiple answers）

	人数 Number	品牌形象 brand image	外型 outlook	价格 price	功能齐备 all-function	图象清晰度 clarity	图象色彩 color	音响效果 sound effect	售后服务 follow-up service	其他 others
样本 Sample	1015	43.6	13.8	41.3	26.6	44.5	27.1	14.3	12.3	1.6
松下/乐声 Panasonic	296	50.0	12.2	31.1	25.3	45.9	33.1	17.6	9.8	2.0
索尼 Sony	130	54.6	10.8	30.8	28.5	52.3	26.2	20.8	6.2	0.0
康佳 Konka	97	45.4	13.4	50.5	23.7	40.2	14.4	10.3	21.6	3.1
东芝 Toshiba	70	44.3	18.6	32.9	27.1	40.0	25.7	11.4	7.1	0.0
日立 Hitachi	68	52.9	7.4	44.1	19.1	48.5	16.2	8.8	13.2	1.5
王牌 TCL	65	23.1	16.9	55.4	29.2	40.0	30.8	13.8	20.0	1.5
创维 Skyworth-RGB	57	31.6	21.1	49.1	22.8	45.6	31.6	7.0	17.5	0.0
长虹 Changhong	48	50.0	18.8	54.2	35.4	41.7	16.7	8.3	14.6	2.1
乐华 Rowa	41	29.3	4.9	65.9	39.0	36.6	24.4	2.4	12.2	4.9

1-6 彩色电视机未来一年购买打算/ Plan for Future Purchasing of a Color TV

1-6-1 有无购买打算/ Whether Planning to Purchase Next Year

	人数 Number	百分比 Percent
是 yes	101	9.8
否 no	930	90.2

n=1031

1-6-2 打算购买的品牌排名/ The Brand of the Planned Purchase Next Year

排名 Brand Ranking	品牌 Brands	人数 Number	百分比 Percent
1	索尼 Sony	20	19.8
2	松下/乐声 Panasonic	19	18.8
3	康佳 Konka	14	13.9
4	长虹 Changhong	7	6.9
4	王牌 TCL	7	6.9
5	东芝 Toshiba	6	5.9
6	创维 Skyworth-RGB	5	5.0

n=101

1-6-3 打算购买的尺寸/ The Screen Size of the Planned Purchase Next Year

	人数 Number	百分比 Percent
14 英寸 inches	2	2.1
16 英寸 inches	1	1.0
18 英寸 inches	0	0.0
20 英寸 inches	0	0.0
21 英寸 inches	16	16.7
22 英寸 inches	1	1.0
24 英寸 inches	0	0.0
25 英寸 inches	16	16.7
27 英寸 inches	1	1.0
28 英寸 inches	2	2.1
29 英寸 inches	40	41.7
31 英寸 inches	1	1.0
32 英寸 inches	0	0.0
33 英寸 inches	6	6.3
34 英寸 inches	6	6.3
34 英寸以上 over 34 inches	2	2.1
其他 others	2	2.1

n=96

1-6-4 打算购买的价格/ The Price of the Planned Purchase Next Year

	人数 Number	百分比 Percent
2000 元或以下 2000 yuan or below	15	15.2
2001～4000 元 yuan	41	41.4
4001～6000 元 yuan	18	18.2
6001～8000 元 yuan	9	9.1
8001～10000 元 yuan	6	6.1
10001～12000 元 yuan	0	0.0
12001～14000 元 yuan	3	3.0
14001～16000 元 yuan	0	0.0
16001～18000 元 yuan	0	0.0
18001～20000 元 yuan	1	1.0
20000 元以上 over 20000 yuan	3	3.0
完全不知道 don't know	3	3.0

n=99

1-7 选购彩色电视机时不同角色的人口特征/ Demographics of the Different Roles in Purchasing a Color TV

注：不同角色可以多选（Multiple answers）

	人数 Number	16-24 岁 Age	25-34 岁 Age	35-44 岁 Age	45-54 岁 Age	55-60 岁 Age
样本 Sample	922	20.2	30.3	25.5	15.7	8.4
男性 Male	439	20.0	29.8	26.0	15.0	9.1
提议者 advocate	85	20.0	34.1	18.8	16.5	10.6
影响者 influence	76	31.6	26.3	18.4	13.2	10.5
决定者 decider	179	8.4	27.9	31.3	21.2	11.2
使用者 user	234	24.4	31.6	23.9	10.7	9.4
女性 Female	483	20.3	30.6	25.1	16.4	7.7
提议者 advocate	104	19.2	28.8	27.9	19.2	4.8
影响者 influence	111	15.3	39.6	24.3	16.2	4.5
决定者 decider	99	11.1	24.2	32.3	23.2	9.1
使用者 user	308	22.7	30.2	24.7	14.6	7.8

1-8 不同消费者层的家中目前拥有品牌/ Brands of Color TV Owned in Household by Market Segments

1-8-1 时尚流行指标/ Fads Popular Index

	人数 Number	第一品牌及百分比 1st/ percent	第二品牌及百分比 2nd/ percent	第三品牌及百分比 3rd/ percent	第四品牌及百分比 4th/ percent
样本 Sample	1010	**松下/乐声 Panasonic(29.4)**	**索尼 Sony(12.9)**	**康佳 Konka(9.4)**	**东芝 Toshiba(7.0)**
平实生活指向 simple living orientation	511	松下/乐声 Panasonic(29.0)	索尼 Sony(13.7)	康佳 Konka(9.6)	日立 Hitachi(7.4)
时尚流行指向 fashion orientation	499	松下/乐声 Panasonic(29.9)	索尼 Sony(12.0)	康佳 Konka(9.2)	东芝 Toshiba(8.0)

1-8-2 广告态度指标/ Advertising attitude Index

	人数 Number	第一品牌及百分比 1st/ percent	第二品牌及百分比 2nd/ percent	第三品牌及百分比 3rd/ percent	第四品牌及百分比 4th/ percent
样本 Sample	1010	**松下/乐声 Panasonic(29.5)**	**索尼 Sony(12.7)**	**康佳 Konka(9.4)**	**东芝 Toshiba(7.0)**
广告淡漠指向 indifferent orientation	329	松下/乐声 Panasonic(30.4)	索尼 Sony(14.3)	康佳 Konka(8.2)	东芝 Toshiba(7.3)
中间层 medium	587	松下/乐声 Panasonic(29.5)	索尼 Sony(11.6)	康佳 Konka(10.2)	日立 Hitachi(7.3)
信赖广告指向 loyal orientation	94	松下/乐声 Panasonic(26.6)	索尼 Sony(13.8)	东芝 Toshiba(9.6)	康佳 Konka(8.5)

1-9 不同消费者层选择彩色电视机时的考虑因素/ Considerations in Choosing from Different Brands by Market Segments

1-9-1 时尚流行指标/ Fads Popular Index

注：本题为多选题，合计百分比超过 100%（Multiple answers）

	人数 Number	品牌形象 brand image	外型 outlook	价格 price	功能齐备 all-function	图象清晰度 clarity	图象色彩 color	音响效果 sound effect	售后服务 follow-up service	其他 others
样本 Sample	1003	43.6	13.8	41.4	26.6	44.6	27.1	14.3	12.3	1.6
平实生活指向 simple living orientation	508	44.3	11.0	45.7	21.1	42.9	28.9	12.8	13.6	1.8
时尚流行指向 fashion orientation	495	42.8	16.6	37.0	32.3	46.3	25.3	15.8	10.9	1.4

1-9-2 广告态度指标/ Advertising Attitude Index

注：本题为多选题，合计百分比超过 100%（Multiple answers）

	人数 Number	品牌形象 brand image	外型 outlook	价格 price	功能齐备 all-function	图象清晰度 clarity	图象色彩 color	音响效果 sound effect	售后服务 follow-up service	其他 others
样本 Sample	**1003**	**43.7**	**14.0**	**41.3**	**26.6**	**44.3**	**26.9**	**14.5**	**12.4**	**1.6**
广告淡漠指向 indifferent orientation	326	40.2	13.2	44.5	25.2	42.9	29.1	15.0	12.9	2.1
中间层 medium	583	44.9	13.4	39.6	28.1	44.9	26.8	14.4	12.3	1.2
信赖广告指向 loyal orientation	94	47.9	20.2	40.4	22.3	44.7	20.2	12.8	10.6	2.1

1-9-3 价格态度指标/ Price Attitude Index

注：本题为多选题，合计百分比超过 100%（Multiple answers）

	人数 Number	品牌形象 brand image	外型 outlook	价格 price	功能齐备 all-function	图象清晰度 clarity	图象色彩 color	音响效果 sound effect	售后服务 follow-up service	其他 others
样本 Sample	**1009**	**43.6**	**13.9**	**41.3**	**26.6**	**44.6**	**27.1**	**14.3**	**12.4**	**1.6**
价格无关心指向 indifferent orientation	184	40.8	9.8	36.4	33.2	42.4	26.6	15.2	14.1	1.6
中间层 medium	539	44.2	15.4	42.1	26.0	43.6	28.2	14.5	11.7	1.7
价格重视指向 careful orientation	286	44.4	13.6	43.0	23.4	47.9	25.2	13.3	12.6	1.4

● 重庆 / Chongqing

1-1 彩色电视机拥有比例/ Proportion of Color TV Owners in the Sample

	人数 Number	百分比 Percent
有 yes	601	96.3
没有 no	23	3.7

n=624

1-2 彩色电视机的拥有量/ Number of Color TV Owned Per Household

	人数 Number	百分比 Percent
1 台 1 set	431	71.7
2 台 2 sets	154	25.6
3 台 3 sets	12	2.0
4 台及以上 4 sets or over	4	0.7

n=601

1-3 理想品牌排名/ Ranking of the Ideal Brands

排名 Brand Ranking	品牌 Brands	人数 Number	百分比 Percent
1	长虹 Changhong	286	45.8
2	康佳 Konka	86	13.8
3	索尼 Sony	49	7.9
4	王牌 TCL	44	7.1
5	松下/乐声 Panasonic	39	6.3
6	东芝 Toshiba	16	2.6
7	飞利浦 Philips	15	2.4
8	日立 Hitachi	13	2.1
8	海尔 Haier	13	2.1
9	熊猫 Panda	10	1.6
9	创维 Skyworth-RGB	10	1.6

n=624

1-4 对家中现有彩色电视机(最近购买的一台)的五个方面的描述/ About the Color TV Most Recently Purchased

1-4-1 家中现有彩色电视机的品牌排名/ Ranking of the Currently Owned Color TV Brands

排名 Brand Ranking	品牌 Brands	人数 Number	百分比 Percent
1	长虹 Changhong	249	41.5
2	康佳 Konka	66	11.0
3	王牌 TCL	34	5.7
4	松下/乐声 Panasonic	27	4.5
5	熊猫 Panda	26	4.3
6	索尼 Sony	23	3.8
7	红岩 Hongyan	17	2.8
7	东芝 Toshiba	17	2.8
8	创维 Skyworth-RGB	14	2.3
9	金雀 Jinque	10	1.7
9	日立 Hitachi	10	1.7
10	三洋 Sanyo	8	1.3

n=600

1-4-2 该彩色电视机的购买时间/ Time of Purchasing of the Currently Owned Color TV

	人数 Number	百分比 Percent
1985 年或以前 1985 or before	24	4.0
1986～1990 年	81	13.5
1991 年	33	5.5
1992 年	37	6.2
1993 年	35	5.8
1994 年	34	5.7
1995 年	41	6.8
1996 年	66	11.0
1997 年	81	13.5
1998 年	88	14.7
1999 年	79	13.2

n=599

1-4-3 该彩色电视机的价格/ The Price of the Currently Owned Color TV

	人数 Number	百分比 Percent
2000 元或以下 2000 yuan or below	133	22.2
2001～4000 元 yuan	334	55.7
4001～6000 元 yuan	53	8.8
6001～8000 元 yuan	28	4.7
8001～10000 元 yuan	14	2.3
10001～12000 元 yuan	14	2.3
12001～14000 元 yuan	7	1.2
14001～16000 元 yuan	2	0.3
16001～18000 元 yuan	1	0.2
18001～20000 元 yuan	1	0.2
20000 元以上 over 20000 yuan	2	0.3
完全不知道 don't know	11	1.8

n=600

1-4-4 该彩色电视机的尺寸/ The Screen Size of the Currently Owned Color TV

	人数 Number	百分比 Percent
14 英寸 inches	8	1.3
16 英寸 inches	1	0.2
18 英寸 inches	56	9.4
20 英寸 inches	26	4.3
21 英寸 inches	216	36.1
22 英寸 inches	8	1.3
24 英寸 inches	7	1.2
25 英寸 inches	81	13.5
27 英寸 inches	1	0.2
28 英寸 inches	7	1.2
29 英寸 inches	177	29.6
31 英寸 inches	2	0.3
32 英寸 inches	2	0.3
33 英寸 inches	2	0.3
34 英寸 inches	4	0.7
34 英寸以上 over 34 inches	0	0.0
其他 others	0	0.0

n=598

1-4-5 该彩色电视机的类型/ The Type of the Currently Owned Color TV

	人数 Number	百分比 Percent
普通屏幕 traditional screen	202	33.8
平面直角 plane screen	323	54.1
超平 super plane screen	63	10.6
纯平 pure plane screen	8	1.3
其他 others	1	0.2

n=597

1-5 选择不同品牌的彩色电视机的考虑因素/ Considerations in Choosing from Different Brands

注：本题为多选题，合计百分比超过 100%（Multiple answers）

	人数 Number	品牌形象 brand image	外型 outlook	价格 price	功能齐备 all-function	图象清晰度 clarity	图象色彩 color	音响效果 sound effect	售后服务 follow-up service	其他 others
样本 Sample	**596**	**46.5**	**14.1**	**38.6**	**24.8**	**40.9**	**21.1**	**9.9**	**17.4**	**3.7**
长虹 Changhong	248	58.1	12.9	37.1	20.2	38.7	17.7	8.1	17.7	3.2
康佳 Konka	66	47.0	16.7	31.8	19.7	42.4	21.2	13.6	36.4	3.0
王牌 TCL	33	45.5	33.3	45.5	21.2	45.5	12.1	12.1	21.2	0.0
松下/乐声 Panasonic	26	46.2	15.4	38.5	46.2	53.8	30.8	15.4	11.5	0.0
熊猫 Panda	26	46.2	11.5	46.2	19.2	34.6	19.2	3.8	11.5	7.7
索尼 Sony	23	73.9	4.3	4.3	21.7	52.2	30.4	4.3	13.0	13.0
红岩 Hongyan	17	11.8	11.8	82.4	11.8	23.5	17.6	11.8	11.8	0.0
东芝 Toshiba	17	58.8	0.0	5.9	47.1	58.8	41.2	17.6	0.0	5.9
创维 Skyworth-RGB	14	42.9	14.3	57.1	7.1	42.9	14.3	14.3	14.3	0.0
金雀 Jinque	10	20.0	10.0	70.0	30.0	20.0	20.0	0.0	30.0	20.0
日立 Hitachi	10	40.0	20.0	30.0	10.0	20.0	20.0	10.0	10.0	0.0
三洋 Sanyo	8	25.0	12.5	12.5	25.0	100.0	37.5	25.0	0.0	0.0

1-6 彩色电视机未来一年购买打算/ Plan for Future Purchasing of a Color TV

1-6-1 有无购买打算/ Whether Planning to Purchase Next Year

	人数 Number	百分比 Percent
是 yes	80	12.8
否 no	544	87.2

n=624

1-6-2 打算购买的品牌排名/ The Brand of the Planned Purchase Next Year

排名 Brand Ranking	品牌 Brands	人数 Number	百分比 Percent
1	长虹 Changhong	24	31.6
2	康佳 Konka	14	18.4
3	索尼 Sony	7	9.2
4	王牌 TCL	6	7.9
5	飞利浦 Philips	5	6.6
6	松下/乐声 Panasonic	4	5.3
7	海尔 Haier	3	3.9

n=76

1-6-3 打算购买的尺寸/ The Screen Size of the Planned Purchase Next Year

	人数 Number	百分比 Percent
14 英寸 inches	0	0.0
16 英寸 inches	1	1.3
18 英寸 inches	0	0.0
20 英寸 inches	2	2.6
21 英寸 inches	3	3.8
22 英寸 inches	0	0.0
24 英寸 inches	0	0.0
25 英寸 inches	19	24.4
27 英寸 inches	0	0.0
28 英寸 inches	1	1.3
29 英寸 inches	28	35.9
31 英寸 inches	0	0.0
32 英寸 inches	2	2.6
33 英寸 inches	1	1.3
34 英寸 inches	13	16.7
34 英寸以上 over 34 inches	6	7.7
其他 others	2	2.6

n=78

1-6-4 打算购买的价格/ The Price of the Planned Purchase Next Year

	人数 Number	百分比 Percent
2000 元或以下 2000 yuan or below	9	11.3
2001～4000 元 yuan	34	42.5
4001～6000 元 yuan	13	16.3
6001～8000 元 yuan	11	13.8
8001～10000 元 yuan	4	5.0
10001～12000 元 yuan	2	2.5
12001～14000 元 yuan	1	1.3
14001～16000 元 yuan	0	0.0
16001～18000 元 yuan	1	1.3
18001～20000 元 yuan	0	0.0
20000 元以上 over 20000 yuan	3	3.8
完全不知道 don't know	2	2.5

n=80

1-7 选购彩色电视机时不同角色的人口特征/ Demographics of the Different Roles in Purchasing a Color TV

注：不同角色可以多选（Multiple answers）

	人数 Number	16-24 岁 Age	25-34 岁 Age	35-44 岁 Age	45-54 岁 Age	55-60 岁 Age
样本 Sample	539	19.1	28.9	24.7	19.1	8.2
男性 Male	279	19.4	29.0	25.1	17.9	8.6
提议者 advocate	70	27.1	28.6	28.6	10.0	5.7
影响者 influence	33	21.2	33.3	15.2	21.2	9.1
决定者 decider	156	6.4	26.9	35.9	20.5	10.3
使用者 user	167	24.0	28.7	23.4	15.6	8.4
女性 Female	260	18.8	28.8	24.2	20.4	7.7
提议者 advocate	79	17.7	25.3	29.1	24.1	3.8
影响者 influence	33	15.2	42.4	21.2	15.2	6.1
决定者 decider	72	6.9	36.1	26.4	25.0	5.6
使用者 user	178	21.3	31.5	21.9	15.7	9.6

1-8 不同消费者层的家中目前拥有品牌/ Brands of Color TV Owned in Household by Market Segments

1-8-1 时尚流行指标/ Fads Popular Index

	人数 Number	第一品牌及百分比 1st/ percent	第二品牌及百分比 2nd/ percent	第三品牌及百分比 3rd/ percent
样本 Sample	592	**长虹 Changhong(41.7)**	**康佳 Konka(11.0)**	**王牌 TCL(5.7)**
平实生活指向 simple living orientation	352	长虹 Changhong(42.3)	康佳 Konka(11.1)	王牌 TCL(6.0)
时尚流行指向 fashion orientation	240	长虹 Changhong(40.8)	康佳 Konka(10.8)	松下/乐声 Panasonic(6.3)

1-8-2 广告态度指标/ Advertising Attitude Index

	人数 Number	第一品牌及百分比 1st/ percent	第二品牌及百分比 2nd/ percent	第三品牌及百分比 3rd/ percent
样本 Sample	594	**长虹 Changhong(41.6)**	**康佳 Konka(11.1)**	**王牌 TCL(5.7)**
广告淡漠指向 indifferent orientation	157	长虹 Changhong(36.9)	康佳 Konka(11.5)	王牌 TCL(8.9)
中间层 medium	356	长虹 Changhong(42.4)	康佳 Konka(10.4)	王牌 TCL(4.8)
信赖广告指向 loyal orientation	81	长虹 Changhong(46.9)	康佳 Konka(13.6)	熊猫 Panda(6.2)

1-8-3 价格态度指标/ Price Attitude Index

	人数 Number	第一品牌及百分比 1st/ percent	第二品牌及百分比 2nd/ percent	第三品牌及百分比 3rd/ percent
样本 Sample	591	**长虹 Changhong(41.5)**	**康佳 Konka(11.0)**	**王牌 TCL(5.8)**
价格无关心指向 indifferent orientation	103	长虹 Changhong(32.0)	东芝 Toshiba(8.7) 索尼 Sony(8.7)	康佳 Konka(7.8) 松下/乐声 Panasonic(7.8)
中间层 medium	267	长虹 Changhong(41.6)	康佳 Konka(12.4)	王牌 TCL(6.7)
价格重视指向 careful orientation	221	长虹 Changhong(45.7)	康佳 Konka(10.9)	熊猫 Panda(5.0) 王牌 TCL(5.0)

1-9 不同消费者层选择彩色电视机时考虑因素/ Considerations in Choosing from Different Brands by Market Segments

1-9-1 时尚流行指标/ Fads Popular Index

注：本题为多选题，合计百分比超过 100%（Multiple answers）

	人数 Number	品牌形象 brand image	外型 outlook	价格 price	功能齐备 all-function	图象清晰度 clarity	图象色彩 color	音响效果 sound effect	售后服务 follow-up service	其他 others
样本 Sample	589	46.5	13.9	38.7	24.8	41.1	21.1	10.0	17.3	3.4
平实生活指向 simple living orientation	351	46.4	13.1	42.2	23.6	40.2	21.1	7.7	18.8	3.1
时尚流行指向 fashion orientation	238	46.6	15.1	33.6	26.5	42.4	21.0	13.4	15.1	3.8

1-9-2 广告态度指标/ Advertising Attitude Index

注：本题为多选题，合计百分比超过 100%（Multiple answers）

	人数 Number	品牌形象 brand image	外型 outlook	价格 price	功能齐备 all-function	图象清晰度 clarity	图象色彩 color	音响效果 sound effect	售后服务 follow-up service	其他 others
样本 Sample	591	46.5	14.2	38.7	24.7	41.3	21.0	10.0	17.4	3.7
广告淡漠指向 indifferent orientation	154	40.3	8.4	44.8	25.3	41.6	18.8	10.4	16.2	6.5
中间层 medium	356	46.3	13.2	35.7	26.1	42.7	23.9	10.1	18.0	3.1
信赖广告指向 loyal orientation	81	59.3	29.6	40.7	17.3	34.6	12.3	8.6	17.3	1.2

1-9-3 价格态度指标/ Price Attitude Index

注：本题为多选题，合计百分比超过 100%（Multiple answers）

	人数 Number	品牌形象 brand image	外型 outlook	价格 price	功能齐备 all-function	图象清晰度 clarity	图象色彩 color	音响效果 sound effect	售后服务 follow-up service	其他 others
样本 Sample	588	46.8	14.1	38.9	24.7	41.0	21.1	10.0	17.3	3.4
价格无关心指向 indifferent orientation	103	48.5	11.7	28.2	31.1	50.5	22.3	12.6	13.6	2.9
中间层 medium	264	47.3	14.4	39.4	26.1	38.6	22.3	11.4	19.7	2.7
价格重视指向 careful orientation	221	45.2	14.9	43.4	19.9	39.4	19.0	7.2	16.3	4.5

● 武汉 / Wuhan

1-1 彩色电视机拥有比例/ Proportion of Color TV Owners in the Sample

	人数 Number	百分比 Percent
有 yes	624	97.2
没有 no	18	2.8

n=642

1-2 彩色电视机的拥有量/ Number of Color TV Owned Per Household

	人数 Number	百分比 Percent
1 台 1 set	444	71.7
2 台 2 sets	162	26.2
3 台 3 sets	11	1.8
4 台及以上 4 sets or over	2	0.3

n=619

1-3 理想品牌排名/ Ranking of the Ideal Brands

排名 Brand Ranking	品牌 Brands	人数 Number	百分比 Percent
1	长虹 Changhong	201	31.4
2	康佳 Konka	108	16.9
3	松下/乐声 Panasonic	52	8.1
4	王牌 TCL	43	6.7
4	索尼 Sony	43	6.7
5	海尔 Haier	37	5.8
6	飞利浦 Philips	32	5.0
7	东芝 Toshiba	18	2.8
8	日立 Hitachi	9	1.4
9	创维 Skyworth-RGB	7	1.1

n=640

1-4 对家中现有彩色电视机(最近购买的一台)的五个方面的描述/ About the Color TV Most Recently Purchased

1-4-1 家中现有彩色电视机的品牌排名/ Ranking of the Currently Owned Color TV Brands

排名 Brand Ranking	品牌 Brands	人数 Number	百分比 Percent
1	长虹 Changhong	148	23.8
2	康佳 Konka	120	19.3
3	王牌 TCL	36	5.8
4	松下/乐声 Panasonic	30	4.8
5	飞利浦 Philips	23	3.7
6	海尔 Haier	22	3.5
7	东芝 Toshiba	19	3.1
8	厦华 Xoceco	18	2.9
9	莺歌 Yingge	16	2.6
9	索尼 Sony	16	2.6
9	佳丽 Jiali	16	2.6
9	日立 Hitachi	16	2.6

n=622

1-4-2 该彩色电视机的购买时间/ The Time of Purchasing of the Currently Owned Color TV

	人数 Number	百分比 Percent
1985 年或以前 1985 or before	31	5.0
1986～1990 年	114	18.3
1991 年	42	6.8
1992 年	26	4.2
1993 年	35	5.6
1994 年	26	4.2
1995 年	48	7.7
1996 年	52	8.4
1997 年	70	11.3
1998 年	82	13.2
1999 年	96	15.4

n=622

1-4-3 该彩色电视机的价格/ The Price of the Currently Owned Color TV

	人数 Number	百分比 Percent
2000 元或以下 2000 yuan or below	127	20.4
2001～4000 元 yuan	362	58.0
4001～6000 元 yuan	70	11.2
6001～8000 元 yuan	18	2.9
8001～10000 元 yuan	9	1.4
10001～12000 元 yuan	7	1.1
12001～14000 元 yuan	2	0.3
14001～16000 元 yuan	2	0.3
16001～18000 元 yuan	4	0.6
18001～20000 元 yuan	2	0.3
20000 元以上 over 20000 yuan	10	1.6
完全不知道 don't know	11	1.8

n=624

1-4-4 该彩色电视机的尺寸/ The Screen Size of the Currently Owned Color TV

	人数 Number	百分比 Percent
14 英寸 inches	16	2.6
16 英寸 inches	2	0.3
18 英寸 inches	68	11.0
20 英寸 inches	39	6.3
21 英寸 inches	220	35.5
22 英寸 inches	6	1.0
24 英寸 inches	9	1.5
25 英寸 inches	109	17.6
27 英寸 inches	0	0.0
28 英寸 inches	5	0.8
29 英寸 inches	134	21.6
31 英寸 inches	2	0.3
32 英寸 inches	1	0.2
33 英寸 inches	0	0.0
34 英寸 inches	5	0.8
34 英寸以上 over 34 inches	2	0.3
其他 others	1	0.2

n=619

1-4-5 该彩色电视机的类型/ The Type of the Currently Owned Color TV

	人数 Number	百分比 Percent
普通屏幕 traditional screen	282	45.3
平面直角 plane screen	264	42.4
超平 super plane screen	64	10.3
纯平 pure plane screen	7	1.1
其他 others	5	0.8

n=622

1-5 选择不同品牌的彩色电视机的考虑因素/ Considerations in Choosing from Different Brands

注：本题为多选题，合计百分比超过 100%（Multiple answers）

	人数 Number	品牌形象 brand image	外型 outlook	价格 price	功能齐备 all-function	图象清晰度 clarity	图象色彩 color	音响效果 sound effect	售后服务 follow-up service	其他 others
样本 Sample	**621**	**49.1**	**17.4**	**42.8**	**29.0**	**39.8**	**19.8**	**11.8**	**18.8**	**5.6**
长虹 Changhong	148	66.9	12.8	40.5	32.4	37.8	14.9	7.4	20.3	4.1
康佳 Konka	120	60.0	19.2	45.8	30.0	30.0	12.5	8.3	23.3	1.7
王牌 TCL	36	33.3	19.4	50.0	41.7	50.0	25.0	13.9	19.4	0.0
松下/乐声 Panasonic	30	53.3	16.7	26.7	43.3	46.7	26.7	20.0	3.3	3.3
飞利浦 Philips	23	56.5	13.0	30.4	30.4	65.2	26.1	8.7	13.0	8.7
海尔 Haier	22	45.5	18.2	31.8	18.2	40.9	13.6	22.7	81.8	0.0
东芝 Toshiba	19	57.9	10.5	31.6	31.6	47.4	36.8	31.6	10.5	0.0
厦华 Xoceco	18	27.8	22.2	77.8	33.3	33.3	27.8	5.6	11.1	5.6
莺歌 Yingge	16	31.3	6.3	31.3	31.3	18.8	12.5	6.3	18.8	12.5
索尼 Sony	16	50.0	18.8	18.8	25.0	68.8	50.0	31.3	6.3	0.0
佳丽 Jiali	16	37.5	31.3	50.0	25.0	31.3	31.3	12.5	12.5	0.0
日立 Hitachi	15	60.0	26.7	20.0	20.0	53.3	6.7	20.0	0.0	13.3

1-6 彩色电视机未来一年购买打算/ Plan for Future Purchasing of a Color TV

1-6-1 有无购买打算/ Whether Planning to Purchase Next Year

	人数 Number	百分比 Percent
是 yes	95	14.8
否 no	547	85.2

n=642

1-6-2 打算购买的品牌排名/ Ranking of the Brand of the Planned Purchase Next Year

排名 Brand Ranking	品牌 Brands	人数 Number	百分比 Percent
1	长虹 Changhong	30	33.7
2	康佳 Konka	13	14.6
3	王牌 TCL	7	7.9
4	海尔 Haier	6	6.7
5	飞利浦 Philips	4	4.5
5	松下/乐声 Panasonic	4	4.5
5	索尼 Sony	4	4.5

n=89

1-6-3 打算购买的尺寸/ The Screen Size of the Planned Purchase Next Year

	人数 Number	百分比 Percent
14 英寸 inches	4	4.3
16 英寸 inches	3	3.3
18 英寸 inches	0	0.0
20 英寸 inches	3	3.3
21 英寸 inches	5	5.4
22 英寸 inches	1	1.1
24 英寸 inches	1	1.1
25 英寸 inches	17	18.5
27 英寸 inches	3	3.3
28 英寸 inches	0	0.0
29 英寸 inches	44	47.8
31 英寸 inches	3	3.3
32 英寸 inches	1	1.1
33 英寸 inches	0	0.0
34 英寸 inches	5	5.4
34 英寸以上 over 34 inches	2	2.2
其他 others	0	0.0

n=92

1-6-4 打算购买的价格/ The Price of the Planned Purchase Next Year

	人数 Number	百分比 Percent
2000 元以下 2000 yuan or below	9	9.8
2001～4000 元 yuan	54	58.7
4001～6000 元 yuan	20	21.7
6001～8000 元 yuan	5	5.4
8001～10000 元 yuan	3	3.3
10001～12000 元 yuan	0	0.0
12001～14000 元 yuan	0	0.0
14001～16000 元 yuan	0	0.0
16001～18000 元 yuan	0	0.0
18001～20000 元 yuan	1	1.1
20000 元以上 over 20000 yuan	0	0.0
完全不知道 don't know	0	0.0

n=92

1-7 选购彩色电视机时不同角色的人口特征/ Demographics of the Different Roles in Purchasing a Color TV

注：不同角色可以多选（Multiple answers）

	人数 Number	16-24 岁 Age	25-34 岁 Age	35-44 岁 Age	45-54 岁 Age	55-60 岁 Age
样本 Sample	574	20.9	28.4	25.1	18.1	7.5
男性 Male	276	21.4	28.6	24.6	17.0	8.3
提议者 advocate	63	23.8	23.8	25.4	22.2	4.8
影响者 influence	38	26.3	31.6	18.4	23.7	0.0
决定者 decider	130	9.2	30.8	31.5	16.9	11.5
使用者 user	179	24.0	28.5	22.9	16.8	7.8
女性 Female	298	20.5	28.2	25.5	19.1	6.7
提议者 advocate	80	21.3	28.7	27.5	16.3	6.3
影响者 influence	41	17.1	24.4	24.4	31.7	2.4
决定者 decider	114	8.8	26.3	34.2	24.6	6.1
使用者 user	213	21.1	25.4	25.4	19.7	8.5

1-8 不同消费者层的家中目前拥有品牌/ Brands of Color TV Owned in Household by Market Segments

1-8-1 时尚流行指标/ Fads Popular Index

	人数 Number	第一品牌及百分比 1st/ percent	第二品牌及百分比 2nd/ percent	第三品牌及百分比 3rd/ percent	第四品牌及百分比 4th/ percent
样本 Sample	613	**长虹 Changhong(23.3)**	**康佳 Konka(19.1)**	**王牌 TCL(5.9)**	**松下/乐声 Panasonic(4.7)**
平实生活指向 simple living orientation	318	长虹 Changhong(21.7)	康佳 Konka(17.6)	松下/乐声 Panasonic(5.3)	王牌 TCL(5.0)
时尚流行指向 fashion orientation	295	长虹 Changhong(25.1)	康佳 Konka(20.7)	王牌 TCL(6.8)	飞利浦 Philips(4.7)

1-8-2 广告态度指标/ Advertising Attitude Index

	人数 Number	第一品牌及百分比 1st/ percent	第二品牌及百分比 2nd/ percent	第三品牌及百分比 3rd/ percent	第四品牌及百分比 4th/ percent
样本 Sample	615	**长虹 Changhong(23.3)**	**康佳 Konka(19.2)**	**王牌 TCL(5.9)**	**松下/乐声 Panasonic(4.9)**
广告淡漠指向 indifferent orientation	181	长虹 Changhong(24.3)	康佳 Konka(17.7)	王牌 TCL(6.1)	飞利浦 Philips(5.0)
中间层 medium	362	长虹 Changhong(23.2)	康佳 Konka(19.9)	王牌 TCL(5.2)	松下/乐声 Panasonic(4.7)
信赖广告指向 loyal orientation	72	长虹 Changhong(20.8)	康佳 Konka(19.4)	王牌 TCL(8.3)	松下/乐声 Panasonic(6.9)

1-8-3 价格态度指标/ Price Attitude Index

	人数	第一品牌及百分比 1st/ percent	第二品牌及百分比 2nd/ percent	第三品牌及百分比 3rd/ percent	第四品牌及百分比 4th/ percent
样本 Sample	614	**长虹 Changhong(23.3)**	**康佳 Konka(19.2)**	**王牌 TCL(5.9)**	**松下/乐声 Panasonic(4.9)**
价格无关心指向 indifferent orientation	82	长虹 Changhong(26.8)	康佳 Konka(18.3)	王牌 TCL(7.3)	海尔 Haier(6.1) 日立 Hitachi(6.1) 松下/乐声 Panasonic(6.1)
中间层 medium	297	长虹 Changhong(24.6)	康佳 Konka(20.9)	王牌 TCL(6.7)	松下/乐声 Panasonic(5.4)
价格重视指向 careful orientation	235	长虹 Changhong(20.4)	康佳 Konka(17.4)	佳丽 Jiali(4.3) 王牌 TCL(4.3)	海尔 Haier(3.8) 松下/乐声 Panasonic(3.8) 东芝 Toshiba(3.8) 创维 Skyworth-RGB(3.8)

1-9 不同消费者层选择彩色电视机时的考虑因素/ Considerations in Choosing from Different Brands by Market Segments

1-9-1 时尚流行指标/ Fads Popular Index

注：本题为多选题，合计百分比超过 100%（Multiple answers）

	人数 Number	品牌形象 brand image	外型 outlook	价格 price	功能齐备 all - function	图象清晰度 clarity	图象色彩 color	音响效果 sound effect	售后服务 follow-up service	其他 others
样本 Sample	614	48.7	17.3	42.7	28.7	39.6	19.9	11.9	18.9	5.7
平实生活指向 simple living orientation	318	46.5	15.4	44.3	26.1	37.1	18.9	11.6	17.0	6.6
时尚流行指向 fashion orientation	296	51.0	19.3	40.9	31.4	42.2	20.9	12.2	20.9	4.7

1-9-2 广告态度指标/ Advertising Attitude Index

注：本题为多选题，合计百分比超过 100%（Multiple answers）

	人数 Number	品牌形象 brand image	外型 outlook	价格 price	功能齐备 all-function	图象清晰度 clarity	图象色彩 color	音响效果 sound effect	售后服务 follow-up service	其他 others
样本 Sample	616	48.5	17.4	42.9	28.7	39.6	19.8	11.9	18.8	5.7
广告淡漠指向 indifferent orientation	180	46.1	16.1	38.3	22.8	33.9	20.0	12.8	19.4	8.3
中间层 medium	363	49.6	17.4	44.4	31.1	41.6	20.4	12.1	19.0	4.7
信赖广告指向 loyal orientation	73	49.3	20.5	46.6	31.5	43.8	16.4	8.2	16.4	4.1

1-9-3 价格态度指标/ Price Attitude Index

注：本题为多选题，合计百分比超过 100%（Multiple answers）

	人数 Number	品牌形象 brand image	外型 outlook	价格 price	功能齐备 all-function	图象清晰度 clarity	图象色彩 color	音响效果 sound effect	售后服务 follow-up service	其他 others
样本 Sample	615	48.5	17.2	42.8	28.8	39.7	19.8	11.9	18.9	5.7
价格无关心指向 indifferent orientation	81	39.5	21.0	39.5	25.9	32.1	19.8	13.6	22.2	1.2
中间层 medium	298	53.0	17.1	40.9	30.5	44.0	20.8	12.1	18.8	5.7
价格重视指向 careful orientation	236	45.8	16.1	46.2	27.5	36.9	18.6	11.0	17.8	7.2

● 西安 / Xi'an

1-1 彩色电视机拥有比例/ Proportion of Color TV Owners in the Sample

	人数 Number	百分比 Percent
有 yes	592	98.5
没有 no	9	1.5

n=601

1-2 彩色电视机的拥有量/ Number of Color TV Owned Per Household

	人数 Number	百分比 Percent
1 台 1 set	434	73.3
2 台 2 sets	146	24.7
3 台 3 sets	12	2.0
4 台及以上 4 sets or over	0	0.0

n=592

1-3 理想品牌排名/ Ranking of the Ideal Brands

排名 Brand Ranking	品牌 Brands	人数 Number	百分比 Percent
1	长虹 Changhong	132	22.0
2	王牌 TCL	104	17.3
3	康佳 Konka	103	17.2
4	松下/乐声 Panasonic	51	8.5
5	索尼 Sony	39	6.5
6	海信 Hisense	32	5.3
7	海尔 Haier	26	4.3
8	黄河 Huanghe	22	3.7
9	东芝 Toshiba	18	3.0
10	飞利浦 Philips	9	1.5

n=600

1-4 对家中现有彩色电视机(最近购买的一台)的五个方面的描述/ About the Color TV Most Recently Purchased

1-4-1 家中现有彩色电视机的品牌排名/ Ranking of the Currently Owned Color TV Brands

排名 Brand Ranking	品牌 Brands	人数 Number	百分比 Percent
1	黄河 Huanghe	117	19.8
2	长虹 Changhong	83	14.0
3	康佳 Konka	77	13.0
4	松下/乐声 Panasonic	39	6.6
4	王牌 TCL	39	6.6
5	如意 Ruyi	26	4.4
6	海信 Hisense	25	4.2
7	海燕 Haiyan	22	3.7
8	索尼 Sony	20	3.4
9	海尔 Haier	12	2.0
10	福日 Hitachi Fujian	11	1.9
10	东芝 Toshiba	11	1.9

n=592

1-4-2 该彩色电视机的购买时间/ The Time of Purchasing of the Currently Owned Color TV

	人数 Number	百分比 Percent
1985 年或以前 1985 or before	40	6.8
1986～1990 年	115	19.4
1991 年	27	4.6
1992 年	19	3.2
1993 年	25	4.2
1994 年	46	7.8
1995 年	36	6.1
1996 年	59	10.0
1997 年	70	11.8
1998 年	76	12.8
1999 年	79	13.3

n=592

1-4-3 该彩色电视机的价格/ The Price of the Currently Owned Color TV

	人数 Number	百分比 Percent
2000 元及以下 2000 yuan or below	148	25.0
2001～4000 元 yuan	310	52.4
4001～6000 元 yuan	84	14.2
6001～8000 元 yuan	21	3.5
8001～10000 元 yuan	10	1.7
10001～12000 元 yuan	7	1.2
12001～14000 元 yuan	2	0.3
14001～16000 元 yuan	0	0.0
16001～18000 元 yuan	1	0.2
18001～20000 元 yuan	0	0.0
20000 元以上 over 20000 yuan	3	0.5
完全不知道 don't know	6	1.0

n=592

1-4-4 该彩色电视机的尺寸/ The Screen Size of the Currently Owned Color TV

	人数 Number	百分比 Percent
14 英寸 inches	11	1.9
16 英寸 inches	0	0.0
18 英寸 inches	123	20.8
20 英寸 inches	34	5.7
21 英寸 inches	140	23.6
22 英寸 inches	11	1.9
24 英寸 inches	8	1.4
25 英寸 inches	91	15.4
27 英寸 inches	1	0.2
28 英寸 inches	5	0.8
29 英寸 inches	158	26.7
31 英寸 inches	1	0.2
32 英寸 inches	1	0.2
33 英寸 inches	1	0.2
34 英寸 inches	5	0.8
34 英寸以上 over 34 inches	1	0.2
其他 others	1	0.2

n=592

1-4-5 该彩色电视机的类型/ The Type of the Currently Owned Color TV

	人数 Number	百分比 Percent
普通屏幕 traditional screen	269	45.4
平面直角 plane screen	269	45.4
超平 super plane screen	40	6.8
纯平 pure plane screen	13	2.2
其他 others	1	0.2

n=592

1-5 选择不同品牌的彩色电视机的考虑因素/ Considerations in Choosing from Different Brands

注：本题为多选题，合计百分比超过 100%（Multiple answers）

	人数 Number	品牌形象 brand image	外型 outlook	价格 price	功能齐备 all-function	图象清晰度 clarity	图象色彩 color	音响效果 sound effect	售后服务 after-sale service	其他 others
样本 Sample	**592**	**41.2**	**10.5**	**37.2**	**23.8**	**42.7**	**18.4**	**11.1**	**17.7**	**3.2**
黄河 Huanghe	117	35.9	6.8	42.7	13.7	44.4	15.4	6.8	13.7	3.4
长虹 Changhong	83	41.0	19.3	41.0	26.5	38.6	10.8	13.3	21.7	1.2
康佳 Konka	77	45.5	7.8	39.0	26.0	41.6	19.5	18.2	24.7	2.6
松下/乐声 Panasonic	39	64.1	10.3	10.3	35.9	43.6	20.5	7.7	5.1	7.7
王牌 TCL	39	41.0	15.4	43.6	28.2	35.9	10.3	17.9	17.9	0.0
如意 Ruyi	26	23.1	3.8	50.0	15.4	42.3	11.5	11.5	15.4	0.0
海信 Hisense	25	40.0	12.0	40.0	24.0	40.0	24.0	8.0	48.0	8.0
海燕 Haiyan	22	22.7	4.5	54.5	18.2	50.0	22.7	4.5	18.2	4.5
索尼 Sony	20	70.0	10.0	5.0	25.0	40.0	15.0	20.0	10.0	5.0
海尔 Haier	12	83.3	8.3	8.3	16.7	66.7	8.3	0.0	25.0	0.0

1-6 彩色电视机未来一年购买打算/ Plan for Future Purchasing of a Color TV

1-6-1 有无购买打算/ Whether Planning to Purchase Next Year

	人数 Number	百分比 Percent
是 yes	59	9.8
否 no	542	90.2

n=601

1-6-2 打算购买的品牌排名/ The Brand of the Planned Purchase Next Year

排名 Brand Ranking	品牌 Brands	人数 Number	百分比 Percent
1	康佳 Konka	16	28.1
2	王牌 TCL	11	19.3
3	长虹 Changhong	10	17.5
4	海尔 Haier	3	5.3
4	海信 Hisense	3	5.3
5	东芝 Toshiba	2	3.5

n=57

1-6-3 打算购买的尺寸/ The Screen Size of the Planned Purchase Next Year

	人数 Number	百分比 Percent
14 英寸 inches	1	1.7
16 英寸 inches	1	1.7
18 英寸 inches	0	0.0
20 英寸 inches	1	1.7
21 英寸 inches	2	3.4
22 英寸 inches	0	0.0
24 英寸 inches	0	0.0
25 英寸 inches	8	13.8
27 英寸 inches	0	0.0
28 英寸 inches	3	5.2
29 英寸 inches	33	56.9
31 英寸 inches	0	0.0
32 英寸 inches	0	0.0
33 英寸 inches	0	0.0
34 英寸 inches	6	10.3
34 英寸以上 over 34 inches	3	5.2
其他 others	0	0.0

n=58

1-6-4 打算购买的价格/ The Price of the Planned Purchase Next Year

	人数 Number	百分比 Percent
2000 元及以下 2000 yuan or below	5	8.5
2001～4000 元 yuan	36	61.0
4001～6000 元 yuan	12	20.3
6001～8000 元 yuan	3	5.1
8001～10000 元 yuan	0	0.0
10001～12000 元 yuan	1	1.7
12001～14000 元 yuan	1	1.7
14001～16000 元 yuan	0	0.0
16001～18000 元 yuan	0	0.0
18001～20000 元 yuan	0	0.0
20000 元以上 over 20000 yuan	1	1.7
完全不知道 don't know	0	0.0

n=59

1-7 选购彩色电视机时不同角色的人口特征/ Demographics of the Different Roles in Purchasing a Color TV

注：不同角色可以多选（Multiple answers）

	人数 Number	16-24 岁 Age	25-34 岁 Age	35-44 岁 Age	45-54 岁 Age	55-60 岁 Age
样本 Sample	534	19.7	30.7	25.7	16.1	7.9
男性 Male	278	19.4	30.9	26.3	15.5	7.9
提议者 advocate	49	16.3	44.9	20.4	14.3	4.1
影响者 influence	28	28.6	35.7	25.0	3.6	7.1
决定者 decider	141	3.5	27.7	35.5	22.0	11.3
使用者 user	157	26.1	27.4	26.8	14.0	5.7
女性 Female	256	19.9	30.5	25.0	16.8	7.8
提议者 advocate	56	19.6	35.7	25.0	12.5	7.1
影响者 influence	58	22.4	32.8	24.1	10.3	10.3
决定者 decider	64	9.4	23.4	35.9	20.3	10.9
使用者 user	159	24.5	30.8	22.0	18.9	3.8

1-8 不同消费者层的家中目前拥有品牌/ Brands of Color TV Owned in Household by Market Segments

1-8-1 时尚流行指标/ Fads Popular Index

	人数 Number	第一品牌及百分比 1st/ percent	第二品牌及百分比 2nd/ percent	第三品牌及百分比 3rd/ percent	第四品牌及百分比 4th/ percent
样本 Sample	590	**黄河 Huanghe(19.7)**	**长虹 Changhong(14.1)**	**康佳 Konka(13.1)**	**松下/乐声 Panasonic(6.6)** **王牌 TCL(6.6)**
平实生活指向 simple living orientation	338	黄河 Huanghe(22.2)	康佳 Konka(13.6)	长虹 Changhong(12.7)	王牌 TCL(5.9) 如意 Ruyi(5.9)
时尚流行指向 fashion orientation	252	黄河 Huanghe(16.3)	长虹 Changhong(15.9)	康佳 Konka(12.3)	松下/乐声 Panasonic(9.1)

1-8-2 广告态度指标/ Advertising Attitude Index

	人数 Number	第一品牌及百分比 1st/ percent	第二品牌及百分比 2nd/ percent	第三品牌及百分比 3rd/ percent	第四品牌及百分比 4th/ percent
样本 Sample	588	**黄河 Huanghe(19.9)**	**长虹 Changhong(13.9)**	**康佳 Konka(13.1)**	**王牌 TCL(6.6)**
广告淡漠指向 indifferent orientation	181	黄河 Huanghe(20.4)	康佳 Konka(12.7)	长虹 Changhong(12.2)	松下/乐声 Panasonic(7.2)
中间层 medium	328	黄河 Huanghe(20.7)	康佳 Konka(14.0)	长虹 Changhong(13.7)	王牌 TCL(6.4)
信赖广告指向 loyal orientation	79	长虹 Changhong(19.0)	黄河 Huanghe(15.2)	康佳 Konka(10.1)	松下/乐声 Panasonic(7.6) 王牌 TCL(7.6)

1-8-3 价格态度指标/ Price Attitude Index

	人数	第一品牌及百分比 1st/ percent	第二品牌及百分比 2nd/ percent	第三品牌及百分比 3rd/ percent	第四品牌及百分比 4th/ percent
样本 Sample	**588**	**黄河 Huanghe(19.9)**	**长虹 Changhong(13.8)**	**康佳 Konka(13.1)**	**松下/乐声 Panasonic(6.6) 王牌 TCL(6.6)**
价格无关心指向 indifferent orientation	139	黄河 Huanghe(14.4)	康佳 Konka(12.2)	长虹 Changhong(10.1)	王牌 TCL(8.6) 松下/乐声 Panasonic(8.6)
中间层 medium	303	黄河 Huanghe(19.5)	长虹 Changhong(14.2)	康佳 Konka(13.5)	松下/乐声 Panasonic(6.9)
价格重视指向 careful orientation	146	黄河 Huanghe(26.0)	长虹 Changhong(16.4)	康佳 Konka(13.0)	王牌 TCL(6.8) 如意 Ruyi(6.8)

1-9 不同消费者层选择彩色电视机时的考虑因素/ Considerations in Choosing from Different Brands by Market Segments

1-9-1 时尚流行指标/ Fads Popular Index

注：本题为多选题，合计百分比超过 100%（Multiple answers）

	人数 Number	品牌形象 brand image	外型 outlook	价格 price	功能齐备 all-function	图象清晰度 clarity	图象色彩 color	音响效果 sound effect	售后服务 follow-up service	其他 others
样本 Sample	**590**	**41.4**	**10.3**	**37.1**	**23.7**	**42.9**	**18.5**	**11.2**	**17.6**	**3.2**
平实生活指向 simple living orientation	338	41.1	8.6	38.8	21.9	41.1	18.6	9.2	16.0	2.7
时尚流行指向 fashion orientation	252	41.7	12.7	34.9	26.2	45.2	18.3	13.9	19.8	4.0

1-9-2 广告态度指标/ Advertising Attitude Index

注：本题为多选题，合计百分比超过 100%（Multiple answers）

	人数 Number	品牌形象 brand image	外型 outlook	价格 price	功能齐备 all-function	图象清晰度 clarity	图象色彩 color	音响效果 sound effect	售后服务 follow-up service	其他 others
样本 Sample	**588**	**41.3**	**10.5**	**37.4**	**23.6**	**42.3**	**18.4**	**11.2**	**17.9**	**3.2**
广告淡漠指向 indifferent orientation	181	42.0	8.3	37.6	20.4	40.9	21.0	13.3	17.1	3.9
中间层 medium	328	39.3	12.2	40.9	24.7	39.9	18.6	10.1	18.3	3.0
信赖广告指向 loyal orientation	79	48.1	8.9	22.8	26.6	55.7	11.4	11.4	17.7	2.5

1-9-3 价格态度指标/ Price Attitude Index

注：本题为多选题，合计百分比超过 100%（Multiple answers）

	人数 Number	品牌形象 brand image	外型 outlook	价格 price	功能齐备 all-function	图象清晰度 clarity	图象色彩 color	音响效果 sound effect	售后服务 follow-up service	其他 others
样本 Sample	**588**	**41.0**	**10.4**	**36.9**	**23.8**	**42.7**	**18.5**	**11.2**	**17.9**	**3.2**
价格无关心指向 indifferent orientation	139	41.7	11.5	36.0	28.8	38.1	20.9	9.4	15.8	5.0
中间层 medium	303	43.2	11.2	33.3	23.1	40.9	19.5	10.9	16.8	2.3
价格重视指向 careful orientation	146	35.6	7.5	45.2	20.5	50.7	14.4	13.7	21.9	3.4

● 沈阳 / Shenyang

1-1 彩色电视机拥有比例/ Proportion of Color TV Owners in the Sample

	人数 Number	百分比 Percent
有 yes	585	97.5
没有 no	15	2.5

n=600

1-2 彩色电视机的拥有量/ Number of Color TV Owned Per Household

	人数 Number	百分比 Percent
1 台 1 set	477	81.8
2 台 2 sets	101	17.3
3 台 3 sets	3	0.5
4 台及以上 4 sets or over	2	0.3

n=583

1-3 理想品牌排名/ Ranking of the Ideal Brands

排名 Brand Ranking	品牌 Brands	人数 Number	百分比 Percent
1	长虹 Changhong	107	17.8
2	松下/乐声 Panasonic	83	13.8
3	索尼 Sony	75	12.5
4	康佳 Konka	61	10.2
5	王牌 TCL	39	6.5
6	高士达/乐金 LG	36	6.0
7	东芝 Toshiba	30	5.0
8	飞利浦 Philips	26	4.3
9	熊猫 Panda	16	2.7
10	三洋 Sanyo	13	2.2
11	日立 Hitachi	9	1.5

n=600

1-4 对家中现有彩色电视机(最近购买的一台)的五个方面的描述/ About the Color TV Most Recently Purchased

1-4-1 家中现有彩色电视机的品牌排名/ Ranking of the Currently Owned Color TV Brands

排名 Brand Ranking	品牌 Brands	人数 Number	百分比 Percent
1	长虹 Changhong	57	9.8
2	松下/乐声 Panasonic	50	8.6
3	康佳 Konka	35	6.0
4	索尼 Sony	30	5.1
5	熊猫 Panda	28	4.8
6	三洋 Sanyo	27	4.6
7	佳丽彩 Jialicai	26	4.5
8	飞利浦 Philips	25	4.3
8	康力 Konic	25	4.3
9	东芝 Toshiba	23	3.9
10	金风 Jinfeng	19	3.3
11	王牌 TCL	18	3.1
12	百花 Baihua	17	2.9
13	沈阳 Shenyang	16	2.7
14	北京 Beijing	14	2.4
14	高士达/乐金 LG	14	2.4
15	日立 Hitachi	13	2.2

n=584

1-4-2 该彩色电视机的购买时间/ The Time of Purchasing of the Currently Owned Color TV

	人数 Number	百分比 Percent
1985 年或以前 1985 or before	44	7.5
1986～1990 年	182	31.2
1991 年	40	6.8
1992 年	23	3.9
1993 年	26	4.5
1994 年	27	4.6
1995 年	29	5.0
1996 年	38	6.5
1997 年	51	8.7
1998 年	63	10.8
1999 年	61	10.4

n=584

1-4-3 该彩色电视机的价格/ The Price of the Currently Owned Color TV

	人数 Number	百分比 Percent
2000 元或以下 2000 yuan or below	151	25.9
2001～4000 元 yuan	303	51.9
4001～6000 元 yuan	60	10.3
6001～8000 元 yuan	30	5.1
8001～10000 元 yuan	9	1.5
10001～12000 元 yuan	8	1.4
12001～14000 元 yuan	6	1.0
14001～16000 元 yuan	1	0.2
16001～18000 元 yuan	3	0.5
18001～20000 元 yuan	0	0.0
20000 元以上 over 20000 yuan	3	0.5
完全不知道 don't know	10	1.7

n=584

1-4-4 该彩色电视机的尺寸/ The Screen Size of the Currently Owned Color TV

	人数 Number	百分比 Percent
14 英寸 inches	11	1.9
16 英寸 inches	5	0.9
18 英寸 inches	97	16.6
20 英寸 inches	83	14.2
21 英寸 inches	194	33.3
22 英寸 inches	15	2.6
24 英寸 inches	10	1.7
25 英寸 inches	67	11.5
27 英寸 inches	1	0.2
28 英寸 inches	1	0.2
29 英寸 inches	96	16.5
31 英寸 inches	0	0.0
32 英寸 inches	0	0.0
33 英寸 inches	0	0.0
34 英寸 inches	1	0.2
34 英寸以上 over 34 inches	1	0.2
其他 others	1	0.2

n=583

1-4-5 该彩色电视机的类型/ The Type of the Currently Owned Color TV

	人数 Number	百分比 Percent
普通屏幕 traditional screen	292	50.0
平面直角 plane screen	255	43.7
超平 super plane screen	32	5.5
纯平 pure plane screen	4	0.7
其他 others	1	0.2

n=584

1-5 选择不同品牌的彩色电视机的考虑因素/ Ranking of the Considerations in Choosing from Different Brands

注：本题为多选题，合计百分比超过 100%（Multiple answers）

	人数 Number	品牌形象 brand image	外型 outlook	价格 price	功能齐备 all-function	图象清晰度 clarity	图象色彩 color	音响效果 sound effect	售后服务 follow-up service	其他 others
样本 Sample	584	41.4	20.9	40.6	26.7	37.5	19.2	10.1	17.1	3.4
长虹 Changhong	57	54.4	14.0	40.4	33.3	31.6	12.3	8.8	22.8	1.8
松下/乐声 Panasonic	50	78.0	20.0	14.0	36.0	36.0	20.0	12.0	6.0	0.0
康佳 Konka	35	54.3	22.9	17.1	25.7	45.7	22.9	11.4	22.9	2.9
索尼 Sony	30	56.7	23.3	10.0	46.7	60.0	26.7	6.7	10.0	0.0
熊猫 Panda	28	39.3	17.9	32.1	42.9	42.9	21.4	3.6	32.1	3.6
三洋 Sanyo	27	51.9	14.8	48.1	14.8	37.0	29.6	11.1	7.4	0.0
佳丽彩 Jialicai	26	23.1	19.2	50.0	30.8	34.6	30.8	11.5	19.2	3.8
飞利浦 Philips	25	60.0	20.0	44.0	20.0	44.0	20.0	16.0	12.0	0.0
康力 Konic	25	32.0	24.0	56.0	20.0	8.0	16.0	4.0	12.0	12.0
东芝 Toshiba	23	43.5	17.4	8.7	43.5	34.8	21.7	8.7	17.4	0.0
金风 Jinfeng	19	15.8	47.4	47.4	15.8	63.2	21.1	15.8	0.0	5.3
王牌 TCL	18	22.2	5.6	38.9	44.4	44.4	16.7	16.7	27.8	5.6

1-6 彩色电视机未来一年购买打算/ Plan for Future Purchasing of a Color TV

1-6-1 有无购买打算/ Whether Planning to Purchase Next Year

	人数 Number	百分比 Percent
是 yes	75	12.5
否 no	523	87.5

n=598

1-6-2 打算购买的品牌排名/ The Brand of the Planned Purchase Next Year

排名 Brand Ranking	品牌 Brands	人数 Number	百分比 Percent
1	长虹 Changhong	20	27.8
2	康佳 Konka	12	16.7
3	高士达/乐金 LG	8	11.1
3	索尼 Sony	8	11.1
4	王牌 TCL	5	6.9
5	飞利浦 Philips	3	4.2
5	松下/乐声 Panasonic	3	4.2

n=72

1-6-3 打算购买的尺寸/ The Screen Size of the Planned Purchase Next Year

	人数 Number	百分比 Percent
14 英寸 inches	1	1.4
16 英寸 inches	2	2.8
18 英寸 inches	0	0.0
20 英寸 inches	3	4.2
21 英寸 inches	4	5.6
22 英寸 inches	3	4.2
24 英寸 inches	2	2.8
25 英寸 inches	13	18.1
27 英寸 inches	1	1.4
28 英寸 inches	1	1.4
29 英寸 inches	36	50.0
31 英寸 inches	1	1.4
32 英寸 inches	1	1.4
33 英寸 inches	0	0.0
34 英寸 inches	3	4.2
34 英寸以上 over 34 inches	1	1.4
其他 others	0	0.0

n=72

1-6-4 打算购买的价格/ The Price of the Planned Purchase Next Year

	人数 Number	百分比 Percent
2000 元或以下 2000 yuan or below	7	9.7
2001～4000 元 yuan	46	63.9
4001～6000 元 yuan	11	15.3
6001～8000 元 yuan	2	2.8
8001～10000 元 yuan	5	6.9
10001～12000 元 yuan	0	0.0
12001～14000 元 yuan	0	0.0
14001～16000 元 yuan	0	0.0
16001～18000 元 yuan	1	1.4
18001～20000 元 yuan	0	0.0
20000 元以上 over 20000 yuan	0	0.0
完全不知道 don't know	0	0.0

n=72

1-7 选购彩色电视机时不同角色的人口特征/ Demographics of the Different Roles in Purchasing a Color TV

注：不同角色可以多选（Multiple answers）

	人数 Number	16-24 岁 Age	25-34 岁 Age	35-44 岁 Age	45-54 岁 Age	55-60 岁 Age
样本 Sample	**525**	**19.2**	**30.7**	**25.7**	**16.6**	**7.8**
男性 Male	**266**	**18.8**	**30.8**	**26.7**	**15.8**	**7.9**
提议者 advocate	50	26.0	34.0	18.0	18.0	4.0
影响者 influence	25	20.0	28.0	28.0	24.0	0.0
决定者 decider	129	8.5	30.2	27.1	22.5	11.6
使用者 user	161	23.0	31.7	27.3	13.0	5.0
女性 Female	**259**	**19.7**	**30.5**	**24.7**	**17.4**	**7.7**
提议者 advocate	50	18.0	40.0	24.0	14.0	4.0
影响者 influence	19	15.8	31.6	36.8	15.8	0.0
决定者 decider	88	10.2	29.5	26.1	21.6	12.5
使用者 user	185	21.1	27.0	25.9	18.9	7.0

1-8 不同消费者层的家中目前拥有品牌/ Brands of Color TV Owned in Household by Market Segments

1-8-1 时尚流行指标/ Fads Popular Index

	人数 Number	第一品牌及百分比 1st/ percent	第二品牌及百分比 2nd/ percent	第三品牌及百分比 3rd/ percent
样本 Sample	**584**	**长虹 Changhong(9.8)**	**松下/乐声 Panasonic(8.6)**	**康佳 Konka(6.0)**
平实生活指向 simple living orientation	283	长虹 Changhong(8.8)	松下/乐声 Panasonic(6.4)	康佳 Konka(5.7)
时尚流行指向 fashion orientation	301	长虹 Changhong(10.6) 松下/乐声 Panasonic(10.6)	索尼 Sony(6.3) 康佳 Konka(6.3)	三洋 Sanyo(6.0)

1-8-2 广告态度指标/ Advertising Attitude Index

	人数 Number	第一品牌及百分比 1st/ percent	第二品牌及百分比 2nd/ percent	第三品牌及百分比 3rd/ percent
样本 Sample	584	**长虹 Changhong(9.8)**	**松下/乐声 Panasonic(8.6)**	**康佳 Konka(6.0)**
广告淡漠指向 indifferent orientation	167	康佳 Konka(7.8)	康力 Konic(7.2)	长虹 Changhong(5.4) 东芝 Toshiba(5.4) 飞利浦 Philips(5.4) 熊猫 Panda(5.4) 索尼 Sony(5.4)
中间层 medium	342	长虹 Changhong(12.0)	松下/乐声 Panasonic(10.2)	索尼 Sony(5.6)
信赖广告指向 loyal orientation	75	松下/乐声 Panasonic(10.7)	长虹 Changhong(9.3) 康佳 Konka(9.3)	佳丽彩 Jialicai(8.0)

1-9 不同消费者层选择彩色电视机时的考虑因素/ Considerations in Choosing from Different Brands by Market Segments

1-9-1 时尚流行指标/ Fads Popular Index

注：本题为多选题，合计百分比超过 100%（Multiple answers）

	人数 Number	品牌形象 brand image	外型 outlook	价格 price	功能齐备 all-function	图象清晰度 clarity	图象色彩 color	音响效果 sound effect	售后服务 follow-up service	其他 others
样本 Sample	585	41.5	20.9	40.7	26.7	37.4	19.1	10.1	17.3	3.4
平实生活指向 simple living orientation	283	35.7	18.7	43.5	22.3	35.7	19.4	9.9	18.4	4.6
时尚流行指向 fashion orientation	302	47.0	22.8	38.1	30.8	39.1	18.9	10.3	16.2	2.3

1-9-2 广告态度指标/ Advertising Attitude Index

注：本题为多选题，合计百分比超过 100%（Multiple answers）

	人数 Number	品牌形象 brand image	外型 outlook	价格 price	功能齐备 all-function	图象清晰度 clarity	图象色彩 color	音响效果 sound effect	售后服务 follow-up service	其他 others
样本 Sample	585	41.5	20.9	40.7	26.7	37.4	19.1	10.1	17.3	3.4
广告淡漠指向 indifferent orientation	167	37.7	21.0	42.5	22.8	38.3	20.4	9.0	21.0	3.0
中间层 medium	343	42.9	18.7	40.2	26.8	38.8	19.8	9.9	15.7	2.3
信赖广告指向 loyal orientation	75	44.0	30.7	38.7	34.7	29.3	13.3	13.3	16.0	9.3

1-9-3 价格态度指标/ Price Attitude Index

注：本题为多选题，合计百分比超过 100%（Multiple answers）

	人数 Number	品牌形象 brand image	外型 outlook	价格 price	功能齐备 all-function	图象清晰度 clarity	图象色彩 color	音响效果 sound effect	售后服务 follow-up service	其他 others
样本 Sample	584	41.6	20.7	40.6	26.5	37.5	19.2	10.1	17.3	3.4
价格无关心指向 indifferent orientation	102	48.0	15.7	30.4	28.4	34.3	17.6	9.8	17.6	2.0
中间层 medium	286	39.9	19.9	40.2	29.4	38.8	16.4	11.9	17.5	3.5
价格重视指向 careful orientation	196	40.8	24.5	46.4	21.4	37.2	24.0	7.7	16.8	4.1

2.电冰箱 / Refrigerator

● 北京 / Beijing

2-1 电冰箱的拥有比例/ Proportion of Refrigerator Owners in the Sample

	人数 Number	百分比 Percent
有 yes	968	95.7
没有 no	44	4.3

n=1012

2-2 电冰箱的拥有量/ Number of Refrigerator Owned Per Household

	人数 Number	百分比 Percent
1 台 1 set	866	91.1
2 台 2 sets	80	8.4
3 台 3 sets	5	0.5
4 台及以上 4 sets or over	0	0.0

n=951

2-3 理想品牌排名/ Ranking of the Ideal Brands

排名 Brand Ranking	品牌 Brands	人数 Number	百分比 Percent
1	海尔 Haier	473	46.8
2	新飞 Frestech	83	8.2
3	雪花 Snowflower	68	6.7
4	容声 Rongsheng	51	5.0
5	伊莱克斯 Electrolux	36	3.6
6	东芝 Toshiba	28	2.8
7	美菱 Meiling	27	2.7
8	松下/乐声 National	26	2.6
9	长岭 Changling	25	2.5
10	万宝 Wanbao	15	1.5
11	西门子 Siemens	11	1.1
12	夏普/声宝 Sharp	10	1.0

n=1011

2-4 对家中现有电冰箱(最近购买的一台)的五个方面的描述/ About the Refrigerator Most Recently Purchased

2-4-1 家中现有电冰箱的品牌排名/ Ranking of the Currently Owned Refrigerator Brands

排名 Brand Ranking	品牌 Brands	人数 Number	百分比 Percent
1	雪花 Snowflower	196	20.3
2	海尔 Haier	129	13.4
3	万宝 Wanbao	75	7.8
4	新飞 Frestech	70	7.2
5	容声 Rongsheng	54	5.6
6	美菱 Meiling	52	5.4
7	长岭 Changling	42	4.3
8	东芝 Toshiba	41	4.2
9	松下/乐声 National	25	2.6

n=966

2-4-2 该电冰箱的购买的时间/ The Time of Purchasing of the Currently Owned Refrigerator

	人数 Number	百分比 Percent
1985 年或以前 1985 or before	130	13.5
1986～1990 年	303	31.5
1991 年	42	4.4
1992 年	40	4.2
1993 年	35	3.6
1994 年	46	4.8
1995 年	58	6.0
1996 年	54	5.6
1997 年	90	9.4
1998 年	86	8.9
1999 年	77	8.0

n=961

2-4-3 该电冰箱的价格/ The Price of the Currently Owned Refrigerator

	人数 Number	百分比 Percent
1000 元或以下 1000 yuan or below	73	7.6
1001～2000 元 yuan	368	38.3
2001～3000 元 yuan	318	33.1
3001～4000 元 yuan	113	11.8
4001～5000 元 yuan	21	2.2
5001～6000 元 yuan	4	0.4
6001～7000 元 yuan	0	0.0
7001～8000 元 yuan	1	0.1
8001～9000 元 yuan	0	0.0
9001～10000 元 yuan	0	0.0
10000 元以上 over 10000 yuan	2	0.2
完全不知道 don't know	61	6.3

n=961

2-4-4 该电冰箱的容积/ The Volume of the Currently Owned Refrigerator

	人数 Number	百分比 Percent
50 立升 (L)	16	1.7
51～100 立升 (L)	56	5.9
101～150 立升(L)	145	15.2
151～200 立升(L)	443	46.6
201～250 立升(L)	220	23.1
251～300 立升(L)	62	6.5
301～350 立升(L)	6	0.6
350 立升以上 over 350 L	3	0.3

n=951

2-4-5 该电冰箱的类型/ The Type of the Currently Owned Refrigerator

	人数 Number	百分比 Percent
单门冰箱 single door	96	10.0
双门冰箱 double doors	824	85.5
分体式双门冰箱 separate double doors	31	3.2
三门冰箱 tri-doors	12	1.2
四门冰箱 four doors	1	0.1

n=964

2-5 选择不同品牌电冰箱时的考虑因素/ Considerations in Choosing from Different Brands

注：本题为多选题，合计百分比超过 100%（Multiple answers）

	人数 Number	品牌形象 brand image	外型 outlook	价格 price	容量大 big volume	省电 save electricity
样本 Sample	**953**	**42.6**	**17.6**	**31.7**	**29.3**	**21.4**
雪花 Snowflower	196	40.3	13.8	45.4	19.9	16.8
海尔 Haier	126	53.2	14.3	17.5	38.1	25.4
万宝 Wanbao	73	41.1	13.7	38.4	16.4	15.1
新飞 Frestech	69	39.1	17.4	23.2	33.3	29.0
容声 Rongsheng	53	43.4	15.1	37.7	41.5	20.8
美菱 Meiling	52	36.5	19.2	42.3	26.9	19.2
长岭 Changling	42	31.0	14.3	26.2	45.2	33.3
东芝 Toshiba	41	75.6	22.0	19.5	22.0	7.3
松下/乐声 National	24	70.8	12.5	16.7	12.5	8.3
伊莱克斯 Electrolux	18	38.9	44.4	11.1	33.3	38.9
白云 Baiyun	17	35.3	35.3	47.1	41.2	35.3
夏普/声宝 Sharp	17	58.8	17.6	23.5	35.3	23.5
扬子 Yangzi	15	20.0	26.7	33.3	33.3	20.0
香雪海 Xiangxuehai	15	46.7	6.7	20.0	26.7	13.3

续前表 continued

	人数 Number	无氟 no fluoride	无霜 no frost	运转噪音低 low noise	售后服务 follow-up service	冷冻室大 big freezing room	其他 others
样本 Sample	953	11.9	7.3	13.3	14.3	9.0	5.0
雪花 Snowflower	196	4.1	3.1	9.2	18.9	8.2	5.6
海尔 Haier	126	23.0	4.8	14.3	36.5	11.9	0.0
万宝 Wanbao	73	2.7	9.6	6.8	12.3	1.4	11.0
新飞 Frestech	69	37.7	8.7	14.5	11.6	18.8	2.9
容声 Rongsheng	53	7.5	1.9	11.3	15.1	9.4	7.5
美菱 Meiling	52	17.3	7.7	25.0	3.8	9.6	3.8
长岭 Changling	42	26.2	19.0	9.5	11.9	9.5	2.4
东芝 Toshiba	41	4.9	9.8	17.1	0.0	0.0	4.9
松下/乐声 National	24	8.3	37.5	8.3	0.0	4.2	8.3
伊莱克斯 Electrolux	18	16.7	0.0	33.3	27.8	5.6	0.0
白云 Baiyun	17	0.0	0.0	23.5	0.0	0.0	11.8
夏普/声宝 Sharp	17	17.6	17.6	5.9	0.0	5.9	5.9
扬子 Yangzi	15	6.7	0.0	13.3	6.7	33.3	0.0
香雪海 Xiangxuehai	15	6.7	0.0	13.3	20.0	6.7	0.0

2-6 电冰箱未来一年购买打算/ Plan for Future Purchasing of a Refrigerator

2-6-1 有无购买打算/ Whether Planning to Purchase Next Year

	人数 Number	百分比 Percent
是 yes	148	14.7
否 no	856	85.3

n=1004

2-6-2 打算购买的品牌排名/ Ranking of the Brands of the Planned Purchase Next Year

排名 Brand Ranking	品牌 Brands	人数 Number	百分比 Percent
1	海尔 Haier	92	62.6
2	新飞 Frestech	13	8.8
3	伊莱克斯 Electrolux	10	6.8

n=147

2-6-3 打算购买的容积/ The Volume of the Planned Purchase Next Year

	人数 Number	百分比 Percent
50 立升(L)	1	0.7
51～100 立升(L)	4	2.8
101～150 立升(L)	13	9.2
151～200 立升(L)	31	22.0
201～250 立升(L)	58	41.1
251～300 立升(L)	22	15.6
301～350 立升(L)	8	5.7
350 立升以上 over 350 L	4	2.8

n=141

2-6-4 打算购买的价格/ The Price of the Planned Purchase Next Year

	人数 Number	百分比 Percent
1000 元或以下 1000 yuan or below	3	2.1
1001～2000 元 yuan	18	12.6
2001～3000 元 yuan	57	39.9
3001～4000 元 yuan	45	31.5
4001～5000 元 yuan	12	8.4
5001～6000 元 yuan	6	4.2
6001～7000 元 yuan	0	0.0
7001～8000 元 yuan	0	0.0
8001～9000 元 yuan	0	0.0
9001～10000 元 yuan	0	0.0
10000 元以上 over 10000 yuan	1	0.7
完全不知道 don't know	1	0.7

n=143

2-7 选购电冰箱时不同角色的人口特征/ Demographics of the Different Roles in Purchasing a Refrigerator

注：不同角色可以多选（Multiple answers）

	人数 Number	16-24 岁 Age	25-34 岁 Age	35-44 岁 Age	45-54 岁 Age	55-60 岁 Age
样本 Sample	**862**	**19.3**	**29.0**	**26.1**	**16.9**	**8.7**
男性 Male	**425**	**19.5**	**28.5**	**27.3**	**16.2**	**8.5**
提议者 advocate	71	14.1	25.4	26.8	25.4	8.5
影响者 influence	36	13.9	25.0	41.7	19.4	0.0
决定者 decider	190	3.7	26.3	33.7	22.1	14.2
使用者 user	323	24.8	27.9	25.1	15.2	7.1
女性 Female	**437**	**19.0**	**29.5**	**24.9**	**17.6**	**8.9**
提议者 advocate	98	15.3	22.4	29.6	17.3	15.3
影响者 influence	45	20.0	35.6	26.7	11.1	6.7
决定者 decider	119	5.0	31.1	31.1	20.2	12.6
使用者 user	351	21.1	27.9	25.1	17.1	8.8

2-8 不同消费者层的家中目前拥有品牌/ Brands of Refrigerator Owned in Household by Market Segments

2-8-1 时尚流行指标/ Fads Popular Index

	人数 Number	第一品牌及百分比 1st/ percent	第二品牌及百分比 2nd/ percent	第三品牌及百分比 3rd/ percent	第四品牌及百分比 4th/ percent
样本 Sample	**954**	**雪花 Snowflower(20.0)**	**海尔 Haier(13.4)**	**万宝 Wanbao(7.8)**	**新飞 Frestech(7.2)**
平实生活指向 simple living orientation	466	雪花 Snowflower(22.7)	海尔 Haier(13.5)	万宝 Wanbao(7.5)	新飞 Frestech(7.1)
时尚流行指向 fashion orientation	488	雪花 Snowflower(17.4)	海尔 Haier(13.3)	万宝 Wanbao(8.0)	新飞 Frestech(7.4)

2-8-2 广告态度指标/ Advertising Attitude Index

	人数 Number	第一品牌及百分比 1st/ percent	第二品牌及百分比 2nd/ percent	第三品牌及百分比 3rd/ percent	第四品牌及百分比 4th/ percent
样本 Sample	**948**	**雪花 Snowflower(20.3)**	**海尔 Haier(13.5)**	**万宝 Wanbao(7.8)**	**新飞 Frestech(7.2)**
广告淡漠指向 indifferent orientation	272	雪花 Snowflower(23.5)	海尔 Haier(13.6)	新飞 Frestech(7.4) 万宝 Wanbao(7.4)	东芝 Toshiba(5.5)
中间层 medium	549	雪花 Snowflower(19.3)	海尔 Haier(13.1)	万宝 Wanbao(8.4)	新飞 Frestech(6.9)
信赖广告指向 loyal orientation	127	雪花 Snowflower(17.3)	海尔 Haier(15.0)	新飞 Frestech(7.9) 美菱 Meiling(7.9)	万宝 Wanbao(6.3)

2-8-3 价格态度指标/ Price Attitude Index

	人数 Number	第一品牌及百分比 1st/ percent	第二品牌及百分比 2nd/ percent	第三品牌及百分比 3rd/ percent	第四品牌及百分比 4th/ percent
样本 Sample	**958**	**雪花 Snowflower(20.4)**	**海尔 Haier(13.4)**	**万宝 Wanbao(7.8)**	**新飞 Frestech(7.3)**
价格无关心指向 indifferent orientation	195	雪花 Snowflower(16.9)	海尔 Haier(15.9)	新飞 Frestech(8.7)	万宝 Wanbao(8.2)
中间层 medium	480	雪花 Snowflower(20.6)	海尔 Haier(15.6)	新飞 Frestech(6.7)	美菱 Meiling(6.5) 万宝 Wanbao(6.5)
价格重视指向 careful orientation	283	雪花 Snowflower(22.3)	万宝 Wanbao(9.9)	海尔 Haier(7.8)	新飞 Frestech(7.4)

2-9 不同消费者层选择电冰箱时的考虑因素/ Considerations in Choosing from Different Brands by Market Segments

2-9-1 时尚流行指标/ Fads Popular Index

注：本题为多选题，合计百分比超过 100%（Multiple answers）

	人数 Number	品牌形象 brand image	外型 outlook	价格 price	容量大 big volume	省电 save electricity
样本 Sample	**941**	**42.8**	**17.5**	**31.5**	**29.2**	**21.0**
平实生活指向 simple living orientation	459	42.9	17.6	30.7	26.4	21.6
时尚流行指向 fashion orientation	482	42.7	17.4	32.2	32.0	20.5

续前表 continued

	人数 Number	无氟 no fluoride	无霜 no frost	运转噪音低 low noise	售后服务 follow-up service	冷冻室大 big freezing room	其他 others
样本 Sample	941	11.9	7.3	13.3	14.3	9.1	5.1
平实生活指向 simple living orientation	459	11.3	7.2	13.7	15.0	7.4	5.2
时尚流行指向 fashion orientation	482	12.4	7.5	12.9	13.7	10.8	5.0

2-9-2 广告态度指标/ Advertising Attitude Index

注：本题为多选题，合计百分比超过 100%（Multiple answers）

	人数 Number	品牌形象 brand image	外型 outlook	价格 price	容量大 big volume	省电 save electricity
样本 Sample	936	42.6	17.8	31.8	29.3	21.5
广告淡漠指向 indifferent orientation	267	38.6	16.9	31.1	24.0	25.1
中间层 medium	542	45.4	17.5	33.0	31.5	19.0
信赖广告指向 loyal orientation	127	39.4	21.3	28.3	30.7	24.4

续前表 continued

	人数 Number	无氟 no fluoride	无霜 no frost	运转噪音低 low noise	售后服务 follow-up service	冷冻室大 big freezing room	其他 others
样本 Sample	936	11.9	7.4	13.4	14.3	9.0	5.1
广告淡漠指向 indifferent orientation	267	10.5	5.6	13.9	16.1	7.9	8.2
中间层 medium	542	12.7	7.7	13.7	13.8	8.7	3.7
信赖广告指向 loyal orientation	127	11.0	9.4	11.0	12.6	12.6	4.7

2-9-3 价格态度指标/ Price Attitude Index

注：本题为多选题，合计百分比超过 100%（Multiple answers）

	人数 Number	品牌形象 brand image	外型 outlook	价格 price	容量大 big volume	省电 save electricity
样本 Sample	946	42.5	17.5	31.8	29.4	21.6
价格无关心指向 indifferent orientation	192	44.8	17.7	22.4	23.4	19.3
中间层 medium	472	44.1	16.5	33.1	31.4	20.6
价格重视指向 careful orientation	282	38.3	19.1	36.2	30.1	24.8

续前表 continued

	人数 Number	无氟 no fluoride	无霜 no frost	运转噪音低 low noise	售后服务 follow-up service	冷冻室大 big freezing room	其他 others
样本 Sample	946	11.9	7.4	13.5	14.4	9.1	4.9
价格无关心指向 indifferent orientation	192	15.1	8.9	14.6	18.2	10.9	5.2
中间层 medium	472	12.1	7.2	14.4	14.2	8.1	4.4
价格重视指向 careful orientation	282	9.6	6.7	11.3	12.1	9.6	5.3

● 上海 / Shanghai

2-1 电冰箱的拥有比例/ Proportion of Refrigerator Owners in the Sample

	人数 Number	百分比 Percent
有 yes	967	95.4
没有 no	47	4.6

n=1014

2-2 电冰箱的拥有量/ Number of Refrigerator Owned Per Household

	人数 Number	百分比 Percent
1 台 1 set	908	94.8
2 台 2 sets	49	5.1
3 台 3 sets	1	0.1
4 台及以上 4 sets or over	0	0.0

n=958

2-3 理想品牌排名/ Ranking of the Ideal Brands

排名 Brand Ranking	品牌 Brands	人数 Number	百分比 Percent
1	海尔 Haier	290	28.6
2	上菱 Shangling	276	27.2
3	双鹿 Shuanglu	91	9.0
4	松下/乐声 National	40	3.9
5	伊莱克斯 Electrolux	33	3.3
6	新飞 Frestech	30	3.0
6	夏普/声宝 Sharp	30	3.0
7	日立 Hitachi	25	2.5
8	三菱 Mitsubishi	23	2.3
9	东芝 Toshiba	20	2.0
10	三星 Samsung	17	1.7

n=1013

2-4 对家中现有电冰箱(最近购买的一台)的五个方面的描述/ About the Refrigerator Most Recently Purchased

2-4-1 家中现有电冰箱的品牌排名/ Ranking of the Currently Owned Refrigerator Brands

排名 Brand Ranking	品牌 Brands	人数 Number	百分比 Percent
1	上菱 Shangling	277	28.7
2	双鹿 Shuanglu	161	16.7
3	海尔 Haier	83	8.6
4	航天 Hangtian	78	8.1
5	香雪海 Xiangxuehai	28	2.9
6	东芝 Toshiba	23	2.4
7	夏普/声宝 Sharp	22	2.3
8	容声 Rongsheng	21	2.2
9	万宝 Wanbao	20	2.1
10	松下/乐声 National	19	2.0
10	益有 Yiyou	19	2.0

n=966

2-4-2 该电冰箱的购买时间/The Time of Purchasing of the Currently Owned Refrigerator

	人数 Number	百分比 Percent
1985 年或以前 1985 or before	50	5.2
1986～1990 年	314	32.6
1991 年	47	4.9
1992 年	48	5.0
1993 年	43	4.5
1994 年	67	7.0
1995 年	69	7.2
1996 年	86	8.9
1997 年	105	10.9
1998 年	77	8.0
1999 年	57	5.9

n=963

2-4-3 该电冰箱的价格/ The Price of the Currently Owned Refrigerator

	人数 Number	百分比 Percent
1000 元或以下 1000 yuan or below	89	9.3
1001～2000 元 yuan	361	37.5
2001～3000 元 yuan	348	36.2
3001～4000 元 yuan	86	8.9
4001～5000 元 yuan	25	2.6
5001～6000 元 yuan	5	0.5
6001～7000 元 yuan	7	0.7
7001～8000 元 yuan	1	0.1
8001～9000 元 yuan	2	0.2
9001～10000 元 yuan	0	0.0
10000 元以上 over 10000 yuan	1	0.1
完全不知道 don't know	37	3.8

n=962

2-4-4 该电冰箱的容积/ The Volume of the Currently Owned Refrigerator

	人数 Number	百分比 Percent
50 立升 (L)	11	1.1
51～100 立升 (L)	42	4.4
101～150 立升(L)	175	18.2
151～200 立升(L)	430	44.7
201～250 立升(L)	245	25.4
251～300 立升(L)	51	5.3
301～350 立升(L)	1	0.1
350 立升以上 over 350 L	8	0.8

n=963

2-4-5 该电冰箱的类型/ The Type of the Currently Owned Refrigerator

	人数 Number	百分比 Percent
单门冰箱 single door	131	13.6
双门冰箱 double doors	771	79.9
分体式双门冰箱 separate double doors	33	3.4
三门冰箱 tri-doors	29	3.0
四门冰箱 four doors	1	0.1

n=965

2-5 选择不同品牌电冰箱时的考虑因素/ Ranking of the Considerations in Choosing From Different Brands

注：本题为多选题，合计百分比超过 100%（Multiple answers）

	人数 Number	品牌形象 brand image	外型 outlook	价格 price	容量大 big volume	省电 save electricity
样本 Sample	960	33.6	16.1	33.6	30.3	25.9
上菱 Shangling	274	36.1	13.9	21.9	33.2	20.4
双鹿 Shuanglu	160	33.8	14.4	46.3	33.8	30.0
海尔 Haier	82	39.0	20.7	24.4	42.7	31.7
航天 Hangtian	78	26.9	11.5	43.6	29.5	26.9
香雪海 Xiangxuehai	28	35.7	14.3	46.4	10.7	21.4
东芝 Toshiba	23	47.8	13.0	30.4	26.1	13.0
夏普/声宝 Sharp	22	54.5	27.3	22.7	27.3	9.1
容声 Rongsheng	21	23.8	19.0	42.9	47.6	28.6
万宝 Wanbao	20	20.0	25.0	30.0	15.0	25.0
松下/乐声 National	19	31.6	21.1	15.8	31.6	42.1
益有 Yiyou	19	26.3	0.0	63.2	26.3	31.6

续前表 continued

	人数 Number	无氟 no florida	无霜 no frost	运转噪音低 low noise	售后服务 follow-up service	冷冻室大 big freezing room	其他 others
样本 Sample	960	9.6	25.3	11.5	12.3	6.5	5.0
上菱 Shangling	274	9.5	50.0	8.8	16.8	5.5	2.9
双鹿 Shuanglu	160	6.3	11.9	8.1	10.6	8.1	2.5
海尔 Haier	82	18.3	22.0	11.0	22.0	3.7	3.7
航天 Hangtian	78	2.6	3.8	7.7	9.0	2.6	7.7
香雪海 Xiangxuehai	28	0.0	7.1	10.7	7.1	10.7	10.7
东芝 Toshiba	23	4.3	13.0	21.7	4.3	8.7	8.7
夏普/声宝 Sharp	22	13.6	27.3	9.1	9.1	18.2	9.1
容声 Rongsheng	21	19.0	28.6	14.3	9.5	4.8	0.0
万宝 Wanbao	20	5.0	10.0	10.0	20.0	0.0	20.0
松下/乐声 National	19	5.3	42.1	5.3	0.0	10.5	5.3
益有 Yiyou	19	5.3	0.0	15.8	5.3	0.0	21.1

2-6 电冰箱未来一年购买打算/ Plan for Future Purchasing of a Refrigerator

2-6-1 有无购买打算/ Whether Planning to Purchase Next Year

	人数 Number	百分比 Percent
是 yes	95	9.4
否 no	915	90.6

n=1010

2-6-2 打算购买的品牌排名/ Ranking of the Brands of the Planned Purchase Next Year

排名 Brand Ranking	品牌 Brands	人数 Number	百分比 Percent
1	海尔 Haier	36	37.9
2	上菱 Shangling	22	23.2
3	夏普/声宝 Sharp	4	4.2
3	西门子 Siemens	4	4.2
4	伊莱克斯 Electrolux	3	3.2
4	新飞 Frestech	3	3.2
4	三星 Samsung	3	3.2

n=95

2-6-3 打算购买的容积/ The Volume of the Planned Purchase Next Year

	人数 Number	百分比 Percent
50 立升(L)	0	0.0
51～100 立升(L)	2	2.2
101～150 立升(L)	3	3.2
151～200 立升(L)	29	31.2
201～250 立升(L)	40	43.0
251～300 立升(L)	14	15.1
301～350 立升(L)	4	4.3
350 立升以上 over 350 L	1	1.1

n=93

2-6-4 打算购买的价格/ The Price of the Planned Purchase Next Year

	人数 Number	百分比 Percent
1000 元或以下 1000 yuan or below	0	0.0
1001～2000 元 yuan	15	16.1
2001～3000 元 yuan	47	50.5
3001～4000 元 yuan	20	21.5
4001～5000 元 yuan	9	9.7
5001～6000 元 yuan	2	2.2
6001～7000 元 yuan	0	0.0
7001～8000 元 yuan	0	0.0
8001～9000 元 yuan	0	0.0
9001～10000 元 yuan	0	0.0
10000 元以上 over 10000 yuan	0	0.0
完全不知道 don't know	0	0.0

n=93

2-7 选购电冰箱时不同角色的人口特征/ The Demographics of Different Roles in Purchasing a Refrigerator

注：不同角色可以多选（Multiple answers）

	人数 Number	16-24 岁 Age	25-34 岁 Age	35-44 岁 Age	45-54 岁 Age	55-60 岁 Age
样本 Sample	874	20.3	28.3	26.7	16.6	8.2
男性 Male	432	19.7	27.5	27.3	17.4	8.1
提议者 advocate	65	21.5	29.2	26.2	20.0	3.1
影响者 influence	50	18.0	22.0	18.0	30.0	12.0
决定者 decider	185	2.7	27.0	37.8	24.3	8.1
使用者 user	264	25.8	25.8	25.4	15.2	8.0
女性 Female	442	20.8	29.0	26.0	15.8	8.4
提议者 advocate	81	23.5	29.6	29.6	13.6	3.7
影响者 influence	61	16.4	24.6	27.9	23.0	8.2
决定者 decider	127	6.3	26.8	39.4	21.3	6.3
使用者 user	291	23.7	27.8	25.1	13.7	9.6

2-8 不同消费者层的家中目前拥有品牌/ Brands of Refrigerator Owned in Household by Market Segments

2-8-1 时尚流行指标/ Fads Popular Index

	人数 Number	第一品牌及百分比 1st/ percent	第二品牌及百分比 2nd/ percent	第三品牌及百分比 3rd/ percent	第四品牌及百分比 4th/ percent
样本 Sample	958	**上菱 Shangling(28.6)**	**双鹿 Shuanglu(16.6)**	**海尔 Haier(8.6)**	**航天 Hangtian(7.9)**
平实生活指向 simple living orientation	442	上菱 Shangling(27.8)	双鹿 Shuanglu(17.4)	航天 Hangtian(10.4)	海尔 Haier(6.6)
时尚流行指向 fashion orientation	516	上菱 Shangling(29.3)	双鹿 Shuanglu(15.9)	海尔 Haier(10.3)	航天 Hangtian(5.8)

2-8-2 广告态度指标/ Advertising Attitude Index

	人数 Number	第一品牌及百分比 1st/ percent	第二品牌及百分比 2nd/ percent	第三品牌及百分比 3rd/ percent	第四品牌及百分比 4th/ percent
样本 Sample	954	**上菱 Shangling(28.5)**	**双鹿 Shuanglu(16.9)**	**海尔 Haier(8.4)**	**航天 Hangtian(8.1)**
广告淡漠指向 indifferent orientation	240	上菱 Shangling(27.9)	双鹿 Shuanglu(13.8)	航天 Hangtian(9.2)	海尔 Haier(7.1)
中间层 medium	583	上菱 Shangling(29.2)	双鹿 Shuanglu(18.0)	海尔 Haier(9.1)	航天 Hangtian(7.5)
信赖广告指向 loyal orientation	131	上菱 Shangling(26.7)	双鹿 Shuanglu(17.6)	航天 Hangtian(8.4)	海尔 Haier(7.6)

2-8-3 价格态度指标/ Price Attitude Index

	人数 Number	第一品牌及百分比 1st/ percent	第二品牌及百分比 2nd/ percent	第三品牌及百分比 3rd/ percent	第四品牌及百分比 4th/ percent
样本 Sample	963	**上菱 Shangling(28.7)**	**双鹿 Shuanglu(16.7)**	**海尔 Haier(8.6)**	**航天 Hangtian(8.0)**
价格无关心指向 indifferent orientation	144	上菱 Shangling(30.6)	双鹿 Shuanglu(17.4)	海尔 Haier(9.0)	航天 Hangtian(6.3)
中间层 medium	500	上菱 Shangling(29.0)	双鹿 Shuanglu(16.6)	海尔 Haier(8.8)	航天 Hangtian(7.6)
价格重视指向 careful orientation	319	上菱 Shangling(27.3)	双鹿 Shuanglu(16.6)	航天 Hangtian(9.4)	海尔 Haier(8.2)

2-9 不同消费者层选择电冰箱时的考虑因素/ Considerations in Choosing from Different Brands by Market Segments

2-9-1 时尚流行指标/ Fads Popular Index

注：本题为多选题，合计百分比超过 100%（Multiple answers）

	人数 Number	品牌形象 brand image	外型 outlook	价格 price	容量大 big volume	省电 save electricity
样本 Sample	953	**33.8**	**15.9**	**33.7**	**30.3**	**26.1**
平实生活指向 simple living orientation	441	34.9	15.2	39.5	26.1	25.9
时尚流行指向 fashion orientation	512	32.8	16.6	28.7	34.0	26.4

续前表 continued

	人数 Number	无氟 no fluoride	无霜 no frost	运转噪音低 low noise	售后服务 follow-up service	冷冻室大 big freezing room	其他 others
样本 Sample	953	**9.7**	**25.3**	**11.5**	**12.1**	**6.4**	**5.0**
平实生活指向 simple living orientation	441	7.0	22.4	9.5	10.4	6.1	6.3
时尚流行指向 fashion orientation	512	11.9	27.7	13.3	13.5	6.6	3.9

2-9-2 广告态度指标/ Advertising Attitude Index

注：本题为多选题，合计百分比超过 100%（Multiple answers）

	人数 Number	品牌形象 brand image	外型 outlook	价格 price	容量大 big volume	省电 save electricity
样本 Sample	949	**33.6**	**16.1**	**33.7**	**30.2**	**26.0**
广告淡漠指向 indifferent orientation	239	31.4	17.2	38.9	27.6	24.7
中间层 medium	580	34.7	15.0	32.4	31.4	26.4
信赖广告指向 loyal orientation	130	33.1	19.2	30.0	30.0	26.9

续前表 continued

	人数 Number	无氟 no fluoride	无霜 no frost	运转噪音低 low noise	售后服务 follow-up service	冷冻室大 big freezing room	其他 others
样本 Sample	949	**9.4**	**25.3**	**11.5**	**12.1**	**6.5**	**4.8**
广告淡漠指向 indifferent orientation	239	7.1	23.4	12.1	10.5	5.9	6.7
中间层 medium	580	9.7	24.8	10.2	12.4	6.2	4.5
信赖广告指向 loyal orientation	130	12.3	30.8	16.2	13.8	9.2	3.1

2-9-3 价格态度指标/ Price Attitude Index

注：本题为多选题，合计百分比超过 100%（Multiple answers）

	人数 Number	品牌形象 brand image	外型 outlook	价格 price	容量大 big volume	省电 save electricity
样本 Sample	958	33.6	16.2	33.6	30.2	26.1
价格无关心指向 indifferent orientation	145	32.4	20.0	24.1	26.9	22.8
中间层 medium	496	35.7	16.3	31.9	31.5	26.4
价格重视指向 careful orientation	317	30.9	14.2	40.7	29.7	27.1

续前表 continued

	人数 Number	无氟 no fluoride	无霜 no frost	运转噪音低 low noise	售后服务 follow-up service	冷冻室大 big freezing room	其他 others
样本 Sample	958	9.6	25.3	11.5	12.3	6.6	5.0
价格无关心指向 indifferent orientation	145	11.0	26.2	15.2	13.1	6.2	4.8
中间层 medium	496	9.7	25.4	12.1	11.7	7.1	4.8
价格重视指向 careful orientation	317	8.8	24.6	8.8	12.9	6.0	5.4

● 广州 / Guangzhou

2-1 电冰箱的拥有比例/ Proportion of Refrigerator Owners in the Sample

	人数 Number	百分比 Percent
有 yes	960	92.8
没有 no	74	7.2

n=1034

2-2 电冰箱的拥有量/ Number of Refrigerator Owned Per Household

	人数 Number	百分比 Percent
1 台 1 set	913	96.0
2 台 2 sets	37	3.9
3 台 3 sets	1	0.1
4 台及以上 4 sets or over	0	0.0

n=951

2-3 理想品牌排名/ Ranking of the Ideal Brands

排名 Brand Ranking	品牌 Brands	人数 Number	百分比 Percent
1	华凌 Hualing	310	30.0
2	容声 Rongsheng	146	14.1
3	万宝 Wanbao	102	9.9
4	海尔 Haier	94	9.1
5	松下/乐声 National	92	8.9
6	东芝 Toshiba	84	8.1
7	日立 Hitachi	45	4.4
8	三菱 Mitsubish	25	2.4
9	科龙 Kelon	18	1.7
10	西门子 Siemens	16	1.5

n=1034

2-4 对家中现有电冰箱(最近购买的一台)的五个方面的描述/ About the Refrigerator Most Recently Purchased

2-4-1 家中现有电冰箱的品牌排名/ Ranking of the Currently Owned Refrigerator Brands

排名 Brand Ranking	品牌 Brands	人数 Number	百分比 Percent
1	华凌 Hualing	256	26.7
2	万宝 Wanbao	183	19.1
3	容声 Rongsheng	179	18.7
4	东芝 Toshiba	82	8.6
5	松下/乐声 National	71	7.4
6	日立 Hitachi	46	4.8
7	海尔 Haier	28	2.9
8	三菱 Mitsubish	18	1.9
9	科龙 Kelon	15	1.6

n=959

2-4-2 该电冰箱的购买时间/ The Time of Purchasing of the Currently Owned Refrigerator

	人数 Number	百分比 Percent
1985 年以前 1985 or before	60	6.3
1986～1990 年	224	23.4
1991 年	71	7.4
1992 年	76	7.9
1993 年	57	5.9
1994 年	89	9.3
1995 年	102	10.6
1996 年	86	9.0
1997 年	97	10.1
1998 年	62	6.5
1999 年	34	3.5

n=958

2-4-3 该电冰箱的价格/ The Price of the Currently Owned Refrigerator

	人数 Number	百分比 Percent
1000 元或以下 1000 yuan or below	58	6.1
1001～2000 元 yuan	265	27.7
2001～3000 元 yuan	371	38.8
3001～4000 元 yuan	118	12.4
4001～5000 元 yuan	26	2.7
5001～6000 元 yuan	15	1.6
6001～7000 元 yuan	5	0.5
7001～8000 元 yuan	5	0.5
8001～9000 元 yuan	1	0.1
9001～10000 元 yuan	0	0.0
10000 元以上 over 10000 yuan	3	0.3
完全不知道 don't know	88	9.2

n=955

2-4-4 该电冰箱的容积/ The Volume of the Currently Owned Refrigerator

	人数 Number	百分比 Percent
50 立升 (L)	24	2.5
51～100 立升 (L)	69	7.3
101～150 立升(L)	237	24.9
151～200 立升(L)	379	39.9
201～250 立升(L)	139	14.6
251～300 立升(L)	56	5.9
301～350 立升(L)	28	2.9
350 立升以上 over 350 L	18	1.9

n=950

2-4-5 该电冰箱的类型/ The Type of the Currently Owned Refrigerator

	人数 Number	百分比 Percent
单门冰箱 single door	66	6.9
双门冰箱 double doors	824	85.8
分体式双门冰箱 separate double doors	22	2.3
三门冰箱 tri-doors	46	4.8
四门冰箱 four doors	2	0.2

n=960

2-5 选择不同品牌电冰箱时的考虑因素/ Considerations in Choosing From Different Brands

注：本题为多选题，合计百分比超过 100%（Multiple answers）

	人数 Number	品牌形象 brand image	外型 outlook	价格 price	容量大 big volume	省电 save electricity
样本 Sample	**951**	**39.3**	**13.0**	**36.9**	**23.2**	**38.1**
华凌 Hualing	252	40.5	13.1	31.0	27.4	39.3
万宝 Wanbao	181	39.8	14.4	51.4	16.6	32.0
容声 Rongsheng	178	33.7	15.7	40.4	20.8	43.8
东芝 Toshiba	82	53.7	13.4	18.3	22.0	31.7
松下/乐声 National	71	50.7	8.5	36.6	21.1	38.0
日立 Hitachi	46	34.8	13.0	26.1	17.4	47.8
海尔 Haier	28	50.0	10.7	28.6	28.6	35.7
三菱 Mitsubish	18	22.2	16.7	50.0	22.2	38.9
科龙 Kelon	15	20.0	0.0	40.0	40.0	40.0

续前表 continued

	人数 Number	无氟 no florida	无霜 no frost	运转噪音低 low noise	售后服务 follow-up service	冷冻室大 big freezing room	其他 others
样本 Sample	**951**	**5.8**	**23.6**	**15.7**	**12.8**	**3.8**	**2.3**
华凌 Hualing	252	6.0	36.9	17.1	15.5	4.0	2.0
万宝 Wanbao	181	5.0	11.0	10.5	13.3	3.9	2.2
容声 Rongsheng	178	8.4	20.8	12.9	10.7	1.7	3.4
东芝 Toshiba	82	1.2	24.4	20.7	6.1	6.1	1.2
松下/乐声 National	71	7.0	26.8	12.7	16.9	4.2	0.0
日立 Hitachi	46	2.2	26.1	13.0	13.0	0.0	2.2
海尔 Haier	28	0.0	21.4	28.6	17.9	0.0	0.0
三菱 Mitsubish	18	5.6	11.1	22.2	16.7	0.0	0.0
科龙 Kelon	15	6.7	26.7	20.0	6.7	6.7	6.7

2-6 电冰箱未来一年购买打算/ Plan for Future Purchasing of a Refrigerator

2-6-1 有无购买打算/ Whether Planning to Purchase Next Year

	人数 Number	百分比 Percent
是 yes	68	6.6
否 no	964	93.4

n=1032

2-6-2 打算购买的品牌排名/ Ranking of the Brands of the Planned Purchase Next Year

排名 Brand Ranking	品牌 Brands	人数 Number	百分比 Percent
1	华凌 Hualing	20	29.4
2	容声 Rongsheng	11	16.2
3	海尔 Haier	8	11.8
4	西门子 Siemens	4	5.9
5	松下/乐声 National	3	4.4

n=68

2-6-3 打算购买的容积/ The Volume of the Planned Purchase Next Year

	人数 Number	百分比 Percent
50 立升(L)	2	3.1
51～100 立升(L)	2	3.1
101～150 立升(L)	10	15.6
151～200 立升(L)	21	32.8
201～250 立升(L)	10	15.6
251～300 立升(L)	10	15.6
301～350 立升(L)	5	7.8
350 立升以上 over 350 L	4	6.3

n=64

2-6-4 打算购买的价格/ The Price of the Planned Purchase Next Year

	人数 Number	百分比 Percent
1000 元或以下 1000 yuan or below	1	1.6
1001～2000 元 yuan	11	17.7
2001～3000 元 yuan	32	51.6
3001～4000 元 yuan	10	16.1
4001～5000 元 yuan	4	6.5
5001～6000 元 yuan	1	1.6
6001～7000 元 yuan	1	1.6
7001～8000 元 yuan	0	0.0
8001～9000 元 yuan	1	1.6
9001～10000 元 yuan	0	0.0
10000 元以上 over 10000 yuan	0	0.0
完全不知道 don't know	1	1.6

n=62

2-7 选购电冰箱时不同角色的人口特征/ Demographics of the Different Roles in Purchasing a Refrigerator

注：不同角色可以多选（Multiple answers）

	人数 Number	16-24 岁 Age	25-34 岁 Age	35-44 岁 Age	45-54 岁 Age	55-60 岁 Age
样本 Sample	871	19.1	29.2	26 6	16.2	9.0
男性 Male	411	20.0	27.7	26 3	16.3	9.7
提议者 advocate	65	21.5	32.3	20 0	12.3	13.8
影响者 influence	61	21.3	23.0	26 2	19.7	9.8
决定者 decider	161	6.2	21.1	35.4	26.1	11.2
使用者 user	241	26.6	29.5	22.8	11.2	10.0
女性 Female	460	18.3	30.4	27.0	16.1	8.3
提议者 advocate	101	16.8	32.7	25.7	19.8	5.0
影响者 influence	87	12.6	37.9	31.0	13.8	4.6
决定者 decider	94	10.6	20.2	31.9	27.7	9.6
使用者 user	297	19.5	30.6	26.9	14.8	8.1

2-8 不同消费者层的家中目前拥有品牌/ Brands of Refrigerator Owned in Household by Market Segments

2-8-1 时尚流行指标/ Fads Popular Index

	人数 Number	第一品牌及百分比 1st/ percent	第二品牌及百分比 2nd/ percent	第三品牌及百分比 3rd/ percent	第四品牌及百分比 4th/ percent	第五品牌及百分比 5th/ percent
样本 Sample	948	**华凌 Hualing(26.5)**	**万宝 Wanbao(19.0)**	**容声 Rongsheng(18.8)**	**东芝 Toshiba(8.6)**	**松下/乐声 National(7.4)**
平实生活指向 simple living orientation	477	华凌 Hualing(24.7)	容声 Rongsheng(21.2)	万宝 Wanbao(20.3)	东芝 Toshiba(7.1)	松下/乐声 National(6.7)
时尚流行指向 fashion orientation	471	华凌 Hualing(28.2)	万宝 Wanbao(17.6)	容声 Rongsheng(16.3)	东芝 Toshiba(10.2)	松下/乐声 National(8.1)

2-8-2 广告态度指标/ Advertising attitude Index

	人数 Number	第一品牌及百分比 1st/ percent	第二品牌及百分比 2nd/ percent	第三品牌及百分比 3rd/ percent	第四品牌及百分比 4th/ percent	第五品牌及百分比 5th/ percent
样本 Sample	948	**华凌 Hualing(26.8)**	**万宝 Wanbao(19.1)**	**容声 Rongsheng(18.7)**	**东芝 Toshiba(8.4)**	**松下/乐声 National(7.4)**
广告淡漠指向 indifferent orientation	308	华凌 Hualing(27.9)	容声 Rongsheng(19.8)	万宝 Wanbao(18.2)	东芝 Toshiba(8.8)	松下/乐声 National(7.1)
中间层 medium	552	华凌 Hualing(26.1)	万宝 Wanbao(19.4)	容声 Rongsheng(19.0)	东芝 Toshiba(7.8)	松下/乐声 National(7.6)
信赖广告指向 loyal orientation	88	华凌 Hualing(27.3)	万宝 Wanbao(20.5)	容声 Rongsheng(12.5)	东芝 Toshiba(11.4)	松下/乐声 National(6.8)

2-8-3 价格态度指标/ Price Attitude Index

	人数 Number	第一品牌及百分比 1st/ percent	第二品牌及百分比 2nd/ percent	第三品牌及百分比 3rd/ percent	第四品牌及百分比 4th/ percent	第五品牌及百分比 5th/ percent
样本 Sample	954	**华凌 Hualing(26.6)**	**万宝 Wanbao(19.2)**	**容声 Rongsheng(18.6)**	**东芝 Toshiba(8.6)**	**松下/乐声 National(7.4)**
价格无关心指向 indifferent orientation	172	华凌 Hualing(25.0)	万宝 Wanbao(22.1)	容声 Rongsheng(17.4)	东芝 Toshiba(6.4) 松下/乐声 National(6.4)	日立 Hitachi(5.2)
中间层 medium	512	华凌 Hualing(25.8)	容声 Rongsheng(20.1)	万宝 Wanbao(19 5)	东芝 Toshiba(8.2)	松下/乐声 National(7.4)
价格重视指向 careful orientation	270	华凌 Hualing(29.3)	万宝 Wanbao(16.7)	容声 Rongsheng(16.3)	东芝 Toshiba(10.7)	松下/乐声 National(8.1)

2-9 不同消费者层选择电冰箱时考虑因素/ Considerations in Choosing from Different Brands by Market Segments

2-9-1 时尚流行指标/ Fads Popular Index

注：本题为多选题，合计百分比超过 100%（Multiple answers）

	人数 Number	品牌形象 brand image	外型 outlook	价格 price	容量大 big volume	省电 save electricity
样本 Sample	942	39.4	13.1	37.0	23.2	38.2
平实生活指向 simple living orientation	476	41.0	10.7	39.7	23.7	35.7
时尚流行指向 fashion orientation	466	37.8	15.5	34.3	22.7	40.8

续前表 continued

	人数 Number	无氟 no fluoride	无霜 no frost	运转噪音低 low noise	售后服务 follow-up service	冷冻室大 big freezing room	其他 others
样本 Sample	942	5.8	23.6	15.8	12.6	3.7	2.3
平实生活指向 simple living orientation	476	5.0	22.1	14.3	14.9	4.0	2.5
时尚流行指向 fashion orientation	466	6.7	25.1	17.4	10.3	3.4	2.1

2-9-2 广告态度指标/ Advertising Attitude Index

注：本题为多选题，合计百分比超过 100%（Multiple answers）

	人数 Number	品牌形象 brand image	外型 outlook	价格 price	容量大 big volume	省电 save electricity
样本 Sample	941	39.5	13.1	37.0	23.2	38.0
广告淡漠指向 indifferent orientation	306	37.6	15.7	38.9	23.2	34.6
中间层 medium	549	40.6	11.8	36.6	23.5	39.5
信赖广告指向 loyal orientation	86	39.5	11.6	32.6	20.9	40.7

续前表 continued

	人数 Number	无氟 no fluoride	无霜 no frost	运转噪音低 low noise	售后服务 follow-up service	冷冻室大 big freezing room	其他 others
样本 Sample	941	5.6	23.4	15.4	12.9	3.8	2.3
广告淡漠指向 indifferent orientation	306	5.9	24.5	13.7	10.5	3.9	2.9
中间层 medium	549	5.5	23.1	16.4	14.6	2.9	1.8
信赖广告指向 loyal orientation	86	5.8	20.9	15.1	10.5	9.3	3.5

2-9-3 价格态度指标/ Price Attitude Index

注：本题为多选题，合计百分比超过 100%（Multiple answers）

	人数 Number	品牌形象 brand image	外型 outlook	价格 price	容量大 big volume	省电 save electricity
样本 Sample	947	39.4	13.1	37.2	23.2	37.9
价格无关心指向 indifferent orientation	172	45.3	4.7	36.6	20.9	34.3
中间层 medium	506	37.0	16.4	36.6	24.5	40.3
价格重视指向 careful orientation	269	40.1	12.3	38.7	22.3	35.7

续前表 continued

	人数 Number	无氟 no fluoride	无霜 no frost	运转噪音低 low noise	售后服务 follow-up service	冷冻室大 big freezing room	其他 others
样本 Sample	947	5.8	23.5	15.7	12.9	3.8	2.3
价格无关心指向 indifferent orientation	172	6.4	17.4	16.9	13.4	4.1	3.5
中间层 medium	506	5.9	24.3	15.2	12.8	3.8	1.8
价格重视指向 careful orientation	269	5.2	26.0	16.0	12.6	3.7	2.6

● 重庆 / Chongqing

2-1 电冰箱的拥有比例/ Proportion of Refrigerator Owners in the Sample

	人数 Number	百分比 Percent
有 yes	555	88.9
没有 no	69	11.1

n=624

2-2 电冰箱的拥有量/ Number of Refrigerator Owned Per Household

	人数 Number	百分比 Percent
1 台 1 set	533	96.0
2 台 2 sets	21	3.8
3 台 3 sets	1	0.2
4 台及以上 4 sets or over	0	0.0

n=555

2-3 理想品牌排名/ Ranking of the Ideal Brands

排名 Brand Ranking	品牌 Brands	人数 Number	百分比 Percent
1	海尔 Haier	227	36.4
2	容声 Rongsheng	135	21.7
3	长岭 Changling	30	4.8
4	美菱 Meiling	19	3.0
5	新飞 Frestech	17	2.7
6	五洲 Wuzhou	16	2.6
7	阿里斯顿 Aliston	12	1.9
8	风华 Fenghua	11	1.8
8	西门子 Siemens	11	1.8
8	松下/乐声 National	11	1.8
9	将军 General	9	1.4
10	华菱 Hualing	8	1.3

n=623

2-4 对家中现有电冰箱(最近购买的一台)的五个方面的描述/ About the Refrigerator Most Recently Purchased

2-4-1 家中现有电冰箱的品牌排名/ Ranking of the Currently Owned Refrigerator Brands

排名 Brand Ranking	品牌 Brands	人数 Number	百分比 Percent
1	容声 Rongsheng	90	16.3
2	五洲 Wuzhou	51	9.2
3	海尔 Haier	43	7.8
4	将军 General	36	6.5
4	阿里斯顿 Aliston	36	6.5
5	长岭 Changling	29	5.2
6	长庆 Changqing	28	5.1
7	美菱 Meiling	26	4.7
8	风华 Fenghua	25	4.5
9	新飞 Frestech	21	3.8
10	白云 Baiyun	15	2.7

n=553

2-4-2 该电冰箱的购买时间/ The Time of Purchasing of the Currently Owned Refrigerator

	人数 Number	百分比 Percent
1985 年或以前 1985 or before	37	6.7
1986～1990 年	177	31.9
1991 年	28	5.1
1992 年	33	6.0
1993 年	31	5.6
1994 年	32	5.8
1995 年	45	8.1
1996 年	34	6.1
1997 年	59	10.6
1998 年	45	8.1
1999 年	33	6.0

n=554

2-4-3 该电冰箱的价格/ The Price of the Currently Owned Refrigerator

	人数 Number	百分比 Percent
1000 元或以下 1000 yuan or below	43	7.7
1001～2000 元 yuan	248	44.7
2001～3000 元 yuan	197	35.5
3001～4000 元 yuan	39	7.0
4001～5000 元 yuan	5	0.9
5001～6000 元 yuan	2	0.4
6001～7000 元 yuan	0	0.0
7001～8000 元 yuan	3	0.5
8001～9000 元 yuan	0	0.0
9001～10000 元 yuan	0	0.0
10000 元以上 over 10000 yuan	0	0.0
完全不知道 don't know	18	3.2

n=555

2-4-4 该电冰箱的容积/ The Volume of the Currently Owned Refrigerator

	人数 Number	百分比 Percent
50 立升 (L)	17	3.1
51～100 立升 (L)	42	7.6
101～150 立升(L)	113	20.5
151～200 立升(L)	270	48.9
201～250 立升(L)	89	16.1
251～300 立升(L)	14	2.5
301～350 立升(L)	3	0.5
350 立升以上 over 350 L	4	0.7

n=552

2-4-5 该电冰箱的类型/ The Type of the Currently Owned Refrigerator

	人数 Number	百分比 Percent
单门冰箱 single door	71	12.8
双门冰箱 double doors	469	84.5
分体式双门冰箱 separate double doors	9	1.6
三门冰箱 tri-doors	5	0.9
四门冰箱 four doors	1	0.2

n=555

2-5 选择不同品牌电冰箱时的考虑因素/ Considerations in Choosing from Different Brands

注：本题为多选题，合计百分比超过 100%（Multiple answers）

	人数 Number	品牌形象 brand image	外型 outlook	价格 price	容量大 big volume	省电 save electricity
样本 Sample	**544**	**34.9**	**16.2**	**38.8**	**30.0**	**21.1**
容声 Rongsheng	89	44.9	21.3	32.6	23.6	28.1
五洲 Wuzhou	49	36.7	6.1	34.7	36.7	26.5
海尔 Haier	43	32.6	18.6	23.3	30.2	20.9
将军 General	36	16.7	11.1	52.8	19.4	8.3
阿里斯顿 Aliston	35	45.7	14.3	22.9	40.0	20.0
长岭 Changling	29	17.2	17.2	27.6	37.9	31.0
长庆 Changqing	28	32.1	10.7	57.1	25.0	7.1
美菱 Meiling	26	34.6	26.9	38.5	34.6	11.5
风华 Fenghua	24	20.8	25.0	45.8	41.7	20.8
新飞 Frestech	21	42.9	28.6	28.6	52.4	23.8

续前表 continued

	人数 Number	无氟 no fluoride	无霜 no frost	运转噪音低 low noise	售后服务 follow-up service	冷冻室大 big freezing room	其他 others
样本 Sample	**544**	**11.0**	**8.1**	**17.5**	**9.7**	**7.9**	**3.5**
容声 Rongsheng	89	21.3	12.4	21.3	18.0	2.2	1.1
五洲 Wuzhou	49	8.2	4.1	14.3	6.1	10.2	2.0
海尔 Haier	43	9.3	11.6	30.2	30.2	9.3	0.0
将军 General	36	8.3	5.6	16.7	2.8	0.0	11.1
阿里斯顿 Aliston	35	0.0	0.0	11.4	14.3	14.3	2.9
长岭 Changling	29	27.6	17.2	24.1	6.9	13.8	0.0
长庆 Changqing	28	0.0	0.0	10.7	0.0	7.1	7.1
美菱 Meiling	26	19.2	11.5	19.2	11.5	11.5	0.0
风华 Fenghua	24	4.2	4.2	16.7	4.2	12.5	0.0
新飞 Frestech	21	28.6	9.5	9.5	4.8	19.0	0.0

2-6 电冰箱未来一年购买打算/ Plan for Future Purchasing of a Refrigerator

2-6-1 有无购买打算/ Whether Planning to Purchase Next Year

	人数 Number	百分比 Percent
是 yes	69	11.1
否 no	552	88.9

n=621

2-6-2 打算购买的品牌排名/ Ranking of the Brands of the Planned Purchase Next Year

排名 Brand Ranking	品牌 Brands	人数 Number	百分比 Percent
1	海尔 Haier	23	34.3
2	容声 Rongsheng	7	10.4
3	春兰 Chunlan	3	4.5
3	西门子 Siemens	3	4.5
3	新飞 Frestech	3	4.5
4	长岭 Changling	2	3.0
4	三菱 Mitsubish	2	3.0
4	松下/乐声 National	2	3.0

n=67

2-6-3 打算购买的容积/ The Volume of the Planned Purchase Next Year

	人数 Number	百分比 Percent
50 立升(L)	2	2.9
51～100 立升(L)	3	4.4
101～150 立升(L)	4	5.9
151～200 立升(L)	22	32.4
201～250 立升(L)	21	30.9
251～300 立升(L)	9	13.2
301～350 立升(L)	6	8.8
350 立升以上 over 350 L	1	1.5

n=68

2-6-4 打算购买的价格/ The Price of the Planned Purchase Next Year

	人数 Number	百分比 Percent
1000 元或以下 1000 yuan or below	2	2.9
1001～2000 元 yuan	10	14.7
2001～3000 元 yuan	27	39.7
3001～4000 元 yuan	19	27.9
4001～5000 元 yuan	4	5.9
5001～6000 元 yuan	2	2.9
6001～7000 元 yuan	0	0.0
7001～8000 元 yuan	2	2.9
8001～9000 元 yuan	0	0.0
9001～10000 元 yuan	0	0.0
10000 元以上 10000 yuan or over	0	0.0
完全不知道 don't know	2	2.9

n=68

2-7 选购电冰箱时不同角色的人口特征/ Demographics of the Different Roles in Purchasing a Refrigerator

注：不同角色可以多选（Multiple answers）

	人数 Number	16-24 岁 Age	25-34 岁 Age	35-44 岁 Age	45-54 岁 Age	55-60 岁 Age
样本 Sample	475	18.5	27.8	24.8	20.4	8.4
男性 Male	241	19.1	25.7	27.0	19.9	8.3
提议者 advocate	59	15.3	27.1	28.8	20.3	8.5
影响者 influence	27	18.5	33.3	14.8	22.2	11.1
决定者 decider	127	7.1	20.5	38.6	24.4	9.4
使用者 user	146	24.7	28.1	23.3	16.4	7.5
女性 Female	234	17.9	29.9	22.6	20.9	8.5
提议者 advocate	61	16.4	26.2	27.9	21.3	8.2
影响者 influence	29	10.3	62.1	10.3	17.2	0.0
决定者 decider	63	1.6	36.5	27.0	28.6	6.3
使用者 user	162	20.4	31.5	21.0	17.9	9.3

2-8 不同消费者层的家中目前拥有品牌/ Brands of Refrigerator Owned in Household by Market Segments

2-8-1 时尚流行指标/ Fads Popular Index

	人数 Number	第一品牌及百分比 1st/ percent	第二品牌及百分比 2nd/ percent	第三品牌及百分比 3rd/ percent	第四品牌及百分比 4th/ percent
样本 Sample	546	**容声 Rongsheng(16.5)**	**五洲 Wuzhou(8.8)**	**海尔 Haier(7.9)**	**将军 General(6.6)** **阿里斯顿 Aliston(6.6)**
平实生活指向 simple living orientation	322	容声 Rongsheng(15.5)	五洲 Wuzhou(8.7)	将军 General(7.1)	阿里斯顿 Aliston(6.8)
时尚流行指向 fashion orientation	224	容声 Rongsheng(17.9)	海尔 Haier(10.3)	五洲 Wuzhou(8.9)	阿里斯顿 Aliston(6.3)

2-8-2 广告态度指标/ Advertising Attitude Index

	人数 Number	第一品牌及百分比 1st/ percent	第二品牌及百分比 2nd/ percent	第三品牌及百分比 3rd/ percent	第四品牌及百分比 4th/ percent
样本 Sample	**548**	**容声 Rongsheng(16.2)**	**五洲 Wuzhou(8.9)**	**海尔 Haier(7.8)**	**将军 General(6.6)** **阿里斯顿 Aliston(6.6)**
广告淡漠指向 indifferent orientation	143	容声 Rongsheng(15.4)	五洲 Wuzhou(10.5)	将军 General(7.7)	阿里斯顿 Aliston(6.3)
中间层 medium	334	容声 Rongsheng(18.3)	海尔 Haier(8.7)	五洲 Wuzhou(7.8)	阿里斯顿 Aliston(6.9)
信赖广告指向 loyal orientation	71	长庆 Changqing(12.7)	五洲 Wuzhou(11.3)	长岭 Changling(8.5) 海尔 Haier(8.5) 容声 Rongsheng(8.5)	新飞 Frestech(5.6) 美菱 Meiling(5.6) 阿里斯顿 Aliston(5.6)

2-8-3 价格态度指标/ Price Attitude Index

	人数 Number	第一品牌及百分比 1st/ percent	第二品牌及百分比 2nd/ percent	第三品牌及百分比 3rd/ percent	第四品牌及百分比 4th/ percent
样本 Sample	**545**	**容声 Rongsheng(16.1)**	**五洲 Wuzhou(9.4)**	**海尔 Haier(7.7)**	**阿里斯顿 Aliston(6.6)** **将军 General(6.6)**
价格无关心指向 indifferent orientation	91	容声 Rongsheng(14.3)	五洲 Wuzhou(11.0)	海尔 Haier(9.9) 阿里斯顿 Aliston(9.9)	将军 General(6.6) 风华 Fenghua(6.6)
中间层 medium	252	容声 Rongsheng(16.7)	五洲 Wuzhou(8.7)	海尔 Haier(7.9)	长庆 Changqing(6.3)
价格重视指向 careful orientation	202	容声 Rongsheng(16.3)	五洲 Wuzhou(9.4)	将军 General(7.4)	海尔 Haier(6.4)

2-9 不同消费者层选择电冰箱时的考虑因素/ Considerations in Choosing from Different Brands by Market Segments

2-9-1 时尚流行指标/ Fads Popular Index

注：本题为多选题，合计百分比超过 100%（Multiple answers）

	人数 Number	品牌形象 brand image	外型 outlook	价格 price	容量大 big volume	省电 save electricity
样本 Sample	**539**	**35.1**	**16.3**	**39.5**	**29.5**	**21.0**
平实生活指向 simple living orientation	318	32.4	14.8	39.6	31.4	21.1
时尚流行指向 fashion orientation	221	38.9	18.6	39.4	26.7	20.8

续前表 continued

	人数 Number	无氟 no fluoride	无霜 no frost	运转噪音低 low noise	售后服务 follow-up service	冷冻室大 big freezing room	其他 others
样本 Sample	**539**	**10.8**	**8.2**	**17.6**	**9.6**	**8.0**	**3.2**
平实生活指向 simple living orientation	318	10.7	7.9	17.0	7.9	8.8	3.1
时尚流行指向 fashion orientation	221	10.9	8.6	18.6	12.2	6.8	3.2

2-9-2 广告态度指标/ Advertising Attitude Index

注：本题为多选题，合计百分比超过 100%（Multiple answers）

	人数 Number	品牌形象 brand image	外型 outlook	价格 price	容量大 big volume	省电 save electricity
样本 Sample	**541**	**34.9**	**16.1**	**38.8**	**29.9**	**21.1**
广告淡漠指向 indifferent orientation	139	30.2	10.8	38.1	33.1	20.9
中间层 medium	331	35.6	18.4	39.0	29.0	20.8
信赖广告指向 loyal orientation	71	40.8	15.5	39.4	28.2	22.5

续前表 continued

	人数 Number	无氟 no fluoride	无霜 no frost	运转噪音低 low noise	售后服务 follow-up service	冷冻室大 big freezing room	其他 others
样本 Sample	**541**	**10.9**	**7.9**	**17.6**	**9.8**	**7.9**	**3.5**
广告淡漠指向 indifferent orientation	139	7.9	7.9	17.3	7.2	7.9	3.6
中间层 medium	331	13.6	7.9	17.8	10.6	7.6	3.6
信赖广告指向 loyal orientation	71	4.2	8.5	16.9	11.3	9.9	2.8

2-9-3 价格态度指标/ Price Attitude Index

注：本题为多选题，合计百分比超过 100%（Multiple answers）

	人数 Number	品牌形象 brand image	外型 outlook	价格 price	容量大 big volume	省电 save electricity
样本 Sample	538	35.1	16.2	39.0	29.6	21.2
价格无关心指向 indifferent orientation	88	44.3	10.2	25.0	27.3	14.8
中间层 medium	249	34.9	19.7	41.4	32.1	19.3
价格重视指向 careful orientation	201	31.3	14.4	42.3	27.4	26.4

续前表 continued

	人数 Number	无氟 no fluoride	无霜 no frost	运转噪音低 low noise	售后服务 follow-up service	冷冻室大 big freezing room	其他 others
样本 Sample	538	11.0	8.2	17.3	9.9	7.6	3.5
价格无关心指向 indifferent orientation	88	12.5	6.8	17.0	18.2	8.0	2.3
中间层 medium	249	10.4	8.0	18.5	7.2	8.8	2.4
价格重视指向 careful orientation	201	10.9	9.0	15.9	9.5	6.0	5.5

● 武汉 / Wuhan

2-1 电冰箱的拥有比例/ Proportion of Refrigerator Owners in the Sample

	人数 Number	百分比 Percent
有 yes	598	93.1
没有 no	44	6.9

n=642

2-2 电冰箱的拥有量/ Number of Refrigerator Owned Per Household

	人数 Number	百分比 Percent
1 台 1 set	553	94.5
2 台 2 sets	32	5.5
3 台 3 sets	0	0.0
4 台及以上 4 sets or over	0	0.0

n=585

2-3 理想品牌排名/ Ranking of the Ideal Brands

排名 Brand Ranking	品牌 Brands	人数 Number	百分比 Percent
1	海尔 Haier	237	37.1
2	容声 Rongsheng	116	18.2
3	新飞 Frestech	24	3.8
4	伊莱克斯 Electrolux	14	2.2
4	西门子 Siemens	14	2.2
4	松下/乐声 National	14	2.2
5	万宝 Wanbao	12	1.9
5	美菱 Meiling	12	1.9
6	东芝 Toshiba	11	1.7
6	科龙 Kelon	11	1.7

n=639

2-4 对家中现有电冰箱(最近购买的一台)的五个方面的描述/ About the Refrigerator Most Recently Purchased

2-4-1 家中现有电冰箱的品牌排名/ Ranking of the Currently Owned Refrigerator Brands

排名 Brand Ranking	品牌 Brands	人数 Number	百分比 Percent
1	容声 Rongsheng	99	16.7
2	白云 Baiyun	55	9.3
3	沙松 Shasong	45	7.6
3	海尔 Haier	45	7.6
4	万宝 Wanbao	44	7.4
5	中意 Zhongyi	26	4.4
6	美菱 Meiling	19	3.2
7	新飞 Frestech	15	2.5
7	松下/乐声 National	15	2.5

n=592

2-4-2 该电冰箱的购买时间/ The Time of Purchasing of the Currently Owned Refrigerator

	人数 Number	百分比 Percent
1985 年或以前 1985 or before	63	10.6
1986～1990 年	237	39.7
1991 年	34	5.7
1992 年	24	4.0
1993 年	35	5.9
1994 年	26	4.4
1995 年	33	5.5
1996 年	33	5.5
1997 年	40	6.7
1998 年	44	7.4
1999 年	28	4.7

n=597

2-4-3 该电冰箱的价格/ The Price of the Currently Owned Refrigerator

	人数 Number	百分比 Percent
1000 元或以下 1000 yuan or below	39	6.5
1001～2000 元 yuan	307	51.4
2001～3000 元 yuan	188	31.5
3001～4000 元 yuan	33	5.5
4001～5000 元 yuan	10	1.7
5001～6000 元 yuan	0	0.0
6001～7000 元 yuan	0	0.0
7001～8000 元 yuan	0	0.0
8001～9000 元 yuan	0	0.0
9001～10000 元 yuan	0	0.0
10000 元以上 over 10000 yuan	0	0.0
完全不知道 don't know	20	3.4

n=597

2-4-4 该电冰箱的容积/ The Volume of the Currently Owned Refrigerator

	人数 Number	百分比 Percent
50 立升 (L)	17	2.9
51～100 立升 (L)	55	9.3
101～150 立升(L)	110	18.6
151～200 立升(L)	309	52.4
201～250 立升(L)	74	12.5
251～300 立升(L)	19	3.2
301～350 立升(L)	3	0.5
350 立升以上 over 350 L	3	0.5

n=590

2-4-5 该电冰箱的类型/ The Type of the Currently Owned Refrigerator

	人数 Number	百分比 Percent
单门冰箱 single door	74	12.4
双门冰箱 double doors	513	86.1
分体式双门冰箱 separate double doors	5	0.8
三门冰箱 tri-doors	4	0.7
四门冰箱 four doors	0	0.0

n=596

2-5 选择不同品牌电冰箱时的考虑因素/ Considerations in Choosing from Different Brands

注：本题为多选题，合计百分比超过 100%（Multiple answers）

	人数 Number	品牌形象 brand image	外型 outlook	价格 price	容量大 big volume	省电 save electricity
样本 Sample	**590**	**38.5**	**21.0**	**39.5**	**25.1**	**28.5**
容声 Rongsheng	99	48.5	19.2	37.4	29.3	35.4
白云 Baiyun	55	36.4	16.4	50.9	27.3	36.4
沙松 Shasong	45	28.9	8.9	37.8	22.2	42.2
海尔 Haier	45	60.0	22.2	24.4	20.0	24.4
万宝 Wanbao	44	43.2	18.2	50.0	13.6	29.5
中意 Zhongyi	26	34.6	50.0	30.8	26.9	7.7
美菱 Meiling	19	31.6	26.3	26.3	36.8	26.3
新飞 Frestech	15	66.7	26.7	20.0	40.0	33.3
松下/乐声 National	15	46.7	40.0	33.3	0.0	26.7

续前表 continued

	人数 Number	无氟 no fluoride	无霜 no frost	运转噪音低 low noise	售后服务 follow-up service	冷冻室大 big freezing room	其他 others
样本 Sample	**590**	**9.8**	**8.5**	**13.7**	**12.7**	**6.3**	**8.3**
容声 Rongsheng	99	16.2	6.1	16.2	16.2	9.1	6.1
白云 Baiyun	55	1.8	3.6	20.0	5.5	3.6	9.1
沙松 Shasong	45	4.4	8.9	15.6	8.9	0.0	6.7
海尔 Haier	45	17.8	11.1	11.1	31.1	11.1	2.2
万宝 Wanbao	44	4.5	20.5	15.9	2.3	0.0	9.1
中意 Zhongyi	26	0.0	7.7	0.0	19.2	7.7	7.7
美菱 Meiling	19	10.5	0.0	31.6	26.3	10.5	0.0
新飞 Frestech	15	26.7	6.7	0.0	20.0	6.7	6.7
松下/乐声 National	15	46.7	40.0	6.7	6.7	0.0	0.0

2-6 电冰箱未来一年购买打算/ Plan for Future Purchasing of a Refrigerator

2-6-1 有无购买打算/ Whether Planning to Purchase Next Year

	人数 Number	百分比 Percent
是 yes	61	9.5
否 no	579	90.5

n=640

2-6-2 打算购买的品牌排名/ Ranking of the Brands of the Planned Purchase Next Year

排名 Brand Ranking	品牌 Brands	人数 Number	百分比 Percent
1	海尔 Haier	31	60.8
2	容声 Rongsheng	4	7.8
3	科龙 Kelon	2	3.9

n=51

2-6-3 打算购买的容积/ The Volume of the Planned Purchase Next Year

	人数 Number	百分比 Percent
50 立升(L)	1	1.8
51～100 立升(L)	2	3.5
101～150 立升(L)	6	10.5
151～200 立升(L)	22	38.6
201～250 立升(L)	15	26.3
251～300 立升(L)	5	8.8
301～350 立升(L)	5	8.8
350 立升以上 over 350 L	1	1.8

n=57

2-6-4 打算购买的价格/ The Price of the Planned Purchase Next Year

	人数 Number	百分比 Percent
1000 元或以下 1000 yuan or below	2	3.6
1001～2000 元 yuan	13	23.2
2001～3000 元 yuan	27	48.2
3001～4000 元 yuan	8	14.3
4001～5000 元 yuan	3	5.4
5001～6000 元 yuan	2	3.6
6001～7000 元 yuan	1	1.8
7001～8000 元 yuan	0	0.0
8001～9000 元 yuan	0	0.0
9001～10000 元 yuan	0	0.0
10000 元以上 over 10000 yuan	0	0.0
完全不知道 don't know	0	0.0

n=56

2-7 选购电冰箱时不同角色的人口特征/ Demographics of the Different Roles in Purchasing a Refrigerator

注：不同角色可以多选（Multiple answers）

	人数 Number	16-24 岁 Age	25-34 岁 Age	35-44 岁 Age	45-54 岁 Age	55-60 岁 Age
样本 Sample	539	19.9	28.9	25.0	18.9	7.2
男性 Male	255	20.4	27.8	25.9	17.6	8.2
提议者 advocate	63	17.5	27.0	22.2	28.6	4.8
影响者 influence	29	34.5	24.1	20.7	17.2	3.4
决定者 decider	107	6.5	28.0	36.4	17.8	11.2
使用者 user	162	23.5	26.5	25.9	16.7	7.4
女性 Female	284	19.4	29.9	24.3	20.1	6.3
提议者 advocate	60	18.3	26.7	30.0	18.3	6.7
影响者 influence	32	9.4	25.0	25.0	37.5	3.1
决定者 decider	103	4.9	27.2	31.1	27.2	9.7
使用者 user	210	21.4	27.1	25.2	19.5	6.7

2-8 不同消费者层的家中目前拥有品牌/ Brands of Refrigerator Owned in Household by Market Segments

2-8-1 时尚流行指标/ Fads Popular Index

	人数 Number	第一品牌及百分比 1st/ percent	第二品牌及百分比 2nd/ percent	第三品牌及百分比 3rd/ percent	第四品牌及百分比 4th/ percent
样本 Sample	582	**容声 Rongsheng(16.8)**	**白云 Baiyun(9.3)**	**沙松 Shasong(7.7)**	**海尔 Haier(7.6)**
平实生活指向 simple living orientation	302	容声 Rongsheng(16.6)	白云 Baiyun(9.6)	海尔 Haier(7.6) 沙松 Shasong(7.6)	万宝 Wanbao(6.3)
时尚流行指向 fashion orientation	280	容声 Rongsheng(17.1)	白云 Baiyun(8.9)	万宝 Wanbao(8.6)	沙松 Shasong(7.9)

2-8-2 广告态度指标/ Advertising Attitude Index

	人数 Number	第一品牌及百分比 1st/ percent	第二品牌及百分比 2nd/ percent	第三品牌及百分比 3rd/ percent	第四品牌及百分比 4th/ percent
样本 Sample	584	**容声 Rongsheng(17.0)**	**白云 Baiyun(9.2)**	**沙松 Shasong(7.7)**	**万宝 Wanbao(7.5)** **海尔 Haier(7.5)**
广告淡漠指向 indifferent orientation	169	容声 Rongsheng(18.3)	沙松 Shasong(10.7)	万宝 Wanbao(10.1)	白云 Baiyun(7.7)
中间层 medium	348	容声 Rongsheng(17.0)	白云 Baiyun(9.5)	海尔 Haier(8.6)	沙松 Shasong(7.2)
信赖广告指向 loyal orientation	67	容声 Rongsheng(13.4)	白云 Baiyun(11.9)	万宝 Wanbao(9.0)	海尔 Haier(7.5)

2-8-3 价格态度指标/ Price Attitude Index

	人数 Number	第一品牌及百分比 1st/ percent	第二品牌及百分比 2nd/ percent	第三品牌及百分比 3rd/ percent	第四品牌及百分比 4th/ percent
样本 Sample	584	**容声 Rongsheng(17.0)**	**白云 Baiyun(9.2)**	**沙松 Shasong(7.7)**	**海尔 Haier(7.5)** **万宝 Wanbao(7.5)**
价格无关心指向 indifferent orientation	77	容声 Rongsheng(19.5)	万宝 Wanbao(11.7)	沙松 Shasong(7.8)	海尔 Haier(6.5)
中间层 medium	280	容声 Rongsheng(15.4)	白云 Baiyun(10.0)	海尔 Haier(9.6)	沙松 Shasong(7.5)
价格重视指向 careful orientation	227	容声 Rongsheng(18.1)	白云 Baiyun(9.7)	沙松 Shasong(7.9)	万宝 Wanbao(6.6)

2-9 不同消费者层选择电冰箱时的考虑因素/ Considerations in Choosing from Different Brands by Market Segments

2-9-1 时尚流行指标/ Fads Popular Index

注：本题为多选题，合计百分比超过 100%（Multiple answers）

	人数 Number	品牌形象 brand image	外型 outlook	价格 price	容量大 big volume	省电 save electricity
样本 Sample	586	38.2	21.2	39.9	25.1	28.3
平实生活指向 simple living orientation	306	40.2	20.9	42.8	23.5	27.8
时尚流行指向 fashion orientation	280	36.1	21.4	36.8	26.8	28.9

续前表 continued

	人数 Number	无氟 no fluoride	无霜 no frost	运转噪音低 low noise	售后服务 follow-up service	冷冻室大 big freezing room	其他 others
样本 Sample	586	9.6	8.2	13.8	12.5	6.1	8.0
平实生活指向 simple living orientation	306	7.8	8.2	12.4	12.4	7.2	8.2
时尚流行指向 fashion orientation	280	11.4	8.2	15.4	12.5	5.0	7.9

2-9-2 广告态度指标/ Advertising Attitude Index

注：本题为多选题，合计百分比超过 100%（Multiple answers）

	人数 Number	品牌形象 brand image	外型 outlook	价格 price	容量大 big volume	省电 save electricity
样本 Sample	588	38.1	21.1	40.0	25.0	28.2
广告淡漠指向 indifferent orientation	170	37.1	21.2	37.1	21.8	23.5
中间层 medium	350	36.6	21.4	39.7	26.9	29.7
信赖广告指向 loyal orientation	68	48.5	19.1	48.5	23.5	32.4

续前表 continued

	人数 Number	无氟 no fluoride	无霜 no frost	运转噪音低 low noise	售后服务 follow-up service	冷冻室大 big freezing room	其他 others
样本 Sample	588	9.5	8.2	13.9	12.4	6.1	8.2
广告淡漠指向 indifferent orientation	170	4.7	7.6	14.7	10.0	4.1	12.9
中间层 medium	350	11.1	8.6	13.1	13.7	7.4	6.6
信赖广告指向 loyal orientation	68	13.2	7.4	16.2	11.8	4.4	4.4

2-9-3 价格态度指标/ Price Attitude Index

注：本题为多选题，合计百分比超过 100%（Multiple answers）

	人数 Number	品牌形象 brand image	外型 outlook	价格 price	容量大 big volume	省电 save electricity
样本 Sample	588	38.1	20.9	39.8	25.0	28.4
价格无关心指向 indifferent orientation	78	44.9	15.4	32.1	21.8	19.2
中间层 medium	281	38.8	24.6	35.9	24.2	27.4
价格重视指向 careful orientation	229	34.9	18.3	47.2	27.1	32.8

续前表 continued

	人数 Number	无氟 no fluoride	无霜 no frost	运转噪音低 low noise	售后服务 follow-up service	冷冻室大 big freezing room	其他 others
样本 Sample	588	9.5	8.2	13.9	12.6	6.1	8.2
价格无关心指向 indifferent orientation	78	9.0	10.3	9.0	12.8	6.4	7.7
中间层 medium	281	9.6	7.1	16.7	14.2	6.0	9.6
价格重视指向 careful orientation	229	9.6	8.7	12.2	10.5	6.1	6.6

● 西安 / Xi'an

2-1 电冰箱的拥有比例/ Proportion of Refrigerator Owners in the Sample

	人数 Number	百分比 Percent
有 yes	502	83.5
没有 no	99	16.5

n=601

2-2 电冰箱的拥有量/ Number of Refrigerator Owned Per Household

	人数 Number	百分比 Percent
1 台 1 set	488	97.2
2 台 2 sets	14	2.8
3 台 3 sets	0	0.0
4 台及以上 4 sets or over	0	0.0

n=502

2-3 理想品牌排名/ Ranking of the Ideal Brands

排名 Brand Ranking	品牌 Brands	人数 Number	百分比 Percent
1	海尔 Haier	246	41.0
2	长岭 Changling	148	24.7
3	容声 Rongsheng	52	8.7
4	新飞 Frestech	22	3.7
5	松下/乐声 National	12	2.0
6	美菱 Meiling	10	1.7
7	伊莱克斯 Electrolux	9	1.5
8	东芝 Toshiba	7	1.2
8	华凌 Hualing	7	1.2
9	上菱 Shangling	6	1.0
10	香雪海 Xiangxuehai	5	0.8
10	西门子 Siemens	5	0.8

n=600

2-4 对家中现有电冰箱(最近购买的一台)的五个方面的描述/ About the Refrigerator Most Recently Purchased

2-4-1 家中现有电冰箱的品牌排名/ Ranking of the Currently Owned Refrigerator Brands

排名 Brand Ranking	品牌 Brands	人数 Number	百分比 Percent
1	长岭 Changling	175	34.9
2	海尔 Haier	63	12.6
3	容声 Rongsheng	31	6.2
4	万宝 Wanbao	20	4.0
5	黄河 Huanghe	19	3.8
6	美菱 Meiling	15	3.0
6	香雪海 Xiangxuehai	15	3.0
7	松下/乐声 National	13	2.6
8	新飞 Frestech	10	2.0
9	上菱 Shangling	9	1.8
10	扬子 Yangzi	8	1.6
10	中意 Zhongyi	8	1.6

n=501

2-4-2 该电冰箱的购买时间/ The Time of Purchasing of the Currently Owned Refrigerator

	人数 Number	百分比 Percent
1985 年或以前 1985 or before	41	8.2
1986～1990 年	143	28.5
1991 年	41	8.2
1992 年	25	5.0
1993 年	38	7.6
1994 年	42	8.4
1995 年	42	8.4
1996 年	37	7.4
1997 年	52	10.4
1998 年	25	5.0
1999 年	15	3.0

n=501

2-4-3 该电冰箱的价格/ The Price of the Currently Owned Refrigerator

	人数 Number	百分比 Percent
1000 元及以下 1000 yuan or below	28	5.6
1001～2000 元 yuan	181	36.1
2001～3000 元 yuan	223	44.4
3001～4000 元 yuan	43	8.6
4001～5000 元 yuan	7	1.4
5001～6000 元 yuan	1	0.2
6001～7000 元 yuan	1	0.2
7001～8000 元 yuan	1	0.2
8001～9000 元 yuan	0	0.0
9001～10000 元 yuan	0	0.0
10000 元以上 over 10000 yuan	0	0.0
完全不知道 don't know	17	3.4

n=502

2-4-4 该电冰箱的容积/ The Volume of the Currently Owned Refrigerator

	人数 Number	百分比 Percent
50 立升(L)	6	1.2
51～100 立升(L)	25	5.0
101～150 立升(L)	73	14.5
151～200 立升(L)	262	52.2
201～250 立升(L)	114	22.7
251～300 立升(L)	21	4.2
301～350 立升(L)	0	0.0
350 立升以上 over 350 L	1	0.2

n=502

2-4-5 该电冰箱的类型/ The Type of the Currently Owned Refrigerator

	人数 Number	百分比 Percent
单门冰箱 single door	49	9.8
双门冰箱 double doors	432	86.1
分体式双门冰箱 separate double doors	12	2.4
三门冰箱 tri-doors	7	1.4
四门冰箱 four doors	2	0.4

n=502

2-5 选择不同品牌电冰箱时的考虑因素/ Considerations in Choosing from Different Brands

注：本题为多选题，合计百分比超过 100%（Multiple answers）

	人数 Number	品牌形象 brand image	外型 outlook	价格 price	容量大 big volume	省电 save electricity
样本 Sample	501	40.3	15.2	36.3	23.4	23.2
长岭 Changling	175	42.3	13.1	37.7	24.0	23.4
海尔 Haier	63	52.4	12.7	20.6	27.0	30.2
容声 Rongsheng	31	35.5	12.9	29.0	25.8	29.0
万宝 Wanbao	20	50.0	15.0	40.0	45.0	25.0
黄河 Huanghe	19	21.1	15.8	47.4	5.3	15.8
美菱 Meiling	15	40.0	26.7	40.0	20.0	6.7
香雪海 Xiangxuehai	15	26.7	0.0	80.0	13.3	6.7
松下/乐声 National	13	76.9	15.4	23.1	23.1	7.7
新飞 Frestech	10	50.0	10.0	10.0	40.0	30.0

续前表 continued

	人数 Number	无氟 no fluoride	无霜 no frost	运转噪音低 low noise	售后服务 follow-up service	冷冻室大 big freezing room	其他 others
样本 Sample	501	12.4	8.2	14.4	12.8	7.8	3.4
长岭 Changling	175	13.1	5.1	9.1	18.9	8.0	2.9
海尔 Haier	63	17.5	12.7	19.0	17.5	7.9	3.2
容声 Rongsheng	31	25.8	16.1	22.6	16.1	9.7	0.0
万宝 Wanbao	20	10.0	10.0	10.0	5.0	5.0	5.0
黄河 Huanghe	19	5.3	10.5	10.5	15.8	0.0	5.3
美菱 Meiling	15	13.3	6.7	13.3	13.3	6.7	0.0
香雪海 Xiangxuehai	15	0.0	6.7	13.3	6.7	6.7	0.0
松下/乐声 National	13	7.7	0.0	7.7	7.7	7.7	0.0
新飞 Frestech	10	30.0	0.0	10.0	0.0	10.0	10.0

2-6 电冰箱未来一年购买打算/ Plan for Future Purchasing of a Refrigerator

2-6-1 有无购买打算/ Whether Planning to Purchase Next Year

	人数 Number	百分比 Percent
是 yes	56	9.3
否 no	545	90.7

n=601

2-6-2 打算购买的品牌排名/ Ranking of the Brands of the Planned Purchase Next Year

排名 Brand Ranking	品牌 Brands	人数 Number	百分比 Percent
1	海尔 Haier	19	35.8
2	长岭 Changling	10	18.9
3	容声 Rongsheng	4	7.5
4	华凌 Hualing	3	5.7
5	上菱 Shangling	2	3.8
5	新飞 Frestech	2	3.8
5	西门子 Siemens	2	3.8

n=53

2-6-3 打算购买的容积/ The Volume of the Planned Purchase Next Year

	人数 Number	百分比 Percent
50 立升(L)	0	0.0
51～100 立升(L)	2	3.6
101～150 立升(L)	8	14.3
151～200 立升(L)	17	30.4
201～250 立升(L)	22	39.3
251～300 立升(L)	7	12.5
301～350 立升(L)	0	0.0
350 立升以上 over 350 L	0	0.0

n=56

2-6-4 打算购买的价格/ The Price of the Planned Purchase Next Year

	人数 Number	百分比 Percent
1000 元及以下 1000 yuan or below	2	3.6
1001～2000 元 yuan	15	26.8
2001～3000 元 yuan	24	42.9
3001～4000 元 yuan	10	17.9
4001～5000 元 yuan	2	3.6
5001～6000 元 yuan	0	0.0
6001～7000 元 yuan	2	3.6
7001～8000 元 yuan	1	1.8
8001～9000 元 yuan	0	0.0
9001～10000 元 yuan	0	0.0
10000 元以上 over 10000 yuan	0	0.0
完全不知道 don't know	0	0.0

n=56

2-7 选购电冰箱时不同角色的人口特征/ Demographics of the Different Roles in Purchasing a Refrigerator

注：不同角色可以多选（Multiple answers）

	人数 Number	16-24 岁 Age	25-34 岁 Age	35-44 岁 Age	45-54 岁 Age	55-60 岁 Age
样本 Sample	447	19.0	28.4	27.1	17.0	8.5
男性 Male	227	18.9	28.2	27.3	17.2	8.4
提议者 advocate	30	23.3	36.7	26.7	13.3	0.0
影响者 influence	27	22.2	29.6	33.3	7.4	7.4
决定者 decider	110	4.5	23.6	34.5	23.6	13.6
使用者 user	130	25.4	28.5	24.6	16.2	5.4
女性 Female	220	19.1	28.6	26.8	16.8	8.6
提议者 advocate	44	18.2	31.8	29.5	11.4	9.1
影响者 influence	43	20.9	37.2	16.3	16.3	9.3
决定者 decider	55	9.1	20.0	41.8	18.2	10.9
使用者 user	130	21.5	29.2	24.6	18.5	6.2

2-8 不同消费者层的家中目前拥有品牌/ Brands of Refrigerator Owned in Household by Market Segments

2-8-1 时尚流行指标/ Fads Popular Index

	人数 Number	第一品牌及百分比 1st/ percent	第二品牌及百分比 2nd/ percent	第三品牌及百分比 3rd/ percent	第四品牌及百分比 4th/ percent
样本 Sample	500	**长岭 Changling(35.0)**	**海尔 Haier(12.6)**	**容声 Rongsheng(6.2)**	**万宝 Wanbao(4.0)**
平实生活指向 simple living orientation	281	长岭 Changling(34.2)	海尔 Haier(13.2)	容声 Rongsheng(8.2)	万宝 Wanbao(3.6) 黄河 Huanghe(3.6)
时尚流行指向 fashion orientation	219	长岭 Changling(36.1)	海尔 Haier(11.9)	万宝 Wanbao(4.6)	美菱 Meiling(4.1) 黄河 Huanghe(4.1)

2-8-2 广告态度指标/ Advertising Attitude Index

	人数 Number	第一品牌及百分比 1st/ percent	第二品牌及百分比 2nd/ percent	第三品牌及百分比 3rd/ percent	第四品牌及百分比 4th/ percent
样本 Sample	498	**长岭 Changling(35.1)**	**海尔 Haier(12.7)**	**容声 Rongsheng(6.2)**	**万宝 Wanbao(4.0)**
广告淡漠指向 indifferent orientation	153	长岭 Changling(35.3)	海尔 Haier(16.3)	容声 Rongsheng(8.5)	黄河 Huanghe(3.9)
中间层 medium	282	长岭 Changling(34.4)	海尔 Haier(12.1)	容声 Rongsheng(5.3)	万宝 Wanbao(3.9)
信赖广告指向 loyal orientation	63	长岭 Changling(38.1)	海尔 Haier(6.3) 万宝 Wanbao(6.3)	容声 Rongsheng(4.8) 香雪海 Xiangxuehai (4.8) 新飞 Frestech(4.8) 黄河 Huanghe(4.8)	美菱 Meiling(3.2) 长风 Changfeng(3.2)

2-8-3 价格态度指标/ Price Attitude Index

	人数 Number	第一品牌及百分比 1st/ percent	第二品牌及百分比 2nd/ percent	第三品牌及百分比 3rd/ percent	第四品牌及百分比 4th/ percent
样本 Sample	498	**长岭 Changling(34.7)**	**海尔 Haier(12.7)**	**容声 Rongsheng(6.2)**	**万宝 Wanbao(4.0)**
价格无关心指向 indifferent orientation	116	长岭 Changling(31.9)	海尔 Haier(12.9)	容声 Rongsheng(6.9)	香雪海 Xiang Xuehai(4.3) 万宝 Wanbao(4.3)
中间层 medium	263	长岭 Changling(35.4)	海尔 Haier(14.8)	黄河 Huanghe(5.3)	万宝 Wanbao(3.8)
价格重视指向 careful orientation	119	长岭 Changling(36.1)	容声 Rongsheng(12.6)	海尔 Haier(7.6)	香雪海 Xiang Xuehai(5.0)

2-9 不同消费者层选择电冰箱时的考虑因素/ Considerations in Choosing from Different Brands by Market Segments

2-9-1 时尚流行指标/ Fads Popular Index

注：本题为多选题，合计百分比超过 100%（Multiple answers）

	人数 Number	品牌形象 brand image	外型 outlook	价格 price	容量大 big volume	省电 save electricity
样本 Sample	501	40.3	15.4	36.3	23.4	23.2
平实生活指向 simple living orientation	282	42.2	13.8	40 8	22.7	20.6
时尚流行指向 fashion orientation	219	37.9	17.4	30 6	24.2	26.5

续前表 continued

	人数 Number	无氟 no fluoride	无霜 no frost	运转噪音低 low noise	售后服务 follow-up service	冷冻室大 big freezing room	其他 others
样本 Sample	501	12.4	8.2	14 2	12.8	8.0	3.4
平实生活指向 simple living orientation	282	10.6	6.4	10 3	11.0	7.8	2.5
时尚流行指向 fashion orientation	219	14.6	10.5	19.2	15.1	8.2	4.6

2-9-2 广告态度指标/ Advertising Attitude Index

注：本题为多选题，合计百分比超过 100%（Multiple answers）

	人数 Number	品牌形象 brand image	外型 outlook	价格 price	容量大 big volume	省电 save electricity
样本 Sample	499	40.3	15.4	36.5	23.4	22.8
广告淡漠指向 indifferent orientation	153	43.8	11.8	41.2	22.9	22.9
中间层 medium	283	35.3	17.7	38.2	23.0	24.4
信赖广告指向 loyal orientation	63	54.0	14.3	17.5	27.0	15.9

续前表 continued

	人数 Number	无氟 no fluoride	无霜 no frost	运转噪音低 low noise	售后服务 follow-up service	冷冻室大 big freezing room	其他 others
样本 Sample	499	12.4	8.2	14.2	12.8	8.0	3.2
广告淡漠指向 indifferent orientation	153	12.4	7.8	1[illegible].8	11.1	9.2	2.6
中间层 medium	283	12.7	8.5	15.2	12.0	6.4	3.5
信赖广告指向 loyal orientation	63	11.1	7.9	15.9	20.6	12.7	3.2

2-9-3 价格态度指标/ Price Attitude Index

注：本题为多选题，合计百分比超过 100%（Multiple answers）

	人数 Number	品牌形象 brand image	外型 outlook	价格 price	容量大 big volume	省电 save electricity
样本 Sample	499	40.3	15.2	36.3	23.2	22.6
价格无关心指向 indifferent orientation	116	44.8	15.5	32.8	24.1	22.4
中间层 medium	264	42.0	15.2	36.4	20.5	22.7
价格重视指向 careful orientation	119	31.9	15.1	39.5	28.6	22.7

续前表 continued

	人数 Number	无氟 no fluoride	无霜 no frost	运转噪音低 low noise	售后服务 follow-up service	冷冻室大 big freezing room	其他 others
样本 Sample	499	12.4	8.2	14.4	12.8	8.0	3.4
价格无关心指向 indifferent orientation	116	12.1	8.6	14.7	10.3	7.8	5.2
中间层 medium	264	12.5	8.0	13.3	13.3	6.4	3.4
价格重视指向 careful orientation	119	12.6	8.4	16.8	14.3	11.8	1.7

● 沈阳 / Shenyang

2-1 电冰箱的拥有比例/ Proportion of Refrigerator Owners in the Sample

	人数 Number	百分比 Percent
有 yes	468	78.0
没有 no	132	22.0

n=600

2-2 电冰箱的拥有量/ Number of Refrigerator Owned Per Household

	人数 Number	百分比 Percent
1 台 1 set	460	98.7
2 台 2 sets	6	1.3
3 台 3 sets	0	0.0
4 台及以上 4 sets or over	0	0.0

n=466

2-3 理想品牌排名/ Ranking of the Ideal Brands

排名 Brand Ranking	品牌 Brands	人数 Number	百分比 Percent
1	海尔 Haier	266	44.3
2	容声 Rongsheng	79	13.2
3	新飞 Frestech	45	7.5
4	伊莱克斯 Electrolux	24	4.0
5	松下/乐声 National	14	2.3
6	沈努西 Shennuxi	13	2.2
7	美菱 Meiling	11	1.8
7	万宝 Wanbao	11	1.8
7	西门子 Siemens	11	1.8
8	扬子 Yangzi	10	1.7
9	日电 Ridian	9	1.5
10	华日 Huari	8	1.3
10	阿里斯顿 Aliston	8	1.3

n=600

2-4 对家中现有电冰箱(最近购买的一台)的五个方面的描述/ About the Refrigerator Most Recently Purchased

2-4-1 家中现有电冰箱的品牌排名/ Ranking of the Currently Owned Refrigerator Brands

排名 Brand Ranking	品牌 Brands	人数 Number	百分比 Percent
1	沈努西 Shennuxi	48	10.3
1	海尔 Haier	48	10.3
2	容声 Rongsheng	47	10.1
3	万宝 Wanbao	33	7.1
4	长城 Changcheng	29	6.2
5	新飞 Frestech	27	5.8
6	美菱 Meiling	18	3.9
7	辽河 Liaohe	17	3.6
7	日电 Ridian	17	3.6
8	华日 Huari	14	3.0
9	吉诺尔 General	13	2.8
10	白云 Baiyun	10	2.1
10	扬子 Yangzi	10	2.1

n=466

2-4-2 该电冰箱的购买时间/ The Time of Purchasing of the Currently Owned Refrigerator

	人数 Number	百分比 Percent
1985 年或以前 1985 or before	28	6.0
1986～1990 年	168	36.0
1991 年	44	9.4
1992 年	30	6.4
1993 年	27	5.8
1994 年	25	5.4
1995 年	26	5.6
1996 年	26	5.6
1997 年	35	7.5
1998 年	26	5.6
1999 年	32	6.9

n=467

2-4-3 该电冰箱的价格/ The Price of the Currently Owned Refrigerator

	人数 Number	百分比 Percent
1000 元或以下 1000 yuan or below	17	3.6
1001～2000 元 yuan	168	36.0
2001～3000 元 yuan	202	43.3
3001～4000 元 yuan	58	12.4
4001～5000 元 yuan	9	1.9
5001～6000 元 yuan	0	0.0
6001～7000 元 yuan	0	0.0
7001～8000 元 yuan	0	0.0
8001～9000 元 yuan	0	0.0
9001～10000 元 yuan	0	0.0
10000 元以上 over 10000 yuan	0	0.0
完全不知道 don't know	13	2.8

n=467

2-4-4 该电冰箱的容积/ The Volume of the Currently Owned Refrigerator

	人数 Number	百分比 Percent
50 立升 (L)	6	1.3
51～100 立升 (L)	26	5.6
101～150 立升(L)	58	12.4
151～200 立升(L)	222	47.6
201～250 立升(L)	134	28.8
251～300 立升(L)	16	3.4
301～350 立升(L)	3	0.6
350 立升以上 over 350 L	1	0.2

n=466

2-4-5 该电冰箱的类型/ The Type of the Currently Owned Refrigerator

	人数 Number	百分比 Percent
单门冰箱 single door	22	4.7
双门冰箱 double doors	429	91.9
分体式双门冰箱 separate double doors	13	2.8
三门冰箱 tri-doors	3	0.6
四门冰箱 four doors	0	0.0

n=467

2-5 选择不同品牌电冰箱时的考虑因素/ Considerations in Choosing from Different Brands

注：本题为多选题，合计百分比超过 100%（Multiple answers）

	人数 Number	品牌形象 brand image	外型 outlook	价格 price	容量大 big volume	省电 save electricity
样本 Sample	465	34.0	17.8	37.2	35.5	20.9
沈努西 Shennuxi	48	41.7	16.7	56.3	31.3	14.6
海尔 Haier	48	50.0	16.7	18.8	35.4	22.9
容声 Rongsheng	47	51.1	17.0	27.7	31.9	21.3
万宝 Wanbao	33	39.4	18.2	51.5	42.4	18.2
长城 Changcheng	29	24.1	6.9	62.1	27.6	17.2
新飞 Frestech	27	29.6	29.6	11.1	37.0	25.9
美菱 Meiling	18	27.8	11.1	44.4	44.4	22.2
辽河 Liaohe	17	11.8	29.4	35.3	70.6	17.6
日电 Ridian	17	17.6	17.6	47.1	41.2	5.9
华日 Huari	14	42.9	28.6	35.7	28.6	7.1

续前表 continued

	人数 Number	无氟 no fluoride	无霜 no frost	运转噪音低 low noise	售后服务 follow-up service	冷冻室大 big freezing room	其他 others
样本 Sample	465	15.5	4.9	14.8	8.0	9.5	3.4
沈努西 Shennuxi	48	8.3	2.1	8.3	4.2	8.3	0.0
海尔 Haier	48	18.8	8.3	16.7	12.5	12.5	2.1
容声 Rongsheng	47	14.9	4.3	23.4	6.4	10.6	0.0
万宝 Wanbao	33	9.1	6.1	9.1	0.0	0.0	3.0
长城 Changcheng	29	0.0	0.0	13.8	3.4	0.0	13.8
新飞 Frestech	27	44.4	3.7	7.4	7.4	11.1	0.0
美菱 Meiling	18	22.2	0.0	16.7	22.2	11.1	0.0
辽河 Liaohe	17	11.8	0.0	0.0	17.6	11.8	5.9
日电 Ridian	17	52.9	0.0	0.0	17.6	17.6	0.0
华日 Huari	14	0.0	0.0	21.4	7.1	14.3	7.1

2-6 电冰箱未来一年购买打算/ Plan for Future Purchasing of a Refrigerator

2-6-1 有无购买打算/ Whether Planning to Purchase Next Year

	人数 Number	百分比 Percent
是 yes	50	8.3
否 no	549	91.7

n=599

2-6-2 打算购买的品牌排名/ Ranking of the Brands of the Planned Purchase Next Year

排名 Brand Ranking	品牌 Brands	人数 Number	百分比 Percent
1	海尔 Haier	27	56.3
2	容声 Rongsheng	8	16.7
3	松下/乐声 National	2	4.2
3	华凌 Hualing	2	4.2
3	伊莱克斯 Electrolux	2	4.2
3	新飞 Frestech	2	4.2

n=48

2-6-3 打算购买的容积/ The Volume of the Planned Purchase Next Year

	人数 Number	百分比 Percent
50 立升(L)	0	0.0
51～100 立升(L)	1	2.1
101～150 立升(L)	2	4.3
151～200 立升(L)	18	38.3
201～250 立升(L)	14	29.8
251～300 立升(L)	9	19.1
301～350 立升(L)	0	0.0
350 立升以上 over 350 L	3	6.4

n=47

2-6-4 打算购买的价格/ The Price of the Planned Purchase Next Year

	人数 Number	百分比 Percent
1000 元或以下 1000 yuan or below	0	0.0
1001～2000 元 yuan	14	29.8
2001～3000 元 yuan	21	44.7
3001～4000 元 yuan	9	19.1
4001～5000 元 yuan	1	2.1
5001～6000 元 yuan	1	2.1
6001～7000 元 yuan	0	0.0
7001～8000 元 yuan	0	0.0
8001～9000 元 yuan	1	2.1
9001～10000 元 yuan	0	0.0
10000 元以上 over 10000 yuan	0	0.0
完全不知道 don't know	0	0.0

n=47

2-7 选购电冰箱时不同角色的人口特征/ Demographics of the Different Roles in Purchasing a Refrigerator

注：不同角色可以多选（Multiple answers）

	人数 Number	16-24 岁 Age	25-34 岁 Age	35-44 岁 Age	45-54 岁 Age	55-60 岁 Age
样本 Sample	409	17.4	30.6	26.9	18.1	7.1
男性 Male	209	16.3	28.2	28.2	19.6	7.7
提议者 advocate	39	5.1	38.5	25.6	25.6	5.1
影响者 influence	12	33.3	25.0	33.3	8.3	0.0
决定者 decider	104	4.8	31.7	26.9	26.0	10.6
使用者 user	128	21.1	28.1	28.1	17.2	5.5
女性 Female	200	18.5	33.0	25.5	16.5	6.5
提议者 advocate	26	11.5	53.8	23.1	11.5	0.0
影响者 influence	12	33.3	25.0	16.7	25.0	0.0
决定者 decider	66	12.1	21.2	37.9	24.2	4.5
使用者 user	150	19.3	32.7	23.3	16.7	8.0

2-8 不同消费者层的家中目前拥有品牌/ Brands of Refrigerator Owned in Household by Market Segments

2-8-1 时尚流行指标/ Fads Popular Index

	人数 Number	第一品牌及百分比 1st/ percent	第二品牌及百分比 2nd/ percent	第三品牌及百分比 3rd/ percent	第四品牌及百分比 4th/ percent
样本 Sample	466	**沈努西 Shennuxi(10.3)** **海尔 Haier(10.3)**	**容声 Rongsheng(10.1)**	**万宝 Wanbao(7.1)**	**长城 Changcheng(6.2)**
平实生活指向 simple living orientation	220	沈努西 Shennuxi(10.0) 海尔 Haier(10.0)	容声 Rongsheng(7.3) 万宝 Wanbao(7.3)	长城 Changcheng(6.4)	新飞 Frestech(5.0)
时尚流行指向 fashion orientation	246	容声 Rongsheng(12.6)	海尔 Haier(10.6) 沈努西 Shennuxi(10.6)	万宝 Wanbao(6.9)	新飞 Frestech(6.5)

2-8-2 广告态度指标/ Advertising Attitude Index

	人数 Number	第一品牌及百分比 1st/ percent	第二品牌及百分比 2nd/ percent	第三品牌及百分比 3rd/ percent	第四品牌及百分比 4th/ percent
样本 Sample	466	**沈努西 Shenbuxi(10.3)** **海尔 Haier(10.3)**	**容声 Rongsheng(10.1)**	**万宝 Wanbao(7.1)**	**长城 Changcheng(6.2)**
广告淡漠指向 indifferent orientation	132	容声 Rongsheng(11.4)	海尔 Haier(10.6)	沈努西 Shennuxi(9.1)	万宝 Wanbao(7.6)
中间层 medium	272	海尔 Haier(10.3)	容声 Rongsheng(9.9)	沈努西 Shennuxi(9.2)	长城 Changcheng(7.7)
信赖广告指向 loyal orientation	62	沈努西 Shennuxi(17.7)	海尔 Haier(9.7)	容声 Rongsheng(8.1)	万宝 Wanbao(6.5)

2-8-3 价格态度指标/ Price Attitude Index

	人数 Number	第一品牌及百分比 1st/ percent	第二品牌及百分比 2nd/ percent	第三品牌及百分比 3rd/ percent	第四品牌及百分比 4th/ percent
样本 Sample	465	**沈努西 Shennuxi(10.3)** **海尔 Haier(10.3)**	**容声 Rongsheng(9.9)**	**万宝 Wanbao(7.1)**	**长城 Changcheng(6.2)**
价格无关心指向 indifferent orientation	78	海尔 Haier(19.2)	容声 Rongsheng(10.3)	沈努西 Shennuxi(9.0)	新飞 Frestech(5.1)
中间层 medium	233	容声 Rongsheng(9.9)	沈努西 Shennuxi(9.4)	海尔 Haier(8.6)	万宝 Wanbao(7.7)
价格重视指向 careful orientation	154	沈努西 Shennuxi(12.3)	容声 Rongsheng(9.7)	海尔 Haier(8.4)	万宝 Wanbao(7.8) 长城 Changcheng(7.8)

2-9 不同消费者层选择电冰箱时的考虑因素/ Considerations in Choosing from Different Brands by Market Segments

2-9-1 时尚流行指标/ Fads Popular Index

注：本题为多选题，合计百分比超过100%（Multiple answers）

	人数 Number	品牌形象 brand image	外型 outlook	价格 price	容量大 big volume	省电 save electricity
样本 Sample	466	33.9	18.0	37.3	35.4	20.8
平实生活指向 simple living orientation	220	32.7	18.2	37.7	39.1	20.5
时尚流行指向 fashion orientation	246	35.0	17.9	37.0	32.1	21.1

续前表 continued

	人数 Number	无氟 no fluoride	无霜 no frost	运转噪音低 low noise	售后服务 follow-up service	冷冻室大 big freezing room	其他 others
样本 Sample	**466**	**15.7**	**4.9**	**14.8**	**7.9**	**9.4**	**3.4**
平实生活指向 simple living orientation	220	17.3	4.1	12.3	10.0	6.4	5.0
时尚流行指向 fashion orientation	246	14.2	5.7	17.1	6.1	12.2	2.0

2-9-2 广告态度指标/ Advertising Attitude Index

注：本题为多选题，合计百分比超过 100%（Multiple answers）

	人数 Number	品牌形象 brand image	外型 outlook	价格 price	容量大 big volume	省电 save electricity
样本 Sample	**466**	**33.9**	**18.0**	**37.3**	**35.4**	**20.8**
广告淡漠指向 indifferent orientation	132	35.6	16.7	36.4	38.6	23.5
中间层 medium	272	32.7	18.8	36.4	34.2	18.8
信赖广告指向 loyal orientation	62	35.5	17.7	43.5	33.9	24.2

续前表 continued

	人数 Number	无氟 no fluoride	无霜 no frost	运转噪音低 low noise	售后服务 follow-up service	冷冻室大 big freezing room	其他 others
样本 Sample	**466**	**15.7**	**4.9**	**14.8**	**7.9**	**9.4**	**3.4**
广告淡漠指向 indifferent orientation	132	15.2	3.0	13.6	11.4	9.1	4.5
中间层 medium	272	14.7	5.9	16.5	6.6	9.6	2.9
信赖广告指向 loyal orientation	62	21.0	4.8	9.7	6.5	9.7	3.2

2-9-3 价格态度指标/ Price Attitude Index

注：本题为多选题，合计百分比超过 100%（Multiple answers）

	人数 Number	品牌形象 brand image	外型 outlook	价格 price	容量大 big volume	省电 save electricity
样本 Sample	**465**	**34.0**	**18.1**	**37.4**	**35.5**	**20.9**
价格无关心指向 indifferent orientation	78	34.6	10.3	21.8	37.2	21.8
中间层 medium	233	35.6	22.3	35.6	33.9	16.7
价格重视指向 careful orientation	154	31.2	15.6	48.1	37.0	26.6

续前表 continued

	人数 Number	无氟 no fluoride	无霜 no frost	运转噪音低 low noise	售后服务 follow-up service	冷冻室大 big freezing room	其他 others
样本 Sample	**465**	**15.7**	**4.9**	**14.8**	**8.0**	**9.2**	**3.4**
价格无关心指向 indifferent orientation	78	19.2	0.0	20.5	7.7	7.7	6.4
中间层 medium	233	15.9	6.4	17.2	6.9	11.6	1.7
价格重视指向 careful orientation	154	13.6	5.2	8.4	9.7	6.5	4.5

3.微波炉 / Microwave Oven

● 北京 / Beijing

3-1 微波炉的拥有比例/ Proportion of Microwave Oven Owners in the Sample

	人数 Number	百分比 Percent
有 yes	548	54.2
没有 no	464	45.8

n=1012

3-2 微波炉的拥有量/ Number of Microwave Oven Owned Per Household

	人数 Number	百分比 Percent
1 台 1 set	527	98.0
2 台 2 sets	11	2.0
3 台 3 sets	0	0.0
4 台及以上 4 sets or over	0	0.0

n=538

3-3 理想品牌排名/ Ranking of the Ideal Brands

排名 Brand Ranking	品牌 Brands	人数 Number	百分比 Percent
1	格兰仕 Galanz	425	42.1
2	松下/乐声 National	111	11.0
3	高士达/乐金 LG	79	7.8
4	夏普/声宝 Sharp	14	1.4
4	海尔 Haier	14	1.4

n=1009

3-4 对家中现有微波炉(最近购买的一台)的四个方面的描述/ About the Microwave Oven Most Recently Purchased

3-4-1 家中现有微波炉的品牌排名/ Ranking of the Currently Owned Microwave Oven Brands

排名 Brand Ranking	品牌 Brands	人数 Number	百分比 Percent
1	格兰仕 Galanz	294	53.8
2	松下/乐声 National	61	11.2
3	高士达/乐金 LG	58	10.6
4	夏普/声宝 Sharp	22	4.0
5	安宝路 Amproluck	11	2.0
6	惠宝 Huibao	9	1.6
6	蚬华 SMC	9	1.6
7	新宝 Sampo	7	1.3
7	三菱 Mitsubishi	7	1.3

n=546

3-4-2 该微波炉的购买时间/ The Time of Purchasing of the Currently Owned Microwave Oven

	人数 Number	百分比 Percent
1985 年或以前 1985 or before	6	1.1
1986～1990 年	17	3.1
1991 年	5	0.9
1992 年	5	0.9
1993 年	8	1.5
1994 年	24	4.4
1995 年	35	6.4
1996 年	64	11.7
1997 年	147	26.9
1998 年	140	25.6
1999 年	95	17.4

n=546

3-4-3 该微波炉的价格/ The Price of the Currently Owned Microwave Oven

	人数 Number	百分比 Percent
1000 元或以下 1000 yuan or below	279	51.1
1001～2000 元 yuan	165	30.2
2001～3000 元 yuan	54	9.9
3001～4000 元 yuan	16	2.9
4001～5000 元 yuan	4	0.7
5000 元以上 over 5000 yuan	1	0.2
完全不知道 don't know	27	4.9

n=546

3-4-4 该微波炉的类型/ The Type of the Currently Owned Microwave Oven

	人数 Number	百分比 Percent
普通型 regular	358	65.6
含烧烤功能 including stewing and baking function	186	34.1
其他 others	2	0.4

n=546

3-5 选择不同品牌微波炉时的考虑因素/ Considerations in Choosing From Different Brands

注：本题为多选题，合计百分比超过 100%（Multiple answers）

	人数 Number	品牌形象 brand image	外型 outlook	价格 price	功率 power	容量大 big volume
样本 Sample	540	46.3	14.6	48.9	15.6	7.0
格兰仕 Galanz	292	47.3	11.3	54.5	16.1	6.5
松下/乐声 National	61	77.0	9.8	19.7	9.8	8.2
高士达/乐金 LG	57	38.6	29.8	59.6	17.5	8.8
夏普/声宝 Sharp	22	45.5	18.2	31.8	4.5	4.5
安宝路 Amproluck	11	36.4	18.2	45.5	9.1	0.0
惠宝 Huibao	8	25.0	37.5	50.0	12.5	0.0
蚬华 SMC	9	33.3	11.1	55.6	11.1	0.0
新宝 Sampo	6	0.0	0.0	83.3	33.3	0.0
三菱 Mitsubishi	7	71.4	42.9	28.6	28.6	28.6

续前表 continued

	人数 Number	内壁材料 inter material	微电脑控制 computer control ability	售后服务 follow-up service	安全 safety	其他 others
样本 Sample	540	8.0	13.9	12.2	12.8	6.7
格兰仕 Galanz	292	8.9	9.6	12.3	14.0	5.5
松下/乐声 National	61	3.3	36.1	6.6	8.2	3.3
高士达/乐金 LG	57	10.5	12.3	12.3	7.0	3.5
夏普/声宝 Sharp	22	4.5	18.2	4.5	9.1	22.7
安宝路 Amproluck	11	0.0	0.0	36.4	9.1	9.1
惠宝 Huibao	8	12.5	37.5	37.5	12.5	0.0
蚬华 SMC	9	0.0	11.1	11.1	22.2	11.1
新宝 Sampo	6	0.0	0.0	16.7	33.3	0.0
三菱 Mitsubishi	7	14.3	0.0	14.3	0.0	0.0

3-6 微波炉未来一年购买打算/ Plan for Future Purchasing of a Microwave Oven

3-6-1 有无购买打算/ Whether Planning to Purchase Next Year

	人数 Number	百分比 Percent
是 yes	114	11.4
否 no	889	88.6

n=1003

3-6-2 打算购买的品牌排名/ Ranking of the Brand of the Planned Purchase Next Year

排名 Brand Ranking	品牌 Brands	人数 Number	百分比 Percent
1	格兰仕 Galanz	66	59.5
2	高士达/乐金 LG	7	6.3
3	松下/乐声 National	3	2.7
4	三洋 Sanyo	2	1.8
4	海尔 Haier	2	1.8
4	惠而浦 Whirlpool	2	1.8
4	日立 Hitachi	2	1.8
4	三星 Samsung	2	1.8

n=111

3-6-3 打算购买的类型/ The Type of the Planned Purchase Next Year

	人数 Number	百分比 Percent
普通型 regular	44	40.4
含烧烤功能 including stewing and baking function	65	59.6
其他 others	0	0.0

n=109

3-6-4 打算购买的价格/ The Price of the Planned Purchase Next Year

	人数 Number	百分比 Percent
1000 元或以下 1000 yuan or below	57	51.8
1001～2000 元 yuan	40	36.4
2001～3000 元 yuan	10	9.1
3001～4000 元 yuan	2	1.8
4001～5000 元 yuan	0	0.0
5000 元以上 over 5000 yuan	0	0.0
完全不知道 don't know	1	0.9

n=110

3-7 选购微波炉时不同角色的人口特征/ Demographics of the Different Roles in Purchasing a Microwave Oven

注：不同角色可以多选（Multiple answers）

	人数 Number	16-24 岁 Age	25-34 岁 Age	35-44 岁 Age	45-54 岁 Age	55-60 岁 Age
样本 Sample	484	20.5	28.5	27.5	15.9	7.6
男性 Male	229	20.5	27.9	26.2	16.2	9.2
提议者 advocate	38	23.7	26.3	23.7	15.8	10.5
影响者 influence	25	32.0	8.0	32.0	24.0	4.0
决定者 decider	92	6.5	31.5	31.5	18.5	12.0
使用者 user	156	26.3	28.8	23.7	15.4	5.8
女性 Female	255	20.4	29.0	23.6	15.7	6.3
提议者 advocate	62	24.2	32.3	25.8	14.5	3.2
影响者 influence	26	19.2	30.8	42.3	3.8	3.8
决定者 decider	77	3.9	41.6	32.5	16.9	5.2
使用者 user	193	22.8	26.9	28.0	15.0	7.3

3-8 不同消费者层的家中目前拥有品牌/ Brands of Microwave Oven Owned in Household by Market Segments

3-8-1 时尚流行指标/ Fads Popular Index

	人数 Number	第一品牌及百分比 1st/ percent	第二品牌及百分比 2nd/ percent	第三品牌及百分比 3rd/ percent	第四品牌及百分比 4th/ percent
样本 Sample	538	**格兰仕 Galanz(53.9)**	**松下/乐声 National(11.3)**	**高士达/乐金 LG(10.4)**	**夏普/声宝 Sharp(3.9)**
平实生活指向 simple living orientation	251	格兰仕 Galanz(51.4)	松下/乐声 National(12.0)	高士达/乐金 LG(8.8)	夏普/声宝 Sharp(4.4)
时尚流行指向 fashion orientation	287	格兰仕 Galanz(56.1)	高士达/乐金 LG(11.8)	松下/乐声 National(10.8)	夏普/声宝 Sharp(3.5)

3-8-2 广告态度指标/ Advertising Attitude Index

	人数 Number	第一品牌及百分比 1st/ percent	第二品牌及百分比 2nd/ percent	第三品牌及百分比 3rd/ percent	第四品牌及百分比 4th/ percent
样本 Sample	538	**格兰仕 Galanz(53.5)**	**松下/乐声 National(11.3)**	**高士达/乐金 LG(10.6)**	**夏普/声宝 Sharp(4.1)**
广告淡漠指向 indifferent orientation	149	格兰仕 Galanz(48.3)	松下/乐声 National(10.7)	高士达/乐金 LG(10.1)	夏普/声宝 Sharp(2.7)
中间层 medium	318	格兰仕 Galanz(55.7)	松下/乐声 National(11.9)	高士达/乐金 LG(11.3)	夏普/声宝 Sharp(4.4)
信赖广告指向 loyal orientation	71	格兰仕 Galanz(54.9)	松下/乐声 National(9.9)	高士达/乐金 LG(8.5)	夏普/声宝 Sharp(5.6)

3-8-3 价格态度指标/ Price Attitude Index

	人数 Number	第一品牌及百分比 1st/ percent	第二品牌及百分比 2nd/ percent	第三品牌及百分比 3rd/ percent	.第四品牌及百分比 4th/ percent
样本 Sample	543	**格兰仕 Galanz(53.8)**	**松下/乐声 National(11.2)**	**高士达/乐金 LG(10.5)**	**夏普/声宝 Sharp(4.1)**
价格无关心指向 indifferent orientation	115	格兰仕 Galanz(47.8)	松下/乐声 National(14.8)	高士达/乐金 LG(8.7)	夏普/声宝 Sharp(5.2)
中间层 medium	287	格兰仕 Galanz(54.4)	松下/乐声 National(11.8)	高士达/乐金 LG(10.5)	夏普/声宝 Sharp(4.9)
价格重视指向 careful orientation	141	格兰仕 Galanz(57.4)	高士达/乐金 LG(12.1)	松下/乐声 National(7.1)	惠宝 Huibao(2.8) 新宝 Sampo(2.8)

3-9 不同消费者层选择微波炉时的考虑因素/ Considerations in Choosing from Different Brands by Market Segments

3-9-1 时尚流行指标/ Fads Popular Index

注：本题为多选题，合计百分比超过 100%（Multiple answers）

	人数 Number	品牌形象 brand image	外型 outlook	价格 price	功率 power	容量大 big volume
样本 Sample	532	45.9	14.7	49.1	15.6	7.0
平实生活指向 simple living orientation	247	44.9	14.6	49.0	14.2	6.5
时尚流行指向 fashion orientation	285	46.7	14.7	49.1	16.8	7.4

续前表 continued

	人数 Number	内壁材料 inter material	微电脑控制 computer control ability	售后服务 follow-up service	安全 safety	其他 others
样本 Sample	532	7.7	13.5	12.2	13.0	6.8
平实生活指向 simple living orientation	247	8.9	10.9	10.9	12.1	10.1
时尚流行指向 fashion orientation	285	6.7	15.8	13.3	13.7	3.9

3-9-2 广告态度指标/ Advertising Attitude Index

注：本题为多选题，合计百分比超过 100%（Multiple answers）

	人数 Number	品牌形象 brand image	外型 outlook	价格 price	功率 power	容量大 big volume
样本 Sample	533	46.2	14.6	49.3	15.4	7.1
广告淡漠指向 indifferent orientation	147	36.7	13.6	48.3	17.0	8.2
中间层 medium	317	50.2	14.8	48.9	14.8	7.3
信赖广告指向 loyal orientation	69	47.8	15.9	53.6	14.5	4.3

续前表 continued

	人数 Number	内壁材料 inter material	微电脑控制 computer control ability	售后服务 follow-up service	安全 safety	其他 others
样本 Sample	533	8.1	13.5	12.2	12.8	6.8
广告淡漠指向 indifferent orientation	147	7.5	11.6	15.0	9.5	10.9
中间层 medium	317	7.3	13.6	12.3	14.5	5.4
信赖广告指向 loyal orientation	69	13.0	17.4	5.8	11.6	4.3

3-9-3 价格态度指标/ Price Attitude Index

注：本题为多选题，合计百分比超过 100%（Multiple answers）

	人数 Number	品牌形象 brand image	外型 outlook	价格 price	功率 power	容量大 big volume
样本 Sample	537	46.0	14.7	48.8	15.6	7.1
价格无关心指向 indifferent orientation	113	43.4	15.0	36.3	11.5	8.0
中间层 medium	284	51.4	15.1	48.2	19.0	7.0
价格重视指向 careful orientation	140	37.1	13.6	60.0	12.1	6.4

续前表 continued

	人数 Number	内壁材料 inter material	微电脑控制 computer control ability	售后服务 follow-up service	安全 safety	其他 others
样本 Sample	537	7.8	14.0	12.3	12.8	6.7
价格无关心指向 indifferent orientation	113	7.1	16.8	14.2	15.9	8.8
中间层 medium	284	8.1	15.1	12.0	12.0	5.6
价格重视指向 careful orientation	140	7.9	9.3	11.4	12.1	7.1

● 上海 / Shanghai

3-1 微波炉的拥有比例/ Proportion of Microwave Oven Owners in the Sample

	人数 Number	百分比 Percent
有 yes	757	74.7
没有 no	257	25.3

n=1014

3-2 微波炉的拥有量/ Number of Microwave Oven Owned Per Household

	人数 Number	百分比 Percent
1 台 1 set	733	98.0
2 台 2 sets	14	1.9
3 台 3 sets	0	0.0
4 台及以上 4 sets or over	1	0.1

n=748

3-3 理想品牌排名/ Ranking of the Ideal Brands

排名 Brand Ranking	品牌 Brands	人数 Number	百分比 Percent
1	格兰仕 Galanz	401	39.6
2	松下/乐声 National	133	13.1
3	高士达/乐金 LG	91	9.0
4	蚬华 SMC	90	8.9
5	三星 Samsung	53	5.2
6	夏普/声宝 Sharp	49	4.8
7	上菱 Shangling	21	2.1
8	三菱 Mitsubish	19	1.9
9	惠而浦 Whirlpool	16	1.6
10	三洋 Sanyo	15	1.5

n=1013

3-4 对家中现有微波炉(最近购买的一台)的四个方面的描述/ About the Microwave Oven Most Recently Purchased

3-4-1 家中现有微波炉的品牌排名/ Ranking of the Currently Owned Microwave Oven Brands

排名 Brand Ranking	品牌 Brands	人数 Number	百分比 Percent
1	格兰仕 Galanz	277	36.7
2	蚬华 SMC	122	16.2
3	松下/乐声 National	54	7.2
4	高士达/乐金 LG	46	6.1
5	夏普/声宝 Sharp	38	5.0
6	飞跃 Feiyue	36	4.8
7	上菱 Shangling	31	4.1
7	三星 Samsung	31	4.1
8	三菱 Mitsubish	19	2.5
9	亚美 Yamei	15	2.0
10	惠而浦 Whirlpool	11	1.5

n=755

3-4-2 该微波炉的购买时间/ The Time of Purchasing of the Currently Owned Microwave Oven

	人数 Number	百分比 Percent
1985 年或以前 1985 or before	6	0.8
1986～1990 年	28	3.7
1991 年	22	2.9
1992 年	22	2.9
1993 年	38	5.1
1994 年	62	8.3
1995 年	114	15.2
1996 年	129	17.2
1997 年	152	20.2
1998 年	130	17.3
1999 年	48	6.4

n=751

3-4-3 该微波炉的价格/ The Price of the Currently Owned Microwave Oven

	人数 Number	百分比 Percent
1000 元或以下 1000 yuan or below	424	56.4
1001～2000 元 yuan	254	33.8
2001～3000 元 yuan	48	6.4
3001～4000 元 yuan	11	1.5
4001～5000 元 yuan	0	0.0
5000 元以上 over 5000 yuan	2	0.3
完全不知道 don't know	13	1.7

n=752

3-4-4 该微波炉的类型/ The Type of the Currently Owned Microwave Oven

	人数 Number	百分比 Percent
普通型 regular	672	89.2
含烧烤功能 including stewing and baking function	78	10.4
其他 others	3	0.4

n=753

3-5 选择不同品牌微波炉时的考虑因素/ Considerations in Choosing from Different Brands

注：本题为多选题，合计百分比超过 100%（Multiple answers）

	人数 Number	品牌形象 brand image	外型 outlook	价格 price	功率 power	容量大 big volume
样本 Sample	749	43.3	10.4	46.5	32.8	10.5
格兰仕 Galanz	275	43.3	9.8	54.9	32.7	12.0
蚬华 SMC	121	47.1	9.9	38.8	29.8	10.7
松下/乐声 National	54	57.4	11.1	20.4	38.9	7.4
高士达/乐金 LG	46	43.5	23.9	50.0	28.3	4.3
夏普/声宝 Sharp	37	62.2	2.7	37.8	29.7	0.0
飞跃 Feiyue	36	41.7	0.0	52.8	25.0	5.6
上菱 Shangling	31	48.4	3.2	74.2	35.5	6.5
三星 Samsung	31	22.6	22.6	48.4	38.7	6.5
三菱 Mitsubish	19	36.8	15.8	36.8	36.8	10.5

续前表 continued

	人数 Number	内壁材料 inter material	微电脑控制 computer control ability	售后服务 follow-up service	安全 safety	其他 others
样本 Sample	749	5.3	10.7	10.7	15.9	4.0
格兰仕 Galanz	275	7.6	6.2	9.8	13.8	1.8
蚬华 SMC	121	2.5	9.1	7.4	14.9	3.3
松下/乐声 National	54	5.6	31.5	1.9	25.9	0.0
高士达/乐金 LG	46	2.2	8.7	17.4	15.2	6.5
夏普/声宝 Sharp	37	5.4	27.0	13.5	16.2	5.4
飞跃 Feiyue	36	0.0	0.0	11.1	16.7	5.6
上菱 Shangling	31	9.7	0.0	25.8	16.1	3.2
三星 Samsung	31	3.2	9.7	22.6	19.4	3.2
三菱 Mitsubish	19	5.3	10.5	26.3	15.8	10.5

3-6 微波炉未来一年购买打算/ Plan for Future Purchasing of a Microwave Oven

3-6-1 有无购买打算/ Whether Planning to Purchase Next Year

	人数 Number	百分比 Percent
是 yes	44	4.3
否 no	969	95.7

n=1013

3-6-2 打算购买的品牌排名/ The Brand of the Planned Purchase Next Year

排名 Brand Ranking	品牌 Brands	人数 Number	百分比 Percent
1	格兰仕 Galanz	21	47.7
2	松下/乐声 National	6	13.6
3	高士达/乐金 LG	4	9.1

n=44

3-6-3 打算购买的类型/ The Type of the Planned Purchase Next Year

	人数 Number	百分比 Percent
普通型 regular	26	59.1
含烧烤功能 including stewing and baking function	15	34.1
其他 others	3	6.8

n=44

3-6-4 打算购买的价格/ The Price of the Planned Purchase Next Year

	人数 Number	百分比 Percent
1000 元或以下 1000 yuan or below	24	54.5
1001～2000 元 yuan	11	25.0
2001～3000 元 yuan	6	13.6
3001～4000 元 yuan	1	2.3
4001～5000 元 yuan	0	0.0
5000 元以上 over 5000 yuan	1	2.3
完全不知道 don't know	1	2.3

n=44

3-7 选购微波炉时不同角色的人口特征/ Demographics of Different Roles in Purchasing a Microwave Oven

注：不同角色可以多选（Multiple answers）

	人数 Number	16-24 岁 Age	25-34 岁 Age	35-44 岁 Age	45-54 岁 Age	55-60 岁 Age
样本 Sample	698	19.5	28.2	27.4	17.0	7.9
男性 Male	339	19.8	26.8	26.5	18.0	8.8
提议者 advocate	54	25.9	22.2	22.2	24.1	5.6
影响者 influence	45	20.0	24.4	24.4	22.2	8.9
决定者 decider	141	5.7	27.0	36.2	22.7	8.5
使用者 user	185	25.9	25.4	23.2	15.1	10.3
女性 Female	359	19.2	29.5	28.1	16.2	7.0
提议者 advocate	64	21.9	32.8	23.4	15.6	6.3
影响者 influence	39	15.4	28.2	33.3	17.9	5.1
决定者 decider	112	8.0	26.8	38.4	23.2	3.6
使用者 user	240	22.5	27.1	28.7	13.3	8.3

3-8 不同消费者层的家中目前拥有品牌/ Brands of Microwave Oven Owned in Household by Market Segments

3-8-1 时尚流行指标/ Fads Popular Index

	人数 Number	第一品牌及百分比 1st/ percent	第二品牌及百分比 2nd/ percent	第三品牌及百分比 3rd/ percent	第四品牌及百分比 4th/ percent
样本 Sample	749	**格兰仕 Galanz(36.7)**	**蚬华 SMC(16.2)**	**松下/乐声 National(7.2)**	**高士达/乐金 LG(6.1)**
平实生活指向 simple living orientation	340	格兰仕 Galanz(37.1)	蚬华 SMC(16.2)	松下/乐声 National(7.1)	飞跃 Feiyue(5.9)
时尚流行指向 fashion orientation	409	格兰仕 Galanz(36.4)	蚬华 SMC(16.1)	松下/乐声 National(7.3)	高士达/乐金 LG(6.8)

3-8-2 广告态度指标/ Advertising Attitude Index

	人数 Number	第一品牌及百分比 1st/ percent	第二品牌及百分比 2nd/ percent	第三品牌及百分比 3rd/ percent	第四品牌及百分比 4th/ percent
样本 Sample	746	**格兰仕 Galanz(36.5)**	**蚬华 SMC(16.0)**	**松下/乐声 National(7.2)**	**高士达/乐金 LG(6.0)**
广告淡漠指向 indifferent orientation	183	格兰仕 Galanz(36.1)	蚬华 SMC(19.7)	松下/乐声 National(6.0)	三星 Samsung(5.5)
中间层 medium	464	格兰仕 Galanz(36.2)	蚬华 SMC(15.1)	松下/乐声 National(7.5)	高士达/乐金 LG(6.7)
信赖广告指向 loyal orientation	99	格兰仕 Galanz(38.4)	蚬华 SMC(13.1)	松下/乐声 National(8.1)	夏普/声宝 Sharp(7.1)

3-8-3 价格态度指标/ Price Attitude Index

	人数 Number	第一品牌及百分比 1st/ percent	第二品牌及百分比 2nd/ percent	第三品牌及百分比 3rd/ percent	第四品牌及百分比 4th/ percent
样本 Sample	753	**格兰仕 Galanz(36.5)**	**蚬华 SMC(16.2)**	**松下/乐声 National(7.2)**	**高士达/乐金 LG(6.1)**
价格无关心指向 indifferent orientation	117	格兰仕 Galanz(35.9)	蚬华 SMC(16.2)	三星 Samsung(8.5)	高士达/乐金 LG(7.7)
中间层 medium	401	格兰仕 Galanz(33.4)	蚬华 SMC(16.2)	松下/乐声 National(10.7)	夏普/声宝 Sharp(6.0) 高士达/乐金 LG(6.0)
价格重视指向 careful orientation	235	格兰仕 Galanz(42.1)	蚬华 SMC(16.2)	高士达/乐金 LG(5.5)	飞跃 Feiyue(5.1)

3-9 不同消费者层选择微波炉时的考虑因素/ Considerations in Choosing from Different Brands by Market Segments

3-9-1 时尚流行指标/ Fads Popular Index

注：本题为多选题，合计百分比超过 100%（Multiple answers）

	人数 Number	品牌形象 brand image	外型 outlook	价格 price	功率 power	容量大 big volume
样本 Sample	745	43.5	10.5	46.3	33.0	10.7
平实生活指向 simple living orientation	341	43.1	7.6	52.5	29.9	10.0
时尚流行指向 fashion orientation	404	43.8	12.9	41.1	35.6	11.4

续前表 continued

	人数 Number	内壁材料 inter material	微电脑控制 computer control ability	售后服务 follow-up service	安全 safety	其他 others
样本 Sample	745	5.4	10.7	10.3	15.7	4.0
平实生活指向 simple living orientation	341	3.8	9.1	12.0	15.5	5.6
时尚流行指向 fashion orientation	404	6.7	12.1	8.9	15.8	2.7

3-9-2 广告态度指标/ Advertising Attitude Index

注：本题为多选题，合计百分比超过 100%（Multiple answers）

	人数 Number	品牌形象 brand image	外型 outlook	价格 price	功率 power	容量大 big volume
样本 Sample	742	43.3	10.1	46.4	33.0	10.4
广告淡漠指向 indifferent orientation	182	37.9	9.9	54.4	31.9	9.9
中间层 medium	461	43.8	9.1	45.6	32.5	10.0
信赖广告指向 loyal orientation	99	50.5	15.2	35.4	37.4	13.1

续前表 continued

	人数 Number	内壁材料 inter material	微电脑控制 computer control ability	售后服务 follow-up service	安全 safety	其他 others
样本 Sample	742	5.3	10.6	10.6	15.9	4.0
广告淡漠指向 indifferent orientation	182	4.4	9.9	11.0	13.7	2.7
中间层 medium	461	5.9	9.5	10.0	16.3	5.0
信赖广告指向 loyal orientation	99	4.0	17.2	13.1	18.2	2.0

3-9-3 价格态度指标/ Price Attitude Index

注：本题为多选题，合计百分比超过 100%（Multiple answers）

	人数 Number	品牌形象 brand image	外型 outlook	价格 price	功率 power	容量大 big volume
样本 Sample	749	43.4	10.4	46.2	32.8	10.7
价格无关心指向 indifferent orientation	118	47.5	15.3	44.1	31.4	8.5
中间层 medium	398	43.5	10.3	44.5	34.4	10.8
价格重视指向 careful orientation	233	41.2	8.2	50.2	30.9	11.6

续前表 continued

	人数 Number	内壁材料 inter material	微电脑控制 computer control ability	售后服务 follow-up service	安全 safety	其他 others
样本 Sample	749	5.3	10.7	10.7	15.9	4.0
价格无关心指向 indifferent orientation	118	2.5	8.5	11.9	22.0	1.7
中间层 medium	398	6.3	12.6	10.1	14.1	2.8
价格重视指向 careful orientation	233	5.2	8.6	11.2	15.9	7.3

● 广州 / Guangzhou

3-1 微波炉的拥有比例/ Proportion of Microwave Oven Owners in the Sample

	人数 Number	百分比 Percent
有 yes	338	32.7
没有 no	696	67.3

n=1034

3-2 微波炉的拥有量/ Number of Microwave Oven Owned Per Household

	人数 Number	百分比 Percent
1 台 1 set	328	98.8
2 台 2 sets	4	1.2
3 台 3 sets	0	0.0
4 台及以上 4 sets or over	0	0.0

n=332

3-3 理想品牌排名/ Ranking of the Ideal Brands

排名 Brand Ranking	品牌 Brands	人数 Number	百分比 Percent
1	格兰仕 Galanz	246	23.8
2	松下/乐声 National	107	10.4
3	蚬华 SMC	44	4.3
4	高士达/乐金 LG	25	2.4
4	惠而浦 Whirlpool	25	2.4
5	夏普/声宝 Sharp	15	1.5
6	三星 Samsung	13	1.3
7	日立 Hitachi	7	0.7
8	飞利浦 Philips	6	0.6
8	万宝 Wanbao	6	0.6

n=1033

3-4 对家中现有微波炉(最近购买的一台)的四个方面的描述/ About the Microwave Oven Most Recently Purchased

3-4-1 家中现有微波炉的品牌排名/ Ranking of the Currently Owned Microwave Oven Brands

排名 Brand Ranking	品牌 Brands	人数 Number	百分比 Percent
1	格兰仕 Galanz	133	39.3
2	松下/乐声 National	60	17.8
3	蚬华 SMC	41	12.1
4	夏普/声宝 Sharp	14	4.1
5	高士达/乐金 LG	13	3.8
6	三星 Samsung	10	3.0
7	惠而浦 Whirlpool	9	2.7
8	日立 Hitachi	7	2.1
9	万和 Wanhe	5	1.5
9	康宝 Kangbao	5	1.5
10	万家乐 Macro	4	1.2

n=338

3-4-2 该微波炉的购买时间/ The Time of Purchasing of the Currently Owned Microwave Oven

	人数 Number	百分比 Percent
1985 年或以前 1985 or before	1	0.3
1986～1990 年	7	2.1
1991 年	5	1.5
1992 年	10	3.0
1993 年	14	4.2
1994 年	27	8.1
1995 年	22	6.6
1996 年	56	16.8
1997 年	83	24.9
1998 年	84	25.1
1999 年	25	7.5

n=334

3-4-3 该微波炉的价格/ The Price of the Currently Owned Microwave Oven

	人数 Number	百分比 Percent
1000 元以下 1000 yuan or below	135	39.9
1001～2000 元 yuan	113	33.4
2001～3000 元 yuan	47	13.9
3001～4000 元 yuan	13	3.8
4001～5000 元 yuan	2	0.6
5000 元以上 over 5000 yuan	1	0.3
完全不知道 don't know	27	8.0

n=338

3-4-4 该微波炉的类型/ The Type of the Currently Owned Microwave Oven

	人数 Number	百分比 Percent
普通型 regular	209	61.8
含烧烤功能 including stewing and baking function	128	37.9
其他 others	1	0.3

n=338

3-5 选择不同品牌微波炉时的考虑因素/ Considerations in Choosing from Different Brands

注：本题为多选题，合计百分比超过 100%（Multiple answers）

	人数 Number	品牌形象 brand image	外型 outlook	价格 price	功率 power	容量大 big volume
样本 Sample	337	44.2	11.6	49.9	16.9	10.1
格兰仕 Galanz	132	42.4	12.1	57.6	15.9	6.1
松下/乐声 National	60	66.7	10.0	21.7	18.3	5.0
蚬华 SMC	41	36.6	9.8	56.1	14.6	12.2
夏普/声宝 Sharp	14	57.1	7.1	21.4	14.3	28.6
高士达/乐金 LG	13	30.8	23.1	46.2	23.1	7.7
三星 Samsung	10	30.0	0.0	40.0	30.0	20.0
惠而浦 Whirlpool	9	66.7	0.0	66.7	11.1	22.2
日立 Hitachi	7	28.6	0.0	57.1	28.6	14.3
万和 Wanhe	5	40.0	60.0	60.0	20.0	0.0
康宝 Kangbao	5	20.0	0.0	80.0	0.0	0.0

续前表 continued

	人数 Number	内壁材料 inter material	微电脑控制 computer control ability	售后服务 follow-up service	安全 safety	其他 others
样本 Sample	337	3.3	18.1	13.6	25.8	2.1
格兰仕 Galanz	132	3.0	15.2	17.4	23.5	3.8
松下/乐声 National	60	6.7	28.3	5.0	25.0	1.7
蚬华 SMC	41	0.0	17.1	19.5	29.3	0.0
夏普/声宝 Sharp	14	0.0	21.4	0.0	28.6	7.1
高士达/乐金 LG	13	7.7	7.7	23.1	23.1	0.0
三星 Samsung	10	0.0	40.0	0.0	50.0	0.0
惠而浦 Whirlpool	9	11.1	11.1	11.1	33.3	0.0
日立 Hitachi	7	0.0	28.6	42.9	28.6	0.0
万和 Wanhe	5	0.0	0.0	20.0	40.0	0.0
康宝 Kangbao	5	0.0	0.0	0.0	20.0	0.0

3-6 微波炉未来一年购买打算/ Plan for Future Purchasing of a Microwave Oven

3-6-1 有无购买打算/ Whether Planning to Purchase Next Year

	人数 Number	百分比 Percent
是 yes	47	4.6
否 no	985	95.4

n=1032

3-6-2 打算购买的品牌排名/ The Brand of the Planned Purchase Next Year

排名 Brand Ranking	品牌 Brands	人数 Number	百分比 Percent
1	格兰仕 Galanz	23	48.9
2	松下/乐声 National	4	8.5
3	高士达/乐金 LG	2	4.3
3	日立 Hitachi	2	4.3

n=47

3-6-3 打算购买的类型/ The Type of the Planned Purchase Next Year

	人数 Number	百分比 Percent
普通型 regular	16	34.8
含烧烤功能 including stewing and baking function	29	63.0
其他 others	1	2.2

n=46

3-6-4 打算购买的价格/ The Price of the Planned Purchase Next Year

	人数 Number	百分比 Percent
1000 元或以下 1000 yuan or below	16	34.8
1001～2000 元 yuan	19	41.3
2001～3000 元 yuan	7	15.2
3001～4000 元 yuan	4	8.7
4001～5000 元 yuan	0	0.0
5000 元以上 over 5000 yuan	0	0.0
完全不知道 don't know	0	0.0

n=46

3-7 选购微波炉时不同角色的人口特征/ Demographics of the Different Roles in Purchasing a Microwave oven

注：不同角色可以多选（Multiple answers）

	人数 Number	16-24 岁 Age	25-34 岁 Age	35-44 岁 Age	45-54 岁 Age	55-60 岁 Age
样本 Sample	309	19.7	25.9	28.8	17.2	8.4
男性 Male	143	22.4	21.7	29.4	16.8	9.8
提议者 advocate	23	21.7	21.7	26.1	13.0	17.4
影响者 influence	28	32.1	28.6	14.3	17.9	7.1
决定者 decider	57	5.3	21.1	40.4	21.1	12.3
使用者 user	75	30.7	18.7	29.3	13.3	8.0
女性 Female	166	17.5	29.5	28.3	17.5	7.2
提议者 advocate	37	16.2	35.1	21.6	21.6	5.4
影响者 influence	32	12.5	37.5	25.0	18.8	6.3
决定者 decider	33	12.1	21.2	42.4	21.2	3.0
使用者 user	108	16.7	28.7	29.6	15.7	9.3

3-8 不同消费者层的家中目前拥有品牌/ Brands of Microwave Oven Owned in Household by Market Segments

3-8-1 时尚流行指标/ Fads Popular Index

	人数 Number	第一品牌及百分比 1st/ percent	第二品牌及百分比 2nd/ percent	第三品牌及百分比 3rd/ percent	第四品牌及百分比 4th/ percent
样本 Sample	334	**格兰仕 Galanz(39.2)**	**松下/乐声 National(18.0)**	**蚬华 SMC(12.0)**	**夏普/声宝 Sharp(4.2)**
平实生活指向 simple living orientation	153	格兰仕 Galanz(46.4)	松下/乐声 National(16.3)	蚬华 SMC(11.1)	高士达/乐金 LG(4.6)
时尚流行指向 fashion orientation	181	格兰仕 Galanz(33.1)	松下/乐声 National(19.3)	蚬华 SMC(12.7)	夏普/声宝 Sharp(5.5)

3-8-2 广告态度指标/ Advertising Attitude Index

	人数 Number	第一品牌及百分比 1st/ percent	第二品牌及百分比 2nd/ percent	第三品牌及百分比 3rd/ percent	第四品牌及百分比 4th/ percent
样本 Sample	335	**格兰仕 Galanz(39.7)**	**松下/乐声 National(17.6)**	**蚬华 SMC(11.6)**	**夏普/声宝 Sharp(4.2)**
广告淡漠指向 indifferent orientation	105	格兰仕 Galanz(39.0)	松下/乐声 National(19.0)	蚬华 SMC(13.3)	高士达/乐金 LG(4.8)
中间层 medium	201	格兰仕 Galanz(40.3)	松下/乐声 National(15.9)	蚬华 SMC(11.9)	夏普/声宝 Sharp(5.0)
信赖广告指向 loyal orientation	29	格兰仕 Galanz(37.9)	松下/乐声 National(24.1)	夏普/声宝 Sharp(3.4) 岭南 1+1(3.4) 爱多 Idall(3.4) 容声 Rongsheng(3.4) 蚬华 SMC(3.4) 万和 Wanhe(3.4) 日立 Hitachi(3.4) 康宝 Kangbao(3.4) 富士宝 Forth(3.4) 飞利浦 Philips(3.4)	

3-8-3 价格态度指标/ Price Attitude Index

	人数 Number	第一品牌及百分比 1st/ percent	第二品牌及百分比 2nd/ percent	第三品牌及百分比 3rd/ percent	第四品牌及百分比 4th/ percent
样本 Sample	336	**格兰仕 Galanz(39.6)**	**松下/乐声 National(17.9)**	**蚬华 SMC(11.9)**	**夏普/声宝 Sharp(4.2)**
价格无关心指向 indifferent orientation	73	格兰仕 Galanz(45.2)	松下/乐声 National(19.2)	蚬华 SMC(6.8)	惠而浦 Whirlpool(5.5)
中间层 medium	175	格兰仕 Galanz(36.6)	松下/乐声 National(16.6)	蚬华 SMC(16.0)	夏普/声宝 Sharp(4.6) 高士达/乐金 LG(4.6)
价格重视指向 careful orientation	88	格兰仕 Galanz(40.9)	松下/乐声 National(19.3)	蚬华 SMC(8.0)	夏普/声宝 Sharp(6.8)

3-9 不同消费者层选择微波炉时的考虑因素/ Considerations in Choosing from Different Brands by Market Segments

3-9-1 时尚流行指标/ Fads Popular Index

注：本题为多选题，合计百分比超过 100%（Multiple answers）

	人数 Number	品牌形象 brand image	外型 outlook	价格 price	功率 power	容量大 big volume
样本 Sample	333	44.1	11.4	49.8	17.1	10.2
平实生活指向 simple living orientation	153	40.5	10.5	54.9	18.3	9.2
时尚流行指向 fashion orientation	180	47.2	12.2	45.6	16.1	11.1

续前表 continued

	人数 Number	内壁材料 inter material	微电脑控制 computer control ability	售后服务 follow-up service	安全 safety	其他 others
样本 Sample	333	3.3	17.7	13.5	25.5	2.1
平实生活指向 simple living orientation	153	2.0	15.0	15.0	24.2	2.0
时尚流行指向 fashion orientation	180	4.4	20.0	12.2	26.7	2.2

3-9-2 广告态度指标/ Advertising Attitude Index

注：本题为多选题，合计百分比超过 100%（Multiple answers）

	人数 Number	品牌形象 brand image	外型 outlook	价格 price	功率 power	容量大 big volume
样本 Sample	334	44.0	11.4	50.3	16.8	10.2
广告淡漠指向 indifferent orientation	105	39.0	12.4	54.3	24.8	7.6
中间层 medium	200	45.0	10.5	51.0	14.5	11.5
信赖广告指向 loyal orientation	29	55.2	13.8	31.0	3.4	10.3

续前表 continued

	人数 Number	内壁材料 inter material	微电脑控制 computer control ability	售后服务 follow-up service	安全 safety	其他 others
样本 Sample	334	3.3	18.0	13.5	26.0	2.1
广告淡漠指向 indifferent orientation	105	2.9	22.9	15.2	24.8	0.0
中间层 medium	200	3.5	15.5	13.5	28.0	2.5
信赖广告指向 loyal orientation	29	3.4	17.2	6.9	17.2	6.9

3-9-3 价格态度指标/ Price Attitude Index

注：本题为多选题，合计百分比超过 100%（Multiple answers）

	人数 Number	品牌形象 brand image	外型 outlook	价格 price	功率 power	容量大 big volume
样本 Sample	335	44.5	11.6	50.1	16.7	10.1
价格无关心指向 indifferent orientation	72	45.8	11.1	55.6	15.3	4.2
中间层 medium	175	42.9	10.3	46.9	15.4	10.3
价格重视指向 careful orientation	88	46.6	14.8	52.3	20.5	14.8

续前表 continued

	人数 Number	内壁材料 inter material	微电脑控制 computer control ability	售后服务 follow-up service	安全 safety	其他 others
样本 Sample	335	3.3	17.9	13.7	25.7	2.1
价格无关心指向 indifferent orientation	72	4.2	13.9	12.5	26.4	1.4
中间层 medium	175	3.4	20.0	14.9	26.9	2.3
价格重视指向 careful orientation	88	2.3	17.0	12.5	22.7	2.3

● 重庆 / Chongqing

3-1 微波炉的拥有比例/ Proportion of Microwave Oven Owners in the Sample

	人数 Number	百分比 Percent
有 yes	108	17.3
没有 no	516	82.7

n=624

3-2 微波炉的拥有量/ Number of Microwave Oven Owned Per Household

	人数 Number	百分比 Percent
1 台 1 set	107	99.1
2 台 2 sets	1	0.9
3 台 3 sets	0	0.0
4 台及以上 4 sets or over	0	0.0

n=108

3-3 理想品牌排名/ Ranking of the Ideal Brands

排名 Brand Ranking	品牌 Brands	人数 Number	百分比 Percent
1	格兰仕 Galanz	225	36.1
2	高士达/乐金 LG	32	5.1
3	松下/乐声 National	19	3.0
4	海尔 Haier	8	1.3
4	格力 Gree	8	1.3
5	飞利浦 Philips	3	0.5
5	万宝 Wanbao	3	0.5
6	容声 Rongsheng	2	0.3
6	三洋 Sanyo	2	0.3
6	科龙 Kelon	2	0.3

N=624

3-4 对家中现有微波炉(最近购买的一台)的四个方面的描述/ About the Microwave Oven Most Recently Purchased

3-4-1 家中现有微波炉的品牌排名/ Ranking of the Currently Owned Microwave Oven Brands

排名 Brand Ranking	品牌 Brands	人数 Number	百分比 Percent
1	格兰仕 Galanz	76	71.0
2	松下/乐声 National	6	5.6
3	高士达/乐金 LG	5	4.7
4	惠宝 Huibao	4	3.7
5	安宝路 Amproluck	3	2.8
6	康宝 Kangbao	2	1.9
6	三洋 Sanyo	2	1.9

N=107

3-4-2 该微波炉的购买时间/ Time of Purchasing of the Currently Owned Microwave Oven

	人数 Number	百分比 Percent
1985 年或以前 1985 or before	1	0.9
1986～1990 年	3	2.8
1991 年	1	0.9
1992 年	0	0.0
1993 年	0	0.0
1994 年	0	0.0
1995 年	4	3.7
1996 年	12	11.1
1997 年	29	26.9
1998 年	36	33.3
1999 年	22	20.4

n=108

3-4-3 该微波炉的价格/ The Price of the Currently Owned Microwave Oven

	人数 Number	百分比 Percent
1000 元或以下 1000 yuan or below	47	43.5
1001～2000 元 yuan	50	46.3
2001～3000 元 yuan	8	7.4
3001～4000 元 yuan	1	0.9
4001～5000 元 yuan	0	0.0
5000 元以上 over 5000 yuan	2	1.9
完全不知道 don't know	0	0.0

n=108

3-4-4 该微波炉的类型/ The Type of the Currently Owned Microwave Oven

	人数 Number	百分比 Percent
普通型 regular	44	40.7
含烧烤功能 including stewing and baking function	64	59.3
其他 others	0	0.0

n=108

3-5 选择不同品牌微波炉时的考虑因素/ Considerations in Choosing from Different Brands

注：本题为多选题，合计百分比超过 100%（Multiple answers）

	人数 Number	品牌形象 brand image	外型 outlook	价格 price	功率 power	容量大 big volume
样本 Sample	107	57.0	15.9	46.7	19.6	9.3
格兰仕 Galanz	76	63.2	11.8	52.6	15.8	5.3
松下/乐声 National	6	66.7	50.0	0.0	33.3	33.3
高士达/乐金 LG	5	40.0	40.0	40.0	0.0	0.0
惠宝 Huibao	4	0.0	25.0	25.0	75.0	25.0
安宝路 Amproluck	3	66.7	0.0	33.3	0.0	0.0
康宝 Kangbao	2	0.0	0.0	100.0	0.0	0.0
三洋 Sanyo	2	100.0	0.0	50.0	0.0	0.0

续前表 continued

	人数 Number	内壁材料 inter material	微电脑控制 computer control ability	售后服务 follow-up service	安全 safety	其他 others
样本 Sample	107	2.8	20.6	17.8	17.8	4.7
格兰仕 Galanz	76	2.6	15.8	22.4	15.8	6.6
松下/乐声 National	6	0.0	83.3	0.0	0.0	0.0
高士达/乐金 LG	5	0.0	40.0	0.0	20.0	0.0
惠宝 Huibao	4	25.0	25.0	0.0	25.0	0.0
安宝路 Amproluck	3	0.0	0.0	33.3	66.7	0.0
康宝 Kangbao	2	0.0	0.0	0.0	0.0	0.0
三洋 Sanyo	2	0.0	0.0	0.0	50.0	0.0

3-6 微波炉未来一年购买打算/ Plan for Future Purchasing of a Microwave Oven

3-6-1 有无购买打算/ Whether Planning to Purchase Next Year

	人数 Number	百分比 Percent
是 yes	53	8.5
否 no	570	91.5

n=623

3-6-2 打算购买的品牌排名/ The Brand of the Planned Purchase Next Year

排名 Brand Ranking	品牌 Brands	人数 Number	百分比 Percent
1	格兰仕 Galanz	39	73.6
2	飞跃 Feiyue	2	3.8
2	高士达/乐金 LG	2	3.8

n=53

3-6-3 打算购买的类型/ The Type of the Planned Purchase Next Year

	人数 Number	百分比 Percent
普通型 regular	13	26.0
含烧烤功能 including stewing and baking function	37	74.0
其他 others	0	0.0

n=50

3-6-4 打算购买的价格/ The Price of the Planned Purchase Next Year

	人数 Number	百分比 Percent
1000 元或以下 1000 yuan or below	29	55.8
1001～2000 元 yuan	17	32.7
2001～3000 元 yuan	4	7.7
3001～4000 元 yuan	0	0.0
4001～5000 元 yuan	1	1.9
5000 元以上 over 5000 yuan	1	1.9
完全不知道 don't know	0	0.0

n=52

3-7 选购微波炉时不同角色的人口特征/ Demographics of the Different Roles in Purchasing a Microwave Oven

注：不同角色可以多选（Multiple answers）

	人数 Number	16-24 岁 Age	25-34 岁 Age	35-44 岁 Age	45-54 岁 Age	55-60 岁 Age
样本 Sample	90	23.3	28.9	15.6	21.1	11.1
男性 Male	39	17.9	28.2	15.4	20.5	17.9
提议者 advocate	8	37.5	37.5	12.5	0.0	12.5
影响者 influence	6	16.7	16.7	16.7	33.3	16.7
决定者 decider	24	16.7	25.0	20.8	20.8	16.7
使用者 user	20	25.0	30.0	10.0	15.0	20.0
女性 Female	51	27.5	29.4	15.7	21.6	5.9
提议者 advocate	11	27.3	18.2	18.2	27.3	9.1
影响者 influence	9	0.0	44.4	22.2	22.2	11.1
决定者 decider	16	6.3	62.5	12.5	18.8	0.0
使用者 user	35	31.4	22.9	17.1	22.9	5.7

3-8 不同消费者层的家中目前拥有品牌/ Brands of Microwave Oven Owned in Household by Market Segments

3-8-1 时尚流行指标/ Fads Popular Index

	人数 Number	第一品牌及百分比 1st/ percent	第二品牌及百分比 2nd/ percent	第三品牌及百分比 3rd/ percent
样本 Sample	101	**格兰仕 Galanz(73.3)**	**高士达/乐金 LG(5.0)** **松下/乐声 National(5.0)**	**惠宝 Huibao(4.0)**
平实生活指向 simple living orientation	52	格兰仕 Galanz(71.2)	惠宝 Huibao(5.8)	三洋 Sanyo(3.8) 高士达/乐金 LG(3.8) 松下/乐声 National(3.8)
时尚流行指向 fashion orientation	49	格兰仕 Galanz(75.5)	高士达/乐金 LG(6.1) 松下/乐声 National(6.1)	安宝路 Amproluck(4.1)

3-8-2 广告态度指标/ Advertising Attitude Index

	人数 Number	第一品牌及百分比 1st/ percent	第二品牌及百分比 2nd/ percent	第三品牌及百分比 3rd/ percent
样本 Sample	106	**格兰仕 Galanz(71.7)**	**高士达/乐金 LG(4.7)** **松下/乐声 National(4.7)**	**惠宝 Huibao(3.8)**
广告淡漠指向 indifferent orientation	28	格兰仕 Galanz(71.4)	高士达/乐金 LG(7.1)	三洋 Sanyo(3.6) 安宝路 Amproluck(3.6) 惠宝 Huibao(3.6) 康宝 Kangbao(3.6) 上菱 Shangling(3.6) 松下/乐声 National(3.6)
中间层 medium	68	格兰仕 Galanz(72.1)	松下/乐声 National(5.9)	惠宝 Huibao(4.4)
信赖广告指向 loyal orientation	10	格兰仕 Galanz(70.0)	安宝路 Amproluck(10.0) 东芝 Toshiba(10.0) 高士达/乐金 LG(10.0)	

3-8-3 价格态度指标/ Price Attitude Index

	人数 Number	第一品牌及百分比 1st/ percent	第二品牌及百分比 2nd/ percent	第三品牌及百分比 3rd/ percent
样本 Sample	106	**格兰仕 Galanz(71.7)**	**高士达/乐金 LG(4.7)** **松下/乐声 National(4.7)**	**惠宝 Huibao(3.8)**
价格无关心指向 indifferent orientation	26	格兰仕 Galanz(65.4)	松下/乐声 National(7.7)	安宝路 Amproluck(3.8) 东芝 Toshiba(3.8) 高士达/乐金 LG(3.8) 惠宝 Huibao(3.8) 康宝 Kangbao(3.8) 上菱 Shangling(3.8)
中间层 medium	51	格兰仕 Galanz(74.5)	高士达/乐金 LG(5.9) 松下/乐声 National(5.9)	三洋 Sanyo(3.9) 安宝路 Amproluck(3.9) 惠宝 Huibao(3.9)
价格重视指向 careful orientation	29	格兰仕 Galanz(72.4)	高士达/乐金 LG(3.4) 惠宝 Huibao(3.4) 三星 Samsung(3.4) 格力 Gree(3.4)	

3-9 不同消费者层选择微波炉时的考虑因素/ Considerations in Choosing from Different Brands by Market Segments

3-9-1 时尚流行指标/ Fads Popular Index

注：本题为多选题，合计百分比超过 100%（Multiple answers）

	人数 Number	品牌形象 brand image	外型 outlook	价格 price	功率 power	容量大 big volume
样本 Sample	102	57.8	15.7	45.1	18.6	8.8
平实生活指向 simple living orientation	52	63.5	19.2	59.6	23.1	9.6
时尚流行指向 fashion orientation	50	52.0	12.0	30.0	14.0	8.0

续前表 continued

	人数 Number	内壁材料 inter material	微电脑控制 computer control ability	售后服务 follow-up service	安全 safety	其他 others
样本 Sample	102	3.9	19.6	18.6	18.6	4.9
平实生活指向 simple living orientation	52	5.8	17.3	17.3	15.4	3.8
时尚流行指向 fashion orientation	50	2.0	22.0	20.0	22.0	6.0

3-9-2 广告态度指标/ Advertising Attitude Index

注：本题为多选题，合计百分比超过 100%（Multiple answers）

	人数 Number	品牌形象 brand image	外型 outlook	价格 price	功率 power	容量大 big volume
样本 Sample	107	57.0	15.9	46.7	18.7	8.4
广告淡漠指向 indifferent orientation	29	51.7	13.8	44.8	13.8	3.4
中间层 medium	68	57.4	14.7	50.0	23.5	10.3
信赖广告指向 loyal orientation	10	70.0	30.0	30.0	0.0	10.0

续前表 continued

	人数 Number	内壁材料 inter material	微电脑控制 computer control ability	售后服务 follow-up service	安全 safety	其他 others
样本 Sample	107	3.7	20.6	17.8	17.8	4.7
广告淡漠指向 indifferent orientation	29	6.9	6.9	13.8	24.1	10.3
中间层 medium	68	2.9	26.5	17.6	17.6	2.9
信赖广告指向 loyal orientation	10	0.0	20.0	30.0	0.0	0.0

3-9-3 价格态度指标/ Price Attitude Index

注：本题为多选题，合计百分比超过 100%（Multiple answers）

	人数 Number	品牌形象 brand image	外型 outlook	价格 price	功率 power	容量大 big volume
样本 Sample	107	57.0	15.9	46.7	18.7	8.4
价格无关心指向 indifferent orientation	26	42.3	15.4	30.8	11.5	11.5
中间层 medium	52	59.6	13.5	53.8	17.3	5.8
价格重视指向 careful orientation	29	65.5	20.7	48.3	27.6	10.3

续前表 continued

	人数 Number	内壁材料 inter material	微电脑控制 computer control ability	售后服务 follow-up service	安全 safety	其他 others
样本 Sample	107	3.7	20.6	17.8	17.8	4.7
价格无关心指向 indifferent orientation	26	0.0	19.2	26.9	19.2	7.7
中间层 medium	52	5.8	19.2	11.5	21.2	5.8
价格重视指向 careful orientation	29	3.4	24.1	20.7	10.3	0.0

武汉 / Wuhan

3-1 微波炉的拥有比例/ Proportion of Microwave Oven Owners in the Sample

	人数 Number	百分比 Percent
有 yes	123	19.2
没有 no	519	80.8

n=642

3-2 微波炉的拥有量/ Number of Microwave Oven Owned Per Household

	人数 Number	百分比 Percent
1 台 1 set	123	100.0
2 台 2 sets	0	0.0
3 台 3 sets	0	0.0
4 台及以上 4 sets or over	0	0.0

n=123

3-3 理想品牌排名/ Ranking of the Ideal Brands

排名 Brand Ranking	品牌 Brands	人数 Number	百分比 Percent
1	格兰仕 Galanz	189	29.6
2	高士达/乐金 LG	49	7.7
3	松下/乐声 National	14	2.2
4	海尔 Haier	13	2.0
5	三星 Samsung	6	0.9
6	蚬华 SMC	3	0.5
6	日立 Hitachi	3	0.5

n=638

3-4 对家中现有微波炉(最近购买的一台)的四个方面的描述/ About the Microwave Oven Most Recently Purchased

3-4-1 家中现有微波炉的品牌排名/ Ranking of the Currently Owned Microwave Oven Brands

排名 Brand Ranking	品牌 Brands	人数 Number	百分比 Percent
1	格兰仕 Galanz	65	53.3
2	高士达/乐金 LG	19	15.6
3	松下/乐声 National	8	6.6
4	三星 Samsung	6	4.9
5	蚬华 SMC	3	2.5
5	夏普/声宝 Sharp	3	2.5
6	惠宝 Huibao	2	1.6
6	安宝路 Amproluck	2	1.6

n=122

3-4-2 该微波炉的购买时间/ The Time of Purchasing of the Currently Owned Microwave Oven

	人数 Number	百分比 Percent
1985 年或以前 1985 or before	0	0.0
1986～1990 年	3	2.4
1991 年	2	1.6
1992 年	3	2.4
1993 年	0	0.0
1994 年	3	2.4
1995 年	2	1.6
1996 年	6	4.9
1997 年	23	18.7
1998 年	49	39.8
1999 年	32	26.0

n=123

3-4-3 该微波炉的价格/ The Price of the Currently Owned Microwave Oven

	人数 Number	百分比 Percent
1000 元或以下 1000 yuan or below	72	58.5
1001～2000 元 yuan	31	25.2
2001～3000 元 yuan	7	5.7
3001～4000 元 yuan	6	4.9
4001～5000 元 yuan	0	0.0
5000 元以上 over 5000 yuan	0	0.0
完全不知道 don't know	7	5.7

n=123

3-4-4 该微波炉的类型/ The Type of the Currently Owned Microwave Oven

	人数 Number	百分比 Percent
普通型 regular	49	40.5
含烧烤功能 including stewing and baking function	71	58.7
其他 others	1	0.8

n=121

3-5 选择不同品牌微波炉时的考虑因素/ Considerations in Choosing From Different Brands

注：本题为多选题，合计百分比超过 100%（Multiple answers）

	人数 Number	品牌形象 brand image	外型 outlook	价格 price	功率 power	容量大 big volume
样本 Sample	122	48.4	15.6	45.9	18.0	10.7
格兰仕 Galanz	65	56.9	18.5	50.8	18.5	10.8
高士达/乐金 LG	19	47.4	10.5	26.3	10.5	5.3
松下/乐声 National	8	62.5	0.0	12.5	37.5	12.5
三星 Samsung	6	33.3	0.0	66.7	33.3	16.7
蚬华 SMC	3	33.3	0.0	33.3	0.0	0.0
夏普/声宝 Sharp	3	33.3	33.3	33.3	33.3	33.3
惠宝 Huibao	2	0.0	50.0	50.0	0.0	0.0
安宝路 Amproluck	2	0.0	0.0	0.0	50.0	0.0

续前表 continued

	人数 Number	内壁材料 inter material	微电脑控制 computer control ability	售后服务 follow-up service	安全 safety	其他 others
样本 Sample	122	6.6	23.0	17.2	13.9	8.2
格兰仕 Galanz	65	4.6	20.0	20.0	10.8	9.2
高士达/乐金 LG	19	10.5	31.6	31.6	0.0	10.5
松下/乐声 National	8	0.0	25.0	0.0	12.5	12.5
三星 Samsung	6	16.7	0.0	16.7	33.3	0.0
蚬华 SMC	3	0.0	33.3	0.0	66.7	0.0
夏普/声宝 Sharp	3	0.0	66.7	0.0	0.0	0.0
惠宝 Huibao	2	0.0	50.0	0.0	0.0	0.0
安宝路 Amproluck	2	50.0	50.0	0.0	50.0	0.0

3-6 微波炉未来一年购买打算/ Plan for Future Purchasing of a Microwave Oven

3-6-1 有无购买打算/ Whether Planning to Purchase Next Year

	人数 Number	百分比 Percent
是 yes	72	11.2
否 no	569	88.8

n=641

3-6-2 打算购买的品牌排名/ The Brand of the Planned Purchase Next Year

排名 Brand Ranking	品牌 Brands	人数 Number	百分比 Percent
1	格兰仕 Galanz	31	48.4
2	高士达/乐金 LG	8	12.5
3	松下/乐声 National	5	7.8
4	海尔 Haier	2	3.1

n=64

3-6-3 打算购买的类型/ The Type of the Planned Purchase Next Year

	人数 Number	百分比 Percent
普通型 regular	21	30.4
含烧烤功能 including stewing and baking function	46	66.7
其他 others	2	2.9

n=69

3-6-4 打算购买的价格/ The Price of the Planned Purchase Next Year

	人数 Number	百分比 Percent
1000 元或以下 1000 yuan or below	38	55.1
1001～2000 元 yuan	21	30.4
2001～3000 元 yuan	8	11.6
3001～4000 元 yuan	1	1.4
4001～5000 元 yuan	0	0.0
5000 元以上 over 5000 yuan	1	1.4
完全不知道 don't know	0	0.0

n=69

3-7 选购微波炉时不同角色的人口特征/ Demographics of the Different Roles in Purchasing a Microwave Oven

注：不同角色可以多选（Multiple answers）

	人数 Number	16-24 岁 Age	25-34 岁 Age	35-44 岁 Age	45-54 岁 Age	55-60 岁 Age
样本 Sample	108	24.1	29.6	19.4	19.4	7.4
男性 Male	45	26.7	22.2	20.0	20.0	11.1
提议者 advocate	11	0.0	18.2	18.2	45.5	18.2
影响者 influence	7	28.6	14.3	42.9	14.3	0.0
决定者 decider	17	5.9	29.4	23.5	17.6	23.5
使用者 user	32	34.4	25.0	18.8	15.6	6.3
女性 Female	63	22.2	34.9	19.0	19.0	4.8
提议者 advocate	15	33.3	26.7	20.0	13.3	6.7
影响者 influence	8	12.5	37.5	12.5	37.5	0.0
决定者 decider	21	4.8	28.6	33.3	28.6	4.8
使用者 user	44	25.0	36.4	18.2	18.2	2.3

3-8 不同消费者层的家中目前拥有品牌/ Brands of Microwave Oven Owned in Household by Market Segments

3-8-1 时尚流行指标/ Fads Popular Index

	人数 Number	第一品牌及百分比 1st/ percent	第二品牌及百分比 2nd/ percent	第三品牌及百分比 3rd/ percent	第四品牌及百分比 4th/ percent
样本 Sample	118	**格兰仕 Galanz(52.5)**	**高士达/乐金 LG(16.1)**	**松下/乐声 National(6.8)**	**三星 Samsung(5.1)**
平实生活指向 simple living orientation	49	格兰仕 Galanz(49.0)	高士达/乐金 LG(12.2)	松下/乐声 National(10.2)	蚬华 SMC(6.1)
时尚流行指向 fashion orientation	69	格兰仕 Galanz(55.1)	高士达/乐金 LG(18.8)	三星 Samsung(5.8)	松下/乐声 National(4.3) 夏普/声宝 Sharp(4.3)

3-8-2 广告态度指标/ Advertising Attitude Index

	人数 Number	第一品牌及百分比 1st/ percent	第二品牌及百分比 2nd/ percent	第三品牌及百分比 3rd/ percent	第四品牌及百分比 4th/ percent
样本 Sample	118	**格兰仕 Galanz(52.5)**	**高士达/乐金 LG(16.1)**	**松下/乐声 National(6.8)**	**三星 Samsung(5.1)**
广告淡漠指向 indifferent orientation	22	格兰仕 Galanz(40.9)	高士达/乐金 LG(27.3)	三星 Samsung(9.1) 蚬华 SMC(9.1)	松下/乐声 National(4.5) 夏普/声宝 Sharp(4.5) 惠普 HP(4.5)
中间层 medium	78	格兰仕 Galanz(55.1)	高士达/乐金 LG(14.1)	松下/乐声 National(5.1)	三星 Samsung(3.8)
信赖广告指向 loyal orientation	18	格兰仕 Galanz(55.6)	松下/乐声 National(16.7)	高士达/乐金 LG(11.1)	长帝 Changdi(5.6) 三星 Samsung(5.6) 万和 Wanhe(5.6)

3-8-3 价格态度指标/ Price Attitude Index

	人数 Number	第一品牌及百分比 1st/ percent	第二品牌及百分比 2nd/ percent	第三品牌及百分比 3rd/ percent	第四品牌及百分比 4th/ percent
样本 Sample	117	**格兰仕 Galanz(52.1)**	**高士达/乐金 LG(16.2)**	**松下/乐声 National(6.8)**	**三星 Samsung(5.1)**
价格无关心指向 indifferent orientation	19	格兰仕 Galanz(52.6)	高士达/乐金 LG(15.8)	松下/乐声 National(10.5)	飞利浦 Philips(5.3) 三星 Samsung(5.3) 万和 Wanhe(5.3) 蚬华 SMC(5.3)
中间层 medium	61	格兰仕 Galanz(49.2)	高士达/乐金 LG(16.4)	三星 Samsung(6.6)	松下/乐声 National(4.9) 夏普/声宝 Sharp(4.9)
价格重视指向 careful orientation	37	格兰仕 Galanz(56.8)	高士达/乐金 LG(16.2)	松下/乐声 National(8.1)	安宝路 Amproluck(2.7) 创力 Chuangli(2.7) 三菱 Mitsubish(2.7) 三星 Samsung(2.7) 希贵 Heygey(2.7) 新天地 Xintiandi(2.7)

3-9 不同消费者层选择微波炉时的考虑因素/ Considerations in Choosing from Different Brands by Market Segments

3-9-1 时尚流行指标/ Fads Popular Index

注：本题为多选题，合计百分比超过 100%（Multiple answers）

	人数 Number	品牌形象 brand image	外型 outlook	价格 price	功率 power	容量大 big volume
样本 Sample	119	48.7	15.1	46.2	17.6	9.2
平实生活指向 simple living orientation	49	44.9	10.2	46.9	12.2	6.1
时尚流行指向 fashion orientation	70	51.4	18.6	45.7	21.4	11.4

续前表 continued

	人数 Number	内壁材料 inter material	微电脑控制 computer control ability	售后服务 follow-up service	安全 safety	其他 others
样本 Sample	119	6.7	23.5	17.6	14.3	7.6
平实生活指向 simple living orientation	49	12.2	24.5	20.4	14.3	8.2
时尚流行指向 fashion orientation	70	2.9	22.9	15.7	14.3	7.1

3-9-2 广告态度指标/ Advertising Attitude Index

注：本题为多选题，合计百分比超过 100%（Multiple answers）

	人数 Number	品牌形象 brand image	外型 outlook	价格 price	功率 power	容量大 big volume
样本 Sample	119	48.7	15.1	46.2	17.6	9.2
广告淡漠指向 indifferent orientation	22	31.8	18.2	40.9	27.3	13.6
中间层 medium	78	51.3	15.4	51.3	14.1	7.7
信赖广告指向 loyal orientation	19	57.9	10.5	31.6	21.1	10.5

续前表 continued

	人数 Number	内壁材料 inter material	微电脑控制 computer control ability	售后服务 follow-up service	安全 safety	其他 others
样本 Sample	119	6.7	23.5	17.6	14.3	7.6
广告淡漠指向 indifferent orientation	22	9.1	27.3	27.3	13.6	4.5
中间层 medium	78	7.7	25.6	11.5	16.7	7.7
信赖广告指向 loyal orientation	19	0.0	10.5	31.6	5.3	10.5

3-9-3 价格态度指标/ Price Attitude Index

注：本题为多选题，合计百分比超过 100%（Multiple answers）

	人数 Number	品牌形象 brand image	外型 outlook	价格 price	功率 power	容量大 big volume
样本 Sample	118	48.3	14.4	45.8	17.8	9.3
价格无关心指向 indifferent orientation	19	68.4	10.5	26.3	5.3	5.3
中间层 medium	62	40.3	17.7	46.8	25.8	8.1
价格重视指向 careful orientation	37	51.4	10.8	54.1	10.8	13.5

续前表 continued

	人数 Number	内壁材料 inter material	微电脑控制 computer control ability	售后服务 follow-up service	安全 safety	其他 others
样本 Sample	118	6.8	23.7	17.8	14.4	7.6
价格无关心指向 indifferent orientation	19	5.3	26.3	15.8	5.3	0.0
中间层 medium	62	8.1	27.4	12.9	19.4	8.1
价格重视指向 careful orientation	37	5.4	16.2	27.0	10.8	10.8

● 西安 / Xi'an

3-1 微波炉的拥有比例/ Proportion of Microwave Oven Owners in the Sample

	人数 Number	百分比 Percent
有 yes	78	13.0
没有 no	523	87.0

n=601

3-2 微波炉的拥有量/ Number of Microwave Oven Owned Per Household

	人数 Number	百分比 Percent
1 台 1 set	78	100.0
2 台 2 sets	0	0.0
3 台 3 sets	0	0.0
4 台及以上 4 sets or over	0	0.0

n=78

3-3 理想品牌排名/ Ranking of the Ideal Brands

排名 Brand Ranking	品牌 Brands	人数 Number	百分比 Percent
1	格兰仕 Galanz	199	33.3
2	松下/乐声 National	26	4.4
3	高士达/乐金 LG	20	3.4
4	万宝 Wanbao	17	2.8
5	海尔 Haier	11	1.8
6	飞利浦 Philips	7	1.2
7	夏普/声宝 Sharp	6	1.0
8	爱得 Aide	3	0.5
8	飞跃 Feiyue	3	0.5

n=597

3-4 对家中现有微波炉(最近购买的一台)的四个方面的描述/ About the Microwave Oven Most Recently Purchased

3-4-1 家中现有微波炉的品牌排名/ Ranking of the Currently Owned Microwave Oven Brands

排名 Brand Ranking	品牌 Brands	人数 Number	百分比 Percent
1	格兰仕 Galanz	36	46.2
2	松下/乐声 National	10	12.8
3	高士达/乐金 LG	7	9.0
4	夏普/声宝 Sharp	5	6.4
5	惠宝 Huibao	4	5.1
6	安宝路 Amproluck	2	2.6
6	飞跃 Feiyue	2	2.6

n=78

3-4-2 该微波炉的购买时间/ The Time of Purchasing of the Currently Owned Microwave Oven

	人数 Number	百分比 Percent
1985 年或以前 1985 or before	0	0.0
1986～1990 年	2	2.6
1991 年	1	1.3
1992 年	1	1.3
1993 年	5	6.4
1994 年	1	1.3
1995 年	7	9.0
1996 年	7	9.0
1997 年	18	23.1
1998 年	22	28.2
1999 年	14	17.9

n=78

3-4-3 该微波炉的价格/ The Price of the Currently Owned Microwave Oven

	人数 Number	百分比 Percent
1000 元及以下 1000 yuan or below	28	35.9
1001～2000 元 yuan	32	41.0
2001～3000 元 yuan	11	14.1
3001～4000 元 yuan	2	2.6
4001～5000 元 yuan	2	2.6
5000 元以上 over 5000 yuan	0	0.0
完全不知道 don't know	3	3.8

n=78

3-4-4 该微波炉的类型/ The Type of the Currently Owned Microwave Oven

	人数 Number	百分比 Percent
普通型 regular	49	62.8
含烧烤功能 including stewing and baking function	29	37.2
其他 others	0	0.0

n=78

3-5 选择不同品牌微波炉时的考虑因素/ Considerations in Choosing from Different Brands

注：本题为多选题，合计百分比超过 100%（Multiple answers）

	人数 Number	品牌形象 brand image	外型 outlook	价格 price	功率 power	容量大 big volume
样本 Sample	**78**	**52.6**	**17.9**	**34.6**	**20.5**	**5.1**
格兰仕 Galanz	36	52.8	11.1	41.7	19.4	5.6
松下/乐声 National	10	60.0	30.0	20.0	20.0	0.0
高士达/乐金 LG	7	57.1	28.6	14.3	14.3	0.0
夏普/声宝 Sharp	5	80.0	20.0	20.0	20.0	20.0
惠宝 Huibao	4	25.0	50.0	25.0	25.0	0.0

续前表 continued

	人数 Number	内壁材料 inter material	微电脑控制 computer control ability	售后服务 follow-up service	安全 safety	其他 others
样本 Sample	**78**	**3.8**	**19.2**	**17.9**	**19.2**	**7.7**
格兰仕 Galanz	36	2.8	11.1	19.4	16.7	8.3
松下/乐声 National	10	0.0	40.0	0.0	40.0	0.0
高士达/乐金 LG	7	0.0	14.3	14.3	14.3	14.3
夏普/声宝 Sharp	5	0.0	0.0	40.0	0.0	0.0
惠宝 Huibao	4	0.0	50.0	50.0	0.0	0.0

3-6 微波炉未来一年购买打算/ Plan for Future Purchasing of a Microwave Oven

3-6-1 有无购买打算/ Whether Planning to Purchase Next Year

	人数 Number	百分比 Percent
是 yes	37	6.2
否 no	564	93.8

n=601

3-6-2 打算购买的品牌排名/ The Brand of the Planned Purchase Next Year

排名 Brand Ranking	品牌 Brands	人数 Number	百分比 Percent
1	格兰仕 Galanz	23	67.6
2	飞跃 Feiyue	2	5.9
2	松下/乐声 National	2	5.9

n=34

3-6-3 打算购买的类型/ The Type of the Planned Purchase Next Year

	人数 Number	百分比 Percent
普通型 regular	15	42.9
含烧烤功能 including stewing and baking function	19	54.3
其他 others	1	2.9

n=35

3-6-4 打算购买的价格/ The Price of the Planned Purchase Next Year

	人数 Number	百分比 Percent
1000 元及以下 1000 yuan or below	15	40.5
1001～2000 元 yuan	16	43.2
2001～3000 元 yuan	4	10.8
3001～4000 元 yuan	2	5.4
4001～5000 元 yuan	0	0.0
5000 元以上 over 5000 yuan	0	0.0
完全不知道 don't know	0	0.0

n=37

3-7 选购微波炉时不同角色的人口特征/ Demographics of the Different Roles in Purchasing a Microwave oven

注：不同角色可以多选（Multiple answers）

	人数 Number	16-24 岁 Age	25-34 岁 Age	35-44 岁 Age	45-54 岁 Age	55-60 岁 Age
样本 Sample	69	27.5	30.4	17.4	14.5	10.1
男性 Male	32	31.3	28.1	18.8	12.5	9.4
提议者 advocate	4	25.0	0.0	75.0	0.0	0.0
影响者 influence	6	33.3	33.3	33.3	0.0	0.0
决定者 decider	12	0.0	16.7	41.7	25.0	16.7
使用者 user	24	41.7	29.2	16.7	4.2	8.3
女性 Female	37	24.3	32.4	16.2	16.2	10.8
提议者 advocate	5	0.0	60.0	20.0	0.0	20.0
影响者 influence	7	14.3	42.9	14.3	14.3	14.3
决定者 decider	10	10.0	40.0	30.0	20.0	0.0
使用者 user	25	32.0	28.0	12.0	16.0	12.0

3-8 不同消费者层的家中目前拥有品牌/ Brands of Microwave Oven Owned in Household by Market Segments

3-8-1 时尚流行指标/ Fads Popular Index

	人数 Number	第一品牌及百分比 1st/ percent	第二品牌及百分比 2nd/ percent	第三品牌及百分比 3rd/ percent	第四品牌及百分比 4th/ percent
样本 Sample	78	**格兰仕 Galanz(46.2)**	**松下/乐声 National(12.8)**	**高士达/乐金 LG(9.0)**	**夏普/声宝 Sharp(6.4)**
平实生活指向 simple living orientation	30	格兰仕 Galanz(60.0)	高士达/乐金 LG(16.7)	松下/乐声 National(10.0)	安宝路 Amproluck(3.3) 惠而浦 Whirlpool(3.3) 春兰 Chunlan(3.3)
时尚流行指向 fashion orientation	48	格兰仕 Galanz(37.5)	松下/乐声 National(14.6)	夏普/声宝 Sharp(10.4)	惠宝 Huibao(8.3)

3-8-2 广告态度指标/ Advertising Attitude Index

	人数 Number	第一品牌及百分比 1st/ percent	第二品牌及百分比 2nd/ percent	第三品牌及百分比 3rd/ percent	第四品牌及百分比 4th/ percent
样本 Sample	77	**格兰仕 Galanz(45.5)**	**松下/乐声 National(13.0)**	**高士达/乐金 LG(9.1)**	**夏普/声宝 Sharp(6.5)**
广告淡漠指向 indifferent orientation	19	格兰仕 Galanz(47.4)	高士达/乐金 LG(10.5) 松下/乐声 National(10.5)	安宝路 Amproluck(5.3) 东芝 Toshiba(5.3) 飞跃 Feiyue(5.3) 惠而浦 Whirlpool(5.3) 夏普/声宝 Sharp(5.3)	
中间层 medium	47	格兰仕 Galanz(46.8)	松下/乐声 National(14.9)	高士达/乐金 LG(10.6)	惠宝 Huibao(6.4)
信赖广告指向 loyal orientation	11	格兰仕 Galanz(36.4)	夏普/声宝 Sharp(18.2)	海尔 Haier(9.1) 惠宝 Huibao(9.1) 松下/乐声 National(9.1) 蚬华 SMC(9.1)	

3-8-3 价格态度指标/ Price Attitude Index

	人数 Number	第一品牌及百分比 1st/ percent	第二品牌及百分比 2nd/ percent	第三品牌及百分比 3rd/ percent	第四品牌及百分比 4th/ percent
样本 Sample	77	**格兰仕 Galanz(45.5)**	**松下/乐声 National(13.0)**	**高士达/乐金 LG(9.1)**	**夏普/声宝 Sharp(6.5)**
价格无关心指向 indifferent orientation	17	格兰仕 Galanz(58.8)	澳柯玛 Aucma(5.9) 海尔 Haier(5.9) 惠宝 Huibao(5.9) 松下/乐声 National(5.9) 蚬华 SMC(5.9) 烤王 Kaowang(5.9) 佳士 Jiashi(5.9)		
中间层 medium	45	格兰仕 Galanz(44.4)	高士达/乐金 LG(13.3)	松下/乐声 National(11.1)	夏普/声宝 Sharp(8.9)
价格重视指向 careful orientation	15	格兰仕 Galanz(33.3)	松下/乐声 National(26.7)	安宝路 Amproluck(13.3)	东芝 Toshiba(6.7) 高士达/乐金 LG(6.7) 三星 Samsung(6.7) 夏普/声宝 Sharp(6.7)

3-9 不同消费者层选择微波炉时的考虑因素/ Considerations in Choosing from Different Brands by Market Segments

3-9-1 时尚流行指标/ Fads Popular Index

注：本题为多选题，合计百分比超过 100%（Multiple answers）

	人数 Number	品牌形象 brand image	外型 outlook	价格 price	功率 power	容量大 big volume
样本 Sample	78	52.6	17.9	34.6	20.5	5.1
平实生活指向 simple living orientation	30	53.3	10.0	50.0	13.3	6.7
时尚流行指向 fashion orientation	48	52.1	22.9	25.0	25.0	4.2

续前表 continued

	人数 Number	内壁材料 inter material	微电脑控制 computer control ability	售后服务 follow-up service	安全 safety	其他 others
样本 Sample	78	3.8	19.2	17.9	19.2	7.7
平实生活指向 simple living orientation	30	3.3	13.3	13.3	13.3	10.0
时尚流行指向 fashion orientation	48	4.2	22.9	20.8	22.9	6.3

3-9-2 广告态度指标/ Advertising Attitude Index

注：本题为多选题，合计百分比超过 100%（Multiple answers）

	人数 Number	品牌形象 brand image	外型 outlook	价格 price	功率 power	容量大 big volume
样本 Sample	77	53.2	18.2	35.1	20.8	5.2
广告淡漠指向 indifferent orientation	19	57.9	5.3	52.6	5.3	5.3
中间层 medium	47	55.3	23.4	29.8	21.3	6.4
信赖广告指向 loyal orientation	11	36.4	18.2	27.3	45.5	0.0

续前表 continued

	人数 Number	内壁材料 inter material	微电脑控制 computer control ability	售后服务 follow-up service	安全 safety	其他 others
样本 Sample	77	3.9	18.2	18.2	19.5	7.8
广告淡漠指向 indifferent orientation	19	10.5	15.8	10.5	21.1	5.3
中间层 medium	47	2.1	23.4	17.0	17.0	6.4
信赖广告指向 loyal orientation	11	0.0	0.0	36.4	27.3	18.2

3-9-3 价格态度指标/ Price Attitude Index

注：本题为多选题，合计百分比超过 100%（Multiple answers）

	人数 Number	品牌形象 brand image	外型 outlook	价格 price	功率 power	容量大 big volume
样本 Sample	77	53.2	18.2	35.1	19.5	5.2
价格无关心指向 indifferent orientation	17	52.9	5.9	41.2	29.4	11.8
中间层 medium	45	57.8	22.2	28.9	17.8	2.2
价格重视指向 careful orientation	15	40.0	20.0	46.7	13.3	6.7

续前表 continued

	人数 Number	内壁材料 inter material	微电脑控制 computer control ability	售后服务 follow-up service	安全 safety	其他 others
样本 Sample	77	3.9	19.5	16.9	18.2	7.8
价格无关心指向 indifferent orientation	17	0.0	11.8	17.6	23.5	17.6
中间层 medium	45	4.4	17.8	17.8	17.8	6.7
价格重视指向 careful orientation	15	6.7	33.3	13.3	13.3	0.0

● 沈阳 / Shenyang

3-1 微波炉的拥有比例/ Proportion of Microwave Oven Owners in the Sample

	人数 Number	百分比 Percent
有 yes	75	12.5
没有 no	525	87.5

n=600

3-2 微波炉的拥有量/ Number of Microwave Oven Owned Per Household

	人数 Number	百分比 Percent
1台 1 set	74	100.0
2台 2 sets	0	0.0
3台 3 sets	0	0.0
4台及以上 4 sets or over	0	0.0

n=74

3-3 理想品牌排名/ Ranking of the Ideal Brands

排名 Brand Ranking	品牌 Brands	人数 Number	百分比 Percent
1	高士达/乐金 LG	168	28.0
2	格兰仕 Galanz	149	24.8
3	松下/乐声 National	24	4.0
4	海尔 Haier	20	3.3
5	容声 Rongsheng	12	2.0
6	三星 Samsung	6	1.0
7	夏普/声宝 Sharp	4	0.7
8	东芝 Toshiba	3	0.5
9	三洋 Sanyo	2	0.3
9	方太 Fotile	2	0.3

n=601

3-4 对家中现有微波炉(最近购买的一台)的四个方面的描述/ About the Microwave Oven Most Recently Purchased

3-4-1 家中现有微波炉的品牌排名/ Ranking of the Currently Owned Microwave Oven Brands

排名 Brand Ranking	品牌 Brands	人数 Number	百分比 Percent
1	格兰仕 Galanz	37	49.3
2	高士达/乐金 LG	13	17.3
3	松下/乐声 National	12	16.0
4	夏普/声宝 Sharp	3	4.0
5	创力 Chuangli	2	2.7

n=75

3-4-2 该微波炉的购买时间/ Time of Purchasing of the Currently Owned Microwave Oven

	人数 Number	百分比 Percent
1985年或以前 1985 or before	0	0.0
1986～1990年	1	1.3
1991年	1	1.3
1992年	0	0.0
1993年	0	0.0
1994年	2	2.7
1995年	5	6.7
1996年	6	8.0
1997年	16	21.3
1998年	23	30.7
1999年	21	28.0

n=75

3-4-3 该微波炉的价格/ The Price of the Currently Owned Microwave Oven

	人数 Number	百分比 Percent
1000元或以下 1000 yuan or below	31	41.3
1001～2000元 yuan	24	32.0
2001～3000元 yuan	14	18.7
3001～4000元 yuan	3	4.0
4001～5000元 yuan	0	0.0
5000元以上 over 5000 yuan	0	0.0
完全不知道 don't know	3	4.0

n=75

3-4-4 该微波炉的类型/ The Type of the Currently Owned Microwave Oven

	人数 Number	百分比 Percent
普通型 regular	25	33.3
含烧烤功能 including stewing and baking function	50	66.7
其他 others	0	0.0

n=75

3-5 选择不同品牌微波炉时的考虑因素/ Considerations in Choosing from Different Brands

注：本题为多选题，合计百分比超过 100%（Multiple answers）

	人数 Number	品牌形象 brand image	外型 outlook	价格 price	功率 power	容量大 big volume
样本 Sample	74	73.0	4.1	31.1	6.8	10.8
格兰仕 Galanz	37	73.0	5.4	29.7	2.7	10.8
高士达/乐金 LG	13	84.6	7.7	46.2	0.0	7.7
松下/乐声 National	12	83.3	0.0	25.0	25.0	0.0

续前表 continued

	人数 Number	内壁材料 inter material	微电脑控制 computer control ability	售后服务 follow-up service	安全 safety	其他 others
样本 Sample	74	2.7	28.4	14.9	10.8	0.0
格兰仕 Galanz	37	5.4	18.9	16.2	5.4	0.0
高士达/乐金 LG	13	0.0	30.8	15.4	7.7	0.0
松下/乐声 National	12	0.0	50.0	8.3	25.0	0.0

3-6 微波炉未来一年购买打算/ Plan for Future Purchasing of a Microwave Oven

3-6-1 有无购买打算/ Whether Planning to Purchase Next Year

	人数 Number	百分比 Percent
是 yes	65	10.9
否 no	531	89.1

n=596

3-6-2 打算购买的品牌排名/ The Brand of the Planned Purchase Next Year

排名 Brand Ranking	品牌 Brands	人数 Number	百分比 Percent
1	格兰仕 Galanz	37	56.9
2	高士达/乐金 LG	14	21.5
3	东芝 Toshiba	2	3.1
3	海尔 Haier	2	3.1
4	飞跃 Feiyue	1	1.5
4	松下/乐声 National	1	1.5
4	新宝 Sampo	1	1.5

n=65

3-6-3 打算购买的类型/ The Type of the Planned Purchase Next Year

	人数 Number	百分比 Percent
普通型 regular	13	20.3
含烧烤功能 including stewing and baking function	51	79.7
其他 others	0	0.0

n=64

3-6-4 打算购买的价格/ The Price of the Planned Purchase Next Year

	人数 Number	百分比 Percent
1000 元或以下 1000 yuan or below	26	40.0
1001～2000 元 yuan	31	47.7
2001～3000 元 yuan	4	6.2
3001～4000 元 yuan	3	4.6
4001～5000 元 yuan	0	0.0
5000 元以上 over 5000 yuan	0	0.0
完全不知道 don't know	1	1.5

n=65

3-7 选购微波炉时不同角色的人口特征/ Demographics of the Different Roles in Purchasing a Microwave Oven

注：不同角色可以多选（Multiple answers）

	人数 Number	16-24 岁 Age	25-34 岁 Age	35-44 岁 Age	45-54 岁 Age	55-60 岁 Age
样本 Sample	70	10.0	40.0	32.9	14.3	2.9
男性 Male	30	10.0	40.0	33.3	13.3	3.3
提议者 advocate	8	25.0	62.5	0.0	12.5	0.0
影响者 influence	0	0.0	0.0	0.0	0.0	0.0
决定者 decider	19	0.0	36.8	47.4	10.5	5.3
使用者 user	11	9.1	54.5	27.3	9.1	0.0
女性 Female	40	10.0	40.0	32.5	15.0	2.5
提议者 advocate	8	12.5	37.5	25.0	25.0	0.0
影响者 influence	5	20.0	20.0	60.0	0.0	0.0
决定者 decider	15	0.0	46.7	40.0	13.3	0.0
使用者 user	26	11.5	34.6	30.8	19.2	3.8

3-8 不同消费者层的家中目前拥有品牌/ Brands of Microwave Oven Owned in Household by Market Segments

3-8-1 时尚流行指标/ Fads Popular Index

	人数 Number	第一品牌及百分比 1st/ percent	第二品牌及百分比 2nd/ percent	第三品牌及百分比 3rd/ percent
样本 Sample	75	**格兰仕 Galanz(49.3)**	**高士达/乐金 LG(17.3)**	**松下/乐声 National(16.0)**
平实生活指向 simple living orientation	28	格兰仕 Galanz(60.7)	高士达/乐金 LG(14.3)	松下/乐声 National(7.1)
时尚流行指向 fashion orientation	47	格兰仕 Galanz(42.6)	松下/乐声 National(21.3)	高士达/乐金 LG(19.1)

3-8-2 广告态度指标/ Advertising Attitude Index

	人数 Number	第一品牌及百分比 1st/ percent	第二品牌及百分比 2nd/ percent	第三品牌及百分比 3rd/ percent
样本 Sample	75	**格兰仕 Galanz(49.3)**	**高士达/乐金 LG(17.3)**	**松下/乐声 National(16.0)**
广告淡漠指向 indifferent orientation	11	格兰仕 Galanz(54.5)	高士达/乐金 LG(27.3)	松下/乐声 National(9.1) 夏普/声宝 Sharp(9.1)
中间层 medium	52	格兰仕 Galanz(48.1)	松下/乐声 National(17.3)	高士达/乐金 LG(15.4)
信赖广告指向 loyal orientation	12	格兰仕 Galanz(50.0)	高士达/乐金 LG(16.7) 松下/乐声 National(16.7)	创力 Chuangli(8.3) 夏普/声宝 Sharp(8.3)

3-8-3 价格态度指标/ Price Attitude Index

	人数 Number	第一品牌及百分比 1st/ percent	第二品牌及百分比 2nd/ percent	第三品牌及百分比 3rd/ percent
样本 Sample	75	**格兰仕 Galanz(49.3)**	**高士达/乐金 LG(17.3)**	**松下/乐声 National(16.0)**
价格无关心指向 indifferent orientation	16	格兰仕 Galanz(56.3)	高士达/乐金 LG(12.5) 松下/乐声 National(12.5)	夏普/声宝 Sharp(6.3) 菊花 Juhua(6.3)
中间层 medium	43	格兰仕 Galanz(48.8)	高士达/乐金 LG(20.9)	松下/乐声 National(16.3)
价格重视指向 careful orientation	16	格兰仕 Galanz(43.8)	松下/乐声 National(18.8)	高士达/乐金 LG(12.5)

3-9 不同消费者层选择微波炉时的考虑因素/ Considerations in Choosing from Different Brands by Market Segments

3-9-1 时尚流行指标/ Fads Popular Index

注：本题为多选题，合计百分比超过 100%（Multiple answers）

	人数 Number	品牌形象 brand image	外型 outlook	价格 price	功率 power	容量大 big volume
样本 Sample	74	73.0	4.1	31.1	6.8	10.8
平实生活指向 simple living orientation	28	75.0	7.1	32.1	0.0	7.1
时尚流行指向 fashion orientation	46	71.7	2.2	30.4	10.9	13.0

续前表 continued

	人数 Number	内壁材料 inter material	微电脑控制 computer control ability	售后服务 follow-up service	安全 safety	其他 others
样本 Sample	74	2.7	28.4	14.9	10.8	0.0
平实生活指向 simple living orientation	28	3.6	21.4	17.9	14.3	0.0
时尚流行指向 fashion orientation	46	2.2	32.6	13.0	8.7	0.0

3-9-2 广告态度指标/ Advertising Attitude Index

注：本题为多选题，合计百分比超过 100%（Multiple answers）

	人数 Number	品牌形象 brand image	外型 outlook	价格 price	功率 power	容量大 big volume
样本 Sample	74	73.0	4.1	31.1	6.8	10.8
广告淡漠指向 indifferent orientation	11	81.8	9.1	36.4	9.1	45.5
中间层 medium	51	70.6	3.9	33.3	7.8	5.9
信赖广告指向 loyal orientation	12	75.0	0.0	16.7	0.0	0.0

续前表 continued

	人数 Number	内壁材料 inter material	微电脑控制 computer control ability	售后服务 follow-up service	安全 safety	其他 others
样本 Sample	74	2.7	28.4	14.9	10.8	0.0
广告淡漠指向 indifferent orientation	11	0.0	45.5	18.2	27.3	0.0
中间层 medium	51	3.9	25.5	13.7	9.8	0.0
信赖广告指向 loyal orientation	12	0.0	25.0	16.7	0.0	0.0

3-9-3 价格态度指标/ Price Attitude Index

注：本题为多选题，合计百分比超过 100%（Multiple answers）

	人数 Number	品牌形象 brand image	外型 outlook	价格 price	功率 power	容量大 big volume
样本 Sample	74	73.0	4.1	31.1	6.8	10.8
价格无关心指向 indifferent orientation	16	81.3	18.8	12.5	0.0	0.0
中间层 medium	42	73.8	0.0	33.3	11.9	11.9
价格重视指向 careful orientation	16	62.5	0.0	43.8	0.0	18.8

续前表 continued

	人数 Number	内壁材料 inter material	微电脑控制 computer control ability	售后服务 follow-up service	安全 safety	其他 others
样本 Sample	74	2.7	28.4	14.9	10.8	0.0
价格无关心指向 indifferent orientation	16	6.3	43.8	12.5	31.3	0.0
中间层 medium	42	2.4	19.0	19.0	4.8	0.0
价格重视指向 careful orientation	16	0.0	37.5	6.3	6.3	0.0

4.洗衣机 / Washing Machine

● 北京 / Beijing

4-1 洗衣机的拥有比例/ Proportion of Washing Machine Owners in the Sample

	人数 Number	百分比 Percent
有 yes	924	91.3
没有 no	88	8.7

n=1012

4-2 洗衣机的拥有量/ Number of Washing Machine Owned Per Household

	人数 Number	百分比 Percent
1台 1 set	848	93.9
2台 2 sets	54	6.0
3台及以上 3 sets or over	1	0.1

n=903

4-3 理想品牌排名/ Ranking of the Ideal Brands

排名 Brand Ranking	品牌 Brands	人数 Number	百分比 Percent
1	小天鹅 Little Swan	374	37.0
2	海尔 Haier	199	19.7
3	小鸭·圣吉奥 Xiaoya	92	9.1
4	白菊 Baiju	42	4.2
5	松下/乐声 National	36	3.6
6	西门子 Siemens	33	3.3
7	荣事达 Rongshida	20	2.0
8	白兰 Bailan	13	1.3
9	海棠 Haitang	12	1.2
9	三洋 Sanyo	12	1.2

n=1012

4-4 对家中现有洗衣机(最近购买的一台)的四个方面的描述/ About the Washing Machine Most Recently Purchased

4-4-1 家中现有洗衣机的品牌排名/ Ranking of the Currently Owned Washing Machine Brands

排名 Brand Ranking	品牌 Brands	人数 Number	百分比 Percent
1	小天鹅 Little Swan	215	23.4
2	白菊 Baiju	177	19.3
3	海尔 Haier	75	8.2
4	白兰 Bailan	56	6.1
5	小鸭·圣吉奥 Xiaoya	43	4.7
6	荣事达 Rongshida	39	4.3
7	海棠 Haitang	32	3.5
8	水仙 Narcissus	28	3.1
9	松下/乐声 National	26	2.8
10	三洋 Sanyo	23	2.5
11	金羚 Jinling	20	2.2

n=917

4-4-2 该洗衣机的购买时间/ The Time of Purchasing of the Currently Owned Washing Machine

	人数 Number	百分比 Percent
1985 年或以前 1985 or before	70	7.6
1986～1990 年	160	17.4
1991 年	32	3.5
1992 年	43	4.7
1993 年	51	5.5
1994 年	61	6.6
1995 年	68	7.4
1996 年	103	11.2
1997 年	144	15.7
1998 年	97	10.5
1999 年	91	9.9

n=920

4-4-3 该洗衣机的价格/ The Price of the Currently Owned Washing Machine

	人数 Number	百分比 Percent
500 元或以下 500 yuan or below	130	14.1
501～1000 元 yuan	254	27.6
1001～1500 元 yuan	154	16.7
1501～2000 元 yuan	144	15.7
2001～2500 元 yuan	92	10.0
2501～3000 元 yuan	54	5.9
3001～3500 元 yuan	26	2.8
3501～4000 元 yuan	10	1.1
4001～4500 元 yuan	5	0.5
4501～5000 元 yuan	3	0.3
5000 元以上 over 5000 yuan	3	0.3
完全不知道 don't know	45	4.9

n=920

4-4-4 该洗衣机的类型/ The Type of the Currently Owned Washing Machine

	人数 Number	百分比 Percent
普通单缸 single basin	47	5.1
普通双缸 double basins	428	46.6
波轮全自动 turbine automatic	290	31.6
滚筒全自动 rolling basin	154	16.8
其他 others	0	0.0

n=919

4-5 选择不同品牌洗衣机时的考虑因素/ Ranking of the Considerations in Choosing from Different Brands

注：本题为多选题，合计百分比超过 100%（Multiple answers）

	人数 Number	品牌形象 brand image	外型 outlook	价格 price	功能齐备 all-function	容量大 big volume	噪音低 low noise	不伤衣料 no damage service	售后服务 follow-up service	其他 others
样本 Sample	**909**	**40.8**	**12.1**	**37.4**	**36.5**	**30.6**	**13.6**	**11.1**	**18.3**	**4.0**
小天鹅 Little Swan	214	47.7	8.9	27.1	40.2	29.9	11.7	9.3	27.6	3.3
白菊 Baiju	175	34.9	10.3	50.3	29.1	29.1	10.3	10.3	12.0	4.6
海尔 Haier	75	53.3	21.3	25.3	32.0	22.7	14.7	9.3	36.0	8.0
白兰 Bailan	54	35.2	9.3	63.0	14.8	25.9	16.7	11.1	7.4	3.7
小鸭・圣吉奥 Xiaoya	43	41.9	7.0	14.0	55.8	27.9	18.6	32.6	18.6	4.7
荣事达 Rongshida	39	38.5	7.7	33.3	41.0	53.8	20.5	12.8	30.8	0.0
海棠 Haitang	32	34.4	12.5	43.8	56.3	34.4	15.6	3.1	12.5	3.1
水仙 Narcissus	28	46.4	7.1	42.9	10.7	53.6	17.9	10.7	10.7	0.0
松下/乐声 National	26	42.3	19.2	30.8	34.6	19.2	15.4	7.7	15.4	11.5
三洋 Sanyo	23	43.5	34.8	47.8	47.8	52.2	13.0	8.7	13.0	0.0
金羚 Jinling	20	50.0	10.0	35.0	65.0	10.0	5.0	15.0	15.0	0.0
西门子 Siemens	14	64.3	7.1	21.4	57.1	14.3	35.7	28.6	14.3	0.0
威力 Weili	13	38.5	15.4	46.2	53.8	38.5	7.7	7.7	7.7	0.0
高宝 Kobo	13	46.2	15.4	53.8	23.1	7.7	23.1	0.0	0.0	0.0
金鱼 Gold Fish	12	8.3	16.7	33.3	33.3	83.3	8.3	16.7	0.0	8.3

4-6 洗衣机未来购买打算/ Plan for Future Purchasing of a Washing Machine

4-6-1 有无购买打算/ Whether Planning to Purchase Next Year

	人数 Number	百分比 Percent
是 yes	126	12.5
否 no	885	87.5

n=1011

4-6-2 打算购买的品牌排名/ Ranking of the Brands of the Planned Purchase Next Year

排名 Brand Ranking	品牌 Brands	人数 Number	百分比 Percent
1	小天鹅 Little Swan	44	35.8
2	海尔 Haier	32	26.0
3	小鸭・圣吉奥 Xiaoya	15	12.2
4	荣事达 Rongshida	4	3.3
5	三洋 Sanyo	2	1.6
5	松下/乐声 National	2	1.6
5	威力 Weili	2	1.6
5	金羚 Jinling	2	1.6

n=123

4-6-3 打算购买的类型/ The Type of the Planned Purchase Next Year

	人数 Number	百分比 Percent
普通单缸 single basin	2	1.6
普通双缸 double basins	14	11.5
波轮全自动 turbine automatic	46	37.7
滚筒全自动 rolling basin	58	47.5
其他 others	2	1.6

n=122

4-6-4 打算购买的价格/ The Price of the Planned Purchase Next Year

	人数 Number	百分比 Percent
500 元或以下 500 yuan or below	2	1.7
501～1000 元 yuan	15	12.4
1001～1500 元 yuan	18	14.9
1501～2000 元 yuan	30	24.8
2001～2500 元 yuan	24	19.8
2501～3000 元 yuan	15	12.4
3001～3500 元 yuan	9	7.4
3501～4000 元 yuan	3	2.5
4001～4500 元 yuan	2	1.7
4501～5000 元 yuan	3	2.5
5000 元以上 over 5000 yuan	0	0.0
完全不知道 don't know	0	0.0

n=121

4-7 选购洗衣机时不同角色的人口特征/ Demographics of the Different Roles in Purchasing a Washing Machine

注：不同角色可以多选（Multiple answers）

	人数 Number	16-24 岁 Age	25-34 岁 Age	35-44 岁 Age	45-54 岁 Age	55-60 岁 Age
样本 Sample	800	17.6	29.6	26.6	17.8	8.4
男性 Male	398	18.1	28.4	28.6	16.8	8.0
提议者 advocate	75	16.0	29.3	25.3	24.0	5.3
影响者 influence	32	15.6	21.9	37.5	18.8	6.3
决定者 decider	166	4.2	23.5	39.8	20.5	12.0
使用者 user	285	22.8	28.8	26.3	15.8	6.3
女性 Female	402	17.2	30.8	24.6	18.7	8.7
提议者 advocate	84	15.5	26.2	31.0	15.5	11.9
影响者 influence	32	25.0	37.5	21.9	12.5	3.1
决定者 decider	131	3.1	34.4	28.2	22.9	11.5
使用者 user	313	19.2	29.7	24.0	18.5	8.6

4-8 不同消费者层的家中目前拥有品牌/ Brands of Washing Machine Owned in Household by Market Segments

4-8-1 时尚流行指标/ Fads Popular Index

	人数 Number	第一品牌及百分比 1st/ percent	第二品牌及百分比 2nd/ percent	第三品牌及百分比 3rd/ percent	第四品牌及百分比 4th/ percent
样本 Sample	905	**小天鹅 Little Swan(23.5)**	**白菊 Baiju(19.2)**	**海尔 Haier(8.2)**	**白兰 Bailan(6.2)**
平实生活指向 simple living orientation	444	小天鹅 Little Swan(22.7)	白菊 Baiju(19.4)	白兰 Bailan(7.4)	海尔 Haier(6.5)
时尚流行指向 fashion orientation	461	小天鹅 Little Swan(24.3)	白菊 Baiju(19.1)	海尔 Haier(9.8)	小鸭·圣吉奥 Xiaoya(5.2)

4-8-2 广告态度指标/ Advertising Attitude Index

	人数 Number	第一品牌及百分比 1st/ percent	第二品牌及百分比 2nd/ percent	第三品牌及百分比 3rd/ percent	第四品牌及百分比 4th/ percent
样本 Sample	902	**小天鹅 Little Swan(23.4)**	**白菊 Baiju(19.4)**	**海尔 Haier(8.1)**	**白兰 Bailan(6.1)**
广告淡漠指向 indifferent orientation	261	小天鹅 Little Swan(23.0)	白菊 Baiju(19.2)	海尔 Haier(10.0)	白兰 Bailan(6.9)
中间层 medium	519	小天鹅 Little Swan(22.9)	白菊 Baiju(18.7)	海尔 Haier(7.7)	白兰 Bailan(6.2)
信赖广告指向 loyal orientation	122	小天鹅 Little Swan(26.2)	白菊 Baiju(23.0)	海尔 Haier(5.7)	海棠 Haitang(4.9) 荣事达 Rongshida(4.9)

4-8-3 价格态度指标/ Price Attitude Index

	人数 Number	第一品牌及百分比 1st/ percent	第二品牌及百分比 2nd/ percent	第三品牌及百分比 3rd/ percent	第四品牌及百分比 4th/ percent
样本 Sample	910	**小天鹅 Little Swan(23.5)**	**白菊 Baiju(19.2)**	**海尔 Haier(8.1)**	**白兰 Bailan(6.2)**
价格无关心指向 indifferent orientation	183	小天鹅 Little Swan(33.9)	白菊 Baiju(14.2)	海尔 Haier(8.7)	荣事达 Rongshida(5.5) 白兰 Bailan(5.5)
中间层 medium	453	小天鹅 Little Swan(20.8)	白菊 Baiju(19.4)	海尔 Haier(7.9)	白兰 Bailan(6.6)
价格重视指向 careful orientation	274	白菊 Baiju(22.3)	小天鹅 Little Swan(21.2)	海尔 Haier(8.0)	白兰 Bailan(5.8)

4-9 不同消费者层选择洗衣机时的考虑因素/ Considerations in Choosing from Different Brands by Market Segments

4-9-1 时尚流行指标/ Fads Popular Index

注：本题为多选题，合计百分比超过 100%（Multiple answers）

	人数 Number	品牌形象 brand image	外型 outlook	价格 price	功能齐备 all-function	容量大 big volume	噪音低 low noise	不伤衣料 no damage	售后服务 follow-up service	其他 others
样本 Sample	903	40.5	12.0	37.4	36.1	30.5	13.8	11.1	18.5	4.1
平实生活指向 simple living orientation	444	38.5	9.0	39.2	34.9	31.1	14.9	9.9	17.3	5.2
时尚流行指向 fashion orientation	459	42.5	14.8	35.7	37.3	29.8	12.9	12.2	19.6	3.1

4-9-2 广告态度指标/ Advertising Attitude Index

注：本题为多选题，合计百分比超过 100%（Multiple answers）

	人数 Number	品牌形象 brand image	外型 outlook	价格 price	功能齐备 all-function	容量大 big volume	噪音低 low noise	不伤衣料 no damage	售后服务 follow-up service	其他 others
样本 Sample	900	40.8	12.0	37.6	36.4	30.6	14.0	10.6	18.4	4.1
广告淡漠指向 indifferent orientation	260	35.0	10.8	37.7	36.2	24.6	13.5	10.0	21.5	5.4
中间层 medium	518	41.9	11.6	38.2	37.1	32.8	14.3	10.4	17.8	3.5
信赖广告指向 loyal orientation	122	48.4	16.4	34.4	34.4	33.6	13.9	12.3	14.8	4.1

4-9-3 价格态度指标/ Price Attitude Index

注：本题为多选题，合计百分比超过 100%（Multiple answers）

	人数 Number	品牌形象 brand image	外型 outlook	价格 price	功能齐备 all-function	容量大 big volume	噪音低 low noise	不伤衣料 no damage	售后服务 follow-up service	其他 others
样本 Sample	908	40.6	12.1	37.4	36.2	30.6	14.0	11.0	18.5	4.1
价格无关心指向 indifferent orientation	181	40.3	11.6	28.7	39.8	23.2	10.5	11.0	26.5	4.4
中间层 medium	452	43.4	12.8	36.9	37.8	32.5	15.7	12.4	17.5	3.8
价格重视指向 careful orientation	275	36.4	11.3	44.0	31.3	32.4	13.5	8.7	14.9	4.4

● 上海 / Shanghai

4-1 洗衣机的拥有比例/ Proportion of Washing Machine Owners in the Sample

	人数 Number	百分比 Percent
有 yes	846	83.4
没有 no	168	16.6

n=1014

4-2 洗衣机的拥有量/ Number of Washing Machine Owned Per Household

	人数 Number	百分比 Percent
1 台 1 set	819	97.8
2 台 2 sets	17	2.0
3 台及以上 3 sets or over	1	0.1

n=837

4-3 理想品牌排名/ Ranking of the Ideal Brands

排名 Brand Ranking	品牌 Brands	人数 Number	百分比 Percent
1	小天鹅 Little Swan	208	20.6
2	水仙 Narcissus	206	20.4
3	海尔 Haier	155	15.3
4	小鸭・圣吉奥 Xiaoya	103	10.2
5	松下/乐声 National	58	5.7
6	日立 Hitachi	54	5.3
7	申花 Shenhua	47	4.6
8	惠而浦 Whirlpool	26	2.6
9	西门子 Siemens	21	2.1
10	高士达/乐金 LG	19	1.9

n=1012

4-4 对家中现有洗衣机(最近购买的一台)的四个方面的描述/ About the Washing Machine Most Recently Purchased

4-4-1 家中现有洗衣机的品牌排名/ Ranking of the Currently Owned Washing Machine Brands

排名 Brand Ranking	品牌 Brands	人数 Number	百分比 Percent
1	水仙 Narcissus	302	35.7
2	小天鹅 Little Swan	98	11.6
3	申花 Shenhua	87	10.3
4	小鸭・圣吉奥 Xiaoya	54	6.4
5	海尔 Haier	50	5.9
6	日立 Hitachi	37	4.4
7	上海 Shanghai	32	3.8
8	松下/乐声 National	26	3.1
9	荣事达 Rongshida	22	2.6
10	惠而浦 Whirlpool	16	1.9

n=845

4-4-2 该洗衣机的购买时间/ The Time of Purchasing of the Currently Owned Washing Machine

	人数 Number	百分比 Percent
1985 年或以前 1985 or before	58	6.9
1986～1990 年	185	22.0
1991 年	40	4.8
1992 年	47	5.6
1993 年	42	5.0
1994 年	57	6.8
1995 年	71	8.5
1996 年	88	10.5
1997 年	108	12.9
1998 年	91	10.8
1999 年	53	6.3

n=840

4-4-3 该洗衣机的价格/ The Price of the Currently Owned Washing Machine

	人数 Number	百分比 Percent
500 元或以下 500 yuan or below	146	17.4
501～1000 元 yuan	290	34.5
1001～1500 元 yuan	111	13.2
1501～2000 元 yuan	97	11.5
2001～2500 元 yuan	93	11.1
2501～3000 元 yuan	35	4.2
3001～3500 元 yuan	17	2.0
3501～4000 元 yuan	7	0.8
4001～4500 元 yuan	10	1.2
4501～5000 元 yuan	3	0.4
5000 元以上 over 5000 yuan	3	0.4
完全不知道 don't know	29	3.4

n=841

4-4-4 该洗衣机的类型/ The Type of the Currently Owned Washing Machine

	人数 Number	百分比 Percent
普通单缸 single basin	58	6.9
普通双缸 double basins	452	53.7
波轮全自动 turbine automatic	170	20.2
滚筒全自动 rolling basin	157	18.6
其他 others	5	0.6

n=842

4-5 选择不同品牌洗衣机时考虑因素/ Considerations in Choosing from Different Brands

注：本题为多选题，合计百分比超过 100%（Multiple answers）

	人数 Number	品牌形象 brand image	外型 outlook	价格 price	功能齐备 all-function	容量大 big volume	噪音低 low noise	不伤衣料 no damage service	售后服务 follow-up service	其他 others
样本 Sample	841	40.7	11.4	38.5	32.6	29.5	14.0	16.3	13.6	3.7
水仙 Narcissus	299	43.1	8.4	41.5	24.1	27.1	12.4	12.7	12.4	3.7
小天鹅 Little Swan	98	48.0	11.2	32.7	42.9	23.5	11.2	22.4	14.3	3.1
申花 Shenhua	87	39.1	13.8	56.3	16.1	29.9	9.2	17.2	11.5	4.6
小鸭・圣吉奥 Xiaoya	54	42.6	9.3	18.5	50.0	37.0	16.7	27.8	20.4	0.0
海尔 Haier	50	28.0	22.0	18.0	48.0	34.0	26.0	24.0	28.0	6.0
日立 Hitachi	37	62.2	18.9	18.9	45.9	24.3	21.6	18.9	10.8	0.0
上海 Shanghai	31	22.6	9.7	64.5	29.0	12.9	16.1	9.7	12.9	0.0
松下/乐声 National	26	38.5	7.7	38.5	53.8	38.5	15.4	11.5	11.5	3.8
荣事达 Rongshida	22	36.4	13.6	27.3	40.9	72.7	22.7	0.0	18.2	0.0
惠而浦 Whirlpool	16	37.5	12.5	37.5	50.0	37.5	25.0	25.0	12.5	0.0

4-6 洗衣机未来购买打算/ Plan for Future Purchasing of a Washing Machine

4-6-1 有无购买打算/ Whether Planning to Purchase Next Year

	人数 Number	百分比 Percent
是 yes	94	9.3
否 no	920	90.7

n=1014

4-6-2 打算购买的品牌排名/ The Brand of the Planned Purchase Next Year

排名 Brand Ranking	品牌 Brands	人数 Number	百分比 Percent
1	海尔 Haier	21	22.6
2	小天鹅 Little Swan	18	19.4
3	小鸭・圣吉奥 Xiaoya	10	10.8
4	水仙 Narcissus	9	9.7
5	惠而浦 Whirlpool	8	8.6
6	松下/乐声 National	6	6.5
7	西门子 Siemens	5	5.4

n=93

4-6-3 打算购买的类型/ The Type of the Planned Purchase Next Year

	人数 Number	百分比 Percent
普通单缸 single basin	3	3.2
普通双缸 double basins	6	6.5
波轮全自动 turbine automatic	35	37.6
滚筒全自动 rolling basin	48	51.6
其他 others	1	1.1

n=93

4-6-4 打算购买的价格/ The Price of the Planned Purchase Next Year

	人数 Number	百分比 Percent
500 元或以下 500 yuan or below	1	1.1
501～1000 元 yuan	10	10.8
1001～1500 元 yuan	11	11.8
1501～2000 元 yuan	28	30.1
2001～2500 元 yuan	22	23.7
2501～3000 元 yuan	9	9.7
3001～3500 元 yuan	2	2.2
3501～4000 元 yuan	2	2.2
4001～4500 元 yuan	4	4.3
4501～5000 元 yuan	3	3.2
5000 元以上 over 5000 yuan	0	0.0
完全不知道 don't know	1	1.1

n=93

4-7 选购洗衣机时不同角色的人口特征/ The Demographics of Different Roles in Purchasing a Washing Machine

注：不同角色可以多选（Multiple answers）

	人数 Number	16-24 岁 Age	25-34 岁 Age	35-44 岁 Age	45-54 岁 Age	55-60 岁 Age
样本 Sample	738	18.2	27.1	27.6	18.3	8.8
男性 Male	352	17.0	26.7	28.4	19.9	8.0
提议者 advocate	48	29.2	16.7	22.9	27.1	4.2
影响者 influence	47	12.8	14.9	31.9	31.9	8.5
决定者 decider	146	4.8	27.4	35.6	24.7	7.5
使用者 user	188	23.4	28.2	25.5	15.4	7.4
女性 Female	386	19.2	27.5	26.9	16.8	9.6
提议者 advocate	60	23.3	28.3	30.0	13.3	5.0
影响者 influence	45	20.0	22.2	22.2	22.2	13.3
决定者 decider	138	7.2	27.5	37.0	19.6	8.7
使用者 user	250	21.2	26.4	28.4	14.0	10.0

4-8 不同消费者层的家中目前拥有品牌/ Brands of Washing Machine Owned in Household by Market Segments

4-8-1 时尚流行指标/ Fads Popular Index

	人数 Number	第一品牌及百分比 1st/ percent	第二品牌及百分比 2nd/ percent	第三品牌及百分比 3rd/ percent	第四品牌及百分比 4th/ percent
样本 Sample	839	**水仙 Narcissus(35.8)**	**小天鹅 Little Swan(11.7)**	**申花 Shenhua(10.4)**	**小鸭・圣吉奥 Xiaoya(6.4)**
平实生活指向 simple living orientation	387	水仙 Narcissus(37.2)	申花 Shenhua(10.6)	小天鹅 Little Swan(9.0)	上海 Shanghai(5.7)
时尚流行指向 fashion orientation	452	水仙 Narcissus(34.5)	小天鹅 Little Swan(13.9)	申花 Shenhua(10.2)	小鸭・圣吉奥 Xiaoya(7.3)

4-8-2 广告态度指标/ Advertising Attitude Index

	人数 Number	第一品牌及百分比 1st/ percent	第二品牌及百分比 2nd/ percent	第三品牌及百分比 3rd/ percent	第四品牌及百分比 4th/ percent
样本 Sample	834	**水仙 Narcissus(35.9)**	**小天鹅 Little Swan(11.6)**	**申花 Shenhua(10.3)**	**小鸭・圣吉奥 Xiaoya(6.4)**
广告淡漠指向 indifferent orientation	217	水仙 Narcissus(36.4)	申花 Shenhua(13.8)	小天鹅 Little Swan(9.2)	海尔 Haier(5.1)
中间层 medium	502	水仙 Narcissus(34.1)	小天鹅 Little Swan(11.6)	申花 Shenhua(10.2)	小鸭・圣吉奥 Xiaoya(7.6)
信赖广告指向 loyal orientation	115	水仙 Narcissus(42.6)	小天鹅 Little Swan(16.5)	海尔 Haier(5.2) 惠而浦 Whirlpool(5.2) 小鸭・圣吉奥 Xiaoya(5.2)	上海 Shanghai(4.3) 申花 Shenhua(4.3)

4-8-3 价格态度指标/ Price Attitude Index

	人数 Number	第一品牌及百分比 1st/ percent	第二品牌及百分比 2nd/ percent	第三品牌及百分比 3rd/ percent	第四品牌及百分比 4th/ percent
样本 Sample	843	**水仙 Narcissus(35.8)**	**小天鹅 Little Swan(11.6)**	**申花 Shenhua(10.3)**	**小鸭・圣吉奥 Xiaoya(6.4)**
价格无关心指向 indifferent orientation	121	水仙 Narcissus(32.2)	小天鹅 Little Swan(12.4)	申花 Shenhua(9.1)	海尔 Haier(8.3)
中间层 medium	449	水仙 Narcissus(35.4)	小天鹅 Little Swan(11.6)	申花 Shenhua(9.6)	小鸭・圣吉奥 Xiaoya(7.3)
价格重视指向 careful orientation	273	水仙 Narcissus(38.1)	申花 Shenhua(12.1)	小天鹅 Little Swan(11.4)	上海 Shanghai(5.5)

4-9 不同消费者层选择洗衣机时的考虑因素/ Considerations in Choosing from Different Brands by Market Segments

4-9-1 时尚流行指标/ Fads Popular Index

注：本题为多选题，合计百分比超过 100%（Multiple answers）

	人数 Number	品牌形象 brand image	外型 outlook	价格 price	功能齐备 all-function	容量大 big volume	噪音低 low noise	不伤衣料 no damage	售后服务 follow-up service	其他 others
样本 Sample	836	40.7	11.5	38.4	32.8	29.5	13.9	16.3	13.3	3.7
平实生活指向 simple living orientation	387	41.9	10.6	41.3	32.6	25.3	11.9	14.2	14.0	4.1
时尚流行指向 fashion orientation	449	39.6	12.2	35.9	33.0	33.2	15.6	18.0	12.7	3.3

4-9-2 广告态度指标/ Advertising Attitude Index

注：本题为多选题，合计百分比超过 100%（Multiple answers）

	人数 Number	品牌形象 brand image	外型 outlook	价格 price	功能齐备 all-function	容量大 big volume	噪音低 low noise	不伤衣料 no damage	售后服务 follow-up service	其他 others
样本 Sample	831	40.8	11.2	38.5	33.0	29.1	13.7	16.1	13.5	3.7
广告淡漠指向 indifferent orientation	216	41.2	13.0	37.5	30.6	24.5	15.3	17.6	12.5	4.6
中间层 medium	500	40.2	9.4	39.8	33.4	29.6	12.4	14.0	14.8	3.6
信赖广告指向 loyal orientation	115	42.6	15.7	34.8	35.7	35.7	16.5	22.6	9.6	2.6

4-9-3 价格态度指标/ Price Attitude Index

注：本题为多选题，合计百分比超过 100%（Multiple answers）

	人数 Number	品牌形象 brand image	外型 outlook	价格 price	功能齐备 all-function	容量大 big volume	噪音低 low noise	不伤衣料 no damage	售后服务 follow-up service	其他 others
样本 Sample	840	40.7	11.4	38.5	32.7	29.5	14.0	16.3	13.5	3.7
价格无关心指向 indifferent orientation	122	40.2	11.5	33.6	30.3	26.2	19.7	15.6	12.3	1.6
中间层 medium	447	41.8	11.2	35.3	33.3	31.8	12.8	14.8	14.3	3.8
价格重视指向 careful orientation	271	39.1	11.8	45.8	32.8	27.3	13.7	19.2	12.5	4.4

● 广州 / Guangzhou

4-1 洗衣机的拥有比例/ Proportion of Washing Machine Owners in the Sample

	人数 Number	百分比 Percent
有 yes	920	89.0
没有 no	114	11.0

n=1034

4-2 洗衣机的拥有量/ Number of Washing Machine Owned Per Household

	人数 Number	百分比 Percent
1 台 1 set	874	96.4
2 台 2 sets	32	3.5
3 台及以上 3 sets or over	1	0.1

n=907

4-3 理想品牌排名/ Ranking of the Ideal Brands

排名 Brand Ranking	品牌 Brands	人数 Number	百分比 Percent
1	海尔 Haier	132	12.8
2	小天鹅 Little Swan	129	12.5
3	威力 Weili	98	9.5
4	松下/乐声 National	97	9.4
5	凤凰 Phoenix	62	6.0
6	金羚 Jinling	56	5.4
7	惠而浦 Whirlpool	45	4.4
8	小鸭・圣吉奥 Xiaoya	40	3.9
9	西门子 Siemens	35	3.4

n=1033

4-4 对家中现有洗衣机(最近购买的一台)的四个方面的描述/ About the Washing Machine Most Recently Purchased

4-4-1 家中现有洗衣机的品牌排名/ Ranking of the Currently Owned Washing Machine Brands

排名 Brand Ranking	品牌 Brands	人数 Number	百分比 Percent
1	威力 Weili	140	15.2
2	凤凰 Phoenix	134	14.6
3	小天鹅 Little Swan	101	11.0
4	金羚 Jinling	76	8.3
5	海尔 Haier	56	6.1
6	松下/乐声 National	54	5.9
7	小鸭・圣吉奥 Xiaoya	41	4.5
8	高宝 Kobo	31	3.4
8	万宝 Wanbao	31	3.4

n=919

4-4-2 该洗衣机的购买时间/ The Time of Purchasing of the Currently Owned Washing Machine

	人数 Number	百分比 Percent
1985 年或以前 1985 or before	34	3.7
1986～1990 年	135	14.8
1991 年	42	4.6
1992 年	64	7.0
1993 年	92	10.1
1994 年	79	8.7
1995 年	104	11.4
1996 年	103	11.3
1997 年	115	12.6
1998 年	80	8.8
1999 年	64	7.0

n=912

4-4-3 该洗衣机的价格/ The Price of the Currently Owned Washing Machine

	人数 Number	百分比 Percent
500 元或以下 500 yuan or below	58	6.3
501～1000 元 yuan	216	23.6
1001～1500 元 yuan	216	23.6
1501～2000 元 yuan	146	15.9
2001～2500 元 yuan	107	11.7
2501～3000 元 yuan	28	3.1
3001～3500 元 yuan	29	3.2
3501～4000 元 yuan	15	1.6
4001～4500 元 yuan	8	0.9
4501～5000 元 yuan	8	0.9
5000 元以上 over 5000 yuan	20	2.2
完全不知道 don't know	65	7.1

n=916

4-4-4 该洗衣机的类型/ The Type of the Currently Owned Washing Machine

	人数 Number	百分比 Percent
普通单缸 single basin	123	13.4
普通双缸 double basins	258	28.1
波轮全自动 turbine automatic	331	36.1
滚筒全自动 rolling basin	201	21.9
其他 others	5	0.5

n=918

4-5 选择不同品牌洗衣机时的考虑因素/ Considerations in Choosing from Different Brands

注：本题为多选题，合计百分比超过 100%（Multiple answers）

	人数 Number	品牌形象 brand image	外型 outlook	价格 price	功能齐备 all-function	容量大 big volume	噪音低 low noise	不伤衣料 no damage service	售后服务 follow-up service	其他 others
样本 Sample	914	31.9	11.3	45.1	36.0	26.5	25.4	15.6	12.7	2.4
威力 Weili	140	30.7	12.9	53.6	25.7	29.3	22.9	11.4	12.1	2.9
凤凰 Phoenix	133	31.6	8.3	51.9	33.8	20.3	28.6	9.8	8.3	1.5
小天鹅 Little Swan	99	28.3	12.1	42.4	46.5	30.3	31.3	15.2	12.1	1.0
金羚 Jinling	76	30.3	3.9	39.5	35.5	34.2	34.2	11.8	17.1	2.6
海尔 Haier	56	37.5	8.9	32.1	43.2	21.4	19.6	25.0	25.0	1.8
松下/乐声 National	54	53.7	5.6	25.9	33.3	31.5	31.5	24.1	9.3	1.9
小鸭・圣吉奥 Xiaoya	40	32.5	12.5	40.0	42.5	42.5	22.5	25.0	17.5	0.0
高宝 Kobo	31	29.0	9.7	61.3	19.4	22.6	22.6	22.6	16.1	3.2
万宝 Wanbao	31	25.8	12.9	71.0	29.0	6.5	12.9	9.7	12.9	0.0

4-6 洗衣机未来购买打算/ Plan for Future Purchasing of a Washing Machine

4-6-1 有无购买打算/ Whether Planning to Purchase Next Year

	人数 Number	百分比 Percent
是 yes	60	5.8
否 no	972	94.2

n=1032

4-6-2 打算购买的品牌排名/ The Brand of the Planned Purchase Next Year

排名 Brand Ranking	品牌 Brands	人数 Number	百分比 Percent
1	海尔 Haier	14	23.7
2	松下/乐声 National	8	13.6
3	惠而浦 Whirlpool	5	8.5
3	威力 Weili	5	8.5
4	小天鹅 Little Swan	4	6.8

n=59

4-6-3 打算购买的类型/ The Type of the Planned Purchase Next Year

	人数 Number	百分比 Percent
普通单缸 single basin	5	8.5
普通双缸 double basins	1	1.7
波轮全自动 turbine automatic	21	35.6
滚筒全自动 rolling basin	32	54.2
其他 others	0	0.0

n=59

4-6-4 打算购买的价格/ The Price of the Planned Purchase Next Year

	人数 Number	百分比 Percent
500 元或以下 500 yuan or below	2	3.4
501～1000 元 yuan	3	5.2
1001～1500 元 yuan	9	15.5
1501～2000 元 yuan	13	22.4
2001～2500 元 yuan	13	22.4
2501～3000 元 yuan	8	13.8
3001～3500 元 yuan	4	6.9
3501～4000 元 yuan	1	1.7
4001～4500 元 yuan	0	0.0
4501～5000 元 yuan	1	1.7
5000 元以上 over 5000 yuan	4	6.9
完全不知道 don't know	0	0.0

n=58

4-7 选购洗衣机时不同角色的人口特征/ Demographics of the Different Roles in Purchasing a Washing Machine

注：不同角色可以多选（Multiple answers）

	人数 Number	16-24 岁 Age	25-34 岁 Age	35-44 岁 Age	45-54 岁 Age	55-60 岁 Age
样本 Sample	**824**	**18.4**	**29.2**	**26.8**	**16.7**	**8.7**
男性 Male	**375**	**18.1**	**29.1**	**26.7**	**16.3**	**9.9**
提议者 advocate	68	14.7	25.0	32.4	13.2	14.7
影响者 influence	53	28.3	24.5	24.5	15.1	7.5
决定者 decider	141	6.4	28.4	29.1	22.7	13.5
使用者 user	198	23.7	33.3	23.7	11.6	7.6
女性 Female	**449**	**18.7**	**29.4**	**26.9**	**17.1**	**7.8**
提议者 advocate	76	19.7	35.5	19.7	18.4	6.6
影响者 influence	66	10.6	36.4	28.8	16.7	7.6
决定者 decider	108	10.2	24.1	35.2	24.1	6.5
使用者 user	301	19.6	28.9	25.6	18.3	7.6

4-8 不同消费者层的家中目前拥有品牌/ Brands of Washing Machine Owned in Household by Market Segments

4-8-1 时尚流行指标/ Fads Popular Index

	人数 Number	第一品牌及百分比 1st/ percent	第二品牌及百分比 2nd/ percent	第三品牌及百分比 3rd/ percent	第四品牌及百分比 4th/ percent
样本 Sample	**909**	**威力 Weili(15.4)**	**凤凰 Phoenix(14.5)**	**小天鹅 Little Swan(11.0)**	**金羚 Jinling(8.3)**
平实生活指向 simple living orientation	456	凤凰 Phoenix(16.4) 威力 Weili(16.4)	小天鹅 Little Swan(9.6)	金羚 Jinling(9.0)	松下/乐声 National(5.7)
时尚流行指向 fashion orientation	453	威力 Weili(14.3)	凤凰 Phoenix(12.6)	小天鹅 Little Swan(12.4)	金羚 Jinling(7.5)

4-8-2 广告态度指标/ Advertising attitude Index

	人数 Number	第一品牌及百分比 1st/ percent	第二品牌及百分比 2nd/ percent	第三品牌及百分比 3rd/ percent	第四品牌及百分比 4th/ percent
样本 Sample	909	**威力 Weili(15.4)**	**凤凰 Phoenix(14.6)**	**小天鹅 Little Swan(10.9)**	**金羚 Jinling(8.4)**
广告淡漠指向 indifferent orientation	291	凤凰 Phoenix(16.5)	威力 Weili(14.4)	小天鹅 Little Swan(13.1)	金羚 Jinling(10.0)
中间层 medium	538	威力 Weili(16.0)	凤凰 Phoenix(13.3)	小天鹅 Little Swan(9.7)	金羚 Jinling(8.2)
信赖广告指向 loyal orientation	80	威力 Weili(15.0)	凤凰 Phoenix(13.3)	海尔 Haier(11.3) 小天鹅 Little Swan(11.3)	松下/乐声 National(6.3)

4-8-3 价格态度指标/ Price Attitude Index

	人数 Number	第一品牌及百分比 1st/ percent	第二品牌及百分比 2nd/ percent	第三品牌及百分比 3rd/ percent	第四品牌及百分比 4th/ percent
样本 Sample	914	**威力 Weili(15.2)**	**凤凰 Phoenix(14.7)**	**小天鹅 Little Swan(10.9)**	**金羚 Jinling(8.2)**
价格无关心指向 indifferent orientation	167	威力 Weili(16.2)	小天鹅 Little Swan(14.4)	凤凰 Phoenix(13.2)	松下/乐声 National(7.2) 金羚 Jinling(7.2)
中间层 medium	485	威力 Weili(14.6)	凤凰 Phoenix(14.4)	小天鹅 Little Swan(10.1)	金羚 Jinling(9.1)
价格重视指向 careful orientation	262	凤凰 Phoenix(16.0)	威力 Weili(15.6)	小天鹅 Little Swan(10.3)	金羚 Jinling(7.3)

4-9 不同消费者层选择洗衣机时考虑因素/ Considerations in Choosing from Different Brands by Market Segments

4-9-1 时尚流行指标/ Fads Popular Index

注：本题为多选题，合计百分比超过 100%（Multiple answers）

	人数 Number	品牌形象 brand image	外型 outlook	价格 price	功能齐备 all-function	容量大 big volume	噪音低 low noise	不伤衣料 no damage	售后服务 follow-up service	其他 others
样本 Sample	905	31.8	11.3	45.2	35.6	26.5	25.5	15.7	12.7	2.4
平实生活指向 simple living orientation	453	32.7	10.4	46.4	34.0	24.5	23.0	15.9	14.3	2.4
时尚流行指向 fashion orientation	452	31.0	12.2	44.0	37.2	28.5	28.1	15.5	11.1	2.4

4-9-2 广告态度指标/ Advertising Attitude Index

注：本题为多选题，合计百分比超过 100%（Multiple answers）

	人数 Number	品牌形象 brand image	外型 outlook	价格 price	功能齐备 all-function	容量大 big volume	噪音低 low noise	不伤衣料 no damage	售后服务 follow-up service	其他 others
样本 Sample	905	32.3	11.2	45.0	35.9	26.2	25.3	15.6	12.6	2.4
广告淡漠指向 indifferent orientation	289	30.4	12.8	46.4	33.9	24.6	26.3	16.3	13.8	1.7
中间层 medium	537	31.8	11.0	43.9	37.2	26.6	24.2	15.6	11.5	3.0
信赖广告指向 loyal orientation	79	41.8	6.3	46.8	34.2	29.1	29.1	12.7	15.2	1.3

4-9-3 价格态度指标/ Price Attitude Index

注：本题为多选题，合计百分比超过 100%（Multiple answers）

	人数 Number	品牌形象 brand image	外型 outlook	价格 price	功能齐备 all-function	容量大 big volume	噪音低 low noise	不伤衣料 no damage	售后服务 follow-up service	其他 others
样本 Sample	910	32.2	11.2	45.3	35.6	26.4	25.5	15.7	12.7	2.4
价格无关心指向 indifferent orientation	167	36.5	11.4	40.1	35.3	21.6	26.3	17.4	13.2	3.0
中间层 medium	482	30.9	11.2	46.1	35.7	25.1	26.6	13.3	13.5	2.7
价格重视指向 careful orientation	261	31.8	11.1	47.1	35.6	31.8	23.0	19.2	11.1	1.5

重庆 / Chongqing

4-1 洗衣机的拥有比例/ Proportion of Washing Machine Owners in the Sample

	人数 Number	百分比 Percent
有 yes	540	86.5
没有 no	84	13.5

n=624

4-2 洗衣机的拥有量/ Number of Washing Machine Owned Per Household

	人数 Number	百分比 Percent
1 台 1 set	523	97.6
2 台 2 sets	13	2.4
3 台及以上 3 sets or over	0	0.0

n=536

4-3 理想品牌排名/ Ranking of the Ideal Brands

排名 Brand Ranking	品牌 Brands	人数 Number	百分比 Percent
1	海尔 Haier	163	26.2
2	小天鹅 Little Swan	161	25.8
3	三峡 Sanxia	151	24.2
4	小鸭・圣吉奥 Xiaoya	22	3.5
5	松下/乐声 National	18	2.9
6	西门子 Siemens	11	1.8
7	金羚 Jinling	8	1.3
8	荣事达 Rongshida	7	1.1

n=623

4-4 对家中现有洗衣机(最近购买的一台)的四个方面的描述/ About the Washing Machine Most Recently Purchased

4-4-1 家中现有洗衣机的品牌排名/ Ranking of the Currently Owned Washing Machine Brands

排名 Brand Ranking	品牌 Brands	人数 Number	百分比 Percent
1	三峡 Sanxia	325	60.4
2	小天鹅 Little Swan	48	8.9
3	海尔 Haier	38	7.1
4	荣事达 Rongshida	15	2.8
5	威力 Weili	12	2.2
5	金羚 Jinling	12	2.2
6	小鸭・圣吉奥 Xiaoya	11	2.0
7	松下/乐声 National	9	1.7
8	航海 Hanghai	8	1.5
9	水仙 Narcissus	5	0.9

n=538

4-4-2 该洗衣机的购买时间/ The Time of Purchasing of the Currently Owned Washing Machine

	人数 Number	百分比 Percent
1985 年或以前 1985 or before	34	6.3
1986～1990 年	140	25.9
1991 年	28	5.2
1992 年	31	5.7
1993 年	34	6.3
1994 年	51	9.4
1995 年	39	7.2
1996 年	50	9.3
1997 年	48	8.9
1998 年	49	9.1
1999 年	36	6.7

n=540

4-4-3 该洗衣机的价格/ The Price of the Currently Owned Washing Machine

	人数 Number	百分比 Percent
500 元或以下 500 yuan or below	167	31.0
501～1000 元 yuan	237	44.1
1001～1500 元 yuan	42	7.8
1501～2000 元 yuan	31	5.8
2001～2500 元 yuan	23	4.3
2501～3000 元 yuan	16	3.0
3001～3500 元 yuan	10	1.9
3501～4000 元 yuan	4	0.7
4001～4500 元 yuan	0	0.0
4501～5000 元 yuan	1	0.2
5000 元以上 over 5000 yuan	1	0.2
完全不知道 don't know	6	1.1

n=538

4-4-4 该洗衣机的类型/ The Type of the Currently Owned Washing Machine

	人数 Number	百分比 Percent
普通单缸 single basins	38	7.1
普通双缸 double basin	397	73.7
波轮全自动 turbine automatic	63	11.7
滚筒全自动 rolling basins	38	7.1
其他 others	3	0.6

n=539

4-5 选择不同品牌洗衣机时考虑因素/ Considerations in Choosing from Different Brands

注：本题为多选题，合计百分比超过 100%（Multiple answers）

	人数 Number	品牌形象 brand image	外型 outlook	价格 price	功能齐备 all-function	容量大 big volume	噪音低 low noise	不伤衣料 no damage service	售后服务 follow-up service	其他 others
样本 Sample	533	41.3	12.6	45.2	28.1	26.8	12.6	9.4	11.6	2.1
三峡 Sanxia	324	40.4	10.2	52.2	20.1	23.5	12.0	6.8	9.6	2.2
小天鹅 Little Swan	47	53.2	17.0	29.8	48.9	25.5	14.9	17.0	10.6	0.0
海尔 Haier	38	57.9	7.9	26.3	31.6	23.7	10.5	13.2	39.5	2.6
荣事达 Rongshida	15	33.3	40.0	33.3	33.3	66.7	26.7	13.3	20.0	6.7
威力 Weili	12	16.7	16.7	41.7	33.3	41.7	25.0	8.3	0.0	0.0
金羚 Jinling	11	45.5	9.1	9.1	72.7	36.4	18.2	27.3	0.0	9.1
小鸭·圣吉奥 Xiaoya	10	50.0	20.0	40.0	80.0	10.0	10.0	20.0	20.0	0.0
松下/乐声 National	9	77.8	44.4	33.3	33.3	33.3	0.0	11.1	0.0	0.0
航海 Hanghai	8	25.0	12.5	50.0	0.0	37.5	0.0	0.0	0.0	0.0
水仙 Narcissus	5	0.0	0.0	80.0	20.0	40.0	20.0	0.0	0.0	0.0
爱德 Aide	4	0.0	0.0	25.0	75.0	50.0	25.0	25.0	0.0	0.0
东芝 Toshiba	4	50.0	50.0	50.0	0.0	25.0	25.0	25.0	0.0	0.0
高士达/乐金 LG	4	50.0	25.0	0.0	75.0	25.0	0.0	0.0	100.0	0.0
金鱼 Goldfish	3	33.3	0.0	33.3	33.3	0.0	0.0	0.0	0.0	0.0

4-6 洗衣机未来购买打算/ Plan for Future Purchasing of a Washing Machine

4-6-1 有无购买打算/ Whether Planning to Purchase Next Year

	人数 Number	百分比 Percent
是 yes	67	10.8
否 no	556	89.2

n=623

4-6-2 打算购买的品牌排名/ The Brand of the Planned Purchase Next Year

排名 Brand Ranking	品牌 Brands	人数 Number	百分比 Percent
1	海尔 Haier	24	35.8
2	小天鹅 Little Swan	20	29.9
3	三峡 Sanxia	6	9.0
4	西门子 Siemens	4	6.0

n=67

4-6-3 打算购买的类型/ The Type of the Planned Purchase Next Year

	人数 Number	百分比 Percent
普通单缸 single basin	1	1.6
普通双缸 double basins	14	22.6
波轮全自动 turbine automatic	20	32.3
滚筒全自动 rolling basin	27	43.5
其他 others	0	0.0

n=62

4-6-4 打算购买的价格/ The Price of the Planned Purchase Next Year

	人数 Number	百分比 Percent
500 元或以下 500 yuan or below	0	0.0
501～1000 元 yuan	15	23.1
1001～1500 元 yuan	12	18.5
1501～2000 元 yuan	14	21.5
2001～2500 元 yuan	11	16.9
2501～3000 元 yuan	5	7.7
3001～3500 元 yuan	2	3.1
3501～4000 元 yuan	2	3.1
4001～4500 元 yuan	1	1.5
4501～5000 元 yuan	0	0.0
5000 元以上 over 5000 yuan	2	3.1
完全不知道 don't know	1	1.5

n=65

4-7 选购洗衣机时不同角色的人口特征/ Demographics of the Different Roles in Purchasing a Washing Machine

注：不同角色可以多选（Multiple answers）

	人数 Number	16-24 岁 Age	25-34 岁 Age	35-44 岁 Age	45-54 岁 Age	55-60 岁 Age
样本 Sample	471	18.5	27.8	24.2	20.6	8.9
男性 Male	236	19.5	26.3	25.4	19.5	9.3
提议者 advocate	64	17.2	29.7	26.6	17.2	9.4
影响者 influence	37	21.6	27.0	21.6	18.9	10.8
决定者 decider	109	5.5	19.3	40.4	26.6	8.3
使用者 user	125	28.8	27.2	20.0	16.8	7.2
女性 Female	235	17.4	29.4	23.0	21.7	8.5
提议者 advocate	58	10.3	32.8	24.1	25.9	6.9
影响者 influence	23	8.7	47.8	8.7	30.4	4.3
决定者 decider	73	6.8	27.4	30.1	30.1	5.5
使用者 user	166	20.5	31.3	21.1	17.5	9.6

4-8 不同消费者层的家中目前拥有品牌/ Brands of Washing Machine Owned in Household by Market Segments

4-8-1 时尚流行指标/ Fads Popular Index

	人数 Number	第一品牌及百分比 1st/ percent	第二品牌及百分比 2nd/ percent	第三品牌及百分比 3rd/ percent	第四品牌及百分比 4th/ percent
样本 Sample	532	**三峡 Sanxia(60.7)**	**小天鹅 Little Swan(8.8)**	**海尔 Haier(6.8)**	**荣事达 Rongshida(2.8)**
平实生活指向 simple living orientation	311	三峡 Sanxia(63.3)	小天鹅 Little Swan(8.4)	海尔 Haier(4.2)	荣事达 Rongshida(2.6) 威力 Weili(2.6)
时尚流行指向 fashion orientation	221	三峡 Sanxia(57.0)	海尔 Haier(10.4)	小天鹅 Little Swan(9.5)	金羚 Jinling(3.6)

4-8-2 广告态度指标/ Advertising Attitude Index

	人数 Number	第一品牌及百分比 1st/ percent	第二品牌及百分比 2nd/ percent	第三品牌及百分比 3rd/ percent	第四品牌及百分比 4th/ percent
样本 Sample	533	**三峡 Sanxia(60.4)**	**小天鹅 Little Swan(9.0)**	**海尔 Haier(6.9)**	**荣事达 Rongshida(2.8)**
广告淡漠指向 indifferent orientation	143	三峡 Sanxia(67.8)	小天鹅 Little Swan(9.1)	威力 Weili(3.5)	海尔 Haier(2.8)
中间层 medium	320	三峡 Sanxia(58.1)	小天鹅 Little Swan(9.1)	海尔 Haier(8.8)	荣事达 Rongshida(3.8)
信赖广告指向 loyal orientation	70	三峡 Sanxia(55.7)	小天鹅 Little Swan(8.6)	海尔 Haier(7.1)	金羚 Jinling(4.3) 荣事达 Rongshida(4.3) 松下/乐声 National(4.3)

4-8-3 价格态度指标/ Price Attitude Index

	人数 Number	第一品牌及百分比 1st/ percent	第二品牌及百分比 2nd/ percent	第三品牌及百分比 3rd/ percent	第四品牌及百分比 4th/ percent
样本 Sample	529	**三峡 Sanxia(60.5)**	**小天鹅 Little Swan(8.9)**	**海尔 Haier(7.0)**	**荣事达 Rongshida(2.6)**
价格无关心指向 indifferent orientation	94	三峡 Sanxia(52.1)	小天鹅 Little Swan(14.9)	海尔 Haier(8.5)	金鱼 Goldfish(3.2) 沙龙 Salon (3.2)
中间层 medium	235	三峡 Sanxia(59.6)	小天鹅 Little Swan(8.9)	海尔 Haier(6.8)	金羚 Jinling(3.8)
价格重视指向 careful orientation	200	三峡 Sanxia(65.5)	海尔 Haier(6.5)	小天鹅 Little Swan(6.0)	荣事达 Rongshida(3.5) 威力 Weili(3.5)

4-9 不同消费者层选择洗衣机时的考虑因素/ Considerations in Choosing from Different Brands by Market Segments

4-9-1 时尚流行指标/ Fads Popular Index

注：本题为多选题，合计百分比超过 100%（Multiple answers）

	人数 Number	品牌形象 brand image	外型 outlook	价格 price	功能齐备 all-function	容量大 big volume	噪音低 low noise	不伤衣料 no damage	售后服务 follow-up service	其他 others
样本 Sample	530	41.1	12.6	45.5	28.1	26.8	12.6	9.2	11.1	2.1
平实生活指向 simple living orientation	311	40.8	11.6	48.9	24.1	29.3	12.9	8.0	10.3	2.6
时尚流行指向 fashion orientation	219	41.6	14.2	40.6	33.8	23.3	12.3	11.0	12.3	1.4

4-9-2 广告态度指标/ Advertising Attitude Index

注：本题为多选题，合计百分比超过 100%（Multiple answers）

	人数 Number	品牌形象 brand image	外型 outlook	价格 price	功能齐备 all-function	容量大 big volume	噪音低 low noise	不伤衣料 no damage	售后服务 follow-up service	其他 others
样本 Sample	530	41.1	12.5	45.5	28.1	27.0	12.6	9.2	11.5	2.1
广告淡漠指向 indifferent orientation	143	33.6	9.1	50.3	32.2	24.5	11.2	7.0	9.8	2.8
中间层 medium	317	43.2	13.2	44.8	26.2	25.6	13.9	10.7	11.7	1.6
信赖广告指向 loyal orientation	70	47.1	15.7	38.6	28.6	38.6	10.0	7.1	14.3	2.9

4-9-3 价格态度指标/ Price Attitude Index

注：本题为多选题，合计百分比超过 100%（Multiple answers）

	人数 Number	品牌形象 brand image	外型 outlook	价格 price	功能齐备 all-function	容量大 big volume	噪音低 low noise	不伤衣料 no damage	售后服务 follow-up service	其他 others
样本 Sample	526	41.3	12.4	45.4	28.1	27.2	12.0	9.1	11.6	2.1
价格无关心指向 indifferent orientation	93	36.6	11.8	33.3	39.8	21.5	16.1	15.1	16.1	1.1
中间层 medium	234	41.9	12.4	45.7	29.1	29.5	11.1	7.7	10.3	3.0
价格重视指向 careful orientation	199	42.7	12.6	50.8	21.6	27.1	11.1	8.0	11.1	1.5

● 武汉 / Wuhan

4-1 洗衣机的拥有比例/ Proportion of Washing Machine Owners in the Sample

	人数 Number	百分比 Percent
有 yes	576	89.7
没有 no	66	10.3

n=642

4-2 洗衣机的拥有量/ Number of Washing Machine Owned Per Household

	人数 Number	百分比 Percent
1 台 1 set	537	94.4
2 台 2 sets	32	5.6
3 台及以上 3 sets or over	0	0.0

n=569

4-3 理想品牌排名/ Ranking of the Ideal Brands

排名 Brand Ranking	品牌 Brands	人数 Number	百分比 Percent
1	小天鹅 Little Swan	207	32.3
2	海尔 Haier	153	23.9
3	荷花 Hehua	46	7.2
4	金羚 Jinling	41	6.4
5	小鸭・圣吉奥 Xiaoya	39	6.1
6	荣事达 Rongshida	13	2.0
7	松下/乐声 National	10	1.6
8	西门子 Siemens	8	1.2
9	威力 Weili	6	0.9
9	高士达/乐金 LG	6	0.9

n=641

4-4 对家中现有洗衣机(最近购买的一台)的四个方面的描述/ About the Washing Machine Most Recently Purchased

4-4-1 家中现有洗衣机的品牌排名/ Ranking of the Currently Owned Washing Machine Brands

排名 Brand Ranking	品牌 Brands	人数 Number	百分比 Percent
1	荷花 Hehua	214	37.2
2	小天鹅 Little Swan	106	18.4
3	金羚 Jinling	80	13.9
4	海尔 Haier	37	6.4
5	小鸭・圣吉奥 Xiaoya	20	3.5
6	荣事达 Rongshida	18	3.1
7	威力 Weili	13	2.3
8	松下/乐声 National	11	1.9

n=575

4-4-2 该洗衣机的购买时间/ The Time of Purchasing of the Currently Owned Washing Machine

	人数 Number	百分比 Percent
1985 年或以前 1985 or before	62	10.8
1986～1990 年	143	24.9
1991 年	29	5.0
1992 年	37	6.4
1993 年	44	7.7
1994 年	38	6.6
1995 年	56	9.7
1996 年	31	5.4
1997 年	49	8.5
1998 年	49	8.5
1999 年	37	6.4

n=575

4-4-3 该洗衣机的价格/ The Price of the Currently Owned Washing Machine

	人数 Number	百分比 Percent
500 元或以下 500 yuan or below	119	20.7
501～1000 元 yuan	168	29.2
1001～1500 元 yuan	119	20.7
1501～2000 元 yuan	63	10.9
2001～2500 元 yuan	42	7.3
2501～3000 元 yuan	13	2.3
3001～3500 元 yuan	11	1.9
3501～4000 元 yuan	8	1.4
4001～4500 元 yuan	5	0.9
4501～5000 元 yuan	0	0.0
5000 元以上 over 5000 yuan	2	0.3
完全不知道 don't know	26	4.5

n=576

4-4-4 该洗衣机的类型/ The Type of the Currently Owned Washing Machine

	人数 Number	百分比 Percent
普通单缸 single basin	89	15.5
普通双缸 double basins	210	36.5
波轮全自动 turbine automatic	196	34.0
滚筒全自动 rolling basin	79	13.7
其他 others	2	0.3

n=576

4-5 选择不同品牌洗衣机时考虑因素/ Considerations in Choosing from Different Brands

注：本题为多选题，合计百分比超过 100%（Multiple answers）

	人数 Number	品牌形象 brand image	外型 outlook	价格 price	功能齐备 all-function	容量大 big volume	噪音低 low noise	不伤衣料 no damage service	售后服务 follow-up service	其他 others
样本 Sample	572	43.4	13.6	43.9	34.4	23.4	16.8	12.6	18.7	8.2
荷花 Hehua	213	40.4	10.3	54.0	21.1	21.6	12.2	7.5	12.7	9.9
小天鹅 Little Swan	106	53.8	17.9	35.8	40.6	15.1	24.5	7.5	24.5	6.6
金羚 Jinling	80	46.3	17.5	33.8	50.0	25.0	17.5	16.3	18.8	2.5
海尔 Haier	37	51.4	16.2	29.7	32.4	24.3	10.8	24.3	40.5	8.1
小鸭・圣吉奥 Xiaoya	20	30.0	15.0	35.0	70.0	20.0	10.0	20.0	55.0	10.0
荣事达 Rongshida	18	61.1	5.6	44.4	27.8	38.9	22.2	5.6	38.9	0.0
威力 Weili	13	23.1	0.0	38.5	38.5	30.8	23.1	15.4	7.7	23.1
松下/乐声 National	11	45.5	27.3	63.6	54.5	54.5	18.2	18.2	0.0	0.0
高士达/乐金 LG	7	14.3	0.0	28.6	71.4	71.4	28.6	57.1	28.6	0.0
日立 Hitachi	7	42.9	0.0	14.3	42.9	0.0	28.6	14.3	0.0	14.3

4-6 洗衣机未来购买打算/ Plan for Future Purchasing of a Washing Machine

4-6-1 有无购买打算/ Whether Planning to Purchase Next Year

	人数 Number	百分比 Percent
是 yes	74	11.5
否 no	568	88.5

n=642

4-6-2 打算购买的品牌排名/ The Brand of the Planned Purchase Next Year

排名 Brand Ranking	品牌 Brands	人数 Number	百分比 Percent
1	小天鹅 Little Swan	25	37.3
2	海尔 Haier	21	31.3
3	小鸭·圣吉奥 Xiaoya	5	7.5
4	荷花 Hehua	4	6.0
5	威力 Weili	2	3.0
5	西门子 Siemens	2	3.0
5	金羚 Jinling	2	3.0
5	海棠 Haitang	2	3.0

n=67

4-6-3 打算购买的类型/ The Type of the Planned Purchase Next Year

	人数 Number	百分比 Percent
普通单缸 single basin	4	5.6
普通双缸 double basins	7	9.7
波轮全自动 turbine automatic	20	27.8
滚筒全自动 rolling basin	41	56.9
其他 others	0	0.0

n=72

4-6-4 打算购买的价格/ The Price of the Planned Purchase Next Year

	人数 Number	百分比 Percent
500 元或以下 500 yuan or below	3	4.2
501～1000 元 yuan	6	8.3
1001～1500 元 yuan	16	22.2
1501～2000 元 yuan	19	26.4
2001～2500 元 yuan	14	19.4
2501～3000 元 yuan	6	8.3
3001～3500 元 yuan	5	6.9
3501～4000 元 yuan	0	0.0
4001～4500 元 yuan	1	1.4
4501～5000 元 yuan	1	1.4
5000 元以上 over 5000 yuan	1	1.4
完全不知道 don't know	0	0.0

n=72

4-7 选购洗衣机时不同角色的人口特征/ Demographics of the Different Roles in Purchasing a Washing Machine

注：不同角色可以多选（Multiple answers）

	人数 Number	16-24 岁 Age	25-34 岁 Age	35-44 岁 Age	45-54 岁 Age	55-60 岁 Age
样本 Sample	**502**	**17.7**	**28.5**	**27.5**	**18.3**	**8.0**
男性 Male	**240**	**18.3**	**25.4**	**29.2**	**17.9**	**9.2**
提议者 advocate	58	13.8	27.6	32.8	22.4	3.4
影响者 influence	42	26.2	23.8	26.2	19.0	4.8
决定者 decider	95	6.3	26.3	36.8	18.9	11.6
使用者 user	142	21.8	21.8	31.7	16.9	7.7
女性 Female	**262**	**17.2**	**31.3**	**26.0**	**18.7**	**6.9**
提议者 advocate	61	14.8	29.5	31.1	18.0	6.6
影响者 influence	32	12.5	28.1	15.6	34.4	9.4
决定者 decider	100	4.0	27.0	37.0	26.0	6.0
使用者 user	201	19.4	29.9	25.9	17.4	7.5

4-8 不同消费者层的家中目前拥有品牌/ Brands of Washing Machine Owned in Household by Market Segments

4-8-1 时尚流行指标/ Fads Popular Index

	人数 Number	第一品牌及百分比 1st/ percent	第二品牌及百分比 2nd/ percent	第三品牌及百分比 3rd/ percent	第四品牌及百分比 4th/ percent
样本 Sample	566	**荷花 Hehua(37.3)**	**小天鹅 Little Swan(18.7)**	**金羚 Jinling(13.6)**	**海尔 Haier(6.5)**
平实生活指向 simple living orientation	295	荷花 Hehua(44.7)	小天鹅 Little Swan(16.9)	金羚 Jinling(10.5)	海尔 Haier(7.1)
时尚流行指向 fashion orientation	271	荷花 Hehua(29.2)	小天鹅 Little Swan(20.7)	金羚 Jinling(17.0)	海尔 Haier(5.9)

4-8-2 广告态度指标/ Advertising Attitude Index

	人数 Number	第一品牌及百分比 1st/ percent	第二品牌及百分比 2nd/ percent	第三品牌及百分比 3rd/ percent	第四品牌及百分比 4th/ percent
样本 Sample	**568**	**荷花 Hehua(37.3)**	**小天鹅 Little Swan(18.7)**	**金羚 Jinling(13.7)**	**海尔 Haier(6.5)**
广告淡漠指向 indifferent orientation	164	荷花 Hehua(39.0)	小天鹅 Little Swan(21.3)	金羚 Jinling(12.2)	海尔 Haier(7.3)
中间层 medium	339	荷花 Hehua(36.6)	小天鹅 Little Swan(18.6)	金羚 Jinling(14.2)	海尔 Haier(5.9)
信赖广告指向 loyal orientation	65	荷花 Hehua(36.9)	金羚 Jinling(15.4)	小天鹅 Little Swan(12.3)	海尔 Haier(7.7)

4-8-3 价格态度指标/ Price Attitude Index

	人数 Number	第一品牌及百分比 1st/ percent	第二品牌及百分比 2nd/ percent	第三品牌及百分比 3rd/ percent	第四品牌及百分比 4th/ percent
样本 Sample	**568**	**荷花 Hehua(37.3)**	**小天鹅 Little Swan(18.5)**	**金羚 Jinling(13.9)**	**海尔 Haier(6.5)**
价格无关心指向 indifferent orientation	76	荷花 Hehua(28.9)	小天鹅 Little Swan(19.7)	金羚 Jinling(13.2)	海尔 Haier(11.8)
中间层 medium	273	荷花 Hehua(33.7)	小天鹅 Little Swan(20.1)	金羚 Jinling(15.0)	海尔 Haier(7.3)
价格重视指向 careful orientation	219	荷花 Hehua(44.7)	小天鹅 Little Swan(16.0)	金羚 Jinling(12.8)	海尔 Haier(3.7) 荣事达 Rongshida(3.7) 小鸭・圣吉奥 Xiaoya(3.7)

4-9 不同消费者层选择洗衣机时的考虑因素/ Considerations in Choosing from Different Brands by Market Segments

4-9-1 时尚流行指标/ Fads Popular Index

注：本题为多选题，合计百分比超过 100%（Multiple answers）

	人数 Number	品牌形象 brand image	外型 outlook	价格 price	功能齐备 all-function	容量大 big volume	噪音低 low noise	不伤衣料 no damage	售后服务 follow-up service	其他 others
样本 Sample	**564**	**43.4**	**13.7**	**44.1**	**34.2**	**23.6**	**16.8**	**12.8**	**18.8**	**8.0**
平实生活指向 simple living orientation	292	44.2	14.7	47.3	31.5	20.2	15.1	10.3	17.8	8.6
时尚流行指向 fashion orientation	272	42.6	12.5	40.8	37.1	27.2	18.8	15.4	19.9	7.4

4-9-2 广告态度指标/ Advertising Attitude Index

注：本题为多选题，合计百分比超过 100%（Multiple answers）

	人数 Number	品牌形象 brand image	外型 outlook	价格 price	功能齐备 all-function	容量大 big volume	噪音低 low noise	不伤衣料 no damage	售后服务 follow-up service	其他 others
样本 Sample	**566**	**43.5**	**13.6**	**44.2**	**34.3**	**23.5**	**16.8**	**12.7**	**18.7**	**8.0**
广告淡漠指向 indifferent orientation	164	43.9	14.6	45.1	28.7	21.3	17.1	11.0	20.7	9.8
中间层 medium	337	43.0	12.2	43.3	38.0	23.7	17.5	12.8	17.5	7.4
信赖广告指向 loyal orientation	65	44.6	18.5	46.2	29.2	27.7	12.3	16.9	20.0	6.2

4-9-3 价格态度指标/ Price Attitude Index

注：本题为多选题，合计百分比超过 100%（Multiple answers）

	人数 Number	品牌形象 brand image	外型 outlook	价格 price	功能齐备 all-function	容量大 big volume	噪音低 low noise	不伤衣料 no damage	售后服务 follow-up service	其他 others
样本 Sample	**566**	**43.5**	**13.6**	**44.0**	**34.3**	**23.5**	**16.8**	**12.7**	**18.9**	**8.0**
价格无关心指向 indifferent orientation	76	44.7	15.8	31.6	36.8	21.1	10.5	13.2	22.4	6.6
中间层 medium	272	44.1	12.9	44.9	37.5	21.3	16.5	12.9	20.6	7.0
价格重视指向 careful orientation	218	42.2	13.8	47.2	29.4	27.1	19.3	12.4	15.6	9.6

● 西安 / Xi'an

4-1 洗衣机的拥有比例/ Proportion of Washing Machine Owners in the Sample

	人数 Number	百分比 Percent
有 yes	546	91.0
没有 no	54	9.0

n=600

4-2 洗衣机的拥有量/ Number of Washing Machine Owned Per Household

	人数 Number	百分比 Percent
1 台 1 set	522	95.6
2 台 2 sets	23	4.2
3 台及以上 3 sets or over	1	0.2

n=546

4-3 理想品牌排名/ Ranking of the Ideal Brands

排名 Brand Ranking	品牌 Brands	人数 Number	百分比 Percent
1	小天鹅 Little Swan	195	32.6
2	海尔 Haier	157	26.2
3	小鸭・圣吉奥 Xiaoya	51	8.5
4	双鸥 Shuang'ou	36	6.0
5	松下/乐声 National	34	5.7
6	荣事达 Rongshida	13	2.2
7	威力 Weili	9	1.5

n=599

4-4 对家中现有洗衣机(最近购买的一台)的四个方面的描述/ About the Washing Machine Most Recently Purchased

4-4-1 家中现有洗衣机的品牌排名/ Ranking of the Currently Owned Washing Machine Brands

排名 Brand Ranking	品牌 Brands	人数 Number	百分比 Percent
1	双鸥 Shuang'ou	118	21.7
2	小天鹅 Little Swan	76	14.0
3	海尔 Haier	44	8.1
4	长风 Changfeng	39	7.2
5	水仙 Narcissus	31	5.7
6	荣事达 Rongshida	28	5.2
7	松下/乐声 National	27	5.0
8	威力 Weili	23	4.2
9	海鸥 Hai'ou	15	2.8
9	小鸭・圣吉奥 Xiaoya	15	2.8

n=543

4-4-2 该洗衣机的购买时间/ The Time of Purchasing of the Currently Owned Washing Machine

	人数 Number	百分比 Percent
1985 年或以前 1985 or before	52	9.5
1986～1990 年	149	27.3
1991 年	36	6.6
1992 年	38	7.0
1993 年	31	5.7
1994 年	35	6.4
1995 年	45	8.3
1996 年	43	7.9
1997 年	53	9.7
1998 年	39	7.2
1999 年	24	4.4

n=545

4-4-3 该洗衣机的价格/ The Price of the Currently Owned Washing Machine

	人数 Number	百分比 Percent
500 元及以下 500 yuan or below	128	23.4
501～1000 元 yuan	220	40.3
1001～1500 元 yuan	66	12.1
1501～2000 元 yuan	49	9.0
2001～2500 元 yuan	35	6.4
2501～3000 元 yuan	17	3.1
3001～3500 元 yuan	6	1.1
3501～4000 元 yuan	3	0.5
4001～4500 元 yuan	2	0.4
4501～5000 元 yuan	2	0.4
5000 元以上 over 5000 yuan	1	0.2
完全不知道 don't know	17	3.1

n=546

4-4-4 该洗衣机的类型/ The Type of the Currently Owned Washing Machine

	人数 Number	百分比 Percent
普通单缸 single basin	82	15.0
普通双缸 double basins	330	60.4
波轮全自动 turbine automatic	81	14.8
滚筒全自动 rolling basin	49	9.0
其他 others	4	0.7

n=546

4-5 选择不同品牌洗衣机时考虑因素/ Considerations in Choosing from Different Brands

注：本题为多选题，合计百分比超过 100%（Multiple answers）

	人数 Number	品牌形象 brand image	外型 outlook	价格 price	功能齐备 all-function	容量大 big volume	噪音低 low noise	不伤衣料 no damage service	售后服务 follow-up service	其他 others
样本 Sample	**543**	**37.8**	**12.5**	**40.7**	**29.8**	**32.2**	**14.2**	**12.0**	**12.0**	**1.5**
双鸥 Shuang'ou	118	36.4	7.6	50.0	19.5	20.3	5.9	11.9	10.2	0.8
小天鹅 Little Swan	76	46.1	9.2	27.6	44.7	32.9	26.3	14.5	19.7	0.0
海尔 Haier	44	56.8	6.8	25.0	29.5	31.8	20.5	11.4	22.7	4.5
长风 Changfeng	39	25.6	17.9	59.0	28.2	30.8	12.8	12.8	5.1	0.0
水仙 Narcissus	31	29.0	12.9	51.6	25.8	45.2	16.1	3.2	6.5	3.2
荣事达 Rongshida	28	35.7	14.3	35.7	35.7	50.0	21.4	7.1	10.7	3.6
松下/乐声 National	27	51.9	14.8	33.3	14.8	40.7	14.8	7.4	14.8	0.0
威力 Weili	23	47.8	8.7	43.5	17.4	30.4	21.7	0.0	4.3	4.3

4-6 洗衣机未来购买打算/ Plan for Future Purchasing of a Washing Machine

4-6-1 有无购买打算/ Whether Planning to Purchase Next Year

	人数 Number	百分比 Percent
是 yes	49	8.2
否 no	551	91.8

n=600

4-6-2 打算购买的品牌排名/ The Brand of the Planned Purchase Next Year

排名 Brand Ranking	品牌 Brands	人数 Number	百分比 Percent
1	小天鹅 Little Swan	16	34.0
2	海尔 Haier	15	31.9
3	小鸭・圣吉奥 Xiaoya	2	4.3
3	松下/乐声 National	2	4.3

n=47

4-6-3 打算购买的类型/ The Type of the Planned Purchase Next Year

	人数 Number	百分比 Percent
普通单缸 single basin	0	0.0
普通双缸 double basins	4	8.3
波轮全自动 turbine automatic	16	33.3
滚筒全自动 rolling basin	28	58.3
其他 others	0	0.0

n=48

4-6-4 打算购买的价格/ The Price of the Planned Purchase Next Year

	人数 Number	百分比 Percent
500 元及以下 500 yuan or below	0	0.0
501～1000 元 yuan	5	10.4
1001～1500 元 yuan	7	14.6
1501～2000 元 yuan	8	16.7
2001～2500 元 yuan	14	29.2
2501～3000 元 yuan	5	10.4
3001～3500 元 yuan	3	6.3
3501～4000 元 yuan	3	6.3
4001～4500 元 yuan	1	2.1
4501～5000 元 yuan	1	2.1
5000 元以上 over 5000 yuan	0	0.0
完全不知道 don't know	1	2.1

n=48

4-7 选购洗衣机时不同角色的人口特征/ Demographics of the Different Roles in Purchasing a Washing Machine

注：不同角色可以多选（Multiple answers）

	人数 Number	16-24 岁 Age	25-34 岁 Age	35-44 岁 Age	45-54 岁 Age	55-60 岁 Age
样本 Sample	478	15.9	29.3	28.0	18.0	8.8
男性 Male	228	14.9	28.9	29.3	17.1	9.2
提议者 advocate	39	17.9	33.3	30.3	15.4	2.6
影响者 influence	22	22.7	31.8	22.7	13.6	9.1
决定者 decider	122	1.6	28.7	36.1	22.1	11.5
使用者 user	111	22.5	27.0	29.7	14.4	6.3
女性 Female	250	16.8	29.6	26.4	18.8	8.4
提议者 advocate	49	12.2	36.7	18.4	24.5	8.2
影响者 influence	43	16.3	34.9	20.9	18.6	9.3
决定者 decider	66	9.1	27.3	34.8	16.7	12.1
使用者 user	152	17.1	27.6	27.0	21.7	6.6

4-8 不同消费者层的家中目前拥有品牌/ Brands of Washing Machine Owned in Household by Market Segments

4-8-1 时尚流行指标/ Fads Popular Index

	人数 Number	第一品牌及百分比 1st/ percent	第二品牌及百分比 2nd/ percent	第三品牌及百分比 3rd/ percent	第四品牌及百分比 4th/ percent
样本 Sample	541	**双鸥 Shuang'ou(21.6)**	**小天鹅 Little Swan(14.0)**	**海尔 Haier(8.1)**	**长风 Changfeng(7.2)**
平实生活指向 simple living orientation	306	双鸥 Shuang'ou(24.2)	小天鹅 Little Swan(14.4)	长风 Changfeng(8.5)	海尔 Haier(6.5)
时尚流行指向 fashion orientation	235	双鸥 Shuang'ou(18.3)	小天鹅 Little Swan(13.6)	海尔 Haier(10.2)	荣事达 Rongshida(6.4) 水仙 Narcissus(6.4)

4-8-2 广告态度指标/ Advertising Attitude Index

	人数 Number	第一品牌及百分比 1st/ percent	第二品牌及百分比 2nd/ percent	第三品牌及百分比 3rd/ percent	第四品牌及百分比 4th/ percent
样本 Sample	539	**双鸥 Shuang'ou(21.9)**	**小天鹅 Little Swan(13.7)**	**海尔 Haier(8.2)**	**长风 Changfeng(7.2)**
广告淡漠指向 indifferent orientation	167	双鸥 Shuang'ou(26.9)	小天鹅 Little Swan(12.6)	海尔 Haier(9.0)	长风 Changfeng(7.2)
中间层 medium	302	双鸥 Shuang'ou(19.5)	小天鹅 Little Swan(13.6)	海尔 Haier(8.3)	水仙 Narcissus(7.9)
信赖广告指向 loyal orientation	70	双鸥 Shuang'ou(20.0)	小天鹅 Little Swan(17.1)	荣事达 Rongshida(7.1) 长风 Changfeng(7.1) 水仙 Narcissus(7.1)	海尔 Haier(5.7)

4-8-3 价格态度指标/ Price Attitude Index

	人数 Number	第一品牌及百分比 1st/ percent	第二品牌及百分比 2nd/ percent	第三品牌及百分比 3rd/ percent	第四品牌及百分比 4th/ percent
样本 Sample	539	**双鸥 Shuang'ou(21.9)**	**小天鹅 Little Swan(13.7)**	**海尔 Haier(8.0)**	**长风 Changfeng(7.2)**
价格无关心指向 indifferent orientation	122	双鸥 Shuang'ou(20.5)	小天鹅 Little Swan(18.9)	海尔 Haier(6.6)	威力 Weili(4.9) 小鸭・圣吉奥 Xiaoya (4.9) 水仙 Narcissus(4.9) 松下/乐声 National(4.9)
中间层 medium	280	双鸥 Shuang'ou(21.1)	小天鹅 Little Swan(11.1)	海尔 Haier(10.4)	长风 Changfeng(7.9)
价格重视指向 careful orientation	137	双鸥 Shuang'ou(24.8)	小天鹅 Little Swan(14.6)	长风 Changfeng(8.8)	松下/乐声 National(6.6)

4-9 不同消费者层选择洗衣机时的考虑因素/ Considerations in Choosing from Different Brands by Market Segments

4-9-1 时尚流行指标/ Fads Popular Index

注：本题为多选题，合计百分比超过100%（Multiple answers）

	人数 Number	品牌形象 brand image	外型 outlook	价格 price	功能齐备 all-function	容量大 big volume	噪音低 low noise	不伤衣料 no damage	售后服务 follow-up service	其他 others
样本 Sample	544	37.7	12.5	41.0	29.6	32.5	14.2	11.9	11.9	1.5
平实生活指向 simple living orientation	307	37.1	11.4	45.3	27.0	28.7	11.1	8.8	10.1	1.3
时尚流行指向 fashion orientation	237	38.4	13.9	35.4	32.9	37.6	18.1	16.0	14.3	1.7

4-9-2 广告态度指标/ Advertising Attitude Index

注：本题为多选题，合计百分比超过 100%（Multiple answers）

	人数 Number	品牌形象 brand image	外型 outlook	价格 price	功能齐备 all-function	容量大 big volume	噪音低 low noise	不伤衣料 no damage	售后服务 follow-up service	其他 others
样本 Sample	542	37.6	12.5	41.3	29.7	32.5	14.0	12.0	12.0	1.5
广告淡漠指向 indifferent orientation	167	37.7	12.0	42.5	32.9	32.3	8.4	9.6	13.2	1.2
中间层 medium	304	34.5	11.2	43.8	29.3	31.9	16.4	13.8	11.5	1.6
信赖广告指向 loyal orientation	71	50.7	19.7	28.2	23.9	35.2	16.9	9.9	11.3	1.4

4-9-3 价格态度指标/ Price Attitude Index

注：本题为多选题，合计百分比超过 100%（Multiple answers）

	人数 Number	品牌形象 brand image	外型 outlook	价格 price	功能齐备 all-function	容量大 big volume	噪音低 low noise	不伤衣料 no damage	售后服务 follow-up service	其他 others
样本 Sample	542	37.8	12.2	41.0	29.9	32.1	14.0	11.8	11.8	1.5
价格无关心指向 indifferent orientation	123	39.8	14.6	36.6	34.1	25.2	17.9	11.4	12.2	3.3
中间层 medium	281	39.1	11.0	38.4	31.0	32.0	12.5	12.1	10.0	1.1
价格重视指向 careful orientation	138	33.3	12.3	50.0	23.9	38.4	13.8	11.6	15.2	0.7

● 沈阳 / Shenyang

4-1 洗衣机的拥有比例/ Proportion of Washing Machine Owners in the Sample

	人数 Number	百分比 Percent
有 yes	489	81.4
没有 no	112	18.6

n=601

4-2 洗衣机的拥有量/ Number of Washing Machine Owned Per Household

	人数 Number	百分比 Percent
1 台 1 set	473	97.3
2 台 2 sets	13	2.7
3 台及以上 3 sets or over	0	0.0

n=486

4-3 理想品牌排名/ Ranking of the Ideal Brands

排名 Brand Ranking	品牌 Brands	人数 Number	百分比 Percent
1	小天鹅 Little Swan	204	33.9
2	海尔 Haier	105	17.5
3	小鸭・圣吉奥 Xiaoya	100	16.6
4	友谊 Friendship	53	8.8
5	水仙 Narcissus	28	4.7
6	西门子 Siemens	16	2.7
7	松下/乐声 National	13	2.2
8	高士达/乐金 LG	9	1.5
9	荣事达 Rongshida	8	1.3

n=601

4-4 对家中现有洗衣机(最近购买的一台)的四个方面的描述/ About the Washing Machine Most Recently Purchased

4-4-1 家中现有洗衣机的品牌排名/ Ranking of the Currently Owned Washing Machine Brands

排名 Brand Ranking	品牌 Brands	人数 Number	百分比 Percent
1	友谊 Friendship	157	32.2
2	小天鹅 Little Swan	51	10.5
3	水仙 Narcissus	49	10.0
4	海尔 Haier	26	5.3
5	航天 Hangtian	22	4.5
6	小鸭・圣吉奥 Xiaoya	21	4.3
7	荣事达 Rongshida	16	3.3
8	夏普/声宝 Sharp	12	2.5
9	松下/乐声 National	11	2.3
10	金羚 Jinling	9	1.8

n=488

4-4-2 该洗衣机的购买时间/ The Time of Purchasing of the Currently Owned Washing Machine

	人数 Number	百分比 Percent
1985 年或以前 1985 or before	67	13.7
1986～1990 年	147	30.1
1991 年	33	6.7
1992 年	19	3.9
1993 年	30	6.1
1994 年	25	5.1
1995 年	36	7.4
1996 年	30	6.1
1997 年	42	8.6
1998 年	31	6.3
1999 年	29	5.9

n=489

4-4-3 该洗衣机的价格/ The Price of the Currently Owned Washing Machine

	人数 Number	百分比 Percent
500 元或以下 500 yuan or below	123	25.2
501～1000 元 yuan	234	47.9
1001～1500 元 yuan	35	7.2
1501～2000 元 yuan	23	4.7
2001～2500 元 yuan	29	5.9
2501～3000 元 yuan	17	3.5
3001～3500 元 yuan	11	2.2
3501～4000 元 yuan	3	0.6
4001～4500 元 yuan	1	0.2
4501～5000 元 yuan	1	0.2
5000 元以上 over 5000 yuan	2	0.4
完全不知道 don't know	10	2.0

n=489

4-4-4 该洗衣机的类型/ The Type of the Currently Owned Washing Machine

	人数 Number	百分比 Percent
普通单缸 single basin	87	17.9
普通双缸 double basins	296	60.8
波轮全自动 turbine automatic	63	12.9
滚筒全自动 rolling basin	39	8.0
其他 others	2	0.4

n=487

4-5 选择不同品牌洗衣机时的考虑因素/ Considerations in Choosing from Different Brands

注：本题为多选题，合计百分比超过 100%（Multiple answers）

	人数 Number	品牌形象 brand image	外型 outlook	价格 price	功能齐备 all-function	容量大 big volume	噪音低 low noise	不伤衣料 no damage service	售后服务 follow-up service	其他 others
样本 Sample	488	34.4	15.2	41.4	34.2	31.8	18.0	12.7	10.5	4.3
友谊 Friendship	157	31.2	15.3	50.3	36.9	29.3	15.9	10.2	7.0	5.1
小天鹅 Little Swan	51	47.1	9.8	21.6	43.1	31.4	21.6	19.6	21.6	2.0
水仙 Narcissus	49	26.5	24.5	44.9	26.5	40.8	22.4	14.3	6.1	2.0
海尔 Haier	26	42.3	15.4	26.9	50.0	11.5	7.7	11.5	15.4	15.4
航天 Hangtian	22	40.9	9.1	77.3	22.7	18.2	13.6	4.5	4.5	4.5
小鸭・圣吉奥 Xiaoya	21	61.9	4.8	14.3	52.4	28.6	9.5	14.3	38.1	0.0
荣事达 Rongshida	16	50.0	18.8	37.5	6.3	50.0	31.3	0.0	25.0	0.0
夏普/声宝 Sharp	12	16.7	8.3	41.7	33.3	50.0	16.7	25.0	25.0	0.0
松下/乐声 National	11	36.4	9.1	36.4	36.4	27.3	45.5	9.1	0.0	0.0

4-6 洗衣机未来一年购买打算/ Plan for Future Purchasing of a Washing Machine

4-6-1 有无购买打算/ Whether Planning to Purchase Next Year

	人数 Number	百分比 Percent
是 yes	48	8.0
否 no	549	92.0

n=597

4-6-2 打算购买的品牌排名/ The Brand of the Planned Purchase Next Year

排名 Brand Ranking	品牌 Brands	人数 Number	百分比 Percent
1	小天鹅 Little Swan	27	56.3
2	海尔 Haier	7	14.6
3	小鸭·圣吉奥 Xiaoya	5	10.4
4	友谊 Friendship	3	6.3

n=48

4-6-3 打算购买的类型/ The Type of the Planned Purchase Next Year

	人数 Number	百分比 Percent
普通单缸 single basin	2	4.3
普通双缸 double basins	6	12.8
波轮全自动 turbine automatic	20	42.6
滚筒全自动 rolling basin	19	40.4
其他 others	0	0.0

n=47

4-6-4 打算购买的价格/ The Price of the Planned Purchase Next Year

	人数 Number	百分比 Percent
500 元或以下 500 yuan or below	0	0.0
501～1000 元 yuan	5	10.4
1001～1500 元 yuan	17	35.4
1501～2000 元 yuan	7	14.6
2001～2500 元 yuan	5	10.4
2501～3000 元 yuan	5	10.4
3001～3500 元 yuan	4	8.3
3501～4000 元 yuan	2	4.2
4001～4500 元 yuan	1	2.1
4501～5000 元 yuan	2	4.2
5000 元以上 over 5000 yuan	0	0.0
完全不知道 don't know	0	0.0

n=48

4-7 选购洗衣机时不同角色的人口特征/ Demographics of the Different Roles in Purchasing a Washing Machine

注：不同角色可以多选（Multiple answers）

	人数 Number	16-24 岁 Age	25-34 岁 Age	35-44 岁 Age	45-54 岁 Age	55-60 岁 Age
样本 Sample	414	15.9	30.7	28.0	17.4	8.0
男性 Male	196	13.8	29.6	30.1	18.4	8.2
提议者 advocate	33	9.1	30.3	30.3	24.2	6.1
影响者 influence	15	40.0	33.3	13.3	13.3	0.0
决定者 decider	93	4.3	30.1	30.1	23.7	11.8
使用者 user	110	15.5	30.9	31.8	16.4	5.5
女性 Female	218	17.9	31.7	26.1	16.5	7.8
提议者 advocate	26	11.5	34.6	38.5	7.7	7.7
影响者 influence	11	9.1	45.5	18.2	27.3	0.0
决定者 decider	76	9.2	28.9	34.2	18.4	9.2
使用者 user	158	19.0	31.6	24.7	16.5	8.2

4-8 不同消费者层的家中目前拥有品牌/ Brands of Washing Machine Owned in Household by Market Segments

4-8-1 时尚流行指标/ Fads Popular Index

	人数 Number	第一品牌及百分比 1st/ percent	第二品牌及百分比 2nd/ percent	第三品牌及百分比 3rd/ percent
样本 Sample	488	**友谊 Friendship(32.2)**	**小天鹅 Little Swan(10.5)**	**水仙 Narcissus(10.0)**
平实生活指向 simple living orientation	235	友谊 Friendship(30.6)	水仙 Narcissus(13.2)	小天鹅 Little Swan(8.9)
时尚流行指向 fashion orientation	253	友谊 Friendship(33.6)	小天鹅 Little Swan(11.9)	水仙 Narcissus(7.1)

4-8-2 广告态度指标/ Advertising Attitude Index

	人数 Number	第一品牌及百分比 1st/ percent	第二品牌及百分比 2nd/ percent	第三品牌及百分比 3rd/ percent
样本 Sample	488	**友谊 Friendship(32.2)**	**小天鹅 Little Swan(10.5)**	**水仙 Narcissus(10.0)**
广告淡漠指向 indifferent orientation	140	友谊 Friendship(28.6)	水仙 Narcissus(10.7)	小天鹅 Little Swan(9.3)
中间层 medium	284	友谊 Friendship(34.5)	小天鹅 Little Swan(9.5)	水仙 Narcissus(8.8)
信赖广告指向 loyal orientation	64	友谊 Friendship(29.7)	小天鹅 Little Swan(17.2)	水仙 Narcissus(14.1)

4-8-3 价格态度指标/ Price Attitude Index

	人数 Number	第一品牌及百分比 1st/ percent	第二品牌及百分比 2nd/ percent	第三品牌及百分比 3rd/ percent
样本 Sample	487	**友谊 Friendship(32.2)**	**小天鹅 Little Swan(10.5)**	**水仙 Narcissus(10.1)**
价格无关心指向 indifferent orientation	87	友谊 Friendship(31.0)	水仙 Narcissus(12.6)	小天鹅 Little Swan(10.3)
中间层 medium	234	友谊 Friendship(31.2)	小天鹅 Little Swan(12.4)	水仙 Narcissus(8.5)
价格重视指向 careful orientation	166	友谊 Friendship(34.3)	水仙 Narcissus(10.8)	小天鹅 Little Swan(7.8)

4-9 不同消费者层选择洗衣机时的考虑因素/ Considerations in Choosing from Different Brands by Market Segments

4-9-1 时尚流行指标/ Fads Popular Index

注：本题为多选题，合计百分比超过 100%（Multiple answers）

	人数 Number	品牌形象 brand image	外型 outlook	价格 price	功能齐备 all-function	容量大 big volume	噪音低 low noise	不伤衣料 no damage	售后服务 follow-up service	其他 others
样本 Sample	489	34.4	15.1	41.3	34.2	31.7	18.2	12.7	10.4	4.3
平实生活指向 simple living orientation	236	31.8	14.8	44.1	33.9	29.7	15.7	13.1	8.9	4.7
时尚流行指向 fashion orientation	253	36.8	15.4	38.7	34.4	33.6	20.6	12.3	11.9	4.0

4-9-2 广告态度指标/ Advertising Attitude Index

注：本题为多选题，合计百分比超过 100%（Multiple answers）

	人数 Number	品牌形象 brand image	外型 outlook	价格 price	功能齐备 all-function	容量大 big volume	噪音低 low noise	不伤衣料 no damage	售后服务 follow-up service	其他 others
样本 Sample	489	34.4	15.1	41.3	34.2	31.7	18.2	12.7	10.4	4.3
广告淡漠指向 indifferent orientation	140	36.4	13.6	50.0	32.1	27.1	16.4	10.7	7.1	6.4
中间层 medium	285	34.0	13.3	36.8	34.7	32 6	20.4	14.0	11.6	3.5
信赖广告指向 loyal orientation	64	31.3	26.6	42.2	35.9	37 5	12.5	10.9	12.5	3.1

4-9-3 价格态度指标/ Price Attitude Index

注：本题为多选题，合计百分比超过 100%（Multiple answers）

	人数 Number	品牌形象 brand image	外型 outlook	价格 price	功能齐备 all-function	容量大 big volume	噪音低 low noise	不伤衣料 no damage	售后服务 follow-up service	其他 others
样本 Sample	488	34.4	15.2	41.2	34.0	31.8	18.2	12.7	10.2	4.3
价格无关心指向 indifferent orientation	87	36.8	14.9	39.1	31.0	21.8	23.0	16.1	4.6	3.4
中间层 medium	235	36.6	14.9	34.0	36.6	33.6	18.3	12.3	11.5	3.8
价格重视指向 careful orientation	166	30.1	15.7	52.4	31.9	34.3	15.7	11.4	11.4	5.4

5.空调 / Air-conditioner

● 北京 / Beijing

5-1 空调的拥有比例/ Proportion of Air-conditioner Owners in the Sample

	人数 Number	百分比 Percent
有 yes	529	52.3
没有 no	483	47.7

n=1012

5-2 空调的拥有量/ Number of Air-conditioner Owned Per Household

	人数 Number	百分比 Percent
1 台 1 set	418	81.3
2 台 2 sets	92	17.9
3 台及以上 3 sets or over	4	0.8

n=514

5-3 理想品牌排名/ Ranking of the Ideal Brands

排名 Brand Ranking	品牌 Brands	人数 Number	百分比 Percent
1	海尔 Haier	271	26.8
2	三菱 Mitsubishi	150	14.9
3	春兰 Chunlan	86	8.5
4	松下/乐声 National	57	5.6
5	格力 Gree	50	5.0
6	古桥 Guqiao	38	3.8
7	高士达/乐金 LG	31	3.1
8	日立 Hitachi	19	1.9
9	科龙 Kelon	18	1.8
10	美的 Meide	17	1.7
11	长虹 Changhong	11	1.1
12	东宝 Dongbao	10	1.0

n=1010

5-4 对家中现有空调(最近购买的一台)的四个方面的描述/ About the Air-conditioner Most Recently Purchased

5-4-1 家中现有空调的品牌排名/ Ranking of the Currently Owned Air-conditioner Brands

排名 Brand Ranking	品牌 Brands	人数 Number	百分比 Percent
1	三菱 Mitsubishi	78	14.8
2	海尔 Haier	66	12.5
3	古桥 Guqiao	61	11.6
4	春兰 Chunlan	50	9.5
5	松下/乐声 National	40	7.6
6	格力 Gree	32	6.1
7	科龙 Kelon	21	4.0
8	美的 Meide	20	3.8
9	高士达/乐金 LG	15	2.8
10	日立 Hitachi	12	2.3
10	海信 Hisense	12	2.3
11	长虹 Changhong	11	2.1
12	东宝 Dongbao	9	1.7

n=528

5-4-2 该空调的购买时间/ The Time of Purchasing of the Currently Owned Air-conditioner

	人数 Number	百分比 Percent
1985 年或以前 1985 or before	5	0.9
1986～1990 年	9	1.7
1991 年	5	0.9
1992 年	9	1.7
1993 年	15	2.8
1994 年	37	7.0
1995 年	51	9.7
1996 年	62	11.7
1997 年	113	21.4
1998 年	95	18.0
1999 年	127	24.1

n=528

5-4-3 该空调的价格/ The Price of the Currently Owned Air-conditioner

	人数 Number	百分比 Percent
1000 元或以下 1000 yuan or below	3	0.6
1001～2500 元 yuan	71	13.5
2501～4000 元 yuan	191	36.3
4001～5500 元 yuan	156	29.7
5501～7000 元 yuan	54	10.3
7001～8500 元 yuan	24	4.6
8501～10000 元 yuan	8	1.5
10001～11500 元 yuan	0	0.0
11501～13000 元 yuan	0	0.0
13001～15000 元 yuan	0	0.0
15000 元以上 over 15000 yuan	0	0.0
完全不知道 don't know	19	3.6

n=526

5-4-4 该空调的类型/ The Type of the Currently Owned Air-conditioner

	人数 Number	百分比 Percent
单冷窗机 window type (cooling)	111	21.1
冷暖窗机 window type (cooling and heating)	33	6.3
单冷壁挂分体机 split type (cooling)	180	34.3
冷暖壁挂分体机 split type (cooling and heating)	189	36.0
单冷柜机 packaged type (cooling)	4	0.8
冷暖柜机 packaged type (cooling and heating)	5	1.0
分体移动空调 mobile/portable type	1	0.2
其他 others	2	0.4

n=525

5-5 选择不同品牌空调时的考虑因素/ Considerations in Choosing from Different Brands

注：本题为多选题，合计百分比超过 100%（Multiple answers）

	人数 Number	品牌形象 brand image	外型 outlook	价格 price	功率 power	省电 save electricity	多功能 multi function	运转噪音低 low noise	售后服务 follow-up service	其他 others
样本 Sample	525	50.9	11.8	32.6	13.7	22.5	15.6	26.1	24.8	3.4
三菱 Mitsubishi	78	66.7	7.7	16.7	11.5	24.4	24.4	34.6	14.1	0.0
海尔 Haier	66	62.1	13.6	36.4	10.6	13.6	19.7	10.6	62.1	0.0
古桥 Guqiao	60	43.3	10.0	50.0	13.3	25.0	3.3	18.3	25.0	3.3
春兰 Chunlan	50	54.0	0.0	32.0	16.0	18.0	20.0	18.0	28.0	2.0
松下/乐声 National	40	55.0	15.0	20.0	17.5	22.5	15.0	52.5	15.0	5.0
格力 Gree	32	46.9	12.5	18.8	12.5	25.0	15.6	37.5	28.1	3.1
科龙 Kelon	21	33.3	19.0	38.1	4.8	19.0	4.8	19.0	19.0	14.3
美的 Meide	20	35.0	0.0	40.0	15.0	20.0	30.0	20.0	20.0	0.0
高士达/乐金 LG	15	20.0	6.7	46.7	13.3	33.3	6.7	40.0	33.3	6.7
日立 Hitachi	12	58.3	41.7	33.3	33.3	16.7	8.3	16.7	8.3	0.0
海信 Hisense	12	58.3	16.7	33.3	8.3	25.0	33.3	25.0	41.7	0.0
长虹 Changhong	11	81.8	27.3	45.5	9.1	18.2	18.2	27.3	18.2	0.0
东宝 Dongbao	9	44.4	11.1	33.3	22.2	22.2	22.2	22.2	11.1	0.0

5-6 空调未来一年购买打算/ Plan for Future Purchasing of an Air-conditioner

5-6-1 有无购买打算/ Whether Planning to Purchase Next Year

	人数 Number	百分比 Percent
是 yes	205	20.3
否 no	804	79.7

n=1009

5-6-2 打算购买的品牌排名/ Ranking of the Brands of the Planned Purchase Next Year

排名 Brand Ranking	品牌 Brands	人数 Number	百分比 Percent
1	海尔 Haier	58	29.3
2	三菱 Mitsubishi	22	11.1
3	春兰 Chunlan	21	10.6
4	格力 Gree	13	6.6
5	高士达/乐金 LG	11	5.6
6	古桥 Guqiao	8	4.0
6	松下/乐声 National	8	4.0
7	美的 Meide	7	3.5

n=198

5-6-3 打算购买的类型/ The Type of the Planned Purchase Next Year

	人数 Number	百分比 Percent
单冷窗机 window type (cooling)	8	4.1
冷暖窗机 window type (cooling and heating)	25	12.7
单冷壁挂分体机 split type (cooling)	39	19.8
冷暖壁挂分体机 split type (cooling and heating)	91	46.2
单冷柜机 packaged type (cooling)	9	4.6
冷暖柜机 packaged type (cooling and heating)	9	4.6
分体移动空调 mobile/portable type	14	7.1
其他 others	2	1.0

n=197

5-6-4 打算购买的价格/ The Price of the Planned Purchase Next Year

	人数 Number	百分比 Percent
1000 元或以下 1000 yuan or below	4	2.0
1001～2500 元 yuan	13	6.6
2501～4000 元 yuan	70	35.7
4001～5500 元 yuan	74	37.8
5501～7000 元 yuan	24	12.2
7001～8500 元 yuan	7	3.6
8501～10000 元 yuan	2	1.0
10001～11500 元 yuan	0	0.0
11501～13000 元 yuan	2	1.0
13001～15000 元 yuan	0	0.0
15000 元以上 over 15000 yuan	0	0.0
完全不知道 don't know	0	0.0

n=196

5-7 选购空调时不同角色的人口特征/ Demographics of the Different Roles in Purchasing an Air-conditioner

注：不同角色可以多选（Multiple answers）

	人数 Number	16-24 岁 Age	25-34 岁 Age	35-44 岁 Age	45-54 岁 Age	55-60 岁 Age
样本 Sample	**494**	**19.0**	**29.8**	**26.9**	**14.6**	**9.7**
男性 Male	**231**	**17.3**	**29.0**	**28.6**	**14.7**	**10.4**
提议者 advocate	46	17.4	34.8	19.6	15.2	13.0
影响者 influence	21	23.8	19.0	33.3	23.8	0.0
决定者 decider	110	7.3	25.5	35.5	17.3	14.5
使用者 user	163	23.3	26.4	28.2	12.9	9.2
女性 Female	**263**	**20.5**	**30.4**	**25.5**	**14.4**	**9.1**
提议者 advocate	62	27.4	27.4	21.0	14.5	9.7
影响者 influence	31	12.9	32.3	38.7	6.5	9.7
决定者 decider	65	6.2	43.1	33.8	13.8	3.1
使用者 user	203	22.7	29.6	24.1	14.3	9.4

5-8 不同消费者层的家中目前拥有品牌/ Brands of Air-conditioner Owned in Household by Market Segments

5-8-1 时尚流行指标/ Fads Popular Index

	人数 Number	第一品牌及百分比 1st/ percent	第二品牌及百分比 2nd/ percent	第三品牌及百分比 3rd/ percent	第四品牌及百分比 4th/ percent
样本 Sample	**524**	**三菱 Mitsubishi(14.9)**	**海尔 Haier(12.6)**	**古桥 Guqiao(11.5)**	**春兰 Chunlan(9.4)**
平实生活指向 simple living orientation	240	三菱 Mitsubishi(14.2)	海尔 Haier(12.1)	古桥 Guqiao(10.4)	春兰 Chunlan(9.6)
时尚流行指向 fashion orientation	284	三菱 Mitsubishi(15.5)	海尔 Haier(13.0)	古桥 Guqiao(12.3)	春兰 Chunlan(9.2)

5-8-2 广告态度指标/ Advertising Attitude Index

	人数 Number	第一品牌及百分比 1st/ percent	第二品牌及百分比 2nd/ percent	第三品牌及百分比 3rd/ percent	第四品牌及百分比 4th/ percent
样本 Sample	**518**	**三菱 Mitsubishi(15.1)**	**海尔 Haier(12.2)**	**古桥 Guqiao(11.6)**	**春兰 Chunlan(9.7)**
广告淡漠指向 indifferent orientation	141	三菱 Mitsubishi(15.6)	古桥 Guqiao(12.8) 海尔 Haier(12.8)	春兰 Chunlan(10.6) 松下/乐声 National(10.6)	格力 Gree(5.0) 科龙 Kelon(5.0)
中间层 medium	303	三菱 Mitsubishi(15.8)	海尔 Haier(11.2)	古桥 Guqiao(9.6)	春兰 Chunlan(9.2)
信赖广告指向 loyal orientation	74	古桥 Guqiao(17.6)	海尔 Haier(14.9)	三菱 Mitsubishi(10.8)	松下/乐声 National(9.5) 春兰 Chunlan(9.5)

5-8-3 价格态度指标/ Price Attitude Index

	人数 Number	第一品牌及百分比 1st/ percent	第二品牌及百分比 2nd/ percent	第三品牌及百分比 3rd/ percent	第四品牌及百分比 4th/ percent
样本 Sample	521	**三菱 Mitsubishi(14.6)**	**海尔 Haier(12.5)**	**古桥 Guqiao(11.7)**	**春兰 Chunlan(9.6)**
价格无关心指向 indifferent orientation	116	三菱 Mitsubishi(15.5)	春兰 Chunlan(14.7)	海尔 Haier(10.3)	格力 Gree(8.6) 古桥 Guqiao(8.6)
中间层 medium	264	三菱 Mitsubishi(15.2)	海尔 Haier(12.1)	古桥 Guqiao(11.7)	春兰 Chunlan(8.3)
价格重视指向 careful orientation	141	海尔 Haier(14.9)	古桥 Guqiao(14.2)	三菱 Mitsubishi(12.8)	春兰 Chunlan(7.8)

5-9 不同消费者层选择空调时的考虑因素/ Considerations in Choosing from Different Brands by Market Segments

5-9-1 时尚流行指标/ Fads Popular Index

注：本题为多选题，合计百分比超过 100%（Multiple answers）

	人数 Number	品牌形象 brand image	外型 outlook	价格 price	功率 power	省电 save electricity	多功能 multi function	运转噪音低 low noise	售后服务 follow-up service	其他 others
样本 Sample	**522**	**50.8**	**11.7**	**32.8**	**13.6**	**22.2**	**15.7**	**25.9**	**24.7**	**3.4**
平实生活指向 simple living orientation	239	50.2	9.2	32.2	11.3	21.3	15.1	24.7	20.9	4.6
时尚流行指向 fashion orientation	283	51.2	13.8	33.2	15.5	23.0	16.3	26.9	27.9	2.5

5-9-2 广告态度指标/ Advertising Attitude Index

注：本题为多选题，合计百分比超过 100%（Multiple answers）

	人数 Number	品牌形象 brand image	外型 outlook	价格 price	功率 power	省电 save electricity	多功能 multi function	运转噪音低 low noise	售后服务 follow-up service	其他 others
样本 Sample	**516**	**51.0**	**11.4**	**33.1**	**13.8**	**22.5**	**15.1**	**26.2**	**24.6**	**3.5**
广告淡漠指向 indifferent orientation	141	48.2	12.1	28.4	12.8	20.6	17.7	26.2	22.7	6.4
中间层 medium	301	50.5	10.3	34.2	16.3	23.9	12.6	27.6	25.2	2.7
信赖广告指向 loyal orientation	74	58.1	14.9	37.8	5.4	20.3	20.3	20.3	25.7	1.4

5-9-3 价格态度指标/ Price Attitude Index

注：本题为多选题，合计百分比超过 100%（Multiple answers）

	人数 Number	品牌形象 brand image	外型 outlook	价格 price	功率 power	省电 save electricity	多功能 multi function	运转噪音低 low noise	售后服务 follow-up service	其他 others
样本 Sample	**519**	**50.9**	**11.8**	**32.4**	**13.9**	**22.0**	**15.6**	**26.0**	**24.9**	**3.5**
价格无关心指向 indifferent orientation	115	52.2	13.9	19.1	13.9	17.4	19.1	31.3	27.0	6.1
中间层 medium	263	51.7	11.4	34.2	14.1	21.7	16.0	25.5	21.7	3.0
价格重视指向 careful orientation	141	48.2	10.6	39.7	13.5	26.2	12.1	22.7	29.1	2.1

● 上海 / Shanghai

5-1 空调的拥有比例/ Proportion of Air-conditioner Owners in the Sample

	人数 Number	百分比 Percent
有 yes	685	67.6
没有 no	329	32.4

n=1014

5-2 空调的拥有量/ Number of Air-conditioner Owned Per Household

	人数 Number	百分比 Percent
1 台 1 set	543	80.3
2 台 2 sets	114	16.9
3 台及以上 3 sets or over	19	2.8

n=676

5-3 理想品牌排名/ Ranking of the Ideal Brands

排名 Brand Ranking	品牌 Brands	人数 Number	百分比 Percent
1	日立 Hitachi	166	16.5
2	三菱 Mitsubishi	148	14.7
3	松下/乐声 National	144	14.3
4	夏普/声宝 Sharp	137	13.6
5	春兰 Chunlan	136	13.5
6	海尔 Haier	69	6.8
7	高士达/乐金 LG	20	2.0
7	大金 Dakin	20	2.0
8	爱特 Aite	19	1.9
9	上菱 Shangling	17	1.7
10	将军 General	10	1.0

n=1009

5-4 对家中现有空调(最近购买的一台)的四个方面的描述/ About the Air-conditioner Most Recently Purchased

5-4-1 家中现有空调的品牌排名/ Ranking of the Currently Owned Air-conditioner Brands

排名 Brand Ranking	品牌 Brands	人数 Number	百分比 Percent
1	春兰 Chunlan	127	18.6
2	夏普/声宝 Sharp	123	18.0
3	日立 Hitachi	83	12.1
4	松下/乐声 National	65	9.5
5	三菱 Mitsubishi	64	9.4
6	爱特 Aite	60	8.8
7	上菱 Shangling	20	2.9
8	奥克斯三星 AUX	17	2.5
9	海尔 Haier	16	2.3

n=684

5-4-2 该空调的购买时间/ The Time of Purchasing of the Currently Owned Air-conditioner

	人数 Number	百分比 Percent
1985 年或以前 1985 or before	1	0.1
1986～1990 年	9	1.3
1991 年	12	1.8
1992 年	21	3.1
1993 年	35	5.1
1994 年	59	8.7
1995 年	101	14.8
1996 年	143	21.0
1997 年	135	19.8
1998 年	102	15.0
1999 年	63	9.3

n=681

5-4-3 该空调的价格/ The Price of the Currently Owned Air-conditioner

	人数 Number	百分比 Percent
1000 元或以下 1000 yuan or below	6	0.9
1001～2500 元 yuan	73	10.7
2501～4000 元 yuan	195	28.6
4001～5500 元 yuan	199	29.2
5501～7000 元 yuan	124	18.2
7001～8500 元 yuan	45	6.6
8501～10000 元 yuan	16	2.3
10001～11500 元 yuan	5	0.7
11501～13000 元 yuan	4	0.6
13001～15000 元 yuan	0	0.0
15000 元以上 over 15000 yuan	2	0.3
完全不知道 don't know	13	1.9

n=682

5-4-4 该空调的类型/ The Type of the Currently Owned Air-conditioner

	人数 Number	百分比 Percent
单冷窗机 window type (cooling)	105	15.4
冷暖窗机 window type (cooling and heating)	74	10.9
单冷壁挂分体机 split type (cooling)	49	7.2
冷暖壁挂分体机 split type (cooling and heating)	416	61.0
单冷柜机 packaged type (cooling)	2	0.3
冷暖柜机 packaged type (cooling and heating)	23	3.4
分体移动空调 mobile/portable type	9	1.3
其他 others	4	0.6

n=682

5-5 选择不同品牌空调时的考虑因素/ Considerations in Choosing from Different Brands

注：本题为多选题，合计百分比超过 100%（Multiple answers）

	人数 Number	品牌形象 brand image	外型 outlook	价格 price	功率 power	省电 save electricity	多功能 multi function	运转噪音低 low noise	售后服务 follow-up service	其他 others
样本 Sample	681	44.8	11.6	34.2	27.0	30.4	13.5	24.2	18.6	3.5
春兰 Chunlan	126	45.2	10.3	43.7	24.6	29.4	11.9	18.3	26.2	3.2
夏普/声宝 Sharp	123	56.1	9.8	27.6	30.9	27.6	13.8	14.6	17.9	2.4
日立 Hitachi	82	47.6	9.8	28.0	34.1	29.3	12.2	34.1	9.8	4.9
松下/乐声 National	65	40.0	16.9	20.0	23.1	27.7	23.1	30.8	12.3	4.6
三菱 Mitsubishi	64	60.9	10.9	17.2	21.9	26.6	17.2	34.4	15.6	1.6
爱特 Aite	60	35.0	10.0	50.0	25.0	41.7	10.0	21.7	16.7	6.7
上菱 Shangling	20	45.0	10.0	35.0	20.0	15.0	15.0	10.0	35.0	0.0
奥克斯三星 AUX	17	29.4	11.8	52.9	17.6	23.5	35.3	23.5	17.6	0.0
海尔 Haier	16	31.3	12.5	12.5	18.8	50.0	0.0	31.3	43.8	0.0

5-6 空调未来一年购买打算/ Plan for Future Purchasing of an Air-conditioner

5-6-1 有无购买打算/ Whether Planning to Purchase Next Year

	人数 Number	百分比 Percent
是 yes	74	7.3
否 no	939	92.7

n=1013

5-6-2 打算购买的品牌排名/ Ranking of the Brands of the Planned Purchase Next Year

排名 Brand Ranking	品牌 Brands	人数 Number	百分比 Percent
1	春兰 Chunlan	19	26.0
2	日立 Hitachi	12	16.4
2	夏普/声宝 Sharp	12	16.4
3	三菱 Mitsubishi	7	9.6
3	松下/乐声 National	7	9.6
4	海尔 Haier	4	5.5
5	海信 Hisense	2	2.7

n=73

5-6-3 打算购买的类型/ The Type of the Planned Purchase Next Year

	人数 Number	百分比 Percent
单冷窗机 window type (cooling)	1	1.4
冷暖窗机 window type (cooling and heating)	3	4.1
单冷壁挂分体机 split type (cooling)	4	5.5
冷暖壁挂分体机 split type (cooling and heating)	53	72.6
单冷柜机 packaged type (cooling)	2	2.7
冷暖柜机 packaged type (cooling and heating)	8	11.0
分体移动空调 mobile/portable type	2	2.7
其他 others	0	0.0

n=73

5-6-4 打算购买的价格/ The Price of the Planned Purchase Next Year

	人数 Number	百分比 Percent
1000 元或以下 1000 yuan or below	0	0.0
1001～2500 元 yuan	4	5.5
2501～4000 元 yuan	19	26.0
4001～5500 元 yuan	31	42.5
5501～7000 元 yuan	12	16.4
7001～8500 元 yuan	4	5.5
8501～10000 元 yuan	2	2.7
10001～11500 元 yuan	0	0.0
11501～13000 元 yuan	0	0.0
13001～15000 元 yuan	0	0.0
15000 元以上 over 15000 yuan	0	0.0
完全不知道 don't know	1	1.4

n=73

5-7 选购空调时不同角色的人口特征/ The Demographics of Different Roles in Purchasing an Air-conditioner

注：不同角色可以多选（Multiple answers）

	人数 Number	16-24 岁 Age	25-34 岁 Age	35-44 岁 Age	45-54 岁 Age	55-60 岁 Age
样本 Sample	635	18.7	30.2	26.6	16.7	7.7
男性 Male	292	18.5	29.8	26.7	17.8	7.2
提议者 advocate	46	17.4	30.4	26.1	21.7	4.3
影响者 influence	40	22.5	25.0	27.5	17.5	7.5
决定者 decider	120	3.3	30.8	34.2	25.0	6.7
使用者 user	167	25.7	29.9	22.2	15.6	6.6
女性 Female	343	19.0	30.6	26.5	15.7	8.2
提议者 advocate	63	22.2	23.8	28.6	22.2	3.2
影响者 influence	56	14.3	23.2	25.0	21.4	16.1
决定者 decider	95	7.4	30.5	34.7	21.1	6.3
使用者 user	224	21.4	32.1	27.2	11.2	8.0

5-8 不同消费者层的家中目前拥有品牌/ Brands of Air-conditioner Owned in Household by Market Segments

5-8-1 时尚流行指标/ Fads Popular Index

	人数 Number	第一品牌及百分比 1st/ percent	第二品牌及百分比 2nd/ percent	第三品牌及百分比 3rd/ percent	第四品牌及百分比 4th/ percent
样本 Sample	679	**春兰 Chunlan(18.6)**	**夏普/声宝 Sharp(18.0)**	**日立 Hitachi(12.2)**	**松下/乐声 National(9.6)**
平实生活指向 simple living orientation	296	春兰 Chunlan(20.3)	夏普/声宝 Sharp(19.9)	日立 Hitachi(14.5)	三菱 Mitsubishi(8.4)
时尚流行指向 fashion orientation	383	春兰 Chunlan(17.2)	夏普/声宝 Sharp(16.4)	松下/乐声 National(12.0)	日立 Hitachi(10.4)

5-8-2 广告态度指标/ Advertising Attitude Index

	人数 Number	第一品牌及百分比 1st/ percent	第二品牌及百分比 2nd/ percent	第三品牌及百分比 3rd/ percent	第四品牌及百分比 4th/ percent
样本 Sample	674	**春兰 Chunlan(18.4)**	**夏普/声宝 Sharp(18.1)**	**日立 Hitachi(12.3)**	**松下/乐声 National(9.5)** **三菱 Mitsubishi(9.5)**
广告淡漠指向 indifferent orientation	161	春兰 Chunlan(18.6)	夏普/声宝 Sharp(15.5)	日立 Hitachi(11.8)	爱特 Aite(10.6)
中间层 medium	417	夏普/声宝 Sharp(19.7)	春兰 Chunlan(17.0)	日立 Hitachi(12.2)	三菱 Mitsubishi(10.6)
信赖广告指向 loyal orientation	96	春兰 Chunlan(24.0)	夏普/声宝 Sharp(15.6)	松下/乐声 National(14.6)	日立 Hitachi(13.5)

5-8-3 价格态度指标/ Price Attitude Index

	人数 Number	第一品牌及百分比 1st/ percent	第二品牌及百分比 2nd/ percent	第三品牌及百分比 3rd/ percent	第四品牌及百分比 4th/ percent
样本 Sample	682	**春兰 Chunlan(18.6)**	**夏普/声宝 Sharp(18.0)**	**日立 Hitachi(12.2)**	**松下/乐声 National(9.5)**
价格无关心指向 indifferent orientation	113	夏普/声宝 Sharp(20.4)	春兰 Chunlan(18.6)	日立 Hitachi(12.4)	松下/乐声 National(9.7)
中间层 medium	363	夏普/声宝 Sharp(17.6)	春兰 Chunlan(16.5)	日立 Hitachi(12.4)	松下/乐声 National(10.2) 三菱 Mitsubishi(10.2)
价格重视指向 careful orientation	206	春兰 Chunlan(22.3)	夏普/声宝 Sharp(17.5)	日立 Hitachi(11.7)	爱特 Aite(8.7)

5-9 不同消费者层选择空调时考虑因素/ Considerations in Choosing from Different Brands by Market Segments

5-9-1 时尚流行指标/ Fads Popular Index

注：本题为多选题，合计百分比超过 100%（Multiple answers）

	人数 Number	品牌形象 brand image	外型 outlook	价格 price	功率 power	省电 save electricity	多功能 multi function	运转噪音低 low noise	售后服务 follow-up service	其他 others
样本 Sample	677	44.6	11.7	34.4	27.2	30.4	13.6	24.4	18.3	3.5
平实生活指向 simple living orientation	297	46.8	8.8	35.4	24.6	30.6	12.8	20.9	16.8	5.4
时尚流行指向 fashion orientation	380	42.9	13.9	33.7	29.2	30.3	14.2	27.1	19.5	2.1

5-9-2 广告态度指标/ Advertising Attitude Index

注：本题为多选题，合计百分比超过 100%（Multiple answers）

	人数 Number	品牌形象 brand image	外型 outlook	价格 price	功率 power	省电 save electricity	多功能 multi function	运转噪音低 low noise	售后服务 follow-up service	其他 others
样本 Sample	672	44.9	11.2	34.4	26.8	30.4	13.4	24.3	18.5	3.6
广告淡漠指向 indifferent orientation	161	46.0	9.9	29.8	28.0	30.4	9.3	25.5	18.6	5.0
中间层 medium	416	44.0	11.8	35.6	27.2	28.6	14.2	22.8	19.0	3.4
信赖广告指向 loyal orientation	95	47.4	10.5	36.8	23.2	37.9	16.8	28.4	15.8	2.1

5-9-3 价格态度指标/ Price Attitude Index

注：本题为多选题，合计百分比超过 100%（Multiple answers）

	人数 Number	品牌形象 brand image	外型 outlook	价格 price	功率 power	省电 save electricity	多功能 multi function	运转噪音低 low noise	售后服务 follow-up service	其他 others
样本 Sample	680	44.9	11.6	34.4	26.9	30.3	13.5	24.3	18.7	3.5
价格无关心指向 indifferent orientation	113	46.0	8.8	31.9	17.7	31.0	17.7	31.9	14.2	3.5
中间层 medium	361	47.1	12.5	33.0	31.6	26.3	11.6	23.0	20.2	2.5
价格重视指向 careful orientation	206	40.3	11.7	38.3	23.8	36.9	14.6	22.3	18.4	5.3

● 广州 / Guangzhou

5-1 空调的拥有比例/ Proportion of Air-conditioner Owners in the Sample

	人数 Number	百分比 Percent
有 yes	624	60.3
没有 no	410	39.7

n=1034

5-2 空调的拥有量/ Number of Air-conditioner Owned Per Household

	人数 Number	百分比 Percent
1 台 1 set	363	58.8
2 台 2 sets	172	27.9
3 台及以上 3 sets or over	82	13.3

n=617

5-3 理想品牌排名/ Ranking of the Ideal Brands

排名 Brand Ranking	品牌 Brands	人数 Number	百分比 Percent
1	三菱 Mitsubishi	140	13.6
2	美的 Meide	122	11.8
3	华凌 Hualing	117	11.3
4	科龙 Kelon	92	8.9
5	松下/乐声 National	82	7.9
6	格力 Gree	81	7.8
7	日立 Hitachi	46	4.5
8	海尔 Haier	40	3.9
9	华宝 Huabao	26	2.5
10	万宝 Wanbao	14	1.4

n=1033

5-4 对家中现有空调(最近购买的一台)的四个方面的描述/ About the Air-conditioner Most Recently Purchased

5-4-1 家中现有空调的品牌排名/ Ranking of the Currently Owned Air-conditioner Brands

排名 Brand Ranking	品牌 Brands	人数 Number	百分比 Percent
1	华凌 Hualing	88	14.1
2	美的 Meide	76	12.2
3	三菱 Mitsubishi	71	11.4
3	科龙 Kelon	71	11.4
4	格力 Gree	60	9.6
5	松下/乐声 National	43	6.9
6	日立 Hitachi	36	5.8
7	华宝 Huabao	22	3.5
8	万宝 Wanbao	21	3.4
9	海尔 Haier	20	3.2

n=622

5-4-2 该空调的购买时间/The Time of Purchasing of the Currently Owned Air-conditioner

	人数 Number	百分比 Percent
1985 年或以前 1985 or before	1	0.2
1986～1990 年	14	2.3
1991 年	8	1.3
1992 年	31	5.0
1993 年	41	6.6
1994 年	70	11.3
1995 年	85	13.8
1996 年	109	17.7
1997 年	115	18.6
1998 年	105	17.0
1999 年	38	6.2

n=617

5-4-3 该空调的价格/ The Price of the Currently Owned Air-conditioner

	人数 Number	百分比 Percent
1000 元或以下 1000 yuan or below	12	1.9
1001～2500 元 yuan	120	19.4
2501～4000 元 yuan	234	37.7
4001～5500 元 yuan	124	20.0
5501～7000 元 yuan	56	9.0
7001～8500 元 yuan	18	2.9
8501～10000 元 yuan	8	1.3
10001～11500 元 yuan	2	0.3
11501～13000 元 yuan	2	0.3
13001～15000 元 yuan	1	0.2
15000 元以上 over 15000 yuan	2	0.3
完全不知道 don't know	41	6.6

n=620

5-4-4 该空调的类型/ The Type of the Currently Owned Air-conditioner

	人数 Number	百分比 Percent
单冷窗机 window type (cooling)	211	34.7
冷暖窗机 window type (cooling and heating)	32	5.3
单冷壁挂分体机 split type (cooling)	237	39.0
冷暖壁挂分体机 split type (cooling and heating)	62	10.2
单冷柜机 packaged type (cooling)	12	2.0
冷暖柜机 packaged type (cooling and heating)	5	0.8
分体移动空调 mobile/portable type	48	7.9
其他 others	1	0.2

n=608

5-5 选择不同品牌空调时的考虑因素/ Considerations in Choosing from Different Brands

注：本题为多选题，合计百分比超过 100%（Multiple answers）

	人数 Number	品牌形象 brand image	外型 outlook	价格 price	功率 power	省电 save electricity	多功能 multi function	运转噪音低 low noise	售后服务 follow-up service	其他 others
样本 Sample	**618**	**39.3**	**11.7**	**37.5**	**16.8**	**40.5**	**14.2**	**36.4**	**17.2**	**1.9**
华凌 Hualing	88	40.9	13.6	28.4	13.6	37.5	12.5	36.4	25.0	1.1
美的 Meide	76	26.3	5.3	43.4	22.4	38.2	17.1	38.2	13.2	2.6
科龙 Kelon	71	38.0	14.1	33.8	15.5	32.4	9.9	39.4	21.1	1.4
三菱 Mitsubishi	69	59.4	7.2	21.7	15.9	44.9	15.9	60.9	10.1	0.0
格力 Gree	60	35.0	20.0	40.0	15.0	41.7	20.0	36.7	16.7	0.0
松下/乐声 National	42	50.0	9.5	33.3	11.9	40.5	16.7	28.6	28.6	7.1
日立 Hitachi	36	47.2	13.9	27.8	22.2	41.7	13.9	33.3	11.1	0.0
华宝 Huabao	22	54.5	13.6	45.5	13.6	31.8	9.1	13.6	27.3	0.0
万宝 Wanbao	21	19.0	4.8	61.9	19.0	47.6	9.5	33.3	14.3	0.0
海尔 Haier	19	52.6	5.3	47.4	10.5	52.6	5.3	42.1	42.1	0.0

5-6 空调未来一年购买打算/ Plan for Future Purchasing of an Air-conditioner

5-6-1 有无购买打算/ Whether Planning to Purchase Next Year

	人数 Number	百分比 Percent
是 yes	79	7.7
否 no	952	92.3

n=1031

5-6-2 打算购买的品牌排名/ The Brand of the Planned Purchase Next Year

排名 Brand Ranking	品牌 Brands	人数 Number	百分比 Percent
1	美的 Meide	13	16.9
2	华凌 Hualing	11	14.3
3	松下/乐声 National	10	13.0
4	科龙 Kelon	9	11.7
5	三菱 Mitsubishi	5	6.5
5	格力 Gree	5	6.5
5	海尔 Haier	5	6.5
6	珍宝 Ogeneral	3	3.9

n=77

5-6-3 打算购买的类型/ The Type of the Planned Purchase Next Year

	人数 Number	百分比 Percent
单冷窗机 window type (cooling)	8	10.3
冷暖窗机 window type (cooling and heating)	10	12.8
单冷壁挂分体机 split type (cooling)	31	39.7
冷暖壁挂分体机 split type (cooling and heating)	7	9.0
单冷柜机 packaged type (cooling)	3	3.8
冷暖柜机 packaged type (cooling and heating)	3	3.8
分体移动空调 mobile/portable type	14	17.9
其他 others	2	2.6

n=78

5-6-4 打算购买的价格/ The Price of the Planned Purchase Next Year

	人数 Number	百分比 Percent
1000 元或以下 1000 yuan or below	2	2.6
1001～2500 元 yuan	15	19.7
2501～4000 元 yuan	40	52.6
4001～5500 元 yuan	8	10.5
5501～7000 元 yuan	8	10.5
7001～8500 元 yuan	2	2.6
8501～10000 元 yuan	0	0.0
10001～11500 元 yuan	0	0.0
11501～13000 元 yuan	0	0.0
13001～15000 元 yuan	0	0.0
15000 元以上 over 15000 yuan	0	0.0
完全不知道 don't know	1	1.3

n=76

5-7 选购空调时不同角色的人口特征/ Demographics of the Different Roles in Purchasing an Air-conditioner

注：不同角色可以多选（Multiple answers）

	人数 Number	16-24 岁 Age	25-34 岁 Age	35-44 岁 Age	45-54 岁 Age	55-60 岁 Age
样本 Sample	**579**	**19.9**	**28.3**	**29.0**	**14.9**	**7.9**
男性 Male	**266**	**18.8**	**25.2**	**32.3**	**15.0**	**8.6**
提议者 advocate	42	19.0	23.8	19.0	23.8	14.3
影响者 influence	43	25.6	27.9	23.3	11.6	11.6
决定者 decider	112	5.4	27.7	38.4	18.8	9.8
使用者 user	140	25.0	22.9	35.7	12.1	4.3
女性 Female	**313**	**20.8**	**31.0**	**26.2**	**14.7**	**7.3**
提议者 advocate	61	21.3	36.1	24.6	14.8	3.3
影响者 influence	58	12.1	31.0	31.0	17.2	8.6
决定者 decider	60	10.0	28.3	35.0	23.3	3.3
使用者 user	204	24.5	28.4	25.0	14.7	7.4

5-8 不同消费者层的家中目前拥有品牌/ Brands of Air-conditioner Owned in Household by Market Segments

5-8-1 时尚流行指标/ Fads Popular Index

	人数 Number	第一品牌及百分比 1st/ percent	第二品牌及百分比 2nd/ percent	第三品牌及百分比 3rd/ percent	第四品牌及百分比 4th/ percent	第五品牌及百分比 5th/ percent
样本 Sample	**614**	**华凌 Hualing(14.3)**	**美的 Meide(12.4)**	**三菱 Mitsubishi(11.4)**	**科龙 Kelon(11.2)**	**格力 Gree(9.8)**
平实生活指向 simple living orientation	292	华凌 Hualing(16.4)	美的 Meide(13.0)	科龙 Kelon(11.0)	三菱 Mitsubishi(9.6)	格力 Gree(9.2)
时尚流行指向 fashion orientation	322	三菱 Mitsubishi(13.0)	华凌 Hualing(12.4)	美的 Meide(11.8)	科龙 Kelon(11.5)	格力 Gree(10.2)

5-8-2 广告态度指标/ Advertising Attitude Index

	人数 Number	第一品牌及百分比 1st/ percent	第二品牌及百分比 2nd/ percent	第三品牌及百分比 3rd/ percent	第四品牌及百分比 4th/ percent	第五品牌及百分比 5th/ percent
样本 Sample	614	**华凌 Hualing(14.2)**	**美的 Meide(12.1)**	**科龙 Kelon(11.6)**	**三菱 Mitsubishi(11.1)**	**格力 Gree(9.8)**
广告淡漠指向 indifferent orientation	187	华凌 Hualing(16.0)	美的 Meide(12.3)	格力 Gree(9.6)	科龙 Kelon(9.1)	三菱 Mitsubishi(8.6)
中间层 medium	364	华凌 Hualing(13.2) 科龙 Kelon(13.2)	三菱 Mitsubishi(12.1)	美的 Meide(11.0)	格力 Gree(9.9)	松下/乐声 National(7.1)
信赖广告指向 loyal orientation	63	美的 Meide(17.5)	华凌 Hualing(14.3)	三菱 Mitsubishi(12.7)	格力 Gree(9.5) 科龙 Kelon(9.5)	日立 Hitachi(6.3)

5-8-3 价格态度指标/ Price Attitude Index

	人数 Number	第一品牌及百分比 1st/ percent	第二品牌及百分比 2nd/ percent	第三品牌及百分比 3rd/ percent	第四品牌及百分比 4th/ percent	第五品牌及百分比 5th/ percent
样本 Sample	618	**华凌 Hualing(14.1)**	**美的 Meide(12.1)**	**三菱 Mitsubishi(11.5) 科龙 Kelon(11.5)**	**格力 Gree(9.7)**	**松下/乐声 National(7.0)**
价格无关心指向 indifferent orientation	125	华凌 Hualing(21.6)	科龙 Kelon(14.4)	美的 Meide(12.8)	三菱 Mitsubishi(7.2) 格力 Gree(7.2) 日立 Hitachi(7.2)	松下/乐声 National(6.4)
中间层 medium	335	三菱 Mitsubishi(13.7)	华凌 Hualing(12.2) 科龙 Kelon(12.2)	美的 Meide(11.9)	格力 Gree(9.9)	松下/乐声 National(7.8)
价格重视指向 careful orientation	158	美的 Meide(12.0) 华凌 Hualing(12.0)	格力 Gree(11.4)	三菱 Mitsubishi(10.1)	科龙 Kelon(7.6)	华宝 Huabao(5.7) 日立 Hitachi(5.7) 松下/乐声 National(5.7)

5-9 不同消费者层选择空调时的考虑因素/ Considerations in Choosing from Different Brands by Market Segments

5-9-1 时尚流行指标/ Fads Popular Index

注：本题为多选题，合计百分比超过 100%（Multiple answers）

	人数 Number	品牌形象 brand image	外型 outlook	价格 price	功率 power	省电 save electricity	多功能 multi function	运转噪音低 low noise	售后服务 follow-up service	其他 others
样本 Sample	612	39.1	11.8	37.3	17.0	40.0	14.5	36.6	17.2	2.0
平实生活指向 simple living orientation	289	38.8	10.4	40.1	14.9	37.0	11.4	41.9	16.6	2.4
时尚流行指向 fashion orientation	323	39.3	13.0	34.7	18.9	42.7	17.3	31.9	17.6	1.5

5-9-2 广告态度指标/ Advertising Attitude Index

注：本题为多选题，合计百分比超过 100%（Multiple answers）

	人数 Number	品牌形象 brand image	外型 outlook	价格 price	功率 power	省电 save electricity	多功能 multi function	运转噪音低 low noise	售后服务 follow-up service	其他 others
样本 Sample	612	39.4	11.9	37.4	16.8	40.5	14.4	36.3	17.0	2.0
广告淡漠指向 indifferent orientation	188	34.6	14.4	39.9	18.6	36.7	14.4	37.8	16.5	1.1
中间层 medium	361	40.2	10.5	37.7	14.7	43.8	13.0	37.4	17.7	2.5
信赖广告指向 loyal orientation	63	49.2	12.7	28.6	23.8	33.3	22.2	25.4	14.3	1.6

5-9-3 价格态度指标/ Price Attitude Index

注：本题为多选题，合计百分比超过 100%（Multiple answers）

	人数 Number	品牌形象 brand image	外型 outlook	价格 price	功率 power	省电 save electricity	多功能 multi function	运转噪音低 low noise	售后服务 follow-up service	其他 others
样本 Sample	616	39.4	11.9	37.7	16.6	40.1	14.4	36.4	17.0	1.9
价格无关心指向 indifferent orientation	124	41.9	13.7	36.3	14.5	34.7	16.9	38.7	19.4	2.4
中间层 medium	334	39.5	10.5	34.7	16.5	41.0	13.8	36.8	18.3	1.8
价格重视指向 careful orientation	158	37.3	13.3	44.9	18.4	42.4	13.9	33.5	12.7	1.9

● 重庆 / Chongqing

5-1 空调的拥有比例/ Proportion of Air-conditioner Owners in the Sample

	人数 Number	百分比 Percent
有 yes	320	51.3
没有 no	304	48.7

n=624

5-2 空调的拥有量/ Number of Air-conditioner Owned Per Household

	人数 Number	百分比 Percent
1 台 1 set	260	81.3
2 台 2 sets	48	15.0
3 台及以上 3 sets or over	12	3.8

n=320

5-3 理想品牌排名/ Ranking of the Ideal Brands

排名 Brand Ranking	品牌 Brands	人数 Number	百分比 Percent
1	格力 Gree	225	36.1
2	春兰 Chunlan	92	14.8
3	海尔 Haier	72	11.6
4	美的 Meide	34	5.5
5	古城 Gucheng	21	3.4
6	科龙 Kelon	17	2.7
7	松下/乐声 National	16	2.6
8	长虹 Changhong	12	1.9

n=623

5-4 对家中现有空调(最近购买的一台)的四个方面的描述/ About the Air-conditioner Most Recently Purchased

5-4-1 家中现有空调的品牌排名/ Ranking of the Currently Owned Air-conditioner Brands

排名 Brand Ranking	品牌 Brands	人数 Number	百分比 Percent
1	格力 Gree	85	26.7
2	春兰 Chunlan	39	12.3
3	美的 Meide	27	8.5
4	科龙 Kelon	17	5.3
4	海尔 Haier	17	5.3
5	万宝 Wanbao	12	3.8
5	松下/乐声 National	12	3.8
6	飞鹿 Feilu	11	3.5
7	爱特 Aite	10	3.1

n=318

5-4-2 该空调的购买时间/ The Time of Purchasing of the Currently Owned Air-conditioner

	人数 Number	百分比 Percent
1985 年或以前 1985 or before	0	0.0
1986～1990 年	9	2.8
1991 年	5	1.6
1992 年	10	3.1
1993 年	20	6.3
1994 年	22	6.9
1995 年	42	13.2
1996 年	51	16.0
1997 年	59	18.6
1998 年	50	15.7
1999 年	50	15.7

n=318

5-4-3 该空调的价格/ The Price of the Currently Owned Air-conditioner

	人数 Number	百分比 Percent
1000 元或以下 1000 yuan or below	5	1.6
1001～2500 元 yuan	120	37.7
2501～4000 元 yuan	141	44.3
4001～5500 元 yuan	19	6.0
5501～7000 元 yuan	9	2.8
7001～8500 元 yuan	10	3.1
8501～10000 元 yuan	4	1.3
10001～11500 元 yuan	3	0.9
11501～13000 元 yuan	0	0.0
13001～15000 元 yuan	0	0.0
15000 元以上 over 15000 yuan	0	0.0
完全不知道 don't know	7	2.2

n=318

5-4-4 该空调的类型/ The Type of the Currently Owned Air-conditioner

	人数 Number	百分比 Percent
单冷窗机 window type (cooling)	227	71.6
冷暖窗机 window type (cooling and heating)	31	9.8
单冷壁挂分体机 split type (cooling)	13	4.1
冷暖壁挂分体机 split type (cooling and heating)	26	8.2
单冷柜机 packaged type (cooling)	5	1.6
冷暖柜机 packaged type (cooling and heating)	11	3.5
分体移动空调 mobile/portable type	3	0.9
其他 others	1	0.3

n=317

5-5 选择不同品牌空调时的考虑因素/ Considerations in Choosing from Different Brands

注：本题为多选题，合计百分比超过 100%（Multiple answers）

	人数 Number	品牌形象 brand image	外型 outlook	价格 price	功率 power	省电 save electricity	多功能 multi function	运转噪音低 low noise	售后服务 follow-up service	其他 others
样本 Sample	316	44.0	13.6	39.9	19.3	25.6	17.4	23.1	13.6	5.1
格力 Gree	84	48.8	15.5	29.8	26.2	32.1	13.1	28.6	14.3	2.4
春兰 Chunlan	39	66.7	2.6	33.3	12.8	17.9	30.8	12.8	25.6	2.6
美的 Meide	27	40.7	11.1	51.9	29.6	18.5	7.4	25.9	11.1	3.7
科龙 Kelon	17	35.3	5.9	41.2	0.0	17.6	5.9	29.4	23.5	5.9
海尔 Haier	16	62.5	12.5	25.0	12.5	18.8	31.3	6.3	31.3	0.0
万宝 Wanbao	12	0.0	33.3	66.7	16.7	41.7	8.3	16.7	16.7	0.0
松下/乐声 National	12	50.0	16.7	33.3	8.3	8.3	33.3	33.3	8.3	8.3
飞鹿 Feilu	11	18.2	27.3	45.5	36.4	27.3	9.1	27.3	9.1	9.1
爱特 Aite	10	20.0	0.0	80.0	40.0	0.0	10.0	10.0	10.0	0.0

5-6 空调未来一年购买打算/ Plan for Future Purchasing of an Air-conditioner

5-6-1 有无购买打算/ Whether Planning to Purchase Next Year

	人数 Number	百分比 Percent
是 yes	67	10.7
否 no	557	89.3

n=624

5-6-2 打算购买的品牌排名/ Ranking of the Brands of the Planned Purchase Next Year

排名 Brand Ranking	品牌 Brands	人数 Number	百分比 Percent
1	格力 Gree	24	36.4
2	春兰 Chunlan	12	18.2
3	海尔 Haier	9	13.6

n=66

5-6-3 打算购买的类型/ The Type of the Planned Purchase Next Year

	人数 Number	百分比 Percent
单冷窗机 window type (cooling)	19	30.6
冷暖窗机 window type (cooling and heating)	8	12.9
单冷壁挂分体机 split type (cooling)	6	9.7
冷暖壁挂分体机 split type (cooling and heating)	8	12.9
单冷柜机 packaged type (cooling)	7	11.3
冷暖柜机 packaged type (cooling and heating)	12	19.4
分体移动空调 mobile/portable type	2	3.2
其他 others	0	0.0

n=62

5-6-4 打算购买的价格/ The Price of the Planned Purchase Next Year

	人数 Number	百分比 Percent
1000 元或以下 1000 yuan or below	1	1.5
1001～2500 元 yuan	16	24.2
2501～4000 元 yuan	21	31.8
4001～5500 元 yuan	7	10.6
5501～7000 元 yuan	8	12.1
7001～8500 元 yuan	5	7.6
8501～10000 元 yuan	6	9.1
10001～11500 元 yuan	0	0.0
11501～13000 元 yuan	0	0.0
13001～15000 元 yuan	0	0.0
15000 元以上 over 15000 yuan	0	0.0
完全不知道 don't know	2	3.0

n=66

5-7 选购空调时不同角色的人口特征/ Demographics of the Different Roles in Purchasing an Air-conditioner

注：不同角色可以多选（Multiple answers）

	人数 Number	16-24 岁 Age	25-34 岁 Age	35-44 岁 Age	45-54 岁 Age	55-60 岁 Age
样本 Sample	**282**	**20.2**	**29.1**	**22.3**	**19.5**	**8.9**
男性 Male	**140**	**20.0**	**27.1**	**25.7**	**17.9**	**9.3**
提议者 advocate	40	20.0	35.0	20.0	12.5	12.5
影响者 influence	17	23.5	35.3	17.6	11.8	11.8
决定者 decider	72	8.3	18.1	41.7	22.2	9.7
使用者 user	85	25.9	28.2	23.5	11.8	10.6
女性 Female	**142**	**20.4**	**31.0**	**19.0**	**21.1**	**8.5**
提议者 advocate	38	15.8	34.2	10.5	28.9	10.5
影响者 influence	20	10.0	40.0	10.0	35.0	5.0
决定者 decider	41	4.9	34.1	31.7	26.8	2.4
使用者 user	99	22.2	32.3	15.2	20.2	10.1

5-8 不同消费者层的家中目前拥有品牌/ Brands of Air-conditioner Owned in Household by Market Segments

5-8-1 时尚流行指标/ Fads Popular Index

	人数 Number	第一品牌及百分比 1st/ percent	第二品牌及百分比 2nd/ percent	第三品牌及百分比 3rd/ percent	第四品牌及百分比 4th/ percent
样本 Sample	**314**	**格力 Gree(27.1)**	**春兰 Chunlan(12.4)**	**美的 Meide(8.6)**	**科龙 Kelon(5.4)** **海尔 Haier(5.4)**
平实生活指向 simple living orientation	179	格力 Gree(28.5)	春兰 Chunlan(14.0)	美的 Meide(8.9)	科龙 Kelon(5.0)
时尚流行指向 fashion orientation	135	格力 Gree(25.2)	春兰 Chunlan(10.4)	美的 Meide(8.1)	海尔 Haier(7.4)

5-8-2 广告态度指标/ Advertising Attitude Index

	人数 Number	第一品牌及百分比 1st/ percent	第二品牌及百分比 2nd/ percent	第三品牌及百分比 3rd/ percent	第四品牌及百分比 4th/ percent
样本 Sample	**314**	**格力 Gree(26.8)**	**春兰 Chunlan(12.1)**	**美的 Meide(8.6)**	**海尔 Haier(5.4)** **科龙 Kelon(5.4)**
广告淡漠指向 indifferent orientation	74	格力 Gree(31.1)	春兰 Chunlan(10.8)	美的 Meide(9.5)	松下/乐声 National(6.8)
中间层 medium	199	格力 Gree(26.1)	春兰 Chunlan(12.6)	美的 Meide(9.0)	科龙 Kelon(5.5) 海尔 Haier(5.5)
信赖广告指向 loyal orientation	41	格力 Gree(22.0)	春兰 Chunlan(12.2)	海尔 Haier(7.3) 科龙 Kelon(7.3)	长虹 Changhong(4.9) 飞鹿 Feilu(4.9) 蓝波・希岛 Raybo(4.9) 美的 Meide(4.9) 日立 Hitachi(4.9) 万宝 Wanbao(4.9)

5-8-3 价格态度指标/ Price Attitude Index

	人数 Number	第一品牌及百分比 1st/ percent	第二品牌及百分比 2nd/ percent	第三品牌及百分比 3rd/ percent	第四品牌及百分比 4th/ percent
样本 Sample	**312**	**格力 Gree(26.9)**	**春兰 Chunlan(12.5)**	**美的 Meide(8.3)**	**海尔 Haier(5.4)**
价格无关心指向 indifferent orientation	65	格力 Gree(21.5)	春兰 Chunlan(13.8)	美的 Meide(7.7)	松下/乐声 National(6.2) 科龙 Kelon(6.2)
中间层 medium	146	格力 Gree(26.0)	美的 Meide(10.3)	春兰 Chunlan(8.9)	海尔 Haier(6.2)
价格重视指向 careful orientation	101	格力 Gree(31.7)	春兰 Chunlan(16.8)	科龙 Kelon(6.9)	美的 Meide(5.9)

5-9 不同消费者层选择空调时的考虑因素/ Considerations in Choosing from Different Brands by Market Segments

5-9-1 时尚流行指标/ Fads Popular Index

注：本题为多选题，合计百分比超过 100%（Multiple answers）

	人数 Number	品牌形象 brand image	外型 outlook	价格 price	功率 power	省电 save electricity	多功能 multi function	运转噪音低 low noise	售后服务 follow-up service	其他 others
样本 Sample	**314**	**44.3**	**13.4**	**39.8**	**19.4**	**25.2**	**17.5**	**23.6**	**13.7**	**4.8**
平实生活指向 simple living orientation	180	47.2	10.6	41.7	17.8	28.9	15.0	24.4	15.6	3.9
时尚流行指向 fashion orientation	134	40.3	17.2	37.3	21.6	20.1	20.9	22.4	11.2	6.0

5-9-2 广告态度指标/ Advertising Attitude Index

注：本题为多选题，合计百分比超过 100%（Multiple answers）

	人数 Number	品牌形象 brand image	外型 outlook	价格 price	功率 power	省电 save electricity	多功能 multi function	运转噪音低 low noise	售后服务 follow-up service	其他 others
样本 Sample	314	43.6	13.4	39.8	19.1	25.8	17.2	23.9	13.4	5.1
广告淡漠指向 indifferent orientation	73	42.5	1.4	38.4	12.3	23.3	20.5	28.8	16.4	4.1
中间层 medium	200	44.5	16.5	40.0	23.0	27.0	16.5	23.5	13.5	5.0
信赖广告指向 loyal orientation	41	41.5	19.5	41.5	12.2	24.4	14.6	17.1	7.3	7.3

5-9-3 价格态度指标/ Price Attitude Index

注：本题为多选题，合计百分比超过 100%（Multiple answers）

	人数 Number	品牌形象 brand image	外型 outlook	价格 price	功率 power	省电 save electricity	多功能 multi function	运转噪音低 low noise	售后服务 follow-up service	其他 others
样本 Sample	312	43.9	13.1	39.4	18.9	26.0	17.3	23.4	13.8	5.1
价格无关心指向 indifferent orientation	65	44.6	12.3	33.8	13.8	24.6	27.7	32.3	9.2	4.6
中间层 medium	146	45.9	13.7	36.3	20.5	27.4	13.7	21.2	14.4	6.2
价格重视指向 careful orientation	101	40.6	12.9	47.5	19.8	24.8	15.8	20.8	15.8	4.0

● 武汉 / Wuhan

5-1 空调的拥有比例/ Proportion of Air-conditioner Owners in the Sample

	人数 Number	百分比 Percent
有 yes	398	62.1
没有 no	243	37.9

n=641

5-2 空调的拥有量/ Number of Air-conditioner Owned Per Household

	人数 Number	百分比 Percent
1 台 1 set	337	85.5
2 台 2 sets	52	13.2
3 台及以上 3 sets or over	5	1.3

n=394

5-3 理想品牌排名/ Ranking of the Ideal Brands

排名 Brand Ranking	品牌 Brands	人数 Number	百分比 Percent
1	格力 Gree	192	29.9
2	海尔 Haier	112	17.4
3	春兰 Chunlan	57	8.9
4	美的 Meide	47	7.3
5	科龙 Kelon	39	6.1
6	三菱 Mitsubishi	16	2.5
7	日立 Hitachi	11	1.7
8	高士达/乐金 LG	9	1.4
9	松下/乐声 National	6	0.9
10	华宝 Huabao	5	0.8

n=642

5-4 对家中现有空调(最近购买的一台)的四个方面的描述/ About the Air-conditioner Most Recently Purchased

5-4-1 家中现有空调的品牌排名/ Ranking of the Currently Owned Air-conditioner Brands

排名 Brand Ranking	品牌 Brands	人数 Number	百分比 Percent
1	格力 Gree	105	26.4
2	美的 Meide	56	14.1
3	科龙 Kelon	40	10.1
4	春兰 Chunlan	31	7.8
5	海尔 Haier	29	7.3
6	日立 Hitachi	12	3.0
7	华宝 Huabao	11	2.8
8	松下/乐声 National	9	2.3
8	蓝波・希岛 Raybo	9	2.3
8	高士达/乐金 LG	9	2.3

n=398

5-4-2 该空调的购买时间/ The Time of Purchasing of the Currently Owned Air-conditioner

	人数 Number	百分比 Percent
1985 年或以前 1985 or before	3	0.8
1986～1990 年	16	4.0
1991 年	4	1.0
1992 年	13	3.3
1993 年	34	8.6
1994 年	56	14.1
1995 年	49	12.3
1996 年	53	13.4
1997 年	70	17.6
1998 年	48	12.1
1999 年	51	12.8

n=397

5-4-3 该空调的价格/ The Price of the Currently Owned Air-conditioner

	人数 Number	百分比 Percent
1000 元或以下 1000 yuan or below	3	0.8
1001～2500 元 yuan	179	45.2
2501～4000 元 yuan	139	35.1
4001～5500 元 yuan	32	8.1
5501～7000 元 yuan	19	4.8
7001～8500 元 yuan	10	2.5
8501～10000 元 yuan	4	1.0
10001～11500 元 yuan	1	0.3
11501～13000 元 yuan	0	0.0
13001～15000 元 yuan	0	0.0
15000 元以上 over 15000 yuan	0	0.0
完全不知道 don't know	9	2.3

n=396

5-4-4 该空调的类型/ The Type of the Currently Owned Air-conditioner

	人数 Number	百分比 Percent
单冷窗机 window type (cooling)	274	69.4
冷暖窗机 window type (cooling and heating)	33	8.4
单冷壁挂分体机 split type (cooling)	32	8.1
冷暖壁挂分体机 split type (cooling and heating)	34	8.6
单冷柜机 packaged type (cooling)	4	1.0
冷暖柜机 packaged type (cooling and heating)	12	3.0
分体移动空调 mobile/portable type	6	1.5
其他 others	0	0.0

n=395

5-5 选择不同品牌空调时的考虑因素/ Considerations in Choosing from Different Brands

注：本题为多选题，合计百分比超过 100%（Multiple answers）

	人数 Number	品牌形象 brand image	外型 outlook	价格 price	功率 power	省电 save electricity	多功能 multi function	运转噪音低 low noise	售后服务 follow-up service	其他 others
样本 Sample	**395**	**44.1**	**13.7**	**47.6**	**20.3**	**29.6**	**13.7**	**23.8**	**23.3**	**5.1**
格力 Gree	104	54.8	16.3	47.1	21.2	27.9	9.6	23.1	24.0	2.9
美的 Meide	55	45.5	14.5	61.8	12.7	30.9	10.9	20.0	23.6	3.6
科龙 Kelon	40	52.5	7.5	50.0	17.5	30.0	15.0	37.5	35.0	2.5
春兰 Chunlan	31	54.8	9.7	48.4	16.1	22.6	29.0	12.9	19.4	3.2
海尔 Haier	29	55.2	3.4	20.7	10.3	27.6	20.7	20.7	55.2	10.3
日立 Hitachi	12	58.3	8.3	25.0	25.0	16.7	33.3	33.3	8.3	0.0
华宝 Huabao	11	18.2	9.1	54.5	36.4	27.3	0.0	45.5	27.3	0.0
松下/乐声 National	9	44.4	11.1	33.3	22.2	33.3	11.1	44.4	0.0	0.0
蓝波・希岛 Raybo	9	22.2	11.1	66.7	11.1	55.6	0.0	0.0	44.4	11.1
高士达/乐金 LG	9	44.4	44.4	66.7	22.2	33.3	22.2	11.1	33.3	0.0

5-6 空调未来一年购买打算/ Plan for Future Purchasing of an Air-conditioner

5-6-1 有无购买打算/ Whether Planning to Purchase Next Year

	人数 Number	百分比 Percent
是 yes	90	14.0
否 no	551	86.0

n=641

5-6-2 打算购买的品牌排名/ Ranking of the Brands of the Planned Purchase Next Year

排名 Brand Ranking	品牌 Brands	人数 Number	百分比 Percent
1	格力 Gree	28	33.3
2	海尔 Haier	24	28.6
3	美的 Meide	5	6.0
4	春兰 Chunlan	4	4.8
4	科龙 Kelon	4	4.8
5	松下/乐声 National	2	2.4

n=84

5-6-3 打算购买的类型/ The Type of the Planned Purchase Next Year

	人数 Number	百分比 Percent
单冷窗机 window type (cooling)	17	19.5
冷暖窗机 window type (cooling and heating)	14	16.1
单冷壁挂分体机 split type (cooling)	12	13.8
冷暖壁挂分体机 split type (cooling and heating)	19	21.8
单冷柜机 packaged type (cooling)	8	9.2
冷暖柜机 packaged type (cooling and heating)	9	10.3
分体移动空调 mobile/portable type	8	9.2
其他 others	0	0.0

n=87

5-6-4 打算购买的价格/ The Price of the Planned Purchase Next Year

	人数 Number	百分比 Percent
1000 元或以下 1000 yuan or below	4	4.6
1001～2500 元 yuan	31	35.6
2501～4000 元 yuan	29	33.3
4001～5500 元 yuan	4	4.6
5501～7000 元 yuan	6	6.9
7001～8500 元 yuan	5	5.7
8501～10000 元 yuan	4	4.6
10001～11500 元 yuan	1	1.1
11501～13000 元 yuan	0	0.0
13001～15000 元 yuan	1	1.1
15000 元以上 over 15000 yuan	0	0.0
完全不知道 don't know	2	2.3

n=87

5-7 选购空调时不同角色的人口特征/ Demographics of the Different Roles in Purchasing an Air-conditioner

注：不同角色可以多选（Multiple answers）

	人数 Number	16-24 岁 Age	25-34 岁 Age	35-44 岁 Age	45-54 岁 Age	55-60 岁 Age
样本 Sample	365	19.2	29.9	26.6	17.3	7.1
男性 Male	163	18.4	28.2	27.6	17.2	8.6
提议者 advocate	48	18.8	25.0	31.3	18.8	6.3
影响者 influence	21	28.6	38.1	28.6	4.8	0.0
决定者 decider	76	1.3	27.6	39.5	19.7	11.8
使用者 user	104	20.2	26.9	29.8	16.3	6.7
女性 Female	202	19.8	31.2	25.7	17.3	5.9
提议者 advocate	44	25.0	36.4	25.0	11.4	2.3
影响者 influence	30	16.7	20.0	30.0	26.7	6.7
决定者 decider	67	10.4	26.9	32.8	26.9	3.0
使用者 user	148	18.2	31.8	26.4	17.6	6.1

5-8 不同消费者层的家中目前拥有品牌/ Brands of Air-conditioner Owned in Household by Market Segments

5-8-1 时尚流行指标/ Fads Popular Index

	人数 Number	第一品牌及百分比 1st/ percent	第二品牌及百分比 2nd/ percent	第三品牌及百分比 3rd/ percent	第四品牌及百分比 4th/ percent
样本 Sample	389	**格力 Gree(26.5)**	**美的 Meide(13.6)**	**科龙 Kelon(10.3)**	**春兰 Chunlan(8.0)**
平实生活指向 simple living orientation	184	格力 Gree(28.3)	美的 Meide(17.4)	科龙 Kelon(8.2)	春兰 Chunlan(7.1)
时尚流行指向 fashion orientation	205	格力 Gree(24.9)	科龙 Kelon(12.2)	美的 Meide(10.2)	春兰 Chunlan(8.8)

5-8-2 广告态度指标/ Advertising Attitude Index

	人数 Number	第一品牌及百分比 1st/ percent	第二品牌及百分比 2nd/ percent	第三品牌及百分比 3rd/ percent	第四品牌及百分比 4th/ percent
样本 Sample	390	**格力 Gree(26.4)**	**美的 Meide(13.6)**	**科龙 Kelon(10.3)**	**春兰 Chunlan(7.9)**
广告淡漠指向 indifferent orientation	108	格力 Gree(28.7)	美的 Meide(13.0)	科龙 Kelon(9.3)	春兰 Chunlan(7.4) 海尔 Haier(7.4)
中间层 medium	240	格力 Gree(25.8)	美的 Meide(14.2)	科龙 Kelon(10.0)	春兰 Chunlan(9.6)
信赖广告指向 loyal orientation	42	格力 Gree(23.8)	科龙 Kelon(14.3)	海尔 Haier(11.9) 美的 Meide(11.9)	东宝 Dongbao(4.8) 汇丰 Huifeng(4.8)

5-8-3 价格态度指标/ Price Attitude Index

	人数 Number	第一品牌及百分比 1st/ percent	第二品牌及百分比 2nd/ percent	第三品牌及百分比 3rd/ percent	第四品牌及百分比 4th/ percent
样本 Sample	390	**格力 Gree(26.4)**	**美的 Meide(13.8)**	**科龙 Kelon(10.3)**	**春兰 Chunlan(7.7)**
价格无关心指向 indifferent orientation	61	格力 Gree(29.5)	美的 Meide(19.7)	春兰 Chunlan(9.8)	海尔 Haier(6.6)
中间层 medium	195	格力 Gree(27.7)	美的 Meide(12.8)	科龙 Kelon(12.3)	海尔 Haier(9.2)
价格重视指向 careful orientation	134	格力 Gree(23.1)	美的 Meide(12.7)	科龙 Kelon(10.4)	春兰 Chunlan(6.7)

5-9 不同消费者层选择空调时的考虑因素/ Considerations in Choosing from Different Brands by Market Segments

5-9-1 时尚流行指标/ Fads Popular Index

注：本题为多选题，合计百分比超过 100%（Multiple answers）

	人数 Number	品牌形象 brand image	外型 outlook	价格 price	功率 power	省电 save electricity	多功能 multi function	运转噪音低 low noise	售后服务 follow-up service	其他 others
样本 Sample	386	44.3	13.2	47.7	20.2	30.3	13.7	24.4	23.3	4.7
平实生活指向 simple living orientation	183	44.8	14.2	54.6	18.0	23.5	14.2	22.4	22.4	4.4
时尚流行指向 fashion orientation	203	43.8	12.3	41.4	22.2	36.5	13.3	26.1	24.1	4.9

5-9-2 广告态度指标/ Advertising Attitude Index

注：本题为多选题，合计百分比超过 100%（Multiple answers）

	人数 Number	品牌形象 brand image	外型 outlook	价格 price	功率 power	省电 save electricity	多功能 multi function	运转噪音低 low noise	售后服务 follow-up service	其他 others
样本 Sample	387	44.2	13.2	47.8	20.2	30.2	13.7	24.3	23.3	4.9
广告淡漠指向 indifferent orientation	107	39.3	15.0	49.5	16.8	30.8	14.0	23.4	25.2	4.7
中间层 medium	238	46.2	12.6	48.3	20.2	30.7	13.9	26.1	21.8	5.0
信赖广告指向 loyal orientation	42	45.2	11.9	40.5	28.6	26.2	11.9	16.7	26.2	4.8

5-9-3 价格态度指标/ Price Attitude Index

注：本题为多选题，合计百分比超过 100%（Multiple answers）

	人数 Number	品牌形象 brand image	外型 outlook	价格 price	功率 power	省电 save electricity	多功能 multi function	运转噪音低 low noise	售后服务 follow-up service	其他 others
样本 Sample	387	44.2	13.2	47.8	20.2	30.2	13.4	24.3	23.5	4.9
价格无关心指向 indifferent orientation	61	44.3	14.8	44.3	14.8	23.0	3.3	23.0	27.9	6.6
中间层 medium	194	45.9	11.3	49.0	22.2	29.9	15.5	24.2	26.3	4.1
价格重视指向 careful orientation	132	41.7	15.2	47.7	19.7	34.1	15.2	25.0	17.4	5.3

● 西安 / Xi'an

5-1 空调的拥有比例/ Proportion of Air-conditioner Owners in the Sample

	人数 Number	百分比 Percent
有 yes	231	38.5
没有 no	369	61.5

n=600

5-2 空调的拥有量/ Number of Air-conditioner Owned Per Household

	人数 Number	百分比 Percent
1 台 1 set	203	87.9
2 台 2 sets	23	10.0
3 台及以上 3 sets or over	5	2.2

n=231

5-3 理想品牌排名/ Ranking of the Ideal Brands

排名 Brand Ranking	品牌 Brands	人数 Number	百分比 Percent
1	海尔 Haier	166	27.8
2	春兰 Chunlan	114	19.1
3	格力 Gree	74	12.4
4	美的 Meide	30	5.0
5	三菱 Mitsubishi	24	4.0
6	松下/乐声 National	19	3.2
7	长岭 Changling	12	2.0
8	科龙 Kelon	11	1.8
9	古城 Gucheng	10	1.7
10	宝花 Baohua	7	1.2

n=597

5-4 对家中现有空调(最近购买的一台)的四个方面的描述/ About the Air-conditioner Most Recently Purchased

5-4-1 家中现有空调的品牌排名/ Ranking of the Currently Owned Air-conditioner Brands

排名 Brand Ranking	品牌 Brands	人数 Number	百分比 Percent
1	海尔 Haier	37	16.1
2	春兰 Chunlan	32	13.9
3	格力 Gree	25	10.9
4	三菱 Mitsubishi	17	7.4
5	松下/乐声 National	14	6.1
6	美的 Meide	13	5.7
7	长岭 Changling	11	4.8
8	科龙 Kelon	10	4.3
9	宝花 Baohua	9	3.9
10	日立 Hitachi	6	2.6

n=230

5-4-2 该空调的购买时间/ The Time of Purchasing of the Currently Owned Air-conditioner

	人数 Number	百分比 Percent
1985 年或以前 1985 or before	0	0.0
1986～1990 年	8	3.5
1991 年	5	2.2
1992 年	9	3.9
1993 年	10	4.3
1994 年	14	6.1
1995 年	32	13.9
1996 年	41	17.7
1997 年	49	21.2
1998 年	32	13.9
1999 年	31	13.4

n=231

5-4-3 该空调的价格/ The Price of the Currently Owned Air-conditioner

	人数 Number	百分比 Percent
1000 元及以下 1000 yuan or below	2	0.9
1001～2500 元 yuan	52	22.5
2501～4000 元 yuan	84	36.4
4001～5500 元 yuan	45	19.5
5501～7000 元 yuan	22	9.5
7001～8500 元 yuan	9	3.9
8501～10000 元 yuan	7	3.0
10001～11500 元 yuan	1	0.4
11501～13000 元 yuan	0	0.0
13001～15000 元 yuan	0	0.0
15000 元以上 over 15000 yuan	0	0.0
完全不知道 don't know	9	3.9

n=231

5-4-4 该空调的类型/ The Type of the Currently Owned Air-conditioner

	人数 Number	百分比 Percent
单冷窗机 window type (cooling)	76	32.9
冷暖窗机 window type (cooling and heating)	15	6.5
单冷壁挂分体机 split type (cooling)	59	25.5
冷暖壁挂分体机 split type (cooling and heating)	59	25.5
单冷柜机 packaged type (cooling)	1	0.4
冷暖柜机 packaged type (cooling and heating)	13	5.6
分体移动空调 mobile/portable type	8	3.5
其他 others	0	0.0

n=231

5-5 选择不同品牌空调时考虑因素/ Considerations in Choosing from Different Brands

注：本题为多选题，合计百分比超过 100%（Multiple answers）

	人数 Number	品牌形象 brand image	外型 outlook	价格 price	功率 power	省电 save electricity	多功能 multi function	运转噪音低 low noise	售后服务 follow-up service	其他 others
样本 Sample	**230**	**45.7**	**13.0**	**31.3**	**20.4**	**29.1**	**14.3**	**23.5**	**22.6**	**2.6**
海尔 Haier	37	48.6	18.9	24.3	16.2	29.7	21.6	21.6	35.1	0.0
春兰 Chunlan	32	43.8	6.3	28.1	18.8	28.1	12.5	15.6	40.6	0.0
格力 Gree	25	76.0	8.0	32.0	12.0	28.0	20.0	40.0	24.0	0.0
三菱 Mitsubishi	17	47.1	5.9	23.5	41.2	35.3	5.9	17.6	17.6	0.0
松下/乐声 National	14	50.0	28.6	21.4	7.1	42.9	21.4	50.0	0.0	7.1
美的 Meide	13	38.5	0.0	38.5	7.7	30.8	23.1	23.1	7.7	0.0
长岭 Changling	11	45.5	0.0	54.5	0.0	45.5	18.2	9.1	27.3	0.0
科龙 Kelon	10	60.0	40.0	10.0	40.0	20.0	20.0	40.0	30.0	0.0

5-6 空调未来一年购买打算/ Plan for Future Purchasing of an Air-conditioner

5-6-1 有无购买打算/ Whether Planning to Purchase Next Year

	人数 Number	百分比 Percent
是 yes	61	10.2
否 no	539	89.8

n=600

5-6-2 打算购买的品牌排名/ Ranking of the Brand of the Planned Purchase Next Year

排名 Brand Ranking	品牌 Brands	人数 Number	百分比 Percent
1	海尔 Haier	16	27.6
2	格力 Gree	12	20.7
3	春兰 Chunlan	9	15.5
4	美的 Meide	4	6.9

n=58

5-6-3 打算购买的类型/ The Type of the Planned Purchase Next Year

	人数 Number	百分比 Percent
单冷窗机 window type (cooling)	4	6.7
冷暖窗机 window type (cooling and heating)	7	11.7
单冷壁挂分体机 split type (cooling)	13	21.7
冷暖壁挂分体机 split type (cooling and heating)	16	26.7
单冷柜机 packaged type (cooling)	4	6.7
冷暖柜机 packaged type (cooling and heating)	12	20.0
分体移动空调 mobile/portable type	4	6.7
其他 others	0	0.0

n=60

5-6-4 打算购买的价格/ The Price of the Planned Purchase Next Year

	人数 Number	百分比 Percent
1000 元或以下 1000 yuan or below	3	5.0
1001～2500 元 yuan	11	18.3
2501～4000 元 yuan	16	26.7
4001～5500 元 yuan	10	16.7
5501～7000 元 yuan	8	13.3
7001～8500 元 yuan	9	15.0
8501～10000 元 yuan	2	3.3
10001～11500 元 yuan	1	1.7
11501～13000 元 yuan	0	0.0
13001～15000 元 yuan	0	0.0
15000 元以上 over 15000 yuan	0	0.0
完全不知道 don't know	0	0.0

n=60

5-7 选购空调时不同角色的人口特征/ Demographics of the Different Roles in Purchasing an Air-conditioner

注：不同角色可以多选（Multiple answers）

	人数 Number	16-24 岁 Age	25-34 岁 Age	35-44 岁 Age	45-54 岁 Age	55-60 岁 Age
样本 Sample	205	20.0	34.6	23.4	16.1	5.9
男性 Male	97	21.6	29.9	26.8	15.5	6.2
提议者 advocate	13	7.7	38.5	30.8	23.1	0.0
影响者 influence	10	20.0	60.0	20.0	0.0	0.0
决定者 decider	54	3.7	27.8	42.6	18.5	7.4
使用者 user	54	35.2	24.1	20.4	16.7	3.7
女性 Female	108	18.5	38.9	20.4	16.7	5.6
提议者 advocate	20	25.0	45.0	15.0	10.0	5.0
影响者 influence	20	5.0	60.0	20.0	5.0	10.0
决定者 decider	19	15.8	31.6	26.3	21.1	5.3
使用者 user	73	20.5	35.6	20.5	19.2	4.1

5-8 不同消费者层的家中目前拥有品牌/ Brands of Air-conditioner Owned in Household by Market Segments

5-8-1 时尚流行指标/ Fads Popular Index

	人数 Number	第一品牌及百分比 1st/ percent	第二品牌及百分比 2nd/ percent	第三品牌及百分比 3rd/ percent	第四品牌及百分比 4th/ percent
样本 Sample	230	**海尔 Haier(16.1)**	**春兰 Chunlan(13.9)**	**格力 Gree(10.9)**	**三菱 Mitsubishi(7.4)**
平实生活指向 simple living orientation	109	海尔 Haier(15.6)	春兰 Chunlan(14.7)	格力 Gree(11.0)	三菱 Mitsubishi(8.3)
时尚流行指向 fashion orientation	121	海尔 Haier(16.5)	春兰 Chunlan(13.2)	格力 Gree(10.7)	松下/乐声 National(8.3)

5-8-2 广告态度指标/ Advertising Attitude Index

	人数 Number	第一品牌及百分比 1st/ percent	第二品牌及百分比 2nd/ percent	第三品牌及百分比 3rd/ percent	第四品牌及百分比 4th/ percent
样本 Sample	230	**海尔 Haier(16.1)**	**春兰 Chunlan(13.9)**	**格力 Gree(10.9)**	**三菱 Mitsubishi(7.4)**
广告淡漠指向 indifferent orientation	59	海尔 Haier(15.3)	春兰 Chunlan(13.6)	三菱 Mitsubishi(11.9) 格力 Gree(11.9)	美的 Meide(8.5)
中间层 medium	138	海尔 Haier(17.4)	春兰 Chunlan(13.8)	格力 Gree(8.7)	松下/乐声 National(8.0)
信赖广告指向 loyal orientation	33	格力 Gree(18.2)	春兰 Chunlan(15.2)	海尔 Haier(12.1)	三菱 Mitsubishi(9.1)

5-8-3 价格态度指标/ Price Attitude Index

	人数 Number	第一品牌及百分比 1st/ percent	第二品牌及百分比 2nd/ percent	第三品牌及百分比 3rd/ percent	第四品牌及百分比 4th/ percent
样本 Sample	229	**海尔 Haier(16.2)**	**春兰 Chunlan(14.0)**	**格力 Gree(10.9)**	**三菱 Mitsubishi(7.4)**
价格无关心指向 indifferent orientation	56	春兰 Chunlan(16.1) 格力 Gree(16.1)	海尔 Haier(8.9)	松下/乐声 National(7.1)	三菱 Mitsubishi(5.4)
中间层 medium	128	海尔 Haier(21.1)	春兰 Chunlan(15.6)	三菱 Mitsubishi(9.4)	格力 Gree(8.6)
价格重视指向 careful orientation	45	格力 Gree(11.1) 海尔 Haier(11.1)	宝花 Baohua(8.9) 松下/乐声 National(8.9)	长岭 Changling(6.7) 春兰 Chunlan(6.7) 美的 Meide(6.7)	三菱 Mitsubishi(4.4) 开利 Carrier(4.4)

5-9 不同消费者层选择空调时的考虑因素/ Considerations in Choosing from Different Brands by Market Segments

5-9-1 时尚流行指标/ Fads Popular Index

注：本题为多选题，合计百分比超过 100%（Multiple answers）

	人数 Number	品牌形象 brand image	外型 outlook	价格 price	功率 power	省电 save electricity	多功能 multi function	运转噪音低 low noise	售后服务 follow-up service	其他 others
样本 Sample	231	45.5	13.4	31.6	20.3	29.0	14.3	23.8	22.5	2.6
平实生活指向 simple living orientation	109	44.0	13.8	33.9	13.8	22.9	13.8	16.5	24.8	2.8
时尚流行指向 fashion orientation	122	46.7	13.1	29.5	26.2	34.4	14.8	30.3	20.5	2.5

5-9-2 广告态度指标/ Advertising Attitude Index

注：本题为多选题，合计百分比超过 100%（Multiple answers）

	人数 Number	品牌形象 brand image	外型 outlook	价格 price	功率 power	省电 save electricity	多功能 multi function	运转噪音低 low noise	售后服务 follow-up service	其他 others
样本 Sample	231	45.5	13.4	31.6	20.3	29.0	14.3	23.8	22.5	2.6
广告淡漠指向 indifferent orientation	60	53.3	15.0	33.3	18.3	26.7	8.3	20.0	16.7	5.0
中间层 medium	138	42.0	10.9	34.8	18.8	28.3	14.5	26.8	25.4	1.4
信赖广告指向 loyal orientation	33	45.5	21.2	15.2	30.3	36.4	24.2	18.2	21.2	3.0

5-9-3 价格态度指标/ Price Attitude Index

注：本题为多选题，合计百分比超过 100%（Multiple answers）

	人数 Number	品牌形象 brand image	外型 outlook	价格 price	功率 power	省电 save electricity	多功能 multi function	运转噪音低 low noise	售后服务 follow-up service	其他 others
样本 Sample	230	45.2	13.0	31.7	20.4	28.7	14.3	23.9	22.6	2.6
价格无关心指向 indifferent orientation	57	47.4	15.8	26.3	17.5	26.3	17.5	26.3	17.5	5.3
中间层 medium	128	50.8	13.3	28.1	23.4	26.6	14.8	22.7	26.6	1.6
价格重视指向 careful orientation	45	26.7	8.9	48.9	15.6	37.8	8.9	24.4	17.8	2.2

● 沈阳 / Shenyang

5-1 空调的拥有比例/ Proportion of Air-conditioner Owners in the Sample

	人数 Number	百分比 Percent
有 yes	27	4.5
没有 no	574	95.5

n=601

5-2 空调的拥有量/ Number of Air-conditioner Owned Per Household

	人数 Number	百分比 Percent
1 台 1 set	25	92.6
2 台 2 sets	2	7.4
3 台及以上 3 sets or over	0	0.0

n=27

5-3 理想品牌排名/ Ranking of the Ideal Brands

排名 Brand Ranking	品牌 Brands	人数 Number	百分比 Percent
1	海尔 Haier	106	17.7
2	高士达/乐金 LG	72	12.0
3	春兰 Chunlan	48	8.0
4	三菱 Mitsubishi	47	7.8
5	三洋 Sanyo	38	6.3
6	松下/乐声 Naticnal	20	3.3
7	格力 Gree	17	2.8
8	科龙 Kelon	8	1.3
9	美的 Meide	7	1.2
10	格兰仕 Galanz	6	1.0

n=600

5-4 对家中现有空调(最近购买的一台)的四个方面的描述/ About the Air-conditioner Most Recently Purchased

5-4-1 家中现有空调的品牌排名/ Ranking of the Currently Owned Air-conditioner Brands

排名 Brand Ranking	品牌 Brands	人数 Number	百分比 Percent
1	三洋 Sanyo	6	22.2
2	三菱 Mitsubishi	5	18.5
3	春兰 Chunlan	4	14.8
4	高士达/乐金 LG	3	11.1
5	格力 Gree	2	7.4
5	海尔 Haier	2	7.4

n=27

5-4-2 该空调的购买时间/ The Time of Purchasing of the Currently Owned Air-conditioner

	人数 Number	百分比 Percent
1985 年或以前 1985 or before	0	0.0
1986～1990 年	0	0.0
1991 年	0	0.0
1992 年	0	0.0
1993 年	0	0.0
1994 年	3	11.1
1995 年	2	7.4
1996 年	3	11.1
1997 年	4	14.8
1998 年	7	25.9
1999 年	8	29.6

n=27

5-4-3 该空调的价格/ The Price of the Currently Owned Air-conditioner

	人数 Number	百分比 Percent
1000 元或以下 1000 yuan or below	1	3.7
1001～2500 元 yuan	2	7.4
2501～4000 元 yuan	6	22.2
4001～5500 元 yuan	6	22.2
5501～7000 元 yuan	5	18.5
7001～8500 元 yuan	2	7.4
8501～10000 元 yuan	1	3.7
10001～11500 元 yuan	1	3.7
11501～13000 元 yuan	0	0.0
13001～15000 元 yuan	1	3.7
15000 元以上 over 15000 yuan	0	0.0
完全不知道 don't know	2	7.4

n=27

5-4-4 该空调的类型/ The Type of the Currently Owned Air-conditioner

	人数 Number	百分比 Percent
单冷窗机 window type (cooling)	5	18.5
冷暖窗机 window type (cooling and heating)	8	29.6
单冷壁挂分体机 split type (cooling)	2	7.4
冷暖壁挂分体机 split type (cooling and heating)	9	33.3
单冷柜机 packaged type (cooling)	0	0.0
冷暖柜机 packaged type (cooling and heating)	0	0.0
分体移动空调 mobile/portable type	3	11.1
其他 others	0	0.0

n=27

5-5 选择不同品牌空调时的考虑因素/ Considerations in Choosing from Different Brands

注：本题为多选题，合计百分比超过 100%（Multiple answers）

	人数 Number	品牌形象 brand image	外型 outlook	价格 price	功率 power	省电 save electricity	多功能 multi function	运转噪音低 low noise	售后服务 follow-up service	其他 others
样本 Sample	**27**	**51.9**	**3.7**	**22.2**	**7.4**	**22.2**	**37.0**	**25.9**	**11.1**	**3.7**
三洋 Sanyo	6	83.3	16.7	0.0	16.7	0.0	16.7	0.0	0.0	0.0
三菱 Mitsubishi	5	80.0	0.0	20.0	20.0	0.0	60.0	40.0	0.0	0.0
春兰 Chunlan	4	25.0	0.0	25.0	0.0	50.0	50.0	0.0	0.0	25.0
高士达/乐金 LG	3	33.3	0.0	33.3	0.0	66.7	33.3	66.7	33.3	0.0
格力 Gree	2	0.0	0.0	0.0	0.0	0.0	50.0	0.0	50.0	0.0
海尔 Haier	2	100.0	0.0	0.0	0.0	0.0	50.0	50.0	50.0	0.0

5-6 空调未来一年购买打算/ Plan for Future Purchasing of an Air-conditioner

5-6-1 有无购买打算/ Whether Planning to Purchase Next Year

	人数 Number	百分比 Percent
是 yes	27	4.5
否 no	572	95.5

n=599

5-6-2 打算购买的品牌排名/ Ranking of the Brand of the Planned Purchase Next Year

排名 Brand Ranking	品牌 Brands	人数 Number	百分比 Percent
1	海尔 Haier	10	37.0
2	三洋 Sanyo	2	7.4
2	春兰 Chunlan	2	7.4
2	高士达/乐金 LG	2	7.4
2	三菱 Mitsubishi	2	7.4
2	松下/乐声 National	2	7.4

n=27

5-6-3 打算购买的类型/ The Type of the Planned Purchase Next Year

	人数 Number	百分比 Percent
单冷窗机 window type (cooling)	1	3.8
冷暖窗机 window type (cooling and heating)	7	26.9
单冷壁挂分体机 split type (cooling)	4	15.4
冷暖壁挂分体机 split type (cooling and heating)	7	26.9
单冷柜机 packaged type (cooling)	1	3.8
冷暖柜机 packaged type (cooling and heating)	1	3.8
分体移动空调 mobile/portable type	5	19.2
其他 others	0	0.0

n=26

5-6-4 打算购买的价格/ The Price of the Planned Purchase Next Year

	人数 Number	百分比 Percent
1000 元或以下 1000 yuan or below	0	0.0
1001～2500 元 yuan	4	14.8
2501～4000 元 yuan	11	40.7
4001～5500 元 yuan	4	14.8
5501～7000 元 yuan	4	14.8
7001～8500 元 yuan	2	7.4
8501～10000 元 yuan	1	3.7
10001～11500 元 yuan	0	0.0
11501～13000 元 yuan	1	3.7
13001～15000 元 yuan	0	0.0
15000 元以上 over 15000 yuan	0	0.0
完全不知道 don't know	0	0.0

n=27

5-7 选购空调时不同角色的人口特征/ Demographics of the Different Roles in Purchasing an Air-conditioner

注：不同角色可以多选（Multiple answers）

	人数 Number	16-24 岁 Age	25-34 岁 Age	35-44 岁 Age	45-54 岁 Age	55-60 岁 Age
样本 Sample	**26**	**11.5**	**50.0**	**23.1**	**11.5**	**3.8**
男性 Male	**11**	**9.1**	**45.5**	**36.4**	**9.1**	**0.0**
提议者 advocate	2	0.0	100.0	0.0	0.0	0.0
影响者 influence	0	0.0	0.0	0.0	0.0	0.0
决定者 decider	5	0.0	40.0	60.0	0.0	0.0
使用者 user	8	12.5	50.0	25.0	12.5	0.0
女性 Female	**15**	**13.3**	**53.3**	**13.3**	**13.3**	**6.7**
提议者 advocate	4	0.0	50.0	0.0	25.0	25.0
影响者 influence	0	0.0	0.0	0.0	0.0	0.0
决定者 decider	3	33.3	33.3	0.0	0.0	33.3
使用者 user	12	16.7	50.0	16.7	8.3	8.3

5-8 不同消费者层的家中目前拥有品牌/ Brands of Air-conditioner Owned in Household by Market Segments

5-8-1 时尚流行指标/ Fads Popular Index

	人数 Number	第一品牌及百分比 1st/ percent	第二品牌及百分比 2nd/ percent	第三品牌及百分比 3rd/ percent
样本 Sample	**27**	**三洋 Sanyo(22.2)**	**三菱 Mitsubishi(18.5)**	**春兰 Chunlan(14.8)**
平实生活指向 simple living orientation	9	三菱 Mitsubishi(33.3)	春兰 Chunlan(22.2)	高士达/乐金 LG(11.1) 美的 Meide(11.1) 三洋 Sanyo(11.1) 澳柯玛 Aucma(11.1)
时尚流行指向 fashion orientation	18	三洋 Sanyo(27.8)	春兰 Chunlan(11.1) 高士达/乐金 LG(11.1) 格力 Gree(11.1) 海尔 Haier(11.1) 三菱 Mitsubishi(11.1)	长虹 Changhong(5.6) 松下/乐声 National(5.6) 好纳斯 Haonasi(5.6)

5-8-2 广告态度指标/ Advertising Attitude Index

	人数 Number	第一品牌及百分比 1st/ percent	第二品牌及百分比 2nd/ percent	第三品牌及百分比 3rd/ percent
样本 Sample	27	**三洋 Sanyo(22.2)**	**三菱 Mitsubishi(18.5)**	**春兰 Chunlan(14.8)**
广告淡漠指向 indifferent orientation	6	春兰 Chunlan(33.3) 三洋 Sanyo(33.3)	格力 Gree(16.7) 三菱 Mitsubishi(16.7)	
中间层 medium	17	高士达/乐金 LG(17.6) 三洋 Sanyo(17.6) 三菱 Mitsubishi(17.6)	海尔 Haier(11.8)	长虹 Changhong(5.9) 春兰 Chunlan(5.9) 格力 Gree(5.9) 美的 Meide(5.9) 澳柯玛 Aucma(5.9) 好纳斯 Haonasi(5.9)
信赖广告指向 loyal orientation	4	春兰 Chunlan(25.0) 三洋 Sanyo(25.0) 松下/乐声 National(25.0) 三菱 Mitsubishi(25.0)		

5-8-3 价格态度指标/ Price Attitude Index

	人数 Number	第一品牌及百分比 1st/ percent	第二品牌及百分比 2nd/ percent	第三品牌及百分比 3rd/ percent
样本 Sample	27	**三洋 Sanyo(22.2)**	**三菱 Mitsubishi(18.5)**	**春兰 Chunlan(14.8)**
价格无关心指向 indifferent orientation	8	春兰 Chunlan(37.5)	三洋 Sanyo(25.0) 三菱 Mitsubishi(25.0)	格力 Gree(12.5)
中间层 medium	11	三洋 Sanyo(18.2)	长虹 Changhong(9.1) 春兰 Chunlan(9.1) 高士达/乐金 LG(9.1) 格力 Gree(9.1) 海尔 Haier(9.1) 美的 Meide(9.1) 三菱 Mitsubishi(9.1) 澳柯玛 Aucma(9.1) 好纳斯 Haonasi(9.1)	
价格重视指向 careful orientation	8	高士达/乐金 LG(25.0) 三洋 Sanyo(25.0) 三菱 Mitsubishi(25.0)	海尔 Haier(12.5) 松下/乐声 National(12.5)	

5-9 不同消费者层选择空调时考虑因素/ Considerations in Choosing from Different Brands by Market Segments

5-9-1 时尚流行指标/ Fads Popular Index

注：本题为多选题，合计百分比超过 100%（Multiple answers）

	人数 Number	品牌形象 brand image	外型 outlook	价格 price	功率 power	省电 save electricity	多功能 multi function	运转噪音低 low noise	售后服务 follow-up service	其他 others
样本 Sample	27	51.9	3.7	22.2	7.4	22.2	37.0	25.9	11.1	3.7
平实生活指向 simple living orientation	9	55.6	11.1	44.4	11.1	22.2	22.2	33.3	11.1	11.1
时尚流行指向 fashion orientation	18	50.0	0.0	11.1	5.6	22.2	44.4	22.2	11.1	0.0

5-9-2 广告态度指标/ Advertising Attitude Index

注：本题为多选题，合计百分比超过 100%（Multiple answers）

	人数 Number	品牌形象 brand image	外型 outlook	价格 price	功率 power	省电 save electricity	多功能 multi function	运转噪音低 low noise	售后服务 follow-up service	其他 others
样本 Sample	27	51.9	3.7	22.2	7.4	22.2	37.0	25.9	11.1	3.7
广告淡漠指向 indifferent orientation	6	33.3	0.0	33.3	0.0	33.3	50.0	16.7	0.0	0.0
中间层 medium	17	58.8	5.9	17.6	11.8	23.5	29.4	23.5	17.6	5.9
信赖广告指向 loyal orientation	4	50.0	0.0	25.0	0.0	0.0	50.0	50.0	0.0	0.0

5-9-3 价格态度指标/ Price Attitude Index

注：本题为多选题，合计百分比超过 100%（Multiple answers）

	人数 Number	品牌形象 brand image	外型 outlook	价格 price	功率 power	省电 save electricity	多功能 multi function	运转噪音低 low noise	售后服务 follow-up service	其他 others
样本 Sample	27	51.9	3.7	22.2	7.4	22.2	37.0	25.9	11.1	3.7
价格无关心指向 indifferent orientation	8	50.0	0.0	25.0	12.5	25.0	50.0	12.5	0.0	12.5
中间层 medium	11	45.5	0.0	27.3	0.0	27.3	27.3	27.3	9.1	0.0
价格重视指向 careful orientation	8	62.5	12.5	12.5	12.5	12.5	37.5	37.5	25.0	0.0

6.录/放像机 / VTR

● 北京 / Beijing

6-1 录放像机的拥有比例/ Proportion of VTR Owners in the Sample

	人数 Number	百分比 Percent
有 yes	574	56.8
没有 no	436	43.2

n=1010

6-2 录放像机的拥有量/ Number of VTR Owned Per Household

	人数 Number	百分比 Percent
1 台 1 set	526	94.1
2 台及以上 2 sets or over	33	5.9

n=559

6-3 理想品牌排名/ Ranking of the Ideal Brands

排名 Brand Ranking	品牌 Brands	人数 Number	百分比 Percent
1	松下/乐声 Panasonic	296	29.3
2	索尼 Sony	76	7.5
3	日立 Hitachi	60	5.9
4	东芝 Toshiba	31	3.1
5	夏普/声宝 Sharp	20	2.0
6	三洋 Sanyo	13	1.3
7	飞利浦 Philips	8	0.8
7	胜利 JVC	8	0.8
8	三星 Samsung	6	0.6

n=1011

6-4 对家中现有录放像机(最近购买的一台)的四个方面的描述/ About the VTR Most Recently Purchased

6-4-1 家中现有录放像机的品牌排名/ Ranking of the Currently Owned VTR Brands

排名 Brand Ranking	品牌 Brands	人数 Number	百分比 Percent
1	松下/乐声 Panasonic	227	39.8
2	日立 Hitachi	86	15.1
3	东芝 Toshiba	41	7.2
4	夏普/声宝 Sharp	36	6.3
5	索尼 Sony	28	4.9
6	高士达/乐金 LG	13	2.3
7	三星 Samsung	10	1.8
7	三洋 Sanyo	10	1.8
7	胜利 JVC	10	1.8

n=570

6-4-2 该录放像机的购买时间/ The Time of Purchasing of the Currently Owned VTR

	人数 Number	百分比 Percent
1985 年或以前 1985 or before	25	4.4
1986～1990 年	179	31.3
1991 年	53	9.3
1992 年	52	9.1
1993 年	53	9.3
1994 年	47	8.2
1995 年	58	10.2
1996 年	47	8.2
1997 年	34	6.0
1998 年	18	3.2
1999 年	5	0.9

n=571

6-4-3 录放像机的价格/ The Price of the Currently Owned VTR

	人数 Number	百分比 Percent
1000 元或以下 1000 yuan or below	29	5.1
1001～2000 元 yuan	116	20.3
2001～3000 元 yuan	180	31.5
3001～4000 元 yuan	156	27.3
4001～5000 元 yuan	44	7.7
5000 元以上 over 5000 yuan	10	1.8
完全不知道 don't know	36	6.3

n=571

6-4-4 该录放像机的类型/ The Type of the Currently Owned VTR

	人数 Number	百分比 Percent
普通放像机 play only VTR	89	15.7
卡拉 OK 放像机 play only karaoke VTR	46	8.1
普通录放像机 VTR	263	46.4
卡拉 OK 录放像机 karaoke VTR	168	29.6
其他 others	1	0.2

n=567

6-5 选择不同品牌录放像机时的考虑因素/ Considerations in Choosing from Different Brands

注：本题为多选题，合计百分比超过 100%（Multiple answers）

	人数 Number	品牌形象 brand image	外型 outlook	价格 price	画质好 clarity	多制式 multi-system
样本 Sample	**562**	**54.3**	**9.4**	**26.3**	**17.4**	**17.3**
松下/乐声 Panasonic	221	63.8	7.2	19.0	17.2	16.3
日立 Hitachi	84	59.5	16.7	25.0	16.7	19.0
东芝 Toshiba	41	46.3	12.2	26.8	22.0	17.1
夏普/声宝 Sharp	36	52.8	2.8	27.8	13.9	25.0
索尼 Sony	28	46.4	7.1	35.7	25.0	14.3
高士达/乐金 LG	13	46.2	15.4	38.5	23.1	7.7
三星 Samsung	10	50.0	0.0	20.0	10.0	20.0
三洋 Sanyo	10	40.0	0.0	30.0	10.0	10.0
胜利 JVC	10	30.0	10.0	20.0	30.0	50.0

续前表 continued

	人数 Number	立体声 stereo	有卡拉 OK 功能 karaoke function	售后服务 follow-up service	功能全 all-functions	其他 others
样本 Sample	**562**	**7.5**	**21.0**	**6.6**	**22.2**	**4.3**
松下/乐声 Panasonic	221	5.9	20.4	7.7	23.5	3.2
日立 Hitachi	84	8.3	22.6	2.4	16.7	3.6
东芝 Toshiba	41	9.8	17.1	4.9	29.3	2.4
夏普/声宝 Sharp	36	11.1	25.0	2.8	13.9	2.8
索尼 Sony	28	7.1	17.9	10.7	28.6	0.0
高士达/乐金 LG	13	0.0	23.1	0.0	15.4	7.7
三星 Samsung	10	0.0	40.0	30.0	40.0	0.0
三洋 Sanyo	10	20.0	30.0	10.0	30.0	10.0
胜利 JVC	10	10.0	0.0	10.0	50.0	10.0

6-6 录放像机未来购买打算/ Plan for Future Purchasing of a VTR

6-6-1 有无购买打算/ Whether Planning to Purchase Next Year

	人数 Number	百分比 Percent
是 yes	16	1.6
否 no	982	98.4

n=998

6-6-2 打算购买的品牌排名/ Ranking of the Brand of the Planned Purchase Next Year

排名 Brand Ranking	品牌 Brands	人数 Number	百分比 Percent
1	松下/乐声 Panasonic	6	37.5
2	东芝 Toshiba	1	6.3
2	万利达 Malata	1	6.3
2	和康 Hekang	1	6.3

N=16

6-6-3 打算购买的类型/ The Type of the Planned Purchase Next Year

	人数 Number	百分比 Percent
普通放像机 play only VTR	4	28.6
卡拉 OK 放像机 play only karaoke VTR	4	28.6
普通录放像机 VTR	4	28.6
卡拉 OK 录放像机 karaoke VTR	2	14.3
其他 others	0	0.0

n=14

6-6-4 打算购买的价格/ The Price of the Planned Purchase Next Year

	人数 Number	百分比 Percent
1000 元或以下 1000 yuan or below	3	23.1
1001～2000 元 yuan	4	30.8
2001～3000 元 yuan	3	23.1
3001～4000 元 yuan	1	7.7
4001～5000 元 yuan	0	0.0
5000 元以上 over 5000 yuan	2	15.4
完全不知道 don't know	0	0.0

n=13

6-7 选购录放像机时不同角色的人口特征/ Demographics of the Different Roles in Purchasing a VTR

注：不同角色可以多选（Multiple answers）

	人数 Number	16-24 岁 Age	25-34 岁 Age	35-44 岁 Age	45-54 岁 Age	55-60 岁 Age
样本 Sample	503	22.1	26.4	27.6	16.9	7.0
男性 Male	261	21.5	24.9	29.1	15.7	8.8
提议者 advocate	43	18.6	25.6	32.6	14.0	9.3
影响者 influence	18	22.2	33.3	16.7	27.8	0.0
决定者 decider	124	4.8	20.2	43.5	20.2	11.3
使用者 user	174	28.7	25.3	26.4	12.6	6.9
女性 Female	242	22.7	28.1	26.0	18.2	5.0
提议者 advocate	40	22.5	35.0	20.0	15.0	7.5
影响者 influence	23	26.1	34.8	30.4	0.0	8.7
决定者 decider	63	9.5	33.3	28.6	20.6	7.9
使用者 user	190	26.3	26.3	26.3	17.4	3.7

6-8 不同消费者层的家中目前拥有品牌/ Brands of VTR Owned in Household by Market Segments

6-8-1 时尚流行指标/ Fads Popular Index

	人数 Number	第一品牌及百分比 1st/ percent	第二品牌及百分比 2nd/ percent	第三品牌及百分比 3rd/ percent	第四品牌及百分比 4th/ percent
样本 Sample	560	**松下/乐声 Panasonic(39.6)**	**日立 Hitachi(14.8)**	**东芝 Toshiba(7.1)**	**夏普/声宝 Sharp(6.4)**
平实生活指向 simple living orientation	258	松下/乐声 Panasonic(38.8)	日立 Hitachi(15.5)	东芝 Toshiba(8.1)	夏普/声宝 Sharp(5.0)
时尚流行指向 fashion orientation	302	松下/乐声 Panasonic(40.4)	日立 Hitachi(14.2)	夏普/声宝 Sharp(7.6)	东芝 Toshiba(6.3)

6-8-2 广告态度指标/ Advertising Attitude Index

	人数 Number	第一品牌及百分比 1st/ percent	第二品牌及百分比 2nd/ percent	第三品牌及百分比 3rd/ percent	第四品牌及百分比 4th/ percent
样本 Sample	561	**松下/乐声 Panasonic(39.9)**	**日立 Hitachi(15.2)**	**东芝 Toshiba(7.1)**	**夏普/声宝 Sharp(6.4)**
广告淡漠指向 indifferent orientation	166	松下/乐声 Panasonic(44.0)	日立 Hitachi(15.1)	东芝 Toshiba(7.2)	夏普/声宝 Sharp(6.0)
中间层 medium	329	松下/乐声 Panasonic(38.6)	日立 Hitachi(16.4)	夏普/声宝 Sharp(7.0)	东芝 Toshiba(6.7)
信赖广告指向 loyal orientation	66	松下/乐声 Panasonic(36.4)	东芝 Toshiba(9.1) 日立 Hitachi(9.1)	高士达/乐金 LG(6.1)	三洋 Sanyo(4.5) 胜利 JVC(4.5) 夏普/声宝 Sharp(4.5)

6-8-3 价格态度指标/ Price Attitude Index

	人数 Number	第一品牌及百分比 1st/ percent	第二品牌及百分比 2nd/ percent	第三品牌及百分比 3rd/ percent	第四品牌及百分比 4th/ percent
样本 Sample	565	**松下/乐声 Panasonic(39.8)**	**日立 Hitachi(15.2)**	**东芝 Toshiba(7.1)**	**夏普/声宝 Sharp(6.4)**
价格无关心指向 indifferent orientation	128	松下/乐声 Panasonic(37.5)	日立 Hitachi(18.0)	东芝 Toshiba(6.3)	索尼 Sony(5.5)
中间层 medium	277	松下/乐声 Panasonic(41.9)	日立 Hitachi(14.1)	夏普/声宝 Sharp(7.9)	东芝 Toshiba(7.6)
价格重视指向 careful orientation	160	松下/乐声 Panasonic(38.1)	日立 Hitachi(15.0)	东芝 Toshiba(6.9)	夏普/声宝 Sharp(5.0)

6-9 不同消费者层选择录放像机时的考虑因素/ Considerations in Choosing from Different Brands by Market Segments

6-9-1 时尚流行指标/ Fads Popular Index

注：本题为多选题，合计百分比超过 100%（Multiple answers）

	人数 Number	品牌形象 brand image	外型 outlook	价格 price	画质好 clarity	多制式 multi-system
样本 Sample	556	54.1	9.5	26.6	17.6	17.3
平实生活指向 simple living orientation	256	53.1	9.0	28.1	16.4	16.4
时尚流行指向 fashion orientation	300	55.0	10.0	25.3	18.7	18.0

续前表 continued

	人数 Number	立体声 stereo	有卡拉 OK 功能 karaoke function	售后服务 follow-up service	功能全 all-function	其他 others
样本 Sample	556	7.2	21.0	6.7	22.1	4.3
平实生活指向 simple living orientation	256	5.9	20.3	7.0	20.7	5.5
时尚流行指向 fashion orientation	300	8.3	21.7	6.3	23.3	3.3

6-9-2 广告态度指标/ Advertising Attitude Index

注：本题为多选题，合计百分比超过 100%（Multiple answers）

	人数 Number	品牌形象 brand image	外型 outlook	价格 price	画质好 clarity	多制式 multi-system
样本 Sample	556	54.3	9.5	26.8	17.8	17.6
广告淡漠指向 indifferent orientation	164	48.2	11.0	26.2	13.4	17.1
中间层 medium	326	56.4	9.5	25.8	19.0	18.7
信赖广告指向 loyal orientation	66	59.1	6.1	33.3	22.7	13.6

续前表 continued

	人数 Number	立体声 stereo	有卡拉 OK 功能 karaoke function	售后服务 follow-up service	功能全 all-function	其他 others
样本 Sample	556	7.2	20.9	6.7	22.5	4.3
广告淡漠指向 indifferent orientation	164	4.3	22.0	11.6	23.8	5.5
中间层 medium	326	8.3	21.2	4.9	20.2	4.0
信赖广告指向 loyal orientation	66	9.1	16.7	3.0	30.3	3.0

6-9-3 价格态度指标/ Price Attitude Index

注：本题为多选题，合计百分比超过 100%（Multiple answers）

	人数 Number	品牌形象 brand image	外型 outlook	价格 price	画质好 clarity	多制式 multi-system
样本 Sample	560	53.9	9.6	26.4	17.7	17.5
价格无关心指向 indifferent orientation	129	51.9	14.0	14.7	16.3	17.1
中间层 medium	274	56.9	7.3	24.8	16.4	19.7
价格重视指向 careful orientation	157	50.3	10.2	38.9	21.0	14.0

续前表 continued

	人数 Number	立体声 stereo	有卡拉 OK 功能 karaoke function	售后服务 follow-up service	功能全 all-functions	其他 others
样本 Sample	560	7.5	21.1	6.4	22.5	4.3
价格无关心指向 indifferent orientation	129	5.4	20.2	8.5	19.4	7.0
中间层 medium	274	10.2	22.3	5.5	25.5	3.6
价格重视指向 careful orientation	157	4.5	19.7	6.4	19.7	3.2

● 上海 / Shanghai

6-1 录放像机的拥有比例/ Proportion of VTR Owners in the Sample

	人数 Number	百分比 Percent
有 yes	479	47.2
没有 no	535	52.8

n=1014

6-2 录放像机的拥有量/ Number of VTR Owned Per Household

	人数 Number	百分比 Percent
1 台 1 set	458	98.1
2 台及以上 2 sets or over	9	1.9

n=467

6-3 理想品牌排名/ Ranking of the Ideal Brands

排名 Brand Ranking	品牌 Brands	人数 Number	百分比 Percent
1	松下/乐声 Panasonic	400	39.9
2	索尼 Sony	84	8.4
3	日立 Hitachi	63	6.3
4	夏普/声宝 Sharp	56	5.6
5	东芝 Toshiba	44	4.4
6	胜利 JVC	23	2.3
7	飞利浦 Philips	14	1.4
8	新科 Shinco	9	0.9
8	三洋 Sanyo	9	0.9
9	爱华 Aiwa	8	0.8
9	高士达/乐金 LG	8	0.8
10	爱多 Idall	7	0.7

n=1002

6-4 对家中现有录放像机(最近购买的一台)的四个方面的描述/ About the VTR Most Recently Purchased

6-4-1 家中现有录放像机的品牌排名/ Ranking of the Currently Owned VTR Brands

排名 Brand Ranking	品牌 Brands	人数 Number	百分比 Percent
1	松下/乐声 Panasonic	205	43.1
2	夏普/声宝 Sharp	53	11.1
3	日立 Hitachi	41	8.6
4	东芝 Toshiba	37	7.8
5	索尼 Sony	27	5.7
6	胜利 JVC	23	4.8
7	爱华 Aiwa	10	2.1
8	富丽 Fuli	9	1.9
9	上海 Shanghai	8	1.7
10	高士达/乐金 LG	7	1.5

n=476

6-4-2 该录放像机的购买时间/ The Time of Purchasing of the Currently Owned VTR

	人数 Number	百分比 Percent
1985 年或以前 1985 or before	19	4.0
1986～1990 年	118	24.8
1991 年	51	10.7
1992 年	52	10.9
1993 年	56	11.8
1994 年	50	10.5
1995 年	45	9.5
1996 年	38	8.0
1997 年	29	6.1
1998 年	18	3.8
1999 年	0	0.0

n=476

6-4-3 录放像机的价格/ The Price of the Currently Owned VTR

	人数 Number	百分比 Percent
1000 元或以下 1000 yuan or below	13	2.7
1001～2000 元 yuan	123	25.8
2001～3000 元 yuan	180	37.8
3001～4000 元 yuan	99	20.8
4001～5000 元 yuan	30	6.3
5000 元以上 over 5000 yuan	8	1.7
完全不知道 don't know	23	4.8

n=476

6-4-4 该录放像机的类型/ The Type of the Currently Owned VTR

	人数 Number	百分比 Percent
普通放像机 play only VTR	123	25.9
卡拉 OK 放像机 play only karaoke VTR	48	10.1
普通录放像机 VTR	224	47.3
卡拉 OK 录放像机 karaoke VTR	77	16.2
其他 others	2	0.4

n=474

6-5 选择不同品牌录放像机时的考虑因素/ Considerations in Choosing from Different Brands

注：本题为多选题，合计百分比超过 100%（Multiple answers）

	人数 Number	品牌形象 brand image	外型 outlook	价格 price	画质好 clarity	多制式 multi-system
样本 Sample	473	55.2	10.1	29.0	27.7	13.5
松下/乐声 Panasonic	204	61.8	8.8	22.5	29.4	15.7
夏普/声宝 Sharp	53	49.1	7.5	30.2	28.3	18.9
日立 Hitachi	40	72.5	10.0	27.5	17.5	12.5
东芝 Toshiba	36	55.6	19.4	27.8	25.0	8.3
索尼 Sony	27	48.1	11.1	37.0	37.0	7.4
胜利 JVC	23	60.9	4.3	26.1	39.1	13.0
爱华 Aiwa	10	10.0	20.0	50.0	0.0	10.0
富丽 Fuli	9	33.3	22.2	55.6	11.1	22.2
上海 Shanghai	8	50.0	0.0	37.5	25.0	25.0
高士达/乐金 LG	7	28.6	14.3	57.1	14.3	0.0

续前表 continued

	人数 Number	立体声 stereo	有卡拉 OK 功能 karaoke function	售后服务 follow-up service	功能全 all-function	其他 others
样本 Sample	473	7.8	18.6	7.6	16.9	2.3
松下/乐声 Panasonic	204	6.4	16.7	6.9	16.7	2.5
夏普/声宝 Sharp	53	5.7	9.4	13.2	20.8	1.9
日立 Hitachi	40	7.5	20.0	7.5	12.5	2.5
东芝 Toshiba	36	2.8	13.9	0.0	27.8	0.0
索尼 Sony	27	3.7	18.5	7.4	14.8	7.4
胜利 JVC	23	4.3	30.4	21.7	13.0	4.3
爱华 Aiwa	10	10.0	30.0	20.0	20.0	0.0
富丽 Fuli	9	11.1	0.0	22.2	11.1	0.0
上海 Shanghai	8	37.5	25.0	0.0	12.5	0.0
高士达/乐金 LG	7	14.3	42.9	0.0	14.3	0.0

6-6 录放像机未来购买打算/ Plan for Future Purchasing of a VTR

6-6-1 有无购买打算/ Whether Planning to Purchase Next Year

	人数 Number	百分比 Percent
是 yes	7	0.7
否 no	1004	99.3

n=1011

6-6-2 打算购买的品牌排名/ The Brand of the Planned Purchase Next Year

排名 Brand Ranking	品牌 Brands	人数 Number	百分比 Percent
1	东芝 Toshiba	1	14.3
1	飞利浦 Philips	1	14.3
1	日立 Hitachi	1	14.3
1	索尼 Sony	1	14.3
1	夏普/声宝 Sharp	1	14.3
1	三菱 Mitsubishi	1	14.3

n=7

6-6-3 打算购买的类型/ The Type of the Planned Purchase Next Year

	人数 Number	百分比 Percent
普通放像机 play only VTR	0	0.0
卡拉 OK 放像机 play only karaoke VTR	1	16.7
普通录放像机 VTR	2	33.3
卡拉 OK 录放像机 karaoke VTR	3	50.0
其他 others	0	0.0

n=6

6-6-4 打算购买的价格/ The Price of the Planned Purchase Next Year

	人数 Number	百分比 Percent
1000 元或以下 1000 yuan or below	0	0.0
1001～2000 元 yuan	1	16.7
2001～3000 元 yuan	3	50.0
3001～4000 元 yuan	0	0.0
4001～5000 元 yuan	1	16.7
5000 元以上 over 5000 yuan	1	16.7
完全不知道 don't know	0	0.0

n=6

6-7 选购录放像机时不同角色的人口特征/ The Demographics of Different Roles in Purchasing a VTR

注：不同角色可以多选（Multiple answers）

	人数 Number	16-24 岁 Age	25-34 岁 Age	35-44 岁 Age	45-54 岁 Age	55-60 岁 Age
样本 Sample	412	22.1	23.8	32.0	16.0	6.1
男性 Male	202	20.3	20.8	34.2	19.8	5.0
提议者 advocate	28	28.6	10.7	35.7	25.0	0.0
影响者 influence	31	22.6	12.9	32.3	25.8	6.5
决定者 decider	95	5.3	22.1	45.3	22.1	5.3
使用者 user	109	25.7	23.9	31.2	16.5	2.8
女性 Female	210	23.8	26.7	30.0	12.4	7.1
提议者 advocate	39	28.2	28.2	25.6	12.8	5.1
影响者 influence	37	18.9	21.6	40.5	13.5	5.4
决定者 decider	51	13.7	23.5	39.2	17.6	5.9
使用者 user	136	25.7	24.3	30.1	11.8	8.1

6-8 不同消费者层的家中目前拥有品牌/ Brands of VTR Owned in Household by Market Segments

6-8-1 时尚流行指标/ Fads Popular Index

	人数 Number	第一品牌及百分比 1st/ percent	第二品牌及百分比 2nd/ percent	第三品牌及百分比 3rd/ percent	第四品牌及百分比 4th/ percent
样本 Sample	471	**松下/乐声 Panasonic(43.1)**	**夏普/声宝 Sharp(11.3)**	**日立 Hitachi(8.5)**	**东芝 Toshiba(7.9)**
平实生活指向 simple living orientation	206	松下/乐声 Panasonic(43.7)	日立 Hitachi(12.1)	夏普/声宝 Sharp(9.2)	东芝 Toshiba(7.8)
时尚流行指向 fashion orientation	265	松下/乐声 Panasonic(42.6)	夏普/声宝 Sharp(12.8)	东芝 Toshiba(7.9)	日立 Hitachi(5.7) 索尼 Sony(5.7)

6-8-2 广告态度指标/ Advertising Attitude Index

	人数 Number	第一品牌及百分比 1st/ percent	第二品牌及百分比 2nd/ percent	第三品牌及百分比 3rd/ percent	第四品牌及百分比 4th/ percent
样本 Sample	470	**松下/乐声 Panasonic(42.6)**	**夏普/声宝 Sharp(11.3)**	**日立 Hitachi(8.7)**	**东芝 Toshiba(7.9)**
广告淡漠指向 indifferent orientation	107	松下/乐声 Panasonic(39.3)	日立 Hitachi(10.3)	夏普/声宝 Sharp(9.3)	索尼 Sony(8.4)
中间层 medium	297	松下/乐声 Panasonic(43.8)	夏普/声宝 Sharp(11.1)	日立 Hitachi(9.1)	东芝 Toshiba(7.1)
信赖广告指向 loyal orientation	66	松下/乐声 Panasonic(42.4)	夏普/声宝 Sharp(15.2)	东芝 Toshiba(13.6)	日立 Hitachi(4.5) 胜利 JVC(4.5) 索尼 Sony(4.5)

6-8-3 价格态度指标/ Price Attitude Index

	人数 Number	第一品牌及百分比 1st/ percent	第二品牌及百分比 2nd/ percent	第三品牌及百分比 3rd/ percent	第四品牌及百分比 4th/ percent
样本 Sample	475	**松下/乐声 Panasonic(43.2)**	**夏普/声宝 Sharp(11.2)**	**日立 Hitachi(8.4)**	**东芝 Toshiba(7.8)**
价格无关心指向 indifferent orientation	67	松下/乐声 Panasonic(41.8)	夏普/声宝 Sharp(9.0)	日立 Hitachi(7.5)	东芝 Toshiba(4.5) 三星 Samsung(4.5) 胜利 JVC(4.5) 索尼 Sony(4.5)
中间层 medium	262	松下/乐声 Panasonic(42.7)	夏普/声宝 Sharp(11.8)	日立 Hitachi(8.4)	东芝 Toshiba(7.6)
价格重视指向 careful orientation	146	松下/乐声 Panasonic(44.5)	夏普/声宝 Sharp(11.0)	东芝 Toshiba(9.6)	日立 Hitachi(8.9)

6-9 不同消费者层选择录放像机时考虑因素/ Considerations in Choosing from Different Brands by Market Segments

6-9-1 时尚流行指标/ Fads Popular Index

注：本题为多选题，合计百分比超过 100%（Multiple answers）

	人数 Number	品牌形象 brand image	外型 outlook	价格 price	画质好 clarity	多制式 multi-system
样本 Sample	471	55.4	10.2	29.1	27.4	13.2
平实生活指向 simple living orientation	207	60.4	9.2	30.0	21.3	10.6
时尚流行指向 fashion orientation	264	51.5	11.0	28.4	32.2	15.2

续前表 continued

	人数 Number	立体声 stereo	有卡拉 OK 功能 karaole function	售后服务 follow-up service	功能全 all-function	其他 others
样本 Sample	471	7.9	18.7	7.6	17.0	2.3
平实生活指向 simple living orientation	207	6.3	17.9	6.3	14.0	1.9
时尚流行指向 fashion orientation	264	9.1	19.3	3.7	19.3	2.7

6-9-2 广告态度指标/ Advertising Attitude Index

注：本题为多选题，合计百分比超过 100%（Multiple answers）

	人数 Number	品牌形象 brand image	外型 outlook	价格 price	画质好 clarity	多制式 multi-system
样本 Sample	470	55.5	9.8	28.9	27.4	13.4
广告淡漠指向 indifferent orientation	108	57.4	10.2	25.9	21.3	13.0
中间层 medium	297	55.6	10.1	29.0	24.6	12.5
信赖广告指向 loyal orientation	65	52.3	7.7	33.8	50.8	18.5

续前表 continued

	人数 Number	立体声 stereo	有卡拉 OK 功能 karaole function	售后服务 follow-up service	功能全 all-function	其他 others
样本 Sample	470	7.7	18.7	7.4	17.0	2.3
广告淡漠指向 indifferent orientation	108	10.2	19.4	5.5	16.7	1.9
中间层 medium	297	6.7	18.5	7.4	16.2	3.0
信赖广告指向 loyal orientation	65	7.7	18.5	10.8	21.5	0.0

6-9-3 价格态度指标/ Price Attitude Index

注：本题为多选题，合计百分比超过 100%（Multiple answers）

	人数 Number	品牌形象 brand image	外型 outlook	价格 price	画质好 clarity	多制式 multi-system
样本 Sample	475	55.2	10.1	29.1	27.6	13.5
价格无关心指向 indifferent orientation	69	62.3	13.0	23.2	27.5	13.0
中间层 medium	259	53.7	10.8	28.2	28.6	15.8
价格重视指向 careful orientation	147	54.4	7.5	33.3	25.9	9.5

续前表 continued

	人数 Number	立体声 stereo	有卡拉 OK 功能 karaole function	售后服务 follow-up service	功能全 all-function	其他 others
样本 Sample	475	7.8	18.7	7.6	16.8	2.3
价格无关心指向 indifferent orientation	69	8.7	11.6	4.3	13.0	2.9
中间层 medium	259	8.5	18.1	8.5	18.1	2.3
价格重视指向 careful orientation	147	6.1	23.1	7.5	16.3	2.0

● 广州 / Guangzhou

6-1 录放像机的拥有比例/ Proportion of VTR Owners in the Sample

	人数 Number	百分比 Percent
有 yes	348	33.7
没有 no	686	66.3

n=1034

6-2 录放像机的拥有量/ Number of VTR Owned Per Household

	人数 Number	百分比 Percent
1 台 1 set	326	96.4
2 台及以上 2 sets or over	12	3.6

n=338

6-3 理想品牌排名/ Ranking of the Ideal Brands

排名 Brand Ranking	品牌 Brands	人数 Number	百分比 Percent
1	松下/乐声 Panasonic	154	14.9
2	索尼 Sony	98	9.5
3	日立 Hitachi	38	3.7
4	东芝 Toshiba	27	2.6
5	夏普/声宝 Sharp	13	1.3
6	爱华 Aiwa	11	1.1
7	先锋 Pioneer	11	1.1
8	三星 Samsung	9	0.9
8	胜利 JVC	9	0.9
9	王牌 TCL	6	0.6

n=1032

6-4 对家中现有录放像机(最近购买的一台)的四个方面的描述/ About the VTR Most Recently Purchased

6-4-1 家中现有录放像机的品牌排名/ Ranking of the Currently Owned VTR Brands

排名 Brand Ranking	品牌 Brands	人数 Number	百分比 Percent
1	松下/乐声 Panasonic	103	29.8
2	日立 Hitachi	42	12.1
3	索尼 Sony	36	10.4
4	东芝 Toshiba	27	7.8
5	夏普/声宝 Sharp	14	4.0
6	先锋 Pioneer	11	3.2
7	富丽 Fuli	9	2.6
8	爱华 Aiwa	7	2.0

n=346

6-4-2 该录放像机的购买时间/ The Time of Purchasing of the Currently Owned VTR

	人数 Number	百分比 Percent
1985 年或以前 1985 or before	12	3.5
1986～1990 年	90	26.2
1991 年	36	10.5
1992 年	26	7.6
1993 年	34	9.9
1994 年	33	9.6
1995 年	30	8.7
1996 年	31	9.0
1997 年	27	7.8
1998 年	20	5.8
1999 年	5	1.5

n=344

6-4-3 录放像机的价格/ The Price of the Currently Owned VTR

	人数 Number	百分比 Percent
1000 元或以下 1000 yuan or below	43	12.4
1001～2000 元 yuan	106	30.6
2001～3000 元 yuan	88	25.4
3001～4000 元 yuan	55	15.9
4001～5000 元 yuan	20	5.8
5000 元以上 over 5000 yuan	8	2.3
完全不知道 don't know	26	7.5

n=346

6-4-4 该录放像机的类型/ The Type of the Currently Owned VTR

	人数 Number	百分比 Percent
普通放像机 play only VTR	108	31.0
卡拉 OK 放像机 play only karaoke VTR	74	21.3
普通录放像机 VTR	111	31.9
卡拉 OK 录放像机 karaoke VTR	54	15.5
其他 others	1	0.3

n=348

6-5 选择不同品牌录放像机时的考虑因素/ Considerations in Choosing from Different Brands

注：本题为多选题，合计百分比超过 100%（Multiple answers）

	人数 Number	品牌形象 brand image	外型 outlook	价格 price	画质好 clarity	多制式 multi-system
样本 Sample	**345**	**38.3**	**10.7**	**36.5**	**31.9**	**13.6**
松下/乐声 Panasonic	103	51.5	10.7	33.0	35.0	14.6
日立 Hitachi	42	35.7	11.9	33.3	23.8	11.9
索尼 Sony	36	36.1	8.3	19.4	52.8	16.7
东芝 Toshiba	27	40.7	7.4	44.4	40.7	7.4
夏普/声宝 Sharp	14	50.0	7.1	28.6	42.9	35.7
先锋 Pioneer	11	45.5	18.2	36.4	0.0	9.1
富丽 Fuli	9	11.1	22.2	77.8	11.1	0.0
爱华 Aiwa	7	42.9	0.0	42.9	42.9	14.3

续前表 continued

	人数 Number	立体声 stereo	有卡拉 OK 功能 karaoke function	售后服务 follow-up service	功能全 all-function	其他 others
样本 Sample	**345**	**10.7**	**20.6**	**5.4**	**24.1**	**2.6**
松下/乐声 Panasonic	103	8.7	19.4	6.8	18.4	1.9
日立 Hitachi	42	9.5	11.9	11.9	23.8	2.4
索尼 Sony	36	27.8	38.9	2.8	25.0	0.0
东芝 Toshiba	27	3.7	7.4	3.7	18.5	7.4
夏普/声宝 Sharp	14	7.1	7.1	7.1	42.9	0.0
先锋 Pioneer	11	18.2	27.3	0.0	54.5	0.0
富丽 Fuli	9	0.0	11.1	0.0	0.0	0.0
爱华 Aiwa	7	0.0	14.3	14.3	42.9	0.0

6-6 录放像机未来购买打算/ Plan for Future Purchasing of a VTR

6-6-1 有无购买打算/ Whether Planning to Purchase Next Year

	人数 Number	百分比 Percent
是 yes	17	1.7
否 no	1012	98.3

n=1029

6-6-2 打算购买的品牌排名/ The Brand of the Planned Purchase Next Year

排名 Brand Ranking	品牌 Brands	人数 Number	百分比 Percent
1	东芝 Toshiba	2	11.8
1	王牌 TCL	2	11.8
2	步步高 BBK	1	5.9
2	宏图 Hongtu	1	5.9
2	山水 Sansui	1	5.9
2	索尼 Sony	1	5.9
2	夏普/声宝 Sharp	1	5.9
2	日立 Hitachi	1	5.9
2	Roly	1	5.9

n=17

6-6-3 打算购买的类型/ The Type of the Planned Purchase Next Year

	人数 Number	百分比 Percent
普通放像机 play only VTR	2	12.5
卡拉 OK 放像机 play only karaoke VTR	7	43.8
普通录放像机 VTR	0	0.0
卡拉 OK 录放像机 karaoke VTR	7	43.8
其他 others	0	0.0

n=16

6-6-4 打算购买的价格/ The Price of the Planned Purchase Next Year

	人数 Number	百分比 Percent
1000 元或以下 1000 yuan or below	3	17.6
1001～2000 元 yuan	7	41.2
2001～3000 元 yuan	3	17.6
3001～4000 元 yuan	2	11.8
4001～5000 元 yuan	2	11.8
5000 元以上 over 5000 yuan	0	0.0
完全不知道 don't know	0	0.0

n=17

6-7 选购录放像机时不同角色的人口特征/ Demographics of the Different Roles in Purchasing a VTR

注：不同角色可以多选（Multiple answers）

	人数 Number	16-24 岁 Age	25-34 岁 Age	35-44 岁 Age	45-54 岁 Age	55-60 岁 Age
样本 Sample	298	20.8	24.8	30.2	17.8	6.4
男性 Male	146	19.9	27.4	26.0	17.1	9.6
提议者 advocate	23	8.7	47.8	21.7	13.0	8.7
影响者 influence	20	35.0	20.0	20.0	20.0	5.0
决定者 decider	63	4.8	25.4	34.9	27.0	7.9
使用者 user	79	25.3	29.1	26.6	10.1	8.9
女性 Female	152	21.7	22.4	34.2	18.4	3.3
提议者 advocate	27	14.8	33.3	22.2	22.2	7.4
影响者 influence	19	15.8	5.3	52.6	26.3	0.0
决定者 decider	35	11.4	22.9	37.1	22.9	5.7
使用者 user	102	23.5	18.6	37.3	17.6	2.9

6-8 不同消费者层的家中目前拥有品牌/ Brands of VTR Owned in Household by Market Segments

6-8-1 时尚流行指标/ Fads Popular Index

	人数 Number	第一品牌及百分比 1st/ percent	第二品牌及百分比 2nd/ percent	第三品牌及百分比 3rd/ percent	第四品牌及百分比 4th/ percent
样本 Sample	342	**松下/乐声 Panasonic(29.8)**	**日立 Hitachi(12.3)**	**索尼 Sony(10.5)**	**东芝 Toshiba(7.6)**
平实生活指向 simple living orientation	175	松下/乐声 Panasonic(29.1)	日立 Hitachi(10.9)	索尼 Sony(9.7)	东芝 Toshiba(7.4)
时尚流行指向 fashion orientation	167	松下/乐声 Panasonic(30.5)	日立 Hitachi(13.8)	索尼 Sony(11.4)	东芝 Toshiba(7.8)

6-8-2 广告态度指标/ Advertising Attitude Index

	人数 Number	第一品牌及百分比 1st/ percent	第二品牌及百分比 2nd/ percent	第三品牌及百分比 3rd/ percent	第四品牌及百分比 4th/ percent
样本 Sample	339	**松下/乐声 Panasonic(30.1)**	**日立 Hitachi(12.4)**	**索尼 Sony(10.6)**	**东芝 Toshiba(7.7)**
广告淡漠指向 indifferent orientation	112	松下/乐声 Panasonic(28.6)	日立 Hitachi(10.7)	索尼 Sony(7.1)	夏普/声宝 Sharp(6.3) 东芝 Toshiba(6.3)
中间层 medium	199	松下/乐声 Panasonic(30.2)	日立 Hitachi(13.1) 索尼 Sony(13.1)	东芝 Toshiba(8.5)	先锋 Pioneer(4.0)
信赖广告指向 loyal orientation	28	松下/乐声 Panasonic(35.7)	日立 Hitachi(14.3)	东芝 Toshiba(7.1) 索尼 Sony(7.1)	奇星 Qixing(3.6) KONES(3.6) 先锋 Pioneer(3.6) 华乐 Huale(3.6) 康佳 Konka(3.6) 三菱 Mitsubishi(3.6)

6-8-3 价格态度指标/ Price Attitude Index

	人数 Number	第一品牌及百分比 1st/ percent	第二品牌及百分比 2nd/ percent	第三品牌及百分比 3rd/ percent	第四品牌及百分比 4th/ percent
样本 Sample	345	**松下/乐声 Panasonic(29.9)**	**日立 Hitachi(12.2)**	**索尼 Sony(10.1)**	**东芝 Toshiba(7.8)**
价格无关心指向 indifferent orientation	58	松下/乐声 Panasonic(25.9)	日立 Hitachi(19.0) 索尼 Sony(19.0)	东芝 Toshiba(8.6)	夏普/声宝 Sharp(5.2)
中间层 medium	176	松下/乐声 Panasonic(33.0)	日立 Hitachi(9.1)	东芝 Toshiba(6.3) 索尼 Sony(6.3)	先锋 Pioneer(4.5) 夏普/声宝 Sharp(4.5)
价格重视指向 careful orientation	111	松下/乐声 Panasonic(27.0)	日立 Hitachi(13.5)	索尼 Sony(11.7)	东芝 Toshiba(9.9)

6-9 不同消费者层选择录放像机时的考虑因素/ Considerations in Choosing from Different Brands by Market Segments

6-9-1 时尚流行指标/ Fads Popular Index

注：本题为多选题，合计百分比超过 100%（Multiple answers）

	人数 Number	品牌形象 brand image	外型 outlook	价格 price	画质好 clarity	多制式 multi-system
样本 Sample	343	39.1	10.5	36.7	31.8	13.7
平实生活指向 simple living orientation	175	33.1	9.7	41.7	32.0	12.6
时尚流行指向 fashion orientation	168	45.2	11.3	31.5	31.5	14.9

续前表 continued

	人数 Number	立体声 stereo	有卡拉 OK 功能 karaoke function	售后服务 follow-up service	功能全 all-function	其他 others
样本 Sample	343	10.8	20.4	6.1	23.9	2.3
平实生活指向 simple living orientation	175	9.1	19.4	4.6	25.1	3.4
时尚流行指向 fashion orientation	168	12.5	21.4	7.7	22.6	1.2

6-9-2 广告态度指标/ Advertising Attitude Index

注：本题为多选题，合计百分比超过 100%（Multiple answers）

	人数 Number	品牌形象 brand image	外型 outlook	价格 price	画质好 clarity	多制式 multi-system
样本 Sample	341	38.4	10.9	36.7	32.0	13.2
广告淡漠指向 indifferent orientation	112	31.3	11.6	46.4	36.6	15.2
中间层 medium	200	40.0	10.5	34.5	32.0	12.5
信赖广告指向 loyal orientation	29	55.2	10.3	13.8	13.8	10.3

续前表 continued

	人数 Number	立体声 stereo	有卡拉 OK 功能 karaoke function	售后服务 follow-up service	功能全 all-function	其他 others
样本 Sample	341	11.1	19.9	5.9	24.0	2.6
广告淡漠指向 indifferent orientation	112	13.4	17.9	3.6	18.8	5.4
中间层 medium	200	9.0	20.5	6.5	27.0	1.5
信赖广告指向 loyal orientation	29	17.2	24.1	10.3	24.1	0.0

6-9-3 价格态度指标/ Price Attitude Index

注：本题为多选题，合计百分比超过 100%（Multiple answers）

	人数 Number	品牌形象 brand image	外型 outlook	价格 price	画质好 clarity	多制式 multi-system
样本 Sample	346	38.7	10.7	36.4	31.5	13.9
价格无关心指向 indifferent orientation	60	41.7	6.7	25.0	33.3	16.7
中间层 medium	176	40.9	8.5	38.6	28.4	13.1
价格重视指向 careful orientation	110	33.6	16.4	39.1	35.5	13.6

续前表 continued

	人数 Number	立体声 stereo	有卡拉 OK 功能 karaoke function	售后服务 follow-up service	功能全 all-function	其他 others
样本 Sample	346	11.0	20.2	6.4	24.0	2.6
价格无关心指向 indifferent orientation	60	15.0	21.7	8.3	28.3	0.0
中间层 medium	176	10.2	22.2	8.5	23.3	2.8
价格重视指向 careful orientation	110	10.0	16.4	1.8	22.7	3.6

● 重庆 / Chongqing

6-1 录放像机的拥有比例/ Proportion of VTR Owners in the Sample

	人数 Number	百分比 Percent
有 yes	140	22.4
没有 no	484	77.6

n=624

6-2 录放像机的拥有量/ Number of VTR Owned Per Household

	人数 Number	百分比 Percent
1 台 1 set	132	95.7
2 台及以上 2 sets or over	6	4.3

n=138

6-3 理想品牌排名/ Ranking of the Ideal Brands

排名 Brand Ranking	品牌 Brands	人数 Number	百分比 Percent
1	松下/乐声 Panasonic	92	14.7
2	索尼 Sony	39	6.3
3	日立 Hitachi	22	3.5
4	新科 Shinco	16	2.6
5	东芝 Toshiba	7	1.1
6	三星 Samsung	6	1.0
7	夏普/声宝 Sharp	5	0.8
7	厦新 Amoisonic	5	0.8
7	步步高 BBK	5	0.8

n=624

6-4 对家中现有录放像机(最近购买的一台)的四个方面的描述/ About the VTR Most Recently Purchased

6-4-1 家中现有录放像机的品牌排名/ Ranking of the Currently Owned VTR Brands

排名 Brand Ranking	品牌 Brands	人数 Number	百分比 Percent
1	松下/乐声 Panasonic	30	21.7
2	日立 Hitashi	13	9.4
3	索尼 Sony	9	6.5
3	东芝 Toshiba	9	6.5
4	夏普/声宝 Sharp	6	4.3
5	富丽 Fuli	5	3.6
6	步步高 BBK	4	2.9
6	爱华 Aiwa	4	2.9
6	长虹 Changhong	4	2.9
6	胜利 JVC	4	2.9

n=138

6-4-2 该录放像机的购买时间/ The Time of Purchasing of the Currently Owned VTR

	人数 Number	百分比 Percent
1985 年或以前 1985 or before	4	2.9
1986～1990 年	23	16.5
1991 年	7	5.0
1992 年	5	3.6
1993 年	14	10.1
1994 年	20	14.4
1995 年	14	10.1
1996 年	9	6.5
1997 年	17	12.2
1998 年	21	15.1
1999 年	5	3.6

n=139

6-4-3 录放像机的价格/ The Price of the Currently Owned VTR

	人数 Number	百分比 Percent
1000 元或以下 1000 yuan or below	17	12.1
1001～2000 元 yuan	49	35.0
2001～3000 元 yuan	29	20.7
3001～4000 元 yuan	32	22.9
4001～5000 元 yuan	4	2.9
5000 元以上 over 5000 yuan	4	2.9
完全不知道 don't know	5	3.6

n=140

6-4-4 该录放像机的类型/ The Type of the Currently Owned VTR

	人数 Number	百分比 Percent
普通放像机 play only VTR	42	30.2
卡拉 OK 放像机 play only karaoke VTR	38	27.3
普通录放像机 VTR	25	18.0
卡拉 OK 录放像机 karaoke VTR	34	24.5
其他 others	0	0.0

n=139

6-5 选择不同品牌录放像机时的考虑因素/ Considerations in Choosing from Different Brands

注：本题为多选题，合计百分比超过 100%（Multiple answers）

	人数 Number	品牌形象 brand image	外型 outlook	价格 price	画质好 clarity	多制式 multi-system
样本 Sample	136	44.1	11.0	27.9	20.6	10.3
松下/乐声 Panasonic	30	73.3	20.0	23.3	26.7	3.3
日立 Hitachi	13	69.2	0.0	23.1	15.4	15.4
索尼 Sony	9	44.4	0.0	11.1	0.0	11.1
东芝 Toshiba	9	55.6	11.1	22.2	0.0	0.0
夏普/声宝 Sharp	6	50.0	16.7	50.0	50.0	33.3
富丽 Fuli	5	20.0	0.0	60.0	20.0	40.0

续前表 continued

	人数 Number	立体声 stereo	有卡拉 OK 功能 karaoke function	售后服务 follow-up service	功能全 all-function	其他 others
样本 Sample	136	13.2	27.9	6.6	22.8	2.9
松下/乐声 Panasonic	30	10.0	20.0	6.7	20.0	0.0
日立 Hitachi	13	0.0	23.1	7.7	38.5	7.7
索尼 Sony	9	33.3	33.3	11.1	33.3	0.0
东芝 Toshiba	9	0.0	33.3	0.0	22.2	0.0
夏普/声宝 Sharp	6	0.0	0.0	0.0	16.7	0.0
富丽 Fuli	5	20.0	0.0	0.0	40.0	0.0

6-6 录放像机未来购买打算/ Plan for Future Purchasing of a VTR

6-6-1 有无购买打算/ Whether Planning to Purchase Next Year

	人数 Number	百分比 Percent
是 yes	12	1.9
否 no	612	98.1

n=624

6-6-2 打算购买的品牌排名/ The Brand of the Planned Purchase Next Year

排名 Brand Ranking	品牌 Brands	人数 Number	百分比 Percent
1	新科 Shinco	3	25.0

n=12

6-6-3 打算购买的类型/ The Type of the Planned Purchase Next Year

	人数 Number	百分比 Percent
普通放像机 play only VTR	0	0.0
卡拉 OK 放像机 play only karaoke VTR	4	33.3
普通录放像机 VTR	4	33.3
卡拉 OK 录放像机 karaoke VTR	4	33.3
其他 others	0	0.0

n=12

6-6-4 打算购买的价格/ The Price of the Planned Purchase Next Year

	人数 Number	百分比 Percent
1000 元或以下 1000 yuan or below	0	0.0
1001～2000 元 yuan	3	25.0
2001～3000 元 yuan	4	33.3
3001～4000 元 yuan	1	8.3
4001～5000 元 yuan	2	16.7
5000 元以上 over 5000 yuan	1	8.3
完全不知道 don't know	1	8.3

n=12

6-7 选购录放像机时不同角色的人口特征/ Demographics of the Different Roles in Purchasing a VTR

注：不同角色可以多选（Multiple answers）

	人数 Number	16-24 岁 Age	25-34 岁 Age	35-44 岁 Age	45-54 岁 Age	55-60 岁 Age
样本 Sample	122	23.8	30.3	19.7	18.0	8.2
男性 Male	67	20.9	31.3	17.9	19.4	10.4
提议者 advocate	13	15.4	46.2	23.1	0.0	15.4
影响者 influence	7	14.3	42.9	28.6	0.0	14.3
决定者 decider	28	3.6	28.6	28.6	28.6	10.7
使用者 user	45	28.9	35.6	11.1	15.6	8.9
女性 Female	55	27.3	29.1	21.8	16.4	5.5
提议者 advocate	11	18.2	45.5	9.1	18.2	9.1
影响者 influence	12	25.0	33.3	16.7	16.7	8.3
决定者 decider	15	6.7	33.3	26.7	33.3	0.0
使用者 user	39	30.8	25.6	23.1	12.8	7.7

6-8 不同消费者层的家中目前拥有品牌/ Brands of VTR Owned in Household by Market Segments

6-8-1 时尚流行指标/ Fads Popular Index

	人数 Number	第一品牌及百分比 1st/ percent	第二品牌及百分比 2nd/ percent	第三品牌及百分比 3rd/ percent
样本 Sample	136	**松下/乐声 Panasonic(21.3)**	**日立 Hitachi(9.6)**	**索尼 Sony(6.6)** **东芝 Toshiba(6.6)**
平实生活指向 simple living orientation	68	松下/乐声 Panasonic(16.2)	日立 Hitachi(13.2)	东芝 Toshiba(5.9) 胜利 JVC(5.9) 索尼 Sony(5.9) 夏普/声宝 Sharp(5.9)
时尚流行指向 fashion orientation	68	松下/乐声 Panasonic(26.5)	东芝 Toshiba(7.4) 索尼 Sony(7.4)	日立 Hitachi(5.9) 长虹 Changhong(5.9)

6-8-2 广告态度指标/ Advertising Attitude Index

	人数 Number	第一品牌及百分比 1st/ percent	第二品牌及百分比 2nd/ percent	第三品牌及百分比 3rd/ percent
样本 Sample	134	**松下/乐声 Panasonic(20.9)**	**日立 Hitachi(9.7)**	**东芝 Toshiba(6.7)** **索尼 Sony(6.7)**
广告淡漠指向 indifferent orientation	33	日立 Hitachi(15.2) 松下/乐声 Panasonic(15.2)	东芝 Toshiba(12.1)	索尼 Sony(9.1)
中间层 medium	83	松下/乐声 Panasonic(21.7)	夏普/声宝 Sharp(7.2) 日立 Hitachi(7.2)	东芝 Toshiba(4.8) 索尼 Sony(4.8)
信赖广告指向 loyal orientation	18	松下/乐声 Panasonic(27.8)	日立 Hitachi(11.1) 索尼 Sony(11.1)	长虹 Changhong(5.6) 玉兔 Yutu(5.6) 万里通 Wanlitong(5.6) 顶天 Dingtian(5.6) 爱华 Aiwa(5.6) 爱浪 Ailang(5.6) 汤姆逊 Tangmuxun(5.6) 胜利 JVC(5.6) 东芝 Toshiba(5.6)

6-8-3 价格态度指标/ Price Attitude Index

	人数 Number	第一品牌及百分比 1st/ percent	第二品牌及百分比 2nd/ percent	第三品牌及百分比 3rd/ percent
样本 Sample	133	**松下/乐声 Panasonic(21.8)**	**日立 Hitachi(9.8)**	**东芝 Toshiba(6.8)**
价格无关心指向 indifferent orientation	34	松下/乐声 Panasonic(20.6)	东芝 Toshiba(14.7)	索尼 Sony(11.8)
中间层 medium	59	松下/乐声 Panasonic(22.0)	日立 Hitachi(16.9)	东芝 Toshiba(6.8)
价格重视指向 careful orientation	40	松下/乐声 Panasonic(22.5)	富丽 Fuli(7.5)	日立 Hitachi(5.0) 胜利 JVC(5.0) 长虹 Changhong(5.0)

6-9 不同消费者层选择录放像机时考虑因素/ Considerations in Choosing from Different Brands by Market Segments

6-9-1 时尚流行指标/ Fads Popular Index

注：本题为多选题，合计百分比超过 100%（Multiple answers）

	人数 Number	品牌形象 brand image	外型 outlook	价格 price	画质好 clarity	多制式 multi-system
样本 Sample	136	43.4	10.3	27.9	20.6	11.0
平实生活指向 simple living orientation	67	43.3	10.4	29.9	17.9	11.9
时尚流行指向 fashion orientation	69	43.5	10.1	26.1	23.2	10.1

续前表 continued

	人数 Number	立体声 stereo	有卡拉 OK 功能 karaoke function	售后服务 follow-up service	功能全 all-function	其他 others
样本 Sample	136	12.5	28.7	6.6	22.8	2.9
平实生活指向 simple living orientation	67	9.0	26.9	6.0	28.4	4.5
时尚流行指向 fashion orientation	69	15.9	30.4	7.2	17.4	1.4

6-9-2 广告态度指标/ Advertising Attitude Index

注：本题为多选题，合计百分比超过 100%（Multiple answers）

	人数 Number	品牌形象 brand image	外型 outlook	价格 price	画质好 clarity	多制式 multi-system
样本 Sample	134	42.5	10.4	28.4	21.6	11.2
广告淡漠指向 indifferent orientation	33	42.4	3.0	30.3	6.1	12.1
中间层 medium	82	41.5	12.2	29.3	26.8	9.8
信赖广告指向 loyal orientation	19	47.4	15.8	21.1	26.3	15.8

续前表 continued

	人数 Number	立体声 stereo	有卡拉 OK 功能 karaoke function	售后服务 follow-up service	功能全 all-function	其他 others
样本 Sample	134	12.7	29.9	6.7	22.4	3.0
广告淡漠指向 indifferent orientation	33	15.2	33.3	6.1	33.3	3.0
中间层 medium	82	9.8	28.0	6.1	14.6	3.7
信赖广告指向 loyal orientation	19	21.1	31.6	10.5	36.8	0.0

6-9-3 价格态度指标/ Price Attitude Index

注：本题为多选题，合计百分比超过 100%（Multiple answers）

	人数 Number	品牌形象 brand image	外型 outlook	价格 price	画质好 clarity	多制式 multi-system
样本 Sample	133	42.9	10.5	27.8	21.8	10.5
价格无关心指向 indifferent orientation	34	44.1	5.9	29.4	11.8	5.9
中间层 medium	58	50.0	5.2	15.5	22.4	8.6
价格重视指向 careful orientation	41	31.7	22.0	43.9	29.3	17.1

续前表 continued

	人数 Number	立体声 stereo	有卡拉 OK 功能 karaoke function	售后服务 follow-up service	功能全 all-function	其他 others
样本 Sample	133	12.8	28.6	6.8	23.3	3.0
价格无关心指向 indifferent orientation	34	14.7	23.5	8.8	32.4	2.9
中间层 medium	58	13.8	29.3	8.6	27.6	5.2
价格重视指向 careful orientation	41	9.8	31.7	2.4	9.8	0.0

● 武汉 / Wuhan

6-1 录放像机的拥有比例/ Proportion of VTR Owners in the Sample

	人数 Number	百分比 Percent
有 yes	189	29.5
没有 no	452	70.5

n=641

6-2 录放像机的拥有量/ Number of VTR Owned Per Household

	人数 Number	百分比 Percent
1 台 1 set	180	97.8
2 台及以上 2 sets or over	4	2.2

n=184

6-3 理想品牌排名/ Ranking of the Ideal Brands

排名 Brand Ranking	品牌 Brands	人数 Number	百分比 Percent
1	松下/乐声 Panasonic	66	10.3
2	索尼 Sony	19	3.0
2	夏普/声宝 Sharp	19	3.0
3	东芝 Toshiba	15	2.3
4	日立 Hitachi	13	2.0
5	三星 Samsung	9	1.4
6	新科 Shinco	7	1.1
7	富丽 Fuli	5	0.8
8	爱华 Aiwa	4	0.6
8	万利达 Malata	4	0.6

n=640

6-4 对家中现有录放像机(最近购买的一台)的四个方面的描述/ About the VTR Most Recently Purchased

6-4-1 家中现有录放像机的品牌排名/ Ranking of the Currently Owned VTR Brands

排名 Brand Ranking	品牌 Brands	人数 Number	百分比 Percent
1	松下/乐声 Panasonic	48	25.8
2	东芝 Toshiba	21	11.3
3	夏普/声宝 Sharp	15	8.1
4	日立 Hitachi	13	7.0
5	富丽 Fuli	12	6.5
6	三星 Samsung	11	5.9
7	索尼 Sony	4	2.2
7	富士 Fuji	4	2.2
7	爱华 Aiwa	4	2.2

n=186

6-4-2 该录放像机的购买时间/ The Time of Purchasing of the Currently Owned VTR

	人数 Number	百分比 Percent
1985 年或以前 1985 or before	5	2.6
1986～1990 年	49	25.9
1991 年	20	10.6
1992 年	25	13.2
1993 年	25	13.2
1994 年	15	7.9
1995 年	18	9.5
1996 年	11	5.8
1997 年	7	3.7
1998 年	9	4.8
1999 年	5	2.6

n=189

6-4-3 录放像机的价格/ The Price of the Currently Owned VTR

	人数 Number	百分比 Percent
1000 元或以下 1000 yuan or below	10	5.3
1001～2000 元 yuan	80	42.3
2001～3000 元 yuan	65	34.4
3001～4000 元 yuan	20	10.6
4001～5000 元 yuan	2	1.1
5000 元以上 over 5000 yuan	4	2.1
完全不知道 don't know	8	4.2

n=189

6-4-4 该录放像机的类型/ The Type of the Currently Owned VTR

	人数 Number	百分比 Percent
普通放像机 play only VTR	66	35.3
卡拉 OK 放像机 play only karaoke VTR	30	16.0
普通录放像机 VTR	60	32.1
卡拉 OK 录放像机 karaoke VTR	31	16.6
其他 others	0	0.0

n=187

6-5 选择不同品牌录放像机时的考虑因素/ Considerations in Choosing from Different Brands

注：本题为多选题，合计百分比超过 100%（Multiple answers）

	人数 Number	品牌形象 brand image	外型 outlook	价格 price	画质好 clarity	多制式 multi-system
样本 Sample	**186**	**46.2**	**10.8**	**32.3**	**27.4**	**11.8**
松下/乐声 Panosonic	48	52.1	10.4	25.0	29.2	12.5
东芝 Toshiba	21	47.6	0.0	19.0	33.3	4.8
夏普/声宝 Sharp	15	60.0	6.7	33.3	20.0	26.7
日立 Hitashi	13	84.6	7.7	23.1	30.8	7.7
富丽 Fuli	12	25.0	0.0	41.7	25.0	0.0
三星 Samsung	11	45.5	27.3	18.2	18.2	36.4
索尼 Sony	4	50.0	0.0	25.0	50.0	25.0
富士 Fuji	4	25.0	50.0	75.0	25.0	0.0
爱华 Aiwa	4	25.0	50.0	25.0	75.0	0.0

续前表 continued

	人数 Number	立体声 stereo	有卡拉 OK 功能 karaoke function	售后服务 follow-up service	功能全 all-function	其他 others
样本 Sample	**186**	**8.1**	**24.2**	**5.4**	**24.7**	**6.5**
松下/乐声 Panosonic	48	12.5	22.9	6.3	29.2	2.1
东芝 Toshiba	21	9.5	9.5	9.5	19.0	14.3
夏普/声宝 Sharp	15	0.0	40.0	6.7	26.7	6.7
日立 Hitashi	13	15.4	15.4	0.0	23.1	0.0
富丽 Fuli	12	0.0	16.7	8.3	33.3	16.7
三星 Samsung	11	0.0	36.4	9.1	18.2	9.1
索尼 Sony	4	0.0	50.0	0.0	25.0	25.0
富士 Fuji	4	0.0	0.0	0.0	25.0	0.0
爱华 Aiwa	4	0.0	50.0	0.0	0.0	0.0

6-6 录放像机未来购买打算/ Plan for Future Purchasing of a VTR

6-6-1 有无购买打算/ Whether Planning to Purchase Next Year

	人数 Number	百分比 Percent
是 yes	7	1.1
否 no	631	98.9

n=638

6-6-2 打算购买的品牌排名/ The Brand of the Planned Purchase Next Year

排名 Brand Ranking	品牌 Brands	人数 Number	百分比 Percent
1	松下/乐声 Panasonic	1	16.7
1	索尼 Sony	1	16.7
1	厦华 Xoceco	1	16.7
1	先锋 Pioneer	1	16.7
1	万利达 Malata	1	16.7

n=6

6-6-3 打算购买的类型/ The Type of the Planned Purchase Next Year

	人数 Number	百分比 Percent
普通放像机 play only VTR	1	16.7
卡拉 OK 放像机 play only karaoke VTR	0	0.0
普通录放像机 VTR	1	16.7
卡拉 OK 录放像机 karaoke VTR	4	66.7
其他 others	0	0.0

n=6

6-6-4 打算购买的价格/ The Price of the Planned Purchase Next Year

	人数 Number	百分比 Percent
1000 元或以下 1000 yuan or below	1	14.3
1001～2000 元 yuan	3	42.9
2001～3000 元 yuan	1	14.3
3001～4000 元 yuan	1	14.3
4001～5000 元 yuan	0	0.0
5000 元以上 over 5000 yuan	1	14.3
完全不知道 don't know	0	0.0

n=7

6-7 选购录放像机时不同角色的人口特征/ Demographics of the Different Roles in Purchasing a VTR

注：不同角色可以多选（Multiple answers）

	人数 Number	16-24 岁 Age	25-34 岁 Age	35-44 岁 Age	45-54 岁 Age	55-60 岁 Age
样本 Sample	**165**	**24.2**	**33.9**	**26.1**	**13.3**	**2.4**
男性 Male	**77**	**26.0**	**29.9**	**26.0**	**15.6**	**2.6**
提议者 advocate	16	18.8	18.8	43.8	18.8	0.0
影响者 influence	12	41.7	25.0	25.0	8.3	0.0
决定者 decider	36	11.1	33.3	33.3	22.2	0.0
使用者 user	53	26.4	26.4	28.3	15.1	3.8
女性 Female	**88**	**22.7**	**37.5**	**26.1**	**11.4**	**2.3**
提议者 advocate	20	25.0	20.0	45.0	10.0	0.0
影响者 influence	13	15.4	30.8	23.1	23.1	7.7
决定者 decider	26	7.7	34.6	34.6	19.2	3.8
使用者 user	65	21.5	36.9	30.8	9.2	1.5

6-8 不同消费者层的家中目前拥有品牌/ Brands of VTR Owned in Household by Market Segments

6-8-1 时尚流行指标/ Fads Popular Index

	人数 Number	第一品牌及百分比 1st/ percent	第二品牌及百分比 2nd/ percent	第三品牌及百分比 3rd/ percent
样本 Sample	**184**	**松下/乐声 Panasonic(26.1)**	**东芝 Toshiba(11.4)**	**夏普/声宝 Sharp(8.2)**
平实生活指向 simple living orientation	77	松下/乐声 Panasonic(24.7)	东芝 Toshiba(11.7)	夏普/声宝 Sharp(9.1)
时尚流行指向 fashion orientation	107	松下/乐声 Panasonic(27.1)	东芝 Toshiba(11.2)	三星 Samsung(7.5) 夏普/声宝 Sharp(7.5)

6-8-2 广告态度指标/ Advertising Attitude Index

	人数 Number	第一品牌及百分比 1st/ percent	第二品牌及百分比 2nd/ percent	第三品牌及百分比 3rd/ percent
样本 Sample	**185**	**松下/乐声 Panasonic(25.9)**	**东芝 Toshiba(11.4)**	**夏普/声宝 Sharp(8.1)**
广告淡漠指向 indifferent orientation	50	松下/乐声 Panasonic(32.0)	东芝 Toshiba(10.0)	日立 Hitachi(6.0) 三星 Samsung(6.0) 万利达 Malata(6.0)
中间层 medium	112	松下/乐声 Panasonic(23.2)	夏普/声宝 Sharp(11.6)	东芝 Toshiba(10.7)
信赖广告指向 loyal orientation	23	松下/乐声 Panasonic(26.1)	东芝 Toshiba(17.4)	日立 Hitachi(8.7)

6-8-3 价格态度指标/ Price Attitude Index

	人数 Number	第一品牌及百分比 1st/ percent	第二品牌及百分比 2nd/ percent	第三品牌及百分比 3rd/ percent
样本 Sample	**184**	**松下/乐声 Panasonic(26.1)**	**东芝 Toshiba(11.4)**	**夏普/声宝 Sharp(8.2)**
价格无关心指向 indifferent orientation	28	松下/乐声 Panasonic(21.4)	东芝 Toshiba(14.3) 三星 Samsung(14.3)	日立 Hitachi(7.1)
中间层 medium	94	松下/乐声 Panasonic(23.4)	东芝 Toshiba(13.8)	夏普/声宝 Sharp(11.7)
价格重视指向 careful orientation	62	松下/乐声 Panasonic(32.3)	东芝 Toshiba(6.5) 日立 Hitachi(6.5)	三星 Samsung(4.8) 夏普/声宝 Sharp(4.8) 飞利浦 Philips(4.8)

6-9 不同消费者层选择录放像机时的考虑因素/ Considerations in Choosing from Different Brands by Market Segments

6-9-1 时尚流行指标/ Fads Popular Index

注：本题为多选题，合计百分比超过 100%（Multiple answers）

	人数 Number	品牌形象 brand image	外型 outlook	价格 price	画质好 clarity	多制式 multi-system
样本 Sample	187	47.1	10.7	33.2	27.3	11.8
平实生活指向 simple living orientation	79	48.1	10.1	31.6	30.4	7.6
时尚流行指向 fashion orientation	108	46.3	11.1	34.3	25.0	14.8

续前表 continued

	人数 Number	立体声 stereo	有卡拉 OK 功能 karaoke function	售后服务 follow-up service	功能全 all-function	其他 others
样本 Sample	187	8.0	25.1	5.3	24.1	5.9
平实生活指向 simple living orientation	79	3.8	24.1	6.3	21.5	7.6
时尚流行指向 fashion orientation	108	11.1	25.9	4.6	25.9	4.6

6-9-2 广告态度指标/ Advertising Attitude Index

注：本题为多选题，合计百分比超过 100%（Multiple answers）

	人数 Number	品牌形象 brand image	外型 outlook	价格 price	画质好 clarity	多制式 multi-system
样本 Sample	188	46.8	10.6	33.0	27.1	11.7
广告淡漠指向 indifferent orientation	50	40.0	8.0	38.0	20.0	14.0
中间层 medium	114	47.4	13.2	34.2	28.1	13.2
信赖广告指向 loyal orientation	24	58.3	4.2	16.7	37.5	0.0

续前表 continued

	人数 Number	立体声 stereo	有卡拉 OK 功能 karaoke function	售后服务 follow-up service	功能全 all-function	其他 others
样本 Sample	188	8.0	25.0	5.3	24.5	5.9
广告淡漠指向 indifferent orientation	50	8.0	22.0	4.0	24.0	6.0
中间层 medium	114	7.9	26.3	6.1	26.3	4.4
信赖广告指向 loyal orientation	24	8.3	25.0	4.2	16.7	12.5

6-9-3 价格态度指标/ Price Attitude Index

注：本题为多选题，合计百分比超过 100%（Multiple answers）

	人数 Number	品牌形象 brand image	外型 outlook	价格 price	画质好 clarity	多制式 multi-system
样本 Sample	187	46.5	10.7	32.6	26.7	11.8
价格无关心指向 indifferent orientation	28	50.0	7.1	25.0	21.4	21.4
中间层 medium	94	47.9	11.7	25.5	30.9	11.7
价格重视指向 careful orientation	65	43.1	10.8	46.2	23.1	7.7

续前表 continued

	人数 Number	立体声 stereo	有卡拉 OK 功能 karaoke function	售后服务 follow-up service	功能全 all-function	其他 others
样本 Sample	187	8.0	25.1	5.3	24.6	5.9
价格无关心指向 indifferent orientation	28	0.0	17.9	3.6	35.7	3.6
中间层 medium	94	10.6	28.7	7.4	23.4	7.4
价格重视指向 careful orientation	65	7.7	23.1	3.1	21.5	4.6

● 西安 / Xi'an

6-1 录放像机的拥有比例/ Proportion of VTR Owners in the Sample

	人数 Number	百分比 Percent
有 yes	167	27.8
没有 no	433	72.2

n=600

6-2 录放像机的拥有量/ Number of VTR Owned Per Household

	人数 Number	百分比 Percent
1 台 1 set	164	98.2
2 台及以上 2 sets or over	3	1.8

n=167

6-3 理想品牌排名/ Ranking of the Ideal Brands

排名 Brand Ranking	品牌 Brands	人数 Number	百分比 Percent
1	松下/乐声 Panasonic	140	23.5
2	索尼 Sony	28	4.7
3	日立 Hitachi	19	3.2
4	东芝 Toshiba	12	2.0
5	夏普/声宝 Sharp	11	1.8
6	步步高 BBK	10	1.7
6	新科 Shinco	10	1.7
7	三星 Samsung	9	1.5
8	爱多 Idall	8	1.3
8	厦新 Amoisonic	8	1.3
9	三洋 Sanyo	6	1.0
10	先科 SAST	5	0.8

n=595

6-4 对家中现有录放像机(最近购买的一台)的四个方面的描述/ About the VTR Most Recently Purchased

6-4-1 家中现有录放像机的品牌排名/ Ranking of the Currently Owned VTR Brands

排名 Brand Ranking	品牌 Brands	人数 Number	百分比 Percent
1	松下/乐声 Panasonic	55	33.7
2	夏普/声宝 Sharp	15	9.2
3	日立 Hitachi	14	8.6
4	富丽 Fuli	8	4.9
5	三星 Samsung	6	3.7
6	爱多 Idall	5	3.1
6	东芝 Toshiba	5	3.1
7	三洋 Sanyo	4	2.5
7	索尼 Sony	4	2.5
7	万利达 Malata	4	2.5
8	飞利浦 Philips	3	1.8

n=163

6-4-2 该录放像机的购买时间/ The Time of Purchasing of the Currently Owned VTR

	人数 Number	百分比 Percent
1985 年或以前 1985 or before	5	3.0
1986～1990 年	21	12.6
1991 年	21	12.6
1992 年	22	13.2
1993 年	16	9.6
1994 年	20	12.0
1995 年	23	13.8
1996 年	14	8.4
1997 年	11	6.6
1998 年	10	6.0
1999 年	4	2.4

n=167

6-4-3 录放像机的价格/ The Price of the Currently Owned VTR

	人数 Number	百分比 Percent
1000 元及以下 1000 yuan or below	14	8.4
1001～2000 元 yuan	50	29.9
2001～3000 元 yuan	49	29.3
3001～4000 元 yuan	34	20.4
4001～5000 元 yuan	10	6.0
5000 元以上 over 5000 yuan	1	0.6
完全不知道 don't know	9	5.4

n=167

6-4-4 该录放像机的类型/ The Type of the Currently Owned VTR

	人数 Number	百分比 Percent
普通放像机 play only VTR	43	25.7
卡拉 OK 放像机 play only karaoke VTR	26	15.6
普通录放像机 VTR	39	23.4
卡拉 OK 录放像机 karaoke VTR	58	34.7
其他 others	1	0.6

n=167

6-5 选择不同品牌录放像机时考虑因素/ Considerations in Choosing from Different Brands

注：本题为多选题，合计百分比超过 100%（Multiple answers）

	人数 Number	品牌形象 brand image	外型 outlook	价格 price	画质好 clarity	多制式 multi-system
样本 Sample	163	45.4	10.4	29.4	25.8	10.4
松下/乐声 Panasonic	55	58.2	10.9	27.3	27.3	7.3
夏普/声宝 Sharp	15	40.0	13.3	40.0	26.7	20.0
日立 Hitachi	14	35.7	14.3	7.1	28.6	14.3
富丽 Fuli	8	25.0	0.0	25.0	25.0	12.5
三星 Samsung	6	83.3	16.7	0.0	16.7	16.7

续前表 continued

	人数 Number	立体声 stereo	有卡拉 OK 功能 karaoke function	售后服务 follow-up service	功能全 all-function	其他 others
样本 Sample	163	11.7	27.6	4.9	21.5	2.5
松下/乐声 Panasonic	55	9.1	18.2	7.3	23.6	1.8
夏普/声宝 Sharp	15	0.0	26.7	0.0	26.7	6.7
日立 Hitachi	14	14.3	35.7	0.0	50.0	0.0
富丽 Fuli	8	12.5	75.0	12.5	0.0	0.0
三星 Samsung	6	16.7	66.7	16.7	0.0	0.0

6-6 录放像机未来购买打算/ Plan for Future Purchasing of a VTR

6-6-1 有无购买打算/ Whether Planning to Purchase Next Year

	人数 Number	百分比 Percent
是 yes	6	1.0
否 no	594	99.0

n=600

6-6-2 打算购买的品牌排名/ The Brand of the Planned Purchase Next Year

排名 Brand Ranking	品牌 Brands	人数 Number	百分比 Percent
1	步步高 BBK	2	33.3
2	华录 Hualu	1	16.7
2	厦新 Amoisonic	1	16.7
2	新科 Shinco	1	16.7

n=6

6-6-3 打算购买的类型/ The Type of the Planned Purchase Next Year

	人数 Number	百分比 Percent
普通放像机 play only VTR	1	16.7
卡拉 OK 放像机 play only karaoke VTR	2	33.3
普通录放像机 VTR	0	0.0
卡拉 OK 录放像机 karaoke VTR	3	50.0
其他 others	0	0.0

n=6

6-6-4 打算购买的价格/ The Price of the Planned Purchase Next Year

	人数 Number	百分比 Percent
1000 元及以下 1000 yuan or below	2	33.3
1001～2000 元 yuan	4	66.7
2001～3000 元 yuan	0	0.0
3001～4000 元 yuan	0	0.0
4001～5000 元 yuan	0	0.0
5000 元以上 over 5000 yuan	0	0.0
完全不知道 don't know	0	0.0

n=6

6-7 选购录放像机时不同角色的人口特征/ Demographics of the Different Roles in Purchasing a VTR

注：不同角色可以多选（Multiple answers）

	人数 Number	16-24 岁 Age	25-34 岁 Age	35-44 岁 Age	45-54 岁 Age	55-60 岁 Age
样本 Sample	149	19.5	30.2	28.9	18.1	3.4
男性 Male	78	23.1	24.4	28.2	20.5	3.8
提议者 advocate	10	20.0	0.0	50.0	30.0	0.0
影响者 influence	5	40.0	0.0	40.0	0.0	20.0
决定者 decider	35	2.9	20.0	54.3	20.0	2.9
使用者 user	49	32.7	26.5	24.5	14.3	2.0
女性 Female	71	15.5	36.6	29.6	15.5	2.8
提议者 advocate	15	13.3	66.7	6.7	6.7	6.7
影响者 influence	10	0.0	60.0	30.0	10.0	0.0
决定者 decider	10	10.0	40.0	30.0	20.0	0.0
使用者 user	48	16.7	33.3	31.3	16.7	2.1

6-8 不同消费者层的家中目前拥有品牌/ Brands of VTR Owned in Household by Market Segments

6-8-1 时尚流行指标/ Fads Popular Index

	人数 Number	第一品牌及百分比 1st/ percent	第二品牌及百分比 2nd/ percent	第三品牌及百分比 3rd/ percent	第四品牌及百分比 4th/ percent
样本 Sample	162	**松下/乐声 Panasonic(34.0)**	**夏普/声宝 Sharp(8.6) 日立 Hitachi(8.6)**	**富丽 Fuli(4.9)**	**三星 Samsung(3.7)**
平实生活指向 simple living orientation	89	松下/乐声 Panasonic(29.2)	夏普/声宝 Sharp(9.0)	日立 Hitachi(7.9)	东芝 Toshiba(4.5) 富丽 Fuli(4.5)
时尚流行指向 fashion orientation	73	松下/乐声 Panasonic(39.7)	日立 Hitachi(9.6)	夏普/声宝 Sharp(8.2)	富丽 Fuli(5.5)

6-8-2 广告态度指标/ Advertising Attitude Index

	人数 Number	第一品牌及百分比 1st/ percent	第二品牌及百分比 2nd/ percent	第三品牌及百分比 3rd/ percent	第四品牌及百分比 4th/ percent
样本 Sample	161	**松下/乐声 Panasonic(33.5)**	**夏普/声宝 Sharp(9.3)**	**日立 Hitashi(8.7)**	**富丽 Fuli(5.0)**
广告淡漠指向 indifferent orientation	42	松下/乐声 Panasonic(23.8)	夏普/声宝 Sharp(14.3)	富丽 Fuli(9.5)	日本 777(4.8) 东芝 Toshiba(4.8)
中间层 medium	95	松下/乐声 Panasonic(34.7)	夏普/声宝 Sharp(9.5) 日立 Hitachi(9.5)	爱多 Idall(4.2) 富丽 Fuli(4.2) 三星 Samsung(4.2)	万利达 Malata(3.2)
信赖广告指向 loyal orientation	24	松下/乐声 Panasonic(45.8)	日立 Hitachi(16.7)	三洋 Sanyo(8.3)	东芝 Toshiba(4.2) 飞利浦 Philips(4.2) 三星 Samsung(4.2) 索尼 Sony(4.2) 步步高 BBK(4.2) 裕新 Yuxing(4.2)

6-8-3 价格态度指标/ Price Attitude Index

	人数 Number	第一品牌及百分比 1st/ percent	第二品牌及百分比 2nd/ percent	第三品牌及百分比 3rd/ percent	第四品牌及百分比 4th/ percent
样本 Sample	161	**松下/乐声 Panasonic(33.5)**	**夏普/声宝 Sharp(9.3)**	**日立 Hitachi(8.7)**	**富丽 Fuli(5.0)**
价格无关心指向 indifferent orientation	35	松下/乐声 Panasonic(45.7)	日立 Hitachi(11.4)	日本 777(5.7)	飞达 Feida(2.9) 富士 Fuji(2.9) 江奎 Jiangkui(2.9) 夏普/声宝 Sharp(2.9) 万利达 Malata(2.9) 三星 Samsung(2.9) 福奈 Funai(2.9) 富丽 Fuli(2.9) 东芝 Toshiba(2.9)
中间层 medium	93	松下/乐声 Panasonic(28.0)	夏普/声宝 Sharp(10.8)	日立 Hitachi(8.6)	富丽 Fuli(5.4) 爱多 Idall(5.4) 三星 Samsung(5.4)
价格重视指向 careful orientation	33	松下/乐声 Panasonic(36.4)	夏普/声宝 Sharp(12.1)	东芝 Toshiba(6.1) 富丽 Fuli(6.1) 日立 Hitachi(6.1) 三洋 Sanyo(6.1)	先科 SAST(3.0) 裕新 Yuxing(3.0) 日本 ORION(3.0) 新星 Xinxing(3.0) 万利达 Malata(3.0) 厦新 Amoisonic(3.0) 索尼 Sony(3.0) 高士达/乐金 LG(3.0)

6-9 不同消费者层选择录放像机时的考虑因素/ Considerations in Choosing from Different Brands by Market Segments

6-9-1 时尚流行指标/ Fads Popular Index

注：本题为多选题，合计百分比超过 100%（Multiple answers）

	人数 Number	品牌形象 brand image	外型 outlook	价格 price	画质好 clarity	多制式 multi-system
样本 Sample	166	45.2	9.6	28.9	25.3	10.2
平实生活指向 simple living orientation	91	39.6	12.1	34.1	19.8	6.6
时尚流行指向 fashion orientation	75	52.0	6.7	22.7	32.0	14.7

续前表 continued

	人数 Number	立体声 stereo	有卡拉 OK 功能 karaoke function	售后服务 follow-up service	功能全 all-function	其他 others
样本 Sample	166	11.4	27.1	4.8	22.3	3.0
平实生活指向 simple living orientation	91	13.2	23.1	6.6	22.0	4.4
时尚流行指向 fashion orientation	75	9.3	32.0	2.7	22.7	1.3

6-9-2 广告态度指标/ Advertising Attitude Index

注：本题为多选题，合计百分比超过 100%（Multiple answers）

	人数 Number	品牌形象 brand image	外型 outlook	价格 price	画质好 clarity	多制式 multi-system
样本 Sample	165	45.5	10.3	29.1	24.8	10.3
广告淡漠指向 indifferent orientation	43	34.9	14.0	48.8	16.3	4.7
中间层 medium	98	46.9	8.2	25.5	25.5	12.2
信赖广告指向 loyal orientation	24	58.3	12.5	8.3	37.5	12.5

续前表 continued

	人数 Number	立体声 stereo	有卡拉 OK 功能 karaoke function	售后服务 follow-up service	功能全 all-function	其他 others
样本 Sample	165	11.5	26.7	4.8	22.4	3.0
广告淡漠指向 indifferent orientation	43	9.3	18.6	4.7	20.9	7.0
中间层 medium	98	14.3	29.6	5.1	21.4	2.0
信赖广告指向 loyal orientation	24	4.2	29.2	4.2	29.2	0.0

6-9-3 价格态度指标/ Price Attitude Index

注：本题为多选题，合计百分比超过 100%（Multiple answers）

	人数 Number	品牌形象 brand image	外型 outlook	价格 price	画质好 clarity	多制式 multi-system
样本 Sample	164	45.1	10.4	28.7	24.4	9.8
价格无关心指向 indifferent orientation	36	58.3	11.1	27.8	22.2	8.3
中间层 medium	95	46.3	7.4	26.3	26.3	10.5
价格重视指向 careful orientation	33	27.3	18.2	36.4	21.2	9.1

续前表 continued

	人数 Number	立体声 stereo	有卡拉 OK 功能 karaoke function	售后服务 follow-up service	功能全 all-function	其他 others
样本 Sample	164	11.6	26.8	4.9	22.6	3.0
价格无关心指向 indifferent orientation	36	11.1	22.2	5.6	16.7	5.6
中间层 medium	95	13.7	22.1	5.3	26.3	3.2
价格重视指向 careful orientation	33	6.1	45.5	3.0	18.2	0.0

● 沈阳 / Shenyang

6-1 录放像机的拥有比例/ Proportion of VTR Owners in the Sample

	人数 Number	百分比 Percent
有 yes	172	28.7
没有 no	428	71.3

n=600

6-2 录放像机的拥有量/ Number of VTR Owned Per Household

	人数 Number	百分比 Percent
1 台 1 set	168	98.2
2 台及以上 2 sets or over	3	1.8

n=171

6-3 理想品牌排名/ Ranking of the Ideal Brands

排名 Brand Ranking	品牌 Brands	人数 Number	百分比 Percent
1	松下/乐声 Panasonic	145	24.2
2	索尼 Sony	36	6.0
3	东芝 Toshiba	21	3.5
4	先科 SAST	16	2.7
4	三洋 Sanyo	16	2.7
5	夏普/声宝 Sharp	13	2.2
6	新科 Shinco	10	1.7
7	飞利浦 Philips	8	1.3
7	高士达/乐金 LG	8	1.3
8	步步高 BBK	7	1.2
8	日立 Hitachi	7	1.2
9	胜利 JVC	5	0.8
9	爱华 Aiwa	5	0.8

n=600

6-4 对家中现有录放像机(最近购买的一台)的四个方面的描述/ About the VTR Most Recently Purchased

6-4-1 家中现有录放像机的品牌排名/ Ranking of the Currently Owned VTR Brands

排名 Brand Ranking	品牌 Brands	人数 Number	百分比 Percent
1	松下/乐声 Panasonic	67	39.2
2	东芝 Toshiba	13	7.6
2	福奈 Funai	13	7.6
3	夏普/声宝 Sharp	9	5.3
4	索尼 Sony	7	4.1
4	三洋 Sanyo	7	4.1
5	日立 Hitachi	6	3.5
6	新科 Shinco	5	2.9
7	胜利 JVC	4	2.3
7	步步高 BBK	4	2.3

n=171

6-4-2 该录放像机的购买时间/ The Time of Purchasing of the Currently Owned VTR

	人数 Number	百分比 Percent
1985 年或以前 1985 or before	3	1.8
1986～1990 年	57	33.3
1991 年	16	9.4
1992 年	13	7.6
1993 年	19	11.1
1994 年	18	10.5
1995 年	15	8.8
1996 年	11	6.4
1997 年	10	5.8
1998 年	6	3.5
1999 年	3	1.8

n=171

6-4-3 录放像机的价格/ The Price of the Currently Owned VTR

	人数 Number	百分比 Percent
1000 元或以下 1000 yuan or below	10	5.8
1001～2000 元 yuan	47	27.3
2001～3000 元 yuan	48	27.9
3001～4000 元 yuan	44	25.6
4001～5000 元 yuan	11	6.4
5000 元以上 over 5000 yuan	5	2.9
完全不知道 don't know	7	4.1

n=172

6-4-4 该录放像机的类型/ The Type of the Currently Owned VTR

	人数 Number	百分比 Percent
普通放像机 play only VTR	60	35.1
卡拉 OK 放像机 play only karaoke VTR	31	18.1
普通录放像机 VTR	45	26.3
卡拉 OK 录放像机 karaoke VTR	35	20.5
其他 others	0	0.0

n=171

6-5 选择不同品牌录放像机时的考虑因素/ Considerations in Choosing from Different Brands

注：本题为多选题，合计百分比超过 100%（Multiple answers）

	人数 Number	品牌形象 brand image	外型 outlook	价格 price	画质好 clarity	多制式 multi-system
样本 Sample	**169**	**46.2**	**9.5**	**30.8**	**23.7**	**11.2**
松下/乐声 Panasonic	66	51.5	7.6	28.8	18.2	10.6
东芝 Toshiba	13	38.5	7.7	30.8	30.8	7.7
福奈 Funai	13	38.5	23.1	38.5	15.4	7.7
夏普/声宝 Sharp	9	66.7	11.1	66.7	33.3	0.0
索尼 Sony	7	42.9	14.3	28.6	28.6	14.3
三洋 Sanyo	6	66.7	0.0	16.7	33.3	0.0
日立 Hitachi	6	50.0	0.0	0.0	16.7	33.3

续前表 continued

	人数 Number	立体声 stereo	有卡拉 OK 功能 karaoke function	售后服务 follow-up service	功能全 all-function	其他 others
样本 Sample	**169**	**9.5**	**22.5**	**8.9**	**24.9**	**3.0**
松下/乐声 Panasonic	66	10.6	22.7	7.6	27.3	1.5
东芝 Toshiba	13	7.7	15.4	0.0	23.1	15.4
福奈 Funai	13	0.0	15.4	30.8	30.8	0.0
夏普/声宝 Sharp	9	0.0	11.1	0.0	44.4	0.0
索尼 Sony	7	28.6	42.9	14.3	0.0	0.0
三洋 Sanyo	6	0.0	33.3	0.0	0.0	0.0
日立 Hitachi	6	0.0	33.3	0.0	50.0	16.7

6-6 录放像机未来一年购买打算/ Plan for Future Purchasing of a VTR

6-6-1 有无购买打算/ Whether Planning to Purchase Next Year

	人数 Number	百分比 Percent
是 yes	1	0.2
否 no	597	99.8

n=598

6-6-2 打算购买的品牌排名/ The Brand of the Planned Purchase Next Year

排名 Brand Ranking	品牌 Brands	人数 Number	百分比 Percent
1	飞利浦 Philips	1	100.0

n=1

6-6-3 打算购买的类型/ The Type of the Planned Purchase Next Year

	人数 Number	百分比 Percent
普通放像机 play only VTR	0	0.0
卡拉 OK 放像机 play only karaoke VTR	0	0.0
普通录放像机 VTR	0	0.0
卡拉 OK 录放像机 karaoke VTR	1	100.0
其他 others	0	0.0

n=1

6-6-4 打算购买的价格/ The Price of the Planned Purchase Next Year

	人数 Number	百分比 Percent
1000 元或以下 1000 yuan or below	0	0.0
1001～2000 元 yuan	1	100.0
2001～3000 元 yuan	0	0.0
3001～4000 元 yuan	0	0.0
4001～5000 元 yuan	0	0.0
5000 元以上 over 5000 yuan	0	0.0
完全不知道 don't know	0	0.0

n=1

6-7 选购录放像机时不同角色的人口特征/ Demographics of the Different Roles in Purchasing a VTR

注：不同角色可以多选（Multiple answers）

	人数 Number	16-24 岁 Age	25-34 岁 Age	35-44 岁 Age	45-54 岁 Age	55-60 岁 Age
样本 Sample	146	19.9	36.3	21.9	17.1	4.8
男性 Male	76	15.8	39.5	19.7	21.1	3.9
提议者 advocate	14	14.3	42.9	14.3	21.4	7.1
影响者 influence	5	40.0	20.0	0.0	40.0	0.0
决定者 decider	38	5.3	39.5	26.3	21.1	7.9
使用者 user	43	18.6	41.9	18.6	20.9	0.0
女性 Female	70	24.3	32.9	24.3	12.9	5.7
提议者 advocate	12	16.7	41.7	8.3	25.0	8.3
影响者 influence	4	25.0	25.0	25.0	0.0	25.0
决定者 decider	19	10.5	36.8	36.8	10.5	5.3
使用者 user	45	28.9	28.9	22.2	11.1	8.9

6-8 不同消费者层的家中目前拥有品牌/ Brands of VTR Owned in Household by Market Segments

6-8-1 时尚流行指标/ Fads Popular Index

	人数 Number	第一品牌及百分比 1st/ percent	第二品牌及百分比 2nd/ percent	第三品牌及百分比 3rd/ percent
样本 Sample	171	**松下/乐声 Panasonic(39.2)**	**东芝 Toshiba(7.6)** **福奈 Funai(7.6)**	**夏普/声宝 Sharp(5.3)**
平实生活指向 simple living orientation	73	松下/乐声 Panasonic(34.2)	福奈 Funai(11.0)	东芝 Toshiba(8.2)
时尚流行指向 fashion orientation	98	松下/乐声 Panasonic(42.9)	东芝 Toshiba(7.1)	福奈 Funai(5.1) 夏普/声宝 Sharp(5.1)

6-8-2 广告态度指标/ Advertising Attitude Index

	人数 Number	第一品牌及百分比 1st/ percent	第二品牌及百分比 2nd/ percent	第三品牌及百分比 3rd/ percent
样本 Sample	171	**松下/乐声 Panasonic(39.2)**	**东芝 Toshiba(7.6)** **福奈 Funai(7.6)**	**夏普/声宝 Sharp(5.3)**
广告淡漠指向 indifferent orientation	47	松下/乐声 Panasonic(40.4)	三洋 Sanyo(6.4)	飞利浦 Philips(4.3) 索尼 Sony(4.3) 夏普/声宝 Sharp(4.3) 东芝 Toshiba(4.3) 新科 Shinco(4.3)
中间层 medium	96	松下/乐声 Panasonic(42.7)	福奈 Funai(10.4)	东芝 Toshiba(7.3)
信赖广告指向 loyal orientation	28	松下/乐声 Panasonic(25.0)	东芝 Toshiba(14.3)	福奈 Funai(7.1) 日立 Hitachi(7.1)

6-8-3 价格态度指标/ Price Attitude Index

	人数 Number	第一品牌及百分比 1st/ percent	第二品牌及百分比 2nd/ percent	第三品牌及百分比 3rd/ percent
样本 Sample	170	**松下/乐声 Panasonic(39.4)**	**福奈 Funai(7.6)**	**东芝 Toshiba(7.1)**
价格无关心指向 indifferent orientation	37	松下/乐声 Panasonic(40.5)	飞利浦 Philips(5.4) 福奈 Funai(5.4) 三洋 Sanyo(5.4) 索尼 Sony(5.4)	康佳 Konka(2.7) 科成达 Kechengda(2.7) 金星 Jinxing(2.7) 三峡 Sanxia(2.7) 珠波 Zhubo(2.7) 新科 Shinco(2.7) 步步高 BBK(2.7) 胜利 JVC(2.7) 三星 Samsung(2.7) 日立 Hitachi(2.7) 健伍 Kenwood(2.7) 东芝 Toshiba(2.7)
中间层 medium	86	松下/乐声 Panasonic(37.2)	夏普/声宝 Sharp(7.0)	东芝 Toshiba(5.8) 福奈 Funai(5.8)
价格重视指向 careful orientation	47	松下/乐声 Panasonic(42.6)	东芝 Toshiba(12.8) 福奈 Funai(12.8)	三洋 Sanyo(6.4) 夏普/声宝 Sharp(6.4)

6-9 不同消费者层选择录放像机时的考虑因素/ Considerations in Choosing from Different Brands by Market Segments

6-9-1 时尚流行指标/ Fads Popular Index

注：本题为多选题，合计百分比超过 100%（Multiple answers）

	人数 Number	品牌形象 brand image	外型 outlook	价格 price	画质好 clarity	多制式 multi-system
样本 Sample	170	**45.9**	**9.4**	**31.2**	**23.5**	**11.2**
平实生活指向 simple living orientation	71	46.5	9.9	32.4	28.2	9.9
时尚流行指向 fashion orientation	99	45.5	9.1	30.3	20.2	12.1

续前表 continued

	人数 Number	立体声 stereo	有卡拉 OK 功能 karaoke function	售后服务 follow-up service	功能全 all-function	其他 others
样本 Sample	170	**9.4**	**22.9**	**8.8**	**24.7**	**2.9**
平实生活指向 simple living orientation	71	11.3	19.7	11.3	26.8	4.2
时尚流行指向 fashion orientation	99	8.1	25.3	7.1	23.2	2.0

6-9-2 广告态度指标/ Advertising Attitude Index

注：本题为多选题，合计百分比超过 100%（Multiple answers）

	人数 Number	品牌形象 brand image	外型 outlook	价格 price	画质好 clarity	多制式 multi-system
样本 Sample	170	**45.9**	**9.4**	**31.2**	**23.5**	**11.2**
广告淡漠指向 indifferent orientation	46	34.8	4.3	41.3	28.3	13.0
中间层 medium	96	51.0	13.5	22.9	22.9	10.4
信赖广告指向 loyal orientation	28	46.4	3.6	42.9	17.9	10.7

续前表 continued

	人数 Number	立体声 stereo	有卡拉 OK 功能 karaoke function	售后服务 follow-up service	功能全 all-function	其他 others
样本 Sample	170	**9.4**	**22.9**	**8.8**	**24.7**	**2.9**
广告淡漠指向 indifferent orientation	46	10.9	23.9	13.0	21.7	0.0
中间层 medium	96	9.4	21.9	8.3	24.0	4.2
信赖广告指向 loyal orientation	28	7.1	25.0	3.6	32.1	3.6

6-9-3 价格态度指标/ Price Attitude Index

注：本题为多选题，合计百分比超过 100%（Multiple answers）

	人数 Number	品牌形象 brand image	外型 outlook	价格 price	画质好 clarity	多制式 multi-system
样本 Sample	**169**	**45.6**	**9.5**	**31.4**	**23.7**	**11.2**
价格无关心指向 indifferent orientation	37	51.4	5.4	16.2	27.0	10.8
中间层 medium	86	39.5	12.8	29.1	25.6	11.6
价格重视指向 careful orientation	46	52.2	6.5	47.8	17.4	10.9

续前表 continued

	人数 Number	立体声 stereo	有卡拉 OK 功能 karaoke function	售后服务 follow-up service	功能全 all-function	其他 others
样本 Sample	**169**	**9.5**	**23.1**	**8.9**	**24.9**	**2.4**
价格无关心指向 indifferent orientation	37	16.2	21.6	8.1	24.3	2.7
中间层 medium	86	9.3	22.1	7.0	23.3	2.3
价格重视指向 careful orientation	46	4.3	26.1	13.0	28.3	2.2

7.音响 / Hi-Fi Stereo

● 北京 / Beijing

7-1 音响的拥有比例/ Proportion of Hi-Fi Stereo Owners in the Sample

	人数 Number	百分比 Percent
有 yes	370	36.6
没有 no	641	63.4

n=1011

7-2 音响的拥有量/ Number of Hi-Fi Stereo Owned Per Household

	人数 Number	百分比 Percent
1 台 1 set	346	95.6
2 台及以上 2 sets or over	16	4.4

n=362

7-3 理想品牌排名/ Ranking of the Ideal Brands

排名 Brand Ranking	品牌 Brands	人数 Number	百分比 Percent
1	索尼 Sony	134	13.3
2	健伍 Kenwood	81	8.0
3	先锋 Pioneer	72	7.1
4	松下 Panasonic	47	4.6
5	爱华 Aiwa	42	4.2
6	飞利浦 Philips	29	2.9
6	山水 Sansui	29	2.9
7	三洋 Sanyo	10	1.0
8	JBL	8	0.8

n=1011

7-4 对家中现有音响(最近购买的一台)的四个方面的描述/ About the Hi-Fi Stereo Most Recently Purchased

7-4-1 家中现有音响的品牌排名/ Ranking of the Currently Owned Hi-Fi Stereo Brands

排名 Brand Ranking	品牌 Brands	人数 Number	百分比 Percent
1	索尼 Sony	48	13.2
2	飞利浦 Philips	32	8.8
3	松下 Panasonic	30	8.2
4	爱华 Aiwa	26	7.1
4	先锋 Pioneer	26	7.1
5	健伍 Kenwood	23	6.3

n=364

7-4-2 该音响的购买时间/ The Time of Purchasing of the Currently Owned Hi-Fi Stereo

	人数 Number	百分比 Percent
1985 年或以前 1985 or before	8	2.2
1986～1990 年	60	16.3
1991 年	19	5.2
1992 年	18	4.9
1993 年	21	5.7
1994 年	36	9.8
1995 年	40	10.9
1996 年	50	13.6
1997 年	49	13.4
1998 年	44	12.0
1999 年	22	6.0

n=367

7-4-3 该音响的价格/ The Price of the Currently Owned Hi-Fi Stereo

	人数 Number	百分比 Percent
1000 元或以下 1000 yuan or below	49	13.3
1001～4000 元 yuan	166	45.0
4001～7000 元 yuan	85	23.0
7001～10000 元 yuan	28	7.6
10001～13000 元 yuan	14	3.8
13001～16000 元 yuan	2	0.5
16001～19000 元 yuan	3	0.8
19001～22000 元 yuan	1	0.3
22001～25000 元 yuan	0	0.0
25001～28000 元 yuan	1	0.3
28001～31000 元 yuan	1	0.3
31000 元以上 over 31000 yuan	1	0.3
完全不知道 don't know	18	4.9

n=369

7-4-4 该音响的类型/ The Type of the Currently Owned Hi-Fi Stereo

	人数 Number	百分比 Percent
普通套装音响 compact Hi-Fi (audio system)	202	55.0
兼容 VCD 套装音响 compact Hi-Fi with VCD	86	23.4
兼容 LD 套装音响 compact Hi-Fi with LD	14	3.8
兼容 LD 和 VCD 套装音响 compact Hi-Fi with LD/VCD	14	3.8
基本功能发烧音响 compact Hi-Fi (audio system)	18	4.9
兼容 VCD 发烧音响 compact Hi-Fi with VCD	14	3.8
兼容 LD 发烧音响 compact Hi-Fi with LD	3	0.8
兼容 LD 和 VCD 发烧音响 compact Hi-Fi with LD/VCD	12	3.3
其他 others	4	1.1

n=367

7-5 选择不同品牌音响时的考虑因素/ Considerations in Choosing from Different Brands

注：本题为多选题，合计百分比超过 100%（Multiple answers）

	人数 Number	品牌形象 brand image	外型 outlook	价格 price	音质 sound effect	遥控功能 remote control	专业声誉 professional prestege
样本 Sample	**357**	**38.9**	**14.3**	**31.9**	**46.8**	**9.2**	**4.8**
索尼 Sony	48	70.8	14.6	18.8	45.8	12.5	4.2
飞利浦 Philips	32	50.0	12.5	37.5	62.5	3.1	0.0
松下 Panasonic	30	46.7	26.7	3.3	50.0	13.3	0.0
爱华 Aiwa	26	46.2	19.2	15.4	53.8	7.7	7.7
先锋 Pioneer	25	60.0	4.0	24.0	48.0	8.0	12.0
健伍 Kenwood	22	45.5	4.5	13.6	54.5	13.6	4.5

续前表 continued

	人数 Number	卡拉 OK 功能 karaoke function	原产地 place of production	功能齐备 all-function	售后服务 follow-up service	其他 others
样本 Sample	**357**	**14.3**	**10.6**	**24.4**	**6.2**	**3.1**
索尼 Sony	48	14.6	14.6	25.0	2.1	2.1
飞利浦 Philips	32	12.5	0.0	15.6	9.4	0.0
松下 Panasonic	30	16.7	13.3	23.3	3.3	0.0
爱华 Aiwa	26	3.8	15.4	23.1	11.5	7.7
先锋 Pioneer	25	12.0	4.0	24.0	8.0	4.0
健伍 Kenwood	22	4.5	31.8	22.7	0.0	9.1

7-6 音响未来购买打算/ Plan for Future Purchasing of a Hi-Fi Stereo

7-6-1 有无购买打算/ Whether Planning to Purchase Next Year

	人数 Number	百分比 Percent
是 yes	68	6.8
否 no	938	93.2

n=1006

7-6-2 打算购买的品牌排名/ Ranking of the Brand of the Planned Purchase Next Year

排名 Brand Ranking	品牌 Brands	人数 Number	百分比 Percent
1	先锋 Pioneer	8	13.8
2	健伍 Kenwood	5	8.6
3	松下 Panasonic	4	6.9
3	飞利浦 Philips	4	6.9

n=58

7-6-3 打算购买的类型/ The Type of the Planned Purchase Next Year

	人数 Number	百分比 Percent
普通套装音响 compact Hi-Fi (audio system)	9	14.3
兼容 VCD 套装音响 compact Hi-Fi with VCD	17	27.0
兼容 LD 套装音响 compact Hi-Fi with LD	2	3.2
兼容 LD 和 VCD 套装音响 compact Hi-Fi with LD/VCD	13	20.6
基本功能发烧音响 compact Hi-Fi (audio system)	5	7.9
兼容 VCD 发烧音响 compact Hi-Fi with VCD	3	4.8
兼容 LD 发烧音响 compact Hi-Fi with LD	2	3.2
兼容 LD 和 VCD 发烧音响 compact Hi-Fi with LD/VCD	12	19.0
其他 others	0	0.0

n=63

7-6-4 打算购买的价格/ The Price of the Planned Purchase Next Year

	人数 Number	百分比 Percent
1000 元或以下 1000 yuan or below	11	17.5
1001～4000 元 yuan	13	20.6
4001～7000 元 yuan	23	36.5
7001～10000 元 yuan	6	9.5
10001～13000 元 yuan	4	6.3
13001～16000 元 yuan	0	0.0
16001～19000 元 yuan	0	0.0
19001～22000 元 yuan	1	1.6
22001～25000 元 yuan	3	4.8
25001～28000 元 yuan	0	0.0
28001～31000 元 yuan	1	1.6
31000 元以上 over 31000 yuan	0	0.0
完全不知道 don't know	1	1.6

n=63

7-7 选购音响时不同角色的人口特征/ Demographics of the Different Roles in Purchasing a Hi-Fi Stereo

注：不同角色可以多选（Multiple answers）

	人数 Number	16-24 岁 Age	25-34 岁 Age	35-44 岁 Age	45-54 岁 Age	55-60 岁 Age
样本 sample	343	19.2	32.1	25.1	14.9	8.7
男性 Male	167	20.4	32.3	25.1	12.6	9.6
提议者 advocate	31	22.6	32.3	35.5	0.0	9.7
影响者 influence	15	26.7	46.7	6.7	6.7	13.3
决定者 decider	88	10.2	25.0	35.2	18.2	11.4
使用者 user	109	24.8	35.8	22.9	11.0	5.5
女性 Female	176	18.2	31.8	25.0	17.0	8.0
提议者 advocate	35	22.9	37.1	22.9	5.7	11.4
影响者 influence	22	22.7	31.8	36.4	4.5	4.5
决定者 decider	50	4.0	44.0	28.0	14.0	10.0
使用者 user	131	20.6	31.3	24.4	17.6	6.1

7-8 不同消费者层的家中目前拥有品牌/ Brands of Hi-Fi Stereo Owned in Household by Market Segments

7-8-1 时尚流行指标/ Fads Popular Index

	人数 Number	第一品牌及百分比 1st/ percent	第二品牌及百分比 2nd/ percent	第三品牌及百分比 3rd/ percent	第四品牌及百分比 4th/ percent
样本 Sample	360	**索尼 Sony(13.1)**	**飞利浦 Philips(8.6)**	**松下 Panasonic(8.3)**	**爱华 Aiwa(7.2)** **先锋 Pioneer(7.2)**
平实生活指向 simple living orientation	154	索尼 Sony(13.0)	飞利浦 Philips(11.0)	爱华 Aiwa(9.7)	先锋 Pioneer(7.1)
时尚流行指向 fashion orientation	206	索尼 Sony(13.1)	松下 Panasonic(9.7)	先锋 Pioneer(7.3) 健伍 Kenwood(7.3)	飞利浦 Philips(6.8)

7-8-2 广告态度指标/ Advertising Attitude Index

	人数 Number	第一品牌及百分比 1st/ percent	第二品牌及百分比 2nd/ percent	第三品牌及百分比 3rd/ percent	第四品牌及百分比 4th/ percent
样本 Sample	**358**	**索尼 Sony(13.4)**	**飞利浦 Philips(8.9)**	**松下 Panasonic(7.8)**	**爱华 Aiwa(7.3) 先锋 Pioneer(7.3)**
广告淡漠指向 indifferent orientation	98	索尼 Sony(15.3)	飞利浦 Philips(8.2) 爱华 Aiwa(8.2) 松下 Panasonic(8.2)	先锋 Pioneer(6.1) 健伍 Kenwood(6.1)	新科 Shinco(3.1) 菲力克 Feilike(3.1) JBL(3.1)
中间层 medium	210	索尼 Sony(14.3)	先锋 Pioneer(9.0)	飞利浦 Philips(8.6)	松下 Panasonic(7.1)
信赖广告指向 loyal orientation	50	爱华 Aiwa(12.0) 飞利浦 Philips(12.0)	松下 Panasonic(10.0)	健伍 Kenwood(8.0) 三洋 Sanyo(8.0)	索尼 Sony(6.0) 夏普/声宝 Sharp(6.0)

7-8-3 价格态度指标/ Price Attitude Index

	人数 Number	第一品牌及百分比 1st/ percent	第二品牌及百分比 2nd/ percent	第三品牌及百分比 3rd/ percent	第四品牌及百分比 4th/ percent
样本 Sample	**360**	**索尼 Sony(13.1)**	**飞利浦 Philips(8.9)**	**松下 Panasonic(8.1)**	**爱华 Aiwa(7.2) 先锋 Pioneer(7.2)**
价格无关心指向 indifferent orientation	85	索尼 Sony(12.9)	松下 Panasonic(8.2) 飞利浦 Philips(8.2) 先锋 Pioneer(8.2)	健伍 Kenwood(5.9)	爱华 Aiwa(4.7) 山水 Sansui(4.7)
中间层 medium	185	索尼 Sony(14.1)	爱华 Aiwa(9.7)	飞利浦 Philips(8.6) 健伍 Kenwood(8.6)	松下 Panasonic(8.1)
价格重视指向 careful orientation	90	索尼 Sony(11.1)	飞利浦 Philips(10.0)	松下 Panasonic(7.8)	先锋 Pioneer(6.7)

7-9 不同消费者层选择音响时的考虑因素/ Considerations in Choosing from Different Brands by Market Segments

7-9-1 时尚流行指标/ Fads Popular Index

注：本题为多选题，合计百分比超过 100%（Multiple answers）

	人数 Number	品牌形象 brand image	外型 outlook	价格 price	音质 sound effect	遥控功能 remote control	专业声誉 professional prestige
样本 Sample	**359**	**39.0**	**14.5**	**31.8**	**46.0**	**9.7**	**4.7**
平实生活指向 simple living orientation	155	38.7	10.3	36.1	40.0	11.0	3.9
时尚流行指向 fashion orientation	204	39.2	17.6	28.4	50.5	8.8	5.4

续前表 continued

	人数 Number	卡拉 OK 功能 karaoke function	原产地 place of production	功能齐备 all-function	售后服务 follow-up service	其他 others
样本 Sample	**359**	**14.5**	**10.6**	**24.0**	**6.1**	**3.3**
平实生活指向 simple living orientation	155	10.3	9.7	27.7	7.1	3.9
时尚流行指向 fashion orientation	204	17.6	11.3	21.1	5.4	2.9

7-9-2 广告态度指向/ Advertising Attitude Index

注：本题为多选题，合计百分比超过 100%（Multiple answers）

	人数 Number	品牌形象 brand image	外型 outlook	价格 price	音质 sound effect	遥控功能 remote control	专业声誉 professional prestige
样本 Sample	**356**	**39.3**	**14.6**	**31.7**	**46.6**	**9.6**	**4.8**
广告淡漠指向 indifferent orientation	96	36.5	14.6	30.2	45.8	14.6	5.2
中间层 medium	210	42.4	11.9	32.9	46.7	8.6	5.2
信赖广告指向 loyal orientation	50	32.0	26.0	30.0	48.0	4.0	2.0

续前表 continued

	人数 Number	卡拉 OK 功能 karaoke function	原产地 place production	功能齐备 all-function	售后服务 follow-up service	其他 others
样本 Sample	**356**	**14.3**	**10.7**	**23.9**	**6.2**	**3.4**
广告淡漠指向 indifferent orientation	96	15.6	14.6	25.0	6.3	5.2
中间层 medium	210	13.8	7.1	24.8	7.1	2.9
信赖广告指向 loyal orientation	50	14.0	18.0	18.0	2.0	2.0

7-9-3 价格态度指向/ Price Attitude Index

注：本题为多选题，合计百分比超过 100%（Multiple answers）

	人数 Number	品牌形象 brand image	外型 outlook	价格 price	音质 sound effect	遥控功能 remote control	专业声誉 professional prestige
样本 Sample	359	39.0	14.8	32.0	46.8	9.5	4.7
价格无关心指向 indifferent orientation	85	40.0	11.8	24.7	51.8	7.1	4.7
中间层 medium	185	42.2	14.1	30.3	48.6	9.2	4.9
价格重视指向 careful orientation	89	31.5	19.1	42.7	38.2	12.4	4.5

续前表 continued

	人数 Number	卡拉 OK 功能 karaoke function	原产地 place of production	功能齐备 all-function	售后服务 follow-up service	其他 others
样本 Sample	359	14.5	10.6	24.2	6.1	3.1
价格无关心指向 indifferent orientation	85	9.4	11.8	21.2	10.6	1.2
中间层 medium	185	14.6	11.4	25.9	5.4	3.8
价格重视指向 careful orientation	89	19.1	7.9	23.6	3.4	3.4

● 上海 / Shanghai

7-1 音响的拥有比例/ Proportion of Hi-Fi Stereo Owners in the Sample

	人数 Number	百分比 Percent
有 yes	343	33.8
没有 no	671	66.2

n=1014

7-2 音响的拥有量/ Number of Hi-Fi Stereo Owned Per Household

	人数 Number	百分比 Percent
1 台 1 set	326	97.0
2 台及以上 2 sets or over	10	3.0

n=336

7-3 理想品牌排名/ Ranking of the Ideal Brands

排名 Brand Ranking	品牌 Brands	人数 Number	百分比 Percent
1	索尼 Sony	162	16.1
2	健伍 Kenwood	103	10.2
3	松下 Panasonic	81	8.1
4	先锋 Pioneer	79	7.9
5	JBL	29	2.9
6	皇冠 Avance	25	2.5
7	飞利浦 Philips	24	2.4
8	爱华 Aiwa	22	2.2
9	胜利 JVC	21	2.1
10	皇后 Queen	19	1.9

n=1005

7-4 对家中现有音响(最近购买的一台)的四个方面的描述/ About the Hi-Fi Stereo Most Recently Purchased

7-4-1 家中现有音响的品牌排名/ Ranking of the Currently Owned Hi-Fi Stereo Brands

排名 Brand Ranking	品牌 Brands	人数 Number	百分比 Percent
1	健伍 Kenwood	34	10.0
2	索尼 Sony	32	9.4
3	先锋 Pioneer	27	7.9
4	奇声 Qisheng	16	4.7
4	松下 Panasonic	16	4.7
5	爱华 Aiwa	15	4.4
6	新科 Shinco	13	3.8
7	JBL	9	2.6
8	多品牌组合机（发烧音响）Combinations	8	2.3
8	飞利浦 Philips	8	2.3
8	皇冠 Avance	8	2.3
9	胜利 JVC	7	2.1
10	迪波 Dibo	6	1.8

n=341

7-4-2 该音响的购买时间/ The Time of Purchasing of the Currently Owned Hi-Fi Stereo

	人数 Number	百分比 Percent
1985 年或以前 1985 or before	2	0.6
1986～1990 年	19	5.7
1991 年	9	2.7
1992 年	20	6.0
1993 年	23	6.8
1994 年	29	8.6
1995 年	41	12.2
1996 年	55	16.4
1997 年	58	17.3
1998 年	52	15.5
1999 年	28	8.3

n=336

7-4-3 该音响的价格/ The Price of the Currently Owned Hi-Fi Stereo

	人数 Number	百分比 Percent
1000 元或以下 1000 yuan or below	24	7.1
1001～4000 元 yuan	107	31.8
4001～7000 元 yuan	76	22.6
7001～10000 元 yuan	51	15.1
10001～13000 元 yuan	32	9.5
13001～16000 元 yuan	11	3.3
16001～19000 元 yuan	10	3.0
19001～22000 元 yuan	7	2.1
22001～25000 元 yuan	4	1.2
25001～28000 元 yuan	1	0.3
28001～31000 元 yuan	0	0.0
31000 元以上 over 31000 yuan	3	0.9
完全不知道 don't know	11	3.3

n=337

7-4-4 该音响的类型/ The Type of the Currently Owned Hi-Fi Stereo

	人数 Number	百分比 Percent
普通套装音响 compact Hi-Fi (audio system)	138	40.9
兼容 VCD 套装音响 compact Hi-Fi with VCD	89	26.4
兼容 LD 套装音响 compact Hi-Fi with LD	18	5.3
兼容 LD 和 VCD 套装音响 compact Hi-Fi with LD/VCD	34	10.1
基本功能发烧音响 compact Hi-Fi (audio system)	28	8.3
兼容 VCD 发烧音响 compact Hi-Fi with VCD	14	4.2
兼容 LD 发烧音响 compact Hi-Fi with LD	2	0.6
兼容 LD 和 VCD 发烧音响 compact Hi-Fi with LD/VCD	9	2.7
其他 others	5	1.5

n=337

7-5 选择不同品牌音响时考虑因素/ Considerations in Choosing from Different Brands

注：本题为多选题，合计百分比超过 100%（Multiple answers）

	人数 Number	品牌形象 brand image	外型 outlook	价格 price	音质 sound effect	遥控功能 remote control	专业声誉 professional prestige
样本 Sample	**335**	**34.3**	**9.3**	**31.9**	**53.1**	**7.5**	**9.9**
健伍 Kenwood	34	52.9	11.8	38.2	55.9	5.9	11.8
索尼 Sony	32	40.6	12.5	37.5	68.8	12.5	18.8
先锋 Pioneer	26	61.5	3.8	11.5	46.2	7.7	7.7
奇声 Qisheng	16	18.8	6.3	25.0	50.0	25.0	0.0
松下 Panasonic	15	33.3	6.7	13.3	60.0	13.3	20.0
爱华 Aiwa	14	35.7	21.4	42.9	42.9	7.1	14.3
新科 Shinco	13	15.4	0.0	46.2	38.5	0.0	0.0
JBL	9	66.7	11.1	44.4	55.6	0.0	22.2
多品牌组合机（发烧音响）Combinations	6	0.0	0.0	33.3	66.7	0.0	16.7
飞利浦 Philips	8	37.5	12.5	37.5	37.5	0.0	12.5
皇冠 Avance	8	50.0	0.0	0.0	62.5	12.5	12.5

续前表 continued

	人数 Number	卡拉 OK 功能 karaoke function	原产地 place production	功能齐备 all-function	售后服务 follow-up service	其他 others
样本 Sample	**335**	**22.1**	**7.8**	**25.7**	**5.4**	**2.1**
健伍 Kenwood	34	5.9	11.8	20.6	0.0	0.0
索尼 Sony	32	15.6	9.4	18.8	6.3	3.1
先锋 Pioneer	26	34.6	11.5	30.8	0.0	3.8
奇声 Qisheng	16	25.0	0.0	50.0	18.8	6.3
松下 Panasonic	15	20.0	26.7	33.3	0.0	0.0
爱华 Aiwa	14	28.6	7.1	35.7	7.1	0.0
新科 Shinco	13	30.8	0.0	30.8	7.7	0.0
JBL	9	33.3	0.0	11.1	11.1	0.0
多品牌组合（发烧音响）Combinations	6	0.0	0.0	33.3	0.0	0.0
飞利浦 Philips	8	12.5	0.0	0.0	0.0	0.0
皇冠 Avance	8	37.5	25.0	25.0	12.5	0.0

7-6 音响未来购买打算/ Plan for Future Purchasing of a Hi-Fi Stereo

7-6-1 有无购买打算/ Whether Planning to Purchase Next Year

	人数 Number	百分比 Percent
是 yes	55	5.4
否 no	957	94.6

n=1012

7-6-2 打算购买的品牌排名/ The Brand of the Planned Purchase Next Year

排名 Brand Ranking	品牌 Brands	人数 Number	百分比 Percent
1	健伍 Kenwood	10	18.9
2	索尼 Sony	4	7.5
2	松下 Panasonic	4	7.5
3	先锋 Pioneer	3	5.7
3	胜利 JVC	3	5.7
3	三洋 Sanyo	3	5.7
4	奇声 Qisheng	2	3.8
4	皇后 Queen	2	3.8
4	JBL	2	3.8

n=53

7-6-3 打算购买的类型/ The Type of the Planned Purchase Next Year

	人数 Number	百分比 Percent
普通套装音响 compact Hi-Fi (audio system)	6	11.1
兼容 VCD 套装音响 compact Hi-Fi with VCD	14	25.9
兼容 LD 套装音响 compact Hi-Fi with LD	3	5.6
兼容 LD 和 VCD 套装音响 compact Hi-Fi with LD/VCD	12	22.2
基本功能发烧音响 compact Hi-Fi (audio system)	8	14.8
兼容 VCD 发烧音响 compact Hi-Fi with VCD	1	1.9
兼容 LD 发烧音响 compact Hi-Fi with LD	1	1.9
兼容 LD 和 VCD 发烧音响 compact Hi-Fi with LD/VCD	9	16.7
其他 others	0	0.0

n=54

7-6-4 打算购买的价格/ The Price of the Planned Purchase Next Year

	人数 Number	百分比 Percent
1000 元或以下 1000 yuan or below	1	1.9
1001～4000 元 yuan	18	33.3
4001～7000 元 yuan	8	14.8
7001～10000 元 yuan	10	18.5
10001～13000 元 yuan	10	18.5
13001～16000 元 yuan	3	5.6
16001～19000 元 yuan	1	1.9
19001～22000 元 yuan	2	3.7
22001～25000 元 yuan	1	1.9
25001～28000 元 yuan	0	0.0
28001～31000 元 yuan	0	0.0
31000 元以上 ove31000 yuan	0	0.0
完全不知道 don't know	0	0.0

n=54

7-7 选购音响时不同角色的人口特征/ The Demographics of Different Roles in Purchasing a Hi-Fi Stereo

注：不同角色可以多选（Multiple answers）

	人数 Number	16-24 岁 Age	25-34 岁 Age	35-44 岁 Age	45-54 岁 Age	55-60 岁 Age
样本 sample	313	18.8	32.6	28.8	14.4	5.4
男性 Male	161	15.5	34.8	29.2	16.1	4.3
提议者 advocate	27	22.2	29.6	14.8	29.6	3.7
影响者 influence	17	17.6	23.5	35.3	17.6	5.9
决定者 decider	80	6.3	38.8	36.3	17.5	1.3
使用者 user	74	25.7	37.8	21.6	9.5	5.4
女性 Female	152	22.4	30.3	28.3	12.5	6.6
提议者 advocate	25	20.0	36.0	28.0	12.0	4.0
影响者 influence	18	22.2	27.8	38.9	5.6	5.6
决定者 decider	46	15.2	30.4	34.8	15.2	4.3
使用者 user	98	25.5	24.5	31.6	11.2	7.1

7-8 不同消费者层的家中目前拥有品牌/ Brands of Hi-Fi Stereo Owned in Household by Market Segments

7-8-1 时尚流行指标/ Fads Popular Index

	人数 Number	第一品牌及百分比 1st/ percent	第二品牌及百分比 2nd/ percent	第三品牌及百分比 3rd/ percent	第四品牌及百分比 4th/ percent	第五品牌及百分比 5th/ percent
样本 Sample	338	**健伍 Kenwood(9.8)**	**索尼 Sony(9.5)**	**先锋 Pioneer(7.7)**	**奇声 Qisheng(4.7)** **松下 Panasonic(4.7)**	**爱华 Aiwa(4.4)**
平实生活指向 simple living orientation	132	健伍 Kenwood(9.8)	先锋 Pioneer(7.6)	索尼 Sony(6.8)	飞利浦 Philips(4.5)	JBL(3.8) 爱华 Aiwa(3.8) 松下 Panasonic(3.8)
时尚流行指向 fashion orientation	206	索尼 Sony(11.2)	健伍 Kenwood(9.7)	先锋 Pioneer(7.8)	奇声 Qisheng(5.8)	松下 Panasonic(5.3)

7-8-2 广告态度指标/ Advertising attitude Index

	人数 Number	第一品牌及百分比 1st/ percent	第二品牌及百分比 2nd/ percent	第三品牌及百分比 3rd/ percent	第四品牌及百分比 4th/ percent	第五品牌及百分比 5th/ percent
样本 Sample	338	**健伍 Kenwood(10.1)**	**索尼 Sony(9.5)**	**先锋 Pioneer(7.7)**	**奇声 Qisheng(4.7)** **松下 Panasonic(4.7)**	**爱华 Aiwa(4.1)**
广告淡漠指向 indifferent orientation	85	新科 shinco(9.4) 健伍 Kenwood(9.4)	索尼 Sony(7.1)	爱华 Aiwa(4.7) 皇冠 Avance(4.7) 先锋 Pioneer(4.7)	飞利浦 Philips(3.5)	狮龙 Sherwood(2.4) 迪波 Dibo(2.4) 星球 Xingqiu(2.4) 马兰士 Malanshi(2.4) 海鸟 Hainiao(2.4) 兰海 Lanhai(2.4) 山水 Sansui(2.4) 三洋 Sanyo(2.4) 大宇 Daewoo(2.4) JBL(2.4)
中间层 medium	198	索尼 Sony(10.6)	健伍 Kenwood(10.1)	先锋 Pioneer(7.6)	奇声 Qisheng(7.1)	松下 Panasonic(5.6)
信赖广告指向 loyal orientation	55	先锋 Pioneer(12.7)	健伍 Kenwood(10.9)	索尼 Sony(9.1)	松下 Panasonic(7.3)	JBL(5.5)

7-8-3 价格态度指标/ Price Attitude Index

	人数 Number	第一品牌及百分比 1st/ percent	第二品牌及百分比 2nd/ percent	第三品牌及百分比 3rd/ percent	第四品牌及百分比 4th/ percent	第五品牌及百分比 5th/ percent
样本 Sample	340	**健伍 Kenwood(10.0)**	**索尼 Sony(9.4)**	**先锋 Pioneer(7.9)**	**松下 Panasonic(4.7)**	**奇声 Qisheng(4.4)** **爱华 Aiwa(4.4)**
价格无关心指向 indifferent orientation	50	爱华 Aiwa(12.0)	索尼 Sony(10.0)	健伍 Kenwood(8.0) 先锋 Pioneer(8.0)	松下 Panasonic(6.0)	皇冠 Avance(4.0) 狮龙 Sherwood(4.0) 马兰士 Malanshi(4.0) 新科 Shinco(4.0)
中间层 medium	201	索尼 Sony(10.9)	先锋 Pioneer(9.0) 健伍 Kenwood(9.0)	新科 Shinco(5.5)	奇声 Qisheng(4.0) 爱华 Aiwa(4.0) 松下 Panasonic(4.0)	
价格重视指向 careful orientation	89	健伍 Kenwood(13.5)	奇声 Qisheng(7.9)	松下 Panasonic(5.6) 索尼 Sony(5.6) 先锋 Pioneer(5.6)	胜利 JVC(4.5) 飞利浦 Philips(4.5)	

7-9 不同消费者层选择音响时的考虑因素/ Considerations in Choosing from Different Brands by Market Segments

7-9-1 时尚流行指标/ Fads Popular Index

注：本题为多选题，合计百分比超过 100%（Multiple answers）

	人数 Number	品牌形象 brand image	外型 outlook	价格 price	音质 sound effect	遥控功能 remote control	专业声誉 professional prestige
样本 Sample	334	34.7	9.3	31.7	52.7	7.2	9.9
平实生活指向 simple living orientation	132	37.9	9.8	33.3	41.7	6.8	12.1
时尚流行指向 fashion orientation	202	32.7	8.9	30.7	59.9	7.4	8.4

续前表 continued

	人数 Number	卡拉 OK 功能 karaoke function	原产地 place of production	功能齐备 all-function	售后服务 follow-up service	其他 others
样本 Sample	334	21.6	7.8	26.0	5.1	2.4
平实生活指向 simple living orientation	132	22.0	4.5	22.0	6.1	2.3
时尚流行指向 fashion orientation	202	21.3	9.9	28.7	4.5	2.5

7-9-2 广告态度指向/ Advertising Attitude Index

注：本题为多选题，合计百分比超过 100%（Multiple answers）

	人数 Number	品牌形象 brand image	外型 outlook	价格 price	音质 sound effect	遥控功能 remote control	专业声誉 professional prestige
样本 Sample	334	34.7	9.3	32.0	52.7	7.5	9.6
广告淡漠指向 indifferent orientation	85	32.9	7.1	25.9	49.4	7.1	11.8
中间层 medium	196	33.7	9 7	35 7	51.0	7.7	9.2
信赖广告指向 loyal orientation	53	41.5	11.3	28 3	64.2	7.5	7.5

续前表 continued

	人数 Number	卡拉 OK 功能 karaoke function	原产地 place of production	功能齐备 all-function	售后服务 follow-up service	其他 others
样本 Sample	334	21.3	7.5	26.0	5.1	2.4
广告淡漠指向 indifferent orientation	85	21.2	7.1	20.0	5.9	4.7
中间层 medium	196	21.9	7.1	28.6	6.1	1.5
信赖广告指向 loyal orientation	53	18.9	9.4	26.4	0.0	1.9

7-9-3 价格态度指向/ Price Attitude Index

注：本题为多选题，合计百分比超过 100%（Multiple answers）

	人数 Number	品牌形象 brand image	外型 outlook	价格 price	音质 sound effect	遥控功能 remote control	专业声誉 professional prestige
样本 Sample	336	34.5	9.2	32.1	52.7	7.4	9.8
价格无关心指向 indifferent orientation	50	38.0	10.0	22.0	58.0	8.0	10.0
中间层 medium	196	33.2	10.7	31.6	51.5	7.1	10.2
价格重视指向 careful orientation	90	35.6	5.6	38.9	52.2	7.8	8.9

续前表 continued

	人数 Number	卡拉 OK 功能 karaoke function	原产地 place of production	功能齐备 all- function	售后服务 follow-up service	其他 others
样本 Sample	336	22.0	7.7	25.9	5.4	2.1
价格无关心指向 indifferent orientation	50	14.0	14.0	28.0	4.0	2.0
中间层 medium	196	25.0	7.7	27.6	7.1	1.5
价格重视指向 careful orientation	90	20.0	4.4	21.1	2.2	3.3

● 广州 / Guangzhou

7-1 音响的拥有比例/ Proportion of Hi-Fi Stereo Owners in the Sample

	人数 Number	百分比 Percent
有 yes	526	50.9
没有 no	508	49.1

n=1034

7-2 音响的拥有量/ Number of Hi-Fi Stereo Owned Per Household

	人数 Number	百分比 Percent
1台 1 set	486	93.8
2台及以上 2 sets or over	32	6.2

n=518

7-3 理想品牌排名/ Ranking of the Ideal Brands

排名 Brand Ranking	品牌 Brands	人数 Number	百分比 Percent
1	索尼 Sony	173	16.8
2	先锋 Pioneer	82	7.9
3	健伍 Kenwood	81	7.8
4	山水 Sansui	39	3.8
5	松下 Panasonic	35	3.4
6	爱华 Aiwa	27	2.6
7	三星 Samsung	10	1.0
7	奇声 Qisheng	10	1.0
8	狮龙 Sherwood	8	0.8
9	天龙 Denon	7	0.7
9	胜利 JVC	7	0.7

n=1032

7-4 对家中现有音响(最近购买的一台)的四个方面的描述/ About the Hi-Fi Stereo Most Recently Purchased

7-4-1 家中现有音响的品牌排名/ Ranking of the Currently Owned Hi-Fi Stereo Brands

排名 Brand Ranking	品牌 Brands	人数 Number	百分比 Percent
1	索尼 Sony	72	13.7
2	先锋 Pioneer	45	8.6
3	健伍 Kenwood	38	7.3
4	松下 Panasonic	31	5.9
5	爱华 Aiwa	30	5.7
6	多品牌组合机（发烧音响）Combinations	28	5.3
7	钻石 Dianmond	13	2.5
8	山水 Sansui	12	2.3
8	奇声 Qisheng	12	2.3
9	三星 Samsung	9	1.7
10	天龙 Denon	8	1.5

n=524

7-4-2 该音响的购买时间/The Time of Purchasing of the Currently Owned Hi-Fi Stereo

	人数 Number	百分比 Percent
1985 年或以前 1985 or before	11	2.1
1986～1990 年	42	8.0
1991 年	15	2.9
1992 年	36	6.8
1993 年	50	9.5
1994 年	46	8.7
1995 年	78	14.8
1996 年	84	16.0
1997 年	80	15.2
1998 年	65	12.4
1999 年	19	3.6

n=526

7-4-3 该音响的价格/ The Price of the Currently Owned Hi-Fi Stereo

	人数 Number	百分比 Percent
1000 元或以下 1000 yuan or below	66	12.6
1001～4000 元 yuan	245	46.8
4001～7000 元 yuan	102	19.5
7001～10000 元 yuan	38	7.3
10001～13000 元 yuan	18	3.4
13001～16000 元 yuan	4	0.8
16001～19000 元 yuan	5	1.0
19001～22000 元 yuan	4	0.8
22001～25000 元 yuan	3	0.6
25001～28000 元 yuan	0	0.0
28001～31000 元 yuan	0	0.0
31000 元或以上 31000 yuan or over	4	0.8
完全不知道 don't know	35	6.7

n=524

7-4-4 该音响的类型/ The Type of the Currently Owned Hi-Fi Stereo

	人数 Number	百分比 Percent
普通套装音响 compact Hi-Fi (audio system)	245	47.0
兼容 VCD 套装音响 compact Hi-Fi with VCD	135	25.9
兼容 LD 套装音响 compact Hi-Fi with LD	18	3.5
兼容 LD 和 VCD 套装音响 compact Hi-Fi with LD/VCD	34	6.5
基本功能发烧音响 compact Hi-Fi (audio system)	36	6.9
兼容 VCD 发烧音响 compact Hi-Fi with VCD	21	4.0
兼容 LD 发烧音响 compact Hi-Fi with LD	6	1.2
兼容 LD 和 VCD 发烧音响 compact Hi-Fi with LD/VCD	13	2.5
其他 others	13	2.5

n=521

7-5 选择不同品牌音响时的考虑因素/ Considerations in Choosing from Different Brands

注：本题为多选题，合计百分比超过 100%（Multiple answers）

	人数 Number	品牌形象 brand image	外型 outlook	价格 price	音质 sound effect	遥控功能 remote control	专业声誉 professional prestige
样本 Sample	**522**	**27.8**	**10.3**	**39.8**	**53.1**	**9.6**	**11.5**
索尼 Sony	72	38.9	13.9	34.7	52.8	5.6	12.5
先锋 Pioneer	44	45.5	6.8	20.5	45.5	11.4	20.5
健伍 Kenwood	38	44.7	5.3	26.3	60.5	7.9	21.1
松下 Panasonic	31	25.8	16.1	41.9	58.1	22.6	9.7
爱华 Aiwa	30	60.0	13.3	30.0	30.0	6.7	16.7
多品牌组合机（发烧音响）Combinations	28	7.1	3.6	42.9	42.9	10.7	10.7
钻石 Diamond	13	15.4	0.0	61.5	53.8	0.0	0.0
山水 Sansui	12	16.7	25.0	41.7	58.3	8.3	25.0
奇声 Qisheng	12	8.3	8.3	41.7	58.3	0.0	8.3

续前表 continued

	人数 Number	卡拉 OK 功能 karaoke function	原产地 place production	功能齐备 all-function	售后服务 follow-up service	其他 others
样本 Sample	**522**	**17.6**	**7.9**	**27.8**	**6.7**	**0.8**
索尼 Sony	72	20.8	9.7	34.7	4.2	0.0
先锋 Pioneer	44	15.9	18.2	22.7	6.8	0.0
健伍 Kenwood	38	13.2	15.8	36.8	7.9	2.6
松下 Panasonic	31	29.0	6.5	35.5	3.2	0.0
爱华 Aiwa	30	16.7	16.7	16.7	0.0	0.0
多品牌组合机（发烧音响）Combinations	28	17.9	0.0	35.7	0.0	7.1
钻石 Diamond	13	7.7	15.4	23.1	7.7	0.0
山水 Sansui	12	16.7	0.0	16.7	0.0	0.0
奇声 Qisheng	12	8.3	8.3	16.7	33.3	8.3

7-6 音响未来购买打算/ Plan for Future Purchasing of a Hi-Fi Stereo

7-6-1 有无购买打算/ Whether Planning to Purchase Next Year

	人数 Number	百分比 Percent
是 yes	55	5.3
否 no	977	94.7

n=1032

7-6-2 打算购买的品牌排名/ The Brand of the Planned Purchase Next Year

排名 Brand Ranking	品牌 Brands	人数 Number	百分比 Percent
1	索尼 Sony	15	27.3
2	健伍 Kenwood	3	5.5
3	先锋 Pioneer	2	3.6
3	东芝 Toshiba	2	3.6
3	牡丹 Peony	2	3.6
3	山水 Sansui	2	3.6
3	松下 Panasonic	2	3.6

n=55

7-6-3 打算购买的类型/ The Type of the Planned Purchase Next Year

	人数 Number	百分比 Percent
普通套装音响 compact Hi-Fi (audio system)	15	27.3
兼容 VCD 套装音响 compact Hi-Fi with VCD	16	29.1
兼容 LD 套装音响 compact Hi-Fi with LD	2	3.6
兼容 LD 和 VCD 套装音响 compact Hi-Fi with LD/VCD	9	16.4
基本功能发烧音响 compact Hi-Fi (audio system)	2	3.6
兼容 VCD 发烧音响 compact Hi-Fi with VCD	2	3.6
兼容 LD 发烧音响 compact Hi-Fi with LD	0	0.0
兼容 LD 和 VCD 发烧音响 compact Hi-Fi with LD/VCD	7	12.7
其他 others	2	3.6

n=55

7-6-4 打算购买的价格/ The Price of the Planned Purchase Next Year

	人数 Number	百分比 Percent
1000 元或以下 1000 yuan or below	3	5.5
1001～4000 元 yuan	34	61.8
4001～7000 元 yuan	6	10.9
7001～10000 元 yuan	3	5.5
10001～13000 元 yuan	7	12.7
13001～16000 元 yuan	0	0.0
16001～19000 元 yuan	0	0.0
19001～22000 元 yuan	2	3.6
22001～25000 元 yuan	0	0.0
25001～28000 元 yuan	0	0.0
28001～31000 元 yuan	0	0.0
31000 元以上 over 31000 yuan	0	0.0
完全不知道 don't know	0	0.0

n=55

7-7 选购音响时不同角色的人口特征/ Demographics of the Different Roles in Purchasing a Hi-Fi Stereo

注：不同角色可以多选（Multiple answers）

	人数 Number	16-24 岁 Age	25-34 岁 Age	35-44 岁 Age	45-54 岁 Age	55-60 岁 Age
样本 sample	476	22.1	29.8	27.9	14.1	6.1
男性 Male	250	20.0	29.2	29.6	14.8	6.4
提议者 advocate	31	22.6	16.1	29.0	19.4	12.9
影响者 influence	37	32.4	27.0	21.6	13.5	5.4
决定者 decider	119	8.4	35.3	31.9	17.6	6.7
使用者 user	136	25.7	30.9	28.7	10.3	4.4
女性 Female	226	24.3	30.5	26.1	13.3	5.8
提议者 advocate	37	24.3	37.8	27.0	8.1	2.7
影响者 influence	56	17.9	28.6	35.7	16.1	1.8
决定者 decider	39	17.9	30.8	30.8	12.8	7.7
使用者 user	141	25.5	28.4	26.2	14.2	5.7

7-8 不同消费者层的家中目前拥有品牌/ Brands of Hi-Fi Stereo Owned in Household by Market Segments

7-8-1 时尚流行指标/ Fads Popular Index

	人数 Number	第一品牌及百分比 1st/ percent	第二品牌及百分比 2nd/ percent	第三品牌及百分比 3rd/ percent	第四品牌及百分比 4th/ percent
样本 Sample	519	**索尼 Sony(13.7)**	**先锋 Pioneer(8.7)**	**健伍 Kenwood(7.3)**	**松下 Panasonic(6.0)**
平实生活指向 simple living orientation	266	索尼 Sony(10.9)	先锋 Pioneer(10.2)	爱华 Aiwa(6.0)	多品牌组合机（发烧音响）Combinations(4.5) 松下 Panasonic(4.5)
时尚流行指向 fashion orientation	253	索尼 Sony(16.6)	健伍 Kenwood(11.5)	松下 Panasonic(7.5)	先锋 Pioneer(7.1)

7-8-2 广告态度指标/ Advertising attitude Index

	人数 Number	第一品牌及百分比 1st/ percent	第二品牌及百分比 2nd/ percent	第三品牌及百分比 3rd/ percent	第四品牌及百分比 4th/ percent
样本 Sample	516	**索尼 Sony(13.6)**	**先锋 Pioneer(8.7)**	**健伍 Kenwood(7.2)**	**松下 Panasonic(6.0)**
广告淡漠指向 indifferent orientation	153	索尼 Sony(13.1)	健伍 Kenwood(6.5) 松下 Panasonic(6.5)	爱华 Aiwa(5.9)	先锋 Pioneer(5.2)
中间层 medium	318	索尼 Sony(14.8)	先锋 Pioneer(10.4)	松下 Panasonic(6.6) 健伍 Kenwood(6.6)	多品牌组合机（发烧音响）Combinations(6.3)
信赖广告指向 loyal orientation	45	健伍 Kenwood(13.3)	先锋 Pioneer(8.9)	索尼 Sony(6.7) 爱华 Aiwa(6.7)	天龙 Denon(4.4) 星河 Xinghe(4.4) 奇星 Qixing(4.4)

7-8-3 价格态度指标/ Price Attitude Index

	人数 Number	第一品牌及百分比 1st/ percent	第二品牌及百分比 2nd/ percent	第三品牌及百分比 3rd/ percent	第四品牌及百分比 4th/ percent
样本 Sample	520	**索尼 Sony(13.8)**	**先锋 Pioneer(8.7)**	**健伍 Kenwood(7.3)**	**松下 Panasonic(6.0)**
价格无关心指向 indifferent orientation	91	索尼 Sony(12.1)	先锋 Pioneer(8.8) 健伍 Kenwood(8.8)	多品牌组合机（发烧音响）Combinations(7.7)	松下 Panasonic(6.6)
中间层 medium	283	索尼 Sony(14.5)	先锋 Pioneer(9.2)	健伍 Kenwood(7.4)	多品牌组合机（发烧音响）Combinations(6.7)
价格重视指向 careful orientation	146	索尼 Sony(13.7)	爱华 Aiwa(8.9)	先锋 Pioneer(7.5)	松下 Panasonic(6.8)

7-9 不同消费者层选择音响时考虑因素/ Considerations in Choosing from Different Brands by Market Segments

7-9-1 时尚流行指标/ Fads Popular Index

注：本题为多选题，合计百分比超过 100%（Multiple answers）

	人数 Number	品牌形象 brand image	外型 outlook	价格 price	音质 sound effect	遥控功能 remote control	专业声誉 professional prestige
样本 Sample	519	27.4	10.6	40.3	53.4	9.6	11.2
平实生活指向 simple living orientation	266	25.9	7.5	41.0	47.7	9.0	11.3
时尚流行指向 fashion orientation	253	28.9	13.8	39.5	59.3	10.3	11.1

续前表 continued

	人数 Number	卡拉 OK 功能 karaoke function	原产地 place of production	功能齐备 all-function	售后服务 follow-up service	其他 others
样本 Sample	519	17.3	8.1	27.9	6.7	0.8
平实生活指向 simple living orientation	266	15.8	8.6	29.3	7.5	1.1
时尚流行指向 fashion orientation	253	19.0	7.5	26.5	5.9	0.4

7-9-2 广告态度指向/ Advertising Attitude Index

注：本题为多选题，合计百分比超过 100%（Multiple answers）

	人数 Number	品牌形象 brand image	外型 outlook	价格 price	音质 sound effect	遥控功能 remote control	专业声誉 professional prestige
样本 Sample	516	27.5	10.7	40.1	53.3	9.5	11.2
广告淡漠指向 indifferent orientation	154	22.1	9.7	38.3	50.0	11.7	11.0
中间层 medium	317	29.7	9.8	41.3	53.9	8.2	11.4
信赖广告指向 loyal orientation	45	31.1	20.0	37.8	60.0	11.1	11.1

续前表 continued

	人数 Number	卡拉 OK 功能 karaoke function	原产地 place of production	功能齐备 all-function	售后服务 follow-up service	其他 others
样本 Sample	516	17.8	7.8	27.7	6.6	0.8
广告淡漠指向 indifferent orientation	154	22.1	7.8	31.2	8.4	0.6
中间层 medium	317	16.4	7.6	26.8	5.7	0.9
信赖广告指向 loyal orientation	45	13.3	8.9	22.2	6.7	0.0

7-9-3 价格态度指向/ Price Attitude Index

注：本题为多选题，合计百分比超过 100%（Multiple answers）

	人数 Number	品牌形象 brand image	外型 outlook	价格 price	音质 sound effect	遥控功能 remote control	专业声誉 professional prestige
样本 Sample	520	27.9	10.6	40.0	53.1	9.6	11.5
价格无关心指向 indifferent orientation	92	25.0	9.8	28.3	54.3	10.9	12.0
中间层 medium	282	28.4	10.6	43.6	58.2	8.5	9.9
价格重视指向 careful orientation	146	28.8	11.0	40.4	42.5	11.0	14.4

续前表 continued

	人数 Number	卡拉 OK 功能 karaoke function	原产地 place of production	功能齐备 all-function	售后服务 follow-up service	其他 others
样本 Sample	520	17.5	8.1	27.9	6.7	0.8
价格无关心指向 indifferent orientation	92	16.3	8.7	39.1	6.5	0.0
中间层 medium	282	16.3	7.1	25.2	6.4	1.1
价格重视指向 careful orientation	146	20.5	9.6	26.0	7.5	0.7

● 重庆 / Chongqing

7-1 音响的拥有比例/ Proportion of Hi-Fi Stereo Owners in the Sample

	人数 Number	百分比 Percent
有 yes	209	33.5
没有 no	415	66.5

n=624

7-2 音响的拥有量/ Number of Hi-Fi Stereo Owned Per Household

	人数 Number	百分比 Percent
1 台 1 set	191	92.3
2 台及以上 2 sets or over	16	7.7

n=207

7-3 理想品牌排名/ Ranking of the Ideal Brands

排名 Brand Ranking	品牌 Brands	人数 Number	百分比 Percent
1	索尼 Sony	37	5.9
2	先锋 Pioneer	34	5.5
3	松下 Panasonic	30	4.8
4	健伍 Kenwood	22	3.5
5	湖山 Hushan	18	2.9
6	新科 Shinco	15	2.4
7	厦新 Amoisonic	9	1.4
7	爱华 Aiwa	9	1.4
8	雅马哈 Yamaha	6	1.0
8	奇声 Qisheng	6	1.0
8	先科 SAST	6	1.0
9	高士 Gaoshi	5	0.8
9	飞利浦 Philips	5	0.8
10	JBL	4	0.6
10	天朗 Tannoy	4	0.6

n=622

7-4 对家中现有音响(最近购买的一台)的四个方面的描述/ About the Hi-Fi Stereo Most Recently Purchased

7-4-1 家中现有音响的品牌排名/ Ranking of the Currently Owned Hi-Fi Stereo Brands

排名 Brand Ranking	品牌 Brands	人数 Number	百分比 Percent
1	先锋 Pioneer	11	5.4
2	奇声 Qisheng	10	4.9
3	爱华 Aiwa	8	3.9
3	索尼 Sony	8	3.9
3	松下 Panasonic	8	3.9
4	多品牌组合机（发烧音响）Combinations	7	3.4
5	联声 Liansheng	6	2.9
5	新科 Shinco	6	2.9
5	健伍 Kenwood	6	2.9

n=204

7-4-2 该音响的购买时间/ The Time of Purchasing of the Currently Owned Hi-Fi Stereo

	人数 Number	百分比 Percent
1985 年或以前 1985 or before	1	0.5
1986～1990 年	4	1.9
1991 年	6	2.9
1992 年	4	1.9
1993 年	10	4.8
1994 年	17	8.2
1995 年	14	6.7
1996 年	31	14.9
1997 年	40	19.2
1998 年	54	26.0
1999 年	27	13.0

n=208

7-4-3 该音响的价格/ The Price of the Currently Owned Hi-Fi Stereo

	人数 Number	百分比 Percent
1000 元或以下 1000 yuan or below	33	15.9
1001～4000 元 yuan	119	57.2
4001～7000 元 yuan	25	12.0
7001～10000 元 yuan	16	7.7
10001～13000 元 yuan	4	1.9
13001～16000 元 yuan	1	0.5
16001～19000 元 yuan	3	1.4
19001～22000 元 yuan	2	1.0
22001～25000 元 yuan	0	0.0
25001～28000 元 yuan	0	0.0
28001～31000 元 yuan	0	0.0
31000 元以上 over 31000 yuan	1	0.5
完全不知道 don't know	4	1.9

n=208

7-4-4 该音响的类型/ The Type of the Currently Owned Hi-Fi Stereo

	人数 Number	百分比 Percent
普通套装音响 compact Hi-Fi (audio system)	86	42.0
兼容 VCD 套装音响 compact Hi-Fi with VCD	67	32.7
兼容 LD 套装音响 compact Hi-Fi with LD	4	2.0
兼容 LD 和 VCD 套装音响 compact Hi-Fi with LD/VCD	19	9.3
基本功能发烧音响 compact Hi-Fi (audio system)	7	3.4
兼容 VCD 发烧音响 compact Hi-Fi with VCD	6	2.9
兼容 LD 发烧音响 compact Hi-Fi with LD	1	0.5
兼容 LD 和 VCD 发烧音响 compact Hi-Fi with LD/VCD	7	3.4
其他 others	8	3.9

n=205

7-5 选择不同品牌音响时的考虑因素/ Considerations in Choosing from Different Brands

注：本题为多选题，合计百分比超过 100%（Multiple answers）

	人数 Number	品牌形象 brand image	外型 outlook	价格 price	音质 sound effect	遥控功能 remote control	专业声誉 professional prestige
样本 Sample	**203**	**18.2**	**11.8**	**38.4**	**50.7**	**12.3**	**2.5**
先锋 Pioneer	11	27.3	0.0	27.3	36.4	18.2	27.3
奇声 Qisheng	10	20.0	10.0	50.0	60.0	10.0	0.0
爱华 Aiwa	8	50.0	0.0	50.0	37.5	25.0	0.0
索尼 Sony	8	37.5	12.5	37.5	37.5	37.5	0.0
松下 Panasonic	8	37.5	25.0	12.5	37.5	12.5	0.0
多品牌组合机（发烧音响）Combinations	7	0.0	0.0	71.4	57.1	0.0	0.0
联声 Liansheng	6	16.7	16.7	66.7	66.7	0.0	0.0
新科 Shinco	6	0.0	0.0	33.3	16.7	16.7	0.0
健伍 Kenwood	6	16.7	50.0	16.7	66.7	33.3	16.7

续前表 continued

	人数 Number	卡拉 OK 功能 karaoke function	原产地 place production	功能齐备 all-function	售后服务 follow-up service	其他 others
样本 Sample	**203**	**32.5**	**4.9**	**24.1**	**3.9**	**3.9**
先锋 Pioneer	11	36.4	9.1	36.4	0.0	0.0
奇声 Qisheng	10	40.0	0.0	40.0	20.0	10.0
爱华 Aiwa	8	12.5	0.0	37.5	12.5	0.0
索尼 Sony	8	50.0	25.0	37.5	0.0	0.0
松下 Panasonic	8	37.5	0.0	25.0	25.0	0.0
多品牌组合机（发烧音响）Combinations	7	14.3	0.0	14.3	0.0	14.3
联声 Liansheng	6	66.7	0.0	16.7	0.0	0.0
新科 Shinco	6	16.7	0.0	33.3	0.0	16.7
健伍 Kenwood	6	16.7	0.0	16.7	0.0	0.0

7-6 音响未来购买打算/ Plan for Future Purchasing of a Hi-Fi Stereo

7-6-1 有无购买打算/ Whether Planning to Purchase Next Year

	人数 Number	百分比 Percent
是 yes	46	7.4
否 no	576	92.6

n=622

7-6-2 打算购买的品牌排名/ The Brand of the Planned Purchase Next Year

排名 Brand Ranking	品牌 Brands	人数 Number	百分比 Percent
1	厦新 Amoisonic	2	4.5
1	达声 Dasheng	2	4.5
1	雅马哈 Yamaha	2	4.5
1	新科 Shinco	2	4.5
1	先锋 Pioneer	2	4.5
1	丽声 CAV	2	4.5
1	健伍 Kenwood	2	4.5

n=44

7-6-3 打算购买的类型/ The Type of the Planned Purchase Next Year

	人数 Number	百分比 Percent
普通套装音响 compact Hi-Fi (audio system)	8	17.4
兼容 VCD 套装音响 compact Hi-Fi with VCD	14	30.4
兼容 LD 套装音响 compact Hi-Fi with LD	1	2.2
兼容 LD 和 VCD 套装音响 compact Hi-Fi with LD/VCD	11	23.9
基本功能发烧音响 compact Hi-Fi (audio system)	2	4.3
兼容 VCD 发烧音响 compact Hi-Fi with VCD	1	2.2
兼容 LD 发烧音响 compact Hi-Fi with LD	0	0.0
兼容 LD 和 VCD 发烧音响 compact Hi-Fi with LD/VCD	5	10.9
其他 others	4	8.7

n=46

7-6-4 打算购买的价格/ The Price of the Planned Purchase Next Year

	人数 Number	百分比 Percent
1000 元或以下 1000 yuan or below	5	10.9
1001～4000 元 yuan	19	41.3
4001～7000 元 yuan	14	30.4
7001～10000 元 yuan	4	8.7
10001～13000 元 yuan	2	4.3
13001～16000 元 yuan	0	0.0
16001～19000 元 yuan	1	2.2
19001～22000 元 yuan	0	0.0
22001～25000 元 yuan	0	0.0
25001～28000 元 yuan	0	0.0
28001～31000 元 yuan	0	0.0
31000 元以上 over 31000 yuan	0	0.0
完全不知道 don't know	1	2.2

n=46

7-7 选购音响时不同角色的人口特征/ Demographics of the Different Roles in Purchasing a Hi-Fi Stereo

注：不同角色可以多选（Multiple answers）

	人数 Number	16-24 岁 Age	25-34 岁 Age	35-44 岁 Age	45-54 岁 Age	55-60 岁 Age
样本 sample	189	22.2	26.5	26.5	18.5	6.3
男性 Male	100	18.0	26.0	31.0	16.0	9.0
提议者 advocate	29	10.3	31.0	27.6	20.7	10.3
影响者 influence	8	0.0	75.0	25.0	0.0	0.0
决定者 decider	48	4.2	25.0	45.3	18.8	6.3
使用者 user	61	23.0	29.5	26.2	11.5	9.8
女性 Female	89	27.0	27.0	21.3	21.3	3.4
提议者 advocate	22	18.2	36.4	27.3	9.1	9.1
影响者 influence	8	0.0	50.0	25.0	12.5	12.5
决定者 decider	22	9.1	36.4	31 8	22.7	0.0
使用者 user	69	30.4	29.0	18 8	18.8	2.9

7-8 不同消费者层的家中目前拥有品牌/ Brands of Hi-Fi Stereo Owned in Household by Market Segments

7-8-1 时尚流行指标/ Fads Popular Index

	人数 Number	第一品牌及百分比 1st/ percent	第二品牌及百分比 2nd/ percent	第三品牌及百分比 3rd/ percent
样本 Sample	201	**先锋 Pioneer(5.0)** **奇声 Qisheng(5.0)**	**索尼 Sony(4.0)** **松下 Panasonic(4.0)**	**爱华 Aiwa(3.5)** **多品牌组合机（发烧音响）Combinations(3.5)**
平实生活指向 simple living orientation	109	多品牌组合机（发烧音响）Combinations(4.6)	爱华 Aiwa(3.7) 松下 Panasonic(3.7)	健伍 Kenwood(2.8) 联声 Liansheng(2.8) 奇声 Qisheng(2.8) 索尼 Sony(2.8) 先锋 Pioneer(2.8)
时尚流行指向 fashion orientation	92	先锋 Pioneer(7.6) 奇声 Qisheng(7.6)	索尼 Sony(5.4)	新科 Shinco(4.3) 松下 Panasonic(4.3)

7-8-2 广告态度指标/ Advertising attitude Index

	人数 Number	第一品牌及百分比 1st/ percent	第二品牌及百分比 2nd/ percent	第三品牌及百分比 3rd/ percent
样本 Sample	203	**先锋 Pioneer(4.9)** **奇声 Qisheng(4.9)**	**爱华 Aiwa(3.9)** **索尼 Sony(3.9)** **松下 Panasonic(3.9)**	**多品牌组合机（发烧音响）Combinations(3.4)**
广告淡漠指向 indifferent orientation	60	先锋 Pioneer(8.3)	爱华 Aiwa(6.7)	湖山 Hushan(5.0) 索尼 Sony(5.0)
中间层 medium	118	多品牌组合机（发烧音响）Combinations(5.1) 奇声 Qisheng(5.1)	新科 Shinco(4.2) 先锋 Pioneer(4.2) 松下 Panasonic(4.2) 联声 Liansheng(4.2)	索尼 Sony(3.4) 健伍 Kenwood(3.4)
信赖广告指向 loyal orientation	25	爱华 Aiwa(8.0) 奇声 Qisheng(8.0)	爱邦 Aibang(4.0) 声视达 Shengshida(4.0) UBL(4.0) 共创 Gongchuang(4.0) Drmeiqi(4.0) 雅特 Yate(4.0) 天机 Tianji(4.0) 恒谊 Hengyi(4.0) 威士博 Weishibo(4.0) 金正 Nitaus(4.0) Jinlun(4.0) 声丽 Shengli(4.0) 美声 Meisheng(4.0) 华声 Huasheng(4.0) 索尼 Sony(4.0) 松下 Panasonic(4.0) 东芝 Toshiba(4.0)	

7-8-3 价格态度指标/ Price Attitude Index

	人数 Number	第一品牌及百分比 1st/ percent	第二品牌及百分比 2nd/ percent	第三品牌及百分比 3rd/ percent
样本 Sample	198	**先锋 Pioneer(5.1)** **奇声 Qisheng(5.1)**	**索尼 Sony(4.0)** **爱华 Aiwa(4.0)** **松下 Panasonic(4.0)**	**联声 Liansheng(3.0)** **健伍 Kenwood(3.0)** **新科 Shinco(3.0)** **多品牌组合机（发烧音响）Combinations(3.0)**
价格无关心指向 indifferent orientation	39	爱华 Aiwa(10.3)	先锋 Pioneer(7.7) 索尼 Sony(7.7)	松下 Panasonic(5.1) GBL(5.1) 新科 Shinco(5.1) 多品牌组合机（发烧音响）Combinations(5.1)
中间层 medium	96	奇声 Qisheng(6.3)	松下 Panasonic(5.2) 先锋 Pioneer(5.2)	湖山 Hushan(3.1) 新科 Shinco(3.1) 联声 Liansheng(3.1) 健伍 Kenwood(3.1) 爱华 Aiwa(3.1)
价格重视指向 careful orientation	63	索尼 Sony(4.8) 奇声 Qisheng(4.8)	先科 SAST(3.2) JBL(3.2) 先锋 Pioneer(3.2) 多品牌组合机（发烧音响）Combinations(3.2) 健伍 Kenwood(3.2) 联声 Liansheng(3.2) 过江龙 Guojiangliong(3.2)	AWL(1.6) 金正 Nintaus(1.6) 兰思 Lansi(1.6) Jinlun(1.6) 美多 Meiduo(1.6) 波比度 Bobidu(1.6) 声霸 Shengba(1.6) 爱邦 Aibang(1.6) 日田 Ritian(1.6) 天机 Tianji(1.6) 永胜 Yongsheng(1.6) 永声 Yongsheng(1.6) Drmeiqi(1.6) 三汇 Sanhui(1.6) Svite(1.6) 思龙 Silong(1.6) JCD(1.6) 香武仕 SunWoods(1.6) 爱华 Aiwa(1.6) 华强 Huaqiang(1.6) 皇冠 Avance(1.6) 科乐 Folo(1.6) 三星 Samsung(1.6) 松下 Panasonic

7-9 不同消费者层选择音响时的考虑因素/ Considerations in Choosing from Different Brands by Market Segments

7-9-1 时尚流行指标/ Fads Popular Index

注：本题为多选题，合计百分比超过 100%（Multiple answers）

	人数 Number	品牌形象 brand image	外型 outlook	价格 price	音质 sound effect	遥控功能 remote control	专业声誉 professional prestige
样本 Sample	205	17.6	11.7	38.5	51.2	11.2	2.0
平实生活指向 simple living orientation	112	15.2	16.1	49.1	50.0	10.7	1.8
时尚流行指向 fashion orientation	93	20.4	6.5	25.8	52.7	11.8	2.2

续前表 continued

	人数 Number	卡拉 OK 功能 karaoke function	原产地 place of production	功能齐备 all-function	售后服务 follow-up service	其他 others
样本 Sample	205	32.2	4.9	23.9	3.9	3.9
平实生活指向 simple living orientation	112	33.0	2.7	19.6	2.7	4.5
时尚流行指向 fashion orientation	93	31.2	7.5	29.0	5.4	3.2

7-9-2 广告态度指向/ Advertising Attitude Index

注：本题为多选题，合计百分比超过 100%（Multiple answers）

	人数 Number	品牌形象 brand image	外型 outlook	价格 price	音质 sound effect	遥控功能 remote control	专业声誉 professional prestige
样本 Sample	207	18.4	11.6	38.2	51.7	11.6	1.9
广告淡漠指向 indifferent orientation	59	15.3	10.2	39.0	47.5	11.9	1.7
中间层 medium	123	18.7	11.4	37.4	55.3	12.2	2.4
信赖广告指向 loyal orientation	25	24.0	16.0	40.0	44.0	8.0	0.0

续前表 continued

	人数 Number	卡拉 OK 功能 karaoke function	原产地 place production	功能齐备 all-function	售后服务 follow-up service	其他 others
样本 Sample	207	31.9	4.8	24.2	3.9	3.9
广告淡漠指向 indifferent orientation	59	23.7	8.5	23.7	5.1	5.1
中间层 medium	123	36.6	2.4	26.0	2.4	1.6
信赖广告指向 loyal orientation	25	28.0	8.0	16.0	8.0	12.0

7-9-3 价格态度指向/ Price Attitude Index

注：本题为多选题，合计百分比超过 100%（Multiple answers）

	人数 Number	品牌形象 brand image	外型 outlook	价格 price	音质 sound effect	遥控功能 remote control	专业声誉 professional prestige
样本 Sample	202	18.3	11.9	38.6	51.0	10.9	2.0
价格无关心指向 indifferent orientation	43	20.9	7.0	34.9	58.1	11.6	2.3
中间层 medium	97	20.6	14.4	37.1	49.5	8.2	3.1
价格重视指向 careful orientation	62	12.9	11.3	43.5	48.4	14.5	0.0

续前表 continued

	人数 Number	卡拉 OK 功能 karaoke function	原产地 place production	功能齐备 all-function	售后服务 follow-up service	其他 others
样本 Sample	202	32.2	4.5	23.3	4.0	4.0
价格无关心指向 indifferent orientation	43	23.3	7.0	25.6	4.7	2.3
中间层 medium	97	30.9	2.1	25.8	4.1	4.1
价格重视指向 careful orientation	62	40.3	6.5	17.7	3.2	4.8

● 武汉 / Wuhan

7-1 音响的拥有比例/ Proportion of Hi-Fi Stereo Owners in the Sample

	人数 Number	百分比 Percent
有 yes	214	33.4
没有 no	426	66.6

n=640

7-2 音响的拥有量/ Number of Hi-Fi Stereo Owned Per Household

	人数 Number	百分比 Percent
1 台 1 set	206	97.2
2 台及以上 2 sets or over	6	2.8

n=212

7-3 理想品牌排名/ Ranking of the Ideal Brands

排名 Brand Ranking	品牌 Brands	人数 Number	百分比 Percent
1	先锋 Pioneer	32	5.0
2	索尼 Sony	26	4.1
3	健伍 Kenwood	17	2.7
4	厦新 Amoisonic	15	2.3
4	新科 Shinco	15	2.3
4	松下 Panasonic	15	2.3
5	飞利浦 Philips	10	1.6
6	三星 Samsung	9	1.4

n=640

7-4 对家中现有音响(最近购买的一台)的四个方面的描述/ About the Hi-Fi Stereo Most Recently Purchased

7-4-1 家中现有音响的品牌排名/ Ranking of the Currently Owned Hi-Fi Stereo Brands

排名 Brand Ranking	品牌 Brands	人数 Number	百分比 Percent
1	长江 Changjiang	17	8.1
2	新科 Shinco	11	5.2
2	厦新 Amoisonic	11	5.2
3	松下 Panasonic	9	4.3
3	先锋 Pioneer	9	4.3
4	奇声 Qisheng	8	3.8
5	夏普/声宝 Sharp	7	3.3
6	康丽 Kangli	6	2.8
6	万利达 Malata	6	2.8

n=211

7-4-2 该音响的购买时间/ The Time of Purchasing of the Currently Owned Hi-Fi Stereo

	人数 Number	百分比 Percent
1985 年或以前 1985 or before	4	1.9
1986～1990 年	31	14.5
1991 年	7	3.3
1992 年	11	5.1
1993 年	13	6.1
1994 年	14	6.5
1995 年	28	13.1
1996 年	27	12.6
1997 年	27	12.6
1998 年	37	17.3
1999 年	15	7.0

n=214

7-4-3 该音响的价格/ The Price of the Currently Owned Hi-Fi Stereo

	人数 Number	百分比 Percent
1000 元或以下 1000 yuan or below	42	19.6
1001～4000 元 yuan	113	52.8
4001～7000 元 yuan	31	14.5
7001～10000 元 yuan	9	4.2
10001～13000 元 yuan	3	1.4
13001～16000 元 yuan	1	0.5
16001～19000 元 yuan	1	0.5
19001～22000 元 yuan	1	0.5
22001～25000 元 yuan	0	0.0
25001～28000 元 yuan	1	0.5
28001～31000 元 yuan	0	0.0
31000 元以上 over 31000 yuan	1	0.5
完全不知道 don't know	11	5.1

n=214

7-4-4 该音响的类型/ The Type of the Currently Owned Hi-Fi Stereo

	人数 Number	百分比 Percent
普通套装音响 compact Hi-Fi (audio system)	108	50.7
兼容 VCD 套装音响 compact Hi-Fi with VCD	73	34.3
兼容 LD 套装音响 compact Hi-Fi with LD	5	2.3
兼容 LD 和 VCD 套装音响 compact Hi-Fi with LD/VCD	8	3.8
基本功能发烧音响 compact Hi-Fi (audio system)	6	2.8
兼容 VCD 发烧音响 compact Hi-Fi with VCD	5	2.3
兼容 LD 发烧音响 compact Hi-Fi with LD	0	0.0
兼容 LD 和 VCD 发烧音响 compact Hi-Fi with LD/VCD	5	2.3
其他 others	3	1.4

n=213

7-5 选择不同品牌音响时的考虑因素/ Considerations in Choosing from Different Brands

注：本题为多选题，合计百分比超过 100%（Multiple answers）

	人数 Number	品牌形象 brand image	外型 outlook	价格 price	音质 sound effect	遥控功能 remote control	专业声誉 professional prestige
样本 Sample	210	36.2	11.9	41.0	49.0	6.7	6.2
长江 Changjiang	17	29.4	17.6	70.6	29.4	0.0	0.0
新科 Shinco	11	54.5	9.1	36.4	36.4	9.1	9.1
厦新 Amoisonic	11	63.6	9.1	63.6	18.2	9.1	9.1
松下 Panasonic	9	55.6	22.2	33.3	33.3	0.0	0.0
先锋 Pioneer	9	66.7	11.1	0.0	66.7	0.0	0.0
奇声 Qisheng	8	37.5	0.0	25.0	100.0	12.5	0.0
夏普/声宝 Sharp	7	42.9	0.0	28.6	57.1	0.0	14.3

续前表 continued

	人数 Number	卡拉 OK 功能 karaoke function	原产地 place production	功能齐备 all-function	售后服务 follow-up service	其他 others
样本 Sample	210	29.5	6.2	21.0	7.1	4.8
长江 Changjiang	17	5.9	17.6	11.3	5.9	5.9
新科 Shinco	11	54.5	0.0	18.2	0.0	0.0
厦新 Amoisonic	11	36.4	0.0	18.2	9.1	0.0
松下 Panasonic	9	33.3	11.1	11.1	0.0	0.0
先锋 Pioneer	9	22.2	22.2	11.1	0.0	0.0
奇声 Qisheng	8	75.0	0.0	12.5	25.0	0.0
夏普/声宝 Sharp	7	42.9	14.3	14.3	0.0	14.3

7-6 音响未来购买打算/ Plan for Future Purchasing of a Hi-Fi Stereo

7-6-1 有无购买打算/ Whether Planning to Purchase Next Year

	人数 Number	百分比 Percent
是 yes	34	5.3
否 no	608	94.7

n=642

7-6-2 打算购买的品牌排名/ The Brand of the Planned Purchase Next Year

排名 Brand Ranking	品牌 Brands	人数 Number	百分比 Percent
1	索尼 Sony	3	10.3
2	奇声 Qisheng	2	6.9
2	松下 Panasonic	2	6.9
2	先锋 Pioneer	2	6.9
2	新科 Shinco	2	6.9

n=29

7-6-3 打算购买的类型/ The Type of the Planned Purchase Next Year

	人数 Number	百分比 Percent
普通套装音响 compact Hi-Fi (audio system)	1	3.2
兼容 VCD 套装音响 compact Hi-Fi with VCD	12	38.7
兼容 LD 套装音响 compact Hi-Fi with LD	2	6.5
兼容 LD 和 VCD 套装音响 compact Hi-Fi with LD/VCD	3	9.7
基本功能发烧音响 compact Hi-Fi (audio system)	3	9.7
兼容 VCD 发烧音响 compact Hi-Fi with VCD	2	6.5
兼容 LD 发烧音响 compact Hi-Fi with LD	2	6.5
兼容 LD 和 VCD 发烧音响 compact Hi-Fi with LD/VCD	3	9.7
其他 others	3	9.7

n=31

7-6-4 打算购买的价格/ The Price of the Planned Purchase Next Year

	人数 Number	百分比 Percent
1000 元以下 1000 yuan or below	4	12.1
1001～4000 元 yuan	18	54.5
4001～7000 元 yuan	6	18.2
7001～10000 元 yuan	2	6.1
10001～13000 元 yuan	2	6.1
13001～16000 元 yuan	0	0.0
16001～19000 元 yuan	0	0.0
19001～22000 元 yuan	1	3.0
22001～25000 元 yuan	0	0.0
25001～28000 元 yuan	0	0.0
28001～31000 元 yuan	0	0.0
31000 元以上 31000 yuan or over	0	0.0
完全不知道 don't know	0	0.0

n=33

7-7 选购音响时不同角色的人口特征/ Demographics of the Different Roles in Purchasing a Hi-Fi Stereo

注：不同角色可以多选（Multiple answers）

	人数 Number	16-24 岁 Age	25-34 岁 Age	35-44 岁 Age	45-54 岁 Age	55-60 岁 Age
样本 sample	195	21.5	37.4	20.5	15.9	4.6
男性 Male	90	25.6	31.1	21.1	15.6	6.7
提议者 advocate	17	11.8	23.5	29.4	35.3	0.0
影响者 influence	9	33.3	11.1	33.3	0.0	22.2
决定者 decider	48	8.3	41.7	29.2	16.7	4.2
使用者 user	52	34.6	23.1	21.2	15.4	5.8
女性 Female	105	18.1	42.9	20.0	16.2	2.9
提议者 advocate	24	25.0	29.2	33.3	8.3	4.2
影响者 influence	17	17.6	29.4	29.4	17.6	5.9
决定者 decider	26	0.0	46.2	23.1	23.1	7.7
使用者 user	78	19.2	42.3	20.5	15.4	2.6

7-8 不同消费者层的家中目前拥有品牌/ Brands of Hi-Fi Stereo Owned in Household by Market Segments

7-8-1 时尚流行指标/ Fads Popular Index

	人数 Number	第一品牌及百分比 1st/ percent	第二品牌及百分比 2nd/ percent	第三品牌及百分比 3rd/ percent
样本 Sample	203	**长江 Changjiang(8.4)**	**厦新 Amoisonic(5.4)**	**先锋 Pioneer(4.4)** **新科 Shinco(4.4)**
平实生活指向 simple living orientation	91	新科 Shinco(5.5)	厦新 Amoisonic(4.4) 康丽 Kangli(4.4) 先锋 Pioneer(4.4)	长江 Changjiang(3.3) 万利达 Malata(3.3) 健伍 Kenwood(3.3)
时尚流行指向 fashion orientation	112	长江 Changjiang(12.5)	厦新 Amoisonic(6.3) 夏普/声宝 Sharp(6.3)	松下 Panasonic(5.4) 奇声 Qisheng(5.4)

7-8-2 广告态度指标/ Advertising Attitude Index

	人数 Number	第一品牌及百分比 1st/ percent	第二品牌及百分比 2nd/ percent	第三品牌及百分比 3rd/ percent
样本 Sample	204	**长江 Changjiang(8.3)**	**厦新 Amoisonic(5.4)**	**先锋 Pioneer(4.4)** **新科 Shinco(4.4)**
广告淡漠指向 indifferent orientation	54	厦新 Amoisonic(7.4)	长江 Changjiang(5.6)	夏普/声宝 Sharp(3.7) 索尼 Sony(3.7) 松下 Panasonic(3.7) 康丽 Kangli(3.7) 飞利浦 Philips(3.7)
中间层 medium	128	长江 Changjiang(8.6)	新科 Shinco(6.3)	松下 Panasonic(4.7)
信赖广告指向 loyal orientation	22	厦新 Amoisonic(13.6) 长江 Changjiang(13.6) 先锋 Pioneer(13.6)	STDING(4.5) KONES(4.5) 金鸡 Jinji(4.5) 国立 Guoli(4.5) 先驱 Xianqu(4.5) 富士达 Fushida(4.5) 蓝光 Languang(4.5) 夏普/声宝 Sharp(4.5) 日立 Hitachi(4.5) 奇声 Qisheng(4.5) JBL(4.5)	

7-8-3 价格态度指标/ Price Attitude Index

	人数 Number	第一品牌及百分比 1st/ percent	第二品牌及百分比 2nd/ percent	第三品牌及百分比 3rd/ percent
样本 Sample	204	长江 Changjiang(8.3)	厦新 Amoisonic(4.9)	先锋 Pioneer(4.4) 新科 Shinco(4.4)
价格无关心指向 indifferent orientation	32	奇声 Qisheng(9.4) 新科 Shinco(9.4)	爱华 Aiwa(6.3) 厦新 Amoisonic(6.3) 松下 Panasonic(6.3) 夏普/声宝 Sharp(6.3) 先锋 Pioneer(6.3)	星河 Xinghe(3.1) 琴润 Qinrun(3.1) 金鹰 Jinying(3.1) 声霸 Shengba(3.1) 先驱 Xianqu(3.1) 万利达 Malata(3.1) 索尼 Sony(3.1) 先科 SAST(3.1) 力之霸 LMB(3.1) 飞利浦 Philips(3.1) 丹特 Dantax(3.1) 长江 Changjiang(3.1) JBL(3.1)
中间层 medium	104	长江 Changjiang(9.6)	松下 Panasonic(5.8)	厦新 Amoisonic(4.8)
价格重视指向 careful orientation	68	长江 Changjiang(8.8)	新科 Shinco(7.4)	先锋 Pioneer(5.9)

7-9 不同消费者层选择音响时的考虑因素/ Considerations in Choosing from Different Brands by Market Segments

7-9-1 时尚流行指标/ Fads Popular Index

注：本题为多选题，合计百分比超过 100%（Multiple answers）

	人数 Number	品牌形象 brand image	外型 outlook	价格 price	音质 sound effect	遥控功能 remote control	专业声誉 professional prestige
样本 Sample	205	35.1	11.7	41.5	49.8	6.3	5.9
平实生活指向 simple living orientation	91	31.9	9.9	48.4	48.4	6.6	6.6
时尚流行指向 fashion orientation	114	37.7	13.2	36.0	50.9	6.1	5.3

续前表 continued

	人数 Number	卡拉 OK 功能 karaoke function	原产地 place of production	功能齐备 all-function	售后服务 follow-up service	其他 others
样本 Sample	205	28.8	5.9	21.5	7.3	4.9
平实生活指向 simple living orientation	91	26.4	3.3	17.6	8.8	3.3
时尚流行指向 fashion orientation	114	30.7	7.9	24.6	6.1	6.1

7-9-2 广告态度指向/ Advertising Attitude Index

注：本题为多选题，合计百分比超过 100%（Multiple answers）

	人数 Number	品牌形象 brand image	外型 outlook	价格 price	音质 sound effect	遥控功能 remote control	专业声誉 professional prestige
样本 Sample	206	35.0	12.1	41.7	49.5	6.3	5.8
广告淡漠指向 indifferent orientation	54	24.1	11.1	44.4	53.7	7.4	11.1
中间层 medium	130	36.9	12.3	42.3	47.7	6.9	4.6
信赖广告指向 loyal orientation	22	50.0	13.6	31.8	50.0	0.0	0.0

续前表 continued

	人数 Number	卡拉 OK 功能 karaoke function	原产地 place production	功能齐备 all-function	售后服务 follow-up service	其他 others
样本 Sample	206	28.6	5.8	21.4	7.3	4.9
广告淡漠指向 indifferent orientation	54	33.3	9.3	16.7	7.4	1.9
中间层 medium	130	27.7	3.8	24.6	8.5	5.4
信赖广告指向 loyal orientation	22	22.7	9.1	13.6	0.0	9.1

7-9-3 价格态度指向/ Price Attitude Index

注：本题为多选题，合计百分比超过 100%（Multiple answers）

	人数 Number	品牌形象 brand image	外型 outlook	价格 price	音质 sound effect	遥控功能 remote control	专业声誉 professional prestige
样本 Sample	206	34.5	12.1	41.3	50.0	5.8	6.3
价格无关心指向 indifferent orientation	31	41.9	16.1	35.5	58.1	9.7	9.7
中间层 medium	106	30.2	10.4	37.7	53.8	5.7	4.7
价格重视指向 careful orientation	69	37.7	13.0	49.3	40.6	4.3	7.2

续前表 continued

	人数 Number	卡拉 OK 功能 karaoke function	原产地 place production	功能齐备 all-function	售后服务 follow-up service	其他 others
样本 Sample	206	28.6	5.8	21.8	7.3	4.9
价格无关心指向 indifferent orientation	31	29.0	6.5	19.4	9.7	3.2
中间层 medium	106	29.2	8.5	24.5	8.5	6.6
价格重视指向 careful orientation	69	27.5	1.4	18.8	4.3	2.9

● 西安 / Xi'an

7-1 音响的拥有比例/ Proportion of Hi-Fi Stereo Owners in the Sample

	人数 Number	百分比 Percent
有 yes	173	28.8
没有 no	427	71.2

n=600

7-2 音响的拥有量/ Number of Hi-Fi Stereo Owned Per Household

	人数 Number	百分比 Percent
1 台 1 set	169	97.7
2 台及以上 2 sets or over	4	2.3

n=173

7-3 理想品牌排名/ Ranking of the Ideal Brands

排名 Brand Ranking	品牌 Brands	人数 Number	百分比 Percent
1	松下 Panasonic	39	6.6
2	索尼 Sony	38	6.4
3	爱华 Aiwa	35	5.9
4	先锋 Pioneer	30	5.0
5	健伍 Kenwood	21	3.5
6	厦新 Amoisonic	12	2.0
6	飞利浦 Philips	12	2.0
7	步步高 BBK	10	1.7
8	三洋 Sanyo	9	1.5
9	先科 SAST	8	1.3
10	新科 Shinco	7	1.2
10	山水 Sansui	7	1.2

n=595

7-4 对家中现有音响(最近购买的一台)的四个方面的描述/ About the Hi-Fi Stereo Most Recently Purchased

7-4-1 家中现有音响的品牌排名/ Ranking of the Currently Owned Hi-Fi Stereo Brands

排名 Brand Ranking	品牌 Brands	人数 Number	百分比 Percent
1	先锋 Pioneer	15	8.7
2	爱华 Aiwa	13	7.6
3	松下 Panasonic	9	5.2
4	索尼 Sony	8	4.7
5	飞利浦 Philips	7	4.1
6	新科 Shinco	6	3.5
6	奇声 Qisheng	6	3.5
7	健伍 Kenwood	5	2.9
8	星河 Xinghe	4	2.3
8	燕舞 Yanwu	4	2.3
8	厦新 Amoisonic	4	2.3

n=172

7-4-2 该音响的购买时间/ The Time of Purchasing of the Currently Owned Hi-Fi Stereo

	人数 Number	百分比 Percent
1985 年或以前 1985 or before	5	2.9
1986～1990 年	10	5.8
1991 年	11	6.4
1992 年	4	2.3
1993 年	20	11.6
1994 年	9	5.2
1995 年	26	15.0
1996 年	22	12.7
1997 年	32	18.5
1998 年	24	13.9
1999 年	10	5.8

n=173

7-4-3 该音响的价格/ The Price of the Currently Owned Hi-Fi Stereo

	人数 Number	百分比 Percent
1000 元及以下 1000 yuan or below	22	12.7
1001～4000 元 yuan	95	54.9
4001～7000 元 yuan	28	16.2
7001～10000 元 yuan	9	5.2
10001～13000 元 yuan	9	5.2
13001～16000 元 yuan	0	0.0
16001～19000 元 yuan	0	0.0
19001～22000 元 yuan	1	0.6
22001～25000 元 yuan	1	0.6
25001～28000 元 yuan	0	0.0
28001～31000 元 yuan	1	0.6
31000 元以上 over 31000 yuan	1	0.6
完全不知道 don't know	6	3.5

n=173

7-4-4 该音响的类型/ The Type of the Currently Owned Hi-Fi Stereo

	人数 Number	百分比 Percent
普通套装音响 compact Hi-Fi (audio system)	76	43.9
兼容 VCD 套装音响 compact Hi-Fi with VCD	49	28.3
兼容 LD 套装音响 compact Hi-Fi with LD	6	3.5
兼容 LD 和 VCD 套装音响 compact Hi-Fi with LD/VCD	15	8.7
基本功能发烧音响 compact Hi-Fi (audio system)	11	6.4
兼容 VCD 发烧音响 compact Hi-Fi with VCD	6	3.5
兼容 LD 发烧音响 compact Hi-Fi with LD	0	0.0
兼容 LD 和 VCD 发烧音响 compact Hi-Fi with LD/VCD	7	4.0
其他 others	3	1.7

n=173

7-5 选择不同品牌音响时考虑因素/ Considerations in Choosing from Different Brands

注：本题为多选题，合计百分比超过 100%（Multiple answers）

	人数 Number	品牌形象 brand image	外型 outlook	价格 price	音质 sound effect	遥控功能 remote control	专业声誉 professional prestige
样本 Sample	**172**	**31.4**	**12.2**	**33.1**	**53.5**	**6.4**	**10.5**
先锋 Pioneer	15	46.7	6.7	26 7	40.0	6.7	6.7
爱华 Aiwa	13	53.8	23.1	23 1	46.2	0.0	15.4
松下 Panasonic	9	33.3	22.2	22 2	66.7	0.0	11.1
索尼 Sony	8	62.5	0.0	12.5	50.0	12.5	37.5
飞利浦 Philips	7	57.1	14.3	42.9	42.9	0.0	0.0

续前表 continued

	人数 Number	卡拉 OK 功能 karaoke function	原产地 place of production	功能齐备 all-function	售后服务 follow-up service	其他 others
样本 Sample	**172**	**14.5**	**8.1**	**27.3**	**5.2**	**2.3**
先锋 Pioneer	15	20.0	13.3	26.7	6.7	0.0
爱华 Aiwa	13	0.0	7.7	30.8	0.0	0.0
松下 Panasonic	9	22.2	22.2	22.2	0.0	0.0
索尼 Sony	8	0.0	25.0	25.0	25.0	0.0
飞利浦 Philips	7	14.3	14.3	28.6	0.0	0.0

7-6 音响未来购买打算/ Plan for Future Purchasing of a Hi-Fi Stereo

7-6-1 有无购买打算/ Whether Planning to Purchase Next Year

	人数 Number	百分比 Percent
是 yes	29	4.8
否 no	570	95.2

n=599

7-6-2 打算购买的品牌排名/ The Brand of the Planned Purchase Next Year

排名 Brand Ranking	品牌 Brands	人数 Number	百分比 Percent
1	山水 Sansui	3	11.5
1	索尼 Sony	3	11.5
2	厦新 Amoisonic	2	7.7
2	步步高 BBK	2	7.7

n=26

7-6-3 打算购买的类型/ The Type of the Planned Purchase Next Year

	人数 Number	百分比 Percent
普通套装音响 compact Hi-Fi (audio system)	6	20.7
兼容 VCD 套装音响 compact Hi-Fi with VCD	7	24.1
兼容 LD 套装音响 compact Hi-Fi with LD	3	10.3
兼容 LD 和 VCD 套装音响 compact Hi-Fi with LD/VCD	4	13.8
基本功能发烧音响 compact Hi-Fi (audio system)	2	6.9
兼容 VCD 发烧音响 compact Hi-Fi with VCD	2	6.9
兼容 LD 发烧音响 compact Hi-Fi with LD	3	10.3
兼容 LD 和 VCD 发烧音响 compact Hi-Fi with LD/VCD	2	6.9
其他 others	0	0.0

n=29

7-6-4 打算购买的价格/ The Price of the Planned Purchase Next Year

	人数 Number	百分比 Percent
1000 元及以下 1000 yuan or below	2	6.9
1001～4000 元 yuan	12	41.4
4001～7000 元 yuan	10	34.5
7001～10000 元 yuan	2	6.9
10001～13000 元 yuan	1	3.4
13001～16000 元 yuan	0	0.0
16001～19000 元 yuan	0	0.0
19001～22000 元 yuan	1	3.4
22001～25000 元 yuan	1	3.4
25001～28000 元 yuan	0	0.0
28001～31000 元 yuan	0	0.0
31000 元以上 over 31000 yuan	0	0.0
完全不知道 don't know	0	0.0

n=29

7-7 选购音响时不同角色的人口特征/ Demographics of the Different Roles in Purchasing a Hi-Fi Stereo

注：不同角色可以多选（Multiple answers）

	人数 Number	16-24 岁 Age	25-34 岁 Age	35-44 岁 Age	45-54 岁 Age	55-60 岁 Age
样本 sample	154	19.5	44.2	20.1	13.0	3.2
男性 Male	87	18.4	40.2	21.8	14.9	4.6
提议者 advocate	11	27.3	36.4	27.3	9.1	0.0
影响者 influence	12	16.7	41.7	25.0	0.0	16.7
决定者 decider	49	8.2	40.8	28.6	20.4	2.0
使用者 user	42	26.2	38.1	19.0	11.9	4.8
女性 Female	67	20.9	49.3	17.9	10.4	1.5
提议者 advocate	12	0.0	58.3	33.3	8.3	0.0
影响者 influence	11	18.2	72.7	0.0	9.1	0.0
决定者 decider	18	22.2	50.0	16.7	11.1	0.0
使用者 user	44	25.0	40.9	20.5	11.4	2.3

7-8 不同消费者层的家中目前拥有品牌/ Brands of Hi-Fi Stereo Owned in Household by Market Segments

7-8-1 时尚流行指标/ Fads Popular Index

	人数 Number	第一品牌及百分比 1st/ percent	第二品牌及百分比 2nd/ percent	第三品牌及百分比 3rd/ percent
样本 Sample	172	**先锋 Pioneer(8.7)**	**爱华 Aiwa(7.6)**	**松下 Panasonic(5.2)**
平实生活指向 simple living orientation	78	爱华 Aiwa(7.7) 先锋 Pioneer(7.7)	索尼 Sony(6.4)	松下 Panasonic(5.1)
时尚流行指向 fashion orientation	94	先锋 Pioneer(9.6)	爱华 Aiwa(7.4)	松下 Panasonic(5.3)

7-8-2 广告态度指标/ Advertising Attitude Index

	人数 Number	第一品牌及百分比 1st/ percent	第二品牌及百分比 2nd/ percent	第三品牌及百分比 3rd/ percent
样本 Sample	172	**先锋 Pioneer(8.7)**	**爱华 Aiwa(7.6)**	**松下 Panasonic(5.2)**
广告淡漠指向 indifferent orientation	41	爱华 Aiwa(9.8) 先锋 Pioneer(9.8)	奇声 Qisheng(7.3) 松下 Panasonic(7.3)	厦新 Amoisonic(4.9) 新科 Shinco(4.9) 燕舞 Yanwu(4.9) 健伍 Kenwood(4.9)
中间层 medium	100	先锋 Pioneer(9.0)	爱华 Aiwa(6.0) 飞利浦 Philips(6.0)	索尼 Sony(5.0)
信赖广告指向 loyal orientation	31	爱华 Aiwa(9.7)	松下 Panasonic(6.5) 索尼 Sony(6.5) 先锋 Pioneer(6.5) 厦新 Amoisonic(6.5)	蓝光 Languang(3.2) 雅顿 Yadun(3.2) 新飞 Xinfei(3.2) 金正 Nintaus(3.2) 红灯 Hongdeng(3.2) 新科 Shinco(3.2) 星河 Xinghe(3.2) 星球 Xingqiu(3.2) 丽声 CAV(3.2) 健伍 Kenwood(3.2) 富声 Fusheng(3.2) 飞利浦 Philips(3.2)

7-8-3 价格态度指标/ Price Attitude Index

	人数 Number	第一品牌及百分比 1st/ percent	第二品牌及百分比 2nd/ percent	第三品牌及百分比 3rd/ percent
样本 Sample	170	**先锋 Pioneer(8.8)**	**爱华 Aiwa(7.6)**	**松下 Panasonic(5.3)**
价格无关心指向 indifferent orientation	50	先锋 Pioneer(10.0)	松下 Panasonic(8.0)	健伍 Kenwood(6.0) 新科 Shinco(6.0)
中间层 medium	87	爱华 Aiwa(10.3)	索尼 Sony(6.9) 飞利浦 Philips(6.9)	先锋 Pioneer(5.7)
价格重视指向 careful orientation	33	先锋 Pioneer(15.2)	爱华 Aiwa(6.1) 奇声 Qisheng(6.1) 先科 SAST(6.1) 星河 Xinghe(6.1)	厦新 Amoisonic(3.0) 飞鸽 Feige(3.0) 金正 Nintaus(3.0) 红灯 Hongdeng(3.0) 冠豪 Guanhao(3.0) 小霸王 Subbor(3.0) 先驱 Xianqu(3.0) 万利达 Malata(3.0) 蓝光 Languan(3.0) 夏普/声宝 Sharp(3.0) 索尼 Sony(3.0) 松下 Panasonic(3.0) 丽声 CAV(3.0) 健伍 Kenwood(3.0) 湖山 Hushan(3.0) 富声 Fusheng(3.0)

7-9 不同消费者层选择音响时考虑因素/ Considerations in Choosing from Different Brands by Market Segments

7-9-1 时尚流行指标/ Fads Popular Index

注：本题为多选题，合计百分比超过 100%（Multiple answers）

	人数 Number	品牌形象 brand image	外型 outlook	价格 price	音质 sound effect	遥控功能 remote control	专业声誉 professional prestige
样本 Sample	173	31.2	12.7	33.5	53.8	6.4	10.4
平实生活指向 simple living orientation	78	34.6	10.3	33.3	44.9	5.1	9.0
时尚流行指向 fashion orientation	95	28.4	14.7	33.7	61.1	7.4	11.6

续前表 continued

	人数 Number	卡拉 OK 功能 karaoke function	原产地 place of production	功能齐备 all-function	售后服务 follow-up service	其他 others
样本 Sample	173	14.5	8.1	27.2	5.2	2.3
平实生活指向 simple living orientation	78	10.3	9.0	26.9	7.7	0.0
时尚流行指向 fashion orientation	95	17.9	7.4	27.4	3.2	4.2

7-9-2 广告态度指向/ Advertising Attitude Index

注：本题为多选题，合计百分比超过 100%（Multiple answers）

	人数 Number	品牌形象 brand image	外型 outlook	价格 price	音质 sound effect	遥控功能 remote control	专业声誉 professional prestige
样本 Sample	173	31.2	12.7	33.5	53.8	6.4	10.4
广告淡漠指向 indifferent orientation	41	34.1	14.6	36.6	48.8	7.3	12.2
中间层 medium	101	31.7	11.9	30.7	52.5	6.9	9.9
信赖广告指向 loyal orientation	31	25.8	12.9	38.7	64.5	3.2	9.7

续前表 continued

	人数 Number	卡拉 OK 功能 karaoke function	原产地 place of production	功能齐备 all-function	售后服务 follow-up service	其他 others
样本 Sample	173	14.5	8.1	27.2	5.2	2.3
广告淡漠指向 indifferent orientation	41	14.6	9.8	22.0	0.0	2.4
中间层 medium	101	14.9	7.9	30.7	7.9	3.0
信赖广告指向 loyal orientation	31	12.9	6.5	22.6	3.2	0.0

7-9-3 价格态度指向/ Price Attitude Index

注：本题为多选题，合计百分比超过 100%（Multiple answers）

	人数 Number	品牌形象 brand image	外型 outlook	价格 price	音质 sound effect	遥控功能 remote control	专业声誉 professional prestige
样本 Sample	171	31.0	12.9	33.3	53.8	6.4	9.9
价格无关心指向 indifferent orientation	50	24.0	12.0	32.0	48.0	2.0	16.0
中间层 medium	87	37.9	6.9	27.6	54.0	8.0	4.6
价格重视指向 careful orientation	34	23.5	29.4	50.0	61.8	8.8	14.7

续前表 continued

	人数 Number	卡拉 OK 功能 karaoke function	原产地 place of production	功能齐备 all-function	售后服务 follow-up service	其他 others
样本 Sample	171	14.6	8.2	26.9	5.3	2.3
价格无关心指向 indifferent orientation	50	14.0	6.0	34.0	2.0	2.0
中间层 medium	87	14.9	9.2	28.7	5.7	3.4
价格重视指向 careful orientation	34	14.7	8.8	11.8	8.8	0.0

● 沈阳 / Shenyang

7-1 音响的拥有比例/ Proportion of Hi-Fi Stereo Owners in the Sample

	人数 Number	百分比 Percent
有 yes	151	25.1
没有 no	450	74.9

n=601

7-2 音响的拥有量/ Number of Hi-Fi Stereo Owned Per Household

	人数 Number	百分比 Percent
1 台 1 set	142	95.3
2 台及以上 2 sets or over	7	4.7

n=149

7-3 理想品牌排名/ Ranking of the Ideal Brands

排名 Brand Ranking	品牌 Brands	人数 Number	百分比 Percent
1	先锋 Pioneer	49	8.2
2	松下 Panasonic	33	5.5
3	先科 SAST	27	4.5
3	新科 Shinco	27	4.5
3	索尼 Sony	27	4.5
4	健伍 Kenwood	22	3.7
5	飞利浦 Philips	20	3.3
6	大宇 Daewoo	18	3.0
7	爱华 Aiwa	17	2.8
8	三洋 Sanyo	12	2.0

n=600

7-4 对家中现有音响(最近购买的一台)的四个方面的描述/ About the Hi-Fi Stereo Most Recently Purchased

7-4-1 家中现有音响的品牌排名/ Ranking of the Currently Owned Hi-Fi Stereo Brands

排名 Brand Ranking	品牌 Brands	人数 Number	百分比 Percent
1	爱华 Aiwa	17	11.3
2	先锋 Pioneer	13	8.7
3	新科 Shinco	12	8.0
4	飞利浦 Philips	10	6.7
5	索尼 Sony	7	4.7
6	先科 SAST	5	3.3
6	健伍 Kenwood	5	3.3
6	松下 Panasonic	5	3.3

n=150

7-4-2 该音响的购买时间/ The Time of Purchasing of the Currently Owned Hi-Fi Stereo

	人数 Number	百分比 Percent
1985 年或以前 1985 or before	2	1.4
1986～1990 年	13	8.8
1991 年	6	4.1
1992 年	7	4.7
1993 年	12	8.1
1994 年	13	8.8
1995 年	21	14.2
1996 年	13	8.8
1997 年	20	13.5
1998 年	27	18.2
1999 年	14	9.5

n=148

7-4-3 该音响的价格/ The Price of the Currently Owned Hi-Fi Stereo

	人数 Number	百分比 Percent
1000 元或以下 1000 yuan or below	31	20.7
1001～4000 元 yuan	69	46.0
4001～7000 元 yuan	25	16.7
7001～10000 元 yuan	8	5.3
10001～13000 元 yuan	6	4.0
13001～16000 元 yuan	2	1.3
16001～19000 元 yuan	3	2.0
19001～22000 元 yuan	0	0.0
22001～25000 元 yuan	0	0.0
25001～28000 元 yuan	0	0.0
28001～31000 元 yuan	0	0.0
31000 元以上 over 31000 yuan	2	1.3
完全不知道 don't know	4	2.7

n=150

7-4-4 该音响的类型/ The Type of the Currently Owned Hi-Fi Stereo

	人数 Number	百分比 Percent
普通套装音响 compact Hi-Fi (audio system)	63	42.3
兼容 VCD 套装音响 compact Hi-Fi with VCD	57	38.3
兼容 LD 套装音响 compact Hi-Fi with LD	5	3.4
兼容 LD 和 VCD 套装音响 compact Hi-Fi with LD/VCD	9	6.0
基本功能发烧音响 compact Hi-Fi (audio system)	4	2.7
兼容 VCD 发烧音响 compact Hi-Fi with VCD	5	3.4
兼容 LD 发烧音响 compact Hi-Fi with LD	0	0.0
兼容 LD 和 VCD 发烧音响 compact Hi-Fi with LD/VCD	4	2.7
其他 others	2	1.3

n=149

7-5 选择不同品牌音响时的考虑因素/ Considerations in Choosing from Different Brands

注：本题为多选题，合计百分比超过 100%（Multiple answers）

	人数 Number	品牌形象 brand image	外型 outlook	价格 price	音质 sound effect	遥控功能 remote control	专业声誉 professional prestige
样本 Sample	150	36.7	9.3	32.0	47.3	14.0	8.0
爱华 Aiwa	17	64.7	11.8	11.8	64.7	17.6	5.9
先锋 Pioneer	13	46.2	0.0	23.1	61.5	15.4	7.7
新科 Shinco	12	50.0	0.0	16.7	33.3	33.3	0.0
飞利浦 Philips	10	60.0	10.0	30.0	50.0	10.0	10.0
索尼 Sony	7	42.9	14.3	0.0	14.3	42.9	0.0

续前表 continued

	人数 Number	卡拉 OK 功能 karaoke function	原产地 place of production	功能齐备 all-function	售后服务 follow-up service	其他 others
样本 Sample	150	25.3	5.3	25.3	3.3	2.0
爱华 Aiwa	17	23.5	11.8	23.5	5.9	0.0
先锋 Pioneer	13	30.8	7.7	38.5	0.0	0.0
新科 Shinco	12	25.0	0.0	41.7	0.0	0.0
飞利浦 Philips	10	20.0	0.0	30.0	0.0	0.0
索尼 Sony	7	28.6	0.0	42.9	0.0	0.0

7-6 音响未来一年购买打算/ Plan for Future Purchasing of a Hi-Fi Stereo

7-6-1 有无购买打算/ Whether Planning to Purchase Next Year

	人数 Number	百分比 Percent
是 yes	26	4.3
否 no	573	95.7

n=599

7-6-2 打算购买的品牌排名/ The Brand of the Planned Purchase Next Year

排名 Brand Ranking	品牌 Brands	人数 Number	百分比 Percent
1	索尼 Sony	4	15.4
2	新科 Shinco	3	11.5
2	先锋 Pioneer	3	11.5
2	松下 Panasonic	3	11.5
3	山水 Sansui	2	7.7
3	大宇 Daewoo	2	7.7

n=26

7-6-3 打算购买的类型/ The Type of the Planned Purchase Next Year

	人数 Number	百分比 Percent
普通套装音响 compact Hi-Fi (audio system)	7	26.9
兼容 VCD 套装音响 compact Hi-Fi with VCD	6	23.1
兼容 LD 套装音响 compact Hi-Fi with LD	1	3.8
兼容 LD 和 VCD 套装音响 compact Hi-Fi with LD/VCD	5	19.2
基本功能发烧音响 compact Hi-Fi (audio system)	1	3.8
兼容 VCD 发烧音响 compact Hi-Fi with VCD	0	0.0
兼容 LD 发烧音响 compact Hi-Fi with LD	2	7.7
兼容 LD 和 VCD 发烧音响 compact Hi-Fi with LD/VCD	4	15.4
其他 others	0	0.0

n=26

7-6-4 打算购买的价格/ The Price of the Planned Purchase Next Year

	人数 Number	百分比 Percent
1000 元或以下 1000 yuan or below	0	0.0
1001～4000 元 yuan	20	76.9
4001～7000 元 yuan	3	11.5
7001～10000 元 yuan	1	3.8
10001～13000 元 yuan	1	3.8
13001～16000 元 yuan	0	0.0
16001～19000 元 yuan	1	3.8
19001～22000 元 yuan	0	0.0
22001～25000 元 yuan	0	0.0
25001～28000 元 yuan	0	0.0
28001～31000 元 yuan	0	0.0
31000 元以上 over 31000 yuan	0	0.0
完全不知道 don't know	0	0.0

n=26

7-7 选购音响时不同角色的人口特征/ Demographics of the Different Roles in Purchasing a Hi-Fi Stereo

注：不同角色可以多选（Multiple answers）

	人数 Number	16-24 岁 Age	25-34 岁 Age	35-44 岁 Age	45-54 岁 Age	55-60 岁 Age
样本 sample	130	18.5	39.2	23.8	11.5	6.9
男性 Male	74	12.2	36.5	29.7	14.9	6.8
提议者 advocate	15	20.0	26.7	26.7	13.3	13.3
影响者 influence	8	25.0	37.5	25.0	12.5	0.0
决定者 decider	44	6.8	47.7	18.2	20.5	6.8
使用者 user	42	16.7	40.5	33.3	7.1	2.4
女性 Female	56	26.8	42.9	16.1	7.1	7.1
提议者 advocate	6	33.3	16.7	0.0	33.3	16.7
影响者 influence	4	25.0	0.0	25.0	25.0	25.0
决定者 decider	16	12.5	50.0	25.0	0.0	12.5
使用者 user	42	31.0	42.9	11.9	9.5	4.8

7-8 不同消费者层的家中目前拥有品牌/ Brands of Hi-Fi Stereo Owned in Household by Market Segments

7-8-1 时尚流行指标/ Fads Popular Index

	人数 Number	第一品牌及百分比 1st/ percent	第二品牌及百分比 2nd/ percent	第三品牌及百分比 3rd/ percent
样本 Sample	150	**爱华 Aiwa(11.3)**	**先锋 Pioneer(8.7)**	**新科 Shinco(8.0)**
平实生活指向 simple living orientation	57	索尼 Sony(10.5) 飞利浦 Philips(10.5)	新科 Shinco(8.8)	松下 Panasonic(5.3)
时尚流行指向 fashion orientation	93	爱华 Aiwa(16.1)	先锋 Pioneer(11.8)	新科 Shinco(7.5)

7-8-2 广告态度指标/ Advertising Attitude Index

	人数 Number	第一品牌及百分比 1st/ percent	第二品牌及百分比 2nd/ percent	第三品牌及百分比 3rd/ percent
样本 Sample	150	**爱华 Aiwa(11.3)**	**先锋 Pioneer(8.7)**	**新科 Shinco(8.0)**
广告淡漠指向 indifferent orientation	37	先锋 Pioneer(10.8)	健伍 Kenwood(8.1) 索尼 Sony(8.1) 新科 Shinco(8.1)	爱华 Aiwa(5.4) 飞利浦 Philips(5.4) 先科 SAST(5.4)
中间层 medium	91	爱华 Aiwa(13.2)	先锋 Pioneer(8.8)	飞利浦 Philips(7.7)
信赖广告指向 loyal orientation	22	新科 Shinco(22.7)	爱华 Aiwa(13.6)	飞利浦 Philips(4.5) 奇声 Qisheng(4.5) 三洋 Sanyo(4.5) 索尼 Sony(4.5) 先锋 Pioneer(4.5) 大宇 Daewoo(4.5) 星球 Xingqiu(4.5) 万利达 Malata(4.5) 声星 Shengxing(4.5) 厦华 Xoceco(4.5) 海尔 Haier(4.5) 百佳 Baijia(4.5) 塞格 Saige(4.5) KADAR(4.5)

7-8-3 价格态度指标/ Price Attitude Index

	人数 Number	第一品牌及百分比 1st/ percent	第二品牌及百分比 2nd/ percent	第三品牌及百分比 3rd/ percent
样本 Sample	150	**爱华 Aiwa(11.3)**	**先锋 Pioneer(8.7)**	**新科 Shinco(8.0)**
价格无关心指向 indifferent orientation	33	先锋 Pioneer(12.1) 爱华 Aiwa(12.1)	飞利浦 Philips(9.1) 新科 Shinco(9.1)	康丽 Kangli(6.1) 健伍 Kenwood(6.1) 索尼 Sony(6.1)
中间层 medium	80	爱华 Aiwa(8.8) 新科 Shinco(8.8)	先锋 Pioneer(6.3)	索尼 Sony(5.0) 先科 SAST(5.0) 飞利浦 Philips(5.0)
价格重视指向 careful orientation	37	爱华 Aiwa(16.2)	先锋 Pioneer(10.8)	松下 Panasonic(8.1) 飞利浦 Philips(8.1)

7-9 不同消费者层选择音响时的考虑因素/ Considerations in Choosing from Different Brands by Market Segments

7-9-1 时尚流行指标/ Fads Popular Index

注：本题为多选题，合计百分比超过 100%（Multiple answers）

	人数 Number	品牌形象 brand image	外型 outlook	价格 price	音质 sound effect	遥控功能 remote control	专业声誉 professional prestige
样本 Sample	150	36.7	9.3	32.0	47.3	14.0	8.0
平实生活指向 simple living orientation	57	36.8	8.8	36.8	38.6	8.8	1.8
时尚流行指向 fashion orientation	93	36.6	9.7	29.0	52.7	17.2	11.8

续前表 continued

	人数 Number	卡拉 OK 功能 karaoke function	原产地 place of production	功能齐备 all-function	售后服务 follow-up service	其他 others
样本 Sample	150	25.3	5.3	25.3	3.3	2.0
平实生活指向 simple living orientation	57	28.1	3.5	24.6	1.8	0.0
时尚流行指向 fashion orientation	93	23.7	6.5	25.8	4.3	3.2

7-9-2 广告态度指向/ Advertising Attitude Index

注：本题为多选题，合计百分比超过 100%（Multiple answers）

	人数 Number	品牌形象 brand image	外型 outlook	价格 price	音质 sound effect	遥控功能 remote control	专业声誉 professional prestige
样本 Sample	150	36.7	9.3	32.0	47.3	14.0	8.0
广告淡漠指向 indifferent orientation	37	35.1	13.5	35.1	45.9	18.9	8.1
中间层 medium	91	38.5	8.8	29.7	48.4	11.0	6.6
信赖广告指向 loyal orientation	22	31.8	4.5	36.4	45.5	18.2	13.6

续前表 continued

	人数 Number	卡拉 OK 功能 karaoke function	原产地 place of production	功能齐备 all-function	售后服务 follow-up service	其他 others
样本 Sample	150	25.3	5.3	25.3	3.3	2.0
广告淡漠指向 indifferent orientation	37	27.0	2.7	32.4	0.0	5.4
中间层 medium	91	25.3	7.7	20.9	4.4	1.1
信赖广告指向 loyal orientation	22	22.7	0.0	31.8	4.5	0.0

7-9-3 价格态度指向/ Price Attitude Index

注：本题为多选题，合计百分比超过 100%（Multiple answers）

	人数 Number	品牌形象 brand image	外型 outlook	价格 price	音质 sound effect	遥控功能 remote control	专业声誉 professional prestige
样本 Sample	150	36.7	9.3	32.0	47.3	14.0	8.0
价格无关心指向 indifferent orientation	33	42.4	12.1	12.1	51.5	18.2	6.1
中间层 medium	80	37.5	8.8	37.5	43.8	11.3	8.8
价格重视指向 careful orientation	37	29.7	8.1	37.8	51.4	16.2	8.1

续前表 continued

	人数 Number	卡拉 OK 功能 karaoke function	原产地 place of production	功能齐备 all-function	售后服务 follow-up service	其他 others
样本 Sample	150	25.3	5.3	25.3	3.3	2.0
价格无关心指向 indifferent orientation	33	24.2	6.1	36.4	0.0	0.0
中间层 medium	80	21.3	5.0	22.5	1.3	3.8
价格重视指向 careful orientation	37	35.1	5.4	21.6	10.8	0.0

8.影碟机 VCD/DVD/SVCD Player

● 北京 / Beijing

8-1 影碟机的拥有比例/ Proportion of VCD Player Owners in the Sample

	人数 Number	百分比 Percent
有 yes	589	58.2
没有 no	423	41.8

n=1012

8-2 影碟机的拥有量/ Number of VCD Player Owned Per Household

	人数 Number	百分比 Percent
1 台 1 set	565	97.1
2 台及以上 2 sets or over	17	2.9

n=582

8-3 理想品牌排名/ Ranking of the Ideal Brands

排名 Brand Ranking	品牌 Brands	人数 Number	百分比 Percent
1	新科 Shinco	99	9.8
2	万利达 Malata	79	7.8
3	爱多 Idall	74	7.3
4	先科 SAST	69	6.8
5	索尼 Sony	59	5.8
6	松下 Panasonic	57	5.6
7	步步高 BBK	40	4.0
8	厦新 Amoisonic	29	2.9
9	金正 Nintaus	20	2.0
9	飞利浦 Philips	20	2.0
10	三星 Samsung	17	1.7
11	新天利 Xintianli	11	1.1

n=1009

8-4 对家中现有影碟机(最近购买的一台)的五个方面的描述/ About the VCD Player Most Recently Purchased

8-4-1 家中现有影碟机的品牌排名/ Ranking of the Currently Owned VCD Player Brands

排名 Brand Ranking	品牌 Brands	人数 Number	百分比 Percent
1	爱多 Idall	83	14.4
2	新科 Shinco	75	13.0
3	万利达 Malata	63	10.9
4	先科 SAST	49	8.5
5	索尼 Sony	35	6.1
6	松下 Panasonic	31	5.4
7	厦新 Amoisonic	23	4.0
8	三星 Samsung	16	2.8
9	飞利浦 Philips	15	2.6
10	新天利 Xintianli	14	2.4
11	德加拉 Thakral	12	2.1
12	金正 Nintaus	10	1.7

n=578

8-4-2 该影碟机的购买时间/ The Time of Purchasing of the Currently Owned VCD Player

	人数 Number	百分比 Percent
1993 年	6	1.0
1994 年	4	0.7
1995 年	20	3.4
1996 年	78	13.4
1997 年	177	30.4
1998 年	199	34.2
1999 年	98	16.8

n=582

8-4-3 该影碟机的价格/ The Price of the Currently Owned VCD Player

	人数 Number	百分比 Percent
1000 元或以下 1000 yuan or below	112	19.2
1001～2000 元 yuan	316	54.3
2001～3000 元 yuan	85	14.6
3001～4000 元 yuan	27	4.6
4001～5000 元 yuan	8	1.4
5001～6000 元 yuan	4	0.7
6001～7000 元 yuan	2	0.3
7001～8000 元 yuan	5	0.9
8001～9000 元 yuan	0	0.0
9001～10000 元 yuan	0	0.0
10000 元以上 over 10000 yuan	0	0.0
完全不知道 don't know	23	4.0

n=582

8-4-4 该影碟机的类型/ The Kind of the Currently Owned VCD Player

	人数 Number	百分比 Percent
VCD 机	532	91.1
DVD 机	14	2.4
CVD 机	3	0.5
SVCD 机	33	5.7
其他 others	2	0.3

n=584

8-4-5 该影碟机的机型/ The Type of the Currently Owned VCD Player

	人数 Number	百分比 Percent
普通机 VCD	403	71.2
自动换碟机 auto disc change	155	27.4
便携式机 portable VCD	5	0.9
其他 others	3	0.5

n=566

8-5 选择不同品牌影碟机时的考虑因素/ Considerations in Choosing from Different Brands

注：本题为多选题，合计百分比超过 100%（Multiple answers）

	人数 Number	品牌形象 brand image	外型 outlook	价格 price	画质好 clarity	纠错能力 correct ability
样本 Sample	**568**	**35.9**	**7.9**	**37.7**	**21.7**	**35.0**
爱多 Idall	82	42.7	2.4	43.9	14.6	34.1
新科 Shinco	74	39.2	6.8	33.8	32.4	37.8
万利达 Malata	61	52.5	8.2	36.1	26.2	50.8
先科 SAST	49	36.7	8.2	44.9	6.1	46.9
索尼 Sony	34	52.9	5.9	26.5	29.4	14.7
松下 Panasonic	30	30.0	16.7	26.7	26.7	16.7
厦新 Amoisonic	22	36.4	4.5	31.8	27.3	45.5
三星 Samsung	16	50.0	6.3	18.8	6.3	12.5
飞利浦 Philips	15	46.7	13.3	40.0	33.3	13.3
新天利 Xintianli	14	14.3	0.0	28.6	14.3	50.0
德加拉 Thakral	12	16.7	8.3	50.0	8.3	50.0
金正 Nintaus	10	40.0	0.0	20.0	20.0	70.0

续前表 continued

	人数 Number	多制式 multi-system	有卡拉 OK 功能 karaoke function	有游戏功能 game function flavored	售后服务 follow-up service	其他 others
样本 Sample	**568**	**7.7**	**30.1**	**4.8**	**9.0**	**4.0**
爱多 Idall	82	4.9	29.3	1.2	4.9	6.1
新科 Shinco	74	10.8	29.7	1.4	12.2	0.0
万利达 Malata	61	4.9	29.5	0.0	6.6	1.6
先科 SAST	49	4.1	34.7	4.1	8.2	0.0
索尼 Sony	34	11.8	23.5	8.8	8.8	5.9
松下 Panasonic	30	6.7	43.3	0.0	10.0	6.7
厦新 Amoisonic	22	4.5	27.3	9.1	9.1	0.0
三星 Samsung	16	12.5	25.0	6.3	12.5	0.0
飞利浦 Philips	15	6.7	40.0	0.0	20.0	0.0
新天利 Xintianli	14	7.1	42.9	35.7	7.1	7.1
德加拉 Thakral	12	8.3	0.0	0.0	8.3	8.3
金正 Nintaus	10	10.0	30.0	10.0	10.0	10.0

8-6 影碟机未来购买打算/ Plan for Future Purchasing of a VCD Player

8-6-1 有无购买打算/ Whether Planning to Purchase Next Year

	人数 Number	百分比 Percent
是 yes	96	9.6
否 no	909	90.4

n=1005

8-6-2 打算购买的品牌排名/ Ranking of the Brands of the Planned Purchase Next Year

排名 Brand Ranking	品牌 Brands	人数 Number	百分比 Percent
1	新科 Shinco	15	17.0
2	先科 SAST	8	9.1
3	万利达 Malata	7	8.0
4	爱多 Idall	6	6.8
5	索尼 Sony	5	5.7
6	松下 Panasonic	4	4.5

n=88

8-6-3 打算购买的机型/ The Type of the Planned Purchase Next Year

	人数 Number	百分比 Percent
VCD 机	27	30.3
DVD 机	52	58.4
CVD 机	2	2.2
SVCD 机	6	6.7
其他 others	2	2.2

n=89

8-6-4 打算购买的价格/ The Price of the Planned Purchase Next Year

	人数 Number	百分比 Percent
1000 元或以下 1000 yuan or below	20	22.7
1001～2000 元 yuan	33	37.5
2001～3000 元 yuan	26	29.5
3001～4000 元 yuan	2	2.3
4001～5000 元 yuan	3	3.4
5001～6000 元 yuan	2	2.3
6001～7000 元 yuan	1	1.1
7001～8000 元 yuan	0	0.0
8001～9000 元 yuan	0	0.0
9001～10000 元 yuan	0	0.0
10000 元以上 over 10000 yuan	0	0.0
完全不知道 don't know	1	1.1

n=88

8-7 选购影碟机时不同角色的人口特征/ Demographics of the Different Roles in Purchasing a VCD Player

注：不同角色可以多选（Multiple answers）

	人数 Number	16-24 岁 Age	25-34 岁 Age	35-44 岁 Age	45-54 岁 Age	55-60 岁 Age
样本 Sample	541	20.7	30.7	26.6	15.2	6.8
男性 Male	268	20.5	30.6	26.9	13.8	8.2
提议者 advocate	47	27.7	27.7	27.7	12.8	4.3
影响者 influence	27	25.9	33.3	29.6	11.1	0.0
决定者 decider	142	12.0	32.4	31.7	13.4	10.6
使用者 user	189	25.4	28.0	25.4	14.3	6.9
女性 Female	273	20.9	30.8	26.4	16.5	5.5
提议者 advocate	53	26.4	24.5	26.4	17.0	5.7
影响者 influence	26	42.3	19.2	19.2	11.5	7.7
决定者 decider	75	13.3	40.0	24.0	17.3	5.3
使用者 user	203	21.2	31.0	28.6	14.8	4.4

8-8 不同消费者层的家中目前拥有品牌/ Brands of VCD Player Owned in Household by Market Segments

8-8-1 时尚流行指标/ Fads Popular Index

	人数 Number	第一品牌及百分比 1st/ percent	第二品牌及百分比 2nd/ percent	第三品牌及百分比 3rd/ percent	第四品牌及百分比 4th/ percent
样本 Sample	571	**爱多 Idall(14.4)**	**新科 Shinco(13.1)**	**万利达 Malata(11.0)**	**先科 SAST(8.6)**
平实生活指向 simple living orientation	259	新科 Shinco(15.1)	爱多 Idall(13.5)	先科 SAST(10.4)	万利达 Malata(8.9)
时尚流行指向 fashion orientation	312	爱多 Idall(15.1)	万利达 Malata(12.8)	新科 Shinco(11.5)	索尼 Sony(7.7)

8-8-2 广告态度指标/ Advertising Attitude Index

	人数 Number	第一品牌及百分比 1st/ percent	第二品牌及百分比 2nd/ percent	第三品牌及百分比 3rd/ percent	第四品牌及百分比 4th/ percent
样本 Sample	**569**	**爱多 Idall(14.2)**	**新科 Shinco(13.2)**	**万利达 Malata(11.1)**	**先科 SAST(8.6)**
广告淡漠指向 indifferent orientation	160	爱多 Idall(13.1)	新科 Shinco(11.9)	先科 SAST(10.0)	万利达 Malata(8.1)
中间层 medium	326	爱多 Idall(14.7) 新科 Shinco(14.7)	万利达 Malata(12.0)	先科 SAST(7.7) 索尼 Sony(7.7)	松下 Panasonic(4.3)
信赖广告指向 loyal orientation	83	爱多 Idall(14.5)	万利达 Malata(13.3)	新科 Shinco(9.6) 先科 SAST(9.6)	松下 Panasonic(7.2)

8-8-3 价格态度指标/ Price Attitude Index

	人数 Number	第一品牌及百分比 1st/ percent	第二品牌及百分比 2nd/ percent	第三品牌及百分比 3rd/ percent	第四品牌及百分比 4th/ percent
样本 Sample	**575**	**爱多 Idall(14.4)**	**新科 Shinco(13.0)**	**万利达 Malata(11.0)**	**先科 SAST(8.3)**
价格无关心指向 indifferent orientation	126	爱多 Idall(11.9)	新科 Shinco(10.3) 先科 SAST(10.3)	万利达 Malata(8.7)	索尼 Sony(7.9)
中间层 medium	289	新科 Shinco(15.6)	爱多 Idall(13.5)	万利达 Malata(10.7)	先科 SAST(6.9) 索尼 Sony(6.9)
价格重视指向 careful orientation	160	爱多 Idall(18.1)	万利达 Malata(13.1)	新科 Shinco(10.6)	先科 SAST(9.4)

8-9 不同消费者层选择影碟机时的考虑因素/ Considerations in Choosing from Different Brands by Market Segments

8-9-1 时尚流行指标/ Fads Popular Index

注：本题为多选题，合计百分比超过 100%（Multiple answers）

	人数 Number	品牌形象 brand image	外型 outlook	价格 price	画质好 clarity	纠错能力 correct ability
样本 Sample	**570**	**35.8**	**7.9**	**37.5**	**21.6**	**35.3**
平实生活指向 simple living orientation	258	34.5	6.2	36.4	21.7	36.4
时尚流行指向 fashion orientation	312	36.9	9.3	38.5	21.5	34.3

续前表 continued

	人数 Number	多制式 multi-system	有卡拉 OK 功能 karaoke function	有游戏功能 game function flavored	售后服务 follow-up service	其他 others
样本 Sample	**570**	**7.7**	**29.6**	**4.9**	**9.1**	**4.0**
平实生活指向 simple living orientation	258	6.6	27.9	4.3	8.1	3.9
时尚流行指向 fashion orientation	312	8.7	31.1	5.4	9.9	4.2

8-9-2 广告态度指向/ Advertising Attitude Index

注：本题为多选题，合计百分比超过 100%（Multiple answers）

	人数 Number	品牌形象 brand image	外型 outlook	价格 price	画质好 clarity	纠错能力 correct ability
样本 Sample	**568**	**36.1**	**8.3**	**38.0**	**21.3**	**34.9**
广告淡漠指向 indifferent orientation	158	31.0	9.5	36.1	21.5	34.8
中间层 medium	325	38.8	8.0	37.5	23.1	36.3
信赖广告指向 loyal orientation	85	35.3	7.1	43.5	14.1	29.4

续前表 continued

	人数 Number	多制式 multi-system	有卡拉 OK 功能 karaoke function	有游戏功能 game function flavored	售后服务 follow-up service	其他 others
样本 Sample	**568**	**7.9**	**29.6**	**4.9**	**9.0**	**3.7**
广告淡漠指向 indifferent orientation	158	5.7	29.1	5.1	9.5	5.1
中间层 medium	325	10.2	29.8	4.0	9.5	2.5
信赖广告指向 loyal orientation	85	3.5	29.4	8.2	5.9	5.9

8-9-3 价格态度指向/ Price Attitude Index

注：本题为多选题，合计百分比超过 100%（Multiple answers）

	人数 Number	品牌形象 brand image	外型 outlook	价格 price	画质好 clarity	纠错能力 correct ability
样本 Sample	574	35.7	8.2	37.8	21.1	35.2
价格无关心指向 indifferent orientation	125	35.2	7.2	35.2	25.6	29.6
中间层 medium	290	34.1	10.0	35.2	21.7	37.9
价格重视指向 careful orientation	159	39.0	5.7	44.7	16.4	34.6

续前表 continued

	人数 Number	多制式 multi-system	有卡拉 OK 功能 karaoke function	有游戏功能 game function flavored	售后服务 follow-up service	其他 others
样本 Sample	574	7.8	29.6	4.9	9.1	4.0
价格无关心指向 indifferent orientation	125	11.2	30.4	4.0	8.0	4.8
中间层 medium	290	6.9	26.9	4.5	10.0	3.1
价格重视指向 careful orientation	159	6.9	34.0	6.3	8.2	5.0

● 上海 / Shanghai

8-1 影碟机的拥有比例/ Proportion of VCD Player Owners in the Sample

	人数 Number	百分比 Percent
有 yes	632	62.3
没有 no	382	37.7

n=1014

8-2 影碟机的拥有量/ Number of VCD Player Owned Per Household

	人数 Number	百分比 Percent
1 台 1 set	598	96.3
2 台及以上 2 sets or over	23	3.7

n=621

8-3 理想品牌排名/ Ranking of the Ideal Brands

排名 Brand Ranking	品牌 Brands	人数 Number	百分比 Percent
1	新科 Shinco	154	15.3
2	松下 Panasonic	113	11.2
3	步步高 BBK	87	8.6
4	索尼 Sony	82	8.1
5	爱多 Idall	75	7.4
6	飞利浦 Philips	69	6.8
7	先科 SAST	50	5.0
8	万利达 Malata	47	4.7
9	三星 Samsung	35	3.5
10	夏普/声宝 Sharp	19	1.9

n=1008

8-4 对家中现有影碟机(最近购买的一台)的五个方面的描述/ About the VCD Player Most Recently Purchased

8-4-1 家中现有影碟机的品牌排名/ Ranking of the Currently Owned VCD Player Brands

排名 Brand Ranking	品牌 Brands	人数 Number	百分比 Percent
1	新科 Shinco	130	20.6
2	爱多 Idall	64	10.2
3	万利达 Malata	48	7.6
4	松下 Panasonic	42	6.7
5	步步高 BBK	36	5.7
6	飞利浦 Philips	29	4.6
7	德加拉 Thakral	27	4.3
8	先科 SAST	26	4.1
9	三星 Samsung	25	4.0
10	上海 Shanghai	17	2.7

n=630

8-4-2 该影碟机的购买时间/ The Time of Purchasing of the Currently Owned VCD Player

	人数 Number	百分比 Percent
1993 年	6	1.0
1994 年	17	2.7
1995 年	37	5.9
1996 年	125	19.9
1997 年	216	34.3
1998 年	153	24.3
1999 年	75	11.9

n=629

8-4-3 该影碟机的价格/ The Price of the Currently Owned VCD Player

	人数 Number	百分比 Percent
1000 元或以下 1000 yuan or below	99	15.7
1001～2000 元 yuan	352	56.0
2001～3000 元 yuan	97	15.4
3001～4000 元 yuan	39	6.2
4001～5000 元 yuan	19	3.0
5001～6000 元 yuan	2	0.3
6001～7000 元 yuan	1	0.2
7001～8000 元 yuan	0	0.0
8001～9000 元 yuan	1	0.2
9001～10000 元 yuan	0	0.0
10000 元以上 over 10000 yuan	1	0.2
完全不知道 don't know	18	2.9

n=629

8-4-4 该影碟机的类型/ The Kind of the Currently Owned VCD Player

	人数 Number	百分比 Percent
VCD 机	592	94.1
DVD 机	17	2.7
CVD 机	3	0.5
SVCD 机	16	2.5
其他 others	1	0.2

n=629

8-4-5 该影碟机的机型/ The Type of the Currently Owned VCD Player

	人数 Number	百分比 Percent
普通机 VCD	460	73.4
自动换碟机 auto disc change	152	24.2
便携式机 portable VCD	11	1.8
其他 others	4	0.6

n=627

8-5 选择不同品牌影碟机时的考虑因素/ Considerations in Choosing from Different Brands

注：本题为多选题，合计百分比超过 100%（Multiple answers）

	人数 Number	品牌形象 brand image	外型 outlook	价格 price	画质好 clarity	纠错能力 correct ability
样本 Sample	627	42.3	8.5	41.9	26.3	29.3
新科 Shinco	130	50.8	5.4	42.3	24.6	26.2
爱多 Idall	64	57.8	1.6	51.6	23.4	40.6
万利达 Malata	48	41.7	2.1	33.3	27.1	37.5
松下 Panasonic	41	53.7	9.8	24.4	26.8	19.5
步步高 BBK	36	50.0	16.7	55.6	27.8	33.3
飞利浦 Philips	29	48.3	24.1	24.1	27.6	34.5
德加拉 Thakral	26	19.2	11.5	80.8	23.1	26.9
先科 SAST	26	30.8	11.5	34.6	11.5	34.6
三星 Samsung	25	60.0	0.0	16.0	28.0	16.0
上海 Shanghai	17	17.6	0.0	58.8	11.8	35.3

续前表 continued

	人数 Number	多制式 multi-system	有卡拉 OK 功能 karaoke function	有游戏功能 game function flavored	售后服务 follow-up service	其他 others
样本 Sample	**627**	**12.3**	**29.5**	**1.0**	**9.3**	**2.1**
新科 Shinco	130	13.8	29.2	0.8	15.4	2.3
爱多 Idall	64	9.4	25.0	0.0	9.4	0.0
万利达 Malata	48	12.5	37.5	0.0	10.4	4.2
松下 Panasonic	41	9.8	24.4	4.9	7.3	0.0
步步高 BBK	36	2.8	13.9	2.8	8.3	0.0
飞利浦 Philips	29	24.1	20.7	0.0	3.4	0.0
德加拉 Thakral	26	3.8	19.2	0.0	3.8	0.0
先科 SAST	26	7.7	42.3	0.0	11.5	11.5
三星 Samsung	25	24.0	48.0	0.0	16.0	0.0
上海 Shanghai	17	23.5	47.1	5.9	0.0	0.0

8-6 影碟机未来购买打算/ Plan for Future Purchasing of a VCD Player

8-6-1 有无购买打算/ Whether Planning to Purchase Next Year

	人数 Number	百分比 Percent
是 yes	49	4.8
否 no	964	95.2

n=1013

8-6-2 打算购买的品牌排名/ The Brand of the Planned Purchase Next Year

排名 Brand Ranking	品牌 Brands	人数 Number	百分比 Percent
1	新科 Shinco	11	22.9
2	飞利浦 Philips	6	12.5
3	松下 Panasonic	5	10.4
4	金正 Nintaus	3	6.3
4	先科 SAST	3	6.3
5	厦新 Amoisonic	2	4.2
5	三星 Samsung	2	4.2
5	步步高 BBK	2	4.2
5	爱华 Aiwa	2	4.2

n=48

8-6-3 打算购买的机型/ The Type of the Planned Purchase Next Year

	人数 Number	百分比 Percent
VCD 机	15	30.6
DVD 机	24	49.0
CVD 机	4	8.2
SVCD 机	4	8.2
其他 others	2	4.1

n=49

8-6-4 打算购买的价格/ The Price of the Planned Purchase Next Year

	人数 Number	百分比 Percent
1000 元或以下 1000 yuan or below	5	10.2
1001～2000 元 yuan	18	36.7
2001～3000 元 yuan	13	26.5
3001～4000 元 yuan	9	18.4
4001～5000 元 yuan	1	2.0
5001～6000 元 yuan	0	0.0
6001～7000 元 yuan	2	4.1
7001～8000 元 yuan	0	0.0
8001～9000 元 yuan	0	0.0
9001～10000 元 yuan	1	2.0
10000 元以上 over 10000 yuan	0	0.0
完全不知道 don't know	0	0.0

n=49

8-7 选购影碟机时不同角色的人口特征/ Demographics of Different Roles in Purchasing a VCD Player

注：不同角色可以多选（Multiple answers）

	人数 Number	16-24 岁 Age	25-34 岁 Age	35-44 岁 Age	45-54 岁 Age	55-60 岁 Age
样本 Sample	575	22.6	32.7	24.7	14.3	5.7
男性 Male	298	23.2	32.6	23.2	14.8	6.4
提议者 advocate	52	30.8	32.7	21.2	15.4	0.0
影响者 influence	35	28 6	28.6	14.3	17.1	11.4
决定者 decider	137	10.2	34.3	30.7	20.4	4.4
使用者 user	169	30.2	29.6	21.3	11.2	7.7
女性 Female	277	22.0	32.9	26.4	13.7	5.1
提议者 advocate	45	31.1	28.9	26.7	13.3	0.0
影响者 influence	39	20.5	25.6	28.2	17.9	7.7
决定者 decider	77	14.3	35.1	28.6	18.2	3.9
使用者 user	183	21.3	33.3	27.9	11.5	6.0

8-8 不同消费者层的家中目前拥有品牌/ Brands of VCD Player Owned in Household by Market Segments

8-8-1 时尚流行指标/ Fads Popular Index

	人数 Number	第一品牌及百分比 1st/ percent	第二品牌及百分比 2nd/ percent	第三品牌及百分比 3rd/ percent	第四品牌及百分比 4th/ percent
样本 Sample	624	**新科 Shinco(20.0)**	**爱多 Idall(10.3)**	**万利达 Malata(7.7)**	**松下 Panasonic(6.7)**
平实生活指向 simple living orientation	259	新科 Shinco(20.1)	万利达 Malata(10.4)	爱多 Idall(9.7)	步步高 BBK(5.8)
时尚流行指向 fashion orientation	365	新科 Shinco(20.0)	爱多 Idall(10.7)	松下 Panasonic(8.5)	万利达 Malata(5.8) 步步高 BBK(5.8)

8-8-2 广告态度指标/ Advertising Attitude Index

	人数 Number	第一品牌及百分比 1st/ percent	第二品牌及百分比 2nd/ percent	第三品牌及百分比 3rd/ percent	第四品牌及百分比 4th/ percent
样本 Sample	622	**新科 Shinco(20.7)**	**爱多 Idall(10.0)**	**万利达 Malata(7.7)**	**松下 Panasonic(6.6)**
广告淡漠指向 indifferent orientation	160	新科 Shinco(19.4)	万利达 Malata(10.6)	飞利浦 Philips(8.1)	爱多 Idall(6.9)
中间层 medium	376	新科 Shinco(21.5)	爱多 Idall(11.2)	万利达 Malata(7.2)	松下 Panasonic(6.4)
信赖广告指向 loyal orientation	86	新科 Shinco(19.8)	松下 Panasonic(11.6)	爱多 Idall(10.5)	先科 SAST(7.0)

8-8-3 价格态度指标/ Price Attitude Index

	人数 Number	第一品牌及百分比 1st/ percent	第二品牌及百分比 2nd/ percent	第三品牌及百分比 3rd/ percent	第四品牌及百分比 4th/ percent
样本 Sample	629	**新科 Shinco(20.7)**	**爱多 Idall(10.2)**	**万利达 Malata(7.6)**	**松下 Panasonic(6.7)**
价格无关心指向 indifferent orientation	103	新科 Shinco(16.5)	万利达 Malata(9.7)	爱多 Idall(8.7)	飞利浦 Philips(7.8)
中间层 medium	349	新科 Shinco(21.5)	爱多 Idall(10.6)	万利达 Malata(6.6)	步步高 BBK(6.3)
价格重视指向 careful orientation	177	新科 Shinco(21.5)	爱多 Idall(10.2)	松下 Panasonic(9.0)	万利达 Malata(8.5)

8-9 不同消费者层选择影碟机时考虑因素/ Considerations in Choosing from Different Brands by Market Segments

8-9-1 时尚流行指标/ Fads Popular Index

注：本题为多选题，合计百分比超过 100%（Multiple answers）

	人数 Number	品牌形象 brand image	外型 outlook	价格 price	画质好 clarity	纠错能力 correct ability
样本 Sample	623	42.4	8.7	41.7	26.2	29.7
平实生活指向 simple living orientation	258	44.6	3.9	41.1	26.0	27.9
时尚流行指向 fashion orientation	365	40.8	12.1	42.2	26.3	31.0

续前表 continued

	人数 Number	多制式 multi-system	有卡拉 OK 功能 karaoke function	有游戏功能 game function flavored	售后服务 follow-up service	其他 others
样本 Sample	623	12.4	29.4	1.0	9.0	2.1
平实生活指向 simple living orientation	258	12.4	29.8	1.6	8.5	1.9
时尚流行指向 fashion orientation	365	12.3	29.0	0.5	9.3	2.2

8-9-2 广告态度指向/ Advertising Attitude Index

注：本题为多选题，合计百分比超过 100%（Multiple answers）

	人数 Number	品牌形象 brand image	外型 outlook	价格 price	画质好 clarity	纠错能力 correct ability
样本 Sample	621	42.5	8.5	41.7	26.1	29.3
广告淡漠指向 indifferent orientation	160	40.0	8.8	40.6	21.9	27.5
中间层 medium	375	44.5	7.7	44.5	25.1	28.3
信赖广告指向 loyal orientation	86	38.4	11.6	31.4	38.4	37.2

续前表 continued

	人数 Number	多制式 multi-system	有卡拉 OK 功能 karaoke function	有游戏功能 game function flavored	售后服务 follow-up service	其他 others
样本 Sample	621	12.2	29.6	1.0	9.2	1.9
广告淡漠指向 indifferent orientation	160	10.0	31.3	2.5	6.3	1.3
中间层 medium	375	13.6	29.1	0.3	10.1	2.7
信赖广告指向 loyal orientation	86	10.5	29.1	1.2	10.5	0.0

8-9-3 价格态度指向/ Price Attitude Index

注：本题为多选题，合计百分比超过 100%（Multiple answers）

	人数 Number	品牌形象 brand image	外型 outlook	价格 price	画质好 clarity	纠错能力 correct ability
样本 Sample	628	42.0	8.6	42.0	26.3	29.5
价格无关心指向 indifferent orientation	102	42.2	7.8	34.3	24.5	33.3
中间层 medium	348	42.0	9.5	41.4	27.9	29.3
价格重视指向 careful orientation	178	42.1	7.3	47.8	24.2	27.5

续前表 continued

	人数 Number	多制式 multi-system	有卡拉 OK 功能 karaoke function	有游戏功能 game function flavored	售后服务 follow-up service	其他 others
样本 Sample	628	12.3	29.6	1.0	9.2	2.1
价格无关心指向 indifferent orientation	102	9.8	25.5	0.0	9.8	1.0
中间层 medium	348	14.1	30.5	1.1	8.6	2.0
价格重视指向 careful orientation	178	10.1	30.3	1.1	10.1	2.8

● 广州 / Guangzhou

8-1 影碟机的拥有比例/ Proportion of VCD Player Owners in the Sample

	人数 Number	百分比 Percent
有 yes	666	64.4
没有 no	368	35.6

n=1034

8-2 影碟机的拥有量/ Number of VCD Player Owned Per Household

	人数 Number	百分比 Percent
1 台 1 set	623	94.8
2 台及以上 2 sets or over	34	5.2

n=657

8-3 理想品牌排名/ Ranking of the Ideal Brands

排名 Brand Ranking	品牌 Brands	人数 Number	百分比 Percent
1	索尼 Sony	169	16.4
2	爱多 Idall	112	10.9
3	松下 Panasonic	69	6.7
4	步步高 BBK	40	3.9
5	三星 Samsung	38	3.7
6	飞利浦 Philips	30	2.9
7	金格川谷 Gynco	28	2.7
8	新科 Shinco	27	2.6
9	先科 SAST	23	2.2
9	蚬华 SMC	23	2.2

n=1032

8-4 对家中现有 (最近购买的一台)的五个方面的描述/ About the VCD Player Most Recently Purchased

8-4-1 家中现有影碟机的品牌排名/ Ranking of the Currently Owned VCD Player Brands

排名 Brand Ranking	品牌 Brands	人数 Number	百分比 Percent
1	爱多 Idall	79	12.2
2	索尼 Sony	70	10.8
3	三星 Samsung	45	6.9
4	松下 Panasonic	39	6.0
5	蚬华 SMC	34	5.2
6	金格川谷 Gynco	33	5.1
7	新科 Shinco	30	4.6
8	先科 SAST	29	4.5
9	步步高 BBK	23	3.5

n=650

8-4-2 该影碟机的购买时间/ The Time of Purchasing of the Currently Owned VCD Player

	人数 Number	百分比 Percent
1993 年	14	2.1
1994 年	19	2.9
1995 年	67	10.1
1996 年	144	21.7
1997 年	198	29.8
1998 年	166	25.0
1999 年	56	8.4

n=664

8-4-3 该影碟机的价格/ The Price of the Currently Owned VCD Player

	人数 Number	百分比 Percent
1000 元或以下 1000 yuan or below	129	19.4
1001～2000 元 yuan	326	49.0
2001～3000 元 yuan	107	16.1
3001～4000 元 yuan	36	5.4
4001～5000 元 yuan	19	2.9
5001～6000 元 yuan	6	0.9
6001～7000 元 yuan	4	0.6
7001～8000 元 yuan	2	0.3
8001～9000 元 yuan	1	0.2
9001～10000 元 yuan	1	0.2
10000 元以上 over 10000 yuan	1	0.2
完全不知道 don't know	33	5.0

n=665

8-4-4 该影碟机的类型/ The Kind of the Currently Owned VCD Player

	人数 Number	百分比 Percent
VCD 机	624	93.8
DVD 机	26	3.9
CVD 机	5	0.8
SVCD 机	7	1.1
其他 others	3	0.5

n=665

8-4-5 该影碟机的机型/ The Type of the Currently Owned VCD Player

	人数 Number	百分比 Percent
普通机 VCD	549	85.0
自动换碟机 auto disc change	90	13.9
便携式机 portable VCD	5	0.8
其他 others	2	0.3

n=646

8-5 选择不同品牌影碟机时的考虑因素/ Considerations in Choosing from Different Brands

注：本题为多选题，合计百分比超过 100%（Multiple answers）

	人数 Number	品牌形象 brand image	外型 outlook	价格 price	画质好 clarity	纠错能力 correct ability
样本 Sample	650	30.9	11.5	49.1	36.6	27.2
爱多 Idall	79	38.0	8.9	36.7	32.9	41.8
索尼 Sony	70	44.3	18.6	35.7	38.6	17.1
三星 Samsung	45	42.2	13.3	46.7	42.2	13.3
松下 Panasonic	39	38.5	7.7	48.7	46.2	28.2
蚬华 SMC	34	29.4	5.9	55.9	26.5	29.4
金格川谷 Gynco	33	42.4	27.3	51.5	42.4	33.3
新科 Shinco	30	36.7	3.3	40.0	50.0	36.7
先科 SAST	29	20.7	13.8	34.5	55.2	37.9
步步高 BBK	23	39.1	8.7	60.9	17.4	34.8

续前表 continued

	人数 Number	多制式 multi-system	有卡拉 OK 功能 karaoke function	有游戏功能 game function flavored	售后服务 follow-up service	其他 others
样本 Sample	650	8.9	33.1	0.9	8.9	1.8
爱多 Idall	79	5.1	32.9	2.5	12.7	3.8
索尼 Sony	70	7.1	31.4	0.0	8.6	4.3
三星 Samsung	45	8.9	26.7	0.0	13.3	0.0
松下 Panasonic	39	12.8	33.3	0.0	2.6	0.0
蚬华 SMC	34	5.9	26.5	0.0	29.4	0.0
金格川谷 Gynco	33	9.1	30.3	0.0	0.0	0.0
新科 Shinco	30	3.3	30.0	0.0	10.0	0.0
先科 SAST	29	10.3	51.7	3.4	13.8	0.0
步步高 BBK	23	4.3	26.1	0.0	4.3	0.0

8-6 影碟机未来购买打算/ Plan for Future Purchasing of a VCD Player

8-6-1 有无购买打算/ Whether Planning to Purchase Next Year

	人数 Number	百分比 Percent
是 yes	49	4.7
否 no	985	95.3

n=1034

8-6-2 打算购买的品牌排名/ The Brand of the Planned Purchase Next Year

排名 Brand Ranking	品牌 Brands	人数 Number	百分比 Percent
1	索尼 Sony	8	16.7
2	爱多 Idall	6	12.5
3	步步高 BBK	5	10.4
4	飞利浦 Philips	4	8.3

n=48

8-6-3 打算购买的机型/ The Type of the Planned Purchase Next Year

	人数 Number	百分比 Percent
VCD 机	15	30.6
DVD 机	31	63.3
CVD 机	2	4.1
SVCD 机	1	2.0
其他 others	0	0.0

n=49

8-6-4 打算购买的价格/ The Price of the Planned Purchase Next Year

	人数 Number	百分比 Percent
1000 元或以下 1000 yuan or below	4	8.3
1001～2000 元 yuan	18	37.5
2001～3000 元 yuan	16	33.3
3001～4000 元 yuan	4	8.3
4001～5000 元 yuan	2	4.2
5001～6000 元 yuan	1	2.1
6001～7000 元 yuan	0	0.0
7001～8000 元 yuan	3	6.3
8001～9000 元 yuan	0	0.0
9001～10000 元 yuan	0	0.0
10000 元以上 over 10000 yuan	0	0.0
完全不知道 don't know	0	0.0

n=48

8-7 选购影碟机时不同角色的人口特征/ Demographics of the Different Roles in Purchasing a VCD Player

注：不同角色可以多选（Multiple answers）

	人数 Number	16-24 岁 Age	25-34 岁 Age	35-44 岁 Age	45-54 岁 Age	55-60 岁 Age
样本 Sample	614	23.3	29.5	26.4	14.3	6.5
男性 Male	322	21.4	28.9	28.6	14.0	7.1
提议者 advocate	53	39.6	34.0	15.1	5.7	5.7
影响者 influence	44	29.5	20.5	27.3	13.6	9.1
决定者 decider	147	11.6	28.6	35.4	18.4	6.1
使用者 user	168	23.8	31.5	26.3	10.1	7.7
女性 Female	292	25.3	30.1	24.0	14.7	5.8
提议者 advocate	51	37.3	29.4	15.7	13.7	3.9
影响者 influence	43	14.0	37.2	27.9	16.3	4.7
决定者 decider	54	18.5	33.3	27.8	14.8	5.6
使用者 user	194	26.3	29.4	24.7	13.9	5.7

8-8 不同消费者层的家中目前拥有品牌/ Brands of VCD Player Owned in Household by Market Segments

8-8-1 时尚流行指标/ Fads Popular Index

	人数 Number	第一品牌及百分比 1st/ percent	第二品牌及百分比 2nd/ percent	第三品牌及百分比 3rd/ percent	第四品牌及百分比 4th/ percent
样本 Sample	642	**爱多 Idall(12.3)**	**索尼 Sony(10.7)**	**三星 Samsung(6.9)**	**松下 Panasonic(5.9)**
平实生活指向 simple living orientation	321	爱多 Idall(12.8)	索尼 Sony(9.3)	金格川谷 Gynco(6.5)	三星 Samsung(6.2)
时尚流行指向 fashion orientation	321	索尼 Sony(12.1)	爱多 Idall(11.8)	松下 Panasonic(8.1)	三星 Samsung(7.5)

8-8-2 广告态度指标/ Advertising Attitude Index

	人数 Number	第一品牌及百分比 1st/ percent	第二品牌及百分比 2nd/ percent	第三品牌及百分比 3rd/ percent	第四品牌及百分比 4th/ percent
样本 Sample	642	**爱多 Idall(12.1)**	**索尼 Sony(10.7)**	**三星 Samsung(6.9)**	**松下 Panasonic(6.1)**
广告淡漠指向 indifferent orientation	196	索尼 Sony(11.7)	爱多 Idall(9.7)	先科 SAST(7.1)	金格川谷 Gynco(6.6)
中间层 medium	391	爱多 Idall(13.3)	索尼 Sony(9.7)	松下 Panasonic(7.7)	三星 Samsung(6.9)
信赖广告指向 loyal orientation	55	索尼 Sony(14.5)	爱多 Idall(12.7)	三星 Samsung(10.9)	新科 Shinco(5.5) 夏普/声宝 Sharp(5.5) 松下 Panasonic(5.5) 步步高 BBK(5.5)

8-8-3 价格态度指标/ Price Attitude Index

	人数 Number	第一品牌及百分比 1st/ percent	第二品牌及百分比 2nd/ percent	第三品牌及百分比 3rd/ percent	第四品牌及百分比 4th/ percent
样本 Sample	645	**爱多 Idall(12.2)**	**索尼 Sony(10.9)**	**三星 Samsung(6.8)**	**松下 Panasonic(6.0)**
价格无关心指向 indifferent orientation	120	爱多 Idall(12.5) 索尼 Sony(12.5)	三星 Samsung(10.0)	先科 SAST(6.7)	蚬华 SMC(5.0)
中间层 medium	349	爱多 Idall(11.2)	索尼 Sony(10.0)	三星 Samsung(6.6)	蚬华 SMC(6.3) 松下 Panasonic(6.3)
价格重视指向 careful orientation	176	爱多 Idall(14.2)	索尼 Sony(11.4)	松下 Panasonic(6.8)	步步高 BBK(5.7) 金格川谷(5.7) Gynco

8-9 不同消费者层选择影碟机时的考虑因素/ Considerations in Choosing from Different Brands by Market Segments

8-9-1 时尚流行指标/ Fads Popular Index

注：本题为多选题，合计百分比超过 100%（Multiple answers）

	人数 Number	品牌形象 brand image	外型 outlook	价格 price	画质好 clarity	纠错能力 correct ability
样本 Sample	658	30.5	11.7	49.8	36.3	26.9
平实生活指向 simple living orientation	331	29.9	11.8	51.7	34.7	27.2
时尚流行指向 fashion orientation	327	31.2	11.6	48.0	37.9	26.6

续前表 continued

	人数 Number	多制式 multi-system	有卡拉 OK 功能 karaoke function	有游戏功能 game function flavored	售后服务 follow-up service	其他 others
样本 Sample	658	8.7	33.0	1.1	8.7	1.8
平实生活指向 simple living orientation	331	9.1	31.1	1.2	8.5	2.1
时尚流行指向 fashion orientation	327	8.3	34.9	0.9	8.9	1.5

8-9-2 广告态度指向/ Advertising Attitude Index

注：本题为多选题，合计百分比超过 100%（Multiple answers）

	人数 Number	品牌形象 brand image	外型 outlook	价格 price	画质好 clarity	纠错能力 correct ability
样本 Sample	658	30.9	11.4	49.4	35.9	27.1
广告淡漠指向 indifferent orientation	202	26.7	11.9	50.5	39.1	24.3
中间层 medium	399	32.1	10.3	49.9	34.6	28.8
信赖广告指向 loyal orientation	57	36.8	17.5	42.1	33.3	24.6

续前表 continued

	人数 Number	多制式 multi-system	有卡拉 OK 功能 karaoke function	有游戏功能 game function flavored	售后服务 follow-up service	其他 others
样本 Sample	658	8.8	33.1	1.1	8.5	1.7
广告淡漠指向 indifferent orientation	202	8.4	37.6	1.0	9.4	1.0
中间层 medium	399	9.0	30.1	0.8	8.3	2.3
信赖广告指向 loyal orientation	57	8.8	38.6	3.5	7.0	0.0

8-9-3 价格态度指向/ Price Attitude Index

注：本题为多选题，合计百分比超过 100%（Multiple answers）

	人数 Number	品牌形象 brand image	外型 outlook	价格 price	画质好 clarity	纠错能力 correct ability
样本 Sample	661	30.9	11.6	49.6	36.0	27.1
价格无关心指向 indifferent orientation	123	35.8	5.7	48.0	35.0	23.6
中间层 medium	357	28.6	13.4	51.0	36.1	28.3
价格重视指向 careful orientation	181	32.0	12.2	48.1	36.5	27.1

续前表 continued

	人数 Number	多制式 multi-system	有卡拉 OK 功能 karaoke function	有游戏功能 game function flavored	售后服务 follow-up service	其他 others
样本 Sample	661	8.8	33.0	1.1	8.9	1.8
价格无关心指向 indifferent orientation	123	6.5	30.1	0.0	8.1	2.4
中间层 medium	357	8.1	32.8	1.1	9.5	2.0
价格重视指向 careful orientation	181	11.6	35.4	1.7	8.3	1.1

● 重庆 / Chongqing

8-1 影碟机的拥有比例/ Proportion of VCD Player Owners in the Sample

	人数 Number	百分比 Percent
有 yes	361	57.9
没有 no	263	42.1

n=624

8-2 影碟机的拥有量/ Number of VCD Player Owned Per Household

	人数 Number	百分比 Percent
1 台 1 set	349	97.5
2 台及以上 2 sets or over	9	2.5

n=358

8-3 理想品牌排名/ Ranking of the Ideal Brands

排名 Brand Ranking	品牌 Brands	人数 Number	百分比 Percent
1	新科 Shinco	110	17.6
2	步步高 BBK	88	14.1
3	爱多 Idall	39	6.3
4	厦新 Amoisonic	31	5.0
5	先科 SAST	29	4.6
6	松下 Panasonic	22	3.5
6	索尼 Sony	22	3.5
7	金正 Nintaus	18	2.9
8	长虹 Changhong	17	2.7
9	万利达 Malata	15	2.4
9	三星 Samsung	15	2.4
10	飞利浦 Philips	14	2.2

n=624

8-4 对家中现有影碟机(最近购买的一台)的五个方面的描述/ About the VCD Player Most Recently Purchased

8-4-1 家中现有影碟机的品牌排名/ Ranking of the Currently Owned VCD Player Brands

排名 Brand Ranking	品牌 Brands	人数 Number	百分比 Percent
1	新科 Shinco	69	19.4
2	步步高 BBK	27	7.6
3	爱多 Idall	25	7.0
4	厦新 Amoisonic	24	6.7
5	三星 Samsung	18	5.1
6	奇声 Qisheng	16	4.5
7	万利达 Malata	13	3.7
8	先科 SAST	11	3.1
8	索尼 Sony	11	3.1
8	松下 Panasonic	11	3.1
9	长虹 Changhong	10	2.8
10	飞利浦 Philips	6	1.7

n=356

8-4-2 该影碟机的购买时间/ The Time of Purchasing of the Currently Owned VCD Player

	人数 Number	百分比 Percent
1993 年	1	0.3
1994 年	7	1.9
1995 年	16	4.5
1996 年	46	12.8
1997 年	126	35.1
1998 年	119	33.1
1999 年	44	12.3

n=359

8-4-3 该影碟机的价格/ The Price of the Currently Owned VCD Player

	人数 Number	百分比 Percent
1000 元或以下 1000 yuan or below	73	20.2
1001～2000 元 yuan	222	61.5
2001～3000 元 yuan	50	13.9
3001～4000 元 yuan	7	1.9
4001～5000 元 yuan	3	0.8
5001～6000 元 yuan	1	0.3
6001～7000 元 yuan	0	0.0
7001～8000 元 yuan	0	0.0
8001～9000 元 yuan	0	0.0
9001～10000 元 yuan	1	0.3
10000 元以上 over10000 yuan	0	0.0
完全不知道 don't know	4	1.1

n=361

8-4-4 该影碟机的类型/ The Kind of the Currently Owned VCD Player

	人数 Number	百分比 Percent
VCD 机	323	90.0
DVD 机	9	2.5
CVD 机	6	1.7
SVCD 机	20	5.6
其他 others	1	0.3

n=359

8-4-5 该影碟机的机型/ The Type of the Currently Owned VCD Player

	人数 Number	百分比 Percent
普通机 VCD	252	72.4
自动换碟机 auto disc change	93	26.7
便携式机 portable VCD	1	0.3
其他 others	2	0.6

n=348

8-5 选择不同品牌影碟机时的考虑因素/ Considerations in Choosing from Different Brands

注：本题为多选题，合计百分比超过 100%（Multiple answers）

	人数 Number	品牌形象 brand image	外型 outlook	价格 price	画质好 clarity	纠错能力 correct ability
样本 Sample	**356**	**32.3**	**10.4**	**36.5**	**25.0**	**37.4**
新科 Shinco	69	37.7	11.6	40.6	26.1	30.4
步步高 BBK	27	29.6	14.8	33.3	29.6	37.0
爱多 Idall	25	44.0	4.0	32.0	24.0	44.0
厦新 Amoisonic	24	37.5	8.3	33.3	33.3	45.8
三星 Samsung	18	61.1	16.7	16.7	33.3	38.9
奇声 Qisheng	16	6.3	6.3	56.3	25.0	37.5
万利达 Malata	13	38.5	7.7	23.1	7.7	30.8
先科 SAST	11	18.2	0.0	36.4	9.1	54.5
索尼 Sony	11	36.4	9.1	18.2	18.2	45.5
松下 Panasonic	11	63.6	27.3	45.5	27.3	18.2
长虹 Changhong	10	60.0	10.0	50.0	20.0	20.0

续前表 continued

	人数 Number	多制式 multi-system	有卡拉 OK 功能 karaoke function	有游戏功能 game function flavored	售后服务 follow-up service	其他 others
样本 Sample	**356**	**7.0**	**30.9**	**2.8**	**6.5**	**3.4**
新科 Shinco	69	5.8	27.5	4.3	7.2	1.4
步步高 BBK	27	0.0	40.7	3.7	7.4	0.0
爱多 Idall	25	8.0	12.0	0.0	8.0	4.0
厦新 Amoisonic	24	16.7	33.3	0.0	16.7	4.2
三星 Samsung	18	5.6	38.9	0.0	11.1	5.6
奇声 Qisheng	16	6.3	31.3	0.0	6.3	18.8
万利达 Malata	13	0.0	15.4	0.0	15.4	0.0
先科 SAST	11	0.0	36.4	0.0	9.1	0.0
索尼 Sony	11	45.5	18.2	0.0	0.0	0.0
松下 Panasonic	11	0.0	18.2	0.0	9.1	9.1
长虹 Changhong	10	0.0	40.0	0.0	10.0	0.0

8-6 影碟机未来购买打算/ Plan for Future Purchasing of a VCD Player

8-6-1 有无购买打算/ Whether Planning to Purchase Next Year

	人数 Number	百分比 Percent
是 yes	56	9.0
否 no	568	91.0

n=624

8-6-2 打算购买的品牌排名/ The Brand of the Planned Purchase Next Year

排名 Brand Ranking	品牌 Brands	人数 Number	百分比 Percent
1	步步高 BBK	8	14.8
2	金正 Nintaus	7	13.0
2	新科 Shinco	7	13.0
3	厦新 Amoisonic	4	7.4
4	先科 SAST	3	5.6
5	索尼 Sony	2	3.7
5	先锋 Pioneer	2	3.7
5	新天利 Xintianli	2	3.7

n=54

8-6-3 打算购买的机型/ The Type of the Planned Purchase Next Year

	人数 Number	百分比 Percent
VCD 机	15	27.3
DVD 机	35	63.6
CVD 机	1	1.8
SVCD 机	4	7.3
其他 others	0	0.0

n=55

8-6-4 打算购买的价格/ The Price of the Planned Purchase Next Year

	人数 Number	百分比 Percent
1000 元或以下 1000 yuan or below	12	21.4
1001～2000 元 yuan	18	32.1
2001～3000 元 yuan	15	26.8
3001～4000 元 yuan	7	12.5
4001～5000 元 yuan	1	1.8
5001～6000 元 yuan	0	0.0
6001～7000 元 yuan	0	0.0
7001～8000 元 yuan	0	0.0
8001～9000 元 yuan	0	0.0
9001～10000 元 yuan	0	0.0
10000 元以上 over 10000 yuan	0	0.0
完全不知道 don't know	3	5.4

n=56

8-7 选购影碟机时不同角色的人口特征/ Demographics of the Different Roles in Purchasing a VCD Player

注：不同角色可以多选（Multiple answers）

	人数 Number	16-24 岁 Age	25-34 岁 Age	35-44 岁 Age	45-54 岁 Age	55-60 岁 Age
样本 Sample	318	22.3	28.0	24.2	19.5	6.0
男性 Male	175	20.0	29.1	25.7	17.7	7.4
提议者 advocate	41	22.0	36.6	19.5	14.6	7.3
影响者 influence	14	14.3	35.7	14.3	28.6	7.1
决定者 decider	91	8.8	29.7	36.3	22.0	3.3
使用者 user	101	27.7	27.7	21.8	12.9	9.9
女性 Female	143	25.2	26.6	22.4	21.7	4.2
提议者 advocate	36	22.2	36.1	16.7	19.4	5.6
影响者 influence	19	21.1	36.8	15.8	21.1	5.3
决定者 decider	35	5.7	37.1	31.4	25.7	0.0
使用者 user	102	27.5	26.5	23.5	17.6	4.9

8-8 不同消费者层的家中目前拥有品牌/ Brands of VCD Player Owned in Household by Market Segments

8-8-1 时尚流行指标/ Fads Popular Index

	人数 Number	第一品牌及百分比 1st/ percent	第二品牌及百分比 2nd/ percent	第三品牌及百分比 3rd/ percent	第四品牌及百分比 4th/ percent
样本 Sample	351	**新科 Shinco(19.7)**	**步步高 BBK(7.7)**	**爱多 Idall(7.1)**	**厦新 Amoisonic(6.6)**
平实生活指向 simple living orientation	190	新科 Shinco(16.3)	厦新 Amoisonic(7.9)	爱多 Idall(7.4)	步步高 BBK(6.3)
时尚流行指向 fashion orientation	161	新科 Shinco(23.6)	步步高 BBK(9.3)	爱多 Idall(6.8)	厦新 Amoisonic(5.0)

8-8-2 广告态度指标/ Advertising Attitude Index

	人数 Number	第一品牌及百分比 1st/ percent	第二品牌及百分比 2nd/ percent	第三品牌及百分比 3rd/ percent	第四品牌及百分比 4th/ percent
样本 Sample	354	**新科 Shinco(19.2)**	**步步高 BBK(7.6)**	**爱多 Idall(7.1)**	**厦新 Amoisonic(6.8)**
广告淡漠指向 indifferent orientation	94	新科 Shinco(22.3)	步步高 BBK(8.5)	爱多 Idall(6.4) 厦新 Amoisonic(6.4) 奇声 Qisheng(6.4)	万利达 Malata(5.3)
中间层 medium	210	新科 Shinco(16.7)	爱多 Idall(8.1)	步步高 BBK(7.6)	厦新 Amoisonic(7.1)
信赖广告指向 loyal orientation	50	新科 Shinco(24.0)	三星 Samsung(8.0)	步步高 BBK(6.0) 厦新 Amoisonic(6.0) 奇声 Qisheng(6.0)	长虹 Changhong(4.0) 飞利浦 Philips(4.0) 爱多 Idall(4.0)

8-8-3 价格态度指标/ Price Attitude Index

	人数 Number	第一品牌及百分比 1st/ percent	第二品牌及百分比 2nd/ percent	第三品牌及百分比 3rd/ percent	第四品牌及百分比 4th/ percent
样本 Sample	351	**新科 Shinco(19.7)**	**步步高 BBK(7.4)**	**爱多 Idall(7.1)**	**厦新 Amoisonic(6.6)**
价格无关心指向 indifferent orientation	71	新科 Shinco(19.7)	步步高 BBK(9.9)	爱多 Idall(5.6) 先科 SAST(5.6) 飞利浦 Philips(5.6) 万利达 Malata(5.6)	厦新 Amoisonic(4.2)
中间层 medium	165	新科 Shinco(21.2)	爱多 Idall(7.3) 厦新 Amoisonic(7.3)	步步高 BBK(6.7)	奇声 Qisheng(5.5) 三星 Samsung(5.5)
价格重视指向 careful orientation	115	新科 Shinco(17.4)	爱多 Idall(7.8)	步步高 BBK(7.0) 厦新 Amoisonic(7.0)	三星 Samsung(6.1)

8-9 不同消费者层选择影碟机时考虑因素/ Considerations in Choosing from Different Brands by Market Segments

8-9-1 时尚流行指标/ Fads Popular Index

注：本题为多选题，合计百分比超过 100%（Multiple answers）

	人数 Number	品牌形象 brand image	外型 outlook	价格 price	画质好 clarity	纠错能力 correct ability
样本 Sample	**356**	**31.7**	**10.4**	**36.2**	**24.7**	**37.1**
平实生活指向 simple living orientation	193	28.0	13.5	39.4	22.8	35.2
时尚流行指向 fashion orientation	163	36.2	6.7	32.5	27.0	39.3

续前表 continued

	人数 Number	多制式 multi-system	有卡拉 OK 功能 karaoke function	有游戏功能 game function flavored	售后服务 follow-up service	其他 others
样本 Sample	**356**	**6.7**	**31.7**	**2.8**	**6.5**	**3.4**
平实生活指向 simple living orientation	193	6.2	31.1	3.1	6.7	5.2
时尚流行指向 fashion orientation	163	7.4	32.5	2.5	6.1	1.2

8-9-2 广告态度指向/ Advertising Attitude Index

注：本题为多选题，合计百分比超过 100%（Multiple answers）

	人数 Number	品牌形象 brand image	外型 outlook	价格 price	画质好 clarity	纠错能力 correct ability
样本 Sample	**359**	**32.0**	**10.3**	**36.2**	**24.8**	**37.6**
广告淡漠指向 indifferent orientation	95	27.4	4.2	42.1	16.8	38.9
中间层 medium	214	30.4	13.6	33.6	25.2	40.7
信赖广告指向 loyal orientation	50	48.0	8.0	36.0	38.0	22.0

续前表 continued

	人数 Number	多制式 multi-system	有卡拉 OK 功能 karaoke function	有游戏功能 game function flavored	售后服务 follow-up service	其他 others
样本 Sample	**359**	**7.0**	**31.8**	**2.8**	**6.4**	**3.3**
广告淡漠指向 indifferent orientation	95	7.4	24.2	4.2	8.4	6.3
中间层 medium	214	6.1	36.0	1.9	7.0	1.4
信赖广告指向 loyal orientation	50	10.0	28.0	4.0	0.0	6.0

8-9-3 价格态度指向/ Price Attitude Index

注：本题为多选题，合计百分比超过 100%（Multiple answers）

	人数 Number	品牌形象 brand image	外型 outlook	价格 price	画质好 clarity	纠错能力 correct ability
样本 Sample	**356**	**32.0**	**10.4**	**36.5**	**25.0**	**37.6**
价格无关心指向 indifferent orientation	73	28.8	4.1	31.5	26.0	43.8
中间层 medium	165	33.3	12.7	33.9	24.8	37.6
价格重视指向 careful orientation	118	32.2	11.0	43.2	24.6	33.9

续前表 continued

	人数 Number	多制式 multi-system	有卡拉 OK 功能 karaoke function	有游戏功能 game function flavored	售后服务 follow-up service	其他 others
样本 Sample	**356**	**6.7**	**31.2**	**2.8**	**6.5**	**3.4**
价格无关心指向 indifferent orientation	73	4.1	28.8	2.7	6.8	4.1
中间层 medium	165	7.9	27.9	3.0	6.1	3.6
价格重视指向 careful orientation	118	6.8	37.3	2.5	6.8	2.5

● 武汉 / Wuhan

8-1 影碟机的拥有比例/ Proportion of VCD Player Owners in the Sample

	人数 Number	百分比 Percent
有 yes	328	51.2
没有 no	313	48.8

n=641

8-2 影碟机的拥有量/ Number of VCD Player Owned Per Household

	人数 Number	百分比 Percent
1 台 1 set	316	96.9
2 台及以上 2 sets or over	10	3.1

n=326

8-3 理想品牌排名/ Ranking of the Ideal Brands

排名 Brand Ranking	品牌 Brands	人数 Number	百分比 Percent
1	厦新 Amoisonic	114	17.8
2	新科 Shinco	91	14.2
3	步步高 BBK	49	7.6
4	万利达 Malata	27	4.2
5	飞利浦 Philips	15	2.3
6	索尼 Sony	14	2.2
6	爱多 Idall	14	2.2
7	三星 Samsung	9	1.4

n=642

8-4 对家中现有影碟机(最近购买的一台)的五个方面的描述/ About the VCD Player Most Recently Purchased

8-4-1 家中现有影碟机的品牌排名/ Ranking of the Currently Owned VCD Player Brands

排名 Brand Ranking	品牌 Brands	人数 Number	百分比 Percent
1	厦新 Amoisonic	67	20.6
2	新科 Shinco	59	18.1
3	万利达 Malata	28	8.6
4	步步高 BBK	23	7.1
5	爱多 Idall	12	3.7
6	松下 Panasonic	10	3.1
7	三星 Samsung	9	2.8
8	飞利浦 Philips	7	2.1
8	奇声 Qisheng	7	2.1
9	先锋 Pioneer	6	1.8

n=326

8-4-2 该影碟机的购买时间/ Time of Purchasing of the Currently Owned VCD Player

	人数 Number	百分比 Percent
1993 年	4	1.2
1994 年	6	1.8
1995 年	27	8.2
1996 年	43	13.1
1997 年	86	26.2
1998 年	99	30.2
1999 年	63	19.2

n=328

8-4-3 该影碟机的价格/ The Price of the Currently Owned VCD Player

	人数 Number	百分比 Percent
1000 元或以下 1000 yuan or below	78	23.8
1001～2000 元 yuan	169	51.5
2001～3000 元 yuan	49	14.9
3001～4000 元 yuan	17	5.2
4001～5000 元 yuan	2	0.6
5001～6000 元 yuan	1	0.3
6001～7000 元 yuan	1	0.3
7001～8000 元 yuan	2	0.6
8001～9000 元 yuan	1	0.3
9001～10000 元 yuan	0	0.0
10000 元以上 over 10000 yuan	1	0.3
完全不知道 don't know	7	2.1

n=328

8-4-4 该影碟机的类型/ The Kind of the Currently Owned VCD Player

	人数 Number	百分比 Percent
VCD 机	301	91.8
DVD 机	3	0.9
CVD 机	2	0.6
SVCD 机	22	6.7
其他 others	0	0.0

n=328

8-4-5 该影碟机的机型/ The Type of the Currently Owned VCD Player

	人数 Number	百分比 Percent
普通机 VCD	239	73.5
自动换碟机 auto disc change	82	25.2
便携式机 portable VCD	2	0.6
其他 others	2	0.6

n=325

8-5 选择不同品牌影碟机时考虑因素/ Considerations in Choosing from Different Brands

注：本题为多选题，合计百分比超过 100%（Multiple answers）

	人数 Number	品牌形象 brand image	外型 outlook	价格 price	画质好 clarity	纠错能力 correct ability
样本 Sample	**326**	**45.4**	**12.6**	**43.9**	**27.0**	**35.0**
厦新 Amoisonic	67	49.3	11.9	49.3	22.4	43.3
新科 Shinco	59	62.7	13.6	35.6	16.9	28.8
万利达 Malata	28	60.7	10.7	28.6	25.0	64.3
步步高 BBK	23	43.5	0.0	56.5	30.4	47.8
爱多 Idall	12	50.0	16.7	58.3	16.7	16.7
松下 Panasonic	10	40.0	10.0	30.0	50.0	30.0
三星 Samsung	9	44.4	22.2	22.2	33.3	44.4
飞利浦 Philips	7	14.3	14.3	42.9	57.1	28.6
奇声 Qisheng	7	14.3	0.0	57.1	42.9	42.9
先锋 Pioneer	6	66.7	0.0	16.7	50.0	33.3

续前表 continued

	人数 Number	多制式 multi-system	有卡拉 OK 功能 karaoke function	有游戏功能 game function flavored	售后服务 follow-up service	其他 others
样本 Sample	**326**	**3.4**	**37.7**	**3.1**	**10.4**	**2.8**
厦新 Amoisonic	67	4.5	32.8	3.0	19.4	3.0
新科 Shinco	59	5.1	30.5	3.4	10.2	1.7
万利达 Malata	28	0.0	50.0	0.0	10.7	0.0
步步高 BBK	23	4.3	30.4	0.0	17.4	0.0
爱多 Idall	12	8.3	33.3	0.0	8.3	0.0
松下 Panasonic	10	0.0	40.0	0.0	0.0	0.0
三星 Samsung	9	0.0	44.4	0.0	0.0	0.0
飞利浦 Philips	7	14.3	28.6	0.0	0.0	0.0
奇声 Qisheng	7	14.3	85.7	0.0	0.0	0.0
先锋 Pioneer	6	0.0	50.0	0.0	0.0	0.0

8-6 影碟机未来购买打算/ Plan for Future Purchasing of a VCD Player

8-6-1 有无购买打算/ Whether Planning to Purchase Next Year

	人数 Number	百分比 Percent
是 yes	58	9.0
否 no	584	91.0

n=642

8-6-2 打算购买的品牌排名/ The Brand of the Planned Purchase Next Year

排名 Brand Ranking	品牌 Brands	人数 Number	百分比 Percent
1	厦新 Amoisonic	15	30.6
2	新科 Shinco	11	22.4
3	飞利浦 Philips	3	6.1
4	厦华 Xoceco	2	4.1
4	万利达 Malata	2	4.1
4	步步高 BBK	2	4.1

n=49

8-6-3 打算购买的机型/ The Type of the Planned Purchase Next Year

	人数 Number	百分比 Percent
VCD 机	19	33.3
DVD 机	31	54.4
CVD 机	1	1.8
SVCD 机	6	10.5
其他 others	0	0.0

n=57

8-6-4 打算购买的价格/ The Price of the Planned Purchase Next Year

	人数 Number	百分比 Percent
1000 元或以下 1000 yuan or below	11	19.3
1001～2000 元 yuan	29	50.9
2001～3000 元 yuan	14	24.6
3001～4000 元 yuan	1	1.8
4001～5000 元 yuan	1	1.8
5001～6000 元 yuan	0	0.0
6001～7000 元 yuan	0	0.0
7001～8000 元 yuan	0	0.0
8001～9000 元 yuan	0	0.0
9001～10000 元 yuan	0	0.0
10000 元以上 over 10000 yuan	1	1.8
完全不知道 don't know	0	0.0

n=57

8-7 选购影碟机时不同角色的人口特征/ Demographics of the Different Roles in Purchasing a VCD Player

注：不同角色可以多选（Multiple answers）

	人数 Number	16-24 岁 Age	25-34 岁 Age	35-44 岁 Age	45-54 岁 Age	55-60 岁 Age
样本 Sample	299	22.4	33.4	25.1	13.0	6.0
男性 Male	149	20.8	31.5	26.8	12.8	8.1
提议者 advocate	37	18.9	29.7	32.4	13.5	5.4
影响者 influence	19	21.1	31.6	21.1	21.1	5.3
决定者 decider	78	11.5	29.5	38.5	14.1	6.4
使用者 user	95	23.2	32.6	22.1	12.6	9.5
女性 Female	150	24.0	35.3	23.3	13.3	4.0
提议者 advocate	44	34.1	31.8	22.7	11.4	0.0
影响者 influence	21	33.3	9.5	28.6	28.6	0.0
决定者 decider	39	12.8	35.9	28.2	20.5	2.6
使用者 user	105	21.9	36.2	27.6	9.5	4.8

8-8 不同消费者层的家中目前拥有品牌/ Brands of VCD Player Owned in Household by Market Segments

8-8-1 时尚流行指标/ Fads Popular Index

	人数 Number	第一品牌及百分比 1st/ percent	第二品牌及百分比 2nd/ percent	第三品牌及百分比 3rd/ percent
样本 Sample	317	**厦新 Amoisonic(20.8)**	**新科 Shinco(18.0)**	**万利达 Malata(8.2)**
平实生活指向 simple living orientation	148	厦新 Amoisonic(21.6)	新科 Shinco(14.2)	万利达 Malata(12.8)
时尚流行指向 fashion orientation	169	新科 Shinco(21.3)	厦新 Amoisonic(20.1)	步步高 BBK(7.7)

8-8-2 广告态度指标/ Advertising Attitude Index

	人数 Number	第一品牌及百分比 1st/ percent	第二品牌及百分比 2nd/ percent	第三品牌及百分比 3rd/ percent
样本 Sample	319	**厦新 Amoisonic(20.7)**	**新科 Shinco(17.9)**	**万利达 Malata(8.5)**
广告淡漠指向 indifferent orientation	85	厦新 Amoisonic(23.5)	新科 Shinco(16.5)	步步高 BBK(8.2) 万利达 Malata(8.2)
中间层 medium	188	厦新 Amoisonic(19.7)	新科 Shinco(18.1)	万利达 Malata(8.0)
信赖广告指向 loyal orientation	46	新科 Shinco(19.6) 厦新 Amoisonic(19.6)	爱多 Idall(10.9) 万利达 Malata(10.9)	步步高 BBK(6.5)

8-8-3 价格态度指标/ Price Attitude Index

	人数 Number	第一品牌及百分比 1st/ percent	第二品牌及百分比 2nd/ percent	第三品牌及百分比 3rd/ percent
样本 Sample	319	厦新 Amoisonic(20.7)	新科 Shinco(17.6)	万利达 Malata(8.8)
价格无关心指向 indifferent orientation	43	新科 Shinco(20.9) 厦新 Amoisonic(20.9)	步步高 BBK(7.0) 松下 Panasonic(7.0) 万利达 Malata(7.0)	爱华 Aiwa(4.7) 三星 Samsung(4.7)
中间层 medium	160	厦新 Amoisonic(26.9)	新科 Shinco(18.1)	步步高 BBK(8.1)
价格重视指向 careful orientation	116	新科 Shinco(15.5)	万利达 Malata(12.9)	厦新 Amoisonic(12.1)

8-9 不同消费者层选择影碟机时的考虑因素/ Considerations in Choosing from Different Brands by Market Segments

8-9-1 时尚流行指标/ Fads Popular Index

注：本题为多选题，合计百分比超过 100%（Multiple answers）

	人数 Number	品牌形象 brand image	外型 outlook	价格 price	画质好 clarity	纠错能力 correct ability
样本 Sample	319	44.8	11.6	43.6	27.6	35.7
平实生活指向 simple living orientation	149	43.0	9.4	47.0	27.5	34.9
时尚流行指向 fashion orientation	170	46.5	13.5	40.6	27.6	36.5

续前表 continued

	人数 Number	多制式 multi-system	有卡拉 OK 功能 karaoke function	有游戏功能 game function flavored	售后服务 follow-up service	其他 others
样本 Sample	319	3.4	37.6	3.1	10.7	2.8
平实生活指向 simple living orientation	149	0.7	35.6	3.4	8.7	3.4
时尚流行指向 fashion orientation	170	5.9	39.4	2.9	12.4	2.4

8-9-2 广告态度指向/ Advertising Attitude Index

注：本题为多选题，合计百分比超过 100%（Multiple answers）

	人数 Number	品牌形象 brand image	外型 outlook	价格 price	画质好 clarity	纠错能力 correct ability
样本 Sample	321	44.5	12.1	43.6	27.4	35.5
广告淡漠指向 indifferent orientation	85	37.6	7.1	52.9	27.1	36.5
中间层 medium	189	47.1	14.8	39.2	29.1	34.9
信赖广告指向 loyal orientation	47	46.8	10.6	44.7	21.3	36.2

续前表 continued

	人数 Number	多制式 multi-system	有卡拉 OK 功能 karaoke function	有游戏功能 game function flavored	售后服务 follow-up service	其他 others
样本 Sample	321	3.4	37.4	3.1	10.6	2.8
广告淡漠指向 indifferent orientation	85	1.2	36.5	1.2	8.2	4.7
中间层 medium	189	3.7	38.6	4.2	9.0	2.1
信赖广告指向 loyal orientation	47	6.4	34.0	2.1	21.3	2.1

8-9-3 价格态度指向/ Price Attitude Index

注：本题为多选题，合计百分比超过 100%（Multiple answers）

	人数 Number	品牌形象 brand image	外型 outlook	价格 price	画质好 clarity	纠错能力 correct ability
样本 Sample	321	44.2	12.5	43.6	27.4	35.8
价格无关心指向 indifferent orientation	43	51.2	11.6	34.9	32.6	27.9
中间层 medium	161	40.4	13.7	41.0	27.3	38.5
价格重视指向 careful orientation	117	47.0	11.1	50.4	25.6	35.0

续前表 continued

	人数 Number	多制式 multi-system	有卡拉 OK 功能 karaoke function	有游戏功能 game function flavored	售后服务 follow-up service	其他 others
样本 Sample	321	3.1	37.4	3.1	10.6	2.8
价格无关心指向 indifferent orientation	43	0.0	37.2	4.7	4.7	4.7
中间层 medium	161	3.7	36.6	1.9	11.2	4.3
价格重视指向 careful orientation	117	3.4	38.5	4.3	12.0	0.0

● 西安 / Xi'an

8-1 影碟机的拥有比例/ Proportion of VCD Player Owners in the Sample

	人数 Number	百分比 Percent
有 yes	284	47.3
没有 no	316	52.7

n=600

8-2 影碟机的拥有量/ Number of VCD Player Owned Per Household

	人数 Number	百分比 Percent
1 台 1 set	280	98.9
2 台及以上 2 sets or over	3	1.1

n=283

8-3 理想品牌排名/ Ranking of the Ideal Brands

排名 Brand Ranking	品牌 Brands	人数 Number	百分比 Percent
1	步步高 BBK	150	25.2
2	新科 Shinco	92	15.4
3	厦新 Amoisonic	70	11.7
4	爱多 Idall	36	6.0
5	万利达 Malata	32	5.4
6	金正 Nintaus	19	3.2
7	索尼 Sony	14	2.3
8	松下 Panasonic	13	2.2
9	先科 SAST	12	2.0

n=596

8-4 对家中现有影碟机(最近购买的一台)的五个方面的描述/ About the VCD Player Most Recently Purchased

8-4-1 家中现有影碟机的品牌排名/ Ranking of the Currently Owned VCD Player Brands

排名 Brand Ranking	品牌 Brands	人数 Number	百分比 Percent
1	新科 Shinco	56	19.9
2	步步高 BBK	43	15.3
3	万利达 Malata	30	10.7
4	厦新 Amoisonic	28	10.0
5	爱多 Idall	23	8.2
6	先科 SAST	14	5.0
7	索尼 Sony	8	2.8
7	松下 Panasonic	8	2.8
8	三星 Samsung	6	2.1
9	金正 Nintaus	5	1.8
9	飞利浦 Philips	5	1.8

n=281

8-4-2 该影碟机的购买时间/ The Time of Purchasing of the Currently Owned VCD Player

	人数 Number	百分比 Percent
1993 年	6	2.1
1994 年	3	1.1
1995 年	17	6.0
1996 年	33	11.6
1997 年	104	36.6
1998 年	79	27.8
1999 年	42	14.8

n=284

8-4-3 该影碟机的价格/ The Price of the Currently Owned VCD Player

	人数 Number	百分比 Percent
1000 元及以下 1000 yuan or below	64	22.6
1001～2000 元 yuan	169	59.7
2001～3000 元 yuan	27	9.5
3001～4000 元 yuan	8	2.8
4001～5000 元 yuan	7	2.5
5001～6000 元 yuan	2	0.7
6001～7000 元 yuan	1	0.4
7001～8000 元 yuan	0	0.0
8001～9000 元 yuan	0	0.0
9001～10000 元 yuan	0	0.0
10000 元以上 over 10000 yuan	0	0.0
完全不知道 don't know	5	1.8

n=283

8-4-4 该影碟机的类型/ The Kind of the Currently Owned VCD Player

	人数 Number	百分比 Percent
VCD 机	260	91.5
DVD 机	6	2.1
CVD 机	4	1.4
SVCD 机	14	4.9
其他 others	0	0.0

n=284

8-4-5 该影碟机的机型/ The Type of the Currently Owned VCD Player

	人数 Number	百分比 Percent
普通机 VCD	208	74.0
自动换碟机 auto disc change	68	24.2
便携式机 portable VCD	2	0.7
其他 others	3	1.1

n=281

8-5 选择不同品牌影碟机时考虑因素/ Considerations in Choosing from Different Brands

注：本题为多选题，合计百分比超过 100%（Multiple answers）

	人数 Number	品牌形象 brand image	外型 outlook	价格 price	画质好 clarity	纠错能力 correct ability
样本 Sample	281	45.2	6.4	32.0	27.8	34.9
新科 Shinco	56	48.2	14.3	26.8	26.8	39.3
步步高 BBK	43	41.9	7.0	44.2	16.3	51.2
万利达 Malata	30	53.3	0.0	33.3	20.0	46.7
厦新 Amoisonic	28	50.0	10.7	35.7	42.9	21.4
爱多 Idall	23	56.5	4.3	17.4	17.4	39.1
先科 SAST	14	42.9	0.0	21.4	28.6	42.9
索尼 Sony	8	62.5	0.0	12.5	25.0	12.5
松下 Panasonic	8	25.0	0.0	50.0	50.0	25.0

续前表 continued

	人数 Number	多制式 multi-system	有卡拉 OK 功能 karaoke function	有游戏功能 game function flavored	售后服务 follow-up service	其他 others
样本 Sample	281	7.8	27.8	4.3	11.7	3.2
新科 Shinco	56	10.7	30.4	1.8	16.1	7.1
步步高 BBK	43	4.7	16.3	0.0	20.9	2.3
万利达 Malata	30	10.0	33.3	3.3	13.3	0.0
厦新 Amoisonic	28	3.6	28.6	3.6	7.1	0.0
爱多 Idall	23	4.3	43.5	0.0	4.3	0.0
先科 SAST	14	0.0	28.6	14.3	7.1	0.0
索尼 Sony	8	0.0	25.0	0.0	25.0	0.0
松下 Panasonic	8	12.5	25.0	25.0	25.0	0.0

8-6 影碟机未来购买打算/ Plan for Future Purchasing of a VCD Player

8-6-1 有无购买打算/ Whether Planning to Purchase Next Year

	人数 Number	百分比 Percent
是 yes	47	7.8
否 no	553	92.2

n=600

8-6-2 打算购买的品牌排名/ The Brand of the Planned Purchase Next Year

排名 Brand Ranking	品牌 Brands	人数 Number	百分比 Percent
1	步步高 BBK	8	18.6
2	新科 Shinco	6	14.0
3	厦新 Amoisonic	5	11.6
4	裕兴 Yuxing	3	7.0
4	先科 SAST	3	7.0
5	爱多 Idall	2	4.7
5	金正 Nintaus	2	4.7

n=43

8-6-3 打算购买的机型/ The Type of the Planned Purchase Next Year

	人数 Number	百分比 Percent
VCD 机	19	41.3
DVD 机	23	50.0
CVD 机	0	0.0
SVCD 机	4	8.7
其他 others	0	0.0

n=46

8-6-4 打算购买的价格/ The Price of the Planned Purchase Next Year

	人数 Number	百分比 Percent
1000 元及以下 1000 yuan or below	12	26.1
1001～2000 元 yuan	22	47.8
2001～3000 元 yuan	9	19.6
3001～4000 元 yuan	2	4.3
4001～5000 元 yuan	1	2.2
5001～6000 元 yuan	0	0.0
6001～7000 元 yuan	0	0.0
7001～8000 元 yuan	0	0.0
8001～9000 元 yuan	0	0.0
9001～10000 元 yuan	0	0.0
10000 元以上 over 10000 yuan	0	0.0
完全不知道 don't know	0	0.0

n=46

8-7 选购影碟机时不同角色的人口特征/ Demographics of the Different Roles in Purchasing a VCD Player

注：不同角色可以多选（Multiple answers）

	人数 Number	16-24 岁 Age	25-34 岁 Age	35-44 岁 Age	45-54 岁 Age	55-60 岁 Age
样本 Sample	255	24.3	38.0	21.2	12.5	3.9
男性 Male	132	26.5	34.8	22.7	10.6	5.3
提议者 advocate	19	26.3	31.6	31.6	5.3	5.3
影响者 influence	16	31.3	25.0	12.5	12.5	18.8
决定者 decider	70	12.9	44.3	28.6	11.4	2.9
使用者 user	65	35.4	26.2	24.6	12.3	1.5
女性 Female	123	22.0	41.5	19.5	14.6	2.4
提议者 advocate	23	17.4	43.5	26.1	13.0	0.0
影响者 influence	23	21.7	56.5	13.0	8.7	0.0
决定者 decider	32	25.0	34.4	25.0	12.5	3.1
使用者 user	75	21.3	41.3	16.0	17.3	4.0

8-8 不同消费者层的家中目前拥有品牌/ Brands of VCD Player Owned in Household by Market Segments

8-8-1 时尚流行指标/ Fads Popular Index

	人数 Number	第一品牌及百分比 1st/ percent	第二品牌及百分比 2nd/ percent	第三品牌及百分比 3rd/ percent	第四品牌及百分比 4th/ percent
样本 Sample	281	**新科 Shinco(19.9)**	**步步高 BBK(15.3)**	**万利达 Malata(10.7)**	**厦新 Amoisonic(10.0)**
平实生活指向 simple living orientation	139	新科 Shinco(18.7)	步步高 BBK(15.1)	厦新 Amoisonic(12.9)	万利达 Malata(10.8)
时尚流行指向 fashion orientation	142	新科 Shinco(21.1)	步步高 BBK(15.5)	万利达 Malata(10.6)	爱多 Idall(8.5)

8-8-2 广告态度指标/ Advertising Attitude Index

	人数 Number	第一品牌及百分比 1st/ percent	第二品牌及百分比 2nd/ percent	第三品牌及百分比 3rd/ percent	第四品牌及百分比 4th/ percent
样本 Sample	**280**	**新科 Shinco(20.0)**	**步步高 BBK(15.4)**	**万利达 Malata(10.7)**	**厦新 Amoisonic(10.0)**
广告淡漠指向 indifferent orientation	76	新科 Shinco(19.7)	步步高 BBK(15.8)	万利达 Malata(13.2)	厦新 Amoisonic(11.8)
中间层 medium	157	新科 Shinco(21.7)	步步高 BBK(14.0)	万利达 Malata(12.1)	厦新 Amoisonic(10.2)
信赖广告指向 loyal orientation	47	步步高 BBK(19.1)	新科 Shinco(14.9)	松下 Panasonic(8.5)	厦新 Amoisonic(6.4)

8-8-3 价格态度指标/ Price Attitude Index

	人数 Number	第一品牌及百分比 1st/ percent	第二品牌及百分比 2nd/ percent	第三品牌及百分比 3rd/ percent	第四品牌及百分比 4th/ percent
样本 Sample	**279**	**新科 Shinco(20.1)**	**步步高 BBK(15.4)**	**万利达 Malata(10.8)**	**厦新 Amoisonic(10.0)**
价格无关心指向 indifferent orientation	77	新科 Shinco(20.8)	万利达 Malata(15.6)	步步高 BBK(11.7)	厦新 Amoisonic(10.4)
中间层 medium	143	新科 Shinco(22.4)	步步高 BBK(13.3)	爱多 Idall(10.5)	厦新 Amoisonic(9.8)
价格重视指向 careful orientation	59	步步高 BBK(25.4)	新科 Shinco(13.6) 万利达 Malata(13.6)	厦新 Amoisonic(10.2)	先科 SAST(8.5)

8-9 不同消费者层选择影碟机时的考虑因素/ Considerations in Choosing from Different Brands by Market Segments

8-9-1 时尚流行指标/ Fads Popular Index

注：本题为多选题，合计百分比超过 100%（Multiple answers）

	人数 Number	品牌形象 brand image	外型 outlook	价格 price	画质好 clarity	纠错能力 correct ability
样本 Sample	**284**	**45.1**	**6.3**	**32.0**	**27.5**	**35.2**
平实生活指向 simple living orientation	139	48.2	7.9	30.2	28.1	35.3
时尚流行指向 fashion orientation	145	42.1	4.8	33.8	26.9	35.2

续前表 continued

	人数 Number	多制式 multi-system	有卡拉 OK 功能 karaoke function	有游戏功能 game function flavored	售后服务 follow-up service	其他 others
样本 Sample	**284**	**7.7**	**27.5**	**4.2**	**11.6**	**3.2**
平实生活指向 simple living orientation	139	7.2	22.3	2.2	13.7	2.9
时尚流行指向 fashion orientation	145	8.3	32.4	6.2	9.7	3.4

8-9-2 广告态度指向/ Advertising Attitude Index

注：本题为多选题，合计百分比超过 100%（Multiple answers）

	人数 Number	品牌形象 brand image	外型 outlook	价格 price	画质好 clarity	纠错能力 correct ability
样本 Sample	**283**	**45.2**	**6.4**	**31.8**	**27.2**	**35.0**
广告淡漠指向 indifferent orientation	76	48.7	5.3	42.1	22.4	35.5
中间层 medium	159	42.8	7.5	28.3	28.3	39.0
信赖广告指向 loyal orientation	48	47.9	4.2	27.1	31.3	20.8

续前表 continued

	人数 Number	多制式 multi-system	有卡拉 OK 功能 karaoke function	有游戏功能 game function flavored	售后服务 follow-up service	其他 others
样本 Sample	**283**	**7.8**	**27.6**	**4.2**	**11.7**	**3.2**
广告淡漠指向 indifferent orientation	76	6.6	28.9	3.9	9.2	1.3
中间层 medium	159	7.5	28.3	3.8	13.2	2.5
信赖广告指向 loyal orientation	48	10.4	22.9	6.3	10.4	8.3

8-9-3 价格态度指向/ Price Attitude Index

注：本题为多选题，合计百分比超过 100%（Multiple answers）

	人数 Number	品牌形象 brand image	外型 outlook	价格 price	画质好 clarity	纠错能力 correct ability
样本 Sample	282	45.0	6.4	31.9	27.3	35.5
价格无关心指向 indifferent orientation	77	40.3	7.8	32.5	26.0	37.7
中间层 medium	146	49.3	6.8	31.5	33.6	32.2
价格重视指向 careful orientation	59	40.7	3.4	32.2	13.6	40.7

续前表 continued

	人数 Number	多制式 multi-system	有卡拉 OK 功能 karaoke function	有游戏功能 game function flavored	售后服务 follow-up service	其他 others
样本 Sample	282	7.8	27.7	4.3	11.3	3.2
价格无关心指向 indifferent orientation	77	10.4	29.9	6.5	9.1	1.3
中间层 medium	146	6.2	26.0	2.7	10.3	3.4
价格重视指向 careful orientation	59	8.5	28.8	5.1	16.9	5.1

● 沈阳 / Shenyang

8-1 影碟机的拥有比例/ Proportion of VCD Player Owners in the Sample

	人数 Number	百分比 Percent
有 yes	196	32.6
没有 no	405	67.4

n=601

8-2 影碟机的拥有量/ Number of VCD Player Owned Per Household

	人数 Number	百分比 Percent
1 台 1 set	191	97.9
2 台及以上 2 sets or over	4	2.1

n=195

8-3 理想品牌排名/ Ranking of the Ideal Brands

排名 Brand Ranking	品牌 Brands	人数 Number	百分比 Percent
1	新科 Shinco	89	14.8
2	步步高 BBK	69	11.5
3	先科 SAST	67	11.2
4	万利达 Malata	55	9.2
5	爱多 Idall	30	5.0
6	索尼 Sony	20	3.3
7	松下 Panasonic	15	2.5
8	飞利浦 Philips	12	2.0
9	三星 Samsung	11	1.8
10	金正 Nintaus	10	1.7

n=600

8-4 对家中现有影碟机(最近购买的一台)的五个方面的描述/ About the VCD Player Most Recently Purchased

8-4-1 家中现有影碟机的品牌排名/ Ranking of the Currently Owned VCD Player Brands

排名 Brand Ranking	品牌 Brands	人数 Number	百分比 Percent
1	新科 Shinco	24	12.3
2	先科 SAST	21	10.8
3	万利达 Malata	20	10.3
4	步步高 BBK	13	6.7
5	爱多 Idall	8	4.1
5	三星 Samsung	8	4.1
5	索尼 Sony	8	4.1
6	松下 Panasonic	5	2.6
7	裕兴 Yuxing	4	2.1
7	飞利浦 Philips	4	2.1

n=195

8-4-2 该影碟机的购买时间/ Time of Purchasing of the Currently Owned VCD Player

	人数 Number	百分比 Percent
1993 年	3	1.5
1994 年	3	1.5
1995 年	11	5.6
1996 年	18	9.2
1997 年	51	26.2
1998 年	65	33.3
1999 年	44	22.6

n=195

8-4-3 该影碟机的价格/ The Price of the Currently Owned VCD Player

	人数 Number	百分比 Percent
1000 元或以下 1000 yuan or below	45	23.0
1001～2000 元 yuan	108	55.1
2001～3000 元 yuan	25	12.8
3001～4000 元 yuan	5	2.6
4001～5000 元 yuan	6	3.1
5001～6000 元 yuan	2	1.0
6001～7000 元 yuan	0	0.0
7001～8000 元 yuan	1	0.5
8001～9000 元 yuan	0	0.0
9001～10000 元 yuan	0	0.0
10000 元以上 over 10000 yuan	3	1.5
完全不知道 don't know	1	0.5

n=196

8-4-4 该影碟机的类型/ The Kind of the Currently Owned VCD Player

	人数 Number	百分比 Percent
VCD 机	176	90.3
DVD 机	2	1.0
CVD 机	5	2.6
SVCD 机	12	6.2
其他 others	0	0.0

n=195

8-4-5 该影碟机的机型/ The Type of the Currently Owned VCD Player

	人数 Number	百分比 Percent
普通机 VCD	129	66.8
自动换碟机 auto disc change	58	30.1
便携式机 portable VCD	2	1.0
其他 others	4	2.1

n=193

8-5 选择不同品牌影碟机时的考虑因素/ Considerations in Choosing from Different Brands

注：本题为多选题，合计百分比超过 100%（Multiple answers）

	人数 Number	品牌形象 brand image	外型 outlook	价格 price	画质好 clarity	纠错能力 correct ability
样本 Sample	194	41.2	12.9	37.6	30.4	33.5
新科 Shinco	24	41.7	16.7	41.7	29.2	45.8
先科 SAST	21	33.3	19.0	38.1	47.6	28.6
万利达 Malata	20	55.0	5.0	50.0	20.0	35.0
步步高 BBK	13	46.2	0.0	30.8	15.4	23.1
爱多 Idall	8	75.0	25.0	25.0	37.5	25.0
三星 Samsung	8	12.5	25.0	12.5	50.0	25.0
索尼 Sony	7	57.1	0.0	42.9	0.0	28.6

续前表 continued

	人数 Number	多制式 multi-system	有卡拉 OK 功能 karaoke function	有游戏功能 game function flavored	售后服务 follow-up service	其他 others
样本 Sample	194	6.7	33.5	5.7	8.8	2.6
新科 Shinco	24	12.5	25.0	8.3	4.2	0.0
先科 SAST	21	0.0	57.1	4.8	14.3	0.0
万利达 Malata	20	10.0	35.0	0.0	20.0	0.0
步步高 BBK	13	7.7	0.0	7.7	15.4	15.4
爱多 Idall	8	0.0	37.5	0.0	0.0	0.0
三星 Samsung	8	12.5	75.0	12.5	0.0	0.0
索尼 Sony	7	0.0	28.6	0.0	0.0	0.0

8-6 影碟机未来一年购买打算/ Plan for Future Purchasing of a VCD Player

8-6-1 有无购买打算/ Whether Planning to Purchase Next Year

	人数 Number	百分比 Percent
是 yes	55	9.2
否 no	545	90.8

n=600

8-6-2 打算购买的品牌排名/ The Brand of the Planned Purchase Next Year

排名 Brand Ranking	品牌 Brands	人数 Number	百分比 Percent
1	新科 Shinco	20	37.0
2	步步高 BBK	6	11.1
2	先科 SAST	6	11.1
3	万利达 Malata	5	9.3
4	金正 Nintaus	2	3.7
4	厦新 Amoisonic	2	3.7

n=54

8-6-3 打算购买的机型/ The Type of the Planned Purchase Next Year

	人数 Number	百分比 Percent
VCD 机	17	32.1
DVD 机	31	58.5
CVD 机	3	5.7
SVCD 机	2	3.8
其他 others	0	0.0

n=53

8-6-4 打算购买的价格/ The Price of the Planned Purchase Next Year

	人数 Number	百分比 Percent
1000 元或以下 1000 yuan or below	6	10.9
1001～2000 元 yuan	26	47.3
2001～3000 元 yuan	18	32.7
3001～4000 元 yuan	2	3.6
4001～5000 元 yuan	1	1.8
5001～6000 元 yuan	0	0.0
6001～7000 元 yuan	0	0.0
7001～8000 元 yuan	1	1.8
8001～9000 元 yuan	0	0.0
9001～10000 元 yuan	0	0.0
10000 元以上 over 10000 yuan	0	0.0
完全不知道 don't know	1	1.8

n=55

8-7 选购影碟机时不同角色的人口特征/ Demographics of the Different Roles in Purchasing a VCD Player

注：不同角色可以多选（Multiple answers）

	人数 Number	16-24 岁 Age	25-34 岁 Age	35-44 岁 Age	45-54 岁 Age	55-60 岁 Age
样本 Sample	175	21.1	32.0	26.9	17.1	2.9
男性 Male	90	16.7	31.1	30.0	18.9	3.3
提议者 advocate	15	20.0	20.0	33.3	20.0	6.7
影响者 influence	4	25.0	25.0	0.0	50.0	0.0
决定者 decider	54	5.6	38.9	31.5	22.2	1.9
使用者 user	48	22.9	27.1	27.1	18.8	4.2
女性 Female	85	25.9	32.9	23.5	15.3	2.4
提议者 advocate	25	36.0	24.0	20.0	16.0	4.0
影响者 influence	4	0.0	50.0	50.0	0.0	0.0
决定者 decider	22	13.6	36.4	31.8	13.6	4.5
使用者 user	56	30.4	30.4	19.6	16.1	3.6

8-8 不同消费者层的家中目前拥有品牌/ Brands of VCD Player Owned in Household by Market Segments

8-8-1 时尚流行指标/ Fads Popular Index

	人数 Number	第一品牌及百分比 1st/ percent	第二品牌及百分比 2nd/ percent	第三品牌及百分比 3rd/ percent
样本 Sample	195	**新科 Shinco(12.3)**	**先科 SAST(10.8)**	**万利达 Malata(10.3)**
平实生活指向 simple living orientation	82	新科 Shinco(12.2)	先科 SAST(9.8)	万利达 Malata(8.5)
时尚流行指向 fashion orientation	113	新科 Shinco(12.4)	先科 SAST(11.5) 万利达 Malata(11.5)	步步高 BBK(8.0)

8-8-2 广告态度指标/ Advertising Attitude Index

	人数 Number	第一品牌及百分比 1st/ percent	第二品牌及百分比 2nd/ percent	第三品牌及百分比 3rd/ percent
样本 Sample	195	**新科 Shinco(12.3)**	**先科 SAST(10.8)**	**万利达 Malata(10.3)**
广告淡漠指向 indifferent orientation	51	万利达 Malata(15.7)	先科 SAST(9.8)	索尼 Sony(7.8)
中间层 medium	114	新科 Shinco(13.2) 先科 SAST(13.2)	万利达 Malata(8.8)	步步高 BBK(7.9)
信赖广告指向 loyal orientation	30	新科 Shinco(20.0)	步步高 BBK(10.0)	索尼 Sony(6.7) 万利达 Malata(6.7) 金格川谷 Gynco(6.7)

8-8-3 价格态度指标/ Price Attitude Index

	人数 Number	第一品牌及百分比 1st/ percent	第二品牌及百分比 2nd/ percent	第三品牌及百分比 3rd/ percent
样本 Sample	195	**新科 Shinco(12.3)**	**先科 SAST(10.8)**	**万利达 Malata(10.3)**
价格无关心指向 indifferent orientation	41	步步高 BBK(12.2) 先科 SAST(12.2)	万利达 Malata(7.3) 新科 Shinco(7.3)	宏图 Hongtu(4.9) 新天利 Xintianli(4.9) 厦新 Amoisonic(4.9) 爱多 Idall(4.9)
中间层 medium	105	新科 Shinco(14.3)	先科 SAST(9.5) 万利达 Malata(9.5)	步步高 BBK(6.7)
价格重视指向 careful orientation	49	万利达 Malata(14.3)	先科 SAST(12.2) 新科 Shinco(12.2)	飞利浦 Philips(6.1)

8-9 不同消费者层选择影碟机时考虑因素/ Considerations in Choosing from Different Brands by Market Segments

8-9-1 时尚流行指标/ Fads Popular Index

注：本题为多选题，合计百分比超过 100%（Multiple answers）

	人数 Number	品牌形象 brand image	外型 outlook	价格 price	画质好 clarity	纠错能力 correct ability
样本 Sample	195	41.0	12.8	37.9	30.3	33.3
平实生活指向 simple living orientation	82	41.5	12.2	47.6	26.8	34.1
时尚流行指向 fashion orientation	113	40.7	13.3	31.0	32.7	32.7

续前表 continued

	人数 Number	多制式 multi-system	有卡拉 OK 功能 karaoke function	有游戏功能 game function flavored	售后服务 follow-up service	其他 others
样本 Sample	195	6.7	33.3	5.6	8.7	2.6
平实生活指向 simple living orientation	82	2.4	32.9	4.9	8.5	2.4
时尚流行指向 fashion orientation	113	9.7	33.6	6.2	8.8	2.7

8-9-2 广告态度指向/ Advertising Attitude Index

注：本题为多选题，合计百分比超过 100%（Multiple answers）

	人数 Number	品牌形象 brand image	外型 outlook	价格 price	画质好 clarity	纠错能力 correct ability
样本 Sample	195	41.0	12.8	37.9	30.3	33.3
广告淡漠指向 indifferent orientation	52	34.6	15.4	48.1	21.2	36.5
中间层 medium	113	44.2	8.8	33.6	33.6	34.5
信赖广告指向 loyal orientation	30	40.0	23.3	36.7	33.3	23.3

续前表 continued

	人数 Number	多制式 multi-system	有卡拉 OK 功能 karaoke function	有游戏功能 game function flavored	售后服务 follow-up service	其他 others
样本 Sample	195	6.7	33.3	5.6	8.7	2.6
广告淡漠指向 indifferent orientation	52	5.8	36.5	1.9	11.5	3.8
中间层 medium	113	7.1	29.2	7.1	8.0	2.7
信赖广告指向 loyal orientation	30	6.7	43.3	6.7	6.7	0.0

8-9-3 价格态度指向/ Price Attitude Index

注：本题为多选题，合计百分比超过 100%（Multiple answers）

	人数 Number	品牌形象 brand image	外型 outlook	价格 price	画质好 clarity	纠错能力 correct ability
样本 Sample	195	41.0	12.8	37.9	30.3	33.3
价格无关心指向 indifferent orientation	42	38.1	11.9	23.8	31.0	33.3
中间层 medium	105	45.7	14.3	33.3	34.3	32.4
价格重视指向 careful orientation	48	33.3	10.4	60.4	20.8	35.4

续前表 continued

	人数 Number	多制式 multi-system	有卡拉 OK 功能 karaoke function	有游戏功能 game function flavored	售后服务 follow-up service	其他 others
样本 Sample	195	6.7	33.3	5.6	8.7	2.6
价格无关心指向 indifferent orientation	42	2.4	28.6	2.4	7.1	2.4
中间层 medium	105	9.5	33.3	7.6	7.6	1.9
价格重视指向 careful orientation	48	4.2	37.5	4.2	12.5	4.2

9.照相机 / Camera

● 北京 / Beijing

9-1 照相机的拥有比例/ Proportion of Camera Owners in the Sample

	人数 Number	百分比 Percent
有 yes	754	74.5
没有 no	258	25.5

n=1012

9-2 照相机的拥有量/ Number of Camera Owned Per Household

	人数 Number	百分比 Percent
1 台 1 set	577	77.9
2 台及以上 2 sets or over	164	22.1

n=741

9-3 理想品牌排名/ Ranking of the Ideal Brands

排名 Brand Ranking	品牌 Brands	人数 Number	百分比 Percent
1	佳能 Canon	156	15.4
2	理光 Ricoh	120	11.9
3	尼康 Nikon	96	9.5
4	奥林巴斯 Olympus	89	8.8
5	美能达 Minolta	28	2.8
6	海鸥 Seagull	22	2.2
7	索尼 Sony	18	1.8
8	柯尼卡 Konica	17	1.7
9	柯达 Kodak	11	1.1
10	三星 Samsung	10	1.0

n=1010

9-4 对家中现有照相机(最近购买的一台)的四个方面的描述/ About the Camera Most Recently Purchased

9-4-1 家中现有照相机的品牌排名/ Ranking of the Currently Owned Camera Brands

排名 Brand Ranking	品牌 Brands	人数 Number	百分比 Percent
1	理光 Ricoh	128	17.1
2	佳能 Canon	87	11.6
3	奥林巴斯 Olympus	85	11.4
4	海鸥 Seagull	53	7.1
5	美能达 Minolta	36	4.8
6	尼康 Nikon	28	3.7
7	柯尼卡 Konica	26	3.5
8	汤姆 Toma	22	2.9
9	凤凰 Phoenix	16	2.1
10	宾得 Pentax	16	2.1

n=747

9-4-2 该照相机的购买时间/ The Time of Purchasing of the Currently Owned Camera

	人数 Number	百分比 Percent
1985 年或以前 1985 or before	62	8.3
1986～1990 年	150	20.1
1991 年	42	5.6
1992 年	29	3.9
1993 年	48	6.4
1994 年	52	7.0
1995 年	68	9.1
1996 年	80	10.7
1997 年	97	13.0
1998 年	71	9.5
1999 年	46	6.2

n=745

9-4-3 该照相机的价格/ The Price of the Currently Owned Camera

	人数 Number	百分比 Percent
1000 元或以下 1000 yuan or below	368	49.1
1001～2000 元 yuan	169	22.5
2001～3000 元 yuan	86	11.5
3001～4000 元 yuan	30	4.0
4001～5000 元 yuan	18	2.4
5001～6000 元 yuan	11	1.5
6001～7000 元 yuan	5	0.7
7001～8000 元 yuan	4	0.5
8001～9000 元 yuan	0	0.0
9001～10000 元 yuan	4	0.5
10000 元以上 over 10000 yuan	5	0.7
完全不知道 don't know	50	6.7

n=750

9-4-4 该照相机的类型/ The Type of the Currently Owned Camera

	人数 Number	百分比 Percent
固定镜头傻瓜相机 set lens simpleton camera	325	43.7
变焦镜头傻瓜相机 zoom lens simpleton camera	216	29.0
机械单镜头反光相机 mechanic single len reflector camera	63	8.5
自动单镜头反光相机 automatic single len reflector camera	46	6.2
手动加自动单反相机 manual or automatic camera	67	9.0
数字相机 digital camera	10	1.3
一次成像相机 one step camera	6	0.8
120 专业相机 120 professional camera	5	0.7
其他 others	6	0.8

n=744

9-5 选择不同品牌照相机时的考虑因素/ Considerations in Choosing from Different Brands

注：本题为多选题，合计百分比超过 100%（Multiple answers）

	人数 Number	品牌形象 brand image	外型 outlook	价格 price	成像质量 picture quality	变焦功能 zooming function	专业声誉 professional prestige
样本 Sample	**733**	**32.3**	**10.6**	**37.9**	**21.6**	**13.0**	**5.0**
理光 Ricoh	125	40.0	12.0	36.0	19.2	12.0	3.2
佳能 Canon	86	46.5	10.5	29.1	22.1	15.1	8.1
奥林巴斯 Olympus	85	44.7	17.6	20.0	18.8	23.5	5.9
海鸥 Seagull	53	34.0	3.8	39.6	26.4	7.5	7.5
美能达 Minolta	36	27.8	5.6	33.3	38.9	36.1	11.1
尼康 Nikon	27	40.7	11.1	25.9	40.7	7.4	18.5
柯尼卡 Konica	26	15.4	15.4	61.5	11.5	3.8	3.8
汤姆 Toma	22	4.5	9.1	50.0	4.5	0.0	0.0
凤凰 Phoenix	16	31.3	0.0	56.3	31.3	12.5	6.3
宾得 Pentax	16	31.3	0.0	25.0	31.3	37.5	6.3
三星 Samsung	15	20.0	6.7	40.0	6.7	26.7	0.0
富士 Fuji	11	36.4	18.2	18.2	27.3	18.2	0.0
雅西卡 Yashica	11	18.2	9.1	27.3	54.5	18.2	0.0
甘光 Ganguang	9	22.2	11.1	55.6	11.1	0.0	11.1

续前表 continued

	人数 Number	操作方便 easy to deal with	原产地 place of production	功能齐备 all-function	售后服务 follow-up service	其他 others
样本 Sample	**733**	**43.1**	**8.7**	**13.4**	**1.6**	**4.9**
理光 Ricoh	125	46.4	11.2	13.6	2.4	2.4
佳能 Canon	86	44.2	9.3	14.0	2.3	3.5
奥林巴斯 Olympus	85	49.4	17.6	16.5	1.2	3.5
海鸥 Seagull	53	26.4	1.9	13.2	1.9	5.7
美能达 Minolta	36	25.0	8.3	25.0	0.0	0.0
尼康 Nikon	27	48.1	11.1	7.4	0.0	3.7
柯尼卡 Konica	26	46.2	7.7	11.5	0.0	3.8
汤姆 Toma	22	54.5	0.0	13.6	0.0	13.6
凤凰 Phoenix	16	31.3	6.3	0.0	0.0	6.3
宾得 Pentax	16	43.8	18.8	31.3	0.0	6.3
三星 Samsung	15	53.3	0.0	26.7	0.0	0.0
富士 Fuji	11	9.1	27.3	0.0	0.0	18.2
雅西卡 Yashica	11	27.3	18.2	36.4	0.0	0.0
甘光 Ganguang	9	66.7	0.0	0.0	11.1	0.0

9-6 照相机未来一年购买打算/ Plan for Future Purchasing of a Camera

9-6-1 有无购买打算/ Whether Planning to Purchase Next Year

	人数 Number	百分比 Percent
是 yes	93	9.3
否 no	911	90.7

n=1004

9-6-2 打算购买的品牌排名/ Ranking of the Brands of the Planned Purchase Next Year

排名 Brand Ranking	品牌 Brands	人数 Number	百分比 Percent
1	佳能 Canon	19	22.1
2	奥林巴斯 Olympus	14	16.3
3	理光 Ricoh	7	8.1
4	尼康 Nikon	6	7.0

n=86

9-6-3 打算购买的类型/ The Type of the Planned Purchase Next Year

	人数 Number	百分比 Percent
固定镜头傻瓜相机 set lens simpleton camera	16	18.2
变焦镜头傻瓜相机 zoom lens simpleton camera	30	34.1
机械单镜头反光相机 mechanic single len reflector camera	3	3.4
自动单镜头反光相机 automatic single len reflector camera	8	9.1
手动加自动单反相机 manual or automatic camera	14	15.9
数字相机 digital camera	14	15.9
一次成像相机 one step camera	1	1.1
120 专业相机 120 professional camera	1	1.1
其他 others	1	1.1

n=88

9-6-4 打算购买的价格/ The Price of the Planned Purchase Next Year

	人数 Number	百分比 Percent
1000 元或以下 1000 yuan or below	20	23.0
1001～2000 元 yuan	24	27.6
2001～3000 元 yuan	20	23.0
3001～4000 元 yuan	7	8.0
4001～5000 元 yuan	5	5.7
5001～6000 元 yuan	6	6.9
6001～7000 元 yuan	1	1.1
7001～8000 元 yuan	1	1.1
8001～9000 元 yuan	1	1.1
9001～10000 元 yuan	1	1.1
10000 元以上 over 10000 yuan	1	1.1
完全不知道 don't know	0	0.0

n=87

9-7 选购照相机时不同角色的人口特征/ Demographics of the Different Roles in Purchasing a Camera

注：不同角色可以多选（Multiple answers）

	人数 Number	16-24 岁 Age	25-34 岁 Age	35-44 岁 Age	45-54 岁 Age	55-60 岁 Age
样本 Sample	**657**	**21.2**	**28.6**	**25.6**	**16.6**	**8.1**
男性 Male	**332**	**22.9**	**26.2**	**26.2**	**16.0**	**8.7**
提议者 advocate	34	17.6	14.7	35.3	20.6	11.8
影响者 influence	25	16.0	28.0	20.0	28.0	8.0
决定者 decider	164	7.9	26.2	36.6	18.3	11.0
使用者 user	236	29.2	27.5	21.6	13.6	8.1
女性 Female	**325**	**19.4**	**31.1**	**24.9**	**17.2**	**7.4**
提议者 advocate	59	16.9	22.0	33.9	22.0	5.1
影响者 influence	30	26.7	33.3	16.7	13.3	10.0
决定者 decider	72	4.2	44.4	31.9	13.9	5.6
使用者 user	246	21.5	29.3	26.8	15.9	6.5

9-8 不同消费者层的家中目前拥有品牌/ Brands of Camera Owned in Household by Market Segments

9-8-1 时尚流行指标/ Fads Popular Index

	人数 Number	第一品牌及百分比 1st/ percent	第二品牌及百分比 2nd/ percent	第三品牌及百分比 3rd/ percent	第四品牌及百分比 4th/ percent
样本 Sample	738	**理光 Ricoh(17.1)**	**佳能 Canon(11.7)**	**奥林巴斯 Olympus(11.4)**	**海鸥 Seagull(7.2)**
平实生活指向 simple living orientation	360	理光 Ricoh(16.7)	奥林巴斯 Olympus(10.3)	佳能 Canon(10.0)	海鸥 Seagull(8.9)
时尚流行指向 fashion orientation	378	理光 Ricoh(17.5)	佳能 Canon(13.2)	奥林巴斯 Olympus(12.4)	海鸥 Seagull(5.6)

9-8-2 广告态度指标/ Advertising Attitude Index

	人数 Number	第一品牌及百分比 1st/ percent	第二品牌及百分比 2nd/ percent	第三品牌及百分比 3rd/ percent	第四品牌及百分比 4th/ percent
样本 Sample	737	**理光 Ricoh(17.2)**	**佳能 Canon(11.8)**	**奥林巴斯 Olympus(11.4)**	**海鸥 Seagull(7.1)**
广告淡漠指向 indifferent orientation	217	理光 Ricoh(15.7)	佳能 Canon(12.4)	奥林巴斯 Olympus(12.0)	海鸥 Seagull(7.4)
中间层 medium	421	理光 Ricoh(17.8)	佳能 Canon(11.9)	奥林巴斯 Olympus(10.2)	海鸥 Seagull(7.1)
信赖广告指向 loyal orientation	99	理光 Ricoh(18.2)	奥林巴斯 Olympus(15.2)	佳能 Canon(10.1)	海鸥 Seagull(6.1)

9-8-3 价格态度指标/ Price Attitude Index

	人数 Number	第一品牌及百分比 1st/ percent	第二品牌及百分比 2nd/ percent	第三品牌及百分比 3rd/ percent	第四品牌及百分比 4th/ percent
样本 Sample	742	**理光 Ricoh(17.3)**	**佳能 Canon(11.7)**	**奥林巴斯 Olympus(11.3)**	**海鸥 Seagull(7.1)**
价格无关心指向 indifferent orientation	155	理光 Ricoh(18.1)	奥林巴斯 Olympus(12.9)	佳能 Canon(12.3)	海鸥 Seagull(6.5)
中间层 medium	374	理光 Ricoh(19.0)	佳能 Canon(12.3)	奥林巴斯 Olympus(12.0)	海鸥 Seagull(5.9)
价格重视指向 careful orientation	213	理光 Ricoh(13.6)	佳能 Canon(10.3)	海鸥 Seagull(9.9)	奥林巴斯 Olympus(8.9)

9-9 不同消费者层选择照相机时的考虑因素/ Considerations in Choosing from Different Brands by Market Segments

9-9-1 时尚流行指标/ Fads Popular Index

注：本题为多选题，合计百分比超过 100%（Multiple answers）

	人数 Number	品牌形象 brand image	外型 outlook	价格 price	成像质量 picture quality	变焦功能 zooming function	专业声誉 professional prestige
样本 Sample	731	32.1	10.7	38.0	21.5	12.9	5.1
平实生活指向 simple living orientation	355	32.1	7.6	40.0	20.6	10.4	5.6
时尚流行指向 fashion orientation	376	32.2	13.6	36.2	22.3	15.2	4.5

续前表 continued

	人数 Number	操作方便 easy to deal with	原产地 place of production	功能齐备 all-functions	售后服务 follow-up service	其他 others
样本 Sample	731	43.4	8.5	13.1	1.6	5.1
平实生活指向 simple living orientation	355	43.4	5.9	12.1	1.1	6.5
时尚流行指向 fashion orientation	376	43.4	10.9	14.1	2.1	3.7

9-9-2 广告态度指标/ Advertising Attitude Index

注：本题为多选题，合计百分比超过 100%（Multiple answers）

	人数 Number	品牌形象 brand image	外型 outlook	价格 price	成像质量 picture quality	变焦功能 zooming function	专业声誉 professional prestige
样本 Sample	730	32.2	10.4	38.4	21.5	12.5	4.9
广告淡漠指向 indifferent orientation	218	25.2	10.1	33.9	25.7	10.1	4.1
中间层 medium	416	34.1	11.3	40.4	20.0	14.2	5.8
信赖广告指向 loyal orientation	96	39.6	7.3	39.6	18.8	10.4	3.1

续前表 continued

	人数 Number	操作方便 easy to deal with	原产地 place of production	功能齐备 all-function	售后服务 follow-up service	其他 others
样本 Sample	730	43.3	8.8	13.3	1.6	4.9
广告淡漠指向 indifferent orientation	218	45.4	8.3	16.1	1.4	7.3
中间层 medium	416	42.3	9.1	11.8	1.7	3.6
信赖广告指向 loyal orientation	96	42.7	8.3	13.5	2.1	5.2

9-9-3 价格态度指标/ Price Attitude Index

注：本题为多选题，合计百分比超过 100%（Multiple answers）

	人数 Number	品牌形象 brand image	外型 outlook	价格 price	成像质量 picture quality	变焦功能 zooming function	专业声誉 professional prestige
样本 Sample	735	32.2	10.5	37.8	21.5	12.9	5.0
价格无关心指向 indifferent orientation	155	28.4	9.0	33.5	26.5	11.6	5.2
中间层 medium	373	34.0	10.5	37.3	20.4	15.0	6.4
价格重视指向 careful orientation	207	31.9	11.6	42.0	19.8	10.1	2.4

续前表 continued

	人数 Number	操作方便 easy to deal with	原产地 place of production	功能齐备 all-function	售后服务 follow-up service	其他 others
样本 Sample	735	43.1	8.6	13.2	1.6	5.0
价格无关心指向 indifferent orientation	155	43.2	12.9	10.3	1.3	6.5
中间层 medium	373	43.7	7.2	13.9	1.3	3.5
价格重视指向 careful orientation	207	42.0	7.7	14.0	2.4	6.8

● 上海 / Shanghai

9-1 照相机的拥有比例/ Proportion of Camera Owners in the Sample

	人数 Number	百分比 Percent
有 yes	490	48.3
没有 no	524	51.7

n=1014

9-2 照相机的拥有量/ Number of Camera Owned Per Household

	人数 Number	百分比 Percent
1 台 1 set	432	89.4
2 台及以上 2 sets or over	51	10.6

n=483

9-3 理想品牌排名/ Ranking of the Ideal Brands

排名 Brand Ranking	品牌 Brands	人数 Number	百分比 Percent
1	佳能 Canon	311	30.9
2	海鸥 Seagull	139	13.8
3	奥林巴斯 Olympus	72	7.1
4	尼康 Nikon	60	6.0
5	理光 Ricoh	55	5.5
6	索尼 Sony	47	4.7
7	美能达 Minolta	35	3.5
8	柯尼卡 Konica	28	2.8
9	柯达 Kodak	19	1.9
10	松下 National	11	1.1

n=1007

9-4 对家中现有照相机(最近购买的一台)的四个方面的描述/ About the Camera Most Recently Purchased

9-4-1 家中现有照相机的品牌排名/ Ranking of the Currently Owned Camera Brands

排名 Brand Ranking	品牌 Brands	人数 Number	百分比 Percent
1	海鸥 Seagull	126	25.8
2	佳能 Canon	101	20.7
3	理光 Ricoh	46	9.4
4	奥林巴斯 Olympus	42	8.6
5	美能达 Minolta	26	5.3
6	柯尼卡 Konica	20	4.1
7	尼康 Nikon	18	3.7
8	汤姆 Toma	10	2.0
9	索尼 Sony	9	1.8
9	凤凰 Phoenix	9	1.8
10	柯达 Kodak	7	1.4

n=488

9-4-2 该照相机的购买时间/ The Time of Purchasing of the Currently Owned Camera

	人数 Number	百分比 Percent
1985 年或以前 1985 or before	37	7.6
1986～1990 年	77	15.8
1991 年	26	5.3
1992 年	20	4.1
1993 年	28	5.7
1994 年	41	8.4
1995 年	61	12.5
1996 年	55	11.3
1997 年	64	13.1
1998 年	59	12.1
1999 年	20	4.1

n=488

9-4-3 该照相机的价格/ The Price of the Currently Owned Camera

	人数 Number	百分比 Percent
1000 元或以下 1000 yuan or below	246	50.3
1001～2000 元 yuan	115	23.5
2001～3000 元 yuan	52	10.6
3001～4000 元 yuan	24	4.9
4001～5000 元 yuan	11	2.2
5001～6000 元 yuan	2	0.4
6001～7000 元 yuan	5	1.0
7001～8000 元 yuan	2	0.4
8001～9000 元 yuan	0	0.0
9001～10000 元 yuan	2	0.4
10000 元以上 over 10000 yuan	1	0.2
完全不知道 don't know	29	5.9

n=489

9-4-4 该照相机的类型/ The Type of the Currently Owned Camera

	人数 Number	百分比 Percent
固定镜头傻瓜相机 set lens simpleton camera	193	39.6
变焦镜头傻瓜相机 zoom lens simpleton camera	135	27.7
机械单镜头反光相机 mechanic single len reflector camera	60	12.3
自动单镜头反光相机 automatic single len reflector camera	38	7.8
手动加自动单反相机 manual or automatic camera	40	8.2
数字相机 digital camera	9	1.8
一次成像相机 one step camera	2	0.4
120 专业相机 120 professional camera	4	0.8
其他 others	6	1.2

n=487

9-5 选择不同品牌照相机时考虑因素/ Considerations in Choosing from Different Brands

注：本题为多选题，合计百分比超过 100%（Multiple answers）

	人数 Number	品牌形象 brand image	外型 outlook	价格 price	成像质量 picture quality	变焦功能 zooming function	专业声誉 professional prestige
样本 Sample	**487**	**39.0**	**11.1**	**33.9**	**23.2**	**17.0**	**7.2**
海鸥 Seagull	126	38.1	11.1	31.7	25.4	11.1	6.3
佳能 Canon	100	45.0	17.0	27.0	17.0	10.0	9.0
理光 Ricoh	46	39.1	8.7	45.7	19.6	13.0	8.7
奥林巴斯 Olympus	42	45.2	7.1	19.0	31.0	33.3	4.8
美能达 Minolta	26	42.3	3.8	30.8	30.8	38.5	15.4
柯尼卡 Konica	20	50.0	5.0	40.0	10.0	0.0	0.0
尼康 Nikon	18	55.6	0.0	5.6	16.7	44.4	16.7
汤姆 Toma	10	0.0	10.0	50.0	10.0	20.0	0.0
索尼 Sony	9	22.2	11.1	33.3	33.3	33.3	0.0
凤凰 Phoenix	9	44.4	11.1	22.2	22.2	11.1	0.0

续前表 continued

	人数 Number	操作方便 easy to deal with	原产地 place of production	功能齐备 all-function	售后服务 follow-up service	其他 others
样本 Sample	**487**	**36.8**	**10.3**	**13.3**	**4.9**	**3.3**
海鸥 Seagull	126	25.4	7.1	13.5	6.3	4.8
佳能 Canon	100	42.0	13.0	17.0	7.0	3.0
理光 Ricoh	46	39.1	8.7	8.7	6.5	4.3
奥林巴斯 Olympus	42	45.2	21.4	11.9	2.4	4.8
美能达 Minolta	26	30.8	11.5	19.2	0.0	0.0
柯尼卡 Konica	20	65.0	10.0	0.0	0.0	0.0
尼康 Nikon	18	38.9	22.2	11.1	5.6	0.0
汤姆 Toma	10	70.0	0.0	10.0	0.0	0.0
索尼 Sony	9	33.3	0.0	33.3	11.1	0.0
凤凰 Phoenix	9	44.4	22.2	11.1	0.0	0.0

9-6 照相机未来一年购买打算/ Plan for Future Purchasing of a Camera

9-6-1 有无购买打算/ Whether Planning to Purchase Next Year

	人数 Number	百分比 Percent
是 yes	48	4.7
否 no	965	95.3

n=1013

9-6-2 打算购买的品牌排名/ Ranking of the Brands of the Planned Purchase Next Year

排名 Brand Ranking	品牌 Brands	人数 Number	百分比 Percent
1	佳能 Canon	21	43.8
2	海鸥 Seagull	5	10.4
2	理光 Ricoh	5	10.4
3	奥林巴斯 Olympus	4	8.3
4	柯尼卡 Konica	2	4.2
4	尼康 Nikon	2	4.2

n=48

9-6-3 打算购买的类型/ The Type of the Planned Purchase Next Year

	人数 Number	百分比 Percent
固定镜头傻瓜相机 set lens simpleton camera	8	18.6
变焦镜头傻瓜相机 zoom lens simpleton camera	15	34.9
机械单镜头反光相机 mechanic single len reflector camera	2	4.7
自动单镜头反光相机 automatic single len reflector camera	6	14.0
手动加自动单反相机 manual or automatic camera	4	9.3
数字相机 digital camera	5	11.6
一次成像相机 one step camera	2	4.7
120 专业相机 120 professional camera	0	0.0
其他 others	1	2.3

n=43

9-6-4 打算购买的价格/ The Price of the Planned Purchase Next Year

	人数 Number	百分比 Percent
1000 元或以下 1000 yuan or below	9	20.0
1001～2000 元 yuan	13	28.9
2001～3000 元 yuan	12	26.7
3001～4000 元 yuan	5	11.1
4001～5000 元 yuan	3	6.7
5001～6000 元 yuan	1	2.2
6001～7000 元 yuan	1	2.2
7001～8000 元 yuan	0	0.0
8001～9000 元 yuan	0	0.0
9001～10000 元 yuan	0	0.0
10000 元以上 over 10000 yuan	1	2.2
完全不知道 don't know	0	0.0

n=45

9-7 选购照相机时不同角色的人口特征/ Demographics of Different Roles in Purchasing a Camera

注：不同角色可以多选（Multiple answers）

	人数 Number	16-24 岁 Age	25-34 岁 Age	35-44 岁 Age	45-54 岁 Age	55-60 岁 Age
样本 Sample	415	19.3	28.9	28.9	16.4	6.5
男性 Male	198	16.2	27.3	31.3	18.2	7.1
提议者 advocate	32	15.6	21.9	40.6	15.6	6.3
影响者 influence	10	20.0	30.0	30.0	10.0	10.0
决定者 decider	97	4.1	24.7	38.1	26.8	6.2
使用者 user	99	22.2	32.3	22.2	16.2	7.1
女性 Female	217	22.1	30.4	26.7	14.7	6.0
提议者 advocate	44	31.8	29.5	22.7	15.9	0.0
影响者 influence	29	10.3	17.2	44.8	17.2	10.3
决定者 decider	60	11.7	30.0	28.3	21.7	8.3
使用者 user	140	24.3	29.3	27.9	12.9	5.7

9-8 不同消费者层的家中目前拥有品牌/ Brands of Camera Owned in Household by Market Segments

9-8-1 时尚流行指标/ Fads Popular Index

	人数 Number	第一品牌及百分比 1st/ percent	第二品牌及百分比 2nd/ percent	第三品牌及百分比 3rd/ percent	第四品牌及百分比 4th/ percent
样本 Sample	485	**海鸥 Seagull(26.0)**	**佳能 Canon(20.4)**	**理光 Ricoh(9.3)**	**奥林巴斯 Olympus(8.7)**
平实生活指向 simple living orientation	204	海鸥 Seagull(30.4)	佳能 Canon(15.2)	理光 Ricoh(14.2)	奥林巴斯 Olympus(7.4)
时尚流行指向 fashion orientation	281	佳能 Canon(24.2)	海鸥 Seagull(22.8)	奥林巴斯 Olympus(9.6)	理光 Ricoh(5.7)

9-8-2 广告态度指标/ Advertising Attitude Index

	人数 Number	第一品牌及百分比 1st/ percent	第二品牌及百分比 2nd/ percent	第三品牌及百分比 3rd/ percent	第四品牌及百分比 4th/ percent
样本 Sample	486	**海鸥 Seagull(25.9)**	**佳能 Canon(20.6)**	**理光 Ricoh(9.5)**	**奥林巴斯 Olympus(8.6)**
广告淡漠指向 indifferent orientation	114	海鸥 Seagull(23.7)	佳能 Canon(15.8)	理光 Ricoh(10.5)	奥林巴斯 Olympus(8.8) 柯尼卡 Konica(8.8) 美能达 Minolta(8.8)
中间层 medium	299	海鸥 Seagull(25.8)	佳能 Canon(21.7)	理光 Ricoh(10.0)	奥林巴斯 Olympus(8.4)
信赖广告指向 loyal orientation	73	海鸥 Seagull(30.1)	佳能 Canon(23.3)	奥林巴斯 Olympus(9.6)	柯达 Kodak(5.5) 柯尼卡 Konica(5.5) 理光 Ricoh(5.5)

9-8-3 价格态度指标/ Price Attitude Index

	人数 Number	第一品牌及百分比 1st/ percent	第二品牌及百分比 2nd/ percent	第三品牌及百分比 3rd/ percent	第四品牌及百分比 4th/ percent
样本 Sample	487	**海鸥 Seagull(25.7)**	**佳能 Canon(20.7)**	**理光 Ricoh(9.4)**	**奥林巴斯 Olympus(8.6)**
价格无关心指向 indifferent orientation	72	海鸥 Seagull(27.8)	佳能 Canon(19.4)	奥林巴 Olympus(13.9)	美能达 Minolta(6.9) 理光 Ricoh(6.9)
中间层 medium	265	海鸥 Seagull(25.3)	佳能 Canon(23.0)	奥林巴 Olympus(10.9)	理光 Ricoh(9.8)
价格重视指向 careful orientation	150	海鸥 Seagull(25.3)	佳能 Canon(17.3)	理光 Ricoh(10.0)	美能达 Minolta(6.0)

9-9 不同消费者层选择照相机时的考虑因素/ Considerations in Choosing from Different Brands by Market Segments

9-9-1 时尚流行指标/ Fads Popular Index

注：本题为多选题，合计百分比超过 100%（Multiple answers）

	人数 Number	品牌形象 brand image	外型 outlook	价格 price	成像质量 picture quality	变焦功能 zooming function	专业声誉 professional prestige
样本 Sample	486	38.9	11.3	34.2	23.0	17.1	7.2
平实生活指向 simple living orientation	204	41.7	5.4	39.7	22.5	16.7	7.4
时尚流行指向 fashion orientation	282	36.9	15.6	30.1	23.4	17.4	7.1

续前表 continued

	人数 Number	操作方便 easy to deal with	原产地 place of production	功能齐备 all-function	售后服务 follow-up service	其他 others
样本 Sample	486	36.4	10.3	13.6	4.7	3.3
平实生活指向 simple living orientation	204	34.3	8.8	11.8	4.9	2.9
时尚流行指向 fashion orientation	282	37.9	11.3	14.9	4.6	3.5

9-9-2 广告态度指标/ Advertising Attitude Index

注：本题为多选题，合计百分比超过 100%（Multiple answers）

	人数 Number	品牌形象 brand image	外型 outlook	价格 price	成像质量 picture quality	变焦功能 zooming function	专业声誉 professional prestige
样本 Sample	487	39.0	11.3	34.1	23.0	16.8	7.2
广告淡漠指向 indifferent orientation	114	38.6	8.8	36.8	20.2	13.2	11.4
中间层 medium	300	39.0	11.7	35.7	20.0	17.3	6.3
信赖广告指向 loyal orientation	73	39.7	13.7	23.3	39.7	20.5	4.1

续前表 continued

	人数 Number	操作方便 easy to deal with	原产地 place of production	功能齐备 all-function	售后服务 follow-up service	其他 others
样本 Sample	487	36.6	10.3	13.3	4.7	3.3
广告淡漠指向 indifferent orientation	114	40.4	9.6	11.4	7.0	3.5
中间层 medium	300	34.3	12.0	15.0	4.3	3.3
信赖广告指向 loyal orientation	73	39.7	4.1	9.6	2.7	2.7

9-9-3 价格态度指标/ Price Attitude Index

注：本题为多选题，合计百分比超过 100%（Multiple answers）

	人数 Number	品牌形象 brand image	外型 outlook	价格 price	成像质量 picture quality	变焦功能 zooming function	专业声誉 professional prestige
样本 Sample	488	38.9	11.3	34.0	23.2	17.0	7.2
价格无关心指向 indifferent orientation	72	41.7	11.1	16.7	27.8	19.4	12.5
中间层 medium	265	38.5	9.4	32.8	21.9	18.1	6.8
价格重视指向 careful orientation	151	38.4	14.6	44.4	23.2	13.9	5.3

续前表 continued

	人数 Number	操作方便 easy to deal with	原产地 place of production	功能齐备 all-function	售后服务 follow-up service	其他 others
样本 Sample	488	36.7	10.2	13.3	4.9	3.3
价格无关心指向 indifferent orientation	72	31.9	8.3	12.5	4.2	6.9
中间层 medium	265	39.2	11.7	14.7	4.9	3.0
价格重视指向 careful orientation	151	34.4	8.6	11.3	5.3	2.0

● 广州 / Guangzhou

9-1 照相机的拥有比例/ Proportion of Camera Owners in the Sample

	人数 Number	百分比 Percent
有 yes	505	48.8
没有 no	529	51.2

n=1034

9-2 照相机的拥有量/ Number of Camera Owned Per Household

	人数 Number	百分比 Percent
1 台 1 set	440	88.5
2 台及以上 2 sets or over	57	11.5

n=497

9-3 理想品牌排名/ Ranking of the Ideal Brands

排名 Brand Ranking	品牌 Brands	人数 Number	百分比 Percent
1	佳能 Canon	142	13.8
2	理光 Ricoh	131	12.7
3	奥林巴斯 Olympus	47	4.6
4	尼康 Nikon	40	3.9
5	美能达 Minolta	22	2.1
6	海鸥 Seagull	20	1.9
6	索尼 Sony	20	1.9
7	宾得 Pentax	17	1.6

n=1031

9-4 对家中现有照相机(最近购买的一台)的四个方面的描述/ About the Camera Most Recently Purchased

9-4-1 家中现有照相机的品牌排名/ Ranking of the Currently Owned Camera Brands

排名 Brand Ranking	品牌 Brands	人数 Number	百分比 Percent
1	理光 Ricoh	102	20.4
2	佳能 Canon	89	17.8
3	奥林巴斯 Olympus	41	8.2
4	珠江 Zhujiang	31	6.2
5	海鸥 Seagull	25	5.0
6	宾得 Pentax	21	4.2
7	尼康 Nikon	16	3.2
8	美能达 Minolta	15	3.0

n=499

9-4-2 该照相机的购买时间/ The Time of Purchasing of the Currently Owned Camera

	人数 Number	百分比 Percent
1985 年或以前 1985 or before	25	5.0
1986～1990 年	57	11.4
1991 年	37	7.4
1992 年	37	7.4
1993 年	45	9.0
1994 年	35	7.0
1995 年	63	12.6
1996 年	67	13.4
1997 年	73	14.6
1998 年	41	8.2
1999 年	20	4.0

n=500

9-4-3 该照相机的价格/ The Price of the Currently Owned Camera

	人数 Number	百分比 Percent
1000 元或以下 1000 yuan or below	251	49.9
1001～2000 元 yuan	112	22.3
2001～3000 元 yuan	54	10.7
3001～4000 元 yuan	23	4.6
4001～5000 元 yuan	10	2.0
5001～6000 元 yuan	9	1.8
6001～7000 元 yuan	3	0.6
7001～8000 元 yuan	1	0.2
8001～9000 元 yuan	1	0.2
9001～10000 元 yuan	1	0.2
10000 元以上 over 10000 yuan	3	0.6
完全不知道 don't know	35	7.0

n=503

9-4-4 该照相机的类型/ The Type of the Currently Owned Camera

	人数 Number	百分比 Percent
固定镜头傻瓜相机 set lens simpleton camera	222	44.3
变焦镜头傻瓜相机 zoom lens simpleton camera	129	25.7
机械单镜头反光相机 mechanic single len reflector camera	32	6.4
自动单镜头反光相机 automatic single len reflector camera	64	12.8
手动加自动单反相机 manual or automatic camera	30	6.0
数字相机 digital camera	10	2.0
一次成像相机 one step camera	2	0.4
120 专业相机 120 professional camera	3	0.6
其他 others	9	1.8

n=501

9-5 选择不同品牌照相机时的考虑因素/ Considerations in Choosing from Different Brands

注：本题为多选题，合计百分比超过 100%（Multiple answers）

	人数 Number	品牌形象 brand image	外型 outlook	价格 price	成像质量 picture quality	变焦功能 zooming function	专业声誉 professional prestige
样本 Sample	498	31.5	11.8	40.6	22.9	17.9	7.4
理光 Ricoh	102	33.3	11.8	47.1	23.5	16.7	8.8
佳能 Canon	88	34.1	12.5	40.9	27.3	18.2	6.8
奥林巴斯 Olympus	41	56.1	17.1	14.6	19.5	17.1	14.6
珠江 Zhujiang	31	16.1	9.7	64.5	12.9	6.5	3.2
海鸥 Seagull	25	28.0	12.0	48.0	28.0	28.0	8.0
宾得 Pentax	21	38.1	9.5	9.5	19.0	38.1	14.3
尼康 Nikon	16	50.0	0.0	18.8	25.0	31.3	6.3
美能达 Minolta	15	60.0	20.0	13.3	26.7	20.0	6.7

续前表 continued

	人数 Number	操作方便 easy to deal with	原产地 place of production	功能齐备 all -function	售后服务 follow-up service	其他 others
样本 Sample	498	42.2	7.4	15.3	2.2	2.4
理光 Ricoh	102	48.0	2.0	12.7	3.9	0.0
佳能 Canon	88	36.4	5.7	13.6	1.1	4.5
奥林巴斯 Olympus	41	58.5	7.3	24.4	0.0	0.0
珠江 Zhujiang	31	45.2	6.5	3.2	3.2	0.0
海鸥 Seagull	25	20.0	4.0	8.0	8.0	0.0
宾得 Pentax	21	52.4	23.8	23.8	0.0	0.0
尼康 Nikon	16	25.0	18.8	31.3	0.0	6.3
美能达 Minolta	15	33.3	13.3	46.7	6.7	0.0

9-6 照相机未来一年购买打算/ Plan for Future Purchasing of a Camera

9-6-1 有无购买打算/ Whether Planning to Purchase Next Year

	人数 Number	百分比 Percent
是 yes	37	3.6
否 no	995	96.4

n=1032

9-6-2 打算购买的品牌排名/ Ranking of the Brands of the Planned Purchase Next Year

排名 Brand Ranking	品牌 Brands	人数 Number	百分比 Percent
1	佳能 Canon	12	32.4
2	理光 Ricoh	9	24.3
3	尼康 Nikon	3	8.1

n=37

9-6-3 打算购买的类型/ The Type of the Planned Purchase Next Year

	人数 Number	百分比 Percent
固定镜头傻瓜相机 set lens simpleton camera	6	16.2
变焦镜头傻瓜相机 zoom lens simpleton camera	13	35.1
机械单镜头反光相机 mechanic single len reflector camera	0	0.0
自动单镜头反光相机 automatic single len reflector camera	4	10.8
手动加自动单反相机 manual or automatic camera	7	18.9
数字相机 digital camera	5	13.5
一次成像相机 one step camera	1	2.7
120 专业相机 120 professional camera	1	2.7
其他 others	0	0.0

n=37

9-6-4 打算购买的价格/ The Price of the Planned Purchase Next Year

	人数 Number	百分比 Percent
1000 元或以下 1000 yuan or below	8	21.6
1001～2000 元 yuan	15	40.5
2001～3000 元 yuan	8	21.6
3001～4000 元 yuan	2	5.4
4001～5000 元 yuan	2	5.4
5001～6000 元 yuan	1	2.7
6001～7000 元 yuan	0	0.0
7001～8000 元 yuan	1	2.7
8001～9000 元 yuan	0	0.0
9001～10000 元 yuan	0	0.0
10000 元以上 over 10000 yuan	0	0.0
完全不知道 don't know	0	0.0

n=37

9-7 选购照相机时不同角色的人口特征/ Demographics of the Different Roles in Purchasing a Camera

注：不同角色可以多选（Multiple answers）

	人数 Number	16-24 岁 Age	25-34 岁 Age	35-44 岁 Age	45-54 岁 Age	55-60 岁 Age
样本 Sample	437	17.6	33.0	24.5	18.3	6.6
男性 Male	220	14.5	34.5	25.9	19.5	5.5
提议者 advocate	22	18.2	31.8	22.7	22.7	4.5
影响者 influence	28	25.0	25.0	17.9	17.9	14.3
决定者 decider	91	7.7	27.5	33.0	26.4	5.5
使用者 user	129	16.3	38.8	26.4	14.7	3.9
女性 Female	217	20.7	31.3	23.0	17.1	7.8
提议者 advocate	42	16.7	33.3	26.2	19.0	4.8
影响者 influence	35	14.3	34.3	22.9	20.0	8.6
决定者 decider	41	12.2	31.7	29.3	24.4	2.4
使用者 user	145	24.1	29.7	21.4	16.6	8.3

9-8 不同消费者层的家中目前拥有品牌/ Brands of Camera Owned in Household by Market Segments

9-8-1 时尚流行指标/ Fads Popular Index

	人数 Number	第一品牌及百分比 1st/ percent	第二品牌及百分比 2nd/ percent	第三品牌及百分比 3rd/ percent	第四品牌及百分比 4th/ percent
样本 Sample	496	**理光 Ricoh(20.2)**	**佳能 Canon(17.9)**	**奥林巴斯 Olympus(8.3)**	**珠江 Zhujiang(6.3)**
平实生活指向 simple living orientation	262	理光 Ricoh(18.7)	佳能 Canon(17.6)	奥林巴斯 Olympus(8.4)	珠江 Zhujiang(5.7)
时尚流行指向 fashion orientation	234	理光 Ricoh(21.8)	佳能 Canon(18.4)	奥林巴斯 Olympus(8.1)	珠江 Zhujiang(6.8)

9-8-2 广告态度指标/ Advertising Attitude Index

	人数 Number	第一品牌及百分比 1st/ percent	第二品牌及百分比 2nd/ percent	第三品牌及百分比 3rd/ percent	第四品牌及百分比 4th/ percent
样本 Sample	492	**理光 Ricoh(20.5)**	**佳能 Canon(17.5)**	**奥林巴斯 Olympus(8.3)**	**珠江 Zhujiang(6.1)**
广告淡漠指向 indifferent orientation	162	佳能 Canon(19.1) 理光 Ricoh(19.1)	海鸥 Seagull(6.2)	珠江 Zhujiang(5.6)	奥林巴斯 Olympus(4.3) 宾得 Pentax(4.3)
中间层 medium	293	理光 Ricoh(21.8)	佳能 Canon(17.7)	奥林巴斯 Olympus(9.6)	珠江 Zhujiang(6.5)
信赖广告指向 loyal orientation	37	奥林巴斯 Olympus(16.2) 理光 Ricoh(16.2)	佳能 Canon(8.1)	珠江 Zhujiang(5.4) 美能达 Minolta(5.4) 柯尼卡 Konica(5.4)	海鸥 Seagull(2.7) 凤凰 Phoenix(2.7) 尼康 Nikon(2.7) 宾得 Pentax(2.7) 奥立克 Olike(2.7)

9-8-3 价格态度指标/ Price Attitude Index

	人数 Number	第一品牌及百分比 1st/ percent	第二品牌及百分比 2nd/ percent	第三品牌及百分比 3rd/ percent	第四品牌及百分比 4th/ percent
样本 Sample	495	**理光 Ricoh(20.4)**	**佳能 Canon(18.0)**	**奥林巴斯 Olympus(8.3)**	**珠江 Zhujiang(6.1)**
价格无关心指向 indifferent orientation	93	理光 Ricoh(23.7)	佳能 Canon(19.4)	珠江 Zhujiang(5.4) 奥林巴斯 Olympus(5.4) 美能达 Minolta(5.4)	宾得 Pentax(4.3) 富士 Fuji(4.3)
中间层 medium	258	佳能 Canon(20.2)	理光 Ricoh(18.6)	奥林巴斯 Olympus(11.2)	珠江 Zhujiang(7.0)
价格重视指向 careful orientation	144	理光 Ricoh(21.5)	佳能 Canon(13.2)	海鸥 Seagull(7.6)	奥林巴斯 Olympus(4.9) 珠江 Zhujiang(4.9)

9-9 不同消费者层选择照相机时考虑因素/ Considerations in Choosing from Different Brands by Market Segments

9-9-1 时尚流行指标/ Fads Popular Index

注：本题为多选题，合计百分比超过 100%（Multiple answers）

	人数 Number	品牌形象 brand image	外型 outlook	价格 price	成像质量 picture quality	变焦功能 zooming function	专业声誉 professional prestige
样本 Sample	**501**	**31.3**	**11.6**	**40.3**	**23.4**	**17.6**	**7.4**
平实生活指向 simple living orientation	265	30.9	12.8	41.1	20.0	13.6	8.3
时尚流行指向 fashion orientation	236	31.8	10.2	39.4	27.1	22.0	6.4

续前表 continued

	人数 Number	操作方便 easy to deal with	原产地 place of production	功能齐备 all- function	售后服务 follow-up service	其他 others
样本 Sample	**501**	**42.3**	**7.4**	**15.6**	**2.2**	**2.8**
平实生活指向 simple living orientation	265	46.0	8.7	12.5	1.5	2.6
时尚流行指向 fashion orientation	236	38.1	5.9	19.1	3.0	3.0

9-9-2 广告态度指标/ Advertising Attitude Index

注：本题为多选题，合计百分比超过 100%（Multiple answers）

	人数 Number	品牌形象 brand image	外型 outlook	价格 price	成像质量 picture quality	变焦功能 zooming function	专业声誉 professional prestige
样本 Sample	**497**	**31.4**	**11.7**	**39.8**	**23.1**	**17.5**	**7.4**
广告淡漠指向 indifferent orientation	163	30.1	11.0	38.7	17.8	14.1	4.9
中间层 medium	295	28.8	12.5	41.4	26.8	19.3	8.8
信赖广告指向 loyal orientation	39	56.4	7.7	33.3	17.9	17.9	7.7

续前表 continued

	人数 Number	操作方便 easy to deal with	原产地 place of production	功能齐备 all- function	售后服务 follow-up service	其他 others
样本 Sample	**497**	**42.5**	**7.4**	**15.5**	**2.0**	**2.8**
广告淡漠指向 indifferent orientation	163	46.6	10.4	14.1	3.7	2.5
中间层 medium	295	40.7	6.1	15.3	1.0	3.1
信赖广告指向 loyal orientation	39	38.5	5.1	23.1	2.6	2.6

9-9-3 价格态度指标/ Price Attitude Index

注：本题为多选题，合计百分比超过 100%（Multiple answers）

	人数 Number	品牌形象 brand image	外型 outlook	价格 price	成像质量 picture quality	变焦功能 zooming function	专业声誉 professional prestige
样本 Sample	**500**	**31.2**	**11.4**	**40.4**	**23.4**	**17.8**	**7.4**
价格无关心指向 indifferent orientation	93	31.2	10.8	29.0	26.9	11.8	6.5
中间层 medium	261	33.7	10.0	40.2	28.0	20.7	7.3
价格重视指向 careful orientation	146	26.7	14.4	47.9	13.0	16.4	8.2

续前表 continued

	人数 Number	操作方便 easy to deal with	原产地 place of production	功能齐备 all- function	售后服务 follow-up service	其他 others
样本 Sample	**500**	**41.8**	**7.4**	**15.6**	**2.2**	**2.8**
价格无关心指向 indifferent orientation	93	41.9	7.5	23.7	3.2	2.2
中间层 medium	261	39.8	6.1	14.9	3.1	3.4
价格重视指向 careful orientation	146	45.2	9.6	11.6	0.0	2.1

● 重庆 / Chongqing

9-1 照相机的拥有比例/ Proportion of Camera Owners in the Sample

	人数 Number	百分比 Percent
有 yes	210	33.7
没有 no	414	66.3

n=624

9-2 照相机的拥有量/ Number of Camera Owned Per Household

	人数 Number	百分比 Percent
1 台 1 set	181	87.0
2 台及以上 2 sets or over	27	13.0

n=208

9-3 理想品牌排名/ Ranking of the Ideal Brands

排名 Brand Ranking	品牌 Brands	人数 Number	百分比 Percent
1	理光 Ricoh	75	12.0
2	佳能 Canon	29	4.6
3	海鸥 Seagull	28	4.5
4	索尼 Sony	21	3.4
5	奥林巴斯 Olympus	20	3.2
6	珠江 Zhujiang	17	2.7
7	松下 National	13	2.1
7	柯尼卡 Konica	13	2.1
7	尼康 Nikon	13	2.1
8	美能达 Minolta	11	1.8
9	凤凰 Phoenix	9	1.4
10	柯达 Kodak	8	1.3
10	三星 Samsung	8	1.3

n=624

9-4 对家中现有照相机(最近购买的一台)的四个方面的描述/ About the Camera Most Recently Purchased

9-4-1 家中现有照相机的品牌排名/ Ranking of the Currently Owned Camera Brands

排名 Brand Ranking	品牌 Brands	人数 Number	百分比 Percent
1	理光 Ricoh	34	16.2
2	珠江 Zhujiang	15	7.1
3	海鸥 Seagull	14	6.7
4	凤凰 Phoenix	12	5.7
5	奥林巴斯 Olympus	11	5.2
5	佳能 Canon	11	5.2
5	汤姆 Toma	11	5.2
6	柯尼卡 Konica	8	3.8
7	美能达 Minolta	6	2.9
7	尼康 Nikon	6	2.9
8	索尼 Sony	5	2.4
9	华莹 Huaying	4	1.9
9	红梅 Hongmei	4	1.9
9	三星 Samsung	4	1.9
10	华夏 Huaxia	3	1.4
10	爱华 Aiwa	3	1.4
10	富士 Fuji	3	1.4

n=210

9-4-2 该照相机的购买时间/ The Time of Purchasing of the Currently Owned Camera

	人数 Number	百分比 Percent
1985 年或以前 1985 or before	18	8.6
1986～1990 年	35	16.7
1991 年	9	4.3
1992 年	10	4.8
1993 年	10	4.8
1994 年	21	10.0
1995 年	20	9.6
1996 年	29	13.9
1997 年	20	9.6
1998 年	26	12.4
1999 年	11	5.3

n=209

9-4-3 该照相机的价格/ The Price of the Currently Owned Camera

	人数 Number	百分比 Percent
1000 元或以下 1000 yuan or below	143	68.1
1001～2000 元 yuan	36	17.1
2001～3000 元 yuan	11	5.2
3001～4000 元 yuan	8	3.8
4001～5000 元 yuan	1	0.5
5001～6000 元 yuan	0	0.0
6001～7000 元 yuan	2	1.0
7001～8000 元 yuan	0	0.0
8001～9000 元 yuan	0	0.0
9001～10000 元 yuan	0	0.0
10000 元以上 over10000 yuan	1	0.5
完全不知道 don't know	8	3.8

n=210

9-4-4 该照相机的类型/ The Type of the Currently Owned Camera

	人数 Number	百分比 Percent
固定镜头傻瓜相机 set lens simpleton camera	103	49.0
变焦镜头傻瓜相机 zoom lens simpleton camera	40	19.0
机械单镜头反光相机 mechanic single len reflector camera	31	14.8
自动单镜头反光相机 automatic single len reflector camera	18	8.6
手动加自动单反相机 manual or automatic camera	10	4.8
数字相机 digital camera	4	1.9
一次成像相机 one step camera	0	0.0
120 专业相机 120 professional camera	2	1.0
其他 others	2	1.0

n=210

9-5 选择不同品牌照相机时考虑因素/ Considerations in Choosing from Different Brands

注：本题为多选题，合计百分比超过 100%（Multiple answers）

	人数 Number	品牌形象 brand image	外型 outlook	价格 price	成像质量 picture quality	变焦功能 zooming function	专业声誉 professional prestige
样本 Sample	**210**	**24.3**	**12.4**	**45.2**	**24.8**	**11.9**	**1.9**
理光 Ricoh	34	32.4	5.9	26.5	23.5	14.7	2.9
珠江 Zhujiang	15	20.0	13.3	46.7	33.3	20.0	0.0
海鸥 Seagull	14	21.4	21.4	50.0	21.4	14.3	0.0
凤凰 Phoenix	12	33.3	0.0	66.7	41.7	0.0	0.0
奥林巴斯 Olympus	11	54.5	45.5	18.2	27.3	27.3	0.0
佳能 Canon	11	63.6	9.1	36.4	63.6	27.3	0.0
汤姆 Toma	11	0.0	27.3	72.7	9.1	0.0	0.0
柯尼卡 Konica	8	25.0	25.0	75.0	37.5	0.0	12.5
美能达 Minolta	6	66.7	0.0	50.0	33.3	33.3	33.3
尼康 Nikon	6	50.0	0.0	33.3	33.3	0.0	0.0
索尼 Sony	5	20.0	20.0	60.0	0.0	20.0	0.0
华莹 Huaying	4	0.0	0.0	50.0	25.0	0.0	0.0
红梅 Hongmei	4	0.0	0.0	75.0	0.0	0.0	0.0
三星 Samsung	4	0.0	25.0	50.0	25.0	0.0	0.0

续前表 continued

	人数 Number	操作方便 easy to deal with	原产地 place of production	功能齐备 all-function	售后服务 follow-up service	其他 others
样本 Sample	**210**	**42.4**	**7.6**	**8.6**	**2.4**	**4.3**
理光 Ricoh	34	44.1	17.6	14.7	2.9	8.8
珠江 Zhujiang	15	33.3	0.0	0.0	0.0	0.0
海鸥 Seagull	14	0.0	0.0	7.1	0.0	0.0
凤凰 Phoenix	12	50.0	0.0	0.0	8.3	0.0
奥林巴斯 Olympus	11	63.6	18.2	9.1	9.1	0.0
佳能 Canon	11	27.3	9.1	18.2	0.0	0.0
汤姆 Toma	11	54.5	9.1	18.2	0.0	0.0
柯尼卡 Konica	8	62.5	25.0	0.0	0.0	0.0
美能达 Minolta	6	33.3	0.0	0.0	0.0	0.0
尼康 Nikon	6	83.3	0.0	0.0	0.0	0.0
索尼 Sony	5	20.0	20.0	20.0	0.0	0.0
华莹 Huaying	4	0.0	0.0	0.0	0.0	25.0
红梅 Hongmei	4	50.0	0.0	0.0	0.0	0.0
三星 Samsung	4	75.0	0.0	50.0	0.0	0.0

9-6 照相机未来一年购买打算/ Plan for Future Purchasing of a Camera

9-6-1 有无购买打算/ Whether Planning to Purchase Next Year

	人数 Number	百分比 Percent
是 yes	29	4.7
否 no	594	95.3

n=623

9-6-2 打算购买的品牌排名/ Ranking of the Brands of the Planned Purchase Next Year

排名 Brand Ranking	品牌 Brands	人数 Number	百分比 Percent
1	理光 Ricoh	5	18.5
2	奥林巴斯 Olympus	4	14.8
3	JEC	2	7.4
3	佳能 Canon	2	7.4

n=27

9-6-3 打算购买的类型/ The Type of the Planned Purchase Next Year

	人数 Number	百分比 Percent
固定镜头傻瓜相机 set lens simpleton camera	6	21.4
变焦镜头傻瓜相机 zoom lens simpleton camera	11	39.3
机械单镜头反光相机 mechanic single len reflector camera	2	7.1
自动单镜头反光相机 automatic single len reflector camera	3	10.7
手动加自动单反相机 manual or automatic camera	2	7.1
数字相机 digital camera	3	10.7
一次成像相机 one step camera	0	0.0
120 专业相机 120 professional camera	0	0.0
其他 others	1	3.6

n=28

9-6-4 打算购买的价格/ The Price of the Planned Purchase Next Year

	人数 Number	百分比 Percent
1000 元或以下 1000 yuan or below	11	39.3
1001～2000 元 yuan	7	25.0
2001～3000 元 yuan	4	14.3
3001～4000 元 yuan	5	17.9
4001～5000 元 yuan	0	0.0
5001～6000 元 yuan	0	0.0
6001～7000 元 yuan	0	0.0
7001～8000 元 yuan	0	0.0
8001～9000 元 yuan	0	0.0
9001～10000 元 yuan	0	0.0
10000 元以上 over10000 yuan	1	3.6
完全不知道 don't know	0	0.0

n=28

9-7 选购照相机时不同角色的人口特征/ Demographics of the Different Roles in Purchasing a Camera

注：不同角色可以多选（Multiple answers）

	人数 Number	16-24 岁 Age	25-34 岁 Age	35-44 岁 Age	45-54 岁 Age	55-60 岁 Age
样本 Sample	173	24.9	31.8	18.5	19.1	5.8
男性 Male	90	21.1	26.7	23.3	20.0	8.9
提议者 advocate	13	7.7	38.5	15.4	30.8	7.7
影响者 influence	4	50.0	50.0	0.0	0.0	0.0
决定者 decider	58	10.3	24.1	31.0	24.1	10.3
使用者 user	48	29.2	27.1	18.8	14.6	10.4
女性 Female	83	28.9	37.3	13.3	18.1	2.4
提议者 advocate	18	22.2	38.9	11.1	22.2	5.6
影响者 influence	6	16.7	16.7	16.7	50.0	0.0
决定者 decider	21	14.3	47.6	14.3	23.8	0.0
使用者 user	55	29.1	40.0	14.5	12.7	3.6

9-8 不同消费者层的家中目前拥有品牌/ Brands of Camera Owned in Household by Market Segments

9-8-1 时尚流行指标/ Fads Popular Index

	人数 Number	第一品牌及百分比 1st/ percent	第二品牌及百分比 2nd/ percent	第三品牌及百分比 3rd/ percent	第四品牌及百分比 4th/ percent
样本 Sample	**204**	**理光 Ricoh(16.2)**	**珠江 Zhujiang(7.4)**	**海鸥 Seagull(6.9)**	**凤凰 Phoenix(5.9)**
平实生活指向 simple living orientation	106	理光 Ricoh(14.2)	珠江 Zhujiang(9.4)	凤凰 Phoenix(7.5) 海鸥 Seagull(7.5)	奥林巴斯 Olympus(4.7)
时尚流行指向 fashion orientation	98	理光 Ricoh(18.4)	汤姆 Toma(7.1)	奥林巴斯 Olympus(6.1) 海鸥 Seagull(6.1)	珠江 Zhujiang(5.1) 佳能 Canon(5.1)

9-8-2 广告态度指标/ Advertising Attitude Index

	人数 Number	第一品牌及百分比 1st/ percent	第二品牌及百分比 2nd/ percent	第三品牌及百分比 3rd/ percent	第四品牌及百分比 4th/ percent
样本 Sample	**207**	**理光 Ricoh(15.9)**	**珠江 Zhujiang(7.2)**	**海鸥 Seagull(6.8)**	**凤凰 Phoenix(5.8)**
广告淡漠指向 indifferent orientation	52	理光 Ricoh(19.2)	珠江 Zhujiang(15.4)	奥林巴斯 Olympus(7.7)	凤凰 Phoenix(5.8) 海鸥 Seagull(5.8)
中间层 medium	130	理光 Ricoh(17.7)	海鸥 Seagull(6.9) 汤姆 Toma(6.9)	凤凰 Phoenix(5.4) 珠江 Zhujiang(5,4) 佳能 Canon(5.4)	奥林巴斯 Olympus(4.6)
信赖广告指向 loyal orientation	25	尼康 Nikon(12.0)	索尼 Sony(8.0) 凤凰 Phoenix(8.0) 海鸥 Seagull(8.0) 美能达 Minolta(8.0)	超能 Chaoneng(4.0) 明佳 Mingjia(4.0) 摄梅 Shemei(4.0) 菲利浦 Philips(4.0) 福兰卡 Franka(4.0) 爱华 Aiwa(4.0) 汤姆 Toma(4.0) 企鹅 Penguin(4.0) 柯尼卡 Konica(4.0) 金拍得丽 Premier(4.0) 佳能 Canon(4.0) 红梅 Hongmei(4.0) 奥林巴斯 Olympus(4.0)	

9-8-3 价格态度指标/ Price Attitude Index

	人数 Number	第一品牌及百分比 1st/ percent	第二品牌及百分比 2nd/ percent	第三品牌及百分比 3rd/ percent	第四品牌及百分比 4th/ percent
样本 Sample	**209**	**理光 Ricoh(16.3)**	**珠江 Zhujiang(7.2)**	**海鸥 Seagull(6.7)**	**凤凰 Phoenix(5.7)**
价格无关心指向 indifferent orientation	48	理光 Ricoh(22.9)	珠江 Zhujiang(12.5)	海鸥 Seagull(6.3) 佳能 Canon(6.3) 柯尼卡 Konica(6.3) 奥林巴斯 Olympus(6.3) 索尼 Sony(6.3)	宾得 Pentax(2.1) 凤凰 Phoenix(2.1) 红梅 Hongmei(2.1) 三星 Samsung(2.1) 汤姆 Toma(2.1) JEC(2.1) 爱华 Aiwa(2.1) 华莹 Huaying(2.1) 摄梅 Shemei(2.1) 汤姆森 Toms(2.1) 超能 Chaoneng(2.1)
中间层 medium	104	理光 Ricoh(15.4)	汤姆 Toma(7.7)	海鸥 Seagull(6.7)	奥林巴斯 Olympus(5.8) 珠江 Zhujiang(5.8) 凤凰 Phoenix(5.8)
价格重视指向 careful orientation	57	理光 Ricoh(12.3)	凤凰 Phoenix(8.8)	海鸥 Seagull(7.0) 佳能 Canon(7.0)	珠江 Zhujiang(5.3) 尼康 Nikon(5.3) 美能达 Minolta(5.3)

9-9 不同消费者层选择照相机时考虑因素/ Considerations in Choosing from Different Brands by Market Segments

9-9-1 时尚流行指标/ Fads Popular Index

注：本题为多选题，合计百分比超过 100%（Multiple answers）

	人数 Number	品牌形象 brand image	外型 outlook	价格 price	成像质量 picture quality	变焦功能 zooming function	专业声誉 professional prestige
样本 Sample	**204**	**23.5**	**12.3**	**45.1**	**25.0**	**11.8**	**2.0**
平实生活指向 simple living orientation	106	24.5	15.1	51.9	27.4	13.2	1.9
时尚流行指向 fashion orientation	98	22.4	9.2	37.8	22.4	10.2	2.0

续前表 continued

	人数 Number	操作方便 easy to deal with	原产地 place of production	功能齐备 all-function	售后服务 follow-up service	其他 others
样本 Sample	204	42.6	7.4	7.8	2.5	4.4
平实生活指向 simple living orientation	106	46.2	5.7	6.6	1.9	2.8
时尚流行指向 fashion orientation	98	38.8	9.2	9.2	3.1	6.1

9-9-2 广告态度指标/ Advertising Attitude Index

注：本题为多选题，合计百分比超过 100%（Multiple answers）

	人数 Number	品牌形象 brand image	外型 outlook	价格 price	成像质量 picture quality	变焦功能 zooming function	专业声誉 professional prestige
样本 Sample	207	24.2	12.1	44.9	25.1	12.1	1.9
广告淡漠指向 indifferent orientation	52	26.9	15.4	36.5	26.9	15.4	1.9
中间层 medium	130	23.1	8.5	48.5	24.6	12.3	2.3
信赖广告指向 loyal orientation	25	24.0	24.0	44.0	24.0	4.0	0.0

续前表 continued

	人数 Number	操作方便 easy to deal with	原产地 place of production	功能齐备 all-function	售后服务 follow-up service	其他 others
样本 Sample	207	42.5	7.7	8.2	2.4	4.3
广告淡漠指向 indifferent orientation	52	38.5	9.6	11.5	1.9	1.9
中间层 medium	130	41.5	7.7	8.5	3.1	6.2
信赖广告指向 loyal orientation	25	56.0	4.0	0.0	0.0	0.0

9-9-3 价格态度指标/ Price Attitude Index

注：本题为多选题，合计百分比超过 100%（Multiple answers）

	人数 Number	品牌形象 brand image	外型 outlook	价格 price	成像质量 picture quality	变焦功能 zooming function	专业声誉 professional prestige
样本 Sample	209	23.9	12.0	45.0	24.9	12.0	1.9
价格无关心指向 indifferent orientation	48	25.0	12.5	29.2	20.8	20.8	2.1
中间层 medium	104	21.2	11.5	47.1	26.9	9.6	2.9
价格重视指向 careful orientation	57	28.1	12.3	54.4	24.6	8.8	0.0

续前表 continued

	人数 Number	操作方便 easy to deal with	原产地 place of production	功能齐备 all-function	售后服务 follow-up service	其他 others
样本 Sample	209	42.6	7.7	8.6	2.4	4.3
价格无关心指向 indifferent orientation	48	43.8	12.5	14.6	0.0	2.1
中间层 medium	104	40.4	6.7	6.7	3.8	5.8
价格重视指向 careful orientation	57	45.6	5.3	7.0	1.8	3.5

● 武汉 / Wuhan

9-1 照相机的拥有比例/ Proportion of Camera Owners in the Sample

	人数 Number	百分比 Percent
有 yes	252	39.3
没有 no	389	60.7

n=641

9-2 照相机的拥有量/ Number of Camera Owned Per Household

	人数 Number	百分比 Percent
1 台 1 set	219	88.3
2 台及以上 2 sets or over	29	11.7

n=248

9-3 理想品牌排名/ Ranking of the Ideal Brands

排名 Brand Ranking	品牌 Brands	人数 Number	百分比 Percent
1	理光 Ricoh	46	7.2
2	佳能 Canon	42	6.5
3	海鸥 Seagull	25	3.9
4	美能达 Minolta	15	2.3
5	尼康 Nikon	13	2.0
6	奥林巴斯 Olympus	12	1.9
7	松下 National	10	1.6
8	柯尼卡 Konica	8	1.2
8	柯达 Kodak	8	1.2
9	索尼 Sony	7	1.1
9	凤凰 Phoenix	7	1.1

n=642

9-4 对家中现有照相机(最近购买的一台)的四个方面的描述/ About the Camera Most Recently Purchased

9-4-1 家中现有照相机的品牌排名/ Ranking of the Currently Owned Camera Brands

排名 Brand Ranking	品牌 Brands	人数 Number	百分比 Percent
1	理光 Ricoh	42	17.2
2	海鸥 Seagull	24	9.8
3	佳能 Canon	22	9.0
4	凤凰 Phoenix	9	3.7
4	汤姆 Toma	9	3.7
5	尼康 Nikon	7	2.9
5	柯尼卡 Konica	7	2.9
6	美能达 Minolta	6	2.5

n=244

9-4-2 该照相机的购买时间/ The Time of Purchasing of the Currently Owned Camera

	人数 Number	百分比 Percent
1985 年以前 1985 or before	29	11.6
1986～1990 年	51	20.5
1991 年	8	3.2
1992 年	10	4.0
1993 年	19	7.6
1994 年	24	9.6
1995 年	28	11.2
1996 年	18	7.2
1997 年	26	10.4
1998 年	22	8.8
1999 年	14	5.6

n=249

9-4-3 该照相机的价格/ The Price of the Currently Owned Camera

	人数 Number	百分比 Percent
1000 元或以下 1000 yuan or below	175	69.7
1001～2000 元 yuan	37	14.7
2001～3000 元 yuan	15	6.0
3001～4000 元 yuan	1	0.4
4001～5000 元 yuan	4	1.6
5001～6000 元 yuan	0	0.0
6001～7000 元 yuan	0	0.0
7001～8000 元 yuan	2	0.8
8001～9000 元 yuan	0	0.0
9001～10000 元 yuan	0	0.0
10000 元以上 over 10000 yuan	0	0.0
完全不知道 don't know	17	6.8

n=251

9-4-4 该照相机的类型/ The Type of the Currently Owned Camera

	人数 Number	百分比 Percent
固定镜头傻瓜相机 set lens simpleton camera	122	48.4
变焦镜头傻瓜相机 zoom lens simpleton camera	47	18.7
机械单镜头反光相机 mechanic single len reflector camera	36	14.3
自动单镜头反光相机 automatic single len reflector camera	20	7.9
手动加自动单反相机 manual or automatic camera	14	5.6
数字相机 digital camera	3	1.2
一次成像相机 one step camera	1	0.4
120 专业相机 120 professional camera	4	1.6
其他 others	5	2.0

n=252

9-5 选择不同品牌照相机时的考虑因素/ Considerations in Choosing from Different Brands

注：本题为多选题，合计百分比超过 100%（Multiple answers）

	人数 Number	品牌形象 brand image	外型 outlook	价格 price	成像质量 picture quality	变焦功能 zooming function	专业声誉 professional prestige
样本 Sample	**243**	**35.4**	**12.3**	**46.9**	**23.9**	**10.3**	**4.9**
理光 Ricoh	41	48.8	9.8	41.5	24.4	9.8	12.2
海鸥 Seagull	24	50.0	4.2	58.3	29.2	8.3	0.0
佳能 Canon	22	22.7	4.5	18.2	31.8	18.2	4.5
凤凰 Phoenix	9	44.4	11.1	44.4	33.3	11.1	11.1
汤姆 Toma	9	11.1	11.1	77.8	11.1	0.0	0.0
尼康 Nikon	7	28.6	14.3	42.9	28.6	14.3	0.0
柯尼卡 Konica	7	71.4	0.0	42.9	28.6	28.6	14.3
美能达 Minolta	6	16.7	16.7	33.3	16.7	33.3	0.0

续前表 continued

	人数 Number	操作方便 easy to deal with	原产地 place of production	功能齐备 all-function	售后服务 follow-up service	其他 others
样本 Sample	**243**	**44.0**	**4.5**	**15.2**	**2.1**	**7.4**
理光 Ricoh	41	51.2	12.2	12.2	0.0	2.4
海鸥 Seagull	24	29.2	0.0	12.5	8.3	12.5
佳能 Canon	22	40.9	0.0	22.7	0.0	13.6
凤凰 Phoenix	9	22.2	0.0	0.0	0.0	0.0
汤姆 Toma	9	66.7	0.0	0.0	0.0	0.0
尼康 Nikon	7	71.4	0.0	0.0	0.0	0.0
柯尼卡 Konica	7	14.3	14.3	28.6	0.0	0.0
美能达 Minolta	6	66.7	0.0	33.3	0.0	0.0

9-6 照相机未来一年购买打算/ Plan for Future Purchasing of a Camera

9-6-1 有无购买打算/ Whether Planning to Purchase Next Year

	人数 Number	百分比 Percent
是 yes	33	5.1
否 no	608	94.9

n=641

9-6-2 打算购买的品牌排名/ Ranking of the Brands of the Planned Purchase Next Year

排名 Brand Ranking	品牌 Brands	人数 Number	百分比 Percent
1	海鸥 Seagull	4	15.4
2	奥林巴斯 Olympus	3	11.5
2	佳能 Canon	3	11.5
3	索尼 Sony	2	7.7
3	理光 Ricoh	2	7.7

n=26

9-6-3 打算购买的类型/ The Type of the Planned Purchase Next Year

	人数 Number	百分比 Percent
固定镜头傻瓜相机 set lens simpleton camera	8	25.0
变焦镜头傻瓜相机 zoom lens simpleton camera	10	31.3
机械单镜头反光相机 mechanic single len reflector camera	2	6.3
自动单镜头反光相机 automatic single len reflector camera	1	3.1
手动加自动单反相机 manual or automatic camera	1	3.1
数字相机 digital camera	7	21.9
一次成像相机 one step camera	1	3.1
120 专业相机 120 professional camera	1	3.1
其他 others	1	3.1

n=32

9-6-4 打算购买的价格/ The Price of the Planned Purchase Next Year

	人数 Number	百分比 Percent
1000 元或以下 1000 yuan or below	11	33.3
1001～2000 元 yuan	11	33.3
2001～3000 元 yuan	6	18.2
3001～4000 元 yuan	2	6.1
4001～5000 元 yuan	1	3.0
5001～6000 元 yuan	1	3.0
6001～7000 元 yuan	0	0.0
7001～8000 元 yuan	0	0.0
8001～9000 元 yuan	0	0.0
9001～10000 元 yuan	0	0.0
10000 元以上 over 10000 yuan	1	3.0
完全不知道 don't know	0	0.0

n=33

9-7 选购照相机时不同角色的人口特征/ Demographics of the Different Roles in Purchasing a Camera

注：不同角色可以多选（Multiple answers）

	人数 Number	16-24 岁 Age	25-34 岁 Age	35-44 岁 Age	45-54 岁 Age	55-60 岁 Age
样本 Sample	215	20.9	31.2	21.9	19.1	7.0
男性 Male	96	19.8	27.1	24.0	17.7	11.5
提议者 advocate	15	0.0	20.0	46.7	20.0	13.3
影响者 influence	8	25.0	37.5	12.5	12.5	12.5
决定者 decider	43	2.3	30.2	34.9	20.9	11.6
使用者 user	64	25.0	25.0	23.4	15.6	10.9
女性 Female	119	21.8	34.5	20.2	20.2	3.4
提议者 advocate	27	11.1	29.6	40.7	18.5	0.0
影响者 influence	11	27.3	9.1	18.2	45.5	0.0
决定者 decider	36	5.6	36.1	25.0	30.6	2.8
使用者 user	90	22.2	35.6	20.0	17.8	4.4

9-8 不同消费者层的家中目前拥有品牌/ Brands of Camera Owned in Household by Market Segments

9-8-1 时尚流行指标/ Fads Popular Index

	人数 Number	第一品牌及百分比 1st/ percent	第二品牌及百分比 2nd/ percent	第三品牌及百分比 3rd/ percent
样本 Sample	242	**理光 Ricoh(17.4)**	**海鸥 Seagull(9.9)**	**佳能 Canon(9.1)**
平实生活指向 simple living orientation	117	理光 Ricoh(17.1)	海鸥 Seagull(12.0)	佳能 Canon(5.1) 尼康 Nikon(5.1)
时尚流行指向 fashion orientation	125	理光 Ricoh(17.6)	佳能 Canon(12.8)	海鸥 Seagull(8.0)

9-8-2 广告态度指标/ Advertising Attitude Index

	人数 Number	第一品牌及百分比 1st/ percent	第二品牌及百分比 2nd/ percent	第三品牌及百分比 3rd/ percent
样本 Sample	242	**理光 Ricoh(17.4)**	**海鸥 Seagull(9.9)**	**佳能 Canon(9.1)**
广告淡漠指向 indifferent orientation	72	海鸥 Seagull(18.1)	理光 Ricoh(11.1)	佳能 Canon(9.7)
中间层 medium	144	理光 Ricoh(20.1)	佳能 Canon(7.6)	海鸥 Seagull(6.9)
信赖广告指向 loyal orientation	26	理光 Ricoh(19.2)	佳能 Canon(15.4)	富士 Fuji(3.8) 海鸥 Seagull(3.8) 虎丘 Huqiu(3.8) 凤凰 Phoenix(3.8) 美能达 Minolta(3.8) 尼康 Nikon(3.8) 汤姆 Toma(3.8) 雅西卡 Yashica(3.8) 索尼 Sony(3.8)

9-8-3 价格态度指标/ Price Attitude Index

	人数 Number	第一品牌及百分比 1st/ percent	第二品牌及百分比 2nd/ percent	第三品牌及百分比 3rd/ percent
样本 Sample	242	**理光 Ricoh(17.4)**	**海鸥 Seagull(9.9)**	**佳能 Canon(9.1)**
价格无关心指向 indifferent orientation	43	理光 Ricoh(14.0)	海鸥 Seagull(9.3) 佳能 Canon(9.3)	奥林巴斯 Olympus(4.7) 凤凰 Phoenix(4.7) 索尼 Sony(4.7) 汤姆 Toma(4.7) 华夏 Huaxia(4.7)
中间层 medium	121	理光 Ricoh(18.2)	海鸥 Seagull(9.9)	佳能 Canon(8.3)
价格重视指向 careful orientation	78	理光 Ricoh(17.9)	海鸥 Seagull(10.3) 佳能 Canon(10.3)	尼康 Nikon(5.1)

9-9 不同消费者层选择照相机时考虑因素/ Considerations in Choosing from Different Brands by Market Segments

9-9-1 时尚流行指标/ Fads Popular Index

注：本题为多选题，合计百分比超过 100%（Multiple answers）

	人数 Number	品牌形象 brand image	外型 outlook	价格 price	成像质量 picture quality	变焦功能 zooming function	专业声誉 professional prestige
样本 Sample	248	34.3	12.5	46.8	23.8	10.1	4.8
平实生活指向 simple living orientation	119	34.5	15.1	52.9	25.2	7.6	3.4
时尚流行指向 fashion orientation	129	34.1	10.1	41.1	22.5	12.4	6.2

续前表 continued

	人数 Number	操作方便 easy to deal with	原产地 place of production	功能齐备 all-function	售后服务 follow-up service	其他 others
样本 Sample	248	45.2	4.0	14.9	2.0	7.3
平实生活指向 simple living orientation	119	46.2	2.5	15.1	2.5	6.7
时尚流行指向 fashion orientation	129	44.2	5.4	14.7	1.6	7.8

9-9-2 广告态度指标/ Advertising Attitude Index

注：本题为多选题，合计百分比超过 100%（Multiple answers）

	人数 Number	品牌形象 brand image	外型 outlook	价格 price	成像质量 picture quality	变焦功能 zooming function	专业声誉 professional prestige
样本 Sample	248	34.3	12.5	46.8	23.8	10.1	4.8
广告淡漠指向 indifferent orientation	73	31.5	12.3	53 4	19.2	8.2	1.4
中间层 medium	146	36.3	12 3	42.5	28.1	11.6	6.2
信赖广告指向 loyal orientation	29	31.0	13 8	51.7	13.8	6.9	6.9

续前表 continued

	人数 Number	操作方便 easy to deal with	原产地 place of production	功能齐备 all-function	售后服务 follow-up service	其他 others
样本 Sample	248	45.2	4.0	14.9	2.0	7.3
广告淡漠指向 indifferent orientation	73	38.4	1.4	15.1	2.7	11.0
中间层 medium	146	47.9	4.8	14.4	2.1	5.5
信赖广告指向 loyal orientation	29	48.3	6.9	17.2	0.0	6.9

9-9-3 价格态度指标/ Price Attitude Index

注：本题为多选题，合计百分比超过 100%（Multiple answers）

	人数 Number	品牌形象 brand image	外型 outlook	价格 price	成像质量 picture quality	变焦功能 zooming function	专业声誉 professional prestige
样本 Sample	248	34.3	12.5	46.8	23.8	10.1	4.8
价格无关心指向 indifferent orientation	43	34.9	11.6	32.6	25.6	18.6	0.0
中间层 medium	127	29.1	16.5	49.6	26.0	7.9	6.3
价格重视指向 careful orientation	78	42.3	6.4	50.0	19.2	9.0	5.1

续前表 continued

	人数 Number	操作方便 easy to deal with	原产地 place of production	功能齐备 all-function	售后服务 follow-up service	其他 others
样本 Sample	248	45.2	4.0	14.9	2.0	7.3
价格无关心指向 indifferent orientation	43	48.8	2.3	11.6	2.3	9.3
中间层 medium	127	44.9	4.7	16.5	2.4	5.5
价格重视指向 careful orientation	78	43.6	3.8	14.1	1.3	9.0

● 西安 / Xi'an

9-1 照相机的拥有比例/ Proportion of Camera Owners in the Sample

	人数 Number	百分比 Percent
有 yes	307	51.2
没有 no	293	48.8

n=600

9-2 照相机的拥有量/ Number of Camera Owned Per Household

	人数 Number	百分比 Percent
1 台 1 set	276	89.9
2 台及以上 2 sets or over	31	10.1

n=307

9-3 理想品牌排名/ Ranking of the Ideal Brands

排名 Brand Ranking	品牌 Brands	人数 Number	百分比 Percent
1	理光 Ricoh	97	16.3
2	佳能 Canon	81	13.6
3	尼康 Nikon	32	5.4
4	海鸥 Seagull	28	4.7
5	奥林巴斯 Olympus	22	3.7
6	美能达 Minolta	16	2.7
7	柯达 Kodak	12	2.0

n=595

9-4 对家中现有照相机(最近购买的一台)的四个方面的描述/ About the Camera Most Recently Purchased

9-4-1 家中现有照相机的品牌排名/ Ranking of the Currently Owned Camera Brands

排名 Brand Ranking	品牌 Brands	人数 Number	百分比 Percent
1	理光 Ricoh	64	20.9
2	海鸥 Seagull	27	8.8
3	佳能 Canon	26	8.5
4	华山 Huashan	21	6.9
5	奥林巴斯 Olympus	17	5.6
5	凤凰 Phoenix	17	5.6
6	尼康 Nikon	11	3.6
6	汤姆 Toma	11	3.6
7	美能达 Minolta	10	3.3
8	柯达 Kodak	6	2.0
8	索尼 Sony	6	2.0

n=306

9-4-2 该照相机的购买时间/ The Time of Purchasing of the Currently Owned Camera

	人数 Number	百分比 Percent
1985 年或以前 1985 or before	26	8.5
1986～1990 年	58	19.0
1991 年	26	8.5
1992 年	22	7.2
1993 年	25	8.2
1994 年	15	4.9
1995 年	26	8.5
1996 年	46	15.0
1997 年	27	8.8
1998 年	24	7.8
1999 年	11	3.6

n=306

9-4-3 该照相机的价格/ The Price of the Currently Owned Camera

	人数 Number	百分比 Percent
1000 元或以下 1000 yuan or below	214	69.9
1001～2000 元 yuan	42	13.7
2001～3000 元 yuan	19	6.2
3001～4000 元 yuan	12	3.9
4001～5000 元 yuan	3	1.0
5001～6000 元 yuan	0	0.0
6001～7000 元 yuan	1	0.3
7001～8000 元 yuan	0	0.0
8001～9000 元 yuan	0	0.0
9001～10000 元 yuan	0	0.0
10000 元以上 over 10000 yuan	1	0.3
完全不知道 don't know	14	4.6

n=306

9-4-4 该照相机的类型/ The Type of the Currently Owned Camera

	人数 Number	百分比 Percent
固定镜头傻瓜相机 set lens simpleton camera	156	51.1
变焦镜头傻瓜相机 zoom lens simpleton camera	53	17.4
机械单镜头反光相机 mechanic single len reflector camera	33	10.8
自动单镜头反光相机 automatic single len reflector camera	27	8.9
手动加自动单反相机 manual or automatic camera	21	6.9
数字相机 digital camera	7	2.3
一次成像相机 one step camera	2	0.7
120 专业相机 120 professional camera	4	1.3
其他 others	2	0.7

n=305

9-5 选择不同品牌照相机时考虑因素/ Considerations in Choosing from Different Brands

注：本题为多选题，合计百分比超过 100%（Multiple answers）

	人数 Number	品牌形象 brand image	外型 outlook	价格 price	成像质量 picture quality	变焦功能 zooming function	专业声誉 professional prestige
样本 Sample	306	28.8	6.5	40.2	26.5	9.2	6.9
理光 Ricoh	64	39.1	4.7	35.9	26.6	3.1	10.9
海鸥 Seagull	27	33.3	7.4	37.0	37.0	18.5	0.0
佳能 Canon	26	53.8	0.0	26.9	26.9	3.8	0.0
华山 Huashan	21	19.0	4.8	57.1	19.0	9.5	4.8
奥林巴斯 Olympus	17	47.1	11.8	29.4	23.5	11.8	23.5
凤凰 Phoenix	17	29.4	0.0	41.2	11.8	17.6	11.8

续前表 continued

	人数 Number	操作方便 easy to deal with	原产地 place of production	功能齐备 all-function	售后服务 follow-up service	其他 others
样本 Sample	306	41.2	6.2	10.8	2.9	1.3
理光 Ricoh	64	45.3	1.6	9.4	1.6	3.1
海鸥 Seagull	27	22.2	0.0	18.5	3.7	0.0
佳能 Canon	26	38.5	3.8	19.2	0.0	0.0
华山 Huashan	21	33.3	0.0	4.8	4.8	0.0
奥林巴斯 Olympus	17	29.4	41.2	29.4	5.9	0.0
凤凰 Phoenix	17	58.8	5.9	11.8	11.8	0.0

9-6 照相机未来一年购买打算/ Plan for Future Purchasing of a Camera

9-6-1 有无购买打算/ Whether Planning to Purchase Next Year

	人数 Number	百分比 Percent
是 yes	33	5.5
否 no	566	94.5

n=599

9-6-2 打算购买的品牌排名/ Ranking of the Brands of the Planned Purchase Next Year

排名 Brand Ranking	品牌 Brands	人数 Number	百分比 Percent
1	佳能 Canon	9	29.0
2	理光 Ricoh	4	12.9
3	海鸥 Seagull	2	6.5

n=31

9-6-3 打算购买的类型/ The Type of the Planned Purchase Next Year

	人数 Number	百分比 Percent
固定镜头傻瓜相机 set lens simpleton camera	11	34.4
变焦镜头傻瓜相机 zoom lens simpleton camera	6	18.8
机械单镜头反光相机 mechanic single len reflector camera	3	9.4
自动单镜头反光相机 automatic single len reflector camera	4	12.5
手动加自动单反相机 manual or automatic camera	3	9.4
数字相机 digital camera	4	12.5
一次成像相机 one step camera	0	0.0
120 专业相机 120 professional camera	1	3.1
其他 others	0	0.0

n=32

9-6-4 打算购买的价格/ The Price of the Planned Purchase Next Year

	人数 Number	百分比 Percent
1000 元或以下 1000 yuan or below	13	40.6
1001～2000 元 yuan	10	31.3
2001～3000 元 yuan	7	21.9
3001～4000 元 yuan	1	3.1
4001～5000 元 yuan	0	0.0
5001～6000 元 yuan	1	3.1
6001～7000 元 yuan	0	0.0
7001～8000 元 yuan	0	0.0
8001～9000 元 yuan	0	0.0
9001～10000 元 yuan	0	0.0
10000 元以上 over 10000 yuan	0	0.0
完全不知道 don't know	0	0.0

n=32

9-7 选购照相机时不同角色的人口特征/ Demographics of the Different Roles in Purchasing a Camera

注：不同角色可以多选（Multiple answers）

	人数 Number	16-24 岁 Age	25-34 岁 Age	35-44 岁 Age	45-54 岁 Age	55-60 岁 Age
样本 Sample	255	20.0	29.0	27.8	15.7	7.5
男性 Male	131	22.9	23.7	29.8	14.5	9.2
提议者 advocate	12	25.0	25.0	33.3	16.7	0.0
影响者 influence	11	36.4	27.3	27.3	9.1	0.0
决定者 decider	66	7.6	22.7	43.9	13.6	12.1
使用者 user	72	27.8	26.4	25.0	15.3	5.6
女性 Female	124	16.9	34.7	25.8	16.9	5.6
提议者 advocate	19	15.8	26.3	26.3	21.1	10.5
影响者 influence	21	19.0	33.3	33.3	9.5	4.8
决定者 decider	25	16.0	36.0	20.0	16.0	12.0
使用者 user	77	20.8	36.4	23.4	18.2	1.3

9-8 不同消费者层的家中目前拥有品牌/ Brands of Camera Owned in Household by Market Segments

9-8-1 时尚流行指标/ Fads Popular Index

	人数 Number	第一品牌及百分比 1st/ percent	第二品牌及百分比 2nd/ percent	第三品牌及百分比 3rd/ percent	第四品牌及百分比 4th/ percent
样本 Sample	306	**理光 Ricoh(20.9)**	**海鸥 Seagull(8.8)**	**佳能 Canon(8.5)**	**华山 Huashan(6.9)**
平实生活指向 simple living orientation	164	理光 Ricoh(17.7)	华山 Huashan(9.1)	海鸥 Seagull(8.5)	佳能 Canon(6.7)
时尚流行指向 fashion orientation	142	理光 Ricoh(24.6)	佳能 Canon(10.6)	海鸥 Seagull(9.2)	奥林巴斯 Olympus(7.0)

9-8-2 广告态度指标/ Advertising Attitude Index

	人数 Number	第一品牌及百分比 1st/ percent	第二品牌及百分比 2nd/ percent	第三品牌及百分比 3rd/ percent	第四品牌及百分比 4th/ percent
样本 Sample	302	**理光 Ricoh(20.9)**	**海鸥 Seagull(8.6)** **佳能 Canon(8.6)**	**华山 Huashan(7.0)**	**奥林巴斯 Olympus(5.6)** **凤凰 Phoenix(5.6)**
广告淡漠指向 indifferent orientation	88	理光 Ricoh(20.5)	凤凰 Phoenix(9.1) 佳能 Canon(9.1)	华山 Huashan(8.0)	海鸥 Seagull(6.8)
中间层 medium	175	理光 Ricoh(20.0)	海鸥 Seagull(10.3)	华山 Huashan(7.4) 奥林巴斯 Olympus(7.4) 佳能 Canon(7.4)	凤凰 Phoenix(4.6)
信赖广告指向 loyal orientation	39	理光 Ricoh(25.6)	佳能 Canon(12.8)	尼康 Nikon(7.7)	海鸥 Seagull(5.1)

9-8-3 价格态度指标/ Price Attitude Index

	人数 Number	第一品牌及百分比 1st/ percent	第二品牌及百分比 2nd/ percent	第三品牌及百分比 3rd/ percent	第四品牌及百分比 4th/ percent
样本 Sample	305	**理光 Ricoh(21.0)**	**海鸥 Seagull(8.9)**	**佳能 Canon(8.5)**	**华山 Huashan(6.9)**
价格无关心指向 indifferent orientation	78	理光 Ricoh(24.4)	华山 Huashan(11.5)	凤凰 Phoenix(7.7) 海鸥 Seagull(7.7)	尼康 Nikon(5.1) 佳能 Canon(5.1) 奥林巴斯 Olympus(5.1)
中间层 medium	156	理光 Ricoh(21.2)	佳能 Canon(10.9)	海鸥 Seagull(9.6)	奥林巴斯 Olympus(7.1)
价格重视指向 careful orientation	71	理光 Ricoh(16.9)	海鸥 Seagull(8.5)	华山 Huashan(7.0) 佳能 Canon(7.0) 凤凰 Phoenix(7.0)	甘光 Ganguang(4.2) 红梅 Hongmei(4.2) 柯达 Kodak(4.2) 汤姆 Toma(4.2)

9-9 不同消费者层选择照相机时的考虑因素/ Considerations in Choosing from Different Brands by Market Segments

9-9-1 时尚流行指标/ Fads Popular Index

注：本题为多选题，合计百分比超过 100%（Multiple answers）

	人数 Number	品牌形象 brand image	外型 outlook	价格 price	成像质量 picture quality	变焦功能 zooming function	专业声誉 professional prestige
样本 Sample	306	28.8	6.5	40.2	26.5	9.2	6.9
平实生活指向 simple living orientation	164	23.2	4.9	48.2	22.6	9.1	5.5
时尚流行指向 fashion orientation	142	35.2	8.5	31.0	31.0	9.2	8.5

续前表 continued

	人数 Number	操作方便 easy to deal with	原产地 place of production	功能齐备 all-function	售后服务 follow-up service	其他 others
样本 Sample	306	41.2	6.2	10.8	2.9	1.3
平实生活指向 simple living orientation	164	43.9	5.5	10.4	2.4	0.6
时尚流行指向 fashion orientation	142	38.0	7.0	11.3	3.5	2.1

9-9-2 广告态度指标/ Advertising Attitude Index

注：本题为多选题，合计百分比超过 100%（Multiple answers）

	人数 Number	品牌形象 brand image	外型 outlook	价格 price	成像质量 picture quality	变焦功能 zooming function	专业声誉 professional prestige
样本 Sample	302	28.5	6.3	40.4	26.5	8.3	7.0
广告淡漠指向 indifferent orientation	88	23.9	3.4	45.5	25.0	5.7	8.0
中间层 medium	175	29.7	9.1	41.1	25.7	9.7	6.3
信赖广告指向 loyal orientation	39	33.3	0.0	25.6	33.3	7.7	7.7

续前表 continued

	人数 Number	操作方便 easy to deal with	原产地 place of production	功能齐备 all-function	售后服务 follow-up service	其他 others
样本 Sample	302	41.7	6.3	10.9	3.0	1.3
广告淡漠指向 indifferent orientation	88	47.7	8.0	10.2	2.3	1.1
中间层 medium	175	40.0	5.1	11.4	2.9	1.1
信赖广告指向 loyal orientation	39	35.9	7.7	10.3	5.1	2.6

9-9-3 价格态度指标/ Price Attitude Index

注：本题为多选题，合计百分比超过 100%（Multiple answers）

	人数 Number	品牌形象 brand image	外型 outlook	价格 price	成像质量 picture quality	变焦功能 zooming function	专业声誉 professional prestige
样本 Sample	305	28.9	6.6	40.0	26.2	9.2	6.9
价格无关心指向 indifferent orientation	78	30.8	3.8	42.3	21.8	10.3	6.4
中间层 medium	156	31.4	8.3	38.5	30.1	8.3	8.3
价格重视指向 careful orientation	71	21.1	5.6	40.8	22.5	9.9	4.2

续前表 continued

	人数 Number	操作方便 easy to deal with	原产地 place of production	功能齐备 all-function	售后服务 follow-up service	其他 others
样本 Sample	305	41.3	5.9	10.8	3.0	1.3
价格无关心指向 indifferent orientation	78	43.6	3.8	7.7	3.8	1.3
中间层 medium	156	37.2	8.3	10.9	1.9	1.3
价格重视指向 careful orientation	71	47.9	2.8	14.1	4.2	1.4

● 沈阳 / Shenyang

9-1 照相机的拥有比例/ Proportion of Camera Owners in the Sample

	人数 Number	百分比 Percent
有 yes	272	45.3
没有 no	328	54.7

n=600

9-2 照相机的拥有量/ Number of Camera Owned Per Household

	人数 Number	百分比 Percent
1 台 1 set	245	91.1
2 台及以上 2 sets or over	24	8.9

n=269

9-3 理想品牌排名/ Ranking of the Ideal Brands

排名 Brand Ranking	品牌 Brands	人数 Number	百分比 Percent
1	理光 Ricoh	104	17.4
2	松下 National	41	6.9
3	佳能 Canon	33	5.5
4	尼康 Nikon	29	4.8
5	海鸥 Seagull	23	3.8
6	奥林巴斯 Olympus	19	3.2
6	索尼 Sony	19	3.2
7	凤凰 Phoenix	16	2.7
8	富士 Fuji	9	1.5

n=598

9-4 对家中现有照相机(最近购买的一台)的四个方面的描述/ About the Camera Most Recently Purchased

9-4-1 家中现有照相机的品牌排名/ Ranking of the Currently Owned Camera Brands

排名 Brand Ranking	品牌 Brands	人数 Number	百分比 Percent
1	理光 Ricoh	40	14.8
2	海鸥 Seagull	26	9.6
3	凤凰 Phoenix	19	7.0
4	奥林巴斯 Olympus	14	5.2
4	佳能 Canon	14	5.2
5	尼康 Nikon	13	4.8
6	汤姆 Toma	9	3.3
7	柯尼卡 Konica	8	3.0
8	松下 National	5	1.9
8	美能达 Minolta	5	1.9

n=270

9-4-2 该照相机的购买时间/ The Time of Purchasing of the Currently Owned Camera

	人数 Number	百分比 Percent
1985 年或以前 1985 or before	26	9.6
1986～1990 年	87	32.1
1991 年	15	5.5
1992 年	15	5.5
1993 年	16	5.9
1994 年	19	7.0
1995 年	21	7.7
1996 年	22	8.1
1997 年	23	8.5
1998 年	13	4.8
1999 年	14	5.2

n=271

9-4-3 该照相机的价格/ The Price of the Currently Owned Camera

	人数 Number	百分比 Percent
1000 元或以下 1000 yuan or below	191	70.5
1001～2000 元 yuan	44	16.2
2001～3000 元 yuan	16	5.9
3001～4000 元 yuan	6	2.2
4001～5000 元 yuan	4	1.5
5001～6000 元 yuan	1	0.4
6001～7000 元 yuan	0	0.0
7001～8000 元 yuan	0	0.0
8001～9000 元 yuan	0	0.0
9001～10000 元 yuan	0	0.0
10000 元以上 over 10000 yuan	1	0.4
完全不知道 don't know	8	3.0

n=271

9-4-4 该照相机的类型/ The Type of the Currently Owned Camera

	人数 Number	百分比 Percent
固定镜头傻瓜相机 set lens simpleton camera	139	51.5
变焦镜头傻瓜相机 zoom lens simpleton camera	50	18.5
机械单镜头反光相机 mechanic single len reflector camera	35	13.0
自动单镜头反光相机 automatic single len reflector camera	20	7.4
手动加自动单反相机 manual or automatic camera	18	6.7
数字相机 digital camera	3	1.1
一次成像相机 one step camera	1	0.4
120 专业相机 120 professional camera	0	0.0
其他 others	4	1.5

n=270

9-5 选择不同品牌照相机时的考虑因素/ Considerations in Choosing from Different Brands

注：本题为多选题，合计百分比超过 100%（Multiple answers）

	人数 Number	品牌形象 brand image	外型 outlook	价格 price	成像质量 picture quality	变焦功能 zooming function	专业声誉 professional prestige
样本 Sample	270	26.7	10.7	41.5	28.1	10.7	3.3
理光 Ricoh	40	40.0	5.0	22.5	30.0	12.5	12.5
海鸥 Seagull	26	23.1	3.8	53.8	19.2	7.7	3.8
凤凰 Phoenix	19	26.3	10.5	47.4	31.6	15.8	0.0
奥林巴斯 Olympus	14	57.1	21.4	28.6	35.7	21.4	0.0
佳能 Canon	14	35.7	14.3	42.9	14.3	21.4	0.0
尼康 Nikon	13	30.8	7.7	30.8	38.5	7.7	7.7
汤姆 Toma	9	0.0	22.2	77.8	22.2	0.0	0.0
柯尼卡 Konica	8	0.0	12.5	62.5	0.0	0.0	0.0

续前表 continued

	人数 Number	操作方便 easy to deal with	原产地 place of production	功能齐备 all-function	售后服务 follow-up service	其他 others
样本 Sample	270	40.0	6.7	14.4	3.7	5.2
理光 Ricoh	40	50.0	10.0	15.0	5.0	5.0
海鸥 Seagull	26	30.8	3.8	19.2	0.0	3.8
凤凰 Phoenix	19	15.8	5.3	21.1	0.0	0.0
奥林巴斯 Olympus	14	28.6	14.3	14.3	0.0	0.0
佳能 Canon	14	57.1	7.1	7.1	7.1	7.1
尼康 Nikon	13	15.4	0.0	23.1	0.0	0.0
汤姆 Toma	9	44.4	11.1	11.1	11.1	0.0
柯尼卡 Konica	8	50.0	12.5	12.5	0.0	0.0

9-6 照相机未来一年购买打算/ Plan for Future Purchasing of a Camera

9-6-1 有无购买打算/ Whether Planning to Purchase Next Year

	人数 Number	百分比 Percent
是 yes	22	3.7
否 no	574	96.3

n=596

9-6-2 打算购买的品牌排名/ Ranking of the Brands of the Planned Purchase Next Year

排名 Brand Ranking	品牌 Brands	人数 Number	百分比 Percent
1	理光 Ricoh	6	27.3
2	佳能 Canon	4	18.2
3	海鸥 Seagull	1	4.5
3	美能达 Minolta	1	4.5
3	尼康 Nikon	1	4.5
3	日立 Hitachi	1	4.5
3	索尼 Sony	1	4.5
3	东芝 Toshiba	1	4.5

n=22

9-6-3 打算购买的类型/ The Type of the Planned Purchase Next Year

	人数 Number	百分比 Percent
固定镜头傻瓜相机 set lens simpleton camera	6	27.3
变焦镜头傻瓜相机 zoom lens simpleton camera	4	18.2
机械单镜头反光相机 mechanic single len reflector camera	0	0.0
自动单镜头反光相机 automatic single len reflector camera	3	13.6
手动加自动单反相机 manual or automatic camera	2	9.1
数字相机 digital camera	5	22.7
一次成像相机 one step camera	2	9.1
120 专业相机 120 professional camera	0	0.0
其他 others	0	0.0

n=22

9-6-4 打算购买的价格/ The Price of the Planned Purchase Next Year

	人数 Number	百分比 Percent
1000 元或以下 1000 yuan or below	6	27.3
1001～2000 元 yuan	5	22.7
2001～3000 元 yuan	5	22.7
3001～4000 元 yuan	2	9.1
4001～5000 元 yuan	2	9.1
5001～6000 元 yuan	0	0.0
6001～7000 元 yuan	1	4.5
7001～8000 元 yuan	0	0.0
8001～9000 元 yuan	0	0.0
9001～10000 元 yuan	1	4.5
10000 元以上 over 10000 yuan	0	0.0
完全不知道 don't know	0	0.0

n=22

9-7 选购照相机时不同角色的人口特征/ Demographics of the Different Roles in Purchasing a Camera

注：不同角色可以多选（Multiple answers）

	人数 Number	16-24 岁 Age	25-34 岁 Age	35-44 岁 Age	45-54 岁 Age	55-60 岁 Age
样本 Sample	238	18.5	33.2	22.7	18.9	6.7
男性 Male	131	16.0	34.4	23.7	18.3	7.6
提议者 advocate	19	31.6	21.1	21.1	26.3	0.0
影响者 influence	3	33.3	33.3	0.0	33.3	0.0
决定者 decider	64	3.1	31.3	28.1	25.0	12.5
使用者 user	82	17.1	40.2	20.7	17.1	4.9
女性 Female	107	21.5	31.8	21.5	19.6	5.6
提议者 advocate	19	21.1	26.3	21.1	26.3	5.3
影响者 influence	3	0.0	33.3	33.3	33.3	0.0
决定者 decider	31	29.0	25.8	19.4	16.1	9.7
使用者 user	75	20.0	34.7	24.0	18.7	2.7

9-8 不同消费者层的家中目前拥有品牌/ Brands of Camera Owned in Household by Market Segments

9-8-1 时尚流行指标/ Fads Popular Index

	人数 Number	第一品牌及百分比 1st/ percent	第二品牌及百分比 2nd/ percent	第三品牌及百分比 3rd/ percent	第四品牌及百分比 4th/ percent
样本 Sample	270	**理光 Ricoh(14.8)**	**海鸥 Seagull(9.6)**	**凤凰 Phoenix(7.0)**	**奥林巴斯 Olympus(5.2)** **佳能 Canon(5.2)**
平实生活指向 simple living orientation	133	海鸥 Seagull(10.5) 理光 Ricoh(10.5)	凤凰 Phoenix(6.0)	汤姆 Toma(5.3)	奥林巴斯 Olympus(4.5) 佳能 Canon(4.5)
时尚流行指向 fashion orientation	137	理光 Ricoh(19.0)	海鸥 Seagull(8.8)	凤凰 Phoenix(8.0)	尼康 Nikon(5.8) 奥林巴斯 Olympus(5.8) 佳能 Canon(5.8)

9-8-2 广告态度指标/ Advertising Attitude Index

	人数 Number	第一品牌及百分比 1st/ percent	第二品牌及百分比 2nd/ percent	第三品牌及百分比 3rd/ percent	第四品牌及百分比 4th/ percent
样本 Sample	270	**理光 Ricoh(14.8)**	**海鸥 Seagull(9.6)**	**凤凰 Phoenix(7.0)**	**奥林巴斯 Olympus(5.2)** **佳能 Canon(5.2)**
广告淡漠指向 indifferent orientation	77	理光 Ricoh(10.4)	凤凰 Phoenix(7.8) 佳能 Canon(7.8)	海鸥 Seagull(6.5)	
中间层 medium	161	理光 Ricoh(14.9)	海鸥 Seagull(11.8)	凤凰 Phoenix(7.5)	奥林巴斯 Olympus(5.6)
信赖广告指向 loyal orientation	32	理光 Ricoh(25.0)	尼康 Nikon(12.5)	海鸥 Seagull(6.3) 奥林巴斯 Olympus(6.3)	凤凰 Phoenix(3.1) 富士 Fuji(3.1) 甘光 Ganguang(3.1) 宾得 Pentax(3.1) 柯尼卡 Konica(3.1) 美能达 Minolta(3.1) 青岛 Qingdao(3.1) 上海 Shanghai(3.1) 汤姆 Toma(3.1) 腾马 Tomr(3.1) 三洋 Sanyang(3.1)

9-8-3 价格态度指标/ Price Attitude Index

	人数 Number	第一品牌及百分比 1st/ percent	第二品牌及百分比 2nd/ percent	第三品牌及百分比 3rd/ percent	第四品牌及百分比 4th/ percent
样本 Sample	269	**理光 Ricoh(14.9)**	**海鸥 Seagull(9.7)**	**凤凰 Phoenix(7.1)**	**奥林巴斯 Olympus(5.2)**
价格无关心指向 indifferent orientation	49	理光 Ricoh(22.4)	奥林巴斯 Olympus(8.2) 海鸥 Seagull(8.2)	佳能 Canon(6.1) 尼康 Nikon(6.1)	美能达 Minolta(4.1) 松下 National(4.1)
中间层 medium	138	理光 Ricoh(12.3)	海鸥 Seagull(8.0)	凤凰 Phoenix(7.2)	尼康 Nikon(5.8)
价格重视指向 careful orientation	82	理光 Ricoh(14.6)	海鸥 Seagull(13.4)	凤凰 Phoenix(9.8)	柯尼卡 Konica(4.9)

9-9 不同消费者层选择照相机时的考虑因素/ Considerations in Choosing from Different Brands by Market Segments

9-9-1 时尚流行指标/ Fads Popular Index

注：本题为多选题，合计百分比超过 100%（Multiple answers）

	人数 Number	品牌形象 brand image	外型 outlook	价格 price	成像质量 picture quality	变焦功能 zooming function	专业声誉 professional prestige
样本 Sample	271	**26.6**	**10.7**	**41.3**	**28.0**	**10.7**	**3.3**
平实生活指向 simple living orientation	133	25.6	12.8	44.4	29.3	8.3	1.5
时尚流行指向 fashion orientation	138	27.5	8.7	38.4	26.8	13.0	5.1

续前表 continued

	人数 Number	操作方便 easy to deal with	原产地 place of production	功能齐备 all-function	售后服务 follow-up service	其他 others
样本 Sample	271	**39.9**	**6.6**	**14.4**	**3.7**	**5.5**
平实生活指向 simple living orientation	133	36.8	6.0	17.3	3.0	7.5
时尚流行指向 fashion orientation	138	42.8	7.2	11.6	4.3	3.6

9-9-2 广告态度指标/ Advertising Attitude Index

注：本题为多选题，合计百分比超过 100%（Multiple answers）

	人数 Number	品牌形象 brand image	外型 outlook	价格 price	成像质量 picture quality	变焦功能 zooming function	专业声誉 professional prestige
样本 Sample	271	**26.6**	**10.7**	**41.3**	**28.0**	**10.7**	**3.3**
广告淡漠指向 indifferent orientation	77	22.1	6.5	54.5	28.6	14.3	1.3
中间层 medium	162	27.2	11.7	37.0	27.8	8.6	3.7
信赖广告指向 loyal orientation	32	34.4	15.6	31.3	28.1	12.5	6.3

续前表 continued

	人数 Number	操作方便 easy to deal with	原产地 place of production	功能齐备 all-function	售后服务 follow-up service	其他 others
样本 Sample	271	**39.9**	**6.6**	**14.4**	**3.7**	**5.5**
广告淡漠指向 indifferent orientation	77	40.3	7.8	18.2	3.9	5.2
中间层 medium	162	39.5	6.8	12.3	4.3	6.2
信赖广告指向 loyal orientation	32	40.6	3.1	15.6	0.0	3.1

9-9-3 价格态度指标/ Price Attitude Index

注：本题为多选题，合计百分比超过 100%（Multiple answers）

	人数 Number	品牌形象 brand image	外型 outlook	价格 price	成像质量 picture quality	变焦功能 zooming function	专业声誉 professional prestige
样本 Sample	270	**26.7**	**10.7**	**41.5**	**27.8**	**10.7**	**3.3**
价格无关心指向 indifferent orientation	49	30.6	6.1	20.4	28.6	14.3	2.0
中间层 medium	139	25.9	15.1	43.2	28.8	9.4	3.6
价格重视指向 careful orientation	82	25.6	6.1	51.2	25.6	11.0	3.7

续前表 continued

	人数 Number	操作方便 easy to deal with	原产地 place of production	功能齐备 all-function	售后服务 follow-up service	其他 others
样本 Sample	**270**	**40.0**	**6.7**	**14.4**	**3.7**	**5.2**
价格无关心指向 indifferent orientation	49	49.0	4.1	18.4	0.0	10.2
中间层 medium	139	38.1	7.9	14.4	3.6	5.8
价格重视指向 careful orientation	82	37.8	6.1	12.2	6.1	1.2

10.胶卷 / Film

● 北京 / Beijing

10-1 最近六个月有无使用的比例/ Proportion of the Sample Using Films in the Last Six Months

	人数 Number	百分比 Percent
是 yes	678	67.0
否 no	334	33.0

n=1012

10-2 样本、男性各年龄层、女性各年龄层最近六个月有无使用的比例/ Proportion of the Sample Using Films in the Last Six Months by the Whole Sample, Age and Gender Groups

	人数 Number	是 yes	否 no
样本 Sample	**1012**	**67.0**	**33.0**
男性 Male	**504**	**63.5**	**36.5**
16~24 岁 Age	105	55.2	44.8
25~34 岁 Age	151	65.6	34.4
35~44 岁 Age	131	64.9	35.1
45~54 岁 Age	77	67.5	32.5
55~60 岁 Age	40	65.0	35.0
女性 Female	**508**	**70.5**	**29.5**
16~24 岁 Age	108	68.5	31.5
25~34 岁 Age	150	74.7	25.3
35~44 岁 Age	124	73.4	26.6
45~54 岁 Age	84	65.5	34.5
55~60 岁 Age	42	61.9	38.1

10-3 最近一次使用的品牌排名/ Ranking of the Film Brands Used Last Time

排名 Brand Ranking	品牌 Brands	人数 Number	百分比 Percent
1	柯达 KODAK	360	53.3
2	富士 FUJI	210	31.1
3	乐凯 LUCKY	98	14.5
4	柯尼卡 KONICA	2	0.3
4	依尔福 ILFORD	2	0.3

n=676

10-4 使用的类型/ The Type of the Film Used

	人数 Number	百分比 Percent
感光度 100（一般常用）ISO100	608	90.7
感光度 200 ISO 200	55	8.2
感光度 400 ISO 400	7	1.0

n=670

10-5 选择不同品牌时考虑的因素/ Considerations in Choosing from Different Brands

注：本题为多选题，合计百分比超过 100%（Multiple answers）

	人数 Number	品牌形象 brand image	包装 package	价格 price	成像质量 picture quality	色彩 color	购买方便 convenience	有专卖店冲印服务 exclusive film developing shop	其他 others
样本 Sample	**672**	**52.1**	**1.8**	**27.8**	**42.4**	**38.8**	**18.0**	**17.1**	**2.1**
柯达 KODAK	358	52.2	2.2	19.6	47.2	45.3	16.5	23.7	1.1
富士 FUJI	209	58.9	1.0	25.4	40.2	34.4	18.7	9.1	2.4
乐凯 LUCKY	97	37.1	2.1	62.9	27.8	22.7	22.7	10.3	5.2
柯尼卡 KONICA	2	50.0	0.0	50.0	0.0	100.0	0.0	0.0	0.0
依尔福 ILFORD	2	50.0	0.0	50.0	100.0	50.0	0.0	0.0	0.0

10-6 样本、男性各年龄层、女性各年龄层一年内的使用量/ How Many Films to be Used in a Year by the Whole Sample, Age and Gender groups

	人数 Number	1 卷	2 卷	3 卷	4 卷	5 卷	6--10 卷	11 卷及以上 11 or over
样本 Sample	672	10.4	22.3	17.4	10.6	15.6	19.3	4.3
男性 Male	317	11.7	22.1	18.6	11.0	13.2	18.6	4.7
16~24 岁 Age	56	14.3	21.4	23.2	12.5	12.5	10.7	5.4
25~34 岁 Age	99	6.1	14.1	23.2	10.1	15.2	27.3	4.0
35~44 岁 Age	84	11.9	27.4	15.5	11.9	10.7	16.7	6.0
45~54 岁 Age	52	15.4	32.7	9.6	11.5	11.5	15.4	3.8
55~60 岁 Age	26	19.2	15.4	19.2	7.7	19.2	15.4	3.8
女性 Female	355	9.3	22.5	16.3	10.1	17.7	20.0	3.9
16~24 岁 Age	74	10.8	16.2	18.9	13.5	20.3	17.6	2.7
25~34 岁 Age	112	4.5	22.3	17.9	12.5	17.9	21.4	3.6
35~44 岁 Age	89	13.5	29.2	14.6	4.5	14.6	20.2	3.4
45~54 岁 Age	54	7.4	25.9	13.0	13.0	18.5	16.7	5.6
55~60 岁 Age	26	15.4	11.5	15.4	3.8	19.2	26.9	7.7

10-7 样本、男性各年龄层、女性各年龄层的购买地点/ Settings of Purchasing Films by the Whole Sample, Age and Gender Groups

	人数 Number	大商场 department store	照片冲洗店 film developing shop	照相器材店 camera equipment shop	就近商店 nearby shop	旅游点 tourist	其他 others
样本 Sample	670	33.1	24.8	11.8	26.9	1.5	1.9
男性 Male	318	36.2	21.7	11.9	26.4	1.9	1.9
16~24 岁 Age	58	25.9	29.3	10.3	29.3	1.7	3.4
25~34 岁 Age	98	35.7	22.4	11.2	30.6	0.0	0.0
35~44 岁 Age	84	45.2	17.9	11.9	22.6	2.4	0.0
45~54 岁 Age	52	28.8	15.4	17.3	26.9	5.8	5.8
55~60 岁 Age	26	46.2	26.9	7.7	15.4	0.0	3.8
女性 Female	352	30.4	27.6	11.6	27.3	1.1	2.0
16~24 岁 Age	73	28.8	34.2	8.2	28.8	0.0	0.0
25~34 岁 Age	110	30.0	33.6	9.1	23.6	1.8	1.8
35~44 岁 Age	89	33.7	18.0	15.7	27.0	2.2	3.4
45~54 岁 Age	54	35.2	18.5	16.7	27.8	0.0	1.9
55~60 岁 Age	26	15.4	34.6	7.7	38.5	0.0	3.8

10-8 下一次打算购买的品牌排名/ Ranking of the Brands of the Planned Purchase Next Time

排名 Brand Ranking	品牌 Brands	人数 Number	百分比 Percent
1	柯达 KODAK	549	56.0
2	富士 FUJI	262	26.7
3	乐凯 LUCKY	133	13.6
4	柯尼卡 KONICA	15	1.5
5	福达 FUDA	7	0.7
6	爱克发 AGFA	6	0.6

n=981

10-9 理想品牌排名/ Ranking of the Ideal Brands

排名 Brand Ranking	品牌 Brands	人数 Number	百分比 Percent
1	柯达 KODAK	583	57.6
2	富士 FUJI	258	25.5
3	乐凯 LUCKY	89	8.8
4	柯尼卡 KONICA	8	0.8
5	爱克发 AGFA	3	0.3

n=1012

10-10 不同消费者层最近一次购买的品牌/ Brands of Purchased Last Time by Market Segments

10-10-1 时尚流行指标/ Fads Popular Index

	人数 Number	第一品牌及百分比 1st/ percent	第二品牌及百分比 2nd/ percent	第三品牌及百分比 3rd/ percent
样本 Sample	665	柯达 KODAK(53.2)	富士 FUJI(30.8)	乐凯 LUCKY(14.7)
平实生活指向 simple living orientation	316	柯达 KODAK(49.4)	富士 FUJI(31.6)	乐凯 LUCKY(18.7)
时尚流行指向 fashion orientation	349	柯达 KODAK(56.7)	富士 FUJI(30.1)	乐凯 LUCKY(11.2)

10-10-2 广告态度指标/ Advertising Attitude Index

	人数 Number	第一品牌及百分比 1st/ percent	第二品牌及百分比 2nd/ percent	第三品牌及百分比 3rd/ percent
样本 Sample	**664**	**柯达 KODAK(53.5)**	**富士 FUJI(30.9)**	**乐凯 LUCKY(14.5)**
广告淡漠指向 indifferent orientation	192	柯达 KODAK(51.6)	富士 FUJI(30.2)	乐凯 LUCKY(17.7)
中间层 medium	387	柯达 KODAK(53.0)	富士 FUJI(31.5)	乐凯 LUCKY(14.2)
信赖广告指向 loyal orientation	85	柯达 KODAK(60.0)	富士 FUJI(29.4)	乐凯 LUCKY(8.2)

10-11 不同消费者层选择胶卷时的考虑因素/ Considerations in Choosing from Different Brands by Market Segments

10-11-1 时尚流行指标/ Fads Popular Index

注：本题为多选题，合计百分比超过 100%（Multiple answers）

	人数 Number	品牌形象 brand image	包装 package	价格 price	成像质量 picture quality	色彩 color	购买方便 convenience	有专卖店冲印服务 exclusive film developing shop	其他 others
样本 Sample	**662**	**52.0**	**1.8**	**27.9**	**42.3**	**39.0**	**18.1**	**17.1**	**2.1**
平实生活指向 simple living orientation	317	51.1	2.2	30.6	43.2	32.2	18.6	15.1	2.5
时尚流行指向 fashion orientation	345	52.8	1.4	25.5	41.4	45.2	17.7	18.8	1.7

10-11-2 广告态度指标/ Advertising Attitude Index

注：本题为多选题，合计百分比超过 100%（Multiple answers）

	人数 Number	品牌形象 brand image	包装 package	价格 price	成像质量 picture quality	色彩 color	购买方便 convenience	有专卖店冲印服务 exclusive film developing shop	其他 others
样本 Sample	**661**	**52.2**	**1.7**	**27.5**	**42.8**	**38.6**	**17.9**	**17.1**	**2.1**
广告淡漠指向 indifferent orientation	191	46.1	1.0	29.3	42.9	37.7	20.9	15.2	3.1
中间层 medium	385	54.3	1.6	28.3	44.2	40.5	16.9	17.7	1.3
信赖广告指向 loyal orientation	85	56.5	3.5	20.0	36.5	31.8	15.3	18.8	3.5

● 上海 / Shanghai

10-1 最近六个月有无使用的比例/ Proportion of the Sample Using Films in the Last Six Months

	人数 Number	百分比 Percent
是 yes	476	46.9
否 no	538	53.1

n=1014

10-2 样本、男性各年龄层、女性各年龄层最近六个月有无使用的比例/ Proportion of the Sample Using Films in the Last Six Months by the Whole Sample, Age and Gender Groups

	人数 Number	是 yes	否 no
样本 Sample	**1014**	**46.9**	**53.1**
男性 Male	**509**	**44.4**	**55.6**
16~24 岁 Age	109	33.9	66.1
25~34 岁 Age	146	54.1	45.9
35~44 岁 Age	130	46.9	53.1
45~54 岁 Age	85	40.0	60.0
55~60 岁 Age	39	38.5	61.5
女性 Female	**505**	**49.5**	**50.5**
16~24 岁 Age	108	47.2	52.8
25~34 岁 Age	144	56.3	43.8
35~44 岁 Age	130	47.7	52.3
45~54 岁 Age	82	43.9	56.1
55~60 岁 Age	41	48.8	51.2

10-3 最近一次使用的品牌排名/ Ranking of the Film Brands Used Last Time

排名 Brand Ranking	品牌 Brands	人数 Number	百分比 Percent
1	柯达 KODAK	401	84.2
2	富士 FUJI	58	12.2
3	柯尼卡 KONICA	7	1.5
4	乐凯 LUCKY	4	0.8
5	爱克发 AGFA	3	0.6

n=476

10-4 使用的类型/ The Type of the Film Used

	人数 Number	百分比 Percent
感光度 100（一般常用）ISO100	403	84.8
感光度 200 ISO 200	62	13.1
感光度 400 ISO 400	10	2.1

n=475

10-5 选择不同品牌时的考虑因素/ Considerations in Choosing from Different Brands

注：本题为多选题，合计百分比超过 100%（Multiple answers）

	人数 Number	品牌形象 brand image	包装 package	价格 price	成像质量 picture quality	色彩 color	购买方便 convenience	有专卖店冲印服务 exclusive film developing shop	其他 others
样本 Sample	**476**	**56.7**	**2.5**	**21.8**	**48.9**	**46.6**	**18.7**	**17.0**	**0.6**
柯达 KODAK	401	60.3	2.7	17.2	50.4	47.1	18.7	19.0	0.2
富士 FUJI	58	36.2	1.7	44.8	41.4	46.6	19.0	8.6	1.7
柯尼卡 KONICA	7	42.9	0.0	57.1	42.9	28.6	28.6	0.0	0.0
乐凯 LUCKY	4	25.0	0.0	75.0	75.0	25.0	0.0	0.0	0.0
爱克发 AGFA	3	100.0	0.0	33.3	0.0	100.0	0.0	0.0	0.0

10-6 样本、男性各年龄层、女性各年龄层一年内的使用量/ How Many Films to be Used in a Year by the Whole Sample, Age and Gender groups

	人数 Number	1 卷	2 卷	3 卷	4 卷	5 卷	6~10 卷	11 卷及以上 11 or over
样本 Sample	**476**	**16.8**	**29.4**	**16.8**	**11.8**	**10.9**	**11.8**	**2.5**
男性 Male	**226**	**12.8**	**31.4**	**16.4**	**11.1**	**11.9**	**13.7**	**2.7**
16~24 岁 Age	37	16.2	40.5	5.4	10.8	13.5	13.5	0.0
25~34 岁 Age	79	7.6	22.8	17.7	15.2	13.9	20.3	2.5
35~44 岁 Age	61	14.8	32.8	18.0	9.8	9.8	11.5	3.3
45~54 岁 Age	34	20.6	32.4	23.5	8.8	5.9	5.9	2.9
55~60 岁 Age	15	6.7	46.7	13.3	0.0	20.0	6.7	6.7
女性 Female	**250**	**20.4**	**27.6**	**17.2**	**12.4**	**10.0**	**10.0**	**2.4**
16~24 岁 Age	51	21.6	25.5	13.7	13.7	9.8	15.7	0.0
25~34 岁 Age	81	11.1	29.6	19.8	13.6	13.6	8.6	3.7
35~44 岁 Age	62	30.6	29.0	27.4	6.5	3.2	3.2	0.0
45~54 岁 Age	36	13.9	27.8	5.6	16.7	16.7	13.9	5.6
55~60 岁 Age	20	35.0	20.0	5.0	15.0	5.0	15.0	5.0

10-7 样本、男性各年龄层、女性各年龄层的购买地点/ Settings of Purchasing Films by the Whole Sample, Age and Gender Groups

	人数 Number	大商场 department store	照片冲洗店 film developing shop	照相器材店 camera equipment shop	就近商店 nearby shop	旅游点 tourist	其他 others
样本 Sample	**473**	**18.0**	**31.9**	**19.0**	**27.3**	**2.1**	**1.7**
男性 Male	**225**	**19.6**	**30.7**	**19.6**	**26.7**	**1.8**	**1.8**
16~24 岁 Age	37	18.9	29.7	18.9	32.4	0.0	0.0
25~34 岁 Age	79	20.3	38.0	15.2	24.1	2.5	0.0
35~44 岁 Age	60	25.0	23.3	16.7	31.7	0.0	3.3
45~54 岁 Age	34	14.7	23.5	29.4	20.6	5.9	5.9
55~60 岁 Age	15	6.7	40.0	33.3	20.0	0.0	0.0
女性 Female	**248**	**16.5**	**33.1**	**18.5**	**27.8**	**2.4**	**1.6**
16~24 岁 Age	51	15.7	41.2	15.7	27.5	0.0	0.0
25~34 岁 Age	80	16.3	27.5	23.8	27.5	2.5	2.5
35~44 岁 Age	61	9.8	32.8	18.0	32.8	3.3	3.3
45~54 岁 Age	36	25.0	33.3	19.4	16.7	5.6	0.0
55~60 岁 Age	20	25.0	35.0	5.0	35.0	0.0	0.0

10-8 下一次打算购买的品牌排名/ Ranking of the Brand of the Planned Purchase Next Time

排名 Brand Ranking	品牌 Brands	人数 Number	百分比 Percent
1	柯达 KODAK	806	81.1
2	富士 FUJI	118	11.9
3	柯尼卡 KONICA	33	3.3
4	乐凯 LUCKY	20	2.0
5	爱克发 AGFA	6	0.6
5	福达 FUDA	6	0.6

n=994

10-9 理想品牌排名/ Ranking of the Ideal Brands

排名 Brand Ranking	品牌 Brands	人数 Number	百分比 Percent
1	柯达 KODAK	865	85.5
2	富士 FUJI	95	9.4
3	柯尼卡 KONICA	18	1.8
4	乐凯 LUCKY	13	1.3
5	爱克发 AGFA	5	0.5

n=1012

10-10 不同消费者层最近一次购买的品牌/ Brands of Purchased Last Time by Market Segments

10-10-1 时尚流行指标/ Fads Popular Index

	人数 Number	第一品牌及百分比 1st/ percent	第二品牌及百分比 2nd/ percent	第三品牌及百分比 3rd/ percent	第四品牌及百分比 4th/ percent
样本 Sample	473	**柯达 KODAK(84.4)**	**富士 FUJI(12.1)**	**柯尼卡 KONICA(1.5)**	**乐凯 LUCKY(0.8)**
平实生活指向 simple living orientation	198	柯达 KODAK(85.4)	富士 FUJI(11.6)	乐凯 LUCKY(1.5)	柯尼卡 KONICA(1.0)
时尚流行指向 fashion orientation	275	柯达 KODAK(83.6)	富士 FUJI(12.4)	柯尼卡 KONICA(1.8)	爱克发 AGFA(1.1)

10-10-2 广告态度指标/ Advertising Attitude Index

	人数 Number	第一品牌及百分比 1st/ percent	第二品牌及百分比 2nd/ percent	第三品牌及百分比 3rd/ percent	第四品牌及百分比 4th/ percent
样本 Sample	471	**柯达 KODAK(84.3)**	**富士 FUJI(12.1)**	**柯尼卡 KONICA(1.5)**	**乐凯 LUCKY(0.8)**
广告淡漠指向 indifferent orientation	115	柯达 KODAK(84.3)	富士 FUJI(9.6)	柯尼卡 KONICA(3.5)	爱克发 AGFA(0.9) 佳能 Canon(0.9)
中间层 medium	284	柯达 KODAK(85.2)	富士 FUJI(12.0)	乐凯 LUCKY(1.4)	爱克发 AGFA(0.7)
信赖广告指向 loyal orientation	72	柯达 KODAK(80.6)	富士 FUJI(16.7)	柯尼卡 KONICA(2.8)	

10-11 不同消费者层选择胶卷时考虑因素/ Considerations in Choosing from Different Brands by Market Segments

10-11-1 时尚流行指标/ Fads Popular Index

注：本题为多选题，合计百分比超过 100%（Multiple answers）

	人数 Number	品牌形象 brand image	包装 package	价格 price	成像质量 picture quality	色彩 color	购买方便 convenience	有专卖店冲印服务 exclusive film developing shop	其他 others
样本 Sample	473	56.9	2.5	21.8	49.0	46.5	18.6	16.9	0.6
平实生活指向 simple living orientation	198	53.5	2.0	24.7	44.9	40.9	20.2	15.7	0.0
时尚流行指向 fashion orientation	275	59.3	2.9	19.6	52.0	50.5	17.5	17.8	1.1

10-11-2 广告态度指标/ Advertising Attitude Index

注：本题为多选题，合计百分比超过 100%（Multiple answers）

	人数 Number	品牌形象 brand image	包装 package	价格 price	成像质量 picture quality	色彩 color	购买方便 convenience	有专卖店冲印服务 exclusive film developing shop	其他 others
样本 Sample	471	56.9	2.3	21.2	49.0	46.5	18.7	17.0	0.6
广告淡漠指向 indifferent orientation	115	46.1	1.7	20.0	47.0	42.6	22.6	13.9	0.0
中间层 medium	284	60.2	2.8	22.2	50.0	45.8	16.2	17.3	1.1
信赖广告指向 loyal orientation	72	61.1	1.4	19.4	48.6	55.6	22.2	20.8	0.0

● 广州 / Guangzhou

10-1 最近六个月有无使用的比例/ Proportion of the Sample Using Films in the Last Six Months

	人数 Number	百分比 Percent
是 yes	495	47.9
否 no	539	52.1

n=1034

10-2 样本、男性各年龄层、女性各年龄层最近六个月有无使用的比例/ Proportion of the Sample Using Films in the Last Six Months by the Whole Sample, Age and Gender Groups

	人数 Number	是 yes	否 no
样本 Sample	1034	47.9	52.1
男性 Male	499	45.1	54.9
16~24 岁 Age	106	27.4	72.6
25~34 岁 Age	150	58.0	42.0
35~44 岁 Age	127	48.8	51.2
45~54 岁 Age	73	50.7	49.3
55~60 岁 Age	43	23.3	76.7
女性 Female	535	50.5	49.5
16~24 岁 Age	112	58.0	42.0
25~34 岁 Age	158	57.0	43.0
35~44 岁 Age	137	48.9	51.1
45~54 岁 Age	87	40.2	59.8
55~60 岁 Age	41	31.7	68.3

10-3 最近一次使用的品牌排名/ Ranking of the Film Brands Used Last Time

排名 Brand Ranking	品牌 Brands	人数 Number	百分比 Percent
1	富士 FUJI	245	49.7
2	柯达 KODAK	223	45.2
3	柯尼卡 KONICA	13	2.6
4	乐凯 LUCKY	6	1.2

n=493

10-4 使用的类型/ The Type of the Film Used

	人数 Number	百分比 Percent
感光度 100（一般常用）ISO100	393	79.9
感光度 200 ISO 200	92	18.7
感光度 400 ISO 400	7	1.4

n=492

10-5 选择不同品牌时的考虑因素/ Considerations in Choosing from Different Brands

注：本题为多选题，合计百分比超过 100%（Multiple answers）

	人数 Number	品牌形象 brand image	包装 package	价格 price	成像质量 picture quality	色彩 color	购买方便 convenience	有专卖店冲印服务 exclusive film developing shop	其他 others
样本 Sample	490	50.8	2.4	32.0	47.8	43.5	20.4	13.5	0.8
富士 FUJI	243	50.6	2.9	29.6	46.1	44.4	20.6	14.0	0.4
柯达 KODAK	222	52.7	2.3	33.8	50.0	42.3	19.8	14.0	0.9
柯尼卡 KONICA	13	46.2	0.0	53.8	53.8	46.2	23.1	0.0	0.0
乐凯 LUCKY	6	33.3	0.0	33.3	33.3	33.3	16.7	16.7	0.0

10-6 样本、男性各年龄层、女性各年龄层一年内的使用量/ How Many Films to be Used in a Year by the Whole Sample, Age and Gender groups

	人数 Number	1 卷	2 卷	3 卷	4 卷	5 卷	6--10 卷	11 卷及以上 11 or over
样本 Sample	495	14.1	25.9	20.4	10.7	9.9	14.3	4.6
男性 Male	225	12.4	25.8	19.1	11.6	9.8	15.1	6.2
16~24 岁 Age	29	6.9	24.1	24.1	3.4	17.2	13.8	10.3
25~34 岁 Age	87	10.3	18.4	17.2	16.1	4.6	27.6	5.7
35~44 岁 Age	62	16.1	35.5	19.4	9.7	12.9	3.2	3.2
45~54 岁 Age	37	13.5	27.0	24.3	10.8	10.8	8.1	5.4
55~60 岁 Age	10	20.0	30.0	0.0	10.0	10.0	10.0	20.0
女性 Female	270	15.6	25.9	21.5	10.0	10.0	13.7	3.3
16~24 岁 Age	65	15.4	23.1	24.6	12.3	9.2	10.8	4.6
25~34 岁 Age	90	8.9	26.7	22.2	12.2	12.2	14.4	3.3
35~44 岁 Age	67	20.9	29.9	23.9	6.0	7.5	10.4	1.5
45~54 岁 Age	35	22.9	20.0	14.3	8.6	5.7	22.9	5.7
55~60 岁 Age	13	15.4	30.8	7.7	7.7	23.1	15.4	0.0

10-7 样本、男性各年龄层、女性各年龄层的购买地点/ Settings of Purchasing Films by the Whole Sample, Age and Gender Groups

	人数 Number	大商场 department store	照片冲洗店 film developing shop	照相器材店 camera equipment shop	就近商店 nearby shop	旅游点 tourist	其他 others
样本 Sample	490	14.1	46.9	13.3	22.7	1.4	1.6
男性 Male	222	13.5	47.3	13.5	23.4	1.8	0.5
16~24 岁 Age	29	13.8	41.4	17.2	20.7	6.9	0.0
25~34 岁 Age	86	14.0	51.2	11.6	19.8	2.3	1.2
35~44 岁 Age	61	14.8	45.9	11.5	27.9	0.0	0.0
45~54 岁 Age	36	11.1	44.4	16.7	27.8	0.0	0.0
55~60 岁 Age	10	10.0	50.0	20.0	20.0	0.0	0.0
女性 Female	268	14.6	46.6	13.1	22.0	1.1	2.6
16~24 岁 Age	64	10.9	54.7	17.2	15.6	0.0	1.6
25~34 岁 Age	89	15.7	48.3	9.0	23.6	0.0	3.4
35~44 岁 Age	67	13.4	40.3	11.9	28.4	4.5	1.5
45~54 岁 Age	35	20.0	54.3	11.4	11.4	0.0	2.9
55~60 岁 Age	13	15.4	7.7	30.8	38.5	0.0	7.7

10-8 下一次打算购买的品牌排名/ The Brand of the Planned Purchase Next Time

排名 Brand Ranking	品牌 Brands	人数 Number	百分比 Percent
1	富士 FUJI	454	44.7
2	柯达 KODAK	451	44.4
3	柯尼卡 KONICA	55	5.4
4	乐凯 LUCKY	21	2.1
5	福达 FUDA	5	0.5
6	爱克发 AGFA	3	0.3

n=1016

10-9 理想品牌排名/ Ranking of the Ideal Brands

排名 Brand Ranking	品牌 Brands	人数 Number	百分比 Percent
1	富士 FUJI	452	43.8
2	柯达 KODAK	448	43.4
3	柯尼卡 KONICA	29	2.8
4	乐凯 LUCKY	9	0.9

n=1032

10-10 不同消费者层最近一次购买的品牌/ Brands of Purchased Last Time by Market Segments

10-10-1 时尚流行指标/ Fads Popular Index

	人数 Number	第一品牌及百分比 1st/ percent	第二品牌及百分比 2nd/ percent	第三品牌及百分比 3rd/ percent	第四品牌及百分比 4th/ percent
样本 Sample	488	富士 FUJI(50.0)	柯达 KODAK(44.9)	柯尼卡 KONICA(2.7)	乐凯 LUCKY(1.2)
平实生活指向 simple living orientation	231	富士 FUJI(51.5)	柯达 KODAK(42.4)	柯尼卡 KONICA(3.0)	乐凯 LUCKY(1.3)
时尚流行指向 fashion orientation	257	富士 FUJI(48.6)	柯达 KODAK(47.1)	柯尼卡 KONICA(2.3)	乐凯 LUCKY(1.2)

10-10-2 广告态度指标/ Advertising attitude Index

	人数 Number	第一品牌及百分比 1st/ percent	第二品牌及百分比 2nd/ percent	第三品牌及百分比 3rd/ percent	第四品牌及百分比 4th/ percent
样本 Sample	485	**富士 FUJI(49.1)**	**柯达 KODAK(46.0)**	**柯尼卡 KONICA(2.7)**	**乐凯 LUCKY(1.2)**
广告淡漠指向 indifferent orientation	157	富士 FUJI(52.9)	柯达 KODAK(40.1)	乐凯 LUCKY(2.5)	柯尼卡 KONICA(1.9)
中间层 medium	287	富士 FUJI(48.8)	柯达 KODAK(47.0)	柯尼卡 KONICA(3.1)	乐凯 LUCKY(0.7)
信赖广告指向 loyal orientation	41	柯达 KODAK(61.0)	富士 FUJI(36.5)	柯尼卡 KONICA(2.4)	

10-11 不同消费者层选择胶卷时的考虑因素/ Considerations in Choosing from Different Brands by Market Segments

10-11-1 时尚流行指标/ Fads Popular Index

注：本题为多选题，合计百分比超过 100%（Multiple answers）

	人数 Number	品牌形象 brand image	包装 package	价格 price	成像质量 picture quality	色彩 color	购买方便 convenience	有专卖店冲印服务 exclusive film developing shop	其他 others
样本 Sample	**487**	**50.7**	**2.5**	**32.2**	**47.6**	**43.5**	**20.5**	**13.3**	**0.8**
平实生活指向 simple living orientation	229	50.7	2.2	32.8	48.0	46.7	18.8	14.0	1.3
时尚流行指向 fashion orientation	258	50.8	2.7	31.8	47.3	40.7	22.1	12.8	0.4

10-11-2 广告态度指标/ Advertising Attitude Index

注：本题为多选题，合计百分比超过 100%（Multiple answers）

	人数 Number	品牌形象 brand image	包装 package	价格 price	成像质量 picture quality	色彩 color	购买方便 convenience	有专卖店冲印服务 exclusive film developing shop	其他 others
样本 Sample	**484**	**50.8**	**2.5**	**32.0**	**47.5**	**43.4**	**20.7**	**13.0**	**0.6**
广告淡漠指向 indifferent orientation	157	47.8	3.8	33.8	43.3	47.1	19.1	14.0	1.3
中间层 medium	284	50.0	1.8	29.9	50.4	44.0	19.0	13.0	0.4
信赖广告指向 loyal orientation	43	67.4	2.3	39.5	44.2	25.6	37.2	9.3	0.0

● 重庆 / Chongqing

10-1 最近六个月有无使用的比例/ Proportion of the Sample Using Films in the Last Six Months

	人数 Number	百分比 Percent
是 yes	242	38.8
否 no	382	61.2

n=624

10-2 样本、男性各年龄层、女性各年龄层最近六个月有无使用的比例/ Proportions of the Sample Using Films in the Last Six Months by the Whole Sample, Age and Gender Groups

	人数 Number	是 yes	否 no
样本 Sample	624	38.8	61.2
男性 Male	314	39.2	60.8
16~24 岁 Age	64	42.2	57.8
25~34 岁 Age	93	45.2	54.8
35~44 岁 Age	75	32.0	68.0
45~54 岁 Age	54	35.2	64.8
55~60 岁 Age	28	39.3	60.7
女性 Female	310	38.4	61.6
16~24 岁 Age	64	57.8	42.2
25~34 岁 Age	90	47.8	52.2
35~44 岁 Age	73	16.4	83.6
45~54 岁 Age	60	35.0	65.0
55~60 岁 Age	23	26.1	73.9

10-3 最近一次使用的品牌排名/ Ranking of the Film Brands Used Last Time

排名 Brand Ranking	品牌 Brands	人数 Number	百分比 Percent
1	柯达 KODAK	142	59.4
2	富士 FUJI	85	35.6
3	乐凯 LUCKY	9	3.8
4	柯尼卡 KONICA	3	1.3

n=239

10-4 使用的类型/ The Type of the Film Used

	人数 Number	百分比 Percent
感光度 100（一般常用）ISO100	203	84.6
感光度 200 ISO 200	31	12.9
感光度 400 ISO 400	6	2.5

n=240

10-5 选择不同品牌时的考虑因素/ Ranking of the Considerations in Choosing from Different Brands

注：本题为多选题，合计百分比超过 100%（Multiple answers）

	人数 Number	品牌形象 brand image	包装 package	价格 price	成像质量 picture quality	色彩 color	购买方便 convenience	有专卖店冲印服务 exclusive film developing shop	其他 others
样本 Sample	236	48.7	2.5	21.6	52.1	39.4	18.2	20.3	0.8
柯达 KODAK	141	48.9	2.1	17.0	55.3	39.0	18.4	24.1	1.4
富士 FUJI	83	51.8	2.4	22.9	49.4	41.0	19.3	14.5	0.0
乐凯 LUCKY	9	22.2	11.1	66.7	44.4	33.3	11.1	11.1	0.0
柯尼卡 KONICA	3	33.3	0.0	66.7	0.0	33.3	0.0	33.3	0.0

10-6 样本、男性各年龄层、女性各年龄层一年内的使用量/ How Many Films to be Used in a Year by the Whole Sample, Age and Gender groups

	人数 Number	1 卷	2 卷	3 卷	4 卷	5 卷	6--10 卷	11 卷及以上 11 or over
样本 Sample	239	15.5	34.3	18.4	7.5	9.6	12.6	2.1
男性 Male	121	15.7	37.2	17.4	8.3	9.9	9.9	1.7
16~24 岁 Age	27	18.5	33.3	7.4	11.1	7.4	22.2	0.0
25~34 岁 Age	42	11.9	42.9	19.0	4.8	16.7	2.4	2.4
35~44 岁 Age	23	13.0	30.4	34.8	8.7	8.7	4.3	0.0
45~54 岁 Age	19	26.3	31.6	15.8	5.3	5.3	15.8	0.0
55~60 岁 Age	10	10.0	50.0	0.0	20.0	0.0	10.0	10.0
女性 Female	118	15.3	31.4	19.5	6.8	9.3	15.3	2.5
16~24 岁 Age	37	13.5	27.0	27.0	8.1	10.8	8.1	5.4
25~34 岁 Age	43	7.0	30.2	16.3	9.3	11.6	23.3	2.3
35~44 岁 Age	11	27.3	36.4	9.1	9.1	0.0	18.2	0.0
45~54 岁 Age	21	28.6	42.9	19.0	0.0	0.0	9.5	0.0
55~60 岁 Age	6	16.7	16.7	16.7	0.0	33.3	16.7	0.0

10-7 样本、男性各年龄层、女性各年龄层的购买地点/ Settings of Purchasing Films by the Whole Sample, Age and Gender Groups

	人数 Number	大商场 department store	照片冲洗店 film developing shop	照相器材店 camera equipment shop	就近商店 nearby shop	旅游点 tourist	其他 others
样本 Sample	238	21.8	46.6	11.8	16.0	3.8	0.0
男性 Male	123	19.5	43.1	13.8	19.5	4.1	0.0
16~24 岁 Age	27	14.8	48.1	14.8	22.2	0.0	0.0
25~34 岁 Age	42	21.4	50.0	7.1	14.3	7.1	0.0
35~44 岁 Age	24	25.0	37.5	12.5	25.0	0.0	0.0
45~54 岁 Age	19	10.5	36.8	21.1	21.1	10.5	0.0
55~60 岁 Age	11	27.3	27.3	27.3	18.2	0.0	0.0
女性 Female	115	24.3	50.4	9.6	12.2	3.5	0.0
16~24 岁 Age	37	21.6	59.5	8.1	10.8	0.0	0.0
25~34 岁 Age	41	22.0	51.2	7.3	17.1	2.4	0.0
35~44 岁 Age	11	27.3	45.5	18.2	0.0	9.1	0.0
45~54 岁 Age	20	35.0	35.0	15.0	10.0	5.0	0.0
55~60 岁 Age	6	16.7	50.0	0.0	16.7	16.7	0.0

10-8 下一次打算购买的品牌排名/ The Brands of the Planned Purchase Next Time

排名 Brand Ranking	品牌 Brands	人数 Number	百分比 Percent
1	柯达 KODAK	368	63.3
2	富士 FUJI	158	27.2
3	乐凯 LUCKY	24	4.1
4	柯尼卡 KONICA	7	1.2
5	福达 FUDA	5	0.9

n=581

10-9 理想品牌排名/ Ranking of the Ideal Brands

排名 Brand Ranking	品牌 Brands	人数 Number	百分比 Percent
1	柯达 KODAK	414	66.3
2	富士 FUJI	148	23.7
3	乐凯 LUCKY	18	2.9
4	柯尼卡 KONICA	3	0.5

n=624

10-10 不同消费者层最近一次购买的品牌/ Brands of Purchased Last Time by Market Segments

10-10-1 时尚流行指标/ Fads Popular Index

	人数 Number	第一品牌及百分比 1st/ percent	第二品牌及百分比 2nd/ percent	第三品牌及百分比 3rd/ percent
样本 Sample	235	**柯达 KODAK(58.7)**	**富士 FUJI(36.2)**	**乐凯 LUCKY(3.8)**
平实生活指向 simple living orientation	122	柯达 KODAK(56.6)	富士 FUJI(38.5)	柯尼卡 KONICA(2.5) 乐凯 LUCKY(2.5)
时尚流行指向 fashion orientation	113	柯达 KODAK(61.1)	富士 FUJI(33.5)	乐凯 LUCKY(5.3)

10-10-2 广告态度指标/ Advertising Attitude Index

	人数 Number	第一品牌及百分比 1st/ percent	第二品牌及百分比 2nd/ percent	第三品牌及百分比 3rd/ percent
样本 Sample	237	**柯达 KODAK(59.5)**	**富士 FUJI(35.4)**	**乐凯 LUCKY(3.8)**
广告淡漠指向 indifferent orientation	56	柯达 KODAK(58.9)	富士 FUJI(33.9)	柯尼卡 KONICA(3.6) 乐凯 LUCKY(3.6)
中间层 medium	155	柯达 KODAK(61.3)	富士 FUJI(34.2)	乐凯 LUCKY(3.9)
信赖广告指向 loyal orientation	26	柯达 KODAK(50.0)	富士 FUJI(46.2)	乐凯 LUCKY(3.8)

10-11 不同消费者层选择胶卷时的考虑因素/ Considerations in Choosing from Different Brands by Market Segments

10-11-1 时尚流行指标/ Fads Popular Index

注：本题为多选题，合计百分比超过 100%（Multiple answers）

	人数 Number	品牌形象 brand image	包装 package	价格 price	成像质量 picture quality	色彩 color	购买方便 convenience	有专卖店冲印服务 exclusive film developing shop	其他 others
样本 Sample	234	49.1	2.6	21.4	52.6	38.5	17.9	19.2	0.9
平实生活指向 simple living orientation	122	47.5	2.5	23.0	51.6	39.3	16.4	18.0	0.8
时尚流行指向 fashion orientation	112	50.9	2.7	19.6	53.6	37.5	19.6	20.5	0.9

10-11-2 广告态度指标/ Advertising Attitude Index

注：本题为多选题，合计百分比超过 100%（Multiple answers）

	人数 Number	品牌形象 brand image	包装 package	价格 price	成像质量 picture quality	色彩 color	购买方便 convenience	有专卖店冲印服务 exclusive film developing shop	其他 others
样本 Sample	236	48.3	2.5	21.6	52.5	39.0	18.2	19.9	0.8
广告淡漠指向 indifferent orientation	56	41.1	3.6	19.6	57.1	39.3	12.5	16.1	0.0
中间层 medium	155	49.0	1.9	22.6	51.0	37.4	20.0	23.2	0.6
信赖广告指向 loyal orientation	25	60.0	4.0	20.0	52.0	48.0	20.0	8.0	4.0

武汉 / Wuhan

10-1 最近六个月有无使用的比例/ Proportion of the Sample Using Films in the Last Six Months

	人数 Number	百分比 Percent
是 yes	243	37.9
否 no	399	62.1

n=642

10-2 样本、男性各年龄层、女性各年龄层最近六个月有无使用的比例/ Proportion of the Sample Using Films in the Last Six Months by the Whole Sample, Age and Gender Groups

	人数 Number	是 yes	否 no
样本 Sample	642	37.9	62.1
男性 Male	311	34.7	65.3
16~24 岁 Age	65	29.2	70.8
25~34 岁 Age	89	42.7	57.3
35~44 岁 Age	80	27.5	72.5
45~54 岁 Age	52	32.7	67.3
55~60 岁 Age	25	48.0	52.0
女性 Female	331	40.8	59.2
16~24 岁 Age	69	46.4	53.6
25~34 岁 Age	96	55.2	44.8
35~44 岁 Age	78	32.1	67.9
45~54 岁 Age	62	33.9	66.1
55~60 岁 Age	26	15.4	84.6

10-3 最近一次使用的品牌排名/ Ranking of the Film Brands Used Last Time

排名 Brand Ranking	品牌 Brands	人数 Number	百分比 Percent
1	柯达 KODAK	160	66.1
2	富士 FUJI	55	22.7
3	乐凯 LUCKY	19	7.9
4	柯尼卡 KONICA	7	2.9

n=242

10-4 使用的类型/ The Type of the Film Used

	人数 Number	百分比 Percent
感光度 100（一般常用）ISO100	198	82.8
感光度 200 ISO 200	33	13.8
感光度 400 ISO 400	8	3.3

n=239

10-5 选择不同品牌时的考虑因素/ Considerations in Choosing from Different Brands

注：本题为多选题，合计百分比超过 100%（Multiple answers）

	人数 Number	品牌形象 brand image	包装 package	价格 price	成像质量 picture quality	色彩 color	购买方便 convenience	有专卖店冲印服务 exclusive film developing shop	其他 others
样本 Sample	240	57.9	4.2	31.7	55.8	38.8	20.8	15.8	1.3
柯达 KODAK	159	67.9	3.8	27.7	56.0	35.8	17.6	17.6	1.3
富士 FUJI	54	46.3	5.6	25.9	57.4	50.0	22.2	14.8	0.0
乐凯 LUCKY	19	26.3	5.3	78.9	47.4	36.8	36.8	5.3	0.0
柯尼卡 KONICA	7	14.3	0.0	42.9	71.4	14.3	42.9	14.3	14.3

10-6 样本、男性各年龄层、女性各年龄层一年内的使用量/ How Many Films to be Used in a Year by the Whole Sample, Age and Gender groups

	人数 Number	1 卷	2 卷	3 卷	4 卷	5 卷	6--10 卷	11 卷及以上 11 or over
样本 Sample	**240**	**22.1**	**30.0**	**15.4**	**9.2**	**10.8**	**10.4**	**2.1**
男性 Male	**106**	**18.9**	**25.5**	**15.1**	**11.3**	**10.4**	**16.0**	**2.8**
16~24 岁 Age	18	16.7	22.2	11.1	11.1	11.1	22.2	5.6
25~34 岁 Age	38	18.4	21.1	10.5	15.8	13.2	18.4	2.6
35~44 岁 Age	21	33.3	23.8	23.8	0.0	9.5	9.5	0.0
45~54 岁 Age	17	11.8	23.5	23.5	17.6	11.8	5.9	5.9
55~60 岁 Age	12	8.3	50.0	8.3	8.3	0.0	25.0	0.0
女性 Female	**134**	**24.6**	**33.6**	**15.7**	**7.5**	**11.2**	**6.0**	**1.5**
16~24 岁 Age	32	21.9	31.3	12.5	9.4	12.5	12.5	0.0
25~34 岁 Age	52	19.2	30.8	25.0	5.8	9.6	5.8	3.8
35~44 岁 Age	25	40.0	36.0	4.0	8.0	12.0	0.0	0.0
45~54 岁 Age	21	19.0	38.1	14.3	9.5	14.3	4.8	0.0
55~60 岁 Age	4	50.0	50.0	0.0	0.0	0.0	0.0	0.0

10-7 样本、男性各年龄层、女性各年龄层的购买地点/ Settings of Purchasing Films by the Whole Sample, Age and Gender Groups

	人数 Number	大商场 department store	照片冲洗店 film developing shop	照相器材店 camera equipment shop	就近商店 nearby shop	旅游点 tourist	其他 others
样本 Sample	**242**	**24.0**	**33.9**	**12.8**	**24.4**	**2.9**	**2.1**
男性 Male	**107**	**24.3**	**31.8**	**15.0**	**25.2**	**2.8**	**0.9**
16~24 岁 Age	19	15.8	42.1	15.8	21.1	5.3	0.0
25~34 岁 Age	38	26.3	34.2	15.8	18.4	2.6	2.6
35~44 岁 Age	21	19.0	23.8	23.8	33.3	0.0	0.0
45~54 岁 Age	17	41.2	23.5	0.0	29.4	5.9	0.0
55~60 岁 Age	12	16.7	33.3	16.7	33.3	0.0	0.0
女性 Female	**135**	**23.7**	**35.6**	**11.1**	**23.7**	**3.0**	**3.0**
16~24 岁 Age	32	25.0	50.0	12.5	6.3	3.1	3.1
25~34 岁 Age	53	26.4	26.4	11.3	32.1	1.9	1.9
35~44 岁 Age	25	24.0	32.0	8.0	28.0	4.0	4.0
45~54 岁 Age	21	19.0	42.9	9.5	23.8	0.0	4.8
55~60 岁 Age	4	0.0	25.0	25.0	25.0	25.0	0.0

10-8 下一次打算购买的品牌排名/ The Brand of the Planned Purchase Next Time

排名 Brand Ranking	品牌 Brands	人数 Number	百分比 Percent
1	柯达 KODAK	396	66.9
2	富士 FUJI	110	18.6
3	乐凯 LUCKY	41	6.9
4	柯尼卡 KONICA	22	3.7
5	福达 FUDA	4	0.7
6	依尔福 ILFORD	2	0.3
6	爱克发 AGFA	2	0.3

n=592

10-9 理想品牌排名/ Ranking of the Ideal Brands

排名 Brand Ranking	品牌 Brands	人数 Number	百分比 Percent
1	柯达 KODAK	402	62.6
2	富士 FUJI	93	14.5
3	乐凯 LUCKY	25	3.9
4	柯尼卡 KONICA	10	1.6

n=642

10-10 不同消费者层最近一次购买的品牌/ Brands of Purchased Last Time by Market Segments

10-10-1 时尚流行指标/ Fads Popular Index

	人数 Number	第一品牌及百分比 1st/ percent	第二品牌及百分比 2nd/ percent	第三品牌及百分比 3rd/ percent	第四品牌及百分比 4th/ percent
样本 Sample	**239**	**柯达 KODAK(65.7)**	**富士 FUJI(23.0)**	**乐凯 LUCKY(7.9)**	**柯尼卡 KONICA(2.9)**
平实生活指向 simple living orientation	111	柯达 KODAK(69.4)	富士 FUJI(20.7)	乐凯 LUCKY(6.3)	柯尼卡 KONICA(2.7)
时尚流行指向 fashion orientation	128	柯达 KODAK(62.5)	富士 FUJI(25.0)	乐凯 LUCKY(9.4)	柯尼卡 KONICA(3.1)

10-10-2 广告态度指标/ Advertising Attitude Index

	人数 Number	第一品牌及百分比 1st/ percent	第二品牌及百分比 2nd/ percent	第三品牌及百分比 3rd/ percent	第四品牌及百分比 4th/ percent
样本 Sample	**239**	**柯达 KODAK(65.7)**	**富士 FUJI(23.0)**	**乐凯 LUCKY(7.9)**	**柯尼卡 KONICA(2.9)**
广告淡漠指向 indifferent orientation	69	柯达 KODAK(72.5)	富士 FUJI(17.4)	乐凯 LUCKY(5.8)	柯尼卡 KONICA(4.3)
中间层 medium	143	柯达 KODAK(62.9)	富士 FUJI(23.8)	乐凯 LUCKY(9.8)	柯尼卡 KONICA(2.8)
信赖广告指向 loyal orientation	27	柯达 KODAK(63.0)	富士 FUJI(33.3)	乐凯 LUCKY(3.7)	

10-11 不同消费者层选择胶卷时的考虑因素/ Considerations in Choosing from Different Brands by Market Segments

10-11-1 时尚流行指标/ Fads Popular Index

注：本题为多选题，合计百分比超过 100%（Multiple answers）

	人数 Number	品牌形象 brand image	包装 package	价格 price	成像质量 picture quality	色彩 color	购买方便 convenience	有专卖店冲印服务 exclusive film developing shop	其他 others
样本 Sample	**237**	**57.8**	**4.2**	**31.6**	**55.3**	**39.2**	**20.3**	**16.0**	**1.3**
平实生活指向 simple living orientation	110	65.5	5.5	29.1	52.7	40.0	21.8	19.1	0.9
时尚流行指向 fashion orientation	127	51.2	3.1	33.9	57.5	38.6	18.9	13.4	1.6

10-11-2 广告态度指标/ Advertising Attitude Index

注：本题为多选题，合计百分比超过 100%（Multiple answers）

	人数 Number	品牌形象 brand image	包装 package	价格 price	成像质量 picture quality	色彩 color	购买方便 convenience	有专卖店冲印服务 exclusive film developing shop	其他 others
样本 Sample	**237**	**57.8**	**4.2**	**31.6**	**55.3**	**39.2**	**20.3**	**16.0**	**1.3**
广告淡漠指向 indifferent orientation	68	58.8	7.4	27.9	52.9	35.3	16.2	17.6	1.5
中间层 medium	143	56.6	2.8	33.6	55.2	42.7	22.4	15.4	1.4
信赖广告指向 loyal orientation	26	61.5	3.8	30.8	61.5	30.8	19.2	15.4	0.0

● 西安 / Xi'an

10-1 最近六个月有无使用的比例/ Proportion of the Sample Using Films in the Last Six Months

	人数 Number	百分比 Percent
是 yes	330	55.0
否 no	270	45.0

n=600

10-2 样本、男性各年龄层、女性各年龄层最近六个月有无使用的比例/ Proportion of the Sample Using Films in the Last Six Months by the Whole Sample, Age and Gender Groups

	人数 Number	是 yes	否 no
样本 Sample	**600**	**55.0**	**45.0**
男性 Male	**301**	**57.5**	**42.5**
16~24 岁 Age	64	60.9	39.1
25~34 岁 Age	91	62.6	37.4
35~44 岁 Age	76	56.6	43.4
45~54 岁 Age	46	47.8	52.2
55~60 岁 Age	24	50.0	50.0
女性 Female	**299**	**52.5**	**47.5**
16~24 岁 Age	61	57.4	42.6
25~34 岁 Age	90	62.2	37.8
35~44 岁 Age	74	44.6	55.4
45~54 岁 Age	49	42.9	57.1
55~60 岁 Age	25	48.0	52.0

10-3 最近一次使用的品牌排名/ Ranking of the Film Brands Used Last Time

排名 Brand Ranking	品牌 Brands	人数 Number	百分比 Percent
1	柯达 KODAK	167	50.9
2	乐凯 LUCKY	83	25.3
3	富士 FUJI	53	16.2
4	柯尼卡 KONICA	20	6.1

n=328

10-4 使用的类型/ The Type of the Film Used

	人数 Number	百分比 Percent
感光度 100（一般常用）ISO100	295	90.2
感光度 200 ISO 200	30	9.2
感光度 400 ISO 400	2	0.6

n=327

10-5 选择不同品牌时的考虑因素/ Considerations in Choosing from Different Brands

注：本题为多选题，合计百分比超过 100%（Multiple answers）

	人数 Number	品牌形象 brand image	包装 package	价格 price	成像质量 picture quality	色彩 color	购买方便 convenience	有专卖店冲印服务 exclusive film developing shop	其他 others
样本 Sample	327	43.4	4.3	32.1	59.0	31.8	15.9	8.9	1.5
柯达 KODAK	167	49.1	5.4	22.2	63.5	33.5	11.4	8.4	1.8
乐凯 LUCKY	83	28.9	3.6	59.0	50.6	22.9	24.1	9.6	2.4
富士 FUJI	53	54.7	3.8	20.8	58.5	39.6	15.1	7.5	0.0
柯尼卡 KONICA	20	25.0	0.0	40.0	70.0	35.0	20.0	15.0	0.0

10-6 样本、男性各年龄层、女性各年龄层一年内的使用量/ How Many Films to be Used in a Year by the Whole Sample, Age and Gender groups

	人数 Number	1 卷	2 卷	3 卷	4 卷	5 卷	6--10 卷	11 卷及以上 11 or over
样本 Sample	327	16.5	28.7	17.7	11.0	10.7	11.6	3.7
男性 Male	171	17.5	28.1	19.3	8.8	10.5	11.7	4.1
16~24 岁 Age	39	10.3	25.6	17.9	7.7	20.5	10.3	7.7
25~34 岁 Age	56	16.1	30.4	19.6	10.7	8.9	8.9	5.4
35~44 岁 Age	42	26.2	26.2	26.2	9.5	4.8	7.1	0.0
45~54 岁 Age	22	22.7	27.3	4.5	4.5	13.6	27.3	0.0
55~60 岁 Age	12	8.3	33.3	25.0	8.3	0.0	16.7	8.3
女性 Female	156	15.4	29.5	16.0	13.5	10.9	11.5	3.2
16~24 岁 Age	35	11.4	34.3	8.6	14.3	14.3	11.4	5.7
25~34 岁 Age	56	8.9	28.6	23.2	12.5	14.3	8.9	3.6
35~44 岁 Age	33	24.2	36.4	15.2	12.1	3.0	6.1	3.0
45~54 岁 Age	21	19.0	19.0	14.3	4.8	14.3	28.6	0.0
55~60 岁 Age	11	27.3	18.2	9.1	36.4	0.0	9.1	0.0

10-7 样本、男性各年龄层、女性各年龄层的购买地点/ Settings of Purchasing Films by the Whole Sample, Age and Gender Groups

	人数 Number	大商场 department store	照片冲洗店 film developing shop	照相器材店 camera equipment shop	就近商店 nearby shop	旅游点 tourist	其他 others
样本 Sample	328	20.7	33.8	19.2	22.3	3.4	0.6
男性 Male	171	22.8	33.9	16.4	23.4	2.9	0.6
16~24 岁 Age	39	20.5	35.9	15.4	25.6	2.6	0.0
25~34 岁 Age	56	19.6	35.7	16.1	25.0	3.6	0.0
35~44 岁 Age	43	27.9	37.2	16.3	16.3	2.3	0.0
45~54 岁 Age	22	27.3	27.3	22.7	18.2	0.0	4.5
55~60 岁 Age	11	18.2	18.2	9.1	45.5	9.1	0.0
女性 Female	157	18.5	33.8	22.3	21.0	3.8	0.6
16~24 岁 Age	35	14.3	45.7	22.9	14.3	2.9	0.0
25~34 岁 Age	56	16.1	33.9	19.6	23.2	7.1	0.0
35~44 岁 Age	33	27.3	30.3	21.2	21.2	0.0	0.0
45~54 岁 Age	21	23.8	23.8	23.8	23.8	4.8	0.0
55~60 岁 Age	12	8.3	25.0	33.3	25.0	0.0	8.3

10-8 下一次打算购买的品牌排名/ The Brand of the Planned Purchase Next Time

排名 Brand Ranking	品牌 Brands	人数 Number	百分比 Percent
1	柯达 KODAK	275	46.8
2	乐凯 LUCKY	144	24.5
3	富士 FUJI	107	18.2
4	柯尼卡 KONICA	48	8.2

n=587

10-9 理想品牌排名/ Ranking of the Ideal Brands

排名 Brand Ranking	品牌 Brands	人数 Number	百分比 Percent
1	柯达 KODAK	343	57.2
2	乐凯 LUCKY	103	17.2
3	富士 FUJI	97	16.2
4	柯尼卡 KONICA	34	5.7

n=600

10-10 不同消费者层最近一次购买的品牌/ Brands of Purchased Last Time by Market Segments

10-10-1 时尚流行指标/ Fads Popular Index

	人数 Number	第一品牌及百分比 1st/ percent	第二品牌及百分比 2nd/ percent	第三品牌及百分比 3rd/ percent	第四品牌及百分比 4th/ percent
样本 Sample	327	**柯达 KODAK(50.8)**	**乐凯 LUCKY(25.4)**	**富士 FUJI(16.2)**	**柯尼卡 KONICA(6.1)**
平实生活指向 simple living orientation	166	柯达 KODAK(48.2)	乐凯 LUCKY(26.5)	富士 FUJI(18.1)	柯尼卡 KONICA(5.4)
时尚流行指向 fashion orientation	161	柯达 KODAK(53.4)	乐凯 LUCKY(24.2)	富士 FUJI(14.3)	柯尼卡 KONICA(6.8)

10-10-2 广告态度指标/ Advertising Attitude Index

	人数 Number	第一品牌及百分比 1st/ percent	第二品牌及百分比 2nd/ percent	第三品牌及百分比 3rd/ percent	第四品牌及百分比 4th/ percent
样本 Sample	325	**柯达 KODAK(51.4)**	**乐凯 LUCKY(25.2)**	**富士 FUJI(16.3)**	**柯尼卡 KONICA(5.5)**
广告淡漠指向 indifferent orientation	96	柯达 KODAK(49.0)	乐凯 LUCKY(26.0)	富士 FUJI(18.8)	柯尼卡 KONICA(4.2)
中间层 medium	183	柯达 KODAK(51.9)	乐凯 LUCKY(24.6)	富士 FUJI(15.3)	柯尼卡 KONICA(7.1)
信赖广告指向 loyal orientation	46	柯达 KODAK(54.3)	乐凯 LUCKY(26.1)	富士 FUJI(15.2)	柯尼卡 KONICA(2.2)

10-11 不同消费者层选择胶卷时的考虑因素/ Considerations in Choosing from Different Brands by Market Segments

10-11-1 时尚流行指标/ Fads Popular Index

注：本题为多选题，合计百分比超过 100%（Multiple answers）

	人数 Number	品牌形象 brand image	包装 package	价格 price	成像质量 picture quality	色彩 color	购买方便 convenience	有专卖店冲印服务 exclusive film developing shop	其他 others
样本 Sample	327	43.4	4.3	32.1	58.7	31.8	15.9	9.2	1.5
平实生活指向 simple living orientation	166	41.6	4.2	34.3	58.4	30.7	13.9	7.8	1.8
时尚流行指向 fashion orientation	161	45.3	4.3	29.8	59.0	32.9	18.0	10.6	1.2

10-11-2 广告态度指标/ Advertising Attitude Index

注：本题为多选题，合计百分比超过 100%（Multiple answers）

	人数 Number	品牌形象 brand image	包装 package	价格 price	成像质量 picture quality	色彩 color	购买方便 convenience	有专卖店冲印服务 exclusive film developing shop	其他 others
样本 Sample	325	43.4	4.3	32.0	58.8	32.0	15.7	9.2	1.5
广告淡漠指向 indifferent orientation	97	41.2	4.1	32.0	58.8	34.0	16.5	11.3	2.1
中间层 medium	183	41.5	4.9	32.8	61.7	32.8	16.4	6.6	1.6
信赖广告指向 loyal orientation	45	55.6	2.2	28.9	46.7	24.4	11.1	15.6	0.0

沈阳 / Shenyang

10-1 最近六个月有无使用的比例/ Proportion of the Sample Using Films in the Last Six Months

	人数 Number	百分比 Percent
是 yes	268	44.6
否 no	333	55.4

n=601

10-2 样本、男性各年龄层、女性各年龄层最近六个月有无使用的比例/ Proportion of the Sample Using Films in the Last Six Months by the Whole Sample, Age and Gender Groups

	人数 Number	是 yes	否 no
样本 Sample	601	44.6	55.4
男性 Male	299	43.8	56.2
16~24 岁 Age	64	35.9	64.1
25~34 岁 Age	89	55.1	44.9
35~44 岁 Age	76	40.8	59.2
45~54 岁 Age	46	37.0	63.0
55~60 岁 Age	24	45.8	54.2
女性 Female	302	45.4	54.6
16~24 岁 Age	64	50.0	50.0
25~34 岁 Age	90	52.2	47.8
35~44 岁 Age	76	39.5	60.5
45~54 岁 Age	48	47.9	52.1
55~60 岁 Age	24	20.8	79.2

10-3 最近一次使用的品牌排名/ Ranking of the Film Brands Used Last Time

排名 Brand Ranking	品牌 Brands	人数 Number	百分比 Percent
1	富士 FUJI	126	47.2
2	柯达 KODAK	118	44.2
3	乐凯 LUCKY	12	4.5
4	爱克发 AGFA	8	3.0
5	柯尼卡 KONICA	2	0.7

n=267

10-4 使用的类型/ The Type of the Film Used

	人数 Number	百分比 Percent
感光度 100（一般常用）ISO100	246	92.5
感光度 200 ISO 200	17	6.4
感光度 400 ISO 400	3	1.1

n=266

10-5 选择不同品牌时的考虑因素/ Considerations in Choosing from Different Brands

注：本题为多选题，合计百分比超过 100%（Multiple answers）

	人数 Number	品牌形象 brand image	包装 package	价格 price	成像质量 picture quality	色彩 color	购买方便 convenience	有专卖店冲印服务 exclusive film developing shop	其他 others
样本 Sample	267	43.8	4.5	28.8	54.3	35.2	19.9	10.5	1.5
富士 FUJI	126	38.9	3.2	29.4	54.0	34.1	20.6	11.9	1.6
柯达 KODAK	118	48.3	6.8	25.4	58.5	36.4	21.2	8.5	0.8
乐凯 LUCKY	12	41.7	0.0	58.3	25.0	41.7	8.3	8.3	0.0
爱克发 AGFA	8	50.0	0.0	12.5	50.0	12.5	0.0	25.0	12.5

10-6 样本、男性各年龄层、女性各年龄层一年内的使用量/ How Many Films to be Used in a Year by the Whole Sample, Age and Gender groups

	人数 Number	1 卷	2 卷	3 卷	4 卷	5 卷	6--10 卷	11 卷及以上 11 or over
样本 Sample	267	17.2	31.8	20.2	9.4	9.0	10.5	1.9
男性 Male	131	16.0	33.6	20.6	8.4	9.2	9.9	2.3
16~24 岁 Age	23	13.0	34.8	39.1	4.3	8.7	0.0	0.0
25~34 岁 Age	49	10.2	30.6	16.3	8.2	12.2	18.4	4.1
35~44 岁 Age	31	25.8	41.9	12.9	6.5	3.2	6.5	3.2
45~54 岁 Age	17	11.8	35.3	23.5	5.9	11.8	11.8	0.0
55~60 岁 Age	11	27.3	18.2	18.2	27.3	9.1	0.0	0.0
女性 Female	136	18.4	30.1	19.9	10.3	8.8	11.0	1.5
16~24 岁 Age	32	9.4	34.4	12.5	15.6	12.5	9.4	6.3
25~34 岁 Age	47	12.8	31.9	23.4	8.5	8.5	14.9	0.0
35~44 岁 Age	30	30.0	20.0	26.7	10.0	3.3	10.0	0.0
45~54 岁 Age	22	22.7	27.3	18.2	9.1	13.6	9.1	0.0
55~60 岁 Age	5	40.0	60.0	0.0	0.0	0.0	0.0	0.0

10-7 样本、男性各年龄层、女性各年龄层的购买地点/ Settings of Purchasing Films by the Whole Sample, Age and Gender Groups

	人数 Number	大商场 department store	照片冲洗店 film developing shop	照相器材店 camera equipment shop	就近商店 nearby shop	旅游点 tourist	其他 others
样本 Sample	266	25.2	23.7	18.4	24.1	5.3	3.4
男性 Male	131	29.0	19.8	15.3	28.2	5.3	2.3
16~24 岁 Age	23	4.3	34.8	17.4	30.4	13.0	0.0
25~34 岁 Age	49	30.6	20.4	16.3	22.4	6.1	4.1
35~44 岁 Age	31	32.3	12.9	12.9	38.7	3.2	0.0
45~54 岁 Age	17	47.1	17.6	11.8	23.5	0.0	0.0
55~60 岁 Age	11	36.4	9.1	18.2	27.3	0.0	9.1
女性 Female	135	21.5	27.4	21.5	20.0	5.2	4.4
16~24 岁 Age	32	21.9	25.0	18.8	15.6	9.4	9.4
25~34 岁 Age	47	21.3	19.1	34.0	19.1	4.3	2.1
35~44 岁 Age	30	16.7	50.0	10.0	16.7	3.3	3.3
45~54 岁 Age	21	28.6	14.3	19.0	28.6	4.8	4.8
55~60 岁 Age	5	20.0	40.0	0.0	40.0	0.0	0.0

10-8 下一次打算购买的品牌排名/ The Brands of the Planned Purchase Next Time

排名 Brand Ranking	品牌 Brands	人数 Number	百分比 Percent
1	柯达 KODAK	276	47.0
2	富士 FUJI	236	40.2
3	乐凯 LUCKY	37	6.3
4	爱克发 AGFA	27	4.6
5	柯尼卡 KONICA	4	0.7
5	福达 FUDA	4	0.7

n=587

10-9 理想品牌排名/ Ranking of the Ideal Brands

排名 Brand Ranking	品牌 Brands	人数 Number	百分比 Percent
1	柯达 KODAK	304	50.6
2	富士 FUJI	227	37.8
3	乐凯 LUCKY	28	4.7
4	爱克发 AGFA	23	3.8
5	柯尼卡 KONICA	2	0.3
5	福达 FUDA	2	0.3

n=601

10-10 不同消费者层最近一次购买的品牌/ Brands of Purchased Last Time by Market Segments

10-10-1 时尚流行指标/ Fads Popular Index

	人数 Number	第一品牌及百分比 1st/ percent	第二品牌及百分比 2nd/ percent	第三品牌及百分比 3rd/ percent	第四品牌及百分比 4th/ percent	第五品牌及百分比 5th/ percent
样本 Sample	267	富士 FUJI(47.2)	柯达 KODAK(44.2)	乐凯 LUCKY(4.5)	爱克发 AGFA(3.0)	柯尼卡 KONICA(0.7)
平实生活指向 simple living orientation	119	柯达 KODAK(47.1)	富士 FUJI(45.4)	爱克发 AGFA(4.2)	乐凯 LUCKY(2.5)	乐凯 LUCKY(0.8)
时尚流行指向 fashion orientation	148	富士 FUJI(48.6)	柯达 KODAK(41.9)	乐凯 LUCKY(6.1)	爱克发 AGFA(2.0)	柯尼卡 KONICA(1.4)

10-10-2 广告态度指标/ Advertising Attitude Index

	人数 Number	第一品牌及百分比 1st/ percent	第二品牌及百分比 2nd/ percent	第三品牌及百分比 3rd/ percent	第四品牌及百分比 4th/ percent	第五品牌及百分比 5th/ percent
样本 Sample	**267**	**富士 FUJI(47.2)**	**柯达 KODAK(44.2)**	**乐凯 LUCKY(4.5)**	**爱克发 AGFA(3.0)**	**柯尼卡 KONICA(0.7)**
广告淡漠指向 indifferent orientation	70	富士 FUJI(50.0)	柯达 KODAK(44.3)	乐凯 LUCKY(4.3)	爱克发 AGFA(1.4)	
中间层 medium	166	富士 FUJI(47.6)	柯达 KODAK(41.6)	乐凯 LUCKY(4.8)	爱克发 AGFA(4.2)	柯尼卡 KONICA(1.2)
信赖广告指向 loyal orientation	31	柯达 KODAK(58.1)	富士 FUJI(38.7)	乐凯 LUCKY(3.2)		

10-11 不同消费者层选择胶卷时考虑因素/ Considerations in Choosing from Different Brands by Market Segments

10-11-1 时尚流行指标/ Fads Popular Index

注：本题为多选题，合计百分比超过 100%（Multiple answers）

	人数 Number	品牌形象 brand image	包装 package	价格 price	成像质量 picture quality	色彩 color	购买方便 convenience	有专卖店冲印服务 exclusive film developing shop	其他 others
样本 Sample	**267**	**43.8**	**4.5**	**28.8**	**54.3**	**35.2**	**19.9**	**10.5**	**1.5**
平实生活指向 simple living orientation	119	42.0	5.0	27.7	61.3	31.9	20.2	10.1	0.8
时尚流行指向 fashion orientation	148	45.3	4.1	29.7	48.6	37.8	19.6	10.8	2.0

10-11-2 广告态度指标/ Advertising Attitude Index

注：本题为多选题，合计百分比超过 100%（Multiple answers）

	人数 Number	品牌形象 brand image	包装 package	价格 price	成像质量 picture quality	色彩 color	购买方便 convenience	有专卖店冲印服务 exclusive film developing shop	其他 others
样本 Sample	**267**	**43.8**	**4.5**	**28.8**	**54.3**	**35.2**	**19.9**	**10.5**	**1.5**
广告淡漠指向 indifferent orientation	70	31.4	5.7	32.9	62.9	34.3	20.0	11.4	0.0
中间层 medium	166	46.4	2.4	26.5	51.2	34.3	19.9	10.8	2.4
信赖广告指向 loyal orientation	31	58.1	12.9	32.3	51.6	41.9	19.4	6.5	0.0

第十二篇　电脑、通讯工具
Part XII　Personal Computer and Telecommunications

- 家用电脑　Personal Computer
- 私人电话　Telephone
- BP 机　Pager
- 移动电话　Mobile Phone

电脑、通讯工具

电脑

微机（包括台式计算机、笔记本电脑和服务器）作为信息产业的重要组成部分，其发展在 1999 年上半年取得较好的成绩，上半年销售量为 223.6 万台，与去年同期相比，增长率为 16.6%；销售额为 249.08 亿元，比去年增长 14.3%。

台式电脑

台式计算机一直是微机的重头戏，其上半年的销售量达到了 204.1 万台，占微机销售总量的 91.2%；销售额为 191.2 亿元，占微机总销售额的 76.8%。台式电脑上半年销售量与去年同期相比增长 15.7%，销售额比去年同期增长 12.8%。

其市场特点如下：

一、国内品牌继续扩大市场，国外品牌蓄势待发，兼容机市场继续萎缩。

面对国外品牌的激烈竞争，国产微机（国内品牌机和国产兼容机）的市场占有率曾一度下滑到 33%。但国内品牌很快就奋起直追，市场占有率逐步上升，到 1999 年上半年已达到 74.2%（国产兼容机 24.3%，国产品牌机 49.9%）。兼容机市场在国产品牌和国外品牌的双重打压下，所占份额逐年下降。兼容机的价格优势被品牌机的价格战冲得七零八落，而品牌机良好的售后服务更是兼容机可望而不可及的，所以，其市场的萎缩也在情理之中。1999 年上半年，其市场份额只有 24.3 %。慧聪信息研究所通过对中国台式ＰＣ厂商公司总部、外商驻华机构的面访调研，获得了厂商的自报销量数据。根据厂商自报销量数据与其他调查所得到的客观市场份额，推算各品牌的市场份额如下：

1998 年中国大陆台式 PC 总量为 342.12 万台，比 1997 年增长 20.3％。销量排名依次为联想（54.77 万台）、IBM（26.27 万台）、方正（25.68 万台）、COMPAQ（24.83 万台），市场份额分别为 16.01％、7.67％、7.51％、7.26％。

二、家用电脑市场未现预计的火爆，商用市场再度升温。

1998 年，政府机构调整和国企改革，使商用电脑市场出现了－0 .6 的负增长，导致商用电脑在台式电脑市场的份额从 79.8%减至 68.4%。而家用电脑在国内厂家的精心培育下，逐步成为介于住房、汽车和家用电器之间的另一消费热点，其市场份额逐年提高，成为带动计算机市场发展的强劲动力。1999 年上半年，国民经济的恢复，政府机构调整的结束，电子商务的带动以及解决 2000 年问题带来的商机，使商用电脑的增长率止跌反涨，达到 7%。而家月市场只是稳定上升，没有惊人表现。1999 年上半年中国台式 PC 的市场构成为：家用电脑 34.4%, 商用电脑 65.6%。尽管商用电脑的市场份额由于家用市场份额的扩大而逐年下滑，但是在近期内，它仍然会占据台式电脑市场的主流，各大厂商依然会重视商用电脑的研发和生产，同时会进一步开拓家用电脑市场。

台式电脑的市场发展特点：

1．产品升级加快，奔腾Ⅲ提前成为主流。

2．“价格战”如火如荼，依然是各大厂商营销策略中的主要手段。

3．销售渠道建设方兴未艾，形式多种多样。

4．服务战愈演愈烈，服务内涵开始演变。

5．绿色、健康和环保逐渐成为消费时尚，也成为厂商开发产品的主打旋律和新的“卖点”。

6．1999 年上半年，解决计算机 2000 年问题进入修改、升级、更新阶段，为市场提供了极好的商机。

7．“维纳斯”计划促进了我国推出“女娲计划”和“3C 联盟”建立，更使中国信息家电市场初露端倪。

笔记本电脑

1999 年上半年中国的笔记本电脑市场呈现出平稳增长的良好态势，并以较高的增长速度成为计算机产品市场中的亮点。销售量为 13.3 万台，比 1998 年上半场增长 29.1%，销售额为 27.5 亿元，同比增长 22.2%。目前笔记本电脑市场的规模并不是很大，从长远发展来看，国内的笔记本电脑市场有着巨大的发展潜力，笔记本电脑技术的发展以及用户需求的增长将使市场的潜力逐步显现出来。目前笔记本电脑市场上品牌已达 30 多种，各品牌新产品开发和市场开拓力度均有所加大，市场竞争日益激烈。1999 年上半年，价格竞争、渠道竞争、服务竞争等成为各厂商竞争市场的主要手段。近年，东芝笔记本电脑在我国市场一直占有 1/4 以上的份额，但是其霸主地位正在受到 IBM、COMPAQ、NEC 等诸多品牌的威胁。在低档产品市场上，我国台湾的产品以及联想、方正、紫光等国产品牌也开始占有越来越重要的地位。

笔记本电脑市场呈现以下特点：

1． 厂商竞争日益激烈，售后服务成为焦点。

2． 新产品、新技术推动市场发展。

3． 笔记本电脑价格趋于降低。

国家拉动内需的政策、政府上网工程的启动以及政府采购行为将对 IT 市场发展有新的促进，同时将带动笔记本电脑市场的发展。1998 年以来，中国笔记本电脑的技术发展比较迅猛，新技术层出不穷，为笔记本电脑市场的发展创造了优越的技术环境。生产工艺日益成熟导致笔记本电脑价格下降，有望刺激用户需求的增长进而推动市场的发展。1998 年下半年国家加大打击走私力度，有效遏制了非法入关渠道，笔记本电脑市场逐渐趋向规范成熟。但笔记本电脑市场的发展也存在消极因素，诸如被普遍关注的 2000 年问题，一些用户目前仍持观望态度，将推迟其购买计划。

（数据来源：《中国计算机报》、《中国电子报》）

电话

随着通讯事业的发展，尤其是对人口众多的农村市场的开拓，电话逐渐走入千家万户，电话机市场需求庞大。据《中国电子报》报道，1996 年 8 月 26 日，中国公用电话交换机容量突破 1 亿门，一举超过日本、德国，形成了仅次于美国的世界第二大电话网络规模，而在 1985 年我国仅排在第 17 位，1998 年局用交换机又增加了 2221 万户，使容量达到 1.35 亿门，中国电话用户的总数达到 1.15 亿户。预计 2000 年，电话交换机 1.9 亿门，城市实现平均每户一部电话。1998 年全国电话普及率为 9.3%，预计今年将达到 11%，国内电话机市场正以每年 1500 万部的速度增长。

据信息产业部统计，国内生产厂家有 300 多家，生产的品种 400 多个，年产量达 1400 多万台。在这些电话机企业中，涌现出了一大批电话机知名品牌，如 TCL、步步高、泰丰、佳信、万德莱等。据《中国电子报》报道，TCL 电话机称雄十载，市场占有率始终保持在 25%—40%之间。国内电话机市场是国货一统天下，但洋品牌已开始为迈进国内电话机市场做准备。

目前电话机市场呈现以下特点：

1．话机功能日趋齐全，款式色彩丰富，名牌产品俏销，市场销售开始向几个主要品牌集中。

2．无绳电话成为竞争焦点。

3．大量的假冒伪劣产品充斥市场。

4．电话机市场过度竞争导致产品质量有所下降。

5．电话机价格战一触即发。

随着电信业的发展，服务的日趋完善，将促使电话机市场异常活跃，电话机将成为新一代竞争热点。电话机市场走势形成新的特点：

1．古典式拨盘电话机又开始走俏。

2．液晶显示按键电话机、无绳电话机在现代家庭中唱主角。

寻呼机

寻呼机自 1984 年进入我国后，在国内以惊人的速度发展，寻呼市场以每年 150%的速度递增。目前中国寻呼用户达 7000 万，但寻呼市场的普及率仅为 6%，仍有很大的发展潜力。目前寻呼业面临着来自移动电话的强大冲击，其冲击主要来自两个方面：一是手机及其服务价格的不断下调，大大削弱了无线寻呼的价格优势；另一方面，越来越多的来电显示、短信息服务等移动电话服务功能，淡化了寻呼机与手机的互补性。1998 年以来寻呼业发展势头逐渐减缓，1998 年全国寻呼机用户仅增长 10%，有的城市还出现了负增长。我国ＢＰ机生产企业于 1990 年开始高速发展，ＢＰ机生产企业的黄金时代大约在 1993 年到 1996 年，其时厂家林立，组装机、自主开发机比比皆是。然而主要由于数字蜂房手机在功能和价值上的优势越来越明显，不断夺走ＢＰ机用户，加上我国经济正处于深化改革和结构调整之中，从 1997 年以后ＢＰ机生产企业的发展跌入了负增长。

目前ＢＰ机生产企业约 80 家。主要的生产企业有天津摩托罗拉、济南浪潮、广东建生、京统、万事达、和桥、顺达、光电、联华、顺霸、波导、中桥、录基、运俊等公司。市场销售额最大的依然是外国产品，从寻呼发射机、寻呼系统到小的寻呼机，市场的主导产品是摩托罗拉、三星等品牌。国产品牌中，最大的波导牌寻呼机年产量仅为 32.5 万台。国内寻呼机市场 70％多被摩托罗拉公司占有；寻呼机 90％多是国外品牌。尽管近年来国产寻呼机的市场份额逐年增加，但技术含量较高的寻呼发射机、中继基站设备和中文寻呼机，我国能生产的企业却寥寥无几，均处于开发与生产起步阶段，且在技术体制和制造工艺上沿袭国外产品结构与模式。摩托罗拉称霸中国寻呼市场的状况仍未改变。

寻呼机市场呈现以下特点：

1．寻呼台恶性竞争。

全国的寻呼台有 1700 多家，为求得生存的规模和更多的利润，不少寻呼台纷纷降价，以接近成本甚至低于成本的价格招揽用户。恶性价格战导致各寻呼台之间无序竞争，降价倾销，虚假广告和非法跑台的现象时有发生，寻呼台的错呼、漏呼、延误呼等问题也成了消费者投诉的热点。

2．用户增速放缓，寻呼台数量减少，技术含量高的服务项目和服务质量开始取代“价格战”成为新的竞争焦点。

3．农村可能成为无线寻呼的潜在广阔市场。

4．随着网络时代的到来，具有新功能的寻呼机将会被人们接受，并得到越来越广泛的应用。

（数据来源：www.chinainfobank.com ）

手机

中国移动电话市场是世界上最活跃的移动电话市场，其发展速度迅猛。据《经济参考报》报道，1998 年全国新增手机用户 1200 万，全国手机用户 2400 万。1999 年上半年新增用户 854 户，手机用户总数亦涨至 3300 多万，位居世界第三。1998 年手机产量多达 1000 万部。1999 年上半年我国手机产量 808 万部。手机普及率低于 2%，手机市场潜力巨大。

国外品牌驰骋中国手机市场，摩托罗拉、诺基亚、爱立信等品牌占据中国手机市场 96%的市场份额，摩托罗拉与诺基亚竞争日趋激烈，国产品牌亦加入竞争行列。1998 年 10 月推出第一个中国品牌手机——科健，1999 年 1 月厦华推出华夏 1 号，此外还有东方通信、康佳、TCL、厦新等。已经推出或将要推出国产手机的企业目前已达 20 多家。深圳是国产手机产量最多的城市。

1998 年手机市场迅速发展。据《工商导报》，截至 98 年底，中国的移动通信 GSM 网覆盖了 330 个地市和 2000 多个县市，与 38 个国家和地区实现了自动漫游。各个通信厂商不断更新技术，推出新一代手机品种、款式、功能都较 1997 年有了进步。1997 年经原邮电部电政司批准进网的手机进网证号发至 172 号，1998 年三季度止包括到期换证和新批入网的已有 100 多个入网证号，年末还批准一些新机进网。经对照，1998 年一些厂家相继推出了一些更加先进的手机机种，如风糜市场的双频手机纷纷亮相，高保真绿色手机也进入市场，中文显示手机走俏神州大地，翻盖小型机更受国人青睐。1998 年有的厂家还推出了顶级“掌中宝”，袖珍机和平民化一些新机种。

纵观 1998 年手机市场之发展，可概述为如下四方面特征：

1．简单化和功能化。简单化是手机用户的一大企盼，目前在市场上推出的手机，几乎都有来电显示、振动提示、录音、大容量储存、与ＢＰ机联号使用功能以及免提拨号通话功能，功能虽多，但使用极为简便。

2．小型化和智能化。近年来进入市场的超小型手机品种越来越多。随着电脑和英特网的发展和普及，可使移动电话功能扩展至收发传真、存取电子邮件、个人信息管理、浏览互联网，成为现代化的移动办公室。

3．个性化和多样化。1998 年摩托罗拉、爱立信、诺基亚、阿尔卡特、萨基姆、松下、三星等公司先后推出了多种颜色的机身，美其名为“随心换”、“时尚手机”博得了女士一族的喜爱。一些厂家还推出了个性化设计手机，单一振铃音变为十多种及音乐声有别于他人，手机屏幕也越做越大。

4．大众化、平民化。一些厂商针对工薪阶层开发的工薪机使手机由“大款”向“布衣”转化，创造了条件。

随着“入关”的脚步声越来越近，电信市场面临开放，国家亦将扶植国产品牌。1999 年初，自主开发 GMS 手机以及推进 CDMA 产业化，已被国家计委和科技部列入了《当前优先发展的高技术产业化重点领域指南》，信息部又筹资 4 亿元，扶植国内企业自主开发手机。

Personal Computer and Telecommunications

Personal Computer

Computers, including desk computers, notebook computers and servers, have been an important part of information industry, gaining a satisfying development in the first half-year in 1999. The sales reached 2.236 million, 16.6% more than the same period of last year. The sales revenue reached 24.908 billion yuan, increasing by 14.3%.

Desk Computer

Desk computer has always been the focus of the computers, whose sales volume in the first half-year of 1999 has reached 2.041 million sets, taking a share of 91.2% of all types of computers. The sales revenue reached 19.12 billion yuan, accounting for 76.8% of the total sales revenue of computers. Desk computers' sales in the first half-year of 1999 is 15.7% more than that of the same period of last year, with sales revenue 12.8% up.

Its market features are as the followings:

1. The Chinese local brands continue to expand the market, foreign brands are getting ready to rush into China market, while the compatible computer market is shrinking.

In face of the severe competition from the foreign rivals, the market share of Chinese computers (both Chinese brands and homemade compatible computers) once declined to 33%. But Chinese brands did not surrender and their market share went up gradually, even reaching 74.2% in the first half-year of 1999 (homemade compatible computers enjoying 24.3% and Chinese brand 49.9%), but the market share for the foreign brand computers is only 25.8%.

Under the double pressure from the national and foreign brands, the compatible computer market has seen a shrinking share of market. The price advantage compatible computers' has been completely destroyed by that of brand computers' price fight while the latter excellent follow-up service is far beyond the reach of the former. It is natural that the compatible computers would face a shrinking. Its market share was only 24.3% in the first half-year of 1999.

Huicong Information Research Institute has carried out a interview research on the headquarters of China desk computer manufactures and agents of foreign manufactures, and collected the data reported by themselves. According to the data and the other objective market share obtained by other ways, the market share of different brands may be estimated as the following:

In 1998, the gross output of desk computer in China mainland were 3.4212 million sets, 20.3% more than that of 1997. And the sales volume rank as that: Legend (547.7 thousand sets), IBM (262.7 thousand sets), Founder (256.8 thousand sets), Compaq (248.3 thousand sets), with their market shares 16.01%, 7.67%, 7.51% and 7.26% respectively.

2. The household computer market has not shown any signs of flourishing while commercial computer market becomes heated again.

In 1998, the government organization radiation and enterprise reform, bring a negative growth of -0.6% to commercial computer market, That lead to desk computer declining from 79.8% to 68.4%. Household computer, under the delicate cultivation of Chinese manufactures, is gradually becoming another consuming focus besides housing, cars and manufactures household appliances. Its market share is promoting yearly, turning out to be a great impetus for the growth of computer market development.

During the first half-year of 1999 the national economy recovered, the ending of radiation of the government's organization, the emerge of e-commerce and the desire to solve the problem brought by the year 2000 give computer manufactures a lot of opportunities. The sales of commercial computers stopped falling and went up to 7%, and its share in computer market also stopped declining sharply. But the household computer is only rising steadily, without something surprising. During this period, the market composition of desk computer in China is that the household computer holds 34.4% and the commercial ones 65.6%.

Although the marketing share of commercial computer has been falling with the expansion of the household ones, however, within a short period, it still will hold the main part of the desk computer. All large computer manufactures will still pay attention to the research and development of the commercial computer when further developing the household computer market.

Desk computer market is developing with such characters:

1. The up-grade of the products is speeding up. Pentium III becomes the main stream in advance.

2. "Price fight" is heated, remaining the key in marketing competition of all the manufactures.

3. The building of distribution channels is still on its rise with versatile manners.

4. Service competition is acting on strongly, with a change in the service content.

5. Green, healthy and environmental-protection have gradually become the consuming fashion. They are also the "selling points" and the key tone in the manufactures' developing products.

6. During the first half-year of 1999, the solution of computer Y2K is entering into the periods of reform, up-grade and innovation, providing a great opportunity for the manufactures.

7. "Venus" project has put forward the introduction of "nuwa Plan" and the set-up of "Three Cs Ally", forming China's IT and household appliances market.

Notebook Computer

In the first half year of 1999, China's notebook computer market had experienced a satisfying state of stable improvement, and became a rising star in the computer market with its high growth speed. Its sales volume reached 133 thousand sets, 29.1% more than that of 1998, and its sales revenue 2.75 billion yuan, 22.2% than before. For the moment, notebook computer market isn't large in scale yet, but there is a great development potential in long term. The technology improvement in it and the growth of users' demands will reveal its marketing potential step by step.

Currently, there are more than 30 brands in notebook computer market. All of them are making more efforts to develop new products and market in the case of more competition. In the first-half year of 1999, manufactures mainly compete in price, channel and services. These years, Toshiba notebook computer has always kept a market share of one fourth in China. But its authority is being challenged by the other brands of IBM, COMPAQ, NEC and so on. In the lower-grade products market, Taiwan products and other Chinese brands of Legend, Founder and Unit Splendour are enjoying a more important status.

In the whole, notebook computer market is taking on the following features:

1. The manufactures' competition is increasingly, focusing on the follow-up services.
2. New products and new technology is pushing forward the development of the market.
3. Notebook computer is tending to be more inexpensive.

The government's policy of stimulating domestic demand, the stating of the government network and the government purchasing will give a new trigger to IT market and also the development of notebook computer market. Since 1998, the technology of China's notebook computer has been sharp with a continuos appearance of new technologies, That has laid a good technical base for the market improvement. The improvement of the production naturally leads to the cut of price, which in turn will push forward the rise in demands and then the market development. During the second half year of 1998, the government enforced the force to fight against smuggling and curbed the illegal impact channels effectively so that notebook computer market tend to be standardized and mature.

But negative factors are also existing in the notebook computer market, such as the common well-noticed Y2K problem. So some consumers are still holding back their purchasing plan to have a clearer thinking.

(Sources: "China COMPUTER" and "China Electronics")

Telephone

With the development of communication business, and esp. the development of the rural market with a big population, telephone is gradually entering into thousands of family, which creates great demands of telephone. According to the report from "China Electronics", on August 26th of 1996, the capacity of China's local switchboards broke through 100 million, surmounting Japan and Germany, jumping to the second biggest telephone network only inferior to America. But in 1985, China was only listed as the 17th. In 1998, another 22.21 million families joined the group of the telephone converters. It brought the volume to 135 million and the Chinese telephone users' number to 115 million. It is estimated that in the year of 2000, the telephone converters will be 190 million, getting the fact that each household in cities will have its own telephone in average. In 1998, the popularity of telephone was 9.3%, and is supposed to be 11% in 1999. Now the domestic telephone market is developing at a rate of 15 million every year.

According to the statistics from the Ministry of Information Industry, over 300 national producers turned up more than 400 types of products and the total output is more than 14 million. Among these telephone enterprises, a lot of famous brands come out such as TCL, BBK, Taifeng, jiaxin and Wandelai and so on. According to the report from

"China Electronics", TCL has stood on the first place in the telephone market for about ten years, with market shares of 25%--40%. National products dominated domestic telephone market, but the foreign brands are making preparation for entering Chinese market.

For the moment, the telephone market is featured as:

1. Telephone products have more and more satisfying variety, with rich color and styles. Famous brands are welcomed so that market sale is concentrating on several main brands.

2. Composite telephone is the focus of the competition.

3. Large numbers of fake or shoddy products are roaring in the market.

4. The vicious competition in the telephone market has led to the decline of the products' quality to some degree.

5. The price fight of telephone market is on the verge of breakout.

With the development of telecommunication, and the daily improvement of the service, the telephone market is activated to a large degree. Telephone will be the new center of the new generation's competition.

The market trends will be going on as:

1. Classical dial telephone will be popular again.

2. Liquid crystal illustrated button-pushing telephone and composite telephone lead the main role in the family.

Pager

Since the entry of Pager to China in 1984, it has been developing at a shocking speed, with its market expanding at a speed of 150% every year. For the moment, the China's pager users have reached a number of 70 million while the popularity in the market is still only 6%, which shows a great potential in development.

Currently, pager industry is facing a serious challenge from the cell phones, which mainly comes up in two terms. On one hand, the price of cell phone and its service decline continuously, which lessen the priority of BP in the same aspect; on the other hand, the functions of cell phone with in-call illustration and short message service which devalue the sense of cooperation between cell phone and BP. In 98, the developing power of BP industry had declined, with a small increasing rate of 10% in 98 and even minus increase in some cities.

Our country's BP producing enterprises began a high-speed development since 90, with a golden time in the period from 1993 to 1996 when factories stood as forests with assembly and independent-developing machinery everywhere. But the digital cell phones are overpowering more and more in the function and value, snapping away a lot of users, which, apart from a deepened reform and organizational adjust in government, brought the BP industry after 97 into a minus development. Recently, there are only 80 enterprises in BP production, who are Motorola in Tianjin, Langchao in Jinan, Jiansheng in Guandong, Jingtong, Wangshida, Heqiao, Shunda, Guandian, Lianhua, Sunba, Bodao, Zhongqiao, Luji and Yunjun.

However, the ones with the major market allots are still foreign products, in lot of aspects of launching equipment of BP, calling system and small BP. The leading brands are Motorola and Sumsang. In the national ones, the top Bodao has an annual output of only 325 thousand. Over 70% market shares are for Motorola, 90% for foreign brands. Although the recent market share for national BP is increasing yearly, the high technological calling-launching equipment, the relay base's equipment and Chinese-illustrated BP are still rare in the national production. The enterprises in China are still in the starting period and so on taking after the foreign products' organization and manners in technology system and working arts. It will keep the same that Motorola enjoys a monopoly in China market.

The BP market is featured as:

1. A malignant competition in BP servers.

There are over 17 million BP servers in the country who are trying to cut down the price for an existence scale and more profits, so to attract the users by a price approaching or lower than the cost. The vicious price fight has led to a messy competition with a continuous phenomenon of devalued selling, cheating advertisement and illegal server changing. While the problems of a mistake, omission and delay in calling also become the usual complaints from consumers.

2. The increase in the number of users is slowing down with a less number of BP servers. High technological service items and service quality have replaced the price fight in being the new competition focus.

3. Countryside maybe becomes a potential broad market for BP.

4. With the coming of internet age, BP owning new functions will be accepted and applied widely.

(Sources:www.chinainfobank.com)

Mobil Phone

The mobile phone market in China is one of the most vigorous in the world, with shocking speed of development. According to the report by "Economic Reference", in1998, the whole country's newly-added mobile phone customers were 12 million and the whole country's customers 24 million. In the early half year of 1999, the newly-added customers were 8.54 million while the whole numbers are 33 million, ranking third in the world. In 1998, the output of mobile phone reached 10 million while in the early half of 1999 it reached 8.08 million. Besides, in terms of the popularity of only 2%, the potential of mobile phone is still great.

The foreign brands are prosperous in the China market. For example, Motorola, Nokia, Ericsson and the sort of brands occupy 96% of the market in China. While Motorola and Nokia are having an accelerating severe competition, the national brands also enter the fight. In October of 1998, the first Chinese brand of mobile phone--Kejian came out. And then Xiahua lunched the Huaxia No.1 in January of 1999. Then followed by Oriental Communication, Konka, TCL, Xiaxing. The enterprises that have or will put forward the national mobile phones are more than 20. Shenzhen is the city with the biggest output of national mobile phone.

In 1998, the mobile phone market is developing sharply. According to "Industry and Commerce Guidance", by the end of 1998, the Chinese mobile communication network GSM had covered 330 cities and over 2000 counties, getting an automatic roaming with 38 countries and areas. Every communication tool producers are keeping on renewing the technology to reform mobile phones with a more developed shape and function than that of 1997. In 1997, the network-entry certificates in mobile phone, which were issued by the former the Electronic Post Department of the Ministry of Post Service had been registered until No.172. While by the third quarter of 98, the number of the registered certificates had been up to over 100, which including the new ones and the old renewed ones, followed by some others by the end of the year. In comparison, some producers had presented some more advanced sorts of mobile phones consequently, such as the double-channeled ones that are popular in the market, the hi-fi environmental-protective ones, the Chinese-displaying ones and the cover-equipped ones. In 1998, the producers even introduced the top "Zhangzhongbao", so called the mini types and the populous ones.

The development of mobile phone market in 1998 can be concluded as the following four features:

First, a preference for simples and much more functional. Being simple is one of the biggest calls from users. For the moment, almost all mobile phones in market are mainly equipped with illustration of in-call message, vibration reminding, recording and a large store of message, featured with the functions of ally with BP in same number and the picking-free dialing system, which are all simple in operation.

Second, the mini-types and intellectual power. For the past years, more and more super mini-typed mobile phones have come to the market in more versatile sorts. With the development and the popularity of PC and internet, the functions of mobile phone have expanded to fax, storing of email, arrangement of personal message and internet exploring, which make it a small mobile office.

Third, emphasis in personality and versatility. In 98, the producers like Motorola, Ericsson, Nokia, Alcatel, Sagem, Panasonic and Sumsang have presented multicolored covering for the mobile phones and even named them "Changeable as will" or "Fashionable Mobil phone" that appeal most to ladies. Some producers also introduced the personal designed products, with more than 10 kinds music ringing instead of the former single one, and a bigger screen.

Fourth, the populaces sense. Some brands are developing some special types for the salaried people which has brought the mobile phone to populace.

With the entering into the WTO around the corner, the electronic communication market is facing an open while the government is still propping the national brands. In the beginning of 1999, the self-developing GMS mobile phones and the promotion of CDMA industrialization, had been enlisted by the National Planning Committee and The Ministry of Science Technology into the "Guidance on Current Emphasis Fields of Priory Developed High Technological Industrialization". And the Ministry of Information collected a proceeds of 400 million yuan to prop up the national brands developed by our enterprises.

1.电脑 / Personal Computer

● 北京 / Beijing

1-1 家用电脑拥有比例/ Personal Computer Ownership

	人数 Number	百分比 Percent
没有 no	685	67.7
有 yes	327	32.3

n=1012

1-2 家用电脑拥有量/ Number of Personal Computer Owned per Household

	人数 Number	百分比 Percent
1 台 set	298	92.8
2 台 sets	22	6.9
3 台及以上 3 sets or over	1	0.3

n=321

1-3 对家中现有电脑（指最近购买的一台）四个方面的描述/ About the Personal Computer Most Recently Purchased

1-3-1 现有品牌排名/ Ranking of the Brands of the Currently Owned Personal Computer

排名 Brand Ranking	品牌 Brands	人数 Number	百分比 Percent
1	兼容机 Compatibility	157	51.0
2	联想 Legend	55	17.9
3	长城 Great Wall	12	3.9
4	康柏 Compaq	8	2.6
5	IBM	6	1.9
6	柏安 Bai'an	5	1.6
6	方正 Founder	5	1.6
7	恒生 Hengsheng	4	1.3
8	飞利浦 Philips	3	1.0
8	东芝 Toshiba	3	1.0
8	同方 Tong Fang	3	1.0
8	四通 Stone	3	1.0
8	宏基 Acer	3	1.0

n=308

1-3-2 该电脑的类型/ The Type of this Personal Computer

	人数 Number	百分比 Percent
台式机 computer	306	95.9
笔记本式 notebook	13	4.1

n=319

1-3-3 该电脑的购买时间/ Time of Purchasing of the Currently Owned Personal Computer

	人数 Number	百分比 Percent
1990 年或以前 1990 or before	2	0.6
1991-1994 年	20	6.3
1995 年	19	6.0
1996 年	36	11.3
1997 年	58	18.2
1998 年	92	28.8
1999 年	92	28.8

n=319

1-3-4 该电脑的价格/ The Price of the Currently Owned Personal Computer

	人数 Number	百分比 Percent
5000 元以下 below 5000 yuan	25	7.9
5000-8000 元 yuan	88	27.7
8000-10000 元 yuan	77	24.2
10000-15000 元 yuan	106	33.3
15000 元以上 over 15000 yuan	22	6.9

n=318

1-4 对该电脑的使用情况/ About the Use of the Personal Computer Most Recently Purchased

1-4-1 该电脑的主要使用者/ Users of This Personal Computer

	人数 Number	自己 myself	自己不用，家里其他人都用 family members use it except me	自己不用，家里其他部分人用 some of family members use it	全家人都用 all of my family use it
样本 Sample	323	41.5	8.4	18.0	32.2
男性 Male	169	48.5	5.3	14.8	31.4
16~24 岁 Age	53	75.5	1.9	1.9	20.8
25~34 岁 Age	44	56.8	2.3	2.3	38.6
35~44 岁 Age	31	29.0	3.2	22.6	45.2
45~54 岁 Age	25	28.0	20.0	32.0	20.0
55~60 岁 Age	16	6.3	6.3	50.0	37.5
女性 Female	154	33.8	11.7	21.4	33.1
16~24 岁 Age	45	80.0	2.2	2.2	15.6
25~34 岁 Age	32	31.3	9.4	12.5	46.9
35~44 岁 Age	38	10.5	21.1	21.1	47.4
45~54 岁 Age	28	7.1	10.7	46.4	35.7
55~60 岁 Age	11	0.0	27.3	63.6	9.1

1-4-2 该电脑是否上因特网/ Whether the Currently Owned Computer is Networked

	人数 Number	百分比 Percent
是 yes	115	35.6
否 no	208	64.4

n=323

1-4-3 上网的目的/ Purpose of Using Internet

注：本题为多选题，合计百分比超过 100%（Multiple answers）

	人次 Person-time	百分比 Percent
收发 E-mail	81	70.4
普通浏览 internet skimming	76	66.1
聊天 Chatting	15	13.0
玩游戏 playing game	10	8.7
听音乐 enjoying music	3	2.6
下载软件 downloading	46	40.0
处理公务 handle business affairs	13	11.3
购物 purchasing	1	0.9
教育（如网络授课）education on line	9	7.8
打电话 telephone call	4	3.5
其他 others	7	6.1

n=115

1-4-4 该电脑的主要用途/ Main Use of this Personal Computer

注：本题为多选题，合计百分比超过 100%（Multiple answers）

	人次 Person-time	百分比 Percent
日常文字处理 daily word processing	130	40.9
玩电脑游戏 computer game	178	56.0
教育学习 education	132	41.5
查阅国际互联网 Internet 信息 internet skimming	59	18.6
接发电子邮件 E-mail sent & receive e-mail	56	17.6
家庭财务、档案管理 family finance or file management	10	3.1
在家处理公务 handle business affairs at home	37	11.6
看 VCD watch VCD	64	20.1
听音乐 enjoy music	31	9.7
图像处理 picture or photo processing	21	6.6
炒股 stock use	30	9.4
其他 others	6	1.9

n=318

1-5 家用电脑未来一年购买打算/ Plan for Future Purchasing of a Personal Computer

1-5-1 是否打算购买/ Whether Planning to Buy a Personal Computer Next Year

	人数 Number	百分比 Percent
打算买 yes	262	26.0
不打算买 no	746	74.0

n=1008

1-5-2 打算购买的品牌/ Ranking of the Brands Planned to Purchase

排名 Brand Ranking	品牌 Brands	人数 Number	百分比 Percent
1	联想 Legend	84	32.8
2	兼容机 Compatibility	41	16.0
3	IBM	32	12.5
4	康柏 Compaq	13	5.1
5	柏安 Bai'an	9	3.5
6	长城 Great Wall	8	3.1
7	惠普 HP	6	2.3
7	东芝 Toshiba	6	2.3
8	飞利浦 Philips	5	2.0
8	四通 Stone	5	2.0

n=256

1-5-3 打算购买的类型/ The Type of the Personal Computer Planned to Purchase

	人数 Number	百分比 Percent
台式机 computer	234	90.7
笔记本式 notebook	24	9.3

n=258

1-6 理想品牌排名/ Ranking of the Ideal Brands of Personal Computer

排名 Brand Ranking	品牌 Brands	人数 Number	百分比 Percent
1	联想 Legend	330	32.6
2	IBM	147	14.5
3	康柏 Compaq	62	6.1
4	苹果 Apple	19	1.9
5	惠普 HP	15	1.5
5	长城 Great Wall	15	1.5
6	飞利浦 Philips	12	1.2
7	方正 Founder	11	1.1
8	四通 Stone	10	1.0
8	宏基 Acer	10	1.0

n=1012

1-7 不同消费者层的理想品牌/ The Ideal Brands by Market Segments

1-7-1 时尚流行指标/ Fads Popular Index

	人数 Number	第一品牌及百分比 1st/ percent	第二品牌及百分比 2nd/ percent	第三品牌及百分比 3rd/ percent
样本 Sample	998	**联想 Legend(32.6)**	**IBM(14.6)**	**康柏 Compaq(6.0)**
平实生活指向 simple living orientation	491	联想 Legend(31.2)	IBM(14.9)	康柏 Compaq(6.7)
时尚流行指向 fashion orientation	507	联想 Legend(33.9)	IBM(14.4)	康柏 Compaq(5.3)

1-7-2 广告态度指标/ Advertising Attitude Index

	人数 Number	第一品牌及百分比 1st/ percent	第二品牌及百分比 2nd/ percent	第三品牌及百分比 3rd/ percent
样本 Sample	994	**联想 Legend(32.3)**	**IBM(14.7)**	**康柏 Compaq(6.1)**
广告淡漠指向 indifferent orientation	289	联想 Legend(32.5)	IBM(13.5)	康柏 Compaq(5.2)
中间层 medium	572	联想 Legend(32.5)	IBM(15.6)	康柏 Compaq(6.6)
信赖广告指向 loyal orientation	133	联想 Legend(30.8)	IBM(13.5)	康柏 Compaq(6.0)

1-7-3 价格态度指标/ Price Attitude Index

	人数 Number	第一品牌及百分比 1st/ percent	第二品牌及百分比 2nd/ percent	第三品牌及百分比 3rd/ percent
样本 Sample	1002	**联想 Legend(32.5)**	**IBM(14.7)**	**康柏 Compaq(6.1)**
价格无关心指向 indifferent orientation	203	联想 Legend(32.5)	IBM(19.7)	康柏 Compaq(6.4)
中间层 medium	501	联想 Legend(34.7)	IBM(15.6)	康柏 Compaq(5.8)
价格重视指向 careful orientation	298	联想 Legend(28.9)	IBM(9.7)	康柏 Compaq(6.4)

● 上海 / Shanghai

1-1 家用电脑拥有比例/ Personal Computer Ownership

	人数 Number	百分比 Percent
没有 no	836	82.4
有 yes	178	17.6

n=1014

1-2 家用电脑拥有量/ Number of Personal Computer Owned per Household

	人数 Number	百分比 Percent
1 台 set	165	93.8
2 台 sets	10	5.7
3 台及以上 3 sets or over	1	0.6

n=176

1-3 对家中现有电脑（指最近购买的一台）四个方面的描述/ About the Personal Computer Most Recently Purchased

1-3-1 现有品牌排名/ Ranking of the Brands of the Currently Owned Personal Computer

排名 Brand Ranking	品牌 Brands	人数 Number	百分比 Percent
1	兼容机 Compatibility	84	48.0
2	东海 Donghai	19	10.9
3	IBM	11	6.3
4	联想 Legend	9	5.1
5	飞利浦 Philips	6	3.4
6	华东 Huadong	5	2.9
7	康柏 Compaq	4	2.3
8	实达 Start	3	1.7
8	方正 Founder	3	1.7
8	宏基 Acer	3	1.7
8	NEC	3	1.7
9	长城 Great Wall	2	1.1
9	虹志 AST	2	1.1
9	苹果 Apple	2	1.1

n=175

1-3-2 该电脑的类型/ The Type of this Personal Computer

	人数 Number	百分比 Percent
台式机 computer	167	96.5
笔记本式 notebook	6	3.5

n=173

1-3-3 该电脑的购买时间/The Time of Purchasing of the Currently Owned Personal Computer

	人数 Number	百分比 Percent
1990 年或以前 1990 or before	0	0.0
1991-1994 年	9	5.1
1995 年	10	5.7
1996 年	19	10.9
1997 年	33	18.9
1998 年	64	36.6
1999 年	40	22.9

n=175

1-3-4 该电脑的价格/ The Price of the Currently Owned Personal Computer

	人数 Number	百分比 Percent
5000 元以下 below 5000 yuan	8	4.6
5000-8000 元 yuan	59	33.7
8000-10000 元 yuan	52	29.7
10000-15000 元 yuan	48	27.4
15000 元以上 over 15000 yuan	8	4.6

n=175

1-4 对该电脑的使用情况/ About the Use of the Personal Computer Most Recently Purchased

1-4-1 该电脑的主要使用者/ Users of This Personal Computer

	人数 Number	自己 myself	自己不用，家里其他人都用 family members use it except me	自己不用，家里其他部分人用 some of family members use it	全家人都用 all of my family use it
样本 Sample	176	47.7	11.9	17.0	23.3
男性 Male	89	61.8	4.5	12.4	21.3
16~24 岁 Age	35	88.6	0.0	0.0	11.4
25~34 岁 Age	18	72.2	5.6	0.0	22.2
35~44 岁 Age	14	42.9	0.0	14.3	42.9
45~54 岁 Age	17	23.5	11.8	41.2	23.5
55~60 岁 Age	5	20.0	20.0	40.0	20.0
女性 Female	87	33.3	19.5	21.8	25.3
16~24 岁 Age	24	58.3	4.2	4.2	33.3
25~34 岁 Age	20	60.0	10.0	5.0	25.0
35~44 岁 Age	14	7.1	28.6	28.6	35.7
45~54 岁 Age	21	9.5	23.8	47.6	19.0
55~60 岁 Age	8	0.0	62.5	37.5	0.0

1-4-2 该电脑是否上因特网/ Whether the Currently Owned Computer is Networked

	人数 Number	百分比 Percent
是 yes	76	43.2
否 no	100	56.8

n=176

1-4-3 上网的目的/ Purpose of Using Internet

注：本题为多选题，合计百分比超过 100%（Multiple answers）

	人次 Person-time	百分比 Percent
收发 E-mail	47	62.7
普通浏览 internet skimming	47	62.7
聊天 Chatting	14	18.7
玩游戏 playing game	14	18.7
听音乐 enjoying music	6	8.0
下载软件 downloading	35	46.7
处理公务 handle business affairs	5	6.7
购物 purchasing	1	1.3
教育（如网络授课）education on line	6	8.0
打电话 telephone call	0	0.0
其他 others	2	2.7

n=75

1-4-4 该电脑的主要用途/ Main Use of this Personal Computer

注：本题为多选题，合计百分比超过 100%（Multiple answers）

	人次 Person-time	百分比 Percent
日常文字处理 daily word processing	57	32.8
玩电脑游戏 computer game	101	58.0
教育学习 education	78	44.8
查阅国际互联网 Internet 信息 internet skimming	42	24.1
接发电子邮件 E-mail sent & receive e-mail	33	19.0
家庭财务、档案管理 family finance or file management	7	4.0
在家处理公务 handle business affairs at home	12	6.9
看 VCD watch VCD	30	17.2
听音乐 enjoy music	26	14.9
图像处理 picture or photo processing	9	5.2
炒股 stock use	17	9.8
其他 others	1	0.6

n=174

1-5 家用电脑未来一年购买打算/ Plan for Future Purchasing of a Personal Computer

1-5-1 是否打算购买/ Whether Planning to Buy a Personal Computer Next Year

	人数 Number	百分比 Percent
打算买 yes	223	22.0
不打算买 no	791	78.0

n=1014

1-5-2 打算购买的品牌/ Ranking of the Brands Planned to Purchase

排名 Brand Ranking	品牌 Brands	人数 Number	百分比 Percent
1	联想 Legend	61	27.6
2	兼容机 Compatibility	41	18.6
3	IBM	40	18.1
4	康柏 Compaq	14	6.3
5	惠普 HP	10	4.5
6	东海 Donghai	9	4.1
7	苹果 Apple	6	2.7
8	NEC	5	2.3
8	东芝 Toshiba	5	2.3
8	飞利浦 Philips	5	2.3
8	西门子 Siemens	5	2.3

n=221

1-5-3 打算购买的类型/ The Type of the Personal Computer Planned to Purchase

	人数 Number	百分比 Percent
台式机 computer	205	92.8
笔记本式 notebook	16	7.2

n=221

1-6 理想品牌排名/ Ranking of the Ideal Brands of Personal Computer

排名 Brand Ranking	品牌 Brands	人数 Number	百分比 Percent
1	联想 Legend	220	21.7
2	IBM	195	19.2
3	东海 Donghai	73	7.2
4	康柏 Compaq	51	5.0
5	苹果 Apple	43	4.2
6	NEC	34	3.4
7	惠普 HP	28	2.8
8	飞利浦 Philips	24	2.4
9	东芝 Toshiba	19	1.9
10	长城 Great Wall	17	1.7
11	西门子 Siemens	16	1.6
12	实达 Start	11	1.1
13	宏基 Acer	8	0.8

n=1013

1-7 不同消费者层理想品牌/ The Ideal Brands by Market Segments

1-7-1 时尚流行指标/ Fads Popular Index

	人数 Number	第一品牌及百分比 1st/ percent	第二品牌及百分比 2nd/ percent	第三品牌及百分比 3rd/ percent
样本 Sample	1004	**联想 Legend(21.5)**	**IBM(19.2)**	**东海 East Sea(7.3)**
平实生活指向 simple living orientation	471	联想 Legend(20.8)	IBM(16.6)	东海 East Sea (8.3)
时尚流行指向 fashion orientation	533	联想 Legend(22.1)	IBM(21.6)	东海 East Sea (6.4)

1-7-2 广告态度指标/ Advertising Attitude Index

	人数 Number	第一品牌及百分比 1st/ percent	第二品牌及百分比 2nd/ percent	第三品牌及百分比 3rd/ percent
样本 Sample	1001	**联想 Legend(21.7)**	**IBM(19.1)**	**东海 East Sea (7.2)**
广告淡漠指向 indifferent orientation	256	联想 Legend(21.5)	IBM(13.7)	东海 East Sea (8.6)
中间层 medium	610	联想 Legend(21.3) IBM(21.3)	东海 East Sea (6.6)	康柏 Compaq(5.1)
信赖广告指向 loyal orientation	135	联想 Legend(23.7)	IBM(19.3)	苹果 Apple(7.4) 东海 East Sea (7.4)

1-7-3 价格态度指标/ Price Attitude Index

	人数 Number	第一品牌及百分比 1st/ percent	第二品牌及百分比 2nd/ percent	第三品牌及百分比 3rd/ percent
样本 Sample	1010	**联想 Legend(21.6)**	**IBM(19.3)**	**东海 East Sea (7.2)**
价格无关心指向 indifferent orientation	151	IBM(24.5)	联想 Legend(18.5)	东海 East Sea (7.9)
中间层 medium	520	联想 Legend(21.5)	IBM(20.6)	东海 East Sea (7.3)
价格重视指向 careful orientation	339	联想 Legend(23.0)	IBM(15.0)	东海 East Sea (6.8)

● 广州 / Guangzhou

1-1 家用电脑拥有比例/ Personal Computer Ownership

	人数 Number	百分比 Percent
没有 no	716	69.2
有 yes	318	30.8

n=1034

1-2 家用电脑拥有量/ Number of Personal Computer Owned per Household

	人数 Number	百分比 Percent
1 台 set	294	93.3
2 台 sets	20	6.3
3 台及以上 3 sets or over	1	0.3

n=315

1-3 对家中现有电脑（指最近购买的一台）四个方面的描述/ About the Personal Computer Most Recently Purchased

1-3-1 现有品牌排名/ Ranking of the Brands of the Currently Owned Personal Computer

排名 Brand Ranking	品牌 Brands	人数 Number	百分比 Percent
1	兼容机 Compatibility	211	66.8
2	联想 Legend	25	7.9
3	IBM	19	6.0
4	飞利浦 Philips	14	4.4
5	NEC	8	2.5

n=316

1-3-2 该电脑的类型/ The Type of this Personal Computer

	人数 Number	百分比 Percent
台式机 computer	306	99.0
笔记本式 notebook	3	1.0

n=309

1-3-3 该电脑的购买时间/ Time of Purchasing of the Currently Owned Personal Computer

	人数 Number	百分比 Percent
1990 年或以前 1990 or before	3	1.0
1991-1994 年	17	5.4
1995 年	21	6.7
1996 年	42	13.3
1997 年	64	20.3
1998 年	99	31.4
1999 年	69	21.9

n=315

1-3-4 该电脑的价格/ The Price of the Currently Owned Personal Computer

	人数 Number	百分比 Percent
5000 元以下 below 5000 yuan	49	15.7
5000-8000 元 yuan	128	41.0
8000-10000 元 yuan	68	21.8
10000-15000 元 yuan	61	19.6
15000 元以上 over 15000 yuan	6	1.9

n=312

1-4 对该电脑的使用情况/ About the Use of the Personal Computer Most Recently Purchased

1-4-1 该电脑的主要使用者/ Users of This Personal Computer

	人数 Number	自己 myself	自己不用，家里其他人都用 family members use it except me	自己不用，家里其他部分人用 some of family members use it	全家人都用 all of my family use it
样本 Sample	316	40.5	10.8	21.5	27.2
男性 Male	164	50.6	9.1	16.5	23.8
16~24 岁 Age	52	80.8	0.0	7.7	11.5
25~34 岁 Age	42	71.4	2.4	2.4	23.8
35~44 岁 Age	31	19.4	9.7	32.3	38.7
45~54 岁 Age	27	18.5	29.6	22.2	29.6
55~60 岁 Age	12	0.0	25.0	50.0	25.0
女性 Female	152	29.6	12.5	27.0	30.9
16~24 岁 Age	44	54.5	2.3	11.4	31.8
25~34 岁 Age	33	27.3	9.1	27.3	36.4
35~44 岁 Age	33	15.2	15.2	27.3	42.4
45~54 岁 Age	30	16.7	26.7	36.7	20.0
55~60 岁 Age	12	16.7	16.7	58.3	8.3

1-4-2 该电脑是否上因特网/ Whether the Currently Owned Computer is Networked

	人数 Number	百分比 Percent
是 yes	78	24.8
否 no	236	75.2

n=314

1-4-3 上网的目的/ Purpose of Using Internet

注：本题为多选题，合计百分比超过 100%（Multiple answers）

	人次 Person-time	百分比 Percent
收发 E-mail	54	70.1
普通浏览 internet skimming	55	71.4
聊天 chatting	13	16.9
玩游戏 playing game	11	14.3
听音乐 enjoying music	2	2.6
下载软件 downloading	34	44.2
处理公务 handle business affairs	11	14.3
购物 purchasing	0	0.0
教育（如网络授课）education on line	2	2.6
打电话 telephone call	1	1.3
其他 others	3	3.9

n=77

1-4-4 该电脑的主要用途/ Main Use of this Personal Computer

注：本题为多选题，合计百分比超过 100%（Multiple answers）

	人次 Person-time	百分比 Percent
日常文字处理 daily word processing	134	43.4
玩电脑游戏 computer game	190	61.5
教育学习 education	140	45.3
查阅国际互联网 Internet 信息 internet skimming	39	12.6
接发电子邮件 E-mail sent & receive e-mail	34	11.0
家庭财务、档案管理 family finance or file management	12	3.9
在家处理公务 handle business affairs at home	23	7.4
看 VCD watch VCD	46	14.9
听音乐 enjoy music	65	21.0
图像处理 picture or photo processing	24	7.8
炒股 stock use	14	4.5
其他 others	8	2.6

n=309

1-5 家用电脑未来一年购买打算/ Plan for Future Purchasing of a Personal Computer

1-5-1 是否打算购买/ Whether Planning to Buy a Personal Computer Next Year

	人数 Number	百分比 Percent
打算买 yes	230	22.3
不打算买 no	802	77.7

n=1032

1-5-2 打算购买的品牌/ Ranking of the Brands Planned to Purchase

排名 Brand Ranking	品牌 Brands	人数 Number	百分比 Percent
1	兼容机 Compatibility	60	26.3
2	联想 Legend	49	21.5
3	IBM	45	19.7
4	飞利浦 Philips	14	6.1
5	苹果 Apple	13	5.7

n=228

1-5-3 打算购买的类型/ The Type of the Personal Computer Planned to Purchase

	人数 Number	百分比 Percent
台式机 computer	209	91.3
笔记本式 notebook	20	8.7

n=229

1-6 理想品牌排名/ Ranking of the Ideal Brands of Personal Computer

排名 Brand Ranking	品牌 Brands	人数 Number	百分比 Percent
1	IBM	244	23.6
2	联想 Legend	187	18.1
3	苹果 Apple	45	4.4
4	康柏 Compaq	38	3.7
5	飞利浦 Philips	30	2.9
6	NEC	26	2.5
7	长城 Great Wall	24	2.3

n=1034

1-7 不同消费者层的理想品牌/ The Ideal Brands by Market Segments

1-7-1 时尚流行指标/ Fads Popular Index

	人数 Number	第一品牌及百分比 1st/ percent	第二品牌及百分比 2nd/ percent	第三品牌及百分比 3rd/ percent
样本 Sample	1022	**IBM(23.9)**	**联想 Legend(17.8)**	**苹果 Apple(4.3)**
平实生活指向 simple living orientation	518	IBM(20.3)	联想 Legend(18.0)	苹果 Apple(3.9)
时尚流行指向 fashion orientation	504	IBM(27.6)	联想 Legend(17.7)	苹果 Apple(4.8)

1-7-2 广告态度指标/ Advertising Attitude Index

	人数 Number	第一品牌及百分比 1st/ percent	第二品牌及百分比 2nd/ percent	第三品牌及百分比 3rd/ percent
样本 Sample	1022	**IBM(23.6)**	**联想 Legend(18.0)**	**苹果 Apple(4.3)**
广告淡漠指向 indifferent orientation	334	IBM(23.7)	联想 Legend(17.4)	苹果 Apple(4.2)
中间层 medium	593	IBM(23.8)	联想 Legend(19.4)	苹果 Apple(4.6)
信赖广告指向 loyal orientation	95	IBM(22.1)	联想 Legend(11.6)	康柏 Compaq(7.4)

1-7-3 价格态度指标/ Price Attitude Index

	人数 Number	第一品牌及百分比 1st/ percent	第二品牌及百分比 2nd/ percent	第三品牌及百分比 3rd/ percent
样本 Sample	1028	**IBM(23.7)**	**联想 Legend(18.2)**	**苹果 Apple(4.4)**
价格无关心指向 indifferent orientation	188	IBM(26.1)	联想 Legend(16.5)	苹果 Apple(5.9)
中间层 medium	549	IBM(26.0)	联想 Legend(17.1)	苹果 Apple(4.2)
价格重视指向 careful orientation	291	联想 Legend(21.3)	IBM(17.9)	苹果 Apple(3.8)

● 重庆 / Chongqing

1-1 家用电脑拥有比例/ Personal Computer Ownership

	人数 Number	百分比 Percent
没有 no	568	91.0
有 yes	56	9.0

n=624

1-2 家用电脑拥有量/ Number of Personal Computer Owned per Household

	人数 Number	百分比 Percent
1 台 set	50	94.3
2 台 sets	3	5.7
3 台及以上 3 sets or over	0	0.0

n=53

1-3 对家中现有电脑（指最近购买的一台）四个方面的描述/ About the Personal Computer Most Recently Purchased

1-3-1 现有品牌排名/ Ranking of the Brands of the Currently Owned Personal Computer

排名 Brand Ranking	品牌 Brands	人数 Number	百分比 Percent
1	兼容机 Compatibility	31	59.6
2	联想 Legend	7	13.5
3	方正 Founder	2	3.8
3	实达 Start	2	3.8
3	爱莎 ASR	2	3.8
3	NEC	2	3.8

n=52

1-3-2 该电脑的类型/ The Type of this Personal Computer

	人数 Number	百分比 Percent
台式机 computer	51	98.1
笔记本式 notebook	1	1.9

n=52

1-3-3 该电脑的购买时间/ Time of Purchasing of the Currently Owned Personal Computer

	人数 Number	百分比 Percent
1990 年或以前 1990 or before	0	0.0
1991-1994 年	1	1.9
1995 年	2	3.8
1996 年	1	1.9
1997 年	7	13.5
1998 年	19	36.5
1999 年	22	42.3

n=52

1-3-4 该电脑的价格/ The Price of the Currently Owned Personal Computer

	人数 Number	百分比 Percent
5000 元以下 below 5000 yuan	5	9.6
5000-8000 元 yuan	22	42.3
8000-10000 元 yuan	10	19.2
10000-15000 元 yuan	14	26.9
15000 元以上 over 15000 yuan	1	1.9

n=52

1-4 对该电脑的使用情况/ About the Use of the Personal Computer Most Recently Purchased

1-4-1 该电脑的主要使用者/ Users of this Personal Computer

	人数 Number	自己 myself	自己不用，家里其他人都用 family members use it except me	自己不用，家里其他部分人用 some of family members use it	全家人都用 all of my family use it
样本 Sample	51	31.4	7.8	31.4	29.4
男性 Male	28	42.9	0.0	32.1	25.0
16~24 岁 Age	6	83.3	0.0	0.0	16.7
25~34 岁 Age	6	33.3	0.0	16.7	50.0
35~44 岁 Age	7	57.1	0.0	28.6	14.3
45~54 岁 Age	3	33.3	0.0	33.3	33.3
55~60 岁 Age	6	0.0	0.0	83.3	16.7
女性 Female	23	17.4	17.4	30.4	34.8
16~24 岁 Age	7	42.9	14.3	14.3	28.6
25~34 岁 Age	5	0.0	0.0	20.0	80.0
35~44 岁 Age	5	20.0	20.0	40.0	20.0
45~54 岁 Age	6	0.0	33.3	50.0	16.7
55~60 岁 Age	0	0.0	0.0	0.0	0.0

1-4-2 该电脑是否上因特网/ Whether the Currently Owned Computer is Networked

	人数 Number	百分比 Percent
是 yes	12	23.1
否 no	40	76.9

n=52

1-4-3 上网的目的/ Purpose of Using Internet

注：本题为多选题，合计百分比超过 100%（Multiple answers）

	人次 Person-time	百分比 Percent
收发 E-mail	6	50.0
普通浏览 internet skimming	9	75.0
聊天 Chatting	2	16.7
玩游戏 playing game	4	33.3
听音乐 enjoying music	0	0.0
下载软件 downloading	3	25.0
处理公务 handle business affairs	3	25.0
购物 purchasing	0	0.0
教育（如网络授课）education on line	2	16.7
打电话 telephone call	0	0.0
其他 others	0	0.0

n=12

1-4-4 该电脑的主要用途/ Main Use of this Personal Computer

注：本题为多选题，合计百分比超过 100%（Multiple answers）

	人次 Person-time	百分比 Percent
日常文字处理 daily word processing	22	42.3
玩电脑游戏 PC game	36	69.2
教育学习 education	21	40.4
查阅国际互联网 Internet 信息 internet skimming	8	15.4
接发电子邮件 E-mail sent & receive e-mail	4	7.7
家庭财务、档案管理 family finance or file management	1	1.9
在家处理公务 handle business affairs at home	4	7.7
看 VCD watch VCD	8	15.4
听音乐 enjoy music	9	17.3
图像处理 picture or photo processing	1	1.9
炒股 stock use	5	9.6
其他 others	3	5.8

n=52

1-5 家用电脑未来一年购买打算/ Plan for Future Purchasing of a Personal Computer

1-5-1 是否打算购买/ Whether Planning to Buy a Personal Computer Next Year

	人数 Number	百分比 Percent
打算买 yes	96	15.4
不打算买 no	528	84.6

n=624

1-5-2 打算购买的品牌/ Ranking of the Brands Planned to Purchase

排名 Brand Ranking	品牌 Brands	人数 Number	百分比 Percent
1	联想 Legend	27	29.7
2	兼容机 Compatibility	17	18.7
3	飞利浦 Philips	8	8.8
4	IBM	6	6.6
5	东芝 Toshiba	5	5.5
6	NEC	4	4.4
7	同方 Tong Fang	3	3.3

n=91

1-5-3 打算购买的类型/ The Type of the Personal Computer Planned to Purchase

	人数 Number	百分比 Percent
台式机 computer	82	92.1
笔记本式 notebook	7	7.9

n=89

1-6 理想品牌排名/ Ranking of the Ideal Brands of Personal Computer

排名 Brand Ranking	品牌 Brands	人数 Number	百分比 Percent
1	联想 Legend	159	25.5
2	长城 Great Wall	28	4.5
3	IBM	26	4.2
4	飞利浦 Philips	23	3.7
5	方正 Founder	13	2.1
6	苹果 Apple	12	1.9
6	TCL	12	1.9
7	东芝 Toshiba	10	1.6
8	NEC	8	1.3
8	同方 Tong Fang	8	1.3
9	康柏 Compaq	7	1.1
10	惠普 HP	6	1.0

n=624

1-7 不同消费者层的理想品牌/ The Ideal Brands by Market Segments

1-7-1 时尚流行指标/ Fads Popular Index

	人数 Number	第一品牌及百分比 1st/ percent	第二品牌及百分比 2nd/ percent	第三品牌及百分比 3rd/ percent
样本 Sample	616	**联想 Legend(25.3)**	**长城 Great Wall(4.4)**	**IBM(4.2)**
平实生活指向 simple living orientation	369	联想 Legend(24.7)	IBM(4.6)	长城 Great Wall(4.3)
时尚流行指向 fashion orientation	247	联想 Legend(26.3)	长城 Great Wall(4.5)	飞利浦 Philips(3.6) IBM(3.6)

1-7-2 广告态度指标/ Advertising Attitude Index

	人数 Number	第一品牌及百分比 1st/ percent	第二品牌及百分比 2nd/ percent	第三品牌及百分比 3rd/ percent
样本 Sample	618	**联想 Legend(25.4)**	**长城 Great Wall(4.4)**	**IBM(4.2)**
广告淡漠指向 indifferent orientation	167	联想 Legend(19.2)	IBM(6.6)	飞利浦 Philips(4.8)
中间层 medium	367	联想 Legend(28.6)	长城 Great Wall(4.1)	方正 Founder(3.3)
信赖广告指向 loyal orientation	84	联想 Legend(23.8)	IBM(7.1)	飞利浦 Philips(6.0) 长城 Great Wall(6.0)

1-7-3 价格态度指标/ Price Attitude Index

	人数 Number	第一品牌及百分比 1st/ percent	第二品牌及百分比 2nd/ percent	第三品牌及百分比 3rd/ percent
样本 Sample	615	**联想 Legend(25.5)**	**长城 Great Wall(4.6)**	**IBM(4.1)**
价格无关心指向 indifferent orientation	106	联想 Legend(28.3)	IBM(8.5)	苹果 Apple(4.7)
中间层 medium	280	联想 Legend(28.6)	长城 Great Wall(5.1)	IBM(4.3)
价格重视指向 careful orientation	229	联想 Legend(20.5)	飞利浦 Philips(5.2)	长城 Great Wall(4.4)

● 武汉 / Wuhan

1-1 家用电脑拥有比例/ Personal Computer Ownership

	人数 Number	百分比 Percent
没有 no	559	87.1
有 yes	83	12.9

n=642

1-2 家用电脑拥有量/ Number of Personal Computer Owned per Household

	人数 Number	百分比 Percent
1 台 set	78	95.1
2 台 sets	3	3.7
3 台及以上 3 sets or over	1	1.2

n=82

1-3 对家中现有电脑（指最近购买的一台）四个方面的描述/ About the Personal Computer Most Recently Purchased

1-3-1 现有品牌排名/ Ranking of the Brands of the Currently Owned Personal Computer

排名 Brand Ranking	品牌 Brands	人数 Number	百分比 Percent
1	兼容机 Compatibility	62	74.7
2	联想 Legend	5	6.0
3	惠普 HP	2	2.4
3	宏基 Acer	2	2.4

n=83

1-3-2 该电脑的类型/ The Type of this Personal Computer

	人数 Number	百分比 Percent
台式机 computer	82	98.8
笔记本式 notebook	1	1.2

n=83

1-3-3 该电脑的购买时间/ Time of Purchasing of the Currently Owned Personal Computer

	人数 Number	百分比 Percent
1990 年或以前 1990 or before	0	0.0
1991-1994 年	4	5.0
1995 年	2	2.5
1996 年	10	12.5
1997 年	20	25.0
1998 年	20	25.0
1999 年	24	30.0

n=80

1-3-4 该电脑的价格/ The Price of the Currently Owned Personal Computer

	人数 Number	百分比 Percent
5000 元以下 below 5000 yuan	11	14.1
5000-8000 元 yuan	38	48.7
8000-10000 元 yuan	17	21.8
10000-15000 元 yuan	10	12.8
15000 元以上 over 15000 yuan	2	2.6

n=78

1-4 对该电脑的使用情况/ About the Use of the Personal Computer Most Recently Purchased

1-4-1 该电脑的主要使用者/ Users of This Personal Computer

	人数 Number	自己 myself	自己不用，家里其他人都用 family members use it except me	自己不用，家里其他部分人用 some of family members use it	全家人都用 all of my family use it
样本 Sample	81	39.5	8.6	22.2	29.6
男性 Male	43	48.8	11.6	16.3	23.3
16~24 岁 Age	18	88.9	0.0	0.0	11.1
25~34 岁 Age	10	40.0	10.0	20.0	30.0
35~44 岁 Age	5	20.0	20.0	20.0	40.0
45~54 岁 Age	8	0.0	37.5	25.0	37.5
55~60 岁 Age	2	0.0	0.0	100.0	0.0
女性 Female	38	28.9	5.3	28.9	36.8
16~24 岁 Age	12	66.7	0.0	8.3	25.0
25~34 岁 Age	7	28.6	0.0	0.0	71.4
35~44 岁 Age	3	0.0	0.0	33.3	66.7
45~54 岁 Age	13	7.7	7.7	53.8	30.8
55~60 岁 Age	3	0.0	33.3	66.7	0.0

1-4-2 该电脑是否上因特网/ Whether the Currently Owned Computer is Networked

	人数 Number	百分比 Percent
是 yes	16	19.3
否 no	67	80.7

n=83

1-4-3 上网的目的/ Purpose of Using Internet

注：本题为多选题，合计百分比超过 100%（Multiple answers）

	人次 Person-time	百分比 Percent
收发 E-mail	12	75.0
普通浏览 internet skimming	9	56.3
聊天 Chatting	1	6.3
玩游戏 playing game	1	6.3
听音乐 enjoying music	0	0.0
下载软件 downloading	7	43.8
处理公务 handle business affairs	0	0.0
购物 purchasing	0	0.0
教育（如网络授课）education on line	3	18.8
打电话 telephone call	2	12.5
其他 others	1	6.3

n=16

1-4-4 该电脑的主要用途/ Main Use of this Personal Computer

注：本题为多选题，合计百分比超过 100%（Multiple answers）

	人次 Person-time	百分比 Percent
日常文字处理 daily word processing	28	33.7
玩电脑游戏 computer game	51	61.4
教育学习 education	52	62.7
查阅国际互联网 Internet 信息 internet skimming	9	10.8
接发电子邮件 E-mail sent & receive e-mail	8	9.6
家庭财务、档案管理 family finance or file management	2	2.4
在家处理公务 handle business affairs at home	4	4.8
看 VCD watch VCD	16	19.3
听音乐 enjoy music	18	21.7
图像处理 picture or photo processing	8	9.6
炒股 stock use	4	4.8
其他 others	0	0.0

n=83

1-5 家用电脑未来一年购买打算/ Plan for Future Purchasing of a Personal Computer

1-5-1 是否打算购买/ Whether Planning to Buy a Personal Computer Next Year

	人数 Number	百分比 Percent
打算买 yes	120	18.7
不打算买 no	521	81.3

n=641

1-5-2 打算购买的品牌/ Ranking of the Brands Planned to Purchase

排名 Brand Ranking	品牌 Brands	人数 Number	百分比 Percent
1	兼容机 Compatibility	44	37.9
2	联想 Legend	26	22.4
4	IBM	9	7.8
5	长城 Great Wall	8	6.9
6	飞利浦 Philips	5	4.3
7	TCL	4	3.4
8	海信 Hisense	2	1.7
8	苹果 Apple	2	1.7

n=116

1-5-3 打算购买的类型/ The Type of the Personal Computer Planned to Purchase

	人数 Number	百分比 Percent
台式机 computer	111	94.1
笔记本式 notebook	7	5.9

n=118

1-6 理想品牌排名/ Ranking of the Ideal Brands of Personal Computer

排名 Brand Ranking	品牌 Brands	人数 Number	百分比 Percent
1	联想 Legend	124	19.3
2	IBM	62	9.7
3	长城 Great Wall	21	3.3
4	飞利浦 Philips	9	1.4
5	苹果 Apple	8	1.2
6	实达 Start	7	1.1
7	惠普 HP	6	0.9
7	康柏 Compaq	6	0.9
7	金长城 Great Wall	6	0.9

n=642

1-7 不同消费者层的理想品牌/ The Ideal Brands by Market Segments

1-7-1 时尚流行指标/ Fads Popular Index

	人数 Number	第一品牌及百分比 1st/ percent	第二品牌及百分比 2nd/ percent	第三品牌及百分比 3rd/ percent
样本 Sample	**632**	**联想 Legend(19.5)**	**IBM(9.8)**	**长城 Great Wall(3.3)**
平实生活指向 simple living orientation	330	联想 Legend(20.0)	IBM(7.9)	苹果 Apple(1.8)
时尚流行指向 fashion orientation	302	联想 Legend(18.9)	IBM(11.9)	长城 Great Wall(5.3)

1-7-2 广告态度指标/ Advertising Attitude Index

	人数 Number	第一品牌及百分比 1st/ percent	第二品牌及百分比 2nd/ percent	第三品牌及百分比 3rd/ percent
样本 Sample	**634**	**联想 Legend(19.4)**	**IBM(9.8)**	**长城 Great Wall(3.3)**
广告淡漠指向 indifferent orientation	188	联想 Legend(16.5)	IBM(8.0)	苹果 Apple(2.1)
中间层 medium	373	联想 Legend(19.8)	IBM(10.5)	长城 Great Wall(4.6)
信赖广告指向 loyal orientation	73	联想 Legend(24.7)	IBM(11.0)	四通 Stone(2.7)

1-7-3 价格态度指标/ Price Attitude Index

	人数 Number	第一品牌及百分比 1st/ percent	第二品牌及百分比 2nd/ percent	第三品牌及百分比 3rd/ percent
样本 Sample	**634**	**联想 Legend(19.4)**	**IBM(9.6)**	**长城 Great Wall(3.3)**
价格无关心指向 indifferent orientation	84	联想 Legend(17.9)	IBM(14.3)	苹果 Apple(3.6)
中间层 medium	306	联想 Legend(21.2)	IBM(9.8)	长城 Great Wall(3.9)
价格重视指向 careful orientation	244	联想 Legend(17.6)	IBM(7.8)	长城 Great Wall(2.9)

● 西安 / Xi'an

1-1 家用电脑拥有比例/ Personal Computer Ownership

	人数 Number	百分比 Percent
没有 no	539	89.8
有 yes	61	10.2

n=600

1-2 家用电脑拥有量/ Number of Personal Computer Owned per Household

	人数 Number	百分比 Percent
1 台 set	59	96.7
2 台 sets	2	3.3
3 台及以上 3 sets or over	0	0.0

n=61

1-3 对家中现有电脑（指最近购买的一台）四个方面的描述/ About the Personal Computer Most Recently Purchased

1-3-1 现有品牌排名/ Ranking of the Brands of the Currently Owned Personal Computer

排名 Brand Ranking	品牌 Brands	人数 Number	百分比 Percent
1	兼容机 Compatibility	41	67.2
2	联想 Legend	6	9.8
3	IPC	2	3.3
3	海信 Hisense	2	3.3

n=61

1-3-2 该电脑的类型/ The Type of this Personal Computer

	人数 Number	百分比 Percent
台式机 computer	59	96.7
笔记本式 notebook	2	3.3

n=61

1-3-3 该电脑的购买时间/ Time of Purchasing of the Currently Owned Personal Computer

	人数 Number	百分比 Percent
1990 年或以前 1990 or before	2	3.3
1991-1994 年	2	3.3
1995 年	8	13.1
1996 年	6	9.8
1997 年	11	18.0
1998 年	19	31.2
1999 年	13	21.3

n=61

1-3-4 该电脑的价格/ The Price of the Currently Owned Personal Computer

	人数 Number	百分比 Percent
5000 元以下 below 5000 yuan	9	15.0
5000-8000 元 yuan	22	36.7
8000-10000 元 yuan	14	23.3
10000-15000 元 yuan	11	18.3
15000 元以上 over 15000 yuan	4	6.7

n=60

1-4 对该电脑的使用情况/ About the Use of the Personal Computer Most Recently Purchased

1-4-1 该电脑的主要使用者/ Users of this Personal Computer

	人数 Number	自己 myself	自己不用，家里其他人都用 family members use it except me	自己不用，家里其他部分人用 some of family members use it	全家人都用 all of my family use it
样本 Sample	61	47.5	11.5	13.1	27.9
男性 Male	41	53.7	12.2	2.4	31.7
16~24 岁 Age	13	84.6	7.7	0.0	7.7
25~34 岁 Age	14	57.1	7.1	0.0	35.7
35~44 岁 Age	10	20.0	20.0	10.0	50.0
45~54 岁 Age	3	0.0	33.3	0.0	66.7
55~60 岁 Age	1	100.0	0.0	0.0	0.0
女性 Female	20	35.0	10.0	35.0	20.0
16~24 岁 Age	3	66.7	0.0	33.3	0.0
25~34 岁 Age	10	50.0	10.0	20.0	20.0
35~44 岁 Age	5	0.0	20.0	40.0	40.0
45~54 岁 Age	2	0.0	0.0	100.0	0.0
55~60 岁 Age	0	0.0	0.0	0.0	0.0

1-4-2 该电脑是否上因特网/ Whether the Currently Owned Computer is Networked

	人数 Number	百分比 Percent
是 yes	16	26.2
否 no	45	73.8

n=61

1-4-3 上网的目的/ Purpose of Using Internet

注：本题为多选题，合计百分比超过 100%（Multiple answers）

	人次 Person-time	百分比 Percent
收发 E-mail	9	56.3
普通浏览 internet skimming	8	50.0
聊天 chatting	1	6.3
玩游戏 playing game	6	37.5
听音乐 enjoying music	1	6.3
下载软件 downloading	7	43.8
处理公务 handle business affairs	3	18.8
购物 purchasing	0	0.0
教育（如网络授课）education on line	2	12.5
打电话 telephone call	1	6.3
其他 others	1	6.3

n=16

1-4-4 该电脑的主要用途/ Main Use of this Personal Computer

注：本题为多选题，合计百分比超过 100%（Multiple answers）

	人次 Person-time	百分比 Percent
日常文字处理 daily word processing	16	26.2
玩电脑游戏 computer game	32	52.5
教育学习 education	31	50.8
查阅国际互联网 Internet 信息 internet skimming	4	6.6
接发电子邮件 E-mail sent & receive e-mail	10	16.4
家庭财务、档案管理 family finance or file management	0	0.0
在家处理公务 handle business affairs at home	5	8.2
看 VCD watch VCD	9	14.8
听音乐 enjoy music	7	11.5
图像处理 picture or photo processing	5	8.2
炒股 stock use	8	13.1
其他 others	1	1.6

n=61

1-5 家用电脑未来一年购买打算/ Plan for Future Purchasing of a Personal Computer

1-5-1 是否打算购买/ Whether Planning to Buy a Personal Computer Next Year

	人数 Number	百分比 Percent
打算买 yes	110	18.3
不打算买 no	490	81.7

n=600

1-5-2 打算购买的品牌/ Ranking of the Brands Planned to Purchase

排名 Brand Ranking	品牌 Brands	人数 Number	百分比 Percent
1	联想 Legend	34	32.1
2	兼容机 Compatibility	22	20.8
3	IBM	7	6.6
3	飞利浦 Philips	7	6.6
4	长城 Great Wall	6	5.7
5	苹果 Apple	4	3.8

n=106

1-5-3 打算购买的类型/ The Type of the Personal Computer Planned to Purchase

	人数 Number	百分比 Percent
台式机 computer	99	90.0
笔记本式 notebook	11	10.0

n=110

1-6 理想品牌排名/ Ranking of the Ideal Brands of Personal Computer

排名 Brand Ranking	品牌 Brands	人数 Number	百分比 Percent
1	联想 Legend	201	33.4
2	IBM	37	6.2
3	长城 Great Wall	24	4.0
4	海信 Hisense	17	2.8
4	康柏 Compaq	17	2.8
5	方正 Founder	12	2.0
6	裕兴 Yuxing	11	1.8

n=601

1-7 不同消费者层的理想品牌/ The Ideal Brands by Market Segments

1-7-1 时尚流行指标/ Fads Popular Index

	人数 Number	第一品牌及百分比 1st/ percent	第二品牌及百分比 2nd/ percent	第三品牌及百分比 3rd/ percent
样本 Sample	599	**联想 Legend(33.2)**	**IBM(6.2)**	**长城 Great Wall(4.0)**
平实生活指向 simple living orientation	341	联想 Legend(32.6)	IBM(4.7)	长城 Great Wall(4.1)
时尚流行指向 fashion orientation	258	联想 Legend(34.1)	IBM(8.1)	长城 Great Wall(3.9)

1-7-2 广告态度指标/ Advertising Attitude Index

	人数 Number	第一品牌及百分比 1st/ percent	第二品牌及百分比 2nd/ percent	第三品牌及百分比 3rd/ percent
样本 Sample	597	**联想 Legend(33.3)**	**IBM(6.2)**	**长城 Great Wall(4.0)**
广告淡漠指向 indifferent orientation	184	联想 Legend(37.0)	长城 Great Wall(5.4)	IBM(3.8)
中间层 medium	334	联想 Legend(32.6)	IBM(7.8)	长城 Great Wall(3.6)
信赖广告指向 loyal orientation	79	联想 Legend(27.8)	IBM(5.1) 裕兴 Yuxing(5.1)	康柏 Compaq(3.8) 四通 Stone(3.8)

1-7-3 价格态度指标/ Price Attitude Index

	人数 Number	第一品牌及百分比 1st/ percent	第二品牌及百分比 2nd/ percent	第三品牌及百分比 3rd/ percent
样本 Sample	597	**联想 Legend(33.5)**	**IBM(6.2)**	**长城 Great Wall(4.0)**
价格无关心指向 indifferent orientation	142	联想 Legend(33.8)	IBM(6.3)	海信 Hisense(3.5)
中间层 medium	306	联想 Legend(34.0)	IBM(6.9)	长城 Great Wall(4.6)
价格重视指向 careful orientation	149	联想 Legend(32.2)	IBM(4.7)	长城 Great Wall(4.0)

● 沈阳 / Shenyang

1-1 家用电脑拥有比例/ Personal Computer Ownership

	人数 Number	百分比 Percent
没有 no	530	88.2
有 yes	71	11.8

n=601

1-2 家用电脑拥有量/ Number of Personal Computer Owned per Household

	人数 Number	百分比 Percent
1 台 set	63	95.5
2 台 sets	3	4.5
3 台及以上 3 sets or over	0	0.0

n=66

1-3 对家中现有电脑（指最近购买的一台）四个方面的描述/ About the Personal Computer Most Recently Purchased

1-3-1 现有品牌排名/ Ranking of the Brands of the Currently Owned Personal Computer

排名 Brand Ranking	品牌 Brands	人数 Number	百分比 Percent
1	兼容机 Compatibility	45	68.2
2	联想 Legend	8	12.1
3	长城 Great Wall	3	4.5
4	浪潮 Langchao	2	3.0
4	飞利浦 Philips	2	3.0

n=66

1-3-2 该电脑的类型/ The Type of this Personal Computer

	人数 Number	百分比 Percent
台式机 computer	63	96.9
笔记本式 notebook	2	3.1

n=65

1-3-3 该电脑的购买时间/ Time of Purchasing of the Currently Owned Personal Computer

	人数 Number	百分比 Percent
1990 年或以前 1990 or before	2	3.0
1991-1994 年	2	3.0
1995 年	2	3.0
1996 年	5	7.6
1997 年	7	10.6
1998 年	25	37.9
1999 年	23	34.8

n=66

1-3-4 该电脑的价格/ The Price of the Currently Owned Personal Computer

	人数 Number	百分比 Percent
5000 元以下 below 5000 yuan	9	13.8
5000-8000 元 yuan	33	50.8
8000-10000 元 yuan	11	16.9
10000-15000 元 yuan	10	15.4
15000 元以上 over 15000 yuan	2	3.1

n=65

1-4 对该电脑的使用情况/ About the Use of the Personal Computer Most Recently Purchased

1-4-1 该电脑的主要使用者/ Users of this Personal Computer

	人数 Number	自己 myself	自己不用，家里其他人都用 family members use it except me	自己不用，家里其他部分人用 some of family members use it	全家人都用 all of my family use it
样本 Sample	66	42.4	15.2	13.6	28.8
男性 Male	41	53.7	9.8	9.8	26.8
16~24 岁 Age	12	91.7	8.3	0.0	0.0
25~34 岁 Age	15	46.7	13.3	0.0	40.0
35~44 岁 Age	7	28.6	14.3	28.6	28.6
45~54 岁 Age	5	0.0	0.0	40.0	60.0
55~60 岁 Age	2	100.0	0.0	0.0	0.0
女性 Female	25	24.0	24.0	20.0	32.0
16~24 岁 Age	8	62.5	12.5	12.5	12.5
25~34 岁 Age	5	20.0	20.0	0.0	60.0
35~44 岁 Age	4	0.0	0.0	25.0	75.0
45~54 岁 Age	7	0.0	57.1	42.9	0.0
55~60 岁 Age	1	0.0	0.0	0.0	100.0

1-4-2 该电脑是否上因特网/ Whether the Currently Owned Computer is Networked

	人数 Number	百分比 Percent
是 yes	14	21.2
否 no	52	78.8

n=66

1-4-3 上网的目的/ Purpose of Using Internet

注：本题为多选题，合计百分比超过 100%（Multiple answers）

	人次 Person-time	百分比 Percent
收发 E-mail	11	78.6
普通浏览 internet skimming	9	64.3
聊天 Chatting	3	21.4
玩游戏 playing game	2	14.3
听音乐 enjoying music	1	7.1
下载软件 downloading	6	42.9
处理公务 handle business affairs	3	21.4
购物 purchasing	0	0.0
教育（如网络授课）education on line	1	7.1
打电话 telephone call	0	0.0
其他 others	0	0.0

n=14

1-4-4 该电脑的主要用途/ Main Use of this Personal Computer

注：本题为多选题，合计百分比超过 100%（Multiple answers）

	人次 Person-time	百分比 Percent
日常文字处理 daily word processing	25	37.9
玩电脑游戏 computer game	30	45.5
教育学习 education	35	53.0
查阅国际互联网信息 internet skimming	10	15.2
接发电子邮件 E-mail sent & receive e-mail	5	7.6
家庭财务、档案管理 family finance or file management	7	10.6
在家处理公务 handle business affairs at home	6	9.1
看 VCD watch VCD	19	28.8
听音乐 enjoy music	11	16.7
图像处理 picture or photo processing	4	6.1
炒股 stock use	8	12.1
其他 others	1	1.5

n=66

1-5 家用电脑未来一年购买打算/ Plan for Future Purchasing of a Personal Computer

1-5-1 是否打算购买/ Whether Planning to Buy a Personal Computer Next Year

	人数 Number	百分比 Percent
打算买 yes	106	17.7
不打算买 no	494	82.3

n=600

1-5-2 打算购买的品牌/ Ranking of the Brands Planned to Purchase

排名 Brand Ranking	品牌 Brands	人数 Number	百分比 Percent
1	联想 Legend	44	41.9
2	兼容机 Compatibility	24	22.9
3	飞利浦 Philips	7	6.7
4	东芝 Toshiba	5	4.8
5	康柏 Compaq	4	3.8
5	长城 Great Wall	4	3.8
6	惠普 HP	3	2.9
6	IBM	3	2.9
7	TCL	2	1.9
7	苹果 Apple	2	1.9
7	同方 Tongfang	2	1.9

n=105

1-5-3 打算购买的类型/ The Type of the Personal Computer Planned to Purchase

	人数 Number	百分比 Percent
台式机 computer	94	90.4
笔记本式 notebook	10	9.6

n=104

1-6 理想品牌排名/ Ranking of the Ideal Brands of Personal Computer

排名 Brand Ranking	品牌 Brands	人数 Number	百分比 Percent
1	联想 Legend	161	26.8
2	IBM	49	8.2
3	东芝 Toshiba	21	3.5
4	长城 Great Wall	19	3.2
5	飞利浦 Philips	17	2.8
6	苹果 Apple	16	2.7
7	裕兴 Yuxing	15	2.5
8	康柏 Compaq	13	2.2
8	兼容机 Compatibility	13	2.2
9	同方 Tongfang	11	1.8

n=600

1-7 不同消费者层的理想品牌/ The Ideal Brands by Market Segments

1-7-1 时尚流行指标/ Fads Popular Index

	人数 Number	第一品牌及百分比 1st/ percent	第二品牌及百分比 2nd/ percent	第三品牌及百分比 3rd/ percent
样本 Sample	600	**联想 Legend(26.8)**	**IBM(8.2)**	**东芝 Toshiba(3.5)**
平实生活指向 simple living orientation	291	联想 Legend(25.4)	IBM(7.6)	长城 Great Wall(4.1)
时尚流行指向 fashion orientation	309	联想 Legend(28.2)	IBM(8.7)	东芝 Toshiba(4.2)

1-7-2 广告态度指标/ Advertising Attitude Index

	人数 Number	第一品牌及百分比 1st/ percent	第二品牌及百分比 2nd/ percent	第三品牌及百分比 3rd/ percent
样本 Sample	600	**联想 Legend(26.8)**	**IBM(8.2)**	**东芝 Toshiba(3.5)**
广告淡漠指向 indifferent orientation	172	联想 Legend(26.7)	IBM(7.6)	东芝 Toshiba(4.1) 长城 Great Wall(4.1)
中间层 medium	353	联想 Legend(26.3)	IBM(8.8)	东芝 Toshiba(3.1) 飞利浦 Philips(3.1) 长城 Great Wall(3.1)
信赖广告指向 loyal orientation	75	联想 Legend(29.3)	IBM(6.7)	苹果 Apple(4.0) 东芝 Toshiba(4.0) 西门子 Siemens(4.0) 同方 Tongfang(4.0)

1-7-3 价格态度指标/ Price Attitude Index

	人数 Number	第一品牌及百分比 1st/ percent	第二品牌及百分比 2nd/ percent	第三品牌及百分比 3rd/ percent
样本 Sample	**599**	**联想 Legend(26.9)**	**IBM(8.2)**	**东芝 Toshiba(3.5)**
价格无关心指向 indifferent orientation	104	联想 Legend(38.5)	IBM(4.8)	康柏 Compaq(3.8) 飞利浦 Philips(3.8) 长城 Great Wall(3.8)
中间层 medium	292	联想 Legend(25.7)	IBM(8.6)	苹果 Apple(4.1)
价格重视指向 careful orientation	203	联想 Legend(22.7)	IBM(9.4)	东芝 Toshiba(4.4)

2.私人电话 / Telephone

● 北京 / Beijing

2-1 私人电话拥有比例/ Telephone Ownership

	人数 Number	百分比 Percent
有 yes	897	88.7
没有 no	114	11.3

n=1011

2-2 家中装有几条电话线/ How Many Telephone lines

	人数 Number	百分比 Percent
1 条 1 line	832	93.4
2 条 2 lines	56	6.3
3 条及以上 3 lines or over	3	0.3

n=891

2-3 电话线的类型/ The Type of the Telephone Line

注：本题为多选题，合计百分比超过 100%（Multiple answers）

	人次 Person-time	百分比 Percent
直线电话 direct	856	95.5
分机电话 extension	46	5.1

n=896

2-4 所使用电话机的种类/ The Type of the Telephone

注：本题为多选题，合计百分比超过 100%（Multiple answers）

	人次 Person-time	百分比 Percent
普通电话 regular telephone	767	85.8
无绳电话（子母机）composite telephone	165	18.5
便携式电话 portable telephone	0	0.0

n=894

2-5 有无安装电话的打算/ Whether Planning to Get a Telephone Next Year

	人数 Number	百分比 Percent
打算 yes	129	13.0
不打算 no	860	87.0

n=989

2-6 打算安装的种类/ The Type Planned to Use

注：本题为多选题，合计百分比超过 100%（Multiple answers）

	人次 Person-time	百分比 Percent
普通电话 regular telephone	76	61.3
无绳电话（子母机）composite telephone	50	40.3
便携式电话 portable telephone	0	0.0

n=124

● 上海 / Shanghai

2-1 私人电话拥有比例/ Telephone Ownership

	人数 Number	百分比 Percent
有 yes	903	89.1
没有 no	111	10.9

n=1014

2-2 家中装有几条电话线/ How Many Telephone lines

	人数 Number	百分比 Percent
1 条 1 line	863	95.6
2 条 2 lines	37	4.1
3 条及以上 3 lines or over	3	0.3

n=903

2-3 电话线的类型/ The Type of the Telephone Line

注：本题为多选题，合计百分比超过 100%（Multiple answers）

	人次 Person-time	百分比 Percent
直线电话 direct	885	98.0
分机电话 extension	22	2.4

n=903

2-4 所使用电话机的种类/ The Type of the Telephone

注：本题为多选题，合计百分比超过 100%（Multiple answers）

	人次 Person-time	百分比 Percent
普通电话 regular telephone	773	85.6
无绳电话（子母机）composite telephone	178	19.7
便携式电话 portable telephone	0	0.0

n=903

2-5 有无安装电话的打算/ Whether Planning to Get a Telephone Next Year

	人数 Number	百分比 Percent
打算 yes	110	10.9
不打算 no	898	89.1

n=1008

2-6 打算安装的种类/ The Type Planned to Use

注：本题为多选题，合计百分比超过 100%（Multiple answers）

	人次 Person-time	百分比 Percent
普通电话 regular telephone	61	56.5
无绳电话（子母机）composite telephone	52	48.1
便携式电话 portable telephone	0	0.0

n=108

● 广州 / Guangzhou

2-1 私人电话拥有比例/ Telephone Ownership

	人数 Number	百分比 Percent
有 yes	913	88.3
没有 no	121	11.7

n=1034

2-2 家中装有几条电话线/ How Many Telephone lines

	人数 Number	百分比 Percent
1 条 1 line	853	93.5
2 条 2 lines	53	5.8
3 条及以上 3 lines or over	6	0.7

n=912

2-3 电话线的类型/ The Type of the Telephone Line

注：本题为多选题，合计百分比超过 100%（Multiple answers）

	人次 Person-time	百分比 Percent
直线电话 direct	881	96.5
分机电话 extension	38	4.2

n=913

2-4 所使用电话机的种类/ The Type of the Telephone

注：本题为多选题，合计百分比超过 100%（Multiple answers）

	人次 Person-time	百分比 Percent
普通电话 regular telephone	811	88.8
无绳电话（子母机）composite telephone	145	15.9
便携式电话 portable telephone	0	0.0

n=913

2-5 有无安装电话的打算/ Whether Planning to Get a Telephone Next Year

	人数 Number	百分比 Percent
打算 yes	141	13.7
不打算 no	887	86.3

n=1028

2-6 打算安装的种类/ The Type Planned to Use

注：本题为多选题，合计百分比超过 100%（Multiple answers）

	人次 Person-time	百分比 Percent
普通电话 regular telephone	94	66.7
无绳电话（子母机）composite telephone	53	37.6
便携式电话 portable telephone	0	0.0

n=141

● 重庆 / Chongqing

2-1 私人电话拥有比例/ Telephone Ownership

	人数 Number	百分比 Percent
有 yes	448	72.1
没有 no	173	27.9

n=621

2-2 家中装有几条电话线/ How Many Telephone lines

	人数 Number	百分比 Percent
1 条 1 line	428	95.7
2 条 2 lines	15	3.4
3 条及以上 3 lines or over	4	0.9

n=447

2-3 电话线的类型/ The Type of the Telephone Line

注：本题为多选题，合计百分比超过 100%（Multiple answers）

	人次 Person-time	百分比 Percent
直线电话 direct	434	96.9
分机电话 extension	16	3.6

n=448

2-4 所使用电话机的种类/ The Type of the Telephone

注：本题为多选题，合计百分比超过 100%（Multiple answers）

	人次 Person-time	百分比 Percent
普通电话 regular telephone	426	95.3
无绳电话（子母机）composite telephone	27	6.0
便携式电话 portable telephone	0	0.0

n=447

2-5 有无安装电话的打算/ Whether Planning to Get a Telephone Next Year

	人数 Number	百分比 Percent
打算 yes	81	13.1
不打算 no	538	86.9

n=619

2-6 打算安装的种类/ The Type Planned to Use

注：本题为多选题，合计百分比超过 100%（Multiple answers）

	人次 Person-time	百分比 Percent
普通电话 regular telephone	63	78.8
无绳电话（子母机）composite telephone	19	23.8
便携式电话 portable telephone	0	0.0

n=80

● 武汉 / Wuhan

2-1 私人电话拥有比例/ Telephone Ownership

	人数 Number	百分比 Percent
有 yes	534	83.3
没有 no	107	16.7

n=641

2-2 家中装有几条电话线/ How Many Telephone lines

	人数 Number	百分比 Percent
1 条 1 line	515	96.6
2 条 2 lines	16	3.0
3 条及以上 3 lines or over	2	0.4

n=533

2-3 电话线的类型/ The Type of the Telephone Line

注：本题为多选题，合计百分比超过 100%（Multiple answers）

	人次 Person-time	百分比 Percent
直线电话 direct	518	97.0
分机电话 extension	21	3.9

n=534

2-4 所使用电话机的种类/ The Type of the Telephone

注：本题为多选题，合计百分比超过 100%（Multiple answers）

	人数 Person-time	百分比 Percent
普通电话 regular telephone	486	91.2
无绳电话（子母机）composite telephone	59	11.1
便携式电话 portable telephone	0	0.0

n=533

2-5 有无安装电话的打算/ Whether Planning to Get a Telephone Next Year

	人数 Number	百分比 Percent
打算 yes	68	10.9
不打算 no	556	89.1

n=624

2-6 打算安装的种类/ The Type Planned to Use

注：本题为多选题，合计百分比超过 100%（Multiple answers）

	人数 Person-time	百分比 Percent
普通电话 regular telephone	38	58.5
无绳电话（子母机）composite telephone	30	46.2
便携式电话 portable telephone	0	0.0

n=65

● 西安 / Xi'an

2-1 私人电话拥有比例/ Telephone Ownership

	人数 Number	百分比 Percent
有 yes	423	70.5
没有 no	177	29.5

n=600

2-2 家中装有几条电话线/ How Many Telephone lines

	人数 Number	百分比 Percent
1 条 1 line	401	95.0
2 条 2 lines	19	4.5
3 条及以上 3 lines or over	2	0.5

n=422

2-3 电话线的类型/ The Type of the Telephone Line

注：本题为多选题，合计百分比超过 100%（Multiple answers）

	人次 Person-time	百分比 Percent
直线电话 direct	410	97.2
分机电话 extension	14	3.3

n=422

2-4 所使用电话机的种类/ The Type of the Telephone

注：本题为多选题，合计百分比超过 100%（Multiple answers）

	人次 Person-time	百分比 Percent
普通电话 regular telephone	370	87.7
无绳电话（子母机） composite telephone	59	14.0
便携式电话 portable telephone	1	0.2

n=422

2-5 有无安装电话的打算/ Whether Planning to Get a Telephone Next Year

	人数 Number	百分比 Percent
打算 yes	92	15.3
不打算 no	508	84.7

n=600

2-6 打算安装的种类/ The Type Planned to Use

注：本题为多选题，合计百分比超过 100%（Multiple answers）

	人次 Person-time	百分比 Percent
普通电话 regular telephone	57	62.0
无绳电话（子母机） composite telephone	35	38.0
便携式电话 portable telephone	0	0.0

n=92

● 沈阳 / Shenyang

2-1 私人电话拥有比例/ Telephone Ownership

	人数 Number	百分比 Percent
有 yes	429	71.4
没有 no	172	28.6

n=601

2-2 家中装有几条电话线/ How Many Telephone lines

	人数 Number	百分比 Percent
1 条 1 line	414	97.0
2 条 2 lines	13	3.0
3 条及以上 3 lines or over	0	0.0

n=427

2-3 电话线的类型/ The Type of the Telephone Line

注：本题为多选题，合计百分比超过 100%（Multiple answers）

	人次 Person-time	百分比 Percent
直线电话 direct	415	97.2
分机电话 extension	14	3.3

n=427

2-4 所使用电话机的种类/ The Type of the Telephone

注：本题为多选题，合计百分比超过 100%（Multiple answers）

	人次 Person-time	百分比 Percent
普通电话 regular telephone	405	94.6
无绳电话（子母机）composite telephone	25	5.8
便携式电话 portable telephone	0	0.0

n=428

2-5 有无安装电话的打算/ Whether Planning to Get a Telephone Next Year

	人数 Number	百分比 Percent
打算 yes	67	11.2
不打算 no	533	88.8

n=600

2-6 打算安装的种类/ The Type Planned to Use

注：本题为多选题，合计百分比超过 100%（Multiple answers）

	人次 Person-time	百分比 Percent
普通电话 regular telephone	49	74.2
无绳电话（子母机）composite telephone	19	28.8
便携式电话 portable telephone	0	0.0

n=66

3.BP 机 / Pager

● 北京 / Beijing

3-1 BP 机拥有比例/ Pagers Ownership

	人数 Number	百分比 Percent
使用 yes	451	44.6
不使用 no	561	55.4

n=1012

3-2 样本、男性各年龄层、女性各年龄层使用 BP 机的比例/ Proportion of the Sample Using Pagers by the Whole Sample, Age and Gender Groups

	人数 Number	使用 yes	不使用 no
样本 Sample	1012	44.6	55.4
男性 Male	504	53.2	46.8
16~24 岁 Age	105	38.1	61.9
25~34 岁 Age	151	64.2	35.8
35~44 岁 Age	131	64.1	35.9
45~54 岁 Age	77	46.8	53.2
55~60 岁 Age	40	27.5	72.5
女性 Female	508	36.0	64.0
16~24 岁 Age	108	40.7	59.3
25~34 岁 Age	150	46.0	54.0
35~44 岁 Age	124	43.5	56.5
45~54 岁 Age	84	17.9	82.1
55~60 岁 Age	42	2.4	97.6

3-3 现用 BP 机的来源/ Source of Obtaining the Currently Owned Pager

	人数 Number	百分比 Percent
自己付费购买 bought by myself	325	72.1
单位配发 offered free by my work unit	109	24.2
其他 others	17	3.8

n=451

3-4 现用 BP 机的品牌排名/ Ranking of the Brands of the Currently Owned Pager

排名 Brand Ranking	品牌 Brands	人数 Number	百分比 Percent
1	摩托罗拉 Motorola	356	80.4
2	松下 Panasonic	16	3.6
3	大洋 Dayang	13	2.9
4	NEC	8	1.8
5	信利 Truly	5	1.1

n=443

3-5 现用 BP 机的种类/ The Type of the Currently Owned Pager

	人数 Number	百分比 Percent
汉字显示型 pages	228	53.8
数字显示型 number signs	196	46.2

n=424

3-6 选择呼台的考虑因素/ Ranking of the Considerations in Choosing the BP Station

注：本题为多选题，合计百分比超过 100%（Multiple answers）

排名 Ranking	考虑因素 Considerations	人次 Person-time	百分比 Percent
1	服务质量好 good service	175	40.1
2	信息接收好 good performance	174	39.9
3	呼台的知名度 awareness of the BP service station	117	26.8
4	覆盖地区广 wide coverage	113	25.9
5	价格 price	97	22.2
6	联网地区多 wide areas connected	80	18.3
7	其他 others	32	7.3
8	有促销 with promotion activities	17	3.9

n=436

3-7 样本、男性各年龄层、女性各年龄层平均每天接收的信息量/ Pieces of Information Received in a Day by the Whole Sample, Age and Gender Groups

	人数 Number	1 条以下 below 1 piece	1-2 条 1-2 pieces	3-4 条 3-4 pieces	5-9 条 5-9 pieces	10-19 条 10-19 pieces	20 条以上 20 pieces or over
样本 Sample	450	13.6	31.3	28.4	16.2	6.4	4.0
男性 Male	267	12.7	29.2	27.7	17.2	7.9	5.2
16~24 岁 Age	40	17.5	37.5	22.5	12.5	5.0	5.0
25~34 岁 Age	97	11.3	34.0	29.9	16.5	4.1	4.1
35~44 岁 Age	83	14.5	22.9	24.1	18.1	14.5	6.0
45~54 岁 Age	36	8.3	27.8	30.6	22.2	2.8	8.3
55~60 岁 Age	11	9.1	9.1	45.5	18.2	18.2	0.0
女性 Female	183	14.8	34.4	29.5	14.8	4.4	2.2
16~24 岁 Age	44	15.9	36.4	27.3	11.4	9.1	0.0
25~34 岁 Age	69	14.5	29.0	30.4	20.3	4.3	1.4
35~44 岁 Age	54	16.7	38.9	29.6	11.1	1.9	1.9
45~54 岁 Age	15	6.7	40.0	26.7	13.3	0.0	13.3
55~60 岁 Age	1	0.0	0.0	100.0	0.0	0.0	0.0

3-8 样本、男性各年龄层、女性各年龄层未来一年有无购买 BP 机的打算/ Whether Planning to Buy a Pager Next Year by the Whole Sample, Age and Gender Groups

	人数 Number	购买 yes	不购买 no
样本 Sample	1005	8.2	91.8
男性 Male	501	8.6	91.4
16~24 岁 Age	105	21.9	78.1
25~34 岁 Age	151	7.3	92.7
35~44 岁 Age	128	5.5	94.5
45~54 岁 Age	77	2.6	97.4
55~60 岁 Age	40	0.0	100.0
女性 Female	504	7.7	92.3
16~24 岁 Age	106	21.7	78.3
25~34 岁 Age	149	4.0	96.0
35~44 岁 Age	124	5.6	94.4
45~54 岁 Age	83	3.6	96.4
55~60 岁 Age	42	0.0	100.0

3-9 打算购买的品牌排名/ Ranking of the Brands planned to Buy

排名 Brand Ranking	品牌 Brands	人数 Number	百分比 Percent
1	摩托罗拉 Motorola	73	89.0
2	NEC	3	3.7
3	松下 Panasonic	1	1.2
3	飞利浦 Philips	1	1.2
3	皮尔・卡丹 Pierre Cardin	1	1.2
3	建生 Jiansheng	1	1.2

n=82

3-10 打算购买的种类/ The Type of the Planned Purchase

	人数 Number	百分比 Percent
汉字显示型 pages	54	65.9
数字显示型 number signs	28	34.1

n=82

3-11 理想品牌排名/ Ranking of the Ideal Brands

排名 Brand Ranking	品牌 Brands	人数 Number	百分比 Percent
1	摩托罗拉 Motorola	682	67.5
2	松下 Panasonic	26	2.6
3	爱立信 Ericsson	7	0.7
4	飞利浦 Philips	4	0.4
5	大洋 Dayang	3	0.3
5	诺基亚 Nokia	3	0.3
5	三星 Samsung	3	0.3

n=1011

3-12 不同消费者层的理想品牌/ The Ideal Brands by Market Segments

3-12-1 时尚流行指标/ Fads Popular Index

	人数 Number	第一品牌及百分比 1st/ percent	第二品牌及百分比 2nd/ percent	第三品牌及百分比 3rd/ percent
样本 Sample	**997**	**摩托罗拉 Motorola(67.3)**	**松下 Panasonic(2.5)**	**爱立信 Ericsson (0.7)**
平实生活指向 simple living orientation	491	摩托罗拉 Motorola(60.9)	松下 Panasonic(3.1)	爱立信 Ericsson (1.2)
时尚流行指向 fashion orientation	506	摩托罗拉 Motorola(73.5)	松下 Panasonic(2.0)	飞利浦 Philips(0.6)

3-12-2 广告态度指标/ Advertising Attitude Index

	人数 Number	第一品牌及百分比 1st/ percent	第二品牌及百分比 2nd/ percent	第三品牌及百分比 3rd/ percent
样本 Sample	**993**	**摩托罗拉 Motorola(67.9)**	**松下 Panasonic(2.3)**	**爱立信 Ericsson (0.7)**
广告淡漠指向 indifferent orientation	289	摩托罗拉 Motorola(62.3)	松下 Panasonic(2.1)	爱立信 Ericsson (1.0)
中间层 medium	572	摩托罗拉 Motorola(70.6)	松下 Panasonic(2.3)	三星 Samsung(0.3) 大洋 Dayang(0.3) 飞利浦 Philips(0.3) 爱立信 Ericsson (0.3)
信赖广告指向 loyal orientation	132	摩托罗拉 Motorola(68.2)	松下 Panasonic(3.0)	爱立信 Ericsson (1.5)

3-12-3 价格态度指标/ Price Attitude Index

	人数 Number	第一品牌及百分比 1st/ percent	第二品牌及百分比 2nd/ percent	第三品牌及百分比 3rd/ percent
样本 Sample	**1001**	**摩托罗拉 Motorola(67.4)**	**松下 Panasonic(2.5)**	**爱立信 Ericsson (0.7)**
价格无关心指向 indifferent orientation	203	摩托罗拉 Motorola(70.0)	松下 Panasonic(3.9)	飞利浦 Philips(1.0) 大洋 Dayang(1.0) 爱立信 Ericsson (1.0)
中间层 medium	500	摩托罗拉 Motorola(73.6)	松下 Panasonic(2.4)	三星 Samsung(0.6) 爱立信 Ericsson (0.6)
价格重视指向 careful orientation	298	摩托罗拉 Motorola(55.4)	松下 Panasonic(1.7)	飞利浦 Philips(0.7) 爱立信 Ericsson (0.7)

● 上海 / Shanghai

3-1 BP 机拥有比例/ Pagers Ownership

	人数 Number	百分比 Percent
使用 yes	309	30.5
不使用 no	705	69.5

n=1014

3-2 样本、男性各年龄层、女性各年龄层使用 BP 机的比例/ Proportion of the Sample Using Pagers by the Whole Sample, Age and Gender Groups

	人数 Number	使用 yes	不使用 no
样本 Sample	**1014**	**30.5**	**69.5**
男性 Male	**509**	**37.5**	**62.5**
16~24 岁 Age	109	29.4	70.6
25~34 岁 Age	146	47.9	52.1
35~44 岁 Age	130	40.8	59.2
45~54 岁 Age	85	38.8	61.2
55~60 岁 Age	39	7.7	92.3
女性 Female	**505**	**23.4**	**76.6**
16~24 岁 Age	108	33.3	66.7
25~34 岁 Age	144	31.3	68.8
35~44 岁 Age	130	19.2	80.8
45~54 岁 Age	82	11.0	89.0
55~60 岁 Age	41	7.3	92.7

3-3 现用 BP 机的来源/ Source of Obtaining the Currently Owned Pager

	人数 Number	百分比 Percent
自己付费购买 bought by myself	224	73.0
单位配发 offered free by my work unit	74	24.1
其他 others	9	2.9

n=307

3-4 现用 BP 机的品牌排名/ Ranking of the Brands of the Currently Owned Pager

排名 Brand Ranking	品牌 Brands	人数 Number	百分比 Percent
1	摩托罗拉 Motorola	243	79.2
2	NEC	13	4.2
3	汇讯 Huixun	7	2.3
4	卡西欧 Casio	6	2.0
5	三星 Samsung	5	1.6
5	松下 Panasonic	5	1.6
6	快译通 Instant-dict	2	0.7
6	卫星 Satellite	2	0.7
6	飞利浦 Philips	2	0.7

n=307

3-5 现用 BP 机的种类/ The Type of the Currently Owned Pager

	人数 Number	百分比 Percent
汉字显示型 pages	87	28.8
数字显示型 number signs	215	71.2

n=302

3-6 选择呼台的考虑因素/ Ranking of the Considerations in Choosing the BP Station

注：本题为多选题，合计百分比超过 100%（Multiple answers）

排名 Ranking	考虑因素 Considerations	人次 Person-time	百分比 Percent
1	信息接收好 good performance	156	50.8
2	呼台的知名度 awareness of the BP service station	83	27.0
2	服务质量好 good service	83	27.0
3	覆盖地区广 wide coverage	77	25.1
4	联网地区多 wide areas connected	72	23.5
5	价格 price	56	18.2
6	其他 others	24	7.8
7	有促销 with promotion activities	17	5.5

n=307

3-7 样本、男性各年龄层、女性各年龄层平均每天接收的信息量/ Pieces of Information Received in a Day by the Whole Sample, Age and Gender Groups

	人数 Number	1 条以下 below 1 piece	1-2 条 1-2 pieces	3-4 条 3-4 pieces	5-9 条 5-9 pieces	10-19 条 10-19 pieces	20 条以上 20 pieces or over
样本 Sample	303	13.2	24.8	34.3	17.2	5.9	4.6
男性 Male	187	11.8	21.9	35.3	17.1	8.0	5.9
16~24 岁 Age	32	12.5	28.1	40.6	9.4	6.3	3.1
25~34 岁 Age	67	14.9	20.9	34.3	13.4	10.4	6.0
35~44 岁 Age	52	9.6	17.3	38.5	17.3	9.6	7.7
45~54 岁 Age	33	9.1	24.2	27.3	30.3	3.0	6.1
55~60 岁 Age	3	0.0	33.3	33.3	33.3	0.0	0.0
女性 Female	116	15.5	29.3	32.8	17.2	2.6	2.6
16~24 岁 Age	36	16.7	16.7	36.1	22.2	2.8	5.6
25~34 岁 Age	43	11.6	39.5	32.6	11.6	4.7	0.0
35~44 岁 Age	25	24.0	36.0	28.0	8.0	0.0	4.0
45~54 岁 Age	9	11.1	22.2	22.2	44.4	0.0	0.0
55~60 岁 Age	3	0.0	0.0	66.7	33.3	0.0	0.0

3-8 样本、男性各年龄层、女性各年龄层未来一年有无购买 BP 机的打算/ Whether Planning to Buy a Pager Next Year by the Whole Sample, Age and Gender Groups

	人数 Number	购买 yes	不购买 no
样本 Sample	1013	5.8	94.2
男性 Male	509	6.7	93.3
16~24 岁 Age	109	16.5	83.5
25~34 岁 Age	146	5.5	94.5
35~44 岁 Age	130	4.6	95.4
45~54 岁 Age	85	1.2	98.8
55~60 岁 Age	39	2.6	97.4
女性 Female	504	5.0	95.0
16~24 岁 Age	108	9.3	90.7
25~34 岁 Age	144	6.9	93.1
35~44 岁 Age	129	1.6	98.4
45~54 岁 Age	82	2.4	97.6
55~60 岁 Age	41	2.4	97.6

3-9 打算购买的品牌排名/ Ranking of the Brands planned to Buy

排名 Brand Ranking	品牌 Brands	人数 Number	百分比 Percent
1	摩托罗拉 Motorola	46	78.0
2	松下 Panasonic	4	6.8
3	NEC	3	5.1
4	飞利浦 Philips	2	3.4
4	卡西欧 Casio	2	3.4
5	三星 Samsung	1	1.7
5	阿波罗 Apollo	1	1.7

n=59

3-10 打算购买的种类/ The Type of the Planned Purchase

	人数 Number	百分比 Percent
汉字显示型 pages	28	47.5
数字显示型 number signs	31	52.5

n=59

3-11 理想品牌排名/ Ranking of the Ideal Brands

排名 Brand Ranking	品牌 Brands	人数 Number	百分比 Percent
1	摩托罗拉 Motorola	709	70.0
2	松下 Panasonic	58	5.7
2	NEC	58	5.7
3	飞利浦 Philips	22	2.2
4	卡西欧 Casio	16	1.6
5	三星 Samsung	11	1.1
6	皮尔·卡丹 Pierre Cardin	3	0.3
6	西门子 Siemens	3	0.3
6	爱立信 Ericsson	3	0.3

n=1013

3-12 不同消费者层的理想品牌/ The Ideal Brands by Market Segments

3-12-1 时尚流行指标/ Fads Popular Index

	人数 Number	第一品牌及百分比 1st/ percent	第二品牌及百分比 2nd/ percent	第三品牌及百分比 3rd/ percent
样本 Sample	1004	**摩托罗拉 Motorola(70.0)**	**松下 Panasonic(5.8)** **NEC(5.8)**	**飞利浦 Philips(2.2)**
平实生活指向 simple living orientation	471	摩托罗拉 Motorola(65.8)	松下 Panasonic(5.5)	NEC(4.5)
时尚流行指向 fashion orientation	533	摩托罗拉 Motorola(73.7)	NEC(6.9)	松下 Panasonic(6.0)

3-12-2 广告态度指标/ Advertising Attitude Index

	人数 Number	第一品牌及百分比 1st/ percent	第二品牌及百分比 2nd/ percent	第三品牌及百分比 3rd/ percent
样本 Sample	1001	**摩托罗拉 Motorola(70.1)**	**松下 Panasonic(5.8)**	**NEC(5.7)**
广告淡漠指向 indifferent orientation	256	摩托罗拉 Motorola(64.1)	松下 Panasonic(7.8)	NEC(4.7)
中间层 medium	610	摩托罗拉 Motorola(72.1)	NEC(5.4)	松下 Panasonic(5.2)
信赖广告指向 loyal orientation	135	摩托罗拉 Motorola(72.6)	NEC(8.9)	松下 Panasonic(4.4)

3-12-3 价格态度指标/ Price Attitude Index

	人数 Number	第一品牌及百分比 1st/ percent	第二品牌及百分比 2nd/ percent	第三品牌及百分比 3rd/ percent
样本 Sample	1010	**摩托罗拉 Motorola(70.1)**	**松下 Panasonic(5.7) NEC(5.7)**	**飞利浦 Philips(2.1)**
价格无关心指向 indifferent orientation	151	摩托罗拉 Motorola(66.9)	松下 Panasonic(7.3)	NEC(6.6)
中间层 medium	520	摩托罗拉 Motorola(72.5)	NEC(6.2)	松下 Panasonic(5.0)
价格重视指向 careful orientation	339	摩托罗拉 Motorola(67.8)	松下 Panasonic(6.2)	NEC(4.7)

● 广州 / Guangzhou

3-1 BP 机拥有比例/ Pagers Ownership

	人数 Number	百分比 Percent
使用 yes	407	39.4
不使用 no	627	60.6

n=1034

3-2 样本、男性各年龄层、女性各年龄层使用 BP 机的比例/ Proportion of the Sample Using Pagers by the Whole Sample, Age and Gender Groups

	人数 Number	使用 yes	不使用 no
样本 Sample	1034	39.4	60.6
男性 Male	499	47.5	52.5
16~24 岁 Age	106	46.2	53.8
25~34 岁 Age	150	60.0	40.0
35~44 岁 Age	127	42.5	57.5
45~54 岁 Age	73	49.3	50.7
55~60 岁 Age	43	18.6	81.4
女性 Female	535	31.8	68.2
16~24 岁 Age	112	45.5	54.5
25~34 岁 Age	158	38.6	61.4
35~44 岁 Age	137	29.2	70.8
45~54 岁 Age	87	18.4	81.6
55~60 岁 Age	41	4.9	95.1

3-3 现用 BP 机的来源/ Source of Obtaining the Currently Owned Pager

	人数 Number	百分比 Percent
自己付费购买 bought by myself	345	85.0
单位配发 offered free by my work unit	41	10.1
其他 others	20	4.9

n=406

3-4 现用 BP 机的品牌排名/ Ranking of the Brands of the Currently Owned Pager

排名 Brand Ranking	品牌 Brands	人数 Number	百分比 Percent
1	摩托罗拉 Motorola	252	62.2
2	NEC	44	10.9
3	松下 Panasonic	40	9.9
4	三星 Samsung	19	4.7
5	大井 OI	8	2.0
6	快译通 Instant-dict	6	1.5
7	雅皇 Yahuang	4	1.0
7	飞利浦 Philips	4	1.0

n=405

3-5 现用 BP 机的种类/ The Type of the Currently Owned Pager

	人数 Number	百分比 Percent
汉字显示型 pages	66	16.8
数字显示型 number signs	328	83.2

n=394

3-6 选择呼台的考虑因素/ Ranking of the Considerations in Choosing the BP Station

注：本题为多选题，合计百分比超过 100%（Multiple answers）

排名 Ranking	考虑因素 Considerations	人次 Person-time	百分比 Percent
1	信息接收好 good performance	175	43.4
2	覆盖地区广 wide coverage	160	39.7
3	价格 price	121	30.0
4	服务质量好 good service	115	28.5
5	呼台的知名度 awareness of the BP service station	101	25.1
6	联网地区多 wide areas connected	92	22.8
7	有促销 with promotion activities	24	6.0
8	其他 others	12	3.0

n=403

3-7 样本、男性各年龄层、女性各年龄层平均每天接收的信息量/ Pieces of Information Received in a Day by the Whole Sample, Age and Gender Groups

	人数 Number	1 条以下 below 1 piece	1-2 条 1-2 pieces	3-4 条 3-4 pieces	5-9 条 5-9 pieces	10-19 条 10-19 pieces	20 条以上 20 pieces or over
样本 Sample	**406**	**16.0**	**35.5**	**33.5**	**11.3**	**3.2**	**0.5**
男性 Male	**236**	**15.7**	**30.9**	**36.0**	**13.6**	**3.4**	**0.4**
16~24 岁 Age	49	14.3	38.8	32.7	12.2	2.0	0.0
25~34 岁 Age	90	16.7	24.4	38.9	15.6	4.4	0.0
35~44 岁 Age	53	17.0	30.2	35.8	13.2	1.9	1.9
45~54 岁 Age	36	11.1	38.9	33.3	13.9	2.8	0.0
55~60 岁 Age	8	25.0	25.0	37.5	0.0	12.5	0.0
女性 Female	**170**	**16.5**	**41.8**	**30.0**	**8.2**	**2.9**	**0.6**
16~24 岁 Age	51	15.7	35.3	37.3	9.8	2.0	0.0
25~34 岁 Age	61	13.1	49.2	27.9	6.6	1.6	1.6
35~44 岁 Age	40	15.0	47.5	25.0	10.0	2.5	0.0
45~54 岁 Age	16	25.0	25.0	31.3	6.3	12.5	0.0
55~60 岁 Age	2	100.0	0.0	0.0	0.0	0.0	0.0

3-8 样本、男性各年龄层、女性各年龄层未来一年有无购买 BP 机的打算/ Whether Planning to Buy a Pager Next Year by the Whole Sample, Age and Gender Groups

	人数 Number	购买 yes	不购买 no
样本 Sample	**1030**	**5.0**	**95.0**
男性 Male	**496**	**5.8**	**94.2**
16~24 岁 Age	106	15.1	84.9
25~34 岁 Age	149	2.7	97.3
35~44 岁 Age	127	4.7	95.3
45~54 岁 Age	73	2.7	97.3
55~60 岁 Age	41	2.4	97.6
女性 Female	**534**	**4.3**	**95.7**
16~24 岁 Age	112	8.9	91.1
25~34 岁 Age	157	3.2	96.8
35~44 岁 Age	137	3.6	96.4
45~54 岁 Age	87	3.4	96.6
55~60 岁 Age	41	0.0	100.0

3-9 打算购买的品牌排名/ Ranking of the Brands planned to Buy

排名 Brand Ranking	品牌 Brands	人数 Number	百分比 Percent
1	摩托罗拉 Motorola	35	67.3
2	三星 Samsung	7	13.5
3	NEC	5	9.6
4	飞利浦 Philips	4	7.7
5	松下 Panasonic	1	1.9

n=52

3-10 打算购买的种类/ The Type of the Planned Purchase

	人数 Number	百分比 Percent
汉字显示型 pages	32	61.5
数字显示型 number signs	20	38.5

n=52

3-11 理想品牌排名/ Ranking of the Ideal Brands

排名 Brand Ranking	品牌 Brands	人数 Number	百分比 Percent
1	摩托罗拉 Motorola	525	50.8
2	NEC	83	8.0
3	松下 Panasonic	61	5.9
4	三星 Samsung	30	2.9
5	飞利浦 Philips	26	2.5

n=1034

3-12 不同消费者层的理想品牌/ The Ideal Brands by Market Segments

3-12-1 时尚流行指标/ Fads Popular Index

	人数 Number	第一品牌及百分比 1st/ percent	第二品牌及百分比 2nd/ percent	第三品牌及百分比 3rd/ percent
样本 Sample	1022	**摩托罗拉 Motorola(50.6)**	**NEC(8.0)**	**松下 Panasonic(6.0)**
平实生活指向 simple living orientation	518	摩托罗拉 Motorola(50.6)	NEC(5.6)	松下 Panasonic(4.8)
时尚流行指向 fashion orientation	504	摩托罗拉 Motorola(50.6)	NEC(10.5)	松下 Panasonic(7.1)

3-12-2 广告态度指标/ Advertising Attitude Index

	人数 Number	第一品牌及百分比 1st/ percent	第二品牌及百分比 2nd/ percent	第三品牌及百分比 3rd/ percent
样本 Sample	1022	**摩托罗拉 Motorola(50.7)**	**NEC(7.9)**	**松下 Panasonic(5.9)**
广告淡漠指向 indifferent orientation	334	摩托罗拉 Motorola(47.3)	NEC(6.0)	松下 Panasonic(5.7)
中间层 medium	593	摩托罗拉 Motorola(51.9)	NEC(8.8)	松下 Panasonic(6.2)
信赖广告指向 loyal orientation	95	摩托罗拉 Motorola(54.7)	NEC(9.5)	松下 Panasonic(4.2)

3-12-3 价格态度指标/ Price Attitude Index

	人数 Number	第一品牌及百分比 1st/ percent	第二品牌及百分比 2nd/ percent	第三品牌及百分比 3rd/ percent
样本 Sample	1028	**摩托罗拉 Motorola(51.0)**	**NEC(8.1)**	**松下 Panasonic(5.8)**
价格无关心指向 indifferent orientation	188	摩托罗拉 Motorola(52.1)	松下 Panasonic(8.5)	NEC(6.4)
中间层 medium	549	摩托罗拉 Motorola(51.0)	NEC(8.9)	松下 Panasonic(5.6)
价格重视指向 careful orientation	291	摩托罗拉 Motorola(50.2)	NEC(7.6)	松下 Panasonic(4.5)

● 重庆 / Chongqing

3-1 BP 机拥有比例/ Pagers Ownership

	人数 Number	百分比 Percent
使用 yes	212	34.0
不使用 no	412	66.0

n=624

3-2 样本、男性各年龄层、女性各年龄层使用 BP 机的比例/ Proportion of the Sample Using Pagers by the Whole Sample, Age and Gender Groups

	人数 Number	使用 yes	不使用 no
样本 Sample	624	34.0	66.0
男性 Male	314	43.0	57.0
16~24 岁 Age	64	39.1	60.9
25~34 岁 Age	93	54.8	45.2
35~44 岁 Age	75	48.0	52.0
45~54 岁 Age	54	29.6	70.4
55~60 岁 Age	28	25.0	75.0
女性 Female	310	24.8	75.2
16~24 岁 Age	64	40.6	59.4
25~34 岁 Age	90	40.0	60.0
35~44 岁 Age	73	15.1	84.9
45~54 岁 Age	60	5.0	95.0
55~60 岁 Age	23	4.3	95.7

3-3 现用 BP 机的来源/ Source of Obtaining the Currently Owned Pager

	人数 Number	百分比 Percent
自己付费购买 bought by myself	165	77.8
单位配发 offered free by my work unit	39	18.4
其他 others	8	3.8

n=212

3-4 现用 BP 机的品牌排名/ Ranking of the Brands of the Currently Owned Pager

排名 Brand Ranking	品牌 Brands	人数 Number	百分比 Percent
1	摩托罗拉 Motorola	106	50.0
2	NEC	47	22.2
3	松下 Panasonic	15	7.1
4	信利 Truly	5	2.4
5	熊猫 Panda	4	1.9
6	雅皇 Yahuang	3	1.4
6	三星 Samsung	3	1.4
7	DDP	2	0.9
7	大洋 Dayang	2	0.9

n=212

3-5 现用 BP 机的种类/ The Type of the Currently Owned Pager

	人数 Number	百分比 Percent
汉字显示型 pages	24	12.2
数字显示型 number signs	173	87.8

n=197

3-6 选择呼台的考虑因素/ Ranking of the Considerations in Choosing the BP Station

注：本题为多选题，合计百分比超过 100%（Multiple answers）

排名 Ranking	考虑因素 Considerations	人次 Person-time	百分比 Percent
1	信息接收好 good performance	97	46.6
2	覆盖地区广 wide coverage	71	34.1
3	服务质量好 good service	60	28.8
4	呼台的知名度 awareness of the BP service station	45	21.6
5	价格 price	38	18.3
6	联网地区多 wide areas connected	35	16.8
7	其他 others	9	4.3
8	有促销 with promotion activities	8	3.8

n=208

3-7 样本、男性各年龄层、女性各年龄层平均每天接收的信息量/ Pieces of Information Received in a Day by the Whole Sample, Age and Gender Groups

	人数 Number	1 条以下 below 1 piece	1-2 条 1-2 pieces	3-4 条 3-4 pieces	5-9 条 5-9 pieces	10-19 条 10-19 pieces	20 条以上 20 pieces or over
样本 Sample	211	2.8	29.4	36.0	25.1	4.7	1.9
男性 Male	135	2.2	31.9	32.6	28.1	4.4	0.7
16~24 岁 Age	25	8.0	60.0	24.0	4.0	4.0	0.0
25~34 岁 Age	51	0.0	19.6	37.3	41.2	2.0	0.0
35~44 岁 Age	36	2.8	30.6	33.3	25.0	8.3	0.0
45~54 岁 Age	16	0.0	25.0	37.5	25.0	6.3	6.3
55~60 岁 Age	7	0.0	42.9	14.3	42.9	0.0	0.0
女性 Female	76	3.9	25.0	42.1	19.7	5.3	3.9
16~24 岁 Age	26	3.8	26.9	50.0	11.5	7.7	0.0
25~34 岁 Age	35	5.7	25.7	40.0	25.7	2.9	0.0
35~44 岁 Age	11	0.0	18.2	36.4	27.3	0.0	18.2
45~54 岁 Age	3	0.0	33.3	33.3	0.0	0.0	33.3
55~60 岁 Age	1	0.0	0.0	0.0	0.0	100.0	0.0

3-8 样本、男性各年龄层、女性各年龄层未来一年有无购买 BP 机的打算/ Whether Planning to Buy a Pager Next Year by the Whole Sample, Age and Gender Groups

	人数 Number	购买 yes	不购买 no
样本 Sample	622	6.6	93.4
男性 Male	313	8.3	91.7
16~24 岁 Age	64	18.8	81.3
25~34 岁 Age	93	8.6	91.4
35~44 岁 Age	74	6.8	93.2
45~54 岁 Age	54	1.9	98.1
55~60 岁 Age	28	0.0	100.0
女性 Female	309	4.9	95.1
16~24 岁 Age	64	10.9	89.1
25~34 岁 Age	89	4.5	95.5
35~44 岁 Age	73	5.5	94.5
45~54 岁 Age	60	0.0	100.0
55~60 岁 Age	23	0.0	100.0

3-9 打算购买的品牌排名/ Ranking of the Brands planned to Buy

排名 Brand Ranking	品牌 Brands	人数 Number	百分比 Percent
1	摩托罗拉 Motorola	28	68.3
2	松下 Panasonic	3	7.3
2	NEC	3	7.3
2	飞利浦 Philips	3	7.3
3	皮尔・卡丹 Pierre Cardin	2	4.9

n=41

3-10 打算购买的种类/ The Type of the Planned Purchase

	人数 Number	百分比 Percent
汉字显示型 pages	10	25.0
数字显示型 number signs	30	75.0

n=40

3-11 理想品牌排名/ Ranking of the Ideal Brands

排名 Brand Ranking	品牌 Brands	人数 Number	百分比 Percent
1	摩托罗拉 Motorola	378	60.6
2	松下 Panasonic	38	6.1
3	NEC	36	5.8
4	飞利浦 Philips	15	2.4
5	三星 Samsung	10	1.6
6	信利 Truly	3	0.5
7	大洋 Dayang	2	0.3
7	TCL	2	0.3

n=624

3-12 不同消费者层的理想品牌/ The Ideal Brands by Market Segments

3-12-1 时尚流行指标/ Fads Popular Index

	人数 Number	第一品牌及百分比 1st/ percent	第二品牌及百分比 2nd/ percent	第三品牌及百分比 3rd/ percent
样本 Sample	616	**摩托罗拉 Motorola(60.7)**	**松下 Panasonic(6.2)**	**NEC(5.7)**
平实生活指向 simple living orientation	369	摩托罗拉 Motorola(58.8)	松下 Panasonic(5.1)	NEC(4.3)
时尚流行指向 fashion orientation	247	摩托罗拉 Motorola(63.6)	松下 Panasonic(7.7) NEC(7.7)	飞利浦 Philips(3.2)

3-12-2 广告态度指标/ Advertising Attitude Index

	人数 Number	第一品牌及百分比 1st/ percent	第二品牌及百分比 2nd/ percent	第三品牌及百分比 3rd/ percent
样本 Sample	618	**摩托罗拉 Motorola(60.2)**	**松下 Panasonic(6.1)**	**NEC(5.8)**
广告淡漠指向 indifferent orientation	167	摩托罗拉 Motorola(58.7)	松下 Panasonic(6.0)	NEC(3.0)
中间层 medium	367	摩托罗拉 Motorola(60.5)	NEC(7.9)	松下 Panasonic(6.5)
信赖广告指向 loyal orientation	84	摩托罗拉 Motorola(61.9)	松下 Panasonic(4.8)	飞利浦 Philips(3.6)

3-12-3 价格态度指标/ Price Attitude Index

	人数 Number	第一品牌及百分比 1st/ percent	第二品牌及百分比 2nd/ percent	第三品牌及百分比 3rd/ percent
样本 Sample	615	**摩托罗拉 Motorola(60.7)**	**松下 Panasonic(6.0)**	**NEC(5.5)**
价格无关心指向 indifferent orientation	106	摩托罗拉 Motorola(67.0)	松下 Panasonic(5.7)	NEC(4.7)
中间层 medium	280	摩托罗拉 Motorola(61.8)	NEC(7.1)	松下 Panasonic(6.4)
价格重视指向 careful orientation	229	摩托罗拉 Motorola(56.3)	松下 Panasonic(5.7)	NEC(3.9)

● 武汉 / Wuhan

3-1 BP 机拥有比例/ Pagers Ownership

	人数 Number	百分比 Percent
使用 yes	184	28.7
不使用 no	458	71.3

n=642

3-2 样本、男性各年龄层、女性各年龄层使用 BP 机的比例/ Proportion of the Sample Using Pagers by the Whole Sample, Age and Gender Groups

	人数 Number	使用 yes	不使用 no
样本 Sample	642	28.7	71.3
男性 Male	311	36.0	64.0
16~24 岁 Age	65	36.9	63.1
25~34 岁 Age	89	55.1	44.9
35~44 岁 Age	80	28.8	71.3
45~54 岁 Age	52	26.9	73.1
55~60 岁 Age	25	8.0	92.0
女性 Female	331	21.8	78.2
16~24 岁 Age	69	39.1	60.9
25~34 岁 Age	96	29.2	70.8
35~44 岁 Age	78	11.5	88.5
45~54 岁 Age	62	12.9	87.1
55~60 岁 Age	26	0.0	100.0

3-3 现用 BP 机的来源/ Source of Obtaining the Currently Owned Pager

	人数 Number	百分比 Percent
自己付费购买 bought by myself	136	73.9
单位配发 offered free by my work unit	41	22.3
其他 others	7	3.8

n=184

3-4 现用 BP 机的品牌排名/ Ranking of the Brands of the Currently Owned Pager

排名 Brand Ranking	品牌 Brands	人数 Number	百分比 Percent
1	摩托罗拉 Motorola	123	67.6
2	大洋 Dayang	13	7.1
3	松下 Panasonic	10	5.5
4	NEC	7	3.8
5	卡西欧 Casio	6	3.3
5	熊猫 Panda	6	3.3
6	信利 Truly	4	2.2

n=182

3-5 现用 BP 机的种类/ The Type of the Currently Owned Pager

	人数 Number	百分比 Percent
汉字显示型 pages	71	39.0
数字显示型 number signs	111	61.0

n=182

3-6 选择呼台的考虑因素/ Ranking of the Considerations in Choosing the BP Station

注：本题为多选题，合计百分比超过 100%（Multiple answers）

排名 Ranking	考虑因素 Considerations	人次 Person-time	百分比 Percent
1	信息接收好 good performance	90	49.2
2	服务质量好 good service	71	38.8
3	呼台的知名度 awareness of the BP service station	56	30.6
4	价格 price	48	26.2
5	覆盖地区广 wide coverage	46	25.1
6	联网地区多 wide areas connected	45	24.6
7	其他 others	9	4.9
8	有促销 with promotion activities	2	1.1

n=183

3-7 样本、男性各年龄层、女性各年龄层平均每天接收的信息量/ Pieces of Information Received in a Day by the Whole Sample, Age and Gender Groups

	人数 Number	1 条以下 below 1 piece	1-2 条 1-2 pieces	3-4 条 3-4 pieces	5-9 条 5-9 pieces	10-19 条 10-19 pieces	20 条以上 20 pieces or over
样本 Sample	184	6.0	33.2	38.0	15.2	6.5	1.1
男性 Male	112	5.4	32.1	34.8	17.9	8.9	0.9
16~24 岁 Age	24	4.2	41.7	33.3	12.5	8.3	0.0
25~34 岁 Age	49	6.1	32.7	26.5	22.4	12.2	0.0
35~44 岁 Age	23	0.0	21.7	47.8	21.7	4.3	4.3
45~54 岁 Age	14	7.1	35.7	50.0	0.0	7.1	0.0
55~60 岁 Age	2	50.0	0.0	0.0	50.0	0.0	0.0
女性 Female	72	6.9	34.7	43.1	11.1	2.8	1.4
16~24 岁 Age	27	3.7	44.4	44.4	7.4	0.0	0.0
25~34 岁 Age	28	10.7	35.7	35.7	10.7	3.6	3.6
35~44 岁 Age	9	11.1	22.2	44.4	22.2	0.0	0.0
45~54 岁 Age	8	0.0	12.5	62.5	12.5	12.5	0.0
55~60 岁 Age	0	0	0	0	0	0	0

3-8 样本、男性各年龄层、女性各年龄层未来一年有无购买 BP 机的打算/ Whether Planning to Buy a Pager Next Year by the Whole Sample, Age and Gender Groups

	人数 Number	购买 yes	不购买 no
样本 Sample	641	7.0	93.0
男性 Male	311	8.0	92.0
16~24 岁 Age	65	16.9	83.1
25~34 岁 Age	89	5.6	94.4
35~44 岁 Age	80	10.0	90.0
45~54 岁 Age	52	1.9	98.1
55~60 岁 Age	25	0.0	100.0
女性 Female	330	6.1	93.9
16~24 岁 Age	69	10.1	89.9
25~34 岁 Age	96	7.3	92.7
35~44 岁 Age	78	2.6	97.4
45~54 岁 Age	61	6.6	93.4
55~60 岁 Age	26	0.0	100.0

3-9 打算购买的品牌排名/ Ranking of the Brands planned to Buy

排名 Brand Ranking	品牌 Brands	人数 Number	百分比 Percent
1	摩托罗拉 Motorola	37	82.2
2	松下 Panasonic	3	6.7

n=45

3-10 打算购买的种类/ The Type of the Planned Purchase

	人数 Number	百分比 Percent
汉字显示型 pages	23	51.1
数字显示型 number signs	22	48.9

n=45

3-11 理想品牌排名/ Ranking of the Ideal Brands

排名 Brand Ranking	品牌 Brands	人数 Number	百分比 Percent
1	摩托罗拉 Motorola	338	52.6
2	松下 Panasonic	15	2.3
3	NEC	10	1.6
4	大洋 Dayang	6	0.9
5	三星 Samsung	3	0.5
5	飞利浦 Philips	3	0.5
6	卡西欧 Casio	2	0.3

n=642

3-12 不同消费者层的理想品牌/ The Ideal Brands by Market Segments

3-12-1 时尚流行指标/ Fads Popular Index

	人数 Number	第一品牌及百分比 1st/ percent	第二品牌及百分比 2nd/ percent	第三品牌及百分比 3rd/ percent
样本 Sample	632	**摩托罗拉 Motorola(52.5)**	**松下 Panasonic(2.4)**	**NEC(1.6)**
平实生活指向 simple living orientation	330	摩托罗拉 Motorola(45.5)	松下 Panascnic(1.8)	NEC(1.2)
时尚流行指向 fashion orientation	302	摩托罗拉 Motorola(60.3)	松下 Panasonic(3.0)	NEC(2.0)

3-12-2 广告态度指标/ Advertising Attitude Index

	人数 Number	第一品牌及百分比 1st/ percent	第二品牌及百分比 2nd/ percent	第三品牌及百分比 3rd/ percent
样本 Sample	634	**摩托罗拉 Motorola(52.4)**	**松下 Panasonic(2.4)**	**NEC(1.6)**
广告淡漠指向 indifferent orientation	188	摩托罗拉 Motorola(46.8)	松下 Panasonic(1.6)	NEC(0.5) 飞利浦 Philips(0.5) 三星 Samsung(0.5)
中间层 medium	373	摩托罗拉 Motorola(53.1)	松下 Panasonic(3.2)	NEC(2.1)
信赖广告指向 loyal orientation	73	摩托罗拉 Motorola(63.0)	大洋 Dayang(2.7)	NEC(1.4) 三星 Samsung(1.4) 爱立信 Ericsson(1.4)

3-12-3 价格态度指标/ Price Attitude Index

	人数 Number	第一品牌及百分比 1st/ percent	第二品牌及百分比 2nd/ percent	第三品牌及百分比 3rd/ percent
样本 Sample	634	**摩托罗拉 Motorola(52.4)**	**松下 Panasonic(2.4)**	**NEC(1.6)**
价格无关心指向 indifferent orientation	84	摩托罗拉 Motorola(59.5)	松下 Panasonic(3.6)	NEC(2.4) 大洋 Dayang(2.4)
中间层 medium	306	摩托罗拉 Motorola(59.5)	松下 Panasonic(2.0)	NEC(1.3)
价格重视指向 careful orientation	244	摩托罗拉 Motorola(41.0)	松下 Panasonic(2.5)	NEC(1.6)

● 西安 / Xi'an

3-1 BP 机拥有比例/ Pagers Ownership

	人数 Number	百分比 Percent
使用 yes	257	42.8
不使用 no	344	57.2

n=601

3-2 样本、男性各年龄层、女性各年龄层使用 BP 机的比例/ Proportion of the Sample Using Pagers by the Whole Sample, Age and Gender Groups

	人数 Number	使用 yes	不使用 no
样本 Sample	601	42.8	57.2
男性 Male	302	53.0	47.0
16~24 岁 Age	64	42.2	57.8
25~34 岁 Age	91	68.1	31.9
35~44 岁 Age	77	63.6	36.4
45~54 岁 Age	46	39.1	60.9
55~60 岁 Age	24	16.7	83.3
女性 Female	299	32.4	67.6
16~24 岁 Age	61	39.3	60.7
25~34 岁 Age	90	44.4	55.6
35~44 岁 Age	74	33.8	66.2
45~54 岁 Age	49	14.3	85.7
55~60 岁 Age	25	4.0	96.0

3-3 现用 BP 机的来源/ Source of Obtaining the Currently Owned Pager

	人数 Number	百分比 Percent
自己付费购买 bought by myself	208	80.9
单位配发 offered free by my work unit	37	14.4
其他 others	12	4.7

n=257

3-4 现用 BP 机的品牌排名/ Ranking of the Brands of the Currently Owned Pager

排名 Brand Ranking	品牌 Brands	人数 Number	百分比 Percent
1	摩托罗拉 Motorola	179	69.9
2	大洋 Dayang	20	7.8
3	松下 Panasonic	11	4.3
4	卡西欧 Casio	9	3.5
5	NEC	3	1.2
5	三星 Samsung	3	1.2
5	熊猫 Panda	3	1.2

n=256

3-5 现用 BP 机的种类/ The Type of the Currently Owned Pager

	人数 Number	百分比 Percent
汉字显示型 pages	77	30.0
数字显示型 number signs	180	70.0

n=257

3-6 选择呼台的考虑因素/ Ranking of the Considerations in Choosing the BP Station

注：本题为多选题，合计百分比超过 100%（Multiple answers）

排名 Ranking	考虑因素 Considerations	人次 Person-time	百分比 Percent
1	信息接收好 good performance	112	43.6
2	覆盖地区广 wide coverage	80	31.1
3	呼台的知名度 awareness of the BP service station	73	28.4
4	服务质量好 good service	69	26.8
5	联网地区多 wide areas connected	68	26.5
6	价格 price	47	18.3
7	其他 others	14	5.4
8	有促销 with promotion activities	12	4.7

n=257

3-7 样本、男性各年龄层、女性各年龄层平均每天接收的信息量/ Pieces of Information Received in a Day by the Whole Sample, Age and Gender Groups

	人数 Number	1 条以下 below 1 piece	1-2 条 1-2 pieces	3-4 条 3-4 pieces	5-9 条 5-9 pieces	10-19 条 10-19 pieces	20 条以上 20 pieces or over
样本 Sample	257	5.4	25.7	40.9	19.5	7.0	1.6
男性 Male	160	6.3	21.9	39.4	21.9	8.8	1.9
16~24 岁 Age	27	3.7	22.2	44.4	18.5	11.1	0.0
25~34 岁 Age	62	9.7	16.1	41.9	22.6	9.7	0.0
35~44 岁 Age	49	4.1	28.6	34.7	16.3	10.2	6.1
45~54 岁 Age	18	0.0	27.8	44.4	27.8	0.0	0.0
55~60 岁 Age	4	25.0	0.0	0.0	75.0	0.0	0.0
女性 Female	97	4.1	32.0	43.3	15.5	4.1	1.0
16~24 岁 Age	24	0.0	45.8	41.7	12.5	0.0	0.0
25~34 岁 Age	40	2.5	27.5	40.0	22.5	5.0	2.5
35~44 岁 Age	25	12.0	24.0	60.0	4.0	0.0	0.0
45~54 岁 Age	7	0.0	28.6	14.3	28.6	28.6	0.0
55~60 岁 Age	1	0.0	100.0	0.0	0.0	0.0	0.0

3-8 样本、男性各年龄层、女性各年龄层未来一年有无购买 BP 机的打算/ Whether Planning to Buy a Pager Next Year by the Whole Sample, Age and Gender Groups

	人数 Number	购买 yes	不购买 no
样本 Sample	601	7.3	92.7
男性 Male	302	7.6	92.4
16~24 岁 Age	64	17.2	82.8
25~34 岁 Age	91	6.6	93.4
35~44 岁 Age	77	5.2	94.8
45~54 岁 Age	46	4.3	95.7
55~60 岁 Age	24	0.0	100.0
女性 Female	299	7.0	93.0
16~24 岁 Age	61	11.5	88.5
25~34 岁 Age	90	11.1	88.9
35~44 岁 Age	74	2.7	97.3
45~54 岁 Age	49	4.1	95.9
55~60 岁 Age	25	0.0	100.0

3-9 打算购买的品牌排名/ Ranking of the Brands planned to Buy

排名 Brand Ranking	品牌 Brands	人数 Number	百分比 Percent
1	摩托罗拉 Motorola	32	72.7
2	大洋 Dayang	4	9.1
3	三星 Samsung	3	6.8
4	飞利浦 Philips	2	4.5

n=44

3-10 打算购买的种类/ The Type of the Planned Purchase

	人数 Number	百分比 Percent
汉字显示型 pages	23	52.3
数字显示型 number signs	21	47.7

n=44

3-11 理想品牌排名/ Ranking of the Ideal Brands

排名 Brand Ranking	品牌 Brands	人数 Number	百分比 Percent
1	摩托罗拉 Motorola	425	70.8
2	松下 Panasonic	19	3.2
2	飞利浦 Philips	19	3.2
3	三星 Samsung	14	2.3
4	大洋 Dayang	11	1.8
5	NEC	7	1.2
6	卡西欧 Casio	5	0.8

n=600

3-12 不同消费者层的理想品牌/ The Ideal Brands by Market Segments

3-12-1 时尚流行指标/ Fads Popular Index

	人数 Number	第一品牌及百分比 1st/ percent	第二品牌及百分比 2nd/ percent	第三品牌及百分比 3rd/ percent
样本 Sample	598	**摩托罗拉 Motorola(70.7)**	**松下 Panasonic(3.2)** **飞利浦 Philips(3.2)**	**三星 Samsung(2.3)**
平实生活指向 simple living orientation	340	摩托罗拉 Motorola(65.6)	松下 Panasonic(3.8)	飞利浦 Philips(3.2) 三星 Samsung(3.2)
时尚流行指向 fashion orientation	258	摩托罗拉 Motorola(77.5)	飞利浦 Philips(3.1)	大洋 Dayang(2.7)

3-12-2 广告态度指标/ Advertising Attitude Index

	人数 Number	第一品牌及百分比 1st/ percent	第二品牌及百分比 2nd/ percent	第三品牌及百分比 3rd/ percent
样本 Sample	596	**摩托罗拉 Motorola(71.0)**	**松下 Panasonic(3.2)**	**飞利浦 Philips(3.0)**
广告淡漠指向 indifferent orientation	184	摩托罗拉 Motorola(69.0)	松下 Panasonic(3.8)	大洋 Dayang(3.3)
中间层 medium	333	摩托罗拉 Motorola(72.7)	飞利浦 Philips(3.0)	松下 Panasonic(2.7)
信赖广告指向 loyal orientation	79	摩托罗拉 Motorola(68.4)	松下 Panasonic(3.8) 飞利浦 Philips(3.8) 大洋 Dayang(3.8)	三星 Samsung(2.5)

3-12-3 价格态度指标/ Price Attitude Index

	人数 Number	第一品牌及百分比 1st/ percent	第二品牌及百分比 2nd/ percent	第三品牌及百分比 3rd/ percent
样本 Sample	596	**摩托罗拉 Motorola(70.8)**	**飞利浦 Philips(3.2)**	**松下 Panasonic(3.0)**
价格无关心指向 indifferent orientation	142	摩托罗拉 Motorola(76.8)	三星 Samsung(3.5)	松下 Panasonic(2.8) 飞利浦 Philips(2.8)
中间层 medium	306	摩托罗拉 Motorola(69.6)	飞利浦 Philips(3.6)	松下 Panasonic(3.3)
价格重视指向 careful orientation	148	摩托罗拉 Motorola(67.6)	三星 Samsung(4.1)	松下 Panasonic(2.7) 飞利浦 Philips(2.7)

● 沈阳 / Shenyang

3-1 BP 机拥有比例/ Pagers Ownership

	人数 Number	百分比 Percent
使用 yes	277	46.2
不使用 no	323	53.8

n=600

3-2 样本、男性各年龄层、女性各年龄层使用 BP 机的比例/ Proportion of the Sample Using Pagers by the Whole Sample, Age and Gender Groups

	人数 Number	使用 yes	不使用 no
样本 Sample	600	46.2	53.8
男性 Male	299	55.5	44.5
16~24 岁 Age	64	46.9	53.1
25~34 岁 Age	89	66.3	33.7
35~44 岁 Age	76	64.5	35.5
45~54 岁 Age	46	52.2	47.8
55~60 岁 Age	24	16.7	83.3
女性 Female	301	36.9	63.1
16~24 岁 Age	64	40.6	59.4
25~34 岁 Age	89	53.9	46.1
35~44 岁 Age	76	38.2	61.8
45~54 岁 Age	48	14.6	85.4
55~60 岁 Age	24	4.2	95.8

3-3 现用 BP 机的来源/ Source of Obtaining the Currently Owned Pager

	人数 Number	百分比 Percent
自己付费购买 bought by myself	225	81.5
单位配发 offered free by my work unit	37	13.4
其他 others	14	5.1

n=276

3-4 现用 BP 机的品牌排名/ Ranking of the Brands of the Currently Owned Pager

排名 Brand Ranking	品牌 Brands	人数 Number	百分比 Percent
1	摩托罗拉 Motorola	218	79.0
2	松下 Panasonic	22	8.0
3	大洋 Dayang	7	2.5
4	卡西欧 Casio	6	2.2
5	NEC	3	1.1

n=276

3-5 现用 BP 机的种类/ The Type of the Currently Owned Pager

	人数 Number	百分比 Percent
汉字显示型 pages	36	13.0
数字显示型 number signs	241	87.0

n=277

3-6 选择呼台的考虑因素/ Ranking of the Considerations in Choosing the BP Station

注：本题为多选题，合计百分比超过 100%（Multiple answers）

排名 Ranking	考虑因素 Considerations	人次 Person-time	百分比 Percent
1	信息接收好 good performance	120	43.3
2	呼台的知名度 awareness of the BP service station	102	36.8
3	服务质量好 good service	91	32.9
4	覆盖地区广 wide coverage	80	28.9
5	联网地区多 wide areas connected	67	24.2
6	价格 price	58	20.9
7	其他 others	10	3.6
8	有促销 with promotion activities	3	1.1

n=277

3-7 样本、男性各年龄层、女性各年龄层平均每天接收的信息量/ Pieces of Information Received in a Day by the Whole Sample, Age and Gender Groups

	人数 Number	1 条以下 below 1 piece	1-2 条 1-2 pieces	3-4 条 3-4 pieces	5-9 条 5-9 pieces	10-19 条 10-19 pieces	20 条以上 20 pieces or over
样本 Sample	277	16.6	32.1	33.9	12.3	3.6	1.4
男性 Male	166	12.7	32.5	33.7	14.5	4.2	2.4
16~24 岁 Age	30	23.3	30.0	26.7	13.3	3.3	3.3
25~34 岁 Age	59	10.2	37.3	33.9	13.6	5.1	0.0
35~44 岁 Age	49	10.2	34.7	32.7	18.4	0.0	4.1
45~54 岁 Age	24	12.5	20.8	45.8	8.3	8.3	4.2
55~60 岁 Age	4	0.0	25.0	25.0	25.0	25.0	0.0
女性 Female	111	22.5	31.5	34.2	9.0	2.7	0.0
16~24 岁 Age	26	11.5	46.2	30.8	11.5	0.0	0.0
25~34 岁 Age	48	25.0	27.1	35.4	10.4	2.1	0.0
35~44 岁 Age	29	20.7	27.6	37.9	6.9	6.9	0.0
45~54 岁 Age	7	57.1	14.3	28.6	0.0	0.0	0.0
55~60 岁 Age	1	0.0	100.0	0.0	0.0	0.0	0.0

3-8 样本、男性各年龄层、女性各年龄层未来一年有无购买 BP 机的打算/ Whether Planning to Buy a Pager Next Year by the Whole Sample, Age and Gender Groups

	人数 Number	购买 yes	不购买 no
样本 Sample	599	6.3	93.7
男性 Male	299	8.7	91.3
16~24 岁 Age	64	12.5	87.5
25~34 岁 Age	89	5.6	94.4
35~44 岁 Age	76	11.8	88.2
45~54 岁 Age	46	8.7	91.3
55~60 岁 Age	24	0.0	100.0
女性 Female	300	4.0	96.0
16~24 岁 Age	64	12.5	87.5
25~34 岁 Age	88	1.1	98.9
35~44 岁 Age	76	2.6	97.4
45~54 岁 Age	48	2.1	97.9
55~60 岁 Age	24	0.0	100.0

3-9 打算购买的品牌排名/ Ranking of the Brands planned to Buy

排名 Brand Ranking	品牌 Brands	人数 Number	百分比 Percent
1	摩托罗拉 Motorola	28	75.7
2	飞利浦 Philips	5	13.5
3	松下 Panasonic	2	5.4
4	NEC	1	2.7
4	三星 Samsung	1	2.7

n=37

3-10 打算购买的种类/ The Type of the Planned Purchase

	人数 Number	百分比 Percent
汉字显示型 pages	17	45.9
数字显示型 number signs	20	54.1

n=37

3-11 理想品牌排名/ Ranking of the Ideal Brands

排名 Brand Ranking	品牌 Brands	人数 Number	百分比 Percent
1	摩托罗拉 Motorola	445	74.2
2	松下 Panasonic	63	10.5
3	飞利浦 Philips	15	2.5
4	卡西欧 Casio	11	1.8
5	三星 Samsung	4	0.7
6	大洋 Dayang	2	0.3
6	NEC	2	0.3

n=600

3-12 不同消费者层的理想品牌/ The Ideal Brands by Market Segments

3-12-1 时尚流行指标/ Fads Popular Index

	人数 Number	第一品牌及百分比 1st/ percent	第二品牌及百分比 2nd/ percent	第三品牌及百分比 3rd/ percent
样本 Sample	**600**	**摩托罗拉 Motorola(74.2)**	**松下 Panasonic(10.5)**	**飞利浦 Philips(2.5)**
平实生活指向 simple living orientation	291	摩托罗拉 Motorola(74.2)	松下 Panasonic(6.5)	飞利浦 Philips(2.4)
时尚流行指向 fashion orientation	309	摩托罗拉 Motorola(74.1)	松下 Panasonic(14.2)	飞利浦 Philips(2.6)

3-12-2 广告态度指标/ Advertising Attitude Index

	人数 Number	第一品牌及百分比 1st/ percent	第二品牌及百分比 2nd/ percent	第三品牌及百分比 3rd/ percent
样本 Sample	**600**	**摩托罗拉 Motorola(74.2)**	**松下 Panasonic(10.5)**	**飞利浦 Philips(2.5)**
广告淡漠指向 indifferent orientation	172	摩托罗拉 Motorola(79.1)	松下 Panasonic(7.0)	卡西欧 Casio(2.3)
中间层 medium	353	摩托罗拉 Motorola(72.0)	松下 Panasonic(11.6)	飞利浦 Philips(2.8)
信赖广告指向 loyal orientation	75	摩托罗拉 Motorola(73.3)	松下 Panasonic(13.3)	飞利浦 Philips(2.7)

3-12-3 价格态度指标/ Price Attitude Index

	人数 Number	第一品牌及百分比 1st/ percent	第二品牌及百分比 2nd/ percent	第三品牌及百分比 3rd/ percent
样本 Sample	**599**	**摩托罗拉 Motorola(74.3)**	**松下 Panasonic(10.4)**	**飞利浦 Philips(2.5)**
价格无关心指向 indifferent orientation	104	摩托罗拉 Motorola(76.9)	松下 Panasonic(7.7)	卡西欧 Casio(3.8)
中间层 medium	292	摩托罗拉 Motorola(75.0)	松下 Panasonic(11.3)	飞利浦 Philips(2.4)
价格重视指向 careful orientation	203	摩托罗拉 Motorola(71.9)	松下 Panasonic(10.3)	飞利浦 Philips(3.4)

4.移动电话 / Mobile Phone

● 北京 / Beijing

4-1 移动电话拥有比例/ Mobile Phones Ownership

	人数 Number	百分比 Percent
使用 yes	236	23.3
不使用 no	776	76.7

n=1012

4-2 现用移动电话的来源/ Source of Obtaining the Currently Owned Mobile Phone

	人数 Number	百分比 Percent
自己付费购买 bought by myself	190	80.9
单位配发 offered free by my work unit	37	15.7
其他 others	8	3.4

n=235

4-3 现用移动电话的品牌排名/ Ranking of the Brands of the Currently Owned Mobile Phone

排名 Brand Ranking	品牌 Brands	人数 Number	百分比 Percent
1	诺基亚 Nokia	75	31.8
2	摩托罗拉 Motorola	74	31.4
3	爱立信 Ericsson	49	20.8
4	西门子 Siemens	15	6.4
5	飞利浦 Philips	7	3.0
6	松下 Panasonic	6	2.5
7	索尼 Sony	3	1.3
8	三星 Samsung	2	0.8

n=236

4-4 选择移动电话时的考虑因素/ Ranking of the Considerations in Choosing the Mobile Phone

注：本题为多选题，合计百分比超过 100%（Multiple answers）

排名 Ranking	考虑因素 Considerations	人次 Person-time	百分比 Percent
1	轻便小巧 light and small	124	52.8
2	价格适中 reasonable price	95	40.4
3	功能多 with multi-function	83	35.3
4	外观 appearance	73	31.1
5	功能新 with new function	39	16.6
6	抗阻能力强 with strong anti-noise power	30	12.8
7	其他 others	10	4.3

n=235

4-5 所使用通讯网的类型/ The Type of the Net the Currently Owned Mobile Phone Used

	人数 Number	百分比 Percent
模拟网 analog net	31	14.0
数字网 digital net	180	81.4
CDMA	10	4.5

n=221

4-6 所使用通讯网的名称/ The Name of the Net the Currently Owned Mobile Phone Used

	人数 Number	百分比 Percent
中国电信网 China Telecom	158	68.7
中国联通网 China Unicom	71	30.9
长城网 the Great Wall Telecom	1	0.4

n=230

4-7 平均每天接收的信息量/ Pieces of Information Received in a Day

	人数 Number	百分比 Percent
1 条以下 below 1 piece	24	10.2
1-2 条 pieces	53	22.6
3-4 条 pieces	68	28.9
5-9 条 pieces	48	20.4
10-19 条 pieces	33	14.0
20 条以上 20 pieces or over	9	3.8

n=235

4-8 平均每天发出的信息量/ Pieces of Information Sent in a Day

	人数 Number	百分比 Percent
1 条以下 below 1 piece	16	6.8
1-2 条 pieces	53	22.6
3-4 条 pieces	70	29.9
5-9 条 pieces	62	26.5
10-19 条 pieces	28	12.0
20 条以上 20 pieces or over	5	2.1

n=234

4-9 未来一年有无购买移动电话的打算/ Whether Planning to Buy a Mobile Phone Next Year

	人数 Number	百分比 Percent
购买 yes	231	23.1
不购买 no	769	76.9

n=1000

4-10 打算购买的品牌/ Ranking of the Brands Planned to Buy

排名 Brand Ranking	品牌 Brands	人数 Number	百分比 Percent
1	诺基亚 Nokia	94	40.9
2	摩托罗拉 Motorola	65	28.3
3	爱立信 Ericsson	39	17.0
4	西门子 Siemens	10	4.3
5	飞利浦 Philips	5	2.2
6	松下 Panosonic	4	1.7
7	NEC	3	1.3
7	阿尔凯特 Alcatel	3	1.3
8	索尼 Sony	2	0.9

n=230

4-11 理想品牌排名/ Ranking of the Ideal Brands

排名 Brand Ranking	品牌 Brands	人数 Number	百分比 Percent
1	诺基亚 Nokia	270	26.7
2	摩托罗拉 Motorola	240	23.7
3	爱立信 Ericsson	166	16.4
4	西门子 Siemens	26	2.6
5	松下 Panasonic	13	1.3
6	飞利浦 Philips	10	1.0
7	索尼 Sony	6	0.6
7	三星 Samsung	6	0.6
8	NEC	5	0.5

n=1012

4-12 不同消费者层的理想品牌/ The Ideal Brands by Market Segments

4-12-1 时尚流行指标/ Fads Popular Index

	人数 Number	第一品牌及百分比 1st/ percent	第二品牌及百分比 2nd/ percent	第三品牌及百分比 3rd/ percent
样本 Sample	**998**	**诺基亚 Nokia(26.6)**	**摩托罗拉 Motorola(23.9)**	**爱立信 Ericsson(16.4)**
平实生活指向 simple living orientation	491	诺基亚 Nokia(25.1)	摩托罗拉 Motorola(22.8)	爱立信 Ericsson(14.5)
时尚流行指向 fashion orientation	507	诺基亚 Nokia(28.0)	摩托罗拉 Motorola(25.0)	爱立信 Ericsson(18.3)

4-12-2 广告态度指标/ Advertising Attitude Index

	人数 Number	第一品牌及百分比 1st/ percent	第二品牌及百分比 2nd/ percent	第三品牌及百分比 3rd/ percent
样本 Sample	**994**	**诺基亚 Nokia(27.0)**	**摩托罗拉 Motorola(23.3)**	**爱立信 Ericsson(16.5)**
广告淡漠指向 indifferent orientation	289	诺基亚 Nokia(26.3)	摩托罗拉 Motorola(17.6)	爱立信 Ericsson(17.3)
中间层 medium	572	诺基亚 Nokia(28.3)	摩托罗拉 Motorola(24.5)	爱立信 Ericsson(17.0)
信赖广告指向 loyal orientation	133	摩托罗拉 Motorola(30.8)	诺基亚 Nokia(22.6)	爱立信 Ericsson(12.8)

4-12-3 价格态度指标/ Price Attitude Index

	人数 Number	第一品牌及百分比 1st/ percent	第二品牌及百分比 2nd/ percent	第三品牌及百分比 3rd/ percent
样本 Sample	1002	**诺基亚 Nokia(26.7)**	**摩托罗拉 Motorola(23.8)**	**爱立信 Ericsson(16.2)**
价格无关心指向 indifferent orientation	203	诺基亚 Nokia(30.5)	摩托罗拉 Motorola(25.1)	爱立信 Ericsson(18.7)
中间层 medium	501	诺基亚 Nokia(29.3)	摩托罗拉 Motorola(26.9)	爱立信 Ericsson(15.4)
价格重视指向 careful orientation	298	诺基亚 Nokia(19.8)	摩托罗拉 Motorola(17.4)	爱立信 Ericsson(15.8)

● 上海 / Shanghai

4-1 移动电话拥有比例/ Mobile Phones Ownership

	人数 Number	百分比 Percent
使用 yes	221	21.8
不使用 no	793	78.2

n=1014

4-2 现用移动电话的来源/ Source of Obtaining the Currently Owned Mobile Phone

	人数 Number	百分比 Percent
自己付费购买 bought by myself	192	86.9
单位配发 offered free by my work unit	23	10.4
其他 others	6	2.7

n=221

4-3 现用移动电话的品牌排名/ Ranking of the Brands of the Currently Owned Mobile Phone

排名 Brand Ranking	品牌 Brands	人数 Number	百分比 Percent
1	爱立信 Ericsson	61	27.7
2	诺基亚 Nokia	56	25.5
3	摩托罗拉 Motorola	55	25.0
4	西门子 Siemens	19	8.6
5	松下 Panasonic	7	3.2
6	三星 Samsung	6	2.7
6	飞利浦 Philips	6	2.7
7	索尼 Sony	2	0.9
7	阿尔凯特 Alcatel	2	0.9
7	NEC	2	0.9

n=220

4-4 选择移动电话时的考虑因素/ Ranking of the Considerations in Choosing the Mobile Phone

注：本题为多选题，合计百分比超过 100%（Multiple answers）

排名 Ranking	考虑因素 Considerations	人次 Person-time	百分比 Percent
1	轻便小巧 light and small	112	50.7
2	价格适中 reasonable price	104	47.1
3	功能多 with multi-function	86	38.9
4	外观 appearance	59	26.7
5	功能新 with new function	39	17.6
6	抗阻能力强 with strong anti-noise power	37	16.7
7	其他 others	8	3.6

n=221

4-5 所使用通讯网的类型/ The Type of the Net the Currently Owned Mobile Phone Used

	人数 Number	百分比 Percent
模拟网 analog net	23	10.5
数字网 digital net	187	85.0
CDMA	10	4.5

n=220

4-6 所使用通讯网的名称/ The Name of the Net the Currently Owned Mobile Phone Used

	人数 Number	百分比 Percent
中国电信网 China Telecom	138	63.0
中国联通网 China Unicom	77	35.2
长城网 the Great Wall Telecom	4	1.8

n=219

4-7 平均每天接收的信息量/ Pieces of Information Received in a Day

	人数 Number	百分比 Percent
1 条以下 below 1 piece	25	11.4
1-2 条 pieces	48	21.8
3-4 条 pieces	74	33.6
5-9 条 pieces	41	18.6
10-19 条 pieces	24	10.9
20 条以上 20 pieces or over	8	3.6

n=220

4-8 平均每天发出的信息量/ Pieces of Information Sent in a Day

	人数 Number	百分比 Percent
1 条以下 below 1 piece	13	5.9
1-2 条 pieces	58	26.2
3-4 条 pieces	74	33.5
5-9 条 pieces	45	20.4
10-19 条 pieces	25	11.3
20 条以上 20 pieces or over	6	2.7

n=221

4-9 未来一年有无购买移动电话的打算/ Whether Planning to Buy a Mobile Phone Next Year

	人数 Number	百分比 Percent
购买 yes	179	17.7
不购买 no	834	82.3

n=1013

4-10 打算购买的品牌/ Ranking of the Brands Planned to Buy

排名 Brand Ranking	品牌 Brands	人数 Number	百分比 Percent
1	诺基亚 Nokia	66	37.1
2	爱立信 Ericsson	43	24.2
3	摩托罗拉 Motorola	41	23.0
4	阿尔凯特 Alcatel	6	3.4
4	NEC	6	3.4
5	西门子 Siemens	5	2.8
6	松下 Panosonic	4	2.2
7	索尼 Sony	2	1.1
7	飞利浦 Philips	2	1.1
8	博世 Busuh	1	0.6

n=178

4-11 理想品牌排名/ Ranking of the Ideal Brands

排名 Brand Ranking	品牌 Brands	人数 Number	百分比 Percent
1	诺基亚 Nokia	276	27.2
2	爱立信 Ericsson	232	22.9
3	摩托罗拉 Motorola	216	21.3
4	西门子 Siemens	60	5.9
5	NEC	54	5.3
6	松下 Panasonic	29	2.9
7	飞利浦 Philips	17	1.7
8	三星 Samsung	12	1.2
9	索尼 Sony	10	1.0
10	阿尔凯特 Alcatel	8	0.8

n=1013

4-12 不同消费者层的理想品牌/ The Ideal Brands by Market Segments

4-12-1 时尚流行指标/ Fads Popular Index

	人数 Number	第一品牌及百分比 1st/ percent	第二品牌及百分比 2nd/ percent	第三品牌及百分比 3rd/ percent
样本 Sample	1004	**诺基亚 Nokia(27.3)**	**爱立信 Ericsson(23.0)**	**摩托罗拉 Motorola(21.2)**
平实生活指向 simple living orientation	471	诺基亚 Nokia(25.7)	爱立信 Ericsson(21.9)	摩托罗拉 Motorola(21.7)
时尚流行指向 fashion orientation	533	诺基亚 Nokia(28.7)	爱立信 Ericsson(24.0)	摩托罗拉 Motorola(20.8)

4-12-2 广告态度指标/ Advertising Attitude Index

	人数 Number	第一品牌及百分比 1st/ percent	第二品牌及百分比 2nd/ percent	第三品牌及百分比 3rd/ percent
样本 Sample	1001	**诺基亚 Nokia(27.3)**	**爱立信 Ericsson(22.7)**	**摩托罗拉 Motorola(21.5)**
广告淡漠指向 indifferent orientation	256	诺基亚 Nokia(25.8)	摩托罗拉 Motorola(21.5)	爱立信 Ericsson(18.0)
中间层 medium	610	诺基亚 Nokia(26.2)	爱立信 Ericsson(24.4)	摩托罗拉 Motorola(22.1)
信赖广告指向 loyal orientation	135	诺基亚 Nokia(34.8)	爱立信 Ericsson(23.7)	摩托罗拉 Motorola(18.5)

4-12-3 价格态度指标/ Price Attitude Index

	人数 Number	第一品牌及百分比 1st/ percent	第二品牌及百分比 2nd/ percent	第三品牌及百分比 3rd/ percent
样本 Sample	1010	**诺基亚 Nokia(27.3)**	**爱立信 Ericsson(23.0)**	**摩托罗拉 Motorola(21.4)**
价格无关心指向 indifferent orientation	151	诺基亚 Nokia(27.8)	爱立信 Ericsson(22.5)	摩托罗拉 Motorola(21.9)
价格重视指向 careful orientation	520	诺基亚 Nokia(28.7)	爱立信 Ericsson(25.0)	摩托罗拉 Motorola(18.8)
价格重视指向 careful orientation	339	摩托罗拉 Motorola(25.1) 诺基亚 Nokia(25.1)	爱立信 Ericsson(20.1)	西门子 Siemens(6.2)

● 广州 / Guangzhou

4-1 移动电话拥有比例/ Mobile Phones Ownership

	人数 Number	百分比 Percent
使用 yes	288	27.9
不使用 no	746	72.1

n=1034

4-2 现用移动电话的来源/ Source of Obtaining the Currently Owned Mobile Phone

	人数 Number	百分比 Percent
自己付费购买 bought by myself	264	91.7
单位配发 offered free by my work unit	15	5.2
其他 others	9	3.1

n=288

4-3 现用移动电话的品牌排名/ Ranking of the Brands of the Currently Owned Mobile Phone

排名 Brand Ranking	品牌 Brands	人数 Number	百分比 Percent
1	诺基亚 Nokia	99	34.4
2	爱立信 Ericsson	81	28.1
3	摩托罗拉 Motorola	74	25.7
4	三星 Samsung	10	3.5
5	西门子 Siemens	9	3.1
6	飞利浦 Philips	6	2.1

n=288

4-4 选择移动电话时的考虑因素/ Ranking of the Considerations in Choosing the Mobile Phone

注：本题为多选题，合计百分比超过 100%（Multiple answers）

排名 Ranking	考虑因素 Considerations	人次 Person-time	百分比 Percent
1	价格适中 reasonable price	151	52.8
1	轻便小巧 light and small	151	52.8
2	功能多 with multi-function	117	40.9
3	外观 appearance	75	26.2
4	功能新 with new function	43	15.0
5	抗阻能力强 with strong anti-noise power	39	13.6
6	其他 others	11	3.8

n=286

4-5 所使用通讯网的类型/ The Type of the Net the Currently Owned Mobile Phone Used

	人数 Number	百分比 Percent
模拟网 analog net	18	6.4
数字网 digital net	254	90.1
CDMA	10	3.5

n=282

4-6 所使用通讯网的名称/ The Name of the Net the Currently Owned Mobile Phone Used

	人数 Number	百分比 Percent
中国电信网 China Telecom	210	73.4
中国联通网 China Unicom	75	26.2
长城网 the Great Wall Telecom	1	0.3

n=286

4-7 平均每天接收的信息量/ Pieces of Information Received in a Day

	人数 Number	百分比 Percent
1 条以下 below 1 piece	21	7.3
1-2 条 pieces	39	13.6
3-4 条 pieces	107	37.3
5-9 条 pieces	76	26.5
10-19 条 pieces	33	11.5
20 条以上 20 pieces or over	11	3.8

n=287

4-8 平均每天发出的信息量/ Pieces of Information Sent in a Day

	人数 Number	百分比 Percent
1 条以下 below 1 piece	21	7.3
1-2 条 pieces	64	22.4
3-4 条 pieces	92	32.2
5-9 条 pieces	75	26.2
10-19 条 pieces	26	9.1
20 条以上 20 pieces or over	8	2.8

n=286

4-9 未来一年有无购买移动电话的打算/ Whether Planning to Buy a Mobile Phone Next Year

	人数 Number	百分比 Percent
购买 yes	205	19.9
不购买 no	826	80.1

n=1031

4-10 打算购买的品牌/ Ranking of the Brands Planned to Buy

排名 Brand Ranking	品牌 Brands	人数 Number	百分比 Percent
1	摩托罗拉 Motorola	66	32.4
2	诺基亚 Nokia	64	31.4
3	爱立信 Ericsson	37	18.1
4	三星 Samsung	20	9.8

n=204

4-11 理想品牌排名/ Ranking of the Ideal Brands

排名 Brand Ranking	品牌 Brands	人数 Number	百分比 Percent
1	诺基亚 Nokia	274	26.5
2	摩托罗拉 Motorola	209	20.2
3	爱立信 Ericsson	197	19.1
4	三星 Samsung	53	5.1
5	西门子 Siemens	30	2.9
6	NEC	29	2.8

n=1033

4-12 不同消费者层的理想品牌/ The Ideal Brands by Market Segments

4-12-1 时尚流行指标/ Fads Popular Index

	人数 Number	第一品牌及百分比 1st/ percent	第二品牌及百分比 2nd/ percent	第三品牌及百分比 3rd/ percent
样本 Sample	1021	**诺基亚 Nokia(26.3)**	**摩托罗拉 Motorola(20.2)**	**爱立信 Ericsson(19.2)**
平实生活指向 simple living orientation	517	诺基亚 Nokia(24.8)	摩托罗拉 Motorola(20.1)	爱立信 Ericsson(18.4)
时尚流行指向 fashion orientation	504	诺基亚 Nokia(28.0)	摩托罗拉 Motorola(20.2)	爱立信 Ericsson(20.0)

4-12-2 广告态度指标/ Advertising Attitude Index

	人数 Number	第一品牌及百分比 1st/ percent	第二品牌及百分比 2nd/ percent	第三品牌及百分比 3rd/ percent
样本 Sample	1021	**诺基亚 Nokia(26.2)**	**摩托罗拉 Motorola(20.4)**	**爱立信 Ericsson(18.9)**
广告淡漠指向 indifferent orientation	334	诺基亚 Nokia(24.9)	爱立信 Ericsson(19.5)	摩托罗拉 Motorola(17.4)
中间层 medium	592	诺基亚 Nokia(27.5)	摩托罗拉 Motorola(21.5)	爱立信 Ericsson(18.6)
信赖广告指向 loyal orientation	95	摩托罗拉 Motorola(24.2)	诺基亚 Nokia(23.2)	爱立信 Ericsson(18.9)

4-12-3 价格态度指标/ Price Attitude Index

	人数 Number	第一品牌及百分比 1st/ percent	第二品牌及百分比 2nd/ percent	第三品牌及百分比 3rd/ percent
样本 Sample	1027	**诺基亚 Nokia(26.5)**	**摩托罗拉 Motorola(20.2)**	**爱立信 Ericsson(19.1)**
价格无关心指向 indifferent orientation	188	诺基亚 Nokia(35.1)	摩托罗拉 Motorola(19.7)	爱立信 Ericsson(16.0)
中间层 medium	549	诺基亚 Nokia(25.9)	摩托罗拉 Motorola(21.9)	爱立信 Ericsson(18.6)
价格重视指向 careful orientation	290	诺基亚 Nokia(22.1) 爱立信 Ericsson(22.1)	摩托罗拉 Motorola(17.2)	三星 Samsung(4.5)

● 重庆 / Chongqing

4-1 移动电话拥有比例/ Mobile Phones Ownership

	人数 Number	百分比 Percent
使用 yes	93	14.9
不使用 no	531	85.1

n=624

4-2 现用移动电话的来源/ Source of Obtaining the Currently Owned Mobile Phone

	人数 Number	百分比 Percent
自己付费购买 bought by myself	82	88.2
单位配发 offered free by my work unit	11	11.8
其他 others	0	0.0

n=93

4-3 现用移动电话的品牌排名/ Ranking of the Brands of the Currently Owned Mobile Phone

排名 Brand Ranking	品牌 Brands	人数 Number	百分比 Percent
1	摩托罗拉 Motorola	32	34.4
2	诺基亚 Nokia	22	23.7
3	爱立信 Ericsson	16	17.2
4	西门子 Siemens	8	8.6
5	松下 Panasonic	5	5.4
5	NEC	5	5.4
6	飞利浦 Philips	2	2.2
6	三星 Samsung	2	2.2

n=93

4-4 选择移动电话时的考虑因素/ Ranking of the Considerations in Choosing the Mobile Phone

注：本题为多选题，合计百分比超过 100%（Multiple answers）

排名 Ranking	考虑因素 Considerations	人次 Person-time	百分比 Percent
1	轻便小巧 light and small	39	42.4
2	价格适中 reasonable price	35	38.0
2	功能多 with multi-function	35	38.0
3	外观 appearance	21	22.8
4	抗阻能力强 with strong anti-noise power	19	20.7
5	功能新 with new function	10	10.9
6	其他 others	6	6.5

n=92

4-5 所使用通讯网的类型/ The Type of the Net the Currently Owned Mobile Phone Used

	人数 Number	百分比 Percent
模拟网 analog net	21	22.8
数字网 digital net	70	76.1
CDMA	1	1.1

n=92

4-6 所使用通讯网的名称/ The Name of the Net the Currently Mobile Phone Used

	人数 Number	百分比 Percent
中国电信网 China Telecom	62	71.3
中国联通网 China Unicom	24	27.6
长城网 the Great Wall Telecom	1	1.1

n=87

4-7 平均每天接收的信息量/ Pieces of Information Received in a Day

	人数 Number	百分比 Percent
1 条以下 below 1 piece	7	7.9
1-2 条 pieces	15	16.9
3-4 条 pieces	34	38.2
5-9 条 pieces	23	25.8
10-19 条 pieces	10	11.2
20 条以上 20 pieces or over	0	0.0

n=89

4-8 平均每天发出的信息量/ Pieces of Information Sent in a Day

	人数 Number	百分比 Percent
1 条以下 below 1 piece	1	1.1
1-2 条 pieces	19	20.9
3-4 条 pieces	30	33.0
5-9 条 pieces	26	28.6
10-19 条 pieces	14	15.4
20 条以上 20 pieces or over	1	1.1

n=91

4-9 未来一年有无购买移动电话的打算/ Whether Planning to Buy a Mobile Phone Next Year

	人数 Number	百分比 Percent
购买 yes	88	14.1
不购买 no	534	85.9

n=622

4-10 打算购买的品牌/ Ranking of the Brands Planned to Buy

排名 Brand Ranking	品牌 Brands	人数 Number	百分比 Percent
1	诺基亚 Nokia	39	44.3
2	摩托罗拉 Motorola	25	28.4
3	爱立信 Ericsson	13	14.8
4	三星 Samsung	4	4.5
5	飞利浦 Philips	3	3.4

n=88

4-11 理想品牌排名/ Ranking of the Ideal Brands

排名 Brand Ranking	品牌 Brands	人数 Number	百分比 Percent
1	摩托罗拉 Motorola	198	31.7
2	诺基亚 Nokia	148	23.7
3	爱立信 Ericsson	79	12.7
4	西门子 Siemens	22	3.5
5	飞利浦 Philips	18	2.9
6	NEC	12	1.9
6	松下 Panasonic	12	1.9
7	三星 Samsung	8	1.3
8	TCL	4	0.6
9	索尼 Sony	3	0.5
10	阿尔凯特 Alcatel	2	0.3

n=624

4-12 不同消费者层的理想品牌/ The Ideal Brands by Market Segments

4-12-1 时尚流行指标/ Fads Popular Index

	人数 Number	第一品牌及百分比 1st/ percent	第二品牌及百分比 2nd/ percent	第三品牌及百分比 3rd/ percent
样本 Sample	616	**摩托罗拉 Motorola(31.8)**	**诺基亚 Nokia(23.5)**	**爱立信 Ericsson(12.8)**
平实生活指向 simple living orientation	369	摩托罗拉 Motorola(33.1)	诺基亚 Nokia(20.9)	爱立信 Ericsson(11.1)
时尚流行指向 fashion orientation	247	摩托罗拉 Motorola(30.0)	诺基亚 Nokia(27.5)	爱立信 Ericsson(15.4)

4-12-2 广告态度指标/ Advertising Attitude Index

	人数 Number	第一品牌及百分比 1st/ percent	第二品牌及百分比 2nd/ percent	第三品牌及百分比 3rd/ percent
样本 Sample	618	**摩托罗拉 Motorola(31.7)**	**诺基亚 Nokia(23.5)**	**爱立信 Ericsson(12.6)**
广告淡漠指向 indifferent orientation	167	摩托罗拉 Motorola(29.3)	诺基亚 Nokia(22.2)	爱立信 Ericsson(17.4)
中间层 medium	367	摩托罗拉 Motorola(33.2)	诺基亚 Nokia(24.3)	爱立信 Ericsson(11.7)
信赖广告指向 loyal orientation	84	摩托罗拉 Motorola(29.8)	诺基亚 Nokia(22.6)	爱立信 Ericsson(7.1)

4-12-3 价格态度指标/ Price Attitude Index

	人数 Number	第一品牌及百分比 1st/ percent	第二品牌及百分比 2nd/ percent	第三品牌及百分比 3rd/ percent
样本 Sample	615	**摩托罗拉 Motorola(31.9)**	**诺基亚 Nokia(23.6)**	**爱立信 Ericsson(12.7)**
价格无关心指向 indifferent orientation	106	诺基亚 Nokia(30.2)	摩托罗拉 Motorola(29.2)	爱立信 Ericsson(17.9)
中间层 medium	280	摩托罗拉 Motorola(31.8)	诺基亚 Nokia(25.7)	爱立信 Ericsson(15.7)
价格重视指向 careful orientation	229	摩托罗拉 Motorola(33.2)	诺基亚 Nokia(17.9)	爱立信 Ericsson(6.6)

● 武汉 / Wuhan

4-1 移动电话拥有比例/ Mobile Phones Ownership

	人数 Number	百分比 Percent
使用 yes	90	14.0
不使用 no	552	86.0

n=642

4-2 现用移动电话的来源/ Source of Obtaining the Currently Owned Mobile Phone

	人数 Number	百分比 Percent
自己付费购买 bought by myself	75	83.3
单位配发 offered free by my work unit	10	11.1
其他 others	5	5.6

n=90

4-3 现用移动电话的品牌排名/ Ranking of the Brands of the Currently Owned Mobile Phone

排名 Brand Ranking	品牌 Brands	人数 Number	百分比 Percent
1	摩托罗拉 Motorola	39	43.8
2	爱立信 Ericsson	19	21.3
3	诺基亚 Nokia	13	14.6
4	西门子 Siemens	7	7.9
5	松下 Panasonic	4	4.5
6	三星 Samsung	3	3.4
7	NEC	2	2.2
8	飞利浦 Philips	1	1.1

n=89

4-4 选择移动电话时的考虑因素/ Ranking of the Considerations in Choosing the Mobile Phone

注：本题为多选题，合计百分比超过 100%（Multiple answers）

排名 Ranking	考虑因素 Considerations	人次 Person-time	百分比 Percent
1	轻便小巧 light and small	54	60.0
2	功能多 with multi-function	42	46.7
3	价格适中 reasonable price	40	44.4
4	外观 appearance	33	36.7
5	抗阻能力强 with strong anti-noise power	14	15.6
6	功能新 with new function	10	11.1
7	其他 others	3	3.3

n=90

4-5 所使用通讯网的类型/ The Type of the Net the Currently Owned Mobile Phone Used

	人数 Number	百分比 Percent
模拟网 analog net	17	18.9
数字网 digital net	71	78.9
CDMA	2	2.2

n=90

4-6 所使用通讯网的名称/ The Name of the Net the Currently Owned Mobile Phone Used

	人数 Number	百分比 Percent
中国电信网 China Telecom	43	48.9
中国联通网 China Unicom	43	48.9
长城网 the Great Wall Telecom	2	2.3

n=88

4-7 平均每天接收的信息量/ Pieces of Information Received in a Day

	人数 Number	百分比 Percent
1 条以下 below 1 piece	9	10.0
1-2 条 pieces	13	14.4
3-4 条 pieces	37	41.1
5-9 条 pieces	20	22.2
10-19 条 pieces	6	6.7
20 条以上 20 pieces or over	5	5.6

n=90

4-8 平均每天发出的信息量/ Pieces of Information Sent in a Day

	人数 Number	百分比 Percent
1 条以下 below 1 piece	2	2.2
1-2 条 pieces	16	17.8
3-4 条 pieces	36	40.0
5-9 条 pieces	25	27.8
10-19 条 pieces	8	8.9
20 条以上 20 pieces or over	3	3.3

n=90

4-9 未来一年有无购买移动电话的打算/ Whether Planning to Buy a Mobile Phone Next Year

	人数 Number	百分比 Percent
购买 yes	92	14.4
不购买 no	549	85.6

n=641

4-10 打算购买的品牌/ Ranking of the Brands Planned to Buy

排名 Brand Ranking	品牌 Brands	人数 Number	百分比 Percent
1	诺基亚 Nokia	29	31.9
2	摩托罗拉 Motorola	28	30.8
3	爱立信 Ericsson	19	20.9
4	飞利浦 Philips	4	4.4
5	松下 Panasonic	2	2.2
5	西门子 Siemens	2	2.2
5	三星 Samsung	2	2.2

n=91

4-11 理想品牌排名/ Ranking of the Ideal Brands

排名 Brand Ranking	品牌 Brands	人数 Number	百分比 Percent
1	摩托罗拉 Motorola	138	21.5
2	诺基亚 Nokia	102	15.9
3	爱立信 Ericsson	99	15.4
4	西门子 Siemens	12	1.9
5	飞利浦 Philips	11	1.7
6	三星 Samsung	9	1.4
7	NEC	4	0.6
7	松下 Panasonic	4	0.6

n=642

4-12 不同消费者层的理想品牌/ The Ideal Brands by Market Segments

4-12-1 时尚流行指标/ Fads Popular Index

	人数 Number	第一品牌及百分比 1st/ percent	第二品牌及百分比 2nd/ percent	第三品牌及百分比 3rd/ percent
样本 Sample	632	**摩托罗拉 Motorola(21.2)**	**诺基亚 Nokia(16.0)**	**爱立信 Ericsson(15.3)**
平实生活指向 simple living orientation	330	摩托罗拉 Motorola(19.1)	诺基亚 Nokia(15.2)	爱立信 Ericsson(11.8)
时尚流行指向 fashion orientation	302	摩托罗拉 Motorola(23.5)	爱立信 Ericsson(19.2)	诺基亚 Nokia(16.9)

4-12-2 广告态度指标/ Advertising Attitude Index

	人数 Number	第一品牌及百分比 1st/ percent	第二品牌及百分比 2nd/ percent	第三品牌及百分比 3rd/ percent
样本 Sample	634	**摩托罗拉 Motorola(21.3)**	**诺基亚 Nokia(15.9)**	**爱立信 Ericsson(15.3)**
广告淡漠指向 indifferent orientation	188	摩托罗拉 Motorola(18.6)	诺基亚 Nokia(16.5)	爱立信 Ericsson(9.0)
中间层 medium	373	摩托罗拉 Motorola(21.4)	爱立信 Ericsson(17.4)	诺基亚 Nokia(15.5)
信赖广告指向 loyal orientation	73	摩托罗拉 Motorola(27.4)	爱立信 Ericsson(20.5)	诺基亚 Nokia(16.4)

4-12-3 价格态度指标/ Price Attitude Index

	人数 Number	第一品牌及百分比 1st/ percent	第二品牌及百分比 2nd/ percent	第三品牌及百分比 3rd/ percent
样本 Sample	634	**摩托罗拉 Motorola(21.3)**	**诺基亚 Nokia(15.9)**	**爱立信 Ericsson(15.3)**
价格无关心指向 indifferent orientation	84	摩托罗拉 Motorola(27.4)	爱立信 Ericsson(21.4)	诺基亚 Nokia(16.7)
中间层 medium	306	摩托罗拉 Motorola(21.9)	诺基亚 Nokia(18.0)	爱立信 Ericsson(16.0)
价格重视指向 careful orientation	244	摩托罗拉 Motorola(18.4)	诺基亚 Nokia(13.1)	爱立信 Ericsson(12.3)

● 西安 / Xi'an

4-1 移动电话拥有比例/ Mobile Phones Ownership

	人数 Number	百分比 Percent
使用 yes	87	14.5
不使用 no	514	85.5

n=601

4-2 现用移动电话的来源/ Source of Obtaining the Currently Owned Mobile Phone

	人数 Number	百分比 Percent
自己付费购买 bought by myself	78	89.7
单位配发 offered free by my work unit	8	9.2
其他 others	1	1.1

n=87

4-3 现用移动电话的品牌排名/ Ranking of the Brands of the Currently Owned Mobile Phone

排名 Brand Ranking	品牌 Brands	人数 Number	百分比 Percent
1	摩托罗拉 Motorola	28	32.2
2	爱立信 Ericsson	21	24.1
3	诺基亚 Nokia	18	20.7
4	三星 Samsung	9	10.3
5	西门子 Siemens	4	4.6
6	飞利浦 Philips	3	3.4
7	松下 Panasonic	2	2.3

n=87

4-4 选择移动电话时的考虑因素/ Ranking of the Considerations in Choosing the Mobile Phone

注：本题为多选题，合计百分比超过 100%（Multiple answers）

排名 Ranking	考虑因素 Considerations	人次 Person-time	百分比 Percent
1	轻便小巧 light and small	46	52.9
2	功能多 with multi-function	31	35.6
2	外观 appearance	31	35.6
3	价格适中 reasonable price	30	34.5
4	功能新 with new function	12	13.8
5	抗阻能力强 with strong anti-noise power	9	10.3
6	其他 others	2	2.3

n=87

4-5 所使用通讯网的类型/ The Type of the Net the Currently Owned Mobile Phone Used

	人数 Number	百分比 Percent
模拟网 analog net	11	12.6
数字网 digital net	65	74.7
CDMA	11	12.6

n=87

4-6 所使用通讯网的名称/ The Name of the Net the Currently Owned Mobile Phone Used

	人数 Number	百分比 Percent
中国电信网 China Telecom	55	64.0
中国联通网 China Unicom	26	30.2
长城网 the Great Wall Telecom	5	5.8

n=86

4-7 平均每天接收的信息量/ Pieces of Information Received in a Day

	人数 Number	百分比 Percent
1 条以下 below 1 piece	3	3.4
1-2 条 pieces	13	14.9
3-4 条 pieces	27	31.0
5-9 条 pieces	17	19.5
10-19 条 pieces	21	24.1
20 条以上 20 pieces or over	6	6.9

n=87

4-8 平均每天发出的信息量/ Pieces of Information Sent in a Day

	人数 Number	百分比 Percent
1 条以下 below 1 piece	2	2.3
1-2 条 pieces	16	18.4
3-4 条 pieces	24	27.6
5-9 条 pieces	19	21.8
10-19 条 pieces	23	26.4
20 条以上 20 pieces or over	3	3.4

n=87

4-9 未来一年有无购买移动电话的打算/ Whether Planning to Buy a Mobile Phone Next Year

	人数 Number	百分比 Percent
购买 yes	81	13.5
不购买 no	519	86.5

n=600

4-10 打算购买的品牌/ Ranking of the Brands Planned to Buy

排名 Brand Ranking	品牌 Brands	人数 Number	百分比 Percent
1	摩托罗拉 Motorola	27	33.3
2	诺基亚 Nokia	20	24.7
3	爱立信 Ericsson	12	14.8
4	松下 Panasonic	7	8.6
5	飞利浦 Philips	6	7.4
6	西门子 Siemens	5	6.2
7	三星 Samsung	3	3.7

n=81

4-11 理想品牌排名/ Ranking of the Ideal Brands

排名 Brand Ranking	品牌 Brands	人数 Number	百分比 Percent
1	摩托罗拉 Motorola	195	32.4
2	诺基亚 Nokia	117	19.5
3	爱立信 Ericsson	82	13.6
4	西门子 Siemens	25	4.2
5	飞利浦 Philips	19	3.2
6	三星 Samsung	14	2.3
7	松下 Panasonic	13	2.2

n=601

4-12 不同消费者层的理想品牌/ The Ideal Brands by Market Segments

4-12-1 时尚流行指标/ Fads Popular Index

	人数 Number	第一品牌及百分比 1st/ percent	第二品牌及百分比 2nd/ percent	第三品牌及百分比 3rd/ percent
样本 Sample	599	**摩托罗拉 Motorola(32.4)**	**诺基亚 Nokia(19.5)**	**爱立信 Ericsson(13.7)**
平实生活指向 simple living orientation	341	摩托罗拉 Motorola(33.1)	诺基亚 Nokia(16.4)	爱立信 Ericsson(12.6)
时尚流行指向 fashion orientation	258	摩托罗拉 Motorola(31.4)	诺基亚 Nokia(23.5)	爱立信 Ericsson(15.1)

4-12-2 广告态度指标/ Advertising Attitude Index

	人数 Number	第一品牌及百分比 1st/ percent	第二品牌及百分比 2nd/ percent	第三品牌及百分比 3rd/ percent
样本 Sample	597	**摩托罗拉 Motorola(32.5)**	**诺基亚 Nokia(19.4)**	**爱立信 Ericsson(13.6)**
广告淡漠指向 indifferent orientation	184	摩托罗拉 Motorola(33.7)	诺基亚 Nokia(17.9)	爱立信 Ericsson(14.1)
中间层 medium	334	摩托罗拉 Motorola(29.3)	诺基亚 Nokia(21.9)	爱立信 Ericsson(14.4)
信赖广告指向 loyal orientation	79	摩托罗拉 Motorola(43.0)	诺基亚 Nokia(12.7)	爱立信 Ericsson(8.9)

4-12-3 价格态度指标/ Price Attitude Index

	人数 Number	第一品牌及百分比 1st/percent	第二品牌及百分比 2nd/percent	第三品牌及百分比 3rd/percent
样本 Sample	597	**摩托罗拉 Motorola(32.7)**	**诺基亚 Nokia(19.3)**	**爱立信 Ericsson(13.4)**
价格无关心指向 indifferent orientation	142	摩托罗拉 Motorola(31.7)	诺基亚 Nokia(21.8)	爱立信 Ericsson(17.6)
中间层 medium	306	摩托罗拉 Motorola(31.0)	诺基亚 Nokia(18.6)	爱立信 Ericsson(13.7)
价格重视指向 careful orientation	149	摩托罗拉 Motorola(36.9)	诺基亚 Nokia(18.1)	爱立信 Ericsson(8.7)

● 沈阳 / Shenyang

4-1 移动电话拥有比例/ Mobile Phones Ownership

	人数 Number	百分比 Percent
使用 yes	137	22.8
不使用 no	463	77.2

n=600

4-2 现用移动电话的来源/ Source of Obtaining the Currently Owned Mobile Phone

	人数 Number	百分比 Percent
自己付费购买 bought by myself	114	83.2
单位配发 offered free by my work unit	17	12.4
其他 others	6	4.4

n=137

4-3 现用移动电话的品牌排名/ Ranking of the Brands of the Currently Owned Mobile Phone

排名 Brand Ranking	品牌 Brands	人数 Number	百分比 Percent
1	诺基亚 Nokia	59	43.1
2	摩托罗拉 Motorola	33	24.1
3	爱立信 Ericsson	28	20.4
4	西门子 Siemens	11	8.0
5	松下 Panasonic	5	3.6
6	华夏 Xdgegd	1	0.7

n=137

4-4 选择移动电话时的考虑因素/ Ranking of the Considerations in Choosing the Mobile Phone

注：本题为多选题，合计百分比超过 100%（Multiple answers）

排名 Ranking	考虑因素 Considerations	人次 Person-time	百分比 Percent
1	功能多 with multi-function	67	49.3
2	价格适中 reasonable price	56	41.2
2	轻便小巧 light and small	56	41.2
3	外观 appearance	37	27.2
4	抗阻能力强 with strong anti-noise power	25	18.4
5	功能新 with new function	19	14.0
6	其他 others	5	3.7

n=136

4-5 所使用通讯网的类型/ The Type of the Net the Currently Owned Mobile Phone Used

	人数 Number	百分比 Percent
模拟网 analog net	24	17.6
数字网 digital net	112	82.4
CDMA	0	0.0

n=136

4-6 所使用通讯网的名称/ The Name of the Net the Currently Owned Mobile Phone Used

	人数 Number	百分比 Percent
中国电信网 China Telecom	85	62.0
中国联通网 China Unicom	52	38.0
长城网 the Great Wall Telecom	0	0.0

n=137

4-7 平均每天接收的信息量/ Pieces of Information Received in a Day

	人数 Number	百分比 Percent
1 条以下 below 1 piece	10	7.3
1-2 条 pieces	30	21.9
3-4 条 pieces	40	29.2
5-9 条 pieces	42	30.7
10-19 条 pieces	12	8.8
20 条以上 20 pieces or over	3	2.2

n=137

4-8 平均每天发出的信息量/ Pieces of Information Sent in a Day

	人数 Number	百分比 Percent
1 条以下 below 1 piece	8	5.8
1-2 条 pieces	21	15.3
3-4 条 pieces	61	44.5
5-9 条 pieces	32	23.4
10-19 条 pieces	14	10.2
20 条以上 20 pieces or over	1	0.7

n=137

4-9 未来一年有无购买移动电话的打算/ Whether Planning to Buy a Mobile Phone Next Year

	人数 Number	百分比 Percent
购买 yes	109	18.2
不购买 no	491	81.8

n=600

4-10 打算购买的品牌/ Ranking of the Brands Planned to Buy

排名 Brand Ranking	品牌 Brands	人数 Number	百分比 Percent
1	诺基亚 Nokia	46	42.6
2	摩托罗拉 Motorola	30	27.8
3	爱立信 Ericsson	19	17.6
4	西门子 Siemens	8	7.4
5	三星 Samsung	3	2.8
6	松下 Panasonic	1	0.9
6	索尼 Sony	1	0.9

n=108

4-11 理想品牌排名/ Ranking of the Ideal Brands

排名 Brand Ranking	品牌 Brands	人数 Number	百分比 Percent
1	诺基亚 Nokia	185	30.8
2	摩托罗拉 Motorola	149	24.8
3	爱立信 Ericsson	120	20.0
4	西门子 Siemens	24	4.0
5	飞利浦 Philips	19	3.2
6	松下 Panasonic	16	2.7
7	三星 Samsung	6	1.0
8	NEC	3	0.5
9	索尼 Sony	2	0.3

n=600

4-12 不同消费者层的理想品牌/ The Ideal Brands by Market Segments

4-12-1 时尚流行指标/ Fads Popular Index

	人数 Number	第一品牌及百分比 1st/ percent	第二品牌及百分比 2nd/ percent	第三品牌及百分比 3rd/ percent
样本 Sample	600	**诺基亚 Nokia(30.8)**	**摩托罗拉 Motorola(24.8)**	**爱立信 Ericsson(20.0)**
平实生活指向 simple living orientation	291	诺基亚 Nokia(31.3)	摩托罗拉 Motorola(23.7)	爱立信 Ericsson(16.5)
时尚流行指向 fashion orientation	309	诺基亚 Nokia(30.4)	摩托罗拉 Motorola(25.9)	爱立信 Ericsson(23.3)

4-12-2 广告态度指标/ Advertising Attitude Index

	人数 Number	第一品牌及百分比 1st/ percent	第二品牌及百分比 2nd/ percent	第三品牌及百分比 3rd/ percent
样本 Sample	600	**诺基亚 Nokia(30.8)**	**摩托罗拉 Motorola(24.8)**	**爱立信 Ericsson(20.0)**
广告淡漠指向 indifferent orientation	172	诺基亚 Nokia(27.9)	摩托罗拉 Motorola(25.6)	爱立信 Ericsson(21.5)
中间层 medium	353	诺基亚 Nokia(32.9)	摩托罗拉 Motorola(23.8)	爱立信 Ericsson(19.5)
信赖广告指向 loyal orientation	75	摩托罗拉 Motorola(28.0) 诺基亚 Nokia(28.0)	爱立信 Ericsson(18.7)	西门子 Siemens(6.7)

4-12-3 价格态度指标/ Price Attitude Index

	人数 Number	第一品牌及百分比 1st/ percent	第二品牌及百分比 2nd/ percent	第三品牌及百分比 3rd/ percent
样本 Sample	599	**诺基亚 Nokia(30.9)**	**摩托罗拉 Motorola(24.9)**	**爱立信 Ericsson(19.9)**
价格无关心指向 indifferent orientation	104	诺基亚 Nokia(38.5)	摩托罗拉 Motorola(27.9)	爱立信 Ericsson(14.4)
中间层 medium	292	诺基亚 Nokia(32.5)	摩托罗拉 Motorola(24.0)	爱立信 Ericsson(22.9)
价格重视指向 careful orientation	203	摩托罗拉 Motorola(24.6) 诺基亚 Nokia(24.6)	爱立信 Ericsson(13.2)	西门子 Siemens(4.4)

第十三篇　住房、汽车、金融、保险
Part XIII　Housing, Car, Finance and Insurance

- 住房　Housing
- 私人汽车　Car
- 储蓄　Deposit
- 信用卡　Credit Card
- 投资　Investment
- 保险　Insurance

住房、汽车、旅游

住房

1998年全国房地产开发完成投资3580亿元，其中土地开发完成投资283亿元，商品房建设完成投资2800亿元。1998年商品房施工面积48473万平方米，比上年增加11.5%，商品房住宅施工面积34292万平方米；98年商品房实际销售面积10662万平方米，比去年增长34.8%，商品住宅销售面积9511万平方米，比去年增长38.08%。（数据来源：《99中国经济年鉴》）1999年，中国房地产市场情况发生了一些变化：一方面，房地产投资额继续快速增长；另一方面，商品房销售增长速度却在放慢。全国房地产业呈现回落态势，但回落幅度在下半年有所减缓。1—5月，房地产投资额为946.7亿元，比去年同期增长21.3%，其中住宅投资额为623.7亿元，增长34.4%，这两个增长速度分别比去年全年增长速度高8.7和10.4个百分点。1—5月份商品房销售面积为2094.5万平方米，商品房销售额为427.7亿元，比去年同期仅增长2.8%，而去年平均增长速度为36.6%。

从7月开始，全国房地产开发回落幅度有所减缓，7月份"国房景气指数"为101.65点，与去年同期相比减少2.10点，比6月份减少0.56点。8月份，"国房景气指数"为101.29点，与去年同期相比减少2.06点。"国房景气指数"总体水平呈现降幅逐缓的发展趋势。其中，空置面积分类指数连续4个月保持下降的势头，成为拉动"国房景气指数"上升的主要因素。1—8月份，全国商品房空置面积达7147万平方米，比去年同期增长21%，增长幅度比前7个月减少1.1个百分点。商品房空置指数为101.86点，比7月份减少1.46点，是今年以来下降幅度最大的一次。这表明国家深化房改的政策和各地消化空置面积的努力已取得初步成效。具体有：

1、1999年3月，中国人民银行颁布的《关于开展个人消费信贷指导意见》指出：所有银行均可向消费者发放贷款，有关住房贷款的首期支付比例也由30%降到20%。随即，各商业银行纷纷出台一系列促进各人住房贷款的措施。

2、1999年6月，中国人民银行7次降息。这给贷款购房者带来的直接效益是利息成本减少，个人住房贷款期限长，实惠多。

3、1999年7月，财政部、国土资源部、建设部制定了《已购公有住房和经济适用房上市出售土地出让金和收益分配管理的若干规定》、《已购公有住房和经济适用住房上市出售管理暂行方法》这一系列规定，使住房二级市场进入了实质性操作阶段。

4、1999年8月，财政部、国家税务总局发出通知，从今年8月1日起对房地产市场的营业税、契税、土地增值税等进行减免政策。税收负担的降低，有力地推动了住房二级市场的发展。

同月，建设部、国家计委等八部委局联手推进住宅产业现代化，提高住宅质量。八部委联合提出，到2005年，解决城镇住宅的工程质量、功能质量通病，初步满足居民对住宅适应性的要求；到2010年,城镇住宅应符合适用、经济、美观的要求，工程质量、功能质量基本满足居民的长期居住需求，居住环境较大改善。

5、除国家出台的一些政策外，各地也为搞好和拓展本地房地产市场、促进流通、倡导住宅消费新理念作了努力：上海首家房地产超市——申大房产超市的营业，我国首家绿色生态小区——北京北潞春小区的开盘销售，以及深圳"瑞达苑"、北京"日月东华"高科技智能住宅的登场……

综上分析，1999年我国房地产业面临着有利的经济发展和宏观政策环境，但能否就认为我国整个房地产市场将以适度快速增长趋势、稳步健康发展、前景一片大好呢？

1、居民仍嫌房价高。据中国社会调查事务所[SSIC]调查发现，72.8%的人表示1000—2000元/平米的房价是可接受的；75.3%的人能承受的总的住房投资在8万元左右。

2、6 万亿元是否能拉动住房消费。央行统计资料显示，到 1998 年底，全国居民储蓄存款余额达 5.34075 万亿元。就此认为中国“普通”百姓手中有很多钱是不明智的：

1）占全国总人口 20%的高收入人储蓄存款占了全国储蓄存款总余额的 50%。

2）在这 6 万亿元储蓄存款中，还有一部分农村信用社、农业银行和邮政储蓄中来自农村农户。

3）企事业单位“小金库”的“公款私存”有增无减。

我国城镇“普通”居民实际储蓄今年 6 月底为 9000 亿元左右，这部分储蓄又有多少份额用于住房消费呢？国家统计局抽样调查显示，为子女上学作准备、自己养老、购房 1998 年所占比例分别为 44%、38.4%和 20.3%；另外，婚丧嫁娶、购买股票、国债、小汽车等，这就可框算出在这 9000 多亿元城镇“普通”居民储蓄存款中真正能用于住房消费的不超过 2000 亿元。

3、“三让”下拉房价的希望别报太大。截止 1998 年底，全国商品房空置 8000 多万平米，“政府让点费、银行让点息、企业让点利”是近期政府有关部门出台的一系列消化积压商品房的思路，但“三让”政策能使房价下降多少呢？就房价中的税费而言，近两年减免近百项，而反映在房价上不过降低了 2%左右。房价的大头是地价、建设安装及市政设施费用，虽然存在一些高利润房，但许多开发商却抱定“永不言降”。所以，目前在“三让”下，房价不会下降太大。

4、个人住房贷款受限颇多。

1）具体经办部门观念陈旧。

2）手续过于繁复、僵化。

3）税收多而滥。

4）担保难觅。

目前，我国房地产交易市场的特点：

1、商品房销售形势持续好转。国家统计局固定资产投资快报显示，1998 年商品房销售面积 10662 万平方米，比 1997 年增长 34.8%，其中商品住宅销售面积 9511 万平方米，比 97 年增长 38.08%。商品房销售额 2135 亿元，比 1997 年增长 36.5%，其中商品住宅销售额 1718.25 亿元，比 97 年增长 41.22%。

2、存量住房交易市场稳步开放。房地产二、三级市场的联动，对盘活存量住房，带动商品房市场的进一步繁荣起了重要的作用。上海市 1998 年存量房地产买卖过户面积达 315 万平方米，比 1997 年增长 94%，成交金额 63.3 亿元，比 1997 年增长 118%。

3、房地产抵押日益活跃。重庆市 1998 年房地产抵押登记 18329 件，抵押面积 1012 万平方米，抵押担保债务价值 106 亿元，分别比 1997 年增长 53%、19%、51%。

4、中介服务继续发展和规范。到 1998 年底，我国房地产估价师已突破 1 万人，初步建立一支适应房地产市场发展的房地产估价师队伍。

5、置换——房市新亮点。置换房，一方面盘活了部分空置的商品房市场；另一方面，满足了人们对住房的多元化、多层次的需求，因此深受老百姓青睐。1998 年，上海房屋置换股份公司签定了置换合同 5502 笔，成交额达 4.3 亿元，而 1999 年一季度，签定的置换合同是去年同期的 11 倍。

我国房地产业发展日益趋向理性化，世纪之交的房地产市场将演示十大趋势：

1、全面步入房地产买方市场。

2、住房产品“领衔主演”房地产市场。

3、经济适用房将成为市场主打产品。

4、购房主体由集团变为个人。

5、住房交易市场日益活跃。

6、住房产品呼唤精品名牌。

7、房地产中介的地位和作用大大提高。

8、物业管理方兴未艾。

9、住房金融迅速发展。

10、房地产市场向小城镇拓展。

家用汽车

1999 年上半年全国轿车厂商的轿车累计销量为 26 万辆，继续保持低速运行态势，各厂家的库存压力较大。到 1999 年 6 月，总库存已增加到 11.1 万辆。这些增量主要是由于红旗、奥迪、捷达和桑塔纳四个车型的三家总经销单位上半年的库存增加。上半年的全国轿车销量仅比去年同玥增长率 2%，特别是二季度轿车销量下降 5.8%。全国大中城市轿车销量大幅度下滑的现象更加严重。

1998 年有上海大众、天津汽车、一汽大众、长安汽车、神龙汽车、一汽集团、北京汽车、西安秦川、广州轿车、贵州航空、江南汽车、吉林江北、海南汽车、一汽顺德、广州本田等 15 家企业生产轿车。至 1998 年底，上海大众汽车公司市场占有率 46.96%，占绝对优势；居第二、第三位的是天津汽车和一汽大众，其市场占有率分别为 18.78%、12.99%。

99 年国内轿车市场出现以下现象：

1、轿车市场目标向高档豪华发展。从 1999 年生产的车型看，其性能与老百姓所希望的经济型轿车的距离不是缩小而是拉大，正向高档豪华型发展。广州标致撤资后，填补空缺的是更高档车型本田雅阁；上海桑塔纳退居二线后，接继车型是别克和帕萨特 B5 轿车；红旗新型 CA7200E3L 的推出。一汽大众 50 万左右的高级奥迪 A6 于 9 月 6 日下线，天津的金夏利已粉墨登场……

2、经济型小轿车大行其道。一方面，高档轿车在纷纷登台，另一方面，经济型轿车以其贴近大众的“平民”特色在私车市场独领风骚，经济型轿车成了市场最眩目的亮点之一。今年以来，夏利、奥拓等品牌的经济型轿车的市场售价已跌破 5 万元大关，并有进一步下降的趋势。1999 年 7 月天津轿车推出低价位的新型环保车以来，出现了多年罕见的排队购车现象。

3、轻型车企业将触角伸向轿车领域，抢占家庭轿车市场。这些轻型车企业分别是：跃进、江铃、庆铃、金杯和哈飞。它们都有汽车巨头作背景，企图在下个世纪能分轿车市场一杯羹，占有一席之地。

4、1999 年中国汽车大战演绎的新主题：环保和节能。各轿车厂家都在致力于改革排放系统、开发双燃料汽油、降低油耗以及改变人们的消费观念。桑塔纳、捷达、富康、切诺基，其改进后的环保车都于 1999 年亮相国内。

回顾 99 年汽车之路，依然存在不利之处：

1、库存增加太快，上半年库存并没有压下去多少。

2、产销率不理想。据《中国经济年鉴》统计，98 年全国轿车产销量分别为 50.71 万辆和 50.83 万辆，产销率在 98%左右游移，而 99 年的情况却令人不甚乐观，如 4 月分的这两个数据为 96.9%和 94%。

3、政策环境变化失衡。一方面，对汽车市场有利好作用的燃油税、购置税难出台；另一方面，排放限制政策却迅速出台，使多年持续高增长、对汽车市场拉动相当大的微客遭遇当头一棒，出现明显的产大于销，库存大幅度增加的局面。

4、刺激内需的政策刚刚见效。一季度工业增加值同比增长 10.1%，比去年增加 1.9 个百分点，但经济增长对汽车需求增长的拉动作月不足且滞后。

5、汽车价格隐性下降。有些汽车虽然功能增加、装置改良而价格却保持不变。

世纪之末，反思我国轿车消费政策和现状，加快其发展，应持有哪些观点呢？

1、轿车以个人消费为主是轿车产业发展的必由之路。

2、 经济型轿车是普及轿车的主力军。 据国家统计局城调总队对北京等 10 个省市区 5000 户居民家庭的最 新调查结果显示：90%以居民家庭认为最合适的轿车价位在 7 万元以下；91.5%的居民家庭认为购车时的附加费应在 4000 元以下；而使用轿车一年的费用，94.7%的家庭认为应在 6000 元以下。这个结果明显提出了绝大多数居民对轿车的购买和使用能力。

3、银行应更广泛和全面地介入轿车市场。自 1998 年建行推出轿车贷款业务后，各商业银行纷纷跟进，然而至 99 年上半年，个人贷款购车只有千余辆，未能起到明显作用。主要原因是贷款条件苛刻。手续繁琐、贷款比例低、期限短、轿车本身不能抵押等条件，极大地限制了人们的购车积极性。

4、尽快上台阶，实现轿车产量的跳跃式增长。加入 WTO，我国轿车产业最多只有 5 年的关税保护期，因此，要尽可能取消阻碍轿车市场发展的限制性消费政策，使轿车工业在关税保护期内尽快达到规模产量，使得购车与更新轿车形成稳定和良性循环的市场需求。

5、各方配合，启动轿车消费市场。我国轿车工业的历史尽管不长，但经过了十几年的发展，已经形成了具有一定开发能力的轿车产业。轿车生产企业与相关配套企业已经具有“一荣俱容荣、一损俱损”的关系。所以要解放思想，从国家、企业、个人各方面配合，启动轿车消费市场。

旅游

旅游业被誉为永不衰落的“朝阳产业”。旅游业领改革开放之先，得改革开放之利，经过 20 年的艰苦创业，从小到大，产业形象日趋鲜明，产业地位不断提高，已形成了一定规模的产业体系，成为国民经济中新兴的增长点，在赚取外汇、拉动内需和服务社会等方面发挥着积极作用，对国民经济和社会发展的贡献也在不断增大。

1998 年，中国接待入境旅游者 6347.84 万人次，是 1978 年 180.92 万人次的 35 倍多，其中，旅华外国人、华侨和港澳台同胞分别是 1978 年的近 40 倍、7 倍和 36 倍；旅游创汇 126.02 亿美元，1978 年仅为 2.63 亿美元；国内旅游者为 6.94 亿人次，国民出游率为 56.4%，国内旅游收入为 2391.18 亿元；1998 年中国旅游业总收入为 3438.6 亿元人民币，占国内生产总值的 4.32%。据世界旅游组织统计，1998 年中国接待入境过夜旅游人数居世界第六，旅游创汇由 1997 年的世界第八位升至第七位。

1999 年前 5 个月全国旅游形势喜人。首先是国际旅游恢复了较快增长。1999 年前四个月来华旅游人数 2301.2 万人次，比去年同期增长 14.33%，其中，外国人 243.02 万人次，增长 10.76%；港澳同胞 1974.5 万人次，增长 14.78%，特别是澳门，3、4 月份入境人数都比去年同期有较大增长，终于走出了 1998 年全年和 1999 年前两个月的持续下降的颓势，非常令人振奋；台湾同胞 79.81 万人次，增长 16.17%，情况也很好。从客源市场看，除非洲游客下降外，其他各洲均有一定增长，在主要客源国中，除俄罗斯、蒙古有较大下降外，日本、韩国、美国、马来西亚、加拿大、印尼、泰国、法国等 8 个国家均实现了两位数增长，其中：日本增长 16.49%，韩国增长 53.11%，美国增长 14.27%，泰国增长 63.46%，印尼增长 79.08%，法国增长 13.68%。1—4 月份，全国国际旅游外汇收入累计测算数为 45 亿美元，比去年同期增长 14%。

国内旅游作为一个新的消费热点，还在继续升温。在 1999 年前几个月之中，已经形成了春节和“五一”两次国内旅游高潮，出现了整体上旅游旺季提前、旅游热点增多的现象。1999 年春节间，出门旅游过年成为一种新时尚，呈现了“南来北往、进城下乡”的繁荣景象。根据国家旅游局的典型调查推算，仅春节期间，全国出门旅游过年的人次就有 1800 万，旅游花费为 140 亿元人民币；“五一”期间又出现了国内旅游新高潮，出游规模甚至高于春节期间，特别是短线旅游、“郊区游”的势头更猛，增幅很大。以北京市为例，怀柔县和密云县在“五一”期间分别接待了 21.17 万人和 5.91 万人次，比去年同期分别增长 28%和 16.3%，黄山、华山、峨嵋山接待的游客也都比去年同期增长 20%以上。组织参观昆明世博会掀起了 1999 年国内旅游的第三个高潮。随着国内旅游市场的日趋兴旺，旅游部门各项措施的及时跟进，国内旅游管理水平也不断提高。如江苏无锡市和广西桂林市演化了“一日游”接待体系改革，上海对旅游市场尝试批发代理制，广东有计划地开发青年旅馆等。国内旅游持续迅猛的发展，不仅可以成为推动我们旅游业整体增长的重要支柱，而且也将在贯彻“扩大内需”的战略中发挥积极而独到的作用。

中国旅游资源极其丰富，中国旅游业年轻又有朝气，潜力十分巨大，发展前景广阔。特别是中部地区旅游资源丰富最具开发价值，是中国旅游业实现跨世纪大发展的后劲所在。此外因全国范围内仍有众多尚未开发的和尚未深度挖掘的景区景点，投资前景也被看好。国家旅游局已确定一批新的重点旅游开发区，如四川九寨沟、云南迪庆、湖北神农架、丝绸之路、长江三峡、内蒙古呼伦贝尔草原等，这些旅游项目都有广阔的投资前景。因此我们有充分的理由相信，21 世纪中国旅游业展现在世界面前的将是一个更为成熟、更加充满希望和活力的产业形象。预计到 2010 年，中国旅游入境人数（含港澳居民）将达 6400－7100 万人次，国际旅游创汇将达 380－430 亿美元；国内旅游在 2001－2010 年间可望保持接待人数每年增长 8%、收入每年增长 15%的水平，到 2010 年，国内旅游人数将达到 20－25 亿人次，国内旅游收入达到 10000－10500 亿元；到 2010 年，我国旅游业总收入将达到 1.3－1.4 万亿元人民币。世界旅游组织预测，2020 年中国将成为世界最大的旅游目的地国和第四大旅游客源国。

Housing, Family Car & Tourism

Housing

In 98, the real estate development had invested 358 billion yuan among which 28.3 billion yuan went for earth development and 280 billion yuan went for commercial housing. In 98, the commercial housing occupied a constructing area of 484.73 million square meters, 11.5% more than last year, and a residence area of 342.92 million square meters. In the same year, the commercial housing were actually sold 106.62 square meters, increasing by 34.8% over last year, and the commercial residence 95.11 million square meters, increasing 38.08%. (sources: “99 China Economy Yearbook”). In 99, there is something changed in the real estate market. On one hand, the investment volume kept growing rapidly, on the other hand, the sales of the commercial housing went slowly . A decline occurred in the whole real estate industry. However, the decline speed slowed down in the second half of the year. From January to May, the investment in the real estate was 94.67 billion yuan, rising by 21.3% over the same period of last year, among which 62.37 billion yuan went for residence, 34.4% more than the last year. These two growth speeds are 8.7% and 10.4% higher than that of the year of 98. During the same period, the sold area was 20.945 million square meters, with sales revenue 42.77 billion yuan, only rising by 2.8% in comparison with the same term of last year, though the average growth speed of last year was 36.6%.

Since July, the decline speed of the real estate development began to slow down. by the “housing prosperity index” for July was 101.65 points, 2.10 points less than the same term last year and 0.56 points less than June. In August, the “housing prosperity index” was 101.29 points, 2.06 points less than that of the same term last year. It showed a tendency in which the dropping speed slowed down. The continuous falling trend for 4 months in the classified index for the vacant housing. From January to August, the vacant area of the country’s commercial housing reached 71.47 million square meters, increasing 21% against the same term of last year, but 1.1% less than previous 7 month in the speed of vacancy growth. The commercial housing’s vacant index was 101.86 points during that period,

1.46 points less than July, it was the biggest declining range this year, which showed a satisfying result from our country's enforcing the housing reform policy and all the parties' efforts in digesting the vacant area. It can be detailed as :

1. In March of 99, the China People's Bank issued "The Instructive Ideas for opening Personal Consuming Credit", pointing out that all banks can grant loan to consumers, and the first housing loan declined 20% from 30%. Soon after, all commercial banks issued a series of measures to push the personal housing loan consequently.

2. In June of 99, the China People's Bank cut the interest for the seventh time, which brought a direct benefit to housing loan borrowers in that they can pay less interest to the bank, and enjoy longer credit term.

3. In July of 99, the Ministry of Finance, the Ministry of Land Resource and the Ministry of Construction jointly developed "Some Regulations over the sales revenue and the profits allocation methods of the purchased public & welfare housing that come to market", "The Momentary regulations over the sales management of the purchased public & welfare housing that come to market", which bring the secondary market of housing into practical operation.

4. In August of 99, the Ministry of Finance and the National Tax General Bureau declared that since August of the year, a policy would be carried out to free or lessen the real estate market's business tax, deed tax and earth VAT. The relief of the tax burden has encouraged powerfully the growth of secondary market of housing.

In the same month, eight ministries, including the Ministry of Construction, the National Auditing Committee had allied in pushing forward the modernization of housing business and the improvement of the residence housing. It has been suggested in ally that by 2005, the common problems existed in construction quality and function should be solved and satisfy the need of the residents. By 2010, the urban lodging will be up to the needs in function, economics and graceful outlook. The quality of the construction and function will satisfy the requirement for long-term living and better environment.

5. Apart from the basic policies issued by the relevant government, all provinces and cities also took efforts in expanding and improving the local real estate market in promoting the house dealing in advocating new residence concepts. For example, the open of Shanghai's first real estate supermarket Shenda real estate supermarket, the first green ecological neighborhood in the country Beijing Beiluchun; and the Shenzhen's "Ruidayuan", Beijing's "Riyuedonghua" the high science-and-tech housing area.

In one word, in 99, our real estate business faced favorable economy development and macro-control environment. Is this, however, can be a reason to say that real estate market will enjoy a great prospect with a stable or healthy development at a reasonable rate? Properly not.

1. The potential housing consumers are still complaining about the high price. Reported by the survey from China Social Survey Inspection Center (SSIC), 72.8% people regarded the housing price of 1000-2000 yuan per square meter acceptable, while 75.3% people can afford an investment of about 80 thousand yuan on housing buying.

2. Whether 6 trillion yuan can pull people to buy houses? The statistics from China Central Bank show that by the end of 98, the deposit remains of the whole country reached 5.34075 trillion yuan. But it's not wise to say that Chinese people have lots of money in hand.

1) The high income segment who account for 20% of the whole country's population shares 50% of the country's total deposit.

2) Among the 6 trillion yuan, there is still a small part from countryside people through countryside credit cooperatives, agricultural banks and postal deposits.

3) The phenomena of depositing institutional fund in the name of individuals becomes more popular instead of being erased.

At the end of this year, the actual amount of deposit from urban ordinary people will climb up to 0.9 trillion yuan.

Then, how much of it will go for house buying. According to the sample survey by National Statistics Bureau, the percentage of deposit for child's education, the pension and house buying in 98 were 44%, 38.4% and 20.3% respectively. Besides, wedding, funeral, stocks buying, national debt buying and car buying would also cost a great deal of deposit. Taking all these into account, of the 0.9 trillion yuan deposit, no more than 0.2 trillion yuan can be spent on housing.

3. The practice of "three cutting" can be expected to cut down the high price of house. By the end of 98, the whole country's house market has got unsold area over 80 million square meters. The idea of "The government cutting down fees for construction was a newly issued policy by the governments in order to digest the stored commercial houses. But how much can this policy cut down the house price? Take the taxes for example. Almost 100 kinds of taxes and fees have been cancelled or lessened in recent years. But all the effort only led to a cut of 2% in the house price in which the main parts are land cost, construction fee, and civil facilities installment. Though there are some houses that sell at high profit margin and their price can be cut down a lot, many land developers still insist on "no cutting". So, in spite of the "three cutting" policy, the house price will not go down in the near future.

4. There are many problems in housing loan, including the old-fashioned concepts of the bankers, the too-complicated and stiff procedures, the unlimited items of fees and taxes and the difficult in finding a bondsman.

For the moment, our real estate market is featured as:

1. A continuous amelioration in commercial house sales. The information about fixed assets from the National Statistics Bureau showed, in 98, the commercial houses were sold 106.62 million square meters, 34.8% more than 97. Among it there was an area of 95.11 million square meters for residence which was 38.08% more than last year. The sales revenue reached 213.5 billion yuan, rising 36.5% over 97, residence sales account for 171.825 billion yuan, rising by 41.22%.

2. A stable open of the stored house market. The allied operation of the second-hand third-hand real estate markets have played an important role in promoting the sales of stored houses and helping the further prosperity of the market. In Shanghai of 98, the ownership-transferred houses got an area of 3.15 million square meters, 94% larger than 97, with a revenue of 6.33 billion yuan, 118% higher than 97.

3. The raise of mortgage on real estate is activating daily. Chongqing had registered 18.329 thousand pieces of such mortgage events in 98, and a mortgaged area of 10.12 million square meters, a mortgaged security debt of 10.6 billion yuan, respectively 53.%, 19%, and 51% increasing than 97.

4. The intermediary service is still developing and being standardized. By the end of 98, the number of our country's real estate appraisers had been over 10 thousand. they formed a group in pace with the development of real estate market.

5. Exchange-- the rising star of the real estate market. On one hand house exchanging stimulates the selling of empty commercial houses, on the other hand, such practice satisfies people's need for the diversity of houses and is therefore welcomed by the mass. In 98, Shanghai House-Exchange Corporation had signed 5.502 thousand contracts, The sales revenue was 430 million yuan. In the first quarter of 99, the number of signed contracts had gone up 11 times as much as that of the same term last year.

Our real estate industry is developing more rationally. And the market facing the overturn of the century will show the following ten tendencies:

1. A buyer's market will form.

2. Houses will play the leading role in the real estate market.

3. The economical house will be the major products.

4. The purchasers will shift from institutions to individuals.
5. The house market will be increasingly active.
6. The elite houses are needed.
7. The intermediary will be more important.
8. The lodging management business will flourish.
9. The housing finance will grow rapidly.
10. The real estate market will make its way to small towns.

Family Car

The accumulated total sales of cars in the first half of 1999 was 260 thousand and the whole business was run at a low speed and was under the pressure of large stock. The total number of cars kept in stock had come to 111 thousand by June of 1999. Such a large stock was mainly caused by the increase of stock of Red Flag, Audi, Jetta and Santana. The sale of the first 6 months of 1999 was merely 2% over that of the same period of last year. The sales of the 2nd quarterof 1999 declined by 5.8%. The dropping of sales of cars was even more serious in the medium or big-sized cities.

There were altogether 15 car manufacturers in 1998, including: Shanghai Volkswagon, Tianjin Qiche, Changan Qiche, Yiqi Volkswagon, Yiqi Group, Beijing Qiche, Xi'an Qinchuang Guangzhou Jiaoche, GuizhouHangkong, Jiangnan Qiche, Jiling Jiangbei, Hainan Qiche, Yiqi Shunde, Guangzhou Itonda, etc. By the end of 1998, Shanghai Volkswagon Corporation had occupied 46.96% of the whole market and taken a dominant role. Tianjin Qiche and Yiqi Volkswagon, the 2nd and 3rd, holding 18.78% and 12.99% of the market.

The current domestic car market of 1999 is as follows:

1. The goal of car market shifts to luxurious cars. From the model cars in 1999, the distance lies in performance was longer instead of big shorter in regard of the economical cars expected by the ordinary consumers. Family cars are becoming more and more luxious. The more luxurious Honda Accord took the place of Guangzhou Peugeot ; Buick and Passate B5 succeed Shanghai Santana ; the new model of Red Flag CA7200E3L was brought forth; the top-grade Audi worthy about 500 thousand RMB rolled down the production line and the Golden Xiali has came up onto the stage.

2. Economical cars are widely accepted. When top-grade cars flourish at the market, the economical cars took advantages with its "ordinary people" personality and has become one of the fascinating focuses at the market. The price of some economical cars such as Alto and Xiali has dropped below 50 thousand RMB since this year and may continue to drop. The new environment-protective model brought forth by Tianjin Qiche in July of 1999 at a low price attracts the customers to lineup to buy it. Such an interest in cars is rather rare in years.

3. Van makers began to step in family car market in attempt to get a share. These van-makers areYuejin, Jiangling, Qingling, Jinbei and Hafei. Being the major van-makers, they try to take a share at family car market in the next century.

4.The new themes at car competition in 1999 is competition environmental protection and energy saving. All the carmakers are working hard to improve outlet system, to explore the use of double fuels, to reduce the use of energy and to change consumers' habits. The new environmental protective models of Santana, Jetta, Citroen, Cherokee all came up to the family car market in 1999.

Looking back at the car market in 1999, we find there are still some disadvantages in this industry:

1. Fast increase of stock. The stock of the first half of year has not been reduced much.

2. Unsatisfied ratio between output and sales. According to the statistic from Chinese Economy Yearbook, the output of home-made cars in 1998 is 507.1 thousand and the number of sole cars is 508.3 thousand. The ratio is about 98%. ut the rate in 1999 is not satisfying, e.g. 96.9% and 94% in April.

3. Unbalance of positive and negative policies from government. The fuel tax and consuming tax which favor car market are slow to be carried out while the rules to restrict theoutlet of cars are quick to be effective. That greatly damaged the market of mini-van which once pulled up the car consumption. As a result, the output has obviously surpassed sales and the cars in stock has increased.

4.The stimulating policy has just come to be effective. The added value of the first quarter is 10.1% more than that of same term last year, and 1.9% more than that of the previous year. But the economic increase is not effective enough to stimulate the demand for cars.

5.The intangibles drop of car price. Some cars are added with some more functions, but still sold at the original price.

At the end of the century, by reviewing the car consuming policy and the current state of can market, we get to know that:

1. Personal consumption of car will be a major encouraging factor in the development of car industry.

2. Economical family cars are the main force to make cars popularized. According to the result of research conducted by National Statistics Bureau on 5000 families in 10 provinces and cities, 90% of the families consider 70 thousand RMB the most suitable price for a car; and 91.5% of them think the added charge to buy a car should be no more than 4000 thousand RMB. As for the fee for using a car for one year, 94.7% of families think the cost should be below 6000RMB. The result tells the acceptable cost to purchase and use cars for most people.

3. Banks should participate car consumption more comprehensively. After the Construction Band introduced car loan in 1998, other banks followed suit immediately. But by the first half of 1999, there were only about 1000 car purchased on loan. Loan policy does not make any obvious influence upon car purchase due to its strict requirement, complicated formalities, short-term low ratio and, the impossibility to raise a mortgage on cars. All these factors greatly restrict the vigor of consumers to buy cars.

4.The car output and quality should be increased by a large margin as quickly as possible. The protective term can only last for 5 years after China's entrance of WTO. Therefore the restrictive policies to hinder the development of car industry should be eliminated in order to help enlarge the car industry scale within 5 years. In this way, the purchase and innovation of cars will form a stable and favorable environment for car industry.

5.All the relevant departments should cooperate to work for the increase of car consumption. Despite of the short history of a dozen years, Chinese car industry got some developing ability. The car manufacturers have set up a close relationship with the suppliers that "one flourishes, all flourish, one crashes, all crashes." Therefore it is necessary for the governments, the manufacturers and the consumers to work together to spur on the car market in China.

Tourism

Tourism is called a rising-sun industry, as it is believed never declining. Tourism, one of the first businesses to respond to and benefited from the reform and open-up policy, has built up its own distinct image and industrial structure and has heightened its status in national economy after 20 years hardship. It takes an active role in earning foreign exchange, stimulating national consumption and serving the society and contributes more and more to national economy and social development.

The tourists came to China is 63.4784 million in 1998, 35 times more than the number of 1.8092 million in 1978. Among them the number of overseas Chinese and Chinese from HongKong, Macao and Taiwan are respectively 40 times, 7 times and 36 times more than those of 1978. The foreign exchange achieved 12.602 billion dollars whereas it was only 263 million dollars in 1978. Chinese travelers were 649 million accounting for 56.4% of the total population, leading to a tourism revenue of 239.118 billion RMB. The gross revenue of tourism in 1998 was 343.86 billion RMB, accounting for 4.32% of the GDP. According to the statistics by the International Tourism Organization, the number of foreign tourists to China in 1998 ranked 6th in the international tourism market. The amount of earned foreign exchange through tourism ranked 7th from the 8th in 1997.

The situation of tourism in the first 5 months of 1999 is satisfactory. The number of tourists to China increases quickly. In the first 4 months, 23.012 million tourists came to voyage in China, 14.33% more than that of the same period in the previous year. Among them 2.4302 million were foreign tourists, 10.76% rising , 19.745 million tourists come from HongKong and Macao, increased by 14.78%. It is exciting that the number of tourists from Macao has been much increased, especially in March and April, whereas the tourist number kept declining last year round and the first 2 months of this year. The number of tourists from Taiwan is 798.1 thousand, increased by 16.17%. As for the tourists resource, the number of tourists from all the continents increased to some degree except that Africa. And for the major tourist resources, except Russia and Mongolia, all the other countries, including Japan, Korea, America, Malaysia, Canada, Indonesia, Thailand, and France, played an increasingly important role in China's tourism market.. The number of tourists from Japan increases 16.49% and the number from Korea, 53.11%, America, 14.27%, Thailand, 63.46%, Indonesia, 79.08%, France, 13.68%. The total foreign exchange revenue produced, by international tourists was estimated as 4.5 billion dollars from January to April, 14% more than that the same period of last year.

Domestic tour, a new consumption preference, keeps rising. In the first several months of this year, there has been two tour upsurges at the Spring Festival and on May 1st. The tourism season comes earlier than previous years and the number of scenes and landscapes grew. It becomes a fashion to go out to celebrate Spring Festival this year. People choose different places of interest in either south or north, either cities or countryside. China's tourism market is flourishing. According to the research by National Tourism Bureau, just during the Spring Festival Season, 18 million people went out to spend their holidays. Their tour expenditure achieved 14 billion RMB. May 1st is another tourism peak , and the number of tourists is even larger. Short-route trip and suburban trip are esp. welcomed and the number of tourists increased greatly. Take Beijing as an example, there were 211.7 thousand and 59.1 thousand tourists to Huairou county and Miyun county, increased by 28% and 16.3% respectively. The number of tourists to Huangshang, Huashan and Ermeishan were 20% more than that of the previous year. The visit to International Fair in Kunming causes the 3rd upsurge of tourism. Along with the flourishing of domestic tourism market and the immediate administrative principles and practices of the relevant government the level of management of domestic tourism has been enhanced. e.g Wuxi Jiangsu and Guiling Guangxi reform their reception system to one-day tour, Shanghai tries the wholesale agency at tourism market, Guangdong opens youth hotels strategically, etc. The stable and fast growth of domestic tourism can not only accelerate the development of the whole tourism industry, but also take active role in carrying out the strategy of stimulating domestic consumption.

China is rich in tourism resources and tourism industry in China is young and energetic. There is a great potential market and a good prospect for it. The exploitation of tourism resources in the middle of China provides the development of Chinese tourism industry with great bank-ups. Meanwhile it is considered prospective to invest to exploit some new places of interest. Some new scenes have been decided by the National Tourism Bureau, including Jiouzhaigou Sichuan, Diqing Yunnan, Shengnongjia Hubei, the Silkroad, the Three Gorges, Hulunbei'er Prairie (Inner Mongolia),etc. Therefore we have sound reason to expect a more mature, vigorous and hopeful Chinese tourism industry in 21st century. It is anticipated that in 2010, the tourists to China will be 6.4– 7.1 million, and will result in an estimated revenue of 3.8—4.3 billion dollars. The number of domestic tourists is expected to grow at 8% per year from 2001 to 2010 and revenue increases at 15% per year. By 2010, the number of domestic tourists will achieve 2—2.5 billion, resulting in 1.05 trillion RMB in revenue; totaling 1.3—1.4 trillion RMB in revenue. It is anticipated by International Tourism Organization that, China will become the first choice for tourists and the 4th largest in the world in 2020.

1.住房 / Housing

● 北京 / Beijing

1-1 目前的住房情况/ The Condition of the Residence Live Currently

注：本题为多选题，合计百分比超过 100%（Multiple answers）

	人次 Person-time	百分比 Percent
租的 rented	176	17.4
单位房，不属自己 owned by my work unit, not mine	327	32.4
单位房，已属自己 bought from my work unit	314	31.1
自己买的 bought by myself	145	14.4
自建 self-built	33	3.3
其他 others	48	4.8

n=1010

1-2 目前的住房面积/ The Area of the Residence Live Currently

	人数 Number	百分比 Percent
$10m^2$ 以下 below $10m^2$	12	1.2
10-19m^2	140	13.9
20-29m^2	100	10.0
30-39m^2	126	12.5
40-49m^2	210	20.9
50-59m^2	204	20.3
60-79m^2	151	15.0
80-99m^2	45	4.5
$100m^2$ 或以上 $100m^2$ or over	17	1.7

n=1005

1-3 有无购房打算/ Whether Planning to Own a Residence

	人数 Number	百分比 Percent
打算买 yes	307	30.3
不打算买 no	705	69.7

n=1012

1-4 打算何时购买/ When to Purchase

	人数 Number	百分比 Percent
1 年以内 in a year	68	22.5
1-2 年 years	59	19.5
2-3 年 years	44	14.6
3-5 年 years	48	15.9
5-7 年 years	33	10.9
7-10 年 years	21	7.0
10 年以后 ten years later	29	9.6

n=302

1-5 打算购买面积/ The Area Planned to Purchase

	人数 Number	百分比 Percent
$40m^2$ 以下 below $40m^2$	14	4.6
40-59m^2	49	16.1
60-79m^2	87	28.5
80-99m^2	71	23.3
100-149m^2	75	24.6
150-199m^2	4	1.3
$200m^2$ 或以上 $200m^2$ or over	5	1.6

n=305

1-6 打算购买的房型/ The Type of Residence to Purchase

	人数 Number	百分比 Percent
只有一间 single room	2	0.7
一房（一厅）1 room 1 sitting-room	12	3.9
二房（一厅）2 rooms 1 sitting-room	129	42.2
二房（二厅）2 rooms 2 sitting-rooms	48	15.7
三房（一厅）3 rooms 1 sitting-room	72	23.5
三房（二厅）3 rooms 2 sitting-rooms	29	9.5
四房（一厅）4 rooms 1 sitting-room	3	1.0
四房（二厅）4 rooms 2 sitting-rooms	9	2.9
其他 others	2	0.7

n=306

1-7 对居住条件的期望/ Expectation to Residence

1-7-1 对居住条件的期望/ Expectation to Residence

	人数 Number	百分比 Percent
高层公寓楼 skyscraper apartment	200	70.7
独门独院的小楼 house	83	29.3

n=283

1-7-2 对居住条件的期望/ Expectation to Residence

	人数 Number	百分比 Percent
地点位于郊区 located in suburb	117	38.5
地点在市区 located in downtown	187	61.5

n=304

1-7-3 对居住条件的期望/ Expectation to Residence

	人数 Number	百分比 Percent
相同面积下房间数多的 more rooms under same size	149	52.1
相同面积下房间数少的 less rooms under same size	137	47.9

n=286

1-7-4 对居住条件的期望/ Expectation to Residence

	人数 Number	百分比 Percent
中式建筑 Chinese-style	220	76.1
西式建筑 western-style	69	23.9

n=289

● 上海 / Shanghai

1-1 目前的住房情况/ The Condition of the Residence Live Currently

注：本题为多选题，合计百分比超过 100%（Multiple answers）

	人次 Person-time	百分比 Percent
租的 rented	336	33.1
单位房，不属自己 owned by my work unit, not mine	201	19.8
单位房，已属自己 bought from my work unit	162	16.0
自己买的 bought by myself	202	19.9
自建 self-built	56	5.5
其他 others	67	6.6

n=1014

1-2 目前的住房面积/ The Area of the Residence Live Currently

	人数 Number	百分比 Percent
10 m² 以下 below 10 m²	14	1.4
10-19m²	223	22.0
20-29 m²	301	29.7
30-39 m²	179	17.7
40-49 m²	81	8.0
50-59 m²	59	5.8
60-79 m²	80	7.9
80-99 m²	43	4.2
100 m² 或以上 100 m² or over	32	3.2

n=1012

1-3 有无购房打算/ Whether Planning to Own a Residence

	人数 Number	百分比 Percent
打算买 yes	320	31.6
不打算买 no	694	68.4

n=1014

1-4 打算何时购买/ When to Purchase

	人数 Number	百分比 Percent
1 年以内 in a year	53	16.6
1-2 年 years	60	18.8
2-3 年 years	69	21.6
3-5 年 years	65	20.4
5-7 年 years	23	7.2
7-10 年 years	21	6.6
10 年以后 ten years later	28	8.8

n=319

1-5 打算购买面积/ The Area Planned to Purchase

	人数 Number	百分比 Percent
40 m²以下 below 40 m²	28	8.8
40-59 m²	69	21.7
60-79 m²	61	19.2
80-99 m²	64	20.1
100-149 m²	80	25.2
150-199 m²	13	4.1
200 m²或以上 200 m² or over	3	0.9

n=318

1-6 打算购买的房型/ The Type of Residence to Purchase

	人数 Number	百分比 Percent
只有一间 single room	4	1.3
一房（一厅）1 room 1 sitting-room	18	5.7
二房（一厅）2 rooms 1 sitting-room	153	48.3
二房（二厅）2 rooms 2 sitting-rooms	41	12.9
三房（一厅）3 rooms 1 sitting-room	61	19.2
三房（二厅）3 rooms 2 sitting-rooms	28	8.8
四房（一厅）4 rooms 1 sitting-room	0	0.0
四房（二厅）4 rooms 2 sitting-rooms	11	3.5
其他 others	1	0.3

n=317

1-7 对居住条件的期望/ Expectation to Residence

1-7-1 对居住条件的期望/ Expectation to Residence

	人数 Number	百分比 Percent
高层公寓楼 skyscraper apartment	196	62.6
独门独院的小楼 house	117	37.4

n=313

1-7-2 对居住条件的期望/ Expectation to Residence

	人数 Number	百分比 Percent
地点位于郊区 located in suburb	75	23.8
地点在市区 located in downtown	240	76.2

n=315

1-7-3 对居住条件的期望/ Expectation to Residence

	人数 Number	百分比 Percent
相同面积下房间数多的 more rooms under same size	164	51.9
相同面积下房间数少的 less rooms under same size	152	48.1

n=316

1-7-4 对居住条件的期望/ Expectation to Residence

	人数 Number	百分比 Percent
中式建筑 Chinese-style	196	63.2
西式建筑 western-style	114	36.8

n=310

● 广州 / Guangzhou

1-1 目前的住房情况/ The Condition of the Residence Live Currently

注：本题为多选题，合计百分比超过 100%（Multiple answers）

	人次 Person-time	百分比 Percent
租的 rented	268	25.9
单位房，不属自己 owned by my work unit, not mine	135	13.1
单位房，已属自己 bought from my work unit	331	32.0
自己买的 bought by myself	171	16.5
自建 self-built	103	10.0
其他 others	44	4.3

n=1034

1-2 目前的住房面积/ The Area of the Residence Live Currently

	人数 Number	百分比 Percent
$10m^2$以下 below $10m^2$	5	0.5
$10\text{-}19m^2$	57	5.6
$20\text{-}29m^2$	128	12.5
$30\text{-}39m^2$	155	15.1
$40\text{-}49m^2$	162	15.8
$50\text{-}59m^2$	166	16.2
$60\text{-}79m^2$	211	20.5
$80\text{-}99m^2$	88	8.6
$100m^2$或以上 $100m^2$ or over	55	5.4

n=1027

1-3 有无购房打算/ Whether Planning to Own a Residence

	人数 Number	百分比 Percent
打算买 yes	299	28.9
不打算买 no	734	71.1

n=1033

1-4 打算何时购买/ When to Purchase

	人数 Number	百分比 Percent
1 年以内 in a year	72	24.2
1-2 年 years	42	14.1
2-3 年 years	45	15.2
3-5 年 years	49	16.5
5-7 年 years	35	11.8
7-10 年 years	17	5.7
10 年以后 ten years later	37	12.5

n=297

1-5 打算购买面积/ The Area Planned to Purchase

	人数 Number	百分比 Percent
$40m^2$以下 below $40m^2$	14	4.7
$40\text{-}59m^2$	51	17.2
$60\text{-}79m^2$	94	31.6
$80\text{-}99m^2$	59	19.9
$100\text{-}149m^2$	71	23.9
$150\text{-}199m^2$	4	1.3
$200m^2$或以上 $200m^2$ or over	4	1.3

n=297

1-6 打算购买的房型/ The Type of Residence to Purchase

	人数 Number	百分比 Percent
只有一间 single room	2	0.7
一房（一厅）1 room 1 sitting-room	6	2.0
二房（一厅）2 rooms 1 sitting-room	117	39.1
二房（二厅）2 rooms 2 sitting-rooms	33	11.0
三房（一厅）3 rooms 1 sitting-room	59	19.7
三房（二厅）3 rooms 2 sitting-rooms	63	21.1
四房（一厅）4 rooms 1 sitting-room	5	1.7
四房（二厅）4 rooms 2 sitting-rooms	13	4.3
其他 others	1	0.3

n=299

1-7 对居住条件的期望/ Expectation to Residence

1-7-1 对居住条件的期望/ Expectation to Residence

	人数 Number	百分比 Percent
高层公寓楼 skyscraper apartment	180	61.4
独门独院的小楼 house	113	38.6

n=293

1-7-2 对居住条件的期望/ Expectation to Residence

	人数 Number	百分比 Percent
地点位于郊区 located in suburb	90	30.4
地点在市区 located in downtown	206	69.6

n=296

1-7-3 对居住条件的期望/ Expectation to Residence

	人数 Number	百分比 Percent
相同面积下房间数多的 more rooms under same size	151	52.8
相同面积下房间数少的 less rooms under same size	135	47.2

n=286

1-7-4 对居住条件的期望/ Expectation to Residence

	人数 Number	百分比 Percent
中式建筑 Chinese-style	207	71.1
西式建筑 western-style	84	28.9

n=291

● 重庆 / Chongqing

1-1 目前的住房情况/ The Condition of the Residence Live Currently

注：本题为多选题，合计百分比超过 100%（Multiple answers）

	人次 Person-time	百分比 Percent
租的 rented	50	8.0
单位房，不属自己 owned by my work unit, not mine	220	35.4
单位房，已属自己 bought from my work unit	199	32.0
自己买的 bought by myself	116	18.6
自建 self-built	20	3.2
其他 others	31	5.0

n=622

1-2 目前的住房面积/ The Area of the Residence Live Currently

	人数 Number	百分比 Percent
10 m² 以下 below 10 m²	4	0.6
10-19m²	34	5.5
20-29 m²	98	15.9
30-39 m²	106	17.2
40-49 m²	103	16.7
50-59 m²	112	18.1
60-79 m²	102	16.5
80-99 m²	35	5.7
100 m² 或以上 100 m² or over	24	3.9

n=618

1-3 有无购房打算/ Whether Planning to Own a Residence

	人数 Number	百分比 Percent
打算买 yes	192	30.8
不打算买 no	431	69.2

n=623

1-4 打算何时购买/ When to Purchase

	人数 Number	百分比 Percent
1 年以内 in a year	33	17.5
1-2 年 years	31	16.4
2-3 年 years	30	15.9
3-5 年 years	32	16.9
5-7 年 years	25	13.2
7-10 年 years	13	6.9
10 年以后 ten years later	25	13.2

n=189

1-5 打算购买面积/ The Area Planned to Purchase

	人数 Number	百分比 Percent
40 m² 以下 below 40 m²	7	3.7
40-59 m²	33	17.4
60-79 m²	35	18.4
80-99 m²	37	19.5
100-149 m²	60	31.6
150-199 m²	11	5.8
200 m² 或以上 200 m²or over	7	3.7

n=190

1-6 打算购买的房型/ The Type of Residence to Purchase

	人数 Number	百分比 Percent
只有一间 single room	1	0.5
一房（一厅）1 room 1 sitting-room	9	4.7
二房（一厅）2 rooms 1 sitting-room	82	42.7
二房（二厅）2 rooms 2 sitting-rooms	13	6.8
三房（一厅）3 rooms 1 sitting-room	40	20.8
三房（二厅）3 rooms 2 sitting-rooms	35	18.2
四房（一厅）4 rooms 1 sitting-room	1	0.5
四房（二厅）4 rooms 2 sitting-rooms	6	3.1
其他 others	5	2.6

n=192

1-7 对居住条件的期望/ Expectation to Residence

1-7-1 对居住条件的期望/ Expectation to Residence

	人数 Number	百分比 Percent
高层公寓楼 skyscraper apartment	138	73.4
独门独院的小楼 house	50	26.6

n=188

1-7-2 对居住条件的期望/ Expectation to Residence

	人数 Number	百分比 Percent
地点位于郊区 located in suburb	95	49.5
地点在市区 located in downtown	97	50.5

n=192

1-7-3 对居住条件的期望/ Expectation to Residence

	人数 Number	百分比 Percent
相同面积下房间数多的 more rooms under same size	95	50.5
相同面积下房间数少的 less rooms under same size	93	49.5

n=188

1-7-4 对居住条件的期望/ Expectation to Residence

	人数 Number	百分比 Percent
中式建筑 Chinese-style	155	82.0
西式建筑 western-style	34	18.0

n=189

● 武汉 / Wuhan

1-1 目前的住房情况/ The Condition of the Residence Live Currently

注：本题为多选题，合计百分比超过 100%（Multiple answers）

	人次 Person-time	百分比 Percent
租的 rented	47	7.3
单位房，不属自己 owned by my work unit, not mine	215	33.6
单位房，已属自己 bought from my work unit	218	34.1
自己买的 bought by myself	69	10.8
自建 self-built	60	9.4
其他 others	44	6.9

n=640

1-2 目前的住房面积/ The Area of the Residence Live Currently

	人数 Number	百分比 Percent
$10m^2$以下 below $10m^2$	3	0.5
$10\text{-}19m^2$	36	5.7
$20\text{-}29m^2$	60	9.4
$30\text{-}39m^2$	114	17.9
$40\text{-}49m^2$	119	18.7
$50\text{-}59m^2$	111	17.4
$60\text{-}79m^2$	121	19.0
$80\text{-}99m^2$	44	6.9
$100m^2$或以上 $100m^2$ or over	29	4.6

n=637

1-3 有无购房打算/ Whether Planning to Own a Residence

	人数 Number	百分比 Percent
打算买 yes	216	33.6
不打算买 no	426	66.4

n=642

1-4 打算何时购买/ When to Purchase

	人数 Number	百分比 Percent
1 年以内 in a year	44	20.7
1-2 年 years	36	16.9
2-3 年 years	34	16.0
3-5 年 years	39	18.3
5-7 年 years	20	9.4
7-10 年 years	15	7.0
10 年以后 ten years later	25	11.7

n=213

1-5 打算购买面积/ The Area Planned to Purchase

	人数 Number	百分比 Percent
$40m^2$ 以下 below $40m^2$	10	4.7
40-59m^2	45	21.2
60-79m^2	60	28.3
80-99m^2	37	17.5
100-149m^2	52	24.5
150-199m^2	7	3.3
$200m^2$ 或以上 $200m^2$ or over	1	0.5

n=212

1-6 打算购买的房型/ The Type of Residence to Purchase

	人数 Number	百分比 Percent
只有一间 single room	1	0.5
一房（一厅）1 room 1 sitting-room	5	2.3
二房（一厅）2 rooms 1 sitting-room	106	49.3
二房（二厅）2 rooms 2 sitting-rooms	32	14.9
三房（一厅）3 rooms 1 sitting-room	31	14.4
三房（二厅）3 rooms 2 sitting-rooms	30	14.0
四房（一厅）4 rooms 1 sitting-room	2	0.9
四房（二厅）4 rooms 2 sitting-rooms	6	2.8
其他 others	2	0.9

n=215

1-7 对居住条件的期望/ Expectation to Residence

1-7-1 对居住条件的期望/ Expectation to Residence

	人数 Number	百分比 Percent
高层公寓楼 skyscraper apartment	121	56.8
独门独院的小楼 house	92	43.2

n=213

1-7-2 对居住条件的期望/ Expectation to Residence

	人数 Number	百分比 Percent
地点位于郊区 located in suburb	55	25.9
地点在市区 located in downtown	157	74.1

n=212

1-7-3 对居住条件的期望/ Expectation to Residence

	人数 Number	百分比 Percent
相同面积下房间数多的 more rooms under same size	97	45.5
相同面积下房间数少的 less rooms under same size	116	54.5

n=213

1-7-4 对居住条件的期望/ Expectation to Residence

	人数 Number	百分比 Percent
中式建筑 Chinese-style	164	77.7
西式建筑 western-style	47	22.3

n=211

西安 / Xi'an

1-1 目前的住房情况/ The Condition of the Residence Live Currently

注：本题为多选题，合计百分比超过 100%（Multiple answers）

	人次 Person-time	百分比 Percent
租的 rented	109	18.1
单位房，不属自己 owned by my work unit, not mine	185	30.8
单位房，已属自己 bought from my work unit	162	27.0
自己买的 bought by myself	119	19.8
自建 self-built	27	4.5
其他 others	11	1.8

n=601

1-2 目前的住房面积/ The Area of the Residence Live Currently

	人数 Number	百分比 Percent
10 m^2 以下 below 10m^2	4	0.7
10-19 m^2	35	5.8
20-29 m^2	42	7.0
30-39 m^2	77	12.8
40-49 m^2	119	19.8
50-59 m^2	106	17.6
60-79 m^2	153	25.5
80-99 m^2	45	7.5
100 m^2 或以上 100 m^2 or over	20	3.3

n=601

1-3 有无购房打算/ Whether Planning to Own a Residence

	人数 Number	百分比 Percent
打算买 yes	208	34.6
不打算买 no	393	65.4

n=601

1-4 打算何时购买/ When to Purchase

	人数 Number	百分比 Percent
1 年以内 in a year	37	17.8
1-2 年 years	41	19.7
2-3 年 years	40	19.2
3-5 年 years	40	19.2
5-7 年 years	21	10.1
7-10 年 years	8	3.8
10 年以后 ten years later	21	10.1

n=208

1-5 打算购买面积/ The Area Planned to Purchase

	人数 Number	百分比 Percent
40m^2 以下 below 40m^2	4	1.9
40-59m^2	29	14.0
60-79m^2	49	23.7
80-99m^2	56	27.1
100-149m^2	58	28.0
150-199m^2	9	4.3
200m^2 或以上 200m^2 or over	2	1.0

n=207

1-6 打算购买的房型/ The Type of Residence to Purchase

	人数 Number	百分比 Percent
只有一间 single room	1	0.5
一房（一厅）1 room 1 sitting-room	5	2.4
二房（一厅）2 rooms 1 sitting-room	75	36.2
二房（二厅）2 rooms 2 sitting-rooms	36	17.4
三房（一厅）3 rooms 1 sitting-room	40	19.3
三房（二厅）3 rooms 2 sitting-rooms	36	17.4
四房（一厅）4 rooms 1 sitting-room	3	1.4
四房（二厅）4 rooms 2 sitting-rooms	9	4.3
其他 others	2	1.0

n=207

1-7 对居住条件的期望/ Expectation to Residence

1-7-1 对居住条件的期望/ Expectation to Residence

	人数 Number	百分比 Percent
高层公寓楼 skyscraper apartment	122	58.9
独门独院的小楼 house	85	41.1

n=207

1-7-2 对居住条件的期望/ Expectation to Residence

	人数 Number	百分比 Percent
地点位于郊区 located in suburb	104	50.0
地点在市区 located in downtown	104	50.0

n=208

1-7-3 对居住条件的期望/ Expectation to Residence

	人数 Number	百分比 Percent
相同面积下房间数多的 more rooms under same size	99	47.8
相同面积下房间数少的 less rooms under same size	108	52.2

n=207

1-7-4 对居住条件的期望/ Expectation to Residence

	人数 Number	百分比 Percent
中式建筑 Chinese-style	175	84.5
西式建筑 western-style	32	15.5

n=207

● 沈阳 / Shenyang

1-1 目前的住房情况/ The Condition of the Residence Live Currently

注：本题为多选题，合计百分比超过 100%（Multiple answers）

	人次 Person-time	百分比 Percent
租的 rented	52	8.7
单位房，不属自己 owned by my work unit, not mine	167	27.9
单位房，已属自己 bought from my work unit	157	26.3
自己买的 bought by myself	176	29.4
自建 self-built	5	0.8
其他 others	45	7.5

n=598

1-2 目前的住房面积/ The Area of the Residence Live Currently

	人数 Number	百分比 Percent
$10m^2$ 以下 below $10m^2$	3	0.5
$10\text{-}19m^2$	56	9.3
$20\text{-}29m^2$	68	11.4
$30\text{-}39m^2$	89	14.9
$40\text{-}49m^2$	114	19.0
$50\text{-}59m^2$	131	21.9
$60\text{-}79m^2$	101	16.9
$80\text{-}99m^2$	21	3.5
$100m^2$ 或以上 $100m^2$ or over	16	2.7

n=599

1-3 有无购房打算/ Whether Planning to Own a Residence

	人数 Number	百分比 Percent
打算买 yes	176	29.4
不打算买 no	423	70.6

n=599

1-4 打算何时购买/ When to Purchase

	人数 Number	百分比 Percent
1 年以内 in a year	15	8.6
1-2 年 years	47	26.9
2-3 年 years	35	20.0
3-5 年 years	38	21.7
5-7 年 years	17	9.7
7-10 年 years	9	5.1
10 年以后 10 years later	14	8.0

n=175

1-5 打算购买面积/ The Area Planned to Purchase

	人数 Number	百分比 Percent
$40m^2$ 以下 below $40m^2$	4	2.3
$40\text{-}59m^2$	31	17.9
$60\text{-}79m^2$	40	23.1
$80\text{-}99m^2$	29	16.8
$100\text{-}149m^2$	59	34.1
$150\text{-}199m^2$	10	5.8
$200m^2$ 或以上 $200m^2$ or over	0	0.0

n=173

1-6 打算购买的房型/ The Type of Residence to Purchase

	人数 Number	百分比 Percent
只有一间 single room	2	1.1
一房（一厅）1 room 1 sitting-room	15	8.6
二房（一厅）2 rooms 1 sitting-room	76	43.4
二房（二厅）2 rooms 2 sitting-rooms	21	12.0
三房（一厅）3 rooms 1 sitting-room	36	20.6
三房（二厅）3 rooms 2 sitting-rooms	18	10.3
四房（一厅）4 rooms 1 sitting-room	1	0.6
四房（二厅）4 rooms 2 sitting-rooms	4	2.3
其他 others	2	1.1

n=175

1-7 对居住条件的期望/ Expectation to Residence

1-7-1 对居住条件的期望/ Expectation to Residence

	人数 Number	百分比 Percent
高层公寓楼 skyscraper apartment	102	60.0
独门独院的小楼 house	68	40.0

n=170

1-7-2 对居住条件的期望/ Expectation to Residence

	人数 Number	百分比 Percent
地点位于郊区 located in suburb	34	19.7
地点在市区 located in downtown	139	80.3

n=173

1-7-3 对居住条件的期望/ Expectation to Residence

	人数 Number	百分比 Percent
相同面积下房间数多的 more rooms under same size	96	55.8
相同面积下房间数少的 less rooms under same size	76	44.2

n=172

1-7-4 对居住条件的期望/ Expectation to Residence

	人数 Number	百分比 Percent
中式建筑 Chinese-style	139	81.3
西式建筑 western-style	32	18.7

n=171

2.家用汽车 / Car

● 北京 / Beijing

2-1 家用汽车拥有比例/ Automobile Ownership

	人数 Number	百分比 Percent
有 yes	86	8.5
没有 no	926	91.5

n=1012

2-2 现用汽车的来源/ Source of Obtaining the Currently Owned Automobile

	人数 Number	百分比 Percent
自家购买的 bought by myself	74	88.1
单位配发使用的 offered by my work unit	10	11.9

n=84

2-3 现用汽车的品牌/ The Brand of the Currently Owned Automobile

排名 Brand Ranking	品牌 Brands	人数 Number	百分比 Percent
1	松花江 Songhuajiang	10	11.9
1	桑塔纳 Santana	10	11.9
2	夏利 Xiali	9	10.7
2	捷达 Jetta	9	10.7
3	昌河 Changhe	8	9.5
3	富康(神龙）Citroen.ZX	8	9.5
4	长安奥拓 Chang'an Alto	7	8.3
5	切诺基 Cherokee	4	4.8

n=84

2-4 该车的购买时间/ The Time of Purchasing the Currently Owned Automobile

	人数 Number	百分比 Percent
1990 年或以前 1990 or before	3	3.6
1991 年	0	0.0
1992 年	4	4.8
1993 年	0	0.0
1994 年	3	3.6
1995 年	8	9.5
1996 年	9	10.7
1997 年	30	35.7
1998 年	20	23.8
1999 年	7	8.3

n=84

2-5 该车在购买时是否是新车/ Whether the First Owner of the Currently Owned Automobile

	人数 Number	百分比 Percent
新车 new	74	87.1
二手车 second-hand	11	12.9

n=85

2-6 有无购车打算/ Whether Planning to Purchase Automobile

	人数 Number	百分比 Percent
打算买 yes	224	22.3
不打算买 no	779	77.7

n=1003

2-7 打算何时购买/ When to Purchase

	人数 Number	百分比 Percent
1 年以内 in a year	15	6.9
1-2 年 years	34	15.7
2-3 年 years	47	21.8
3-5 年 years	49	22.7
5-7 年 years	28	13.0
7-10 年 years	21	9.7
10 年以后 ten years later	22	10.2

n=216

2-8 打算购买的品牌/ The Brand of the Planned Purchase

排名 Brand Ranking	品牌 Brands	人数 Number	百分比 Percent
1	捷达 Jetta	20	21.3
2	富康(神龙）Citroen.ZX	19	20.2
3	桑塔纳 Santana	12	12.8
4	夏利 Xiali	7	7.4
5	长安奥拓 Chang'an Alto	5	5.3

n=94

2-9 计划用于购车的花费/ The Expense of the Automobile Planned to Purchase

	人数 Number	百分比 Percent
5 万元以下 below 50 thousands yuan	9	9.7
5-10 万元 50-100 thousands yuan	30	32.3
10-15 万元 100-150 thousands yuan	25	26.9
15-20 万元 150-200 thousands yuan	18	19.4
20-30 万元 200-300 thousands yuan	7	7.5
30-50 万元 300-500 thousands yuan	2	2.2
50-100 万元 500 thousands-1 million yuan	0	0.0
100 万元以上 over 1 million yuan	2	2.2

n=93

2-10 理想品牌排名/ Ranking of the Ideal Brands

排名 Brand Ranking	品牌 Brands	人数 Number	百分比 Percent
1	奔驰 Mercedes-Benz	242	24.4
2	宝马 BMW	120	12.1
3	富康(神龙）Citroen.ZX	80	8.1
4	桑塔纳 Santana	69	7.0
5	本田 Honda	35	3.5
6	奥迪 Audi	31	3.1
6	法拉利 Ferrari	31	3.1
7	捷达 Jetta	29	2.9
7	红旗 Hongqi	25	2.5
7	卡迪拉克 Cadillac	25	2.5
7	大众 Volkswagen	25	2.5
8	劳斯莱斯 R&R	22	2.2

n=990

2-11 不同消费者层的理想品牌/ The Ideal Brands by Market Segments

2-11-1 时尚流行指标/ Fads Popular Index

	人数	第一品牌及百分比 1st/ percent	第二品牌及百分比 2nd/ percent	第三品牌及百分比 3rd/ percent
样本 Sample	976	**奔驰 Mercedes-Benz(24.2)**	**宝马 BMW(12.2)**	**富康(神龙）Citroen.ZX(8.1)**
平实生活指向 simple living orientation	482	奔驰 Mercedes-Benz(23.7)	宝马 BMW(11.0)	富康(神龙）Citroen.ZX(9.1)
时尚流行指向 fashion orientation	494	奔驰 Mercedes-Benz(24.7)	宝马 BMW(13.4)	富康(神龙）Citroen.ZX(7.1)

2-11-2 广告态度指标/ Advertising Attitude Index

	人数	第一品牌及百分比 1st/ percent	第二品牌及百分比 2nd/ percent	第三品牌及百分比 3rd/ percent
样本 Sample	973	**奔驰 Mercedes-Benz(24.5)**	**宝马 BMW(12.0)**	**富康(神龙）Citroen.ZX(8.1)**
广告淡漠指向 indifferent orientation	282	奔驰 Mercedes-Benz(23.0)	宝马 BMW(10.6)	富康(神龙）Citroen.ZX(6.4)
中间层 medium	562	奔驰 Mercedes-Benz(24.4)	宝马 BMW(12.8)	富康(神龙）Citroen.ZX(9.6)
信赖广告指向 loyal orientation	129	奔驰 Mercedes-Benz(27.9)	宝马 BMW(11.6)	桑塔纳 Santana(8.5)

2-11-3 价格态度指标/ Price Attitude Index

	人数	第一品牌及百分比 1st/ percent	第二品牌及百分比 2nd/ percent	第三品牌及百分比 3rd/ percent
样本 Sample	980	**奔驰 Mercedes-Benz(24.4)**	**宝马 BMW(12.2)**	**富康(神龙）Citroen.ZX(8.0)**
价格无关心指向 indifferent orientation	200	奔驰 Mercedes-Benz(26.0)	宝马 BMW(15.0)	桑塔纳 Santana(7.0)
中间层 medium	490	奔驰 Mercedes-Benz(24.1)	宝马 BMW(12.0)	富康(神龙）Citroen.ZX(8.4)
价格重视指向 careful orientation	290	奔驰 Mercedes-Benz(23.8)	宝马 BMW(10.7)	富康(神龙）Citroen.ZX(9.0)

● 上海 / Shanghai

2-1 家用汽车拥有比例/ Automobile Ownership

	人数 Number	百分比 Percent
有 yes	11	1.1
没有 no	1003	98.9

n=1014

2-2 现用汽车的来源/ Source of Obtaining the Currently Owned Automobile

	人数 Number	百分比 Percent
自家购买的 bought by myself	6	54.5
单位配发使用的 offered by my work unit	5	45.5

n=11

2-3 现用汽车的品牌/ The Brand of the Currently Owned Automobile

排名 Brand Ranking	品牌 Brands	人数 Number	百分比 Percent
1	桑塔纳 Santana	6	60.0
2	尼桑 Nissan	2	20.0
3	奥迪 Audi	1	10.0
3	雪佛莱 Chevrolet	1	10.0

n=10

2-4 该车的购买时间/ The Time of Purchasing the Currently Owned Automobile

	人数 Number	百分比 Percent
1990 年或以前 1990 or before	0	0.0
1991 年	0	0.0
1992 年	1	10.0
1993 年	1	10.0
1994 年	2	20.0
1995 年	0	0.0
1996 年	0	0.0
1997 年	2	20.0
1998 年	2	20.0
1999 年	2	20.0

n=10

2-5 该车在购买时是否是新车/ Whether the First Owner of the Currently Owned Automobile

	人数 Number	百分比 Percent
新车 new	8	80.0
二手车 second-hand	2	20.0

n=10

2-6 有无购车打算/ Whether Planning to Purchase Automobile

	人数 Number	百分比 Percent
打算买 yes	74	7.3
不打算买 no	938	92.7

n=1012

2-7 打算何时购买/ When to Purchase

	人数 Number	百分比 Percent
1 年以内 in a year	2	2.8
1-2 年 years	5	7.0
2-3 年 years	6	8.5
3-5 年 years	12	16.9
5-7 年 years	17	23.9
7-10 年 years	10	14.1
10 年以后 ten years later	19	26.8

n=71

2-8 打算购买的品牌/ The Brand of the Planned Purchase

排名 Brand Ranking	品牌 Brands	人数 Number	百分比 Percent
1	桑塔纳 Santana	6	46.2
2	别克 Buick	3	23.1
3	富康(神龙） Citroen.ZX	1	7.7
3	尼桑 Nissan	1	7.7
3	北旅 Beilv	1	7.7

n=13

2-9 计划用于购车的花费/ The Expense of the Automobile Planned to Purchase

	人数 Number	百分比 Percent
5 万元以下 below 50 thousands yuan	0	0.0
5-10 万元 50-100 thousands yuan	5	38.5
10-15 万元 100-150 thousands yuan	1	7.7
15-20 万元 150-200 thousands yuan	3	23.1
20-30 万元 200-300 thousands yuan	4	30.8
30-50 万元 300-500 thousands yuan	0	0.0
50-100 万元 500 thousands-1 million yuan	0	0.0
100 万元以上 over 1 million yuan	0	0.0

n=13

2-10 理想品牌排名/ Ranking of the Ideal Brands

排名 Brand Ranking	品牌 Brands	人数 Number	百分比 Percent
1	别克 Buick	259	25.6
2	桑塔纳 Santana	183	18.1
3	奔驰 Mercedes-Benz	160	15.8
4	奥迪 Audi	55	5.4
5	宝马 BMW	52	5.1
6	劳斯莱斯 R&R	40	4.0
7	红旗 Hongqi	28	2.8
8	丰田 Toyota	26	2.6
9	法拉利 Ferrari	25	2.5
10	林肯 Lincoln	24	2.4
11	卡迪拉克 Cadillac	20	2.0
12	福特 Ford	12	1.2
13	大众 Volkswagen	10	1.0
14	本田 Honda	8	0.8

n=1010

2-11 不同消费者层的理想品牌/ The Ideal Brands by Market Segments

2-11-1 时尚流行指标/ Fads Popular Index

	人数 Number	第一品牌及百分比 1st/ percent	第二品牌及百分比 2nd/ percent	第三品牌及百分比 3rd/ percent
样本 Sample	1001	**别克 Buick（25.6)**	**桑塔纳 Santana（18.1)**	**奔驰 Mercedes-Benz（16.0)**
平实生活指向 simple living orientation	470	别克 Buick（23.8)	桑塔纳 Santana（21.3)	奔驰 Mercedes-Benz（14.7)
时尚流行指向 fashion orientation	531	别克 Buick（27.1)	奔驰 Mercedes-Benz（17.1)	桑塔纳 Santana（15.3)

2-11-2 广告态度指标/ Advertising Attitude Index

	人数 Number	第一品牌及百分比 1st/ percent	第二品牌及百分比 2nd/ percent	第三品牌及百分比 3rd/ percent
样本 Sample	998	**别克 Buick（25.7)**	**桑塔纳 Santana（18.2)**	**奔驰 Mercedes-Benz（15.9)**
广告淡漠指向 indifferent orientation	256	别克 Buick（24.6)	桑塔纳 Santana（18.4)	奔驰 Mercedes-Benz（14.5)
中间层 medium	607	别克 Buick（25.9)	桑塔纳 Santana（18.1)	奔驰 Mercedes-Benz（17.3)
信赖广告指向 loyal orientation	135	别克 Buick（26.7)	桑塔纳 Santana（18.5)	奔驰 Mercedes-Benz（12.6)

2-11-3 价格态度指标/ Price Attitude Index

	人数 Number	第一品牌及百分比 1st/ percent	第二品牌及百分比 2nd/ percent	第三品牌及百分比 3rd/ percent
样本 Sample	1007	**别克 Buick（25.7)**	**桑塔纳 Santana（18.1)**	**奔驰 Mercedes-Benz（15.9)**
价格无关心指向 indifferent orientation	151	别克 Buick（25.8)	奔驰 Mercedes-Benz（17.2)	桑塔纳 Santana（13.2)
中间层 medium	518	别克 Buick（24.9)	奔驰 Mercedes-Benz（17.6)	桑塔纳 Santana（15.3)
价格重视指向 careful orientation	338	别克 Buick（26.9)	桑塔纳 Santana（24.6)	奔驰 Mercedes-Benz（12.7)

● 广州 / Guangzhou

2-1 家用汽车拥有比例/ Automobile Ownership

	人数 Number	百分比 Percent
有 yes	13	1.3
没有 no	1021	98.7

n=1034

2-2 现用汽车的来源/ Source of Obtaining the Currently Owned Automobile

	人数 Number	百分比 Percent
自家购买的 bought by myself	12	92.3
单位配发使用的 offered by my work unit	1	7.7

n=13

2-3 现用汽车的品牌/ The Brand of the Currently Owned Automobile

排名 Brand Ranking	品牌 Brands	人数 Number	百分比 Percent
1	铃木 Suzuki	2	15.4
1	本田 Honda	2	15.4
2	五菱 Wuling	1	7.7
2	松花江 Songhuajiang	1	7.7
2	吉林 Jilin	1	7.7
2	三菱 Mitsubishi	1	7.7
2	捷达 Jetta	1	7.7
2	皇冠 Crown	1	7.7
2	大众 Volkswagen	1	7.7
2	长安奥拓 Chang'an Alto	1	7.7
2	标致 Peugeot	1	7.7

n=13

2-4 该车的购买时间/ The Time of Purchasing the Currently Owned Automobile

	人数 Number	百分比 Percent
1990 年或以前 1990 or before	0	0.0
1991 年	0	0.0
1992 年	0	0.0
1993 年	0	0.0
1994 年	0	0.0
1995 年	3	23.1
1996 年	0	0.0
1997 年	6	46.2
1998 年	1	7.7
1999 年	3	23.1

n=13

2-5 该车在购买时是否是新车/ Whether the First Owner of the Currently Owned Automobile

	人数 Number	百分比 Percent
新车 new	7	53.8
二手车 second-hand	6	46.2

n=13

2-6 有无购车打算/ Whether Planning to Purchase Automobile

	人数 Number	百分比 Percent
打算买 yes	87	8.5
不打算买 no	942	91.5

n=1029

2-7 打算何时购买/ When to Purchase

	人数 Number	百分比 Percent
1 年以内 in a year	3	3.5
1-2 年 years	8	9.4
2-3 年 years	14	16.5
3-5 年 years	10	11.8
5-7 年 years	18	21.2
7-10 年 years	16	18.8
10 年以后 ten years later	16	18.8

n=85

2-8 打算购买的品牌/ The Brand of the Planned Purchase

排名 Brand Ranking	品牌 Brands	人数 Number	百分比 Percent
1	本田 Honda	7	28.0
2	昌河 Changhe	3	12.0
3	宝马 BMW	2	8.0
3	捷达 Jetta	2	8.0

n=25

2-9 计划用于购车的花费/ The Expense of the Automobile Planned to Purchase

	人数 Number	百分比 Percent
5 万元以下 below 50 thousands yuan	2	8.0
5-10 万元 50-100 thousands yuan	10	40.0
10-15 万元 100-150 thousands yuan	2	8.0
15-20 万元 150-200 thousands yuan	5	20.0
20-30 万元 200-300 thousands yuan	5	20.0
30-50 万元 300-500thousands yuan	0	0.0
50-100 万元 500thousands-1 million yuan	1	4.0

n=25

2-10 理想品牌排名/ Ranking of the Ideal Brands

排名 Brand Ranking	品牌 Brands	人数 Number	百分比 Percent
1	奔驰 Mercedes-Benz	257	24.9
2	宝马 BMW	136	13.2
3	本田 Honda	57	5.5
4	丰田 Toyota	51	4.9
5	法拉利 Ferrari	45	4.4
6	劳斯莱斯 R&R	41	4.0
7	桑塔纳 Santana	23	2.2
8	三菱 Mitsubishi	21	2.0
9	奥迪 Audi	20	1.9
10	凌志 Lexus	18	1.7

n=1032

2-11 不同消费者层的理想品牌/ The Ideal Brands by Market Segments

2-11-1 时尚流行指标/ Fads Popular Index

	人数 Number	第一品牌及百分比 1st/ percent	第二品牌及百分比 2nd/ percent	第三品牌及百分比 3rd/ percent
样本 Sample	1020	**奔驰 Mercedes-Benz(25.0)**	**宝马 BMW(13.2)**	**本田 Honda(5.6)**
平实生活指向 simple living orientation	518	奔驰 Mercedes-Benz(24.3)	宝马 BMW(12.0)	本田 Honda(5.6)
时尚流行指向 fashion orientation	502	奔驰 Mercedes-Benz(25.7)	宝马 BMW(14.5)	法拉利 Ferrari(6.2)

2-11-2 广告态度指标/ Advertising Attitude Index

	人数 Number	第一品牌及百分比 1st/ percent	第二品牌及百分比 2nd/ percent	第三品牌及百分比 3rd/ percent
样本 Sample	1020	**奔驰 Mercedes-Benz(24.8)**	**宝马 BMW(12.9)**	**本田 Honda(5.6)**
广告淡漠指向 indifferent orientation	334	奔驰 Mercedes-Benz(24.9)	宝马 BMW(13.2)	本田 Honda(6.9)
中间层 medium	591	奔驰 Mercedes-Benz(25.4)	宝马 BMW(12.9)	丰田 Toyota(5.2)
信赖广告指向 loyal orientation	95	奔驰 Mercedes-Benz(21.1)	宝马 BMW(12.6)	本田 Honda(5.3) 劳斯莱斯 R&R(5.3) 丰田 Toyota(5.3)

2-11-3 价格态度指标/ Price Attitude Index

	人数 Number	第一品牌及百分比 1st/ percent	第二品牌及百分比 2nd/ percent	第三品牌及百分比 3rd/ percent
样本 Sample	1026	**奔驰 Mercedes-Benz(25.0)**	**宝马 BMW(13.2)**	**本田 Honda(5.6)**
价格无关心指向 indifferent orientation	188	奔驰 Mercedes-Benz(28.7)	宝马 BMW(13.8)	法拉利 Ferrari(5.9)
中间层 medium	547	奔驰 Mercedes-Benz(25.2)	宝马 BMW(14.8)	丰田 Toyota(5.3) 本田 Honda(5.3)
价格重视指向 careful orientation	291	奔驰 Mercedes-Benz(22.3)	宝马 BMW(9.6)	本田 Honda(6.5)

● 重庆 / Chongqing

2-1 家用汽车拥有比例/ Automobile Ownership

	人数 Number	百分比 Percent
有 yes	11	1.8
没有 no	612	98.2

n=623

2-2 现用汽车的来源/ Source of Obtaining the Currently Owned Automobile

	人数 Number	百分比 Percent
自家购买的 bought by myself	10	90.9
单位配发使用的 offered by my work unit	1	9.1

n=11

2-3 现用汽车的品牌/ The Brand of the Currently Owned Automobile

排名 Brand Ranking	品牌 Brands	人数 Number	百分比 Percent
1	桑塔纳 Santana	4	36.4
2	长安奥拓 Chang'an Alto	3	27.3

n=11

2-4 该车的购买时间/ Time of Purchasing of the Currently Owned Automobile

	人数 Number	百分比 Percent
1990 年或以前 1990 or before	0	0.0
1991 年	0	0.0
1992 年	0	0.0
1993 年	0	0.0
1994 年	0	0.0
1995 年	1	9.1
1996 年	3	27.3
1997 年	0	0.0
1998 年	6	54.5
1999 年	1	9.1

n=11

2-5 该车在购买时是否是新车/ Whether the First Owner of the Currently Owned Automobile

	人数 Number	百分比 Percent
新车 new	9	81.8
二手车 second-hand	2	18.2

n=11

2-6 有无购车打算/ Whether Planning to Purchase Automobile

	人数 Number	百分比 Percent
打算买 yes	35	5.7
不打算买 no	583	94.3

n=618

2-7 打算何时购买/ When to Purchase

	人数 Number	百分比 Percent
1 年以内 in a year	4	11.8
1-2 年 years	3	8.8
2-3 年 years	2	5.9
3-5 年 years	5	14.7
5-7 年 years	4	11.8
7-10 年 years	6	17.6
10 年以后 ten years later	10	29.4

n=34

2-8 打算购买的品牌/ The Brand of the Planned Purchase

排名 Brand Ranking	品牌 Brands	人数 Number	百分比 Percent
1	桑塔纳 Santana	3	33.3
2	宝马 BMW	1	11.1
2	本田 Honda	1	11.1
2	长安奥拓 Chang'an Alto	1	11.1
2	红旗 Hongqi	1	11.1
2	拉达 Lada	1	11.1

n=9

2-9 计划用于购车的花费/ The Expense of the Automobile Planned to Purchase

	人数 Number	百分比 Percent
5 万元以下 below yuan 50 thousands	0	0.0
5-10 万元 50-100 thousands yuan	2	22.2
10-15 万元 100-150 thousands yuan	2	22.2
15-20 万元 150-200 thousands yuan	2	22.2
20-30 万元 200-300 thousands yuan	1	11.1
30-50 万元 300-500 thousands yuan	1	11.1
50-100 万元 500 thousands-1 million yuan	1	11.1
100 万元以上 over 1 million yuan	0	0.0

n=9

2-10 理想品牌排名/ Ranking of the Ideal Brands

排名 Brand Ranking	品牌 Brands	人数 Number	百分比 Percent
1	奔驰 Mercedes-Benz	153	24.7
2	宝马 BMW	67	10.8
3	桑塔纳 Santana	62	10.0
4	红旗 Hongqi	56	9.0
5	劳斯莱斯 R&R	29	4.7
6	长安奥拓 Chang'an Alto	22	3.5
7	丰田 Toyota	18	2.9
8	法拉利 Ferrari	12	1.9
9	林肯 Lincoln	9	1.5
10	本田 Honda	7	1.1
10	大众 Volkswagen	7	1.1
10	富康(神龙) Citroen.ZX	7	1.1
10	奥迪 Audi	7	1.1

n=620

2-11 不同消费者层的理想品牌/ The Ideal Brands by Market Segments

2-11-1 时尚流行指标/ Fads Popular Index

	人数 Number	第一品牌及百分比 1st/ percent	第二品牌及百分比 2nd/ percent	第三品牌及百分比 3rd/ percent
样本 Sample	612	**奔驰 Mercedes-Benz(24.8)**	**宝马 BMW(10.8)**	**桑塔纳 Santana(10.1)**
平实生活指向 simple living orientation	367	奔驰 Mercedes-Benz(22.6)	桑塔纳 Santana(11.4) 红旗 Hongqi(11.4)	宝马 BMW(8.4)
时尚流行指向 fashion orientation	245	奔驰 Mercedes-Benz(28.2)	宝马 BMW(14.3)	桑塔纳 Santana(8.2) 劳斯莱斯 R&R(8.2)

2-11-2 广告态度指标/ Advertising Attitude Index

	人数 Number	第一品牌及百分比 1st/ percent	第二品牌及百分比 2nd/ percent	第三品牌及百分比 3rd/ percent
样本 Sample	614	**奔驰 Mercedes-Benz(24.4)**	**宝马 BMW(10.9)**	**桑塔纳 Santana(9.9)**
广告淡漠指向 indifferent orientation	166	奔驰 Mercedes-Benz(23.5)	桑塔纳 Santana(12.0)	红旗 Hongqi(10.2)
中间层 medium	364	奔驰 Mercedes-Benz(24.7)	宝马 BMW(11.5)	桑塔纳 Santana(9.9)
信赖广告指向 loyal orientation	84	奔驰 Mercedes-Benz(25.0)	宝马 BMW(11.9)	红旗 Hongqi(9.5)

2-11-3 价格态度指标/ Price Attitude Index

	人数 Number	第一品牌及百分比 1st/ percent	第二品牌及百分比 2nd/ percent	第三品牌及百分比 3rd/ percent
样本 Sample	611	**奔驰 Mercedes-Benz(25.0)**	**宝马 BMW(10.5)**	**桑塔纳 Santana(10.1)**
价格无关心指向 indifferent orientation	105	奔驰 Mercedes-Benz(29.5)	宝马 BMW(16.2)	劳斯莱斯 R&R(9.5)
中间层 medium	277	奔驰 Mercedes-Benz(27.4)	宝马 BMW(10.8)	桑塔纳 Santana(9.7)
价格重视指向 careful orientation	229	奔驰 Mercedes-Benz(20.1)	桑塔纳 Santana(12.2)	红旗 Hongqi(11.8)

● 武汉 / Wuhan

2-1 家用汽车拥有比例/ Automobile Ownership

	人数 Number	百分比 Percent
有 yes	4	0.6
没有 no	638	99.4

n=642

2-2 现用汽车的来源/ Source of Obtaining the Currently Owned Automobile

	人数 Number	百分比 Percent
自家购买的 bought by myself	4	100.0
单位配发使用的 offered by my work unit	0	0.0

n=4

2-3 现用汽车的品牌/ The Brand of the Currently Owned Automobile

排名 Brand Ranking	品牌 Brands	人数 Number	百分比 Percent
1	富康(神龙) Citroen.ZX	2	50.0
2	万山 Wanshan	1	25.0

n=4

2-4 该车的购买时间/ Time of Purchasing of the Currently Owned Automobile

	人数 Number	百分比 percent
1990 年或以前 1990 or before	0	0.0
1991 年	0	0.0
1992 年	0	0.0
1993 年	0	0.0
1994 年	0	0.0
1995 年	0	0.0
1996 年	0	0.0
1997 年	0	0.0
1998 年	2	50.0
1999 年	2	50.0

n=4

2-5 该车在购买时是否是新车/ Whether the First Owner of the Currently Owned Automobile

	人数 Number	百分比 Percent
新车 new	3	75.0
二手车 second-hand	1	25.0

n=4

2-6 有无购车打算/ Whether Planning to Purchase Automobile

	人数 Number	百分比 Percent
打算买 yes	38	5.9
不打算买 no	601	94.1

n=639

2-7 打算何时购买/ When to Purchase

	人数 Number	百分比 Percent
1 年以内 in a year	1	2.7
1-2 年 years	1	2.7
2-3 年 years	8	21.6
3-5 年 years	8	21.6
5-7 年 years	9	24.3
7-10 年 years	4	10.8
10 年以后 ten years later	6	16.2

n=37

2-8 打算购买的品牌/ Ranking of the Brand of the Planned Purchase

排名 Brand Ranking	品牌 Brands	人数 Number	百分比 Percent
1	富康(神龙) Citroen.ZX	3	33.3
2	奥迪 Audi	1	11.1
2	本田 Honda	1	11.1
2	长安奥拓 Chang'an Alto	1	11.1
2	丰田 Toyota	1	11.1
2	卡迪拉克 Cadillac	1	11.1
2	夏利 Xiali	1	11.1

n=9

2-9 计划用于购车的花费/ The Expense of the Automobile Planned to Purchase

	人数 Number	百分比 Percent
5 万元以下 below 50 thousands yuan	2	20.0
5-10 万元 50-100 thousands yuan	2	20.0
10-15 万元 100-150 thousands yuan	2	20.0
15-20 万元 150-200 thousands yuan	2	20.0
20-30 万元 200-300 thousands yuan	0	0.0
30-50 万元 300-500 thousands yuan	1	10.0
50-100 万元 500 thousands-1 million yuan	1	10.0
100 万元以上 over 1 million yuan	0	0.0

n=10

2-10 理想品牌排名/ Ranking of the Ideal Brands

排名 Brand Ranking	品牌 Brands	人数 Number	百分比 Percent
1	奔驰 Mercedes-Benz	96	15.1
2	富康(神龙) Citroen.ZX	82	12.9
3	桑塔纳 Santana	34	5.4
3	宝马 BMW	34	5.4
4	红旗 Hongqi	26	4.1
5	奥迪 Audi	22	3.5
6	劳斯莱斯 R&R	20	3.1
7	丰田 Toyota	18	2.8
8	法拉利 Ferrari	17	2.7
9	林肯 Lincoln	14	2.2
9	本田 Honda	14	2.2

n=635

2-11 不同消费者层的理想品牌/ The Ideal Brands by Market Segments

2-11-1 时尚流行指标/ Fads Popular Index

	人数 Number	第一品牌及百分比 1st/ percent	第二品牌及百分比 2nd/ percent	第三品牌及百分比 3rd/ percent
样本 Sample	625	**奔驰 Mercedes-Benz(15.0)**	**富康(神龙)Citroen.ZX(12.6)**	**宝马 BMW(5.4)**
平实生活指向 simple living orientation	324	奔驰 Mercedes-Benz(13.3)	富康(神龙)Citroen.ZX(12.3)	红旗 Hongqi(5.9)
时尚流行指向 fashion orientation	301	奔驰 Mercedes-Benz(16.9)	富康(神龙)Citroen.ZX(13.0)	宝马 BMW(6.6)

2-11-2 广告态度指标/ Advertising Attitude Index

	人数 Number	第一品牌及百分比 1st/ percent	第二品牌及百分比 2nd/ percent	第三品牌及百分比 3rd/ percent
样本 Sample	627	**奔驰 Mercedes-Benz(15.0)**	**富康(神龙)Citroen.ZX (12.6)**	**桑塔纳 Santana(5.4)** **宝马 BMW(5.4)**
广告淡漠指向 indifferent orientation	186	奔驰 Mercedes-Benz(15.6)	富康(神龙)Citroen.ZX (9.1)	红旗 Hongqi(6.5)
中间层 medium	368	富康(神龙)Citroen.ZX (14.1) 奔驰 Mercedes-Benz(14.1)	宝马 BMW(5.7)	桑塔纳 Santana(5.2)
信赖广告指向 loyal orientation	73	奔驰 Mercedes-Benz(17.8)	富康(神龙)Citroen.ZX (13.7)	桑塔纳 Santana(9.6)

2-11-3 价格态度指标/ Price Attitude Index

	人数 Number	第一品牌及百分比 1st/ percent	第二品牌及百分比 2nd/ percent	第三品牌及百分比 3rd/ percent
样本 Sample	627	**奔驰 Mercedes-Benz(15.2)**	**富康(神龙)Citroen.ZX (12.6)**	**桑塔纳 Santana(5.4)** **宝马 BMW(5.4)**
价格无关心指向 indifferent orientation	83	奔驰 Mercedes-Benz(18.1)	富康(神龙)Citroen.ZX (10.8)	宝马 BMW(7.2)
中间层 medium	302	奔驰 Mercedes-Benz(18.2)	富康(神龙)Citroen.ZX (10.3)	桑塔纳 Santana(6.0)
价格重视指向 careful orientation	242	富康(神龙)Citroen.ZX (16.1)	奔驰 Mercedes-Benz(10.3)	红旗 Hongqi(6.6)

● 西安 / Xi'an

2-1 家用汽车拥有比例/ Automobile Ownership

	人数 Number	百分比 Percent
有 yes	8	1.3
没有 no	593	98.7

n=601

2-2 现用汽车的来源/ Source of Obtaining the Currently Owned Automobile

	人数 Number	百分比 Percent
自家购买的 bought by myself	7	87.5
单位配发使用的 offered by my work unit	1	12.5

n=8

2-3 现用汽车的品牌/ Ranking of the Brands of the Currently Owned Automobile

排名 Brand Ranking	品牌 Brands	人数 Number	百分比 Percent
1	捷达 Jetta	2	25.0
1	昌河 Changhe	2	25.0
2	尼桑 Nissan	1	12.5
2	桑塔纳 Santana	1	12.5
2	依维柯 Iveco	1	12.5
2	海南马自达 HaiNan Mazda	1	12.5

n=8

2-4 该车的购买时间/ Time of Purchasing of the Currently Owned Automobile

	人数 Number	百分比 percent
1990 年或以前 1990 or before	0	0.0
1991 年	0	0.0
1992 年	0	0.0
1993 年	0	0.0
1994 年	1	12.5
1995 年	0	0.0
1996 年	2	25.0
1997 年	3	37.5
1998 年	2	25.0
1999 年	0	0.0

n=8

2-5 该车在购买时是否是新车/ Whether the First Owner of the Currently Owned Automobile

	人数 Number	百分比 Percent
新车 new	4	50.0
二手车 second-hand	4	50.0

n=8

2-6 有无购车打算/ Whether Planning to Purchase Automobile

	人数 Number	百分比 Percent
打算买 yes	47	7.8
不打算买 no	554	92.2

n=601

2-7 打算何时购买/ When to Purchase

	人数 Number	百分比 Percent
1 年以内 in a year	4	8.5
1-2 年 years	8	17.0
2-3 年 years	9	19.1
3-5 年 years	8	17.0
5-7 年 years	9	19.1
7-10 年 years	4	8.5
10 年以后 ten years later	5	10.6

n=47

2-8 打算购买的品牌/ Ranking of the Brand of the Planned Purchase

排名 Brand Ranking	品牌 Brands	人数 Number	百分比 Percent
1	桑塔纳 Santana	9	42.9
2	三菱 Mitsubishi	3	14.3

n=21

2-9 计划用于购车的花费/ The Expense of the Automobile Planned to Purchase

	人数 Number	百分比 Percent
5 万元以下 below 50 thousands yuan	3	14.3
5-10 万元 50-100 thousands yuan	5	23.8
10-15 万元 100-150 thousands yuan	5	23.8
15-20 万元 150-200 thousands yuan	5	23.8
20-30 万元 200-300 thousands yuan	2	9.5
30-50 万元 300-500 thousands yuan	1	4.8
50-100 万元 500 thousands-1 million yuan	0	0.0
100 万元以上 over 1 million yuan	0	0.0

n=21

2-10 理想品牌排名/ Ranking of the Ideal Brands

排名 Brand Ranking	品牌 Brands	人数 Number	百分比 Percent
1	奔驰 Mercedes-Benz	132	22.0
2	桑塔纳 Santana	91	15.1
3	宝马 BMW	43	7.2
4	红旗 Hongqi	38	6.3
5	丰田 Toyota	32	5.3
6	奥迪 Audi	30	5.0
7	劳斯莱斯 R&R	27	4.5
8	林肯 Lincoln	17	2.8
9	夏利 Xiali	14	2.3
10	富康(神龙) Citroen.ZX	13	2.2

n=601

2-11 不同消费者层的理想品牌/ The Ideal Brands by Market Segments

2-11-1 时尚流行指标/ Fads Popular Index

	人数 Number	第一品牌及百分比 1st/ percent	第二品牌及百分比 2nd/ percent	第三品牌及百分比 3rd/ percent
样本 Sample	599	**奔驰 Mercedes-Benz(21.9)**	**桑塔纳 Santana(15.2)**	**宝马 BMW(7.2)**
平实生活指向 simple living orientation	341	奔驰 Mercedes-Benz(20.8)	桑塔纳 Santana(15.8)	红旗 Hongqi(7.0)
时尚流行指向 fashion orientation	258	奔驰 Mercedes-Benz(23.3)	桑塔纳 Santana(14.3)	宝马 BMW(8.5)

2-11-2 广告态度指标/ Advertising Attitude Index

	人数 Number	第一品牌及百分比 1st/ percent	第二品牌及百分比 2nd/ percent	第三品牌及百分比 3rd/ percent
样本 Sample	597	**奔驰 Mercedes-Benz(22.1)**	**桑塔纳 Santana(15.2)**	**宝马 BMW(7.2)**
广告淡漠指向 indifferent orientation	184	奔驰 Mercedes-Benz(22.8)	桑塔纳 Santana(13.6)	丰田 Toyota(9.2)
中间层 medium	334	奔驰 Mercedes-Benz(23.7)	桑塔纳 Santana(12.9)	红旗 Hongqi(8.4)
信赖广告指向 loyal orientation	79	桑塔纳 Santana(29.1)	奔驰 Mercedes-Benz(13.9)	宝马 BMW(8.9)

2-11-3 价格态度指标/ Price Attitude Index

	人数 Number	第一品牌及百分比 1st/ percent	第二品牌及百分比 2nd/ percent	第三品牌及百分比 3rd/ percent
样本 Sample	597	**奔驰 Mercedes-Benz(21.8)**	**桑塔纳 Santana(15.2)**	**宝马 BMW(7.2)**
价格无关心指向 indifferent orientation	142	奔驰 Mercedes-Benz(30.3)	桑塔纳 Santana(14.1)	宝马 BMW(12.7)
中间层 medium	306	奔驰 Mercedes-Benz(20.6)	桑塔纳 Santana(14.7)	红旗 Hongqi(8.2)
价格重视指向 careful orientation	149	桑塔纳 Santana(17.4)	奔驰 Mercedes-Benz(16.1)	红旗 Hongqi(6.0)

● 沈阳 / Shenyang

2-1 家用汽车拥有比例/ Automobile Ownership

	人数 Number	百分比 Percent
有 yes	4	0.7
没有 no	596	99.3

n=600

2-2 现用汽车的来源/ Source of Obtaining the Currently Owned Automobile

	人数 Number	百分比 Percent
自家购买的 bought by myself	4	100.0
单位配发使用的 offered by my work unit	0	0.0

n=4

2-3 现用汽车的品牌/ Ranking of the Brand of the Currently Owned Automobile

排名 Brand Ranking	品牌 Brands	人数 Number	百分比 Percent
1	捷达 Jetta	2	50.0
1	拉达 Lada	2	50.0

n=4

2-4 该车的购买时间/ The Time of Purchasing the Currently Owned Automobile

	人数 Number	百分比 percent
1990 年或以前 1990 or before	0	0.0
1991 年	0	0.0
1992 年	0	0.0
1993 年	0	0.0
1994 年	1	33.3
1995 年	0	0.0
1996 年	0	0.0
1997 年	0	0.0
1998 年	2	66.7
1999 年	0	0.0

n=3

2-5 该车在购买时是否是新车/ Whether the First Owner of the Currently Owned Automobile

	人数 Number	百分比 Percent
新车 new	3	75.0
二手车 second-hand	1	25.0

n=4

2-6 有无购车打算/ Whether Planning to Purchase Automobile

	人数 Number	百分比 Percent
打算买 yes	54	9.0
不打算买 no	546	91.0

n=600

2-7 打算何时购买/ When to Purchase

	人数 Number	百分比 Percent
1 年以内 in a year	2	3.8
1-2 年 years	1	1.9
2-3 年 years	11	21.2
3-5 年 years	10	19.2
5-7 年 years	9	17.3
7-10 年 years	4	7.7
10 年以后 10 years later	15	28.8

n=52

2-8 打算购买的品牌/ The Brand of the Planned Purchase

排名 Brand Ranking	品牌 Brands	人数 Number	百分比 Percent
1	桑塔纳 Santana	4	33.3
2	富康(神龙) Citroen.ZX	3	25.0
3	别克 Buick	1	8.3
3	红旗 Hongqi	1	8.3
3	昌河 Changhe	1	8.3
3	夏利王 Xialiwang	1	8.3

n=12

2-9 计划用于购车的花费/ The Expense of the Automobile Planned to Purchase

	人数 Number	百分比 Percent
5 万元以下 below 50 thousands yuan	4	28.6
5-10 万元 50-100 thousands yuan	3	21.4
10-15 万元 100-150 thousands yuan	3	21.4
15-20 万元 150-200 thousands yuan	3	21.4
20-30 万元 200-300 thousands yuan	0	0.0
30-50 万元 300-500 thousands yuan	1	7.1
50-100 万元 500 thousands-1 million yuan	0	0.0
100 万元以上 over 1 million yuan	0	0.0

n=14

2-10 理想品牌排名/ Ranking of the Ideal Brands

排名 Brand Ranking	品牌 Brands	人数 Number	百分比 Percent
1	奔驰 Mercedes-Benz	206	34.6
2	桑塔纳 Santana	57	9.6
3	红旗 Hongqi	56	9.4
4	宝马 BMW	43	7.2
5	奥迪 Audi	42	7.1
6	林肯 Lincoln	29	4.9
7	丰田 Toyota	26	4.4
8	别克 Buick	19	3.2
9	卡迪拉克 Cadillac	18	3.0
10	捷达 Jetta	11	1.8

n=595

2-11 不同消费者层的理想品牌/ The Ideal Brands by Market Segments

2-11-1 时尚流行指标/ Fads Popular Index

	人数 Number	第一品牌及百分比 1st/ percent	第二品牌及百分比 2nd/ percent	第三品牌及百分比 3rd/ percent	第四品牌及百分比 4th/ percent
样本 Sample	595	**奔驰 Mercedes-Benz(34.6)**	**桑塔纳 Santana(9.6)**	**红旗 Hongqi(9.4)**	**宝马 BMW(7.2)**
平实生活指向 simple living orientation	287	奔驰 Mercedes-Benz(30.0)	桑塔纳 Santana(10.1)	红旗 Hongqi(8.7)	宝马 BMW(8.4)
时尚流行指向 fashion orientation	308	奔驰 Mercedes-Benz(39.0)	红旗 Hongqi(10.1)	桑塔纳 Santana(9.1)	奥迪 Audi(6.5)

2-11-2 广告态度指标/ Advertising Attitude Index

	人数 Number	第一品牌及百分比 1st/ percent	第二品牌及百分比 2nd/ percent	第三品牌及百分比 3rd/ percent	第四品牌及百分比 4th/ percent
样本 Sample	595	**奔驰 Mercedes-Benz(34.6)**	**桑塔纳 Santana(9.6)**	**红旗 Hongqi(9.4)**	**宝马 BMW(7.2)**
广告淡漠指向 indifferent orientation	170	奔驰 Mercedes-Benz(34.7)	红旗 Hongqi(12.4)	桑塔纳 Santana(8.8)	林肯 Lincoln(5.9)
中间层 medium	352	奔驰 Mercedes-Benz(34.4)	桑塔纳 Santana(10.5)	宝马 BMW(8.2)	红旗 Hongqi(8.0)
信赖广告指向 loyal orientation	73	奔驰 Mercedes-Benz(35.6)	红旗 Hongqi(9.6)	奥迪 Audi(8.2) 宝马 BMW(8.2)	桑塔纳 Santana(6.8)

2-11-3 价格态度指标/ Price Attitude Index

	人数 Number	第一品牌及百分比 1st/ percent	第二品牌及百分比 2nd/ percent	第三品牌及百分比 3rd/ percent	第四品牌及百分比 4th/ percent
样本 Sample	594	**奔驰 Mercedes-Benz(34.7)**	**桑塔纳 Santana(9.4) 红旗 Hongqi(9.4)**	**宝马 BMW(7.2)**	**奥迪 Audi(7.1)**
价格无关心指向 indifferent orientation	103	奔驰 Mercedes-Benz(29.1)	桑塔纳 Santana(11.7)	宝马 BMW(8.7) 丰田 Toyota(8.7)	林肯 Lincoln(7.8)
中间层 medium	291	奔驰 Mercedes-Benz(39.9)	红旗 Hongqi(10.3)	桑塔纳 Santana(8.2) 宝马 BMW(8.2)	奥迪 Audi(5.2)
价格重视指向 careful orientation	200	奔驰 Mercedes-Benz(30.0)	奥迪 Audi(10.5)	桑塔纳 Santana(10.0)	红旗 Hongqi(9.5)

3.储蓄 / Deposit

● 北京 / Beijing

3-1 有没有参加储蓄/ Whether Have Deposit in Bank

	人数 Number	百分比 Percent
有 yes	945	93.4
没有 no	67	6.6

n=1012

3-2 现用的储蓄单位排名/ Ranking of the Banks Currently Used

注：本题为多选题，合计百分比超过 100%（Multiple answers）

排名 Brand Ranking	品牌 Brands	人次 Person-time	百分比 Percent
1	工商银行 Industrial & Commercial Bank of China	809	85.6
2	建设银行 Construction Bank of China	246	26.0
3	中国银行 Bank of China	150	15.9
4	农业银行 Agricultural Bank of China	65	6.9
5	邮政储蓄 Postal Saving	49	5.2
6	城市合作银行/商业银行 Commercial Bank	39	4.1
7	交通银行 Bank of Communications	32	3.4
8	招商银行 China Merchants Bank	10	1.1
9	其他	6	0.6

n=945

3-3 选择储蓄单位的考虑因素/ Ranking of the Considerations of Choosing a Bank

注：本题为多选题，合计百分比超过 100%（Multiple answers）

排名 Ranking	考虑因素 Considerations	人次 Person-time	百分比 Percent
1	就近 close to reach	748	79.7
2	营业网点多 wide- spread business points	251	26.8
3	手续便捷 simple procedure	206	22.0
4	信誉好 good credit	190	20.3
5	服务态度好 good service	118	12.6
6	单位指定的 assigned by the work unit	115	12.3
7	营业时间长 long business time	94	10.0
8	有优惠条件 with preferential terms	6	0.6
8	其他 others	6	0.6

n=938

3-4 储蓄的目的/ The Purpose of Deposit

注：本题为多选题，合计百分比超过 100%（Multiple answers）

	人次 Person-time	百分比 Percent
为了将来孩子上学用 for children's future education	384	41.0
为了将来孩子结婚用 for children's marriage	84	9.0
为了自己结婚用 for my marriage	53	5.7
为了买房子 to buy houses	202	21.6
为了买车 to buy a car	106	11.3
为了退休后的生活 for retired life	250	26.7
以备意外的急用 for urgent use	547	58.4
其他 others	50	5.3

n=937

3-5 未来一年储蓄程度的增减/ Increase or Decrease the Amount of Deposit in the Coming Year

	人数 Number	百分比 Percent
增加 increase	242	24.6
减少 decrease	205	20.8
和今年差不多 about the same	209	21.2
不一定 not sure	273	27.7
不参加 won't save money any longer	55	5.6

n=984

3-6 打算选择的储蓄单位排名/ Ranking of the Banks Planned to Use in the Coming Year

注：本题为多选题，合计百分比超过 100%（Multiple answers）

排名 Brand Ranking	品牌 Brands	人次 Person-time	百分比 Percent
1	工商银行 Industrial & Commercial Bank of China	771	83.8
2	建设银行 Construction Bank of China	232	25.2
3	中国银行 Bank of China	160	17.4
4	农业银行 Agricultural Bank of China	53	5.8
5	邮政储蓄 Postal Saving	43	4.7
6	城市合作银行/商业银行 Commercial Bank	31	3.4
7	交通银行 Bank of Communications	24	2.6
8	招商银行 China Merchants Bank	11	1.2
9	其他 others	3	0.3

n=920

● 上海 / Shanghai

3-1 有没有参加储蓄/ Whether Have Deposit in Bank

	人数 Number	百分比 Percent
有 yes	870	85.8
没有 no	144	14.2

n=1014

3-2 现用的储蓄单位排名/ Ranking of the Banks Currently Used

注：本题为多选题，合计百分比超过 100%（Multiple answers）

排名 Brand Ranking	品牌 Brands	人次 Person-time	百分比 Percent
1	工商银行 Industrial & Commercial Bank of China	704	80.9
2	建设银行 Construction Bank of China	152	17.5
3	中国银行 Bank of China	144	16.6
4	农业银行 Agricultural Bank of China	83	9.5
5	邮政储蓄 Postal Saving	61	7.0
6	交通银行 Bank of Communications	58	6.7
7	城市合作银行/商业银行 Commercial Bank	55	6.3
8	招商银行 China Merchants Bank	9	1.0
9	浦东发展银行 Pu Dong Development Bank	4	0.5
10	上海银行 Shanghai Bank	3	0.3

n=870

3-3 选择储蓄单位的考虑因素/ Ranking of the Considerations of Choosing a Bank

注：本题为多选题，合计百分比超过 100%（Multiple answers）

排名 Ranking	考虑因素 Considerations	人次 Person-time	百分比 Percent
1	就近 close to reach	671	77.1
2	手续便捷 simple procedure	207	23.8
3	营业网点多 wide- spread business points	193	22.2
4	信誉好 good credit	155	17.8
5	服务态度好 good service	118	13.6
6	单位指定的 assigned by the work unit	112	12.9
7	营业时间长 long business time	110	12.6
8	有优惠条件 with preferential terms	10	1.1
9	其他 others	4	0.5

n=870

3-4 储蓄的目的/ The Purpose of Deposit

注：本题为多选题，合计百分比超过 100%（Multiple answers）

	人次 Person-time	百分比 Percent
为了将来孩子上学用 for children's future education	341	39.2
为了将来孩子结婚用 for children's marriage	112	12.9
为了自己结婚用 for my marriage	87	10.0
为了买房子 to buy houses	229	26.3
为了买车 to buy a car	37	4.3
为了退休后的生活 for retired life	238	27.4
以备意外的急用 for urgent use	525	60.3
其他 others	18	2.1

n=870

3-5 未来一年储蓄程度的增减/ Increase or Decrease the Amount of Deposit in the Coming Year

	人数 Number	百分比 Percent
增加 increase	168	16.7
减少 decrease	198	19.6
和今年差不多 about the same	221	21.9
不一定 not sure	275	27.3
不参加 won't save money any longer	147	14.6

n=1009

3-6 打算选择的储蓄单位排名/ Ranking of the Banks Planned to Use in the Coming Year

注：本题为多选题，合计百分比超过 100%（Multiple answers）

排名 Brand Ranking	品牌 Brands	人次 Person-time	百分比 Percent
1	工商银行 Industrial & Commercial Bank of China	643	75.3
2	中国银行 Bank of China	165	19.3
3	建设银行 Construction Bank of China	153	17.9
4	农业银行 Agricultural Bank of China	69	8.1
5	城市合作银行/商业银行 Commercial Bank	56	6.6
6	交通银行 Bank of Communications	51	6.0
7	邮政储蓄 Postal Saving	50	5.9
8	浦东发展银行 Pu Dong Development Bank	4	0.5
8	招商银行 China Merchants Bank	4	0.5

n=854

● 广州 / Guangzhou

3-1 有没有参加储蓄/ Whether Have Deposit in Bank

	人数 Number	百分比 Percent
有 yes	935	90.4
没有 no	99	9.6

n=1034

3-2 现用的储蓄单位排名/ Ranking of the Banks Currently Used

注：本题为多选题，合计百分比超过 100%（Multiple answers）

排名 Brand Ranking	品牌 Brands	人次 Person-time	百分比 Percent
1	工商银行 Industrial & Commercial Bank of China	706	75.5
2	建设银行 Construction Bank of China	422	45.1
3	中国银行 Bank of China	300	32.1
4	农业银行 Agricultural Bank of China	158	16.9
5	邮政储蓄 Post saving	39	4.2
6	城市合作银行/商业银行 Commercial Bank	27	2.9
7	交通银行 Bank of Communications	18	1.9

n=935

3-3 选择储蓄单位的考虑因素/ Ranking of the Considerations of Choosing a Bank

注：本题为多选题，合计百分比超过 100%（Multiple answers）

排名 Ranking	考虑因素 Considerations	人次 Person-time	百分比 Percent
1	就近 close to reach	689	74.0
2	营业网点多 wide- spread business points	287	30.8
3	手续便捷 simple procedure	266	28.6
4	信誉好 good credit	219	23.5
5	服务态度好 good service	170	18.3
6	单位指定的 assigned by the work unit	94	10.1
7	营业时间长 long business time	84	9.0
8	有优惠条件 with preferential terms	21	2.3
9	其他 others	5	0.5

n=931

3-4 储蓄的目的/ The Purpose of Deposit

注：本题为多选题，合计百分比超过 100%（Multiple answers）

	人次 Person-time	百分比 Percent
为了将来孩子上学用 for children's future education	348	37.3
为了将来孩子结婚用 for children's marriage	67	7.2
为了自己结婚用 for my marriage	63	6.7
为了买房子 to buy houses	154	16.5
为了买车 to buy a car	44	4.7
为了退休后的生活 for retired life	253	27.1
以备意外的急用 for urgent use	603	64.6
其他 others	53	5.7

n=934

3-5 未来一年储蓄程度的增减/ Increase or Decrease the Amount of Deposit in the Coming Year

	人数 Number	百分比 Percent
增加 increase	213	20.7
减少 decrease	139	13.5
和今年差不多 about the same	255	24.8
不一定 not sure	306	29.7
不参加 won't save money any longer	117	11.4

n=1030

3-6 打算选择的储蓄单位排名/ Ranking of the Banks Planned to Use in the Coming Year

注：本题为多选题，合计百分比超过 100%（Multiple answers）

排名 Brand Ranking	品牌 Brands	人次 Person-time	百分比 Percent
1	工商银行 Industrial & Commercial Bank of China	636	70.6
2	建设银行 Construction Bank of China	391	43.4
3	中国银行 Bank of China	278	30.9
4	农业银行 Agricultural Bank of China	114	12.7
5	城市合作银行/商业银行 Commercial Bank	27	3.0
6	邮政储蓄 Post saving	23	2.6
7	交通银行 Bank of Communications	19	2.1

n=901

● 重庆 / Chongqing

3-1 有没有参加储蓄/ Whether Have Deposit in Bank

	人数 Number	百分比 Percent
有 yes	492	78.8
没有 no	132	21.2

n=624

3-2 现用的储蓄单位排名/ Ranking of the Banks Currently Used

注：本题为多选题，合计百分比超过 100%（Multiple answers）

排名 Brand Ranking	品牌 Brands	人次 Person-time	百分比 Percent
1	工商银行 Industrial & Commercial Bank of China	326	66.3
2	建设银行 Construction Bank of China	118	24.0
3	交通银行 Bank of Communications	84	17.1
4	农业银行 Agricultural Bank of China	78	15.9
5	中国银行 Bank of China	62	12.6
6	邮政储蓄 Postal saving	22	4.4
7	城市合作银行/商业银行 Commercial Bank	10	2.0
8	招商银行 China Merchants Bank	6	1.2
9	信用社 Credit Union	4	0.8

n=492

3-3 选择储蓄单位的考虑因素/ Ranking of Considerations of Choosing a Bank

注：本题为多选题，合计百分比超过 100%（Multiple answers）

排名 Ranking	考虑因素 Considerations	人次 Person-time	百分比 Percent
1	就近 close to reach	263	54.5
2	信誉好 good credit	181	37.5
3	营业网点多 wide- spread business points	136	28.2
4	手续便捷 simple procedure	118	24.4
5	服务态度好 good service	104	21.5
6	营业时间长 long business time	43	8.9
6	单位指定的 assigned by the work unit	43	8.9
7	有优惠条件 with preferential terms	10	2.1
8	其他 others	8	1.7

n=483

3-4 储蓄的目的/ The Purpose of Deposit

注：本题为多选题，合计百分比超过 100%（Multiple answers）

	人次 Person-time	百分比 Percent
为了将来孩子上学用 for children's future education	205	42.4
为了将来孩子结婚用 for children's marriage	30	6.2
为了自己结婚用 for my marriage	32	6.6
为了买房子 to buy houses	106	21.9
为了买车 to buy a car	17	3.5
为了退休后的生活 for retired life	114	23.6
以备意外的急用 for urgent use	313	64.7
其他 others	21	4.3

n=484

3-5 未来一年储蓄程度的增减/ Increase or Decrease the Amount of Deposit in the Coming Year

	人数 Number	百分比 Percent
增加 increase	144	23.4
减少 decrease	68	11.0
和今年差不多 about the same	96	15.6
不一定 not sure	162	26.3
不参加 won't save money any longer	146	23.7

n=616

3-6 打算选择的储蓄单位排名/ Ranking of the Banks Planned to Use in the Coming Year

注：本题为多选题，合计百分比超过 100%（Multiple answers）

排名 Brand Ranking	品牌 Brands	人次 Person-time	百分比 Percent
1	工商银行 Industrial & Commercial Bank of China	304	65.0
2	建设银行 Construction Bank of China	115	24.6
3	中国银行 Bank of China	84	17.9
4	交通银行 Bank of Communications	71	15.2
5	农业银行 Agricultural Bank of China	66	14.1
6	邮政储蓄 Postal saving	21	4.5
7	招商银行 China Merchants Bank	11	2.4
8	城市合作银行/商业银行 Commercial Bank	9	1.9

n=468

● 武汉 / Wuhan

3-1 有没有参加储蓄/ Whether Have Deposit in Bank

	人数 Number	百分比 Percent
有 yes	520	81.0
没有 no	122	19.0

n=642

3-2 现用的储蓄单位排名/ Ranking of the Banks Currently Used

注：本题为多选题，合计百分比超过 100%（Multiple answers）

排名 Brand Ranking	品牌 Brands	人次 Person-time	百分比 Percent
1	工商银行 Industrial & Commercial Bank of China	290	55.8
2	建设银行 Construction Bank of China	199	38.3
3	农业银行 Agricultural Bank of China	94	18.1
4	中国银行 Bank of China	77	14.8
5	交通银行 Bank of Communications	44	8.5
6	邮政储蓄 Postal Saving	35	6.7
7	城市合作银行/商业银行 Commercial Bank	24	4.6
8	招商银行 China Merchants Bank	7	1.3

n=520

3-3 选择储蓄单位的考虑因素/ Ranking of the Considerations of Choosing a Bank

注：本题为多选题，合计百分比超过 100%（Multiple answers）

排名 Ranking	考虑因素 Considerations	人次 Person-time	百分比 Percent
1	就近 close to reach	409	79.1
2	信誉好 good credit	122	23.6
3	手续便捷 simple procedure	117	22.6
4	营业网点多 wide- spread business points	102	19.7
5	服务态度好 good service	94	18.2
6	单位指定的 assigned by the work unit	86	16.6
7	营业时间长 long business time	54	10.4
8	有优惠条件 with preferential terms	10	1.9
9	其他 others	6	1.2

n=517

3-4 储蓄的目的/ The Purpose of Deposit

注：本题为多选题，合计百分比超过 100%（Multiple answers）

	人次 Person-time	百分比 Percent
为了将来孩子上学用 for children's future education	257	49.8
为了将来孩子结婚用 for children's marriage	79	15.3
为了自己结婚用 for my marriage	47	9.1
为了买房子 to buy houses	113	21.9
为了买车 to buy a car	15	2.9
为了退休后的生活 for retired life	129	25.0
以备意外的急用 for urgent use	296	57.4
其他 others	26	5.0

n=516

3-5 未来一年储蓄程度的增减/ Increase or Decrease the Amount of Deposit in the Coming Year

	人数 Number	百分比 Percent
增加 increase	132	20.6
减少 decrease	88	13.7
和今年差不多 about the same	112	17.5
不一定 not sure	179	27.9
不参加 won't save money any longer	130	20.3

n=641

3-6 打算选择的储蓄单位排名/ Ranking of the Banks Planned to Use in the Coming Year

注：本题为多选题，合计百分比超过 100%（Multiple answers）

排名 Brand Ranking	品牌 Brands	人次 Person-time	百分比 Percent
1	工商银行 Industrial & Commercial Bank of China	277	54.7
2	建设银行 Construction Bank of China	187	37.0
3	中国银行 Bank of China	108	21.3
4	农业银行 Agricultural Bank of China	84	16.6
5	交通银行 Bank of Communications	39	7.7
6	邮政储蓄 Postal Saving	29	5.7
7	城市合作银行/商业银行 Commercial Bank	16	3.2
8	招商银行 China Merchants Bank	6	1.2

n=506

● 西安 / Xi'an

3-1 有没有参加储蓄/ Whether Have Deposit in Bank

	人数 Number	百分比 Percent
有 yes	468	77.9
没有 no	133	22.1

n=601

3-2 现用的储蓄单位排名/ Ranking of the Banks Currently Used

注：本题为多选题，合计百分比超过 100%（Multiple answers）

排名 Brand Ranking	品牌 Brands	人次 Person-time	百分比 Percent
1	工商银行 Industrial & Commercial Bank of China	294	62.8
2	建设银行 Construction Bank of China	137	29.3
3	中国银行 Bank of China	83	17.7
4	农业银行 Agricultural Bank of China	64	13.7
5	交通银行 Bank of Communications	25	5.3
6	邮政储蓄 Postal saving	19	4.1
7	城市合作银行/商业银行 Commercial Bank	18	3.8
8	招商银行 China Merchants Bank	7	1.5

n=468

3-3 选择储蓄单位的考虑因素/ Ranking of the Considerations of Choosing a Bank

注：本题为多选题，合计百分比超过 100%（Multiple answers）

排名 Ranking	考虑因素 Considerations	人次 Person-time	百分比 Percent
1	就近 close to reach	343	73.4
2	信誉好 good credit	123	26.3
3	手续便捷 simple procedure	97	20.8
4	服务态度好 good service	75	16.1
5	营业网点多 wide- spread business points	64	13.7
6	营业时间长 long business time	44	9.4
7	单位指定的 assigned by the work unit	28	6.0
8	有优惠条件 with preferential terms	6	1.3
9	其他 others	3	0.6

n=467

3-4 储蓄的目的/ The Purpose of Deposit

注：本题为多选题，合计百分比超过 100%（Multiple answers）

	人次 Person-time	百分比 Percent
为了将来孩子上学用 for children's future education	214	45.8
为了将来孩子结婚用 for children's marriage	84	18.0
为了自己结婚用 for my marriage	32	6.9
为了买房子 to buy houses	121	25.9
为了买车 to buy a car	23	4.9
为了退休后的生活 for retired life	103	22.1
以备意外的急用 for urgent use	248	53.1
其他 others	20	4.3

n=467

3-5 未来一年储蓄程度的增减/ Increase or Decrease the Amount of Deposit in the Coming Year

	人数 Number	百分比 Percent
增加 increase	133	22.2
减少 decrease	100	16.7
和今年差不多 about the same	98	16.3
不一定 not sure	144	24.0
不参加 won't save money any longer	125	20.8

n=600

3-6 打算选择的储蓄单位排名/ Ranking of the Banks Planned to Use in the Coming Year

注：本题为多选题，合计百分比超过 100%（Multiple answers）

排名 Brand Ranking	品牌 Brands	人次 Person-time	百分比 Percent
1	工商银行 Industrial & Commercial Bank of China	288	61.0
2	建设银行 Construction Bank of China	138	29.2
3	中国银行 Bank of China	95	20.1
4	农业银行 Agricultural Bank of China	50	10.6
5	交通银行 Bank of Communications	34	7.2
6	邮政储蓄 Postal saving	17	3.6
7	城市合作银行/商业银行 Commercial Bank	15	3.2
8	招商银行 China Merchants Bank	4	0.8

n=472

沈阳 / Shenyang

3-1 有没有参加储蓄/ Whether Have Deposit in Bank

	人数 Number	百分比 Percent
有 yes	506	84.2
没有 no	95	15.8

n=601

3-2 现用的储蓄单位排名/ Ranking of the Banks Currently Used

注：本题为多选题，合计百分比超过 100%（Multiple answers）

排名 Brand Ranking	品牌 Brands	人次 Person-time	百分比 Percent
1	工商银行 Industrial & Commercial Bank of China	289	57.1
2	建设银行 Construction Bank of China	153	30.2
3	中国银行 Bank of China	83	16.4
4	农业银行 Agricultural Bank of China	72	14.2
5	招商银行 China Merchants Bank	30	5.9
6	交通银行 Bank of Communications	26	5.1
7	城市合作银行/商业银行 Commercial Bank	25	4.9
8	邮政储蓄 Postal Saving	17	3.4
9	其他 others	5	1.0
10	钢花银行 Ganghua Bank	1	0.2

n=506

3-3 选择储蓄单位的考虑因素/ Ranking of the Considerations of Choosing a Bank

注：本题为多选题，合计百分比超过 100%（Multiple answers）

排名 Ranking	考虑因素 Considerations	人次 Person-time	百分比 Percent
1	就近 close to reach	354	71.1
2	信誉好 good credit	132	26.5
3	服务态度好 good service	111	22.3
4	手续便捷 simple procedure	101	20.3
5	营业网点多 wide- spread business points	94	18.9
6	营业时间长 long business time	79	15.9
7	单位指定的 assigned by the work unit	28	5.6
8	有优惠条件 with preferential terms	12	2.4
9	其他 others	1	0.2

n=498

3-4 储蓄的目的/ The Purpose of Deposit

注：本题为多选题，合计百分比超过 100%（Multiple answers）

	人次 Person-time	百分比 Percent
为了将来孩子上学用 for children's future education	245	49.3
为了将来孩子结婚用 for children's marriage	93	18.7
为了自己结婚用 for my marriage	41	8.2
为了买房子 to buy houses	78	15.7
为了买车 to buy a car	15	3.0
为了退休后的生活 for retired life	118	23.7
以备意外的急用 for urgent use	297	59.8
其他 others	18	3.6

n=497

3-5 未来一年储蓄程度的增减/ Increase or Decrease the Amount of Deposit in the Coming Year

	人数 Number	百分比 Percent
增加 increase	160	26.8
减少 decrease	132	22.1
和今年差不多 about the same	63	10.6
不一定 not sure	149	25.0
不参加 won't save money any longer	93	15.6

n=597

3-6 打算选择的储蓄单位排名/ Ranking of the Banks Planned to Use in the Coming Year

注：本题为多选题，合计百分比超过 100%（Multiple answers）

排名 Brand Ranking	品牌 Brands	人次 Person-time	百分比 Percent
1	工商银行 Industrial & Commercial Bank of China	294	58.9
2	建设银行 Construction Bank of China	162	32.5
3	中国银行 Bank of China	85	17.0
4	农业银行 Agricultural Bank of China	64	12.8
5	招商银行 China Merchants Bank	27	5.4
6	交通银行 Bank of Communications	26	5.2
6	城市合作银行/商业银行 Commercial Bank	26	5.2
7	邮政储蓄 Postal Saving	21	4.2
8	其他 others	4	0.8

n=499

4.信用卡 / Credit Card

● 北京 / Beijing

4-1 拥有信用卡的比例/ Credit Card Ownership

	人数 Number	百分比 Percent
有 yes	303	30.0
没有 no	707	70.0

n=1010

4-2 拥有信用卡的品牌/ Ranking of the Brands of the Credit Card Currently Owned

注：本题为多选题，合计百分比可能超过 100%（Multiple answers）

排名 Brand Ranking	品牌 Brands	人次 Person-time	百分比 Percent
1	牡丹卡 Peony Card	198	66.0
2	龙卡 Long Card	84	28.0
3	一卡通 Yikatong	66	22.0
4	长城卡 Great Wall Card	55	18.3
5	金穗卡 Kins Card	12	4.0
6	太平洋卡 Pacific Card	7	2.3
7	浦江卡 Pujiang Card	5	1.7

n=300

4-3 未来一年有无使用信用卡的打算/ Whether Planning to Use a Credit Card in the Coming Year

	人数 Number	百分比 Percent
是 yes	364	36.3
否 no	639	63.7

n=1003

4-4 打算使用的品牌/ Ranking of the Brands of the Credit Card Planned to Use

注：本题为多选题，合计百分比可能超过 100%（Multiple answers）

排名 Brand Ranking	品牌 Brands	人次 Person-time	百分比 Percent
1	牡丹卡 Peony Card	215	60.2
2	长城卡 Great Wall Card	100	28.0
3	龙卡 Long Card	98	27.5
4	一卡通 Yikatong	95	26.6
5	金穗卡 Kins Card	19	5.3
6	太平洋卡 Pacific Card	6	1.7
7	浦江卡 Pujiang Card	4	1.1

n=357

4-5 不同消费者层拥有信用卡的比例/ Credit Card Ownership by Market Segments

4-5-1 时尚流行指标/ Fads Popular Index

	人数 Number	有 yes	没有 no
样本 Sample	996	29.7	70.3
平实生活指向 simple living orientation	489	28.2	71.8
时尚流行指向 fashion orientation	507	31.2	68.8

4-5-2 信息交流指标/ Information Communication Index

	人数 Number	有 yes	没有 no
样本 Sample	1002	29.7	70.3
信息消极指向 negative orientation	63	20.6	79.4
中间层 medium	521	31.7	68.3
信息积极指向 active orientation	418	28.7	71.3

4-6 不同消费者层打算使用信用卡的比例/ Whether Planning to Using a Credit Card in Coming Year by Market Segments

4-6-1 时尚流行指标/ Fads Popular Index

	人数 Number	是 yes	否 no
样本 Sample	989	36.2	63.8
平实生活指向 simple living orientation	486	30.7	69.3
时尚流行指向 fashion orientation	503	41.6	58.4

4-6-2 信息交流指标/ Information Communication Index

	人数 Number	是 yes	否 no
样本 Sample	996	36.0	64.0
信息消极指向 negative orientation	63	17.5	82.5
中间层 medium	517	39.7	60.3
信息积极指向 active orientation	416	34.4	65.6

● 上海 / Shanghai

4-1 拥有信用卡的比例/ Credit Card Ownership

	人数 Number	百分比 Percent
有 yes	314	31.0
没有 no	700	69.0

n=1014

4-2 拥有信用卡的品牌/ Ranking of the Brands of the Credit Card Currently Owned

注：本题为多选题，合计百分比可能超过 100%（Multiple answers）

排名 Brand Ranking	品牌 Brands	人次 Person-time	百分比 Percent
1	牡丹卡 Peony Card	141	45.2
2	龙卡 Long Card	89	28.5
3	浦江卡 Pujiang Card	87	27.9
4	一卡通 Yikatong	56	17.9
5	长城卡 Great Wall Card	43	13.8
6	太平洋卡 Pacific Card	26	8.3
7	金穗卡 Kins Card	11	3.5
8	东方卡 Dongfang Card	8	2.6

n=312

4-3 未来一年有无使用信用卡的打算/ Whether Planning to Use a Credit Card in the Coming Year

	人数 Number	百分比 Percent
是 yes	334	33.0
否 no	679	67.0

n=1013

4-4 打算使用的品牌/ Ranking of the Brands of the Credit Card Planned to Use

注：本题为多选题，合计百分比可能超过 100%（Multiple answers）

排名 Brand Ranking	品牌 Brands	人次 Person-time	百分比 Percent
1	牡丹卡 Peony Card	142	42.8
2	龙卡 Long Card	100	30.1
3	一卡通 Yikatong	86	25.9
4	长城卡 Great Wall Card	60	18.1
5	浦江卡 Pujiang Card	53	16.0
6	太平洋卡 Pacific Card	27	8.1
7	金穗卡 Kins Card	19	5.7
8	东方卡 Dongfang Card	8	2.4
9	VISA	3	0.9

n=332

4-5 不同消费者层拥有信用卡的比例/ Credit Card Ownership by Market Segments

4-5-1 时尚流行指标/ Fads Popular Index

	人数 Number	有 yes	没有 no
样本 Sample	1005	30.8	69.2
平实生活指向 simple living orientation	471	25.1	74.9
时尚流行指向 fashion orientation	534	36.0	64.0

4-5-2 信息交流指标/ Information Communication Index

	人数 Number	有 yes	没有 no
样本 Sample	1005	31.1	68.9
信息消极指向 negative orientation	55	18.2	81.8
中间层 medium	576	30.9	69.1
信息积极指向 active orientation	374	33.4	66.6

4-6 不同消费者层打算使用信用卡的比例/ Whether Planning to Using a Credit Card in Coming Year by Market Segments

4-6-1 时尚流行指标/ Fads Popular Index

	人数 Number	是 yes	否 no
样本 Sample	1004	33.1	66.9
平实生活指向 simple living orientation	470	25.1	74.9
时尚流行指向 fashion orientation	534	40.1	59.9

4-6-2 信息交流指标/ Information Communication Index

	人数 Number	是 yes	否 no
样本 Sample	1004	33.2	66.8
信息消极指向 negative orientation	54	20.4	79.6
中间层 medium	576	32.6	67.4
信息积极指向 active orientation	374	35.8	64.2

● 广州 / Guangzhou

4-1 拥有信用卡的比例/ Credit Card Ownership

	人数 Number	百分比 Percent
有 yes	255	24.7
没有 no	778	75.3

n=1033

4-2 拥有信用卡的品牌/ Ranking of the Brands of the Credit Card Currently Owned

注：本题为多选题，合计百分比可能超过 100%（Multiple answers）

排名 Brand Ranking	品牌 Brands	人次 Person-time	百分比 Percent
1	牡丹卡 Peony Card	142	55.9
2	龙卡 Long Card	100	39.4
3	长城卡 Great Wall Card	66	26.0
4	金穗卡 Kins Card	28	11.0
5	一卡通 Yikatong	17	6.7
6	太平洋卡 Pacific Card	5	2.0

n=254

4-3 未来一年有无使用信用卡的打算/ Whether Planning to Use a Credit Card in the Coming Year

	人数 Number	百分比 Percent
是 yes	283	27.6
否 no	744	72.4

n=1027

4-4 打算使用的品牌/ Ranking of the Brands of the Credit Card Planned to Use

注：本题为多选题，合计百分比可能超过 100%（Multiple answers）

排名 Brand Ranking	品牌 Brands	人次 Person-time	百分比 Percent
1	牡丹卡 Peony Card	161	57.3
2	长城卡 Great Wall Card	99	35.2
3	龙卡 Long Card	90	32.0
4	一卡通 Yikatong	42	14.9
5	金穗卡 Kins Card	29	10.3
6	太平洋卡 Pacific Card	6	2.1

n=281

4-5 不同消费者层拥有信用卡的比例/ Credit Card Ownership by Market Segments

4-5-1 时尚流行指标/ Fads Popular Index

	人数 Number	有 yes	没有 no
样本 Sample	1021	**24.4**	**75.6**
平实生活指向 simple living orientation	518	20.7	79.3
时尚流行指向 fashion orientation	503	28.2	71.8

4-5-2 信息交流指标/ Information Communication Index

	人数 Number	有 yes	没有 no
样本 Sample	1025	**24.6**	**75.4**
信息消极指向 negative orientation	111	18.0	82.0
中间层 medium	662	25.1	74.9
信息积极指向 active orientation	252	26.2	73.8

4-6 不同消费者层打算使用信用卡的比例/ Whether Planning to Using a Credit Card in Coming Year by Market Segments

4-6-1 时尚流行指标/ Fads Popular Index

	人数 Number	是 yes	否 no
样本 Sample	1015	**27.2**	**72.8**
平实生活指向 simple living orientation	516	23.1	76.9
时尚流行指向 fashion orientation	499	31.5	68.5

4-6-2 信息交流指标/ Information Communication Index

	人数 Number	是 yes	否 no
样本 Sample	1019	**27.3**	**72.7**
信息消极指向 negative orientation	111	16.2	83.8
中间层 medium	659	28.1	71.9
信息积极指向 active orientation	249	30.1	69.9

● 重庆 / Chongqing

4-1 拥有信用卡的比例/ Credit Card Ownership

	人数 Number	百分比 Percent
有 yes	172	27.7
没有 no	449	72.3

n=621

4-2 拥有信用卡的品牌/ Ranking of the Brands of the Credit Card Currently Owned

注：本题为多选题，合计百分比可能超过 100%（Multiple answers）

排名 Brand Ranking	品牌 Brands	人次 Person-time	百分比 Percent
1	牡丹卡 Peony Card	105	61.0
2	太平洋卡 Pacific Card	44	25.6
2	一卡通 Yikatong	44	25.6
3	龙卡 Long Card	35	20.3
4	长城卡 Great Wall Card	10	5.8
5	金穗卡 Kins Card	6	3.5

n=172

4-3 未来一年有无使用信用卡的打算/ Whether Planning to Use a Credit Card in the Coming Year

	人数 Number	百分比 Percent
是 yes	193	31.4
否 no	422	68.6

n=615

4-4 打算使用的品牌/ Ranking of the Brands of the Credit Card Planned to Use

注：本题为多选题，合计百分比可能超过 100%（Multiple answers）

排名 Brand Ranking	品牌 Brands	人次 Person-time	百分比 Percent
1	牡丹卡 Peony Card	122	63.9
2	一卡通 Yikatong	60	31.4
3	太平洋卡 Pacific Card	49	25.7
4	龙卡 Long Card	40	20.9
5	长城卡 Great Wall Card	23	12.0
6	金穗卡 Golden Card	12	6.3
7	浦江卡 Pujiang Card	3	1.6

n=191

4-5 不同消费者层拥有信用卡的比例/ Credit Card Ownership by Market Segments

4-5-1 时尚流行指标/ Fads Popular Index

	人数 Number	有 yes	没有 no
样本 Sample	613	27.7	72.3
平实生活指向 simple living orientation	367	23.2	76.8
时尚流行指向 fashion orientation	246	34.6	65.4

4-5-2 信息交流指标/ Information Communication Index

	人数 Number	有 yes	没有 no
样本 Sample	612	27.9	72.1
信息消极指向 negative orientation	45	22.2	77.8
中间层 medium	339	25.7	74.3
信息积极指向 active orientation	228	32.5	67.5

4-6 不同消费者层打算使用信用卡的比例/ Whether Planning to Using a Credit Card in Coming Year by Market Segments

4-6-1 时尚流行指标/ Fads Popular Index

	人数 Number	是 yes	否 no
样本 Sample	607	31.5	68.5
平实生活指向 simple living orientation	363	23.7	76.3
时尚流行指向 fashion orientation	244	43.0	57.0

4-6-2 信息交流指标/ Information Communication Index

	人数 Number	是 yes	否 no
样本 Sample	606	31.5	68.5
信息消极指向 negative orientation	45	22.2	77.8
中间层 medium	333	30.0	70.0
信息积极指向 active orientation	228	35.5	64.5

● 武汉 / Wuhan

4-1 拥有信用卡的比例/ Credit Card Ownership

	人数 Number	百分比 Percent
有 yes	128	19.9
没有 no	514	80.1

n=642

4-2 拥有信用卡的品牌/ Ranking of the Brands of the Credit Card Currently Owned

注：本题为多选题，合计百分比可能超过 100%（Multiple answers）

排名 Brand Ranking	品牌 Brands	人次 Person-time	百分比 Percent
1	龙卡 Long Card	44	34.4
2	牡丹卡 Peony Card	39	30.5
3	一卡通 Yikatong	36	28.1
4	长城卡 Great Wall Card	16	12.5
5	金穗卡 Kins Card	8	6.3
6	太平洋卡 Pacific Card	6	4.7
7	灵通卡 Lingtong Card	1	0.8

n=128

4-3 未来一年有无使用信用卡的打算/ Whether Planning to Use a Credit Card in the Coming Year

	人数 Number	百分比 Percent
是 yes	143	22.3
否 no	499	77.7

n=642

4-4 打算使用的品牌/ Ranking of the Brands of the Credit Card Planned to Use

注：本题为多选题，合计百分比可能超过 100%（Multiple answers）

排名 Brand Ranking	品牌 Brands	人次 Person-time	百分比 Percent
1	牡丹卡 Peony Card	50	35.7
2	一卡通 Yikatong	48	34.3
3	龙卡 Long Card	44	31.4
4	长城卡 Great Wall Card	23	16.4
5	金穗卡 Kins Card	11	7.9
6	太平洋卡 Pacific Card	7	5.0
7	灵通卡 Lingtong Card	1	0.7

n=140

4-5 不同消费者层拥有信用卡的比例/ Credit Card Ownership by Market Segments

4-5-1 时尚流行指标/ Fads Popular Index

	人数 Number	有 yes	没有 no
样本 Sample	632	19.6	80.4
平实生活指向 simple living orientation	330	16.4	83.6
时尚流行指向 fashion orientation	302	23.2	76.8

4-5-2 信息交流指标/ Information Communication Index

	人数 Number	有 yes	没有 no
样本 Sample	631	19.7	80.3
信息消极指向 negative orientation	46	17.4	82.6
中间层 medium	363	19.6	80.4
信息积极指向 active orientation	222	20.3	79.7

4-6 不同消费者层打算使用信用卡的比例/ Whether Planning to Using a Credit Card in Coming Year by Market Segments

4-6-1 时尚流行指标/ Fads Popular Index

	人数 Number	是 yes	否 no
样本 Sample	632	22.0	78.0
平实生活指向 simple living orientation	330	17.0	83.0
时尚流行指向 fashion orientation	302	27.5	72.5

4-6-2 信息交流指标/ Information Communication Index

	人数 Number	是 yes	否 no
样本 Sample	631	21.9	78.1
信息消极指向 negative orientation	46	13.0	87.0
中间层 medium	363	20.7	79.3
信息积极指向 active orientation	222	25.7	74.3

● 西安 / Xi'an

4-1 拥有信用卡的比例/ Credit Card Ownership

	人数 Number	百分比 Percent
有 yes	82	13.6
没有 no	519	86.4

n=601

4-2 拥有信用卡的品牌/ Ranking of the Brands of the Credit Card Currently Owned

注：本题为多选题，合计百分比可能超过 100%（Multiple answers）

排名 Brand Ranking	品牌 Brands	人次 Person-time	百分比 Percent
1	龙卡 Long Card	32	39.0
2	一卡通 Yikatong	29	35.4
3	长城卡 Great Wall Card	23	28.0
4	牡丹卡 Peony Card	15	18.3
5	金穗卡 Kins Card	11	13.4
6	太平洋卡 Pacific Card	8	9.8

n=82

4-3 未来一年有无使用信用卡的打算/ Whether Planning to Use a Credit Card in the Coming Year

	人数 Number	百分比 Percent
是 yes	110	18.3
否 no	491	81.7

n=601

4-4 打算使用的品牌/ Ranking of the Brands of the Credit Card Planned to Use

注：本题为多选题，合计百分比可能超过 100%（Multiple answers）

排名 Brand Ranking	品牌 Brands	人次 Person-time	百分比 Percent
1	一卡通 Yikatong	44	40.4
2	龙卡 Long Card	37	33.9
3	长城卡 Great Wall Card	32	29.4
4	牡丹卡 Peony Card	30	27.5
5	金穗卡 Kins Card	8	7.3
5	太平洋卡 Pacific Card	8	7.3

n=109

4-5 不同消费者层拥有信用卡的比例/ Credit Card Ownership by Market Segments

4-5-1 时尚流行指标/ Fads Popular Index

	人数 Number	有 yes	没有 no
样本 Sample	599	13.7	86.3
平实生活指向 simple living orientation	341	10.6	89.4
时尚流行指向 fashion orientation	258	17.8	82.2

4-5-2 信息交流指标/ Information Communication Index

	人数 Number	有 yes	没有 no
样本 Sample	**599**	**13.7**	**86.3**
信息消极指向 negative orientation	69	10.1	89.9
中间层 medium	340	13.5	86.5
信息积极指向 active orientation	190	15.3	84.7

4-6 不同消费者层打算使用信用卡的比例/ Whether Planning to Using a Credit Card in Coming Year by Market Segments

4-6-1 时尚流行指标/ Fads Popular Index

	人数 Number	是 yes	否 no
样本 Sample	**599**	**18.4**	**81.6**
平实生活指向 simple living orientation	341	15.0	85.0
时尚流行指向 fashion orientation	258	22.9	77.1

4-6-2 信息交流指标/ Information Communication Index

	人数 Number	是 yes	否 no
样本 Sample	**599**	**18.4**	**81.6**
信息消极指向 negative orientation	69	10.1	89.9
中间层 medium	340	18.5	81.5
信息积极指向 active orientation	190	21.1	78.9

● 沈阳 / Shenyang

4-1 拥有信用卡的比例/ Credit Card Ownership

	人数 Number	百分比 Percent
有 yes	152	25.3
没有 no	449	74.7

n=601

4-2 拥有信用卡的品牌/ Ranking of the Brands of the Credit Card Currently Owned

注：本题为多选题，合计百分比可能超过 100%（Multiple answers）

排名 Brand Ranking	品牌 Brands	人次 Person-time	百分比 Percent
1	一卡通 Yikatong	98	64.5
2	龙卡 Long Card	60	39.5
3	牡丹卡 Peony Card	17	11.2
4	长城卡 Great Wall Card	15	9.9
5	金穗卡 Kins Card	14	9.2
6	太平洋卡 Pacific Card	12	7.9

n=152

4-3 未来一年有无使用信用卡的打算/ Whether Planning to Use a Credit Card in the Coming Year

	人数 Number	百分比 Percent
是 yes	197	32.9
否 no	402	67.1

n=599

4-4 打算使用的品牌/ Ranking of the Brands of the Credit Card Planned to Use

注：本题为多选题，合计百分比可能超过 100%（Multiple answers）

排名 Brand Ranking	品牌 Brands	人次 Person-time	百分比 Percent
1	一卡通 Yikatong	133	67.5
2	龙卡 Long Card	72	36.5
3	牡丹卡 Peony Card	33	16.8
4	长城卡 Great Wall Card	30	15.2
5	金穗卡 Kins Card	21	10.7
6	太平洋卡 Pacific Card	10	5.1

n=197

4-5 不同消费者层拥有信用卡的比例/ Credit Card Ownership by Market Segments

4-5-1 时尚流行指标/ Fads Popular Index

	人数 Number	有 yes	没有 no
样本 Sample	601	25.3	74.7
平实生活指向 simple living orientation	292	22.3	77.7
时尚流行指向 fashion orientation	309	28.2	71.8

4-5-2 信息交流指标/ Information Communication Index

	人数 Number	有 yes	没有 no
样本 Sample	600	25.3	74.7
信息消极指向 negative orientation	55	12.7	87.3
中间层 medium	313	24.9	75.1
信息积极指向 active orientation	232	28.9	71.1

4-6 不同消费者层打算使用信用卡的比例/ Whether Planning to Using a Credit Card in the Coming Year by Market Segments

4-6-1 时尚流行指标/ Fads Popular Index

	人数 Number	是 yes	否 no
样本 Sample	599	32.9	67.1
平实生活指向 simple living orientation	291	26.8	73.2
时尚流行指向 fashion orientation	308	38.6	61.4

4-6-2 信息交流指标/ Information Communication Index

	人数 Number	是 yes	否 no
样本 Sample	598	32.9	67.1
信息消极指向 negative orientation	55	16.4	83.6
中间层 medium	312	33.3	66.7
信息积极指向 active orientation	231	36.4	63.6

5.投资 / Investment

● 北京 / Beijing

5-1 目前参与的投资形式/ The Kinds of the Investment Involved in Currently

注：本题为多选题，合计百分比超过 100%（Multiple answers）

	人次 Person-time	百分比 Percent
债券（如国库券等）bond	232	23.0
股票 stock	228	22.6
外汇 foreign exchange	50	5.0
期货 futures	3	0.3
基金 fund	19	1.9
收藏 collection	73	7.2
其他 others	9	0.9
都没有 not involved in	564	55.9

n=1009

5-2 未来一年打算参与的投资形式/ The Kinds of Investment Planning to Involve in Next Year

注：本题为多选题，合计百分比超过 100%（Multiple answers）

	人次 Person-time	百分比 Percent
债券（如国库券等）bond	168	16.8
股票 stock	239	23.9
外汇 foreign exchange	47	4.7
期货 futures	2	0.2
基金 fund	23	2.3
收藏 collection	69	6.9
其他 others	581	58.1

n=1000

● 上海 / Shanghai

5-1 目前参与的投资形式/ The Kinds of the Investment Involved in Currently

注：本题为多选题，合计百分比超过 100%（Multiple answers）

	人次 Person-time	百分比 Percent
债券（如国库券等）bond	201	19.8
股票 stock	402	39.6
外汇 foreign exchange	44	4.3
期货 futures	3	0.3
基金 fund	47	4.6
收藏 collection	27	2.7
其他 others	2	0.2
都没有 not involved in	503	49.6

n=1014

5-2 未来一年打算参与的投资形式/ The Kinds of Investment Planning to Involve in Next Year

注：本题为多选题，合计百分比可能超过 100%（Multiple answers）

	人次 Person-time	百分比 Percent
债券（如国库券等）bond	184	18.2
股票 stock	368	36.4
外汇 foreign exchange	49	4.8
期货 futures	4	0.4
基金 fund	61	6.0
收藏 collection	27	2.7
其他 others	2	0.2
都不参加 won't involve in	523	51.7

n=1012

● 广州 / Guangzhou

5-1 目前参与的投资形式/ The Kinds of the Investment Involved in Currently

注：本题为多选题，合计百分比超过 100%（Multiple answers）

	人次 Person-time	百分比 Percent
债券（如国库券等）bond	111	10.7
股票 stock	195	18.9
外汇 foreign exchange	14	1.4
期货 futures	2	0.2
基金 fund	18	1.7
收藏 collection	34	3.3
其他 others	3	0.3
都没有 not involved in	745	72.1

n=1033

5-2 未来一年打算参与的投资形式/ The Kinds of Investment Planning to Involve in Next Year

注：本题为多选题，合计百分比超过 100%（Multiple answers）

	人次 Person-time	百分比 Percent
债券（如国库券等）bond	106	10.3
股票 stock	205	19.9
外汇 foreign exchange	20	1.9
期货 futures	5	0.5
基金 fund	23	2.2
收藏 collection	32	3.1
其他 others	735	71.4
都不参加 won't involve in	5	0.5

n=1030

● 重庆 / Chongqing

5-1 目前参与的投资形式/ The Kinds of the Investment Involved in Currently

注：本题为多选题，合计百分比超过 100%（Multiple answers）

	人次 Person-time	百分比 Percent
债券（如国库券等）bond	44	7.1
股票 stock	147	23.6
外汇 foreign exchange	4	0.6
期货 futures	0	0.0
基金 fund	7	1.1
收藏 collection	23	3.7
其他 others	3	0.5
都没有 not involved in	439	70.4

n=624

5-2 未来一年打算参与的投资形式/ The Kinds of Investment Planning to Involve in Next Year

注：本题为多选题，合计百分比超过 100%（Multiple answers）

	人次 Person-time	百分比 Percent
债券（如国库券等）bond	45	7.3
股票 stock	130	21.1
外汇 foreign exchange	5	0.8
期货 futures	3	0.5
基金 fund	5	0.8
收藏 collection	21	3.4
其他 others	457	74.1
都不参加 won't involve in	3	0.5

n=617

● 武汉 / Wuhan

5-1 目前参与的投资形式/ The Kinds of the Investment Involved in Currently

注：本题为多选题，合计百分比超过 100%（Multiple answers）

	人次 Person-time	百分比 Percent
债券（如国库券等）bond	79	12.3
股票 stock	122	19.0
外汇 foreign exchange	12	1.9
期货 futures	0	0.0
基金 fund	9	1.4
收藏 collection	36	5.6
其他 others	3	0.5
都没有 not involved in	449	69.9

n=642

5-2 未来一年打算参与的投资形式/ The Kinds of Investment Planning to Involve in Next Year

注：本题为多选题，合计百分比超过 100%（Multiple answers）

	人次 Person-time	百分比 Percent
债券（如国库券等）bond	66	10.3
股票 stock	105	16.4
外汇 foreign exchange	11	1.7
期货 futures	2	0.3
基金 fund	12	1.9
收藏 collection	42	6.6
其他 others	7	1.1
都不参加 won't involve in	464	72.4

n=641

● 西安 / Xi'an

5-1 目前参与的投资形式/ The Kinds of the Investment Involved in Currently

注：本题为多选题，合计百分比超过 100%（Multiple answers）

	人次 Person-time	百分比 Percent
债券（如国库券等）bond	75	12.5
股票 stock	131	21.8
外汇 foreign exchange	9	1.5
期货 futures	3	0.5
基金 fund	3	0.5
收藏 collection	30	5.0
其他 others	6	1.0
都没有 not involved in	404	67.2

n=601

5-2 未来一年打算参与的投资形式/ The Kinds of Investment Planning to Involve in Next Year

注：本题为多选题，合计百分比超过 100%（Multiple answers）

	人次 Person-time	百分比 Percent
债券（如国库券等）bond	68	11.3
股票 stock	119	19.8
外汇 foreign exchange	8	1.3
期货 futures	4	0.7
基金 fund	6	1.0
收藏 collection	23	3.8
其他 others	6	1.0
都不参加 won't involve in	417	69.4

n=601

● 沈阳 / Shenyang

5-1 目前参与的投资形式/ The Kinds of the Investment Involved in Currently

注：本题为多选题，合计百分比超过 100%（Multiple answers）

	人次 Person-time	百分比 Percent
债券（如国库券等）bond	53	8.8
股票 stock	99	16.5
外汇 foreign exchange	6	1.0
期货 futures	1	0.2
基金 fund	13	2.2
收藏 collection	22	3.7
其他 others	3	0.5
都没有 not involved in	453	75.4

n=601

5-2 未来一年打算参与的投资形式/ The Kinds of Investment Planning to Involve in Next Year

注：本题为多选题，合计百分比超过 100%（Multiple answers）

	人次 Person-time	百分比 Percent
债券（如国库券等）bond	57	9.5
股票 stock	99	16.5
外汇 foreign exchange	7	1.2
期货 futures	4	0.7
基金 fund	14	2.3
收藏 collection	21	3.5
其他 others	4	0.7
都不参加 won't involve in	452	75.2

n=601

6.保险 / Insurance

北京 / Beijing

6-1 参与保险的比例/ Whether Have Bought One Kind of Insurance

	人数 Number	百分比 Percent
参加了 yes	512	50.6
没有参加 no	500	49.4

n=1012

6-2 参加的险种/ The Kinds of the Insurance Bought Already

注：本题为多选题，合计百分比超过 100%（Multiple answers）

	人次 Person-time	百分比 Percent
家庭财产保险 family property	94	18.6
意外保险 accident	127	25.1
健康医疗保险 medical	168	33.2
子女类保险 children security	161	31.8
养老金保险 stipend	207	40.9
人寿保险 life	129	25.5
其他 others	7	1.4

n=506

6-3 参加的保险公司/ Ranking of the Insurance Companies Chosen

注：本题为多选题，合计百分比超过 100%（Multiple answers）

排名 Brand Ranking	保险公司 Insurance Companies	人次 Person-time	百分比 Percent
1	平安保险公司 Ping'an Insurance Co. of China	202	40.2
2	中国人民保险公司 China People's Insurance Co.,Ltd	125	24.9
3	太平洋保险公司 China Pacific Insurance Co.,Ltd.	103	20.5
4	中国人寿 China Life Insurance Co.,Ltd	59	11.7
5	新华人寿 Xinhua Life Insurance Co.Ltd.	34	6.8
6	泰康人寿 Taikang Life Insurance Co.,Ltd .	18	3.6
7	社会保险局 Social Insurance	4	0.8
7	友邦 Youbang Insurance Co.,Ltd.	4	0.8

n=503

6-4 选择保险公司的考虑因素/ Ranking of the Considerations of Choosing an Insurance Company

注：本题为多选题，合计百分比超过 100%（Multiple answers）

排名 Ranking	考虑因素 Considerations	人次 Person-time	百分比 Percent
1	单位指定的 assigned by the working unit	185	36.6
2	信誉好 good credit	144	28.5
3	人员推销 personal selling	103	20.4
4	亲友推荐 introduced by relatives & friends	95	18.8
5	服务态度好 good service	82	16.2
6	手续便捷 simple procedure	66	13.1
7	就近 close to reach	46	9.1
8	有优惠条件 with preferential terms	28	5.5
9	其他 others	10	2.0

n=505

6-5 未来一年有无参加保险的打算/ Whether Planning to Buy Insurance in the Coming Year

	人数 Number	百分比 Percent
是 yes	280	27.8
否 no	506	50.1
不一定 not sure	223	22.1

n=1009

6-6 打算参加的险种/ The Kinds of the Insurance Planned to Buy

注：本题为多选题，合计百分比超过 100%（Multiple answers）

	人次 Person-time	百分比 Percent
家庭财产保险 family property	52	18.8
意外保险 accidental hurt of human body	71	25.6
健康医疗保险 serious disease	117	42.2
子女类保险 children security	78	28.2
养老金保险 stipend	106	38.3
人寿保险 life	68	24.5
其他 others	9	3.2

n=277

6-7 打算参加的保险公司/ Ranking of the Insurance Companies Planned to Choose

注：本题为多选题，合计百分比超过 100%（Multiple answers）

排名 Brand Ranking	保险公司 Insurance Companies	人次 Person-time	百分比 Percent
1	平安保险公司 Ping'an Insurance Co. of China	92	33.2
2	中国人民保险公司 China People's Insurance Co.,Ltd	87	31.4
3	太平洋保险公司 China Pacific Insurance Co.,Ltd.	59	21.3
4	中国人寿 China Life Insurance Co.,Ltd	53	19.1
5	新华人寿 Xinhua Life Insurance Co.Ltd.	23	8.3
6	泰康人寿 Taikang Life Insurance Co.,Ltd .	18	6.5
7	友邦 Youbang Insurance Co.,Ltd.	7	2.5

n=277

● 上海 / Shanghai

6-1 参与保险的比例/ Whether Have Bought One Kind of Insurance

	人数 Number	百分比 Percent
参加了 yes	526	51.9
没有参加 no	488	48.1

n=1014

6-2 参加的险种/ The Kinds of the Insurance Bought Already

注：本题为多选题，合计百分比超过 100%（Multiple answers）

	人次 Person-time	百分比 Percent
家庭财产保险 family property	55	10.5
意外保险 accident	97	18.4
健康医疗保险 medical	143	27.2
子女类保险 children security	173	32.9
养老金保险 stipend	223	42.4
人寿保险 life	210	39.9
其他 others	3	0.6

n=526

6-3 参加的保险公司/ Ranking of the Insurance Companies Chosen

注：本题为多选题，合计百分比超过 100%（Multiple answers）

排名 Brand Ranking	保险公司 Insurance Companies	人次 Person-time	百分比 Percent
1	平安保险公司 Ping'an Insurance Co. of China	236	45.0
2	中国人民保险公司 China People's Insurance Co.,Ltd	127	24.2
3	太平洋保险公司 China Pacific Insurance Co.,Ltd.	113	21.5
4	中国人寿 China Life Insurance Co.,Ltd	73	13.9
5	友邦 Youbang Insurance Co.,Ltd.	69	13.1
6	泰康人寿 Taikang Life Insurance Co.,Ltd .	5	1.0
7	中宏 Zhonghong	4	0.8
8	新华人寿 Xinhua Life Insurance Co.Ltd.	2	0.4

n=525

6-4 选择保险公司的考虑因素/ Ranking of the Considerations of Choosing an Insurance Company

注：本题为多选题，合计百分比超过 100%（Multiple answers）

排名 Ranking	考虑因素 Considerations	人次 Person-time	百分比 Percent
1	信誉好 good credit	177	33.7
2	人员推销 personal selling	158	30.1
3	服务态度好 good service	134	25.5
4	亲友推荐 introduced by relatives & friends	100	19.0
5	单位指定的 assigned by the working unit	99	18.9
6	就近 close to reach	68	13.0
7	手续便捷 simple procedure	59	11.2
8	有优惠条件 with preferential terms	57	10.9
9	其他 others	5	1.0

n=525

6-5 未来一年有无参加保险的打算/ Whether Planning to Buy Insurance in the Coming Year

	人数 Number	百分比 Percent
是 yes	223	22.0
否 no	556	54.9
不一定 not sure	234	23.1

n=1013

6-6 打算参加的险种/ The Kinds of the Insurance Planned to Buy

注：本题为多选题，合计百分比超过 100%（Multiple answers）

	人次 Person-time	百分比 Percent
家庭财产保险 family property	41	18.4
意外保险 accidental hurt of human body	50	22.4
健康医疗保险 serious disease	105	47.1
子女类保险 children security	54	24.2
养老金保险 stipend	105	47.1
人寿保险 life	61	27.4
其他 others	2	0.9

n=223

6-7 打算参加的保险公司/ Ranking of the Insurance Companies Planned to Choose

注：本题为多选题，合计百分比超过 100%（Multiple answers）

排名 Brand Ranking	保险公司 Insurance Companies	人次 Person-time	百分比 Percent
1	平安保险公司 Ping'an Insurance Co. of China	93	41.9
2	太平洋保险公司 China Pacific Insurance Co.,Ltd.	62	27.9
2	中国人民保险公司 China People's Insurance Co.,Ltd	62	27.9
3	中国人寿 China Life Insurance Co.,Ltd	38	17.1
4	友邦 Youbang Insurance Co.,Ltd.	27	12.2
5	泰康人寿 Taikang Life Insurance Co.,Ltd .	3	1.4

n=222

● 广州 / Guangzhou

6-1 参与保险的比例/ Whether Have Bought One Kind of Insurance

	人数 Number	百分比 Percent
参加了 yes	422	40.8
没有参加 no	612	59.2

n=1034

6-2 参加的险种/ The Kinds of the Insurance Bought Already

注：本题为多选题，合计百分比超过 100%（Multiple answers）

	人次 Person-time	百分比 Percent
家庭财产保险 family property	43	10.2
意外保险 accident	123	29.2
健康医疗保险 medical	125	29.7
子女类保险 children security	122	29.0
养老金保险 stipend	175	41.6
人寿保险 life	140	33.3
其他 others	3	0.7

n=421

6-3 参加的保险公司/ Ranking of the Insurance Companies Chosen

注：本题为多选题，合计百分比超过 100%（Multiple answers）

排名 Brand Ranking	保险公司 Insurance Companies	人次 Person-time	百分比 Percent
1	中国人民保险公司 China People's Insurance Co.,Ltd	136	32.5
2	平安保险公司 Ping'an Insurance Co. of China	120	28.7
3	中国人寿 China Life Insurance Co.,Ltd	112	26.8
4	友邦 Youbang Insurance Co.,Ltd.	51	12.2
5	太平洋保险公司 China Pacific Insurance Co.,Ltd.	50	12.0

n=418

6-4 选择保险公司的考虑因素/ Ranking of the Considerations of Choosing an Insurance Company

注：本题为多选题，合计百分比超过 100%（Multiple answers）

排名 Ranking	考虑因素 Considerations	人次 Person-time	百分比 Percent
1	信誉好 good credit	201	48.0
2	单位指定的 assigned by the working unit	107	25.5
3	服务态度好 good service	94	22.4
4	人员推销 personal selling	82	19.6
5	亲友推荐 introduced by relatives & friends	75	17.9
6	手续便捷 simple procedure	50	11.9
7	有优惠条件 with preferential terms	39	9.3
8	就近 close to reach	21	5.0
9	其他 others	4	1.0

n=419

6-5 未来一年有无参加保险的打算/ Whether Planning to Buy Insurance in the Coming Year

	人数 Number	百分比 Percent
是 yes	222	21.5
否 no	471	45.6
不一定 not sure	341	33.0

n=1034

6-6 打算参加的险种/ The Kinds of the Insurance Planned to Buy

注：本题为多选题，合计百分比超过 100%（Multiple answers）

	人次 Person-time	百分比 Percent
家庭财产保险 family property	29	13.1
意外保险 accidental hurt of human body	65	29.4
健康医疗保险 serious disease	95	43.0
子女类保险 children security	53	24.0
养老金保险 stipend	78	35.3
人寿保险 life	76	34.4
其他 others	2	0.9

n=221

6-7 打算参加的保险公司/ Ranking of the Insurance Companies Planned to Choose

注：本题为多选题，合计百分比超过 100%（Multiple answers）

排名 Brand Ranking	保险公司 Insurance Companies	人次 Person-time	百分比 Percent
1	中国人民保险公司 China People's Insurance Co.,Ltd	76	34.2
2	中国人寿 China Life Insurance Co.,Ltd	62	27.9
3	平安保险公司 Ping'an Insurance Co. of China	51	23.0
4	友邦 Youbang Insurance Co.,Ltd.	42	18.9
5	太平洋保险公司 China Pacific Insurance Co.,Ltd.	25	11.3

n=222

● 重庆 / Chongqing

6-1 参与保险的比例/ Whether Have Bought One Kind of Insurance

	人数 Number	百分比 Percent
参加了 yes	184	29.5
没有参加 no	440	70.5

n=624

6-2 参加的险种/ The Kinds of the Insurance Bought Already

注：本题为多选题，合计百分比超过 100%（Multiple answers）

	人次 Person-time	百分比 Percent
家庭财产保险 family property	17	9.2
意外保险 accident	44	23.9
健康医疗保险 medical	60	32.6
子女类保险 children security	46	25.0
养老金保险 stipend	70	38.0
人寿保险 life	38	20.7
其他 others	2	1.1

n=184

6-3 参加的保险公司/ Ranking of the Insurance Companies Chosen

注：本题为多选题，合计百分比超过 100%（Multiple answers）

排名 Brand Ranking	保险公司 Insurance Companies	人次 Person-time	百分比 Percent
1	平安保险公司 Ping'an Insurance Co. of China	63	34.4
2	中国人寿 China Life Insurance Co.,Ltd	49	26.8
2	太平洋保险公司 China Pacific Insurance Co.,Ltd.	49	26.8
3	中国人民保险公司 China People's Insurance Co.,Ltd	48	26.2
4	社会保险局 Social Insurance	2	1.1

n=183

6-4 选择保险公司的考虑因素/ Ranking of the Considerations of Choosing an Insurance Company

注：本题为多选题，合计百分比超过 100%（Multiple answers）

排名 Ranking	考虑因素 Considerations	人次 Person-time	百分比 Percent
1	信誉好 good credit	70	38.5
2	人员推销 personal selling	47	25.8
3	单位指定的 assigned by the working unit	44	24.2
4	服务态度好 good service	38	20.9
5	亲友推荐 introduced by relatives & friends	33	18.1
6	手续便捷 simple procedure	21	11.5
7	就近 close to reach	13	7.1
8	有优惠条件 with preferential terms	10	5.5
9	其他 others	1	0.5

n=182

6-5 未来一年有无参加保险的打算/ Whether Planning to Buy Insurance in the Coming Year

	人数 Number	百分比 Percent
是 yes	122	19.6
否 no	344	55.2
不一定 not sure	157	25.2

n=623

6-6 打算参加的险种/ The Kind of the Insurance Planned to Buy

注：本题为多选题，合计百分比超过 100%（Multiple answers）

	人次 Person-time	百分比 Percent
家庭财产保险 family property	14	11.5
意外保险 accidental hurt of human body	36	29.5
健康医疗保险 serious disease	44	36.1
子女类保险 children security	28	23.0
养老金保险 stipend	37	30.3
人寿保险 life	26	21.3
其他 others	3	2.5

n=122

6-7 打算参加的保险公司/ Ranking of the Insurance Companies Planned to Choose

注：本题为多选题，合计百分比超过 100%（Multiple answers）

排名 Brand Ranking	保险公司 Insurance Companies	人次 Person-time	百分比 Percent
1	中国人寿 China Life Insurance Co.,Ltd	42	34.4
2	中国人民保险公司 China People's Insurance Co.,Ltd	41	33.6
3	平安保险公司 Ping'an Insurance Co. of China	35	28.7
4	太平洋保险公司 China Pacific Insurance Co.,Ltd.	31	25.4

n=122

● 武汉 / Wuhan

6-1 参与保险的比例/ Whether Have Bought One Kind of Insurance

	人数 Number	百分比 Percent
参加了 yes	235	36.6
没有参加 no	407	63.4

n=642

6-2 参加的险种/ The Kinds of the Insurance Bought Already

注：本题为多选题，合计百分比超过 100%（Multiple answers）

	人次 Person-time	百分比 Percent
家庭财产保险 family property	21	8.9
意外保险 accident	28	11.9
健康医疗保险 medical	50	21.3
子女类保险 children security	93	39.6
养老金保险 stipend	96	40.9
人寿保险 life	62	26.4
其他 others	6	2.6

n=235

6-3 参加的保险公司/ Ranking of the Insurance Companies Chosen

注：本题为多选题，合计百分比超过 100%（Multiple answers）

排名 Brand Ranking	保险公司 Insurance Companies	人次 Person-time	百分比 Percent
1	中国人寿 China Life Insurance Co.,Ltd	75	32.2
2	平安保险公司 Ping'an Insurance Co. of China	71	30.5
3	中国人民保险公司 China People's Insurance Co.,Ltd	70	30.0
4	太平洋保险公司 China Pacific Insurance Co.,Ltd.	27	11.6
5	泰康人寿 Taikang Life Insurance Co.,Ltd .	5	2.1

n=233

6-4 选择保险公司的考虑因素/ Ranking of the Considerations of Choosing an Insurance Company

注：本题为多选题，合计百分比超过 100%（Multiple answers）

排名 Ranking	考虑因素 Considerations	人次 Person-time	百分比 Percent
1	人员推销 personal selling	71	30.3
2	单位指定的 assigned by the working unit	64	27.4
3	信誉好 good credit	55	23.5
4	服务态度好 good service	44	18.8
5	亲友推荐 introduced by relatives & friends	40	17.1
6	手续便捷 simple procedure	29	12.4
7	就近 close to reach	27	11.5
8	有优惠条件 with preferential terms	24	10.3
9	其他 others	6	2.6

n=234

6-5 未来一年有无参加保险的打算/ Whether Planning to Buy Insurance in the Coming Year

	人数 Number	百分比 Percent
是 yes	141	22.0
否 no	387	60.3
不一定 not sure	114	17.8

n=642

6-6 打算参加的险种/ The Kinds of the Insurance Planned to Buy

注：本题为多选题，合计百分比超过 100%（Multiple answers）

	人次 Person-time	百分比 Percent
家庭财产保险 family property	19	13.5
意外保险 accidental hurt of human body	22	15.6
健康医疗保险 serious disease	64	45.4
子女类保险 children security	37	26.2
养老金保险 stipend	48	34.0
人寿保险 life	42	29.8
其他 others	3	2.1

n=141

6-7 打算参加的保险公司/ Ranking of the Insurance Companies Planned to Choose

注：本题为多选题，合计百分比超过 100%（Multiple answers）

排名 Brand Ranking	保险公司 Insurance Companies	人次 Person-time	百分比 Percent
1	中国人寿 China Life Insurance Co.,Ltd	61	43.3
2	中国人民保险公司 China People's Insurance Co.,Ltd	52	36.9
3	太平洋保险公司 China Pacific Insurance Co.,Ltd.	27	19.1
3	平安保险公司 Ping'an Insurance Co. of China	27	19.1
4	泰康人寿 Taikang Life Insurance Co.,Ltd .	7	5.0
5	友邦 Youbang Insurance Co.,Ltd.	2	1.4

n=141

● 西安 / Xi'an

6-1 参与保险的比例/ Whether Have Bought One Kind of Insurance

	人数 Number	百分比 Percent
参加了 yes	253	42.1
没有参加 no	348	57.9

n=601

6-2 参加的险种/ The Kinds of the Insurance Bought Already

注：本题为多选题，合计百分比超过 100%（Multiple answers）

	人次 Person-time	百分比 Percent
家庭财产保险 family property	27	10.7
意外保险 accident	52	20.6
健康医疗保险 medical	56	22.1
子女类保险 children security	93	36.8
养老金保险 stipend	80	31.6
人寿保险 life	82	32.4
其他 others	1	0.4

n=253

6-3 参加的保险公司/ Ranking of the Insurance Companies Chosen

注：本题为多选题，合计百分比超过 100%（Multiple answers）

排名 Brand Ranking	保险公司 Insurance Companies	人次 Person-time	百分比 Percent
1	太平洋保险公司 China Pacific Insurance Co.,Ltd.	98	38.9
2	中国人民保险公司 China People's Insurance Co.,Ltd	69	27.4
3	平安保险公司 Ping'an Insurance Co. of China	61	24.2
4	中国人寿 China Life Insurance Co.,Ltd	54	21.4

n=252

6-4 选择保险公司的考虑因素/ Ranking of the Considerations of Choosing an Insurance Company

注：本题为多选题，合计百分比超过 100%（Multiple answers）

排名 Ranking	考虑因素 Considerations	人次 Person-time	百分比 Percent
1	人员推销 personal selling	73	28.9
2	信誉好 good credit	71	28.1
3	单位指定的 assigned by the working unit	62	24.5
4	亲友推荐 introduced by relatives & friends	47	18.6
5	服务态度好 good service	42	16.6
6	手续便捷 simple procedure	36	14.2
7	就近 close to reach	24	9.5
8	有优惠条件 with preferential terms	15	5.9
9	其他 others	4	1.6

n=253

6-5 未来一年有无参加保险的打算/ Whether Planning to Buy Insurance in the Coming Year

	人数 Number	百分比 Percent
是 yes	147	24.5
否 no	298	49.6
不一定 not sure	156	26.0

n=601

6-6 打算参加的险种/ The Kinds of the Insurance Planned to Buy

注：本题为多选题，合计百分比超过 100%（Multiple answers）

	人次 Person-time	百分比 Percent
家庭财产保险 family property	27	10.7
意外保险 accidental hurt of human body	52	20.6
健康医疗保险 serious disease	56	22.1
子女类保险 children security	93	36.8
养老金保险 stipend	80	31.6
人寿保险 life	82	32.4
其他 others	1	0.4

n=253

6-7 打算参加的保险公司/ Ranking of the Insurance Companies Planned to Choose

注：本题为多选题，合计百分比超过 100%（Multiple answers）

排名 Brand Ranking	保险公司 Insurance Companies	人次 Person-time	百分比 Percent
1	太平洋保险公司 China Pacific Insurance Co.,Ltd.	56	38.6
2	中国人民保险公司 China People's Insurance Co.,Ltd	42	29.0
3	平安保险公司 Ping'an Insurance Co. of China	41	28.3
4	中国人寿 China Life Insurance Co.,Ltd	38	26.2

n=145

● 沈阳 / Shenyang

6-1 参与保险的比例/ Whether Have Bought One Kind of Insurance

	人数 Number	百分比 Percent
参加了 yes	226	37.6
没有参加 no	375	62.4

n=601

6-2 参加的险种/ The Kinds of the Insurance Bought Already

注：本题为多选题，合计百分比超过 100%（Multiple answers）

	人次 Person-time	百分比 Percent
家庭财产保险 family property	27	11.9
意外保险 accident	52	23.0
健康医疗保险 medical	51	22.6
子女类保险 children security	62	27.4
养老金保险 stipend	89	39.4
人寿保险 life	60	26.5
其他 others	5	2.2

n=226

6-3 参加的保险公司/ Ranking of the Insurance Companies Chosen

注：本题为多选题，合计百分比超过 100%（Multiple answers）

排名 Brand Ranking	保险公司 Insurance Companies	人次 Person-time	百分比 Percent
1	中国人寿 China Life Insurance Co.,Ltd	93	41.2
2	平安保险公司 Ping'an Insurance Co. of China	77	34.1
3	中国人民保险公司 China People's Insurance Co.,Ltd	50	22.1
4	太平洋保险公司 China Pacific Insurance Co.,Ltd.	18	8.0
5	友邦 Youbang Insurance Co.,Ltd.	3	1.3

n=226

6-4 选择保险公司的考虑因素/ Ranking of the Considerations of Choosing an Insurance Company

注：本题为多选题，合计百分比超过 100%（Multiple answers）

排名 Ranking	考虑因素 Considerations	人次 Person-time	百分比 Percent
1	单位指定的 assigned by the working unit	86	38.4
2	信誉好 good credit	61	27.2
3	人员推销 personal selling	40	17.9
4	服务态度好 good service	34	15.2
5	亲友推荐 introduced by relatives & friends	31	13.8
6	有优惠条件 with preferential terms	23	10.3
7	手续便捷 simple procedure	21	9.4
8	就近 close to reach	14	6.3
9	其他 others	8	3.6

n=224

6-5 未来一年有无参加保险的打算/ Whether Planning to Buy Insurance in the Coming Year

	人数 Number	百分比 Percent
是 yes	155	25.8
否 no	324	53.9
不一定 not sure	122	20.3

n=601

6-6 打算参加的险种/ The Kinds of the Insurance Planned to Buy

注：本题为多选题，合计百分比超过 100%（Multiple answers）

	人次 Person-time	百分比 Percent
家庭财产保险 family property	19	12.3
意外保险 accidental hurt of human body	38	24.5
健康医疗保险 serious disease	43	27.7
子女类保险 children security	31	20.0
养老金保险 stipend	62	40.0
人寿保险 life	47	30.3
其他 others	1	0.6

n=155

6-7 打算参加的保险公司/ Ranking of the Insurance Companies Planned to Choose

注：本题为多选题，合计百分比超过 100%（Multiple answers）

排名 Brand Ranking	保险公司 Insurance Companies	人次 Person-time	百分比 Percent
1	中国人寿 China Life Insurance Co.,Ltd	76	49.0
2	平安保险公司 Ping'an Insurance Co. of China	59	38.1
3	中国人民保险公司 China People's Insurance Co.,Ltd	39	25.2
4	太平洋保险公司 China Pacific Insurance Co.,Ltd.	13	8.4

n=155

第十四篇　饮食、购物场所
Part XIV　Restaurant and Shopping Places

- 百货公司、购物中心　Department Store, Shopping Center
- 超市　Supermarket
- 西式快餐店　Western-style Fast-food Restaurant

饮食、购物场所

百货公司/购物中心

大商场以设施齐全、商品丰富、购物环境好而受到消费者青睐。全国主要大型商场市场销售在 1998 年继续以低于社会商品零售总额增长速度的态势发展。1998 年全国 286 家大型商场实现商品销售总额 1069.64 亿元，比 1997 年同期增长 0.29%；商品零售额实现 852.13 亿元，同比增长 2.62%，增长速度为近年来的最低点。在 286 家大型商场中，1998 年销售增长速度比 1997 年同期下降的有 168 家，占 60.14%，其中销售同比下降 10%以上的大商场 115 家，下降 20% 以上的商场有 76 家； 零售额增长速度比 1997 年同期下降的有 164 家，占 57.345%，其中，同比下降 10%以上的有 115 家，同比下降 20% 以上的有 75 家。在 286 家大型零售商场中，商品销售总额超亿元的有 221 家，其中超 10 亿元的只有 22 家；零售额超亿元的有 208 家，其中超 10 亿元的仅有 8 家。1998 年度 286 家大型零售商场总体实现利润总额 22.25 亿元，比 1997 年同期下降 16.93%，有 136 家商场利润总额比 1997 年同期下降，占 47.55%，亏损企业有 53 家，占 18.53%。（数据来源：《99 中国经济年鉴》）

据内贸部统计，1999 年上半年，全国大型百货商场的经营利润继续下滑，其中零售利润下降了 2.8%，批发利润下降了 4.7%，利润负增长的 117 家，亏损的仅 50 家。与利润下滑相反，销售成本增加、管理费用增长。1999 年上半年上市公司年报显示，在划分的 12 个行业中，百货零售企业排在最后一名，近 70 家百货零售企业利润总额 同比下降 31.82%，每股平均利润仅有几分钱。以北京和上海为例：北京市现有大中型百货商场 109 家，亏损面已近 30%，近 20%的商场利润为零，北京大型商场的平均利润率已不足 2%；上海现有大中型百货商场 230 余家，全市商业企业平均利润率也由以往的 3.5%降至 1.2%左右。

大型商场出现效益滑坡的现象是有其深层次原因的：

1、盲目建设导致数量膨胀，商业平均利润摊薄。

2、买方市场和消费分流的特征日趋明显，越来越多的消费者非商品支出比重日益加大，消费者的购买力出现了分流。

3、布局过于集中，且呈现趋同化经营。大商场一般集中在中心商业区，相同档次的商场直接竞争，导致购买力分流和效益下降。大而全的统一模式使众多商场找不准自己的定位，竞争空间日益狭窄。

4、结构失衡，网点布局不合理。从当前零售市场的形势看，在很多大城市里，百货商店、购物中心等零售业态已出现过剩的趋势，而在很多中小城市，商业网点则相对不足。

加入 WTO，我国大型商场要想抵御外来零售巨头的入侵，重构自身的核心竞争能力，必须在经营观念、经营方式上实现由传统向现代的转化，具体体现在以下几个方面：

1、树立主力商品概念，在竞争战略上采用别具一格和品质领先战略，集中经营适合该业态和企业自身的商品。据国家内贸部信息，1—9 月份城市大型百货商场销售增长较大的前几种商品依次为：冷热饮水机、25 英寸以上彩电、燃气灶、彩色电视机、消毒柜、滚筒洗衣机、西裤、女装、T 恤衫和空调。

2、改革落后的经营方式。现在大型商场普遍采用与厂商联营方式，在付款方式上是售后付款，在利润来源上是按销售额倒扣，其最大的弊端是抬高了售价，降低了竞争力。

3、加快自身的连锁化经营。我国连锁商店基本上限于超市、连锁店、专业店等业态，百货商店导入连锁经营的还相当少，这显然与零售业的发展趋势是不相吻和的。

由于城市的扩大、大型商场的迅速发展，城市多级商业中心模式已经形成。大部分国有商场向着大型化、综合化方向发展。许多过去只以专营店经营为主的品种或经营形式也进入了大型商场，如家具、食品超市等。

最明显的变化是一些时令商品或微利商品如袋装、盒装鲜菜、速冻食品等上市伊始就出现在大型商场中。除此之外，绝大多数商场还打破了以往单一柜台式的经营方式，基本形成了柜台式、开架式、店中店相结合的综合经营方式。

现今，消费支出的多元化使居民的消费心态趋向成熟，大商场应该卖消费者随意性购买的商品，而定向购买的商品应划归专业店和超市。业态和商品的性质注定了这种分工的合理性。这是一种零售商业发展的趋势。因此，今后大型商场的发展应放弃对商场单体数量的过分追求，注重商场的集团化，规模化。

超市

超级市场以经营食品和日用杂货为主，因其经营的商品品种多、品牌全、挑选余地大，并且在挑选时可以不受干扰；同时明码标价、自选商品、产品规范、货款电脑结算、实行连锁经营，统一采购和配置，因此，在我国在经济发展较快、人均收入水平较高的地区，超市已成为消费者日常购物主要场所。

超市在 1999 年继续以连锁经营的形式发展。连锁经营的主要特征是分散经营，统一管理。它最早于 19 世纪初出现在美国，20 世纪在英、美、日等国获得迅猛发展。连锁经营统一采购配送商品、统一经营管理的模式可有效减少中间环节，降低进货成本，降低流通价格并有利于杜绝假冒伪劣商品，净化流通秩序，生产企业不再承担风险，以销定产，同时超市买断商品所承担的风险由此也得到补偿，进货价格相对较低，消费者也从中受益。1995 年以来，这种经营方式在我国零售业得到很大发展，连锁店的形式已发展成超市、便利店、仓储式商场、综合商场等多种形式。

1998 年，全国连锁经营销售额已达 1000 亿元，其中超市、便利店、大型综合超市、仓储商场销售额为 600 亿元，比去年增长 43%，约占社会消费品零售总额的 5%左右。1998 年，年销售额超过亿元的连锁企业 71 家，比上年增加 27%；过亿元企业总销售额达 344 亿元，比上年增长 115%。上海市连锁店营业额突破 185 亿元，占全市零售额的 12.6%。上海联华、华联超市公司，店铺数分别达到 359 个和 360 个，销售额分别为 3.8 亿元和 3 亿元，利润分别为 4000 万元和 4200 万元。连锁网络正在由城市向周边农村市场发展，一些连锁企业已有半数左右店铺开在县镇。如广东省东莞市美佳连锁超市 38 个店铺中，31 个开在乡镇。特许连锁成为企业扩张的重要方式，据连锁经营协会统计，1/3 以上的会员企业都有特许加盟店。

据 1999 年 11 月在上海召开的'99 中国连锁业会议上得到的数据，1999 年底，我国的连锁企业达 1500 家，店铺达到 2.6 万个，销售额可突破 1500 亿元。8 年前，上海联华超市公司开设了第一家超市门店，当时还很少有人知晓“连锁经营”。而如今联华超市的连锁门店已达 600 家，连锁网络已跨出上海，在江苏、浙江、安徽等省布点设店，企业规模和效益同步发展，资产总额已突破 10 亿元；1998 年实现销售 42 亿元，1999 年 1 月到 10 月已实现销售 65 亿元。我国连锁企业在当前扩大内需、开拓市场中有了突飞猛进的发展，连锁经营已成为我国商业服务领域最具生命力的经营方式。

仓储式商店成为连锁经营中被广泛应用的一种业态，经营面积在几千平方米以上的大型综合超市开始在大城市出现，一些区域型的百货商场也开始改造成大型综合超市，连锁店的经营范围也从家电、服装、鞋业，扩展到药品、汽车、建材等产品。国外著名超市集团的特大型超市的单个商场面积达 1 万平方米，一般大型超市的商场面积在 5000 平方米以上，中型的为 3000 平方米，小型的也有 1000 平方米左右。而我国，一方面，一般超市的经营面积大都在 500 平方米左右，处在超市发展的初级阶段；另一方面，近年却兴起一股兴建大型超市热，如武汉汉口从太平洋路到车站路不到 10 公里的沿线一带，就集中了 6 家营业面积在 5000 平方米的大型超市，最近的两家仅距 1 公里多，造成了恶性循环。

由于受到资金、人才、管理水平等多方面的限制，超市的计算机应用大都处于初级阶段，硬件设施极需继续引进和完善。我国超市虽已普遍采用了电子收银机，但是条码技术、POS 系统、计算机网络尚处在开发阶段。商品编码技术落后，致使我国超市的管理不尽人意。另外我国绝大多数超市防止偷盗的办法仍停留在“靠人盯”的阶段，既增加了管理成本，又难以取得良好效果，先进的电子监控设备或其它现代化手段的应用更是寥寥无几。

从 1992 年我国开放零售业市场开始到现在，国外的一些大型零售集团如美国的沃尔玛、法国的家乐福、德国的麦德龙、荷兰的万客隆、日本的伊藤洋华堂、马来西亚的百盛都已进入中国。1999 年 11 月 15 日，中美签署就中国加入世贸组织的双边协议，入世基本已成定局。加入 WTO 以后，市场准入将逐步开放，世界零售业巨霸将会更踊跃地进入中国，它们强大的信息优势、资金优势、管理优势、规模经营形成的价格优势和服务优势，将对本已惨淡经营的中国大型零售商业企业带来重大的冲击。

快 餐

在我国现阶段经济发展的情况下，快餐业的发展满足了人们对进餐吃饱、吃好、省钱、省时、享受舒适环境的需求，并间接地促进了我国其他相关行业的极大发展。快餐业在中国的年增幅达 20%，被经济学家称之为中国商品市场和劳务市场最大、最具吸引力的产业之一。国家内贸局提供的材料表明，1998 年全国餐饮业实现营业额 2783 亿元，同比增长 15.7%，发展速度居国民经济各行业前列。其中快餐业的发展对整个餐饮业的推动最为明显。据国家统计局数字显示，1999 年 1—6 月，我国全社会餐饮业实现营业额 1458 亿元，比去年同期增长 13.6%，继续保持较高的增长势头，但增长幅度比去年同期下降 2.5%。

中式快餐的发展总是一波一波的。七年前，上海的荣华基向肯德基叫板，接着河南红高粱又向麦当劳挑战，他们几乎于一夜之间走红全国，可旋既又销声匿迹。1998 年 7 月开始的麦当劳与肯德基之战，在 1999 年的中国快餐的乡土舞台上还在打来打去。虽然在京沪穗三大城市，以北京的阿德鸭快餐店、红高粱、上海的新亚大包为代表的中式快餐，再次向洋快餐发起了反攻，但与洋快餐在中国的快餐的扩张速度相比，仍难与之抗衡。美国的肯德基和麦当劳在中国已经分别开了 200 多家分店，并获得了惊人的效益。截至 1999 年 1 月，单是肯德基在中国大陆的投资总额已达 2.27 亿美元，投资范围遍及 15 个省、70 个城市和地区，共计 300 多个网点。（《中国质量报》99.4.30）以上海为例，肯德基在上海有 52 家网点，年营业额高达 5—6 亿元人民币，1999 年上半年广告投入 678 万元；麦当劳目前在上海有 25 家店，今年上半年广告投入 843 万元。

虽然当前中式快餐已有了一定的经营规模和发展优势，但如果用标准化制作、工业化生产、连锁式经营等现代快餐特征来衡量，大多数中式快餐还远远未达到要求。再与 12 亿人的饮食消费相比较，其发展步伐还是太慢，究其原因主要有：

1、现代中式快餐的发展时间不如西式快餐长，这使洋快餐不论从投资规模到品牌效应都要比中式快餐强。麦当劳和肯德基都是国际知名品牌，在未进入中国市场前就已经家喻户晓，再加大规模广告投入，使之成为年轻人特别是孩子趋之若鹜的消费场所。以深圳为例，麦当劳和肯德基在深圳的投资总额分别为 2973 万美元和 1020 万美元，平均单店投资额分别为 85 万美元和 73 万美元。而中式快餐面点王，投资不过 2000 万人民币，单店投资仅 150 万人民币。

2、缺乏合理的组织秩序和成熟的理论指导。以红高粱为例，因缺乏体系化的严格管理和严密的财务制度，不到 5 年，从郑州到北京，再到上海、天津，麦当劳旁边傲然挺立的一棵棵红高粱便象多米诺骨牌一样应风倒地。

3、中式产品的自然特点，很难搞标准化制作。

4、快餐的优势在于“连锁”，而中式快餐店主们主观上缺乏“连锁”观念，客观上由于资金、管理水平、原料供应等诸多原因的制约，不能广泛的形成“连锁”经营局面。

5、中式快餐经营者们对人员的培训与管理力度不够。

6、餐饮市场由卖方市场走向买方市场，只重价格不重质量的做法只能使快餐企业走向倒闭。无论肯德基还是麦当劳都要求其所售饮料温度 4℃左右，汉堡包在 13 分钟内售出，否则就必须丢弃，中式快餐都远未能此严格程度。

西式快餐源于工业文明，而中式快餐则根植于东方农业文化，各自代表不同的文化背景和社会背景，要发展中式快餐业应取长补短，那么中式快餐向洋快餐学什么呢？

首先，要学习洋快餐标准化、工厂化的生产方式，像洋快餐一样锁定味道，改变目前仅凭师傅掌握火候而没有定质定量的科学标准，一品千味、一店千味的小作坊状况。

其次，学习洋快餐的运转机制和管理模式。麦当劳和肯德基与其供应商唇齿合作的运转机制和标准化的管理模式，保证了产品从种植、生产、加工的源头就是标准化了的。

更为关键的是，中式快餐急需改变目前直营直销方式，学习洋快餐特许连锁经营的扩张模式，走规模经营之路。

Restaurant and Shopping Places

Department store / shopping center

Consumers prefer to long-sized stores for their complete facilities, abundant choices of goods and pleasant surroundings. In 1998, the sales in major large-sized stores in China continue to grow more slowly than that of the gross retail. In 1998, the gross sale of merchandise in 286 stores reached 106.964 billion yuan in China, 0.29% down than the same term in 1997; The retail revenue 85.213 billion yuan, 2.62% up compared with that of last year. But the growth rates was the lowest in recent years. Among the large-sized department stores, 168 went down in growth speed compared with 1997, accounting for 60.14%. There were 115 stores whose sale commodity dropped 10%, 76 stores dropped 20%. 164 declined in retail revenue, accounting for 57.3%, compared with last year, among which 115 stores dropped 10% and 75 stores dropped 20%. Among the 286 long-sized depart 208 retail sale exceed 0.1billion in sale exceed, and only 8 stores exceed 1 billion. The gross profit in these large-sized stores has reached 2.225 billion and dropped 16.93% than that of 1997, 136 stores declined in gross profit, accounting for 47.55%, 53 stores lost and accounting for 18.53%.(Sources: '99 China Economic Yearbook)

According to the statistic of China Civil Trade Bureau, in the first half of 1999, the management profit in large-sized stores in China continued to decline , in which, the retail profit dropped 2.8% , whole-sale profit dropped 4.7%. 117 stores grew negatively and 50 lost. On the contrary, the sale and management costs rose . Accounting to annual report on the companies that are brought to the market, in the first half of 1999, retail store ranked in the last in the divided 12 businesses, nearly 70 stores has dropped 31.82% in retail profit compared with that of the same term last year, the average profit per stock is only several fen. Take Beijing and Shanghai for examples, there are 109 large and middle stores in Beijing, but 30% among them are in deficit and almost 20% has naught profit. There are 230 large and middle stores in Shanghai, but the average profit in them has dropped from 3.5% to 1.2%.

The drop of profit in large-stores has some profound reasons as the following:

1. Blind construction has caused the increase of stores, and thus lead to decreasing profit.

2. The buyer's market has formed and fragmentation in market is obvious, more and more consumers spend more money on non-goods. There come fragmentation in consumer's buying power.

3. The concentrated layout and the similar management. Large stores generally assemble in commercial centers and stores in same class compete directly with each other, which break up consumers' buying power and decline profit. Many stores haven't define their positions because of the general model. The competition becomes even more severe.

4. The framework is out of balance, and the outlet arrangement need to be reasonable. Taking the present retail

situation into consideration, there are too many department stores and shopping centers in many big cities, while the outlet are not enough in small cities.

After joining in WTO, large-sized stores must shift the traditional philosophy of management and marketing to the modern ones in order to rebuild and strengthen the abilities to defense the challenge from the famous stores abroad and to be more competitive. Specifically speaking, they should carry out the following practices:

1. Establish concept of mainstream goods, make the competitive strategy unique and quality of commodity prominent, focus goods that match the business and its development. The information from the National Civil Trade Bureau shows, from January to September , the goods that rank first in terms of sales growth are hot & cool water-fountain, color TV-set over 25 inch, gas ovens, disinfector, trousers, apparel for woman, T-shirt and air-conditioners .

2. Reform the backward management, by now, many large-sized stores employ the way of combined marketing with manufacturers, stores pay the manufactures after sell the goods, by doing so, the main problems are the rise of prices and the weakness in competition and offer the profit on the basis of sale volume.

3. Accelerate the chained management. The chains market is limited to supermarket, chain branches and specialty shops, it is rare in department stores. Clearly this is far from matching the developing trend in retail business.

As the expansion of cities, the large-scaled stores multistage commercial centers have come into form in cities. Most state-owned stores grow even the larger and more comprehensive. Many commodities which had mainly sold in specialty shops can be bought in large-sized stores now, e.g. furniture and food supermarket etc. Its most obvious changes are that some seasonal food and slim-profit commodities, such as packaged vegetables, frozen food are sold in those large stores as soon as they come to market. Besides, most department stores gave up the model of simply counter-selling, and has formed a mix of counters, self-services and shop-within-shops..

At present, the diversity in expenditures has made consumers psychography more sophisticated. Large-scaled stores should sell such goods that consumers can buy whenever they want, and directory should be sold in specialty shops or supermarkets. The nature of the business and goods conform that it is reasonable. This is in the trend of the development of retail business. Therefore, in the future, the development for large-sized stores should stress the characteristics of group and scale instead of quantity justly.

Supermarket

Food and sundry good daily necessities are the major goods sold in supermarket. All these make supermarkets the daily shopping places for consumers in the areas where the economy develops quickly and the people are better paid. In the supermarket, there are a large variety of brands of goods to choose freely, and consumers can choose whatever they like without being interrupted. Meanwhile the prices are clearly marked, customers serve themselves, goods are standardized computer handles accounts, supermarkets operate in chains and buy and distribute goods in at one time.

The supermarket keeps developing in 1999 in chains. The major features of chains management are the decentralized managing and central control. It first appeared in America in the early 19th century and it developed quickly in England, America and Japan in 20th century. Goods are purchased together and then allocated to outlet. Therefore there are fewer middle links and the purchasing cost can drop. It can help prevent and poor quality goods, regulate distribution system, lessen the risk in production, and define production according to the sales. Meanwhile supermarkets are compensated by doing so. They enjoy lower purchasing prices and transfer the benefit to consumers. Such kind of operation has developed greatly in Chinese retail business since 1995, and there have been various forms by now such as supermarkets, convenientmalls and shopping centers.

The total sales of chains of 1998, was 100 billion yuan, among which 60 billion came from all kinds of supermarkets, 43% up than the previous year accounting for about 5% of the total amount of sales of consumer goods. In 1998 there were 71 chains companies whose annual sales surpasses 100 million, 27% up the previous year. The total sales of all these enterprises comes to 34.4 billion yuan, 115% more than that of last year. The sales volume of the chains shops in Shanghai broke the record of 18.5 billion yuan, 12.6% of the total retail revenues of Shanghai. The number of chains shops of Shanghai Lianhua and Hualian supermarket reached 359 and 360 respectively and the sales are 0.38 billion yuan and 0.3 billion yuan, producing the profit of 40 million and 42million yuan. The chains shops are expanded from urban areas to the rural areas around them. And a half of some chains shops are in towns. For example among the 38 Meijia chains outlets of Dongguan in Guangdong province, 31 are in the countryside. Franchise is the major way for company to expand. According to the statistics given by Chains Business Association, more than 1/3 of its members have franchise shops (Sources: '99 Chinese Economic Yearbook).

According to the data taken from the 99 Chinese Chains Industry Conference held in Shanghai in November, 1999, there are 1500 chains enterprises in China at the end of 1999 and the total number of outlets are 26 thousand. The sales is expected to surpass 15 million yuan. Lianhua in Shanghai run the first supermarket 8 years ago when people knew what chains business was. Nowadays chains members of Lianhua has come to 600 (some even outside Shanghai) with the total assets over 1 billion yuan. Their sales of 1998 was 4.2 billion yuan and 6.5 billion yuan from January to October in 1999. Chinese chains industry has developed greatly against the background of enlarging domestic demand for good sand exploring market. Chains businesses by now become the most energetic way of management in Chinese services field.

Mall is a widely employed form of chains business, large-sized comprehensive supermarkets with a business space over thousand square meters begin to appear in large cities, and some regional stores are transformed to supermarkets. Their scope of business has extended from household electrical appliances, clothing and shoes to medicines, cars and building materials. The business space of some famous foreign hyper market can be 10 thousand m^2 and the business space of general large-sized supermarkets is about 5000 m^2, that of the medium-sized is 3000 m^2 and that of the small-sized is about 1000 m^2 . However in China, the supermarkets are at their early stage and the business space of most of the supermarkets is 500 m^2, much smaller than that in foreign countries. On the other hand, the enthusiasm in opening up supermarkets creates vicious competition. For example in Wuhan Hankou, along the 10km.s road from Pacific Road to Station Road, there are 6 supermarkets with business space over 5000 m^2. The closest two are no more than 1km away from each other.

Restricted by capitals, human resource and management level, the utilization of most computers are at the early stage and the hardware and equipment still need to be introduced and bettered. Although electronic cashier is widely adopted in supermarkets, the bar code technology, POS system and computer network are still at the developing stage. The backwardness of goods coding causes the unsatisfactory management in supermarkets. Apart from it, in most Chinese supermarkets, it still depends on shop assistants to prevent goods stealing. The way increase managing cost, but cannot fulfill the desired aim satisfactorily. The advanced electronic supervising equipment and other modern methods are rarely found.

Since the opening up of Chinese retail business, some large retail groups from abroad have come to China, such as Welma from America, Carrifree from France, Medlonfrom Germany, Makro from Holand, ItoYoKado from Japan, Parkson from Malaysia. On Nov 15, 1999 the bilateral agreement about China's joining in WTO.

China is expected to officially join in WTO soon. After that, Chinese market will gradually open up to the whole world, and the super retail companies will rush to China. Their great advantages in information, capital, management, price and service will challenge Chinese large-sized retail companies which is now keeping going by pain-taking efforts under difficult circumstances.

Fast food

Under the current economy developing in our country, fast food is playing a more important role in satisfying people by being tasty, economical, efficient while providing comfortable surroundings . It indirectly triggers the rapid growth of other industries. Fast food business, with a yearly growth rate of 20% in China, has been deemed by economists as one of the biggest and most striking segment among the Chinese merchandise and labor market . According to the Country Civil Trade Bureau, in 1998, the restaurant industry in the whole county has got a revenue of 278.3 billion yuan , 15.7% rise over the previous year. Its growth speed was the fastest among all the businesses. And fast food is the most major factor in pushing the whole industry. According to the statistics by National Statistics Bureau, the whole industry has a revenue of 145.8 billion yuan , from January to July in 1999, increasing 13.6% over the same term of the previous year in amount , while keeping an upward tendency, but the growth rate has fallen by 2.5%.

The development of Chinese-style fast food always has its ups and downs. Seven years ago, Ronghua Chicken of Shanghai tried to challenge Kentucky Chicken. Red Kaoliang of Henan province challenged MacDolald . These Chinese brands became popular overnight but collapse soon. The fight between MacDolald and Kentucky, beginning on July 1998, still goes in China's fast food market. In the three metropolitan cities: Beijing, Shanghai and Guangdong, Chinese fast food represented by A'de Duck, Red Kaoliang of Beijing, Xingya Bag of Shanghai, and Da XiHao of Guangdong, has put up another retaliation toward foreign rivals. These Chinese fast food, however, can not compete successfully with its foreign rivals in terms of expansion rate. Kentucky and Macdonald's have opened 200 franchisees respectively, and have got a striking effectiveness. By January, 1999, Kentucky, has invested in China Mainland as much as 227 million dollars, including 15 provinces, 70 cities. More than 300 outlets have been set up. ("China Quality", April 30th, 1999) Take Shanghai for example, Kentucky has set up 52 outlets there, earning a yearly revenue as high as 500-600 million yuan. Their total advertising expenditures went for 6.78 million yuan the first half of 1999, while Macdonald's has set up 25 franchises, spending 8.43 million yuan in advertising at the same time.

Even having gained a certain management scale and development advantage, most Chinese fast food business are still far from being up to the standards in terms of standardization, industrialization and chains management . And when compared with the food consuming of the 1.2 billion people in China , the growth of fast food is too slow . That's because :

1.Chinese fast food doesn't enjoy a marketing history as long as its foreign rivals .So the foreign fast food businesses are strong both in investment scale and brand effect . Macdonald's and Kentucky are both international famous brands , being well known long before entering China. They spent much on advertising and naturally became a favorite of the youth, esp. the kids . For instance, in Shengzhen , the investment of McDonalds's and Kentucky are 29.73 million US dollars and 10.20 million US dollars,0.85 respectively to 0.73 million US dollars for a single franchise. On the other hand, Chinese "Pastry King "is invested only 20 million RMB yuan , with single franchise 1.5 million yuan only.

2.There is no reasonable organizational order and sophisticated principles. Red Gaoliang is typical. Due to the lack in systematic management and the strict financial control, within 5 years, through cities like Zhengzhou, Beijing,

Shanghai, Tianjin, the Chinese fast food formerly standing beside Macdonald's and Kentucky had been lashed down like Domino while Macdonald's still goes well.

3.The nature of Chinese food makes it difficult for standardization.

4.The advantage of fast food roots in chains. While Chinese fast food owners are weak in this sense. The incapability of forming a wide-range of chains will results from the objective reasons in funds, poor management level, the supply and so on.

5.The training of the staffs from the owners are far not enough.

6.The restaurant market has shifted from seller-control to buyer-control, Being only price-concerned without quality will end any fast food restaurant. Macdonalds or Kentucky require all drinks be kept 4℃or so and hamburgers be sold within 13 minutes , or deserting them. Such a critical control in quality is rare in Chinese fast food business.

Western-style fast food originated from the industrial civilization while Chinese one from agricultural culture. They represent different cultural and social backgrounds. To develop Chinese food, there are much to learn from the rivals :

First, take the standardization and industrialization in producing and aim at one taste of the food . The case that the cook decides the food taste based on fire without following any standard must be modified. One food with different taste from time to time and one restaurant serving many different food will surely hinder the growth of Chinese fast food business , and must also be changed.

Second, follow the management and operation models of foreign counterparts. The close cooperation between Macdonald's or Kentucky and their suppliers, and the standardized administration have secured the standardization of all parts: from plantation, production to processing.

Last and not the least, Chinese fast food business should change its direct –selling way and pick up the expansion mode by licensing chains franchises in order to build its way of large-scale marketing.

1.百货公司 / Department Store / Shopping Center

● 北京 / Beijing

1-1 最近三个月是否去过百货公司/购物中心的比例/ Proportion of the Sample Visiting Department Stores/Shopping Centers in the Last Three Months

	人数 Number	百分比 Percent
去过 yes	827	81.7
没去过 no	185	18.3

n=1012

1-2 最常去的百货公司/购物中心排名/ Ranking of the Department Stores/Shopping Centers Visited Most Frequently

注：本题为多选题，合计百分比超过100%（Multiple answers）

排名 Brand Ranking	品牌 Brands	人次 Person-time	百分比 Percent
1	西单购物中心 Xidan Shopping Center	176	21.5
2	蓝岛 Blue Island	149	18.2
3	西单商场 Xidan Department Store	124	15.1
4	王府井百货大楼 Wangfujing Department Store	118	14.4
5	城乡贸易中心 Chengxiang Trade Center	116	14.1
6	双安商场 Shuang'an Department Store	101	12.3
7	百盛 Parkson Shopping Center	92	11.2
8	复兴商业城 Fuxing Commercial City	85	10.4
9	长安商场 Chang'an Department Store	74	9.0
10	庄胜崇光 Sogo	65	7.9
11	华联商厦 Hualian Department Store	63	7.7
12	新东安市场 Sun Dong'an Plaza	61	7.4
13	当代商城 Beijing Modern Plaza	44	5.4
14	赛特 Scitech Plaza	40	4.9
15	天桥商场 Tianqiao Department Store	39	4.8

n=820

1-3 样本、男性各年龄层、女性各年龄层最近三个月是否去过百货公司/购物中心的比例/ Whether Having Visited Department Stores/Shopping Centers in the Last Three Months by the Whole Sample, Age and Gender Groups

	人数 Number	去过 yes	没去过 no
样本 Sample	1012	81.7	18.3
男性 Male	504	76.8	23.2
16~24 岁 Age	105	85.7	14.3
25~34 岁 Age	151	80.1	19.9
35~44 岁 Age	131	75.6	24.4
45~54 岁 Age	77	64.9	35.1
55~60 岁 Age	40	67.5	32.5
女性 Female	508	86.6	13.4
16~24 岁 Age	108	91.7	8.3
25~34 岁 Age	150	88.0	12.0
35~44 岁 Age	124	87.9	12.1
45~54 岁 Age	84	84.5	15.5
55~60 岁 Age	42	69.0	31.0

1-4 样本、男性各年龄层、女性各年龄层最近三个月去百货公司/购物中心的频率/ Frequencies of Visiting Department Stores/Shopping Centers in the Last Three Months by the Whole Sample, Age and Gender Groups

	人数 Number	一周 1 次或以上 once a week or over	两周 1 次左右 about once every two weeks	约一个月 1 次 about once a month	两三个月 1 次及以下 once every 2 or 3 months or below
样本 Sample	**823**	**27.9**	**29.6**	**31.0**	**11.4**
男性 Male	**386**	**23.8**	**28.5**	**34.7**	**13.0**
16~24 岁 Age	90	20.0	36.7	30.0	13.3
25~34 岁 Age	121	26.4	26.4	38.0	9.1
35~44 岁 Age	98	16.3	28.6	37.8	17.3
45~54 岁 Age	50	38.0	28.0	24.0	10.0
55~60 岁 Age	27	25.9	11.1	44.4	18.5
女性 Female	**437**	**31.6**	**30.7**	**27.7**	**10.1**
16~24 岁 Age	99	35.4	37.4	21.2	6.1
25~34 岁 Age	131	31.3	34.4	24.4	9.9
35~44 岁 Age	109	25.7	28.4	35.8	10.1
45~54 岁 Age	69	36.2	20.3	31.9	11.6
55~60 岁 Age	29	31.0	24.1	24.1	20.7

1-5 去百货公司/购物中心购物的种类/ Categories of Visiting Department Stores/Shopping Centers in the Last Three Months

注：本题为多选题，合计百分比超过 100%（Multiple answers）

	人次 Person-time	百分比 Percent
化妆/保养品 cosmetic	118	14.5
首饰 jewelry	15	1.8
鞋/帽/袜类 shoes/caps/socks	161	19.7
成人服装 adult clothes	351	43.0
童装 kid's clothes	47	5.8
内衣 underwear	52	6.4
布匹 cloth	7	0.9
玩具/婴儿用品 toy/infant's product	20	2.5
箱包皮具 bag & suitcase	14	1.7
体育用品 sports facilities	38	4.7
日用品 daily necessities	268	32.8
厨房用品 kitchen utensil	38	4.7
家用器皿 household appliance	14	1.7
家具/室内装饰 furniture	5	0.6
家用电器 household electronic products	46	5.6
图书 books	64	7.8
文具 stationary	33	4.0
音像制品 video & audio	68	8.3
食品 food	271	33.2
饮料 beverage	71	8.7
酒 alcohol drink	16	2.0
烟 cigarette	23	2.8
调味品 flavoring	35	4.3
菜蔬类 vegetable	22	2.7
水果 fruit	21	2.6
配菜 blend dish	7	0.9
其他 others	17	2.1

n=816

1-6 样本、男性各年龄层、女性各年龄层常与谁一起去百货公司/购物中心/ With Whom When Visiting Department Stores/Shopping Centers by the Whole Sample, Age and Gender Groups

	人数 Number	和家人或亲戚 family members & relatives	和朋友 friends	和同事/同学 colleagues or schoolmates	单独 single
样本 Sample	823	55.3	14.2	10.2	20.3
男性 Male	387	58.7	15.8	8.3	17.3
16~24 岁 Age	90	23.3	34.4	26.7	15.6
25~34 岁 Age	121	60.3	19.0	4.1	16.5
35~44 岁 Age	99	70.7	7.1	3.0	19.2
45~54 岁 Age	50	86.0	0.0	0.0	14.0
55~60 岁 Age	27	74.1	0.0	0.0	25.9
女性 Female	436	52.3	12.8	11.9	22.9
16~24 岁 Age	98	39.8	26.5	27.6	6.1
25~34 岁 Age	131	55.7	12.2	10.7	21.4
35~44 岁 Age	108	54.6	6.5	9.3	29.6
45~54 岁 Age	70	55.7	8.6	1.4	34.3
55~60 岁 Age	29	62.1	3.4	0.0	34.5

1-7 选择百货公司/购物中心的考虑因素/ Ranking of the Considerations of Choosing a Department Store/Shopping Center

注：本题为多选题，合计百分比超过 100%（Multiple answers）

排名 Ranking	考虑因素 Considerations	人次 Person-time	百分比 Percent
1	交通便利 convenient transportation	527	64.0
2	价格适中 reasonable price	314	38.1
3	质量可靠 reliable quality	309	37.5
4	商品种类齐全 wide range of choices	264	32.0
5	就近 close to reach	185	22.5
6	服务态度好 good service	70	8.5
7	退换商品方便 easy replacement	64	7.8
8	经常有促销活动 promotion	47	5.7
9	空间宽敞 wide space	44	5.3
10	室内外装潢设计现代化 modern decoration	36	4.4
11	提供餐饮休息配套服务 providing dining & rest service	26	3.2
12	可送货上门 goods deliver in	18	2.2
13	有大量进口商品 lots of imported goods	11	1.3
14	大型商品保修 reparation guarantee for expensive items	7	0.8
15	其他 others	6	0.7

n=824

1-8 重度消费者的人口分布/ Demographics of the Heavy Consumers

	人数 Number	16-24 岁 Age	25-34 岁 Age	35-44 岁 Age	45-54 岁 Age	55-60 岁 Age
样本 Sample	474	25.9	31.6	21.7	15.2	5.5
男性 Male	202	25.2	31.7	21.8	16.3	5.0
一周 1 次或以上 once a week or over	92	19.6	34.8	17.4	20.7	7.6
两周 1 次左右 about once every two weeks	110	30.0	29.1	25.5	12.7	2.7
女性 Female	272	26.5	31.6	21.7	14.3	5.9
一周 1 次或以上 once a week or over	138	25.4	29.7	20.3	18.1	6.5
两周 1 次左右 about once every two weeks	134	27.6	33.6	23.1	10.4	5.2

1-9 不同消费者层常去的百货公司/购物中心/ Department Stores/Shopping Centers Visited Most Frequently by Market Segments

1-9-1 时尚流行指标/ Fads Popular Index

注：本题为多选题，合计百分比超过 100%（Multiple answers）

	人数	第一品牌及百分比 1st/ percent	第二品牌及百分比 2nd/ percent	第三品牌及百分比 3rd/ percent	第四品牌及百分比 4th/ percent
样本 Sample	810	**西单购物中心 Xidan Shopping Center(21.4)**	**蓝岛 Blue Island(18.3)**	**西单商场 Xidan Department Store(15.2)**	**王府井百货大楼 Wangfujing Department Store(14.3)**
平实生活指向 simple living orientation	373	西单购物中心 Xidan Shopping Center(19.0)	蓝岛 Blue Island(17.4)	王府井百货大楼 Wangfujing Department Store(16.1)	城乡贸易中心 Chengxiang Trade Center(15.8)
时尚流行指向 fashion orientation	437	西单购物中心 Xidan Shopping Center(23.3)	蓝岛 Blue Island(19.0)	西单商场 Xidan Department Store(14.9)	百盛 Parkson Shopping Center(13.0) 双安商场 Shuang'an Department Store(13.0)

1-9-2 价格态度指标/ Price Attitude Index

注：本题为多选题，合计百分比超过 100%（Multiple answers）

	人数	第一品牌及百分比 1st/ percent	第二品牌及百分比 2nd/ percent	第三品牌及百分比 3rd/ percent	第四品牌及百分比 4th/ percent
样本 Sample	814	**西单购物中心 Xidan Shopping Center(21.5)**	**蓝岛 Blue Island(18.1)**	**西单商场 Xidan Department Store(15.1)**	**王府井百货大楼 Wangfujing Department Store(14.3)**
价格无关心指向 indifferent orientation	172	西单购物中心 Xidan Shopping Center(24.4)	蓝岛 Blue Island(19.8)	城乡贸易中心 Chengxiang Trade Center(15.1)	西单商场 Xidan Department Store(14.5)
中间层 medium	407	西单购物中心 Xidan Shopping Center(21.6)	蓝岛 Blue Island(17.9)	西单商场 Xidan Department Store(14.7)	双安商场 Shuang'an Department Store(13.3)
价格重视指向 careful orientation	235	王府井百货大楼 Wangfujing Department Store(20.0)	西单购物中心 Xidan Shopping Center(19.1)	蓝岛 Blue Island(17.0)	西单商场 Xidan Department Store(16.2)

1-10 重度消费者的消费者层构成/ The Composition of the Heavy Consumers

1-10-1 时尚流行指标/ Fads popular Index

	人数 Number	平实生活指向 simple living orientation	时尚流行指向 fashion orientation
样本 Sample	466	38.4	61.6
一周 1 次或以上 once a week or over	226	34.1	65.9
两周 1 次左右 about once every two weeks	240	42.5	57.5

1-10-2 价格态度指标/ Price Attitude Index

	人数 Number	价格无关心指向 indifferent orientation	中间层 medium	价格重视指向 careful orientation
样本 Sample	470	20.2	50.9	28.9
一周 1 次或以上 once a week or over	228	19.3	50.4	30.3
两周 1 次左右 about once every two weeks	242	21.1	51.2	27.7

● 上海 / Shanghai

1-1 最近三个月是否去过百货公司/购物中心的比例/ Proportion of the Sample Visiting Department Stores/Shopping Centers in the Last Three Months

	人数 Number	百分比 Percent
去过 yes	771	76.0
没去过 no	243	24.0

n=1014

1-2 最常去的百货公司/购物中心排名/ Ranking of the Department Stores/Shopping Centers Visited Most Frequently

注：本题为多选题，合计百分比超过 100%（Multiple answers）

排名 Brand Ranking	品牌 Brands	人次 Person-time	百分比 Percent
1	一百 Shanghai No.1 Department Store	243	31.5
2	太平洋百货 Pacific Shopping Center	200	25.9
3	华联商厦 Hualian Department Store	193	25.0
4	新世界 New World	180	23.3
5	百盛 Parkson Shopping Center	149	19.3
6	八百伴 New Century	101	13.1
7	东方商厦 Orient Shopping Center	86	11.2
8	六百 Shanghai No.6 Department Store	73	9.5
9	七百 Shanghai No.7 Department Store	69	8.9
10	伊势丹 Istan	63	8.2
11	香港名店街 HongKong Mingdianjie	60	7.8
12	迪美购物中心 Dimei Shopping Center	33	4.3
13	豫园 Yuyuan Department Store	31	4.0
14	佳士客 Jusco	26	3.4
15	精品商厦 Jingpin Department Store	24	3.1

n=771

1-3 样本、男性各年龄层、女性各年龄层最近三个月是否去过百货公司/购物中心的比例/ Whether Having Visited Department Stores/Shopping Centers in the Last Three Months by the Whole Sample, Age and Gender Groups

	人数 Number	去过 yes	没去过 no
样本 Sample	1014	76.0	24.0
男性 Male	509	72.9	27.1
16~24 岁 Age	109	77.1	22.9
25~34 岁 Age	146	76.0	24.0
35~44 岁 Age	130	73.1	26.9
45~54 岁 Age	85	64.7	35.3
55~60 岁 Age	39	66.7	33.3
女性 Female	505	79.2	20.8
16~24 岁 Age	108	91.7	8.3
25~34 岁 Age	144	85.4	14.6
35~44 岁 Age	130	75.4	24.6
45~54 岁 Age	82	70.7	29.3
55~60 岁 Age	41	53.7	46.3

1-4 样本、男性各年龄层、女性各年龄层最近三个月去百货公司/购物中心的频率/ Frequencies of Visiting Department Stores/Shopping Centers in the Last Three Months by the Whole Sample, Age and Gender Groups

	人数 Number	一周 1 次或以上 once a week or over	两周 1 次左右 about once every two weeks	约一个月 1 次 about once a month	两三个月 1 次及以下 once every 2 or 3 months or below
样本 Sample	771	24.3	26.2	36.2	13.4
男性 Male	371	21.3	24.8	39.9	14.0
16~24 岁 Age	84	20.2	33.3	35.7	10.7
25~34 岁 Age	111	20.7	28.8	42.3	8.1
35~44 岁 Age	95	21.1	15.8	40.0	23.2
45~54 岁 Age	55	21.8	21.8	43.6	12.7
55~60 岁 Age	26	26.9	19.2	34.6	19.2
女性 Female	400	27.0	27.5	32.8	12.8
16~24 岁 Age	99	28.3	28.3	32.3	11.1
25~34 岁 Age	123	22.8	28.5	37.4	11.4
35~44 岁 Age	98	31.6	20.4	35.7	12.2
45~54 岁 Age	58	27.6	29.3	22.4	20.7
55~60 岁 Age	22	22.7	45.5	22.7	9.1

1-5 去百货公司/购物中心购物的种类/ Categories of Visiting Department Stores/Shopping Centers in the Last Three Months

注：本题为多选题，合计百分比超过 100%（Multiple answers）

	人次 Person-time	百分比 Percent
化妆/保养品 cosmetic	116	15.1
首饰 jewelry	21	2.7
鞋/帽/袜类 shoes/caps/socks	154	20.0
成人服装 adult clothes	439	57.0
童装 kid's clothes	62	8.1
内衣 underwear	34	4.4
布匹 cloth	2	0.3
玩具/婴儿用品 toy/infant's product	28	3.6
箱包皮具 bag & suitcase	20	2.6
体育用品 sports facilities	27	3.5
日用品 daily necessities	206	26.8
厨房用品 kitchen utensil	24	3.1
家用器皿 household appliance	13	1.7
家具/室内装饰 furniture	13	1.7
家用电器 household electronic products	56	7.3
图书 books	56	7.3
文具 stationary	33	4.3
音像制品 video & audio	53	6.9
食品 food	173	22.5
饮料 beverage	54	7.0
酒 alcohol drink	13	1.7
烟 cigarette	16	2.1
调味品 flavoring	31	4.0
菜蔬类 vegetable	17	2.2
水果 fruit	25	3.2
配菜 blend dish	6	0.8
其他 others	21	2.7

n=770

1-6 样本、男性各年龄层、女性各年龄层常与谁一起去百货公司/购物中心/ With Whom When Visiting Department Stores/Shopping Centers by the Whole Sample, Age and Gender Groups

	人数 Number	和家人或亲戚 family members & relatives	和朋友 friends	和同事/同学 colleagues or schoolmates	单独 single
样本 Sample	770	55.7	22.7	10.1	11.4
男性 Male	371	56.9	23.5	6.5	13.2
16~24 岁 Age	84	25.0	46.4	20.2	8.3
25~34 岁 Age	111	37.8	35.1	5.4	21.6
35~44 岁 Age	95	82.1	8.4	1.1	8.4
45~54 岁 Age	55	89.1	1.8	0.0	9.1
55~60 岁 Age	26	80.8	0.0	0.0	19.2
女性 Female	399	54.6	22.1	13.5	9.8
16~24 岁 Age	99	30.3	38.4	26.3	5.1
25~34 岁 Age	123	51.2	24.4	13.0	11.4
35~44 岁 Age	97	69.1	13.4	7.2	10.3
45~54 岁 Age	58	74.1	6.9	6.9	12.1
55~60 岁 Age	22	68.2	13.6	4.5	13.6

1-7 选择百货公司/购物中心的考虑因素/ Ranking of the Considerations of Choosing a Department Store/Shopping Center

注：本题为多选题，合计百分比超过 100%（Multiple answers）

排名 Ranking	考虑因素 Considerations	人次 Person-time	百分比 Percent
1	交通便利 convenient transportation	456	59.1
2	质量可靠 reliable quality	365	47.3
3	价格适中 reasonable price	247	32.0
3	商品种类齐全 wide range of choices	247	32.0
4	服务态度好 good service	110	14.3
5	就近 close to reach	95	12.3
6	经常有促销活动 promotion	91	11.8
7	空间宽敞 wide space	70	9.1
8	室内外装潢设计现代化 modern decoration	34	4.4
9	退换商品方便 easy replacement	29	3.8
10	提供餐饮休息配套服务 providing dining & rest service	19	2.5
11	有大量进口商品 lots of imported goods	16	2.1
11	可送货上门 goods deliver in	16	2.1
12	大型商品保修 reparation guarantee for expensive items	13	1.7
13	其他 others	5	0.6

n=771

1-8 重度消费者的人口分布/ Demographics of the Heavy Consumers

	人数 Number	16-24 岁 Age	25-34 岁 Age	35-44 岁 Age	45-54 岁 Age	55-60 岁 Age
样本 Sample	**389**	**26.0**	**30.3**	**22.1**	**14.7**	**6.9**
男性 Male	**171**	**26.3**	**32.2**	**20.5**	**14.0**	**7.0**
一周 1 次或以上 once a week or over	79	21.5	29.1	25.3	15.2	8.9
两周 1 次左右 about once every two weeks	92	30.4	34.8	16.3	13.0	5.4
女性 Female	**218**	**25.7**	**28.9**	**23.4**	**15.1**	**6.9**
一周 1 次或以上 once a week or over	108	25.9	25.9	28.7	14.8	4.6
两周 1 次左右 about once every two weeks	110	25.5	31.8	18.2	15.5	9.1

1-9 不同消费者层常去的百货公司/购物中心/ Department Stores/Shopping Centers Visited Most Frequently by Market Segments

1-9-1 时尚流行指标/ Fads Popular Index

注：本题为多选题，合计百分比超过 100%（Multiple answers）

	人数 Number	第一品牌及百分比 1st/ percent	第二品牌及百分比 2nd/ percent	第三品牌及百分比 3rd/ percent	第四品牌及百分比 4th / percent
样本 Sample	**763**	**一百 Shanghai No.1 Department Store(31.5)**	**太平洋百货 Pacific Shopping Center(26.1)**	**华联商厦 Hualian Department Store(25.0)**	**新世界 New World(23.3)**
平实生活指向 simple living orientation	321	一百 Shanghai No.1 Department Store(39.6)	华联商厦 Hualian Department Store(27.4)	新世界 New World(22.7)	太平洋百货 Pacific Shopping Center(16.5)
时尚流行指向 fashion orientation	442	太平洋百货 Pacific Shopping Center(33.0)	一百 Shanghai No.1 Department Store(25.6)	百盛 Parkson Shopping Center(23.8) 新世界 New World(23.8)	华联商厦 Hualian Department Store(23.3)

1-9-2 价格态度指标/ Price Attitude Index

注：本题为多选题，合计百分比超过 100%（Multiple answers）

	人数 Number	第一品牌及百分比 1st/ percent	第二品牌及百分比 2nd/ percent	第三品牌及百分比 3rd/ percent	第四品牌及百分比 4th / percent
样本 Sample	770	**一百 Shanghai No.1 Department Store(31.6)**	**太平洋百货 Pacific Shopping Center(25.8)**	**华联商厦 Hualian Department Store(25.1)**	**新世界 New World(23.4)**
价格无关心指向 indifferent orientation	116	新世界 New World(31.9)	太平洋百货 Pacific Shopping Center(31.0)	一百 Shanghai No.1 Department Store(24.1)	华联商厦 Hualian Department Store(21.6) 百盛 Parkson Shopping Center(21.6)
中间层 medium	406	一百 Shanghai No.1 Department Store(30.0)	太平洋百货 Pacific Shopping Center(27.6)	华联商厦 Hualian Department Store(23.2)	新世界 New World(21.2)
价格重视指向 careful orientation	248	一百 Shanghai No.1 Department Store(37.5)	华联商厦 Hualian Department Store(29.8)	新世界 New World(23.0)	太平洋百货 Pacific Shopping Center(20.6)

1-10 重度消费者的消费者层构成/ The Composition of the Heavy Consumers

1-10-1 时尚流行指标/ Fads popular Index

	人数 Number	平实生活指向 simple living orientation	时尚流行指向 fashion orientation
样本 Sample	386	35.5	64.5
一周 1 次或以上 once a week or over	185	30.3	69.7
两周 1 次左右 about once every two weeks	201	40.3	59.7

1-10-2 价格态度指标/ Price Attitude Index

	人数 Number	价格无关心指向 indifferent orientation	中间层 medium	价格重视指向 careful orientation
样本 Sample	388	15.5	51.8	32.7
一周 1 次或以上 once a week or over	187	15.0	52.9	32.1
两周 1 次左右 about once every two weeks	201	15.9	50.7	33.3

● 广州 / Guangzhou

1-1 最近三个月是否去过百货公司/购物中心的比例/ Proportion of the Sample Visiting Department Stores/Shopping Centers in the Last Three Months

	人数 Number	百分比 Percent
去过 yes	825	79.8
没去过 no	209	20.2

n=1034

1-2 最常去的百货公司/购物中心排名/ Ranking of the Department Stores/Shopping Centers Visited Most Frequently

注：本题为多选题，合计百分比超过 100%（Multiple answers）

排名 Brand Ranking	品牌 Brands	人次 Person-time	百分比 Percent
1	广州百货大厦 Guangzhou Merchandise Building	357	43.4
2	天河城购物广场 Teem Plaza	206	25.1
3	新大新百货大厦 XDX Merchandise Building	204	24.8
4	吉之岛 Jusco	171	20.8
5	东山百货大厦 Dongshan Merchandise Building	137	16.7
6	海珠 Haizhu	115	14.0
7	永安 Yong'an	104	12.7

n=822

1-3 样本、男性各年龄层、女性各年龄层最近三个月是否去过百货公司/购物中心的比例/ Whether Having Visited Department Stores/Shopping Centers in the Last Three Months by the Whole Sample, Age and Gender Groups

	人数 Number	去过 yes	没去过 no
样本 Sample	1034	79.8	20.2
男性 Male	499	74.1	25.9
16~24 岁 Age	106	66.0	34.0
25~34 岁 Age	150	84.0	16.0
35~44 岁 Age	127	75.6	24.4
45~54 岁 Age	73	74.0	26.0
55~60 岁 Age	43	55.8	44.2
女性 Female	535	85.0	15.0
16~24 岁 Age	112	89.3	10.7
25~34 岁 Age	158	87.3	12.7
35~44 岁 Age	137	88.3	11.7
45~54 岁 Age	87	80.5	19.5
55~60 岁 Age	41	63.4	36.6

1-4 样本、男性各年龄层、女性各年龄层最近三个月去百货公司/购物中心的频率/ Frequencies of Visiting Department Stores/Shopping Centers in the Last Three Months by the Whole Sample, Age and Gender Groups

	人数 Number	一周 1 次或以上 once a week or over	两周 1 次左右 about once every two weeks	约一个月 1 次 about once a month	两三个月 1 次及以下 once every 2 or 3 months or below
样本 Sample	824	24.8	34.0	30.9	10.3
男性 Male	370	20.0	33.0	33.8	13.2
16~24 岁 Age	70	18.6	37.1	31.4	12.9
25~34 岁 Age	126	19.8	38.9	31.7	9.5
35~44 岁 Age	96	20.8	21.9	39.6	17.7
45~54 岁 Age	54	14.8	37.0	29.6	18.5
55~60 岁 Age	24	33.3	25.0	37.5	4.2
女性 Female	454	28.6	34.8	28.6	7.9
16~24 岁 Age	100	25.0	43.0	24.0	8.0
25~34 岁 Age	138	34.1	33.3	25.4	7.2
35~44 岁 Age	120	30.8	33.3	30.0	5.8
45~54 岁 Age	70	20.0	32.9	40.0	7.1
55~60 岁 Age	26	26.9	23.1	26.9	23.1

1-5 去百货公司/购物中心购物的种类/ Categories of Visiting Department Stores/Shopping Centers in the Last Three Months

注：本题为多选题，合计百分比超过 100%（Multiple answers）

	人次 Person-time	百分比 Percent
化妆/保养品 cosmetic	118	14.4
首饰 jewelry	20	2.4
鞋/帽/袜类 shoes/caps/socks	83	10.1
成人服装 adult clothes	223	27.3
童装 kid's clothes	47	5.7
内衣 underwear	20	2.4
布匹 cloth	2	0.2
玩具/婴儿用品 toy/infant's product	36	4.4
箱包皮具 bag & suitcase	7	0.9
体育用品 sports facilities	39	4.8
日用品 daily necessities	380	46.5
厨房用品 kitchen utensil	62	7.6
家用器皿 household appliance	43	5.3
家具/室内装饰 furniture	14	1.7
家用电器 household electronic products	46	5.6
图书 books	37	4.5
文具 stationary	59	7.2
音像制品 video & audio	32	3.9
食品 food	269	32.9
饮料 beverage	91	11.1
酒 alcohol drink	9	1.1
烟 cigarette	15	1.8
调味品 flavoring	43	5.3
菜蔬类 vegetable	12	1.5
水果 fruit	9	1.1
配菜 blend dish	6	0.7
其他 others	16	2.0

n=818

1-6 样本、男性各年龄层、女性各年龄层常与谁一起去百货公司/购物中心/ With Whom When Visiting Department Stores/Shopping Centers by the Whole Sample, Age and Gender Groups

	人数 Number	和家人或亲戚 family members & relatives	和朋友 friends	和同事/同学 colleagues or schoolmates	单独 single
样本 Sample	819	53.0	23.2	9.2	14.7
男性 Male	367	54.0	22.6	7.1	16.3
16~24 岁 Age	70	32.9	30.0	21.4	15.7
25~34 岁 Age	126	42.9	39.7	3.2	14.3
35~44 岁 Age	95	73.7	8.4	1.1	16.8
45~54 岁 Age	53	67.9	5.7	11.3	15.1
55~60 岁 Age	23	65.2	4.3	0.0	30.4
女性 Female	452	52.2	23.7	10.8	13.3
16~24 岁 Age	99	25.3	42.4	29.3	3.0
25~34 岁 Age	138	49.3	27.5	8.0	15.2
35~44 岁 Age	120	65.8	15.0	6.7	12.5
45~54 岁 Age	69	60.9	11.6	1.4	26.1
55~60 岁 Age	26	84.6	3.8	0.0	11.5

1-7 选择百货公司/购物中心的考虑因素/ Ranking of the Considerations of Choosing a Department Store/Shopping Center

注：本题为多选题，合计百分比超过 100%（Multiple answers）

排名 Ranking	考虑因素 Considerations	人次 Person-time	百分比 Percent
1	交通便利 convenient transportation	399	48.4
2	质量可靠 reliable quality	391	47.5
3	商品种类齐全 wide range of choices	267	32.4
4	价格适中 reasonable price	249	30.2
5	服务态度好 good service	152	18.4
6	就近 close to reach	127	15.4
7	空间宽敞 wide space	95	11.5
8	室内外装潢设计现代化 modern decoration	35	4.2
9	退换商品方便 easy replacement	27	3.3
10	经常有促销活动 promotion	25	3.0
11	大型商品保修 reparation guarantee for expensive items	21	2.5
11	提供餐饮休息配套服务 providing dining & rest service	21	2.5
12	可送货上门 goods deliver in	17	2.1
13	有大量进口商品 lots of imported goods	12	1.5
14	其他 others	7	0.8

n=824

1-8 重度消费者的人口分布/ Demographics of the Heavy Consumers

	人数 Number	16-24 岁 Age	25-34 岁 Age	35-44 岁 Age	45-54 岁 Age	55-60 岁 Age
样本 Sample	484	22.1	34.5	24.4	13.4	5.6
男性 Male	196	19.9	37.8	20.9	14.3	7.1
一周 1 次或以上 once a week or over	74	17.6	33.8	27.0	10.8	10.8
两周 1 次左右 about once every two weeks	122	21.3	40.2	17.2	16.4	4.9
女性 Female	288	23.6	32.3	26.7	12.8	4.5
一周 1 次或以上 once a week or over	130	19.2	36.2	23.5	10.8	5.4
两周 1 次左右 about once every two weeks	158	27.2	29.1	25.3	14.6	3.8

1-9 不同消费者层常去的百货公司/购物中心// Department Stores/Shopping Centers Visited Most Frequently by Market Segments

1-9-1 时尚流行指标/ Fads Popular Index

注：本题为多选题，合计百分比超过 100%（Multiple answers）

	人数 Number	第一品牌及百分比 1st/ percent	第二品牌及百分比 2nd/ percent	第三品牌及百分比 3rd/ percent
样本 Sample	811	**广州百货大厦 Guangzhou Merchandise Building(43.2)**	**天河城购物广场 Teem Plaza(25.0)**	**新大新百货大厦 XDX Merchandise Building(24.8)**
平实生活指向 simple living orientation	397	广州百货大厦 Guangzhou Merchandise Building(39.5)	天河城购物广场 Teem Plaza(24.7)	新大新百货大厦 XDX Merchandise Building(24.4)
时尚流行指向 fashion orientation	414	广州百货大厦 Guangzhou Merchandise Building(46.6)	天河城购物广场 Teem Plaza(25.4)	新大新百货大厦 XDX Merchandise Building(25.1)

1-9-2 价格态度指标/ Price Attitude Index

注：本题为多选题，合计百分比超过 100%（Multiple answers）

	人数 Number	第一品牌及百分比 1st/ percent	第二品牌及百分比 2nd/ percent	第三品牌及百分比 3rd/ percent
样本 Sample	817	**广州百货大厦 Guangzhou Merchandise Building(43.5)**	**天河城购物广场 Teem Plaza(25.2)**	**新大新百货大厦 XDX Merchandise Building(24.7)**
价格无关心指向 indifferent orientation	146	广州百货大厦 Guangzhou Merchandise Building(44.5)	天河城购物广场 Teem Plaza(36.3)	吉之岛 Jusco(22.6)
中间层 medium	437	广州百货大厦 Guangzhou Merchandise Building(45.1)	新大新百货大厦 XDX Merchandise Building(26.5)	天河城购物广场 Teem Plaza(22.9)
价格重视指向 careful orientation	234	广州百货大厦 Guangzhou Merchandise Building(39.7)	新大新百货大厦 XDX Merchandise Building(23.5)	天河城购物广场 Teem Plaza(22.6)

1-10 重度消费者的消费者层构成/ The Composition of the Heavy Consumers

1-10-1 时尚流行指标/ Fads popular Index

	人数 Number	平实生活指向 simple living orientation	时尚流行指向 fashion orientation
样本 Sample	477	46.1	53.9
一周 1 次或以上 once a week or over	201	43.3	56.7
两周 1 次左右 about once every two weeks	276	48.2	51.8

1-10-2 价格态度指标/ Price Attitude Index

	人数 Number	价格无关心指向 indifferent orientation	中间层 medium	价格重视指向 careful orientation
样本 Sample	480	17.7	54.8	27.5
一周 1 次或以上 once a week or over	202	14.9	53.0	32.2
两周 1 次左右 about once every two weeks	278	19.8	56.1	24.1

● 重庆 / Chongqing

1-1 最近三个月是否去过百货公司/购物中心的比例/ Proportion of the Sample Visiting Department Stores/Shopping Centers in the Last Three Months

	人数 Number	百分比 Percent
去过 yes	464	74.4
没去过 no	160	25.6

n=624

1-2 最常去的百货公司/购物中心排名/ Ranking of the Department Stores/Shopping Centers Visited Most Frequently

注：本题为多选题，合计百分比超过 100%（Multiple answers）

排名 Brand Ranking	品牌 Brands	人次 Person-time	百分比 Percent
1	重百 Chongqing Department Store	282	60.8
2	立丹百货 Lidan	61	13.1
3	沙坪坝百货公司 Shapingba Department Store	49	10.6
4	百盛 Parkson Shopping Center	42	9.1
5	富安百货 Mega Department Store	39	8.4
6	阳光百货 Sunshine Department Store	27	5.8
6	两路口百货公司 Lianglukou	27	5.8
7	渝北商场 Yubei	23	5.0
7	观音桥百货公司 Guanyinqiao	23	5.0
8	友谊 Friendship	22	4.7
9	重庆商业大厦 Chongqing Shangye	19	4.1
10	惠工百货 Huigong	15	3.2

n=464

1-3 样本、男性各年龄层、女性各年龄层最近三个月是否去过百货公司/购物中心的比例/ Whether Having Visited Department Stores/Shopping Centers in the Last Three Months by the Whole Sample, Age and Gender Groups

	人数 Number	去过 yes	没去过 no
样本 Sample	624	74.4	25.6
男性 Male	314	70.4	29.6
16~24 岁 Age	64	82.8	17.2
25~34 岁 Age	93	72.0	28.0
35~44 岁 Age	75	66.7	33.3
45~54 岁 Age	54	61.1	38.9
55~60 岁 Age	28	64.3	35.7
女性 Female	310	78.4	21.6
16~24 岁 Age	64	96.9	3.1
25~34 岁 Age	90	81.1	18.9
35~44 岁 Age	73	75.3	24.7
45~54 岁 Age	60	66.7	33.3
55~60 岁 Age	23	56.5	43.5

1-4 样本、男性各年龄层、女性各年龄层最近三个月去百货公司/购物中心的频率/ Frequencies of Visiting Department Stores/Shopping Centers in the Last Three Months by the Whole Sample, Age and Gender Groups

	人数 Number	一周 1 次或以上 once a week or over	两周 1 次左右 about once every two weeks	约一个月 1 次 about once a month	两三个月 1 次及以下 once every 2 or 3 months or below
样本 Sample	462	29.4	30.3	29.7	10.6
男性 Male	220	23.6	28.6	35.5	12.3
16~24 岁 Age	52	19.2	30.8	36.5	13.5
25~34 岁 Age	67	16.4	23.9	47.8	11.9
35~44 岁 Age	50	30.0	34.0	24.0	12.0
45~54 岁 Age	33	27.3	33.3	30.3	9.1
55~60 岁 Age	18	38.9	16.7	27.8	16.7
女性 Female	242	34.7	31.8	24.4	9.1
16~24 岁 Age	62	40.3	32.3	24.2	3.2
25~34 岁 Age	72	38.9	38.9	15.3	6.9
35~44 岁 Age	55	36.4	30.9	27.3	5.5
45~54 岁 Age	40	22.5	25.0	27.5	25.0
55~60 岁 Age	13	15.4	15.4	53.8	15.4

1-5 去百货公司/购物中心购物的种类/ Categories of Visiting Department Stores/Sh●pping Centers in the Last Three Months

注：本题为多选题，合计百分比超过 100%（Multiple answers）

	人次 Person-time	百分比 Percent
化妆/保养品 cosmetic	67	14.6
首饰 jewelry	18	3.9
鞋/帽/袜类 shoes/caps/socks	60	13.1
成人服装 adult clothes	171	37.3
童装 kid's clothes	18	3.9
内衣 underwear	14	3.1
布匹 cloth	2	0.4
玩具/婴儿用品 toy/infant's product	14	3.1
箱包皮具 bag & suitcase	8	1.7
体育用品 sports facilities	9	2.0
日用品 daily necessities	194	42.3
厨房用品 kitchen utensil	19	4.1
家用器皿 household appliance	14	3.1
家具/室内装饰 furniture	7	1.5
家用电器 household electronic products	37	8.1
图书 books	14	3.1
文具 stationary	25	5.4
音像制品 video & audio	14	3.1
食品 food	126	27.5
饮料 beverage	39	8.5
酒 alcohol drink	11	2.4
烟 cigarette	5	1.1
调味品 flavoring	32	7.0
菜蔬类 vegetable	4	0.9
水果 fruit	5	1.1
配菜 blend dish	3	0.7
其他 others	18	3.9

n=459

1-6 样本、男性各年龄层、女性各年龄层常与谁一起去百货公司/购物中心/ With Whom When Visiting Department Stores/Shopping Centers by the Whole Sample, Age and Gender Groups

	人数 Number	和家人或亲戚 family members & relatives	和朋友 friends	和同事/同学 colleagues or schoolmates	单独 single
样本 Sample	462	57.1	17.1	9.5	16.2
男性 Male	221	60.2	14.5	8.6	16.7
16~24 岁 Age	53	34.0	26.4	28.3	11.3
25~34 岁 Age	67	56.7	20.9	4.5	17.9
35~44 岁 Age	50	78.0	2.0	2.0	18.0
45~54 岁 Age	33	66.7	9.1	0.0	24.2
55~60 岁 Age	18	88.9	0.0	0.0	11.1
女性 Female	241	54.4	19.5	10.4	15.8
16~24 岁 Age	61	36.1	36.1	16.4	11.5
25~34 岁 Age	72	58.3	20.8	11.1	9.7
35~44 岁 Age	55	63.6	10.9	7.3	18.2
45~54 岁 Age	40	65.0	10.0	2.5	22.5
55~60 岁 Age	13	46.2	0.0	15.4	38.5

1-7 选择百货公司/购物中心的考虑因素/ Ranking of the Considerations of Choosing a Department Store/Shopping Center

注：本题为多选题，合计百分比超过 100%（Multiple answers）

排名 Ranking	考虑因素 Considerations	人次 Person-time	百分比 Percent
1	质量可靠 reliable quality	293	63.3
2	交通便利 convenient transportation	170	36.7
3	价格适中 reasonable price	153	33.0
4	商品种类齐全 wide range of choices	137	29.6
5	服务态度好 good service	103	22.2
6	就近 close to reach	39	8.4
7	空间宽敞 wide space	34	7.3
8	室内外装潢设计现代化 modern decoration	33	7.1
9	退换商品方便 easy replacement	29	6.3
10	经常有促销活动 promotion	18	3.9
10	大型商品保修 reparation guarantee for expensive items	18	3.9
11	可送货上门 goods deliver in	13	2.8
12	提供餐饮休息配套服务 providing dining & rest service	12	2.6
13	有大量进口商品 lots of imported goods	5	1.1
13	其他 others	5	1.1

n=463

1-8 重度消费者的人口分布/ Demographics of the Heavy Consumers

	人数 Number	16-24 岁 Age	25-34 岁 Age	35-44 岁 Age	45-54 岁 Age	55-60 岁 Age
样本 Sample	276	25.7	30.1	25.0	14.1	5.1
男性 Male	115	22.6	23.5	27.8	17.4	8.7
一周 1 次或以上 once a week or over	52	19.2	21.2	28.8	17.3	13.5
两周 1 次左右 about once every two weeks	63	25.4	25.4	27.0	17.5	4.8
女性 Female	161	28.0	34.8	23.0	11.8	2.5
一周 1 次或以上 once a week or over	84	29.8	33.3	23.8	10.7	2.4
两周 1 次左右 about once every two weeks	77	26.0	36.4	22.1	13.0	2.6

1-9 不同消费者层常去的百货公司/购物中心// Department Stores/Shopping Centers Visited Most Frequently by Market Segments

1-9-1 时尚流行指标/ Fads Popular Index

注：本题为多选题，合计百分比超过 100%（Multiple answers）

	人数 Number	第一品牌及百分比 1st/ percent	第二品牌及百分比 2nd/ percent	第三品牌及百分比 3rd/ percent
样本 Sample	458	**重百 Chongqing Department store (60.5)**	**立丹百货 Lidan(13.3)**	**沙坪坝百货公司 Shapingba Department Store (10.7)**
平实生活指向 simple living orientation	241	重百 Chongqing Department Store (62.2)	沙坪坝百货公司 Shapingba Department Store(13.7)	立丹百货 Lidan(11.6)
时尚流行指向 fashion orientation	217	重百 Chongqing Department Store (58.5)	立丹百货 Lidan(15.2)	富安百货 Mega Department Store(12.9)

1-9-2 价格态度指标/ Price Attitude Index

注：本题为多选题，合计百分比超过 100%（Multiple answers）

	人数 Number	第一品牌及百分比 1st/ percent	第二品牌及百分比 2nd/ percent	第三品牌及百分比 3rd/ percent
样本 Sample	460	**重百 Chongqing Department Store (61.1)**	**立丹百货 Lidan(13.0)**	**沙坪坝百货公司 Shapingba Department Store(10.4)**
价格无关心指向 indifferent orientation	82	重百 Chongqing Department Store(54.9)	百盛 Parkson Shopping Center(14.6)	沙坪坝百货公司 Shapingba Department Store(12.2)
中间层 medium	215	重百 Chongqing Department Store(62.8)	立丹百货 Lidan(14.0)	富安百货 Mega Department Store(10.2)
价格重视指向 careful orientation	163	重百 Chongqing Department Store(62.0)	立丹百货 Lidan(13.5)	沙坪坝百货公司 Shapingba Department Store(10.4)

1-10 重度消费者的消费者层构成/ The Composition of the Heavy Consumers

1-10-1 时尚流行指标/ Fads popular Index

	人数 Number	平实生活指向 simple living orientation	时尚流行指向 fashion orientation
样本 Sample	274	46.7	53.3
一周 1 次或以上 once a week or over	134	46.3	53.7
两周 1 次左右 about once every two weeks	140	47.1	52.9

1-10-2 价格态度指标/ Price Attitude Index

	人数 Number	价格无关心指向 indifferent orientation	中间层 medium	价格重视指向 careful orientation
样本 Sample	272	18.8	49.6	31.6
一周 1 次或以上 once a week or over	133	20.3	51.1	28.6
两周 1 次左右 about once every two weeks	139	17.3	48.2	34.5

● 武汉 / Wuhan

1-1 最近三个月是否去过百货公司/购物中心的比例/ Proportion of the Sample Visiting Department Stores/Shopping Centers in the Last Three Months

	人数 Number	百分比 Percent
去过 yes	509	79.3
没去过 no	133	20.7

n=642

1-2 最常去的百货公司/购物中心排名/ Ranking of the Department Stores/Shopping Centers Visited Most Frequently

注：本题为多选题，合计百分比超过 100%（Multiple answers）

排名 Brand Ranking	品牌 Brands	人次 Person-time	百分比 Percent
1	武汉广场 Wuhan Square	222	43.7
2	佳丽广场 Jiali Square	150	29.5
3	王府井百货大楼 Wangfujing Department Store	103	20.3
4	中南商业大楼 Zhongnan Department Store	97	19.1
5	亚贸广场 Yamao Square	89	17.5
6	青山商城 Qingshan Department Store	65	12.8
7	武汉商场 Wuhan Department Store	64	12.6
8	汉阳商场 Hanyang Department Store	61	12.0
9	中心百货 Centeral Department Store	41	8.1
10	中商广场 Zhongshang Square	32	6.3

n=508

1-3 样本、男性各年龄层、女性各年龄层最近三个月是否去过百货公司/购物中心的比例/ Whether having Visited Department Stores/Shopping Centers in the Last Three Months by the Whole Sample, Age and Gender Groups

	人数 Number	去过 yes	没去过 no
样本 Sample	642	79.3	20.7
男性 Male	311	74.6	25.4
16~24 岁 Age	65	83.1	16.9
25~34 岁 Age	89	82.0	18.0
35~44 岁 Age	80	58.8	41.3
45~54 岁 Age	52	80.8	19.2
55~60 岁 Age	25	64.0	36.0
女性 Female	331	83.7	16.3
16~24 岁 Age	69	88.4	11.6
25~34 岁 Age	96	91.7	8.3
35~44 岁 Age	78	79.5	20.5
45~54 岁 Age	62	85.5	14.5
55~60 岁 Age	26	50.0	50.0

1-4 样本、男性各年龄层、女性各年龄层最近三个月去百货公司/购物中心的频率/ Frequencies of Visiting Department Stores/Shopping Centers in the Last Three Months by the Whole Sample, Age and Gender Groups

	人数 Number	一周 1 次或以上 once a week or over	两周 1 次左右 about once two weeks	约一个月 1 次 about once a month	两三个月 1 次及以下 once 2 or 3 months or below
样本 Sample	507	24.3	27.6	35.1	13.0
男性 Male	232	23.3	24.1	37.9	14.7
16~24 岁 Age	54	27.8	29.6	35.2	7.4
25~34 岁 Age	73	27.4	21.9	38.4	12.3
35~44 岁 Age	47	12.8	23.4	46.8	17.0
45~54 岁 Age	42	21.4	23.8	33.3	21.4
55~60 岁 Age	16	25.0	18.8	31.3	25.0
女性 Female	275	25.1	30.5	32.7	11.6
16~24 岁 Age	61	37.7	36.1	21.3	4.9
25~34 岁 Age	88	26.1	35.2	33.0	5.7
35~44 岁 Age	61	21.3	24.6	42.6	11.5
45~54 岁 Age	53	17.0	22.6	37.7	22.6
55~60 岁 Age	12	8.3	33.3	16.7	41.7

1-5 去百货公司/购物中心购物的种类/ Categories of Visiting Department Stores/Shopping Centers in the Last Three Months

注：本题为多选题，合计百分比超过 100%（Multiple answers）

	人次 Person-time	百分比 Percent
化妆/保养品 cosmetic	92	18.3
首饰 jewelry	15	3.0
鞋/帽/袜类 shoes/caps/socks	98	19.4
成人服装 adult clothes	281	55.8
童装 kid's clothes	40	7.9
内衣 underwear	26	5.2
布匹 cloth	1	0.2
玩具/婴儿用品 toy/infant's product	12	2.4
箱包皮具 bag & suitcase	10	2.0
体育用品 sports facilities	9	1.8
日用品 daily necessities	170	33.7
厨房用品 kitchen utensil	31	6.2
家用器皿 household appliance	7	1.4
家具/室内装饰 furniture	3	0.6
家用电器 household electronic products	29	5.8
图书 books	29	5.8
文具 stationary	26	5.2
音像制品 video & audio	16	3.2
食品 food	122	24.2
饮料 beverage	22	4.4
酒 alcohol drink	6	1.2
烟 cigarette	10	2.0
调味品 flavoring	31	6.2
菜蔬类 vegetable	12	2.4
水果 fruit	5	1.0
配菜 blend dish	4	0.8
其他 others	15	3.0

n=504

1-6 样本、男性各年龄层、女性各年龄层常与谁一起去百货公司/购物中心/ With Whom When Visiting Department Stores/Shopping Centers by the Whole Sample, Age and Gender Groups

	人数 Number	和家人或亲戚 family members & relatives	和朋友 friends	和同事/同学 colleagues or schoolmates	单独 single
样本 Sample	505	54.3	17.8	10.7	17.2
男性 Male	230	53.9	17.4	8.7	20.0
16~24 岁 Age	54	25.9	33.3	27.8	13.0
25~34 岁 Age	72	43.1	29.2	5.6	22.2
35~44 岁 Age	47	83.0	2.1	2.1	12.8
45~54 岁 Age	42	69.0	0.0	0.0	31.0
55~60 岁 Age	15	73.3	0.0	0.0	26.7
女性 Female	275	54.5	18.2	12.4	14.9
16~24 岁 Age	60	26.7	38.3	28.3	6.7
25~34 岁 Age	88	62.5	18.2	11.4	8.0
35~44 岁 Age	62	62.9	6.5	6.5	24.2
45~54 岁 Age	52	59.6	13.5	3.8	23.1
55~60 岁 Age	13	69.2	0.0	7.7	23.1

1-7 选择百货公司/购物中心的考虑因素/ Ranking of the Considerations of Choosing a Department Store/Shopping Center

注：本题为多选题，合计百分比超过 100%（Multiple answers）

排名 Ranking	考虑因素 Considerations	人次 Person-time	百分比 Percent
1	交通便利 convenient transportation	346	68.2
2	质量可靠 reliable quality	219	43.2
3	价格适中 reasonable price	192	37.9
4	商品种类齐全 wide range of choices	143	28.2
5	就近 close to reach	102	20.1
6	服务态度好 good service	53	10.5
7	室内外装潢设计现代化 modern decoration	42	8.3
8	经常有促销活动 promotion	37	7.3
9	空间宽敞 wide space	28	5.5
10	退换商品方便 easy replacement	26	5.1
11	提供餐饮休息配套服务 providing dining & rest service	16	3.2
12	有大量进口商品 lots of imported goods	7	1.4
13	大型商品保修 reparation guarantee for expensive items	5	1.0
14	可送货上门 goods deliver in	3	0.6
14	其他 others	3	0.6

n=507

1-8 重度消费者的人口分布/ Demographics of the Heavy Consumers

	人数 Number	16-24 岁 Age	25-34 岁 Age	35-44 岁 Age	45-54 岁 Age	55-60 岁 Age
样本 Sample	263	28.9	34.2	17.1	15.2	4.6
男性 Male	110	28.2	32.7	15.5	17.3	6.4
一周 1 次或以上 once a week or over	54	27.8	37.0	11.1	16.7	7.4
两周 1 次左右 about once two weeks	56	28.6	28.6	19.6	17.9	5.4
女性 Female	153	29.4	35.3	18.3	13.7	3.3
一周 1 次或以上 once a week or over	69	33.3	33.3	18.8	13.0	1.4
两周 1 次左右 about once two weeks	84	26.2	36.9	17.9	14.3	4.8

1-9 不同消费者层常去的百货公司/购物中心// Department Stores/Shopping Centers Visited Most Frequently by Market Segments

1-9-1 时尚流行指标/ Fads Popular Index

注：本题为多选题，合计百分比超过 100%（Multiple answers）

	人数 Number	第一品牌及百分比 1st/ percent	第二品牌及百分比 2nd/ percent	第三品牌及百分比 3rd/ percent	第四品牌及百分比 4th/ percent
样本 Sample	499	**武汉广场 Wuhan Square(43.5)**	**佳丽广场 Jiali Square(29.9)**	**王府井百货大楼 Wangfujing Department Store(19.8)**	**中南商业大楼 Zhongnan Department Store(19.2)**
平实生活指向 simple living orientation	248	武汉广场 Wuhan Square(39.9)	佳丽广场 Jiali Square(23.0)	中南商业大楼 Zhongnan Department Store(19.8)	亚贸广场 Yamao Square(19.0)
时尚流行指向 fashion orientation	251	武汉广场 Wuhan Square(47.0)	佳丽广场 Jiali Square(36.7)	王府井百货大楼 Wangfujing Department Store(23.9)	中南商业大楼 Zhongnan Department Store(18.7)

1-9-2 价格态度指标/ Price Attitude Index

注：本题为多选题，合计百分比超过 100%（Multiple answers）

	人数 Number	第一品牌及百分比 1st/ percent	第二品牌及百分比 2nd/ percent	第三品牌及百分比 3rd/ percent	第四品牌及百分比 4th/ percent
样本 Sample	501	**武汉广场 Wuhan Square(43.1)**	**佳丽广场 Jiali Square(29.7)**	**王府井百货大楼 Wangfujing Department Store(20.0)**	**中南商业大楼 Zhongnan Department Store(19.2)**
价格无关心指向 indifferent orientation	67	武汉广场 Wuhan Square(46.3)	佳丽广场 Jiali Square(26.9)	王府井百货大楼 Wangfujing Department Store(20.9)	亚贸广场 Yamao Square(19.4)
中间层 medium	251	武汉广场 Wuhan Square(47.4)	佳丽广场 Jiali Square(33.9)	王府井百货大楼 Wangfujing Department Store(23.5)	中南商业大楼 Zhongnan Department Store(22.7)
价格重视指向 careful orientation	183	武汉广场 Wuhan Square(36.1)	佳丽广场 Jiali Square(25.1)	亚贸广场 Yamao Square(15.8)	青山商城 Qingshan Department Store(15.3)

1-10 重度消费者的消费者层构成/ The Composition of the Heavy Consumers

1-10-1 时尚流行指标/ Fads popular Index

	人数 Number	平实生活指向 simple living orientation	时尚流行指向 fashion orientation
样本 Sample	256	39.1	60.9
一周 1 次或以上 once a week or over	121	30.6	69.4
两周 1 次左右 about once every two weeks	135	46.7	53.3

1-10-2 价格态度指标/ Price Attitude Index

	人数 Number	价格无关心指向 indifferent orientation	中间层 medium	价格重视指向 careful orientation
样本 Sample	257	13.2	52.9	33.9
一周 1 次或以上 once a week or over	121	15.7	52.9	31.4
两周 1 次左右 about once every two weeks	136	11.0	52.9	36.0

● 西安 / Xi'an

1-1 最近三个月是否去过百货公司/购物中心的比例/ Proportion of the Sample Visiting Department Stores/Shopping Centers in the Last Three Months

	人数 Number	百分比 Percent
去过 yes	474	78.9
没去过 no	127	21.1

n=601

1-2 最常去的百货公司/购物中心排名/ Ranking of the Department Stores/Shopping Centers Visited Most Frequently

注：本题为多选题，合计百分比超过 100%（Multiple answers）

排名 Brand Ranking	品牌 Brands	人次 Person-time	百分比 Percent
1	开元商厦 Xi'an Kaiyuan Shopping Center	268	56.5
2	民生商厦 Minsheng Shopping Center	263	55.5
3	百盛 Parkson Shopping Center	108	22.8
4	世纪金花商厦 Century Ginwa Shopping Center	79	16.7
5	唐城商厦 Tangcheng Department Store	78	16.5
6	军区商场 Armyman Service Society Shanxi Province. Military Sub	51	10.8
7	秋林商厦 Qiuling Shopping Center	31	6.5
8	北大街商场 Beidajie Shop	25	5.3
9	西安商业大厦 Xi'an Shopping Center	19	4.0
10	太白商厦 Taibai Shopping Center	17	3.6

n=474

1-3 样本、男性各年龄层、女性各年龄层最近三个月是否去过百货公司/购物中心的比例/ Whether having Visited Department Stores/Shopping Centers in the Last Three Months by the Whole Sample, Age and Gender Group

	人数 Number	去过 yes	没去过 no
样本 Sample	601	78.9	21.1
男性 Male	302	73.5	26.5
16~24 岁 Age	64	71.9	28.1
25~34 岁 Age	91	83.5	16.5
35~44 岁 Age	77	72.7	27.3
45~54 岁 Age	46	60.9	39.1
55~60 岁 Age	24	66.7	33.3
女性 Female	299	84.3	15.7
16~24 岁 Age	61	85.2	14.8
25~34 岁 Age	90	85.6	14.4
35~44 岁 Age	74	79.7	20.3
45~54 岁 Age	49	85.7	14.3
55~60 岁 Age	25	88.0	12.0

1-4 样本、男性各年龄层、女性各年龄层最近三个月去百货公司/购物中心的频率/ Frequencies of Visiting Department Stores/Shopping Centers in the Last Three Months by the Whole Sample, Age and Gender Groups

	人数 Number	一周 1 次或以上 once a week or over	两周 1 次左右 about once every two weeks	约一个月 1 次 about once a month	两三个月 1 次及以下 once every 2 or 3 months or below
样本 Sample	473	21.8	30.2	38.3	9.7
男性 Male	222	20.7	31.1	37.8	10.4
16~24 岁 Age	46	21.7	19.6	47.8	10.9
25~34 岁 Age	76	18.4	36.8	34.2	10.5
35~44 岁 Age	56	26.8	25.0	37.5	10.7
45~54 岁 Age	28	14.3	42.9	32.1	10.7
55~60 岁 Age	16	18.8	37.5	37.5	6.3
女性 Female	251	22.7	29.5	38.6	9.2
16~24 岁 Age	52	21.2	40.4	32.7	5.8
25~34 岁 Age	77	33.8	26.0	35.1	5.2
35~44 岁 Age	59	8.5	23.7	50.8	16.9
45~54 岁 Age	42	23.8	42.9	28.6	4.8
55~60 岁 Age	21	23.8	4.8	52.4	19.0

1-5 去百货公司/购物中心购物的种类/ Categories of Visiting Department Stores/Shopping Centers in the Last Three Months

注：本题为多选题，合计百分比超过 100%（Multiple answers）

	人次 Person-time	百分比 Percent
化妆/保养品 cosmetic	87	18.4
首饰 jewelry	18	3.8
鞋/帽/袜类 shoes/caps/socks	71	15.0
成人服装 adult clothes	158	33.3
童装 kid's clothes	26	5.5
内衣 underwear	33	7.0
布匹 cloth	3	0.6
玩具/婴儿用品 toy/infant's product	13	2.7
箱包皮具 bag & suitcase	3	0.6
体育用品 sports facilities	10	2.1
日用品 daily necessities	190	40.1
厨房用品 kitchen utensil	18	3.8
家用器皿 household appliance	19	4.0
家具/室内装饰 furniture	3	0.6
家用电器 household electronic products	28	5.9
图书 books	26	5.5
文具 stationary	20	4.2
音像制品 video & audio	12	2.5
食品 food	136	28.7
饮料 beverage	40	8.4
酒 alcohol drink	14	3.0
烟 cigarette	17	3.6
调味品 flavoring	27	5.7
菜蔬类 vegetable	5	1.1
水果 fruit	7	1.5
配菜 blend dish	5	1.1
其他 others	10	2.1

n=474

1-6 样本、男性各年龄层、女性各年龄层常与谁一起去百货公司/购物中心/ With Whom When Visiting Department Stores/Shopping Centers by the Whole Sample, Age and Gender Groups

	人数 Number	和家人或亲戚 family members & relatives	和朋友 friends	和同事/同学 colleagues or schoolmates	单独 single
样本 Sample	473	61.1	18.2	9.9	10.8
男性 Male	222	62.2	14.4	10.4	13.1
16~24 岁 Age	46	26.1	28.3	37.0	8.7
25~34 岁 Age	76	63.2	17.1	6.6	13.2
35~44 岁 Age	56	78.6	5.4	1.8	14.3
45~54 岁 Age	28	71.4	10.7	0.0	17.9
55~60 岁 Age	16	87.5	0.0	0.0	12.5
女性 Female	251	60.2	21.5	9.6	8.8
16~24 岁 Age	51	39.2	41.2	19.6	0.0
25~34 岁 Age	77	51.9	27.3	9.1	11.7
35~44 岁 Age	59	67.8	13.6	8.5	10.2
45~54 岁 Age	42	73.8	9.5	2.4	14.3
55~60 岁 Age	22	90.9	0.0	4.5	4.5

1-7 选择百货公司/购物中心的考虑因素/ Ranking of the Considerations of Choosing a Department Store/Shopping Center

注：本题为多选题，合计百分比超过 100%（Multiple answers）

排名 Ranking	考虑因素 Considerations	人次 Person-time	百分比 Percent
1	质量可靠 reliable quality	303	63.9
2	交通便利 convenient transportation	229	48.3
3	商品种类齐全 wide range of choices	164	34.6
4	价格适中 reasonable price	140	29.5
5	服务态度好 good service	56	11.8
6	就近 close to reach	49	10.3
7	空间宽敞 wide space	36	7.6
8	经常有促销活动 promotion	31	6.5
9	退换商品方便 easy replacement	23	4.9
10	室内外装潢设计现代化 modern decoration	15	3.2
11	大型商品保修 reparation guarantee for expensive items	10	2.1
12	可送货上门 goods deliver in	6	1.3
13	其他 others	4	0.8
13	提供餐饮休息配套服务 providing dining & rest service	4	0.8
13	有大量进口商品 lots of imported goods	4	0.8

n=474

1-8 重度消费者的人口分布/ Demographics of the Heavy Consumers

	人数 Number	16-24 岁 Age	25-34 岁 Age	35-44 岁 Age	45-54 岁 Age	55-60 岁 Age
样本 Sample	246	20.7	35.8	19.5	17.9	6.1
男性 Male	115	16.5	36.5	25.2	13.9	7.8
一周 1 次或以上 once a week or over	46	21.7	30.4	32.6	8.7	6.5
两周 1 次左右 about once every two weeks	69	13.0	40.6	20.3	17.4	8.7
女性 Female	131	24.4	35.1	14.5	21.4	4.6
一周 1 次或以上 once a week or over	57	19.3	45.6	8.8	17.5	8.8
两周 1 次左右 about once every two weeks	74	28.4	27.0	18.9	24.3	1.4

1-9 不同消费者层常去的百货公司/购物中心// Department Stores/Shopping Centers Visited Most Frequently by Market Segments

1-9-1 时尚流行指标/ Fads Popular Index

注：本题为多选题，合计百分比超过 100%（Multiple answers）

	人数 Number	第一品牌及百分比 1st/ percent	第二品牌及百分比 2nd/ percent	第三品牌及百分比 3rd/ percent
样本 Sample	**472**	**开元商厦 Xi'an Kaiyuan Shopping Center (56.8)**	**民生商厦 Minsheng Shopping Center (55.7)**	**百盛 Parkson Shopping Center (22.9)**
平实生活指向 simple living orientation	253	开元商厦 Xi'an Kaiyuan Shopping Center(55.7)	民生商厦 Minsheng Shopping Center (53.0)	百盛 Parkson Shopping Center(19.4)
时尚流行指向 fashion orientation	219	民生商厦 Minsheng Shopping Center(58.9)	开元商厦 Xi'an Kaiyuan Shopping Center (58.0)	百盛 Parkson Shopping Center(26.9)

1-9-2 价格态度指标/ Price Attitude Index

注：本题为多选题，合计百分比超过 100%（Multiple answers）

	人数 Number	第一品牌及百分比 1st/ percent	第二品牌及百分比 2nd/ percent	第三品牌及百分比 3rd/ percent
样本 Sample	**471**	**开元商厦 Xi'an Kaiyuan Shopping Center (56.5)**	**民生商厦 Minsheng Shopping Center (55.4)**	**百盛 Parkson Shopping Center(22.7)**
价格无关心指向 indifferent orientation	115	民生商厦 Minsheng Shopping Center(62.6)	开元商厦 Xi'an Kaiyuan Shopping Center (59.1)	百盛 Parkson Shopping Center(27.0)
中间层 medium	250	开元商厦 Xi'an Kaiyuan Shopping Center (56.8)	民生商厦 Minsheng Shopping Center(54.0)	百盛 Parkson Shopping Center(19.2)
价格重视指向 careful orientation	106	开元商厦 Xi'an Kaiyuan Shopping Center (52.8)	民生商厦 Minsheng Shopping Center(50.9)	百盛 Parkson Shopping Center(26.4)

1-10 重度消费者的消费者层构成/ The Composition of the Heavy Consumers

1-10-1 时尚流行指标/ Fads popular Index

	人数 Number	平实生活指向 simple living orientation	时尚流行指向 fashion orientation
样本 Sample	**245**	**49.8**	**50.2**
一周 1 次或以上 once a week or over	103	53.4	46.6
两周 1 次左右 about once every two weeks	142	47.2	52.8

1-10-2 价格态度指标/ Price Attitude Index

	人数 Number	价格无关心指向 indifferent orientation	中间层 medium	价格重视指向 careful orientation
样本 Sample	**246**	**23.2**	**54.1**	**22.8**
一周 1 次或以上 once a week or over	103	17.5	56.3	26.2
两周 1 次左右 about once every two weeks	143	27.3	52.4	20.3

● 沈阳 / Shenyang

1-1 最近三个月是否去过百货公司/购物中心的比例/ Proportion of the Sample Visiting Department Stores/Shopping Centers in the Last Three Months

	人数 Number	百分比 Percent
去过 yes	448	74.5
没去过 no	153	25.5

n=601

1-2 最常去的百货公司/购物中心排名/ Ranking of the Department Stores/Shopping Centers Visited Most Frequently

注：本题为多选题，合计百分比超过 100%（Multiple answers）

排名 Brand Ranking	品牌 Brands	人次 Person-time	百分比 Percent
1	中兴—沈阳商业大厦 Zhongxing Shenyang Commercial Building	243	54.2
2	沈阳商业城 Shenyang Shopping Center	174	38.8
3	东亚商业广场 Dongya	137	30.6
4	联营公司 Lianying	111	24.8
5	铁西百货大楼 Tiexi Department Store	76	17.0
6	鹏利 Top Glory Square	68	15.2
7	铁西商业大厦 Tiexi	41	9.2
8	和平商场 Heping	30	6.7
9	沈阳百货大楼 Shenyang Department Store	22	4.9
10	皇姑五一商场 Huang Gu Wu Yi Shopping Center	18	4.0
11	朝鲜族百货大楼 Chao Xian Zu Department Store	11	2.5

n=448

1-3 样本、男性各年龄层、女性各年龄层最近三个月是否去过百货公司/购物中心的比例/ Whether Having Visited Department Stores/Shopping Centers in the Last Three Months by the Whole Sample, Age and Gender Groups

	人数 Number	去过 yes	没去过 no
样本 Sample	601	74.5	25.5
男性 Male	299	71.2	28.8
16~24 岁 Age	64	79.7	20.3
25~34 岁 Age	89	83.1	16.9
35~44 岁 Age	76	59.2	40.8
45~54 岁 Age	46	65.2	34.8
55~60 岁 Age	24	54.2	45.8
女性 Female	302	77.8	22.2
16~24 岁 Age	64	84.4	15.6
25~34 岁 Age	90	85.6	14.4
35~44 岁 Age	76	76.3	23.7
45~54 岁 Age	48	70.8	29.2
55~60 岁 Age	24	50.0	50.0

1-4 样本、男性各年龄层、女性各年龄层最近三个月去百货公司/购物中心的频率/ Frequencies of Visiting Department Stores/Shopping Centers in the Last Three Months by the Whole Sample, Age and Gender Groups

	人数 Number	一周 1 次或以上 once a week or over	两周 1 次左右 about once every two weeks	约一个月 1 次 about once a month	两三个月 1 次及以下 once every 2 or 3 months or below
样本 Sample	447	17.0	29.1	36.9	17.0
男性 Male	213	13.6	26.3	41.3	18.8
16~24 岁 Age	51	11.8	25.5	45.1	17.6
25~34 岁 Age	74	14.9	35.1	35.1	14.9
35~44 岁 Age	45	13.3	31.1	37.8	17.8
45~54 岁 Age	30	6.7	6.7	53.3	33.3
55~60 岁 Age	13	30.8	7.7	46.2	15.4
女性 Female	234	20.1	31.6	32.9	15.4
16~24 岁 Age	54	27.8	29.6	27.8	14.8
25~34 岁 Age	77	24.7	35.1	31.2	9.1
35~44 岁 Age	57	14.0	33.3	42.1	10.5
45~54 岁 Age	34	8.8	23.5	35.3	32.4
55~60 岁 Age	12	16.7	33.3	16.7	33.3

1-5 去百货公司/购物中心购物的种类/ Categories of Visiting Department Stores/Shopping Centers in the Last Three Months

注：本题为多选题，合计百分比超过 100%（Multiple answers）

	人次 Person-time	百分比 Percent
化妆/保养品 cosmetic	76	17.1
首饰 jewelry	13	2.9
鞋/帽/袜类 shoes/caps/socks	115	25.8
成人服装 adult clothes	177	39.8
童装 kid's clothes	30	6.7
内衣 underwear	20	4.5
布匹 cloth	8	1.8
玩具/婴儿用品 toy/infant's product	16	3.6
箱包皮具 bag & suitcase	5	1.1
体育用品 sports facilities	9	2.0
日用品 daily necessities	137	30.8
厨房用品 kitchen utensil	19	4.3
家用器皿 household appliance	8	1.8
家具/室内装饰 furniture	2	0.4
家用电器 household electronic products	24	5.4
图书 books	22	4.9
文具 stationary	12	2.7
音像制品 video & audio	13	2.9
食品 food	118	26.5
饮料 beverage	43	9.7
酒 alcohol drink	9	2.0
烟 cigarette	15	3.4
调味品 flavoring	22	4.9
菜蔬类 vegetable	7	1.6
水果 fruit	11	2.5
配菜 blend dish	1	0.2
其他 others	12	2.7

n=445

1-6 样本、男性各年龄层、女性各年龄层常与谁一起去百货公司/购物中心/ With Whom When Visiting Department Stores/Shopping Centers by the Whole Sample, Age and Gender Groups

	人数 Number	和家人或亲戚 family members & relatives	和朋友 friends	和同事/同学 colleagues or schoolmates	单独 single
样本 Sample	448	49.6	21.0	10.7	18.8
男性 Male	213	52.1	18.8	12.7	16.4
16~24 岁 Age	51	21.6	43.1	21.6	13.7
25~34 岁 Age	74	52.7	17.6	14.9	14.9
35~44 岁 Age	45	66.7	4.4	4.4	24.4
45~54 岁 Age	30	73.3	6.7	6.7	13.3
55~60 岁 Age	13	69.2	7.7	7.7	15.4
女性 Female	235	47.2	23.0	8.9	20.9
16~24 岁 Age	54	31.5	46.3	18.5	3.7
25~34 岁 Age	77	50.6	19.5	11.7	18.2
35~44 岁 Age	58	53.4	17.2	3.4	25.9
45~54 岁 Age	34	50.0	8.8	0.0	41.2
55~60 岁 Age	12	58.3	8.3	0.0	33.3

1-7 选择百货公司/购物中心的考虑因素/ Considerations of Choosing a Department Store/Shopping Center

注：本题为多选题，合计百分比超过 100%（Multiple answers）

排名 Ranking	考虑因素 Considerations	人次 Person-time	百分比 Percent
1	质量可靠 reliable quality	267	59.7
2	交通便利 convenient transportation	230	51.5
3	价格适中 reasonable price	158	35.3
4	商品种类齐全 wide range of choices	125	28.0
5	服务态度好 good service	76	17.0
6	退换商品方便 easy replacement	52	11.6
7	就近 close to reach	49	11.0
8	空间宽敞 wide space	23	5.1
9	大型商品保修 reparation guarantee for expensive items	16	3.6
10	可送货上门 goods deliver in	12	2.7
11	室内外装潢设计现代化 modern decoration	10	2.2
12	提供餐饮休息配套服务 providing dining & rest service	7	1.6
12	经常有促销活动 promotion	7	1.6
13	其他 others	6	1.3
14	有大量进口商品 lots of imported goods	2	0.4

n=447

1-8 重度消费者的人口分布/ Demographics of the Heavy Consumers

	人数 Number	16-24 岁 Age	25-34 岁 Age	35-44 岁 Age	45-54 岁 Age	55-60 岁 Age
样本 Sample	206	24.3	40.3	22.8	7.3	5.3
男性 Male	85	22.4	43.5	23.5	4.7	5.9
一周 1 次或以上 once a week or over	29	20.7	37.9	20.7	6.9	13.8
两周 1 次左右 about once every two weeks	56	23.2	46.4	25.0	3.6	1.8
女性 Female	121	25.6	38.0	22.3	9.1	5.0
一周 1 次或以上 once a week or over	47	31.9	40.4	17.0	6.4	4.3
两周 1 次左右 about once every two weeks	74	21.6	36.5	25.7	10.8	5.4

1-9 不同消费者层常去的百货公司/购物中心// Department Stores/Shopping Centers Visited Most Frequently by Market Segments

1-9-1 时尚流行指标/ Fads Popular Index

注：本题为多选题，合计百分比超过 100%（Multiple answers）

	人数 Number	第一品牌及百分比 1st/ percent	第二品牌及百分比 2nd/ percent	第三品牌及百分比 3rd/ percent	第四品牌及百分比 4th/ percent
样本 Sample	448	**中兴-沈阳商业大厦 Zhongxing Shenyang Commercial Building (54.2)**	**沈阳商业城 Shenyang Shopping Center(38.8)**	**东亚商业广场 Dongya(30.6)**	**联营公司 Lianying(24.8)**
平实生活指向 simple living orientation	196	中兴-沈阳商业大厦 Zhongxing Shenyang Commercial Building (50.5)	沈阳商业城 Shenyang Shopping Center(36.2)	东亚商业广场 Dongya(30.1)	联营公司 Lianying(25.0)
时尚流行指向 fashion orientation	252	中兴-沈阳商业大厦 Zhongxing Shenyang Commercial Building (57.1)	沈阳商业城 Shenyang Shopping Center(40.9)	东亚商业广场 Dongya(31.0)	联营公司 Lianying(24.6)

1-9-2 价格态度指标/ Price Attitude Index

注：本题为多选题，合计百分比超过 100%（Multiple answers）

	人数 Number	第一品牌及百分比 1st/ percent	第二品牌及百分比 2nd/ percent	第三品牌及百分比 3rd/ percent	第四品牌及百分比 4th/ percent
样本 Sample	447	**中兴-沈阳商业大厦 Zhongxing Shenyang Commercial Building (54.4)**	**沈阳商业城 Shenyang Shopping Center (38.9)**	**东亚商业广场 Dongya(30.6)**	**联营公司 Lianying(24.8)**
价格无关心指向 indifferent orientation	79	中兴-沈阳商业大厦 Zhongxing Shenyang Commercial Building (48.1)	沈阳商业城 Shenyang Shopping Center (36.7) 东亚商业广场 Dongya(36.7)	联营公司 Lianying (17.7)	鹏利 Top Glory Square (8.9) 铁西百货大楼 Tiexi Department Store(8.9) 和平商场 Heping(8.9)
中间层 medium	217	中兴-沈阳商业大厦 Zhongxing Shenyang Commercial Building (56.2)	沈阳商业城 Shenyang Shopping Center(41.9)	东亚商业广场 Dongya(30.4)	联营公司 Lianying (25.3)
价格重视指向 careful orientation	151	中兴-沈阳商业大厦 Zhongxing Shenyang Commercial Building (55.0)	沈阳商业城 Shenyang Shopping Center (35.8)	联营公司 Lianying (27.8) 东亚商业广场 Dongya(27.8)	铁西百货大楼 Tiexi Department Store(19.2)

1-10 重度消费者的消费者层构成/ The Composition of the Heavy Consumers

1-10-1 时尚流行指标/ Fads popular Index

	人数 Number	平实生活指向 simple living orientation	时尚流行指向 fashion orientation
样本 Sample	206	**32.0**	**68.0**
一周 1 次或以上 once a week or over	76	35.5	64.5
两周 1 次左右 about once every two weeks	130	30.0	70.0

1-10-2 价格态度指标/ Price Attitude Index

	人数 Number	价格无关心指向 indifferent orientation	中间层 medium	价格重视指向 careful orientation
样本 Sample	206	**15.0**	**53.4**	**31.6**
一周 1 次或以上 once a week or over	76	14.5	47.4	38.2
两周 1 次左右 about once every two weeks	130	15.4	56.9	27.7

2.超市 / Supermarket

● 北京 / Beijing

2-1 最近三个月是否去过超市的比例/ Proportion of the Sample Visiting Supermarkets in the Last Three Months

	人数 Number	百分比 Percent
去过 yes	889	87.8
没去过 no	123	12.2

n=1012

2-2 最常去的超市排名/ Ranking of the Supermarkets Visited Most Frequently

注：本题为多选题，合计百分比超过 100%（Multiple answers）

排名 Brand Ranking	品牌 Brands	人次 Person-time	百分比 Percent
1	家乐福/创益佳 Carrefour	156	17.6
2	万客隆 Makro	152	17.1
3	华普超市 Jian	140	15.8
4	天客隆 Tiankelong	126	14.2
5	亿客隆 Yikelong	121	13.6
6	利客隆 Likelong	108	12.2
7	城市之光 Glory of the City	104	11.7
8	物美 Wu Mart	79	8.9
9	京客隆 Warehouse Shopping City	76	8.6
10	好邻居 Good Neighbour Supermarket	50	5.6
10	顺天府 Shuntianfu	50	5.6
11	西客隆 Xikelong	49	5.5
12	望京购物中心 Wangjing	43	4.8
13	明珠超市 Mingzhu	35	3.9
14	普尔斯马特 Price Smart	32	3.6
15	华堂商场 Ito Yokado	30	3.4

n=887

2-3 样本、男性各年龄层、女性各年龄层最近三个月是否去过超市的比例/ Whether Having Visited Supermarkets in the Last Three Months by the Whole Sample, Age and Gender Groups

	人数 Number	去过 yes	没去过 no
样本 Sample	1012	87.8	12.2
男性 Male	504	81.2	18.8
16~24 岁 Age	105	83.8	16.2
25~34 岁 Age	151	85.4	14.6
35~44 岁 Age	131	80.2	19.8
45~54 岁 Age	77	71.4	28.6
55~60 岁 Age	40	80.0	20.0
女性 Female	508	94.5	5.5
16~24 岁 Age	108	96.3	3.7
25~34 岁 Age	150	96.0	4.0
35~44 岁 Age	124	95.2	4.8
45~54 岁 Age	84	92.9	7.1
55~60 岁 Age	42	85.7	14.3

2-4 样本、男性各年龄层、女性各年龄层最近三个月去超市的频率/ Frequencies of Visiting Supermarkets in the Last Three Months by the Whole Sample, Age and Gender Groups

	人数 Number	一周 3 次或以上 three times a week or over	一周 1～2 次 once or twice a week	两周 1 次左右 about once every two weeks	约一个月 1 次 about once a month	两三个月 1 次及以下 once every 2 or 3 months or below
样本 Sample	886	11.7	40.4	28.2	16.4	3.3
男性 Male	407	8.8	39.1	28.3	18.9	4.9
16~24 岁 Age	88	12.5	34.1	29.5	21.6	2.3
25~34 岁 Age	129	5.4	44.2	30.2	16.3	3.9
35~44 岁 Age	104	12.5	31.7	27.9	20.2	7.7
45~54 岁 Age	54	7.4	48.1	22.2	14.8	7.4
55~60 岁 Age	32	3.1	40.6	28.1	25.0	3.1
女性 Female	479	14.2	41.5	28.2	14.2	1.9
16~24 岁 Age	104	16.3	30.8	43.3	7.7	1.9
25~34 岁 Age	143	16.8	48.3	24.5	8.4	2.1
35~44 岁 Age	118	11.9	41.5	24.6	20.3	1.7
45~54 岁 Age	78	7.7	43.6	23.1	24.4	1.3
55~60 岁 Age	36	19.4	41.7	22.2	13.9	2.8

2-5 去超市购物的种类/ Categories of Visiting Supermarkets in the Last Three Months

注：本题为多选题，合计百分比超过 100%（Multiple answers）

	人次 Person-time	百分比 Percent
化妆/保养品 cosmetic	53	6.1
首饰 jewelry	1	0.1
鞋/帽/袜类 shoes/caps/socks	34	3.9
成人服装 adult clothes	37	4.2
童装 kid's clothes	10	1.1
内衣 underwear	26	3.0
布匹 cloth	1	0.1
玩具/婴儿用品 toy/infant's product	17	1.9
箱包皮具 bag & suitcase	3	0.3
体育用品 sports facilities	10	1.1
日用品 daily necessities	475	54.2
厨房用品 kitchen utensil	49	5.6
家用器皿 household appliance	9	1.0
家具/室内装饰 furniture	2	0.2
家用电器 household electronic products	17	1.9
图书 books	16	1.8
文具 stationary	23	2.6
音像制品 video & audio	22	2.5
食品 food	640	73.1
饮料 beverage	244	27.9
酒 alcohol drink	47	5.4
烟 cigarette	16	1.8
调味品 flavoring	123	14.0
菜蔬类 vegetable	50	5.7
水果 fruit	31	3.5
配菜 blend dish	17	1.9
其他 others	6	0.7

n=876

2-6 样本、男性各年龄层、女性各年龄层常与谁一起去超市/ With Whom When Visiting Supermarkets by the Whole Sample, Age and Gender Groups

	人数 Number	和家人或亲戚 family members & relatives	和朋友 friends	和同事/同学 colleagues or schoolmates	单独 single
样本 Sample	885	58.3	8.9	5.6	27.1
男性 Male	408	63.0	10.8	3.4	22.8
16~24 岁 Age	87	41.4	27.6	12.6	18.4
25~34 岁 Age	129	61.2	10.9	0.8	27.1
35~44 岁 Age	105	71.4	5.7	1.0	21.9
45~54 岁 Age	55	78.2	0.0	1.8	20.0
55~60 岁 Age	32	75.0	0.0	0.0	25.0
女性 Female	477	54.3	7.3	7.5	30.8
16~24 岁 Age	103	54.4	13.6	20.4	11.7
25~34 岁 Age	143	54.5	7.7	4.9	32.9
35~44 岁 Age	118	56.8	3.4	6.8	33.1
45~54 岁 Age	78	52.6	6.4	0.0	41.0
55~60 岁 Age	35	48.6	2.9	0.0	48.6

2-7 选择超市的考虑因素/ Ranking of the Considerations of Choosing a Supermarket

注：本题为多选题，合计百分比超过 100%（Multiple answers）

排名 Ranking	考虑因素 Considerations	人次 Person-time	百分比 Percent
1	交通便利 convenient transportation	539	60.8
2	价格适中 reasonable price	519	58.5
3	就近 close to reach	272	30.7
4	商品种类齐全 wide range of choices	256	28.9
5	质量可靠 reliable quality	233	26.3
6	经常有促销活动 promotion	44	5.0
7	服务态度好 good service	40	4.5
8	空间宽敞 wide space	39	4.4
9	退换商品方便 easy replacement	19	2.1
10	有大量进口商品 lots of imported goods	5	0.6
11	其他 others	4	0.5
11	室内外装潢设计现代化 modern decoration	4	0.5
12	可送货上门 goods deliver in	2	0.2
13	大型商品保修 reparation guarantee for expensive items	1	0.1
13	提供餐饮休息配套服务 providing dining & rest service	1	0.1

n=887

2-8 重度消费者的人口分布/ Demographics of the Heavy Consumers

	人数 Number	16-24 岁 Age	25-34 岁 Age	35-44 岁 Age	45-54 岁 Age	55-60 岁 Age
样本 Sample	712	22.6	32.4	23.5	14.0	7.4
男性 Male	310	21.6	33.2	24.2	13.5	7.4
一周 3 次或以上 three times a week or over	36	30.6	19.4	36.1	11.1	2.8
一周 1～2 次 once or twice a week	159	18.9	35.8	20.8	16.4	8.2
两周 1 次左右 about once every two weeks	115	22.6	33.9	25.2	10.4	7.8
女性 Female	402	23.4	31.8	22.9	14.4	7.5
一周 3 次或以上 three times a week or over	68	25.0	35.3	20.6	8.8	10.3
一周 1～2 次 once or twice a week	199	16.1	34.7	24.6	17.1	7.5
两周 1 次左右 about once every two weeks	135	33.3	25.9	21.5	13.3	5.9

2-9 不同消费者层常去的超市/ Supermarkets Visited Most Frequently by Market Segments

2-9-1 时尚流行指标/ Fads Popular Index

注：本题为多选题，合计百分比超过 100%（Multiple answers）

	人数	第一品牌及百分比 1st/ percent	第二品牌及百分比 2nd/ percent	第三品牌及百分比 3rd / percent	第四品牌及百分比 4th/ percent
样本 Sample	**874**	**家乐福/创益佳 Carrefour(17.4)**	**万客隆 Makro(17.0)**	**华普超市 Jian(15.4)**	**天客隆 Tiankelong(14.1)**
平实生活指向 simple living orientation	408	万客隆 Makro(15.7)	亿客隆 Yikelong (15.2)	家乐福/创益佳 Carrefour(14.7)	天客隆 Tiankelong(13.7)
时尚流行指向 fashion orientation	466	家乐福/创益佳 Carrefour(19.7)	万客隆 Makro(18.2)	华普超市 Jian(17.4)	天客隆 Tiankelong(14.4)

2-9-2 价格态度指标/ Price Attitude Index

注：本题为多选题，合计百分比超过 100%（Multiple answers）

	人数	第一品牌及百分比 1st/ percent	第二品牌及百分比 2nd/ percent	第三品牌及百分比 3rd/ percent	第四品牌及百分比 4th/ percent
样本 Sample	**877**	**家乐福/创益佳 Carrefour(17.6)**	**万客隆 Makro(17.1)**	**华普超市 Jian(15.7)**	**天客隆 Tiankelong(14.3)**
价格无关心指向 indifferent orientation	182	家乐福/创益佳 Carrefour(19.8)	万客隆 Makro(14.8) 天客隆 Tiankelong(14.8)	亿客隆 Yikelong (13.7)	华普超市 Jian(13.2)
中间层 medium	431	华普超市 Jian(18.1)	家乐福/创益佳 Carrefour(17.4)	万客隆 Makro(17.2)	天客隆 Tiankelong(13.9)
价格重视指向 careful orientation	264	万客隆 Makro(18.6)	家乐福/创益佳 Carrefour(16.3) 亿客隆 Yikelong (16.3)	天客隆 Tiankelong(14.4)	城市之光 Glory of the City(14.0)

2-10 重度消费者的消费者层构成/ The Composition of the Heavy Consumers

2-10-1 时尚流行指标/ Fads popular Index

	人数 Number	平实生活指向 simple living orientation	时尚流行指向 fashion orientation
样本 Sample	**701**	**42.8**	**57.2**
一周 3 次或以上 3 times or over a week	104	41.3	58.7
一周 1～2 次 once or twice a week	349	41.5	58.5
两周 1 次左右 once every two weeks	248	45.2	54.8

2-10-2 价格态度指标/ Price Attitude Index

	人数 Number	价格无关心指向 indifferent orientation	中间层 medium	价格重视指向 careful orientation
样本 Sample	**704**	**21.0**	**49.9**	**29.1**
一周 3 次或以上 3 times or over a week	103	18.4	53.4	28.2
一周 1～2 次 once or twice a week	351	21.4	46.4	32.2
两周 1 次左右 once every two weeks	250	21.6	53.2	25.2

● 上海 / Shanghai

2-1 最近三个月是否去过超市的比例/ Proportion of the Sample Visiting Supermarkets in the Last Three Months

	人数 Number	百分比 Percent
去过 yes	970	95.7
没去过 no	44	4.3

n=1014

2-2 最常去的超市排名/ Ranking of the Supermarkets Visited Most Frequently

注：本题为多选题，合计百分比超过 100%（Multiple answers）

排名 Brand Ranking	品牌 Brands	人次 Person-time	百分比 Percent
1	华联 Hualian	486	50.1
2	联华 Lianhua	407	42.0
3	家乐福/创益佳 Carrefour	335	34.5
4	农工商 Nonggongshang	305	31.4
5	易初莲花 Lotus	165	17.0
6	顶顶鲜 Tops	91	9.4
7	百佳超市 Park'n	80	8.2
8	麦德龙 Matro	71	7.3
9	易买得 Yimaide	49	5.1
10	捷强 Jieqiang	45	4.6
11	乐购 Legou	19	2.0
11	欧尚 Ougou	19	2.0
12	家家乐 Jiajiale	18	1.9
13	农工商小豆苗 Nong Gong Shang Xiao Dou Miao	13	1.3
14	东方超值 Dong Fang Chao Zhi	12	1.2
15	星地 Xingdi	10	1.0

n=970

2-3 样本、男性各年龄层、女性各年龄层最近三个月是否去过超市的比例/ Whether Having Visited Supermarkets in the Last Three Months by the Whole Sample, Age and Gender Groups

	人数 Number	去过 yes	没去过 no
样本 Sample	1014	95.7	4.3
男性 Male	509	94.1	5.9
16~24 岁 Age	109	91.7	8.3
25~34 岁 Age	146	94.5	5.5
35~44 岁 Age	130	95.4	4.6
45~54 岁 Age	85	92.9	7.1
55~60 岁 Age	39	97.4	2.6
女性 Female	505	97.2	2.8
16~24 岁 Age	108	95.4	4.6
25~34 岁 Age	144	99.3	0.7
35~44 岁 Age	130	98.5	1.5
45~54 岁 Age	82	100.0	0.0
55~60 岁 Age	41	85.4	14.6

2-4 样本、男性各年龄层、女性各年龄层最近三个月去超市的频率/ Frequencies of Visiting Supermarkets in the Last Three Months by the Whole Sample, Age and Gender Groups

	人数 Number	一周 3 次或以上 3 times a week or over	一周 1~2 次 once or twice a week	两周 1 次左右 about once every two weeks	约一个月 1 次 about once a month	两三个月 1 次及以下 once every 2 or 3 months or below
样本 Sample	967	24.5	45.1	18.9	9.8	1.7
男性 Male	479	21.7	45.5	19.0	10.9	2.9
16~24 岁 Age	100	19.0	48.0	17.0	11.0	5.0
25~34 岁 Age	138	26.1	40.6	22.5	8.0	2.9
35~44 岁 Age	124	17.7	48.4	16.9	15.3	1.6
45~54 岁 Age	79	19.0	49.4	20.3	10.1	1.3
55~60 岁 Age	38	31.6	39.5	15.8	7.9	5.3
女性 Female	488	27.3	44.7	18.9	8.8	0.4
16~24 岁 Age	103	34.0	38.8	17.5	9.7	0.0
25~34 岁 Age	140	30.0	40.7	19.3	10.0	0.0
35~44 岁 Age	128	18.8	52.3	21.9	7.0	0.0
45~54 岁 Age	82	25.6	47.6	17.1	7.3	2.4
55~60 岁 Age	35	31.4	42.9	14.3	11.4	0.0

2-5 去超市购物的种类/ Categories of Visiting Supermarkets in the Last Three Months

注：本题为多选题，合计百分比超过 100%（Multiple answers）

	人次 Person-time	百分比 Percent
化妆/保养品 cosmetic	63	6.5
首饰 jewelry	7	0.7
鞋/帽/袜类 shoes/caps/socks	28	2.9
成人服装 adult clothes	25	2.6
童装 kid's clothes	4	0.4
内衣 underwear	24	2.5
布匹 cloth	0	0.0
玩具/婴儿用品 toy/infant's product	12	1.2
箱包皮具 bag & suitcase	2	0.2
体育用品 sports facilities	11	1.1
日用品 daily necessities	513	53.2
厨房用品 kitchen utensil	78	8.1
家用器皿 household appliance	12	1.2
家具/室内装饰 furniture	3	0.3
家用电器 household electronic products	10	1.0
图书 books	9	0.9
文具 stationary	21	2.2
音像制品 video & audio	28	2.9
食品 food	674	69.8
饮料 beverage	339	35.1
酒 alcohol drink	48	5.0
烟 cigarette	51	5.3
调味品 flavoring	201	20.8
菜蔬类 vegetable	112	11.6
水果 fruit	66	6.8
配菜 blend dish	45	4.7
其他 others	4	0.4

n=965

2-6 样本、男性各年龄层、女性各年龄层常与谁一起去超市/ With Whom When Visiting Supermarket by the Whole Sample, Age and Gender Groups

	人数 Number	和家人或亲戚 family members & relatives	和朋友 friends	和同事/同学 colleagues or schoolmates	单独 single
样本 Sample	963	61.1	8.2	5.4	25.3
男性 Male	477	59.3	9.4	5.0	26.2
16~24 岁 Age	99	43.4	18.2	16.2	22.2
25~34 岁 Age	138	47.1	15.9	3.6	33.3
35~44 岁 Age	124	71.0	3.2	0.8	25.0
45~54 岁 Age	79	77.2	1.3	2.5	19.0
55~60 岁 Age	37	70.3	0.0	0.0	29.7
女性 Female	486	62.8	7.0	5.8	24.5
16~24 岁 Age	102	52.0	17.6	11.8	18.6
25~34 岁 Age	142	64.8	8.5	5.6	21.1
35~44 岁 Age	127	66.9	2.4	4.7	26.0
45~54 岁 Age	80	68.8	1.3	2.5	27.5
55~60 岁 Age	35	57.1	0.0	0.0	42.9

2-7 选择超市的考虑因素/ Ranking of the Considerations of Choosing a Supermarket

注：本题为多选题，合计百分比超过 100%（Multiple answers）

排名 Ranking	考虑因素 Considerations	人次 Person-time	百分比 Percent
1	交通便利 convenient transportation	585	60.4
2	价格适中 reasonable price	547	56.4
3	商品种类齐全 wide range of choices	346	35.7
4	质量可靠 reliable quality	311	32.1
5	就近 close to reach	253	26.1
6	经常有促销活动 promotion	89	9.2
7	服务态度好 good service	62	6.4
8	空间宽敞 wide space	53	5.5
9	退换商品方便 easy replacement	16	1.7
10	室内外装潢设计现代化 modern decoration	7	0.7
11	可送货上门 goods deliver in	6	0.6
12	有大量进口商品 lots of imported goods	5	0.5
12	提供餐饮休息配套服务 providing dining & rest service	5	0.5
13	其他 others	4	0.4
14	大型商品保修 reparation guarantee for expensive items	2	0.2

n=969

2-8 重度消费者的人口分布/ Demographics of the Heavy Consumers

	人数 Number	16-24 岁 Age	25-34 岁 Age	35-44 岁 Age	45-54 岁 Age	55-60 岁 Age
样本 Sample	856	20.7	29.1	25.9	16.8	7.5
男性 Male	413	20.3	29.8	24.9	16.9	8.0
一周 3 次或以上 three times a week or over	104	18.3	34.6	21.2	14.4	11.5
一周 1～2 次 once or twice a week	218	22.0	25.7	27.5	17.9	6.9
两周 1 次左右 about once every two weeks	91	18.7	34.1	23.1	17.6	6.6
女性 Female	443	21.0	28.4	26.9	16.7	7.0
一周 3 次或以上 three times a week or over	133	26.3	31.6	18.0	15.8	8.3
一周 1～2 次 once or twice a week	218	18.3	26.1	30.7	17.9	6.9
两周 1 次左右 about once every two weeks	92	19.6	29.3	30.4	15.2	5.4

2-9 不同消费者层常去的超市/ Supermarkets Visited Most Frequently by Market Segments

2-9-1 时尚流行指标/ Fads Popular Index

注：本题为多选题，合计百分比超过 100%（Multiple answers）

	人数	第一品牌及百分比 1st/ percent	第二品牌及百分比 2nd/ percent	第三品牌及百分比 3rd/ percent	第四品牌及百分比 4th / percent
样本 Sample	961	**华联 Hualian（49.9）**	**联华 Lianhua（42.0）**	**家乐福/创益佳 Carrefour（34.5）**	**农工商 Nonggongshang（31.2）**
平实生活指向 simple living orientation	448	华联 Hualian（52.9）	联华 Lianhua（44.0）	农工商 Nonggongshang （31.7）	家乐福/创益佳 Carrefour（30.4）
时尚流行指向 fashion orientation	513	华联 Hualian（47.4）	联华 Lianhua（40.4）	家乐福/创益佳 Carrefour（38.2）	农工商 Nonggongshang （30.8）

2-9-2 价格态度指标/ Price Attitude Index

注：本题为多选题，合计百分比超过 100%（Multiple answers）

	人数	第一品牌及百分比 1st/ percent	第二品牌及百分比 2nd/ percent	第三品牌及百分比 3rd/ percent	第四品牌及百分比 4th / percent
样本 Sample	968	**华联 Hualian（50.1）**	**联华 Lianhua（42.0）**	**家乐福/创益佳 Carrefour（34.4）**	**农工商 Nonggongshang（31.4）**
价格无关心指向 indifferent orientation	139	华联 Hualian（53.2）	联华 Lianhua（41.0）	家乐福/创益佳 Carrefour（35.3）	农工商 Nonggongshang （27.3）
中间层 medium	504	华联 Hualian（48.8）	联华 Lianhua（39.7）	家乐福/创益佳 Carrefour（35.5）	农工商 Nonggongshang （31.0）
价格重视指向 careful orientation	325	华联 Hualian（50.8）	联华 Lianhua（46.2）	农工商 Nonggongshang （33.8）	家乐福/创益佳 Carrefour（32.3）

2-10 重度消费者的消费者层构成/ The Composition of the Heavy Consumers

2-10-1 时尚流行指标/ Fads popular Index

	人数 Number	平实生活指向 simple living orientation	时尚流行指向 fashion orientation
样本 Sample	**667**	**44.2**	**55.8**
一周 3 次或以上 3 times a week or over	236	41.1	58.9
一周 1~2 次 once or twice a week	431	45.9	54.1

2-10-2 价格态度指标/ Price Attitude Index

	人数 Number	价格无关心指向 indifferent orientation	中间层 medium	价格重视指向 careful orientation
样本 Sample	**672**	**15.3**	**52.5**	**32.1**
一周 3 次或以上 3 times a week or over	237	15.2	54.9	30.0
一周 1~2 次 once or twice a week	435	15.4	51.3	33.3

● 广州 / Guangzhou

2-1 最近三个月是否去过超市的比例/ Proportion of the Sample Visiting Supermarkets in the Last Three Months

	人数 Number	百分比 Percent
去过 yes	844	81.6
没去过 no	190	18.4

n=1034

2-2 最常去的超市排名/ Ranking of the Supermarkets Visited Most Frequently

注：本题为多选题，合计百分比超过 100%（Multiple answers）

排名 Brand Ranking	品牌 Brands	人次 Person-time	百分比 Percent
1	好又多 Trust-mart	401	47.6
2	岛内价 Daoneijia	265	31.4
3	百佳超市 Park'n	165	19.6
4	天河城吉之岛 Jusco	161	19.1
5	正大万客隆 Chia Tai Makro	110	13.0
6	胜佳 Shengjia	88	10.4
7	广客隆 Guangkelong	66	7.8
8	宏城 Home City	61	7.2

n=843

2-3 样本、男性各年龄层、女性各年龄层最近三个月是否去过超市的比例/ Whether Having Visited Supermarkets in the Last Three Months by the Whole Sample, Age and Gender Groups

	人数 Number	去过 yes	没去过 no
样本 Sample	**1034**	**81.6**	**18.4**
男性 Male	**499**	**75.6**	**24.4**
16~24 岁 Age	106	72.6	27.4
25~34 岁 Age	150	79.3	20.7
35~44 岁 Age	127	77.2	22.8
45~54 岁 Age	73	78.1	21.9
55~60 岁 Age	43	60.5	39.5
女性 Female	**535**	**87.3**	**12.7**
16~24 岁 Age	112	92.9	7.1
25~34 岁 Age	158	90.5	9.5
35~44 岁 Age	137	87.6	12.4
45~54 岁 Age	87	79.3	20.7
55~60 岁 Age	41	75.6	24.4

2-4 样本、男性各年龄层、女性各年龄层最近三个月去超市的频率/ Frequencies of Visiting Supermarkets in the Last Three Months by the Whole Sample, Age and Gender Groups

	人数 Number	一周 3 次或以上 3 times a week or over	一周 1～2 次 once or twice a week	两周 1 次左右 about once every two weeks	约一个月 1 次 about once a month	两三个月 1 次及以下 once every 2 or 3 months or below
样本 Sample	841	6.7	34.0	30.0	23.1	6.3
男性 Male	377	5.6	27.3	32.1	28.6	6.4
16~24 岁 Age	77	7.8	27.3	37.7	19.5	7.8
25~34 岁 Age	119	5.0	28.6	37.8	22.7	5.9
35~44 岁 Age	98	2.0	31.6	27.6	30.6	8.2
45~54 岁 Age	57	7.0	17.5	24.6	45.6	5.3
55~60 岁 Age	26	11.5	26.9	23.1	38.5	0.0
女性 Female	464	7.5	39.4	28.2	18.5	6.3
16~24 岁 Age	103	6.8	38.8	32.0	16.5	5.8
25~34 岁 Age	143	9.1	44.1	24.5	18.2	4.2
35~44 岁 Age	119	8.4	42.0	28.6	15.1	5.9
45~54 岁 Age	68	4.4	22.1	38.2	23.5	11.8
55~60 岁 Age	31	6.5	48.4	9.7	29.0	6.5

2-5 去超市购物的种类/ Categories of Visiting Supermarkets in the Last Three Months

注：本题为多选题，合计百分比超过 100%（Multiple answers）

	人次 Person-time	百分比 Percent
化妆/保养品 cosmetic	63	7.6
首饰 jewelry	5	0.6
鞋/帽/袜类 shoes/caps/socks	21	2.5
成人服装 adult clothes	41	4.9
童装 kid's clothes	13	1.6
内衣 underwear	11	1.3
布匹 cloth	0	0.0
玩具/婴儿用品 toy/infant's product	16	1.9
箱包皮具 bag & suitcase	3	0.4
体育用品 sports facilities	7	0.8
日用品 daily necessities	493	59.2
厨房用品 kitchen utensil	63	7.6
家用器皿 household appliance	17	2.0
家具/室内装饰 furniture	3	0.4
家用电器 household electronic products	14	1.7
图书 books	8	1.0
文具 stationary	29	3.5
音像制品 video & audio	6	0.7
食品 food	559	67.1
饮料 beverage	209	25.1
酒 alcohol drink	25	3.0
烟 cigarette	27	3.2
调味品 flavoring	86	10.3
菜蔬类 vegetable	21	2.5
水果 fruit	21	2.5
配菜 blend dish	25	3.0
其他 others	7	0.8

n=833

2-6 样本、男性各年龄层、女性各年龄层常与谁一起去超市/ With Whom When Visiting Supermarket by the Whole Sample, Age and Gender Groups

	人数 Number	和家人或亲戚 family members & relatives	和朋友 friends	和同事/同学 colleagues or schoolmates	单独 single
样本 Sample	**835**	**52.0**	**19.4**	**8.6**	**20.0**
男性 Male	**372**	**53.0**	**17.2**	**6.7**	**23.1**
16~24 岁 Age	77	37.7	26.0	16.9	19.5
25~34 岁 Age	116	38.8	25.9	6.0	29.3
35~44 岁 Age	98	71.4	8.2	4.1	16.3
45~54 岁 Age	55	65.5	9.1	1.8	23.6
55~60 岁 Age	26	65.4	3.8	0.0	30.8
女性 Female	**463**	**51.2**	**21.2**	**10.2**	**17.5**
16~24 岁 Age	103	37.9	30.1	26.2	5.8
25~34 岁 Age	142	55.6	23.9	4.2	16.2
35~44 岁 Age	118	58.5	16.9	7.6	16.9
45~54 岁 Age	69	47.8	14.5	7.2	30.4
55~60 岁 Age	31	54.8	9.7	0.0	35.5

2-7 选择超市的考虑因素/ Ranking of the Considerations of Choosing a Supermarket

注：本题为多选题，合计百分比超过 100%（Multiple answers）

排名 Ranking	考虑因素 Considerations	人次 Person-time	百分比 Percent
1	价格适中 reasonable price	510	60.6
2	交通便利 convenient transportation	376	44.7
3	商品种类齐全 wide range of choices	301	35.7
4	质量可靠 reliable quality	248	29.5
5	就近 close to reach	179	21.3
6	服务态度好 good service	85	10.1
7	空间宽敞 wide space	58	6.9
8	经常有促销活动 promotion	49	5.8
9	室内外装潢设计现代化 modern decoration	12	1.4
9	有大量进口商品 lots of imported goods	12	1.4
10	退换商品方便 easy replacement	9	1.1
11	可送货上门 goods deliver in	7	0.8
12	大型商品保修 reparation guarantee for expensive items	5	0.6
13	其他 others	4	0.5
13	提供餐饮休息配套服务 providing dining & rest service	4	0.5

n=842

2-8 重度消费者的人口分布/ Demographics of the Heavy Consumers

	人数 Number	16-24 岁 Age	25-34 岁 Age	35-44 岁 Age	45-54 岁 Age	55-60 岁 Age
样本 Sample	**594**	**22.9**	**33.0**	**25.9**	**12.1**	**6.1**
男性 Male	**245**	**22.9**	**34.7**	**24.5**	**11.4**	**6.5**
一周 3 次或以上 three times a week or over	21	28.6	28.6	9.5	19.0	14.3
一周 1～2 次 once or twice a week	103	20.4	33.0	30.1	9.7	6.8
两周 1 次左右 about once every two weeks	121	24.0	37.2	22.3	11.6	5.0
女性 Female	**349**	**22.9**	**31.8**	**26.9**	**12.6**	**5.7**
一周 3 次或以上 three times a week or over	35	20.0	37.1	28.6	8.6	5.7
一周 1～2 次 once or twice a week	183	21.9	34.4	27.3	8.2	8.2
两周 1 次左右 about once every two weeks	131	25.2	26.7	26.0	19.8	2.3

2-9 不同消费者层常去的超市/ Supermarkets Visited Most Frequently by Market Segments

2-9-1 时尚流行指标/ Fads Popular Index

注：本题为多选题，合计百分比超过 100%（Multiple answers）

	人数 Number	第一品牌及百分比 1st/ percent	第二品牌及百分比 2nd/ percent	第三品牌及百分比 3rd/ percent
样本 Sample	832	**好又多 Trust-mart(47.6)**	**岛内价 Daoneijia(31.5)**	**百佳超市 Park'n(19.7)**
平实生活指向 simple living orientation	416	好又多 Trust-mart(46.6)	岛内价 Daoneijia(27.9)	天河城吉之岛 Jusco(19.5)
时尚流行指向 fashion orientation	416	好又多 Trust-mart(48.6)	岛内价 Daoneijia (35.1)	百佳超市 Park'n(20.9)

2-9-2 价格态度指标/ Price Attitude Index

注：本题为多选题，合计百分比超过 100%（Multiple answers）

	人数 Number	第一品牌及百分比 1st/ percent	第二品牌及百分比 2nd/ percent	第三品牌及百分比 3rd/ percent
样本 Sample	838	**好又多 Trust-mart(47.5)**	**岛内价 Daoneijia (31.4)**	**百佳超市 Park'n(19.6)**
价格无关心指向 indifferent orientation	148	好又多 Trust-mart(47.3)	天河城吉之岛 Jusco(27.7)	岛内价 Daoneijia (25.0)
中间层 medium	454	好又多 Trust-mart(46.9)	岛内价 Daoneijia (33.7)	百佳超市 Park'n(19.2)
价格重视指向 careful orientation	236	好又多 Trust-mart(48.7)	岛内价 Daoneijia (30.9)	百佳超市 Park'n(20.8)

2-10 重度消费者的消费者层构成/ The Composition of the Heavy Consumers

2-10-1 时尚流行指标/ Fads popular Index

	人数 Number	平实生活指向 simple living orientation	时尚流行指向 fashion orientation
样本 Sample	**337**	**47.8**	**52.2**
一周 3 次或以上 3 times a week or over	55	52.7	47.3
一周 1~2 次 once or twice a week	282	46.8	53.2

2-10-2 价格态度指标/ Price Attitude Index

	人数 Number	价格无关心指向 indifferent orientation	中间层 medium	价格重视指向 careful orientation
样本 Sample	**339**	**17.1**	**55.5**	**27.4**
一周 3 次或以上 3 times a week or over	55	16.4	54.5	29.1
一周 1~2 次 once or twice a week	284	17.3	55.6	27.1

● 重庆 / Chongqing

2-1 最近三个月是否去过超市的比例/ Proportion of the Sample Visiting Supermarkets in the Last Three Months

	人数 Number	百分比 Percent
去过 yes	445	71.4
没去过 no	178	28.6

n=623

2-2 最常去的超市排名/ Ranking of the Supermarkets Visited Most Frequently

注：本题为多选题，合计百分比超过 100%（Multiple answers）

排名 Brand Ranking	品牌 Brands	人次 Person-time	百分比 Percent
1	家乐福/创益佳 Carrefour	319	71.7
2	山城（平价）超市 Shancheng	82	18.4
3	新世纪超市 Xinshiji	79	17.8
4	重百百汇超市 Baihui	48	10.8
5	沙百司超市 Shabaisi	26	5.8
6	十点利 Shidianli	24	5.4
7	阳光 Yangguang	14	3.1
8	惠工食品超市 Huigong	12	2.7
9	群鹰超市 Qunying	6	1.3
10	重百沙坪商场 Shaping Branch	5	1.1
10	十分利 Shifenli	5	1.1

n=445

2-3 样本、男性各年龄层、女性各年龄层最近三个月是否去过超市的比例/ Whether Having Visited Supermarkets in the Last Three Months by the Whole Sample, Age and Gender Groups

	人数 Number	去过 yes	没去过 no
样本 Sample	**623**	**71.4**	**28.6**
男性 Male	**314**	**68.2**	**31.8**
16~24 岁 Age	64	76.6	23.4
25~34 岁 Age	93	78.5	21.5
35~44 岁 Age	75	66.7	33.3
45~54 岁 Age	54	50.0	50.0
55~60 岁 Age	28	53.6	46.4
女性 Female	**309**	**74.8**	**25.2**
16~24 岁 Age	63	93.7	6.3
25~34 岁 Age	90	76.7	23.3
35~44 岁 Age	73	76.7	23.3
45~54 岁 Age	60	58.3	41.7
55~60 岁 Age	23	52.2	47.8

2-4 样本、男性各年龄层、女性各年龄层最近三个月去超市的频率/ Frequencies of Visiting Supermarkets in the Last Three Months by the Whole Sample, Age and Gender Groups

	人数 Number	一周 3 次或以上 3 times a week or over	一周 1~2 次 once or twice a week	两周 1 次左右 about once every two weeks	约一个月 1 次 about once a month	两三个月 1 次及以下 once every 2 or 3 months or below
样本 Sample	**442**	**5.7**	**30.3**	**31.2**	**24.0**	**8.8**
男性 Male	**213**	**4.2**	**30.0**	**31.0**	**26.3**	**8.5**
16~24 岁 Age	49	0.0	40.8	22.4	26.5	10.2
25~34 岁 Age	72	2.8	26.4	36.1	29.2	5.6
35~44 岁 Age	50	10.0	32.0	34.0	20.0	4.0
45~54 岁 Age	27	3.7	18.5	25.9	33.3	18.5
55~60 岁 Age	15	6.7	26.7	33.3	20.0	13.3
女性 Female	**229**	**7.0**	**30.6**	**31.4**	**21.8**	**9.2**
16~24 岁 Age	58	10.3	32.8	34.5	17.2	5.2
25~34 岁 Age	69	1.4	37.7	31.9	21.7	7.2
35~44 岁 Age	56	5.4	28.6	32.1	25.0	8.9
45~54 岁 Age	34	17.6	17.6	23.5	23.5	17.6
55~60 岁 Age	12	0.0	25.0	33.3	25.0	16.7

2-5 去超市购物的种类/ Categories of Visiting Supermarkets in the Last Three Months

注：本题为多选题，合计百分比超过 100%（Multiple answers）

	人次 Person-time	百分比 Percent
化妆/保养品 cosmetic	19	4.3
首饰 jewelry	3	0.7
鞋/帽/袜类 shoes/caps/socks	14	3.1
成人服装 adult clothes	24	5.4
童装 kid's clothes	8	1.8
内衣 underwear	9	2.0
布匹 cloth	0	0.0
玩具/婴儿用品 toy/infant's product	11	2.5
箱包皮具 bag & suitcase	4	0.9
体育用品 sports facilities	5	1.1
日用品 daily necessities	227	51.0
厨房用品 kitchen utensil	24	5.4
家用器皿 household appliance	9	2.0
家具/室内装饰 furniture	0	0.0
家用电器 household electronic products	4	0.9
图书 books	10	2.2
文具 stationary	19	4.3
音像制品 video & audio	13	2.9
食品 food	272	61.1
饮料 beverage	91	20.4
酒 alcohol drink	16	3.6
烟 cigarette	4	0.9
调味品 flavoring	63	14.2
菜蔬类 vegetable	19	4.3
水果 fruit	13	2.9
配菜 blend dish	10	2.2
其他 others	7	1.6

n=445

2-6 样本、男性各年龄层、女性各年龄层常与谁一起去超市/ With Whom When Visiting Supermarket by the Whole Sample, Age and Gender Groups

	人数 Number	和家人或亲戚 family members & relatives	和朋友 friends	和同事/同学 colleagues or schoolmates	单独 single
样本 Sample	**441**	**56.2**	**18.8**	**7.7**	**17.2**
男性 Male	**212**	**57.5**	**17.0**	**7.5**	**17.9**
16~24 岁 Age	49	30.6	24.5	24.5	20.4
25~34 岁 Age	72	52.8	23.6	4.2	19.4
35~44 岁 Age	49	79.6	10.2	0.0	10.2
45~54 岁 Age	27	66.7	7.4	0.0	25.9
55~60 岁 Age	15	80.0	0.0	6.7	13.3
女性 Female	**229**	**55.0**	**20.5**	**7.9**	**16.6**
16~24 岁 Age	59	35.6	44.1	10.2	10.2
25~34 岁 Age	68	67.6	10.3	7.4	14.7
35~44 岁 Age	55	56.4	18.2	9.1	16.4
45~54 岁 Age	35	65.7	11.4	2.9	20.0
55~60 岁 Age	12	41.7	0.0	8.3	50.0

2-7 选择超市的考虑因素/ Ranking of the Considerations of Choosing a Supermarket

注：本题为多选题，合计百分比超过 100%（Multiple answers）

排名 Ranking	考虑因素 Considerations	人次 Person-time	百分比 Percent
1	价格适中 reasonable price	284	64.3
2	质量可靠 reliable quality	198	44.8
3	商品种类齐全 wide range of choices	181	41.0
4	交通便利 convenient transportation	154	34.8
5	服务态度好 good service	55	12.4
6	就近 close to reach	41	9.3
7	空间宽敞 wide space	35	7.9
8	经常有促销活动 promotion	26	5.9
9	室内外装潢设计现代化 modern decoration	11	2.5
10	提供餐饮休息配套服务 providing dining & rest service	7	1.6
10	退换商品方便 easy replacement	7	1.6
11	其他 others	5	1.1
12	大型商品保修 reparation guarantee for expensive items	4	0.9
13	有大量进口商品 lots of imported goods	3	0.7
14	可送货上门 goods deliver in	1	0.2

n=442

2-8 重度消费者的人口分布/ Demographics of the Heavy Consumers

	人数 Number	16-24 岁 Age	25-34 岁 Age	35-44 岁 Age	45-54 岁 Age	55-60 岁 Age
样本 Sample	297	25.6	32.3	25.3	11.1	5.7
男性 Male	139	22.3	33.8	27.3	9.4	7.2
一周 3 次或以上 three times a week or over	9	0.0	22.2	55.6	11.1	11.1
一周 1～2 次 once or twice a week	64	31.3	29.7	25.0	7.8	6.3
两周 1 次左右 about once every two weeks	66	16.7	39.4	25.8	10.6	7.6
女性 Female	158	28.5	31.0	23.4	12.7	4.4
一周 3 次或以上 three times a week or over	16	37.5	6.3	18.8	37.5	0.0
一周 1～2 次 once or twice a week	70	27.1	37.1	22.9	8.6	4.3
两周 1 次左右 about once every two weeks	72	27.8	30.6	25.0	11.1	5.6

2-9 不同消费者层常去的超市/ Supermarkets Visited Most Frequently by Market Segments

2-9-1 时尚流行指标/ Fads Popular Index

注：本题为多选题，合计百分比超过 100%（Multiple answers）

	人数 Number	第一品牌及百分比 1st/ percent	第二品牌及百分比 2nd/ percent	第三品牌及百分比 3rd/ percent	第四品牌及百分比 4th/ percent
样本 Sample	437	**家乐福/创益佳 Carrefour(71.4)**	**山城（平价）超市 Shancheng(18.8)**	**新世纪超市 Xishiji(17.6)**	**重百百汇超市 Baihui(11.0)**
平实生活指向 simple living orientation	236	家乐福/创益佳 Carrefour(64.4)	山城（平价）超市 Shancheng(24.2)	新世纪超市 Xinshiji(14.8)	重百百汇超市 Baihui(9.7)
时尚流行指向 fashion orientation	201	家乐福/创益佳 Carrefour(79.6)	新世纪超市 Xinshiji(20.9)	山城（平价）超市 Shancheng(12.4) 重百百汇超市 Baihui(12.4)	沙百司超市 Shabaisi(7.5)

2-9-2 价格态度指标/ Price Attitude Index

注：本题为多选题，合计百分比超过 100%（Multiple answers）

	人数 Number	第一品牌及百分比 1st/ percent	第二品牌及百分比 2nd/ percent	第三品牌及百分比 3rd/ percent	第四品牌及百分比 4th/ percent
样本 Sample	441	**家乐福/创益佳 Carrefour(71.7)**	**山城（平价）超市 Shancheng(18.4)**	**新世纪超市 Xinshiji(17.7)**	**重百百汇超市 Baihui(10.7)**
价格无关心指向 indifferent orientation	77	家乐福/创益佳 Carrefour(74.0)	新世纪超市 Xinshiji (20.8)	山城（平价）超市 Shancheng(14.3)	重百百汇超市 Baihui(10.4)
中间层 medium	213	家乐福/创益佳 Carrefour(73.7)	山城（平价）超市 Shancheng(18.8)	新世纪超市 Xinshiji (15.0)	重百百汇超市 Baihui(9.4)
价格重视指向 careful orientation	151	家乐福/创益佳 Carrefour(67.5)	山城（平价）超市 Shancheng(19.9) 新世纪超市 Xinshiji (19.9)	重百百汇超市 Baihui(12.6)	十点利 Shidianli(7.3)

2-10 重度消费者的消费者层构成/ Composition of the Heavy Consumers

2-10-1 时尚流行指标/ Fads popular Index

	人数 Number	平实生活指向 simple living orientation	时尚流行指向 fashion orientation
样本 Sample	292	**52.4**	**47.6**
一周 3 次或以上 3 times or over a week	25	44.0	56.0
一周 1～2 次 once or twice a week	133	48.9	51.1
两周 1 次左右 about once a week	134	57.5	42.5

2-10-2 价格态度指标/ Price Attitude Index

	人数 Number	价格无关心指向 indifferent orientation	中间层 medium	价格重视指向 careful orientation
样本 Sample	293	**18.4**	**47.8**	**33.8**
一周 3 次或以上 3 times or over a week	24	16.7	37.5	45.8
一周 1～2 次 once or twice a week	134	20.9	49.3	29.9
两周 1 次左右 about once a week	135	16.3	48.1	35.6

● 武汉 / Wuhan

2-1 最近三个月是否去过超市的比例/ Proportion of the Sample Visiting Supermarkets in the Last Three Months

	人数 Number	百分比 Percent
去过 yes	473	73.9
没去过 no	167	26.1

n=640

2-2 最常去的超市排名/ Ranking of the Supermarkets Visited Most Frequently

注：本题为多选题，合计百分比超过 100%（Multiple answers）

排名 Brand Ranking	品牌 Brands	人次 Person-time	百分比 Percent
1	华联 Hualian	162	34.2
2	徐东平价 Xu Dong Ping Jia	161	34.0
3	家乐福/创益佳 Carrefour	76	16.1
4	大师量贩店 Dashi Supermarket	62	13.1
5	家家乐 Jiajiale	52	11.0
6	中百仓储 Zhong Bai Cang Chu	47	9.9
7	金田 Jintian	43	9.1
8	百盛量贩店 Parkson	42	8.9
9	佰汇 Baihui	38	8.0

n=473

2-3 样本、男性各年龄层、女性各年龄层最近三个月是否去过超市的比例/ Whether having Visited Supermarkets in the Last Three Months by the Whole Sample, Age and Gender Groups

	人数 Number	去过 yes	没去过 no
样本 Sample	640	73.9	26.1
男性 Male	310	67.1	32.9
16~24 岁 Age	65	69.2	30.8
25~34 岁 Age	89	78.7	21.3
35~44 岁 Age	80	58.8	41.3
45~54 岁 Age	52	67.3	32.7
55~60 岁 Age	24	45.8	54.2
女性 Female	330	80.3	19.7
16~24 岁 Age	68	91.2	8.8
25~34 岁 Age	96	85.4	14.6
35~44 岁 Age	78	84.6	15.4
45~54 岁 Age	62	69.4	30.6
55~60 岁 Age	26	46.2	53.8

2-4 样本、男性各年龄层、女性各年龄层最近三个月去超市的频率/ Frequencies of Visiting Supermarkets in the Last Three Months by the Whole Sample, Age and Gender Groups

	人数 Number	一周 3 次或以上 three times a week or over	一周 1~2 次 once or twice a week	两周 1 次左右 about once every two weeks	约一个月 1 次 about once a month	两三个月 1 次及以下 once every 2 or 3 months or below
样本 Sample	471	6.2	23.8	32.1	25.1	13.0
男性 Male	207	2.9	22.7	35.3	23.2	15.9
16~24 岁 Age	45	2.2	26.7	35.6	17.8	17.8
25~34 岁 Age	69	4.3	29.0	31.9	23.2	11.6
35~44 岁 Age	47	4.3	17.0	34.0	27.7	17.0
45~54 岁 Age	35	0.0	11.4	45.7	25.7	17.1
55~60 岁 Age	11	0.0	27.3	27.3	18.2	27.3
女性 Female	264	8.7	24.6	29.5	26.5	10.6
16~24 岁 Age	62	14.5	29.0	33.9	19.4	3.2
25~34 岁 Age	82	9.8	25.6	36.6	20.7	7.3
35~44 岁 Age	66	4.5	22.7	24.2	33.3	15.2
45~54 岁 Age	42	4.8	21.4	21.4	35.7	16.7
55~60 岁 Age	12	8.3	16.7	16.7	33.3	25.0

2-5 去超市购物的种类/ Categories of Visiting Supermarkets in the Last Three Months

注：本题为多选题，合计百分比超过 100%（Multiple answers）

	人次 Person-time	百分比 Percent
化妆/保养品 cosmetic	47	10.0
首饰 jewelry	4	0.8
鞋/帽/袜类 shoes/caps/socks	30	6.4
成人服装 adult clothes	51	10.8
童装 kid's clothes	11	2.3
内衣 underwear	16	3.4
布匹 cloth	0	0.0
玩具/婴儿用品 toy/infant's product	9	1.9
箱包皮具 bag & suitcase	6	1.3
体育用品 sports facilities	4	0.8
日用品 daily necessities	256	54.2
厨房用品 kitchen utensil	50	10.6
家用器皿 household appliance	12	2.5
家具/室内装饰 furniture	3	0.6
家用电器 household electronic products	14	3.0
图书 books	10	2.1
文具 stationary	17	3.6
音像制品 video & audio	8	1.7
食品 food	267	56.6
饮料 beverage	91	19.3
酒 alcohol drink	11	2.3
烟 cigarette	13	2.8
调味品 flavoring	89	18.9
菜蔬类 vegetable	26	5.5
水果 fruit	13	2.8
配菜 blend dish	12	2.5
其他 others	4	0.8

n=472

2-6 样本、男性各年龄层、女性各年龄层常与谁一起去超市/ With Whom When Visiting Supermarket by the Whole Sample, Age and Gender Groups

	人数 Number	和家人或亲戚 family members & relatives	和朋友 friends	和同事/同学 colleagues or schoolmates	单独 single
样本 Sample	467	56.7	14.3	9.0	19.9
男性 Male	207	56.5	14.5	7.7	21.3
16~24 岁 Age	45	26.7	31.1	24.4	17.8
25~34 岁 Age	70	54.3	21.4	4.3	20.0
35~44 岁 Age	47	76.6	2.1	2.1	19.1
45~54 岁 Age	35	71.4	0.0	2.9	25.7
55~60 岁 Age	10	60.0	0.0	0.0	40.0
女性 Female	260	56.9	14.2	10.0	18.8
16~24 岁 Age	60	38.3	23.3	28.3	10.0
25~34 岁 Age	80	62.5	15.0	6.3	16.3
35~44 岁 Age	66	63.6	9.1	3.0	24.2
45~54 岁 Age	42	64.3	9.5	2.4	23.8
55~60 岁 Age	12	50.0	8.3	8.3	33.3

2-7 选择超市的考虑因素/ Ranking of the Considerations of Choosing a Supermarket

注：本题为多选题，合计百分比超过 100%（Multiple answers）

排名 Ranking	考虑因素 Considerations	人次 Person-time	百分比 Percent
1	交通便利 convenient transportation	308	65.1
2	价格适中 reasonable price	303	64.1
3	质量可靠 reliable quality	152	32.1
4	商品种类齐全 wide range of choices	148	31.3
5	就近 close to reach	112	23.7
6	服务态度好 good service	36	7.6
6	经常有促销活动 promotion	36	7.6
7	空间宽敞 wide space	23	4.9
8	提供餐饮休息配套服务 providing dining & rest service	12	2.5
9	其他 others	7	1.5
10	退换商品方便 easy replacement	5	1.1
10	室内外装潢设计现代化 modern decoration	5	1.1
11	有大量进口商品 lots of imported goods	4	0.8
12	可送货上门 goods deliver in	2	0.4
13	大型商品保修 reparation guarantee for expensive items	1	0.2

n=473

2-8 重度消费者的人口分布/ Demographics of the Heavy Consumers

	人数 Number	16-24 岁 Age	25-34 岁 Age	35-44 岁 Age	45-54 岁 Age	55-60 岁 Age
样本 Sample	**292**	**26.4**	**35.6**	**20.5**	**13.7**	**3.8**
男性 Male	**126**	**23.0**	**35.7**	**20.6**	**15.9**	**4.8**
一周 3 次或以上 3 times or over a week	6	16.7	50.0	33.3	0.0	0.0
一周 1～2 次 once or twice a week	47	25.5	42.6	17.0	8.5	6.4
两周 1 次左右 once every two weeks	73	21.9	30.1	21.9	21.9	4.1
女性 Female	**166**	**28.9**	**35.5**	**20.5**	**12.0**	**3.0**
一周 3 次或以上 3 times or over a week	23	39.1	34.8	13.0	8.7	4.3
一周 1～2 次 once or twice a week	65	27.7	32.3	23.1	13.8	3.1
两周 1 次左右 once every two weeks	78	26.9	38.5	20.5	11.5	2.6

2-9 不同消费者层常去的超市/ Supermarkets Visited Most Frequently by Market Segments

2-9-1 时尚流行指标/ Fads Popular Index

注：本题为多选题，合计百分比超过 100%（Multiple answers）

	人数 Number	第一品牌及百分比 1st/ percent	第二品牌及百分比 2nd/ percent	第三品牌及百分比 3rd/ percent
样本 Sample	**468**	**华联 Hualian(34.2)** **徐东平价 Xu Dong Ping Jia(34.2)**	**家乐福/创益佳 Carrefour(16.2)**	**大师量贩店 Dashi Supermarket(12.6)**
平实生活指向 simple living orientation	226	徐东平价 Xu Dong Ping Jia(36.3)	华联 Hualian(32.3)	家家乐 Jiajiale(12.4) 家乐福/创益佳 Carrefour(12.4)
时尚流行指向 fashion orientation	242	华联 Hualian(36.0)	徐东平价 Xu Dong Ping Jia(32.2)	家乐福/创益佳 Carrefour(19.8)

2-9-2 价格态度指标/ Price Attitude Index

注：本题为多选题，合计百分比超过 100%（Multiple answers）

	人数 Number	第一品牌及百分比 1st/ percent	第二品牌及百分比 2nd/ percent	第三品牌及百分比 3rd/ percent
样本 Sample	**470**	**华联 Hualian(34.3)**	**徐东平价 Xu Dong Ping Jia(34.0)**	**家乐福/创益佳 Carrefour(16.2)**
价格无关心指向 indifferent orientation	57	徐东平价 Xu Dong Ping Jia(40.4)	华联 Hualian(29.8)	大师量贩店 Dashi Supermarket(14.0)
中间层 medium	236	华联 Hualian(35.2)	徐东平价 Xu Dong Ping Jia(32.2)	家乐福/创益佳 Carrefour(16.9)
价格重视指向 careful orientation	177	华联 Hualian(34.5) 徐东平价 Xu Dong Ping Jia(34.5)	家乐福/创益佳 Carrefour(16.9)	家家乐 Jiajiale(13.0)

2-10 重度消费者的消费者层构成/ The Composition of the Heavy Consumers

2-10-1 时尚流行指标/ Fads popular Index

	人数 Number	平实生活指向 simple living orientation	时尚流行指向 fashion orientation
样本 Sample	288	43.8	56.3
一周 3 次或以上 3 times or over a week	28	25.0	75.0
一周 1～2 次 once or twice a week	110	40.9	59.1
两周 1 次左右 once every two weeks	150	49.3	50.7

2-10-2 价格态度指标/ Price Attitude Index

	人数 Number	价格无关心指向 indifferent orientation	中间层 medium	价格重视指向 careful orientation
样本 Sample	289	14.9	50.9	34.3
一周 3 次或以上 3 times or over a week	28	17.9	60.7	21.4
一周 1～2 次 once or twice a week	111	17.1	47.7	35.1
两周 1 次左右 once every two weeks	150	12.7	51.3	36.0

● 西安 / Xi'an

2-1 最近三个月是否去过超市的比例/ Proportion of the Sample Visiting Supermarkets in the Last Three Months

	人数 Number	百分比 Percent
去过 yes	401	66.7
没去过 no	200	33.3

n=601

2-2 最常去的超市排名/ Ranking of the Supermarkets Visited Most Frequently

注：本题为多选题，合计百分比超过 100%（Multiple answers）

排名 Brand Ranking	品牌 Brands	人次 Person-time	百分比 Percent
1	海星 Haixing	181	45.1
2	友谊 Friendship Supermarket	73	18.2
3	家世界 Home Club	61	15.2
4	百隆 Shanxi Bailong Linked	48	12.0
5	好又多 Trust-mart	47	11.7
6	好邻居 Good Neighbour Supermarket	22	5.5
7	百盛超市 Parkson	18	4.5
8	世纪金花 Century Ginwa	9	2.2
9	通汇平价超市 Tonghui	7	1.7

n=401

2-3 样本、男性各年龄层、女性各年龄层最近三个月是否去过超市的比例/ Whether Having Visited Supermarkets in the Last Three Months by the Whole Sample, Age and Gender Groups

	人数 Number	去过 yes	没去过 no
样本 Sample	601	66.7	33.3
男性 Male	302	63.2	36.8
16~24 岁 Age	64	62.5	37.5
25~34 岁 Age	91	67.0	33.0
35~44 岁 Age	77	62.3	37.7
45~54 岁 Age	46	54.3	45.7
55~60 岁 Age	24	70.8	29.2
女性 Female	299	70.2	29.8
16~24 岁 Age	61	82.0	18.0
25~34 岁 Age	90	75.6	24.4
35~44 岁 Age	74	62.2	37.8
45~54 岁 Age	49	65.3	34.7
55~60 岁 Age	25	56.0	44.0

2-4 样本、男性各年龄层、女性各年龄层最近三个月去超市的频率/ Frequencies of Visiting Supermarkets in the Last Three Months by the Whole Sample, Age and Gender Groups

	人数 Number	一周 3 次或以上 three times a week or over	一周 1～2 次 once or twice a week	两周 1 次左右 about once every two weeks	约一个月 1 次 about once a month	两三个月 1 次及以下 once every 2 or 3 months or below
样本 Sample	401	5.7	26.4	25.9	32.4	9.5
男性 Male	191	4.7	23.6	24.6	37.2	9.9
16~24 岁 Age	40	12.5	25.0	27.5	30.0	5.0
25~34 岁 Age	61	4.9	23.0	27.9	32.8	11.5
35~44 岁 Age	48	2.1	33.3	18.8	37.5	8.3
45~54 岁 Age	25	0.0	12.0	20.0	48.0	20.0
55~60 岁 Age	17	0.0	11.8	29.4	52.9	5.9
女性 Female	210	6.7	29.0	27.1	28.1	9.0
16~24 岁 Age	50	8.0	28.0	26.0	32.0	6.0
25~34 岁 Age	68	7.4	38.2	25.0	23.5	5.9
35~44 岁 Age	46	8.7	15.2	26.1	39.1	10.9
45~54 岁 Age	32	3.1	31.3	31.3	21.9	12.5
55~60 岁 Age	14	0.0	28.6	35.7	14.3	21.4

2-5 去超市购物的种类/ Categories of Visiting Supermarkets in the Last Three Months

注：本题为多选题，合计百分比超过 100%（Multiple answers）

	人次 Person-time	百分比 Percent
化妆/保养品 cosmetic	42	10.5
首饰 jewelry	1	0.2
鞋/帽/袜类 shoes/caps/socks	14	3.5
成人服装 adult clothes	18	4.5
童装 kid's clothes	6	1.5
内衣 underwear	9	2.2
布匹 cloth	1	0.2
玩具/婴儿用品 toy/infant's product	8	2.0
箱包皮具 bag & suitcase	2	0.5
体育用品 sports facilities	2	0.5
日用品 daily necessities	188	46.9
厨房用品 kitchen utensil	26	6.5
家用器皿 household appliance	13	3.2
家具/室内装饰 furniture	3	0.7
家用电器 household electronic products	6	1.5
图书 books	12	3.0
文具 stationary	17	4.2
音像制品 video & audio	5	1.2
食品 food	223	55.6
饮料 beverage	98	24.4
酒 alcohol drink	11	2.7
烟 cigarette	9	2.2
调味品 flavoring	44	11.0
菜蔬类 vegetable	3	0.7
水果 fruit	5	1.2
配菜 blend dish	5	1.2
其他 others	10	2.5

n=401

2-6 样本、男性各年龄层、女性各年龄层常与谁一起去超市/ With Whom When Visiting Supermarket by the Whole Sample, Age and Gender Groups

	人数 Number	和家人或亲戚 family members & relatives	和朋友 friends	和同事/同学 colleagues or schoolmates	单独 single
样本 Sample	401	59.4	15.2	10.0	15.5
男性 Male	191	62.8	15.2	8.4	13.6
16~24 岁 Age	40	27.5	37.5	27.5	7.5
25~34 岁 Age	61	59.0	14.8	4.9	21.3
35~44 岁 Age	48	79.2	4.2	4.2	12.5
45~54 岁 Age	25	80.0	12.0	0.0	8.0
55~60 岁 Age	17	88.2	0.0	0.0	11.8
女性 Female	210	56.2	15.2	11.4	17.1
16~24 岁 Age	50	44.0	28.0	20.0	8.0
25~34 岁 Age	68	54.4	14.7	11.8	19.1
35~44 岁 Age	46	60.9	8.7	13.0	17.4
45~54 岁 Age	32	65.6	12.5	0.0	21.9
55~60 岁 Age	14	71.4	0.0	0.0	28.6

2-7 选择超市的考虑因素/ Ranking of the Considerations of Choosing a Supermarket

注：本题为多选题，合计百分比超过 100%（Multiple answers）

排名 Ranking	考虑因素 Considerations	人次 Person-time	百分比 Percent
1	交通便利 convenient transportation	189	47.1
2	价格适中 reasonable price	182	45.4
3	质量可靠 reliable quality	169	42.1
4	商品种类齐全 wide range of choices	129	32.2
5	就近 close to reach	63	15.7
6	空间宽敞 wide space	32	8.0
7	服务态度好 good service	27	6.7
8	经常有促销活动 promotion	18	4.5
9	室内外装潢设计现代化 modern decoration	14	3.5
10	退换商品方便 easy replacement	9	2.2
11	其他 others	4	1.0
11	可送货上门 goods deliver in	4	1.0
12	大型商品保修 reparation guarantee for expensive items	3	0.7
12	提供餐饮休息配套服务 providing dining & rest service	3	0.7
13	有大量进口商品 lots of imported goods	2	0.5

n=401

2-8 重度消费者的人口分布/ Demographics of the Heavy Consumers

	人数 Number	16-24 岁 Age	25-34 岁 Age	35-44 岁 Age	45-54 岁 Age	55-60 岁 Age
样本 Sample	233	24.5	35.2	21.0	12.4	6.9
男性 Male	101	25.7	33.7	25.7	7.9	6.9
一周 3 次或以上 three times a week or over	9	55.6	33.3	11.1	0.0	0.0
一周 1～2 次 once or twice a week	45	22.2	31.1	35.6	6.7	4.4
两周 1 次左右 about once every two weeks	47	23.4	36.2	19.1	10.6	10.6
女性 Female	132	23.5	36.4	17.4	15.9	6.8
一周 3 次或以上 three times a week or over	14	28.6	35.7	28.6	7.1	0.0
一周 1～2 次 once or twice a week	61	23.0	42.6	11.5	16.4	6.6
两周 1 次左右 about once every two weeks	57	22.8	29 8	21.1	17.5	8.8

2-9 不同消费者层常去的超市/ Supermarkets Visited Most Frequently by Market Segments

2-9-1 时尚流行指标/ Fads Popular Index

注：本题为多选题，合计百分比超过 100%（Multiple answers）

	人数 Number	第一品牌及百分比 1st/ percent	第二品牌及百分比 2nd/ percent	第三品牌及百分比 3rd/ percent
样本 Sample	400	**海星 Haixing(45.0)**	**友谊 Friendship Supermarket(18.3)**	**家世界 Home Club(15.3)**
平实生活指向 simple living orientation	210	海星 Haixing(43.8)	友谊 Friendship Supermarket(19.5)	家世界 Home Club(15.7)
时尚流行指向 fashion orientation	190	海星 Haixing(46.3)	友谊 Friendship Supermarket(16.8)	家世界 Home Club(14.7)

2-9-2 价格态度指标/ Price Attitude Index

注：本题为多选题，合计百分比超过 100%（Multiple answers）

	人数 Number	第一品牌及百分比 1st/ percent	第二品牌及百分比 2nd/ percent	第三品牌及百分比 3rd/ percent
样本 Sample	398	**海星 Haixing(45.0)**	**友谊 Friendship Supermarket(17.8)**	**家世界 Home Club(15.3)**
价格无关心指向 indifferent orientation	97	海星 Haixing(49.5)	友谊 Friendship Supermarket(21.6)	百隆 Shanxi Bailong Linked(13.4)
中间层 medium	204	海星 Haixing(44.1)	友谊 Friendship Supermarket(16.2)	好又多 Trust-mart(14.7)
价格重视指向 careful orientation	97	海星 Haixing(42.3)	家世界 Home Club(22.7)	友谊 Friendship Supermarket(17.5)

2-10 重度消费者的消费者层构成/ The Composition of the Heavy Consumers

2-10-1 时尚流行指标/ Fads popular Index

	人数 Number	平实生活指向 simple living orientation	时尚流行指向 fashion orientation
样本 Sample	233	49.8	50.2
一周 3 次或以上 3 times or over a week	23	43.5	56.5
一周 1～2 次 once or twice a week	106	51.9	48.1
两周 1 次左右 once every two weeks	104	49.0	51.0

2-10-2 价格态度指标/ Price Attitude Index

	人数 Number	价格无关心指向 indifferent orientation	中间层 medium	价格重视指向 careful orientation
样本 Sample	230	24.8	54.3	20.9
一周 3 次或以上 3 times or over a week	23	17.4	52.2	30.4
一周 1～2 次 once or twice a week	105	23.8	60.0	16.2
两周 1 次左右 once every two weeks	102	27.5	49.0	23.5

● 沈阳 / Shenyang

2-1 最近三个月是否去过超市的比例/ Proportion of the Sample Visiting Supermarkets in the Last Three Months

	人数 Number	百分比 Percent
去过 yes	480	79.9
没去过 no	121	20.1

n=601

2-2 最常去的超市排名/ Ranking of the Supermarkets Visited Most Frequently

注：本题为多选题，合计百分比超过 100%（Multiple answers）

排名 Brand Ranking	品牌 Brands	人次 Person-time	百分比 Percent
1	家乐福/创益佳 Carrefour	271	56.5
2	银泰 In Time	97	20.2
3	客来多 Kelaiduo	96	20.0
4	中辰超市 Zhongchen	64	13.3
4	再就业 Zaijiuye	64	13.3
5	百佳超市 Park'n	58	12.1
6	沁园春超市 Qin Yuan Chun Market	47	9.8
7	天天超市 Tiantian	24	5.0
8	信盟便利店 Civic Moon Shop	12	2.5
9	芳草地 Fangcaodi	11	2.3
9	九千家超市 Jiuqianjia	11	2.3
10	大卖场 Damaichang	7	1.5
10	满客隆 Mankelong	7	1.5
10	中诚超市 Zhongcheng	7	1.5

n=480

2-3 样本、男性各年龄层、女性各年龄层最近三个月是否去过超市的比例/ Whether Having Visited Supermarkets in the Last Three Months by the Whole Sample, Age and Gender Groups

	人数 Number	去过 yes	没去过 no
样本 Sample	601	79.9	20.1
男性 Male	299	74.6	25.4
16~24 岁 Age	64	76.6	23.4
25~34 岁 Age	89	84.3	15.7
35~44 岁 Age	76	67.1	32.9
45~54 岁 Age	46	76.1	23.9
55~60 岁 Age	24	54.2	45.8
女性 Female	302	85.1	14.9
16~24 岁 Age	64	92.2	7.8
25~34 岁 Age	90	87.8	12.2
35~44 岁 Age	76	85.5	14.5
45~54 岁 Age	48	79.2	20.8
55~60 岁 Age	24	66.7	33.3

2-4 样本、男性各年龄层、女性各年龄层最近三个月去超市的频率/ Frequencies of Visiting Supermarkets in the Last Three Months by the Whole Sample, Age and Gender Groups

	人数 Number	一周 3 次或以上 three times a week or over	一周 1～2 次 once or twice a week	两周 1 次左右 about once every two weeks	约一个月 1 次 about once a month	两三个月 1 次及以下 once every 2 or 3 months or below
样本 Sample	479	7.7	27.8	29.4	26.1	9.0
男性 Male	222	7.7	25.2	27.0	28.8	11.3
16~24 岁 Age	49	6.1	22.4	30.6	28.6	12.2
25~34 岁 Age	75	10.7	33.3	28.0	20.0	8.0
35~44 岁 Age	51	5.9	19.6	23.5	35.3	15.7
45~54 岁 Age	34	0.0	17.6	29.4	44.1	8.8
55~60 岁 Age	13	23.1	30.8	15.4	15.4	15.4
女性 Female	257	7.8	30.0	31.5	23.7	7.0
16~24 岁 Age	59	6.8	39.0	25.4	25.4	3.4
25~34 岁 Age	79	13.9	31.6	34.2	17.7	2.5
35~44 岁 Age	65	0.0	30.8	40.0	20.0	9.2
45~54 岁 Age	38	10.5	15.8	21.1	34.2	18.4
55~60 岁 Age	16	6.3	18.8	31.3	37.5	6.3

2-5 去超市购物的种类/ Categories of Visiting Supermarkets in the Last Three Months

注：本题为多选题，合计百分比超过 100%（Multiple answers）

	人次 Person-time	百分比 Percent
化妆/保养品 cosmetic	54	11.3
首饰 jewelry	2	0.4
鞋/帽/袜类 shoes/caps/socks	20	4.2
成人服装 adult clothes	16	3.3
童装 kid's clothes	8	1.7
内衣 underwear	12	2.5
布匹 cloth	0	0.0
玩具/婴儿用品 toy/infant's product	9	1.9
箱包皮具 bag & suitcase	1	0.2
体育用品 sports facilities	4	0.8
日用品 daily necessities	230	48.0
厨房用品 kitchen utensil	51	10.6
家用器皿 household appliance	3	0.6
家具/室内装饰 furniture	1	0.2
家用电器 household electronic products	0	0.0
图书 books	9	1.9
文具 stationary	15	3.1
音像制品 video & audio	3	0.6
食品 food	312	65.1
饮料 beverage	143	29.9
酒 alcohol drink	18	3.8
烟 cigarette	12	2.5
调味品 flavoring	87	18.2
菜蔬类 vegetable	8	1.7
水果 fruit	13	2.7
配菜 blend dish	5	1.0
其他 others	7	1.5

n=479

2-6 样本、男性各年龄层、女性各年龄层常与谁一起去超市/ With Whom When Visiting Supermarket by the Whole Sample, Age and Gender Groups

	人数 Number	和家人或亲戚 family members & relatives	和朋友 friends	和同事/同学 colleagues or schoolmates	单独 single
样本 Sample	479	51.8	17.1	10.2	20.9
男性 Male	223	51.6	16.6	10.8	21.1
16~24 岁 Age	49	12.2	40.8	30.6	16.3
25~34 岁 Age	75	50.7	18.7	8.0	22.7
35~44 岁 Age	51	74.5	2.0	3.9	19.6
45~54 岁 Age	35	68.6	5.7	2.9	22.9
55~60 岁 Age	13	69.2	0.0	0.0	30.8
女性 Female	256	52.0	17.6	9.8	20.7
16~24 岁 Age	58	29.3	34.5	22.4	13.8
25~34 岁 Age	79	51.9	15.2	7.6	25.3
35~44 岁 Age	65	64.6	9.2	7.7	18.5
45~54 岁 Age	38	55.3	15.8	2.6	26.3
55~60 岁 Age	16	75.0	6.3	0.0	18.8

2-7 选择超市的考虑因素/ Ranking of the Considerations of Choosing a Supermarket

注：本题为多选题，合计百分比超过 100%（Multiple answers）

排名 Ranking	考虑因素 Considerations	人次 Person-time	百分比 Percent
1	价格适中 reasonable price	280	58.6
2	质量可靠 reliable quality	238	49.8
3	交通便利 convenient transportation	233	48.7
4	商品种类齐全 wide range of choices	143	29.9
5	就近 close to reach	82	17.2
6	服务态度好 good service	51	10.7
7	空间宽敞 wide space	33	6.9
8	经常有促销活动 promotion	14	2.9
9	退换商品方便 easy replacement	11	2.3
10	其他 others	5	1.0
11	提供餐饮休息配套服务 providing dining & rest service	4	0.8
11	室内外装潢设计现代化 modern decoration	4	0.8
12	可送货上门 goods deliver in	2	0.4
13	有大量进口商品 lots of imported goods	1	0.2

n=478

2-8 重度消费者的人口分布/ Demographics of the Heavy Consumers

	人数 Number	16-24 岁 Age	25-34 岁 Age	35-44 岁 Age	45-54 岁 Age	55-60 岁 Age
样本 Sample	311	22.8	37.6	22.8	10.9	5.8
男性 Male	133	21.8	40.6	18.8	12.0	6.8
一周 3 次或以上 3 times a week or over	17	17.6	47.1	17.6	0.0	17.6
一周 1～2 次 once or twice a week	56	19.6	44.6	17.9	10.7	7.1
两周 1 次左右 about once every two weeks	60	25.0	35.0	20.0	16.7	3.3
女性 Female	178	23.6	35.4	25.8	10.1	5.1
一周 3 次或以上 3 times a week or over	20	20.0	55.0	0.0	20.0	5.0
一周 1～2 次 once or twice a week	77	29.9	32.5	26.0	7.8	3.9
两周 1 次左右 about once every two weeks	81	18.5	33.3	32.1	9.9	6.2

2-9 不同消费者层常去的超市/ Supermarkets Visited Most Frequently by Market Segments

2-9-1 时尚流行指标/ Fads Popular Index

注：本题为多选题，合计百分比超过 100%（Multiple answers）

	人数 Number	第一品牌及百分比 1st/ percent	第二品牌及百分比 2nd/ percent	第三品牌及百分比 3rd/ percent	第四品牌及百分比 4th/ percent
样本 Sample	480	**家乐福/创益佳 Carrefour(56.5)**	**银泰 In Time(20.2)**	**客来多 Kelaiduo(20.0)**	**中辰超市 Zhongchen(13.3) 再就业 Zaijiuye(13.3)**
平实生活指向 simple living orientation	207	家乐福/创益佳 Carrefour(54.1)	客来多 Kelaiduo(17.4)	银泰 In Time(16.9)	中辰超市 Zhongchen(14.5)
时尚流行指向 fashion orientation	273	家乐福/创益佳 Carrefour(58.2)	银泰 In Time(22.7)	客来多 Kelaiduo(22.0)	再就业 Zaijiuye(12.8)

2-9-2 价格态度指标/ Price Attitude Index

注：本题为多选题，合计百分比超过 100%（Multiple answers）

	人数 Number	第一品牌及百分比 1st/ percent	第二品牌及百分比 2nd/ percent	第三品牌及百分比 3rd/ percent	第四品牌及百分比 4th/ percent
样本 Sample	479	**家乐福/创益佳 Carrefour(56.6)**	**银泰 In Time(20.3)**	**客来多 Kelaiduo(20.0)**	**中辰超市 Zhongchen(13.4) 再就业 Zaijiuye(13.4)**
价格无关心指向 indifferent orientation	84	家乐福/创益佳 Carrefour(54.8)	百佳超市 Park'n(21.4) 客来多 Kelaiduo(21.4)	银泰 In Time(19.0) 中辰超市 Zhongchen(19.0)	再就业 Zaijiuye(13.1) 沁园春超市 Qin Yuan Chun Market (13.1)
中间层 medium	239	家乐福/创益佳 Carrefour(57.7)	客来多 Kelaiduo(21.8)	银泰 In Time(19.7)	中辰超市 Zhongchen(11.7) 再就业 Zaijiuye(11.7)
价格重视指向 careful orientation	156	家乐福/创益佳 Carrefour(55.8)	银泰 In Time(21.8)	客来多 Kelaiduo(16.7)	再就业 Zaijiuye(16.0)

2-10 重度消费者的消费者层构成/ The Composition of the Heavy Consumers

2-10-1 时尚流行指标/ Fads popular Index

	人数 Number	平实生活指向 simple living orientation	时尚流行指向 fashion orientation
样本 Sample	311	**38.9**	**61.1**
一周 3 次或以上 3 times or over a week	37	40.5	59.5
一周 1～2 次 once or twice a week	133	36.1	63.9
两周 1 次左右 once every two weeks	141	41.1	58.9

2-10-2 价格态度指标/ Price Attitude Index

	人数 Number	价格无关心指向 indifferent orientation	中间层 medium	价格重视指向 careful orientation
样本 Sample	310	**17.1**	**52.6**	30.3
一周 3 次或以上 3 times or over a week	37	27.0	43.2	29.7
一周 1～2 次 once or twice a week	133	13.5	51.9	34.6
两周 1 次左右 once every two weeks	140	17.9	55.7	26.4

3.西式快餐店 / Western-style Fast-food Restaurant

● 北京 / Beijing

3-1 最近三个月是否去过西式快餐店的比例/ Proportion of the Sample Visiting Western-style Fast-food Restaurants in the Last Three Months

	人数 Number	百分比 Percent
去过 yes	514	50.8
没去过 no	498	49.2

n=1012

3-2 最常去的西式快餐店排名/ Ranking of the Western-style Fast-food Restaurants Visited Most Frequently

注：本题为多选题，合计百分比超过 100%（Multiple answers）

排名 Brand Ranking	品牌 Brands	人次 Person-time	百分比 Percent
1	麦当劳 Macdonald's	460	89.5
2	肯德基 KFC	390	75.9
3	必胜客 Pizza Hut	57	11.1
4	艾德熊 A&W	49	9.5
5	罗杰斯 Roasters	30	5.8
6	乐天利 Lotte	23	4.5
7	大磨坊 De'lifrance	12	2.3
8	德克士 Dicos	8	1.6
9	芳香鸡 CFC	6	1.2

n=514

3-3 样本、男性各年龄层、女性各年龄层最近三个月是否去过西式快餐店的比例/ Whether Having Visited Western-style Fast-food Restaurants in the Last Three Months by the Whole Sample, Age and Gender Groups

	人数 Number	去过 yes	没去过 no
样本 Sample	1012	50.8	49.2
男性 Male	504	45.2	54.8
16~24 岁 Age	105	61.0	39.0
25~34 岁 Age	151	55.6	44.4
35~44 岁 Age	131	44.3	55.7
45~54 岁 Age	77	20.8	79.2
55~60 岁 Age	40	15.0	85.0
女性 Female	508	56.3	43.7
16~24 岁 Age	108	81.5	18.5
25~34 岁 Age	150	62.7	37.3
35~44 岁 Age	124	56.5	43.5
45~54 岁 Age	84	31.0	69.0
55~60 岁 Age	42	19.0	81.0

3-4 样本、男性各年龄层、女性各年龄层最近三个月去西式快餐店的频率/ Frequencies of Visiting Western-style Fast-food Restaurants in the Last Three Months by the Whole Sample, Age and Gender Groups

	人数 Number	一周 1 次或以上 once a week or over	两周 1 次左右 about once every two weeks	约一个月 1 次 about once a month	两三个月 1 次及以下 once every 2 or 3 months or below
样本 Sample	512	12.5	30.9	35.9	20.7
男性 Male	227	11.5	30.8	34.8	22.9
16~24 岁 Age	64	7.8	35.9	34.4	21.9
25~34 岁 Age	84	9.5	29.8	45.2	15.5
35~44 岁 Age	58	19.0	27.6	25.9	27.6
45~54 岁 Age	15	6.7	33.3	26.7	33.3
55~60 岁 Age	6	16.7	16.7	0.0	66.7
女性 Female	285	13.3	30.9	36.8	18.9
16~24 岁 Age	88	18.2	33.0	35.2	13.6
25~34 岁 Age	93	9.7	36.6	35.5	18.3
35~44 岁 Age	70	12.9	28.6	38.6	20.0
45~54 岁 Age	26	15.4	15.4	42.3	26.9
55~60 岁 Age	8	0.0	12.5	37.5	50.0

3-5 样本、男性各年龄层、女性各年龄层最近一次在西式快餐店的花费/ Expense in the Most Recent Visit to Western-style Fast-food Restaurant by the Whole Sample, Age and Gender Groups

	人数 Number	10元及以下 10 yuan or below	11-20元 yuan	21-30元 yuan	31-40元 yuan	41-50元 yuan	51-70元 yuan	71-100元 yuan	100元以上 over 100 yuan
样本 Sample	513	1.2	19.7	36.1	13.8	16.4	6.4	5.3	1.2
男性 Male	227	1.3	20.3	27.3	16.7	18.5	6.6	7.9	1.3
16~24岁 Age	63	1.6	20.6	20.6	14.3	27.0	6.3	6.3	3.2
25~34岁 Age	84	0.0	22.6	31.0	14.3	17.9	9.5	3.6	1.2
35~44岁 Age	58	3.4	20.7	27.6	20.7	12.1	3.4	12.1	0.0
45~54岁 Age	16	0.0	0.0	31.3	31.3	18.8	0.0	18.8	0.0
55~60岁 Age	6	0.0	33.3	33.3	0.0	0.0	16.7	16.7	0.0
女性 Female	286	1.0	19.2	43.0	11.5	14.7	6.3	3.1	1.0
16~24岁 Age	88	1.1	22.7	46.6	9.1	10.2	5.7	2.3	2.3
25~34岁 Age	94	2.1	18.1	47.9	10.6	13.8	5.3	2.1	0.0
35~44岁 Age	70	0.0	11.4	40.0	15.7	17.1	10.0	5.7	0.0
45~54岁 Age	26	0.0	34.6	26.9	7.7	23.1	3.8	0.0	3.8
55~60岁 Age	8	0.0	12.5	25.0	25.0	25.0	0.0	12.5	0.0

3-6 样本、男性各年龄层、女性各年龄层常与谁一起去西式快餐店/ With Whom When Visiting Western-style Fast-food Restaurant by the Whole Sample, Age and Gender Groups

	人数 Number	和家人或亲戚 family members & relatives	和朋友 friends	和同事/同学 colleagues or schoolmates	单独 single
样本 Sample	510	56.5	25.9	11.2	6.5
男性 Male	226	50.4	32.3	9.7	7.5
16~24岁 Age	64	15.6	50.0	25.0	9.4
25~34岁 Age	83	50.6	37.3	2.4	9.6
35~44岁 Age	57	78.9	14.0	3.5	3.5
45~54岁 Age	16	81.3	6.3	6.3	6.3
55~60岁 Age	6	66.7	16.7	16.7	0.0
女性 Female	284	61.3	20.8	12.3	5.6
16~24岁 Age	88	19.3	42.0	34.1	4.5
25~34岁 Age	93	79.6	11.8	3.2	5.4
35~44岁 Age	69	87.0	7.2	2.9	2.9
45~54岁 Age	26	65.4	19.2	0.0	15.4
55~60岁 Age	8	75.0	12.5	0.0	12.5

3-7 样本、男性各年龄层、女性各年龄层对就餐方式的喜好/ Preferred Categories of Western-style Fast-food Restaurant by the Whole Sample, Age and Gender Groups

	人数 Number	外卖 take-out	店内吃 in the restaurant
样本 Sample	512	6.1	93.9
男性 Male	226	5.8	94.2
16~24岁 Age	64	3.1	96.9
25~34岁 Age	84	6.0	94.0
35~44岁 Age	56	7.1	92.9
45~54岁 Age	16	12.5	87.5
55~60岁 Age	6	0.0	100.0
女性 Female	286	6.3	93.7
16~24岁 Age	88	3.4	96.6
25~34岁 Age	94	7.4	92.6
35~44岁 Age	70	7.1	92.9
45~54岁 Age	26	11.5	88.5
55~60岁 Age	8	0.0	100.0

3-8 选择西式快餐店的考虑因素/ Ranking of the Considerations of Choosing a Western-style Fast-food Restaurant

注：本题为多选题，合计百分比超过 100%（Multiple answers）

排名 Ranking	考虑因素 Considerations	人次 Person-time	百分比 Percent
1	口味好 good taste	269	52.4
2	卫生 clean	244	47.6
3	就近 close to reach	223	43.5
4	方便、迅速 convenient and quickly	208	40.5
5	价格适中 reasonable price	72	14.0
6	服务态度好 good services	64	12.5
7	店面布置有特色 special display in the restaurant	37	7.2
8	有特色活动（如生日餐等）special activities (birthday party e	28	5.5
9	其他 others	10	1.9

n=513

3-9 重度消费者的人口分布/ Demographics of the Heavy Consumers

	人数 Number	16-24 岁 Age	25-34 岁 Age	35-44 岁 Age	45-54 岁 Age	55-60 岁 Age
样本 Sample	222	32.9	34.2	25.2	6.3	1.4
男性 Male	96	29.2	34.4	28.1	6.3	2.1
一周 1 次或以上 once a week or over	26	19.2	30.8	42.3	3.8	3.8
两周 1 次左右 about once every two weeks	70	32.9	35.7	22.9	7.1	1.4
女性 Female	126	35.7	34.1	23.0	6.3	0.8
一周 1 次或以上 once a week or over	38	42.1	23.7	23.7	10.5	0.0
两周 1 次左右 about once every two weeks	88	33.0	38.6	22.7	4.5	1.1

3-10 不同消费者层常去的西式快餐店/ Western Style Fast-food Restaurants Visited Most Frequently by Market Segments

3-10-1 时尚流行指标/ Fads Popular Index

注：本题为多选题，合计百分比超过 100%（Multiple answers）

	人数	第一品牌及百分比 1st/ percent	第二品牌及百分比 2nd/ percent	第三品牌及百分比 3rd/ percent	第四品牌及百分比 4th / percent
样本 Sample	508	**麦当劳 Macdonald's(89.8)**	**肯德基 KFC(75.8)**	**必胜客 Pizza Hut(11.2)**	**艾德熊 A&W(9.4)**
平实生活指向 simple living orientation	210	麦当劳 Macdonald's(88.6)	肯德基 KFC(75.2)	艾德熊 A&W(10.0)	必胜客 Pizza Hut(8.1)
时尚流行指向 fashion orientation	298	麦当劳 Macdonald's(90.6)	肯德基 KFC(76.2)	必胜客 Pizza Hut(13.4)	艾德熊 A&W(9.1)

3-10-2 价格态度指标/ Price Attitude Index

注：本题为多选题，合计百分比超过 100%（Multiple answers）

	人数	第一品牌及百分比 1st/ percent	第二品牌及百分比 2nd/ percent	第三品牌及百分比 3rd/ percent	第四品牌及百分比 4th/ percent
样本 Sample	511	**麦当劳 Macdonald's(89.4)**	**肯德基 KFC(75.9)**	**必胜客 Pizza Hut(11.2)**	**艾德熊 A&W(9.6)**
价格无关心指向 indifferent orientation	123	麦当劳 Macdonald's(92.7)	肯德基 KFC(72.4)	必胜客 Pizza Hut(12.2)	艾德熊 A&W(11.4)
中间层 medium	272	麦当劳 Macdonald's(88.2)	肯德基 KFC(78.7)	必胜客 Pizza Hut(11.4)	艾德熊 A&W(9.2)
价格重视指向 careful orientation	116	麦当劳 Macdonald's(88.8)	肯德基 KFC(73.3)	必胜客 Pizza Hut(9.5)	艾德熊 A&W(8.6)

3-11 重度消费者的消费者层构成/ The Composition of the Heavy Consumers

3-11-1 时尚流行指标/ Fads popular Index

	人数 Number	平实生活指向 simple living orientation	时尚流行指向 fashion orientation
样本 Sample	222	37.8	62.2
一周 1 次或以上 once a week or over	64	29.7	70.3
两周 1 次左右 about once every two weeks	158	41.1	58.9

3-11-2 价格态度指标/ Price Attitude Index

	人数 Number	价格无关心指向 indifferent orientation	中间层 medium	价格重视指向 careful orientation
样本 Sample	221	25.8	51.6	22.6
一周 1 次或以上 once a week or over	64	29.7	43.8	26.6
两周 1 次左右 about once every two weeks	157	24.2	54.8	21.0

● 上海 / Shanghai

3-1 最近三个月是否去过西式快餐店的比例/ Proportion of the Sample Visiting Western-style Fast-food Restaurants in the Last Three Months

	人数 Number	百分比 Percent
去过 yes	495	48.8
没去过 no	519	51.2

n=1014

3-2 最常去的西式快餐店排名/ Ranking of the Western-style Fast-food Restaurants Visited Most Frequently

注：本题为多选题，合计百分比超过 100%（Multiple answers）

排名 Brand Ranking	品牌 Brands	人次 Person-time	百分比 Percent
1	肯德基 KFC	449	91.1
2	麦当劳 Macdonald's	358	72.6
3	必胜客 Pizza Hut	122	24.7
4	芳香鸡 CFC	6	1.2
5	德克士 Dicos	3	0.6
5	比飒利 Bisali	3	0.6

n=493

3-3 样本、男性各年龄层、女性各年龄层最近三个月是否去过西式快餐店的比例/ Whether Having Visited Western-style Fast-food Restaurants in the Last Three Months by the Whole Sample, Age and Gender Groups

	人数 Number	去过 yes	没去过 no
样本 Sample	1014	48.8	51.2
男性 Male	509	45.4	54.6
16~24 岁 Age	109	67.0	33.0
25~34 岁 Age	146	57.5	42.5
35~44 岁 Age	130	33.8	66.2
45~54 岁 Age	85	24.7	75.3
55~60 岁 Age	39	23.1	76.9
女性 Female	505	52.3	47.7
16~24 岁 Age	108	77.8	22.2
25~34 岁 Age	144	61.1	38.9
35~44 岁 Age	130	43.1	56.9
45~54 岁 Age	82	26.8	73.2
55~60 岁 Age	41	34.1	65.9

3-4 样本、男性各年龄层、女性各年龄层最近三个月去西式快餐店的频率/ Frequencies of Visiting Western-style Fast-food Restaurants in the Last Three Months by the Whole Sample, Age and Gender Groups

	人数 Number	一周 1 次或以上 once a week or over	两周 1 次左右 about once every two weeks	约一个月 1 次 about once a month	两三个月 1 次及以下 once every 2 or 3 months or below
样本 Sample	491	8.4	31.0	39.7	21.0
男性 Male	229	7.4	36.2	35.8	20.5
16~24 岁 Age	73	12.3	38.4	32.9	16.4
25~34 岁 Age	84	6.0	35.7	39.3	19.0
35~44 岁 Age	43	7.0	32.6	39.5	20.9
45~54 岁 Age	20	0.0	45.0	25.0	30.0
55~60 岁 Age	9	0.0	22.2	33.3	44.4
女性 Female	262	9.2	26.3	43.1	21.4
16~24 岁 Age	83	13.3	30.1	43.4	13.3
25~34 岁 Age	87	8.0	29.9	47.1	14.9
35~44 岁 Age	56	8.9	17.9	41.1	32.1
45~54 岁 Age	22	4.5	22.7	27.3	45.5
55~60 岁 Age	14	0.0	21.4	50.0	28.6

3-5 样本、男性各年龄层、女性各年龄层最近一次在西式快餐店的花费/ Expense in the Most Recent Visit to Western-style Fast-food Restaurant by the Whole Sample, Age and Gender Groups

	人数 Number	10 元及以下 10 yuan or below	11-20 元 11-20 yuan	21-30 元 21-30 yuan	31-40 元 31-40 yuan	41-50 元 41-50 yuan	51-70 元 51-70 yuan	71-100 元 71-100 yuan	100 元以上 over 100 yuan
样本 Sample	493	1.2	25.4	46.5	9.5	13.0	2.2	2.2	0.0
男性 Male	229	1.3	24.9	43.7	11.4	13.5	2.2	3.1	0.0
16~24 岁 Age	73	2.7	23.3	41.1	9.6	16.4	2.7	4.1	0.0
25~34 岁 Age	84	1.2	22.6	46.4	8.3	16.7	1.2	3.6	0.0
35~44 岁 Age	43	0.0	32.6	46.5	14.0	4.7	2.3	0.0	0.0
45~54 岁 Age	20	0.0	25.0	40.0	20.0	10.0	5.0	0.0	0.0
55~60 岁 Age	9	0.0	22.2	33.3	22.2	11.1	0.0	11.1	0.0
女性 Female	264	1.1	25.8	48.9	8.0	12.5	2.3	1.5	0.0
16~24 岁 Age	84	2.4	22.6	44.0	9.5	16.7	2.4	2.4	0.0
25~34 岁 Age	88	1.1	25.0	51.1	8.0	13.6	1.1	0.0	0.0
35~44 岁 Age	56	0.0	21.4	58.9	5.4	7.1	3.6	3.6	0.0
45~54 岁 Age	22	0.0	36.4	45.5	4.5	9.1	4.5	0.0	0.0
55~60 岁 Age	14	0.0	50.0	28.6	14.3	7.1	0.0	0.0	0.0

3-6 样本、男性各年龄层、女性各年龄层常与谁一起去西式快餐店/ With Whom When Visiting Western-style Fast-food Restaurant by the Whole Sample, Age and Gender Groups

	人数 Number	和家人或亲戚 family members & relatives	和朋友 friends	和同事/同学 colleagues or schoolmates	单独 single
样本 Sample	491	52.3	30.8	14.9	2.0
男性 Male	227	48.5	34.4	14.1	3.1
16~24 岁 Age	72	12.5	51.4	34.7	1.4
25~34 岁 Age	84	46.4	44.0	6.0	3.6
35~44 岁 Age	43	86.0	7.0	2.3	4.7
45~54 岁 Age	20	85.0	5.0	5.0	5.0
55~60 岁 Age	8	100.0	0.0	0.0	0.0
女性 Female	264	55.7	27.7	15.5	1.1
16~24 岁 Age	84	11.9	48.8	38.1	1.2
25~34 岁 Age	88	67.0	27.3	5.7	0.0
35~44 岁 Age	56	87.5	5.4	5.4	1.8
45~54 岁 Age	22	77.3	18.2	0.0	4.5
55~60 岁 Age	14	85.7	7.1	7.1	0.0

3-7 样本、男性各年龄层、女性各年龄层对就餐方式的喜好/ Preferred Categories of Western-style Fast-food Restaurant by the Whole Sample, Age and Gender Groups

	人数 Number	外卖 take-out	店内吃 in the restaurant
样本 Sample	**493**	**5.3**	**94.7**
男性 Male	**229**	**7.0**	**93.0**
16~24 岁 Age	73	6.8	93.2
25~34 岁 Age	84	4.8	95.2
35~44 岁 Age	43	9.3	90.7
45~54 岁 Age	20	10.0	90.0
55~60 岁 Age	9	11.1	88.9
女性 Female	**264**	**3.8**	**96.2**
16~24 岁 Age	84	2.4	97.6
25~34 岁 Age	88	4.5	95.5
35~44 岁 Age	56	3.6	96.4
45~54 岁 Age	22	4.5	95.5
55~60 岁 Age	14	7.1	92.9

3-8 选择西式快餐店的考虑因素/ Ranking of the Considerations of Choosing a Western-style Fast-food Restaurant

注：本题为多选题，合计百分比超过 100%（Multiple answers）

排名 Ranking	考虑因素 Considerations	人次 Person-time	百分比 Percent
1	口味好 good taste	290	58.9
2	卫生 clean	184	37.4
2	方便、迅速 convenient and quickly	184	37.4
3	就近 close to reach	172	35.0
4	价格适中 reasonable price	82	16.7
5	服务态度好 good services	75	15.2
6	店面布置有特色 special display in the restaurant	60	12.2
7	有特色活动（如生日餐等）special activities (birthday party e	13	2.6
8	其他 others	12	2.4

n=492

3-9 重度消费者的人口分布/ Demographics of the Heavy Consumers

	人数 Number	16-24 岁 Age	25-34 岁 Age	35-44 岁 Age	45-54 岁 Age	55-60 岁 Age
样本 Sample	**193**	**37.8**	**35.2**	**16.6**	**7.8**	**2.6**
男性 Male	**100**	**37.0**	**35.0**	**17.0**	**9.0**	**2.0**
一周 1 次或以上 once a week or over	17	52.9	29.4	17.6	0.0	0.0
两周 1 次左右 about once every two weeks	83	33.7	36.1	16.9	10.8	2.4
女性 Female	**93**	**38.7**	**35.5**	**16.1**	**6.5**	**3.2**
一周 1 次或以上 once a week or over	24	45.8	29.2	20.8	4.2	0.0
两周 1 次左右 about once every two weeks	69	36.2	37.7	14.5	7.2	4.3

3-10 不同消费者层常去的西式快餐店/ Western Style Fast-food Restaurants Visited Most Frequently by Market Segments

3-10-1 时尚流行指标/ Fads Popular Index

注：本题为多选题，合计百分比超过 100%（Multiple answers）

	人数 Number	第一品牌及百分比 1st/ percent	第二品牌及百分比 2nd/ percent	第三品牌及百分比 3rd/ percent
样本 Sample	**490**	**肯德基 KFC(91.0)**	**麦当劳 Macdonald's(72.7)**	**必胜客 Pizza Hut(24.7)**
平实生活指向 simple living orientation	164	肯德基 KFC(89.6)	麦当劳 Macdonald's(69.5)	必胜客 Pizza Hut(15.9)
时尚流行指向 fashion orientation	326	肯德基 KFC(91.7)	麦当劳 Macdonald's(74.2)	必胜客 Pizza Hut(29.1)

3-10-2 价格态度指标/ Price Attitude Index

注：本题为多选题，合计百分比超过 100%（Multiple answers）

	人数 Number	第一品牌及百分比 1st/ percent	第二品牌及百分比 2nd/ percent	第三品牌及百分比 3rd/ percent
样本 Sample	492	**肯德基 KFC(91.3)**	**麦当劳 Macdonald's(72.6)**	**必胜客 Pizza Hut(24.8)**
价格无关心指向 indifferent orientation	85	肯德基 KFC(94.1)	麦当劳 Macdonald's(70.6)	必胜客 Pizza Hut(27.1)
中间层 medium	277	肯德基 KFC(91.0)	麦当劳 Macdonald's(72.6)	必胜客 Pizza Hut(25.3)
价格重视指向 careful orientation	130	肯德基 KFC(90.0)	麦当劳 Macdonald's(73.8)	必胜客 Pizza Hut(22.3)

3-11 重度消费者的消费者层构成/ The Composition of the Heavy Consumers

3-11-1 时尚流行指标/ Fads popular Index

	人数 Number	平实生活指向 simple living orientation	时尚流行指向 fashion orientation
样本 Sample	192	26.0	74.0
一周 1 次或以上 once a week or over	41	24.4	75.6
两周 1 次左右 about once every two weeks	151	26.5	73.5

3-11-2 价格态度指标/ Price Attitude Index

	人数 Number	价格无关心指向 indifferent orientation	中间层 medium	价格重视指向 careful orientation
样本 Sample	193	22.8	58.0	19.2
一周 1 次或以上 once a week or over	41	17.1	65.9	17.1
两周 1 次左右 about once every two weeks	152	24.3	55.9	19.7

● 广州 / Guangzhou

3-1 最近三个月是否去过西式快餐店的比例/ Proportion of the Sample Visiting Western-style Fast-food Restaurants in the Last Three Months

	人数 Number	百分比 Percent
去过 yes	547	52.9
没去过 no	487	47.1

n=1034

3-2 最常去的西式快餐店排名/ Ranking of the Western-style Fast-food Restaurants Visited Most Frequently

注：本题为多选题，合计百分比超过 100%（Multiple answers）

排名 Brand Ranking	品牌 Brands	人次 Person-time	百分比 Percent
1	麦当劳 Macdonald's	486	89.0
2	肯德基 KFC	350	64.1
3	必胜客 Pizza Hut	104	19.0
4	添美食 Pimmy's	37	6.8
5	大西豪 Daxihao	36	6.6
6	大快活 Firewood	27	4.9

n=546

3-3 样本、男性各年龄层、女性各年龄层最近三个月是否去过西式快餐店的比例/ Whether Having Visited Western-style Fast-food Restaurants in the Last Three Months by the Whole Sample, Age and Gender Groups

	人数 Number	去过 yes	没去过 no
样本 Sample	1034	52.9	47.1
男性 Male	499	49.3	50.7
16~24 岁 Age	106	62.3	37.7
25~34 岁 Age	150	60.0	40.0
35~44 岁 Age	127	45.7	54.3
45~54 岁 Age	73	30.1	69.9
55~60 岁 Age	43	23.3	76.7
女性 Female	535	56.3	43.7
16~24 岁 Age	112	71.4	28.6
25~34 岁 Age	158	64.6	35.4
35~44 岁 Age	137	57.7	42.3
45~54 岁 Age	87	36.8	63.2
55~60 岁 Age	41	19.5	80.5

3-4 样本、男性各年龄层、女性各年龄层最近三个月去西式快餐店的频率/ Frequencies of Visiting Western-style Fast-food Restaurants in the Last Three Months by the Whole Sample, Age and Gender Groups

	人数 Number	一周 1 次或以上 once a week or over	两周 1 次左右 about once every two weeks	约一个月 1 次 about once a month	两三个月 1 次及以下 once every 2 or 3 months or below
样本 Sample	542	10.0	29.0	41.5	19.6
男性 Male	243	9.9	25.9	43.6	20.6
16~24 岁 Age	66	18.2	22.7	47.0	12.1
25~34 岁 Age	89	6.7	31.5	47.2	14.6
35~44 岁 Age	56	7.1	23.2	41.1	28.6
45~54 岁 Age	22	4.5	27.3	27.3	40.9
55~60 岁 Age	10	10.0	10.0	40.0	40.0
女性 Female	299	10.0	31.4	39.8	18.7
16~24 岁 Age	79	12.7	44.3	30.4	12.7
25~34 岁 Age	102	11.8	30.4	37.3	20.6
35~44 岁 Age	78	7.7	23.1	50.0	19.2
45~54 岁 Age	32	3.1	25.0	40.6	31.3
55~60 岁 Age	8	12.5	25.0	62.5	0.0

3-5 样本、男性各年龄层、女性各年龄层最近一次在西式快餐店的花费/ Expense in the Most Recent Visit to Western-style Fast-food Restaurant by the Whole Sample, Age and Gender Groups

	人数 Number	10 元及以下 10 yuan or below	11-20 元 yuan	21-30 元 yuan	31-40 元 yuan	41-50 元 yuan	51-70 元 yuan	71-100 元 yuan	100 元以上 over 100 yuan
样本 Sample	546	5.5	49.6	36.1	4.9	3.5	0.2	0.2	0.0
男性 Male	246	3.7	46.7	40.7	5.3	3.7	0.0	0.0	0.0
16~24 岁 Age	66	1.5	43.9	39.4	7.6	7.6	0.0	0.0	0.0
25~34 岁 Age	90	2.2	44.4	46.7	3.3	3.3	0.0	0.0	0.0
35~44 岁 Age	58	5.2	50.0	39.7	3.4	1.7	0.0	0.0	0.0
45~54 岁 Age	22	4.5	50.0	36.4	9.1	0.0	0.0	0.0	0.0
55~60 岁 Age	10	20.0	60.0	10.0	10.0	0.0	0.0	0.0	0.0
女性 Female	300	7.0	52.0	32.3	4.7	3.3	0.3	0.3	0.0
16~24 岁 Age	79	6.3	49.4	35.4	2.5	5.1	1.3	0.0	0.0
25~34 岁 Age	102	7.8	52.0	30.4	7.8	1.0	0.0	1.0	0.0
35~44 岁 Age	79	3.8	49.4	36.7	5.1	5.1	0.0	0.0	0.0
45~54 岁 Age	32	15.6	62.5	18.8	0.0	3.1	0.0	0.0	0.0
55~60 岁 Age	8	0.0	62.5	37.5	0.0	0.0	0.0	0.0	0.0

3-6 样本、男性各年龄层、女性各年龄层常与谁一起去西式快餐店/ With Whom When Visiting Western-style Fast-food Restaurant by the Whole Sample, Age and Gender Groups

	人数 Number	和家人或亲戚 family members & relatives	和朋友 friends	和同事/同学 colleagues or schoolmates	单独 single
样本 Sample	**538**	**54.5**	**28.8**	**13.8**	**3.0**
男性 Male	**241**	**47.3**	**34.0**	**15.4**	**3.3**
16~24 岁 Age	62	19.4	51.6	24.2	4.8
25~34 岁 Age	89	34.8	43.8	15.7	5.6
35~44 岁 Age	58	84.5	13.8	1.7	0.0
45~54 岁 Age	22	68.2	9.1	22.7	0.0
55~60 岁 Age	10	70.0	10.0	20.0	0.0
女性 Female	**297**	**60.3**	**24.6**	**12.5**	**2.7**
16~24 岁 Age	80	23.8	46.3	28.8	1.3
25~34 岁 Age	101	65.3	21.8	7.9	5.0
35~44 岁 Age	76	80.3	10.5	7.9	1.3
45~54 岁 Age	32	81.3	15.6	0.0	3.1
55~60 岁 Age	8	87.5	12.5	0.0	0.0

3-7 样本、男性各年龄层、女性各年龄层对就餐方式的喜好/ Preferred Categories of Western-style Fast-food Restaurant by the Whole Sample, Age and Gender Groups

	人数 Number	外卖 take-out	店内吃 in the restaurant
样本 Sample	**545**	**4.8**	**95.2**
男性 Male	**245**	**3.7**	**96.3**
16~24 岁 Age	66	6.1	93.9
25~34 岁 Age	90	3.3	96.7
35~44 岁 Age	57	1.8	98.2
45~54 岁 Age	22	4.5	95.5
55~60 岁 Age	10	0.0	100.0
女性 Female	**300**	**5.7**	**94.3**
16~24 岁 Age	80	7.5	92.5
25~34 岁 Age	101	5.0	95.0
35~44 岁 Age	79	1.3	98.7
45~54 岁 Age	32	15.6	84.4
55~60 岁 Age	8	0.0	100.0

3-8 选择西式快餐店的考虑因素/ Ranking of the Considerations of Choosing a Western-style Fast-food Restaurant

注：本题为多选题，合计百分比超过 100%（Multiple answers）

排名 Ranking	考虑因素 Considerations	人次 Person-time	百分比 Percent
1	口味好 good taste	314	57.9
2	卫生 clean	222	41.0
3	就近 close to reach	197	36.3
4	方便、迅速 convenient and quickly	187	34.5
5	服务态度好 good services	110	20.3
6	价格适中 reasonable price	73	13.5
7	店面布置有特色 special display in the restaurant	43	7.9
8	有特色活动（如生日餐等）special activities (birthday party e	29	5.4
9	其他 others	9	1.7

n=542

3-9 重度消费者的人口分布/ Demographics of the Heavy Consumers

	人数 Number	16-24 岁 Age	25-34 岁 Age	35-44 岁 Age	45-54 岁 Age	55-60 岁 Age
样本 Sample	211	34.1	36.5	19.4	7.6	2.4
男性 Male	87	31.0	39.1	19.5	8.0	2.3
一周 1 次或以上 once a week or over	24	50.0	25.0	16.7	4.2	4.2
两周 1 次左右 about once every two weeks	63	23.8	44.4	20.6	9.5	1.6
女性 Female	124	36.3	34.7	19.4	7.3	2.4
一周 1 次或以上 once a week or over	30	33.3	40.0	20.0	3.3	3.3
两周 1 次左右 about once every two weeks	94	37.2	33.0	19.1	8.5	2.1

3-10 不同消费者层常去的西式快餐店/ Western Style Fast-food Restaurants Visited Most Frequently by Market Segments

3-10-1 时尚流行指标/ Fads Popular Index

注：本题为多选题，合计百分比超过 100%（Multiple answers）

	人数 Number	第一品牌及百分比 1st/ percent	第二品牌及百分比 2nd/ percent	第三品牌及百分比 3rd/ percent	第四品牌及百分比 4th/ percent
样本 Sample	541	**麦当劳 Macdonald's(89.1)**	**肯德基 KFC(64.1)**	**必胜客 Pizza Hut(19.0)**	**添美食 Pimmy's(6.8)**
平实生活指向 simple living orientation	226	麦当劳 Macdonald's(86.7)	肯德基 KFC(60.2)	必胜客 Pizza Hut(12.4)	添美食 Pimmy's(6.2)
时尚流行指向 fashion orientation	315	麦当劳 Macdonald's(90.8)	肯德基 KFC(67.0)	必胜客 Pizza Hut(23.8)	大西豪 Daxihao(7.6)

3-10-2 价格态度指标/ Price Attitude Index

注：本题为多选题，合计百分比超过 100%（Multiple answers）

	人数 Number	第一品牌及百分比 1st/ percent	第二品牌及百分比 2nd/ percent	第三品牌及百分比 3rd/ percent	第四品牌及百分比 4th/ percent
样本 Sample	544	**麦当劳 Macdonald's(89.0)**	**肯德基 KFC(64.2)**	**必胜客 Pizza Hut(19.1)**	**添美食 Pimmy's(6.8)**
价格无关心指向 indifferent orientation	104	麦当劳 Macdonald's(92.3)	肯德基 KFC(59.6)	必胜客 Pizza Hut(21.2)	大西豪 Daxihao(6.7)
中间层 medium	300	麦当劳 Macdonald's(90.0)	肯德基 KFC(65.3)	必胜客 Pizza Hut(20.3)	大西豪 Daxihao(7.0) 添美食 Pimmy's(7.0)
价格重视指向 careful orientation	140	麦当劳 Macdonald's(84.3)	肯德基 KFC(65.0)	必胜客 Pizza Hut(15.0)	添美食 Pimmy's(7.1)

3-11 重度消费者的消费者层构成/ The Composition of the Heavy Consumers

3-11-1 时尚流行指标/ Fads popular Index

	人数 Number	平实生活指向 simple living orientation	时尚流行指向 fashion orientation
样本 Sample	209	33.0	67.0
一周 1 次或以上 once a week or over	53	28.3	71.7
两周 1 次左右 about once every two weeks	156	34.6	65.4

3-11-2 价格态度指标/ Price Attitude Index

	人数 Number	价格无关心指向 indifferent orientation	中间层 medium	价格重视指向 careful orientation
样本 Sample	211	20.9	55.9	23.2
一周 1 次或以上 once a week or over	54	14.8	59.3	25.9
两周 1 次左右 about once every two weeks	157	22.9	54.8	22.3

● 重庆 / Chongqing

3-1 最近三个月是否去过西式快餐店的比例/ Proportion of the Sample Visiting Western-style Fast-food Restaurants in the Last Three Months

	人数 Number	百分比 Percent
去过 yes	130	20.8
没去过 no	494	79.2

n=624

3-2 最常去的西式快餐店排名/ Ranking of the Western-style Fast-food Restaurants Visited Most Frequently

注：本题为多选题，合计百分比超过 100%（Multiple answers）

排名 Brand Ranking	品牌 Brands	人次 Person-time	百分比 Percent
1	肯德基 KFC	105	80.8
2	德克士 Dicos	79	60.8

n=130

3-3 样本、男性各年龄层、女性各年龄层最近三个月是否去过西式快餐店的比例/ Whether Having Visited Western-style Fast-food Restaurants in the Last Three Months by the Whole Sample, Age and Gender Groups

	人数 Number	去过 yes	没去过 no
样本 Sample	**624**	**20.8**	**79.2**
男性 Male	314	19.4	80.6
16~24 岁 Age	64	29.7	70.3
25~34 岁 Age	93	22.6	77.4
35~44 岁 Age	75	12.0	88.0
45~54 岁 Age	54	14.8	85.2
55~60 岁 Age	28	14.3	85.7
女性 Female	310	22.3	77.7
16~24 岁 Age	64	42.2	57.8
25~34 岁 Age	90	27.8	72.2
35~44 岁 Age	73	12.3	87.7
45~54 岁 Age	60	13.3	86.7
55~60 岁 Age	23	0.0	100.0

3-4 样本、男性各年龄层、女性各年龄层最近三个月去西式快餐店的频率/ Frequencies of Visiting Western-style Fast-food Restaurants in the Last Three Months by the Whole Sample, Age and Gender Groups

	人数 Number	一周 1 次或以上 once a week or over	两周 1 次左右 about once every two weeks	约一个月 1 次 about once a month	两三个月 1 次及以下 once every 2 or 3 months or below
样本 Sample	**130**	**6.2**	**16.2**	**41.5**	**36.2**
男性 Male	61	6.6	14.8	37.7	41.0
16~24 岁 Age	19	10.5	10.5	36.8	42.1
25~34 岁 Age	21	4.8	19.0	52.4	23.8
35~44 岁 Age	9	11.1	11.1	22.2	55.6
45~54 岁 Age	8	0.0	25.0	25.0	50.0
55~60 岁 Age	4	0.0	0.0	25.0	75.0
女性 Female	69	5.8	17.4	44.9	31.9
16~24 岁 Age	27	11.1	22.2	48.1	18.5
25~34 岁 Age	25	4.0	12.0	36.0	48.0
35~44 岁 Age	9	0.0	11.1	55.6	33.3
45~54 岁 Age	8	0.0	25.0	50.0	25.0
55~60 岁 Age	0	0.0	0.0	0.0	0

3-5 样本、男性各年龄层、女性各年龄层最近一次在西式快餐店的花费/ Expense in the Most Recent Visit to Western-style Fast-food Restaurant by the Whole Sample, Age and Gender Groups

	人数 Number	10 元及以下 10 yuan or below	11-20 元 yuan	21-30 元 yuan	31-40 元 yuan	41-50 元 yuan	51-70 元 yuan	71-100 元 yuan	100 元以上 over 100 yuan
样本 Sample	130	3.8	30.8	26.9	9.2	13.8	4.6	3.1	7.7
男性 Male	61	6.6	16.4	32.8	9.8	14.8	6.6	3.3	9.8
16~24 岁 Age	19	10.5	10.5	36.8	5.3	21.1	10.5	0.0	5.3
25~34 岁 Age	21	4.8	19.0	19.0	23.8	19.0	4.8	4.8	4.8
35~44 岁 Age	9	11.1	11.1	55.6	0.0	11.1	0.0	0.0	11.1
45~54 岁 Age	8	0.0	25.0	37.5	0.0	0.0	0.0	12.5	25.0
55~60 岁 Age	4	0.0	25.0	25.0	0.0	0.0	25.0	0.0	25.0
女性 Female	69	1.4	43.5	21.7	8.7	13.0	2.9	2.9	5.8
16~24 岁 Age	27	0.0	44.4	33.3	7.4	11.1	0.0	3.7	0.0
25~34 岁 Age	25	0.0	40.0	12.0	12.0	16.0	8.0	4.0	8.0
35~44 岁 Age	9	0.0	33.3	11.1	11.1	22.2	0.0	0.0	22.2
45~54 岁 Age	8	12.5	62.5	25.0	0.0	0.0	0.0	0.0	0.0
55~60 岁 Age	0	0	0	0	0	0	0	0	0

3-6 样本、男性各年龄层、女性各年龄层常与谁一起去西式快餐店/ With Whom When Visiting Western-style Fast-food Restaurant by the Whole Sample, Age and Gender Groups

	人数 Number	和家人或亲戚 family members & relatives	和朋友 friends	和同事/同学 colleagues or schoolmates	单独 single
样本 Sample	130	48.5	34.6	12.3	4.6
男性 Male	61	39.3	37.7	13.1	9.8
16~24 岁 Age	19	10.5	42.1	31.6	15.8
25~34 岁 Age	21	38.1	47.6	9.5	4.8
35~44 岁 Age	9	44.4	44.4	0.0	11.1
45~54 岁 Age	8	87.5	0.0	0.0	12.5
55~60 岁 Age	4	75.0	25.0	0.0	0.0
女性 Female	69	56.5	31.9	11.6	0.0
16~24 岁 Age	27	11.1	66.7	22.2	0.0
25~34 岁 Age	25	80.0	16.0	4.0	0.0
35~44 岁 Age	9	88.9	0.0	11.1	0.0
45~54 岁 Age	8	100.0	0.0	0.0	0.0
55~60 岁 Age	0	0.0	0.0	0.0	0.0

3-7 样本、男性各年龄层、女性各年龄层对就餐方式的喜好/ Preferred Categories of Western-style Fast-food Restaurant by the Whole Sample, Age and Gender Groups

	人数 Number	外卖 take-out	店内吃 in the restaurant
样本 Sample	130	6.9	93.1
男性 Male	61	8.2	91.8
16~24 岁 Age	19	5.3	94.7
25~34 岁 Age	21	4.8	95.2
35~44 岁 Age	9	22.2	77.8
45~54 岁 Age	8	12.5	87.5
55~60 岁 Age	4	0.0	100.0
女性 Female	69	5.8	94.2
16~24 岁 Age	27	7.4	92.6
25~34 岁 Age	25	4.0	96.0
35~44 岁 Age	9	11.1	88.9
45~54 岁 Age	8	0.0	100.0
55~60 岁 Age	0	0.0	0.0

3-8 选择西式快餐店的考虑因素/ Ranking of the Considerations of Choosing a Western-style Fast-food Restaurant

注：本题为多选题，合计百分比超过 100%（Multiple answers）

排名 Ranking	考虑因素 Considerations	人次 Person-time	百分比 Percent
1	口味好 good taste	86	67.2
2	卫生 clean	52	40.6
3	店面布置有特色 special display in the restaurant	35	27.3
3	方便、迅速 convenient and quickly	35	27.3
4	服务态度好 good services	22	17.2
4	有特色活动（如生日餐等）special activities (birthday party etc.)	22	17.2
5	价格适中 reasonable price	18	14.1
6	就近 close to reach	11	8.6
7	其他 others	4	3.1

n=128

3-9 重度消费者的人口分布/ Demographics of the Heavy Consumers

	人数 Number	16-24 岁 Age	25-34 岁 Age	35-44 岁 Age	45-54 岁 Age	55-60 岁 Age
样本 Sample	29	44.8	31.0	10.3	13.8	0.0
男性 Male	13	30.8	38.5	15.4	15.4	0.0
一周 1 次或以上 once a week or over	4	50.0	25.0	25.0	0.0	0.0
两周 1 次左右 about once every two weeks	9	22.2	44.4	11.1	22.2	0.0
女性 Female	16	56.3	25.0	6.3	12.5	0.0
一周 1 次或以上 once a week or over	4	75.0	25.0	0.0	0.0	0.0
两周 1 次左右 about once every two weeks	12	50.0	25.0	8.3	16.7	0.0

3-10 不同消费者层常去的西式快餐店/ Western Style Fast-food Restaurants Visited Most Frequently by Market Segments

3-10-1 时尚流行指标/ Fads Popular Index

注：本题为多选题，合计百分比超过 100%（Multiple answers）

	人数 Number	第一品牌及百分比 1st/ percent	第二品牌及百分比 2nd/ percent	第三品牌及百分比 3rd/ percent
样本 Sample	128	**肯德基 KFC(80.5)**	**德克士 Dicos(60.9)**	**芳香鸡 CFC(0.8) 美国乡村鸡 Mei Guo Xiang Chun Ji(0.8) 开心汤姆 HAPPY TOM(0.8)**
平实生活指向 simple living orientation	51	肯德基 KFC(82.4)	德克士 Dicos(56.9)	美国乡村鸡 Mei Guo Xiang Chun Ji (2.0)
时尚流行指向 fashion orientation	77	肯德基 KFC(79.2)	德克士 Dicos(63.6)	芳香鸡 CFC(1.3) 开心汤姆 HAPPY TOM(1.3)

3-10-2 价格态度指标/ Price Attitude Index

注：本题为多选题，合计百分比超过 100%（Multiple answers）

	人数 Number	第一品牌及百分比 1st/ percent	第二品牌及百分比 2nd/ percent	第三品牌及百分比 3rd/ percent
样本 Sample	128	**肯德基 KFC(80.5)**	**德克士 Dicos(60.2)**	**芳香鸡 CFC(0.8) 美国乡村鸡 Mei Guo Xiang Chun Ji(0.8) 开心汤姆 HAPPY TOM(0.8)**
价格无关心指向 indifferent orientation	37	肯德基 KFC(75.7)	德克士 Dicos(59.5)	美国乡村鸡 Mei Guo Xiang Chun Ji(2.7) 开心汤姆 HAPPY TOM(2.7)
中间层 medium	67	肯德基 KFC(83.6)	德克士 Dicos(61.2)	芳香鸡 CFC(1.5)
价格重视指向 careful orientation	24	肯德基 KFC(79.2)	德克士 Dicos(58.3)	

3-11 重度消费者的消费者层构成/ The Composition of the Heavy Consumers

3-11-1 时尚流行指标/ Fads popular Index

	人数 Number	平实生活指向 simple living orientation	时尚流行指向 fashion orientation
样本 Sample	29	31.0	69.0
一周 1 次或以上 once a week or over	8	37.5	62.5
两周 1 次左右 about once every two weeks	21	28.6	71.4

3-11-2 价格态度指标/ Price Attitude Index

	人数 Number	价格无关心指向 indifferent orientation	中间层 medium	价格重视指向 careful orientation
样本 Sample	29	51.7	37.9	10.3
一周 1 次或以上 once a week or over	8	62.5	37.5	0.0
两周 1 次左右 about once every two weeks	21	47.6	38.1	14.3

● 武汉 / Wuhan

3-1 最近三个月是否去过西式快餐店的比例/ Proportion of the Sample Visiting Western-style Fast-food Restaurants in the Last Three Months

	人数 Number	百分比 Percent
去过 yes	216	33.8
没去过 no	423	66.2

n=639

3-2 最常去的西式快餐店排名/ Ranking of the Western-style Fast-food Restaurants Visited Most Frequently

注：本题为多选题，合计百分比超过 100%（Multiple answers）

排名 Brand Ranking	品牌 Brands	人次 Person-time	百分比 Percent
1	肯德基 KFC	185	85.6
2	麦当劳 Macdonald's	183	84.7
3	德克士 Dicos	9	4.2

n=216

3-3 样本、男性各年龄层、女性各年龄层最近三个月是否去过西式快餐店的比例/ Whether having Visited Western-style Fast-food Restaurants in the Last Three Months by the Whole Sample, Age and Gender Groups

	人数 Number	去过 yes	没去过 no
样本 Sample	639	33.8	66.2
男性 Male	310	31.0	69.0
16~24 岁 Age	65	55.4	44.6
25~34 岁 Age	89	46.1	53.9
35~44 岁 Age	80	15.0	85.0
45~54 岁 Age	52	11.5	88.5
55~60 岁 Age	24	4.2	95.8
女性 Female	329	36.5	63.5
16~24 岁 Age	68	63.2	36.8
25~34 岁 Age	95	55.8	44.2
35~44 岁 Age	78	14.1	85.9
45~54 岁 Age	62	17.7	82.3
55~60 岁 Age	26	7.7	92.3

3-4 样本、男性各年龄层、女性各年龄层最近三个月去西式快餐店的频率/ Frequencies of Visiting Western-style Fast-food Restaurants in the Last Three Months by the Whole Sample, Age and Gender Groups

	人数 Number	一周 1 次或以上 once a week or over	两周 1 次左右 about once two weeks	约一个月 1 次 about once a month	两三个月 1 次及以下 once 2 or 3 months or below
样本 Sample	216	10.6	21.3	39.4	28.7
男性 Male	96	9.4	24.0	38.5	28.1
16~24 岁 Age	36	5.6	19.4	44.4	30.6
25~34 岁 Age	41	17.1	22.0	36.6	24.4
35~44 岁 Age	12	0.0	33.3	41.7	25.0
45~54 岁 Age	6	0.0	50.0	16.7	33.3
55~60 岁 Age	1	0.0	0.0	0.0	100.0
女性 Female	120	11.7	19.2	40.0	29.2
16~24 岁 Age	43	9.3	27.9	44.2	18.6
25~34 岁 Age	53	15.1	17.0	47.2	20.8
35~44 岁 Age	11	9.1	18.2	9.1	63.6
45~54 岁 Age	11	9.1	0.0	27.3	63.6
55~60 岁 Age	2	0.0	0.0	0.0	100.0

3-5 样本、男性各年龄层、女性各年龄层最近一次在西式快餐店的花费/ Expense in the Most Recent Visit to Western-style Fast-food Restaurant by the Whole Sample, Age and Gender Groups

	人数 Number	10 元及以下 10 yuan or below	11-20 元 yuan	21-30 元 yuan	31-40 元 yuan	41-50 元 yuan	51-70 元 yuan	71-100 元 yuan	100 元以上 over 100 yuan
样本 Sample	216	6.0	44.0	30.1	5.6	11.1	1.4	1.9	0.0
男性 Male	96	3.1	39.6	25.0	9.4	17.7	2.1	3.1	0.0
16~24 岁 Age	36	2.8	47.2	22.2	11.1	13.9	0.0	2.8	0.0
25~34 岁 Age	41	2.4	39.0	26.8	7.3	19.5	2.4	2.4	0.0
35~44 岁 Age	12	8.3	16.7	33.3	16.7	16.7	8.3	0.0	0.0
45~54 岁 Age	6	0.0	50.0	16.7	0.0	16.7	0.0	16.7	0.0
55~60 岁 Age	1	0.0	0.0	0.0	0.0	100.0	0.0	0.0	0.0
女性 Female	120	8.3	47.5	34.2	2.5	5.8	0.8	0.8	0.0
16~24 岁 Age	43	7.0	55.8	30.2	0.0	4.7	2.3	0.0	0.0
25~34 岁 Age	53	7.5	43.4	35.8	5.7	7.5	0.0	0.0	0.0
35~44 岁 Age	11	9.1	36.4	54.5	0.0	0.0	0.0	0.0	0.0
45~54 岁 Age	11	0.0	54.5	27.3	0.0	9.1	0.0	9.1	0.0
55~60 岁 Age	2	100.0	0.0	0.0	0.0	0.0	0.0	0.0	0.0

3-6 样本、男性各年龄层、女性各年龄层常与谁一起去西式快餐店/ With Whom When Visiting Western-style Fast-food Restaurant by the Whole Sample, Age and Gender Groups

	人数 Number	和家人或亲戚 family members & relatives	和朋友 friends	和同事/同学 colleagues or schoolmates	单独 single
样本 Sample	215	48.4	35.3	13.5	2.8
男性 Male	95	38.9	43.2	13.7	4.2
16~24 岁 Age	36	8.3	63.9	25.0	2.8
25~34 岁 Age	41	41.5	43.9	7.3	7.3
35~44 岁 Age	11	90.9	0.0	9.1	0.0
45~54 岁 Age	6	100.0	0.0	0.0	0.0
55~60 岁 Age	1	100.0	0.0	0.0	0.0
女性 Female	120	55.8	29.2	13.3	1.7
16~24 岁 Age	43	11.6	55.8	30.2	2.3
25~34 岁 Age	53	73.6	20.8	3.8	1.9
35~44 岁 Age	11	100.0	0.0	0.0	0.0
45~54 岁 Age	11	90.9	0.0	9.1	0.0
55~60 岁 Age	2	100.0	0.0	0.0	0.0

3-7 样本、男性各年龄层、女性各年龄层对就餐方式的喜好/ Preferred Categories of Western-style Fast-food Restaurant by the Whole Sample, Age and Gender Groups

	人数 Number	外卖 take-out	店内吃 in the restaurant
样本 Sample	216	2.8	97.2
男性 Male	96	3.1	96.9
16~24 岁 Age	36	2.8	97.2
25~34 岁 Age	41	0.0	100.0
35~44 岁 Age	12	0.0	100.0
45~54 岁 Age	6	33.3	66.7
55~60 岁 Age	1	0.0	100.0
女性 Female	120	2.5	97.5
16~24 岁 Age	43	2.3	97.7
25~34 岁 Age	53	1.9	98.1
35~44 岁 Age	11	0.0	100.0
45~54 岁 Age	11	9.1	90.9
55~60 岁 Age	2	0.0	100.0

3-8 选择西式快餐店的考虑因素/ Ranking of the Considerations of Choosing a Western-style Fast-food Restaurant

注：本题为多选题，合计百分比超过 100%（Multiple answers）

排名 Ranking	考虑因素 Considerations	人次 Person-time	百分比 Percent
1	口味好 good taste	124	57.7
2	卫生 clean	98	45.6
3	方便、迅速 convenient and quickly	74	34.4
4	就近 close to reach	51	23.7
4	服务态度好 good services	51	23.7
4	店面布置有特色 special display in the restaurant	51	23.7
5	价格适中 reasonable price	35	16.3
6	有特色活动（如生日餐等）special activities (birthday party etc.)	18	8.4
7	其他 others	8	3.7

n=215

3-9 重度消费者的人口分布/ Demographics of the Heavy Consumers

	人数 Number	16-24 岁 Age	25-34 岁 Age	35-44 岁 Age	45-54 岁 Age	55-60 岁 Age
样本 Sample	69	36.2	47.8	10.1	5.8	0.0
男性 Male	32	28.1	50.0	12.5	9.4	0.0
一周 1 次或以上 once a week or over	9	22.2	77.8	0.0	0.0	0.0
两周 1 次左右 about once two weeks	23	30.4	39.1	17.4	13.0	0.0
女性 Female	37	43.2	45.9	8.1	2.7	0.0
一周 1 次或以上 once a week or over	14	28.6	57.1	7.1	7.1	0.0
两周 1 次左右 about once two weeks	23	52.2	39.1	8.7	0.0	0.0

3-10 不同消费者层常去的西式快餐店/ Western Style Fast-food Restaurants Visited Most Frequently by Market Segments

3-10-1 时尚流行指标/ Fads Popular Index

注：本题为多选题，合计百分比超过 100%（Multiple answers）

	人数 Number	第一品牌及百分比 1st/ percent	第二品牌及百分比 2nd/ percent	第三品牌及百分比 3rd/ percent
样本 Sample	212	**肯德基 KFC(85.4)**	**麦当劳 Macdonald's(84.9)**	**德克士 Dicos(4.2)**
平实生活指向 simple living orientation	85	麦当劳 Macdonald's(82.4)	肯德基 KFC(76.5)	德克士 Dicos(4.7)
时尚流行指向 fashion orientation	127	肯德基 KFC(91.3)	麦当劳 Macdonald's(86.6)	德克士 Dicos(3.9)

3-10-2 价格态度指标/ Price Attitude Index

注：本题为多选题，合计百分比超过 100%（Multiple answers）

	人数 Number	第一品牌及百分比 1st/ percent	第二品牌及百分比 2nd/ percent	第三品牌及百分比 3rd/ percent
样本 Sample	212	**肯德基 KFC(85.4)**	**麦当劳 Macdonald's(84.9)**	**德克士 Dicos(4.2)**
价格无关心指向 indifferent orientation	35	麦当劳 Macdonald's(82.9)	肯德基 KFC(77.1)	德克士 Dicos(5.7)
中间层 medium	122	肯德基 KFC(86.1)	麦当劳 Macdonald's(82.8)	德克士 Dicos(4.9)
价格重视指向 careful orientation	55	麦当劳 Macdonald's(90.9)	肯德基 KFC(89.1)	德克士 Dicos(1.8)

3-11 重度消费者的消费者层构成/ The Composition of the Heavy Consumers

3-11-1 时尚流行指标/ Fads popular Index

	人数 Number	平实生活指向 simple living orientation	时尚流行指向 fashion orientation
样本 Sample	68	29.4	70.6
一周 1 次或以上 once a week or over	22	27.3	72.7
两周 1 次左右 about once every two weeks	46	30.4	69.6

3-11-2 价格态度指标/ Price Attitude Index

	人数 Number	价格无关心指向 indifferent orientation	中间层 medium	价格重视指向 careful orientation
样本 Sample	67	19.4	58.2	22.4
一周 1 次或以上 once a week or over	22	18.2	45.5	36.4
两周 1 次左右 about once every two weeks	45	20.0	64.4	15.6

● 西安 / Xi'an

3-1 最近三个月是否去过西式快餐店的比例/ Proportion of the Sample Visiting Western-style Fast-food Restaurants in the Last Three Months

	人数 Number	百分比 Percent
去过 yes	169	28.1
没去过 no	432	71.9

n=601

3-2 最常去的西式快餐店排名/ Ranking of the Western-style Fast-food Restaurants Visited Most Frequently

注：本题为多选题，合计百分比超过 100%（Multiple answers）

排名 Brand Ranking	品牌 Brands	人次 Person-time	百分比 Percent
1	肯德基 KFC	158	94.0
2	德克士 Dicos	48	28.6
3	大磨坊 De'lifrance	3	1.8
4	堡之碧 B & B	2	1.2

n=168

3-3 样本、男性各年龄层、女性各年龄层最近三个月是否去过西式快餐店的比例/ Whether Having Visited Western-style Fast-food Restaurants in the Last Three Months by the Whole Sample, Age and Gender Groups

	人数 Number	去过 yes	没去过 no
样本 Sample	601	28.1	71.9
男性 Male	302	26.2	73.8
16~24 岁 Age	64	37.5	62.5
25~34 岁 Age	91	18.7	81.3
35~44 岁 Age	77	37.7	62.3
45~54 岁 Age	46	13.0	87.0
55~60 岁 Age	24	12.5	87.5
女性 Female	299	30.1	69.9
16~24 岁 Age	61	34.4	65.6
25~34 岁 Age	90	42.2	57.8
35~44 岁 Age	74	28.4	71.6
45~54 岁 Age	49	10.2	89.8
55~60 岁 Age	25	20.0	80.0

3-4 样本、男性各年龄层、女性各年龄层最近三个月去西式快餐店的频率/ Frequencies of Visiting Western-style Fast-food Restaurants in the Last Three Months by the Whole Sample, Age and Gender Groups

	人数 Number	一周 1 次或以上 once a week or over	两周 1 次左右 about once every two weeks	约一个月 1 次 about once a month	两三个月 1 次及以下 once every 2 or 3 months or below
样本 Sample	168	5.4	20.2	46.4	28.0
男性 Male	79	7.6	20.3	45.6	26.6
16~24 岁 Age	24	4.2	20.8	58.3	16.7
25~34 岁 Age	17	5.9	29.4	23.5	41.2
35~44 岁 Age	29	10.3	17.2	48.3	24.1
45~54 岁 Age	6	16.7	16.7	50.0	16.7
55~60 岁 Age	3	0.0	0.0	33.3	66.7
女性 Female	89	3.4	20.2	47.2	29.2
16~24 岁 Age	21	0.0	19.0	47.6	33.3
25~34 岁 Age	38	7.9	23.7	47.4	21.1
35~44 岁 Age	21	0.0	14.3	42.9	42.9
45~54 岁 Age	5	0.0	20.0	60.0	20.0
55~60 岁 Age	4	0.0	25.0	50.0	25.0

3-5 样本、男性各年龄层、女性各年龄层最近一次在西式快餐店的花费/ Expense in the Most Recent Visit to Western-style Fast-food Restaurant by the Whole Sample, Age and Gender Groups

	人数 Number	10 元及以下 10 yuan or below	11-20 元 yuan	21-30 元 yuan	31-40 元 yuan	41-50 元 yuan	51-70 元 yuan	71-100 元 yuan	100 元以上 over 100 yuan
样本 Sample	169	0.6	18.3	33.1	11.2	21.9	3.6	9.5	1.8
男性 Male	79	0.0	15.2	29.1	12.7	22.8	2.5	15.2	2.5
16~24 岁 Age	24	0.0	16.7	25.0	8.3	25.0	4.2	16.7	4.2
25~34 岁 Age	17	0.0	17.6	41.2	17.6	0.0	0.0	23.5	0.0
35~44 岁 Age	29	0.0	13.8	31.0	17.2	27.6	3.4	6.9	0.0
45~54 岁 Age	6	0.0	0.0	16.7	0.0	50.0	0.0	16.7	16.7
55~60 岁 Age	3	0.0	33.3	0.0	0.0	33.3	0.0	33.3	0.0
女性 Female	90	1.1	21.1	36.7	10.0	21.1	4.4	4.4	1.1
16~24 岁 Age	21	4.8	14.3	38.1	19.0	14.3	4.8	4.8	0.0
25~34 岁 Age	38	0.0	23.7	36.8	7.9	23.7	5.3	0.0	2.6
35~44 岁 Age	21	0.0	14.3	28.6	9.5	28.6	4.8	14.3	0.0
45~54 岁 Age	5	0.0	40.0	60.0	0.0	0.0	0.0	0.0	0.0
55~60 岁 Age	5	0.0	40.0	40.0	0.0	20.0	0.0	0.0	0.0

3-6 样本、男性各年龄层、女性各年龄层常与谁一起去西式快餐店/ With Whom When Visiting Western-style Fast-food Restaurant by the Whole Sample, Age and Gender Groups

	人数 Number	和家人或亲戚 family members & relatives	和朋友 friends	和同事/同学 colleagues or schoolmates	单独 single
样本 Sample	168	61.3	29.2	7.1	2.4
男性 Male	79	58.2	29.1	10.1	2.5
16~24 岁 Age	24	16.7	50.0	29.2	4.2
25~34 岁 Age	17	58.8	35.3	5.9	0.0
35~44 岁 Age	29	82.8	13.8	0.0	3.4
45~54 岁 Age	6	83.3	16.7	0.0	0.0
55~60 岁 Age	3	100.0	0.0	0.0	0.0
女性 Female	89	64.0	29.2	4.5	2.2
16~24 岁 Age	21	38.1	57.1	4.8	0.0
25~34 岁 Age	37	64.9	27.0	2.7	5.4
35~44 岁 Age	21	76.2	19.0	4.8	0.0
45~54 岁 Age	5	80.0	0.0	20.0	0.0
55~60 岁 Age	5	100.0	0.0	0.0	0.0

3-7 样本、男性各年龄层、女性各年龄层对就餐方式的喜好/ Preferred Categories of Western-style Fast-food Restaurant by the Whole Sample, Age and Gender Groups

	人数 Number	外卖 take-out	店内吃 in the restaurant
样本 Sample	169	3.6	96.4
男性 Male	79	1.3	98.7
16~24 岁 Age	24	0.0	100.0
25~34 岁 Age	17	0.0	100.0
35~44 岁 Age	29	0.0	100.0
45~54 岁 Age	6	16.7	83.3
55~60 岁 Age	3	0.0	100.0
女性 Female	90	5.6	94.4
16~24 岁 Age	21	4.8	95.2
25~34 岁 Age	38	5.3	94.7
35~44 岁 Age	21	9.5	90.5
45~54 岁 Age	5	0.0	100.0
55~60 岁 Age	5	0.0	100.0

3-8 选择西式快餐店的考虑因素/ Ranking of the Considerations of Choosing a Western-style Fast-food Restaurant

注：本题为多选题，合计百分比超过 100%（Multiple answers）

排名 Ranking	考虑因素 Considerations	人次 Person-time	百分比 Percent
1	口味好 good taste	103	60.9
2	卫生 clean	87	51.5
3	方便、迅速 convenient and quickly	55	32.5
4	就近 close to reach	34	20.1
5	服务态度好 good services	31	18.3
6	店面布置有特色 special display in the restaurant	25	14.8
7	有特色活动（如生日餐等）special activities (birthday party e	16	9.5
8	价格适中 reasonable price	15	8.9
9	其他 others	2	1.2

n=169

3-9 重度消费者的人口分布/ Demographics of the Heavy Consumers

	人数 Number	16-24 岁 Age	25-34 岁 Age	35-44 岁 Age	45-54 岁 Age	55-60 岁 Age
样本 Sample	43	23.3	41.9	25.6	7.0	2.3
男性 Male	22	27.3	27.3	36.4	9.1	0.0
一周 1 次或以上 once a week or over	6	16.7	16.7	50.0	16.7	0.0
两周 1 次左右 about once every two weeks	16	31.3	31.3	31.3	6.3	0.0
女性 Female	21	19.0	57.1	14.3	4.8	4.8
一周 1 次或以上 once a week or over	3	0.0	100.0	0.0	0.0	0.0
两周 1 次左右 about once every two weeks	18	22.2	50.0	16.7	5.6	5.6

3-10 不同消费者层常去的西式快餐店/ Western Style Fast-food Restaurants Visited Most Frequently by Market Segments

3-10-1 时尚流行指标/ Fads Popular Index

注：本题为多选题，合计百分比超过 100%（Multiple answers）

	人数 Number	第一品牌及百分比 1st/ percent	第二品牌及百分比 2nd/ percent	第三品牌及百分比 3rd/ percent
样本 Sample	168	**肯德基 KFC(94.0)**	**德克士 Dicos(28.6)**	**大磨坊 De'lifrance(1.8)**
平实生活指向 simple living orientation	63	肯德基 KFC(93.7)	德克士 Dicos(19.0)	大磨坊 De'lifrance(1.6) 乐天利 Lotte(1.6)
时尚流行指向 fashion orientation	105	肯德基 KFC(94.3)	德克士 Dicos(34.3)	大磨坊 De'lifrance(1.9) 堡之碧 B & B(1.9)

3-10-2 价格态度指标/ Price Attitude Index

注：本题为多选题，合计百分比超过 100%（Multiple answers）

	人数 Number	第一品牌及百分比 1st/ percent	第二品牌及百分比 2nd/ percent	第三品牌及百分比 3rd/ percent
样本 Sample	165	**肯德基 KFC(93.9)**	**德克士 Dicos(29.1)**	**大磨坊 De'lifrance(1.8)**
价格无关心指向 indifferent orientation	46	肯德基 KFC(93.5)	德克士 Dicos(32.6)	大磨坊 De'lifrance(2.2) 乐天利 Lotte(2.2)
中间层 medium	86	肯德基 KFC(95.3)	德克士 Dicos(27.9)	大磨坊 De'lifrance(2.3) 堡之碧 B & B(2.3)
价格重视指向 careful orientation	33	肯德基 KFC(90.9)	德克士 Dicos(27.3)	

3-11 重度消费者的消费者层构成/ The Composition of the Heavy Consumers

3-11-1 时尚流行指标/ Fads popular Index

	人数 Number	平实生活指向 simple living orientation	时尚流行指向 fashion orientation
样本 Sample	43	30.2	69.8
一周 1 次或以上 once a week or over	9	44.4	55.6
两周 1 次左右 about once every two weeks	34	26.5	73.5

3-11-2 价格态度指标/ Price Attitude Index

	人数 Number	价格无关心指向 indifferent orientation	中间层 medium	价格重视指向 careful orientation
样本 Sample	42	28.6	57.1	14.3
一周 1 次或以上 once a week or over	9	11.1	55.6	33.3
两周 1 次左右 about once every two weeks	33	33.3	57.6	9.1

● 沈阳 / Shenyang

3-1 最近三个月是否去过西式快餐店的比例/ Proportion of the Sample Visiting Western-style Fast-food Restaurants in the Last Three Months

	人数 Number	百分比 Percent
去过 yes	175	29.1
没去过 no	426	70.9

n=601

3-2 最常去的西式快餐店排名/ Ranking of the Western-style Fast-food Restaurants Visited Most Frequently

注：本题为多选题，合计百分比超过 100%（Multiple answers）

排名 Brand Ranking	品牌 Brands	人次 Person-time	百分比 Percent
1	肯德基 KFC	140	80.0
2	麦当劳 Macdonald's	102	58.3
3	加州牛肉面 California Beef Noodle King	33	18.9
4	顶好快餐 Dinghao	8	4.6
5	都市快车 City Cyclone	5	2.9

n=175

3-3 样本、男性各年龄层、女性各年龄层最近三个月是否去过西式快餐店的比例/ Whether Having Visited Western-style Fast-food Restaurants in the Last Three Months by the Whole Sample, Age and Gender Groups

	人数 Number	去过 yes	没去过 no
样本 Sample	**601**	**29.1**	**70.9**
男性 Male	**299**	**28.4**	**71.6**
16~24 岁 Age	64	37.5	62.5
25~34 岁 Age	89	40.4	59.6
35~44 岁 Age	76	22.4	77.6
45~54 岁 Age	46	15.2	84.8
55~60 岁 Age	24	4.2	95.8
女性 Female	**302**	**29.8**	**70.2**
16~24 岁 Age	64	45.3	54.7
25~34 岁 Age	90	36.7	63.3
35~44 岁 Age	76	30.3	69.7
45~54 岁 Age	48	8.3	91.7
55~60 岁 Age	24	4.2	95.8

3-4 样本、男性各年龄层、女性各年龄层最近三个月去西式快餐店的频率/ Frequencies of Visiting Western-style Fast-food Restaurants in the Last Three Months by the Whole Sample, Age and Gender Groups

	人数 Number	一周 1 次或以上 once a week or over	两周 1 次左右 about once every two weeks	约一个月 1 次 about once a month	两三个月 1 次及以下 once every 2 or 3 months or below
样本 Sample	**175**	**6.9**	**18.9**	**40.0**	**34.3**
男性 Male	**85**	**7.1**	**14.1**	**41.2**	**37.6**
16~24 岁 Age	24	8.3	20.8	50.0	20.8
25~34 岁 Age	36	5.6	11.1	38.9	44.4
35~44 岁 Age	17	5.9	17.6	35.3	41.2
45~54 岁 Age	7	14.3	0.0	42.9	42.9
55~60 岁 Age	1	0.0	0.0	0.0	100.0
女性 Female	**90**	**6.7**	**23.3**	**38.9**	**31.1**
16~24 岁 Age	29	13.8	20.7	41.4	24.1
25~34 岁 Age	33	6.1	24.2	30.3	39.4
35~44 岁 Age	23	0.0	30.4	39.1	30.4
45~54 岁 Age	4	0.0	0.0	75.0	25.0
55~60 岁 Age	1	0.0	0.0	100.0	0.0

3-5 样本、男性各年龄层、女性各年龄层最近一次在西式快餐店的花费/ Expense in the Most Recent Visit to Western-style Fast-food Restaurant by the Whole Sample, Age and Gender Groups

	人数 Number	10元及以下 10 yuan or below	11-20 元 yuan	21-30 元 yuan	31-40 元 yuan	41-50 元 yuan	51-70 元 yuan	71-100 元 yuan	100 元以上 over 100 yuan
样本 Sample	175	2.9	28.0	33.1	6.3	12.0	8.0	6.9	2.9
男性 Male	85	2.4	27.1	34.1	2.4	10.6	9.4	10.6	3.5
16~24 岁 Age	24	4.2	25.0	41.7	4.2	12.5	4.2	4.2	4.2
25~34 岁 Age	36	2.8	16.7	36.1	0.0	11.1	13.9	13.9	5.6
35~44 岁 Age	17	0.0	35.3	23.5	0.0	11.8	11.8	17.6	0.0
45~54 岁 Age	7	0.0	57.1	28.6	14.3	0.0	0.0	0.0	0.0
55~60 岁 Age	1	0.0	100.0	0.0	0.0	0.0	0.0	0.0	0.0
女性 Female	90	3.3	28.9	32.2	10.0	13.3	6.7	3.3	2.2
16~24 岁 Age	29	0.0	31.0	31.0	13.8	13.8	6.9	0.0	3.4
25~34 岁 Age	33	3.0	30.3	27.3	9.1	12.1	6.1	9.1	3.0
35~44 岁 Age	23	8.7	21.7	34.8	8.7	17.4	8.7	0.0	0.0
45~54 岁 Age	4	0.0	50.0	50.0	0.0	0.0	0.0	0.0	0.0
55~60 岁 Age	1	0.0	0.0	100.0	0.0	0.0	0.0	0.0	0.0

3-6 样本、男性各年龄层、女性各年龄层常与谁一起去西式快餐店/ With Whom When Visiting Western-style Fast-food Restaurant by the Whole Sample, Age and Gender Groups

	人数 Number	和家人或亲戚 family members & relatives	和朋友 friends	和同事/同学 colleagues or schoolmates	单独 single
样本 Sample	174	52.9	31.0	13.8	2.3
男性 Male	85	44.7	37.6	14.1	3.5
16~24 岁 Age	24	8.3	58.3	29.2	4.2
25~34 岁 Age	36	44.4	44.4	8.3	2.8
35~44 岁 Age	17	70.6	11.8	11.8	5.9
45~54 岁 Age	7	100.0	0.0	0.0	0.0
55~60 岁 Age	1	100.0	0.0	0.0	0.0
女性 Female	89	60.7	24.7	13.5	1.1
16~24 岁 Age	29	24.1	44.8	31.0	0.0
25~34 岁 Age	32	71.9	21.9	3.1	3.1
35~44 岁 Age	23	82.6	8.7	8.7	0.0
45~54 岁 Age	4	100.0	0.0	0.0	0.0
55~60 岁 Age	1	100.0	0.0	0.0	0.0

3-7 样本、男性各年龄层、女性各年龄层对就餐方式的喜好/ Preferred Categories of Western-style Fast-food Restaurant by the Whole Sample, Age and Gender Groups

	人数 Number	外卖 take-out	店内吃 in the restaurant
样本 Sample	175	8.6	91.4
男性 Male	85	7.1	92.9
16~24 岁 Age	24	4.2	95.8
25~34 岁 Age	36	2.8	97.2
35~44 岁 Age	17	23.5	76.5
45~54 岁 Age	7	0.0	100.0
55~60 岁 Age	1	0.0	100.0
女性 Female	90	10.0	90.0
16~24 岁 Age	29	10.3	89.7
25~34 岁 Age	33	6.1	93.9
35~44 岁 Age	23	8.7	91.3
45~54 岁 Age	4	25.0	75.0
55~60 岁 Age	1	100.0	0.0

3-8 选择西式快餐店的考虑因素/ Ranking of the Considerations of Choosing a Western-style Fast-food Restaurant

注：本题为多选题，合计百分比超过 100%（Multiple answers）

排名 Ranking	考虑因素 Considerations	人次 Person-time	百分比 Percent
1	口味好 good taste	110	62.9
2	卫生 clean	67	38.3
3	方便、迅速 convenient and quickly	65	37.1
4	就近 close to reach	35	20.0
5	价格适中 reasonable price	30	17.1
6	服务态度好 good services	25	14.3
7	店面布置有特色 special display in the restaurant	19	10.9
8	有特色活动（如生日餐等）special activities (birthday party e	15	8.6
9	其他 others	8	4.6

n=175

3-9 重度消费者的人口分布/ Demographics of the Heavy Consumers

	人数 Number	16-24 岁 Age	25-34 岁 Age	35-44 岁 Age	45-54 岁 Age	55-60 岁 Age
样本 Sample	45	37.8	35.6	24.4	2.2	0.0
男性 Male	18	38.9	33.3	22.2	5.6	0.0
一周 1 次或以上 once a week or over	6	33.3	33.3	16.7	16.7	0.0
两周 1 次左右 about once every two weeks	12	41.7	33.3	25.0	0.0	0.0
女性 Female	27	37.0	37.0	25.9	0.0	0.0
一周 1 次或以上 once a week or over	6	66.7	33.3	0.0	0.0	0.0
两周 1 次左右 about once every two weeks	21	28.6	38.1	33.3	0.0	0.0

3-10 不同消费者层常去的西式快餐店/ Western Style Fast-food Restaurants Visited Most Frequently by Market Segments

3-10-1 时尚流行指标/ Fads Popular Index

注：本题为多选题，合计百分比超过 100%（Multiple answers）

	人数 Number	第一品牌及百分比 1st/ percent	第二品牌及百分比 2nd/ percent	第三品牌及百分比 3rd/ percent
样本 Sample	175	**肯德基 KFC(80.0)**	**麦当劳 Macdonald's(58.3)**	**加州牛肉面 California Beef Noodle King (18.9)**
平实生活指向 simple living orientation	56	肯德基 KFC(78.6)	麦当劳 Macdonald's(57.1)	加州牛肉面 California Beef Noodle King(14.3)
时尚流行指向 fashion orientation	119	肯德基 KFC(80.7)	麦当劳 Macdonald's(58.8)	加州牛肉面 California Beef Noodle King(21.0)

3-10-2 价格态度指标/ Price Attitude Index

注：本题为多选题，合计百分比超过 100%（Multiple answers）

	人数 Number	第一品牌及百分比 1st/ percent	第二品牌及百分比 2nd/ percent	第三品牌及百分比 3rd/ percent
样本 Sample	175	**肯德基 KFC(80.0)**	**麦当劳 Macdonald s(58.3)**	**加州牛肉面 California Beef Noodle King (18.9)**
价格无关心指向 indifferent orientation	38	肯德基 KFC(71.1)	麦当劳 Macdonald's(55.3)	加州牛肉面 California Beef Noodle King(18.4)
中间层 medium	100	肯德基 KFC(84.0)	麦当劳 Macdonald's(61.0)	加州牛肉面 California Beef Noodle King(20.0)
价格重视指向 careful orientation	37	肯德基 KFC(78.4)	麦当劳 Macdonald's(54.1)	加州牛肉面 California Beef Noodle King(16.2)

3-11 重度消费者的消费者层构成/ The Composition of the Heavy Consumers

3-11-1 时尚流行指标/ Fads popular Index

	人数 Number	平实生活指向 simple living orientation	时尚流行指向 fashion orientation
样本 Sample	45	22.2	77.8
一周 1 次或以上 once a week or over	12	0.0	100.0
两周 1 次左右 about once every two weeks	33	30.3	69.7

3-11-2 价格态度指标/ Price Attitude Index

	人数 Number	价格无关心指向 indifferent orientation	中间层 medium	价格重视指向 careful orientation
样本 Sample	45	26.7	57.8	15.6
一周 1 次或以上 once a week or over	12	50.0	33.3	16.7
两周 1 次左右 about once every two weeks	33	18.2	66.7	15.2

《2000 IMI 消费行为与生活形态年鉴 》读者意见征询问卷

年鉴的读者朋友：您好！

请您根据您对年鉴的使用情况填写下面问卷，便于我们在下一次年鉴编辑中进行改进。谢谢！

	非常满意	比较满意	一般	比较不满意	非常不满意	不满意部分的补充说明
对全书的整体评价	5	4	3	2	1	
第一篇 七城市基本情况与样本结构	5	4	3	2	1	
第二篇 消费者分析	5	4	3	2	1	
第三篇 消费者日常生活形态	5	4	3	2	1	
第四篇 媒介分析	5	4	3	2	1	
第五篇 食品	5	4	3	2	1	
第六篇 饮料	5	4	3	2	1	
第七篇 烟酒	5	4	3	2	1	
第八篇 洗涤日用品	5	4	3	2	1	
第九篇 化妆品、卫生用品	5	4	3	2	1	
第十篇 药品、营养保健品	5	4	3	2	1	
第十一篇 家用电器、照相器材	5	4	3	2	1	
第十二篇 电脑、通讯工具	5	4	3	2	1	
第十三篇 住房、汽车、金融、保险	5	4	3	2	1	
第十四篇 饮食、购物场所	5	4	3	2	1	

A. 在将来的 IMI 年鉴中 您最希望增加的产品类别有：	
B. 在将来的 IMI 年鉴中 您最希望增加的研究城市有：	
C. 其他改进意见	

请留下您和贵单位的联系方式，我们将为您及时提供 IMI 项目研究的相关资料：

您的姓名：________ 职务：________ 公司名称：________

联系电话：________ 传真：________ 公司地址：________

电子邮件：________ ________（邮编：____）

请将该问卷填答以后通过邮寄或传真给 IMI 年鉴编辑部：

地址：北京广播学院 IMI 年鉴编辑部（邮编：100024）

电话：8610-6576-8137　传真：8610-6577-9823　E-mail：2000info@imiyearbook.com

IMI Beijing　Feb.2000

《2000 IMI Consumer Behaviours & Life Patterns Yearbook》
Readership Survey

Thank you for using this edition of IMI yearbook. To help us improve the editing level, please complete the questionnaire with your opinions on this book. Any of your suggestions will be appreciated. Thank you for your cooperation.

	Perfect	Good	Fair	Weak	Poor	Areas you hope IMI yearbook to improve (Please specify)
Evaluation of the whole book	5	4	3	2	1	
Part 1 The General Market Conditions of the Seven Cities and Sample Compositions	5	4	3	2	1	
Part 2 Consumer Analysis	5	4	3	2	1	
Part 3 Consumers Everyday Life	5	4	3	2	1	
Part 4 Media Exposure	5	4	3	2	1	
Part 5 Food	5	4	3	2	1	
Part 6 Beverage	5	4	3	2	1	
Part 7 Alcohol Products and Cigarette	5	4	3	2	1	
Part 8 Household Necessities	5	4	3	2	1	
Part 9 Cosmetics and Napkins	5	4	3	2	1	
Part 10 Medicine and Health Care Products	5	4	3	2	1	
Part 11 Home Electronic Products	5	4	3	2	1	
Part 12 Personal Computer and Tele-communications	5	4	3	2	1	
Part 13 Housing, Car, Finance and Insurance	5	4	3	2	1	
Part 14 Restaurant and Shopping Places	5	4	3	2	1	

A. **Product categories** you hope to be added in IMI yearbook:	
B. **Cities** you hope to be added in IMI yearbook:	
C. **Other suggestions**: (Please specify)	

Please Send Us the Address of Yours or Your Company. We Will Provide the Related Materials When Available.

Name: ____________ Title: ____________ Name of your company: ____________________

Tel: ______________ Fax: ____________ Address: ____________________

E-mail Address: ____________________ ____________ (Postal code:)

Please Mail or Fax Your Reply to *The Editorial Department of IMI Yearbook*:

Address: IMI. Beijing Broadcasting Institute Postal Code: 100024

Tel: 8610-6576-8137 Fax: 8610-6577-9823 E-mail Address: 2000info@imiyearbook.com

IMI Beijing Feb.2000

请关注

IMI 年鉴在积累四年数据的基础上，在 2000 年推出更为深入的客户服务领域：

专项研究报告：IMI 年鉴的专项研究报告分析角度有三。

角度之一：**IMI“品牌-消费者”**研究

该角度专项研究报告的基本内容：

- ✧ 品牌竞争分析：主要品牌的市场占有率、本品牌的市场地位、品牌忠诚度等
- ✧ 本品牌与竞争品牌消费群分析：使用本品牌的消费者都是什么样的人，有什么样的行为和心理特征，媒介接触习惯如何，与其它品牌的消费者相比是否具有鲜明的特点；
- ✧ 重度消费者分析：本类产品的大量/主要消费者是谁，有什么样的行为特征和心理取向，媒介接触习惯如何；
- ✧ 本类产品的市场现状及发展趋势分析：普及率、使用情况、需求状况等；
- ✧ 结合以上信息进行品牌定位、目标市场锁定与媒介传达之关联分析。

角度之二：**IMI“媒介-受众”**研究

该角度专项研究报告的基本内容：

- ✧ 媒介竞争分析：城市主要媒介的分布、该媒介的市场背景以及媒介忠诚度等；
- ✧ 该媒介与当地竞争者的受众群分析：接触该媒介的受众群都是什么样的人，有什么样的行为和心理特征，与其它竞争媒介的受众相比是否有鲜明的特点；
- ✧ 忠诚受众群分析：该媒介的忠诚受众构成，忠诚受众的商品消费表现，有什么样的行为特征和心理取向，以及媒介接触习惯如何；
- ✧ 结合以上信息进行媒介定位、目标受众市场锁定与媒介传达之关联分析。

角度之三："IMI 生活者群体"研究

"IMI 生活者"的划分主要以人口的基本特征为划分指标，以其中的一个变量或两个变量对人群进行界定，关于这个界定的特殊生活者群类（"IMI 生活者群体"）可以进行有关商品的消费行为以及生活态度核心理趋向等方面的重点研究。例如我们可以针对上海地区的 25—35 岁的生活者进行有关的数据分析和描述。

专项报告的详细介绍和案例请参看 IMI 年鉴的 CD—ROM）

专项报告的表现形式：

精确的资料表格 + 直观的各类图形 + 客观的文字分析

关于 IMI 年鉴（数据库）有任何需求或疑问，请与我们联系：

地址：北京建国门内大街 8 号中粮广场 A 座 524-526 室

电话：010-65239812　010-65239814

传真：010-65239813

Email:2000sale@imiyearbook.com

http:/\www.imiyearbook.com

勘 误 表

627 页 4-4 表"不同学历的读者经常阅读的杂志"有误，请参看下表。

4-4 不同学历的读者经常阅读的杂志/ Frequently Read Magazines by Educational Levels

注：本题为多选题，合计百分比超过 100%（Multiple answers）

	人数 Number	上海电视 Shanghai TV	读者 Duzhe	青年一代 Qing Nian Yi Dai	现代家庭 Modern Family	知音 Bosom Friend	大众医学 Popular Medicine	世界时装之苑 ELLE
样本 Sample	505	23.8	16.6	12.9	12.7	9.1	6.7	4.8
小学及以下 Primary School or Below	3	33.3	0.0	33.3	33.3	0.0	0.0	0.0
初中 Middle School	98	22.4	11.2	15.3	9.2	11.2	8.2	1.0
高中/中专/技校 High School/Technical Secondary School	270	29.3	15.9	10.7	11.9	10.4	6.7	6.7
大学专科 2-3 Year College	90	11.1	21.1	18.9	17.8	4.4	7.8	3.3
大学本科 4-5 Year College	40	17.5	25.0	7.5	12.5	5.0	2.5	2.5
研究生或以上 Graduate or Above	4	25.0	25.0	0.0	25.0	25.0	0.0	25.0

ISBN 7-81004-859-7

9 787810 048590 >

责任编辑：姜树琪　韩旺辰　陈友军

图书在版编目（CIP）数据

2000IMI 消费行为与生活形态年鉴/北京创研研究所编.
北京：北京广播学院出版社，2000.3
ISBN 7-81004-859-7

I.I…　II.北…　III.①消费形式—中国—年鉴②生活方式—中国—年鉴　IV. D669.3-54

中国版本图书馆 CIP 数据核字（2000）第 14398 号

2000IMI 消费行为与生活形态年鉴
（上下卷）
北京广播学院出版社发行
新华书店经销
煤炭工业出版社印刷厂印刷
889×1194 毫米 16 开 155.25 印张 3870 千字
2000 年 2 月第 1 版 2000 年 2 月第 1 次印刷
印数：1-3000 册
ISBN 7-81004-859-7/G・504
定价：2000.00 元

2000IMI消费行为与生活形态年鉴

北京·上海·广州·重庆·武汉·西安·沈阳

IMI（创研）市场信息研究所　　人民日报华泰投资管理有限公司
北京广播学院广告学系　　《国际广告》杂志社

上卷

Y&D Marketing Service LTD.
北京华泰创研数据有限公司

北京广播学院出版社

1-7 样本、男性各年龄层、女性各年龄层的品牌习惯/ Brand Habit in Consuming Carbonated Beverage by the Whole Sample, Age and Gender Groups

	人数 Number	基本固定饮用一个牌子 used in only one brand	比较固定地饮用两个或三个牌子 used in two or three brands	基本上不太固定牌子 no brand preference
样本 Sample	783	44.6	44.3	11.1
男性 Male	384	45.8	41.7	12.5
16~24 岁 Age	94	52.1	39.4	8.5
25~34 岁 Age	130	47.7	42.3	10.0
35~44 岁 Age	98	41.8	39.8	18.4
45~54 岁 Age	42	35.7	54.8	9.5
55~60 岁 Age	20	45.0	30.0	25.0
女性 Female	399	43.4	46.9	9.8
16~24 岁 Age	97	38.1	50.5	11.3
25~34 岁 Age	124	46.8	48.4	4.8
35~44 岁 Age	96	45.8	44.8	9.4
45~54 岁 Age	58	43.1	43.1	13.8
55~60 岁 Age	24	37.5	41.7	20.8

【5】 Some of the questions can have more than one answer. For those questions, we used different calculating methods according to different questions. Some percentage show the effective numbers of respondents. This may add the percentage of chosen items up to over 100%; Some percentage show the total respondents, and this adds the percentage of chosen items up to 100%. For those questions with more than one answer, we generally explain the effective sample and the percentage calculating methods. For example, the analysis of considerations for purchasing carbonated beverage. See the following table.

1-8 选择该类商品的考虑因素/ Ranking of the Considerations in Purchasing

注：本题为多选题，合计百分比超过 100%（Multiple answers）

排名 Ranking	考虑因素 Considerations	人次 Person-time	百分比 Percent
1	口味好 pleasant taste	552	70.6
2	有名的牌子 famous brand	310	39.6
3	价格适中 reasonable price	219	28.0
4	生产日期 date of producing	158	20.2
5	购买方便 easy to buy	129	16.5
6	只是由于习惯 out of habit	99	12.7
7	广告影响 influence of advertising	82	10.5
8	单位发的 offered by the working unit	54	6.9
9	有优惠条件 with preferential terms	23	2.9
10	别人送的 given by other people	21	2.7
11	包装吸引人 appealing package	12	1.5
12	朋友推荐 introduction of friends	7	0.9
13	售货员介绍 introduced by the shop assistants	2	0.3
13	其它 others	2	0.3

n=782

The first line indicates that among the 782 respondents who answered this question, 552 took "pleasant taste "into their considerations when purchased the beverage, counting for 70.6% of the effective sample.(n=782 means the effective sample)

【6】 Please note the actual meaning of percentage in the tables when read them. See the following table.

Shanghai, Guangzhou, Chongqing, Wuhan, Xi'an and **Shenyang**, which are presented as the same names. Here, let's take the output of beverage consumption in Beijing for an example.

【2】 The headline of the tables are generally the same as the question in the questionnaire. The items in the first line are the possible answers to the question. For example, table 1-5 in Beijing category, the question in the questionnaire is 'Whether purchased carbonated beverage in the last 3 months?', the given answers are 1) yes or 2) no . The headline and the first line of the table indicate it.

1-5 样本、男性各年龄层、女性各年龄层最近三个月有无购买的比例/ Purchasing in the Last Three Months by the Whole Sample, Age and Gender Groups

	人数 Number	买过 yes	没买过 no
样本 Sample	1011	71.8	28.2
男性 Male	504	70.0	30.0
16~24 岁 Age	105	82.9	17.1
25~34 岁 Age	151	78.1	21.9
35~44 岁 Age	131	68.7	31.3
45~54 岁 Age	77	54.5	45.5
55~60 岁 Age	40	40.0	60.0
女性 Female	507	73.6	26.4
16~24 岁 Age	108	86.1	13.9
25~34 岁 Age	150	78.0	22.0
35~44 岁 Age	124	75.0	25.0
45~54 岁 Age	84	61.9	38.1
55~60 岁 Age	41	43.9	56.1

【3】 The data of table 1-5 presents the cross-analysis output of the questions with age and gender. Except the figures in 'number' item, all the other figures in the table should be expressed as '%'. But, in order to make them easy to read, the '%' is omitted. All the percentage should refer to line percentage (to the figures on the left) when is not particularly noted. The three lines of block figures in the above table show that in the last 3 months, 71.8% people of the sample bought carbonated beverage, 28.2% did not. Among them, 70.0% males did while 30.0% males did not; 73.6% females did while 26.4% females did not. There are more females buying carbonated beverage than males. But the difference is small. The last line shows that in the last 3 months, 43.9% females aged 55-60 bought carbonated beverage, 56.1% did not. Compared with the percentage for the ' bought' and ' not-bought' females in the sample (73.6% and 26.4%), the percentage of females aged 55-60 who bought carbonated beverage is much lower than other females in the sample, lowest among all ages. The percentage of male aged 16-24 who bought carbonated beverage counts for 86.1%, higher than the other ages. The other analysis is explained much the same way.

【4】 Not all the questions are answered by the respondents. We regard them as missing value when analyze that question. Only those who answered the question are taken into account in the items of 'people' and 'percentage'. For example, in analyzing carbonated beverage brand habits, only 783 respondents answered the question, therefore, only those 783 people are included in the analysis. See the following table.

1-3 样本、男性各年龄层、女性各年龄层的常用品牌/ The Most Frequently Used Brands by the Whole Sample, Age and Gender Groups

	人数 Number	第一品牌及百分比 1st/ percent	第二品牌及百分比 2nd/ percent	第三品牌及百分比 3rd/ percent	第四品牌及百分比 4th/ percent
样本 Sample	**780**	**可口可乐 Coca-cola(59.2)**	**雪碧 Sprite(11.4)**	**百事可乐 Pepsi(7.9)**	**北冰洋 Beibingyang(5.8)**
男性 Male	**381**	**可口可乐 Coca-cola(60.1)**	**雪碧 Sprite(10.2)**	**百事可乐 Pepsi(8.7)**	**北冰洋 Beibingyang(5.8)**
16~24 岁 Age	94	可口可乐 Coca-cola(58.5)	百事可乐 Pepsi(9.6) 北冰洋 Beibingyang(9.6)	醒目 Smart(5.3) 雪碧 Sprite(5.3)	健力宝 Jianlibao(3.2)
25~34 岁 Age	130	可口可乐 Coca-cola(65.4)	雪碧 Sprite(11.5)	百事可乐 Pepsi(6.9)	美年达 Mirinda(4.6)
35~44 岁 Age	96	可口可乐 Coca-cola(55.2)	百事可乐 Pepsi(11.5)	雪碧 Sprite(10.4)	北冰洋 Beibingyang(4.2)
45~54 岁 Age	41	可口可乐 Coca-cola(58.5)	北冰洋 Beibingyang(9.8) 雪碧 Sprite(9.8)	百事可乐 Pepsi(7.3)	美年达 Mirinda(4.9)
55~60 岁 Age	20	可口可乐 Coca-cola(60.0)	雪碧 Sprite(25.0)	北冰洋 Beibingyang(10.0)	百事可乐 Pepsi(5.0)
女性 Female	**399**	**可口可乐 Coca-cola(58.4)**	**雪碧 Sprite(12.5)**	**百事可乐 Pepsi(7.3)**	**北冰洋 Beibingyang(5.8)**
16~24 岁 Age	97	可口可乐 Coca-cola(54.6)	百事可乐 Pepsi(17.5)	美年达 Mirinda(6.2)	醒目 Smart(5.2)
25~34 岁 Age	124	可口可乐 Coca-cola(66.1)	雪碧 Sprite(11.3)	北冰洋 Beibingyang(5.6)	百事可乐 Pepsi(4.8)
35~44 岁 Age	96	可口可乐 Coca-cola(54.2)	雪碧 Sprite(18.8)	北冰洋 Beibingyang(8.3)	百事可乐 Pepsi(3.1) 健力宝 Jianlibao(3.1)
45~54 岁 Age	58	可口可乐 Coca-cola(58.6)	雪碧 Sprite(17.2)	北冰洋 Beibingyang(8.6)	百事可乐 Pepsi(5.2) 美年达 Mirinda(5.2)
55~60 岁 Age	24	可口可乐 Coca-cola(50.0)	雪碧 Sprite(25.0)	北冰洋 Beibingyang(8.3) 美年达 Mirinda(8.3)	非常可乐 Future(4.2) 北京 Beijing(4.2)

表中有两个问题要加以注意：第一，每一行的百分比相加不等于百分之百。原因是我们只选取了排名在前三位、前四位或前五位的品牌列表，其它品牌未列出。第二，最后一行数字中，55~60 岁的只有 24 人，第二品牌的百分比是 25.0%，第三品牌的百分比是 8.3%，如果只看百分比，两者相差了 16.7 个百分比，考虑到其基数 24 较小，计算其实际人数，第二品牌是 6 个人，第三品牌是 2 个人，两者只差了 4 个人。对于基数很小的百分比在阅读时要特别注意，这种百分比只能作为参考，其意义一般不大。作者将这类百分比列出是为了统一格式。

【7】有关品牌的问题，有些被访者的答案可能是“不确定”或“没注意品牌”，比如“请问您最常食用的饼干是什么牌的？”，有些被访者记不清品牌，回答“不确定”，经追问后也还是“不确定”，对于这种事实情况，为了不影响其他品牌的市场占有率，在数据计算时没有将其变为缺失，也就是说，这种“不确定”的品牌仍然占据了一定的比例，但因为这种“不确定”的回答信息太模糊，研究价值不大，所以没有将它列在表内。

Data Explanation

Most of the data output of this yearbook are presented in the form of tables. In order to make the tables simpler and more readable, most of them are made similar in format. Meanwhile, the presentation of the analysis output is made consistent. We hereby present the understanding method as follows. For these tables special both in format and content, they have their own special explanation in the book.

【1】 This book is classified by product category, under each category list the data outputs of **Beijing,**

1-7 样本、男性各年龄层、女性各年龄层的品牌习惯/ Brand Habit in Consuming Carbonated Beverage by the Whole Sample, Age and Gender Groups

	人数 Number	基本固定饮用一个牌子 used in only one brand	比较固定地饮用两个或三个牌子 used in two or three brands	基本上不太固定牌子 no brand preference
样本 Sample	783	44.6	44.3	11.1
男性 Male	384	45.8	41.7	12.5
16~24 岁 Age	94	52.1	39.4	8.5
25~34 岁 Age	130	47.7	42.3	10.0
35~44 岁 Age	98	41.8	39.8	18.4
45~54 岁 Age	42	35.7	54.8	9.5
55~60 岁 Age	20	45.0	30.0	25.0
女性 Female	399	43.4	46.9	9.8
16~24 岁 Age	97	38.1	50.5	11.3
25~34 岁 Age	124	46.8	48.4	4.8
35~44 岁 Age	96	45.8	44.8	9.4
45~54 岁 Age	58	43.1	43.1	13.8
55~60 岁 Age	24	37.5	41.7	20.8

【5】问卷中有一部分题目是多选题，对于多选题，根据题目的不同，百分比的算法也不同。有的百分比是对填选该题的有效人数计算的，这样计算得到的所有选项的百分比之和有可能超过 100%；有的百分比是对总人次计算的，这样计算得到的所有选项的百分比之和仍然等于 100%。对于多选题，在分析时一般都加注了有效样本量或百分比的计算方法，请读者在阅读表格时留意表格注解。例如对选择碳酸饮料的考虑因素的分析，见下表。

1-8 选择该类商品的考虑因素/ Ranking of the Considerations in Purchasing

注：本题为多选题，合计百分比超过 100%（Multiple answers）

排名 Ranking	考虑因素 Considerations	人次 Person-time	百分比 Percent
1	口味好 pleasant taste	552	70.6
2	有名的牌子 famous brand	310	39.6
3	价格适中 reasonable price	219	28.0
4	生产日期 date of producing	158	20.2
5	购买方便 easy to buy	129	16.5
6	只是由于习惯 out of habit	99	12.7
7	广告影响 influence of advertising	82	10.5
8	单位发的 offered by the working unit	54	6.9
9	有优惠条件 with preferential terms	23	2.9
10	别人送的 given by other people	21	2.7
11	包装吸引人 appealing package	12	1.5
12	朋友推荐 introduction of friends	7	0.9
13	售货员介绍 introduced by the shop assistants	2	0.3
13	其它 others	2	0.3

n=782

第一行数字表示，在回答了该题的 782 人中，考虑因素之一是“口味好”的有 552 人次，占有效样本量的 70.6%（表末的“n=782”为有效样本量）。

【6】在阅读表格时要注意表格中百分比的实际含义。看下面的表格。

数据说明

本年鉴数据结果多以表格形式出现。为方便读者查阅，大多数表格形式相似，数据分析结果的表示方法也力求统一。在这里给出一般的解读方法，那些形式或内容比较特别的表格在书中已经加了注解。

【1】本书以商品为主要分类项，每类商品的内容下都分列北京、上海、广州、重庆、武汉、西安、沈阳七城市各自的数据结果，以“**●北京（Beijing）**”、“**●上海（Shanghai）**”、“**●广州（Guangzhou）**”、“**●重庆（Chongqing）**”“**●武汉（Wuhan）**”、“**●西安（Xi’an）**”、“**●沈阳（Shenyang）**”作为区别标志。下面以北京地区饮料类的结果举例说明。

【2】书中表格的标题一般就是调查时问卷所问的问题，表头所列的项目即该问题的所有可能选项。比如“饮料类”的表 1-5，问卷中的问题是最近三个月有无购买过碳酸饮料，供选择的答案是 1.买过，2.没买过。表格的标题和表头对此做了提示。

1-5 样本、男性各年龄层、女性各年龄层最近三个月有无购买的比例/ Purchasing in the Last Three Months by the Whole Sample, Age and Gender Groups

	人数 Number	买过 yes	没买过 no
样本 Sample	**1011**	**71.8**	**28.2**
男性 Male	**504**	**70.0**	**30.0**
16~24 岁 Age	105	82.9	17.1
25~34 岁 Age	151	78.1	21.9
35~44 岁 Age	131	68.7	31.3
45~54 岁 Age	77	54.5	45.5
55~60 岁 Age	40	40.0	60.0
女性 Female	**507**	**73.6**	**26.4**
16~24 岁 Age	108	86.1	13.9
25~34 岁 Age	150	78.0	22.0
35~44 岁 Age	124	75.0	25.0
45~54 岁 Age	84	61.9	38.1
55~60 岁 Age	41	43.9	56.1

【3】表 1-5 中的数据是该问题与年龄和性别作交互分析的结果。表中除人数（人次）对应的数字以外的数都是百分比，为了简洁易读，都没有标上百分号。如果没有特别注明，百分比都是指的行百分比（对左边数字而言的百分比）。上表中的三行黑体数字表示，样本中有 71.8%的人最近三个月买过碳酸饮料，28.2%的人没有买过；其中男性中有 70.0%的人最近三个月买过碳酸饮料，30.0%的人没有买过；女性中有 73.6%的人最近三个月买过碳酸饮料，26.4%的人没有买过；由此可以看到，女性买过的比例略高于男性，但差别不大。最后一行数字表示，55~60 岁的女性中，43.9%的人最近三个月买过碳酸饮料，56.1%的人没有买过，与样本中女性买过和没有买过的百分比（73.6%和 26.4%）相比，55~60 岁的女性买过碳酸饮料的比例比样本女性要低得多，是各年龄层中最低的。而 16~24 岁的女性买过碳酸饮料的百分比是 86.1%，比其它各年龄层的比例都高，是各年龄层中最高的。书中其他表格的分析类似。

【4】有些问题不是所有被访者都做了回答，对于没有回答该题的人分析时做缺失处理，人数和百分比的计算只对回答该问题的人进行。比如对碳酸饮料的品牌习惯的分析，只有 783 人填答了此题，所以分析是对这 783 个人进行的。见下表。

【5】 **Date of Conducting:** Oct.28 / 1999 — Dec. 4 / 1999

【6】 **Total Effective Samples:**

Beijing	1012	Shanghai	1014
Guangzhou	1034	Chongqing	624
Wuhan	642	Xi'an	601
Shenyang	601		

Total: 5528

Sampling Explanation

【1】 **Methods of Sampling:** Multi-level Mixed Random Sampling

【2】 **Areas:** Beijing, Shanghai, Guangzhou, Chongqing, Wuhan, Xi'an, Shenyang. Districts of each city conducted research:

City	No of Districts conducted research	Names of Districts
Beijing	8	Dongcheng District, Xicheng District, Chongwen District, Xuanwu District, Chaoyang District, Haidian District, Fengtai District, Shijingshan District
Shanghai	13	Huangpu District, Nanshi District, Luwan District, Xuhui District, Changning District, Jing'an District, Putuo District, Zhabei District, Hongkou District, Yangpu District, Baoshan District, Minhang District, Pudong District
Guangzhou	5	Dongshan District, Liwan District, Yuexiu District, Haizhu District, Tianhe District
Chongqing	6	Yuzhong District, Dadukou District, Jiangbei District, Shapingba District, Jiulongpo District, Nan'an District
Wuhan	7	Jiang'an District, Jianghan District, Qiaokou District, Hanyang District, Wuchang District, Qingshan District, Hongshan District
Xi'an	7	Xincheng District, Beilin District, Lianhu District, Baqiao District, Weiyang District, Yanta District, Yanliang District
Shenyang	5	Heping District, Shenhe District, Dadong District, Huanggu District, Tiexi District

【3】 **Respondents:** Registered citizens aged 16-60 living in town in the above 7 cities. The sample panels for Guangzhou and Wuhan are based on the urban Neighbourhood Namelist published by local Statistic Bureaus(1998 data),and the sample panel for the other 5 cities are selected on the basis of Neighbourhood Namelist issued by the National Statistic Bureau (Data of 1996). Age and gender are taken as the controlled variables. Samples are chosen according to population ratio of each town and neighbourhood, first going to the neighbourhood, and to household, and finally define the respondents at random number.

【4】 **Interviewing method:** Household retaining questionnaire

(Interviewers deliver and collect questionnaire within 3 days with attitude & media questions completed on the site)

抽样说明

【1】**抽样方法**：多级混合随机抽样

【2】**调查区域**：北京、上海、广州、重庆、武汉、西安、沈阳七城市主要城区。每城市所调查的城区如下：

城市	调查城区数	调查城区
北京	8	东城区、西城区、崇文区、宣武区、朝阳区、海淀区、丰台区、石景山区
上海	13	黄浦区、南市区、卢湾区、徐汇区、长宁区、静安区、普陀区、闸北区、虹口区、杨浦区、宝山区、闵行区、浦东新区
广州	5	东山区、荔湾区、越秀区、海珠区、天河区
重庆	6	渝中区、大渡口区、江北区、沙坪坝区、九龙坡区、南岸区
武汉	7	江岸区、江汉区、硚口区、汉阳区、武昌区、青山区、洪山区
西安	7	新城区、碑林区、莲湖区、灞桥区、未央区、雁塔区、阎良区
沈阳	5	和平区、沈河区、大东区、皇姑区、铁西区

【3】**调查对象**：北京、上海、广州、重庆、武汉、西安、沈阳七城市被抽取的城区中，有该城市户口的16-60岁的居民。广州和武汉以当地统计局出版的城市居委会名录（1998年数据）为抽样框，其余五个城市以国家统计局提供的城市居委会名录（1996年数据）为抽样框，抽样时以性别和年龄作为控制变量，按照每个城区和居委会的人口比例抽取样本，先抽取到居委会，再到户，最后用随机数字表确定调查对象。

【4】**访问方式**：入户留置式问卷访问

（访问员在三日内完成问卷的入户发送与回收，其中态度性问题和媒介问题面访完成）

【5】**执行时间**：1999年10月28日—1999年12月4日

【6】**有效样本量**：北京1012　上海1014　广州1034　重庆624　武汉642　西安601　沈阳601

七城市共5528个样本

有限公司以及沈阳北方经济咨询有限公司等同仁单位深致谢意！

参加年鉴背景文章资料收集和撰写工作的还有北京广播学院广告学系99级研究生李莉，苗春霞，张宇鹏，李萍同学；同时也感谢钟静老师在最后的校对和编辑中付出的辛勤劳动；感谢廖文梅同学为年鉴所做的资料整理工作。特别感谢程坪老师在各种文章资料的翻译工作上提供的大量帮助。

在去年这个时间，我们以“数据农人”自称，为 IMI 年鉴的开拓事业感到骄傲同时，也多少感到寂寞。事业发展，规模扩大，然而，我们初衷不改，每当数据整合成年鉴出版，我们就向社会明言：公开所有的数据库，并为学术研究机构和大专院校无偿提供数据服务。

1.继续出版每年一期的《IMI 消费行为与生活形态年鉴》；

今年推出的 2000 年鉴同时附带 CD-ROM，所提供的表格和数据在 Word 和 Excel 中可以进行进一步的编辑。

2.向用户（企业和公司）提供更为专业和深入的专项研究报告（专项研究报告的详细的介绍请见年鉴封底和 CD—ROM）；

IMI 年鉴印刷出版物的分析架构主要以性别和年龄两个基本指标为支架，进行有关消费行为与品牌的重点分析，从去年开始的针对企业和公司的专项研究报告，在数据分析处理的深度以及数据涵盖面上都比 IMI 年鉴更为深入。专项研究报告的分析角度可以针对市场上该商品的主要竞争品牌，同时也可以针对某一消费群体（使用人口特征变量、或消费行为变量以及生活形态变量，都可以进行消费群体的划分）进行更为深入的挖掘，再加上 4 年的数据资料比较分析，可以更有针对性的为客户提供一对一的服务

3. “IMI 年鉴数据综合分析系统”的推出（(详细介绍在 CD-ROM 中)

IMI 年鉴计划在今年 6 月份推出“IMI 年鉴数据综合分析系统”，即数据库加分析软件套装。目前市面上通用的数据分析软件专业性太强，对大多数从事营销、广告、市场研究的人员来说，掌握起来有一定难度。而“IMI 年鉴综合分析系统”在大量的消费者数据的基础上，配套的分析软件全中文操作，操作界面非常简单，分析方法非常实用，是进行消费者研究时必备的数据库软件。

（三）

像历年一样，到这里我们要感谢对 IMI 年鉴提供了大量帮助的单位和个人：

首先，我们非常感谢人民日报华泰投资管理有限公司对 IMI 年鉴的鼎力支持。IMI（创研）市场信息研究所与华泰公司合作注册了——北京华泰创研数据有限公司，负责 IMI 年鉴的发行和后续相关产品的开发，使 IMI 年鉴事业运作更加专业化、市场化。

我们非常感谢香港中文大学的潘忠党教授、魏然教授、梁永炽教授。从第一部年鉴开始，三位教授多次飞赴北京，为年鉴的调查问卷，研究框架以及分析方法与 IMI 研究人员进行蹉商研讨，他们向 IMI 研究人员介绍最新的学术成果，也积极向海外推介 IMI 年鉴，为 IMI 年鉴架设通往国际的桥梁。

同时我们也非常感谢清华紫光集团的光盘中心。目前该中心的研究人员除了维护“IMI 年鉴编辑软件系统”工作之外，同时正在开发“IMI 年鉴数据综合分析系统”，并计划于 2000 年 6 月份正式面市。届时推出的 “IMI 年鉴数据综合分析系统”将涵盖更大量的数据，同时配有更为实用的分析系统，界面非常友好，全中文操作，直接提高使用者对于 IMI 年鉴的基础数据处理和综合分析能力。

在本年鉴的实地执行过程中，我们继续得到当地调查公司的大力支持：这里向上海东方市场调查公司，广州三思市场调查研究公司，重庆腾博市场调研咨询有限公司，武汉格兰德市场调查公司，西安新兰德市场调查

序　　言

（一）

倏忽之间IMI年鉴已经跨进了第五个年头。

1996年，第一部IMI年鉴呱呱落地，我们本着“信息共享”的精神，凭借国内外各界人士的鼎力支持，着手开拓和耕耘消费领域的数据采集和数据分析这片处女地，追溯其源，来自两个方面的需求直接触动着我们：

首先，源自我们自身的需求，从80年代末开始，我们已经开始通过各种市场调查收集汇总有关数据，然而，对应环境的变化，这些点滴积累还是“杯水车薪”。我们的队伍中不乏长年从事科研和教学的专业人员，然而，面对社会环境的急剧变化，我们深感市场数据的匮乏。各种经济研究，营销策划需要大量的相关数据，同样，专业教学也存在这种需求。

其次，源自同行和社会的需求。90年代，产品积压、供过于求已经成为不争的事实。政府呼唤“内需”，企业寻求“点子”，面对这种环境，我们清醒地认识到，无论是“策划大师”长袖善舞，还是“MBA”学子意气风发，要捕捉市场机会，要启动消费需求，生活者的消费行为和生活形态的动态数据是基础之中的基础。

正因为是基础的基础，所以年鉴事业做得异常艰辛。专业方面无数的课题有待我们攻克，而资金筹措，销售发行网络的建立，更让我们煞费苦心。然而，回顾五年历程，天大的难题一一攻克，年鉴事业不断进步发展，究其原因，是因为我们始终恪守IMI年鉴经营的三大理念：第一，CREATIVE （创造性的市场研究）；第二，NETWORK（网络沟通，个体与个体，个体与组织相互沟通）；第三，OPENSYSTEM（信息公开，资源共享）。

凭籍着创造性理念，IMI年鉴事业无论在整体发展还是在具体操作层面，不断求新创新，IMI年鉴的调查规模从第一年的三大城市扩展到2000年版的七大城市；IMI年鉴的研究领域从消费者的个体延伸到消费者的家庭以及社会背景；IMI年鉴的调查手段在坚持入户调查的同时，开发了新的电话网络调查系统。IMI年鉴之所以能够生存而且至今保持中国唯一的消费年鉴，最重要的理白就是：IMI年鉴不只是一个传统意义上的“信息情报商品”，它是根植于“网络性”和“公开性”的时代产物，并将“信息取之于社会还原于社会”、“整合各方力量，沟通互动”的经营理念用于实践。我们欣喜地看到，越来越多的国内外的专家学者参与IMI年鉴工作，在使用IMI年鉴数据同时，也为年鉴提供崭新的研究思路和方法；越来越多的厂家企业与IMI年鉴建立关系，他们往往在年鉴数据的基础之上，提出自己特殊的要求，寻求数据背后更多的信息；越来越多的投资者、网络经营者关注IMI年鉴，谋求在更加宽广的领域与IMI年鉴合作。

（二）

2000 IMI消费者年鉴继续扩大城市规模，考虑到地域代表性，增加了东北城市沈阳，样本量也由原来的4800扩大到今年的5500。今年IMI年鉴将进一步开拓客户服务领域：

《2000 IMI 消费行为与生活形态年鉴 》

研究机构、研究编辑人员

项目总统筹 北京华泰创研数据有限公司

研究机构 IMI（创研）市场信息研究所
人民日报华泰投资管理有限公司
北京广播学院广告学系
《国际广告》杂志社

项目总负责 郭东风（人民日报华泰投资管理有限公司董事长）
黄升民（北京广播学院广告学系教授）

项目策划 黄升民（北京广播学院广告学系教授）
丁俊杰（北京广播学院广告学系副教授）
刘立宾（国际广告杂志社社长兼主编）

编委会成员 黄升民 丁俊杰 郭东风 刘立宾 安军 王冰

研究人员 黄升民 丁俊杰 王冰 黄京华 李彩云 张津 黄伶俐 方宁 金川

《2000 IMI 消费行为与生活形态年鉴 》编辑部

编辑部主任 黄京华
编辑部副主任 李彩云
技术总负责 黄京华
编辑部成员 黄京华 李彩云 张津 林琳 黄伶俐 方宁 金川 邓创仪 方钰淳 盛慧云 吴月潇 马凌 马劲松 李萍 刘荣 吕静 吴南 李兆平 郝婷 聂靓 马芳

1-3 样本、男性各年龄层、女性各年龄层的常用品牌/ The Most Frequently Used Brands by the Whole Sample, Age and Gender Groups

	人数 Number	第一品牌及百分比 1st/ percent	第二品牌及百分比 2nd/ percent	第三品牌及百分比 3rd/ percent	第四品牌及百分比 4th/ percent
样本 Sample	780	**可口可乐 Coca-cola(59.2)**	**雪碧 Sprite(11.4)**	**百事可乐 Pepsi(7.9)**	**北冰洋 Beibingyang(5.8)**
男性 Male	381	**可口可乐 Coca-cola(60.1)**	**雪碧 Sprite(10.2)**	**百事可乐 Pepsi(8.7)**	**北冰洋 Beibingyang(5.8)**
16~24 岁 Age	94	可口可乐 Coca-cola(58.5)	百事可乐 Pepsi(9.6) 北冰洋 Beibingyang(9.6)	醒目 Smart(5.3) 雪碧 Sprite(5.3)	健力宝 Jianlibao(3.2)
25~34 岁 Age	130	可口可乐 Coca-cola(65.4)	雪碧 Sprite(11.5)	百事可乐 Pepsi(6.9)	美年达 Mirinda(4.6)
35~44 岁 Age	96	可口可乐 Coca-cola(55.2)	百事可乐 Pepsi(11.5)	雪碧 Sprite(10.4)	北冰洋 Beibingyang(4.2)
45~54 岁 Age	41	可口可乐 Coca-cola(58.5)	北冰洋 Beibingyang(9.8) 雪碧 Sprite(9.8)	百事可乐 Pepsi(7.3)	美年达 Mirinda(4.9)
55~60 岁 Age	20	可口可乐 Coca-cola(60.0)	雪碧 Sprite(25.0)	北冰洋 Beibingyang(10.0)	百事可乐 Pepsi(5.0)
女性 Female	399	**可口可乐 Coca-cola(58.4)**	**雪碧 Sprite(12.5)**	**百事可乐 Pepsi(7.3)**	**北冰洋 Beibingyang(5.8)**
16~24 岁 Age	97	可口可乐 Coca-cola(54.6)	百事可乐 Pepsi(17.5)	美年达 Mirinda(6.2)	醒目 Smart(5.2)
25~34 岁 Age	124	可口可乐 Coca-cola(66.1)	雪碧 Sprite(11.3)	北冰洋 Beibingyang(5.6)	百事可乐 Pepsi(4.8)
35~44 岁 Age	96	可口可乐 Coca-cola(54.2)	雪碧 Sprite(18.8)	北冰洋 Beibingyang(8.3)	百事可乐 Pepsi(3.1) 健力宝 Jianlibao(3.1)
45~54 岁 Age	58	可口可乐 Coca-cola(58.6)	雪碧 Sprite(17.2)	北冰洋 Beibingyang(8.6)	百事可乐 Pepsi(5.2) 美年达 Mirinda(5.2)
55~60 岁 Age	24	可口可乐 Coca-cola(50.0)	雪碧 Sprite(25.0)	北冰洋 Beibingyang(8.3) 美年达 Mirinda(8.3)	非常可乐 Future(4.2) 北京 Beijing(4.2)

Be careful about two problems in this table: 1) the percentage in the first line does not add up to 100%, because we only choose the first 3 or 4 or 5 brands, excluding the other brands; 2)there are only 24 people aged 55-60 in the last line. The percentage for the second brand is 25.0%; the 3rd 8.3%. If we only. look at the percentage, the difference between the 2nd brand and the 3rd brand is 16.7; But as the base is as small as 24 people, when we count the actual people, the 2nd brand comes 6 people, and the 3rd 2 people. The difference is only 4 people. For such percentage resulted from small bases, readers must be very careful. Such percentage can only be used as reference, bearing little meaning. We list them in the book for the purpose of consistency and unity.

【7】 In terms of question about brand name, some respondents may answer uncertainly or paid no attention. e.g. "What is the brand of cookie you choose most often?" According to this question some respondents may reply uncertainly, and after probing they insisted the same answer. It is really a kind of phenomena in market. In order not to affect other brand's market share, we did not count them as missing values. That is, all these uncertain brands have occupied some places in brand ranking, but we did not list them because of their vague information and low value of study.

Beijing

东城区 Dongcheng
23.4万户(10 000 households)
63.3万人(10 000 persons)

西城区 Xicheng
28.1万户(10 000 households)
79.2万人(10 000 persons)

崇文区 Chongwen
15.7万户(10 000 households)
42.0万人(10 000 persons)

宣武区 Xuanwu
20.0万户(10 000 households)
56.4万人(10 000 persons)

朝阳区 Chaoyang
53.1万户(10 000 households)
146.4万人(10 000 persons)

海淀区 Haidian
48.6万户(10 000 households)
152.6万人(10 000 persons)

丰台区 Fengtai
29.2万户(10 000 households)
79.5万人(10 000 persons)

石景山区 Shijingshan
11.0万户(10 000 households)
32.4万人(10 000 persons)

人口概况 SUMMARY

总人口 Total Population (10000 persons)	1223.4万人
总户数 Total Households (10000 households)	383.4万户
平均每户人口 Per Households (1 person)	2.85人
男女性别比 Sex Ratio	1.026

经济发展 ECONOMIC DEVELOPMENT

国内生产总值 Gross Domestic Product (100 000 000 yuan)	2009.9亿元
对外贸易出口 Value of Exports (USD 100 000 000)	28.29亿美元
工业企业个数 Number of Industrial Enterprises(unit)	30160个
职工年平均工资 Average Annual Wage for Staff and Workers (yuan)	12300元

居民生活 URBAN HOUSEHOLDS

城市居民平均每人居住面积 Per Capita Living Space (sq.m)	10.03平方米
城市居民燃气用户 Households With Access To Gas(10,000 households)	247.3万户
城市居民每人每天生活用水 Living Consumption Per Day (kg)	238.2公斤
城市每年平均生活用电量 Daily Annual Iiving Electrioity Consumption(1000,0 kmh)	294045万千瓦/小时

消费情况 CONSUMER INDICATORS

社会消费品零售总额 Total Retail Sales of Consumer Goods (100 000 000 yuan)	1195.2亿元
城市居民人均生活费收入 Annual Discretionary Income for Urban Households (yuan)	8471.98元
城市居民人均生活费支出 Lliving Expenditure Per Capita for Urban Households (yuan)	6970.83元
城市居民储蓄存款余额 Urban Savings Deposit (100 000 000 yuan)	2287.2亿元

★以上均为1998年统计数据

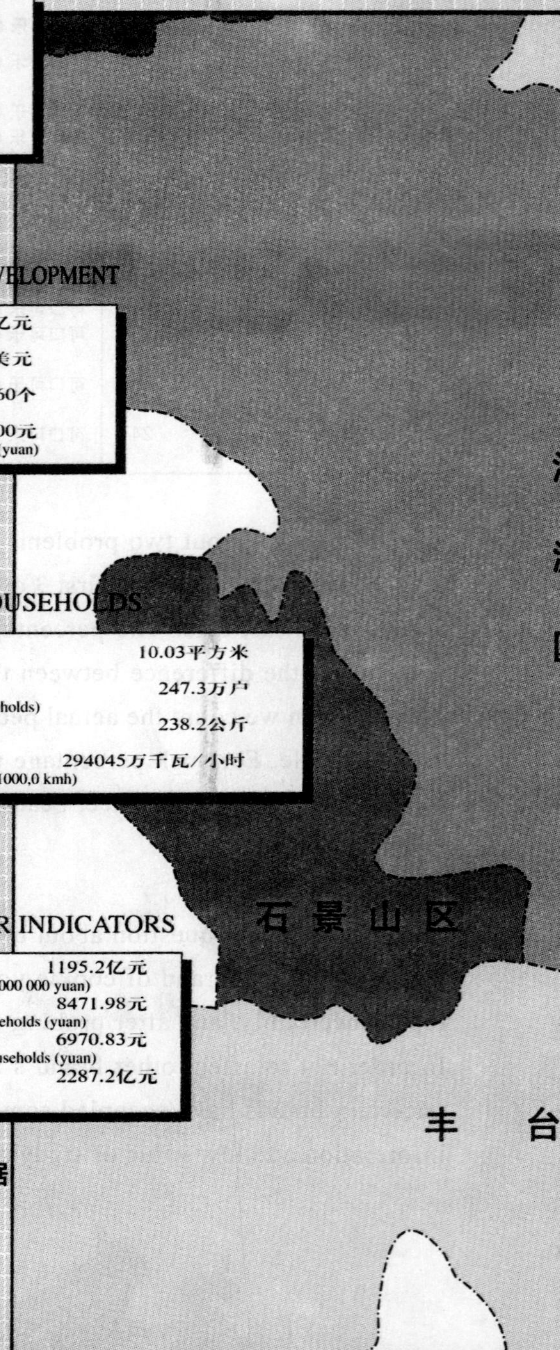

北京地区 图例

区县界　总户数
北京市区　总人口

北京地区概况图

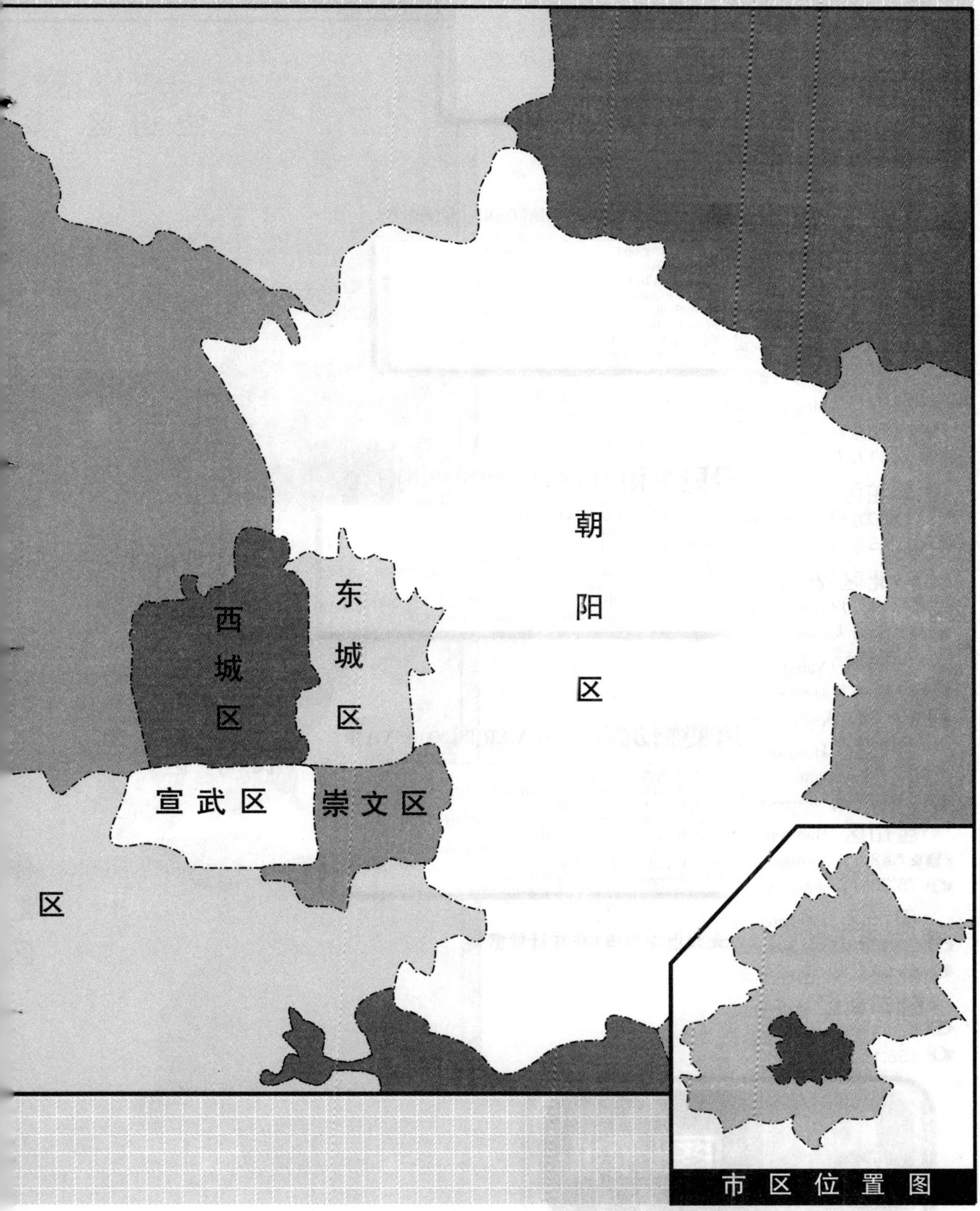

Shanghai

黄浦区 Huangpu
8.33万户(10 000 households)
24.91万人(10 000 persons)

南市区 Nanshi
16.30万户(10 000 households)
44.69万人(10 000 persons)

卢湾区 Luwan
13.51万户(10 000 households)
36.80万人(10 000 persons)

徐汇区 Xuhui
30.41万户(10 000 households)
84.79万人(10 000 persons)

长宁区 Changning
22.19万户(10 000 households)
61.07万人(10 000 persons)

静安区 Jing'an
13.18万户(10 000 households)
37.31万人(10 000 persons)

普陀区 Putuo
29.60万户(10 000 households)
83.45万人(10 000 persons)

闸北区 Zhabei
25.14万户(10 000 households)
68.65万人(10 000 persons)

杨浦区 Yangpu
37.61万户(10 000 households)
108.03万人(10 000 persons)

虹口区 Hongkou
29.33万户(10 000 households)
79.97万人(10 000 persons)

宝山区 Baoshan
27.42万户(10 000 households)
75.30万人(10 000 persons)

闵行区 Minhang
20.96万户(10 000 households)
59.34万人(10 000 persons)

浦东新区 Pudong
56.39万户(10 000 households)
156.18万人(10 000 persons)

人口概况 SUMMARY

总人口 Total Population (10000 persons)	1306.58万人
总户数 Total Households (10000 households)	465.72万户
平均每户人口 Per Households (1 person)	2.8人
男女性别比 Sex Ratio	1.016

经济发展 ECONOMIC DEVELOPMENT

国内生产总值 Gross Domestic Product (100 000 000 yuan)	3688.2亿元
对外贸易出口 Value of Exports (USD 100 000 000)	163.28亿美元
工业企业个数 Number of Industrial Enterprises(unit)	22450个
职工年平均工资 Average Annual Wage for Staff and Workers (yuan)	12059元

居民生活 URBAN HOUSEHOLDS

城市居民平均每人居住面积 Per Capita Living Space (sq.m)	9.7平方米
城市居民燃气用户 Households With Access to Gas (10 000households)	247.18万户
城市居民年生活用水量 Daily Tap Water Consumption (10 000 000 cu.m)	11.55亿立方米
城市年生活用电量 Average Annual Living Electricity Consumption (100 000 000 kwh)	121.54亿千瓦/小时

消费情况 CONSUMER INDICATORS

社会消费品零售总额 Total Retail Sales of Consumer Goods (100 000 000 yuan)	1471.03亿元
城市居民人均生活费收入 Annual Discretionary Income for Urban Households (yuan)	8773.1元
城市居民人均消费性支出 Annual Lliving Expenditure Per Capita for Urban Households (yuan)	6866.41元
城市居民储蓄存款余额 Urban Savings Deposit (100 000 000 yuan)	2372.94亿元

★以上均为1998年统计数据

上海地区 图例

区县界
上海市区
总户数
总人口

上海地区概况图

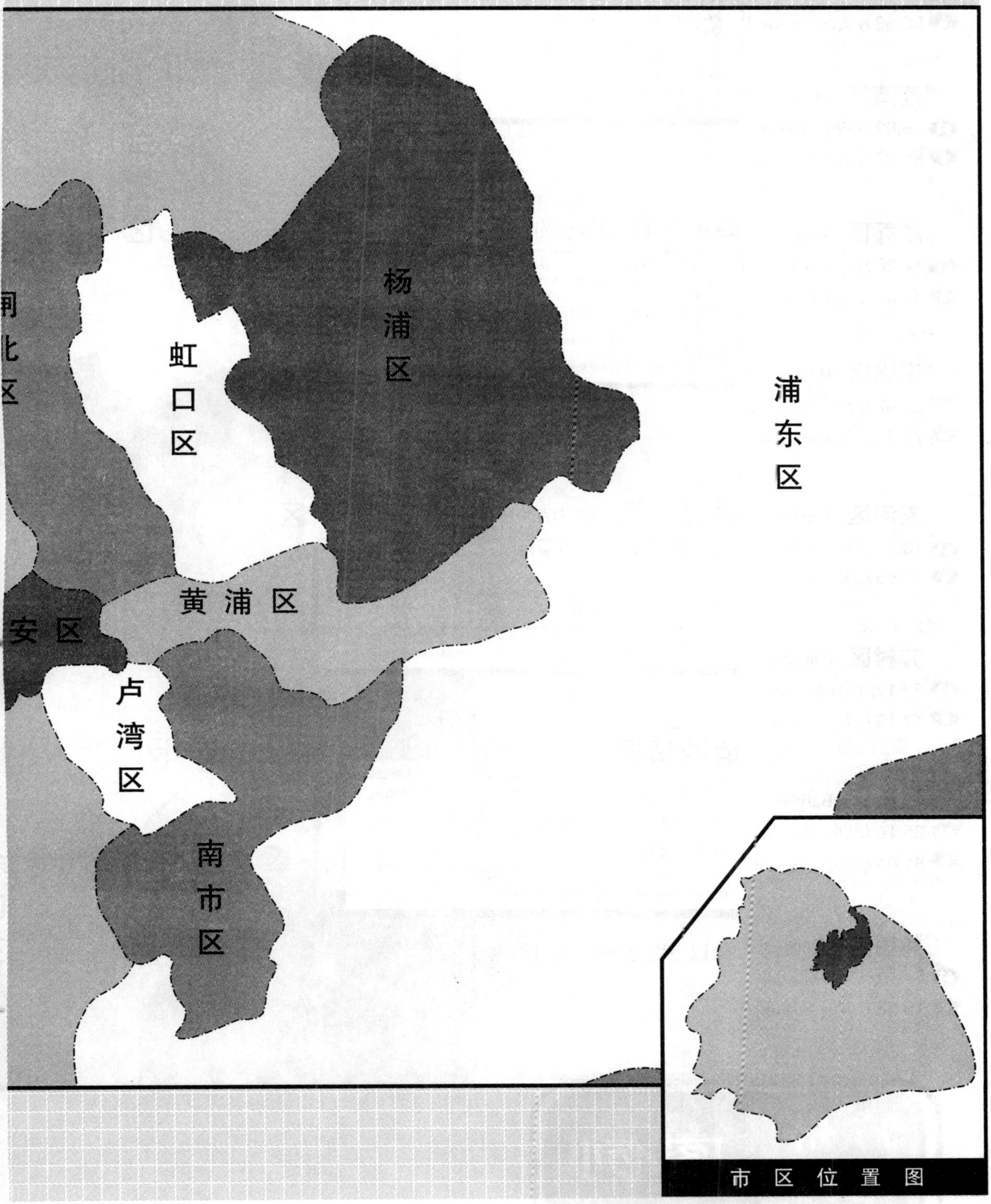

Guangzhou

东山区 Dongshan
17.44万户(10 000 households)
58.58万人(10 000 persons)

荔湾区 Liwan
16.92万户(10 000 households)
51.87万人(10 000 persons)

越秀区 Yuexiu
14.20万户(10 000 households)
44.07万人(10 000 persons)

海珠区 Haizhu
23.87万户(10 000 households)
76.40万人(10 000 persons)

天河区 Tianhe
13.74万户(10 000 households)
47.56万人(10 000 persons)

芳村区 Fangcun
5.61万户(10 000 households)
17.19万人(10 000 persons)

白云区 Baiyun
25.14万户(10 000 households)
81.04万人(10 000 persons)

黄埔区 Huangpu
6.04万户(10 000 households)
19.33万人(10 000 persons)

人口概况 SUMMARY

总人口 Total Population (10000 persons)	674.14万人
总户数 Total Households (10000 households)	200.6279万户
平均每户人口 Per Households (1 person)	3.36人
男女性别比 Sex Ratio	1.06

经济发展 ECONOMIC DEVELOPMENT

国内生产总值 Gross Domestic Product (100 000 000 yuan)	1841.61亿元
对外贸易出口 Value of Exports (USD 100 000 000)	80.17亿美元
工业企业个数 Number of Industrial Enterprises(unit)	40163个
职工年平均工资 Average Annual Wage for Staff and Workers (yuan)	14318元

居民生活 URBAN HOUSEHOLDS

城市居民平均每人居住面积 Per Capita Living Space (sq.m)	11.55平方米
城市居民燃气用户 Households With Access to Gas (10 000 households)	44.71万户
城市居民每人每天用水量 Per Capita Daily Consumption of Water for Residential Use (liter)	567升
城市每年平均生活用电量 Average Annual Living Electricity Consumption (10 000 kwh)	222910万千瓦/小时

消费情况 CONSUMER INDICATORS

社会消费品零售总额 Total Retail Sales of Consumer Goods (100 000 000 yuan)	904.57亿元
城市居民人均生活费收入 Annual Discretionary Income for Urban Households (yuan)	11255.7元
城市居民人均生活费支出 Annual Lliving Expenditure Per Capita for Urban Households (yuan)	9422.33元
城市居民储蓄存款余额 Urban Savings Deposit (100 000 000 yuan)	1882.22亿元

★以上均为1998年统计数据

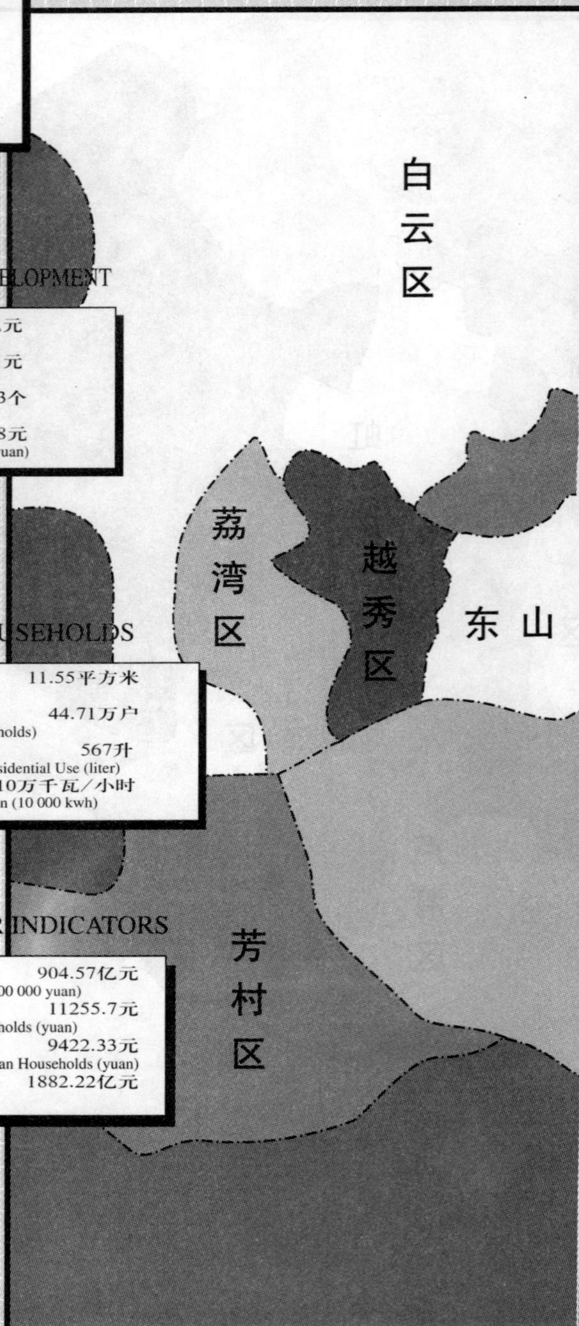

广州地区 图例

- —·—·— 区县界
- 广州市区
- 总户数
- 总人口

广州地区概况图

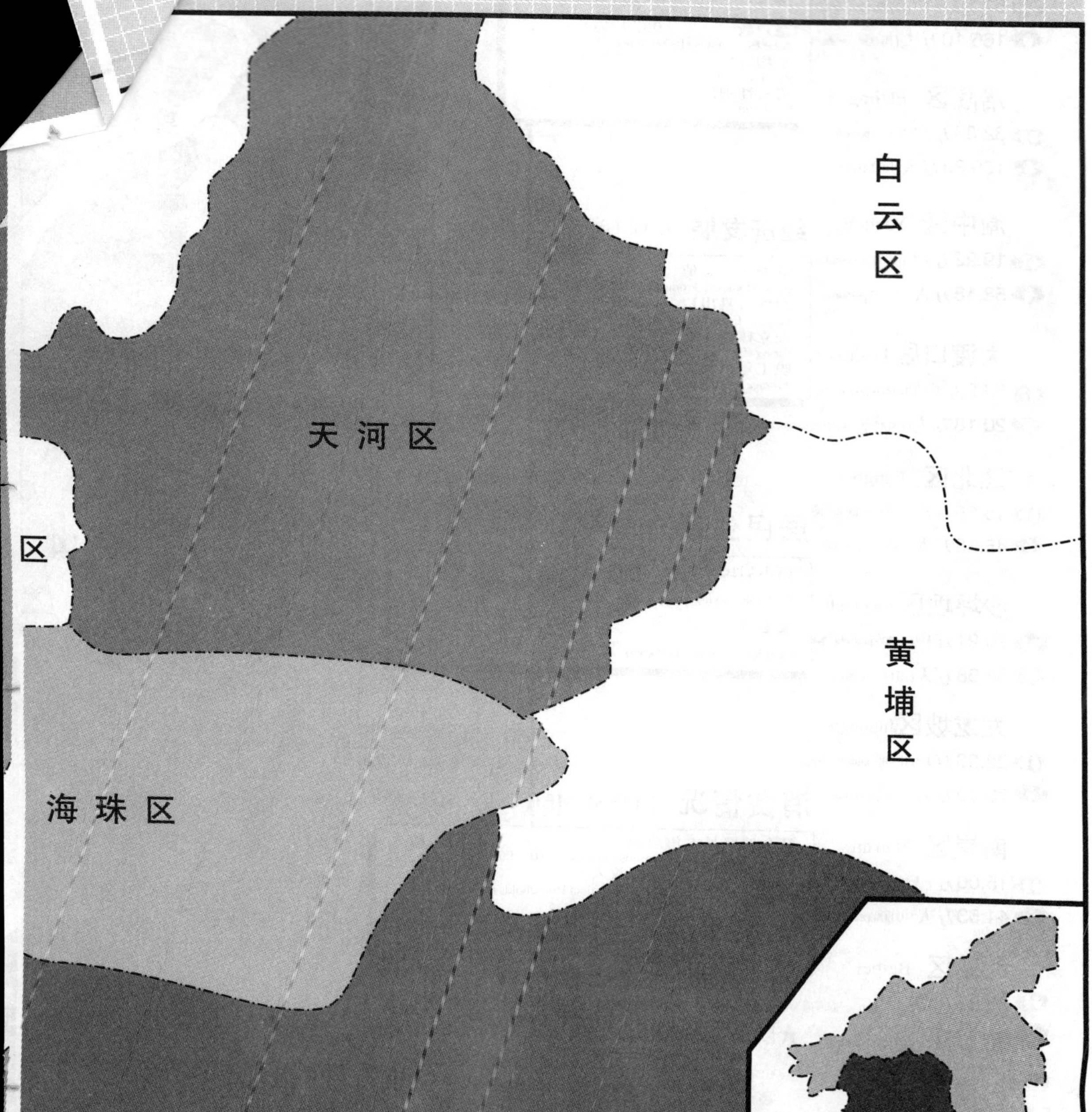

Chongqing

万州区 Wanzhou
51.39万户(10 000 households)
165.10万人(10 000 persons)

涪陵区 FUling
32.88万户(10 000 households)
109.23万人(10 000 persons)

渝中区 Yuzhong
19.22万户(10 000 households)
58.18万人(10 000 persons)

大渡口区 Dadukou
6.62万户(10 000 households)
20.18万人(10 000 persons)

江北区 Jiangbei
15.09万户(10 000 households)
45.18万人(10 000 persons)

沙坪坝区 Shapingba
20.21万户(10 000 households)
64.68万人(10 000 persons)

九龙坡区 Jiulongpo
22.53万户(10 000 households)
70.10万人(10 000 persons)

南岸区 Nan'an
15.06万户(10 000 households)
44.53万人(10 000 persons)

北碚区 Beibei
20.23万户(10 000 households)
63.17万人(10 000 persons)

巴南区 Banan
27.20万户(10 000 households)
86.11万人(10 000 persons)

人口概况 SUMMARY

总人口 Total Population (10000 persons)	3059.69万人
总户数 Total Households (10000 households)	907.17万户
平均每户 Per Households (1 person)	3.37人
男女性别比 Sex Ratio	1.09

经济发展 ECONOMIC DEVELOPMENT

国内生产总值 Gross Domestic Product (100 000 000 yuan)	1429.3亿元
对外贸易出口 Value of Exports (USD 10 000)	51411万美元
独立核算工业企业数 Number of Industrial Enterprises with Independent Accounting System(unit)	2000个(新口径)
职工年平均工资 Average Annual Wage for Staff and Workers (yuan)	5710元

居民生活 URBAN HOUSEHOLDS

城市居民平均每人居住面积 Per Capita Living Space (sq.m)	9.21平方米
发电量 Electricity (100 000 000 kwh)	60.9亿千瓦/小时

消费情况 CONSUMER INDICATORS

社会消费品零售总额 Total Retail Sales of Consumer Goods (100 000 000 yuan)	1815亿元
城市居民人均可支配收入 Annual Discretionary Income for Urban Households (yuan)	5467元
城市居民人均消费性支出 Annual Lliving Expenditure Per Capita for Urban Households (yuan)	4894.54元
城市居民储蓄存款余额 Urban Savings Deposit (100 000 000 yuan)	724.54亿元

★以上均为1998年统计数据

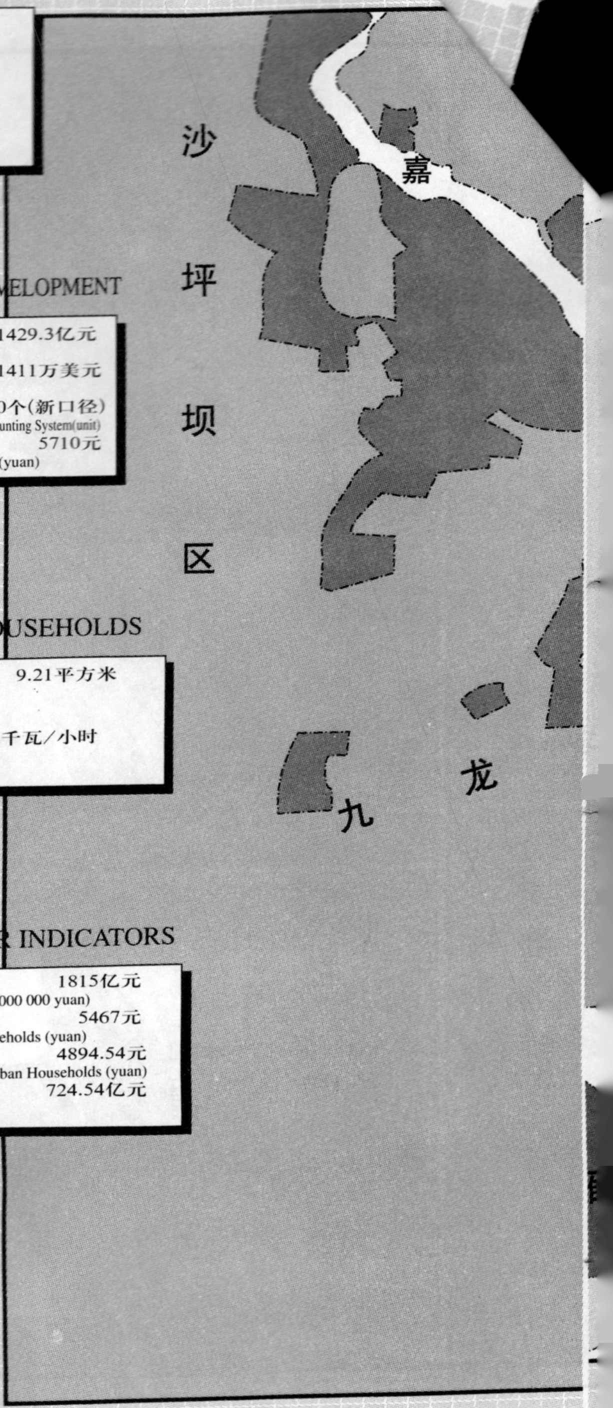

重庆地区 图例

区县界
重庆市区
总户数
总人口

重庆地区概况图

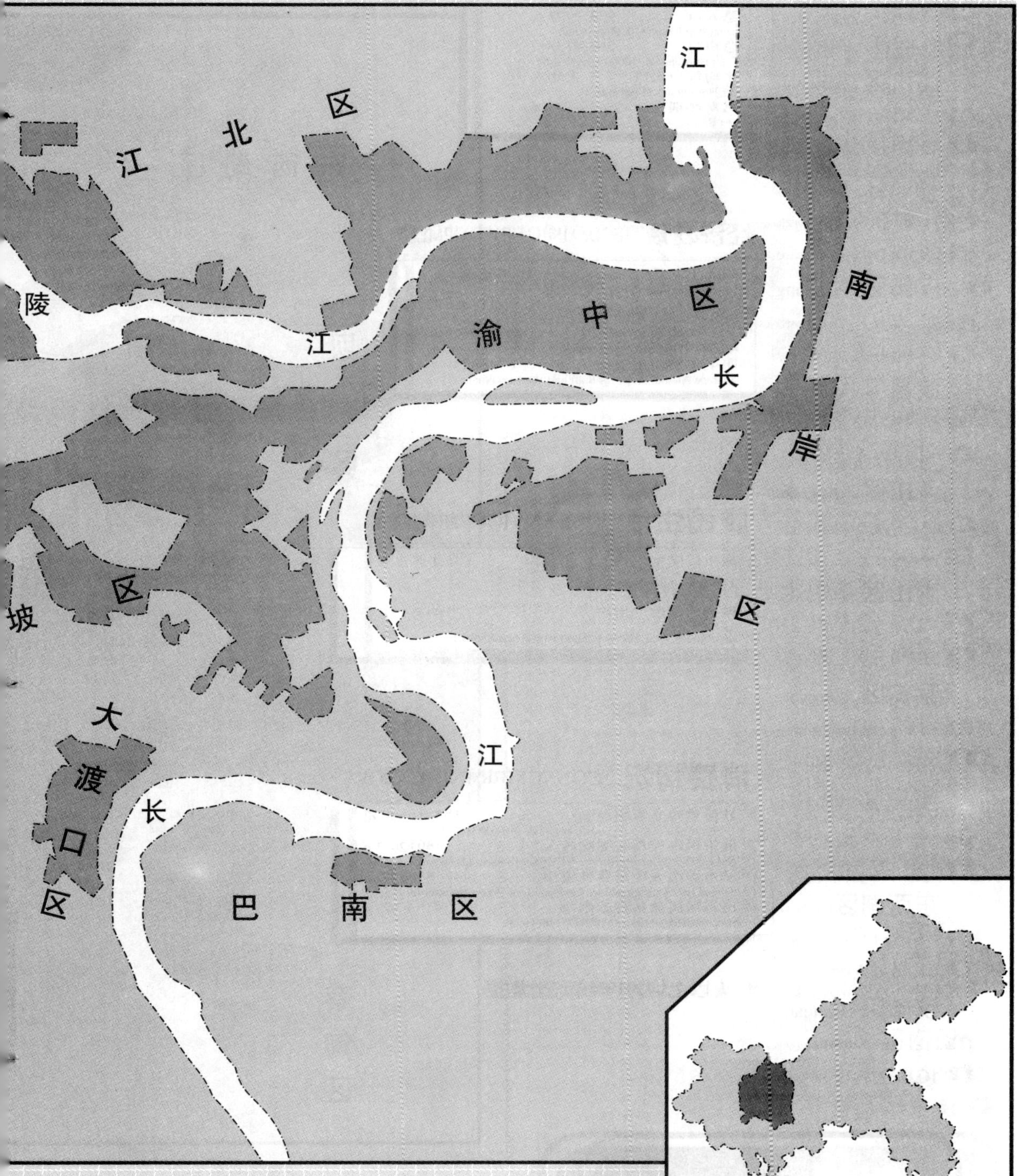

Wuhan

江岸区 Jiang'an

19.56万户(10 000 households)

61.28万人(10 000 persons)

江汉区 Jianghan

14.05万户(10 000 households)

45.14万人(10 000 persons)

硚口区 Qiaokou

16.91万户(10 000 households)

53.09万人(10 000 persons)

汉阳区 Hanyang

11.88万户(10 000 households)

37.86万人(10 000 persons)

武昌区 Wuchang

24.18万户(10 000 households)

82.11万人(10 000 persons)

青山区 Qingshan

11.70万户(10 000

households)

洪山区 Hongshan

13.59万户(10 000 households)

58.60万人(10 000 persons)

蔡甸区 Caidian

13.94万户(10 000 households)

53.26万人(10 000 persons)

江夏区 Jiangxia

16.75万户(10 000 households)

64.44万人(10 000 persons)

东西湖区 Dongxihu

7.56万户(10 000 households)

21.55万人(10 000 persons)

汉南区 Hannan

3.22万户(10 000 households)

10.62万人(10 000 persons)

人口概况 SUMMARY

总人口 Total Population (10000 persons)	731.79万人
总户数 Total Households (10000 households)	205.43万户
平均每户人口 Per Households (1 person)	3.56人
男女性别比 Sex Ratio	1.06

经济发展 ECONOMIC DEVELOPMENT

国内生产总值 Gross Domestic Product (100 000 000 yuan)	1015.89亿元
对外贸易出口 Value of Exports (USD 100 000 000)	10.8亿美元
工业企业个数 Number of Industrial Enterprises(unit)	40553个
职工年平均工资 Average Annual Wage for Staff and Workers (yuan)	6746元

居民生活 URBAN HOUSEHOLDS

城市居民平均每人居住面积 Per Capita Living Space (sq.m)	8.1平方米
城市居民燃气用户 Households With Access to Gas (10 000 households)	83万户

消费情况 CONSUMER INDICATORS

社会消费品零售总额 Total Retail Sales of Consumer Goods (10 000 yuan)	5273168万元
城市居民人均可支配收入 Annual Discretionary Income for Urban Households (yuan)	5912.52元
城市居民人均消费性支出 Annual Lliving Expenditure Per Capita for Urban Households (yuan)	5264.40元
城市居民储蓄存款余额 Urban Savings Deposit (100 000 000 yuan)	455.35亿元

★以上均为1998年统计数据

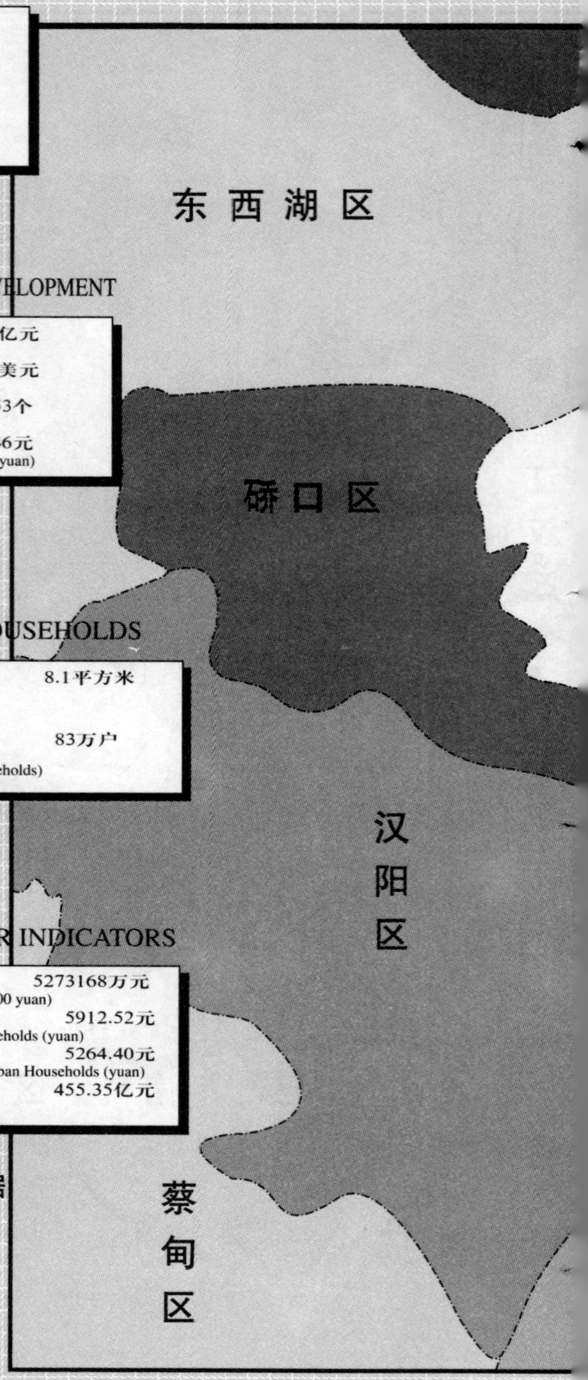

武汉地区 图例

区县界

武汉市区

总户数

总人口

武汉地区概况图

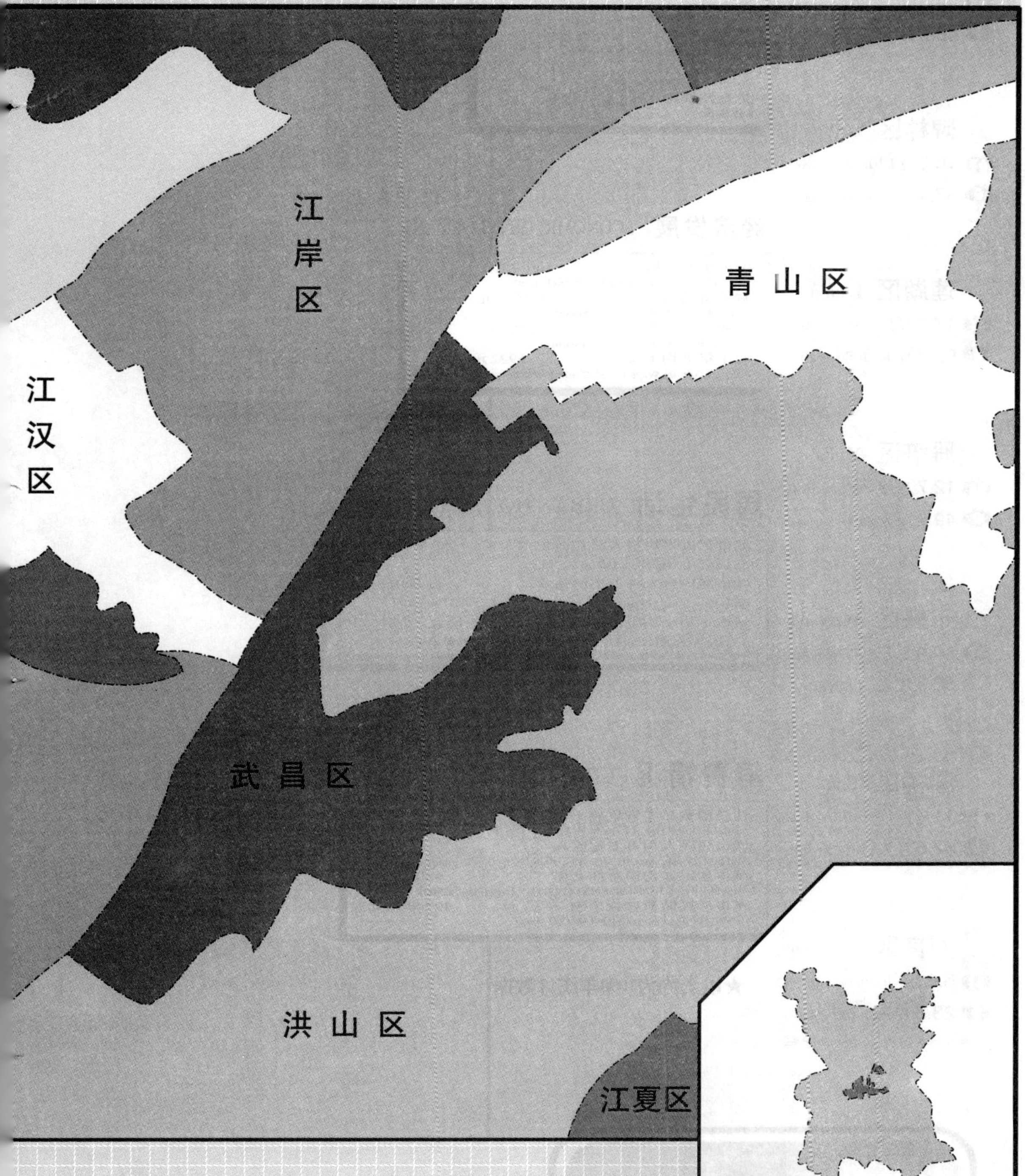

Xi'an

新城区 Xincheng

14.5万户(10 000 households)

46.9万人(10 000 persons)

碑林区 Beilin

16.6万户(10 000 households)

57.4万人(10 000 persons)

莲湖区 Lianhu

17.8万户(10 000 households)

57.2万人(10 000 persons)

雁塔区 Yanta

12.7万户(10 000 households)

49.2万人(10 000 persons)

未央区 Weiyang

10.4万户(10 000 households)

36.3万人(10 000 persons)

灞桥区 Baqiao

11.3万户(10 000 households)

42.6万人(10 000 persons)

阎良区 Yanliang

5.9万户(10 000 households)

23.0万人(10 000 persons)

人口概况 SUMMARY

总人口 Total Population (10000 persons)	668.22万人
总户数 Total Households (10000 households)	178.9万户
平均每户人口 Per Households (1 person)	3.74人
男女性别比 Sex Ratio	1.068

经济发展 ECONOMIC DEVELOPMENT

国内生产总值 Gross Domestic Product(100 000 000 yuan)	560.4亿元
对外贸易出口 Value of Exports (USD 100 000 000)	2.42亿美元
工业企业个数 Number of Industrial Enterprises(unit)	45979个
职工年平均工资 Average Annual Wage for Staff and Workers (yuan)	6922元

居民生活 URBAN HOUSEHOLDS

城市居民平均每人居住面积 Per Capita Living Space (sq.m)	8.6平方米
城市居民每人每天生活用水 Per Capita Daily Consumption of Water for Residential Use (liter)	11.03升
城市每年平均生活用电量 Average Annual Living Electricity Consumption (10 000 kwh)	473202万千瓦/小时

消费情况 CONSUMER INDICATORS

社会消费品零售总额 Total Retail Sales of Consumer Goods (100 000 000 yuan)	271.84亿元
城市居民人均可支配收入 Annual Discretionary Income for Urban Households (yuan)	5669元
城市居民人均消费性支出 Annual Lliving Expenditure Per Capita for Urban Households (yuan)	4806.60元
城市居民储蓄存款余额 Urban Savings Deposit (100 000 000 yuan)	499.68亿元

★以上均为1998年统计数据

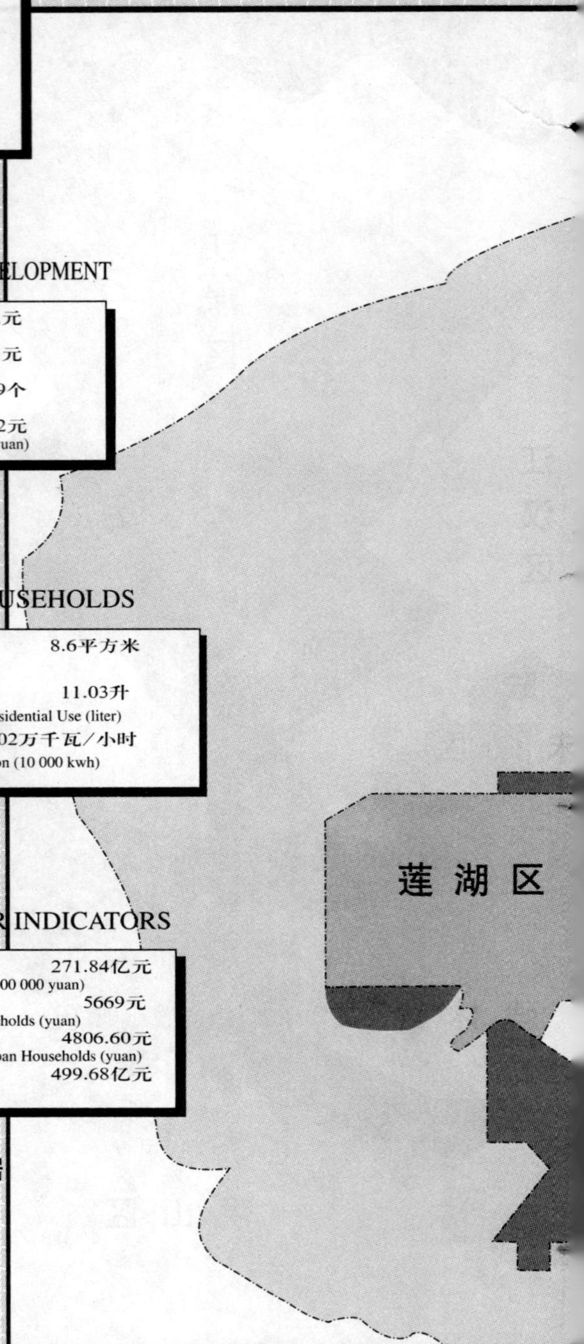

西安地区 图例

区县界　　总户数

西安市区　　总人口

西安地区概况图

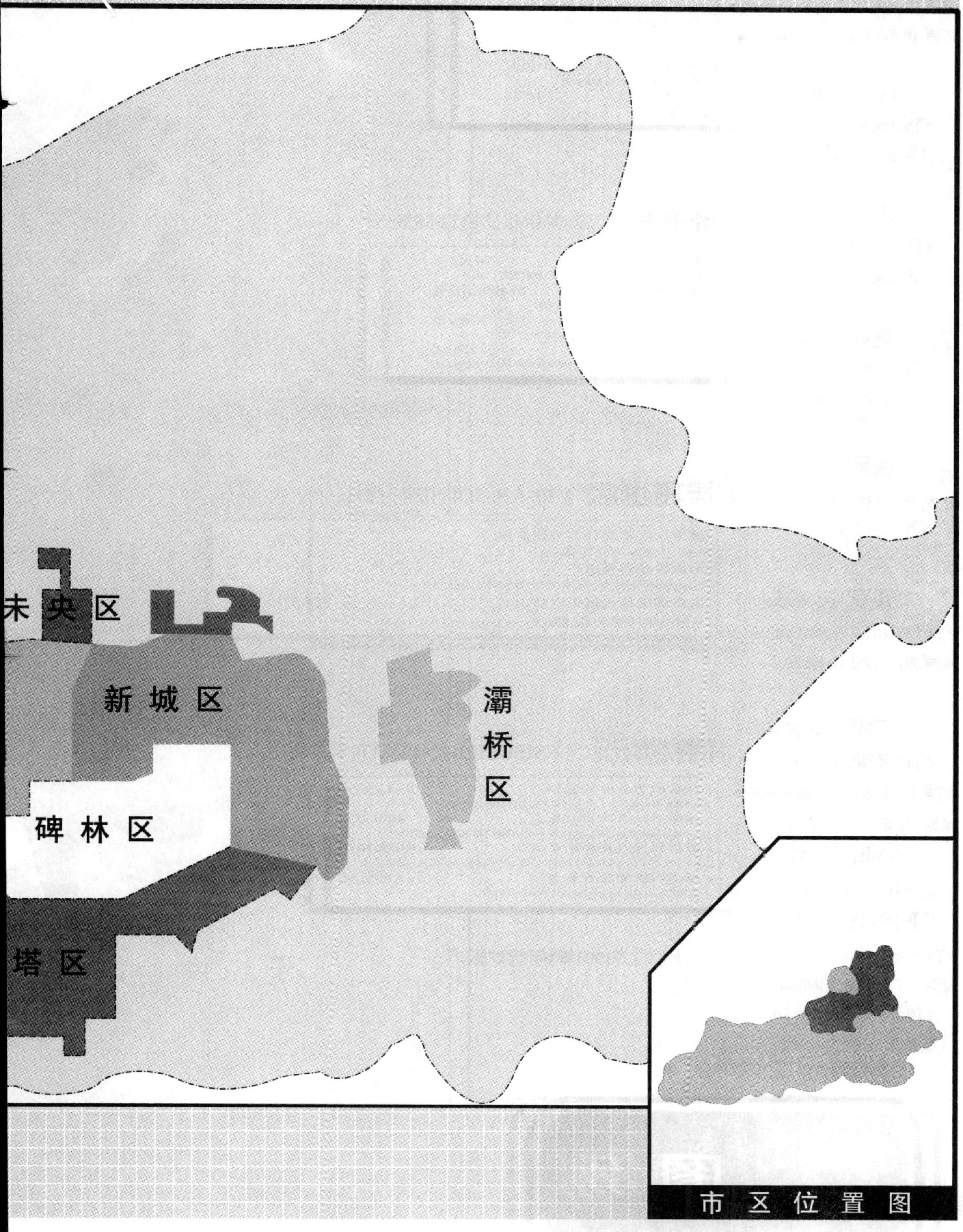

Shenyang

和平 Heping

20.11万户(10 000 households)

63.42万人(10 000 persons)

沈河 Shenhe

19.40万户(10 000 households)

59.55万人(10 000 persons)

大东 Dadong

20.26万户(10 000 households)

63.20万人(10 000 persons)

皇姑 Huanggu

21.62万户(10 000 households)

69.63万人(10 000 persons)

铁西 Tiexi

23.84万户(10 000 households)

75.03万人(10 000 persons)

苏家屯 Sujiatun

12.67万户(10 000 households)

41.26万人(10 000 persons)

东陵 Dongling

12.58万户(10 000 households)

40.87万人(10 000 persons)

新城子 Xinchengzi

8.76万户(10 000 households)

29.75万人(10 000 persons)

于洪 Yuhong

11.16万户(10 000 households)

37.28万人(10 000 persons)

人口概况 SUMMARY

总人口 Total Population (10000 persons)	674.86万人
总户数 Total Households (10000 households)	207.9万户
平均每户人口 Per Households (1 person)	3.25人
男女性别比 Sex Ratio	1.03

经济发展 ECONOMIC DEVELOPMENT

国内生产总值 Gross Domestic Product (100 000 000 yuan)	941亿元
对外贸易出口 Value of Exports (USD 10 000)	89490万美元
工业企业个数 Number of Industrial Enterprises(unit)	54980个
职工年平均工资 Average Annual Wage for Staff and Workers (yuan)	6090元

居民生活 URBAN HOUSEHOLDS

城市居民平均每人居住面积 Per Capita Living Space (sq.m)	7.77平方米
城市居民燃气用户 Households With Access To Gas(10,000 households)	73.7万户
城市居民每人每天生活用水 Living Consumption Per Day (L)	254.2升

消费情况 CONSUMER INDICATORS

社会消费品零售总额 Total Retail Sales of Consumer Goods (100 000 000 yuan)	473.3亿元
城市居民人均可支配收入 Annual Discretionary Income for Urban Households (yuan)	4931.6元
城市居民人均消费性支出 Lliving Expenditure Per Capita for Urban Households (yuan)	4639.58元
城市居民储蓄存款余额 Urban Savings Deposit (100 000 000 yuan)	735.80亿元

★以上均为1998年统计数据

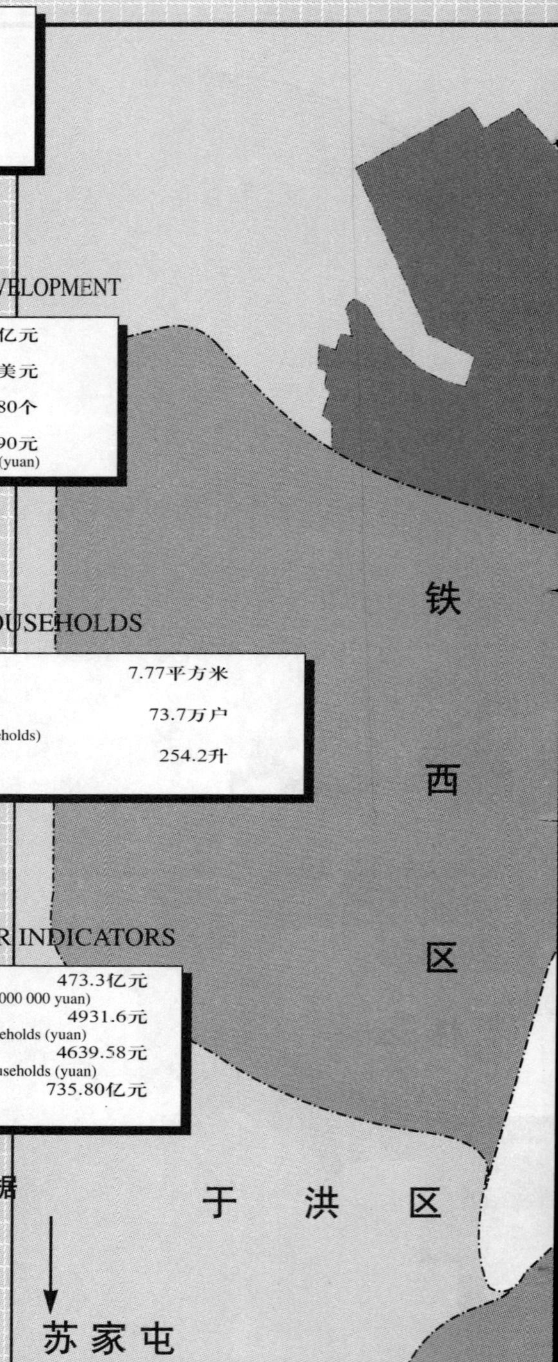

沈阳地区 图例

区县界　　总户数

沈阳市区　　总人口

沈阳地区概况图

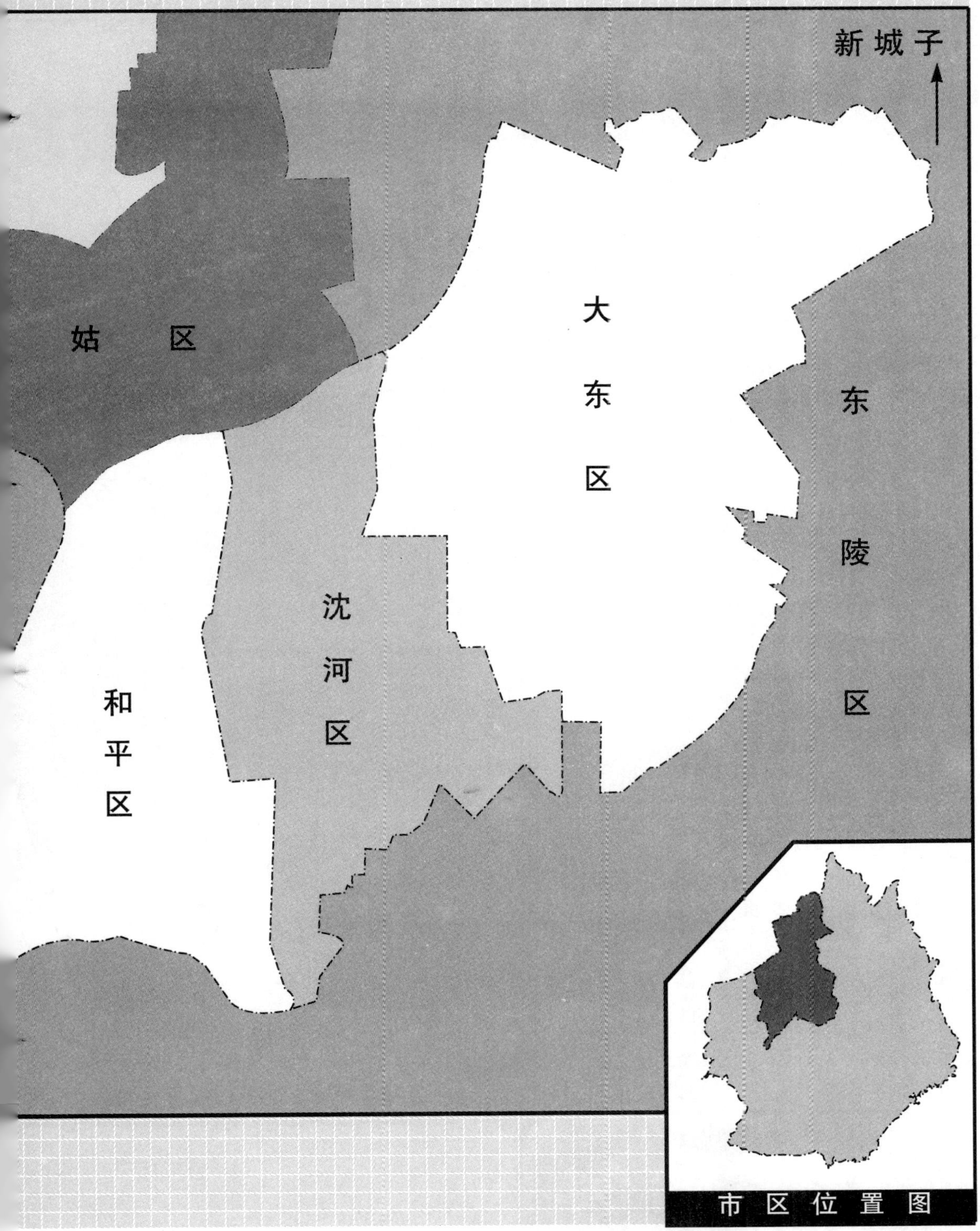

目　　录

上　卷

第一篇　七城市基本情况与样本结构

第二篇 消费者分析

第三篇 消费者日常生活形态

第四篇　媒介分析

第五篇 食品

第六篇 饮料

下 卷

第七篇 烟酒

第八篇　洗涤日用品

第九篇　化妆品、卫生用品

第十篇 药品、营养保健品

第十篇　药品、营养保健品

第十一篇　家用电器、照相器材

第十二篇 电脑、通讯工具

第十三篇　住房、汽车、金融、保险

第十四篇　饮食、购物场所

Contents

Part I The General Market Conditions of the Seven Cities and Sample Compositions

Part II Consumer Analysis

Part III Consumers' Everyday Life

Part IV Media Exposure

Part V Food

Part VI Beverage

Part XIII Housing, Car, Finance and Insurance

第一篇　七城市基本情况与样本结构

Part I　The General Market Conditions of the Seven Cities and Sample Compositions

- 基本状况　The General Market Conditions
  - 北京　Beijing
  - 上海　Shanghai
  - 广州　Guangzhou
  - 重庆　Chongqing
  - 武汉　Wuhan
  - 西安　Xi'an
  - 沈阳　Shenyang
- 样本结构　Sample Compositions
  - 北京　Beijing
  - 上海　Shanghai
  - 广州　Guangzhou
  - 重庆　Chongqing
  - 武汉　Wuhan
  - 西安　Xi'an
  - 沈阳　Shenyang

1 北京市基本情况

The General Market Conditions of Beijing

1-1 人口概况 / General Demographic Characteristics

据 1998 人口抽样调查统计，全市人口出生率 6‰，人口死亡率为 5.3‰，人口自然增长率 0.7‰，比上年下降 1.2 个千分点。年末在京居住半年以上常住人口 1245.6 万人，比上年增加 5.6 万人。据公安部门统计，年末户籍人口为 1091.5 万人，其中男性人口数为 552.6 万人，女性人口数为 538.9 万人，男女之比为 1.02：1。全市家庭总户数为 22669 户，其中城区为 6192 户。人口密度为 647 人/平方公里，其中城区和近郊区的人口密度分别为 27358 人/平方公里和 3196 人/平方公里，宣武区的人口密度最大，为 32620 人/平方公里，丰台区的人口密度最小，为 2612 人/平方公里。

According to the sample population survey in 1998, the birth rate of the population was 6 per thousand ,the death rate was 5.3 per thousand, The natural growth rate of the population was 0.7 per thousand, down 1.2 thousand point over the previous year. The resident population was 12.456 million (population living in Beijing for more than six months), 56000 more than the previous year.

According to statistics from the public security department, the registered population was 10.915 million by the end of 1998, 5.526 million male, 5.389 million female, the sex ratio was 1.02:1 (male=100). By the end of 1998, there were 22669 households in the city, 6192 households in the city districts. The population density was 647 person/sq.km, the figure of city districts and suburban districts was 27358 person/sq.km and 3196 person/sq.km. The population density of Xuanwu district was the largest, 32620 person/sq.km; and that figure of Fengtai district was the smallest, 2612 person/sq.km.

北京地区历年人口变动图（万人）

Total Population Change in Main Years of Beijing（10000 persons）

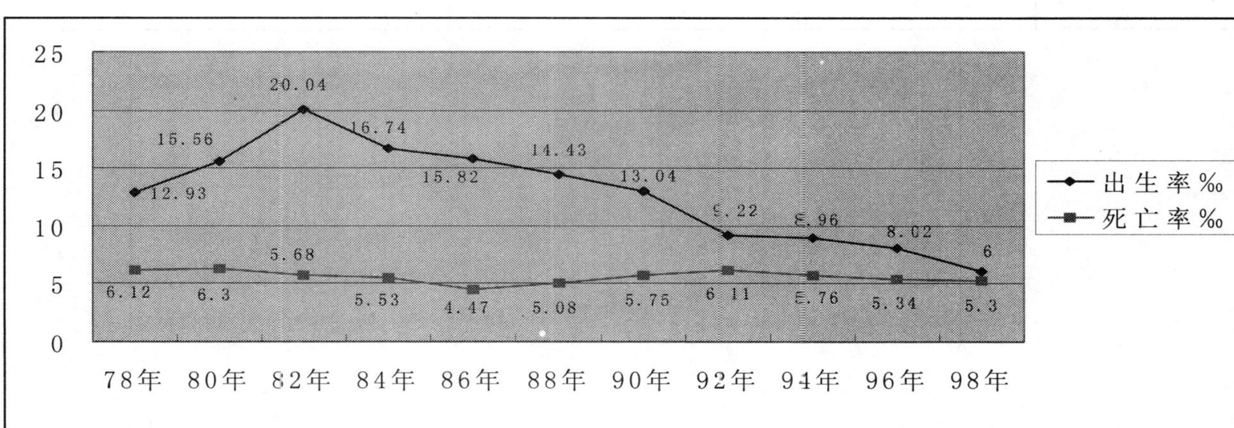

注：本章数据全部摘自《北京统计年鉴 1999 》/Resource:"'99Statistical Yearbook of Beijing"

1-1-1 北京 1998 年人口情况一览表 / List of Population in 1998 of Beijing City

地 区 Region		土地面积（平方公里）Land Area (sq.km)	人口密度（人/平方公里）Population Density (person/sq.km)	常住人口（万人）Permanent (10000 persons)	非农业户（万人）Non-Agricultural	总户数（万户）Total Households (10000 households)	非农业户（万户）Non-Agricultural (10000 households)
全市	Total	16807.8	647	1091.5	733.7	383.4	259.2
城区	City Proper	87.1	27358	240.9	240.9	87.2	87.2
东城区	Dongcheng	24.7	25609	63.3	63.3	23.4	23.4
西城区	Xicheng	30.0	26387	79.2	79.2	28.1	28.1
崇文区	chongwen	15.9	26449	42.0	42.0	15.7	15.7
宣武区	xuanwu	16.5	32620	56.4	56.4	20.0	20.0
近郊区	Near Suburbs	1282.8	3196	410.9	362.0	141.9	121.7
朝阳区	Chaoyang	470.8	3110	146.4	126.9	53.1	44.7
丰台区	Fengtai	304.2	2612	79.5	64.7	29.2	23.4
石景山区	Shijingshan	81.8	3842	32.4	30.8	11.0	10.3
海淀区	Haidian	426.0	3582	152.6	139.6	48.6	43.3

续上表（continued）

地 区 Region		常住人口 男（万人）Permanent Residents Male (10000 person)	常住人口 女（万人）Permanent Residents Female (10000 person)	1998 年出生人数（人）Number of Birth (person)	1998 年死亡人数（人）Number of Death (person)	1998 自然增加人数（人）Number of Natural Growth (person)
全市	Total	552.6	538.9	66892	75247	-8355
城区	City Proper	121.6	119.3	8838	19148	−10310
东城区	Dongcheng	31.6	31.7	2472	4538	−2066
西城区	Xicheng	39.7	39.5	3085	5687	−2602
崇文区	Chongwen	21.0	21.0	1326	3897	−2571
宣武区	Xuanwu	29.3	27.1	1955	5026	−3071
近郊区	Near suburbs	210.5	200.4	20042	25184	-5142
朝阳区	Chaoyang	74.6	71.8	6911	8652	-1741
丰台区	Fengtai	40.5	39.0	4146	6678	-2532
石景山区	Shijingshan	17.1	15.3	1522	2239	-717
海淀区	Haidian	78.3	74.3	7463	7615	-152

1-1-2 北京市人口年龄构成及性别比（人口变动情况抽样调查资料）/ Age and Gender Composition（From the Result of the Migration Survey）

年龄段 Age Group	抽样人口数（人） Number of Persons Sampled (person)			占抽样人口数的比重（%） Percentage (%)			性别比 Sex Ratio （女=100） (Male=100)
	合计 Total	男 Male	女 Female	合计 Total	男 Male	女 Female	
总计 Total	71486	36417	35069	100	50.94	49.06	103.84
0-4 岁	2295	1191	1104	3.21	1.67	1.54	107.88
5-9 岁	3857	2004	1853	5.39	2.80	2.59	108.15
10-14 岁	5096	2615	2481	7.[illegible]3	3.66	3.47	105.40
15-19 岁	5178	2605	2573	7.24	3.64	3.60	101.24
20-24 岁	4769	2597	2172	6.67	3.63	3.04	119.57
25-29 岁	5930	2974	2956	8.30	4.16	4.14	100.61
30-34 岁	6540	3302	3238	9.[illegible]5	4.62	4.53	101.98
35-39 岁	7755	3963	3792	10.84	5.54	5.30	104.51
40-44 岁	7643	3866	3777	10.69	5.41	5.28	102.36
45-49 岁	5836	3015	2821	8.[illegible]7	4.22	3.95	106.88
50-54 岁	3562	1899	1663	4.99	2.66	2.33	114.19
55-59 岁	3014	1460	1554	4.21	2.04	2.17	93.95
60-64 岁	3575	1748	1827	5.01	2.45	2.56	95.68
65-69 岁	2798	1438	1360	3.91	2.01	1.90	105.74
70-74 岁	1867	915	952	2.61	1.28	1.33	96.11
75-79 岁	996	492	504	1.40	0.69	0.71	97.62
80-84 岁	514	218	296	0.71	0.30	0.41	73.65
85-89 岁	197	90	107	0.28	0.13	0.15	84.11
90 岁及以上	64	24	39	0.09	0.03	0.06	64.10

1-1-3 北京市历年人口变动情况 / Migration of Beijing City

年 份 Year	年底总人口（万人） Total population (10000 persons)	按性别分 Grouped by Sex		按农业、非农业分 Grouped by Agriculture and Non-Agriculture		人口出生率（‰） Birth Rate	人口死亡率（‰） Death Rate	人口自然增长率（‰） Natural Growth Rate
		男 Male	女 Female	农业人口 Agricultural	非农业人口 Non-agricultural			
1978	872	443	429	393	479	12.93	6.12	6.81
1979	897	455	442	387	510	13.67	5.92	7.75
1980	904	458	446	383	521	15.56	6.30	9.26
1981	919	466	453	386	533	16.93	6.02	10.91
1982	935	474	461	391	544	20.04	5.68	14.36
1983	950	483	467	393	557	15.63	5.49	10.14
1984	965	491	474	395	570	16.74	5.53	11.21
1985	981	500	481	395	586	15.45	5.75	9.70
1986	1028	524	504	407	621	15.82	4.47	11.35
1987	1047	525	522	410	637	17.29	5.40	11.89
1988	1061	534	527	411	650	14.43	5.08	9.35
1989	1075	538	537	431	664	12.84	5.53	7.49
1990	1086	545	541	413	673	13.04	5.75	7.23
1991	1094	547	547	411	683	8.03	5.82	2.21
1992	1102	554	548	410	692	9.22	6.11	3.11
1993	1112	559	553	405	707	9.35	6.16	3.19
1994	1125	564	561	400	725	8.96	5.76	3.20
1995	1251	627	624	436	815	7.92	5.12	2.80
1996	1259	639	620	430	829	8.02	5.34	2.68
1997	1240	551	535	363	723	7.91	6.02	1.89
1998	1224	552.6	538.9	357.8	733.7	6.0	5.3	0.7

注：1982-1989 年数据是根据 1982、1990 两年人口普查数据调整的，1990 年以后数据是人口变动抽样调查数，其余年份数据为户籍统计数。

1-2 经济发展 / Economic Development

1998 年北京市完成全年经济增长 9%的目标、国民经济继续保持“高增长，低通胀”的良好发展态势。1998 年全市实现国民生产总值 200.9 亿元，按可比价格计算，比上年增长 9.7%。

全市经济继续保持“三、二、一”的增长格局，第三产业继续保持领先增长。全年第一产业实现增加值 87 亿元，比上年增长 1.8%，第二产业全年实现增加值 790.8 亿元，比上年增长 9.6%；第三产业继续成为促进经济发展的增长点，全年实现增加值达到 1132.1 亿元，比上年增长 10.5%，比全市经济增速高 0.8 个百分点，占国内生产总值的比重为 56.3%。

全年实现工业增加值 614 亿元，比上年增长 9.1%，其中年销售收入在 500 万元及以上企业实现增加值 540 亿元,增长 10.5%。建筑业全年实现增加值 176.8 亿元，按可比价格计算增长 12.4%，增速比上年提高 7.3 个百分点。

邮电通信业发展突飞猛进。年末本地公众电话交换机总容量达到 686 万门，比上年增长 25.6%。电信业务稳步增长，其中计算机互联网络用户，数字数据网用户增长迅速，市区电话普及率达到 69 部/百人，比上年增加 13 部，移动电话用户 116.7 万户，新增 50 万户。

全年批发、零售贸易和餐饮业实现增加值 207.8 亿元，比上年增长 4.5%。金融、保险业实现增加值 271.95 亿元，比上年增加 8.62%。全市金融机构累计回笼资金 70.7 亿元，创历史最好水平。

房地产业逐渐走出调整期，市场销售渐旺。全年房地产开发实现增加值 68.1 亿元，比上年增加 55.8%。房地产施工面积 3499.1 万平方米，比上年增长 21.6%。其中商品住宅 376.8 万平方米，比上年增长 47.1%；竣工面积 842.8 万平方米，比上年增长 23.5%。市场销售看好，全年销售商品房 409.1 万平方米（建筑面积），增长 40.6%，其中销售商品住宅 376.8 万平方米，比上年增长 47.1%。商品房销售额 216 亿元，增长 31.6%。

全年利用外资 28.7 亿美元，其中外商直接投资额 20.7 亿美元，增长 29.6%；非投资性对外借款 5.7 亿美元，下降 12.0%。

旅游规模不断扩大。全年接待海外旅游者 220.1 万人次，比上年下降 4.2%。全年旅游外汇收入 23.8 亿美元，比上年增长 6%。随着人民生活水平的不断提高，来京旅游的国内游客达到 8731 万人次，增长 8.4%。全市宾馆饭店客房出租率 55%。

In 1998,the national economy continued to keep a good tendency of “High Growth and Low Inflation.” According to primary statistics, the city‘s Gross Domestic Product (GDP) accomplished in 1998 was 20.09 billion yuan, a growth of 9.7 percent over the previous year at comparable prices.

The service sector continued to contribute the most, industry the second most and agriculture the third most to the city‘s economic development. The achieved added value of primary industry was 8.7 billion yuan, up 1.8%, the secondary industry was 79.08 billion yuan, up 9.6%, the teriary industry was 113.21 billion yuan, up 10.5%, and the service sector continued to keep the lead in the growth rate, accounting for 56.3 percent of the GDP.

The added value accomplished by industry annually was 61.4 billion yuan, up 9.1percent over the previous year. The industrial enterprises with more than 5 million yuan achieved the added value of 54 billion, up 10.5 percent.The added value accomplished by construction was17.68 billion yuan, a growth of 7.3 percent over the previous year at comparable prices.

Post and telecommunications developed rapidly. By the end of the year, the total capacity of local public telephone exchanges reached 6.86 million gates, up 25.6 percent over the previous year. The turnover of communication rose steadily. Of which, the number of subscribers of computer networks and data networks increased rapidly. By the end of the year, every 100 residents owned 69 telephone sets, up 13 sets. And the number of mobile telephone was 1,167,000, up 500,000.

The achieved added value of wholesale, retail trade and catering is 20.78 billion yuan, up 4.5% over the previous year. The achieved added value of finance and insuring was 27.195 billion yuan, up 8.62%. The currency withdrawn by the finance organization was 7.07 billion yuan, attaining the top level of the history.

Real estate gradually bid farewell to the adjustment period and the market was thriving, Investment in the development of real estate was 6.81 billion yuan, up 55.8 percent over the previous year. The construction area of the real estate sector was 34.991 million square meters, up 21.6%. Of which, the housing area was 3.768 million square meters, up 47.1 percent over the previous year; the completed area was 8 428 million square meters, up 23.5 percent over the previous year. Sales on the real estate market were hot. The total sales areas of completed houses were 4.091 million square meters (construction area), up 40.6 percent. Of which, the sales areas of completed houses were 3.768 million square meters, up 47.1 percent, the total sales was 21.6 billion yuan, up 31.6%.

The total foreign capital utilized was 2.87 billion dollar, of which the direct investment was2.07 billion, up 29.6%, the un-invested foreign loan was 0.57 billion dollar, down 12.0%.

Tourism continued to be expanded and international tourism developed healthily. The number of foreign tourists for 1998 was 2.201 million, down 4.2 percent over 1997. Earnings in foreign exchange reached 2.38 billion US dollars, up 6 percent over the previous year. With gradual improvement of people's living standards, the number of domestic tourist to Beijing reached 87.31 million, up 8.4 percent. The occupancy rate of the city's hotels was 55 percent.

1-2-1 主要年份国内生产总值 / Gross National Product in Main Years

单位：亿元 (100 000 000 yuan)

年 份 Year	国内生产总值 Gross Domestic Product	第一产业 Primary Industry	第二产业 Secondary Industry	工业 Industry	建筑业 Construction	第三产业 Tertiary Industry	运输邮电业 Transportation,Post and Telecommunications	商业 Wholesale, Retail and Catering	人均国内生产总值（元） Per Capital Gross Domestic Products (yuan)
1978	108.84	5.63	77.43	70.22	7.21	25.78	7.00	8.28	1290
1979	120.11	5.17	85.18	77.37	7.81	29.76	6.55	8.79	1391
1980	139.07	6.07	95.79	86.94	8.85	37.21	6.96	11.01	1582
1981	139.15	6.67	92.52	82.71	9.81	40.02	7.60	11.86	1558
1982	154.94	10.34	99.79	89.30	10.49	44.81	8.25	11.05	1704
1983	183.13	12.85	112.65	98.76	13.89	57.63	9.06	13.63	1977
1984	216.61	14.85	130.68	113.99	16.69	71.08	10.43	18.37	2308
1985	257.12	17.81	153.66	130.65	23.01	85.65	12.74	25.89	2704
1986	284.86	19.14	165.75	141.17	24.58	99.97	14.98	27.99	2955
1987	326.82	24.31	182.59	154.54	28.05	119.92	17.70	27.21	3338
1988	410.22	37.07	221.27	189.48	31.79	151.88	19.03	39.07	4125
1989	455.96	38.53	252.23	212.83	39.40	165.20	18.72	34.77	4499
1990	500.82	43.88	262.39	219.27	43.12	194.55	23.96	43.85	3224
1991	598.89	45.52	291.53	255.59	35.94	261.84	29.61	65.65	5781
1992	709.10	48.67	345.91	292.97	52.94	314.52	35.49	85.41	6805
1993	863.53	53.57	414.79	334.00	80.79	395.17	37.58	113.88	8240
1994	1084.03	74.77	499.84	405.11	94.73	509.42	61.55	146.62	10265
1995	1394.89	81.44	615.17	503.71	111.46	693.28	83.55	174.70	13073
1996	1615.73	83.46	683.14	541.41	141.73	849.13	113.78	187.59	15044
1997	1810.09	84.85	738.56	588.36	150.20	985.68	135.79	202.45	16735
1998	2011.31	86.56	786.85	610.66	176.19	1137.9	154.45	207.33	18478

1-2-2 社会消费品零售总额 / Retail Sales of Consumer Goods

单位：亿元 (100 000 000 yuan)

年 · 份 Year	社会消费品零售额 Total Retail Sales of Consumer Goods	按行业分 By Sector				按类别分 By Tape			
		批发零售贸易业 Wholesale and Retail Trade	餐饮业 Catering	制造业 Manufact-uring	其它行业 Others	食品类 Food	衣着类 Clothing	日用品类 Daily Used Articles	燃料类 Fuels
1978	44.17	40.67	1.73	1.24	0.52	18.03	8.86	12.41	1.34
1979	52.20	47.34	2.11	2.10	0.53	20.38	11.08	15.67	1.46
1980	61.32	53.48	2.73	3.52	1.15	24.36	12.94	18.78	1.59
1981	68.82	57.83	3.53	5.10	1.70	27.19	14.08	21.86	1.72
1982	73.31	61.41	3.72	5.45	1.98	28.94	13.29	24.21	1.70
1983	83.57	70.40	4.01	5.98	2.33	32.89	15.17	27.89	1.85
1984	101.66	85.61	4.72	7.76	2.68	38.05	18.00	36.96	2.18
1985	127.90	106.47	6.00	9.58	3.08	47.15	21.40	50.30	2.82
1986	146.46	119.28	8.11	8.90	3.90	57.38	21.59	57.06	3.32
1987	176.59	140.24	10.68	11.96	5.46	72.37	25.59	67.32	3.68
1988	234.30	186.36	16.10	13.87	7.16	92.04	32.99	93.88	4.11
1989	266.73	213.06	16.50	15.43	9.04	108.06	31.58	106.27	5.81
1990	307.66	247.72	19.30	14.31	10.19	121.96	40.62	123.27	7.18
1991	357.75	286.21	22.89	16.75	11.91	138.51	47.06	146.62	7.72
1992	430.01	333.71	30.82	19.41	17.07	165.49	57.19	174.81	10.28
1993	531.79	393.00	44.62	28.65	22.29	192.01	84.00	241.50	14.28
1994	666.98	481.49	54.20	25.33	11.79	246.42	108.99	294.58	16.99
1995	826.98	584.86	63.04	29.57	8.09	353.01	120.90	337.48	15.59
1996	969.66	691.23	71.92	38.09	29.27	413.06	142.03	397.30	17.27
1997	1051.53	709.44	72.42	56.32	213.29	389.68	104.58	492.15	29.13
1998	1195.21	865.71	81.82	63.75	183.94	347.89	145.50	664.88	36.95

注：1993 年以前是社会商品零售总额，1993 年以后是社会消费品零售总额。/Note: Data before 1993 refers to total retail sales of commodity and data after 1993 refers to total retail sales of consumer goods.

1-2-3 各城区国民经济主要指标一览表 / List of Major Economic Indicators in Districts of Beijing

项　目 Item	东城区 Dongcheng	西城区 Xicheng	崇文区 Chongwen	宣武区 xuanwu	朝阳区 Chaoyang	丰台区 Fengtai	石景山区 Shijingshan	海淀区 Haidian
常住户籍人口（万人） Permanent residents (person)	63.3	79.2	42.0	56.4	146.4	79.5	32.4	152.6
自然增加人数 Number of Natural Growth	-2066	-2602	-2571	-3071	-1741	-2532	-717	-152
职工平均工资（元） Average Wage for Staff and Workers (yuan)	13462	13970	11432	11908	13203	10074	10380	13840
社会消费品零售总额（万元） Total Retail Sales of Consumer Goods	706419	974557	357645	423989	1483969	599632	306219	2388971
食品类（万元） Food (10000 yuan)	271561	267432	117083	137626	348733	249481	160954	417534
衣着类（万元） Clothing (10000 yuan)	101142	185988	50765	40942	227047	42115	14069	108324
日用品类（万元） Daily Use Articles (10000 yuan)	327852	517994	187129	242348	851798	284436	124027	1842938
燃料类（万元） Fuels (10000 yuan)	5864	3143	2668	3073	56391	23600	7169	2017

1-3 居民生活 / Living Conditions of the Residents

全市再就业工程取得进展。全年下岗职工 16.96 万人，其中 10.21 万人实现了再就业，下岗职工在就业率 60.2%；富余人员分流安置率 72.9%。年末城镇失业登记 2.95 万人，登记失业率 0.66%。社会保障制度改革稳步推进，全市养老统筹覆盖面为 95%，失业保险统筹覆盖面为 94%，地方企业大病医疗统筹覆盖面为 85.2%，分别比上年增加 12.6 个、9.7 个和 12.2 个百分点。

城乡人民收入明显提高，生活质量进一步改善。全市职工平均工资 12300 元，比上年增长 11.6%，扣除价格因素影响，实际增长 9%。全市城镇居民人均可支配收入 8472 元，比上年增长 8.4%，扣除价格因素，实际增长 5.9%，人均消费性支出为 6970.8 元，比上年同期增长 6.7%。

城乡居民储蓄继续增加，到年末，城乡居民储蓄存款余额达 2287.2 亿元，比年初增加 312 亿元。其中城镇居民储蓄存款余额达 2063.2 亿元，比年初增加 292.4 亿元：农民储蓄存款余额达 224 亿元，比年初增加 19.6 亿元。居民居住条件得到改善。城镇居民人均使用面积达到 14.86 平方米，比上年增加 3.5%，农民人均生活用房面积 27.6 平方米，比年初增加 0.7%。

New progress was made in the re-employment project and the reform if the social insurance system, The unemployed and laid–off people were handled by the municipal government properly, and1,021,000 of the 1,696,000 laid–people in the year were handled. The rearrangement rate in urban districts was 60.2 percent. The social insurance system further improved, The city's planning on the pension scheme, serious sick and health care and unemployment reached 95 percent, 94 percent and 85.2 percent respectively, up 12.6,9.7 and 12.2 percent respectively, playing an active role for social stabilization.

The income of urban and rural residents increased obviously and the living quality was further upgraded. The annual per capita wage of the city's employees was 12,300 yuan,up11.6 percent over the previous year. Eliminating the price factor, the actual growth was 9 percent. The per capita of living income was 8472 yuan ,up 8.4%,eliminating the price factor, the actual growth was 5.9%, the per capita of living expenditure was 6970.4 yuan , up 6.7% over the same time of the pervious year.

The savings of the urban and rural residents continued to grow. By the end of 1999, their savings reached 228.72 billion yuan, or 31.2 billion yuan more than the beginning of the year. Of which, 206.32 billion yuan were savings of urban and township residents, and increased 29.24 billion yuan from the beginning of the year; 22.4 billion yuan belonged to the rural residents, increasing 1.96 billion yuan as compared to the beginning of the year. The residents' housing conditions witnessed further improvements. The per capita housing space in the urban area reached 14.86 square meters and increased 3.5 percent over the previous year, and the per capita housing space in the rural area 27.6 square meters, up 0.7 square meters compared with the beginning of the year.

1-3-1 平均每人主要社会经济活动 / Major Economic Indicators Per Capita

项 目	Item	单位 Unit	1998	1997	1998 为 1997 的百分比 1998 as % of 1997
社会消费品零售总额	Retail Sales of Consumer Goods	元（yuan）	110980.4	9722.0	112.9
食品	Food	元（yuan）	3196.0	3602.8	88.7
衣着	Clothing	元 (yuan)	1336.7	1299.7	102.8
用品	Daily Used Articles	元 (yuan)	6108.2	4550.2	134.2
主要消费品零售量	Retail Sales of Consumer Goods				
粮食	Grain	公斤 (kg)	109.8	215.4	51.0
食用植物油	Edible Vegetable Oil	公斤 (kg)	25.1	31.4	79.9
猪肉	Pork	公斤 (kg)	20.2	30.0	67.3
鲜蛋	Fresh Eggs	公斤 (kg)	8.7	11.5	75.7
水产品	Aquatic	公斤 (kg)	15.4	24.1	63.9
棉布	Cotton	米 (meter)	0.46	0.47	97.9
邮电	Postal and telecommunications				
邮寄函件	Mail	件 (unit)	46.6	50.2	92.8
城市公用事业	Urban				
日生活用水量	Daily Residential Use of Water	公斤 (kg)	238.2	229.0	104.0
城市居民居住面积	Living Space of Urban Residence	平方米 (sq.m)	10.03	9.66	103.8
平均每千人拥有公共交通车量	Possession of Public Traffic Vehicle Per 1000 Persons	辆 (unit)	0.99	0.97	102.1
乘坐公共电汽车次数	Times of Riding Bus or Trolley	次 (times)	342.2	320.5	106.8
人均公共绿地面积	Public Green Areas	平方米 (sq.m)	9.0	7.8	115.0
卫生	Health				
平均每千人拥有医生	Number of Doctors Per 1000 Persons	人 (person)	4.76	5.06	94.1
平均每千人拥有医院床位	Number of Beds Per 1000 Persons	张 (unit)	6.13	6.06	101.2
人民生活	People's Livelihood				
职工年平均工资	Annual Average Wage	元 (yuan)	12285.0	11019.0	111.5
居民家庭生活费收入	Annual Living Income of Urban Residence	元 (yuan)	8472.0	7813.1	108.4
农民家庭纯收入	Annual Net Income of Rural Residence	元 (yuan)	4028.9	3762.4	107.1
城市居民储蓄存款余额	Saving Deposit of Urban and Rural	元 (yuan)	20954.5	18196.8	115.2
城镇居民	Urban	元 (yuan)	28120.3	24504.0	114.8
农村居民	Rural	元 (yuan)	6260.5	5632.7	111.1

1-3-2 历年职工年平均工资变化情况 / Changes in the Average Annual Wage for Staff and Workers in Main Years

（单位：元）

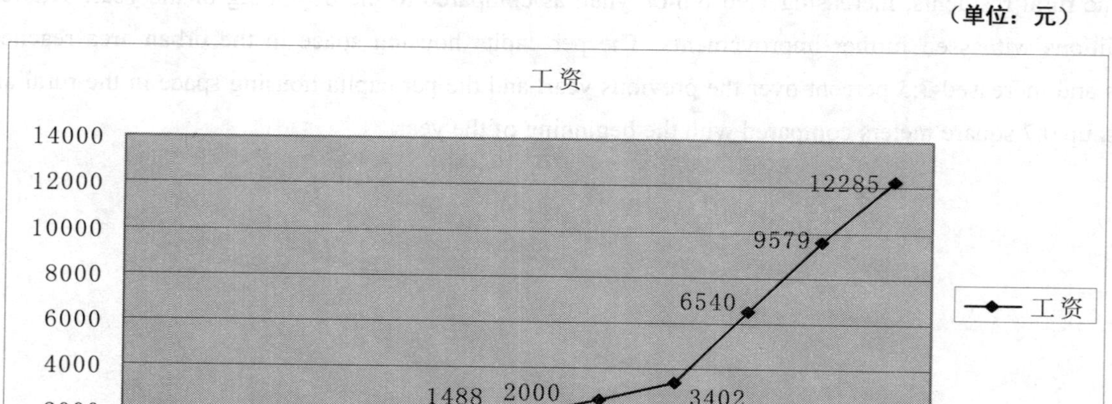

1-3-3 1000 户居民家庭平均每百户耐用消费品年末拥有情况一览表 / List of Per 100 Household Year-end Possession of Durable Consumer yuan Goods of 1000 Urban Households

项 目	Item	单位 Unit	总平均 Average	低收入户 Low Income	中等偏下收入户 Medium-Low Income	中等收入户 Medium Income	中等偏上收入户 Medium-High Income	高收入户 High Income	1998 为 1997 的% 1998 as % of 1997
自行车	Bicycles	辆 (unit)	221	232	223	225	218	208	105.5
电风扇	Electric Fans	台 (set)	145	136	130	153	147	160	105.4
电冰箱	Refrigerators	台 (set)	105.4	102	104	106	104	111.00	101.2
冰柜	Freezers	台 (set)	15.60	11	15	15	18	18	94
洗衣机	Washing machines	台 (set)	102.2	94	104	106	100	107	101.6
彩电	Color TV Sets	台 (set)	133.2	122	124	141	130	149	107.6
录放像机	Video recorders	台 (set)	59.8	52	52	58	69	68	106.8
家用电脑	Game-Computers	台 (set)	15	9	17	15	10	24	123.0
组合音响	Hi-fi Systems	套 (set)	22.2	11	24	20	24	32	114.4
照相机	Cameras	架 (set)	95.2	71	94	88	108	114	107.9
微波炉	Microwave Stove	台 (set)	37.2	21	36	32	43	53	144.2
空调器	Air-Conditioners	台 (set)	34	16	32	16	38	67	125.0
淋浴热水器	Showers	个 (set)	65.4	39	54	60	79	94	112.0
排油烟机	Range Hoods	台 (set)	59.4	36	46	60	70	85	105.3
吸尘器	Dust Catcher	台 (set)	23.4	16	15	17	37	32	97.5
电炊具	Electric Cooking	台 (set)	68.6	49	50	69	77	97	127.0
摩托车	Motorcycles	辆 (unit)	3.8	3	1	4	4	7	90.5

1-3-4 居民收入、支出、储蓄情况一览表 / List of Income, Expenditure and Savings Deposit of Urban Household

年份 Year	城镇居民家庭平均每人每年（元） Annual Income Per Capita of Urban Households (yuan)			农村居民家庭平均每人每年（元） Annual Income Per Capita of Rural Households (yuan)			城镇储蓄（亿元） Urban Savings Deposit (100 000 000 yuan)	农户储蓄（亿元） Rural Saving Deposit (100 000 000 yuan)	人均储蓄（元） Saving Deposit Per Capita (yuan)
	全部收入 Total	生活费收入 Living Income	生活消费支出 Living Expenditure	纯收入 Net Income	总支出 Total Expenditure	生活消费支出 Living Expenditure			
1978	450.18	365.40	359.86	225	219	185	8.90	0.43	107.09
1979	491.54	414.95	408.66	250	235	205	10.44	0.63	123.04
1980	599.40	501.36	490.44	308	290	257	13.33	1.06	159.20
1981	619.57	514.14	511.43	361	351	307	15.74	1.65	189.23
1982	668.06	561.05	534.82	430	411	346	19.19	2.58	232.55
1983	716.60	590.47	574.06	519	499	384	25.11	4.70	312.49
1984	837.65	693.70	666.75	664	559	435	32.14	6.67	401.42
1985	1158.84	907.72	923.32	775	726	510	42.24	9.45	522.70
1986	1317.33	1067.52	1067.38	823	857	645	55.62	12.95	664.52
1987	1413.24	1181.87	1147.60	916	943	706	75.19	17.79	871.38
1988	1767.67	1436.97	1455.55	1063	1246	883	90.55	21.09	1032.98
1989	1899.57	1787.08	1520.41	1231	1356	976	133.75	28.26	1597.76
1990	2067.33	1787.08	1646.05	1297	1372	981	188.03	38.59	2208.73
1991	2359.88	2040.43	1860.17	1422	1585	1100	249.88	48.30	2878.21
1992	2813.10	2363.68	2134.65	1569	1684	1179	328.21	59.61	3721.93
1993	3935.39	3296.04	2939.60	1855	1714	1309	482.48	78.18	5349.78
1994	5585.88	4731.24	4134.12	2422	2175	1676	745.88	107.33	8079.62
1995	6748.68	5868.36	5019.76	3224	3080	2433	1111.50	142.46	11757.61
1996	7945.78	6885.48	5729.45	3580	3272	2656	1528.41	178.56	15839.09
1997	8741.71	7813.11	6531.81	3762	3379	2795	1770.91	204.36	18188.77
1998	10098.23	8471.98	6970.83	4028	3617	2945	2063.19	224.00	20954.54

2　上海市基本情况

The General Market Conditions of Shanghai

2-1　人口概况 / General Demographic Characteristics

1998 年末上海市总人口（户籍人口）为 1306.58 万人。全市人口出生率为 4.7‰，死亡率为 7.8‰，自然增长率为-3.1‰。1998 年上海人口占全国总人口的 1%。在全市总人口中，男性为 658.22 万人，占 50.4%，农业人口为 352.93 万人，占 27%。

1998 年末上海市家庭总户数 465.72 万户，平均每户家庭人口 2.8 人。全市人口密度每平方公里为 2061 人，其中市区每平方公里为 3296 人，郊县每平方公里为 763 人。人口分布继续由中心城区向边缘地区转移。全市人口密度最高的南市区达每平方公里 56791 人，比上年减少 1442 人。

上海人口平均寿命男性为 75.06 岁，女性为 79.02 岁，分别比 1978 年提高 4.37 岁和 4.24 岁，高于世界平均水平和中等收入国家水平，接近主要发达国家水平。

By the end of 1998, Shanghai had a population (with residence cards) of 13,065,800. In 1998, the birth rate stood at 0.47%, mortality rate 0.78% and the natural growth rate –0.31 %. The city's population accounted for 1% of the nation's total. Of the city's population, 6,582,200 were male or 50.4% of the total and 3,529,300 belonged to the agricultural population or 27.8% of the total.

By the end of 1998, there were 4,657,200 households in the city with an average family having 2.8 members. The city's average population density reached 2,061 persons per square kilometer, with the figure in the urban area standing at 3,296 persons per square kilometer and the rural figure 763 persons per square kilometer .However, the population is continuing to spread from downtown areas to suburban areas. Nanshi District reported the highest population density of 56,791 persons per square kilometer, 1,442 persons less than that of the previous year.

The city's average life expectancy grew to 75.06 years for men and 79.02 years for women, 4.37 and 4.24 years longer than the 1978 figures, respectively. So, the city's average life expectancy was higher than the level of the world average and that of the middle–income countries and close to that of economically advanced countries.

注：本章数据全部摘自《上海统计年鉴 1999》/Resource: ″'99 Statistical Yearbook of Shanghai″

上海历年人口变动图（‰）

Population Change in Main Years of Shanghai（‰）

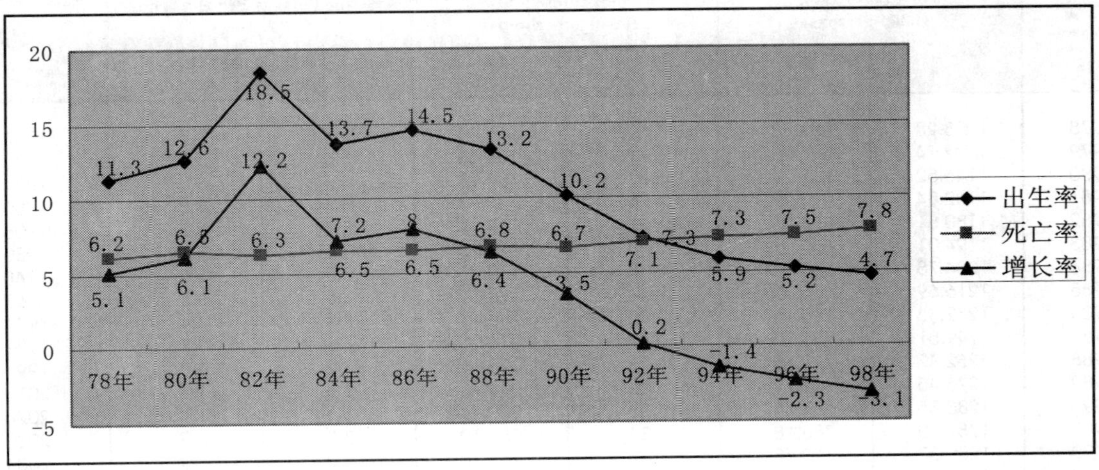

2-1-1 上海市 1998 年人口情况一览表 / List of Population in 1998 of Shanghai City

地区 Region		土地面积（平方公里）Land Area (sq.km)	总户数（万户）Total Households (10000 households)	年底总人口（万人）Total population (10000 persons)	平均每户人口（人）Average Persons Per Household	人口密度（人/平方里）Population Density (person/sq.km)	出生人数（万人）Birth (10000persons)
全市	Total	6340.50	465.72	1306.58	2.8	2061	6.17
城区	Urban District	3248.7	378.79	1070.62	2.8	3296	4.77
黄浦区	Huangpu	4.54	8.33	24.91	3.0	54862	0.09
南市区	Nanshi	7.87	16.30	44.69	2.7	56791	0.24
卢湾区	Luwan	8.05	13.51	36.80	2.7	45710	0.14
徐汇区	Xuhui	54.76	30.41	84.79	2.8	15483	0.33
长宁区	Changning	38.30	22.19	61.07	2.8	15945	0.23
静安区	Jing'an	7.62	13.18	37.31	2.8	48968	0.14
普陀区	Putuo	54.83	29.60	83.45	2.8	15220	0.31
闸北区	Zhabei	29.26	25.14	68.65	2.7	23460	0.25
虹口区	Hongkou	23.48	29.33	79.97	2.7	34058	0.31
杨浦区	Yangpu	60.73	37.61	108.03	2.9	17789	0.42
浦东新区	Pudong New Area	522.75	56.39	156.18	2.8	2988	0.70
闵行区	Minhang	371.68	20.96	59.34	2.8	1597	0.31
嘉定区	Jiading	458.80	14.98	47.41	3.2	1033	0.28
宝山区	Baoshan	415.27	27.42	75.30	2.7	1813	0.35
金山区	Jinshan	586.05	17.22	53.69	3.1	916	0.37
松江区	songjiang	604.71	16.22	49.03	3.0	811	0.30

2-1-2 上海市历年人口变动情况 / Migration of Shanghai in Main Years

年 份 Year	年底总人口（万人）Total population (10000 persons)		总户数（万户）Total Households (10000 households)		平均每户人口（人）Average Persons Per Household (Person)		人口密度（人/平方公里）Population Density (person/sq.km)	
		市区 District		市区 District		市区 District		市区 District
1978	1098.28	557.38	291.69	151.84	3.8	3.7	1776	35153
1979	1132.14	591.45	296.71	154.58	3.8	3.8	1830	37301
1980	1146.52	601.29	303.87	157.96	3.8	3.8	1854	37922
1981	1162.84	613.39	314.56	162.68	3.7	3.8	1880	27520
1982	1180.51	626.84	321.71	167.54	3.7	3.7	1908	27230
1983	1194.01	639.07	330.60	173.03	3.6	3.7	1930	27762
1984	1204.78	688.13	340.78	189.72	3.5	3.6	1948	19716
1985	1216.69	698.30	351.72	197.39	3.5	3.5	1967	19889
1986	1232.33	710.16	364.92	206.47	3.4	3.4	1944	18915
1987	1249.51	721.77	380.19	216.25	3.3	3.3	1971	19225
1988	1262.42	732.65	394.95	226.11	3.2	3.2	1991	19514
1989	1276.45	777.79	406.82	244.41	3.1	3.2	2013	10388
1990	1283.35	783.48	415.28	250.71	3.1	3.1	2024	10464
1991	1287.20	786.18	425.84	259.19	3.0	3.0	2030	10483
1992	1289.37	792.75	431.67	265.70	3.0	3.0	2034	10003
1993	1294.74	948.01	438.69	318.56	3.0	3.0	2042	4609
1994	1298.81	953.04	444.38	323.79	2.9	2.9	2048	4633
1995	1301.37	956.66	450.76	329.88	2.9	2.9	2052	4651
1996	1304.43	961.02	457.49	336.30	2.9	2.9	2057	4672
1997	1305.46	1018.59	461.40	357.67	2.8	2.8	2059	3854
1998	1306.58	1070.62	465.72	378.79	2.8	2.8	2061	3296

2-1-3 上海市历年人口出生率、死亡率及自然增长率/ Birth Rate, Death Rate and National Growth Rate of Population

年 份 Year	出生人数（人）Number of Birth (person)	人口出生率（‰）Birth Rate	死亡人数（人）Number of Death (person)	人口死亡率（‰）Death Rate	自然增加人（人）Number of Natural Growth (person)	人口自然增长率（‰）Natural Growth Rate
1978	12.36	11.3	6.82	6.2	5.54	5.1
1979	13.76	12.3	6.81	6.1	6.95	6.2
1980	14.31	11.8	7.39	6.5	6.92	5.3
1981	19.38	16.8	7.44	6.5	11.94	10.3
1982	21.68	18.5	7.35	6.3	14.33	12.2
1983	17.80	15.4	8.19	6.9	9.61	8.5
1984	16.38	13.7	7.82	6.5	8.56	7.2
1985	15.43	12.7	8.10	6.7	7.33	6.0
1986	17.75	14.5	7.93	6.5	9.81	8.0
1987	19.02	15.3	8.27	6.7	10.75	8.6
1988	16.53	13.2	8.47	6.8	8.06	6.4
1989	15.91	12.5	8.43	6.6	7.48	5.9
1990	13.12	10.2	8.63	6.7	4.49	3.5
1991	10.08	7.8	8.56	6.7	1.52	1.1
1992	9.37	7.3	9.10	7.1	0.27	0.2
1993	8.40	6.5	9.40	7.3	-1.00	-0.8
1994	7.63	5.9	9.42	7.3	-1.79	-1.4
1995	7.11	5.5	9.79	7.5	-2.68	-2.0
1996	6.79	5.2	9.77	7.5	-2.98	-2.3
1997	6.42	4.9	9.57	7.3	-3.15	-2.4
1998	6.17	4.7	10.13	7.8	-3.96	-3.1

2-2 经济发展 / Economic Development

1998 年，上海国民经济运行状况良好，实现了持续、快速、健康发展。全年实现国内生产总值 3688.2 亿元，按可比价格计算，比上年增长 10.1%。其中，第一产业实现增加值 78.5 亿元，增长 2.2%，占国内生产总值的比重为 2.1%，比上年下降 0.2 个百分点；第二产业实现增加值 1847.2 亿元，增长 8.2%，占国内生产总值比重的 50.1%，比上年下降 2 个百分点；第三产业实现增加值 1762.5 亿元，增长 14.3%，第三产业增加值占国内生产总值的比重达到 47.8%，比上年提高 2.3 个百分点。全市人均国内生产总值达到 28240 元，全市财政收入完成 1146 亿元，比上年增长 7%。全年商品零售价格水平比上年下降 4.9%，居民消费价格水平与上年持平。

1998 年，上海积极贯彻中央适度从紧的财政政策和货币政策，市场在上年低涨幅、低价位的基础上进一步回落，再次呈现了物价上涨率低于经济增长率的良好势头。全年商品零售价格指数 95.1，比上年回落 3.7 个百分点；居民消费价格指数 100，比上年回落 2.8 个百分点。在居民消费价格指数中，食品类指数下降 2.3%，衣着类下降 7%，家庭设备及用品类下降 6.9%，医疗保健类上涨 2.6%，交通和通信工具类下降 5.1%，娱乐、教育、文化用品类下降 7.2%，居住类上涨 13.4%，服务项目类上涨 14.4%。在商品零售价格指数中，绝大部分商品价格涨幅比上年有明显回落。其中，燃料、食品、服装价格涨幅分别比上年回落了 14.7、10.3 和 9.9 个百分点。

1998 年，上海口岸进出口商品总额 636.4 亿美元，比上年增长 8.4%，其中，出口总额 374.6 亿美元，增长 12%；进口总额 261.8 亿美元，增长 3.8 %。按海关口径统计全年本市外贸出口总值 163.28 亿美元，比上年增长 10.9%，其中，出口总值 159.56 亿美元，增长 5.9%；进口总值 153.88 亿美元，增长 4.5%。

旅游业以上海的都市文化为依托，调整好管理体制，积极吸引国内外游客，形成“大旅游”的新格局。1998 年，全年旅游产业增加值 172 亿元，比上年增加 7.7%。全年共接待 170 多个国家和地区的旅游者 152.71 万人次，其中，外国人 117.55 万人次，港、澳、台同胞 30.09 万人次。全年接待国内旅游者 7098 万人次，比上年增长 4.7%。

商贸系统不断深化改革，国内贸易稳步发展，消费品市场繁荣活跃。全年社会消费品零售总额 1471.03 亿元，比上年增长 11%。各种经济成分的商业全面发展。国有商业企业商品零售额 590.92 亿元，比上年增长 10.5%；集体商业企业商品零售额 417.01 亿元，增长 8.3%；私营经济零售额 59.48 亿元，增长 6.8%。各类商品销售全面增长。全年社会消费品零售总额中，食品类商品零售额为 604.21 亿元，比上年增长 13.5%；衣着类商品零售额为 197.44 亿元，增长 6.1%；用品类商品零售额为 659.24 亿元，增长 10.3%。高档、耐用消费品和小型家用电器销售量均有不同幅度的增长。彩色电视机比上年增长 24.1%，家用电冰箱增长 17.9%，家用洗衣机增长 22.2%，摄像机增长 39.8%，摩托车增长 73.1%。

大力发展连锁商业，兴建各类连锁超市、便民店，使市民家庭购物更加方便快捷。至 1998 年末，全市连锁商业网点达到 2900 家，连锁超市门店 1150 家。

In 1998,the city reported sustained, rapid and sound economic development. Its total GDP reached 368.82 billion yuan, up 10.1% from the previous year according to the comparable prices. Of which, the achieved added value of the primary industry was 7.85 billion yuan, up 2.2%, accounting for 2.1%, lower 0.2 percent .The figures with the secondary industry stood at 184.72 billion yuan, 8.2%, 50.1% and 2%, respectively. However, the tertiary industry achieved added value of 176.25 billion yuan, up 14.3% over 1997 and accounting for 47.8% of the city’s total GDP or 0.23 percentage point lower than that of the previous year. In the year, the city’s average per capita GDP reached 28,240 yuan, the city’s revenue stood at 114.6 billion yuan, up 7%. Of the whole 1998, the price level of the commodity retail sales as 4.9% lower than last year, the price level of residents’ consumption keeping the same level as last year.

In 1998,Shanghai followed the Central Government’s moderate financial and monetary austerity policies and further reduced the level of price hikes. As a result, the price hike level was well put under control and it was lower than the economic growth rate. In the whole year of 1998, the price index of the commodity retail sales was 95.1, dropping by 3.7 percentage points from the figure of the previous year. The price index of residents’ consumption stood at 100, down 2.8 percentage points, Of the price indexes of residents’ consumption, the figure with food was down 2.3

percent; clothing was down 7%; household appliances and articles was down 6.9%; medical and health products was up 2.6%; transport and telecommunications tools was down 5.1%; recreation, education and stationary was down 7.2%; housing was up 13.4%; and services was up 14.4%. Among the indexes of commodity retail sales, the price hikes for most commodities slowed down noticeably. For instance, the price hike levels of fuels, food and clothing declined by 14.7, 10.3 and 9.9 percentage points, respectively, from the previous year.

In 1998, the city reported new growth in imports and exports, with the total value of commodities passing through Shanghai Port reaching 63.64 billion US dollars, up 8.4%, and the import 26.18 billion US dollars, up 3.8%, the export 37.46 billion US dollars up 12%. In 1998 the city's total import ant export of foreign trade amounted to 16.328 billion US dollars, rising by 10.9% over 1998. Of the city's total, the export was valued at 15.956 billion US dollars, up 5.9%, and the import 15.388 billion US dollars, up 4.5%, too.

By resorting to the metropolitan culture of the city, Shanghai has made great efforts to attract tourists from both at home and abroad. The added value of the tourism stood at 17.2 billion yuan, up 7.7 percent. The city received 1.5271 million overseas tourists from more than 170 countries and regions in 1998. Of the total, the number of foreign travelers reached 1.1755 million, and the number of tourists from Hong Kong, Macao and Taiwan hit 300,900. Of the whole year, 70.98 million tourists came to Shanghai, up 4.7%.

The year of 1998 saw a brisk market with retail sales of consumer goods totaled 147.103 billion yuan, up 11% over the previous year. The growth covered all types of enterprises. The state-owned commercial enterprises reported a retail turnover of 59.092 billion yuan, up 10.5% over 1997; the collective enterprises recorded a 8.3 % growth to 41.701 billion yuan; the private businesses posted a 6.8% increase to 5.948 billion yuan. The growth also covered all commodities. Of the total retail sales of consumer goods in the year, food items 60.421 billion yuan, up 13.5%; clothing 19.744 billion yuan, up 6.1%; household necessities 65.924 billion yuan, up 10.3%.. High–grade and durable consumer goods and small household electric appliances all reported sales growth. The sales of color TV sets went up by 24.1% over the previous year, refrigeratores by 17.9%, washing-machines by 22.2%, vidicons by 39.8% and motorcycles by 73.1%.

While chain–stores and supermarkets became popular in Shanghai, efforts were made to increase the number of their outlets and improve the quality of their services to offer more conveniences to local residents, At the end of 1998, Shanghai had a total of 2900 chain-stores outlets, and of 1150 supermarkets.

2-2-1 社会经济主要指标平均每人水平 / Per Capita Main Social and Economic Indicators

年 份 Year	国内生产总值（元）Gross Domestic Products (yuan)	社会消费品零售额（元）Retail Sales of Consumer Goods (yuan)	职工年平均工资（元）Average Annual Wages of Staff and Workers (yuan)	城市居民家庭生活费收入（元）Annual Living income of Urban Residence	城市居民消费性支出（元）Living Expenditure of Urban Residence
1979	2568	612	784	—	—
1980	2738	706	873	560	553
1981	2813	768	870	589	585
1982	2877	766	883	606	576
1983	2963	848	897	641	615
1984	3259	1032	1110	787	726
1985	3355	1432	1416	1012	992
1986	4008	1608	1689	1215	1170
1987	4396	1815	1893	1347	1282
1988	5161	2355	2277	1616	1648
1989	5489	2610	2608	1860	1812
1990	5910	2608	2917	2050	1936
1991	6955	2973	3375	2334	2167
1992	8652	3608	4273	2842	2509
1993	11700	4814	5650	4057	3530
1994	15204	5944	7401	5566	4669
1995	18943	7461	9279	6822	5868
1996	22275	8913	10663	7721	6763
1997	25750	10155	11425	8439	6820
1998	28240	11263	12059	8773	6866

续上表（continued）

年 份 Year	市区居住面积（平方米）Living Space of Urban Areas (sq.m)	市区公共绿地面积（平方米）Urban Public Green Areas (sq.m)	每万人拥有 Per 10 000 Population		
			公共车辆（辆）Buses (unit)	大学生（人）University Students (person)	医院床位（张）Beds in Hospitals (unit)
1978	4.5	0.47	2.7	46	43
1979	4.3	0.47	3.1	60	43
1980	4.4	0.44	3.2	67	43
1981	4.5	0.46	3.4	78	43
1982	4.7	0.45	3.6	71	44
1983	4.9	0.45	3.7	66	44
1984	4.7	0.47	3.9	75	44
1985	5.4	0.71	4.2	89	44
1986	6.0	0.90	4.5	95	44
1987	6.2	0.93	4.7	98	45
1988	6.3	0.96	4.8	102	47
1989	6.4	0.96	4.8	99	48
1990	6.6	1.02	4.9	94	48
1991	6.7	1.07	5.1	91	49
1992	6.9	1.15	5.3	93	50
1993	7.3	1.15	5.4	101	52
1994	7.5	1.40	5.7	108	52
1995	8.0	1.69	8.9	110	51
1996	8.7	1.92	10.2	113	52
1997	9.3	2.41	10.9	118	52
1998	9.7	2.96	11.7	126	52

2-2-2 主要年份国内生产总值 / Gross Domestic Product in Main Years

单位：亿元 (100 000 000 yuan)

年 份 Year	国内生产总值 Gross Domestic Product	第一产业 Primary Industry	第二产业 Secondary Industry	第三产业 Tertiary Industry	人均国内生产总值 Gross Domestic Product Per Capita (yuan)
1978	272.81	11.00	211.05	50.76	2498
1979	286.43	11.39	221.21	53.83	2568
1980	311.89	10.10	236.10	65.69	2738
1981	324.76	10.58	244.34	69.84	2813
1982	337.07	13.31	249.32	74.44	2877
1983	351.81	13.52	255.32	82.97	2963
1984	390.85	17.26	275.37	98.22	3259
1985	466.75	19.53	325.63	121.59	3855
1986	490.83	19.69	336.02	135.12	4008
1987	545.46	21.60	364.38	159.48	4396
1988	648.30	27.36	433.05	187.89	5161
1989	696.54	29.63	466.18	200.73	5489
1990	756.45	32.60	482.68	241.17	5910
1991	893.77	33.36	551.34	309.07	6955
1992	1114.32	34.16	677.39	402.77	8652
1993	1511.61	38.21	900.33	573.07	11700
1994	1971.92	48.59	1143.24	780.09	15204
1995	2462.57	61.68	1409.85	991.04	18943
1996	2902.20	71.58	1582.50	1248.12	22275
1997	3360.21	75.80	1754.39	1530.02	25750
1998	3688.20	78.50	1847.20	1762.50	28240

2-2-3 社会消费品零售总额 / Retail Sales of Consumer Goods

单位：亿元 (100 000 000 yuan)

年 份 Year	社会消费品零售总额 Retail Sales of Consumer Goods	按商品用途分 By Use			
		食品类 Food	衣着类 Clothing	用品类 Articles	燃料类 Fuels
1978	54.10	26.51	11.60	15.16	0.83
1979	68.28	30.05	16.07	21.28	0.88
1980	80.43	34.30	19.75	25.44	0.94
1981	88.73	38.78	21.27	27.73	0.95
1982	89.80	40.72	19.57	28.52	0.99
1983	100.68	44.21	22.31	33.17	0.99
1984	123.72	50.18	27.71	44.81	1.02
1985	173.39	64.08	35.51	72.70	1.10
1986	196.84	76.99	39.38	79.31	1.16
1987	225.25	91.01	42.52	90.41	1.31
1988	295.83	119.36	53.66	121.17	1.64
1989	331.38	140.03	51.95	137.70	1.70
1990	333.86	142.15	52.33	137.23	2.15
1991	382.06	162.82	52.91	163.30	3.03
1992	464.82	190.70	67.04	202.83	4.25
1993	624.30	254.13	93.90	280.42	4.85
1994	770.74	306.85	114.84	343.18	5.87
1995	970.04	384.08	142.58	436.40	6.98
1996	1161.30	462.71	165.76	524.69	8.14
1997	1325.21	532.12	186.04	597.64	9.41
1998	1471.03	604.21	197.44	659.24	10.29

2-3 居民生活 / Living Conditions of the Residents

1998 年末全社会从业人员为 836.21 万人，比上年减少 11.04 万人。年末全市职工人数 412.61 万人，比上年减少 22.66 万人，其中国有单位职工 259.07 万人，集体单位职工 59.81 万人，其他所有制单位职工 93.73 万人。全年全市城镇新安置就业人员 26.73 万人。目前城镇失业人数 15.96 万人，城镇登记失业率 2.9%，比上年提高了 0.1 个百分点。

从业人员三次产业结构发生变化。从业人员主要向第三产业转移，年末比重上升到 41.5%，比上年增加 3.3 个百分点；第一产业从业人员比重比上一年略有增加，达 12.4%；而第二产业从业人员比重比上一年减少 6 个百分点，为 46%。

城乡人民生活继续得到改善，居民收入稳定增长。1998 年，上海市从业人员报酬达到 535.51 亿元，其中，国有经济单位从业人员为 330.7 亿元。1998 年，上海市职工工资总额达到 510.35 亿元，比上年增长 0.05%；全市职工年平均工资为 12059 元，增长 7.1%。在职工工资总额中，国有经济单位工资总额为 353.69 亿元，增长 5.5%；企业工资总额为 330.1 亿元，外商投资企业工资总额为 74.96 亿元。

据抽样调查统计，1998 年城市居民家庭人均年生活费收入 8773.1 元，比上年增长 4%。按收入水平分组，年人均生活费收入在 3000 元以下的家庭占总户数的比重为 1%；收入在 3000-4000 元之间的占 3.2%；收入在 4000-5000 元之间的占 4.4%；收入在 5000-6000 元之间的占 9.2%；收入在 6000-7000 元之间的占 14.6%；收入在 7000-8000 元之间的占 12.4%；收入在 8000-9000 元之间的占 15%；收入在 9000-10000 元之间的占 11.2%，收入在 10000 元以上的占 29%。随着收入水平的稳步提高，上海居民家庭年人均消费性支出继续增加，1998 年，城市居民家庭年人均消费性支出为 6866.41 元，比上年增长 0.7%，其中，食品类支出为 3467.96 元，占总支出的比重为 50.5%，比上年提高了 1 个百分点。

1998 年，上海郊县农民家庭年人均纯收入为 5407 元，比上年增长 2.5%；农民家庭年人均生活消费支出 4923.53 元，比上年增长 0.6%。

城乡居民储蓄存款继续增加。至 1998 年末上海市城乡居民储蓄存款余额 2372.94 亿元，人均储蓄存款达 18161 元。

By the end of 1998, the city employed a total of 8,362,100 people, 110400 less than last year. The year–end number of staff and workers amounted to 4,126,100, 226,600 less than the figure of the previous year. Of the total number of staff and workers, 2,590,700 were hired by state–owned work units; 598,100 were employed by collectively–owned work units; 937,300 were on the payroll of work units of other types of ownership. In 1998, the city found jobs for 267,300 people in the urban area. The number of unemployed was159,600, representing a registered unemployment rate of 2.9% in the urban area, 0.1% higher than 1997.

Employment changes continue in employment in the tertiary industry climbed to 41.5%, 3.3 percentage points higher that the previous year, The figure with the primary industry edged up to 12.4% and the figure with the secondary industry dropped by 6 percentage points to 46%.

The living standards of residents living in both urban and rural areas have continued to improve and their incomes keep growing steadily. In 1998, the pay for the city's employees totaled 53.551 billion yuan including 33.07 billion yuan for employees of state–owned work units. In the same year, the salaries paid to staff and workers in the city totaled 51.035 billion yuan, up 0.05% from the previous year, with an average per capita annual salary reaching 12,059 yuan, up 7.1%. Of the total,the pay for employees of state-owned work units were 35.369 billion yuan,up 5.5%; the salaries paid to staff and the figures with the foreign-invested enterprises were 7.496 billion yuan.

According to statistics from a sample survey, in 1998 the average per capita annual income among the city's urban families reached 8,773.1 yuan, 4% higher than that of 1997. A breakdown of income levels indicates that families with per capita annual income below 3,000 yuan accounted for 1.0% of the total; families of the 3,000-4,000 yuan category made up 3.2% of the total; families at the 4,000-5,000 yuan level were 4.4% of the total; families in the 5,000-6,000 yuan group 9.2%; families of 6,000-7,000 yuan 14.6%; families of 7,000-8,000 yuan 12.4%; families of 8,000-9,000 yuan 15%; families of 9,000-10,000 yuan 11.2%; and families with per capita annual income above 10,000 amounted to 29% of the total. Along with the steady increase in their incomes, the local families have also seen increase in the average per capita annual consumption expenditures. In 1998 an average urban resident's annual consumption expenditure reached 6,886.41 yuan, 0.7% more than the 1997 figure. Of the total, expenditure on food was 3,467.96 yuan or 50.5%, 1 percentage point higher than that of the previous year.

In 1998, an average per capita annual net income of the city's farmers stood at 5,407 yuan, 2.5% more than in 1997. The average per capita living expenses hit 4,923.53 yuan, 0.6% more than the figure of the previous year.

The amount of urban and rural residents' savings deposits continues to grow. By the end of 1998, the balance of their savings deposits totaled 2,372.94 billion yuan, per savings deposits 18161 yuan.

上海地区主要年份职工工资收入（单位：元）

Average Wages of Staff and Workers of Shanghai (yuan)

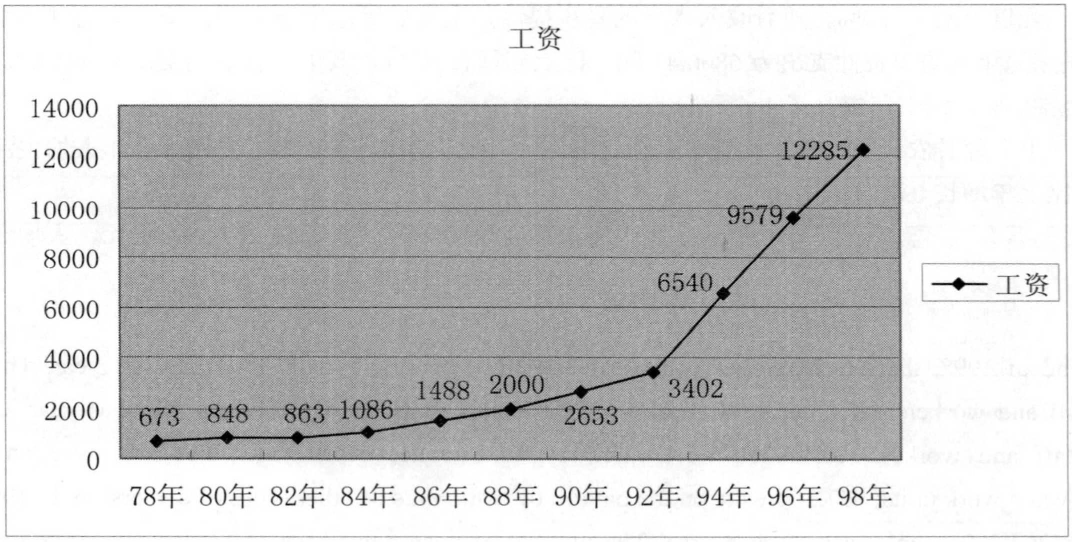

2-3-1 主要年份平均每百户城市居民家中耐用消费品年末拥有情况一览表 / List of Urban Household Year-end Possession of Durable Consumer Goods Per 100 Households in Main Years

商品名称	Item	单位 Unit	1990	1995	1996	1997	1998
自行车	Bicycle	辆 (unit)	114	115	124	125	132.8
助力自行车	Scooter	辆 (unit)	—	4.8	7.2	7.2	13.0
摩托车	Motorcycle	辆 (unit)	—	0.8	1.0	1.2	1.4
收录音机	Recorder	台 (set)	100	89	99	82	82.2
彩色电视机	Color TV Set	台 (set)	77	109	113	119	128.2
录放相机	Video Recorder	台 (set)	14	49	51	52	48.8
影碟机	VCD Player	台 (set)	—	—	—	15.2	25.4
组合音响	Stereo System	台 (set)	1	13	15	18	21.2
家用空调器	Household Air Conditioner	台 (set)	—	33	50	62	68.6
热水沐浴器	Water Heater	台 (set)	—	37	42	51	53.8
微波炉	Microwave	台 (set)	—	33	45	55	62.8
个人计算机	Personal Computer	台 (set)	—	2.2	5.2	8.6	13.2
电风扇	Electric Fan	台 (set)	187	216	224	228	229
电冰箱	Household Refrigerator	台 (set)	88	98	101	102	103
洗衣机	Washing Machine	台 (set)	72	78	82	87	91.6
照相机	Camera	架 (set)	44	52	52	54	58.6
摄像机	Video Camera	架 (set)	—	1.4	2.0	1.4	2.6
钢琴	Piano	架 (set)	—	2.2	2.4	2.0	2.6
移动电话	Mobile Phone	台 (set)	—	—	0.8	2.4	6.0

2-3-2 自来水、煤（液化）气供应和交通情况 / Tap Water, Gas and Liquefied Petroleum Supply and Public Transportation

项目	Item	单位 Unit	1994	1995	1996	1997	1998
煤气	**Gas Supply**						
销售量	Total	亿立方米	14.88	15.83	17.07	17.04	17.25
生产用	Production Use	亿立方米	3.94	3.71	3.44	3.06	2.72
生活用	Residential	亿立方米 (10^8 cu.m)	10.91	12.10	13.60	13.95	14.48
家庭用气户数	Households With Access to Gas	万户 (1000)	169.10	192.69	206.69	226.12	247.18
液化石油气	**Liquefied Petroleum Gas**						
销售量	Total Sales Volume	万吨 (10000 tons)	122801	205460	231807	262180	260127
家庭用气	Residential Use	万吨 (10000 tons)	65392	166912	191929	204942	189656
家庭用气户数	Households With Access Gas	万户 (10000)	55.77	153.93	174.14	196.30	219.50
自来水	**Tap Water**						
售水总量	Sakes Volume of Tap Water	亿立方米 (10^8 cu.m)	14.18	19.04	19.79	19.81	20.08
生活用水	Residential Use	亿立方米 (10^8 cu.m)	7.78	10.28	10.77	11.24	11.55
平均每日用水量	Daily Tap Water Consumption	万立方米 (10000)	388.49	521.64	540.71	542.74	—
公共交通	**Public Transit**						
年末营运公共车辆	Operating Pubic Vehicles	辆 (unit)	7415	11637	13323	14207	15282
公共汽车	Buses	辆 (unit)	6617	10884	12715	13655	14764
全年运客总量	Passengers Carried Yearly	亿人次 (10^8personstimes)	52.37	51.35	23.07	23.78	24.88

2-3-3 文化卫生事业情况一览表 / List of the Culture and Health Facilities in Shanghai

项 目 Item	单 位 Unit	数 量 Number	项 目 Item	单 位 Unit	数 量 Number
一、电影放映单位 Film projection Units	个 (unit)	466	五、电视台 Television Stations	座 (set)	3
影剧院 Cinemas and Theatres	个 (unit)	263	自办节目 Self-produced Programs	套 (set)	12
剧院 Theatres	个 (unit)	38	平均每周播出时间 Program house Per Week	小时 (hour)	890
艺术表演团体 Art Performance Troupes	个 (unit)	31	电视人口覆盖率 Population Coverage Rate	%	100
二、群众艺术馆 Mass Art Centers	个 (unit)	3	六、广播电台 Broadcasting Stations	座 (set)	2
文化馆 Cultural Palaces	个 (unit)	43	自办节目 Self-produced Programs	套 (set)	21
			平均每周播出时间 Program house Per Week	小时 (hour)	305
三、图书馆 Public Libraries	个 (unit)	32	广播人口覆盖率 Population Coverage Rate	%	100
总藏书量 Collection	万册、件 (10000)	4809			
读者人数 Readers	万人次 (10000)	1170	七、医疗卫生机构数 Heath Care Institutions	个 (unit)	4637
			床位数 Hospital Beds	张 (bed)	70175
四、博物馆、纪念馆 Museums and Memorial Halls	个 (unit)	12	卫生技术人员 Medical Professionals	人 (person)	108358

3　广州市基本情况

The General Market Conditions of Guangzhou

3-1 人口概况 / General Demographic Characteristics

广州市下辖八个区，四个县级市，土地面积 7434.4 平方公里，1998 年总人口 674.14 万人，比 1997 年增加 7.65 万人，增长率为 1.15%，增幅比上年的 1.59%下降了 0.44 个百分点。其中：市区人口 399.30 万人，比上年增加 3.65 万人，增长率为 0.92%，增幅比 97 年下降 0.48 个百分点；四个县级市人口为 274.84 万人，比 97 年增加 4 万人，增长率为 1.48%，增幅比 97 年下降 0.39 个百分点。

1998 年末，全市非农业人口为 417.28 万人，占总人口的比重为 61.90%，比上年上升 0.25 个百分点；增长率为 1.56%，比总人口的增长率高出 0.4 个百分点。随着近年来城市整体规划的实施、基础建设的发展，老城区人口继续向外扩散，越秀区、荔湾区、东山区人口占市区人口的比重由上年的 6.73%、7.85%和 8.76%，分别下降为 6.56%、7.70%和 8.70%；天河区、白云区、芳村区则由上年的 7.04%、12.21%和 2.53%，分别上升为 7.15%、12.27%和 2.55%。

1998 年全市迁入人口为 14.06 万人，比上年增加 0.11 万人，迁出人口为 9.41 万人，比上年增加 1.14 万人；迁移净增人口为 4.65 万人，比上年减少 1.03 万人。“九五”期间，广州人口出生率逐年下降。据市计生委 98 年报统计人口出生率为 10.80‰，比 1997 年的 11.58‰减少了 0.78 个千分点，比“八五”时期的 14.13‰下降了 3.33 个千分点。

广州市的综合经济实力对外来人口仍有较强的吸引力，1998 年广州市的外来人口波动在 175 万人左右，按照市公安局办理外来人口暂住证的统计，从来源地区分：省外的占 62 66%，省内的占 36.36%，来自港澳、国外的占 0.98%；从来穗目的分类：务工务农的占 61.99%，经商的占 7.74%，从事服务业的占 9.82%，投亲访友和旅游观光的占 15.21%，其他的占 5.24%。

Guangzhou city which is composed of 8 districts and 4 county boroughs, covers 7434.4 square kilometers. It has a population of 6,741,400 in the year of 1998, 76,500 people more than 1997, up 1.15%, 0.44 percentage point lower than that of the previous year. Urban population reached 3993000 people, 36500 more than last year; up 0.92%, 0.48 percentage point lower than that of the previous year. The four county boroughts population of Guangzhou is 2,748,400 people more than last year, up 1.48%, 0.39 percentage point lower than that of 1997.

By the end of 1998, the population of non-agricultural people is 4.1728 million, 61.90% of the total population, 0.25 higher than that of last year, up 1.56%, 0.41% higher than the growth rate of the total population. With the development of the city, people live in the old districts move to the outsides. The population of Yuexiu. Liwan and Dongshan districts are 6.56%, 7.70% and 8.70% of the total number, but those of last year are 6.73%,7.85% and 8.76%. The population of Tianhe .Baiyun .Fangcun districts are 7.15%,12.27%and 2.55%, and those of last year are 7.04%,12.21% and 2.53%.

By the end of 1998, the figure of residential registration reach 140,600 people, 1,100 more than last year, the people moved out was 46,500, 10,300 less than last year. The birth rate and the natural growth rate continued fall steadily. In 1998, the birth rate was 10.8‰, 0.078 percentage point lower than 11.58‰ of last year, 0.333 percentage point lower than 14.13‰ of “the period of 85”.

注：本章数据全部摘自《广州统计年鉴 1999》/Resource:″'99 Statistical Yearbook of Guangzhou″

The reform of the economic construction continued to deepen in 1998, the rapidly economic development still attracted more and more people from other provinces. By the end of 1998, about 1,750,000 people moved in Guangzhou.All these people can be categoried by the place they are from, 36.36% of the total population were Guangzhou native, about 62.66%, were from other provinces, 0.98% from HongKong, Macao, Taiwan and other countries.

And by the popose they come to Guangzhou, about 61.99% were engaged in industry and farming, 7.74% were in business purposes, 9.82% were in services, 15.21 % came from visiting or sight-seeing, 5.24% were engaged in other items.

3-1-1 广州市 1998 年人口情况一览表 / List of Population in 1998 of Gungzhou City

地 区 Region	土地面积（平方公里）Land Area (sq.km)	年底总人口（人）Total population (person)	非农业人口（人）Non-Agricultural (person)	总户数（户）Total Households (household)	非农业户（户）Non-Agricultural (household)	人口密度（人/平方里）Population Density (person/sq.km)
全市 Total	7434.4	6741400	4172824	2006279	1359135	907
市区 Urban	1443.6	3993008	3306277	1229635	1038709	2766
东山区 Dongshan	17.2	586736	585382	174444	174269	34113
荔湾区 Liwan	11.8	519239	516927	169184	168296	44003
越秀区 Yuexiu	8.9	441896	440689	141985	141985	49651
海珠区 Haizhu	90.4	769384	699313	238723	218601	8511
天河区 Tianhe	108.3	481625	420151	137442	118913	4447
芳村区 Fangcun	42.6	172129	135994	56133	45115	4041
白云区 Baiyun	1042.7	827243	362504	251365	128124	793
黄埔区 Huangpu	121.7	194756	145322	60359	43406	1600

续上表（continued）

地 区 Region	人口出生率（‰）Birth Rate	人口死亡率（‰）Death Rate	人口自然增长率（‰）Natural Growth Rate	男（人）Male (person)	女（人）Female(person)
全市 Total	10.10	6.11	3.99	3469164	3272236
城区 Urban	7.79	6.57	1.22	2081552	1911456
东山区 Dongshan	7.32	5.87	1.45	301776	284960
荔湾区 Liwan	5.43	8.33	-2.9	264475	254764
越秀区 Yuexiu	6.06	7.89	-1.83	222632	219264
海珠区 Haizhu	6.42	6.55	-0.13	405685	363699
天河区 Tianhe	8.82	4.60	4.22	258054	223571
芳村区 Fangcun	7.85	8.49	-0.64	91540	80589
白云区 Baiyun	9.98	6.51	3.47	431602	395641
黄埔区 Huangpu	13.16	4.29	8.87	105788	88968

3-1-2 广州市历年人口变动情况 / Migration of Guangzhou in Main Years

年份 Year	总户数（户） Total Households (household)	非农业户（户） Non-Agricultural (household)	年底总人口（人） Total population (person)	非农业人口 Non-Agricultural	人口出生率（‰） Birth Rate	人口死亡率（‰） Death Rate
1952	678722	302173	2719141	1348971	—	—
1957	811439	424157	3377586	1864029	39.49	7.12
1962	864664	460369	3702454	2114263	38.78	6.80
1965	888576	476709	3985070	2189776	27.01	5.25
1970	979764	514287	4185363	2089540	23.79	5.46
1975	1071998	552155	4591000	2182326	16.94	5.95
1978	1145925	597366	4828961	2321421	15.46	5.32
1980	1162717	637899	5018638	2560391	16.25	5.57
1985	1369170	813157	5449820	2956158	16.59	5.36
1990	1641063	1028780	5942534	3413860	14.97	5.49
1991	1674843	1058625	6022186	3482920	13.15	5.09
1992	1721098	1098388	6122016	3558383	13.11	5.53
1993	1824611	1219882	6236647	3753872	13.35	5.60
1994	1831663	1219312	6370241	3872396	12.47	5.29
1995	1871173	1246205	6433241	3952759	11.82	5.57
1996	1905305	1274665	6532967	4032704	12.03	5.71
1997	1945526	1306327	6629339	4108639	11.37	5.40
1998	2006279	1359135	6704699	4172824	10.10	6.11

3-2 经济发展 / Economic Development

1998年，广州市国民经济运行状况良好，全年实现年内生产总值1341.61亿元，比上年增长13.1%。其中，第一产业增加值88.88亿元，增长4%；第二产业增加值826.43亿元，增长12.6%；第三产业增加值926.30亿元，增长14.7%。衡量综合经济势力水平的重要标志—人均国内生产总值达2.75万元，增长11.6%。全年工业增加值716.56亿元，比上年增长13.0%，其中完成工业总产值2520.75亿元，比上年增长13.9%。全年农业增加值90.06亿元；农业总产值154.02亿元，比上年增长4.6%；社会消费品零售总额904.57亿元、固定资产投资额746亿元、外贸出口总额80.18亿美元，分别比上年增长12.7%、13.6%和6.4%。

广州在全省的社会经济发展中占有重要地位。国内生产总值占全省的23.2%，其中农业增加值、工业增加值、第三产业增加值分别占全省的8.8%、20.5%和31.6%。全社会固定资产投资额、社会消费品零售总额、海关出口总额分别占全省的28.4%、27.8%和13.7%。

房地产商品住宅建设加快发展。全年商品住宅完成投资148.66亿元，比上年增长22.3%，增幅比上年提高8.1个百分点，占全市房地产开发投资额的55.31%。商品住宅施工面积2100.89万平方米，比上年增长16.5%，占商品房施工面积的66%；商品住宅竣工面积602.79万平方米，增长19.3%，占商品房施工面积的79.7%。

广州面对亚洲金融危机对外经贸的影响，适时调整出口产品结构，推动了外贸出口市场向多元化发展。全年外贸进出口总值130.63亿美元，比上年增长12.5%。其中进口总值50.45亿美元，增长24%；出口总值80.18亿美元，增长6.4%。全年实际利用外资30.45亿美元，比上年增长5.2%，其中外商直接投资27.16亿美元，增长9.5%。1998年末，广州地区金融机构本外币各项存款余额4562.69亿元比上年末增加714.64亿元，增长18.6%；本外币各项贷款余额2994.94亿元，比上年末增加312.77亿元，增长11.7%。

Guangzhou's total GDP accomplished 184.161 billion-yuan in 1998, up 13.1% than last year. The primary industry achieved added value of 8.888 billion yuan, up 4%; the figure with the secondary industry stood at 82.643 billion yuan, up 12.6%; the tertiary industry achieved added value of 92.630 billion yuan, up 14.7%. In this year, the city's average per capita GDP reached 27,500 yuan, up 11.6%. The industry added value was 71.656 billion yuan, up 13.0%, the achieved value was 252.075 billion yuan , up 13.9%. The agriculture added value of 9.006 billion yuan, the gross output value of agriculture was 15.402 billion yuan, up 4.6%; the retail sales of consumer goods was 90.457 billion yuan, investment in fixed assets was 74.6 billion yuan, and the total exports were 8.018 billion US dollars, up 12.7%. 13.6% and 6.4%.

Guangzhou is important to the economic development of the province, the gross domestic product accounts for 23.2%, of which, the added value of agriculture. industry and service sector account for 8.8%.20.5% and 31.6%. The investment in fixed assets. the retail sales consumer goods, the customers total exports, account for 28.4%, 27.8% and 13.7%. separately.

The development of real estate is rapid. The achieved investment of housing amounted to 14.866 billion yuan, up 22.3%, 8.1 percent more than last year, accounted for 55.31% of the gross real estate development. The construction area of the housing was 210.089 million square meters, up 16.5%, accounted for 66%, the completed area was 60.279 million square meters, up 19.3%, accounted for 79.7%.

In 1998 the city's total important export of foreign trade amounted to 13.063 billion US dollars, rising by 12.5% over 1998. Of the city's total, the export was valued at 8.018 billion US dollars, up 6.4%, and the import 5.045 billion US dollars, up 24%. In 1998, the amount of foreign capital actually used was 3.045 billion US dollars, up 5.2%, of which, the direct foreign investments was 2.716 billion US dollars, up 9.5%, the domestic and foreign loans amounted to 299.494 billion yuan, 31.277 billion more than last year and up 11.7%.

3-2-1 主要年份国内生产总值（按当年价格计算）/ Gross Domestic Products in Main Years（Calculated from the Price of 1998）

单位：万元 (10 000 yuan)

年 份 Year	国内生产总值 Gross Domestic Product	第一产业 Primary Industry	第二产业 Secondary Industry			第三产业 Tertiary Industry
				工业 Industry	建筑业 Construction	
1952	53910	10787	16940	16434	506	26183
1957	111836	14952	51153	46088	5065	45731
1962	124147	20314	61196	56196	5000	42637
1965	180348	25033	101444	93401	8043	53871
1970	266600	31234	170872	164979	5893	64494
1975	366351	44318	227351	219739	7612	94682
1978	430947	50287	252479	243585	8894	128181
1980	575497	62438	313734	295337	18397	199325
1985	1243623	120449	658130	577048	81082	465044
1990	3195952	257288	1362975	1180978	181997	1575689
1991	3866741	281734	1799166	1582970	216196	1785841
1992	5107027	356399	2413129	2120096	293033	2337499
1993	7408369	475960	3517151	3055304	461847	3415258
1994	9761829	606222	4567537	3883405	684132	4588070
1995	12430697	734606	5801945	4959398	842547	5894146
1996	14449358	811630	6753844	5814566	939278	6883884
1997	16462567	857155	7661529	6661968	999561	7943883
1998	18416025	888763	8264307	7142835	1121472	9262982

3-2-2 各城区国民经济主要指标一览表 / List of Major Economic Indicators in Districts of Guangzhou

项　目 Item	单　位 Unit	东山区 Dongshan	荔湾区 Liwan	越秀区 Yuexiu	海珠区 Haizhu	天河区 Tianhe	芳村区 Fangcun	白云区 Baiyun	黄埔区 Huangpu
年末总人口 Year-end Population	万人 (10000 persons)	58.7	51.9	44.2	76.93	48.2	17.2	82.7	19.5
国内生产总值 Gross Domestic Product	亿元 (10^8 yuan)	22.0	33.4	20.6	44.3	68.0	17.4	103.3	21.9
财政收入 Financial Revenue	亿元 (10^8 yuan)	5.45	4.12	4.59	4.61	5.86	2.77	7.96	2.55
年末职工人数 Number of Staff and Works	万人 (10000 persons)	5.25	6.86	5.49	7.87	4.13	2.23	3.38	3.19
全年工资总额 Total Annual Wage	亿元 (10^8 yuan)	6.19	7.25	5.87	8.38	5.37	2.67	4.87	4.17
职工平均工资 Average Wage for Staff and Workers	元 (yuan)	11784	10777	10696	10613	13322	11962	14118	13393
社会消费品零售总额 Retail Sales of Consumer Goods	万元 (10000 yuan)	546643	655368	375887	393615	800682	118680	588943	137436
实际利用外资 Foreign Capital Absorbed	万美元 (USD 10000)	3179	1697	6827	2492	5560	2869	7653	5050
外贸出口总值 Total Export Value	万美元 (USD 10000)	4277	3189	3747	22691	24459	11386	56798	40919
小学在校学生数 Students Enrollment of Primary Schools	万人 (10000 persons)	4.31	3.97	3.24	6.32	5.01	1.66	11.24	2.05
幼儿园在园人数 Children Enrollment of Kinder Gardens	万人 (10000 persons)	1.86	1.26	1.09	2.45	1.97	0.68	3.41	0.91
医院数 Number of Hospital	个 (unit)	6	9	9	8	5	4	3	4
私营个体经济企业户数 Number of Self-employment Enterprises	户 (household)	8813	12667	13466	15748	19046	5922	34768	8343
乡镇企业总收入 Total Income of Township Enterprises	亿元 (10^8 yuan)	—	—	—	52.8	72.3	26.7	223.8	41.1
乡镇企业总产值 Gross Output Value of Township Enterprises	亿元 (10^8 yuan)	—	—	—	29.88	42.0	21.4	166.9	37.1

3-3 居民生活 / Living Conditions of the Residents

年末全市总人口 674.14 万人，比上年末增加 7.65 万人。劳动力结构进一步调整，全市从业人员 444.07 万人，第一、二、三产业分别占 21.04%、38.34%、40.62%。年末职工总人数 196.51 万人，比上年末减少 3.30 万人；城镇私营从业人员和个体劳动者 63.34 万人，比上年增加 5.58 万人。

居民实际收入增加。全市居民年人均可支配收入 11256 元，比上年增长 7.8%，剔除价格变动因素，实际增长 10.3%。消费结构发生变化，居民用于食品的支出增长放缓；用于文艺教育、旅游、居住的支出明显增加；大屏幕彩电、电脑、组合音响、影碟机等新一代耐用消费品已进入居民家庭。农村居民年人均纯收入 5629 元，增长 1.50 %，剔除价格变动因素，实际增长 3.56 %。全市职工工资总额 283.14 亿元，比上年增长 8.2 %。职工年平均工资 14318 元，增长 9.1 %，剔除价格变动因素，实际增长 11.7 %。

城乡居民居住条件有所改善，城市居民人均居住面积从上年的 10.79 平方米提高到本年的 11.7 平方米；农村居民人均居住面积由上年的 32.21 平方米提高到本年的 35.73 平方米。

1998 年，广州市消费品市场保持稳定发展，各种大型商场、超市、连锁店、仓储式商场有较大发展。全年社会消费品零售总额 904.57 亿元，比上年增长 12.7%，剔除商品零售价格变动因素，实际增长 17.0%。其中，城镇消费品零售额为 830.65 亿元，增长 12.7%；农村消费品零售额为 73.92 亿元，增长 12.3%。分行业看，贸易业零售额 601.06 亿元，增长 12.8%，餐饮业零售额 158.38 亿元，增长 14.2%。市场规模扩大，商品购销不断增长。全年集市贸易成交额 361.14 亿元，比上年增长 22.7%；成交额超亿元的大型集市贸易市场 31 个。

The city had a total population of 6.7414 million people in 1998, 76500more than the end of last year. The adjustment of labor force extended. There were 4.4407 million people were employed, representing 21.04%, 38.34%, 40.62% of the primary, secondary and tertiary industry, respectively. By the end of the year, the number of staff and workers reached 1.9651 million, 33000 less than last year and the figure of private workers and self-employed workers reached 633400 people, 55,800 more than that of 1997.

The actual income of residents increased. In 1998, the average per capita annual income of the city's residents was actually 11256 yuan, up 7.8%. Eliminating the price factor, the actual growth was 10.3%. Consumption structure changed. The expenditure on food decreased while the figure of education of arts, tourism and residence increased obviously. A large amount of family bought lots of high—grade electric appliance, such as large scale color TV set, computer, Hi-Fi and laser disc player, etc. In 1998, the average per capita annual income among rural residents reached 5629 yuan, up 1.50 %. Eliminating the price factor, the actual growth was 3.56%. The total pay for the staff and workers reached 28.314 billion yuan, up 8.2% than the year of 1997.The annual per capita wage of the city's employees was 14318 yuan, up 9.1%, eliminating the price factor, actually grew 11.7%.

The residential conditions both in urban and rural area were improved. The per capita residential space in the urban area reached 11.7 square meters from 10.79 square meters last year and the figure in the rural area reached35.73 square meters from 32.21 square meters of the year 1997.

In 1998, the city's consumer market kept a good tendency. New progress was made in shopping-centers, supermarkets, chain-stores, etc. And the retail sales of consumer goods totaled were 90.457billion yuan, up 12.7%. Eliminating the price factor, it actually grew 17.0%. Of which, the figure in urban area was 830.65 billion yuan, up 12.7 %., and the figure in rural sales of wholesale and retail business was 7.392 billion yuan, up 12.3%, and the figure of catering was 36.114 billion yuan, up 22.7%. The scale of market was enlarged and transactions were increased. There were 31 huge retail stores whose income reached over 0.1 billion yuan.

3-3-1 城市居民家庭平均每人每月生活费收入和消费性支出情况 / Urban Household Monthly Income Available for Living Standards and Consumer Expenditures

单位：元 (yuan)

项 目 Item	1978	1980	1985	1990	1995	1997
期初手存现金 Deposits in Cash Year-beginning	—	**12.05**	**34.21**	**283.96**	**530.44**	**658.85**
生活费收入 Living Income	**36.84**	**46.21**	**87.21**	**216.09**	**712.77**	**820.60**
消费性支出 Consumption Spending	**36.65**	**43.42**	**84.29**	**200.80**	**633.48**	**730.67**
购买商品支出 Expenditures of Goods	**32.65**	**40.19**	**76.14**	**176.27**	**514.32**	**563.95**
食品 Food	22.73	30.81	53.13	122.83	321.25	362.91
衣着 Clothing	3.47	4.48	5.94	13.94	44.77	48.08
日用品 Daily Use Articles	—	2.05	9.24	17.16	70.88	60.38
文化娱乐用品 Good for Recreational and Cultural	—	1.04	4.19	8.79	28.53	39.58
书报杂志 Books, Newspaper and Magazines	—	0.30	0.85	1.83	5.03	6.83
药品及医疗用品 Medicine	—	0.31	0.88	2.54	17.21	21.72
房屋及建筑材料 Housing and Building Materials			0.39	4.13	13.97	11.97
燃料 Fuels	1.24	0.63	0.89	3.21	7.22	8.40
其他商品 Others	—	0.57	0.63	1.84	5.46	4.08
非商品支出 Non-Expenditures of Goods	**4.00**	**3.23**	**8.15**	**24.53**	**119.16**	**166.72**
房租 Rent	—	0.70	0.92	1.37	4.82	17.03
水费 Water	—	—	0.35	0.82	2.71	4.18
电费 Electricity	—	—	1.54	5.09	15.91	22.02
煤气费 Gas	—	—	—	0.21	3.49	5.81
市内交通费 Transportation	—	—	0.84	1.64	9.14	11.34
其他交通费 Other Transportation	—	—	0.58	1.74	7.24	9.68
邮电费 Postal and Telecommunications	—	0.03	0.11	0.68	10.34	15.45
医疗保健费 Medicines and Medical Services		0.22	0.22	0.80	3.18	5.21
学杂费 Tuition Fee	—	0.15	0.70	2.61	16.82	30.75
保育费 Child-care Fee	—	0.32	0.43	1.19	3.85	4.07
文娱费 Recreation	—	0.21	0.61	2.03	8.15	8.96
修理服务费 Repair and Services	—	0.36	1.75	5.18	28.51	25.46
其他支出 Others	—	0.25	0.70	1.17	5.00	6.76
期末手存现金 Deposits in Cash Year-end	—	**15.20**	**74.02**	**386.10**	**1122.55**	**826.76**

3-3-2 主要年份平均每百户城市居民家中耐用消费品年末拥有情况一览表 / List of Urban Household Year-end Possession of Durable Consumer Goods Per 100 Households in Main Years

项 目 Item		单位 Unit	1990	1995	1997	1998
组合家具	Systems	套 (set)	51.7	55.0	55.4	57.4
自行车	Bicycles	辆 (unit)	191.7	190.7	189.0	173.2
电风扇	Electric Fans	台 (set)	335.7	326.0	322.6	297.8
洗衣机	Washing machines	台 (set)	87.3	105.0	100.6	98.8
电冰箱	Refrigerators	台 (set)	87.3	102.3	101.8	101.6
摩托车	Motorcycles	台 (set)	4.0	12.7	16.8	22.8
彩电	Color TV Sets	台 (set)	88.7	111.0	134.4	140.6
黑白电视机	Black and Write TV Sets	台 (set)	36.7	16.7	—	—
立体声收录机	Recorder	台 (set)	44.7	36.0	—	61.2
照相机	Cameras	架 (set)	33.7	66.0	75.0	73.6
中高档乐器 Middle-High Grade Musical Instrument		台 (set)	8.3	13.7	9.6	8.6
空调器	Air-Conditioners	台 (set)	1.3	57.3	99.2	107.4
电炊具	Electric Cooking	台 (set)	128.3	160.3	139.8	150.0
组合音响	Hi-fi Systems	套 (set)	17.3	40.7	55.4	55.4
录放像机	Videorecorders	台 (set)	31.0	63.0	52.8	50.6

3-3-3 基础服务事业主要指标一览表 / List of Major Indicators of the Basic Service Facilities

项 目 Item	单 位 Unit	1995（市区）(Urban)	1997（市区）(Urban)	1998（市区）(Urban)
交通 Transportation				
铁路客运量（发送量）Passenger Transported by Railway	万人 (10000 person)	2306	2363	2453
公路客运量 Passenger Transported by Highway	万人 (10000 person)	5074	4594	5279
水路客运量 Passenger Transported by Waterway	万人 (10000 person)	378	209	68
航空客运量 Passenger Transported by Civil Aviation	万人 (10000 person)	480	468	436
邮电 Postal and Telecommunication				
年末邮电局所数 Number of Post and Telecommunications Offices	所 (unit)	328	461	478
邮电业务总量 Sales Volume of Posts and Telecommunication	万元 (10000 yuan)	363243	576651	684932
报纸发行量 Circulation of newspaper	万份 (10000 copies)	175583	163378	153396
杂志发行量 Circulation of Magazine	万份 (10000 copies)	4837	4884	5015
年末电话机数 Number of Telephone	部 (unit)	1589281	1711124	1865318
市话 Number of Telephone in Urban	部 (unit)	1589281	1711124	1865318
移动电话期末户数 Number of Mobile Telephone Users	户 (household)	227985	5447666	837980
无线寻呼期末户数 Number of Radio Pager users	户 (household)	844200	1201342	1272766
服务 Service				
每千人拥有的贸易网点数 Per 1000 Population Possession of Trade Outlets	个 (unit)	33	35	33.5
每千人拥有的餐饮网点数 Per 1000 Population Possession of Catering outlets	个(unit)	3	3	2.6
每千人拥有的服务网点数 Per 1000 Population Possession of Service Outlets	个(unit)	5	5	5.5

3-3-4 城市公共事业主要指标一览表 / List of Major Indicators of the Public Service

项 目 Item	单 位 Unit	1995	1997	1998
城市供水 Urban Water Supply				
全年供水量 Total Water Supply	万立方米 (10000 sq.m)	124184	122953	122294
全年售水量 Sales of volume	立万方米 (10000 sq.m)	110899	108510	108602
生活用水 Living Consumption	万立方米 (10000 sq.m)	73522	78098	80453
年末用水人数 Number of User Year-end	万人 (10000 persons)	372	383	391
用水普及 Percentage of Population Using Water	%	98.20	98.63	98.94
平均每人每天用水量（按市区用水人口） Per Capita Daily Water Consumption (in Urban)	升 (liter)	544	585	567
平均每人每天用水量（按用水人口） Per Capita Daily Water Consumption	升 (liter)	541	559	564
城市用电 Urban Electricity Condition				
全市供电总量 Total Electricity Supply	万千瓦·时 (1000 kwh)	1329050	1536644	1681543
城乡居民生活用电（全市） Residential Use of Rural and Urban Household (city)	万千瓦·时 (1000 kwh)	252491	301610	347175
城市居民生活用电（全市） Residential Use of Urban Household (city)	万千瓦·时 (1000 kwh)	177549	196283	222910
市区供电总量 Urban Electricity Supply	万千瓦·时 (1000 kwh)	958143	1100404	1201077
城乡居民生活用电（市区） Residential Use of Rural and Urban Household (Urban)	万千瓦·时 (1000 kwh)	189711	222980	260692
城市居民生活用电（市区） Residential Use of Urban Household (Urban)	万千瓦·时(1000 kwh)	147861	163909	197799
城市用气 Urban Gas				
液化气供应量 Liquefied Petroleum Gas Supply	吨 (ton)	127334	151719	154126
家庭使用 Household Use	吨 (ton)	102818	92244	94752
居民液化气使用户数 Households with Access to Liquefied Petroleum Gas	户 (household)	448295	440630	447119
煤气销售量 Sales Volume of Gas	万立方米 (10000 sq.m)	7078	7952	8641
家庭使用 Household Use	万立方米 (10000 sq.m)	6724	7326	7774
居民煤气使用户数 Households with Access to Liquefied Petroleum Gas	户 (household)	256705	312840	346135
按人口计算气化率 Population with Access to Gas	%	86.60	90.63	91.89
住宅 housing				
年末实有住宅居住面积 Living Space of Areas	万平方米 (10000 sq.m)	3043.65	3524.18	3817.17
平均每人居住面积 Per Capita Living Space	平方米 (sq.m)	9.61	10.79	11.55

3-3-5 文化、娱乐事业主要指标一览表 / List of Major Indicators of the Culture and Entertainment Facilities

项 目	Item	单 位 Unit	1997（市区）(Urban)	1998 (市区) (Urban)
电影艺术	**Art of Film**			
电影院	Cinemas	间 (unit)	27	29
电影映出场次	Showing	场 (time)	76391	62266
电影观众人数	Spectators	万人次 (10000 persons-times)	342	395
艺术表演	**Art Performance**			
艺术表演团体	Art Performance Troupes	个 (unit)	18	18
艺术表演场所	Places	间 (unit)	36	38
艺术表演演出场次	Showing	场 (time)	5420	4771
艺术表演观众人次	Spectators	万人次 (10000 persons-times)	288	276
广播电视	**Broadcasting And Television**			
广播电台	Broadcasting Stations	座 (set)	4	4
广播节目套数	Broadcasting Program Sets	套 (set)	12	12
平均日播音	Broadcasting Hours Per Week	小时:分 (hour: minute)	191: 55	191:55
广播覆盖人口率	Population Coverage Rate	%	100	100
电视台	Television Stations	座 (set)	3	3
电视节目套数	Television Program Sets	套 (set)	5	5
平均周播放时间	Program Hours Per Week	小时:分 (hour: minute)	407: 24	526:26
电视覆盖人口率	Population Coverage Rate	%	100	100
社会群众文化	**Mass Culture**			
公共图书馆	Public Libraries	间 (unit)	11	11
公共图书馆藏书	Collection	万册 (10000 copies)	670	719
群众艺术馆、文化馆	Mass Art Centers and Culture Centers	间 (unit)	10	10
图书发行量	Circulation of Books	万册 (10000 copies)	7237	7565
博物馆	Museums and Memorial Halls	个 (unit)	20	20
纪念馆	Memorial Halls	个 (unit)	13	13
文物单位	History Relic	个 (unit)	4	4
卡拉	OK Karoke Room	间 (unit)	691	631
音乐茶座	Music room	间 (unit)	30	28
歌舞厅	Singing and Dance Room	间 (unit)	51	32
出版	**Published**			
全年出版报纸	Newspaper Published			
种数	Number of Publications	种 (special)	75	71
总印数	Total Printed	万份 (10000 copies)	173890	190173
全年出版图书	Books Published			
种数	Number of Publications	种 (special)	3939	3681
总印数	Total Printed	万册 (10000 copies)	39596	32343
全年出版杂志刊物	Magazines			
种数	Number of Publications	种 (special)	260	254
总印数	Total Printed	万册 (10000 copies)	20669	21127

4 重庆市基本情况

The General Market Conditions of Chongqing

4-1 人口概况 / General Demographic Characteristics

1998年，全市人口出生率为11.64‰，死亡率为7.09‰，自然增长率为4.55‰。年末全市总人口为3059.69万人，比上年增加16.77万人，增长0.55%。年末全市总户数907.17万户，平均每户人口3.37人。全市人口密度为每平方公里371人。

劳动就业工作得到加强。1998年，全市各级政府采取多种措施解决就业问题，年末全市从业人员达到1686.71万人，比上年末减少0.19%，其中城镇从业人员369.76万人，比上年末增长0.21%。在城镇从业人员中，职工人数278.25万人，比上年末下降3.82%；三资企业和城镇私营、个体从业人员115.03万人，比上年末增长25.85%。1997年末全市39.64万企业下岗人员中，已有21.3万人通过多种渠道、各种方式实现了再就业，再就业率达53.8%，1998年，再就业工作再上新台阶，又有12.96万国有企业下岗人员实现再就业，其中绝大部分为自谋生路。

In 1998, the birth rate was 11.64‰ and the mortality rate was 7.09‰, the natural growth rate was 4.55‰. By the end of the year, the total population of Chongqing was 30.5969 million, increased 167,700 than 1997, up by 0.55%, there are 9.0717 million families with an average people of 3.37. The density of population was 371 people per square kilometer.

Employment work was strengthened. In 1998, governments at all levels adopted many measures to solve employment problems. By the year's end, the number of employees was 16.867 million, down 0.19% over the end of the previous year, including 3.6976 million employees urban districts, up 0.21% over the end of the previous year. Among employees in urban districts, staff and workers reached 2.7825 million, down 3.82 percent over the end of the previous year; employees in foreign-funded enterprises, private enterprises and self-employed economy reached 1150300 persons, up 25.85 percent over the end of the previous year. 213,000 persons of the 396,400 laid-off workers in 1997, have found new jobs through various channels and by various means. Reemployment rate was 53.8%. By the year's end, 129,6C0 workers of state-owned enterprises found new jobs.

注：本章数据全部摘自《重庆统计年鉴1999》/Resource:"'99 Statistical Yearbook of Chongqing"

4-1-1 重庆市1998年人口情况一览表 / List of Population in 1998 of Chongqing City

地区 Region		土地面积（平方公里） Land Area (sq. km)	人口密度（人/平方公里） Density of Population (person/sq.·km)	出生率（‰） Birth Rate	死亡率（‰） Mortality Rate	自然增长率（‰） Natural Growth Rate
全市总计 Total		82402.95	371	11.64	7.09	4.55
万州区	Wanzhou	3457.00	478	11.36	7.53	3.83
涪陵区	Fuling	2946.00	371	9.54	5.87	3.67
渝中区	Yuzhong	21.90	26566	5.16	7.91	-2.75
大渡口区	Dadukou	94.39	2138	7.87	7.87	0
江北区	Jiangbei	213.52	2116	6.67	8.23	-1.56
沙坪坝区	Shapingba	383.45	1687	6.82	6.82	0
九龙坡区	Jiulongpo	443.03	1582	8.06	6.05	2.02
南岸区	Nan'an	278.78	1597	7.67	8.80	-1.13
北碚区	Beibei	755.42	836	11.44	7.47	3.97
万盛区	Wansheng	565.58	471	14.30	6.40	7.90
双桥区	Shuangqiao	37.48	1110	16.91	4.83	12.08
渝北区	Yubei	1452.03	546	9.24	6.20	3.04
巴南区	Banan	1830.30	470	8.83	7.09	1.74

续上表（continued）

地区 Region		年末总人口（万人） Year--End Total Population (10000 persons)	男性占人口比重（%） Male Proportion	女性占人口比重（%） Female Proportion	户数（万户） Households (10000 households)	平均每户人口（人） Population Per Household (person)
全市总计	Total	3059.69	52.19	47.81	907.17	3.37
万州区	Wanzhou	165.10	51.65	48.35	51.39	3.21
涪陵区	Fuling	109.23	51.65	48.35	32.88	3.32
渝中区	Yuzhong	58.18	50.77	49.23	19.22	3.03
大渡口区	Dadukou	20.18	50.35	49.65	6.62	3.05
江北区	Jiangbei	45.18	51.04	48.96	15.09	2.99
沙坪坝区	Shapingba	64.68	51.28	48.72	20.21	3.20
九龙坡区	Jiulongpo	70.10	51.13	48.87	22.53	3.11
南岸区	Nan'an	44.53	50.80	49.20	15.06	2.96
北碚区	Beibei	63.17	51.42	48.58	20.23	3.12
万盛区	Wansheng	26.64	50.49	49.51	7.43	3.59
双桥区	Shuangqiao	4.16	52.16	47.84	1.18	3.52
渝北区	Yubei	79.31	51.78	48.22	26.42	3.00
巴南区	Banan	86.11	51.90	48.10	27.20	3.17

4-2 经济发展 / Economic Development

据初步统计，1998年全市实现国内生产总值1429.26亿元，按可比价格计算比上年增长5.9%，其中：第一产业减少5.84亿元，减少1.9%；第二产业增加值21.98亿元，增长3.9%，第三产业增加值63.02亿元，增长19.3%。人均国内生产总值达到4684元。

邮电通信保持迅猛发展势头，全年完成邮电业务总量3.46亿元，比上年增长48.2%。截止1998年底市话交换机容量198.04万门，农话交换机容量68.17万门，住宅电话93.32万户，移动电话用户407311户，无线寻呼用户712421户。

1998年，全市实现社会消费品零售总额553.7亿元，比上年增长9.02%。1998年，社会消费品零售总额中公有制经济所占比重为32.4%，非公有制经济的比重为67.7%。

市场物价涨幅持续回落。1998年全市城市商品零售价格总指数为94.5%，比上年回落7.2个百分点，居民消费价格总指数为96.4%，比上年回落6.9个百分点。

全年外贸进出口总值（海关口径）10.34亿美元，实际利用外资金额5.53亿美元。

1998年，全年接待海外旅游者16.34万人次，旅游外汇收入0.88亿美元，分别比上年下降36.9%和16.2%。

According to primary statistics, the city's gross domestic product (GDP) of the year was 142.926 billion yuan, up by 5.9 percent over the previous year at comparable prices. Of this total, the value-reduced of the primary industry was 0.584 billion yuan, down by 1.9 percent; the value-added of the secondary industry was 2.198 billion yuan, up by 3.9 percent; the value-added of the tertiary industry was 6.302 billion yuan, up by 19.3 percent. Per capita GDP amounted to 4684 yuan.

Posts and telecommunications industry developed rapidly. The total business transaction accomplished in 1998 was 0.346 billion yuan, up 48.2 percent. By the end of 1998, the capacity of local telephone converters reached 1,980,438 lines; the capacity of rural telephone exchanges was 681,710 lines; the number of residential telephone subscribers was 933,154, the number of mobile telephone subscribers was 407,311; and the number of subscriber of pageing service was712, 421.

In 1998, the total retail states of consumer goods reached 55.37 billion, increased by 9.02%. The state-owned enterprises account for 32.4% of the retail states of consumer goods, and the non-state-owned shared 67.7%.

The market prices continued to decline in 1998. In this year, the general retail price index was 94.5%, which was 7.2% below the previous year. And the general consumer price index was 96.4% , which was 6.9% below 1997.

During 1998 the total volume of export and import (Statistics of the Customs) was 1.034 billion US dollars. The actual utilization of foreign capital was 0.55billion US dollars.

In the year 1998, Chongqing received overseas tourists of 163,400 person-time, and incomes of foreign exchange from tourism accounted for 88 million US dollars, down 36.9% and 16.2% respectively.

4-2-1 国民经济主要指标 / Major Indicators of National Economics

项 目 Item	单 位 Unit	1997年	1998年	指 数 Index 1997=100
年末总人口 Year-end Population	**万人（10000 persons）**	3042.92	3059.7	100.6
非农业人口 Non-Agriculture Population	万人（10000 persons）	594.58	614.03	103.3
社会从业人员 Employment	万人（10000 persons）	1689.89	1686.7	99.8
国内生产总值（现价） Gross Domestic Product(current prices)	**亿元（100 000 000 yuan）**	1350.10	1429.3	105.9
第一产业 Primary Industry	亿元（100 000 000 yuan）	304.51	298.7	98.1
第二产业 Secondary Industry	亿元（100 000 000 yuan）	563.40	585.4	103.9
第三产业 Tertiary Industry	亿元（100 000 000 yuan）	482.19	545.21	113.1
人均国内生产总值 Per Capita Gross Domestic Product	**元（yuan）**	4452.0	4684	105.2
工农业总产值（1990年不变价） Gross Output Value of Industry and Agriculture (1990 constant prices)	亿元（100 000 000 yuan）	1381.35	1407.7	101.9
农林牧渔业总产值（1990年不变价） Gross Output Value of Farming, Forestry, Animal Husbandry and Fishery (1990 constant prices)	亿元（100 000 000 yuan）	231.05	236.7	102.4
工业总产值（1990年不变价） Gross Industrial Output Value (current prices)	亿元（100 000 000 yuan）	1150.29	1170.97	101.8
全社会固定资产投资总额 Total Investment in Fixed Assets	亿元（100 000 000 yuan）	370.95	498.2	134.3
全社会房屋竣工面积 Floor Space Completed	万平方米（10000 sq.m）	4301.96	4284.9	99.6
住宅 Residential Building	万平方米（10000 sq.m）	3363.04	3267.9	97.2
社会消费品零售总额 Retail Sales of Consumer Goods	万元（10000 yuan）	5079315	5536961	109
外贸进出口总值 Total Exports and Imports	万美元（USD 10000）	163178	140266	116.3
国际旅游人数 Number of Tourists Number of international Tourism	万人次（10000 person-times）	10548	8837	83.8
全部职工平均货币工资 Average Monetary Wage of Staff and Workers	元（yuan）	5502	5710	103.8
城市居民人均可支配收入 Per Capita Disposable Income of Urban Residents	元（yuan）	5323	5467	102.7
医院 Hospitals	个（unit）	2553	3171	124.2
医院病床数 Number of Hospital Beds	张（unit）	69591	65934	94.7
卫生技术人员 Number of Medical Technical Personnel	个（unit）	88423	88769	100.4

4-2-2 主要国民经济指标平均每人水平 / Per Capita Main Indicators of National Economics

项 目 Item		单 位 Unit	1997年	1998年
国内生产总值（当年价） Gross Domestic Product (current prices)		元 (yuan)	4452.0	4684.0
工农业总产值 Gross Output Value of Industry and Agriculture (current prices)		元 (yuan)	4555.0	4613.0
工业总产值 Gross Output Value of Industry		元 (yuan)	3793.0	3838.0
农业总产值 Gross Output Value of Agriculture		元 (yuan)	762.0	775.0
地方预算内财政收入 Local Financial Revenue in Budget		元 (yuan)	246.0	281.0
主要农产品产量 Output of Major Farm Products				
粮食	Grain	公斤 (kg)	391.0	379.0
油料	Oil-Bearing Gropes	公斤 (kg)	7.7	8.2
猪肉	Pork	公斤 (kg)	39.5	39.9
水果	Fruits	公斤 (kg)	20.0	24.3
主要工业产品产量	Output of Major Industrial Products			
布	Cloth	米 (m)	17.6	13.1
机制纸及纸板	Machine-Made Paper and Paperboards	公斤 (kg)	7.7	6.5
发电量	Electricity	千瓦时 (kwh)	488.5	520.0
原煤	Coal	公斤 (kg)	966.4	843.6
钢	Steel	公斤 (kg)	45.8	53.7
钢材	Steel Products	公斤 (kg)	39.8	42.9
水泥	Cement	公斤 (kg)	322.3	384.6
社会消费品零售总额 Retail Sales of Consumer Goods		元 (yuan)	1675.0	1815.0
职工平均货币工资 Average Monetary Wage of Staff and Workers		元 (yuan)	5502.0	5710.0
城镇居民家庭可支配收入 Disposable Income of Urban Residents		元 (yuan)	5323.0	5467.0
农村居民人均纯收入 Per Capita Net Income of Rural Residents		元 (yuan)	1643.0	1720.0
城乡居民储蓄存款 Urban and Rural Residents Savings Deposits		元 (yuan)	1915.0	2375.0

4-3 居民生活 / Living Conditions of the Residents

1998年末，全市职工平均工资为5710元，比上年增长3.8%。城市居民人均可支配收入5467元，比上年增长2.7%，农民人均纯收入1720元，比上年增长4.7%。居民储蓄存款余额达到724.54亿元，比年初增长24.6%。

城市居民居住条件进一步改善，人均居住面积达到9.23平方米。使用天然气的居民1998年达到了96%。

By the year's end, the city's average wage of staff and workers was 5710 yuan, up 3.8 percent. The annual per capita disposable income of urban households was 5467 yuan, up 2.7 percent. The per capita net income of rural household was 1720 yuan, up 4.7 percent. The savings of residents reached 72.45 billion yuan, up 24.6 percent over the beginning of the year.

Housing conditions for urban residents further improved. The per capita residential space was 9.23 square meters. 96% of the total urban families were provided with the natural gas in Chongqing.

4-3-1 人民物质文化生活情况一览表 / List of the Living Standards of Residents Material and Culture Life

项目 Item		单位 Unit	1997年	1998年	指数 Index 1997=100
城乡居民收入 Income of Urban and Rural Residents					
职工平均工资 Average Wages of Staff and Workers		元 (yuan)	5502	5710	103.8
城镇居民人均可支配收入 Per Capita Disposable Income of Urban Residents(constant prices)		元 (yuan)	5323	5467	102.7
农民人均纯收入 Per Capita Net Income of Rural Residents		元 (yuan)	1643	1720	104.7
每人每年生活消费 Per Capita Annual Average Consumption for Living					
城乡居民消费水平（现价） Level of Urban and Rural Residents(constant prices)		元 (yuan)	2211	2052	107.7
农业居民	Agriculture Residents	元 (yuan)	1388	1363	98.2
非农业居民	Non-agriculture Residents	元 (yuan)	5646	5711	101.2
粮食	Grain	公斤 (kg)	211.43	204.74	96.8
食用植物油	Edible Plant Oil	公斤 (kg)	6.05	6.63	109.6
猪肉	Pork	公斤 (kg)	23.47	29.20	124.4
食糖	Sugar	公斤 (kg)	2.08	2.18	104.8
家禽	Poultry	公斤 (kg)	2.87	2.97	103.5
鲜蛋	Fresh Eggs	公斤 (kg)	4.90	5.32	108.6
蔬菜	Vegetable	公斤 (kg)	160.08	158.08	98.6
布（含化纤布） Cloth (Including Chemical Fibber Cloth)		米 (m)	1.02	0.99	97.1
消费品零售总额 Retail Sales of Consumer Goods		元 (yuan)	1675	1815	108.4

续上表（continued）

平均每人居住面积（抽样调查） **Per Capita Floor Space of Residential Buildings(sample survey)**				
城镇住房面积 Urban address	平方米 (sq.m)	8.65	9.21	106.5
农村住房面积 Rural Areas	平方米 (sq.m)	24.74	26.39	106.7
邮电 **Postal and Telecommunication Services**				
每万人拥有电话 Telephone Sets Owned per 10000 Persons	部 (unit)	419	503	120
每人平均交寄函件 Number of Letters Mailed per Person	件 (unit)	4.01	4.17	104
储蓄 **Savings**				
城乡居民储蓄存款余额 Balance of Savings Deposit of Rural and Urban Residents	亿元 (10^8 yuan)	581. 30	724.54	124.6
平均每人储蓄存款余额 Per Capita Balance of saving deposit	元 (yuan)	1915	2375	124
教育、生活 **Education and Living**				
每万人拥有大学生 Number of University Students per 10000 Persons	人(person)	27.62	27.26	98.7
每百户城市家庭拥有电视机 Number of TV sets per 100 Urban households	台 (unit)	107.00	116.67	109.0
每百户城市家庭拥有收录机 Number of Recorders per 100 Urban households	台 (unit)	43.67	50.00	114.5
每百户农村家庭拥有电视机 Number of TV sets per 100 rural Households	台 (unit)	81.13	87.40	107.7
每百户农村家庭拥有收录机 Number of Recorders per 100 Rural Households	台 (unit)	19.13	21.20	110.8
卫生 **Public Health**				
每万人拥有医院病床 Number of Hospital Beds per 10000 Persons	张 (unit)	22. 81	21.61	99.1
每万人拥有医生 Number of Doctors per 10000 Persons	人 (person)	14.24	14.27	100.2
就业（抽样调查） **Employment (Sample Survey)**				
城镇居民平均每户就业人数 Number of Employees per Household of Urban Residents	人 (person)	1.92	1.86	96.9

4-3-2 城镇居民家庭平均每人全年消费支出及构成 / Urban Household Per Capita Annual Consumer Expenditures

单位：元（yuan）

项 目 Item	总平均 Average	最低收入户 Lowest Income Households	低收入户 Low Income Households	中等偏下户 Lower Middle Income Households
消费支出 Expenditures for Consumption	4894. 54	2593.37	3448.77	3968.07
食品 Food	2179.20	1480.08	1890.63	2015.97
#粮食 Grain	193.12	174.59	225.22	197.15
油脂 Oil and Fat	90.71	78.69	104.82	89.19
肉禽及制品 Meat , Poultry and Related Products	488.37	353.66	480.63	472.69
蛋类 Egg	78.49	62.19	65.83	74.83
菜类 Vegetable	211.27	162.13	226.77	221.40
奶及奶制品 Milk and Dairy Products	80.05	48.03	54.29	69.12
衣着 Clothing	571.69	224.43	353.86	398.77
#服装 Garments	414.92	148.84	260.35	281.96
家庭设备及服务 Household Facilities, Articles and Services	461.25	118.41	129.06	284.51
医疗保健 Medicine and Medical services	185.90	84.40	143.13	115.63
交通及通讯 Transportation and Communication	337.83	126.52	166.51	246.57
娱乐、教育文化服务 Recreation, Education and Cultural Services	604.78	226.09	317.93	453.69
居住 Residence	354.66	251.73	367.68	295.46
杂项商品与服务 Miscellaneous Commodities and Services	199.23	81.71	79.97	157.47
消费支出构成 Composition of Expenditures for Consumption				
食品 Food	44.5	57.1	54.8	50.8
衣着 Clothing	11.7	8.7	10.3	10.0
家庭设备及服务 Household Facilities, Articles and Services	9.4	4.6	3.7	7.2
医疗保健 Medicine and Medical Services	3.8	3.3	4.2	2.9
交通与通讯 Transportation and Communication	6.9	4.9	4.8	6.2
娱乐教育文化服务 Recreation, Education and Cultural Services	12.4	8.7	9.2	11.4
居住 Residence	7.2	9.7	10.7	7.4
杂项商品与服务 Miscellaneous Commodities and Services	4.1	3.2	2.3	4.0

续上表（continued）

项目 Item		中等收入户 Middle Income Households	中等偏上户 Upper Middle Income Households	高收入户 High Income Households	最高收入户 Highest Income Households
消费支出	**Expenditures for Consumption**	**4587.47**	**5635.33**	**7191.19**	**7905.32**
食品	Food	2157.02	2414.21	2692.76	2607.78
#粮食	Grain	194.53	183.90	200.81	179.28
油脂	Oil and Fats	92.32	87.70	102.00	83.97
肉禽及制品	Meat, Poultry and Related Products	502.33	506.30	551.72	540.65
蛋类	Egg	75.78	83.66	101.84	88.53
菜类	Vegetables	216.30	202.19	218.67	203.59
奶及奶制品类	Milk and Dairy Products	79.44	97.40	113.20	96.60
衣着	Clothing	537.41	689.75	908.88	1084.53
#服装	Garments	392.93	492.07	693.64	793.91
家庭设备及服务	Household Facilities, Articles and Services	375.19	502.84	1026.31	1153.75
医疗保健	Medicine and Medical Services	164.53	269.38	273.57	286.81
交通及通讯	Transportation and Communications	360.11	408.90	552.72	560.04
娱乐教育文化服务	Recreation, Education and Cultural Services	520.28	725.44	997.25	1227.20
居住	Residence	334.00	372.83	397.49	554.66
杂项商品与服务	Miscellaneous Commodities and Services	138.93	251.98	342.21	430.55
消费支出构成	**Composition of Expenditures for Consumption**				
食品	Food	47.0	42.8	37.4	33.0
衣着	Clothing	11.7	12.2	12.60	13.7
家庭设备及服务	Household Facilities, Articles and Services	8.2	8.9	14.3	14.6
医疗保健	Medicine and Medical Services	3.6	4.8	3.8	3.6
交通与通讯	Transportation and Communication	7.8	7.3	7.7	7.2
娱乐教育文化服务	Recreation, Education and Cultural Services	11.3	12.9	13.9	15.5
居住	Residence	7.3	6.6	5.5	7.0
杂项商品与服务	Miscellaneous Commodities and Services	3.0	4.5	4.8	5.4

4-3-3 主要年份平均每百户城镇居民家中耐用消费品年末拥有情况一览表 / List of Urban Household Year-end Possession of Durable Consumer Goods Per 100 Households in Main Years

品名 Item		单位 Unit	1997年	1998年	指数 Index 1997=100
缝纫机	Sewing Machine	架 (unit)	51.00	45.67	89.5
洗衣机	Washing Machine	台 (unit)	89.67	95.00	105.9
电风扇	Electric Fan	台 (unit)	205.67	209.33	101.8
电冰箱	Refrigerator	台 (Unit)	98.67	98.00	99.3
彩色电视机	Color TV Set	台 (Unit)	107.00	116.67	109.0
组合音响	Hi-fi Stereo Component System	套 (set)	15.33	25.00	163.1
收录机	Radio Cassette Player	台 (unit)	43.67	50.00	114.5
照相机	Camera	台 (unit)	53.33	58.67	110.0
中高档乐器	Medium and High Grade Musical Instrument	件 (piece)	8.76	11.33	130.7
空调器	Air Conditioner	台 (unit)	59.33	68.33	115.2

4-3-4 交通、邮电情况一览表 / Transportation and Postal Communications

项目 Item	1997年	1998年	指数 Index 1997=100
民用车辆拥有量（辆） Total Civil Motor Vehicles (vehicle)	282865	329972	116.7
#私人拥有量（辆） Private Owned	34771	64916	186.7
民用船舶拥有量（辆） Civil Transport Vessels	5744	5471	95.3
#私人拥有量（艘） Private Owned (vessel)	3029	2880	95.1
旅客周转量总计（万人次） Total Passenger-Kilometers (10000 person times)	2388433	2476181	103.7
铁路（万人次） Railway (10000 person times)	483000	491700	101.8
公路（万人次） Highway (10000 person times)	1288392	1455763	113.0
水路（万人次） Waterway (10000 person times)	509570	351451	69.0
民航（万人次） Civil Aviation (10000 person times)	107471	177267	164.9
年末市内电话（户） Local(urban)Telephone Subscribers at year-end(subscriber)	961438	1214929	126.4
#住宅电话（户） Residential Telephone Subscribers(subscriber)	630434	933154	148.0
年末无线寻呼用户（户） Number of Subscribers of Paging Service at year-end (subscriber)	468444	712421	152.1
年末移动电话用户（户） Number of Mobile Telephone Subscribers (subscriber)	191494	407311	213.0
平均每百人邮电业务量（元） Total Revenue from Postal and Telecommunication Services per 100 Persons (yuan)	7673	11306	147.4
平均每人每年发函件数（件） Annual Average Number of Letters Mailed per Capita (piece)	4.0	4.16	104.0
平均每人每年定报刊数（份） Annual Average Number of Newspapers and Magazines Subscribed per Capita (piece)	9.2	10.10	109.8
平均每百人拥有电话机部数（部） Number of Telephone Sets Owned per 100 persons(unit)	4.2	6.75	160.7

5 武汉市基本情况

The General Market Conditions of Wuhan

5-1 人口概况 / General Demographic Characteristics

1998 年末，武汉人口总数为 7317907 人，其中城区人口 3803724 人，郊区人口 321707 人，市郊人口 3192476 人。年末全市总户数 2054327 户，平均每户人口 3.56 人，其中城区平均每户 3.39 人，郊区平均每户 4.03 人。人口出生率为 8.38‰，死亡率为 6.11‰，自然增长率由上年的 3.01‰下降到 2.27‰。全年净迁移人口 37133 人。全市人口密度为每平方公里 864 人，其中城区每平方公里 4404 人，郊区每平方公里 421 人，市郊每平方公里 467 人。密度最大的是江汉区，每平方公里 13504 人。密度最小的是江夏区，每平方公里 321 人。

1998 年末，全市有职工 202.37 万人，比上年下降 2.7%；职工工资总额 1353726 万元，增长 5.7%。社会从业人员 415.20 万人，增长 0.8%。

By the end of 1998, the total population of Wuhan was 7317907, and 380372 of the total were from urban area, 321707 from suburbs, and 3192476 from the ajacent suberbs. Totally there were 2054327 families in the city, with an average family member of 3.56. Of which, rural family had 4.03 members and urban family had 3.39 members. The birthrate stood at 8.38‰, mortality rate 6.11‰, and the natural growth rate declined to 2.27‰ from 3.01‰ last year. During the whole year, about 37133 people moved into and out the city. The city's average population density reached 864 persons per square kilometer, with the figure in urban area standing at 4404 persons per square kilometer, 421 in suburbs per square kilometer and the rural figure was 467 persons per square kilometer. JiangHan District reported the highest population density of 13504 persons per square kilometer while Jiangxia district reported the lowest population density of 321 per square kilometer.

By the end of 1998, the city's stuff and workers amounted to 2.0237 million, 2.7% fewer than the last year. The total payment for the stuff workers was 13.54 billion yuan, up 5.7%. The city employed a totaled 4.152 million, up 0.8%.

注：本章数据全部摘自《武汉统计年鉴 1999》/ Resource: " '99Statistical Yearbook of Wuhan "

5-1-1 武汉市 1998 年人口情况一览表 / List of Population in 1998 of Wuhan City

地 区 Region		土地面积（平方公里）Land Area (sq.km)	人口密度（人/平方公里）Population Density (person/sq.km)	1998 年		1997 年	
				户数（户）Households (Household)	年末人口（人）Year-end Population (Person)	户数（户）Households (Household)	年末人口（人）Year-end Population (Person)
总计	Total	8467.11	864	2054327	7317907	2012794	7239017
江岸区	Jiang'an	64.24	9539	195625	612778	194187	609371
江汉区	Jianghan	33.43	13504	140447	451433	139753	450361
桥口区	Qiaokou	46.40	11442	169097	530917	168735	531082
汉阳区	Hanyang	91.50	4138	118842	378614	120074	380518
武昌区	Wuchang	81.22	10110	241777	821115	238910	813354
青山区	Qingshan	45.13	9369	117000	422835	114720	418867
洪山区	Hongshan	501.70	1168	135871	586032	134013	567094
蔡甸区	Caidian	1091.00	488	139432	532569	141496	516299
江夏区	Jiangxia	2008.98	321	167531	644373	165439	626485
东西湖区	Dongxihu	495.51	435	75647	215541	78952	212203
汉南区	Hannan	268.00	396	32219	106166	30244	105712
黄陂县	Huangpi	2261.00	481	273653	1086950	268920	1077660
新洲县	Xinzhou	1479.00	628	225418	928584	215502	920011

5-1-2 人口构成及人口变动 / Composition and Changes of Population

指标 Item		单位 Unit	全市 Total		市区 District		市辖县 County	
			1997	1998	1997	1998	1997	1998
总人口	Total Population	人（Person）	7239017	7317907	5241346	5302373	1997671	2015534
男	Male	人（Person）	3691383	3760109	2673371	2730308	1018012	1029801
女	Female	人（Person）	3468031	3557798	2499129	2572065	968902	985733
农业人口	Agriculture Population	人（Person）	3004357	3033640	1351680	1364388	1652677	1669252
非农业人口	Non-agriculture Population	人（Person）	4155057	4284267	3820820	3911824	334234	372443
出生人口	Birth Population	人（Person）	64687	61014	45398	43324	19289	17690
死亡人口	Death Population	人（Person）	43001	44460	31286	32473	11715	11987
自然增长人口	Natural Growth	人（Person）	21686	16554	14112	10851	7574	5703
出生率	Birth Rate	‰	8.98	8.38	8.72	8.22	9.68	8.82
死亡率	Death Rate	‰	5.97	6.11	6.01	6.16	5.88	5.97
自然增长率	Natural Growth Rate	‰	3.01	2.27	2.71	2.06	3.80	2.85

5-1-3 武汉市人口年龄构成及性别比（人口变动情况抽样调查资料） / Age and Gender Composition（From the Result of the Migration Survey）

年龄段 Age Group	全市 Total			市区 District		
	合计 Total	男 Male	女 Female	合计 Total	男 Male	女 Female
总计 Total	**7317907**	**3760109**	**3557798**	**5302373**	**2730308**	**2572065**
0-4	283278	153396	129882	173010	91873	81137
5-9	495149	260475	234674	309393	162202	147191
10-14	579996	299977	280019	387424	200140	187284
15-19	667560	347077	320483	502210	262248	239962
20-24	643835	349976	293859	478775	267720	211055
25-29	652284	334513	317771	466590	243937	222563
30-34	643133	329642	313491	456729	236594	220135
35-39	652830	334177	318653	509999	261772	248227
40-44	673730	341911	327819	522995	25570	257425
45-49	528173	270221	257952	383260	200551	182709
50-54	382645	198215	184430	271362	139991	131371
55-59	293150	149056	144194	205601	102470	103131
60-64	279955	138724	141231	213755	10423	109732
65-69	223889	113151	110798	171379	86969	84410
70-74	155664	74653	81011	118972	56959	62013
75-79	93910	40574	53336	70046	29920	40126
80-84	47744	17932	29812	35609	13032	22577
85-89	16530	5412	11118	12084	3644	8440
90-94	3694	955	2739	2630	596	2034
95-99	709	164	545	505	92	413
100 岁及以上 100 and above	48	8	40	42	5	37

5-1-4 武汉市历年人口变动情况 / Migration of Wuhan City

年份 Year	总户数 Total Households			总人口数 Total Population		
	全市 Total	市区 District	市辖县 County	全市 Total	市区 District	市辖县 County
1978	1242830	779952	467238	5482880	3322161	2160719
1979	1265333	805526	459807	5583605	3433589	2150016
1980	1295255	830192	465063	5672307	3509273	2163034
1981	1354643	874370	480273	5779010	3597711	2181299
1982	1394258	909938	484320	5869748	3670204	2199544
1983	1431570	941572	489998	5943953	3727202	2216751
1984	1468146	973558	494618	6605880	3780639	2225241
1985	1513285	1004550	508735	6083925	3837778	2246147
1986	1569960	1045759	524201	6199553	3941133	258420
1987	1618773	1090338	528435	6293398	4023135	2270263
1988	1679344	1125273	554071	6417236	4107710	2135526
1989	1736160	1164641	517519	6532563	4172870	2359693
1990	1788289	1202528	585761	6697458	4245531	2451927
1991	1847598	1249019	598579	6770312	4290091	2480221
1992	1882288	1274475	607813	6844645	4313477	2513618
1993	1908980	1293022	615886	6916923	4376387	2540536
1994	1942012	1370771	631241	7000050	4436130	2563920
1995	1963446	1326770	636676	7100100	4494872	2605528
1996	1991734	1502525	489209	7159414	5172500	1986914
1997	2012794	1528372	484422	7239017	5241346	1997671
1998	2054327	1555256	499071	7317907	5302373	2015534

5-2 经济发展 / Economic Development

1998 年，武汉市国民经济及各项事业保持良好发展态势，城市综合实力进一步增强。全年实现国内生产总值 1015.89 亿元，按可比价格计算，比上年增长 13.0%，其中第一产业完成增加值 79.85 亿元，增长 4.2%；第二产业完成增加值 453.72 亿元，增长 11.9%；第三产业完成增加值 482.32 亿元，增长 16.0%。全市人均国内生产总值达到 13957.41 元，比上年增加 1284.75 元，增长 10.1%。三种产业增加值占国内生产总值的比重由 1997 年 8.6, 46.3, 45.1 变化为 7.9, 44.7, 47.4，第三产业占比提高了 2.3 个百分点。财政收入占国内生产总值的比重达到 9.9%。

全年实现社会消费品零售总额 527.3 亿元，比上年增长 15.5%，量贩店、平价店、连锁店等商业经营业态迅速扩展。

1998 年全市共接待海外旅游者 15.1 万人次，比上年减少 51.1%，国际旅游（外汇）收入 5613 万美元，减少 48.9%。

年末金融机构各项存款余额 1285.3 亿元，比年初增长 15.4 亿元，其中城镇居民储蓄存款余额 425.5 亿元，增长 20.6%。截止 1998 年末，全市有证券交易场所 81 个，全市证券交易额 1240.3 亿元，比上年下降 40.1%。

In 1998, the local economy of Wuhan city keeped a good developing tendency, and city economic strength was enlarged. Its total GDP reached 101.89 billion yuan, up 13.0% from the previous year according to the comparable prices. The primary industry achieved added value of 7.985 billion yuan, up 4.2% over 1997 and accounted for 7.9% of the city's total GDP, 0.7% lower than that of 1997. The figures with the secondary industry stood at 45.372 billion yuan, 11.9% more than 1997, and accounted for 44.7% of the city's total GDP, 1.6% lower than that of 1997. As for the tertiary industry, it achieved added value of 48.232 billion yuan, up 16.0% over 1997. The tertiary industry accounted for 47.4% of the city's total GDP from 45.1% of 1997, or 2.3 percentage point higher than that of the previous year. The total financial revenue accounted for 9.9% of the city's total GDP.

In 1998, the social retail sales volume surpassed 52.73 billion yuan, up 15.5%. Many shopping centers of large scale, retail sales supermarkets and chain stores got prosperous and spread widely and quickly.

In 1998, the city received 151,000 overseas tourists, 51.1% fewer than the previous year, and earned 56.13 million US dollars, down 48.9%.

By the end of 1998, the volume of the city's financial institutions savings were 128,53 billion yuan, 1.54 billion yuan more than that of the beginning of this year. Of which, 42.55 billion yuan were savings of urban and township residents, increased 20.6%. By the end of 1998, there were 81 securities institutions in the city, and the sum of securities institution transactions reached 124.03 billion yuan down 40.1% over last year.

5-2-1 主要年份国内生产总值 / Gross Domestic Product in Main Years

年份 Year	国内生产 Domestic Product 总值（亿元）Gross (100 million yuan)	第一产业 Primary Industry	第二产业 Secondary Industry	第三产业 Tertiary Industry	构成（%）Composition	第一产业 Primary Industry	第二产业 Secondary Industry	第三产业 Tertiary Industry	人均国内生产总值（元）Per Capita Gross Domestic Products (yuan)
1990	176.83	27.50	92.04	57.29	100.0	15.6	52.0	32.4	2673
1991	207.95	25.65	99.98	82.32	100.0	12.3	48.1	39.6	3144
1992	255.42	30.44	122.56	102.42	100.0	11.9	48.0	40.1	3752
1993	357.23	35.87	177.46	143.90	100.0	10.0	49.7	40.3	5192
1994	485.76	44.01	242.62	199.13	100.0	9.1	49.9	41.0	6980
1995	606.91	60.74	294.67	251.50	100.0	10.0	48.6	41.4	8609
1996	782.13	71.61	366.19	344.33	100.0	9.2	46.8	44.0	10970
1997	912.33	78.79	422.06	411.48	100.0	8.6	46.3	45.1	12673
1998	1015.89	79.85	453.72	482.32	100.0	7.9	44.7	47.4	13957

5-2-2 社会消费品零售总额 / Retail Sales of Consumer Goods

年份 Year	消费品零售总额（万元）Total Retail Consume Goods (10000 yuan)	指数（上年=100）Item	年份 Year	消费品零售总额（万元）Total Retail of Consume Goods (10000 yuan)	指数（上年=100）Item
1952	41082	——	1975	127036	108.2
1953	54166	131.8	1976	132784	104.5
1954	51675	95.4	1977	139750	105.2
1955	52224	101.1	1978	157086	112.4
1956	72538	138.9	1979	179840	114.5
1957	77584	107.0	1980	219490	122.0
1958	83757	108.0	1981	244985	111.6
1959	92593	110.5	1982	266412	108.7
1960	98845	106.8	1983	296380	111.2
1961	88515	89.5	1984	362100	122.2
1962	87404	98.7	1985	486210	134.3
1963	80004	91.5	1986	534432	109.9
1964	80766	101.0	1987	636886	119.2
1965	80921	100.2	1988	833627	130.9
1966	86446	106.8	1989	932510	111.9
1967	94690	109.5	1990	957229	102.7
1968	96140	1051.5	1991	1091230	114.0
1969	95908	99.8	1992	1235498	113.2
1970	95631	99.7	1993	17505498	138.0
1971	96836	101.3	1994	2345541	13 7.5
1972	104620	108.0	1995	3026064	129.0
1973	114218	109.2	1996	3800808	125.6
1974	117409	102.8	1997	4565445	120.1
			1998	5273168	115.5

5-3 居民生活 / Living Conditions of the Residents

全年城区居民人均可支配收入 5912.52 元，增长 6.1%，剔除价格因素比上年同期增长 9%。城区居民食品支出占消费支出的比重即恩格尔系数为 44.5%，比上年下降 5.3 个百分点。居民家庭收入水平有了一定提高，但贫富悬殊仍在不断加大。下岗待业人员增多，职工收入增长受到一定限制。

1998 年居民消费增长主要由设备及用品、娱乐文教、居住的大幅增长所带动。

全年商品零售价格和居民消费价格总水平分别比上年下降 3.8%和 2.6%，是从 1975 年以来首次出现的价格水平的负增长。分类别看，价格水平下降的有食品（为 95.5%），衣着（为 91.4%），医疗保健（为 98.6%），交通和通讯工具（为 92.7%）和娱乐教育文化用品（为 94.4%）等五个大类；价格水平上涨的有居住（为 101.6%）

和服务项目（为 109.0%）等两大类。

In 1998, the average per capita annual income of the city actually reached 5912.52 yuan, 6.1% more than that of last year. Eliminating the price factor, the actual growth was 9.0%. The outlay on food in urban area represented 44.5% of the total expenditure (Engle Index), 5.3 percentage lowers than the previous year. Although the family earned more, discrepancy of resident's income continued to enlarge in 1998. The number of laid-off people increased, and living conditions of some low-income families descended.

In 1998, the consumption increase was mainly exalted by the great increase of appliance, entertainment, education and housing.

The level of retail sales price and resident's consumer price decreased 3.8% and 2.6% than the previous year respectively. And it was the first depress year in term of price from 1975. The price of food item lowered by 95.5%, clothing items 91.4%, medicine and healthy items 98.6%, traffic and communication items lowered by 92.7%, and recreation and sports items decreased 94.4% than last year. However, housing prices advanced by 101.6% and service industry 109.0% up.

5-3-1 城镇居民不同收入层次家庭年人均收支情况 / Urban Household Annual Revenue and Expend Per Capita by Level of Income

单位:元 (yuan)

项 目 Item	合计 Total	最低收入户 Lowest Income	低收入户 Low Income	中等偏下收入户 Medium-Low Income	中等收入户 Medium Income	中等偏上收入户 Medium-High Income	高收入户 High Income	最高收入户 Highest Income
初期手存现金	319642.0	17380.4	21789.8	52724.0	59197.1	86508.7	30323.7	51718.0
可支配收入 Discretionary Income	11266857.8	510024.4	746831.1	1826357.9	2269935.2	2564886.3	1485334.3	1863488.3
实际收入 Real Income	11287417.0	513049.4	748431.1	1830077.9	2274133.6	2568676.3	1487251.2	1865797.2
职工收入 Staff and Workers	7129550.6	312718.0	434305.1	1119294.0	1458259.9	1883234.7	985864.5	935864.3
储蓄贷款收入 Savings and lending Income	1967551.0	59053.3	54807.3	270978.4	487648.1	492365.7	264601.4	338096.5
实际支出 Real Expenditures	11104474.9	533615.6	761724.5	1884263.4	2413260.0	2609061.5	1387645.4	1514904.2
消费支出 Consumption Expenditures	10031887.9	516422.1	721392.5	1704233.0	2180793.1	2347224.5	1278845.4	1282977.0
食品 Food	4468163.7	298064.1	399186.0	887301.2	942351.5	960070.1	507567.3	473623.3
衣着 Clothing	1174966.5	29590.5	63514.8	175047.8	294052.2	290542.1	188824.8	133394.1
家庭设备用品及服务 Household Facilities, Articles and Services	808188.0	11917.6	26185.6	81354.0	153777.6	230844.9	105213.1	198895.2
医疗保健 Medicine and Medical Services	391643.3	22154.6	33188.3	64816.1	75964.0	92222.2	55670.6	47627.2
交通和通讯 Transportation and Communication	448150.3	13509.0	29078.8	75706.3	98959.4	101969.0	63699.4	65228.2
娱乐教育文化服务 Recreation, Education and Cultural Services	1058673.0	47912.0	58330.9	159193.8	214515.1	274988.7	181189.2	122543.0
居住 Residence	1286494.7	79950.3	92987.5	203331.2	327827.7	300629.9	110915.4	170812.4
杂项商品和服务 Miscellaneous, Commodities and Services	395608.1	13323.8	18920.4	57482.4	73305.4	95957.3	65765.3	70853.3
储蓄贷款支出 Savings and Lending Expenditures	1976712.35	36427.42	31058.03	190716.26	304296.09	434547.23	335158.76	644508.56
期末手存现金	493422.8	19440.2	32245.7	78800.6	103422.8	103942.0	59372.1	96199.0

5-3-2 历年职工年平均工资变化情况 / Changes in the Average Annual Wage for Staff and Workers in Main Years

单位：元（yuan）

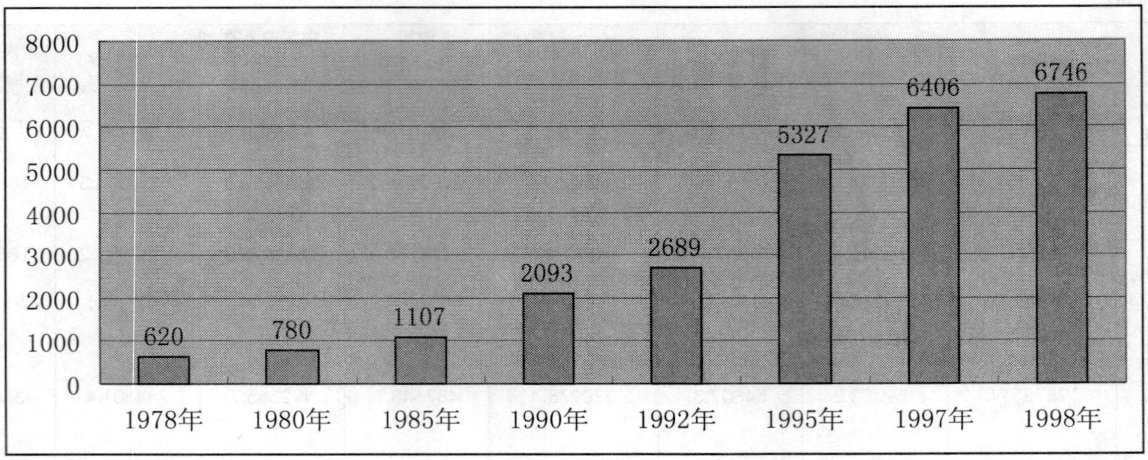

5-3-3 自来水、煤（液化）气供应和交通情况 / Tap Water, Gas and Liquefied Petroleum Supply and Public Transportation

项 目 Item		单 位 Unit	1992	1993	1994	1995	1996	1997	1998
煤气	**Gas Supply**								
供气总量	Total	万立方米 (10000 cu.m)	46433	110499	88444	134952	125880	16130	17635
家庭用量	Use by Household	万立方米 (10000 cu.m)	11109	12500	14411	17252	17695	15264	17130
家庭用户	Household	户 (household)	…	…	…	…	257173	277437	298058
用气人口	Population with Access to Gas	万人 (10000 Person)	61	69	78	81.5	82.3	91.1	103.9
液化石油	**Liquefied Petroleum Gas**								
供气总量	Total	吨 (ton)	36538	36538	47610	53009	72827	68667	78500
家庭用量	Use by Household	吨 (ton)	32321	32321	46763	52434	72454	68667	78500
家庭用户	Household	户 (household)	…	…	…	…	563370	497657	528043
用气人口	Population with Access to Gas	万人 (10000 Person)	67.1	102.6	127.0	143.7	162.4	169.1	170.8
自来水	**Tap Water**								
人均生活用水量	Consumption of Tap Water for Residential Use	升 (liter)	35.8	309.0	319.0	340.0	335.1	309.4	316.0
自来水普及率	Percentage of Population Using Tap Water	%	97.0	98.0	98.1	100.0	100.0	100.0	100.0
公共交通	**Public Transit**								
每万人拥有公共交通车量	Possession of Public Traffic Vichle Per 10000 Persons	辆 (unit)	9.1	8.8	7.7	11.8	12.0	12.9	14.0
公共汽车	Buses	辆 (unit)	1674	1675	…	…	3259	4113	4410
电车	Trolley bus	辆(unit)	307	289	…	…	242	242	254
出租汽车	Taxis	辆(unit)	4930	6459	10512	10719	12236	12600	12290

5-3-4 城市居民家庭平均每百户耐用消费品年末拥有情况一览表 / List of Urban Household Year-end Possession of Durable Consumer Goods Per 100 Households

项 目 Item		单位 Unit	合计 Total	最低收入户 Lowest Income	低收入户 Low Income	中等偏下收入户 Medium-Low Income	中等收入户 Medium Income	中等偏上收入户 Medium-High Income	高收入户 High Income	最高收入户 Highest Income
自行车	Bicycles	辆 (unit)	140. 00	113. 33	140. 00	140. 83	160. 00	135. 00	160. 00	115. 00
电风扇	Electric Fans	台 (set)	247. 50	190. 00	225. 00	223. 33	260. 00	244. 17	333. 33	271. 67
电冰箱	Refrigerators	台 (set)	99. 50	85. 00	95. 00	96. 67	101. 67	100. 83	100. 00	116. 67
冰柜	Freezers	台 (set)	3. 67	5. 00	5. 00	——	2. 50	6. 67	1. 67	6. 67
洗衣机	Washing machines	台 (set)	99. 83	83. 33	95. 00	95. 83	94. 17	103. 33	111. 67	121. 67
彩电	Color TV Sets	台 (set)	107. 17	91. 67	103. 33	102. 50	108. 33	106. 67	120. 00	121. 67
录放像机	Videorecorders	台 (set)	31. 67	21. 67	30. 00	31. 67	27. 50	38. 33	43. 33	26. 67
家用电脑	Game-Computers	台 (set)	4. 67	1. 67	——	4. 17	3. 33	5. 00	10. 00	10. 00
组合音响	Hi-Fi Systems	套 (set)	23. 50	11. 67	13. 33	20. 00	19. 17	27. 50	43. 33	33. 33
立体声收录机	StereoRecorders	台 (set)	51. 33	35. 00	38. 33	60. 83	46. 67	59. 17	43. 33	63. 33
照相机	Cameras	架 (set)	49. 00	18. 33	31. 67	43. 33	48. 33	60. 83	70. 00	65. 00
电炊具	Electric Cooking	台 (set)	61. 00	36. 67	31. 67	48. 33	69. 17	70. 83	51. 67	113. 33
空调器	Air-Conditioners	台 (set)	61. 50	25. 00	31. 67	59. 17	66. 67	68. 33	85. 00	85. 00
淋浴热水器	Showers	个 (set)	56. 67	25. 00	26. 67	49. 17	61, 67	66. 67	75. 00	85. 00
排油烟机	Range Hoods	台 (set)	41. 67	31. 67	23. 33	35. 83	46. 67	47. 50	53. 33	48. 33
吸尘器	Dust Catcher	台 (set)	8. 33	3. 33	3. 33	7. 50	6. 67	7. 50	18. 33	15. 00
摩托车	Motorcycles	辆 (unit)	4. 67	1. 67	1. 67	——	6. 67	10. 00	6. 67	3. 33

5-3-5 文化卫生事业情况一览表 / List of the Culture and Health Facilities in Wuhan

项目 Item	单位 Unit	数量 Number	项目 Item	单位 Unit	数量 number
一，剧场 Theatres	个 (unit)	18	平均每周播出时间 Program house Per Week	小时 (hour)	656
艺术表演团体 Art Performance Troupes	个 (unit)	21	电视人口覆盖率 Population Coverage Rate	%	96.2
二、群众艺术馆 Mass Art Centers	个 (unit)	3	六、广播电台 Broadcasting Stations	座 (set)	4
文化馆 Cultural Palaces	个 (unit)	20	自办节目 Self-produced Programs	套 (set)	13
			平均每周播出时间 Program house Per Week	小时 (hour)	215
三、图书馆 Public Libraries	个 (unit)	17	广播人口覆盖率 Population Coverage Rate	%	96
总藏书量 Collection	万册、件 (10000)	704.6			
读者人数 Readers	万人次 (10000)	1103	七、医疗卫生机构数 Heath Care Institutions	个 (unit)	1165
			床位数 Hospital Beds	张 (bed)	32961
四、博物馆、纪念馆 Museums and Memorial Halls	个 (unit)		卫生技术人员 Medical Professionals	人 (person)	56556

6 西安市基本情况

The General Market Conditions of Xi'an

6-1 人口概况 / General Demographic Characteristics

1998 年全市人口出生率为 9.62‰，比上年下降 0.76 个千分点，死亡率为 4.66‰，比上年下降 0.09 个千分点，人口自然增长率为 4.95‰，比上年下降 0.69 个千分点。年末全市总人口 668.21 万人。

1998 年全市共安置城镇就业人员 8.81 万人，年末全市职工人数为 177.2 万人，其中国有单位职工 106.06 万人，集体经济单位职工 21.50 万人，其它经济类型单位 13.93 万人。城镇个体劳动者 35.71 万人。

In 1998, the city's birth rate stood at 0.962%, 0.076 percentage point lower than last year, the mortality rate stood at 0.466%, 0.009 percentage point lower, and the natural growth rate stood at 0.495%, 0.069 percentage point lower . By the end of 1998, the city had a population of 6682168 people.

In 1998, the city found jobs for 88100 people. The year-end number of staff and workers amounted to 1,772,000 people. Of the total number of staff and workers, 1060600 were hired by state-owned work unites, 215,000 were employed by collecting-owned work units, 139300 were on the Dayroll of work units of other types of ownership, and 357100 were self-employed workers.

6-1-1 西安市 1998 年人口情况一览表 / List of Population in 1998 of Xi'an City

地 区 Region	土地面积（平方公里）Land Area (sq.km)	人口密度（人/平方公里）Population Density (person/sq.km)	总人口（人）Total Population (person)	非农业人口（人）Non-Agriculture Population (person)	总户数（户）Total Households (household)
全市 Total	**9983**	**669**	**6682168**	**2717526**	**1788797**
市区 Urban	1964	1926	3782534	2400224	1057402
新城 Xincheng	31	15151	469681	458034	145486
碑林 Beilin	22	26130	574869	563709	165558
莲湖 Lianhu	38	15065	572472	537679	178116
灞桥 Baqiao	322	1323	426020	155464	113348
未央 Weiyang	261	1393	363559	160081	103975
雁塔 Yanta	152	3242	492721	347896	127190
阎良 Yanliang	240	961	230742	71927	58714

注：本章数据全部摘自《西安统计年鉴 1999》/ Resource: '99 statisical Yearbook of Xi'an'

续上表（continued）

地 区 Region	常住人口 Permanent Residents		出生人数（人）Number of Birth (person)	死亡人数（人）Number of Death (person)	自然增加人数（人）Number of Natural Growth (person)
	男（人）Male (person)	女（人）Female (person)			
全市 Total	3450190	3231978	63962	31007	32955
市区 Urban	1949725	1832809	33168	14025	19143
新城 Xincheng	241526	228155	3712	2113	1599
碑林 Beiling	304781	295533	4054	1618	2436
莲湖 Lianhu	295533	276939	4842	1704	3138
灞桥 Baqiao	215714	210306	4517	1922	2595
未央 Weiyang	104044	179515	3523	1588	1935
雁塔 Yanta	259085	233636	4150	1168	2982
阎良 Yanliang	117527	113115	2266	838	1428

6-1-2 主要年份人口、人口密度和人口发展情况 / Population, Population Density and Population Changes In Main Year

单位: 人（person）

年份 Year	总人口 Total Population		女性人口数 Female	非农业人口数 Non-Agricultural	人口密度（人/平方公里）Population Density (person/sq.km)	指数（上年 100）Index (previous year=100)	
		市区 Urban				全市 Total	市区 Urban
1952	2529228	924220	188059	575090	254	102.6	103.1
1957	3272826	1470085	1505793	1110763	328	103.2	104.6
1965	4000502	1798785	1907420	1363855	401	102.5	103.4
1970	4351197	1881235	2104689	1391166	436	101.9	101.4
1975	4783889	2024530	2318153	1531027	480	101.2	100.3
1978	4980995	2101455	2418216	1599849	499	101.7	102.7
1980	5119053	2211871	2492612	1723476	513	101.4	102.6
1985	5531132	2457581	2683953	2019043	554	101.6	102.2
1986	5639673	2517950	2732976	2059200	565	101.9	102.5
1987	5744588	2576926	2781213	2102533	575	101.9	102.3
1988	5853479	2649366	2836814	2169917	587	101.9	102.8
1989	5973588	2708002	2894424	2225428	598	102.0	102.2
1990	6088901	2756677	2952879	2269836	610	101.9	101.8
1991	6154777	2788918	2981337	2303534	617	101.1	101.2
1992	6231978	2830135	3019204	2364545	624	101.3	101.5
1993	6309145	2878247	3052996	2403467	632	101.2	101.7
1994	6394544	2931624	3091700	2483546	641	101.4	101.9
1995	6482079	2982684	3134575	2557090	645	101.4	101.7
1996	6548724	3033056	3165968	2612786	653	101.0	101.7
1997	6620578	3734917	3201816	2675156	663	101.1	101.6
1998	6682168	3782534	3231978	2717526	669	100.9	101.3

6-1-3 西安市历年人口变动情况 / Migration of Xi'an City

年份 Year	出生人数（人） Number of Birth (person)	出生率（‰） Birth Rate	死亡人数（人） Number of Death (person)	死亡率（‰） Death Rate	迁入人口（人） Move in from outside (person)	迁出人口（人） Move out (person)	自然增长率（‰） Natural Growth Rate
1952	76754	30.74	22138	8.86	——	——	21.87
1957	122737	38.19	27612	8.57	252926	229226	29.52
1965	115340	29.19	33590	8.50	131109	108302	20.69
1970	120511	27.96	23448	5.44	68775	83854	22.53
1975	90628	19.04	31699	6.66	89840	91562	12.38
1978	78051	15.80	30151	6.10	111222	78684	9.70
1980	65864	12.96	31930	6.28	133560	96364	6.68
1985	89451	16.30	30085	5.48	115957	87364	10.82
1986	101360	18.15	27777	4.97	117893	83933	13.17
1987	97578	17.14	28288	4.97	125790	92551	12.17
1988	94213	16.24	28905	4.98	135421	89708	11.26
1989	117822	19.92	30379	5.13	127270	101451	14.78
1990	123972	20.55	34469	5.72	118160	98604	14.84
1991	87267	14.25	32615	5.33	89788	60935	8.93
1992	89750	14.49	33928	5.48	139397	95444	9.01
1993	92509	14.75	33707	5.38	114950	83262	9.38
1994	80760	12.71	31584	4.97	134042	85854	7.74
1995	76929	11.95	32061	4.98	144054	88468	6.97
1996	72620	11.15	34111	5.24	119435	88757	5.91
1997	68268	10.38	31247	4.75	125751	86225	5.64
1998	63962	9.62	31007	4.66	108865	83567	4.95

6-2 经济发展 / Economic Development

1998 年全年实现国民生产总值 560.4 亿元，按可比价格计算比上年增长 13.5%，其中第一产业增加值 52 亿元，第二产业增加值 248.3 亿元，第三产业增加值 260.1 亿元，分别比 1997 年增长 4.8%、18.6%和 9.5%。邮电通信事业继续迅速发展。年末市话交换机总容量 119.60 万门，比上年增长 17.82%；电话机数达 91.30 万部，住宅电话用户 56.07 万户，比上年增长 27.09%。公用电话、无线寻呼及通讯能力大幅度提高，年末公用电话达 19900 部，比上年增长 42.14%，其中磁卡电话 1800 部，移动通讯用户 10.2 万户。

市场繁荣，购销两旺。1998 年，全市共有批发、零售贸易和餐饮业网点 12.83 万个，从业人员 70.20 万人，分别比上年增长 9.24%和 17.34%。全年实现社会消费品零售总额 271.85 亿元，比上年增长 8.93%。

物价趋于平稳，涨幅回落。1998 年商品零售物价总指数下降 4.5%，居民消费价格总值数下降 2.1%。

对外经济贸易面临严峻的形式。1998 年，市属进出口总值比去年下降 30.63%，其中出口总值下降 20.61%。旅游事业有较快的发展。全年接待海外旅游者 47.78 万人，全年旅游收入 1.94 亿美元。

In 1998, the city's National Product (GNP) accomplished 56.04 billion yuan. Up 13.5% over the previous year at comparable prices. Of which, the added value of the primary industry was 5.2 billion, and the figure of the secondary industry was 24.83 billion yuan, the figure of the tertiary industry was 26.01 billion yuan, 4.8%, 18.6% and 9.5% respectively over that of 1997.

Post and telecommunications developed rapidly. By the end of the year, the total capacity of the local telephone exchanges reached 1,196,000, up 17.82% over the previous year. The number of subscribers telephones was 913,000, 560,700 of them were resident telephones, up 27.09%. The turnover of communication rose rapidly. By the end of 1998, there were 19900 public telephone sets, up 42.14%. Of which, 1800 were IC card telephone. And there were 102,000 mobile telephones.

The market continued to keep a good tendency. By the end of 1998, Xi'an had a total of 128300 wholesale, retail and catering outlets，employing 702000 people. The total retail sales was 27.185 billion yuan, up 8.93%.

The total social retail sales come up to 27.185 billion yuan, and the total consumer price index decreased by 2.1%.

There was difficult in foreign economic relation and trade. The total import and export in 1998 was down 30.63%. Of which, the total export was down 20.61%. Tourism of the city developed rapidly. In 1998, the city received 477,800 overseas tourists. Income earned was 0.194 billion US dollars.

6-2-1 主要年份国内生产总值 / Gross Domestic Product in Main Years

单位：亿元 (100 000 000 yuan)

年 份 Year	国内生产总值 Gross Domestic Product	第一产业 Primary Industry	第二产业 Secondary Industry	第三产业 Tertiary Industry	人均国内生产总值 Gross Domestic Product Per Capita (yuan)
1952	3.37	1.59	0.88	0.900	135
1957	8.02	2.09	3.97	1.96	249
1965	12.76	2.62	7.22	2.92	323
1970	17.76	3.13	10.95	3.67	412
1975	21.33	4.14	12.63	4.56	448
1978	25.35	4.83	14.59	5.93	513
1980	31.66	4.73	18.69	8.24	623
1983	35.89	5.22	20.14	10.53	674
1984	44.14	7.45	24.17	12.52	817
1985	57.58	8.76	30.83	17.99	1049
1986	65.78	9.59	33.86	22.33	1178
1987	80.16	10.73	37.69	31.74	1409
1988	99.22	11.47	46.58	41.17	1711
1989	109.38	12.78	48.91	47.69	1861
1990	116.51	13.94	50.15	52.42	1949
1991	136.14	17.17	57.06	61.91	2245
1992	164.85	18.78	69.22	76.85	2688
1993	229.56	22.58	110.88	96.10	3688
1994	276.25	31.68	114.70	129.87	4377
1995	330.35	41.40	125.33	163.62	5156
1996	410.42	46.46	161.36	202.60	6322
1997	500.55	51.33	209.71	239.62	7602
1998	557.15	51.91	247.62	257.62	8376

6-2-2 国民经济主要指标 / Main National Economic Indicators

项 目 Item		单 位 Unit	1995 年	1996 年	1997 年	1998 年
年末总人口	Year-end Population	万人 (10 000 persons)	648.21	654.87	662.06	668.22
人口自然增长率	Natural Growth Rate	‰	6.97	5.91	5.64	4.95
城乡居民储蓄存款余额	Residential Deposits	万元 (10 000 yuan)	2914647	3940163	3587774	4996845
职工平均工资	Average Wage of Staff and Workers	元 (yuan)	4763	5407	5785	6051
社会消费品零售总额	Retail Sales of Consumer Goods	万元 (10 000 yuan)	1802190	2128247	2495611	2718469
平均生活用水	Living Consumption of Tap Water Per Day	升/人日 (liter/person day)	138	239.5	140.22	147.16
城市居民生活用电	Electricity Consumption by Urban Households	万度 (10000 kwh)	44286	47370	75907	76211
液化石油气使用人口	Person with Access to Liquefied Petroleum Gas	万人 (10 000 persons)	94.5	100.82	91.98	93.10
煤气使用人口	Person with Access to Gas	万人 (10 000 persons)	25.8	27.43	26.52	27.37
公共汽车数	Buses	辆 (unit)	811	877	1031	1458
无轨电车	Trolley Buses	辆 (unit)	166	151	138	115
公路客运量	Passengers Carried	万人 (10 000 persons)	6128	6802	6167	6948
出租客汽车	Taxi					
年末营运车辆数	Operating Vehicles	辆 (unit)	1277	1324	1382	1501
客运量	Passengers Carried	万人次(10 000 person.times)	1023	1365	28453	31908
邮电业务总量	Revenue from Postal and Telecommunications Services	万元 (10 000 yuan)	76450	104566	137236	204927
年末电话机数	Year-end Number of Telephones	个 (unit)	482461	585527	722287	801418
医院	Hospitals	个 (unit)	368	316	211	223
医院床位数	Hospital Beds	张 (bed)	28265	26126	25693	26314
医生	Doctors	人 (person)	18648	14607	11933	18728

6-3 居民生活 / Living Conditions of the Residents

人民生活水平进一步提高。据对城乡居民家庭抽样调查，1998 年城镇居民人均可支配收入 5669 元；其中，生活费收入 5284 元，增长 5.26%。城乡居民耐用消费品继续增加。城镇每百户家庭拥有空调 39.3 台，电冰箱 93.0 台，增加 5 台；录放像机 27.7 台；照相机 46.3 台。

1998 年，全市城乡居民储蓄存款大幅度增加。年末居民储蓄存款余额 499.68 亿元，比上年末净增 66.12 亿元，增长 15.3%。城乡居民居住条件继续改善。城市居民人均居住面积 9.96 平方米，比上年增加 0.48 平方米。

Now progress was made in the people's living conditions. According to a simple survey, to both urban and rural families in 1998, the average per capital annual income of the city was 5669 yuan. Of which, income of living was 5284 yuan, up 5.26%. More and more families had electric appliances. In the urban area, about every 100 people owned 39.3 air-conditioners; 93 refrigerators, 5 more than 1997; 27.7 video recorders and 46.3 cameras.

In 1998, the amount of urban and rural residents' saving deposits increased a lot. By the end of 1998, the balance of their savings deposits totaled 49.968 billion yuan.6.612 billion yuan more than the end of 1997, up 15.3%. The residents' housing conditions witnessed further improvements. The per capita housing space in the urban area reached 9.96 square meters and increased 0.48 square meters over the previous year.

6-3-1 城镇居民家庭基本情况 / Basic Indicators of Urban Household, 1998

单位：元（yuan）

项目	Items	1995	1996	1997	1998
年人均实际	**Annual Real Income Per Capita**	**4169.97**	**5049.59**	**5371.56**	**5697.03**
生活费收入	Living Income	3913.51	4712.25	5020	5284
年人均实际支出	**Annual Real Expenditure Per Capita**	**4324.23**	**4949.38**	**5318.10**	**5723.83**
消费性支出	Living Expenditures	3766.28	4434.33	4752.61	4806.60
食品	Food	1682.77	1889.86	1934.44	1910.93
衣着	Clothing	477.32	558.00	525.83	449.58
设备用品及服务	Facilities, Articles and Services	517.82	519.75	517.50	546.23
医疗保健	Medicine and Medical Services	123.09	180.24	217.28	287.70
交通和通讯	Transportation and Communications	210.13	275.55	304.05	264.68
娱乐教育文化服务	Recreation, Education and Cultural Services	340.74	418.14	594.73	585.08
居住	Residence	244.30	407.38	449.88	534.81
杂项商品和服务	Miscellaneous Commodities and Services	170.11	185.41	208.90	227.60
非消费性支出	Non-Living Expenditures	556.88	514.97	565.41	917.20
人均期末手存现金	**Average Per Capita Deposits in Cash**	**247.84**	**349.56**	**366.08**	**383.32**
人均年可支配收入	**Annual Discretionary Income Per Capita**	**4152.56**	**5022.94**	**5344.14**	**5669.59**

注：调查人数为 300 人/ total sample: 300

6-3-2 城镇居民不同收入层次家庭年人均收支情况 / Urban Household Annual Revenue and Expend Per Capita by Level of Income, 1998

单位:元 (yuan)

项 目 Items	总平均 Average	最低收入户 Lowest Income Family	低收入户 Low Income Family	中等偏下收入户 Medium-Low Income Family	中等收入户 Medium Income Family	中等偏上收入户 Medium-High Income Family	高收入户 High Income Family	最高收入户 Highest Income Family
实际收入 Real Income	**5697.03**	**2296.81**	**3197.45**	**4281.37**	**5558.42**	**6811.29**	**8678.84**	**12802.53**
国有单位职工工资 Wages of Staff and Workers of State-owned Units	3046.82	1063.35	1345.63	2361.14	3382.48	4155.78	4408.99	5298.40
集体单位职工工资 Wages of Staff and Workers of Collective-Owned Units	173.43	89.88	326.06	184.00	190.58	153.65	0	267.34
其它所有制职工工资 Wages of Staff and Workers of Other Ownership Units	72.06	4.85	0	28.93	46.96	48.10	262.06	306.70
离退休再就业者收入 Income of Retired Veteran Careers	85.96	23.17	45.93	46.45	73.68	93.97	203.71	227.76
储蓄贷款收入 Saving and Landing Income	**1345.88**	**415.55**	**801.59**	**1191.99**	**1041.94**	**1376.37**	**1485.85**	**4801.10**
提取储蓄存款 Saving Deposits	978.90	165.59	535.94	649.80	810.00	1153.72	1131.12	3723.45
期末手存现金 Deposits in Cash	383.32	164.52	195.98	330.32	342.95	433.45	572.29	915.42
实际支出 Real Expenditures	**5723.83**	**2469.86**	**3744.36**	**4541.84**	**5445.22**	**6698.74**	**7945.59**	**12827.50**
消费性支出 Living Expenditures	4806.60	2302.89	3281.75	3825.00	4804.05	5901.53	6237.50	9364.35
食品 Food	1910.93	1195.96	1545.02	1664.40	1897.73	2099.79	2465.85	3180.47
衣着 Clothing	449.58	157.08	285.17	336.39	543.17	574.85	605.09	720.11
设备用品及服务 Facilities, Articles and Services	546.23	102.17	180.39	317.00	447.84	821.17	715.37	1824.27
医疗保健 Medicine and Medical Services	287.70	87.94	110.35	235.02	340.20	272.41	525.95	624.15
交通和通讯 Transportation and Communications	264.68	90.34	1487.91	192.01	286.73	335.07	381.29	541.54
娱乐教育文化服务 Recreation, Education and Cultural Services	585.08	278.01	382.51	444.58	612.14	857.44	609.11	984.81
居住 Residence	534.81	341.53	476.37	488.36	524.71	569.80	611.76	908.91
杂项商品和服务 Miscellaneous Commodities and Services	227.60	49.85	153.01	147.23	151.54	371.00	323.09	580.09
非消费性指出 Non-Living Expenditures	917.20	166.98	462.61	716.80	641.12	797.11	1708.09	3463.15
储蓄贷款支出 Expenditures of Saving Loans	**1320.50**	**320.88**	**292.14**	**943.17**	**1251.73**	**1434.36**	**2119.90**	**4455.21**
存入储蓄款 Saving Deposits	724.12	49.70	75.06	459.80	588.09	819.79	1231.34	3038.52
其它借贷支出 Others	362.56	206.38	146.87	230.01	486.59	366.60	507.54	786.39

6-3-3 城镇居民家庭平均每百户耐用消费品年末拥有情况一览表 / List of Urban Household Year-end Possession of Durable Consumer Goods Per 100 Households

项 目 Item		单 位 Unit	1994	1995	1996	1997	1998
自行车	Bicycles	辆 (unit)	188.7	195.7	201.0	196.3	188.6
电风扇	Electric Fans	台 (set)	165.3	177.7	185.3	186.7	180.3
电冰箱	Refrigerators	台 (set)	80.0	82.7	87.7	88.7	92.7
冰柜	Freezers	台 (set)	0.7	1.0	1.0	1.7	1.0
洗衣机	Washing machines	台 (set)	94.7	96.3	95.3	97.7	98.7
彩电	Color TV Sets	台 (set)	99.7	100.7	106.0	110.0	113.6
录放像机	Video Recorders	台 (set)	16.0	17.0	22.3	22.3	27.7
组合音响	Hi-Fi Systems	套 (set)	7.3	7.7	5.3	8.0	10.7
收录机	Recorders	台 (set)	25.0	22.3	21.7	67.0	60.7
照相机	Cameras	架 (set)	45.0	44.7	48.0	44.0	46.3
空调器	Air-Conditioners	台 (set)	11.3	18.0	26.0	31.0	39.3
淋浴热水器	Showers	台 (set)	31.0	36.0	43.3	43.7	50.3
排油烟机	Range Hoods	个 (set)	35.7	41.7	51.0	53.3	61.0
吸尘器	Dust Catcher	台 (set)	8.7	7.3	7.3	8.3	8.7
电炊具	Electric Cooking	台 (set)	46.3	56.0	70.7	90.3	96.0
摩托车	Motorcycles	台 (set)	1.7	1.7	3.0	2.0	2.3

6-3-4 人民物质文化生活水平 / Improvement of People's Materiel and Cultural Life

项 目 Item	单 位 Unit	1995	1996	1997	1998
非农业居民消费水平 Non-Agricultural Resident's Consumption	元 (yuan)	5168	5930	7073	7508
城镇居民家庭人均生活费收入 Urban Household Per Capita Annual Living Income	元 (yuan)	3914	4712	5020	5284
全部职工年平均工资 Average Wage for Staff and Workers	元 (yuan)	4763	5407	5785	6922
城镇居民人均居住面积 Living Space of Urban Residence	平方米 (sq.m)	9.18	9.70	9.48	9.96
每百万人拥有公共汽车 Number of Buses Per 1 000 000 Persons	辆 (unit)	3.30	3.42	2.14	2.18
年底城乡居民储蓄存款余额 Saving Deposit of Urban and Rural Residence	万元 (10 000 yuan)	2914647	3940163	4335626	4996845
平均每人储蓄存款余额 Saving Deposit Per Capita	元 (yuan)	4527	6047	6547	7478
每百户拥有电视机 Number of TV Sets Per 1 000 000 Persons	部 (ton)	114	115	110.0	114.0
每百户拥有电冰箱 Number of Refrigerators Per 1 000 000 Persons	部 (ton)	83	88	88.7	93.0
每百户拥有录音机 Number of Recorders Per 1 000 000 Persons	部 (ton)	70	75	67.0	61.0
每万人拥有病床 Number of Beds Per 10 000 Persons	张 (bed)	50	49	47	43
每万人拥有医生 Number of Doctors Per 10 000 Persons	人 (person)	29	22	18	28
平均每人生活用水量 Living Consumption of Tap Water Per Person	吨 (ton)	138	87	84	85
家用煤气普及率 Percentage of Population Using Gas	%	55.7	58.0	58.1	70.1

7　沈阳市基本情况

The General Market Conditions of Shenyang

7-1 人口概况 / General Demographic Characteristics

1998 年全市人口出生率为 6.47‰，比上年下降 0.88 个千分点，死亡率为 6.34‰, 比上年下降 0.1 个千分点，人口自然增长率为 0.13‰，比上年下降 0.81 个千分点。年末全市总人口 674.9 万人，比上年增加 1.1 万人，人口密度为平均每平方公里 520 人。年末全市总户数 2079385 户，平均每户 3.25 人。

1998 年，国有企业下岗职工人数 7.3 万人左右。全市共有 3.3 万名符合条件的下岗职工进入再就业服务中心，其中有 9700 人实现了再就业。全市共有 19.4 万人次实现了就业和再就业，城镇登记失业率为 2.33%。

In 1998, the city's birth rate stood at 6.47‰, 0.088 percentage point lower than last year, the mortality rate stood at 6.34‰, 0.01 percentage lower. And the natural growth rate stood at 0. 13‰, 0.081percentage point lower than last year. By the end of 1998, the city had population of 6749000 people, 11000 more than the previous year.

In 1998, 73,000 workers of state-owned enterprises were laid off, and 33,000 of them registered in the city re-employment center. And the center found jobs for 9700 people. Totally there were 194,000 person re-employed This year, the registered city unemployment rate stood at 2.33%.

7-1-1 沈阳市 1998 年人口情况一览表 / List of Population in 1998 of Shenyang City

地　区 Region	土地面积（平方公里） Land Area (sq.km)	人口密度（人/平方公里） Population Density (person/sq.km)	总人口（人） Total Population (person)	总户数（户） Total Households (household)
全市　Total	**12980**	**520**	**6748628**	**2079385**
市区　Urban	3495	1375	4799851	1503949
和平　Heping	21	30228	634156	201143
沈河　Shenhe	18	33046	595510	193966
大东　Dadong	49	12889	632031	202616
皇姑　Huanggu	37	18717	696309	216171
铁西　Tiexi	39	19228	750312	238421
苏家屯　Sujiatun	777	530	412556	126692
东陵　Dongling	931	438	408672	125798
新城子　Xinchengzi	849	351	297524	87554
于洪　Yuhong	774	481	372781	111588

注：本章数据全部摘自《沈阳统计年鉴 1999》/ Resource: " '99Statistical Yearbook of Shenyang "

续上表（continued）

地　区 Region	出生人数（人） Number of Birth (person)	死亡人数（人） Number of Death (person)	自然增加人数（人） Number of Natural Growth (person)
全市　Total	43627	42760	867
市区　Urban	25690	31079	-5389
和平　Heping	2990	4186	-1196
沈河　Shenhe	2842	4073	-1231
大东　Dadong	2844	4517	-1673
皇姑　Huanggu	3264	4135	-871
铁西　Tiexi	3081	5191	-2110
苏家屯 Sujiatun	3058	2507	551
东陵　Dongling	3060	2160	900
新城子 Xinchengzi	2110	1953	157
于洪　Yuhong	2441	2357	84

7-1-2 主要年份人口和人口发展情况 / Population and Population Changes In Main Yeas

单位：人 (person)

年份 Year	总人口 Total Population	男性人口数 Male	女性人口数 Female	非农业人口数 Non-Agricultural
1949	2942443	1548628	1393815	1146037
1952	3295179	1753754	1541425	1532143
1957	4251709	2221391	2020318	2496548
1962	4376555	2251101	2125454	2557846
1965	4845081	2492378	2352703	2802761
1970	4897417	2504140	2393277	2354246
1975	5187372	2640878	2546494	2486913
1978	5404700	2751185	2653515	2647980
1980	5667669	2881247	2786422	3035817
1985	6063377	3084886	2978491	3514272
1986	6146920	3131072	3015848	3596125
1987	6233631	3175569	3058062	3678993
1988	6311426	3214789	3096637	3794998
1989	6398844	3257768	3141076	3852962
1990	6460649	3282141	3178508	3888112
1991	6500783	3302924	3197859	3943593
1992	6531658	3316833	3214825	3983260
1993	6576562	3340944	3235618	4051036
1994	6623656	3361344	3262312	4104353
1995	6667917	3384270	3283647	4150775
1996	6710376	3401134	3309242	4198267
1997	6737910	3412197	3325713	4226270
1998	6748628	3416423	3332205	4242201

7-1-3 沈阳市历年人口变动情况 / Migration of Shenyang City

年份 Year	出生人数（人） Number of Birth (person)	出生率（‰） Birth Rate	死亡人数（人） Number of Death (person)	死亡率（‰） Death Rate	自然增长率（‰） Natural Growth Rate
1978	94007	17.7	27959	5.3	12.5
1980	86089	15.4	30846	5.5	9.9
1985	81526	13.5	34028	5.6	7.9
1986	90411	14.8	32970	5.4	9.2
1987	100949	16.3	34202	5.5	10.8
1988	92244	14.7	35578	5.6	9.0
1989	86756	13.7	35844	5.6	8.0
1990	79799	12.4	37894	5.9	6.5
1991	58894	9.1	36257	5.6	3.6
1992	59179	9.1	38545	5.9	3.2
1993	59620	9.1	404111	6.2	2.9
1994	60310	9.1	41373	6.3	2.9
1995	53100	8.0	40957	6.2	1.8
1996	52466	7.8	43268	6.5	1.4
1997	49443	7.4	43118	6.4	0.9
1998	43627	6.5	42760	6.3	0.1

7-2 经济发展 / Economic Development

1998 年全年实现国内生产总值 941 亿元，按可比价格计算比上年增长 10.6%，其中第一产业增加值 65 亿元，第二产业增加值 410 亿元，第三产业增加值 466 亿元，分别比 1997 年增长 11.8%、11.0%和 9.8%。

邮电通信事业继续迅速发展。累计电话交换机总容量 172.7 万门。电话机数达 136.17 万部，住宅电话用户 98.4 万户，比上年增长 17.9%。无线寻呼用户 138.3 万户，比上年增加 35.7 万户，移动电话用户 40.97 万户，增加 20.3 万户。

1998 年，全市消费市场购销略显平淡。全年实现社会消费品零售总额 473.3 亿元，比上年增长 11.5%。其中批发零售贸易销售 353.9 亿元，餐饮业 47.4 亿元，制造业 23.5 亿元，其它行业 48.4 亿元。在消费品市场中，国有经济零售额 99.4 亿元，比上年增长 7.0%。物价呈下降趋势。1998 年商品零售物价总指数为 96.5%，居民消费价格总值数为 99.0%。

1998 年，市属进出口总值 156091 万美元，比 1997 年增长 8.4%，其中进口总值 66601 万美元，出口总值 89490 万美元，分别增长 39.8%和下降 6.1%。旅游事业有较快的发展。全年接待海外旅游者 12.1 万人，比上年增长 1.7%，全年旅游收入 6007 万美元，比上年增长 9.3%。

In 1998,the city's Gross Domestic Product (GDP) accomplished 94.1 billion-yuan, 10.6% up over the previous year at comparable prices. Of which, the added value of the primary industry was 6.5 billion, and the figure of the secondary industry was 41.0 billion yuan, the figure of the tertiary industry was 46.6 billion yuan, up 11.8%, 11.0% and 9.8% than 1997 respectively.

Post and telecommunications developed rapidly. By the end of the year, the total capacity of the local telephone exchanges reached 1.727 million and 1.36 million telephones totally in Shenyang, of which 0.984 million was residential telephones, 17.9% more than 1997. And there were 409.7 thousand mobile telephones in 1998, 203 thousand more than 1997. As for the number of pageing subscribers reached to 1.383 million, which was 357 thausand more than that of 1997.

The consuming market was not good in 1998. By the end of 1998, Shenyang had a total consumption of 47.33 billion yuan, 11.5% more than 1997. Wholesale and retail shared 35.39 billion, food industry 4.74 billion, manufacturing industry 2.35 billion and others 4.84 billion. In the consumption market, the state-owned economy shared 9.94 billion, which was 7.0% up than 1997. The price kept a stable down tendency. In the whole year of 1998, the price index of the commodity retail sales was 96.5%, and the price index of resident's consumption stood at 99.0%.

New progress was made in foreign trade. The total import and export in 1998 was 1.5609 billion US dollars, up 8.4%. Of which, the total import reached to 0.666 billion and export reached 0.8949 billion US dollars, up 39.8% and down 6.1% respectively. Tourism of the city developed rapidly. In 1998, the city received 121,000 overseas tourists, up 1.7% over 1997. Income earned was 60.07 million US dollars, up 9.3% over the previous year.

7-2-1 主要年份国内生产总值 / Gross National Product in Main Years

单位：亿元 (100 000 000 yuan)

年 份 Year	国内生产总值 Gross Domestic Product	第一产业 Primary Industry	第二产业 Secondary Industry	第三产业 Tertiary Industry
1978	43.6	4.0	28.7	10.9
1980	56.7	6.5	36.3	13.9
1981	54.7	7.5	32.2	15.0
1982	61.2	8.2	37.2	15.8
1983	77.5	12.1	42.3	23.1
1984	92.9	13.5	51.7	27.7
1985	109.8	10.7	63.1	36.0
1986	125.2	11.6	72.1	41.5
1987	153.7	14.6	85.3	53.8
1988	193.0	20.1	99.3	73.6
1989	217.1	16.4	110.4	90.3
1990	234.5	23.8	107.1	103.6
1991	254.3	25.4	113.4	115.5
1992	325.4	29.3	150.6	145.5
1993	425.2	34.9	199.8	190.5
1994	556.3	44.6	257.2	254.5
1995	682.5	51.2	303.7	327.7
1996	764.4	54.7	329.5	380.2
1997	851.1	58.6	375.0	417.5
1998	938.8	64.9	412.2	461.7

7-2-2 国民经济主要指标 / Main National Economic Indicators

项　目 Item		单　位 Unit	1995 年	1996 年	1997 年	1998 年
年末总人口	Year-end Population	万人 (10 000 persons)	666.8	671.0	673.8	647.9
人口自然增长率	Natural Growth Rate	‰	1.8	1.4	0.9	0.1
城乡居民储蓄存款余额	Residential Deposits	亿元 (100 000 000 yuan)	468.9	580.7	689.1	809.5
职工平均工资 Average Wage of Staff and Workers		元 (yuan)	4900	5198	5801	6090
社会消费品零售总额 Retail Sales of Consumer Goods		万元 (10 000 yuan)	295.4	365.5	424.6	473.3
生活用水量 Living Consumption of Tap Water		万吨 (10 000 ton)	34485	36915	36530	35964
城市居民生活用电 Electricity Consumption by Urban Households		万度 (10 000 kwh)	114697	132920	142428	149219
公路客运量	Passengers Carried	万人 (10 000 persons)	7747	6589	5375	4753
出租客汽车	Taxi	辆 (unit)	13641	13550	14325	16104
年末营运车辆数	Operating Vehicles	辆 (unit)	2562	2241	2539	2462
客运量	Passengers Carried	万人次 (10 000 person.times)	54640	61568	62505	61985
邮电业务总量 Revenue from Postal and Telecommunications Services		万元 (10 000 yuan)	119095	152734	171756	197460
年末电话机数 Year-end Number of Telephones		万个 (10 000unit)	76.15	100.64	119.34	136.17
医院	Hospitals	个 (unit)	374	373	373	369
医院床位数	Hospital Beds	张 (bed)	37344	35411	35300	36929
医生	Doctors	万人 (10 000person)	2.2	2.1	2.1	2.0

7-3 居民生活 / Living Conditions of the Residents

人民生活进一步提高。据对城乡居民家庭抽样调查，1998 年城镇居民人均可支配收 4931.6 元，比上年增长 4.6%，剔除物价下降因素，实际增长 5.7%。

1998 年，全市城乡居民储蓄存款大幅度增加。年末居民储蓄存款余额 809.48 亿元，比上年末净增 120.40 亿元，其中城镇居民储蓄存款余额 735.80 亿元；农村居民储蓄存款余额 73.68 亿元。城乡居民居住条件继续改善。城市居民人均居住面积 7.77 平方米，比上年增加 0.26 平方米。

Now progress was made in the people's living conditions. According to a sample survey, to both urban and rural families in 1998, the average per capital manageable annual income of the city was 4931.6 yuan, up 4.6% than last year. Eliminating the price inflation, the actual growth was 5.7%.

In 1998, the amount of urban and rural residents' saves deposits increased a lot. By the end of 1998, the balance of their savings deposits totaled 80.95 billion yuan, which was 12.04 billion yuan more than that of 1997. Of which, the figure of urban residents was 73.58 billion yuan, and the figure of rural residents was 7.368 billion yuan. The residents' housing conditions witnessed further improvements. The per capita housing space in the urban area reached 7.77 square meters and increased 0.26 square meter over the previous year.

7-3-1 城镇居民家庭基本情况 / Basic Indicators of Urban Household, 1998

单位：元（yuan）

项 目	Item	1995	1996	1997	1998
年人均实际收入	**Annual Real Income Per Capita**	**4083.58**	**4360.00**	**4737.32**	**4954.56**
生活费收入	Living Income	3720.79	4006.17	——	——
年人均实际支出	**Annual Real Expenditure Per Capita**	**4352.86**	**4399.18**	**5227.72**	**5417.62**
消费性支出	Living Expenditures	3766.36	3858.34	4217.49	4639.58
食品	Food	1903.00	1923.12	1955.36	1918.92
衣着	Clothing	615.03	582.72	613.55	601.56
设备用品及服务	Facilities, Articles and Services	203.22	193.81	208.07	478.51
医疗保健	Medicine and Medical Services	110.68	126.15	180.46	233.59
交通和通讯	Transportation and Communications	170.52	191.88	201.50	246.93
娱乐教育文化服务	Recreation, Education and Cultural Services	413.46	441.20	578.82	591.49
居住	Residence	211.22	265.81	306.56	372.20
杂项商品和服务	Miscellaneous Commodities and Services	139.23	133.65	173.17	196.38
非消费性支出	Non-Living Expenditures	586.42	540.84	1010.23	778.04
人均年可支配收入	**Annual Discretionary Income Per Capita**	**4082.61**	**4352.60**	**4713.52**	**4931.60**

7-3-2 城镇居民家庭平均每百户耐用消费品年末购买情况一览表 / List of Urban Household Year-end purchase of Durable Consumer Goods Per 100 Households

项 目	Item	单 位 Unit	1994	1995	1996	1997	1998
自行车	Bicycles	辆 (unit)	14.8	13.8	11.0	10.2	10.6
电风扇	Electric Fans	台 (set)	3.2	2.4	0.6	4.4	2.2
电冰箱	Refrigerators	台 (set)	0.6	1.4	1.2	1.4	2.2
冰柜	Freezers	台 (set)	0.4	0.4	0.4	0.2	0.2
洗衣机	Washing machines	台 (set)	1.4	1.8	1.4	3.0	2.6
彩电	Color TV Sets	台 (set)	1.0	0.4	0.6	2.2	5.2
录放像机	Video Recorders	台 (set)	1.8	0.2	0.8	0.2	0.2
游戏机	Video Game Player	台 (set)	1.2	0.8	0.4	——	——
组合音响	Hi-Fi Systems	套 (set)	1.0	1.4	0.8	1.0	2.0
收录机	Recorders	台 (set)	1.0	2.6	3.0	2.8	1.6
照相机	Cameras	架 (set)	1.6	0.5	1.2	0.4	0.6
淋浴热水器	Showers	台 (set)	7.2	6.6	3.8	5.2	5.2
排油烟机	Range Hoods	个 (set)	4.0	5.2	4.4	3.6	6.6
吸尘器	Dust Catcher	台 (set)	1.2	0.4	0.4	0.4	0.6
电炊具	Electric Cooking	台 (set)	6.2	6.4	4.0	6.0	7.8
摩托车	Motorcycles	台 (set)	0.2	0.0	0.2	0.4	0.2

7-3-3 人民物质文化生活水平 / Improvement of People's Materiel and Cultural Life

项 目 Item		单 位 Unit	1995	1996	1997	1998
全部职工年平均工资	Average Wage for Staff and Workers	元 (yuan)	4900	5198	5801	6090
城镇居民人均居住面积	Living Space of Urban Residence	平方米 (sq.m)	6.87	7.22	7.51	7.77
年底城乡居民储蓄存款余额	Saving Deposit of Urban and Rural Residence	亿元 (100 000 000 yuan)	468.86	580.68	689.08	809.48
平均每人储蓄存款余额	Saving Deposit per Capita	元 (yuan)	7029	8681	10227	11994
每百户拥有彩色电视机	Number of color TV Sets per 1 000 000 Persons	部 (ton)	94.0	95.4	100.6	108.0
每百户拥有电冰箱	Number of Refrigerators per 1 000 000 Persons	部 (ton)	78.2	78.8	82.2	84.2
每百户拥有录音机	Number of Recorders per 1 000 000 Persons	部 (ton)	84.0	78.2	73.8	66.0
每千人拥有病床	Number of Beds per 1 000 Persons	张 (bed)	5.8	5.7	5.7	5.7
每千人拥有医生	Number of Doctors per 1 000 Persons	人 (person)	3.3	3.2	3.1	3.0

8 北京市样本结构 / The Sample Compositions of Beijing

8-1 性别构成/ Gender Composition

	有效样本量 Total	男性 Male	女性 Female
人数 Number	1012	504	508
百分比 Percent	100.0	49.8	50.2

8-2 年龄构成/ Age Composition

	有效样本量 Total	16-24 岁 Age	25-34 岁 Age	35-44 岁 Age	45-54 岁 Age	55-60 岁 Age
人数 Number	1012	213	301	255	161	82
百分比 Percent	100.0	21.0	29.7	25.2	15.9	8.1

8-3 学历构成/ Educational Composition

	有效样本量 Total	小学及以下 Primary School or Below	初中 Middle School	高中/中专/技校 High School/ Technical Secondary School	大学专科 2-3 Year College	大学本科 4-5 Year College	研究生或以上 Graduate or Above
人数 Number	1008	31	168	436	208	148	17
百分比 Percent	100.0	3.1	16.7	43.3	20.6	14.7	1.7

8-4 职业构成/ Occupational Composition

	有效样本量 Total	劳务职 Labor	技能职 Skill	服务职 Service	事务职 Assistance	销售职 Marketing	技术职 Technique	技术类以外的专门职 Professional Outside Technique	自由职业者 Free Lance
人数 Number	1007	105	102	77	33	45	80	112	8
百分比 Percent	100.0	10.4	10.1	7.6	3.3	4.5	7.9	11.1	0.8

续前表 continued

	有效样本量 Total	企业/公司管理人员 Manager	行政管理人员/公务员 Administrator	经营者 Businessman	个体户 Self-employed Labor	军警 Military & Police	高中/中专/技校学生 High School/ Technical Secondary School Student
人数 Number	1007	67	63	14	27	6	88
百分比 Percent	100.0	6.7	6.3	1.4	2.7	0.6	8.7

续前表 continued

	有效样本量 Total	大学生 College Student	研究生 Graduate Student	家庭主妇 Housewife	离退休人员 Retired	下岗、待业人员 Unemployed	其他 Others
人数 Number	1007	42	3	11	61	45	18
百分比 Percent	100.0	4.2	0.3	1.1	6.1	4.5	1.8

8-5 婚姻状况/ Marital Status Composition

	有效样本量 Total	已婚 Married	未婚 Single	离异 Divorced	丧偶 Widowed
人数 Number	1007	679	299	21	8
百分比 Percent	100.0	67.4	29.7	2.1	0.8

8-6 家庭常住人口数/ Number of Regular Household Members

	有效样本量 Total	1 人 1 People	2 人 2 People	3 人 3 People	4 人 4 People	5 人 5 People	6 人 6 People	7 人以上 7 People Above
人数 Number	1011	32	131	539	169	94	32	14
百分比 Percent	100.0	3.2	13.0	53.3	16.7	9.3	3.2	1.4

8-7 个人平均月收入/ Individual Monthly Income

	有效样本量 Total	无收入 no income	500 元以下 below 500 yuan	501-1000 元 yuan	1001-1500 元 yuan	1501-2000 元 yuan	2001-3000 元 yuan	3001-4000 元 yuan	4001-5000 元 yuan	5000 元以上 over 5000 yuan
人数 Number	1000	151	94	272	245	118	90	8	6	16
百分比 Percent	100.0	15.1	9.4	27.2	24.5	11.8	9.0	0.8	0.6	1.6

8-8 家庭平均月总收入/ Household Monthly Income

	有效样本量 Total	500 元以下 below 500 yuan	501-1000 元 yuan	1001-1500 元 yuan	1501-2000 元 yuan	2001-3000 元 yuan	3001-4000 元 yuan	4001-6000 元 yuan	6001-8000 元 yuan	8000 元以上 over 8000 yuan
人数 Number	1004	17	65	147	192	358	95	78	16	36
百分比 Percent	100.0	1.7	6.5	14.6	19.1	35.7	9.5	7.8	1.6	3.6

9 上海市样本结构 / Sample Compositions of Shanghai

9-1 性别构成/ Gender Composition

	有效样本量 Total	男性 Male	女性 Female
人数 Number	1014	509	505
百分比 Percent	100.0	50.2	49.8

9-2 年龄构成/ Age Composition

	有效样本量 Total	16-24 岁 Age	25-34 岁 Age	35-44 岁 Age	45-54 岁 Age	55-60 岁 Age
人数 Number	1014	217	290	260	167	80
百分比 Percent	100.0	21.4	28.6	25.6	16.5	7.9

9-3 学历构成/ Educational Composition

	有效样本量 Total	小学及以下 Primary School or Below	初中 Middle School	高中/中专/技校 High School/ Technical Secondary School	大学专科 2-3 Year College	大学本科 4-5 Year College	研究生或以上 Graduate or Above
人数 Number	1011	22	266	510	138	68	7
百分比 Percent	100.0	2.2	26.3	50.4	13.6	6.7	0.7

9-4 职业构成/ Occupational Composition

	有效样本量 Total	劳务职 Labor	技能职 Skill	服务职 Service	事务职 Assistance	销售职 Marketing	技术职 Techni que	技术类以外的专门职 Professional Outside Technique	自由职业者 Free Lance
人数 Number	1013	153	104	83	41	38	54	76	12
百分比 Percent	100.0	15.1	10.3	8.2	4.0	3.8	5.3	7.5	1.2

续前表 continued

	有效样本量 Total	企业/公司管理人员 Manager	行政管理人员/公务员 Administrator	经营者 Businessman	个体户 Self-employed Labor	军警 Military & Police	高中/中专/技校学生 High School/ Technical Secondary School Student
人数 Number	1013	54	34	9	31	3	76
百分比 Percent	100.0	5.3	3.4	0.9	3.1	0.3	7.5

续前表 continued

	有效样本量 Total	大学生 College Student	研究生 Graduate Student	家庭主妇 Housewife	离退休人员 Retired	下岗、待业人员 Unemployed	其他 Others
人数 Number	1013	32	2	7	84	98	22
百分比 Percent	100.0	3.2	0.2	0.7	8.3	9.7	2.2

9-5 婚姻状况/ Marital Status Composition

	有效样本量 Total	已婚 Married	未婚 Single	离异 Divorced	丧偶 Widowed
人数 Number	1007	646	340	13	8
百分比 Percent	100.0	64.2	33.8	1.3	0.8

9-6 家庭常住人口数/ Number of Regular Household Members

	有效样本量 Total	1 人 1 People	2 人 2 People	3 人 3 People	4 人 4 People	5 人 5 People	6 人 6 People	7 人或以上 7 People or Above
人数 Number	1014	25	89	569	189	112	18	12
百分比 Percent	100.0	2.5	8.8	56.1	18.6	11.0	1.8	1.2

9-7 个人平均月收入/ Individual Monthly Income

	有效样本量 Total	无收入 no income	500元以下 below 500 yuan	501-1000元 yuan	1001-1500元 yuan	1501-2000元 yuan	2001-3000元 yuan	3001-4000元 yuan	4001-5000元 yuan	5000元以上 over 5000 yuan
人数 Number	1009	156	104	298	237	97	93	12	6	6
百分比 Percent	100.0	15.5	10.3	29.5	23.5	9.7	9.3	1.2	0.6	0.6

9-8 家庭平均月总收入/ Household Monthly Income

	有效样本量 Total	500元以下 below 500 yuan	501-1000元 yuan	1001-1500元 yuan	1501-2000元 yuan	2001-3000元 yuan	3001-4000元 yuan	4001-6000元 yuan	6001-8000元 yuan	8000元以上 over 8000 yuan
人数 Number	1011	18	72	147	165	367	101	97	16	28
百分比 Percent	100.0	1.8	7.1	14.5	16.3	36.3	1.0	9.6	1.6	2.8

10 广州市样本结构/ Sample Compositions of Guangzhou

10-1 性别构成/ Gender Composition

	有效样本量 Total	男性 Male	女性 Female
人数 Number	1034	499	535
百分比 Percent	100.0	48.3	51.7

10-2 年龄构成/ Age Composition

	有效样本量 Total	16-24岁 Age	25-34岁 Age	35-44岁 Age	45-54岁 Age	55-60岁 Age
人数 Number	1034	218	308	264	160	84
百分比 Percent	100.0	21.1	29.8	25.5	15.5	8.1

10-3 学历构成/ Educational Composition

	有效样本量 Total	小学及以下 Primary School or Below	初中 Middle School	高中/中专/技校 High School/ Technical Secondary School	大学专科 2-3 Year College	大学本科 4-5 Year College	研究生或以上 Graduate or Above
人数 Number	1024	53	219	508	129	103	12
百分比 Percent	100.0	5.2	21.4	49.6	12.6	10.1	1.2

10-4 职业构成/ Occupational Composition

	有效样本量 Total	劳务职 Labor	技能职 Skill	服务职 Service	事务职 Assistance	销售职 Marketing	技术职 Technique	技术类以外的专门职 Professional Outside Technique	自由职业者 Free Lance
人数 Number	1032	109	83	76	37	56	48	80	9
百分比 Percent	100.0	10.6	8.0	7.4	3.6	5.4	4.7	7.8	0.9

续前表 continued

	有效样本量 Total	企业/公司管理人员 Manager	行政管理人员/公务员 Administrator	经营者 Businessman	个体户 Self-employed Labor	军警 Military & Police	高中/中专/技校学生 High School/ Technical Secondary School Student
人数 Number	1032	42	44	20	62	4	83
百分比 Percent	100.0	4.1	4.3	1.9	6.0	0.4	8.0

续前表 continued

	有效样本量 Total	大学生 College Student	研究生 Graduate Student	家庭主妇 Housewife	离退休人员 Retired	下岗、待业人员 Unemployed	其他 Others
人数 Number	1032	62	1	30	57	112	17
百分比 Percent	100.0	6.0	0.1	2.9	5.5	10.9	1.6

10-5 婚姻状况/ Marital Status Composition

	有效样本量 Total	已婚 Married	未婚 Single	离异 Divorced	丧偶 Widowed
人数 Number	1011	651	335	5	20
百分比 Percent	100.0	64.4	33.1	0.5	2.0

10-6 家庭常住人口数/ Number of Regular Household Members

	有效样本量 Total	1人 1 People	2人 2 People	3人 3 People	4人 4 People	5人 5 People	6人 6 People	7人或以上 7 People or Above
人数 Number	1034	24	104	459	243	118	42	44
百分比 Percent	100.0	2.3	10.1	44.4	23.5	11.4	4.1	4.3

10-7 个人平均月收入/ Individual Monthly Income

	有效样本量 Total	无收入 no income	500元以下 below 500 yuan	501-1000元 yuan	1001-1500元 yuan	1501-2000元 yuan	2001-3000元 yuan	3001-4000元 yuan	4001-5000元 yuan	5000元以上 over 5000 yuan
人数 Number	1030	216	98	231	232	98	121	16	10	8
百分比 Percent	100.0	21.0	9.5	22.4	22.5	9.5	11.7	1.6	1.0	0.8

10-8 家庭平均月总收入/ Household Monthly Income

	有效样本量 Total	500元以下 below 500 yuan	501-1000元 yuan	1001-1500元 yuan	1501-2000元 yuan	2001-3000元 yuan	3001-4000元 yuan	4001-6000元 yuan	6001-8000元 yuan	8000元以上 over 8000 yuan
人数 Number	1027	27	71	134	163	373	116	89	23	31
百分比 Percent	100.0	2.67	6.9	13.0	15.9	36.3	11.3	8.7	2.2	3.0

11 重庆市样本结构/ Sample Composition of Chongqing

11-1 性别构成/ Gender Composition

	有效样本量 Total	男性 Male	女性 Female
人数 Number	624	314	310
百分比 Percent	100.0	50.3	49.7

11-2 年龄构成/ Age Composition

	有效样本量 Total	16-24岁 Age	25-34岁 Age	35-44岁 Age	45-54岁 Age	55-60岁 Age
人数 Number	624	128	183	148	114	51
百分比 Percent	100.0	20.5	29.3	23.7	18.3	8.2

11-3 学历构成/ Educational Compositon

	有效样本量 Total	小学及以下 Primary School or Below	初中 Middle School	高中/中专/技校 High School/ Technical Secondary School	大学专科 2-3 Year College	大学本科 4-5 Year College	研究生或以上 Graduate or Above
人数 Number	622	60	200	246	83	32	1
百分比 Percent	100.0	9.6	32.2	39.5	13.3	5.1	0.2

11-4 职业构成/ Occupational Composition

	有效样本量 Total	劳务职 Labor	技能职 Skill	服务职 Service	事务职 Assistance	销售职 Marke-ting	技术职 Technique	技术类以外的专门职 Professional Outside Technique	自由职业者 Free Lance
人数 Number	623	95	57	43	7	14	27	37	4
百分比 Percent	100.0	15.2	9.1	6.9	1.1	2.2	4.3	5.9	0.6

续前表 continued

	有效样本量 Total	企业/公司管理人员 Manager	行政管理人员/公务员 Administrator	经营者 Businessman	个体户 Self-employed Labor	军警 Military & Police	高中/中专/技校学生 High School/ Technical Secondary School Student
人数 Number	623	22	12	4	53	1	54
百分比 Percent	100.0	3.5	1.9	0.6	8.5	0.2	8.7

续前表 continued

	有效样本量 Total	大学生 College Student	研究生 Graduate Student	家庭主妇 Housewife	离退休人员 Retired	下岗、待业人员 Unemployed	其他 Others
人数 Number	623	14	0	19	62	89	9
百分比 Percent	100.0	2.2	0.0	3.0	10.0	14.3	1.4

11-5 婚姻状况/ Marital Status Composition

	有效样本量 Total	已婚 Married	未婚 Single	离异 Divorced	丧偶 Widowed
人数 Number	617	415	172	25	5
百分比 Percent	100.0	67.3	27.9	4.1	0.8

11-6 家庭常住人口数/ Number of Regular Household Members

	有效样本量 Total	1人 1 People	2人 2 People	3人 3 People	4人 4 People	5人 5 People	6人 6 People	7人或以上 7 People or Above
人数 Number	624	9	70	314	123	73	28	7
百分比 Percent	100.0	1.4	11.2	50.3	19.7	11.7	4.5	1.1

11-7 个人平均月收入/ Individual Monthly Income

	有效样本量 Total	无收入 no income	500元以下 below 500 yuan	501-1000元 yuan	1001-1500元 yuan	1501-2000元 yuan	2001-3000元 yuan	3001-4000元 yuan	4001-5000元 yuan	5000元以上 over 5000 yuan
人数 Number	622	127	213	194	57	16	12	1	1	1
百分比 Percent	100.0	20.4	34.2	31.2	9.2	2.6	1.9	0.2	0.2	0.2

11-8 家庭平均月总收入/ Household Monthly Income

	有效样本量 Total	500元以下 below 500 yuan	501-1000元 yuan	1001-1500元 yuan	1501-2000元 yuan	2001-3000元 yuan	3001-4000元 yuan	4001-6000元 yuan	6001-8000元 yuan	8000元以上 over 8000 yuan
人数 Number	623	69	190	165	88	91	6	9	2	3
百分比 Percent	100.0	11.1	30.5	26.5	14.1	14.6	1.0	1.4	0.3	0.5

12 武汉市样本结构 / Sample Compositions of Wuhan

12-1 性别构成/ Gender Composition

	有效样本量 Total	男性 Male	女性 Female
人数 Number	642	311	331
百分比 Percent	100.0	48.4	51.6

12-2 年龄构成/ Age Composition

	有效样本量 Total	16-24岁 Age	25-34岁 Age	35-44岁 Age	45-54岁 Age	55-60岁 Age
人数 Number	642	134	185	158	114	51
百分比 Percent	100.0	20.9	28.8	24.6	17.8	7.9

12-3 学历构成/ Educational Composition

	有效样本量 Total	小学及以下 Primary School or Below	初中 Middle School	高中/中专/技校 High School/ Technical Secondary School	大学专科 2-3 Year College	大学本科 4-5 Year College	研究生或以上 Graduate or Above
人数 Number	641	29	155	285	112	55	5
百分比 Percent	100.0	4.5	24.2	44.5	17.5	8.6	0.8

12-4 职业构成/ Occupational Composition

	有效样本量 Total	劳务职 Labor	技能职 Skill	服务职 Service	事务职 Assistance	销售职 Marketing	技术职 Technique	技术类以外的专门职 Professional Outside Technique	自由职业者 Free Lance
人数 Number	635	77	53	42	17	18	28	54	4
百分比 Percent	100.0	12.1	8.3	6.6	2.7	2.8	4.4	8.5	0.6

续前表 continued

	有效样本量 Total	企业/公司管理人员 Manager	行政管理人员/公务员 Administrator	经营者 Businessman	个体户 Self-employed Labor	军警 Military & Police	高中/中专/技校学生 High School/ Technical Secondary School Student
人数 Number	635	28	35	8	31	0	28
百分比 Percent	100.0	4.4	5.5	1.3	4.9	0.0	4.4

续前表 continued

	有效样本量 Total	大学生 College Student	研究生 Graduate Student	家庭主妇 Housewife	离退休人员 Retired	下岗、待业人员 Unemployed	其他 Others
人数 Number	635	33	0	7	51	102	19
百分比 Percent	100.0	5.2	0.0	1.1	8.0	16.1	3.0

12-5 婚姻状况/ Marital Status Composition

	有效样本量 Total	已婚 Married	未婚 Single	离异 Divorced	丧偶 Widowed
人数 Number	634	426	186	8	14
百分比 Percent	100.0	67.2	29.3	1.3	2.2

12-6 家庭常住人口数/ Number of Regular Household Members

	有效样本量 Total	1人 1 People	2人 2 People	3人 3 People	4人 4 People	5人 5 People	6人 6 People	7人或以上 7 People or Above
人数 Number	642	12	67	333	125	69	18	18
百分比 Percent	100.0	1.9	10.4	51.9	19.5	10.7	2.8	2.8

12-7 各人平均月收入/ Individual Monthly Income

	有效样本量 Total	无收入 no income	500元以下 below 500 yuan	501-1000元 yuan	1001-1500元 yuan	1501-2000元 yuan	2001-3000元 yuan	3001-4000元 yuan	4001-5000元 yuan	5000元以上 over 5000 yuan
人数 Number	641	112	196	229	68	19	15	1	1	0
百分比 Percent	100．0	17.5	30.6	35.7	10.6	3.0	2.3	0.2	0.2	0.0

12-8 家庭平均月总收入/ Household Monthly Income

	有效样本量 Total	500元以下 below 500 yuan	501-1000元 yuan	1001-1500元 yuan	1501-2000元 yuan	2001-3000元 yuan	3001-4000元 yuan	4001-6000元 yuan	6001-8000元 yuan	8000元以上 over 8000 yuan
人数 Number	641	51	169	151	99	145	17	9	0	0
百分比 Percent	100．0	8.0	26.4	23.6	15.4	22.6	2.7	1.4	0.0	0.0

13 西安市样本结构 / Sample Composition of Xi'an

13-1 性别构成/ Gender Composition

	有效样本量 Total	男性 Male	女性 Female
人数 Number	601	302	299
百分比 Percent	100.0	50.2	49.8

13-2 年龄构成/ Age Composition

	有效样本量 Total	16-24岁 Age	25-34岁 Age	35-44岁 Age	45-54岁 Age	55-60岁 Age
人数 Number	601	125	181	151	95	49
百分比 Percent	100.0	20.8	30.1	25.1	15.8	8.2

13-3 学历构成/ Educational Composition

	有效样本量 Total	小学及以下 Primary School or Below	初中 Middle School	高中/中专/技校 High school/ Technical Secondary School	大学专科 2-3 Year College	大学本科 4-5 Year College	研究生或以上 Graduate or Above
人数 Number	598	16	122	283	113	59	5
百分比 Percent	100.0	2.7	20.4	47.3	18.9	9.9	0.8

13-4 职业构成/ Occupational Composition

	有效样本量 Total	劳务职 Labor	技能职 Skill	服务职 Service	事务职 Assistance	销售职 Marketing	技术职 Technique	技术类以外的专门职 Professional Outside Technique	自由职业者 Free Lance
人数 Number	600	96	49	43	6	18	43	59	6
百分比 Percent	100.0	16.0	8.2	7.2	1.0	3.0	7.2	9.8	1.0

续前表 continued

	有效样本量 Total	企业/公司管理人员 Manager	行政管理人员/公务员 Administrator	经营者 Businessman	个体户 Self-employed Labor	军警 Military & Police	高中/中专/技校学生 High school/ Technical Secondary School Student
人数 Number	600	29	24	6	42	4	41
百分比 Percent	100.0	4.8	4.0	1.0	7.0	0.7	6.8

续前表 continued

	有效样本量 Total	大学生 College Student	研究生 Graduate student	家庭主妇 Housewife	离退休人员 Retired	下岗、待业人员 Unemployed	其他 Others
人数 Number	600	24	2	11	49	47	1
百分比 Percent	100.0	4.0	0.3	1.8	8.2	7.8	0.2

13-5 婚姻状况/ Marital Status Composition

	有效样本量 Total	已婚 Married	未婚 Single	离异 Divorced	丧偶 Widowed
人数 Number	597	424	151	16	6
百分比 Percent	100.0	71.0	25.3	2.7	1.0

13-6 家庭常住人口数/ Number of Regular Household Members

	有效样本量 Total	1人 1 People	2人 2 People	3人 3 People	4人 4 People	5人 5 People	6人 6 People	7人及以上 7 People or Above
人数 Number	601	12	61	298	140	58	24	8
百分比 Percent	100.0	2.0	10.1	49.6	23.3	9.7	4.0	1.3

13-7 各人平均月收入/ Individual Monthly Income

	有效样本量 Total	无收入 no income	500元以下 below 500 yuan	501-1000元 yuan	1001-1500元 yuan	1501-2000元 yuan	2001-3000元 yuan	3001-4000元 yuan	4001-5000元 yuan	5000元以上 over 5000 yuan
人数 Number	600	104	176	239	53	11	6	5	4	2
百分比 Percent	100.0	17.3	29.3	39.8	8.8	1.8	1.0	0.8	0.7	0.3

13-8 家庭平均月总收入/ Household Monthly Income

	有效样本量 Total	500元以下 below 500 yuan	501-1000元 yuan	1001-1500元 yuan	1501-2000元 yuan	2001-3000元 yuan	3001-4000元 yuan	4001-6000元 yuan	6001-8000元 yuan	8000元以上 over 8000 yuan
人数 Number	600	33	166	189	89	93	14	11	1	4
百分比 Percent	100.0	5.5	27.7	31.5	14.8	15.5	2.3	1.8	0.2	0.7

14 沈阳市样本结构 / Sample Compositions of Shenyang

14-1 性别构成/ Gender Composition

	有效样本量 Total	男性 Male	女性 Female
人数 Number	601	299	302
百分比 Percent	100.0	49.8	50.2

14-2 年龄构成/ Age Composition

	有效样本量 Total	16-24岁 Age	25-34岁 Age	35-44岁 Age	45-54岁 Age	55-60岁 Age
人数 Number	601	128	179	152	94	48
百分比 Percent	100.0	21.3	29.8	25.3	15.6	8.0

14-3 学历构成/ Educational Composition

	有效样本量 Total	小学及以下 Primary School or Below	初中 Middle School	高中/中专/技校 High School/ Technical Secondary School	大学专科 2-3 Year College	大学本科 4-5 Year College	研究生或以上 Graduate or Above
人数 Number	601	17	211	227	91	52	3
百分比 Percent	100.0	2.8	35.1	37.8	15.1	8.7	0.5

14-4 职业构成/ Occupational Composition

	有效样本量 Total	劳务职 Labor	技能职 Skill	服务职 Service	事务职 Assistance	销售职 Marketing	技术职 Technique	技术类以外的专门职 Professional Outside Technique	自由职业者 Free Lance
人数 Number	601	81	64	45	10	17	27	44	2
百分比 Percent	100.0	13.5	10.6	7.5	1.7	2.8	4.5	7.3	0.3

续前表 continued

	有效样本量 Total	企业/公司管理人员 Manager	行政管理人员/公务员 Administrator	经营者 Businessman	个体户 Self-employed Labor	军警 Military & Police	高中/中专/技校学生 High School/ Technical Secondary School Student
人数 Number	601	33	18	7	46	4	52
百分比 Percent	100.0	5.5	3.0	1.2	7.7	0.7	8.7

续前表 continued

	有效样本量 Total	大学生 College Student	研究生 Graduate Student	家庭主妇 Housewife	离退休人员 Retired	下岗、待业人员 Unemployed	其他 Others
人数 Number	601	18	0	18	34	68	13
百分比 Percent	100.0	3.0	0.0	3.0	5.7	11.3	2.2

14-5 婚姻状况/ Marital Status Composition

	有效样本量 Total	已婚 Married	未婚 Single	离异 Divorced	丧偶 Widowed
人数 Number	594	404	168	10	12
百分比 Percent	100.0	68.0	28.3	1.7	2.0

14-6 家庭常住人口数/ Number of Regular Household Members

	有效样本量 Total	1人 1 People	2人 2 People	3人 3 People	4人 4 People	5人 5 People	6人 6 People	7人以上 7 People or Above
人数 Number	601	8	68	343	106	56	14	6
百分比 Percent	100.0	1.3	11.3	57.1	17.6	9.3	2.3	1.0

14-7 个人平均月收入/ Individual Monthly Income

	有效样本量 Total	无收入 no income	500元以下 below 500 yuan	501-1000元 yuan	1001-1500元 yuan	1501-2000元 yuan	2001-3000元 yuan	3001-4000元 yuan	4001-5000元 yuan	5000元以上 over 5000 yuan
人数 Number	599	134	180	218	46	8	13	0	0	0
百分比 Percent	100	22.4	30.1	36.4	7.7	1.3	2.2	0.0	0.0	0.0

14-8 家庭平均月总收入/ Household Monthly Income

	有效样本量 Total	500元以下 below 500 yuan	501-1000元 yuan	1001-1500元 yuan	1501-2000元 yuan	2001-3000元 yuan	3001-4000元 yuan	4001-6000元 yuan	6001-8000元 yuan	8000元以上 over 8000 yuan
人数 Number	601	53	217	162	80	79	6	4	0	0
百分比 Percent	100	8.8	36.1	27.0	13.3	13.1	1.0	0.7	0.0	0.0

第二篇　消费者分析
Part II　Consumer Analysis

- 消费者层划分方法
  Method Used for the Consumer Segmentation
- 北京消费者层　Market Segmentation in Beijing
- 上海消费者层　Market Segmentation in Shanghai
- 广州消费者层　Market Segmentation in Guangzhou
- 重庆消费者层　Market Segmentation in Chongqing
- 武汉消费者层　Market Segmentation in Wuhan
- 西安消费者层　Market Segmentation in Xi'an
- 沈阳消费者层　Market Segmentation in Shenyang

1. 消费者层划分方法概述

98/99 年鉴中我们用因子分析和变量累加的方法确立了五个综合指标，然后用这五个综合指标的得分高低作为划分消费者层的依据。今年我们将继续沿用这种方法来划分消费者层。为了保持研究的延续性，我们只对有关流行与时尚、饮食与健康、购物与消费、广告、信息这五方面的 61 种说法，做了因子分析。其中每一种说法的取值为 1，2，3，4，5。1 代表非常不同意，2 代表比较不同意，3 代表不一定，4 代表比较同意，5 代表非常同意，总之，分值越高表示越同意，分值越低表示越不同意。对七个城市的所有数据所做的因子分析结果如下表所示：

因子构成及因子命名

因子及命名	变量	因子负荷	方差贡献率（%）	累计方差贡献率（%）
因子 1：时尚流行	在别人眼里我是个时髦的人	0.707	10.398	10.398
	流行与实用之间我比较看重流行	0.645		
	我刻意打扮是为了发挥自己的个性	0.641		
	我时常尝试新的发型	0.634		
	我很注意流行的趋势	0.613		
	我很注意自己的外表修饰	0.568		
	我购买一种新产品或者享受新的服务一般都比别人早	0.491		
因子 2：信赖广告	购买商品时还是以有广告的品牌比较可靠	0.679	6.547	16.946
	我觉得做过电视广告的商品有亲切感	0.659		
	广告是可以信赖的	0.650		
	广告中的信息对我做购物决定起了很大的作用	0.638		
因子 3：品质与名牌	我宁愿多花一点钱购买品质较好的东西	0.724	6.468	23.414
	即使价格贵一些，我还是喜欢买名牌产品	0.621		
	对于想要的东西，价格贵一些也会买	0.613		
	我认为名牌的商品品质比较好	0.558		
因子 4：信息交流	我经常从朋友那里听到各种各样的信息	0.627	5.787	29.200
	得到新信息后我会立即告诉别人	0.618		
	我觉得好的东西一定会向别人推荐	0.591		
	别人想做什么的时候通常会找我出主意	0.567		
因子 5：消费消极	我对跟自己无关的话题不关心	0.673	5.549	34.749
	真正的好产品不需要做广告	0.641		
	我宁愿自己做饭而不愿去买现成的食物	0.541		
	我的服饰和装扮多年来基本上没有多大改变	0.481		
因子 6：健康营养	我很注意饮食的营养平衡	0.721	5.431	40.180
	我经常吃一些维生素等保健品来补充营养	0.709		
	我会刻意去吃对健康美容有益的食物	0.581		
因子 7：重视价格	对于有些想要的东西我会等到降价或特卖时才买	0.648	5.290	45.470
	买东西时我经常货比三家	0.637		
	购买商品时我考虑的因素主要是价格	0.564		
因子 8：崇尚西方	我向往欧美等先进国家的生活方式	0.681	5.254	50.724
	我偏好西方的艺术文化	0.632		
	当我使用外国产品时心理多少会有满足感	0.604		

因子分析剔除了相关性不太强的变量，从因子构成及因子命名表中可以看到，剩下的 32 个变量，主要反映了八个方面的信息，我们从中选取了**时尚流行、信赖广告、健康营养、重视价格、信息交流**这五个因子作为分层的指标，根据指标的不同取值划分消费者层。由于每个指标包含的变量个数不同，每个指标的取值也略有不同，下面依次说明。（要注意的是，与 98/99 年鉴相比，时尚流行因子的变量构成有一定的变化，信息交流因子是一个新的因子。）

- 时尚流行指标

时尚流行指标由构成时尚流行因子 7 个变量组成：

在别人眼里我是个时髦的人

流行与实用之间我比较看重流行

我刻意打扮是为了发挥自己的个性

我时常尝试新的发型

我很注意流行的趋势

我很注意自己的外表修饰

我购买一种新产品或者享受新的服务一般都比别人早

由于每一个变量的分值都是 1 至 5 分，且都是分值越低表示越不同意，分值越高表示越同意，将这 7 个变量的得分累加，即得到时尚流行指标的累加得分，其取值范围是 7 至 35 分。如果将累加得分除以变量数 7，指标的得分也在 1 至 5 分之间，由指标得分的大小可以知道消费者对时尚流行的重视程度：指标得分在 1 到 2 之间的（2 不算在内）表示不重视时尚流行；指标得分在 2 到 3 之间的（3 不算在内）表示不太重视时尚流行；指标得分在 3 到 4 之间的（4 不算在内）表示比较重视时尚流行；指标得分在 4 到 5 之间的表示重视时尚流行。

- 广告态度指标

广告态度指标由构成信赖广告因子的 4 个变量组成：

购买商品时还是以有广告的品牌比较可靠

我觉得做过电视广告的商品有亲切感

广告是可以信赖的

广告中的信息对我做购物决定起了很大的作用

广告态度指标的得分由上述 4 个变量的得分累加，再除以 4。则指标的得分也在 1 至 5 分之间，由指标得分的大小可以知道消费者对广告的信赖程度：指标得分在 1 到 2 之间的（2 不算在内）表示不信赖广告；指标得分在 2 到 3 之间的（3 不算在内）表示不太信赖广告；指标得分在 3 到 4 之间的（4 不算在内）表示比较信赖广告；指标得分在 4 到 5 之间的表示信赖广告。

- 饮食健康指标

饮食健康指标由构成健康营养因子的 3 个变量组成：

我很注意饮食的营养平衡

我经常吃一些维生素等保健品来补充营养

我会刻意去吃对健康美容有益的食物

饮食健康指标的得分由上述 3 个变量的得分累加，再除以 3。则指标的得分也在 1 至 5 分之间，由指标得分的大小可以知道消费者在饮食上对健康营养的重视程度：指标得分在 1 到 2 之间的（2 不算在内）表示不重视健康营养；指标得分在 2 到 3 之间的（3 不算在内）表示不太重视健康营养；指标得分在 3 到 4 之间的（4 不算在内）表示比较重视健康营养；指标得分在 4 到 5 之间的表示重视健康营养。

- 价格态度指标

价格态度指标由构成重视价格因子的 3 个变量组成：

对于有些想要的东西我会等到降价或特卖时才买

买东西时我经常货比三家

购买商品时我考虑的因素主要是价格

价格态度指标的得分由上述 3 个变量的得分累加，再除以 3。则指标的得分也在 1 至 5 分之间，由指标得分的大小可以知道消费者在购物时对价格的重视程度：指标得分在 1 到 2 之间的（2 不算在内）表示不重视价格；指标得分在 2 到 3 之间的（3 不算在内）表示不太重视价格；指标得分在 3 到 4 之间的（4 不算在内）表示比较重视价格；指标得分在 4 到 5 之间的表示重视价格。

- 信息交流指标

信息交流指标由构成信息交流因子的 4 个变量组成：

我经常从朋友那里听到各种各样的信息

得到新信息后我会立即告诉别人

我觉得好的东西一定会向别人推荐

别人想做什么的时候通常会找我出主意

信息交流指标的得分由上述 4 个变量的得分累加，再除以 4。则指标的得分也在 1 至 5 分之间，由指标得分的大小可以知道消费者信息交流的程度：指标得分在 1 到 2 之间的（2 不算在内）表示信息交流不积极；指标得分在 2 到 3 之间的（3 不算在内）表示信息交流不太积极；指标得分在 3 到 4 之间的（4 不算在内）表示信息交流比较积极；指标得分在 4 到 5 之间的表示信息交流积极。

在确定了分层指标后就可以根据指标的不同取值范围划分消费者层。对于上述的五个指标，较为直接的分层办法就是，按照每个指标取值的 4 个层次将消费者分为 4 层。但是由于有些指标的取值在 1 到 2 之间的消费者个案数较少，有些指标的取值在 4 到 5 之间的消费者个案数较少，上述的分层会导致有些消费者层人数太少，不便于分析。所以对有些指标将取值为 1 到 2 和 2 到 3 的消费者合并为一层，对有些指标将取值为 3 到 4 和 4 到 5 的消费者合并为一层。每个指标的分层方法和各层的意义如下：

- 用时尚流行指标划分消费者层

对于所有七个城市，时尚流行指标将消费者划分为两个消费者层。该指标取值为 1 到 3 的消费者（取值为 1 到 2 和 2 到 3 的消费者合并为一层）为一个消费者层，命名为“平实生活指向”消费者层；该指标取值为 3 到 5 的消费者（取值为 3 到 4 和 4 到 5 的消费者合并为一层）为一个消费者层，命名为“时尚流行指向”消费者层。

- 用广告态度指标划分消费者层

对于所有七个城市，广告态度指标将消费者划分为三个消费者层。该指标取值为 1 到 3 的消费者（取值为 1 到 2 和 2 到 3 的消费者合并为一层）为一个消费者层，命名为“广告淡漠指向”消费者层；该指标取值为 3 到 4 的消费者为一个消费者层，命名为“中间层”；该指标取值为 4 到 5 的消费者为一个消费者层，命名为“信赖广告指向”消费者层。

- 用饮食健康指标划分消费者层

对于所有七个城市，饮食健康指标将消费者划分为三个消费者层。该指标取值为 1 到 3 的消费者（取值为 1 到 2 和 2 到 3 的消费者合并为一层）为一个消费者层，命名为“饮食‘温饱’指向”消费者层；该指标取值为 3 到 4 的消费者为一个消费者层，命名为“中间层”；该指标取值为 4 到 5 的消费者为一个消费者层，命名为“健康营养指向”消费者层。

- 用价格态度指标划分消费者层

对于所有七个城市，价格态度指标将消费者划分为三个消费者层。该指标取值为 1 到 3 的消费者（取值为 1 到 2 和 2 到 3 的消费者合并为一层）为一个消费者层，命名为“价格无关心指向”消费者层；该指标取值为 3 到 4 的消费者为一个消费者层，命名为“中间层”；该指标取值为 4 到 5 的消费者为一个消费者层，命名为“价格重视指向”消费者层。

- 用信息交流指标划分消费者层

对于所有七个城市，信息交流指标将消费者划分为三个消费者层。该指标取值为 1 到 3 的消费者（取值为 1 到 2 和 2 到 3 的消费者合并为一层）为一个消费者层，命名为“信息消极指向”消费者层；该指标取值为 3 到 4 的消费者为一个消费者层，命名为“中间层”；该指标取值为 4 到 5 的消费者为一个消费者层，命名为“信息积极指向”消费者层。

对于以上的消费者分层方法，有以下几点说明：

（1）综合指标的选取

以上综合指标的选取主要考虑与去年的一致性，总的来说变化不大。但是由于消费者分层指标及各指标所包含的变量并没有最后确定，还处于探索阶段，因此在指标的选取和变量的选取上都有一些变化，读者要注意与上期年鉴对比分析。

（2）缺失值

由于用于累加的题项有缺失值，累加后的综合指标自然会有缺失值存在。而且参与累加的题项只要有一个有缺失，综合指标就会是缺失值，所以综合指标的缺失值数会比每一个题目的缺失值多。

（3）消费者层的应用

限于篇幅及是否必要，除用时尚流行指标划分的消费者层应用于所有类别商品的分析外，用其他指标划分的消费者层的应用，根据商品的不同是有选择的。

Method Used for the Consumer Segmentation

We developed 5 comprehensive indexes by factor analysis and variable cumulation in our 98/99 yearbook. Then we used the scores for the indexes as the base for segment consumers. We are going to continue the same segmentation way. To be continuation, we only analyses factors about 61 sayings with 5 major categories concerning fade, food &

drink, shopping &consuming, advertising and information. The score for each saying is defined as 1.2.3.4.and 5. Score 1 represents much disagreement, score 2 represents somewhat disagreement, score 3 represents uncertainty, score 4 represents somewhat agreement, score 5 represents much agreement. The higher the score, the more the respondent agrees. The output of the factor analysis for the 7 cities'data comes as the following table.

Factors & Names	Variables	Factor Loading	Pct of Var (%)	Cut Pct (%)
Factor1: Fads & Popular	I am regarded a fashionable person by others	0. 707	10. 398	10. 398
	I prefer fade between fade and practicability	0. 645		
	I dress up on purpose to show my personality	0. 641		
	I often try new hairstyle	0. 634		
	I pay much attention to fashionable trends	0. 613		
	I do mind my own appearance	0. 568		
	I often buy or enjoy a new product or a new service earlier than others	0. 491		
Factor2: Believing in Advertising	When purchasing goods, those advertised brands are more reliable	0. 679	6. 547	16. 946
	I feel dear to those products which run TV commercials	0. 659		
	Advertising can be trusted	0. 650		
	The massage in advertising is very important in my buying decision	0. 638		
Factor3: Quality & Famous Brand	I prefer paying more for products with better quality	0. 724	6. 468	23. 414
	I will buy the item I like even if it is higher in price	0. 621		
	I would like to buy famous brands even if they are higher in price	0. 613		
	I think famous brands are of better quality	0. 558		
Factor4: Information Communication	I often heard all kinds of information from friends	0. 627	5. 787	29. 200
	I will immediately tell the new information to others once I get it	0. 618		
	I will recommend items which I feel good	0. 591		
	I often play the role of a consultant	0. 567		
Factor5: Negative Consumption	I don't care for the topics not associated with me	0. 673	5. 549	34. 749
	Real good products needn't run advertising	0. 641		
	I prefer cooking by myself to buying ready food	0. 541		
	My look and clothes have been kept unchanged basically	0. 481		
Factor6: Health & Nutrition	I care much about the balance of nutrition of food	0. 721	5. 431	40. 180
	I often take some vitamins to supply nutrition	0. 709		
	I would like to take food that is good to health or beauty on purpose	0. 581		
Factor7: Price-consciousness	For the goods I want to buy, I can wait till they are on sale	0. 648	5. 290	45. 470
	I often compare goods sold at different stores	0. 637		
	Price is my main consideration when I purchase goods	0. 564		
Factor8: Appreciating Western Countries	I appreciate the life style of the developed western countries	0. 681	5. 254	50. 724
	I prefer western arts and culture	0. 632		
	I feel somewhat satisfied when I use imported products	0. 604		

Variables with little relevance are omitted in factor analysis. The table of factor structure and factor naming has indicated that the other 32 variables mainly reflect information about 8 aspects. We select "fads & popular, believing in advertising, health & nutrition, price-consciousness and Information Communication" as the indexes for our hierarchy and consumers segmentation according to different scores. As each index contains different number of variables, the scores come out a little different.

(Note: compared with 98/99 yearbook, the variables composition for the fads & popular factor has changed. information communication factor is also an added one.)

- Fads & Popular Index

Fads and popular factor is composed of 7 variables.

I am regarded a fashionable person by others

I prefer fade between fade and practicability

I dress up on purpose to show my personality

I often try new hairstyle

I pay much attention to fashionable trends

I do mind my own appearance

I often buy or enjoy a new product or a new service earlier than others

Because each variable scores from 1 to 5, the lower the score, the more disagreement it shows. Cumulating the scores of the 7 variables, we get the cumulative score of fads & popular index, which scores 7~35. If dividing the cum score by the number of variables (7), the index can get 1~5 score. From the score, we can get to know how consumers look at fads & popular. Scoring 1~2 (excluding 2) means consumers do not care about fads & popular; scoring 2~3 (excluding 3) means consumers do not care much; scoring 3~4 (excluding 4) means consumers care a little; Scoring 4~5 means that consumers care much.

- Ad. Attitude Index

Advertising attitude index includes 4 variables:

When purchasing goods, those advertised brands are more reliable

I feel dear to those products which run TV commercials

Advertising can be trusted

The massage in advertising is very important in my buying decision

Scores of index also go between 1 to 5. From the scores of the index, we may get to know how much consumers believe in advertising. Scoring 1~2 (excluding 2) means consumers do not believe in advertising; scoring 2~3 (excluding 3) means consumers do not believe in advertising very much; scoring 3~4 (excluding 4) means consumers somewhat believe in advertising and scoring 4~5 means consumers believe in advertising.

- Food & Drink Index

This index is composed of 3 variables:

I care much about the balance of nutrition of food

I often take some vitamins to supply nutrition

I would like to take food that is good to health or beauty on purpose

The scores of this index come from the cumulative scores divided by 3, running from 1~5. From the scores, we can get to know how the consumers regard the importance of nutrition of food. Scoring 1~2 (excluding 2) means consumers do not care about nutrition & health; scoring 2~3 (excluding 3) means consumers do not care too much; scoring 3~4 (excluding 4) means consumers care a little; and scoring 4~5 means consumers care nutrition and health very much.

- Price Attitude Index

This index is composed of 3 variables:

For the goods I want to buy, I can wait till they are on sale

I often compare goods sold at different stores

Price is my main consideration when I purchase goods

The score of this index comes from the cumulative scores divided by 3, running from 1 to 5. From the scores we can get to know how consumers care about the price when they make buying-decision: scoring 1~2 (excluding 2) means consumers do not care about price; scoring 2~3 (excluding 3) means consumers do not care too much; scoring 3~4 (excluding 4) means consumers care a little; and scoring 4~5 means consumers care very much.

- Information Communication Index

This index is composed of 4 variables that make up the negative factors:

I often heard all kinds of information from friends

I will immediately tell the new information to others once I get it

I will recommend items which I feel good

I often play the role of a consultant

The score of this index comes from cumulative scores divided by 4, running from 1 to 5. From the scores, we can get to know the degree of the information exchanging: scoring 1~2 (excluding 2) means consumers are not active in exchanging information; scoring 2~3 (excluding 3) means consumers are not active too much; scoring 3~4 (excluding 4) means consumers are somewhat active in exchanging information; and scoring 4~5 means consumers are active.

After the hierarchical indexes are set, the consumers can be segmented based on different scores. For the about 5 indexes, the direct way of segmentation is to put consumers into 4 segments according to the 4 score of each index. But as sometimes there are few cases scoring 1-2, or 4-5, the above hierarchical method will lead to few cases in that segment. That will do not favor the analysis. Thus, we sometimes combine the consumers scoring 1-2, 2-3,3-4, or 4-5 The hierarchical methods and importance of each segment are as follows.

- Segmenting Consumers by Fads & Popular Index

  For all the 7 cities, fads & popular index segments consumers into 2 segments: 1)"simple living orientation" segment, representing people scoring 1-3; and 2)"popular orientation" segment scoring 3-5.

- Segmenting Consumers by Advertising Attitude Index

  For all the 7 cities this index segments consumers into 3 segments: 1)"indifferent orientation" segment, representing people scoring 1-3; and 2) "medium" segment, scoring 3-4; and 3) "loyal orientation" segment, scoring 4-5.

- Segmenting Consumers by Food & Drink Index
  For all the 7 cities, this index segments consumers into 3 segments: 1)"basic" segment, representing people scoring 1,2 and 3; 2) "medium" segment, scoring3,4; and 3)"healthy & nutritious orientation" segment, scoring 4 and 5.

- Segmenting Consumers by Price Attitude Index
  For all the 7 cities, this index segments consumers into 3 segments: 1)"price-indifferent" segment, representing people scoring 1-3; 2)"medium" segment, scoring 3-4; and 3)"price-careful" segment, scoring 4-5.

- Segmenting Consumers by Information Communication Index
  For all the 7 cities, this index segment consumers into 3 segments: 1)"negative orientation", representing people scoring 1-3; 2)"medium", scoring 3-4; and 3)"active orientation" scoring 4-5.

Notes:

1)Comprehensive index selection

When selecting comprehensive indexes, we take the similar index out of the same considerations as last year. But because the final variables of the index for consumer hierarchy and each segment have not been decided yet, Therefore, there are some changes in the selection of both the indexes and the variables.

2)Missing value

Because the questions used in calculation contain missing value, there must be missing value in the cumulative comprehensive indexes. Even one missing value in the question will lead to missing value in the comprehensive index. Therefore , there will be more missing value in comprehensive indexes than in each question.

3)The application of consumers hierarchy

Due to the limits of length and necessity, we only applied: "fads & popular" index to all the product categories. As for the other products using different hierarchical methods, we decide to use the index or not according to different products.

2.北京消费者层 / Market Segmentation in Beijing

1. 时尚流行指标/ Fads Popular Index

1-1 不同消费者层的性别构成/ Gender Composition of Market Segments

	人数 Number	男性 Male	女性 Female
样本 Sample	998	49.8	50.2
平实生活指向 simple living orientation	491	55.8	44.2
时尚流行指向 fashion orientation	507	44.0	56.0

1-2 不同消费者层的年龄构成/ Age Composition of Market Segments

	人数 Number	16-24 岁 Age	25-34 岁 Age	35-44 岁 Age	45-54 岁 Age	55-60 岁 Age
样本 Sample	998	20.8	30.1	25.2	15.8	8.1
平实生活指向 simple living orientation	491	16.3	27.5	25.5	19.3	11.4
时尚流行指向 fashion orientation	507	25.2	32.5	24.9	12.4	4.9

1-3 不同消费者层的学历构成/ Educational Composition of Market Segments

	人数 Number	小学以下 Primary School or Below	初中 Middle School	高中/中专/技校 High School/ Technical Secondary School	大学专科 2-3Year College	大学本科 4-5Year College	研究生或以上 Graduate or Above
样本 Sample	994	3.1	16.6	43.2	20.6	14.8	1.7
平实生活指向 simple living orientation	489	5.5	17.6	36.6	21.1	17.0	2.2
时尚流行指向 fashion orientation	505	0.8	15.6	49.5	20.2	12.7	1.2

1-4 不同消费者层的职业构成/ Occupational Composition of Market Segments

	人数 Number	劳务职 Labor	技能职 Skill	服务职 Service	事务职 Assistance	销售职 Marketing	技术职 Technique	技术类以外的专门职 Professional Outside Technique
样本 Sample	993	10.4	10.1	7.6	3.2	4.4	8.0	11.3
平实生活指向 simple living orientation	488	12.7	10.7	5.9	2.3	3.5	10.0	10.0
时尚流行指向 fashion orientation	505	8.1	9.5	9.1	4.2	5.3	5.9	12.5

续前表 continued

	人数 Number	自由职业者 Free Lance	企业/公司管理人员 Manager	行政管理人员/公务员 Administrator	经营者 Businessman	个体户 Self-employed Labor	军警 Military&police
样本 Sample	993	0.8	6.6	6.3	1.4	2.7	0.6
平实生活指向 simple living orientation	488	0.6	7.0	6.8	1.4	2.5	0.8
时尚流行指向 fashion orientation	505	1.0	6.3	5.9	1.4	3.0	0.4

续前表 continued

	人数 Number	高中/中专/技校学生 High school/ Secondary School Student	大学生 College Student	研究生 Graduate Student	家庭主妇 Housewife	离退休人员 Retired	下岗、待业人员 Unemployed	其它 Others
样本 Sample	993	8.7	4.1	0.3	1.1	6.0	4.5	1.8
平实生活指向 simple living orientation	488	5.9	4.3	0.2	1.2	7.4	4.5	2.3
时尚流行指向 fashion orientation	505	11.3	4.0	0.4	1.0	4.8	4.6	1.4

1-5 不同消费者层的婚姻状况/ Marital Status of Market Segments

	人数 Number	已婚 Married	未婚 Single	离异 Divorced	丧偶 Widowed
样本 Sample	994	67.5	29.6	2.1	0.8
平实生活指向 simple living orientation	490	73.3	23.5	2.2	1.0
时尚流行指向 fashion orientation	504	61.9	35.5	2.0	0.6

1-6 不同消费者层的个人月收入/ Individual Monthly Income of Market Segments

	有效样本量 Total	无收入 no income	500 元以下 below 500 yuan	501-1000 元 yuan	1001-1500 元 yuan	1501-2000 元 yuan	2001-3000 元 yuan	3001-4000 元 yuan	4001-5000 元 yuan	5000 元以上 over 5000 yuan
样本 Sample	986	15.0	9.4	27.2	24.4	11.9	9.0	0.8	0.6	1.6
平实生活指向 simple living orientation	486	12.3	10.5	30.9	24.5	10.7	8.6	0.8	0.4	1.2
时尚流行指向 fashion orientation	500	17.6	8.4	23.6	24.4	13.0	9.4	0.8	0.8	2.0

2.广告态度指标/ Advertising Attitude Index

2-1 不同消费者层的性别构成/ Gender Composition of Market Segments

	人数 Number	男性 Male	女性 Female
样本 Sample	994	50.0	50.0
广告淡漠指向 indifferent orientation	289	58.5	41.5
中间层 medium	572	48.8	51.2
信赖广告指向 loyal orientation	133	36.8	63.2

2-2 不同消费者层的年龄构成/ Age Composition of Market Segments

	人数 Number	16-24 岁 Age	25-34 岁 Age	35-44 岁 Age	45-54 岁 Age	55-60 岁 Age
样本 Sample	994	20.9	29.9	25.1	15.9	8.2
广告淡漠指向 indifferent orientation	289	23.2	21.1	26.3	20.8	8.7
中间层 medium	572	20.1	33.4	24.8	14.2	7.5
信赖广告指向 loyal orientation	133	19.5	33.8	23.3	12.8	10.5

2-3 不同消费者层的学历构成/ Educational Composition of Market Segments

	人数 Number	小学以下 Primary School or Below	初中 Middle School	高中/中专/技校 High School/ Technical Secondary School	大学专科 2-3Year College	大学本科 4-5Year College	研究生或以上 Graduate or Above
样本 Sample	990	3.1	16.9	42.4	20.9	14.9	1.7
广告淡漠指向 indifferent orientation	288	3.1	18.4	46.2	18.8	12.2	1.4
中间层 medium	570	2.8	15.1	40.9	23.5	15.8	1.9
信赖广告指向 loyal orientation	132	4.5	21.2	40.9	14.4	17.4	1.5

2-4 不同消费者层的职业构成/ Occupational Composition of Market Segments

	人数 Number	劳务职 Labor	技能职 Skill	服务职 Service	事务职 Assistance	销售职 Marketing	技术职 Technique	技术类以外的专门职 Professional Outside Technique
样本 Sample	989	10.5	10.0	7.5	3.3	4.4	8.1	11.2
广告淡漠指向 indifferent orientation	286	11.2	11.2	8.0	3.1	2.8	9.1	8.4
中间层 medium	570	10.0	10.2	7.7	3.3	5.3	8.1	12.6
信赖广告指向 loyal orientation	133	11.3	6.8	5.3	3.8	4.5	6.0	11.3

续前表 continued

	人数 Number	自由职业者 Free Lance	企业/公司管理人员 Manager	行政管理人员/公务员 Administrator	经营者 Businessman	个体户 Self-employed Labor	军警 Military&police
样本 Sample	989	0.8	6.7	6.2	1.4	2.6	0.6
广告淡漠指向 indifferent orientation	286	0.7	7.3	4.2	1.0	3.5	0.0
中间层 medium	570	1.1	6.3	7.4	1.6	1.8	0.7
信赖广告指向 loyal orientation	133	0.0	6.8	5.3	1.5	4.5	1.5

续前表 continued

	人数 Number	高中/中专/技校学生 High school/ Secondary School Student	大学生 College Student	研究生 Graduate Student	家庭主妇 Housewife	离退休人员 Retired	下岗、待业人员 Unemployed	其它 Others
样本 Sample	989	8.5	4.2	0.3	1.1	6.2	4.6	1.7
广告淡漠指向 indifferent orientation	286	9.4	4.2	0.3	0.3	6.3	5.6	3.1
中间层 medium	570	7.9	4.0	0.4	1.1	5.6	4.0	1.1
信赖广告指向 loyal orientation	133	9.0	5.3	0.0	3.0	8.3	4.5	1.5

2-5 不同消费者层的婚姻状况/ Marital Status of Market Segments

	人数 Number	已婚 Married	未婚 Single	离异 Divorced	丧偶 Widowed
样本 Sample	989	67.4	29.6	2.1	0.8
广告淡漠指向 indifferent orientation	287	64.8	31.0	3.1	1.0
中间层 medium	569	68.2	29.5	1.9	0.4
信赖广告指向 loyal orientation	133	69.9	27.1	0.8	2.3

2-6 不同消费者层的个人月收入/ Individual Monthly Income of Market Segments

	有效样本量 Total	无收入 no income	500 元以下 below 500 yuan	501-1000 元 yuan	1001-1500 元 yuan	1501-2000 元 yuan	2001-3000 元 yuan	3001-4000 元 yuan	4001-5000 元 yuan	5000 元以上 over 5000 yuan
样本 Sample	983	15.1	9.2	27.4	24.4	12.0	9.1	0.8	0.6	1.5
广告淡漠指向 indifferent orientation	284	16.2	10.2	26.8	23.2	13.7	7.7	0.4	0.0	1.8
中间层 medium	567	13.9	8.3	28.2	24.3	10.8	10.6	1.2	1.1	1.6
信赖广告指向 loyal orientation	132	17.4	10.6	25.0	27.3	13.6	5.3	0.0	0.0	0.8

3.饮食健康指标/ Foods & Drink Quality Index

3-1 不同消费者层的性别构成/ Gender Composition of Market Segments

	人数 Number	男性 Male	女性 Female
样本 Sample	1006	49.8	50.2
饮食“温饱”指向 "basic" orientation	292	64.0	36.0
中间层 medium	477	50.1	49.9
健康营养指向 health & nutrition orientation	237	31.6	68.4

3-2 不同消费者层的年龄构成/ Age Composition of Market Segments

	人数 Number	16-24 岁 Age	25-34 岁 Age	35-44 岁 Age	45-54 岁 Age	55-60 岁 Age
样本 Sample	1006	21.0	29.7	25.1	16.0	8.2
饮食"温饱"指向 "basic" orientation	292	27.4	32.5	22.9	10.6	6.5
中间层 medium	477	19.3	33.5	23.5	17.0	6.7
健康营养指向 health & nutrition orientation	237	16.5	18.6	31.2	20.7	13.1

3-3 不同消费者层的学历构成/ Educational Composition of Market Segments

	人数 Number	小学以下 Primary School or Below	初中 Middle School	高中/中专/技校 High School/ Technical Secondary School	大学专科 2-3Year College	大学本科 4-5Year College	研究生或以上 Graduate or Above
样本 Sample	1002	3.1	16.8	43.1	20.6	14.8	1.7
饮食"温饱"指向 "basic" orientation	290	3.8	15.9	42.1	20.0	16.9	1.4
中间层 medium	475	2.3	17.9	42.9	18.5	16.2	2.1
健康营养指向 health & nutrition orientation	237	3.8	15.6	44.7	25.3	9.3	1.3

3-4 不同消费者层的职业构成/ Occupational Composition of Market Segments

	人数 Number	劳务职 Labor	技能职 Skill	服务职 Service	事务职 Assistance	销售职 Marketing	技术职 Technique	技术类以外的专门职 Professional Outside Technique
样本 Sample	1001	10.5	10.2	7.6	3.2	4.5	8.0	11.0
饮食"温饱"指向 "basic" orientation	289	9.3	10.0	8.3	2.1	2.4	11.1	6.6
中间层 medium	476	12.2	10.9	6.5	2.9	5.0	7.1	10.9
健康营养指向 health & nutrition orientation	236	8.5	8.9	8.9	5.1	5.9	5.9	16.5

续前表 continued

	人数 Number	自由职业者 Free Lance	企业/公司管理人员 Manager	行政管理人员/公务员 Administrator	经营者 Businessman	个体户 Self-employed Labor	军警 Military&police
样本 Sample	1001	0.8	6.7	6.3	1.4	2.7	0.6
饮食"温饱"指向 "basic" orientation	289	0.7	7.6	6.9	2.1	3.1	0.0
中间层 medium	476	1.1	6.3	5.7	1.3	2.7	1.1
健康营养指向 health & nutrition orientation	236	0.4	6.4	6.8	0.8	2.1	0.4

续前表 continued

	人数 Number	高中/中专/技校学生 High school/ Secondary School Student	大学生 College Student	研究生 Graduate Student	家庭主妇 Housewife	离退休人员 Retired	下岗、待业人员 Unemployed	其它 Others
样本 Sample	1001	8.7	4.2	0.3	1.1	6.1	4.4	1.8
饮食"温饱"指向 "basic" orientation	289	11.4	5.5	0.3	1.0	4.5	5.2	1.7
中间层 medium	476	8.2	4.0	0.4	1.3	5.9	4.6	1.9
健康营养指向 health & nutrition orientation	236	6.4	3.0	0.0	0.8	8.5	3.0	1.7

3-5 不同消费者层的婚姻状况/ Marital Status of Market Segments

	人数 Number	已婚 Married	未婚 Single	离异 Divorced	丧偶 Widowed
样本 Sample	1001	67.4	29.7	2.1	0.8
饮食"温饱"指向 "basic" orientation	292	61.3	38.0	0.7	0.0
中间层 medium	474	67.7	29.1	2.1	1.1
健康营养指向 health & nutrition orientation	235	74.5	20.4	3.8	1.3

3-6 不同消费者层的个人月收入/ Individual Monthly Income of Market Segments

	有效样本量 Total	无收入 no income	500 元以下 below 500 yuan	501-1000 元 yuan	1001-1500 元 yuan	1501-2000 元 yuan	2001-3000 元 yuan	3001-4000 元 yuan	4001-5000 元 yuan	5000 元以上 over 5000 yuan
样本 Sample	994	15.0	9.5	27.4	24.4	11.8	9.0	0.8	0.6	1.6
饮食"温饱"指向 "basic" orientation	288	18.1	8.3	28.1	23.3	11.8	6.6	1.0	1.4	1.4
中间层 medium	470	15.5	9.1	26.8	25.5	11.1	9.1	0.2	0.4	2.1
健康营养指向 health & nutrition orientation	236	10.2	11.4	27.5	23.7	13.1	11.4	1.7	0.0	0.8

4.价格态度指标/ Price Attitude Index

4-1 不同消费者层的性别构成/ Gender Composition of Market Segments

	人数 Number	男性 Male	女性 Female
样本 Sample	1002	49.7	50.3
价格无关心指向 indifferent orientation	203	54.7	45.3
中间层 medium	501	52.1	47.9
价格重视指向 careful orientation	298	42.3	57.7

4-2 不同消费者层的年龄构成/ Age Composition of Market Segments

	人数 Number	16-24 岁 Age	25-34 岁 Age	35-44 岁 Age	45-54 岁 Age	55-60 岁 Age
样本 Sample	1002	21.2	29.5	25.2	15.9	8.2
价格无关心指向 indifferent orientation	203	29.6	28.1	24.6	12.3	5.4
中间层 medium	501	22.2	34.3	24.0	13.0	6.6
价格重视指向 careful orientation	298	13.8	22.5	27.9	23.2	12.8

4-3 不同消费者层的学历构成/ Educational Composition of Market Segments

	人数 Number	小学以下 Primary School or Below	初中 Middle School	高中/中专/技校 High School/ Technical Secondary School	大学专科 2-3Year College	大学本科 4-5Year College	研究生或以上 Graduate or Above
样本 Sample	998	3.1	16.6	43.3	20.5	14.7	1.7
价格无关心指向 indifferent orientation	201	1.0	11.4	44.8	24.4	15.9	2.5
中间层 medium	499	2.0	13.6	44.5	21.0	17.0	1.8
价格重视指向 careful orientation	298	6.4	25.2	40.3	17.1	10.1	1.0

4-4 不同消费者层的职业构成/ Occupational Composition of Market Segments

	人数 Number	劳务职 Labor	技能职 Skill	服务职 Service	事务职 Assistance	销售职 Marketing	技术职 Technique	技术类以外的专门职 Professional Outside Technique
样本 Sample	997	10.4	10.1	7.6	3.3	4.4	8.0	10.9
价格无关心指向 indifferent orientation	201	7.0	7.5	6.5	2.5	3.0	11.9	15.4
中间层 medium	498	9.4	9.6	7.2	4.0	4.8	8.6	9.6
价格重视指向 careful orientation	298	14.4	12.8	9.1	2.7	4.7	4.4	10.1

续前表 continued

	人数 Number	自由职业者 Free Lance	企业/公司管理人员 Manager	行政管理人员/公务员 Administrator	经营者 Businessman	个体户 Self-employed Labor	军警 Military&police
样本 Sample	997	0.8	6.6	6.3	1.4	2.6	0.6
价格无关心指向 indifferent orientation	201	2.0	6.0	6.0	4.5	1.5	0.5
中间层 medium	498	0.6	8.6	6.4	0.8	3.2	0.6
价格重视指向 careful orientation	298	0.3	3.7	6.4	0.3	2.3	0.7

续前表 continued

	人数 Number	高中/中专/技校学生 High school/ Secondary School Student	大学生 College Student	研究生 Graduate Student	家庭主妇 Housewife	离退休人员 Retired	下岗、待业人员 Unemployed	其它 Others
样本 Sample	997	8.8	4.2	0.3	1.1	6.0	4.5	1.8
价格无关心指向 indifferent orientation	201	11.9	4.0	0.5	0.5	3.0	3.0	3.0
中间层 medium	498	10.6	4.0	0.2	1.4	4.0	4.6	1.4
价格重视指向 careful orientation	298	3.7	4.7	0.3	1.0	11.4	5.4	1.7

4-5 不同消费者层的婚姻状况/ Marital Status of Market Segments

	人数 Number	已婚 Married	未婚 Single	离异 Divorced	丧偶 Widowed
样本 Sample	998	67.2	29.9	2.1	0.8
价格无关心指向 indifferent orientation	203	60.1	36.9	2.0	1.0
中间层 medium	499	65.3	32.9	1.6	0.2
价格重视指向 careful orientation	296	75.3	19.9	3.0	1.7

4-6 不同消费者层的个人月收入/ Individual Monthly Income of Market Segments

	有效样本量 Total	无收入 no income	500 元以下 below 500 yuan	501-1000 元 yuan	1001-1500 元 yuan	1501-2000 元 yuan	2001-3000 元 yuan	3001-4000 元 yuan	4001-5000 元 yuan	5000 元以上 over 5000 yuan
样本 Sample	990	15.3	9.4	27.2	24.6	11.6	9.0	0.8	0.6	1.5
价格无关心指向 indifferent orientation	201	18.4	4.5	16.4	27.4	19.4	10.9	1.0	1.5	0.5
中间层 medium	492	16.1	8.9	25.6	25.8	10.2	10.2	0.6	0.6	2.0
价格重视指向 careful orientation	297	11.8	13.5	37.0	20.9	8.8	5.7	1.0	0.0	1.3

5.信息交流指标/ Information Communication Index

5-1 不同消费者层的性别构成/ Gender Composition of Market Segments

	人数 Number	男性 Male	女性 Female
样本 Sample	1004	50.0	50.0
信息消极指向 negative orientation	63	66.7	33.3
中间层 medium	523	54.9	45.1
信息积极指向 active orientation	418	41.4	58.6

5-2 不同消费者层的年龄构成/ Age Composition of Market Segments

	人数 Number	16-24 岁 Age	25-34 岁 Age	35-44 岁 Age	45-54 岁 Age	55-60 岁 Age
样本 Sample	1004	21.2	29.6	25.2	15.9	8.1
信息消极指向 negative orientation	63	17.5	25.4	25.4	22.2	9.5
中间层 medium	523	22.6	34.8	22.9	13.4	6.3
信息积极指向 active orientation	418	20.1	23.7	28.0	18.2	10.0

5-3 不同消费者层的学历构成/ Educational Composition of Market Segments

	人数 Number	小学以下 Primary School or Below	初中 Middle School	高中/中专/技校 High School/ Technical Secondary School	大学专科 2-3Year College	大学本科 4-5Year College	研究生或以上 Graduate or Above
样本 Sample	1000	3.1	16.8	43.3	20.5	14.7	1.6
信息消极指向 negative orientation	63	9.5	20.6	33.3	20.6	14.3	1.6
中间层 medium	519	2.1	14.8	42.2	21.0	18.1	1.7
信息积极指向 active orientation	418	3.3	18.7	46.2	19.9	10.5	1.4

5-4 不同消费者层的职业构成/ Occupational Composition of Market Segments

	人数 Number	劳务职 Labor	技能职 Skill	服务职 Service	事务职 Assistance	销售职 Marketing	技术职 Technique	技术类以外的专门职 Professional Outside Technique
样本 Sample	999	10.4	10.1	7.6	3.3	4.5	8.0	11.1
信息消极指向 negative orientation	62	19.4	4.8	1.6	3.2	1.6	6.5	6.5
中间层 medium	519	9.4	10.2	7.5	3.5	5.2	10.8	10.0
信息积极指向 active orientation	418	10.3	10.8	8.6	3.[illegible]	4.1	4.8	13.2

续前表 continued

	人数 Number	自由职业者 Free Lance	企业/公司管理人员 Manager	行政管理人员/公务员 Administrator	经营者 Businessman	个体户 Self-employed Labor	军警 Military&police
样本 Sample	999	0.8	6.7	6.2	1.3	2.7	0.6
信息消极指向 negative orientation	62	3.2	1.6	3.2	0.0	4.8	1.6
中间层 medium	519	0.6	6.9	6.7	1.3	2.5	0.8
信息积极指向 active orientation	418	0.7	7.2	6.0	1.4	2.6	0.2

续前表 continued

	人数 Number	高中/中专/技校学生 High school/ Secondary School Student	大学生 College Student	研究生 Graduate Student	家庭主妇 Housewife	离退休人员 Retired	下岗、待业人员 Unemployed	其它 Others
样本 Sample	999	8.8	4.2	0.3	1.1	6.1	4.4	1.7
信息消极指向 negative orientation	62	4.8	8.1	1.6	0.0	8.1	14.5	4.8
中间层 medium	519	9.6	3.9	0.2	1.5	4.2	3.7	1.3
信息积极指向 active orientation	418	8.4	4.1	0.2	0.7	8.1	3.8	1.7

5-5 不同消费者层的婚姻状况/ Marital Status of Market Segments

	人数 Number	已婚 Married	未婚 Single	离异 Divorced	丧偶 Widowed
样本 Sample	999	67.6	29.8	1.9	0.7
信息消极指向 negative orientation	62	71.0	25.8	1.6	1.6
中间层 medium	522	64.9	33.3	1.3	0.4
信息积极指向 active orientation	415	70.4	26.0	2.7	1.0

5-6 不同消费者层的个人月收入/ Individual Monthly Income of Market Segments

	有效样本量 Total	无收入 no income	500 元以下 below 500 yuan	501-1000 元 yuan	1001-1500 元 yuan	1501-2000 元 yuan	2001-3000 元 yuan	3001-4000 元 yuan	4001-5000 元 yuan	5000 元以上 over 5000 yuan
样本 Sample	994	15.2	9.4	27.4	24.3	11.7	9.1	0.8	0.6	1.6
信息消极指向 negative orientation	414	14.0	9.7	28.7	22.7	13.0	9.4	1.0	0.0	1.4
中间层 medium	517	15.5	9.1	26.3	25.1	10.6	9.7	0.6	1.2	1.9
信息积极指向 active orientation	63	20.6	9.5	27.0	28.6	11.1	1.6	1.6	0.0	0.0

3.上海消费者层/ Market Segmentation in Shanghai

1. 时尚流行指标/ Fads Popular Index

1-1 不同消费者层的性别构成/ Gender Composition of Market Segments

	人数 Number	男性 Male	女性 Female
样本 Sample	1005	50.0	50.0
平实生活指向 simple living orientation	471	52.9	47.1
时尚流行指向 fashion orientation	534	47.6	52.4

1-2 不同消费者层的年龄构成/ Age Composition of Market Segments

	人数 Number	16-24 岁 Age	25-34 岁 Age	35-44 岁 Age	45-54 岁 Age	55-60 岁 Age
样本 Sample	1005	21.4	28.6	25.6	16.6	7.9
平实生活指向 simple living orientation	471	12.7	22.9	28.5	23.8	12.1
时尚流行指向 fashion orientation	534	29.0	33.5	23.0	10.3	4.1

1-3 不同消费者层的学历构成/ Educational Composition of Market Segments

	人数 Number	小学以下 Primary School or Below	初中 Middle School	高中/中专/技校 High School/ Technical Secondary School	大学专科 2-3Year College	大学本科 4-5Year College	研究生或以上 Graduate or Above
样本 Sample	1002	2.2	26.1	50.5	13.7	6.8	0.7
平实生活指向 simple living orientation	470	4.0	34.7	42.3	12.3	6.2	0.4
时尚流行指向 fashion orientation	532	0.6	18.6	57.7	14.8	7.3	0.9

1-4 不同消费者层的职业构成/ Occupational Composition of Market Segments

	人数 Number	劳务职 Labor	技能职 Skill	服务职 Service	事务职 Assistance	销售职 Marketing	技术职 Technique	技术类以外的专门职 Professional Outside Technique
样本 Sample	1004	15.2	10.3	8.2	4.1	3.7	5.4	7.5
平实生活指向 simple living orientation	471	18.0	11.0	6.8	3.8	3.0	5.9	6.8
时尚流行指向 fashion orientation	533	12.8	9.6	9.4	4.3	4.3	4.9	8.1

续前表 continued

	人数 Number	自由职业者 Free Lance	企业/公司管理人员 Manager	行政管理人员/公务员 Administrator	经营者 Businessman	个体户 Self-employed Labor	军警 Military&police
样本 Sample	1004	1.2	5.4	3.4	0.9	3.1	0.3
平实生活指向 simple living orientation	471	1.3	3.6	3.4	0.6	3.4	0.0
时尚流行指向 fashion orientation	533	1.1	6.9	3.4	1.1	2.8	0.6

续前表 continued

	人数 Number	高中/中专/技校学生 High school/ Secondary School Student	大学生 College Student	研究生 Graduate Student	家庭主妇 Housewife	离退休人员 Retired	下岗、待业人员 Unemployed	其它 Other
样本 Sample	1004	7.5	3.2	0.2	0.7	8.4	9.4	2.2
平实生活指向 simple living orientation	471	5.1	1.9	0.0	0.4	14.0	8.3	2.5
时尚流行指向 fashion orientation	533	9.6	4.3	0.4	0.9	3.4	10.3	1.9

1-5 不同消费者层的婚姻状况/ Marital Status of Market Segments

	人数 Number	已婚 Married	未婚 Single	离异 Divorced	丧偶 Widowed
样本 Sample	998	64.2	33.8	1.2	0.8
平实生活指向 simple living orientation	468	75.0	22.2	1.7	1.1
时尚流行指向 fashion orientation	530	54.7	44.0	0.8	0.6

1-6 不同消费者层的个人月收入/ Individual Monthly Income of Market Segments

	有效样本量 Total	无收入 no income	500 元以下 below 500 yuan	501-1000 元 yuan	1001-1500 元 yuan	1501-2000 元 yuan	2001-3000 元 yuan	3001-4000 元 yuan	4001-5000 元 yuan	5000 元以上 over 5000 yuan
样本 Sample	1000	15.4	10.1	29.8	23.4	9.7	9.2	1.2	0.6	0.6
平实生活指向 simple living orientation	469	10.9	11.7	37.5	22.6	8.3	7.5	0.6	0.9	0.0
时尚流行指向 fashion orientation	531	19.4	8.7	23.0	24.1	10.9	10.7	1.7	0.4	1.1

2. 广告态度指标/ Advertising Attitude Index

2-1 不同消费者层的性别构成/ Gender Composition of Market Segments

	人数 Number	男性 Male	女性 Female
样本 Sample	1002	49.9	50.1
广告淡漠指向 indifferent orientation	256	50.4	49.6
中间层 medium	611	50.9	49.1
信赖广告指向 loyal orientation	135	44.4	55.6

2-2 不同消费者层的年龄构成/ Age Composition of Market Segments

	人数 Number	16-24 岁 Age	25-34 岁 Age	35-44 岁 Age	45-54 岁 Age	55-60 岁 Age
样本 Sample	1002	21.4	28.4	25.6	16.7	7.9
广告淡漠指向 indifferent orientation	256	19.9	25.8	26.6	17.6	10.2
中间层 medium	611	20.1	29.0	26.5	16.5	7.9
信赖广告指向 loyal orientation	135	29.6	31.1	20.0	15.6	3.7

2-3 不同消费者层的学历构成/ Educational Composition of Market Segments

	人数 Number	小学以下 Primary School or Below	初中 Middle School	高中/中专/技校 High School/ Technical Secondary School	大学专科 2-3Year College	大学本科 4-5Year College	研究生或以上 Graduate or Above
样本 Sample	999	2.2	26.3	50.6	13.7	6.6	0.6
广告淡漠指向 indifferent orientation	256	2.3	28.5	50.4	12.9	5.9	0.0
中间层 medium	608	2.1	24.3	51.2	14.3	7.2	0.8
信赖广告指向 loyal orientation	135	2.2	31.1	48.1	12.6	5.2	0.7

2-4 不同消费者层的职业构成/ Occupational Composition of Market Segments

	人数 Number	劳务职 Labor	技能职 Skill	服务职 Service	事务职 Assistance	销售职 Marketing	技术职 Technique	技术类以外的专门职 Professional Outside Technique
样本 Sample	1001	15.0	10.2	8.2	4.0	3.8	5.3	7.6
广告淡漠指向 indifferent orientation	256	18.0	5.9	6.3	3.9	4.7	6.3	6.3
中间层 medium	610	14.1	11.8	8.9	4.3	3.4	5.1	7.9
信赖广告指向 loyal orientation	135	13.3	11.1	8.9	3.0	3.7	4.4	8.9

续前表 continued

	人数 Number	自由职业者 Free Lance	企业/公司管理人员 Manager	行政管理人员/公务员 Administrator	经营者 Businessman	个体户 Self-employed Labor	军警 Military&police
样本 Sample	1001	1.2	5.3	3.4	0.9	3.1	0.3
广告淡漠指向 indifferent orientation	256	0.8	3.9	3.9	1.2	4.3	0.4
中间层 medium	610	1.3	5.9	3.4	1.0	2.3	0.3
信赖广告指向 loyal orientation	135	1.5	5.2	2.2	0.0	4.4	0.0

续前表 continued

	人数 Number	高中/中专/技校学生 High school/ Secondary School Student	大学生 College Student	研究生 Graduate Student	家庭主妇 Housewife	离退休人员 Retired	下岗、待业人员 Unemployed	其它 Other
样本 Sample	1001	**7.6**	**3.2**	**0.1**	**0.7**	**8.3**	**9.7**	**2.2**
广告淡漠指向 indifferent orientation	256	7.0	2.3	0.0	0.8	10.2	11.7	2.3
中间层 medium	610	7.4	3.8	0.0	0.7	8.2	8.5	1.8
信赖广告指向 loyal orientation	135	9.6	2.2	0.7	0.7	5.2	11.1	3.7

2-5 不同消费者层的婚姻状况/ Marital Status of Market Segments

	人数 Number	已婚 Married	未婚 Single	离异 Divorced	丧偶 Widowed
样本 Sample	995	**64.5**	**33.4**	**1.3**	**0.8**
广告淡漠指向 indifferent orientation	255	67.1	31.4	1.2	0.4
中间层 medium	606	64.0	33.5	1.3	1.2
信赖广告指向 loyal orientation	134	61.9	36.6	1.5	0.0

2-6 不同消费者层的个人月收入/ Individual Monthly Income of Market Segments

	有效样本量 Total	无收入 no income	500 元以下 below 500 yuan	501-1000 元 yuan	1001-1500 元 yuan	1501-2000 元 yuan	2001-3000 元 yuan	3001-4000 元 yuan	4001-5000 元 yuan	5000 元以上 over 5000 yuan
样本 Sample	997	**15.5**	**10.4**	**29.3**	**23.5**	**9.7**	**9.1**	**1.2**	**0.6**	**0.6**
广告淡漠指向 indifferent orientation	256	17.6	10.2	30.1	25.0	7.8	7.8	1.2	0.0	0.4
中间层 medium	607	14.2	10.7	30.3	22.9	9.6	9.2	1.5	0.8	0.8
信赖广告指向 loyal orientation	134	17.9	9.7	23.1	23.1	14.2	11.2	0.0	0.7	0.0

3. 饮食健康指标/ Foods &Drink Quality Index

3-1 不同消费者层的性别构成/ Gender Composition of Market Segments

	人数 Number	男性 Male	女性 Female
样本 Sample	1009	**50.1**	**49.9**
饮食"温饱"指向 "basic" orientation	240	57.9	42.1
中间层 medium	495	49.9	50.1
健康营养指向 health & nutrition orientation	274	43.8	56.2

3-2 不同消费者层的年龄构成/ Age Composition of Market Segments

	人数 Number	16-24 岁 Age	25-34 岁 Age	35-44 岁 Age	45-54 岁 Age	55-60 岁 Age
样本 Sample	1009	**21.3**	**28.7**	**25.5**	**16.6**	**7.9**
饮食"温饱"指向 "basic" orientation	240	22.9	22.5	25.8	20.8	7.9
中间层 medium	495	22.0	32.1	23.0	15.4	7.5
健康营养指向 health & nutrition orientation	274	18.6	28.1	29.6	15.0	8.8

3-3 不同消费者层的学历构成/ Educational Composition of Market Segments

	人数 Number	小学以下 Primary School or Below	初中 Middle School	高中/中专/技校 High School/ Technical Secondary School	大学专科 2-3Year College	大学本科 4-5Year College	研究生或以上 Graduate or Above
样本 Sample	1006	2.2	26.3	50.5	13.7	6.7	0.6
饮食"温饱"指向 "basic" orientation	238	5.9	33.2	44.5	10.5	5.9	0.0
中间层 medium	494	1.2	26.1	49.0	16.4	6.3	1.0
健康营养指向 health & nutrition orientation	274	0.7	20.8	58.4	11.7	8.0	0.4

3-4 不同消费者层的职业构成/ Occupational Composition of Market Segments

	人数 Number	劳务职 Labor	技能职 Skill	服务职 Service	事务职 Assistance	销售职 Marketing	技术职 Technique	技术类以外的专门职 Professional Outside Technique
样本 Sample	1008	15.2	10.3	8.0	4.1	3.8	5.4	7.5
饮食"温饱"指向 "basic" orientation	240	17.5	9.6	6.3	3.3	2.5	3.8	4.2
中间层 medium	494	16.0	10.9	7.5	4.9	4.0	5.5	7.9
健康营养指向 health & nutrition orientation	274	11.7	9.9	10.6	3.3	4.4	6.6	9.9

续前表 continued

	人数 Number	自由职业者 Free Lance	企业/公司管理人员 Manager	行政管理人员/公务员 Administrator	经营者 Businessman	个体户 Self-employed Labor	军警 Military&police
样本 Sample	1008	1.2	5.3	3.4	0.8	3.1	0.3
饮食"温饱"指向 "basic" orientation	240	1.3	3.8	3.8	0.8	5.8	0.4
中间层 medium	494	1.2	6.3	2.4	0.6	1.8	0.2
健康营养指向 health & nutrition orientation	274	1.1	4.7	4.7	1.1	2.9	0.4

续前表 continued

	人数 Number	高中/中专/技校学生 High school/ Secondary School Student	大学生 College Student	研究生 Graduate Student	家庭主妇 Housewife	离退休人员 Retired	下岗、待业人员 Unemployed	其它 Other
样本 Sample	1008	7.5	3.1	0.2	0.7	8.3	9.7	2.2
饮食"温饱"指向 "basic" orientation	240	10.0	1.7	0.0	0.4	10.4	13.3	1.3
中间层 medium	494	7.9	3.8	0.4	0.6	7.9	8.1	2.0
健康营养指向 health & nutrition orientation	274	4.7	2.9	0.0	1.1	7.3	9.5	3.3

3-5 不同消费者层的婚姻状况/ Marital Status of Market Segments

	人数 Number	已婚 Married	未婚 Single	离异 Divorced	丧偶 Widowed
样本 Sample	1002	64.2	33.7	1.3	0.8
饮食"温饱"指向 "basic" orientation	239	61.5	36.8	1.3	0.4
中间层 medium	491	63.7	33.8	1.4	1.0
健康营养指向 health & nutrition orientation	272	67.3	30.9	1.1	0.7

3-6 不同消费者层的个人月收入/ Individual Monthly Income of Market Segments

	有效样本量 Total	无收入 no income	500 元以下 below 500 yuan	501-1000 元 yuan	1001-1500 元 yuan	1501-2000 元 yuan	2001-3000 元 yuan	3001-4000 元 yuan	4001-5000 元 yuan	5000 元以上 over 5000 yuan
样本 Sample	1004	15.4	10.2	29.7	23.6	9.7	9.3	1.0	0.6	0.6
饮食"温饱"指向 "basic" orientation	238	16.4	12.6	29.4	24.4	8 4	6.7	0.0	1.3	0.8
中间层 medium	493	16.4	8.7	32.3	23.3	7 7	9.5	1.2	0.6	0.2
健康营养指向 health & nutrition orientation	273	12.8	10.6	25.3	23.4	14 3	11.0	1.5	0.0	1.1

4. 价格态度指标/ Price Attitude Index

4-1 不同消费者层的性别构成/ Gender Composition of Market Segments

	人数 Number	男性 Male	女性 Female
样本 Sample	1011	50.1	49.9
价格无关心指向 indifferent orientation	151	58.3	41.7
中间层 medium	521	51.6	48.4
价格重视指向 careful orientation	339	44.2	55.8

4-2 不同消费者层的年龄构成/ Age Composition of Market Segments

	人数 Number	16-24 岁 Age	25-34 岁 Age	35-44 岁 Age	45-54 岁 Age	55-60 岁 Age
样本 Sample	1011	21.4	28.6	25.6	16.5	7.9
价格无关心指向 indifferent orientation	151	30.5	32.5	19.2	11.3	6.6
中间层 medium	521	24.0	30.1	25.9	13.6	6.3
价格重视指向 careful orientation	339	13.3	24.5	23.0	23.3	10.9

4-3 不同消费者层的学历构成/ Educational Composition of Market Segments

	人数 Number	小学以下 Primary School or Below	初中 Middle School	高中/中专/技校 High School/ Technical Secondary School	大学专科 2-3Year College	大学本科 4-5Year College	研究生或以上 Graduate or Above
样本 Sample	1008	2.2	26.4	50.4	13.6	6.7	0.7
价格无关心指向 indifferent orientation	149	2.7	24.2	49.0	15.4	8.7	0.0
中间层 medium	521	0.6	20.5	54.1	15.5	8.1	1.2
价格重视指向 careful orientation	338	4.4	36.4	45.3	9.8	3.8	0.3

4-4 不同消费者层的职业构成/ Occupational Composition of Market Segments

	人数 Number	劳务职 Labor	技能职 Skill	服务职 Service	事务职 Assistance	销售职 Marketing	技术职 Technique	技术类以外的专门职 Professional Outside Technique
样本 Sample	1010	15.0	10.3	8.2	4.1	3.8	5.3	7.5
价格无关心指向 indifferent orientation	150	10.0	11.3	4.7	2.7	4.0	6.7	8.0
中间层 medium	521	14.4	9.8	6.7	4.4	5.2	6.9	9.0
价格重视指向 careful orientation	339	18.3	10.6	12.1	4.1	1.5	2.4	5.0

续前表 continued

	人数 Number	自由职业者 Free Lance	企业/公司管理人员 Manager	行政管理人员/公务员 Administrator	经营者 Businessman	个体户 Self-employed Labor	军警 Military&police
样本 Sample	1010	1.2	5.3	3.4	0.9	3.0	0.3
价格无关心指向 indifferent orientation	150	1.3	4.0	4.0	1.3	4.0	0.0
中间层 medium	521	1.2	6.9	4.2	0.8	2.7	0.6
价格重视指向 careful orientation	339	1.2	3.5	1.8	0.9	2.9	0.0

续前表 continued

	人数 Number	高中/中专/技校学生 High school /Secondary School Student	大学生 College Student	研究生 Graduate Student	家庭主妇 Housewife	离退休人员 Retired	下岗、待业人员 Unemployed	其它 Other
样本 Sample	1010	7.5	3.1	0.2	0.7	8.3	9.7	2.2
价格无关心指向 indifferent orientation	150	14.7	2.0	0.0	0.7	6.0	12.0	2.7
中间层 medium	521	7.1	4.4	0.4	0.6	5.4	7.7	1.7
价格重视指向 careful orientation	339	5.0	1.5	0.0	0.9	13.9	11.8	2.7

4-5 不同消费者层的婚姻状况/ Marital Status of Market Segments

	人数 Number	已婚 Married	未婚 Single	离异 Divorced	丧偶 Widowed
样本 Sample	1004	64.2	33.7	1.3	0.8
价格无关心指向 indifferent orientation	150	54.0	44.0	2.0	0.0
中间层 medium	518	61.8	36.5	1.2	0.6
价格重视指向 careful orientation	336	72.6	24.7	1.2	1.5

4-6 不同消费者层的个人月收入/ Individual Monthly Income of Market Segments

	有效样本量 Total	无收入 no income	500 元以下 below 500 yuan	501-1000 元 yuan	1001-1500 元 yuan	1501-2000 元 yuan	2001-3000 元 yuan	3001-4000 元 yuan	4001-5000 元 yuan	5000 元以上 over 5000 yuan
样本 Sample	1006	15.4	10.3	29.5	23.6	9.5	9.2	1.2	0.6	0.6
价格无关心指向 indifferent orientation	149	22.8	6.0	22.1	19.5	8.1	16.8	2.0	1.3	1.3
中间层 medium	519	15.2	9.2	27.0	24.1	12.3	9.6	1.3	0.6	0.6
价格重视指向 careful orientation	338	12.4	13.9	36.7	24.6	5.9	5.3	0.6	0.3	0.3

5. 信息交流指标/ Information Communication Index

5-1 不同消费者层的性别构成/ Gender Composition of Market Segments

	人数 Number	男性 Male	女性 Female
样本 Sample	1005	50.4	49.6
信息消极指向 negative orientation	55	45.5	54.5
中间层 medium	576	51.2	48.8
信息积极指向 active orientation	374	50.0	50.0

5-2 不同消费者层的年龄构成/ Age Composition of Market Segments

	人数 Number	16-24 岁 Age	25-34 岁 Age	35-44 岁 Age	45-54 岁 Age	55-60 岁 Age
样本 Sample	1005	21.5	28.5	25.5	16.6	8.0
信息消极指向 negative orientation	55	12.7	34.5	18.2	20.0	14.5
中间层 medium	576	21.2	27.3	26.7	16.5	8.3
信息积极指向 active orientation	374	23.3	29.4	24.5	16.3	6.4

5-3 不同消费者层的学历构成/ Educational Composition of Market Segments

	人数 Number	小学以下 Primary School or Below	初中 Middle School	高中/中专/技校 High School /Technical Secondary School	大学专科 2-3Year College	大学本科 4-5Year College	研究生或以上 Graduate or Above
样本 Sample	1002	2.2	26.1	50.4	13.8	6.8	0.7
信息消极指向 negative orientation	54	11.1	29.6	50.0	5.6	3.7	0.0
中间层 medium	575	1.7	26.3	48.7	14.8	7.5	1.0
信息积极指向 active orientation	373	1.6	25.5	53.1	13.4	6.2	0.3

5-4 不同消费者层的职业构成/ Occupational Composition of Market Segments

	人数 Number	劳务职 Labor	技能职 Skill	服务职 Service	事务职 Assistance	销售职 Marketing	技术职 Technique	技术类以外的专门职 Professional Outside Technique
样本 Sample	1004	15.0	10.3	8.2	4.0	3.8	5.4	7.5
信息消极指向 negative orientation	55	18.2	5.5	10.9	1.8	1.8	7.3	9.1
中间层 medium	576	14.8	10.6	6.8	4.3	3.5	6.1	6.4
信息积极指向 active orientation	373	15.0	10.5	9.9	3.8	4.6	4.0	8.8

续前表 continued

	人数 Number	自由职业者 Free Lance	企业/公司管理人员 Manager	行政管理人员/公务员 Administrator	经营者 Businessman	个体户 Self-employed Labor	军警 Military&police
样本 Sample	1004	1.2	5.4	3.4	0.9	3.1	0.3
信息消极指向 negative orientation	55	3.6	0.0	1.8	0.0	1.8	0.0
中间层 medium	576	0.7	5.7	4.2	0.7	2.8	0.3
信息积极指向 active orientation	373	1.6	5.6	2.4	1.3	3.8	0.3

续前表 continued

	人数 Number	高中/中专/技校学生 High school/ Secondary School Student	大学生 College Student	研究生 Graduate Student	家庭主妇 Housewife	离退休人员 Retired	下岗、待业人员 Unemployed	其它 Other
样本 Sample	1004	7.6	3.1	0.2	0.6	8.4	9.7	2.2
信息消极指向 negative orientation	55	1.8	0.0	0.0	3.6	14.5	10.9	7.3
中间层 medium	576	7.8	3.5	0.3	0.5	9.0	9.9	2.1
信息积极指向 active orientation	373	8.0	2.9	0.0	0.3	6.4	9.1	1.6

5-5 不同消费者层的婚姻状况/ Marital Status of Market Segments

	人数 Number	已婚 Married	未婚 Single	离异 Divorced	丧偶 Widowed
样本 Sample	998	64.0	33.9	1.3	0.8
信息消极指向 negative orientation	55	70.9	27.3	1.8	0.0
中间层 medium	570	64.2	33.2	1.4	1.2
信息积极指向 active orientation	373	62.7	35.9	1.1	0.3

5-6 不同消费者层的个人月收入/ Individual Monthly Income of Market Segments

	有效样本量 Total	无收入 no income	500 元以下 below 500 yuan	501-1000 元 yuan	1001-1500 元 yuan	1501-2000 元 yuan	2001-3000 元 yuan	3001-4000 元 yuan	4001-5000 元 yuan	5000 元以上 over 5000 yuan
样本 Sample	1000	15.5	10.2	29.5	23.4	9.7	9.3	1.2	0.6	0.6
信息积极指向 active orientation	55	16.4	10.9	41.8	16.4	5.5	9.1	0.0	0.0	0.0
中间层 medium	574	15.2	10.5	30.5	24.7	8.0	8.2	1.6	0.9	0.5
信息消极指向 negative orientation	371	15.9	9.7	26.1	22.4	12.9	11.1	0.8	0.3	0.8

4.广州消费者层 / Market Segmentation in Guangzhou

1. 时尚流行指标/ Fads Popular Index

1-1 不同消费者层的性别构成/ Gender Composition of Market Segments

	人数 Number	男性 Male	女性 Female
样本 Sample	1022	48.3	51.7
平实生活指向 simple living orientation	518	52.5	47.5
时尚流行指向 fashion orientation	504	44.0	56.0

1-2 不同消费者层的年龄构成/ Age Composition of Market Segments

	人数 Number	16-24 岁 Age	25-34 岁 Age	35-44 岁 Age	45-54 岁 Age	55-60 岁 Age
样本 Sample	1022	21.0	29.9	25.4	15.5	8.1
平实生活指向 simple living orientation	518	12.7	27.2	28.0	19.7	12.4
时尚流行指向 fashion orientation	504	29.6	32.7	22.8	11.1	3.8

1-3 不同消费者层的学历构成/ Educational Composition of Market Segments

	人数 Number	小学以下 Primary School or Below	初中 Middle School	高中/中专/技校 High School/ Technical Secondary School	大学专科 2-3Year College	大学本科 4-5Year College	研究生或以上 Graduate or Above
样本 Sample	1012	5.2	21.1	49.6	12.7	10.1	1.2
平实生活指向 simple living orientation	512	7.8	23.0	47.1	10.2	10.4	1.6
时尚流行指向 fashion orientation	500	2.6	19.2	52.2	15.4	9.8	0.8

1-4 不同消费者层的职业构成/ Occupational Composition of Market Segments

	人数 Number	劳务职 Labor	技能职 Skill	服务职 Service	事务职 Assistance	销售职 Marketing	技术职 Technique	技术类以外的专门职 Professional Outside Technique
样本 Sample	1020	10.7	7.9	7.2	3.6	5.5	4.7	7.8
平实生活指向 simple living orientation	517	13.5	8.3	6.0	3.9	5.8	5.8	7.5
时尚流行指向 fashion orientation	503	7.8	7.6	8.3	3.4	5.2	3.6	8.2

续前表 continued

	人数 Number	自由职业者 Free Lance	企业/公司管理人员 Manager	行政管理人员/公务员 Administrator	经营者 Businessman	个体户 Self-employed Labor	军警 Military&Police
样本 Sample	1020	0.8	4.0	4.2	2.0	6.1	0.4
平实生活指向 simple living orientation	517	0.6	3.9	4.3	1.9	6.0	0.6
时尚流行指向 fashion orientation	503	1.0	4.2	4 2	2.0	6.2	0.2

续前表 continued

	人数 Number	高中/中专/技校学生 High School/ Technical Secondary School Student	大学生 College Student	研究生 Graduate Student	家庭主妇 Housewife	离退休人员 Retired	下岗、待业人员 Unemployed	其他 Others
样本 Sample	1020	8.0	6.0	0.1	2.9	5.6	10.8	1.7
平实生活指向 simple living orientation	517	4.3	4.1	0.0	2.5	7.9	11.4	1.7
时尚流行指向 fashion orientation	503	11.9	8.0	0.2	3.4	3.2	10.1	1.6

1-5 不同消费者层的婚姻状况/ Marital Status of Market Segments

	人数 Number	已婚 Married	未婚 Single	离异 Divorced	丧偶 Widowed
样本 Sample	999	64.4	33.2	0.5	1.9
平实生活指向 simple living orientation	502	72.3	23.5	0.8	3.4
时尚流行指向 fashion orientation	497	56.3	43.1	0.2	0.4

2.广告态度指标 / Advertising Attitude Index

2-1 不同消费者层的性别构成/ Gender Composition of Market Segments

	人数 Number	男性 Male	女性 Female
样本 Sample	1022	48.4	51.6
广告淡漠指向 indifferent orientation	334	52.4	47.6
中间层 medium	593	46.7	53.3
信赖广告指向 loyal orientation	95	45.3	54.7

2-2 不同消费者层的年龄构成/ Age Composition of Market Segments

	人数 Number	16-24 岁 Age	25-34 岁 Age	35-44 岁 Age	45-54 岁 Age	55-60 岁 Age
样本 Sample	1022	21.1	29.6	25.7	15.4	8.1
广告淡漠指向 indifferent orientation	334	16.8	26.0	28.7	17.4	11.1
中间层 medium	593	23.4	32.2	23.4	13.7	7.3
信赖广告指向 loyal orientation	95	22.1	26.3	29.5	18.9	3.2

2-3 不同消费者层的学历构成/ Educational Composition of Market Segments

	人数 Number	小学以下 Primary School or Below	初中 Middle School	高中/中专/技校 High School/ Technical Secondary School	大学专科 2-3Year College	大学本科 4-5Year College	研究生或以上 Graduate or Above
样本 Sample	1012	5.1	21.3	49.6	12.5	10.2	1.2
广告淡漠指向 indifferent orientation	329	7.6	18.2	51.1	10.9	10.0	2.1
中间层 medium	590	4.2	21.7	49.0	14.1	10.2	0.8
信赖广告指向 loyal orientation	93	2.2	30.1	48.4	8.6	10.8	0.0

2-4 不同消费者层的职业构成/ Occupational Composition of Market Segments

	人数 Number	劳务职 Labor	技能职 Skill	服务职 Service	事务职 Assistance	销售职 Marketing	技术职 Technique	技术类以外的专门职 Professional Outside Technique
样本 Sample	1020	10.6	8.1	7.1	3.6	5.4	4.6	7.8
广告淡漠指向 indifferent orientation	334	12.0	9.0	7.2	3.0	4.8	6.9	7.5
中间层 medium	591	10.3	7.1	6.9	3.7	6.3	3.4	8.0
信赖广告指向 loyal orientation	95	7.4	11.6	7.4	5.3	2.1	4.2	8.4

续前表 continued

	人数 Number	自由职业者 Free Lance	企业/公司管理人员 Manager	行政管理人员/公务员 Administrator	经营者 Businessman	个体户 Self-employed Labor	军警 Military&Police
样本 Sample	1020	0.9	4.0	4.3	2.0	6.1	0.4
广告淡漠指向 indifferent orientation	334	0.9	3.6	5.4	2.1	5.4	0.0
中间层 medium	591	0.8	4.1	3.6	1.9	6.1	0.7
信赖广告指向 loyal orientation	95	1.1	5.3	5.3	2.1	8.4	0.0

续前表 continued

	人数 Number	高中/中专/技校学生 High School/ Technical Secondary School Student	大学生 College Student	研究生 Graduate Student	家庭主妇 Housewife	离退休人员 Retired	下岗、待业人员 Unemployed	其他 Others
样本 Sample	1020	8.1	6.1	0.1	2.9	5.5	10.7	1.7
广告淡漠指向 indifferent orientation	334	7.5	3.9	0.0	3.3	7.5	8.7	1.5
中间层 medium	591	8.3	7.4	0.2	3.0	4.6	12.0	1.7
信赖广告指向 loyal orientation	95	9.5	5.3	0.0	1.1	4.2	9.5	2.1

2-5 不同消费者层的婚姻状况/ Marital Status of Market Segments

	人数 Number	已婚 Married	未婚 Single	离异 Divorced	丧偶 Widowed
样本 Sample	999	64.5	33.0	0.5	2.0
广告淡漠指向 indifferent orientation	326	67.8	30.1	0.3	1.8
中间层 medium	580	62.8	34.5	0.5	2.2
信赖广告指向 loyal orientation	93	63.4	34.4	1.1	1.1

3.饮食健康指标 / Foods & Drink Quality Index

3-1 不同消费者层的性别构成/ Gender Composition of Market Segments

	人数 Number	男性 Male	女性 Female
样本 Sample	1029	48.4	51.6
饮食"温饱"指向 "basic" orientation	299	58.2	41.8
中间层 medium	546	47.3	52.7
健康营养指向 health & nutrition orientation	184	35.9	64.1

3-2 不同消费者层的年龄构成/ Age Composition of Market Segments

	人数 Number	16-24 岁 Age	25-34 岁 Age	35-44 岁 Age	45-54 岁 Age	55-60 岁 Age
样本 Sample	1029	21.1	29.9	25.5	15.5	8.1
饮食"温饱"指向 "basic" orientation	299	21.4	28.8	23.1	18.4	8.4
中间层 medium	546	21.4	31.1	26.0	12.5	9.0
健康营养指向 health & nutrition orientation	184	19.6	28.3	27.7	19.6	4.9

3-3 不同消费者层的学历构成/ Educational Composition of Market Segments

	人数 Number	小学以下 Primary School or Below	初中 Middle School	高中/中专/技校 High School/ Technical Secondary School	大学专科 2-3Year College	大学本科 4-5Year College	研究生或以上 Graduate or Above
样本 Sample	1019	5.2	21.3	49.8	12.6	10.0	1.2
饮食"温饱"指向 "basic" orientation	298	8.4	21.1	45.3	12.1	11.4	1.7
中间层 medium	540	4.6	20.4	51.3	13.1	9.4	1.1
健康营养指向 health & nutrition orientation	181	1.7	24.3	52.5	11.6	9.4	0.6

3-4 不同消费者层的职业构成/ Occupational Composition of Market Segments

	人数 Number	劳务职 Labor	技能职 Skill	服务职 Service	事务职 Assistance	销售职 Marketing	技术职 Technique	技术类以外的专门职 Professional Outside Technique
样本 Sample	1027	10.6	8.1	7.4	3.6	5.5	4.7	7.7
饮食"温饱"指向 "basic" orientation	299	10.4	8.4	7.0	3.3	6.7	6.7	6.4
中间层 medium	545	11.2	8.1	6.6	3.9	5.5	4.0	6.6
健康营养指向 health & nutrition orientation	183	9.3	7.7	10.4	3.3	3.3	3.3	13.1

续前表 continued

	人数 Number	自由职业者 Free Lance	企业/公司管理人员 Manager	行政管理人员/公务员 Administrator	经营者 Businessman	个体户 Self-employed Labor	军警 Military&Police
样本 Sample	1027	0.9	4.1	4.3	1.9	6.0	0.4
饮食"温饱"指向 "basic" orientation	299	0.7	3.7	4.0	3.0	6.7	0.0
中间层 medium	545	1.1	3.9	4.0	1.5	5.9	0.6
健康营养指向 health & nutrition orientation	183	0.5	5.5	5.5	1.6	5.5	0.5

续前表 continued

	人数 Number	高中/中专/技校学生 High School/ Technical Secondary School Student	大学生 College Student	研究生 Graduate Student	家庭主妇 Housewife	离退休人员 Retired	下岗、待业人员 Unemployed	其他 Others
样本 Sample	1027	8.0	6.0	0.1	2.7	5.6	10.8	1.7
饮食"温饱"指向 "basic" orientation	299	7.0	6.0	0.3	3.3	4.7	11.4	0.3
中间层 medium	545	8.6	6.4	0.0	2.6	5.5	11.9	2.2
健康营养指向 health & nutrition orientation	183	7.7	4.9	0.0	2.2	7.1	6.6	2.2

3-5 不同消费者层的婚姻状况/ Marital Status of Market Segments

	人数 Number	已婚 Married	未婚 Single	离异 Divorced	丧偶 Widowed
样本 Sample	1006	64.3	33.2	0.5	2.0
饮食"温饱"指向 "basic" orientation	289	60.9	36.0	0.3	2.8
中间层 medium	535	65.2	32.7	0.4	1.7
健康营养指向 health & nutrition orientation	182	67.0	30.2	1.1	1.6

4.价格态度指标/ Price Attitude Index

4-1 不同消费者层的性别构成/ Gender Composition of Market Segments

	人数 Number	男性 Male	女性 Female
样本 Sample	1028	48.2	51.8
价格无关心指向 indifferent orientation	188	53.2	46.8
中间层 medium	549	49.9	50.1
价格重视指向 careful orientation	291	41.9	58.1

4-2 不同消费者层的年龄构成/ Age Composition of Market Segments

	人数 Number	16-24 岁 Age	25-34 岁 Age	35-44 岁 Age	45-54 岁 Age	55-60 岁 Age
样本 Sample	1028	21.2	29.7	25.5	15.6	8.1
价格无关心指向 indifferent orientation	188	23.4	33.5	22.3	14.4	6.4
中间层 medium	549	22.4	30.1	24.4	14.6	8.6
价格重视指向 careful orientation	291	17.5	26.5	29.6	18.2	8.2

4-3 不同消费者层的学历构成/ Educational Composition of Market Segments

	人数 Number	小学以下 Primary School or Below	初中 Middle School	高中/中专/技校 High School/ Technical Secondary School	大学专科 2-3Year College	大学本科 4-5Year College	研究生或以上 Graduate or Above
样本 Sample	1018	5.2	21.4	49.6	12.5	10.1	1.2
价格无关心指向 indifferent orientation	186	4.3	13.4	48.9	14.5	15.6	3.2
中间层 medium	542	4.6	24.0	48.2	12.7	9.4	1.1
价格重视指向 careful orientation	290	6.9	21.7	52.8	10.7	7.9	0.0

4-4 不同消费者层的职业构成/ Occupational Composition of Market Segments

	人数 Number	劳务职 Labor	技能职 Skill	服务职 Service	事务职 Assistance	销售职 Marketing	技术职 Technique	技术类以外的专门职 Professional Outside Technique
样本 Sample	1026	10.6	8.0	7.3	3.6	5.4	4.7	7.8
价格无关心指向 indifferent orientation	188	8.5	5.3	6.4	3.7	6.9	5.9	9.0
中间层 medium	548	9.5	9.7	7.7	2.6	5.5	4.7	8.4
价格重视指向 careful orientation	290	14.1	6.6	7.2	5.5	4.1	3.8	5.9

续前表 continued

	人数 Number	自由职业者 Free Lance	企业/公司管理人员 Manager	行政管理人员/公务员 Administrator	经营者 Businessman	个体户 Self-employed Labor	军警 Military&Police
样本 Sample	1026	0.9	4.1	4.2	1.9	6.0	0.4
价格无关心指向 indifferent orientation	188	0.5	4.3	5.3	2.7	6.4	0.5
中间层 medium	548	0.9	4.4	4.0	1.8	5.8	0.2
价格重视指向 careful orientation	290	1.0	3.4	3.8	1.7	6.2	0.7

续前表 continued

	人数 Number	高中/中专/技校学生 High School/ Technical Secondary School Student	大学生 College Student	研究生 Graduate Student	家庭主妇 Housewife	离退休人员 Retired	下岗、待业人员 Unemployed	其他 Others
样本 Sample	1026	8.1	6.0	0.1	2.8	5.6	10.8	1.7
价格无关心指向 indifferent orientation	188	7.4	8.5	0.0	2.1	3.7	10.6	2.1
中间层 medium	548	8.8	4.9	0.2	2.9	5.7	10.6	1.8
价格重视指向 careful orientation	290	7.2	6.6	0.0	3.1	6.6	11.4	1.0

4-5 不同消费者层的婚姻状况/ Marital Status of Market Segments

	人数 Number	已婚 Married	未婚 Single	离异 Divorced	丧偶 Widowed
样本 Sample	1005	64.2	33.3	0.5	2.0
价格无关心指向 indifferent orientation	181	59.7	38.7	0.0	1.7
中间层 medium	538	63.9	34.8	0.4	0.9
价格重视指向 careful orientation	286	67.5	27.3	1.0	4.2

5.信息交流指标 / Information Communication Index

5-1 不同消费者层的性别构成/ Gender Composition of Market Segments

	人数 Number	男性 Male	女性 Female
样本 Sample	1026	48.1	51.9
信息消极指向 negative orientation	111	51.4	48.6
中间层 medium	662	49.4	50.6
信息积极指向 active orientation	253	43.5	56.5

5-2 不同消费者层的年龄构成/ Age Composition of Market Segments

	人数 Number	16-24 岁 Age	25-34 岁 Age	35-44 岁 Age	45-54 岁 Age	55-60 岁 Age
样本 Sample	1026	21.1	29.7	25.6	15.4	8.2
信息消极指向 negative orientation	111	10.8	23.4	23.8	19.8	17.1
中间层 medium	662	22.5	30.5	25.5	13.7	7.7
信息积极指向 active orientation	253	21.7	30.4	24.5	17.8	5.5

5-3 不同消费者层的学历构成/ Educational Composition of Market Segments

	人数 Number	小学以下 Primary School or Below	初中 Middle School	高中/中专/技校 High School/ Technical Secondary School	大学专科 2-3Year College	大学本科 4-5Year College	研究生或以上 Graduate or Above
样本 Sample	1016	5.2	21.4	49.6	12.5	10.1	1.2
信息消极指向 negative orientation	109	13.8	20.2	53.2	4.6	7.3	0.9
中间层 medium	656	4.6	22.1	47.7	13.6	10.4	1.7
信息积极指向 active orientation	251	3.2	19.9	53.0	13.1	10.8	0.0

5-4 不同消费者层的职业构成/ Occupational Composition of Market Segments

	人数 Number	劳务职 Labor	技能职 Skill	服务职 Service	事务职 Assistance	销售职 Marketing	技术职 Technique	技术类以外的专门职 Professional Outside Technique
样本 Sample	1024	10.6	7.8	7.3	3.6	5.5	4.6	7.8
信息消极指向 negative orientation	111	17.1	6.3	7.2	5.4	4.5	2.7	1.8
中间层 medium	660	10.0	8.2	7.0	4.1	4.8	5.2	8.0
信息积极指向 active orientation	253	9.5	7.5	8.3	1.6	7.5	4.0	9.9

续前表 continued

	人数 Number	自由职业者 Free Lance	企业/公司管理人员 Manager	行政管理人员/公务员 Administrator	经营者 Businessman	个体户 Self-employed Labor	军警 Military&Police
样本 Sample	1024	0.9	4.0	4.3	2.0	6.1	0.4
信息消极指向 negative orientation	111	2.7	0.9	3.6	4.5	3.6	0.9
中间层 medium	660	0.2	4.7	4.1	1.7	6.1	0.3
信息积极指向 active orientation	253	2.0	3.6	5.1	1.6	7.1	0.4

续前表 continued

	人数 Number	高中/中专/技校学生 High School/ Technical Secondary School Student	大学生 College Student	研究生 Graduate Student	家庭主妇 Housewife	离退休人员 Retired	下岗、待业人员 Unemployed	其他 Others
样本 Sample	1024	8.1	6.1	0.1	2.8	5.6	10.8	1.7
信息消极指向 negative orientation	111	1.8	2.7	0.0	5.4	9.9	17.1	1.8
中间层 medium	660	9.1	6.5	0.2	2.3	5.2	10.5	2.1
信息积极指向 active orientation	253	8.3	6.3	0.0	3.2	4.7	9.1	0.4

5-5 不同消费者层的婚姻状况/ Marital Status of Market Segments

	人数 Number	已婚 Married	未婚 Single	离异 Divorced	丧偶 Widowed
样本 Sample	1003	64.5	33.0	0.5	2.0
信息消极指向 negative orientation	108	71.3	23.1	0.0	5.6
中间层 medium	646	64.1	33.9	0.5	1.5
信息积极指向 active orientation	249	62.7	34.9	0.8	1.6

5.重庆消费者层 / Market Segmentation in Chongqing

1.时尚流行指标/ Fads Popular Index

1-1 不同消费者层的性别构成/ Gender Composition of Market Segments

	人数 Number	男性 Male	女性 Female
样本 Sample	616	50.3	49.7
平实生活指向 simple living orientation	369	54.7	45.3
时尚流行指向 fashion orientation	247	43.7	56.3

1-2 不同消费者层的年龄构成/ Age Composition of Market Segments

	人数	16-24 岁 Age	25-34 岁 Age	35-44 岁 Age	45-54 岁 Age	55-60 岁 Age
样本 Sample	616	20.5	29.5	23.7	18.5	7.8
平实生活指向 simple living orientation	369	12.7	26.3	27.9	21.7	11.4
时尚流行指向 fashion orientation	247	32.0	34.4	17.4	13.8	2.4

1-3 不同消费者层的学历构成/ Educational Composition of Market Segments

	人数 Number	小学以下 Primary School or Below	初中 Middle School	高中/中专/技校 High School/ Technical Secondary School	大学专科 2-3Year College	大学本科 4-5Year College	研究生或以上 Graduate or Above
样本 Sample	614	9.6	32.6	39.4	13.2	5.0	0.2
平实生活指向 simple living orientation	368	13.3	33.4	35.9	11.1	6.0	0.3
时尚流行指向 fashion orientation	246	4.1	31.3	44.7	16.3	3.7	0.0

1-4 不同消费者层的职业构成/ Occupational Composition of Market Segments

	人数 Number	劳务职 Labor	技能职 Skill	服务职 Service	事务职 Assistance	销售职 Marketing	技术职 Technique	技术类以外的专门职 Professional Outside Technique
样本 Sample	615	15.3	9.3	7.0	1.1	2.3	4.2	6.0
平实生活指向 simple living orientation	369	16.3	10.8	5.4	0.8	2.4	4.3	6.0
时尚流行指向 fashion orientation	246	13.8	6.9	9.3	1 6	2.0	4.1	6.1

续前表 continued

	人数 Number	自由职业者 Free Lance	企业/公司管理人员 Manager	行政管理人员/公务员 Administrator	经营者 Businessman	个体户 Self-employed Labor	军警 Military &Police
样本 Sample	615	0.7	3.4	2 0	0.5	8.6	0.2
平实生活指向 simple living orientation	369	0.5	4.1	1 9	0.5	8.4	0.3
时尚流行指向 fashion orientation	246	0.8	2.4	2 0	0.4	8.9	0.0

续前表 continued

	人数 Number	高中/中专/技校学生 High School/ Technical Secondary School Student	大学生 College Student	研究生 Graduate Student	家庭主妇 Housewife	离退休人员 Retired	下岗、待业人员 Unemployed	其他 Others
样本 Sample	615	8.6	2.1	0.0	3.1	9.9	14.5	1.3
平实生活指向 simple living orientation	369	4.3	1.1	0.0	4.3	12.2	14.9	1.4
时尚流行指向 fashion orientation	246	15.0	3.7	0.0	1.2	6.5	13.8	1.2

1-5 不同消费者层的婚姻状况/ Marital Status of Market Segments

	人数 Number	已婚 Married	未婚 Single	离异 Divorced	丧偶 Widowed
样本 Sample	609	67.3	27.9	4.1	0.7
平实生活指向 simple living orientation	365	77.5	17.8	3.8	0.8
时尚流行指向 fashion orientation	244	52.0	43.0	4.5	0.4

1-6 不同消费者层的个人月收入/ Individual Monthly Income of Market Segments

	有效样本量 Total	无收入 no income	500 元以下 below 500 yuan	501-1000 元 yuan	1001-1500 元 yuan	1501-2000 元 yuan	2001-3000 元 yuan	3001-4000 元 yuan	4001-5000 元 yuan	5000 元以上 over 5000 yuan
样本 Sample	614	20.4	34.5	31.3	9.0	2.6	2.0	0.2	0.2	0.0
平实生活指向 simple living orientation	369	15.4	39.0	33.9	9.2	1.6	0.8	0.0	0.0	0.0
时尚流行指向 fashion orientation	245	27.8	27.8	27.3	8.6	4.1	3.7	0.4	0.4	0.0

2. 广告态度指标/ Advertising Attitude Index

2-1 不同消费者层的性别构成/ Gender Composition of Market Segments

	人数 Number	男性 Male	女性 Female
样本 Sample	618	50.5	49.5
广告淡漠指向 indifferent orientation	167	61.7	38.3
中间层 medium	367	46.9	53.1
信赖广告指向 loyal orientation	84	44.0	56.0

2-2 不同消费者层的年龄构成/ Age Composition of Market Segments

	人数	16-24 岁 Age	25-34 岁 Age	35-44 岁 Age	45-54 岁 Age	55-60 岁 Age
样本 Sample	618	20.7	29.1	23.8	18.3	8.1
广告淡漠指向 indifferent orientation	167	17.4	25.1	24.6	22.8	10.2
中间层 medium	367	23.2	30.0	23.2	15.5	8.2
信赖广告指向 loyal orientation	84	16.7	33.3	25.0	21.4	3.6

2-3 不同消费者层的学历构成/ Educational Composition of Market Segments

	人数 Number	小学以下 Primary School or Below	初中 Middle School	高中/中专/技校 High School/ Technical Secondary School	大学专科 2-3Year College	大学本科 4-5Year College	研究生或以上 Graduate or Above
样本 Sample	616	9.4	32.3	39.6	13.5	5.0	0.2
广告淡漠指向 indifferent orientation	166	15.1	28.3	40.4	10.2	6.0	0.0
中间层 medium	366	6.6	32.8	40.2	15.0	5.2	0.3
信赖广告指向 loyal orientation	84	10.7	38.1	35.7	13.1	2.4	0.0

2-4 不同消费者层的职业构成/ Occupational Composition of Market Segments

	人数 Number	劳务职 Labor	技能职 Skill	服务职 Service	事务职 Assistance	销售职 Marketing	技术职 Technique	技术类以外的专门职 Professional Outside Technique
样本 Sample	617	15.4	9.1	6.8	1.1	2.3	4.4	5.8
广告淡漠指向 indifferent orientation	167	13.2	10.8	7.2	0.6	3.0	4.8	6.0
中间层 medium	367	15.0	8.4	8.2	1.6	2.5	4.1	6.8
信赖广告指向 loyal orientation	83	21.7	8.4	0.0	0.0	0.0	4.8	1.2

续前表 continued

	人数 Number	自由职业者 Free Lance	企业/公司管理人员 Manager	行政管理人员/公务员 Administrator	经营者 Businessman	个体户 Self-employed Labor	军警 Military &Police
样本 Sample	617	0.6	3.6	1.9	0.6	8.4	0.2
广告淡漠指向 indifferent orientation	167	0.0	6.0	1.8	0.6	9.0	0.6
中间层 medium	367	0.8	2.5	1.9	0.5	7.6	0.0
信赖广告指向 loyal orientation	83	1.2	3.6	2.4	1.2	10.8	0.0

续前表 continued

	人数 Number	高中/中专/技校学生 High School/ Technical Secondary School Student	大学生 College Student	研究生 Graduate Student	家庭主妇 Housewife	离退休人员 Retired	下岗、待业人员 Unemployed	其他 Others
样本 Sample	617	8.8	2.3	0.0	2.9	9.9	14.4	1.5
广告淡漠指向 indifferent orientation	167	9.0	0.0	0.0	3.6	10.8	12.0	1.2
中间层 medium	367	9.0	3.5	0.0	2.5	9.8	13.9	1.4
信赖广告指向 loyal orientation	83	7.2	1.2	0.0	3.5	8.4	21.7	2.4

2-5 不同消费者层的婚姻状况/ Marital Status of Market Segments

	人数 Number	已婚 Married	未婚 Single	离异 Divorced	丧偶 Widowed
样本 Sample	611	66.9	28.2	4.1	0.8
广告淡漠指向 indifferent orientation	163	71.8	25.8	1.8	0.6
中间层 medium	364	64.3	30.2	4.7	0.8
信赖广告指向 loyal orientation	84	69.0	23.8	6.0	1.2

2-6 不同消费者层的个人月收入/ Individual Monthly Income of Market Segments

	有效样本量 Total	无收入 no income	500 元以下 below 500 yuan	501-1000 元 yuan	1001-1500 元 yuan	1501-2000 元 yuan	2001-3000 元 yuan	3001-4000 元 yuan	4001-5000 元 yuan	5000 元以上 over 5000 yuan
样本 Sample	616	20.3	34.4	31.3	8.9	2.6	1.9	0.2	0.2	0.2
广告淡漠指向 indifferent orientation	166	18.1	35.5	31.9	10.2	2.4	1.8	0.0	0.0	0.0
中间层 medium	366	21.9	33.3	31.1	9.0	2.5	1.6	0.3	0.3	0.0
信赖广告指向 loyal orientation	84	17.9	36.9	31.0	6.0	3.6	3.6	0.0	0.0	1.2

3. 饮食健康指标/ Foods & Drink Quality Index

3-1 不同消费者层的性别构成/ Gender Composition of Market Segments

	人数 Number	男性 Male	女性 Female
样本 Sample	618	50.3	49.7
饮食"温饱"指向 "basic" orientation	233	60.5	39.5
中间层 medium	261	47.5	52.5
健康营养指向 health & nutrition orientation	124	37.1	62.9

3-2 不同消费者层的年龄构成/ Age Composition of Market Segments

	人数	16-24 岁 Age	25-34 岁 Age	35-44 岁 Age	45-54 岁 Age	55-60 岁 Age
样本 Sample	618	20.7	29.4	23.5	18.3	8.1
饮食"温饱"指向 "basic" orientation	233	17.6	29.6	23.6	19.3	9.9
中间层 medium	261	22.6	31.8	23.8	15.3	6.5
健康营养指向 health & nutrition orientation	124	22.6	24.2	22.6	22.6	8.1

3-3 不同消费者层的学历构成/ Educational Composition of Market Segments

	人数 Number	小学以下 Primary School or Below	初中 Middle School	高中/中专/技校 High School/ Technical Secondary School	大学专科 2-3Year College	大学本科 4-5Year College	研究生或以上 Graduate or Above
样本 Sample	616	9.6	32.5	39.4	13.1	5.2	0.2
饮食"温饱"指向 "basic" orientation	233	13.3	33.5	37.8	11.2	4.3	0.0
中间层 medium	259	7.3	28.2	44.0	13.5	6.6	0.4
健康营养指向 health & nutrition orientation	124	7.3	39.5	33.1	16.1	4.0	0.0

3-4 不同消费者层的职业构成/ Occupational Composition of Market Segments

	人数 Number	劳务职 Labor	技能职 Skill	服务职 Service	事务职 Assistance	销售职 Marketing	技术职 Technique	技术类以外的专门职 Professional Outside Technique
样本 Sample	617	15.2	9.2	7.0	1.1	2.3	4.4	5.5
饮食"温饱"指向 "basic" orientation	233	15.0	11.2	4.3	0.4	2.6	3.9	3.4
中间层 medium	261	14.9	8.8	9.6	1.5	1.5	4.6	8.0
健康营养指向 health & nutrition orientation	123	16.3	6.5	6.5	1.6	3.3	4.9	4.1

续前表 continued

	人数 Number	自由职业者 Free Lance	企业/公司管理人员 Manager	行政管理人员/公务员 Administrator	经营者 Businessman	个体户 Self-employed Labor	军警 Military &Police
样本 Sample	617	0.6	3.6	1.9	0.6	8.6	0.2
饮食"温饱"指向 "basic" orientation	233	0.4	3.9	0.4	0.9	8.6	0.0
中间层 medium	261	1.1	3.4	2.3	0.4	8.0	0.4
健康营养指向 health & nutrition orientation	123	0.0	3.3	4.1	0.8	9.8	0.0

续前表 continued

	人数 Number	高中/中专/技校学生 High School/ Technical Secondary School Student	大学生 College Student	研究生 Graduate Student	家庭主妇 Housewife	离退休人员 Retired	下岗、待业人员 Unemployed	其他 Others
样本 Sample	617	8.8	2.3	0.0	3.1	9.9	14.3	1.5
饮食“温饱”指向 "basic" orientation	233	8.2	2.1	0.0	4.7	10.7	18.0	1.3
中间层 medium	261	10.0	1.9	0.0	2.3	7.3	11.9	1.9
健康营养指向 health & nutrition orientation	123	7.3	3.3	0.0	1.6	13.8	12.2	0.8

3-5 不同消费者层的婚姻状况/ Marital Status of Market Segments

	人数 Number	已婚 Married	未婚 Single	离异 Divorced	丧偶 Widowed
样本 Sample	611	67.1	28.0	4.1	0.8
饮食“温饱”指向 "basic" orientation	230	68.7	27.0	3.9	0.4
中间层 medium	258	66.3	29.8	3.5	0.4
健康营养指向 health & nutrition orientation	123	65.9	26.0	5.7	2.4

3-6 不同消费者层的个人月收入/ Individual Monthly Income of Market Segments

	有效样本量 Total	无收入 no income	500 元以下 below 500 yuan	501-1000 元 yuan	1001-1500 元 yuan	1501-2000 元 yuan	2001-3000 元 yuan	3001-4000 元 yuan	4001-5000 元 yuan	5000 元以上 over 5000 yuan
样本 Sample	616	20.6	34.4	31.0	8.9	2.6	1.9	0.2	0.2	0.2
饮食“温饱”指向 "basic" orientation	233	21.0	39.1	26.6	9.0	3.0	0.9	0.0	0.4	0.0
中间层 medium	259	20.8	31.7	34.7	7.7	2.7	2.3	0.0	0.0	0.0
健康营养指向 health & nutrition orientation	124	19.4	31.5	31.5	11.3	1.6	3.2	0.8	0.0	0.8

4. 价格态度指标/ Price Attitude Index

4-1 不同消费者层的性别构成/ Gender Composition of Market Segments

	人数 Number	男性 Male	女性 Female
样本 Sample	615	50.4	49.6
价格无关心指向 indifferent orientation	106	62.3	37.7
中间层 medium	280	56.1	43.9
价格重视指向 careful orientation	229	38.0	62.0

4-2 不同消费者层的年龄构成/ Age Composition of Market Segments

	人数 Number	16-24 岁 Age	25-34 岁 Age	35-44 岁 Age	45-54 岁 Age	55-60 岁 Age
样本 Sample	615	20.5	29.3	23.7	18.4	8.1
价格无关心指向 indifferent orientation	106	31.1	30.2	21.7	10.4	6.6
中间层 medium	280	24.6	28.9	24.6	15.4	6.4
价格重视指向 careful orientation	229	10.5	29.3	23.6	25.8	10.9

4-3 不同消费者层的学历构成/ Educational Composition of Market Segments

	人数 Number	小学以下 Primary School or Below	初中 Middle School	高中/中专/技校 High School/ Technical Secondary School	大学专科 2-3Year College	大学本科 4-5Year College	研究生或以上 Graduate or Above
样本 Sample	613	9.6	32.3	39.5	13.4	5.1	0.2
价格无关心指向 indifferent orientation	105	6.7	23.8	42.9	16.2	10.5	0.0
中间层 medium	280	7.9	29.6	41.8	15.7	4.6	0.4
价格重视指向 careful orientation	228	13.2	39.5	35.1	9.2	3.1	0.0

4-4 不同消费者层的职业构成/ Occupational Composition of Market Segments

	人数 Number	劳务职 Labor	技能职 Skill	服务职 Service	事务职 Assistance	销售职 Marketing	技术职 Technique	技术类以外的专门职 Professional Outside Technique
样本 Sample	614	15.3	9.1	7.0	1.0	2.3	4.2	6.0
价格无关心指向 indifferent orientation	106	7.5	10.4	3.8	1.9	2.8	0.9	6.6
中间层 medium	280	15.7	9.3	8.2	1.4	3.6	6.4	4.3
价格重视指向 careful orientation	228	18.4	8.3	7.0	0.0	0.4	3.1	7.9

续前表 continued

	人数 Number	自由职业者 Free Lance	企业/公司管理人员 Manager	行政管理人员/公务员 Administrator	经营者 Businessman	个体户 Self-employed Labor	军警 Military &Police
样本 Sample	614	0.7	3.4	2.0	0.7	8.6	0.2
价格无关心指向 indifferent orientation	106	0.9	5.7	2.8	0.9	17.0	0.9
中间层 medium	280	0.7	3.6	1.8	0.7	7.1	0.0
价格重视指向 careful orientation	228	0.4	2.2	1.8	0.4	6.6	0.0

续前表 continued

	人数 Number	高中/中专/技校学生 High School/ Technical Secondary School Student	大学生 College Student	研究生 Graduate Student	家庭主妇 Housewife	离退休人员 Retired	下岗、待业人员 Unemployed	其他 Others
样本 Sample	614	8.6	2.3	0.0	3.1	9.9	14.2	1.5
价格无关心指向 indifferent orientation	106	15.1	3.8	0.0	1.9	4.7	11.3	0.9
中间层 medium	280	9.6	2.5	0.0	2.1	7.5	13.6	1.8
价格重视指向 careful orientation	228	4.4	1.3	0.0	4.8	15.4	16.2	1.3

4-5 不同消费者层的婚姻状况/ Marital Status of Market Segments

	人数 Number	已婚 Married	未婚 Single	离异 Divorced	丧偶 Widowed
样本 Sample	608	66.9	28.1	4.1	0.8
价格无关心指向 indifferent orientation	106	58.5	37.7	2.8	0.9
中间层 medium	274	62.4	35.0	2.6	0.0
价格重视指向 careful orientation	228	76.3	15.4	6.6	1.8

4-6 不同消费者层的个人月收入/ Individual Monthly Income of Market Segments

	有效样本量 Total	无收入 no income	500 元以下 below 500 yuan	501-1000 元 yuan	1001-1500 元 yuan	1501-2000 元 yuan	2001-3000 元 yuan	3001-4000 元 yuan	4001-5000 元 yuan	5000 元以上 over 5000 yuan
样本 Sample	613	20.4	34.3	31.3	9.0	2.6	2.0	0.2	0.2	0.2
价格无关心指向 indifferent orientation	105	21.9	25.7	25.7	14.3	6.7	4.8	0.0	0.0	1.0
中间层 medium	280	21.8	29.6	35.7	8.2	2.5	1.8	0.0	0.4	0.0
价格重视指向 careful orientation	228	18.0	43.9	28.5	7.5	C.9	0.9	0.4	0.0	0.0

5. 信息交流指标/ Information Communication Index

5-1 不同消费者层的性别构成/ Gender Composition of Market Segments

	人数 Number	男性 Male	女性 Female
样本 Sample	615	50.7	49.3
信息消极指向 negative orientation	47	53.2	46.8
中间层 medium	339	54.3	45.7
信息积极指向 active orientation	229	45.0	55.0

5-2 不同消费者层的年龄构成/ Age Composition of Market Segments

	人数	16-24 岁 Age	25-34 岁 Age	35-44 岁 Age	45-54 岁 Age	55-60 岁 Age
样本 Sample	615	20.5	29.3	23.6	18.5	8.1
信息消极指向 negative orientation	47	25.5	23.4	19.1	14.9	17.0
中间层 medium	339	20.4	28.9	23.3	19.5	8.0
信息积极指向 active orientation	229	19.7	31.0	24.9	17.9	6.6

5-3 不同消费者层的学历构成/ Educational Composition of Market Segments

	人数 Number	小学以下 Primary School or Below	初中 Middle School	高中/中专/技校 Hign School/Technical Secondary School	大学专科 2-3Year College	大学本科 4-5Year College	研究生或以上 Graduate or Above
样本 Sample	613	9.6	32.3	39.3	13.4	5.2	0.2
信息消极指向 negative orientation	47	10.6	46.8	29.8	10.6	2.1	0.0
中间层 medium	338	10.1	29.3	39.1	15.7	5.6	0.3
信息积极指向 active orientation	228	8.8	33.8	41.7	10.5	5.3	0.0

5-4 不同消费者层的职业构成/ Occupational Composition of Market Segments

	人数 Number	劳务职 Labor	技能职 Skill	服务职 Service	事务职 Assistance	销售职 Marketing	技术职 Technique	技术类以外的专门职 Professional Outside Technique
样本 Sample	614	15.3	9.3	7.0	1.1	2.1	4.4	5.9
信息消极指向 negative orientation	47	14.9	12.8	8.5	0.0	2.1	0.0	2.1
中间层 medium	339	14.2	9.1	6.2	1.5	1.2	5.0	7.1
信息积极指向 active orientation	228	17.1	8.8	7.9	0.9	3.5	4.4	4.8

续前表 continued

	人数 Number	自由职业者 Free Lance	企业/公司管理人员 Manager	行政管理人员/公务员 Administrator	经营者 Businessman	个体户 Self-employed Labor	军警 Military &Police
样本 Sample	614	0.7	3.6	2.0	0.5	8.6	0.2
信息消极指向 negative orientation	47	0.0	4.3	2.1	0.0	4.3	0.0
中间层 medium	339	1.2	4.4	2.7	0.6	9.4	0.3
信息积极指向 active orientation	228	0.0	2.2	0.9	0.4	8.3	0.0

续前表 continued

	人数 Number	高中/中专/技校学生 High School/Technical Secondary School Student	大学生 College Student	研究生 Graduate Student	家庭主妇 Housewife	离退休人员 Retired	下岗、待业人员 Unemployed	其他 Others
样本 Sample	614	8.6	2.1	0.0	3.1	9.9	14.2	1.5
信息消极指向 negative orientation	47	8.5	0.0	0.0	10.6	12.8	17.0	0.0
中间层 medium	339	9.4	2.1	0.0	1.8	10.3	12.4	1.2
信息积极指向 active orientation	228	7.5	2.6	0.0	3.5	8.8	16.2	2.2

5-5 不同消费者层的婚姻状况/ Marital Status of Market Segments

	人数 Number	已婚 Married	未婚 Single	离异 Divorced	丧偶 Widowed
样本 Sample	608	67.3	27.8	4.1	0.8
信息消极指向 negative orientation	47	70.2	27.7	2.1	0.0
中间层 medium	333	69.4	27.6	2.4	0.6
信息积极指向 active orientation	228	63.6	28.1	7.0	1.3

5-6 不同消费者层的个人月收入/ Individual Monthly Income of Market Segments

	有效样本量 Total	无收入 no income	500 元以下 below 500 yuan	501-1000 元 yuan	1001-1500 元 yuan	1501-2000 元 yuan	2001-3000 元 yuan	3001-4000 元 yuan	4001-5000 元 yuan	5000 元以上 over 5000 yuan
样本 Sample	613	20.1	34.3	31.5	9.1	2.6	2.0	0.2	0.2	0.2
信息积极指向 active orientation	47	27.7	36.2	31.9	0.0	2.1	2.1	0.0	0.0	0.0
中间层 medium	338	19.5	31.4	32.0	12.1	2.1	2.4	0.0	0.3	0.3
信息消极指向 negative orientation	228	19.3	38.2	30.7	6.6	3.5	1.3	0.4	0.0	0.0

6.武汉消费者层 / Market Segmentation in Wuhan

1.时尚流行指标/ Fads Popular Index

1-1 不同消费者层的性别构成/ Gender Composition of Market Segments

	人数 Number	男性 Male	女性 Female
样本 Sample	632	48.3	51.7
平实生活指向 simple living orientation	330	51.2	48.8
时尚流行指向 fashion orientation	302	45.0	55.0

1-2 不同消费者层的年龄构成/ Age Composition of Market Segments

	人数 Number	16-24 岁 Age	25-34 岁 Age	35-44 岁 Age	45-54 岁 Age	55-60 岁 Age
样本 Sample	632	21.0	28.5	24.8	17.7	7.9
平实生活指向 simple living orientation	330	16.7	24.2	26.4	21.2	11.5
时尚流行指向 fashion orientation	302	25.8	33.1	23.2	13.9	4.0

1-3 不同消费者层的学历构成/ Educational Composition of Market Segments

	人数 Number	小学以下 Primary School or Below	初中 Middle School	高中/中专/技校 High School/ Technical Secondary School	大学专科 2-3Year College	大学本科 4-5Year College	研究生或以上 Graduate or Above
样本 Sample	631	4.6	24.2	44.5	17.4	8.4	0.8
平实生活指向 simple living orientation	329	6.1	25.5	45.3	13.4	9.1	0.6
时尚流行指向 fashion orientation	302	3.0	22.8	43.7	21.9	7.6	1.0

1-4 不同消费者层的职业构成/ Occupational Composition of Market Segments

	人数 Number	劳务职 Labor	技能职 Skill	服务职 Service	事务职 Assistance	销售职 Marketing	技术职 Technique	技术类以外的专门职 Professional Outside Technique
样本 Sample	625	12.2	8.3	6.6	2.7	2.7	4.5	8.2
平实生活指向 simple living orientation	327	13.8	7.0	6.1	3.1	1.5	5.5	7.6
时尚流行指向 fashion orientation	298	10.4	9.7	7.0	2.3	4.0	3.4	8.7

续前表 continued

	人数 Number	自由职业者 Free Lance	企业/公司管理人员 Manager	行政管理人员/公务员 Administrator	经营者 Businessman	个体户 Self-employed Labor	军警 Military &Police
样本 Sample	625	0.6	4.5	5.6	1.3	5.0	0.0
平实生活指向 simple living orientation	327	0.6	3.4	6.1	1.8	4.0	0.0
时尚流行指向 fashion orientation	298	0.7	5.7	5.0	0.7	6.0	0.0

续前表 continued

	人数 Number	高中/中专/技校学生 High School/ Technical Secondary School Student	大学生 College Student	研究生 Graduate Student	家庭主妇 Housewife	离退休人员 Retired	下岗、待业人员 Unemployed	其他 Others
样本 Sample	625	4.5	5.1	0.0	1.1	7.8	16.3	3.0
平实生活指向 simple living orientation	327	4.9	3.4	0.0	1.2	11.6	15.3	3.1
时尚流行指向 fashion orientation	298	4.0	7.0	0.0	1.0	3.7	17.4	3.0

1-5 不同消费者层的婚姻状况/ Marital Status of Market Segments

	人数 Number	已婚 Married	未婚 Single	离异 Divorced	丧偶 Widowed
样本 Sample	625	67.2	29.3	1.3	2.2
平实生活指向 simple living orientation	329	70.5	24.6	1.2	3.6
时尚流行指向 fashion orientation	296	63.5	34.5	1.4	0.7

1-6 不同消费者层的个人月收入/ Individual Monthly Income of Market Segments

	有效样本量 Total	无收入 no income	500 元以下 below 500 yuan	501-1000 元 yuan	1001-1500 元 yuan	1501-2000 元 yuan	2001-3000 元 yuan	3001-4000 元 yuan	4001-5000 元 yuan	5000 元以上 over 5000 yuan
样本 Sample	631	17.7	30.6	35.8	10.5	3.0	2.1	0.2	0.2	0.0
平实生活指向 simple living orientation	329	15.5	34.3	37.7	9.4	1.5	1.2	0.0	0.3	0.0
时尚流行指向 fashion orientation	302	20.2	26.5	33.8	11.6	4.6	3.0	0.3	0.0	0.0

2.广告态度指标/ Advertising Attitude Index

2-1 不同消费者层的性别构成/ Gender Composition of Market Segments

	人数 Number	男性 Male	女性 Female
样本 Sample	634	48.4	51.6
广告淡漠指向 indifferent orientation	188	53.2	46.8
中间层 medium	373	47.2	52.8
信赖广告指向 loyal orientation	73	42.5	57.5

2-2 不同消费者层的年龄构成/ Age Composition of Market Segments

	人数 Number	16-24 岁 Age	25-34 岁 Age	35-44 岁 Age	45-54 岁 Age	55-60 岁 Age
样本 Sample	634	21.0	28.5	24.9	17.7	7.9
广告淡漠指向 indifferent orientation	188	15.4	22.9	32.4	20.2	9.0
中间层 medium	373	22.0	31.1	22.0	17.2	7.8
信赖广告指向 loyal orientation	73	30.1	30.1	20.5	13.7	5.5

2-3 不同消费者层的学历构成/ Educational Composition of Market Segments

	人数 Number	小学以下 Primary School or Below	初中 Middle School	高中/中专/技校 High School/ Technical Secondary School	大学专科 2-3Year College	大学本科 4-5Year College	研究生或以上 Graduate or Above
样本 Sample	633	4.6	24.3	44.5	17.4	8.4	0.8
广告淡漠指向 indifferent orientation	188	6.4	25.0	42.0	16.0	9.6	1.1
中间层 medium	372	3.0	23.1	47.6	17.2	8.6	0.5
信赖广告指向 loyal orientation	73	8.2	28.8	35.6	21.9	4.1	1.4

2-4 不同消费者层的职业构成/ Occupational Composition of Market Segments

	人数 Number	劳务职 Labor	技能职 Skill	服务职 Service	事务职 Assistance	销售职 Marketing	技术职 Technique	技术类以外的专门职 Professional Outside Technique
样本 Sample	627	12.3	8.5	6.5	2.7	2.7	4.5	8.1
广告淡漠指向 indifferent orientation	186	11.3	7.5	5.9	3.8	3.2	6.5	8.6
中间层 medium	368	12.2	8.7	7.3	2.4	2.4	4.1	8.2
信赖广告指向 loyal orientation	73	15.1	9.6	4.1	1.4	2.7	1.4	6.8

续前表 continued

	人数 Number	自由职业者 Free Lance	企业/公司管理人员 Manager	行政管理人员/公务员 Administrator	经营者 Businessman	个体户 Self-employed Labor	军警 Military & Police
样本 Sample	627	0.6	4.5	5 6	1.3	4.9	0.0
广告淡漠指向 indifferent orientation	186	0.0	4.3	4 8	0.0	7.5	0.0
中间层 medium	368	0.8	5.2	6.3	1.9	3.0	0.0
信赖广告指向 loyal orientation	73	1.4	1.4	4.1	1.4	8.2	0.0

续前表 continued

	人数 Number	高中/中专/技校学生 High School/ Technical Secondary School Student	大学生 College Student	研究生 Graduate Student	家庭主妇 Housewife	离退休人员 Retired	下岗、待业人员 Unemployed	其他 Others
样本 Sample	627	4.5	5.1	0.0	[illegible].1	7.8	16.3	3.0
广告淡漠指向 indifferent orientation	186	3.8	3.8	0.0	[illegible].1	9.1	16.1	2.7
中间层 medium	368	5.2	4.9	0.0	0.8	7.9	15.2	3.5
信赖广告指向 loyal orientation	73	2.7	9.6	0.0	2.7	4.1	21.9	1.4

2-5 不同消费者层的婚姻状况/ Marital Status of Market Segments

	人数 Number	已婚 Married	未婚 Single	离异 Divorced	丧偶 Widowed
样本 Sample	627	67.3	29.2	1.3	2.2
广告淡漠指向 indifferent orientation	185	71.9	22.7	1.1	4.3
中间层 medium	369	65.0	32.0	1.6	1.4
信赖广告指向 loyal orientation	73	67.1	31.5	0.0	1.4

2-6 不同消费者层的个人月收入/ Individual Monthly Income of Market Segments

	有效样本量 Total	无收入 no income	500 元以下 below 500 yuan	501-1000 元 yuan	1001-1500 元 yuan	1501-2000 元 yuan	2001-3000 元 yuan	3001-4000 元 yuan	4001-5000 元 yuan	5000 元以上 over 5000 yuan
样本 Sample	633	17.7	30.6	35.9	10.4	3.0	2.1	0.2	0.2	0.0
广告淡漠指向 indifferent orientation	188	12.2	36.2	37.2	12.2	2.1	0.0	0.0	0.0	0.0
中间层 medium	372	17.2	28.5	37.4	10.2	3.2	3.0	0.3	0.3	0.0
信赖广告指向 loyal orientation	73	34.2	27.4	24.7	6.8	4.1	2.7	0.0	0.0	0.0

3.饮食健康指标/ Fads & Drink Quality Index

3-1 不同消费者层的性别构成/ Gender Composition of Market Segments

	人数 Number	男性 Male	女性 Female
样本 Sample	631	48.5	51.5
饮食"温饱"指向 "basic" orientation	220	57.3	42.7
中间层 medium	284	46.8	53.2
健康营养指向 health & nutrition orientation	127	37.0	63.0

3-2 不同消费者层的年龄构成/ Age Composition of Market Segments

	人数 Number	16-24 岁 Age	25-34 岁 Age	35-44 岁 Age	45-54 岁 Age	55-60 岁 Age
样本 Sample	631	20.9	28.7	25.0	17.4	7.9
饮食"温饱"指向 "basic" orientation	220	22.7	27.7	25.5	15.0	9.1
中间层 medium	284	22.5	28.9	25.4	16.5	6.7
健康营养指向 health & nutrition orientation	127	14.2	29.9	23.6	23.6	8.7

3-3 不同消费者层的学历构成/ Educational Composition of Market Segments

	人数 Number	小学以下 Primary School or Below	初中 Middle School	高中/中专/技校 High School/ Technical Secondary School	大学专科 2-3Year College	大学本科 4-5Year College	研究生或以上 Graduate or Above
样本 Sample	630	4.6	24.1	44.4	17.6	8.4	0.8
饮食"温饱"指向 "basic" orientation	220	6.4	28.6	39.5	14.1	9.5	1.8
中间层 medium	283	4.2	21.9	45.6	20.5	7.4	0.4
健康营养指向 health & nutrition orientation	127	2.4	21.3	50.4	17.3	8.7	0.0

3-4 不同消费者层的职业构成/ Occupational Composition of Market Segments

	人数 Number	劳务职 Labor	技能职 Skill	服务职 Service	事务职 Assistance	销售职 Marketing	技术职 Technique	技术类以外的专门职 Professional Outside Technique
样本 Sample	624	12.2	8.3	6.7	2.7	2.7	4.5	8.2
饮食"温饱"指向 "basic" orientation	218	10.6	9.6	6.4	3.7	4.1	4.1	4.1
中间层 medium	281	13.9	7.5	7.8	2.5	1.4	5.0	10.7
健康营养指向 health & nutrition orientation	125	11.2	8.0	4.8	1.6	3.2	4.0	9.6

续前表 continued

	人数 Number	自由职业者 Free Lance	企业/公司管理人员 Manager	行政管理人员/公务员 Administrator	经营者 Businessman	个体户 Self-employed Labor	军警 Military &Police
样本 Sample	624	0.6	4.5	5.6	1.3	5.0	0.0
饮食"温饱"指向 "basic" orientation	218	0.9	2.8	5.5	0.9	6.0	0.0
中间层 medium	281	0.4	4.3	5.7	1.4	3.6	0.0
健康营养指向 health & nutrition orientation	125	0.8	8.0	5.6	1.6	6.4	0.0

续前表 continued

	人数 Number	高中/中专/技校学生 High School/ Technical Secondary School Student	大学生 College Student	研究生 Graduate Student	家庭主妇 Housewife	离退休人员 Retired	下岗、待业人员 Unemployed	其他 Others
样本 Sample	624	4.5	5.1	0.0	1.1	7.7	16.2	3.0
饮食"温饱"指向 "basic" orientation	218	5.0	5.5	0.0	0.9	8.7	18.3	2.8
中间层 medium	281	3.9	6.0	0.0	1.4	6.8	17.1	0.7
健康营养指向 health & nutrition orientation	125	4.8	2.4	0.0	0.8	8.0	10.4	8.8

3-5 不同消费者层的婚姻状况/ Marital Status of Market Segments

	人数 Number	已婚 Married	未婚 Single	离异 Divorced	丧偶 Widowed
样本 Sample	623	67.3	29.2	1.3	2.2
饮食"温饱"指向 "basic" orientation	218	61.9	32.6	1.8	3.7
中间层 medium	279	67.4	30.5	1.1	1.1
健康营养指向 health & nutrition orientation	126	76.2	20.6	0.8	2.4

3-6 不同消费者层的个人月收入/ Individual Monthly Income of Market Segments

	有效样本量 Total	无收入 no income	500元以下 below 500 yuan	501-1000元 yuan	1001-1500元 yuan	1501-2000元 yuan	2001-3000元 yuan	3001-4000元 yuan	4001-5000元 yuan	5000元以上 over 5000 yuan
样本 Sample	630	17.6	30.8	35.7	10.5	3.0	2.1	0.2	0.2	0.0
饮食"温饱"指向 "basic" orientation	220	18.6	33.6	34.1	8.2	2.3	2.7	0.0	0.5	0.0
中间层 medium	283	18.7	28.6	38.2	11.0	2.5	1.1	0.0	0.0	0.0
健康营养指向 health & nutrition orientation	127	13.4	30.7	33.1	13.4	5.5	3.1	0.8	0.0	0.0

4.价格态度指标/ Price Attitude Index

4-1 不同消费者层的性别构成/ Gender Composition of Market Segments

	人数 Number	男性 Male	女性 Female
样本 Sample	634	48.6	51.4
价格无关心指向 indifferent orientation	84	66.7	33.3
中间层 medium	306	49.0	51.0
价格重视指向 careful orientation	244	41.8	58.2

4-2 不同消费者层的年龄构成/ Age Composition of Market Segments

	人数 Number	16-24岁 Age	25-34岁 Age	35-44岁 Age	45-54岁 Age	55-60岁 Age
样本 Sample	634	20.8	28.7	24.9	17.7	7.9
价格无关心指向 indifferent orientation	84	26.2	26.2	28.6	11.9	7.1
中间层 medium	306	27.1	32.4	22.2	12.4	5.9
价格重视指向 careful orientation	244	11.1	25.0	27.0	26.2	10.7

4-3 不同消费者层的学历构成/ Educational Composition of Market Segments

	人数 Number	小学以下 Primary School or Below	初中 Middle School	高中/中专/技校 High School/ Technical Secondary School	大学专科 2-3Year College	大学本科 4-5Year College	研究生或以上 Graduate or Above
样本 Sample	633	4.6	24.3	44.4	17.5	8.4	0.8
价格无关心指向 indifferent orientation	84	0.0	19.0	44.0	19.0	14.3	3.6
中间层 medium	306	2.3	18.3	49.0	20.3	9.5	0.7
价格重视指向 careful orientation	243	9.1	33.7	38.7	13.6	4.9	0.0

4-4 不同消费者层的职业构成/ Occupational Composition of Market Segments

	人数 Number	劳务职 Labor	技能职 Skill	服务职 Service	事务职 Assistance	销售职 Marketing	技术职 Technique	技术类以外的专门职 Professional Outside Technique
样本 Sample	627	12.3	8.5	6.7	2.7	2.7	4.5	8.1
价格无关心指向 indifferent orientation	84	9.5	4.8	8.3	4.8	1.2	2.4	11.9
中间层 medium	300	10.3	9.7	7.0	2.7	4.7	6.0	8.0
价格重视指向 careful orientation	243	15.6	8.2	5.8	2.1	0.8	3.3	7.0

续前表 continued

	人数 Number	自由职业者 Free Lance	企业/公司管理人员 Manager	行政管理人员/公务员 Administrator	经营者 Businessman	个体户 Self-employed Labor	军警 Military & Police
样本 Sample	627	0.6	4.5	5.6	1.3	4.9	0.0
价格无关心指向 indifferent orientation	84	0.0	2.4	9.5	2.4	7.1	0.0
中间层 medium	300	1.0	5.3	5.3	1.7	3.7	0.0
价格重视指向 careful orientation	243	0.4	4.1	4.5	0.4	5.8	0.0

续前表 continued

	人数 Number	高中/中专/技校学生 High School/ Technical Secondary School Student	大学生 College Student	研究生 Graduate Student	家庭主妇 Housewife	离退休人员 Retired	下岗、待业人员 Unemployed	其他 Others
样本 Sample	627	4.3	5.1	0.0	1.1	7.8	16.3	3.0
价格无关心指向 indifferent orientation	84	8.3	7.1	0.0	0.0	2.4	15.5	2.4
中间层 medium	300	4.7	6.0	0.0	1.0	5.3	15.7	2.0
价格重视指向 careful orientation	243	2.5	3.3	0.0	1.6	12.8	17.3	4.5

4-5 不同消费者层的婚姻状况/ Marital Status of Market Segments

	人数 Number	已婚 Married	未婚 Single	离异 Divorced	丧偶 Widowed
样本 Sample	626	67.4	29.1	1.3	2.2
价格无关心指向 indifferent orientation	84	60.7	36.9	0.0	2.4
中间层 medium	302	60.3	36.8	1.0	2.0
价格重视指向 careful orientation	240	78.8	16.7	2.1	2.5

4-6 不同消费者层的个人月收入/ Individual Monthly Income of Market Segments

	有效样本量 Total	无收入 no income	500 元以下 below 500 yuan	501-1000 元 yuan	1001-1500 元 yuan	1501-2000 元 yuan	2001-3000 元 yuan	3001-4000 元 yuan	4001-5000 元 yuan	5000 元以上 over 5000 yuan
样本 Sample	633	17.5	30.6	35.9	10.6	3.0	2.1	0.2	0.2	0.0
价格无关心指向 indifferent orientation	84	17.9	23.8	29.8	17.9	6.0	3.6	0.0	1.2	0.0
中间层 medium	305	19.0	25.2	38.4	12.5	2.0	2.6	0.3	0.0	0.0
价格重视指向 careful orientation	244	15.6	39.8	34.8	5.7	3.3	0.8	0.0	0.0	0.0

5.信息交流指标/ Information Communication Index

5-1 不同消费者层的性别构成/ Gender Composition of Market Segments

	人数 Number	男性 Male	女性 Female
样本 Sample	631	48.3	51.7
信息消极指向 negative orientation	46	39.1	60.9
中间层 medium	363	52.3	47.7
信息积极指向 active orientation	222	43.7	56.3

5-2 不同消费者层的年龄构成/ Age Composition of Market Segments

	人数 Number	16-24 岁 Age	25-34 岁 Age	35-44 岁 Age	45-54 岁 Age	55-60 岁 Age
样本 Sample	631	20.9	28.7	25.0	17.4	7.9
信息消极指向 negative orientation	46	10.9	17.4	26.1	23.9	21.7
中间层 medium	363	21.8	31.7	23.7	16.8	6.1
信息积极指向 active orientation	222	21.6	26.1	27.0	17.1	8.1

5-3 不同消费者层的学历构成/ Educational Composition of Market Segments

	人数 Number	小学以下 Primary School or Below	初中 Middle School	高中/中专/技校 High School/ Technical Secondary School	大学专科 2-3Year College	大学本科 4-5Year College	研究生或以上 Graduate or Above
样本 Sample	630	4.4	24.4	44.8	17.3	8.4	0.6
信息消极指向 negative orientation	46	10.9	41.3	34.8	6.5	6.5	0.0
中间层 medium	362	3.9	21.8	46.1	18.2	9.1	0.8
信息积极指向 active orientation	222	4.1	25.2	44.6	18.0	7.7	0.5

5-4 不同消费者层的职业构成/ Occupational Composition of Market Segments

	人数 Number	劳务职 Labor	技能职 Skill	服务职 Service	事务职 Assistance	销售职 Marketing	技术职 Technique	技术类以外的专门职 Professional Outside Technique
样本 Sample	624	12.3	8.5	6.7	2.7	2.7	4.3	8.2
信息消极指向 negative orientation	46	13.0	13.0	4.3	2.2	4.3	2.2	2.2
中间层 medium	358	12.0	7.8	8.1	3.4	2.8	4.2	7.8
信息积极指向 active orientation	220	12.7	8.6	5.0	1.8	2.3	5.0	10.0

续前表 continued

	人数 Number	自由职业者 Free Lance	企业/公司管理人员 Manager	行政管理人员/公务员 Administrator	经营者 Businessman	个体户 Self-employed Labor	军警 Military & Police
样本 Sample	624	0.6	4.3	5.4	1.3	5.0	0.0
信息消极指向 negative orientation	46	0.0	0.0	2.2	0.0	6.5	0.0
中间层 medium	358	0.8	4.7	5.3	0.8	4.2	0.0
信息积极指向 active orientation	220	0.5	4.5	6.4	2.3	5.9	0.0

续前表 continued

	人数 Number	高中/中专/技校学生 High School/ Technical Secondary School Student	大学生 College Student	研究生 Graduate Student	家庭主妇 Housewife	离退休人员 Retired	下岗、待业人员 Unemployed	其他 Others
样本 Sample	624	4.5	5.1	0.0	1.1	7.7	16.3	3.0
信息消极指向 negative orientation	46	6.5	4.3	0.0	0.0	17.4	19.6	2.2
中间层 medium	358	4.7	5.0	0.0	1.4	7.0	17.3	2.5
信息积极指向 active orientation	220	3.6	5.5	0.0	0.9	6.8	14.1	4.1

5-5 不同消费者层的婚姻状况/ Marital Status of Market Segments

	人数 Number	已婚 Married	未婚 Single	离异 Divorced	丧偶 Widowed
样本 Sample	623	67.3	29.2	1.3	2.2
信息消极指向 negative orientation	46	76.1	21.7	0.0	2.2
中间层 medium	356	63.5	32.0	2.0	2.5
信息积极指向 active orientation	221	71.5	26.2	0.5	1.8

5-6 不同消费者层的个人月收入/ Individual Monthly Income of Market Segments

	有效样本量 Total	无收入 no income	500 元以下 below 500 yuan	501-1000 元 yuan	1001-1500 元 yuan	1501-2000 元 yuan	2001-3000 元 yuan	3001-4000 元 yuan	4001-5000 元 yuan	5000 元以上 over 5000 yuan
样本 Sample	630	17.8	30.6	35.9	10.3	3.0	2.1	0.2	0.2	0.0
信息积极指向 active orientation	46	19.6	47.8	26.1	6.5	0.0	0.0	0.0	0.0	0.0
中间层 medium	362	17.1	29.3	39.0	9.4	3.3	1.7	0.0	0.3	0.0
信息消极指向 negative orientation	222	18.5	29.3	32.9	12.6	3.2	3.2	0.5	0.0	0.0

7.西安消费者层 / Market Segmentation in Xi'an

1. 时尚流行指标/ Fads Popular Index

1-1 不同消费者层的性别构成/ Gender Composition of Market Segments

	人数 Number	男性 Male	女性 Female
样本 Sample	599	50.4	49.6
平实生活指向 simple living orientation	341	54.0	46.0
时尚流行指向 fashion orientation	258	45.7	54.3

1-2 不同消费者层的年龄构成/ Age Composition of Market Segments

	人数	16-24 岁 Age	25-34 岁 Age	35-44 岁 Age	45-54 岁 Age	55-60 岁 Age
样本 Sample	599	20.9	30.2	25.0	15.7	8.2
平实生活指向 simple living orientation	341	16.7	24.3	27.3	19.9	11.7
时尚流行指向 fashion orientation	258	26.4	38.0	22.1	10.1	3.5

1-3 不同消费者层的学历构成/ Educational Composition of Market Segments

	人数 Number	小学以下 Primary School or Below	初中 Middle School	高中/中专/技校 High school/ Technical Secondary School	大学专科 2-3 Year College	大学本科 4-5 Year College	研究生或以上 Graduate or Above
样本 Sample	596	2.7	20.3	47.3	19.0	9.9	0.8
平实生活指向 simple living orientation	340	3.8	23.5	45.9	16.5	9.1	1.2
时尚流行指向 fashion orientation	256	1.2	16.0	49.2	22.3	10.9	0.4

1-4 不同消费者层的职业构成/ Occupational Composition of Market Segments

	人数 Number	劳务职 Labor	技能职 Skill	服务职 Service	事务职 Assistance	销售职 Marketing	技术职 Technique	技术类以外的专门职 Professional Outside Technique
样本 Sample	598	15.9	8.2	7.2	1.0	3.0	7.2	9.9
平实生活指向 simple living orientation	341	18.5	8.2	7.3	0.9	2.9	7.6	8.5
时尚流行指向 fashion orientation	257	12.5	8.2	7.0	1.2	3.1	6.6	11.7

续前表 continued

	人数 Number	自由职业者 Free Lance	企业/公司管理人员 Manager	行政管理人员/公务员 Administrator	经营者 Businessman	个体户 Self-employed Labor	军警 Military & Police
样本 Sample	598	1.0	4.8	4.0	1.0	7.0	0.7
平实生活指向 simple living orientation	341	0.3	4.7	4.1	0.9	5.0	0.6
时尚流行指向 fashion orientation	257	1.9	5.1	3.9	1.2	9.7	0.8

续前表 continued

	人数 Number	高中/中专/技校 High School /Technical Secondary School Student	大学生 College Student	研究生 Graduate Student	家庭主妇 Housewife	离退休人员 Retired	下岗、待业人员 Unemployed	其他 Others
样本 Sample	598	6.9	4.0	0.3	1.7	8.2	7.9	0.2
平实生活指向 simple living orientation	341	5.3	4.4	0.3	1.8	11.4	7.3	0.0
时尚流行指向 fashion orientation	257	8.9	3.5	0.4	1.6	3.9	8.6	0.4

1-5 不同消费者层的婚姻状况/ Marital Status of Market Segments

	人数 Number	已婚 Married	未婚 Single	离异 Divorced	丧偶 Widowed
样本 Sample	595	422	151	16	6
平实生活指向 simple living orientation	338	259	66	8	5
时尚流行指向 fashion orientation	257	163	85	8	1

1-6 不同消费者层的个人月收入/ Individual Monthly Income of Market Segments

	有效样本量 Total	无收入 no income	500 元以下 below 500 yuan	501-1000 元 yuan	1001-1500 元 yuan	1501-2000 元 yuan	2001-3000 元 yuan	3001-4000 元 yuan	4001-5000 元 yuan	5000 元以上 over 5000 yuan
样本 Sample	598	17.4	29.3	39.8	8.9	1.8	1.0	0.8	0.7	0.3
平实生活指向 simple living orientation	341	16.1	34.3	39.9	6.5	1.5	0.6	0.6	0.3	0.3
时尚流行指向 fashion orientation	257	19.1	22.6	39.7	12.1	2.3	1.6	1.2	1.2	0.4

2. 广告态度指标/ Advertising Attitude Index

2-1 不同消费者层的性别构成/ Gender Composition of Market Segments

	人数 Number	男性 Male	女性 Female
样本 Sample	597	50.3	49.7
广告淡漠指向 indifferent orientation	184	50.5	49.5
中间层 medium	334	50.6	49.4
信赖广告指向 loyal orientation	79	48.1	51.9

2-2 不同消费者层的年龄构成/ Age Composition of Market Segments

	人数 Number	16-24 岁 Age	25-34 岁 Age	35-44 岁 Age	45-54 岁 Age	55-60 岁 Age
样本 Sample	597	20.8	30.2	25.3	15.6	8.2
广告淡漠指向 indifferent orientation	184	17.4	27.2	27.7	14.7	13.0
中间层 medium	334	21.9	32.6	23.4	16.5	5.7
信赖广告指向 loyal orientation	79	24.1	26.6	27.8	13.9	7.6

2-3 不同消费者层的学历构成/ Educational Composition of Market Segments

	人数 Number	小学以下 Primary School or Below	初中 Middle School	高中/中专/技校 High school/ Technical Secondary School	大学专科 2-3 Year College	大学本科 4-5 Year College	研究生或以上 Graduate or Above
样本 Sample	594	2.7	20.4	47.3	18.9	9.9	0.8
广告淡漠指向 indifferent orientation	184	2.7	20.7	48.4	20.1	7.1	1.1
中间层 medium	332	2.7	19.6	46.4	18.4	12.3	0.6
信赖广告指向 loyal orientation	78	2.6	23.1	48.7	17.9	6.4	1.3

2-4 不同消费者层的职业构成/ Occupational Composition of Market Segments

	人数 Number	劳务职 Labor	技能职 Skill	服务职 Service	事务职 Assistance	销售职 Marketing	技术职 Technique	技术类以外的专门职 Professional Outside Technique
样本 Sample	596	16.1	8.2	7.0	1.0	3.0	7.2	9.9
广告淡漠指向 indifferent orientation	184	17.4	8.7	9.8	0.5	3.3	4.3	8.7
中间层 medium	334	14.4	8.4	5.7	1.5	3.3	8.7	11.4
信赖广告指向 loyal orientation	78	20.5	6.4	6.4	0.0	1.3	7.7	6.4

续前表 continued

	人数 Number	自由职业者 Free Lance	企业/公司管理人员 Manager	行政管理人员/公务员 Administrator	经营者 Businessman	个体户 Self-employed Labor	军警 Military & Police
样本 Sample	596	1.0	4.9	4.0	0.8	7.0	0.7
广告淡漠指向 indifferent orientation	184	0.5	3.8	7.1	1.1	5.4	0.0
中间层 medium	334	0.9	5.4	1.8	0.9	7.8	0.9
信赖广告指向 loyal orientation	78	2.6	5.1	6.4	0.0	7.7	1.3

续前表 continued

	人数 Number	高中/中专/技校 High School /Technical Secondary School Student	大学生 College Student	研究生 Graduate Student	家庭主妇 Housewife	离退休人员 Retired	下岗、待业人员 Unemployed	其他 Others
样本 Sample	**596**	**6.9**	**4.0**	**0.3**	**1.8**	**7.9**	**7.9**	**0.2**
广告淡漠指向 indifferent orientation	184	4.9	4.3	0.5	1.6	9.8	8.2	0.0
中间层 medium	334	7.8	3.6	0.3	2.4	6.6	8.1	0.3
信赖广告指向 loyal orientation	78	7.7	5.1	0.0	0.0	9.0	6.4	0.0

2-5 不同消费者层的婚姻状况/ Marital Status of Market Segments

	人数 Number	已婚 Married	未婚 Single	离异 Divorced	丧偶 Widowed
样本 Sample	**593**	**71.0**	**25.3**	**2.7**	**1.0**
广告淡漠指向 indifferent orientation	181	74.0	22.1	1.7	2.2
中间层 medium	333	69.1	26.7	3.6	0.6
信赖广告指向 loyal orientation	79	72.2	26.6	1.3	0.0

2-6 不同消费者层的个人月收入/ Individual Monthly Income of Market Segments

	有效样本量 Total	无收入 no income	500元以下 below 500 yuan	501-1000元 yuan	1001-1500元 yuan	1501-2000元 yuan	2001-3000元 yuan	3001-4000元 yuan	4001-5000元 yuan	5000元以上 over 5000 yuan
样本 Sample	**596**	**17.3**	**29.4**	**39.9**	**8.9**	**1.8**	**0.8**	**0.8**	**0.7**	**0.3**
广告淡漠指向 indifferent orientation	184	15.8	31.5	41.3	7.6	1.6	0.5	0.5	0.5	0.5
中间层 medium	334	18.0	28.4	38.6	10.2	1.5	1.2	0.9	0.9	0.3
信赖广告指向 loyal orientation	78	17.9	28.2	42.3	6.4	3.8	0.0	1.3	0.0	0.0

3. 饮食健康指标/ Foods & Drink Index

3-1 不同消费者层的性别构成/ Gender Composition of Market Segments

	人数 Number	男性 Male	女性 Female
样本 Sample	**601**	**50.2**	**49.8**
饮食"温饱"指向 "basic" orientation	233	59.2	40.8
中间层 medium	272	46.0	54.0
健康营养指向 health & nutrition orientation	96	40.6	59.4

3-2 不同消费者层的年龄构成/ Age Composition of Market Segments

	人数 Number	16-24岁 Age	25-34岁 Age	35-44岁 Age	45-54岁 Age	55-60岁 Age
样本 Sample	**601**	**20.8**	**30.1**	**25.1**	**15.8**	**8.2**
饮食"温饱"指向 "basic" orientation	233	20.6	27.0	25.8	16.7	9.9
中间层 medium	272	21.3	34.9	24.6	13.6	5.5
健康营养指向 health & nutrition orientation	96	19.8	24.0	25.0	19.8	11.5

3-3 不同消费者层的学历构成/ Educational Composition of Market Segments

	人数 Number	小学以下 Primary School or Below	初中 Middle School	高中/中专/技校 High school/ Technical Secondary School	大学专科 2-3 Year College	大学本科 4-5 Year College	研究生或以上 Graduate or Above
样本 Sample	598	2.7	20.4	47.3	18.9	9.9	0.8
饮食"温饱"指向 "basic" orientation	233	4.3	26.2	40.3	18.9	8.6	1.7
中间层 medium	270	1.9	14.1	54.1	19.6	10.0	0.4
健康营养指向 health & nutrition orientation	95	1.1	24.2	45.3	16.8	12.6	0.0

3-4 不同消费者层的职业构成/ Occupational Composition of Market Segments

	人数 Number	劳务职 Labor	技能职 Skill	服务职 Service	事务职 Assistance	销售职 Marketing	技术职 Technique	技术类以外的专门职 Professional Outside Technique
样本 Sample	600	16.0	8.2	7.2	1.0	3.0	7.2	9.8
饮食"温饱"指向 "basic" orientation	232	19.4	8.2	6.5	0.4	2.2	8.2	5.6
中间层 medium	272	14.7	9.6	8.5	1.1	2.9	7.7	12.1
健康营养指向 health & nutrition orientation	96	11.5	4.2	5.2	2.1	5.2	3.1	13.5

续前表 continued

	人数 Number	自由职业者 Free Lance	企业/公司管理人员 Manager	行政管理人员/公务员 Administrator	经营者 Businessman	个体户 Self-employed Labor	军警 Military & Police
样本 Sample	600	1.0	4.8	4.0	1.0	7.0	0.7
饮食"温饱"指向 "basic" orientation	232	0.9	3.4	5.2	0.9	5.6	0.0
中间层 medium	272	0.4	5.1	2.6	1.1	8.1	0.7
健康营养指向 health & nutrition orientation	96	3.1	7.3	5.2	1.0	7.3	2.1

续前表 continued

	人数 Number	高中/中专/技校 High School/ Technical Secondary School Student	大学生 College Student	研究生 Graduate Student	家庭主妇 Housewife	离退休人员 Retired	下岗、待业人员 Unemployed	其他 Others
样本 Sample	600	6.8	4.0	0.3	1.8	8.2	7.8	0.2
饮食"温饱"指向 "basic" orientation	232	7.8	6.0	0.4	1.7	9.5	7.8	0.4
中间层 medium	272	6.3	2.6	0.4	1.5	6.6	8.1	0.0
健康营养指向 health & nutrition orientation	96	6.3	3.1	0.0	3.1	9.4	7.3	0.0

3-5 不同消费者层的婚姻状况/ Marital Status of Market Segments

	人数 Number	已婚 Married	未婚 Single	离异 Divorced	丧偶 Widowed
样本 Sample	597	71.0	25.3	2.7	1.0
饮食"温饱"指向 "basic" orientation	231	69.3	25.1	3.9	1.7
中间层 medium	272	71.7	25.7	2.2	0.4
健康营养指向 health & nutrition orientation	94	73.4	24.5	1.1	1.1

3-6 不同消费者层的个人月收入/ Individual Monthly Income of Market Segments

	有效样本量 Total	无收入 no income	500元以下 below 500 yuan	501-1000元 yuan	1001-1500元 yuan	1501-2000元 yuan	2001-3000元 yuan	3001-4000元 yuan	4001-5000元 yuan	5000元以上 over 5000 yuan
样本 Sample	600	17.3	29.3	39.8	8.8	1.8	1.0	0.8	0.7	0.3
饮食"温饱"指向 "basic" orientation	233	21.5	27.0	42.5	5.6	1.7	1.3	0.0	0.0	0.4
中间层 medium	271	13.7	32.1	37.3	11.1	2.6	0.7	1.8	0.7	0.0
健康营养指向 health & nutrition orientation	96	17.7	27.1	40.6	10.4	0.0	1.0	0.0	2.1	1.0

4. 价格态度指标/ Price Attitude Index

4-1 不同消费者层的性别构成/ Gender Composition of Market Segments

	人数 Number	男性 Male	女性 Female
样本 Sample	597	49.9	50.1
价格无关心指向 indifferent orientation	142	60.6	39.4
中间层 medium	306	48.7	51.3
价格重视指向 careful orientation	149	42.3	57.7

4-2 不同消费者层的年龄构成/ Age Composition of Market Segments

	人数 Number	16-24岁 Age	25-34岁 Age	35-44岁 Age	45-54岁 Age	55-60岁 Age
样本 Sample	597	20.8	30.2	25.0	15.9	8.2
价格无关心指向 indifferent orientation	142	26.8	37.3	21.8	8.5	5.6
中间层 medium	306	21.9	32.0	21.2	17.6	7.2
价格重视指向 careful orientation	149	12.8	19.5	35.6	19.5	12.8

4-3 不同消费者层的学历构成/ Educational Composition of Market Segments

	人数 Number	小学以下 Primary School or Below	初中 Middle School	高中/中专/技校 High school/ Technical Secondary School	大学专科 2-3 Year College	大学本科 4-5 Year College	研究生或以上 Graduate or Above
样本 Sample	594	2.5	20.4	47.6	18.9	9.9	0.7
价格无关心指向 indifferent orientation	141	1.4	16.3	46.8	24.8	10.6	0.0
中间层 medium	304	2.0	18.1	46.4	20.1	12.8	0.7
价格重视指向 careful orientation	149	4.7	28.9	51.0	10.7	3.4	1.3

4-4 不同消费者层的职业构成/ Occupational Composition of Market Segments

	人数 Number	劳务职 Labor	技能职 Skill	服务职 Service	事务职 Assistance	销售职 Marketing	技术职 Technique	技术类以外的专门职 Professional Outside Technique
样本 Sample	596	15.9	8.1	7.2	1.0	3.0	7.0	9.9
价格无关心指向 indifferent orientation	142	12.0	8.5	7.0	1.4	2.1	9.2	10.6
中间层 medium	305	15.7	8.2	9.2	1.0	3.3	7.2	11.1
价格重视指向 careful orientation	149	20.1	7.4	3.4	0.7	3.4	4.7	6.7

续前表 continued

	人数 Number	自由职业者 Free Lance	企业/公司管理人员 Manager	行政管理人员/公务员 Administrator	经营者 Businessman	个体户 Self-employed Labor	军警 Military & Police
样本 Sample	596	1.0	4.9	3.9	1.0	7.0	0.7
价格无关心指向 indifferent orientation	142	0.0	6.3	2.8	2.1	6.3	0.0
中间层 medium	305	1.6	3.9	4.6	1.0	6.6	1.3
价格重视指向 careful orientation	149	0.7	5.4	3.4	0.0	8.7	0.0

续前表 continued

	人数 Number	高中/中专/技校 High School /Technical Secondary School Student	大学生 College Student	研究生 Graduate Student	家庭主妇 Housewife	离退休人员 Retired	下岗、待业人员 Unemployed	其他 Others
样本 Sample	596	6.9	4.0	0.3	1.8	8.2	7.9	0.2
价格无关心指向 indifferent orientation	142	10.6	2.8	0.0	2.8	3.5	11.3	0.7
中间层 medium	305	6.9	5.6	0.7	1.3	5.9	4.9	0.0
价格重视指向 careful orientation	149	3.4	2.0	0.0	2.0	17.4	10.7	0.0

4-5 不同消费者层的婚姻状况/ Marital Status of Market Segments

	人数 Number	已婚 Married	未婚 Single	离异 Divorced	丧偶 Widowed
样本 Sample	593	71.0	25.3	2.7	1.0
价格无关心指向 indifferent orientation	142	62.0	35.2	2.8	0.0
中间层 medium	303	71.0	25.1	3.0	1.0
价格重视指向 careful orientation	148	79.7	16.2	2.0	2.0

4-6 不同消费者层的个人月收入/ Individual Monthly Income of Market Segments

	有效样本量 Total	无收入 no income	500 元以下 below 500 yuan	501-1000 元 yuan	1001-1500 元 yuan	1501-2000 元 yuan	2001-3000 元 yuan	3001-4000 元 yuan	4001-5000 元 yuan	5000 元以上 over 5000 yuan
样本 Sample	596	17.3	29.5	40.1	8.6	1.8	1.0	0.8	0.7	0.2
价格无关心指向 indifferent orientation	141	23.4	22.7	33.3	11.3	3.5	2.1	2.8	0.7	0.0
中间层 medium	306	16.7	25.2	45.1	9.5	1.6	0.3	0.3	1.0	0.3
价格重视指向 careful orientation	149	12.8	45.0	36.2	4.0	0.7	1.3	0.0	0.0	0.0

5. 信息交流指标/ Information Communication Index

5-1 不同消费者层的性别构成/ Gender Composition of Market Segments

	人数 Number	男性 Male	女性 Female
样本 Sample	599	50.4	49.6
信息消极指向 negative orientation	69	59.4	40.6
中间层 medium	340	48.5	51.5
信息积极指向 active orientation	190	50.5	49.5

5-2 不同消费者层的年龄构成/ Age Composition of Market Segments

	人数 Number	16-24 岁 Age	25-34 岁 Age	35-44 岁 Age	45-54 岁 Age	55-60 岁 Age
样本 Sample	599	20.9	30.2	25.2	15.7	8.0
信息消极指向 negative orientation	69	20.3	29.0	21.7	18.8	10.1
中间层 medium	340	19.7	34.4	23.2	15.6	7.1
信息积极指向 active orientation	190	23.2	23.2	30.0	14.7	8.9

5-3 不同消费者层的学历构成/ Educational Composition of Market Segments

	人数 Number	小学以下 Primary School or Below	初中 Middle School	高中/中专/技校 High school/ Technical Secondary School	大学专科 2-3 Year College	大学本科 4-5 Year College	研究生或以上 Graduate or Above
样本 Sample	596	2.7	20.3	47.3	19.0	9.9	0.8
信息消极指向 negative orientation	69	4.3	18.8	50.7	15.9	10.1	0.0
中间层 medium	337	1.8	22.0	46.3	18.4	10.7	0.9
信息积极指向 active orientation	190	3.7	17.9	47.9	21.1	8.4	1.1

5-4 不同消费者层的职业构成/ Occupational Composition of Market Segments

	人数 Number	劳务职 Labor	技能职 Skill	服务职 Service	事务职 Assistance	销售职 Marketing	技术职 Technique	技术类以外的专门职 Professional Outside Technique
样本 Sample	598	16.1	8.2	7.2	1.0	3.0	7.2	9.9
信息消极指向 negative orientation	69	18.8	10.1	4.3	1.4	2.9	7.2	8.7
中间层 medium	340	14.7	7.6	10.0	0.9	3.5	6.8	11.5
信息积极指向 active orientation	189	17.5	8.5	3.2	1.1	2.1	7.9	7.4

续前表 continued

	人数 Number	自由职业者 Free Lance	企业/公司管理人员 Manager	行政管理人员/公务员 Administrator	经营者 Businessman	个体户 Self-employed Labor	军警 Military & Police
样本 Sample	598	1.0	4.8	3.8	1.0	7.0	0.7
信息消极指向 negative orientation	69	0.0	2.9	4.3	1.4	8.7	0.0
中间层 medium	340	0.9	5.0	3.8	1.5	6.8	0.3
信息积极指向 active orientation	189	1.6	5.3	3.7	0.0	6.9	1.6

续前表 continued

	人数 Number	高中/中专/技校 High School /Technical Secondary School Student	大学生 College Student	研究生 Graduate Student	家庭主妇 Housewife	离退休人员 Retired	下岗、待业人员 Unemployed	其他 Others
样本 Sample	598	6.9	4.0	0.3	1.7	8.2	7.9	0.2
信息消极指向 negative orientation	69	8.7	1.4	0.0	5.8	2.9	10.1	0.0
中间层 medium	340	5.6	3.8	0.3	1.8	7.1	7.9	0.3
信息积极指向 active orientation	189	8.5	5.3	0.5	0.0	12.2	6.9	0.0

5-5 不同消费者层的婚姻状况/ Marital Status of Market Segments

	人数 Number	已婚 Married	未婚 Single	离异 Divorced	丧偶 Widowed
样本 Sample	596	71.0	25.3	2.7	1.0
信息消极指向 negative orientation	68	76.5	20.6	2.9	0.0
中间层 medium	340	71.8	24.4	3.2	0.6
信息积极指向 active orientation	188	67.6	28.7	1.6	2.1

5-6 不同消费者层的个人月收入/ Individual Monthly Income of Market Segments

	有效样本量 Total	无收入 no income	500 元以下 below 500 yuan	501-1000 元 yuan	1001-1500 元 yuan	1501-2000 元 yuan	2001-3000 元 yuan	3001-4000 元 yuan	4001-5000 元 yuan	5000 元以上 over 5000 yuan
样本 Sample	598	17.4	29.4	39.6	8.9	1.8	1.0	0.8	0.7	0.3
信息积极指向 active orientation	69	23.2	20.3	43.5	8.7	2.9	0.0	0.0	1.4	0.0
中间层 medium	339	16.5	30.4	38.9	9.1	1.2	1.5	0.9	0.9	0.6
信息消极指向 negative orientation	190	16.8	31.1	39.5	8.4	2.6	0.5	1.1	0.0	0.0

8.沈阳消费者层 / Market Segmentation in Shenyang

1. 时尚流行指标/ Fads Popular Index

1-1 不同消费者层的性别构成/ Gender Composition of Market Segments

	人数 Number	男性 Male	女性 Female
样本 Sample	601	49.8	50.2
平实生活指向 simple living orientation	292	56.5	43.5
时尚流行指向 fashion orientation	309	43.4	56.6

1-2 不同消费者层的年龄构成/ Age Composition of Market Segments

	人数 Number	16-24 岁 Age	25-34 岁 Age	35-44 岁 Age	45-54 岁 Age	55-60 岁 Age
样本 Sample	601	21.3	29.8	25.3	15.6	8.0
平实生活指向 simple living orientation	292	14.7	28.1	25.0	20.2	12.0
时尚流行指向 fashion orientation	309	27.5	31.4	25.6	11.3	4.2

1-3 不同消费者层的学历构成/ Educational Composition of Market Segments

	人数 Number	小学以下 Primary School or Below	初中 Middle School	高中/中专/技校 High School/ Technical Secondary School	大学专科 2-3Year College	大学本科 4-5Year College	研究生或以上 Graduate or Above
样本 Sample	601	2.8	35.1	37.8	15.1	8.7	0.5
平实生活指向 simple living orientation	292	4.8	39.7	30.5	15.1	9.9	0.0
时尚流行指向 fashion orientation	309	1.0	30.7	44.7	15.2	7.4	1.0

1-4 不同消费者层的职业构成/ Occupational Composition of Market Segments

	人数 Number	劳务职 Labor	技能职 Skill	服务职 Service	事务职 Assistance	销售职 Marketing	技术职 Technique	技术类以外的专门职 Professional Outside Technique
样本 Sample	601	13.5	10.6	7.5	1.7	2.8	4.5	7.3
平实生活指向 simple living orientation	292	14.0	10.6	5.1	1.7	2.4	5.8	4.8
时尚流行指向 fashion orientation	309	12.9	10.7	9.7	1.6	3.2	3.2	9.7

续前表 continued

	人数 Number	自由职业者 Free Lance	企业/公司管理人员 Manager	行政管理人员/公务员 Administrator	经营者 Businessman	个体户 Self-employed Labor	军警 Military & Police
样本 Sample	601	0.3	5.5	3.0	1.2	7.7	0.7
平实生活指向 simple living orientation	292	0.3	7.2	3.1	1.0	7.2	0.7
时尚流行指向 fashion orientation	309	0.3	3.9	2.9	1.3	8.1	0.6

续前表 continued

	人数 Number	高中/中专/技校学生 High School/ Technical Secondary School Student	大学生 College Student	研究生 Graduate Student	家庭主妇 Housewife	离退休人员 Retired	下岗、待业人员 Unemployed	其他 Others
样本 Sample	601	8.7	3.0	0.0	3.0	5.7	11.3	2.2
平实生活指向 simple living orientation	292	7.5	3.1	0.0	4.5	6.8	13.0	1.0
时尚流行指向 fashion orientation	309	9.7	2.9	0.0	1.6	4.5	9.7	3.2

1-5 不同消费者层的婚姻状况/ Marital Status of Market Segments

	人数 Number	已婚 Married	未婚 Single	离异 Divorced	丧偶 Widowed
样本 Sample	594	68.0	28.3	1.7	2.0
平实生活指向 simple living orientation	289	72.7	23.2	2.1	2.1
时尚流行指向 fashion orientation	305	63.6	33.1	1.3	2.0

1-6 不同消费者层的个人月收入/ Individual Monthly Income of Market Segments

	有效样本量 Total	无收入 no income	500 元以下 below 500 yuan	501-1000 元 yuan	1001-1500 元 yuan	1501-2000 元 yuan	2001-3000 元 yuan	3001-4000 元 yuan	4001-5000 元 yuan	5000 元以上 over 5000 yuan
样本 Sample	599	22.4	30.1	36.4	7.7	1.3	2.2	0.0	0.0	0.0
平实生活指向 simple living orientation	291	22.3	29.6	35.7	8.2	1.7	2.4	0.0	0.0	0.0
时尚流行指向 fashion orientation	308	22.4	30.5	37.0	7.1	1.0	1.9	0.0	0.0	0.0

2. 广告态度指标/ Advertising Attitude Index

2-1 不同消费者层的性别构成/ Gender Composition of Market Segments

	人数 Number	男性 Male	女性 Female
样本 Sample	601	49.8	50.2
广告淡漠指向 indifferent orientation	172	57.0	43.0
中间层 medium	354	44.4	55.6
信赖广告指向 loyal orientation	75	58.7	41.3

2-2 不同消费者层的年龄构成/ Age Composition of Market Segments

	人数 Number	16-24 岁 Age	25-34 岁 Age	35-44 岁 Age	45-54 岁 Age	55-60 岁 Age
样本 Sample	601	21.3	29.8	25.3	15.6	8.0
广告淡漠指向 indifferent orientation	172	23.3	23.8	25.2	17.4	9.3
中间层 medium	354	21.5	32.2	25.1	13.8	7.3
信赖广告指向 loyal orientation	75	16.0	32.0	24.0	20.0	8.0

2-3 不同消费者层的学历构成/ Educational Composition of Market Segments

	人数 Number	小学以下 Primary School or Below	初中 Middle School	高中/中专/技校 High School/ Technical Secondary School	大学专科 2-3Year College	大学本科 4-5Year College	研究生或以上 Graduate or Above
样本 Sample	601	2.8	35.1	37.8	15.1	8.7	0.5
广告淡漠指向 indifferent orientation	172	2.9	40.1	38.4	8.7	9.9	0.0
中间层 medium	354	3.1	31.4	38.7	16.9	9.0	0.8
信赖广告指向 loyal orientation	75	1.3	41.3	32.0	21.3	4.0	0.0

2-4 不同消费者层的职业构成/ Occupational Composition of Market Segments

	人数 Number	劳务职 Labor	技能职 Skill	服务职 Service	事务职 Assistance	销售职 Marketing	技术职 Technique	技术类以外的专门职 Professional Outside Technique
样本 Sample	601	13.5	10.6	7.5	1.7	2.8	4.5	7.3
广告淡漠指向 indifferent orientation	172	14.5	12.8	7.0	1.2	0.6	3.5	8.1
中间层 medium	354	12.7	9.6	7.3	1.4	3.7	5.9	6.2
信赖广告指向 loyal orientation	75	14.7	10.7	9.3	4.0	4.0	0.0	10.7

续前表 continued

	人数 Number	自由职业者 Free Lance	企业/公司管理人员 Manager	行政管理人员/公务员 Administrator	经营者 Businessman	个体户 Self-employed Labor	军警 Military &Police
样本 Sample	601	0.3	5.5	3.0	1.2	7.7	0.7
广告淡漠指向 indifferent orientation	172	0.6	7.6	1.7	0.6	5.8	0.6
中间层 medium	354	0.3	4.5	3.7	0.8	9.3	0.8
信赖广告指向 loyal orientation	75	0.0	5.3	2.7	4.0	4.0	0.0

续前表 continued

	人数 Number	高中/中专/技校学生 High School/ Technical Secondary School Student	大学生 College Student	研究生 Graduate Student	家庭主妇 Housewife	离退休人员 Retired	下岗、待业人员 Unemployed	其他 Others
样本 Sample	601	8.7	3.0	0.0	3.0	5.7	11.3	2.2
广告淡漠指向 indifferent orientation	172	8.7	2.9	0.0	4.1	5.2	12.8	1.7
中间层 medium	354	9.3	3.1	0.0	2.3	5.4	11.3	2.3
信赖广告指向 loyal orientation	75	5.3	2.7	0.0	4.0	8.0	8.0	2.7

2-5 不同消费者层的婚姻状况/ Marital Status of Market Segments

	人数 Number	已婚 Married	未婚 Single	离异 Divorced	丧偶 Widowed
样本 Sample	594	68.0	28.3	1.7	2.0
广告淡漠指向 indifferent orientation	170	66.5	30.6	0.6	2.4
中间层 medium	349	67.3	28.7	2.3	1.7
信赖广告指向 loyal orientation	75	74.7	21.3	1.3	2.7

2-6 不同消费者层的个人月收入/ Individual Monthly Income of Market Segments

	有效样本量 Total	无收入 no income	500元以下 below 500 yuan	501-1000元 yuan	1001-1500元 yuan	1501-2000元 yuan	2001-3000元 yuan	3001-4000元 yuan	4001-5000元 yuan	5000元以上 over 5000 yuan
样本 Sample	599	22.4	30.1	36.4	7.7	1.3	2.2	0.0	0.0	0.0
广告淡漠指向 indifferent orientation	172	22.7	25.6	40.1	7.6	1.2	2.9	0.0	0.0	0.0
中间层 medium	352	22.7	31.8	34.9	7.7	1.1	1.7	0.0	0.0	0.0
信赖广告指向 loyal orientation	75	20.0	32.0	34.7	8.0	2.7	2.7	0.0	0.0	0.0

3. 饮食健康指标/ Foods & Drink Index

3-1 不同消费者层的性别构成/ Gender Composition of Market Segments

	人数 Number	男性 Male	女性 Female
样本 Sample	601	49.8	50.2
饮食"温饱"指向 "basic" orientation	193	59.1	40.9
中间层 medium	265	45.7	54.3
健康营养指向 health & nutrition orientation	143	44.8	55.2

3-2 不同消费者层的年龄构成/ Age Composition of Market Segments

	人数 Number	16-24岁 Age	25-34岁 Age	35-44岁 Age	45-54岁 Age	55-60岁 Age
样本 Sample	601	21.3	29.8	25.3	15.6	8.0
饮食"温饱"指向 "basic" orientation	193	17.1	33.7	24.4	16.1	8.8
中间层 medium	265	23.0	29.4	25.7	14.3	7.5
健康营养指向 health & nutrition orientation	143	23.8	25.2	25.9	17.5	7.7

3-3 不同消费者层的学历构成/ Educational Composition of Market Segments

	人数 Number	小学以下 Primary School or Below	初中 Middle School	高中/中专/技校 High School/ Technical Secondary School	大学专科 2-3Year College	大学本科 4-5Year College	研究生或以上 Graduate or Above
样本 Sample	601	2.8	35.1	37.8	15.1	8.7	0.5
饮食"温饱"指向 "basic" orientation	193	2.1	38.9	33.2	14.5	10.9	0.5
中间层 medium	265	3.8	31.3	40.8	15.5	7.9	0.8
健康营养指向 health & nutrition orientation	143	2.1	37.1	38.5	15.4	7.0	0.0

3-4 不同消费者层的职业构成/ Occupational Composition of Market Segments

	人数 Number	劳务职 Labor	技能职 Skill	服务职 Service	事务职 Assistance	销售职 Marketing	技术职 Technique	技术类以外的专门职 Professional Outside Technique
样本 Sample	601	13.5	10.6	7.5	1.7	2.8	4.5	7.3
饮食"温饱"指向 "basic" orientation	193	17.1	9.8	5.2	2.1	1.6	6.2	3.1
中间层 medium	265	12.1	12.1	6.4	1.5	3.0	4.2	9.4
健康营养指向 health & nutrition orientation	143	11.2	9.1	12.6	1.4	4.2	2.8	9.1

续前表 continued

	人数 Number	自由职业者 Free Lance	企业/公司管理人员 Manager	行政管理人员/公务员 Administrator	经营者 Businessman	个体户 Self-employed Labor	军警 Military &Police
样本 Sample	**601**	**0.3**	**5.5**	**3.0**	**1.2**	**7.7**	**0.7**
饮食"温饱"指向 "basic" orientation	193	1.0	5.7	3.1	2.1	8.3	1.0
中间层 medium	265	0.0	5.7	4.2	0.4	8.3	0.8
健康营养指向 health & nutrition orientation	143	0.0	4.9	0.7	1.4	5.6	0.0

续前表 continued

	人数 Number	高中/中专/技校学生 High School/ Technical Secondary School Student	大学生 College Student	研究生 Graduate Student	家庭主妇 Housewife	离退休人员 Retired	下岗、待业人员 Unemployed	其他 Others
样本 Sample	**601**	**8.7**	**3.0**	**0.0**	**3.0**	**5.7**	**11.3**	**2.2**
饮食"温饱"指向 "basic" orientation	193	7.3	3.6	0.0	3.6	5.7	11.9	1.6
中间层 medium	265	9.1	1.9	0.0	2.6	4.9	10.6	3.0
健康营养指向 health & nutrition orientation	143	9.8	4.2	0.0	2.8	7.0	11.9	1.4

3-5 不同消费者层的婚姻状况/ Marital Status of Market Segments

	人数 Number	已婚 Married	未婚 Single	离异 Divorced	丧偶 Widowed
样本 Sample	**594**	**68.0**	**28.3**	**1.7**	**2.0**
饮食"温饱"指向 "basic" orientation	192	69.8	26.0	1.6	2.6
中间层 medium	260	68.5	28.8	1.5	1.2
健康营养指向 health & nutrition orientation	142	64.8	30.3	2.1	2.8

3-6 不同消费者层的个人月收入/ Individual Monthly Income of Market Segments

	有效样本量 Total	无收入 no income	500 元以下 below 500 yuan	501-1000 元 yuan	1001-1500 元 yuan	1501-2000 元 yuan	2001-3000 元 yuan	3001-4000 元 yuan	4001-5000 元 yuan	5000 元以上 over 5000 yuan
样本 Sample	**599**	**22.4**	**30.1**	**36.4**	**7.7**	**1.3**	**2.2**	**0.0**	**0.0**	**0.0**
饮食"温饱"指向 "basic" orientation	192	19.8	30.2	36.5	8.3	1.0	4.2	0.0	0.0	0.0
中间层 medium	265	22.6	28.3	38.9	7.9	0.8	1.5	0.0	0.0	0.0
健康营养指向 health & nutrition orientation	142	25.4	33.1	31.7	6.3	2.8	0.7	0.0	0.0	0.0

4. 价格态度指标/ Price Attitude Index

4-1 不同消费者层的性别构成/ Gender Composition of Market Segments

	人数 Number	男性 Male	女性 Female
样本 Sample	**600**	**49.7**	**50.3**
价格无关心指向 indifferent orientation	105	67.6	32.4
中间层 medium	292	49.7	50.3
价格重视指向 careful orientation	203	40.4	59.6

4-2 不同消费者层的年龄构成/ Age Composition of Market Segments

	人数 Number	16-24 岁 Age	25-34 岁 Age	35-44 岁 Age	45-54 岁 Age	55-60 岁 Age
样本 Sample	600	21.3	29.7	25.3	15.7	8.0
价格无关心指向 indifferent orientation	105	27.6	35.2	2[illegible].0	12.4	3.8
中间层 medium	292	24.0	32.5	26.0	10.6	6.8
价格重视指向 careful orientation	203	14.3	22.7	26.6	24.6	11.8

4-3 不同消费者层的学历构成/ Educational Composition of Market Segments

	人数 Number	小学以下 Primary School or Below	初中 Middle School	高中/中专/技校 High School/ Technical Secondary School	大学专科 2-3Year College	大学本科 4-5Year College	研究生或以上 Graduate or Above
样本 Sample	600	2.8	35.2	37.8	15.0	8.7	0.5
价格无关心指向 indifferent orientation	105	1.0	20.0	43.8	19.0	16.2	0.0
中间层 medium	292	1.7	33.2	40.1	15.8	8.2	1.0
价格重视指向 careful orientation	203	5.4	45.8	31.5	11.8	5.4	0.0

4-4 不同消费者层的职业构成/ Occupational Composition of Market Segments

	人数 Number	劳务职 Labor	技能职 Skill	服务职 Service	事务职 Assistance	销售职 Marketing	技术职 Technique	技术类以外的专门职 Professional Outside Technique
样本 Sample	600	13.5	10.7	7.5	1.7	2.8	4.5	7.3
价格无关心指向 indifferent orientation	105	3.8	9.5	7.6	1.0	4.8	6.7	6.7
中间层 medium	292	16.8	9.2	8.2	2.1	2.7	4.8	7.9
价格重视指向 careful orientation	203	13.8	13.3	6.4	1.5	2.0	3.0	6.9

续前表 continued

	人数 Number	自由职业者 Free Lance	企业/公司管理人员 Manager	行政管理人员/公务员 Administrator	经营者 Businessman	个体户 Self-employed Labor	军警 Military & Police
样本 Sample	600	0.3	5.5	3.0	1.2	7.7	0.7
价格无关心指向 indifferent orientation	105	1.9	10.5	3.8	1.0	8.6	0.0
中间层 medium	292	0.0	6.2	3.1	1.7	7.9	0.7
价格重视指向 careful orientation	203	0.0	2.0	2.5	0.5	6.9	1.0

续前表 continued

	人数 Number	高中/中专/技校学生 High School/ Technical Secondary School Student	大学生 College Student	研究生 Graduate Student	家庭主妇 Housewife	离退休人员 Retired	下岗、待业人员 Unemployed	其他 Others
样本 Sample	600	8.7	3.0	0.0	3.0	5.7	11.2	2.2
价格无关心指向 indifferent orientation	105	12.4	4.8	0.0	0.0	2.9	14.3	0.0
中间层 medium	292	9.2	2.1	0.0	1.7	3.4	10.3	2.1
价格重视指向 careful orientation	203	5.9	3.4	0.0	6.4	10.3	10.8	3.4

4-5 不同消费者层的婚姻状况/ Marital Status of Market Segments

	人数 Number	已婚 Married	未婚 Single	离异 Divorced	丧偶 Widowed
样本 Sample	593	68.0	28.3	1.7	2.0
价格无关心指向 indifferent orientation	104	61.5	36.5	1.0	1.0
中间层 medium	287	66.2	31.7	1.7	0.3
价格重视指向 careful orientation	202	73.8	19.3	2.0	5.0

4-6 不同消费者层的个人月收入/ Individual Monthly Income of Market Segments

	有效样本量 Total	无收入 no income	500 元以下 below 500 yuan	501-1000 元 yuan	1001-1500 元 yuan	1501-2000 元 yuan	2001-3000 元 yuan	3001-4000 元 yuan	4001-5000 元 yuan	5000 元以上 over 5000 yuan
样本 Sample	598	22.4	29.9	36.5	7.7	1.3	2.2	0.0	0.0	0.0
价格无关心指向 indifferent orientation	104	26.9	20.2	33.7	11.5	1.0	6.7	0.0	0.0	0.0
中间层 medium	292	21.2	26.7	39.7	8.2	2.1	2.1	0.0	0.0	0.0
价格重视指向 careful orientation	202	21.8	39.6	33.2	5.0	0.5	0.0	0.0	0.0	0.0

5. 信息交流指标/ Information Communication Index

5-1 不同消费者层的性别构成/ Gender Composition of Market Segments

	人数 Number	男性 Male	女性 Female
样本 Sample	600	49.8	50.2
信息消极指向 negative orientation	55	47.3	52.7
中间层 medium	313	48.2	51.8
信息积极指向 active orientation	232	52.6	47.4

5-2 不同消费者层的年龄构成/ Age Composition of Market Segments

	人数 Number	16-24 岁 Age	25-34 岁 Age	35-44 岁 Age	45-54 岁 Age	55-60 岁 Age
样本 Sample	600	21.3	29.7	25.3	15.7	8.0
信息消极指向 negative orientation	55	27.3	29.1	29.1	10.9	3.6
中间层 medium	313	22.4	28.4	26.5	15.3	7.3
信息积极指向 active orientation	232	18.5	31.5	22.8	17.2	9.9

5-3 不同消费者层的学历构成/ Educational Composition of Market Segments

	人数 Number	小学以下 Primary School or Below	初中 Middle School	高中/中专/技校 High School/ Technical Secondary School	大学专科 2-3Year College	大学本科 4-5Year College	研究生或以上 Graduate or Above
样本 Sample	600	2.8	35.0	37.8	15.2	8.7	0.5
信息消极指向 negative orientation	55	0.0	49.1	38.2	9.1	3.6	0.0
中间层 medium	313	3.2	33.5	38.0	15.3	9.3	0.6
信息积极指向 active orientation	232	3.0	33.6	37.5	16.4	9.1	0.4

5-4 不同消费者层的职业构成/ Occupational Composition of Market Segments

	人数 Number	劳务职 Labor	技能职 Skill	服务职 Service	事务职 Assistance	销售职 Marketing	技术职 Technique	技术类以外的专门职 Professional Outside Technique
样本 Sample	600	13.5	10.5	7.5	1.7	2.8	4.5	7.3
信息消极指向 negative orientation	55	20.0	3.6	9.1	1.8	1.8	1.8	1.8
中间层 medium	313	12.8	11.2	7.7	1.6	3.5	6.7	7.0
信息积极指向 active orientation	232	12.9	11.2	6.9	1.7	2.2	2.2	9.1

续前表 continued

	人数 Number	自由职业者 Free Lance	企业/公司管理人员 Manager	行政管理人员/公务员 Administrator	经营者 Businessman	个体户 Self-employed Labor	军警 Military &Police
样本 Sample	600	0.3	5.5	3.0	1.2	7.7	0.7
信息消极指向 negative orientation	55	1.8	1.8	1.8	1.8	9.1	0.0
中间层 medium	313	0.0	6.1	3.2	0.6	6.1	0.6
信息积极指向 active orientation	232	0.4	5.6	3.0	1.7	9.5	0.9

续前表 continued

	人数 Number	高中/中专/技校学生 High School/ Technical Secondary School Student	大学生 College Student	研究生 Graduate Student	家庭主妇 Housewife	离退休人员 Retired	下岗、待业人员 Unemployed	其他 Others
样本 Sample	600	8.7	3.0	0.0	3.0	5.7	11.3	2.2
信息消极指向 negative orientation	55	16.4	0.0	0.0	1.8	3.6	20.0	1.8
中间层 medium	313	9.3	2.9	0.0	3.2	5.8	10.2	1.6
信息积极指向 active orientation	232	6.0	3.9	0.0	3.0	6.0	10.8	3.0

5-5 不同消费者层的婚姻状况/ Marital Status of Market Segments

	人数 Number	已婚 Married	未婚 Single	离异 Divorced	丧偶 Widowed
样本 Sample	594	68.0	28.3	1.7	2.0
信息消极指向 negative orientation	55	63.6	36.4	0.0	0.0
中间层 medium	307	65.5	30.3	2.0	2.3
信息积极指向 active orientation	232	72.4	23.7	1.7	2.2

5-6 不同消费者层的个人月收入/ Individual Monthly Income of Market Segments

	有效样本量 Total	无收入 no income	500 元以下 below 500 yuan	501-1000 元 yuan	1001-1500 元 yuan	1501-2000 元 yuan	2001-3000 元 yuan	3001-4000 元 yuan	4001-5000 元 yuan	5000 元以上 over 5000 yuan
样本 Sample	598	22.4	30.1	36.3	7.7	1.3	2.2	0.0	0.0	0.0
信息积极指向 active orientation	55	30.9	29.1	32.7	5.5	0.0	1.8	0.0	0.0	0.0
中间层 medium	311	22.2	30.2	37.3	7.4	1.6	1.3	0.0	0.0	0.0
信息消极指向 negative orientation	232	20.7	30.2	35.8	8.6	1.3	3.4	0.0	0.0	0.0

第三篇　消费者日常生活形态
Part III　Consumers' Everyday Life

- 电器及耐用消费品拥有情况
  Possession of Home Electronic and Durable Products
- 服务性产品消费情况　Services Usage
- 消费信息接触情况　Consuming Information Contact
- 休闲活动　Leisure Activities
- 旅游　Travel
- 社会、生活态度　Attitudes and Values

1. 电器及耐用消费品拥有情况
Possession of Home Electronic and Durable Products

● 北京 / Beijing

1-1 家中现在拥有电器及耐用消费品排名/ Ranking of the Home Electronic and Durable Products Presently Possessed

注：本题为多选题，合计百分比超过 100%（Multiple answers）

		人次 Person-time	百分比 Percent
1	彩色电视机 color TV	1000	98.8
2	电冰箱 refrigerator	968	95.7
3	电风扇 electronic fan	935	92.4
4	洗衣机 washing machine	924	91.3
5	录音机 recorder	842	83.2
6	照相机 camera	754	74.5
7	磁带随身听 walkman	724	71.5
8	抽油烟机 kitchen ventilator	713	70.5
9	煤气热水器 gas water heater	608	60.1
10	影碟机 VCD player	589	58.2
11	录/放像机 VTR	574	56.7
12	微波炉 microwave oven	548	54.2
13	空调机 air-conditioner	529	52.3
14	电子游戏机 video game player	466	46.0
15	吸尘器 vacuum cleaner	389	38.4
16	电热水壶 electronic thermos	370	36.6
16	音响 Hi-Fi stereo	370	36.6
17	电暖气 electronic heater	288	28.5
18	榨汁机 juice extractor	262	25.9
18	加湿器 humidifier	262	25.9
19	饮水机 water dispenser	225	22.2
20	电热水器 electronic water heater	222	21.9
21	冰柜 freezers	209	20.7
22	电子辞典 quick-machine interpreter	203	20.1
23	CD 随身听 Discman	174	17.2
24	电烤箱 electric oven	165	16.3
25	食物加工机 food processor	148	14.6
26	摄像机 video camera	105	10.4
27	空气净化器 air purifier	97	9.6
28	煤气烤箱 gas oven	95	9.4
29	数码相机 digital camera	88	8.7
30	摩托车 motorcycle	77	7.6
31	消毒碗柜 cooking utensil sterilize	68	6.7
31	DVD	68	6.7
32	传真机 fax-machine	44	4.3
33	钢琴 piano	39	3.9
34	MD	20	2.0
35	洗碗机 dish washer	18	1.8
35	烘干机 dryer	18	1.8
36	数字摄像机 digital video camera	17	1.7

n=1012

1-2 计划未来一年内购买的电器及耐用消费品排名/ Ranking of the Home Electronic and Durable Products to be Purchased Next Year

注：本题为多选题，合计百分比超过 100%（Multiple answers）

		人次 Person-time	百分比 Percent
1	空调机 air-conditioner	198	19.6
2	饮水机 water dispenser	178	17.6
3	彩色电视机 color TV	147	14.5
4	电冰箱 refrigerator	131	12.9
5	洗衣机 washing machine	121	12.0
6	DVD	119	11.8
7	微波炉 microwave oven	108	10.7
8	摄像机 video camera	93	9.2
9	影碟机 VCD player	92	9.1
10	照相机 camera	88	8.7
11	数码相机 digital camera	87	8.6
12	榨汁机 juice extractor	85	8.4
12	抽油烟机 kitchen ventilator	85	8.4
12	加湿器 humidifier	85	8.4
13	消毒碗柜 cooking utensil sterilize	74	7.3
14	空气净化器 air purifier	70	6.9
15	电热水器 electronic water heater	68	6.7
15	电子辞典 quick-machine interpreter	68	6.7
15	电烤箱 electric oven	68	6.7
16	音响 Hi-Fi stereo	66	6.5
17	CD 随身听 Discman	64	6.3
18	电热水壶 electronic thermos	61	6.0
19	煤气热水器 gas water heater	52	5.1
20	电暖气 electronic heater	50	4.9
21	吸尘器 vacuum cleaner	47	4.6
22	食物加工机 food processor	43	4.2
23	传真机 fax-machine	42	4.2
24	洗碗机 dish washer	40	4.0
25	冰柜 freezers	38	3.8
26	数字摄像机 digital video camera	32	3.2
27	MD	30	3.0
28	摩托车 motorcycle	29	2.9
29	烘干机 dryer	19	1.9
29	磁带随身听 walkman	19	1.9
30	钢琴 piano	17	1.7
31	录/放像机 VTR	15	1.5
32	录音机 recorder	13	1.3
33	电风扇 electronic fan	10	1.0
34	电子游戏机 video game player	8	0.8
34	煤气烤箱 gas oven	8	0.8

n=1012

● 上海 / Shanghai

1-1 家中现在拥有电器及耐用消费品排名/ Ranking of the Home Electronic and Durable Products Presently Possessed

注：本题为多选题，合计百分比超过 100%（Multiple answers）

排名 Ranking		人次 Person-time	百分比 Percent
1	彩色电视机 color TV	1000	98.6
2	电冰箱 refrigerator	967	95.4
3	电风扇 electronic fan	959	94.6
4	洗衣机 washing machine	846	83.4
5	录音机 recorder	802	79.1
6	微波炉 microwave oven	757	74.7
7	空调机 air-conditioner	685	67.6
8	磁带随身听 walkman	642	63.3
9	影碟机 VCD player	632	62.3
10	抽油烟机 kitchen ventilator	620	61.1
11	煤气热水器 gas water heater	575	56.7
12	电暖气 electronic heater	534	52.7
13	照相机 camera	490	48.3
14	吸尘器 vacuum cleaner	483	47.6
15	录/放像机 VTR	479	47.2
16	电子游戏机 video game player	445	43.9
17	饮水机 water dispenser	409	40.3
18	电热水壶 electronic thermos	343	33.8
18	音响 Hi-Fi stereo	343	33.8
19	榨汁机 juice extractor	224	22.1
20	电子辞典 quick-machine interpreter	186	18.3
21	CD 随身听 Discman	177	17.5
22	电热水器 electronic water heater	142	14.0
23	空气净化器 air purifier	135	13.3
24	食物加工机 food professor	128	12.6
25	电烤箱 electronic oven	111	10.9
26	数码相机 digital camera	65	6.4
27	冰柜 freezers	63	6.2
27	消毒碗柜 cooking utensil sterilize	63	6.2
28	摄像机 video camera	56	5.5
29	DVD	48	4.7
30	摩托车 motorcycle	47	4.6
31	传真机 fax-machine	37	3.6
31	钢琴 piano	37	3.6
32	烘干机 dryer	32	3.2
33	加湿器 humidifier	25	2.5
34	MD	18	1.8
35	洗碗机 dish washer	16	1.6
36	数字摄像机 digital video camera	12	1.2
37	煤气烤箱 gas oven	9	0.9

n=1014

1-2 计划未来一年内购买的电器及耐用消费品排名/ Ranking of the Home Electronic and Durable Products to be Purchased Next Year

注：本题为多选题，合计百分比超过 100%（Multiple answers）

排名 Ranking		人次 Person-time	百分比 Percent
1	饮水机 water dispenser	158	15.6
2	彩色电视机 color TV	130	12.8
3	DVD	125	12.3
4	数码相机 digital camera	116	11.4
5	消毒碗柜 cooking utensil sterilize	111	10.9
6	CD 随身听 Discman	109	10.7
7	洗衣机 washing machine	94	9.3
8	电冰箱 refrigerator	93	9.2
9	榨汁机 juice extractor	92	9.1
10	摄像机 video camera	86	8.5
11	空气净化器 air purifier	84	8.3
11	电子辞典 quick-machine interpreter	84	8.3
12	洗碗机 dish washer	82	8.1
13	煤气热水器 gas water heater	79	7.8
14	吸尘器 vacuum cleaner	78	7.7
15	空调机 air-conditioner	74	7.3
16	抽油烟机 kitchen ventilator	67	6.6
17	食物加工机 food professor	61	6.0
18	音响 Hi-Fi stereo	55	5.4
19	烘干机 dryer	51	5.0
20	电热水器 electronic water heater	50	4.9
21	影碟机 VCD player	49	4.8
22	照相机 camera	48	4.7
23	传真机 fax-machine	45	4.4
24	摩托车 motorcycle	44	4.3
24	微波炉 microwave oven	44	4.3
25	电热水壶 electronic thermos	42	4.1
25	电暖气 electronic heater	42	4.1
25	电烤箱 electronic oven	42	4.1
26	MD	39	3.8
27	数字摄像机 digital video camera	37	3.6
28	加湿器 humidifier	31	3.1
29	冰柜 freezers	28	2.8
30	钢琴 piano	20	2.0
31	磁带随身听 walkman	18	1.8
32	录音机 recorder	15	1.5
32	电子游戏机 video game player	15	1.5
33	煤气烤箱 gas oven	10	1.0
34	电风扇 electronic fan	7	0.7
34	录/放像机 VTR	7	0.7

n=1014

● 广州 / Guangzhou

1-1 家中现在拥有电器及耐用消费品排名/ Ranking of the Home Electronic and Durable Products Presently Possessed

注：本题为多选题，合计百分比超过 100%（Multiple answers）

		人次 Person-time	百分比 Percent
1	彩色电视机 color TV	1022	98.8
2	电风扇 electronic fan	986	95.4
3	电冰箱 refrigerator	960	92.8
4	洗衣机 washing machine	920	89.0
5	煤气热水器 gas water heater	754	72.9
6	录音机 recorder	712	68.9
7	影碟机 VCD player	666	64.4
8	抽油烟机 kitchen ventilator	655	63.3
9	消毒碗柜 cooking utensil sterilize	631	61.0
10	空调机 air-conditioner	624	60.3
11	音响 Hi-Fi stereo	526	50.9
12	照相机 camera	505	48.8
13	电热水壶 electronic thermos	448	43.3
14	磁带随身听 walkman	443	42.8
15	电子游戏机 video game player	384	37.1
16	录/放像机 VTR	348	33.7
17	微波炉 microwave oven	338	32.7
18	摩托车 motorcycle	320	30.9
19	CD 随身听 Discman	228	22.1
20	榨汁机 juice extractor	198	19.1
20	电热水器 electronic water heater	198	19.1
21	冰柜 freezers	194	18.8
22	饮水机 water dispenser	170	16.4
23	电子辞典 quick-machine interpreter	160	15.5
24	电暖气 electronic heater	135	13.1
25	数码相机 digital camera	114	11.0
26	DVD	99	9.6
27	吸尘器 vacuum cleaner	96	9.3
28	电烤箱 electronic oven	76	7.4
29	摄像机 video camera	58	5.6
30	洗碗机 dish washer	47	4.5
30	烘干机 dryer	47	4.5
31	空气净化器 air purifier	45	4.4
32	食物加工机 food processor	43	4.2
33	传真机 fax-machine	36	3.5
34	MD	32	3.1
35	钢琴 piano	22	2.1
36	加湿器 humidifier	13	1.3
37	数字摄像机 digital video camera	12	1.2
38	煤气烤箱 gas oven	4	0.4

n=1034

1-2 计划未来一年内购买的电器及耐用消费品排名/ Ranking of the Home Electronic and Durable Products to be Purchased Next Year

注：本题为多选题，合计百分比超过 100%（Multiple answers）

		人次 Person-time	百分比 Percent
1	饮水机 water dispenser	165	16.0
2	DVD	129	12.5
3	消毒碗柜 cooking utensil sterilize	99	9.6
3	彩色电视机 color TV	99	9.6
4	CD 随身听 Discman	97	9.4
5	数码相机 digital camera	81	7.8
6	洗碗机 dish washer	80	7.7
7	空调机 air-conditioner	75	7.3
8	抽油烟机 kitchen ventilator	74	7.2
9	榨汁机 juice extractor	71	6.9
10	电冰箱 refrigerator	68	6.6
11	摩托车 motorcycle	66	6.4
11	电子辞典 quick-machine interpreter	66	6.4
12	洗衣机 washing machine	60	5.8
13	吸尘器 vacuum cleaner	56	5.4
13	MD	56	5.4
14	音响 Hi-Fi stereo	55	5.3
15	电暖气 electronic heater	52	5.0
16	电热水器 electronic water heater	49	4.7
16	摄像机 video camera	49	4.7
16	传真机 fax-machine	49	4.7
16	影碟机 VCD player	49	4.7
17	微波炉 microwave oven	47	4.5
18	电热水壶 electronic thermos	42	4.1
19	空气净化器 air purifier	41	4.0
20	电烤箱 electronic oven	39	3.8
21	照相机 camera	37	3.6
22	煤气热水器 gas water heater	35	3.4
22	数字摄像机 digital video camera	35	3.4
22	钢琴 piano	35	3.4
23	烘干机 dryer	31	3.0
24	磁带随身听 walkman	28	2.7
25	冰柜 freezers	25	2.4
25	食物加工机 food processor	25	2.4
26	加湿器 humidifier	22	2.1
27	电子游戏机 video game player	21	2.0
28	录/放像机 VTR	17	1.6
29	煤气烤箱 gas oven	16	1.5
30	电风扇 electronic fan	15	1.5
31	录音机 recorder	14	1.4

n=1034

● 重庆 / Chongqing

1-1 家中现在拥有电器及耐用消费品排名/ Ranking of the Home Electronic and Durable Products Presently Possessed

注：本题为多选题，合计百分比超过 100%（Multiple answers）

		人次 Person-time	百分比 Percent
1	电风扇 electronic fan	609	97.6
2	彩电 color TV	601	96.3
3	电冰箱 refrigerator	555	88.5
4	洗衣机 washing machine	540	86.5
5	影碟机 VCD player	361	57.9
6	煤气热水器 gas water heater	324	51.9
7	空调机 air-conditioner	320	51.3
8	录音机 recorder	318	51.0
9	磁带随身听 walkman	286	45.8
10	电热水壶 electronic thermos	246	39.4
11	电暖气 electronic heater	217	34.8
12	照相机 camera	210	33.7
13	音响 Hi-Fi stereo	209	33.5
14	电子游戏机 video game player	195	31.3
15	抽油烟机 kitchen ventilator	187	30.0
16	录/放像机 VTR	140	22.4
17	榨汁机 juice extractor	111	17.8
18	微波炉 microwave oven	108	17.3
19	电热水器 electronic water heater	97	15.5
20	饮水机 water dispenser	96	15.4
21	冰柜 freezers	68	10.9
22	DVD	51	8.2
23	食物加工机 food processor	42	6.7
24	吸尘器 vacuum cleaner	40	6.4
25	电烤箱 electric oven	37	5.9
26	数码相机 digital camera	30	4.8
27	电子辞典 quick-machine interpreter	28	4.5
28	CD 随身听 Discman	23	3.7
29	摩托车 motorcycle	19	3.0
30	消毒碗柜 cooking utensil sterilize	18	2.9
31	烘干机 dryer	14	2.2
32	摄像机 video camera	14	2.2
32	空气净化器 air purifier	13	2.1
33	加湿器 humidifier	10	1.6
34	传真机 fax-machine	6	1.0
35	钢琴 piano	5	0.8
36	MD	3	0.5
37	洗碗机 dish washer	2	0.3
37	煤气烤箱 gas oven	2	0.3
38	数字摄像机 digital video camera	1	0.2

n=624

1-2 计划未来一年内购买的电器及耐用消费品排名/ Ranking of the Home Electronic and Durable Products to be Purchased Next Year

注：本题为多选题，合计百分比超过 100%（Multiple answers）

		人次 Person-time	百分比 Percent
1	彩电 color TV	80	12.8
2	DVD	71	11.4
3	电冰箱 refrigerator	69	11.1
4	洗衣机 washing machine	66	10.6
4	空调机 air-conditioner	66	10.6
5	饮水机 water dispenser	64	10.3
6	影碟机 VCD player	56	9.0
7	微波炉 microwave oven	53	8.5
8	消毒碗柜 cooking utensil sterilize	46	7.4
8	音响 Hi-Fi stereo	46	7.4
9	抽油烟机 kitchen ventilator	44	7.1
10	电暖气 electronic heater	32	5.1
11	CD 随身听 Discman	31	5.0
12	电烤箱 electric oven	30	4.8
13	照相机 camera	29	4.7
14	榨汁机 juice extractor	28	4.5
15	电热水器 electronic water heater	27	4.3
15	数码相机 digital camera	27	4.3
16	电子辞典 quick-machine interpreter	24	3.8
17	电热水壶 electronic thermos	23	3.7
17	吸尘器 vacuum cleaner	23	3.7
17	摩托车 motorcycle	23	3.7
18	摄像机 video camera	22	3.5
19	洗碗机 dish washer	20	3.2
20	煤气热水器 gas water heater	19	3.0
21	空气净化器 air purifier	17	2.7
21	食物加工机 food processor	17	2.7
22	磁带随身听 walkman	15	2.4
23	烘干机 dryer	13	2.1
24	录/放像机 VTR	12	1.9
25	冰柜 freezers	11	1.8
25	电子游戏机 video game player	11	1.8
25	传真机 fax-machine	11	1.8
26	录音机 recorder	9	1.4
27	数字摄像机 digital video camera	7	1.1
28	煤气烤箱 gas oven	6	1.0
29	电风扇 electronic fan	5	0.8
30	加湿器 humidifier	4	0.6
30	MD	4	0.6
31	钢琴 piano	3	0.5

n=624

● 武汉 / Wuhan

1-1 家中现在拥有电器及耐用消费品排名/ Ranking of the Home Electronic and Durable Products Presently Possessed

注：本题为多选题，合计百分比超过 100%（Multiple answers）

		人次 Person-time	百分比 Percent
1	电风扇 electronic fan	625	97.4
2	彩电 color TV	624	97.2
3	电冰箱 refrigerator	598	93.1
4	洗衣机 washing machine	576	89.7
5	录音机 recorder	461	71.8
6	空调机 air-conditioner	398	62.0
7	磁带随身听 walkman	377	58.7
8	影碟机 VCD player	328	51.1
9	抽油烟机 kitchen ventilator	303	47.2
9	电暖气 electronic heater	303	47.2
10	煤气热水器 gas water heater	293	45.6
11	电热水壶 electronic thermos	272	42.4
12	照相机 camera	252	39.3
13	电子游戏机 video game player	219	34.1
14	音响 Hi-Fi stereo	214	33.3
15	录/放像机 VTR	189	29.4
16	电热水器 electronic water heater	150	23.4
17	微波炉 microwave oven	123	19.2
18	饮水机 water dispenser	91	14.2
19	消毒碗柜 cooking utensil sterilize	87	13.6
20	榨汁机 juice extractor	75	11.7
21	摩托车 motorcycle	68	10.6
22	冰柜 freezers	65	10.1
22	吸尘器 vacuum cleaner	65	10.1
23	CD 随身听 Discman	61	9.5
24	电烤箱 electronic oven	60	9.3
25	电子辞典 quick-machine interpreter	44	6.9
26	DVD	33	5.1
26	食物加工机 food processor	33	5.1
27	空气净化器 air purifier	21	3.3
27	数码相机 digital camera	21	3.3
28	摄像机 video camera	20	3.1
29	MD	12	1.9
30	烘干机 dryer	11	1.7
31	钢琴 piano	10	1.6
32	洗碗机 dish washer	9	1.4
33	传真机 fax-machine	7	1.1
34	数字摄像机 digital video camera	4	0.6
34	煤气烤箱 gas oven	4	0.6
35	加湿器 humidifier	3	0.5

n=642

1-2 计划未来一年内购买的电器及耐用消费品排名/ Ranking of the Home Electronic and Durable Products to be Purchased Next Year

注：本题为多选题，合计百分比超过 100%（Multiple answers）

		人次 Person-time	百分比 Percent
1	彩电 color TV	95	14.8
2	空调机 air-conditioner	89	13.9
3	电热水器 electronic water heater	79	12.3
4	消毒碗柜 cooking utensil sterilize	76	11.8
5	洗衣机 washing machine	74	11.5
6	微波炉 microwave oven	72	11.2
7	DVD	71	11.1
8	电冰箱 refrigerator	61	9.5
9	影碟机 VCD player	58	9.0
10	饮水机 water dispenser	57	8.9
11	摩托车 motorcycle	45	7.0
12	榨汁机 juice extractor	40	6.2
12	电烤箱 electronic oven	40	6.2
13	抽油烟机 kitchen ventilator	38	5.9
14	洗碗机 dish washer	36	5.6
15	音响 Hi-Fi stereo	34	5.3
16	照相机 camera	33	5.1
17	电热水壶 electronic thermos	29	4.5
18	数码相机 digital camera	27	4.2
19	电暖气 electronic heater	24	3.7
19	空气净化器 air purifier	24	3.7
19	CD 随身听 Discman	24	3.7
19	摄像机 video camera	24	3.7
20	电子辞典 quick-machine interpreter	23	3.6
21	煤气热水器 gas water heater	17	2.6
21	吸尘器 vacuum cleaner	17	2.6
22	录音机 recorder	11	1.7
22	传真机 fax-machine	11	1.7
23	磁带随身听 walkman	10	1.6
24	加湿器 humidifier	9	1.4
24	烘干机 dryer	9	1.4
24	电子游戏机 video game player	9	1.4
25	冰柜 freezers	8	1.2
25	食物加工机 food processor	8	1.2
26	录/放像机 VTR	7	1.1
27	钢琴 piano	6	0.9
28	电风扇 electronic fan	4	0.6
28	MD	4	0.6
28	数字摄像机 digital video camera	4	0.6
29	煤气烤箱 gas oven	3	0.5

n=642

● 西安 / Xi'an

1-1 家中现在拥有电器及耐用消费品排名/ Ranking of the Home Electronic and Durable Products Presently Possessed

注：本题为多选题，合计百分比超过100%（Multiple answers）

		人次 Person-time	百分比 Percent
1	彩电 color TV	592	98.5
2	洗衣机 washing machine	546	90.8
3	电风扇 electronic fan	527	87.7
4	电冰箱 refrigerator	502	83.5
5	录音机 recorder	415	69.1
6	抽油烟机 kitchen ventilator	354	58.9
7	照相机 camera	307	51.1
8	磁带随身听 walkman	300	49.9
9	影碟机 VCD player	284	47.3
10	电热水壶 electronic thermos	262	43.6
11	空调机 air-conditioner	231	38.4
12	电热水器 electronic water heater	225	37.4
13	音响 Hi-Fi stereo	173	28.8
14	电暖气 electronic heater	169	28.1
15	电子游戏机 video game player	168	28.0
16	录/放像机 VTR	167	27.8
17	煤气热水器 gas water heater	126	21.0
18	饮水机 water dispenser	114	19.0
19	摩托车 motorcycle	113	18.8
20	微波炉 microwave oven	78	13.0
21	吸尘器 vacuum cleaner	66	11.0
22	榨汁机 juice extractor	63	10.5
23	冰柜 freezers	61	10.1
24	电烤箱 electronic oven	46	7.7
25	食物加工机 food processor	45	7.5
26	CD 随身听 Discman	42	7.0
27	电子辞典 quick-machine interpreter	38	6.3
28	加湿器 humidifier	27	4.5
29	DVD	27	4.5
29	数码相机 digital camera	26	4.3
30	消毒碗柜 cooking utensil sterilize	24	4.0
31	摄像机 video camera	23	3.8
32	MD	18	3.0
33	空气净化器 air purifier	15	2.5
34	传真机 fax-machine	9	1.5
35	钢琴 piano	7	1.2
36	数字摄像机 digital video camera	4	0.7
36	煤气烤箱 gas oven	4	0.7
37	洗碗机 dish washer	3	0.5
38	烘干机 dryer	2	0.3

n=601

1-2 计划未来一年内购买的电器及耐用消费品排名/ Ranking of the Home Electronic and Durable Products to be Purchased Next Year

注：本题为多选题，合计百分比超过 100%（Multiple answers）

		人次 Person-time	百分比 Percent
1	DVD	72	12.0
2	空调机 air-conditioner	61	10.1
3	消毒碗柜 cooking utensil sterilize	60	10.0
3	摩托车 motorcycle	60	10.0
4	彩电 color TV	59	9.8
5	饮水机 water dispenser	57	9.5
6	抽油烟机 kitchen ventilator	56	9.3
6	电冰箱 refrigerator	56	9.3
7	洗衣机 washing machine	49	8.2
8	影碟机 VCD player	47	7.8
9	电热水器 electronic water heater	37	6.2
9	微波炉 microwave oven	37	6.2
10	照相机 camera	33	5.5
11	榨汁机 juice extractor	31	5.2
11	电暖气 electronic heater	31	5.2
11	电烤箱 electronic oven	31	5.2
12	数码相机 digital camera	29	4.8
12	音响 Hi-Fi stereo	29	4.8
13	洗碗机 dish washer	28	4.7
13	加湿器 humidifier	28	4.7
14	吸尘器 vacuum cleaner	27	4.5
14	摄像机 video camera	27	4.5
15	电子辞典 quick-machine interpreter	24	4.0
16	CD 随身听 Discman	23	3.8
17	电热水壶 electronic thermos	21	3.5
18	空气净化器 air purifier	16	2.7
19	冰柜 freezers	15	2.5
20	煤气热水器 gas water heater	12	2.0
20	磁带随身听 walkman	12	2.0
21	电子游戏机 video game player	11	1.8
22	电风扇 electronic fan	10	1.7
23	食物加工机 food processor	9	1.5
24	传真机 fax-machine	8	1.3
24	钢琴 piano	8	1.3
25	烘干机 dryer	7	1.2
25	录音机 recorder	7	1.2
26	MD	6	1.0
26	数字摄像机 digital video camera	6	1.0
26	录/放像机 VTR	6	1.0
27	煤气烤箱 gas oven	3	0.5

n=601

● 沈阳 / Shenyang

1-1 家中现在拥有电器及耐用消费品排名/ Ranking of the Home Electronic and Durable Products Presently Possessed

注：本题为多选题，合计百分比超过 100%（Multiple answers）

排名 Ranking		人次 Person-time	百分比 Percent
1	彩色电视机 color TV	585	97.3
2	洗衣机 washing machine	489	81.4
3	电冰箱 refrigerator	468	77.9
4	抽油烟机 kitchen ventilator	444	73.9
5	录音机 recorder	422	70.2
6	电风扇 electronic fan	398	66.2
7	磁带随身听 walkman	308	51.2
8	照相机 camera	272	45.3
9	影碟机 VCD player	196	32.6
10	吸尘器 vacuum cleaner	192	31.9
11	电热水壶 electronic thermos	179	29.8
12	电热水器 electronic water heater	178	29.6
13	电子游戏机 video game player	176	29.3
14	煤气热水器 gas water heater	173	28.8
15	录/放像机 VTR	172	28.6
16	电暖气 electronic heater	159	26.5
17	音响 Hi-Fi stereo	151	25.1
18	饮水机 water dispenser	85	14.1
19	微波炉 microwave oven	75	12.5
20	冰柜 freezers	71	11.8
21	榨汁机 juice extractor	59	9.8
22	摩托车 motorcycle	46	7.7
23	CD 随身听 Discman	38	6.3
24	加湿器 humidifier	29	4.8
25	DVD	28	4.7
25	电烤箱 electronic oven	28	4.7
26	空调机 air-conditioner	27	4.5
27	电子辞典 quick-machine interpreter	25	4.2
28	数码相机 digital camera	21	3.5
29	消毒碗柜 cooking utensil sterilize	20	3.3
30	摄像机 video camera	18	3.0
31	钢琴 piano	13	2.2
32	食物加工机 food processor	11	1.8
33	空气净化器 air purifier	9	1.5
34	MD	8	1.3
34	传真机 fax-machine	8	1.3
35	烘干机 dryer	6	1.0
36	数字摄像机 digital video camera	5	0.8
37	洗碗机 dish washer	4	0.7
38	煤气烤箱 gas oven	0	0.0

n=601

1-2 计划未来一年内购买的电器及耐用消费品排名/ Ranking of the Home Electronic and Durable Products to be Purchased Next Year

注：本题为多选题，合计百分比超过 100%（Multiple answers）

排名 Ranking		人次 Person-time	百分比 Percent
1	饮水机 water dispenser	85	14.1
2	彩色电视机 color TV	71	11.8
3	DVD	70	11.6
4	微波炉 microwave oven	62	10.3
5	影碟机 VCD player	54	9.0
6	电热水器 electronic water heater	53	8.8
7	电冰箱 refrigerator	47	7.8
7	洗衣机 washing machine	47	7.8
8	抽油烟机 kitchen ventilator	40	6.7
9	电烤箱 electronic oven	39	6.5
10	消毒碗柜 cooking utensil sterilize	36	6.0
11	吸尘器 vacuum cleaner	33	5.5
12	摄像机 video camera	29	4.8
13	榨汁机 juice extractor	27	4.5
13	CD 随身听 Discman	27	4.5
14	电风扇 electronic fan	26	4.3
14	电子辞典 quick-machine interpreter	26	4.3
14	空调机 air-conditioner	26	4.3
15	电热水壶 electronic thermos	25	4.2
15	电暖气 electronic heater	25	4.2
16	音响 Hi-Fi stereo	24	4.0
17	摩托车 motorcycle	22	3.7
18	数码相机 digital camera	21	3.5
18	照相机 camera	21	3.5
19	洗碗机 dish washer	18	3.0
19	加湿器 humidifier	18	3.0
20	冰柜 freezers	16	2.7
21	煤气热水器 gas water heater	15	2.5
22	空气净化器 air purifier	11	1.8
23	数字摄像机 digital video camera	10	1.7
23	电子游戏机 video game player	10	1.7
23	传真机 fax-machine	10	1.7
24	磁带随身听 walkman	9	1.5
24	食物加工机 food processor	9	1.5
25	钢琴 piano	8	1.3
26	烘干机 dryer	6	1.0
26	MD	6	1.0
27	煤气烤箱 gas oven	3	0.5
28	录音机 recorder	1	0.2
28	录/放像机 VTR	1	0.2

n=601

2. 服务性产品消费情况 / Services Usage

● 北京 / Beijing

2-1 最近一年内使用过的服务项目排名/ Ranking of the Services have Used Last Year

注：本题为多选题，合计百分比超过 100%（Multiple answers）

排名 Ranking	服务项目 Service Items	人次 Person-time	百分比 Percent
1	有线电视 cable TV	909	91.2
2	国内长途电话 domestic long-distance call	761	76.3
3	体育场馆 stadium	377	37.8
4	高档餐厅就餐 dining in first-class restaurant	371	37.2
5	付费电话信息服务 telephone information service	298	29.9
6	VCD/录像带出租 renting VCD & videotape	282	28.3
7	邮政速递 express mail service	250	25.1
8	美容厅/院 beauty parlor	230	23.1
9	网上浏览 internet skimming	206	20.7
10	KTV 包厢 KTV room	202	20.3
11	器械健身 gym equipment	197	19.8
12	电子邮件 e-mail	174	17.5
13	国际长途电话 international long-distance call	173	17.4
14	电视购物 TV shopping	141	14.1
15	电脑发传真 fax through computer	128	12.8
16	网吧 internet cafe	95	9.5
17	汽车租赁 renting car	89	8.9
18	小时工 household service counted in hours	72	7.2

n=997

2-2 计划未来一年使用的服务项目排名/ Ranking of the Services Planned to Use Next Year

注：本题为多选题，合计百分比超过 100%（Multiple answers）

排名 Ranking	服务项目 Service Items	人次 Person-time	百分比 Percent
1	网上浏览 internet skimming	177	32.4
2	电视购物 TV shopping	146	26.7
3	电子邮件 e-mail	145	26.5
4	器械健身 gym equipment	137	25.0
5	电脑发传真 fax through computer	113	20.7
6	小时工 household service counted in hours	95	17.4
7	体育场馆 stadium	90	16.5
8	汽车租赁 renting car	88	16.1
9	国际长途电话 international long-distance call	76	13.9
10	网吧 internet cafe	59	10.8
11	美容厅/院 beauty parlor	58	10.6
11	邮政速递 express mail service	58	10.6
12	高档餐厅就餐 dining in first-class restaurant	44	8.0
13	付费电话信息服务 telephone information service	42	7.7
14	电视购物 TV shopping	34	6.2
14	VCD/录像带出租 renting VCD & videotape	34	6.2
15	国内长途电话 domestic long-distance call	31	5.7
16	KTV 包厢 KTV room	19	3.5

n=547

2-3 样本、男性各年龄层、女性各年龄层过去一年内使用的服务/ Services Used Last Year by the Whole Sample, Age and Gender Groups

注：本题为多选题，合计百分比超过 100%（Multiple answers）

	人数 Number	国际长途电话 international long-distance call	国内长途电话 domestic long-distance call	电脑发传真 fax through computer	电子邮件 e-mail	网上浏览 internet skimming	邮政速递 express mail service
样本 Sample	**997**	**17.4**	**76.3**	**12.8**	**17.5**	**20.7**	**25.1**
男性 Male	**499**	**19.0**	**76.6**	**15.0**	**20.0**	**22.8**	**27.1**
16~24 岁 Age	104	14.4	65.4	17.3	31.7	35.6	23.1
25~34 岁 Age	150	23.3	80.0	22.0	28.7	32.7	36.7
35~44 岁 Age	131	22.9	78.6	11.5	10.7	11.5	24.4
45~54 岁 Age	75	14.7	81.3	9.3	8.0	10.7	18.7
55~60 岁 Age	39	10.3	76.9	5.1	10.3	12.8	25.6
女性 Female	**498**	**15.7**	**76.1**	**10.6**	**14.9**	**18.5**	**23.1**
16~24 岁 Age	106	13.2	75.5	10.4	18.9	26.4	22.6
25~34 岁 Age	148	16.9	79.1	14.9	23.6	25.0	31.1
35~44 岁 Age	120	18.3	79.2	11.7	9.2	14.2	20.0
45~54 岁 Age	83	10.8	68.7	7.2	6.0	9.6	18.1
55~60 岁 Age	41	19.5	73.2	0.0	7.3	4.9	14.6

续前表 continued

	人数 Number	付费电话信息服务 telephone information service	电视购物 TV shopping	KTV 包厢 KTV room	有线电视 cable TV	高档餐厅就餐 dinning in first-class restaurant	美容厅/院 beauty parlor
样本 Sample	**997**	**29.9**	**14.1**	**20.3**	**91.2**	**37.2**	**23.1**
男性 Male	**499**	**29.1**	**10.2**	**23.2**	**90.6**	**39.5**	**17.0**
16~24 岁 Age	104	35.6	9.6	22.1	88.5	29.8	17.3
25~34 岁 Age	150	36.0	10.0	36.0	90.0	54.0	28.0
35~44 岁 Age	131	22.9	12.2	21.4	90.8	42.0	13.7
45~54 岁 Age	75	18.7	9.3	8.0	92.0	25.3	9.3
55~60 岁 Age	39	25.6	7.7	12.8	94.9	28.2	0.0
女性 Female	**498**	**30.7**	**18.1**	**17.3**	**91.8**	**34.9**	**29.1**
16~24 岁 Age	106	37.7	21.7	22.6	87.7	29.2	22.6
25~34 岁 Age	148	38.5	15.5	25.7	92.6	45.9	38.5
35~44 岁 Age	120	24.2	15.0	14.2	92.5	39.2	39.2
45~54 岁 Age	83	21.7	25.3	7.2	92.8	24.1	16.9
55~60 岁 Age	41	22.0	12.2	2.4	95.1	19.5	7.3

续前表 continued

	人数 Number	体育场馆 stadium	VCD/录像带出租 renting VCD & videotape	小时工 household service counted in hours	汽车租赁 renting car	器械健身 gym equipment	网吧 internet cafe
样本 Sample	**997**	**37.8**	**28.3**	**7.2**	**8.9**	**19.8**	**9.5**
男性 Male	**499**	**43.5**	**29.7**	**5.2**	**10.0**	**20.2**	**14.0**
16~24 岁 Age	104	62.5	43.3	7.7	7.7	26.0	49.0
25~34 岁 Age	150	46.0	36.0	5.3	18.0	22.7	10.0
35~44 岁 Age	131	37.4	23.7	4.6	6.9	18.3	0.8
45~54 岁 Age	75	26.7	18.7	4.0	0.0	16.0	4.0
55~60 岁 Age	39	35.9	10.3	2.6	15.4	10.3	0.0
女性 Female	**498**	**32.1**	**26.9**	**9.2**	**7.8**	**19.3**	**5.0**
16~24 岁 Age	106	50.9	30.2	6.6	7.5	19.8	14.2
25~34 岁 Age	148	36.5	37.2	12.2	11.5	18.2	2.0
35~44 岁 Age	120	30.8	22.5	10.0	6.7	20.8	4.2
45~54 岁 Age	83	14.5	19.3	7.2	7.2	18.1	2.4
55~60 岁 Age	41	7.3	9.8	7.3	0.0	19.5	0.0

2-4 样本、男性各年龄层、女性各年龄层计划未来一年内使用的服务/ Services to be Used Next Year by the Whole Sample, Age and Gender Groups

注：本题为多选题，合计百分比超过 100%（Multiple answers）

	人数 Number	国际长途电话 international long-distance call	国内长途电话 domestic long-distance call	电脑发传真 fax through computer	电子邮件 e-mail	网上浏览 internet skimming	邮政速递 express mail service
样本 Sample	547	13.9	5.7	20.7	26.5	32.4	10.6
男性 Male	277	15.2	6.5	22.4	26.4	32.9	10.1
16~24 岁 Age	77	13.0	5.2	24.7	35.1	40.3	10.4
25~34 岁 Age	88	15.9	8.0	18.2	19.3	25.0	9.1
35~44 岁 Age	64	7.8	4.7	23.4	31.3	42.2	10.9
45~54 岁 Age	33	24.2	9.1	21.2	15.2	21.2	9.1
55~60 岁 Age	15	33.3	6.7	33.3	26.7	26.7	13.3
女性 Female	270	12.6	4.8	18.9	26.7	31.9	11.1
16~24 岁 Age	77	10.4	5.2	24.7	31.2	45.5	11.7
25~34 岁 Age	96	16.7	5.2	16.7	21.9	29.2	8.3
35~44 岁 Age	60	10.0	1.7	15.0	28.3	20.0	13.3
45~54 岁 Age	28	10.7	10.7	21.4	32.1	28.6	14.3
55~60 岁 Age	9	11.1	0.0	11.1	11.1	33.3	11.1

续前表 continued

	人数 Number	付费电话信息服务 telephone information service	电视购物 TV shopping	KTV 包厢 KTV room	有线电视 cable TV	高档餐厅就餐 dinning in first-class restaurant	美容厅/院 beauty parlor
样本 Sample	547	7.7	26.7	3.5	6.2	8.0	10.6
男性 Male	277	9.7	28.5	4.7	7.2	7.9	7.6
16~24 岁 Age	77	10.4	20.8	7.8	7.8	11.7	7.8
25~34 岁 Age	88	8.0	33.0	4.5	6.8	6.8	9.1
35~44 岁 Age	64	14.1	28.1	4.7	7.8	4.7	9.4
45~54 岁 Age	33	3.0	33.3	0.0	3.0	9.1	3.0
55~60 岁 Age	15	13.3	33.3	0.0	13.3	6.7	0.0
女性 Female	270	5.6	24.8	2.2	5.2	8.1	13.7
16~24 岁 Age	77	9.1	27.3	5.2	9.1	11.7	18.2
25~34 岁 Age	96	4.2	22.9	2.1	3.1	3.1	15.6
35~44 岁 Age	60	3.3	25.0	0.0	5.0	6.7	6.7
45~54 岁 Age	28	7.1	17.9	0.0	3.6	17.9	14.3
55~60 岁 Age	9	0.0	44.4	0.0	0.0	11.1	0.0

续前表 continued

	人数 Number	体育场馆 stadium	VCD/录像带出租 renting VCD & videotape	小时工 household service counted in hours	汽车租赁 renting car	器械健身 gym equipment	网吧 internet cafe
样本 Sample	547	16.5	6.2	17.4	16.1	25.0	10.8
男性 Male	277	16.6	8.7	13.4	18.4	24.9	9.4
16~24 岁 Age	77	10.4	10.4	6.5	23.4	19.5	13.0
25~34 岁 Age	88	20.5	5.7	18.2	18.2	31.8	8.0
35~44 岁 Age	64	21.9	12.5	14.1	20.3	23.4	12.5
45~54 岁 Age	33	12.1	6.1	21.2	9.1	21.2	3.0
55~60 岁 Age	15	13.3	6.7	0.0	6.7	26.7	0.0
女性 Female	270	16.3	3.7	21.5	13.7	25.2	12.2
16~24 岁 Age	77	15.6	5.2	20.8	13.0	32.5	20.8
25~34 岁 Age	96	16.7	1.0	20.8	18.8	24.0	13.5
35~44 岁 Age	60	13.3	5.0	23.3	6.7	21.7	3.3
45~54 岁 Age	28	17.9	3.6	21.4	17.9	21.4	7.1
55~60 岁 Age	9	33.3	11.1	22.2	0.0	11.1	0.0

2-5 不同消费者层最近一年内使用过的服务/ Services Used Last Year by Market Segments

2-5-1 时尚流行指标/ Fads Popular Index

注：本题为多选题，合计百分比超过 100%（Multiple answers）

	人数 Number	国际长途电话 international long-distance call	国内长途电话 domestic long-distance call	电脑发传真 fax through computer	电子邮件 e-mail	网上浏览 internet skimming	邮政速递 express mail service
样本 Sample	984	17.3	76.4	12.9	17.7	20.9	25.3
平实生活指向 simple living orientation	483	16.1	75.2	12.4	17.4	20.1	24.4
时尚流行指向 fashion orientation	501	18.4	77.6	13.4	18.0	21.8	26.1

续前表 continued

	人数 Number	付费电话信息服务 telephone information service	电视购物 TV shopping	KTV 包厢 KTV room	有线电视 cable TV	高档餐厅就餐 dinning in first-class restaurant	美容厅/院 beauty parlor
样本 Sample	984	30.2	14.1	20.4	91.3	37.4	23.2
平实生活指向 simple living orientation	483	27.1	13.0	16.1	91.1	30.8	14.7
时尚流行指向 fashion orientation	501	33.1	15.2	24.6	91.4	43.7	31.3

续前表 continued

	人数 Number	体育场馆 stadium	VCD/录像带出租 renting VCD & videotape	小时工 household service counted in hours	汽车租赁 renting car	器械健身 gym equipment	网吧 internet cafe
样本 Sample	984	37.8	28.3	7.2	8.9	19.9	9.6
平实生活指向 simple living orientation	483	34.6	26.9	6.4	7.7	18.8	8.1
时尚流行指向 fashion orientation	501	40.9	29.5	8.0	10.2	21.0	11.0

2-5-2 信息交流指标/ Information Communication Index

注：本题为多选题，合计百分比超过 100%（Multiple answers）

	人数 Number	国际长途电话 international long-distance call	国内长途电话 domestic long-distance call	电脑发传真 fax through computer	电子邮件 e-mail	网上浏览 internet skimming	邮政速递 express mail service
样本 Sample	989	17.4	76.3	12.6	17.1	20.3	25.0
信息消极指向 negative orientation	63	11.1	73.0	1.6	4.8	4.8	14.3
中间层 medium	516	18.4	74.8	13.4	18.0	22.5	25.0
信息积极指向 active orientation	410	17.1	78.8	13.4	17.8	20.0	26.6

续前表 continued

	人数 Number	付费电话信息服务 telephone information service	电视购物 TV shopping	KTV 包厢 KTV room	有线电视 cable TV	高档餐厅就餐 dinning in first-class restaurant	美容厅/院 beauty parlor
样本 Sample	989	29.6	14.2	20.3	91.4	37.3	23.0
信息消极指向 negative orientation	63	14.3	11.1	7.9	92.1	19.0	9.5
中间层 medium	516	30.2	12.2	20.7	90.5	36.0	21.7
信息积极指向 active orientation	410	31.2	17.1	21.7	92.4	41.7	26.6

续前表 continued

	人数 Number	体育场馆 stadium	VCD/录像带出租 renting VCD & videotape	小时工 household service counted in hours	汽车租赁 renting car	器械健身 gym equipment	网吧 internet cafe
样本 Sample	989	37.9	28.2	7.0	8.9	19.8	9.6
信息消极指向 negative orientation	63	19.0	23.8	3.2	4.8	15.9	7.9
中间层 medium	516	39.9	28.7	7.8	9.1	16.9	10.1
信息积极指向 active orientation	410	38.3	28.3	6.6	9.3	24.1	9.3

2-6 不同消费者层计划未来一年内使用的服务/ Services to be Used Next Year by Market Segments

2-6-1 时尚流行指标/ Fads Popular Index

注：本题为多选题，合计百分比超过 100%（Multiple answers）

	人数 Number	国际长途电话 international long-distance call	国内长途电话 domestic long-distance call	电脑发传真 fax through computer	电子邮件 e-mail	网上浏览 internet skimming	邮政速递 express mail service
样本 Sample	539	14.1	5.8	20.6	26.5	32.1	10.4
平实生活指向 simple living orientation	248	15.7	7.3	21.4	27.4	29.0	10.9
时尚流行指向 fashion orientation	291	12.7	4.5	19.9	25.8	34.7	10.0

续前表 continued

	人数 Number	付费电话信息服务 telephone information service	电视购物 TV shopping	KTV 包厢 KTV room	有线电视 cable TV	高档餐厅就餐 dinning in first-class restaurant	美容厅/院 beauty parlor
样本 Sample	539	7.8	26.5	3.3	6.1	8.2	10.6
平实生活指向 simple living orientation	248	6.5	23.8	2.4	6.5	8.1	9.3
时尚流行指向 fashion orientation	291	8.9	28.9	4.1	5.8	8.2	11.7

续前表 continued

	人数 Number	体育场馆 stadium	VCD/录像带出租 renting VCD & videotape	小时工 household service counted in hours	汽车租赁 renting car	器械健身 gym equipment	网吧 internet cafe
样本 Sample	539	16.3	6.3	17.4	16.3	25.0	10.8
平实生活指向 simple living orientation	248	17.7	6.5	18.1	15.7	20.6	8.5
时尚流行指向 fashion orientation	291	15.1	6.2	16.8	16.8	28.9	12.7

2-6-2 信息交流指标/ Information Communication Index

注：本题为多选题，合计百分比超过 100%（Multiple answers）

	人数 Number	国际长途电话 international long-distance call	国内长途电话 domestic long-distance call	电脑发传真 fax through computer	电子邮件 e-mail	网上浏览 internet skimming	邮政速递 express mail service
样本 Sample	544	13.8	5.5	20.6	26.3	32.2	10.7
信息消极指向 negative orientation	25	20.0	0.0	24.0	32.0	44.0	8.0
中间层 medium	280	13.2	7.5	21.8	27.1	31.1	10.4
信息积极指向 active orientation	239	13.8	3.8	18.8	24.7	32.2	11.3

续前表 continued

	人数 Number	付费电话信息服务 telephone information service	电视购物 TV shopping	KTV 包厢 KTV room	有线电视 cable TV	高档餐厅就餐 dinning in first-class restaurant	美容厅/院 beauty parlor
样本 Sample	544	7.7	26.5	3.5	6.1	7.9	10.5
信息消极指向 negative orientation	25	0.0	24.0	0.0	0.0	8.0	8.0
中间层 medium	280	9.6	26.4	3.9	7.5	9.6	12.1
信息积极指向 active orientation	239	6.3	26.8	3.3	5.0	5.9	8.8

续前表 continued

	人数 Number	体育场馆 stadium	VCD/录像带出租 renting VCD & videotape	小时工 household service counted in hours	汽车租赁 renting car	器械健身 gym equipment	网吧 internet cafe
样本 Sample	544	16.5	6.3	17.5	16.2	25.0	10.8
信息消极指向 negative orientation	25	16.0	4.0	8.0	20.0	8.0	8.0
中间层 medium	280	16.8	5.7	17.5	15.4	28.2	12.1
信息积极指向 active orientation	239	16.3	7.1	18.4	16.7	23.0	9.6

● 上海 / Shanghai

2-1 最近一年内使用过的服务项目排名/ Ranking of the Services have been Used Last Year

注：本题为多选题，合计百分比超过 100%（Multiple answers）

排名 Ranking	服务项目 Service Items	人次 Person-time	百分比 Percent
1	有线电视 cable TV	919	92.1
2	国内长途电话 domestic long-distance call	699	70.0
3	VCD/录像带出租 renting VCD & videotape	372	37.3
4	高档餐厅就餐 dining in first-class restaurant	330	33.1
5	体育场馆 stadium	266	26.7
6	KTV 包厢 KTV room	259	26.0
7	付费电话信息服务 telephone information service	234	23.4
8	美容厅/院 beauty parlor	183	18.3
9	邮政速递 express mail service	171	17.1
10	器械健身 gym equipment	143	14.3
11	国际长途电话 international long-distance call	135	13.5
12	网上浏览 internet skimming	131	13.1
13	网吧 internet cafe	113	11.3
14	电子邮件 e-mail	105	10.5
15	电脑发传真 fax through computer	78	7.8
16	汽车租赁 renting car	74	7.4
17	电视购物 TV shopping	61	6.1
17	小时工 household service counted in hours	61	6.1

n=998

2-2 计划未来一年使用的服务项目排名/ Ranking of the Services Planned to Use Next Year

注：本题为多选题，合计百分比超过 100%（Multiple answers）

排名 Ranking	服务项目 Service Items	人次 Person-time	百分比 Percent
1	网上浏览 internet skimming	227	32.9
2	电子邮件 e-mail	185	26.8
3	电视购物 TV shopping	168	24.3
4	器械健身 gym equipment	158	22.9
5	电脑发传真 fax through computer	127	18.4
6	美容厅/院 beauty parlor	101	14.6
7	小时工 household service counted in hours	100	14.5
8	网吧 internet cafe	93	13.5
8	高档餐厅就餐 dining in first-class restaurant	93	13.5
9	体育场馆 stadium	90	13.0
10	汽车租赁 renting car	80	11.6
11	邮政速递 express mail service	79	11.4
12	付费电话信息服务 telephone information service	78	11.3
13	国际长途电话 international long-distance call	72	10.4
14	VCD/录像带出租 renting VCD & videotape	55	8.0
15	KTV 包厢 KTV room	47	6.8
16	国内长途电话 domestic long-distance call	34	4.9
17	电视购物 TV shopping	25	3.6

n=691

2-3 样本、 男性各年龄层、 女性各年龄层过去一年内使用的服务/ Services Used Last Year by the Whole Sample, Age and Gender Groups

注：本题为多选题，合计百分比超过 100%（Multiple answers）

	人数 Number	国际长途电话 international long-distance call	国内长途电话 domestic long-distance call	电脑发传真 fax through computer	电子邮件 e-mail	网上浏览 internet skimming	邮政速递 express mail service
样本 Sample	998	13.5	70.0	7.8	10.5	13.1	17.1
男性 Male	499	13.0	72.3	9.2	12.0	16.2	18.2
16~24 岁 Age	108	8.3	59.3	9.3	19.4	26.9	15.7
25~34 岁 Age	145	13.1	77.9	9.7	15.9	19.3	19.3
35~44 岁 Age	128	14.1	72.7	7.8	7.0	9.4	18.0
45~54 岁 Age	82	14.6	79.3	13.4	6.1	11.0	20.7
55~60 岁 Age	36	19.4	72.2	2.8	5.6	8.3	16.7
女性 Female	499	14.0	67.7	6.4	9.0	10.0	16.0
16~24 岁 Age	106	12.3	66.0	8.5	12.3	18.9	24.5
25~34 岁 Age	143	14.7	66.4	9.8	13.3	13.3	17.5
35~44 岁 Age	129	16.3	69.0	4.7	5.4	3.1	13.2
45~54 岁 Age	81	13.6	74.1	2.5	7.4	8.6	8.6
55~60 岁 Age	40	10.0	60.0	2.5	0.0	0.0	12.5

续前表 continued

	人数 Number	付费电话信息服务 telephone information service	电视购物 TV shopping	KTV 包厢 KTV room	有线电视 cable TV	高档餐厅就餐 dinning in first-class restaurant	美容厅/院 beauty parlor
样本 Sample	998	23.4	6.1	26.0	92.1	33.1	18.3
男性 Male	499	25.1	4.8	28.9	92.2	34.9	15.4
16~24 岁 Age	108	26.9	3.7	33.3	88.0	34.3	12.0
25~34 岁 Age	145	26.2	5.5	40.0	96.6	46.2	26.9
35~44 岁 Age	128	18.0	1.6	20.3	93.0	26.6	10.9
45~54 岁 Age	82	34.1	11.0	26.8	91.5	39.0	11.0
55~60 岁 Age	36	19.4	2.8	5.6	86.1	11.1	5.6
女性 Female	499	21.8	7.4	23.0	92.0	31.3	21.2
16~24 岁 Age	106	27.4	5.7	39.6	84.9	34.0	26.4
25~34 岁 Age	143	23.1	11.9	35.0	92.3	42.0	35.0
35~44 岁 Age	129	26.4	7.8	11.6	96.9	29.5	18.6
45~54 岁 Age	81	14.8	3.7	9.9	91.4	18.5	3.7
55~60 岁 Age	40	2.5	2.5	0.0	95.0	17.5	2.5

续前表 continued

	人数 Number	体育场馆 stadium	VCD/录像带出租 renting VCD & videotape	小时工 household service counted in hours	汽车租赁 renting car	器械健身 gym equipment	网吧 internet cafe
样本 Sample	998	26.7	37.3	6.1	7.4	14.3	11.3
男性 Male	499	36.3	41.1	4.6	7.4	16.4	18.0
16~24 岁 Age	108	53.7	55.6	4.6	7.4	25.0	43.5
25~34 岁 Age	145	38.6	53.8	4.8	11.0	20.0	24.8
35~44 岁 Age	128	30.5	25.0	3.1	4.7	9.4	3.9
45~54 岁 Age	82	26.8	32.9	4.9	6.1	14.6	1.2
55~60 岁 Age	36	16.7	22.2	8.3	5.6	5.6	2.8
女性 Female	499	17.0	33.5	7.6	7.4	12.2	4.6
16~24 岁 Age	106	31.1	43.4	9.4	6.6	13.2	14.2
25~34 岁 Age	143	17.5	46.9	7.7	7.7	18.9	2.8
35~44 岁 Age	129	10.1	25.6	4.7	9.3	6.2	0.8
45~54 岁 Age	81	11.1	17.3	6.2	6.2	12.3	2.5
55~60 岁 Age	40	12.5	17.5	15.0	5.0	5.0	2.5

2-4 样本、男性各年龄层、女性各年龄层计划未来一年内使用的服务/ Services to be Used Next Year by the Whole Sample, Age and Gender Groups

注：本题为多选题，合计百分比超过 100%（Multiple answers）

	人数 Number	国际长途电话 international long-distance call	国内长途电话 domestic long-distance call	电脑发传真 fax through computer	电子邮件 e-mail	网上浏览 internet skimming	邮政速递 express mail service
样本 Sample	691	10.4	4.9	18.4	26.8	32.9	11.4
男性 Male	353	13.6	3.1	20.7	28.9	34.0	12.2
16~24 岁 Age	90	12.2	3.3	34.4	47.8	47.8	14.4
25~34 岁 Age	114	11.4	4.4	19.3	23.7	32.5	12.3
35~44 岁 Age	80	15.0	2.5	11.3	12.5	22.5	8.8
45~54 岁 Age	56	21.4	0.0	16.1	32.1	32.1	12.5
55~60 岁 Age	13	0.0	7.7	15.4	30.8	30.8	15.4
女性 Female	338	7.1	6.8	16.0	24.6	31.7	10.7
16~24 岁 Age	92	9.8	7.6	28.3	44.6	46.7	10.9
25~34 岁 Age	110	7.3	7.3	11.8	13.6	27.3	10.0
35~44 岁 Age	78	6.4	6.4	12.8	24.4	29.5	6.4
45~54 岁 Age	42	4.8	2.4	7.1	11.9	19.0	23.8
55~60 岁 Age	16	0.0	12.5	12.5	18.8	18.8	0.0

续前表 continued

	人数 Number	付费电话信息服务 telephone information service	电视购物 TV shopping	KTV 包厢 KTV room	有线电视 cable TV	高档餐厅就餐 dinning in first-class restaurant	美容厅/院 beauty parlor
样本 Sample	691	11.3	24.3	6.8	3.6	13.5	14.6
男性 Male	353	11.0	24.4	5.7	3.7	11.9	7.1
16~24 岁 Age	90	10.0	36.7	8.9	5.6	15.6	6.7
25~34 岁 Age	114	11.4	23.7	6.1	0.9	7.9	9.6
35~44 岁 Age	80	7.5	16.3	2.5	5.0	12.5	5.0
45~54 岁 Age	56	16.1	19.6	1.8	3.6	14.3	3.6
55~60 岁 Age	13	15.4	15.4	15.4	7.7	7.7	15.4
女性 Female	338	11.5	24.3	8.0	3.6	15.1	22.5
16~24 岁 Age	92	7.6	30.4	8.7	6.5	15.2	21.7
25~34 岁 Age	110	10.0	23.6	9.1	2.7	18.2	23.6
35~44 岁 Age	78	16.7	20.5	9.0	1.3	12.8	29.5
45~54 岁 Age	42	16.7	21.4	4.8	2.4	14.3	11.9
55~60 岁 Age	16	6.3	18.8	0.0	6.3	6.3	12.5

续前表 continued

	人数 Number	体育场馆 stadium	VCD/录像带出租 renting VCD & videotape	小时工 household service counted in hours	汽车租赁 renting car	器械健身 gym equipment	网吧 internet cafe
样本 Sample	691	13.0	8.0	14.5	11.6	22.9	13.5
男性 Male	353	15.6	7.4	12.2	13.9	22.4	13.6
16~24 岁 Age	90	15.6	5.6	10.0	15.6	18.9	21.1
25~34 岁 Age	114	15.8	6.1	14.9	16.7	27.2	15.8
35~44 岁 Age	80	13.8	8.8	5.0	15.0	21.3	7.5
45~54 岁 Age	56	14.3	7.1	19.6	3.6	17.9	5.4
55~60 岁 Age	13	30.8	23.1	15.4	15.4	30.8	15.4
女性 Female	338	10.4	8.6	16.9	9.2	23.4	13.3
16~24 岁 Age	92	15.2	12.0	19.6	12.0	32.6	25.0
25~34 岁 Age	110	9.1	4.5	17.3	10.0	21.8	11.8
35~44 岁 Age	78	7.7	10.3	19.2	10.3	20.5	10.3
45~54 岁 Age	42	11.9	7.1	2.4	0.0	14.3	2.4
55~60 岁 Age	16	0.0	12.5	25.0	6.3	18.8	0.0

2-5 不同消费者层最近一年内使用过的服务/ Services Used Last Year by Market Segments

2-5-1 时尚流行指标/ Fads Popular Index

注：本题为多选题，合计百分比超过 100%（Multiple answers）

	人数 Number	国际长途电话 international long-distance call	国内长途电话 domestic long-distance call	电脑发传真 fax through computer	电子邮件 e-mail	网上浏览 internet skimming	邮政速递 express mail service
样本 Sample	989	13.5	70.0	7.9	10.6	13.2	17.2
平实生活指向 simple living orientation	460	11.5	68.3	5.4	8.7	12.2	15.2
时尚流行指向 fashion orientation	529	15.3	71.5	10.0	12.3	14.2	18.9

续前表 continued

	人数 Number	付费电话信息服务 telephone information service	电视购物 TV shopping	KTV 包厢 KTV room	有线电视 cable TV	高档餐厅就餐 dinning in first-class restaurant	美容厅/院 beauty parlor
样本 Sample	989	23.5	6.2	26.1	92.0	33.3	18.4
平实生活指向 simple living orientation	460	21.3	4.6	14.3	93.0	24.6	8.7
时尚流行指向 fashion orientation	529	25.3	7.6	36.3	91.1	40.8	26.8

续前表 continued

	人数 Number	体育场馆 stadium	VCD/录像带出租 renting VCD&videotape	小时工 household service counted in hours	汽车租赁 renting car	器械健身 gym equipment	网吧 internet cafe
样本 Sample	989	26.7	37.4	6.2	7.5	14.5	11.3
平实生活指向 simple living orientation	460	21.7	29.6	5.2	4.8	9.8	7.2
时尚流行指向 fashion orientation	529	31.0	44.2	7.0	9.8	18.5	14.9

2-5-2 信息交流指标/ Information Communication Index

注：本题为多选题，合计百分比超过 100%（Multiple answers）

	人数 Number	国际长途电话 international long-distance call	国内长途电话 domestic long-distance call	电脑发传真 fax through computer	电子邮件 e-mail	网上浏览 internet skimming	邮政速递 express mail service
样本 Sample	989	13.7	70.1	7.9	10.6	13.2	17.3
信息消极指向 negative orientation	54	9.3	63.0	3.7	9.3	9.3	11.1
中间层 medium	568	13.0	68.8	7.6	10.9	13.7	15.8
信息积极指向 active orientation	367	15.3	73.0	9.0	10.4	13.1	20.4

续前表 continued

	人数 Number	付费电话信息服务 telephone information service	电视购物 TV shopping	KTV 包厢 KTV room	有线电视 cable TV	高档餐厅就餐 dinning in first-class restaurant	美容厅/院 beauty parlor
样本 Sample	**989**	**23.6**	**6.2**	**26.2**	**92.0**	**33.3**	**18.3**
信息消极指向 negative orientation	54	7.4	3.7	14.8	90.7	22.2	11.1
中间层 medium	568	21.7	7.2	24.5	90.1	29.8	17.4
信息积极指向 active orientation	367	28.9	4.9	30.5	95.1	40.3	20.7

续前表 continued

	人数 Number	体育场馆 stadium	VCD/录像带出租 renting VCD&videotape	小时工 household service counted in hours	汽车租赁 renting car	器械健身 gym equipment	网吧 internet cafe
样本 Sample	**989**	**26.8**	**37.2**	**6.0**	**7.4**	**14.4**	**11.3**
信息消极指向 negative orientation	54	14.8	27.8	1.9	1.9	11.1	11.1
中间层 medium	568	24.6	32.7	5.8	6.9	12.9	10.6
信息积极指向 active orientation	367	31.9	45.5	6.8	9.0	17.2	12.5

2-6 不同消费者层计划未来一年内使用的服务/ Services to be Used Next Year by Market Segments

2-6-1 时尚流行指标/ Fads Popular Index

注：本题为多选题，合计百分比超过 100%（Multiple answers）

	人数 Number	国际长途电话 international long-distance call	国内长途电话 domestic long-distance call	电脑发传真 fax through computer	电子邮件 e-mail	网上浏览 internet skimming	邮政速递 express mail service
样本 Sample	**687**	**10.5**	**4.9**	**18.2**	**26.6**	**32.6**	**11.4**
平实生活指向 simple living orientation	286	11.5	5.9	18.9	26.9	29.7	12.2
时尚流行指向 fashion orientation	401	9.7	4.2	17.7	26.4	34.7	10.7

续前表 continued

	人数 Number	付费电话信息服务 telephone information service	电视购物 TV shopping	KTV 包厢 KTV room	有线电视 cable TV	高档餐厅就餐 dinning in first-class restaurant	美容厅/院 beauty parlor
样本 Sample	**687**	**11.2**	**24.2**	**6.7**	**3.6**	**13.2**	**14.7**
平实生活指向 simple living orientation	286	12.6	21.7	7.7	3.8	15.0	11.2
时尚流行指向 fashion orientation	401	10.2	25.9	6.0	3.5	12.0	17.2

续前表 continued

	人数 Number	体育场馆 stadium	VCD/录像带出租 renting VCD&videotape	小时工 household service counted in hours	汽车租赁 renting car	器械健身 gym equipment	网吧 internet cafe
样本 Sample	**687**	**13.0**	**7.9**	**14.4**	**11.5**	**22.6**	**13.4**
平实生活指向 simple living orientation	286	14.7	8.0	14.7	9.4	20.3	12.2
时尚流行指向 fashion orientation	401	11.7	7.7	14.2	13.0	24.2	14.2

2-6-2 信息交流指标/ Information Communication Index

注：本题为多选题，合计百分比超过 100%（Multiple answers）

	人数 Number	国际长途电话 international long-distance call	国内长途电话 domestic long-distance call	电脑发传真 fax through computer	电子邮件 e-mail	网上浏览 internet skimming	邮政速递 express mail service
样本 Sample	685	10.2	4.8	18.4	26.9	33.0	11.2
信息消极指向 negative orientation	26	15.4	3.8	11.5	11.5	23.1	11.5
中间层 medium	399	10.3	6.0	17.0	26.8	31.6	11.8
信息积极指向 active orientation	260	9.6	3.1	21.2	28.5	36.2	10.4

续前表 continued

	人数 Number	付费电话信息服务 telephone information service	电视购物 TV shopping	KTV 包厢 KTV room	有线电视 cable TV	高档餐厅就餐 dinning in first-class restaurant	美容厅/院 beauty parlor
样本 Sample	685	11.1	24.2	6.9	3.6	13.6	14.5
信息消极指向 negative orientation	26	11.5	38.5	3.8	7.7	7.7	15.4
中间层 medium	399	9.8	19.5	7.8	4.5	16.3	15.3
信息积极指向 active orientation	260	13.1	30.0	5.8	1.9	10.0	13.1

续前表 continued

	人数 Number	体育场馆 stadium	VCD/录像带出租 renting VCD&videotape	小时工 household service counted in hours	汽车租赁 renting car	器械健身 gym equipment	网吧 internet cafe
样本 Sample	685	13.0	7.9	14.5	11.7	22.9	13.6
信息消极指向 negative orientation	26	7.7	0.0	15.4	15.4	7.7	3.8
中间层 medium	399	12.8	9.0	13.3	10.3	22.1	12.8
信息积极指向 active orientation	260	13.8	6.9	16.2	13.5	25.8	15.8

● 广州 / Guangzhou

2-1 最近一年内使用过的服务项目排名/ Ranking of the Services have Used Last Year

注：本题为多选题，合计百分比超过 100%（Multiple answers）

排名 Ranking	服务项目 Service Items	人次 Person-time	百分比 Percent
1	有线电视 cable TV	926	90.6
2	国内长途电话 domestic long-distance call	713	69.8
3	高档餐厅就餐 dining in first-class restaurant	356	34.8
4	国际长途电话 international long-distance call	259	25.3
5	体育场馆 stadium	258	25.2
6	VCD/录像带出租 renting VCD & videotape	196	19.2
7	美容厅/院 beauty parlor	185	18.1
8	邮政速递 express mail service	180	17.6
9	付费电话信息服务 telephone information service	168	16.4
10	网上浏览 internet skimming	140	13.7
11	器械健身 gym equipment	138	13.5
12	KTV 包厢 KTV room	132	12.9
13	电子邮件 e-mail	128	12.5
14	电脑发传真 fax through computer	58	5.7
15	网吧 internet cafe	54	5.3
16	小时工 household service counted in hours	49	4.8
17	汽车租赁 renting car	48	4.7
18	电视购物 TV shopping	27	2.6

n=1022

2-2 计划未来一年使用的服务项目排名/ Ranking of the Services Planned to Use Next Year

注：本题为多选题，合计百分比超过 100%（Multiple answers）

排名 Ranking	服务项目 Service Items	人次 Person-time	百分比 Percent
1	网上浏览 internet skimming	205	36.9
2	电子邮件 e-mail	167	30.0
3	电脑发传真 fax through computer	127	22.8
4	电视购物 TV shopping	118	21.2
5	器械健身 gym equipment	113	20.3
6	网吧 internet cafe	90	16.2
7	高档餐厅就餐 dining in first-class restaurant	88	15.8
8	国际长途电话 international long-distance call	69	12.4
9	邮政速递 express mail service	65	11.7
10	小时工 household service counted in hours	63	11.3
11	体育场馆 stadium	62	11.2
12	美容厅/院 beauty parlor	57	10.3
13	汽车租赁 renting car	53	9.5
14	付费电话信息服务 telephone information service	49	8.8
15	国内长途电话 domestic long-distance call	41	7.4
16	VCD/录像带出租 renting VCD & videotape	35	6.3
17	KTV 包厢 KTV room	27	4.9
18	电视购物 TV shopping	13	2.3

n=556

2-3 样本、男性各年龄层、女性各年龄层过去一年内使用的服务/ Services Used Last Year by the Whole Sample, Age and Gender Groups

注：本题为多选题，合计百分比超过 100%（Multiple answers）

	人数 Number	国际长途电话 international long-distance call	国内长途电话 domestic long-distance call	电脑发传真 fax through computer	电子邮件 e-mail	网上浏览 internet skimming	邮政速递 express mail service
样本 Sample	1022	25.3	69.8	5.7	12.5	13.7	17.6
男性 Male	493	24.1	71.2	6.1	14.8	17.4	17.6
16~24 岁 Age	105	22.9	71.4	5.7	29.5	34.3	19.0
25~34 岁 Age	148	27.7	78.4	12.2	18.9	23.0	25.7
35~44 岁 Age	126	24.6	64.3	2.4	6.3	5.6	12.7
45~54 岁 Age	72	22.2	70.8	2.8	6.9	11.1	12.5
55~60 岁 Age	42	16.7	66.7	2.4	2.4	2.4	9.5
女性 Female	529	26.5	68.4	5.3	10.4	10.2	17.6
16~24 岁 Age	111	26.1	55.9	9.0	24.3	24.3	25.2
25~34 岁 Age	157	26.8	75.2	8.9	11.5	12.1	22.3
35~44 岁 Age	136	29.4	70.6	1.5	4.4	2.9	14.0
45~54 岁 Age	85	28.2	69.4	1.2	3.5	3.5	10.6
55~60 岁 Age	40	12.5	67.5	2.5	2.5	2.5	5.0

续前表 continued

	人数 Number	付费电话信息服务 telephone information service	电视购物 TV shopping	KTV 包厢 KTV room	有线电视 cable TV	高档餐厅就餐 dinning in first-class restaurant	美容厅/院 beauty parlor
样本 Sample	1022	16.4	2.6	12.9	90.6	34.8	18.1
男性 Male	493	13.0	2.6	17.4	91.5	35.7	10.3
16~24 岁 Age	105	13.3	3.8	21.0	88.6	40.0	7.6
25~34 岁 Age	148	15.5	4.1	24.3	90.5	42.6	15.5
35~44 岁 Age	126	11.9	1.6	14.3	95.2	31.0	10.3
45~54 岁 Age	72	11.1	1.4	11.1	90.3	33.3	5.6
55~60 岁 Age	42	9.5	0.0	4.8	92.9	19.0	7.1
女性 Female	529	19.7	2.6	8.7	89.8	34.0	25.3
16~24 岁 Age	111	32.4	4.5	13.5	80.2	41.4	25.2
25~34 岁 Age	157	17.2	1.9	11.5	94.3	38.2	35.7
35~44 岁 Age	136	18.4	3.7	8.1	94.1	37.5	25.0
45~54 岁 Age	85	12.9	0.0	1.2	89.4	16.5	16.5
55~60 岁 Age	40	12.5	2.5	2.5	85.0	22.5	5.0

续前表 continued

	人数 Number	体育场馆 stadium	VCD/录像带出租 renting VCD & videotape	小时工 household service counted in hours	汽车租赁 renting car	器械健身 gym equipment	网吧 internet cafe
样本 Sample	1022	25.2	19.2	4.8	4.7	13.5	5.3
男性 Male	493	30.0	19.9	4.5	5.5	16.6	7.7
16~24 岁 Age	105	46.7	25.7	8.6	4.8	23.8	21.0
25~34 岁 Age	148	39.9	25.7	4.7	4.7	19.6	9.5
35~44 岁 Age	126	18.3	17.5	3.2	3.2	9.5	1.6
45~54 岁 Age	72	18.1	9.7	1.4	11.1	16.7	0.0
55~60 岁 Age	42	9.5	9.5	2.4	7.1	9.5	0.0
女性 Female	529	20.8	18.5	5.1	4.0	10.6	3.0
16~24 岁 Age	111	40.5	27.9	10.8	7.2	17.1	10.8
25~34 岁 Age	157	20.4	19.1	5.1	5.1	8.9	1.9
35~44 岁 Age	136	16.9	14.7	1.5	0.0	8.1	0.7
45~54 岁 Age	85	10.6	14.1	3.5	3.5	11.8	0.0
55~60 岁 Age	40	2.5	12.5	5.0	5.0	5.0	0.0

2-4 样本、男性各年龄层、女性各年龄层计划未来一年内使用的服务/ Services to be Used Next Year by the Whole Sample, Age and Gender Groups

注：本题为多选题，合计百分比超过 100%（Multiple answers）

	人数 Number	国际长途电话 international long-distance call	国内长途电话 domestic long-distance call	电脑发传真 fax through computer	电子邮件 e-mail	网上浏览 internet skimming	邮政速递 express mail service
样本 Sample	556	12.4	7.4	22.8	30.0	36.9	11.7
男性 Male	287	11.1	8.0	25.4	30.3	35.5	16.0
16~24 岁 Age	75	24.0	6.7	41.3	38.7	50.7	20.0
25~34 岁 Age	96	6.3	6.3	21.9	36.5	34.4	14.6
35~44 岁 Age	62	4.8	11.3	21.0	16.1	29.0	11.3
45~54 岁 Age	36	11.1	5.6	11.1	25.0	19.4	25.0
55~60 岁 Age	18	5.6	16.7	22.2	22.2	33.3	5.6
女性 Female	269	13.8	6.7	20.1	29.7	38.3	7.1
16~24 岁 Age	76	17.1	7.9	25.0	40.8	53.9	6.6
25~34 岁 Age	88	10.2	3.4	14.8	25.0	33.0	5.7
35~44 岁 Age	64	15.6	7.8	25.0	29.7	39.1	10.9
45~54 岁 Age	32	9.4	6.3	12.5	21.9	25.0	6.3
55~60 岁 Age	9	22.2	22.2	22.2	11.1	0.0	0.0

续前表 continued

	人数 Number	付费电话信息服务 telephone information service	电视购物 TV shopping	KTV 包厢 KTV room	有线电视 cable TV	高档餐厅就餐 dinning in first-class restaurant	美容厅/院 beauty parlor
样本 Sample	556	8.8	21.2	4.9	2.3	15.8	10.3
男性 Male	287	9.4	19.2	3.1	2.4	17.1	4.5
16~24 岁 Age	75	14.7	24.0	6.7	1.3	16.0	4.0
25~34 岁 Age	96	7.3	21.9	1.0	3.1	15.6	5.2
35~44 岁 Age	62	8.1	11.3	3.2	4.8	14.5	1.6
45~54 岁 Age	36	5.6	11.1	0.0	0.0	25.0	11.1
55~60 岁 Age	18	11.1	27.8	5.6	0.0	22.2	0.0
女性 Female	269	8.2	23.4	6.7	2.2	14.5	16.4
16~24 岁 Age	76	6.6	23.7	10.5	5.3	14.5	17.1
25~34 岁 Age	88	10.2	25.0	6.8	0.0	18.2	14.8
35~44 岁 Age	64	9.4	21.9	6.3	1.6	9.4	18.8
45~54 岁 Age	32	6.3	18.8	0.0	3.1	18.8	15.6
55~60 岁 Age	9	0.0	33.3	0.0	0.0	0.0	11.1

续前表 continued

	人数 Number	体育场馆 stadium	VCD/录像带出租 renting VCD & videotape	小时工 household service counted in hours	汽车租赁 renting car	器械健身 gym equipment	网吧 internet cafe
样本 Sample	556	11.2	6.3	11.3	9.5	20.3	16.2
男性 Male	287	12.2	4.9	9.8	11.5	20.2	15.3
16~24 岁 Age	75	8.0	9.3	12.0	12.0	25.3	26.7
25~34 岁 Age	96	12.5	1.0	11.5	18.8	21.9	13.5
35~44 岁 Age	62	12.9	6.5	6.5	8.1	16.1	6.5
45~54 岁 Age	36	19.4	0.0	8.3	0.0	11.1	11.1
55~60 岁 Age	18	11.1	11.1	5.6	5.6	22.2	16.7
女性 Female	269	10.0	7.8	13.0	7.4	20.4	17.1
16~24 岁 Age	76	10.5	13.2	14.5	10.5	25.0	30.3
25~34 岁 Age	88	11.4	6.8	19.3	6.8	21.6	15.9
35~44 岁 Age	64	9.4	7.8	9.4	9.4	21.9	9.4
45~54 岁 Age	32	6.3	0.0	0.0	0.0	6.3	9.4
55~60 岁 Age	9	11.1	0.0	11.1	0.0	11.1	0.0

2-5 不同消费者层最近一年内使用过的服务/ Services Used Last Year by Market Segments

2-5-1 时尚流行指标/ Fads Popular Index

注：本题为多选题，合计百分比超过 100%（Multiple answers）

	人数 Number	国际长途电话 international long-distance call	国内长途电话 domestic long-distance call	电脑发传真 fax through computer	电子邮件 e-mail	网上浏览 internet skimming	邮政速递 express mail service
样本 Sample	1010	25.5	69.8	5.7	12.7	13.9	17.7
平实生活指向 simple living orientation	512	22.5	68.2	5.3	11.1	12.3	16.2
时尚流行指向 fashion orientation	498	28.7	71.5	6.2	14.3	15.5	19.3

续前表 continued

	人数 Number	付费电话信息服务 telephone information service	电视购物 TV shopping	KTV 包厢 KTV room	有线电视 cable TV	高档餐厅就餐 dinning in first-class restaurant	美容厅/院 beauty parlor
样本 Sample	1010	16.6	2.7	13.0	90.7	34.8	18.1
平实生活指向 simple living orientation	512	13.5	2.0	10.5	92.8	31.1	11.9
时尚流行指向 fashion orientation	498	19.9	3.4	15.5	88.6	38.6	24.5

续前表 continued

	人数 Number	体育场馆 stadium	VCD/录像带出租 renting VCD& videotape	小时工 household service counted in hours	汽车租赁 renting car	器械健身 gym equipment	网吧 internet cafe
样本 Sample	1010	25.3	19.3	4.7	4.8	13.5	5.3
平实生活指向 simple living orientation	512	19.5	16.2	2.5	4.5	10.7	2.3
时尚流行指向 fashion orientation	498	31.3	22.5	6.8	5.0	16.3	8.4

2-5-2 信息交流指标/ Information Communication Index

注：本题为多选题，合计百分比超过 100%（Multiple answers）

	人数 Number	国际长途电话 international long-distance call	国内长途电话 domestic long-distance call	电脑发传真 fax through computer	电子邮件 e-mail	网上浏览 internet skimming	邮政速递 express mail service
样本 Sample	1014	25.4	69.7	5.7	12.3	13.6	17.5
信息消极指向 negative orientation	108	17.6	59.3	3.7	6.5	10.2	10.2
中间层 medium	657	25.7	69.3	5.6	12.8	12.9	16.4
信息积极指向 active orientation	249	28.1	75.5	6.8	13.7	16.9	23.3

续前表 continued

	人数 Number	付费电话信息服务 telephone information service	电视购物 TV shopping	KTV 包厢 KTV room	有线电视 cable TV	高档餐厅就餐 dinning in first-class restaurant	美容厅/院 beauty parlor
样本 Sample	1014	16.5	2.6	13.0	90.6	34.9	18.0
信息消极指向 negative orientation	108	13.0	2.8	5.6	88.0	23.1	12.0
中间层 medium	657	15.4	3.3	12.2	91.0	33.2	17.0
信息积极指向 active orientation	249	20.9	0.4	18.5	90.8	44.6	23.3

续前表 continued

	人数 Number	体育场馆 stadium	VCD/录像带出租 renting VCD& videotape	小时工 household service counted in hours	汽车租赁 renting car	器械健身 gym equipment	网吧 internet cafe
样本 Sample	1014	25.0	19.1	4.7	4.7	13.4	5.2
信息消极指向 negative orientation	108	9.3	13.9	2.8	2.8	6.5	0.9
中间层 medium	657	26.3	17.7	3.7	4.4	12.8	6.1
信息积极指向 active orientation	249	28.5	25.3	8.4	6.4	18.1	4.8

2-6 不同消费者层计划未来一年内使用的服务/ Services to be Used Next Year by Market Segments

2-6-1 时尚流行指标/ Fads Popular Index

注：本题为多选题，合计百分比超过 100%（Multiple answers）

	人数 Number	国际长途电话 international long-distance call	国内长途电话 domestic long-distance call	电脑发传真 fax through computer	电子邮件 e-mail	网上浏览 internet skimming	邮政速递 express mail service
样本 Sample	550	12.5	7.5	22.9	29.8	36.9	11.6
平实生活指向 simple living orientation	249	12.4	8.4	23.7	26.9	34.1	8.8
时尚流行指向 fashion orientation	301	12.6	6.6	22.3	32.2	39.2	14.0

续前表 continued

	人数 Number	付费电话信息服务 telephone information service	电视购物 TV shopping	KTV 包厢 KTV room	有线电视 cable TV	高档餐厅就餐 dinning in first-class restaurant	美容厅/院 beauty parlor
样本 Sample	550	8.9	21.1	4.7	2.4	16.0	10.4
平实生活指向 simple living orientation	249	6.8	19.3	4.4	0.8	18.9	8.8
时尚流行指向 fashion orientation	301	10.6	22.6	5.0	3.7	13.6	11.6

续前表 continued

	人数 Number	体育场馆 stadium	VCD/录像带出租 renting VCD& videotape	小时工 household service counted in hours	汽车租赁 renting car	器械健身 gym equipment	网吧 internet cafe
样本 Sample	550	11.3	6.4	11.5	9.6	20.5	16.4
平实生活指向 simple living orientation	249	13.7	6.4	10.8	10.8	16.9	13.7
时尚流行指向 fashion orientation	301	9.3	6.3	12.0	8.6	23.6	18.6

2-6-2 信息交流指标/ Information Communication Index

注：本题为多选题，合计百分比超过 100%（Multiple answers）

	人数 Number	国际长途电话 international long-distance call	国内长途电话 domestic long-distance call	电脑发传真 fax through computer	电子邮件 e-mail	网上浏览 internet skimming	邮政速递 express mail service
样本 Sample	550	12.4	7.3	22.7	30.0	36.7	11.5
信息消极指向 negative orientation	57	14.0	8.8	19.3	19.3	24.6	8.8
中间层 medium	362	12.4	8.0	24.3	34.0	41.2	12.7
信息积极指向 active orientation	131	11.5	4.6	19.8	23.7	29.8	9.2

续前表 continued

	人数 Number	付费电话信息服务 telephone information service	电视购物 TV shopping	KTV 包厢 KTV room	有线电视 cable TV	高档餐厅就餐 dinning in first-class restaurant	美容厅/院 beauty parlor
样本 Sample	550	8.7	21.3	4.7	2.4	15.6	10.4
信息消极指向 negative orientation	57	7.0	26.3	3.5	1.8	19.3	10.5
中间层 medium	362	8.0	20.2	5.2	2.5	13.3	11.0
信息积极指向 active orientation	131	11.5	22.1	3.8	2.3	20.6	8.4

续前表 continued

	人数 Number	体育场馆 stadium	VCD/录像带出租 renting VCD& videotape	小时工 household service counted in hours	汽车租赁 renting car	器械健身 gym equipment	网吧 internet cafe
样本 Sample	550	11.1	6.4	11.5	9.3	20.4	16.4
信息消极指向 negative orientation	57	14.0	10.5	7.0	5.3	22.8	5.3
中间层 medium	362	9.1	5.2	10.8	9.1	20.4	16.9
信息积极指向 active orientation	131	15.3	7.6	15.3	11.5	19.1	19.8

● 重庆 / Chongqing

2-1 最近一年内使用过的服务项目排名/ Ranking of the Services have Used Last Year

注：本题为多选题，合计百分比超过 100%（Multiple answers）

排名 Ranking	服务项目 Service Items	人次 Person-time	百分比 Percent
1	有线电视 cable TV	587	94.4
2	国内长途电话 domestic long-distance call	421	67.7
3	VCD/录像带出租 renting VCD & videotape	302	48.6
4	高档餐厅就餐 dining in first-class restaurant	176	28.3
5	体育场馆 stadium	154	24.8
6	邮政速递 express mail service	114	18.3
6	付费电话信息服务 telephone information service	114	18.3
7	美容厅/院 beauty parlor	86	13.8
8	器械健身 gym equipment	42	6.8
9	KTV 包厢 KTV room	37	5.9
10	电子邮件 e-mail	31	5.0
11	汽车租赁 renting car	27	4.3
11	国际长途电话 international long-distance call	27	4.3
12	网上浏览 internet skimming	26	4.2
13	电脑发传真 fax through computer	23	3.7
13	网吧 internet cafe	23	3.7
14	电视购物 TV shopping	18	2.9
15	小时工 household service counted in hours	13	2.1

n=622

2-2 计划未来一年使用的服务项目排名/ Ranking of the Services Planned to Use Next Year

注：本题为多选题，合计百分比超过 100%（Multiple answers）

排名 Ranking	服务项目 Service Items	人次 Person-time	百分比 Percent
1	网上浏览 internet skimming	87	28.7
2	器械健身 gym equipment	73	24.1
3	电子邮件 e-mail	65	21.5
4	高档餐厅就餐 dining in first-class restaurant	58	19.1
5	电脑发传真 fax through computer	55	18.2
6	美容厅/院 beauty parlor	52	17.2
7	电视购物 TV shopping	51	16.8
8	网吧 internet cafe	48	15.8
9	体育场馆 stadium	41	13.5
10	国际长途电话 international long-distance call	34	11.2
11	邮政速递 express mail service	31	10.2
11	汽车租赁 renting car	31	10.2
11	国内长途电话 domestic long-distance call	31	10.2
12	付费电话信息服务 telephone information service	26	8.6
13	小时工 household service counted in hours	25	8.3
14	VCD/录像带出租 renting VCD & videotape	17	5.6
14	KTV 包厢 KTV room	17	5.6
15	电视购物 TV shopping	3	1.0

n=303

2-3 样本、男性各年龄层、女性各年龄层过去一年内使用的服务/ Services Used Last Year by the Whole Sample, Age and Gender Groups

注：本题为多选题，合计百分比超过 100%（Multiple answers）

	人数 Number	国际长途电话 international long-distance call	国内长途电话 domestic long-distance call	电脑发传真 fax through computer	电子邮件 e-mail	网上浏览 internet skimming	邮政速递 express mail service
样本 Sample	622	4.3	67.7	3.7	5.0	4.2	18.3
男性 Male	312	3.8	66.0	5.8	4.8	6.4	16.0
16~24 岁 Age	64	3.1	54.7	4.7	7.8	15.6	20.3
25~34 岁 Age	93	4.3	73.1	8.6	5.4	8.6	19.4
35~44 岁 Age	73	5.5	71.2	5.5	2.7	0.0	13.7
45~54 岁 Age	54	3.7	63.0	3.7	3.7	1.9	9.3
55~60 岁 Age	28	0.0	60.7	3.6	3.6	3.6	14.3
女性 Female	310	4.8	69.4	1.6	5.2	1.9	20.6
16~24 岁 Age	64	10.9	70.3	3.1	15.6	9.4	31.3
25~34 岁 Age	90	5.6	80.0	2.2	5.6	0.0	27.8
35~44 岁 Age	73	1.4	56.2	0.0	1.4	0.0	9.6
45~54 岁 Age	60	1.7	73.3	1.7	0.0	0.0	13.3
55~60 岁 Age	23	4.3	56.5	0.0	0.0	0.0	17.4

续前表 continued

	人数 Number	付费电话信息服务 telephone information service	电视购物 TV shopping	KTV 包厢 KTV room	有线电视 cable TV	高档餐厅就餐 dinning in first-class restaurant	美容厅/院 beauty parlor
样本 Sample	622	18.3	2.9	5.9	94.4	28.3	13.8
男性 Male	312	16.7	2.2	6.7	96.5	31.4	8.7
16~24 岁 Age	64	20.3	6.3	3.1	98.4	21.9	9.4
25~34 岁 Age	93	12.9	2.2	14.0	95.7	37.6	12.9
35~44 岁 Age	73	19.2	0.0	8.2	94.5	43.8	8.2
45~54 岁 Age	54	14.8	0.0	0.0	98.1	20.4	3.7
55~60 岁 Age	28	17.9	3.6	0.0	96.4	21.4	3.6
女性 Female	310	20.0	3.5	5.2	92.3	25.2	19.0
16~24 岁 Age	64	21.9	1.6	12.5	90.6	32.8	20.3
25~34 岁 Age	90	24.4	5.6	7.8	91.1	33.3	33.3
35~44 岁 Age	73	17.8	2.7	1.4	95.9	16.4	12.3
45~54 岁 Age	60	16.7	3.3	0.0	88.3	18.3	11.7
55~60 岁 Age	23	13.0	4.3	0.0	100.0	17.4	0.0

续前表 continued

	人数 Number	体育场馆 stadium	VCD/录像带出租 renting VCD & videotape	小时工 household service counted in hours	汽车租赁 renting car	器械健身 gym equipment	网吧 internet cafe
样本 Sample	622	24.8	48.6	2.1	4.3	6.8	3.7
男性 Male	312	30.8	49.0	2.6	4.8	6.1	5.8
16~24 岁 Age	64	40.6	51.6	0.0	3.1	6.3	10.9
25~34 岁 Age	93	32.3	58.1	4.3	1.1	6.5	10.8
35~44 岁 Age	73	39.7	47.9	4.1	6.8	6.8	0.0
45~54 岁 Age	54	14.8	37.0	0.0	7.4	1.9	0.0
55~60 岁 Age	28	10.7	39.3	3.6	10.7	10.7	3.6
女性 Female	310	18.7	48.1	1.6	3.9	7.4	1.6
16~24 岁 Age	64	39.1	70.3	3.1	3.1	14.1	6.3
25~34 岁 Age	90	16.7	51.1	3.3	7.8	5.6	0.0
35~44 岁 Age	73	12.3	41.1	0.0	0.0	5.5	1.4
45~54 岁 Age	60	8.3	41.7	0.0	3.3	5.0	0.0
55~60 岁 Age	23	17.4	13.0	0.0	4.3	8.7	0.0

2-4 样本、男性各年龄层、女性各年龄层计划未来一年内使用的服务/ Services to be Used Next Year by the Whole Sample, Age and Gender Groups

注：本题为多选题，合计百分比超过 100%（Multiple answers）

	人数 Number	国际长途电话 international long-distance call	国内长途电话 domestic long-distance call	电脑发传真 fax through computer	电子邮件 e-mail	网上浏览 internet skimming	邮政速递 express mail service
样本 Sample	303	11.2	10.2	18.2	21.5	28.7	10.2
男性 Male	151	11.9	11.3	21.9	29.1	34.4	11.9
16~24 岁 Age	45	8.9	20.0	22.2	35.6	35.6	13.3
25~34 岁 Age	49	14.3	6.1	20.4	28.6	32.7	12.2
35~44 岁 Age	31	16.1	12.9	25.8	29.0	48.4	12.9
45~54 岁 Age	17	5.9	0.0	23.5	17.6	23.5	5.9
55~60 岁 Age	9	11.1	11.1	11.1	22.2	11.1	11.1
女性 Female	152	10.5	9.2	14.5	13.8	23.0	8.6
16~24 岁 Age	43	14.0	4.7	20.9	23.3	39.5	7.0
25~34 岁 Age	50	10.0	4.0	14.0	10.0	22.0	8.0
35~44 岁 Age	31	3.2	16.1	12.9	9.7	12.9	12.9
45~54 岁 Age	23	13.0	17.4	8.7	13.0	13.0	8.7
55~60 岁 Age	5	20.0	20.0	0.0	0.0	0.0	0.0

续前表 continued

	人数 Number	付费电话信息服务 telephone information service	电视购物 TV shopping	KTV 包厢 KTV room	有线电视 cable TV	高档餐厅就餐 dinning in first-class restaurant	美容厅/院 beauty parlor
样本 Sample	303	8.6	16.8	5.6	1.0	19.1	17.2
男性 Male	151	10.6	13.9	9.3	0.0	16.6	8.6
16~24 岁 Age	45	8.9	15.6	15.6	0.0	11.1	6.7
25~34 岁 Age	49	6.1	10.2	10.2	0.0	12.2	12.2
35~44 岁 Age	31	12.9	3.2	3.2	0.0	12.9	3.2
45~54 岁 Age	17	17.6	23.5	0.0	0.0	41.2	11.8
55~60 岁 Age	9	22.2	44.4	11.1	0.0	33.3	11.1
女性 Female	152	6.6	19.7	2.0	2.0	21.7	25.7
16~24 岁 Age	43	7.0	27.9	2.3	0.0	18.6	27.9
25~34 岁 Age	50	8.0	18.0	2.0	4.0	22.0	28.0
35~44 岁 Age	31	6.5	12.9	0.0	0.0	16.1	25.8
45~54 岁 Age	23	4.3	21.7	4.3	4.3	26.1	21.7
55~60 岁 Age	5	0.0	0.0	0.0	0.0	60.0	0.0

续前表 continued

	人数 Number	体育场馆 stadium	VCD/录像带出租 renting VCD & videotape	小时工 household service counted in hours	汽车租赁 renting car	器械健身 gym equipment	网吧 internet cafe
样本 Sample	303	13.5	5.6	8.3	10.2	24.1	15.8
男性 Male	151	20.5	2.6	7.9	14.6	27.8	21.2
16~24 岁 Age	45	13.3	0.0	6.7	17.8	28.9	31.1
25~34 岁 Age	49	20.4	0.0	10.2	22.4	28.6	20.4
35~44 岁 Age	31	19.4	6.5	0.0	6.5	29.0	16.1
45~54 岁 Age	17	41.2	11.8	11.8	0.0	17.6	11.8
55~60 岁 Age	9	22.2	0.0	22.2	11.1	33.3	11.1
女性 Female	152	6.6	8.6	8.6	5.9	20.4	10.5
16~24 岁 Age	43	2.3	4.7	7.0	7.0	18.6	23.3
25~34 岁 Age	50	8.0	10.0	6.0	6.0	24.0	8.0
35~44 岁 Age	31	3.2	9.7	6.5	6.5	12.9	3.2
45~54 岁 Age	23	17.4	8.7	21.7	4.3	26.1	4.3
55~60 岁 Age	5	0.0	20.0	0.0	0.0	20.0	0.0

2-5 不同消费者层最近一年内使用过的服务/ Services Used Last Year by Market Segments

2-5-1 时尚流行指标/ Fads Popular Index

注：本题为多选题，合计百分比超过 100%（Multiple answers）

	人数 Number	国际长途电话 international long-distance call	国内长途电话 domestic long-distance call	电脑发传真 fax through computer	电子邮件 e-mail	网上浏览 internet skimming	邮政速递 express mail service
样本 Sample	614	4.2	67.8	3.7	5.0	4.2	18.2
平实生活指向 simple living orientation	367	1.9	64.6	2.2	3.5	2.5	14.7
时尚流行指向 fashion orientation	247	7.7	72.5	6.1	7.3	6.9	23.5

续前表 continued

	人数 Number	付费电话信息服务 telephone information service	电视购物 TV shopping	KTV 包厢 KTV room	有线电视 cable TV	高档餐厅就餐 dinning in first-class restaurant	美容厅/院 beauty parlor
样本 Sample	614	18.2	2.8	6.0	94.3	28.3	14.0
平实生活指向 simple living orientation	367	14.4	1.6	2.2	94.6	21.0	6.8
时尚流行指向 fashion orientation	247	23.9	4.5	11.7	93.9	39.3	24.7

续前表 continued

	人数 Number	体育场馆 stadium	VCD/录像带出租 renting VCD &videotape	小时工 household service counted in hours	汽车租赁 renting car	器械健身 gym equipment	网吧 internet cafe
样本 Sample	614	24.6	48.4	2.1	4.1	6.8	3.6
平实生活指向 simple living orientation	367	18.0	37.9	0.8	3.0	4.4	1.9
时尚流行指向 fashion orientation	247	34.4	64.0	4.0	5.7	10.5	6.1

2-5-2 信息交流指标/ Information Communication Index

注：本题为多选题，合计百分比超过 100%（Multiple answers）

	人数 Number	国际长途电话 international long-distance call	国内长途电话 domestic long-distance call	电脑发传真 fax through computer	电子邮件 e-mail	网上浏览 internet skimming	邮政速递 express mail service
样本 Sample	613	4.2	68.4	3.6	4.9	4.2	18.4
信息消极指向 negative orientation	47	0.0	55.3	4.3	2.1	0.0	14.9
中间层 medium	338	5.0	66.9	3.0	4.4	5.0	15.4
信息积极指向 active orientation	228	3.9	73.2	4.4	6.1	3.9	23.7

续前表 continued

	人数 Number	付费电话信息服务 telephone information service	电视购物 TV shopping	KTV 包厢 KTV room	有线电视 cable TV	高档餐厅就餐 dinning in first-class restaurant	美容厅/院 beauty parlor
样本 Sample	613	18.6	2.9	6.0	94.3	28.5	13.9
信息消极指向 negative orientation	47	17.0	0.0	10.6	95.7	25.5	10.6
中间层 medium	338	15.7	2.1	4.1	93.5	25.7	12.4
信息积极指向 active orientation	228	23.2	4.8	7.9	95.2	33.3	16.7

续前表 continued

	人数 Number	体育场馆 stadium	VCD/录像带出租 renting VCD &videotape	小时工 household service counted in hours	汽车租赁 renting car	器械健身 gym equipment	网吧 internet cafe
样本 Sample	613	25.0	48.6	2.1	4.4	6.9	3.4
信息消极指向 negative orientation	47	8.5	38.3	2.1	4.3	10.6	0.0
中间层 medium	338	25.7	48.2	2.1	4.4	5.3	3.3
信息积极指向 active orientation	228	27.2	51.3	2.2	4.4	8.3	4.4

2-6 不同消费者层计划未来一年内使用的服务/ Services to be Used Next Year by Market Segments

2-6-1 时尚流行指标/ Fads Popular Index

注：本题为多选题，合计百分比超过 100%（Multiple answers）

	人数 Number	国际长途电话 international long-distance call	国内长途电话 domestic long-distance call	电脑发传真 fax through computer	电子邮件 e-mail	网上浏览 internet skimming	邮政速递 express mail service
样本 Sample	298	11.1	10.1	18.1	21.5	28.5	10.1
平实生活指向 simple living orientation	148	10.8	10.1	14.9	15.5	25.7	10.1
时尚流行指向 fashion orientation	150	11.3	10.0	21.3	27.3	31.3	10.0

续前表 continued

	人数 Number	付费电话信息服务 telephone information service	电视购物 TV shopping	KTV 包厢 KTV room	有线电视 cable TV	高档餐厅就餐 dinning in first-class restaurant	美容厅/院 beauty parlor
样本 Sample	298	8.4	16.8	5.4	1.0	19.1	17.1
平实生活指向 simple living orientation	148	5.4	14.9	4.1	1.4	17.6	16.9
时尚流行指向 fashion orientation	150	11.3	18.7	6.7	0.7	20.7	17.3

续前表 continued

	人数 Number	体育场馆 stadium	VCD/录像带出租 renting VCD& videotape	小时工 household service counted in hours	汽车租赁 renting car	器械健身 gym equipment	网吧 internet cafe
样本 Sample	298	13.4	5.7	7.4	10.1	23.5	15.8
平实生活指向 simple living orientation	148	18.2	8.8	8.8	8.8	23.0	10.1
时尚流行指向 fashion orientation	150	8.7	2.7	6.0	11.3	24.0	21.3

2-6-2 信息交流指标/ Information Communication Index

注：本题为多选题，合计百分比可能超过 100%（Multiple answers）

	人数 Number	国际长途电话 international long-distance call	国内长途电话 domestic long-distance call	电脑发传真 fax through computer	电子邮件 e-mail	网上浏览 internet skimming	邮政速递 express mail service
样本 Sample	298	11.1	10.1	18.1	21.1	28.5	10.1
信息消极指向 negative orientation	18	5.6	5.6	11.1	16.7	22.2	0.0
中间层 medium	159	10.1	10.7	18.9	25.2	30.2	9.4
信息积极指向 active orientation	121	13.2	9.9	18.2	16.5	27.3	12.4

续前表 continued

	人数 Number	付费电话信息服务 telephone information service	电视购物 TV shopping	KTV 包厢 KTV room	有线电视 cable TV	高档餐厅就餐 dinning in first-class restaurant	美容厅/院 beauty parlor
样本 Sample	**298**	**8.4**	**16.4**	**5.4**	**1.0**	**19.1**	**16.4**
信息消极指向 negative orientation	18	11.1	22.2	11.1	0.0	16.7	27.8
中间层 medium	159	7.5	16.4	5.0	1.3	18.9	15.7
信息积极指向 active orientation	121	9.1	15.7	5.0	0.8	19.8	15.7

续前表 continued

	人数 Number	体育场馆 stadium	VCD/录像带出租 renting VCD& videotape	小时工 household service counted in hours	汽车租赁 renting car	器械健身 gym equipment	网吧 internet cafe
样本 Sample	**298**	**13.4**	**5.4**	**8.1**	**9.7**	**24.2**	**15.4**
信息消极指向 negative orientation	18	16.7	5.6	5.6	0.0	11.1	27.8
中间层 medium	159	14.5	5.7	8.2	10.7	27.0	11.9
信息积极指向 active orientation	121	11.6	5.0	8.3	9.9	22.3	18.2

● 武汉 / Wuhan

2-1 最近一年内使用过的服务项目排名/ Ranking of the Services have Used Last Year

注：本题为多选题，合计百分比超过 100%（Multiple answers）

排名 Ranking	服务项目 Service Items	人次 Person-time	百分比 Percent
1	有线电视 cable TV	562	90.1
2	国内长途电话 domestic long-distance call	436	69.9
3	VCD/录像带出租 renting VCD & videotape	271	43.4
4	高档餐厅就餐 dining in first-class restaurant	209	33.5
5	付费电话信息服务 telephone information service	159	25.5
6	KTV 包厢 KTV room	134	21.5
7	邮政速递 express mail service	132	21.2
8	体育场馆 stadium	124	19.9
9	美容厅/院 beauty parlor	105	16.8
10	汽车租赁 renting car	72	11.5
11	网吧 internet cafe	51	8.2
12	网上浏览 internet skimming	46	7.4
13	器械健身 gym equipment	44	7.1
14	电脑发传真 fax through computer	40	6.4
14	国际长途电话 international long-distance call	40	6.4
15	电子邮件 e-mail	36	5.8
16	电视购物 TV shopping	20	3.2
17	小时工 household service counted in hours	18	2.9

n=624

2-2 计划未来一年使用的服务项目排名/ Ranking of the Services Planned to Use Next Year

注：本题为多选题，合计百分比超过 100%（Multiple answers）

排名 Ranking	服务项目 Service Items	人次 Person-time	百分比 Percent
1	网上浏览 internet skimming	94	28.3
2	器械健身 gym equipment	81	24.4
3	电视购物 TV shopping	62	18.7
4	电子邮件 e-mail	59	17.8
5	网吧 internet cafe	53	16.0
6	电脑发传真 fax through computer	49	14.8
7	美容厅/院 beauty parlor	40	12.0
8	高档餐厅就餐 dining in first-class restaurant	35	10.5
9	体育场馆 stadium	32	9.6
9	小时工 household service counted in hours	32	9.6
10	国内长途电话 domestic long-distance call	30	9.0
11	VCD/录像带出租 renting VCD & videotape	23	6.9
11	汽车租赁 renting car	23	6.9
12	电视购物 TV shopping	22	6.6
13	邮政速递 express mail service	21	6.3
14	付费电话信息服务 telephone information service	20	6.0
15	国际长途电话 international long-distance call	18	5.4
16	KTV 包厢 KTV room	13	3.9

n=332

2-3 样本、 男性各年龄层、 女性各年龄层过去一年内使用的服务/ Services Used Last Year by the Whole Sample, Age and Gender Groups

注：本题为多选题，合计百分比超过 100%（Multiple answers）

	人数 Number	国际长途电话 international long-distance call	国内长途电话 domestic long-distance call	电脑发传真 fax through computer	电子邮件 e-mail	网上浏览 internet skimming	邮政速递 express mail service
样本 Sample	**624**	**6.4**	**69.9**	**6.4**	**5.8**	**7.4**	**21.2**
男性 Male	**306**	**7.2**	**72.2**	**7.5**	**8.5**	**11.4**	**24.2**
16~24 岁 Age	65	3.1	64.6	6.2	15.4	23.1	27.7
25~34 岁 Age	89	9.0	79.8	9.0	11.2	11.2	31.5
35~44 岁 Age	76	3.9	69.7	6.6	2.6	2.6	18.4
45~54 岁 Age	52	11.5	71.2	5.3	7.7	15.4	17.3
55~60 岁 Age	24	12.5	75.0	12.5	0.0	0.0	20.8
女性 Female	**318**	**5.7**	**67.6**	**5.3**	**3.1**	**3.5**	**18.2**
16~24 岁 Age	67	4.5	61.2	9.0	6.0	7.5	17.9
25~34 岁 Age	94	6.4	86.2	7.4	6.4	5.3	21.3
35~44 岁 Age	74	4.1	56.8	1.4	0.0	0.0	21.6
45~54 岁 Age	61	8.2	59.0	4.9	0.0	1.6	14.8
55~60 岁 Age	22	4.5	68.2	0.0	0.0	0.0	4.5

续前表 continued

	人数 Number	付费电话信息服务 telephone information service	电视购物 TV shopping	KTV 包厢 KTV room	有线电视 cable TV	高档餐厅就餐 dinning in first-class restaurant	美容厅/院 beauty parlor
样本 Sample	**624**	**25.5**	**3.2**	**2[illegible].5**	**90.1**	**33.5**	**16.8**
男性 Male	**306**	**28.4**	**2.6**	**24.8**	**88.9**	**36.6**	**14.4**
16~24 岁 Age	65	33.8	3.1	36.9	90.8	36.9	18.5
25~34 岁 Age	89	31.5	1.1	32.6	88.8	49.4	21.3
35~44 岁 Age	76	27.6	3.9	19.7	82.9	28.9	13.2
45~54 岁 Age	52	21.2	1.9	11.5	98.1	28.8	5.8
55~60 岁 Age	24	20.8	4.2	8.3	83.3	29.2	0.0
女性 Female	**318**	**22.6**	**3.8**	**13.2**	**91.2**	**30.5**	**19.2**
16~24 岁 Age	67	22.4	6.0	32.8	91.0	34.3	23.9
25~34 岁 Age	94	29.8	5.3	25.6	89.4	44.7	34.0
35~44 岁 Age	74	24.3	4.1	8.1	90.5	20.3	13.5
45~54 岁 Age	61	14.8	0.0	8.2	95.1	24.6	3.3
55~60 岁 Age	22	9.1	0.0	0.0	90.9	9.1	4.5

续前表 continued

	人数 Number	体育场馆 stadium	VCD/录像带出租 renting VCD & videotape	小时工 household service counted in hours	汽车租赁 renting car	器械健身 gym equipment	网吧 internet cafe
样本 Sample	624	19.9	43.4	2.9	11.5	7.1	8.2
男性 Male	306	27.5	48.0	2.0	10.1	8.2	11.4
16~24 岁 Age	65	36.9	60.0	1.5	9.2	16.9	35.4
25~34 岁 Age	89	31.5	59.6	3.4	7.9	9.0	11.2
35~44 岁 Age	76	26.3	40.8	1.3	15.8	6.6	1.3
45~54 岁 Age	52	19.2	38.5	0.0	5.8	1.9	1.9
55~60 岁 Age	24	8.3	16.7	4.2	12.5	0.0	0.0
女性 Female	318	12.6	39.0	3.8	12.9	6.0	5.0
16~24 岁 Age	67	14.9	50.7	0.0	14.9	9.0	16.4
25~34 岁 Age	94	13.8	47.9	8.5	22.3	9.6	4.3
35~44 岁 Age	74	12.2	27.0	5.4	2.7	2.7	0.0
45~54 岁 Age	61	11.5	32.8	0.0	6.6	3.3	1.6
55~60 岁 Age	22	4.5	22.7	0.0	18.2	0.0	0.0

2-4 样本、男性各年龄层、女性各年龄层计划未来一年内使用的服务/ Services to be Used Next Year by the Whole Sample, Age and Gender Groups

注：本题为多选题，合计百分比超过 100%（Multiple answers）

	人数 Number	国际长途电话 international long-distance call	国内长途电话 domestic long-distance call	电脑发传真 fax through computer	电子邮件 e-mail	网上浏览 internet skimming	邮政速递 express mail service
样本 Sample	332	5.4	9.0	14.8	17.8	28.3	6.3
男性 Male	167	7.8	8.4	15.6	18.6	29.3	9.0
16~24 岁 Age	48	4.2	8.3	22.9	29.2	39.6	10.4
25~34 岁 Age	54	11.1	9.3	20.4	20.4	37.0	11.1
35~44 岁 Age	37	8.1	10.8	5.4	5.4	8.1	8.1
45~54 岁 Age	23	8.7	4.3	8.7	17.4	26.1	4.3
55~60 岁 Age	5	0.0	0.0	0.0	0.0	20.0	0.0
女性 Female	165	3.0	9.7	13.9	17.0	27.3	3.6
16~24 岁 Age	49	2.0	12.2	16.3	28.6	34.7	4.1
25~34 岁 Age	53	1.9	1.9	11.3	11.3	28.3	5.7
35~44 岁 Age	41	2.4	14.6	12.2	7.3	12.2	2.4
45~54 岁 Age	18	11.1	16.7	16.7	22.2	38.9	0.0
55~60 岁 Age	4	0.0	0.0	25.0	25.0	25.0	0.0

续前表 continued

	人数 Number	付费电话信息服务 telephone information service	电视购物 TV shopping	KTV 包厢 KTV room	有线电视 cable TV	高档餐厅就餐 dinning in first-class restaurant	美容厅/院 beauty parlor
样本 Sample	332	6.0	18.7	3.9	6.6	10.5	12.0
男性 Male	167	7.2	21.0	5.4	6.0	10.8	5.4
16~24 岁 Age	48	6.3	25.0	10.4	4.2	16.7	6.3
25~34 岁 Age	54	5.6	16.7	5.6	5.6	7.4	7.4
35~44 岁 Age	37	5.4	16.2	2.7	10.8	10.8	5.4
45~54 岁 Age	23	13.0	30.4	0.0	4.3	8.7	0.0
55~60 岁 Age	5	20.0	20.0	0.0	0.0	0.0	0.0
女性 Female	165	4.8	16.4	2.4	7.3	10.3	18.8
16~24 岁 Age	49	4.1	16.3	0.0	2.0	2.0	20.4
25~34 岁 Age	53	5.7	17.0	1.9	7.5	11.3	22.6
35~44 岁 Age	41	4.9	12.2	7.3	17.1	17.1	19.5
45~54 岁 Age	18	5.6	27.8	0.0	0.0	16.7	5.6
55~60 岁 Age	4	0.0	0.0	0.0	0.0	0.0	0.0

续前表 continued

	人数 Number	体育场馆 stadium	VCD/录像带出租 renting VCD & videotape	小时工 household service counted in hours	汽车租赁 renting car	器械健身 gym equipment	网吧 internet cafe
样本 Sample	332	9.6	6.9	9.6	6.9	24.4	16.0
男性 Male	167	13.2	6.0	10.8	9.0	23.4	16.2
16~24 岁 Age	48	12.5	2.1	14.6	6.3	25.0	27.1
25~34 岁 Age	54	14.8	3.7	9.3	14.8	25.9	18.5
35~44 岁 Age	37	13.5	16.2	13.5	5.4	18.9	2.7
45~54 岁 Age	23	13.0	4.3	4.3	8.7	17.4	13.0
55~60 岁 Age	5	0.0	0.0	0.0	0.0	40.0	0.0
女性 Female	165	6.1	7.9	8.5	4.8	25.5	15.8
16~24 岁 Age	49	12.2	4.1	8.2	4.1	30.6	28.6
25~34 岁 Age	53	3.8	7.5	7.5	3.8	22.6	15.1
35~44 岁 Age	41	4.9	7.3	9.8	4.9	26.8	7.3
45~54 岁 Age	18	0.0	11.1	5.6	0.0	22.2	5.6
55~60 岁 Age	4	0.0	50.0	25.0	50.0	0.0	0.0

2-5 不同消费者层最近一年内使用过的服务/ Services Used Last Year by Market Segments

2-5-1 时尚流行指标/ Fads Popular Index

注：本题为多选题，合计百分比超过 100%（Multiple answers）

	人数 Number	国际长途电话 international long-distance call	国内长途电话 domestic long-distance call	电脑发传真 fax through computer	电子邮件 e-mail	网上浏览 internet skimming	邮政速递 express mail service
样本 Sample	616	6.3	69.8	6.5	5.8	7.5	20.9
平实生活指向 simple living orientation	318	6.6	67.9	6.9	5.0	7.2	20.8
时尚流行指向 fashion orientation	298	6.0	71.8	6.0	6.7	7.7	21.1

续前表 continued

	人数 Number	付费电话信息服务 telephone information service	电视购物 TV shopping	KTV 包厢 KTV room	有线电视 cable TV	高档餐厅就餐 dinning in first-class restaurant	美容厅/院 beauty parlor
样本 Sample	616	25.6	3.2	21.1	89.9	33.0	16.6
平实生活指向 simple living orientation	318	21.7	1.6	16.4	89.0	26.7	10.1
时尚流行指向 fashion orientation	298	29.9	5.0	26.2	90.9	39.6	23.5

续前表 continued

	人数 Number	体育场馆 stadium	VCD/录像带出租 renting VCD & videotape	小时工 household service counted in hours	汽车租赁 renting car	器械健身 gym equipment	网吧 internet cafe
样本 Sample	616	19.6	43.3	2.9	11.5	7.0	8.3
平实生活指向 simple living orientation	318	18.6	37.4	2.5	11.3	5.0	5.3
时尚流行指向 fashion orientation	298	20.8	49.7	3.4	11.7	9.1	11.4

2-5-2 信息交流指标/ Information Communication Index

注：本题为多选题，合计百分比超过 100%（Multiple answers）

	人数 Number	国际长途电话 international long-distance call	国内长途电话 domestic long-distance call	电脑发传真 fax through computer	电子邮件 e-mail	网上浏览 internet skimming	邮政速递 express mail service
样本 Sample	615	6.3	69.9	6.5	5.9	7.3	20.8
信息消极指向 negative orientation	41	0.0	58.5	4.9	0.0	4.9	9.8
中间层 medium	356	5.1	68.5	5.1	5.9	7.0	23.0
信息积极指向 active orientation	218	9.6	74.3	9.2	6.9	8.3	19.3

续前表 continued

	人数 Number	付费电话信息服务 telephone information service	电视购物 TV shopping	KTV 包厢 KTV room	有线电视 cable TV	高档餐厅就餐 dinning in first-class restaurant	美容厅/院 beauty parlor
样本 Sample	615	25.4	3.3	21.3	89.9	33.2	16.6
信息消极指向 negative orientation	41	12.2	2.4	12.2	82.9	19.5	14.6
中间层 medium	356	23.9	2.0	22.5	91.0	31.5	16.0
信息积极指向 active orientation	218	30.3	5.5	21.1	89.4	38.5	17.9

续前表 continued

	人数 Number	体育场馆 stadium	VCD/录像带出租 renting VCD&videotape	小时工 household service counted in hours	汽车租赁 renting car	器械健身 gym equipment	网吧 internet cafe
样本 Sample	615	19.5	43.1	2.9	11.4	6.8	8.1
信息消极指向 negative orientation	41	9.8	26.8	2.4	9.8	2.4	4.9
中间层 medium	356	19.4	41.3	2.0	10.7	5.6	7.9
信息积极指向 active orientation	218	21.6	49.1	4.6	12.8	9.6	9.2

2-6 不同消费者层计划未来一年内使用的服务/ Services to be Used Next Year by Market Segments

2-6-1 时尚流行指向/ Fads Popular Index

注：本题为多选题，合计百分比超过 100%（Multiple answers）

	人数 Number	国际长途电话 international long-distance call	国内长途电话 domestic long-distance call	电脑发传真 fax through computer	电子邮件 e-mail	网上浏览 internet skimming	邮政速递 express mail service
样本 Sample	327	5.5	9.2	14.7	17.7	28.1	6.4
平实生活指向 simple living orientation	166	6.6	8.4	12.7	15.7	25.9	6.6
时尚流行指向 fashion orientation	161	4.3	9.9	16.8	19.9	30.4	6.2

续前表 continued

	人数 Number	付费电话信息服务 telephone information service	电视购物 TV shopping	KTV 包厢 KTV room	有线电视 cable TV	高档餐厅就餐 dinning in first-class restaurant	美容厅/院 beauty parlor
样本 Sample	327	5.8	18.3	4.0	6.7	10.7	12.2
平实生活指向 simple living orientation	166	4.2	18.1	3.6	10.8	10.2	9.0
时尚流行指向 fashion orientation	161	7.5	18.6	4.3	2.5	11.2	15.5

续前表 continued

	人数 Number	体育场馆 stadium	VCD/录像带出租 renting VCD&videotape	小时工 household service counted in hours	汽车租赁 renting car	器械健身 gym equipment	网吧 internet cafe
样本 Sample	327	9.8	7.0	9.8	6.7	24.2	15.6
平实生活指向 simple living orientation	166	6.0	6.0	10.2	6.6	21.1	13.9
时尚流行指向 fashion orientation	161	13.7	8.1	9.3	6.8	27.3	17.4

2-6-2 信息交流指标/ Information Communication Index

注：本题为多选题，合计百分比超过 100%（Multiple answers）

	人数 Number	国际长途电话 international long-distance call	国内长途电话 domestic long-distance call	电脑发传真 fax through computer	电子邮件 e-mail	网上浏览 internet skimming	邮政速递 express mail service
样本 Sample	327	5.5	9.2	14.4	17.4	28.4	6.4
信息消极指向 negative orientation	20	0.0	5.0	20.0	25.0	45.0	15.0
中间层 medium	191	5.2	9.9	13.1	17.3	27.2	7.3
信息积极指向 active orientation	116	6.9	8.6	15.5	16.4	27.6	3.4

续前表 continued

	人数 Number	付费电话信息服务 telephone information service	电视购物 TV shopping	KTV 包厢 KTV room	有线电视 cable TV	高档餐厅就餐 dinning in first-class restaurant	美容厅/院 beauty parlor
样本 Sample	327	5.8	18.3	3 7	6.7	10.4	12.2
信息消极指向 negative orientation	20	5.0	10.0	5 0	10.0	5.0	5.0
中间层 medium	191	3.7	18.3	3.7	6.3	11.5	11.0
信息积极指向 active orientation	116	9.5	19.8	3.4	6.9	9.5	15.5

续前表 continued

	人数 Number	体育场馆 stadium	VCD/录像带出租 renting VCD&videotape	小时工 household service counted in hours	汽车租赁 renting car	器械健身 gym equipment	网吧 internet cafe
样本 Sample	327	9.8	7.0	9.8	6.7	24.5	15.3
信息消极指向 negative orientation	20	10.0	5.0	20.0	10.0	20.0	25.0
中间层 medium	191	9.9	7.3	7.9	5.8	23.6	14.1
信息积极指向 active orientation	116	9.5	6.9	11.2	7.8	26.7	15.5

● 西安 / Xi'an

2-1 最近一年内使用过的服务项目排名/ Ranking of the Services have Used Last Year

注：本题为多选题，合计百分比超过 100%（Multiple answers）

排名 Ranking	服务项目 Service Items	人次 Person-time	百分比 Percent
1	有线电视 cable TV	528	89.5
2	国内长途电话 domestic long-distance call	473	80.2
3	VCD/录像带出租 renting VCD & videotape	183	31.0
4	高档餐厅就餐 dining in first-class restaurant	138	23.4
5	邮政速递 express mail service	115	19.5
6	体育场馆 stadium	114	19.3
7	付费电话信息服务 telephone information service	101	17.1
8	美容厅/院 beauty parlor	89	15.1
9	KTV 包厢 KTV room	57	9.7
10	网吧 internet cafe	48	8.1
11	网上浏览 internet skimming	42	7.1
12	器械健身 gym equipment	36	6.1
13	电子邮件 e-mail	34	5.8
13	国际长途电话 international long-distance call	34	5.8
14	电脑发传真 fax through computer	28	4.7
15	电视购物 TV shopping	27	4.6
16	汽车租赁 renting car	25	4.2
17	小时工 household service counted in hours	9	1.5

n=590

2-2 计划未来一年使用的服务项目排名/ Ranking of the Services Planned to Use Next Year

注：本题为多选题，合计百分比超过 100%（Multiple answers）

排名 Ranking	服务项目 Service Items	人次 Person-time	百分比 Percent
1	网上浏览 internet skimming	88	24.6
2	器械健身 gym equipment	77	21.6
3	电子邮件 e-mail	72	20.2
4	电视购物 TV shopping	67	18.8
5	网吧 internet cafe	55	15.4
5	体育场馆 stadium	55	15.4
6	美容厅/院 beauty parlor	48	13.4
7	高档餐厅就餐 dining in first-class restaurant	46	12.9
8	电脑发传真 fax through computer	44	12.3
9	汽车租赁 renting car	32	9.0
10	电视购物 TV shopping	29	8.1
11	小时工 household service counted in hours	27	7.6
12	邮政速递 express mail service	23	6.4
12	VCD/录像带出租 renting VCD & videotape	23	6.4
13	国际长途电话 international long-distance call	22	6.2
14	付费电话信息服务 telephone information service	15	4.2
15	国内长途电话 domestic long-distance call	13	3.6
15	KTV 包厢 KTV room	13	3.6

n=357

2-3 样本、 男性各年龄层、 女性各年龄层过去一年内使用的服务/ Services Used Last Year by the Whole Sample, Age and Gender Groups

注：本题为多选题，合计百分比超过 100%（Multiple answers）

	人数 Number	国际长途电话 international long-distance call	国内长途电话 domestic long-distance call	电脑发传真 fax through computer	电子邮件 e-mail	网上浏览 internet skimming	邮政速递 express mail service
样本 Sample	590	5.8	80.2	4.7	5.8	7.1	19.5
男性 Male	298	7.0	78.5	6.0	6.7	9.1	20.8
16~24 岁 Age	63	7.9	76.2	6.3	15.9	17.5	23.8
25~34 岁 Age	89	4.5	84.3	10.1	7.9	11.2	19.1
35~44 岁 Age	76	7.9	76.3	3.9	1.3	3.9	22.4
45~54 岁 Age	46	8.7	71.7	0.0	2.2	4.3	21.7
55~60 岁 Age	24	8.3	83.3	8.3	4.2	4.2	12.5
女性 Female	292	4.5	81.8	3.4	4.8	5.1	18.2
16~24 岁 Age	61	8.2	77.0	3.3	6.6	13.1	26.2
25~34 岁 Age	89	3.4	85.4	5.6	9.0	4.5	24.7
35~44 岁 Age	73	1.4	76.7	0.0	0.0	1.4	8.2
45~54 岁 Age	46	6.5	87.0	6.5	4.3	2.2	13.0
55~60 岁 Age	23	4.3	87.0	0.0	0.0	4.3	13.0

续前表 continued

	人数 Number	付费电话信息服务 telephone information service	电视购物 TV shopping	KTV 包厢 KTV room	有线电视 cable TV	高档餐厅就餐 dinning in first-class restaurant	美容厅/院 beauty parlor
样本 Sample	590	17.1	4.6	9.7	89.5	23.4	15.1
男性 Male	298	19.5	4.0	10.7	91.3	25.5	9.7
16~24 岁 Age	63	7.9	3.2	17.5	85.7	20.6	3.2
25~34 岁 Age	89	22.5	0.0	11.2	89.9	30.3	15.7
35~44 岁 Age	76	19.7	6.6	10.5	94.7	27.6	11.8
45~54 岁 Age	46	26.1	6.5	6.5	93.5	19.6	6.5
55~60 岁 Age	24	25.0	8.3	0.0	95.8	25.0	4.2
女性 Female	292	14.7	5.1	8.6	87.7	21.2	20.5
16~24 岁 Age	61	14.8	6.6	9.8	83.6	26.2	27.9
25~34 岁 Age	89	20.2	6.7	18.0	91.0	34.8	30.3
35~44 岁 Age	73	9.6	1.4	2.7	91.8	6.8	12.3
45~54 岁 Age	46	13.0	4.3	2.2	89.1	13.0	10.9
55~60 岁 Age	23	13.0	8.7	0.0	69.6	17.4	8.7

续前表 continued

	人数 Number	体育场馆 stadium	VCD/录像带出租 renting VCD & videotape	小时工 household service counted in hours	汽车租赁 renting car	器械健身 gym equipment	网吧 internet cafe
样本 Sample	590	19.3	31.0	1.5	4.2	6.1	8.1
男性 Male	298	25.2	35.2	2.0	3.4	8.1	13.4
16~24 岁 Age	63	33.3	42.9	3.2	3.2	14.3	31.7
25~34 岁 Age	89	25.8	41.6	0.0	2.2	6.7	15.7
35~44 岁 Age	76	23.7	35.5	2.6	5.3	5.3	6.6
45~54 岁 Age	46	13.0	21.7	2.2	2.2	10.9	2.2
55~60 岁 Age	24	29.2	16.7	4.2	4.2	0.0	0.0
女性 Female	292	13.4	26.7	1.0	5.1	4.1	2.7
16~24 岁 Age	61	19.7	26.2	1.6	3.3	6.6	8.2
25~34 岁 Age	89	18.0	39.3	2.2	9.0	0.0	3.4
35~44 岁 Age	73	4.1	16.4	0.0	0.0	4.1	0.0
45~54 岁 Age	46	10.9	30.4	0.0	4.3	6.5	0.0
55~60 岁 Age	23	13.0	4.3	0.0	13.0	8.7	0.0

2-4 样本、男性各年龄层、女性各年龄层计划未来一年内使用的服务/ Services to be Used Next Year by the Whole Sample, Age and Gender Groups

注：本题为多选题，合计百分比超过 100%（Multiple answers）

	人数 Number	国际长途电话 international long-distance call	国内长途电话 domestic long-distance call	电脑发传真 fax through computer	电子邮件 e-mail	网上浏览 internet skimming	邮政速递 express mail service
样本 Sample	357	6.2	3.6	12.3	20.2	24.6	6.4
男性 Male	185	4.9	3.8	13.0	25.9	30.8	8.1
16~24 岁 Age	47	2.1	6.4	12.8	36.2	51.1	6.4
25~34 岁 Age	56	8.9	1.8	12.5	19.6	25.0	3.6
35~44 岁 Age	46	6.5	4.3	15.2	26.1	23.9	13.0
45~54 岁 Age	24	0.0	4.2	12.5	20.8	33.3	4.2
55~60 岁 Age	12	0.0	0.0	8.3	25.0	0.0	25.0
女性 Female	172	7.6	3.5	11.6	14.0	18.0	4.7
16~24 岁 Age	46	8.7	2.2	15.2	19.6	28.3	0.0
25~34 岁 Age	64	6.3	3.1	17.2	12.5	17.2	3.1
35~44 岁 Age	28	7.1	3.6	3.6	3.6	14.3	10.7
45~54 岁 Age	22	4.5	4.5	4.5	13.6	9.1	4.5
55~60 岁 Age	12	16.7	8.3	0.0	25.0	8.3	16.7

续前表 continued

	人数 Number	付费电话信息服务 telephone information service	电视购物 TV shopping	KTV 包厢 KTV room	有线电视 cable TV	高档餐厅就餐 dinning in first-class restaurant	美容厅/院 beauty parlor
样本 Sample	357	4.2	18.8	3.6	8.1	12.9	13.4
男性 Male	185	2.7	16.8	3.8	7.6	11.4	4.9
16~24 岁 Age	47	6.4	8.5	4.3	8.5	12.8	6.4
25~34 岁 Age	56	0.0	19.6	3.6	10.7	7.1	5.4
35~44 岁 Age	46	2.2	19.6	4.3	6.5	8.7	4.3
45~54 岁 Age	24	4.2	25.0	0.0	4.2	25.0	4.2
55~60 岁 Age	12	0.0	8.3	8.3	0.0	8.3	0.0
女性 Female	172	5.8	20.9	3.5	8.7	14.5	22.7
16~24 岁 Age	46	4.3	23.9	6.5	4.3	17.4	28.3
25~34 岁 Age	64	6.3	28.1	3.1	3.1	14.1	26.6
35~44 岁 Age	28	7.1	14.3	3.6	14.3	7.1	28.6
45~54 岁 Age	22	4.5	9.1	0.0	22.7	18.2	4.5
55~60 岁 Age	12	8.3	8.3	0.0	16.7	16.7	0.0

续前表 continued

	人数 Number	体育场馆 stadium	VCD/录像带出租 renting VCD & videotape	小时工 household service counted in hours	汽车租赁 renting car	器械健身 gym equipment	网吧 internet cafe
样本 Sample	357	15.4	6.4	7.6	9.0	21.6	15.4
男性 Male	185	22.7	5.4	7.0	11.4	18.9	16.2
16~24 岁 Age	47	29.8	2.1	6.4	8.5	21.3	36.2
25~34 岁 Age	56	17.9	5.4	7.1	17.9	14.3	5.4
35~44 岁 Age	46	23.9	8.7	6.5	10.9	17.4	17.4
45~54 岁 Age	24	20.8	8.3	8.3	4.2	20.8	4.2
55~60 岁 Age	12	16.7	0.0	8.3	8.3	33.3	8.3
女性 Female	172	7.6	7.6	8.1	6.4	24.4	14.5
16~24 岁 Age	46	13.0	6.5	10.9	6.5	30.4	28.3
25~34 岁 Age	64	6.3	6.3	7.8	9.4	23.4	7.8
35~44 岁 Age	28	7.1	10.7	7.1	7.1	10.7	10.7
45~54 岁 Age	22	0.0	13.6	0.0	0.0	27.3	13.6
55~60 岁 Age	12	8.3	0.0	16.7	0.0	33.3	8.3

2-5 不同消费者层最近一年内使用过的服务/ Services Used Last Year by Market Segments

2-5-1 时尚流行指标/ Fads Popular Index

注：本题为多选题，合计百分比超过 100%（Multiple answers）

	人数 Number	国际长途电话 international long-distance call	国内长途电话 domestic long-distance call	电脑发传真 fax through computer	电子邮件 e-mail	网上浏览 internet skimming	邮政速递 express mail service
样本 Sample	588	5.8	80.4	4.8	5.8	7.1	19.6
平实生活指向 simple living orientation	335	3.3	77.9	3.3	4.2	6.0	14.9
时尚流行指向 fashion orientation	253	9.1	83.8	6.7	7.9	8.7	25.7

续前表 continued

	人数 Number	付费电话信息服务 telephone information service	电视购物 TV shopping	KTV 包厢 KTV room	有线电视 cable TV	高档餐厅就餐 dinning in first-class restaurant	美容厅/院 beauty parlor
样本 Sample	588	17.2	4.6	9.7	89.5	23.5	15.1
平实生活指向 simple living orientation	335	12.8	3.0	4.2	90.7	15.2	6.0
时尚流行指向 fashion orientation	253	22.9	6.7	17.0	87.7	34.4	27.3

续前表 continued

	人数 Number	体育场馆 stadium	VCD/录像带出租 renting VCD & videotape	小时工 household service counted in hours	汽车租赁 renting car	器械健身 gym equipment	网吧 internet cafe
样本 Sample	588	19.4	31.1	1.5	4.3	6.1	8.2
平实生活指向 simple living orientation	335	16.4	22.7	0.9	4.2	3.9	6.0
时尚流行指向 fashion orientation	253	23.3	42.3	2.4	4.3	9.1	11.1

2-5-2 信息交流指标/ Information Communication Index

注：本题为多选题，合计百分比超过 100%（Multiple answers）

	人数 Number	国际长途电话 international long-distance call	国内长途电话 domestic long-distance call	电脑发传真 fax through computer	电子邮件 e-mail	网上浏览 internet skimming	邮政速递 express mail service
样本 Sample	588	5.8	80.3	4.8	5.8	7.1	19.6
信息消极指向 negative orientation	69	7.2	87.0	1.4	7.2	7.2	17.4
中间层 medium	334	5.1	77.5	6.3	6.0	7.8	19.8
信息积极指向 active orientation	185	6.5	82.7	3.2	4.9	5.9	20.0

续前表 continued

	人数 Number	付费电话信息务 telephone information service	电视购物 TV shopping	KTV 包厢 KTV room	有线电视 cable TV	高档餐厅就餐 dinning in first-class restaurant	美容厅/院 beauty parlor
样本 Sample	588	17.2	4.6	9.7	89.6	23.5	15.1
信息消极指向 negative orientation	69	10.1	5.8	1.4	92.8	18.8	7.2
中间层 medium	334	18.0	3.9	8.4	89.8	22.5	14.1
信息积极指向 active orientation	185	18.4	5.4	15.1	88.1	27.0	20.0

续前表 continued

	人数 Number	体育场馆 stadium	VCD/录像带出租 renting VCD & videotape	小时工 household service counted in hours	汽车租赁 renting car	器械健身 gym equipment	网吧 internet cafe
样本 Sample	588	19.4	31.1	1.5	4.3	6.1	8.2
信息消极指向 negative orientation	69	14.5	27.5	1.4	7.2	1.4	1.4
中间层 medium	334	18.3	30.2	1.5	3.3	4.8	9.0
信息积极指向 active orientation	185	23.2	34.1	1.6	4.9	10.3	9.2

2-6 不同消费者层计划未来一年内使用的服务/ Services to be Used Next Year by Market Segments

2-6-1 时尚流行指标/ Fads Popular Index

注：本题为多选题，合计百分比超过 100%（Multiple answers）

	人数 Number	国际长途电话 international long-distance call	国内长途电话 domestic long-distance call	电脑发传真 fax through computer	电子邮件 e-mail	网上浏览 internet skimming	邮政速递 express mail service
样本 Sample	357	6.2	3.6	12.3	20.2	24.6	6.4
平实生活指向 simple living orientation	184	5.4	4.3	10.3	19.6	22.3	7.6
时尚流行指向 fashion orientation	173	6.9	2.9	14.5	20.8	27.2	5.2

续前表 continued

	人数 Number	付费电话信息服务 telephone information service	电视购物 TV shopping	KTV 包厢 KTV room	有线电视 cable TV	高档餐厅就餐 dinning in first-class restaurant	美容厅/院 beauty parlor
样本 Sample	357	4.2	18.8	3.6	8.1	12.9	13.4
平实生活指向 simple living orientation	184	3.3	17.4	3.3	9.8	15.8	12.5
时尚流行指向 fashion orientation	173	5.2	20.2	4.0	6.4	9.8	14.5

续前表 continued

	人数 Number	体育场馆 stadium	VCD/录像带出租 renting VCD & videotape	小时工 household service counted in hours	汽车租赁 renting car	器械健身 gym equipment	网吧 internet cafe
样本 Sample	357	15.4	6.4	7.6	9.0	21.6	15.4
平实生活指向 simple living orientation	184	16.8	7.1	6.5	8.7	18.5	13.6
时尚流行指向 fashion orientation	173	13.9	5.8	8.7	9.2	24.9	17.3

2-6-2 信息交流指标/ Information Communication Index

注：本题为多选题，合计百分比超过 100%（Multiple answers）

	人数 Number	国际长途电话 international long-distance call	国内长途电话 domestic long-distance call	电脑发传真 fax through computer	电子邮件 e-mail	网上浏览 internet skimming	邮政速递 express mail service
样本 Sample	357	6.2	3.6	12.3	20.2	24.6	6.4
信息消极指向 negative orientation	46	8.7	0.0	13.0	15.2	13.0	6.5
中间层 medium	200	5.5	5.5	11.0	17.5	25.0	5.5
信息积极指向 active orientation	111	6.3	1.8	14.4	27.0	28.8	8.1

续前表 continued

	人数 Number	付费电话信息服务 telephone information service	电视购物 TV shopping	KTV 包厢 KTV room	有线电视 cable TV	高档餐厅就餐 dinning in first-class restaurant	美容厅/院 beauty parlor
样本 Sample	357	4.2	18.8	3.6	8.1	12.9	13.4
信息消极指向 negative orientation	46	10.9	19.6	4.3	2.2	15.2	15.2
中间层 medium	200	4.0	20.0	3.5	9.0	11.5	13.5
信息积极指向 active orientation	111	1.8	16.2	3.6	9.0	14.4	12.6

续前表 continued

	人数 Number	体育场馆 stadium	VCD/录像带出租 renting VCD & videotape	小时工 household service counted in hours	汽车租赁 renting car	器械健身 gym equipment	网吧 internet cafe
样本 Sample	357	15.4	6.4	7.6	9.0	21.6	15.4
信息消极指向 negative orientation	46	30.4	10.9	8.7	6.5	26.1	13.0
中间层 medium	200	12.0	5.5	6.0	8.5	18.0	13.0
信息积极指向 active orientation	111	15.3	6.3	9.9	10.8	26.1	20.7

● 沈阳 / Shenyang

2-1 最近一年内使用过的服务项目排名/ Ranking of the Services have Used Last Year

注：本题为多选题，合计百分比超过 100%（Multiple answers）

排名 Ranking	服务项目 Service Items	人次 Person-time	百分比 Percent
1	国内长途电话 domestic long-distance call	411	76.0
2	有线电视 cable TV	360	66.5
3	VCD/录像带出租 renting VCD & videotape	227	42.0
4	高档餐厅就餐 dining in first-class restaurant	204	37.7
5	KTV 包厢 KTV room	190	35.1
6	体育场馆 stadium	160	29.6
7	付费电话信息服务 telephone information service	152	28.1
8	邮政速递 express mail service	88	16.3
9	美容厅/院 beauty parlor	64	11.8
10	器械健身 gym equipment	51	9.4
11	汽车租赁 renting car	46	8.5
12	电子邮件 e-mail	45	8.3
13	网上浏览 internet skimming	43	7.9
14	电脑发传真 fax through computer	41	7.6
15	国际长途电话 international long-distance call	34	6.3
16	电视购物 TV shopping	30	5.5
17	网吧 internet cafe	29	5.4
18	小时工 household service counted in hours	13	2.4

n=541

2-2 计划未来一年使用的服务项目排名/ Ranking of the Services Planned to Use Next Year

注：本题为多选题，合计百分比超过 100%（Multiple answers）

排名 Ranking	服务项目 Service Items	人次 Person-time	百分比 Percent
1	电视购物 TV shopping	88	28.2
2	器械健身 gym equipment	81	26.0
3	网上浏览 internet skimming	66	21.2
4	美容厅/院 beauty parlor	53	17.0
5	网吧 internet cafe	50	16.0
6	体育场馆 stadium	42	13.5
7	高档餐厅就餐 dining in first-class restaurant	41	13.1
8	电视购物 TV shopping	40	12.8
9	电子邮件 e-mail	39	12.5
10	电脑发传真 fax through computer	37	11.9
11	国际长途电话 international long-distance call	26	8.3
12	付费电话信息服务 telephone information service	25	8.0
13	国内长途电话 domestic long-distance call	23	7.4
14	小时工 household service counted in hours	20	6.4
15	汽车租赁 renting car	18	5.8
16	邮政速递 express mail service	17	5.4
17	VCD/录像带出租 renting VCD & videotape	15	4.8
18	KTV 包厢 KTV room	10	3.2

n=312

2-3 样本、 男性各年龄层、 女性各年龄层过去一年内使用的服务/ Services Used Last Year by the Whole Sample, Age and Gender Groups

注：本题为多选题，合计百分比超过 100%（Multiple answers）

	人数 Number	国际长途电话 international long-distance call	国内长途电话 domestic long-distance call	电脑发传真 fax through computer	电子邮件 e-mail	网上浏览 internet skimming	邮政速递 express mail service
样本 Sample	541	6.3	76.0	7.6	8.3	7.9	16.3
男性 Male	276	5.1	76.8	8.7	10.1	10.1	17.0
16~24 岁 Age	61	3.3	62.3	4.9	9.8	13.1	14.8
25~34 岁 Age	88	10.2	83.0	12.5	15.9	18.2	27.3
35~44 岁 Age	68	2.9	73.5	4.4	7.4	4.4	14.7
45~54 岁 Age	41	2.4	85.4	12.2	4.9	2.4	7.3
55~60 岁 Age	18	0.0	88.9	11.1	5.6	0.0	5.6
女性 Female	265	7.5	75.1	6.4	6.4	5.7	15.5
16~24 岁 Age	61	13.1	73.8	8.2	11.5	11.5	21.3
25~34 岁 Age	80	8.8	77.5	10.0	7.5	7.5	26.3
35~44 岁 Age	71	4.2	77.5	1.4	2.8	2.8	4.2
45~54 岁 Age	37	5.4	67.6	8.1	5.4	0.0	10.8
55~60 岁 Age	16	0.0	75.0	0.0	0.0	0.0	0.0

续前表 continued

	人数 Number	付费电话信息服务 telephone information service	电视购物 TV shopping	KTV 包厢 KTV room	有线电视 cable TV	高档餐厅就餐 dinning in first-class restaurant	美容厅/院 beauty parlor
样本 Sample	541	28.1	5.5	35.1	66.5	37.7	11.8
男性 Male	276	31.2	4.7	41.7	67.8	40.9	4.3
16~24 岁 Age	61	34.4	8.2	32.8	70.5	32.8	8.2
25~34 岁 Age	88	36.4	3.4	55.7	70.5	52.3	4.5
35~44 岁 Age	68	38.2	4.4	47.1	61.8	47.1	4.4
45~54 岁 Age	41	12.2	4.9	29.3	75.6	26.8	0.0
55~60 岁 Age	18	11.1	0.0	11.1	50.0	22.2	0.0
女性 Female	265	24.9	6.4	28.3	65.3	34.3	19.6
16~24 岁 Age	61	41.0	6.6	24.6	67.2	26.2	26.2
25~34 岁 Age	80	26.3	7.5	37.5	63.8	38.8	26.3
35~44 岁 Age	71	16.9	8.5	32.4	56.3	45.1	18.3
45~54 岁 Age	37	18.9	2.7	13.5	81.1	21.6	5.4
55~60 岁 Age	16	6.3	0.0	12.5	68.8	25.0	0.0

续前表 continued

	人数 Number	体育场馆 stadium	VCD/录像带出租 renting VCD & videotape	小时工 household service counted in hours	汽车租赁 renting car	器械健身 gym equipment	网吧 internet cafe
样本 Sample	541	29.6	42.0	2.4	8.5	9.4	5.4
男性 Male	276	39.1	46.0	2.5	10.1	12.0	7.6
16~24 岁 Age	61	52.5	63.9	4.9	11.5	23.0	18.0
25~34 岁 Age	88	39.8	50.0	0.0	11.4	10.2	9.1
35~44 岁 Age	68	35.3	39.7	1.5	5.9	7.4	2.9
45~54 岁 Age	41	31.7	36.6	4.9	9.8	9.8	0.0
55~60 岁 Age	18	22.2	11.1	5.6	16.7	5.6	0.0
女性 Female	265	19.6	37.7	2.3	6.8	6.8	3.0
16~24 岁 Age	61	29.5	54.1	3.3	8.2	16.4	8.2
25~34 岁 Age	80	23.8	43.8	2.5	7.5	3.8	1.3
35~44 岁 Age	71	15.5	33.8	1.4	5.6	2.8	2.8
45~54 岁 Age	37	5.4	18.9	2.7	5.4	5.4	0.0
55~60 岁 Age	16	12.5	6.3	0.0	6.3	6.3	0.0

2-4 样本、男性各年龄层、女性各年龄层计划未来一年内使用的服务/ Services to be Used Next Year by the Whole Sample, Age and Gender Groups

注：本题为多选题，合计百分比超过 100%（Multiple answers）

	人数 Number	国际长途电话 international long-distance call	国内长途电话 domestic long-distance call	电脑发传真 fax through computer	电子邮件 e-mail	网上浏览 internet skimming	邮政速递 express mail service
样本 Sample	312	8.3	7.4	11.9	12.5	21.2	5.4
男性 Male	163	12.3	8.6	12.3	17.2	21.5	4.9
16~24 岁 Age	47	10.6	12.8	8.5	23.4	31.9	4.3
25~34 岁 Age	46	19.6	2.2	21.7	21.7	21.7	6.5
35~44 岁 Age	40	5.0	10.0	10.0	15.0	15.0	7.5
45~54 岁 Age	23	8.7	13.0	8.7	4.3	17.4	0.0
55~60 岁 Age	7	28.6	0.0	0.0	0.0	0.0	0.0
女性 Female	149	4.0	6.0	11.4	7.4	20.8	6.0
16~24 岁 Age	42	7.1	7.1	31.0	16.7	35.7	7.1
25~34 岁 Age	48	4.2	10.4	8.3	4.2	20.8	2.1
35~44 岁 Age	37	0.0	0.0	0.0	2.7	13.5	10.8
45~54 岁 Age	16	6.3	0.0	0.0	6.3	6.3	0.0
55~60 岁 Age	6	0.0	16.7	0.0	0.0	0.0	16.7

续前表 continued

	人数 Number	付费电话信息服务 telephone information service	电视购物 TV shopping	KTV 包厢 KTV room	有线电视 cable TV	高档餐厅就餐 dinning in first-class restaurant	美容厅/院 beauty parlor
样本 Sample	312	8.0	12.8	3.2	28.2	13.1	17.0
男性 Male	163	8.6	11.0	3.1	27.0	16.0	4.9
16~24 岁 Age	47	2.1	10.6	2.1	10.6	10.6	2.1
25~34 岁 Age	46	10.9	13.0	2.2	28.3	26.1	8.7
35~44 岁 Age	40	7.5	10.0	5.0	37.5	15.0	5.0
45~54 岁 Age	23	17.4	8.7	4.3	34.8	13.0	4.3
55~60 岁 Age	7	14.3	14.3	0.0	42.9	0.0	0.0
女性 Female	149	7.4	14.8	3.4	29.5	10.1	30.2
16~24 岁 Age	42	9.5	11.9	4.8	23.8	11.9	26.2
25~34 岁 Age	48	2.1	12.5	2.1	27.1	8.3	35.4
35~44 岁 Age	37	10.8	18.9	2.7	32.4	13.5	40.5
45~54 岁 Age	16	6.3	12.5	6.3	43.8	6.3	6.3
55~60 岁 Age	6	16.7	33.3	0.0	33.3	0.0	16.7

续前表 continued

	人数 Number	体育场馆 stadium	VCD/录像带出租 renting VCD & videotape	小时工 household service counted in hours	汽车租赁 renting car	器械健身 gym equipment	网吧 internet cafe
样本 Sample	312	13.5	4.8	6.4	5.8	26.0	16.0
男性 Male	163	16.6	4.9	6.1	8.0	25.8	15.3
16~24 岁 Age	47	17.0	2.1	8.5	6.4	25.5	23.4
25~34 岁 Age	46	17.4	4.3	6.5	19.6	30.4	17.4
35~44 岁 Age	40	17.5	7.5	5.0	2.5	27.5	10.0
45~54 岁 Age	23	17.4	4.3	4.3	0.0	21.7	8.7
55~60 岁 Age	7	0.0	14.3	0.0	0.0	0.0	0.0
女性 Female	149	10.1	4.7	6.7	3.4	26.2	16.8
16~24 岁 Age	42	19.0	7.1	7.1	4.8	28.6	35.7
25~34 岁 Age	48	4.2	4.2	6.3	4.2	33.3	10.4
35~44 岁 Age	37	5.4	2.7	5.4	2.7	18.9	8.1
45~54 岁 Age	16	18.8	6.3	6.3	0.0	18.8	12.5
55~60 岁 Age	6	0.0	0.0	16.7	0.0	16.7	0.0

2-5 不同消费者层最近一年内使用过的服务/ Services Used Last Year by Market Segments

2-5-1 时尚流行指标/ Fads Popular Index

注：本题为多选题，合计百分比超过 100%（Multiple answers）

	人数 Number	国际长途电话 international long-distance call	国内长途电话 domestic long-distance call	电脑发传真 fax through computer	电子邮件 e-mail	网上浏览 internet skimming	邮政速递 express mail service
样本 Sample	541	6.3	76.0	7.6	8.3	7.9	16.3
平实生活指向 simple living orientation	249	4.8	75.5	6.8	7.6	8.8	14.1
时尚流行指向 fashion orientation	292	7.5	76.4	8.2	8.9	7.2	18.2

续前表 continued

	人数 Number	付费电话信息服务 telephone information service	电视购物 TV shopping	KTV 包厢 KTV room	有线电视 cable TV	高档餐厅就餐 dinning in first-class restaurant	美容厅/院 beauty parlor
样本 Sample	541	28.1	5.5	35.1	66.5	37.7	11.8
平实生活指向 simple living orientation	249	25.7	4.4	32.9	69.1	31.7	4.4
时尚流行指向 fashion orientation	292	30.1	6.5	37.0	64.4	42.8	18.2

续前表 continued

	人数 Number	体育场馆 stadium	VCD/录像带出租 renting VCD & videotape	小时工 household service counted in hours	汽车租赁 renting car	器械健身 gym equipment	网吧 internet cafe
样本 Sample	541	29.6	42.0	2.4	8.5	9.4	5.4
平实生活指向 simple living orientation	249	27.3	33.3	2.0	8.8	5.2	3.2
时尚流行指向 fashion orientation	292	31.5	49.3	2.7	8.2	13.0	7.2

2-5-2 信息交流指标/ Information Communication Index

注：本题为多选题，合计百分比超过 100%（Multiple answers）

	人数 Number	国际长途电话 international long-distance call	国内长途电话 domestic long-distance call	电脑发传真 fax through computer	电子邮件 e-mail	网上浏览 internet skimming	邮政速递 express mail service
样本 Sample	540	6.3	75.9	7.6	8.3	8.0	16.1
信息消极指向 negative orientation	45	6.7	84.4	2.2	4.4	6.7	4.4
中间层 medium	284	6.3	69.4	7.4	10.6	8.1	17.3
信息积极指向 active orientation	211	6.2	82.9	9.0	6.2	8.1	17.1

续前表 continued

	人数 Number	付费电话信息服务 telephone information service	电视购物 TV shopping	KTV 包厢 KTV room	有线电视 cable TV	高档餐厅就餐 dinning in first-class restaurant	美容厅/院 beauty parlor
样本 Sample	540	28.1	5.6	35.2	66.7	37.8	11.7
信息消极指向 negative orientation	45	17.8	4.4	20.0	64.4	24.4	4.4
中间层 medium	284	28.5	5.6	33.8	67.3	35.9	9.2
信息积极指向 active orientation	211	29.9	5.7	40.3	66.4	43.1	16.6

续前表 continued

	人数 Number	体育场馆 stadium	VCD/录像带出租 renting VCD &videotape	小时工 household service counted in hours	汽车租赁 renting car	器械健身 gym equipment	网吧 internet cafe
样本 Sample	540	29.6	42.0	2.4	8.5	9.4	5.4
信息消极指向 negative orientation	45	15.6	31.1	0.0	6.7	0.0	2.2
中间层 medium	284	29.9	43.0	2.1	7.0	8.1	5.3
信息积极指向 active orientation	211	32.2	43.1	3.3	10.9	13.3	6.2

2-6 不同消费者层计划未来一年内使用的服务/ Services to be Used Next Year by Market Segments

2-6-1 时尚流行指标/ Fads Popular Index

注：本题为多选题，合计百分比超过 100%（Multiple answers）

	人数 Number	国际长途电话 international long-distance call	国内长途电话 domestic long-distance call	电脑发传真 fax through computer	电子邮件 e-mail	网上浏览 internet skimming	邮政速递 express mail service
样本 Sample	312	8.3	7.4	11.9	12.5	21.2	5.4
平实生活指向 simple living orientation	136	8.8	8.8	12.5	11.0	19.1	7.4
时尚流行指向 fashion orientation	176	8.0	6.3	11.4	13.6	22.7	4.0

续前表 continued

	人数 Number	付费电话信息服务 telephone information service	电视购物 TV shopping	KTV 包厢 KTV room	有线电视 cable TV	高档餐厅就餐 dinning in first-class restaurant	美容厅/院 beauty parlor
样本 Sample	312	8.0	12.8	3.2	28.2	13.1	17.0
平实生活指向 simple living orientation	136	8.8	12.5	2.2	34.6	14.7	13.2
时尚流行指向 fashion orientation	176	7.4	13.1	4.0	23.3	11.9	19.9

续前表 continued

	人数 Number	体育场馆 stadium	VCD/录像带出租 renting VCD &videotape	小时工 household service counted in hours	汽车租赁 renting car	器械健身 gym equipment	网吧 internet cafe
样本 Sample	312	13.5	4.8	6.4	5.8	26.0	16.0
平实生活指向 simple living orientation	136	12.5	6.6	5.1	4.4	22.1	14.0
时尚流行指向 fashion orientation	176	14.2	3.4	7.4	6.8	29.0	17.6

2-6-2 信息交流指标/ Information Communication Index

注：本题为多选题，合计百分比超过 100%（Multiple answers）

	人数 Number	国际长途电话 international long-distance call	国内长途电话 domestic long-distance call	电脑发传真 fax through computer	电子邮件 e-mail	网上浏览 internet skimming	邮政速递 express mail service
样本 Sample	311	8.4	7.4	11.9	12.5	21.2	5.5
信息消极指向 negative orientation	19	5.3	5.3	15.8	21.1	26.3	5.3
中间层 medium	175	9.7	9.7	9.1	10.9	17.7	4.6
信息积极指向 active orientation	117	6.8	4.3	15.4	13.7	25.6	6.8

续前表 continued

	人数 Number	付费电话信息服务 telephone information service	电视购物 TV shopping	KTV 包厢 KTV room	有线电视 cable TV	高档餐厅就餐 dinning in first-class restaurant	美容厅/院 beauty parlor
样本 Sample	311	8.0	12.9	3.2	28.0	12.9	17.0
信息消极指向 negative orientation	19	5.3	15.8	5.3	47.4	5.3	15.8
中间层 medium	175	5.7	12.6	3.4	26.9	14.9	21.1
信息积极指向 active orientation	117	12.0	12.8	2.6	26.5	11.1	11.1

续前表 continued

	人数 Number	体育场馆 stadium	VCD/录像带出租 renting VCD &videotape	小时工 household service counted in hours	汽车租赁 renting car	器械健身 gym equipment	网吧 internet cafe
样本 Sample	311	13.5	4.8	6.1	5.8	25.7	16.1
信息消极指向 negative orientation	19	15.8	0.0	0.0	0.0	26.3	15.8
中间层 medium	175	13.1	4.0	6.9	6.3	32.0	16.6
信息积极指向 active orientation	117	13.7	6.8	6.0	6.0	16.2	15.4

3. 消费信息接触情况 / Consuming Information Contact

● 北京 / Beijing

3-1 样本、男性各年龄层、女性各年龄层对电视、音响等视听设备的信息接触情况/ Information Contact about Video & Audio Equipment by the Whole Sample, Age and Gender Groups

注：本题为多选题，合计百分比超过 100%（Multiple answers）

	人数 Number	不管买还是不买，想看看 just have a look, without a definite purpose of buying or not	阅读有关的杂志和专门报道 reading magazines related & special reports	相互口头传播信息 communicate information orally among people	经常看这种商品的广告 often watch advertise-ments about such kinds of goods	购买这种商品的新类型 buy the latest type of such kinds of goods	过去在这种商品上花了不少钱 used to spend much money on such kinds of goods	今后愿意在这方面花钱 willing to spend money on such items in future	不关注这方面的信息 don't care about such items
样本 Sample	1007	56.1	25.6	22.0	40.0	18.3	33.2	32.9	13.8
男性 Male	502	60.6	29.9	24.7	42.8	19.5	34.5	36.1	10.8
16~24 岁 Age	104	60.6	27.9	23.1	44.2	23.1	23.1	42.3	9.6
25~34 岁 Age	151	61.6	29.8	24.5	36.4	19.2	35.1	33.1	7.3
35~44 岁 Age	130	57.7	32.3	24.6	45.4	17.7	41.5	32.3	10.8
45~54 岁 Age	77	62.3	29.9	29.9	48.1	18.2	36.4	39.0	14.3
55~60 岁 Age	40	62.5	27.5	20.0	45.0	20.0	35.0	37.5	20.0
女性 Female	505	51.7	21.4	19.4	37.2	17.0	31.9	29.7	16.8
16~24 岁 Age	107	47.7	17.8	21.5	35.5	13.1	23.4	30.8	14.0
25~34 岁 Age	149	54.4	13.4	16.1	36.2	20.8	27.5	31.5	13.4
35~44 岁 Age	124	54.8	31.5	23.4	38.7	19.4	37.1	33.9	14.5
45~54 岁 Age	84	48.8	23.8	14.3	38.1	13.1	35.7	22.6	17.9
55~60 岁 Age	41	48.8	24.4	24.4	39.0	14.6	46.3	22.0	41.5

3-2 样本、男性各年龄层、女性各年龄层对冰箱、洗衣机等白色家电的信息接触情况/ Information Contact about "White Home Electronic Products" by the Whole Sample, Age and Gender Groups

注：本题为多选题，合计百分比超过 100%（Multiple answers）

	人数 Number	不管买还是不买，想看看 just have a look, without a definite purpose of buying or not	阅读有关的杂志和专门报道 reading magazines related & special reports	相互口头传播信息 communicate information orally among people	经常看这种商品的广告 often watch advertise-ments about such kinds of goods	购买这种商品的新类型 buy the latest type of such kinds of goods	过去在这种商品上花了不少钱 used to spend much money on such kinds of goods	今后愿意在这方面花钱 willing to spend money on such items in future	不关注这方面的信息 don't care about such items
样本 Sample	996	37.4	16.7	16.8	29.9	17.8	24.6	26.8	28.1
男性 Male	493	37.9	17.6	16.6	29.4	18.9	21.3	25.8	29.0
16~24 岁 Age	104	26.0	11.5	9.6	26.0	19.2	11.5	21.2	38.5
25~34 岁 Age	145	33.8	16.6	15.9	25.5	16.6	19.3	24.8	26.2
35~44 岁 Age	128	46.9	17.2	21.1	33.6	22.7	25.0	29.7	23.4
45~54 岁 Age	77	45.5	27.3	16.9	32.5	15.6	27.3	26.0	28.6
55~60 岁 Age	39	41.0	20.5	23.1	33.3	20.5	30.8	28.2	33.3
女性 Female	503	37.0	15.7	16.9	30.4	16.7	27.8	27.8	27.2
16~24 岁 Age	105	32.4	12.4	13.3	28.6	12.4	16.2	17.1	35.2
25~34 岁 Age	148	31.1	10.8	15.5	25.0	14.2	22.3	26.4	30.4
35~44 岁 Age	124	46.0	23.4	17.7	32.3	18.5	38.7	33.9	20.2
45~54 岁 Age	84	34.5	13.1	16.7	29.8	16.7	29.8	29.8	23.8
55~60 岁 Age	42	47.6	23.8	28.6	50.0	31.0	40.5	38.1	23.8

3-3 样本、男性各年龄层、女性各年龄层对电脑等通讯工具的信息接触情况/ Information Contact about Computer & Telecommunications by the Whole Sample, Age and Gender Groups

注：本题为多选题，合计百分比超过 100%（Multiple answers）

	人数 Number	不管买还是不买，想看看 just have a look, without a definite purpose of buying or not	阅读有关的杂志和专门报道 reading magazines related & special reports	相互口头传播信息 communicate information orally among people	经常看这种商品的广告 often watch advertisements about such kinds of goods	购买这种商品的新类型 buy the latest type of such kinds of goods	过去在这种商品上花了不少钱 used to spend much money on such kinds of goods	今后愿意在这方面花钱 willing to spend money on such items in future	不关注这方面的信息 don't care about such items
样本 Sample	1008	40.3	31.5	23.5	30.4	16.4	14.9	43.5	25.8
男性 Male	501	45.7	36.5	28.1	34.7	19.0	17.6	44.3	23.2
16~24 岁 Age	104	57.7	54.8	49.0	51.0	30.8	31.7	58.7	6.7
25~34 岁 Age	150	42.7	36.7	26.0	36.0	18.0	12.7	49.3	20.7
35~44 岁 Age	131	47.3	35.9	26.0	31.3	19.8	13.7	43.5	22.9
45~54 岁 Age	77	43.1	24.7	16.9	26.0	7.8	15.6	31.2	31.2
55~60 岁 Age	39	15.4	12.8	10.3	15.4	10.3	15.4	15.4	61.5
女性 Female	507	34.9	26.6	18.9	26.0	13.8	12.2	42.6	28.4
16~24 岁 Age	108	45.4	37.0	32.4	37.0	16.7	15.7	52.8	9.3
25~34 岁 Age	149	34.9	26.8	18.1	22.1	14.8	7.4	46.3	22.8
35~44 岁 Age	124	37.1	28.2	16.9	30.6	13.7	16.1	46.8	22.6
45~54 岁 Age	84	25.0	16.7	10.7	16.7	8.3	13.1	29.8	54.8
55~60 岁 Age	42	21.4	14.3	9.5	16.7	14.3	7.1	16.7	61.9

3-4 样本、男性各年龄层、女性各年龄层对家用轿车的信息接触情况/ Information Contact about Family Car by the Whole Sample, Age and Gender Groups

注：本题为多选题，合计百分比超过 100%（Multiple answers）

	人数 Number	不管买还是不买，想看看 just have a look, without a definite purpose of buying or not	阅读有关的杂志和专门报道 reading magazines related & special reports	相互口头传播信息 communicate information orally among people	经常看这种商品的广告 often watch advertisements about such kinds of goods	购买这种商品的新类型 buy the latest type of such kinds of goods	过去在这种商品上花了不少钱 used to spend much money on such kinds of goods	今后愿意在这方面花钱 willing to spend money on such items in future	不关注这方面的信息 don't care about such items
样本 Sample	1004	32.1	22.6	17.5	22.3	4.3	5.0	24.3	45.5
男性 Male	500	38.4	30.6	22.2	29.4	4.2	5.4	28.4	36.8
16~24 岁 Age	105	43.8	35.2	21.0	33.3	3.8	2.9	35.2	28.6
25~34 岁 Age	151	41.7	39.1	29.1	34.4	6.0	4.6	36.4	25.2
35~44 岁 Age	127	39.4	23.6	21.3	26.0	4.7	8.7	26.8	37.0
45~54 岁 Age	77	33.8	26.0	15.6	27.3	2.6	5.2	13.0	53.2
55~60 岁 Age	40	17.5	17.5	15.0	15.0	0.0	5.0	15.0	70.0
女性 Female	504	25.8	14.7	12.9	15.3	4.4	4.6	20.2	54.2
16~24 岁 Age	107	28.0	23.4	17.8	14.0	6.5	2.8	24.3	49.5
25~34 岁 Age	148	36.5	17.6	14.9	18.9	2.7	4.1	27.0	36.5
35~44 岁 Age	124	21.8	12.1	10.5	16.9	5.6	8.9	18.5	58.1
45~54 岁 Age	83	9.6	4.8	4.8	6.0	1.2	1.2	8.4	79.5
55~60 岁 Age	42	26.2	9.5	16.7	19.0	7.1	4.8	14.3	66.7

3-5 样本、男性各年龄层、女性各年龄层对高级家具的信息接触情况/ Information Contact about First-class Furniture by the Whole Sample, Age and Gender Groups

注：本题为多选题，合计百分比超过 100%（Multiple answers）

	人数 Number	不管买还是不买，想看看 just have a look, without a definite purpose of buying or not	阅读有关的杂志和专门报道 reading magazines related & special reports	相互口头传播信息 communicate information orally among people	经常看这种商品的广告 often watch advertise-ments about such kinds of goods	购买这种商品的新类型 buy the latest type of such kinds of goods	过去在这种商品上花了不少钱 used to spend much money on such kinds of goods	今后愿意在这方面花钱 willing to spend money on such items in future	不关注这方面的信息 don't care about such items
样本 Sample	**995**	**29.8**	**13.6**	**8.6**	**15.2**	**7.0**	**7.8**	**18.9**	**51.6**
男性 Male	**494**	**28.1**	**11.9**	**8.7**	**15.6**	**7.7**	**7.5**	**17.4**	**53.4**
16~24 岁 Age	101	19.8	6.9	6.9	15.8	7.9	1.0	13.9	57.4
25~34 岁 Age	149	32.2	10.7	6.7	14.8	6.0	8.1	17.4	47.7
35~44 岁 Age	127	29.9	15.0	11.0	16.5	7.1	10.2	18.1	51.2
45~54 岁 Age	77	31.2	16.9	9.1	19.5	9.1	6.5	22.1	55.8
55~60 岁 Age	40	22.5	10.0	12.5	7.5	12.5	15.0	15.0	67.5
女性 Female	**501**	**31.5**	**15.2**	**8.6**	**14.8**	**6.4**	**8.2**	**20.4**	**49.7**
16~24 岁 Age	104	30.8	21.2	7.7	14.4	4.8	5.8	26.9	42.3
25~34 岁 Age	149	30.2	11.4	6.7	10.1	5.4	8.1	19.5	49.0
35~44 岁 Age	123	36.6	13.8	13.8	22.8	7.3	11.4	21.1	48.0
45~54 岁 Age	83	26.5	18.1	4.8	13.3	8.4	3.6	14.5	57.8
55~60 岁 Age	42	33.3	11.9	9.5	11.9	7.1	14.3	16.7	59.5

3-6 样本、男性各年龄层、女性各年龄层对西服和时装的信息接触情况/ Information Contact about Business Suit & Fashion by the Whole Sample, Age and Gender Groups

注：本题为多选题，合计百分比超过 100%（Multiple answers）

	人数 Number	不管买还是不买，想看看 just have a look, without a definite purpose of buying or not	阅读有关的杂志和专门报道 reading magazines related & special reports	相互口头传播信息 communicate information orally among people	经常看这种商品的广告 often watch advertise-ments about such kinds of goods	购买这种商品的新类型 buy the latest type of such kinds of goods	过去在这种商品上花了不少钱 used to spend much money on such kinds of goods	今后愿意在这方面花钱 willing to spend money on such items in future	不关注这方面的信息 don't care about such items
样本 Sample	**1005**	**44.9**	**21.7**	**19.1**	**23.8**	**17.7**	**22.9**	**32.3**	**32.3**
男性 Male	**500**	**36.0**	**13.6**	**13.0**	**17.6**	**13.0**	**20.6**	**31.0**	**40.8**
16~24 岁 Age	104	36.5	19.2	21.2	16.3	19.2	19.2	36.5	35.6
25~34 岁 Age	151	36.4	11.9	10.6	17.2	14.6	25.2	34.4	31.8
35~44 岁 Age	128	35.9	7.8	10.2	17.2	8.6	19.5	27.3	43.8
45~54 岁 Age	77	39.0	18.2	7.8	18.2	14.3	18.2	31.2	49.4
55~60 岁 Age	40	27.5	15.0	20.0	22.5	2.5	15.0	15.0	62.5
女性 Female	**505**	**53.7**	**29.7**	**25.1**	**29.9**	**22.4**	**25.1**	**33.7**	**24.0**
16~24 岁 Age	107	52.3	38.3	26.2	31.8	24.3	26.2	45.8	13.1
25~34 岁 Age	149	59.1	30.2	26.8	29.5	23.5	26.8	36.2	18.8
35~44 岁 Age	123	55.3	26.8	27.6	35.8	26.0	26.0	36.6	22.8
45~54 岁 Age	84	47.6	26.2	16.7	22.6	14.3	17.9	17.9	35.7
55~60 岁 Age	42	45.2	21.4	26.2	23.8	19.0	28.6	16.7	50.0

3-7 样本、男性各年龄层、女性各年龄层对酒精饮料的信息接触情况/ Information Contact about Alcohol Drinks by the Whole Sample, Age and Gender Groups

注：本题为多选题，合计百分比超过 100%（Multiple answers）

	人数 Number	不管买还是不买，想看看 just have a look, without a definite purpose of buying or not	阅读有关的杂志和专门报道 reading magazines related & special reports	相互口头传播信息 communicate information orally among people	经常看这种商品的广告 often watch advertisements about such kinds of goods	购买这种商品的新类型 buy the latest type of such kinds of goods	过去在这种商品上花了不少钱 used to spend much money on such kinds of goods	今后愿意在这方面花钱 willing to spend money on such items in future	不关注这方面的信息 don't care about such items
样本 Sample	988	17.7	7.7	10.3	15.9	7.2	17.9	15.7	58.0
男性 Male	494	21.9	9.5	13.4	18.2	8.1	23.5	20.6	51.0
16~24 岁 Age	103	16.5	5.8	7.8	17.5	7.8	15.5	15.5	54.4
25~34 岁 Age	149	15.4	5.4	11.4	17.4	5.4	23.5	18.1	50.3
35~44 岁 Age	127	29.9	14.2	21.3	22.0	11.0	30.7	29.1	44.1
45~54 岁 Age	75	26.7	13.3	12.0	16.0	8.0	22.7	21.3	50.7
55~60 岁 Age	40	25.0	12.5	12.5	15.0	10.0	22.5	15.0	67.5
女性 Female	494	13.6	5.9	7.3	13.6	6.3	12.3	10.7	65.0
16~24 岁 Age	103	8.7	6.8	6.8	16.5	9.7	11.7	8.7	62.1
25~34 岁 Age	147	14.3	3.4	8.2	13.6	6.1	12.2	9.5	65.3
35~44 岁 Age	120	11.7	9.2	9.2	15.8	6.7	17.5	14.2	62.5
45~54 岁 Age	82	15.9	4.9	4.9	7.3	2.4	7.3	9.8	70.7
55~60 岁 Age	42	23.8	4.8	4.8	11.9	4.8	9.5	11.9	66.7

3-8 样本、男性各年龄层、女性各年龄层对 CD 唱片及音乐带的信息接触情况/ Information Contact about CD & Music Cassette by the Whole Sample, Age and Gender Groups

注：本题为多选题，合计百分比超过 100%（Multiple answers）

	人数 Number	不管买还是不买，想看看 just have a look, without a definite purpose of buying or not	阅读有关的杂志和专门报道 reading magazines related & special reports	相互口头传播信息 communicate information orally among people	经常看这种商品的广告 often watch advertisements about such kinds of goods	购买这种商品的新类型 buy the latest type of such kinds of goods	过去在这种商品上花了不少钱 used to spend much money on such kinds of goods	今后愿意在这方面花钱 willing to spend money on such items in future	不关注这方面的信息 don't care about such items
样本 Sample	996	40.5	21.8	21.0	19.3	19.6	27.5	30.6	34.1
男性 Male	494	40.1	20.4	19.4	18.0	17.2	26.7	30.4	35.8
16~24 岁 Age	105	56.2	38.1	41.0	27.6	28.6	42.9	48.6	13.3
25~34 岁 Age	147	41.5	19.0	12.9	15.6	20.4	29.9	29.9	29.9
35~44 岁 Age	127	33.1	11.8	16.5	12.6	9.4	15.0	20.5	44.9
45~54 岁 Age	76	34.2	18.4	13.2	19.7	11.8	25.0	23.7	52.6
55~60 岁 Age	39	25.6	10.3	7.7	15.4	10.3	12.8	28.2	56.4
女性 Female	502	40.8	23.1	22.5	20.5	21.9	28.3	30.9	32.5
16~24 岁 Age	107	57.9	47.7	42.1	35.5	42.1	51.4	48.6	5.6
25~34 岁 Age	148	39.2	20.3	21.6	16.9	18.2	27.0	27.0	27.0
35~44 岁 Age	121	36.4	17.4	16.5	19.0	15.7	22.3	29.8	43.0
45~54 岁 Age	84	28.6	8.3	7.1	6.0	11.9	15.5	17.9	53.6
55~60 岁 Age	42	40.5	16.7	23.8	28.6	21.4	16.7	28.6	47.6

3-9 样本、男性各年龄层、女性各年龄层对护肤品和化妆品的信息接触情况/ Information Contact about Skin Cream & Cosmetics by the Whole Sample, Age and Gender Groups

注：本题为多选题，合计百分比超过 100%（Multiple answers）

	人数 Number	不管买还是不买，想看看 just have a look, without a definite purpose of buying or not	阅读有关的杂志和专门报道 reading magazines related & special reports	相互口头传播信息 communicate information orally among people	经常看这种商品的广告 often watch advertise-ments about such kinds of goods	购买这种商品的新类型 buy the latest type of such kinds of goods	过去在这种商品上花了不少钱 used to spend much money on such kinds of goods	今后愿意在这方面花钱 willing to spend money on such items in future	不关注这方面的信息 don't care about such items
样本 Sample	1001	31.8	20.1	19.2	30.5	15.9	22.5	28.3	42.4
男性 Male	496	14.7	7.1	4.8	15.9	4.8	8.1	12.1	68.1
16~24 岁 Age	103	12.6	3.9	6.8	13.6	1.0	4.9	9.7	72.8
25~34 岁 Age	150	14.0	8.7	4.7	23.3	7.3	7.3	12.0	60.0
35~44 岁 Age	127	20.5	10.2	4.7	15.7	7.9	13.4	15.7	65.4
45~54 岁 Age	76	11.8	5.3	3.9	7.9	2.6	7.9	13.2	76.3
55~60 岁 Age	40	10.0	2.5	2.5	10.0	0.0	2.5	5.0	80.0
女性 Female	505	48.5	32.9	33.3	44.8	26.7	36.6	44.2	17.0
16~24 岁 Age	107	43.0	47.7	40.2	54.2	29.9	29.0	49.5	9.3
25~34 岁 Age	149	55.7	31.5	34.9	43.6	30.2	42.3	48.3	10.7
35~44 岁 Age	123	54.5	33.3	35.8	48.8	30.1	41.5	48.8	14.6
45~54 岁 Age	84	42.9	23.8	25.0	38.1	19.0	34.5	35.7	25.0
55~60 岁 Age	42	31.0	16.7	19.0	26.2	11.9	26.2	19.0	50.0

3-10 样本、男性各年龄层、女性各年龄层对香波等洗涤用品的信息接触情况/ Information Contact about Shampoo & Detergent Cassette by the Whole Sample, Age and Gender Groups

注：本题为多选题，合计百分比超过 100%（Multiple answers）

	人数 Number	不管买还是不买，想看看 just have a look, without a definite purpose of buying or not	阅读有关的杂志和专门报道 reading magazines related & special reports	相互口头传播信息 communicate information orally among people	经常看这种商品的广告 often watch advertise-ments about such kinds of goods	购买这种商品的新类型 buy the latest type of such kinds of goods	过去在这种商品上花了不少钱 used to spend much money on such kinds of goods	今后愿意在这方面花钱 willing to spend money on such items in future	不关注这方面的信息 don't care about such items
样本 Sample	1001	30.6	15.2	19.8	33.4	21.8	23.8	29.2	34.8
男性 Male	497	18.9	8.0	8.9	21.5	12.1	14.5	19.7	53.3
16~24 岁 Age	103	15.5	4.9	10.7	17.5	10.7	12.6	13.6	59.2
25~34 岁 Age	150	18.0	8.7	6.0	29.3	10.7	13.3	21.3	40.7
35~44 岁 Age	128	21.9	8.6	11.7	19.5	14.8	18.8	25.0	53.1
45~54 岁 Age	77	16.9	5.2	6.5	16.9	13.0	11.7	13.0	67.5
55~60 岁 Age	39	25.6	17.9	10.3	17.9	10.3	15.4	25.6	59.0
女性 Female	504	42.1	22.2	30.6	45.0	31.3	32.9	38.5	16.5
16~24 岁 Age	107	34.6	27.1	26.2	51.4	33.6	24.3	34.6	15.9
25~34 岁 Age	148	37.8	18.2	29.1	40.5	28.4	29.7	34.5	17.6
35~44 岁 Age	123	50.4	25.2	37.4	49.6	36.6	38.2	43.1	13.0
45~54 岁 Age	84	41.7	15.5	23.8	34.5	23.8	40.5	40.5	15.5
55~60 岁 Age	42	52.4	28.6	40.5	52.4	35.7	35.7	45.2	26.2

3-11 样本、男性各年龄层、女性各年龄层对外出就餐的信息接触情况/ Information Contact about Dinning Out by the Whole Sample, Age and Gender Groups

注：本题为多选题，合计百分比超过 100%（Multiple answers）

	人数 Number	阅读有关的杂志和专门报道 reading magazines related and special reports	相互口头传播信息 communicate information orally among people	经常看这种服务的广告 often watch advertise-ments about such kind of service	尝试这种服务的新类型 try using the latest type of such kinds of service	过去在这种服务上花了不少钱 used to spend much money on such kinds of service	今后愿意在这方面花钱 willing to spend money on such items in future	不关注这方面的信息 don't care about such items
样本 Sample	1003	18.0	28.9	16.1	23.7	31.3	29.7	33.1
男性 Male	498	18.5	27.7	13.5	21.3	33.3	30.7	32.7
16~24 岁 Age	103	15.5	26.2	10.7	20.4	23.3	27.2	34.0
25~34 岁 Age	148	16.9	32.4	12.2	18.9	45.3	31.8	27.7
35~44 岁 Age	130	21.5	26.9	14.6	24.6	32.3	32.3	29.2
45~54 岁 Age	77	20.8	26.0	16.9	18.2	32.5	35.1	37.7
55~60 岁 Age	40	17.5	20.0	15.0	27.5	20.0	22.5	50.0
女性 Female	505	17.6	30.1	18.6	26.1	29.3	28.7	33.5
16~24 岁 Age	107	24.3	30.8	19.6	27.1	33.6	22.4	27.1
25~34 岁 Age	149	16.8	35.6	21.5	30.2	28.9	26.8	26.8
35~44 岁 Age	124	16.1	31.5	17.7	29.0	36.3	38.7	28.2
45~54 岁 Age	84	14.3	19.0	7.1	17.9	19.0	23.8	50.0
55~60 岁 Age	41	14.6	26.8	31.7	17.1	19.5	31.7	56.1

3-12 样本、男性各年龄层、女性各年龄层对旅行的信息接触情况/ Information Contact about Travelling by the Whole Sample, Age and Gender Groups

注：本题为多选题，合计百分比超过 100%（Multiple answers）

	人数 Number	阅读有关的杂志和专门报道 reading magazines related and special reports	相互口头传播信息 communicate information orally among people	经常看这种服务的广告 often watch advertise-ments about such kind of service	尝试这种服务的新类型 try using the latest type of such kinds of service	过去在这种服务上花了不少钱 used to spend much money on such kinds of service	今后愿意在这方面花钱 willing to spend money on such items in future	不关注这方面的信息 don't care about such items
样本 Sample	1004	35.5	30.2	26.8	18.5	25.3	47.8	26.8
男性 Male	499	35.3	29.7	25.7	16.4	27.7	45.9	26.9
16~24 岁 Age	105	35.2	22.9	23.8	21.9	29.5	43.8	26.7
25~34 岁 Age	149	38.3	30.2	20.1	12.8	24.2	50.3	22.8
35~44 岁 Age	128	32.8	35.2	31.3	15.6	33.6	42.2	25.0
45~54 岁 Age	77	35.1	32.5	31.2	15.6	27.3	41.6	33.8
55~60 岁 Age	40	32.5	22.5	22.5	20.0	17.5	55.0	35.0
女性 Female	505	35.6	30.7	27.9	20.6	23.0	49.7	26.7
16~24 岁 Age	107	38.3	28.0	31.8	22.4	22.4	55.1	18.7
25~34 岁 Age	149	40.9	36.2	23.5	15.4	20.1	53.0	19.5
35~44 岁 Age	124	36.3	29.8	32.3	24.2	29.0	50.0	26.6
45~54 岁 Age	84	27.4	26.2	22.6	20.2	19.0	38.1	41.7
55~60 岁 Age	41	24.4	29.3	31.7	24.4	24.4	46.3	43.9

3-13 样本、男性各年龄层、女性各年龄层对音乐会的信息接触情况/ Information Contact about Concert by the Whole Sample, Age and Gender Groups

注：本题为多选题，合计百分比超过 100%（Multiple answers）

	人数 Number	阅读有关的杂志和专门报道 reading magazines related and special reports	相互口头传播信息 communicate information orally among people	经常看这种服务的广告 often watch advertise-ments about such kind of service	尝试这种服务的新类型 try using the latest type of such kinds of service	过去在这种服务上花了不少钱 used to spend much money on such kinds of service	今后愿意在这方面花钱 willing to spend money on such items in future	不关注这方面的信息 don't care about such items
样本 Sample	**992**	**21.7**	**14.3**	**13.1**	**10.0**	**7.2**	**21.8**	**55.8**
男性 Male	**493**	**22.1**	**12.8**	**12.8**	**9.9**	**7.3**	**19.5**	**58.4**
16~24 岁 Age	103	28.2	18.4	16.5	14.6	6.8	25.2	51.5
25~34 岁 Age	149	19.5	12.1	14.8	7.4	6.0	20.8	51.7
35~44 岁 Age	127	17.3	11.0	10.2	8.7	7.1	17.3	62.2
45~54 岁 Age	75	26.7	12.0	10.7	10.7	12.0	18.7	69.3
55~60 岁 Age	39	23.1	7.7	7.7	10.3	5.1	7.7	69.2
女性 Female	**499**	**21.2**	**15.8**	**13.4**	**10.0**	**7.0**	**24.0**	**53.3**
16~24 岁 Age	106	29.2	29.2	17.0	11.3	8.5	40.6	35.8
25~34 岁 Age	146	24.0	13.7	11.6	7.5	5.5	18.5	51.4
35~44 岁 Age	123	18.7	14.6	16.3	10.6	8.1	26.8	52.8
45~54 岁 Age	83	9.6	6.0	7.2	8.4	3.6	10.8	74.7
55~60 岁 Age	41	22.0	12.2	14.6	17.1	12.2	19.5	63.4

3-14 样本、男性各年龄层、女性各年龄层对电影的信息接触情况/ Information Contact about Movie by the Whole Sample, Age and Gender Groups

注：本题为多选题，合计百分比超过 100%（Multiple answers）

	人数 Number	阅读有关的杂志和专门报道 reading magazines related and special reports	相互口头传播信息 communicate information orally among people	经常看这种服务的广告 often watch advertise-ments about such kind of service	尝试这种服务的新类型 try using the latest type of such kinds of service	过去在这种服务上花了不少钱 used to spend much money on such kinds of service	今后愿意在这方面花钱 willing to spend money on such items in future	不关注这方面的信息 don't care about such items
样本 Sample	**995**	**32.6**	**27.1**	**22.0**	**12.8**	**19.8**	**21.5**	**40.5**
男性 Male	**494**	**31.6**	**24.9**	**20.4**	**12.8**	**19.6**	**22.9**	**42.7**
16~24 岁 Age	105	49.5	38.1	33.3	24.8	37.1	42.9	18.1
25~34 岁 Age	149	31.5	33.6	20.1	8.7	21.5	25.5	30.9
35~44 岁 Age	124	22.6	12.9	10.5	8.1	10.5	9.7	65.3
45~54 岁 Age	77	26.0	14.3	23.4	13.0	11.7	15.6	54.5
55~60 岁 Age	39	23.1	15.4	12.8	10.3	10.3	15.4	59.0
女性 Female	**501**	**33.5**	**29.3**	**23.6**	**12.8**	**20.0**	**20.2**	**38.3**
16~24 岁 Age	105	54.3	44.8	29.5	19.0	30.5	39.0	13.3
25~34 岁 Age	148	34.5	32.4	25.0	10.1	16.2	14.2	34.5
35~44 岁 Age	123	25.2	19.5	22.8	12.2	20.3	21.1	45.5
45~54 岁 Age	84	21.4	21.4	15.5	8.3	15.5	10.7	52.4
55~60 岁 Age	41	26.8	24.4	22.0	17.1	14.6	9.8	65.9

3-15 样本、男性各年龄层、女性各年龄层对戏剧或戏曲的信息接触情况/ Information Contact about Drama or Opera by the Whole Sample, Age and Gender Groups

注：本题为多选题，合计百分比超过 100%（Multiple answers）

	人数 Number	阅读有关的杂志和专门报道 reading magazines related and special reports	相互口头传播信息 communicate information orally among people	经常看这种服务的广告 often watch advertisements about such kind of service	尝试这种服务的新类型 try using the latest type of such kinds of service	过去在这种服务上花了不少钱 used to spend much money on such kinds of service	今后愿意在这方面花钱 willing to spend money on such items in future	不关注这方面的信息 don't care about such items
样本 Sample	992	11.5	7.2	8.8	4.3	4.7	8.4	77.2
男性 Male	490	12.0	5.7	7.8	3.5	5.1	8.2	79.0
16~24 岁 Age	101	7.9	5.0	5.9	4.0	4.0	10.9	78.2
25~34 岁 Age	150	8.0	2.0	4.0	1.3	2.0	4.7	86.0
35~44 岁 Age	122	9.8	5.7	4.9	1.6	3.3	4.9	83.6
45~54 岁 Age	77	23.4	10.4	16.9	7.8	10.4	13.0	68.8
55~60 岁 Age	40	22.5	12.5	17.5	7.5	15.0	15.0	60.0
女性 Female	502	11.0	8.6	9.8	5.2	4.4	8.6	75.5
16~24 岁 Age	107	7.5	2.8	5.6	3.7	3.7	6.5	82.2
25~34 岁 Age	148	6.8	3.4	8.8	2.0	1.4	7.4	80.4
35~44 岁 Age	123	11.4	8.1	8.9	6.5	3.3	7.3	77.2
45~54 岁 Age	83	14.5	15.7	10.8	6.0	7.2	10.8	67.5
55~60 岁 Age	41	26.8	29.3	24.4	14.6	14.6	17.1	51.2

3-16 样本、男性各年龄层、女性各年龄层对蹦迪的信息接触情况/ Information Contact about Disco by the Whole Sample, Age and Gender Groups

注：本题为多选题，合计百分比超过 100%（Multiple answers）

	人数 Number	阅读有关的杂志和专门报道 reading magazines related and special reports	相互口头传播信息 communicate information orally among people	经常看这种服务的广告 often watch advertisements about such kind of service	尝试这种服务的新类型 try using the latest type of such kinds of service	过去在这种服务上花了不少钱 used to spend much money on such kinds of service	今后愿意在这方面花钱 willing to spend money on such items in future	不关注这方面的信息 don't care about such items
样本 Sample	1002	5.3	8.1	3.6	6.7	6.5	7.5	79.7
男性 Male	500	6.2	6.6	3.0	6.8	4.8	7.6	81.0
16~24 岁 Age	105	12.4	19.0	6.7	11.4	6.7	16.2	66.7
25~34 岁 Age	150	7.3	6.0	2.7	12.7	8.0	10.7	72.0
35~44 岁 Age	128	2.3	2.3	1.6	1.6	3.9	3.1	90.6
45~54 岁 Age	77	2.6	1.3	1.3	0.0	0.0	0.0	96.1
55~60 岁 Age	40	5.0	0.0	2.5	2.5	0.0	2.5	92.5
女性 Female	502	4.4	9.6	4.2	6.6	8.2	7.4	78.5
16~24 岁 Age	106	12.3	24.5	7.5	17.0	16.0	17.9	54.7
25~34 岁 Age	148	3.4	6.8	4.1	4.1	9.5	8.1	77.7
35~44 岁 Age	123	2.4	8.1	4.1	4.1	5.7	2.4	83.7
45~54 岁 Age	84	0.0	1.2	1.2	3.6	2.4	2.4	92.9
55~60 岁 Age	41	2.4	2.4	2.4	2.4	2.4	2.4	97.6

3-17 样本、男性各年龄层、女性各年龄层对现场观赏体育比赛的信息接触情况/ Information Contact about Enjoying Live Sports by the Whole Sample, Age and Gender Groups

注：本题为多选题，合计百分比超过 100%（Multiple answers）

	人数 Number	阅读有关的杂志和专门报道 reading magazines related and special reports	相互口头传播信息 communicate information orally among people	经常看这种服务的广告 often watch advertisements about such kind of service	尝试这种服务的新类型 try using the latest type of such kinds of service	过去在这种服务上花了不少钱 used to spend much money on such kinds of service	今后愿意在这方面花钱 willing to spend money on such items in future	不关注这方面的信息 don't care about such items
样本 Sample	996	28.2	20.7	18.0	9.8	13.3	27.1	47.9
男性 Male	494	36.4	28.3	23.7	13.2	18.6	35.2	35.0
16~24 岁 Age	103	42.7	34.0	27.2	19.4	25.2	49.5	21.4
25~34 岁 Age	148	31.8	26.4	21.6	9.5	14.9	33.8	33.1
35~44 岁 Age	128	34.4	22.7	21.1	12.5	17.2	35.2	40.6
45~54 岁 Age	76	43.4	32.9	30.3	11.8	19.7	26.3	39.5
55~60 岁 Age	39	30.8	30.8	17.9	15.4	17.9	20.5	51.3
女性 Female	502	20.1	13.1	12.4	6.6	8.0	19.1	60.6
16~24 岁 Age	104	30.8	20.2	9.6	7.7	9.6	30.8	42.3
25~34 岁 Age	150	16.7	8.7	10.0	4.0	4.7	14.0	64.7
35~44 岁 Age	123	18.7	13.8	14.6	8.1	8.9	19.5	62.6
45~54 岁 Age	84	16.7	10.7	13.1	4.8	8.3	16.7	67.9
55~60 岁 Age	41	17.1	14.6	19.5	12.2	12.2	12.2	70.7

3-18 样本、男性各年龄层、女性各年龄层对运动健身的信息接触情况/ Information Contact about Gym by the Whole Sample, Age and Gender Groups

注：本题为多选题，合计百分比超过 100%（Multiple answers）

	人数 Number	阅读有关的杂志和专门报道 reading magazines related and special reports	相互口头传播信息 communicate information orally among people	经常看这种服务的广告 often watch advertisements about such kind of service	尝试这种服务的新类型 try using the latest type of such kinds of service	过去在这种服务上花了不少钱 used to spend much money on such kinds of service	今后愿意在这方面花钱 willing to spend money on such items in future	不关注这方面的信息 don't care about such items
样本 Sample	995	24.6	15.9	16.5	16.7	13.7	41.5	35.7
男性 Male	494	23.9	15.2	15.2	15.0	14.6	42.7	35.8
16~24 岁 Age	102	27.5	16.7	12.7	15.7	19.6	53.9	25.5
25~34 岁 Age	149	23.5	12.8	14.1	16.1	15.4	51.0	26.2
35~44 岁 Age	127	16.5	14.2	13.4	15.7	11.8	34.6	44.1
45~54 岁 Age	77	28.6	19.5	23.4	10.4	11.7	29.9	48.1
55~60 岁 Age	39	30.8	15.4	15.4	15.4	12.8	33.3	48.7
女性 Female	501	25.3	16.6	17.8	18.4	12.8	40.3	35.5
16~24 岁 Age	105	24.8	19.0	15.2	22.9	14.3	55.2	22.9
25~34 岁 Age	148	20.3	10.1	14.9	10.8	10.1	40.5	39.2
35~44 岁 Age	123	26.0	16.3	19.5	20.3	13.8	42.3	35.8
45~54 岁 Age	83	26.5	18.1	14.5	18.1	10.8	22.9	42.2
55~60 岁 Age	42	40.5	31.0	35.7	28.6	19.0	31.0	40.5

3-19 样本、男性各年龄层、女性各年龄层对技能学习的信息接触情况/ Information Contact about Studying Skills by the Whole Sample, Age and Gender Groups

注：本题为多选题，合计百分比超过 100%（Multiple answers）

	人数 Number	阅读有关的杂志和专门报道 reading magazines related and special reports	相互口头传播信息 communicate information orally among people	经常看这种服务的广告 often watch advertise-ments about such kind of service	尝试这种服务的新类型 try using the latest type of such kinds of service	过去在这种服务上花了不少钱 used to spend much money on such kinds of service	今后愿意在这方面花钱 willing to spend money on such items in future	不关注这方面的信息 don't care about such items
样本 Sample	993	31.0	16.9	16.4	12.5	17.9	40.8	37.4
男性 Male	491	33.4	16.9	16.1	11.0	18.9	43.0	35.6
16~24 岁 Age	103	41.7	29.1	19.4	11.7	26.2	55.3	21.4
25~34 岁 Age	147	35.4	12.9	15.6	10.9	19.7	55.8	25.2
35~44 岁 Age	125	28.8	12.0	16.8	12.0	18.4	35.2	41.6
45~54 岁 Age	76	27.6	13.2	13.2	9.2	13.2	25.0	53.9
55~60 岁 Age	40	30.0	22.5	12.5	10.0	10.0	22.5	57.5
女性 Female	502	28.7	16.9	16.7	13.9	16.9	38.6	39.0
16~24 岁 Age	105	34.3	21.9	25.7	18.1	26.7	52.4	23.8
25~34 岁 Age	148	33.8	18.2	14.9	15.5	15.5	46.6	29.7
35~44 岁 Age	124	29.8	16.1	17.7	14.5	16.9	35.5	37.1
45~54 岁 Age	84	17.9	15.5	11.9	8.3	10.7	25.0	59.5
55~60 岁 Age	41	14.6	4.9	7.3	7.3	9.8	12.2	75.6

3-20 样本、男性各年龄层、女性各年龄层对外语学习的信息接触情况/ Information Contact about Studying Foreign Languages by the Whole Sample, Age and Gender Groups

注：本题为多选题，合计百分比超过 100%（Multiple answers）

	人数 Number	阅读有关的杂志和专门报道 reading magazines related and special reports	相互口头传播信息 communicate information orally among people	经常看这种服务的广告 often watch advertise-ments about such kind of service	尝试这种服务的新类型 try using the latest type of such kinds of service	过去在这种服务上花了不少钱 used to spend much money on such kinds of service	今后愿意在这方面花钱 willing to spend money on such items in future	不关注这方面的信息 don't care about such items
样本 Sample	999	22.5	11.0	11.0	8.0	13.6	35.3	49.6
男性 Male	498	19.9	9.4	8.8	7.4	11.8	32.5	53.4
16~24 岁 Age	104	38.5	25.0	15.4	11.5	18.3	51.9	27.9
25~34 岁 Age	148	19.6	8.8	10.1	10.1	13.5	44.6	41.2
35~44 岁 Age	130	16.2	3.8	5.4	5.4	10.8	25.4	63.1
45~54 岁 Age	77	7.8	3.9	7.8	3.9	5.2	10.4	77.9
55~60 岁 Age	39	7.7	0.0	0.0	0.0	5.1	2.6	87.2
女性 Female	501	25.1	12.6	13.2	8.6	15.4	38.1	45.9
16~24 岁 Age	106	43.4	23.6	24.5	17.0	32.1	64.2	12.3
25~34 岁 Age	149	31.5	14.1	12.8	9.4	12.1	43.6	38.9
35~44 岁 Age	122	19.7	10.7	13.1	4.1	13.9	36.1	47.5
45~54 岁 Age	83	7.2	3.6	3.6	4.8	7.2	13.3	79.5
55~60 岁 Age	41	7.3	2.4	4.9	4.9	4.9	7.3	85.4

3-21 不同消费者层对电视、音响等视听设备的信息接触情况/ Information Contact about Video & Audio Equipment by Market Segments

注：本题为多选题，合计百分比超过 100%（Multiple answers）

	人数 Number	不管买还是不买，想看看 just have a look, without a definite purpose of buying or not	阅读有关的杂志和专门报道 reading magazines related & special reports	相互口头传播信息 communicate information orally among people	经常看这种商品的广告 often watch advertisements about such kind of goods	购买这种商品的新类型 buy the latest type of such kinds of goods	过去在这种商品上花了不少钱 used to spending much money on such kinds of goods	今后愿意在这方面花钱 willing to spend money on such items in future	不关注这方面的信息 don't care about such items
样本 Sample	993	56.2	25.5	22.3	40.0	18.3	33.0	33.0	13.8
平实生活指向 simple living orientation	487	55.2	23.0	20.5	37.4	16.6	30.4	29.4	16.4
时尚流行指向 fashion orientation	506	57.1	27.9	23.9	42.5	20.0	35.6	36.6	11.3

3-22 不同消费者层对冰箱、洗衣机等白色家电的信息接触情况/ Information Contact about "White Home Electronic Products" by Market Segments

注：本题为多选题，合计百分比超过 100%（Multiple answers）

	人数 Number	不管买还是不买，想看看 just have a look, without a definite purpose of buying or not	阅读有关的杂志和专门报道 reading magazines related & special reports	相互口头传播信息 communicate information orally among people	经常看这种商品的广告 often watch advertisements about such kind of goods	购买这种商品的新类型 buy the latest type of such kinds of goods	过去在这种商品上花了不少钱 used to spend much money on such kinds of goods	今后愿意在这方面花钱 willing to spend money on such items in future	不关注这方面的信息 don't care about such items
样本 Sample	982	37.3	16.9	16.7	29.8	17.7	24.6	26.8	28.1
平实生活指向 simple living orientation	482	37.1	14.3	15.4	26.8	15.6	24.7	25.1	29.3
时尚流行指向 fashion orientation	500	37.4	19.4	18.0	32.8	19.8	24.6	28.4	27.0

3-23 不同消费者层对电脑等通讯工具的信息接触情况/ Information Contact about Computer & Telecommunications by Market Segments

注：本题为多选题，合计百分比超过 100%（Multiple answers）

	人数 Number	不管买还是不买，想看看 just have a look, without a definite purpose of buying or not	阅读有关的杂志和专门报道 reading magazines related & special reports	相互口头传播信息 communicate information orally among people	经常看这种商品的广告 often watch advertisements about such kind of goods	购买这种商品的新类型 buy the latest type of such kinds of goods	过去在这种商品上花了不少钱 used to spend much money on such kinds of goods	今后愿意在这方面花钱 willing to spend money on such items in future	不关注这方面的信息 don't care about such items
样本 Sample	994	40.2	31.9	23.6	30.4	16.5	14.9	43.5	25.9
平实生活指向 simple living orientation	489	37.8	30.3	22.9	28.2	14.5	13.7	40.5	31.3
时尚流行指向 fashion orientation	505	42.6	33.5	24.4	32.5	18.4	16.0	46.3	20.6

3-24 不同消费者层对家用轿车的信息接触情况/ Information Contact about Family Car by Market Segments

注：本题为多选题，合计百分比超过 100%（Multiple answers）

	人数 Number	不管买还是不买，想看看 just have a look, without a definite purpose of buying or not	阅读有关的杂志和专门报道 reading magazines related & special reports	相互口头传播信息 communicate information orally among people	经常看这种商品的广告 often watch advertisements about such kind of goods	购买这种商品的新类型 buy the latest type of such kinds of goods	过去在这种商品上花了不少钱 used to spend much money on such kinds of goods	今后愿意在这方面花钱 willing to spend money on such items in future	不关注这方面的信息 don't care about such items
样本 Sample	990	32.0	22.6	17.7	22.3	4.3	4.8	24.3	45.8
平实生活指向 simple living orientation	486	30.2	21.2	15.8	17.5	2.3	2.9	21.4	52.3
时尚流行指向 fashion orientation	504	33.7	24.0	19.4	27.0	6.3	6.7	27.2	39.5

3-25 不同消费者层对高级家具的信息接触情况/ Information Contact about First-class Furniture by Market Segments

注：本题为多选题，合计百分比超过 100%（Multiple answers）

	人数 Number	不管买还是不买，想看看 just have a look, without a definite purpose of buying or not	阅读有关的杂志和专门报道 reading magazines related & special reports	相互口头传播信息 communicate information orally among people	经常看这种商品的广告 often watch advertisements about such kind of goods	购买这种商品的新类型 buy the latest type of such kinds of goods	过去在这种商品上花了不少钱 used to spend much money on such kinds of goods	今后愿意在这方面花钱 willing to spend money on such items in future	不关注这方面的信息 don't care about such items
样本 Sample	982	29.9	13.5	8.8	15.3	7.0	7.9	18.9	51.5
平实生活指向 simple living orientation	481	27.2	11.9	6.4	11.4	5.6	7.5	16.2	57.4
时尚流行指向 fashion orientation	501	32.5	15.2	11.0	19.0	8.4	8.4	21.6	45.9

3-26 不同消费者层对西服和时装的信息接触情况/ Information Contact about Business Suit & Fashion by Market Segments

注：本题为多选题，合计百分比超过 100%（Multiple answers）

	人数 Number	不管买还是不买，想看看 just have a look, without a definite purpose of buying or not	阅读有关的杂志和专门报道 reading magazines related & special reports	相互口头传播信息 communicate information orally among people	经常看这种商品的广告 often watch advertisements about such kind of goods	购买这种商品的新类型 buy the latest type of such kinds of goods	过去在这种商品上花了不少钱 used to spend much money on such kinds of goods	今后愿意在这方面花钱 willing to spend money on such items in future	不关注这方面的信息 don't care about such items
样本 Sample	991	45.0	21.8	19.2	23.3	17.8	23.0	32.1	32.3
平实生活指向 simple living orientation	486	36.8	16.0	12.8	16.9	10.7	15.0	23.9	44.9
时尚流行指向 fashion orientation	505	52.9	27.3	25.3	30.5	24.6	30.7	40.0	20.2

3-27 不同消费者层对酒精饮料的信息接触情况/ Information Contact about Alcohol Drinks by Market Segments

注：本题为多选题，合计百分比超过 100%（Multiple answers）

	人数 Number	不管买还是不买，想看看 just have a look, without a definite purpose of buying or not	阅读有关的杂志和专门报道 reading magazines related & special reports	相互口头传播信息 communicate information orally among people	经常看这种商品的广告 often watch advertisements about such kind of goods	购买这种商品的新类型 buy the latest type of such kinds of goods	过去在这种商品上花了不少钱 used to spend much money on such kinds of goods	今后愿意在这方面花钱 willing to spend money on such items in future	不关注这方面的信息 don't care about such items
样本 Sample	**975**	**17.6**	**7.7**	**10.4**	**16.0**	**7.2**	**18.2**	**15.8**	**57.7**
平实生活指向 simple living orientation	480	16.9	5.8	9.0	13.5	6.0	17.5	14.6	60.4
时尚流行指向 fashion orientation	495	18.4	9.5	11.7	18.4	8.3	18.8	17.0	55.2

3-28 不同消费者层对 CD 唱片及音乐带的信息接触情况/ Information Contact about CD & Music Cassette by Market Segments

注：本题为多选题，合计百分比超过 100%（Multiple answers）

	人数 Number	不管买还是不买，想看看 just have a look, without a definite purpose of buying or not	阅读有关的杂志和专门报道 reading magazines related & special reports	相互口头传播信息 communicate information orally among people	经常看这种商品的广告 often watch advertisements about such kind of goods	购买这种商品的新类型 buy the latest type of such kinds of goods	过去在这种商品上花了不少钱 used to spend much money on such kinds of goods	今后愿意在这方面花钱 willing to spend money on such items in future	不关注这方面的信息 don't care about such items
样本 Sample	**982**	**40.5**	**21.8**	**21.0**	**19.3**	**19.7**	**27.6**	**30.7**	**34.0**
平实生活指向 simple living orientation	481	36.0	16.6	17.5	15.0	14.6	21.4	27.4	41.2
时尚流行指向 fashion orientation	501	44.9	26.7	24.4	23.6	24.6	33.5	33.7	27.1

3-29 不同消费者层对护肤品和化妆品的信息接触情况/ Information Contact about Skin Cream & Cosmetics by Market Segments

注：本题为多选题，合计百分比超过 100%（Multiple answers）

	人数 Number	不管买还是不买，想看看 just have a look, without a definite purpose of buying or not	阅读有关的杂志和专门报道 reading magazines related & special reports	相互口头传播信息 communicate information orally among people	经常看这种商品的广告 often watch advertisements about such kind of goods	购买这种商品的新类型 buy the latest type of such kinds of goods	过去在这种商品上花了不少钱 used to spend much money on such kinds of goods	今后愿意在这方面花钱 willing to spend money on such items in future	不关注这方面的信息 don't care about such items
样本 Sample	**987**	**31.8**	**20.2**	**19.0**	**30.6**	**15.9**	**22.5**	**28.2**	**42.4**
平实生活指向 simple living orientation	484	23.8	13.4	13.8	23.1	10.1	14.3	20.9	52.3
时尚流行指向 fashion orientation	503	39.6	26.6	24.1	37.8	21.5	30.4	35.2	32.8

3-30 不同消费者层对香波等洗涤用品的信息接触情况/ Information Contact about Shampoo & Detergent by Market Segments

注：本题为多选题，合计百分比超过 100%（Multiple answers）

	人数 Number	不管买还是不买，想看看 just have a look, without a definite purpose of buying or not	阅读有关的杂志和专门报道 reading magazines related & special reports	相互口头传播信息 communicate information orally among people	经常看这种商品的广告 often watch advertisements about such kind of goods	购买这种商品的新类型 buy the latest type of such kinds of goods	过去在这种商品上花了不少钱 used to spend much money on such kinds of goods	今后愿意在这方面花钱 willing to spend money on such items in future	不关注这方面的信息 don't care about such items
样本 Sample	987	30.5	15.2	20.0	33.5	21.9	23.9	29.4	34.7
平实生活指向 simple living orientation	483	24.4	11.0	15.3	30.0	16.8	20.5	25.5	39.3
时尚流行指向 fashion orientation	504	36.3	19.2	24.4	36.9	26.8	27.2	33.1	30.2

3-31 不同消费者层对外出就餐的信息接触情况/ Information Contact about Dinning Out by Market Segments

注：本题为多选题，合计百分比超过 100%（Multiple answers）

	人数 Number	阅读有关的杂志和专门报道 reading magazines related and special reports	相互口头传播信息 communicate information orally among people	经常看这种服务的广告 often watch advertisements about such kind of service	尝试这种服务的新类型 try using the latest type of such kinds of service	过去在这种服务上花了不少钱 used to spend much money on such kinds of service	今后愿意在这方面花钱 willing to spend money on such items in future	不关注这方面的信息 don't care about such items
样本 Sample	989	18.0	28.8	16.2	23.8	31.2	29.8	33.2
平实生活指向 simple living orientation	486	17.1	25.3	12.6	18.3	27.2	25.9	39.3
时尚流行指向 fashion orientation	503	18.9	32.2	19.7	29.0	35.2	33.6	27.2

3-32 不同消费者层对旅行的信息接触情况/ Information Contact about Travelling by Market Segments

注：本题为多选题，合计百分比超过 100%（Multiple answers）

	人数 Number	阅读有关的杂志和专门报道 reading magazines related and special reports	相互口头传播信息 communicate information orally among people	经常看这种服务的广告 often watch advertisements about such kind of service	尝试这种服务的新类型 try using the latest type of such kinds of service	过去在这种服务上花了不少钱 used to spend much money on such kinds of service	今后愿意在这方面花钱 willing to spend money on such items in future	不关注这方面的信息 don't care about such items
样本 Sample	991	35.6	30.3	26.7	18.6	25.4	47.9	27.0
平实生活指向 simple living orientation	488	32.4	27.7	24.2	14.8	22.1	44.9	32.2
时尚流行指向 fashion orientation	503	38.8	32.8	29.2	22.3	28.6	50.9	22.1

3-33 不同消费者层对音乐会的信息接触情况/ Information Contact about Concert by Market Segments

注：本题为多选题，合计百分比超过 100%（Multiple answers）

	人数 Number	阅读有关的杂志和专门报道 reading magazines related and special reports	相互口头传播信息 communicate information orally among people	经常看这种服务的广告 often watch advertise-ments about such kind of service	尝试这种服务的新类型 try using the latest type of such kinds of service	过去在这种服务上花了不少钱 used to spend much money on such kinds of service	今后愿意在这方面花钱 willing to spend money on such items in future	不关注这方面的信息 don't care about such items
样本 Sample	979	21.8	14.3	13.2	10.1	7.3	21.9	55.7
平实生活指向 simple living orientation	481	19.3	10.8	11.2	6.7	5.4	18.9	59.9
时尚流行指向 fashion orientation	498	24.1	17.7	15.1	13.5	9.0	24.7	51.6

3-34 不同消费者层对电影的信息接触情况/ Information Contact about Movie by Market Segments

注：本题为多选题，合计百分比超过 100%（Multiple answers）

	人数 Number	阅读有关的杂志和专门报道 reading magazines related and special reports	相互口头传播信息 communicate information orally among people	经常看这种服务的广告 often watch advertise-ments about such kind of service	尝试这种服务的新类型 try using the latest type of such kinds of service	过去在这种服务上花了不少钱 used to spend much money on such kinds of service	今后愿意在这方面花钱 willing to spend money on such items in future	不关注这方面的信息 don't care about such items
样本 Sample	982	32.7	27.2	22.1	12.9	20.1	21.6	40.4
平实生活指向 simple living orientation	481	27.0	24.9	18.5	8.7	17.5	19.5	45.3
时尚流行指向 fashion orientation	501	38.1	29.3	25.5	17.0	22.6	23.6	35.7

3-35 不同消费者层对戏剧或戏曲的信息接触情况/ Information Contact about Drama or Opera by Market Segments

注：本题为多选题，合计百分比超过 100%（Multiple answers）

	人数 Number	阅读有关的杂志和专门报道 reading magazines related and special reports	相互口头传播信息 communicate information orally among people	经常看这种服务的广告 often watch advertise-ments about such kind of service	尝试这种服务的新类型 try using the latest type of such kinds of service	过去在这种服务上花了不少钱 used to spend much money on such kinds of service	今后愿意在这方面花钱 willing to spend money on such items in future	不关注这方面的信息 don't care about such items
样本 Sample	979	11.6	7.3	8.9	4.4	4.8	8.5	76.9
平实生活指向 simple living orientation	481	12.1	8.3	8.7	4.0	6.0	7.1	76.1
时尚流行指向 fashion orientation	498	11.2	6.2	9.0	4.8	3.6	9.8	77.7

3-36 不同消费者层对蹦迪的信息接触情况/ Information Contact about Disco by Market Segments

注：本题为多选题，合计百分比超过 100%（Multiple answers）

	人数 Number	阅读有关的杂志和专门报道 reading magazines related and special reports	相互口头传播信息 communicate information orally among people	经常看这种服务的广告 often watch advertise-ments about such kind of service	尝试这种服务的新类型 try using the latest type of such kinds of service	过去在这种服务上花了不少钱 used to spend much money on such kinds of service	今后愿意在这方面花钱 willing to spend money on such items in future	不关注这方面的信息 don't care about such items
样本 Sample	988	5.3	8.0	3.6	6.6	6.5	7.4	79.9
平实生活指向 simple living orientation	486	2.9	2.9	1.9	3.5	1.4	3.9	89.1
时尚流行指向 fashion orientation	502	7.6	12.9	5.4	9.6	11.4	10.8	70.9

3-37 不同消费者层对现场观赏体育比赛的信息接触情况/ Information Contact about Enjoying Live Sports by Market Segments

注：本题为多选题，合计百分比超过 100%（Multiple answers）

	人数 Number	阅读有关的杂志和专门报道 reading magazines related and special reports	相互口头传播信息 communicate information orally among people	经常看这种服务的广告 often watch advertise-ments about such kind of service	尝试这种服务的新类型 try using the latest type of such kinds of service	过去在这种服务上花了不少钱 used to spend much money on such kinds of service	今后愿意在这方面花钱 willing to spend money on such items in future	不关注这方面的信息 don't care about such items
样本 Sample	**983**	**28.2**	**20.8**	**18.0**	**10.0**	**13.3**	**27.2**	**47.9**
平实生活指向 simple living orientation	484	27.5	18.2	16.1	6.8	11.8	27.9	49.8
时尚流行指向 fashion orientation	499	28.9	23.2	19.8	13.0	14.8	26.5	46.1

3-38 不同消费者层对运动健身的信息接触情况/ Information Contact about Gym by Market Segments

注：本题为多选题，合计百分比超过 100%（Multiple answers）

	人数 Number	阅读有关的杂志和专门报道 reading magazines related and special reports	相互口头传播信息 communicate information orally among people	经常看这种服务的广告 often watch advertise-ments about such kind of service	尝试这种服务的新类型 try using the latest type of such kinds of service	过去在这种服务上花了不少钱 used to spend much money on such kinds of service	今后愿意在这方面花钱 willing to spend money on such items in future	不关注这方面的信息 don't care about such items
样本 Sample	**983**	**24.8**	**16.0**	**16.6**	**16.9**	**13.7**	**41.5**	**35.5**
平实生活指向 simple living orientation	485	21.2	14.0	14.6	13.4	12.6	37.9	39.0
时尚流行指向 fashion orientation	498	28.3	17.9	18.5	20.3	14.9	45.0	32.1

3-39 不同消费者层对技能学习的信息接触情况/ Information Contact about Studying Skills by Market Segments

注：本题为多选题，合计百分比超过 100%（Multiple answers）

	人数 Number	阅读有关的杂志和专门报道 reading magazines related and special reports	相互口头传播信息 communicate information orally among people	经常看这种服务的广告 often watch advertise-ments about such kind of service	尝试这种服务的新类型 try using the latest type of such kinds of service	过去在这种服务上花了不少钱 used to spend much money on such kinds of service	今后愿意在这方面花钱 willing to spend money on such items in future	不关注这方面的信息 don't care about such items
样本 Sample	**980**	**31.1**	**17.1**	**16.5**	**12.7**	**18.2**	**40.9**	**37.1**
平实生活指向 simple living orientation	480	25.6	15.4	14.6	10.6	16.9	36.5	42.7
时尚流行指向 fashion orientation	500	36.4	18.8	18.4	14.6	19.4	45.2	31.8

3-40 不同消费者层对外语学习的信息接触情况/ Information Contact about Studying Foreign Languages by Market Segments

注：本题为多选题，合计百分比超过 100%（Multiple answers）

	人数 Number	阅读有关的杂志和专门报道 reading magazines related and special reports	相互口头传播信息 communicate information orally among people	经常看这种服务的广告 often watch advertise-ments about such kind of service	尝试这种服务的新类型 try using the latest type of such kinds of service	过去在这种服务上花了不少钱 used to spend much money on such kinds of service	今后愿意在这方面花钱 willing to spend money on such items in future	不关注这方面的信息 don't care about such items
样本 Sample	**986**	**22.3**	**11.2**	**11.1**	**8.0**	**13.8**	**35.2**	**49.8**
平实生活指向 simple living orientation	486	19.3	10.3	9.9	8.6	14.6	31.3	54.1
时尚流行指向 fashion orientation	500	25.2	12.0	12.2	7.4	13.0	39.0	45.6

● 上海 / Shanghai

3-1 样本、男性各年龄层、女性各年龄层对电视、音响等视听设备的信息接触情况/ Information Contact about Video & Audio Equipment by the Whole Sample, Age and Gender Groups

注：本题为多选题，合计百分比超过 100%（Multiple answers）

	人数 Number	不管买还是不买想看看 just have a look, without a definite purpose of buying or not	阅读有关的杂志和专门报道 reading magazines related & special reports	相互口头传播信息 communicate information orally among people	经常看这种商品的广告 often watch advertisements about such kinds of goods	购买这种商品的新类型 buy the latest type of such kinds of goods	过去在这种商品上花了不少钱 used to spend much money on such kinds of goods	今后愿意在这方面花钱 willing to spend money on such items in future	不关注这方面的信息 don't care about such items
样本 Sample	**1012**	**55.2**	**26.2**	**21.4**	**32.7**	**12.6**	**25.5**	**27.4**	**14.4**
男性 Male	**508**	**60.0**	**29.1**	**24.0**	**35.4**	**14.6**	**26.6**	**33.3**	**9.1**
16~24 岁 Age	109	56.9	29.4	23.9	44.0	20.2	18.3	34.9	7.3
25~34 岁 Age	146	58.9	28.8	15.1	28.1	13.0	21.9	28.1	10.3
35~44 岁 Age	129	64.3	24.8	24.8	34.9	12.4	29.5	32.6	7.8
45~54 岁 Age	85	64.7	42.4	41.2	43.5	16.5	38.8	42.4	3.5
55~60 岁 Age	39	48.7	15.4	17.9	23.1	7.7	30.8	30.8	25.6
女性 Female	**504**	**50.4**	**23.2**	**18.8**	**30.0**	**10.7**	**24.4**	**21.4**	**19.8**
16~24 岁 Age	108	53.7	25.0	14.8	25.0	12.0	14.8	24.1	16.7
25~34 岁 Age	144	53.5	20.1	20.1	33.3	8.3	21.5	16.7	20.1
35~44 岁 Age	130	51.5	25.4	24.6	34.6	11.5	33.1	26.9	11.5
45~54 岁 Age	82	48.8	25.6	19.5	25.6	17.1	34.1	22.0	25.6
55~60 岁 Age	40	30.0	17.5	5.0	25.0	0.0	12.5	12.5	42.5

3-2 样本、男性各年龄层、女性各年龄层对冰箱、洗衣机等白色家电的信息接触情况/ Information Contact about "White Home Electronic Products" by the Whole Sample, Age and Gender Groups

注：本题为多选题，合计百分比超过 100%（Multiple answers）

	人数 Number	不管买还是不买想看看 just have a look, without a definite purpose of buying or not	阅读有关的杂志和专门报道 reading magazines related & special reports	相互口头传播信息 communicate information orally among people	经常看这种商品的广告 often watch advertisements about such kinds of goods	购买这种商品的新类型 buy the latest type of such kinds of goods	过去在这种商品上花了不少钱 used to spend much money on such kinds of goods	今后愿意在这方面花钱 willing to spend money on such items in future	不关注这方面的信息 don't care about such items
样本 Sample	**1002**	**39.7**	**21.1**	**18.2**	**28.9**	**12.4**	**21.4**	**20.9**	**22.4**
男性 Male	**502**	**40.4**	**20.1**	**17.3**	**28.1**	**14.3**	**23.3**	**22.7**	**20.7**
16~24 岁 Age	108	32.4	23.1	14.8	27.8	11.1	13.9	15.7	27.8
25~34 岁 Age	144	37.5	16.7	11.8	25.0	13.2	18.8	23.6	20.8
35~44 岁 Age	128	47.7	21.9	20.3	24.2	13.3	27.3	23.4	15.6
45~54 岁 Age	84	40.5	25.0	26.2	39.3	22.6	33.3	29.8	16.7
55~60 岁 Age	38	50.0	7.9	15.8	28.9	13.2	31.6	21.1	26.3
女性 Female	**500**	**39.0**	**22.0**	**19.0**	**29.8**	**10.4**	**19.4**	**19.0**	**24.0**
16~24 岁 Age	107	29.9	20.6	17.8	21.5	14.0	13.1	13.1	30.8
25~34 岁 Age	142	35.2	19.0	22.5	35.9	9.2	14.8	16.2	26.1
35~44 岁 Age	128	45.3	25.8	18.8	32.8	12.5	27.3	27.3	13.3
45~54 岁 Age	82	47.6	24.4	22.0	29.3	9.8	28.0	23.2	22.0
55~60 岁 Age	41	39.0	19.5	4.9	22.0	0.0	9.8	9.8	36.6

3-3 样本、男性各年龄层、女性各年龄层对电脑等通讯工具的信息接触情况/ Information Contact about Computer & Telecommunications by the Whole Sample, Age and Gender Groups

注：本题为多选题，合计百分比超过 100%（Multiple answers）

	人数 Number	不管买还是不买想看看 just have a look, without a definite purpose of buying or not	阅读有关的杂志和专门报道 reading magazines related & special reports	相互口头传播信息 communi-cate informa-tion orally among people	经常看这种商品的广告 often watch advertise-ments about such kinds of goods	购买这种商品的新类型 buy the latest type of such kinds of goods	过去在这种商品上花了不少钱 used to spend much money on such kinds of goods	今后愿意在这方面花钱 willing to spend money on such items in future	不关注这方面的信息 don't care about such items
样本 Sample	1011	37.9	25.6	19.4	21.4	11.6	10.6	37.2	27.3
男性 Male	508	42.7	29.3	20.3	23.2	11.8	11.0	40.7	23.6
16~24 岁 Age	109	52.3	46.8	38.5	39.4	20.2	18.3	47.7	10.1
25~34 岁 Age	146	44.5	30.1	17.1	21.2	11.6	7.5	43.2	17.8
35~44 岁 Age	129	40.3	20.2	12.4	15.5	6.2	7.8	41.9	29.5
45~54 岁 Age	85	40.0	29.4	20.0	25.9	15.3	11.8	42.4	27.1
55~60 岁 Age	39	23.1	7.7	7.7	5.1	0.0	12.8	5.1	56.4
女性 Female	503	33.0	21.9	18.5	19.5	11.3	10.1	33.6	31.0
16~24 岁 Age	107	39.3	31.8	22.4	24.3	20.6	11.2	40.2	16.8
25~34 岁 Age	144	36.8	22.2	20.1	17.4	9.7	8.3	39.6	27.8
35~44 岁 Age	129	35.7	20.9	17.1	20.2	3.9	7.0	34.1	30.2
45~54 岁 Age	82	20.7	14.6	17.1	18.3	18.3	20.7	25.6	40.2
55~60 岁 Age	41	19.5	12.2	9.8	14.6	2.4	2.4	9.8	63.4

3-4 样本、男性各年龄层、女性各年龄层对家用轿车的信息接触情况/ Information Contact about Family Car by the Whole Sample, Age and Gender Groups

注：本题为多选题，合计百分比超过 100%（Multiple answers）

	人数 Number	不管买还是不买想看看 just have a look, without a definite purpose of buying or not	阅读有关的杂志和专门报道 reading magazines related & special reports	相互口头传播信息 communi-cate informa-tion orally among people	经常看这种商品的广告 often watch advertise-ments about such kinds of goods	购买这种商品的新类型 buy the latest type of such kinds of goods	过去在这种商品上花了不少钱 used to spend much money on such kinds of goods	今后愿意在这方面花钱 willing to spend money on such items in future	不关注这方面的信息 don't care about such items
样本 Sample	1011	22.1	11.8	6.0	10.3	3.0	1.1	10.7	62.8
男性 Male	508	23.6	14.2	7.1	12.4	3.7	0.8	12.2	57.5
16~24 岁 Age	109	28.4	16.5	9.2	14.7	2.8	0.9	17.4	53.2
25~34 岁 Age	145	26.2	17.9	9.7	13.1	4.8	0.0	15.2	48.3
35~44 岁 Age	130	19.2	13.1	4.6	13.1	4.6	0.8	7.7	61.5
45~54 岁 Age	85	25.9	10.6	7.1	11.8	2.4	2.4	10.6	62.4
55~60 岁 Age	39	10.3	5.1	0.0	2.6	2.6	0.0	5.1	79.5
女性 Female	503	20.5	9.3	5.0	8.2	2.2	1.4	9.1	68.2
16~24 岁 Age	107	30.8	17.8	7.5	9.3	1.9	0.9	15.0	53.3
25~34 岁 Age	144	27.1	12.5	4.9	9.0	4.2	2.8	10.4	58.3
35~44 岁 Age	129	12.4	5.4	4.7	6.2	0.8	0.0	8.5	76.7
45~54 岁 Age	82	13.4	2.4	4.9	7.3	2.4	2.4	3.7	84.1
55~60 岁 Age	41	9.8	2.4	0.0	9.8	0.0	0.0	2.4	82.9

3-5 样本、男性各年龄层、女性各年龄层对高级家具的信息接触情况/ Information Contact about First-class Furniture by the Whole Sample, Age and Gender Groups

注：本题为多选题，合计百分比超过 100%（Multiple answers）

	人数 Number	不管买还是不买想看看 just have a look, without a definite purpose of buying or not	阅读有关的杂志和专门报道 reading magazines related & special reports	相互口头传播信息 communi-cate informa-tion orally among people	经常看这种商品的广告 often watch advertise-ments about such kinds of goods	购买这种商品的新类型 buy the latest type of such kinds of goods	过去在这种商品上花了不少钱 used to spend much money on such kinds of goods	今后愿意在这方面花钱 willing to spend money on such items in future	不关注这方面的信息 don't care about such items
样本 Sample	1010	26.0	12.3	6.9	12.0	5.0	4.1	16.7	52.8
男性 Male	507	22.9	12.8	6.5	9.9	3.9	3.6	14.8	54.0
16~24 岁 Age	109	13.8	12.8	5.5	6.4	6.4	4.6	12.8	61.5
25~34 岁 Age	145	30.3	13.1	6.2	8.3	2.1	4.1	17.9	45.5
35~44 岁 Age	130	16.2	14.6	6.9	13.1	5.4	2.3	17.7	53.8
45~54 岁 Age	84	39.3	14.3	10.7	14.3	3.6	4.8	13.1	46.4
55~60 岁 Age	39	7.7	2.6	0.0	5.1	0.0	0.0	2.6	82.1
女性 Female	503	29.2	11.7	7.4	14.1	6.0	4.6	18.7	51.5
16~24 岁 Age	108	29.6	13.0	8.3	14.8	5.6	3.7	19.4	47.2
25~34 岁 Age	143	37.8	13.3	9.8	15.4	8.4	4.9	21.0	42.0
35~44 岁 Age	129	27.1	9.3	5.4	10.9	3.9	6.2	20.9	54.3
45~54 岁 Age	82	19.5	11.0	6.1	14.6	4.9	3.7	15.9	64.6
55~60 岁 Age	41	24.4	12.2	4.9	17.1	7.3	2.4	7.3	61.0

3-6 样本、男性各年龄层、女性各年龄层对西服和时装的信息接触情况/ Information Contact about Business Suit & Fashion by the Whole Sample, Age and Gender Groups

注：本题为多选题，合计百分比超过 100%（Multiple answers）

	人数 Number	不管买还是不买想看看 just have a look, without a definite purpose of buying or not	阅读有关的杂志和专门报道 reading magazines related & special reports	相互口头传播信息 communi-cate informa-tion orally among people	经常看这种商品的广告 often watch advertise-ments about such kinds of goods	购买这种商品的新类型 buy the latest type of such kinds of goods	过去在这种商品上花了不少钱 used to spend much money on such kinds of goods	今后愿意在这方面花钱 willing to spend money on such items in future	不关注这方面的信息 don't care about such items
样本 Sample	1010	43.7	19.2	18.7	20.9	16.4	22.8	31.4	23.0
男性 Male	507	36.5	15.2	17.2	18.3	15.2	20.5	30.6	26.0
16~24 岁 Age	109	36.7	14.7	21.1	22.9	22.0	12.8	31.2	24.8
25~34 岁 Age	145	42.1	20.0	19.3	17.2	15.2	25.5	34.5	13.1
35~44 岁 Age	129	34.9	15.5	13.2	17.1	10.9	20.2	33.3	31.8
45~54 岁 Age	85	35.3	10.6	18.8	18.8	16.5	27.1	25.9	29.4
55~60 岁 Age	39	23.1	7.7	7.7	12.8	7.7	10.3	15.4	51.3
女性 Female	503	50.9	23.3	20.3	23.5	17.7	25.0	32.2	19.9
16~24 岁 Age	108	50.9	25.9	23.1	26.9	24.1	28.7	40.7	8.3
25~34 岁 Age	143	58.0	30.8	25.9	27.3	23.1	35.0	32.2	9.8
35~44 岁 Age	129	51.2	20.2	17.8	20.2	14.7	23.3	36.4	24.0
45~54 岁 Age	82	46.3	15.9	17.1	19.5	11.0	17.1	24.4	32.9
55~60 岁 Age	41	34.1	14.6	7.3	19.5	4.9	2.4	12.2	46.3

3-7 样本、男性各年龄层、女性各年龄层对酒精饮料的信息接触情况/ Information Contact about Alcohol Drinks by the Whole Sample, Age and Gender Groups

注：本题为多选题，合计百分比超过 100%（Multiple answers）

	人数 Number	不管买还是不买想看看 just have a look, without a definite purpose of buying or not	阅读有关的杂志和专门报道 reading magazines related & special reports	相互口头传播信息 communicate information orally among people	经常看这种商品的广告 often watch advertisements about such kinds of goods	购买这种商品的新类型 buy the latest type of such kinds of goods	过去在这种商品上花了不少钱 used to spend much money on such kinds of goods	今后愿意在这方面花钱 willing to spend money on such items in future	不关注这方面的信息 don't care about such items
样本 Sample	1008	18.9	8.1	12.2	16.7	10.3	15.8	16.7	50.3
男性 Male	506	22.1	8.7	15.2	18.2	9.9	20.8	21.1	42.1
16~24 岁 Age	107	19.6	9.3	16.8	24.3	13.1	16.8	16.8	48.6
25~34 岁 Age	146	24.0	11.0	18.5	21.2	11.0	21.2	19.9	32.2
35~44 岁 Age	129	22.5	6.2	13.2	14.7	7.8	21.7	26.4	45.0
45~54 岁 Age	85	27.1	7.1	12.9	16.5	9.4	27.1	22.4	43.5
55~60 岁 Age	39	10.3	10.3	10.3	5.1	5.1	12.8	17.9	48.7
女性 Female	502	15.7	7.6	9.2	15.1	10.8	10.8	12.2	58.6
16~24 岁 Age	107	14.0	4.7	10.3	20.6	18.7	7.5	6.5	50.5
25~34 岁 Age	143	15.4	9.8	9.8	16.1	8.4	10.5	13.3	53.8
35~44 岁 Age	129	20.2	10.9	11.6	15.5	11.6	14.7	19.4	57.4
45~54 岁 Age	82	15.9	4.9	6.1	11.0	6.1	13.4	11.0	65.9
55~60 岁 Age	41	7.3	2.4	2.4	4.9	4.9	2.4	2.4	85.4

3-8 样本、男性各年龄层、女性各年龄层对 CD 唱片及音乐带的信息接触情况/ Information Contact about CD & Music Cassette by the Whole Sample, Age and Gender Groups

注：本题为多选题，合计百分比超过 100%（Multiple answers）

	人数 Number	不管买还是不买想看看 just have a look, without a definite purpose of buying or not	阅读有关的杂志和专门报道 reading magazines related & special reports	相互口头传播信息 communicate information orally among people	经常看这种商品的广告 often watch advertisements about such kinds of goods	购买这种商品的新类型 buy the latest type of such kinds of goods	过去在这种商品上花了不少钱 used to spend much money on such kinds of goods	今后愿意在这方面花钱 willing to spend money on such items in future	不关注这方面的信息 don't care about such items
样本 Sample	1012	37.3	21.1	21.0	20.0	20.7	28.4	33.9	26.7
男性 Male	509	39.3	25.0	24.6	20.2	23.0	30.1	35.4	22.8
16~24 岁 Age	109	51.4	42.2	45.0	33.0	38.5	45.9	45.0	4.6
25~34 岁 Age	146	37.7	28.8	25.3	17.8	19.2	31.5	32.9	13.7
35~44 岁 Age	130	37.7	19.2	13.8	19.2	19.2	20.0	36.9	30.0
45~54 岁 Age	85	40.0	15.3	22.4	17.6	23.5	30.6	38.8	30.6
55~60 岁 Age	39	15.4	2.6	5.1	2.6	5.1	12.8	5.1	66.7
女性 Female	503	35.2	17.3	17.5	19.7	18.3	26.6	32.4	30.6
16~24 岁 Age	108	48.1	27.8	31.5	26.9	34.3	38.9	44.4	8.3
25~34 岁 Age	142	40.1	16.9	19.0	17.6	19.7	29.6	33.1	23.2
35~44 岁 Age	130	30.8	15.4	11.5	18.5	13.1	27.7	37.7	32.3
45~54 岁 Age	82	24.4	14.6	12.2	18.3	8.5	14.6	19.5	51.2
55~60 岁 Age	41	19.5	2.4	4.9	14.6	7.3	4.9	7.3	68.3

3-9 样本、男性各年龄层、女性各年龄层对护肤品和化妆品的信息接触情况/ Information Contact about Skin Cream & Cosmetics by the Whole Sample, Age and Gender Groups

注：本题为多选题，合计百分比超过 100%（Multiple answers）

	人数 Number	不管买还是不买想看看 just have a look, without a definite purpose of buying or not	阅读有关的杂志和专门报道 reading magazines related & special reports	相互口头传播信息 communicate information orally among people	经常看这种商品的广告 often watch advertisements about such kinds of goods	购买这种商品的新类型 buy the latest type of such kinds of goods	过去在这种商品上花了不少钱 used to spend much money on such kinds of goods	今后愿意在这方面花钱 willing to spend money on such items in future	不关注这方面的信息 don't care about such items
样本 Sample	1011	31.5	18.8	16.7	25.4	15.3	20.3	25.2	41.1
男性 Male	507	15.8	8.5	6.7	11.8	7.1	7.7	11.0	63.9
16~24 岁 Age	107	14.0	12.1	5.6	13.1	3.7	6.5	9.3	68.2
25~34 岁 Age	146	17.8	11.0	9.6	11.6	10.3	7.5	10.3	55.5
35~44 岁 Age	130	14.6	4.6	5.4	13.8	4.6	11.5	12.3	65.4
45~54 岁 Age	85	15.3	8.2	5.9	10.6	8.2	5.9	12.9	65.9
55~60 岁 Age	39	17.9	2.6	5.1	5.1	10.3	2.6	10.3	74.4
女性 Female	504	47.2	29.2	26.8	39.1	23.6	32.9	39.5	18.3
16~24 岁 Age	108	49.1	31.5	31.5	43.5	32.4	34.3	46.3	11.1
25~34 岁 Age	144	52.8	38.9	32.6	44.4	28.5	39.6	42.4	6.9
35~44 岁 Age	130	49.2	27.7	27.7	36.2	23.1	38.5	44.6	16.9
45~54 岁 Age	82	42.7	22.0	15.9	40.2	14.6	24.4	31.7	30.5
55~60 岁 Age	40	25.0	7.5	12.5	15.0	2.5	5.0	10.0	57.5

3-10 样本、男性各年龄层、女性各年龄层对香波等洗涤用品的信息接触情况/ Information Contact about Shampoo & Detergent Cassette by the Whole Sample, Age and Gender Groups

注：本题为多选题，合计百分比超过 100%（Multiple answers）

	人数 Number	不管买还是不买想看看 just have a look, without a definite purpose of buying or not	阅读有关的杂志和专门报道 reading magazines related & special reports	相互口头传播信息 communicate information orally among people	经常看这种商品的广告 often watch advertisements about such kinds of goods	购买这种商品的新类型 buy the latest type of such kinds of goods	过去在这种商品上花了不少钱 used to spend much money on such kinds of goods	今后愿意在这方面花钱 willing to spend money on such items in future	不关注这方面的信息 don't care about such items
样本 Sample	1012	33.3	15.6	16.8	27.2	20.0	22.6	28.9	31.2
男性 Male	508	21.5	7.7	7.3	15.2	10.8	12.4	17.3	50.6
16~24 岁 Age	109	16.5	10.1	8.3	16.5	11.0	11.9	15.6	50.5
25~34 岁 Age	146	23.3	8.2	8.9	17.1	14.4	13.0	19.2	45.2
35~44 岁 Age	130	21.5	6.9	5.4	16.9	5.4	14.6	18.5	49.2
45~54 岁 Age	84	27.4	7.1	6.0	13.1	13.1	10.7	16.7	56.0
55~60 岁 Age	39	15.4	2.6	7.7	2.6	10.3	7.7	12.8	64.1
女性 Female	504	45.2	23.6	26.4	39.3	29.2	32.9	40.5	11.7
16~24 岁 Age	108	38.9	18.5	24.1	38.9	31.5	30.6	38.0	11.1
25~34 岁 Age	143	49.7	28.0	28.7	46.9	35.0	33.6	42.0	1.4
35~44 岁 Age	130	46.2	28.5	30.0	38.5	31.5	40.8	49.2	10.0
45~54 岁 Age	82	48.8	22.0	22.0	39.0	22.0	30.5	36.6	22.0
55~60 岁 Age	41	36.6	9.8	22.0	17.1	9.8	17.1	22.0	34.1

3-11 样本、男性各年龄层、女性各年龄层对外出就餐的信息接触情况/ Information Contact about Dinning Out by the Whole Sample, Age and Gender Groups

注：本题为多选题，合计百分比超过 100%（Multiple answers）

	人数 Number	阅读有关的杂志和专门报道 reading magazines related and special reports	相互口头传播信息 communicate information orally among people	经常看这种服务的广告 often watch advertisem-ents about such kinds of service	尝试这种服务的新类型 try using the latest type of such kinds of service	过去在这种服务上花了不少钱 used to spend much money on such kinds of service	今后愿意在这方面花钱 willing to spend money on such items in future	不关注这方面的信息 don't care about such items
样本 Sample	1013	21.6	28.0	19.3	23.9	24.0	30.6	24.9
男性 Male	508	21.9	28.7	17.9	26.0	25.4	30.9	22.4
16~24 岁 Age	109	25.7	32.1	16.5	25.7	16.5	30.3	17.4
25~34 岁 Age	146	28.8	31.5	18.5	28.1	43.2	28.8	15.1
35~44 岁 Age	129	17.8	19.4	17.8	26.4	18.6	29.5	28.7
45~54 岁 Age	85	17.6	36.5	20.0	28.2	21.2	37.6	22.4
55~60 岁 Age	39	7.7	23.1	15.4	12.8	15.4	30.8	43.6
女性 Female	505	21.4	27.3	20.8	21.8	22.6	30.3	27.3
16~24 岁 Age	108	25.9	29.6	25.9	28.7	20.4	31.5	18.5
25~34 岁 Age	144	24.3	31.9	25.7	29.2	32.6	31.9	20.1
35~44 岁 Age	130	23.1	26.9	17.7	18.5	21.5	36.9	24.6
45~54 岁 Age	82	14.6	22.0	15.9	8.5	14.6	19.5	48.8
55~60 岁 Age	41	7.3	17.1	9.8	14.6	12.2	22.0	41.5

3-12 样本、男性各年龄层、女性各年龄层对旅行的信息接触情况/ Information Contact about Travelling by the Whole Sample, Age and Gender Groups

注：本题为多选题，合计百分比超过 100%（Multiple answers）

	人数 Number	阅读有关的杂志和专门报道 reading magazines related and special reports	相互口头传播信息 communicate information orally among people	经常看这种服务的广告 often watch advertise-ments about such kinds of service	尝试这种服务的新类型 try using the latest type of such kinds of service	过去在这种服务上花了不少钱 used to spend much money on such kinds of service	今后愿意在这方面花钱 willing to spend money on such items in future	不关注这方面的信息 don't care about such kinds of service
样本 Sample	1008	29.5	23.0	20.3	15.4	18.3	42.5	25.6
男性 Male	506	31.6	21.1	20.2	17.0	19.8	43.7	22.9
16~24 岁 Age	109	33.9	16.5	17.4	22.0	17.4	38.5	23.9
25~34 岁 Age	144	36.1	29.2	22.9	16.0	25.0	46.5	12.5
35~44 岁 Age	129	29.5	19.4	20.9	10.9	17.1	45.7	27.1
45~54 岁 Age	85	29.4	22.4	22.4	20.0	18.8	44.7	29.4
55~60 岁 Age	39	20.5	7.7	10.3	20.5	17.9	38.5	30.8
女性 Female	502	27.3	24.9	20.5	13.7	16.7	41.2	28.3
16~24 岁 Age	107	29.0	30.8	19.6	15.9	16.8	44.9	19.6
25~34 岁 Age	142	33.1	26.8	21.8	18.3	22.5	53.5	18.3
35~44 岁 Age	130	27.7	21.5	19.2	10.8	16.2	40.8	28.5
45~54 岁 Age	82	22.0	24.4	22.0	9.8	12.2	26.8	46.3
55~60 岁 Age	41	12.2	14.6	19.5	9.8	7.3	19.5	48.8

3-13 样本、男性各年龄层、女性各年龄层对音乐会的信息接触情况/ Information Contact about Concert by the Whole Sample, Age and Gender Groups

注：本题为多选题，合计百分比超过 100%（Multiple answers）

	人数 Number	阅读有关的杂志和专门报道 reading magazines related and special reports	相互口头传播信息 communicate information orally among people	经常看这种服务的广告 often watch advertise-ments about such kinds of service	尝试这种服务的新类型 try using the latest type of such kinds of service	过去在这种服务上花了不少钱 used to spend much money on such kinds of service	今后愿意在这方面花钱 willing to spend money on such items in future	不关注这方面的信息 don't care about such kinds of service
样本 Sample	1007	22.5	14.8	14.2	8.6	7.0	18.1	50.6
男性 Male	505	22.6	14.5	12.7	8.5	6.9	18.2	50.7
16~24 岁 Age	108	34.3	20.4	17.6	13.9	5.6	26.9	32.4
25~34 岁 Age	143	23.1	16.1	18.2	7.0	9.8	18.9	40.6
35~44 岁 Age	130	19.2	10.8	8.5	7.7	6.9	13.8	60.8
45~54 岁 Age	85	17.6	15.3	7.1	9.4	5.9	18.8	60.0
55~60 岁 Age	39	10.3	2.6	5.1	0.0	2.6	5.1	84.6
女性 Female	502	22.5	15.1	15.7	8.8	7.0	17.9	50.6
16~24 岁 Age	107	27.1	22.4	23.4	17.8	14.0	30.8	29.0
25~34 岁 Age	144	31.3	20.1	16.0	9.7	9.0	20.1	41.0
35~44 岁 Age	128	21.9	10.2	14.8	4.7	3.9	18.0	53.9
45~54 岁 Age	82	9.8	7.3	12.2	4.9	2.4	6.1	75.6
55~60 岁 Age	41	7.3	9.8	4.9	2.4	0.0	0.0	80.5

3-14 样本、男性各年龄层、女性各年龄层对电影的信息接触情况/ Information Contact about Movie by the Whole Sample, Age and Gender Groups

注：本题为多选题，合计百分比超过 100%（Multiple answers）

	人数 Number	阅读有关的杂志和专门报道 reading magazines related and special reports	相互口头传播信息 communicate information orally among people	经常看这种服务的广告 often watch advertise-ments about such kinds of service	尝试这种服务的新类型 try using the latest type of such kinds of service	过去在这种服务上花了不少钱 used to spend much money on such kinds of service	今后愿意在这方面花钱 willing to spend money on such items in future	不关注这方面的信息 don't care about such kinds of service
样本 Sample	1012	31.2	24.1	24.2	10.5	17.9	25.2	34.0
男性 Male	508	31.9	27.6	24.8	9.8	19.1	26.8	31.7
16~24 岁 Age	109	47.7	45.9	37.6	11.9	29.4	40.4	9.2
25~34 岁 Age	145	37.2	29.7	23.4	9.0	21.4	23.4	26.2
35~44 岁 Age	130	28.5	20.0	25.4	8.5	13.8	23.8	35.4
45~54 岁 Age	85	15.3	18.8	17.6	12.9	15.3	28.2	47.1
55~60 岁 Age	39	15.4	12.8	7.7	5.1	7.7	7.7	69.2
女性 Female	504	30.6	20.6	23.6	11.1	16.7	23.6	36.3
16~24 岁 Age	108	40.7	28.7	22.2	19.4	27.8	35.2	16.7
25~34 岁 Age	144	39.6	27.1	32.6	11.8	22.2	25.7	27.8
35~44 岁 Age	130	22.3	16.2	20.8	7.7	10.0	23.1	42.3
45~54 岁 Age	81	21.0	12.3	21.0	6.2	9.9	12.3	55.6
55~60 岁 Age	41	17.1	7.3	9.8	7.3	2.4	9.8	61.0

3-15 样本、男性各年龄层、女性各年龄层对戏剧或戏曲的信息接触情况/ Information Contact about Drama or Opera by the Whole Sample, Age and Gender Groups

注：本题为多选题，合计百分比超过 100%（Multiple answers）

	人数 Number	阅读有关的杂志和专门报道 reading magazines related and special reports	相互口头传播信息 communicate information orally among people	经常看这种服务的广告 often watch advertisements about such kinds of service	尝试这种服务的新类型 try using the latest type of such kinds of service	过去在这种服务上花了不少钱 used to spend much money on such kinds of service	今后愿意在这方面花钱 willing to spend money on such items in future	不关注这方面的信息 don't care about such kinds of service
样本 Sample	**1005**	**13.8**	**10.7**	**8.7**	**5.4**	**5.5**	**10.0**	**68.3**
男性 Male	**506**	**12.1**	**8.7**	**8.1**	**6.3**	**5.3**	**8.9**	**70.9**
16~24 岁 Age	109	7.3	5.5	2.8	5.5	3.7	5.5	81.7
25~34 岁 Age	144	6.9	2.8	5.6	3.5	3.5	3.5	79.9
35~44 岁 Age	129	17.8	10.9	10.1	5.4	5.4	11.6	67.4
45~54 岁 Age	85	16.5	15.3	14.1	11.8	7.1	14.1	56.5
55~60 岁 Age	39	15.4	17.9	12.8	10.3	12.8	17.9	51.3
女性 Female	**499**	**15.6**	**12.8**	**9.2**	**4.4**	**5.6**	**11.0**	**65.5**
16~24 岁 Age	106	8.5	4.7	5.7	5.7	4.7	11.3	73.6
25~34 岁 Age	142	16.9	8.5	5.6	3.5	3.5	7.7	70.4
35~44 岁 Age	128	16.4	18.0	10.2	4.7	5.5	12.5	63.3
45~54 岁 Age	82	18.3	17.1	12.2	3.7	8.5	12.2	62.2
55~60 岁 Age	41	22.0	24.4	22.0	4.9	9.8	14.6	41.5

3-16 样本、男性各年龄层、女性各年龄层对蹦迪的信息接触情况/ Information Contact about Disco by the Whole Sample, Age and Gender Groups

注：本题为多选题，合计百分比超过 100%（Multiple answers）

	人数 Number	阅读有关的杂志和专门报道 reading magazines related and special reports	相互口头传播信息 communicate information orally among people	经常看这种服务的广告 often watch advertisements about such kinds of service	尝试这种服务的新类型 try using the latest type of such kinds of service	过去在这种服务上花了不少钱 used to spend much money on such kinds of service	今后愿意在这方面花钱 willing to spend money on such items in future	不关注这方面的信息 don't care about such kinds of service
样本 Sample	**1009**	**7.3**	**7.7**	**4.6**	**8.3**	**5.3**	**9.2**	**73.3**
男性 Male	**506**	**7.3**	**7.9**	**5.1**	**8.7**	**6.3**	**10.3**	**70.4**
16~24 岁 Age	108	12.0	14.8	12.0	16.7	9.3	20.4	45.4
25~34 岁 Age	145	9.0	10.3	5.5	11.0	11.7	16.6	60.7
35~44 岁 Age	129	6.2	7.0	3.1	4.7	3.1	3.9	79.8
45~54 岁 Age	85	2.4	0.0	1.2	4.7	1.2	1.2	91.8
55~60 岁 Age	39	2.6	0.0	0.0	0.0	0.0	0.0	97.4
女性 Female	**503**	**7.4**	**7.6**	**4.0**	**8.0**	**4.2**	**8.2**	**76.3**
16~24 岁 Age	108	12.0	12.0	7.4	22.2	9.3	18.5	52.8
25~34 岁 Age	143	11.2	9.8	3.5	9.1	4.2	9.1	70.6
35~44 岁 Age	130	3.1	6.2	3.1	1.5	2.3	3.8	86.2
45~54 岁 Age	82	4.9	2.4	2.4	1.2	2.4	3.7	92.7
55~60 岁 Age	40	0.0	2.5	2.5	0.0	0.0	0.0	95.0

3-17 样本、男性各年龄层、女性各年龄层对现场观赏体育比赛的信息接触情况/ Information Contact about Enjoying Live Sports by the Whole Sample, Age and Gender Groups

注：本题为多选题，合计百分比超过 100%（Multiple answers）

	人数 Number	阅读有关的杂志和专门报道 reading magazines related and special reports	相互口头传播信息 communicate information orally among people	经常看这种服务的广告 often watch advertise-ments about such kinds of service	尝试这种服务的新类型 try using the latest type of such kinds of service	过去在这种服务上花了不少钱 used to spend much money on such kinds of service	今后愿意在这方面花钱 willing to spend money on such items in future	不关注这方面的信息 don't care about such kinds of service
样本 Sample	1011	27.9	21.3	18.2	8.6	10.0	22.9	44.5
男性 Male	508	36.8	28.3	23.4	10.6	14.0	30.3	31.5
16~24 岁 Age	108	37.0	36.1	27.8	17.6	19.4	43.5	15.7
25~34 岁 Age	146	37.0	28.8	19.9	11.0	13.0	28.8	30.8
35~44 岁 Age	130	41.5	27.7	23.1	6.2	13.8	31.5	33.1
45~54 岁 Age	85	37.6	28.2	31.8	11.8	14.1	22.4	32.9
55~60 岁 Age	39	17.9	7.7	7.7	2.6	2.6	12.8	69.2
女性 Female	503	18.9	14.1	12.9	6.6	6.0	15.5	57.7
16~24 岁 Age	108	20.4	21.3	16.7	7.4	8.3	27.8	39.8
25~34 岁 Age	144	20.1	13.2	11.1	9.0	6.3	8.3	56.9
35~44 岁 Age	130	20.0	12.3	10.8	6.9	3.1	17.7	63.8
45~54 岁 Age	81	18.5	13.6	16.0	2.5	9.9	14.8	63.0
55~60 岁 Age	40	7.5	5.0	10.0	2.5	0.0	2.5	77.5

3-18 样本、男性各年龄层、女性各年龄层对运动健身的信息接触情况/ Information Contact about Gym by the Whole Sample, Age and Gender Groups

注：本题为多选题，合计百分比超过 100%（Multiple answers）

	人数 Number	阅读有关的杂志和专门报道 reading magazines related and special reports	相互口头传播信息 communicate information orally among people	经常看这种服务的广告 often watch advertise-ments about such kinds of service	尝试这种服务的新类型 try using the latest type of such kinds of service	过去在这种服务上花了不少钱 used to spend much money on such kinds of service	今后愿意在这方面花钱 willing to spend money on such items in future	不关注这方面的信息 don't care about such kinds of service
样本 Sample	1012	23.7	17.6	16.1	15.2	9.7	34.0	36.5
男性 Male	509	26.5	17.7	14.9	15.9	11.6	36.0	34.4
16~24 岁 Age	109	34.9	25.7	11.0	22.9	21.1	48.6	19.3
25~34 岁 Age	146	26.0	17.8	13.7	15.1	13.7	43.2	26.0
35~44 岁 Age	130	23.1	13.8	16.2	10.8	6.2	26.9	43.1
45~54 岁 Age	85	29.4	15.3	24.7	18.8	9.4	28.2	42.4
55~60 岁 Age	39	10.3	12.8	5.1	10.3	0.0	20.5	61.5
女性 Female	503	20.9	17.5	17.3	14.5	7.8	32.0	38.6
16~24 岁 Age	107	25.2	15.0	21.5	19.6	11.2	43.0	23.4
25~34 岁 Age	143	19.6	16.1	14.0	17.5	7.7	35.7	32.9
35~44 岁 Age	130	20.0	19.2	13.8	13.8	7.7	27.7	46.9
45~54 岁 Age	82	23.2	22.0	26.8	8.5	4.9	25.6	45.1
55~60 岁 Age	41	12.2	14.6	9.8	4.9	4.9	17.1	58.5

3-19 样本、男性各年龄层、女性各年龄层对技能学习的信息接触情况/ Information Contact about Studying Skills by the Whole Sample, Age and Gender Groups

注：本题为多选题，合计百分比超过 100%（Multiple answers）

	人数 Number	阅读有关的杂志和专门报道 reading magazines related and special reports	相互口头传播信息 communicate information orally among people	经常看这种服务的广告 often watch advertisements about such kinds of service	尝试这种服务的新类型 try using the latest type of such kinds of service	过去在这种服务上花了不少钱 used to spend much money on such kinds of service	今后愿意在这方面花钱 willing to spend money on such items in future	不关注这方面的信息 don't care about such kinds of service
样本 Sample	**1009**	**25.5**	**16.2**	**15.6**	**11.4**	**11.8**	**35.2**	**40.8**
男性 Male	**507**	**26.4**	**17.4**	**13.6**	**10.7**	**11.8**	**38.3**	**39.4**
16~24 岁 Age	109	39.4	25.7	17.4	12.8	16.5	54.1	22.0
25~34 岁 Age	145	24.1	14.5	10.3	10.3	15.9	46.2	29.0
35~44 岁 Age	129	21.7	17.1	17.1	10.9	10.1	32.6	47.3
45~54 岁 Age	85	29.4	20.0	10.6	11.8	4.7	27.1	47.1
55~60 岁 Age	39	7.7	0.0	10.3	2.6	5.1	7.7	84.6
女性 Female	**502**	**24.5**	**14.9**	**17.5**	**12.2**	**11.8**	**32.1**	**42.2**
16~24 岁 Age	107	28.0	17.8	24.3	20.6	18.7	47.7	21.5
25~34 岁 Age	143	30.8	16.8	19.6	12.6	18.2	42.0	27.3
35~44 岁 Age	130	24.6	15.4	13.8	10.0	7.7	28.5	49.2
45~54 岁 Age	82	15.9	13.4	13.4	9.8	3.7	14.6	67.1
55~60 岁 Age	40	10.0	2.5	12.5	0.0	0.0	2.5	77.5

3-20 样本、男性各年龄层、女性各年龄层对外语学习的信息接触情况/ Information Contact about Studying Foreign Languages by the Whole Sample, Age and Gender Groups

注：本题为多选题，合计百分比超过 100%（Multiple answers）

	人数 Number	阅读有关的杂志和专门报道 reading magazines related and special reports	相互口头传播信息 communicate information orally among people	经常看这种服务的广告 often watch advertisements about such kinds of service	尝试这种服务的新类型 try using the latest type of such kinds of service	过去在这种服务上花了不少钱 used to spend much money on such kinds of service	今后愿意在这方面花钱 willing to spend money on such items in future	不关注这方面的信息 don't care about such kinds of service
样本 Sample	**1013**	**20.8**	**11.1**	**10.9**	**8.2**	**12.2**	**33.1**	**49.4**
男性 Male	**509**	**21.4**	**11.8**	**9.4**	**7.5**	**11.6**	**35.0**	**49.1**
16~24 岁 Age	109	33.9	26.6	11.0	16.5	29.4	56.9	20.2
25~34 岁 Age	146	24.0	11.0	12.3	6.8	11.0	46.6	35.6
35~44 岁 Age	130	12.3	6.9	6.9	4.6	7.7	25.4	62.3
45~54 岁 Age	85	20.0	5.9	9.4	4.7	1.2	11.8	72.9
55~60 岁 Age	39	10.3	2.6	2.6	0.0	0.0	12.8	84.6
女性 Female	**504**	**20.2**	**10.3**	**12.3**	**8.9**	**12.9**	**31.2**	**49.6**
16~24 岁 Age	108	36.1	20.4	24.1	14.8	25.0	59.3	13.9
25~34 岁 Age	143	25.9	12.6	15.4	9.8	17.5	41.3	34.3
35~44 岁 Age	130	14.6	8.5	6.2	9.2	7.7	17.7	63.8
45~54 岁 Age	82	4.9	1.2	3.7	3.7	2.4	11.0	84.1
55~60 岁 Age	41	7.3	0.0	7.3	0.0	2.4	4.9	82.9

3-21 不同消费者层对电视、音响等视听设备的信息接触情况/ Information Contact about Video&Audio Equipment by Market Segments

注：本题为多选题，合计百分比超过 100%（Multiple answers）

	人数 Number	不管买还是不买想看看 just have a look, without a definite purpose of buying or not	阅读有关的杂志和专门报道 reading magazines related & special reports	相互口头传播信息 communicate information orally among people	经常看这种商品的广告 often watch advertisements about such kinds of goods	购买这种商品的新类型 buy the latest type of such kinds of goods	过去在这种商品上花了不少钱 used to spend much money on such kinds of goods	今后愿意在这方面花钱 willing to spend money on such items in future	不关注这方面的信息 don't care about such items
样本 Sample	1003	54.9	26.2	21.4	32.9	12.7	25.6	27.3	14.5
平实生活指向 simple living orientation	470	53.0	22.3	20.4	33.0	10.6	24.5	25.7	18.7
时尚流行指向 fashion orientation	533	56.7	29.6	22.3	32.8	14.4	26.6	28.7	10.7

3-22 不同消费者层对冰箱、洗衣机等白色家电的信息接触情况/ Information Contact about "White Home Electronic Products" by Market Segments

注：本题为多选题，合计百分比超过 100%（Multiple answers）

	人数 Number	不管买还是不买想看看 just have a look, without a definite purpose of buying or not	阅读有关的杂志和专门报道 reading magazines related & special reports	相互口头传播信息 communicate information orally among people	经常看这种商品的广告 often watch advertisements about such kinds of goods	购买这种商品的新类型 buy the latest type of such kinds of goods	过去在这种商品上花了不少钱 used to spend much money on such kinds of goods	今后愿意在这方面花钱 willing to spend money on such items in future	不关注这方面的信息 don't care about such items
样本 Sample	993	39.6	20.8	18.1	29.1	12.4	21.5	20.8	22.3
平实生活指向 simple living orientation	466	38.4	19.7	16.3	28.8	10.5	22.3	20.0	25.1
时尚流行指向 fashion orientation	527	40.6	21.8	19.7	29.4	14.0	20.7	21.6	19.7

3-23 不同消费者层对电脑等通讯工具的信息接触情况/ Information Contact about Computer & Telecommunications by Market Segments

注：本题为多选题，合计百分比超过 100%（Multiple answers）

	人数 Number	不管买还是不买想看看 just have a look, without a definite purpose of buying or not	阅读有关的杂志和专门报道 reading magazines related & special reports	相互口头传播信息 communicate information orally among people	经常看这种商品的广告 often watch advertisements about such kinds of goods	购买这种商品的新类型 buy the latest type of such kinds of goods	过去在这种商品上花了不少钱 used to spend much money on such kinds of goods	今后愿意在这方面花钱 willing to spend money on such items in future	不关注这方面的信息 don't care about such items
样本 Sample	1002	38.0	25.6	19.3	21.5	11.5	10.6	37.3	27.1
平实生活指向 simple living orientation	470	32.8	22.8	15.3	18.9	8.9	10.0	30.9	36.8
时尚流行指向 fashion orientation	532	42.7	28.2	22.7	23.7	13.7	11.1	43.0	18.6

3-24 不同消费者层对家用轿车的信息接触情况/ Information Contact about Family Car by Market Segments

注：本题为多选题，合计百分比超过 100%（Multiple answers）

	人数 Number	不管买还是买，想看看 just have a look, without a definite purpose of buying or not	阅读有关的杂志和专门报道 reading magazines related & special reports	相互口头传播信息 communicate information orally among people	经常看这种商品的广告 often watch advertisements about such kinds of goods	购买这种商品的新类型 buy the latest type of such kinds of goods	过去在这种商品上花了不少钱 used to spend much money on such kinds of goods	今后愿意在这方面花钱 willing to spend money on such items in future	不关注这方面的信息 don't care about such items
样本 Sample	1002	22.1	11.9	6.0	10.3	3.0	1.1	10.7	62.9
平实生活指向 simple living orientation	470	18.5	9.4	4.3	7.7	1.7	0.6	8.1	69.4
时尚流行指向 fashion orientation	532	25.2	14.1	7.5	12.6	4.1	1.5	13.0	57.1

3-25 不同消费者层对高级家具的信息接触情况/ Information Contact about First-class Furniture by Market Segments

注：本题为多选题，合计百分比超过 100%（Multiple answers）

	人数 Number	不管买还是不买想看看 just have a look, without a definite purpose of buying or not	阅读有关的杂志和专门报道 reading magazines related & special reports	相互口头传播信息 communicate information orally among people	经常看这种商品的广告 often watch advertisements about such kinds of goods	购买这种商品的新类型 buy the latest type of such kinds of goods	过去在这种商品上花了不少钱 used to spend much money on such kinds of goods	今后愿意在这方面花钱 willing to spend money on such items in future	不关注这方面的信息 don't care about such items
样本 Sample	1001	26.1	12.2	6.9	11.8	4.9	4.1	16.7	52.8
平实生活指向 simple living orientation	470	21.3	9.8	5.1	11.3	2.3	2.3	11.1	61.3
时尚流行指向 fashion orientation	531	30.3	14.3	8.5	12.2	7.2	5.6	21.7	45.4

3-26 不同消费者层对西服和时装的信息接触情况/ Information Contact about Business Suit & Fashion by Market Segments

注：本题为多选题，合计百分比超过 100%（Multiple answers）

	人数 Number	不管买还是不买想看看 just have a look, without a definite purpose of buying or not	阅读有关的杂志和专门报道 reading magazines related & special reports	相互口头传播信息 communicate information orally among people	经常看这种商品的广告 often watch advertisements about such kinds of goods	购买这种商品的新类型 buy the latest type of such kinds of goods	过去在这种商品上花了不少钱 used to spend much money on such kinds of goods	今后愿意在这方面花钱 willing to spend money on such items in future	不关注这方面的信息 don't care about such items
样本 Sample	1001	43.7	19.1	18.7	20.9	16.3	22.9	31.4	23.2
平实生活指向 simple living orientation	469	37.7	13.0	13.2	17.1	10.0	13.9	25.2	33.5
时尚流行指向 fashion orientation	532	48.9	24.4	23.5	24.2	21.8	30.8	36.8	14.1

3-27 不同消费者层对酒精饮料的信息接触情况/ Information Contact about Alcohol Drinks by Market Segments

注：本题为多选题，合计百分比超过 100%（Multiple answers）

	人数 Number	不管买还是不买想看看 just have a look, without a definite purpose of buying or not	阅读有关的杂志和专门报道 reading magazines related & special reports	相互口头传播信息 communicate informatio n orally among people	经常看这种商品的广告 often watch advertise-ments about such kinds of goods	购买这种商品的新类型 buy the latest type of such kinds of goods	过去在这种商品上花了不少钱 used to spend much money on such kinds of goods	今后愿意在这方面花钱 willing to spend money on such items in future	不关注这方面的信息 don't care about such items
样本 Sample	999	19.1	8.2	12.3	16.7	10.3	15.8	16.6	50.3
平实生活指向 simple living orientation	470	16.4	8.1	11.9	13.8	8.1	14.3	15.7	56.4
时尚流行指向 fashion orientation	529	21.6	8.3	12.7	19.3	12.3	17.2	17.4	44.8

3-28 不同消费者层对 CD 唱片及音乐带的信息接触情况/ Information Contact about CD & Music Cassette by Market Segments

注：本题为多选题，合计百分比超过 100%（Multiple answers）

	人数 Number	不管买还是不买想看看 just have a look, without a definite purpose of buying or not	阅读有关的杂志和专门报道 reading magazines related & special reports	相互口头传播信息 communicate informa-tion orally among people	经常看这种商品的广告 often watch advertise-ments about such kinds of goods	购买这种商品的新类型 buy the latest type of such kinds of goods	过去在这种商品上花了不少钱 used to spend much money on such kinds of goods	今后愿意在这方面花钱 willing to spend money on such items in future	不关注这方面的信息 don't care about such items
样本 Sample	1003	37.3	21.0	20.8	19.9	20.6	28.3	34.0	26.7
平实生活指向 simple living orientation	471	29.1	17.2	16.1	16.3	14.0	19.5	26.8	40.1
时尚流行指向 fashion orientation	532	44.5	24.4	25.0	23.1	26.5	36.1	40.4	14.8

3-29 不同消费者层对护肤品和化妆品的信息接触情况/ Information Contact about Skin Cream & Cosmetics by Market Segments

注：本题为多选题，合计百分比超过 100%（Multiple answers）

	人数 Number	不管买还是不买想看看 just have a look, without a definite purpose of buying or not	阅读有关的杂志和专门报道 reading magazines related & special reports	相互口头传播信息 communicate informa-tion orally among people	经常看这种商品的广告 often watch advertise-ments about such kinds of goods	购买这种商品的新类型 buy the latest type of such kinds of goods	过去在这种商品上花了不少钱 used to spend much money on such kinds of goods	今后愿意在这方面花钱 willing to spend money on such items in future	不关注这方面的信息 don't care about such items
样本 Sample	1002	31.5	18.7	16.7	25.3	15.1	20.3	25.4	41.3
平实生活指向 simple living orientation	471	25.7	13.0	11.7	19.5	7.9	11.3	17.2	52.9
时尚流行指向 fashion orientation	531	36.7	23.7	21.1	30.5	21.5	28.2	32.8	31.1

3-30 不同消费者层对香波等洗涤用品的信息接触情况/ Information Contact about Shampoo & Detergent by Market Segments

注：本题为多选题，合计百分比超过 100%（Multiple answers）

	人数 Number	不管买还是不买想看看 just have a look, without a definite purpose of buying or not	阅读有关的杂志和专门报道 reading magazines related & special reports	相互口头传播信息 communicate information orally among people	经常看这种商品的广告 often watch advertisements about such kinds of goods	购买这种商品的新类型 buy the latest type of such kinds of goods	过去在这种商品上花了不少钱 used to spend much money on such kinds of goods	今后愿意在这方面花钱 willing to spend money on such items in future	不关注这方面的信息 don't care about such items
样本 Sample	1003	33.4	15.6	16.8	27.0	20.1	22.6	29.0	31.4
平实生活指向 simple living orientation	471	29.9	11.9	12.5	21.2	12.7	17.8	24.6	38.9
时尚流行指向 fashion orientation	532	36.5	18.8	20.7	32.1	26.7	26.9	32.9	24.8

3-31 不同消费者层对外出就餐的信息接触情况/ Information Contact about Dinning Out by Market Segments

注：本题为多选题，合计百分比超过 100%（Multiple answers）

	人数 Number	阅读有关的杂志和专门报道 reading magazines related and special reports	相互口头传播信息 communicate information orally among people	经常看这种服务的广告 often watch advertisements about such kinds of service	尝试这种服务的新类型 try using the latest type of such kinds of service	过去在这种服务上花了不少钱 used to spend much money on such kinds of service	今后愿意在这方面花钱 willing to spend money on such items in future	不关注这方面的信息 don't care about such items
样本 Sample	1004	21.5	27.9	19.2	23.8	24.2	30.7	24.9
平实生活指向 simple living orientation	470	17.0	25.1	17.2	18.1	18.9	24.9	35.1
时尚流行指向 fashion orientation	534	25.5	30.3	21.0	28.8	28.8	35.8	15.9

3-32 不同消费者层对旅行的信息接触情况/ Information Contact about Travelling by Market Segments

注：本题为多选题，合计百分比超过 100%（Multiple answers）

	人数 Number	阅读有关的杂志和专门报道 reading magazines related and special reports	相互口头传播信息 communicate information orally among people	经常看这种服务的广告 often watch advertisements about such kinds of service	尝试这种服务的新类型 try using the latest type of such kinds of service	过去在这种服务上花了不少钱 used to spend much money on such kinds of service	今后愿意在这方面花钱 willing to spend money on such items in future	不关注这方面的信息 don't care about such kinds of service
样本 Sample	999	29.2	23.2	20.3	15.4	18.3	42.5	25.6
平实生活指向 simple living orientation	467	27.0	20.1	22.3	13.1	15.2	37.0	31.9
时尚流行指向 fashion orientation	532	31.2	25.9	18.6	17.5	21.1	47.4	20.1

3-33 不同消费者层对音乐会的信息接触情况/ Information Contact about Concert by Market Segments

注：本题为多选题，合计百分比超过 100%（Multiple answers）

	人数 Number	阅读有关的杂志和专门报道 reading magazines related and special reports	相互口头传播信息 communicate information orally among people	经常看这种服务的广告 often watch advertisements about such kinds of service	尝试这种服务的新类型 try using the latest type of such kinds of service	过去在这种服务上花了不少钱 used to spend much money on such kinds of service	今后愿意在这方面花钱 willing to spend money on such items in future	不关注这方面的信息 don't care about such kinds of service
样本 Sample	998	22.6	14.8	14.2	8.7	7.0	18.1	50.6
平实生活指向 simple living orientation	468	17.9	12.0	12.8	4.7	4.3	10.9	62.4
时尚流行指向 fashion orientation	530	26.8	17.4	15.5	12.3	9.4	24.5	40.2

3-34 不同消费者层对电影的信息接触情况/ Information Contact about Movie by Market Segments

注：本题为多选题，合计百分比可能超过 100%（Multiple answers）

	人数 Number	阅读有关的杂志和专门报道 reading magazines related and special reports	相互口头传播信息 communicate information orally among people	经常看这种服务的广告 often watch advertisements about such kinds of service	尝试这种服务的新类型 try using the latest type of such kinds of service	过去在这种服务上花了不少钱 used to spend much money on such kinds of service	今后愿意在这方面花钱 willing to spend money on such items in future	不关注这方面的信息 don't care about such kinds of service
样本 Sample	1003	31.3	24.3	24.2	10.6	17.8	25.2	34.0
平实生活指向 simple living orientation	470	27.9	21.9	23.4	7.9	13.4	19.6	43.6
时尚流行指向 fashion orientation	533	34.3	26.5	25.0	12.9	21.8	30.2	25.5

3-35 不同消费者层对戏剧或戏曲的信息接触情况/ Information Contact about Drama or Opera by Market Segments

注：本题为多选题，合计百分比超过 100%（Multiple answers）

	人数 Number	阅读有关的杂志和专门报道 reading magazines related and special reports	相互口头传播信息 communicate information orally among people	经常看这种服务的广告 often watch advertisements about such kinds of service	尝试这种服务的新类型 try using the latest type of such kinds of service	过去在这种服务上花了不少钱 used to spend much money on such kinds of service	今后愿意在这方面花钱 willing to spend money on such items in future	不关注这方面的信息 don't care about such kinds of service
样本 Sample	996	13.8	10.7	8.6	5.3	5.5	9.9	68.3
平实生活指向 simple living orientation	468	15.0	13.0	10.0	5.3	4.9	9.8	66.2
时尚流行指向 fashion orientation	528	12.7	8.7	7.4	5.3	6.1	10.0	70.1

3-36 不同消费者层对蹦迪的信息接触情况/ Information Contact about Disco by Market Segments

注：本题为多选题，合计百分比超过 100%（Multiple answers）

	人数 Number	阅读有关的杂志和专门报道 reading magazines related and special reports	相互口头传播信息 communicate information orally among people	经常看这种服务的广告 often watch advertisements about such kinds of service	尝试这种服务的新类型 try using the latest type of such kinds of service	过去在这种服务上花了不少钱 used to spend much money on such kinds of service	今后愿意在这方面花钱 willing to spend money on such items in future	不关注这方面的信息 don't care about such kinds of service
样本 Sample	1000	7.3	7.8	4.5	8.2	5.3	9.3	73.5
平实生活指向 simple living orientation	469	2.1	2.8	2.8	4.3	1.3	3.8	86.6
时尚流行指向 fashion orientation	531	11.9	12.2	6.0	11.7	8.9	14.1	62.0

3-37 不同消费者层对现场观赏体育比赛的信息接触情况/ Information Contact about Enjoying Live Sports by Market Segments

注：本题为多选题，合计百分比可能超过 100%（Multiple answers）

	人数 Number	阅读有关的杂志和专门报道 reading magazines related and special reports	相互口头传播信息 communicate information orally among people	经常看这种服务的广告 often watch advertisements about such kinds of service	尝试这种服务的新类型 try using the latest type of such kinds of service	过去在这种服务上花了不少钱 used to spend much money on such kinds of service	今后愿意在这方面花钱 willing to spend money on such items in future	不关注这方面的信息 don't care about such kinds of service
样本 Sample	1002	27.8	21.4	18.4	8.7	10.1	23.0	44.5
平实生活指向 simple living orientation	470	26.0	19.8	16.4	6.2	7.0	21.3	49.6
时尚流行指向 fashion orientation	532	29.5	22.7	20.1	10.9	12.8	24.4	40.0

3-38 不同消费者层对运动健身的信息接触情况/ Information Contact about Gym by Market Segments

注：本题为多选题，合计百分比可能超过 100%（Multiple answers）

	人数 Number	阅读有关的杂志和专门报道 reading magazines related and special reports	相互口头传播信息 communicate information orally among people	经常看这种服务的广告 often watch advertise-ments about such kinds of service	尝试这种服务的新类型 try using the latest type of such kinds of service	过去在这种服务上花了不少钱 used to spend much money on such kinds of service	今后愿意在这方面花钱 willing to spend money on such items in future	不关注这方面的信息 don't care about such kinds of service
样本 Sample	1003	23.7	17.7	16.3	15.3	9.8	34.0	36.4
平实生活指向 simple living orientation	470	20.4	15.7	16.4	13.8	5.3	27.4	45.1
时尚流行指向 fashion orientation	533	26.6	19.5	16.1	16.5	13.7	39.8	28.7

3-39 不同消费者层对技能学习的信息接触情况/ Information Contact about Studying Skills by Market Segments

注：本题为多选题，合计百分比超过 100%（Multiple answers）

	人数 Number	阅读有关的杂志和专门报道 reading magazines related and special reports	相互口头传播信息 communicate information orally among people	经常看这种服务的广告 often watch advertise-ments about such kinds of service	尝试这种服务的新类型 try using the latest type of such kinds of service	过去在这种服务上花了不少钱 used to spend much money on such kinds of service	今后愿意在这方面花钱 willing to spend money on such items in future	不关注这方面的信息 don't care about such kinds of service
样本 Sample	1000	25.5	16.2	15.5	11.4	11.8	35.4	40.7
平实生活指向 simple living orientation	469	22.6	14.1	13.2	9.8	9.2	29.2	47.3
时尚流行指向 fashion orientation	531	28.1	18.1	17.5	12.8	14.1	40.9	34.8

3-40 不同消费者层对外语学习的信息接触情况/ Information Contact about Studying Foreign Languages by Market Segments

注：本题为多选题，合计百分比超过 100%（Multiple answers）

	人数 Number	阅读有关的杂志和专门报道 reading magazines related and special reports	相互口头传播信息 communicate information orally among people	经常看这种服务的广告 often watch advertise-ments about such kinds of service	尝试这种服务的新类型 try using the latest type of such kinds of service	过去在这种服务上花了不少钱 used to spend much money on such kinds of service	今后愿意在这方面花钱 willing to spend money on such items in future	不关注这方面的信息 don't care about such kinds of service
样本 Sample	1004	20.8	11.2	10.8	8.1	12.3	33.3	49.3
平实生活指向 simple living orientation	470	13.6	7.0	6.8	5.1	8.5	25.5	62.8
时尚流行指向 fashion orientation	534	27.2	14.8	14.2	10.7	15.5	40.1	37.5

● 广州 / Guangzhou

3-1 样本、男性各年龄层、女性各年龄层对电视、音响等视听设备的信息接触情况/ Information Contact about Video & Audio Equipment by the Whole Sample, Age and Gender Groups

注：本题为多选题，合计百分比超过 100%（Multiple answers）

	人数 Number	不管买还是不买，想看看 just have a look, without a definite purpose of buying or not	阅读有关的杂志和专门报道 reading magazines related & special reports	相互口头传播信息 communicate information orally among people	经常看这种商品的广告 often watch advertise-ments about such kinds of goods	购买这种商品的新类型 buy the latest type of such kinds of goods	过去在这种商品上花了不少钱 used to spend much money on such kinds of goods	今后愿意在这方面花钱 willing to spend money on such items in future	不关注这方面的信息 don't care about such items
样本 Sample	1034	48.1	16.5	14.8	21.6	8.4	19.2	19.7	21.1
男性 Male	499	53.7	20.2	18.0	22.8	8.8	20.4	23.8	15.2
16~24 岁 Age	106	52.8	20.8	23.6	21.7	11.3	10.4	22.6	16.0
25~34 岁 Age	150	62.0	24.0	17.3	26.7	8.7	20.0	30.7	13.3
35~44 岁 Age	127	49.6	15.7	15.7	22.0	7.9	22.8	18.9	15.7
45~54 岁 Age	73	57.5	23.3	21.9	26.0	9.6	26.0	23.3	11.0
55~60 岁 Age	43	32.6	14.0	7.0	9.3	4.7	30.2	18.6	25.6
女性 Female	535	42.8	13.1	11.8	20.4	8.0	18.1	15.9	26.5
16~24 岁 Age	112	40.2	15.2	12.5	26.8	8.0	17.9	14.3	18.8
25~34 岁 Age	158	46.8	13.9	13.3	15.2	8.2	17.1	15.8	22.8
35~44 岁 Age	137	43.1	13.9	10.9	23.4	12.4	15.3	16.8	26.3
45~54 岁 Age	87	44.8	11.5	13.8	21.8	3.4	21.8	19.5	31.0
55~60 岁 Age	41	29.3	4.9	2.4	9.8	2.4	24.4	9.8	53.7

3-2 样本、男性各年龄层、女性各年龄层对冰箱、洗衣机等白色家电的信息接触情况/ Information Contact about "White Home Electronic Products" by the Whole Sample, Age and Gender Groups

注：本题为多选题，合计百分比超过 100%（Multiple answers）

	人数 Number	不管买还是不买，想看看 just have a look, without a definite purpose of buying or not	阅读有关的杂志和专门报道 reading magazines related & special reports	相互口头传播信息 communicate information orally among people	经常看这种商品的广告 often watch advertise-ments about such kinds of goods	购买这种商品的新类型 buy the latest type of such kinds of goods	过去在这种商品上花了不少钱 used to spend much money on such kinds of goods	今后愿意在这方面花钱 willing to spend money on such items in future	不关注这方面的信息 don't care about such items
样本 Sample	1028	31.0	10.2	10.5	16.4	8.0	16.9	16.0	31.5
男性 Male	494	31.4	11.5	10.3	15.0	7.5	16.4	18.6	31.0
16~24 岁 Age	106	27.4	13.2	12.3	12.3	5.7	10.4	12.3	42.5
25~34 岁 Age	149	28.2	14.1	8.1	16.8	9.4	17.4	22.1	29.5
35~44 岁 Age	124	38.7	6.5	8.1	17.7	5.6	16.9	20.2	22.6
45~54 岁 Age	72	34.7	18.1	15.3	13.9	12.5	19.4	19.4	25.0
55~60 岁 Age	43	25.6	2.3	11.6	9.3	2.3	20.9	16.3	41.9
女性 Female	534	30.7	9.0	10.7	17.8	8.4	17.4	13.5	32.0
16~24 岁 Age	111	25.2	5.4	8.1	19.8	7.2	11.7	8.1	33.3
25~34 岁 Age	158	34.2	7.0	12.7	13.9	5.7	16.5	15.2	30.4
35~44 岁 Age	137	27.7	12.4	12.4	20.4	11.7	17.5	17.5	30.7
45~54 岁 Age	87	35.6	13.8	8.0	19.5	10.3	21.8	14.9	31.0
55~60 岁 Age	41	31.7	4.9	9.8	14.6	7.3	26.8	4.9	41.5

3-3 样本、男性各年龄层、女性各年龄层对电脑等通讯工具的信息接触情况/ Information Contact about Computer & Telecommunications by the Whole Sample, Age and Gender Groups

注：本题为多选题，合计百分比超过 100%（Multiple answers）

	人数 Number	不管买还是不买，想看看 just have a look, without a definite purpose of buying or not	阅读有关的杂志和专门报道 reading magazines related & special reports	相互口头传播信息 communicate information orally among people	经常看这种商品的广告 often watch advertisements about such kinds of goods	购买这种商品的新类型 buy the latest type of such kinds of goods	过去在这种商品上花了不少钱 used to spend much money on such kinds of goods	今后愿意在这方面花钱 willing to spend money on such items in future	不关注这方面的信息 don't care about such items
样本 Sample	**1034**	**29.3**	**22.0**	**14.7**	**18.6**	**8.9**	**11.0**	**28.1**	**33.9**
男性 Male	**499**	**35.1**	**25.7**	**19.0**	**24.0**	**9.2**	**14.4**	**33.1**	**27.1**
16~24 岁 Age	106	50.0	40.6	34.0	41.5	10.4	18.9	44.3	9.4
25~34 岁 Age	150	40.0	28.0	20.7	27.3	14.0	16.0	39.3	19.3
35~44 岁 Age	127	30.7	19.7	10.2	15.7	5.5	10.2	26.8	33.9
45~54 岁 Age	73	26.0	19.2	17.8	17.8	9.6	13.7	26.0	37.0
55~60 岁 Age	43	9.3	9.3	4.7	4.7	0.0	11.6	14.0	60.5
女性 Female	**535**	**23.9**	**18.5**	**10.7**	**13.5**	**8.6**	**7.9**	**23.6**	**40.4**
16~24 岁 Age	112	33.9	31.3	14.3	22.3	11.6	9.8	35.7	14.3
25~34 岁 Age	158	25.9	15.8	11.4	11.4	9.5	7.0	27.2	38.6
35~44 岁 Age	137	20.4	15.3	10.9	12.4	8.8	5.8	19.7	42.3
45~54 岁 Age	87	21.8	18.4	6.9	12.6	5.7	10.3	16.1	55.2
55~60 岁 Age	41	4.9	4.9	4.9	2.4	2.4	7.3	4.9	80.5

3-4 样本、男性各年龄层、女性各年龄层对家用轿车的信息接触情况/ Information Contact about Family Car by the Whole Sample, Age and Gender Groups

注：本题为多选题，合计百分比超过 100%（Multiple answers）

	人数 Number	不管买还是不买，想看看 just have a look, without a definite purpose of buying or not	阅读有关的杂志和专门报道 reading magazines related & special reports	相互口头传播信息 communicate information orally among people	经常看这种商品的广告 often watch advertisements about such kinds of goods	购买这种商品的新类型 buy the latest type of such kinds of goods	过去在这种商品上花了不少钱 used to spend much money on such kinds of goods	今后愿意在这方面花钱 willing to spend money on such items in future	不关注这方面的信息 don't care about such items
样本 Sample	**1033**	**19.6**	**11.7**	**6.5**	**10.2**	**1.5**	**1.4**	**8.7**	**62.1**
男性 Male	**499**	**23.2**	**16.6**	**7.6**	**12.0**	**1.0**	**1.4**	**11.0**	**55.5**
16~24 岁 Age	106	23.6	21.7	9.4	18.9	0.9	1.9	14.2	46.2
25~34 岁 Age	150	33.3	19.3	9.3	15.3	0.0	0.7	14.7	46.7
35~44 岁 Age	127	22.0	17.3	4.7	10.2	3.1	2.4	9.4	52.0
45~54 岁 Age	73	12.3	9.6	8.2	4.1	0.0	0.0	4.1	79.5
55~60 岁 Age	43	9.3	4.7	4.7	2.3	0.0	2.3	7.0	79.1
女性 Female	**534**	**16.1**	**7.1**	**5.4**	**8.4**	**2.1**	**1.3**	**6.6**	**68.4**
16~24 岁 Age	112	21.4	12.5	7.1	12.5	1.8	1.8	7.1	52.7
25~34 岁 Age	157	21.7	7.0	7.0	7.0	1.9	1.3	7.0	67.5
35~44 岁 Age	137	13.1	6.6	5.1	10.2	2.2	1.5	8.8	70.1
45~54 岁 Age	87	10.3	4.6	3.4	5.7	3.4	1.1	4.6	74.7
55~60 岁 Age	41	2.4	0.0	0.0	2.4	0.0	0.0	0.0	95.1

3-5 样本、男性各年龄层、女性各年龄层对高级家具的信息接触情况/ Information Contact about First-class Furniture by the Whole Sample, Age and Gender Groups

注：本题为多选题，合计百分比超过 100%（Multiple answers）

	人数 Number	不管买还是不买，想看看 just have a look, without a definite purpose of buying or not	阅读有关的杂志和专门报道 reading magazines related & special reports	相互口头传播信息 communicate information orally among people	经常看这种商品的广告 often watch advertisements about such kinds of goods	购买这种商品的新类型 buy the latest type of such kinds of goods	过去在这种商品上花了不少钱 used to spend much money on such kinds of goods	今后愿意在这方面花钱 willing to spend money on such items in future	不关注这方面的信息 don't care about such items
样本 Sample	**1032**	**31.8**	**9.5**	**6.6**	**11.5**	**4.8**	**6.3**	**16.2**	**44.1**
男性 Male	**498**	**29.5**	**7.8**	**5.2**	**10.6**	**5.4**	**5.8**	**15.3**	**47.6**
16~24 岁 Age	106	26.4	9.4	1.9	12.3	4.7	0.9	10.4	47.2
25~34 岁 Age	150	34.0	8.7	6.7	13.3	8.7	9.3	25.3	39.3
35~44 岁 Age	126	28.6	8.7	7.1	11.1	4.8	5.6	11.1	48.4
45~54 岁 Age	73	31.5	5.5	4.1	4.1	4.1	5.5	12.3	56.2
55~60 岁 Age	43	20.9	2.3	4.7	7.0	0.0	7.0	9.3	60.5
女性 Female	**534**	**33.9**	**11.0**	**7.9**	**12.4**	**4.3**	**6.7**	**17.0**	**40.8**
16~24 岁 Age	112	33.0	13.4	3.6	15.2	5.4	3.6	18.8	33.9
25~34 岁 Age	157	37.6	12.7	10.2	16.6	3.2	5.1	21.0	35.0
35~44 岁 Age	137	35.8	9.5	8.8	9.5	6.6	9.5	16.8	40.1
45~54 岁 Age	87	31.0	10.3	9.2	9.2	3.4	10.3	13.8	46.0
55~60 岁 Age	41	22.0	4.9	4.9	4.9	0.0	4.9	4.9	73.2

3-6 样本、男性各年龄层、女性各年龄层对西服和时装的信息接触情况/ Information Contact about Business Suit & Fashion by the Whole Sample, Age and Gender Groups

注：本题为多选题，合计百分比超过 100%（Multiple answers）

	人数 Number	不管买还是不买，想看看 just have a look, without a definite purpose of buying or not	阅读有关的杂志和专门报道 reading magazines related & special reports	相互口头传播信息 communicate information orally among people	经常看这种商品的广告 often watch advertisements about such kinds of goods	购买这种商品的新类型 buy the latest type of such kinds of goods	过去在这种商品上花了不少钱 used to spend much money on such kinds of goods	今后愿意在这方面花钱 willing to spend money on such items in future	不关注这方面的信息 don't care about such items
样本 Sample	**1034**	**34.1**	**11.9**	**13.2**	**13.0**	**11.3**	**15.8**	**24.5**	**34.1**
男性 Male	**499**	**28.5**	**8.4**	**7.6**	**10.4**	**8.2**	**13.2**	**21.8**	**42.5**
16~24 岁 Age	106	30.2	15.1	10.4	14.2	13.2	10.4	21.7	40.6
25~34 岁 Age	150	35.3	5.3	6.7	10.7	8.0	14.7	30.7	30.7
35~44 岁 Age	127	26.8	7.9	5.5	11.8	5.5	14.2	16.5	46.5
45~54 岁 Age	73	24.7	9.6	9.6	5.5	5.5	13.7	17.8	53.4
55~60 岁 Age	43	11.6	2.3	7.0	4.7	9.3	11.6	14.0	58.1
女性 Female	**535**	**39.4**	**15.1**	**18.5**	**15.3**	**14.2**	**18.1**	**26.9**	**26.4**
16~24 岁 Age	112	42.0	19.6	17.9	13.4	20.5	17.0	30.4	17.0
25~34 岁 Age	158	42.4	15.8	22.2	20.9	15.8	25.3	34.2	18.4
35~44 岁 Age	137	43.8	16.8	19.0	17.5	13.9	16.8	24.8	23.4
45~54 岁 Age	87	34.5	9.2	14.9	8.0	9.2	14.9	20.7	36.8
55~60 岁 Age	41	17.1	7.3	12.2	7.3	2.4	4.9	9.8	70.7

3-7 样本、男性各年龄层、女性各年龄层对酒精饮料的信息接触情况/ Information Contact about Alcohol Drinks by the Whole Sample, Age and Gender Groups

注：本题为多选题，合计百分比超过 100%（Multiple answers）

	人数 Number	不管买还是不买，想看看 just have a look, without a definite purpose of buying or not	阅读有关的杂志和专门报道 reading magazines related & special reports	相互口头传播信息 communicate information orally among people	经常看这种商品的广告 often watch advertisements about such kinds of goods	购买这种商品的新类型 buy the latest type of such kinds of goods	过去在这种商品上花了不少钱 used to spend much money on such kinds of goods	今后愿意在这方面花钱 willing to spend money on such items in future	不关注这方面的信息 don't care about such items
样本 Sample	1028	13.4	3.8	9.5	8.0	4.5	12.0	12.2	58.3
男性 Male	497	15.7	4.4	10.9	7.6	5.6	14.9	14.9	52.3
16~24 岁 Age	106	13.2	4.7	15.1	6.6	6.6	15.1	17.0	50.9
25~34 岁 Age	149	16.8	6.7	8.1	8.1	4.0	18.1	16.8	49.7
35~44 岁 Age	127	18.1	3.1	11.8	10.2	7.1	15.7	13.4	47.2
45~54 岁 Age	72	18.1	1.4	11.1	4.2	2.8	6.9	9.7	61.1
55~60 岁 Age	43	7.0	4.7	7.0	7.0	9.3	14.0	16.3	65.1
女性 Female	531	11.3	3.2	8.3	8.3	3.4	9.2	9.6	63.8
16~24 岁 Age	111	13.5	3.6	5.4	10.8	3.6	9.0	6.3	63.1
25~34 岁 Age	156	13.5	4.5	8.3	7.7	5.1	7.1	10.9	62.8
35~44 岁 Age	136	11.0	2.9	9.6	9.6	2.2	9.6	9.6	62.5
45~54 岁 Age	87	9.2	2.3	8.0	6.9	3.4	14.9	13.8	64.4
55~60 岁 Age	41	2.4	0.0	12.2	2.4	0.0	4.9	4.9	73.2

3-8 样本、男性各年龄层、女性各年龄层对 CD 唱片及音乐带的信息接触情况/ Information Contact about CD & Music Cassette by the Whole Sample, Age and Gender Groups

注：本题为多选题，合计百分比超过 100%（Multiple answers）

	人数 Number	不管买还是不买，想看看 just have a look, without a definite purpose of buying or not	阅读有关的杂志和专门报道 reading magazines related & special reports	相互口头传播信息 communicate information orally among people	经常看这种商品的广告 often watch advertisements about such kinds of goods	购买这种商品的新类型 buy the latest type of such kinds of goods	过去在这种商品上花了不少钱 used to spend much money on such kinds of goods	今后愿意在这方面花钱 willing to spend money on such items in future	不关注这方面的信息 don't care about such items
样本 Sample	1031	33.2	12.7	15.0	13.2	14.0	22.5	27.8	31.4
男性 Male	498	37.3	13.3	16.7	13.5	15.5	23.9	30.3	29.3
16~24 岁 Age	106	47.2	26.4	27.4	23.6	25.5	34.9	44.3	10.4
25~34 岁 Age	149	37.6	10.7	17.4	11.4	12.8	22.8	30.2	26.2
35~44 岁 Age	127	39.4	6.3	7.9	8.7	15.0	18.9	22.0	34.6
45~54 岁 Age	73	31.5	15.1	21.9	13.7	15.1	23.3	31.5	39.7
55~60 岁 Age	43	16.3	7.0	4.7	9.3	2.3	16.3	18.6	53.5
女性 Female	533	29.3	12.2	13.5	12.9	12.6	21.2	25.5	33.4
16~24 岁 Age	111	38.7	18.0	21.6	19.8	14.4	40.5	31.5	5.4
25~34 岁 Age	157	29.9	14.0	15.3	14.0	15.9	21.0	28.7	27.4
35~44 岁 Age	137	28.5	8.8	9.5	10.2	10.2	13.9	18.2	39.4
45~54 岁 Age	87	21.8	10.3	11.5	11.5	10.3	17.2	31.0	51.7
55~60 岁 Age	41	19.5	4.9	2.4	2.4	7.3	2.4	9.8	73.2

3-9 样本、男性各年龄层、女性各年龄层对护肤品和化妆品的信息接触情况/ Information Contact about Skin Cream & Cosmetics by the Whole Sample, Age and Gender Groups

注：本题为多选题，合计百分比超过 100%（Multiple answers）

	人数 Number	不管买还是不买，想看看 just have a look, without a definite purpose of buying or not	阅读有关的杂志和专门报道 reading magazines related & special reports	相互口头传播信息 communicate information orally among people	经常看这种商品的广告 often watch advertisements about such kinds of goods	购买这种商品的新类型 buy the latest type of such kinds of goods	过去在这种商品上花了不少钱 used to spend much money on such kinds of goods	今后愿意在这方面花钱 willing to spend money on such items in future	不关注这方面的信息 don't care about such items
样本 Sample	1029	23.9	11.8	13.6	17.0	11.6	16.3	23.0	45.7
男性 Male	495	9.3	4.2	4.4	7.5	5.3	5.3	10.1	72.3
16~24 岁 Age	106	11.3	2.8	5.7	8.5	4.7	2.8	10.4	66.0
25~34 岁 Age	149	10.7	6.7	5.4	8.1	5.4	5.4	13.4	65.1
35~44 岁 Age	125	10.4	3.2	4.8	8.8	8.0	6.4	8.8	79.2
45~54 岁 Age	72	4.2	2.8	1.4	2.8	2.8	8.3	8.3	79.2
55~60 岁 Age	43	4.7	4.7	2.3	7.0	2.3	2.3	4.7	81.4
女性 Female	534	37.5	18.7	22.1	25.8	17.4	26.6	35.0	21.0
16~24 岁 Age	112	43.8	24.1	24.1	32.1	21.4	33.0	42.9	10.7
25~34 岁 Age	158	42.4	23.4	27.2	33.5	22.8	35.4	43.0	12.0
35~44 岁 Age	137	38.0	19.0	21.9	19.0	14.6	24.8	27.7	19.7
45~54 岁 Age	86	29.1	8.1	18.6	17.4	12.8	14.0	32.6	31.4
55~60 岁 Age	41	17.1	7.3	4.9	19.5	4.9	7.3	12.2	65.9

3-10 样本、男性各年龄层、女性各年龄层对香波等洗涤用品的信息接触情况/ Information Contact about Shampoo & Detergent Cassette by the Whole Sample, Age and Gender Groups

注：本题为多选题，合计百分比超过 100%（Multiple answers）

	人数 Number	不管买还是不买，想看看 just have a look, without a definite purpose of buying or not	阅读有关的杂志和专门报道 reading magazines related & special reports	相互口头传播信息 communicate information orally among people	经常看这种商品的广告 often watch advertisements about such kinds of goods	购买这种商品的新类型 buy the latest type of such kinds of goods	过去在这种商品上花了不少钱 used to spend much money on such kinds of goods	今后愿意在这方面花钱 willing to spend money on such items in future	不关注这方面的信息 don't care about such items
样本 Sample	1034	24.8	7.5	13.8	18.2	13.9	16.9	24.1	36.7
男性 Male	499	16.8	4.2	7.6	10.6	7.8	11.0	16.0	56.1
16~24 岁 Age	106	17.0	4.7	11.3	9.4	8.5	3.8	13.2	53.8
25~34 岁 Age	150	17.3	4.0	8.7	11.3	9.3	12.7	18.7	55.3
35~44 岁 Age	127	18.1	3.1	5.5	11.8	7.1	15.7	16.5	54.3
45~54 岁 Age	73	13.7	5.5	5.5	11.0	5.5	6.8	11.0	63.0
55~60 岁 Age	43	16.3	4.7	4.7	7.0	7.0	16.3	20.9	58.1
女性 Female	535	32.1	10.7	19.6	25.2	19.6	22.4	31.6	18.5
16~24 岁 Age	112	29.5	11.6	14.3	26.8	17.0	22.3	31.3	17.9
25~34 岁 Age	158	36.7	12.7	19.6	28.5	22.2	29.1	33.5	14.6
35~44 岁 Age	137	32.8	11.7	21.9	24.8	21.2	16.1	26.3	17.5
45~54 岁 Age	87	31.0	8.0	24.1	17.2	20.7	20.7	39.1	19.5
55~60 岁 Age	41	22.0	2.4	17.1	26.8	9.8	22.0	26.8	36.6

3-11 样本、男性各年龄层、女性各年龄层对外出就餐的信息接触情况/ Information Contact about Dinning Out by the Whole Sample, Age and Gender Groups

注：本题为多选题，合计百分比超过 100%（Multiple answers）

	人数 Number	阅读有关的杂志和专门报道 reading magazines related and special reports	相互口头传播信息 communicate information orally among people	经常看这种服务的广告 often watch advertise-ments about such kinds of service	尝试这种服务的新类型 buy the latest type of such kinds of service	过去在这种服务上花了不少钱 used to spend much money on such kinds of service	今后愿意在这方面花钱 willing to spend money on such items in future	不关注这方面的信息 don't care about such items
样本 Sample	**1030**	**13.1**	**22.5**	**9.5**	**17.8**	**20.4**	**25.9**	**30.7**
男性 Male	**496**	**13.1**	**20.6**	**8.7**	**16.5**	**21.8**	**25.4**	**31.9**
16~24 岁 Age	106	7.5	24.5	4.7	17.9	15.1	18.9	35.8
25~34 岁 Age	149	14.1	16.1	6.7	21.5	24.2	33.6	28.9
35~44 岁 Age	127	15.0	23.6	9.4	12.5	21.3	22.8	29.9
45~54 岁 Age	71	14.1	23.9	18.3	14.1	18.3	19.7	36.6
55~60 岁 Age	43	16.3	11.6	7.0	11.5	37.2	30.2	30.2
女性 Female	**534**	**13.1**	**24.3**	**10.3**	**18.9**	**19.1**	**26.4**	**29.6**
16~24 岁 Age	112	13.4	23.2	13.4	25.9	20.5	22.3	17.9
25~34 岁 Age	157	16.6	26.1	13.4	21.0	22.9	29.3	25.5
35~44 岁 Age	137	11.7	24.8	8.8	14.5	16.1	28.5	30.7
45~54 岁 Age	87	12.6	26.4	6.9	14.9	16.1	28.7	37.9
55~60 岁 Age	41	4.9	14.6	2.4	14.5	17.1	14.6	56.1

3-12 样本、男性各年龄层、女性各年龄层对旅行的信息接触情况/ Information Contact about Travelling by the Whole Sample, Age and Gender Groups

注：本题为多选题，合计百分比超过 100%（Multiple answers）

	人数 Number	阅读有关的杂志和专门报道 reading magazines related and special reports	相互口头传播信息 communicate information orally among people	经常看这种服务的广告 often watch advertise-ments about such kinds of service	尝试这种服务的新类型 try using the latest type of such kinds of service	过去在这种服务上花了不少钱 used to spend much money on such kinds of service	今后愿意在这方面花钱 willing to spend money on such items in future	不关注这方面的信息 don't care about such kinds of service
样本 Sample	**1033**	**24.8**	**17.9**	**18.7**	**12.1**	**15.8**	**40.4**	**25.7**
男性 Male	**499**	**22.6**	**15.4**	**15.8**	**11.2**	**16.0**	**40.7**	**28.3**
16~24 岁 Age	106	27.4	15.1	15.1	9.4	12.3	39.6	26.4
25~34 岁 Age	150	26.0	17.3	16.7	14.7	20.0	46.7	24.0
35~44 岁 Age	127	18.1	13.4	13.4	9.4	11.0	41.7	29.9
45~54 岁 Age	73	21.9	15.1	21.9	11.0	20.5	28.8	38.4
55~60 岁 Age	43	14.0	16.3	11.6	9.3	18.6	39.5	25.6
女性 Female	**534**	**26.8**	**20.2**	**21.3**	**12.9**	**15.5**	**40.1**	**23.2**
16~24 岁 Age	112	29.5	17.9	20.5	13.4	15.2	41.1	15.2
25~34 岁 Age	158	31.0	24.1	27.2	19.0	17.7	45.6	15.2
35~44 岁 Age	137	24.8	16.8	20.4	10.9	14.6	35.0	29.9
45~54 岁 Age	86	23.3	24.4	15.1	7.0	15.1	39.5	30.2
55~60 岁 Age	41	17.1	14.6	17.1	7.3	12.2	34.1	39.0

3-13 样本、男性各年龄层、女性各年龄层对音乐会的信息接触情况/ Information Contact about Concert by the Whole Sample, Age and Gender Groups

注：本题为多选题，合计百分比超过 100%（Multiple answers）

	人数 Number	阅读有关的杂志和专门报道 reading magazines related and special reports	相互口头传播信息 communicate information orally among people	经常看这种服务的广告 often watch advertisements about such kinds of service	尝试这种服务的新类型 try using the latest type of such kinds of service	过去在这种服务上花了不少钱 used to spend much money on such kinds of service	今后愿意在这方面花钱 willing to spend money on such items in future	不关注这方面的信息 don't care about such kinds of service
样本 Sample	**1032**	**14.0**	**10.9**	**7.8**	**8.1**	**5.0**	**15.3**	**59.7**
男性 Male	**499**	**12.4**	**8.8**	**7.4**	**6.8**	**5.4**	**15.6**	**62.1**
16~24 岁 Age	106	19.8	16.0	8.5	12.3	9.4	18.9	47.2
25~34 岁 Age	150	13.3	8.0	8.7	6.0	6.0	22.0	53.3
35~44 岁 Age	127	8.7	7.9	7.9	3.1	2.4	11.8	73.2
45~54 岁 Age	73	8.2	6.8	6.8	6.8	5.5	6.8	78.1
55~60 岁 Age	43	9.3	0.0	0.0	7.0	2.3	11.6	69.8
女性 Female	**533**	**15.4**	**12.8**	**8.3**	**9.4**	**4.7**	**15.0**	**57.4**
16~24 岁 Age	112	25.9	19.6	8.0	17.9	4.5	22.3	34.8
25~34 岁 Age	157	17.8	12.7	10.8	8.9	4.5	16.6	56.1
35~44 岁 Age	136	11.0	13.2	11.0	8.1	8.1	17.6	56.6
45~54 岁 Age	87	5.7	8.0	3.4	3.4	1.1	5.7	78.2
55~60 岁 Age	41	12.2	2.4	0.0	4.9	2.4	0.0	82.9

3-14 样本、男性各年龄层、女性各年龄层对电影的信息接触情况/ Information Contact about Movie by the Whole Sample, Age and Gender Groups

注：本题为多选题，合计百分比超过 100%（Multiple answers）

	人数 Number	阅读有关的杂志和专门报道 reading magazines related and special reports	相互口头传播信息 communicate information orally among people	经常看这种服务的广告 often watch advertisements about such kinds of service	尝试这种服务的新类型 try using the latest type of such kinds of service	过去在这种服务上花了不少钱 used to spend much money on such kinds of service	今后愿意在这方面花钱 willing to spend money on such items in future	不关注这方面的信息 don't care about such kinds of service
样本 Sample	**1027**	**18.1**	**11.8**	**11.7**	**7.1**	**10.0**	**15.1**	**52.7**
男性 Male	**495**	**18.2**	**9.5**	**11.5**	**7.5**	**11.9**	**14.9**	**54.7**
16~24 岁 Age	104	33.7	11.5	18.3	15.4	22.1	26.9	34.6
25~34 岁 Age	150	20.0	14.0	12.7	6.0	14.0	20.7	47.3
35~44 岁 Age	125	9.6	4.8	4.8	4.8	8.8	8.0	67.2
45~54 岁 Age	73	9.6	8.2	12.3	4.1	4.1	2.7	71.2
55~60 岁 Age	43	14.0	4.7	9.3	7.0	2.3	7.0	65.1
女性 Female	**532**	**18.0**	**13.9**	**11.8**	**6.8**	**8.3**	**15.2**	**50.8**
16~24 岁 Age	110	27.3	27.3	15.5	14.5	14.5	25.5	16.4
25~34 岁 Age	157	16.6	14.6	13.4	6.4	9.6	18.5	52.2
35~44 岁 Age	137	21.9	9.5	10.9	4.4	5.8	8.8	54.7
45~54 岁 Age	87	9.2	9.2	11.5	3.4	4.6	12.6	67.8
55~60 岁 Age	41	4.9	0.0	0.0	2.4	2.4	2.4	87.8

3-15 样本、男性各年龄层、女性各年龄层对戏剧或戏曲的信息接触情况/ Information Contact about Drama or Opera by the Whole Sample, Age and Gender Groups

注：本题为多选题，合计百分比超过 100%（Multiple answers）

	人数 Number	阅读有关的杂志和专门报道 reading magazines related and special reports	相互口头传播信息 communicate information orally among people	经常看这种服务的广告 often watch advertisements about such kinds of service	尝试这种服务的新类型 try using the latest type of such kinds of service	过去在这种服务上花了不少钱 used to spend much money on such kinds of service	今后愿意在这方面花钱 willing to spend money on such items in future	不关注这方面的信息 don't care about such kinds of service
样本 Sample	**1033**	**7.3**	**5.8**	**3.4**	**3.3**	**3.2**	**4.5**	**79.2**
男性 Male	**499**	**6.4**	**5.2**	**3.2**	**2.0**	**2.8**	**4.2**	**80.8**
16~24 岁 Age	106	8.5	4.7	0.0	0.9	0.9	2.8	83.0
25~34 岁 Age	150	4.7	3.3	2.7	2.0	2.0	2.0	84.7
35~44 岁 Age	127	5.5	3.9	3.1	0.8	2.4	3.1	84.3
45~54 岁 Age	73	6.8	5.5	6.8	1.4	1.4	5.5	75.3
55~60 岁 Age	43	9.3	16.3	7.0	9.3	14.0	16.3	60.5
女性 Female	**534**	**8.1**	**6.4**	**3.6**	**4.5**	**3.6**	**4.9**	**77.7**
16~24 岁 Age	112	5.4	3.6	4.5	6.3	2.7	2.7	80.4
25~34 岁 Age	157	4.5	3.2	3.8	2.5	3.8	4.5	86.0
35~44 岁 Age	137	8.8	6.6	0.7	2.9	0.7	2.9	81.0
45~54 岁 Age	87	16.1	10.3	5.7	5.7	4.6	6.9	66.7
55~60 岁 Age	41	9.8	17.1	4.9	9.8	12.2	14.6	51.2

3-16 样本、男性各年龄层、女性各年龄层对蹦迪的信息接触情况/ Information Contact about Disco by the Whole Sample, Age and Gender Groups

注：本题为多选题，合计百分比超过 100%（Multiple answers）

	人数 Number	阅读有关的杂志和专门报道 reading magazines related and special reports	相互口头传播信息 communicate information orally among people	经常看这种服务的广告 often watch advertisements about such kinds of service	尝试这种服务的新类型 try using the latest type of such kinds of service	过去在这种服务上花了不少钱 used to spend much money on such kinds of service	今后愿意在这方面花钱 willing to spend money on such items in future	不关注这方面的信息 don't care about such kinds of service
样本 Sample	**1031**	**4.3**	**3.8**	**2.5**	**6.6**	**3.7**	**5.0**	**80.4**
男性 Male	**498**	**3.8**	**3.6**	**2.4**	**5.8**	**3.4**	**4.2**	**81.3**
16~24 岁 Age	106	9.4	7.5	2.8	5.7	5.7	6.6	68.9
25~34 岁 Age	149	4.0	4.0	2.0	8.1	4.7	6.0	79.2
35~44 岁 Age	127	1.6	0.8	3.9	5.5	1.6	1.6	86.6
45~54 岁 Age	73	0.0	2.7	1.4	1.4	2.7	2.7	91.8
55~60 岁 Age	43	2.3	2.3	0.0	7.0	0.0	2.3	86.0
女性 Female	**533**	**4.7**	**3.9**	**2.6**	**7.3**	**3.9**	**5.8**	**79.5**
16~24 岁 Age	112	6.3	9.8	1.8	15.2	7.1	13.4	58.9
25~34 岁 Age	156	5.1	2.6	3.2	5.[illegible]	3.2	5.1	82.7
35~44 岁 Age	137	5.1	2.2	1.5	6.6	2.9	3.6	85.4
45~54 岁 Age	87	3.4	2.3	4.6	5.7	4.6	3.4	83.9
55~60 岁 Age	41	0.0	2.4	2.4	0.0	0.0	0.0	95.1

3-17 样本、男性各年龄层、女性各年龄层对现场观赏体育比赛的信息接触情况/ Information Contact about Enjoying Live Sports by the Whole Sample, Age and Gender Groups

注：本题为多选题，合计百分比超过 100%（Multiple answers）

	人数 Number	阅读有关的杂志和专门报道 reading magazines related and special reports	相互口头传播信息 communicate information orally among people	经常看这种服务的广告 often watch advertise-ments about such kinds of service	尝试这种服务的新类型 try using the latest type of such kinds of service	过去在这种服务上花了不少钱 used to spend much money on such kinds of service	今后愿意在这方面花钱 willing to spend money on such items in future	不关注这方面的信息 don't care about such kinds of service
样本 Sample	**1033**	**16.2**	**10.6**	**8.1**	**5.6**	**5.8**	**15.6**	**58.3**
男性 Male	**498**	**22.5**	**14.9**	**9.4**	**6.4**	**8.6**	**22.3**	**46.4**
16~24 岁 Age	106	33.0	18.9	10.4	10.4	10.4	27.4	34.0
25~34 岁 Age	150	24.7	14.7	9.3	5.3	10.0	26.0	40.0
35~44 岁 Age	127	17.3	18.1	11.8	5.5	4.7	17.3	47.2
45~54 岁 Age	72	16.7	8.3	9.7	5.6	9.7	25.0	62.5
55~60 岁 Age	43	14.0	7.0	0.0	4.7	9.3	7.0	69.8
女性 Female	**535**	**10.3**	**6.5**	**6.9**	**4.9**	**3.2**	**9.3**	**69.3**
16~24 岁 Age	112	16.1	8.0	9.8	8.0	4.5	9.8	59.8
25~34 岁 Age	158	7.0	4.4	7.6	3.2	5.1	13.9	68.4
35~44 岁 Age	137	10.2	8.0	5.8	6.6	2.2	8.0	70.8
45~54 岁 Age	87	9.2	8.0	6.9	2.3	1.1	5.7	73.6
55~60 岁 Age	41	9.8	2.4	0.0	2.4	0.0	2.4	85.4

3-18 样本、男性各年龄层、女性各年龄层对运动健身的信息接触情况/ Information Contact about Gym by the Whole Sample, Age and Gender Groups

注：本题为多选题，合计百分比超过 100%（Multiple answers）

	人数 Number	阅读有关的杂志和专门报道 reading magazines related and special reports	相互口头传播信息 communicate information orally among people	经常看这种服务的广告 often watch advertise-ments about such kinds of service	尝试这种服务的新类型 try using the latest type of such kinds of service	过去在这种服务上花了不少钱 used to spend much money on such kinds of service	今后愿意在这方面花钱 willing to spend money on such items in future	不关注这方面的信息 don't care about such kinds of service
样本 Sample	**1031**	**12.9**	**8.2**	**7.9**	**12.3**	**9.2**	**27.0**	**46.3**
男性 Male	**496**	**13.5**	**7.7**	**7.9**	**11.3**	**11.1**	**32.3**	**42.9**
16~24 岁 Age	106	17.9	13.2	11.3	16.0	16.0	34.0	28.3
25~34 岁 Age	150	18.0	7.3	9.3	12.0	18.0	44.7	32.7
35~44 岁 Age	125	9.6	6.4	7.2	12.0	4.8	26.4	51.2
45~54 岁 Age	72	9.7	5.6	2.8	6.9	1.4	20.8	59.7
55~60 岁 Age	43	4.7	2.3	4.7	2.3	9.3	20.9	62.8
女性 Female	**535**	**12.3**	**8.8**	**7.9**	**13.3**	**7.5**	**22.1**	**49.3**
16~24 岁 Age	112	17.9	10.7	8.0	16.1	10.7	21.4	35.7
25~34 岁 Age	158	8.9	6.3	12.7	13.3	9.5	25.3	50.0
35~44 岁 Age	137	14.6	9.5	5.8	15.3	6.6	24.1	49.6
45~54 岁 Age	87	6.9	8.0	3.4	12.6	3.4	18.4	59.8
55~60 岁 Age	41	14.6	12.2	4.9	0.0	2.4	12.2	61.0

3-19 样本、男性各年龄层、女性各年龄层对技能学习的信息接触情况/ Information Contact about Studying Skills by the Whole Sample, Age and Gender Groups

注：本题为多选题，合计百分比超过 100%（Multiple answers）

	人数 Number	阅读有关的杂志和专门报道 reading magazines related and special reports	相互口头传播信息 communicate information orally among people	经常看这种服务的广告 often watch advertisements about such kinds of service	尝试这种服务的新类型 try using the latest type of such kinds of service	过去在这种服务上花了不少钱 used to spend much money on such kinds of service	今后愿意在这方面花钱 willing to spend money on such items in future	不关注这方面的信息 don't care about such kinds of service
样本 Sample	1033	19.6	9.9	7.2	8.0	8.0	28.9	44.4
男性 Male	499	21.2	8.6	7.0	8.8	9.2	32.3	41.3
16~24 岁 Age	106	32.1	14.2	6.6	6.6	13.2	35.8	25.5
25~34 岁 Age	150	23.3	9.3	7.3	10.0	12.0	44.7	32.0
35~44 岁 Age	127	15.7	4.7	8.7	8.7	7.1	28.3	45.7
45~54 岁 Age	73	15.1	9.6	6.8	6.8	5.5	21.9	61.6
55~60 岁 Age	43	14.0	2.3	2.3	14.0	2.3	9.3	65.1
女性 Female	534	18.0	11.0	7.3	7.3	6.9	25.8	47.4
16~24 岁 Age	112	25.9	15.2	8.9	7.1	7.1	33.0	28.6
25~34 岁 Age	158	20.3	13.9	9.5	10.1	8.9	35.4	38.6
35~44 岁 Age	136	14.7	8.1	5.9	5.1	8.1	21.3	51.5
45~54 岁 Age	87	13.8	5.7	6.9	8.0	4.6	16.1	65.5
55~60 岁 Age	41	7.3	9.8	0.0	2.4	0.0	4.9	80.5

3-20 样本、男性各年龄层、女性各年龄层对外语学习的信息接触情况/ Information Contact about Studying Foreign Languages by the Whole Sample, Age and Gender Groups

注：本题为多选题，合计百分比超过 100%（Multiple answers）

	人数 Number	阅读有关的杂志和专门报道 reading magazines related and special reports	相互口头传播信息 communicate information orally among people	经常看这种服务的广告 often watch advertisements about such kinds of service	尝试这种服务的新类型 try using the latest type of such kinds of service	过去在这种服务上花了不少钱 used to spend much money on such kinds of service	今后愿意在这方面花钱 willing to spend money on such items in future	不关注这方面的信息 don't care about such kinds of service
样本 Sample	1034	14.3	6.3	6.8	6.5	6.8	25.9	56.7
男性 Male	499	13.0	6.0	6.2	5.8	8.0	27.3	57.3
16~24 岁 Age	106	27.4	12.3	10.4	8.5	10.4	47.2	30.2
25~34 岁 Age	150	12.7	7.3	6.7	4.7	10.0	36.0	47.3
35~44 岁 Age	127	5.5	0.8	5.5	4.7	5.5	16.5	71.7
45~54 岁 Age	73	11.0	6.8	2.7	5.5	9.6	9.6	79.5
55~60 岁 Age	43	4.7	0.0	2.3	7.0	0.0	9.3	79.1
女性 Female	535	15.5	6.5	7.3	7.1	5.6	24.7	56.1
16~24 岁 Age	112	38.4	13.4	10.7	11.6	12.5	47.3	17.9
25~34 岁 Age	158	12.0	6.3	8.2	10.8	5.1	25.9	55.1
35~44 岁 Age	137	7.3	2.9	5.1	2.9	4.4	19.7	67.9
45~54 岁 Age	87	10.3	5.7	6.9	4.6	2.3	11.5	73.6
55~60 岁 Age	41	4.9	2.4	2.4	0.0	0.0	2.4	87.8

3-21 不同消费者层对电视、音响等视听设备的信息接触情况/ Information Contact about Video & Audio Equipment by Market Segments

注：本题为多选题，合计百分比超过 100%（Multiple answers）

	人数 Number	不管买还是不买，想看看 just have a look, without a definite purpose of buying or not	阅读有关的杂志和专门报道 reading magazines related & special reports	相互口头传播信息 communicate information orally among people	经常看这种商品的广告 often watch advertisements about such kinds of goods	购买这种商品的新类型 buy the latest type of such kinds of goods	过去在这种商品上花了不少钱 used to spend much money on such kinds of goods	今后愿意在这方面花钱 willing to spend money on such items in future	不关注这方面的信息 don't care about such items
样本 Sample	1022	48.0	16.7	14.5	21.4	8.3	19.4	20.0	21.1
平实生活指向 simple living orientation	518	48.8	16.8	12.9	18.9	6.9	20.1	19.5	23.2
时尚流行指向 fashion orientation	504	47.2	16.7	16.1	24.0	9.7	18.7	20.4	19.0

3-22 不同消费者层对冰箱、洗衣机等白色家电的信息接触情况/ Information Contact about "White Home Electronic Products" by Market Segments

注：本题为多选题，合计百分比超过 100%（Multiple answers）

	人数 Number	不管买还是不买，想看看 just have a look, without a definite purpose of buying or not	阅读有关的杂志和专门报道 reading magazines related & special reports	相互口头传播信息 communicate information orally among people	经常看这种商品的广告 often watch advertisements about such kinds of goods	购买这种商品的新类型 buy the latest type of such kinds of goods	过去在这种商品上花了不少钱 used to spend much money on such kinds of goods	今后愿意在这方面花钱 willing to spend money on such items in future	不关注这方面的信息 don't care about such items
样本 Sample	1016	30.9	10.2	10.4	16.4	8.1	17.1	15.9	31.5
平实生活指向 simple living orientation	515	31.7	8.2	9.7	15.0	6.2	18.8	17.7	31.7
时尚流行指向 fashion orientation	501	30.1	12.4	11.2	18.0	10.0	15.4	14.2	31.3

3-23 不同消费者层对电脑等通讯工具的信息接触情况/ Information Contact about Computer & Telecommunications by Market Segments

注：本题为多选题，合计百分比超过 100%（Multiple answers）

	人数 Number	不管买还是不买，想看看 just have a look, without a definite purpose of buying or not	阅读有关的杂志和专门报道 reading magazines related & special reports	相互口头传播信息 communicate information orally among people	经常看这种商品的广告 often watch advertisements about such kinds of goods	购买这种商品的新类型 buy the latest type of such kinds of goods	过去在这种商品上花了不少钱 used to spend much money on such kinds of goods	今后愿意在这方面花钱 willing to spend money on such items in future	不关注这方面的信息 don't care about such items
样本 Sample	1022	29.4	21.9	14.6	18.4	9.0	11.2	28.5	34.0
平实生活指向 simple living orientation	518	27.0	21.6	12.4	15.3	6.8	12.5	27.2	39.6
时尚流行指向 fashion orientation	504	31.7	22.2	16.9	21.6	11.3	9.7	29.8	28.2

3-24 不同消费者层对家用轿车的信息接触情况/ Information Contact about Family Car by Market Segments

注：本题为多选题，合计百分比超过 100%（Multiple answers）

	人数 Number	不管买还是不买，想看看 just have a look, without a definite purpose of buying or not	阅读有关的杂志和专门报道 reading magazines related & special reports	相互口头传播信息 communicate information orally among people	经常看这种商品的广告 often watch advertisements about such kinds of goods	购买这种商品的新类型 buy the latest type of such kinds of goods	过去在这种商品上花了不少钱 used to spend much money on such kinds of goods	今后愿意在这方面花钱 willing to spend money on such items in future	不关注这方面的信息 don't care about such items
样本 Sample	1021	19.6	11.9	6.4	10.3	1.6	1.3	8.8	62.1
平实生活指向 simple living orientation	517	18.2	11.2	5.4	8.[illegible]	1.5	1.2	6.4	67.3
时尚流行指向 fashion orientation	504	21.0	12.5	7.3	12.5	1.6	1.4	11.3	56.7

3-25 不同消费者层对高级家具的信息接触情况/ Information Contact about First-class Furniture by Market Segments

注：本题为多选题，合计百分比超过 100%（Multiple answers）

	人数 Number	不管买还是不买，想看看 just have a look, without a definite purpose of buying or not	阅读有关的杂志和专门报道 reading magazines related & special reports	相互口头传播信息 communicate information orally among people	经常看这种商品的广告 often watch advertisements about such kinds of goods	购买这种商品的新类型 buy the latest type of such kinds of goods	过去在这种商品上花了不少钱 used to spend much money on such kinds of goods	今后愿意在这方面花钱 willing to spend money on such items in future	不关注这方面的信息 don't care about such items
样本 Sample	1020	31.9	9.4	6.6	11.6	4.8	6.4	16.3	44.0
平实生活指向 simple living orientation	517	30.9	7.7	5.6	7.7	4.4	6.2	14.7	50.1
时尚流行指向 fashion orientation	503	32.8	11.1	7.6	15.5	5.2	6.6	17.9	37.8

3-26 不同消费者层对西服和时装的信息接触情况/ Information Contact about Business Suit & Fashion by Market Segments

注：本题为多选题，合计百分比超过 100%（Multiple answers）

	人数 Number	不管买还是不买，想看看 just have a look, without a definite purpose of buying or not	阅读有关的杂志和专门报道 reading magazines related & special reports	相互口头传播信息 communicate information orally among people	经常看这种商品的广告 often watch advertisements about such kinds of goods	购买这种商品的新类型 buy the latest type of such kinds of goods	过去在这种商品上花了不少钱 used to spend much money on such kinds of goods	今后愿意在这方面花钱 willing to spend money on such items in future	不关注这方面的信息 don't care about such items
样本 Sample	1022	34.2	11.9	13.3	13.0	11.4	15.9	24.6	34.1
平实生活指向 simple living orientation	518	30.9	7.9	9.1	8.7	7.3	12.2	19.3	43.6
时尚流行指向 fashion orientation	504	37.7	16.1	17.7	17.5	15.5	19.6	30.0	24.4

3-27 不同消费者层对酒精饮料的信息接触情况/ Information Contact about Alcohol Drinks by Market Segments

注：本题为多选题，合计百分比超过 100%（Multiple answers）

	人数 Number	不管买还是不买，想看看 just have a look, without a definite purpose of buying or not	阅读有关的杂志和专门报道 reading magazines related & special reports	相互口头传播信息 communicate information orally among people	经常看这种商品的广告 often watch advertisements about such kinds of goods	购买这种商品的新类型 buy the latest type of such kinds of goods	过去在这种商品上花了不少钱 used to spend much money on such kinds of goods	今后愿意在这方面花钱 willing to spend money on such items in future	不关注这方面的信息 don't care about such items
样本 Sample	1016	13.4	3.7	9.5	8.0	4.5	11.9	12.1	58.3
平实生活指向 simple living orientation	516	13.8	3.5	9.5	7.8	4.1	11.6	13.2	58.9
时尚流行指向 fashion orientation	500	13.0	4.0	9.6	8.2	5.0	12.2	11.0	57.6

3-28 不同消费者层对 CD 唱片及音乐带的信息接触情况/ Information Contact about CD & Music Cassette by Market Segments

注：本题为多选题，合计百分比超过 100%（Multiple answers）

	人数 Number	不管买还是不买，想看看 just have a look, without a definite purpose of buying or not	阅读有关的杂志和专门报道 reading magazines related & special reports	相互口头传播信息 communicate information orally among people	经常看这种商品的广告 often watch advertisements about such kinds of goods	购买这种商品的新类型 buy the latest type of such kinds of goods	过去在这种商品上花了不少钱 used to spend much money on such kinds of goods	今后愿意在这方面花钱 willing to spend money on such items in future	不关注这方面的信息 don't care about such items
样本 Sample	1019	33.1	12.8	15.1	13.2	13.9	22.5	28.0	31.3
平实生活指向 simple living orientation	516	30.2	10.7	12.2	11.2	12.8	18.8	25.4	39.3
时尚流行指向 fashion orientation	503	36.0	14.9	18.1	15.3	15.1	26.2	30.6	23.1

3-29 不同消费者层对护肤品和化妆品的信息接触情况/ Information Contact about Skin Cream & Cosmetics by Market Segments

注：本题为多选题，合计百分比超过 100%（Multiple answers）

	人数 Number	不管买还是不买，想看看 just have a look, without a definite purpose of buying or not	阅读有关的杂志和专门报道 reading magazines related & special reports	相互口头传播信息 communicate information orally among people	经常看这种商品的广告 often watch advertisements about such kinds of goods	购买这种商品的新类型 buy the latest type of such kinds of goods	过去在这种商品上花了不少钱 used to spend much money on such kinds of goods	今后愿意在这方面花钱 willing to spend money on such items in future	不关注这方面的信息 don't care about such items
样本 Sample	1017	23.7	11.7	13.6	16.8	11.5	16.0	23.0	45.8
平实生活指向 simple living orientation	516	19.4	7.0	8.9	11.8	8.3	9.5	17.8	55.4
时尚流行指向 fashion orientation	501	28.1	16.6	18.4	22.0	14.8	22.8	28.3	35.9

3-30 不同消费者层对香波等洗涤用品的信息接触情况/ Information Contact about Shampoo & Detergent by Market Segments

注：本题为多选题，合计百分比超过 100%（Multiple answers）

	人数 Number	不管买还是不买，想看看 just have a look, without a definite purpose of buying or not	阅读有关的杂志和专门报道 reading magazines related & special reports	相互口头传播信息 communicate information orally among people	经常看这种商品的广告 often watch advertisements about such kinds of goods	购买这种商品的新类型 buy the latest type of such kinds of goods	过去在这种商品上花了不少钱 used to spend much money on such kinds of goods	今后愿意在这方面花钱 willing to spend money on such items in future	不关注这方面的信息 don't care about such items
样本 Sample	1022	24.7	7.3	13.8	18.1	13.9	16.8	24.1	36.7
平实生活指向 simple living orientation	518	22.8	4.6	12.7	15.8	10.8	17.0	23.7	39.8
时尚流行指向 fashion orientation	504	26.6	10.1	14.9	20.4	17.1	16.7	24.4	33.5

3-31 不同消费者层对外出就餐的信息接触情况/ Information Contact about Dinning Out by Market Segments

注：本题为多选题，合计百分比超过 100%（Multiple answers）

	人数 Number	阅读有关的杂志和专门报道 reading magazines related and special reports	相互口头传播信息 communicate information orally among people	经常看这种服务的广告 often watch advertisements about such kinds of service	尝试这种服务的新类型 try using the latest type of such kinds of service	过去在这种服务上花了不少钱 used to spend much money on such kinds of service	今后愿意在这方面花钱 willing to spend money on such items in future	不关注这方面的信息 don't care about such items
样本 Sample	1018	13.0	22.4	9.5	17.9	20.5	25.8	30.7
平实生活指向 simple living orientation	517	12.4	20.5	8.5	14.1	18.8	24.0	35.4
时尚流行指向 fashion orientation	501	13.6	24.4	10.6	21.8	22.4	27.7	25.9

3-32 不同消费者层对旅行的信息接触情况/ Information Contact about Travelling by Market Segments

注：本题为多选题，合计百分比超过 100%（Multiple answers）

	人数 Number	阅读有关的杂志和专门报道 reading magazines related and special reports	相互口头传播信息 communicate information orally among people	经常看这种服务的广告 often watch advertisements about such kinds of service	尝试这种服务的新类型 try using the latest type of such kinds of service	过去在这种服务上花了不少钱 used to spend much money on such kinds of service	今后愿意在这方面花钱 willing to spend money on such items in future	不关注这方面的信息 don't care about such items
样本 Sample	1021	24.7	17.9	18.6	12.2	15.9	40.3	25.7
平实生活指向 simple living orientation	517	21.9	15.1	14.7	10.8	15.5	40.0	31.1
时尚流行指向 fashion orientation	504	27.6	20.8	22.6	13.7	16.3	40.5	20.0

3-33 不同消费者层对音乐会的信息接触情况/ Information Contact about Concert by Market Segments

注：本题为多选题，合计百分比超过 100%（Multiple answers）

	人数 Number	阅读有关的杂志和专门报道 reading magazines related and special reports	相互口头传播信息 communicate information orally among people	经常看这种服务的广告 often watch advertisements about such kinds of service	尝试这种服务的新类型 try using the latest type of such kinds of service	过去在这种服务上花了不少钱 used to spend much money on such kinds of service	今后愿意在这方面花钱 willing to spend money on such items in future	不关注这方面的信息 don't care about such items
样本 Sample	1020	13.9	10.9	7.8	8.2	5.0	15.2	59.8
平实生活指向 simple living orientation	517	10.6	6.6	5.2	5.6	3.3	11.0	69.8
时尚流行指向 fashion orientation	503	17.3	15.3	10.5	10.9	6.8	19.5	49.5

3-34 不同消费者层对电影的信息接触情况/ Information Contact about Movie by Market Segments

注：本题为多选题，合计百分比超过 100%（Multiple answers）

	人数 Number	阅读有关的杂志和专门报道 reading magazines related and special reports	相互口头传播信息 communicate information orally among people	经常看这种服务的广告 often watch advertise-ments about such kinds of service	尝试这种服务的新类型 try using the latest type of such kinds of service	过去在这种服务上花了不少钱 used to spend much money on such kinds of service	今后愿意在这方面花钱 willing to spend money on such items in future	不关注这方面的信息 don't care about such items
样本 Sample	1015	18.1	11.9	11.7	7.2	10.0	15.1	52.6
平实生活指向 simple living orientation	516	14.9	8.7	8.5	5.8	7.8	14.0	61.2
时尚流行指向 fashion orientation	499	21.4	15.2	15.0	8.6	12.4	16.2	43.7

3-35 不同消费者层对戏剧或戏曲的信息接触情况/ Information Contact about Drama or Opera by Market Segments

注：本题为多选题，合计百分比超过 100%（Multiple answers）

	人数 Number	阅读有关的杂志和专门报道 reading magazines related and special reports	相互口头传播信息 communicate information orally among people	经常看这种服务的广告 often watch advertise-ments about such kinds of service	尝试这种服务的新类型 try using the latest type of such kinds of service	过去在这种服务上花了不少钱 used to spend much money on such kinds of service	今后愿意在这方面花钱 willing to spend money on such items in future	不关注这方面的信息 don't care about such items
样本 Sample	1021	7.3	5.8	3.4	3.3	3.2	4.6	79.0
平实生活指向 simple living orientation	517	7.0	5.6	3.3	3.1	3.7	5.4	78.9
时尚流行指向 fashion orientation	504	7.7	6.0	3.6	3.6	2.8	3.8	79.2

3-36 不同消费者层对蹦迪的信息接触情况/ Information Contact about Disco by Market Segments

注：本题为多选题，合计百分比超过 100%（Multiple answers）

	人数 Number	阅读有关的杂志和专门报道 reading magazines related and special reports	相互口头传播信息 communicate information orally among people	经常看这种服务的广告 often watch advertise-ments about such kinds of service	尝试这种服务的新类型 try using the latest type of such kinds of service	过去在这种服务上花了不少钱 used to spend much money on such kinds of service	今后愿意在这方面花钱 willing to spend money on such items in future	不关注这方面的信息 don't care about such items
样本 Sample	1019	4.3	3.8	2.6	6.7	3.6	5.1	80.3
平实生活指向 simple living orientation	517	2.9	2.1	1.7	4.4	1.4	2.1	88.0
时尚流行指向 fashion orientation	502	5.8	5.6	3.4	9.0	6.0	8.2	72.3

3-37 不同消费者层对现场观赏体育比赛的信息接触情况/ Information Contact about Enjoying Live Sports by Market Segments

注：本题为多选题，合计百分比超过 100%（Multiple answers）

	人数 Number	阅读有关的杂志和专门报道 reading magazines related and special reports	相互口头传播信息 communicate information orally among people	经常看这种服务的广告 often watch advertise-ments about such kinds of service	尝试这种服务的新类型 try using the latest type of such kinds of service	过去在这种服务上花了不少钱 used to spend much money on such kinds of service	今后愿意在这方面花钱 willing to spend money on such items in future	不关注这方面的信息 don't care about such items
样本 Sample	1021	16.2	10.6	8.2	5.5	5.8	15.7	58.3
平实生活指向 simple living orientation	518	15.4	9.8	8.3	3.9	4.4	13.9	62.9
时尚流行指向 fashion orientation	503	16.9	11.3	8.2	7.2	7.2	17.5	53.5

3-38 不同消费者层对运动健身的信息接触情况/ Information Contact about Gym by Market Segments

注：本题为多选题，合计百分比超过 100%（Multiple answers）

	人数 Number	阅读有关的杂志和专门报道 reading magazines related and special reports	相互口头传播信息 communicate information orally among people	经常看这种服务的广告 often watch advertise-ments about such kinds of service	尝试这种服务的新类型 try using the latest type of such kinds of service	过去在这种服务上花了不少钱 used to spend much money on such kinds of service	今后愿意在这方面花钱 willing to spend money on such items in future	不关注这方面的信息 don't care about such items
样本 Sample	1019	12.9	8.1	7.8	12.3	9.2	27.0	46.5
平实生活指向 simple living orientation	517	10.6	7.0	7.0	11.0	7.2	22.2	54.7
时尚流行指向 fashion orientation	502	15.1	9.4	8.6	13.5	11.4	31.9	38.0

3-39 不同消费者层对技能学习的信息接触情况/ Information Contact about Studying Skills by Market Segments

注：本题为多选题，合计百分比超过 100%（Multiple answers）

	人数 Number	阅读有关的杂志和专门报道 reading magazines related and special reports	相互口头传播信息 communicate information orally among people	经常看这种服务的广告 often watch advertise-ments about such kinds of service	尝试这种服务的新类型 try using the latest type of such kinds of service	过去在这种服务上花了不少钱 used to spend much money on such kinds of service	今后愿意在这方面花钱 willing to spend money on such items in future	不关注这方面的信息 don't care about such items
样本 Sample	1021	19.6	9.9	7.2	7.9	7.9	29.1	44.5
平实生活指向 simple living orientation	517	19.0	9.5	6.2	8.7	5.8	26.1	49.1
时尚流行指向 fashion orientation	504	20.2	10.3	8.3	7.1	10.1	32.1	39.7

3-40 不同消费者层对外语学习的信息接触情况/ Information Contact about Studying Foreign Languages by Market Segments

注：本题为多选题，合计百分比超过 100%（Multiple answers）

	人数 Number	阅读有关的杂志和专门报道 reading magazines related and special reports	相互口头传播信息 communicate information orally among people	经常看这种服务的广告 often watch advertise-ments about such kinds of service	尝试这种服务的新类型 try using the latest type of such kinds of service	过去在这种服务上花了不少钱 used to spend much money on such kinds of service	今后愿意在这方面花钱 willing to spend money on such items in future	不关注这方面的信息 don't care about such items
样本 Sample	1022	14.3	6.4	6.7	6.4	6.8	25.9	56.8
平实生活指向 simple living orientation	518	12.0	4.1	5.6	5.4	4.8	20.1	66.0
时尚流行指向 fashion orientation	504	16.7	8.7	7.7	7.3	8.9	31.9	47.4

● 重庆 / Chongqing

3-1 样本、男性各年龄层、女性各年龄层对电视、音响等视听设备的信息接触情况/ Information Contact about Video & Audio Equipment by the Whole Sample, Age and Gender Groups

注：本题为多选题，合计百分比超过 100%（Multiple answers）

	人数 Number	不管买还是不买，想看看 just have a look, without a definite purpose of buying or not	阅读有关的杂志和专门报道 reading magazines related & special reports	相互口头传播信息 communicate information orally among people	经常看这种商品的广告 often watch advertisements about such kinds of goods	购买这种商品的新类型 buy the latest type of such kinds of goods	过去在这种商品上花了不少钱 used to spend much money on such kinds of goods	今后愿意在这方面花钱 willing to spend money on such items in future	不关注这方面的信息 don't care about such items
样本 Sample	623	62.9	25.8	23.6	39.2	10.8	32.1	33.5	13.8
男性 Male	313	68.1	30.0	25.9	41.5	12.5	32.6	38.7	10.9
16~24 岁 Age	64	62.5	23.4	20.3	28.1	7.8	10.9	35.9	10.9
25~34 岁 Age	92	72.8	37.0	23.9	40.2	15.2	33.7	40.2	4.3
35~44 岁 Age	75	73.3	32.0	33.3	52.0	13.3	38.7	48.0	12.0
45~54 岁 Age	54	68.5	22.2	24.1	44.4	13.0	44.4	37.0	7.4
55~60 岁 Age	28	50.0	32.1	28.6	42.9	10.7	39.3	17.9	35.7
女性 Female	310	57.7	21.6	21.3	36.8	9.0	31.6	28.4	16.8
16~24 岁 Age	64	57.8	25.0	20.3	40.6	10.9	20.3	26.6	15.6
25~34 岁 Age	90	61.1	21.1	27.8	34.4	11.1	35.6	32.2	11.1
35~44 岁 Age	73	57.5	20.5	15.1	35.6	6.8	32.9	27.4	17.8
45~54 岁 Age	60	56.7	25.0	16.7	30.0	8.3	31.7	26.7	21.7
55~60 岁 Age	23	47.8	8.7	30.4	56.5	4.3	43.5	26.1	26.1

3-2 样本、男性各年龄层、女性各年龄层对冰箱、洗衣机等白色家电的信息接触情况/ Information Contact about "White Home Electronic Products" by the Whole Sample, Age and Gender Groups

注：本题为多选题，合计百分比超过 100%（Multiple answers）

	人数 Number	不管买还是不买，想看看 just have a look, without a definite purpose of buying or not	阅读有关的杂志和专门报道 reading magazines related & special reports	相互口头传播信息 communicate information orally among people	经常看这种商品的广告 often watch advertisements about such kinds of goods	购买这种商品的新类型 buy the latest type of such kinds of goods	过去在这种商品上花了不少钱 used to spend much money on such kinds of goods	今后愿意在这方面花钱 willing to spend money on such items in future	不关注这方面的信息 don't care about such items
样本 Sample	621	46.1	18.0	17.7	34.0	8.9	27.4	28.7	23.3
男性 Male	312	45.5	20.2	18.3	33.3	10.6	27.2	32.7	21.2
16~24 岁 Age	64	28.1	10.9	9.4	18.8	6.3	7.8	25.0	34.4
25~34 岁 Age	92	45.7	25.0	17.4	32.6	15.2	28.3	35.9	15.2
35~44 岁 Age	74	56.8	21.6	25.7	44.6	12.2	32.4	37.8	16.2
45~54 岁 Age	54	53.7	18.5	18.5	37.0	5.6	35.2	31.5	11.1
55~60 岁 Age	28	39.3	25.0	21.4	32.1	10.7	39.3	28.6	42.9
女性 Female	309	46.6	15.9	17.2	34.6	7.1	27.5	24.6	25.6
16~24 岁 Age	64	45.3	20.3	10.9	32.8	6.3	17.2	20.3	28.1
25~34 岁 Age	90	44.4	14.4	20.0	33.3	7.8	24.4	24.4	23.3
35~44 岁 Age	72	52.8	19.4	16.7	34.7	6.9	31.9	27.8	25.0
45~54 岁 Age	60	50.0	11.7	15.0	33.3	8.3	28.3	30.0	21.7
55~60 岁 Age	23	30.4	8.7	30.4	47.8	4.3	52.2	13.0	39.1

3-3 样本、男性各年龄层、女性各年龄层对电脑等通讯工具的信息接触情况/ Information Contact about Computer & Telecommunications by the Whole Sample, Age and Gender Groups

注：本题为多选题，合计百分比超过 100%（Multiple answers）

	人数 Number	不管买还是不买，想看看 just have a look, without a definite purpose of buying or not	阅读有关的杂志和专门报道 reading magazines related & special reports	相互口头传播信息 communicate information orally among people	经常看这种商品的广告 often watch advertisements about such kinds of goods	购买这种商品的新类型 buy the latest type of such kinds of goods	过去在这种商品上花了不少钱 used to spend much money on such kinds of goods	今后愿意在这方面花钱 willing to spend money on such items in future	不关注这方面的信息 don't care about such items
样本 Sample	623	24.4	17.2	11.6	15.6	4.8	5.8	28.9	53.8
男性 Male	314	30.6	22.6	15.6	20.7	7.3	8.3	36.0	44.9
16~24 岁 Age	64	45.3	29.7	29.7	25.0	9.4	7.8	53.1	18.8
25~34 岁 Age	93	32.3	26.9	14.0	22.6	6.5	14.0	41.9	37.6
35~44 岁 Age	75	33.3	21.3	13.3	24.0	13.3	8.0	40.0	46.7
45~54 岁 Age	54	18.5	13.0	9.3	14.8	0.0	0.0	14.8	68.5
55~60 岁 Age	28	7.1	14.3	7.1	7.1	3.6	7.1	7.1	78.6
女性 Female	309	18.1	11.7	7.4	10.4	2.3	3.2	21.7	62.8
16~24 岁 Age	64	23.4	21.9	9.4	14.1	6.3	4.7	29.7	45.3
25~34 岁 Age	89	22.5	11.2	10.1	11.2	1.1	4.5	29.2	57.3
35~44 岁 Age	73	20.5	11.0	4.1	8.2	2.7	2.7	17.8	67.1
45~54 岁 Age	60	10.0	6.7	8.3	6.7	0.0	1.7	11.7	76.7
55~60 岁 Age	23	0.0	0.0	0.0	13.0	0.0	0.0	8.7	82.6

3-4 样本、男性各年龄层、女性各年龄层对家用轿车的信息接触情况/ Information Contact about Family Car by the Whole Sample, Age and Gender Groups

注：本题为多选题，合计百分比超过 100%（Multiple answers）

	人数 Number	不管买还是不买，想看看 just have a look, without a definite purpose of buying or not	阅读有关的杂志和专门报道 reading magazines related & special reports	相互口头传播信息 communicate information orally among people	经常看这种商品的广告 often watch advertisements about such kinds of goods	购买这种商品的新类型 buy the latest type of such kinds of goods	过去在这种商品上花了不少钱 used to spend much money on such kinds of goods	今后愿意在这方面花钱 willing to spend money on such items in future	不关注这方面的信息 don't care about such items
样本 Sample	619	18.9	12.3	8.2	9.9	1.6	1.1	9.2	70.1
男性 Male	313	24.0	16.6	13.4	12.8	1.9	0.6	11.2	62.9
16~24 岁 Age	64	34.4	23.4	21.9	17.2	1.6	0.0	17.2	42.2
25~34 岁 Age	93	29.0	19.4	14.0	15.1	2.2	1.1	11.8	55.9
35~44 岁 Age	75	21.3	17.3	12.0	10.7	2.7	0.0	10.7	70.7
45~54 岁 Age	53	15.1	9.4	9.4	11.3	1.9	0.0	9.4	77.4
55~60 岁 Age	28	7.1	3.6	3.6	3.6	0.0	3.6	0.0	85.7
女性 Female	306	13.7	7.8	2.9	6.9	1.3	1.6	7.2	77.5
16~24 岁 Age	63	27.0	15.9	4.8	3.2	0.0	1.6	14.3	60.3
25~34 岁 Age	87	17.2	12.6	4.6	10.3	2.3	3.4	9.2	69.0
35~44 岁 Age	73	9.6	4.1	1.4	8.2	1.4	1.4	2.7	84.9
45~54 岁 Age	60	3.3	0.0	1.7	3.3	1.7	0.0	5.0	93.3
55~60 岁 Age	23	4.3	0.0	0.0	8.7	0.0	0.0	0.0	91.3

3-5 样本、男性各年龄层、女性各年龄层对高级家具的信息接触情况/ Information Contact about First-class Furniture by the Whole Sample, Age and Gender Groups

注：本题为多选题，合计百分比超过 100%（Multiple answers）

	人数 Number	不管买还是不买，想看看 just have a look, without a definite purpose of buying or not	阅读有关的杂志和专门报道 reading magazines related & special reports	相互口头传播信息 communicate information orally among people	经常看这种商品的广告 often watch advertisements about such kinds of goods	购买这种商品的新类型 buy the latest type of such kinds of goods	过去在这种商品上花了不少钱 used to spend much money on such kinds of goods	今后愿意在这方面花钱 willing to spend money on such items in future	不关注这方面的信息 don't care about such items
样本 Sample	**618**	**35.9**	**9.2**	**9.1**	**11.5**	**4.4**	**6.5**	**26.2**	**46.4**
男性 Male	**311**	**34.7**	**10.6**	**9.0**	**11.3**	**4.2**	**7.1**	**25.4**	**46.9**
16~24 岁 Age	63	28.6	7.9	7.9	9.5	3.2	1.6	23.8	55.6
25~34 岁 Age	93	35.5	16.1	8.6	10.8	3.2	3.2	31.2	35.5
35~44 岁 Age	73	42.5	12.3	15.1	11.0	5.5	11.0	24.7	42.5
45~54 岁 Age	54	31.5	5.6	3.7	14.8	5.6	14.8	20.4	57.4
55~60 岁 Age	28	32.1	3.6	7.1	10.7	3.6	7.1	21.4	57.1
女性 Female	**307**	**37.1**	**7.8**	**9.1**	**11.7**	**4.6**	**5.9**	**27.0**	**45.9**
16~24 岁 Age	63	39.7	11.1	6.3	9.5	4.8	1.6	36.5	42.9
25~34 岁 Age	88	46.6	9.1	14.8	14.8	4.5	9.1	28.4	35.2
35~44 岁 Age	73	41.1	6.8	8.2	13.7	5.5	5.5	28.8	46.6
45~54 岁 Age	60	25.0	5.0	6.7	6.7	3.3	5.0	20.0	56.7
55~60 岁 Age	23	13.0	4.3	4.3	13.0	4.3	8.7	8.7	65.2

3-6 样本、男性各年龄层、女性各年龄层对西服和时装的信息接触情况/ Information Contact about Business Suit & Fashion by the Whole Sample, Age and Gender Groups

]注：本题为多选题，合计百分比超过 100%（Multiple answers）

	人数 Number	不管买还是不买，想看看 just have a look, without a definite purpose of buying or not	阅读有关的杂志和专门报道 reading magazines related & special reports	相互口头传播信息 communicate information orally among people	经常看这种商品的广告 often watch advertise-ments about such kinds of goods	购买这种商品的新类型 buy the latest type of such kinds of goods	过去在这种商品上花了不少钱 used to spend much money on such kinds of goods	今后愿意在这方面花钱 willing to spend money on such items in future	不关注这方面的信息 don't care about such items
样本 Sample	**622**	**45.5**	**18.5**	**19.9**	**22.8**	**14.1**	**21.4**	**40.0**	**28.8**
男性 Male	**314**	**43.6**	**14.0**	**14.6**	**19.7**	**13.4**	**20.1**	**36.0**	**31.5**
16~24 岁 Age	64	37.5	17.2	17.2	23.4	23.4	15.6	29.7	26.6
25~34 岁 Age	93	53.8	18.3	14.0	18.3	10.8	22.6	47.3	19.4
35~44 岁 Age	75	42.7	9.3	16.0	20.0	9.3	25.3	38.7	36.0
45~54 岁 Age	54	33.3	9.3	11.1	16.7	13.0	16.7	31.5	44.4
55~60 岁 Age	28	46.4	14.3	14.3	21.4	10.7	14.3	14.3	46.4
女性 Female	**308**	**47.4**	**23.1**	**25.3**	**26.0**	**14.9**	**22.7**	**44.2**	**26.0**
16~24 岁 Age	64	48.4	40.6	28.1	28.1	17.2	29.7	59.4	9.4
25~34 岁 Age	90	54.4	23.3	30.0	30.0	17.8	25.6	51.1	15.6
35~44 岁 Age	72	51.4	19.4	25.0	22.2	12.5	15.3	40.3	33.3
45~54 岁 Age	59	40.7	15.3	16.9	25.4	11.9	20.3	30.5	39.0
55~60 岁 Age	23	21.7	4.3	21.7	17.4	13.0	21.7	21.7	56.5

3-7 样本、男性各年龄层、女性各年龄层对酒精饮料的信息接触情况/ Information Contact about Alcohol Drinks by the Whole Sample, Age and Gender Groups

注：本题为多选题，合计百分比超过 100%（Multiple answers）

	人数 Number	不管买还是不买，想看看 just have a look, without a definite purpose of buying or not	阅读有关的杂志和专门报道 reading magazines related & special reports	相互口头传播信息 communicate information orally among people	经常看这种商品的广告 often watch advertisements about such kinds of goods	购买这种商品的新类型 buy the latest type of such kinds of goods	过去在这种商品上花了不少钱 used to spend much money on such kinds of goods	今后愿意在这方面花钱 willing to spend money on such items in future	不关注这方面的信息 don't care about such items
样本 Sample	**615**	**21.1**	**6.0**	**11.4**	**16.4**	**6.5**	**17.2**	**20.0**	**51.9**
男性 Male	**310**	**24.2**	**6.8**	**14.5**	**16.8**	**7.1**	**20.6**	**26.1**	**42.3**
16~24 岁 Age	62	11.3	8.1	9.7	9.7	4.8	12.9	21.0	54.8
25~34 岁 Age	92	29.3	7.6	10.9	17.4	5.4	20.7	30.4	35.9
35~44 岁 Age	74	32.4	5.4	20.3	21.6	9.5	27.0	31.1	35.1
45~54 岁 Age	54	22.2	5.6	22.2	20.4	11.1	22.2	27.8	38.9
55~60 岁 Age	28	17.9	7.1	7.1	10.7	3.6	17.9	7.1	60.7
女性 Female	**305**	**18.0**	**5.2**	**8.2**	**16.1**	**5.9**	**13.8**	**13.8**	**61.6**
16~24 岁 Age	63	15.9	9.5	12.7	19.0	11.1	15.9	12.7	54.0
25~34 岁 Age	89	22.5	5.6	9.0	16.9	4.5	16.9	16.9	53.9
35~44 岁 Age	71	16.9	5.6	7.0	12.7	2.8	9.9	8.5	71.8
45~54 岁 Age	59	13.6	1.7	5.1	13.6	5.1	6.8	15.3	71.2
55~60 岁 Age	23	21.7	0.0	4.3	21.7	8.7	26.1	17.4	56.5

3-8 样本、男性各年龄层、女性各年龄层对 CD 唱片及音乐带的信息接触情况/ Information Contact about CD & Music Cassette by the Whole Sample, Age and Gender Groups

注：本题为多选题，合计百分比超过 100%（Multiple answers）

	人数 Number	不管买还是不买，想看看 just have a look, without a definite purpose of buying or not	阅读有关的杂志和专门报道 reading magazines related & special reports	相互口头传播信息 communicate information orally among people	经常看这种商品的广告 often watch advertisements about such kinds of goods	购买这种商品的新类型 buy the latest type of such kinds of goods	过去在这种商品上花了不少钱 used to spend much money on such kinds of goods	今后愿意在这方面花钱 willing to spend money on such items in future	不关注这方面的信息 don't care about such items
样本 Sample	**616**	**36.5**	**14.1**	**15.3**	**14.1**	**15.3**	**21.6**	**30.2**	**42.0**
男性 Male	**312**	**36.9**	**17.0**	**15.7**	**15.7**	**18.6**	**21.5**	**32.4**	**42.0**
16~24 岁 Age	64	50.0	37.5	28.1	28.1	40.6	32.8	56.3	14.1
25~34 岁 Age	92	40.2	16.3	16.3	17.4	16.3	23.9	33.7	32.6
35~44 岁 Age	74	37.8	8.1	10.8	9.5	14.9	20.3	28.4	50.0
45~54 岁 Age	54	25.9	13.0	11.1	11.1	9.3	14.8	18.5	63.0
55~60 岁 Age	28	14.3	3.6	7.1	7.1	3.6	3.6	10.7	75.0
女性 Female	**304**	**36.2**	**11.2**	**14.8**	**12.5**	**11.8**	**21.7**	**28.0**	**42.1**
16~24 岁 Age	64	46.9	23.4	31.3	23.4	20.3	39.1	40.6	15.6
25~34 岁 Age	88	39.8	12.5	15.9	10.2	10.2	23.9	25.0	34.1
35~44 岁 Age	71	36.6	8.5	7.0	11.3	9.9	16.9	26.8	52.1
45~54 岁 Age	58	27.6	3.4	8.6	6.9	8.6	10.3	24.1	58.6
55~60 岁 Age	23	13.0	0.0	4.3	8.7	8.7	8.7	17.4	73.9

3-9 样本、男性各年龄层、女性各年龄层对护肤品和化妆品的信息接触情况/ Information Contact about Skin Cream & Cosmetics by the Whole Sample, Age and Gender Groups

注：本题为多选题，合计百分比超过 100%（Multiple answers）

	人数 Number	不管买还是不买，想看看 just have a look, without a definite purpose of buying or not	阅读有关的杂志和专门报道 reading magazines related & special reports	相互口头传播信息 communicate information orally among people	经常看这种商品的广告 often watch advertisements about such kinds of goods	购买这种商品的新类型 buy the latest type of such kinds of goods	过去在这种商品上花了不少钱 used to spend much money on such kinds of goods	今后愿意在这方面花钱 willing to spend money on such items in future	不关注这方面的信息 don't care about such items
样本 Sample	623	27.6	14.9	15.7	20.7	11.7	17.8	26.3	55.7
男性 Male	314	8.9	7.0	5.7	8.9	3.2	5.7	6.7	81.5
16~24 岁 Age	64	3.1	6.3	6.3	7.8	1.6	1.6	4.7	81.3
25~34 岁 Age	93	8.6	7.5	4.3	6.5	2.2	7.5	9.7	81.7
35~44 岁 Age	75	14.7	9.3	8.0	12.0	5.3	6.7	6.7	81.3
45~54 岁 Age	54	11.1	5.6	7.4	14.8	5.6	9.3	7.4	74.1
55~60 岁 Age	28	3.6	3.6	0.0	0.0	0.0	0.0	0.0	96.4
女性 Female	309	46.6	23.0	25.9	32.7	20.4	30.1	46.3	29.4
16~24 岁 Age	64	48.4	28.1	25.0	37.5	25.0	29.7	57.8	15.6
25~34 岁 Age	90	56.7	28.9	28.9	34.4	21.1	40.0	52.2	15.6
35~44 岁 Age	73	50.7	21.9	30.1	35.6	19.2	31.5	50.7	30.1
45~54 岁 Age	59	32.2	15.3	20.3	22.0	16.9	16.9	28.8	50.8
55~60 岁 Age	23	26.1	8.7	17.4	30.4	17.4	21.7	21.7	65.2

3-10 样本、男性各年龄层、女性各年龄层对香波等洗涤用品的信息接触情况/ Information Contact about Shampoo & Detergent Cassette by the Whole Sample, Age and Gender Groups

注：本题为多选题，合计百分比超过 100%（Multiple answers）

	人数 Number	不管买还是不买，想看看 just have a look, without a definite purpose of buying or not	阅读有关的杂志和专门报道 reading magazines related & special reports	相互口头传播信息 communicate information orally among people	经常看这种商品的广告 often watch advertisements about such kinds of goods	购买这种商品的新类型 buy the latest type of such kinds of goods	过去在这种商品上花了不少钱 used to spend much money on such kinds of goods	今后愿意在这方面花钱 willing to spend money on such items in future	不关注这方面的信息 don't care about such items
样本 Sample	622	35.4	11.7	16.4	29.6	17.0	29.9	37.9	33.8
男性 Male	313	20.4	6.7	8.0	17.6	8.9	19.5	24.6	52.7
16~24 岁 Age	64	10.9	4.7	9.4	15.6	9.4	10.9	15.6	59.4
25~34 岁 Age	93	19.4	5.4	4.3	11.8	6.5	22.6	28.0	53.8
35~44 岁 Age	74	25.7	5.4	12.2	23.0	8.1	24.3	29.7	48.6
45~54 岁 Age	54	22.2	11.1	9.3	22.2	11.1	20.4	27.8	44.4
55~60 岁 Age	28	28.6	10.7	3.6	17.9	14.3	14.3	14.3	60.7
女性 Female	309	50.5	16.8	24.9	41.7	25.2	40.5	51.5	14.6
16~24 岁 Age	64	37.5	15.6	28.1	39.1	31.3	32.8	45.3	15.6
25~34 岁 Age	90	55.6	18.9	20.0	43.3	22.2	44.4	54.4	10.0
35~44 岁 Age	73	60.3	23.3	28.8	42.5	24.7	47.9	56.2	15.1
45~54 岁 Age	59	45.8	11.9	27.1	40.7	23.7	33.9	50.8	15.3
55~60 岁 Age	23	47.8	4.3	17.4	43.5	26.1	39.1	43.5	26.1

3-11 样本、男性各年龄层、女性各年龄层对外出就餐的信息接触情况/ Information Contact about Dinning Out by the Whole Sample, Age and Gender Groups

注：本题为多选题，合计百分比超过 100%（Multiple answers）

	人数 Number	阅读有关的杂志和专门报道 reading magazines related and special reports	相互口头传播信息 communicate information orally among people	经常看这种服务的广告 often watch advertisements about such kinds of service	尝试这种服务的新类型 buy the latest type of such kinds of service	过去在这种服务上花了不少钱 used to spend much money on such kinds of service	今后愿意在这方面花钱 willing to spend money on such items in future	不关注这方面的信息 don't care about such items
样本 Sample	**617**	**14.9**	**22.5**	**12.6**	**13.3**	**22.4**	**31.9**	**40.5**
男性 Male	**310**	**15.5**	**22.9**	**12.9**	**13.2**	**25.8**	**38.4**	**35.8**
16~24 岁 Age	64	12.5	12.5	7.8	12.5	17.2	39.1	34.4
25~34 岁 Age	92	17.4	25.0	13.0	14.1	32.6	40.2	33.7
35~44 岁 Age	73	20.5	34.2	17.8	19.2	37.0	50.7	16.4
45~54 岁 Age	54	13.0	24.1	14.8	5.6	20.4	29.6	48.1
55~60 岁 Age	27	7.4	7.4	7.4	11.1	3.7	14.8	74.1
女性 Female	**307**	**14.3**	**22.1**	**12.4**	**13.4**	**18.9**	**25.4**	**45.3**
16~24 岁 Age	64	18.8	18.8	12.5	23.4	18.8	35.9	28.1
25~34 岁 Age	89	18.0	29.2	13.5	10.1	20.2	25.8	36.0
35~44 岁 Age	73	12.3	21.9	13.7	12.3	17.8	27.4	53.4
45~54 岁 Age	58	6.9	17.2	8.6	12.1	17.2	10.3	62.1
55~60 岁 Age	23	13.0	17.4	13.0	4.3	21.7	26.1	60.9

3-12 样本、男性各年龄层、女性各年龄层对旅行的信息接触情况/ Information Contact about Travelling by the Whole Sample, Age and Gender Groups

注：本题为多选题，合计百分比超过 100%（Multiple answers）

	人数 Number	阅读有关的杂志和专门报道 reading magazines related and special reports	相互口头传播信息 communicate information orally among people	经常看这种服务的广告 often watch advertisements about such kinds of service	尝试这种服务的新类型 try using the latest type of such kinds of service	过去在这种服务上花了不少钱 used to spend much money on such kinds of service	今后愿意在这方面花钱 willing to spend money on such items in future	不关注这方面的信息 don't care about such kinds of service
样本 Sample	**621**	**25.1**	**20.9**	**15.9**	**9.7**	**17.9**	**46.2**	**35.3**
男性 Male	**312**	**24.7**	**20.8**	**16.0**	**9.3**	**16.3**	**47.4**	**35.3**
16~24 岁 Age	63	19.0	14.3	15.9	9.5	6.3	52.4	25.4
25~34 岁 Age	92	31.5	25.0	16.3	9.8	19.6	52.2	28.3
35~44 岁 Age	75	21.3	17.3	14.7	10.7	22.7	46.7	44.0
45~54 岁 Age	54	27.8	29.6	22.2	5.6	18.5	44.4	35.2
55~60 岁 Age	28	17.9	14.3	7.1	10.7	7.1	28.6	57.1
女性 Female	**309**	**25.6**	**21.0**	**15.9**	**10.0**	**19.4**	**45.0**	**35.3**
16~24 岁 Age	64	31.3	20.3	14.1	17.2	18.8	53.1	20.3
25~34 岁 Age	90	28.9	22.2	20.0	7.8	17.8	50.0	30.0
35~44 岁 Age	73	23.3	17.8	12.3	8.2	19.2	35.6	45.2
45~54 岁 Age	59	23.7	22.0	15.3	8.5	20.3	47.5	40.7
55~60 岁 Age	23	8.7	26.1	17.4	8.7	26.1	26.1	52.2

3-13 样本、男性各年龄层、女性各年龄层对音乐会的信息接触情况/ Information Contact about Concert by the Whole Sample, Age and Gender Groups

注：本题为多选题，合计百分比超过 100%（Multiple answers）

	人数 Number	阅读有关的杂志和专门报道 reading magazines related and special reports	相互口头传播信息 communicate information orally among people	经常看这种服务的广告 often watch advertisements about such kinds of service	尝试这种服务的新类型 try using the latest type of such kinds of service	过去在这种服务上花了不少钱 used to spend much money on such kinds of service	今后愿意在这方面花钱 willing to spend money on such items in future	不关注这方面的信息 don't care about such kinds of service
样本 Sample	618	16.2	10.4	10.0	5.2	5.7	17.0	65.7
男性 Male	311	13.8	10.0	9.3	5.5	4.5	16.7	67.8
16~24 岁 Age	64	18.8	20.3	10.9	6.3	3.1	18.8	53.1
25~34 岁 Age	91	13.2	11.0	13.2	5.5	3.3	18.7	64.8
35~44 岁 Age	75	13.3	4.0	5.3	6.7	9.3	21.3	69.3
45~54 岁 Age	54	14.8	9.3	11.1	3.7	3.7	11.1	74.1
55~60 岁 Age	27	3.7	0.0	0.0	3.7	0.0	3.7	96.3
女性 Female	307	18.6	10.7	10.7	4.9	6.8	17.3	63.5
16~24 岁 Age	64	31.3	18.8	9.4	9.4	6.3	29.7	43.8
25~34 岁 Age	90	17.8	13.3	13.3	4.4	10.0	17.8	61.1
35~44 岁 Age	73	12.3	6.8	9.6	4.1	2.7	13.7	72.6
45~54 岁 Age	57	17.5	7.0	10.5	3.5	7.0	12.3	71.9
55~60 岁 Age	23	8.7	0.0	8.7	0.0	8.7	4.3	78.3

3-14 样本、男性各年龄层、女性各年龄层对电影的信息接触情况/ Information Contact about Movie by the Whole Sample, Age and Gender Groups

注：本题为多选题，合计百分比超过 100%（Multiple answers）

	人数 Number	阅读有关的杂志和专门报道 reading magazines related and special reports	相互口头传播信息 communicate information orally among people	经常看这种服务的广告 often watch advertisements about such kinds of service	尝试这种服务的新类型 try using the latest type of such kinds of service	过去在这种服务上花了不少钱 used to spend much money on such kinds of service	今后愿意在这方面花钱 willing to spend money on such items in future	不关注这方面的信息 don't care about such kinds of service
样本 Sample	619	24.2	19.4	16.5	7.1	16.0	24.9	46.8
男性 Male	312	22.1	17.0	13.1	6.7	15.4	23.4	46.5
16~24 岁 Age	64	37.5	26.6	28.1	17.2	23.4	37.5	20.3
25~34 岁 Age	91	24.2	23.1	7.7	4.4	17.6	24.2	44.0
35~44 岁 Age	75	12.0	8.0	8.0	6.7	12.0	18.7	57.3
45~54 岁 Age	54	13.5	14.8	11.1	0.0	9.3	18.5	57.4
55~60 岁 Age	28	14.3	3.6	14.3	3.6	10.7	10.7	64.3
女性 Female	307	26.4	21.8	19.9	7.5	16.6	26.4	47.2
16~24 岁 Age	64	45.3	37.5	25.0	15.6	26.6	50.0	18.8
25~34 岁 Age	89	24.7	23.6	20.2	5.6	19.1	30.3	47.2
35~44 岁 Age	73	26.0	19.2	23.3	9.6	15.1	19.2	52.1
45~54 岁 Age	58	17.2	10.3	12.1	1.7	5.2	8.6	62.1
55~60 岁 Age	23	4.3	8.7	13.0	0.0	13.0	13.0	73.9

3-15 样本、男性各年龄层、女性各年龄层对戏剧或戏曲的信息接触情况/ Information Contact about Drama or Opera by the Whole Sample, Age and Gender Groups

注：本题为多选题，合计百分比超过 100%（Multiple answers）

	人数 Number	阅读有关的杂志和专门报道 reading magazines related and special reports	相互口头传播信息 communicate information orally among people	经常看这种服务的广告 often watch advertisements about such kinds of service	尝试这种服务的新类型 try using the latest type of such kinds of service	过去在这种服务上花了不少钱 used to spend much money on such kinds of service	今后愿意在这方面花钱 willing to spend money on such items in future	不关注这方面的信息 don't care about such kinds of service
样本 Sample	615	4.4	4.2	2.8	1.3	2.9	4.9	88.3
男性 Male	311	3.2	4.2	1.9	1.6	3.5	5.5	87.8
16~24 岁 Age	64	1.6	1.6	0.0	1.6	0.0	0.0	95.3
25~34 岁 Age	92	1.1	0.0	1.1	1.1	0.0	3.3	93.5
35~44 岁 Age	75	5.3	2.7	2.7	4.0	6.7	6.7	88.0
45~54 岁 Age	52	1.9	9.6	3.8	0.0	7.7	13.5	78.8
55~60 岁 Age	28	10.7	17.9	3.6	0.0	7.1	7.1	67.9
女性 Female	304	5.6	4.3	3.6	1.0	2.3	4.3	88.8
16~24 岁 Age	61	8.2	6.6	1.6	0.0	1.6	4.9	90.2
25~34 岁 Age	89	3.4	0.0	3.4	0.0	1.1	2.2	93.3
35~44 岁 Age	73	6.8	5.5	2.7	1.4	2.7	2.7	90.4
45~54 岁 Age	58	5.2	5.2	1.7	0.0	1.7	3.4	87.9
55~60 岁 Age	23	4.3	8.7	17.4	8.7	8.7	17.4	65.2

3-16 样本、男性各年龄层、女性各年龄层对蹦迪的信息接触情况/ Information Contact about Disco by the Whole Sample, Age and Gender Groups

注：本题为多选题，合计百分比超过 100%（Multiple answers）

	人数 Number	阅读有关的杂志和专门报道 reading magazines related and special reports	相互口头传播信息 communicate information orally among people	经常看这种服务的广告 often watch advertisements about such kinds of service	尝试这种服务的新类型 try using the latest type of such kinds of service	过去在这种服务上花了不少钱 used to spend much money on such kinds of service	今后愿意在这方面花钱 willing to spend money on such items in future	不关注这方面的信息 don't care about such kinds of service
样本 Sample	618	4.7	5.7	4.4	3.9	6.1	10.2	80.6
男性 Male	309	2.9	4.9	4.5	3.9	6.8	10.0	81.2
16~24 岁 Age	63	7.9	11.1	11.1	4.8	12.7	25.4	52.4
25~34 岁 Age	92	4.3	8.7	5.4	8.7	10.9	14.1	77.2
35~44 岁 Age	74	0.0	0.0	0.0	1.4	2.7	1.4	94.6
45~54 岁 Age	52	0.0	0.0	3.8	0.0	1.9	1.9	94.2
55~60 岁 Age	28	0.0	0.0	0.0	0.0	0.0	0.0	100.0
女性 Female	309	6.5	6.5	4.2	3.9	5.5	10.4	79.9
16~24 岁 Age	63	19.0	20.6	11.1	12.7	12.7	30.2	44.4
25~34 岁 Age	90	5.6	4.4	2.2	2.2	7.8	12.2	77.8
35~44 岁 Age	73	4.1	2.7	4.1	2.7	2.7	2.7	93.2
45~54 岁 Age	60	0.0	1.7	0.0	0.0	0.0	0.0	98.3
55~60 岁 Age	23	0.0	0.0	4.3	0.0	0.0	0.0	95.7

3-17 样本、男性各年龄层、女性各年龄层对现场观赏体育比赛的信息接触情况/ Information Contact about Enjoying Live Sports by the Whole Sample, Age and Gender Groups

注：本题为多选题，合计百分比超过 100%（Multiple answers）

	人数 Number	阅读有关的杂志和专门报道 reading magazines related and special reports	相互口头传播信息 communicate information orally among people	经常看这种服务的广告 often watch advertisements about such kinds of service	尝试这种服务的新类型 try using the latest type of such kinds of service	过去在这种服务上花了不少钱 used to spend much money on such kinds of service	今后愿意在这方面花钱 willing to spend money on such items in future	不关注这方面的信息 don't care about such kinds of service
样本 Sample	619	22.9	19.1	13.9	5.8	13.1	27.6	53.3
男性 Male	312	32.1	26.9	18.9	9.3	17.9	38.5	37.8
16~24 岁 Age	63	42.9	27.0	27.0	12.7	27.0	42.9	22.2
25~34 岁 Age	92	31.5	31.5	18.5	7.6	18.5	46.7	32.6
35~44 岁 Age	75	37.3	33.3	17.3	10.7	17.3	42.7	34.7
45~54 岁 Age	54	22.2	18.5	14.8	7.4	11.1	29.6	51.9
55~60 岁 Age	28	14.3	10.7	14.3	7.1	10.7	7.1	71.4
女性 Female	307	13.7	11.1	8.8	2.3	8.1	16.6	69.1
16~24 岁 Age	63	25.4	17.5	7.9	3.2	7.9	30.2	50.8
25~34 岁 Age	90	14.4	13.3	13.3	2.2	11.1	20.0	63.3
35~44 岁 Age	73	11.0	9.6	9.6	4.1	11.0	9.6	79.5
45~54 岁 Age	58	8.6	6.9	3.4	0.0	0.0	6.9	79.3
55~60 岁 Age	23	0.0	0.0	4.3	0.0	8.7	13.0	82.6

3-18 样本、男性各年龄层、女性各年龄层对运动健身的信息接触情况/ Information Contact about Gym by the Whole Sample, Age and Gender Groups

注：本题为多选题，合计百分比超过 100%（Multiple answers）

	人数 Number	阅读有关的杂志和专门报道 reading magazines related and special reports	相互口头传播信息 communicate information orally among people	经常看这种服务的广告 often watch advertisements about such kinds of service	尝试这种服务的新类型 try using the latest type of such kinds of service	过去在这种服务上花了不少钱 used to spend much money on such kinds of service	今后愿意在这方面花钱 willing to spend money on such items in future	不关注这方面的信息 don't care about such kinds of service
样本 Sample	619	16.0	12.1	9.9	8.1	7.4	28.6	56.1
男性 Male	311	14.8	9.3	8.7	7.1	8.0	30.2	56.6
16~24 岁 Age	62	24.2	9.7	11.3	11.3	9.7	46.8	33.9
25~34 岁 Age	93	14.0	10.8	9.7	5.4	9.7	34.4	55.9
35~44 岁 Age	75	9.3	6.7	6.7	8.0	6.7	20.0	68.0
45~54 岁 Age	53	11.3	7.5	7.5	3.8	3.8	18.9	69.8
55~60 岁 Age	28	17.9	14.3	7.1	7.1	10.7	28.6	53.6
女性 Female	308	17.2	14.9	11.0	9.1	6.8	26.9	55.5
16~24 岁 Age	63	27.0	19.0	7.9	20.6	7.9	44.4	31.7
25~34 岁 Age	90	16.7	17.8	14.4	5.6	7.8	25.6	56.7
35~44 岁 Age	73	12.3	5.5	6.8	5.5	6.8	19.2	68.5
45~54 岁 Age	59	16.9	16.9	15.3	6.8	6.8	23.7	57.6
55~60 岁 Age	23	8.7	17.4	8.7	8.7	0.0	17.4	69.6

3-19 样本、男性各年龄层、女性各年龄层对技能学习的信息接触情况/ Information Contact about Studying Skills by the Whole Sample, Age and Gender Groups

注：本题为多选题，合计百分比超过 100%（Multiple answers）

	人数 Number	阅读有关的杂志和专门报道 reading magazines related and special reports	相互口头传播信息 communicate information orally among people	经常看这种服务的广告 often watch advertisements about such kinds of service	尝试这种服务的新类型 try using the latest type of such kinds of service	过去在这种服务上花了不少钱 used to spend much money on such kinds of service	今后愿意在这方面花钱 willing to spend money on such items in future	不关注这方面的信息 don't care about such kinds of service
样本 Sample	**621**	**16.9**	**9.2**	**8.1**	**6.0**	**8.2**	**30.3**	**55.9**
男性 Male	**313**	**19.5**	**10.9**	**9.6**	**5.8**	**9.6**	**35.5**	**50.2**
16~24 岁 Age	63	27.0	9.5	4.8	4.8	7.9	44.4	30.2
25~34 岁 Age	93	20.4	10.8	8.6	4.3	7.5	44.1	43.0
35~44 岁 Age	75	17.3	13.3	12.0	9.3	14.7	37.3	53.3
45~54 岁 Age	54	16.7	9.3	14.8	3.7	11.1	18.5	66.7
55~60 岁 Age	28	10.7	10.7	7.1	7.1	3.6	14.3	78.6
女性 Female	**308**	**14.3**	**7.5**	**6.5**	**6.2**	**6.8**	**25.0**	**61.7**
16~24 岁 Age	64	25.0	15.6	10.9	9.4	12.5	46.9	32.8
25~34 岁 Age	90	17.8	5.6	6.7	8.9	7.8	31.1	54.4
35~44 岁 Age	73	8.2	6.8	4.1	5.5	6.8	15.1	75.3
45~54 岁 Age	58	10.3	5.2	3.4	1.7	1.7	10.3	79.3
55~60 岁 Age	23	0.0	0.0	8.7	0.0	0.0	8.7	82.6

3-20 样本、男性各年龄层、女性各年龄层对外语学习的信息接触情况/ Information Contact about Studying Foreign Languages by the Whole Sample, Age and Gender Groups

注：本题为多选题，合计百分比超过 100%（Multiple answers）

	人数 Number	阅读有关的杂志和专门报道 reading magazines related and special reports	相互口头传播信息 communicate information orally among people	经常看这种服务的广告 often watch advertisements about such kinds of service	尝试这种服务的新类型 try using the latest type of such kinds of service	过去在这种服务上花了不少钱 used to spend much money on such kinds of service	今后愿意在这方面花钱 willing to spend money on such items in future	不关注这方面的信息 don't care about such kinds of service
样本 Sample	**619**	**8.4**	**4.8**	**2.9**	**2.7**	**5.8**	**16.5**	**76.6**
男性 Male	**312**	**9.3**	**3.5**	**2.9**	**1.5**	**5.1**	**17.6**	**76.0**
16~24 岁 Age	64	25.0	9.4	9.4	4.7	12.5	45.3	39.1
25~34 岁 Age	93	10.8	3.2	2.2	2.2	7.5	24.7	66.7
35~44 岁 Age	74	1.4	1.4	0.0	0.0	1.4	2.7	97.3
45~54 岁 Age	54	1.9	1.9	1.9	0.0	0.0	1.9	96.3
55~60 岁 Age	27	3.7	0.0	0.0	0.0	0.0	0.0	96.3
女性 Female	**307**	**7.5**	**6.2**	**2.9**	**3.9**	**6.5**	**15.3**	**77.2**
16~24 岁 Age	63	23.8	19.0	7.9	12.7	20.6	39.7	41.3
25~34 岁 Age	90	5.6	3.3	1.1	2.2	4.4	15.6	77.8
35~44 岁 Age	73	2.7	2.7	1.4	1.4	2.7	4.1	91.8
45~54 岁 Age	58	1.7	3.4	1.7	1.7	1.7	8.6	89.7
55~60 岁 Age	23	0.0	0.0	4.3	0.0	0.0	0.0	95.7

3-21 不同消费者层对电视、音响等视听设备的信息接触情况/ Information Contact about Video & Audio Equipment by Market Segments

注：本题为多选题，合计百分比超过 100%（Multiple answers）

	人数 Number	不管买还是不买，想看看 just have a look, without a definite purpose of buying or not	阅读有关的杂志和专门报道 reading magazines related & special reports	相互口头传播信息 communicate information orally among people	经常看这种商品的广告 often watch advertisements about such kinds of goods	购买这种商品的新类型 buy the latest type of such kinds of goods	过去在这种商品上花了不少钱 used to spend much money on such kinds of goods	今后愿意在这方面花钱 willing to spend money on such items in future	不关注这方面的信息 don't care about such items
样本 Sample	615	63.3	26.0	23.6	39.2	10.6	32.2	33.8	13.7
平实生活指向 simple living orientation	368	63.6	23.4	22.8	39.4	8.7	34.2	32.6	14.1
时尚流行指向 fashion orientation	247	62.8	30.0	24.7	38.9	13.4	29.1	35.6	13.0

3-22 不同消费者层对冰箱、洗衣机等白色家电的信息接触情况/ Information Contact about "White Home Electronic Products" by Market Segments

注：本题为多选题，合计百分比超过 100%（Multiple answers）

	人数 Number	不管买还是不买，想看看 just have a look, without a definite purpose of buying or not	阅读有关的杂志和专门报道 reading magazines related & special reports	相互口头传播信息 communicate information orally among people	经常看这种商品的广告 often watch advertisements about such kinds of goods	购买这种商品的新类型 buy the latest type of such kinds of goods	过去在这种商品上花了不少钱 used to spend much money on such kinds of goods	今后愿意在这方面花钱 willing to spend money on such items in future	不关注这方面的信息 don't care about such items
样本 Sample	613	46.5	18.1	17.8	34.1	8.8	27.7	28.5	23.0
平实生活指向 simple living orientation	367	45.8	15.5	18.8	33.8	6.8	28.9	28.3	23.7
时尚流行指向 fashion orientation	246	47.6	22.0	16.3	34.6	11.8	26.0	28.9	22.0

3-23 不同消费者层对电脑等通讯工具的信息接触情况/ Information Contact about Computer & Telecommunications by Market Segments

注：本题为多选题，合计百分比超过 100%（Multiple answers）

	人数 Number	不管买还是不买，想看看 just have a look, without a definite purpose of buying or not	阅读有关的杂志和专门报道 reading magazines related & special reports	相互口头传播信息 communicate information orally among people	经常看这种商品的广告 often watch advertisements about such kinds of goods	购买这种商品的新类型 buy the latest type of such kinds of goods	过去在这种商品上花了不少钱 used to spend much money on such kinds of goods	今后愿意在这方面花钱 willing to spend money on such items in future	不关注这方面的信息 don't care about such items
样本 Sample	615	24.2	16.9	11.5	15.8	4.9	5.7	28.8	54.3
平实生活指向 simple living orientation	369	19.2	12.7	10.0	13.3	3.5	5.4	25.7	62.6
时尚流行指向 fashion orientation	246	31.7	23.2	13.8	19.5	6.9	6.1	33.3	41.9

3-24 不同消费者层对家用轿车的信息接触情况/ Information Contact about Family Car by Market Segments

注：本题为多选题，合计百分比超过 100%（Multiple answers）

	人数 Number	不管买还是不买，想看看 just have a look, without a definite purpose of buying or not	阅读有关的杂志和专门报道 reading magazines related & special reports	相互口头传播信息 communicate information orally among people	经常看这种商品的广告 often watch advertisements about such kinds of goods	购买这种商品的新类型 buy the latest type of such kinds of goods	过去在这种商品上花了不少钱 used to spend much money on such kinds of goods	今后愿意在这方面花钱 willing to spend money on such items in future	不关注这方面的信息 don't care about such items
样本 Sample	611	19.0	12.3	8.2	9.8	1.5	1.1	9.2	69.9
平实生活指向 simple living orientation	367	12.0	7.6	7.1	6.3	0.5	0.3	5.4	78.7
时尚流行指向 fashion orientation	244	29.5	19.3	9.8	14.3	2.9	2.5	14.8	56.6

3-25 不同消费者层对高级家具的信息接触情况/ Information Contact about First-class Furniture by Market Segments

注：本题为多选题，合计百分比超过 100%（Multiple answers）

	人数 Number	不管买还是不买，想看看 just have a look, without a definite purpose of buying or not	阅读有关的杂志和专门报道 reading magazines related & special reports	相互口头传播信息 communicate information orally among people	经常看这种商品的广告 often watch advertisements about such kinds of goods	购买这种商品的新类型 buy the latest type of such kinds of goods	过去在这种商品上花了不少钱 used to spend much money on such kinds of goods	今后愿意在这方面花钱 willing to spend money on such items in future	不关注这方面的信息 don't care about such items
样本 Sample	611	36.3	9.3	9.2	11.6	4.4	6.4	26.5	46.0
平实生活指向 simple living orientation	367	30.0	7.4	7.4	9.3	1.9	4.6	21.3	54.2
时尚流行指向 fashion orientation	244	45.9	12.3	11.9	15.2	8.2	9.0	34.4	33.6

3-26 不同消费者层对西服和时装的信息接触情况/ Information Contact about Business Suit & Fashion by Market Segments

注：本题为多选题，合计百分比超过 100%（Multiple answers）

	人数 Number	不管买还是不买，想看看 just have a look, without a definite purpose of buying or not	阅读有关的杂志和专门报道 reading magazines related & special reports	相互口头传播信息 communicate information orally among people	经常看这种商品的广告 often watch advertisements about such kinds of goods	购买这种商品的新类型 buy the latest type of such kinds of goods	过去在这种商品上花了不少钱 used to spend much money on such kinds of goods	今后愿意在这方面花钱 willing to spend money on such items in future	不关注这方面的信息 don't care about such items
样本 Sample	614	46.1	18.6	20.2	23.0	14.3	21.3	40.2	28.3
平实生活指向 simple living orientation	367	40.3	13.4	16.3	18.0	8.7	12.0	34.3	37.6
时尚流行指向 fashion orientation	247	54.7	26.3	25.9	30.4	22.7	35.2	49.0	14.6

3-27 不同消费者层对酒精饮料的信息接触情况/ Information Contact about Alcohol Drinks by Market Segments

注：本题为多选题，合计百分比超过 100%（Multiple answers）

	人数 Number	不管买还是不买，想看看 just have a look, without a definite purpose of buying or not	阅读有关的杂志和专门报道 reading magazines related & special reports	相互口头传播信息 communicate information orally among people	经常看这种商品的广告 often watch advertisements about such kinds of goods	购买这种商品的新类型 buy the latest type of such kinds of goods	过去在这种商品上花了不少钱 used to spend much money on such kinds of goods	今后愿意在这方面花钱 willing to spend money on such items in future	不关注这方面的信息 don't care about such items
样本 Sample	607	21.4	6.1	11.5	16.5	6.3	17.3	20.3	51.7
平实生活指向 simple living orientation	362	21.0	5.0	12.4	14.4	5.0	15.5	19.6	53.0
时尚流行指向 fashion orientation	245	22.0	7.8	10.2	19.6	8.2	20.0	21.2	49.8

3-28 不同消费者层对 CD 唱片及音乐带的信息接触情况/ Information Contact about CD & Music Cassette by Market Segments

注：本题为多选题，合计百分比超过 100%（Multiple answers）

	人数 Number	不管买还是不买，想看看 just have a look, without a definite purpose of buying or not	阅读有关的杂志和专门报道 reading magazines related & special reports	相互口头传播信息 communicate information orally among people	经常看这种商品的广告 often watch advertisements about such kinds of goods	购买这种商品的新类型 buy the latest type of such kinds of goods	过去在这种商品上花了不少钱 used to spend much money on such kinds of goods	今后愿意在这方面花钱 willing to spend money on such items in future	不关注这方面的信息 don't care about such items
样本 Sample	608	36.7	14.3	15.5	14.3	15.0	21.5	30.6	42.1
平实生活指向 simple living orientation	363	29.8	8.0	9.6	9.6	10.2	16.0	24.2	53.2
时尚流行指向 fashion orientation	245	46.9	23.7	24.1	21.2	22.0	29.8	40.0	25.7

3-29 不同消费者层对护肤品和化妆品的信息接触情况/ Information Contact about Skin Cream & Cosmetics by Market Segments

注：本题为多选题，合计百分比超过 100%（Multiple answers）

	人数 Number	不管买还是不买，想看看 just have a look, without a definite purpose of buying or not	阅读有关的杂志和专门报道 reading magazines related & special reports	相互口头传播信息 communicate information orally among people	经常看这种商品的广告 often watch advertisements about such kinds of goods	购买这种商品的新类型 buy the latest type of such kinds of goods	过去在这种商品上花了不少钱 used to spend much money on such kinds of goods	今后愿意在这方面花钱 willing to spend money on such items in future	不关注这方面的信息 don't care about such items
样本 Sample	615	27.6	15.1	15.9	21.0	11.7	18.0	26.7	55.4
平实生活指向 simple living orientation	368	20.1	10.6	12.5	15.2	7.9	12.8	20.7	66.0
时尚流行指向 fashion orientation	247	38.9	21.9	21.1	29.6	17.4	25.9	35.6	39.7

3-30 不同消费者层对香波等洗涤用品的信息接触情况/ Information Contact about Shampoo & Detergent by Market Segments

注：本题为多选题，合计百分比超过 100%（Multiple answers）

	人数 Number	不管买还是不买，想看看 just have a look, without a definite purpose of buying or not	阅读有关的杂志和专门报道 reading magazines related & special reports	相互口头传播信息 communicate information orally among people	经常看这种商品的广告 often watch advertisements about such kinds of goods	购买这种商品的新类型 buy the latest type of such kinds of goods	过去在这种商品上花了不少钱 used to spend much money on such kinds of goods	今后愿意在这方面花钱 willing to spend money on such items in future	不关注这方面的信息 don't care about such items
样本 Sample	614	35.8	11.9	16.6	29.6	17.1	30.3	38.4	33.4
平实生活指向 simple living orientation	368	34.5	10.3	14.7	27.2	14.1	26.1	36.7	35.9
时尚流行指向 fashion orientation	246	37.8	14.2	19.5	33.3	21.5	36.6	41.1	29.7

3-31 不同消费者层对外出就餐的信息接触情况/ Information Contact about Dinning Out by Market Segments

注：本题为多选题，合计百分比超过 100%（Multiple answers）

	人数 Number	阅读有关的杂志和专门报道 reading magazines related and special reports	相互口头传播信息 communicate information orally among people	经常看这种服务的广告 often watch advertisements about such kinds of service	尝试这种服务的新类型 try using the latest type of such kinds of service	过去在这种服务上花了不少钱 used to spend much money on such kinds of service	今后愿意在这方面花钱 willing to spend money on such items in future	不关注这方面的信息 don't care about such items
样本 Sample	610	15.1	22.8	12.8	13.3	22.5	32.0	40.3
平实生活指向 simple living orientation	364	9.6	19.8	10.4	9.3	18.1	29.7	48.9
时尚流行指向 fashion orientation	246	23.2	27.2	16.3	19.1	28.9	35.4	27.6

3-32 不同消费者层对旅行的信息接触情况/ Information Contact about Travelling by Market Segments

注：本题为多选题，合计百分比超过 100%（Multiple answers）

	人数 Number	阅读有关的杂志和专门报道 reading magazines related and special reports	相互口头传播信息 communicate information orally among people	经常看这种服务的广告 often watch advertisements about such kinds of service	尝试这种服务的新类型 try using the latest type of such kinds of service	过去在这种服务上花了不少钱 used to spend much money on such kinds of service	今后愿意在这方面花钱 willing to spend money on such items in future	不关注这方面的信息 don't care about such kinds of service
样本 Sample	613	25.0	20.7	16.2	9.8	17.9	46.3	35.4
平实生活指向 simple living orientation	367	19.3	18.0	13.4	5.5	13.4	41.7	43.3
时尚流行指向 fashion orientation	246	33.3	24.8	20.3	14.6	24.8	53.3	23.6

3-33 不同消费者层对音乐会的信息接触情况/ Information Contact about Concert by Market Segments

注：本题为多选题，合计百分比超过 100%（Multiple answers）

	人数 Number	阅读有关的杂志和专门报道 reading magazines related and special reports	相互口头传播信息 communicate information orally among people	经常看这种服务的广告 often watch advertisements about such kinds of service	尝试这种服务的新类型 try using the latest type of such kinds of service	过去在这种服务上花了不少钱 used to spend much money on such kinds of service	今后愿意在这方面花钱 willing to spend money on such items in future	不关注这方面的信息 don't care about such kinds of service
样本 Sample	610	16.4	10.5	10.2	5.1	5.6	17.0	65.7
平实生活指向 simple living orientation	363	9.4	5.5	6.6	3.6	3.9	12.7	76.0
时尚流行指向 fashion orientation	247	26.7	17.8	15.4	7.3	8.1	23.5	50.6

3-34 不同消费者层对电影的信息接触情况/ Information Contact about Movie by Market Segments

注：本题为多选题，合计百分比超过 100%（Multiple answers）

	人数 Number	阅读有关的杂志和专门报道 reading magazines related and special reports	相互口头传播信息 communicate information orally among people	经常看这种服务的广告 often watch advertisements about such kinds of service	尝试这种服务的新类型 try using the latest type of such kinds of service	过去在这种服务上花了不少钱 used to spend much money on such kinds of service	今后愿意在这方面花钱 willing to spend money on such items in future	不关注这方面的信息 don't care about such kinds of service
样本 Sample	611	24.2	19.5	16.5	7.0	16.0	24.7	47.1
平实生活指向 simple living orientation	366	19.4	15.6	14.8	6.3	12.0	23.5	52.2
时尚流行指向 fashion orientation	245	31.4	25.3	19.2	8.2	22.0	26.5	39.6

3-35 不同消费者层对戏剧或戏曲的信息接触情况/ Information Contact about Drama or Opera by Market Segments

注：本题为多选题，合计百分比超过 100%（Multiple answers）

	人数 Number	阅读有关的杂志和专门报道 reading magazines related and special reports	相互口头传播信息 communicate information orally among people	经常看这种服务的广告 often watch advertisements about such kinds of service	尝试这种服务的新类型 try using the latest type of such kinds of service	过去在这种服务上花了不少钱 used to spend much money on such kinds of service	今后愿意在这方面花钱 willing to spend money on such items in future	不关注这方面的信息 don't care about such kinds of service
样本 Sample	607	4.3	4.3	2.8	1.3	3.0	4.9	88.3
平实生活指向 simple living orientation	362	4.4	5.5	2.2	1.7	3.6	4.7	87.3
时尚流行指向 fashion orientation	245	4.1	2.4	3.7	0.8	2.0	5.3	89.8

3-36 不同消费者层对蹦迪的信息接触情况/ Information Contact about Disco by Market Segments

注：本题为多选题，合计百分比超过 100%（Multiple answers）

	人数 Number	阅读有关的杂志和专门报道 reading magazines related and special reports	相互口头传播信息 communicate information orally among people	经常看这种服务的广告 often watch advertisements about such kinds of service	尝试这种服务的新类型 try using the latest type of such kinds of service	过去在这种服务上花了不少钱 used to spend much money on such kinds of service	今后愿意在这方面花钱 willing to spend money on such items in future	不关注这方面的信息 don't care about such kinds of service
样本 Sample	610	4.6	5.6	4.4	3.9	6.2	10.3	80.7
平实生活指向 simple living orientation	365	1.1	1.9	1.9	1.4	1.6	4.7	90.7
时尚流行指向 fashion orientation	245	9.8	11.0	8.2	7.8	13.1	18.8	65.7

3-37 不同消费者层对现场观赏体育比赛的信息接触情况/ Information Contact about Enjoying Live Sports by Market Segments

注：本题为多选题，合计百分比超过 100%（Multiple answers）

	人数 Number	阅读有关的杂志和专门报道 reading magazines related and special reports	相互口头传播信息 communicate information orally among people	经常看这种服务的广告 often watch advertisements about such kinds of service	尝试这种服务的新类型 try using the latest type of such kinds of service	过去在这种服务上花了不少钱 used to spend much money on such kinds of service	今后愿意在这方面花钱 willing to spend money on such items in future	不关注这方面的信息 don't care about such kinds of service
样本 Sample	611	23.2	19.1	14.1	5.7	12.9	27.5	53.4
平实生活指向 simple living orientation	365	19.7	17.0	11.8	4.9	12.3	26.0	57.3
时尚流行指向 fashion orientation	246	28.5	22.4	17.5	6.9	13.8	29.7	47.6

3-38 不同消费者层对运动健身的信息接触情况/ Information Contact about Gym by Market Segments

注：本题为多选题，合计百分比超过 100%（Multiple answers）

	人数 Number	阅读有关的杂志和专门报道 reading magazines related and special reports	相互口头传播信息 communicate information orally among people	经常看这种服务的广告 often watch advertisements about such kinds of service	尝试这种服务的新类型 try using the latest type of such kinds of service	过去在这种服务上花了不少钱 used to spend much money on such kinds of service	今后愿意在这方面花钱 willing to spend money on such items in future	不关注这方面的信息 don't care about such kinds of service
样本 Sample	**611**	**16.2**	**12.1**	**10.0**	**8.0**	**7.5**	**28.8**	**56.0**
平实生活指向 simple living orientation	365	12.3	9.9	7.7	4.1	4.9	22.7	64.9
时尚流行指向 fashion orientation	246	22.0	15.4	13.4	13.8	11.4	37.8	42.7

3-39 不同消费者层对技能学习的信息接触情况/ Information Contact about Studying Skills by Market Segments

注：本题为多选题，合计百分比超过 100%（Multiple answers）

	人数 Number	阅读有关的杂志和专门报道 reading magazines related and special reports	相互口头传播信息 communicate information orally among people	经常看这种服务的广告 often watch advertisements about such kinds of service	尝试这种服务的新类型 try using the latest type of such kinds of service	过去在这种服务上花了不少钱 used to spend much money on such kinds of service	今后愿意在这方面花钱 willing to spend money on such items in future	不关注这方面的信息 don't care about such kinds of service
样本 Sample	**613**	**17.1**	**9.1**	**8.2**	**5.9**	**8.2**	**30.3**	**55.8**
平实生活指向 simple living orientation	366	15.0	8.2	6.8	5.2	7.4	26.8	61.2
时尚流行指向 fashion orientation	247	20.2	10.5	10.1	6.9	9.3	35.6	47.8

3-40 不同消费者层对外语学习的信息接触情况/ Information Contact about Studying Foreign Languages by Market Segments

注：本题为多选题，合计百分比超过 100%（Multiple answers）

	人数 Number	阅读有关的杂志和专门报道 reading magazines related and special reports	相互口头传播信息 communicate information orally among people	经常看这种服务的广告 often watch advertisements about such kinds of service	尝试这种服务的新类型 try using the latest type of such kinds of service	过去在这种服务上花了不少钱 used to spend much money on such kinds of service	今后愿意在这方面花钱 willing to spend money on such items in future	不关注这方面的信息 don't care about such kinds of service
样本 Sample	**611**	**8.2**	**4.9**	**2.9**	**2.8**	**5.9**	**16.5**	**76.8**
平实生活指向 simple living orientation	365	4.7	3.3	1.9	1.4	3.6	10.7	85.8
时尚流行指向 fashion orientation	246	13.4	7.3	4.5	4.9	9.3	25.2	63.4

● 武汉 / Wuhan

3-1 样本、男性各年龄层、女性各年龄层对电视、音响等视听设备的信息接触情况/ Information Contact about Video & Audio Equipment by the Whole Sample, Age and Gender Groups

注：本题为多选题，合计百分比超过 100%（Multiple answers）

	人数 Number	不管买还是不买，想看看 just have a look, without a definite purpose of buying or not	阅读有关的杂志和专门报道 reading magazines related & special reports	相互口头传播信息 communicate information orally among people	经常看这种商品的广告 often watch advertisements about such kinds of goods	购买这种商品的新类型 buy the latest type of such kinds of goods	过去在这种商品上花了不少钱 used to spend much money on such kinds of goods	今后愿意在这方面花钱 willing to spend money on such items in future	不关注这方面的信息 don't care about such items
样本 Sample	640	65.3	37.0	32.7	49.4	19.2	33.8	39.4	10.8
男性 Male	310	70.0	42.3	32.6	50.0	21.6	33.9	43.9	8.4
16~24 岁 Age	65	69.2	50.8	43.1	60.0	16.9	12.3	56.9	4.6
25~34 岁 Age	89	76.4	42.7	31.5	51.7	25.8	38.2	40.4	6.7
35~44 岁 Age	80	72.5	33.8	27.5	46.3	20.0	46.3	40.0	8.8
45~54 岁 Age	52	59.6	46.2	30.8	48.1	23.1	30.8	40.4	9.6
55~60 岁 Age	24	62.5	37.5	29.2	33.3	20.8	41.7	41.7	20.8
女性 Female	330	60.9	32.1	32.7	48.8	17.0	33.6	35.2	13.0
16~24 岁 Age	68	63.2	32.4	30.9	50.0	10.3	20.6	39.7	10.3
25~34 岁 Age	96	65.6	33.3	36.5	53.1	19.8	49.0	38.5	9.4
35~44 岁 Age	78	65.4	29.5	37.2	48.7	19.2	29.5	38.5	7.7
45~54 岁 Age	62	51.6	35.5	33.9	45.2	19.4	35.5	29.0	21.0
55~60 岁 Age	26	46.2	26.9	7.7	38.5	11.5	19.2	15.4	30.8

3-2 样本、男性各年龄层、女性各年龄层对冰箱、洗衣机等白色家电的信息接触情况/ Information Contact about "White Home Electronic Products" by the Whole Sample, Age and Gender Groups

注：本题为多选题，合计百分比超过 100%（Multiple answers）

	人数 Number	不管买还是不买，想看看 just have a look, without a definite purpose of buying or not	阅读有关的杂志和专门报道 reading magazines related & special reports	相互口头传播信息 communicate information orally among people	经常看这种商品的广告 often watch advertisements about such kinds of goods	购买这种商品的新类型 buy the latest type of such kinds of goods	过去在这种商品上花了不少钱 used to spend much money on such kinds of goods	今后愿意在这方面花钱 willing to spend money on such items in future	不关注这方面的信息 don't care about such items
样本 Sample	634	50.0	25.4	23.8	39.1	17.7	27.6	31.2	22.9
男性 Male	306	49.7	27.5	19.9	35.3	17.6	25.2	32.0	25.8
16~24 岁 Age	65	38.5	26.2	15.4	35.4	12.3	10.8	33.8	26.2
25~34 岁 Age	86	55.8	30.2	22.1	37.2	20.9	22.1	34.9	24.4
35~44 岁 Age	80	50.0	21.3	21.3	35.0	16.3	36.3	31.3	22.5
45~54 岁 Age	51	47.1	33.3	21.6	35.3	17.6	29.4	27.5	29.4
55~60 岁 Age	24	62.5	29.2	16.7	29.2	25.0	29.2	29.2	33.3
女性 Female	328	50.3	23.5	27.4	42.7	17.7	29.9	30.5	20.1
16~24 岁 Age	68	42.6	20.6	27.9	42.6	13.2	22.1	36.8	22.1
25~34 岁 Age	95	58.9	22.1	28.4	51.6	20.0	38.9	26.3	14.7
35~44 岁 Age	77	54.5	24.7	26.0	42.9	23.4	32.5	39.0	14.3
45~54 岁 Age	62	43.5	29.0	33.9	33.9	17.7	24.2	27.4	27.4
55~60 岁 Age	26	42.3	19.2	11.5	30.8	3.8	23.1	11.5	34.6

3-3 样本、男性各年龄层、女性各年龄层对电脑等通讯工具的信息接触情况/ Information Contact about Computer & Telecommunications by the Whole Sample, Age and Gender Groups

注：本题为多选题，合计百分比超过 100%（Multiple answers）

	人数 Number	不管买还是不买，想看看 just have a look, without a definite purpose of buying or not	阅读有关的杂志和专门报道 reading magazines related & special reports	相互口头传播信息 communicate information orally among people	经常看这种商品的广告 often watch advertisements about such kinds of goods	购买这种商品的新类型 buy the latest type of such kinds of goods	过去在这种商品上花了不少钱 used to spend much money on such kinds of goods	今后愿意在这方面花钱 willing to spend money on such items in future	不关注这方面的信息 don't care about such items
样本 Sample	638	42.3	29.5	23.8	27.6	13.9	9.1	39.2	34.5
男性 Male	310	49.0	32.3	28.4	31.6	15.8	10.3	42.6	28.7
16~24 岁 Age	65	52.3	52.3	47.7	56.9	18.5	13.8	61.5	7.7
25~34 岁 Age	89	61.8	36.0	29.2	34.8	21.3	14.6	47.2	21.3
35~44 岁 Age	80	42.5	22.5	17.5	13.8	5.0	5.0	31.3	42.5
45~54 岁 Age	52	40.4	21.2	23.1	25.0	17.3	7.7	32.7	32.7
55~60 岁 Age	24	33.3	20.8	20.8	25.0	20.8	8.3	33.3	58.3
女性 Female	328	36.0	26.8	19.5	23.8	12.2	7.9	36.0	39.9
16~24 岁 Age	68	47.1	48.5	27.9	29.4	16.2	11.8	51.5	13.2
25~34 岁 Age	96	44.8	30.2	25.0	30.2	14.6	8.3	40.6	33.3
35~44 岁 Age	77	31.2	22.1	14.3	20.8	7.8	2.6	28.6	46.8
45~54 岁 Age	61	24.6	13.1	13.1	18.0	11.5	9.8	32.8	54.1
55~60 岁 Age	26	15.4	3.8	7.7	7.7	7.7	7.7	7.7	80.8

3-4 样本、男性各年龄层、女性各年龄层对家用轿车的信息接触情况/ Information Contact about Family Car by the Whole Sample, Age and Gender Groups

注：本题为多选题，合计百分比超过 100%（Multiple answers）

	人数 Number	不管买还是不买，想看看 just have a look, without a definite purpose of buying or not	阅读有关的杂志和专门报道 reading magazines related & special reports	相互口头传播信息 communicate information orally among people	经常看这种商品的广告 often watch advertisements about such kinds of goods	购买这种商品的新类型 buy the latest type of such kinds of goods	过去在这种商品上花了不少钱 used to spend much money on such kinds of goods	今后愿意在这方面花钱 willing to spend money on such items in future	不关注这方面的信息 don't care about such items
样本 Sample	636	22.0	14.5	11.8	13.4	2.7	2.0	9.0	64.3
男性 Male	309	29.1	21.4	18.1	18.1	4.2	1.9	11.3	54.0
16~24 岁 Age	65	44.6	24.6	23.1	29.2	4.6	3.1	16.9	35.4
25~34 岁 Age	89	32.6	29.2	23.6	18.0	5.6	2.2	12.4	49.4
35~44 岁 Age	79	24.1	20.3	15.2	16.5	0.0	1.3	13.9	54.4
45~54 岁 Age	52	19.2	11.5	11.5	11.5	7.7	1.9	1.9	71.2
55~60 岁 Age	24	12.5	8.3	8.3	8.3	4.2	0.0	4.2	83.3
女性 Female	327	15.3	8.0	5.8	8.9	1.2	2.1	6.7	74.0
16~24 岁 Age	68	27.9	10.3	2.9	14.7	1.5	2.9	10.3	57.4
25~34 岁 Age	95	20.0	12.6	11.6	12.6	2.1	4.2	12.6	62.1
35~44 岁 Age	77	13.0	7.8	3.9	6.5	1.3	1.3	3.9	81.8
45~54 岁 Age	61	0.0	1.6	4.9	3.3	0.0	0.0	0.0	93.4
55~60 岁 Age	26	7.7	0.0	0.0	0.0	0.0	0.0	0.0	92.3

3-5 样本、男性各年龄层、女性各年龄层对高级家具的信息接触情况/ Information Contact about First-class Furniture by the Whole Sample, Age and Gender Groups

注：本题为多选题，合计百分比超过 100%（Multiple answers）

	人数 Number	不管买还是不买，想看看 just have a look, without a definite purpose of buying or not	阅读有关的杂志和专门报道 reading magazines related & special reports	相互口头传播信息 communicate information orally among people	经常看这种商品的广告 often watch advertisements about such kinds of goods	购买这种商品的新类型 buy the latest type of such kinds of goods	过去在这种商品上花了不少钱 used to spend much money on such kinds of goods	今后愿意在这方面花钱 willing to spend money on such items in future	不关注这方面的信息 don't care about such items
样本 Sample	**637**	**37.5**	**14.0**	**11.0**	**16.5**	**8.6**	**6.0**	**23.7**	**48.0**
男性 Male	**308**	**36.4**	**13.6**	**11.7**	**15.9**	**8.8**	**4.9**	**24.0**	**47.4**
16~24 岁 Age	65	32.3	13.8	10.8	24.6	7.7	4.6	27.7	41.5
25~34 岁 Age	88	46.6	18.2	10.2	11.4	11.4	4.5	25.0	39.8
35~44 岁 Age	79	39.2	11.4	13.9	17.7	6.3	6.3	24.1	46.8
45~54 岁 Age	52	23.1	9.6	9.6	13.5	5.8	0.0	15.4	61.5
55~60 岁 Age	24	29.2	12.5	16.7	8.3	16.7	12.5	29.2	62.5
女性 Female	**329**	**38.6**	**14.3**	**10.3**	**17.0**	**8.5**	**7.0**	**23.4**	**48.6**
16~24 岁 Age	68	42.6	16.2	8.8	20.6	14.7	2.9	27.9	41.2
25~34 岁 Age	96	45.8	14.6	14.6	22.9	8.3	15.6	31.3	40.6
35~44 岁 Age	78	43.6	15.4	9.0	12.8	7.7	1.3	23.1	48.7
45~54 岁 Age	61	24.6	14.8	9.8	13.1	6.6	6.6	13.1	55.7
55~60 岁 Age	26	19.2	3.8	3.8	7.7	0.0	3.8	7.7	80.8

3-6 样本、男性各年龄层、女性各年龄层对西服和时装的信息接触情况/ Information Contact about Business Suit & Fashion by the Whole Sample, Age and Gender Groups

注：本题为多选题，合计百分比超过 100%（Multiple answers）

	人数 Number	不管买还是不买想看看 just have a look, without a definite purpose of buying or not	阅读有关的杂志和专门报道 reading magazines related & special reports	相互口头传播信息 communicate information orally among people	经常看这种商品的广告 often watch advertisements about such kinds of goods	购买这种商品的新类型 buy the latest type of such kinds of goods	过去在这种商品上花了不少钱 used to spend much money on such kinds of goods	今后愿意在这方面花钱 willing to spend money on such items in future	不关注这方面的信息 don't care about such items
样本 Sample	**638**	**64.1**	**25.4**	**29.3**	**33.2**	**28.1**	**31.5**	**45.1**	**16.8**
男性 Male	**309**	**58.9**	**20.4**	**24.3**	**27.5**	**24.3**	**27.8**	**46.0**	**19.1**
16~24 岁 Age	65	58.5	24.6	33.8	36.9	30.8	26.2	55.4	10.8
25~34 岁 Age	88	67.0	25.0	25.0	26.1	26.1	38.6	51.1	12.5
35~44 岁 Age	80	55.0	17.5	21.3	26.3	25.0	23.8	45.0	20.0
45~54 岁 Age	52	53.8	13.5	13.5	21.2	11.5	13.5	30.8	32.7
55~60 岁 Age	24	54.2	16.7	29.2	25.0	25.0	37.5	37.5	33.3
女性 Female	**329**	**69.0**	**30.1**	**34.0**	**38.6**	**31.6**	**35.0**	**44.4**	**14.6**
16~24 岁 Age	68	63.2	47.1	35.3	50.0	44.1	44.1	48.5	10.3
25~34 岁 Age	96	84.4	36.5	37.5	41.7	42.7	47.9	51.0	2.1
35~44 岁 Age	78	69.2	23.1	38.5	43.6	29.5	26.9	47.4	12.8
45~54 岁 Age	61	62.3	16.4	29.5	21.3	14.8	24.6	37.7	23.0
55~60 岁 Age	26	42.3	15.4	15.4	23.1	3.8	11.5	15.4	57.7

3-7 样本、男性各年龄层、女性各年龄层对酒精饮料的信息接触情况/ Information Contact about Alcohol Drinks by the Whole Sample, Age and Gender Groups

注：本题为多选题，合计百分比超过 100%（Multiple answers）

	人数 Number	不管买还是不买，想看看 just have a look, without a definite purpose of buying or not	阅读有关的杂志和专门报道 reading magazines related & special reports	相互口头传播信息 communicate information orally among people	经常看这种商品的广告 often watch advertisements about such kinds of goods	购买这种商品的新类型 buy the latest type of such kinds of goods	过去在这种商品上花了不少钱 used to spend much money on such kinds of goods	今后愿意在这方面花钱 willing to spend money on such items in future	不关注这方面的信息 don't care about such items
样本 Sample	631	22.2	10.9	11.7	19.3	11.4	15.5	19.2	54.4
男性 Male	305	25.2	11.8	13.8	20.0	11.5	17.7	22.3	48.9
16~24 岁 Age	65	12.3	10.8	12.3	21.5	13.8	7.7	16.9	53.8
25~34 岁 Age	87	28.7	13.8	16.1	18.4	8.0	18.4	25.3	47.1
35~44 岁 Age	77	28.6	10.4	13.0	19.5	13.0	24.7	22.1	46.8
45~54 岁 Age	52	32.7	11.5	13.5	19.2	9.6	17.3	23.1	44.2
55~60 岁 Age	24	20.8	12.5	12.5	25.0	16.7	20.8	25.0	58.3
女性 Female	326	19.3	10.1	9.8	18.7	11.3	13.5	16.3	59.5
16~24 岁 Age	67	17.9	14.9	10.4	14.9	11.9	13.4	22.4	52.2
25~34 岁 Age	95	25.3	11.6	9.5	25.3	17.9	17.9	17.9	55.8
35~44 岁 Age	78	16.7	6.4	11.5	15.4	7.7	12.8	11.5	62.8
45~54 岁 Age	60	15.0	6.7	8.3	16.7	6.7	10.0	15.0	63.3
55~60 岁 Age	26	19.2	11.5	7.7	19.2	7.7	7.7	11.5	73.1

3-8 样本、男性各年龄层、女性各年龄层对 CD 唱片及音乐带的信息接触情况/ Information Contact about CD & Music Cassette by the Whole Sample, Age and Gender Groups

注：本题为多选题，合计百分比超过 100%（Multiple answers）

	人数 Number	不管买还是不买，想看看 just have a look, without a definite purpose of buying or not	阅读有关的杂志和专门报道 reading magazines related & special reports	相互口头传播信息 communicate information orally among people	经常看这种商品的广告 often watch advertisements about such kinds of goods	购买这种商品的新类型 buy the latest type of such kinds of goods	过去在这种商品上花了不少钱 used to spend much money on such kinds of goods	今后愿意在这方面花钱 willing to spend money on such items in future	不关注这方面的信息 don't care about such items
样本 Sample	635	40.3	21.3	20.2	23.1	22.4	22.8	36.4	36.5
男性 Male	307	38.8	21.8	20.8	21.5	22.1	23.5	36.5	35.5
16~24 岁 Age	65	58.5	43.1	40.0	33.8	41.5	35.4	58.5	9.2
25~34 岁 Age	88	42.0	21.6	17.0	19.3	19.3	22.7	36.4	29.5
35~44 岁 Age	78	30.8	9.0	16.7	15.4	15.4	17.9	28.2	47.4
45~54 岁 Age	52	25.0	19.2	11.5	21.2	15.4	19.2	25.0	46.2
55~60 岁 Age	24	29.2	12.5	16.7	16.7	16.7	20.8	29.2	66.7
女性 Female	328	41.8	20.7	19.5	24.7	22.6	22.3	36.3	37.5
16~24 岁 Age	68	64.7	38.2	27.9	35.3	35.3	41.2	55.9	13.2
25~34 岁 Age	96	53.1	22.9	25.0	27.1	33.3	32.3	39.6	26.0
35~44 岁 Age	77	26.0	11.7	10.4	20.8	13.0	9.1	35.1	46.8
45~54 岁 Age	61	29.5	14.8	16.4	16.4	13.1	11.5	21.3	54.1
55~60 岁 Age	26	15.4	7.7	11.5	19.2	0.0	0.0	11.5	76.9

3-9 样本、男性各年龄层、女性各年龄层对护肤品和化妆品的信息接触情况/ Information Contact about Skin Cream & Cosmetics by the Whole Sample, Age and Gender Groups

注：本题为多选题，合计百分比超过 100%（Multiple answers）

	人数 Number	不管买还是不买，想看看 just have a look, without a definite purpose of buying or not	阅读有关的杂志和专门报道 reading magazines related & special reports	相互口头传播信息 communicate information orally among people	经常看这种商品的广告 often watch advertisements about such kinds of goods	购买这种商品的新类型 buy the latest type of such kinds of goods	过去在这种商品上花了不少钱 used to spend much money on such kinds of goods	今后愿意在这方面花钱 willing to spend money on such items in future	不关注这方面的信息 don't care about such items
样本 Sample	634	33.6	22.2	21.3	30.8	18.5	20.3	26.5	46.4
男性 Male	306	17.0	8.2	6.2	12.7	5.9	6.5	8.2	72.5
16~24 岁 Age	64	12.5	4.7	7.8	17.2	7.8	4.7	7.8	68.8
25~34 岁 Age	88	23.9	14.8	9.1	15.9	8.0	8.0	9.1	67.0
35~44 岁 Age	78	15.4	5.1	1.3	9.0	2.6	7.7	9.0	74.4
45~54 岁 Age	52	15.4	5.8	7.7	11.5	5.8	5.8	7.7	76.9
55~60 岁 Age	24	12.5	8.3	4.2	4.2	4.2	4.2	4.2	87.5
女性 Female	328	49.1	35.4	35.4	47.6	30.2	33.2	43.6	22.0
16~24 岁 Age	68	51.5	58.8	52.9	57.4	41.2	48.5	61.8	7.4
25~34 岁 Age	96	62.5	33.3	38.5	57.3	38.5	43.8	46.9	10.4
35~44 岁 Age	77	53.2	39.0	39.0	45.5	33.8	27.3	46.8	16.9
45~54 岁 Age	61	32.8	21.3	19.7	37.7	11.5	19.7	31.1	42.6
55~60 岁 Age	26	19.2	3.8	3.8	15.4	3.8	3.8	3.8	69.2

3-10 样本、男性各年龄层、女性各年龄层对香波等洗涤用品的信息接触情况/ Information Contact about Shampoo & Detergent Cassette by the Whole Sample, Age and Gender Groups

注：本题为多选题，合计百分比超过 100%（Multiple answers）

	人数 Number	不管买还是不买，想看看 just have a look, without a definite purpose of buying or not	阅读有关的杂志和专门报道 reading magazines related & special reports	相互口头传播信息 communicate information orally among people	经常看这种商品的广告 often watch advertisements about such kinds of goods	购买这种商品的新类型 buy the latest type of such kinds of goods	过去在这种商品上花了不少钱 used to spend much money on such kinds of goods	今后愿意在这方面花钱 willing to spend money on such items in future	不关注这方面的信息 don't care about such items
样本 Sample	636	38.1	20.3	22.2	33.6	27.0	26.7	36.2	33.0
男性 Male	307	24.1	12.4	12.1	18.9	16.0	18.2	20.8	52.8
16~24 岁 Age	64	18.8	12.5	12.5	25.0	10.9	14.1	18.8	54.7
25~34 岁 Age	88	28.4	17.0	13.6	19.3	22.7	23.9	28.4	44.3
35~44 岁 Age	79	26.6	6.3	10.1	16.5	15.2	16.5	17.7	54.4
45~54 岁 Age	52	23.1	15.4	13.5	19.2	13.5	17.3	19.2	53.8
55~60 岁 Age	24	16.7	8.3	8.3	8.3	12.5	16.7	12.5	70.8
女性 Female	329	51.1	27.7	31.6	47.4	37.4	34.7	50.5	14.6
16~24 岁 Age	68	47.1	38.2	42.6	55.9	39.7	45.6	60.3	7.4
25~34 岁 Age	96	59.4	26.0	26.0	47.9	43.8	34.4	47.9	11.5
35~44 岁 Age	78	53.8	29.5	37.2	51.3	37.2	39.7	62.8	6.4
45~54 岁 Age	61	44.3	23.0	24.6	41.0	34.4	23.0	37.7	23.0
55~60 岁 Age	26	38.5	11.5	23.1	26.9	15.4	19.2	26.9	50.0

3-11 样本、男性各年龄层、女性各年龄层对外出就餐的信息接触情况/ Information Contact about Dinning Out by the Whole Sample, Age and Gender Groups

注：本题为多选题，合计百分比超过 100%（Multiple answers）

	人数 Number	阅读有关的杂志和专门报道 reading magazines related and special reports	相互口头传播信息 communicate information orally among people	经常看这种服务的广告 often watch advertisements about such kinds of service	尝试这种服务的新类型 buy the latest type of such kinds of service	过去在这种服务上花了不少钱 used to spend much money on such kinds of service	今后愿意在这方面花钱 willing to spend money on such items in future	不关注这方面的信息 don't care about such items
样本 Sample	**634**	**14.7**	**25.7**	**13.2**	**22.7**	**23.8**	**30.3**	**39.6**
男性 Male	**307**	**14.3**	**25.7**	**12.7**	**22.8**	**24.1**	**29.0**	**35.8**
16~24 岁 Age	65	20.0	32.3	10.8	18.5	23.1	38.5	24.6
25~34 岁 Age	87	17.2	32.2	14.9	34.5	32.2	39.1	25.3
35~44 岁 Age	79	7.6	22.8	12.7	19.0	26.6	21.5	43.0
45~54 岁 Age	52	9.6	15.4	7.7	15.4	9.6	11.5	50.0
55~60 岁 Age	24	20.8	16.7	20.8	20.8	20.8	29.2	50.0
女性 Female	**327**	**15.0**	**25.7**	**13.8**	**22.6**	**23.5**	**31.5**	**43.1**
16~24 岁 Age	68	14.7	26.5	13.2	29.4	32.4	42.6	25.0
25~34 岁 Age	95	21.1	34.7	17.9	32.6	34.7	43.2	28.4
35~44 岁 Age	78	15.4	24.4	11.5	16.7	12.8	24.4	55.1
45~54 岁 Age	60	8.3	16.7	13.3	13.3	16.7	20.0	55.0
55~60 岁 Age	26	7.7	15.4	7.7	7.7	7.7	7.7	80.8

3-12 样本、男性各年龄层、女性各年龄层对旅行的信息接触情况/ Information Contact about Travelling by the Whole Sample, Age and Gender Groups

注：本题为多选题，合计百分比超过 100%（Multiple answers）

	人数 Number	阅读有关的杂志和专门报道 reading magazines related and special reports	相互口头传播信息 communicate information orally among people	经常看这种服务的广告 often watch advertisements about such kinds of service	尝试这种服务的新类型 try using the latest type of such kinds of service	过去在这种服务上花了不少钱 used to spend much money on such kinds of service	今后愿意在这方面花钱 willing to spend money on such items in future	不关注这方面的信息 don't care about such kinds of service
样本 Sample	**636**	**32.1**	**26.7**	**25.5**	**21.9**	**20.3**	**50.2**	**31.9**
男性 Male	**308**	**29.5**	**24.0**	**26.3**	**18.8**	**20.5**	**47.7**	**33.4**
16~24 岁 Age	65	36.9	26.2	24.6	16.9	21.5	46.2	27.7
25~34 岁 Age	88	31.8	30.7	29.5	21.6	19.3	56.8	23.9
35~44 岁 Age	79	21.5	19.0	25.3	17.7	21.5	43.0	39.2
45~54 岁 Age	52	28.8	17.3	23.1	17.3	17.3	40.4	44.2
55~60 岁 Age	24	29.2	25.0	29.2	20.8	25.0	50.0	41.7
女性 Female	**328**	**34.5**	**29.3**	**24.7**	**24.7**	**20.1**	**52.4**	**30.5**
16~24 岁 Age	68	51.5	32.4	32.4	25.0	22.1	69.1	8.8
25~34 岁 Age	95	38.9	32.6	27.4	34.7	26.3	64.2	20.0
35~44 岁 Age	78	32.1	24.4	24.4	14.1	17.9	41.0	38.5
45~54 岁 Age	61	21.3	34.4	21.3	29.5	18.0	45.9	39.3
55~60 岁 Age	26	11.5	11.5	3.8	7.7	3.8	15.4	80.8

3-13 样本、男性各年龄层、女性各年龄层对音乐会的信息接触情况/ Information Contact about Concert by the Whole Sample, Age and Gender Groups

注：本题为多选题，合计百分比超过 100%（Multiple answers）

	人数 Number	阅读有关的杂志和专门报道 reading magazines related and special reports	相互口头传播信息 communicate information orally among people	经常看这种服务的广告 often watch advertisements about such kinds of service	尝试这种服务的新类型 try using the latest type of such kinds of service	过去在这种服务上花了不少钱 used to spend much money on such kinds of service	今后愿意在这方面花钱 willing to spend money on such items in future	不关注这方面的信息 don't care about such kinds of service
样本 Sample	637	21.8	15.5	13.2	9.6	6.1	20.1	58.1
男性 Male	308	23.4	16.6	13.0	10.1	6.2	23.4	55.8
16~24 岁 Age	65	35.4	23.1	13.8	13.8	7.7	29.2	44.6
25~34 岁 Age	88	21.6	12.5	11.4	9.1	5.7	21.6	54.5
35~44 岁 Age	79	16.5	22.8	15.2	8.9	6.3	25.3	55.7
45~54 岁 Age	52	21.2	3.8	7.7	1.9	1.9	15.4	65.4
55~60 岁 Age	24	25.0	20.8	20.8	25.0	12.5	25.0	70.8
女性 Female	329	20.4	14.6	13.4	9.1	6.1	17.0	60.2
16~24 岁 Age	68	32.4	14.7	14.7	13.2	2.9	23.5	47.1
25~34 岁 Age	96	24.0	12.5	15.6	8.3	10.4	21.9	52.1
35~44 岁 Age	78	15.4	17.9	10.3	7.7	5.1	12.8	66.7
45~54 岁 Age	61	14.8	18.0	14.8	11.5	4.9	13.1	67.2
55~60 岁 Age	26	3.8	3.8	7.7	0.0	3.8	3.8	88.5

3-14 样本、男性各年龄层、女性各年龄层对电影的信息接触情况/ Information Contact about Movie by the Whole Sample, Age and Gender Groups

注：本题为多选题，合计百分比超过 100%（Multiple answers）

	人数 Number	阅读有关的杂志和专门报道 reading magazines related and special reports	相互口头传播信息 communicate information orally among people	经常看这种服务的广告 often watch advertisements about such kinds of service	尝试这种服务的新类型 try using the latest type of such kinds of service	过去在这种服务上花了不少钱 used to spend much money on such kinds of service	今后愿意在这方面花钱 willing to spend money on such items in future	不关注这方面的信息 don't care about such kinds of service
样本 Sample	638	26.5	25.9	22.4	13.2	13.2	22.7	48.9
男性 Male	309	25.6	24.6	19.1	10.7	12.3	24.6	49.2
16~24 岁 Age	65	38.5	43.1	32.3	18.5	20.0	46.2	29.2
25~34 岁 Age	88	30.7	34.1	20.5	10.2	15.9	26.1	42.0
35~44 岁 Age	80	18.8	10.0	12.5	8.8	6.3	15.0	60.0
45~54 岁 Age	52	17.3	15.4	15.4	5.8	5.8	15.4	55.8
55~60 岁 Age	24	12.5	8.3	8.3	8.3	12.5	12.5	79.2
女性 Female	329	27.4	27.1	25.5	15.5	14.0	21.0	48.6
16~24 岁 Age	68	50.0	44.1	41.2	30.9	29.4	42.6	17.6
25~34 岁 Age	96	33.3	30.2	26.0	15.6	17.7	24.0	44.8
35~44 岁 Age	78	21.8	14.1	16.7	14.1	7.7	10.3	62.8
45~54 岁 Age	61	11.5	31.1	26.2	6.6	3.3	13.1	55.7
55~60 岁 Age	26	0.0	0.0	7.7	0.0	3.8	3.8	84.6

3-15 样本、男性各年龄层、女性各年龄层对戏剧或戏曲的信息接触情况/ Information Contact about Drama or Opera by the Whole Sample, Age and Gender Groups

注：本题为多选题，合计百分比超过 100%（Multiple answers）

	人数 Number	阅读有关的杂志和专门报道 reading magazines related and special reports	相互口头传播信息 communicate information orally among people	经常看这种服务的广告 often watch advertisements about such kinds of service	尝试这种服务的新类型 try using the latest type of such kinds of service	过去在这种服务上花了不少钱 used to spend much money on such kinds of service	今后愿意在这方面花钱 willing to spend money on such items in future	不关注这方面的信息 don't care about such kinds of service
样本 Sample	636	10.8	7.5	7.9	4.2	3.3	6.1	80.3
男性 Male	309	11.0	6.8	7.4	2.6	4.2	6.8	80.3
16~24 岁 Age	65	10.8	1.5	3.1	1.5	3.1	1.5	87.7
25~34 岁 Age	88	2.3	0.0	4.5	0.0	1.1	1.1	94.3
35~44 岁 Age	80	7.5	11.3	7.5	3.8	6.3	10.0	75.0
45~54 岁 Age	52	23.1	9.6	11.5	3.8	0.0	7.7	65.4
55~60 岁 Age	24	29.2	25.0	20.8	8.3	20.8	29.2	58.3
女性 Female	327	10.7	8.3	8.3	5.8	2.4	5.5	80.4
16~24 岁 Age	67	7.5	3.0	3.0	4.5	0.0	1.5	89.6
25~34 岁 Age	95	11.6	5.3	9.5	5.3	3.2	4.2	84.2
35~44 岁 Age	78	6.4	3.8	3.8	2.6	1.3	2.6	87.2
45~54 岁 Age	61	16.4	21.3	19.7	8.2	1.6	13.1	60.7
55~60 岁 Age	26	15.4	15.4	3.8	15.4	11.5	11.5	69.2

3-16 样本、男性各年龄层、女性各年龄层对蹦迪的信息接触情况/ Information Contact about Disco by the Whole Sample, Age and Gender Groups

注：本题为多选题，合计百分比超过 100%（Multiple answers）

	人数 Number	阅读有关的杂志和专门报道 reading magazines related and special reports	相互口头传播信息 communicate information orally among people	经常看这种服务的广告 often watch advertisements about such kinds of service	尝试这种服务的新类型 try using the latest type of such kinds of service	过去在这种服务上花了不少钱 used to spend much money on such kinds of service	今后愿意在这方面花钱 willing to spend money on such items in future	不关注这方面的信息 don't care about such kinds of service
样本 Sample	634	5.2	6.3	4.6	7.6	5.2	9.9	80.0
男性 Male	306	5.2	5.9	4.6	8.5	6.9	9.2	79.1
16~24 岁 Age	65	15.4	15.4	12.3	16.9	20.0	21.5	52.3
25~34 岁 Age	87	4.6	5.7	2.3	13.8	5.7	11.5	75.9
35~44 岁 Age	78	1.3	2.6	3.8	2.6	2.6	3.8	89.7
45~54 岁 Age	52	1.9	0.0	0.0	0.0	0.0	1.9	96.2
55~60 岁 Age	24	0.0	4.2	4.2	4.2	4.2	0.0	91.7
女性 Female	328	5.2	6.7	4.6	6.7	3.7	10.7	80.8
16~24 岁 Age	68	13.2	14.7	4.4	16.2	8.8	25.0	57.4
25~34 岁 Age	95	5.3	6.3	6.3	8.4	4.2	13.7	77.9
35~44 岁 Age	78	1.3	2.6	1.3	2.6	1.3	5.1	93.6
45~54 岁 Age	61	3.3	6.6	6.6	1.6	1.6	1.6	88.5
55~60 岁 Age	26	0.0	0.0	3.8	0.0	0.0	0.0	96.2

3-17 样本、男性各年龄层、女性各年龄层对现场观赏体育比赛的信息接触情况/ Information Contact about Enjoying Live Sports by the Whole Sample, Age and Gender Groups

注：本题为多选题，合计百分比超过 100%（Multiple answers）

	人数 Number	阅读有关的杂志和专门报道 reading magazines related and special reports	相互口头传播信息 communicate information orally among people	经常看这种服务的广告 often watch advertisements about such kinds of service	尝试这种服务的新类型 try using the latest type of such kinds of service	过去在这种服务上花了不少钱 used to spend much money on such kinds of service	今后愿意在这方面花钱 willing to spend money on such items in future	不关注这方面的信息 don't care about such kinds of service
样本 Sample	**635**	**30.9**	**26.9**	**20.8**	**11.5**	**9.6**	**25.5**	**46.9**
男性 Male	**308**	**41.9**	**38.3**	**26.6**	**13.3**	**14.9**	**37.7**	**31.8**
16~24 岁 Age	65	50.8	44.6	35.4	23.1	12.3	41.5	21.5
25~34 岁 Age	88	39.8	34.1	21.6	10.2	15.9	45.5	29.5
35~44 岁 Age	79	39.2	44.3	29.1	15.2	19.0	38.0	30.4
45~54 岁 Age	52	44.2	32.7	19.2	1.9	9.6	32.7	36.5
55~60 岁 Age	24	29.2	29.2	29.2	16.7	16.7	8.3	62.5
女性 Female	**327**	**20.5**	**16.2**	**15.3**	**9.8**	**4.6**	**14.1**	**61.2**
16~24 岁 Age	67	25.4	17.9	9.0	10.4	6.0	22.4	52.2
25~34 岁 Age	95	22.1	18.9	18.9	11.6	7.4	16.8	60.0
35~44 岁 Age	78	16.7	15.4	15.4	7.7	2.6	11.5	64.1
45~54 岁 Age	61	23.0	14.8	21.3	8.2	3.3	9.8	59.0
55~60 岁 Age	26	7.7	7.7	3.8	11.5	0.0	0.0	84.6

3-18 样本、男性各年龄层、女性各年龄层对运动健身的信息接触情况/ Information Contact about Gym by the Whole Sample, Age and Gender Groups

注：本题为多选题，合计百分比超过 100%（Multiple answers）

	人数 Number	阅读有关的杂志和专门报道 reading magazines related and special reports	相互口头传播信息 communicate information orally among people	经常看这种服务的广告 often watch advertisements about such kinds of service	尝试这种服务的新类型 try using the latest type of such kinds of service	过去在这种服务上花了不少钱 used to spend much money on such kinds of service	今后愿意在这方面花钱 willing to spend money on such items in future	不关注这方面的信息 don't care about such kinds of service
样本 Sample	**635**	**24.6**	**17.8**	**20.3**	**15.9**	**7.4**	**32.6**	**46.1**
男性 Male	**307**	**29.6**	**17.6**	**22.1**	**16.9**	**9.1**	**36.2**	**42.3**
16~24 岁 Age	65	44.6	27.7	26.2	32.3	13.8	49.2	21.5
25~34 岁 Age	88	23.9	12.5	17.0	15.9	8.0	37.5	38.6
35~44 岁 Age	78	26.9	16.7	24.4	14.1	6.4	30.8	48.7
45~54 岁 Age	52	25.0	11.5	19.2	3.8	7.7	30.8	55.8
55~60 岁 Age	24	29.2	25.0	29.2	16.7	12.5	25.0	62.5
女性 Female	**328**	**19.8**	**18.0**	**18.6**	**14.9**	**5.8**	**29.3**	**49.7**
16~24 岁 Age	68	29.4	25.0	20.6	16.2	7.4	47.1	27.9
25~34 岁 Age	96	16.7	16.7	15.6	13.5	4.2	31.3	55.2
35~44 岁 Age	78	23.1	17.9	23.1	15.4	5.1	26.9	51.3
45~54 岁 Age	60	15.0	16.7	21.7	13.3	8.3	20.0	53.3
55~60 岁 Age	26	7.7	7.7	3.8	19.2	3.8	3.8	73.1

3-19 样本、男性各年龄层、女性各年龄层对技能学习的信息接触情况/ Information Contact about Studying Skills by the Whole Sample, Age and Gender Groups

注：本题为多选题，合计百分比超过 100%（Multiple answers）

	人数 Number	阅读有关的杂志和专门报道 reading magazines related and special reports	相互口头传播信息 communicate information orally among people	经常看这种服务的广告 often watch advertise-ments about such kinds of service	尝试这种服务的新类型 try using the latest type of such kinds of service	过去在这种服务上花了不少钱 used to spend much money on such kinds of service	今后愿意在这方面花钱 willing to spend money on such items in future	不关注这方面的信息 don't care about such kinds of service
样本 Sample	**635**	**29.0**	**18.6**	**16.7**	**13.5**	**12.6**	**33.2**	**46.9**
男性 Male	**307**	**31.9**	**18.9**	**17.6**	**12.4**	**13.4**	**32.9**	**45.3**
16~24 岁 Age	65	38.5	26.2	23.1	20.0	18.5	47.7	32.3
25~34 岁 Age	86	36.0	20.9	23.3	16.3	18.6	46.5	33.7
35~44 岁 Age	80	26.3	13.8	10.0	7.5	10.0	18.8	58.8
45~54 岁 Age	52	30.8	17.3	15.4	7.7	7.7	25.0	44.2
55~60 岁 Age	24	20.8	12.5	12.5	4.2	4.2	8.3	79.2
女性 Female	**328**	**26.2**	**18.3**	**15.9**	**14.6**	**11.9**	**33.5**	**48.5**
16~24 岁 Age	68	44.1	30.9	25.0	25.0	17.6	58.8	23.5
25~34 岁 Age	95	36.8	24.2	21.1	23.2	20.0	38.9	35.8
35~44 岁 Age	78	16.7	11.5	9.0	6.4	3.8	28.2	60.3
45~54 岁 Age	61	11.5	11.5	9.8	3.3	6.6	16.4	65.6
55~60 岁 Age	26	3.8	0.0	7.7	7.7	3.8	3.8	84.6

3-20 样本、男性各年龄层、女性各年龄层对外语学习的信息接触情况/ Information Contact about Studying Foreign Languages by the Whole Sample, Age and Gender Groups

注：本题为多选题，合计百分比超过 100%（Multiple answers）

	人数 Number	阅读有关的杂志和专门报道 reading magazines related and special reports	相互口头传播信息 communicate information orally among people	经常看这种服务的广告 often watch advertise-ments about such kinds of service	尝试这种服务的新类型 try using the latest type of such kinds of service	过去在这种服务上花了不少钱 used to spend much money on such kinds of service	今后愿意在这方面花钱 willing to spend money on such items in future	不关注这方面的信息 don't care about such kinds of service
样本 Sample	**635**	**18.0**	**10.4**	**9.6**	**6.1**	**6.9**	**26.0**	**63.3**
男性 Male	**306**	**18.6**	**8.8**	**8.8**	**4.9**	**5.9**	**23.9**	**64.4**
16~24 岁 Age	65	30.8	15.4	18.5	6.2	9.2	38.5	40.0
25~34 岁 Age	87	25.3	12.6	11.5	8.0	9.2	34.5	54.0
35~44 岁 Age	79	8.9	3.8	2.5	3.8	2.5	11.4	83.5
45~54 岁 Age	51	11.8	2.0	2.0	0.0	2.0	15.7	72.5
55~60 岁 Age	24	8.3	8.3	8.3	4.2	4.2	4.2	87.5
女性 Female	**329**	**17.3**	**11.9**	**10.3**	**7.3**	**7.9**	**28.0**	**62.3**
16~24 岁 Age	68	39.7	25.0	23.5	17.6	14.7	66.2	20.6
25~34 岁 Age	96	17.7	13.5	12.5	8.3	9.4	29.2	57.3
35~44 岁 Age	78	6.4	6.4	2.6	2.6	2.6	14.1	82.1
45~54 岁 Age	61	11.5	4.9	6.6	1.6	6.6	11.5	77.0
55~60 岁 Age	26	3.8	3.8	0.0	3.8	3.8	3.8	96.2

3-21 不同消费者层对电视、音响等视听设备的信息接触情况/ Information Contact about Video & Audio Equipment by Market Segments

注：本题为多选题，合计百分比超过 100%（Multiple answers）

	人数 Number	不管买还是不买，想看看 just have a look, without a definite purpose of buying or not	阅读有关的杂志和专门报道 reading magazines related & special reports	相互口头传播信息 communicate information orally among people	经常看这种商品的广告 often watch advertisements about such kinds of goods	购买这种商品的新类型 buy the latest type of such kinds of goods	过去在这种商品上花了不少钱 used to spend much money on such kinds of goods	今后愿意在这方面花钱 willing to spend money on such items in future	不关注这方面的信息 don't care about such items
样本 Sample	632	65.3	36.7	32.4	49.4	19.0	33.7	39.4	10.8
平实生活指向 simple living orientation	330	62.4	31.5	31.5	44.8	14.2	32.7	36.4	12.4
时尚流行指向 fashion orientation	302	68.5	42.4	33.4	54.3	24.2	34.8	42.7	8.9

3-22 不同消费者层对冰箱、洗衣机等白色家电的信息接触情况/ Information Contact about "White Home Electronic Products" by Market Segments

注：本题为多选题，合计百分比超过 100%（Multiple answers）

	人数 Number	不管买还是不买，想看看 just have a look, without a definite purpose of buying or not	阅读有关的杂志和专门报道 reading magazines related & special reports	相互口头传播信息 communicate information orally among people	经常看这种商品的广告 often watch advertisements about such kinds of goods	购买这种商品的新类型 buy the latest type of such kinds of goods	过去在这种商品上花了不少钱 used to spend much money on such kinds of goods	今后愿意在这方面花钱 willing to spend money on such items in future	不关注这方面的信息 don't care about such items
样本 Sample	626	49.8	24.9	23.2	39.1	17.6	27.6	31.3	23.0
平实生活指向 simple living orientation	325	48.6	22.5	22.2	35.7	13.2	26.8	30.8	25.5
时尚流行指向 fashion orientation	301	51.2	27.6	24.3	42.9	22.3	28.6	31.9	20.3

3-23 不同消费者层对电脑等通讯工具的信息接触情况/ Information Contact about Computer & Telecommunications by Market Segments

注：本题为多选题，合计百分比超过 100%（Multiple answers）

	人数 Number	不管买还是不买，想看看 just have a look, without a definite purpose of buying or not	阅读有关的杂志和专门报道 reading magazines related & special reports	相互口头传播信息 communicate information orally among people	经常看这种商品的广告 often watch advertisements about such kinds of goods	购买这种商品的新类型 buy the latest type of such kinds of goods	过去在这种商品上花了不少钱 used to spend much money on such kinds of goods	今后愿意在这方面花钱 willing to spend money on such items in future	不关注这方面的信息 don't care about such items
样本 Sample	631	42.3	29.3	23.8	27.6	13.9	8.9	39.5	34.5
平实生活指向 simple living orientation	330	36.4	23.9	19.4	22.1	11.2	7.0	35.8	41.2
时尚流行指向 fashion orientation	301	48.8	35.2	28.6	33.6	16.9	11.0	43.5	27.2

3-24 不同消费者层对家用轿车的信息接触情况/ Information Contact about Family Car by Market Segments

注：本题为多选题，合计百分比超过 100%（Multiple answers）

	人数 Number	不管买还是不买，想看看 just have a look, without a definite purpose of buying or not	阅读有关的杂志和专门报道 reading magazines related & special reports	相互口头传播信息 communicate information orally among people	经常看这种商品的广告 often watch advertisements about such kinds of goods	购买这种商品的新类型 buy the latest type of such kinds of goods	过去在这种商品上花了不少钱 used to spend much money on such kinds of goods	今后愿意在这方面花钱 willing to spend money on such items in future	不关注这方面的信息 don't care about such items
样本 Sample	629	21.8	14.1	11.1	13.4	2.7	2.1	8.6	64.7
平实生活指向 simple living orientation	329	19.8	12.5	8.8	8.8	2.1	1.5	7.6	70.2
时尚流行指向 fashion orientation	300	24.0	16.0	13.7	18.3	3.3	2.7	9.7	58.7

3-25 不同消费者层对高级家具的信息接触情况/ Information Contact about First-class Furniture by Market Segments

注：本题为多选题，合计百分比超过 100%（Multiple answers）

	人数 Number	不管买还是不买，想看看 just have a look, without a definite purpose of buying or not	阅读有关的杂志和专门报道 reading magazines related & special reports	相互口头传播信息 communicate information orally among people	经常看这种商品的广告 often watch advertisements about such kinds of goods	购买这种商品的新类型 buy the latest type of such kinds of goods	过去在这种商品上花了不少钱 used to spend much money on such kinds of goods	今后愿意在这方面花钱 willing to spend money on such items in future	不关注这方面的信息 don't care about such items
样本 Sample	631	37.2	14.1	10.9	16.2	8.6	5.9	23.5	48.3
平实生活指向 simple living orientation	329	32.5	10.6	8.8	11.9	5.2	4.6	17.6	55.6
时尚流行指向 fashion orientation	302	42.4	17.9	13.2	20.9	12.3	7.3	29.8	40.4

3-26 不同消费者层对西服和时装的信息接触情况/ Information Contact about Business Suit & Fashion by Market Segments

注：本题为多选题，合计百分比超过 100%（Multiple answers）

	人数 Number	不管买还是不买，想看看 just have a look, without a definite purpose of buying or not	阅读有关的杂志和专门报道 reading magazines related & special reports	相互口头传播信息 communicate information orally among people	经常看这种商品的广告 often watch advertisements about such kinds of goods	购买这种商品的新类型 buy the latest type of such kinds of goods	过去在这种商品上花了不少钱 used to spend much money on such kinds of goods	今后愿意在这方面花钱 willing to spend money on such items in future	不关注这方面的信息 don't care about such items
样本 Sample	632	63.8	25.2	29.1	33.1	27.8	31.3	44.9	16.9
平实生活指向 simple living orientation	330	55.5	17.9	21.8	23.9	18.5	20.3	36.4	25.5
时尚流行指向 fashion orientation	302	72.8	33.1	37.1	43.0	38.1	43.4	54.3	7.6

3-27 不同消费者层对酒精饮料的信息接触情况/ Information Contact about Alcohol Drinks by Market Segments

注：本题为多选题，合计百分比超过 100%（Multiple answers）

	人数 Number	不管买还是不买，想看看 just have a look, without a definite purpose of buying or not	阅读有关的杂志和专门报道 reading magazines related & special reports	相互口头传播信息 communicate information orally among people	经常看这种商品的广告 often watch advertisements about such kinds of goods	购买这种商品的新类型 buy the latest type of such kinds of goods	过去在这种商品上花了不少钱 used to spend much money on such kinds of goods	今后愿意在这方面花钱 willing to spend money on such items in future	不关注这方面的信息 don't care about such items
样本 Sample	625	21.9	10.9	11.5	19.0	11.2	15.5	18.7	54.7
平实生活指向 simple living orientation	327	18.0	8.0	8.6	15.6	8.6	15.3	17.1	58.1
时尚流行指向 fashion orientation	298	26.2	14.1	14.8	22.8	14.1	15.8	20.5	51.0

3-28 不同消费者层对 CD 唱片及音乐带的信息接触情况/ Information Contact about CD & Music Cassette by Market Segments

注：本题为多选题，合计百分比超过 100%（Multiple answers）

	人数 Number	不管买还是不买，想看看 just have a look, without a definite purpose of buying or not	阅读有关的杂志和专门报道 reading magazines related & special reports	相互口头传播信息 communicate information orally among people	经常看这种商品的广告 often watch advertisements about such kinds of goods	购买这种商品的新类型 buy the latest type of such kinds of goods	过去在这种商品上花了不少钱 used to spend much money on such kinds of goods	今后愿意在这方面花钱 willing to spend money on such items in future	不关注这方面的信息 don't care about such items
样本 Sample	629	40.1	21.3	20.2	23.2	22.4	22.6	36.4	36.6
平实生活指向 simple living orientation	329	32.8	17.0	15.8	17.3	17.3	17.3	28.6	45.0
时尚流行指向 fashion orientation	300	48.0	26.0	25.0	29.7	28.0	28.3	45.0	27.3

3-29 不同消费者层对护肤品和化妆品的信息接触情况/ Information Contact about Skin Cream & Cosmetics by Market Segments

注：本题为多选题，合计百分比超过 100%（Multiple answers）

	人数 Number	不管买还是不买，想看看 just have a look, without a definite purpose of buying or not	阅读有关的杂志和专门报道 reading magazines related & special reports	相互口头传播信息 communicate information orally among people	经常看这种商品的广告 often watch advertisements about such kinds of goods	购买这种商品的新类型 buy the latest type of such kinds of goods	过去在这种商品上花了不少钱 used to spend much money on such kinds of goods	今后愿意在这方面花钱 willing to spend money on such items in future	不关注这方面的信息 don't care about such items
样本 Sample	628	33.4	22.3	21.2	30.7	18.5	20.4	26.6	46.5
平实生活指向 simple living orientation	329	22.8	15.2	13.7	22.8	9.4	12.8	17.6	58.1
时尚流行指向 fashion orientation	299	45.2	30.1	29.4	39.5	28.4	28.8	36.5	33.8

3-30 不同消费者层对香波等洗涤用品的信息接触情况/ Information Contact about Shampoo & Detergent by Market Segments

注：本题为多选题，合计百分比超过 100%（Multiple answers）

	人数 Number	不管买还是不买，想看看 just have a look, without a definite purpose of buying or not	阅读有关的杂志和专门报道 reading magazines related & special reports	相互口头传播信息 communicate information orally among people	经常看这种商品的广告 often watch advertisements about such kinds of goods	购买这种商品的新类型 buy the latest type of such kinds of goods	过去在这种商品上花了不少钱 used to spend much money on such kinds of goods	今后愿意在这方面花钱 willing to spend money on such items in future	不关注这方面的信息 don't care about such items
样本 Sample	630	37.6	20.2	22.1	33.7	27.0	26.7	36.2	33.2
平实生活指向 simple living orientation	330	32.7	13.9	17.6	28.2	20.0	23.0	30.3	38.2
时尚流行指向 fashion orientation	300	43.0	27.0	27.0	39.7	34.7	30.7	42.7	27.7

3-31 不同消费者层对外出就餐的信息接触情况/ Information Contact about Dinning Out by Market Segments

注：本题为多选题，合计百分比超过 100%（Multiple answers）

	人数 Number	阅读有关的杂志和专门报道 reading magazines related and special reports	相互口头传播信息 communicate information orally among people	经常看这种服务的广告 often watch advertisements about such kinds of service	尝试这种服务的新类型 try using the latest type of such kinds of service	过去在这种服务上花了不少钱 used to spend much money on such kinds of service	今后愿意在这方面花钱 willing to spend money on such items in future	不关注这方面的信息 don't care about such items
样本 Sample	628	14.2	25.5	12.9	22.3	23.7	30.3	39.8
平实生活指向 simple living orientation	328	12.2	21.6	11.0	17.4	18.6	23.8	47.9
时尚流行指向 fashion orientation	300	16.3	29.7	15.0	27.7	29.3	37.3	31.0

3-32 不同消费者层对旅行的信息接触情况/ Information Contact about Travelling by Market Segments

注：本题为多选题，合计百分比超过 100%（Multiple answers）

	人数 Number	阅读有关的杂志和专门报道 reading magazines related and special reports	相互口头传播信息 communicate information orally among people	经常看这种服务的广告 often watch advertisements about such kinds of service	尝试这种服务的新类型 try using the latest type of such kinds of service	过去在这种服务上花了不少钱 used to spend much money on such kinds of service	今后愿意在这方面花钱 willing to spend money on such items in future	不关注这方面的信息 don't care about such kinds of service
样本 Sample	631	31.7	26.1	25.0	21.2	19.8	49.9	32.2
平实生活指向 simple living orientation	329	27.4	23.1	23.7	16.7	16.4	44.7	39.2
时尚流行指向 fashion orientation	302	36.4	29.5	26.5	26.2	23.5	55.6	24.5

3-33 不同消费者层对音乐会的信息接触情况/ Information Contact about Concert by Market Segments

注：本题为多选题，合计百分比超过 100%（Multiple answers）

	人数 Number	阅读有关的杂志和专门报道 reading magazines related and special reports	相互口头传播信息 communicate information orally among people	经常看这种服务的广告 often watch advertisements about such kinds of service	尝试这种服务的新类型 try using the latest type of such kinds of service	过去在这种服务上花了不少钱 used to spend much money on such kinds of service	今后愿意在这方面花钱 willing to spend money on such items in future	不关注这方面的信息 don't care about such kinds of service
样本 Sample	631	21.6	15.4	12.8	9.5	6.0	19.8	58.5
平实生活指向 simple living orientation	329	17.6	11.9	10.6	5.8	4.9	16.1	65.7
时尚流行指向 fashion orientation	302	25.8	19.2	15.2	13.6	7.3	23.8	50.7

3-34 不同消费者层对电影的信息接触情况/ Information Contact about Movie by Market Segments

注：本题为多选题，合计百分比超过 100%（Multiple answers）

	人数 Number	阅读有关的杂志和专门报道 reading magazines related and special reports	相互口头传播信息 communicate information orally among people	经常看这种服务的广告 often watch advertise-ments about such kinds of service	尝试这种服务的新类型 try using the latest type of such kinds of service	过去在这种服务上花了不少钱 used to spend much money on such kinds of service	今后愿意在这方面花钱 willing to spend money on such items in future	不关注这方面的信息 don't care about such kinds of service
样本 Sample	632	26.4	25.8	22.3	13.0	13.1	22.5	48.9
平实生活指向 simple living orientation	330	23.6	22.1	18.5	10.3	8.8	19.7	54.8
时尚流行指向 fashion orientation	302	29.5	29.8	26.5	15.9	17.9	25.5	42.4

3-35 不同消费者层对戏剧或戏曲的信息接触情况/ Information Contact about Drama or Opera by Market Segments

注：本题为多选题，合计百分比超过 100%（Multiple answers）

	人数 Number	阅读有关的杂志和专门报道 reading magazines related and special reports	相互口头传播信息 communicate information orally among people	经常看这种服务的广告 often watch advertise-ments about such kinds of service	尝试这种服务的新类型 try using the latest type of such kinds of service	过去在这种服务上花了不少钱 used to spend much money on such kinds of service	今后愿意在这方面花钱 willing to spend money on such items in future	不关注这方面的信息 don't care about such kinds of service
样本 Sample	630	10.6	7.3	7.8	4.1	3.3	6.0	80.6
平实生活指向 simple living orientation	329	10.9	6.4	8.2	3.3	2.1	5.8	81.2
时尚流行指向 fashion orientation	301	10.3	8.3	7.3	5.0	4.7	6.3	80.1

3-36 不同消费者层对蹦迪的信息接触情况/ Information Contact about Disco by Market Segments

注：本题为多选题，合计百分比超过 100%（Multiple answers）

	人数 Number	阅读有关的杂志和专门报道 reading magazines related and special reports	相互口头传播信息 communicate information orally among people	经常看这种服务的广告 often watch advertise-ments about such kinds of service	尝试这种服务的新类型 try using the latest type of such kinds of service	过去在这种服务上花了不少钱 used to spend much money on such kinds of service	今后愿意在这方面花钱 willing to spend money on such items in future	不关注这方面的信息 don't care about such kinds of service
样本 Sample	628	4.9	6.4	4.5	7.5	5.3	10.0	80.1
平实生活指向 simple living orientation	328	2.7	3.0	2.4	3.7	1.8	4.6	89.3
时尚流行指向 fashion orientation	300	7.3	10.0	6.7	11.7	9.0	16.0	70.0

3-37 不同消费者层对现场观赏体育比赛的信息接触情况/ Information Contact about Enjoying Live Sports by Market Segments

注：本题为多选题，合计百分比超过 100%（Multiple answers）

	人数 Number	阅读有关的杂志和专门报道 reading magazines related and special reports	相互口头传播信息 communicate information orally among people	经常看这种服务的广告 often watch advertise-ments about such kinds of service	尝试这种服务的新类型 try using the latest type of such kinds of service	过去在这种服务上花了不少钱 used to spend much money on such kinds of service	今后愿意在这方面花钱 willing to spend money on such items in future	不关注这方面的信息 don't care about such kinds of service
样本 Sample	629	30.7	26.7	20.5	11.3	9.4	25.4	47.1
平实生活指向 simple living orientation	329	28.3	24.0	17.3	8.8	7.0	22.5	50.8
时尚流行指向 fashion orientation	300	33.3	29.7	24.0	14.0	12.0	28.7	43.0

3-38 不同消费者层对运动健身的信息接触情况/ Information Contact about Gym by Market Segments

注：本题为多选题，合计百分比超过 100%（Multiple answers）

	人数 Number	阅读有关的杂志和专门报道 reading magazines related and special reports	相互口头传播信息 communicate information orally among people	经常看这种服务的广告 often watch advertisements about such kinds of service	尝试这种服务的新类型 try using the latest type of such kinds of service	过去在这种服务上花了不少钱 used to spend much money on such kinds of service	今后愿意在这方面花钱 willing to spend money on such items in future	不关注这方面的信息 don't care about such kinds of service
样本 Sample	629	24.6	18.0	20.0	15.9	7.3	32.6	46.3
平实生活指向 simple living orientation	330	21.8	17.0	19.7	12.7	6.1	30.0	50.3
时尚流行指向 fashion orientation	299	27.8	19.1	20.4	19.4	8.7	35.5	41.8

3-39 不同消费者层对技能学习的信息接触情况/ Information Contact about Studying Skills by Market Segments

注：本题为多选题，合计百分比超过 100%（Multiple answers）

	人数 Number	阅读有关的杂志和专门报道 reading magazines related and special reports	相互口头传播信息 communicate information orally among people	经常看这种服务的广告 often watch advertisements about such kinds of service	尝试这种服务的新类型 try using the latest type of such kinds of service	过去在这种服务上花了不少钱 used to spend much money on such kinds of service	今后愿意在这方面花钱 willing to spend money on such items in future	不关注这方面的信息 don't care about such kinds of service
样本 Sample	629	28.6	18.3	16.4	13.2	12.6	33.2	47.2
平实生活指向 simple living orientation	329	26.4	16.4	14.3	10.0	9.7	29.5	50.2
时尚流行指向 fashion orientation	300	31.0	20.3	18.7	16.7	15.7	37.3	44.0

3-40 不同消费者层对外语学习的信息接触情况/ Information Contact about Studying Foreign Languages by Market Segments

注：本题为多选题，合计百分比超过 100%（Multiple answers）

	人数 Number	阅读有关的杂志和专门报道 reading magazines related and special reports	相互口头传播信息 communicate information orally among people	经常看这种服务的广告 often watch advertisements about such kinds of service	尝试这种服务的新类型 try using the latest type of such kinds of service	过去在这种服务上花了不少钱 used to spend much money on such kinds of service	今后愿意在这方面花钱 willing to spend money on such items in future	不关注这方面的信息 don't care about such kinds of service
样本 Sample	630	17.8	10.2	9.4	6.0	6.8	25.9	63.7
平实生活指向 simple living orientation	329	18.2	8.8	7.3	4.9	6.4	23.7	66.0
时尚流行指向 fashion orientation	301	17.3	11.6	11.6	7.3	7.3	28.2	61.1

● 西安 / Xi'an

3-1 样本、男性各年龄层、女性各年龄层对电视、音响等视听设备的信息接触情况/ Information Contact about Video & Audio Equipment by the Whole Sample, Age and Gender Groups

注：本题为多选题，合计百分比超过 100%（Multiple answers）

	人数 Number	不管买还是不买，想看看 just have a look, without a definite purpose of buying or not	阅读有关的杂志和专门报道 reading magazines related & special reports	相互口头传播信息 communicate information orally among people	经常看这种商品的广告 often watch advertisements about such kinds of goods	购买这种商品的新类型 buy the latest type of such kinds of goods	过去在这种商品上花了不少钱 used to spend much money on such kinds of goods	今后愿意在这方面花钱 willing to spend money on such items in future	不关注这方面的信息 don't care about such items
样本 Sample	598	48.3	19.7	18.2	36.6	10.5	22.2	19.4	18.4
男性 Male	300	54.3	24.3	19.0	40.0	12.7	23.7	20.7	15.0
16~24 岁 Age	64	56.3	20.3	18.8	42.2	7.8	7.8	17.2	14.1
25~34 岁 Age	89	61.8	20.2	12.4	29.2	5.6	23.6	19.1	15.7
35~44 岁 Age	77	54.5	24.7	24.7	48.1	16.9	33.8	24.7	11.7
45~54 岁 Age	46	52.2	41.3	23.9	45.7	26.1	37.0	23.9	10.9
55~60 岁 Age	24	25.0	16.7	16.7	37.5	12.5	8.3	16.7	33.3
女性 Female	298	42.3	15.1	17.4	33.2	8.4	20.8	18.1	21.8
16~24 岁 Age	61	41.0	11.5	18.0	34.4	8.2	11.5	19.7	19.7
25~34 岁 Age	89	43.8	19.1	23.6	34.8	6.7	19.1	16.9	19.1
35~44 岁 Age	74	45.9	13.5	23.0	36.5	10.8	28.4	14.9	16.2
45~54 岁 Age	49	38.8	12.2	6.1	22.4	8.2	22.4	20.4	30.6
55~60 岁 Age	25	36.0	20.0	0.0	36.0	8.0	24.0	24.0	36.0

3-2 样本、男性各年龄层、女性各年龄层对冰箱、洗衣机等白色家电的信息接触情况/ Information Contact about "White Home Electronic Products" by the Whole Sample, Age and Gender Groups

注：本题为多选题，合计百分比超过 100%（Multiple answers）

	人数 Number	不管买还是不买，想看看 just have a look, without a definite purpose of buying or not	阅读有关的杂志和专门报道 reading magazines related & special reports	相互口头传播信息 communicate information orally among people	经常看这种商品的广告 often watch advertisements about such kinds of goods	购买这种商品的新类型 buy the latest type of such kinds of goods	过去在这种商品上花了不少钱 used to spend much money on such kinds of goods	今后愿意在这方面花钱 willing to spend money on such items in future	不关注这方面的信息 don't care about such items
样本 Sample	601	31.4	15.5	17.1	30.0	9.5	16.8	16.1	30.1
男性 Male	302	32.1	18.5	18.5	32.1	11.6	18.5	16.9	28.1
16~24 岁 Age	64	23.4	12.5	9.4	34.4	6.3	7.8	10.9	32.8
25~34 岁 Age	91	29.7	16.5	16.5	24.2	8.8	16.5	17.6	29.7
35~44 岁 Age	77	40.3	18.2	22.1	32.5	16.9	24.7	22.1	26.0
45~54 岁 Age	46	32.6	28.3	28.3	37.0	19.6	30.4	15.2	26.1
55~60 岁 Age	24	37.5	25.0	20.8	45.8	4.2	12.5	16.7	20.8
女性 Female	299	30.8	12.4	15.7	27.8	7.4	15.1	15.4	32.1
16~24 岁 Age	61	23.0	13.1	6.6	24.6	9.8	6.6	16.4	37.7
25~34 岁 Age	90	33.3	12.2	13.3	33.3	4.4	17.8	13.3	31.1
35~44 岁 Age	74	29.7	9.5	25.7	28.4	6.8	18.9	13.5	27.0
45~54 岁 Age	49	36.7	10.2	16.3	22.4	12.2	12.2	16.3	34.7
55~60 岁 Age	25	32.0	24.0	16.0	24.0	4.0	20.0	24.0	32.0

3-3 样本、男性各年龄层、女性各年龄层对电脑等通讯工具的信息接触情况/ Information Contact about Computer & Telecommunications by the Whole Sample, Age and Gender Groups

注：本题为多选题，合计百分比超过 100%（Multiple answers）

	人数 Number	不管买还是不买，想看看 just have a look, without a definite purpose of buying or not	阅读有关的杂志和专门报道 reading magazines related & special reports	相互口头传播信息 communicate informatio n orally among people	经常看这种商品的广告 often watch advertisements about such kinds of goods	购买这种商品的新类型 buy the latest type of such kinds of goods	过去在这种商品上花了不少钱 used to spend much money on such kinds of goods	今后愿意在这方面花钱 willing to spend money on such items in future	不关注这方面的信息 don't care about such items
样本 Sample	600	29.2	20.2	17.5	21.8	7.7	4.7	27.3	37.8
男性 Male	301	33.9	25.6	20.9	28.2	11.6	7.3	31.9	27.6
16~24 岁 Age	63	39.7	31.7	28.6	31.7	11.1	11.1	41.3	11.1
25~34 岁 Age	91	31.9	31.9	19.8	29.7	13.2	8.8	36.3	20.9
35~44 岁 Age	77	33.8	18.2	18.2	23.4	9.1	3.9	29.9	36.4
45~54 岁 Age	46	41.3	21.7	23.9	32.6	15.2	8.7	23.9	37.0
55~60 岁 Age	24	12.5	16.7	8.3	20.8	8.3	0.0	12.5	50.0
女性 Female	299	24.4	14.7	14.0	15.4	3.7	2.0	22.7	48.2
16~24 岁 Age	61	36.1	21.3	21.3	23.0	1.6	3.3	34.4	26.2
25~34 岁 Age	90	27.8	16.7	14.4	21.1	3.3	2.2	28.9	36.7
35~44 岁 Age	74	23.0	12.2	13.5	9.5	6.8	2.7	14.9	56.8
45~54 岁 Age	49	14.3	8.2	6.1	8.2	0.0	0.0	18.4	71.4
55~60 岁 Age	25	8.0	12.0	12.0	8.0	8.0	0.0	4.0	72.0

3-4 样本、男性各年龄层、女性各年龄层对家用轿车的信息接触情况/ Information Contact about Family Car by the Whole Sample, Age and Gender Groups

注：本题为多选题，合计百分比超过 100%（Multiple answers）

	人数 Number	不管买还是不买，想看看 just have a look, without a definite purpose of buying or not	阅读有关的杂志和专门报道 reading magazines related & special reports	相互口头传播信息 communicate information orally among people	经常看这种商品的广告 often watch advertisements about such kinds of goods	购买这种商品的新类型 buy the latest type of such kinds of goods	过去在这种商品上花了不少钱 used to spend much money on such kinds of goods	今后愿意在这方面花钱 willing to spend money on such items in future	不关注这方面的信息 don't care about such items
样本 Sample	599	17.9	10.5	9.0	12.2	2.2	1.7	11.0	61.9
男性 Male	300	23.7	16.3	13.0	15.7	2.3	1.7	16.7	51.0
16~24 岁 Age	62	29.0	24.2	14.5	14.5	0.0	0.0	14.5	46.8
25~34 岁 Age	91	25.3	16.5	13.2	15.4	5.5	3.3	19.8	45.1
35~44 岁 Age	77	24.7	16.9	15.6	15.6	1.3	1.3	19.5	48.1
45~54 岁 Age	46	17.4	8.7	13.0	21.7	2.2	2.2	13.0	58.7
55~60 岁 Age	24	12.5	8.3	0.0	8.3	0.0	0.0	8.3	79.2
女性 Female	299	12.0	4.7	5.0	8.7	2.0	1.7	5.4	72.9
16~24 岁 Age	61	19.7	6.6	4.9	9.8	3.3	0.0	4.9	63.9
25~34 岁 Age	90	18.9	6.7	6.7	7.8	3.3	4.4	11.1	62.2
35~44 岁 Age	74	2.7	0.0	2.7	9.5	1.4	1.4	0.0	87.8
45~54 岁 Age	49	8.2	4.1	4.1	8.2	0.0	0.0	2.0	75.5
55~60 岁 Age	25	4.0	8.0	8.0	8.0	0.0	0.0	8.0	84.0

3-5 样本、男性各年龄层、女性各年龄层对高级家具的信息接触情况/ Information Contact about First-class Furniture by the Whole Sample, Age and Gender Groups

注：本题为多选题，合计百分比超过 100%（Multiple answers）

	人数 Number	不管买还是不买，想看看 just have a look, without a definite purpose of buying or not	阅读有关的杂志和专门报道 reading magazines related & special reports	相互口头传播信息 communicate information orally among people	经常看这种商品的广告 often watch advertisements about such kinds of goods	购买这种商品的新类型 buy the latest type of such kinds of goods	过去在这种商品上花了不少钱 used to spend much money on such kinds of goods	今后愿意在这方面花钱 willing to spend money on such items in future	不关注这方面的信息 don't care about such items
样本 Sample	601	28.1	7.8	7.8	10.3	4.8	3.7	17.1	49.9
男性 Male	302	25.5	8.9	7.9	11.6	6.3	4.6	17.9	48.3
16~24 岁 Age	64	17.2	6.3	7.8	10.9	4.7	1.6	15.6	59.4
25~34 岁 Age	91	23.1	11.0	8.8	12.1	8.8	11.0	24.2	40.7
35~44 岁 Age	77	37.7	10.4	7.8	11.7	3.9	2.6	19.5	44.2
45~54 岁 Age	46	17.4	8.7	10.9	13.0	10.9	2.2	13.0	52.2
55~60 岁 Age	24	33.3	4.2	0.0	8.3	0.0	0.0	4.2	54.2
女性 Female	299	30.8	6.7	7.7	9.0	3.3	2.7	16.4	51.5
16~24 岁 Age	61	27.9	6.6	6.6	8.2	4.9	4.9	23.0	45.9
25~34 岁 Age	90	37.8	11.1	12.2	10.0	4.4	5.6	18.9	41.1
35~44 岁 Age	74	24.3	4.1	1.4	6.8	1.4	0.0	12.2	60.8
45~54 岁 Age	49	32.7	2.0	8.2	10.2	2.0	0.0	10.2	59.2
55~60 岁 Age	25	28.0	8.0	12.0	12.0	4.0	0.0	16.0	60.0

3-6 样本、男性各年龄层、女性各年龄层对西服和时装的信息接触情况/ Information Contact about Business Suit & Fashion by the Whole Sample, Age and Gender Groups

注：本题为多选题，合计百分比超过 100%（Multiple answers）

	人数 Number	不管买还是不买，想看看 just have a look, without a definite purpose of buying or not	阅读有关的杂志和专门报道 reading magazines related & special reports	相互口头传播信息 communicate information orally among people	经常看这种商品的广告 often watch advertisements about such kinds of goods	购买这种商品的新类型 buy the latest type of such kinds of goods	过去在这种商品上花了不少钱 used to spend much money on such kinds of goods	今后愿意在这方面花钱 willing to spend money on such items in future	不关注这方面的信息 don't care about such items
样本 Sample	601	40.8	17.6	17.0	19.3	15.3	17.6	25.3	29.0
男性 Male	302	32.1	11.6	9.9	13.9	10.9	15.9	25.2	35.8
16~24 岁 Age	64	31.3	10.9	10.9	10.9	6.3	20.3	28.1	34.4
25~34 岁 Age	91	30.8	12.1	11.0	13.2	15.4	16.5	26.4	27.5
35~44 岁 Age	77	31.2	13.0	7.8	15.6	7.8	16.9	32.5	35.1
45~54 岁 Age	46	37.0	10.9	8.7	17.4	13.0	15.2	17.4	43.5
55~60 岁 Age	24	33.3	8.3	12.5	12.5	12.5	0.0	4.2	58.3
女性 Female	299	49.5	23.7	24.1	24.7	19.7	19.4	25.4	22.1
16~24 岁 Age	61	50.8	29.5	23.0	31.1	23.0	27.9	37.7	8.2
25~34 岁 Age	90	63.3	31.1	30.0	27.8	26.7	23.3	28.9	11.1
35~44 岁 Age	74	50.0	18.9	29.7	24.3	10.8	14.9	17.6	27.0
45~54 岁 Age	49	34.7	14.3	10.2	16.3	18.4	14.3	22.4	36.7
55~60 岁 Age	25	24.0	16.0	16.0	16.0	16.0	8.0	12.0	52.0

3-7 样本、男性各年龄层、女性各年龄层对酒精饮料的信息接触情况/ Information Contact about Alcohol Drinks by the Whole Sample, Age and Gender Groups

注：本题为多选题，合计百分比超过 100%（Multiple answers）

	人数 Number	不管买还是不买，想看看 just have a look, without a definite purpose of buying or not	阅读有关的杂志和专门报道 reading magazines related & special reports	相互口头传播信息 communicate information orally among people	经常看这种商品的广告 often watch advertisements about such kinds of goods	购买这种商品的新类型 buy the latest type of such kinds of goods	过去在这种商品上花了不少钱 used to spend much money on such kinds of goods	今后愿意在这方面花钱 willing to spend money on such items in future	不关注这方面的信息 don't care about such items
样本 Sample	**598**	**16.6**	**6.7**	**14.9**	**20.9**	**8.4**	**16.6**	**12.7**	**47.2**
男性 Male	**301**	**20.9**	**8.6**	**16.6**	**19.6**	**10.0**	**21.9**	**17.9**	**38.5**
16~24 岁 Age	64	10.9	4.7	7.8	15.6	10.9	14.1	12.5	50.0
25~34 岁 Age	91	19.8	8.8	14.3	17.6	11.0	18.7	17.6	36.3
35~44 岁 Age	77	33.8	9.1	23.4	24.7	11.7	29.9	22.1	31.2
45~54 岁 Age	46	17.4	4.3	17.4	21.7	2.2	26.1	17.4	37.0
55~60 岁 Age	23	17.4	26.1	26.1	17.4	13.0	21.7	21.7	43.5
女性 Female	**297**	**12.1**	**4.7**	**13.1**	**22.2**	**6.7**	**11.1**	**7.4**	**55.9**
16~24 岁 Age	61	13.1	3.3	11.5	26.2	4.9	9.8	9.8	50.8
25~34 岁 Age	89	13.5	4.5	12.4	20.2	7.9	9.0	6.7	57.3
35~44 岁 Age	73	8.2	5.5	16.4	26.0	2.7	6.8	5.5	57.5
45~54 岁 Age	49	20.4	8.2	14.3	18.4	14.3	18.4	8.2	53.1
55~60 岁 Age	25	0.0	0.0	8.0	16.0	4.0	20.0	8.0	64.0

3-8 样本、男性各年龄层、女性各年龄层对 CD 唱片及音乐带的信息接触情况/ Information Contact about CD & Music Cassette by the Whole Sample, Age and Gender Groups

注：本题为多选题，合计百分比超过 100%（Multiple answers）

	人数 Number	不管买还是不买，想看看 just have a look, without a definite purpose of buying or not	阅读有关的杂志和专门报道 reading magazines related & special reports	相互口头传播信息 communicate information orally among people	经常看这种商品的广告 often watch advertisements about such kinds of goods	购买这种商品的新类型 buy the latest type of such kinds of goods	过去在这种商品上花了不少钱 used to spend much money on such kinds of goods	今后愿意在这方面花钱 willing to spend money on such items in future	不关注这方面的信息 don't care about such items
样本 Sample	**598**	**26.4**	**13.5**	**14.5**	**13.0**	**12.4**	**13.7**	**18.1**	**42.8**
男性 Male	**302**	**25.2**	**14.9**	**13.2**	**13.6**	**12.6**	**15.9**	**20.5**	**41.4**
16~24 岁 Age	64	39.1	25.0	21.9	18.8	20.3	23.4	35.9	15.6
25~34 岁 Age	91	25.3	15.4	13.2	17.6	12.1	17.6	22.0	40.7
35~44 岁 Age	77	19.5	7.8	10.4	9.1	10.4	13.0	15.6	44.2
45~54 岁 Age	46	21.7	15.2	13.0	13.0	13.0	15.2	15.2	52.2
55~60 岁 Age	24	12.5	8.3	0.0	0.0	0.0	0.0	0.0	83.3
女性 Female	**296**	**27.7**	**12.2**	**15.9**	**12.5**	**12.2**	**11.5**	**15.5**	**44.3**
16~24 岁 Age	61	44.3	19.7	31.1	16.4	16.4	18.0	23.0	14.8
25~34 岁 Age	90	27.8	13.3	20.0	14.4	20.0	11.1	18.9	34.4
35~44 岁 Age	71	19.7	7.0	5.6	9.9	5.6	11.3	9.9	62.0
45~54 岁 Age	49	22.4	8.2	6.1	6.1	2.0	8.2	10.2	63.3
55~60 岁 Age	25	20.0	12.0	12.0	16.0	12.0	4.0	12.0	64.0

3-9 样本、男性各年龄层、女性各年龄层对护肤品和化妆品的信息接触情况/ Information Contact about Skin Cream & Cosmetics by the Whole Sample, Age and Gender Groups

注：本题为多选题，合计百分比超过 100%（Multiple answers）

	人数 Number	不管买还是不买，想看看 just have a look, without a definite purpose of buying or not	阅读有关的杂志和专门报道 reading magazines related & special reports	相互口头传播信息 communicate information orally among people	经常看这种商品的广告 often watch advertisements about such kinds of goods	购买这种商品的新类型 buy the latest type of such kinds of goods	过去在这种商品上花了不少钱 used to spend much money on such kinds of goods	今后愿意在这方面花钱 willing to spend money on such items in future	不关注这方面的信息 don't care about such items
样本 Sample	599	28.5	14.4	16.5	27.5	11.2	16.0	21.7	44.7
男性 Male	301	9.6	4.0	3.7	14.0	4.3	4.3	7.6	73.4
16~24 岁 Age	64	9.4	7.8	6.3	20.3	7.8	1.6	7.8	65.6
25~34 岁 Age	91	8.8	4.4	3.3	9.9	3.3	5.5	6.6	73.6
35~44 岁 Age	76	10.5	0.0	2.6	11.8	2.6	3.9	5.3	80.3
45~54 岁 Age	46	8.7	6.5	4.3	17.4	6.5	6.5	15.2	71.7
55~60 岁 Age	24	12.5	0.0	0.0	12.5	0.0	4.2	4.2	75.0
女性 Female	298	47.7	24.8	29.5	41.3	18.1	27.9	35.9	15.8
16~24 岁 Age	61	54.1	37.7	32.8	44.3	26.2	39.3	49.2	1.6
25~34 岁 Age	90	58.9	27.8	33.3	44.4	18.9	31.1	42.2	6.7
35~44 岁 Age	74	54.1	24.3	33.8	45.9	16.2	29.7	36.5	10.8
45~54 岁 Age	49	30.6	16.3	14.3	30.6	16.3	14.3	16.3	40.8
55~60 岁 Age	24	4.2	0.0	25.0	29.2	4.2	8.3	16.7	50.0

3-10 样本、男性各年龄层、女性各年龄层对香波等洗涤用品的信息接触情况/ Information Contact about Shampoo & Detergent Cassette by the Whole Sample, Age and Gender Groups

注：本题为多选题，合计百分比超过 100%（Multiple answers）

	人数 Number	不管买还是不买，想看看 just have a look, without a definite purpose of buying or not	阅读有关的杂志和专门报道 reading magazines related & special reports	相互口头传播信息 communicate information orally among people	经常看这种商品的广告 often watch advertisements about such kinds of goods	购买这种商品的新类型 buy the latest type of such kinds of goods	过去在这种商品上花了不少钱 used to spend much money on such kinds of goods	今后愿意在这方面花钱 willing to spend money on such items in future	不关注这方面的信息 don't care about such items
样本 Sample	600	28.5	9.2	17.5	32.0	15.7	15.2	20.5	35.2
男性 Male	302	13.6	4.6	5.3	21.9	8.6	6.6	12.6	59.6
16~24 岁 Age	64	9.4	7.8	3.1	26.6	14.1	3.1	14.1	53.1
25~34 岁 Age	91	9.9	2.2	6.6	16.5	6.6	6.6	12.1	64.8
35~44 岁 Age	77	19.5	1.3	2.6	27.3	6.5	10.4	14.3	57.1
45~54 岁 Age	46	15.2	10.9	6.5	17.4	10.9	8.7	10.9	63.0
55~60 岁 Age	24	16.7	4.2	12.5	20.8	4.2	0.0	8.3	58.3
女性 Female	298	43.6	13.8	29.9	42.3	22.8	23.8	28.5	10.4
16~24 岁 Age	61	42.6	11.5	29.5	42.6	23.0	26.2	34.4	4.9
25~34 岁 Age	89	44.9	13.5	28.1	49.4	21.3	21.3	30.3	10.1
35~44 岁 Age	74	48.6	17.6	37.8	36.5	25.7	23.0	24.3	8.1
45~54 岁 Age	49	34.7	16.3	24.5	36.7	18.4	24.5	30.6	18.4
55~60 岁 Age	25	44.0	4.0	24.0	44.0	28.0	28.0	16.0	16.0

3-11 样本、男性各年龄层、女性各年龄层对外出就餐的信息接触情况/ Information Contact about Dinning Out by the Whole Sample, Age and Gender Groups

注：本题为多选题，合计百分比超过 100%（Multiple answers）

	人数 Number	阅读有关的杂志和专门报道 reading magazines related and special reports	相互口头传播信息 communicate information orally among people	经常看这种服务的广告 often watch advertisements about such kinds of service	尝试这种服务的新类型 buy the latest type of such kinds of service	过去在这种服务上花了不少钱 used to spend much money on such kinds of service	今后愿意在这方面花钱 willing to spend money on such items in future	不关注这方面的信息 don't care about such items
样本 Sample	601	11.5	24.5	15.0	18.6	20.3	27.5	35.1
男性 Male	302	11.6	21.5	14.6	18.2	23.2	27.2	33.4
16~24 岁 Age	64	7.8	17.2	12.5	14.1	10.9	25.0	37.5
25~34 岁 Age	91	7.7	30.8	13.2	19.8	26.4	30.8	28.6
35~44 岁 Age	77	7.8	16.9	19.5	20.8	33.8	26.0	33.8
45~54 岁 Age	46	26.1	17.4	13.0	23.9	23.9	28.3	32.6
55~60 岁 Age	24	20.8	20.8	12.5	4.2	8.3	20.8	41.7
女性 Female	299	11.4	27.4	15.4	19.1	17.4	27.8	36.8
16~24 岁 Age	61	11.5	21.3	18.0	19.7	16.4	34.4	31.1
25~34 岁 Age	90	13.3	45.6	18.9	28.9	28.9	33.3	15.6
35~44 岁 Age	74	9.5	21.6	14.9	13.5	12.2	25.7	48.6
45~54 岁 Age	49	12.2	16.3	10.2	10.2	6.1	18.4	55.1
55~60 岁 Age	25	8.0	16.0	8.0	16.0	16.0	16.0	56.0

3-12 样本、男性各年龄层、女性各年龄层对旅行的信息接触情况/ Information Contact about Travelling by the Whole Sample, Age and Gender Groups

注：本题为多选题，合计百分比超过 100%（Multiple answers）

	人数 Number	阅读有关的杂志和专门报道 reading magazines related and special reports	相互口头传播信息 communicate information orally among people	经常看这种服务的广告 often watch advertisements about such kinds of service	尝试这种服务的新类型 try using the latest type of such kinds of service	过去在这种服务上花了不少钱 used to spend much money on such kinds of service	今后愿意在这方面花钱 willing to spend money on such items in future	不关注这方面的信息 don't care about such kinds of service
样本 Sample	600	24.5	24.3	16.2	14.7	14.8	46.3	26.5
男性 Male	302	23.5	24.8	17.2	16.6	17.5	46.0	25.8
16~24 岁 Age	64	20.3	21.9	15.6	25.0	12.5	46.9	28.1
25~34 岁 Age	91	24.2	29.7	18.7	12.1	16.5	58.2	15.4
35~44 岁 Age	77	23.4	24.7	15.6	15.6	19.5	40.3	29.9
45~54 岁 Age	46	21.7	21.7	17.4	15.2	26.1	34.8	34.8
55~60 岁 Age	24	33.3	20.8	20.8	16.7	12.5	37.5	29.2
女性 Female	298	25.5	23.8	15.1	12.8	12.1	46.6	27.2
16~24 岁 Age	61	29.5	26.2	11.5	16.4	8.2	54.1	19.7
25~34 岁 Age	90	32.2	31.1	16.7	13.3	13.3	53.3	17.8
35~44 岁 Age	74	16.2	23.0	14.9	12.2	10.8	43.2	31.1
45~54 岁 Age	48	20.8	12.5	14.6	10.4	10.4	39.6	35.4
55~60 岁 Age	25	28.0	16.0	20.0	8.0	24.0	28.0	52.0

3-13 样本、男性各年龄层、女性各年龄层对音乐会的信息接触情况/ Information Contact about Concert by the Whole Sample, Age and Gender Groups

注：本题为多选题，合计百分比超过 100%（Multiple answers）

	人数 Number	阅读有关的杂志和专门报道 reading magazines related and special reports	相互口头传播信息 communicate information orally among people	经常看这种服务的广告 often watch advertisements about such kinds of service	尝试这种服务的新类型 try using the latest type of such kinds of service	过去在这种服务上花了不少钱 used to spend much money on such kinds of service	今后愿意在这方面花钱 willing to spend money on such items in future	不关注这方面的信息 don't care about such kinds of service
样本 Sample	600	14.7	13.2	10.8	7.2	5.8	11.7	60.8
男性 Male	301	13.6	11.3	11.6	8.3	7.0	10.3	62.1
16~24 岁 Age	64	18.8	29.7	18.8	12.5	4.7	15.6	42.2
25~34 岁 Age	91	9.9	7.7	8.8	9.9	6.6	9.9	67.0
35~44 岁 Age	76	17.1	5.3	6.6	6.6	9.2	9.2	67.1
45~54 岁 Age	46	13.0	6.5	17.4	4.3	8.7	8.7	65.2
55~60 岁 Age	24	4.2	4.2	8.3	4.2	4.2	4.2	75.0
女性 Female	299	15.7	15.1	10.0	6.0	4.7	13.0	59.5
16~24 岁 Age	61	19.7	24.6	9.8	9.8	4.9	19.7	44.3
25~34 岁 Age	90	21.1	15.6	14.4	8.9	4.4	13.3	50.0
35~44 岁 Age	74	17.6	10.8	8.1	1.4	5.4	8.1	67.6
45~54 岁 Age	49	4.1	12.2	8.2	6.1	4.1	14.3	71.4
55~60 岁 Age	25	4.0	8.0	4.0	0.0	4.0	8.0	84.0

3-14 样本、男性各年龄层、女性各年龄层对电影的信息接触情况/ Information Contact about Movie by the Whole Sample, Age and Gender Groups

注：本题为多选题，合计百分比超过 100%（Multiple answers）

	人数 Number	阅读有关的杂志和专门报道 reading magazines related and special reports	相互口头传播信息 communicate information orally among people	经常看这种服务的广告 often watch advertisements about such kinds of service	尝试这种服务的新类型 try using the latest type of such kinds of service	过去在这种服务上花了不少钱 used to spend much money on such kinds of service	今后愿意在这方面花钱 willing to spend money on such items in future	不关注这方面的信息 don't care about such kinds of service
样本 Sample	601	26.5	21.3	17.3	12.0	16.3	16.0	41.4
男性 Male	302	28.1	18.2	17.2	13.2	16.9	17.5	40.4
16~24 岁 Age	64	42.2	37.5	25.0	14.1	31.3	23.4	17.2
25~34 岁 Age	91	31.9	18.7	9.9	15.4	12.1	18.7	40.7
35~44 岁 Age	77	26.0	10.4	15.6	10.4	14.3	13.0	46.8
45~54 岁 Age	46	13.0	13.0	26.1	15.2	19.6	17.4	47.8
55~60 岁 Age	24	12.5	0.0	12.5	8.3	0.0	12.5	66.7
女性 Female	299	24.7	24.4	17.4	10.7	15.7	14.4	42.5
16~24 岁 Age	61	36.1	32.8	26.2	16.4	19.7	21.3	23.0
25~34 岁 Age	90	27.8	35.6	22.2	13.3	23.3	21.1	28.9
35~44 岁 Age	74	23.0	12.2	14.9	6.8	12.2	8.1	58.1
45~54 岁 Age	49	10.2	16.3	6.1	4.1	6.1	6.1	61.2
55~60 岁 Age	25	20.0	16.0	8.0	12.0	8.0	8.0	56.0

3-15 样本、男性各年龄层、女性各年龄层对戏剧或戏曲的信息接触情况/ Information Contact about Drama or Opera by the Whole Sample, Age and Gender Groups

注：本题为多选题，合计百分比超过 100%（Multiple answers）

	人数 Number	阅读有关的杂志和专门报道 reading magazines related and special reports	相互口头传播信息 communicate information orally among people	经常看这种服务的广告 often watch advertisements about such kinds of service	尝试这种服务的新类型 try using the latest type of such kinds of service	过去在这种服务上花了不少钱 used to spend much money on such kinds of service	今后愿意在这方面花钱 willing to spend money on such items in future	不关注这方面的信息 don't care about such kinds of service
样本 Sample	**601**	**10.6**	**8.2**	**6.7**	**6.5**	**5.7**	**6.3**	**74.7**
男性 Male	**302**	**10.6**	**6.3**	**6.0**	**5.6**	**5.0**	**4.3**	**76.2**
16~24 岁 Age	64	7.8	3.1	4.7	1.6	1.6	1.6	82.8
25~34 岁 Age	91	8.8	1.1	4.4	3.3	6.6	0.0	83.5
35~44 岁 Age	77	6.5	2.6	5.2	5.2	3.9	6.5	80.5
45~54 岁 Age	46	6.5	13.0	6.5	10.9	6.5	4.3	71.7
55~60 岁 Age	24	45.8	33.3	16.7	16.7	8.3	20.8	25.0
女性 Female	**299**	**10.7**	**10.0**	**7.4**	**7.4**	**6.4**	**8.4**	**73.2**
16~24 岁 Age	61	4.9	1.6	0.0	3.3	0.0	0.0	91.8
25~34 岁 Age	90	7.8	4.4	6.7	4.4	3.3	3.3	81.1
35~44 岁 Age	74	8.1	6.8	6.8	8.1	4.1	4.1	81.1
45~54 岁 Age	49	18.4	22.4	12.2	12.2	12.2	26.5	49.0
55~60 岁 Age	25	28.0	36.0	20.0	16.0	28.0	24.0	24.0

3-16 样本、男性各年龄层、女性各年龄层对蹦迪的信息接触情况/ Information Contact about Disco by the Whole Sample, Age and Gender Groups

注：本题为多选题，合计百分比超过 100%（Multiple answers）

	人数 Number	阅读有关的杂志和专门报道 reading magazines related and special reports	相互口头传播信息 communicate information orally among people	经常看这种服务的广告 often watch advertisements about such kinds of service	尝试这种服务的新类型 try using the latest type of such kinds of service	过去在这种服务上花了不少钱 used to spend much money on such kinds of service	今后愿意在这方面花钱 willing to spend money on such items in future	不关注这方面的信息 don't care about such kinds of service
样本 Sample	**600**	**2.7**	**7.0**	**3.0**	**7.3**	**6.3**	**6.8**	**76.7**
男性 Male	**301**	**2.0**	**5.6**	**2.3**	**6.6**	**5.3**	**5.6**	**78.4**
16~24 岁 Age	63	6.3	15.9	3.2	17.5	4.8	9.5	58.7
25~34 岁 Age	91	2.2	5.5	4.4	3.3	7.7	9.9	73.6
35~44 岁 Age	77	0.0	1.3	1.3	3.9	6.5	2.6	87.0
45~54 岁 Age	46	0.0	2.2	0.0	6.5	0.0	0.0	91.3
55~60 岁 Age	24	0.0	0.0	0.0	0.0	4.2	0.0	95.8
女性 Female	**299**	**3.3**	**8.4**	**3.7**	**8.0**	**7.4**	**8.0**	**74.9**
16~24 岁 Age	61	8.2	18.0	6.6	8.2	8.2	26.2	47.5
25~34 岁 Age	90	3.3	8.9	5.6	16.7	14.4	7.8	65.6
35~44 岁 Age	74	1.4	2.7	1.4	2.7	4.1	1.4	90.5
45~54 岁 Age	49	0.0	0.0	0.0	2.0	0.0	0.0	98.0
55~60 岁 Age	25	4.0	16.0	4.0	4.0	4.0	0.0	84.0

3-17 样本、男性各年龄层、女性各年龄层对现场观赏体育比赛的信息接触情况/ Information Contact about Enjoying Live Sports by the Whole Sample, Age and Gender Groups

注：本题为多选题，合计百分比超过 100%（Multiple answers）

	人数 Number	阅读有关的杂志和专门报道 reading magazines related and special reports	相互口头传播信息 communicate information orally among people	经常看这种服务的广告 often watch advertisements about such kinds of service	尝试这种服务的新类型 try using the latest type of such kinds of service	过去在这种服务上花了不少钱 used to spend much money on such kinds of service	今后愿意在这方面花钱 willing to spend money on such items in future	不关注这方面的信息 don't care about such kinds of service
样本 Sample	598	25.1	19.9	14.4	8.4	11.7	20.7	48.5
男性 Male	300	33.0	28.0	22.0	10.7	15.7	29.0	33.7
16~24 岁 Age	64	29.7	40.6	23.4	9.4	14.1	31.3	23.4
25~34 岁 Age	90	35.6	26.7	18.9	10.0	17.8	34.4	34.4
35~44 岁 Age	77	39.0	23.4	28.6	11.7	16.9	22.1	29.9
45~54 岁 Age	45	33.3	31.1	17.8	15.6	17.8	31.1	42.2
55~60 岁 Age	24	12.5	8.3	16.7	4.2	4.2	20.8	54.2
女性 Female	298	17.1	11.7	6.7	6.0	7.7	12.4	63.4
16~24 岁 Age	60	20.0	11.7	3.3	3.3	8.3	25.0	55.0
25~34 岁 Age	90	15.6	15.6	6.7	7.8	5.6	7.8	62.2
35~44 岁 Age	74	20.3	9.5	12.2	4.1	9.5	13.5	62.2
45~54 岁 Age	49	10.2	6.1	4.1	6.1	4.1	8.2	79.6
55~60 岁 Age	25	20.0	16.0	4.0	12.0	16.0	4.0	60.0

3-18 样本、男性各年龄层、女性各年龄层对运动健身的信息接触情况/ Information Contact about Gym by the Whole Sample, Age and Gender Groups

注：本题为多选题，合计百分比超过 100%（Multiple answers）

	人数 Number	阅读有关的杂志和专门报道 reading magazines related and special reports	相互口头传播信息 communicate information orally among people	经常看这种服务的广告 often watch advertisements about such kinds of service	尝试这种服务的新类型 try using the latest type of such kinds of service	过去在这种服务上花了不少钱 used to spend much money on such kinds of service	今后愿意在这方面花钱 willing to spend money on such items in future	不关注这方面的信息 don't care about such kinds of service
样本 Sample	601	18.5	13.6	11.6	12.3	7.3	26.0	43.9
男性 Male	302	17.9	12.6	10.9	12.6	8.6	27.2	43.4
16~24 岁 Age	64	17.2	18.8	15.6	17.2	12.5	39.1	25.0
25~34 岁 Age	91	22.0	8.8	5.5	14.3	12.1	26.4	42.9
35~44 岁 Age	77	15.6	10.4	13.0	9.1	2.6	23.4	48.1
45~54 岁 Age	46	17.4	10.9	13.0	13.0	8.7	23.9	58.7
55~60 岁 Age	24	12.5	20.8	8.3	4.2	4.2	16.7	50.0
女性 Female	299	19.1	14.7	12.4	12.0	6.0	24.7	44.5
16~24 岁 Age	61	24.6	14.8	13.1	16.4	0.0	36.1	29.5
25~34 岁 Age	90	21.1	13.3	8.9	12.2	5.6	31.1	44.4
35~44 岁 Age	74	16.2	17.6	16.2	5.4	4.1	17.6	52.7
45~54 岁 Age	49	10.2	10.2	8.2	12.2	6.1	18.4	51.0
55~60 岁 Age	25	24.0	20.0	20.0	20.0	28.0	8.0	44.0

3-19 样本、男性各年龄层、女性各年龄层对技能学习的信息接触情况/ Information Contact about Studying Skills by the Whole Sample, Age and Gender Groups

注：本题为多选题，合计百分比超过 100%（Multiple answers）

	人数 Number	阅读有关的杂志和专门报道 reading magazines related and special reports	相互口头传播信息 communicate information orally among people	经常看这种服务的广告 often watch advertisements about such kinds of service	尝试这种服务的新类型 try using the latest type of such kinds of service	过去在这种服务上花了不少钱 used to spend much money on such kinds of service	今后愿意在这方面花钱 willing to spend money on such items in future	不关注这方面的信息 don't care about such kinds of service
样本 Sample	600	21.2	12.8	12.2	9.5	10.3	32.2	44.7
男性 Male	301	23.6	14.6	15.9	8.6	12.6	32.6	42.2
16~24 岁 Age	63	28.6	17.5	15.9	6.3	17.5	36.5	30.2
25~34 岁 Age	91	24.2	12.1	15.4	9.9	12.1	38.5	45.1
35~44 岁 Age	77	19.5	15.6	9.1	5.2	6.5	35.1	45.5
45~54 岁 Age	46	28.3	17.4	30.4	15.2	19.6	26.1	37.0
55~60 岁 Age	24	12.5	8.3	12.5	8.3	8.3	4.2	62.5
女性 Female	299	18.7	11.0	8.4	10.4	8.0	31.8	47.2
16~24 岁 Age	61	34.4	18.0	14.8	6.6	4.9	49.2	24.6
25~34 岁 Age	90	18.9	14.4	8.9	13.3	5.6	44.4	33.3
35~44 岁 Age	74	14.9	8.1	4.1	8.1	10.8	24.3	62.2
45~54 岁 Age	49	12.2	6.1	8.2	12.2	12.2	12.2	65.3
55~60 岁 Age	25	4.0	0.0	4.0	12.0	8.0	4.0	72.0

3-20 样本、男性各年龄层、女性各年龄层对外语学习的信息接触情况/ Information Contact about Studying Foreign Languages by the Whole Sample, Age and Gender Groups

注：本题为多选题，合计百分比超过 100%（Multiple answers）

	人数 Number	阅读有关的杂志和专门报道 reading magazines related and special reports	相互口头传播信息 communicate information orally among people	经常看这种服务的广告 often watch advertisements about such kinds of service	尝试这种服务的新类型 try using the latest type of such kinds of service	过去在这种服务上花了不少钱 used to spend much money on such kinds of service	今后愿意在这方面花钱 willing to spend money on such items in future	不关注这方面的信息 don't care about such kinds of service
样本 Sample	601	13.6	6.0	3.5	3.7	7.0	23.0	64.6
男性 Male	302	14.9	4.0	3.3	3.3	6.3	24.5	62.6
16~24 岁 Age	64	23.4	7.8	1.6	4.7	17.2	48.4	32.8
25~34 岁 Age	91	17.6	2.2	7.7	4.4	3.3	22.0	62.6
35~44 岁 Age	77	11.7	5.2	1.3	1.3	3.9	23.4	68.8
45~54 岁 Age	46	10.9	2.2	2.2	4.3	2.2	8.7	78.3
55~60 岁 Age	24	0.0	0.0	0.0	0.0	4.2	4.2	91.7
女性 Female	299	12.4	8.0	3.7	4.0	7.7	21.4	66.6
16~24 岁 Age	61	23.0	24.6	6.6	8.2	14.8	49.2	32.8
25~34 岁 Age	90	13.3	5.6	3.3	3.3	6.7	21.1	62.2
35~44 岁 Age	74	9.5	5.4	4.1	5.4	9.5	14.9	78.4
45~54 岁 Age	49	8.2	0.0	0.0	0.0	2.0	4.1	87.8
55~60 岁 Age	25	0.0	0.0	4.0	0.0	0.0	8.0	88.0

3-21 不同消费者层对电视、音响等视听设备的信息接触情况/ Information Contact about Video & Audio Equipment by Market Segments

注：本题为多选题，合计百分比超过 100%（Multiple answers）

	人数 Number	不管买还是不买，想看看 just have a look, without a definite purpose of buying or not	阅读有关的杂志和专门报道 reading magazines related & special reports	相互口头传播信息 communicate information orally among people	经常看这种商品的广告 often watch advertisements about such kinds of goods	购买这种商品的新类型 buy the latest type of such kinds of goods	过去在这种商品上花了不少钱 use to spend much money on such kinds of goods	今后愿意在这方面花钱 willing to spend money on such items in future	不关注这方面的信息 don't care about such items
样本 Sample	596	48.5	19.8	18.3	36.7	10.6	22.0	19.3	18.5
平实生活指向 simple living orientation	339	46.6	19.5	17.7	38.3	9.7	21.2	17.7	18.6
时尚流行指向 fashion orientation	257	51.0	20.2	19.1	34.6	11.7	23.0	21.4	18.3

3-22 不同消费者层对冰箱、洗衣机等白色家电的信息接触情况/ Information Contact about "White Home Electronic Products" by Market Segments

注：本题为多选题，合计百分比超过 100%（Multiple answers）

	人数 Number	不管买还是不买，想看看 just have a look, without a definite purpose of buying or not	阅读有关的杂志和专门报道 reading magazines related & special reports	相互口头传播信息 communicate information orally among people	经常看这种商品的广告 often watch advertisements about such kinds of goods	购买这种商品的新类型 buy the latest type of such kinds of goods	过去在这种商品上花了不少钱 use to spend much money on such kinds of goods	今后愿意在这方面花钱 willing to spend money on such items in future	不关注这方面的信息 don't care about such items
样本 Sample	599	31.4	15.5	17.0	30.1	9.5	16.9	16.2	30.2
平实生活指向 simple living orientation	341	31.1	15.8	19.6	30.2	8.5	16.7	15.0	28.2
时尚流行指向 fashion orientation	258	31.8	15.1	13.6	29.8	10.9	17.1	17.8	32.9

3-23 不同消费者层对电脑等通讯工具的信息接触情况/ Information Contact about Computer & Telecommunications by Market Segments

注：本题为多选题，合计百分比超过 100%（Multiple answers）

	人数 Number	不管买还是不买，想看看 just have a look, without a definite purpose of buying or not	阅读有关的杂志和专门报道 reading magazines related & special reports	相互口头传播信息 communicate information orally among people	经常看这种商品的广告 often watch advertisements about such kinds of goods	购买这种商品的新类型 buy the latest type of such kinds of goods	过去在这种商品上花了不少钱 use to spend much money on such kinds of goods	今后愿意在这方面花钱 willing to spend money on such items in future	不关注这方面的信息 don't care about such items
样本 Sample	598	29.3	20.2	17.6	21.7	7.7	4.7	27.4	37.8
平实生活指向 simple living orientation	340	27.1	18.5	16.5	20.3	7.6	2.9	22.9	44.4
时尚流行指向 fashion orientation	258	32.2	22.5	19.0	23.6	7.8	7.0	33.3	29.1

3-24 不同消费者层对家用轿车的信息接触情况/ Information Contact about Family Car by Market Segments

注：本题为多选题，合计百分比超过 100%（Multiple answers）

	人数 Number	不管买还是不买，想看看 just have a look, without a definite purpose of buying or not	阅读有关的杂志和专门报道 reading magazines related & special reports	相互口头传播信息 communicate information orally among people	经常看这种商品的广告 often watch advertise-ments about such kinds of goods	购买这种商品的新类型 buy the latest type of such kinds of goods	过去在这种商品上花了不少钱 use to spend much money on such kinds of goods	今后愿意在这方面花钱 willing to spend money on such items in future	不关注这方面的信息 don't care about such items
样本 Sample	597	17.9	10.6	9.0	12.2	2.2	1.7	11.1	61.8
平实生活指向 simple living orientation	339	14.5	8.6	9.1	11.8	1.8	1.2	8.8	65.8
时尚流行指向 fashion orientation	258	22.5	13.2	8.9	12.8	2.7	2.3	14.0	56.6

3-25 不同消费者层对高级家具的信息接触情况/ Information Contact about First-class Furniture by Market Segments

注：本题为多选题，合计百分比超过 100%（Multiple answers）

	人数 Number	不管买还是不买，想看看 just have a look, without a definite purpose of buying or not	阅读有关的杂志和专门报道 reading magazines related & special reports	相互口头传播信息 communicate information orally among people	经常看这种商品的广告 often watch advertise-ments about such kinds of goods	购买这种商品的新类型 buy the latest type of such kinds of goods	过去在这种商品上花了不少钱 use to spend much money on such kinds of goods	今后愿意在这方面花钱 willing to spend money on such items in future	不关注这方面的信息 don't care about such items
样本 Sample	599	28.2	7.8	7.8	10.2	4.8	3.7	17.2	49.9
平实生活指向 simple living orientation	341	25.5	7.6	7.0	10.0	3.8	3.5	17.0	52.8
时尚流行指向 fashion orientation	258	31.8	8.1	8.9	10.5	6.2	3.9	17.4	46.1

3-26 不同消费者层对西服和时装的信息接触情况/ Information Contact about Business Suit & Fashion by Market Segments

注：本题为多选题，合计百分比超过 100%（Multiple answers）

	人数 Number	不管买还是不买，想看看 just have a look, without a definite purpose of buying or not	阅读有关的杂志和专门报道 reading magazines related & special reports	相互口头传播信息 communicate information orally among people	经常看这种商品的广告 often watch advertise-ments about such kinds of goods	购买这种商品的新类型 buy the latest type of such kinds of goods	过去在这种商品上花了不少钱 use to spend much money on such kinds of goods	今后愿意在这方面花钱 willing to spend money on such items in future	不关注这方面的信息 don't care about such items
样本 Sample	599	40.7	17.7	17.0	19.4	15.2	17.5	25.4	29.0
平实生活指向 simple living orientation	341	36.4	15.2	12.9	19.1	12.3	12.0	19.1	36.7
时尚流行指向 fashion orientation	258	46.5	20.9	22.5	19.8	19.0	24.8	33.7	19.0

3-27 不同消费者层对酒精饮料的信息接触情况/ Information Contact about Alcohol Drinks by Market Segments

注：本题为多选题，合计百分比超过 100%（Multiple answers）

	人数 Number	不管买还是不买，想看看 just have a look, without a definite purpose of buying or not	阅读有关的杂志和专门报道 reading magazines related & special reports	相互口头传播信息 communicate information orally among people	经常看这种商品的广告 often watch advertise-ments about such kinds of goods	购买这种商品的新类型 buy the latest type of such kinds of goods	过去在这种商品上花了不少钱 use to spend much money on such kinds of goods	今后愿意在这方面花钱 willing to spend money on such items in future	不关注这方面的信息 don't care about such items
样本 Sample	596	16.6	6.7	14.9	21.0	8.2	16.6	12.6	47.3
平实生活指向 simple living orientation	338	17.8	6.5	16.9	20.1	7.1	18.0	14.5	44.7
时尚流行指向 fashion orientation	258	15.1	7.0	12.4	22.1	9.7	14.7	10.1	50.8

3-28 不同消费者层对 CD 唱片及音乐带的信息接触情况/ Information Contact about CD & Music Cassette by Market Segments

注：本题为多选题，合计百分比超过 100%（Multiple answers）

	人数 Number	不管买还是不买，想看看 just have a look, without a definite purpose of buying or not	阅读有关的杂志和专门报道 reading magazines related & special reports	相互口头传播信息 communicate information orally among people	经常看这种商品的广告 often watch advertise-ments about such kinds of goods	购买这种商品的新类型 buy the latest type of such kinds of goods	过去在这种商品上花了不少钱 use to spend much money on such kinds of goods	今后愿意在这方面花钱 willing to spend money on such items in future	不关注这方面的信息 don't care about such items
样本 Sample	596	26.5	13.6	14.6	13.1	12.4	13.6	18.0	43.0
平实生活指向 simple living orientation	338	21.3	11.8	12.1	10.1	10.7	11.5	15.4	50.9
时尚流行指向 fashion orientation	258	33.3	15.9	17.8	17.1	14.7	16.3	21.3	32.6

3-29 不同消费者层对护肤品和化妆品的信息接触情况/ Information Contact about Skin Cream & Cosmetics by Market Segments

注：本题为多选题，合计百分比超过 100%（Multiple answers）

	人数 Number	不管买还是不买，想看看 just have a look, without a definite purpose of buying or not	阅读有关的杂志和专门报道 reading magazines related & special reports	相互口头传播信息 communicate information orally among people	经常看这种商品的广告 often watch advertise-ments about such kinds of goods	购买这种商品的新类型 buy the latest type of such kinds of goods	过去在这种商品上花了不少钱 use to spend much money on such kinds of goods	今后愿意在这方面花钱 willing to spend money on such items in future	不关注这方面的信息 don't care about such items
样本 Sample	597	28.5	14.4	16.4	27.6	11.2	15.9	21.6	44.9
平实生活指向 simple living orientation	341	23.8	10.3	12.3	22.6	8.5	10.9	15.5	52.8
时尚流行指向 fashion orientation	256	34.8	19.9	21.9	34.4	14.8	22.7	29.7	34.4

3-30 不同消费者层对香波等洗涤用品的信息接触情况/ Information Contact about Shampoo & Detergent by Market Segments

注：本题为多选题，合计百分比超过 100%（Multiple answers）

	人数 Number	不管买还是不买，想看看 just have a look, without a definite purpose of buying or not	阅读有关的杂志和专门报道 reading magazines related & special reports	相互口头传播信息 communicate information orally among people	经常看这种商品的广告 often watch advertisements about such kinds of goods	购买这种商品的新类型 buy the latest type of such kinds of goods	过去在这种商品上花了不少钱 use to spend much money on such kinds of goods	今后愿意在这方面花钱 willing to spend money on such items in future	不关注这方面的信息 don't care about such items
样本 Sample	598	28.4	9.2	17.6	32.1	15.6	15.2	20.6	35.3
平实生活指向 simple living orientation	340	29.1	7.1	15.6	27.9	12.4	12.9	18.2	40.6
时尚流行指向 fashion orientation	258	27.5	12.0	20.2	37.6	19.8	18.2	23.6	28.3

3-31 不同消费者层对外出就餐的信息接触情况/ Information Contact about Dinning Out by Market Segments

注：本题为多选题，合计百分比超过 100%（Multiple answers）

	人数 Number	阅读有关的杂志和专门报道 reading magazines related and special reports	相互口头传播信息 communicate information orally among people	经常看这种服务的广告 often watch advertisements about such kinds of service	尝试这种服务的新类型 try using the latest type of such kinds of service	过去在这种服务上花了不少钱 used to spend much money on such kinds of service	今后愿意在这方面花钱 willing to spend money on such items in future	不关注这方面的信息 don't care about such items
样本 Sample	599	11.5	24.5	15.0	18.7	20.4	27.4	35.1
平实生活指向 simple living orientation	341	10.0	21.4	10.6	13.8	13.8	21.7	43.7
时尚流行指向 fashion orientation	258	13.6	28.7	20.9	25.2	29.1	34.9	23.6

3-32 不同消费者层对旅行的信息接触情况/ Information Contact about Travelling by Market Segments

注：本题为多选题，合计百分比超过 100%（Multiple answers）

	人数 Number	阅读有关的杂志和专门报道 reading magazines related and special reports	相互口头传播信息 communicate information orally among people	经常看这种服务的广告 often watch advertisements about such kinds of service	尝试这种服务的新类型 try using the latest type of such kinds of service	过去在这种服务上花了不少钱 used to spend much money on such kinds of service	今后愿意在这方面花钱 willing to spend money on such items in future	不关注这方面的信息 don't care about such kinds of service
样本 Sample	599	24.5	24.4	16.2	14.7	14.9	46.4	26.4
平实生活指向 simple living orientation	341	23.2	21.1	13.8	13.2	10.6	42.5	29.9
时尚流行指向 fashion orientation	258	26.4	28.7	19.4	16.7	20.5	51.6	21.7

3-33 不同消费者层对音乐会的信息接触情况/ Information Contact about Concert by Market Segments

注：本题为多选题，合计百分比超过 100%（Multiple answers）

	人数 Number	阅读有关的杂志和专门报道 reading magazines related and special reports	相互口头传播信息 communicate information orally among people	经常看这种服务的广告 often watch advertisements about such kinds of service	尝试这种服务的新类型 try using the latest type of such kinds of service	过去在这种服务上花了不少钱 used to spend much money on such kinds of service	今后愿意在这方面花钱 willing to spend money on such items in future	不关注这方面的信息 don't care about such kinds of service
样本 Sample	598	14.7	13.0	10.9	7.2	5.9	11.7	60.9
平实生活指向 simple living orientation	340	12.9	11.8	8.2	6.5	5.0	8.8	66.8
时尚流行指向 fashion orientation	258	17.1	14.7	14.3	8.1	7.0	15.5	53.1

3-34 不同消费者层对电影的信息接触情况/ Information Contact about Movie by Market Segments

注：本题为多选题，合计百分比超过 100%（Multiple answers）

	人数 Number	阅读有关的杂志和专门报道 reading magazines related and special reports	相互口头传播信息 communicate information orally among people	经常看这种服务的广告 often watch advertise-ments about such kinds of service	尝试这种服务的新类型 try using the latest type of such kinds of service	过去在这种服务上花了不少钱 used to spend much money on such kinds of service	今后愿意在这方面花钱 willing to spend money on such items in future	不关注这方面的信息 don't care about such kinds of service
样本 Sample	**599**	**26.5**	**21.4**	**17.4**	**11.9**	**16.2**	**16.0**	**41.4**
平实生活指向 simple living orientation	341	25.5	21.7	16.4	11.4	13.5	16.1	44.0
时尚流行指向 fashion orientation	258	27.9	20.9	18.6	12.4	19.8	15.9	38.0

3-35 不同消费者层对戏剧或戏曲的信息接触情况/ Information Contact about Drama or Opera by Market Segments

注：本题为多选题，合计百分比超过 100%（Multiple answers）

	人数 Number	阅读有关的杂志和专门报道 reading magazines related and special reports	相互口头传播信息 communicate information orally among people	经常看这种服务的广告 often watch advertisements about such kinds of service	尝试这种服务的新类型 try using the latest type of such kinds of service	过去在这种服务上花了不少钱 used to spend much money on such kinds of service	今后愿意在这方面花钱 willing to spend money on such items in future	不关注这方面的信息 don't care about such kinds of service
样本 Sample	**599**	**10.7**	**8.2**	**6.7**	**6.5**	**5.7**	**6.3**	**74.6**
平实生活指向 simple living orientation	341	11.7	11.4	7.0	8.5	6.7	7.9	69.5
时尚流行指向 fashion orientation	258	9.3	3.9	6.2	3.9	4.3	4.3	81.4

3-36 不同消费者层对蹦迪的信息接触情况/ Information Contact about Disco by Market Segments

注：本题为多选题，合计百分比超过 100%（Multiple answers）

	人数 Number	阅读有关的杂志和专门报道 reading magazines related and special reports	相互口头传播信息 communicate information orally among people	经常看这种服务的广告 often watch advertise-ments about such kinds of service	尝试这种服务的新类型 try using the latest type of such kinds of service	过去在这种服务上花了不少钱 used to spend much money on such kinds of service	今后愿意在这方面花钱 willing to spend money on such items in future	不关注这方面的信息 don't care about such kinds of service
样本 Sample	**598**	**2.7**	**7.0**	**3.0**	**7.4**	**6.4**	**6.9**	**76.6**
平实生活指向 simple living orientation	340	1.2	4.1	2.1	3.8	4.1	5.0	83.5
时尚流行指向 fashion orientation	258	4.7	10.9	4.3	12.0	9.3	9.3	67.4

3-37 不同消费者层对现场观赏体育比赛的信息接触情况/ Information Contact about Enjoying Live Sports by Market Segments

注：本题为多选题，合计百分比超过 100%（Multiple answers）

	人数 Number	阅读有关的杂志和专门报道 reading magazines related and special reports	相互口头传播信息 communicate information orally among people	经常看这种服务的广告 often watch advertise-ments about such kinds of service	尝试这种服务的新类型 try using the latest type of such kinds of service	过去在这种服务上花了不少钱 used to spend much money on such kinds of service	今后愿意在这方面花钱 willing to spend money on such items in future	不关注这方面的信息 don't care about such kinds of service
样本 Sample	**596**	**25.0**	**19.8**	**14.4**	**8.4**	**11.7**	**20.8**	**48.5**
平实生活指向 simple living orientation	340	25.0	19.7	15.3	9.4	12.4	21.5	48.5
时尚流行指向 fashion orientation	256	25.0	19.9	13.3	7.0	10.9	19.9	48.4

3-38 不同消费者层对运动健身的信息接触情况/ Information Contact about Gym by Market Segments

注：本题为多选题，合计百分比超过 100%（Multiple answers）

	人数 Number	阅读有关的杂志和专门报道 reading magazines related and special reports	相互口头传播信息 communicate information orally among people	经常看这种服务的广告 often watch advertise-ments about such kinds of service	尝试这种服务的新类型 try using the latest type of such kinds of service	过去在这种服务上花了不少钱 used to spend much money on such kinds of service	今后愿意在这方面花钱 willing to spend money on such items in future	不关注这方面的信息 don't care about such kinds of service
样本 Sample	599	18.4	13.5	11.7	12.4	7.3	26.0	44.1
平实生活指向 simple living orientation	341	17.3	13.2	10.6	10.3	7.0	23.2	47.8
时尚流行指向 fashion orientation	258	19.8	14.0	13.2	15.1	7.8	29.8	39.1

3-39 不同消费者层对技能学习的信息接触情况/ Information Contact about Studying Skills by Market Segments

注：本题为多选题，合计百分比超过 100%（Multiple answers）

	人数 Number	阅读有关的杂志和专门报道 reading magazines related and special reports	相互口头传播信息 communicate information orally among people	经常看这种服务的广告 often watch advertise-ments about such kinds of service	尝试这种服务的新类型 try using the latest type of such kinds of service	过去在这种服务上花了不少钱 used to spend much money on such kinds of service	今后愿意在这方面花钱 willing to spend money on such items in future	不关注这方面的信息 don't care about such kinds of service
样本 Sample	598	21.2	12.7	12.2	9.5	10.2	32.3	44.8
平实生活指向 simple living orientation	341	18.5	11.1	10.3	9.7	10.0	26.1	50.4
时尚流行指向 fashion orientation	257	24.9	14.8	14.8	9.3	10.5	40.5	37.4

3-40 不同消费者层对外语学习的信息接触情况/ Information Contact about Studying Foreign Languages by Market Segments

注：本题为多选题，合计百分比超过 100%（Multiple answers）

	人数 Number	阅读有关的杂志和专门报道 reading magazines related and special reports	相互口头传播信息 communicate information orally among people	经常看这种服务的广告 often watch advertise-ments about such kinds of service	尝试这种服务的新类型 try using the latest type of such kinds of service	过去在这种服务上花了不少钱 used to spend much money on such kinds of service	今后愿意在这方面花钱 willing to spend money on such items in future	不关注这方面的信息 don't care about such kinds of service
样本 Sample	599	13.7	6.0	3.5	3.7	6.8	22.9	64.8
平实生活指向 simple living orientation	341	10.3	5.6	2.9	4.1	7.3	19.1	70.7
时尚流行指向 fashion orientation	258	18.2	6.6	4.3	3.1	6.2	27.9	57.0

● 沈阳 / Shenyang

3-1 样本、男性各年龄层、女性各年龄层对电视、音响等视听设备的信息接触情况/ Information Contact about Video & Audio Equipment by the Whole Sample, Age and Gender Groups

注：本题为多选题，合计百分比超过 100%（Multiple answers）

	人数 Number	不管买还是不买，想看看 just have a look, without a definite purpose of buying or not	阅读有关的杂志和专门报道 reading magazines related & special reports	相互口头传播信息 communicate information orally among people	经常看这种商品的广告 often watch advertise-ments about such kinds of goods	购买这种商品的新类型 buy the latest type of such kinds of goods	过去在这种商品上花了不少钱 used to spend much money on such kinds of goods	今后愿意在这方面花钱 willing to spend money on such items in future	不关注这方面的信息 don't care about such items
样本 Sample	601	58.4	29.3	31.4	40.4	14.6	23.8	31.1	15.6
男性 Male	299	61.9	30.4	30.8	39.8	14.4	24.1	32.8	14.0
16~24 岁 Age	64	67.2	23.4	21.9	32.8	10.9	21.9	25.0	10.9
25~34 岁 Age	89	64.0	38.2	34.8	38.2	12.4	25.8	42.7	13.5
35~44 岁 Age	76	57.9	31.6	36.8	40.8	14.5	25.0	28.9	18.4
45~54 岁 Age	46	60.9	28.3	26.1	47.8	21.7	21.7	32.6	10.9
55~60 岁 Age	24	54.2	20.8	29.2	45.8	16.7	25.0	29.2	16.7
女性 Female	302	55.0	28.1	32.1	41.1	14.9	23.5	29.5	17.2
16~24 岁 Age	64	48.4	29.7	29.7	37.5	20.3	17.2	26.6	15.6
25~34 岁 Age	90	50.0	23.3	25.6	33.3	8.9	21.1	27.8	22.2
35~44 岁 Age	76	60.5	31.6	31.6	46.1	17.1	27.6	34.2	14.5
45~54 岁 Age	48	66.7	31.3	45.8	50.0	18.8	29.2	35.4	10.4
55~60 岁 Age	24	50.0	25.0	37.5	45.8	8.3	25.0	16.7	25.0

3-2 样本、男性各年龄层、女性各年龄层对冰箱、洗衣机等白色家电的信息接触情况/ Information Contact about "White Home Electronic Products" by the Whole Sample, Age and Gender Groups

注：本题为多选题，合计百分比超过 100%（Multiple answers）

	人数 Number	不管买还是不买，想看看 just have a look, without a definite purpose of buying or not	阅读有关的杂志和专门报道 reading magazines related & special reports	相互口头传播信息 communicate information orally among people	经常看这种商品的广告 often watch advertise-ments about such kinds of goods	购买这种商品的新类型 buy the latest type of such kinds of goods	过去在这种商品上花了不少钱 used to spend much money on such kinds of goods	今后愿意在这方面花钱 willing to spend money on such items in future	不关注这方面的信息 don't care about such items
样本 Sample	601	43.9	19.1	21.6	29.8	10.1	19.3	19.8	25.6
男性 Male	299	44.8	19.4	20.7	28.1	8.4	20.4	19.4	25.1
16~24 岁 Age	64	37.5	9.4	9.4	20.3	3.1	15.6	14.1	35.9
25~34 岁 Age	89	47.2	27.0	24.7	27.0	9.0	19.1	24.7	28.1
35~44 岁 Age	76	46.1	22.4	26.3	32.9	9.2	23.7	19.7	14.5
45~54 岁 Age	46	47.8	17.4	21.7	26.1	10.9	26.1	17.4	23.9
55~60 岁 Age	24	45.8	12.5	16.7	41.7	12.5	16.7	16.7	20.8
女性 Female	302	43.0	18.9	22.5	31.5	11.9	18.2	20.2	26.2
16~24 岁 Age	64	31.3	17.2	23.4	28.1	18.8	10.9	18.8	31.3
25~34 岁 Age	90	41.1	12.2	12.2	20.0	5.6	18.9	17.8	32.2
35~44 岁 Age	76	48.7	26.3	23.7	36.8	11.8	19.7	23.7	19.7
45~54 岁 Age	48	52.1	18.8	33.3	39.6	10.4	27.1	18.8	20.8
55~60 岁 Age	24	45.8	25.0	33.3	50.0	20.8	12.5	25.0	20.8

3-3 样本、男性各年龄层、女性各年龄层对电脑等通讯工具的信息接触情况/ Information Contact about Computer & Telecommunications by the Whole Sample, Age and Gender Groups

注：本题为多选题，合计百分比超过 100%（Multiple answers）

	人数 Number	不管买还是不买，想看看 just have a look, without a definite purpose of buying or not	阅读有关的杂志和专门报道 reading magazines related & special reports	相互口头传播信息 communicate information orally among people	经常看这种商品的广告 often watch advertise-ments about such kinds of goods	购买这种商品的新类型 buy the latest type of such kinds of goods	过去在这种商品上花了不少钱 used to spend much money on such kinds of goods	今后愿意在这方面花钱 willing to spend money on such items in future	不关注这方面的信息 don't care about such items
样本 Sample	601	36.3	28.1	23.6	24.6	10.1	8.0	31.4	36.4
男性 Male	299	40.1	31.1	27.1	26.1	9.7	12.0	32.8	31.8
16~24 岁 Age	64	64.1	43.8	43.8	37.5	14.1	18.8	42.2	14.1
25~34 岁 Age	89	38.2	37.1	27.0	24.7	10.1	10.1	40.4	28.1
35~44 岁 Age	76	30.3	26.3	19.7	23.7	9.2	10.5	21.1	44.7
45~54 岁 Age	46	32.6	17.4	21.7	17.4	4.3	10.9	32.6	30.4
55~60 岁 Age	24	29.2	16.7	16.7	25.0	8.3	8.3	16.7	54.2
女性 Female	302	32.5	25.2	20.2	23.2	10.6	4.0	30.1	41.1
16~24 岁 Age	64	48.4	32.8	29.7	26.6	15.6	7.8	42.2	20.3
25~34 岁 Age	90	32.2	26.7	15.6	18.9	12.2	2.2	26.7	41.1
35~44 岁 Age	76	31.6	22.4	19.7	31.6	9.2	1.3	32.9	39.5
45~54 岁 Age	48	22.9	20.8	18.8	20.8	6.3	6.3	22.9	56.3
55~60 岁 Age	24	12.5	16.7	16.7	8.3	4.2	4.2	16.7	70.8

3-4 样本、男性各年龄层、女性各年龄层对家用轿车的信息接触情况/ Information Contact about Family Car by the Whole Sample, Age and Gender Groups

注：本题为多选题，合计百分比超过 100%（Multiple answers）

	人数 Number	不管买还是不买，想看看 just have a look, without a definite purpose of buying or not	阅读有关的杂志和专门报道 reading magazines related & special reports	相互口头传播信息 communicate information orally among people	经常看这种商品的广告 often watch advertise-ments about such kinds of goods	购买这种商品的新类型 buy the latest type of such kinds of goods	过去在这种商品上花了不少钱 used to spend much money on such kinds of goods	今后愿意在这方面花钱 willing to spend money on such items in future	不关注这方面的信息 don't care about such items
样本 Sample	601	21.5	16.1	13.3	12.6	3.0	1.5	10.1	60.6
男性 Male	299	26.8	21.7	17.4	15.7	4.0	1.0	12.7	51.5
16~24 岁 Age	64	29.7	25.0	18.8	18.8	4.7	3.1	15.6	42.2
25~34 岁 Age	89	32.6	30.3	27.0	24.7	5.6	1.1	19.1	40.4
35~44 岁 Age	76	26.3	17.1	11.8	10.5	3.9	0.0	5.3	59.2
45~54 岁 Age	46	21.7	13.0	10.9	8.7	2.2	0.0	13.0	60.9
55~60 岁 Age	24	8.3	12.5	8.3	4.2	0.0	0.0	4.2	75.0
女性 Female	302	16.2	10.6	9.3	9.6	2.0	2.0	7.6	69.5
16~24 岁 Age	64	32.8	18.8	15.6	14.1	4.7	3.1	12.5	56.3
25~34 岁 Age	90	16.7	11.1	8.9	10.0	1.1	0.0	8.9	65.6
35~44 岁 Age	76	9.2	5.3	9.2	6.6	2.6	3.9	6.6	72.4
45~54 岁 Age	48	8.3	10.4	6.3	10.4	0.0	2.1	4.2	81.3
55~60 岁 Age	24	8.3	4.2	0.0	4.2	0.0	0.0	0.0	87.5

3-5 样本、男性各年龄层、女性各年龄层对高级家具的信息接触情况/ Information Contact about First-class Furniture by the Whole Sample, Age and Gender Groups

注：本题为多选题，合计百分比超过 100%（Multiple answers）

	人数 Number	不管买还是不买，想看看 just have a look, without a definite purpose of buying or not	阅读有关的杂志和专门报道 reading magazines related & special reports	相互口头传播信息 communicate information orally among people	经常看这种商品的广告 often watch advertise-ments about such kinds of goods	购买这种商品的新类型 buy the latest type of such kinds of goods	过去在这种商品上花了不少钱 used to spend much money on such kinds of goods	今后愿意在这方面花钱 willing to spend money on such items in future	不关注这方面的信息 don't care about such items
样本 Sample	**600**	**30.3**	**13.8**	**8.0**	**12.0**	**5.0**	**4.7**	**14.8**	**53.3**
男性 Male	**298**	**28.9**	**11.4**	**6.4**	**11.1**	**3.4**	**4.7**	**14.8**	**54.4**
16~24 岁 Age	63	23.8	6.3	4.8	7.9	4.8	4.8	15.9	58.7
25~34 岁 Age	89	33.7	16.9	6.7	19.1	5.6	6.7	20.2	41.6
35~44 岁 Age	76	32.9	9.2	6.6	9.2	1.3	3.9	13.2	57.9
45~54 岁 Age	46	23.9	10.9	6.5	4.3	2.2	4.3	10.9	63.0
55~60 岁 Age	24	20.8	12.5	8.3	8.3	0.0	0.0	4.2	62.5
女性 Female	**302**	**31.8**	**16.2**	**9.6**	**12.9**	**6.6**	**4.6**	**14.9**	**52.3**
16~24 岁 Age	64	32.8	23.4	10.9	12.5	9.4	4.7	18.8	43.8
25~34 岁 Age	90	36.7	11.1	10.0	12.2	4.4	3.3	12.2	47.8
35~44 岁 Age	76	31.6	15.8	7.9	13.2	5.3	5.3	17.1	52.6
45~54 岁 Age	48	27.1	20.8	10.4	14.6	8.3	8.3	16.7	60.4
55~60 岁 Age	24	20.8	8.3	8.3	12.5	8.3	0.0	4.2	75.0

3-6 样本、男性各年龄层、女性各年龄层对西服和时装的信息接触情况/ Information Contact about Business Suit & Fashion by the Whole Sample, Age and Gender Groups

注：本题为多选题，合计百分比超过 100%（Multiple answers）

	人数 Number	不管买还是不买，想看看 just have a look, without a definite purpose of buying or not	阅读有关的杂志和专门报道 reading magazines related & special reports	相互口头传播信息 communicate information orally among people	经常看这种商品的广告 often watch advertise-ments about such kinds of goods	购买这种商品的新类型 buy the latest type of such kinds of goods	过去在这种商品上花了不少钱 used to spend much money on such kinds of goods	今后愿意在这方面花钱 willing to spend money on such items in future	不关注这方面的信息 don't care about such items
样本 Sample	**601**	**50.4**	**22.3**	**26.3**	**26.0**	**21.8**	**27.8**	**31.9**	**24.0**
男性 Male	**299**	**46.2**	**15.4**	**19.7**	**21.1**	**17.4**	**22.1**	**28.8**	**28.1**
16~24 岁 Age	64	45.3	14.1	17.2	20.3	15.6	18.8	34.4	28.1
25~34 岁 Age	89	51.7	21.3	24.7	27.0	23.6	25.8	39.3	21.3
35~44 岁 Age	76	39.5	17.1	14.5	17.1	19.7	21.1	15.8	31.6
45~54 岁 Age	46	50.0	6.5	19.6	19.6	13.0	30.4	30.4	26.1
55~60 岁 Age	24	41.7	8.3	25.0	16.7	0.0	4.2	12.5	45.8
女性 Female	**302**	**54.6**	**29.1**	**32.8**	**30.8**	**26.2**	**33.4**	**35.1**	**19.9**
16~24 岁 Age	64	48.4	37.5	31.3	28.1	32.8	37.5	35.9	18.8
25~34 岁 Age	90	62.2	26.7	34.4	26.7	28.9	34.4	37.8	12.2
35~44 岁 Age	76	59.2	30.3	36.8	40.8	30.3	38.2	40.8	14.5
45~54 岁 Age	48	50.0	29.2	25.0	29.2	14.6	27.1	29.2	31.3
55~60 岁 Age	24	37.5	12.5	33.3	25.0	8.3	16.7	16.7	45.8

3-7 样本、男性各年龄层、女性各年龄层对酒精饮料的信息接触情况/ Information Contact about Alcohol Drinks by the Whole Sample, Age and Gender Groups

注：本题为多选题，合计百分比超过 100%（Multiple answers）

	人数 Number	不管买还是不买，想看看 just have a look, without a definite purpose of buying or not	阅读有关的杂志和专门报道 reading magazines related & special reports	相互口头传播信息 communicate information orally among people	经常看这种商品的广告 often watch advertise-ments about such kinds of goods	购买这种商品的新类型 buy the latest type of such kinds of goods	过去在这种商品上花了不少钱 used to spend much money on such kinds of goods	今后愿意在这方面花钱 willing to spend money on such items in future	不关注这方面的信息 don't care about such items
样本 Sample	600	21.8	9.5	13.5	18.5	11.5	17.3	16.2	49.2
男性 Male	298	25.8	11.1	15.8	21.5	11.7	24.8	22.5	39.3
16~24 岁 Age	64	21.9	7.8	6.3	18.8	9.4	10.9	15.6	51.6
25~34 岁 Age	88	27.3	12.5	22.7	27.3	12.5	21.6	23.9	28.4
35~44 岁 Age	76	22.4	11.8	11.8	17.1	10.5	30.3	23.7	43.4
45~54 岁 Age	46	30.4	13.0	15.2	15.2	10.9	41.3	23.9	34.8
55~60 岁 Age	24	33.3	8.3	29.2	33.3	20.8	25.0	29.2	41.7
女性 Female	302	17.9	7.9	11.3	15.6	11.3	9.9	9.9	58.9
16~24 岁 Age	64	17.2	15.6	12.5	14.1	17.2	10.9	10.9	57.8
25~34 岁 Age	90	14.4	6.7	8.9	10.0	11.1	5.6	6.7	62.2
35~44 岁 Age	76	23.7	6.6	15.8	26.3	10.5	15.8	14.5	43.4
45~54 岁 Age	48	18.8	4.2	8.3	16.7	8.3	10.4	10.4	68.8
55~60 岁 Age	24	12.5	4.2	8.3	4.2	4.2	4.2	4.2	79.2

3-8 样本、男性各年龄层、女性各年龄层对 CD 唱片及音乐带的信息接触情况/ Information Contact about CD & Music Cassette by the Whole Sample, Age and Gender Groups

注：本题为多选题，合计百分比超过 100%（Multiple answers）

	人数 Number	不管买还是不买，想看看 just have a look, without a definite purpose of buying or not	阅读有关的杂志和专门报道 reading magazines related & special reports	相互口头传播信息 communicate information orally among people	经常看这种商品的广告 often watch advertise-ments about such kinds of goods	购买这种商品的新类型 buy the latest type of such kinds of goods	过去在这种商品上花了不少钱 used to spend much money on such kinds of goods	今后愿意在这方面花钱 willing to spend money on such items in future	不关注这方面的信息 don't care about such items
样本 Sample	601	34.4	17.0	20.6	18.3	16.5	21.6	24.5	37.9
男性 Male	299	36.8	18.4	22.7	18.1	17.4	20.4	26.8	34.1
16~24 岁 Age	64	54.7	35.9	37.5	34.4	31.3	42.2	45.3	7.8
25~34 岁 Age	89	39.3	20.2	25.8	18.0	21.3	20.2	33.7	25.8
35~44 岁 Age	76	30.3	13.2	18.4	13.2	9.2	14.5	15.8	43.4
45~54 岁 Age	46	34.8	6.5	10.9	8.7	8.7	8.7	17.4	45.7
55~60 岁 Age	24	4.2	4.2	8.3	8.3	8.3	4.2	4.2	83.3
女性 Female	302	32.1	15.6	18.5	18.5	15.6	22.8	22.2	41.7
16~24 岁 Age	64	50.0	26.6	28.1	32.8	32.8	43.8	39.1	20.3
25~34 岁 Age	90	30.0	10.0	13.3	14.4	10.0	17.8	17.8	42.2
35~44 岁 Age	76	25.0	15.8	19.7	14.5	13.2	19.7	21.1	40.8
45~54 岁 Age	48	31.3	16.7	18.8	22.9	14.6	16.7	16.7	58.3
55~60 岁 Age	24	16.7	4.2	8.3	0.0	0.0	8.3	8.3	66.7

3-9 样本、男性各年龄层、女性各年龄层对护肤品和化妆品的信息接触情况/ Information Contact about Skin Cream & Cosmetics by the Whole Sample, Age and Gender Groups

注：本题为多选题，合计百分比超过 100%（Multiple answers）

	人数 Number	不管买还是不买，想看看 just have a look, without a definite purpose of buying or not	阅读有关的杂志和专门报道 reading magazines related & special reports	相互口头传播信息 communicate information orally among people	经常看这种商品的广告 often watch advertise-ments about such kinds of goods	购买这种商品的新类型 buy the latest type of such kinds of goods	过去在这种商品上花了不少钱 used to spend much money on such kinds of goods	今后愿意在这方面花钱 willing to spend money on such items in future	不关注这方面的信息 don't care about such items
样本 Sample	601	35.9	18.3	21.5	27.6	17.0	22.0	27.0	41.8
男性 Male	299	13.4	6.0	7.7	13.4	5.0	5.7	9.0	67.2
16~24 岁 Age	64	4.7	3.1	6.3	10.9	6.3	4.7	7.8	76.6
25~34 岁 Age	89	19.1	10.1	13.5	15.7	7.9	6.7	9.0	56.2
35~44 岁 Age	76	13.2	2.6	3.9	9.2	3.9	7.9	11.8	71.1
45~54 岁 Age	46	19.6	8.7	6.5	13.0	2.2	4.3	10.9	67.4
55~60 岁 Age	24	4.2	4.2	4.2	25.0	0.0	0.0	0.0	70.8
女性 Female	302	58.3	30.5	35.1	41.7	28.8	38.1	44.7	16.6
16~24 岁 Age	64	64.1	32.8	28.1	53.1	35.9	32.8	46.9	7.8
25~34 岁 Age	90	68.9	31.1	40.0	42.2	32.2	44.4	53.3	5.6
35~44 岁 Age	76	61.8	40.8	40.8	46.1	30.3	47.4	47.4	10.5
45~54 岁 Age	48	37.5	18.8	33.3	29.2	22.9	29.2	35.4	39.6
55~60 岁 Age	24	33.3	12.5	20.8	20.8	4.2	16.7	16.7	54.2

3-10 样本、男性各年龄层、女性各年龄层对香波等洗涤用品的信息接触情况/ Information Contact about Shampoo & Detergent Cassette by the Whole Sample, Age and Gender Groups

注：本题为多选题，合计百分比超过 100%（Multiple answers）

	人数 Number	不管买还是不买，想看看 just have a look, without a definite purpose of buying or not	阅读有关的杂志和专门报道 reading magazines related & special reports	相互口头传播信息 communicate information orally among people	经常看这种商品的广告 often watch advertise-ments about such kinds of goods	购买这种商品的新类型 buy the latest type of such kinds of goods	过去在这种商品上花了不少钱 used to spend much money on such kinds of goods	今后愿意在这方面花钱 willing to spend money on such items in future	不关注这方面的信息 don't care about such items
样本 Sample	601	41.3	15.1	20.0	30.1	22.5	24.6	30.1	30.6
男性 Male	299	22.4	7.4	9.4	17.7	12.4	11.7	17.7	49.2
16~24 岁 Age	64	18.8	7.8	10.9	15.6	10.9	9.4	14.1	57.8
25~34 岁 Age	89	27.0	7.9	12.4	19.1	13.5	13.5	20.2	36.0
35~44 岁 Age	76	22.4	3.9	3.9	9.2	17.1	13.2	19.7	57.9
45~54 岁 Age	46	23.9	10.9	8.7	23.9	8.7	10.9	19.6	45.7
55~60 岁 Age	24	12.5	8.3	12.5	33.3	4.2	8.3	8.3	54.2
女性 Female	302	59.9	22.8	30.5	42.4	32.5	37.4	42.4	12.3
16~24 岁 Age	64	54.7	21.9	23.4	45.3	37.5	28.1	37.5	17.2
25~34 岁 Age	90	58.9	16.7	27.8	42.2	32.2	36.7	47.8	6.7
35~44 岁 Age	76	68.4	30.3	34.2	43.4	31.6	52.6	47.4	6.6
45~54 岁 Age	48	58.3	22.9	39.6	43.8	33.3	37.5	39.6	14.6
55~60 岁 Age	24	54.2	25.0	29.2	29.2	20.8	16.7	25.0	33.3

3-11 样本、男性各年龄层、女性各年龄层对外出就餐的信息接触情况/ Information Contact about Dinning Out by the Whole Sample, Age and Gender Groups

注：本题为多选题，合计百分比超过 100%（Multiple answers）

	人数 Number	阅读有关的杂志和专门报道 reading magazines related and special reports	相互口头传播信息 communicate information orally among people	经常看这种服务的广告 often watch advertise-ments about such kinds of service	尝试这种服务的新类型 try using the latest type of such kinds of service	过去在这种服务上花了不少钱 used to spend much money on such kinds of service	今后愿意在这方面花钱 willing to spend money on such items in future	不关注这方面的信息 don't care about such items
样本 Sample	600	20.5	20.8	15.0	21.0	23.2	28.8	34.5
男性 Male	299	20.1	20.4	15.7	20.1	28.8	32.4	34.4
16~24 岁 Age	64	20.3	10.9	9.4	10.9	20.3	29.7	45.3
25~34 岁 Age	89	19.1	25.8	21.3	22.5	37.1	40.4	21.3
35~44 岁 Age	76	22.4	22.4	15.8	26.3	30.3	31.6	35.5
45~54 岁 Age	46	17.4	19.6	13.0	17.4	28.3	28.3	37.0
55~60 岁 Age	24	20.8	20.8	16.7	20.8	16.7	20.8	45.8
女性 Female	301	20.9	21.3	14.3	21.9	17.6	25.2	34.6
16~24 岁 Age	63	27.0	22.2	17.5	23.8	20.6	31.7	28.6
25~34 岁 Age	90	17.8	17.8	10.0	26.7	16.7	22.2	28.9
35~44 岁 Age	76	22.4	28.9	14.5	19.7	17.1	27.6	26.3
45~54 岁 Age	48	16.7	18.8	16.7	18.8	16.7	25.0	50.0
55~60 岁 Age	24	20.8	12.5	16.7	12.5	16.7	12.5	66.7

3-12 样本、男性各年龄层、女性各年龄层对旅行的信息接触情况/ Information Contact about Travelling by the Whole Sample, Age and Gender Groups

注：本题为多选题，合计百分比超过 100%（Multiple answers）

	人数 Number	阅读有关的杂志和专门报道 reading magazines related and special reports	相互口头传播信息 communicate information orally among people	经常看这种服务的广告 often watch advertise-ments about such kinds of service	尝试这种服务的新类型 try using the latest type of such kinds of service	过去在这种服务上花了不少钱 used to spend much money on such kinds of service	今后愿意在这方面花钱 willing to spend money on such items in future	不关注这方面的信息 don't care about such items
样本 Sample	601	25.6	23.1	18.5	19.5	20.3	42.3	28.3
男性 Male	299	25.4	20.7	19.1	17.7	21.4	44.8	27.4
16~24 岁 Age	64	15.6	9.4	17.2	10.9	12.5	42.2	37.5
25~34 岁 Age	89	31.5	32.6	23.6	24.7	30.3	53.9	15.7
35~44 岁 Age	76	28.9	14.5	13.2	15.8	22.4	36.8	32.9
45~54 岁 Age	46	28.3	26.1	21.7	13.0	19.6	47.8	19.6
55~60 岁 Age	24	12.5	16.7	20.8	25.0	12.5	37.5	41.7
女性 Female	302	25.8	25.5	17.9	21.2	19.2	39.7	29.1
16~24 岁 Age	64	34.4	25.0	15.6	25.0	21.9	43.8	21.9
25~34 岁 Age	90	28.9	30.0	12.2	17.8	14.4	42.2	25.6
35~44 岁 Age	76	21.1	27.6	18.4	22.4	22.4	35.5	27.6
45~54 岁 Age	48	18.8	20.8	29.2	25.0	16.7	43.8	37.5
55~60 岁 Age	24	20.8	12.5	20.8	12.5	25.0	25.0	50.0

3-13 样本、男性各年龄层、女性各年龄层对音乐会的信息接触情况/ Information Contact about Concert by the Whole Sample, Age and Gender Groups

注：本题为多选题，合计百分比超过 100%（Multiple answers）

	人数 Number	阅读有关的杂志和专门报道 reading magazines related and special reports	相互口头传播信息 communicate information orally among people	经常看这种服务的广告 often watch advertisements about such kinds of service	尝试这种服务的新类型 try using the latest type of such kinds of service	过去在这种服务上花了不少钱 used to spend much money on such kinds of service	今后愿意在这方面花钱 willing to spend money on such items in future	不关注这方面的信息 don't care about such items
样本 Sample	**600**	**14.2**	**11.7**	**13.8**	**9.2**	**5.5**	**14.7**	**59.0**
男性 Male	**298**	**12.1**	**10.7**	**11.7**	**10.4**	**6.7**	**11.7**	**61.4**
16~24 岁 Age	64	17.2	15.6	15.6	14.1	6.3	17.2	46.9
25~34 岁 Age	89	10.1	12.4	10.1	10.1	4.5	12.4	61.8
35~44 岁 Age	75	12.0	6.7	12.0	9.3	10.7	10.7	64.0
45~54 岁 Age	46	10.9	10.9	6.5	10.9	6.5	8.7	65.2
55~60 岁 Age	24	8.3	4.2	16.7	4.2	4.2	4.2	83.3
女性 Female	**302**	**16.2**	**12.6**	**15.9**	**7.9**	**4.3**	**17.5**	**56.6**
16~24 岁 Age	64	23.4	20.3	20.3	9.4	3.1	28.1	40.6
25~34 岁 Age	90	11.1	5.6	12.2	5.6	2.2	17.8	60.0
35~44 岁 Age	76	17.1	14.5	14.5	10.5	6.6	13.2	55.3
45~54 岁 Age	48	18.8	14.6	20.8	10.4	6.3	16.7	60.4
55~60 岁 Age	24	8.3	8.3	12.5	0.0	4.2	4.2	83.3

3-14 样本、男性各年龄层、女性各年龄层对电影的信息接触情况/ Information Contact about Movie by the Whole Sample, Age and Gender Groups

注：本题为多选题，合计百分比超过 100%（Multiple answers）

	人数 Number	阅读有关的杂志和专门报道 reading magazines related and special reports	相互口头传播信息 communicate information orally among people	经常看这种服务的广告 often watch advertisements about such kinds of service	尝试这种服务的新类型 try using the latest type of such kinds of service	过去在这种服务上花了不少钱 used to spend much money on such kinds of service	今后愿意在这方面花钱 willing to spend money on such items in future	不关注这方面的信息 don't care about such items
样本 Sample	**600**	**22.5**	**18.8**	**18.3**	**13.5**	**17.3**	**19.0**	**45.5**
男性 Male	**298**	**23.2**	**16.1**	**17.4**	**14.1**	**18.5**	**20.5**	**44.6**
16~24 岁 Age	63	39.7	33.3	30.2	20.6	27.0	31.7	14.3
25~34 岁 Age	89	29.2	16.9	19.1	20.2	18.0	23.6	39.3
35~44 岁 Age	76	11.8	9.2	5.3	3.9	18.4	13.2	57.9
45~54 岁 Age	46	13.0	6.5	19.6	8.7	13.0	15.2	60.9
55~60 岁 Age	24	12.5	8.3	12.5	16.7	8.3	12.5	70.8
女性 Female	**302**	**21.9**	**21.5**	**19.2**	**12.9**	**16.2**	**17.5**	**46.4**
16~24 岁 Age	64	37.5	37.5	20.3	14.1	26.6	31.3	26.6
25~34 岁 Age	90	23.3	13.3	21.1	14.4	17.8	15.6	46.7
35~44 岁 Age	76	14.5	19.7	14.5	7.9	11.8	13.2	48.7
45~54 岁 Age	48	16.7	20.8	20.8	20.8	8.3	12.5	56.3
55~60 岁 Age	24	8.3	16.7	20.8	4.2	12.5	12.5	70.8

3-15 样本、男性各年龄层、女性各年龄层对戏剧或戏曲的信息接触情况/ Information Contact about Drama or Opera by the Whole Sample, Age and Gender Groups

注：本题为多选题，合计百分比超过 100%（Multiple answers）

	人数 Number	阅读有关的杂志和专门报道 reading magazines related and special reports	相互口头传播信息 communicate information orally among people	经常看这种服务的广告 often watch advertise-ments about such kinds of service	尝试这种服务的新类型 try using the latest type of such kinds of service	过去在这种服务上花了不少钱 used to spend much money on such kinds of service	今后愿意在这方面花钱 willing to spend money on such items in future	不关注这方面的信息 don't care about such items
样本 Sample	601	10.5	7.5	8.3	4.5	2.5	4.0	79.0
男性 Male	299	6.0	4.3	4.7	3.7	1.3	2.0	85.3
16~24 岁 Age	64	1.6	1.6	4.7	3.1	0.0	3.1	90.6
25~34 岁 Age	89	2.2	3.4	2.2	2.2	0.0	0.0	91.0
35~44 岁 Age	76	6.6	3.9	3.9	3.9	1.3	2.6	86.8
45~54 岁 Age	46	10.9	4.3	2.2	4.3	0.0	0.0	78.3
55~60 岁 Age	24	20.8	16.7	20.8	8.3	12.5	8.3	58.3
女性 Female	302	14.9	10.6	11.9	5.3	3.6	6.0	72.8
16~24 岁 Age	64	9.4	3.1	4.7	3.1	3.1	6.3	81.3
25~34 岁 Age	90	4.4	3.3	5.6	1.1	0.0	2.2	86.7
35~44 岁 Age	76	13.2	7.9	9.2	6.6	1.3	2.6	75.0
45~54 岁 Age	48	31.3	22.9	27.1	10.4	6.3	16.7	45.8
55~60 岁 Age	24	41.7	41.7	33.3	12.5	20.8	8.3	45.8

3-16 样本、男性各年龄层、女性各年龄层对蹦迪的信息接触情况/ Information Contact about Disco by the Whole Sample, Age and Gender Groups

注：本题为多选题，合计百分比超过 100%（Multiple answers）

	人数 Number	阅读有关的杂志和专门报道 reading magazines related and special reports	相互口头传播信息 communicate information orally among people	经常看这种服务的广告 often watch advertise-ments about such kinds of service	尝试这种服务的新类型 try using the latest type of such kinds of service	过去在这种服务上花了不少钱 used to spend much money on such kinds of service	今后愿意在这方面花钱 willing to spend money on such items in future	不关注这方面的信息 don't care about such items
样本 Sample	601	4.3	5.5	3.2	6.8	4.7	7.3	81.5
男性 Male	299	2.3	4.7	2.7	6.4	6.4	8.0	80.3
16~24 岁 Age	64	4.7	14.1	3.1	10.9	12.5	25.0	50.0
25~34 岁 Age	89	4.5	4.5	4.5	11.2	6.7	6.7	79.8
35~44 岁 Age	76	0.0	1.3	0.0	1.3	3.9	1.3	93.4
45~54 岁 Age	46	0.0	0.0	4.3	2.2	4.3	2.2	91.3
55~60 岁 Age	24	0.0	0.0	0.0	0.0	0.0	0.0	100.0
女性 Female	302	6.3	6.3	3.6	7.3	3.0	6.6	82.8
16~24 岁 Age	64	20.3	17.2	7.8	21.9	10.9	18.8	53.1
25~34 岁 Age	90	3.3	3.3	1.1	3.3	0.0	4.4	86.7
35~44 岁 Age	76	1.3	3.9	2.6	3.9	0.0	2.6	90.8
45~54 岁 Age	48	2.1	2.1	4.2	2.1	2.1	2.1	95.8
55~60 岁 Age	24	4.2	4.2	4.2	4.2	4.2	4.2	95.8

3-17 样本、男性各年龄层、女性各年龄层对现场观赏体育比赛的信息接触情况/ Information Contact about Enjoying Live Sports by the Whole Sample, Age and Gender Groups

注：本题为多选题，合计百分比超过 100%（Multiple answers）

	人数 Number	阅读有关的杂志和专门报道 reading magazines related and special reports	相互口头传播信息 communicate information orally among people	经常看这种服务的广告 often watch advertisements about such kinds of service	尝试这种服务的新类型 try using the latest type of such kinds of service	过去在这种服务上花了不少钱 used to spend much money on such kinds of service	今后愿意在这方面花钱 willing to spend money on such items in future	不关注这方面的信息 don't care about such items
样本 Sample	**601**	**34.1**	**27.5**	**22.5**	**11.8**	**12.0**	**19.6**	**42.1**
男性 Male	**299**	**45.5**	**33.4**	**28.1**	**17.4**	**18.7**	**28.8**	**28.1**
16~24 岁 Age	64	50.0	29.7	32.8	15.6	14.1	37.5	25.0
25~34 岁 Age	89	50.6	37.1	25.8	20.2	22.5	31.5	30.3
35~44 岁 Age	76	42.1	39.5	27.6	19.7	21.1	23.7	25.0
45~54 岁 Age	46	43.5	30.4	26.1	8.7	19.6	30.4	23.9
55~60 岁 Age	24	29.2	16.7	29.2	20.8	8.3	8.3	45.8
女性 Female	**302**	**22.8**	**21.5**	**16.9**	**6.3**	**5.3**	**10.6**	**56.0**
16~24 岁 Age	64	18.8	23.4	20.3	7.8	10.9	15.6	50.0
25~34 岁 Age	90	23.3	17.8	11.1	4.4	2.2	4.4	54.4
35~44 岁 Age	76	25.0	25.0	15.8	6.6	6.6	17.1	53.9
45~54 岁 Age	48	27.1	22.9	27.1	8.3	2.1	8.3	62.5
55~60 岁 Age	24	16.7	16.7	12.5	4.2	4.2	4.2	70.8

3-18 样本、男性各年龄层、女性各年龄层对运动健身的信息接触情况/ Information Contact about Gym by the Whole Sample, Age and Gender Groups

注：本题为多选题，合计百分比超过 100%（Multiple answers）

	人数 Number	阅读有关的杂志和专门报道 reading magazines related and special reports	相互口头传播信息 communicate information orally among people	经常看这种服务的广告 often watch advertisements about such kinds of service	尝试这种服务的新类型 try using the latest type of such kinds of service	过去在这种服务上花了不少钱 used to spend much money on such kinds of service	今后愿意在这方面花钱 willing to spend money on such items in future	不关注这方面的信息 don't care about such items
样本 Sample	**600**	**19.5**	**17.7**	**15.8**	**15.0**	**7.0**	**26.7**	**43.2**
男性 Male	**298**	**19.1**	**16.4**	**14.1**	**15.8**	**8.1**	**28.5**	**41.3**
16~24 岁 Age	64	17.2	18.8	12.5	21.9	12.5	40.6	32.8
25~34 岁 Age	88	21.6	18.2	20.5	19.3	8.0	31.8	37.5
35~44 岁 Age	76	18.4	15.8	7.9	10.5	5.3	17.1	48.7
45~54 岁 Age	46	23.9	10.9	15.2	10.9	6.5	26.1	45.7
55~60 岁 Age	24	8.3	16.7	12.5	12.5	8.3	25.0	45.8
女性 Female	**302**	**19.9**	**18.9**	**17.5**	**14.2**	**6.0**	**24.8**	**45.0**
16~24 岁 Age	64	26.6	25.0	28.1	21.9	9.4	29.7	20.3
25~34 岁 Age	90	12.2	11.1	13.3	11.1	6.7	27.8	48.9
35~44 岁 Age	76	23.7	19.7	13.2	10.5	6.6	23.7	51.3
45~54 岁 Age	48	20.8	22.9	18.8	12.5	0.0	14.6	54.2
55~60 岁 Age	24	16.7	20.8	16.7	20.8	4.2	25.0	58.3

3-19 样本、男性各年龄层、女性各年龄层对技能学习的信息接触情况/ Information Contact about Studying Skills by the Whole Sample, Age and Gender Groups

注：本题为多选题，合计百分比超过 100%（Multiple answers）

	人数 Number	阅读有关的杂志和专门报道 reading magazines related and special reports	相互口头传播信息 communicate information orally among people	经常看这种服务的广告 often watch advertisements about such kinds of service	尝试这种服务的新类型 try using the latest type of such kinds of service	过去在这种服务上花了不少钱 used to spend much money on such kinds of service	今后愿意在这方面花钱 willing to spend money on such items in future	不关注这方面的信息 don't care about such items
样本 Sample	601	23.5	15.0	15.1	11.6	12.1	27.3	46.8
男性 Male	299	22.7	15.4	14.7	12.4	11.7	31.1	45.5
16~24 岁 Age	64	29.7	18.8	17.2	17.2	9.4	50.0	23.4
25~34 岁 Age	89	30.3	19.1	15.7	14.6	16.9	36.0	37.1
35~44 岁 Age	76	17.1	13.2	15.8	11.8	9.2	26.3	52.6
45~54 岁 Age	46	15.2	15.2	10.9	6.5	10.9	15.2	63.0
55~60 岁 Age	24	8.3	0.0	8.3	4.2	8.3	8.3	79.2
女性 Female	302	24.2	14.6	15.6	10.9	12.6	23.5	48.0
16~24 岁 Age	64	32.8	23.4	17.2	20.3	18.8	34.4	31.3
25~34 岁 Age	90	20.0	13.3	14.4	8.9	12.2	22.2	51.1
35~44 岁 Age	76	25.0	15.8	17.1	11.8	13.2	26.3	42.1
45~54 岁 Age	48	25.0	8.3	16.7	6.3	10.4	18.8	58.3
55~60 岁 Age	24	12.5	4.2	8.3	0.0	0.0	0.0	79.2

3-20 样本、男性各年龄层、女性各年龄层对外语学习的信息接触情况/ Information Contact about Studying Foreign Languages by the Whole Sample, Age and Gender Groups

注：本题为多选题，合计百分比超过 100%（Multiple answers）

	人数 Number	阅读有关的杂志和专门报道 reading magazines related and special reports	相互口头传播信息 communicate information orally among people	经常看这种服务的广告 often watch advertisements about such kinds of service	尝试这种服务的新类型 try using the latest type of such kinds of service	过去在这种服务上花了不少钱 used to spend much money on such kinds of service	今后愿意在这方面花钱 willing to spend money on such items in future	不关注这方面的信息 don't care about such items
样本 Sample	600	18.8	9.3	8.2	7.5	9.3	23.8	57.7
男性 Male	298	17.4	8.1	6.7	6.0	8.7	23.2	59.4
16~24 岁 Age	64	32.8	20.3	9.4	10.9	20.3	50.0	26.6
25~34 岁 Age	89	20.2	7.9	6.7	6.7	6.7	24.7	58.4
35~44 岁 Age	75	12.0	5.3	8.0	5.3	2.7	14.7	65.3
45~54 岁 Age	46	6.5	0.0	4.3	0.0	6.5	4.3	80.4
55~60 岁 Age	24	4.2	0.0	0.0	4.2	8.3	8.3	91.7
女性 Female	302	20.2	10.6	9.6	8.9	9.9	24.5	56.0
16~24 岁 Age	64	43.8	20.3	21.9	20.3	31.3	42.2	26.6
25~34 岁 Age	90	17.8	11.1	5.6	6.7	4.4	30.0	51.1
35~44 岁 Age	76	11.8	7.9	6.6	9.2	6.6	17.1	65.8
45~54 岁 Age	48	8.3	6.3	8.3	2.1	2.1	12.5	77.1
55~60 岁 Age	24	16.7	0.0	4.2	0.0	0.0	4.2	79.2

3-21 不同消费者层对电视、音响等视听设备的信息接触情况/ Information Contact about Video & Audio Equipment by Market Segments

注：本题为多选题，合计百分比超过 100%（Multiple answers）

	人数 Number	不管买还是不买，想看看 just have a look, without a definite purpose of buying or not	阅读有关的杂志和专门报道 reading magazines related & special reports	相互口头传播信息 communicate information orally among people	经常看这种商品的广告 often watch advertisements about such kinds of goods	购买这种商品的新类型 buy the latest type of such kinds of goods	过去在这种商品上花了不少钱 used to spend much money on such kinds of goods	今后愿意在这方面花钱 willing to spend money on such items in future	不关注这方面的信息 don't care about such items
样本 Sample	601	58.4	29.3	31.4	40.4	14.6	23.8	31.1	15.6
平实生活指向 simple living orientation	292	56.8	26.4	29.8	38.0	11.3	19.9	30.1	17.1
时尚流行指向 fashion orientation	309	59.9	32.0	33.0	42.7	17.8	27.5	32.0	14.2

3-22 不同消费者层对冰箱、洗衣机等白色家电的信息接触情况/ Information Contact about "White Home Electronic Products" by Market Segments

注：本题为多选题，合计百分比超过 100%（Multiple answers）

	人数 Number	不管买还是不买，想看看 just have a look, without a definite purpose of buying or not	阅读有关的杂志和专门报道 reading magazines related & special reports	相互口头传播信息 communicate information orally among people	经常看这种商品的广告 often watch advertisements about such kinds of goods	购买这种商品的新类型 buy the latest type of such kinds of goods	过去在这种商品上花了不少钱 used to spend much money on such kinds of goods	今后愿意在这方面花钱 willing to spend money on such items in future	不关注这方面的信息 don't care about such items
样本 Sample	601	43.9	19.1	21.6	29.8	10.1	19.3	19.8	25.6
平实生活指向 simple living orientation	292	42.8	13.4	20.5	25.7	7.2	15.8	17.1	27.7
时尚流行指向 fashion orientation	309	45.0	24.6	22.7	33.7	12.9	22.7	22.3	23.6

3-23 不同消费者层对电脑等通讯工具的信息接触情况/ Information Contact about Computer & Telecommunications by Market Segments

注：本题为多选题，合计百分比超过 100%（Multiple answers）

	人数 Number	不管买还是不买，想看看 just have a look, without a definite purpose of buying or not	阅读有关的杂志和专门报道 reading magazines related & special reports	相互口头传播信息 communicate information orally among people	经常看这种商品的广告 often watch advertisements about such kinds of goods	购买这种商品的新类型 buy the latest type of such kinds of goods	过去在这种商品上花了不少钱 used to spend much money on such kinds of goods	今后愿意在这方面花钱 willing to spend money on such items in future	不关注这方面的信息 don't care about such items
样本 Sample	601	36.3	28.1	23.6	24.6	10.1	8.0	31.4	36.4
平实生活指向 simple living orientation	292	29.5	22.6	21.2	18.5	8.6	8.2	29.8	41.4
时尚流行指向 fashion orientation	309	42.7	33.3	25.9	30.4	11.7	7.8	33.0	31.7

3-24 不同消费者层对家用轿车的信息接触情况/ Information Contact about Family Car by Market Segments

注：本题为多选题，合计百分比超过 100%（Multiple answers）

	人数 Number	不管买还是不买，想看看 just have a look, without a definite purpose of buying or not	阅读有关的杂志和专门报道 reading magazines related & special reports	相互口头传播信息 communicate information orally among people	经常看这种商品的广告 often watch advertise-ments about such kinds of goods	购买这种商品的新类型 buy the latest type of such kinds of goods	过去在这种商品上花了不少钱 used to spend much money on such kinds of goods	今后愿意在这方面花钱 willing to spend money on such items in future	不关注这方面的信息 don't care about such items
样本 Sample	601	21.5	16.1	13.3	12.6	3.0	1.5	10.1	60.6
平实生活指向 simple living orientation	292	16.1	12.3	9.9	9.2	1.0	0.3	8.9	66.4
时尚流行指向 fashion orientation	309	26.5	19.7	16.5	15.9	4.9	2.6	11.3	55.0

3-25 不同消费者层对高级家具的信息接触情况/ Information Contact about First-class Furniture by Market Segments

注：本题为多选题，合计百分比超过 100%（Multiple answers）

	人数 Number	不管买还是不买，想看看 just have a look, without a definite purpose of buying or not	阅读有关的杂志和专门报道 reading magazines related & special reports	相互口头传播信息 communicate information orally among people	经常看这种商品的广告 often watch advertise-ments about such kinds of goods	购买这种商品的新类型 buy the latest type of such kinds of goods	过去在这种商品上花了不少钱 used to spend much money on such kinds of goods	今后愿意在这方面花钱 willing to spend money on such items in future	不关注这方面的信息 don't care about such items
样本 Sample	600	30.3	13.8	8.0	12.0	5.0	4.7	14.8	53.3
平实生活指向 simple living orientation	291	25.4	10.7	5.8	8.6	2.4	4.1	14.1	59.1
时尚流行指向 fashion orientation	309	35.0	16.8	10.0	15.2	7.4	5.2	15.5	47.9

3-26 不同消费者层对西服和时装的信息接触情况/ Information Contact about Business Suit & Fashion by Market Segments

注：本题为多选题，合计百分比超过 100%（Multiple answers）

	人数 Number	不管买还是不买，想看看 just have a look, without a definite purpose of buying or not	阅读有关的杂志和专门报道 reading magazines related & special reports	相互口头传播信息 communicate information orally among people	经常看这种商品的广告 often watch advertise-ments about such kinds of goods	购买这种商品的新类型 buy the latest type of such kinds of goods	过去在这种商品上花了不少钱 used to spend much money on such kinds of goods	今后愿意在这方面花钱 willing to spend money on such items in future	不关注这方面的信息 don't care about such items
样本 Sample	601	50.4	22.3	26.3	26.0	21.8	27.8	31.9	24.0
平实生活指向 simple living orientation	292	42.8	14.4	19.5	18.2	14.7	20.2	25.7	32.5
时尚流行指向 fashion orientation	309	57.6	29.8	32.7	33.3	28.5	35.0	37.9	15.9

3-27 不同消费者层对酒精饮料的信息接触情况/ Information Contact about Alcohol Drinks by Market Segments

注：本题为多选题，合计百分比超过 100%（Multiple answers）

	人数 Number	不管买还是不买，想看看 just have a look, without a definite purpose of buying or not	阅读有关的杂志和专门报道 reading magazines related & special reports	相互口头传播信息 communicate information orally among people	经常看这种商品的广告 often watch advertise-ments about such kinds of goods	购买这种商品的新类型 buy the latest type of such kinds of goods	过去在这种商品上花了不少钱 used to spend much money on such kinds of goods	今后愿意在这方面花钱 willing to spend money on such items in future	不关注这方面的信息 don't care about such items
样本 Sample	600	21.8	9.5	13.5	18.5	11.5	17.3	16.2	49.2
平实生活指向 simple living orientation	291	21.3	7.2	12.7	16.8	10.7	19.9	17.9	49.5
时尚流行指向 fashion orientation	309	22.3	11.7	14.2	20.1	12.3	14.9	14.6	48.9

3-28 不同消费者层对 CD 唱片及音乐带的信息接触情况/ Information Contact about CD & Music Cassette by Market Segments

注：本题为多选题，合计百分比超过 100%（Multiple answers）

	人数 Number	不管买还是不买，想看看 just have a look, without a definite purpose of buying or not	阅读有关的杂志和专门报道 reading magazines related & special reports	相互口头传播信息 communicate information orally among people	经常看这种商品的广告 often watch advertise-ments about such kinds of goods	购买这种商品的新类型 buy the latest type of such kinds of goods	过去在这种商品上花了不少钱 used to spend much money on such kinds of goods	今后愿意在这方面花钱 willing to spend money on such items in future	不关注这方面的信息 don't care about such items
样本 Sample	601	34.4	17.0	20.6	18.3	16.5	21.6	24.5	37.9
平实生活指向 simple living orientation	292	28.1	14.0	18.2	12.7	13.7	13.7	20.2	46.6
时尚流行指向 fashion orientation	309	40.5	19.7	23.0	23.6	19.1	29.1	28.5	29.8

3-29 不同消费者层对护肤品和化妆品的信息接触情况/ Information Contact about Skin Cream & Cosmetics by Market Segments

注：本题为多选题，合计百分比超过 100%（Multiple answers）

	人数 Number	不管买还是不买，想看看 just have a look, without a definite purpose of buying or not	阅读有关的杂志和专门报道 reading magazines related & special reports	相互口头传播信息 communicate information orally among people	经常看这种商品的广告 often watch advertise-ments about such kinds of goods	购买这种商品的新类型 buy the latest type of such kinds of goods	过去在这种商品上花了不少钱 used to spend much money on such kinds of goods	今后愿意在这方面花钱 willing to spend money on such items in future	不关注这方面的信息 don't care about such items
样本 Sample	601	35.9	18.3	21.5	27.6	17.0	22.0	27.0	41.8
平实生活指向 simple living orientation	292	26.4	13.0	15.1	22.6	8.6	16.1	18.8	49.0
时尚流行指向 fashion orientation	309	45.0	23.3	27.5	32.4	24.9	27.5	34.6	35.0

3-30 不同消费者层对香波等洗涤用品的信息接触情况/ Information Contact about Shampoo & Detergent by Market Segments

注：本题为多选题，合计百分比超过 100%（Multiple answers）

	人数 Number	不管买还是不买，想看看 just have a look, without a definite purpose of buying or not	阅读有关的杂志和专门报道 reading magazines related & special reports	相互口头传播信息 communicate information orally among people	经常看这种商品的广告 often watch advertise-ments about such kinds of goods	购买这种商品的新类型 buy the latest type of such kinds of goods	过去在这种商品上花了不少钱 used to spend much money on such kinds of goods	今后愿意在这方面花钱 willing to spend money on such items in future	不关注这方面的信息 don't care about such items
样本 Sample	601	41.3	15.1	20.0	30.1	22.5	24.6	30.1	30.6
平实生活指向 simple living orientation	292	37.0	12.0	14.0	25.7	16.8	20.2	24.0	36.6
时尚流行指向 fashion orientation	309	45.3	18.1	25.6	34.3	27.8	28.8	35.9	24.9

3-31 不同消费者层对外出就餐的信息接触情况/ Information Contact about Dinning Out by Market Segments

注：本题为多选题，合计百分比超过 100%（Multiple answers）

	人数 Number	阅读有关的杂志和专门报道 reading magazines related and special reports	相互口头传播信息 communicate information orally among people	经常看这种服务的广告 often watch advertise-ments about such kinds of service	尝试这种服务的新类型 try using the latest type of such kinds of service	过去在这种服务上花了不少钱 used to spend much money on such kinds of service	今后愿意在这方面花钱 willing to spend money on such items in future	不关注这方面的信息 don't care about such items
样本 Sample	600	20.5	20.8	15.0	21.0	23.2	28.8	34.5
平实生活指向 simple living orientation	292	15.4	18.2	12.0	17.1	19.5	25.7	42.1
时尚流行指向 fashion orientation	308	25.3	23.4	17.9	24.7	26.6	31.8	27.3

3-32 不同消费者层对旅行的信息接触情况/ Information Contact about Travelling by Market Segments

注：本题为多选题，合计百分比超过 100%（Multiple answers）

	人数 Number	阅读有关的杂志和专门报道 reading magazines related and special reports	相互口头传播信息 communicate information orally among people	经常看这种服务的广告 often watch advertise-ments about such kinds of service	尝试这种服务的新类型 try using the latest type of such kinds of service	过去在这种服务上花了不少钱 used to spend much money on such kinds of service	今后愿意在这方面花钱 willing to spend money on such items in future	不关注这方面的信息 don't care about such items
样本 Sample	601	25.6	23.1	18.5	19.5	20.3	42.3	28.3
平实生活指向 simple living orientation	292	20.9	18.8	14.4	16.4	16.8	40.1	34.2
时尚流行指向 fashion orientation	309	30.1	27.2	22.3	22.3	23.6	44.3	22.7

3-33 不同消费者层对音乐会的信息接触情况/ Information Contact about Concert by Market Segments

注：本题为多选题，合计百分比超过 100%（Multiple answers）

	人数 Number	阅读有关的杂志和专门报道 reading magazines related and special reports	相互口头传播信息 communicate information orally among people	经常看这种服务的广告 often watch advertise-ments about such kinds of service	尝试这种服务的新类型 try using the latest type of such kinds of service	过去在这种服务上花了不少钱 used to spend much money on such kinds of service	今后愿意在这方面花钱 willing to spend money on such items in future	不关注这方面的信息 don't care about such items
样本 Sample	600	14.2	11.7	13.8	9.2	5.5	14.7	59.0
平实生活指向 simple living orientation	292	8.6	8.6	7.9	8.9	3.1	10.6	67.8
时尚流行指向 fashion orientation	308	19.5	14.6	19.5	9.4	7.8	18.5	50.6

3-34 不同消费者层对电影的信息接触情况/ Information Contact about Movie by Market Segments

注：本题为多选题，合计百分比超过 100%（Multiple answers）

	人数 Number	阅读有关的杂志和专门报道 reading magazines related and special reports	相互口头传播信息 communicate information orally among people	经常看这种服务的广告 often watch advertise-ments about such kinds of service	尝试这种服务的新类型 try using the latest type of such kinds of service	过去在这种服务上花了不少钱 used to spend much money on such kinds of service	今后愿意在这方面花钱 willing to spend money on such items in future	不关注这方面的信息 don't care about such items
样本 Sample	600	22.5	18.8	18.3	13.5	17.3	19.0	45.5
平实生活指向 simple living orientation	292	17.5	16.8	15.4	13.0	13.7	14.7	51.7
时尚流行指向 fashion orientation	308	27.3	20.8	21.1	14.0	20.8	23.1	39.6

3-35 不同消费者层对戏剧或戏曲的信息接触情况/ Information Contact about Drama or Opera by Market Segments

注：本题为多选题，合计百分比超过 100%（Multiple answers）

	人数 Number	阅读有关的杂志和专门报道 reading magazines related and special reports	相互口头传播信息 communicate information orally among people	经常看这种服务的广告 often watch advertise-ments about such kinds of service	尝试这种服务的新类型 try using the latest type of such kinds of service	过去在这种服务上花了不少钱 used to spend much money on such kinds of service	今后愿意在这方面花钱 willing to spend money on such items in future	不关注这方面的信息 don't care about such items
样本 Sample	601	10.5	7.5	8.3	4.5	2.5	4.0	79.0
平实生活指向 simple living orientation	292	12.0	10.3	7.9	5.8	2.7	4.5	77.1
时尚流行指向 fashion orientation	309	9.1	4.9	8.7	3.2	2.3	3.6	80.9

3-36 不同消费者层对蹦迪的信息接触情况/ Information Contact about Disco by Market Segments

注：本题为多选题，合计百分比超过 100%（Multiple answers）

	人数 Number	阅读有关的杂志和专门报道 reading magazines related and special reports	相互口头传播信息 communicate information orally among people	经常看这种服务的广告 often watch advertise-ments about such kinds of service	尝试这种服务的新类型 try using the latest type of such kinds of service	过去在这种服务上花了不少钱 used to spend much money on such kinds of service	今后愿意在这方面花钱 willing to spend money on such items in future	不关注这方面的信息 don't care about such items
样本 Sample	601	4.3	5.5	3.2	6.8	4.7	7.3	81.5
平实生活指向 simple living orientation	292	1.7	2.4	1.4	3.1	1.0	2.7	92.1
时尚流行指向 fashion orientation	309	6.8	8.4	4.9	10.4	8.1	11.7	71.5

3-37 不同消费者层对现场观赏体育比赛的信息接触情况/ Information Contact about Enjoying Live Sports by Market Segments

注：本题为多选题，合计百分比超过 100%（Multiple answers）

	人数 Number	阅读有关的杂志和专门报道 reading magazines related and special reports	相互口头传播信息 communicate information orally among people	经常看这种服务的广告 often watch advertise-ments about such kinds of service	尝试这种服务的新类型 try using the latest type of such kinds of service	过去在这种服务上花了不少钱 used to spend much money on such kinds of service	今后愿意在这方面花钱 willing to spend money on such items in future	不关注这方面的信息 don't care about such items
样本 Sample	601	34.1	27.5	22.5	11.8	12.0	19.6	42.1
平实生活指向 simple living orientation	292	31.8	23.3	20.5	11.0	10.3	18.5	46.2
时尚流行指向 fashion orientation	309	36.2	31.4	24.3	12.6	13.6	20.7	38.2

3-38 不同消费者层对运动健身的信息接触情况/ Information Contact about Gym by Market Segments

注：本题为多选题，合计百分比超过 100%（Multiple answers）

	人数 Number	阅读有关的杂志和专门报道 reading magazines related and special reports	相互口头传播信息 communicate information orally among people	经常看这种服务的广告 often watch advertisements about such kinds of service	尝试这种服务的新类型 try using the latest type of such kinds of service	过去在这种服务上花了不少钱 used to spend much money on such kinds of service	今后愿意在这方面花钱 willing to spend money on such items in future	不关注这方面的信息 don't care about such items
样本 Sample	**600**	**19.5**	**17.7**	**15.8**	**15.0**	**7.0**	**26.7**	**43.2**
平实生活指向 simple living orientation	291	16.2	17.2	12.7	13.4	5.2	22.7	49.8
时尚流行指向 fashion orientation	309	22.7	18.1	18.8	16.5	8.7	30.4	36.9

3-39 不同消费者层对技能学习的信息接触情况/ Information Contact about Studying Skills by Market Segments

注：本题为多选题，合计百分比超过 100%（Multiple answers）

	人数 Number	阅读有关的杂志和专门报道 reading magazines related and special reports	相互口头传播信息 communicate information orally among people	经常看这种服务的广告 often watch advertisements about such kinds of service	尝试这种服务的新类型 try using the latest type of such kinds of service	过去在这种服务上花了不少钱 used to spend much money on such kinds of service	今后愿意在这方面花钱 willing to spend money on such items in future	不关注这方面的信息 don't care about such items
样本 Sample	**601**	**23.5**	**15.0**	**15.1**	**11.6**	**12.1**	**27.3**	**46.8**
平实生活指向 simple living orientation	292	22.9	13.4	14.0	10.3	9.9	25.3	49.0
时尚流行指向 fashion orientation	309	23.9	16.5	16.2	12.9	14.2	29.1	44.7

3-40 不同消费者层对外语学习的信息接触情况/ Information Contact about Studying Foreign Languages by Market Segments

注：本题为多选题，合计百分比超过 100%（Multiple answers）

	人数 Number	阅读有关的杂志和专门报道 reading magazines related and special reports	相互口头传播信息 communicate information orally among people	经常看这种服务的广告 often watch advertisements about such kinds of service	尝试这种服务的新类型 try using the latest type of such kinds of service	过去在这种服务上花了不少钱 used to spend much money on such kinds of service	今后愿意在这方面花钱 willing to spend money on such items in future	不关注这方面的信息 don't care about such items
样本 Sample	**600**	**18.8**	**9.3**	**8.2**	**7.5**	**9.3**	**23.8**	**57.7**
平实生活指向 simple living orientation	292	17.8	7.9	6.2	5.8	8.2	20.5	63.0
时尚流行指向 fashion orientation	308	19.8	10.7	10.1	9.1	10.4	26.9	52.6

4．休闲活动 / Leisure Activities

● 北京 / Beijing

4-1 常做的休闲活动排名/ Ranking of the Frequently Engaged Activities

注：本题为多选题，合计百分比超过 100%（Multiple answers）

排名 Ranking	活动项目 Activity Items	人次 Person-time	百分比 Percent
1	看书 reading	837	83.4
2	逛街购物 shopping	665	66.3
3	听音乐 enjoying music	617	61.5
4	去动物园或公园 going to the park or zoo	496	49.5
5	打羽毛球 badminton	446	44.5
6	慢跑 jogging	374	37.3
7	游泳 swimming	359	35.8
8	看展览会 visiting exhibition	342	34.1
9	看电影 going to movie	341	34.0
10	唱卡拉 OK Karaoke	334	33.3
11	打麻将 mah-jong	314	31.3
12	打乒乓球 table-tennis	286	28.5
13	国内一天往返的旅行 short journey that can be back in a day	285	28.4
14	登山 mountain climbing	282	28.1
15	打保龄球 bowling	278	27.7
16	国内一天以上的旅行 domestic travel	269	26.8
17	打游戏机 playing video game	260	25.9
18	电脑游戏 playing PC game	255	25.4
19	种花盆栽 horticulture	248	24.7
20	去博物馆或美术馆 going to museum or art gallery	202	20.1
21	郊游露营 outing & camping	190	18.9
22	打篮球 basketball	167	16.7
23	开汽车兜风 going out for a driving	162	16.2
24	听演唱会/音乐会 attending concert	161	16.1
25	编织裁剪 knitting & tailoring	153	15.3
26	钓鱼 fishing	143	14.3
27	酒吧/咖啡屋/茶秀 going to cafe or bar	138	13.8
28	绘画书法 drawing & calligraphy	126	12.6
29	踢足球 soccer	117	11.7
30	滚轴溜冰 rolling skating	109	10.9
31	跳迪斯科 disco	87	8.7
32	打网球 tennis	79	7.9
33	扭秧歌/木兰拳/交谊舞 doing the YangKo	74	7.4
34	乐器演奏 playing musical instrument	67	6.7
35	滑冰 skating	48	4.8
36	玩滑板 skateboarding	14	1.4
37	打高尔夫球 golf	13	1.3
38	海外旅行 overseas travel	11	1.1

n=1003

4-2 想做的休闲活动排名/ Ranking of the Desired Activities

注：本题为多选题，合计百分比超过 100%（Multiple answers）

排名 Ranking	活动项目 Activity Items	人次 Person-time	百分比 Percent
1	海外旅行 overseas travel	349	40.2
2	郊游露营 outing & camping	301	34.7
3	打网球 tennis	295	34.0
4	听演唱会/音乐会 attending concert	283	32.6
5	国内一天以上的旅行 domestic travel	276	31.8
6	登山 mountain climbing	260	30.0
7	打保龄球 bowling	237	27.3
8	开汽车兜风 going out for a driving	221	25.5
9	去博物馆或美术馆 going to museum or art gallery	196	22.6
10	游泳 swimming	195	22.5
11	国内一天往返的旅行 short journey that can be back in a day	163	18.8
12	看电影 going to movie	162	18.7
13	钓鱼 fishing	159	18.3
14	滑冰 skating	154	17.7
15	打高尔夫球 golf	153	17.6
16	看展览会 visiting exhibition	145	16.7
17	绘画书法 drawing & calligraphy	143	16.5
18	慢跑 jogging	131	15.1
19	打羽毛球 badminton	127	14.6
19	打乒乓球 table-tennis	127	14.6
20	去动物园或公园 going to the park or zoo	118	13.6
21	种花盆栽 horticulture	113	13.0
22	乐器演奏 playing musical instrument	107	12.3
23	酒吧/咖啡屋/茶秀 going to cafe or bar	103	11.9
24	听音乐 enjoying music	90	10.4
25	滚轴溜冰 rolling skating	85	9.8
26	电脑游戏 playing PC game	84	9.7
27	跳迪斯科 disco	79	9.1
27	打篮球 basketball	79	9.1
28	踢足球 soccer	77	8.9
29	唱卡拉 OK Karaoke	75	8.6
30	扭秧歌/木兰拳/交谊舞 doing the YangKo	69	7.9
30	玩滑板 skateboarding	69	7.9
31	编织裁剪 knitting & tailoring	67	7.7
32	打麻将 mah-jong	66	7.6
33	逛街购物 shopping	61	7.0
34	看书 reading	54	6.2
35	打游戏机 playing video game	53	6.1

n=868

4-3 样本、男性各年龄层、女性各年龄层常做的活动/ Frequently Engaged Activities by the Whole Sample, Age and Gender Groups

注：本题为多选题，合计百分比超过 100%（Multiple answers）

	人数 Number	打网球 tennis	打高尔夫球 golf	打羽毛球 badmin-ton	打保龄球 bowling	踢足球 soccer	打篮球 basket-ball	打乒乓球 table tennis	慢跑 jogging	玩滑板 skate boarding	跳迪斯科 disco
样本 Sample	1003	7.9	1.3	44.5	27.7	11.7	16.7	28.5	37.3	1.4	8.7
男性 Male	499	8.2	1.0	43.1	32.5	21.4	23.8	38.7	38.1	2.2	7.6
16~24 岁 Age	105	9.5	1.0	52.4	37.1	49.5	61.0	43.8	40.0	8.6	13.3
25~34 岁 Age	151	10.6	0.0	50.3	43.0	23.2	17.2	43.7	29.8	0.0	11.3
35~44 岁 Age	128	7.0	2.3	37.5	29.7	10.9	14.1	39.8	32.0	0.8	4.7
45~54 岁 Age	75	4.0	1.3	34.7	21.3	8.0	12.0	28.0	48.0	1.3	1.3
55~60 岁 Age	40	7.5	0.0	25.0	10.0	0.0	5.0	22.5	65.0	0.0	0.0
女性 Female	504	7.5	1.6	45.8	23.0	2.0	9.5	18.5	36.5	0.6	9.7
16~24 岁 Age	108	13.9	1.9	75.9	25.9	1.9	31.5	19.4	46.3	2.8	12.0
25~34 岁 Age	147	8.8	0.0	43.5	35.4	4.1	4.8	19.0	32.0	0.0	10.9
35~44 岁 Age	124	4.8	1.6	40.3	21.8	0.8	2.4	19.4	29.0	0.0	8.1
45~54 岁 Age	84	3.6	4.8	29.8	9.5	1.2	4.8	15.5	40.5	0.0	3.6
55~60 岁 Age	41	2.4	0.0	24.4	2.4	0.0	0.0	17.1	41.5	0.0	17.1

续前表 continued

	人数 Number	打麻将 mah-jong	游泳 swim-ming	滚轴溜冰 rolling skating	滑冰 skating	钓鱼 fishing	登山 mountain climbing	听音乐 enjoying music	看电影 going to movie	打游戏机 playing video game	编织裁剪 knitting & tailoring
样本 Sample	1003	31.3	35.8	10.9	4.8	14.3	28.1	61.5	34.0	25.9	15.3
男性 Male	499	35.9	39.5	9.2	6.8	21.0	27.7	57.7	32.5	32.1	1.0
16~24 岁 Age	105	28.6	41.9	30.5	10.5	21.9	32.4	77.1	53.3	66.7	0.0
25~34 岁 Age	151	40.4	45.0	6.0	6.0	17.2	25.8	60.9	39.7	33.8	0.0
35~44 岁 Age	128	39.8	40.6	2.3	8.6	27.3	28.1	46.1	18.8	21.9	0.8
45~54 岁 Age	75	36.0	36.0	2.7	2.7	20.0	26.7	48.0	22.7	8.0	2.7
55~60 岁 Age	40	25.0	15.0	0.0	2.5	15.0	22.5	50.0	12.5	12.5	5.0
女性 Female	504	26.8	32.1	12.5	2.8	7.5	28.6	65.3	35.5	19.8	29.4
16~24 岁 Age	108	18.5	53.7	47.2	7.4	5.6	32.4	84.3	59.3	30.6	8.3
25~34 岁 Age	147	35.4	35.4	6.1	2.0	8.8	25.2	64.6	35.4	24.5	21.8
35~44 岁 Age	124	31.5	29.8	1.6	1.6	10.5	28.2	56.5	29.8	15.3	34.7
45~54 岁 Age	84	25.0	16.7	1.2	1.2	4.8	33.3	58.3	20.2	13.1	57.1
55~60 岁 Age	41	7.3	2.4	0.0	0.0	4.9	22.0	58.5	22.0	2.4	39.0

续前表 continued

	人数 Number	种花盆栽 horticulture	看书 reading	绘画书法 drawing & calligraphy	乐器演奏 playing musical instrument	开汽车兜风 going out for a driving	逛街购物 shopping	郊游露营 outing & camping	海外旅行 overseas travel	国内一天以上的旅行 domestic travel
样本 Sample	1003	15.3	24.7	83.4	12.6	6.7	16.2	66.3	18.9	1.1
男性 Male	499	1.0	19.2	84.4	11.2	8.4	23.8	52.3	19.4	1.2
16~24 岁 Age	105	0.0	2.9	84.8	16.2	15.2	15.2	52.4	18.1	1.9
25~34 岁 Age	151	0.0	11.9	80.8	9.3	6.6	33.8	58.3	17.9	0.7
35~44 岁 Age	128	0.8	22.7	86.7	7.8	3.9	26.6	49.2	23.4	2.3
45~54 岁 Age	75	2.7	37.3	89.3	9.3	12.0	20.0	53.3	18.7	0.0
55~60 岁 Age	40	5.0	45.0	80.0	20.0	5.0	7.5	37.5	17.5	0.0
女性 Female	504	29.4	30.2	82.5	13.9	5.0	8.5	80.2	18.5	1.0
16~24 岁 Age	108	8.3	5.6	87.0	28.7	8.3	8.3	80.6	18.5	0.9
25~34 岁 Age	147	21.8	21.8	87.1	10.2	3.4	8.8	81.6	17.0	0.7
35~44 岁 Age	124	34.7	35.5	83.9	8.1	4.0	16.1	78.2	17.7	0.0
45~54 岁 Age	84	57.1	54.8	72.6	10.7	2.4	0.0	76.2	20.2	2.4
55~60 岁 Age	41	39.0	58.5	70.7	12.2	9.8	2.4	87.8	22.0	2.4

续前表 continued

	人数 Number	国内一天往返的旅行 short journey that can be back in a day	看展览会 visiting exhibition	听演唱会/音乐会 attending concert	扭秧歌/木兰拳/交谊舞 doing the YangKo	去博物馆或美术馆 going to museum or art gallery	唱卡拉OK karaoke	去动物园或公园 going to park or zoo	酒吧/咖啡屋/茶秀 going to cafe or bar	电脑游戏 playing PC game
样本 Sample	1003	26.8	28.4	34.1	16.1	7.4	20.1	33.3	49.5	13.8
男性 Male	499	29.1	28.1	36.9	15.2	4.4	21.0	33.7	43.1	17.0
16~24 岁 Age	105	20.0	21.0	39.0	18.1	2.9	22.9	38.1	38.1	26.7
25~34 岁 Age	151	31.1	28.5	31.8	15.2	2.0	15.9	45.0	39.7	20.5
35~44 岁 Age	128	35.2	35.9	39.8	14.8	4.7	26.6	33.6	53.1	15.6
45~54 岁 Age	75	28.0	26.7	37.3	12.0	6.7	18.7	16.0	41.3	5.3
55~60 岁 Age	40	27.5	22.5	40.0	15.0	12.5	22.5	12.5	40.0	5.0
女性 Female	504	24.6	28.8	31.3	16.9	10.3	19.2	32.9	55.8	10.5
16~24 岁 Age	108	23.1	31.5	25.9	18.5	3.7	20.4	36.1	55.6	16.7
25~34 岁 Age	147	21.1	29.3	28.6	16.3	4.1	16.3	37.4	55.1	14.3
35~44 岁 Age	124	30.6	28.2	33.1	16.1	17.7	22.6	37.9	48.4	8.9
45~54 岁 Age	84	25.0	28.6	38.1	16.7	10.7	20.2	25.0	56.0	2.4
55~60 岁 Age	41	22.0	22.0	36.6	17.1	26.8	14.6	9.8	80.5	2.4

4-4 样本、男性各年龄层、女性各年龄层想做的活动/ Desired Activities by the Whole Sample, Age and Gender Groups

注：本题为多选题，合计百分比超过 100%（Multiple answers）

	人数 Number	打网球 tennis	打高尔夫球 golf	打羽毛球 badminton	打保龄球 bowling	踢足球 soccer	打篮球 basketball	打乒乓球 table-tennis	慢跑 jogging	玩滑板 skate boarding	跳迪斯科 disco
样本 Sample	**868**	**34.0**	**17.6**	**14.6**	**27.3**	**8.9**	**9.1**	**14.6**	**15.1**	**7.9**	**9.1**
男性 Male	**431**	**33.2**	**22.5**	**15.1**	**25.5**	**14.2**	**11.8**	**15.1**	**16.2**	**9.3**	**8.4**
16~24 岁 Age	99	55.6	30.3	17.2	36.4	19.2	12.1	16.2	16.2	26.3	18.2
25~34 岁 Age	127	41.7	27.6	15.7	22.8	15.7	11.0	9.4	15.0	5.5	7.9
35~44 岁 Age	108	21.3	19.4	15.7	25.0	12.0	15.7	13.0	22.2	5.6	3.7
45~54 岁 Age	65	10.8	13.8	10.8	16.9	12.3	9.2	24.6	10.8	1.5	4.6
55~60 岁 Age	32	15.6	6.3	12.5	21.9	3.1	6.3	21.9	12.5	0.0	3.1
女性 Female	**437**	**34.8**	**12.8**	**14.2**	**29.1**	**3.7**	**6.4**	**14.2**	**14.0**	**6.6**	**9.8**
16~24 岁 Age	103	62.1	26.2	7.8	45.6	8.7	12.6	15.5	8.7	16.5	20.4
25~34 岁 Age	130	38.5	12.3	13.1	22.3	3.8	3.1	13.8	16.2	5.4	7.7
35~44 岁 Age	105	21.9	8.6	18.1	27.6	1.9	9.5	18.1	18.1	2.9	5.7
45~54 岁 Age	65	15.4	6.2	16.9	24.6	0.0	0.0	10.8	15.4	3.1	9.2
55~60 岁 Age	34	14.7	0.0	20.6	17.6	0.0	2.9	5.9	5.9	0.0	0.0

续前表 continued

	人数 Number	打麻将 mah-jong	游泳 swimming	滚轴溜冰 rolling skating	滑冰 skating	钓鱼 fishing	登山 mountain climbing	听音乐 enjoying music	看电影 going to movie	打游戏机 playing video game	编织裁剪 knitting & tailoring
样本 Sample	**868**	**7.6**	**22.5**	**9.8**	**17.7**	**18.3**	**30.0**	**10.4**	**18.7**	**6.1**	**7.7**
男性 Male	**431**	**6.5**	**23.9**	**10.4**	**16.7**	**24.4**	**29.0**	**9.7**	**19.0**	**6.7**	**3.2**
16~24 岁 Age	99	11.1	27.3	22.2	27.3	26.3	33.3	10.1	24.2	10.1	5.1
25~34 岁 Age	127	4.7	19.7	11.0	18.1	28.3	33.9	7.1	19.7	7.1	1.6
35~44 岁 Age	108	7.4	25.9	6.5	17.6	24.1	24.1	13.0	16.7	5.6	3.7
45~54 岁 Age	65	3.1	26.2	3.1	4.6	20.0	23.1	9.2	13.8	3.1	1.5
55~60 岁 Age	32	3.1	18.8	0.0	0.0	12.5	25.0	9.4	18.8	6.3	6.3
女性 Female	**437**	**8.7**	**21.1**	**9.2**	**18.8**	**12.4**	**30.9**	**11.0**	**18.3**	**5.5**	**12.1**
16~24 岁 Age	103	12.6	21.4	22.3	38.8	19.4	35.0	3.9	20.4	10.7	15.5
25~34 岁 Age	130	4.6	31.5	10.8	19.2	9.2	32.3	13.8	17.7	3.1	16.2
35~44 岁 Age	105	7.6	21.0	2.9	11.4	13.3	27.6	16.2	19.0	4.8	6.7
45~54 岁 Age	65	7.7	9.2	0.0	6.2	12.3	26.2	10.8	16.9	6.2	10.8
55~60 岁 Age	34	17.6	2.9	0.0	2.9	0.0	32.4	5.9	14.7	0.0	5.9

续前表 continued

	人数 Number	种花盆栽 horticulture	看书 reading	绘画书法 drawing & calligraphy	乐器演奏 playing musical instrument	开汽车兜风 going out for a driving	逛街购物 shopping	郊游露营 outing & camping	海外旅行 overseas travel	国内一天以上的旅行 domestic travel
样本 Sample	**868**	**7.7**	**13.0**	**6.2**	**16.5**	**12.3**	**25.5**	**7.0**	**34.7**	**40.2**
男性 Male	**431**	**3.2**	**10.7**	**5.3**	**13.7**	**13.0**	**27.8**	**6.7**	**33.4**	**40.8**
16~24 岁 Age	99	5.1	11.1	7.1	9.1	25.3	40.4	10.1	45.5	42.4
25~34 岁 Age	127	1.6	9.4	7.9	9.4	7.9	33.1	7.1	39.4	50.4
35~44 岁 Age	108	3.7	10.2	1.9	15.7	12.0	27.8	5.6	22.2	41.7
45~54 岁 Age	65	1.5	15.4	4.6	16.9	4.6	7.7	4.6	27.7	29.2
55~60 岁 Age	32	6.3	6.3	3.1	31.3	15.6	9.4	3.1	21.9	18.8
女性 Female	**437**	**12.1**	**15.3**	**7.1**	**19.2**	**11.7**	**23.1**	**7.3**	**35.9**	**39.6**
16~24 岁 Age	103	15.5	16.5	3.9	21.4	23.3	39.8	3.9	51.5	60.2
25~34 岁 Age	130	16.2	16.9	5.4	20.0	11.5	28.5	10.0	41.5	37.7
35~44 岁 Age	105	6.7	15.2	8.6	20.0	5.7	10.5	9.5	27.6	33.3
45~54 岁 Age	65	10.8	7.7	10.8	16.9	7.7	13.8	4.6	27.7	27.7
55~60 岁 Age	34	5.9	20.6	11.8	11.8	2.9	8.8	5.9	8.8	26.5

续前表 continued

	人数 Number	国内一天往返的旅行 short journey that can be back in a day	看展览会 visiting exhibition	听演唱会/音乐会 attending concert	扭秧歌/木兰拳/交谊舞 doing the YangKo	去博物馆或美术馆 going to museum or art gallery	唱卡拉OK karaoke	去动物园或公园 going to park or zoo	酒吧/咖啡屋/茶秀 going to cafe or bar	电脑游戏 playing PC game
样本 Sample	868	31.8	18.8	16.7	32.6	7.9	22.6	8.6	13.6	11.9
男性 Male	431	31.6	19.3	17.2	31.1	4.6	20.6	8.6	14.2	10.4
16~24 岁 Age	99	36.4	20.2	17.2	41.4	3.0	24.2	4.0	22.2	13.1
25~34 岁 Age	127	33.1	17.3	15.7	30.7	4.7	17.3	10.2	11.8	16.5
35~44 岁 Age	108	28.7	16.7	16.7	27.8	7.4	18.5	10.2	8.3	9.3
45~54 岁 Age	65	27.7	24.6	23.1	24.6	4.6	24.6	12.3	15.4	1.5
55~60 岁 Age	32	28.1	21.9	12.5	25.0	0.0	21.9	3.1	15.6	0.0
女性 Female	437	32.0	18.3	16.2	34.1	11.2	24.5	8.7	13.0	13.3
16~24 岁 Age	103	44.7	26.2	18.4	52.4	7.8	28.2	7.8	9.7	28.2
25~34 岁 Age	130	34.6	14.6	14.6	32.3	9.2	23.8	9.2	15.4	15.4
35~44 岁 Age	105	23.8	14.3	13.3	26.7	14.3	22.9	8.6	14.3	5.7
45~54 岁 Age	65	23.1	15.4	15.4	24.6	13.8	20.0	10.8	10.8	4.6
55~60 岁 Age	34	26.5	26.5	26.5	26.5	14.7	29.4	5.9	14.7	0.0

4-5 不同消费者常做的休闲活动/ Frequently Engaged Activities by Market Segments

4-5-1 时尚流行指标/ Fads Popular Index

注：本题为多选题，合计百分比超过 100%（Multiple answers）

	人数 Number	打网球 tennis	打高尔夫球 golf	打羽毛球 badmin-ton	打保龄球 bowling	踢足球 soccer	打篮球 basket-ball	打乒乓球 table tennis	慢跑 jogging	玩滑板 skateboarding	跳迪斯科 disco
样本 Sample	989	8.0	1.2	44.6	28.0	11.6	16.6	28.4	37.2	1.3	8.6
平实生活指向 simple living orientation	485	7.0	0.4	40.6	22.1	11.1	14.6	27.0	36.5	1.0	3.3
时尚流行指向 fashion orientation	504	8.9	2.0	48.4	33.7	12.1	18.5	29.8	37.9	1.6	13.7

续前表 continued

	人数 Number	打麻将 mah-jong	游泳 swim-ming	滚轴溜冰 rolling skating	滑冰 skating	钓鱼 fishing	登山 moun-tain climbing	听音乐 enjoying music	看电影 going to movie	打游戏机 playing video game	编织裁剪 knitting & tailor-ing
样本 Sample	989	31.2	36.1	10.8	4.8	14.5	28.2	61.6	34.4	26.1	15.3
平实生活指向 simple living orientation	485	30.5	30.9	6.2	4.5	13.0	26.2	57.1	29.1	24.5	15.7
时尚流行指向 fashion orientation	504	31.9	41.1	15.3	5.0	15.9	30.2	65.9	39.5	27.6	14.9

续前表 continued

	人数 Number	种花盆栽 horticul-ture	看书 reading	绘画书法 drawing & calligra-phy	乐器演奏 playing musical instru-ment	开汽车兜风 going out for a driving	逛街购物 shopping	郊游露营 outing & camping	海外旅行 overseas travel	国内一天以上的旅行 domestic travel
样本 Sample	989	15.3	24.8	83.4	12.6	6.6	16.3	66.4	19.1	1.1
平实生活指向 simple living orientation	485	15.7	27.8	82.9	10.7	6.6	12.2	58.8	15.5	0.4
时尚流行指向 fashion orientation	504	14.9	21.8	83.9	14.5	6.5	20.2	73.8	22.6	1.8

续前表 continued

	人数 Number	国内一天往返的旅行 short journey that can be back in a day	看展览会 visiting exhibition	听演唱会/音乐会 attending concert	扭秧歌/木兰拳/交谊舞 doing the YangKo	去博物馆或美术馆 going to museum or art gallery	唱卡拉OK karaoke	去动物园或公园 going to park or zoo	酒吧/咖啡屋/茶秀 going to cafe or bar	电脑游戏 playing PC game
样本 Sample	989	26.8	28.4	34.2	16.3	7.3	20.2	33.4	49.4	25.6
平实生活指向 simple living orientation	485	21.9	25.2	34.6	12.2	6.4	19.0	23.9	49.3	23.5
时尚流行指向 fashion orientation	504	31.5	31.5	33.7	20.2	8.1	21.4	42.5	49.6	27.6

4-5-2 信息交流指标/ Information Communication Index

注：本题为多选题，合计百分比超过 100%（Multiple answers）

	人数 Number	打网球 tennis	打高尔夫球 golf	打羽毛球 badminton	打保龄球 bowling	踢足球 soccer	打篮球 basketball	打乒乓球 table tennis	慢跑 jogging	玩滑板 skateboarding	跳迪斯科 disco
样本 Sample	995	7.8	1.3	44.6	27.9	11.7	16.7	28.6	37.4	1.4	8.7
信息消极指向 negative orientation	61	3.3	0.0	27.9	14.8	9.8	16.4	19.7	27.9	1.6	4.9
中间层 medium	519	8.3	1.0	43.4	27.9	12.1	16.6	26.2	34.9	1.2	5.6
信息积极指向 active orientation	415	8.0	1.9	48.7	29.9	11.3	16.9	33.0	41.9	1.7	13.3

续前表 continued

	人数 Number	打麻将 mah-jong	游泳 swimming	滚轴溜冰 rolling skating	滑冰 skating	钓鱼 fishing	登山 mountain climbing	听音乐 enjoying music	看电影 going to movie	打游戏机 playing video game	编织裁剪 knitting & tailoring
样本 Sample	995	31.5	36.1	11.0	4.8	14.2	28.3	61.4	34.1	26.0	15.3
信息消极指向 negative orientation	61	32.8	32.8	9.8	3.3	13.1	13.1	50.8	27.9	18.0	8.2
中间层 medium	519	29.5	33.9	9.8	4.2	12.9	27.0	59.7	30.8	25.6	12.7
信息积极指向 active orientation	415	33.7	39.3	12.5	5.8	15.9	32.3	65.1	39.0	27.7	19.5

续前表 continued

	人数 Number	种花盆栽 horticulture	看书 reading	绘画书法 drawing & calligraphy	乐器演奏 playing musical instrument	开汽车兜风 going out for a driving	逛街购物 shopping	郊游露营 outing & camping	海外旅行 overseas travel	国内一天以上的旅行 domestic travel
样本 Sample	995	15.3	24.7	83.3	12.7	6.7	16.3	66.3	19.1	1.1
信息消极指向 negative orientation	61	8.2	16.4	70.5	6.6	4.9	11.5	52.5	8.2	1.6
中间层 medium	519	12.7	20.6	83.0	11.2	6.4	14.5	61.7	15.4	0.8
信息积极指向 active orientation	415	19.5	31.1	85.5	15.4	7.5	19.3	74.2	25.3	1.4

续前表 continued

	人数 Number	国内一天往返的旅行 short journey that can be back in a day	看展览会 visiting exhibition	听演唱会/音乐会 attending concert	扭秧歌/木兰拳/交谊舞 doing the YangKo	去博物馆或美术馆 going to museum or art gallery	唱卡拉OK karaoke	去动物园或公园 going to park or zoo	酒吧/咖啡屋/茶秀 going to cafe or bar	电脑游戏 playing PC game
样本 Sample	995	26.9	28.4	34.1	16.1	7.3	20.3	33.4	49.7	25.3
信息消极指向 negative orientation	61	14.8	18.0	21.3	1.6	6.6	14.8	18.0	50.8	13.1
中间层 medium	519	26.0	26.8	31.4	15.6	5.2	18.3	30.4	46.6	26.2
信息积极指向 active orientation	415	29.9	32.0	39.3	18.8	10.[illegible]	23.6	39.3	53.5	26.0

4-6 不同消费者层想做的休闲活动/ Desired Activities by Market Segments

4-6-1 时尚流行指标/ Fads Popular Index

注：本题为多选题，合计百分比超过 100%（Multiple answers）

	人数 Number	打网球 tennis	打高尔夫球 golf	打羽毛球 badminton	打保龄球 bowling	踢足球 soccer	打篮球 basketball	打乒乓球 table tennis	慢跑 jogging	玩滑板 skateboarding	跳迪斯科 disco
样本 Sample	856	33.9	17.4	14.6	27.2	8.9	9.2	14.6	15.1	7.8	9.1
平实生活指向 simple living orientation	412	29.4	13.8	15.0	25.5	7.8	8.3	15.5	13.6	4.9	8.0
时尚流行指向 fashion orientation	444	38.1	20.7	14.2	28.8	9.9	10.1	13.7	16.4	10.6	10.1

续前表 continued

	人数 Number	打麻将 mah-jong	游泳 swimming	滚轴溜冰 rolling skating	滑冰 skating	钓鱼 fishing	登山 mountain climbing	听音乐 enjoying music	看电影 going to movie	打游戏机 playing video game	编织裁剪 knitting & tailoring
样本 Sample	856	7.2	22.1	9.7	17.8	18.1	29.9	10.4	18.5	6.1	7.8
平实生活指向 simple living orientation	412	7.3	22.3	9.0	17.2	20.1	28.6	10.0	18.4	5.1	7.5
时尚流行指向 fashion orientation	444	7.2	21.8	10.4	18.2	16.2	31.1	10.8	18.5	7.0	8.1

续前表 continued

	人数 Number	种花盆栽 horticulture	看书 reading	绘画书法 drawing & calligraphy	乐器演奏 playing musical instrument	开汽车兜风 going out for a driving	逛街购物 shopping	郊游露营 outing & camping	海外旅行 overseas travel	国内一天以上的旅行 domestic travel
样本 Sample	856	7.8	13.0	6.3	16.6	12.3	25.4	7.0	34.5	40.2
平实生活指向 simple living orientation	412	7.5	11.2	6.1	15.5	11.7	23.1	8.0	35.4	36.2
时尚流行指向 fashion orientation	444	8.1	14.6	6.5	17.6	12.8	27.5	6.1	33.6	43.9

续前表 continued

	人数 Number	国内一天往返的旅行 short journey that can be back in a day	看展览会 visiting exhibition	听演唱会/音乐会 attending concert	扭秧歌/木兰拳/交谊舞 doing the YangKo	去博物馆或美术馆 going to museum or art gallery	唱卡拉OK karaoke	去动物园或公园 going to park or zoo	酒吧/咖啡屋/茶秀 going to cafe or bar	电脑游戏 playing PC game
样本 Sample	856	31.9	18.8	16.7	32.5	8.1	22.8	8.4	13.8	9.8
平实生活指向 simple living orientation	412	34.7	21.4	16.7	31.3	6.8	25.2	9.7	13.6	6.8
时尚流行指向 fashion orientation	444	29.3	16.4	16.7	33.6	9.2	20.5	7.2	14.0	12.6

4-6-2 信息交流指标/ Information Communication Index

注：本题为多选题，合计百分比超过 100%（Multiple answers）

	人数 Number	打网球 tennis	打高尔夫球 golf	打羽毛球 badminton	打保龄球 bowling	踢足球 soccer	打篮球 basketball	打乒乓球 table tennis	慢跑 jogging	玩滑板 skateboarding	跳迪斯科 disco
样本 Sample	861	34.3	17.8	14.6	27.2	8.9	9.1	14.6	15.0	8.0	9.1
信息消极指向 negative orientation	42	19.0	14.3	11.9	26.2	11.9	9.5	11.9	14.3	11.9	11.9
中间层 medium	460	33.3	18.9	12.8	27.6	9.1	9.3	13.9	17.2	7.4	8.3
信息积极指向 active orientation	359	37.3	16.7	17.3	26.7	8.4	8.6	15.9	12.3	8.4	9.7

续前表 continued

	人数 Number	打麻将 mah-jong	游泳 swim-ming	滚轴溜冰 rolling skating	滑冰 skating	钓鱼 fishing	登山 moun-tain climbing	听音乐 enjoying music	看电影 going to movie	打游戏机 playing video game	编织裁剪 knitting & tailor-ing
样本 Sample	861	7.7	22.4	9.9	17.5	18.4	29.7	10.3	18.6	6.2	7.8
信息消极指向 negative orientation	42	9.5	16.7	9.5	16.7	16.7	31.0	9.5	19.0	14.3	11.9
中间层 medium	460	5.0	26.5	10.7	17.8	20.9	30.0	11.1	21.5	5.4	6.5
信息积极指向 active orientation	359	10.9	17.8	8.9	17.3	15.3	29.2	9.5	14.8	6.1	8.9

续前表 continued

	人数 Number	种花盆栽 horticul-ture	看书 reading	绘画书法 drawing & calligra-phy	乐器演奏 playing musical instru-ment	开汽车兜风 going out for a driving	逛街购物 shopping	郊游露营 outing & camping	海外旅行 overseas travel	国内一天以上的旅行 domestic travel
样本 Sample	861	7.8	13.0	6.2	16.3	12.1	25.4	7.0	34.7	40.4
信息消极指向 negative orientation	42	11.9	7.1	7.1	14.3	16.7	9.5	4.8	23.8	23.8
中间层 medium	460	6.5	12.0	7.0	13.9	11.5	27.4	8.0	39.3	39.1
信息积极指向 active orientation	359	8.9	15.0	5.0	19.5	12.3	24.8	5.8	30.1	44.0

续前表 continued

	人数 Number	国内一天往返的旅行 short journey that can be back in a day	看展览会 visiting exhibi-tion	听演唱会/音乐会 attending concert	扭秧歌/木兰拳/交谊舞 doing the YangKo	去博物馆或美术馆 going to museum or art gallery	唱卡拉OK karaoke	去动物园或公园 going to park or zoo	酒吧/咖啡屋/茶秀 going to cafe or bar	电脑游戏 playing PC game
样本 Sample	861	31.8	18.7	16.7	32.8	8.0	22.6	8.6	13.5	9.8
信息消极指向 negative orientation	42	21.4	11.9	7.1	23.8	4.8	19.0	9.5	9.5	11.9
中间层 medium	460	33.3	18.9	15.7	32.4	7.0	21.1	8.0	14.8	9.1
信息积极指向 active orientation	359	31.2	19.2	19.2	34.3	9.7	25.1	9.2	12.3	10.3

● 上海 / Shanghai

4-1 常做的休闲活动排名/ Ranking of the Frequently Engaged Activities

注：本题为多选题，合计百分比可能超过 100%（Multiple answers）

排名 Ranking	活动项目 Activity Items	人次 Person-time	百分比 Percent
1	看书 reading	786	78.1
2	逛街购物 shopping	684	68.0
3	听音乐 enjoying music	603	59.9
4	唱卡拉 OK Karaoke	405	40.3
5	看电影 going to movie	366	36.4
6	打保龄球 bowling	339	33.7
7	打麻将 mah-jong	324	32.2
8	去动物园或公园 going to the park or zoo	306	30.4
9	打游戏机 playing video game	299	29.7
10	打羽毛球 badminton	272	27.0
11	电脑游戏 playing PC game	236	23.5
12	打乒乓球 table-tennis	235	23.4
13	种花盆栽 horticulture	232	23.1
14	游泳 swimming	225	22.4
15	慢跑 jogging	214	21.3
16	酒吧/咖啡屋/茶秀 going to cafe or bar	208	20.7
17	国内一天以上的旅行 domestic travel	206	20.5
18	看展览会 visiting exhibition	203	20.2
19	国内一天往返的旅行 short journey that can be back in a day	158	15.7
20	编织裁剪 knitting & tailoring	157	15.6
21	去博物馆或美术馆 going to museum or art gallery	131	13.0
21	打篮球 basketball	131	13.0
22	听演唱会/音乐会 attending concert	122	12.1
22	踢足球 soccer	122	12.1
23	跳迪斯科 disco	115	11.4
24	郊游露营 outing & camping	110	10.9
25	滚轴溜冰 rolling skating	98	9.7
26	绘画书法 drawing & calligraphy	91	9.0
27	扭秧歌/木兰拳/交谊舞 doing the YangKo	67	6.7
28	打网球 tennis	62	6.2
29	钓鱼 fishing	54	5.4
30	开汽车兜风 going out for a driving	49	4.9
31	乐器演奏 playing musical instrument	33	3.3
32	登山 mountain climbing	32	3.2
33	滑冰 skating	29	2.9
34	海外旅行 overseas travel	17	1.7
35	玩滑板 skateboarding	14	1.4
36	打高尔夫球 golf	11	1.1

n=1006

4-2 想做的休闲活动排名/ Ranking of the Desired Activities

注：本题为多选题，合计百分比可能超过 100%（Multiple answers）

排名 Ranking	活动项目 Activity Items	人次 Person-time	百分比 Percent
1	海外旅行 overseas travel	361	40.2
2	国内一天以上的旅行 domestic travel	341	38.0
3	打网球 tennis	277	30.9
4	听演唱会/音乐会 attending concert	254	28.3
5	郊游露营 outing & camping	247	27.5
6	登山 mountain climbing	236	26.3
7	国内一天往返的旅行 short journey that can be back in a day	217	24.2
8	开汽车兜风 going out for a driving	197	22.0
9	钓鱼 fishing	183	20.4
10	看展览会 visiting exhibition	172	19.2
11	去博物馆或美术馆 going to museum or art gallery	167	18.6
12	看电影 going to movie	163	18.2
13	打高尔夫球 golf	161	17.9
14	慢跑 jogging	152	16.9
15	去动物园或公园 going to the park or zoo	146	16.3
16	游泳 swimming	143	15.9
16	种花盆栽 horticulture	143	15.9
17	打保龄球 bowling	132	14.7
18	唱卡拉 OK Karaoke	116	12.9
19	绘画书法 drawing & calligraphy	108	12.0
20	打羽毛球 badminton	101	11.3
21	跳迪斯科 disco	94	10.5
22	乐器演奏 playing musical instrument	89	9.9
23	电脑游戏 playing PC game	87	9.7
23	打乒乓球 table-tennis	87	9.7
24	踢足球 soccer	85	9.5
25	滑冰 skating	84	9.4
25	酒吧/咖啡屋/茶秀 going to cafe or bar	84	9.4
26	听音乐 enjoying music	81	9.0
27	玩滑板 skateboarding	79	8.8
28	滚轴溜冰 rolling skating	77	8.6
28	扭秧歌/木兰拳/交谊舞 doing the YangKo	77	8.6
29	编织裁剪 knitting & tailoring	73	8.1
30	打麻将 mah-jong	71	7.9
31	打篮球 basketball	60	6.7
32	逛街购物 shopping	59	6.6
33	打游戏机 playing video game	39	4.3
34	看书 reading	31	3.5

n=897

4-3 样本、男性各年龄层、女性各年龄层常做的活动/ Frequently Engaged Activities by the Whole Sample, Age and Gender Groups

注：本题为多选题，合计百分比超过 100%（Multiple answers）

	人数 Number	打网球 tennis	打高尔夫球 golf	打羽毛球 badminton	打保龄球 bowling	踢足球 soccer	打篮球 basketball	打乒乓球 table tennis	慢跑 jogging	玩滑板 skateboarding	跳迪斯科 disco
样本 Sample	**1006**	**6.2**	**1.1**	**27.0**	**33.7**	**12.1**	**13.0**	**23.4**	**21.3**	**1.4**	**11.4**
男性 Male	**505**	**7.9**	**1.4**	**28.7**	**41.0**	**22.4**	**20.8**	**30.5**	**22.6**	**2.0**	**13.3**
16~24 岁 Age	109	12.8	2.8	51.4	54.1	59.6	59.6	51.4	34.9	5.5	20.2
25~34 岁 Age	146	9.6	0.7	32.9	55.5	19.9	17.1	35.6	15.8	2.1	21.2
35~44 岁 Age	127	6.3	1.6	14.2	32.3	7.9	3.9	17.3	15.0	0.0	8.7
45~54 岁 Age	85	2.4	1.2	18.8	22.4	8.2	7.1	17.6	25.9	0.0	3.5
55~60 岁 Age	38	5.3	0.0	18.4	18.4	5.3	10.5	23.7	31.6	2.6	0.0
女性 Female	**501**	**4.4**	**0.8**	**25.3**	**26.3**	**[illegible].8**	**5.2**	**16.2**	**20.0**	**0.8**	**9.6**
16~24 岁 Age	107	15.9	0.9	43.0	51.4	[illegible].9	14.0	27.1	25.2	2.8	22.4
25~34 岁 Age	143	2.8	1.4	28.0	37.1	0.7	2.8	20.3	10.5	0.0	10.5
35~44 岁 Age	130	0.0	0.0	16.9	12.3	3.1	5.4	13.1	22.3	0.8	5.4
45~54 岁 Age	81	1.2	0.0	16.0	8.6	2.5	0.0	7.4	19.8	0.0	1.2
55~60 岁 Age	40	0.0	2.5	15.0	2.5	0.0	0.0	0.0	32.5	0.0	2.5

续前表 continued

	人数 Number	打麻将 mah-jong	游泳 swimming	滚轴溜冰 rolling skating	滑冰 skating	钓鱼 fishing	登山 mountain climbing	听音乐 enjoying music	看电影 going to movie	打游戏机 playing video game	编织裁剪 knitting & tailoring
样本 Sample	**1006**	**32.2**	**22.4**	**9.7**	**2.9**	**5.4**	**3.2**	**59.9**	**36.4**	**29.7**	**15.3**
男性 Male	**505**	**36.8**	**30.3**	**11.1**	**3.4**	**7.7**	**4.0**	**60.8**	**37.2**	**37.8**	**1.0**
16~24 岁 Age	109	19.3	41.3	33.9	7.3	9.2	5.5	76.1	55.0	81.7	0.0
25~34 岁 Age	146	36.3	30.1	7.5	2.7	8.2	3.4	61.6	43.8	36.3	0.0
35~44 岁 Age	127	44.9	29.9	3.1	2.4	5.5	2.4	53.5	27.6	25.2	0.0
45~54 岁 Age	85	50.6	24.7	1.2	2.4	7.1	5.9	60.0	27.1	17.6	2.7
55~60 岁 Age	38	31.6	13.2	7.9	0.0	10.5	2.6	39.5	15.8	5.3	5.0
女性 Female	**501**	**27.5**	**14.4**	**8.4**	**2.4**	**3.0**	**2.4**	**59.1**	**35.5**	**21.6**	**29.4**
16~24 岁 Age	107	19.6	27.1	30.8	8.4	4.7	6.5	80.4	62.6	42.1	8.3
25~34 岁 Age	143	33.6	11.9	4.2	2.1	2.1	2.8	64.3	43.4	24.5	21.8
35~44 岁 Age	130	31.5	17.7	2.3	0.0	3.1	0.8	51.5	23.8	16.2	34.7
45~54 岁 Age	81	21.0	3.7	0.0	0.0	1.2	0.0	48.1	16.0	8.6	57.1
55~60 岁 Age	40	27.5	0.0	0.0	0.0	5.0	0.0	30.0	12.5	0.0	39.0

续前表 continued

	人数 Number	种花盆栽 horticulture	看书 reading	绘画书法 drawing & calligraphy	乐器演奏 playing musical instrument	开汽车兜风 going out for a driving	逛街购物 shopping	郊游露营 outing & camping	海外旅行 overseas travel	国内一天以上的旅行 domestic travel
样本 Sample	**1006**	**15.6**	**23.1**	**78.1**	**9.0**	**3.3**	**4.9**	**68.0**	**10.9**	**1.7**
男性 Male	**505**	**1.2**	**22.2**	**79.4**	**10.1**	**4.2**	**6.9**	**59.2**	**12.1**	**1.4**
16~24 岁 Age	109	0.9	6.4	79.8	15.6	2.8	3.7	62.4	13.8	0.0
25~34 岁 Age	146	2.1	18.5	82.2	6.2	7.5	8.2	55.5	12.3	2.7
35~44 岁 Age	127	1.6	23.6	76.4	6.3	3.1	9.4	59.8	9.4	0.8
45~54 岁 Age	85	0.0	36.5	76.5	10.6	0.0	7.1	60.0	12.9	2.4
55~60 岁 Age	38	0.0	44.7	84.2	21.1	7.9	2.6	60.5	13.2	0.0
女性 Female	**501**	**30.1**	**24.0**	**76.8**	**8.0**	**2.4**	**2.8**	**76.8**	**9.8**	**2.0**
16~24 岁 Age	107	5.6	11.2	86.0	16.8	4.7	4.7	82.2	15.0	0.0
25~34 岁 Age	143	23.8	18.2	82.5	4.9	2.1	4.2	81.8	8.4	2.8
35~44 岁 Age	130	39.2	28.5	73.1	6.9	0.0	2.3	76.2	10.8	2.3
45~54 岁 Age	81	49.4	33.3	67.9	6.2	2.5	0.0	75.3	6.2	2.5
55~60 岁 Age	40	50.0	45.0	62.5	2.5	5.0	0.0	50.0	5.0	2.5

续前表 continued

	人数 Number	国内一天往返的旅行 short journey that can be back in a day	看展览会 visiting exhibitin	听演唱会/音乐会 attending concert	扭秧歌/木兰拳/交谊舞 doing the YangKo	去博物馆或美术馆 going to museum or art gallery	唱卡拉OK karaoke	去动物园或公园 going to park or zoo	酒吧/咖啡屋/茶秀 going to cafe or bar	电脑游戏 playing PC game
样本 Sample	**1006**	**20.5**	**15.7**	**20.2**	**12.1**	**6.7**	**13.0**	**40.3**	**30.4**	**20.7**
男性 Male	**505**	**22.0**	**17.0**	**24.2**	**13.3**	**3.8**	**14.7**	**43.6**	**30.1**	**24.4**
16~24 岁 Age	109	17.4	17.4	28.4	14.7	2.8	19.3	53.2	34.9	32.1
25~34 岁 Age	146	19.9	16.4	23.3	16.4	4.1	13.0	56.2	30.8	37.0
35~44 岁 Age	127	23.6	16.5	22.0	12.6	3.9	9.4	40.9	26.0	15.7
45~54 岁 Age	85	28.2	18.8	28.2	11.8	5.9	20.0	29.4	30.6	14.1
55~60 岁 Age	38	23.7	15.8	13.2	2.6	0.0	13.2	7.9	26.3	5.3
女性 Female	**501**	**19.0**	**14.4**	**16.2**	**11.0**	**9.6**	**11.4**	**36.9**	**30.7**	**17.0**
16~24 岁 Age	107	17.8	11.2	22.4	18.7	0.9	21.5	56.1	29.0	38.3
25~34 岁 Age	143	24.5	19.6	12.6	10.5	9.1	6.3	50.3	34.3	23.8
35~44 岁 Age	130	18.5	13.8	13.1	6.2	7.7	10.0	30.0	31.5	5.4
45~54 岁 Age	81	16.0	13.6	18.5	12.3	16.0	11.1	14.8	28.4	3.7
55~60 岁 Age	40	10.0	7.5	17.5	5.0	27.5	7.5	5.0	25.0	0.0

4-4 样本、男性各年龄层、女性各年龄层想做的活动/ Desired Activities by the Whole Sample, Age and Gender Groups

注：本题为多选题，合计百分比超过 100%（Multiple answers）

	人数 Number	打网球 tennis	打高尔夫球 golf	打羽毛球 badminton	打保龄球 bowling	踢足球 soccer	打篮球 basket-ball	打乒乓球 table-tennis	慢跑 jogging	玩滑板 skate-boarding	跳迪斯科 disco
样本 Sample	**897**	**30.9**	**17.9**	**11.3**	**14.7**	**9.5**	**6.7**	**9.7**	**16.9**	**8.8**	**10.5**
男性 Male	**459**	**34.0**	**23.7**	**10.7**	**14.6**	**14.8**	**8.3**	**12.2**	**19.6**	**11.3**	**8.7**
16~24 岁 Age	103	51.5	33.0	7.8	14.6	10.7	7.8	6.8	16.5	30.1	19.4
25~34 岁 Age	138	47.8	34.1	8.7	10.1	16.7	8.7	13.8	18.8	9.4	7.2
35~44 岁 Age	113	19.5	10.6	15.0	15.0	19.5	11.5	16.8	23.9	3.5	4.4
45~54 岁 Age	74	17.6	17.6	13.5	24.3	13.5	6.8	13.5	21.6	5.4	2.7
55~60 岁 Age	31	6.5	9.7	6.5	9.7	6.5	0.0	3.2	12.9	0.0	9.7
女性 Female	**438**	**27.6**	**11.9**	**11.9**	**14.8**	**3.9**	**5.0**	**7.1**	**14.2**	**6.2**	**12.3**
16~24 岁 Age	105	48.6	29.5	12.4	16.2	12.4	11.4	11.4	14.3	19.0	19.0
25~34 岁 Age	131	36.6	9.2	13.0	11.5	0.8	3.8	6.1	13.7	3.1	16.0
35~44 岁 Age	109	15.6	6.4	16.5	21.1	2.8	2.8	8.3	11.9	2.8	10.1
45~54 岁 Age	67	6.0	3.0	6.0	9.0	0.0	3.0	3.0	13.4	0.0	1.5
55~60 岁 Age	26	3.8	0.0	0.0	15.4	0.0	0.0	0.0	26.9	0.0	3.8

续前表 continued

	人数 Number	打麻将 mah-jong	游泳 swimming	滚轴溜冰 rolling skating	滑冰 skating	钓鱼 fishing	登山 mountain climbing	听音乐 enjoying music	看电影 going to movie	打游戏机 playing video game	编织裁剪 knitting & tailoring
样本 Sample	**897**	**7.9**	**15.9**	**8.6**	**9.4**	**20.4**	**26.3**	**9.0**	**18.2**	**4.3**	**8.1**
男性 Male	**459**	**6.3**	**17.6**	**9.8**	**10.5**	**26.1**	**29.0**	**7.6**	**15.3**	**3.7**	**3.9**
16~24 岁 Age	103	3.9	11.7	19.4	20.4	28.2	39.8	4.9	12.6	2.9	9.7
25~34 岁 Age	138	8.0	22.5	10.9	10.1	26.1	30.4	5.8	10.9	4.3	3.6
35~44 岁 Age	113	8.0	23.0	5.3	7.1	26.5	28.3	9.7	23.0	4.4	0.9
45~54 岁 Age	74	5.4	12.2	5.4	4.1	20.3	17.6	9.5	16.2	2.7	2.7
55~60 岁 Age	31	3.2	9.7	0.0	6.5	32.3	16.1	12.9	12.9	3.2	0.0
女性 Female	**438**	**9.6**	**14.2**	**7.3**	**8.2**	**14.4**	**23.5**	**10.5**	**21.2**	**5.0**	**12.6**
16~24 岁 Age	105	11.4	23.8	14.3	20.0	25.7	44.8	6.7	14.3	9.5	19.0
25~34 岁 Age	131	9.2	16.8	10.7	5.3	13.0	22.9	7.6	16.8	3.1	14.5
35~44 岁 Age	109	11.0	7.3	1.8	7.3	10.1	14.7	16.5	32.1	5.5	9.2
45~54 岁 Age	67	7.5	7.5	1.5	0.0	11.9	11.9	14.9	22.4	3.0	7.5
55~60 岁 Age	26	3.8	7.7	0.0	0.0	0.0	7.7	3.8	23.1	0.0	3.8

续前表 continued

	人数 Number	种花盆栽 horti-culture	看书 reading	绘画书法 drawing & calli-graphy	乐器演奏 playing musical instrument	开汽车兜风 going out for a driving	逛街购物 shopping	郊游露营 outing & camping	海外旅行 overseas travel	国内一天以上的旅行 domestic travel
样本 Sample	**897**	**8.1**	**15.9**	**3.5**	**12.0**	**9.9**	**22.0**	**6.6**	**27.5**	**40.2**
男性 Male	**459**	**3.9**	**13.7**	**4.1**	**12.2**	**10.7**	**25.5**	**7.0**	**27.7**	**38.8**
16~24 岁 Age	103	9.7	17.5	1.9	11.7	16.5	40.8	7.8	35.0	45.6
25~34 岁 Age	138	3.6	8.0	2.2	15.9	11.6	28.3	7.2	34.8	44.9
35~44 岁 Age	113	0.9	16.8	3.5	8.0	6.2	22.1	4.4	22.1	31.9
45~54 岁 Age	74	2.7	17.6	10.8	12.2	6.8	13.5	8.1	21.6	36.5
55~60 岁 Age	31	0.0	6.5	6.5	12.9	12.9	3.2	9.7	6.5	19.4
女性 Female	**438**	**12.6**	**18.3**	**2.7**	**11.9**	**9.1**	**18.3**	**6.2**	**27.4**	**41.8**
16~24 岁 Age	105	19.0	22.9	1.0	16.2	18.1	27.6	2.9	39.0	61.0
25~34 岁 Age	131	14.5	16.0	3.1	16.0	7.6	23.7	4.6	32.1	51.1
35~44 岁 Age	109	9.2	14.7	4.6	5.5	6.4	11.9	7.3	18.3	32.1
45~54 岁 Age	67	7.5	23.9	3.0	9.0	4.5	10.4	10.4	23.9	14.9
55~60 岁 Age	26	3.8	11.5	0.0	7.7	3.8	0.0	11.5	3.8	26.9

续前表 continued

	人数 Number	国内一天往返的旅行 short journey that can be back in a day	看展览会 visiting exhibition	听演唱会/音乐会 attending concert	扭秧歌/木兰拳/交谊舞 doing the YangKo	去博物馆或美术馆 going to museum or art gallery	唱卡拉OK karaoke	去动物园或公园 going to park or zoo	酒吧/咖啡屋/茶秀 going to cafe or bar	电脑游戏 playing PC game
样本 Sample	897	38.0	24.2	19.2	28.3	8.6	18.6	12.9	16.3	9.4
男性 Male	459	37.9	22.4	17.9	25.1	6.3	17.6	11.8	15.3	9.4
16~24 岁 Age	103	29.1	22.3	12.6	37.9	5.8	16.5	15.5	12.6	12.6
25~34 岁 Age	138	37.7	22.5	20.3	28.3	5.8	19.6	8.0	14.5	10.9
35~44 岁 Age	113	41.6	22.1	17.7	21.2	6.2	20.4	16.8	19.5	9.7
45~54 岁 Age	74	40.5	28.4	16.2	12.2	6.8	12.2	10.8	10.8	4.1
55~60 岁 Age	31	48.4	9.7	29.0	12.9	9.7	16.1	0.0	22.6	3.2
女性 Female	438	38.1	26.0	20.5	31.7	11.0	19.6	14.2	17.4	9.4
16~24 岁 Age	105	43.8	25.7	21.9	41.9	13.3	17.1	14.3	20.0	14.3
25~34 岁 Age	131	34.4	19.8	19.1	33.6	7.6	21.4	9.9	11.5	10.7
35~44 岁 Age	109	34.9	28.4	22.0	30.3	11.0	17.4	20.2	21.1	8.3
45~54 岁 Age	67	40.3	34.3	22.4	17.9	13.4	22.4	11.9	22.4	4.5
55~60 岁 Age	26	42.3	26.9	11.5	23.1	11.5	23.1	15.4	7.7	0.0

4-5 不同消费者层常做的休闲活动/ Frequently Engaged Activities by Market Segments

4-5-1 时尚流行指标/ Fads Popular Index

注：本题为多选题，合计百分比可能超过 100%（Multiple answers）

	人数 Number	打网球 tennis	打高尔夫球 golf	打羽毛球 bad-minton	打保龄球 bowling	踢足球 soccer	打篮球 basket-ball	打乒乓球 table-tennis	慢跑 jogging	玩滑板 skate-boarding	跳迪斯科 disco
样本 Sample	997	6.2	1.1	27.1	33.9	12.2	12.9	23.3	21.4	1.4	11.5
平实生活指向 simple living orientation	464	4.3	0.0	23.3	22.0	8.4	8.8	15.5	20.7	0.9	4.5
时尚流行指向 fashion orientation	533	7.9	2.1	30.4	44.3	15.6	16.5	30.0	22.0	1.9	17.6

续前表 continued

	人数 Number	打麻将 mah-jong	游泳 swim-ming	滚轴溜冰 rolling skating	滑冰 skating	钓鱼 fishing	登山 mountain climbing	听音乐 enjoy-ing music	看电影 going to movie	打游戏机 playing video game	编织裁剪 knitting & tailor-ing
样本 Sample	997	32.0	22.3	9.7	2.9	5.4	3.2	59.8	36.2	29.7	15.7
平实生活指向 simple living orientation	464	30.8	17.5	4.3	0.9	4.3	2.2	51.9	25.4	20.7	20.7
时尚流行指向 fashion orientation	533	33.0	26.5	14.4	4.7	6.4	4.1	66.6	45.6	37.5	11.4

续前表 continued

	人数 Number	种花盆栽 horticul-ture	看书 reading	绘画书法 drawing & Calli-graphy	乐器演奏 playing musical instru-ment	开汽车兜风 going out for a driving	逛街购物 shopping	郊游露营 outing & camping	海外旅行 overseas travel	国内一天以上的旅行 domestic travel
样本 Sample	997	15.7	23.3	78.0	9.1	3.3	4.9	67.9	11.0	1.6
平实生活指向 simple living orientation	.464	20.7	27.6	77.6	7.3	2.4	2.4	62.7	7.5	0.9
时尚流行指向 fashion orientation	533	11.4	19.5	78.4	10.7	4.1	7.1	72.4	14.1	2.3

续前表 continued

	人数 Number	国内一天往返的旅行 short journey that can be back in a day	看展览会 visiting exhibition	听演唱会/音乐会 attending concert	扭秧歌/木兰拳/交谊舞 doing the YangKo	去博物馆或美术馆 going to museum or art gallery	唱卡拉OK karaoke	去动物园或公园 going to park or zoo	酒吧/咖啡屋/茶秀 going to cafe or bar	电脑游戏 playing PC game
样本 Sample	997	20.6	15.7	20.2	12.1	6.7	13.0	40.3	30.3	23.5
平实生活指向 simple living orientation	464	15.7	11.2	19.4	6.9	6.7	11.2	26.3	28.9	15.9
时尚流行指向 fashion orientation	533	24.8	19.7	20.8	16.7	6.8	14.6	52.5	31.5	30.0

4-5-2 信息交流指标/ Information Communication Index

注：本题为多选题，合计百分比可能超过 100%（Multiple answers）

	人数 Number	打网球 tennis	打高尔夫球 golf	打羽毛球 bad-minton	打保龄球 bowling	踢足球 soccer	打篮球 basket-ball	打乒乓球 table tennis	慢跑 jogging	玩滑板 skate boarding	跳迪斯科 disco
样本 Sample	997	6.2	1.1	27.0	33.8	12.1	13.0	23.3	21.3	1.3	11.4
信息消极指向 negative orientation	52	7.7	1.9	19.2	21.2	7.7	5.8	9.6	9.6	1.9	7.7
中间层 medium	571	5.8	1.1	25.0	31.5	12.3	13.7	21.2	19.8	1.4	10.9
信息积极指向 active orientation	374	6.7	1.1	31.0	39.0	12.6	13.1	28.3	25.1	1.1	12.8

续前表 continued

	人数 Number	打麻将 mah-jong	游泳 swimm-ing	滚轴溜冰 rolling skating	滑冰 skating	钓鱼 fishing	登山 mountain climbing	听音乐 enjoy-ing music	看电影 going to movie	打游戏机 playing video game	编织裁剪 knitting & tailor-ing
样本 Sample	997	32.2	22.3	9.6	2.8	5.4	3.2	59.8	36.4	29.7	15.1
信息消极指向 negative orientation	52	26.9	11.5	3.8	3.8	3.8	5.8	44.2	19.2	26.9	28.8
中间层 medium	571	31.2	21.2	8.1	1.8	4.6	1.8	57.8	36.8	26.8	14.9
信息积极指向 active orientation	374	34.5	25.4	12.8	4.3	7.0	5.1	65.0	38.2	34.5	13.6

续前表 continued

	人数 Number	种花盆栽 horticul-ture	看书 reading	绘画书法 drawing & calligra-phy	乐器演奏 playing musical instru-ment	开汽车兜风 going out for a driving	逛街购物 shopping	郊游露营 outing & camping	海外旅行 overseas travel	国内一天以上的旅行 domestic travel
样本 Sample	997	15.1	23.1	78.2	9.1	3.3	4.8	67.9	10.9	1.7
信息消极指向 negative orientation	52	28.8	25.0	67.3	1.9	5.8	1.9	50.0	11.5	1.9
中间层 medium	571	14.9	20.3	76.7	8.2	2.6	4.0	65.1	8.1	1.6
信息积极指向 active orientation	374	13.6	27.0	82.1	11.5	4.0	6.4	74.6	15.2	1.9

续前表 continued

	人数 Number	国内一天往返的旅行 short journey that can be back in a day	看展览会 visiting exhibition	听演唱会/音乐会 attending concert	扭秧歌/木兰拳/交谊舞 doing the YangKo	去博物馆或美术馆 going to museum or art gallery	唱卡拉OK karaoke	去动物园或公园 going to park or zoo	酒吧/咖啡屋/茶秀 going to cafe or bar	电脑游戏 playing PC game
样本 Sample	997	20.6	15.7	20.1	12.0	6.6	13.0	40.2	30.2	23.6
信息消极指向 negative orientation	52	9.6	7.7	15.4	7.7	13.5	3.8	28.8	17.3	17.3
中间层 medium	571	17.9	15.1	17.9	10.9	5.4	12.1	37.1	28.7	22.2
信息积极指向 active orientation	374	26.2	17.9	24.1	14.4	7.5	15.8	46.5	34.2	26.5

4-6 不同消费者层想做的休闲活动/ Desired Activities by Market Segments

4-6-1 时尚流行指标/ Fads Popular Index

注：本题为多选题，合计百分比超过 100%（Multiple answers）

	人数 Number	打网球 tennis	打高尔夫球 golf	打羽毛球 bad-minton	打保龄球 bowling	踢足球 soccer	打篮球 basket-ball	打乒乓球 table tennis	慢跑 jogging	玩滑板 skate boarding	跳迪斯科 disco
样本 Sample	889	30.9	18.0	11.2	14.6	9.3	6.7	9.8	17.1	8.8	10.5
平实生活指向 simple living orientation	400	23.0	12.5	9.0	16.5	6.8	6.3	10.0	17.5	5.3	7.8
时尚流行指向 fashion orientation	489	37.4	22.5	13.1	13.1	11.5	7.2	9.6	16.8	11.7	12.7

续前表 continued

	人数 Number	打麻将 mah-jong	游泳 swimming	滚轴溜冰 rolling skating	滑冰 skating	钓鱼 fishing	登山 mountain climbing	听音乐 enjoy-ing music	看电影 going to movie	打游戏机 playing video game	编织裁剪 knitting & tailor-ing
样本 Sample	889	7.9	15.9	8.7	9.4	20.2	26.2	9.0	18.1	4.4	8.1
平实生活指向 simple living orientation	400	8.0	16.5	7.5	6.3	19.8	20.0	11.8	21.0	4.0	6.8
时尚流行指向 fashion orientation	489	7.8	15.3	9.6	12.1	20.7	31.3	6.7	15.7	4.7	9.2

续前表 continued

	人数 Number	种花盆栽 horticul-ture	看书 reading	绘画书法 drawing & calligra-phy	乐器演奏 playing musical instru-ment	开汽车兜风 going out for a driving	逛街购物 shopping	郊游露营 outing & camping	海外旅行 overseas travel	国内一天以上的旅行 domestic travel
样本 Sample	889	8.1	15.9	3.5	12.0	9.9	22.2	6.4	27.7	40.3
平实生活指向 simple living orientation	400	6.8	14.5	4.3	11.3	9.8	16.8	9.0	25.8	32.5
时尚流行指向 fashion orientation	489	9.2	17.0	2.9	12.7	10.0	26.6	4.3	29.2	46.6

续前表 continued

	人数 Number	国内一天往返的旅行 short journey that can be back in a day	看展览会 visiting exhibition	听演唱会/音乐会 attending concert	扭秧歌/木兰拳/交谊舞 doing the YangKo	去博物馆或美术馆 going to museum or art gallery	唱卡拉OK karaoke	去动物园或公园 going to park or zoo	酒吧/咖啡屋/茶秀 going to cafe or bar	电脑游戏 playing PC game
样本 Sample	889	38.1	24.2	19.2	28.1	8.7	18.6	12.9	16.2	9.7
平实生活指向 simple living orientation	400	43.5	28.3	20.0	23.5	8.5	19.8	14.3	15.8	5.5
时尚流行指向 fashion orientation	489	33.7	20.9	18.6	31.9	8.8	17.6	11.9	16.6	13.1

4-6-2 信息交流指标/ Information Communication Index

注：本题为多选题，合计百分比可能超过 100%（Multiple answers）

	人数 Number	打网球 tennis	打高尔夫球 golf	打羽毛球 bad-minton	打保龄球 bowling	踢足球 soccer	打篮球 basket-ball	打乒乓球 table tennis	慢跑 jogging	玩滑板 skate-boarding	跳迪斯科 disco
样本 Sample	888	31.1	17.9	11.4	14.6	9.5	6.8	9.7	17.0	8.9	10.4
信息消极指向 negative orientation	36	11.1	11.1	2.8	2.8	13.9	8.3	8.3	19.4	2.8	2.8
中间层 medium	510	28.4	15.5	9.0	14.9	8.6	5.9	9.0	17.8	7.8	9.8
信息积极指向 active orientation	342	37.1	22.2	15.8	15.5	10.2	7.9	10.8	15.5	11.1	12.0

续前表 continued

	人数 Number	打麻将 mah-jong	游泳 swimm-ing	滚轴溜冰 rolling skating	滑冰 skating	钓鱼 fishing	登山 mountain climbing	听音乐 enjoy-ing music	看电影 going to movie	打游戏机 playing video game	编织裁剪 knitting & tailor-ing
样本 Sample	888	7.9	16.1	8.7	9.5	20.5	26.2	9.1	17.9	4.3	8.2
信息消极指向 negative orientation	36	11.1	5.6	2.8	2.8	22.2	16.7	11.1	11.1	5.6	2.8
中间层 medium	510	9.0	16.3	9.2	8.4	20.4	26.5	9.2	18.6	4.5	9.0
信息积极指向 active orientation	342	5.8	17.0	8.5	11.7	20.5	26.9	8.8	17.5	3.8	7.6

续前表 continued

	人数 Number	种花盆栽 horticul-ture	看书 reading	绘画书法 drawing & calligra-phy	乐器演奏 playing musical instrume nt	开汽车兜风 going out for a driving	逛街购物 shopping	郊游露营 outing & camping	海外旅行 overseas travel	国内一天以上的旅行 domestic travel
样本 Sample	888	8.2	15.9	3.4	12.0	10.0	22.1	6.6	27.5	40.2
信息消极指向 negative orientation	36	2.8	13.9	5.6	13.9	5.6	13.9	2.8	13.9	30.6
中间层 medium	510	9.0	15.9	2.9	12.4	8.8	21.6	8.4	26.1	39.4
信息积极指向 active orientation	342	7.6	16.1	3.8	11.4	12.3	23.7	4.4	31.0	42.4

续前表 continued

	人数 Number	国内一天往返的旅行 short journey that can be back in a day	看展览会 visiting exhibition	听演唱会/音乐会 attending concert	扭秧歌/木兰拳/交谊舞 doing the YangKo	去博物馆或美术馆 going to museum or art gallery	唱卡拉OK karaoke	去动物园或公园 going to park or zoo	酒吧/咖啡屋/茶秀 going to cafe or bar	电脑游戏 playing PC game
样本 Sample	888	38.1	24.0	19.1	28.5	8.7	18.6	13.0	16.4	9.6
信息消极指向 negative orientation	36	30.6	30.6	16.7	13.9	5.6	13.9	5.6	13.9	11.1
中间层 medium	510	37.1	20.8	18.2	26.5	7.8	19.8	13.7	15.9	9.0
信息积极指向 active orientation	342	40.4	28.1	20.8	33.0	10.2	17.3	12.6	17.5	10.2

● 广州 / Guangzhou

4-1 常做的休闲活动排名/ Ranking of the Frequently Engaged Activities

注：本题为多选题，合计百分比超过 100%（Multiple answers）

排名 Ranking	活动项目 Activity Items	人次 Person-time	百分比 Percent
1	看书 reading	697	68.3
2	逛街购物 shopping	658	64.5
3	听音乐 enjoying music	536	52.5
4	唱卡拉 OK Karaoke	417	40.9
5	去动物园或公园 going to the park or zoo	414	40.6
6	打麻将 mah-jong	384	37.6
7	打羽毛球 badminton	347	34.0
8	慢跑 jogging	335	32.8
9	打游戏机 playing video game	256	25.1
10	打乒乓球 table-tennis	252	24.7
11	游泳 swimming	250	24.5
12	看电影 going to movie	243	23.8
13	电脑游戏 playing PC game	224	22.0
14	种花盆栽 horticulture	200	19.6
15	国内一天以上的旅行 domestic travel	190	18.6
16	酒吧/咖啡屋/茶秀 going to cafe or bar	175	17.2
17	登山 mountain climbing	171	16.8
17	打篮球 basketball	171	16.8
18	国内一天往返的旅行 short journey that can be back in a day	160	15.7
19	打保龄球 bowling	152	14.9
20	看展览会 visiting exhibition	136	13.3
21	踢足球 soccer	120	11.8
22	听演唱会/音乐会 attending concert	111	10.9
23	跳迪斯科 disco	108	10.6
24	滚轴溜冰 rolling skating	84	8.2
25	郊游露营 outing & camping	82	8.0
26	编织裁剪 knitting & tailoring	78	7.6
26	去博物馆或美术馆 going to museum or art gallery	78	7.6
27	绘画书法 drawing & calligraphy	68	6.7
28	钓鱼 fishing	66	6.5
29	开汽车兜风 going out for a driving	63	6.2
30	打网球 tennis	61	6.0
31	扭秧歌/木兰拳/交谊舞 doing the YangKo	41	4.0
32	滑冰 skating	36	3.5
33	乐器演奏 playing musical instrument	31	3.0
34	海外旅行 overseas travel	19	1.9
35	打高尔夫球 golf	11	1.1
35	玩滑板 skateboarding	11	1.1

n=1020

4-2 想做的休闲活动排名/ Ranking of the Desired Activities

注：本题为多选题，合计百分比超过 100%（Multiple answers）

排名 Ranking	活动项目 Activity Items	人次 Person-time	百分比 Percent
1	海外旅行 overseas travel	424	48.4
2	国内一天以上的旅行 domestic travel	351	40.1
3	打网球 tennis	284	32.4
4	听演唱会/音乐会 attending concert	262	29.9
5	郊游露营 outing & camping	239	27.3
6	打保龄球 bowling	225	25.7
7	开汽车兜风 going out for a driving	220	25.1
8	登山 mountain climbing	198	22.6
9	打高尔夫球 golf	197	22.5
10	国内一天往返的旅行 short journey that can be back in a day	190	21.7
11	钓鱼 fishing	167	19.1
12	游泳 swimming	150	17.1
13	滑冰 skating	136	15.5
14	种花盆栽 horticulture	125	14.3
15	看展览会 visiting exhibition	124	14.2
16	看电影 going to movie	117	13.4
17	打羽毛球 badminton	114	13.0
18	打乒乓球 table-tennis	110	12.6
19	去博物馆或美术馆 going to museum or art gallery	108	12.3
20	去动物园或公园 going to the park or zoo	105	12.0
21	电脑游戏 playing PC game	104	11.9
22	酒吧/咖啡屋/茶秀 going to cafe or bar	103	11.8
23	玩滑板 skateboarding	101	11.5
24	跳迪斯科 disco	99	11.3
25	乐器演奏 playing musical instrument	95	10.8
25	滚轴溜冰 rolling skating	95	10.8
26	唱卡拉 OK Karaoke	94	10.7
27	听音乐 enjoying music	92	10.5
28	慢跑 jogging	78	8.9
29	扭秧歌/木兰拳/交谊舞 doing the YangKo	76	8.7
30	绘画书法 drawing & calligraphy	71	8.1
31	编织裁剪 knitting & tailoring	70	8.0
31	打篮球 basketball	70	8.0
32	踢足球 soccer	68	7.8
33	打麻将 mah-jong	61	7.0
34	打游戏机 playing video game	54	6.2
35	逛街购物 shopping	51	5.8
36	看书 reading	33	3.8

n=876

4-3 样本、男性各年龄层、女性各年龄层常做的活动/ Frequently Engaged Activities by the Whole Sample, Age and Gender Groups

注：本题为多选题，合计百分比超过 100%（Multiple answers）

	人数 Number	打网球 tennis	打高尔夫球 golf	打羽毛球 badminton	打保龄球 bowling	踢足球 soccer	打篮球 basket-ball	打乒乓球 table tennis	慢跑 jogging	玩滑板 skateboarding	跳迪斯科 disco
样本 Sample	1020	6.0	1.1	34.0	14.9	11.8	16.8	24.7	32.8	1.1	10.6
男性 Male	490	7.8	1.2	30.0	19.0	22.0	25.1	30.0	31.6	1.4	11.2
16~24 岁 Age	106	8.5	0.9	49.1	24.5	50.0	65.1	47.2	34.9	5.7	19.8
25~34 岁 Age	148	14.2	2.0	34.5	27.0	24.3	19.6	29.1	27.7	0.0	14.2
35~44 岁 Age	124	4.8	0.0	25.8	16.1	8.1	10.5	25.8	25.0	0.8	6.5
45~54 岁 Age	70	2.9	2.9	12.9	5.7	7.1	14.3	22.9	35.7	0.0	4.3
55~60 岁 Age	42	0.0	0.0	7.1	7.1	9.5	4.8	14.3	50.0	0.0	4.8
女性 Female	530	4.3	0.9	37.7	11.1	2.3	9.1	19.8	34.0	0.8	10.0
16~24 岁 Age	112	12.5	0.9	66.1	18.8	0.9	23.2	30.4	36.6	2.7	17.0
25~34 岁 Age	158	3.8	0.6	34.8	12.7	1.3	3.8	17.7	24.1	0.0	9.5
35~44 岁 Age	134	1.5	2.2	40.3	10.4	3.7	9.0	25.4	35.8	0.0	9.0
45~54 岁 Age	86	1.2	0.0	16.3	4.7	4.7	4.7	9.3	39.5	1.2	4.7
55~60 岁 Age	40	0.0	0.0	7.5	0.0	0.0	0.0	2.5	47.5	0.0	7.5

续前表 continued

	人数 Number	打麻将 mah-jong	游泳 swim-ming	滚轴溜冰 rolling skating	滑冰 skating	钓鱼 fishing	登山 mountain climbing	听音乐 enjoy-ing music	看电影 going to movie	打游戏机 playing video game	编织裁剪 knitting & tailoring
样本 Sample	1020	37.6	24.5	8.2	3.5	6.5	16.8	52.5	23.8	25.1	7.6
男性 Male	490	40.6	27.1	8.0	3.7	9.2	16.3	53.7	23.9	32.0	0.8
16~24 岁 Age	106	40.6	36.8	18.9	8.5	8.5	16.0	73.6	38.7	68.9	0.0
25~34 岁 Age	148	37.2	31.8	7.4	3.4	8.8	15.5	54.1	29.1	38.5	1.4
35~44 岁 Age	124	50.0	23.4	4.0	2.4	11.3	16.1	48.4	16.9	15.3	0.8
45~54 岁 Age	70	41.4	20.0	2.9	1.4	4.3	15.7	44.3	7.1	8.6	0.0
55~60 岁 Age	42	23.8	9.5	2.4	0.0	14.3	21.4	33.3	16.7	4.8	2.4
女性 Female	530	34.9	22.1	8.5	3.4	4.0	17.2	51.5	23.8	18.7	14.0
16~24 岁 Age	112	31.3	33.9	27.7	9.8	5.4	20.5	74.1	50.0	39.3	10.7
25~34 岁 Age	158	31.6	19.6	3.2	3.2	4.4	17.7	51.9	19.6	20.3	5.1
35~44 岁 Age	134	43.3	26.9	4.5	1.5	4.5	11.2	51.5	21.6	14.2	17.2
45~54 岁 Age	86	29.1	11.6	3.5	0.0	1.2	18.6	34.9	9.3	4.7	27.9
55~60 岁 Age	40	42.5	5.0	0.0	0.0	2.5	22.5	22.5	5.0	0.0	17.5

续前表 continued

	人数 Number	种花盆栽 horticul-ture	看书 reading	绘画书法 drawing & calligra-phy	乐器演奏 playing musical instru-ment	开汽车兜风 going out for a driving	逛街购物 shopping	郊游露营 outing & camping	海外旅行 overseas travel	国内一天以上的旅行 domestic travel
样本 Sample	1020	7.6	19.6	68.3	6.7	3.0	6.2	64.5	8.0	1.9
男性 Male	490	0.8	12.9	69.0	6.3	2.7	9.2	49.8	8.0	1.4
16~24 岁 Age	106	0.0	5.7	81.1	14.2	6.6	8.5	57.5	8.5	1.9
25~34 岁 Age	148	1.4	8.8	73.0	6.1	2.0	14.2	51.4	12.8	1.4
35~44 岁 Age	124	0.8	15.3	59.7	2.4	1.6	8.9	48.4	4.8	0.0
45~54 岁 Age	70	0.0	18.6	68.6	2.9	1.4	4.3	45.7	7.1	2.9
55~60 岁 Age	42	2.4	28.6	52.4	4.8	0.0	2.4	35.7	0.0	2.4
女性 Female	530	14.0	25.8	67.7	7.0	3.4	3.4	78.1	8.1	2.3
16~24 岁 Age	112	10.7	17.0	81.3	15.2	8.0	7.1	82.1	10.7	0.9
25~34 岁 Age	158	5.1	22.2	72.8	6.3	1.9	4.4	83.5	8.9	1.3
35~44 岁 Age	134	17.2	32.8	64.2	4.5	3.7	2.2	76.1	9.0	5.2
45~54 岁 Age	86	27.9	27.9	54.7	4.7	1.2	0.0	69.8	5.8	2.3
55~60 岁 Age	40	17.5	37.5	50.0	0.0	0.0	0.0	70.0	0.0	0.0

续前表 continued

	人数 Number	国内一天往返的旅行 short journey that can be back in a day	看展览会 visiting exhibition	听演唱会/音乐会 atten-ding concert	扭秧歌/木兰拳/交谊舞 doing the YangKo	去博物馆或美术馆 going to museum or art gallery	唱卡拉OK karaoke	去动物园或公园 going to park or zoo	酒吧/咖啡屋/茶秀 going to cafe or bar	电脑游戏 playing PC game
样本 Sample	1020	18.6	15.7	13.3	10.9	4.0	7.6	40.9	40.6	17.2
男性 Male	490	17.6	15.3	14.7	10.8	2.4	8.8	43.5	37.6	20.0
16~24 岁 Age	106	17.0	14.2	15.1	14.2	0.0	7.5	47.2	26.4	22.6
25~34 岁 Age	148	18.2	13.5	16.2	12.2	1.4	9.5	50.7	40.5	33.8
35~44 岁 Age	124	16.9	11.3	8.9	12.1	3.2	6.5	46.8	41.1	15.3
45~54 岁 Age	70	20.0	22.9	21.4	5.7	4.3	14.3	32.9	32.9	4.3
55~60 岁 Age	42	14.3	23.8	14.3	2.4	7.1	7.1	16.7	52.4	4.8
女性 Female	530	19.6	16.0	12.1	10.9	5.5	6.6	38.5	43.4	14.5
16~24 岁 Age	112	23.2	15.2	12.5	23.2	4.5	8.9	57.1	36.6	32.1
25~34 岁 Age	158	19.6	19.6	13.3	6.3	4.4	6.3	37.3	44.9	12.0
35~44 岁 Age	134	21.6	17.9	14.2	14.2	6.0	6.7	44.8	46.3	13.4
45~54 岁 Age	86	15.1	10.5	7.0	2.3	3.5	5.8	18.6	39.5	4.7
55~60 岁 Age	40	12.5	10.0	10.0	2.5	15.0	2.5	12.5	55.0	0.0

4-4 样本、男性各年龄层、女性各年龄层想做的活动/ Desired Activities by the Whole Sample, Age and Gender Groups

注：本题为多选题，合计百分比超过 100%（Multiple answers）

	人数 Number	打网球 tennis	打高尔夫球 golf	打羽毛球 badminton	打保龄球 bowling	踢足球 soccer	打篮球 basket ball	打乒乓球 table tennis	慢跑 jogging	玩滑板 skateboarding	跳迪斯科 disco
样本 Sample	**876**	**32.4**	**22.5**	**13.0**	**25.7**	**7.8**	**8.0**	**12.6**	**8.9**	**11.5**	**11.3**
男性 Male	**431**	**31.1**	**26.5**	**12.8**	**23.2**	**9.3**	**7.4**	**11.8**	**8.8**	**13.5**	**10.9**
16~24 岁 Age	101	53.5	31.7	13.9	28.7	13.9	6.9	11.9	5.9	26.7	17.8
25~34 岁 Age	135	31.1	31.9	11.1	23.7	9.6	9.6	11.1	5.2	16.3	11.1
35~44 岁 Age	105	22.9	22.9	11.4	22.9	10.5	6.7	10.5	15.2	3.8	7.6
45~54 岁 Age	59	20.3	15.3	18.6	20.3	0.0	5.1	16.9	5.1	5.1	5.1
55~60 岁 Age	31	6.5	19.4	9.7	9.7	6.5	6.5	9.7	19.4	6.5	9.7
女性 Female	**445**	**33.7**	**18.7**	**13.3**	**28.1**	**6.3**	**8.5**	**13.3**	**9.0**	**9.7**	**11.7**
16~24 岁 Age	105	56.2	29.5	8.6	40.0	10.5	18.1	12.4	7.6	20.0	23.8
25~34 岁 Age	145	35.9	18.6	21.4	24.8	5.5	6.2	16.6	9.7	8.3	6.2
35~44 岁 Age	102	28.4	16.7	9.8	28.4	4.9	2.0	11.8	10.8	6.9	8.8
45~54 岁 Age	69	13.0	10.1	11.6	24.6	5.8	11.6	14.5	10.1	4.3	13.0
55~60 岁 Age	24	4.2	4.2	4.2	4.2	0.0	0.0	0.0	0.0	0.0	0.0

续前表 continued

	人数 Number	打麻将 mah-jong	游泳 swimming	滚轴溜冰 rolling skating	滑冰 skating	钓鱼 fishing	登山 mountian climbing	听音乐 enjoying music	看电影 going to movie	打游戏机 playing video game	编织裁剪 knitting & tailoring
样本 Sample	**876**	**7.0**	**17.1**	**10.8**	**15.5**	**19.1**	**22.6**	**10.5**	**13.4**	**6.2**	**8.0**
男性 Male	**431**	**5.3**	**18.1**	**10.4**	**16.2**	**21.6**	**21.6**	**9.3**	**11.6**	**4.9**	**3.0**
16~24 岁 Age	101	8.9	23.8	18.8	22.8	22.3	27.7	10.9	17.8	7.9	4.0
25~34 岁 Age	135	4.4	14.1	16.3	20.7	25.9	25.2	8.1	9.6	4.4	2.2
35~44 岁 Age	105	2.9	19.0	2.9	10.5	14.3	14.3	9.5	9.5	5.7	3.8
45~54 岁 Age	59	5.1	13.6	0.0	8.5	22.0	15.3	8.5	8.5	0.0	1.7
55~60 岁 Age	31	6.5	22.6	3.2	9.7	22.6	22.6	9.7	12.9	3.2	3.2
女性 Female	**445**	**8.5**	**16.2**	**11.2**	**14.8**	**16.6**	**23.6**	**11.7**	**15.1**	**7.4**	**12.8**
16~24 岁 Age	105	15.2	23.8	21.9	28.6	27.6	28.6	7.6	14.3	7.6	20.0
25~34 岁 Age	145	7.6	17.9	9.7	11.0	15.2	27.6	9.0	14.5	9.7	12.4
35~44 岁 Age	102	6.9	11.8	8.8	12.7	9.8	18.6	13.7	17.6	4.9	9.8
45~54 岁 Age	69	4.3	10.1	5.8	8.7	17.4	18.8	20.3	15.9	8.7	10.1
55~60 岁 Age											

续前表 continued

	人数 Number	种花盆栽 horticulture	看书 reading	绘画书法 drawing & calligraphy	乐器演奏 playing musical instrument	开汽车兜风 going out for a driving	逛街购物 shopping	郊游露营 outing & camping	海外旅行 overseas travel	国内一天以上的旅行 domestic travel
样本 Sample	**876**	**8.0**	**14.3**	**3.8**	**8.1**	**10.8**	**25.1**	**5.8**	**27.3**	**48.4**
男性 Male	**431**	**3.0**	**13.0**	**2.6**	**7.2**	**10.2**	**26.9**	**6.5**	**25.1**	**49.7**
16~24 岁 Age	101	4.0	12.9	2.0	4.0	12.9	39.6	7.9	42.6	52.5
25~34 岁 Age	135	2.2	14.1	3.0	8.9	11.1	31.9	5.9	22.2	56.3
35~44 岁 Age	105	3.8	11.4	1.9	5.7	7.6	21.9	6.7	20.0	46.7
45~54 岁 Age	59	1.7	11.9	0.0	8.5	10.2	15.3	6.8	18.6	45.8
55~60 岁 Age	31	3.2	16.1	9.7	12.9	6.5	3.2	3.2	9.7	29.0
女性 Female	**445**	**12.8**	**15.5**	**4.9**	**9.0**	**11.5**	**23.4**	**5.2**	**29.4**	**47.2**
16~24 岁 Age	105	20.0	15.2	6.7	12.4	20.0	33.3	3.8	47.6	53.3
25~34 岁 Age	145	12.4	14.5	4.8	6.9	9.0	26.2	3.4	29.0	46.9
35~44 岁 Age	102	9.8	15.7	3.9	9.8	9.8	23.5	6.9	25.5	47.1
45~54 岁 Age	69	10.1	14.5	5.8	7.2	8.7	10.1	7.2	15.9	40.6
55~60 岁 Age	24	4.2	25.0	0.0	8.3	4.2	0.0	8.3	8.3	41.7

续前表 continued

	人数 Number	国内一天往返的旅行 short journey that can be back in a day	看展览会 visiting exhibition	听演唱会/音乐会 attending concert	扭秧歌/木兰拳/交谊舞 doing the YangKo	去博物馆或美术馆 going to museum or art gallery	唱卡拉OK karaoke	去动物园或公园 going to park or zoo	酒吧/咖啡屋/茶秀 going to cafe or bar	电脑游戏 playing PC game
样本 Sample	876	40.1	21.7	14.2	29.9	8.7	12.3	10.7	12.0	11.8
男性 Male	431	37.4	19.7	13.0	27.4	7.7	11.4	8.6	10.7	10.0
16~24 岁 Age	101	36.6	21.8	12.9	40.6	7.9	16.8	13.9	12.9	18.8
25~34 岁 Age	135	37.0	19.3	12.6	34.8	8.9	13.3	7.4	8.9	8.1
35~44 岁 Age	105	38.1	19.0	13.3	16.2	4.8	7.6	7.6	9.5	6.7
45~54 岁 Age	59	37.3	20.3	16.9	15.3	8.5	8.5	5.1	13.6	6.8
55~60 岁 Age	31	38.7	16.1	6.5	12.9	9.7	3.2	6.5	9.7	6.5
女性 Female	445	42.7	23.6	15.3	32.4	9.7	13.3	12.8	13.3	13.5
16~24 岁 Age	105	45.7	23.8	17.1	41.0	12.4	21.0	16.2	15.2	26.7
25~34 岁 Age	145	44.1	25.5	13.8	32.4	5.5	9.7	14.5	12.4	9.0
35~44 岁 Age	102	39.2	19.6	17.6	33.3	12.7	11.8	9.8	12.7	11.8
45~54 岁 Age	69	40.6	24.6	15.9	27.5	13.0	13.0	13.0	17.4	8.7
55~60 岁 Age	24	41.7	25.0	4.2	4.2	0.0	8.3	0.0	0.0	4.2

4-5 不同消费层常做的休闲活动/ Frequently Engaged Activities by Market Segments

4-5-1 时尚流行指标/ Fads Popular Index

注：本题为多选题，合计百分比超过 100%（Multiple answers）

	人数 Number	打网球 tennis	打高尔夫球 golf	打羽毛球 badminton	打保龄球 bowling	踢足球 soccer	打篮球 basketball	打乒乓球 table tennis	慢跑 jogging	玩滑板 skate boarding	跳迪斯科 disco
样本 Sample	1008	6.0	1.1	34.1	15.1	11.7	16.8	24.7	33.0	1.1	10.5
平实生活指向 simple living orientation	507	4.7	0.6	29.2	10.8	8.3	13.0	22.9	34.1	0.8	5.7
时尚流行指向 fashion orientation	501	7.2	1.6	39.1	19.4	15.2	20.6	26.5	31.9	1.4	15.4

续前表 continued

	人数 Number	打麻将 mah-jong	游泳 swimming	滚轴溜冰 rolling skating	滑冰 skating	钓鱼 fishing	登山 mountain climbing	听音乐 enjoying music	看电影 going to movie	打游戏机 playing video game	编织裁剪 knitting & tailoring
样本 Sample	1008	37.4	24.7	8.3	3.6	6.4	17.0	52.5	23.9	25.0	7.7
平实生活指向 simple living orientation	507	35.3	20.9	3.9	1.0	5.7	16.8	45.8	18.3	18.3	7.9
时尚流行指向 fashion orientation	501	39.5	28.5	12.8	6.2	7.2	17.2	59.3	29.5	31.7	7.6

续前表 continued

	人数 Number	种花盆栽 horticulture	看书 reading	绘画书法 drawing & calligraphy	乐器演奏 playing musical instrument	开汽车兜风 going out for a driving	逛街购物 shopping	郊游露营 outing & camping	海外旅行 overseas travel	国内一天以上的旅行 domestic travel
样本 Sample	1008	7.7	19.4	68.1	6.6	3.0	6.3	64.8	8.0	1.8
平实生活指向 simple living orientation	507	7.9	20.9	66.7	5.7	0.8	5.1	57.6	6.5	1.0
时尚流行指向 fashion orientation	501	7.6	18.0	69.5	7.6	5.2	7.4	72.1	9.6	2.6

续前表 continued

	人数 Number	国内一天往返的旅行 short journey that can be back in a day	看展览会 visiting exhibition	听演唱会/音乐会 attending concert	扭秧歌/木兰拳/交谊舞 doing the YangKo	去博物馆或美术馆 going to museum or art gallery	唱卡拉OK karaoke	去动物园或公园 going to park or zoo	酒吧/咖啡屋/茶秀 going to cafe or bar	电脑游戏 playing PC game
样本 Sample	1008	18.7	15.9	13.4	10.9	4.1	7.7	40.8	41.0	22.0
平实生活指向 simple living orientation	507	15.8	14.2	13.6	6.5	3.2	7.7	31.4	42.6	16.8
时尚流行指向 fashion orientation	501	21.6	17.6	13.2	15.4	5.0	7.8	50.3	39.3	27.3

4-5-2 信息交流指标/ Information Communication Index

注：本题为多选题，合计百分比超过 100%（Multiple answers）

	人数 Number	打网球 tennis	打高尔夫球 golf	打羽毛球 badminton	打保龄球 bowling	踢足球 soccer	打篮球 basketball	打乒乓球 table tennis	慢跑 jogging	玩滑板 skate boarding	跳迪斯科 disco
样本 Sample	1012	6.0	1.1	33.8	15.0	11.7	16.8	24.6	32.7	1.1	10.4
信息消极指向 negative orientation	104	7.7	1.0	22.1	8.7	11.5	14.4	16.3	29.8	1.0	7.7
中间层 medium	658	6.1	0.9	33.3	15.3	12.6	17.6	23.9	31.9	0.9	10.2
信息积极指向 active orientation	250	5.2	1.6	40.0	16.8	9.2	15.6	30.0	36.0	1.6	12.0

续前表 continued

	人数 Number	打麻将 mah-jong	游泳 swimming	滚轴溜冰 rolling skating	滑冰 skating	钓鱼 fishing	登山 mountain climbing	听音乐 enjoying music	看电影 going to movie	打游戏机 playing video game	编织裁剪 knitting & tailoring
样本 Sample	1012	37.6	24.6	8.2	3.6	5.5	16.8	52.6	23.9	24.9	7.5
信息消极指向 negative orientation	104	39.4	16.3	6.7	1.9	2.9	16.3	39.4	20.2	12.5	7.7
中间层 medium	658	36.8	23.1	7.4	3.3	6.8	15.5	52.6	23.7	25.7	6.8
信息积极指向 active orientation	250	39.2	32.0	10.8	4.8	7.2	20.4	58.0	26.0	28.0	9.2

续前表 continued

	人数 Number	种花盆栽 horticulture	看书 reading	绘画书法 drawing & calligraphy	乐器演奏 playing musical instrument	开汽车兜风 going out for a driving	逛街购物 shopping	郊游露营 outing & camping	海外旅行 overseas travel	国内一天以上的旅行 domestic travel
样本 Sample	1012	7.5	19.6	68.4	6.5	2.9	6.1	64.6	8.0	1.9
信息消极指向 negative orientation	104	7.7	15.4	50.0	5.8	1.0	5.8	56.7	3.8	1.0
中间层 medium	658	6.8	19.0	67.8	5.8	2.9	5.6	63.5	7.6	1.5
信息积极指向 active orientation	250	9.2	22.8	77.6	8.8	3.6	7.6	70.8	10.8	3.2

续前表 continued

	人数 Number	国内一天往返的旅行 short journey that can be back in a day	看展览会 visiting exhibition	听演唱会/音乐会 attending concert	扭秧歌/木兰拳/交谊舞 doing the YangKo	去博物馆或美术馆 going to museum or art gallery	唱卡拉OK karaoke	去动物园或公园 going to park or zoo	酒吧/咖啡屋/茶秀 going to cafe or bar	电脑游戏 playing PC game
样本 Sample	1012	18.5	15.5	13.2	11.0	4.1	7.6	40.7	40.9	21.9
信息消极指向 negative orientation	104	9.6	11.5	7.7	6.7	1.0	6.7	29.8	41.3	9.6
中间层 medium	658	18.5	14.6	12.9	10.8	3.8	6.4	40.0	38.8	23.3
信息积极指向 active orientation	250	22.0	19.6	16.4	13.2	6.0	11.2	47.2	46.4	23.6

4-6 不同消费者层想做的休闲活动/ Desired Activities by Market Segments

4-6-1 时尚流行指标/ Fads Popular Index

注：本题为多选题，合计百分比超过 100%（Multiple answers）

	人数 Number	打网球 tennis	打高尔夫球 golf	打羽毛球 badminton	打保龄球 bowling	踢足球 soccer	打篮球 basketball	打乒乓球 table tennis	慢跑 jogging	玩滑板 skateboarding	跳迪斯科 disco
样本 Sample	866	32.6	22.3	13.0	25.6	7.7	8.1	12.7	9.0	11.5	11.3
平实生活指向 simple living orientation	430	24.9	19.1	14.4	24.4	7.2	6.5	14.4	9.8	7.9	10.0
时尚流行指向 fashion orientation	436	40.1	25.5	11.7	26.8	8.3	9.6	11.0	8.3	15.1	12.6

续前表 continued

	人数 Number	打麻将 mahjong	游泳 swimming	滚轴溜冰 rolling skating	滑冰 skating	钓鱼 fishing	登山 mountain climbing	听音乐 enjoying music	看电影 going to movie	打游戏机 playing video game	编织裁剪 knitting & tailoring
样本 Sample	866	6.9	17.2	10.9	15.6	19.1	22.5	10.4	13.3	6.2	8.0
平实生活指向 simple living orientation	430	5.1	15.6	11.4	14.2	15.1	22.1	9.5	12.8	5.6	6.5
时尚流行指向 fashion orientation	436	8.7	18.8	10.3	17.0	22.9	22.9	11.2	13.8	6.9	9.4

续前表 continued

	人数 Number	种花盆栽 horticulture	看书 reading	绘画书法 drawing & calligraphy	乐器演奏 playing musical instrument	开汽车兜风 going out for a driving	逛街购物 shopping	郊游露营 outing & camping	海外旅行 overseas travel	国内一天以上的旅行 domestic travel
样本 Sample	866	8.0	14.4	3.8	8.1	11.0	25.1	5.9	27.5	48.4
平实生活指向 simple living orientation	430	6.5	14.9	3.3	8.6	9.5	19.1	7.7	24.2	47.7
时尚流行指向 fashion orientation	436	9.4	14.0	4.4	7.6	12.4	31.0	4.1	30.7	49.1

续前表 continued

	人数 Number	国内一天往返的旅行 short journey that can be back in a day	看展览会 visiting exhibition	听演唱会/音乐会 attending concert	扭秧歌/木兰拳/交谊舞 doing the YangKo	去博物馆或美术馆 going to museum or art gallery	唱卡拉OK karaoke	去动物园或公园 going to park or zoo	酒吧/咖啡屋/茶秀 going to cafe or bar	电脑游戏 playing PC game
样本 Sample	866	40.2	21.8	14.1	29.9	8.7	12.5	10.7	11.8	11.9
平实生活指向 simple living orientation	430	40.2	21.6	13.0	26.0	8.4	13.3	11.2	13.7	9.8
时尚流行指向 fashion orientation	436	40.1	22.0	15.1	33.7	8.9	11.7	10.3	9.9	14.0

4-6-2 信息交流指标/ Information Communication Index

注：本题为多选题，合计百分比超过 100%（Multiple answers）

	人数 Number	打网球 tennis	打高尔夫球 golf	打羽毛球 badminton	打保龄球 bowling	踢足球 soccer	打篮球 basketball	打乒乓球 table tennis	慢跑 jogging	玩滑板 skate boarding	跳迪斯科 disco
样本 Sample	871	32.1	22.4	13.1	25.6	7.7	7.9	12.5	9.0	11.5	11.1
信息消极指向 negative orientation	89	18.0	27.0	18.0	22.5	4.5	4.5	10.1	11.2	9.0	11.2
中间层 medium	565	33.1	21.9	13.1	25.7	7.4	8.1	11.7	8.7	11.3	10.4
信息积极指向 active orientation	217	35.5	21.7	11.1	26.7	9.7	8.8	15.7	8.8	12.9	12.9

续前表 continued

	人数 Number	打麻将 mah-jong	游泳 swim-ming	滚轴溜冰 rolling skating	滑冰 skating	钓鱼 fishing	登山 moun-tain climbing	听音乐 enjoy-ing music	看电影 going to movie	打游戏机 playing video game	编织裁剪 knitting & tailor-ing
样本 Sample	**871**	**7.0**	**17.0**	**10.8**	**15.4**	**18.8**	**22.5**	**10.6**	**13.3**	**6.1**	**8.0**
信息消极指向 negative orientation	89	3.4	16.9	5.6	13.5	20.2	14.6	11.2	9.0	6.7	3.4
中间层 medium	565	8.3	17.3	11.5	15.0	18.2	24.2	9.9	14.2	6.0	9.0
信息积极指向 active orientation	217	5.1	16.1	11.1	17.1	19.8	21.2	12.0	12.9	6.0	7.4

续前表 continued

	人数 Number	种花盆栽 horti-culture	看书 reading	绘画书法 drawing & calligra-phy	乐器演奏 playing musical instru-ment	开汽车兜风 going out for a driving	逛街购物 shopping	郊游露营 outing & camping	海外旅行 overseas travel	国内一天以上的旅行 domestic travel
样本 Sample	**871**	**8.0**	**14.2**	**3.8**	**8.2**	**10.9**	**25.1**	**5.9**	**27.2**	**48.3**
信息消极指向 negative orientation	89	3.4	11.2	2.2	4.5	5.6	16.9	9.0	27.0	47.2
中间层 medium	565	9.0	13.6	4.8	8.5	10.6	25.3	6.0	25.5	47.3
信息积极指向 active orientation	217	7.4	17.1	1.8	8.8	13.8	28.1	4.1	31.8	51.6

续前表 continued

	人数 Number	国内一天往返的旅行 short journey that can be back in a day	看展览会 visiting exhibi-tion	听演唱会/音乐会 attending concert	扭秧歌/木兰拳/交谊舞 doing the YangKo	去博物馆或美术馆 going to museum or art gallery	唱卡拉OK karaoke	去动物园或公园 going to park or zoo	酒吧/咖啡屋/茶秀 going to cafe or bar	电脑游戏 playing PC game
样本 Sample	**871**	**40.2**	**21.8**	**14.2**	**30.0**	**8.6**	**12.3**	**10.8**	**11.9**	**11.7**
信息消极指向 negative orientation	89	34.8	13.5	12.4	21.3	7.9	7.9	14.6	11.2	12.4
中间层 medium	565	41.2	22.7	14.2	28.7	8.0	13.3	9.9	12.0	11.7
信息积极指向 active orientation	217	39.6	23.0	15.2	36.9	10.6	11.5	11.5	12.0	11.5

● 重庆 / Chongqing

4-1 常做的休闲活动排名/ Ranking of the Frequently Engaged Activities

注：本题为多选题，合计百分比可能超过 100%（Multiple answers）

排名 Ranking	活动项目 Activity Items	人次 Person-time	百分比 Percent
1	看书 reading	436	70.6
2	逛街购物 shopping	405	65.5
3	听音乐 enjoying music	374	60.5
4	打麻将 mah-jong	314	50.8
5	唱卡拉 OK Karaoke	273	44.2
6	去动物园或公园 going to the park or zoo	226	36.6
7	打游戏机 playing video game	164	26.5
8	打羽毛球 badminton	160	25.9
9	看电影 going to movie	158	25.6
10	慢跑 jogging	152	24.6
11	游泳 swimming	149	24.1
12	编织裁剪 knitting & tailoring	123	19.9
13	打乒乓球 table-tennis	114	18.4
14	国内一天以上的旅行 domestic travel	99	16.0
15	电脑游戏 playing PC game	96	15.5
16	钓鱼 fishing	95	15.4
17	种花盆栽 horticulture	94	15.2
18	看展览会 visiting exhibition	93	15.0
19	登山 mountain climbing	88	14.2
20	酒吧/咖啡屋/茶秀 going to cafe or bar	85	13.8
21	国内一天往返的旅行 short journey that can be back in a day	75	12.1
22	跳迪斯科 disco	69	11.2
23	郊游露营 outing & camping	68	11.0
24	听演唱会/音乐会 attending concert	67	10.8
25	踢足球 soccer	66	10.7
26	打篮球 basketball	60	9.7
27	滑冰 skating	41	6.6
28	扭秧歌/木兰拳/交谊舞 doing the YangKo	39	6.3
29	绘画书法 drawing & calligraphy	37	6.0
29	去博物馆或美术馆 going to museum or art gallery	37	6.0
29	打保龄球 bowling	37	6.0
30	滚轴溜冰 rolling skating	35	5.7
31	开汽车兜风 going out for a driving	27	4.4
31	打网球 tennis	27	4.4
32	乐器演奏 playing musical instrument	16	2.6
33	玩滑板 skateboarding	5	0.8
34	海外旅行 overseas travel	4	0.6
34	打高尔夫球 golf	4	0.6

n=618

4-2 想做的休闲活动排名/ Ranking of the Desired Activities

注：本题为多选题，合计百分比可能超过 100%（Multiple answers）

排名 Ranking	活动项目 Activity Items	人次 Person-time	百分比 Percent
1	国内一天以上的旅行 domestic travel	206	39.8
2	海外旅行 overseas travel	156	30.2
3	听演唱会/音乐会 attending concert	154	29.8
4	郊游露营 outing & camping	145	28.0
5	国内一天往返的旅行 short journey that can be back in a day	140	27.1
6	打网球 tennis	125	24.2
7	登山 mountain climbing	119	23.0
8	钓鱼 fishing	107	20.7
9	打保龄球 bowling	101	19.5
10	看电影 going to movie	99	19.1
11	开汽车兜风 going out for a driving	92	17.8
12	去动物园或公园 going to the park or zoo	91	17.6
13	去博物馆或美术馆 going to museum or art gallery	82	15.9
14	看展览会 visiting exhibition	81	15.7
15	游泳 swimming	80	15.5
16	种花盆栽 horticulture	78	15.1
17	打羽毛球 badminton	66	12.8
18	打高尔夫球 golf	62	12.0
19	滑冰 skating	56	10.8
20	打乒乓球 table-tennis	50	9.7
21	绘画书法 drawing & calligraphy	48	9.3
22	电脑游戏 playing PC game	46	8.9
23	跳迪斯科 disco	40	7.7
24	慢跑 jogging	39	7.5
24	打篮球 basketball	39	7.5
24	酒吧/咖啡屋/茶秀 going to cafe or bar	39	7.5
25	听音乐 enjoying music	38	7.4
25	唱卡拉 OK Karaoke	38	7.4
26	编织裁剪 knitting & tailoring	33	6.4
26	玩滑板 skateboarding	33	6.4
26	扭秧歌/木兰拳/交谊舞 doing the YangKo	33	6.4
27	踢足球 soccer	30	5.8
28	逛街购物 shopping	29	5.6
29	乐器演奏 playing musical instrument	28	5.4
30	滚轴溜冰 rolling skating	26	5.0
31	看书 reading	22	4.3
32	打麻将 mah-jong	20	3.9
33	打游戏机 playing video game	11	2.1

n=517

4-3 样本、男性各年龄层、女性各年龄层常做的活动/ Frequently Engaged Activities by the Whole Sample, Age and Gender Groups

注：本题为多选题，合计百分比超过 100%（Multiple answers）

	人数 Number	打网球 tennis	打高尔夫球 golf	打羽毛球 bad-minton	打保龄球 bowling	踢足球 soccer	打篮球 basket-ball	打乒乓球 table-tennis	慢跑 jogging	玩滑板 skate-boarding	跳迪斯科 disco
样本 Sample	618	4.4	0.6	25.9	6.0	10.7	9.7	18.4	24.6	0.8	11.2
男性 Male	310	4.8	1.0	23.9	6.1	19.4	15.5	21.6	23.5	1.6	9.4
16~24 岁 Age	64	6.3	1.6	31.3	3.1	60.9	46.9	43.8	31.3	7.8	14.1
25~34 岁 Age	92	5.4	0.0	27.2	8.7	16.3	12.0	15.2	19.6	0.0	15.2
35~44 岁 Age	73	5.5	1.4	24.7	9.6	5.5	5.5	23.3	20.5	0.0	5.5
45~54 岁 Age	53	3.8	1.9	15.1	1.9	1.9	3.8	9.4	20.8	0.0	1.9
55~60 岁 Age	28	0.0	0.0	10.7	3.6	3.6	3.6	10.7	32.1	0.0	3.6
女性 Female	308	3.9	0.3	27.9	5.8	1.9	3.9	15.3	25.6	0.0	13.0
16~24 岁 Age	64	4.7	1.6	54.7	12.5	3.1	9.4	40.6	35.9	0.0	25.0
25~34 岁 Age	89	6.7	0.0	27.0	9.0	4.5	4.5	14.6	16.9	0.0	15.7
35~44 岁 Age	73	1.4	0.0	23.3	1.4	0.0	2.7	8.2	17.8	0.0	5.5
45~54 岁 Age	60	0.0	0.0	10.0	1.7	0.0	0.0	3.3	31.7	0.0	8.3
55~60 岁 Age	22	9.1	0.0	18.2	0.0	0.0	0.0	0.0	40.9	0.0	4.5

续前表 continued

	人数 Number	打麻将 mah-jong	游泳 swimming	滚轴溜冰 rolling skating	滑冰 skating	钓鱼 fishing	登山 mountain climbing	听音乐 enjoying music	看电影 going to movie	打游戏机 playing video game	编织裁剪 kniting & tailoring
样本 Sample	618	50.8	24.1	5.7	6.6	15.4	14.2	60.5	25.6	26.5	19.9
男性 Male	310	51.3	33.5	6.8	5.5	25.8	11.6	59.7	25.5	30.6	0.6
16~24 岁 Age	64	32.8	53.1	20.3	12.5	15.6	10.9	67.2	43.8	65.6	0.0
25~34 岁 Age	92	56.5	38.0	7.6	6.5	25.0	10.9	60.9	27.2	32.6	1.1
35~44 岁 Age	73	54.8	30.1	0.0	4.1	31.5	12.3	63.0	20.5	21.9	0.0
45~54 岁 Age	53	52.8	17.0	1.9	0.0	30.2	11.3	52.8	9.4	9.4	1.9
55~60 岁 Age	28	64.3	14.3	0.0	0.0	28.6	14.3	42.9	21.4	7.1	0.0
女性 Female	308	50.3	14.6	4.5	7.8	4.9	16.9	61.4	25.6	22.4	39.3
16~24 岁 Age	64	45.3	26.6	17.2	21.9	1.6	25.0	87.5	57.8	50.0	17.2
25~34 岁 Age	89	55.1	18.0	3.4	9.0	6.7	16.9	65.2	25.8	28.1	33.7
35~44 岁 Age	73	56.2	9.6	0.0	2.7	6.8	8.2	60.3	13.7	9.6	50.7
45~54 岁 Age	60	48.3	6.7	0.0	0.0	3.3	20.0	40.0	13.3	8.3	53.3
55~60 岁 Age	22	31.8	4.5	0.0	0.0	4.5	13.6	31.8	4.5	0.0	50.0

续前表 continued

	人数 Number	种花盆栽 horticulture	看书 reading	绘画书法 drawing & calligraphy	乐器演奏 playing musical instrument	开汽车兜风 going out for a driving	逛街购物 shopping	郊游露营 outing & camping	海外旅行 overseas travel	国内一天以上的旅行 domestic travel
样本 Sample	618	19.9	15.2	70.6	6.0	2.6	4.4	65.5	11.0	0.6
男性 Male	310	0.6	14.5	71.6	5.2	1.9	5.5	51.6	10.0	1.0
16~24 岁 Age	64	0.0	3.1	65.6	6.3	1.6	1.6	50.0	9.4	0.0
25~34 岁 Age	92	1.1	8.7	78.3	5.4	3.3	6.5	54.3	9.8	1.1
35~44 岁 Age	73	0.0	20.5	71.2	4.1	2.7	9.6	46.6	13.7	0.0
45~54 岁 Age	53	1.9	20.8	62.3	1.9	0.0	3.8	66.0	9.4	3.8
55~60 岁 Age	28	0.0	32.1	82.1	10.7	0.0	3.6	32.1	3.6	0.0
女性 Female	308	39.3	15.9	69.5	6.8	3.2	3.2	79.5	12.0	0.3
16~24 岁 Age	64	17.2	10.9	82.8	18.8	9.4	3.1	89.1	20.3	0.0
25~34 岁 Age	89	33.7	13.5	77.5	4.5	0.0	7.9	82.0	15.7	1.1
35~44 岁 Age	73	50.7	11.0	60.3	2.7	2.7	1.4	71.2	6.8	0.0
45~54 岁 Age	60	53.3	25.0	60.0	5.0	1.7	0.0	76.7	6.7	0.0
55~60 岁 Age	22	50.0	31.8	54.5	0.0	4.5	0.0	77.3	4.5	0.0

续前表 continued

	人数 Number	国内一天往返的旅行 short journey that can be back in a day	看展览会 visiting exhibition	听演唱会/音乐会 attending concert	扭秧歌/木兰拳/交谊舞 doing the YangKo	去博物馆或美术馆 going to museum or art gallery	唱卡拉OK karaoke	去动物园或公园 going to park or zoo	酒吧/咖啡屋/茶秀 going to cafe or bar	电脑游戏 Playing PC game
样本 Sample	618	16.0	12.1	15.0	10.8	6.3	6.0	44.2	36.6	13.8
男性 Male	310	17.7	11.9	15.2	11.9	4.2	5.2	43.9	32.9	14.8
16~24 岁 Age	64	7.8	7.8	17.2	18.8	1.6	4.7	48.4	26.6	17.2
25~34 岁 Age	92	19.6	10.9	14.1	9.8	3.3	3.3	58.7	29.3	21.7
35~44 岁 Age	73	28.8	19.2	19.2	16.4	5.5	9.6	38.4	38.4	13.7
45~54 岁 Age	53	11.3	9.4	11.3	7.5	7.5	3.8	35.8	39.6	3.8
55~60 岁 Age	28	17.9	10.7	10.7	0.0	3.6	3.6	14.3	32.1	10.7
女性 Female	308	14.3	12.3	14.9	9.7	8.4	6.8	44.5	40.3	12.7
16~24 岁 Age	64	18.8	17.2	18.8	15.6	1.6	9.4	64.1	42.2	26.6
25~34 岁 Age	89	18.0	12.4	14.6	14.6	5.6	5.6	50.6	49.4	18.0
35~44 岁 Age	73	4.1	4.1	13.7	6.8	4.1	6.8	39.7	35.6	4.1
45~54 岁 Age	60	18.3	16.7	15.0	1.7	25.0	6.7	31.7	31.7	3.3
55~60 岁 Age	22	9.1	13.6	9.1	4.5	9.1	4.5	13.6	36.4	4.5

4-4 样本、男性各年龄层、女性各年龄层想做的活动/ Desired Activities by the Whole Sample, Age and Gender Groups

注：本题为多选题，合计百分比超过 100%（Multiple answers）

	人数 Number	打网球 tennis	打高尔夫球 golf	打羽毛球 badminton	打保龄球 bowling	踢足球 soccer	打篮球 basket-ball	打乒乓球 table-tennis	慢跑 jogging	玩滑板 skate-boarding	跳迪斯科 disco
样本 Sample	**517**	**24.2**	**12.0**	**12.8**	**19.5**	**5.8**	**7.5**	**9.7**	**7.5**	**6.4**	**7.7**
男性 Male	**261**	**26.1**	**16.5**	**13.8**	**24.9**	**9.6**	**10.0**	**9.6**	**8.4**	**8.4**	**8.0**
16~24 岁 Age	56	41.1	23.2	10.7	32.1	14.3	8.9	5.4	7.1	26.8	19.6
25~34 岁 Age	78	24.4	23.1	17.9	24.4	14.1	6.4	14.1	6.4	6.4	5.1
35~44 岁 Age	63	23.8	12.7	11.1	23.8	3.2	9.5	4.8	6.3	1.6	7.9
45~54 岁 Age	42	16.7	4.8	16.7	21.4	4.8	19.0	16.7	14.3	0.0	0.0
55~60 岁 Age	22	18.2	9.1	9.1	18.2	9.1	9.1	4.5	13.6	4.5	4.5
女性 Female	**256**	**22.3**	**7.4**	**11.7**	**14.1**	**2.0**	**5.1**	**9.8**	**6.6**	**4.3**	**7.4**
16~24 岁 Age	57	38.6	15.8	7.0	24.6	7.0	8.8	5.3	5.3	14.0	10.5
25~34 岁 Age	81	18.5	7.4	16.0	12.3	0.0	4.9	12.3	2.5	2.5	6.2
35~44 岁 Age	55	20.0	3.6	9.1	14.5	1.8	3.6	14.5	5.5	1.8	5.5
45~54 岁 Age	49	16.3	4.1	14.3	8.2	0.0	4.1	4.1	14.3	0.0	8.2
55~60 岁 Age	14	7.1	0.0	7.1	0.0	0.0	0.0	14.3	14.3	0.0	7.1

续前表 continued

	人数 Number	打麻将 mah-jong	游泳 swim-ming	滚轴溜冰 rolling skating	滑冰 skating	钓鱼 fishing	登山 moun-tain climbing	听音乐 enjoy-ing music	看电影 going to movie	打游戏机 playing video game	编织裁剪 knit-ting & tailor-ing
样本 Sample	**517**	**3.9**	**15.5**	**5.0**	**10.8**	**20.7**	**23.0**	**7.4**	**19.1**	**2.1**	**6.4**
男性 Male	**261**	**3.8**	**13.0**	**6.1**	**10.3**	**27.2**	**24.5**	**8.4**	**15.7**	**1.9**	**2.3**
16~24 岁 Age	56	3.6	8.9	12.5	17.9	30.4	28.6	5.4	14.3	3.6	3.6
25~34 岁 Age	78	3.8	15.4	5.1	16.7	28.2	26.9	11.5	12.8	0.0	2.6
35~44 岁 Age	63	3.2	14.3	4.8	4.8	25.4	22.2	7.9	22.2	0.0	0.0
45~54 岁 Age	42	4.8	9.5	2.4	0.0	26.2	16.7	11.9	19.0	2.4	2.4
55~60 岁 Age	22	4.5	18.2	4.5	4.5	22.7	27.3	0.0	4.5	9.1	4.5
女性 Female	**256**	**3.9**	**18.0**	**3.9**	**11.3**	**14.1**	**21.5**	**6.3**	**22.7**	**2.3**	**10.5**
16~24 岁 Age	57	3.5	26.3	5.3	24.6	17.5	35.1	3.5	15.8	1.8	8.8
25~34 岁 Age	81	8.6	22.2	4.9	16.0	14.8	25.9	6.2	28.4	3.7	16.0
35~44 岁 Age	55	1.8	12.7	3.6	3.6	9.1	9.1	1.8	20.0	1.8	5.5
45~54 岁 Age	49	0.0	8.2	2.0	0.0	14.3	14.3	10.2	24.5	2.0	8.2
55~60 岁 Age	14	0.0	14.3	0.0	0.0	14.3	14.3	21.4	21.4	0.0	14.3

续前表 continued

	人数 Number	种花盆栽 horticul-ture	看书 reading	绘画书法 drawing & calligra-phy	乐器演奏 playing musical instru-ment	开汽车兜风 going out for a driving	逛街购物 shopping	郊游露营 outing & camping	海外旅行 overseas travel	国内一天以上的旅行 domestic travel
样本 Sample	**517**	**6.4**	**15.1**	**4.3**	**9.3**	**5.4**	**17.8**	**5.6**	**28.0**	**30.2**
男性 Male	**261**	**2.3**	**12.6**	**3.1**	**11.1**	**6.9**	**24.1**	**7.3**	**28.0**	**33.0**
16~24 岁 Age	56	3.6	8.9	3.6	12.5	8.9	39.3	5.4	39.3	33.9
25~34 岁 Age	78	2.6	10.3	1.3	7.7	5.1	29.5	6.4	32.1	39.7
35~44 岁 Age	63	0.0	9.5	4.8	7.9	4.8	17.5	9.5	23.8	28.6
45~54 岁 Age	42	2.4	21.4	2.4	9.5	4.8	11.9	4.8	21.4	28.6
55~60 岁 Age	22	4.5	22.7	4.5	31.8	18.2	9.1	13.6	9.1	27.3
女性 Female	**256**	**10.5**	**17.6**	**5.5**	**7.4**	**3.9**	**11.3**	**3.9**	**28.1**	**27.3**
16~24 岁 Age	57	8.8	17.5	7.0	5.3	8.8	24.6	0.0	38.6	36.8
25~34 岁 Age	81	16.0	17.3	2.5	8.6	4.9	14.8	6.2	32.1	28.4
35~44 岁 Age	55	5.5	21.8	10.9	5.5	1.8	3.6	3.6	23.6	25.5
45~54 岁 Age	49	8.2	12.2	2.0	12.2	0.0	2.0	4.1	14.3	20.4
55~60 岁 Age	14	14.3	21.4	7.1	0.0	0.0	0.0	7.1	28.6	14.3

续前表 continued

	人数 Number	国内一天往返的旅行 short journey that can be back in a day	看展览会 visiting exhibition	听演唱会/音乐会 attending concert	扭秧歌/木兰拳/交谊舞 doing the YangKo	去博物馆或美术馆 going to museum or art gallery	唱卡拉OK karaoke	去动物园或公园 going to park or zoo	酒吧/咖啡屋/茶秀 going to cafe or bar	电脑游戏 Playing PC game
样本 Sample	517	39.8	27.1	15.7	29.8	6.4	15.9	7.4	17.6	7.5
男性 Male	261	39.5	28.0	18.0	28.7	3.4	15.3	7.7	16.9	6.5
16~24 岁 Age	56	39.3	23.2	19.6	37.5	3.6	16.1	5.4	12.5	5.4
25~34 岁 Age	78	46.2	30.8	20.5	35.9	2.6	15.4	9.0	12.8	5.1
35~44 岁 Age	63	36.5	27.0	12.7	15.9	4.8	15.9	7.9	19.0	4.8
45~54 岁 Age	42	45.2	26.2	21.4	31.0	0.0	11.9	9.5	19.0	14.3
55~60 岁 Age	22	13.6	36.4	13.6	13.6	9.1	18.2	4.5	31.8	4.5
女性 Female	256	40.2	26.2	13.3	30.9	9.4	16.4	7.0	18.4	8.6
16~24 岁 Age	57	28.1	19.3	17.5	50.9	1.8	17.5	3.5	10.5	15.8
25~34 岁 Age	81	46.9	29.6	12.3	30.9	4.9	13.6	8.6	17.3	8.6
35~44 岁 Age	55	38.2	27.3	10.9	23.6	16.4	12.7	9.1	18.2	7.3
45~54 岁 Age	49	42.9	28.6	14.3	22.4	18.4	24.5	8.2	24.5	4.1
55~60 岁 Age	14	50.0	21.4	7.1	7.1	7.1	14.3	0.0	35.7	0.0

4-5 不同消费层常做的休闲活动/ Frequently Engaged Activities by Market Segments

4-5-1 时尚流行指标/ Fads Popular Index

注：本题为多选题，合计百分比超过 100%（Multiple answers）

	人数 Number	打网球 tennis	打高尔夫球 golf	打羽毛球 badminton	打保龄球 bowling	踢足球 soccer	打篮球 basketball	打乒乓球 table tennis	慢跑 jogging	玩滑板 skateboarding	跳迪斯科 disco
样本 Sample	610	4.3	0.7	25.7	5.9	10.5	9.3	18.5	24.4	0.8	11.0
平实生活指向 simple living orientation	364	3.0	0.3	20.3	3.3	8.0	5.8	14.0	23.4	0.5	4.4
时尚流行指向 fashion orientation	246	6.1	1.2	33.7	9.8	14.2	14.6	25.2	26.0	1.2	20.7

续前表 continued

	人数 Number	打麻将 mahjong	游泳 swimming	滚轴溜冰 rolling skating	滑冰 skating	钓鱼 fishing	登山 mountain climbing	听音乐 enjoying music	看电影 going to movie	打游戏机 playing video game	编织裁剪 knitting & tailoring
样本 Sample	610	51.0	24.3	5.7	6.7	15.4	14.3	60.7	25.4	26.4	20.0
平实生活指向 simple living orientation	364	50.0	18.7	2.7	3.6	15.4	12.1	51.1	17.3	18.7	22.5
时尚流行指向 fashion orientation	246	52.4	32.5	10.2	11.4	15.4	17.5	74.8	37.4	37.8	16.3

续前表 continued

	人数 Number	种花盆栽 horticulture	看书 reading	绘画书法 drawing & calligraphy	乐器演奏 playing musical instrument	开汽车兜风 going out for a driving	逛街购物 shopping	郊游露营 outing & camping	海外旅行 overseas travel	国内一天以上的旅行 domestic travel
样本 Sample	610	20.0	14.8	70.2	5.9	2.6	4.3	65.7	11.1	0.7
平实生活指向 simple living orientation	364	22.5	14.6	69.0	4.4	1.6	3.0	60.7	9.1	0.8
时尚流行指向 fashion orientation	246	16.3	15.0	72.0	8.1	4.1	6.1	73.2	14.2	0.4

续前表 continued

	人数 Number	国内一天往返的旅行 short journey that can be back in a day	看展览会 visiting exhibition	听演唱会/音乐会 attending concert	扭秧歌/木兰拳/交谊舞 doing the YangKo	去博物馆或美术馆 going to museum or art gallery	唱卡拉OK Karaoke	去动物园或公园 going to park or zoo	酒吧/咖啡屋/茶秀 going to cafe or bar	电脑游戏 Playing PC game
样本 Sample	610	16.1	12.1	14.9	10.7	6.4	5.7	44.3	36.7	15.2
平实生活指向 simple living orientation	364	10.4	8.8	12.6	6.3	6.9	4.1	34.3	34.3	9.9
时尚流行指向 fashion orientation	246	24.4	17.1	18.3	17.1	5.7	8.1	58.9	40.2	23.2

4-5-2 信息交流指标/ Information Communication Index

注：本题为多选题，合计百分比超过 100%（Multiple answers）

	人数 Number	打网球 tennis	打高尔夫球 golf	打羽毛球 badminton	打保龄球 bowling	踢足球 soccer	打篮球 basketball	打乒乓球 table tennis	慢跑 jogging	玩滑板 skateboarding	跳迪斯科 disco
样本 Sample	609	4.4	0.7	25.9	6.1	10.5	9.5	18.2	24.6	0.8	11.2
信息消极指向 negative orientation	46	2.2	0.0	13.0	0.0	10.9	6.5	10.9	23.9	0.0	4.3
中间层 medium	335	3.9	0.0	24.8	5.1	10.1	10.1	18.2	20.0	1.2	11.6
信息积极指向 active orientation	228	5.7	1.8	30.3	8.8	11.0	9.2	19.7	31.6	0.4	11.8

续前表 continued

	人数 Number	打麻将 mah-jong	游泳 swimming	滚轴溜冰 rolling skating	滑冰 skating	钓鱼 fishing	登山 mountain climbing	听音乐 enjoying music	看电影 going to movie	打游戏机 playing video game	编织裁剪 knitting & tailoring
样本 Sample	609	50.4	24.3	5.7	6.6	15.4	14.4	60.8	25.5	26.3	19.5
信息消极指向 negative orientation	46	65.2	23.9	2.2	6.5	17.4	8.7	50.0	21.7	21.7	13.0
中间层 medium	335	47.8	21.8	5.1	5.4	15.8	11.6	57.3	21.8	25.1	18.8
信息积极指向 active orientation	228	51.3	28.1	7.5	8.3	14.5	19.7	68.0	31.6	28.9	21.9

续前表 continued

	人数 Number	种花盆栽 horticulture	看书 reading	绘画书法 drawing & calligraphy	乐器演奏 playing musical instrument	开汽车兜风 going out for a driving	逛街购物 shopping	郊游露营 outing & camping	海外旅行 overseas travel	国内一天以上的旅行 domestic travel
样本 Sample	609	19.5	15.1	70.4	5.9	2.6	4.4	65.5	11.2	0.7
信息消极指向 negative orientation	46	13.0	6.5	63.0	2.2	0.0	6.5	60.9	0.0	2.2
中间层 medium	335	18.8	13.4	69.6	4.5	1.8	4.5	60.6	10.7	0.6
信息积极指向 active orientation	228	21.9	19.3	73.2	8.8	4.4	3.9	73.7	14.0	0.4

续前表 continued

	人数 Number	国内一天往返的旅行 short journey that can be back in a day	看展览会 visiting exhibition	听演唱会/音乐会 attending concert	扭秧歌/木兰拳/交谊舞 doing the YangKo	去博物馆或美术馆 going to museum or art gallery	唱卡拉OK karaoke	去动物园或公园 going to park or zoo	酒吧/咖啡屋/茶秀 going to cafe or bar	电脑游戏 Playing PC game
样本 Sample	609	16.3	12.3	15.3	10.8	6.4	6.1	44.2	36.9	15.3
信息消极指向 negative orientation	46	10.9	6.5	4.3	6.5	2.2	0.0	28.3	30.4	8.7
中间层 medium	335	14.0	9.6	13.7	8.7	6.0	6.0	41.2	31.0	15.5
信息积极指向 active orientation	228	20.6	17.5	19.7	14.9	7.9	7.5	51.8	46.9	16.2

4-6 不同消费者层想做的休闲活动/ Desired Activities by Market Segments

4-6-1 时尚流行指标/ Fads Popular Index

注：本题为多选题，合计百分比超过 100%（Multiple answers）

	人数 Number	打网球 tennis	打高尔夫球 golf	打羽毛球 bad-minton	打保龄球 bowling	踢足球 soccer	打篮球 basket-ball	打乒乓球 table tennis	慢跑 jogging	玩滑板 skatebo arding	跳迪斯科 disco
样本 Sample	510	23.9	11.8	12.7	19.6	5.9	7.6	9.8	7.6	6.3	7.6
平实生活指向 simple living orientation	291	17.5	6.5	12.7	15.5	6.5	7.6	11.0	10.0	2.4	5.8
时尚流行指向 fashion orientation	219	32.4	18.7	12.8	25.1	5.0	7.8	8.2	4.6	11.4	10.0

续前表 continued

	人数 Number	打麻将 mah-jong	游泳 swimmi ng	滚轴溜冰 rolling skating	滑冰 skating	钓鱼 fishing	登山 moun-tain clim-bing	听音乐 enjoy-ing music	看电影 going to movie	打游戏机 playing video game	编织裁剪 knitting & tailoring
样本 Sample	510	3.9	15.1	4.9	10.6	20.8	22.5	7.5	19.0	2.0	6.3
平实生活指向 simple living orientation	291	5.2	13.4	2.7	7.9	20.6	20.3	10.0	19.9	2.1	5.2
时尚流行指向 fashion orientation	219	2.3	17.4	7.8	14.2	21.0	25.6	4.1	17.8	1.8	7.8

续前表 continued

	人数 Number	种花盆栽 horticul-ture	看书 reading	绘画书法 drawing & calligra-phy	乐器演奏 playing musical instru-ment	开汽车兜风 going out for a driving	逛街购物 shopping	郊游露营 outing & camping	海外旅行 overseas travel	国内一天以上的旅行 domestic travel
样本 Sample	510	6.3	15.1	4.3	9.2	5.1	17.8	5.3	27.5	29.8
平实生活指向 simple living orientation	291	5.2	15.5	5.2	10.7	5.2	11.0	6.5	23.0	25.1
时尚流行指向 fashion orientation	219	7.8	14.6	3.2	7.3	5.0	26.9	3.7	33.3	36.1

续前表 continued

	人数 Number	国内一天往返的旅行 short journey that can be back in a day	看展览会 visiting exhibi-tion	听演唱会/音乐会 attending concert	扭秧歌/木兰拳/交谊舞 doing the YangKo	去博物馆或美术馆 going to museum or art gallery	唱卡拉OK karaoke	去动物园或公园 going to park or zoo	酒吧/咖啡屋/茶秀 going to cafe or bar	电脑游戏 Playing PC game
样本 Sample	510	39.8	27.1	15.7	29.6	6.3	15.9	7.5	17.6	8.8
平实生活指向 simple living orientation	291	38.8	27.1	15.8	25.1	5.8	17.5	9.3	22.3	6.5
时尚流行指向 fashion orientation	219	41.1	26.9	15.5	35.6	6.8	13.7	5.0	11.4	11.9

4-6-2 信息交流指标/ Information Communication Index

注：本题为多选题，合计百分比超过 100%（Multiple answers）

	人数 Number	打网球 tennis	打高尔夫球 golf	打羽毛球 badmin ton	打保龄球 bowling	踢足球 soccer	打篮球 basket-ball	打乒乓球 table tennis	慢跑 jogging	玩滑板 skatebo arding	跳迪斯科 disco
样本 Sample	510	24.1	11.8	12.5	19.2	5.9	7.6	9.6	7.6	6.3	7.8
信息消极指向 negative orientation	33	12.1	6.1	12.1	18.2	9.1	18.2	9.1	6.1	6.1	6.1
中间层 medium	275	25.1	10.9	10.5	17.8	7.6	8.0	10.2	8.4	5.8	9.1
信息积极指向 active orientation	202	24.8	13.9	15.3	21.3	3.0	5.4	8.9	6.9	6.9	6.4

续前表 continued

	人数 Number	打麻将 mah-jong	游泳 swim-ming	滚轴溜冰 rolling skating	滑冰 skating	钓鱼 fishing	登山 moun-tain clim-bing	听音乐 enjoying music	看电影 going to movie	打游戏机 playing video game	编织裁剪 knitting & tailoring
样本 Sample	510	3.9	15.5	4.9	10.8	21.0	22.9	7.3	19.2	2.2	6.3
信息消极指向 negative orientation	33	3.0	12.1	3.0	3.0	12.1	15.2	9.1	18.2	0.0	9.1
中间层 medium	275	4.4	16.0	3.6	13.5	22.2	21.8	7.6	17.5	2.9	6.2
信息积极指向 active orientation	202	3.5	15.3	6.9	8.4	20.8	25.7	6.4	21.8	1.5	5.9

续前表 continued

	人数 Number	种花盆栽 horticul-ture	看书 reading	绘画书法 drawing & calligra-phy	乐器演奏 playing musical instru-ment	开汽车兜风 going out for a driving	逛街购物 shopping	郊游露营 outing & camping	海外旅行 overseas travel	国内一天以上的旅行 domestic travel
样本 Sample	510	6.3	15.1	4.3	9.4	5.3	17.6	5.7	28.0	30.4
信息消极指向 negative orientation	33	9.1	9.1	3.0	6.1	3.0	18.2	3.0	27.3	30.3
中间层 medium	275	6.2	15.6	4.4	11.6	5.1	18.2	7.6	28.4	29.8
信息积极指向 active orientation	202	5.9	15.3	4.5	6.9	5.9	16.8	3.5	27.7	31.2

续前表 continued

	人数 Number	国内一天往返的旅行 short journey that can be back in a day	看展览会 visiting exhibi-tion	听演唱会/音乐会 attending concert	扭秧歌/木兰拳/交谊舞 doing the YangKo	去博物馆或美术馆 going to museum or art gallery	唱卡拉OK karaoke	去动物园或公园 going to park or zoo	酒吧/咖啡屋/茶秀 going to cafe or bar	电脑游戏 Playing PC game
样本 Sample	510	39.8	27.3	15.5	29.6	6.3	15.7	7.3	17.6	9.0
信息消极指向 negative orientation	33	39.4	36.4	12.1	30.3	3.0	18.2	6.1	30.3	9.1
中间层 medium	275	38.9	25.8	14.2	28.0	5.8	12.0	8.7	17.5	10.5
信息积极指向 active orientation	202	41.1	27.7	17.8	31.7	7.4	20.3	5.4	15.8	6.9

● 武汉 / Wuhan

4-1 常做的休闲活动排名/ Ranking of the Frequently Engaged Activities

注：本题为多选题，合计百分比超过 100%（Multiple answers）

排名 Ranking	活动项目 Activity Items	人次 Person-time	百分比 Percent
1	看书 reading	492	78.2
2	逛街购物 shopping	446	70.9
3	听音乐 enjoying music	369	58.7
4	唱卡拉 OK Karaoke	280	44.5
5	去动物园或公园 going to the park or zoo	267	42.4
6	打麻将 mah-jong	240	38.2
7	慢跑 jogging	207	32.9
8	打羽毛球 badminton	205	32.6
9	看电影 going to movie	177	28.1
10	游泳 swimming	172	27.3
11	打游戏机 playing video game	156	24.8
12	打乒乓球 table-tennis	151	24.0
13	编织裁剪 knitting & tailoring	136	21.6
14	电脑游戏 playing PC game	132	21.0
15	种花盆栽 horticulture	126	20.0
16	国内一天以上的旅行 domestic travel	124	19.7
17	看展览会 visiting exhibition	98	15.6
18	打篮球 basketball	90	14.3
19	打保龄球 bowling	89	14.1
20	酒吧/咖啡屋/茶秀 going to cafe or bar	87	13.8
21	国内一天往返的旅行 short journey that can be back in a day	83	13.2
22	听演唱会/音乐会 attending concert	77	12.2
22	绘画书法 drawing & calligraphy	77	12.2
23	钓鱼 fishing	74	11.8
23	滚轴溜冰 rolling skating	74	11.8
24	踢足球 soccer	72	11.4
25	扭秧歌/木兰拳/交谊舞 doing the YangKo	62	9.9
26	跳迪斯科 disco	61	9.7
27	郊游露营 outing & camping	53	8.4
28	登山 mountain climbing	47	7.5
29	打网球 tennis	44	7.0
30	开汽车兜风 going out for a driving	43	6.8
31	乐器演奏 playing musical instrument	25	4.0
32	去博物馆或美术馆 going to museum or art gallery	24	3.8
33	滑冰 skating	19	3.0
34	打高尔夫球 golf	7	1.1
35	海外旅行 overseas travel	6	1.0
36	玩滑板 skateboarding	4	0.6

n=629

4-2 想做的休闲活动排名/ Ranking of the Desired Activities

注：本题为多选题，合计百分比超过 100%（Multiple answers）

排名 Ranking	活动项目 Activity Items	人次 Person-time	百分比 Percent
1	国内一天以上的旅行 domestic travel	198	37.4
2	海外旅行 overseas travel	176	33.3
3	郊游露营 outing & camping	146	27.6
4	打网球 tennis	141	26.7
5	听演唱会/音乐会 attending concert	140	26.5
6	登山 mountain climbing	118	22.3
7	打保龄球 bowling	117	22.1
8	国内一天往返的旅行 short journey that can be back in a day	110	20.8
9	开汽车兜风 going out for a driving	98	18.5
10	看展览会 visiting exhibition	97	18.3
11	钓鱼 fishing	96	18.1
12	去博物馆或美术馆 going to museum or art gallery	93	17.6
13	去动物园或公园 going to the park or zoo	83	15.7
14	游泳 swimming	79	14.9
15	看电影 going to movie	73	13.8
16	种花盆栽 horticulture	72	13.6
17	打羽毛球 badminton	64	12.1
18	绘画书法 drawing & calligraphy	63	11.9
19	打高尔夫球 golf	62	11.7
20	慢跑 jogging	60	11.3
21	打乒乓球 table-tennis	55	10.4
21	唱卡拉 OK Karaoke	55	10.4
22	电脑游戏 playing PC game	52	9.8
23	听音乐 enjoying music	49	9.3
24	乐器演奏 playing musical instrument	48	9.1
25	滑冰 skating	47	8.9
26	酒吧/咖啡屋/茶秀 going to cafe or bar	46	8.7
27	扭秧歌/木兰拳/交谊舞 doing the YangKo	40	7.6
27	踢足球 soccer	40	7.6
28	滚轴溜冰 rolling skating	38	7.2
28	玩滑板 skateboarding	38	7.2
29	跳迪斯科 disco	37	7.0
30	编织裁剪 knitting & tailoring	36	6.8
30	打麻将 mah-jong	36	6.8
31	打篮球 basketball	29	5.5
32	逛街购物 shopping	21	4.0
33	看书 reading	19	3.6
34	打游戏机 playing video game	15	2.8

n=529

4-3 样本、男性各年龄层、女性各年龄层常做的活动/ Frequently Engaged Activities by the Whole Sample, Age and Gender Groups

注：本题为多选题，合计百分比超过 100%（Multiple answers）

	人数 Number	打网球 tennis	打高尔夫球 golf	打羽毛球 badmin-ton	打保龄球 bowling	踢足球 soccer	打篮球 basket-ball	打乒乓球 table-tennis	慢跑 jogging	玩滑板 skate-boarding	跳迪斯科 disco
样本 Sample	629	7.0	1.1	32.6	14.1	11.4	14.3	24.0	32.9	0.6	9.7
男性 Male	306	7.2	0.7	31.7	19.0	22.5	21.6	34.3	35.3	1.0	9.5
16~24 岁 Age	65	10.8	0.0	53.8	29.2	49.2	60.0	53.8	46.2	4.6	20.0
25~34 岁 Age	87	13.8	0.0	33.3	25.3	35.6	17.2	44.8	32.2	0.0	11.5
35~44 岁 Age	79	2.5	2.5	19.0	16.5	7.6	10.1	22.8	26.6	0.0	5.1
45~54 岁 Age	51	0.0	0.0	29.4	7.8	0.0	5.9	23.5	33.3	0.0	2.0
55~60 岁 Age	24	4.2	0.0	12.5	0.0	0.0	4.2	4.2	50.0	0.0	4.2
女性 Female	323	6.8	1.5	33.4	9.6	0.9	7.4	14.2	30.7	0.3	9.9
16~24 岁 Age	68	16.2	2.9	55.9	14.7	2.9	23.5	26.5	33.8	1.5	22.1
25~34 岁 Age	95	7.4	1.1	36.8	14.7	0.0	2.1	15.8	21.1	0.0	10.5
35~44 岁 Age	78	2.6	2.6	23.1	5.1	0.0	2.6	9.0	24.4	0.0	3.8
45~54 岁 Age	60	3.3	0.0	23.3	5.0	1.7	6.7	6.7	45.0	0.0	6.7
55~60 岁 Age	22	0.0	0.0	13.6	0.0	0.0	0.0	9.1	45.5	0.0	0.0

续前表 continued

	人数 Number	打麻将 mah-jongg	游泳 swimming	滚轴溜冰 rolling skating	滑冰 skating	钓鱼 fishing	登山 mountain climbing	听音乐 enjoying music	看电影 going to movie	打游戏机 playing video game	编织裁剪 knitting & tailoring
样本 Sample	629	38.2	27.3	11.8	3.0	11.8	7.5	58.7	28.1	24.8	21.6
男性 Male	306	41.5	37.3	13.7	3.3	20.9	8.5	58.5	28.8	32.0	0.7
16~24 岁 Age	65	27.7	55.4	41.5	12.3	9.2	6.2	80.0	47.7	72.3	0.0
25~34 岁 Age	87	51.7	37.9	16.1	1.1	31.0	16.1	60.9	40.2	44.8	1.1
35~44 岁 Age	79	43.0	40.5	1.3	1.3	20.3	2.5	51.9	11.4	8.9	0.0
45~54 岁 Age	51	39.2	21.6	0.0	0.0	25.5	3.9	47.1	15.7	5.9	2.0
55~60 岁 Age	24	41.7	8.3	0.0	0.0	8.3	16.7	37.5	20.8	8.3	0.0
女性 Female	323	35.0	18.0	9.9	2.8	3.1	6.5	58.8	27.6	18.0	41.5
16~24 岁 Age	68	27.9	32.4	38.2	10.3	2.9	13.2	72.1	54.4	48.5	7.4
25~34 岁 Age	95	32.6	22.1	6.3	2.1	3.2	5.3	62.1	26.3	15.8	38.9
35~44 岁 Age	78	51.3	11.5	0.0	0.0	3.8	5.1	53.8	11.5	5.1	62.8
45~54 岁 Age	60	28.3	8.3	0.0	0.0	3.3	3.3	53.3	25.0	8.3	55.0
55~60 岁 Age	22	27.3	4.5	0.0	0.0	0.0	4.5	36.4	13.6	4.5	45.0

续前表 continued

	人数 Number	种花盆栽 horticulture	看书 reading	绘画书法 drawing & calligraphy	乐器演奏 playing musical instrument	开汽车兜风 going out for a driving	逛街购物 shopping	郊游露营 outing & camping	海外旅行 overseas travel	国内一天以上的旅行 domestic travel
样本 Sample	629	21.6	20.0	78.2	12.2	4.0	6.8	70.9	8.4	1.0
男性 Male	306	0.7	16.0	78.8	11.4	3.3	10.1	59.5	7.8	1.0
16~24 岁 Age	65	0.0	3.1	89.2	12.3	4.6	4.6	61.5	4.6	0.0
25~34 岁 Age	87	1.1	12.6	85.1	8.0	2.3	18.4	62.1	10.3	2.3
35~44 岁 Age	79	0.0	8.9	60.8	7.6	1.3	12.7	54.4	7.6	1.3
45~54 岁 Age	51	2.0	39.2	78.4	17.6	5.9	2.0	54.9	7.8	0.0
55~60 岁 Age	24	0.0	37.5	87.5	20.8	4.2	4.2	70.8	8.3	0.0
女性 Female	323	41.5	23.8	77.7	13.0	4.6	3.7	81.7	9.0	0.9
16~24 岁 Age	68	7.4	11.8	94.1	35.3	11.8	2.9	82.4	8.8	1.5
25~34 岁 Age	95	38.9	25.3	81.1	13.7	4.2	9.5	92.6	14.7	2.1
35~44 岁 Age	78	62.8	19.2	67.9	2.6	0.0	1.3	82.1	5.1	0.0
45~54 岁 Age	60	55.0	38.3	71.7	5.0	5.0	0.0	70.0	6.7	0.0
55~60 岁 Age	22	45.5	31.8	63.6	0.0	0.0	0.0	63.6	4.5	0.0

续前表 continued

	人数 Number	国内一天往返的旅行 short journey that can be back in a day	看展览会 visiting exhibition	听演唱会/音乐会 attending concert	扭秧歌/木兰拳/交谊舞 doing the YangKo	去博物馆或美术馆 going to museum or art gallery	唱卡拉OK karaoke	去动物园或公园 going to park or zoo	酒吧/咖啡屋/茶秀 going to cafe or bar	电脑游戏 playing PC game
样本 Sample	629	19.7	13.2	15.6	12.2	9.9	3.8	44.5	42.4	13.8
男性 Male	306	20.9	13.7	20.6	11.8	8.2	4.6	48.0	41.5	16.0
16~24 岁 Age	65	15.4	15.4	27.7	10.8	4.6	3.1	67.7	46.2	29.2
25~34 岁 Age	87	31.0	20.7	20.7	10.3	6.9	3.4	57.5	49.4	21.8
35~44 岁 Age	79	15.2	8.9	17.7	15.2	6.3	5.1	40.5	34.2	10.1
45~54 岁 Age	51	19.6	7.8	15.7	7.8	5.9	5.9	31.4	33.3	3.9
55~60 岁 Age	24	20.8	12.5	20.8	16.7	33.3	8.3	20.8	41.7	4.2
女性 Female	323	18.6	12.7	10.8	12.7	11.5	3.1	41.2	43.3	11.8
16~24 岁 Age	68	13.2	7.4	13.2	7.4	1.5	4.4	67.6	41.2	25.0
25~34 岁 Age	95	27.4	18.9	12.6	15.8	10.5	3.2	48.4	58.9	17.9
35~44 岁 Age	78	16.7	10.3	9.0	11.5	10.3	2.6	34.6	38.5	5.1
45~54 岁 Age	60	16.7	13.3	8.3	15.0	21.7	3.3	23.3	30.0	0.0
55~60 岁 Age	22	9.1	9.1	9.1	13.6	22.7	0.0	0.0	36.4	0.0

4-4 样本、男性各年龄层、女性各年龄层想做的活动/ Desired Activities by the Whole Sample, Age and Gender Groups

注：本题为多选题，合计百分比超过 100%（Multiple answers）

	人数 Number	打网球 tennis	打高尔夫球 golf	打羽毛球 badminton	打保龄球 bowling	踢足球 soccer	打篮球 basketball	打乒乓球 table-tennis	慢跑 jogging	玩滑板 skate-boarding	跳迪斯科 disco
样本 Sample	529	26.7	11.7	12.1	22.1	7.6	5.5	10.4	11.3	7.2	7.0
男性 Male	252	28.6	14.7	13.5	24.6	13.9	8.7	12.3	13.5	8.3	5.6
16~24 岁 Age	59	47.5	23.7	15.3	33.9	15.3	10.2	6.8	10.2	23.7	10.2
25~34 岁 Age	77	33.8	20.8	15.6	26.0	14.3	13.0	15.6	6.5	7.8	7.8
35~44 岁 Age	64	17.2	7.8	15.6	17.2	20.3	6.3	10.9	15.6	1.6	3.1
45~54 岁 Age	39	17.9	2.6	5.1	23.1	5.1	5.1	15.4	25.6	0.0	0.0
55~60 岁 Age	13	0.0	7.7	7.7	15.4	0.0	0.0	15.4	23.1	0.0	0.0
女性 Female	277	24.9	9.0	10.8	19.9	1.8	2.5	8.7	9.4	6.1	8.3
16~24 岁 Age	67	49.3	16.4	6.0	37.3	3.0	6.0	4.5	6.0	17.9	11.9
25~34 岁 Age	82	30.5	13.4	14.6	19.5	2.4	2.4	11.0	6.1	6.1	11.0
35~44 岁 Age	67	10.4	3.0	14.9	16.4	1.5	0.0	10.4	11.9	0.0	3.0
45~54 岁 Age	47	8.5	2.1	8.5	6.4	0.0	2.1	10.6	12.8	0.0	8.5
55~60 岁 Age	14	0.0	0.0	0.0	0.0	0.0	0.0	0.0	21.4	0.0	0.0

续前表 continued

	人数 Number	打麻将 mah-jongg	游泳 swimming	滚轴溜冰 rolling skating	滑冰 skating	钓鱼 fishing	登山 mountain climbing	听音乐 enjoying music	看电影 going to movie	打游戏机 playing video game	编织裁剪 knitting & tailoring
样本 Sample	529	6.8	14.9	7.2	8.9	18.1	22.3	9.3	13.8	2.8	6.8
男性 Male	252	7.1	17.5	6.7	9.9	23.4	24.6	6.3	13.5	3.2	1.6
16~24岁 Age	59	5.1	15.3	13.6	20.3	30.5	44.1	5.1	11.9	3.4	3.4
25~34岁 Age	77	6.5	24.7	7.8	14.3	20.8	23.4	5.2	13.0	3.9	1.3
35~44岁 Age	64	6.3	14.1	4.7	3.1	20.3	15.6	6.3	12.5	4.7	0.0
45~54岁 Age	39	15.4	12.8	0.0	0.0	17.9	15.4	12.8	20.5	0.0	2.6
55~60岁 Age	13	0.0	15.4	0.0	0.0	38.5	15.4	0.0	7.7	0.0	0.0
女性 Female	277	6.5	12.6	7.6	7.9	13.4	20.2	11.9	14.1	2.5	11.6
16~24岁 Age	67	4.5	23.9	16.4	23.9	22.4	43.3	6.0	10.4	6.0	16.4
25~34岁 Age	82	7.3	12.2	8.5	4.9	17.1	18.3	14.6	22.0	1.2	9.8
35~44岁 Age	67	7.5	7.5	4.5	1.5	7.5	4.5	16.4	9.0	1.5	11.9
45~54岁 Age	47	4.3	8.5	0.0	0.0	4.3	14.9	10.6	10.6	2.1	6.4
55~60岁 Age	14	14.3	0.0	0.0	7.1	7.1	14.3	7.1	21.4	0.0	14.3

续前表 continued

	人数 Number	种花盆栽 horticulture	看书 reading	绘画书法 drawing & calligraphy	乐器演奏 playing musical instrument	开汽车兜风 going out for a driving	逛街购物 shopping	郊游露营 outing & camping	海外旅行 overseas travel	国内一天以上的旅行 domestic travel
样本 Sample	529	6.8	13.6	3.6	11.9	9.1	18.5	4.0	27.6	33.3
男性 Male	252	1.6	12.3	3.2	15.1	10.3	23.8	3.2	27.0	29.8
16~24 岁 Age	59	3.4	6.8	0.0	16.9	16.9	35.6	3.4	40.7	37.3
25~34 岁 Age	77	1.3	9.1	2.6	19.5	10.4	26.0	2.6	27.3	41.6
35~44 岁 Age	64	0.0	15.6	6.3	7.8	4.7	20.3	4.7	23.4	25.0
45~54 岁 Age	39	2.6	20.5	5.1	17.9	7.7	15.4	2.6	15.4	10.3
55~60 岁 Age	13	0.0	15.4	0.0	7.7	15.4	0.0	0.0	15.4	7.7
女性 Female	277	11.6	14.8	4.0	9.0	7.9	13.7	4.7	28.2	36.5
16~24 岁 Age	67	16.4	17.9	0.0	10.4	19.4	22.4	4.5	50.7	50.7
25~34 岁 Age	82	9.8	8.5	4.9	12.2	9.8	18.3	4.9	28.0	42.7
35~44 岁 Age	67	11.9	16.4	3.0	6.0	0.0	10.4	3.0	25.4	25.4
45~54 岁 Age	47	6.4	19.1	8.5	6.4	2.1	2.1	6.4	6.4	29.8
55~60 岁 Age	14	14.3	14.3	7.1	7.1	0.0	0.0	7.1	7.1	7.1

续前表 continued

	人数 Number	国内一天往返的旅行 short journey that can be back in a day	看展览会 visiting exhibition	听演唱会/音乐会 attending concert	扭秧歌/木兰拳/交谊舞 doing the YangKo	去博物馆或美术馆 going to museum or art gallery	唱卡拉OK karaoke	去动物园或公园 going to park or zoo	酒吧/咖啡屋/茶秀 going to cafe or bar	电脑游戏 playing PC game
样本 Sample	529	37.4	20.8	18.3	26.5	7.6	17.6	10.4	15.7	8.7
男性 Male	252	38.5	18.7	19.8	25.8	8.3	21.0	9.5	15.1	9.5
16~24 岁 Age	59	37.3	20.3	22.0	37.3	5.1	23.7	10.2	10.2	15.3
25~34 岁 Age	77	44.2	23.4	22.1	28.6	10.4	19.5	2.6	13.0	13.0
35~44 岁 Age	64	35.9	14.1	14.1	18.8	7.8	17.2	15.6	21.9	6.3
45~54 岁 Age	39	43.6	15.4	25.6	17.9	10.3	25.6	15.4	17.9	0.0
55~60 岁 Age	13	7.7	15.4	7.7	15.4	7.7	23.1	0.0	7.7	7.7
女性 Female	277	36.5	22.7	17.0	27.1	6.9	14.4	11.2	16.2	7.9
16~24 岁 Age	67	40.3	23.9	20.9	37.3	4.5	20.9	6.0	11.9	17.9
25~34 岁 Age	82	42.7	26.8	22.0	29.3	11.0	15.9	12.2	12.2	8.5
35~44 岁 Age	67	32.8	17.9	13.4	19.4	6.0	7.5	11.9	20.9	3.0
45~54 岁 Age	47	31.9	25.5	12.8	25.5	4.3	12.8	14.9	19.1	2.1
55~60 岁 Age	14	14.3	7.1	0.0	7.1	7.1	14.3	14.3	28.6	0.0

4-5 不同消费者层常做的休闲活动/ Frequently Engaged Activities by Market Segments

4-5-1 时尚流行指标/ Fads Popular Index

注：本题为多选题，合计百分比超过 100%（Multiple answers）

	人数 Number	打网球 tennis	打高尔夫球 golf	打羽毛球 badminton	打保龄球 bowling	踢足球 soccer	打篮球 basketball	打乒乓球 table-tennis	慢跑 jogging	玩滑板 skate-boarding	跳迪斯科 disco
样本 Sample	624	6.9	1.1	32.4	14.1	11.4	14.4	23.7	32.9	0.6	9.8
平实生活指向 simple living orientation	323	6.2	0.9	28.2	10.5	10.2	13.9	20.7	33.4	0.0	5.3
时尚流行指向 fashion orientation	301	7.6	1.3	36.9	17.9	12.6	15.0	26.9	32.2	1.3	14.6

续前表 continued

	人数 Number	打麻将 mah-jong	游泳 swimming	滚轴溜冰 rolling skating	滑冰 skating	钓鱼 fishing	登山 mountain climbing	听音乐 enjoying music	看电影 going to movie	打游戏机 playing video game	编织裁剪 knitting & tailoring
样本 Sample	624	38.0	27.4	11.5	3.0	11.5	7.4	58.3	28.2	24.7	21.5
平实生活指向 simple living orientation	323	36.2	25.1	7.4	2.8	11.1	6.8	54.8	21.1	21.1	22.0
时尚流行指向 fashion orientation	301	39.9	29.9	15.9	3.3	12.0	8.0	62.1	35.9	28.6	20.9

续前表 continued

	人数 Number	种花盆栽 horticulture	看书 reading	绘画书法 drawing & calligraphy	乐器演奏 playing musical instrument	开汽车兜风 going out for a driving	逛街购物 shopping	郊游露营 outing & camping	海外旅行 overseas travel	国内一天以上的旅行 domestic travel
样本 Sample	624	21.5	20.0	78.2	12.0	4.0	6.7	70.8	8.5	1.0
平实生活指向 simple living orientation	323	22.0	21.4	76.8	10.2	2.8	4.6	62.5	6.5	0.3
时尚流行指向 fashion orientation	301	20.9	18.6	79.7	14.0	5.3	9.0	79.7	10.6	1.7

续前表 continued

	人数 Number	国内一天往返的旅行 short journey that can be back in a day	看展览会 visiting exhibition	听演唱会/音乐会 attending concert	扭秧歌/木兰拳/交谊舞 doing the YangKo	去博物馆或美术馆 going to museum or art gallery	唱卡拉OK karaoke	去动物园或公园 going to park or zoo	酒吧/咖啡屋/茶秀 going to cafe or bar	电脑游戏 playing PC game
样本 Sample	**624**	**19.7**	**13.0**	**15.4**	**11.9**	**9.9**	**3.8**	**44.6**	**42.3**	**20.8**
平实生活指向 simple living orientation	323	17.0	12.4	13.9	9.0	7.1	3.7	33.4	39.6	17.0
时尚流行指向 fashion orientation	301	22.6	13.6	16.9	15.0	13.0	4.0	56.5	45.2	24.9

4-5-2 信息交流指标/ Information Communication Index

注：本题为多选题，合计百分比超过 100%（Multiple answers）

	人数 Number	打网球 tennis	打高尔夫球 golf	打羽毛球 badminton	打保龄球 bowling	踢足球 soccer	打篮球 basketball	打乒乓球 table-tennis	慢跑 jogging	玩滑板 skate-boarding	跳迪斯科 disco
样本 Sample	**623**	**6.7**	**1.1**	**32.6**	**14.0**	**11.4**	**14.1**	**23.9**	**32.9**	**0.6**	**9.8**
信息消极指向 negative orientation	42	4.8	0.0	23.8	9.5	7.1	4.8	11.9	28.6	0.0	7.1
中间层 medium	359	5.8	1.1	31.2	15.3	13.1	15.6	23.4	30.1	0.8	8.6
信息积极指向 active orientation	222	8.6	1.4	36.5	12.6	9.5	13.5	27.0	38.3	0.5	12.2

续前表 continued

	人数 Number	打麻将 mah-jong	游泳 swimming	滚轴溜冰 rolling skating	滑冰 skating	钓鱼 fishing	登山 mountain climbing	听音乐 enjoying music	看电影 going to movie	打游戏机 playing video game	编织裁剪 knitting & tailoring
样本 Sample	**623**	**38.4**	**27.4**	**11.7**	**3.0**	**11.9**	**7.5**	**58.6**	**28.3**	**24.6**	**21.7**
信息消极指向 negative orientation	42	35.7	28.6	7.1	2.4	4.8	4.8	50.0	23.8	19.0	21.4
中间层 medium	359	36.5	26.7	10.3	3.6	11.4	5.8	56.5	29.5	26.2	19.8
信息积极指向 active orientation	222	41.9	28.4	14.9	2.3	14.0	10.8	63.5	27.0	23.0	24.8

续前表 continued

	人数 Number	种花盆栽 horticulture	看书 reading	绘画书法 drawing & calligraphy	乐器演奏 playing musical instrument	开汽车兜风 going out for a driving	逛街购物 shopping	郊游露营 outing & camping	海外旅行 overseas travel	国内一天以上的旅行 domestic travel
样本 Sample	**623**	**21.7**	**20.2**	**78.5**	**12.2**	**4.0**	**6.7**	**70.8**	**8.5**	**1.0**
信息消极指向 negative orientation	42	21.4	19.0	61.9	16.7	0.0	0.0	64.3	11.9	0.0
中间层 medium	359	19.8	18.1	76.6	9.7	2.5	7.0	65.7	6.4	1.1
信息积极指向 active orientation	222	24.8	23.9	84.7	15.3	7.2	7.7	80.2	11.3	0.9

续前表 continued

	人数 Number	国内一天往返的旅行 short journey that can be back in a day	看展览会 visiting exhibition	听演唱会/音乐会 attending concert	扭秧歌/木兰拳/交谊舞 doing the YangKo	去博物馆或美术馆 going to museum or art gallery	唱卡拉OK karaoke	去动物园或公园 going to park or zoo	酒吧/咖啡屋/茶秀 going to cafe or bar	电脑游戏 playing PC game
样本 Sample	**623**	**19.4**	**13.2**	**15.6**	**12.0**	**9.5**	**3.9**	**44.5**	**42.5**	**20.9**
信息消极指向 negative orientation	42	7.1	4.8	2.4	16.7	7.1	0.0	33.3	42.9	11.9
中间层 medium	359	17.5	10.3	13.1	9.7	7.5	3.3	43.2	37.9	20.9
信息积极指向 active orientation	222	24.8	19.4	22.1	14.9	13.1	5.4	48.6	50.0	22.5

4-6 不同消费者层想做的休闲活动/ Desired Activities by Market Segments

4-6-1 时尚流行指标/ Fads Popular Index

注：本题为多选题，合计百分比超过 100%（Multiple answers）

	人数 Number	打网球 tennis	打高尔夫球 golf	打羽毛球 badmin-ton	打保龄球 bowling	踢足球 soccer	打篮球 basket-ball	打乒乓球 table-tennis	慢跑 jogging	玩滑板 skate-boarding	跳迪斯科 disco
样本 Sample	526	26.6	11.8	12.2	22.1	7.4	5.3	10.5	11.4	7.2	6.8
平实生活指向 simple living orientation	257	21.0	9.7	13.2	21.4	8.2	4.7	8.9	13.6	6.6	3.5
时尚流行指向 fashion orientation	269	32.0	13.8	11.2	22.7	6.7	5.9	11.9	9.3	7.8	10.0

续前表 continued

	人数 Number	打麻将 mah-jong	游泳 swim-ming	滚轴溜冰 rolling skating	滑冰 skating	钓鱼 fishing	登山 mountain climbing	听音乐 enjoying music	看电影 going to movie	打游戏机 playing video game	编织裁剪 knitting & tailoring
样本 Sample	526	6.8	15.0	7.2	8.9	18.1	22.2	9.3	13.7	2.9	6.8
平实生活指向 simple living orientation	257	8.6	16.0	6.2	8.2	17.9	20.6	10.9	15.6	3.1	5.8
时尚流行指向 fashion orientation	269	5.2	14.1	8.2	9.7	18.2	23.8	7.8	11.9	2.6	7.8

续前表 continued

	人数 Number	种花盆栽 horticul-ture	看书 reading	绘画书法 drawing & calligraphy	乐器演奏 playing musical instru-ment	开汽车兜风 going out for a driving	逛街购物 shopping	郊游露营 outing & camping	海外旅行 overseas travel	国内一天以上的旅行 domestic travel
样本 Sample	526	6.8	13.7	3.6	12.0	9.1	18.4	4.0	27.6	33.5
平实生活指向 simple living orientation	257	5.8	14.0	4.7	12.1	8.9	13.6	4.7	28.4	28.0
时尚流行指向 fashion orientation	269	7.8	13.4	2.6	11.9	9.3	23.0	3.3	26.8	38.7

续前表 continued

	人数 Number	国内一天往返的旅行 short journey that can be back in a day	看展览会 visiting exhibi-tion	听演唱会/音乐会 attending concert	扭秧歌/木兰拳/交谊舞 doing the YangKo	去博物馆或美术馆 going to museum or art gallery	唱卡拉OK karaoke	去动物园或公园 going to park or zoo	酒吧/咖啡屋/茶秀 going to cafe or bar	电脑游戏 playing PC game
样本 Sample	526	37.5	20.9	18.4	26.6	7.6	17.7	10.3	15.8	9.9
平实生活指向 simple living orientation	257	37.4	22.6	17.9	25.7	8.2	18.3	12.1	19.5	8.2
时尚流行指向 fashion orientation	269	37.5	19.3	19.0	27.5	7.1	17.1	8.6	12.3	11.5

4-6-2 信息交流指标/ Information Communication Index

注：本题为多选题，合计百分比超过 100%（Multiple answers）

	人数 Number	打网球 tennis	打高尔夫球 golf	打羽毛球 badmin-ton	打保龄球 bowling	踢足球 soccer	打篮球 basket-ball	打乒乓球 table-tennis	慢跑 jogging	玩滑板 skate-boarding	跳迪斯科 disco
样本 Sample	525	26.7	11.4	12.0	22.1	7.4	5.3	10.1	11.2	7.0	6.9
信息消极指向 negative orientation	30	23.3	13.3	16.7	20.0	0.0	3.3	6.7	6.7	6.7	3.3
中间层 medium	300	26.3	13.0	11.7	20.7	8.3	5.3	9.3	11.7	7.3	5.3
信息积极指向 active orientation	195	27.7	8.7	11.8	24.6	7.2	5.6	11.8	11.3	6.7	9.7

续前表 continued

	人数 Number	打麻将 mah-jong	游泳 swimming	滚轴溜冰 rolling skating	滑冰 skating	钓鱼 fishing	登山 mountain climbing	听音乐 enjoying music	看电影 going to movie	打游戏机 playing video game	编织裁剪 knitting & tailoring
样本 Sample	525	6.9	14.9	7.2	8.8	17.7	22.3	9.3	13.7	2.9	6.9
信息消极指向 negative orientation	30	6.7	3.3	3.3	6.7	30.0	20.0	3.3	10.0	0.0	3.3
中间层 medium	300	8.3	16.7	7.7	10.0	16.7	24.3	9.7	12.7	2.7	6.3
信息积极指向 active orientation	195	4.6	13.8	7.2	7.2	17.4	19.5	9.7	15.9	3.6	8.2

续前表 continued

	人数 Number	种花盆栽 horticulture	看书 reading	绘画书法 drawing & calligraphy	乐器演奏 playing musical instrument	开汽车兜风 going out for a driving	逛街购物 shopping	郊游露营 outing & camping	海外旅行 overseas travel	国内一天以上的旅行 domestic travel
样本 Sample	525	6.9	13.7	3.6	12.0	9.0	18.5	4.0	27.4	33.1
信息消极指向 negative orientation	30	3.3	16.7	6.7	6.7	10.0	16.7	3.3	13.3	33.3
中间层 medium	300	6.3	13.3	4.0	11.3	8.3	19.7	5.0	28.3	30.0
信息积极指向 active orientation	195	8.2	13.8	2.6	13.8	9.7	16.9	2.6	28.2	37.9

续前表 continued

	人数 Number	国内一天往返的旅行 short journey that can be back in a day	看展览会 visiting exhibition	听演唱会/音乐会 attending concert	扭秧歌/木兰拳/交谊舞 doing the YangKo	去博物馆或美术馆 going to museum or art gallery	唱卡拉OK karaoke	去动物园或公园 going to park or zoo	酒吧/咖啡屋/茶秀 going to cafe or bar	电脑游戏 playing PC game
样本 Sample	525	37.7	21.0	18.5	26.5	7.4	17.5	10.3	15.4	9.9
信息消极指向 negative orientation	30	33.3	20.0	6.7	6.7	6.7	13.3	10.0	23.3	6.7
中间层 medium	300	34.7	18.7	17.3	25.0	7.0	18.3	9.0	14.3	9.3
信息积极指向 active orientation	195	43.1	24.6	22.1	31.8	8.2	16.9	12.3	15.9	11.3

● 西安 / Xi'an

4-1 常做的休闲活动排名/ Ranking of the Frequently Engaged Activities

注：本题为多选题，合计百分比可能超过 100%（Multiple answers）

排名 Ranking	活动项目 Activity Items	人次 Person-time	百分比 Percent
1	看书 reading	468	78.8
2	逛街购物 shopping	338	56.9
3	听音乐 enjoying music	322	54.2
4	打麻将 mah-jong	248	41.8
5	去动物园或公园 going to the park or zoo	218	36.7
6	看电影 going to movie	211	35.5
7	打羽毛球 badminton	207	34.8
8	慢跑 jogging	181	30.5
9	唱卡拉 OK Karaoke	180	30.3
10	游泳 swimming	149	25.1
11	打乒乓球 table-tennis	145	24.4
12	打游戏机 playing video game	126	21.2
13	编织裁剪 knitting & tailoring	124	20.9
14	种花盆栽 horticulture	118	19.9
15	电脑游戏 playing PC game	106	17.8
16	打篮球 basketball	94	15.8
17	看展览会 visiting exhibition	93	15.7
18	国内一天以上的旅行 domestic travel	91	15.3
19	登山 mountain climbing	69	11.6
20	打保龄球 bowling	68	11.4
20	踢足球 soccer	68	11.4
21	酒吧/咖啡屋/茶秀 going to cafe or bar	66	11.1
22	钓鱼 fishing	64	10.8
23	国内一天往返的旅行 short journey that can be back in a day	63	10.6
24	跳迪斯科 disco	61	10.3
24	去博物馆或美术馆 going to museum or art gallery	61	10.3
24	绘画书法 drawing & calligraphy	61	10.3
24	听演唱会/音乐会 attending concert	61	10.3
25	郊游露营 outing & camping	50	8.4
26	扭秧歌/木兰拳/交谊舞 doing the YangKo	49	8.2
27	滚轴溜冰 rolling skating	39	6.6
28	开汽车兜风 going out for a driving	34	5.7
29	滑冰 skating	26	4.4
30	打网球 tennis	25	4.2
31	乐器演奏 playing musical instrument	21	3.5
32	玩滑板 skateboarding	11	1.9
33	海外旅行 overseas travel	5	0.8
33	打高尔夫球 golf	5	0.8

n=594

4-2 想做的休闲活动排名/ Ranking of the Desired Activities

注：本题为多选题，合计百分比可能超过 100%（Multiple answers）

排名 Ranking	活动项目 Activity Items	人次 Person-time	百分比 Percent
1	国内一天以上的旅行 domestic travel	200	37.5
2	海外旅行 overseas travel	138	25.9
3	登山 mountain climbing	132	24.8
4	郊游露营 outing & camping	129	24.2
5	打保龄球 bowling	123	23.1
6	打网球 tennis	109	20.5
7	开汽车兜风 going out for a driving	105	19.7
8	听演唱会/音乐会 attending concert	95	17.8
9	国内一天往返的旅行 short journey that can be back in a day	91	17.1
10	钓鱼 fishing	82	15.4
11	游泳 swimming	81	15.2
12	种花盆栽 horticulture	75	14.1
13	去动物园或公园 going to the park or zoo	73	13.7
14	看电影 going to movie	64	12.0
15	打高尔夫球 golf	61	11.4
16	看展览会 visiting exhibition	59	11.1
17	慢跑 jogging	53	9.9
17	绘画书法 drawing & calligraphy	53	9.9
18	去博物馆或美术馆 going to museum or art gallery	52	9.8
19	滑冰 skating	49	9.2
20	打乒乓球 table-tennis	46	8.6
21	电脑游戏 playing PC game	45	8.4
22	乐器演奏 playing musical instrument	44	8.3
23	打羽毛球 badminton	40	7.5
24	唱卡拉 OK Karaoke	38	7.1
25	逛街购物 shopping	33	6.2
25	踢足球 soccer	33	6.2
25	酒吧/咖啡屋/茶秀 going to cafe or bar	33	6.2
26	听音乐 enjoying music	32	6.0
27	打篮球 basketball	26	4.9
28	跳迪斯科 disco	25	4.7
28	玩滑板 skateboarding	25	4.7
28	扭秧歌/木兰拳/交谊舞 doing the YangKo	25	4.7
29	打麻将 mah-jong	23	4.3
30	编织裁剪 knitting & tailoring	22	4.1
31	打游戏机 playing video game	21	3.9
32	滚轴溜冰 rolling skating	20	3.8
33	看书 reading	12	2.3

n=533

4-3 样本、男性各年龄层、女性各年龄层常做的活动/ Frequently Engaged Activities by the Whole Sample, Age and Gender Groups

注：本题为多选题，合计百分比超过 100%（Multiple answers）

	人数 Number	打网球 tennis	打高尔夫球 golf	打羽毛球 badminton	打保龄球 bowling	踢足球 soccer	打篮球 basketball	打乒乓球 table tennis	慢跑 jogging	玩滑板 skate boarding	跳迪斯科 disco
样本 Sample	594	4.2	0.8	34.8	11.4	11.4	15.8	24.4	30.5	1.9	10.3
男性 Male	295	4.7	1.0	35.9	14.6	20.0	25.8	30.8	30.8	2.0	7.5
16~24 岁 Age	64	9.4	1.6	48.4	12.5	50.0	59.4	56.3	26.6	6.3	14.1
25~34 岁 Age	91	7.7	0.0	36.3	22.0	17.6	24.2	31.9	29.7	0.0	12.1
35~44 岁 Age	76	0.0	1.3	38.2	9.2	10.5	10.5	14.5	27.6	2.6	2.6
45~54 岁 Age	42	2.4	2.4	19.0	14.3	7.1	16.7	31.0	35.7	0.0	0.0
55~60 岁 Age	22	0.0	0.0	22.7	9.1	0.0	4.5	9.1	50.0	0.0	0.0
女性 Female	299	3.7	0.7	33.8	8.4	3.0	6.0	18.1	30.1	1.7	13.0
16~24 岁 Age	61	4.9	1.6	49.2	9.8	6.6	13.1	42.6	36.1	6.6	14.8
25~34 岁 Age	90	7.8	0.0	32.2	14.4	2.2	3.3	23.3	16.7	1.1	16.7
35~44 岁 Age	74	0.0	1.4	33.8	4.1	4.1	6.8	6.8	28.4	0.0	12.2
45~54 岁 Age	49	0.0	0.0	22.4	4.1	0.0	2.0	4.1	42.9	0.0	8.2
55~60 岁 Age	25	4.0	0.0	24.0	4.0	0.0	4.0	0.0	44.0	0.0	8.0

续前表 continued

	人数 Number	打麻将 mah-jong	游泳 swimming	滚轴溜冰 rolling skating	滑冰 skating	钓鱼 fishing	登山 mountain climbing	听音乐 enjoying music	看电影 going to movie	打游戏机 playing video game	编织裁剪 knitting & tailoring
样本 Sample	594	41.8	25.1	6.6	4.4	10.8	11.6	54.2	35.5	21.2	20.9
男性 Male	295	47.5	29.5	8.5	5.4	14.9	13.6	53.6	37.3	28.8	1.0
16~24 岁 Age	64	29.7	37.5	25.0	15.6	10.9	21.9	78.1	56.3	50.0	0.0
25~34 岁 Age	91	54.9	30.8	8.8	4.4	15.4	13.2	48.4	39.6	33.0	3.3
35~44 岁 Age	76	65.8	35.5	1.3	2.6	17.1	9.2	46.1	31.6	21.1	0.0
45~54 岁 Age	42	35.7	11.9	0.0	0.0	21.4	9.5	50.0	21.4	11.9	0.0
55~60 岁 Age	22	27.3	13.6	0.0	0.0	4.5	13.6	36.4	22.7	9.1	0.0
女性 Female	299	36.1	20.7	4.7	3.3	6.7	9.7	54.8	33.8	13.7	40.5
16~24 岁 Age	61	21.3	31.1	14.8	9.8	13.1	19.7	72.1	55.7	14.8	13.1
25~34 岁 Age	90	42.2	30.0	2.2	3.3	11.1	7.8	62.2	38.9	16.7	32.2
35~44 岁 Age	74	39.2	17.6	2.7	0.0	1.4	8.1	51.4	27.0	16.2	59.5
45~54 岁 Age	49	30.6	6.1	2.0	2.0	2.0	8.2	40.8	18.4	6.1	53.1
55~60 岁 Age	25	52.0	0.0	0.0	0.0	0.0	0.0	24.0	12.0	8.0	56.0

续前表 continued

	人数 Number	种花盆栽 horticulture	看书 reading	绘画书法 drawing & calligraphy	乐器演奏 playing musical instrument	开汽车兜风 going out for a driving	逛街购物 shopping	郊游露营 outing & camping	海外旅行 overseas travel	国内一天以上的旅行 domestic travel
样本 Sample	594	20.9	19.9	78.8	10.3	3.5	5.7	56.9	8.4	0.8
男性 Male	295	1.0	13.6	79.0	12.9	5.1	9.5	40.7	9.5	1.0
16~24 岁 Age	64	0.0	4.7	87.5	14.1	14.1	10.9	35.9	10.9	1.6
25~34 岁 Age	91	3.3	12.1	71.4	11.0	2.2	11.0	49.5	11.0	0.0
35~44 岁 Age	76	0.0	11.8	78.9	11.8	0.0	7.9	38.2	9.2	1.3
45~54 岁 Age	42	0.0	11.9	78.6	14.3	4.8	11.9	42.9	9.5	2.4
55~60 岁 Age	22	0.0	54.5	86.4	18.2	9.1	0.0	22.7	0.0	0.0
女性 Female	299	40.5	26.1	78.6	7.7	2.0	2.0	72.9	7.4	0.7
16~24 岁 Age	61	13.1	11.5	85.2	16.4	8.2	1.6	75.4	8.2	1.6
25~34 岁 Age	90	32.2	21.1	83.3	6.7	0.0	3.3	80.0	8.9	1.1
35~44 岁 Age	74	59.5	27.0	77.0	6.8	1.4	1.4	68.9	4.1	0.0
45~54 岁 Age	49	53.1	36.7	65.3	2.0	0.0	2.0	69.4	8.2	0.0
55~60 岁 Age	25	56.0	56.0	76.0	4.0	0.0	0.0	60.0	8.0	0.0

续前表 continued

	人数 Number	国内一天往返的旅行 short journey that can be back in a day	看展览会 visiting exhibition	听演唱会/音乐会 attending concert	扭秧歌/木兰拳/交谊舞 doing the YangKo	去博物馆或美术馆 going to museum or art gallery	唱卡拉OK karaoke	去动物园或公园 going to park or zoo	酒吧/咖啡屋/茶秀 going to cafe or bar	电脑游戏 playing PC game
样本 Sample	594	15.3	10.6	15.7	10.3	8.2	10.3	30.3	36.7	11.1
男性 Male	295	15.9	11.5	16.9	11.5	6.4	12.9	31.2	33.2	14.6
16~24 岁 Age	64	18.8	9.4	15.6	20.3	3.1	18.8	34.4	26.6	17.2
25~34 岁 Age	91	14.3	12.1	16.5	11.0	5.5	13.2	37.4	37.4	23.1
35~44 岁 Age	76	15.8	9.2	14.5	9.2	6.6	6.6	32.9	32.9	9.2
45~54 岁 Age	42	16.7	19.0	19.0	4.8	4.8	14.3	21.4	28.6	9.5
55~60 岁 Age	22	13.6	9.1	27.3	9.1	22.7	13.6	9.1	45.5	0.0
女性 Female	299	14.7	9.7	14.4	9.0	10.0	7.7	29.4	40.1	7.7
16~24 岁 Age	61	18.0	9.8	11.5	9.8	6.6	4.9	32.8	39.3	13.1
25~34 岁 Age	90	14.4	10.0	10.0	6.7	5.6	5.6	37.8	51.1	13.3
35~44 岁 Age	74	14.9	12.2	21.6	13.5	10.8	13.5	36.5	25.7	1.4
45~54 岁 Age	49	12.2	8.2	14.3	8.2	14.3	4.1	12.2	36.7	4.1
55~60 岁 Age	25	12.0	4.0	16.0	4.0	24.0	12.0	4.0	52.0	0.0

4-4 样本、男性各年龄层、女性各年龄层想做的活动/ Desired Activities by the Whole Sample, Age and Gender Groups

注：本题为多选题，合计百分比超过 100%（Multiple answers）

	人数 Number	打网球 tennis	打高尔夫球 golf	打羽毛球 badminton	打保龄球 bowling	踢足球 soccer	打篮球 basketball	打乒乓球 table tennis	慢跑 jogging	玩滑板 skate boarding	跳迪斯科 disco
样本 Sample	533	20.5	11.4	7.5	23.1	6.2	4.9	8.6	9.9	4.7	4.7
男性 Male	268	21.6	14.9	6.0	26.5	9.7	6.7	8.6	10.1	6.0	3.4
16~24 岁 Age	58	24.1	15.5	8.6	22.4	8.6	1.7	6.9	1.7	10.3	3.4
25~34 岁 Age	82	26.8	12.2	6.1	24.4	12.2	7.3	6.1	8.5	8.5	6.1
35~44 岁 Age	71	22.5	11.3	4.2	32.4	9.9	8.5	12.7	11.3	1.4	1.4
45~54 岁 Age	39	10.3	23.1	5.1	25.6	7.7	12.8	12.8	15.4	2.6	2.6
55~60 岁 Age	18	11.1	22.2	5.6	27.8	5.6	0.0	0.0	27.8	5.6	0.0
女性 Female	265	19.2	7.9	9.1	19.6	2.6	3.0	8.7	9.8	3.4	6.0
16~24 岁 Age	54	33.3	16.7	9.3	37.0	5.6	5.6	5.6	9.3	9.3	13.0
25~34 岁 Age	86	24.4	9.3	7.0	20.9	3.5	0.0	8.1	8.1	2.3	8.1
35~44 岁 Age	64	15.6	3.1	6.3	12.5	0.0	4.7	10.9	14.1	1.6	3.1
45~54 岁 Age	41	2.4	2.4	17.1	14.6	2.4	4.9	12.2	9.8	2.4	0.0
55~60 岁 Age	20	5.0	5.0	10.0	0.0	0.0	0.0	5.0	5.0	0.0	0.0

续前表 continued

	人数 Number	打麻将 mah-jong	游泳 swimming	滚轴溜冰 rolling skating	滑冰 skating	钓鱼 fishing	登山 mountain climbing	听音乐 enjoying music	看电影 going to movie	打游戏机 playing video game	编织裁剪 knitting & tailoring
样本 Sample	533	4.3	15.2	3.8	9.2	15.4	24.8	6.0	12.0	3.9	4.1
男性 Male	268	2.6	16.4	2.6	10.4	25.4	29.1	6.0	11.6	5.2	1.9
16~24 岁 Age	58	3.4	22.4	3.4	17.2	19.0	36.2	1.7	10.3	6.9	3.4
25~34 岁 Age	82	2.4	14.6	2.4	15.9	23.0	30.5	6.1	12.2	4.9	1.2
35~44 岁 Age	71	0.0	11.3	1.4	4.2	23.2	29.6	9.9	11.3	5.6	2.8
45~54 岁 Age	39	2.6	23.1	5.1	5.1	28.2	25.6	2.6	12.8	5.1	0.0
55~60 岁 Age	18	11.1	11.1	0.0	0.0	16.7	5.6	11.1	11.1	0.0	0.0
女性 Female	265	6.0	14.0	4.9	7.9	5.3	20.4	6.0	12.5	2.6	6.4
16~24 岁 Age	54	5.6	16.7	14.8	22.2	5.6	24.1	7.4	11.1	7.4	5.6
25~34 岁 Age	86	5.8	20.9	5.8	7.0	3.5	24.4	3.5	12.8	3.5	7.0
35~44 岁 Age	64	3.1	12.5	0.0	4.7	6.3	17.2	6.3	9.4	0.0	6.3
45~54 岁 Age	41	14.6	2.4	0.0	0.0	4.9	17.1	0.0	17.1	0.0	7.3
55~60 岁 Age	20	0.0	5.0	0.0	0.0	10.0	10.0	25.0	15.0	0.0	5.0

续前表 continued

	人数 Number	种花盆栽 horticulture	看书 reading	绘画书法 drawing & calligraphy	乐器演奏 playing musical instrument	开汽车兜风 going out for a driving	逛街购物 shopping	郊游露营 outing & camping	海外旅行 overseas travel	国内一天以上的旅行 domestic travel
样本 Sample	533	4.1	14.1	2.3	9.9	8.3	19.7	6.2	24.2	25.9
男性 Male	268	1.9	11.9	1.5	8.2	7.5	23.5	4.5	22.4	29.5
16~24 岁 Age	58	3.4	10.3	0.0	5.2	8.6	24.1	1.7	37.9	36.2
25~34 岁 Age	82	1.2	12.2	1.2	3.7	8.5	29.3	4.9	14.6	30.5
35~44 岁 Age	71	2.8	9.9	0.0	9.9	5.6	19.7	5.6	19.7	31.0
45~54 岁 Age	39	0.0	15.4	7.7	15.4	5.1	23.1	5.1	25.6	17.9
55~60 岁 Age	18	0.0	16.7	0.0	16.7	11.1	11.1	5.6	11.1	22.2
女性 Female	265	6.4	16.2	3.0	11.7	9.1	15.8	7.9	26.0	22.3
16~24 岁 Age	54	5.6	14.8	0.0	16.7	14.8	27.8	7.4	40.7	40.7
25~34 岁 Age	86	7.0	10.5	3.5	5.8	7.0	18.6	2.3	27.9	20.9
35~44 岁 Age	64	6.3	20.3	3.1	12.5	10.9	12.5	15.6	26.6	17.2
45~54 岁 Age	41	7.3	22.0	4.9	9.8	4.9	7.3	7.3	12.2	12.2
55~60 岁 Age	20	5.0	20.0	5.0	25.0	5.0	0.0	10.0	5.0	15.0

续前表 continued

	人数 Number	国内一天往返的旅行 short journey that can be back in a day	看展览会 visiting exhibition	听演唱会/音乐会 attending concert	扭秧歌/木兰拳/交谊舞 doing the YangKo	去博物馆或美术馆 going to museum or art gallery	唱卡拉 OK karaoke	去动物园或公园 going to park or zoo	酒吧/咖啡屋/茶秀 going to cafe or bar	电脑游戏 playing PC game
样本 Sample	533	37.5	17.1	11.1	17.8	4.7	9.8	7.1	13.7	6.2
男性 Male	268	34.3	16.8	11.2	16.8	4.1	11.2	6.7	15.3	5.2
16~24 岁 Age	58	31.0	15.5	13.8	22.4	6.9	10.3	15.5	13.8	10.3
25~34 岁 Age	82	36.6	24.4	8.5	12.2	6.1	6.1	3.7	14.6	4.9
35~44 岁 Age	71	35.2	15.5	12.7	18.3	2.8	11.3	7.0	12.7	5.6
45~54 岁 Age	39	38.5	10.3	7.7	23.1	0.0	10.3	2.6	20.5	0.0
55~60 岁 Age	18	22.2	5.6	16.7	0.0	0.0	38.9	0.0	22.2	0.0
女性 Female	265	40.8	17.4	10.9	18.9	5.3	8.3	7.5	12.1	7.2
16~24 岁 Age	54	42.6	24.1	13.0	25.9	3.7	14.8	18.5	9.3	11.1
25~34 岁 Age	86	39.5	15.1	11.6	18.6	0.0	7.0	5.8	10.5	8.1
35~44 岁 Age	64	39.1	15.6	3.1	15.6	7.8	7.8	4.7	14.1	9.4
45~54 岁 Age	41	46.3	22.0	14.6	17.1	9.8	7.3	4.9	12.2	0.0
55~60 岁 Age	20	35.0	5.0	20.0	15.0	15.0	0.0	0.0	20.0	0.0

4-5 不同消费者常做的休闲活动/ Frequently Engaged Activities by Market Segments

4-5-1 时尚流行指标/ Fads Popular Index

注：本题为多选题，合计百分比超过100%（Multiple answers）

	人数 Number	打网球 tennis	打高尔夫球 golf	打羽毛球 badminton	打保龄球 bowling	踢足球 soccer	打篮球 basket-ball	打乒乓球 table-tennis	慢跑 jogging	玩滑板 skate-boarding	跳迪斯科 disco
样本 Sample	592	4.2	0.8	34.8	11.5	11.5	15.9	24.5	30.4	1.9	10.3
平实生活指向 simple living orientation	335	3.0	0.6	30.4	6.9	10.7	14.3	21.8	32.2	1.2	5.1
时尚流行指向 fashion orientation	257	5.8	1.2	40.5	17.5	12.5	17.9	28.0	28.0	2.7	17.1

续前表 continued

	人数 Number	打麻将 mah-jong	游泳 swimming	滚轴溜冰 rolling skating	滑冰 skating	钓鱼 fishing	登山 mountain climbing	听音乐 enjoying music	看电影 going to movie	打游戏机 playing video game	编织裁剪 knitting & tailoring
样本 Sample	592	41.7	25.2	6.6	4.4	10.8	11.7	54.1	35.5	21.3	20.6
平实生活指向 simple living orientation	335	39.1	18.8	4.8	3.6	8.1	8.4	43.6	29.0	17.0	20.9
时尚流行指向 fashion orientation	257	45.1	33.5	8.9	5.4	14.4	16.0	67.7	44.0	26.8	20.2

续前表 continued

	人数 Number	种花盆栽 horticulture	看书 reading	绘画书法 drawing & calligraphy	乐器演奏 playing musical instrument	开汽车兜风 going out for a driving	逛街购物 shopping	郊游露营 outing & camping	海外旅行 oversea s travel	国内一天以上的旅行 domestic travel
样本 Sample	592	20.6	19.6	78.9	10.3	3.5	5.7	56.9	8.4	0.8
平实生活指向 simple living orientation	335	20.9	20.9	78.5	8.1	1.8	4.5	51.0	6.9	0.3
时尚流行指向 fashion orientation	257	20.2	17.9	79.4	13.2	5.8	7.4	64.6	10.5	1.6

续前表 continued

	人数 Number	国内一天往返的旅行 short journey that can be back in a day	看展览会 visiting exhibition	听演唱会/音乐会 attending concert	扭秧歌/木兰拳/交谊舞 doing the YangKo	去博物馆或美术馆 going to museum or art gallery	唱卡拉OK karaoke	去动物园或公园 going to park or zoo	酒吧/咖啡屋/茶秀 going to cafe or bar	电脑游戏 playing PC game
样本 Sample	592	15.4	10.6	15.7	10.3	8.3	10.3	30.4	36.7	17.9
平实生活指向 simple living orientation	335	9.6	7.8	14.3	6.9	7.5	9.3	20.3	35.5	14.9
时尚流行指向 fashion orientation	257	23.0	14.4	17.5	14.8	9.3	11.7	43.6	38.1	21.8

4-5-2 信息交流指标/ Information Communication Index

注：本题为多选题，合计百分比超过100%（Multiple answers）

	人数 Number	打网球 tennis	打高尔夫球 golf	打羽毛球 bad-minion	打保龄球 bowling	踢足球 soccer	打篮球 basket-ball	打乒乓球 table-tennis	慢跑 jogging	玩滑板 skate-boarding	跳迪斯科 disco
样本 Sample	592	4.2	0.8	34.8	11.5	11.5	15.9	24.5	30.4	1.9	10.3
信息消极指向 negative orientation	68	4.4	0.0	36.8	7.4	19.1	17.6	35.3	30.9	0.0	7.4
中间层 medium	336	4.5	0.6	32.4	10.4	11.3	15.2	22.3	27.4	1.5	9.2
信息积极指向 active orientation	188	3.7	1.6	38.3	14.9	9.0	16.5	24.5	35.6	3.2	13.3

续前表 continued

	人数 Number	打麻将 mah-jong	游泳 swimming	滚轴溜冰 rolling skating	滑冰 skating	钓鱼 fishing	登山 mountain climbing	听音乐 enjoying music	看电影 going to movie	打游戏机 playing video game	编织裁剪 knitting & tailoring
样本 Sample	592	41.9	25.2	6.6	4.4	10.8	11.7	54.2	35.5	21.3	20.8
信息消极指向 negative orientation	68	33.8	13.2	2.9	1.5	7.4	4.4	29.4	17.6	16.2	10.3
中间层 medium	336	40.2	25.6	6.3	4.8	11.0	10.4	59.2	38.1	20.2	21.1
信息积极指向 active orientation	188	47.9	28.7	8.5	4.8	11.7	16.5	54.3	37.2	25.0	23.9

续前表 continued

	人数 Number	种花盆栽 horticulture	看书 reading	绘画书法 drawing & calligraphy	乐器演奏 playing musical instrument	开汽车兜风 going out for a driving	逛街购物 shopping	郊游露营 outing & camping	海外旅行 overseas travel	国内一天以上的旅行 domestic travel
样本 Sample	592	20.8	19.8	78.7	10.3	3.5	5.7	57.1	8.4	0.8
信息消极指向 negative orientation	68	10.3	19.1	67.6	10.3	1.5	2.9	38.2	0.0	0.0
中间层 medium	336	21.1	18.2	77.1	9.8	2.7	4.2	56.5	8.0	0.9
信息积极指向 active orientation	188	23.9	22.9	85.6	11.2	5.9	9.6	64.9	12.2	1.1

续前表 continued

	人数 Number	国内一天往返的旅行 short journey that can be back in a day	看展览会 visiting exhibition	听演唱会/音乐会 attending concert	扭秧歌/木兰拳/交谊舞 doing the YangKo	去博物馆或美术馆 going to museum or art gallery	唱卡拉OK karaoke	去动物园或公园 going to park or zoo	酒吧/咖啡屋/茶秀 going to cafe or bar	电脑游戏 playing PC game
样本 Sample	592	15.4	10.6	15.7	10.3	8.3	10.3	30.4	36.7	17.9
信息消极指向 negative orientation	68	8.8	7.4	8.8	8.8	13.2	10.3	16.2	39.7	14.7
中间层 medium	336	14.0	9.8	13.7	8.6	7.1	7.7	31.3	36.3	16.4
信息积极指向 active orientation	188	20.2	13.3	21.8	13.8	8.5	14.9	34.0	36.2	21.8

4-6 不同消费者层想做的休闲活动/ Desired Activities by Market Segments

4-6-1 时尚流行指标/ Fads Popular Index

注：本题为多选题，合计百分比超过100%（Multiple answers）

	人数 Number	打网球 tennis	打高尔夫球 golf	打羽毛球 badminton	打保龄球 bowling	踢足球 soccer	打篮球 basketball	打乒乓球 table-tennis	慢跑 jogging	玩滑板 skate-boarding	跳迪斯科 disco
样本 Sample	531	20.5	11.5	7.5	23.2	6.2	4.9	8.7	10.0	4.7	4.7
平实生活指向 simple living orientation	293	15.4	7.2	6.8	19.1	4.8	3.4	6.1	10.9	4.8	3.8
时尚流行指向 fashion orientation	238	26.9	16.8	8.4	28.2	8.0	6.7	11.8	8.8	4.6	5.9

续前表 continued

	人数 Number	打麻将 mah-jong	游泳 swimming	滚轴溜冰 rolling skating	滑冰 skating	钓鱼 fishing	登山 mountain climbing	听音乐 enjoying music	看电影 going to movie	打游戏机 playing video game	编织裁剪 knitting & tailoring
样本 Sample	531	4.3	15.1	3.8	9.2	15.4	24.7	6.0	12.1	4.0	4.1
平实生活指向 simple living orientation	293	5.1	12.3	3.1	9.9	17.7	24.6	8.2	14.0	4.1	2.7
时尚流行指向 fashion orientation	238	3.4	18.5	4.6	8.4	12.6	24.8	3.4	9.7	3.8	5.9

续前表 continued

	人数 Number	种花盆栽 horticulture	看书 reading	绘画书法 drawing & calligraphy	乐器演奏 playing musical instrument	开汽车兜风 going out for a driving	逛街购物 shopping	郊游露营 outing & camping	海外旅行 overseas travel	国内一天以上的旅行 domestic travel
样本 Sample	531	4.1	14.1	2.3	10.0	8.3	19.8	6.0	24.1	26.0
平实生活指向 simple living orientation	293	2.7	15.0	2.0	9.6	8.2	16.0	6.8	18.1	23.2
时尚流行指向 fashion orientation	238	5.9	13.0	2.5	10.5	8.4	24.4	5.0	31.5	29.4

续前表 continued

	人数 Number	国内一天往返的旅行 short journey that can be back in a day	看展览会 visiting exhibition	听演唱会/音乐会 attending concert	扭秧歌/木兰拳/交谊舞 doing the YangKo	去博物馆或美术馆 going to museum or art gallery	唱卡拉OK karaoke	去动物园或公园 going to park or zoo	酒吧/咖啡屋/茶秀 going to cafe or bar	电脑游戏 playing PC game
样本 Sample	531	37.5	17.1	11.1	17.7	4.7	9.8	7.2	13.7	8.5
平实生活指向 simple living orientation	293	38.6	17.7	11.9	16.4	4.1	10.6	7.2	19.1	7.5
时尚流行指向 fashion orientation	238	36.1	16.4	10.1	19.3	5.5	8.8	7.1	7.1	9.7

4-6-2 信息交流指标/ Information Communication Index

注：本题为多选题，合计百分比超过100%（Multiple answers）

	人数 Number	打网球 tennis	打高尔夫球 golf	打羽毛球 badminton	打保龄球 bowling	踢足球 soccer	打篮球 basket-ball	打乒乓球 table-tennis	慢跑 jogging	玩滑板 skate-boarding	跳迪斯科 disco
样本 Sample	531	20.5	11.5	7.5	23.2	6.2	4.9	8.7	10.0	4.7	4.7
信息消极指向 negative orientation	61	16.4	14.8	1.6	21.3	4.9	1.6	0.0	13.1	6.6	4.9
中间层 medium	304	19.4	10.2	8.2	22.7	6.3	3.6	9.9	9.9	4.9	4.6
信息积极指向 active orientation	166	24.1	12.7	8.4	24.7	6.6	8.4	9.6	9.0	3.6	4.8

续前表 continued

	人数 Number	打麻将 mah-jong	游泳 swimming	滚轴溜冰 rolling skating	滑冰 skating	钓鱼 fishing	登山 mountain climbing	听音乐 enjoying music	看电影 going to movie	打游戏机 playing video game	编织裁剪 knitting & tailoring
样本 Sample	531	4.3	15.3	3.8	9.2	15.4	24.9	6.0	12.1	4.0	4.1
信息消极指向 negative orientation	61	1.6	14.8	3.3	23.0	18.0	23.0	18.0	18.0	4.9	3.3
中间层 medium	304	5.3	17.8	3.9	5.9	14.1	25.0	2.6	11.2	4.9	3.6
信息积极指向 active orientation	166	3.6	10.8	3.6	10.2	15.9	25.3	7.8	11.4	1.8	5.4

续前表 continued

	人数 Number	种花盆栽 horticulture	看书 reading	绘画书法 drawing & calligraphy	乐器演奏 playing musical instrument	开汽车兜风 going out for a driving	逛街购物 shopping	郊游露营 outing & camping	海外旅行 overseas travel	国内一天以上的旅行 domestic travel
样本 Sample	531	4.1	13.9	2.3	10.0	8.3	19.8	6.0	24.1	26.0
信息消极指向 negative orientation	61	3.3	9.8	0.0	8.2	6.6	21.3	6.6	14.8	29.5
中间层 medium	304	3.6	12.2	3.3	9.9	7.6	20.4	6.3	24.7	24.3
信息积极指向 active orientation	166	5.4	18.7	1.2	10.8	10.2	18.1	5.4	26.5	27.7

续前表 continued

	人数 Number	国内一天往返的旅行 short journey that can be back in a day	看展览会 visiting exhibition	听演唱会/音乐会 attending concert	扭秧歌/木兰拳/交谊舞 doing the YangKo	去博物馆或美术馆 going to museum or art gallery	唱卡拉OK karaoke	去动物园或公园 going to park or zoo	酒吧/咖啡屋/茶秀 going to cafe or bar	电脑游戏 playing PC game
样本 Sample	531	37.7	17.1	11.1	17.9	4.7	9.8	7.2	13.7	8.5
信息消极指向 negative orientation	61	37.7	18.0	8.2	14.3	3.3	8.2	3.3	21.3	3.3
中间层 medium	304	38.8	20.7	11.2	18.4	4.3	11.2	7.2	13.2	8.9
信息积极指向 active orientation	166	35.5	10.2	12.0	18.1	6.0	7.8	8.4	12.0	9.6

● 沈阳 / Shenyang

4-1 常做的休闲活动排名/ Ranking of the Frequently Engaged Activities

注：本题为多选题，合计百分比超过 100%（Multiple answers）

排名 Ranking	活动项目 Activity Items	人次 Person-time	百分比 Percent
1	看书 reading	481	81.3
2	逛街购物 shopping	377	63.7
3	听音乐 enjoying music	341	57.6
4	唱卡拉 OK Karaoke	278	47.0
5	去动物园或公园 going to the park or zoo	265	44.8
6	打麻将 mah-jong	243	41.0
7	打羽毛球 badminton	228	38.5
8	慢跑 jogging	204	34.5
9	游泳 swimming	183	30.9
10	看电影 going to movie	167	28.2
11	种花盆栽 horticulture	164	27.7
12	打游戏机 playing video game	151	25.5
13	国内一天以上的旅行 domestic travel	120	20.3
14	打乒乓球 table-tennis	117	19.8
15	编织裁剪 knitting & tailoring	116	19.6
16	电脑游戏 playing PC game	114	19.3
17	看展览会 visiting exhibition	112	18.9
18	打篮球 basketball	109	18.4
19	国内一天往返的旅行 short journey that can be back in a day	105	17.7
20	打保龄球 bowling	92	15.5
21	踢足球 soccer	87	14.7
22	听演唱会/音乐会 attending concert	73	12.3
23	郊游露营 outing & camping	60	10.1
24	跳迪斯科 disco	59	10.0
25	酒吧/咖啡屋/茶秀 going to cafe or bar	58	9.8
26	绘画书法 drawing & calligraphy	54	9.1
27	滑冰 skating	53	9.0
28	钓鱼 fishing	52	8.8
29	去博物馆或美术馆 going to museum or art gallery	50	8.4
30	登山 mountain climbing	44	7.4
31	开汽车兜风 going out for a driving	43	7.3
32	扭秧歌/木兰拳/交谊舞 doing the YangKo	42	7.1
32	滚轴溜冰 rolling skating	42	7.1
33	乐器演奏 playing musical instrument	35	5.9
34	打网球 tennis	25	4.2
35	海外旅行 overseas travel	5	0.8
35	玩滑板 skateboarding	5	0.8
36	打高尔夫球 golf	3	0.5

n=592

4-2 想做的休闲活动排名/ Ranking of the Desired Activities

注：本题为多选题，合计百分比超过 100%（Multiple answers）

排名 Ranking	活动项目 Activity Items	人次 Person-time	百分比 Percent
1	国内一天以上的旅行 domestic travel	168	33.7
2	海外旅行 overseas travel	166	33.3
3	郊游露营 outing & camping	162	32.5
4	开汽车兜风 going out for a driving	135	27.1
5	打保龄球 bowling	130	26.1
6	打网球 tennis	123	24.7
6	国内一天往返的旅行 short journey that can be back in a day	123	24.7
6	登山 mountain climbing	123	24.7
7	听演唱会/音乐会 attending concert	121	24.3
8	游泳 swimming	99	19.9
9	打高尔夫球 golf	86	17.3
10	看展览会 visiting exhibition	84	16.9
10	钓鱼 fishing	84	16.9
11	看电影 going to movie	66	13.3
12	去博物馆或美术馆 going to museum or art gallery	64	12.9
13	慢跑 jogging	62	12.4
14	滑冰 skating	60	12.0
15	种花盆栽 horticulture	57	11.4
15	去动物园或公园 going to the park or zoo	57	11.4
16	酒吧/咖啡屋/茶秀 going to cafe or bar	54	10.8
17	听音乐 enjoying music	52	10.4
18	唱卡拉 OK Karaoke	49	9.8
18	打羽毛球 badminton	49	9.8
18	绘画书法 drawing & calligraphy	49	9.8
19	电脑游戏 playing PC game	45	9.0
19	打乒乓球 table-tennis	45	9.0
20	玩滑板 skateboarding	40	8.0
21	乐器演奏 playing musical instrument	38	7.6
21	踢足球 soccer	38	7.6
22	打麻将 mah-jong	36	7.2
23	跳迪斯科 disco	33	6.6
24	逛街购物 shopping	30	6.0
25	扭秧歌/木兰拳/交谊舞 doing the YangKo	28	5.6
26	打篮球 basketball	26	5.2
27	编织裁剪 knitting & tailoring	23	4.6
28	看书 reading	20	4.0
29	滚轴溜冰 rolling skating	16	3.2
30	打游戏机 playing video game	15	3.0

n=498

4-3 样本、男性各年龄层、女性各年龄层常做的活动/ Frequently Engaged Activities by the Whole Sample, Age and Gender Groups

注：本题为多选题，合计百分比超过 100%（Multiple answers）

	人数 Number	打网球 tennis	打高尔夫球 golf	打羽毛球 bad-minton	打保龄球 bowling	踢足球 soccer	打篮球 basket ball	打乒乓球 table tennis	慢跑 jogging	玩滑板 skate boarding	跳迪斯科 disco
样本 Sample	592	4.2	0.5	38.5	15.5	14.7	18.4	19.8	34.5	0.8	10.0
男性 Male	295	5.4	1.0	40.0	20.0	26.8	28.5	30.8	39.0	1.0	8.5
16~24 岁 Age	64	7.8	0.0	54.7	18.8	68.8	71.9	43.8	48.4	1.6	20.3
25~34 岁 Age	89	10.1	0.0	44.9	28.1	29.2	22.5	29.2	37.1	2.2	11.2
35~44 岁 Age	74	2.7	2.7	31.1	21.6	10.8	17.6	31.1	29.7	0.0	1.4
45~54 岁 Age	44	0.0	2.3	38.6	11.4	2.3	9.1	25.0	31.8	0.0	2.3
55~60 岁 Age	24	0.0	0.0	12.5	4.2	0.0	4.2	12.5	62.5	0.0	0.0
女性 Female	297	3.0	0.0	37.0	11.1	2.7	8.4	8.8	30.0	0.7	11.4
16~24 岁 Age	64	4.7	0.0	57.8	14.1	4.7	26.6	14.1	50.0	3.1	29.7
25~34 岁 Age	87	2.3	0.0	31.0	19.5	2.3	1.1	10.3	16.1	0.0	4.6
35~44 岁 Age	76	3.9	0.0	47.4	9.2	2.6	7.9	6.6	28.9	0.0	2.6
45~54 岁 Age	47	2.1	0.0	14.9	0.0	2.1	2.1	6.4	29.8	0.0	14.9
55~60 岁 Age	23	0.0	0.0	13.0	0.0	0.0	0.0	0.0	30.4	0.0	8.7

续前表 continued

	人数 Number	打麻将 mah-jong	游泳 swimming	滚轴溜冰 rolling skating	滑冰 skating	钓鱼 fishing	登山 mountain climbing	听音乐 enjoying music	看电影 going to movie	打游戏机 playing video game	编织裁剪 knitting & tailoring
样本 Sample	**592**	**41.0**	**30.9**	**7.1**	**9.0**	**8.8**	**7.4**	**57.6**	**28.2**	**25.5**	**19.6**
男性 Male	**295**	**48.1**	**34.9**	**8.5**	**11.2**	**13.9**	**7.8**	**55.6**	**28.1**	**34.6**	**1.7**
16~24 岁 Age	64	48.4	43.8	28.1	21.9	4.7	4.7	78.1	62.5	70.3	0.0
25~34 岁 Age	89	59.6	34.8	4.5	12.4	20.2	11.2	51.7	28.1	43.8	2.2
35~44 岁 Age	74	44.6	40.5	4.1	8.1	17.6	5.4	44.6	10.8	20.3	1.4
45~54 岁 Age	44	40.9	25.0	0.0	4.5	9.1	9.1	52.3	11.4	6.8	4.5
55~60 岁 Age	24	29.2	12.5	0.0	0.0	12.5	8.3	50.0	20.8	0.0	0.0
女性 Female	**297**	**34.0**	**26.9**	**5.7**	**6.7**	**3.7**	**7.1**	**59.6**	**28.3**	**16.5**	**37.4**
16~24 岁 Age	64	34.4	45.3	18.8	15.6	4.7	10.9	73.4	56.3	37.5	15.6
25~34 岁 Age	87	41.4	27.6	3.4	8.0	4.6	9.2	62.1	25.3	18.4	36.8
35~44 岁 Age	76	34.2	28.9	2.6	3.9	5.3	6.6	57.9	14.5	6.6	42.1
45~54 岁 Age	47	21.3	10.6	0.0	0.0	0.0	2.1	51.1	27.7	6.4	57.4
55~60 岁 Age	23	30.4	0.0	0.0	0.0	0.0	0.0	34.8	8.7	4.3	43.5

续前表 continued

	人数 Number	种花盆栽 horticulture	看书 reading	绘画书法 drawing & calligraphy	乐器演奏 playing musical instrument	开汽车兜风 going out for a driving	逛街购物 shopping	郊游露营 outing & camping	海外旅行 overseas travel	国内一天以上的旅行 domestic travel
样本 Sample	**592**	**19.6**	**27.7**	**81.3**	**9.1**	**5.9**	**7.3**	**63.7**	**10.1**	**0.8**
男性 Male	**295**	**1.7**	**23.4**	**82.0**	**11.2**	**6.8**	**11.5**	**51.9**	**11.9**	**1.7**
16~24 岁 Age	64	0.0	3.1	90.6	18.8	10.9	4.7	51.6	7.8	1.6
25~34 岁 Age	89	2.2	13.5	82.0	10.1	7.9	16.9	53.9	16.9	3.4
35~44 岁 Age	74	1.4	31.1	75.7	8.1	5.4	13.5	55.4	10.8	0.0
45~54 岁 Age	44	4.5	43.2	84.1	13.6	0.0	9.1	47.7	15.9	2.3
55~60 岁 Age	24	0.0	54.2	75.0	0.0	8.3	8.3	41.7	0.0	0.0
女性 Female	**297**	**37.4**	**32.0**	**80.5**	**7.1**	**5.1**	**3.0**	**75.4**	**8.4**	**0.0**
16~24 岁 Age	64	15.6	20.3	92.2	18.8	15.6	3.1	81.3	7.8	0.0
25~34 岁 Age	87	36.8	23.0	83.9	3.4	1.1	5.7	75.9	6.9	0.0
35~44 岁 Age	76	42.1	31.6	77.6	6.6	3.9	2.6	80.3	10.5	0.0
45~54 岁 Age	47	57.4	46.8	70.2	2.1	2.1	0.0	72.3	12.8	0.0
55~60 岁 Age	23	43.5	69.6	65.2	0.0	0.0	0.0	47.8	0.0	0.0

续前表 continued

	人数 Number	国内一天往返的旅行 short journey that can be back in a day	看展览会 visiting exhibition	听演唱会/音乐会 attending concert	扭秧歌/木兰拳/交谊舞 doing the YangKo	去博物馆或美术馆 going to museum or art gallery	唱卡拉OK karaoke	去动物园或公园 going to park or zoo	酒吧/咖啡屋/茶秀 going to cafe or bar	电脑游戏 playing PC game
样本 Sample	**592**	**20.3**	**17.7**	**18.9**	**12.3**	**7.1**	**8.4**	**47.0**	**44.8**	**9.8**
男性 Male	**295**	**23.7**	**21.0**	**19.7**	**10.5**	**4.4**	**9.5**	**49.2**	**42.4**	**12.9**
16~24 岁 Age	64	17.2	12.5	14.1	12.5	0.0	9.4	56.3	46.9	14.1
25~34 岁 Age	89	33.7	29.2	23.6	11.2	4.5	9.0	56.2	38.2	18.0
35~44 岁 Age	74	24.3	17.6	17.6	9.5	4.1	10.8	50.0	45.9	13.5
45~54 岁 Age	44	13.6	22.7	27.3	11.4	4.5	11.4	43.2	40.9	2.3
55~60 岁 Age	24	20.8	20.8	12.5	4.2	16.7	4.2	12.5	37.5	8.3
女性 Female	**297**	**16.8**	**14.5**	**18.2**	**14.1**	**9.8**	**7.4**	**44.8**	**47.1**	**6.7**
16~24 岁 Age	64	21.9	10.9	25.0	21.9	7.8	15.6	56.3	45.3	10.9
25~34 岁 Age	87	13.8	12.6	14.9	13.8	5.7	4.6	50.6	43.7	8.0
35~44 岁 Age	76	19.7	23.7	19.7	13.2	10.5	6.6	50.0	55.3	6.6
45~54 岁 Age	47	14.9	12.8	14.9	8.5	10.6	4.3	27.7	44.7	2.1
55~60 岁 Age	23	8.7	4.3	13.0	8.7	26.1	4.3	8.7	43.5	0.0

4-4 样本、男性各年龄层、女性各年龄层想做的活动/ Desired Activities by the Whole Sample, Age and Gender Groups

注：本题为多选题，合计百分比超过 100%（Multiple answers）

	人数 Number	打网球 tennis	打高尔夫球 golf	打羽毛球 bad-minton	打保龄球 bowling	踢足球 soccer	打篮球 basket ball	打乒乓球 table tennis	慢跑 jogging	玩滑板 skate boarding	跳迪斯科 disco
样本 Sample	498	24.7	17.3	9.8	26.1	7.6	5.2	9.0	12.4	8.0	6.6
男性 Male	253	26.5	20.9	11.5	31.2	13.0	7.1	10.7	12.3	10.3	5.1
16~24 岁 Age	62	38.7	25.8	11.3	33.9	11.3	9.7	11.3	4.8	27.4	11.3
25~34 岁 Age	79	30.4	26.6	12.7	41.8	17.7	8.9	17.7	13.9	10.1	5.1
35~44 岁 Age	63	23.8	19.0	15.9	28.6	12.7	3.2	4.8	15.9	1.6	1.6
45~54 岁 Age	34	11.8	11.8	2.9	14.7	8.8	8.8	5.9	20.6	0.0	0.0
55~60 岁 Age	15	0.0	0.0	6.7	13.3	6.7	0.0	6.7	0.0	0.0	6.7
女性 Female	245	22.9	13.5	8.2	20.8	2.0	3.3	7.3	12.7	5.7	8.2
16~24 岁 Age	60	43.3	25.0	13.3	43.3	3.3	6.7	8.3	11.7	16.7	16.7
25~34 岁 Age	77	27.3	13.0	9.1	14.3	0.0	2.6	10.4	13.0	1.3	5.2
35~44 岁 Age	59	11.9	13.6	5.1	16.9	5.1	3.4	5.1	15.3	3.4	6.8
45~54 岁 Age	38	5.3	0.0	2.6	7.9	0.0	0.0	5.3	10.5	2.6	2.6
55~60 岁 Age	11	0.0	0.0	9.1	9.1	0.0	0.0	0.0	9.1	0.0	9.1

续前表 continued

	人数 Number	打麻将 mah-jong	游泳 swim-ming	滚轴溜冰 rolling skating	滑冰 skating	钓鱼 fishing	登山 mountain climbing	听音乐 enjoy-ing music	看电影 going to movie	打游戏机 playing video game	编织裁剪 knitting & tailoring
样本 Sample	498	7.2	19.9	3.2	12.0	16.9	24.7	10.4	13.3	3.0	4.6
男性 Male	253	7.5	18.6	4.7	11.9	22.5	28.9	8.7	11.5	3.2	1.2
16~24 岁 Age	62	4.8	21.0	8.1	19.4	25.3	43.5	8.1	8.1	1.6	3.2
25~34 岁 Age	79	6.3	25.3	7.6	12.7	27.3	35.4	11.4	19.0	5.1	1.3
35~44 岁 Age	63	12.7	15.9	1.6	9.5	15.9	17.5	6.3	9.5	4.8	0.0
45~54 岁 Age	34	8.8	8.8	0.0	5.9	17.6	17.6	8.8	5.9	0.0	0.0
55~60 岁 Age	15	0.0	6.7	0.0	0.0	20.0	6.7	6.7	6.7	0.0	0.0
女性 Female	245	6.9	21.2	1.6	12.2	11.0	20.4	12.2	15.1	2.9	8.2
16~24 岁 Age	60	3.3	25.0	6.7	23.3	23.3	36.7	8.3	15.0	5.0	11.7
25~34 岁 Age	77	6.5	26.0	0.0	13.0	6.5	16.9	9.1	14.3	1.3	5.2
35~44 岁 Age	59	10.2	23.7	0.0	6.8	8.5	16.9	22.0	18.6	5.1	6.8
45~54 岁 Age	38	7.9	7.9	0.0	5.3	5.3	13.2	7.9	7.9	0.0	10.5
55~60 岁 Age	11	9.1	0.0	0.0	0.0	9.1	0.0	18.2	27.3	0.0	9.1

续前表 continued

	人数 Number	种花盆栽 horti-culture	看书 reading	绘画书法 drawing & calligraphy	乐器演奏 playing musical instru-ment	开汽车兜风 going out for a driving	逛街购物 shopping	郊游露营 outing & camping	海外旅行 overseas travel	国内一天以上的旅行 domestic travel
样本 Sample	498	4.6	11.4	4.0	9.8	7.6	27.1	6.0	32.5	33.3
男性 Male	253	1.2	9.1	4.3	11.1	9.5	29.6	5.9	31.2	32.4
16~24 岁 Age	62	3.2	6.5	0.0	12.9	19.4	46.8	3.2	43.5	38.7
25~34 岁 Age	79	1.3	10.1	3.8	12.7	10.1	30.4	6.3	29.1	36.7
35~44 岁 Age	63	0.0	11.1	7.9	11.1	4.8	27.0	6.3	27.0	27.0
45~54 岁 Age	34	0.0	2.9	8.8	2.9	2.9	14.7	8.8	26.5	26.5
55~60 岁 Age	15	0.0	20.0	0.0	13.3	0.0	0.0	6.7	20.0	20.0
女性 Female	245	8.2	13.9	3.7	8.6	5.7	24.5	6.1	33.9	34.3
16~24 岁 Age	60	11.7	18.3	1.7	13.3	15.0	51.7	5.0	53.3	48.3
25~34 岁 Age	77	5.2	10.4	7.8	7.8	0.0	24.7	7.8	27.3	32.5
35~44 岁 Age	59	6.8	13.6	1.7	3.4	5.1	11.9	6.8	28.8	33.9
45~54 岁 Age	38	10.5	10.5	2.6	5.3	5.3	2.6	2.6	23.7	23.7
55~60 岁 Age	11	9.1	27.3	0.0	27.3	0.0	18.2	9.1	36.4	9.1

续前表 continued

	人数 Number	国内一天往返的旅行 short journey that can be back in a day	看展览会 visiting exhibition	听演唱会/音乐会 attending concert	扭秧歌/木兰拳/交谊舞 doing the YangKo	去博物馆或美术馆 going to museum or art gallery	唱卡拉OK karaoke	去动物园或公园 going to park or zoo	酒吧/咖啡屋/茶秀 going to cafe or bar	电脑游戏 playing PC game
样本 Sample	498	33.7	24.7	16.9	24.3	5.6	12.9	9.8	11.4	10.8
男性 Male	253	31.6	24.5	18.2	25.3	3.6	12.6	9.1	12.3	12.3
16~24 岁 Age	62	27.4	21.0	24.2	35.5	1.6	17.7	11.3	9.7	22.6
25~34 岁 Age	79	36.7	21.5	17.7	29.1	1.3	16.5	11.4	12.7	13.9
35~44 岁 Age	63	25.4	20.6	15.9	19.0	4.8	6.3	4.8	9.5	6.3
45~54 岁 Age	34	35.3	35.3	8.8	11.8	5.9	5.9	2.9	14.7	5.9
55~60 岁 Age	15	40.0	46.7	26.7	20.0	13.3	13.3	20.0	26.7	0.0
女性 Female	245	35.9	24.9	15.5	23.3	7.8	13.1	10.6	10.6	9.4
16~24 岁 Age	60	31.7	31.7	13.3	28.3	3.3	18.3	11.7	6.7	26.7
25~34 岁 Age	77	42.9	26.0	11.7	19.5	2.6	11.7	10.4	11.7	5.2
35~44 岁 Age	59	28.8	20.3	15.3	22.0	10.2	6.8	13.6	8.5	1.7
45~54 岁 Age	38	31.6	18.4	26.3	21.1	21.1	18.4	5.3	15.8	5.3
55~60 岁 Age	11	63.6	27.3	18.2	36.4	9.1	9.1	9.1	18.2	0.0

4-5 不同消费者层常做的休闲活动/ Frequently Engaged Activities by Market Segments

4-5-1 时尚流行指标/ Fads Popular Index

注：本题为多选题，合计百分比超过 100%（Multiple answers）

	人数 Number	打网球 tennis	打高尔夫球 golf	打羽毛球 bad-minton	打保龄球 bowling	踢足球 soccer	打篮球 basket ball	打乒乓球 table tennis	慢跑 jogging	玩滑板 skate boarding	跳迪斯科 disco
样本 Sample	592	4.2	0.5	38.5	15.5	14.7	18.4	19.8	34.5	0.8	10.0
平实生活指向 simple living orientation	286	2.8	0.7	33.6	9.8	11.5	14.7	18.5	29.7	0.3	3.1
时尚流行指向 fashion orientation	306	5.6	0.3	43.1	20.9	17.6	21.9	20.9	38.9	1.3	16.3

续前表 continued

	人数 Number	打麻将 mah-jong	游泳 swim-ming	滚轴溜冰 rolling skating	滑冰 skating	钓鱼 fishing	登山 mountain climbing	听音乐 enjoying music	看电影 going to movie	打游戏机 playing video game	编织裁剪 knitting & tailoring
样本 Sample	592	41.0	30.9	7.1	9.0	8.8	7.4	57.6	28.2	25.5	19.6
平实生活指向 simple living orientation	286	32.9	25.2	3.5	6.6	8.4	5.6	51.7	23.1	19.6	17.1
时尚流行指向 fashion orientation	306	48.7	36.3	10.5	11.1	9.2	9.2	63.1	33.0	31.0	21.9

续前表 continued

	人数 Number	种花盆栽 horti-culture	看书 reading	绘画书法 drawing & calligraphy	乐器演奏 playing musical instru-ment	开汽车兜风 going out for a driving	逛街购物 shopping	郊游露营 outing & camping	海外旅行 overseas travel	国内一天以上的旅行 domestic travel
样本 Sample	592	19.6	27.7	81.3	9.1	5.9	7.3	63.7	10.1	0.8
平实生活指向 simple living orientation	286	17.1	29.7	80.1	9.1	6.3	5.2	51.7	8.4	0.0
时尚流行指向 fashion orientation	306	21.9	25.8	82.4	9.2	5.6	9.2	74.8	11.8	1.6

续前表 continued

	人数 Number	国内一天往返的旅行 short journey that can be back in a day	看展览会 visiting exhibition	听演唱会/音乐会 attending concert	扭秧歌/木兰拳/交谊舞 doing the Yang Ko	去博物馆或美术馆 going to museum or art gallery	唱卡拉OK karaoke	去动物园或公园 going to park or zoo	酒吧/咖啡屋/茶秀 going to cafe or bar	电脑游戏 playing PC game
样本 Sample	592	20.3	17.7	18.9	12.3	7.1	8.4	47.0	44.8	19.3
平实生活指向 simple living orientation	286	14.3	16.1	16.1	8.7	6.6	7.0	31.8	39.2	16.4
时尚流行指向 fashion orientation	306	25.8	19.3	21.6	15.7	7.5	9.8	61.1	50.0	21.9

4-5-2 信息交流指标/ Information Communication Index

注：本题为多选题，合计百分比超过 100%（Multiple answers）

	人数 Number	打网球 tennis	打高尔夫球 golf	打羽毛球 bad-minton	打保龄球 bowling	踢足球 soccer	打篮球 basket ball	打乒乓球 table tennis	慢跑 jogging	玩滑板 skate boarding	跳迪斯科 disco
样本 Sample	591	4.2	0.5	38.4	15.6	14.7	18.4	19.8	34.5	0.8	10.0
信息消极指向 negative orientation	54	0.0	0.0	27.8	7.4	13.0	16.7	14.8	25.9	0.0	5.6
中间层 medium	308	4.9	0.6	39.6	14.6	14.6	18.5	21.1	32.8	0.6	9.7
信息积极指向 active orientation	229	4.4	0.4	39.3	18.8	15.3	18.8	19.2	38.9	1.3	11.4

续前表 continued

	人数 Number	打麻将 mah-jong	游泳 swim-ming	滚轴溜冰 rolling skating	滑冰 skating	钓鱼 fishing	登山 mountain climbing	听音乐 enjoying music	看电影 going to movie	打游戏机 playing video game	编织裁剪 knitting & tailoring
样本 Sample	591	40.9	30.8	7.1	9.0	8.3	7.4	57.7	28.3	25.5	19.6
信息消极指向 negative orientation	54	31.5	27.8	1.9	9.3	5.6	1.9	46.3	24.1	18.5	16.7
中间层 medium	308	42.2	28.9	8.4	9.4	6.8	6.2	57.8	30.5	27.3	21.4
信息积极指向 active orientation	229	41.5	34.1	6.6	8.3	12.2	10.5	60.3	26.2	24.9	17.9

续前表 continued

	人数 Number	种花盆栽 horti culture	看书 reading	绘画书法 drawing & calligraphy	乐器演奏 playing musical instru-ment	开汽车兜风 going out for a driving	逛街购物 shopping	郊游露营 outing & camping	海外旅行 overseas travel	国内一天以上的旅行 domestic travel
样本 Sample	591	19.6	27.7	81.2	9.0	5.8	7.3	63.8	10.2	0.8
信息消极指向 negative orientation	54	16.7	11.1	79.6	7.4	3.7	3.7	57.4	3.7	0.0
中间层 medium	308	21.4	25.6	81.2	10.1	6.5	6.8	64.9	9.1	0.6
信息积极指向 active orientation	229	17.9	34.5	81.7	7.9	5.2	8.7	63.8	13.1	1.3

续前表 continued

	人数 Number	国内一天往返的旅行 short journey that can be back in a day	看展览会 visiting exhibition	听演唱会/音乐会 attending concert	扭秧歌/木兰拳/交谊舞 doing the Yang Ko	去博物馆或美术馆 going to museum or art gallery	唱卡拉OK karaoke	去动物园或公园 going to park or zoo	酒吧/咖啡屋/茶秀 going to cafe or bar	电脑游戏 playing PC game
样本 Sample	591	20.3	17.8	19.0	12.4	7.1	8.5	47.0	44.7	19.3
信息消极指向 negative orientation	54	11.1	13.0	11.1	9.3	3.7	1.9	25.9	31.5	11.1
中间层 medium	308	17.5	16.2	16.6	12.3	5.2	8.8	47.4	43.8	22.1
信息积极指向 active orientation	229	26.2	21.0	24.0	13.1	10.5	9.6	51.5	48.9	17.5

4-6 不同消费者层想做的休闲活动/ Desired Activities by Market Segments

4-6-1 时尚流行指标/ Fads Popular Index

注：本题为多选题，合计百分比超过 100%（Multiple answers）

	人数 Number	打网球 tennis	打高尔夫球 golf	打羽毛球 bad minton	打保龄球 bowling	踢足球 soccer	打篮球 basket ball	打乒乓球 table tennis	慢跑 jogging	玩滑板 skate boarding	跳迪斯科 disco
样本 Sample	498	24.7	17.3	9.8	26.1	7.6	5.2	9.0	12.4	8.0	6.6
平实生活指向 simple living orientation	230	20.9	12.6	7.8	25.7	8.7	6.1	10.9	13.9	4.8	3.9
时尚流行指向 fashion orientation	268	28.0	21.3	11.6	26.5	6.7	4.5	7.5	11.2	10.8	9.0

续前表 continued

	人数 Number	打麻将 mah-jong	游泳 swim-ming	滚轴溜冰 rolling skating	滑冰 skating	钓鱼 fishing	登山 mountain climbing	听音乐 enjoying music	看电影 going to movie	打游戏机 playing video game	编织裁剪 knitting & tailoring
样本 Sample	498	7.2	19.9	3.2	12.0	16.9	24.7	10.4	13.3	3.0	4.6
平实生活指向 simple living orientation	230	8.3	16.5	3.5	9.6	15.7	21.7	11.7	14.3	3.0	5.7
时尚流行指向 fashion orientation	268	6.3	22.8	3.0	14.2	17.9	27.2	9.3	12.3	3.0	3.7

续前表 continued

	人数 Number	种花盆栽 horti-culture	看书 reading	绘画书法 drawing & calligraphy	乐器演奏 playing musical instrument	开汽车兜风 going out for a driving	逛街购物 shopping	郊游露营 outing & camping	海外旅行 overseas travel	国内一天以上的旅行 domestic travel
样本 Sample	498	4.6	11.4	4.0	9.8	7.6	27.1	6.0	32.5	33.3
平实生活指向 simple living orientation	230	5.7	10.0	5.2	9.6	7.0	23.5	6.1	29.6	28.3
时尚流行指向 fashion orientation	268	3.7	12.7	3.0	10.1	8.2	30.2	6.0	35.1	37.7

续前表 continued

	人数 Number	国内一天往返的旅行 short journey that can be back in a day	看展览会 visiting exhibition	听演唱会/音乐会 attending concert	扭秧歌/木兰拳/交谊舞 doing the Yang Ko	去博物馆或美术馆 going to museum or art gallery	唱卡拉OK karaoke	去动物园或公园 going to park or zoo	酒吧/咖啡屋/茶秀 going to cafe or bar	电脑游戏 playing PC game
样本 Sample	498	33.7	24.7	16.9	24.3	5.6	12.9	9.8	11.4	9.0
平实生活指向 simple living orientation	230	34.8	27.0	17.0	22.6	4.8	14.3	9.6	14.8	7.8
时尚流行指向 fashion orientation	268	32.8	22.8	16.8	25.7	6.3	11.6	10.1	8.6	10.1

4-6-2 信息交流指标/ Information Communication Index

注：本题为多选题，合计百分比超过 100%（Multiple answers）

	人数 Number	打网球 tennis	打高尔夫球 golf	打羽毛球 bad-minton	打保龄球 bowling	踢足球 soccer	打篮球 basket ball	打乒乓球 table tennis	慢跑 jogging	玩滑板 skate boarding	跳迪斯科 disco
样本 Sample	497	24.5	17.1	9.9	26.0	7.6	5.2	8.9	12.3	8.0	6.4
信息消极指向 negative orientation	41	29.3	12.2	17.1	31.7	9.8	7.3	14.6	17.1	7.3	7.3
中间层 medium	259	24.7	18.5	9.7	27.4	8.1	6.2	9.3	10.4	8.5	6.9
信息积极指向 active orientation	197	23.4	16.2	8.6	22.8	6.6	3.6	7.1	13.7	7.6	5.6

续前表 continued

	人数 Number	打麻将 mah-jong	游泳 swim-ming	滚轴溜冰 rolling skating	滑冰 skating	钓鱼 fishing	登山 mountain climbing	听音乐 enjoying music	看电影 going to movie	打游戏机 playing video game	编织裁剪 knitting & tailoring
样本 Sample	497	7.2	19.9	3.2	11.9	16.7	24.5	10.3	13.1	3.0	4.6
信息消极指向 negative orientation	41	9.8	22.0	7.3	12.2	26.8	24.4	14.6	19.5	7.3	4.9
中间层 medium	259	4.6	21.2	3.5	13.9	15.8	27.4	11.6	10.8	1.9	2.7
信息积极指向 active orientation	197	10.2	17.8	2.0	9.1	15.7	20.8	7.6	14.7	3.6	7.1

续前表 continued

	人数 Number	种花盆栽 horti-culture	看书 reading	绘画书法 drawing & calligraphy	乐器演奏 playing musical instru-ment	开汽车兜风 going out for a driving	逛街购物 shopping	郊游露营 outing & camping	海外旅行 overseas travel	国内一天以上的旅行 domestic travel
样本 Sample	497	4.6	11.3	4.0	9.9	7.6	27.0	6.0	32.4	33.2
信息消极指向 negative orientation	41	4.9	12.2	4.9	4.9	4.9	34.1	4.9	36.6	39.0
中间层 medium	259	2.7	9.7	2.3	8.1	7.7	28.2	6.2	35.9	35.1
信息积极指向 active orientation	197	7.1	13.2	6.1	13.2	8.1	23.9	6.1	26.9	29.4

续前表 continued

	人数 Number	国内一天往返的旅行 short journey that can be back in a day	看展览会 visiting exhibition	听演唱会/音乐会 attending concert	扭秧歌/木兰拳/交谊舞 doing the Yang Ko	去博物馆或美术馆 going to museum or art gallery	唱卡拉OK karaoke	去动物园或公园 going to park or zoo	酒吧/咖啡屋/茶秀 going to cafe or bar	电脑游戏 playing PC game
样本 Sample	497	33.6	24.5	16.7	24.1	5.4	12.7	9.7	11.5	8.9
信息消极指向 negative orientation	41	26.8	29.3	12.2	17.1	7.3	9.8	12.2	12.2	12.2
中间层 medium	259	35.5	24.3	18.5	27.0	4.2	14.7	9.7	11.2	9.7
信息积极指向 active orientation	197	32.5	23.9	15.2	21.8	6.6	10.7	9.1	11.7	7.1

5. 旅游 / Travel

● 北京 / Beijing

5-1 最近一年内是否外出旅游过的比例/ Proportion of the Sample Traveling Out or Not Last Year

	人数 Number	百分比 Percent
是 yes	482	47.7
否 no	529	52.3

n=1011

5-2 样本、男性各年龄层、女性各年龄层最近一年内是否外出旅游过/ Traveling Out or Not Last Year by the Whole Sample, Age and Gender Groups

	人数 Number	是 yes	否 no
样本 Sample	1011	47.7	52.3
男性 Male	504	44.0	56.0
16~24 岁 Age	105	41.0	59.0
25~34 岁 Age	151	47.7	52.3
35~44 岁 Age	131	46.6	53.4
45~54 岁 Age	77	39.0	61.0
55~60 岁 Age	40	40.0	60.0
女性 Female	507	51.3	48.7
16~24 岁 Age	108	59.3	40.7
25~34 岁 Age	150	54.7	45.3
35~44 岁 Age	124	48.4	51.6
45~54 岁 Age	84	39.3	60.7
55~60 岁 Age	41	51.2	48.8

5-3 旅游的地区/ Area Visited Last Year

注：本题为多选题，合计百分比超过 100%（Multiple answers）

	人次 Person-time	百分比 Percent
省内 in the province	336	70.4
省外 out of the province	285	59.7
海外 overseas	25	5.2

n=477

5-4 旅游的次数/ Number of Trips Taken Last Year

5-4-1 旅游的次数（省内）/ Number of Trips Taken Last Year (in the Province)

	人数 Number	百分比 Percent
1 次 once	97	28.9
2 次 twice	79	23.5
3 次 times	69	20.5
4-5 次 times	40	11.9
6 次及以上 6 times or over	51	15.2

n=336

5-4-2 旅游的次数（省外）/ Number of Trips Taken Last Year (out of the Province)

	人数 Number	百分比 Percent
1 次 once	165	57.9
2 次 twice	75	26.3
3 次 times	24	8.4
4-5 次 times	13	4.6
6 次及以上 6 times or over	8	2.8

n=285

5-4-3 旅游的次数（海外）/ Number of Trips Taken Last Year (overseas)

	人数 Number	百分比 Percent
1 次 once	18	72.0
2 次 twice	4	16.0
3 次 times	3	12.0
4-5 次 times	0	0.0
6 次及以上 6 times or over	0	0.0

n=25

5-5 样本、男性各年龄层、女性各年龄层最近一年内旅游是和谁一起去的/ With Whom When Traveling Last Year by the Whole Sample, Age and Gender Groups

注：本题为多选题，合计百分比超过 100%（Multiple answers）

	人数 Number	自己一个人 single	和家人 with family members	和朋友/同事/同学 with friends or colleagues or classmates	其他 others
样本 Sample	480	8.5	62.3	54.0	0.4
男性 Male	222	12.6	56.3	57.7	0.9
16~24 岁 Age	43	7.0	39.5	83.7	0.0
25~34 岁 Age	72	12.5	51.4	59.7	1.4
35~44 岁 Age	61	13.1	67.2	47.5	0.0
45~54 岁 Age	30	16.7	63.3	50.0	3.3
55~60 岁 Age	16	18.8	68.8	31.3	0.0
女性 Female	258	5.0	67.4	50.8	0.0
16~24 岁 Age	63	1.6	55.6	66.7	0.0
25~34 岁 Age	81	1.2	70.4	51.9	0.0
35~44 岁 Age	60	8.3	71.7	46.7	0.0
45~54 岁 Age	33	12.1	69.7	39.4	0.0
55~60 岁 Age	21	9.5	76.2	28.6	0.0

5-6 最近一年内旅游是否参加了旅游团/ Whether Having Attended Touring Party Last Year

	人数 Number	百分比 Percent
是 yes	68	14.4
否 no	405	85.6

n=473

5-7 样本、男性各年龄层、女性各年龄层未来一年内是否打算外出旅游/ Whether to Plan to Travel Next Year by the Whole Sample, Age and Gender Groups

	人数 Number	是 yes	否 no
样本 Sample	1005	60.0	40.0
男性 Male	502	60.8	39.2
16~24 岁 Age	103	60.2	39.8
25~34 岁 Age	151	72.2	27.8
35~44 岁 Age	131	61.8	38.2
45~54 岁 Age	77	46.8	53.2
55~60 岁 Age	40	42.5	57.5
女性 Female	503	59.2	40.8
16~24 岁 Age	107	64.5	35.5
25~34 岁 Age	149	71.8	28.2
35~44 岁 Age	124	55.6	44.4
45~54 岁 Age	82	40.2	59.8
55~60 岁 Age	41	48.8	51.2

5-8 未来一年内打算旅游的地区/ Area Planned to Travel Next Year

注：本题为多选题，合计百分比超过 100%（Multiple answers）

	人次 Person-time	百分比 Percent
省内 in the province	183	30.4
省外 out of the province	469	78.0
海外(含台港澳及国外) overseas	104	17.3

n=601

5-9 未来一年内旅游是否打算参加旅游团/ Whether to Attend Touring Party in the Planned Trip Next Year

	人数 Number	百分比 Percent
是 yes	137	22.8
否 no	296	49.3
不一定 indefinite	167	27.8

n=600

5-10 不同消费者层最近一年内是否外出旅游过的比例/ Proportion of the Sample Traveling Out or Not Last Year by Market Segments

5-10-1 时尚流行指标 Fads Popular Index

	人数 Number	是 yes	否 no
样本 Sample	997	47.7	52.3
平实生活指向 simple living orientation	490	43.7	56.3
时尚流行指向 fashion orientation	507	51.7	48.3

5-10-2 信息交流指标/ Information Communication Index

	人数 Number	是 yes	否 no
样本 Sample	1003	47.9	52.1
信息消极指向 negative orientation	63	28.6	71.4
中间层 medium	523	47.8	52.2
信息积极指向 active orientation	417	50.8	49.2

5-11 不同消费者层未来一年内是否打算外出旅游的比例/ Whether to Plan to Travel Next Year by Market Segments

5-11-1 时尚流行指标 Fads Popular Index

	人数 Number	是 yes	否 no
样本 Sample	991	60.0	40.0
平实生活指向 simple living orientation	488	52.9	47.1
时尚流行指向 fashion orientation	503	67.0	33.0

5-11-2 信息交流指标/ Information Communication Index

	人数 Number	是 yes	否 no
样本 Sample	997	60.3	39.7
信息消极指向 negative orientation	63	36.5	63.5
中间层 medium	519	61.5	38.5
信息积极指向 active orientation	415	62.4	37.6

● 上海 / Shanghai

5-1 最近一年内是否外出旅游过的比例/ Proportion of the Sample Traveling Out or Not Last Year

	人数 Number	百分比 Percent
是 yes	366	36.2
否 no	646	63.8

n=1012

5-2 样本、男性各年龄层、女性各年龄层最近一年内是否外出旅游过/ Traveling Out or Not Last Year by the Whole Sample, Age and Gender Groups

	人数 Number	是 yes	否 no
样本 Sample	1012	36.2	63.8
男性 Male	508	36.4	63.6
16~24 岁 Age	109	37.6	62.4
25~34 岁 Age	146	43.8	56.2
35~44 岁 Age	130	26.2	73.8
45~54 岁 Age	84	41.7	58.3
55~60 岁 Age	39	28.2	71.8
女性 Female	504	35.9	64.1
16~24 岁 Age	107	42.1	57.9
25~34 岁 Age	144	44.4	55.6
35~44 岁 Age	130	29.2	70.8
45~54 岁 Age	82	28.0	72.0
55~60 岁 Age	41	26.8	73.2

5-3 旅游的地区/ Area Visited Last Year

注：本题为多选题，合计百分比超过 100%（Multiple answers）

	人次 Person-time	百分比 Percent
省内 in the province	120	33.1
省外 out of the province	299	82.6
海外 overseas	21	5.8

n=362

5-4 旅游的次数/ Number of Trips Taken Last Year

5-4-1 旅游的次数（省内）/ Number of Trips Taken Last Year (in the Province)

	人数 Number	百分比 Percent
1 次 once	53	44.2
2 次 twice	33	27.5
3 次 times	19	15.8
4-5 次 times	11	9.2
6 次及以上 6 times or over	4	3.3

n=120

5-4-2 旅游的次数（省外）/ Number of Trips Taken Last Year (out of the Province)

	人数 Number	百分比 Percent
1 次 once	136	45.5
2 次 twice	104	34.8
3 次 times	29	9.7
4-5 次 times	24	8.0
6 次及以上 6 times or over	6	2.0

n=299

5-4-3 旅游的次数（海外）/ Number of Trips Taken Last Year (overseas)

	人数 Number	百分比 Percent
1 次 once	15	71.4
2 次 twice	5	23.8
3 次 times	1	4.8
4-5 次 times	0	0.0
6 次及以上 6 times or over	0	0.0

n=21

5-5 样本、男性各年龄层、女性各年龄层最近一年内旅游是和谁一起去的/ With Whom When Traveling Last Year by the Whole Sample, Age and Gender Groups

注：本题为多选题，合计百分比超过 100%（Multiple answers）

	人数 Number	自己一个人 single	和家人 with family members	和朋友/同事/同学 with friends or colleagues or classmates	其他 others
样本 Sample	365	6.3	55.1	54.0	0.8
男性 Male	184	8.2	48.4	59.2	1.1
16~24 岁 Age	41	0.0	46.3	65.9	0.0
25~34 岁 Age	64	9.4	39.1	68.8	1.6
35~44 岁 Age	34	11.8	61.8	58.8	0.0
45~54 岁 Age	34	11.8	50.0	44.1	0.0
55~60 岁 Age	11	9.1	63.6	27.3	9.1
女性 Female	181	4.4	61.9	48.6	0.6
16~24 岁 Age	45	2.2	46.7	66.7	2.2
25~34 岁 Age	64	6.3	56.3	53.1	0.0
35~44 岁 Age	38	0.0	81.6	23.7	0.0
45~54 岁 Age	23	8.7	78.3	39.1	0.0
55~60 岁 Age	11	9.1	54.5	54.5	0.0

5-6 最近一年内旅游是否参加了旅游团/ Whether Having Attended Touring Party Last Year

	人数 Number	百分比 Percent
是 yes	84	23.6
否 no	272	76.4

n=356

5-7 样本、男性各年龄层、女性各年龄层未来一年内是否打算外出旅游/ Whether to Plan to Travel Next Year by the Whole Sample, Age and Gender Groups

	人数 Number	是 yes	否 no
样本 Sample	1014	52.2	47.8
男性 Male	509	55.0	45.0
16~24 岁 Age	109	48.6	51.4
25~34 岁 Age	146	61.0	39.0
35~44 岁 Age	130	56.9	43.1
45~54 岁 Age	85	54.1	45.9
55~60 岁 Age	39	46.2	53.8
女性 Female	505	49.3	50.7
16~24 岁 Age	108	62.0	38.0
25~34 岁 Age	144	59.0	41.0
35~44 岁 Age	130	43.8	56.2
45~54 岁 Age	82	34.1	65.9
55~60 岁 Age	41	29.3	70.7

5-8 未来一年内打算旅游的地区/ Area Planned to Travel Next Year

注：本题为多选题，合计百分比超过 100%（Multiple answers）

	人次 Person-time	百分比 Percent
省内 in the province	79	15.0
省外 out of the province	434	82.2
海外(含台港澳及国外) overseas	122	23.1

n=528

5-9 未来一年内旅游是否打算参加旅游团/ Whether to Attend Touring Party in the Planned Trip Next Year

	人数 Number	百分比 Percent
是 yes	169	32.1
否 no	190	36.1
不一定 indefinite	168	31.9

n=527

5-10 不同消费者层最近一年内是否外出旅游过的比例/ Proportion of the Sample Traveling Out or Not Last Year by Market Segments

5-10-1 时尚流行指标 Fads Popular Index

	人数 Number	是 yes	否 no
样本 Sample	**1003**	**36.1**	**63.9**
平实生活指向 simple living orientation	469	30.5	69.5
时尚流行指向 fashion orientation	534	41.0	59.0

5-10-2 信息交流指标/ Information Communication Index

	人数 Number	是 yes	否 no
样本 Sample	**1003**	**36.4**	**63.6**
信息消极指向 negative orientation	55	20.0	80.0
中间层 medium	574	35.0	65.0
信息积极指向 active orientation	374	40.9	59.1

5-11 不同消费者层未来一年内是否打算外出旅游的比例/ Whether to Planning to Travel Next Year by Market Segments

5-11-1 时尚流行指标 Fads Popular Index

	人数 Number	是 yes	否 no
样本 Sample	**1005**	**52.1**	**47.9**
平实生活指向 simple living orientation	471	47.6	52.4
时尚流行指向 fashion orientation	534	56.2	43.8

5-11-2 信息交流指标/ Information Communication Index

	人数 Number	是 yes	否 no
样本 Sample	**1005**	**52.3**	**47.7**
信息消极指向 negative orientation	55	32.7	67.3
中间层 medium	576	50.3	49.7
信息积极指向 active orientation	374	58.3	41.7

● 广州 / Guangzhou

5-1 最近一年内是否外出过的比例/ Proportion of the Sample Traveling Out or Not Last Year

	人数 Number	百分比 Percent
是 yes	409	39.6
否 no	625	60.4

n=1034

5-2 样本、男性各年龄层、女性各年龄层最近一年内是否外出旅游过/ Traveling Out or Not Last Year by the Whole Sample, Age and Gender Groups

	人数 Number	是 yes	否 no
样本 Sample	1034	39.6	60.4
男性 Male	499	36.1	63.9
16~24 岁 Age	106	46.2	53.8
25~34 岁 Age	150	34.7	65.3
35~44 岁 Age	127	29.9	70.1
45~54 岁 Age	73	32.9	67.1
55~60 岁 Age	43	39.5	60.5
女性 Female	535	42.8	57.2
16~24 岁 Age	112	53.6	46.4
25~34 岁 Age	158	47.5	52.5
35~44 岁 Age	137	40.1	59.9
45~54 岁 Age	87	29.9	70.1
55~60 岁 Age	41	31.7	68.3

5-3 旅游的地区/ Area Visited Last Year

注：本题为多选题，合计百分比超过 100%（Multiple answers）

	人次 Person-time	百分比 Percent
省内 in the province	315	79.3
省外 out of the province	160	40.3
海外 overseas	37	9.3

n=397

5-4 旅游的次数/ Number of Trips Taken Last Year

5-4-1 旅游的次数（省内）/ Number of Trips Taken Last Year (in the Province)

	人数 Number	百分比 Percent
1 次 once	147	46.7
2 次 twice	89	28.3
3 次 times	42	13.3
4-5 次 times	30	9.5
6 次及以上 6 times or over	7	2.2

n=315

5-4-2 旅游的次数（省外）/ Number of Trips Taken Last Year (out of the Province)

	人数 Number	百分比 Percent
1 次 once	108	67.5
2 次 twice	43	26.9
3 次 times	6	3.8
4-5 次 times	3	1.9
6 次及以上 6 times or over	0	0.0

n=160

5-4-3 旅游的次数（海外）/ Number of Trips Taken Last Year (overseas)

	人数 Number	百分比 Percent
1 次 once	26	70.3
2 次 twice	5	13.5
3 次 times	6	16.2
4-5 次 times	0	0.0
6 次及以上 6 times or over	0	0.0

n=37

5-5 样本、男性各年龄层、女性各年龄层最近一年内旅游是和谁一起去的/ With Whom When Traveling Last Year by the Whole Sample, Age and Gender Groups

注：本题为多选题，合计百分比超过 100%（Multiple answers）

	人数 Number	自己一个人 single	和家人 with family members	和朋友/同事/同学 with friends or colleagues or classmates	其他 others
样本 Sample	401	9.5	50.9	56.1	0.7
男性 Male	177	12.4	40.7	64.4	1.1
16~24 岁 Age	48	16.7	27.1	70.8	0.0
25~34 岁 Age	52	9.6	32.7	75.0	1.9
35~44 岁 Age	37	10.8	59.5	48.6	0.0
45~54 岁 Age	23	0.0	39.1	65.2	4.3
55~60 岁 Age	17	29.4	64.7	47.1	0.0
女性 Female	224	7.1	58.9	49.6	0.4
16~24 岁 Age	59	3.4	44.1	67.8	1.7
25~34 岁 Age	74	12.2	60.8	45.9	0.0
35~44 岁 Age	54	9.3	70.4	33.3	0.0
45~54 岁 Age	25	0.0	56.0	52.0	0.0
55~60 岁 Age	12	0.0	75.0	50.0	0.0

5-6 最近一年内旅游是否参加了旅游团/ Whether Having Attended Touring Party Last Year

	人数 Number	百分比 Percent
是 yes	162	40.6
否 no	237	59.4

n=399

5-7 样本、男性各年龄层、女性各年龄层未来一年内是否打算外出旅游/ Whether to Planning to Travel Next Year by the Whole Sample, Age and Gender Groups

	人数 Number	是 yes	否 no
样本 Sample	1033	52.8	47.2
男性 Male	498	51.0	49.0
16~24 岁 Age	106	53.8	46.2
25~34 岁 Age	150	57.3	42.7
35~44 岁 Age	126	50.0	50.0
45~54 岁 Age	73	39.7	60.3
55~60 岁 Age	43	44.2	55.8
女性 Female	535	54.4	45.6
16~24 岁 Age	112	67.9	32.1
25~34 岁 Age	158	57.6	42.4
35~44 岁 Age	137	52.6	47.4
45~54 岁 Age	87	42.5	57.5
55~60 岁 Age	41	36.6	63.4

5-8 未来一年内打算旅游的地区/ Area Planned to Travel Next Year

注：本题为多选题，合计百分比超过 100%（Multiple answers）

	人次 Person-time	百分比 Percent
省内 in the province	142	26.2
省外 out of the province	371	68.3
海外(含台港澳及国外) overseas	172	31.7

n=543

5-9 未来一年内旅游是否打算参加旅游团/ Whether to Attend Touring Party in the Planned Trip Next Year

	人数 Number	百分比 Percent
是 yes	266	48.9
否 no	135	24.8
不一定 indefinite	143	26.3

n=544

5-10 不同消费者层最近一年内是否外出旅游过的比例/ Proportion of the Sample Traveling Out or Not Last Year by Market Segments

5-10-1 时尚流行指标 Fads Popular Index

	人数 Number	是 yes	否 no
样本 Sample	1022	**39.5**	**60.5**
平实生活指向 simple living orientation	518	34.9	65.1
时尚流行指向 fashion orientation	504	44.2	55.8

5-10-2 信息交流指标/ Information Communication Index

	人数 Number	是 yes	否 no
样本 Sample	1026	**39.4**	**60.6**
信息消极指向 negative orientation	111	20.7	79.3
中间层 medium	662	38.5	61.5
信息积极指向 active orientation	253	49.8	50.2

5-11 不同消费者层未来一年内是否打算外出旅游的比例/ Whether to Planning to Travel Next Year by Market Segments

5-11-1 时尚流行指标 Fads Popular Index

	人数 Number	是 yes	否 no
样本 Sample	1021	**52.8**	**47.2**
平实生活指向 simple living orientation	517	48.2	51.8
时尚流行指向 fashion orientation	504	57.5	42.5

5-11-2 信息交流指标/ Information Communication Index

	人数 Number	是 yes	否 no
样本 Sample	1025	**52.6**	**47.4**
信息消极指向 negative orientation	111	41.4	58.6
中间层 medium	661	50.7	49.3
信息积极指向 active orientation	253	62.5	37.5

● 重庆 / Chongqing

5-1 最近一年内是否外出旅游过的比例/ Proportion of the Sample Traveling Out or Not Last Year

	人数 Number	百分比 Percent
是 yes	199	31.9
否 no	424	68.1

n=623

5-2 样本、男性各年龄层、女性各年龄层最近一年内是否外出旅游过/ Traveling Out or Not Last Year by the Whole Sample, Age and Gender Groups

	人数 Number	是 yes	否 no
样本 Sample	623	31.9	68.1
男性 Male	313	30.4	69.6
16~24 岁 Age	64	21.9	78.1
25~34 岁 Age	93	40.9	59.1
35~44 岁 Age	75	26.7	73.3
45~54 岁 Age	54	29.6	70.4
55~60 岁 Age	27	25.9	74.1
女性 Female	310	33.5	66.5
16~24 岁 Age	64	46.9	53.1
25~34 岁 Age	90	36.7	63.3
35~44 岁 Age	73	20.5	79.5
45~54 岁 Age	60	30.0	70.0
55~60 岁 Age	23	34.8	65.2

5-3 旅游的地区/ Area Visited Last Year

注：本题为多选题，合计百分比超过 100%（Multiple answers）

	人次 Person-time	百分比 Percent
省内 in the province	141	71.6
省外 out of the province	90	45.7
海外 overseas	3	1.5

n=197

5-4 旅游的次数/ Number of Trips Taken Last Year

5-4-1 旅游的次数（省内）/ Number of Trips Taken Last Year (in the Province)

	人数 Number	百分比 Percent
1 次 once	72	51.1
2 次 twice	40	28.4
3 次 times	11	7.8
4-5 次 times	10	7.1
6 次及以上 6 times or over	8	5.7

n=141

5-4-2 旅游的次数（省外）/ Number of Trips Taken Last Year (out of the Province)

	人数 Number	百分比 Percent
1 次 once	47	52.2
2 次 twice	29	32.2
3 次 times	9	10.0
4-5 次 times	4	4.4
6 次及以上 6 times or over	1	1.1

n=90

5-4-3 旅游的次数（海外）/ Number of Trips Taken Last Year (overseas)

	人数 Number	百分比 Percent
1 次 once	1	33.3
2 次 twice	1	33.3
3 次 times	1	33.3
4-5 次 times	0	0.0
6 次及以上 6 times or over	0	0.0

n=3

5-5 样本、男性各年龄层、女性各年龄层最近一年内旅游是和谁一起去的/ With Whom When Traveling Last Year by the Whole Sample, Age and Gender Groups

注：本题为多选题，合计百分比超过 100%（Multiple answers）

	人数 Number	自己一个人 single	和家人 with family members	和朋友/同事/同学 with friends or colleagues or classmates	其他 others
样本 Sample	198	8.1	49.5	53.5	0.5
男性 Male	94	8.5	44.7	58.5	1.1
16~24 岁 Age	14	7.1	50.0	71.4	0.0
25~34 岁 Age	38	15.8	28.9	73.7	0.0
35~44 岁 Age	20	5.0	50.0	45.0	5.0
45~54 岁 Age	15	0.0	53.3	46.7	0.0
55~60 岁 Age	7	0.0	85.7	14.3	0.0
女性 Female	104	7.7	53.8	49.0	0.0
16~24 岁 Age	30	13.3	50.0	53.3	0.0
25~34 岁 Age	33	0.0	69.7	39.4	0.0
35~44 岁 Age	15	0.0	60.0	53.3	0.0
45~54 岁 Age	18	16.7	33.3	55.6	0.0
55~60 岁 Age	8	12.5	37.5	50.0	0.0

5-6 最近一年内旅游是否参加了旅游团/ Whether Having Attended Touring Party Last Year

	人数 Number	百分比 Percent
是 yes	40	20.7
否 no	153	79.3

n=193

5-7 样本、男性各年龄层、女性各年龄层未来一年内是否打算外出旅游/ Whether to Plan to Travel Next Year by the Whole Sample, Age and Gender Groups

	人数 Number	是 yes	否 no
样本 Sample	621	42.8	57.2
男性 Male	311	41.2	58.8
16~24 岁 Age	64	43.8	56.3
25~34 岁 Age	92	50.0	50.0
35~44 岁 Age	75	41.3	58.7
45~54 岁 Age	53	28.3	71.7
55~60 岁 Age	27	29.6	70.4
女性 Female	310	44.5	55.5
16~24 岁 Age	64	59.4	40.6
25~34 岁 Age	90	48.9	51.1
35~44 岁 Age	73	37.0	63.0
45~54 岁 Age	60	38.3	61.7
55~60 岁 Age	23	26.1	73.9

5-8 未来一年内打算旅游的地区/ Area Planned to Travel Next Year

注：本题为多选题，合计百分比超过 100%（Multiple answers）

	人次 Person-time	百分比 Percent
省内 in the province	108	40.6
省外 out of the province	182	68.4
海外(含台港澳及国外) overseas	20	7.5

n=266

5-9 未来一年内旅游是否打算参加旅游团/ Whether to Attend Touring Party in the Planned Trip Next Year

	人数 Number	百分比 Percent
是 yes	60	22.6
否 no	132	49.6
不一定 indefinite	74	27.8

n=266

5-10 不同消费者层最近一年内是否外出旅游过的比例/ Proportion of the Sample Traveling Out or Not Last Year by Market Segments

5-10-1 时尚流行指标 Fads Popular Index

	人数 Number	是 yes	否 no
样本 Sample	616	32.0	68.0
平实生活指向 simple living orientation	369	23.3	76.7
时尚流行指向 fashion orientation	247	44.9	55.1

5-10-2 信息交流指标/ Information Communication Index

	人数 Number	是 yes	否 no
样本 Sample	615	31.9	68.1
信息消极指向 negative orientation	47	14.9	85.1
中间层 medium	339	31.6	68.4
信息积极指向 active orientation	229	35.8	64.2

5-11 不同消费者层未来一年内是否打算外出旅游的比例/ Whether to Plan to Travel Next Year by Market Segments

5-11-1 时尚流行指标 Fads Popular Index

	人数 Number	是 yes	否 no
样本 Sample	614	42.8	57.2
平实生活指向 simple living orientation	368	34.2	65.8
时尚流行指向 fashion orientation	246	55.7	44.3

5-11-2 信息交流指标/ Information Communication Index

	人数 Number	是 yes	否 no
样本 Sample	613	43.2	56.8
信息消极指向 negative orientation	47	19.1	80.9
中间层 medium	338	43.2	56.8
信息积极指向 active orientation	228	48.2	51.8

● 武汉 / Wuhan

5-1 最近一年内是否外出旅游过的比例/ Proportion of the Sample Traveling Out or Not Last Year

	人数 Number	百分比 Percent
是 yes	196	30.8
否 no	440	69.2

n=636

5-2 样本、男性各年龄层、女性各年龄层最近一年内是否外出旅游过/ Traveling Out or Not Last Year by the Whole Sample, Age and Gender Groups

	人数 Number	是 yes	否 no
样本 Sample	636	30.8	69.2
男性 Male	308	25.6	74.4
16~24 岁 Age	65	23.1	76.9
25~34 岁 Age	87	35.6	64.4
35~44 岁 Age	80	18.8	81.3
45~54 岁 Age	52	26.9	73.1
55~60 岁 Age	24	16.7	83.3
女性 Female	328	35.7	64.3
16~24 岁 Age	68	39.7	60.3
25~34 岁 Age	96	45.8	54.2
35~44 岁 Age	78	32.1	67.9
45~54 岁 Age	60	28.3	71.7
55~60 岁 Age	26	15.4	84.6

5-3 旅游的地区/ Area Visited Last Year

注：本题为多选题，合计百分比超过 100%（Multiple answers）

	人次 Person-time	百分比 Percent
省内 in the province	118	60.5
省外 out of the province	132	67.7
海外 overseas	23	11.8

n=195

5-4 旅游的次数/ Number of Trips Taken Last Year

5-4-1 旅游的次数（省内）/ Number of Trips Taken Last Year (in the Province)

	人数 Number	百分比 Percent
1 次 once	69	58.5
2 次 twice	24	20.3
3 次 times	10	8.5
4-5 次 times	13	11.0
6 次及以上 6 times or over	2	1.7

n=118

5-4-2 旅游的次数（省外）/ Number of Trips Taken Last Year (out of the Province)

	人数 Number	百分比 Percent
1 次 once	68	51.5
2 次 twice	49	37.1
3 次 times	11	8.3
4-5 次 times	4	3.0
6 次及以上 6 times or over	0	0.0

n=132

5-4-3 旅游的次数（海外）/ Number of Trips Taken Last Year (overseas)

	人数 Number	百分比 Percent
1 次 once	6	26.1
2 次 twice	12	52.2
3 次 times	5	21.7
4-5 次 times	0	0.0
6 次及以上 6 times or over	0	0.0

n=23

5-5 样本、男性各年龄层、女性各年龄层最近一年内旅游是和谁一起去的/ With Whom When Traveling Last Year by the Whole Sample, Age and Gender Groups

注：本题为多选题，合计百分比超过 100%（Multiple answers）

	人数 Number	自己一个人 single	和家人 with family members	和朋友/同事/同学 with friends or colleagues or classmates	其他 others
样本 Sample	194	11.9	56.2	46.4	1.0
男性 Male	78	23.1	39.7	60.3	0.0
16~24 岁 Age	15	20.0	26.7	60.0	0.0
25~34 岁 Age	30	13.3	30.0	73.3	0.0
35~44 岁 Age	15	20.0	53.3	60.0	0.0
45~54 岁 Age	14	35.7	57.1	42.9	0.0
55~60 岁 Age	4	75.0	50.0	25.0	0.0
女性 Female	116	4.3	67.2	37.1	1.7
16~24 岁 Age	27	3.7	48.1	55.6	0.0
25~34 岁 Age	44	4.5	68.2	31.8	2.3
35~44 岁 Age	24	0.0	87.5	29.2	0.0
45~54 岁 Age	17	11.8	76.5	23.5	0.0
55~60 岁 Age	4	0.0	25.0	75.0	25.0

5-6 最近一年内旅游是否参加了旅游团/ Whether Having Attended Touring Party Last Year

	人数 Number	百分比 Percent
是 yes	45	23.9
否 no	143	76.1

n=188

5-7 样本、男性各年龄层、女性各年龄层未来一年内是否打算外出旅游/ Whether to Plan to Travel Next Year by the Whole Sample, Age and Gender Groups

	人数 Number	是 yes	否 no
样本 Sample	634	49.5	50.5
男性 Male	308	50.6	49.4
16~24 岁 Age	65	55.4	44.6
25~34 岁 Age	87	63.2	36.8
35~44 岁 Age	80	43.8	56.3
45~54 岁 Age	52	38.5	61.5
55~60 岁 Age	24	41.7	58.3
女性 Female	326	48.5	51.5
16~24 岁 Age	68	60.3	39.7
25~34 岁 Age	96	58.3	41.7
35~44 岁 Age	76	38.2	61.8
45~54 岁 Age	60	43.3	56.7
55~60 岁 Age	26	23.1	76.9

5-8 未来一年内打算旅游的地区/ Area Planned to Travel Next Year

注：本题为多选题，合计百分比超过 100%（Multiple answers）

	人次 Person-time	百分比 Percent
省内 in the province	66	21.2
省外 out of the province	266	85.3
海外(含台港澳及国外) overseas	32	10.3

n=312

5-9 未来一年内旅游是否打算参加旅游团/ Whether to Attend Touring Party in the Planned Trip Next Year

	人数 Number	百分比 Percent
是 yes	66	21.0
否 no	183	58.3
不一定 indefinite	65	20.7

n=314

5-10 不同消费者层最近一年内是否外出旅游过的比例/ Proportion of the Sample Traveling Out or Not Last Year by Market Segments

5-10-1 时尚流行指标 Fads Popular Index

	人数 Number	是 yes	否 no
样本 Sample	**632**	**30.7**	**69.3**
平实生活指向 simple living orientation	330	28.5	71.5
时尚流行指向 fashion orientation	302	33.1	66.9

5-10-2 信息交流指标/ Information Communication Index

	人数 Number	是 yes	否 no
样本 Sample	**631**	**30.6**	**69.4**
信息消极指向 negative orientation	46	23.9	76.1
中间层 medium	363	27.3	72.7
信息积极指向 active orientation	222	37.4	62.6

5-11 不同消费者层未来一年内是否打算外出旅游的比例/ Whether to Plan to Travel Next Year by Market Segments

5-11-1 时尚流行指标 Fads Popular Index

	人数 Number	是 yes	否 no
样本 Sample	**630**	**49.4**	**50.6**
平实生活指向 simple living orientation	329	43.5	56.5
时尚流行指向 fashion orientation	301	55.8	44.2

5-11-2 信息交流指标/ Information Communication Index

	人数 Number	是 yes	否 no
样本 Sample	**629**	**49.3**	**50.7**
信息消极指向 negative orientation	46	28.3	71.7
中间层 medium	362	47.0	53.0
信息积极指向 active orientation	221	57.5	42.5

● 西安 / Xi'an

5-1 最近一年内是否外出旅游过的比例/ Proportion of the Sample Traveling Out or Not Last Year

	人数 Number	百分比 Percent
是 yes	204	33.9
否 no	397	66.1

n=601

5-2 样本、男性各年龄层、女性各年龄层最近一年内是否外出旅游过/ Traveling Out or Not Last Year by the Whole Sample, Age and Gender Groups

	人数 Number	是 yes	否 no
样本 Sample	601	33.9	66.1
男性 Male	302	34.1	65.9
16~24 岁 Age	64	46.9	53.1
25~34 岁 Age	91	41.8	58.2
35~44 岁 Age	77	23.4	76.6
45~54 岁 Age	46	26.1	73.9
55~60 岁 Age	24	20.8	79.2
女性 Female	299	33.8	66.2
16~24 岁 Age	61	42.6	57.4
25~34 岁 Age	90	40.0	60.0
35~44 岁 Age	74	27.0	73.0
45~54 岁 Age	49	22.4	77.6
55~60 岁 Age	25	32.0	68.0

5-3 旅游的地区/ Area Visited Last Year

注：本题为多选题，合计百分比超过 100%（Multiple answers）

	人次 Person-time	百分比 Percent
省内 in the province	130	63.7
省外 out of the province	120	58.8
海外 overseas	3	1.5

n=204

5-4 旅游的次数/ Number of Trips Taken Last Year

5-4-1 旅游的次数（省内）/ Number of Trips Taken Last Year (in the Province)

	人数 Number	百分比 Percent
1 次 once	70	53.8
2 次 twice	26	20.0
3 次 times	13	10.0
4-5 次 times	10	7.7
6 次及以上 6 times or over	11	8.5

n=130

5-4-2 旅游的次数（省外）/ Number of Trips Taken Last Year (out of the Province)

	人数 Number	百分比 Percent
1 次 once	80	66.7
2 次 twice	29	24.2
3 次 times	5	4.2
4-5 次 times	5	4.2
6 次及以上 6 times or over	1	0.8

n=120

5-4-3 旅游的次数（海外）/ Number of Trips Taken Last Year (overseas)

	人数 Number	百分比 Percent
1 次 once	1	33.3
2 次 twice	1	33.3
3 次 times	1	33.3
4-5 次 times	0	0.0
6 次及以上 6 times or over	0	0.0

n=3

5-5 样本、男性各年龄层、女性各年龄层最近一年内旅游是和谁一起去的/ With Whom When Traveling Last Year by the Whole Sample, Age and Gender Groups

注：本题为多选题，合计百分比超过 100%（Multiple answers）

	人数 Number	自己一个人 single	和家人 with family members	和朋友/同事/同学 with friends or colleagues or classmates	其他 others
样本 Sample	203	11.3	50.2	50.7	0.5
男性 Male	103	8.7	45.6	55.3	0.0
16~24 岁 Age	30	13.3	30.0	70.0	0.0
25~34 岁 Age	38	0.0	47.4	55.3	0.0
35~44 岁 Age	18	16.7	50.0	50.0	0.0
45~54 岁 Age	12	16.7	58.3	41.7	0.0
55~60 岁 Age	5	0.0	80.0	20.0	0.0
女性 Female	100	14.0	55.0	46.0	1.0
16~24 岁 Age	26	11.5	46.2	65.4	0.0
25~34 岁 Age	36	8.3	61.1	41.7	0.0
35~44 岁 Age	20	15.0	45.0	55.0	5.0
45~54 岁 Age	10	20.0	60.0	30.0	0.0
55~60 岁 Age	8	37.5	75.0	0.0	0.0

5-6 最近一年内旅游是否参加了旅游团/ Whether Having Attended Touring Party Last Year

	人数 Number	百分比 Percent
是 yes	20	10.0
否 no	180	90.0

n=200

5-7 样本、男性各年龄层、女性各年龄层未来一年内是否打算外出旅游/ Whether to Planning to Travel Next Year by the Whole Sample, Age and Gender Groups

	人数 Number	是 yes	否 no
样本 Sample	600	46.0	54.0
男性 Male	302	43.7	56.3
16~24 岁 Age	64	54.7	45.3
25~34 岁 Age	91	49.5	50.5
35~44 岁 Age	77	35.1	64.9
45~54 岁 Age	46	34.8	65.2
55~60 岁 Age	24	37.5	62.5
女性 Female	298	48.3	51.7
16~24 岁 Age	60	58.3	41.7
25~34 岁 Age	90	53.3	46.7
35~44 岁 Age	74	44.6	55.4
45~54 岁 Age	49	32.7	67.3
55~60 岁 Age	25	48.0	52.0

5-8 未来一年内打算旅游的地区/ Area Planned to Travel Next Year

注：本题为多选题，合计百分比超过 100%（Multiple answers）

	人次 Person-time	百分比 Percent
省内 in the province	52	18.9
省外 out of the province	226	82.2
海外(含台港澳及国外) overseas	26	9.5

n=275

5-9 未来一年内旅游是否打算参加旅游团/ Whether to Attend Touring Party in the Planned Trip Next Year

	人数 Number	百分比 Percent
是 yes	53	19.3
否 no	151	54.9
不一定 indefinite	71	25.8

n=275

5-10 不同消费者层最近一年内是否外出旅游过的比例/ Proportion of the Sample Traveling Out or Not Last Year by Market Segments

5-10-1 时尚流行指标 Fads Popular Index

	人数 Number	是 yes	否 no
样本 Sample	**599**	**34.1**	**65.9**
平实生活指向 simple living orientation	341	25.5	74.5
时尚流行指向 fashion orientation	258	45.3	54.7

5-10-2 信息交流指标/ Information Communication Index

	人数 Number	是 yes	否 no
样本 Sample	**599**	**34.1**	**65.9**
信息消极指向 negative orientation	69	21.7	78.3
中间层 medium	340	32.4	67.6
信息积极指向 active orientation	190	41.6	58.4

5-11 不同消费者层未来一年内是否打算外出旅游的比例/ Whether to Planning to Travel Next Year by Market Segments

5-11-1 时尚流行指标 Fads Popular Index

	人数 Number	是 yes	否 no
样本 Sample	**598**	**46.2**	**53.8**
平实生活指向 simple living orientation	341	37.5	62.5
时尚流行指向 fashion orientation	257	57.6	42.4

5-11-2 信息交流指标/ Information Communication Index

	人数 Number	是 yes	否 no
样本 Sample	**598**	**46.2**	**53.8**
信息消极指向 negative orientation	69	26.1	73.9
中间层 medium	339	46.3	53.7
信息积极指向 active orientation	190	53.2	46.8

● 沈阳 / Shenyang

5-1 最近一年内是否外出旅游过的比例/ Proportion of the Sample Traveling Out or Not Last Year

	人数 Number	百分比 Percent
是 yes	245	40.8
否 no	356	59.2

n=601

5-2 样本、男性各年龄层、女性各年龄层最近一年内是否外出旅游过/ Traveling Out or Not Last Year by the Whole Sample, Age and Gender Groups

	人数 Number	是 yes	否 no
样本 Sample	601	40.8	59.2
男性 Male	299	40.5	59.5
16~24 岁 Age	64	35.9	64.1
25~34 岁 Age	89	55.1	44.9
35~44 岁 Age	76	35.5	64.5
45~54 岁 Age	46	34.8	65.2
55~60 岁 Age	24	25.0	75.0
女性 Female	302	41.1	58.9
16~24 岁 Age	64	48.4	51.6
25~34 岁 Age	90	43.3	56.7
35~44 岁 Age	76	39.5	60.5
45~54 岁 Age	48	35.4	64.6
55~60 岁 Age	24	29.2	70.8

5-3 旅游的地区/ Area Visited Last Year

注：本题为多选题，合计百分比超过 100%（Multiple answers）

	人次 Person-time	百分比 Percent
省内 in the province	199	81.9
省外 out of the province	79	32.5
海外 overseas	4	1.6

n=243

5-4 旅游的次数/ Number of Trips Taken Last Year

5-4-1 旅游的次数（省内）/ Number of Trips Taken Last Year (in the Province)

	人数 Number	百分比 Percent
1 次 once	113	56.8
2 次 twice	51	25.6
3 次 times	19	9.5
4-5 次 times	13	6.5
6 次及以上 6 times or over	3	1.5

n=199

5-4-2 旅游的次数（省外）/ Number of Trips Taken Last Year (out of the Province)

	人数 Number	百分比 Percent
1 次 once	48	60.8
2 次 twice	20	25.3
3 次 times	6	7.6
4-5 次 times	4	5.1
6 次及以上 6 times or over	1	1.3

n=79

5-4-3 旅游的次数（海外）/ Number of Trips Taken Last Year (overseas)

	人数 Number	百分比 Percent
1 次 once	2	50.0
2 次 twice	2	50.0
3 次 times	0	0.0
4-5 次 times	0	0.0
6 次及以上 6 times or over	0	0.0

n=4

5-5 样本、男性各年龄层、女性各年龄层最近一年内旅游是和谁一起去的/ With Whom When Traveling Last Year by the Whole Sample, Age and Gender Groups

注：本题为多选题，合计百分比超过 100%（Multiple answers）

	人数 Number	自己一个人 single	和家人 with family members	和朋友/同事/同学 with friends or colleagues or classmates	其他 others
样本 Sample	243	6.6	53.9	50.6	0.0
男性 Male	120	10.8	42.5	59.2	0.0
16~24 岁 Age	22	4.5	31.8	63.6	0.0
25~34 岁 Age	49	16.3	38.8	59.2	0.0
35~44 岁 Age	27	7.4	40.7	66.7	0.0
45~54 岁 Age	16	12.5	62.5	43.8	0.0
55~60 岁 Age	6	0.0	66.7	50.0	0.0
女性 Female	123	2.4	65.0	42.3	0.0
16~24 岁 Age	31	3.2	48.4	61.3	0.0
25~34 岁 Age	39	2.6	69.2	38.5	0.0
35~44 岁 Age	30	0.0	80.0	30.0	0.0
45~54 岁 Age	16	6.3	75.0	25.0	0.0
55~60 岁 Age	7	0.0	28.6	71.4	0.0

5-6 最近一年内旅游是否参加了旅游团/ Whether Having Attended Touring Party Last Year

	人数 Number	百分比 Percent
是 yes	20	8.4
否 no	218	91.6

n=238

5-7 样本、男性各年龄层、女性各年龄层未来一年内是否打算外出旅游/ Whether to Plan to Travel Next Year by the Whole Sample, Age and Gender Groups

	人数 Number	是 yes	否 no
样本 Sample	601	55.7	44.3
男性 Male	299	56.9	43.1
16~24 岁 Age	64	53.1	46.9
25~34 岁 Age	89	69.7	30.3
35~44 岁 Age	76	52.6	47.4
45~54 岁 Age	46	54.3	45.7
55~60 岁 Age	24	37.5	62.5
女性 Female	302	54.6	45.4
16~24 岁 Age	64	62.5	37.5
25~34 岁 Age	90	58.9	41.1
35~44 岁 Age	76	57.9	42.1
45~54 岁 Age	48	45.8	54.2
55~60 岁 Age	24	25.0	75.0

5-8 未来一年内打算旅游的地区/ Area Planned to Travel Next Year

注：本题为多选题，合计百分比超过 100%（Multiple answers）

	人次 Person-time	百分比 Percent
省内 in the province	151	45.2
省外 out of the province	218	65.3
海外(含台港澳及国外) overseas	36	10.8

n=334

5-9 未来一年内旅游是否打算参加旅游团/ Whether to Attend Touring Party in the Planned Trip Next Year

	人数 Number	百分比 Percent
是 yes	41	12.3
否 no	205	61.7
不一定 indefinite	86	25.9

n=332

5-10 不同消费者层最近一年内是否外出旅游过的比例/ Proportion of the Sample Traveling Out or Not Last Year by Market Segments

5-10-1 时尚流行指标/ Fads Popular Index

	人数 Number	是 yes	否 no
样本 Sample	601	40.8	59.2
平实生活指向 simple living orientation	292	33.6	66.4
时尚流行指向 fashion orientation	309	47.6	52.4

5-10-2 信息交流指标/ Information Communication Index

	人数 Number	是 yes	否 no
样本 Sample	600	40.7	59.3
信息消极指向 negative orientation	55	29.1	70.9
中间层 medium	313	38.0	62.0
信息积极指向 active orientation	232	47.0	53.0

5-11 不同消费者层未来一年内是否打算外出旅游的比例/ Whether to Plan to Travel Next Year by Market Segments

5-11-1 时尚流行指标/ Fads Popular Index

	人数 Number	是 yes	否 no
样本 Sample	601	55.7	44.3
平实生活指向 simple living orientation	292	48.6	51.4
时尚流行指向 fashion orientation	309	62.5	37.5

5-11-2 信息交流指标/ Information Communication Index

	人数 Number	是 yes	否 no
样本 Sample	600	55.7	44.3
信息消极指向 negative orientation	55	36.4	63.6
中间层 medium	313	52.1	47.9
信息积极指向 active orientation	232	65.1	34.9

6. 社会、生活态度 / Attitudes and Values

● 北京 / Beijing

6-1 饮食与健康// Diet/ Nutrition/ Health

	均值 Mean	样本量 N
我很注意饮食以防发胖 I care much not to be over weight	3.66	1010
我一周有三天以上不吃早饭 I cancel breakfast for half days in a week	2.40	1011
我的一日三餐都很规律 I take regular meal 3 times a day	3.74	1008
与西餐相比我更喜欢中式餐饮 Compared with western food, I prefer Chinese food	4.09	1010
我经常购买半成品食品、冷冻食品等容易加工的食品 I often buy food that is easy to cook such as ready-made food, frozen food or cooked food	3.06	1011
我经常吃一些维生素等保健品来补充营养 I often take some vitamins to supply nutrition	2.97	1009
我会刻意去吃对健康美容有益的食物 I would like to take food that is good to health or beauty on purpose	3.13	1009
我宁愿自己做饭而不愿去买现成的食物 I prefer doing cooking myself to buying cooked food	3.20	1012
我很注意饮食的营养平衡 I care much about the balance of nutrition of food	3.71	1012
我经常到麦当劳之类的快餐店吃东西 I often eat at fast-food restaurant like Macdonald's	2.85	1011
我很注意包装上有关添加剂、生产日期的说明 I do pay attention to the instruction of ingredients, and producing date on the package of the food	4.23	1011

6-2 时尚与流行// Fashion/ Style/ Preference for Foreign Product

	均值 Mean	样本量 N
我希望过流行、时髦、休闲的生活 I desired to live a modern, fashionable and casual life	3.39	1004
我很注意流行的趋势 I care for fads	3.18	1009
我向往欧美等先进国家的生活方式 I appreciate the life style of the developed western countries such as USA	2.87	1004
我很注意自己的外表修饰 I do mind my appearance and dressing	3.77	1007
我时常尝试新的发型 I often try new hairstyle	2.27	1011
我的服饰和装扮多年来基本上没有多大改变 I tend to keep my dressing style for years almost without any change	3.48	1011
吸引异性的注目是我很喜欢的感觉 I feel good to attract the attention of the opposite gender	2.81	1008
流行与实用之间我比较看重流行 I care more about fads between fashion and usage	2.65	1012
我觉得自己的品味与众不同 I think my taste is unique	3.20	1010
当我使用外国产品时心理多少会有满足感 I feel somewhat satisfied when I use imported products	2.79	1005
我偏好西方的艺术文化 I prefer western arts and culture	2.76	1011
在别人眼里我是个时髦的人 I am regarded a fashionable person by others	2.58	1008
我刻意打扮是为了发挥自己的个性 I dress up on purpose to show my personality	3.03	1011
我希望过非常浪漫的生活 I hope to live a very romantic life	3.24	1008

6-3 购物与消费// Shopping/ Consumption

	均值 Mean	样本量 N
我经常有冲动性购买 I often buy goods on impulse	2.88	1009
我认为名牌的商品品质比较好 I think famous brands are of better quality	3.91	1011
选购物品时我喜欢尝试新品牌、新产品 I like to try new brands and new products	3.35	1008
买东西时我经常货比三家 I often compare goods sold at different stores	3.60	1009
我经常购买具有独特风格的产品 I often purchase goods of unique style	3.17	1005
购买商品时我考虑的因素主要是价格 Price is my main consideration when I purchase goods	3.42	1008
与其把旧的东西拿去修理不如买新的 I would rather buy a new product than repair it	3.47	1009
为了买汽车和房子，我可以选择银行贷款的方式 In order to buy a car or a house, I can accept the way of loan	2.91	1009
我宁愿多花一点钱购买品质较好的东西 I prefer paying more for products with better quality	4.22	1010
即使价格贵一些，我还是喜欢买名牌产品 I would like to buy famous brands even if they are higher in price	3.43	1011
为节省时间和精力，我愿意花些钱购买某些产品或服务 In order to save time and energy, I'd like to pay more to buy related service and goods	3.42	1010
对于想要的东西，价格贵一些也会买 I will buy the item I like even if it is higher in price	3.83	1010
选购物品时我不喜欢更换品牌 I do not like change brands when I buy the goods	3.36	1008
我非常注意商店的气氛、布置及格调 I mind the atmosphere, setting and tone of the store	3.69	1009
对于有些想要的东西我会等到降价或特卖时才买 For the goods I want to buy, I can wait till they are on sale	3.30	1009

6-4 金钱与投资// Money Management

	均值 Mean	样本量 N
我常搞不清钱花到哪儿去了 I often wonder where I spent my money	2.99	1007
我认为节省开支比拼命挣钱重要 I think it more important to save money than to earn money hard	3.22	1005
我觉得自己对于金融投资方面的知识太少了 I think I know too little about financial investment	3.95	1009
我认为把钱用于投资股票是很危险的事情 I think investing money in stock is very dangerous	3.55	1011
相对于买股票我宁愿把钱存进银行 Compared with buying stocks, I prefer depositing my money in the bank	3.52	1008
我用信用卡购买许多东西 I buy many things with my credit cards	2.17	1005
经济上的安定对我来说很重要 Financial security is very important to me	4.39	1008
我是家里主要理财的人 I am the main financial manager of my family	3.24	1009

6-5 家庭与婚姻// Family/ Home/ Sex Roles

	均值 Mean	样本量 N
家庭是我生活的重心 Family is the main factor in my life	4.18	1006
家庭生活不一定要有小孩 Children do not matter much to my family life	2.62	1006
女人的主要任务是给家人一个快乐的家 Woman's main duty is to make the family happy	3.69	1012
男人应比女人能干 Man is supposed to be more able than woman	3.62	1012
我可以接受女方比男方学历高的婚姻观念 I can accept the idea that the wife holds higher academic degree than the husband	3.55	1010
男性也应该做家务 Husband should also share some housework	4.29	1008
我认为应该让孩子独立自主地成长 I think children should be let to grow independently	4.54	1008
我对老了以后的生活常常感到不安 I often feel restless about my aged life	2.97	1008
结婚仪式应该选在吉利的日子举行 Wedding ceremony should be held on the propitious date	3.89	1011
我赞同年轻人结婚后和父母分开住 I agree that the young couple does not live together with their parents	4.02	1010

6-6 工作与休闲// Work/ Living/ Spare time

	均值 Mean	样本量 N
工作的最佳报酬应该是成就感 The achievements are the best payment for my work	3.89	1003
工作上只要能获得好评价，不轻易换工作 As long as I am satisfied with my work, I will not change my job	3.71	1009
我喜欢安定有保障的工作 I like safe and secured job	4.18	1009
工作稍一懈怠我就会有落后于人的感觉 I feel I am falling behind whenever I am a little bit careless and lazy	3.77	1010
闲着没事做我会觉得不自在 I feel restless to idle away without doing anything	3.86	1008
比起做公司的一般职员我更喜欢独立的工作 I prefer being self-employed to being employed by others as an average staff	3.99	1009
山中或湖边的小屋最适合假期休闲 Huts in the mountain or besides the lake are best for leisure life	4.02	1010
即使会影响收入，我也希望有更多自己的时间 I'd like to have more private time even if that will decrease my earnings	3.47	1010
我宁愿住在市区，而不愿住在郊区 I prefer living in the suburbs to the town	3.50	1009
为了挣更多的钱我宁愿牺牲休闲 I would like sacrifice my leisure time to earn more money	3.21	1008
为了享受休闲，多花一些钱也是值得的 It's worth more to enjoying leisure life	3.56	1010

6-7 自我评价// Self-confidence/ Self-actualization

	均值 Mean	样本量 N
我凡事喜欢自己来，不喜欢依赖别人 I like to do things myself and don't like to depend on others	4.20	1008
与他人相比我认为自己具备更重要的素质 Compared with other people, I think I am of better nature	3.82	1008
我还没有达到自己的目标 I haven't reached my goal yet	4.28	1010
我喜欢被看作领导者 I'd like to be regarded as a leader	2.93	1007
我经常在生活中为自己确立更高的目标 I often set a higher goal for myself in the life	3.96	1011
我总觉得我的能力不如别人 I always feel inferior to others in term of ability	2.54	1012
不管做什么只要我喜欢便是享受 No matter what to do, I would enjoy it if I like it	4.17	1012
我想过有别于以往的人生 I once desire a different life	3.49	1005
我总是想尝试以前没有尝试的东西，接受新的挑战 I always try new things and would like to face new challenge	3.69	1012
我会有效地安排时间，协调好工作与休闲 I can effectively arrange my time, and make good balance between my work and rest	4.02	1007
我关心各种信息并能得到相关的信息和知识 I pay attention to various information and can get related information and knowledge	3.69	1007
我做事一向有计划 I always plan my things well	3.79	1010
我经常能从工作和生活中获得成就感和满足感 I often feel satisfied with my work and life	3.77	1010
在社交活动中我是比较活跃的分子 I am an active member in social life	3.23	1011
为了前途我会辛苦得去进修某些课程和训练 I'd like to take some hard training or courses in order to get a better future	3.71	1012
只要有一些自己的生活空间，我会觉得很满足 I will feel satisfied when I have a certain private living space	4.13	1011

6-8 关于广告// Advertising

	均值 Mean	样本量 N
对自己关心的商品类别，会比较注意其广告 I pay attention to the advertising of those categories that I care	3.84	1010
我觉得做过电视广告的商品有亲切感 I feel dear to those products which run TV commercials	3.26	1007
我为了了解社会的流行、潮流而关心广告 I pay attention to advertising to get to know the social fads and trends	3.16	1011
广告中的信息对我做购物决定起了很大的作用 The massage in advertising is very important factor in my buying decision	3.28	1004
如果这个广告我不喜欢，我就不会购买其相关产品 If I don't like the advertising, I will not buy the advertised products	3.52	1009
当电视出现广告时，我通常会换台 I often change channels when commercials appear on the TV screen	3.62	1012
真正的好产品不需要做广告 Real good products needn't run advertising	3.59	1011
购买商品时还是以有广告的品牌比较可靠 When purchasing goods, those advertised brands are more reliable	3.40	1007
广告是可以信赖的 Advertising can be trusted	2.78	1011
专家推荐的产品应该不会有错 Authority-endorsed products should be good	3.22	1009
广告反映了时代的潮流 Advertising reflects social trends	3.80	1010

6-9 关于信息寻求// Information Seeking

	均值 Mean	样本量 N
我经常从朋友那里听到各种各样的信息 I often get various kinds of information from my friends	3.72	1008
我劝导别人的情况比自己被别人劝导的情况多 I persuade other people more often than others persuade me	3.60	1007
得到新信息后我会立即告诉别人 I will immediately tell the new information I get to other people	3.70	1012
别人想做什么的时候通常会找我出主意 Other people like to consult me when they want to do something	3.47	1011
我觉得好的东西一定会向别人推荐 I will recommend the things that I think good to others	4.07	1009
我购买一种新产品或者享受新的服务一般都比别人早 I often buy or enjoy a new product or a new service earlier than others	3.00	1011
我对跟自己无关的话题不关心 I don't care for the topics not associated with me	3.59	1011
对于流行或新产品的情况，不知道也没有关系 It doesn't matter to me not to know the fads and new products	3.25	1007
当某种商品或服务成为议论的话题时，我也会去尝试 When a product or service becomes the topic of like, I will try it	3.36	1011
我觉得自己能够与新潮流、新信息保持同步 I think I can keep pace with the new fads and new products	3.37	1006

6-10 关注的社会问题// Social Concern

	均值 Mean	样本量 N
政府机构改革问题 Government Structure Reform	3.59	1009
人民币、股票、经济动向 RMB, stock market and economic movement	3.45	1009
东南亚经济危机和中国商业环境的恶化 Economic crisis in Southeast Asia and the deterioration of Chinese business situation	3.17	1002
中国人口问题 Chinese population	3.24	1005
地球变暖等环境问题 The environmental problem such as the earth becomes warmer	3.45	1002
地震、火灾、洪水等自然灾害及救济措施 Earthquake, fire, flood and the remedies	3.71	1002
克隆技术等生物技术的发展 The biological development such as cloning sheep	2.69	1007
爱滋病等疑难病症的扩散情况 The spread out of difficult and complicated diseases such as AIDS	2.91	1008
消费者保护法等围绕商品安全性的问题 Acts and regulation concerning product safety to protect consumers	3.72	1005
塑料瓶、容器及包装品的再生利用问题 The recycling and reuse of plastic bottles, containers and packages	3.18	1004
希望工程的情况 The Hope Project in China	3.34	1007
因特网、电脑时代的生活及其影响 The life in the age of Internet, computer and their influences	3.06	1006
下岗职工问题 The problem of workers out of work	3.65	1004
医疗改革等社会保险制度问题 The social security such as health and care security	4.02	1010
住房改革问题 the Housing Reform	4.08	1010

6-11 对目前生活状态的满意程度// Satisfaction Degree about Current Life State

	均值 Mean	样本量 N
家庭 Family	4.07	1009
工作 Work	3.44	987
消费 Consumption	3.25	1007
休闲娱乐 Relaxation and Entertainment	3.11	1004
人际关系 Interpersonal Relationship	3.67	1008
综合 Overall	3.51	1004

● 上海 / Shanghai

6-1 饮食与健康// Diet/ Nutrition/ Health

	均值 Mean	样本量 N
我很注意饮食以防发胖 I care much not to be over weight	3.50	1014
我一周有三天以上不吃早饭 I cancel breakfast for half days in a week	2.07	1012
我的一日三餐都很规律 I take regular meal 3 times a day	3.89	1014
与西餐相比我更喜欢中式餐饮 Compared with western food, I prefer Chinese food	3.94	1014
我经常购买半成品食品、冷冻食品等容易加工的食品 I often buy food that is easy to cook such as ready-made food, frozen food or cooked food	3.31	1012
我经常吃一些维生素等保健品来补充营养 I often take some vitamins to supply nutrition	3.22	1013
我会刻意去吃对健康美容有益的食物 I would like to take food that is good to health or beauty on purpose	3.10	1012
我宁愿自己做饭而不愿去买现成的食物 I prefer doing cooking myself to buying cooked food	3.25	1013
我很注意饮食的营养平衡 I care much about the balance of nutrition of food	3.76	1012
我经常到麦当劳之类的快餐店吃东西 I often eat at fast-food restaurant like McDonald's	2.87	1013
我很注意包装上有关添加剂、生产日期的说明 I do pay attention to the instruction of ingredients, and producing date on the package of the food	4.13	1014

6-2 时尚与流行// Fashion/ Style/ Preference for Foreign Product

	均值 Mean	样本量 N
我希望过流行、时髦、休闲的生活 I desired to live a modern, fashionable and casual life	3.37	1014
我很注意流行的趋势 I care for fads	3.15	1011
我向往欧美等先进国家的生活方式 I appreciate the life style of the developed western countries such as USA	3.10	1012
我很注意自己的外表修饰 I do mind my appearance and dressing	3.75	1010
我时常尝试新的发型 I often try new hairstyle	2.52	1014
我的服饰和装扮多年来基本上没有多大改变 I tend to keep my dressing style for years almost without any change	3.50	1014
吸引异性的注目是我很喜欢的感觉 I feel good to attract the attention of the opposite gender	2.87	1013
流行与实用之间我比较看重流行 I care more about fads between fashion and usage	2.61	1012
我觉得自己的品味与众不同 I think my taste is unique	3.17	1013
当我使用外国产品时心理多少会有满足感 I feel somewhat satisfied when I use imported products	3.06	1014
我偏好西方的艺术文化 I prefer western arts and culture	2.86	1012
在别人眼里我是个时髦的人 I am regarded a fashionable person by others	2.70	1014
我刻意打扮是为了发挥自己的个性 I dress up on purpose to show my personality	2.93	1014
我希望过非常浪漫的生活 I hope to live a very romantic life	3.25	1013

6-3 购物与消费// Shopping/ Consumption

	均值 Mean	样本量 N
我经常有冲动性购买 I often buy goods on impulse	2.89	1010
我认为名牌的商品品质比较好 I think famous brands are of better quality	3.88	1013
选购物品时我喜欢尝试新品牌、新产品 I like to try new brands and new products	3.38	1012
买东西时我经常货比三家 I often compare goods sold at different stores	3.69	1014
我经常购买具有独特风格的产品 I often purchase goods of unique style	3.18	1012
购买商品时我考虑的因素主要是价格 Price is my main consideration when I purchase goods	3.55	1014
与其把旧的东西拿去修理不如买新的 I would rather buy a new product than repair it	3.24	1014
为了买汽车和房子，我可以选择银行贷款的方式 In order to buy a car or a house, I can accept the way of loan	3.20	1011
我宁愿多花一点钱购买品质较好的东西 I prefer paying more for products with better quality	4.04	1013
即使价格贵一些，我还是喜欢买名牌产品 I would like to buy famous brands even if they are higher in price	3.27	1012
为节省时间和精力，我愿意花些钱购买某些产品或服务 In order to save time and energy, I'd like to pay more to buy related service and goods	3.41	1013
对于想要的东西，价格贵一些也会买 I will buy the item I like even if it is higher in price	3.72	1014
选购物品时我不喜欢更换品牌 I do not like change brands when I buy the goods	3.33	1011
我非常注意商店的气氛、布置及格调 I mind the atmosphere, setting and tone of the store	3.74	1013
对于有些想要的东西我会等到降价或特卖时才买 For the goods I want to buy, I can wait till they are on sale	3.36	1011

6-4 金钱与投资// Money Management

	均值 Mean	样本量 N
我常搞不清钱花到哪儿去了 I often wonder where I spent my money	2.88	1009
我认为节省开支比拼命挣钱重要 I think it more important to save money than to earn money hard	3.15	1010
我觉得自己对于金融投资方面的知识太少了 I think I know too little about financial investment	3.81	1012
我认为把钱用于投资股票是很危险的事情 I think investing money in stock is very dangerous	3.26	1011
相对于买股票我宁愿把钱存进银行 Compared with buying stocks, I prefer depositing my money in the bank	3.22	1012
我用信用卡购买许多东西 I buy many things with my credit cards	2.28	1012
经济上的安定对我来说很重要 Financial security is very important to me	4.33	1014
我是家里主要理财的人 I am the main financial manager of my family	3.36	1013

6-5 家庭与婚姻// Family/ Home/ Sex Roles

	均值 Mean	样本量 N
家庭是我生活的重心 Family is the main factor in my life	4.20	1013
家庭生活不一定要有小孩 Children do not matter much to my family life	2.44	1012
女人的主要任务是给家人一个快乐的家 Woman's main duty is to make the family happy	3.72	1014
男人应比女人能干 Man is supposed to be more able than woman	3.48	1013
我可以接受女方比男方学历高的婚姻观 I can accept the idea that the wife holds higher academic degree than the husband	3.54	1014
男性也应该做家务 Husband should also share some housework	4.13	1012
我认为应该让孩子独立自主地成长 I think children should be let to grow independently	4.41	1013
我对老了以后的生活常常感到不安 I often feel restless about my aged life	2.86	1014
结婚仪式应该选在吉利的日子举行 Wedding ceremony should be held on the propitious date	3.97	1013
我赞同年轻人结婚后和父母分开住 I agree that the young couple does not live together with their parents	3.96	1012

6-6 工作与休闲// Work/ Living/ Spare time

	均值 Mean	样本量 N
工作的最佳报酬应该是成就感 The achievements are the best payment for my work	3.87	1013
工作上只要能获得好评价，不轻易换工作 As long as I am satisfied with my work, I will not change my job	3.77	1012
我喜欢安定有保障的工作 I like safe and secured job	4.28	1013
工作稍一懈怠我就会有落后于人的感觉 I feel I am falling behind whenever I am a little bit careless and lazy	3.62	1010
闲着没事做我会觉得不自在 I feel restless to idle away without doing anything	3.74	1014
比起做公司的一般职员我更喜欢独立的工作 I prefer being self-employed to being employed by others as an average staff	3.79	1014
山中或湖边的小屋最适合假期休闲 Huts in the mountain or besides the lake are best for leisure life	3.95	1012
即使会影响收入，我也希望有更多自己的时间 I'd like to have more private time even if that will decrease my earnings	3.41	1012
我宁愿住在市区，而不愿住在郊区 I prefer living in the suburbs to the town	3.62	1012
为了挣更多的钱我宁愿牺牲休闲 I would like sacrifice my leisure time to earn more money	3.25	1014
为了享受休闲，多花一些钱也是值得的 It's worth more to enjoying leisure life	3.41	1012

6-7 自我评价// Self-confidence/ Self-actualization

	均值 Mean	样本量 N
我凡事喜欢自己来，不喜欢依赖别人 I like to do things myself and don't like to depend on others	4.13	1011
与他人相比我认为自己具备更重要的素质 Compared with other people, I think I am of better nature	3.84	1011
我还没有达到自己的目标 I haven't reached my goal yet	4.12	1013
我喜欢被看作领导者 I'd like to be regarded as a leader	3.12	1012
我经常在生活中为自己确立更高的目标 I often set a higher goal for myself in the life	3.89	1014
我总觉得我的能力不如别人 I always feel inferior to others in term of ability	2.65	1014
不管做什么只要我喜欢便是享受 No matter what to do, I would enjoy it if I like it	3.94	1014
我想过有别于以往的人生 I once desire a different life	3.48	1012
我总是想尝试以前没有尝试的东西，接受新的挑战 I always try new things and would like to face new challenge	3.57	1014
我会有效地安排时间，协调好工作与休闲 I can effectively arrange my time, and make good balance between my work and rest	4.00	1013
我关心各种信息并能得到相关的信息和知识 I pay attention to various information and can get related information and knowledge	3.63	1012
我做事一向有计划 I always plan my things well	3.82	1014
我经常能从工作和生活中获得成就感和满足感 I often feel satisfied with my work and life	3.64	1013
在社交活动中我是比较活跃的分子 I am an active member in social life	3.26	1013
为了前途我会辛苦得去进修某些课程和训练 I'd like to take some hard training or courses in order to get a better future	3.60	1013
只要有一些自己的生活空间，我会觉得很满足 I will feel satisfied when I have a certain private living space	4.01	1013

6-8 关于广告// Advertising

	均值 Mean	样本量 N
对自己关心的商品类别，会比较注意其广告 I pay attention to the advertising of those categories that I care	3.93	1012
我觉得做过电视广告的商品有亲切感 I feel dear to those products which run TV commercials	3.38	1012
我为了了解社会的流行、潮流而关心广告 I pay attention to advertising to get to know the social fads and trends	3.23	1013
广告中的信息对我做购物决定起了很大的作用 The massage in advertising is very important factor in my buying decision	3.29	1008
如果这个广告我不喜欢，我就不会购买其相关产品 If I don't like the advertising, I will not buy the advertised products	3.54	1012
当电视出现广告时，我通常会换台 I often change channels when commercials appear on the TV screen	3.41	1014
真正的好产品不需要做广告 Real good products needn't run advertising	3.65	1010
购买商品时还是以有广告的品牌比较可靠 When purchasing goods, those advertised brands are more reliable	3.35	1010
广告是可以信赖的 Advertising can be trusted	2.84	1014
专家推荐的产品应该不会有错 Authority-endorsed products should be good	3.29	1013
广告反映了时代的潮流 Advertising reflects social trends	3.70	1013

6-9 关于信息寻求// Information Seeking

	均值 Mean	样本量 N
我经常从朋友那里听到各种各样的信息 I often get various kinds of information from my friends	3.73	1011
我劝导别人的情况比自己被别人劝导的情况多 I persuade other people more often than others persuade me	3.45	1012
得到新信息后我会立即告诉别人 I will immediately tell the new information I get to other people	3.69	1014
别人想做什么的时候通常会找我出主意 Other people like to consult me when they want to do something	3.38	1011
我觉得好的东西一定会向别人推荐 I will recommend the things that I think good to others	4.03	1011
我购买一种新产品或者享受新的服务一般都比别人早 I often buy or enjoy a new product or a new service earlier than others	3.00	1014
我对跟自己无关的话题不关心 I don't care for the topics not associated with me	3.52	1013
对于流行或新产品的情况，不知道也没有关系 It doesn't matter to me not to know the fads and new products	3.07	1014
当某种商品或服务成为议论的话题时，我也会去尝试 When a product or service becomes the topic of like, I will try it	3.43	1014
我觉得自己能够与新潮流、新信息保持同步 I think I can keep pace with the new fads and new products	3.23	1012

6-10 关注的社会问题// Social Concern

	均值 Mean	样本量 N
政府机构改革问题 Government Structure Reform	3.43	1011
人民币、股票、经济动向 RMB, stock market and economic movement	3.48	1011
东南亚经济危机和中国商业环境的恶化 Economic crisis in Southeast Asia and the deterioration of Chinese business situation	3.09	1011
中国人口问题 Chinese population	2.90	1010
地球变暖等环境问题 The environmental problem such as the earth becomes warmer	2.93	1008
地震、火灾、洪水等自然灾害及救济措施 Earthquake, fire, flood and the remedies	3.44	1009
克隆技术等生物技术的发展 The biological development such as cloning sheep	2.55	1009
爱滋病等疑难病症的扩散情况 The spread out of difficult and complicated diseases such as AIDS	2.54	1009
消费者保护法等围绕商品安全性的问题 Acts and regulation concerning product safety to protect consumers	3.56	1010
塑料瓶、容器及包装品的再生利用问题 The recycling and reuse of plastic bottles, containers and packages	2.78	1011
希望工程的情况 The Hope Project in China	3.18	1009
因特网、电脑时代的生活及其影响 The life in the age of Internet, computer and their influences	2.96	1011
下岗职工问题 The problem of workers out of work	3.64	1010
医疗改革等社会保险制度问题 The social security such as health and care security	4.00	1011
住房改革问题 the Housing Reform	4.03	1011

6-11 对目前生活状态的满意程度// Satisfaction Degree about Current Life State

	均值 Mean	样本量 N
家庭 Family	4.07	1011
工作 Work	3.37	974
消费 Consumption	3.24	1011
休闲娱乐 Relaxation and Entertainment	3.21	1007
人际关系 Interpersonal Relationship	3.75	1011
综合 Overall	3.55	1007

● 广州 / Guangzhou

6-1 饮食与健康// Diet/ Nutrition/ Health

	均值 Mean	样本量 N
我很注意饮食以防发胖 I care much not to be over weight	3.55	1033
我一周有三天以上不吃早饭 I cancel breakfast for half days in a week	2.23	1032
我的一日三餐都很规律 I take regular meal 3 times a day	3.83	1031
与西餐相比我更喜欢中式餐饮 Compared with western food, I prefer Chinese food	3.87	1033
我经常购买半成品食品、冷冻食品等容易加工的食品 I often buy food that is easy to cook such as ready-made food, frozen food or cooked food	3.09	1031
我经常吃一些维生素等保健品来补充营养 I often take some vitamins to supply nutrition	2.95	1032
我会刻意去吃对健康美容有益的食物 I would like to take food that is good to health or beauty on purpose	3.00	1033
我宁愿自己做饭而不愿去买现成的食物 I prefer doing cooking myself to buying cooked food	3.29	1033
我很注意饮食的营养平衡 I care much about the balance of nutrition of food	3.69	1032
我经常到麦当劳之类的快餐店吃东西 I often eat at fast-food restaurant like McDonald's	2.81	1033
我很注意包装上有关添加剂、生产日期的说明 I do pay attention to the instruction of ingredients, and producing date on the package of the food	3.94	1033

6-2 时尚与流行// Fashion/ Style/ Preference for Foreign Product

	均值 Mean	样本量 N
我希望过流行、时髦、休闲的生活 I desired to live a modern, fashionable and casual life	3.43	1034
我很注意流行的趋势 I care for fads	3.05	1033
我向往欧美等先进国家的生活方式 I appreciate the life style of the developed western countries such as USA	3.03	1029
我很注意自己的外表修饰 I do mind my appearance and dressing	3.58	1031
我时常尝试新的发型 I often try new hairstyle	2.48	1031
我的服饰和装扮多年来基本上没有多大改变 I tend to keep my dressing style for years almost without any change	3.33	1034
吸引异性的注目是我很喜欢的感觉 I feel good to attract the attention of the opposite gender	2.84	1032
流行与实用之间我比较看重流行 I care more about fads between fashion and usage	2.66	1034
我觉得自己的品味与众不同 I think my taste is unique	3.02	1034
当我使用外国产品时心理多少会有满足感 I feel somewhat satisfied when I use imported products	2.91	1032
我偏好西方的艺术文化 I prefer western arts and culture	2.67	1032
在别人眼里我是个时髦的人 I am regarded a fashionable person by others	2.66	1031
我刻意打扮是为了发挥自己的个性 I dress up on purpose to show my personality	2.82	1034
我希望过非常浪漫的生活 I hope to live a very romantic life	3.24	1033

6-3 购物与消费// Shopping/ Consumption

	均值 Mean	样本量 N
我经常有冲动性购买 I often buy goods on impulse	2.95	1032
我认为名牌的商品品质比较好 I think famous brands are of better quality	3.69	1034
选购物品时我喜欢尝试新品牌、新产品 I like to try new brands and new products	3.30	1033
买东西时我经常货比三家 I often compare goods sold at different stores	3.49	1032
我经常购买具有独特风格的产品 I often purchase goods of unique style	3.11	1031
购买商品时我考虑的因素主要是价格 Price is my main consideration when I purchase goods	3.49	1034
与其把旧的东西拿去修理不如买新的 I would rather buy a new product than repair it	3.09	1034
为了买汽车和房子，我可以选择银行贷款的方式 In order to buy a car or a house, I can accept the way of loan	2.86	1033
我宁愿多花一点钱购买品质较好的东西 I prefer paying more for products with better quality	3.94	1032
即使价格贵一些，我还是喜欢买名牌产品 I would like to buy famous brands even if they are higher in price	3.24	1033
为节省时间和精力，我愿意花些钱购买某些产品或服务 In order to save time and energy, I'd like to pay more to buy related service and goods	3.27	1032
对于想要的东西，价格贵一些也会买 I will buy the item I like even if it is higher in price	3.51	1030
选购物品时我不喜欢更换品牌 I do not like change brands when I buy the goods	3.18	1029
我非常注意商店的气氛、布置及格调 I mind the atmosphere, setting and tone of the store	3.44	1027
对于有些想要的东西我会等到降价或特卖时才买 For the goods I want to buy, I can wait till they are on sale	3.29	1030

6-4 金钱与投资// Money Management

	均值 Mean	样本量 N
我常搞不清钱花到哪儿去了 I often wonder where I spent my money	2.99	1034
我认为节省开支比拼命挣钱重要 I think it more important to save money than to earn money hard	3.19	1033
我觉得自己对于金融投资方面的知识太少了 I think I know too little about financial investment	3.75	1032
我认为把钱用于投资股票是很危险的事情 I think investing money in stock is very dangerous	3.40	1032
相对于买股票我宁愿把钱存进银行 Compared with buying stocks, I prefer depositing my money in the bank	3.53	1033
我用信用卡购买许多东西 I buy many things with my credit cards	2.25	1029
经济上的安定对我来说很重要 Financial security is very important to me	4.22	1031
我是家里主要理财的人 I am the main financial manager of my family	3.14	1031

6-5 家庭与婚姻// Family/ Home/ Sex Roles

	均值 Mean	样本量 N
家庭是我生活的重心 Family is the main factor in my life	4.04	1032
家庭生活不一定要有小孩 Children do not matter much to my family life	2.48	1031
女人的主要任务是给家人一个快乐的家 Woman's main duty is to make the family happy	3.66	1032
男人应比女人能干 Man is supposed to be more able than woman	3.25	1032
我可以接受女方比男方学历高的婚姻观念 I can accept the idea that the wife holds higher academic degree than the husband	3.56	1032
男性也应该做家务 Husband should also share some housework	4.03	1031
我认为应该让孩子独立自主地成长 I think children should be let to grow independently	4.20	1031
我对老了以后的生活常常感到不安 I often feel restless about my aged life	2.90	1032
结婚仪式应该选在吉利的日子举行 Wedding ceremony should be held on the propitious date	3.98	1034
我赞同年轻人结婚后和父母分开住 I agree that the young couple does not live together with their parents	3.55	1032

6-6 工作与休闲// Work/ Living/ Spare time

	均值 Mean	样本量 N
工作的最佳报酬应该是成就感 The achievements are the best payment for my work	3.75	1034
工作上只要能获得好评价，不轻易换工作 As long as I am satisfied with my work, I will not change my job	3.58	1034
我喜欢安定有保障的工作 I like safe and secured job	4.13	1034
工作稍一懈怠我就会有落后于人的感觉 I feel I am falling behind whenever I am a little bit careless and lazy	3.46	1031
闲着没事做我会觉得不自在 I feel restless to idle away without doing anything	3.58	1030
比起做公司的一般职员我更喜欢独立的工作 I prefer being self-employed to being employed by others as an average staff	3.65	1032
山中或湖边的小屋最适合假期休闲 Huts in the mountain or besides the lake are best for leisure life	3.92	1034
即使会影响收入，我也希望有更多自己的时间 I'd like to have more private time even if that will decrease my earnings	3.26	1030
我宁愿住在市区，而不愿住在郊区 I prefer living in the suburbs to the town	3.44	1032
为了挣更多的钱我宁愿牺牲休闲 I would like sacrifice my leisure time to earn more money	3.27	1033
为了享受休闲，多花一些钱也是值得的 It's worth more to enjoying leisure life	3.42	1034

6-7 自我评价// Self-confidence/ Self-actualization

	均值 Mean	样本量 N
我凡事喜欢自己来，不喜欢依赖别人 I like to do things myself and don't like to depend on others	3.88	1033
与他人相比我认为自己具备更重要的素质 Compared with other people, I think I am of better nature	3.43	1032
我还没有达到自己的目标 I haven't reached my goal yet	3.91	1032
我喜欢被看作领导者 I'd like to be regarded as a leader	2.97	1033
我经常在生活中为自己确立更高的目标 I often set a higher goal for myself in the life	3.69	1033
我总觉得我的能力不如别人 I always feel inferior to others in term of ability	2.75	1034
不管做什么只要我喜欢便是享受 No matter what to do, I would enjoy it if I like it	3.73	1033
我想过有别于以往的人生 I once desire a different life	3.48	1034
我总是想尝试以前没有尝试的东西，接受新的挑战 I always try new things and would like to face new challenge	3.41	1031
我会有效地安排时间，协调好工作与休闲 I can effectively arrange my time, and make good balance between my work and rest	3.75	1033
我关心各种信息并能得到相关的信息和知识 I pay attention to various information and can get related information and knowledge	3.48	1029
我做事一向有计划 I always plan my things well	3.68	1034
我经常能从工作和生活中获得成就感和满足感 I often feel satisfied with my work and life	3.51	1032
在社交活动中我是比较活跃的分子 I am an active member in social life	3.10	1031
为了前途我会辛苦得去进修某些课程和训练 I'd like to take some hard training or courses in order to get a better future	3.48	1033
只要有一些自己的生活空间，我会觉得很满足 I will feel satisfied when I have a certain private living space	3.73	1034

6-8 关于广告// Advertising

	均值 Mean	样本量 N
对自己关心的商品类别，会比较注意其广告 I pay attention to the advertising of those categories that I care	3.65	1034
我觉得做过电视广告的商品有亲切感 I feel dear to those products which run TV commercials	3.22	1031
我为了了解社会的流行、潮流而关心广告 I pay attention to advertising to get to know the social fads and trends	3.09	1034
广告中的信息对我做购物决定起了很大的作用 The massage in advertising is very important factor in my buying decision	3.11	1033
如果这个广告我不喜欢，我就不会购买其相关产品 If I don't like the advertising, I will not buy the advertised products	3.28	1033
当电视出现广告时，我通常会换台 I often change channels when commercials appear on the TV screen	3.48	1034
真正的好产品不需要做广告 Real good products needn't run advertising	3.37	1033
购买商品时还是以有广告的品牌比较可靠 When purchasing goods, those advertised brands are more reliable	3.29	1027
广告是可以信赖的 Advertising can be trusted	2.78	1033
专家推荐的产品应该不会有错 Authority-endorsed products should be good	3.06	1029
广告反映了时代的潮流 Advertising reflects social trends	3.57	1029

6-9 关于信息寻求// Information Seeking

	均值 Mean	样本量 N
我经常从朋友那里听到各种各样的信息 I often get various kinds of information from my friends	3.54	1033
我劝导别人的情况比自己被别人劝导的情况多 I persuade other people more often than others persuade me	3.25	1030
得到新信息后我会立即告诉别人 I will immediately tell the new information I get to other people	3.50	1033
别人想做什么的时候通常会找我出主意 Other people like to consult me when they want to do something	3.18	1032
我觉得好的东西一定会向别人推荐 I will recommend the things that I think good to others	3.86	1030
我购买一种新产品或者享受新的服务一般都比别人早 I often buy or enjoy a new product or a new service earlier than others	2.90	1032
我对跟自己无关的话题不关心 I don't care for the topics not associated with me	3.38	1033
对于流行或新产品的情况，不知道也没有关系 It doesn't matter to me not to know the fads and new products	3.08	1030
当某种商品或服务成为议论的话题时，我也会去尝试 When a product or service becomes the topic of like, I will try it	3.38	1033
我觉得自己能够与新潮流、新信息保持同步 I think I can keep pace with the new fads and new products	3.12	1033

6-10 关注的社会问题// Social Concern

	均值 Mean	样本量 N
政府机构改革问题 Government Structure Reform	3.49	1033
人民币、股票、经济动向 RMB, stock market and economic movement	3.36	1032
东南亚经济危机和中国商业环境的恶化 Economic crisis in Southeast Asia and the deterioration of Chinese business situation	3.16	1033
中国人口问题 Chinese population	3.14	1033
地球变暖等环境问题 The environmental problem such as the earth becomes warmer	3.11	1028
地震、火灾、洪水等自然灾害及救济措施 Earthquake, fire, flood and the remedies	3.43	1031
克隆技术等生物技术的发展 The biological development such as cloning sheep	2.55	1028
爱滋病等疑难病症的扩散情况 The spread out of difficult and complicated diseases such as AIDS	2.79	1028
消费者保护法等围绕商品安全性的问题 Acts and regulation concerning product safety to protect consumers	3.52	1031
塑料瓶、容器及包装品的再生利用问题 The recycling and reuse of plastic bottles, containers and packages	2.87	1032
希望工程的情况 The Hope Project in China	3.17	1031
因特网、电脑时代的生活及其影响 The life in the age of Internet, computer and their influences	2.98	1030
下岗职工问题 The problem of workers out of work	3.80	1032
医疗改革等社会保险制度问题 The social security such as health and care security	3.93	1032
住房改革问题 the Housing Reform	3.90	1031

6-11 对目前生活状态的满意程度// Satisfaction Degree about Current Life State

	均值 Mean	样本量 N
家庭 Family	3.88	1030
工作 Work	3.36	1015
消费 Consumption	3.26	1031
休闲娱乐 Relaxation and Entertainment	3.27	1028
人际关系 Interpersonal Relationship	3.63	1031
综合 Overall	3.48	1026

● 重庆 / Chongqing

6-1 饮食与健康// Diet/ Nutrition/ Health

	均值 Mean	样本量 N
我很注意饮食以防发胖 I care much not to be over weight	3.09	623
我一周有三天以上不吃早饭 I cancel breakfast for half days in a week	2.39	620
我的一日三餐都很规律 I take regular meal 3 times a day	3.71	621
与西餐相比我更喜欢中式餐饮 Compared with western food, I prefer Chinese food	3.99	617
我经常购买半成品食品、冷冻食品等容易加工的食品 I often buy food that is easy to cook such as ready-made food, frozen food or cooked food	2.70	623
我经常吃一些维生素等保健品来补充营养 I often take some vitamins to supply nutrition	2.88	621
我会刻意去吃对健康美容有益的食物 I would like to take food that is good to health or beauty on purpose	2.82	622
我宁愿自己做饭而不愿去买现成的食物 I prefer doing cooking myself to buying cooked food	3.53	623
我很注意饮食的营养平衡 I care much about the balance of nutrition of food	3.55	621
我经常到麦当劳之类的快餐店吃东西 I often eat at fast-food restaurant like McDonald's	1.97	620
我很注意包装上有关添加剂、生产日期的说明 I do pay attention to the instruction of ingredients, and producing date on the package of the food	4.09	621

6-2 时尚与流行// Fashion/ Style/ Preference for Foreign Product

	均值 Mean	样本量 N
我希望过流行、时髦、休闲的生活 I desired to live a modern, fashionable and casual life	3.33	621
我很注意流行的趋势 I care for fads	2.96	622
我向往欧美等先进国家的生活方式 I appreciate the life style of the developed western countries such as USA	2.82	621
我很注意自己的外表修饰 I do mind my appearance and dressing	3.59	620
我时常尝试新的发型 I often try new hairstyle	2.24	622
我的服饰和装扮多年来基本上没有多大改变 I tend to keep my dressing style for years almost without any change	3.60	622
吸引异性的注目是我很喜欢的感觉 I feel good to attract the attention of the opposite gender	2.66	618
流行与实用之间我比较看重流行 I care more about fads between fashion and usage	2.43	623
我觉得自己的品味与众不同 I think my taste is unique	3.09	621
当我使用外国产品时心理多少会有满足感 I feel somewhat satisfied when I use imported products	2.61	618
我偏好西方的艺术文化 I prefer western arts and culture	2.46	620
在别人眼里我是个时髦的人 I am regarded a fashionable person by others	2.46	621
我刻意打扮是为了发挥自己的个性 I dress up on purpose to show my personality	2.74	622
我希望过非常浪漫的生活 I hope to live a very romantic life	3.25	620

6-3 购物与消费// Shopping/ Consumption

	均值 Mean	样本量 N
我经常有冲动性购买 I often buy goods on impulse	2.73	621
我认为名牌的商品品质比较好 I think famous brands are of better quality	3.81	622
选购物品时我喜欢尝试新品牌、新产品 I like to try new brands and new products	3.27	620
买东西时我经常货比三家 I often compare goods sold at different stores	3.79	622
我经常购买具有独特风格的产品 I often purchase goods of unique style	2.90	622
购买商品时我考虑的因素主要是价格 Price is my main consideration when I purchase goods	3.62	623
与其把旧的东西拿去修理不如买新的 I would rather buy a new product than repair it	3.03	622
为了买汽车和房子，我可以选择银行贷款的方式 In order to buy a car or a house, I can accept the way of loan	2.64	622
我宁愿多花一点钱购买品质较好的东西 I prefer paying more for products with better quality	4.12	621
即使价格贵一些，我还是喜欢买名牌产品 I would like to buy famous brands even if they are higher in price	3.31	621
为节省时间和精力，我愿意花些钱购买某些产品或服务 In order to save time and energy, I'd like to pay more to buy related service and goods	3.08	619
对于想要的东西，价格贵一些也会买 I will buy the item I like even if it is higher in price	3.70	622
选购物品时我不喜欢更换品牌 I do not like change brands when I buy the goods	3.36	621
我非常注意商店的气氛、布置及格调 I mind the atmosphere, setting and tone of the store	3.57	621
对于有些想要的东西我会等到降价或特卖时才买 For the goods I want to buy, I can wait till they are on sale	3.25	616

6-4 金钱与投资// Money Management

	均值 Mean	样本量 N
我常搞不清钱花到哪儿去了 I often wonder where I spent my money	2.93	622
我认为节省开支比拼命挣钱重要 I think it more important to save money than to earn money hard	3.33	620
我觉得自己对于金融投资方面的知识太少了 I think I know too little about financial investment	3.93	621
我认为把钱用于投资股票是很危险的事情 I think investing money in stock is very dangerous	3.51	622
相对于买股票我宁愿把钱存进银行 Compared with buying stocks, I prefer depositing my money in the bank	3.51	623
我用信用卡购买许多东西 I buy many things with my credit cards	1.99	614
经济上的安定对我来说很重要 Financial security is very important to me	4.44	622
我是家里主要理财的人 I am the main financial manager of my family	3.27	622

6-5 家庭与婚姻// Family/ Home/ Sex Roles

	均值 Mean	样本量 N
家庭是我生活的重心 Family is the main factor in my life	4.22	622
家庭生活不一定要有小孩 Children do not matter much to my family life	2.21	620
女人的主要任务是给家人一个快乐的家 Woman's main duty is to make the family happy	3.79	620
男人应比女人能干 Man is supposed to be more able than woman	3.50	620
我可以接受女方比男方学历高的婚姻观念 I can accept the idea that the wife holds higher academic degree than the husband	3.56	622
男性也应该做家务 Husband should also share some housework	4.19	621
我认为应该让孩子独立自主地成长 I think children should be let to grow independently	4.48	622
我对老了以后的生活常常感到不安 I often feel restless about my aged life	2.94	623
结婚仪式应该选在吉利的日子举行 Wedding ceremony should be held on the propitious date	3.90	620
我赞同年轻人结婚后和父母分开住 I agree that the young couple does not live together with their parents	3.83	621

6-6 工作与休闲// Work/ Living/ Spare time

	均值 Mean	样本量 N
工作的最佳报酬应该是成就感 The achievements are the best payment for my work	3.65	619
工作上只要能获得好评价，不轻易换工作 As long as I am satisfied with my work, I will not change my job	3.68	619
我喜欢安定有保障的工作 I like safe and secured job	4.28	621
工作稍一懈怠我就会有落后于人的感觉 I feel I am falling behind whenever I am a little bit careless and lazy	3.58	620
闲着没事做我会觉得不自在 I feel restless to idle away without doing anything	3.71	622
比起做公司的一般职员我更喜欢独立的工作 I prefer being self-employed to being employed by others as an average staff	3.76	623
山中或湖边的小屋最适合假期休闲 Huts in the mountain or besides the lake are best for leisure life	3.91	620
即使会影响收入，我也希望有更多自己的时间 I'd like to have more private time even if that will decrease my earnings	3.35	620
我宁愿住在市区，而不愿住在郊区 I prefer living in the suburbs to the town	3.23	622
为了挣更多的钱我宁愿牺牲休闲 I would like sacrifice my leisure time to earn more money	3.39	621
为了享受休闲，多花一些钱也是值得的 It's worth more to enjoying leisure life	3.25	619

6-7 自我评价// Self-confidence/ Self-actualization

	均值 Mean	样本量 N
我凡事喜欢自己来，不喜欢依赖别人 I like to do things myself and don't like to depend on others	4.15	620
与他人相比我认为自己具备更重要的素质 Compared with other people, I think I am of better nature	3.58	619
我还没有达到自己的目标 I haven't reached my goal yet	4.19	623
我喜欢被看作领导者 I'd like to be regarded as a leader	2.90	622
我经常在生活中为自己确立更高的目标 I often set a higher goal for myself in the life	3.82	622
我总觉得我的能力不如别人 I always feel inferior to others in term of ability	2.65	622
不管做什么只要我喜欢便是享受 No matter what to do, I would enjoy it if I like it	3.93	623
我想过有别于以往的人生 I once desire a different life	3.41	620
我总是想尝试以前没有尝试的东西，接受新的挑战 I always try new things and would like to face new challenge	3.49	622
我会有效地安排时间，协调好工作与休闲 I can effectively arrange my time, and make good balance between my work and rest	3.88	619
我关心各种信息并能得到相关的信息和知识 I pay attention to various information and can get related information and knowledge	3.49	621
我做事一向有计划 I always plan my things well	3.91	622
我经常能从工作和生活中获得成就感和满足感 I often feel satisfied with my work and life	3.52	622
在社交活动中我是比较活跃的分子 I am an active member in social life	3.28	622
为了前途我会辛苦得去进修某些课程和训练 I'd like to take some hard training or courses in order to get a better future	3.31	621
只要有一些自己的生活空间，我会觉得很满足 I will feel satisfied when I have a certain private living space	3.99	622

6-8 关于广告// Advertising

	均值 Mean	样本量 N
对自己关心的商品类别，会比较注意其广告 I pay attention to the advertising of those categories that I care	3.71	621
我觉得做过电视广告的商品有亲切感 I feel dear to those products which run TV commercials	3.21	621
我为了了解社会的流行、潮流而关心广告 I pay attention to advertising to get to know the social fads and trends	3.14	620
广告中的信息对我做购物决定起了很大的作用 The massage in advertising is very important factor in my buying decision	3.23	622
如果这个广告我不喜欢，我就不会购买其相关产品 If I don't like the advertising, I will not buy the advertised products	3.45	623
当电视出现广告时，我通常会换台 I often change channels when commercials appear on the TV screen	3.52	623
真正的好产品不需要做广告 Real good products needn't run advertising	3.59	623
购买商品时还是以有广告的品牌比较可靠 When purchasing goods, those advertised brands are more reliable	3.41	621
广告是可以信赖的 Advertising can be trusted	2.92	623
专家推荐的产品应该不会有错 Authority-endorsed products should be good	3.15	619
广告反映了时代的潮流 Advertising reflects social trends	3.63	618

6-9 关于信息寻求// Information Seeking

	均值 Mean	样本量 N
我经常从朋友那里听到各种各样的信息 I often get various kinds of information from my friends	3.67	619
我劝导别人的情况比自己被别人劝导的情况多 I persuade other people more often than others persuade me	3.44	622
得到新信息后我会立即告诉别人 I will immediately tell the new information I get to other people	3.72	622
别人想做什么的时候通常会找我出主意 Other people like to consult me when they want to do something	3.27	622
我觉得好的东西一定会向别人推荐 I will recommend the things that I think good to others	4.02	620
我购买一种新产品或者享受新的服务一般都比别人早 I often buy or enjoy a new product or a new service earlier than others	2.77	623
我对跟自己无关的话题不关心 I don't care for the topics not associated with me	3.56	623
对于流行或新产品的情况，不知道也没有关系 It doesn't matter to me not to know the fads and new products	3.15	621
当某种商品或服务成为议论的话题时，我也会去尝试 When a product or service becomes the topic of like, I will try it	3.40	621
我觉得自己能够与新潮流、新信息保持同步 I think I can keep pace with the new fads and new products	3.16	618

6-10 关注的社会问题// Social Concern

	均值 Mean	样本量 N
政府机构改革问题 Government Structure Reform	3.34	622
人民币、股票、经济动向 RMB, stock market and economic movement	3.11	623
东南亚经济危机和中国商业环境的恶化 Economic crisis in Southeast Asia and the deterioration of Chinese business situation	2.85	620
中国人口问题 Chinese population	3.05	623
地球变暖等环境问题 The environmental problem such as the earth becomes warmer	2.88	622
地震、火灾、洪水等自然灾害及救济措施 Earthquake, fire, flood and the remedies	3.52	619
克隆技术等生物技术的发展 The biological development such as cloning sheep	2.04	620
爱滋病等疑难病症的扩散情况 The spread out of difficult and complicated diseases such as AIDS	2.60	621
消费者保护法等围绕商品安全性的问题 Acts and regulation concerning product safety to protect consumers	3.67	623
塑料瓶、容器及包装品的再生利用问题 The recycling and reuse of plastic bottles, containers and packages	2.72	622
希望工程的情况 The Hope Project in China	3.16	622
因特网、电脑时代的生活及其影响 The life in the age of Internet, computer and their influences	2.51	619
下岗职工问题 The problem of workers out of work	3.98	621
医疗改革等社会保险制度问题 The social security such as health and care security	4.03	623
住房改革问题 the Housing Reform	4.03	621

6-11 对目前生活状态的满意程度// Satisfaction Degree about Current Life State

	均值 Mean	样本量 N
家庭 Family	3.80	622
工作 Work	3.10	577
消费 Consumption	3.14	621
休闲娱乐 Relaxation and Entertainment	3.21	621
人际关系 Interpersonal Relationship	3.66	622
综合 Overall	3.46	618

● 武汉 / Wuhan

6-1 饮食与健康// Diet/ Nutrition/ Health

	均值 Mean	样本量 N
我很注意饮食以防发胖 I care much not to be over weight	3.34	635
我一周有三天以上不吃早饭 I cancel breakfast for half days in a week	2.03	636
我的一日三餐都很规律 I take regular meal 3 times a day	3.82	633
与西餐相比我更喜欢中式餐饮 Compared with western food, I prefer Chinese food	4.08	635
我经常购买半成品食品、冷冻食品等容易加工的食品 I often buy food that is easy to cook such as ready-made food, frozen food or cooked food	2.92	635
我经常吃一些维生素等保健品来补充营养 I often take some vitamins to supply nutrition	2.86	633
我会刻意去吃对健康美容有益的食物 I would like to take food that is good to health or beauty on purpose	3.00	633
我宁愿自己做饭而不愿去买现成的食物 I prefer doing cooking myself to buying cooked food	3.44	635
我很注意饮食的营养平衡 I care much about the balance of nutrition of food	3.54	635
我经常到麦当劳之类的快餐店吃东西 I often eat at fast-food restaurant like McDonalds	2.47	634
我很注意包装上有关添加剂、生产日期的说明 I do pay attention to the instruction of ingredients, and producing date on the package of the food	4.07	635

6-2 时尚与流行// Fashion/ Style/ Preference for Foreign Product

	均值 Mean	样本量 N
我希望过流行、时髦、休闲的生活 I desired to live a modern, fashionable and casual life	3.28	635
我很注意流行的趋势 I care for fads	3.11	635
我向往欧美等先进国家的生活方式 I appreciate the life style of the developed western countries such as USA	2.71	632
我很注意自己的外表修饰 I do mind my appearance and dressing	3.67	635
我时常尝试新的发型 I often try new hairstyle	2.35	634
我的服饰和装扮多年来基本上没有多大改变 I tend to keep my dressing style for years almost without any change	3.55	634
吸引异性的注目是我很喜欢的感觉 I feel good to attract the attention of the opposite gender	2.66	634
流行与实用之间我比较看重流行 I care more about fads between fashion and usage	2.57	635
我觉得自己的品味与众不同 I think my taste is unique	3.09	635
当我使用外国产品时心理多少会有满足感 I feel somewhat satisfied when I use imported products	2.66	635
我偏好西方的艺术文化 I prefer western arts and culture	2.61	635
在别人眼里我是个时髦的人 I am regarded a fashionable person by others	2.68	635
我刻意打扮是为了发挥自己的个性 I dress up on purpose to show my personality	2.83	634
我希望过非常浪漫的生活 I hope to live a very romantic life	3.10	635

6-3 购物与消费// Shopping/ Consumption

	均值 Mean	样本量 N
我经常有冲动性购买 I often buy goods on impulse	2.80	634
我认为名牌的商品品质比较好 I think famous brands are of better quality	3.68	634
选购物品时我喜欢尝试新品牌、新产品 I like to try new brands and new products	3.30	635
买东西时我经常货比三家 I often compare goods sold at different stores	3.80	635
我经常购买具有独特风格的产品 I often purchase goods of unique style	3.06	634
购买商品时我考虑的因素主要是价格 Price is my main consideration when I purchase goods	3.60	635
与其把旧的东西拿去修理不如买新的 I would rather buy a new product than repair it	3.17	635
为了买汽车和房子，我可以选择银行贷款的方式 In order to buy a car or a house, I can accept the way of loan	2.91	634
我宁愿多花一点钱购买品质较好的东西 I prefer paying more for products with better quality	4.05	635
即使价格贵一些，我还是喜欢买名牌产品 I would like to buy famous brands even if they are higher in price	3.23	635
为节省时间和精力，我愿意花些钱购买某些产品或服务 In order to save time and energy, I'd like to pay more to buy related service and goods	3.19	634
对于想要的东西，价格贵一些也会买 I will buy the item I like even if it is higher in price	3.58	635
选购物品时我不喜欢更换品牌 I do not like change brands when I buy the goods	3.23	635
我非常注意商店的气氛、布置及格调 I mind the atmosphere, setting and tone of the store	3.68	634
对于有些想要的东西我会等到降价或特卖时才买 For the goods I want to buy, I can wait till they are on sale	3.39	635

6-4 金钱与投资// Money Management

	均值 Mean	样本量 N
我常搞不清钱花到哪儿去了 I often wonder where I spent my money	3.12	636
我认为节省开支比拼命挣钱重要 I think it more important to save money than to earn money hard	3.41	636
我觉得自己对于金融投资方面的知识太少了 I think I know too little about financial investment	3.89	634
我认为把钱用于投资股票是很危险的事情 I think investing money in stock is very dangerous	3.50	633
相对于买股票我宁愿把钱存进银行 Compared with buying stocks, I prefer depositing my money in the bank	3.59	635
我用信用卡购买许多东西 I buy many things with my credit cards	2.05	635
经济上的安定对我来说很重要 Financial security is very important to me	4.39	634
我是家里主要理财的人 I am the main financial manager of my family	3.26	635

6-5 家庭与婚姻// Family/ Home/ Sex Roles

	均值 Mean	样本量 N
家庭是我生活的重心 Family is the main factor in my life	4.24	635
家庭生活不一定要有小孩 Children do not matter much to my family life	2.18	634
女人的主要任务是给家人一个快乐的家 Woman's main duty is to make the family happy	3.82	635
男人应比女人能干 Man is supposed to be more able than woman	3.42	635
我可以接受女方比男方学历高的婚姻观念 I can accept the idea that the wife holds higher academic degree than the husband	3.55	633
男性也应该做家务 Husband should also share some housework	4.12	634
我认为应该让孩子独立自主地成长 I think children should be let to grow independently	4.46	634
我对老了以后的生活常常感到不安 I often feel restless about my aged life	3.09	635
结婚仪式应该选在吉利的日子举行 Wedding ceremony should be held on the propitious date	3.89	635
我赞同年轻人结婚后和父母分开住 I agree that the young couple does not live together with their parents	3.85	635

6-6 工作与休闲// Work/ Living/ Spare time

	均值 Mean	样本量 N
工作的最佳报酬应该是成就感 The achievements are the best payment for my work	3.90	635
工作上只要能获得好评价，不轻易换工作 As long as I am satisfied with my work, I will not change my job	3.67	635
我喜欢安定有保障的工作 I like safe and secured job	4.27	635
工作稍一懈怠我就会有落后于人的感觉 I feel I am falling behind whenever I am a little bit careless and lazy	3.70	635
闲着没事做我会觉得不自在 I feel restless to idle away without doing anything	3.90	635
比起做公司的一般职员我更喜欢独立的工作 I prefer being self-employed to being employed by others as an average staff	3.90	633
山中或湖边的小屋最适合假期休闲 Huts in the mountain or besides the lake are best for leisure life	3.86	635
即使会影响收入，我也希望有更多自己的时间 I'd like to have more private time even if that will decrease my earnings	3.27	634
我宁愿住在市区，而不愿住在郊区 I prefer living in the suburbs to the town	3.54	635
为了挣更多的钱我宁愿牺牲休闲 I would like sacrifice my leisure time to earn more money	3.42	635
为了享受休闲，多花一些钱也是值得的 It's worth more to enjoying leisure life	3.25	634

6-7 自我评价// Self-confidence/ Self-actualization

	均值 Mean	样本量 N
我凡事喜欢自己来，不喜欢依赖别人 I like to do things myself and don't like to depend on others	4.20	635
与他人相比我认为自己具备更重要的素质 Compared with other people, I think I am of better nature	3.65	635
我还没有达到自己的目标 I haven't reached my goal yet	4.20	635
我喜欢被看作领导者 I'd like to be regarded as a leader	3.01	634
我经常在生活中为自己确立更高的目标 I often set a higher goal for myself in the life	3.87	635
我总觉得我的能力不如别人 I always feel inferior to others in term of ability	2.71	635
不管做什么只要我喜欢便是享受 No matter what to do, I would enjoy it if I like it	3.97	633
我想过有别于以往的人生 I once desire a different life	3.44	633
我总是想尝试以前没有尝试的东西，接受新的挑战 I always try new things and would like to face new challenge	3.53	635
我会有效地安排时间，协调好工作与休闲 I can effectively arrange my time, and make good balance between my work and rest	3.92	635
我关心各种信息并能得到相关的信息和知识 I pay attention to various information and can get related information and knowledge	3.57	635
我做事一向有计划 I always plan my things well	3.84	634
我经常能从工作和生活中获得成就感和满足感 I often feel satisfied with my work and life	3.59	635
在社交活动中我是比较活跃的分子 I am an active member in social life	3.24	635
为了前途我会辛苦得去进修某些课程和训练 I'd like to take some hard training or courses in order to get a better future	3.47	634
只要有一些自己的生活空间，我会觉得很满足 I will feel satisfied when I have a certain private living space	4.01	633

6-8 关于广告// Advertising

	均值 Mean	样本量 N
对自己关心的商品类别，会比较注意其广告 I pay attention to the advertising of those categories that I care	3.83	634
我觉得做过电视广告的商品有亲切感 I feel dear to those products which run TV commercials	3.14	634
我为了了解社会的流行、潮流而关心广告 I pay attention to advertising to get to know the social fads and trends	3.15	635
广告中的信息对我做购物决定起了很大的作用 The massage in advertising is very important factor in my buying decision	3.28	635
如果这个广告我不喜欢，我就不会购买其相关产品 If I don't like the advertising, I will not buy the advertised products	3.53	633
当电视出现广告时，我通常会换台 I often change channels when commercials appear on the TV screen	3.68	635
真正的好产品不需要做广告 Real good products needn't run advertising	3.71	634
购买商品时还是以有广告的品牌比较可靠 When purchasing goods, those advertised brands are more reliable	3.32	635
广告是可以信赖的 Advertising can be trusted	2.75	635
专家推荐的产品应该不会有错 Authority-endorsed products should be good	3.18	634
广告反映了时代的潮流 Advertising reflects social trends	3.73	634

6-9 关于信息寻求// Information Seeking

	均值 Mean	样本量 N
我经常从朋友那里听到各种各样的信息 I often get various kinds of information from my friends	3.60	635
我劝导别人的情况比自己被别人劝导的情况多 I persuade other people more often than others persuade me	3.46	635
得到新信息后我会立即告诉别人 I will immediately tell the new information I get to other people	3.67	634
别人想做什么的时候通常会找我出主意 Other people like to consult me when they want to do something	3.34	634
我觉得好的东西一定会向别人推荐 I will recommend the things that I think good to others	3.99	634
我购买一种新产品或者享受新的服务一般都比别人早 I often buy or enjoy a new product or a new service earlier than others	2.93	635
我对跟自己无关的话题不关心 I don't care for the topics not associated with me	3.64	635
对于流行或新产品的情况，不知道也没有关系 It doesn't matter to me not to know the fads and new products	3.18	633
当某种商品或服务成为议论的话题时，我也会去尝试 When a product or service becomes the topic of like, I will try it	3.25	634
我觉得自己能够与新潮流、新信息保持同步 I think I can keep pace with the new fads and new products	3.13	635

6-10 关注的社会问题// Social Concern

	均值 Mean	样本量 N
政府机构改革问题 Government Structure Reform	3.56	623
人民币、股票、经济动向 RMB, stock market and economic movement	3.29	623
东南亚经济危机和中国商业环境的恶化 Economic crisis in Southeast Asia and the deterioration of Chinese business situation	3.01	623
中国人口问题 Chinese population	3.28	623
地球变暖等环境问题 The environmental problem such as the earth becomes warmer	3.23	622
地震、火灾、洪水等自然灾害及救济措施 Earthquake, fire, flood and the remedies	3.74	623
克隆技术等生物技术的发展 The biological development such as cloning sheep	2.51	623
爱滋病等疑难病症的扩散情况 The spread out of difficult and complicated diseases such as AIDS	2.82	623
消费者保护法等围绕商品安全性的问题 Acts and regulation concerning product safety to protect consumers	3.71	623
塑料瓶、容器及包装品的再生利用问题 The recycling and reuse of plastic bottles, containers and packages	3.05	623
希望工程的情况 The Hope Project in China	3.43	623
因特网、电脑时代的生活及其影响 The life in the age of Internet, computer and their influences	2.91	622
下岗职工问题 The problem of workers out of work	4.04	622
医疗改革等社会保险制度问题 The social security such as health and care security	4.17	623
住房改革问题 the Housing Reform	4.13	623

6-11 对目前生活状态的满意程度// Satisfaction Degree about Current Life State

	均值 Mean	样本量 N
家庭 Family	3.89	620
工作 Work	3.16	604
消费 Consumption	3.11	618
休闲娱乐 Relaxation and Entertainment	3.00	619
人际关系 Interpersonal Relationship	3.66	620
综合 Overall	3.48	618

● 西安 / Xi'an

6-1 饮食与健康// Diet/ Nutrition/ Health

	均值 Mean	样本量 N
我很注意饮食以防发胖 I care much not to be over weight	3.16	600
我一周有三天以上不吃早饭 I cancel breakfast for half days in a week	2.46	601
我的一日三餐都很规律 I take regular meal 3 times a day	3.62	601
与西餐相比我更喜欢中式餐饮 Compared with western food, I prefer Chinese food	3.99	600
我经常购买半成品食品、冷冻食品等容易加工的食品 I often buy food that is easy to cook such as ready-made food, frozen food or cooked food	2.81	601
我经常吃一些维生素等保健品来补充营养 I often take some vitamins to supply nutrition	2.78	601
我会刻意去吃对健康美容有益的食物 I would like to take food that is good to health or beauty on purpose	2.94	601
我宁愿自己做饭而不愿去买现成的食物 I prefer doing cooking myself to buying cooked food	3.18	601
我很注意饮食的营养平衡 I care much about the balance of nutrition of food	3.45	601
我经常到麦当劳之类的快餐店吃东西 I often eat at fast-food restaurant like McDonald's	2.14	601
我很注意包装上有关添加剂、生产日期的说明 I do pay attention to the instruction of ingredients, and producing date on the package of the food	4.02	601

6-2 时尚与流行// Fashion/ Style/ Preference for Foreign Product

	均值 Mean	样本量 N
我希望过流行、时髦、休闲的生活 I desired to live a modern, fashionable and casual life	3.27	600
我很注意流行的趋势 I care for fads	2.97	600
我向往欧美等先进国家的生活方式 I appreciate the life style of the developed western countries such as USA	2.79	601
我很注意自己的外表修饰 I do mind my appearance and dressing	3.58	601
我时常尝试新的发型 I often try new hairstyle	2.34	600
我的服饰和装扮多年来基本上没有多大改变 I tend to keep my dressing style for years almost without any change	3.40	601
吸引异性的注目是我很喜欢的感觉 I feel good to attract the attention of the opposite gender	2.73	601
流行与实用之间我比较看重流行 I care more about fads between fashion and usage	2.59	601
我觉得自己的品味与众不同 I think my taste is unique	3.10	600
当我使用外国产品时心理多少会有满足感 I feel somewhat satisfied when I use imported products	2.55	601
我偏好西方的艺术文化 I prefer western arts and culture	2.46	600
在别人眼里我是个时髦的人 I am regarded a fashionable person by others	2.53	601
我刻意打扮是为了发挥自己的个性 I dress up on purpose to show my personality	2.74	601
我希望过非常浪漫的生活 I hope to live a very romantic life	3.25	600

6-3 购物与消费// Shopping/ Consumption

	均值 Mean	样本量 N
我经常有冲动性购买 I often buy goods on impulse	2.83	601
我认为名牌的商品品质比较好 I think famous brands are of better quality	3.78	601
选购物品时我喜欢尝试新品牌、新产品 I like to try new brands and new products	3.24	601
买东西时我经常货比三家 I often compare goods sold at different stores	3.65	600
我经常购买具有独特风格的产品 I often purchase goods of unique style	2.95	601
购买商品时我考虑的因素主要是价格 Price is my main consideration when I purchase goods	3.41	601
与其把旧的东西拿去修理不如买新的 I would rather buy a new product than repair it	3.04	600
为了买汽车和房子，我可以选择银行贷款的方式 In order to buy a car or a house, I can accept the way of loan	2.74	600
我宁愿多花一点钱购买品质较好的东西 I prefer paying more for products with better quality	3.97	601
即使价格贵一些，我还是喜欢买名牌产品 I would like to buy famous brands even if they are higher in price	3.18	601
为节省时间和精力，我愿意花些钱购买某些产品或服务 In order to save time and energy, I'd like to pay more to buy related service and goods	3.20	600
对于想要的东西，价格贵一些也会买 I will buy the item I like even if it is higher in price	3.56	601
选购物品时我不喜欢更换品牌 I do not like change brands when I buy the goods	3.32	601
我非常注意商店的气氛、布置及格调 I mind the atmosphere, setting and tone of the store	3.45	600
对于有些想要的东西我会等到降价或特卖时才买 For the goods I want to buy, I can wait till they are on sale	2.96	598

6-4 金钱与投资// Money Management

	均值 Mean	样本量 N
我常搞不清钱花到哪儿去了 I often wonder where I spent my money	3.14	601
我认为节省开支比拼命挣钱重要 I think it more important to save money than to earn money hard	3.00	600
我觉得自己对于金融投资方面的知识太少了 I think I know too little about financial investment	3.63	601
我认为把钱用于投资股票是很危险的事情 I think investing money in stock is very dangerous	3.44	601
相对于买股票我宁愿把钱存进银行 Compared with buying stocks, I prefer depositing my money in the bank	3.45	600
我用信用卡购买许多东西 I buy many things with my credit cards	1.87	601
经济上的安定对我来说很重要 Financial security is very important to me	4.24	601
我是家里主要理财的人 I am the main financial manager of my family	3.36	601

6-5 家庭与婚姻// Family/ Home/ Sex Roles

	均值 Mean	样本量 N
家庭是我生活的重心 Family is the main factor in my life	4.10	601
家庭生活不一定要有小孩 Children do not matter much to my family life	2.21	600
女人的主要任务是给家人一个快乐的家 Woman's main duty is to make the family happy	3.75	601
男人应比女人能干 Man is supposed to be more able than woman	3.61	600
我可以接受女方比男方学历高的婚姻观念 I can accept the idea that the wife holds higher academic degree than the husband	3.68	601
男性也应该做家务 Husband should also share some housework	3.97	601
我认为应该让孩子独立自主地成长 I think children should be let to grow independently	4.29	600
我对老了以后的生活常常感到不安 I often feel restless about my aged life	2.91	600
结婚仪式应该选在吉利的日子举行 Wedding ceremony should be held on the propitious date	3.98	601
我赞同年轻人结婚后和父母分开住 I agree that the young couple does not live together with their parents	3.81	601

6-6 工作与休闲// Work/ Living/ Spare time

	均值 Mean	样本量 N
工作的最佳报酬应该是成就感 The achievements are the best payment for my work	3.79	601
工作上只要能获得好评价，不轻易换工作 As long as I am satisfied with my work, I will not change my job	3.60	601
我喜欢安定有保障的工作 I like safe and secured job	4.03	601
工作稍一懈怠我就会有落后于人的感觉 I feel I am falling behind whenever I am a little bit careless and lazy	3.61	599
闲着没事做我会觉得不自在 I feel restless to idle away without doing anything	3.65	601
比起做公司的一般职员我更喜欢独立的工作 I prefer being self-employed to being employed by others as an average staff	3.82	601
山中或湖边的小屋最适合假期休闲 Huts in the mountain or besides the lake are best for leisure life	3.77	600
即使会影响收入，我也希望有更多自己的时间 I'd like to have more private time even if that will decrease my earnings	3.32	600
我宁愿住在市区，而不愿住在郊区 I prefer living in the suburbs to the town	3.32	601
为了挣更多的钱我宁愿牺牲休闲 I would like sacrifice my leisure time to earn more money	3.24	601
为了享受休闲，多花一些钱也是值得的 It's worth more to enjoying leisure life	3.26	601

6-7 自我评价// Self-confidence/ Self-actualization

	均值 Mean	样本量 N
我凡事喜欢自己来，不喜欢依赖别人 I like to do things myself and don't like to depend on others	4.05	601
与他人相比我认为自己具备更重要的素质 Compared with other people, I think I am of better nature	3.66	600
我还没有达到自己的目标 I haven't reached my goal yet	4.01	601
我喜欢被看作领导者 I'd like to be regarded as a leader	3.01	601
我经常在生活中为自己确立更高的目标 I often set a higher goal for myself in the life	3.83	601
我总觉得我的能力不如别人 I always feel inferior to others in term of ability	2.57	601
不管做什么只要我喜欢便是享受 No matter what to do, I would enjoy it if I like it	3.90	601
我想过有别于以往的人生 I once desire a different life	3.48	601
我总是想尝试以前没有尝试的东西，接受新的挑战 I always try new things and would like to face new challenge	3.50	601
我会有效地安排时间，协调好工作与休闲 I can effectively arrange my time, and make good balance between my work and rest	3.80	600
我关心各种信息并能得到相关的信息和知识 I pay attention to various information and can get related information and knowledge	3.46	601
我做事一向有计划 I always plan my things well	3.74	601
我经常能从工作和生活中获得成就感和满足感 I often feel satisfied with my work and life	3.57	600
在社交活动中我是比较活跃的分子 I am an active member in social life	3.14	601
为了前途我会辛苦得去进修某些课程和训练 I'd like to take some hard training or courses in order to get a better future	3.48	600
只要有一些自己的生活空间，我会觉得很满足 I will feel satisfied when I have a certain private living space	3.88	601

6-8 关于广告// Advertising

	均值 Mean	样本量 N
对自己关心的商品类别，会比较注意其广告 I pay attention to the advertising of those categories that I care	3.76	601
我觉得做过电视广告的商品有亲切感 I feel dear to those products which run TV commercials	3.29	600
我为了了解社会的流行、潮流而关心广告 I pay attention to advertising to get to know the social fads and trends	3.03	601
广告中的信息对我做购物决定起了很大的作用 The massage in advertising is very important factor in my buying decision	3.27	600
如果这个广告我不喜欢，我就不会购买其相关产品 If I don't like the advertising, I will not buy the advertised products	3.53	601
当电视出现广告时，我通常会换台 I often change channels when commercials appear on the TV screen	3.54	601
真正的好产品不需要做广告 Real good products needn't run advertising	3.23	601
购买商品时还是以有广告的品牌比较可靠 When purchasing goods, those advertised brands are more reliable	3.36	599
广告是可以信赖的 Advertising can be trusted	2.77	601
专家推荐的产品应该不会有错 Authority-endorsed products should be good	3.08	601
广告反映了时代的潮流 Advertising reflects social trends	3.60	600

6-9 关于信息寻求// Information Seeking

	均值 Mean	样本量 N
我经常从朋友那里听到各种各样的信息 I often get various kinds of information from my friends	3.58	600
我劝导别人的情况比自己被别人劝导的情况多 I persuade other people more often than others persuade me	3.38	601
得到新信息后我会立即告诉别人 I will immediately tell the new information I get to other people	3.55	601
别人想做什么的时候通常会找我出主意 Other people like to consult me when they want to do something	3.28	601
我觉得好的东西一定会向别人推荐 I will recommend the things that I think good to others	3.94	600
我购买一种新产品或者享受新的服务一般都比别人早 I often buy or enjoy a new product or a new service earlier than others	2.92	601
我对跟自己无关的话题不关心 I don't care for the topics not associated with me	3.51	600
对于流行或新产品的情况，不知道也没有关系 It doesn't matter to me not to know the fads and new products	3.07	599
当某种商品或服务成为议论的话题时，我也会去尝试 When a product or service becomes the topic of like, I will try it	3.28	600
我觉得自己能够与新潮流、新信息保持同步 I think I can keep pace with the new fads and new products	3.11	601

6-10 关注的社会问题// Social Concern

	均值 Mean	样本量 N
政府机构改革问题 Government Structure Reform	3.50	600
人民币、股票、经济动向 RMB, stock market and economic movement	3.36	600
东南亚经济危机和中国商业环境的恶化 Economic crisis in Southeast Asia and the deterioration of Chinese business situation	3.08	600
中国人口问题 Chinese population	3.29	600
地球变暖等环境问题 The environmental problem such as the earth becomes warmer	3.11	600
地震、火灾、洪水等自然灾害及救济措施 Earthquake, fire, flood and the remedies	3.66	600
克隆技术等生物技术的发展 The biological development such as cloning sheep	2.53	600
爱滋病等疑难病症的扩散情况 The spread out of difficult and complicated diseases such as AIDS	2.66	600
消费者保护法等围绕商品安全性的问题 Acts and regulation concerning product safety to protect consumers	3.67	600
塑料瓶、容器及包装品的再生利用问题 The recycling and reuse of plastic bottles, containers and packages	2.93	600
希望工程的情况 The Hope Project in China	3.37	600
因特网、电脑时代的生活及其影响 The life in the age of Internet, computer and their influences	2.91	600
下岗职工问题 The problem of workers out of work	3.84	600
医疗改革等社会保险制度问题 The social security such as health and care security	4.02	600
住房改革问题 the Housing Reform	4.09	600

6-11 对目前生活状态的满意程度// Satisfaction Degree about Current Life State

	均值 Mean	样本量 N
家庭 Family	4.00	598
工作 Work	3.18	584
消费 Consumption	3.09	598
休闲娱乐 Relaxation and Entertainment	2.97	597
人际关系 Interpersonal Relationship	3.64	596
综合 Overall	3.40	597

● 沈阳 / Shenyang

6-1 饮食与健康// Diet/ Nutrition/ Health

	均值 Mean	样本量 N
我很注意饮食以防发胖 I care much not to be over weight	3.51	599
我一周有三天以上不吃早饭 I cancel breakfast for half days in a week	2.24	601
我的一日三餐都很规律 I take regular meal 3 times a day	3.78	601
与西餐相比我更喜欢中式餐饮 Compared with western food, I prefer Chinese food	4.01	601
我经常购买半成品食品、冷冻食品等容易加工的食品 I often buy food that is easy to cook such as ready-made food, frozen food or cooked food	2.82	600
我经常吃一些维生素等保健品来补充营养 I often take some vitamins to supply nutrition	2.91	601
我会刻意去吃对健康美容有益的食物 I would like to take food that is good to health or beauty on purpose	3.10	601
我宁愿自己做饭而不愿去买现成的食物 I prefer doing cooking myself to buying cooked food	3.43	601
我很注意饮食的营养平衡 I care much about the balance of nutrition of food	3.66	601
我经常到麦当劳之类的快餐店吃东西 I often eat at fast-food restaurant like McDonald's	2.37	601
我很注意包装上有关添加剂、生产日期的说明 I do pay attention to the instruction of ingredients, and producing date on the package of the food	4.17	601

6-2 时尚与流行// Fashion/ Style/ Preference for Foreign Product

	均值 Mean	样本量 N
我希望过流行、时髦、休闲的生活 I desired to live a modern, fashionable and casual life	3.41	600
我很注意流行的趋势 I care for fads	3.10	601
我向往欧美等先进国家的生活方式 I appreciate the life style of the developed western countries such as USA	2.89	601
我很注意自己的外表修饰 I do mind my appearance and dressing	3.83	601
我时常尝试新的发型 I often try new hairstyle	2.38	601
我的服饰和装扮多年来基本上没有多大改变 I tend to keep my dressing style for years almost without any change	3.52	600
吸引异性的注目是我很喜欢的感觉 I feel good to attract the attention of the opposite gender	2.61	601
流行与实用之间我比较看重流行 I care more about fads between fashion and usage	2.66	601
我觉得自己的品味与众不同 I think my taste is unique	3.24	601
当我使用外国产品时心理多少会有满足感 I feel somewhat satisfied when I use imported products	2.74	601
我偏好西方的艺术文化 I prefer western arts and culture	2.53	601
在别人眼里我是个时髦的人 I am regarded a fashionable person by others	2.62	601
我刻意打扮是为了发挥自己的个性 I dress up on purpose to show my personality	2.99	601
我希望过非常浪漫的生活 I hope to live a very romantic life	3.37	601

6-3 购物与消费// Shopping/ Consumption

	均值 Mean	样本量 N
我经常有冲动性购买 I often buy goods on impulse	2.70	601
我认为名牌的商品品质比较好 I think famous brands are of better quality	3.76	601
选购物品时我喜欢尝试新品牌、新产品 I like to try new brands and new products	3.36	599
买东西时我经常货比三家 I often compare goods sold at different stores	3.82	600
我经常购买具有独特风格的产品 I often purchase goods of unique style	3.24	599
购买商品时我考虑的因素主要是价格 Price is my main consideration when I purchase goods	3.49	601
与其把旧的东西拿去修理不如买新的 I would rather buy a new product than repair it	3.17	601
为了买汽车和房子，我可以选择银行贷款的方式 In order to buy a car or a house, I can accept the way of loan	2.75	600
我宁愿多花一点钱购买品质较好的东西 I prefer paying more for products with better quality	4.16	600
即使价格贵一些，我还是喜欢买名牌产品 I would like to buy famous brands even if they are higher in price	3.29	601
为节省时间和精力，我愿意花些钱购买某些产品或服务 In order to save time and energy, I'd like to pay more to buy related service and goods	3.20	601
对于想要的东西，价格贵一些也会买 I will buy the item I like even if it is higher in price	3.61	601
选购物品时我不喜欢更换品牌 I do not like change brands when I buy the goods	3.37	601
我非常注意商店的气氛、布置及格调 I mind the atmosphere, setting and tone of the store	3.55	601
对于有些想要的东西我会等到降价或特卖时才买 For the goods I want to buy, I can wait till they are on sale	3.17	601

6-4 金钱与投资// Money Management

	均值 Mean	样本量 N
我常搞不清钱花到哪儿去了 I often wonder where I spent my money	3.07	601
我认为节省开支比拼命挣钱重要 I think it more important to save money than to earn money hard	3.20	601
我觉得自己对于金融投资方面的知识太少了 I think I know too little about financial investment	3.81	600
我认为把钱用于投资股票是很危险的事情 I think investing money in stock is very dangerous	3.58	601
相对于买股票我宁愿把钱存进银行 Compared with buying stocks, I prefer depositing my money in the bank	3.57	601
我用信用卡购买许多东西 I buy many things with my credit cards	2.19	601
经济上的安定对我来说很重要 Financial security is very important to me	4.34	601
我是家里主要理财的人 I am the main financial manager of my family	3.24	601

6-5 家庭与婚姻// Family/ Home/ Sex Roles

	均值 Mean	样本量 N
家庭是我生活的重心 Family is the main factor in my life	4.26	601
家庭生活不一定要有小孩 Children do not matter much to my family life	2.54	601
女人的主要任务是给家人一个快乐的家 Woman's main duty is to make the family happy	3.90	601
男人应比女人能干 Man is supposed to be more able than woman	3.66	601
我可以接受女方比男方学历高的婚姻观念 I can accept the idea that the wife holds higher academic degree than the husband	3.45	601
男性也应该做家务 Husband should also share some housework	4.12	601
我认为应该让孩子独立自主地成长 I think children should be let to grow independently	4.40	601
我对老了以后的生活常常感到不安 I often feel restless about my aged life	3.08	601
结婚仪式应该选在吉利的日子举行 Wedding ceremony should be held on the propitious date	4.07	601
我赞同年轻人结婚后和父母分开住 I agree that the young couple does not live together with their parents	3.96	599

6-6 工作与休闲// Work/ Living/ Spare time

	均值 Mean	样本量 N
工作的最佳报酬应该是成就感 The achievements are the best payment for my work	3.85	598
工作上只要能获得好评价，不轻易换工作 As long as I am satisfied with my work, I will not change my job	3.59	600
我喜欢安定有保障的工作 I like safe and secured job	4.24	601
工作稍一懈怠我就会有落后于人的感觉 I feel I am falling behind whenever I am a little bit careless and lazy	3.66	600
闲着没事做我会觉得不自在 I feel restless to idle away without doing anything	3.67	600
比起做公司的一般职员我更喜欢独立的工作 I prefer being self-employed to being employed by others as an average staff	3.96	601
山中或湖边的小屋最适合假期休闲 Huts in the mountain or besides the lake are best for leisure life	3.99	601
即使会影响收入，我也希望有更多自己的时间 I'd like to have more private time even if that will decrease my earnings	3.41	601
我宁愿住在市区，而不愿住在郊区 I prefer living in the suburbs to the town	3.65	600
为了挣更多的钱我宁愿牺牲休闲 I would like sacrifice my leisure time to earn more money	3.41	601
为了享受休闲，多花一些钱也是值得的 It's worth more to enjoying leisure life	3.29	601

6-7 自我评价// Self-confidence/ Self-actualization

	均值 Mean	样本量 N
我凡事喜欢自己来，不喜欢依赖别人 I like to do things myself and don't like to depend on others	4.17	601
与他人相比我认为自己具备更重要的素质 Compared with other people, I think I am of better nature	3.73	601
我还没有达到自己的目标 I haven't reached my goal yet	4.22	601
我喜欢被看作领导者 I'd like to be regarded as a leader	3.09	601
我经常在生活中为自己确立更高的目标 I often set a higher goal for myself in the life	4.01	601
我总觉得我的能力不如别人 I always feel inferior to others in term of ability	2.58	601
不管做什么只要我喜欢便是享受 No matter what to do, I would enjoy it if I like it	3.93	601
我想过有别于以往的人生 I once desire a different life	3.46	601
我总是想尝试以前没有尝试的东西，接受新的挑战 I always try new things and would like to face new challenge	3.64	601
我会有效地安排时间，协调好工作与休闲 I can effectively arrange my time, and make good balance between my work and rest	3.97	601
我关心各种信息并能得到相关的信息和知识 I pay attention to various information and can get related information and knowledge	3.58	601
我做事一向有计划 I always plan my things well	3.89	600
我经常能从工作和生活中获得成就感和满足感 I often feel satisfied with my work and life	3.77	598
在社交活动中我是比较活跃的分子 I am an active member in social life	3.26	600
为了前途我会辛苦得去进修某些课程和训练 I'd like to take some hard training or courses in order to get a better future	3.61	601
只要有一些自己的生活空间，我会觉得很满足 I will feel satisfied when I have a certain private living space	4.01	600

6-8 关于广告// Advertising

	均值 Mean	样本量 N
对自己关心的商品类别，会比较注意其广告 I pay attention to the advertising of those categories that I care	3.65	600
我觉得做过电视广告的商品有亲切感 I feel dear to those products which run TV commercials	3.27	601
我为了了解社会的流行、潮流而关心广告 I pay attention to advertising to get to know the social fads and trends	3.11	601
广告中的信息对我做购物决定起了很大的作用 The massage in advertising is very important factor in my buying decision	3.25	601
如果这个广告我不喜欢，我就不会购买其相关产品 If I don't like the advertising, I will not buy the advertised products	3.44	601
当电视出现广告时，我通常会换台 I often change channels when commercials appear on the TV screen	3.64	600
真正的好产品不需要做广告 Real good products needn't run advertising	3.60	600
购买商品时还是以有广告的品牌比较可靠 When purchasing goods, those advertised brands are more reliable	3.31	601
广告是可以信赖的 Advertising can be trusted	2.87	601
专家推荐的产品应该不会有错 Authority-endorsed products should be good	3.19	601
广告反映了时代的潮流 Advertising reflects social trends	3.72	601

6-9 关于信息寻求// Information Seeking

	均值 Mean	样本量 N
我经常从朋友那里听到各种各样的信息 I often get various kinds of information from my friends	3.65	600
我劝导别人的情况比自己被别人劝导的情况多 I persuade other people more often than others persuade me	3.51	601
得到新信息后我会立即告诉别人 I will immediately tell the new information I get to other people	3.68	601
别人想做什么的时候通常会找我出主意 Other people like to consult me when they want to do something	3.36	601
我觉得好的东西一定会向别人推荐 I will recommend the things that I think good to others	4.04	601
我购买一种新产品或者享受新的服务一般都比别人早 I often buy or enjoy a new product or a new service earlier than others	3.04	601
我对跟自己无关的话题不关心 I don't care for the topics not associated with me	3.48	601
对于流行或新产品的情况，不知道也没有关系 It doesn't matter to me not to know the fads and new products	3.03	601
当某种商品或服务成为议论的话题时，我也会去尝试 When a product or service becomes the topic of like, I will try it	3.29	601
我觉得自己能够与新潮流、新信息保持同步 I think I can keep pace with the new fads and new products	3.27	601

6-10 关注的社会问题// Social Concern

	均值 Mean	样本量 N
政府机构改革问题 Government Structure Reform	3.48	600
人民币、股票、经济动向 RMB, stock market and economic movement	3.13	600
东南亚经济危机和中国商业环境的恶化 Economic crisis in Southeast Asia and the deterioration of Chinese business situation	2.92	599
中国人口问题 Chinese population	3.12	600
地球变暖等环境问题 The environmental problem such as the earth becomes warmer	3.16	600
地震、火灾、洪水等自然灾害及救济措施 Earhquake, fire, flood and the remedies	3.61	600
克隆技术等生物技术的发展 The biological development such as cloning sheep	2.48	599
爱滋病等疑难病症的扩散情况 The spread out of difficult and complicated diseases such as AIDS	2.61	600
消费者保护法等围绕商品安全性的问题 Acts and regulation concerning product safety to protect consumers	3.59	600
塑料瓶、容器及包装品的再生利用问题 The recycling and reuse of plastic bottles, containers and packages	3.01	600
希望工程的情况 The Hope Project in China	3.48	600
因特网、电脑时代的生活及其影响 The life in the age of Internet, computer and their influences	2.90	599
下岗职工问题 The problem of workers out of work	3.92	600
医疗改革等社会保险制度问题 The social security such as health and care security	4.02	600
住房改革问题 the Housing Reform	4.07	600

6-11 对目前生活状态的满意程度// Satisfaction Degree about Current Life State

	均值 Mean	样本量 N
家庭 Family	4.09	600
工作 Work	3.32	558
消费 Consumption	3.21	599
休闲娱乐 Relaxation and Entertainment	3.15	599
人际关系 Interpersonal Relationship	3.80	600
综合 Overall	3.57	599

第四篇　媒介分析
Part IV　Media Exposure

- 电视　Television
- 广播　Radio
- 报纸　Newspapers
- 杂志　Magazines
- 电影　Movies
- 体育赛事　Sports Event
- 交通工具　Transportation

1.电视 / Television

● 北京 / Beijing

1-1 样本、男性各年龄层、女性各年龄层平时是否接触电视媒介/ Exposure to Television by the Whole Sample, Age and Gender Groups

	人数 Number	从来不看 never	收看 yes
样本 Sample	1012	2.5	97.5
男性 Male	504	2.0	98.0
16~24 岁 Age	105	2.9	97.1
25~34 岁 Age	151	2.6	97.4
35~44 岁 Age	131	1.5	98.5
45~54 岁 Age	77	0.0	100.0
55~60 岁 Age	40	2.5	97.5
女性 Female	508	3.0	97.0
16~24 岁 Age	108	4.6	95.4
25~34 岁 Age	150	4.0	96.0
35~44 岁 Age	124	2.4	97.6
45~54 岁 Age	84	1.2	98.8
55~60 岁 Age	42	0.0	100.0

1-2 一周内不同时间收看电视的时间长短/ The Average Time Spending on Watching TV Per Day

1-2-1 一周内不同时间收看电视的时间长短(周一到周四)/ The Average Time Spending on Watching TV Per Day(Monday-Thursday)

	人数 Number	百分比 Percent
大约半小时或以下 about 1/2 hour or below	83	8.5
大约 1 小时 about 1 hour	168	17.2
大约 2 小时 about 2 hours	223	22.8
大约 3 小时 about 3 hours	192	19.7
大约 4 小时 about 4 hours	135	13.8
大约 5 小时 about 5 hours	62	6.3
大约 6 小时 about 6 hours	32	3.3
大约 7 小时 about 7 hours	15	1.5
大约 8 小时 about 8 hours	4	0.4
大约 9 小时 about 9 hours	2	0.2
大约 10 小时或以上 about 10 hours or over	9	0.9
记不清/不知道 can't remember	10	1.0
没有收看 didn't watch	42	4.3

n=977

1-2-2 一周内不同时间收看电视的时间长短(周五)/ The Average Time Spending on Watching TV Per Day(Friday)

	人数 Number	百分比 Percent
大约半小时或以下 about 1/2 hour or below	59	6.1
大约 1 小时 about 1 hour	127	13.1
大约 2 小时 about 2 hours	196	20.2
大约 3 小时 about 3 hours	215	22.2
大约 4 小时 about 4 hours	155	16.0
大约 5 小时 about 5 hours	83	8.6
大约 6 小时 about 6 hours	40	4.1
大约 7 小时 about 7 hours	19	2.0
大约 8 小时 about 8 hours	13	1.3
大约 9 小时 about 9 hours	6	0.6
大约 10 小时或以上 about 10 hours or over	14	1.4
记不清/不知道 can't remember	11	1.1
没有收看 didn't watch	31	3.2

n=969

1-2-3 一周内不同时间收看电视的时间长短(周六)/ The Average Time Spending on Watching TV Per Day(Saturday)

	人数 Number	百分比 Percent
大约半小时或以下 about 1/2 hour or below	41	4.2
大约 1 小时 about 1 hour	102	10.4
大约 2 小时 about 2 hours	175	17.9
大约 3 小时 about 3 hours	188	19.2
大约 4 小时 about 4 hours	153	15.6
大约 5 小时 about 5 hours	109	11.1
大约 6 小时 about 6 hours	60	6.1
大约 7 小时 about 7 hours	37	3.8
大约 8 小时 about 8 hours	26	2.7
大约 9 小时 about 9 hours	13	1.3
大约 10 小时或以上 about 10 hours or over	41	4.2
记不清/不知道 can't remember	12	1.2
没有收看 didn't watch	21	2.1

n=978

1-2-4 一周内不同时间收看电视的时间长短(周日)/ The Average Time Spending on Watching TV Per Day(Sunday)

	人数 Number	百分比 Percent
大约半小时或以下 about 1/2 hour or below	36	3.7
大约 1 小时 about 1 hour	104	10.6
大约 2 小时 about 2 hours	182	18.6
大约 3 小时 about 3 hours	173	17.7
大约 4 小时 about 4 hours	156	16.0
大约 5 小时 about 5 hours	113	11.6
大约 6 小时 about 6 hours	59	6.0
大约 7 小时 about 7 hours	39	4.0
大约 8 小时 about 8 hours	27	2.8
大约 9 小时 about 9 hours	13	1.3
大约 10 小时或以上 about 10 hours or over	37	3.8
记不清/不知道 can't remember	16	1.6
没有收看 didn't watch	22	2.3

n=977

1-3 经常收看的电视台/ Ranking of the Most Favorite TV Channels

注：本题为多选题，合计百分比超过 100%（Multiple answers）

排名 Brand Ranking	频道 Channels	人次 Person-time	百分比 Percent
1	北京有线 1 台（影视频道）Beijing Cable 1	603	61.3
2	中央 1 台 CCTV-1	511	52.0
3	北京 1 台 Beijing TV 1	423	43.0
4	中央 6 台 CCTV-6	218	22.2
5	中央 5 台 CCTV-5	197	20.0
6	湖南卫视 Hunan Satellite	132	13.4
7	北京 2 台 Beijing TV 2	126	12.8
8	中央 2 台 CCTV-2	97	9.9
9	北京有线 3 台（体育频道）Beijing Cable 3	95	9.7
10	北京有线 2 台（信息频道）Beijing Cable 2	77	7.8
11	中央 8 台 CCTV-8	68	6.9
12	凤凰卫视 Phoenix Channel	63	6.4
13	北京有线 4 台（生活频道）Beijing Cable 4	53	5.4
14	中央 3 台 CCTV-3	46	4.7
15	北京 3 台 Beijing TV 3	28	2.8
16	浙江卫视 Zhejiang Satellite	20	2.0
17	中央 4 台 CCTV-4	16	1.6
18	山东卫视 Shandong Satellite	14	1.4
19	中央 7 台 CCTV-7	12	1.2
20	贵州卫视 Guizhou Satellite	10	1.0
21	四川卫视 Sichuan Satellite	9	0.9
22	云南卫视 Yunnan Satellite	7	0.7
23	广西卫视 Guangxi Satellite	6	0.6
23	河北电视台 Hebei TV 1	6	0.6
24	河南卫视 Henan Satellite	5	0.5

n=983

1-4 样本、男性各年龄层、女性各年龄层最喜欢收看的频道/ The Most Favorite TV Channels by the Whole Sample, Age and Gender Groups

注：本题为多选题，合计百分比超过 100%（Multiple answers）

	人数 Number	北京有线1台（影视频道）Beijing Cable 1	中央1台 CCTV-1	北京1台 Beijing TV 1	中央6台 CCTV-6	中央5台 CCTV-5	湖南卫视 Hunan Satellite	北京2台 Beijing TV 2
样本 Sample	**983**	**61.3**	**52.0**	**43.0**	**22.2**	**20.0**	**13.4**	**12.8**
男性 Male	**492**	**51.2**	**53.3**	**42.9**	**23.6**	**30.7**	**7.7**	**10.6**
16~24 岁 Age	102	59.8	32.4	29.4	26.5	30.4	12.7	13.7
25~34 岁 Age	146	50.0	49.3	44.5	26.7	38.4	7.5	9.6
35~44 岁 Age	129	49.6	61.2	41.1	20.9	30.2	4.7	13.2
45~54 岁 Age	76	50.0	67.1	51.3	25.0	25.0	7.9	5.3
55~60 岁 Age	39	41.0	69.2	61.5	10.3	15.4	5.1	7.7
女性 Female	**491**	**71.5**	**50.7**	**43.2**	**20.8**	**9.4**	**19.1**	**15.1**
16~24 岁 Age	103	84.5	23.3	37.9	21.4	7.8	32.0	24.3
25~34 岁 Age	144	75.7	47.9	31.3	27.1	7.6	25.0	8.3
35~44 岁 Age	119	61.3	61.3	57.1	15.1	10.9	14.3	19.3
45~54 岁 Age	83	68.7	63.9	43.4	21.7	12.0	8.4	12.0
55~60 岁 Age	42	59.5	71.4	57.1	11.9	9.5	2.4	9.5

续前表 continued

	人数 Number	中央2台 CCTV-2	北京有线3台（体育频道）Beijing Cable 3	北京有线2台（信息频道）Beijing Cable 2	中央8台 CCTV-8	凤凰卫视 Phoenix Channel	北京有线4台（生活频道）Beijing Cable 4
样本 Sample	**983**	**9.9**	**9.7**	**7.8**	**6.9**	**6.4**	**5.4**
男性 Male	**492**	**12.4**	**15.4**	**8.1**	**5.9**	**5.7**	**6.1**
16~24 岁 Age	102	10.8	26.5	18.6	3.9	5.9	1.0
25~34 岁 Age	146	15.1	15.1	2.7	5.5	6.2	6.8
35~44 岁 Age	129	10.1	12.4	7.8	6.2	7.0	10.9
45~54 岁 Age	76	10.5	9.2	5.3	5.3	5.3	2.6
55~60 岁 Age	39	17.9	10.3	7.7	12.8	0.0	7.7
女性 Female	**491**	**7.3**	**3.9**	**7.5**	**7.9**	**7.1**	**4.7**
16~24 岁 Age	103	2.9	5.8	17.5	1.0	7.8	1.9
25~34 岁 Age	144	5.6	4.9	5.6	10.4	9.0	6.9
35~44 岁 Age	119	7.6	3.4	6.7	6.7	7.6	7.6
45~54 岁 Age	83	15.7	2.4	3.6	7.2	3.6	2.4
55~60 岁 Age	42	7.1	0.0	0.0	21.4	4.8	0.0

续前表 continued

	人数 Number	中央3台 CCTV-3	北京3台 Beijing TV 3	浙江卫视 Zhejiang Satellite	中央4台 CCTV-4	山东卫视 Shandong Satellite	中央7台 CCTV-7
样本 Sample	**983**	**4.7**	**2.8**	**2.0**	**1.6**	**1.4**	**1.2**
男性 Male	**492**	**4.5**	**1.2**	**1.8**	**1.4**	**1.0**	**1.6**
16~24 岁 Age	102	6.9	2.9	0.0	1.0	1.0	1.0
25~34 岁 Age	146	4.1	0.7	1.4	0.7	1.4	3.4
35~44 岁 Age	129	2.3	0.0	3.1	1.6	0.8	0.8
45~54 岁 Age	76	6.6	2.6	0.0	3.9	1.3	0.0
55~60 岁 Age	39	2.6	0.0	7.7	0.0	0.0	2.6
女性 Female	**491**	**4.9**	**4.5**	**2.2**	**1.8**	**1.8**	**0.8**
16~24 岁 Age	103	4.9	4.9	2.9	0.0	3.9	1.0
25~34 岁 Age	144	7.6	5.6	2.1	3.5	1.4	0.7
35~44 岁 Age	119	0.8	0.8	0.0	0.8	0.8	1.7
45~54 岁 Age	83	6.0	7.2	1.2	2.4	1.2	0.0
55~60 岁 Age	42	4.8	4.8	9.5	2.4	2.4	0.0

续前表 continued

	人数 Number	贵州卫视 Guizhou Satellite	四川卫视 Sichuan Satellite	云南卫视 Yunnan Satellite	广西卫视 Guangxi Satellite	河北电视台 Hebei TV 1	河南卫视 -Henan Satellite
样本 Sample	983	1.0	0.9	0.7	0.6	0.6	0.5
男性 Male	492	0.4	1.0	0.6	0.0	0.8	0.6
16~24 岁 Age	102	0.0	1.0	1.0	0.0	0.0	1.0
25~34 岁 Age	146	0.0	1.4	0.7	0.0	1.4	0.0
35~44 岁 Age	129	0.8	0.8	0.8	0.0	0.8	0.8
45~54 岁 Age	76	1.3	1.3	0.0	0.0	0.0	1.3
55~60 岁 Age	39	0.0	0.0	0.0	0.0	2.6	0.0
女性 Female	491	1.6	0.8	0.8	1.2	0.4	0.4
16~24 岁 Age	103	0.0	1.9	0.0	3.9	0.0	1.0
25~34 岁 Age	144	2.1	1.4	1.4	0.7	0.7	0.0
35~44 岁 Age	119	1.7	0.0	0.8	0.8	0.0	0.0
45~54 岁 Age	83	2.4	0.0	1.2	0.0	1.2	0.0
55~60 岁 Age	42	2.4	0.0	0.0	0.0	0.0	2.4

1-5 经常收看的电视频道/ Ranking of the Most Favorite TV Channels

1-5-1 经常收看的电视频道(周一--周四)/ Ranking of the Most Favorite TV Channels(Monday--Thursday)

注：本题为多选题，合计百分比超过 100%（Multiple answers）

排名 Brand Ranking	频道 Channels	人次 Person-time	百分比 Percent
1	北京有线 1 台（影视频道）Beijing Cable 1	608	64.5
2	中央 1 台 CCTV-1	593	63.0
3	北京 1 台 Beijing TV 1	522	55.4
4	中央 6 台 CCTV-6	297	31.5
5	北京 2 台 Beijing TV 2	259	27.5
6	中央 5 台 CCTV-5	248	26.3
7	中央 2 台 CCTV-2	188	20.0
8	湖南卫视 Hunan Satellite	182	19.3
9	中央 8 台 CCTV-8	177	18.8
10	北京有线 3 台（体育频道）Beijing Cable 3	173	18.4
11	北京有线 4 台（生活频道）Beijing Cable 4	151	16.0
12	北京有线 2 台（信息频道）Beijing Cable 2	144	15.3
13	北京 3 台 Beijing TV 3	122	13.0
14	浙江卫视 Zhejiang Satellite	113	12.0
15	中央 3 台 CCTV-3	106	11.3
16	四川卫视 Sichuan Satellite	96	10.2
16	山东卫视 Shandong Satellite	96	10.2
17	河北电视台 Hebei TV 1	81	8.6
18	凤凰卫视 Phoenix Channel	76	8.1
19	贵州卫视 Guizhou Satellite	65	6.9
20	云南卫视 Yunnan Satellite	62	6.6
21	中央 4 台 CCTV-4	57	6.1
22	中央 7 台 CCTV-7	53	5.6
23	广西卫视 Guangxi Satellite	48	5.1
24	中国教育台 China Education TV 1	32	3.4
25	福建东南卫视 Fujian Satellite Southeast Channel	30	3.2

n=942

1-5-2 经常收看的电视频道(周五)/ Ranking of the Most Favorite TV Channels(Friday)

注：本题为多选题，合计百分比超过 100%（Multiple answers）

排名 Brand Ranking	频道 Channels	人次 Person-time	百分比 Percent
1	北京有线 1 台（影视频道）Beijing Cable 1	602	63.6
2	中央 1 台 CCTV-1	580	61.3
3	北京 1 台 Beijing TV 1	491	51.9
4	中央 6 台 CCTV-6	299	31.6
5	北京 2 台 Beijing TV 2	254	26.8
6	中央 5 台 CCTV-5	238	25.2
7	湖南卫视 Hunan Satellite	200	21.1
8	中央 2 台 CCTV-2	178	18.8
9	中央 8 台 CCTV-8	173	18.3
10	北京有线 3 台（体育频道）Beijing Cable 3	164	17.3
11	北京有线 2 台（信息频道）Beijing Cable 2	144	15.2
12	北京有线 4 台（生活频道）Beijing Cable 4	133	14.1
13	浙江卫视 Zhejiang Satellite	115	12.2
13	北京 3 台 Beijing TV 3	115	12.2
14	中央 3 台 CCTV-3	109	11.5
15	四川卫视 Sichuan Satellite	95	10.0
16	山东卫视 Shandong Satellite	83	8.8
17	河北电视台 Hebei TV 1	77	8.1
18	凤凰卫视 Phoenix Channel	76	8.0
19	云南卫视 Yunnan Satellite	66	7.0
20	贵州卫视 Guizhou Satellite	61	6.4
21	中央 4 台 CCTV-4	59	6.2
22	中央 7 台 CCTV-7	51	5.4
23	广西卫视 Guangxi Satellite	47	5.0
24	福建东南卫视 Fujian Satellite Southeast Channel	30	3.2
25	广东卫视 Guangdong Satellite	29	3.1

n=946

1-5-3 经常收看的电视频道(周六)/ Ranking of the Most Favorite TV Channels(Saturday)

注：本题为多选题，合计百分比超过 100%（Multiple answers）

排名 Brand Ranking	频道 Channels	人次 Person-time	百分比 Percent
1	北京有线 1 台（影视频道）Beijing Cable 1	623	64.8
2	中央 1 台 CCTV-1	578	60.1
3	北京 1 台 Beijing TV 1	495	51.5
4	中央 6 台 CCTV-6	312	32.5
5	湖南卫视 Hunan Satellite	299	31.1
6	北京 2 台 Beijing TV 2	256	26.6
7	中央 5 台 CCTV-5	249	25.9
8	中央 2 台 CCTV-2	189	19.7
9	北京有线 3 台（体育频道）Beijing Cable 3	180	18.7
10	中央 8 台 CCTV-8	165	17.2
11	北京有线 2 台（信息频道）Beijing Cable 2	146	15.2
12	北京有线 4 台（生活频道）Beijing Cable 4	144	15.0
13	浙江卫视 Zhejiang Satellite	127	13.2
14	北京 3 台 Beijing TV 3	124	12.9
15	中央 3 台 CCTV-3	108	11.2
16	四川卫视 Sichuan Satellite	99	10.3
17	山东卫视 Shandong Satellite	93	9.7
18	凤凰卫视 Phoenix Channel	86	8.9
19	河北电视台 Hebei TV 1	83	8.6
20	云南卫视 Yunnan Satellite	70	7.3
21	贵州卫视 Guizhou Satellite	68	7.1
22	中央 7 台 CCTV-7	62	6.5
23	中央 4 台 CCTV-4	55	5.7
24	广西卫视 Guangxi Satellite	51	5.3
25	福建东南卫视 Fujian Satellite Southeast Channel	37	3.9

n=961

1-5-4 经常收看的电视频道(周日)/ Ranking of the Most Favorite TV Channels(Sunday)

注：本题为多选题，合计百分比超过 100%（Multiple answers）

排名 Brand Ranking	频道 Channels	人次 Person-time	百分比 Percent
1	北京有线 1 台（影视频道）Beijing Cable 1	606	63.5
2	中央 1 台 CCTV-1	579	60.7
3	北京 1 台 Beijing TV 1	489	51.3
4	中央 6 台 CCTV-6	317	33.2
5	北京 2 台 Beijing TV 2	252	26.4
6	中央 5 台 CCTV-5	250	26.2
7	湖南卫视 Hunan Satellite	245	25.7
8	中央 2 台 CCTV-2	202	21.2
9	北京有线 3 台（体育频道）Beijing Cable 3	182	19.1
10	中央 8 台 CCTV-8	168	17.6
11	北京有线 4 台（生活频道）Beijing Cable 4	145	15.2
12	北京有线 2 台（信息频道）Beijing Cable 2	142	14.9
13	浙江卫视 Zhejiang Satellite	129	13.5
14	北京 3 台 Beijing TV 3	128	13.4
15	中央 3 台 CCTV-3	112	11.7
16	四川卫视 Sichuan Satellite	95	10.0
17	山东卫视 Shandong Satellite	92	9.6
18	凤凰卫视 Phoenix Channel	85	8.9
19	河北电视台 Hebei TV 1	82	8.6
20	云南卫视 Yunnan Satellite	74	7.8
21	贵州卫视 Guizhou Satellite	67	7.0
22	中央 7 台 CCTV-7	61	6.4
23	中央 4 台 CCTV-4	55	5.8
24	广西卫视 Guangxi Satellite	50	5.2
25	广东卫视 Guangdong Satellite	34	3.6
25	福建东南卫视 Fujian Satellite Southeast Channel	34	3.6
25	中国教育台 China Education TV 1	34	3.6

n=954

1-6 经常收看的电视节目/ Ranking of the Most Favorite TV Programs

注：本题为多选题，合计百分比超过 100%（Multiple answers）

排名 Ranking	电视节目 TV Programs	人次 Person-time	百分比 Percent
1	国内新闻 national news	610	63.0
2	国际新闻 international news	555	57.3
3	体育新闻 sports news	312	32.2
4	港台电视剧 TV play(HK.Taiwan)	285	29.4
5	新闻评论 news comments	231	23.9
6	港台影片 film from HK.Taiwan	221	22.8
7	综艺节目 comprehensive arts	216	22.3
8	国外影片 overseas film	209	21.6
9	国内电视剧 TV play(inland)	196	20.2
10	MTV/音乐节目 MTV/music	173	17.9
11	天气预报 weather forecast	148	15.3
12	赛事报道 games report	119	12.3
13	国内影片 inland film	112	11.6
14	体育专栏节目 sports feature	105	10.8
15	本地新闻 local news	101	10.4
16	谈话节目 Talk Show	91	9.4
17	金融股市 finance & stock	86	8.9
18	军事类节目 military program	80	8.3
19	经济新闻 economic news	78	8.1
20	国外电视剧 overseas TV play	63	6.5
21	曲艺节目 folk art	60	6.2
22	经济信息 economic information	53	5.5
23	科教类节目 scientific education	52	5.4
24	电视直销 direct sale on TV	41	4.2
25	少儿节目 children's program	33	3.4
25	女性节目 women's program	33	3.4
26	消费指南 consumption guide	32	3.3
27	戏曲/戏剧 opera	30	3.1
28	专题类节目 special report	19	2.0
29	广告 advertising	11	1.1
30	舞蹈节目 dancing program	6	0.6
30	其他 others	6	0.6

n=968

1-7 样本、男性各年龄层、女性各年龄层经常收看的电视节目/ The Most Favorite TV Programs by the Whole Sample, Age and Gender Groups

注：本题为多选题，合计百分比超过 100%（Multiple answers）

	人数 Number	国内新闻 national news	国际新闻 international news	新闻评论 news comments	本地新闻 local news	谈话节目 Talk Show	经济新闻 economic news
样本 Sample	968	63.0	29.4	57.3	22.8	10.4	8.1
男性 Male	487	65.9	16.6	66.9	19.5	9.4	11.1
16~24 岁 Age	99	36.4	26.3	42.4	38.4	2.0	9.1
25~34 岁 Age	146	65.8	21.2	66.4	22.6	7.5	14.4
35~44 岁 Age	128	78.9	7.8	80.5	13.3	14.8	7.8
45~54 岁 Age	75	76.0	14.7	69.3	5.3	10.7	16.0
55~60 岁 Age	39	79.5	7.7	82.1	7.7	15.4	5.1
女性 Female	481	60.1	42.4	47.6	26.2	11.4	5.0
16~24 岁 Age	101	28.7	64.4	27.7	57.4	2.0	3.0
25~34 岁 Age	139	57.6	41.7	55.4	21.6	8.6	7.2
35~44 岁 Age	119	73.9	36.1	47.9	21.8	17.6	6.7
45~54 岁 Age	80	73.8	32.5	58.8	11.3	12.5	2.5
55~60 岁 Age	42	78.6	28.6	47.6	7.1	23.8	2.4

续前表 continued

	人数 Number	经济信息 economic information	金融股市 finance & stock	电视直销 direct sale on TV	消费指南 consumption guide	体育新闻 sports news	赛事报道 games report
样本 Sample	968	5.5	8.9	4.2	3.3	32.2	12.3
男性 Male	487	6.4	10.1	2.1	1.6	47.6	19.5
16~24 岁 Age	99	7.1	5.1	1.0	2.0	54.5	26.3
25~34 岁 Age	146	4.8	15.1	1.4	3.4	46.6	19.2
35~44 岁 Age	128	9.4	11.7	3.9	0.8	48.4	17.2
45~54 岁 Age	75	2.7	5.3	1.3	0.0	44.0	17.3
55~60 岁 Age	39	7.7	7.7	2.6	0.0	38.5	15.4
女性 Female	481	4.6	7.7	6.4	5.0	16.6	5.0
16~24 岁 Age	101	2.0	1.0	2.0	2.0	19.8	5.0
25~34 岁 Age	139	4.3	10.1	10.1	9.4	13.7	3.6
35~44 岁 Age	119	7.6	14.3	6.7	6.7	15.1	4.2
45~54 岁 Age	80	6.3	6.3	5.0	1.3	21.3	6.3
55~60 岁 Age	42	0.0	0.0	7.1	0.0	14.3	9.5

续前表 continued

	人数 Number	体育专栏节目 sports feature	国内电视剧 TV play(inland)	港台电视剧 TV play (HK.Taiwan)	国外电视剧 overseas TV play	国内影片 inland film	国外影片 overseas film
样本 Sample	968	10.8	20.2	29.4	6.5	11.6	21.6
男性 Male	487	15.2	16.8	16.6	3.7	10.9	22.0
16~24 岁 Age	99	29.3	3.0	26.3	1.0	9.1	36.4
25~34 岁 Age	146	14.4	14.4	21.2	3.4	12.3	20.5
35~44 岁 Age	128	10.2	19.5	7.8	3.9	7.0	15.6
45~54 岁 Age	75	10.7	28.0	14.7	6.7	17.3	22.7
55~60 岁 Age	39	7.7	30.8	7.7	5.1	10.3	10.3
女性 Female	481	6.4	23.7	42.4	9.4	12.3	21.2
16~24 岁 Age	101	8.9	13.9	64.4	9.9	16.8	28.7
25~34 岁 Age	139	7.9	20.9	41.7	11.5	8.6	30.9
35~44 岁 Age	119	5.0	21.8	36.1	5.9	8.4	15.1
45~54 岁 Age	80	6.3	33.8	32.5	10.0	13.8	11.3
55~60 岁 Age	42	0.0	42.9	28.6	9.5	21.4	7.1

续前表 continued

	人数 Number	港台影片 film from HK.Taiwan	天气预报 weather forecast	广告 advertising	MTV/音乐节目 MTV/music	舞蹈节目 dancing program	曲艺节目 folk art	戏曲/戏剧 opera
样本 Sample	968	22.8	15.3	1.1	17.9	0.6	6.2	3.1
男性 Male	487	19.5	12.7	1.2	12.5	0.4	6.0	3.3
16~24 岁 Age	99	38.4	13.1	2.0	37.4	0.0	1.0	2.0
25~34 岁 Age	146	22.6	8.2	1.4	13.7	0.0	5.5	2.1
35~44 岁 Age	128	13.3	17.2	0.8	2.3	0.8	4.7	0.8
45~54 岁 Age	75	5.3	13.3	0.0	0.0	0.0	14.7	5.3
55~60 岁 Age	39	7.7	12.8	2.6	2.6	2.6	7.7	15.4
女性 Female	481	26.2	17.9	1.0	23.3	0.8	6.4	2.9
16~24 岁 Age	101	57.4	8.9	1.0	53.5	2.0	1.0	1.0
25~34 岁 Age	139	21.6	17.3	1.4	24.5	0.7	3.6	0.7
35~44 岁 Age	119	21.8	21.8	0.8	12.6	0.8	6.7	0.8
45~54 岁 Age	80	11.3	22.5	0.0	7.5	0.0	12.5	7.5
55~60 岁 Age	42	7.1	21.4	2.4	7.1	0.0	16.7	11.9

续前表 continued

	人数 Number	综艺节目 comprehensive arts	军事类节目 military program	专题类节目 special report	科教类节目 scientific education	少儿节目 children's program	女性节目 women's program	其他 others
样本 Sample	968	22.3	8.3	2.0	5.4	3.4	3.4	0.6
男性 Male	487	14.8	13.8	2.3	7.2	2.1	0.2	0.4
16~24 岁 Age	99	12.1	14.1	0.0	10.1	5.1	0.0	0.0
25~34 岁 Age	146	17.1	16.4	2.1	4.8	1.4	0.7	0.7
35~44 岁 Age	128	10.2	12.5	3.1	8.6	0.8	0.0	0.0
45~54 岁 Age	75	20.0	14.7	5.3	4.0	2.7	0.0	0.0
55~60 岁 Age	39	17.9	5.1	0.0	10.3	0.0	0.0	2.6
女性 Female	481	29.9	2.7	1.7	3.5	4.8	6.7	0.8
16~24 岁 Age	101	34.7	0.0	1.0	3.0	5.0	5.0	1.0
25~34 岁 Age	139	24.5	3.6	1.4	3.6	9.4	9.4	0.7
35~44 岁 Age	119	32.8	0.8	3.4	5.0	4.2	6.7	1.7
45~54 岁 Age	80	30.0	7.5	0.0	2.5	0.0	6.3	0.0
55~60 岁 Age	42	28.6	2.4	2.4	2.4	0.0	2.4	0.0

1-8 不同学历的观众收看电视节目的偏好/ Program Preference by Educational Levels

注：本题为多选题，合计百分比超过 100%（Multiple answers）

	人数 Number	国内新闻 national news	国际新闻 international news	新闻评论 news comments	本地新闻 local news	谈话节目 Talk Show	经济新闻 economic news
样本 Sample	964	63.1	57.4	24.0	10.5	9.4	7.9
小学及以下 Primary School or Below	28	67.9	39.3	10.7	17.9	3.6	10.7
初中 Middle School	161	64.6	57.8	21.1	11.2	4.3	5.6
高中/中专/技校 High School/Technical Secondary School	418	62.7	51.2	20.8	11.5	10.0	2.6
大学专科 2-3 Year College	199	63.8	68.8	28.1	9.0	12.6	13.1
大学本科 4-5 Year College	143	59.4	62.2	34.3	7.7	9.1	16.8
研究生或以上 Graduate or Above	15	73.3	60.0	13.3	6.7	20.0	20.0

续前表 continued

	人数 Number	经济信息 economic information	金融股市 finance & stock	电视直销 direct sale on TV	消费指南 consumption guide	体育新闻 sports news	赛事报道 games report
样本 Sample	**964**	**5.5**	**8.8**	**4.3**	**3.3**	**32.3**	**12.2**
小学及以下 Primary School or Below	28	0.0	3.6	0.0	0.0	17.9	3.6
初中 Middle School	161	3.7	6.2	8.1	3.1	29.8	15.5
高中/中专/技校 High School/Technical Secondary School	418	2.6	5.7	5.3	4.5	32.1	12.0
大学专科 2-3 Year College	199	9.5	14.6	2.0	1.5	33.2	12.6
大学本科 4-5 Year College	143	10.5	14.7	0.7	3.5	35.7	11.2
研究生或以上 Graduate or Above	15	13.3	0.0	6.7	0.0	46.7	6.7

续前表 continued

	人数 Number	体育专栏节目 sports feature	国内电视剧 TV play(inland)	港台电视剧 TV play (HK.Taiwan)	国外电视剧 overseas TV play	国内影片 inland film	国外影片 overseas film
样本 Sample	**964**	**10.8**	**20.3**	**29.5**	**6.5**	**11.6**	**21.6**
小学及以下 Primary School or Below	28	7.1	42.9	28.6	10.7	28.6	0.0
初中 Middle School	161	8.7	32.3	29.8	9.9	16.8	10.6
高中/中专/技校 High School/Technical Secondary School	418	12.2	19.6	34.9	5.5	11.7	18.7
大学专科 2-3 Year College	199	9.0	15.1	27.1	7.5	11.1	29.6
大学本科 4-5 Year College	143	11.9	13.3	18.9	4.2	4.2	32.9
研究生或以上 Graduate or Above	15	13.3	6.7	6.7	0.0	0.0	46.7

续前表 continued

	人数 Number	港台影片 film from HK.Taiwan	天气预报 weather forecast	广告 advertising	MTV/音乐节目 MTV/music	舞蹈节目 dancing program	曲艺节目 folk art	戏曲/戏剧 opera
样本 Sample	**964**	**22.8**	**15.4**	**1.1**	**17.9**	**0.6**	**6.2**	**3.1**
小学及以下 Primary School or Below	28	17.9	21.4	3.6	7.1	0.0	17.9	7.1
初中 Middle School	161	20.5	16.8	0.6	9.3	1.2	9.3	4.3
高中/中专/技校 High School/Technical Secondary School	418	29.2	15.8	1.4	23.9	0.7	6.2	3.6
大学专科 2-3 Year College	199	17.1	13.6	0.5	12.6	0.0	4.0	2.0
大学本科 4-5 Year College	143	18.2	14.7	1.4	19.6	0.0	4.2	1.4
研究生或以上 Graduate or Above	15	0.0	6.7	0.0	20.0	6.7	0.0	0.0

续前表 continued

	人数 Number	综艺节目 comprehensive arts	军事类节目 military program	专题类节目 special report	科教类节目 scientific education	少儿节目 children's program	女性节目 women's program	其他 others
样本 Sample	**964**	**22.3**	**8.3**	**2.0**	**5.4**	**3.4**	**3.4**	**0.6**
小学及以下 Primary School or Below	28	25.0	7.1	0.0	3.6	3.6	0.0	0.0
初中 Middle School	161	28.0	9.3	2.5	3.1	1.2	3.7	0.0
高中/中专/技校 High School/Technical Secondary School	418	21.5	7.9	1.0	5.5	5.0	3.8	1.0
大学专科 2-3 Year College	199	22.1	7.5	3.0	6.5	2.0	2.0	0.5
大学本科 4-5 Year College	143	18.2	9.1	2.1	5.6	3.5	4.9	0.0
研究生或以上 Graduate or Above	15	20.0	13.3	13.3	13.3	0.0	0.0	6.7

1-9 经常收看电视时段/ Weekday Times Slots of Television Exposure

注：本题为多选题，合计百分比超过 100%（Multiple answers）

时间段 times slots	周一--周四(%) (Monday--Thursday)	周五(%) (Friday)	周六(%) (Saturday)	周日(%) (Sunday)
样本量 Sample	n=943	n=950	n=965	n=965
0:00-0:30	1.9	1.8	2.3	2.1
0:30-1:00	1.6	1.5	1.9	1.8
1:00-1:30	1.1	1.1	1.2	1.2
1:30-2:00	1.1	0.9	0.9	1.1
2:00-2:30	0.2	0.3	0.4	0.6
2:30-3:00	0.2	0.2	0.3	0.3
3:00-3:30	0.1	0.1	0.1	0.3
3:30-4:00	0.1	0.1	0.1	0.2
4:00-4:30	0.1	0.3	0.2	0.1
4:30-5:00	0.2	0.3	0.4	0.3
5:00-5:30	0.2	0.2	0.2	0.2
5:30-6:00	0.6	0.6	0.7	0.7
6:00-6:30	1.7	1.3	1.1	1.2
6:30-7:00	3.2	2.4	1.7	1.8
7:00-7:30	5.8	4.3	4.0	4.2
7:30-8:00	4.1	3.3	4.0	5.2
8:00-8:30	3.0	3.4	5.5	5.9
8:30-9:00	3.0	3.6	8.1	8.4
9:00-9:30	5.1	5.4	15.6	17.3
9:30-10:00	6.0	6.1	17.6	19.1
10:00-10:30	8.2	7.4	21.8	22.1
10:30-11:00	6.6	6.6	19.9	20.7
11:00-11:30	6.3	6.3	16.7	17.8
11:30-12:00	6.5	6.7	15.9	16.7
12:00-12:30	10.9	10.4	16.4	16.9
12:30-13:00	6.4	6.5	10.2	10.6
13:00-13:30	4.1	5.3	9.1	8.5
13:30-14:00	3.1	4.6	9.4	9.4
14:00-14:30	3.0	4.1	12.2	12.0
14:30-15:00	2.8	4.0	12.7	12.3
15:00-15:30	3.8	5.4	14.0	13.8
15:30-16:00	3.6	5.4	14.1	13.7
16:00-16:30	3.5	5.4	13.8	13.1
16:30-17:00	3.0	4.4	12.0	11.3
17:00-17:30	4.3	5.5	11.1	10.8
17:30-18:00	6.9	7.7	11.6	11.6
18:00-18:30	19.8	20.0	21.3	21.8
18:30-19:00	35.2	35.8	36.6	36.2
19:00-19:30	63.5	63.7	64.2	64.2
19:30-20:00	58.2	61.6	64.7	64.7
20:00-20:30	60.9	67.5	70.5	68.7
20:30-21:00	57.2	65.3	69.2	66.2
21:00-21:30	52.3	61.4	66.3	62.6
21:30-22:00	43.1	52.7	57.0	52.4
22:00-22:30	28.6	36.9	40.7	35.1
22:30-23:00	19.5	26.3	29.5	24.5
23:00-23:30	11.0	15.1	16.6	14.3
23:30-24:00	7.8	10.5	11.7	9.8

1-10 不同消费者层平时是否接触电视媒介/ TV Exposure by Market Segments

1-10-1 时尚流行指标/ Fads Popular Index

	人数 Number	从来不看 never	收看 yes
样本 Sample	998	2.4	97.6
平实生活指向 simple living orientation	491	1.8	98.2
时尚流行指向 fashion orientation	507	3.0	97.0

1-10-2 广告态度指标/ Advertising Attitude Index

	人数 Number	从来不看 never	收看 yes
样本 Sample	994	2.5	97.5
广告淡漠指向 indifferent orientation	289	2.1	97.9
中间层 medium	572	2.3	97.7
信赖广告指向 loyal orientation	133	4.5	95.5

1-11 不同消费者层收看电视频道的偏好/ Channel Preference by Market Segments

1-11-1 时尚流行指标/ Fads Popular Index

注：本题为多选题，合计百分比超过 100%（Multiple answers）

	人数 Number	北京有线1台（影视频道）Beijing Cable 1	中央1台 CCTV-1	北京1台 Beijing TV 1	中央6台 CCTV-6	中央5台 CCTV-5	湖南卫视 Hunan Satellite	北京2台 Beijing TV 2
样本 Sample	970	61.2	52.2	43.0	22.4	19.8	13.5	12.9
平实生活指向 simple living orientation	481	56.1	58.8	41.4	22.0	22.7	9.6	11.2
时尚流行指向 fashion orientation	489	66.3	45.6	44.6	22.7	17.0	17.4	14.5

续前表 continued

	人数 Number	中央2台 CCTV-2	北京有线3台（体育频道）Beijing Cable 3	北京有线2台（信息频道）Beijing Cable 2	中央8台 CCTV-8	凤凰卫视 Phoenix Channel	北京有线4台（生活频道）Beijing Cable 4
样本 Sample	970	10.0	9.6	7.9	6.9	6.3	5.3
平实生活指向 simple living orientation	481	11.4	9.6	8.1	8.7	6.4	4.8
时尚流行指向 fashion orientation	489	8.6	9.6	7.8	5.1	6.1	5.7

续前表 continued

	人数 Number	中央3台 CCTV-3	北京3台 Beijing TV 3	浙江卫视 Zhejiang Satellite	中央4台 CCTV-4	山东卫视 Shandong Satellite	中央7台 CCTV-7
样本 Sample	970	4.7	2.8	2.1	1.6	1.4	1.2
平实生活指向 simple living orientation	481	5.0	2.5	1.2	1.7	1.0	1.7
时尚流行指向 fashion orientation	489	4.5	3.1	2.9	1.6	1.8	0.8

续前表 continued

	人数 Number	贵州卫视 Guizhou Satellite	四川卫视 Sichuan Satellite	云南卫视 Yunnan Satellite	广西卫视 Guangxi Satellite	河北电视台 Hebei TV 1	河南卫视 Henan Satellite
样本 Sample	970	1.0	0.8	0.7	0.6	0.6	0.5
平实生活指向 simple living orientation	481	0.4	0.8	0.2	0.2	1.0	0.6
时尚流行指向 fashion orientation	489	1.6	0.8	1.2	1.0	0.2	0.4

1-11-2 广告态度指标/ Advertising Attitude Index

注：本题为多选题，合计百分比超过 100%（Multiple answers）

	人数 Number	北京有线1台（影视频道）Beijing Cable 1	中央1台 CCTV-1	北京1台 Beijing TV 1	中央6台 CCTV-6	中央5台 CCTV-5	湖南卫视 Hunan Satellite	北京2台 Beijing TV 2
样本 Sample	965	61.2	52.0	43.4	22.2	20.1	13.3	12.8
广告淡漠指向 indifferent orientation	283	59.4	48.4	43.8	19.4	21.9	8.5	15.9
中间层 medium	556	60.6	53.6	44.6	22.8	20.0	14.4	12.2
信赖广告指向 loyal orientation	126	68.3	53.2	37.3	25.4	16.7	19.0	8.7

续前表 continued

	人数 Number	中央2台 CCTV-2	北京有线3台（体育频道）Beijing Cable 3	北京有线2台（信息频道）Beijing Cable 2	中央8台 CCTV-8	凤凰卫视 Phoenix Channel	北京有线4台（生活频道）Beijing Cable 4
样本 Sample	965	9.9	9.4	7.8	6.9	6.4	5.4
广告淡漠指向 indifferent orientation	283	9.9	11.3	9.9	7.1	5.7	6.7
中间层 medium	556	10.3	8.5	7.2	7.2	6.7	4.5
信赖广告指向 loyal orientation	126	8.7	9.5	5.6	5.6	7.1	6.3

续前表 continued

	人数 Number	中央3台 CCTV-3	北京3台 Beijing TV 3	浙江卫视 Zhejiang Satellite	中央4台 CCTV-4	山东卫视 Shandong Satellite	中央7台 CCTV-7
样本 Sample	965	4.8	2.8	2.1	1.7	1.5	1.2
广告淡漠指向 indifferent orientation	283	4.2	3.2	2.1	2.1	1.4	0.7
中间层 medium	556	5.2	2.0	2.0	1.1	1.6	1.8
信赖广告指向 loyal orientation	126	4.0	5.6	2.4	3.2	0.8	0.0

续前表 continued

	人数 Number	贵州卫视 Guizhou Satellite	四川卫视 Sichuan Satellite	云南卫视 Yunnan Satellite	广西卫视 Guangxi Satellite	河北电视台 Hebei TV 1	河南卫视 Henan Satellite
样本 Sample	965	1.0	0.9	0.7	0.5	0.5	0.5
广告淡漠指向 indifferent orientation	283	1.1	2.1	0.4	0.7	0.7	1.1
中间层 medium	556	0.9	0.5	0.9	0.5	0.4	0.4
信赖广告指向 loyal orientation	126	1.6	0.0	0.8	0.0	0.8	0.0

1-12 不同消费者层收看电视节目的偏好/ Program Preference by Market Segments

1-12-1 时尚流行指标/ Fads Popular Index

注：本题为多选题，合计百分比超过 100%（Multiple answers）

	人数 Number	国内新闻 national news	国际新闻 international news	新闻评论 news comments	本地新闻 local news	谈话节目 Talk Show	经济新闻 economic news
样本 Sample	955	63.0	57.4	23.9	10.6	9.3	8.0
平实生活指向 simple living orientation	474	64.8	60.8	23.0	9.9	9.1	8.9
时尚流行指向 fashion orientation	481	61.3	54.1	24.7	11.2	9.6	7.1

续前表 continued

	人数 Number	经济信息 economic information	金融股市 finance & stock	电视直销 direct sale on TV	消费指南 consumption guide	体育新闻 sports news	赛事报道 games report
样本 Sample	955	5.4	8.8	4.3	3.4	32.4	12.4
平实生活指向 simple living orientation	474	6.1	9.5	3.2	2.7	34.6	13.3
时尚流行指向 fashion orientation	481	4.8	8.1	5.4	4.0	30.1	11.4

续前表 continued

	人数 Number	体育专栏节目 sports feature	国内电视剧 TV play (inland)	港台电视剧 TV play (HK.Taiwan)	国外电视剧 overseas TV play	国内影片 inland film	国外影片 overseas film
样本 Sample	955	10.9	20.4	29.0	6.6	11.5	21.3
平实生活指向 simple living orientation	474	11.8	20.7	22.8	6.8	13.1	20.3
时尚流行指向 fashion orientation	481	10.0	20.2	35.1	6.4	10.0	22.2

续前表 continued

	人数 Number	港台影片 film from HK.Taiwan	天气预报 weather forecast	广告 advertising	MTV/音乐节目 MTV/music	舞蹈节目 dancing program	曲艺节目 folk art	戏曲/戏剧 opera
样本 Sample	955	22.6	15.3	1.2	17.9	0.6	6.3	3.1
平实生活指向 simple living orientation	474	17.1	17.7	0.6	13.1	0.2	7.2	4.0
时尚流行指向 fashion orientation	481	28.1	12.9	1.7	22.7	1.0	5.4	2.3

续前表 continued

	人数 Number	综艺节目 comprehensive arts	军事类节目 military program	专题类节目 special report	科教类节目 scientific education	少儿节目 children's program	女性节目 women's program	其他 others
样本 Sample	955	22.5	8.3	2.0	5.4	3.5	3.5	0.6
平实生活指向 simple living orientation	474	20.9	7.4	2.7	5.9	3.6	2.1	0.8
时尚流行指向 fashion orientation	481	24.1	9.1	1.2	5.0	3.3	4.8	0.4

1-12-2 广告态度指标/ Advertising Attitude Index

注：本题为多选题，合计百分比超过100%（Multiple answers）

	人数 Number	国内新闻 national news	国际新闻 international news	新闻评论 news comments	本地新闻 local news	谈话节目 Talk Show	经济新闻 economic news
样本 Sample	951	63.1	57.8	24.2	10.6	9.6	8.1
广告淡漠指向 indifferent orientation	277	59.2	59.9	21.3	9.4	10.8	9.0
中间层 medium	549	65.8	58.1	26.4	12.0	9.1	8.2
信赖广告指向 loyal orientation	125	60.0	52.0	20.8	7.2	8.8	5.6

续前表 continued

	人数 Number	经济信息 economic information	金融股市 finance & stock	电视直销 direct sale on TV	消费指南 consumption guide	体育新闻 sports news	赛事报道 games report
样本 Sample	951	5.6	9.0	4.2	3.3	32.1	12.2
广告淡漠指向 indifferent orientation	277	5.8	8.7	1.4	3.2	32.9	12.6
中间层 medium	549	6.2	9.7	4.7	3.1	31.0	11.5
信赖广告指向 loyal orientation	125	2.4	7.2	8.0	4.0	35.2	14.4

续前表 continued

	人数 Number	体育专栏节目 sports feature	国内电视剧 TV play (inland)	港台电视剧 TV play (HK.Taiwan)	国外电视剧 overseas TV play	国内影片 inland film	国外影片 overseas film
样本 Sample	951	10.9	20.0	29.3	6.6	11.7	21.9
广告淡漠指向 indifferent orientation	277	13.4	19.1	27.1	10.1	12.3	24.2
中间层 medium	549	10.4	20.0	29.5	5.8	11.5	22.2
信赖广告指向 loyal orientation	125	8.0	21.6	33.6	2.4	11.2	15.2

续前表 continued

	人数 Number	港台影片 film from HK.Taiwan	天气预报 weather forecast	广告 advertising	MTV/音乐节目 MTV/music	舞蹈节目 dancing program	曲艺节目 folk art	戏曲/戏剧 opera
样本 Sample	951	22.6	15.0	1.2	17.7	0.6	6.3	3.0
广告淡漠指向 indifferent orientation	277	21.3	17.0	0.4	14.1	0.4	6.5	3.2
中间层 medium	549	20.8	14.2	1.1	19.1	0.7	6.0	2.7
信赖广告指向 loyal orientation	125	33.6	14.4	3.2	19.2	0.8	7.2	4.0

续前表 continued

	人数 Number	综艺节目 comprehensive arts	军事类节目 military program	专题类节目 special report	科教类节目 scientific education	少儿节目 children's program	女性节目 women's program	其他 others
样本 Sample	951	21.9	8.3	2.0	5.5	3.4	3.5	0.6
广告淡漠指向 indifferent orientation	277	17.7	6.9	1.8	7.2	2.9	1.4	0.7
中间层 medium	549	22.6	9.1	2.0	5.6	2.9	3.6	0.5
信赖广告指向 loyal orientation	125	28.0	8.0	2.4	0.8	6.4	7.2	0.8

● 上海 / Shanghai

1-1 样本、男性各年龄层、女性各年龄层平时是否接触电视媒介/ Exposure to Television by the Whole Sample, Age and Gender Groups

	人数 Number	从来不看 never	收看 yes
样本 Sample	1014	3.4	96.6
男性 Male	509	3.3	96.7
16~24 岁 Age	109	6.4	93.6
25~34 岁 Age	146	4.1	95.9
35~44 岁 Age	130	1.5	98.5
45~54 岁 Age	85	1.2	98.8
55~60 岁 Age	39	2.6	97.4
女性 Female	505	3.4	96.6
16~24 岁 Age	108	5.6	94.4
25~34 岁 Age	144	1.4	98.6
35~44 岁 Age	130	3.8	96.2
45~54 岁 Age	82	2.4	97.6
55~60 岁 Age	41	4.9	95.1

1-2 一周内不同时间收看电视的时间长短/ The Average Time Spending on Watching TV Per Day

1-2-1 一周内不同时间收看电视的时间长短(周一到周四)/ The Average Time Spending on Watching TV Per Day(Monday-Thursday)

	人数 Number	百分比 Percent
大约半小时或以下 about 1/2 hour or below	64	6.5
大约 1 小时 about 1 hour	199	20.3
大约 2 小时 about 2 hours	279	28.5
大约 3 小时 about 3 hours	224	22.9
大约 4 小时 about 4 hours	83	8.5
大约 5 小时 about 5 hours	36	3.7
大约 6 小时 about 6 hours	16	1.6
大约 7 小时 about 7 hours	6	0.6
大约 8 小时 about 8 hours	4	0.4
大约 9 小时 about 9 hours	4	0.4
大约 10 小时或以上 about 10 hours or over	4	0.4
记不清/不知道 can't remember	18	1.8
没有收看 didn't watch	42	4.3

n=979

1-2-2 一周内不同时间收看电视的时间长短(周五)/ The Average Time Spending on Watching TV Per Day(Friday)

	人数 Number	百分比 Percent
大约半小时或以下 about 1/2 hour or below	48	4.9
大约 1 小时 about 1 hour	145	14.9
大约 2 小时 about 2 hours	249	25.5
大约 3 小时 about 3 hours	242	24.8
大约 4 小时 about 4 hours	128	13.1
大约 5 小时 about 5 hours	63	6.5
大约 6 小时 about 6 hours	32	3.3
大约 7 小时 about 7 hours	12	1.2
大约 8 小时 about 8 hours	7	0.7
大约 9 小时 about 9 hours	4	0.4
大约 10 小时或以上 about 10 hours or over	5	0.5
记不清/不知道 can't remember	20	2.0
没有收看 didn't watch	21	2.2

n=976

1-2-3 一周内不同时间收看电视的时间长短(周六)/ The Average Time Spending on Watching TV Per Day(Saturday)

	人数 Number	百分比 Percent
大约半小时或以下 about 1/2 hour or below	38	3.9
大约 1 小时 about 1 hour	114	11.7
大约 2 小时 about 2 hours	213	21.8
大约 3 小时 about 3 hours	235	24.1
大约 4 小时 about 4 hours	137	14.0
大约 5 小时 about 5 hours	78	8.0
大约 6 小时 about 6 hours	55	5.6
大约 7 小时 about 7 hours	32	3.3
大约 8 小时 about 8 hours	19	1.9
大约 9 小时 about 9 hours	7	0.7
大约 10 小时或以上 about 10 hours or over	16	1.6
记不清/不知道 can't remember	21	2.1
没有收看 didn't watch	12	1.2

n=977

1-2-4 一周内不同时间收看电视的时间长短(周日)/ The Average Time Spending on Watching TV Per Day(Sunday)

	人数 Number	百分比 Percent
大约半小时或以下 about 1/2 hour or below	38	3.9
大约 1 小时 about 1 hour	116	11.9
大约 2 小时 about 2 hours	213	21.8
大约 3 小时 about 3 hours	228	23.4
大约 4 小时 about 4 hours	146	15.0
大约 5 小时 about 5 hours	69	7.1
大约 6 小时 about 6 hours	50	5.1
大约 7 小时 about 7 hours	34	3.5
大约 8 小时 about 8 hours	17	1.7
大约 9 小时 about 9 hours	15	1.5
大约 10 小时或以上 about 10 hours or over	16	1.6
记不清/不知道 can't remember	21	2.2
没有收看 didn't watch	13	1.3

n=976

1-3 经常收看的电视台/ Ranking of the Most Favorite TV Channels

注：本题为多选题，合计百分比超过 100%（Multiple answers）

排名 Brand Ranking	频道 Channels	人次 Person-time	百分比 Percent
1	东方台 20 频道 Oriental TV Channel 20	572	58.5
2	上海台 8 频道 Shanghai TV Channel 8	493	50.5
3	上海有线影视台 Shanghai Cable Movies Channel	450	46.1
4	东方台 33 频道 Oriental TV Channel 33	283	29.0
5	中央 1 台 CCTV-1	221	22.6
6	上海有线体育台 Shanghai Cable Sports Channel	199	20.4
7	上海台 14 频道 Shanghai TV Channel 14	170	17.4
8	上海有线音乐台 Shanghai Cable Music Channel	128	13.1
9	上海有线新闻台 Shanghai Cable Information Channel	93	9.5
10	上海有线戏剧台 Shanghai Cable Drama Channel	76	7.8
11	上海教育电视 26 频道 Shanghai Education TV 26	33	3.4
12	凤凰卫视 Phoenix Channel	24	2.5
13	上海卫视 Shanghai Satellite	22	2.3
13	中央 2 台 CCTV-2	22	2.3
14	中央 4 台 CCTV-4	12	1.2
16	贵州卫视 Guizhou Satellite	6	0.6
16	中央 8 台 CCTV-8	6	0.6
17	中央 6 台 CCTV-6	5	0.5

n=977

1-4 样本、男性各年龄层、女性各年龄层最喜欢收看的频道/ The Most Favorite TV Channels by the Whole Sample, Age and Gender Groups

注：本题为多选题，合计百分比超过 100%（Multiple answers）

	人数 Number	东方台 20 频道 Oriental TV Channel 20	上海台 8 频道 Shanghai TV Channel 8	上海有线影视台 Shanghai Cable Movies Channel	东方台 33 频道 Oriental TV Channel 33	中央 1 台 CCTV-1	上海有线体育台 Shanghai Cable Sports Channel
样本 Sample	977	58.5	50.5	46.1	29.0	22.6	20.4
男性 Male	491	57.0	46.2	38.7	26.1	28.3	34.6
16~24 岁 Age	101	55.4	34.7	44.6	33.7	12.9	44.6
25~34 岁 Age	140	58.6	40.7	42.9	27.1	23.6	34.3
35~44 岁 Age	128	61.7	50.8	39.1	24.2	39.1	27.3
45~54 岁 Age	84	57.1	59.5	28.6	17.9	38.1	34.5
55~60 岁 Age	38	39.5	52.6	28.9	26.3	28.9	34.2
女性 Female	486	60.1	54.7	53.5	31.9	16.9	6.0
16~24 岁 Age	102	60.8	47.1	47.1	36.3	10.8	6.9
25~34 岁 Age	142	59.9	54.2	60.6	34.5	13.4	4.9
35~44 岁 Age	124	63.7	55.6	62.1	29.0	18.5	7.3
45~54 岁 Age	79	55.7	60.8	45.6	29.1	21.5	5.1
55~60 岁 Age	39	56.4	61.5	33.3	25.6	30.8	5.1

续前表 continued

	人数 Number	上海台 14 频道 Shanghai TV Channel 14	上海有线音乐台 Shanghai Cable Music Channel	上海有线新闻台 Shanghai Cable Information Channel	上海有线戏剧台 Shanghai Cable Drama Channel	上海教育电视 26 频道 Shanghai Education TV 26	凤凰卫视 Phoenix Channel
样本 Sample	977	17.4	13.1	9.5	7.8	3.4	2.5
男性 Male	491	15.5	11.8	12.4	6.5	2.2	1.8
16~24 岁 Age	101	13.9	30.7	7.9	3.0	0.0	1.0
25~34 岁 Age	140	15.0	14.3	13.6	2.1	3.6	1.4
35~44 岁 Age	128	17.2	3.1	10.9	2.3	2.3	3.1
45~54 岁 Age	84	15.5	3.6	19.0	10.7	1.2	2.4
55~60 岁 Age	38	15.8	0.0	10.5	36.8	5.3	0.0
女性 Female	486	19.3	14.4	6.6	9.1	4.5	3.1
16~24 岁 Age	102	25.5	38.2	6.9	2.9	2.9	2.0
25~34 岁 Age	142	21.8	12.7	3.5	4.2	7.7	4.9
35~44 岁 Age	124	13.7	4.8	6.5	5.6	3.2	1.6
45~54 岁 Age	79	15.2	7.6	10.1	20.3	5.1	3.8
55~60 岁 Age	39	20.5	2.6	10.3	30.8	0.0	2.6

续前表 continued

	人数 Number	上海卫视 Shanghai Satellite	中央 2 台 CCTV-2	中央 4 台 CCTV-4	贵州卫视 Guizhou Satellite	中央 8 台 CCTV-8	中央 6 台 CCTV-6
样本 Sample	977	2.3	2.3	1.2	0.6	0.6	0.5
男性 Male	491	1.6	3.1	1.6	0.8	0.2	0.4
16~24 岁 Age	101	2.0	2.0	0.0	1.0	1.0	1.0
25~34 岁 Age	140	2.1	3.6	2.1	0.7	0.0	0.7
35~44 岁 Age	128	1.6	3.1	1.6	1.6	0.0	0.0
45~54 岁 Age	84	1.2	3.6	1.2	0.0	0.0	0.0
55~60 岁 Age	38	0.0	2.6	5.3	0.0	0.0	0.0
女性 Female	486	2.9	1.4	0.8	0.4	1.0	0.6
16~24 岁 Age	102	0.0	1.0	0.0	0.0	2.9	1.0
25~34 岁 Age	142	1.4	0.7	0.7	0.0	0.7	0.0
35~44 岁 Age	124	4.0	1.6	0.8	1.6	0.8	0.0
45~54 岁 Age	79	6.3	1.3	0.0	0.0	0.0	2.5
55~60 岁 Age	39	5.1	5.1	5.1	0.0	0.0	0.0

1-5 经常收看的电视频道/ The Most Favorite TV Channels

1-5-1 经常收看的电视频道(周一--周四)/ Ranking of the Most Favorite TV Channels(Monday--Thursday)

注：本题为多选题，合计百分比超过 100%（Multiple answers）

排名 Brand Ranking	频道 Channels	人次 Person-time	百分比 Percent
1	东方台 20 频道 Oriental TV Channel 20	662	68.2
2	上海台 8 频道 Shanghai TV Channel 8	621	64.0
3	上海有线影视台 Shanghai Cable Movies Channel	547	56.3
4	东方台 33 频道 Oriental TV Channel 33	537	55.3
5	上海台 14 频道 Shanghai TV Channel 14	457	47.1
6	中央 1 台 CCTV-1	343	35.3
7	上海有线体育台 Shanghai Cable Sports Channel	300	30.9
8	上海有线音乐台 Shanghai Cable Music Channel	214	22.0
9	上海有线新闻台 Shanghai Cable Information Channel	188	19.4
10	上海有线戏剧台 Shanghai Cable Drama Channel	166	17.1
11	上海教育电视 26 频道 Shanghai Education TV 26	90	9.3
12	中央 2 台 CCTV-2	61	6.3
13	上海卫视 Shanghai Satellite	36	3.7
14	中央 4 台 CCTV-4	27	2.8

n=971

1-5-2 经常收看的电视频道(周五)/ Ranking of the Most Favorite TV Channels(Friday)

注：本题为多选题，合计百分比超过 100%（Multiple answers）

排名 Brand Ranking	频道 Channels	人次 Person-time	百分比 Percent
1	东方台 20 频道 Oriental TV Channel 20	685	70.6
2	上海台 8 频道 Shanghai TV Channel 8	622	64.1
3	东方台 33 频道 Oriental TV Channel 33	567	58.5
4	上海有线影视台 Shanghai Cable Movies Channel	556	57.3
5	上海台 14 频道 Shanghai TV Channel 14	477	49.2
6	中央 1 台 CCTV-1	339	34.9
7	上海有线体育台 Shanghai Cable Sports Channel	321	33.1
8	上海有线音乐台 Shanghai Cable Music Channel	236	24.3
9	上海有线新闻台 Shanghai Cable Information Channel	189	19.5
10	上海有线戏剧台 Shanghai Cable Drama Channel	178	18.4
11	上海教育电视 26 频道 Shanghai Education TV 26	90	9.3
12	中央 2 台 CCTV-2	62	6.4
13	上海卫视 Shanghai Satellite	36	3.7
14	中央 4 台 CCTV-4	26	2.7
14	中央 8 台 CCTV-8	26	2.7
15	凤凰卫视 Phoenix Channel	20	2.1

n=970

1-5-3 经常收看的电视频道(周六)/ Ranking of the Most Favorite TV Channels(Saturday)

注：本题为多选题，合计百分比超过 100%（Multiple answers）

排名 Brand Ranking	频道 Channels	人次 Person-time	百分比 Percent
1	东方台 20 频道 Oriental TV Channel 20	708	72.7
2	上海台 8 频道 Shanghai TV Channel 8	635	65.2
3	东方台 33 频道 Oriental TV Channel 33	591	60.7
4	上海有线影视台 Shanghai Cable Movies Channel	569	58.4
5	上海台 14 频道 Shanghai TV Channel 14	497	51.0
6	中央 1 台 CCTV-1	352	36.1
7	上海有线体育台 Shanghai Cable Sports Channel	328	33.7
8	上海有线音乐台 Shanghai Cable Music Channel	252	25.9
9	上海有线新闻台 Shanghai Cable Information Channel	195	20.0
10	上海有线戏剧台 Shanghai Cable Drama Channel	183	18.8
11	教育电视 26 频道 Shanghai Education TV 26	94	9.7
12	中央 2 台 CCTV-2	74	7.6
13	上海卫视 Shanghai Satellite	35	3.6
14	中央 4 台 CCTV-4	30	3.1
15	中央 8 台 CCTV-8	26	2.7

n=974

1-5-4 经常收看的电视频道(周日)/ Ranking of the Most Favorite TV Channels(Sunday)

注：本题为多选题，合计百分比超过 100%（Multiple answers）

排名 Brand Ranking	频道 Channels	人次 Person-time	百分比 Percent
1	东方台 20 频道 Oriental TV Channel 20	703	72.4
2	上海台 8 频道 Shanghai TV Channel 8	633	65.2
3	东方台 33 频道 Oriental TV Channel 33	570	58.7
4	上海有线影视台 Shanghai Cable Movies Channel	567	58.4
5	上海台 14 频道 Shanghai TV Channel 14	495	51.0
6	中央 1 台 CCTV-1	353	36.4
7	上海有线体育台 Shanghai Cable Sports Channel	326	33.6
8	上海有线音乐台 Shanghai Cable Music Channel	250	25.7
9	上海有线新闻台 Shanghai Cable Information Channel	196	20.2
10	上海有线戏剧台 Shanghai Cable Drama Channel	185	19.1
11	上海教育电视 26 频道 Shanghai Education TV 26	89	9.2
12	中央 2 台 CCTV-2	74	7.6
13	上海卫视 Shanghai Satellite	35	3.6
14	中央 4 台 CCTV-4	33	3.4
15	中央 8 台 CCTV-8	26	2.7

n=971

1-6 经常收看的电视节目/ Ranking of the Most Favorite TV Programs

注：本题为多选题，合计百分比超过 100%（Multiple answers）

排名 Ranking	电视节目 TV Programs	人次 Person-time	百分比 Percent
1	国内新闻 national news	639	65.5
2	国际新闻 international news	491	50.3
3	港台电视剧 TV play(HK.Taiwan)	398	40.8
4	体育新闻 sports news	322	33.0
5	国内电视剧 TV play(inland)	238	24.4
6	港台影片 film from HK.Taiwan	227	23.3
7	综艺节目 comprehensive arts	192	19.7
8	MTV/音乐节目 MTV/music	184	18.9
9	国外影片 overseas film	171	17.5
10	新闻评论 news comments	157	16.1
11	赛事报道 games report	127	13.0
12	本地新闻 local news	124	12.7
13	天气预报 weather forecast	121	12.4
14	金融股市 finance & stock	120	12.3
15	体育专栏节目 sports feature	104	10.7
16	国外电视剧 overseas TV play	94	9.6
17	戏曲/戏剧 opera	83	8.5
17	谈话节目 Talk Show	83	8.5
18	国内影片 inland film	77	7.9
19	经济新闻 economic news	55	5.6
20	曲艺节目 folk art	53	5.4
20	女性节目 women's program	53	5.4
21	军事类节目 military program	51	5.2
22	经济信息 economic information	40	4.1
22	科教类节目 scientific education	40	4.1
23	消费指南 consumption guide	30	3.1
24	少儿节目 children's program	26	2.7
25	电视直销 direct sale on TV	19	1.9
25	专题类节目 special report	19	1.9
26	舞蹈节目 dancing program	13	1.3
27	广告 advertising	12	1.2
28	其他 others	6	0.6

n=976

1-7 样本、男性各年龄层、女性各年龄层经常收看的电视节目/ The Most Favorite TV Programs by the Whole Sample, Age and Gender Groups

注：本题为多选题，合计百分比超过 100%（Multiple answers）

	人数 Number	国内新闻 national news	国际新闻 international news	新闻评论 news comments	本地新闻 local news	谈话节目 Talk Show	经济新闻 economic news
样本 Sample	976	65.5	40.8	50.3	23.3	12.7	5.6
男性 Male	489	72.6	25.8	60.3	17.4	14.7	8.0
16~24 岁 Age	102	49.0	35.3	38.2	34.3	6.9	2.0
25~34 岁 Age	139	64.7	23.0	58.3	17.3	16.5	10.1
35~44 岁 Age	126	84.9	27.0	69.8	11.9	15.9	6.3
45~54 岁 Age	84	94.0	17.9	77.4	7.1	20.2	11.9
55~60 岁 Age	38	76.3	23.7	57.9	13.2	13.2	13.2
女性 Female	487	58.3	55.9	40.2	29.2	10.7	3.3
16~24 岁 Age	102	36.3	64.7	28.4	50.0	7.8	3.9
25~34 岁 Age	141	47.5	66.0	37.6	30.5	7.8	2.1
35~44 岁 Age	125	72.0	48.0	49.6	23.2	12.8	2.4
45~54 岁 Age	80	73.8	47.5	41.3	13.8	13.8	6.3
55~60 岁 Age	39	79.5	38.5	48.7	20.5	15.4	2.6

续前表 continued

	人数 Number	经济信息 economic information	金融股市 finance & stock	电视直销 direct sale on TV	消费指南 consumption guide	体育新闻 sports news	赛事报道 games report
样本 Sample	976	4.1	12.3	1.9	3.1	33.0	13.0
男性 Male	489	5.5	13.1	0.8	2.0	51.9	22.5
16~24 岁 Age	102	2.9	9.8	2.0	1.0	62.7	32.4
25~34 岁 Age	139	5.0	12.2	1.4	1.4	54.7	23.0
35~44 岁 Age	126	5.6	15.9	0.0	3.2	48.4	13.5
45~54 岁 Age	84	8.3	16.7	0.0	2.4	46.4	22.6
55~60 岁 Age	38	7.9	7.9	0.0	2.6	36.8	23.7
女性 Female	487	2.7	11.5	3.1	4.1	14.0	3.5
16~24 岁 Age	102	1.0	5.9	4.9	4.9	14.7	2.0
25~34 岁 Age	141	3.5	12.1	6.4	4.3	7.8	3.5
35~44 岁 Age	125	3.2	11.2	0.8	4.8	16.0	3.2
45~54 岁 Age	80	3.8	21.3	0.0	3.8	21.3	6.3
55~60 岁 Age	39	0.0	5.1	0.0	0.0	12.8	2.6

续前表 continued

	人数 Number	体育专栏节目 sports feature	国内电视剧 TV play(inland)	港台电视剧 TV play (HK.Taiwan)	国外电视剧 overseas TV play	国内影片 inland film	国外影片 overseas film
样本 Sample	976	10.7	24.4	40.8	9.6	7.9	17.5
男性 Male	489	18.8	16.4	25.8	7.6	5.9	16.6
16~24 岁 Age	102	31.4	11.8	35.3	2.9	2.9	24.5
25~34 岁 Age	139	21.6	11.5	23.0	10.8	5.0	17.3
35~44 岁 Age	126	13.5	20.6	27.0	12.7	10.3	12.7
45~54 岁 Age	84	9.5	17.9	17.9	1.2	4.8	15.5
55~60 岁 Age	38	13.2	28.9	23.7	5.3	5.3	7.9
女性 Female	487	2.5	32.4	55.9	11.7	9.9	18.5
16~24 岁 Age	102	3.9	10.8	64.7	14.7	10.8	27.5
25~34 岁 Age	141	2.1	29.8	66.0	12.8	12.1	24.8
35~44 岁 Age	125	2.4	37.6	48.0	12.0	8.8	14.4
45~54 岁 Age	80	2.5	46.3	47.5	6.3	8.8	3.8
55~60 岁 Age	39	0.0	53.8	38.5	10.3	5.1	15.4

续前表 continued

	人数 Number	港台影片 film from HK.Taiwan	天气预报 weather forecast	广告 advertising	MTV/音乐节目 MTV/music	舞蹈节目 dancing program	曲艺节目 folk art	戏曲/戏剧 opera
样本 Sample	976	23.3	12.4	1.2	18.9	1.3	5.4	8.5
男性 Male	489	17.4	8.6	0.8	16.6	0.8	5.3	5.7
16~24 岁 Age	102	34.3	5.9	1.0	38.2	2.9	2.0	1.0
25~34 岁 Age	139	17.3	5.8	0.7	23.7	0.0	3.6	2.2
35~44 岁 Age	126	11.9	7.9	0.8	4.0	0.0	4.8	4.8
45~54 岁 Age	84	7.1	14.3	1.2	3.6	0.0	8.3	7.1
55~60 岁 Age	38	13.2	15.8	0.0	2.6	2.6	15.8	31.6
女性 Female	487	29.2	16.2	1.6	21.1	1.8	5.5	11.3
16~24 岁 Age	102	50.0	14.7	2.9	53.9	2.9	1.0	2.9
25~34 岁 Age	141	30.5	15.6	0.7	22.7	1.4	3.5	4.3
35~44 岁 Age	125	23.2	19.2	0.0	7.2	0.8	8.0	10.4
45~54 岁 Age	80	13.8	13.8	3.8	7.5	2.5	10.0	21.3
55~60 岁 Age	39	20.5	17.9	2.6	2.6	2.6	7.7	41.0

续前表 continued

	人数 Number	综艺节目 comprehensive arts	军事类节目 military program	专题类节目 special report	科教类节目 scientific education	少儿节目 children's program	女性节目 women's program	其他 others
样本 Sample	**976**	**19.7**	**5.2**	**1.9**	**4.1**	**2.7**	**5.4**	**0.6**
男性 Male	**489**	**11.7**	**9.8**	**1.6**	**5.1**	**1.4**	**0.4**	**0.6**
16~24 岁 Age	102	13.7	11.8	1.0	5.9	3.9	0.0	1.0
25~34 岁 Age	139	11.5	11.5	2.2	7.9	1.4	1.4	0.7
35~44 岁 Age	126	14.3	10.3	2.4	2.4	0.8	0.0	0.0
45~54 岁 Age	84	6.0	4.8	1.2	6.0	0.0	0.0	0.0
55~60 岁 Age	38	10.5	7.9	0.0	0.0	0.0	0.0	2.6
女性 Female	**487**	**27.7**	**0.6**	**2.3**	**3.1**	**3.9**	**10.5**	**0.6**
16~24 岁 Age	102	31.4	1.0	2.0	4.9	3.9	13.7	0.0
25~34 岁 Age	141	27.7	0.0	2.1	2.8	5.7	15.6	1.4
35~44 岁 Age	125	24.8	0.0	1.6	3.2	4.8	8.0	0.8
45~54 岁 Age	80	26.3	0.0	5.0	1.3	1.3	5.0	0.0
55~60 岁 Age	39	30.8	5.1	0.0	2.6	0.0	2.6	0.0

1-8 不同学历的观众收看电视节目的偏好/ Program Preference by Educational levels

注：本题为多选题，合计百分比超过 100%（Multiple answers）

	人数 Number	国内新闻 national news	国际新闻 international news	新闻评论 news comments	本地新闻 local news	谈话节目 Talk Show	经济新闻 economic news
样本 Sample	**973**	**65.5**	**50.2**	**16.0**	**12.7**	**8.4**	**5.4**
小学及以下 Primary School or Below	21	66.7	33.3	19.0	23.8	4.8	0.0
初中 Middle School	258	70.2	50.0	11.6	12.0	6.2	5.0
高中/中专/技校 High School/Technical Secondary School	491	62.1	46.8	13.6	12.6	6.3	5.5
大学专科 2-3 Year College	134	65.7	59.0	26.1	14.2	17.9	6.7
大学本科 4-5 Year College	64	68.8	60.9	28.1	10.9	15.6	6.3
研究生或以上 Graduate or Above	5	100.0	80.0	40.0	0.0	0.0	0.0

续前表 continued

	人数 Number	经济信息 economic information	金融股市 finance & stock	电视直销 direct sale on TV	消费指南 consumption guide	体育新闻 sports news	赛事报道 games report
样本 Sample	**973**	**4.0**	**12.2**	**2.0**	**3.1**	**32.9**	**13.1**
小学及以下 Primary School or Below	21	0.0	4.8	0.0	0.0	9.5	4.8
初中 Middle School	258	2.3	11.6	1.9	3.5	30.2	11.6
高中/中专/技校 High School/Technical Secondary School	491	3.9	12.4	2.2	3.1	34.4	14.1
大学专科 2-3 Year College	134	8.2	15.7	1.5	1.5	33.6	11.9
大学本科 4-5 Year College	64	4.7	7.8	1.6	6.3	35.9	15.6
研究生或以上 Graduate or Above	5	0.0	20.0	0.0	0.0	60.0	20.0

续前表 continued

	人数 Number	体育专栏节目 sports feature	国内电视剧 TV play(inland)	港台电视剧 TV play (HK.Taiwan)	国外电视剧 overseas TV play	国内影片 inland film	国外影片 overseas film
样本 Sample	**973**	**10.7**	**24.5**	**40.9**	**9.6**	**7.9**	**17.6**
小学及以下 Primary School or Below	21	0.0	57.1	57.1	9.5	4.8	4.8
初中 Middle School	258	5.8	34.5	44.2	8.1	10.1	10.9
高中/中专/技校 High School/Technical Secondary School	491	13.0	21.2	43.4	10.4	7.7	19.8
大学专科 2-3 Year College	134	11.9	17.9	30.6	9.0	5.2	25.4
大学本科 4-5 Year College	64	12.5	14.1	25.0	10.9	7.8	14.1
研究生或以上 Graduate or Above	5	20.0	0.0	40.0	0.0	0.0	40.0

续前表 continued

	人数 Number	港台影片 film from HK.Taiwan	天气预报 weather forecast	广告 advertising	MTV/音乐节目 MTV/music	舞蹈节目 dancing program	曲艺节目 folk art	戏曲/戏剧 opera
样本 Sample	**973**	**23.3**	**12.4**	**1.2**	**18.9**	**1.3**	**5.4**	**8.5**
小学及以下 Primary School or Below	21	23.8	4.8	0.0	0.0	4.8	19.0	42.9
初中 Middle School	258	18.2	13.6	1.2	9.7	0.8	8.5	14.3
高中/中专/技校 High School/Technical Secondary School	491	29.9	12.2	1.4	22.4	1.6	3.7	5.3
大学专科 2-3 Year College	134	17.2	11.9	1.5	25.4	0.7	4.5	4.5
大学本科 4-5 Year College	64	7.8	14.1	0.0	21.9	1.6	4.7	7.8
研究生或以上 Graduate or Above	5	0.0	0.0	0.0	20.0	0.0	0.0	0.0

续前表 continued

	人数 Number	综艺节目 comprehensive arts	军事类节目 military program	专题类节目 special report	科教类节目 scientific education	少儿节目 children's program	女性节目 women's program	其他 others
样本 Sample	**973**	**19.6**	**5.2**	**2.0**	**4.1**	**2.7**	**5.4**	**0.6**
小学及以下 Primary School or Below	21	28.6	0.0	0.0	0.0	4.8	9.5	0.0
初中 Middle School	258	17.1	5.4	3.1	3.9	2.3	5.8	0.8
高中/中专/技校 High School/Technical Secondary School	491	21.4	5.5	0.8	4.1	2.9	5.3	0.8
大学专科 2-3 Year College	134	14.2	3.7	3.0	5.2	1.5	5.2	0.0
大学本科 4-5 Year College	64	23.4	7.8	4.7	4.7	3.1	4.7	0.0
研究生或以上 Graduate or Above	5	40.0	0.0	0.0	0.0	20.0	0.0	0.0

1-9 经常收看电视时段/ Weekday Times Slots of Television Exposure

注：本题为多选题，合计百分比超过 100%（Multiple answers）

时间段 times slots	周一--周四(%) (Monday--Thursday)	周五(%) (Friday)	周六(%) (Saturday)	周日(%) (Sunday)
样本量 Sample	n=979	n=975	n=977	n=977
0:00-0:30	1.1	1.3	1.4	1.3
0:30-1:00	1.0	0.9	1.2	1.2
1:00-1:30	1.2	0.9	1.2	0.9
1:30-2:00	0.5	0.3	0.6	0.4
2:00-2:30	0.2	0.2	0.3	0.2
2:30-3:00	0.3	0.3	0.3	0.3
3:00-3:30	0.2	0.2	0.2	0.3
3:30-4:00	0.1	0.1	0.3	0.2
4:00-4:30	0.0	0.1	0.1	0.1
4:30-5:00	0.0	0.0	0.0	0.0
5:00-5:30	0.2	0.1	0.1	0.1
5:30-6:00	0.3	0.4	0.1	0.3
6:00-6:30	0.6	0.7	0.2	0.1
6:30-7:00	0.3	0.5	0.3	0.5
7:00-7:30	3.7	3.4	3.3	3.2
7:30-8:00	2.3	2.4	2.8	2.6
8:00-8:30	2.1	2.6	4.4	4.9
8:30-9:00	2.6	2.3	5.8	5.4
9:00-9:30	4.7	4.7	10.7	10.8
9:30-10:00	5.0	5.8	12.3	12.7
10:00-10:30	5.1	5.7	14.4	15.1
10:30-11:00	4.6	5.5	13.3	14.7
11:00-11:30	4.3	4.4	10.5	11.9
11:30-12:00	4.3	3.7	9.7	11.5
12:00-12:30	5.2	5.4	11.3	11.9
12:30-13:00	3.1	3.6	8.6	8.7
13:00-13:30	2.8	4.4	10.6	11.2
13:30-14:00	3.3	4.8	12.9	13.6
14:00-14:30	4.6	6.1	14.5	15.9
14:30-15:00	4.3	5.7	12.9	14.5
15:00-15:30	3.2	4.2	10.8	11.2
15:30-16:00	2.6	3.4	9.0	9.4
16:00-16:30	1.8	2.5	6.7	7.2
16:30-17:00	2.1	2.4	5.9	6.8
17:00-17:30	3.5	3.9	6.1	7.0
17:30-18:00	6.2	6.6	9.0	9.2
18:00-18:30	21.2	22.5	23.6	23.4
18:30-19:00	42.9	44.8	46.1	46.6
19:00-19:30	62.0	66.6	67.0	67.6
19:30-20:00	62.1	69.1	70.2	70.4
20:00-20:30	61.9	71.4	74.0	73.4
20:30-21:00	53.1	62.9	66.3	64.4
21:00-21:30	38.2	49.3	53.3	50.8
21:30-22:00	27.0	38.3	41.7	38.1
22:00-22:30	13.7	20.6	23.7	20.7
22:30-23:00	8.4	14.6	15.6	13.4
23:00-23:30	4.1	7.4	7.8	6.6
23:30-24:00	2.8	4.6	5.0	4.1

1-10 不同消费者层平时是否接触电视媒介/ TV Exposure by Market Segments

1-10-1 时尚流行指标/ Fads Popular Index

	人数 Number	从来不看 never	收看 yes
样本 Sample	1005	**3.4**	**96.6**
平实生活指向 simple living orientation	471	2.3	97.7
时尚流行指向 fashion orientation	534	4.3	95.7

1-10-2 广告态度指标/ Advertising Attitude Index

	人数 Number	从来不看 never	收看 yes
样本 Sample	1002	**3.3**	**96.7**
广告淡漠指向 indifferent orientation	256	3.1	96.9
中间层 medium	611	2.9	97.1
信赖广告指向 loyal orientation	135	5.2	94.8

1-11 不同消费者层收看电视频道的偏好/ Channel Preference by Market Segments

1-11-1 时尚流行指标/ Fads Popular Index

注：本题为多选题，合计百分比超过 100%（Multiple answers）

	人数 Number	东方台 20 频道 Oriental TV Channel 20	上海台 8 频道 Shanghai TV Channel 8	上海有线影视台 Shanghai Cable Movies Channel	东方台 33 频道 Oriental TV Channel 33	中央 1 台 CCTV-1	上海有线体育台 Shanghai Cable Sports Channel
样本 Sample	968	58.6	50.3	46.0	29.1	22.6	20.6
平实生活指向 simple living orientation	458	56.6	53.1	46.9	31.2	26.0	18.8
时尚流行指向 fashion orientation	510	60.4	47.8	45.1	27.3	19.6	22.2

续前表 continued

	人数 Number	上海台 14 频道 Shanghai TV Channel 14	上海有线音乐台 Shanghai Cable Music Channel	上海有线新闻台 Shanghai Cable Information Channel	上海有线戏剧台 Shanghai Cable Drama Channel	上海教育电视 26 频道 Shanghai Education TV 26	凤凰卫视 Phoenix Channel
样本 Sample	968	17.4	13.2	9.6	7.7	3.1	2.5
平实生活指向 simple living orientation	458	16.8	6.1	9.8	10.5	3.1	2.4
时尚流行指向 fashion orientation	510	17.8	19.6	9.4	5.3	3.1	2.5

续前表 continued

	人数 Number	上海卫视 Shanghai Satellite	中央 2 台 CCTV-2	中央 4 台 CCTV-4	贵州卫视 Guizhou Satellite	中央 8 台 CCTV-8	中央 6 台 CCTV-6
样本 Sample	968	2.3	2.3	1.2	0.6	0.6	0.5
平实生活指向 simple living orientation	458	2.4	2.6	2.0	0.4	0.4	0.7
时尚流行指向 fashion orientation	510	2.2	2.0	0.6	0.8	0.8	0.4

1-11-2 广告态度指标/ Advertising Attitude Index

注：本题为多选题，合计百分比超过 100%（Multiple answers）

	人数 Number	东方台 20 频道 Oriental TV Channel 20	上海台 8 频道 Shanghai TV Channel 8	上海有线影视台 Shanghai Cable Movies Channel	东方台 33 频道 Oriental TV Channel 33	中央 1 台 CCTV-1	上海有线体育台 Shanghai Cable Sports Channel
样本 Sample	966	58.3	50.4	46.0	29.0	22.5	20.3
广告淡漠指向 indifferent orientation	248	54.0	50.4	44.0	29.4	25.0	18.5
中间层 medium	590	61.0	50.7	46.6	29.0	21.2	21.4
信赖广告指向 loyal orientation	128	53.9	49.2	46.9	28.1	23.4	18.8

续前表 continued

	人数 Number	上海台 14 频道 Shanghai TV Channel 14	上海有线音乐台 Shanghai Cable Music Channel	上海有线新闻台 Shanghai Cable Information Channel	上海有线戏剧台 Shanghai Cable Drama Channel	上海教育电视 26 频道 Shanghai Education TV 26	凤凰卫视 Phoenix Channel
样本 Sample	966	17.5	13.3	9.6	7.8	3.4	2.5
广告淡漠指向 indifferent orientation	248	19.0	12.9	9.7	11.3	3.6	2.4
中间层 medium	590	15.9	12.0	9.8	6.4	3.2	2.4
信赖广告指向 loyal orientation	128	21.9	19.5	8.6	7.0	3.9	3.1

续前表 continued

	人数 Number	上海卫视 Shanghai Satellite	中央2台 CCTV-2	中央4台 CCTV-4	贵州卫视 Guizhou Satellite	中央8台 CCTV-8	中央6台 CCTV-6
样本 Sample	966	2.3	2.3	1.2	0.6	0.6	0.5
广告淡漠指向 indifferent orientation	248	2.8	2.4	2.0	0.0	0.4	0.8
中间层 medium	590	1.9	2.5	1.0	1.0	0.7	0.5
信赖广告指向 loyal orientation	128	3.1	0.8	0.8	0.0	0.8	0.0

1-12 不同消费者层收看电视节目的偏好/ Program Preference by Market Segments

1-12-1 时尚流行指标/ Fads Popular Index

注：本题为多选题，合计百分比超过100%。(Multiple answers)

	人数 Number	国内新闻 national news	国际新闻 international news	新闻评论 news comments	本地新闻 local news	谈话节目 Talk Show	经济新闻 economic news
样本 Sample	967	65.5	50.4	15.9	12.8	8.5	5.6
平实生活指向 simple living orientation	459	71.0	55.3	14.8	14.6	7.6	4.6
时尚流行指向 fashion orientation	508	60.4	45.9	16.9	11.2	9.3	6.5

续前表 continued

	人数 Number	经济信息 economic information	金融股市 finance & stock	电视直销 direct sale on TV	消费指南 consumption guide	体育新闻 sports news	赛事报道 games report
样本 Sample	967	4.1	12.2	2.0	3.1	33.3	13.0
平实生活指向 simple living orientation	459	3.9	12.6	0.4	1.5	33.3	13.9
时尚流行指向 fashion orientation	508	4.3	11.8	3.3	4.5	33.3	12.2

续前表 continued

	人数 Number	体育专栏节目 sports feature	国内电视剧 TV play(inland)	港台电视剧 TV play (HK.Taiwan)	国外电视剧 overseas TV play	国内影片 inland film	国外影片 overseas film
样本 Sample	967	10.8	24.3	40.6	9.6	7.9	17.5
平实生活指向 simple living orientation	459	10.9	28.1	36.4	7.6	7.6	17.4
时尚流行指向 fashion orientation	508	10.6	20.9	44.5	11.4	8.1	17.5

续前表 continued

	人数 Number	港台影片 film from HK.Taiwan	天气预报 weather forecast	广告 advertising	MTV/音乐节目 MTV/music	舞蹈节目 dancing program	曲艺节目 folk art	戏曲/戏剧 opera
样本 Sample	967	23.3	12.4	1.2	18.9	1.3	5.5	8.5
平实生活指向 simple living orientation	459	18.1	14.2	1.7	9.2	1.3	8.1	11.8
时尚流行指向 fashion orientation	508	28.0	10.8	0.8	27.8	1.4	3.1	5.5

续前表 continued

	人数 Number	综艺节目 comprehensive arts	军事类节目 military program	专题类节目 special report	科教类节目 scientific education	少儿节目 children's program	女性节目 women's program	其他 others
样本 Sample	967	19.9	5.2	2.0	4.1	2.7	5.5	0.6
平实生活指向 simple living orientation	459	19.0	5.7	2.0	4.8	3.1	3.3	0.7
时尚流行指向 fashion orientation	508	20.7	4.7	2.0	3.5	2.4	7.5	0.6

1-12-2 广告态度指标/ Advertising Attitude Index

注：本题为多选题，合计百分比超过 100%（Multiple answers）

	人数 Number	国内新闻 national news	国际新闻 international news	新闻评论 news comments	本地新闻 local news	谈话节目 Talk Show	经济新闻 economic news
样本 Sample	965	65.7	50.6	16.1	12.6	8.5	5.5
广告淡漠指向 indifferent orientation	248	66.1	46.0	14.5	13.3	8.5	5.2
中间层 medium	590	66.9	52.2	15.8	12.5	8.5	5.6
信赖广告指向 loyal orientation	127	59.1	52.0	20.5	11.8	8.7	5.5

续前表 continued

	人数 Number	经济信息 economic information	金融股市 finance & stock	电视直销 direct sale on TV	消费指南 consumption guide	体育新闻 sports news	赛事报道 games report
样本 Sample	965	4.1	12.3	2.0	3.0	32.6	13.2
广告淡漠指向 indifferent orientation	248	4.4	12.5	0.8	3.6	32.7	14.5
中间层 medium	590	4.4	12.2	2.2	2.9	32.5	12.9
信赖广告指向 loyal orientation	127	2.4	12.6	3.1	2.4	33.1	11.8

续前表 continued

	人数 Number	体育专栏节目 sports feature	国内电视剧 TV play(inland)	港台电视剧 TV play (HK.Taiwan)	国外电视剧 overseas TV play	国内影片 inland film	国外影片 overseas film
样本 Sample	965	10.7	24.5	40.6	9.7	7.9	17.5
广告淡漠指向 indifferent orientation	248	11.3	22.6	34.7	8.1	6.5	19.4
中间层 medium	590	11.2	25.8	41.5	10.7	8.5	17.8
信赖广告指向 loyal orientation	127	7.1	22.0	48.0	8.7	7.9	12.6

续前表 continued

	人数 Number	港台影片 film from HK.Taiwan	天气预报 weather forecast	广告 advertising	MTV/音乐节目 MTV/music	舞蹈节目 dancing program	曲艺节目 folk art	戏曲/戏剧 opera
样本 Sample	965	23.0	12.2	1.2	18.8	1.3	5.4	8.5
广告淡漠指向 indifferent orientation	248	23.8	14.1	0.8	15.7	2.0	8.9	10.1
中间层 medium	590	21.7	12.4	0.8	18.1	1.0	4.4	7.5
信赖广告指向 loyal orientation	127	27.6	7.9	3.9	27.6	1.6	3.1	10.2

续前表 continued

	人数 Number	综艺节目 comprehensive arts	军事类节目 military program	专题类节目 special report	科教类节目 scientific education	少儿节目 children's program	女性节目 women's program	其他 others
样本 Sample	965	19.6	5.1	2.0	4.1	2.7	5.5	0.6
广告淡漠指向 indifferent orientation	248	16.5	8.1	3.2	4.8	3.6	3.2	0.0
中间层 medium	590	20.3	4.2	1.9	3.6	2.2	5.4	1.0
信赖广告指向 loyal orientation	127	22.0	3.1	0.0	5.5	3.1	10.2	0.0

● 广州 / Guangzhou

1-1 样本、男性各年龄层、女性各年龄层平时是否接触电视媒介/ Exposure to Television by the Whole Sample, Age and Gender Groups

	人数 Number	从来不看 never	收看 yes
样本 Sample	1033	1.6	98.4
男性 Male	499	2.8	97.2
16~24 岁 Age	106	2.8	97.2
25~34 岁 Age	150	2.7	97.3
35~44 岁 Age	127	3.1	96.9
45~54 岁 Age	73	1.4	98.6
55~60 岁 Age	43	4.7	95.3
女性 Female	534	0.6	99.4
16~24 岁 Age	112	1.8	98.2
25~34 岁 Age	158	0.0	100.0
35~44 岁 Age	136	0.0	100.0
45~54 岁 Age	87	0.0	100.0
55~60 岁 Age	41	2.4	97.6

1-2 一周内不同时间收看电视的时间长短/ The Average Time Spending on Watching TV Per Day

1-2-1 一周内不同时间收看电视的时间长短(周一到周四)/ The Average Time Spending on Watching TV Per Day(Monday--Thursday)

	人数 Number	百分比 Percent
大约半小时或以下 about 1/2 hour or below	71	7.0
大约 1 小时 about 1 hour	186	18.3
大约 2 小时 about 2 hours	224	22.1
大约 3 小时 about 3 hours	188	18.5
大约 4 小时 about 4 hours	127	12.5
大约 5 小时 about 5 hours	71	7.0
大约 6 小时 about 6 hours	44	4.3
大约 7 小时 about 7 hours	11	1.1
大约 8 小时 about 8 hours	12	1.2
大约 9 小时 about 9 hours	8	0.8
大约 10 小时或以上 about 10 hours or over	21	2.1
记不清/不知道 can't remember	20	2.0
没有收看 didn't watch	31	3.1

n=1014

1-2-2 一周内不同时间收看电视的时间长短(周五)/ The Average Time Spending on Watching TV Per Day(Friday)

	人数 Number	百分比 Percent
大约半小时或以下 about 1/2 hour or below	58	5.7
大约 1 小时 about 1 hour	154	15.3
大约 2 小时 about 2 hours	217	21.5
大约 3 小时 about 3 hours	204	20.2
大约 4 小时 about 4 hours	143	14.2
大约 5 小时 about 5 hours	89	8.8
大约 6 小时 about 6 hours	44	4.4
大约 7 小时 about 7 hours	22	2.2
大约 8 小时 about 8 hours	12	1.2
大约 9 小时 about 9 hours	7	0.7
大约 10 小时或以上 about 10 hours or over	21	2.1
记不清/不知道 can't remember	23	2.3
没有收看 didn't watch	15	1.5

n=1009

1-2-3 一周内不同时间收看电视的时间长短(周六)/ The Average Time Spending on Watching TV Per Day(Saturday)

	人数 Number	百分比 Percent
大约半小时或以下 about 1/2 hour or below	50	4.9
大约 1 小时 about 1 hour	134	13.2
大约 2 小时 about 2 hours	198	19.5
大约 3 小时 about 3 hours	205	20.2
大约 4 小时 about 4 hours	150	14.8
大约 5 小时 about 5 hours	101	10.0
大约 6 小时 about 6 hours	49	4.8
大约 7 小时 about 7 hours	29	2.9
大约 8 小时 about 8 hours	26	2.6
大约 9 小时 about 9 hours	11	1.1
大约 10 小时或以上 about 10 hours or over	25	2.5
记不清/不知道 can't remember	23	2.3
没有收看 didn't watch	13	1.3

n=1014

1-2-4 一周内不同时间收看电视的时间长短(周日)/ The Average Time Spending on Watching TV Per Day(Sunday)

	人数 Number	百分比 Percent
大约半小时或以下 about 1/2 hour or below	50	4.9
大约 1 小时 about 1 hour	141	13.9
大约 2 小时 about 2 hours	201	19.8
大约 3 小时 about 3 hours	202	19.9
大约 4 小时 about 4 hours	143	14.1
大约 5 小时 about 5 hours	96	9.5
大约 6 小时 about 6 hours	52	5.1
大约 7 小时 about 7 hours	27	2.7
大约 8 小时 about 8 hours	24	2.4
大约 9 小时 about 9 hours	17	1.7
大约 10 小时或以上 about 10 hours or over	22	2.2
记不清/不知道 can't remember	24	2.4
没有收看 didn't watch	16	1.6

n=1015

1-3 经常收看的电视台/ Ranking of the Most Favorite TV Channels

注：本题为多选题，合计百分比超过 100%（Multiple answers）

排名 Brand Ranking	频道 Channels	人次 Person-time	百分比 Percent
1	翡翠台 TADETVB	838	82.7
2	本港台 HOMEATV	775	76.5
3	广州电视台 Guangzhou TV	207	20.4
4	明珠台 PEARL	157	15.5
5	珠江台 Zhujiang TV	133	13.1
6	广东有线影视台 Guangdong Cable Movies Channel	127	12.5
7	中央 1 台 CCTV-1	118	11.6
8	广东有线体育台 Guangdong Cable Sports Channel	79	7.8
9	凤凰卫视 Phoenix Channel	68	6.7
10	广州有线体育台 Guangzhou Cable Sports Channel	58	5.7
11	广东卫视 Guangdong Satellite	56	5.5
12	亚洲台 WORLD	54	5.3
13	中央 5 台 CCTV-5	32	3.2
14	商台 Guangdong Business TV	19	1.9
15	中央 6 台 CCTV-6	18	1.8
15	广州有线大众影视台 Guangzhou Cable Movies Channel	18	1.8
15	广东经济台 Guangdong Economic TV	18	1.8
16	广州有线新闻台 Guangzhou Cable News Channel	17	1.7
17	广东有线信息台 Guangdong Cable Information Channel	15	1.5
18	广州有线文艺台 Guangzhou Entertainment Channel	12	1.2
18	广东有线都市台 Guangdong Cable City Channel	12	1.2
19	中央 2 台 CCTV-2	10	1.0
20	广东有线购物频道 Guangdong Cable Shopping Channel	9	0.9
21	中央 3 台 CCTV-3	8	0.8
21	广州有线公安台 Guangzhou Cable Public Security Channel	8	0.8

n=1013

1-4 样本、男性各年龄层、女性各年龄层最喜欢收看的频道/ The Most Favorite TV Channels by the Whole Sample, Age and Gender Groups

注：本题为多选题，合计百分比超过 100%（Multiple answers）

	人数 Number	翡翠台 TADETVB	本港台 HOMEATV	广州电视台 Guangzhou TV	明珠台 PEARL	珠江台 Zhujiang TV	广东有线影视台 Guangdong Cable Movies Channel
样本 Sample	1013	82.7	76.5	20.4	15.5	13.1	12.5
男性 Male	484	78.5	72.5	18.8	15.1	12.8	10.5
16~24 岁 Age	103	85.4	76.7	11.7	22.3	3.9	9.7
25~34 岁 Age	146	72.6	67.1	20.5	17.1	9.6	9.6
35~44 岁 Age	122	83.6	75.4	22.1	12.3	13.1	11.5
45~54 岁 Age	72	73.6	70.8	19.4	9.7	22.2	12.5
55~60 岁 Age	41	75.6	75.6	19.5	7.3	29.3	9.8
女性 Female	529	86.6	80.2	21.9	15.9	13.4	14.4
16~24 岁 Age	110	90.9	75.5	13.6	32.7	11.8	15.5
25~34 岁 Age	157	85.4	84.7	21.7	15.9	8.3	15.3
35~44 岁 Age	136	87.5	77.9	24.3	8.8	14.0	16.2
45~54 岁 Age	86	82.6	86.0	30.2	9.3	18.6	10.5
55~60 岁 Age	40	85.0	70.0	20.0	7.5	25.0	10.0

续前表 continued

	人数 Number	中央 1 台 CCTV-1	广东有线体育台 Guangdong Cable Sports Channel	凤凰卫视 Phoenix Channel	广州有线体育台 Guangzhou Cable Sports Channel	广东卫视 Guangdong Satellite	亚洲台 WORLD
样本 Sample	1013	11.6	7.8	6.7	5.7	5.5	5.3
男性 Male	484	12.8	13.2	4.8	9.9	6.0	4.3
16~24 岁 Age	103	6.8	18.4	3.9	23.3	1.0	4.9
25~34 岁 Age	146	17.1	14.4	7.5	6.8	5.5	5.5
35~44 岁 Age	122	9.8	9.8	1.6	6.6	9.0	4.1
45~54 岁 Age	72	19.4	12.5	5.6	5.6	9.7	4.2
55~60 岁 Age	41	9.8	7.3	4.9	4.9	4.9	0.0
女性 Female	529	10.6	2.8	8.5	1.9	5.1	6.2
16~24 岁 Age	110	4.5	3.6	15.5	1.8	3.6	5.5
25~34 岁 Age	157	13.4	3.2	6.4	1.9	6.4	9.6
35~44 岁 Age	136	9.6	2.9	8.1	1.5	4.4	5.1
45~54 岁 Age	86	11.6	2.3	5.8	1.2	3.5	2.3
55~60 岁 Age	40	17.5	0.0	5.0	5.0	10.0	7.5

续前表 continued

	人数 Number	中央 5 台 CCTV-5	商台 Guangdong Business TV	中央 6 台 CCTV-6	广州有线大众影视台 Guangzhou Cable Movies Channel	广东经济台 Guangdong Economic TV	广州有线新闻台 Guangzhou Cable News Channel
样本 Sample	1013	3.2	1.9	1.8	1.8	1.8	1.7
男性 Male	484	5.6	2.5	1.4	1.4	2.1	2.1
16~24 岁 Age	103	8.7	1.0	1.0	1.9	0.0	0.0
25~34 岁 Age	146	4.8	2.7	0.7	0.7	3.4	2.7
35~44 岁 Age	122	3.3	4.1	2.5	2.5	3.3	2.5
45~54 岁 Age	72	6.9	0.0	1.4	1.4	1.4	1.4
55~60 岁 Age	41	4.9	4.9	2.4	0.0	0.0	4.9
女性 Female	529	0.9	1.3	2.1	2.1	1.5	1.3
16~24 岁 Age	110	0.9	1.8	0.0	3.6	0.9	0.0
25~34 岁 Age	157	2.5	1.3	1.3	0.6	0.6	1.3
35~44 岁 Age	136	0.0	2.2	4.4	1.5	0.7	2.2
45~54 岁 Age	86	0.0	0.0	3.5	4.7	2.3	1.2
55~60 岁 Age	40	0.0	0.0	0.0	0.0	7.5	2.5

续前表 continued

	人数 Number	广东有线信息台 Guangdong Cable Information Channel	广州有线文艺台 Guangzhou Entertainment Channel	广东有线都市台 Guangdong Cable City Channel	中央2台 CCTV-2	广东有线购物频道 Guangdong Cable Shopping Channel	中央3台 CCTV-3	广州有线公安台 Guangzhou Cable Public Security Channel
样本 Sample	1013	1.5	1.2	1.2	1.0	0.9	0.8	0.8
男性 Male	484	1.9	0.4	1.9	1.0	0.4	0.8	1.2
16~24 岁 Age	103	1.0	0.0	1.9	1.0	1.0	0.0	1.0
25~34 岁 Age	146	1.4	0.7	2.1	0.0	0.0	0.7	1.4
35~44 岁 Age	122	0.8	0.8	2.5	0.8	0.0	0.8	0.8
45~54 岁 Age	72	2.8	0.0	1.4	4.2	0.0	2.8	1.4
55~60 岁 Age	41	7.3	0.0	0.0	0.0	2.4	0.0	2.4
女性 Female	529	1.1	1.9	0.6	0.9	1.3	0.8	0.4
16~24 岁 Age	110	0.0	1.8	0.9	0.0	2.7	0.0	0.0
25~34 岁 Age	157	1.3	1.9	0.0	0.6	0.0	0.6	0.0
35~44 岁 Age	136	2.2	1.5	0.7	2.2	2.2	1.5	1.5
45~54 岁 Age	86	1.2	3.5	1.2	0.0	0.0	0.0	0.0
55~60 岁 Age	40	0.0	0.0	0.0	2.5	2.5	2.5	0.0

1-5 经常收看的电视频道/ The Most Favorite TV Channels

1-5-1 经常收看的电视频道(周一--周四)/ Ranking of the Most Favorite TV Channels(Monday--Thursday)

注：本题为多选题，合计百分比超过 100%（Multiple answers）

排名 Brand Ranking	频道 Channels	人次 Person-time	百分比 Percent
1	翡翠台 TADETVB	832	83.7
2	本港台 HOMEATV	794	79.9
3	广州电视台 Guangzhou TV	249	25.1
4	珠江台 Zhujiang TV	230	23.1
5	明珠台 PEARL	218	21.9
5	广东有线影视台 Guangdong Cable Movies Channel	218	21.9
6	中央 1 台 CCTV-1	204	20.5
7	广东卫视 Guangdong Satellite	155	15.6
8	亚洲台 WORLD	143	14.4
9	凤凰卫视 Phoenix Channel	135	13.6
10	广东有线体育台 Guangdong Cable Sports Channel	124	12.5
11	广州有线体育台 Guangzhou Cable Sports Channel	85	8.6
12	广东经济台 Guangdong Economic TV	52	5.2
13	商台 Guangdong Business TV	47	4.7
14	中央 5 台 CCTV-5	46	4.6
15	广东有线都市台 Guangdong Cable City Channel	43	4.3

n=994

1-5-2 经常收看的电视频道(周五)/ Ranking of the Most Favorite TV Channels(Friday)

注：本题为多选题，合计百分比超过 100%（Multiple answers）

排名 Brand Ranking	频道 Channels	人次 Person-time	百分比 Percent
1	本港台 HOMEATV	736	73.9
2	广东卫视 Guangdong Satellite	696	69.9
3	翡翠台 TADETVB	625	62.8
4	明珠台 PEARL	215	21.6
5	广州电视台 Guangzhou TV	191	19.2
6	珠江台 Zhujiang TV	184	18.5
7	广东有线影视台 Guangdong Cable Movies Channel	153	15.4
8	中央 1 台 CCTV-1	139	14.0
9	凤凰卫视 Phoenix Channel	134	13.5
10	亚洲台 WORLD	130	13.1
11	广东有线体育台 Guangdong Cable Sports Channel	97	9.7
12	广州有线体育台 Guangzhou Cable Sports Channel	83	8.3
13	广东经济台 Guangdong Economic TV	48	4.8
14	中央 5 台 CCTV-5	46	4.6
15	商台 Guangdong Business TV	45	4.5

n=996

1-5-3 经常收看的电视频道(周六)/ Ranking of the Most Favorite TV Channels(Saturday)

注：本题为多选题，合计百分比超过 100%（Multiple answers）

排名 Brand Ranking	频道 Channels	人次 Person-time	百分比 Percent
1	翡翠台 TADETVB	836	83.4
2	本港台 HOMEATV	804	80.2
3	明珠台 PEARL	260	25.9
4	广州电视台 Guangzhou TV	217	21.7
5	珠江台 Zhujiang TV	211	21.1
6	广东有线影视台 Guangdong Cable Movies Channel	200	20.0
7	中央 1 台 CCTV-1	181	18.1
8	亚洲台 WORLD	168	16.8
9	广东卫视 Guangdong Satellite	155	15.5
10	凤凰卫视 Phoenix Channel	151	15.1
11	广东有线体育台 Guangdong Cable Sports Channel	136	13.6
12	广州有线体育台 Guangzhou Cable Sports Channel	90	9.0
13	中央 5 台 CCTV-5	54	5.4
14	广东经济台 Guangdong Economic TV	43	4.3
15	商台 Guangdcng Business TV	41	4.1

n=1002

1-5-4 经常收看的电视频道(周日)/ Ranking of the Most Favorite TV Channels(Sunday)

注：本题为多选题，合计百分比超过 100%（Multiple answers）

排名 Brand Ranking	频道 Channels	人次 Person-time	百分比 Percent
1	翡翠台 TADETVB	834	83.3
2	本港台 HOMEATV	791	79.0
3	明珠台 PEARL	245	24.5
4	珠江台 Zhujiang TV	212	21.2
4	广州电视台 Guangzhou TV	212	21.2
5	广东有线影视台 Guangdong Cable Movies Channel	189	18.9
6	中央 1 台 CCTV-1	179	17.9
7	亚洲台 WORLD	164	16.4
8	凤凰卫视 Phoenix Channel	149	14.9
9	广东卫视 Guangdong Satellite	144	14.4
10	广东有线体育台 Guangdong Cable Sports Channel	131	13.1
11	广州有线体育台 Guangzhou Cable Sports Channel	87	8.7
12	中央 5 台 CCTV-5	56	5.6
13	广东经济台 Guangdong Economic TV	41	4.1
14	商台 Guangdong Business TV	39	3.9
14	广东有线都市台 Guangdong Cable City Channel	39	3.9
15	中央 6 台 CCTV-6	38	3.8

n=1001

1-6 经常收看的电视节目/ Ranking of the Most Favorite TV Programs

注：本题为多选题，合计百分比超过 100%（Multiple answers）

排名 Ranking	电视节目 TV Programs	人次 Person-time	百分比 Percent
1	国内新闻 national news	644	64.3
2	港台电视剧 TV play(HK.Taiwan)	586	58.5
3	国际新闻 international news	547	54.6
4	港台影片 film from HK.Taiwan	391	39.0
5	体育新闻 sports news	255	25.4
6	本地新闻 local news	254	25.3
7	MTV/音乐节目 MTV/music	155	15.5
8	国外影片 overseas film	152	15.2
9	综艺节目 comprehensive arts	130	13.0
10	新闻评论 news comments	129	12.9
11	国内电视剧 TV play(inland)	108	10.8
12	天气预报 weather forecast	104	10.4
13	体育专栏节目 sports feature	103	10.3
14	赛事报道 games report	84	8.4
15	国内影片 inland film	78	7.8
16	金融股市 finance & stock	70	7.0
17	军事类节目 military program	54	5.4
18	女性节目 women's program	53	5.3
19	国外电视剧 overseas TV play	47	4.7
20	经济新闻 economic news	41	4.1
21	经济信息 economic information	38	3.8
22	少儿节目 children's program	26	2.6
23	戏曲/戏剧 opera	25	2.5
23	谈话节目 Talk Show	25	2.5
24	消费指南 consumption guide	24	2.4
25	曲艺节目 folk art	18	1.8
25	科教类节目 scientific education	18	1.8
26	专题类节目 special report	15	1.5
27	广告 advertising	13	1.3
27	舞蹈节目 dancing program	13	1.3
28	其他 others	6	0.6
29	电视直销 direct sale on TV	2	0.2

n=1002

1-7 样本、男性各年龄层、女性各年龄层经常收看的电视节目/ The Most Favorite TV Programs by the Whole Sample, Age and Gender Groups

注：本题为多选题，合计百分比超过 100%（Multiple answers）

	人数 Number	国内新闻 national news	国际新闻 international news	新闻评论 news comments	本地新闻 local news	谈话节目 Talk Show	经济新闻 economic news
样本 Sample	1002	64.3	58.5	54.6	39.0	25.3	4.1
男性 Male	477	69.0	46.1	62.3	34.6	27.0	5.7
16~24 岁 Age	102	43.1	48.0	48.0	41.2	21.6	2.9
25~34 岁 Age	145	69.0	41.4	62.1	43.4	28.3	6.2
35~44 岁 Age	119	79.0	49.6	68.1	26.1	32.8	5.0
45~54 岁 Age	71	88.7	46.5	76.1	25.4	26.8	11.3
55~60 岁 Age	40	70.0	47.5	57.5	27.5	20.0	2.5
女性 Female	525	60.0	69.7	47.6	43.0	23.8	2.7
16~24 岁 Age	107	40.2	68.2	33.6	54.2	15.0	0.0
25~34 岁 Age	157	64.3	70.1	52.9	43.9	23.6	1.9
35~44 岁 Age	134	67.9	69.4	51.5	36.6	22.4	5.2
45~54 岁 Age	87	59.8	74.7	50.6	41.4	33.3	3.4
55~60 岁 Age	40	70.0	62.5	45.0	35.0	32.5	2.5

续前表 continued

	人数 Number	经济信息 economic information	金融股市 finance & stock	电视直销 direct sale on TV	消费指南 consumption guide	体育新闻 sports news	赛事报道 games report
样本 Sample	1002	3.8	7.0	0.2	2.4	25.4	8.4
男性 Male	477	5.2	9.2	0.2	1.3	40.9	14.9
16~24 岁 Age	102	4.9	2.0	1.0	1.0	54.9	25.5
25~34 岁 Age	145	6.9	13.1	0.0	0.7	40.0	16.6
35~44 岁 Age	119	3.4	10.1	0.0	1.7	34.5	7.6
45~54 岁 Age	71	7.0	8.5	0.0	2.8	42.3	11.3
55~60 岁 Age	40	2.5	12.5	0.0	0.0	25.0	10.0
女性 Female	525	2.5	5.0	0.2	3.4	11.4	2.5
16~24 岁 Age	107	0.9	3.7	0.0	5.6	17.8	1.9
25~34 岁 Age	157	2.5	5.7	0.6	3.8	12.1	3.2
35~44 岁 Age	134	5.2	5.2	0.0	2.2	9.7	1.5
45~54 岁 Age	87	0.0	4.6	0.0	1.1	6.9	2.3
55~60 岁 Age	40	2.5	5.0	0.0	5.0	7.5	5.0

续前表 continued

	人数 Number	体育专栏节目 sports feature	国内电视剧 TV play (inland)	港台电视剧 play (HK.Taiwan)	国外电视剧 overseas TV play	国内影片 inland film	国外影片 overseas film
样本 Sample	1002	10.3	10.8	58.5	4.7	7.8	15.2
男性 Male	477	17.2	8.6	46.1	3.1	7.5	15.3
16~24 岁 Age	102	29.4	4.9	48.0	4.9	3.9	15.7
25~34 岁 Age	145	16.6	4.8	41.4	2.8	6.9	19.3
35~44 岁 Age	119	10.1	12.6	49.6	2.5	11.8	12.6
45~54 岁 Age	71	14.1	9.9	46.5	2.8	7.0	12.7
55~60 岁 Age	40	15.0	17.5	47.5	2.5	7.5	12.5
女性 Female	525	4.0	12.8	69.7	6.1	8.0	15.0
16~24 岁 Age	107	4.7	6.5	68.2	7.5	6.5	26.2
25~34 岁 Age	157	3.2	13.4	70.1	5.7	7.6	18.5
35~44 岁 Age	134	3.0	8.2	69.4	7.5	7.5	9.7
45~54 岁 Age	87	3.4	19.5	74.7	3.4	12.6	9.2
55~60 岁 Age	40	10.0	27.5	62.5	5.0	5.0	2.5

续前表 continued

	人数 Number	港台影片 TV film from HK.Taiwan	天气预报 weather forecast	广告 advertising	MTV/音乐节目 MTV/music	舞蹈节目 dancing program	曲艺节目 folk art	戏曲/戏剧 opera
样本 Sample	1002	39.0	10.4	1.3	15.5	1.3	1.8	2.5
男性 Male	477	34.6	5.5	0.2	12.8	0.6	1.7	1.9
16~24 岁 Age	102	41.2	5.9	0.0	31.4	1.0	0.0	0.0
25~34 岁 Age	145	43.4	4.1	0.0	11.7	0.0	2.1	0.7
35~44 岁 Age	119	26.1	8.4	0.8	5.9	0.0	1.7	0.8
45~54 岁 Age	71	25.4	4.2	0.0	4.2	1.4	2.8	2.8
55~60 岁 Age	40	27.5	2.5	0.0	5.0	2.5	2.5	12.5
女性 Female	525	43.0	14.9	2.3	17.9	1.9	1.9	3.0
16~24 岁 Age	107	54.2	9.3	3.7	53.3	4.7	0.0	0.9
25~34 岁 Age	157	43.9	13.4	3.2	12.7	2.5	1.3	1.3
35~44 岁 Age	134	36.6	17.9	1.5	9.0	0.7	1.5	1.5
45~54 岁 Age	87	41.4	19.5	1.1	5.7	0.0	4.6	3.4
55~60 岁 Age	40	35.0	15.0	0.0	0.0	0.0	5.0	20.0

续前表 continued

	人数 Number	综艺节目 comprehensive arts	军事类节目 military program	专题类节目 special report	科教类节目 scientific education	少儿节目 children's program	女性节目 women's program	其他 others
样本 Sample	1002	13.0	5.4	1.5	1.8	2.6	5.3	0.6
男性 Male	477	7.1	9.2	1.5	1.3	1.3	0.4	0.2
16~24 岁 Age	102	9.8	11.8	3.9	2.9	1.0	1.0	0.0
25~34 岁 Age	145	9.0	13.1	0.7	0.7	1.4	0.7	0.0
35~44 岁 Age	119	3.4	5.0	1.7	0.0	1.7	0.0	0.8
45~54 岁 Age	71	7.0	4.2	0.0	1.4	1.4	0.0	0.0
55~60 岁 Age	40	5.0	10.0	0.0	2.5	0.0	0.0	0.0
女性 Female	525	18.3	1.9	1.5	2.3	3.8	9.7	1.0
16~24 岁 Age	107	22.4	3.7	1.9	1.9	2.8	10.3	0.9
25~34 岁 Age	157	19.1	1.9	2.5	1.9	6.4	9.6	0.0
35~44 岁 Age	134	19.4	1.5	0.0	3.0	3.0	11.2	0.0
45~54 岁 Age	87	12.6	1.1	1.1	3.4	2.3	8.0	2.3
55~60 岁 Age	40	12.5	0.0	2.5	0.0	2.5	7.5	5.0

1-8 不同学历的观众收看电视节目的偏好/ Program Preference by Educational Levels

注：本题为多选题，合计百分比超过 100%（Multiple answers）

	人数 Number	国内新闻 national news	国际新闻 international news	新闻评论 news comments	本地新闻 local news	谈话节目 Talk Show	经济新闻 economic news
样本 Sample	992	64.1	54.8	13.0	25.3	2.5	4.0
小学及以下 Primary School or Below	53	47.2	39.6	1.9	22.6	0.0	1.9
初中 Middle School	212	64.6	52.4	10.4	24.1	0.9	2.4
高中/中专/技校 High School/Technical Secondary School	491	63.7	53.6	12.8	26.9	3.1	3.5
大学专科 2-3 Year College	126	67.5	65.1	16.7	24.6	1.6	8.7
大学本科 4-5 Year College	98	66.3	60.2	21.4	23.5	4.1	5.1
研究生或以上 Graduate or Above	12	91.7	66.7	8.3	16.7	16.7	8.3

续前表 continued

	人数 Number	经济信息 economic information	金融股市 finance & stock	电视直销 direct sale on TV	消费指南 consumption guide	体育新闻 sports news	赛事报道 games report
样本 Sample	992	3.8	7.1	0.2	2.4	25.7	8.5
小学及以下 Primary School or Below	53	3.8	5.7	0.0	1.9	9.4	5.7
初中 Middle School	212	4.2	3.8	0.9	2.8	20.3	5.2
高中/中专/技校 High School/Technical Secondary School	491	3.1	6.9	0.0	2.6	25.5	7.5
大学专科 2-3 Year College	126	4.8	14.3	0.0	2.4	32.5	11.9
大学本科 4-5 Year College	98	4.1	7.1	0.0	1.0	39.8	17.3
研究生或以上 Graduate or Above	12	16.7	0.0	0.0	0.0	16.7	8.3

续前表 continued

	人数 Number	体育专栏节目 sports feature	国内电视剧 TV play(inland)	港台电视剧 play (HK.Taiwan)	国外电视剧 overseas TV play	国内影片 inland film	国外影片 overseas film
样本 Sample	**992**	**10.3**	**10.7**	**58.4**	**4.7**	**7.9**	**15.3**
小学及以下 Primary School or Below	53	1.9	30.2	69.8	3.8	13.2	7.5
初中 Middle School	212	10.8	16.5	61.8	4.7	10.4	10.4
高中/中专/技校 High School/Technical Secondary School	491	8.6	9.0	61.5	4.1	7.5	14.1
大学专科 2-3 Year College	126	15.9	5.6	46.8	5.6	5.6	23.8
大学本科 4-5 Year College	98	16.3	3.1	44.9	5.1	4.1	24.5
研究生或以上 Graduate or Above	12	0.0	8.3	50.0	25.0	8.3	25.0

续前表 continued

	人数 Number	港台影片 film from HK.Taiwan	天气预报 weather forecast	广告 advertising	MTV/音乐节目 MTV/music	舞蹈节目 dancing program	曲艺节目 folk art	戏曲/戏剧 opera
样本 Sample	**992**	**39.0**	**10.3**	**1.2**	**15.3**	**1.3**	**1.7**	**2.4**
小学及以下 Primary School or Below	53	47.2	5.7	0.0	5.7	0.0	3.8	13.2
初中 Middle School	212	40.1	12.7	0.9	12.7	1.4	3.3	1.9
高中/中专/技校 High School/Technical Secondary School	491	42.2	10.6	1.6	16.1	1.8	1.0	2.2
大学专科 2-3 Year College	126	34.1	7.1	0.8	17.5	0.8	2.4	0.0
大学本科 4-5 Year College	98	25.5	9.2	1.0	20.4	0.0	0.0	1.0
研究生或以上 Graduate or Above	12	16.7	16.7	0.0	8.3	0.0	0.0	8.3

续前表 continued

	人数 Number	综艺节目 comprehensive arts	军事类节目 military program	专题类节目 special report	科教类节目 scientific education	少儿节目 children's program	女性节目 women's program	其他 others
样本 Sample	**992**	**12.8**	**5.4**	**1.4**	**1.8**	**2.6**	**5.2**	**0.6**
小学及以下 Primary School or Below	53	9.4	3.8	0.0	7.5	3.8	3.8	3.8
初中 Middle School	212	9.9	7.1	0.9	0.0	3.8	4.7	0.9
高中/中专/技校 High School/Technical Secondary School	491	13.2	4.5	1.4	1.8	3.1	6.3	0.2
大学专科 2-3 Year College	126	18.3	7.1	2.4	0.8	0.8	5.6	0.0
大学本科 4-5 Year College	98	10.2	6.1	2.0	4.1	0.0	2.0	1.0
研究生或以上 Graduate or Above	12	25.0	0.0	0.0	0.0	0.0	0.0	0.0

1-9 经常收看电视时段/ Weekday Times Slots of Television Exposure

注：本题为多选题，合计百分比超过 100%（Multiple answers）

时间段 times slots	周一—周四（%）(Monday—Thursday)	周五（%）(Friday)	周六（%）(Saturday)	周日（%）(Sunday)
样本量 Sample	n=1010	n=1011	n=1014	n=1014
0:00-0:30	1.5	1.6	2.0	1.8
0:30-1:00	1.2	1.2	1.5	1.4
1:00-1:30	1.0	0.9	1.5	1.2
1:30-2:00	0.7	0.9	1.1	0.8
2:00-2:30	0.5	0.3	0.5	0.4
2:30-3:00	0.5	0.3	0.4	0.3
3:00-3:30	0.3	0.4	0.3	0.2
3:30-4:00	0.4	0.4	0.4	0.5
4:00-4:30	0.4	0.4	0.4	0.5
4:30-5:00	0.2	0.2	0.5	0.6
5:00-5:30	0.2	0.1	0.3	0.3
5:30-6:00	0.2	0.2	0.2	0.3
6:00-6:30	1.4	1.2	1.1	1.3
6:30-7:00	2.6	2.3	1.7	1.8
7:00-7:30	4.1	3.7	3.4	3.1
7:30-8:00	4.3	4.4	4.6	4.5
8:00-8:30	3.4	3.5	4.6	4.7
8:30-9:00	3.5	3.4	4.6	4.1
9:00-9:30	4.8	4.5	7.0	6.4
9:30-10:00	5.1	5.4	7.8	7.9
10:00-10:30	5.9	6.4	10.7	9.8
10:30-11:00	6.1	6.8	10.8	10.8
11:00-11:30	7.7	8.1	12.6	12.0
11:30-12:00	9.8	9.7	14.7	14.2
12:00-12:30	17.1	16.9	19.2	19.0
12:30-13:00	14.7	14.0	16.9	17.4
13:00-13:30	10.3	9.6	15.5	16.1
13:30-14:00	6.4	6.8	12.1	13.1
14:00-14:30	4.2	4.5	9.2	10.1
14:30-15:00	3.8	4.4	8.4	8.7
15:00-15:30	3.3	3.7	6.6	6.6
15:30-16:00	2.7	3.1	5.7	5.9
16:00-16:30	2.6	3.1	5.5	5.9
16:30-17:00	3.1	3.4	5.8	5.8
17:00-17:30	4.5	4.7	6.6	7.1
17:30-18:00	6.5	6.7	8.0	8.2
18:00-18:30	28.7	28.6	28.5	28.6
18:30-19:00	41.5	41.7	41.2	41.5
19:00-19:30	58.0	58.4	59.6	59.2
19:30-20:00	62.6	64.7	63.6	63.2
20:00-20:30	66.0	69.7	69.4	69.7
20:30-21:00	64.1	68.8	70.0	68.9
21:00-21:30	60.3	65.0	66.9	65.6
21:30-22:00	55.2	59.3	61.5	60.4
22:00-22:30	41.4	45.8	48.8	46.2
22:30-23:00	25.5	30.1	33.6	31.8
23:00-23:30	12.1	15.3	17.5	16.5
23:30-24:00	5.5	7.2	8.9	8.6

1-10 不同消费者层平时是否接触电视媒介/ TV Exposure by Market Segments

1-10-1 时尚流行指标/ Fads Popular Index

	人数 Number	从来不看 never	收看 yes
样本 Sample	1021	1.7	98.3
平实生活指向 simple living orientation	518	1.5	98.5
时尚流行指向 fashion orientation	503	1.8	98.2

1-10-2 广告态度指标/ Advertising Attitude Index

	人数 Number	从来不看 never	收看 yes
样本 Sample	1021	1.7	98.3
广告淡漠指向 indifferent orientation	334	0.9	99.1
中间层 medium	593	2.0	98.0
信赖广告指向 loyal orientation	94	2.1	97.9

1-11 不同消费者层收看电视频道的偏好/ Channel Preference by Market Segments

1-11-1 时尚流行指标/ Fads Popular Index

注：本题为多选题，合计百分比超过 100%（Multiple answers）

	人数 Number	翡翠台 TADETVB	本港台 HOMEATV	广州电视台 Guangzhou TV	明珠台 PEARL	珠江台 Zhujiang TV	广东有线影视台 Guangdong Cable Movies Channel
样本 Sample	1001	82.8	76.4	20.7	15.6	13.3	12.4
平实生活指向 simple living orientation	508	80.3	74.4	21.3	12.6	15.7	13.4
时尚流行指向 fashion orientation	493	85.4	78.5	20.1	18.7	10.8	11.4

续前表 continued

	人数 Number	中央 1 台 CCTV-1	广东有线体育台 Guangdong Cable Sports Channel	凤凰卫视 Phoenix Channel	广州有线体育台 Guangzhou Cable Sports Channel	广东卫视 Guangdong Satellite	亚洲台 WORLD
样本 Sample	1001	11.7	7.6	6.8	5.7	5.5	5.4
平实生活指向 simple living orientation	508	14.8	7.9	5.7	3.9	7.1	4.9
时尚流行指向 fashion orientation	493	8.5	7.3	7.9	7.5	3.9	5.9

续前表 continued

	人数 Number	中央 5 台 CCTV-5	商台 Guangdong Business TV	中央 6 台 CCTV-6	广州有线大众影视台 Guangzhou Cable Movies Channel	广东经济台 Guangdong Economic TV	广州有线新闻台 Guangzhou Cable News Channel
样本 Sample	1001	3.2	1.9	1.7	1.8	1.8	1.6
平实生活指向 simple living orientation	508	3.5	2.2	1.4	1.6	2.4	2.0
时尚流行指向 fashion orientation	493	2.8	1.6	2.0	2.0	1.2	1.2

续前表 continued

	人数 Number	广东有线信息台 Guangdong Cable Information Channel	广州有线文艺台 Guangzhou Entertain-ment Channel	广东有线都市台 Guangdong Cable City Channel	中央 2 台 CCTV-2	广东有线购物频道 Guangdong Cable Shopping Channel	中央 3 台 CCTV-3	广州有线公安台 Guangzhou Cable Public Security Channel
样本 Sample	1001	1.4	1.2	1.2	1.0	0.8	0.8	0.8
平实生活指向 simple living orientation	508	1.0	1.4	1.2	1.8	0.2	1.6	0.8
时尚流行指向 fashion orientation	493	1.8	1.0	1.2	0.2	1.4	0.0	0.8

1-11-2 广告态度指标/ Advertising Attitude Index

注：本题为多选题，合计百分比超过 100%（Multiple answers）

	人数 Number	翡翠台 TADETVB	本港台 HOMEATV	广州电视台 Guangzhou TV	明珠台 PEARL	珠江台 Zhujiang TV	广东有线影视台 Guangdong Cable Movies Channel
样本 Sample	1002	82.6	76.3	20.5	15.4	13.3	12.6
广告淡漠指向 indifferent orientation	331	79.8	73.7	21.5	13.3	13.3	15.1
中间层 medium	580	83.4	77.2	21.0	16.0	12.6	10.5
信赖广告指向 loyal orientation	91	87.9	80.2	13.2	18.7	17.6	16.5

续前表 continued

	人数 Number	中央 1 台 CCTV-1	广东有线体育台 Guangdong Cable Sports Channel	凤凰卫视 Phoenix Channel	广州有线体育台 Guangzhou Cable Sports Channel	亚洲台 WORLD	广东卫视 Guangdong Satellite
样本 Sample	1002	11.7	7.8	6.7	5.8	5.4	5.5
广告淡漠指向 indifferent orientation	331	12.7	6.9	7.3	4.5	5.1	6.6
中间层 medium	580	11.4	8.6	6.2	7.2	4.8	5.2
信赖广告指向 loyal orientation	91	9.9	5.5	7.7	1.1	9.9	3.3

续前表 continued

	人数 Number	中央 5 台 CCTV-5	商台 Guangdong Business TV	中央 6 台 CCTV-6	广州有线大众影视台 Guangzhou Cable Movies Channel	广东经济台 Guangdong Economic TV	广州有线新闻台 Guangzhou Cable News Channel
样本 Sample	1002	3.1	1.9	1.8	1.8	1.8	1.7
广告淡漠指向 indifferent orientation	331	3.9	1.5	2.1	0.6	2.7	1.5
中间层 medium	580	2.8	2.1	1.7	2.2	1.4	1.9
信赖广告指向 loyal orientation	91	2.2	2.2	1.1	3.3	1.1	1.1

续前表 continued

	人数 Number	广东有线信息台 Guangdong Cable Information Channel	广州有线文艺台 Guangzhou Entertain-ment Channel	广东有线都市台 Guangdong Cable City Channel	中央 2 台 CCTV-2	广东有线购物频道 Guangdong Cable Shopping Channel	中央 3 台 CCTV-3	广州有线公安台 Guangzhou Cable Public Security Channel
样本 Sample	1002	1.5	1.2	1.2	0.9	0.9	0.8	0.8
广告淡漠指向 indifferent orientation	331	1.2	1.5	1.5	0.9	0.6	1.5	1.5
中间层 medium	580	1.6	0.9	0.9	0.9	1.2	0.5	0.5
信赖广告指向 loyal orientation	91	2.2	2.2	2.2	1.1	0.0	0.0	0.0

1-12 不同消费者层收看电视节目的偏好/ Program Preference by Market Segments

1-12-1 时尚流行指标/ Fads Popular Index

注：本题为多选题，合计百分比超过 100%（Multiple answers）

	人数 Number	国内新闻 national news	国际新闻 international news	新闻评论 news comments	本地新闻 local news	谈话节目 Talk Show	经济新闻 economic news
样本 Sample	990	64.4	54.8	12.7	25.6	2.5	4.0
平实生活指向 simple living orientation	505	69.1	59.2	14.5	28.7	1.4	4.4
时尚流行指向 fashion orientation	485	59.6	50.3	10.9	22.3	3.7	3.7

续前表 continued

	人数 Number	经济信息 economic information	金融股市 finance & stock	电视直销 direct sale on TV	消费指南 consumption guide	体育新闻 sports news	赛事报道 games report
样本 Sample	990	3.7	6.8	0.2	2.4	25.4	8.3
平实生活指向 simple living orientation	505	4.4	7.5	0.0	1.4	24.6	7.7
时尚流行指向 fashion orientation	485	3.1	6.0	0.4	3.5	26.2	8.9

续前表 continued

	人数 Number	体育专栏节目 sports feature	国内电视剧 TV play(inland)	港台电视剧 TV play (HK.Taiwan)	国外电视剧 overseas TV play	国内影片 inland film	国外影片 overseas film
样本 Sample	990	10.1	10.6	58.6	4.7	7.8	15.4
平实生活指向 simple living orientation	505	10.5	12.9	57.2	4.0	7.9	15.0
时尚流行指向 fashion orientation	485	9.7	8.2	60.0	5.6	7.6	15.7

续前表 continued

	人数 Number	港台影片 film from HK.Taiwan	天气预报 weather forecast	广告 advertising	MTV/音乐节目 MTV/music	舞蹈节目 dancing program	曲艺节目 folk art	戏曲/戏剧 opera
样本 Sample	990	38.9	10.3	1.3	15.7	1.2	1.7	2.5
平实生活指向 simple living orientation	505	31.9	10.3	0.4	11.3	0.6	2.4	3.6
时尚流行指向 fashion orientation	485	46.2	10.3	2.3	20.2	1.9	1.0	1.4

续前表 continued

	人数 Number	综艺节目 comprehensive arts	军事类节目 military program	专题类节目 special report	科教类节目 scientific education	少儿节目 children's program	女性节目 women's program	其他 others
样本 Sample	990	13.0	5.4	1.4	1.8	2.5	5.3	0.6
平实生活指向 simple living orientation	505	11.9	6.1	1.8	2.2	3.2	4.4	1.2
时尚流行指向 fashion orientation	485	14.2	4.5	1.0	1.4	1.9	6.2	0.0

1-12-2 广告态度指标/ Advertising Attitude Index

注：本题为多选题，合计百分比超过 100%（Multiple answers）

	人数 Number	国内新闻 national news	国际新闻 international news	新闻评论 news comments	本地新闻 local news	谈话节目 Talk Show	经济新闻 economic news
样本 Sample	990	64.5	54.7	12.6	25.3	2.5	4.1
广告淡漠指向 indifferent orientation	329	66.0	55.9	15.5	24.9	2.4	5.5
中间层 medium	571	64.8	56.4	10.3	24.2	2.8	3.0
信赖广告指向 loyal orientation	90	57.8	40.0	16.7	33.3	1.1	6.7

续前表 continued

	人数 Number	经济信息 economic information	金融股市 finance & stock	电视直销 direct sale on TV	消费指南 consumption guide	体育新闻 sports news	赛事报道 games report
样本 Sample	990	3.8	7.0	0.2	2.2	25.6	8.5
广告淡漠指向 indifferent orientation	329	3.6	7.0	0.0	1.2	27.1	5.8
中间层 medium	571	4.0	7.4	0.4	2.5	25.6	10.0
信赖广告指向 loyal orientation	90	3.3	4.4	0.0	4.4	20.0	8.9

续前表 continued

	人数 Number	体育专栏节目 sports feature	国内电视剧 TV play(inland)	港台电视剧 TV play (HK.Taiwan)	国外电视剧 overseas TV play	国内影片 inland film	国外影片 overseas film
样本 Sample	990	10.2	10.8	58.4	4.6	7.8	15.2
广告淡漠指向 indifferent orientation	329	10.6	11.2	52.0	4.0	6.7	12.2
中间层 medium	571	11.0	10.7	61.1	4.7	8.2	17.2
信赖广告指向 loyal orientation	90	3.3	10.0	64.4	6.7	8.9	13.3

续前表 continued

	人数 Number	港台影片 film from (HK.Taiwan)	天气预报 weather forecast	广告 advertising	MTV/音乐节目 MTV/music	舞蹈节目 dancing program	曲艺节目 folk art	戏曲/戏剧 opera
样本 Sample	990	38.7	10.4	1.3	15.5	1.3	1.8	2.5
广告淡漠指向 indifferent orientation	329	36.5	10.9	0.6	12.5	3.0	2.4	2.7
中间层 medium	571	38.5	10.9	1.6	15.6	0.5	1.2	2.8
信赖广告指向 loyal orientation	90	47.8	5.6	2.2	25.6	0.0	3.3	0.0

续前表 continued

	人数 Number	综艺节目 comprehensive arts	军事类节目 military program	专题类节目 special report	科教类节目 scientific education	少儿节目 children's program	女性节目 women's program	其他 others
样本 Sample	990	12.8	5.5	1.5	1.8	2.6	4.9	0.6
广告淡漠指向 indifferent orientation	329	11.9	7.0	1.2	3.0	2.7	4.3	1.2
中间层 medium	571	12.8	5.1	1.9	1.4	2.8	4.6	0.4
信赖广告指向 loyal orientation	90	16.7	2.2	0.0	0.0	1.1	10.0	0.0

● 重庆 / Chongqing

1-1 样本、男性各年龄层、女性各年龄层平时是否接触电视媒介/ Exposure to Television by the Whole Sample, Age and Gender Groups

	人数 Number	从来不看 never	收看 yes
样本 Sample	623	2.4	97.6
男性 Male	313	3.2	96.8
16~24 岁 Age	64	4.7	95.3
25~34 岁 Age	93	3.2	96.8
35~44 岁 Age	75	5.3	94.7
45~54 岁 Age	54	0.0	100.0
55~60 岁 Age	27	0.0	100.0
女性 Female	310	1.6	98.4
16~24 岁 Age	64	4.7	95.3
25~34 岁 Age	90	0.0	100.0
35~44 岁 Age	73	2.7	97.3
45~54 岁 Age	60	0.0	100.0
55~60 岁 Age	23	0.0	100.0

1-2 一周内不同时间收看电视的时间长短/ The Average Time Spending on Watching TV Per Day

1-2-1 一周内不同时间收看电视的时间长短(周一到周四)/ The Average Time Spending on Watching TV Per Day(Monday-Thursday)

	人数 Number	百分比 Percent
大约半小时或以下 about 1/2 hour or below	20	3.3
大约 1 小时 about 1 hour	63	10.5
大约 2 小时 about 2 hours	125	20.8
大约 3 小时 about 3 hours	120	19.9
大约 4 小时 about 4 hours	91	15.1
大约 5 小时 about 5 hours	63	10.5
大约 6 小时 about 6 hours	26	4.3
大约 7 小时 about 7 hours	15	2.7
大约 8 小时 about 8 hours	13	3.0
大约 9 小时 about 9 hours	11	1.8
大约 10 小时或以上 about 10 hours or over	17	2.8
记不清/不知道 can't remember	15	2.5
没有收看 didn't watch	17	2.8

n=602

1-2-2 一周内不同时间收看电视的时间长短(周五)/ The Average Time Spending on Watching TV Per Day(Friday)

	人数 Number	百分比 Percent
大约半小时或以下 about 1/2 hour or below	17	2.8
大约 1 小时 about 1 hour	47	7.8
大约 2 小时 about 2 hours	102	16.9
大约 3 小时 about 3 hours	121	20.0
大约 4 小时 about 4 hours	95	15.7
大约 5 小时 about 5 hours	84	13.9
大约 6 小时 about 6 hours	45	7.5
大约 7 小时 about 7 hours	16	2.6
大约 8 小时 about 8 hours	23	3.8
大约 9 小时 about 9 hours	10	1.7
大约 10 小时或以上 about 10 hours or over	18	3.0
记不清/不知道 can't remember	17	2.8
没有收看 didn't watch	9	1.5

n=604

1-2-3 一周内不同时间收看电视的时间长短(周六)/ The Average Time Spending on Watching TV Per Day(Saturday)

	人数 Number	百分比 Percent
大约半小时或以下 about 1/2 hour or below	9	1.5
大约 1 小时 about 1 hour	43	7.1
大约 2 小时 about 2 hours	92	15.2
大约 3 小时 about 3 hours	114	18.8
大约 4 小时 about 4 hours	94	15.5
大约 5 小时 about 5 hours	92	15.2
大约 6 小时 about 6 hours	50	8.3
大约 7 小时 about 7 hours	24	4.0
大约 8 小时 about 8 hours	26	4.3
大约 9 小时 about 9 hours	11	1.8
大约 10 小时或以上 about 10 hours or over	30	5.0
记不清/不知道 can't remember	13	2.1
没有收看 didn't watch	7	1.2

n=605

1-2-4 一周内不同时间收看电视的时间长短(周日)/ The Average Time Spending on Watching TV Per Day(Sunday)

	人数 Number	百分比 Percent
大约半小时或以下 about 1/2 hour or below	12	2.0
大约 1 小时 about 1 hour	54	8.9
大约 2 小时 about 2 hours	87	14.4
大约 3 小时 about 3 hours	117	19.3
大约 4 小时 about 4 hours	90	14.9
大约 5 小时 about 5 hours	89	14.7
大约 6 小时 about 6 hours	51	8.4
大约 7 小时 about 7 hours	19	3.1
大约 8 小时 about 8 hours	22	3.6
大约 9 小时 about 9 hours	15	2.5
大约 10 小时或以上 about 10 hours or over	32	5.3
记不清/不知道 can't remember	13	2.1
没有收看 didn't watch	4	0.7

n=605

1-3 经常收看的电视台/ Ranking of the Most Favorite TV Channels

注：本题为多选题，合计百分比超过 100%（Multiple answers）

排名 Brand Ranking	频道 Channels	人次 Person-time	百分比 Percent
1	重庆有线 1 台 Chongqing Cable 1	334	55.3
2	中央 1 台 CCTV-1	280	46.4
3	重庆 1 台 Chongqing TV 1	198	32.8
4	重庆有线 4 台 Chongqing Cable 4	160	26.5
5	中央 6 台 CCTV-6	117	19.4
6	中央 5 台 CCTV-5	101	16.7
7	湖南卫视 Hunan Satellite	78	12.9
8	重庆有线 5 台 Chongqing Cable 5	61	10.1
9	重庆有线 3 台 Chongqing Cable 3	59	9.8
10	中央 2 台 CCTV-2	46	7.6
11	重庆 2 台 Chongqing TV 2	45	7.5
12	中央 8 台 CCTV-8	40	6.6
13	浙江卫视 Zhejiang Satellite	34	5.6
14	福建东南卫视 Fujian Satellite Southeast Channel	33	5.5
15	广东卫视 Guangdong Satellite	22	3.6
16	中央 4 台 CCTV-4	20	3.3
17	中央 3 台 CCTV-3	19	3.1
18	四川卫视 Sichuan Satellite	18	3.0
19	中央 7 台 CCTV-7	9	1.5
19	凤凰卫视 Phoenix Channel	9	1.5
19	山东卫视 Shandong Satellite	9	1.5
20	中国教育台 China Education TV 1	7	1.2
20	湖北卫视 Hubei Satellite	7	1.2
20	新疆卫视 Xinjiang Satellite	7	1.2
20	云南卫视 Yunnan Satellite	7	1.2

n=604

1-4 样本、男性各年龄层、女性各年龄层最喜欢收看的频道/ The Most Favorite TV Channels by the Whole Sample, Age and Gender Groups

注：本题为多选题，合计百分比超过 100%（Multiple answers）

	人数 Number	重庆有线 1 台 Chongqing Cable 1	中央 1 台 CCTV-1	重庆 1 台 Chongqing TV 1	重庆有线 4 台 Chongqing Cable 4	中央 6 台 CCTV-6	中央 5 台 CCTV-5
样本 Sample	604	55.3	46.4	32.8	26.5	19.4	16.7
男性 Male	301	48.8	50.5	28.9	18.3	21.6	28.6
16~24 岁 Age	60	48.3	30.0	20.0	18.3	21.7	41.7
25~34 岁 Age	90	52.2	46.7	27.8	17.8	22.2	37.8
35~44 岁 Age	70	51.4	57.1	35.7	20.0	20.0	20.0
45~54 岁 Age	54	42.6	57.4	35.2	18.5	24.1	13.0
55~60 岁 Age	27	44.4	77.8	22.2	14.8	18.5	22.2
女性 Female	303	61.7	42.2	36.6	34.7	17.2	5.0
16~24 岁 Age	60	66.7	18.3	23.3	40.0	15.0	1.7
25~34 岁 Age	90	63.3	42.2	35.6	35.6	22.2	3.3
35~44 岁 Age	70	70.0	44.3	37.1	44.3	17.1	4.3
45~54 岁 Age	60	48.3	61.7	41.7	18.3	15.0	11.7
55~60 岁 Age	23	52.2	47.8	60.9	30.4	8.7	4.3

续前表 continued

	人数 Number	湖南卫视 Hunan Satellite	重庆有线 5 台 Chongqing Cable 5	重庆有线 3 台 Chongqing Cable 3	中央 2 台 CCTV-2	重庆 2 台 Chongqing TV 2	中央 8 台 CCTV-8
样本 Sample	604	12.9	10.1	9.8	7.6	7.5	6.6
男性 Male	301	10.0	11.0	9.0	9.6	7.3	6.6
16~24 岁 Age	60	11.7	13.3	25.0	5.0	10.0	0.0
25~34 岁 Age	90	12.2	12.2	6.7	10.0	2.2	8.9
35~44 岁 Age	70	11.4	7.1	7.1	8.6	10.0	4.3
45~54 岁 Age	54	7.4	11.1	1.9	13.0	7.4	5.6
55~60 岁 Age	27	0.0	11.1	0.0	14.8	11.1	22.2
女性 Female	303	15.8	9.2	10.6	5.6	7.6	6.6
16~24 岁 Age	60	30.0	11.7	23.3	3.3	11.7	6.7
25~34 岁 Age	90	16.7	10.0	10.0	3.3	3.3	7.8
35~44 岁 Age	70	7.1	8.6	2.9	4.3	10.0	2.9
45~54 岁 Age	60	16.7	5.0	3.3	15.0	8.3	6.7
55~60 岁 Age	23	0.0	13.0	21.7	0.0	4.3	13.0

续前表 continued

	人数 Number	浙江卫视 Zhejiang Satellite	福建东南卫视 Fujian Satellite Southeast Channel	广东卫视 Guangdong Satellite	中央 4 台 CCTV-4	中央 3 台 CCTV-3	四川卫视 Sichuan Satellite
样本 Sample	604	5.6	5.5	3.6	3.3	3.1	3.0
男性 Male	301	3.7	4.0	4.0	4.0	3.7	3.7
16~24 岁 Age	60	6.7	5.0	6.7	1.7	0.0	5.0
25~34 岁 Age	90	1.1	3.3	2.2	2.2	3.3	1.1
35~44 岁 Age	70	1.4	5.7	7.1	2.9	2.9	5.7
45~54 岁 Age	54	9.3	3.7	1.9	5.6	11.1	3.7
55~60 岁 Age	27	0.0	0.0	0.0	14.8	0.0	3.7
女性 Female	303	7.6	6.9	3.3	2.6	2.6	2.3
16~24 岁 Age	60	8.3	6.7	8.3	3.3	1.7	0.0
25~34 岁 Age	90	8.9	7.8	3.3	3.3	1.1	2.2
35~44 岁 Age	70	2.9	4.3	1.4	2.9	2.9	5.7
45~54 岁 Age	60	6.7	11.7	1.7	1.7	3.3	1.7
55~60 岁 Age	23	17.4	0.0	0.0	0.0	8.7	0.0

续前表 continued

	人数 Number	中央 7 台 CCTV-7	凤凰卫视 Phoenix Channel	山东卫视 Shandong Satellite	中国教育台 China Education TV 1	湖北卫视 Hubei Satellite	新疆卫视 Xinjiang Satellite	云南卫视 Yunnan Satellite
样本 Sample	604	1.5	1.5	1.5	1.2	1.2	1.2	1.2
男性 Male	301	2.3	1.7	1.3	1.7	1.7	1.7	1.7
16~24 岁 Age	60	1.7	5.0	1.7	1.7	5.0	5.0	1.7
25~34 岁 Age	90	2.2	2.2	1.1	2.2	2.2	1.1	1.1
35~44 岁 Age	70	4.3	0.0	0.0	2.9	0.0	1.4	1.4
45~54 岁 Age	54	0.0	0.0	1.9	0.0	0.0	0.0	3.7
55~60 岁 Age	27	3.7	0.0	3.7	0.0	0.0	0.0	0.0
女性 Female	303	0.7	1.3	1.7	0.7	0.7	0.7	0.7
16~24 岁 Age	60	0.0	5.0	0.0	0.0	0.0	0.0	1.7
25~34 岁 Age	90	0.0	1.1	4.4	0.0	1.1	1.1	0.0
35~44 岁 Age	70	1.4	0.0	1.4	1.4	0.0	1.4	1.4
45~54 岁 Age	60	1.7	0.0	0.0	0.0	1.7	0.0	0.0
55~60 岁 Age	23	0.0	0.0	0.0	4.3	0.0	0.0	0.0

1-5 经常收看的电视频道/ The Most Favorite TV Channels

1-5-1 经常收看的电视频道(周一--周四)/ Ranking of the Most Favorite TV Channels(Monday--Thursday)

注：本题为多选题，合计百分比超过 100%（Multiple answers）

排名 Brand Ranking	频道 Channels	人次 Person-time	百分比 Percent
1	重庆有线 1 台 Chongqing Cable 1	390	66.9
2	中央 1 台 CCTV-1	381	65.4
3	重庆 1 台 Chongqing TV 1	255	43.7
4	重庆有线 4 台 Chongqing Cable 4	225	38.6
5	中央 6 台 CCTV-6	169	29.0
6	中央 5 台 CCTV-5	149	25.6
7	重庆有线 5 台 Chongqing Cable 5	132	22.6
8	重庆 2 台 Chongqing TV 2	124	21.3
9	浙江卫视 Zhejiang Satellite	116	19.9
10	重庆有线 3 台 Chongqing Cable 3	113	19.4
11	中央 2 台 CCTV-2	107	18.4
12	湖南卫视 Hunan Satellite	106	18.2
13	中央 8 台 CCTV-8	98	16.8
14	四川卫视 Sichuan Satellite	87	14.9
15	广东卫视 Guangdong Satellite	70	12.0

n=583

1-5-2 经常收看的电视频道(周五)/ Ranking of the Most Favorite TV Channels(Friday)

注：本题为多选题，合计百分比超过 100%（Multiple answers）

排名 Brand Ranking	频道 Channels	人次 Person-time	百分比 Percent
1	重庆有线 1 台 Chongqing Cable 1	392	66.7
2	中央 1 台 CCTV-1	371	63.1
3	重庆 1 台 Chongqing TV 1	249	42.3
4	重庆有线 4 台 Chongqing Cable 4	229	38.9
5	中央 6 台 CCTV-6	170	28.9
6	中央 5 台 CCTV-5	149	25.3
7	重庆有线 5 台 Chongqing Cable 5	136	23.1
8	湖南卫视 Hunan Satellite	122	20.7
9	重庆 2 台 Chongqing TV 2	121	20.6
10	重庆有线 3 台 Chongqing Cable 3	119	20.2
11	浙江卫视 Zhejiang Satellite	111	18.9
12	中央 2 台 CCTV-2	104	17.7
13	中央 8 台 CCTV-8	100	17.0
14	四川卫视 Sichuan Satellite	88	15.0
15	广东卫视 Guangdong Satellite	76	12.9

n=588

1-5-3 经常收看的电视频道(周六)/ Ranking of the Most Favorite TV Channels(Saturday)

注：本题为多选题，合计百分比超过 100%（Multiple answers）

排名 Brand Ranking	频道 Channels	人次 Person-time	百分比 Percent
1	重庆有线 1 台 Chongqing Cable 1	396	67.1
2	中央 1 台 CCTV-1	366	62.0
3	重庆 1 台 Chongqing TV 1	246	41.7
4	重庆有线 4 台 Chongqing Cable 4	227	38.5
5	中央 6 台 CCTV-6	177	30.0
6	中央 5 台 CCTV-5	159	26.9
7	湖南卫视 Hunan Satellite	147	24.9
8	重庆有线 5 台 Chongqing Cable 5	136	23.1
9	重庆 2 台 Chongqing TV 2	123	20.8
10	重庆有线 3 台 Chongqing Cable 3	120	20.3
11	浙江卫视 Zhejiang Satellite	118	20.0
12	中央 2 台 CCTV-2	105	17.8
13	中央 8 台 CCTV-8	100	16.9
14	四川卫视 Sichuan Satellite	89	15.1
15	广东卫视 Guangdong Satellite	78	13.2

n=590

1-5-4 经常收看的电视频道(周日)/ Ranking of the Most favorite TV Channels(Sunday)

注：本题为多选题，合计百分比超过 100%（Multiple answers）

排名 Brand Ranking	频道 Channels	人次 Person-time	百分比 Percent
1	重庆有线 1 台 Chongqing Cable 1	390	66.2
2	中央 1 台 CCTV-1	365	62.0
3	重庆 1 台 Chongqing TV 1	241	40.9
4	重庆有线 4 台 Chongqing Cable 4	223	37.9
5	中央 6 台 CCTV-6	172	29.2
6	中央 5 台 CCTV-5	158	26.8
7	重庆有线 5 台 Chongqing Cable 5	134	22.8
8	湖南卫视 Hunan Satellite	124	21.1
9	重庆 2 台 Chongqing TV 2	121	20.5
10	浙江卫视 Zhejiang Satellite	117	19.9
11	重庆有线 3 台 Chongqing Cable 3	115	19.5
12	中央 2 台 CCTV-2	102	17.3
13	中央 8 台 CCTV-8	98	16.6
14	四川卫视 Sichuan Satellite	95	16.1
15	广东卫视 Guangdong Satellite	77	13.1

n=589

1-6 经常收看的电视节目/ Ranking of the Most Favorite TV Programs

注：本题为多选题，合计百分比超过 100%（Multiple answers）

排名 Ranking	电视节目 TV Programs	人次 Person-time	百分比 Percent
1	国内新闻 national news	372	61.6
2	国际新闻 international news	293	48.5
3	港台电视剧 TV play(HK. Taiwan)	192	31.8
4	体育新闻 sports news	170	28.1
5	本地新闻 local news	169	28.0
6	国内电视剧 TV play(inland)	144	23.8
7	综艺节目 comprehensive arts	140	23.2
8	MTV/音乐节目 MTV/music	130	21.5
9	港台影片 film from HK. Taiwan	126	20.9
10	赛事报道 games report	79	13.1
11	国内影片 inland film	78	12.9
12	体育专栏节目 sports feature	74	12.3
13	国外影片 overseas film	71	11.8
14	新闻评论 news comments	68	11.3
15	女性节目 women's program	57	9.4
15	军事类节目 military program	57	9.4
16	谈话节目 Talk Show	52	8.6
17	天气预报 weather forecast	45	7.5
18	经济新闻 economic news	42	7.0
19	经济信息 economic information	38	6.3
20	金融股市 finance & stock	36	6.0
21	国外电视剧 overseas TV play	32	5.3
22	消费指南 consumption guide	20	3.3
23	舞蹈节目 dancing program	19	3.1
24	科教类节目 scientific education	17	2.8
25	曲艺节目 folk art	14	2.3
26	少儿节目 children's program	13	2.2
27	戏曲/戏剧 opera	11	1.8
28	其他 others	10	1.7
29	电视直销 direct sale on TV	6	1.0
30	广告 advertising	5	0.8
31	专题类节目 special report	4	0.7

n=604

1-7 样本、男性各年龄层、女性各年龄层经常收看的电视节目/ The Most Favorite TV Programs by the Whole Sample, Age and Gender Groups

注：本题为多选题，合计百分比超过 100%（Multiple answers）

	人数 Number	国内新闻 national news	国际新闻 international news	新闻评论 news comments	本地新闻 local news	谈话节目 Talk Show	经济新闻 economic news
样本 Sample	604	61.6	31.8	48.5	20.9	28.0	7.0
男性 Male	302	65.6	16.6	59.9	18.5	25.8	8.9
16~24 岁 Age	60	30.0	25.0	31.7	38.3	5.0	6.7
25~34 岁 Age	90	65.6	15.6	58.9	21.1	30.0	10.0
35~44 岁 Age	71	76.1	14.1	73.2	9.9	26.8	8.5
45~54 岁 Age	54	79.6	13.0	70.4	9.3	38.9	11.1
55~60 岁 Age	27	88.9	14.8	70.4	7.4	29.6	7.4
女性 Female	302	57.6	47.0	37.1	23.2	30.1	5.0
16~24 岁 Age	59	40.7	71.2	23.7	40.7	16.9	1.7
25~34 岁 Age	89	62.9	49.4	40.4	24.7	29.2	4.5
35~44 岁 Age	71	56.3	49.3	35.2	22.5	35.2	8.5
45~54 岁 Age	60	68.3	25.0	45.0	11.7	33.3	6.7
55~60 岁 Age	23	56.5	26.1	43.5	4.3	43.5	0.0

续前表 continued

	人数 Number	经济信息 economic information	金融股市 finance & stock	电视直销 direct sale on TV	消费指南 consumption guide	体育新闻 sports news	赛事报道 games report
样本 Sample	604	6.3	6.0	1.0	3.3	28.1	13.1
男性 Male	302	7.6	6.3	0.3	1.3	44.0	22.8
16~24 岁 Age	60	1.7	0.0	1.7	0.0	70.0	43.3
25~34 岁 Age	90	8.9	10.0	0.0	0.0	47.8	22.2
35~44 岁 Age	71	9.9	7.0	0.0	2.8	38.0	19.7
45~54 岁 Age	54	13.0	7.4	0.0	1.9	25.9	7.4
55~60 岁 Age	27	0.0	3.7	0.0	3.7	25.9	18.5
女性 Female	302	5.0	5.6	1.7	5.3	12.3	3.3
16~24 岁 Age	59	5.1	3.4	3.4	1.7	10.2	0.0
25~34 岁 Age	89	3.4	5.6	3.4	5.6	13.5	3.4
35~44 岁 Age	71	7.0	8.5	0.0	7.0	11.3	4.2
45~54 岁 Age	60	5.0	5.0	0.0	5.0	16.7	6.7
55~60 岁 Age	23	4.3	4.3	0.0	8.7	4.3	0.0

续前表 continued

	人数 Number	体育专栏节目 sports feature	国内电视剧 TV play(inland)	港台电视剧 TV play (HK.Taiwan)	国外电视剧 overseas TV play	国内影片 inland film	国外影片 overseas film
样本 Sample	604	12.3	23.8	31.8	5.3	12.9	11.8
男性 Male	302	21.5	19.2	16.6	4.0	12.6	12.3
16~24 岁 Age	60	36.7	6.7	25.0	6.7	6.7	11.7
25~34 岁 Age	90	23.3	11.1	15.6	1.1	12.2	14.4
35~44 岁 Age	71	22.5	18.3	14.1	5.6	9.9	11.3
45~54 岁 Age	54	9.3	33.3	13.0	3.7	18.5	14.8
55~60 岁 Age	27	3.7	48.1	14.8	3.7	22.2	3.7
女性 Female	302	3.0	28.5	47.0	6.6	13.2	11.3
16~24 岁 Age	59	3.4	11.9	71.2	6.8	3.4	22.0
25~34 岁 Age	89	2.2	21.3	49.4	7.9	10.1	11.2
35~44 岁 Age	71	2.8	35.2	49.3	7.0	16.9	9.9
45~54 岁 Age	60	5.0	35.0	25.0	3.3	16.7	6.7
55~60 岁 Age	23	0.0	60.9	26.1	8.7	30.4	0.0

续前表 continued

	人数 Number	港台影片 film from HK. Taiwan	天气预报 weather forecast	广告 advertising	MTV/音乐节目 MTV/music	舞蹈节目 dancing program	曲艺节目 folk art	戏曲/戏剧 opera
样本 Sample	604	20.9	7.5	0.8	21.5	3.1	2.3	1.8
男性 Male	302	18.5	5.3	0.7	17.9	0.7	2.0	0.7
16~24 岁 Age	60	38.3	1.7	1.7	51.7	0.0	0.0	0.0
25~34 岁 Age	90	21.1	5.6	0.0	16.7	0.0	0.0	0.0
35~44 岁 Age	71	9.9	4.2	1.4	8.5	0.0	4.2	0.0
45~54 岁 Age	54	9.3	9.3	0.0	3.7	3.7	3.7	3.7
55~60 岁 Age	27	7.4	7.4	0.0	0.0	0.0	3.7	0.0
女性 Female	302	23.2	9.6	1.0	25.2	5.6	2.6	3.0
16~24 岁 Age	59	40.7	5.1	1.7	64.4	3.4	0.0	0.0
25~34 岁 Age	89	24.7	12.4	0.0	25.8	3.4	2.2	1.1
35~44 岁 Age	71	22.5	8.5	1.4	9.9	7.0	1.4	2.8
45~54 岁 Age	60	11.7	13.3	1.7	10.0	8.3	5.0	3.3
55~60 岁 Age	23	4.3	4.3	0.0	8.7	8.7	8.7	17.4

续前表 continued

	人数 Number	综艺节目 comprehen-sive arts	军事类节目 military program	专题类节目 special report	科教类节目 scientific education	少儿节目 children's program	女性节目 women's program	其他 others
样本 Sample	604	23.2	9.4	0.7	2.8	2.2	9.4	1.7
男性 Male	302	12.3	15.9	0.3	4.3	0.3	0.7	2.3
16~24 岁 Age	60	11.7	16.7	0.0	5.0	0.0	0.0	1.7
25~34 岁 Age	90	12.2	20.0	0.0	5.6	0.0	2.2	3.3
35~44 岁 Age	71	12.7	12.7	0.0	2.8	1.4	0.0	1.4
45~54 岁 Age	54	7.4	11.1	1.9	3.7	0.0	0.0	3.7
55~60 岁 Age	27	22.2	18.5	0.0	3.7	0.0	0.0	0.0
女性 Female	302	34.1	3.0	1.0	1.3	4.0	18.2	1.0
16~24 岁 Age	59	39.0	1.7	0.0	1.7	6.8	20.3	0.0
25~34 岁 Age	89	39.3	3.4	1.1	2.2	5.6	21.3	1.1
35~44 岁 Age	71	32.4	5.6	2.8	0.0	2.8	19.7	0.0
45~54 岁 Age	60	25.0	1.7	0.0	1.7	0.0	15.0	1.7
55~60 岁 Age	23	30.4	0.0	0.0	0.0	4.3	4.3	4.3

1-8 不同学历的观众收看电视节目的偏好/ Program Preference by Educational Levels

注：本题为多选题，合计百分比超过 100%（Multiple answers）

	人数 Number	国内新闻 national news	国际新闻 international news	新闻评论 news comments	本地新闻 local news	谈话节目 Talk Show	经济新闻 economic news
样本 Sample	602	61.6	48.5	11.3	28.1	8.6	7.0
小学及以下 Primary School or Below	58	48.3	50.0	10.3	24.1	0.0	1.7
初中 Middle School	194	64.4	51.0	11.3	33.0	7.2	8.8
高中/中专/技校 HighSchool/Technical Secondary School	239	58.6	43.1	10.0	26.8	7.9	3.8
大学专科 2-3 Year College	79	68.4	49.4	12.7	22.8	15.2	13.9
大学本科 4-5 Year College	31	74.2	67.7	16.1	29.0	22.6	12.9
研究生或以上 Graduate or Above	1	100.0	100.0	100.0	0.0	0.0	0.0

续前表 continued

	人数 Number	经济信息 economic information	金融股市 finance & stock	电视直销 direct sale on TV	消费指南 consumption guide	体育新闻 sports news	赛事报道 games report
样本 Sample	**602**	**6.3**	**6.0**	**1.0**	**3.3**	**28.1**	**13.0**
小学及以下 Primary School or Below	58	5.2	0.0	0.0	1.7	10.3	5.2
初中 Middle School	194	4.6	4.6	1.5	5.2	22.2	9.8
高中/中专/技校 HighSchool/Technical Secondary School	239	5.0	8.4	1.3	3.3	31.4	15.5
大学专科 2-3 Year College	79	15.2	8.9	0.0	1.3	36.7	17.7
大学本科 4-5 Year College	31	6.5	0.0	0.0	0.0	48.4	16.1
研究生或以上 Graduate or Above	1	0.0	0.0	0.0	0.0	100.0	0.0

续前表 continued

	人数 Number	体育专栏节目 sports feature	国内电视剧 TV play(inland)	港台电视剧 TV play (HK. Taiwan)	国外电视剧 overseas TV play	国内影片 inland film	国外影片 overseas film
样本 Sample	**602**	**12.1**	**23.9**	**31.7**	**5.3**	**13.0**	**11.8**
小学及以下 Primary School or Below	58	8.6	44.8	25.9	3.4	22.4	10.3
初中 Middle School	194	9.3	26.8	30.4	6.7	18.6	9.3
高中/中专/技校 HighSchool/Technical Secondary School	239	14.2	20.1	39.3	5.9	9.2	13.0
大学专科 2-3 Year College	79	16.5	17.7	22.8	2.5	6.3	19.0
大学本科 4-5 Year College	31	6.5	12.9	16.1	3.2	6.5	3.2
研究生或以上 Graduate or Above	1	100.0	0.0	0.0	0.0	0.0	0.0

续前表 continued

	人数 Number	港台影片 film from HK. Taiwan	天气预报 weather forecast	广告 advertising	MTV/音乐节目 MTV/music	舞蹈节目 dancing program	曲艺节目 folk art	戏曲/戏剧 opera
样本 Sample	**602**	**20.8**	**7.5**	**0.8**	**21.6**	**3.2**	**2.3**	**1.8**
小学及以下 Primary School or Below	58	17.2	1.7	0.0	6.9	1.7	3.4	6.9
初中 Middle School	194	23.2	8.8	0.0	18.0	3.1	2.6	2.1
高中/中专/技校 HighSchool/Technical Secondary School	239	23.8	7.9	1.7	26.8	3.3	2.1	0.8
大学专科 2-3 Year College	79	10.1	6.3	1.3	25.3	3.8	2.5	1.3
大学本科 4-5 Year College	31	16.1	9.7	0.0	22.6	3.2	0.0	0.0
研究生或以上 Graduate or Above	1	0.0	0.0	0.0	0.0	0.0	0.0	0.0

续前表 continued

	人数 Number	综艺节目 comprehensive arts	军事类节目 military program	专题类节目 special report	科教类节目 scientific education	少儿节目 children's program	女性节目 women's program	其他 others
样本 Sample	**602**	**23.1**	**9.5**	**0.7**	**2.8**	**2.2**	**9.5**	**1.7**
小学及以下 Primary School or Below	58	19.0	8.6	0.0	1.7	3.4	3.4	6.9
初中 Middle School	194	23.7	7.2	0.5	2.1	1.5	9.3	0.5
高中/中专/技校 HighSchool/Technical Secondary School	239	25.1	11.3	0.4	2.5	3.3	11.3	0.8
大学专科 2-3 Year College	79	20.3	11.4	1.3	5.1	0.0	8.9	3.8
大学本科 4-5 Year College	31	19.4	6.5	3.2	6.5	0.0	9.7	0.0
研究生或以上 Graduate or Above	1	0.0	0.0	0.0	0.0	0.0	0.0	0.0

1-9 经常收看电视时段/ Weekday Times Slots of Television Exposure

注：本题为多选题，合计百分比超过 100%（Multiple answers）

时间段 times slots	周一--周四(%) (Monday--Thursday)	周五(%) (Friday)	周六(%) (Saturday)	周日(%) (Sunday)
样本量 Sample	n=597	n=600	n=603	n=605
0:00-0:30	3.2	3.2	3.5	3.1
0:30-1:00	3.0	2.8	3.2	3.0
1:00-1:30	2.5	2.5	2.5	2.1
1:30-2:00	1.8	2.3	2.0	2.0
2:00-2:30	1.0	1.0	1.0	1.0
2:30-3:00	0.8	0.8	0.8	0.8
3:00-3:30	0.5	0.7	0.5	0.5
3:30-4:00	0.3	0.2	0.3	0.3
4:00-4:30	0.3	0.2	0.3	0.3
4:30-5:00	0.3	0.2	0.3	0.2
5:00-5:30	0.0	0.0	0.0	0.0
5:30-6:00	0.0	0.0	0.0	0.2
6:00-6:30	0.2	0.0	0.0	0.0
6:30-7:00	1.2	1.0	0.8	0.8
7:00-7:30	1.8	2.5	2.8	2.6
7:30-8:00	2.8	3.2	3.6	3.5
8:00-8:30	3.9	4.3	4.8	4.8
8:30-9:00	3.7	4.2	5.3	5.5
9:00-9:30	5.9	5.8	7.1	7.6
9:30-10:00	6.5	6.7	8.5	9.3
10:00-10:30	8.7	9.7	12.4	13.2
10:30-11:00	7.9	9.3	12.8	13.9
11:00-11:30	7.0	8.8	12.6	13.7
11:30-12:00	7.7	8.3	12.6	13.7
12:00-12:30	15.1	13.7	17.4	17.5
12:30-13:00	11.2	11.2	13.3	14.2
13:00-13:30	9.9	10.7	13.6	13.9
13:30-14:00	8.5	9.3	11.8	12.2
14:00-14:30	8.4	9.7	12.9	13.4
14:30-15:00	7.7	8.8	12.4	12.6
15:00-15:30	7.2	9.3	13.6	14.2
15:30-16:00	7.4	8.2	12.4	13.4
16:00-16:30	6.9	7.2	11.4	12.7
16:30-17:00	5.5	6.5	9.6	11.2
17:00-17:30	5.2	6.0	9.0	9.6
17:30-18:00	7.0	7.7	9.5	9.3
18:00-18:30	12.7	13.8	15.4	15.2
18:30-19:00	16.6	19.5	20.9	19.3
19:00-19:30	59.5	58.5	60.7	59.2
19:30-20:00	62.3	62.8	65.2	63.8
20:00-20:30	69.5	72.2	73.6	71.4
20:30-21:00	70.9	75.0	76.3	73.6
21:00-21:30	64.0	70.3	73.5	70.2
21:30-22:00	58.6	66.3	69.2	65.8
22:00-22:30	43.7	52.5	55.4	51.2
22:30-23:00	34.5	41.0	43.3	38.8
23:00-23:30	21.3	24.5	26.4	24.5
23:30-24:00	15.9	18.8	20.2	18.5

1-10 不同消费者层平时是否接触电视媒介/ TV Exposure by Market Segments

1-10-1 时尚流行指标/ Fads Popular Index

	人数 Number	从来不看 never	收看 yes
样本 Sample	616	2.4	97.6
平实生活指向 simple living orientation	369	2.2	97.8
时尚流行指向 fashion orientation	247	2.8	97.2

1-10-2 广告态度指标/ Advertising Attitude Index

	人数 Number	从来不看 never	收看 yes
样本 Sample	618	2.4	97.6
广告淡漠指向 indifferent orientation	167	1.8	98.2
中间层 medium	367	3.0	97.0
信赖广告指向 loyal orientation	84	1.2	98.8

1-11 不同消费者层收看电视频道的偏好/ Channel Preference by Market Segments

1-11-1 时尚流行指标/ Fads Popular Index

注：本题为多选题，合计百分比超过 100%（Multiple answers）

	人数 Number	重庆有线 1 台 Chongqing Cable 1	中央 1 台 CCTV-1	重庆 1 台 Chongqing TV 1	重庆有线 4 台 Chongqing Cable 4	中央 6 台 CCTV-6	中央 5 台 CCTV-5
样本 Sample	597	54.9	46.2	33.2	26.3	19.4	16.6
平实生活指向 simple living orientation	360	54.7	52.2	36.7	24.2	19.4	17.2
时尚流行指向 fashion orientation	237	55.3	37.1	27.8	29.5	19.4	15.6

续前表 continued

	人数 Number	湖南卫视 Hunan Satellite	重庆有线 5 台 Chongqing Cable 5	重庆有线 3 台 Chongqing Cable 3	中央 2 台 CCTV-2	重庆 2 台 Chongqing TV 2	中央 8 台 CCTV-8
样本 Sample	597	13.1	10.1	9.7	7.7	7.5	6.7
平实生活指向 simple living orientation	360	8.3	9.4	8.1	7.2	7.8	6.4
时尚流行指向 fashion orientation	237	20.3	11.0	12.2	8.4	7.2	7.2

续前表 continued

	人数 Number	浙江卫视 Zhejiang Satellite	福建东南卫视 Fujian Satellite Southeast Channel	广东卫视 Guangdong Satellite	中央 4 台 CCTV-4	中央 3 台 CCTV-3	四川卫视 Sichuan Satellite
样本 Sample	597	5.7	5.4	3.7	3.4	3.0	2.8
平实生活指向 simple living orientation	360	4.4	5.3	2.2	3.9	3.9	2.2
时尚流行指向 fashion orientation	237	7.6	5.5	5.9	2.5	1.7	3.8

续前表 continued

	人数 Number	中央 7 台 CCTV-7	凤凰卫视 Phoenix Channel	山东卫视 Shandong Satellite	中国教育台 China Education TV 1	湖北卫视 Hubei Satellite	新疆卫视 Xinjiang Satellite	云南卫视 Yunnan Satellite
样本 Sample	597	1.5	1.5	1.5	1.2	1.2	1.2	1.2
平实生活指向 simple living orientation	360	1.7	0.6	1.1	0.8	1.1	1.4	0.8
时尚流行指向 fashion orientation	237	1.3	3.0	2.1	1.7	1.3	0.8	1.7

1-11-2 广告态度指标/ Advertising Attitude Index

注：本题为多选题，合计百分比超过 100%（Multiple answers）

	人数 Number	重庆有线 1 台 Chongqing Cable 1	中央 1 台 CCTV-1	重庆 1 台 Chongqing TV 1	重庆有线 4 台 Chongqing Cable 4	中央 6 台 CCTV-6	中央 5 台 CCTV-5
样本 Sample	599	55.3	46.2	32.7	26.5	19.4	16.9
广告淡漠指向 indifferent orientation	161	49.1	46.6	36.6	25.5	16.8	21.1
中间层 medium	355	56.6	45.4	31.8	25.9	20.8	15.2
信赖广告指向 loyal orientation	83	61.4	49.4	28.9	31.3	18.1	15.7

续前表 continued

	人数 Number	湖南卫视 Hunan Satellite	重庆有线 5 台 Chongqing Cable 5	重庆有线 3 台 Chongqing Cable 3	中央 2 台 CCTV-2	重庆 2 台 Chongqing TV 2	中央 8 台 CCTV-8
样本 Sample	599	13.0	10.2	9.7	7.5	7.5	6.5
广告淡漠指向 indifferent orientation	161	13.0	9.3	5.0	8.1	10.6	5.6
中间层 medium	355	14.1	10.1	12.1	5.9	7.0	7.0
信赖广告指向 loyal orientation	83	8.4	12.0	8.4	13.3	3.6	6.0

续前表 continued

	人数 Number	浙江卫视 Zhejiang Satellite	福建东南卫视 Fujian Satellite Southeast Channel	广东卫视 Guangdong Satellite	中央 4 台 CCTV-4	中央 3 台 CCTV-3	四川卫视 Sichuan Satellite
样本 Sample	599	5.7	5.5	3.7	3.3	3.0	3.0
广告淡漠指向 indifferent orientation	161	4.3	3.7	2.5	3.7	5.0	1.9
中间层 medium	355	5.9	5.6	4.8	2.8	2.3	3.7
信赖广告指向 loyal orientation	83	7.2	8.4	1.2	4.8	2.4	2.4

续前表 continued

	人数 Number	中央 7 台 CCTV-7	凤凰卫视 Phoenix Channel	山东卫视 Shandong Satellite	中国教育台 China Education TV 1	湖北卫视 Hubei Satellite	新疆卫视 Xinjiang Satellite	云南卫视 Yunnan Satellite
样本 Sample	599	1.5	1.5	1.5	1.2	1.2	1.2	1.2
广告淡漠指向 indifferent orientation	161	2.5	1.9	1.2	1.9	1.9	0.6	1.9
中间层 medium	355	0.8	1.7	1.7	1.1	1.1	1.4	1.1
信赖广告指向 loyal orientation	83	2.4	0.0	1.2	0.0	0.0	1.2	0.0

1-12 不同消费者层收看电视节目的偏好/ Program Preference by Market Segments

1-12-1 时尚流行指标/ Fads Popular Index

注：本题为多选题，合计百分比超过 100%（Multiple answers）

	人数 Number	国内新闻 national news	国际新闻 international news	新闻评论 news comments	本地新闻 local news	谈话节目 Talk Show	经济新闻 economic news
样本 Sample	597	61.8	48.2	11.1	28.0	8.5	6.7
平实生活指向 simple living orientation	360	66.1	51.7	11.9	31.7	7.8	7.5
时尚流行指向 fashion orientation	237	55.3	43.0	9.7	22.4	9.7	5.5

续前表 continued

	人数 Number	经济信息 economic information	金融股市 finance & stock	电视直销 direct sale on TV	消费指南 consumption guide	体育新闻 sports news	赛事报道 games report
样本 Sample	**597**	**6.2**	**6.0**	**1.0**	**3.2**	**28.0**	**13.2**
平实生活指向 simple living orientation	360	5.0	5.3	0.6	2.5	27.5	10.0
时尚流行指向 fashion orientation	237	8.0	7.2	1.7	4.2	28.7	18.1

续前表 continued

	人数 Number	体育专栏节目 sports feature	国内电视剧 TV play(inland)	港台电视剧 TV play (HK. Taiwan)	国外电视剧 overseas TV play	国内影片 inland film	国外影片 overseas film
样本 Sample	**597**	**12.4**	**24.1**	**31.8**	**5.4**	**13.1**	**11.6**
平实生活指向 simple living orientation	360	11.4	28.6	29.4	3.6	15.6	10.8
时尚流行指向 fashion orientation	237	13.9	17.3	35.4	8.0	9.3	12.7

续前表 continued

	人数 Number	港台影片 film from HK. Taiwan	天气预报 weather forecast	广告 advertising	MTV/音乐节目 MTV/music	舞蹈节目 dancing program	曲艺节目 folk art	戏曲/戏剧 opera
样本 Sample	**597**	**20.6**	**7.5**	**0.8**	**21.4**	**3.2**	**2.3**	**1.8**
平实生活指向 simple living orientation	360	16.9	9.4	0.6	14.7	3.6	3.1	2.5
时尚流行指向 fashion orientation	237	26.2	4.6	1.3	31.6	2.5	1.3	0.8

续前表 continued

	人数 Number	综艺节目 comprehensive arts	军事类节目 military program	专题类节目 special report	科教类节目 scientific education	少儿节目 children's program	女性节目 women's program	其他 others
样本 Sample	**597**	**23.1**	**9.2**	**0.7**	**2.8**	**2.2**	**9.2**	**1.7**
平实生活指向 simple living orientation	360	21.9	8.9	0.3	3.1	2.2	7.5	1.7
时尚流行指向 fashion orientation	237	24.9	9.7	1.3	2.5	2.1	11.8	1.7

1-12-2 广告态度指标/ Advertising Attitude Index

注：本题为多选题，合计百分比超过 100%（Multiple answers）

	人数 Number	国内新闻 national news	国际新闻 international news	新闻评论 news comments	本地新闻 local news	谈话节目 Talk Show	经济新闻 economic news
样本 Sample	**599**	**61.6**	**48.4**	**11.0**	**28.0**	**8.5**	**7.0**
广告淡漠指向 indifferent orientation	164	62.8	53.7	8.5	29.3	7.3	4.3
中间层 medium	352	60.2	46.0	13.1	25.3	7.7	7.1
信赖广告指向 loyal orientation	83	65.1	48.2	7.2	37.3	14.5	12.0

续前表 continued

	人数 Number	经济信息 economic information	金融股市 finance & stock	电视直销 direct sale on TV	消费指南 consumption guide	体育新闻 sports news	赛事报道 games report
样本 Sample	**599**	**6.3**	**6.0**	**1.0**	**3.3**	**28.4**	**13.2**
广告淡漠指向 indifferent orientation	164	3.0	2.4	0.6	2.4	33.5	16.5
中间层 medium	352	8.8	8.2	0.9	4.0	26.7	10.8
信赖广告指向 loyal orientation	83	2.4	3.6	2.4	2.4	25.3	16.9

续前表 continued

	人数 Number	体育专栏节目 sports feature	国内电视剧 TV play(inland)	港台影片 TV play (HK. Taiwan)	国外电视剧 overseas TV play	国内影片 inland film	国外影片 overseas film
样本 Sample	599	12.4	23.7	31.7	5.3	13.0	11.9
广告淡漠指向 indifferent orientation	164	18.3	25.6	27.4	5.5	11.6	11.6
中间层 medium	352	10.5	23.0	32.4	6.0	14.8	13.4
信赖广告指向 loyal orientation	83	8.4	22.9	37.3	2.4	8.4	6.0

续前表 continued

	人数 Number	港台电视剧 film from HK. Taiwan	天气预报 weather forecast	广告 advertising	MTV/音乐节目 MTV/music	舞蹈节目 dancing program	曲艺节目 folk art	戏曲/戏剧 opera
样本 Sample	599	20.7	7.5	0.8	21.4	3.2	2.3	1.8
广告淡漠指向 indifferent orientation	164	15.9	6.7	0.0	20.1	2.4	3.0	1.8
中间层 medium	352	23.6	7.1	0.6	21.0	3.1	2.0	1.4
信赖广告指向 loyal orientation	83	18.1	10.8	3.6	25.3	4.8	2.4	3.6

续前表 continued

	人数 Number	综艺节目 comprehensive arts	军事类节目 military program	专题类节目 special report	科教类节目 scientific education	少儿节目 children's program	女性节目 women's program	其他 others
样本 Sample	599	23.2	9.5	0.7	2.7	2.2	9.3	1.7
广告淡漠指向 indifferent orientation	164	13.4	11.0	0.6	1.8	1.2	7.9	2.4
中间层 medium	352	25.9	9.4	0.9	3.4	3.1	9.9	1.4
信赖广告指向 loyal orientation	83	31.3	7.2	0.0	1.2	0.0	9.6	1.2

● 武汉 / Wuhan

1-1 样本、男性各年龄层、女性各年龄层平时是否接触电视媒介/ Exposure to Television by the Whole Sample, Age and Gender Groups

	人数 Number	从来不看 never	收看 yes
样本 Sample	635	4.4	95.6
男性 Male	308	3.9	96.1
16~24 岁 Age	65	7.7	92.3
25~34 岁 Age	87	3.4	96.6
35~44 岁 Age	80	3.8	96.3
45~54 岁 Age	52	1.9	98.1
55~60 岁 Age	24	0.0	100.0
女性 Female	327	4.9	95.1
16~24 岁 Age	68	2.9	97.1
25~34 岁 Age	95	3.2	96.8
35~44 岁 Age	78	3.8	96.2
45~54 岁 Age	60	5.0	95.0
55~60 岁 Age	26	19.2	80.8

1-2 一周内不同时间收看电视的时间长短/ The Average Time Spending on Watching TV Per Day

1-2-1 一周内不同时间收看电视的时间长短(周一到周四)/ The Average Time Spending on Watching TV Per Day(Monday-Thursday)

	人数 Number	百分比 Percent
大约半小时或以下 about 1/2 hour or below	38	6.3
大约 1 小时 about 1 hour	103	17.0
大约 2 小时 about 2 hours	163	26.9
大约 3 小时 about 3 hours	143	23.6
大约 4 小时 about 4 hours	71	11.7
大约 5 小时 about 5 hours	30	4.9
大约 6 小时 about 6 hours	21	3.5
大约 7 小时 about 7 hours	4	0.7
大约 8 小时 about 8 hours	4	0.7
大约 9 小时 about 9 hours	1	0.2
大约 10 小时或以上 about 10 hours or over	6	1.0
记不清/不知道 can't remember	4	0.7
没有收看 didn't watch	19	3.1

n=607

1-2-2 一周内不同时间收看电视的时间长短(周五)/ The Average Time Spending on Watching TV Per Day(Friday)

	人数 Number	百分比 Percent
大约半小时或以下 about 1/2 hour or below	27	4.5
大约 1 小时 about 1 hour	71	11.7
大约 2 小时 about 2 hours	144	23.8
大约 3 小时 about 3 hours	142	23.4
大约 4 小时 about 4 hours	85	14.0
大约 5 小时 about 5 hours	67	11.1
大约 6 小时 about 6 hours	30	5.0
大约 7 小时 about 7 hours	6	1.0
大约 8 小时 about 8 hours	3	0.5
大约 9 小时 about 9 hours	3	0.5
大约 10 小时或以上 about 10 hours or over	7	1.2
记不清/不知道 can't remember	6	1.0
没有收看 didn't watch	15	2.5

n=606

1-2-3 一周内不同时间收看电视的时间长短(周六)/ The Average Time Spending on Watching TV Per Day(Saturday)

	人数 Number	百分比 Percent
大约半小时或以下 about 1/2 hour or below	14	2.3
大约 1 小时 about 1 hour	75	12.4
大约 2 小时 about 2 hours	125	20.6
大约 3 小时 about 3 hours	135	22.3
大约 4 小时 about 4 hours	99	16.3
大约 5 小时 about 5 hours	55	9.1
大约 6 小时 about 6 hours	37	6.1
大约 7 小时 about 7 hours	11	1.8
大约 8 小时 about 8 hours	11	1.8
大约 9 小时 about 9 hours	6	1.0
大约 10 小时或以上 about 10 hours or over	16	2.6
记不清/不知道 can't remember	6	1.0
没有收看 didn't watch	16	2.6

n=606

1-2-4 一周内不同时间收看电视的时间长短(周日)/ The Average Time Spending on Watching TV Per Day(Sunday)

	人数 Number	百分比 Percent
大约半小时或以下 about 1/2 hour or below	15	2.5
大约 1 小时 about 1 hour	79	13.1
大约 2 小时 about 2 hours	118	19.5
大约 3 小时 about 3 hours	140	23.1
大约 4 小时 about 4 hours	94	15.5
大约 5 小时 about 5 hours	56	9.3
大约 6 小时 about 6 hours	32	5.3
大约 7 小时 about 7 hours	17	2.8
大约 8 小时 about 8 hours	12	2.0
大约 9 小时 about 9 hours	7	1.2
大约 10 小时或以上 about 10 hours or over	14	2.3
记不清/不知道 can't remember	6	1.0
没有收看 didn't watch	15	2.5

n=605

1-3 经常收看的电视台/ Ranking of the Most Favorite TV Channels

注：本题为多选题，合计百分比超过 100%（Multiple answers）

排名 Brand Ranking	频道 Channels	人次 Person-time	百分比 Percent
1	中央 1 台 CCTV-1	325	53.5
2	湖北经济台 Hubei Economic TV	160	26.4
3	武汉有线综艺台 Wuhan Cable General Channel	141	23.2
4	武汉 1 台 Wuhan TV 1	134	22.1
5	中央 5 台 CCTV-5	132	21.7
6	中央 6 台 CCTV-6	115	18.9
7	武汉有线影视台 Wuhan Cable Movies Channel	90	14.8
8	武汉 2 台 Wuhan TV 2	80	13.2
9	武汉有线体育台 Wuhan Cable Sports Channel	55	9.1
10	武汉有线资讯台 Wuhan Cable Information Channel	54	8.9
11	湖北卫视 Hubei Satellite	48	7.9
12	中央 8 台 CCTV-8	44	7.2
12	湖北有线影视台 Hubei Cable Movies Channel	44	7.2
12	湖南卫视 Hunan Satellite	44	7.2
13	中央 2 台 CCTV-2	43	7.1
14	湖北电视台 Hubei TV	40	6.6
15	湖北有线综艺台 Hubei Cable General Channel	33	5.4
16	凤凰卫视 Phoenix Channel	25	4.1
17	中央 3 台 CCTV-3	21	3.5
18	广东卫视 Guangdong Satellite	16	2.6
19	浙江卫视 Zhejiang Satellite	14	2.3
19	上海卫视 Shanghai Satellite	14	2.3
20	中央 4 台 CCTV-4	12	2.0
21	硚口有线 Qiaokou Cable	11	1.8
22	福建东南卫视 Fujian Satellite Southeast Channel	10	1.6

n=607

1-4 样本、男性各年龄层、女性各年龄层最喜欢收看的频道/ The Most Favorite TV Channels by the Whole Sample, Age and Gender Groups

注：本题为多选题，合计百分比超过 100%（Multiple answers）

	人数 Number	中央 1 台 CCTV-1	湖北经济台 Hubei Economic TV	武汉有线综艺台 Wuhan Cable General Channel	武汉 1 台 Wuhan TV 1	中央 5 台 CCTV-5	中央 6 台 CCTV-6
样本 Sample	**607**	**53.5**	**26.4**	**23.2**	**22.1**	**21.7**	**18.9**
男性 Male	**296**	**58.1**	**18.6**	**17.2**	**18.6**	**35.5**	**25.0**
16~24 岁 Age	60	18.3	36.7	16.7	13.3	36.7	25.0
25~34 岁 Age	84	54.8	10.7	22.6	19.0	36.9	27.4
35~44 岁 Age	77	72.7	18.2	15.6	22.1	36.4	26.0
45~54 岁 Age	51	78.4	7.8	11.8	17.6	35.3	29.4
55~60 岁 Age	24	79.2	25.0	16.7	20.8	25.0	4.2
女性 Female	**311**	**49.2**	**33.8**	**28.9**	**25.4**	**8.7**	**13.2**
16~24 岁 Age	66	13.6	42.4	40.9	22.7	10.6	15.2
25~34 岁 Age	92	51.1	29.3	32.6	23.9	6.5	14.1
35~44 岁 Age	75	54.7	40.0	33.3	24.0	4.0	8.0
45~54 岁 Age	57	78.9	19.3	12.3	29.8	15.8	15.8
55~60 岁 Age	21	52.4	42.9	4.8	33.3	9.5	14.3

续前表 continued

	人数 Number	武汉有线影视台 Wuhan Cable Movies Channel	武汉 2 台 Wuhan TV 2	武汉有线体育台 Wuhan Cable Sports Channel	武汉有线资讯台 Wuhan Cable Information Channel	湖北卫视 Hubei Satellite	中央 8 台 CCTV-8
样本 Sample	607	14.8	13.2	9.1	8.9	7.9	7.2
男性 Male	296	15.2	9.8	14.9	11.5	6.4	7.8
16~24 岁 Age	60	25.0	11.7	21.7	10.0	3.3	5.0
25~34 岁 Age	84	17.9	4.8	14.3	14.3	4.8	7.1
35~44 岁 Age	77	13.0	11.7	16.9	10.4	9.1	7.8
45~54 岁 Age	51	5.9	13.7	5.9	15.7	3.9	13.7
55~60 岁 Age	24	8.3	8.3	12.5	0.0	16.7	4.2
女性 Female	311	14.5	16.4	3.5	6.4	9.3	6.8
16~24 岁 Age	66	25.8	16.7	4.5	10.6	13.6	4.5
25~34 岁 Age	92	14.1	15.2	3.3	7.6	7.6	9.8
35~44 岁 Age	75	13.3	16.0	4.0	2.7	13.3	4.0
45~54 岁 Age	57	5.3	17.5	1.8	5.3	3.5	8.8
55~60 岁 Age	21	9.5	19.0	4.8	4.8	4.8	4.8

续前表 continued

	人数 Number	湖北有线影视台 Hubei Cable Movies Channel	湖南卫视 Hunan Satellite	中央 2 台 CCTV-2	湖北电视台 Hubei TV	湖北有线综艺台 Hubei Cable General Channel	凤凰卫视 Phoenix Channel
样本 Sample	607	7.2	7.2	7.1	6.6	5.4	4.1
男性 Male	296	8.4	4.1	5.7	5.1	4.1	4.1
16~24 岁 Age	60	15.0	6.7	5.0	5.0	5.0	5.0
25~34 岁 Age	84	9.5	6.0	14.3	1.2	6.0	2.4
35~44 岁 Age	77	5.2	0.0	0.0	6.5	2.6	5.2
45~54 岁 Age	51	5.9	3.9	3.9	9.8	2.0	5.9
55~60 岁 Age	24	4.2	4.2	0.0	4.2	4.2	0.0
女性 Female	311	6.1	10.3	8.4	8.0	6.8	4.2
16~24 岁 Age	66	7.6	18.2	10.6	3.0	7.6	3.0
25~34 岁 Age	92	9.8	9.8	4.3	9.8	8.7	3.3
35~44 岁 Age	75	2.7	8.0	5.3	14.7	6.7	2.7
45~54 岁 Age	57	5.3	7.0	15.8	3.5	3.5	8.8
55~60 岁 Age	21	0.0	4.8	9.5	4.8	4.8	4.8

续前表 continued

	人数 Number	中央 3 台 CCTV-3	广东卫视 Guangdong Satellite	浙江卫视 Zhejiang Satellite	上海卫视 Shanghai Satellite	中央 4 台 CCTV-4	硚口有线 Qiaokou Cable	福建东南卫视 Fujian Satellite Southeast Channel
样本 Sample	607	3.5	2.6	2.3	2.3	2.0	1.8	1.6
男性 Male	296	2.7	2.4	2.0	1.0	2.7	2.0	0.7
16~24 岁 Age	60	5.0	1.7	0.0	1.7	3.3	3.3	1.7
25~34 岁 Age	84	0.0	1.2	3.6	1.2	2.4	2.4	1.2
35~44 岁 Age	77	0.0	0.0	1.3	0.0	2.6	2.6	0.0
45~54 岁 Age	51	3.9	2.0	2.0	2.0	3.9	0.0	0.0
55~60 岁 Age	24	12.5	16.7	4.2	0.0	0.0	0.0	0.0
女性 Female	311	4.2	2.9	2.6	3.5	1.3	1.6	2.6
16~24 岁 Age	66	3.0	6.1	0.0	3.0	1.5	0.0	1.5
25~34 岁 Age	92	3.3	2.2	4.3	2.2	0.0	1.1	4.3
35~44 岁 Age	75	5.3	4.0	2.7	1.3	1.3	4.0	0.0
45~54 岁 Age	57	3.5	0.0	1.8	10.5	1.8	1.8	3.5
55~60 岁 Age	21	9.5	0.0	4.8	0.0	4.8	0.0	4.8

1-5 经常收看的电视频道/ The Most Favorite TV Channels

1-5-1 经常收看的电视频道(周一--周四)/ Ranking of the Most Favorite TV Channels(Monday--Thursday)

注：本题为多选题，合计百分比超过 100%（Multiple answers）

排名 Brand Ranking	频道 Channels	人次 Person-time	百分比 Percent
1	中央 1 台 CCTV-1	417	69.6
2	武汉 1 台 Wuhan TV 1	235	39.2
3	湖北经济台 Hubei Economic TV	203	33.9
4	武汉有线综艺台 Wuhan Cable General Channel	197	32.9
5	武汉 2 台 Wuhan TV 2	178	29.7
6	中央 6 台 CCTV-6	173	28.9
7	中央 5 台 CCTV-5	171	28.5
8	武汉有线影视台 Wuhan Cable Movies Channel	160	26.7
9	湖北卫视 Hubei Satellite	122	20.4
10	武汉有线体育台 Wuhan Cable Sports Channel	106	17.7
11	中央 8 台 CCTV-8	100	16.7
12	武汉有线资讯台 Wuhan Cable Information Channel	99	16.5
13	中央 2 台 CCTV-2	95	15.9
14	湖北电视台 Hubei TV	81	13.5
15	湖北有线综艺台 Hubei Cable General Channel	75	12.5

n=599

1-5-2 经常收看的电视频道(周五)/ Ranking of the Most Favorite TV Channels(Friday)

注：本题为多选题，合计百分比超过 100%（Multiple answers）

排名 Brand Ranking	频道 Channels	人次 Person-time	百分比 Percent
1	中央 1 台 CCTV-1	406	67.9
2	武汉 1 台 Wuhan TV 1	219	36.6
3	湖北经济台 Hubei Economic TV	200	33.4
4	武汉有线综艺台 Wuhan Cable General Channel	195	32.6
5	武汉 2 台 Wuhan TV 2	175	29.3
6	中央 5 台 CCTV-5	167	27.9
7	中央 6 台 CCTV-6	164	27.4
8	武汉有线影视台 Wuhan Cable Movies Channel	159	26.6
9	湖北卫视 Hubei Satellite	131	21.9
10	武汉有线体育台 Wuhan Cable Sports Channel	107	17.9
11	武汉有线资讯台 Wuhan Cable Information Channel	93	15.6
12	中央 8 台 CCTV-8	92	15.4
12	中央 2 台 CCTV-2	92	15.4
13	湖南卫视 Hunan Satellite	84	14.0
14	湖北有线影视台 Hubei Cable Movies Channel	78	13.0
15	湖北电视台 Hubei TV	77	12.9

n=598

1-5-3 经常收看的电视频道(周六)/ Ranking of the Most Favorite TV Channels(Saturday)

注：本题为多选题，合计百分比超过 100%（Multiple answers）

排名 Brand Ranking	频道 Channels	人次 Person-time	百分比 Percent
1	中央 1 台 CCTV-1	410	68.7
2	武汉 1 台 Wuhan TV 1	219	36.7
3	湖北经济台 Hubei Economic TV	202	33.8
4	武汉有线综艺台 Wuhan Cable General Channel	198	33.2
5	武汉 2 台 Wuhan TV 2	175	29.3
6	中央 6 台 CCTV-6	168	28.1
7	中央 5 台 CCTV-5	161	27.0
8	武汉有线影视台 Wuhan Cable Movies Channel	155	26.0
9	湖北卫视 Hubei Satellite	128	21.4
10	武汉有线体育台 Wuhan Cable Sports Channel	107	17.9
11	湖南卫视 Hunan Satellite	106	17.8
12	武汉有线资讯台 Wuhan Cable Information Channel	94	15.7
13	中央 2 台 CCTV-2	92	15.4
14	中央 8 台 CCTV-8	90	15.1
15	湖北电视台 Hubei TV	79	13.2

n=597

1-5-4 经常收看的电视频道(周日)/ Ranking of the Most Favorite TV Channels(Sunday)

注：本题为多选题，合计百分比超过 100%（Multiple answers）

排名 Brand Ranking	频道 Channels	人次 Person-time	百分比 Percent
1	中央 1 台 CCTV-1	405	68.3
2	武汉 1 台 Wuhan TV 1	212	35.8
3	湖北经济台 Hubei Economic TV	202	34.1
4	武汉有线综艺台 Wuhan Cable General Channel	200	33.7
5	中央 6 台 CCTV-6	167	28.2
6	武汉 2 台 Wuhan TV 2	166	28.0
7	中央 5 台 CCTV-5	163	27.5
8	武汉有线影视台 Wuhan Cable Movies Channel	158	26.6
9	湖北卫视 Hubei Satellite	129	21.8
10	武汉有线体育台 Wuhan Cable Sports Channel	102	17.2
11	中央 2 台 CCTV-2	94	15.9
12	武汉有线资讯台 Wuhan Cable Information Channel	92	15.5
13	湖南卫视 Hunan Satellite	91	15.3
13	中央 8 台 CCTV-8	91	15.3
14	湖北电视台 Hubei TV	77	13.0
15	湖北有线影视台 Hubei Cable Movies Channel	73	12.3

n=593

1-6 经常收看的电视节目/ Ranking of the Most Favorite TV Programs

注：本题为多选题，合计百分比超过 100%（Multiple answers）

排名 Ranking	电视节目 TV Programs	人次 Person-time	百分比 Percent
1	国内新闻 national news	365	60.4
2	国际新闻 international news	308	51.0
3	港台电视剧 TV play(HK.Taiwan)	212	35.1
3	体育新闻 sports news	212	35.1
4	综艺节目 comprehensive arts	180	29.8
5	港台影片 film from HK.Taiwan	130	21.5
6	国内电视剧 TV play(inland)	125	20.7
7	MTV/音乐节目 MTV/music	124	20.5
8	新闻评论 news comments	113	18.7
9	国外影片 overseas film	102	16.9
10	赛事报道 games report	88	14.6
11	本地新闻 local news	85	14.1
11	天气预报 weather forecast	85	14.1
12	国内影片 inland film	68	11.3
13	体育专栏节目 sports feature	66	10.9
14	军事类节目 military program	57	9.4
15	曲艺节目 folk art	50	8.3
16	谈话节目 Talk Show	47	7.8
17	金融股市 finance & stock	46	7.6
18	经济新闻 economic news	44	7.3
19	女性节目 women's program	34	5.6
19	国外电视剧 overseas TV play	34	5.6
20	经济信息 economic information	28	4.6
21	消费指南 consumption guide	27	4.5
22	少儿节目 children's program	21	3.5
23	戏曲/戏剧 opera	19	3.1
23	科教类节目 scientific education	19	3.1
24	舞蹈节目 dancing program	14	2.3
25	电视直销 direct sale on TV	11	1.8
26	其他 others	9	1.5
27	专题类节目 special report	8	1.3
28	广告 advertising	4	0.7

n=604

1-7 样本、男性各年龄层、女性各年龄层经常收看的电视节目/ The Most Favorite TV Programs by the Whole Sample, Age and Gender Groups

注：本题为多选题，合计百分比超过 100%（Multiple answers）

	人数 Number	国内新闻 national news	国际新闻 international news	新闻评论 news comments	本地新闻 local news	谈话节目 Talk Show	经济新闻 economic news
样本 Sample	604	60.4	35.1	51.0	21.5	14.1	7.3
男性 Male	294	65.6	23.1	61.6	18.7	13.3	7.8
16~24 岁 Age	59	32.2	40.7	44.1	37.3	8.5	6.8
25~34 岁 Age	83	67.5	15.7	61.4	20.5	12.0	9.6
35~44 岁 Age	77	71.4	23.4	67.5	15.6	15.6	6.5
45~54 岁 Age	51	86.3	13.7	78.4	5.9	15.7	5.9
55~60 岁 Age	24	79.2	25.0	50.0	4.2	16.7	12.5
女性 Female	310	55.5	46.5	41.0	24.2	14.8	6.8
16~24 岁 Age	66	24.2	66.7	22.7	50.0	7.6	1.5
25~34 岁 Age	92	53.3	42.4	32.6	25.0	8.7	9.8
35~44 岁 Age	75	65.3	48.0	54.7	14.7	21.3	6.7
45~54 岁 Age	56	76.8	30.4	57.1	8.9	21.4	10.7
55~60 岁 Age	21	71.4	38.1	42.9	14.3	23.8	0.0

续前表 continued

	人数 Number	经济信息 economic information	金融股市 finance & stock	电视直销 direct sale on TV	消费指南 consumption guide	体育新闻 sports news	赛事报道 games report
样本 Sample	604	4.6	7.6	1.8	4.5	35.1	14.6
男性 Male	294	6.5	8.8	0.7	2.4	53.7	25.2
16~24 岁 Age	59	5.1	3.4	1.7	6.8	50.8	32.2
25~34 岁 Age	83	9.6	14.5	1.2	2.4	60.2	21.7
35~44 岁 Age	77	6.5	7.8	0.0	1.3	54.5	28.6
45~54 岁 Age	51	2.0	11.8	0.0	0.0	49.0	21.6
55~60 岁 Age	24	8.3	0.0	0.0	0.0	45.8	16.7
女性 Female	310	2.9	6.5	2.9	6.5	17.4	4.5
16~24 岁 Age	66	1.5	3.0	4.5	10.6	19.7	4.5
25~34 岁 Age	92	4.3	8.7	3.3	6.5	15.2	2.2
35~44 岁 Age	75	2.7	6.7	2.7	4.0	18.7	6.7
45~54 岁 Age	56	3.6	7.1	1.8	7.1	17.9	5.4
55~60 岁 Age	21	0.0	4.8	0.0	0.0	14.3	4.8

续前表 continued

	人数 Number	体育专栏节目 sports feature	国内电视剧 TV play(inland)	港台电视剧 TV play (HK.Taiwan)	国外电视剧 overseas TV play	国内影片 inland film	国外影片 overseas film
样本 Sample	604	10.9	20.7	35.1	5.6	11.3	16.9
男性 Male	294	17.7	15.3	23.1	4.8	10.2	17.0
16~24 岁 Age	59	16.9	6.8	40.7	6.8	5.1	22.0
25~34 岁 Age	83	19.3	7.2	15.7	2.4	6.0	25.3
35~44 岁 Age	77	20.8	16.9	23.4	5.2	15.6	15.6
45~54 岁 Age	51	11.8	31.4	13.7	5.9	17.6	5.9
55~60 岁 Age	24	16.7	25.0	25.0	4.2	4.2	4.2
女性 Female	310	4.5	25.8	46.5	6.5	12.3	16.8
16~24 岁 Age	66	3.0	13.6	66.7	9.1	7.6	25.8
25~34 岁 Age	92	1.1	18.5	42.4	6.5	9.8	23.9
35~44 岁 Age	75	9.3	24.0	48.0	5.3	16.0	9.3
45~54 岁 Age	56	7.1	42.9	30.4	5.4	17.9	10.7
55~60 岁 Age	21	0.0	57.1	38.1	4.8	9.5	0.0

续前表 continued

	人数 Number	港台影片 film from HK.Taiwan	天气预报 weather forecast	广告 advertising	MTV/音乐节目 MTV/music	舞蹈节目 dancing program	曲艺节目 folk art	戏曲/戏剧 opera
样本 Sample	604	21.5	14.1	0.7	20.5	2.3	8.3	3.1
男性 Male	294	18.7	9.5	0.3	15.3	0.3	7.5	2.7
16~24 岁 Age	59	37.3	5.1	0.0	42.4	1.7	5.1	0.0
25~34 岁 Age	83	20.5	9.6	0.0	14.5	0.0	7.2	0.0
35~44 岁 Age	77	15.6	9.1	0.0	6.5	0.0	3.9	2.6
45~54 岁 Age	51	5.9	15.7	2.0	3.9	0.0	11.8	5.9
55~60 岁 Age	24	4.2	8.3	0.0	4.2	0.0	16.7	12.5
女性 Female	310	24.2	18.4	1.0	25.5	4.2	9.0	3.5
16~24 岁 Age	66	50.0	7.6	1.5	59.1	1.5	6.1	0.0
25~34 岁 Age	92	25.0	19.6	2.2	27.2	6.5	9.8	2.2
35~44 岁 Age	75	14.7	24.0	0.0	16.0	1.3	6.7	0.0
45~54 岁 Age	56	8.9	17.9	0.0	5.4	8.9	10.7	12.5
55~60 岁 Age	21	14.3	28.6	0.0	0.0	0.0	19.0	9.5

续前表 continued

	人数 Number	综艺节目 comprehensive arts	军事类节目 military program	专题类节目 special report	科教类节目 scientific education	少儿节目 children's program	女性节目 women's program	其他 others
样本 Sample	604	29.8	9.4	1.3	3.1	3.5	5.6	1.5
男性 Male	294	18.7	17.3	2.0	3.4	1.0	0.0	2.0
16~24 岁 Age	59	30.5	20.3	1.7	6.8	3.4	0.0	0.0
25~34 岁 Age	83	24.1	19.3	2.4	3.6	0.0	0.0	0.0
35~44 岁 Age	77	6.5	18.2	1.3	1.3	0.0	0.0	2.6
45~54 岁 Age	51	11.8	11.8	3.9	2.0	0.0	0.0	5.9
55~60 岁 Age	24	25.0	12.5	0.0	4.2	4.2	0.0	4.2
女性 Female	310	40.3	1.9	0.6	2.9	5.8	11.0	1.0
16~24 岁 Age	66	39.4	0.0	0.0	3.0	7.6	10.6	1.5
25~34 岁 Age	92	48.9	1.1	1.1	5.4	7.6	17.4	0.0
35~44 岁 Age	75	38.7	4.0	1.3	0.0	6.7	12.0	1.3
45~54 岁 Age	56	35.7	1.8	0.0	3.6	0.0	1.8	1.8
55~60 岁 Age	21	23.8	4.8	0.0	0.0	4.8	4.8	0.0

1-8 不同学历的观众收看电视节目的偏好/ Program Preference by Educational Levels

注：本题为多选题，合计百分比超过 100%（Multiple answers）

	人数 Number	国内新闻 national news	国际新闻 international news	新闻评论 news comments	本地新闻 local news	谈话节目 Talk Show	经济新闻 economic news
样本 Sample	603	60.5	51.1	18.7	13.9	7.8	7.3
小学及以下 Primary School or Below	24	62.5	33.3	0.0	20.8	4.2	8.3
初中 Middle School	143	65.0	48.3	17.5	20.3	2.1	9.1
高中/中专/技校 High School/Technical Secondary School	273	55.7	48.7	17.6	13.9	7.0	6.2
大学专科 2-3 Year College	107	61.7	56.1	23.4	7.5	15.9	5.6
大学本科 4-5 Year College	51	68.6	64.7	25.5	5.9	11.8	7.8
研究生或以上 Graduate or Above	5	80.0	100.0	40.0	20.0	20.0	40.0

续前表 continued

	人数 Number	经济信息 economic information	金融股市 finance & stock	电视直销 direct sale on TV	消费指南 consumption guide	体育新闻 sports news	赛事报道 games report
样本 Sample	**603**	**4.6**	**7.5**	**1.8**	**4.5**	**35.2**	**14.6**
小学及以下 Primary School or Below	24	0.0	4.2	0.0	0.0	12.5	12.5
初中 Middle School	143	3.5	4.2	2.1	6.3	31.5	10.5
高中/中专/技校 High School/Technical Secondary School	273	5.1	7.0	2.6	4.0	39.6	17.2
大学专科 2-3 Year College	107	2.8	12.1	0.9	5.6	32.7	13.1
大学本科 4-5 Year College	51	11.8	11.8	0.0	2.0	37.3	17.6
研究生或以上 Graduate or Above	5	0.0	0.0	0.0	0.0	40.0	0.0

续前表 continued

	人数 Number	体育专栏节目 sports feature	国内电视剧 TV play(inland)	港台电视剧 TV play (HK.Taiwan)	国外电视剧 overseas TV play	国内影片 inland film	国外影片 overseas film
样本 Sample	**603**	**10.9**	**20.6**	**35.0**	**5.6**	**11.3**	**16.9**
小学及以下 Primary School or Below	24	4.2	70.8	58.3	8.3	20.8	4.2
初中 Middle School	143	9.8	26.6	37.1	7.0	17.5	11.9
高中/中专/技校 High School/Technical Secondary School	273	12.1	17.2	37.4	5.1	9.5	15.4
大学专科 2-3 Year College	107	12.1	12.1	27.1	6.5	9.3	27.1
大学本科 4-5 Year College	51	7.8	15.7	25.5	2.0	3.9	23.5
研究生或以上 Graduate or Above	5	20.0	20.0	0.0	0.0	0.0	20.0

续前表 continued

	人数 Number	港台影片 film from HK.Taiwan	天气预报 weather forecast	广告 advertising	MTV/音乐节目 MTV/music	舞蹈节目 dancing program	曲艺节目 folk art	戏曲/戏剧 opera
样本 Sample	**603**	**21.4**	**14.1**	**0.7**	**20.6**	**2.3**	**8.3**	**3.2**
小学及以下 Primary School or Below	24	8.3	12.5	0.0	0.0	4.2	8.3	12.5
初中 Middle School	143	20.3	17.5	0.0	11.9	1.4	13.3	4.2
高中/中专/技校 High School/Technical Secondary School	273	26.4	12.8	1.1	22.0	2.9	7.7	2.6
大学专科 2-3 Year College	107	17.8	13.1	0.0	30.8	2.8	6.5	1.9
大学本科 4-5 Year College	51	13.7	15.7	2.0	27.5	0.0	2.0	2.0
研究生或以上 Graduate or Above	5	0.0	0.0	0.0	0.0	0.0	0.0	0.0

续前表 continued

	人数 Number	综艺节目 comprehensive arts	军事类节目 military program	专题类节目 special report	科教类节目 scientific education	少儿节目 children's program	女性节目 women's program	其他 others
样本 Sample	603	29.9	9.5	1.3	3.2	3.5	5.6	1.5
小学及以下 Primary School or Below	24	20.8	4.2	4.2	0.0	0.0	0.0	0.0
初中 Middle School	143	32.9	7.0	0.7	1.4	4.2	5.6	2.1
高中/中专/技校 High School/Technical Secondary School	273	28.9	11.4	1.1	2.6	4.0	5.9	1.5
大学专科 2-3 Year College	107	35.5	6.5	1.9	5.6	1.9	6.5	0.0
大学本科 4-5 Year College	51	19.6	13.7	2.0	5.9	3.9	5.9	3.9
研究生或以上 Graduate or Above	5	20.0	20.0	0.0	20.0	0.0	0.0	0.0

1-9 经常收看电视时段/ Weekday Times Slots of Television Exposure

注：本题为多选题，合计百分比可能超过 100%（Multiple answers）

时间段 times slots	周一--周四(%) (Monday--Thursday)	周五(%) (Friday)	周六(%) (Saturday)	周日(%) (Sunday)
样本量 Sample	n=604	n=605	n=604	n=603
0:00-0:30	2.2	2.5	2.2	2.3
0:30-1:00	2.0	2.3	2.2	2.3
1:00-1:30	1.3	1.5	1.7	1.8
1:30-2:00	1.5	1.7	1.8	1.8
2:00-2:30	0.3	0.3	0.7	0.7
2:30-3:00	0.3	0.3	0.7	0.7
3:00-3:30	0.0	0.0	0.3	0.3
3:30-4:00	0.0	0.0	0.0	0.0
4:00-4:30	0.0	0.0	0.0	0.0
4:30-5:00	0.0	0.0	0.0	0.0
5:00-5:30	0.0	0.0	0.0	0.0
5:30-6:00	0.0	0.0	0.0	0.0
6:00-6:30	0.3	0.5	0.7	0.3
6:30-7:00	0.5	0.5	0.8	0.7
7:00-7:30	2.6	2.0	2.5	2.5
7:30-8:00	2.5	1.7	2.0	2.3
8:00-8:30	1.7	1.3	2.0	2.3
8:30-9:00	1.8	1.2	2.3	3.0
9:00-9:30	4.8	4.3	7.6	8.6
9:30-10:00	5.8	5.6	9.4	9.8
10:00-10:30	6.8	6.1	10.8	10.9
10:30-11:00	5.5	5.5	9.1	9.0
11:00-11:30	4.1	4.1	7.9	7.8
11:30-12:00	3.6	4.3	8.3	8.3
12:00-12:30	9.1	8.4	11.9	11.6
12:30-13:00	7.0	6.9	7.9	8.8
13:00-13:30	4.5	4.6	7.0	7.8
13:30-14:00	3.3	4.0	6.0	6.6
14:00-14:30	5.0	6.3	8.9	10.1
14:30-15:00	5.8	6.6	9.9	11.1
15:00-15:30	5.0	6.3	10.4	11.1
15:30-16:00	4.8	6.0	9.8	10.8
16:00-16:30	3.5	3.8	7.3	8.6
16:30-17:00	3.0	4.0	6.6	7.5
17:00-17:30	4.3	4.1	5.8	5.8
17:30-18:00	5.1	5.1	6.6	6.6
18:00-18:30	11.6	14.4	14.2	14.9
18:30-19:00	21.2	23.5	23.2	23.2
19:00-19:30	68.9	70.6	68.4	68.0
19:30-20:00	65.6	70.9	70.2	69.2
20:00-20:30	62.7	70.2	71.2	69.2
20:30-21:00	59.9	67.4	68.0	66.3
21:00-21:30	50.0	58.7	61.4	59.0
21:30-22:00	43.0	52.4	55.5	53.6
22:00-22:30	26.0	35.5	37.3	34.3
22:30-23:00	18.5	27.3	28.6	25.4
23:00-23:30	9.9	15.0	15.6	13.9
23:30-24:00	7.0	11.2	11.1	10.4

1-10 不同消费者层平时是否接触电视媒介/ TV Exposure by Market Segments

1-10-1 时尚流行指标/ Fads Popular Index

	人数 Number	从来不看 never	收看 yes
样本 Sample	632	4.4	95.6
平实生活指向 simple living orientation	330	5.2	94.8
时尚流行指向 fashion orientation	302	3.6	96.4

1-10-2 广告态度指标/ Advertising Attitude Index

	人数 Number	从来不看 never	收看 yes
样本 Sample	634	4.4	95.6
广告淡漠指向 indifferent orientation	188	9.6	90.4
中间层 medium	373	2.4	97.6
信赖广告指向 loyal orientation	73	1.4	98.6

1-11 不同消费者层收看电视频道的偏好/ Channel Preference by Market Segments

1-11-1 时尚流行指标/ Fads Popular Index

注：本题为多选题，合计百分比超过 100%（Multiple answers）

	人数 Number	中央 1 台 CCTV-1	湖北经济台 Hubei Economic TV	武汉有线综艺台 Wuhan Cable General Channel	武汉 1 台 Wuhan TV 1	中央 5 台 CCTV-5	中央 6 台 CCTV-6
样本 Sample	604	53.8	26.5	23.2	22.2	21.5	18.7
平实生活指向 simple living orientation	313	58.8	25.6	18.5	23.0	22.7	18.2
时尚流行指向 fashion orientation	291	48.5	27.5	28.2	21.3	20.3	19.2

续前表 continued

	人数 Number	武汉有线影视台 Wuhan Cable Movies Channel	武汉 2 台 Wuhan TV 2	武汉有线体育台 Wuhan Cable Sports Channel	武汉有线资讯台 Wuhan Cable Information Channel	湖北卫视 Hubei Satellite	中央 8 台 CCTV-8
样本 Sample	604	14.7	13.2	8.9	8.9	7.8	7.3
平实生活指向 simple living orientation	313	13.4	14.7	8.9	8.9	8.6	8.9
时尚流行指向 fashion orientation	291	16.2	11.7	8.9	8.9	6.9	5.5

续前表 continued

	人数 Number	湖北有线影视台 Hubei Cable Movies Channel	湖南卫视 Hunan Satellite	中央 2 台 CCTV-2	湖北电视台 Hubei TV	湖北有线综艺台 Hubei Cable General Channel	凤凰卫视 Phoenix Channel
样本 Sample	604	7.3	7.3	7.1	6.6	5.5	4.1
平实生活指向 simple living orientation	313	6.4	4.8	8.3	8.0	5.1	3.8
时尚流行指向 fashion orientation	291	8.2	10.0	5.8	5.2	5.8	4.5

续前表 continued

	人数 Number	中央 3 台 CCTV-3	广东卫视 Guangdong Satellite	浙江卫视 Zhejiang Satellite	上海卫视 Shanghai Satellite	中央 4 台 CCTV-4	硚口有线 Qiaokou Cable	福建东南卫视 Fujian Satellite Southeast Channel
样本 Sample	604	3.5	2.6	2.3	2.3	2.0	1.8	1.7
平实生活指向 simple living orientation	313	4.2	1.9	2.2	1.9	2.2	1.6	1.0
时尚流行指向 fashion orientation	291	2.7	3.4	2.4	2.7	1.7	2.1	2.4

1-11-2 广告态度指标/ Advertising Attitude Index

注：本题为多选题，合计百分比超过 100%（Multiple answers）

	人数 Number	中央 1 台 CCTV-1	湖北经济台 Hubei Economic TV	武汉有线综艺台 Wuhan Cable General Channel	武汉 1 台 Wuhan TV 1	中央 5 台 CCTV-5	中央 6 台 CCTV-6
样本 Sample	606	53.6	26.4	23.3	22.1	21.8	19.0
广告淡漠指向 indifferent orientation	170	54.1	22.4	17.6	20.6	25.9	24.1
中间层 medium	364	55.2	27.2	26.4	22.0	21.2	17.3
信赖广告指向 loyal orientation	72	44.4	31.9	20.8	26.4	15.3	15.3

续前表 continued

	人数 Number	武汉有线影视台 Wuhan Cable Movies Channel	武汉 2 台 Wuhan TV 2	武汉有线体育台 Wuhan Cable Sports Channel	武汉有线资讯台 Wuhan Cable Information Channel	湖北卫视 Hubei Satellite	中央 8 台 CCTV-8
样本 Sample	606	14.7	13.2	8.9	8.9	7.8	7.3
广告淡漠指向 indifferent orientation	170	13.5	15.9	10.0	11.2	9.4	5.3
中间层 medium	364	14.8	10.2	7.7	8.8	7.1	7.7
信赖广告指向 loyal orientation	72	16.7	22.2	12.5	4.2	6.9	9.7

续前表 continued

	人数 Number	湖北有线影视台 Hubei Cable Movies Channel	湖南卫视 Hunan Satellite	中央 2 台 CCTV-2	湖北电视台 Hubei TV	湖北有线综艺台 Hubei Cable General Channel	凤凰卫视 Phoenix Channel
样本 Sample	606	7.3	7.3	7.1	6.6	5.4	4.1
广告淡漠指向 indifferent orientation	170	6.5	8.2	6.5	10.0	7.1	2.4
中间层 medium	364	7.7	6.9	7.1	5.8	4.4	5.5
信赖广告指向 loyal orientation	72	6.9	6.9	8.3	2.8	6.9	1.4

续前表 continued

	人数 Number	中央 3 台 CCTV-3	广东卫视 Guangdong Satellite	浙江卫视 Zhejiang Satellite	上海卫视 Shanghai Satellite	中央 4 台 CCTV-4	硚口有线 Qiaokou Cable	福建东南卫视 Fujian Satellite Southeast Channel
样本 Sample	606	3.5	2.6	2.3	2.3	2.0	1.8	1.7
广告淡漠指向 indifferent orientation	170	2.4	2.4	1.8	1.2	0.6	0.6	1.2
中间层 medium	364	4.4	3.0	3.0	1.9	2.5	1.9	1.4
信赖广告指向 loyal orientation	72	1.4	1.4	0.0	6.9	2.8	4.2	4.2

1-12 不同消费者层收看电视节目的偏好/ Program Preference by Market Segments

1-12-1 时尚流行指标/ Fads Popular Index

注：本题为多选题，合计百分比超过 100%（Multiple answers）

	人数 Number	国内新闻 national news	国际新闻 international news	新闻评论 news comments	本地新闻 local news	谈话节目 Talk Show	经济新闻 economic news
样本 Sample	601	60.4	51.1	18.6	14.1	7.8	7.3
平实生活指向 simple living orientation	312	64.1	52.9	16.3	14.1	6.4	8.0
时尚流行指向 fashion orientation	289	56.4	49.1	21.1	14.2	9.3	6.6

续前表 continued

	人数 Number	经济信息 economic information	金融股市 finance & stock	电视直销 direct sale on TV	消费指南 consumption guide	体育新闻 sports news	赛事报道 games report
样本 Sample	601	4.7	7.7	1.8	4.5	34.8	14.6
平实生活指向 simple living orientation	312	4.8	7.7	1.0	2.9	36.2	14.4
时尚流行指向 fashion orientation	289	4.5	7.6	2.8	6.2	33.2	14.9

续前表 continued

	人数 Number	体育专栏节目 sports feature	国内电视剧 TV play(inland)	港台电视剧 TV play (HK.Taiwan)	国外电视剧 overseas TV play	国内影片 inland film	国外影片 overseas film
样本 Sample	601	11.0	20.8	34.9	5.7	11.1	17.0
平实生活指向 simple living orientation	312	10.3	25.6	33.0	5.4	13.1	15.4
时尚流行指向 fashion orientation	289	11.8	15.6	37.0	5.9	9.0	18.7

续前表 continued

	人数 Number	港台影片 film from HK.Taiwan	天气预报 weather forecast	广告 advertising	MTV/音乐节目 MTV/music	舞蹈节目 dancing program	曲艺节目 folk art	戏曲/戏剧 opera
样本 Sample	601	21.5	14.0	0.7	20.5	2.3	8.3	3.0
平实生活指向 simple living orientation	312	17.0	14.4	0.6	17.6	2.6	9.0	4.8
时尚流行指向 fashion orientation	289	26.3	13.5	0.7	23.5	2.1	7.6	1.0

续前表 continued

	人数 Number	综艺节目 comprehensive arts	军事类节目 military program	专题类节目 special report	科教类节目 scientific education	少儿节目 children's program	女性节目 women's program	其他 others
样本 Sample	601	30.0	9.5	1.3	3.2	3.5	5.7	1.5
平实生活指向 simple living orientation	312	23.4	11.5	1.6	2.6	4.2	4.8	1.9
时尚流行指向 fashion orientation	289	37.0	7.3	1.0	3.8	2.8	6.6	1.0

1-12-2 广告态度指标/ Advertising Attitude Index

注：本题为多选题，合计百分比超过 100%（Multiple answers）

	人数 Number	国内新闻 national news	国际新闻 international news	新闻评论 news comments	本地新闻 local news	谈话节目 Talk Show	经济新闻 economic news
样本 Sample	603	60.4	51.5	18.7	14.1	7.8	7.3
广告淡漠指向 indifferent orientation	170	64.1	51.8	18.8	17.1	6.5	8.2
中间层 medium	361	60.4	52.1	18.8	12.7	7.8	6.6
信赖广告指向 loyal orientation	72	51.4	44.4	18.1	13.9	11.1	8.3

续前表 continued

	人数 Number	经济信息 economic information	金融股市 finance & stock	电视直销 direct sale on TV	消费指南 consumption guide	体育新闻 sports news	赛事报道 games report
样本 Sample	603	4.6	7.6	1.8	4.5	35.0	14.6
广告淡漠指向 indifferent orientation	170	4.7	5.9	1.2	2.9	33.5	15.9
中间层 medium	361	5.0	9.1	1.7	3.3	35.7	15.0
信赖广告指向 loyal orientation	72	2.8	4.2	4.2	13.9	34.7	9.7

续前表 continued

	人数 Number	体育专栏节目 sports feature	国内电视剧 TV play(inland)	港台电视剧 TV play (HK.Taiwan)	国外电视剧 overseas TV play	国内影片 inland film	国外影片 overseas film
样本 Sample	603	10.9	20.7	35.0	5.6	11.3	16.9
广告淡漠指向 indifferent orientation	170	13.5	20.0	30.0	5.3	12.4	18.8
中间层 medium	361	11.1	19.7	35.2	5.3	10.8	16.6
信赖广告指向 loyal orientation	72	4.2	27.8	45.8	8.3	11.1	13.9

续前表 continued

	人数 Number	港台影片 film from HK.Taiwan	天气预报 weather forecast	广告 advertising	MTV/音乐节目 MTV/music	舞蹈节目 dancing program	曲艺节目 folk art	戏曲/戏剧 opera
样本 Sample	603	21.6	14.1	0.7	20.4	2.3	8.3	3.2
广告淡漠指向 indifferent orientation	170	16.5	12.4	0.6	16.5	2.9	8.8	4.1
中间层 medium	361	22.4	15.0	0.6	21.6	2.5	8.9	3.3
信赖广告指向 loyal orientation	72	29.2	13.9	1.4	23.6	0.0	4.2	0.0

续前表 continued

	人数 Number	综艺节目 comprehensive arts	军事类节目 military program	专题类节目 special report	科教类节目 scientific education	少儿节目 children's program	女性节目 women's program	其他 others
样本 Sample	603	29.9	9.5	1.3	3.2	3.5	5.6	1.5
广告淡漠指向 indifferent orientation	170	24.1	11.2	3.5	2.9	4.1	4.7	4.1
中间层 medium	361	31.9	8.9	0.6	3.0	3.3	6.1	0.6
信赖广告指向 loyal orientation	72	33.3	8.3	0.0	4.2	2.8	5.6	0.0

● 西安 / Xi'an

1-1 样本、男性各年龄层、女性各年龄层平时是否接触电视媒介/ Exposure to Television by the Whole Sample, Age and Gender Groups

	人数 Number	从来不看 never	收看 yes
样本 Sample	601	3.2	96.8
男性 Male	302	3.6	96.4
16~24 岁 Age	64	4.7	95.3
25~34 岁 Age	91	4.4	95.6
35~44 岁 Age	77	1.3	98.7
45~54 岁 Age	46	2.2	97.8
55~60 岁 Age	24	8.3	91.7
女性 Female	299	2.7	97.3
16~24 岁 Age	61	6.6	93.4
25~34 岁 Age	90	0.0	100.0
35~44 岁 Age	74	2.7	97.3
45~54 岁 Age	49	4.1	95.9
55~60 岁 Age	25	0.0	100.0

1-2 一周内不同时间收看电视的时间长短/ The Average Time Spending on Watching TV Per Day

1-2-1 一周内不同时间收看电视的时间长短(周一到周四)/ The Average Time Spending on Watching TV Per Day(Monday-Thursday)

	人数 Number	百分比 Percent
大约半小时或以下 about 1/2 hour or below	29	5.0
大约 1 小时 about 1 hour	63	10.8
大约 2 小时 about 2 hours	139	23.9
大约 3 小时 about 3 hours	130	22.3
大约 4 小时 about 4 hours	98	16.8
大约 5 小时 about 5 hours	34	5.8
大约 6 小时 about 6 hours	27	4.6
大约 7 小时 about 7 hours	7	1.2
大约 8 小时 about 8 hours	1	0.2
大约 9 小时 about 9 hours	4	0.7
大约 10 小时或以上 about 10 hours or over	4	0.7
记不清/不知道 can't remember	18	3.1
没有收看 didn't watch	28	4.8

n=582

1-2-2 一周内不同时间收看电视的时间长短(周五)/ The Average Time Spending on Watching TV Per Day(Friday)

	人数 Number	百分比 Percent
大约半小时或以下 about 1/2 hour or below	18	3.1
大约 1 小时 about 1 hour	54	9.3
大约 2 小时 about 2 hours	105	18.0
大约 3 小时 about 3 hours	137	23.5
大约 4 小时 about 4 hours	112	19.2
大约 5 小时 about 5 hours	60	10.3
大约 6 小时 about 6 hours	27	4.6
大约 7 小时 about 7 hours	14	2.4
大约 8 小时 about 8 hours	2	0.3
大约 9 小时 about 9 hours	2	0.3
大约 10 小时或以上 about 10 hours or over	14	2.4
记不清/不知道 can't remember	16	2.7
没有收看 didn't watch	21	3.6

n=582

1-2-3 一周内不同时间收看电视的时间长短(周六)/ The Average Time Spending on Watching TV Per Day(Saturday)

	人数 Number	百分比 Percent
大约半小时或以下 about 1/2 hour or below	13	2.2
大约 1 小时 about 1 hour	37	6.4
大约 2 小时 about 2 hours	97	16.7
大约 3 小时 about 3 hours	115	19.8
大约 4 小时 about 4 hours	123	22.0
大约 5 小时 about 5 hours	67	11.5
大约 6 小时 about 6 hours	42	7.2
大约 7 小时 about 7 hours	17	2.9
大约 8 小时 about 8 hours	10	1.7
大约 9 小时 about 9 hours	6	1.0
大约 10 小时或以上 about 10 hours or over	25	4.3
记不清/不知道 can't remember	17	2.9
没有收看 didn't watch	8	1.4

n=582

1-2-4 一周内不同时间收看电视的时间长短(周日)/ The Average Time Spending on Watching TV Per Day(Sunday)

	人数 Number	百分比 Percent
大约半小时或以下 about 1/2 hour or below	9	1.5
大约 1 小时 about 1 hour	44	7.6
大约 2 小时 about 2 hours	102	17.5
大约 3 小时 about 3 hours	111	19.1
大约 4 小时 about 4 hours	106	18.2
大约 5 小时 about 5 hours	71	12.2
大约 6 小时 about 6 hours	45	7.7
大约 7 小时 about 7 hours	15	2.6
大约 8 小时 about 8 hours	12	2.1
大约 9 小时 about 9 hours	6	1.0
大约 10 小时或以上 about 10 hours or over	24	4.1
记不清/不知道 can't remember	21	3.6
没有收看 didn't watch	16	2.7

n=582

1-3 经常收看的电视台/ Ranking of the Most Favorite TV Channels

注：本题为多选题，合计百分比超过 100%（Multiple answers）

排名 Brand Ranking	频道 Channels	人次 Person-time	百分比 Percent
1	中央 1 台 CCTV-1	380	65.3
2	西安 2 台 Xi'an TV 2	114	19.6
3	中央 6 台 CCTV-6	112	19.2
4	西安有线影视台 Xi'an Cable Movies Channel	93	16.0
5	陕西有线影视台 Shaanxi Cable Movies Channel	92	15.8
6	中央 5 台 CCTV-5	89	15.3
7	凤凰卫视 Phoenix Channel	83	14.3
8	西安有线综合台 Xi'an Cable General Channel	78	13.4
9	中央 8 台 CCTV-8	76	13.1
10	陕西 1 台 Shaanxi TV 1	67	11.5
11	西安 1 台 Xi'an TV 1	66	11.3
12	中央 2 台 CCTV-2	59	10.1
13	西安有线生活台 Xi'an Cable Life Channel	37	6.4
14	山东卫视 Shandong Satellite	36	6.2
15	陕西 2 台 Shaanxi TV2	30	5.2
16	西安有线体育台 Xi'an Cable Sports Channel	26	4.5
16	湖南卫视 Hunan Satellite	26	4.5
17	中央 3 台 CCTV-3	21	3.6
18	陕西有线娱乐台 Shaanxi Cable Entertainment Channel	19	3.3
19	河南卫视 Henan Satellite	18	3.1
20	陕西有线体育台 Shaanxi Cable Sports Channel	17	2.9
20	陕西卫视 Shaanxi Satellite	17	2.9
21	陕西 3 台 Shaanxi TV 3	16	2.7

n=582

1-4 样本、男性各年龄层、女性各年龄层最喜欢收看的频道/ The Most Favorite TV Channels by the Whole Sample, Age and Gender Groups

注：本题为多选题，合计百分比超过 100%（Multiple answers）

	人数 Number	中央 1 台 CCTV-1	西安 2 台 Xi'an TV 2	中央 6 台 CCTV-6	西安有线影视台 Xi'an Cable Movies Channel	陕西有线影视台 Shaanxi Cable Movies Channel
样本 Sample	582	65.3	19.6	19.2	16.0	15.8
男性 Male	291	67.4	16.8	19.6	15.1	16.8
16~24 岁 Age	61	60.7	18.0	16.4	19.7	19.7
25~34 岁 Age	87	62.1	20.7	28.7	13.8	21.8
35~44 岁 Age	76	68.4	18.4	14.5	14.5	10.5
45~54 岁 Age	45	73.3	8.9	17.8	11.1	11.1
55~60 岁 Age	22	90.9	9.1	13.6	18.2	22.7
女性 Female	291	63.2	22.3	18.9	16.8	14.8
16~24 岁 Age	57	49.1	26.3	19.3	19.3	14.0
25~34 岁 Age	90	64.4	30.0	14.4	24.4	23.3
35~44 岁 Age	72	52.8	16.7	26.4	13.9	11.1
45~54 岁 Age	47	83.0	19.1	19.1	8.5	10.6
55~60 岁 Age	25	84.0	8.0	12.0	8.0	4.0

续前表 continued

	人数 Number	中央 5 台 CCTV-5	凤凰卫视 Phoenix Channel	西安有线综合台 Xi'an Cable General Channel	中央 8 台 CCTV-8	陕西 1 台 Shaanxi TV 1	西安 1 台 Xi'an TV 1
样本 Sample	582	15.3	14.3	13.4	13.1	11.5	11.3
男性 Male	291	25.4	15.8	13.1	8.2	10.7	10.7
16~24 岁 Age	61	24.6	21.3	9.8	11.5	8.2	14.8
25~34 岁 Age	87	29.9	17.2	5.7	3.4	11.5	8.0
35~44 岁 Age	76	26.3	11.8	21.1	9.2	6.6	7.9
45~54 岁 Age	45	22.2	15.6	15.6	11.1	11.1	17.8
55~60 岁 Age	22	13.6	9.1	18.2	9.1	27.3	4.5
女性 Female	291	5.2	12.7	13.7	17.9	12.4	12.0
16~24 岁 Age	57	1.8	14.0	17.5	17.5	8.8	5.3
25~34 岁 Age	90	6.7	16.7	10.0	12.2	11.1	6.7
35~44 岁 Age	72	9.7	12.5	16.7	25.0	4.2	18.1
45~54 岁 Age	47	2.1	6.4	14.9	14.9	21.3	17.0
55~60 岁 Age	25	0.0	8.0	8.0	24.0	32.0	20.0

续前表 continued

	人数 Number	中央 2 台 CCTV-2	西安有线生活台 Xi'an Cable Life Channel	山东卫视 Shandong Satellite	陕西 2 台 Shaanxi TV 2	西安有线体育台 Xi'an Cable Sports Channel	湖南卫视 Hunan Satellite
样本 Sample	582	10.1	6.4	6.2	5.2	4.5	4.5
男性 Male	291	10.7	4.5	5.8	3.4	5.8	3.1
16~24 岁 Age	61	1.6	4.9	3.3	3.3	13.1	1.6
25~34 岁 Age	87	13.8	4.6	3.4	0.0	5.7	2.3
35~44 岁 Age	76	10.5	5.3	9.2	3.9	5.3	7.9
45~54 岁 Age	45	15.6	2.2	8.9	8.9	0.0	0.0
55~60 岁 Age	22	13.6	4.5	4.5	4.5	0.0	0.0
女性 Female	291	9.6	8.2	6.5	6.9	3.1	5.8
16~24 岁 Age	57	3.5	10.5	12.3	17.5	8.8	10.5
25~34 岁 Age	90	6.7	11.1	4.4	0.0	1.1	5.6
35~44 岁 Age	72	11.1	5.6	8.3	8.3	1.4	4.2
45~54 岁 Age	47	14.9	4.3	4.3	4.3	2.1	6.4
55~60 岁 Age	25	20.0	8.0	0.0	8.0	4.0	0.0

续前表 continued

	人数 Number	中央 3 台 CCTV-3	陕西有线娱乐台 Shaanxi Cable Entertainment Channel	河南卫视 Henan Satellite	陕西有线体育台 Shaanxi Cable Sports Channel	陕西卫视 Shaanxi Satellite	陕西 3 台 Shaanxi TV 3
样本 Sample	582	3.6	3.3	3.1	2.9	2.9	2.7
男性 Male	291	3.4	3.1	1.7	4.1	2.4	2.4
16~24 岁 Age	61	1.6	1.6	1.6	3.3	0.0	4.9
25~34 岁 Age	87	2.3	4.6	1.1	6.9	3.4	1.1
35~44 岁 Age	76	2.6	2.6	1.3	1.3	3.9	1.3
45~54 岁 Age	45	6.7	2.2	2.2	2.2	2.2	4.4
55~60 岁 Age	22	9.1	4.5	4.5	9.1	0.0	0.0
女性 Female	291	3.8	3.4	4.5	1.7	3.4	3.1
16~24 岁 Age	57	3.5	5.3	3.5	5.3	0.0	5.3
25~34 岁 Age	90	3.3	3.3	5.6	2.2	3.3	1.1
35~44 岁 Age	72	5.6	2.8	6.9	0.0	5.6	1.4
45~54 岁 Age	47	0.0	2.1	2.1	0.0	4.3	6.4
55~60 岁 Age	25	8.0	4.0	0.0	0.0	4.0	4.0

1-5 经常收看的电视频道/ Ranking of the Most Favorite TV Channels

1-5-1 经常收看的电视频道(周一--周四)/ Ranking of the Most Favorite TV Channels(Monday--Thursday)

注：本题为多选题，合计百分比超过 100%（Multiple answers）

排名 Brand Ranking	频道 Channels	人次 Person-time	百分比 Percent
1	中央 1 台 CCTV-1	410	71.1
2	西安 2 台 Xi'an TV 2	180	31.2
3	中央 6 台 CCTV-6	154	26.7
4	中央 5 台 CCTV-5	125	21.7
5	西安有线综合台 Xi'an Cable General Channel	123	21.3
6	西安有线影视台 Xi'an Cable Movies Channel	122	21.1
7	中央 2 台 CCTV-2	121	21.0
8	西安 1 台 Xi'an TV 1	120	20.8
9	陕西有线影视台 Shaanxi Cable Movies Channel	117	20.3
10	中央 8 台 CCTV-8	114	19.8
11	凤凰卫视 Phoenix Channel	106	18.4
12	陕西 1 台 Shaanxi TV 1	88	15.3
13	山东卫视 Shandong Satellite	78	13.5
14	西安有线生活台 Xi'an Cable Life Channel	63	10.9
15	西安有线体育台 Xi'an Cable Sports Channel	61	10.6

n=577

1-5-2 经常收看的电视频道(周五)/ Ranking of the Most Favorite TV Channels(Friday)

注：本题为多选题，合计百分比超过 100%（Multiple answers）

排名 Brand Ranking	频道 Channels	人次 Person-time	百分比 Percent
1	中央 1 台 CCTV-1	399	69.0
2	西安 2 台 Xi'an TV 2	184	31.8
3	中央 6 台 CCTV-6	155	26.8
4	西安有线影视台 Xi'an Cable Movies Channel	131	22.7
5	西安有线综合台 Xi'an Cable General Channel	126	21.8
5	中央 5 台 CCTV-5	126	21.8
6	西安 1 台 Xi'an TV 1	125	21.6
7	陕西有线影视台 Shaanxi Cable Movies Channel	120	20.8
8	中央 2 台 CCTV-2	117	20.2
9	中央 8 台 CCTV-8	113	19.6
10	凤凰卫视 Phoenix Channel	106	18.3
11	陕西 1 台 Shaanxi TV 1	93	16.1
12	山东卫视 Shandong Satellite	75	13.0
13	西安有线体育台 Xi'an Cable Sports Channel	60	10.4
13	西安有线生活台 Xi'an Cable Life Channel	60	10.4
14	湖南卫视 Hunan Satellite	58	10.0
15	陕西 2 台 Shaanxi TV 2	55	9.5

n=578

1-5-3 经常收看的电视频道(周六)/ Ranking of the Most Favorite TV Channels(Saturday)

注：本题为多选题，合计百分比超过 100%（Multiple answers）

排名 Brand Ranking	频道 Channels	人次 Person-time	百分比 Percent
1	中央 1 台 CCTV-1	407	70.5
2	西安 2 台 Xi'an TV 2	192	33.3
3	中央 6 台 CCTV-6	165	28.6
4	西安有线影视台 Xi'an Cable Movies Channel	137	23.7
5	陕西有线影视台 Shaanxi Cable Movies Channel	134	23.2
6	中央 8 台 CCTV-8	129	22.4
7	西安有线综合台 Xi'an Cable General Channel	128	22.2
8	西安 1 台 Xi'an TV 1	124	21.5
9	中央 5 台 CCTV-5	123	21.3
10	中央 2 台 CCTV-2	122	21.1
11	凤凰卫视 Phoenix Channel	119	20.6
12	陕西 1 台 Shaanxi TV 1	100	17.3
13	山东卫视 Shandong Satellite	82	14.2
14	湖南卫视 Hunan Satellite	73	12.7
15	西安有线生活台 Xi'an Cable Life Channel	67	11.6

n=577

1-5-4 经常收看的电视频道(周日)/ Ranking of the Most favorite TV Channels(Sunday)

注：本题为多选题，合计百分比超过 100%（Multiple answers）

排名 Brand Ranking	频道 Channels	人次 Person-time	百分比 Percent
1	中央 1 台 CCTV-1	401	69.5
2	西安 2 台 Xi'an TV 2	192	33.3
3	中央 6 台 CCTV-6	155	26.9
4	西安有线影视台 Xi'an Cable Movies Channel	132	22.9
5	陕西有线影视台 Shaanxi Cable Movies Channel	130	22.5
6	西安有线综合台 Xi'an Cable General Channel	125	21.7
7	西安 1 台 Xi'an TV 1	124	21.5
8	中央 8 台 CCTV-8	123	21.3
9	中央 5 台 CCTV-5	122	21.1
10	中央 2 台 CCTV-2	118	20.5
10	凤凰卫视 Phoenix Channel	118	20.5
11	陕西 1 台 Shaanxi TV 1	95	16.5
12	山东卫视 Shandong Satellite	81	14.0
13	湖南卫视 Hunan Satellite	66	11.4
14	西安有线体育台 Xi'an Cable Sports Channel	63	10.9
15	陕西 2 台 Shaanxi TV 2	62	10.7
15	西安有线生活台 Xi'an Cable Life Channel	62	10.7

n=577

1-6 经常收看的电视节目/ Ranking of the Most Favorite TV Programs

注：本题为多选题，合计百分比超过 100%（Multiple answers）

排名 Ranking	电视节目 TV Programs	人次 Person-time	百分比 Percent
1	国内新闻 national news	370	63.6
2	国际新闻 international news	278	47.8
3	综艺节目 comprehensive arts	160	27.5
4	体育新闻 sports news	156	26.8
5	国内电视剧 TV play(inland)	150	25.8
6	港台电视剧 TV play(HK.Taiwan)	132	22.7
7	港台影片 film from HK.Taiwan	129	22.2
8	新闻评论 news comments	125	21.5
9	国内影片 inland film	92	15.8
10	天气预报 weather forecast	90	15.5
10	本地新闻 local news	90	15.5
11	MTV/音乐节目 MTV/music	88	15.1
12	国外影片 overseas film	79	13.6
13	赛事报道 games report	73	12.5
14	曲艺节目 folk art	58	10.0
15	体育专栏节目 sports feature	56	9.6
16	军事类节目 military program	44	7.6
17	金融股市 finance & stock	42	7.2
17	谈话节目 Talk Show	42	7.2
18	国外电视剧 overseas TV play	39	6.7
19	戏曲/戏剧 opera	38	6.5
19	经济新闻 economic news	38	6.5
20	经济信息 economic information	32	5.5
21	女性节目 women's program	25	4.3
22	消费指南 consumption guide	20	3.4
23	少儿节目 children's program	15	2.6
24	舞蹈节目 dancing program	13	2.2
25	专题类节目 special report	7	1.2
25	科教类节目 scientific education	7	1.2
26	广告 advertising	6	1.0
27	电视直销 direct sale on TV	5	0.9
27	其他 others	5	0.9

n=582

1-7 样本、男性各年龄层、女性各年龄层经常收看的电视节目/ The Most Favorite TV Programs by the Whole Sample, Age and Gender Groups

注：本题为多选题，合计百分比超过 100%（Multiple answers）

	人数 Number	国内新闻 national news	国际新闻 international news	新闻评论 news comments	本地新闻 local news	谈话节目 Talk Show	经济新闻 economic news
样本 Sample	**582**	**63.6**	**22.7**	**47.8**	**22.2**	**15.5**	**6.5**
男性 Male	**291**	**67.7**	**13.7**	**56.0**	**21.3**	**16.2**	**9.3**
16~24 岁 Age	61	49.2	21.3	44.3	42.6	9.8	1.6
25~34 岁 Age	87	67.8	17.2	56.3	18.4	17.2	10.3
35~44 岁 Age	76	71.1	11.8	56.6	18.4	14.5	10.5
45~54 岁 Age	45	73.3	6.7	66.7	13.3	22.2	8.9
55~60 岁 Age	22	95.5	0.0	63.6	0.0	22.7	22.7
女性 Female	**291**	**59.5**	**31.6**	**39.5**	**23.0**	**14.8**	**3.8**
16~24 岁 Age	57	36.8	42.1	28.1	36.8	5.3	7.0
25~34 岁 Age	90	56.7	43.3	36.7	25.6	11.1	5.6
35~44 岁 Age	72	68.1	30.6	43.1	20.8	18.1	0.0
45~54 岁 Age	47	72.3	12.8	53.2	12.8	19.1	2.1
55~60 岁 Age	25	72.0	4.0	40.0	8.0	32.0	4.0

续前表 continued

	人数 Number	经济信息 economic information	金融股市 finance & stock	电视直销 direct sale on TV	消费指南 consumption guide	体育新闻 sports news	赛事报道 games report
样本 Sample	582	5.5	7.2	0.9	3.4	26.8	12.5
男性 Male	291	7.9	10.0	0.3	2.7	40.9	22.0
16~24 岁 Age	61	4.9	4.9	0.0	1.6	45.9	31.1
25~34 岁 Age	87	2.3	10.3	1.1	2.3	39.1	25.3
35~44 岁 Age	76	13.2	18.4	0.0	2.6	42.1	21.1
45~54 岁 Age	45	13.3	4.4	0.0	6.7	42.2	11.1
55~60 岁 Age	22	9.1	4.5	0.0	0.0	27.3	9.1
女性 Female	291	3.1	4.5	1.4	4.1	12.7	3.1
16~24 岁 Age	57	5.3	3.5	0.0	5.3	21.1	5.3
25~34 岁 Age	90	4.4	3.3	3.3	2.2	13.3	0.0
35~44 岁 Age	72	2.8	9.7	1.4	5.6	11.1	5.6
45~54 岁 Age	47	0.0	2.1	0.0	4.3	8.5	2.1
55~60 岁 Age	25	0.0	0.0	0.0	4.0	4.0	4.0

续前表 continued

	人数 Number	体育专栏节目 sports feature	国内电视剧 TV play(inland)	港台电视剧 TV play (HK.Taiwan)	国外电视剧 overseas TV play	国内影片 inland film	国外影片 overseas film
样本 Sample	582	9.6	25.8	22.7	6.7	15.8	13.6
男性 Male	291	15.5	17.2	13.7	6.5	13.1	14.8
16~24 岁 Age	61	21.3	9.8	21.3	4.9	14.8	21.3
25~34 岁 Age	87	18.4	14.9	17.2	2.3	11.5	16.1
35~44 岁 Age	76	17.1	13.2	11.8	9.2	11.8	11.8
45~54 岁 Age	45	4.4	31.1	6.7	13.3	15.6	13.3
55~60 岁 Age	22	4.5	31.8	0.0	4.5	13.6	4.5
女性 Female	291	3.8	34.4	31.6	6.9	18.6	12.4
16~24 岁 Age	57	5.3	19.3	42.1	12.3	12.3	22.8
25~34 岁 Age	90	6.7	27.8	43.3	7.8	16.7	16.7
35~44 岁 Age	72	2.8	50.0	30.6	6.9	16.7	6.9
45~54 岁 Age	47	0.0	42.6	12.8	0.0	31.9	6.4
55~60 岁 Age	25	0.0	32.0	4.0	4.0	20.0	0.0

续前表 continued

	人数 Number	港台影片 film from HK.Taiwan	天气预报 weather forecast	广告 advertising	MTV/音乐节目 MTV/music	舞蹈节目 dancing program	曲艺节目 folk art	戏曲/戏剧 opera
样本 Sample	582	22.2	15.5	1.0	15.1	2.2	10.0	6.5
男性 Male	291	21.3	8.2	0.7	12.7	0.7	8.2	3.1
16~24 岁 Age	61	42.6	4.9	3.3	37.7	0.0	6.6	0.0
25~34 岁 Age	87	18.4	6.9	0.0	5.7	0.0	6.9	1.1
35~44 岁 Age	76	18.4	10.5	0.0	7.9	1.3	7.9	1.3
45~54 岁 Age	45	13.3	11.1	0.0	6.7	2.2	6.7	6.7
55~60 岁 Age	22	0.0	9.1	0.0	0.0	0.0	22.7	18.2
女性 Female	291	23.0	22.7	1.4	17.5	3.8	11.7	10.0
16~24 岁 Age	57	36.8	7.0	0.0	40.4	10.5	3.5	0.0
25~34 岁 Age	90	25.6	23.3	1.1	24.4	3.3	8.9	3.3
35~44 岁 Age	72	20.8	22.2	0.0	6.9	2.8	15.3	5.6
45~54 岁 Age	47	12.8	27.7	2.1	2.1	0.0	12.8	23.4
55~60 岁 Age	25	8.0	48.0	8.0	0.0	0.0	28.0	44.0

续前表 continued

	人数 Number	综艺节目 comprehensive arts	军事类节目 military program	专题类节目 special report	科教类节目 scientific education	少儿节目 children's program	女性节目 women's program	其他 others
样本 Sample	582	27.5	7.6	1.2	1.2	2.6	4.3	0.9
男性 Male	291	18.2	10.3	1.7	0.7	1.0	0.0	0.7
16~24 岁 Age	61	8.2	14.8	3.3	0.0	1.6	0.0	0.0
25~34 岁 Age	87	23.0	4.6	0.0	1.1	0.0	0.0	1.1
35~44 岁 Age	76	27.6	10.5	1.3	1.3	1.3	0.0	0.0
45~54 岁 Age	45	11.1	15.6	2.2	0.0	2.2	0.0	0.0
55~60 岁 Age	22	9.1	9.1	4.5	0.0	0.0	0.0	4.5
女性 Female	291	36.8	4.8	0.7	1.7	4.1	8.6	1.0
16~24 岁 Age	57	43.9	7.0	1.8	1.8	3.5	8.8	0.0
25~34 岁 Age	90	40.0	3.3	0.0	0.0	5.6	10.0	1.1
35~44 岁 Age	72	36.1	2.8	0.0	2.8	5.6	11.1	1.4
45~54 岁 Age	47	25.5	10.6	2.1	4.3	0.0	6.4	2.1
55~60 岁 Age	25	32.0	0.0	0.0	0.0	4.0	0.0	0.0

1-8 不同学历的观众收看电视节目的偏好/ Program Preference by Educational Levels

注：本题为多选题，合计百分比超过 100%（Multiple answers）

	人数 Number	国内新闻 national news	国际新闻 international news	新闻评论 news comments	本地新闻 local news	谈话节目 Talk Show	经济新闻 economic news
样本 Sample	579	63.7	47.7	21.6	15.5	7.3	6.4
小学及以下 Primary School or Below	15	53.3	40.0	20.0	6.7	6.7	0.0
初中 Middle School	121	65.3	43.0	19.8	24.8	3.3	4.1
高中/中专/技校 High School/Technical Secondary School	274	62.4	46.4	16.1	14.2	7.3	6.2
大学专科 2-3 Year College	107	66.4	54.2	28.0	9.3	10.3	8.4
大学本科 4-5 Year College	57	64.9	52.6	38.6	17.5	8.8	8.8
研究生或以上 Graduate or Above	5	60.0	60.0	40.0	0.0	20.0	20.0

续前表 continued

	人数 Number	经济信息 economic information	金融股市 finance & stock	电视直销 direct sale on TV	消费指南 consumption guide	体育新闻 sports news	赛事报道 games report
样本 Sample	579	5.2	7.1	0.9	3.5	26.9	12.6
小学及以下 Primary School or Below	15	0.0	0.0	0.0	0.0	13.3	20.0
初中 Middle School	121	3.3	2.5	0.0	5.0	26.4	10.7
高中/中专/技校 High School/Technical Secondary School	274	6.2	8.4	0.7	4.0	21.9	12.8
大学专科 2-3 Year College	107	4.7	11.2	0.9	1.9	36.4	13.1
大学本科 4-5 Year College	57	7.0	5.3	3.5	1.8	36.8	12.3
研究生或以上 Graduate or Above	5	0.0	0.0	0.0	0.0	40.0	20.0

续前表 continued

	人数 Number	体育专栏节目 sports feature	国内电视剧 TV play(inland)	港台电视剧 TV play (HK.Taiwan)	国外电视剧 overseas TV play	国内影片 inland film	国外影片 overseas film
样本 Sample	**579**	**9.7**	**25.9**	**22.8**	**6.7**	**15.9**	**13.3**
小学及以下 Primary School or Below	15	6.7	33.3	20.0	20.0	13.3	6.7
初中 Middle School	121	10.7	29.8	18.2	6.6	19.8	8.3
高中/中专/技校 High School/Technical Secondary School	274	10.2	29.2	26.6	6.6	16.8	12.0
大学专科 2-3 Year College	107	10.3	19.6	19.6	5.6	10.3	18.7
大学本科 4-5 Year College	57	5.3	14.0	21.1	7.0	14.0	22.8
研究生或以上 Graduate or Above	5	0.0	0.0	20.0	0.0	20.0	0.0

续前表 continued

	人数 Number	港台影片 film from HK.Taiwan	天气预报 weather forecast	广告 advertising	MTV/音乐节目 MTV/music	舞蹈节目 dancing program	曲艺节目 folk art	戏曲/戏剧 opera
样本 Sample	**579**	**22.1**	**15.5**	**1.0**	**15.2**	**2.2**	**10.0**	**6.6**
小学及以下 Primary School or Below	15	13.3	26.7	0.0	0.0	0.0	33.3	46.7
初中 Middle School	121	21.5	20.7	2.5	11.6	0.8	12.4	11.6
高中/中专/技校 High School/Technical Secondary School	274	26.6	14.6	0.7	15.3	3.6	9.1	3.3
大学专科 2-3 Year College	107	18.7	12.1	0.9	19.6	1.9	10.3	4.7
大学本科 4-5 Year College	57	12.3	12.3	0.0	19.3	0.0	3.5	5.3
研究生或以上 Graduate or Above	5	0.0	20.0	0.0	0.0	0.0	0.0	0.0

续前表 continued

	人数 Number	综艺节目 comprehensive arts	军事类节目 military program	专题类节目 special report	科教类节目 scientific education	少儿节目 children's program	女性节目 women's program	其他 others
样本 Sample	**579**	**27.6**	**7.4**	**1.2**	**1.2**	**2.6**	**4.3**	**0.9**
小学及以下 Primary School or Below	15	13.3	0.0	0.0	0.0	0.0	0.0	0.0
初中 Middle School	121	28.9	8.3	1.7	1.7	1.7	4.1	0.0
高中/中专/技校 High School/Technical Secondary School	274	23.0	6.9	1.1	1.1	3.3	5.5	1.1
大学专科 2-3 Year College	107	32.7	8.4	0.0	1.9	2.8	2.8	1.9
大学本科 4-5 Year College	57	38.6	8.8	1.8	0.0	1.8	3.5	0.0
研究生或以上 Graduate or Above	5	60.0	0.0	20.0	0.0	0.0	0.0	0.0

1-9 经常收看电视时段/ Weekday Times Slots of Television Exposure

注：本题为多选题，合计百分比超过 100%（Multiple answers）

时间段 times slots	周一--周四(%) (Monday--Thursday)	周五(%) (Friday)	周六(%) (Saturday)	周日(%) (Sunday)
样本量 Sample	n=578	n=580	n=580	n=578
0:00-0:30	2.4	2.9	3.3	3.3
0:30-1:00	2.1	2.2	2.8	2.2
1:00-1:30	1.7	1.7	1.9	1.4
1:30-2:00	1.6	1.6	1.7	1.2
2:00-2:30	0.3	0.5	0.7	0.7
2:30-3:00	0.2	0.2	0.2	0.3
3:00-3:30	0.0	0.0	0.0	0.2
3:30-4:00	0.0	0.0	0.0	0.2
4:00-4:30	0.0	0.0	0.2	0.2
4:30-5:00	0.0	0.2	0.2	0.2
5:00-5:30	0.0	0.3	0.2	0.2
5:30-6:00	0.2	0.3	0.3	0.3
6:00-6:30	0.5	0.5	0.7	0.7
6:30-7:00	1.2	1.7	1.9	2.1
7:00-7:30	5.5	5.2	5.7	5.5
7:30-8:00	4.7	5.2	5.7	5.4
8:00-8:30	3.8	4.8	6.0	6.1
8:30-9:00	4.3	5.5	7.4	7.1
9:00-9:30	4.3	6.6	11.7	11.9
9:30-10:00	4.3	6.4	13.8	13.0
10:00-10:30	6.4	7.9	16.9	16.6
10:30-11:00	5.4	8.1	16.0	16.3
11:00-11:30	4.3	7.4	14.5	15.1
11:30-12:00	5.5	7.6	15.3	16.1
12:00-12:30	16.1	16.7	22.1	22.8
12:30-13:00	9.5	10.2	14.8	15.9
13:00-13:30	6.4	6.7	12.6	14.0
13:30-14:00	4.5	5.0	10.0	11.2
14:00-14:30	3.6	4.3	9.1	10.0
14:30-15:00	3.6	4.1	9.1	9.9
15:00-15:30	3.8	4.0	8.8	9.9
15:30-16:00	3.3	3.6	8.6	9.7
16:00-16:30	3.3	3.8	8.8	8.8
16:30-17:00	3.6	4.0	8.3	8.8
17:00-17:30	4.7	5.7	9.8	10.0
17:30-18:00	5.0	6.4	10.9	11.2
18:00-18:30	16.1	18.4	20.5	20.8
18:30-19:00	27.0	28.3	30.5	30.1
19:00-19:30	65.1	65.5	66.2	64.7
19:30-20:00	63.3	66.4	69.1	66.1
20:00-20:30	67.1	70.9	74.7	70.8
20:30-21:00	67.1	71.9	77.1	72.3
21:00-21:30	59.2	68.1	74.1	69.4
21:30-22:00	49.5	59.8	64.7	59.9
22:00-22:30	34.1	43.6	49.1	44.3
22:30-23:00	22.1	30.7	35.7	31.8
23:00-23:30	12.3	16.4	18.4	16.1
23:30-24:00	9.7	12.4	13.6	11.2

1-10 不同消费者层平时是否接触电视媒介/ TV Exposure by Market Segments

1-10-1 时尚流行指标/ Fads Popular Index

	人数 Number	从来不看 never	收看 yes
样本 Sample	599	3.2	96.8
平实生活指向 simple living orientation	341	3.2	96.8
时尚流行指向 fashion orientation	258	3.1	96.9

1-10-2 广告态度指标/ Advertising Attitude Index

	人数 Number	从来不看 never	收看 yes
样本 Sample	597	3.0	97.0
广告淡漠指向 indifferent orientation	184	4.9	95.1
中间层 medium	334	2.4	97.6
信赖广告指向 loyal orientation	79	1.3	98.7

1-11 不同消费者层收看电视频道的偏好/ Channel Preference by Market Segments

1-11-1 时尚流行指标/ Fads Popular Index

注：本题为多选题，合计百分比超过 100%（Multiple answers）

	人数 Number	中央 1 台 CCTV-1	西安 2 台 Xi'an TV 2	中央 6 台 CCTV-6	西安有线影视台 Xi'an Cable Movies Channel	陕西有线影视台 Shaanxi Cable Movies Channel
样本 Sample	580	65.3	19.7	19.1	15.9	15.9
平实生活指向 simple living orientation	330	69.1	17.3	19.1	14.2	17.0
时尚流行指向 fashion orientation	250	60.4	22.8	19.2	18.0	14.4

续前表 continued

	人数 Number	中央 5 台 CCTV-5	凤凰卫视 Phoenix Channel	西安有线综合台 Xi'an Cable General Channel	中央 8 台 CCTV-8	陕西 1 台 Shaanxi TV 1	西安 1 台 Xi'an TV 1
样本 Sample	580	15.3	14.3	13.3	13.1	11.4	11.4
平实生活指向 simple living orientation	330	16.1	11.8	12.7	15.5	11.5	13.6
时尚流行指向 fashion orientation	250	14.4	17.6	14.0	10.0	11.2	8.4

续前表 continued

	人数 Number	中央 2 台 CCTV-2	西安有线生活台 Xi'an Cable Life Channel	山东卫视 Shandong Satellite	陕西 2 台 Shaanxi TV 2	西安有线体育台 Xi'an Cable Sports Channel	湖南卫视 Hunan Satellite
样本 Sample	580	10.2	6.4	6.2	5.2	4.5	4.5
平实生活指向 simple living orientation	330	10.6	6.4	6.4	6.1	3.3	2.7
时尚流行指向 fashion orientation	250	9.6	6.4	6.0	4.0	6.0	6.8

续前表 continued

	人数 Number	中央 3 台 CCTV-3	陕西有线娱乐台 Shaanxi Cable Entertainment Channel	河南卫视 Henan Satellite	陕西有线体育台 Shaanxi Cable Sports Channel	陕西卫视 Shaanxi Satellite	陕西 3 台 Shaanxi TV 3
样本 Sample	580	3.6	3.3	3.1	2.9	2.8	2.8
平实生活指向 simple living orientation	330	1.8	2.1	2.1	0.9	3.6	3.3
时尚流行指向 fashion orientation	250	6.0	4.8	4.4	5.6	1.6	2.0

1-11-2 广告态度指标/ Advertising Attitude Index

注：本题为多选题，合计百分比超过 100%（Multiple answers）

	人数 Number	中央 1 台 CCTV-1	西安 2 台 Xi'an TV 2	中央 6 台 CCTV-6	西安有线影视台 Xi'an Cable Movies Channel	陕西有线影视台 Shaanxi Cable Movies Channel
样本 Sample	579	65.1	19.5	19.3	16.1	15.9
广告淡漠指向 indifferent orientation	175	68.0	20.0	17.7	18.3	16.6
中间层 medium	326	66.3	19.6	18.7	15.3	16.6
信赖广告指向 loyal orientation	78	53.8	17.9	25.6	14.1	11.5

续前表 continued

	人数 Number	中央5台 CCTV-5	凤凰卫视 Phoenix Channel	西安有线综合台 Xi'an Cable General Channel	中央8台 CCTV-8	陕西1台 Shaanxi TV 1	西安1台 Xi'an TV 1
样本 Sample	579	15.2	14.3	13.3	13.1	11.2	11.4
广告淡漠指向 indifferent orientation	175	12.0	9.7	12.0	17.1	12.0	8.6
中间层 medium	326	15.3	16.0	14.4	11.3	10.7	13.8
信赖广告指向 loyal orientation	78	21.8	17.9	11.5	11.5	11.5	7.7

续前表 continued

	人数 Number	中央2台 CCTV-2	西安有线生活台 Xi'an Cable Life Channel	山东卫视 Shandong Satellite	陕西2台 Shaanxi TV 2	西安有线体育台 Xi'an Cable Sports Channel	湖南卫视 Hunan Satellite
样本 Sample	579	10.2	6.4	6.2	5.2	4.5	4.5
广告淡漠指向 indifferent orientation	175	12.0	6.9	7.4	6.9	5.1	2.9
中间层 medium	326	9.5	6.1	6.1	4.9	4.3	5.5
信赖广告指向 loyal orientation	78	9.0	6.4	3.8	2.6	3.8	3.8

续前表 continued

	人数 Number	中央3台 CCTV-3	陕西有线娱乐台 Shaanxi Cable Entertainment Channel	河南卫视 Henan Satellite	陕西有线体育台 Shaanxi Cable Sports Channel	陕西卫视 Shaanxi Satellite	陕西3台 Shaanxi TV 3
样本 Sample	579	3.6	3.3	3.1	2.9	2.9	2.8
广告淡漠指向 indifferent orientation	175	4.6	3.4	2.3	1.1	5.1	3.4
中间层 medium	326	2.5	3.1	3.7	3.7	2.5	2.8
信赖广告指向 loyal orientation	78	6.4	3.8	2.6	3.8	0.0	1.3

1-12 不同消费者层收看电视节目的偏好/ Program Preference by Market Segments

1-12-1 时尚流行指标/ Fads Popular Index

注：本题为多选题，合计百分比超过 100%（Multiple answers）

	人数 Number	国内新闻 national news	国际新闻 international news	新闻评论 news comments	本地新闻 local news	谈话节目 Talk Show	经济新闻 economic news
样本 Sample	580	63.4	47.8	21.6	15.5	7.2	6.6
平实生活指向 simple living orientation	330	70.9	48.8	20.9	18.2	6.7	6.7
时尚流行指向 fashion orientation	250	53.6	46.4	22.4	12.0	8.0	6.4

续前表 continued

	人数 Number	经济信息 economic information	金融股市 finance & stock	电视直销 direct sale on TV	消费指南 consumption guide	体育新闻 sports news	赛事报道 games report
样本 Sample	580	5.5	7.2	0.9	3.4	26.9	12.6
平实生活指向 simple living orientation	330	5.8	6.4	0.3	3.0	27.6	13.3
时尚流行指向 fashion orientation	250	5.2	8.4	1.6	4.0	26.0	11.6

续前表 continued

	人数 Number	体育专栏节目 sports feature	国内电视剧 TV play(inland)	港台电视剧 TV play (HK.Taiwan)	国外电视剧 overseas TV play	国内影片 inland film	国外影片 overseas film
样本 Sample	582	9.6	25.8	22.7	6.7	15.8	13.6
平实生活指向 simple living orientation	330	8.5	27.3	19.4	6.7	17.9	11.5
时尚流行指向 fashion orientation	250	11.2	23.6	26.8	6.8	12.8	16.4

续前表 continued

	人数 Number	港台影片 film from HK.Taiwan	天气预报 weather forecast	广告 advertising	MTV/音乐节目 MTV/music	舞蹈节目 dancing program	曲艺节目 folk art	戏曲/戏剧 opera
样本 Sample	582	22.2	15.5	1.0	15.1	2.2	10.0	6.5
平实生活指向 simple living orientation	330	19.4	18.2	0.9	7.3	1.2	12.1	9.1
时尚流行指向 fashion orientation	250	25.6	12.0	1.2	25.6	3.6	7.2	3.2

续前表 continued

	人数 Number	综艺节目 comprehensive arts	军事类节目 military program	专题类节目 special report	科教类节目 scientific education	少儿节目 children's program	女性节目 women's program	其他 others
样本 Sample	582	27.5	7.6	1.2	1.2	2.6	4.3	0.9
平实生活指向 simple living orientation	330	22.7	7.3	1.2	1.5	2.1	3.9	0.9
时尚流行指向 fashion orientation	250	34.0	8.0	1.2	0.8	3.2	4.8	0.8

● 沈阳 / Shenyang

1-1 样本、男性各年龄层、女性各年龄层平时是否接触电视媒介/ Exposure to Television by the Whole Sample, Age and Gender Groups

	人数 Number	从来不看 never	收看 yes
样本 Sample	601	2.0	98.0
男性 Male	299	2.7	97.3
16~24 岁 Age	64	1.6	98.4
25~34 岁 Age	89	2.2	97.8
35~44 岁 Age	76	2.6	97.4
45~54 岁 Age	46	6.5	93.5
55~60 岁 Age	24	0.0	100.0
女性 Female	302	1.3	98.7
16~24 岁 Age	64	3.1	96.9
25~34 岁 Age	90	0.0	100.0
35~44 岁 Age	76	1.3	98.7
45~54 岁 Age	48	2.1	97.9
55~60 岁 Age	24	0.0	100.0

1-2 一周内不同时间收看电视的时间长短/ The Average Time Spending on Watching TV Per Day

1-2-1 一周内不同时间收看电视的时间长短(周一到周四)/ The Average Time Spending on Watching TV Per Day (Monday-Thursday)

	人数 Number	百分比 Percent
大约半小时或以下 about 1/2 hour or below	28	4.8
大约 1 小时 about 1 hour	88	14.9
大约 2 小时 about 2 hours	153	26.0
大约 3 小时 about 3 hours	128	21.7
大约 4 小时 about 4 hours	84	14.3
大约 5 小时 about 5 hours	49	8.3
大约 6 小时 about 6 hours	18	3.1
大约 7 小时 about 7 hours	9	1.5
大约 8 小时 about 8 hours	10	1.7
大约 9 小时 about 9 hours	7	1.2
大约 10 小时或以上 about 10 hours or over	8	1.4
记不清/不知道 can't remember	0	0.0
没有收看 didn't watch	7	1.2

n=589

1-2-2 一周内不同时间收看电视的时间长短(周五)/ The Average Time Spending on Watching TV Per Day (Friday)

	人数 Number	百分比 Percent
大约半小时或以下 about 1/2 hour or below	23	3.9
大约 1 小时 about 1 hour	69	11.7
大约 2 小时 about 2 hours	144	24.4
大约 3 小时 about 3 hours	129	21.9
大约 4 小时 about 4 hours	73	12.4
大约 5 小时 about 5 hours	61	10.4
大约 6 小时 about 6 hours	31	5.3
大约 7 小时 about 7 hours	13	2.2
大约 8 小时 about 8 hours	11	1.9
大约 9 小时 about 9 hours	6	1.0
大约 10 小时或以上 about 10 hours or over	14	2.4
记不清/不知道 can't remember	1	0.2
没有收看 didn't watch	14	2.4

n=589

1-2-3 一周内不同时间收看电视的时间长短(周六)/ The Average Time Spending on Watching TV Per Day (Saturday)

	人数 Number	百分比 Percent
大约半小时或以下 about 1/2 hour or below	18	3.1
大约 1 小时 about 1 hour	52	8.8
大约 2 小时 about 2 hours	112	19.0
大约 3 小时 about 3 hours	99	16.8
大约 4 小时 about 4 hours	85	14.4
大约 5 小时 about 5 hours	86	14.6
大约 6 小时 about 6 hours	41	7.0
大约 7 小时 about 7 hours	27	4.6
大约 8 小时 about 8 hours	18	3.1
大约 9 小时 about 9 hours	11	1.9
大约 10 小时或以上 about 10 hours or over	29	4.9
记不清/不知道 can't remember	1	0.2
没有收看 didn't watch	10	1.7

n=589

1-2-4 一周内不同时间收看电视的时间长短(周日)/ The Average Time Spending on Watching TV Per Day (Sunday)

	人数 Number	百分比 Percent
大约半小时或以下 about 1/2 hour or below	19	3.2
大约 1 小时 about 1 hour	56	9.5
大约 2 小时 about 2 hours	108	18.3
大约 3 小时 about 3 hours	93	15.8
大约 4 小时 about 4 hours	85	14.4
大约 5 小时 about 5 hours	85	14.4
大约 6 小时 about 6 hours	39	6.6
大约 7 小时 about 7 hours	30	5.1
大约 8 小时 about 8 hours	21	3.6
大约 9 小时 about 9 hours	10	1.7
大约 10 小时或以上 about 10 hours or over	30	5.1
记不清/不知道 can't remember	2	0.3
没有收看 didn't watch	11	1.9

n=589

1-3 经常收看的电视台/ Ranking of the Most Favorite TV Channels

注：本题为多选题，合计百分比超过 100%（Multiple answers）

排名 Brand Ranking	频道 Channels	人次 Person-time	百分比 Percent
1	中央 1 台 CCTV-1	329	56.0
2	辽宁卫视 Liaoning Satellite	286	48.6
3	沈阳一台 Shenyang TV 1	268	45.6
4	中央 6 台 CCTV-6	116	19.7
5	辽宁北方台 Liaoning North Channel	112	19.0
6	中央 5 台 CCTV-5	92	15.6
7	辽宁有线一台 Liaoning Cable 1	84	14.3
8	沈阳三台 Shenyang TV 3	69	11.7
9	沈阳二台 Shenyang TV 2	64	10.9
10	辽宁有线二台 Liaoning Cable 1	49	8.3
11	中央 8 台 CCTV-8	38	6.5
12	中央 2 台 CCTV-2	37	6.3
13	辽宁教育台 Liaoning Education TV	36	6.1
14	凤凰卫视 Phoenix Channel	15	2.6
15	沈阳五台 Shenyang TV 5	14	2.4
16	沈阳四台 Shenyang TV 4	12	2.0
17	安徽卫视 Anhui Satellite	11	1.9
18	中央 4 台 CCTV-4	9	1.5
19	四川卫视 Sichuan Satellite	7	1.2
19	湖南卫视 Hunan Satellite	7	1.2
19	山东卫视 Shandong Satellite	7	1.2
20	浙江卫视 Zhejiang Satellite	6	1.0
20	福建东南卫视 Fujian Satellite Southeast Channel	6	1.0
21	中央 7 台 CCTV-7	5	0.9

n=588

1-4 样本、男性各年龄层、女性各年龄层最喜欢收看的频道/ The Most Favorite TV Channels by the Whole Sample, Age and Gender Groups

注：本题为多选题，合计百分比超过 100%（Multiple answers）

	人数 Number	中央 1 台 CCTV-1	辽宁卫视 Liaoning Satellite	沈阳一台 Shenyang TV 1	中央 6 台 CCTV-6	辽宁北方台 Liaoning North Channel	中央 5 台 CCTV-5
样本 Sample	**588**	**56.0**	**48.6**	**45.6**	**19.7**	**19.0**	**15.6**
男性 Male	**290**	**56.9**	**47.6**	**42.8**	**21.4**	**17.2**	**26.2**
16~24 岁 Age	63	19.0	44.4	38.1	25.4	28.6	33.3
25~34 岁 Age	86	53.5	38.4	29.1	25.6	10.5	31.4
35~44 岁 Age	74	73.0	52.7	58.1	18.9	14.9	18.9
45~54 岁 Age	43	69.8	58.1	44.2	14.0	20.9	25.6
55~60 岁 Age	24	95.8	54.2	54.2	16.7	12.5	12.5
女性 Female	**298**	**55.0**	**49.7**	**48.3**	**18.1**	**20.8**	**5.4**
16~24 岁 Age	62	32.3	38.7	43.5	19.4	17.7	6.5
25~34 岁 Age	90	54.4	53.3	43.3	16.7	24.4	6.7
35~44 岁 Age	75	62.7	57.3	50.7	16.0	22.7	2.7
45~54 岁 Age	47	70.2	48.9	55.3	21.3	8.5	6.4
55~60 岁 Age	24	62.5	41.7	58.3	20.8	33.3	4.2

续前表 continued

	人数 Number	辽宁有线一台 Liaoning Cable 1	沈阳三台 Shenyang TV 3	沈阳二台 Shenyang TV 2	辽宁有线二台 Liaoning Cable 2	中央 8 台 CCTV-8	中央 2 台 CCTV-2
样本 Sample	**588**	**14.3**	**11.7**	**10.9**	**8.3**	**6.5**	**6.3**
男性 Male	**290**	**14.8**	**14.5**	**7.2**	**9.7**	**6.2**	**4.8**
16~24 岁 Age	63	20.6	17.5	11.1	17.5	4.8	0.0
25~34 岁 Age	86	23.3	23.3	7.0	11.6	8.1	7.0
35~44 岁 Age	74	10.8	8.1	4.1	5.4	5.4	6.8
45~54 岁 Age	43	2.3	9.3	4.7	4.7	4.7	4.7
55~60 岁 Age	24	4.2	4.2	12.5	4.2	8.3	4.2
女性 Female	**298**	**13.8**	**9.1**	**14.4**	**7.0**	**6.7**	**7.7**
16~24 岁 Age	62	24.2	16.1	22.6	8.1	11.3	8.1
25~34 岁 Age	90	14.4	10.0	12.2	8.9	5.6	3.3
35~44 岁 Age	75	10.7	5.3	17.3	4.0	2.7	9.3
45~54 岁 Age	47	8.5	8.5	6.4	10.6	8.5	10.6
55~60 岁 Age	24	4.2	0.0	8.3	0.0	8.3	12.5

续前表 continued

	人数 Number	辽宁教育台 Liaoning Education TV	凤凰卫视 Phoenix Channel	沈阳五台 Shenyang TV 5	沈阳四台 Shenyang TV 4	安徽卫视 Anhui Satellite	中央 4 台 CCTV-4
样本 Sample	588	6.1	2.6	2.4	2.0	1.9	1.5
男性 Male	290	3.4	2.4	3.8	2.1	0.3	0.7
16~24 岁 Age	63	6.3	3.2	4.8	1.6	1.6	0.0
25~34 岁 Age	86	1.2	4.7	5.8	1.2	0.0	1.2
35~44 岁 Age	74	4.1	1.4	1.4	1.4	0.0	1.4
45~54 岁 Age	43	2.3	0.0	4.7	4.7	0.0	0.0
55~60 岁 Age	24	4.2	0.0	0.0	4.2	0.0	0.0
女性 Female	298	8.7	2.7	1.0	2.0	3.4	2.3
16~24 岁 Age	62	8.1	6.5	3.2	1.6	6.5	0.0
25~34 岁 Age	90	10.0	0.0	0.0	3.3	4.4	3.3
35~44 岁 Age	75	9.3	2.7	1.3	1.3	0.0	2.7
45~54 岁 Age	47	10.6	2.1	0.0	2.1	2.1	2.1
55~60 岁 Age	24	0.0	4.2	0.0	0.0	4.2	4.2

续前表 continued

	人数 Number	四川卫视 Sichuan Satellite	湖南卫视 Hunan Satellite	山东卫视 Shandong Satellite	浙江卫视 Zhejiang Satellite	福建东南卫视 Fujian Satellite Southeast Channel	中央 7 台 CCTV-7
样本 Sample	588	1.2	1.2	1.2	1.0	1.0	0.9
男性 Male	290	1.0	1.4	1.4	0.7	1.7	1.0
16~24 岁 Age	63	1.6	0.0	4.8	0.0	4.8	1.6
25~34 岁 Age	86	1.2	3.5	1.2	1.2	1.2	1.2
35~44 岁 Age	74	0.0	0.0	0.0	1.4	0.0	0.0
45~54 岁 Age	43	2.3	2.3	0.0	0.0	2.3	2.3
55~60 岁 Age	24	0.0	0.0	0.0	0.0	0.0	0.0
女性 Female	298	1.3	1.0	1.0	1.3	0.3	0.7
16~24 岁 Age	62	3.2	1.6	1.6	1.6	0.0	0.0
25~34 岁 Age	90	0.0	1.1	1.1	0.0	1.1	1.1
35~44 岁 Age	75	2.7	0.0	1.3	1.3	0.0	0.0
45~54 岁 Age	47	0.0	2.1	0.0	4.3	0.0	0.0
55~60 岁 Age	24	0.0	0.0	0.0	0.0	0.0	4.2

1-5 经常收看的电视频道/ The Most Favorite TV Channels

1-5-1 经常收看的电视频道(周一--周四)/ Ranking of the Most Favorite TV Channels(Monday--Thursday)

注：本题为多选题，合计百分比超过 100%（Multiple answers）

排名 Brand Ranking	频道 Channels	人次 Person-time	百分比 Percent
1	中央 1 台 CCTV-1	389	66.6
2	沈阳一台 Shenyang TV 1	332	56.8
3	辽宁卫视 Liaoning Satellite	322	55.1
4	辽宁北方台 Liaoning North Channel	169	28.9
5	沈阳二台 Shenyang TV 2	134	22.9
6	中央 6 台 CCTV-6	131	22.4
7	辽宁有线一台 Liaoning Cable 1	124	21.2
8	中央 5 台 CCTV-5	108	18.5
9	沈阳三台 Shenyang TV 3	97	16.6
10	辽宁有线二台 Liaoning Cable 1	86	14.7
11	辽宁教育台 Liaoning Education TV	82	14.0
12	中央 2 台 CCTV-2	76	13.0
13	中央 8 台 CCTV-8	67	11.5

n=584

1-5-2 经常收看的电视频道(周五)/ Ranking of the Most Favorite TV Channels(Friday)

注：本题为多选题，合计百分比超过 100%（Multiple answers）

排名 Brand Ranking	频道 Channels	人次 Person-time	百分比 Percent
1	中央 1 台 CCTV-1	367	63.4
2	沈阳一台 Shenyang TV 1	327	56.5
3	辽宁卫视 Liaoning Satellite	313	54.1
4	辽宁北方台 Liaoning North Channel	173	29.9
5	沈阳二台 Shenyang TV 2	132	22.8
6	中央 6 台 CCTV-6	128	22.1
7	辽宁有线一台 Liaoning Cable 1	121	20.9
8	中央 5 台 CCTV-5	111	19.2
9	沈阳三台 Shenyang TV 3	96	16.6
10	辽宁有线二台 Liaoning Cable 1	85	14.7
10	辽宁教育台 Liaoning Education TV	85	14.7
11	中央 2 台 CCTV-2	81	14.0
12	中央 8 台 CCTV-8	62	10.7

n=579

1-5-3 经常收看的电视频道(周六)/ Ranking of the Most Favorite TV Channels(Saturday)

注：本题为多选题，合计百分比超过 100%（Multiple answers）

排名 Brand Ranking	频道 Channels	人次 Person-time	百分比 Percent
1	中央 1 台 CCTV-1	367	63.1
2	沈阳一台 Shenyang TV 1	339	58.2
3	辽宁卫视 Liaoning Satellite	328	56.4
4	辽宁北方台 Liaoning North Channel	178	30.6
5	中央 6 台 CCTV-6	134	23.0
6	沈阳二台 Shenyang TV 2	131	22.5
7	辽宁有线一台 Liaoning Cable 1	128	22.0
8	中央 5 台 CCTV-5	113	19.4
9	沈阳三台 Shenyang TV 3	102	17.5
10	辽宁有线二台 Liaoning Cable 1	87	14.9
11	辽宁教育台 Liaoning Education TV	82	14.1
12	中央 2 台 CCTV-2	81	13.9

n=582

1-5-4 经常收看的电视频道(周日)/ Ranking of the Most Favorite TV Channels(Sunday)

注：本题为多选题，合计百分比超过 100%（Multiple answers）

排名 Brand Ranking	频道 Channels	人次 Person-time	百分比 Percent
1	中央 1 台 CCTV-1	375	64.5
2	沈阳一台 Shenyang TV 1	331	57.0
3	辽宁卫视 Liaoning Satellite	330	56.8
4	辽宁北方台 Liaoning North Channel	185	31.8
5	中央 6 台 CCTV-6	134	23.1
6	沈阳二台 Shenyang TV 2	133	22.9
7	辽宁有线一台 Liaoning Cable 1	124	21.3
8	中央 5 台 CCTV-5	113	19.4
9	沈阳三台 Shenyang TV 3	97	16.7
10	辽宁有线二台 Liaoning Cable 1	84	14.5
10	辽宁教育台 Liaoning Education TV	84	14.5
11	中央 2 台 CCTV-2	81	13.9
12	中央 8 台 CCTV-8	65	11.2

n=581

1-6 经常收看的电视节目/ Ranking of the Most Favorite TV Programs

注：本题为多选题，合计百分比超过 100%（Multiple answers）

排名 Ranking	电视节目 TV Programs	人次 Person-time	百分比 Percent
1	国内新闻 national news	370	63.1
2	国际新闻 international news	299	51.0
3	港台电视剧 TV play(HK.Taiwan)	195	33.3
4	体育新闻 sports news	188	32.1
5	国内电视剧 TV play(inland)	156	26.6
6	综艺节目 comprehensive arts	150	25.6
7	新闻评论 news comments	134	22.9
8	港台影片 film from HK.Taiwan	130	22.2
9	天气预报 weather forecast	123	21.0
10	本地新闻 local news	91	15.5
11	MTV/音乐节目 MTV/music	84	14.3
12	体育专栏节目 sports feature	76	13.0
13	赛事报道 games report	72	12.3
14	国外影片 overseas film	65	11.1
15	国内影片 inland film	63	10.8
16	国外电视剧 overseas TV play	44	7.5
17	军事类节目 military program	38	6.5
18	曲艺节目 folk art	37	6.3
19	经济新闻 economic news	32	5.5
20	金融股市 finance & stock	30	5.1

n=586

1-7 样本、男性各年龄层、女性各年龄层经常收看的电视节目/ The Most Favorite TV Programs by the Whole Sample, Age and Gender Groups

注：本题为多选题，合计百分比超过 100%（Multiple answers）

	人数 Number	国内新闻 national news	国际新闻 international news	新闻评论 news comments	本地新闻 local news	谈话节目 Talk Show	经济新闻 economic news
样本 Sample	586	63.1	33.3	51.0	22.2	15.5	5.5
男性 Male	290	65.2	20.0	57.6	22.8	17.2	5.9
16~24 岁 Age	62	25.8	35.5	30.6	46.8	9.7	0.0
25~34 岁 Age	87	62.1	19.5	55.2	31.0	10.3	5.7
35~44 岁 Age	74	81.1	18.9	63.5	9.5	20.3	5.4
45~54 岁 Age	43	83.7	11.6	74.4	4.7	23.3	11.6
55~60 岁 Age	24	95.8	0.0	87.5	4.2	41.7	12.5
女性 Female	296	61.1	46.3	44.6	21.6	13.9	5.1
16~24 岁 Age	61	26.2	63.9	27.9	49.2	3.3	1.6
25~34 岁 Age	90	60.0	53.3	36.7	17.8	12.2	5.6
35~44 岁 Age	75	76.0	41.3	54.7	21.3	18.7	5.3
45~54 岁 Age	47	72.3	27.7	57.4	4.3	19.1	6.4
55~60 岁 Age	23	87.0	26.1	60.9	0.0	21.7	8.7

续前表 continued

	人数 Number	经济信息 economic information	金融股市 finance & stock	电视直销 direct sale on TV	消费指南 consumption guide	体育新闻 sports news	赛事报道 games report
样本 Sample	586	3.8	5.1	2.0	3.6	32.1	12.3
男性 Male	290	5.2	6.6	0.7	1.7	53.4	22.4
16~24 岁 Age	62	1.6	3.2	1.6	1.6	64.5	41.9
25~34 岁 Age	87	5.7	8.0	1.1	0.0	48.3	28.7
35~44 岁 Age	74	5.4	6.8	0.0	1.4	54.1	10.8
45~54 岁 Age	43	2.3	9.3	0.0	2.3	53.5	11.6
55~60 岁 Age	24	16.7	4.2	0.0	8.3	41.7	4.2
女性 Female	296	2.4	3.7	3.4	5.4	11.1	2.4
16~24 岁 Age	61	1.6	0.0	4.9	6.6	11.5	3.3
25~34 岁 Age	90	0.0	3.3	0.0	4.4	14.4	2.2
35~44 岁 Age	75	2.7	6.7	6.7	8.0	10.7	2.7
45~54 岁 Age	47	6.4	6.4	4.3	4.3	4.3	2.1
55~60 岁 Age	23	4.3	0.0	0.0	0.0	13.0	0.0

续前表 continued

	人数 Number	体育专栏节目 sports feature	国内电视剧 TV play(inland)	港台电视剧 TV play (HK.Taiwan)	国外电视剧 overseas TV play	国内影片 inland film	国外影片 overseas film
样本 Sample	**586**	**13.0**	**26.6**	**33.3**	**7.5**	**10.8**	**11.1**
男性 Male	**290**	**22.1**	**15.5**	**20.0**	**5.5**	**11.7**	**11.7**
16~24 岁 Age	62	35.5	6.5	35.5	3.2	11.3	14.5
25~34 岁 Age	87	25.3	12.6	19.5	6.9	9.2	16.1
35~44 岁 Age	74	17.6	18.9	18.9	5.4	12.2	9.5
45~54 岁 Age	43	9.3	14.0	11.6	7.0	18.6	9.3
55~60 岁 Age	24	12.5	41.7	0.0	4.2	8.3	0.0
女性 Female	**296**	**4.1**	**37.5**	**46.3**	**9.5**	**9.8**	**10.5**
16~24 岁 Age	61	4.9	36.1	63.9	6.6	11.5	13.1
25~34 岁 Age	90	4.4	38.9	53.3	13.3	8.9	12.2
35~44 岁 Age	75	4.0	29.3	41.3	9.3	8.0	12.0
45~54 岁 Age	47	2.1	36.2	27.7	10.6	10.6	6.4
55~60 岁 Age	23	4.3	65.2	26.1	0.0	13.0	0.0

续前表 continued

	人数 Number	港台影片 film from HK.Taiwan	天气预报 weather forecast	广告 advertising	MTV/音乐节目 MTV/music	舞蹈节目 dancing program	曲艺节目 folk art	戏曲/戏剧 opera
样本 Sample	**586**	**22.2**	**21.0**	**1.2**	**14.3**	**1.5**	**6.3**	**3.6**
男性 Male	**290**	**22.8**	**15.5**	**1.0**	**11.7**	**0.7**	**6.2**	**2.4**
16~24 岁 Age	62	46.8	14.5	1.6	40.3	1.6	3.2	0.0
25~34 岁 Age	87	31.0	13.8	1.1	8.0	1.1	11.5	1.1
35~44 岁 Age	74	9.5	18.9	1.4	1.4	0.0	2.7	1.4
45~54 岁 Age	43	4.7	16.3	0.0	0.0	0.0	4.7	2.3
55~60 岁 Age	24	4.2	12.5	0.0	4.2	0.0	8.3	16.7
女性 Female	**296**	**21.6**	**26.4**	**1.4**	**16.9**	**2.4**	**6.4**	**4.7**
16~24 岁 Age	61	49.2	13.1	1.6	50.8	3.3	3.3	0.0
25~34 岁 Age	90	17.8	37.8	1.1	13.3	1.1	6.7	0.0
35~44 岁 Age	75	21.3	22.7	1.3	6.7	2.7	5.3	1.3
45~54 岁 Age	47	4.3	19.1	0.0	2.1	4.3	12.8	17.0
55~60 岁 Age	23	0.0	43.5	4.3	4.3	0.0	4.3	21.7

续前表 continued

	人数 Number	综艺节目 comprehensive arts	军事类节目 military program	专题类节目 special report	科教类节目 scientific education	少儿节目 children's program	女性节目 women's program	其他 others
样本 Sample	**586**	**25.6**	**6.5**	**0.7**	**2.2**	**4.3**	**2.9**	**0.3**
男性 Male	**290**	**17.6**	**12.8**	**0.7**	**2.8**	**2.4**	**0.3**	**0.3**
16~24 岁 Age	62	25.8	11.3	0.0	1.6	3.2	0.0	0.0
25~34 岁 Age	87	20.7	17.2	2.3	3.4	3.4	0.0	1.1
35~44 岁 Age	74	10.8	13.5	0.0	4.1	2.7	0.0	0.0
45~54 岁 Age	43	16.3	9.3	0.0	2.3	0.0	2.3	0.0
55~60 岁 Age	24	8.3	4.2	0.0	0.0	0.0	0.0	0.0
女性 Female	**296**	**33.4**	**0.3**	**0.7**	**1.7**	**6.1**	**5.4**	**0.3**
16~24 岁 Age	61	47.5	0.0	0.0	3.3	6.6	4.9	0.0
25~34 岁 Age	90	32.2	1.1	1.1	1.1	10.0	5.6	1.1
35~44 岁 Age	75	29.3	0.0	1.3	1.3	4.0	6.7	0.0
45~54 岁 Age	47	31.9	0.0	0.0	2.1	2.1	6.4	0.0
55~60 岁 Age	23	17.4	0.0	0.0	0.0	4.3	0.0	0.0

1-8 不同学历的观众收看电视节目的偏好/ Program Preference by Educational Levels

注：本题为多选题，合计百分比超过 100%（Multiple answers）

	人数 Number	国内新闻 national news	国际新闻 international news	新闻评论 news comments	本地新闻 local news	谈话节目 Talk Show	经济新闻 economic news
样本 Sample	586	63.1	51.0	22.9	15.5	4.8	5.5
小学及以下 Primary School or Below	17	64.7	52.9	35.3	23.5	0.0	5.9
初中 Middle School	209	67.5	53.6	25.4	16.7	4.3	4.3
高中/中专/技校 High School/Technical Secondary School	217	54.8	46.5	17.5	13.8	3.2	4.6
大学专科 2-3 Year College	89	66.3	55.1	29.2	15.7	7.9	7.9
大学本科 4-5 Year College	51	74.5	51.0	19.6	15.7	9.8	7.8
研究生或以上 Graduate or Above	3	66.7	66.7	33.3	0.0	0.0	33.3

续前表 continued

	人数 Number	经济信息 economic information	金融股市 finance & stock	电视直销 direct sale on TV	消费指南 consumption guide	体育新闻 sports news	赛事报道 games report
样本 Sample	586	3.8	5.1	2.0	3.6	32.1	12.3
小学及以下 Primary School or Below	17	5.9	0.0	0.0	0.0	11.8	0.0
初中 Middle School	209	1.0	1.9	1.9	3.8	25.4	8.1
高中/中专/技校 High School/Technical Secondary School	217	4.1	6.9	1.8	4.1	37.8	12.9
大学专科 2-3 Year College	89	6.7	5.6	3.4	2.2	31.5	18.0
大学本科 4-5 Year College	51	7.8	11.8	2.0	2.0	43.1	19.6
研究生或以上 Graduate or Above	3	0.0	0.0	0.0	33.3	33.3	33.3

续前表 continued

	人数 Number	体育专栏节目 sports feature	国内电视剧 TV play(inland)	港台电视剧 TV play (HK.Taiwan)	国外电视剧 overseas TV play	国内影片 inland film	国外影片 overseas film
样本 Sample	586	13.0	26.6	33.3	7.5	10.8	11.1
小学及以下 Primary School or Below	17	5.9	52.9	17.6	17.6	11.8	0.0
初中 Middle School	209	10.5	36.4	35.9	7.2	13.4	8.6
高中/中专/技校 High School/Technical Secondary School	217	14.7	22.6	34.6	7.4	10.1	9.2
大学专科 2-3 Year College	89	16.9	18.0	28.1	10.1	10.1	19.1
大学本科 4-5 Year College	51	11.8	11.8	33.3	2.0	3.9	17.6
研究生或以上 Graduate or Above	3	0.0	0.0	0.0	0.0	0.0	33.3

续前表 continued

	人数 Number	港台影片 film from HK.Taiwan	天气预报 weather forecast	广告 advertising	MTV/音乐节目 MTV/music	舞蹈节目 dancing program	曲艺节目 folk art	戏曲/戏剧 opera
样本 Sample	**586**	**22.2**	**21.0**	**1.2**	**14.3**	**1.5**	**6.3**	**3.6**
小学及以下 Primary School or Below	17	5.9	29.4	5.9	0.0	0.0	11.8	17.6
初中 Middle School	209	13.4	23.9	1.0	7.2	0.0	10.5	5.7
高中/中专/技校 High School/Technical Secondary School	217	31.3	20.3	0.5	22.6	3.2	4.6	2.3
大学专科 2-3 Year College	89	27.0	14.6	3.4	14.6	1.1	2.2	1.1
大学本科 4-5 Year College	51	17.6	21.6	0.0	11.8	2.0	2.0	0.0
研究生或以上 Graduate or Above	3	0.0	0.0	0.0	33.3	0.0	0.0	0.0

续前表 continued

	人数 Number	综艺节目 comprehensive arts	军事类节目 military program	专题类节目 special report	科教类节目 scientific education	少儿节目 children's program	女性节目 women's program	其他 others
样本 Sample	**586**	**25.6**	**6.5**	**0.7**	**2.2**	**4.3**	**2.9**	**0.3**
小学及以下 Primary School or Below	17	11.8	5.9	0.0	0.0	0.0	0.0	0.0
初中 Middle School	209	21.1	5.7	0.0	1.0	4.8	3.3	0.0
高中/中专/技校 High School/Technical Secondary School	217	30.0	7.4	0.5	3.2	6.5	2.8	0.5
大学专科 2-3 Year College	89	27.0	5.6	1.1	4.5	0.0	3.4	1.1
大学本科 4-5 Year College	51	29.4	7.8	2.0	0.0	2.0	0.0	0.0
研究生或以上 Graduate or Above	3	0.0	0.0	33.3	0.0	0.0	33.3	0.0

1-9 经常收看电视时段/ Weekday Times Slots of Television Exposure

注：本题为多选题，合计百分比超过 100%（Multiple answers）

时间段 times slots	周一--周四(%) (Monday--Thursday)	周五(%) (Friday)	周六(%) (Saturday)	周日(%) (Sunday)
样本量 Sample	n=589	n=588	n=588	n=589
0:00-0:30	0.3	0.5	1.4	0.8
0:30-1:00	0.3	0.5	0.9	0.7
1:00-1:30	0.0	0.0	0.2	0.2
1:30-2:00	0.2	0.0	0.0	0.2
2:00-2:30	0.0	0.0	0.0	0.0
2:30-3:00	0.0	0.0	0.0	0.0
3:00-3:30	0.0	0.0	0.0	0.0
3:30-4:00	0.0	0.0	0.2	0.2
4:00-4:30	0.3	0.3	0.5	0.5
4:30-5:00	0.5	0.5	0.5	0.5
5:00-5:30	0.5	0.5	0.7	0.7
5:30-6:00	1.0	0.9	1.0	1.0
6:00-6:30	2.7	2.6	2.4	2.5
6:30-7:00	5.6	5.3	5.6	5.8
7:00-7:30	7.6	8.0	10.2	10.0
7:30-8:00	7.6	7.0	9.9	10.4
8:00-8:30	9.8	9.5	13.8	13.4
8:30-9:00	11.0	10.4	15.6	15.8
9:00-9:30	12.1	12.6	21.1	22.1
9:30-10:00	11.0	11.9	22.3	22.9
10:00-10:30	10.5	11.2	26.5	30.6
10:30-11:00	9.3	10.7	25.5	29.7
11:00-11:30	9.2	9.9	21.4	24.4
11:30-12:00	7.8	8.3	16.7	19.5
12:00-12:30	7.1	7.5	12.4	14.4
12:30-13:00	5.9	6.1	9.0	10.0
13:00-13:30	7.6	8.7	12.4	13.8
13:30-14:00	7.6	9.4	13.3	13.9
14:00-14:30	7.5	9.2	15.6	16.1
14:30-15:00	6.8	8.8	14.3	14.6
15:00-15:30	6.3	7.3	13.3	13.9
15:30-16:00	5.8	7.1	13.9	14.1
16:00-16:30	4.6	5.3	11.7	11.9
16:30-17:00	4.6	5.4	10.4	10.2
17:00-17:30	6.8	8.7	12.2	12.1
17:30-18:00	9.5	11.6	13.3	12.9
18:00-18:30	24.8	25.9	27.2	27.0
18:30-19:00	40.6	40.5	41.2	40.9
19:00-19:30	72.8	72.8	73.6	73.0
19:30-20:00	75.7	75.0	77.2	76.4
20:00-20:30	73.0	74.7	76.7	74.9
20:30-21:00	62.6	66.5	69.0	67.4
21:00-21:30	47.4	52.9	54.3	53.3
21:30-22:00	32.3	36.7	37.9	37.5
22:00-22:30	17.5	19.7	21.8	21.4
22:30-23:00	9.8	12.1	13.8	12.7
23:00-23:30	4.4	6.3	7.7	6.6
23:30-24:00	2.0	3.2	4.3	3.4

1-10 不同消费者层平时是否接触电视媒介/ TV Exposure by Market Segments

1-10-1 时尚流行指标/ Fads Popular Index

	人数 Number	从来不看 never	收看 yes
样本 Sample	601	2.0	98.0
平实生活指向 simple living orientation	292	1.7	98.3
时尚流行指向 fashion orientation	309	2.3	97.7

1-10-2 广告态度指标/ Advertising Attitude Index

	人数 Number	从来不看 never	收看 yes
样本 Sample	601	2.0	98.0
广告淡漠指向 indifferent orientation	172	1.7	98.3
中间层 medium	354	2.3	97.7
信赖广告指向 loyal orientation	75	1.3	98.7

1-11 不同消费者层收看电视频道的偏好/ Channel Preference by Market Segments

1-11-1 时尚流行指标/ Fads Popular Index

注：本题为多选题，合计百分比超过 100%（Multiple answers）

	人数 Number	中央 1 台 CCTV-1	辽宁卫视 Liaoning Satellite	沈阳一台 Shenyang TV 1	中央 6 台 CCTV-6	辽宁北方台 Liaoning North Channel	中央 5 台 CCTV-5
样本 Sample	588	56.0	48.6	45.6	19.7	19.0	15.6
平实生活指向 simple living orientation	286	59.4	48.3	47.2	21.0	14.7	17.1
时尚流行指向 fashion orientation	302	52.6	49.0	44.0	18.5	23.2	14.2

续前表 continued

	人数 Number	辽宁有线一台 Liaoning Cable 1	沈阳三台 Shenyang TV 3	沈阳二台 Shenyang TV 2	辽宁有线二台 Liaoning Cable 1	中央 8 台 CCTV-8	中央 2 台 CCTV-2
样本 Sample	588	14.3	11.7	10.9	8.3	6.5	6.3
平实生活指向 simple living orientation	286	12.9	12.2	10.1	8.4	5.9	5.9
时尚流行指向 fashion orientation	302	15.6	11.3	11.6	8.3	7.0	6.6

续前表 continued

	人数 Number	辽宁教育台 Liaoning Education TV	凤凰卫视 Phoenix Channel	沈阳五台 Shenyang TV 5	沈阳四台 Shenyang TV 4	安徽卫视 Anhui Satellite	中央 4 台 CCTV-4
样本 Sample	588	6.1	2.6	2.4	2.0	1.9	1.5
平实生活指向 simple living orientation	286	4.5	1.7	3.5	1.4	1.7	0.7
时尚流行指向 fashion orientation	302	7.6	3.3	1.3	2.6	2.0	2.3

续前表 continued

	人数 Number	四川卫视 Sichuan Satellite	湖南卫视 Hunan Satellite	山东卫视 Shandong Satellite	浙江卫视 Zhejiang Satellite	福建东南卫视 Fujian Satellite Southeast Channel	中央 7 台 CCTV-7
样本 Sample	588	1.2	1.2	1.2	1.0	1.0	0.9
平实生活指向 simple living orientation	286	0.7	1.4	0.7	1.7	0.3	0.7
时尚流行指向 fashion orientation	302	1.7	1.0	1.7	0.3	1.7	1.0

1-11-2 广告态度指标/ Advertising Attitude Index

注：本题为多选题，合计百分比超过 100%（Multiple answers）

	人数 Number	中央 1 台 CCTV-1	辽宁卫视 Liaoning Satellite	沈阳一台 Shenyang TV 1	中央 6 台 CCTV-6	辽宁北方台 Liaoning North Channel	中央 5 台 CCTV-5
样本 Sample	588	56.0	48.6	45.6	19.7	19.0	15.6
广告淡漠指向 indifferent orientation	169	55.6	45.0	44.4	18.9	18.9	12.4
中间层 medium	345	55.1	51.0	45.8	21.7	19.1	15.7
信赖广告指向 loyal orientation	74	60.8	45.9	47.3	12.2	18.9	23.0

续前表 continued

	人数 Number	辽宁有线一台 Liaoning Cable 1	沈阳三台 Shenyang TV 3	沈阳二台 Shenyang TV 2	辽宁有线二台 Liaoning Cable 1	中央 8 台 CCTV-8	中央 2 台 CCTV-2
样本 Sample	588	14.3	11.7	10.9	8.3	6.5	6.3
广告淡漠指向 indifferent orientation	169	11.8	13.0	16.0	9.5	6.5	5.3
中间层 medium	345	14.5	11.3	8.7	7.8	7.0	7.0
信赖广告指向 loyal orientation	74	18.9	10.8	9.5	8.1	4.1	5.4

续前表 continued

	人数 Number	辽宁教育台 Liaoning Education TV	凤凰卫视 Phoenix Channel	沈阳五台 Shenyang TV 5	沈阳四台 Shenyang TV 4	安徽卫视 Anhui Satellite	中央 4 台 CCTV-4
样本 Sample	588	6.1	2.6	2.4	2.0	1.9	1.5
广告淡漠指向 indifferent orientation	169	5.9	3.0	1.8	1.8	2.4	0.0
中间层 medium	345	6.1	2.0	2.3	2.3	1.4	2.0
信赖广告指向 loyal orientation	74	6.8	4.1	4.1	1.4	2.7	2.7

续前表 continued

	人数 Number	四川卫视 Sichuan Satellite	湖南卫视 Hunan Satellite	山东卫视 Shandong Satellite	浙江卫视 Zhejiang Satellite	福建东南卫视 Fujian Satellite Southeast Channel	中央 7 台 CCTV-7
样本 Sample	588	1.2	1.2	1.2	1.0	1.0	0.9
广告淡漠指向 indifferent orientation	169	1.2	1.8	1.8	1.2	1.2	0.6
中间层 medium	345	1.2	0.6	1.2	1.2	1.2	0.9
信赖广告指向 loyal orientation	74	1.4	2.7	0.0	0.0	0.0	1.4

1-12 不同消费者层收看电视节目的偏好/ Program Preference by Market Segments

1-12-1 时尚流行指标/ Fads Popular Index

注：本题为多选题，合计百分比超过 100%（Multiple answers）

	人数 Number	国内新闻 national news	国际新闻 international news	新闻评论 news comments	本地新闻 local news	谈话节目 Talk Show	经济新闻 economic news
样本 Sample	586	63.1	51.0	22.9	15.5	4.8	5.5
平实生活指向 simple living orientation	285	69.5	57.9	25.6	16.5	3.5	5.3
时尚流行指向 fashion orientation	301	57.1	44.5	20.3	14.6	6.0	5.6

续前表 continued

	人数 Number	经济信息 economic information	金融股市 finance & stock	电视直销 direct sale on TV	消费指南 consumption guide	体育新闻 sports news	赛事报道 games report
样本 Sample	586	3.8	5.1	2.0	3.6	32.1	12.3
平实生活指向 simple living orientation	285	3.9	4.9	1.4	2.1	32.6	12.3
时尚流行指向 fashion orientation	301	3.7	5.3	2.7	5.0	31.6	12.3

续前表 continued

	人数 Number	体育专栏节目 sports feature	国内电视剧 TV play(inland)	港台电视剧 TV play (HK.Taiwan)	国外电视剧 overseas TV play	国内影片 inland film	国外影片 overseas film
样本 Sample	586	13.0	26.6	33.3	7.5	10.8	11.1
平实生活指向 simple living orientation	285	13.0	30.9	26.7	8.1	10.9	11.6
时尚流行指向 fashion orientation	301	13.0	22.6	39.5	7.0	10.6	10.6

续前表 continued

	人数 Number	港台影片 film from HK.Taiwan	天气预报 weather forecast	广告 advertising	MTV/音乐节目 MTV/music	舞蹈节目 dancing program	曲艺节目 folk art	戏曲/戏剧 opera
样本 Sample	586	22.2	21.0	1.2	14.3	1.5	6.3	3.6
平实生活指向 simple living orientation	285	19.6	20.7	1.4	10.2	0.4	6.7	4.9
时尚流行指向 fashion orientation	301	24.6	21.3	1.0	18.3	2.7	6.0	2.3

续前表 continued

	人数 Number	综艺节目 comprehensive arts	军事类节目 military program	专题类节目 special report	科教类节目 scientific education	少儿节目 children's program	女性节目 women's program	其他 others
样本 Sample	586	25.6	6.5	0.7	2.2	4.3	2.9	0.3
平实生活指向 simple living orientation	285	18.9	7.4	0.4	2.5	3.5	1.4	0.4
时尚流行指向 fashion orientation	301	31.9	5.6	1.0	2.0	5.0	4.3	0.3

1-12-2 广告态度指标/ Advertising Attitude Index

注：本题为多选题，合计百分比超过 100%（Multiple answers）

	人数 Number	国内新闻 national news	国际新闻 international news	新闻评论 news comments	本地新闻 local news	谈话节目 Talk Show	经济新闻 economic news
样本 Sample	586	63.1	51.0	22.9	15.5	4.8	5.5
广告淡漠指向 indifferent orientation	168	58.9	51.2	22.0	19.0	7.1	5.4
中间层 medium	345	63.5	49.3	23.2	13.6	3.8	4.9
信赖广告指向 loyal orientation	73	71.2	58.9	23.3	16.4	4.1	8.2

续前表 continued

	人数 Number	经济信息 economic information	金融股市 finance & stock	电视直销 direct sale on TV	消费指南 consumption guide	体育新闻 sports news	赛事报道 games report
样本 Sample	586	3.8	5.1	2.0	3.6	32.1	12.3
广告淡漠指向 indifferent orientation	168	3.0	4.8	3.0	3.0	31.0	11.9
中间层 medium	345	4.1	4.9	1.4	3.2	31.9	12.8
信赖广告指向 loyal orientation	73	4.1	6.8	2.7	6.8	35.6	11.0

续前表 continued

	人数 Number	体育专栏节目 sports feature	国内电视剧 TV play(inland)	港台电视剧 TV play (HK.Taiwan)	国外电视剧 overseas TV play	国内影片 inland film	国外影片 overseas film
样本 Sample	586	13.0	26.6	33.3	7.5	10.8	11.1
广告淡漠指向 indifferent orientation	168	12.5	31.5	31.0	7.1	8.3	6.5
中间层 medium	345	12.2	27.5	35.4	8.1	12.8	13.6
信赖广告指向 loyal orientation	73	17.8	11.0	28.8	5.5	6.8	9.6

续前表 continued

	人数 Number	港台影片 film from HK.Taiwan	天气预报 weather forecast	广告 advertising	MTV/音乐节目 MTV/music	舞蹈节目 dancing program	曲艺节目 folk art	戏曲/戏剧 opera
样本 Sample	586	22.2	21.0	1.2	14.3	1.5	6.3	3.6
广告淡漠指向 indifferent orientation	168	20.2	25.0	1.2	14.9	1.8	7.1	4.8
中间层 medium	345	22.6	18.6	1.2	15.4	1.4	5.8	2.9
信赖广告指向 loyal orientation	73	24.7	23.3	1.4	8.2	1.4	6.8	4.1

续前表 continued

	人数 Number	综艺节目 comprehensive arts	军事类节目 military program	专题类节目 special report	科教类节目 scientific education	少儿节目 children's program	女性节目 women's program	其他 others
样本 Sample	586	25.6	6.5	0.7	2.2	4.3	2.9	0.3
广告淡漠指向 indifferent orientation	168	22.6	6.0	0.6	1.8	4.2	1.2	0.6
中间层 medium	345	24.9	6.7	0.9	2.9	4.6	3.8	0.0
信赖广告指向 loyal orientation	73	35.6	6.8	0.0	0.0	2.7	2.7	1.4

1-12-2 广告态度指标/ Advertising Attitude Index

注：本题为多选题，合计百分比超过 100%（Multiple answers）

	人数 Number	国内新闻 national news	国际新闻 international news	新闻评论 news comments	本地新闻 local news	谈话节目 Talk Show	经济新闻 economic news
样本 Sample	582	63.6	47.8	21.5	15.5	7.2	6.5
广告淡漠指向 indifferent orientation	175	67.4	44.6	19.4	18.9	6.3	10.9
中间层 medium	326	63.2	48.8	22.7	12.9	7.1	5.2
信赖广告指向 loyal orientation	78	55.1	48.7	20.5	19.2	10.3	2.6

续前表 continued

	人数 Number	经济信息 economic information	金融股市 finance & stock	电视直销 direct sale on TV	消费指南 consumption guide	体育新闻 sports news	赛事报道 games report
样本 Sample	582	5.5	7.2	0.9	3.4	26.8	12.5
广告淡漠指向 indifferent orientation	175	5.1	9.7	0.6	1.7	30.9	11.4
中间层 medium	326	5.8	7.1	1.2	4.0	24.8	11.7
信赖广告指向 loyal orientation	78	3.8	2.6	0.0	5.1	25.6	17.9

续前表 continued

	人数 Number	体育专栏节目 sports feature	国内电视剧 TV play(inland)	港台电视剧 film from HK.Taiwan	国外电视剧 overseas TV play	国内影片 inland film	国外影片 overseas film
样本 Sample	582	9.6	25.8	22.7	6.7	15.8	13.6
广告淡漠指向 indifferent orientation	175	8.0	25.7	21.1	4.6	17.7	8.6
中间层 medium	326	9.8	23.9	23.6	8.6	14.4	17.8
信赖广告指向 loyal orientation	78	12.8	33.3	23.1	3.8	17.9	7.7

续前表 continued

	人数 Number	港台影片 TV play (HK.Taiwan)	天气预报 weather forecast	广告 advertising	MTV/音乐节目 MTV/music	舞蹈节目 dancing program	曲艺节目 folk art	戏曲/戏剧 opera
样本 Sample	582	22.2	15.5	1.0	15.1	2.2	10.0	6.5
广告淡漠指向 indifferent orientation	175	14.3	17.1	1.1	5.7	1.1	13.1	9.7
中间层 medium	326	26.7	16.0	0.9	18.7	2.8	8.6	5.8
信赖广告指向 loyal orientation	78	21.8	10.3	1.3	21.8	2.6	9.0	2.6

续前表 continued

	人数 Number	综艺节目 comprehen-sive arts	军事类节目 military program	专题类节目 special report	科教类节目 scientific education	少儿节目 children's program	女性节目 women's program	其他 others
样本 Sample	582	27.5	7.6	1.2	1.2	2.6	4.3	0.9
广告淡漠指向 indifferent orientation	175	26.3	6.3	2.3	1.1	2.3	4.0	1.1
中间层 medium	326	28.5	8.3	0.9	1.5	3.1	4.3	0.6
信赖广告指向 loyal orientation	78	26.9	6.4	0.0	0.0	1.3	5.1	1.3

2.广播 / Radio

● 北京 / Beijing

2-1 样本、男性各年龄层、女性各年龄层平时是否接触广播媒介/ Radio Listening by the Whole Sample, Age and Gender Groups

	人数 Number	从来不听 never	收听 yes
样本 Sample	1008	54.3	45.7
男性 Male	504	50.2	49.8
16~24 岁 Age	105	50.5	49.5
25~34 岁 Age	151	49.7	50.3
35~44 岁 Age	131	55.7	44.3
45~54 岁 Age	77	45.5	54.5
55~60 岁 Age	40	42.5	57.5
女性 Female	504	58.3	41.7
16~24 岁 Age	107	37.4	62.6
25~34 岁 Age	148	65.5	34.5
35~44 岁 Age	123	63.4	36.6
45~54 岁 Age	84	69.0	31.0
55~60 岁 Age	42	50.0	50.0

2-2 一周内不同时间收听广播的时间长短/ The Average Time Spending on Listening Radio Per Day

2-2-1 一周内不同时间收听广播的时间长短（周一到周四）/ The Average Time Spending on Listening Radio Per Day (Monday—Thursday)

	人数 Number	百分比 Percent
大约半小时或以下 about 1/2 hour or below	156	34.7
大约 1 小时 about 1 hour	151	33.6
大约 2 小时 about 2 hours	60	13.3
大约 3 小时 about 3 hours	28	6.2
大约 4 小时 about 4 hours	6	1.3
大约 5 小时 about 5 hours	2	0.4
大约 6 小时 about 6 hours	4	0.9
大约 7 小时 about 7 hours	1	0.2
大约 8 小时 about 8 hours	0	0.0
大约 9 小时 about 9 hours	1	0.2
大约 10 小时或以上 about 10 hours or over	3	0.7
记不清/不知道 can't remember	11	2.4
没有收听 didn't listen	27	6.0

n=450

2-2-2 一周内不同时间收听广播的时间长短（周五）/ The Average Time Spending on Listening Radio Per Day (Friday)

	人数 Number	百分比 Percent
大约半小时或以下 about 1/2 hour or below	126	29.3
大约 1 小时 about 1 hour	127	29.5
大约 2 小时 about 2 hours	59	13.7
大约 3 小时 about 3 hours	31	7.2
大约 4 小时 about 4 hours	7	1.6
大约 5 小时 about 5 hours	2	0.5
大约 6 小时 about 6 hours	4	0.9
大约 7 小时 about 7 hours	1	0.2
大约 8 小时 about 8 hours	0	0.0
大约 9 小时 about 9 hours	0	0.0
大约 10 小时或以上 about 10 hours or over	2	0.5
记不清/不知道 can't remember	14	3.3
没有收听 didn't listen	57	13.3

n=430

2-2-3 一周内不同时间收听广播的时间长短（周六）/ The Average Time Spending on Listening Radio Per Day (Saturday)

	人数 Number	百分比 Percent
大约半小时或以下 about 1/2 hour or below	102	24.1
大约 1 小时 about 1 hour	127	30.0
大约 2 小时 about 2 hours	55	13.0
大约 3 小时 about 3 hours	30	7.1
大约 4 小时 about 4 hours	10	2.4
大约 5 小时 about 5 hours	4	0.9
大约 6 小时 about 6 hours	4	0.9
大约 7 小时 about 7 hours	1	0.2
大约 8 小时 about 8 hours	1	0.2
大约 9 小时 about 9 hours	0	0.0
大约 10 小时或以上 about 10 hours or over	1	0.2
记不清/不知道 can't remember	15	3.5
没有收听 didn't listen	73	17.3

n=423

2-2-4 一周内不同时间收听广播的时间长短（周日）/ The Average Time Spending on Listening Radio Per Day (Sunday)

	人数 Number	百分比 Percent
大约半小时或以下 about 1/2 hour or below	103	24.3
大约 1 小时 about 1 hour	128	30.2
大约 2 小时 about 2 hours	54	12.7
大约 3 小时 about 3 hours	33	7.8
大约 4 小时 about 4 hours	9	2.1
大约 5 小时 about 5 hours	5	1.2
大约 6 小时 about 6 hours	4	0.9
大约 7 小时 about 7 hours	1	0.2
大约 8 小时 about 8 hours	1	0.2
大约 9 小时 about 9 hours	0	0.0
大约 10 小时或以上 about 10 hours or over	1	0.2
记不清/不知道 can't remember	14	3.3
没有收听 didn't listen	71	16.7

n=424

2-3 经常收听的广播频道排名/ Ranking of the Most Favorite Radio Channels

注：本题为多选题，合计百分比超过 100%（Multiple answers）

排名 Brand Ranking	频道 Channels	人次 Person-time	百分比 Percent
1	北京音乐台 Beijing Music Channel	273	61.6
2	北京文艺台 Beijing Literature & Art Channel	164	37.0
3	北京交通台 Beijing Traffic Channel	159	35.9
4	中央人民广播电台 China National Radio (CNR)	149	33.6
5	北京新闻台 Beijing News Channel	126	28.4
6	中国国际广播电台 China Radio International (CRI)	93	21.0
7	北京经济台 Beijing Economic Channel	55	12.4
8	中央人民广播电台调频立体声 Leisure FM CNR	54	12.2

n=443

2-4 样本、男性各年龄层、女性各年龄层经常收听的广播频道/ The Most Favorite Radio Channels by the Whole Sample, Age and Gender Groups

注：本题为多选题，合计百分比超过 100%（Multiple answers）

	人数 Number	北京音乐台 Beijing Music Channel	北京文艺台 Beijing Literature & Art Channel	北京交通台 Beijing Traffic Channel	中央人民广播电台 China National Radio (CNR)	北京新闻台 Beijing News Channel	中国国际广播电台 China Radio International (CRI)	北京经济台 Beijing Economic Channel
样本 Sample	443	61.6	37.0	35.9	33.6	28.4	21.0	12.4
男性 Male	240	56.3	34.2	39.2	35.4	27.1	18.8	11.7
16~24 岁 Age	51	74.5	60.8	33.3	25.5	3.9	33.3	5.9
25~34 岁 Age	74	66.2	32.4	45.9	24.3	18.9	23.0	18.9
35~44 岁 Age	54	46.3	18.5	46.3	44.4	38.9	14.8	9.3
45~54 岁 Age	41	36.6	26.8	36.6	43.9	51.2	4.9	7.3
55~60 岁 Age	20	40.0	30.0	15.0	60.0	35.0	5.0	15.0
女性 Female	203	68.0	40.4	32.0	31.5	30.0	23.6	13.3
16~24 岁 Age	66	89.4	69.7	25.8	19.7	10.6	42.4	4.5
25~34 岁 Age	50	86.0	24.0	40.0	20.0	24.0	32.0	18.0
35~44 岁 Age	41	56.1	24.4	31.7	36.6	39.0	2.4	14.6
45~54 岁 Age	26	26.9	30.8	30.8	57.7	57.7	7.7	23.1
55~60 岁 Age	20	30.0	30.0	35.0	55.0	55.0	5.0	15.0

续前表 continued

	人数 Number	中央人民广播电台调频立体声 Leisure FM CNR	BBC	河北人民广播电台 Hebei People's Radio	VOA	天津人民广播电台 Tianjin People's Radio	北京教育台 Beijing Education Channel
样本 Sample	443	12.2	1.4	1.4	1.1	1.1	0.5
男性 Male	240	12.1	2.1	2.1	1.7	1.3	0.4
16~24 岁 Age	51	15.7	2.0	2.0	0.0	2.0	0.0
25~34 岁 Age	74	8.1	4.1	0.0	4.1	0.0	1.4
35~44 岁 Age	54	16.7	1.9	3.7	1.9	1.9	0.0
45~54 岁 Age	41	7.3	0.0	4.9	0.0	2.4	0.0
55~60 岁 Age	20	15.0	0.0	0.0	0.0	0.0	0.0
女性 Female	203	12.3	0.5	0.5	0.5	1.0	0.5
16~24 岁 Age	66	9.1	0.0	0.0	0.0	0.0	0.0
25~34 岁 Age	50	10.0	2.0	0.0	2.0	0.0	0.0
35~44 岁 Age	41	14.6	0.0	0.0	0.0	0.0	2.4
45~54 岁 Age	26	19.2	0.0	0.0	0.0	7.7	0.0
55~60 岁 Age	20	15.0	0.0	5.0	0.0	0.0	0.0

2-5 经常收听的广播电台/ The Most Favorite Radio Channels

2-5-1 经常收听的广播电台（周一到周四）/ Ranking of the Most Favorite Radio Channels (Monday—Thursday)

注：本题为多选题，合计百分比超过 100%（Multiple answers）

排名 Brand Ranking	频道 Channels	人次 Person-time	百分比 Percent
1	北京音乐台 Beijing Music Channel	212	49.6
2	北京交通台 Beijing Traffic Channel	136	31.9
2	中央人民广播电台 China National Radio (CNR)	136	31.9
3	北京文艺台 Beijing Literature & Art Channel	117	27.4
4	北京新闻台 Beijing News Channel	115	26.9
5	中国国际广播电台 China Radio International (CRI)	82	19.2
6	中央人民广播电台调频立体声 Leisure FM (CNR)	56	13.1
7	北京经济台 Beijing Economic Channel	50	11.7
8	BBC	9	2.1
9	河北人民广播电台 Hebei People's Radio	8	1.9
10	通州人民广播电台 Tongzhou People's Radio	5	1.2
10	VOA	5	1.2
11	天津人民广播电台 Tianjin People's Radio	3	0.7

n=427

2-5-2 经常收听的广播电台（周五）/ Ranking of the Most Favorite Radio Channels (Friday)

注：本题为多选题，合计百分比超过 100%（Multiple answers）

排名 Brand Ranking	频道 Channels	人次 Person-time	百分比 Percent
1	北京音乐台 Beijing Music Channel	179	44.0
2	中央人民广播电台 China National Radio (CNR)	125	30.7
3	北京交通台 Beijing Traffic Channel	116	28.5
4	北京新闻台 Beijing News Channel	107	26.3
5	北京文艺台 Beijing Literature & Art Channel	98	24.1
6	中国国际广播电台 China Radio International (CRI)	69	17.0
7	中央人民广播电台调频立体声 Leisure FM CNR	52	12.8
8	北京经济台 Beijing Economic Channel	46	11.3
9	河北人民广播电台 Hebei People's Radio	8	2.0
9	BBC	8	2.0
10	通州人民广播电台 Tongzhou People's Radio	4	1.0
10	天津人民广播电台 Tianjin People's Radio	4	1.0
10	VOA	4	1.0

n=407

2-5-3 经常收听的广播电台（周六）/ Ranking of the Most Favorite Radio Channels (Saturday)

注：本题为多选题，合计百分比超过 100%（Multiple answers）

排名 Brand Ranking	频道 Channels	人次 Person-time	百分比 Percent
1	北京音乐台 Beijing Music Channel	179	45.3
2	中央人民广播电台 China National Radio (CNR)	118	29.9
3	北京新闻台 Beijing News Channel	100	25.3
4	北京交通台 Beijing Traffic Channel	98	24.8
5	北京文艺台 Beijing Literature & Art Channel	91	23.0
6	中国国际广播电台 China Radio International (CRI)	70	17.7
7	中央人民广播电台调频立体声 Leisure FM CNR	50	12.7
8	北京经济台 Beijing Economic Channel	44	11.1
9	BBC	7	1.8
10	河北人民广播电台 Hebei People's Radio	6	1.5
11	天津人民广播电台 Tianjin People's Radio	5	1.3
12	VOA	4	1.0
13	通州人民广播电台 Tongzhou People's Radio	3	0.8

n=395

2-5-4 经常收听的广播电台（周日）/ Ranking of the Most Favorite Radio Channels (Sunday)

注：本题为多选题，合计百分比超过 100%（Multiple answers）

排名 Brand Ranking	频道 Channels	人次 Person-time	百分比 Percent
1	北京音乐台 Beijing Music Channel	177	45.6
2	中央人民广播电台 China National Radio (CNR)	116	29.9
3	北京交通台 Beijing Traffic Channel	97	25.0
4	北京新闻台 Beijing News Channel	94	24.2
5	北京文艺台 Beijing Literature & Art Channel	82	21.1
6	中国国际广播电台 China Radio International (CRI)	65	16.8
7	中央人民广播电台调频立体声 Leisure FM CNR	50	12.9
8	北京经济台 Beijing Economic Channel	46	11.9
9	河北人民广播电台 Hebei People's Radio	6	1.5
10	BBC	6	1.5
11	天津人民广播电台 Tianjin People's Radio	4	1.0
11	VOA	4	1.0
12	通州人民广播电台 Tongzhou People's Radio	3	0.8

n=388

2-6 经常收听的广播节目/ Ranking of the Most Favorite Radio Programs

注：本题为多选题，合计百分比超过 100%（Multiple answers）

排名 Ranking	广播节目 Radio Programs	人次 Person-time	百分比 Percent
1	国内新闻 national news	217	48.4
2	国际新闻 international news	184	41.1
3	港台流行音乐 HK.Taiwan pop music	161	35.9
4	曲艺相声 folk arts	149	33.3
5	天气预报 weather forecast	147	32.8
6	国内流行音乐 inland pop music	116	25.9
7	欧美流行音乐 Europe pop music	113	25.2
8	体育节目 sports	70	15.6
9	交通信息 transportation report	68	15.2
10	评书 storytelling	67	15.0
11	医疗保健 medicare	64	14.3
12	热点话题评说 hot topic	57	12.7
13	古典音乐欣赏 classic music	43	9.6
14	外语教学 language teaching	40	8.9
15	经济信息 economic information report	38	8.5
16	股市信息 stock information	28	6.3
17	点播节目 call-in program	25	5.6
18	戏曲节目 traditional opera	24	5.4
18	教育节目 educational news	24	5.4
19	广播剧 radio play	21	4.7
20	其他 others	10	2.2
21	有奖问答 contest	7	1.6
22	少儿节目 children's program	4	0.9

n=448

2-7 样本、男性各年龄层、女性各年龄层经常收听的广播节目/ The Most Favorite Radio Programs by the Whole Sample, Age and Gender Groups

注：本题为多选题，合计百分比超过 100%（Multiple answers）

	人数 Number	国内新闻 national news	国际新闻 international news	天气预报 weather forecast	经济信息 economic information report	交通信息 transportation report	教育节目 educational program
样本 Sample	448	48.4	41.1	32.8	8.5	15.2	5.4
男性 Male	243	51.0	47.3	27.6	10.3	19.8	3.3
16~24 岁 Age	51	29.4	31.4	21.6	2.0	9.8	5.9
25~34 岁 Age	74	40.5	43.2	24.3	16.2	31.1	2.7
35~44 岁 Age	53	62.3	49.1	30.2	11.3	22.6	0.0
45~54 岁 Age	42	76.2	61.9	40.5	11.9	19.0	7.1
55~60 岁 Age	23	60.9	65.2	21.7	4.3	0.0	0.0
女性 Female	205	45.4	33.7	39.0	6.3	9.8	7.8
16~24 岁 Age	65	21.5	18.5	21.5	3.1	6.2	3.1
25~34 岁 Age	50	44.0	36.0	38.0	10.0	20.0	12.0
35~44 岁 Age	43	55.8	37.2	37.2	4.7	9.3	14.0
45~54 岁 Age	26	69.2	53.8	73.1	11.5	0.0	3.8
55~60 岁 Age	21	71.4	42.9	57.1	4.8	9.5	4.8

续前表 continued

	人数 Number	热点话题评说 hot topics	外语教学 foreign languages teaching	广播剧 radio play	古典音乐欣赏 classic music	欧美流行音乐 Europe & America pop music	港台流行音乐 HK. Taiwan pop music
样本 Sample	**448**	**12.7**	**8.9**	**4.7**	**9.6**	**25.2**	**35.9**
男性 Male	**243**	**12.3**	**5.8**	**3.3**	**8.6**	**22.6**	**30.5**
16~24 岁 Age	51	9.8	11.8	5.9	13.7	49.0	62.7
25~34 岁 Age	74	10.8	9.5	4.1	6.8	33.8	41.9
35~44 岁 Age	53	13.2	1.9	0.0	3.8	9.4	15.1
45~54 岁 Age	42	14.3	0.0	4.8	7.1	0.0	2.4
55~60 岁 Age	23	17.4	0.0	0.0	17.4	0.0	8.7
女性 Female	**205**	**13.2**	**12.7**	**6.3**	**10.7**	**28.3**	**42.4**
16~24 岁 Age	65	15.4	21.5	10.8	18.5	56.9	76.9
25~34 岁 Age	50	12.0	18.0	4.0	8.0	36.0	48.0
35~44 岁 Age	43	11.6	7.0	2.3	9.3	4.7	27.9
45~54 岁 Age	26	19.2	0.0	7.7	0.0	3.8	3.8
55~60 岁 Age	21	4.8	0.0	4.8	9.5	0.0	0.0

续前表 continued

	人数 Number	国内流行音乐 inland pop music	戏曲节目 traditional opera	曲艺相声 folk arts	评书 storytelling	医疗保健 medicare
样本 Sample	**448**	**25.9**	**5.4**	**33.3**	**15.0**	**14.3**
男性 Male	**243**	**21.0**	**5.8**	**39.9**	**20.2**	**9.5**
16~24 岁 Age	51	29.4	0.0	51.0	25.5	3.9
25~34 岁 Age	74	32.4	2.7	36.5	24.3	8.1
35~44 岁 Age	53	15.1	3.8	32.1	15.1	11.3
45~54 岁 Age	42	4.8	2.4	45.2	14.3	9.5
55~60 岁 Age	23	8.7	39.1	34.8	17.4	21.7
女性 Female	**205**	**31.7**	**4.9**	**25.4**	**8.8**	**20.0**
16~24 岁 Age	65	36.9	0.0	23.1	9.2	3.1
25~34 岁 Age	50	32.0	2.0	20.0	10.0	20.0
35~44 岁 Age	43	34.9	4.7	18.6	4.7	25.6
45~54 岁 Age	26	19.2	15.4	38.5	7.7	38.5
55~60 岁 Age	21	23.8	14.3	42.9	14.3	38.1

续前表 continued

	人数 Number	点播节目 call-in program	少儿节目 children's program	体育节目 sports	有奖问答 contest	其他 others
样本 Sample	**448**	**5.6**	**0.9**	**15.6**	**1.6**	**6.3**
男性 Male	**243**	**2.5**	**0.0**	**22.6**	**0.8**	**7.0**
16~24 岁 Age	51	2.0	0.0	29.4	2.0	3.9
25~34 岁 Age	74	2.7	0.0	17.6	1.4	14.9
35~44 岁 Age	53	0.0	0.0	22.6	0.0	5.7
45~54 岁 Age	42	7.1	0.0	26.2	0.0	0.0
55~60 岁 Age	23	0.0	0.0	17.4	0.0	4.3
女性 Female	**205**	**9.3**	**2.0**	**7.3**	**2.4**	**5.4**
16~24 岁 Age	65	10.8	1.5	7.7	1.5	0.0
25~34 岁 Age	50	8.0	6.0	6.0	4.0	8.0
35~44 岁 Age	43	18.6	0.0	4.7	4.7	14.0
45~54 岁 Age	26	0.0	0.0	11.5	0.0	3.8
55~60 岁 Age	21	0.0	0.0	9.5	0.0	0.0

2-8 不同学历的听众收听的广播节目的偏好/ Program Preference by Educational Levels

注：本题为多选题，合计百分比超过 100%（Multiple answers）

	人数 Number	国内新闻 national news	国际新闻 international news	天气预报 weather forecast	经济信息 economic information report	交通信息 transportation report	教育节目 educational program
样本 Sample	**446**	**48.2**	**40.8**	**32.7**	**8.5**	**15.2**	**5.4**
小学及以下 Primary School or Below	12	58.3	50.0	41.7	0.0	16.7	0.0
初中 Middle School	67	58.2	44.8	37.3	9.0	14.9	3.0
高中/中专/技校 High School/Technical Secondary School	183	45.4	31.1	31.1	3.8	18.0	7.7
大学专科 2-3 Year College	108	46.3	43.5	31.5	11.1	13.9	3.7
大学本科 4-5 Year College	70	44.3	52.9	32.9	17.1	10.0	5.7
研究生或以上 Graduate or Above	6	83.3	83.3	33.3	16.7	16.7	0.0

续前表 continued

	人数 Number	热点话题评说 hot topics	外语教学 foreign languages teaching	广播剧 radio play	古典音乐欣赏 classic music	欧美流行音乐 Europe & America pop music	港台流行音乐 HK.Taiwan pop music
样本 Sample	**446**	**12.6**	**9.0**	**4.7**	**9.6**	**25.3**	**36.1**
小学及以下 Primary School or Below	12	0.0	0.0	0.0	0.0	0.0	0.0
初中 Middle School	67	11.9	3.0	6.0	3.0	3.0	16.4
高中/中专/技校 High School/Technical Secondary School	183	14.2	6.0	6.6	9.3	26.2	44.3
大学专科 2-3 Year College	108	15.7	8.3	4.6	9.3	27.8	38.9
大学本科 4-5 Year College	70	7.1	22.9	0.0	20.0	42.9	38.6
研究生或以上 Graduate or Above	6	0.0	33.3	0.0	0.0	50.0	0.0

续前表 continued

	人数 Number	国内流行音乐 inland pop music	戏曲节目 traditional opera	曲艺相声 folk arts	评书 storytelling	医疗保健 medicare
样本 Sample	**446**	**26.0**	**5.4**	**33.2**	**15.0**	**14.3**
小学及以下 Primary School or Below	12	33.3	16.7	41.7	16.7	16.7
初中 Middle School	67	20.9	10.4	38.8	19.4	22.4
高中/中专/技校 High School/Technical Secondary School	183	26.8	6.0	37.2	15.8	9.8
大学专科 2-3 Year College	108	25.9	2.8	31.5	14.8	19.4
大学本科 4-5 Year College	70	28.6	1.4	21.4	8.6	8.6
研究生或以上 Graduate or Above	6	16.7	0.0	0.0	16.7	33.3

续前表 continued

	人数 Number	点播节目 call-in program	少儿节目 children's program	体育节目 sports	有奖问答 contest	其他 others
样本 Sample	446	5.6	0.9	15.5	1.6	6.3
小学及以下 Primary School or Below	12	8.3	0.0	0.0	0.0	0.0
初中 Middle School	67	3.0	0.0	11.9	1.5	7.5
高中/中专/技校 High School/Technical Secondary School	183	8.2	1.6	21.9	2.2	4.4
大学专科 2-3 Year College	108	5.6	0.9	11.1	1.9	12.0
大学本科 4-5 Year College	70	0.0	0.0	11.4	0.0	2.9
研究生或以上 Graduate or Above	6	16.7	0.0	16.7	0.0	0.0

2-9 经常收听广播时段/ Weekday Times Slots of Radio Listening

注：本题为多选题，合计百分比超过 100%（Multiple answers）

时间段 times slots	周一到周四(%) (Monday—Thursday)	周五(%) (Friday)	周六(%) (Saturday)	周日(%) (Sunday)
样本量 Sample	n=436	n=412	n=396	n=393
0:00-0:30	0.7	0.5	1.0	0.8
0:30-1:00	0.7	0.2	0.5	0.5
1:00-1:30	0.5	0.0	0.3	0.0
1:30-2:00	0.0	0.0	0.5	0.3
2:00-2:30	0.0	0.0	0.3	0.5
2:30-3:00	0.0	0.0	0.5	0.5
3:00-3:30	0.0	0.2	0.0	0.0
3:30-4:00	0.2	0.0	0.0	0.3
4:00-4:30	0.0	0.0	0.0	0.0
4:30-5:00	0.0	0.0	0.0	0.3
5:00-5:30	0.7	0.7	0.5	0.5
5:30-6:00	0.7	0.7	0.8	1.0
6:00-6:30	6.9	6.8	5.1	4.6
6:30-7:00	18.8	18.4	13.9	13.2
7:00-7:30	20.2	21.1	18.2	18.1
7:30-8:00	13.3	11.9	10.4	10.7
8:00-8:30	10.8	11.7	11.6	11.7
8:30-9:00	7.8	8.0	9.6	9.7
9:00-9:30	7.3	6.8	8.6	8.1
9:30-10:00	6.2	6.1	8.1	7.9
10:00-10:30	5.7	4.6	7.3	7.6
10:30-11:00	4.8	3.4	5.8	5.6
11:00-11:30	5.5	4.1	6.3	6.4
11:30-12:00	6.4	6.3	7.3	7.6
12:00-12:30	12.8	12.4	14.1	14.0
12:30-13:00	11.9	10.0	11.9	12.2
13:00-13:30	7.1	6.6	7.6	7.6
13:30-14:00	5.5	4.6	5.1	5.1
14:00-14:30	4.1	3.4	3.8	3.8
14:30-15:00	4.1	4.1	4.3	4.1
15:00-15:30	4.4	3.9	4.0	4.6
15:30-16:00	3.4	2.7	3.8	3.6
16:00-16:30	4.6	4.1	4.5	4.8
16:30-17:00	5.5	4.9	3.8	4.1
17:00-17:30	8.0	7.0	5.6	4.8
17:30-18:00	7.3	6.8	4.8	4.8
18:00-18:30	6.0	5.6	5.3	4.8
18:30-19:00	4.6	4.6	4.0	4.1
19:00-19:30	8.7	8.7	8.8	9.4
19:30-20:00	7.6	7.5	7.6	7.6
20:00-20:30	5.5	4.6	5.3	6.1
20:30-21:00	4.4	4.4	4.0	4.8
21:00-21:30	10.1	9.7	10.4	10.4
21:30-22:00	11.7	11.2	11.9	11.7
22:00-22:30	11.9	11.9	12.9	13.7
22:30-23:00	11.5	11.9	12.1	12.7
23:00-23:30	5.3	6.3	6.8	6.4
23:30-24:00	3.4	4.1	4.5	3.8

2-10 样本、男性各年龄层、女性各年龄层是否打过热线电话参与节目/ Call-in Hot-time Telephone to Take Part in the Program by the Whole Sample, Age and Gender Groups

	人数 Number	打过 yes	没打过 no
样本 Sample	442	12.4	87.6
男性 Male	240	12.1	87.9
16~24 岁 Age	52	15.4	84.6
25~34 岁 Age	71	11.3	88.7
35~44 岁 Age	53	13.2	86.8
45~54 岁 Age	42	9.5	90.5
55~60 岁 Age	22	9.1	90.9
女性 Female	202	12.9	87.1
16~24 岁 Age	65	13.8	86.2
25~34 岁 Age	50	18.0	82.0
35~44 岁 Age	42	9.5	90.5
45~54 岁 Age	25	8.0	92.0
55~60 岁 Age	20	10.0	90.0

2-11 不同消费者层平时是否接触广播媒介/ Radio Exposure by Market Segments

2-11-1 时尚流行指标/ Fads Popular Index

	人数 Number	从来不听 never	收听 yes
样本 Sample	994	54.5	45.5
平实生活指向 simple living orientation	489	56.2	43.8
时尚流行指向 fashion orientation	505	52.9	47.1

2-11-2 广告态度指标/ Advertising Attitude Index

	人数 Number	从来不听 never	收听 yes
样本 Sample	990	54.2	45.8
广告淡漠指向 indifferent orientation	288	57.6	42.4
中间层 medium	571	50.4	49.6
信赖广告指向 loyal orientation	131	63.4	36.6

2-12 不同消费者层收听广播频道的偏好/ Channel Preference by Market Segments

2-12-1 时尚流行指标/ Fads Popular Index

注：本题为多选题，合计百分比超过 100%（Multiple answers）

	人数 Number	北京音乐台 Beijing Music Channel	北京文艺台 Beijing Literature & Art Channel	北京交通台 Beijing Traffic Channel	中央人民广播电台 China National Radio (CNR)	北京新闻台 Beijing News Channel	中国国际广播电台 China Radio International (CRI)	北京经济台 Beijing Economic Channel
样本 Sample	434	61.8	36.9	35.9	32.9	28.3	20.7	12.7
平实生活指向 simple living orientation	205	57.6	34.1	33.2	37.1	29.8	22.0	10.2
时尚流行指向 fashion orientation	229	65.5	39.3	38.4	29.3	27.1	19.7	14.8

续前表 continued

	人数 Number	中央人民广播电台调频立体声 Leisure FM CNR	BBC	河北人民广播电台 Hebei People's Radio	VOA	天津人民广播电台 Tianjin People's Radio	北京教育台 Beijing Education Channel
样本 Sample	434	11.8	1.4	1.4	1.2	1.2	0.5
平实生活指向 simple living orientation	205	14.1	1.5	2.0	2.4	1.0	0.5
时尚流行指向 fashion orientation	229	9.6	1.3	0.9	0.0	1.3	0.4

2-12-2 广告态度指标/ Advertising Attitude Index

注：本题为多选题，合计百分比超过 100%（Multiple answers）

	人数 Number	北京音乐台 Beijing Music Channel	北京文艺台 Beijing Literature & Art Channel	北京交通台 Beijing Traffic Channel	中央人民广播电台 China National Radio (CNR)	北京新闻台 Beijing News Channel	中国国际广播电台 China Radio International (CRI)	北京经济台 Beijing Economic Channel
样本 Sample	**435**	**61.8**	**37.5**	**36.3**	**34.0**	**28.0**	**20.7**	**12.6**
广告淡漠指向 indifferent orientation	118	55.1	32.2	33.9	40.7	30.5	22.9	11.9
中间层 medium	272	65.8	39.7	36.8	30.1	25.7	20.6	12.9
信赖广告指向 loyal orientation	45	55.6	37.8	40.0	40.0	35.6	15.6	13.3

续前表 continued

	人数 Number	中央人民广播电台调频立体声 Leisure FM CNR	BBC	河北人民广播电台 Hebei People's Radio	VOA	天津人民广播电台 Tianjin People's Radio	北京教育台 Beijing Education Channel
样本 Sample	**435**	**12.4**	**1.4**	**1.4**	**1.1**	**1.1**	**0.5**
广告淡漠指向 indifferent orientation	118	12.7	1.7	0.8	1.7	0.8	0.0
中间层 medium	272	12.5	1.5	1.1	1.1	1.1	0.7
信赖广告指向 loyal orientation	45	11.1	0.0	4.4	0.0	2.2	0.0

2-13 不同消费者层收看广播节目的偏好/ Program Preference by Market Segments

2-13-1 时尚流行指标/ Fads Popular Index

注：本题为多选题，合计百分比超过 100%（Multiple answers）

	人数 Number	国内新闻 national news	国际新闻 international news	天气预报 weather forecast	经济信息 economic information	交通信息 transportation report	教育节目 educational program
样本 Sample	**439**	**48.5**	**41.5**	**32.6**	**8.7**	**15.5**	**5.5**
平实生活指向 simple living orientation	203	54.2	49.3	34.0	6.9	14.8	4.4
时尚流行指向 fashion orientation	236	43.6	34.7	31.4	10.2	16.1	6.4

续前表 continued

	人数 Number	热点话题评说 hot topics	外语教学 foreign languages teaching	广播剧 radio play	古典音乐欣赏 classic music	欧美流行音乐 Europe & America pop music	港台流行音乐 HK.Taiwan pop music
样本 Sample	**439**	**12.5**	**9.1**	**4.6**	**9.8**	**25.1**	**35.8**
平实生活指向 simple living orientation	203	12.8	9.4	3.9	9.9	19.7	25.1
时尚流行指向 fashion orientation	236	12.3	8.9	5.1	9.7	29.7	44.9

续前表 continued

	人数 Number	国内流行音乐 inland pop music	戏曲节目 traditional opera	曲艺相声 folk art	评书 storytelling	医疗保健 medicare
样本 Sample	**439**	**25.7**	**5.2**	**32.6**	**15.0**	**14.4**
平实生活指向 simple living orientation	203	19.7	6.4	35.0	18.7	15.3
时尚流行指向 fashion orientation	236	30.9	4.2	30.5	11.9	13.6

续前表 continued

	人数 Number	点播节目 call-in program	少儿节目 children's program	体育节目 sports	有奖问答 contest	其他 others
样本 Sample	**439**	**5.7**	**0.9**	**15.5**	**1.4**	**6.4**
平实生活指向 simple living orientation	203	4.9	0.5	17.7	1.5	6.4
时尚流行指向 fashion orientation	236	6.4	1.3	13.6	1.3	6.4

2-13-2 广告态度指标/ Advertising Attitude Index

注：本题为多选题，合计百分比超过 100%（Multiple answers）

	人数 Number	国内新闻 national news	国际新闻 international news	天气预报 weather forecast	经济信息 economic information	交通信息 transportation report	教育节目 educational program
样本 Sample	**440**	**48.6**	**41.6**	**32.7**	**8.6**	**15.2**	**5.2**
广告淡漠指向 indifferent orientation	118	47.5	42.4	30.5	7.6	14.4	5.9
中间层 medium	275	48.4	41.8	32.7	9.5	14.2	4.4
信赖广告指向 loyal orientation	47	53.2	38.3	38.3	6.4	23.4	8.5

续前表 continued

	人数 Number	热点话题评说 hot topics	外语教学 foreign languages teaching	广播剧 radio play	古典音乐欣赏 classic music	欧美流行音乐 Europe & America pop music	港台流行音乐 HK.Taiwan pop music
样本 Sample	**440**	**13.0**	**9.1**	**4.8**	**9.8**	**25.5**	**36.1**
广告淡漠指向 indifferent orientation	118	14.4	5.9	5.9	8.5	22.9	32.2
中间层 medium	275	13.5	10.5	4.0	10.9	25.5	36.0
信赖广告指向 loyal orientation	47	6.4	8.5	6.4	6.4	31.9	46.8

续前表 continued

	人数 Number	国内流行音乐 inland pop music	戏曲节目 traditional opera	曲艺相声 folk art	评书 storytelling	医疗保健 medicare
样本 Sample	**440**	**25.9**	**5.2**	**33.6**	**15.2**	**14.3**
广告淡漠指向 indifferent orientation	118	22.9	5.9	33.1	16.9	15.3
中间层 medium	275	27.6	4.7	34.5	15.6	14.2
信赖广告指向 loyal orientation	47	23.4	6.4	29.8	8.5	12.8

续前表 continued

	人数 Number	点播节目 call-in program	少儿节目 children's program	体育节目 sports	有奖问答 contest	其他 others
样本 Sample	**440**	**5.7**	**0.7**	**15.5**	**1.6**	**6.4**
广告淡漠指向 indifferent orientation	118	6.8	0.8	16.1	1.7	6.8
中间层 medium	275	5.8	0.4	14.5	1.8	6.5
信赖广告指向 loyal orientation	47	2.1	2.1	19.1	0.0	4.3

● 上海 / Shanghai

2-1 样本、男性各年龄层、女性各年龄层平时是否接触广播媒介/ Radio Listening by the Whole Sample, Age and Gender Groups

	人数 Number	从来不听 never	收听 yes
样本 Sample	**1013**	**56.8**	**43.2**
男性 Male	**509**	**57.2**	**42.8**
16~24 岁 Age	109	56.0	44.0
25~34 岁 Age	146	65.1	34.9
35~44 岁 Age	130	56.2	43.8
45~54 岁 Age	85	52.9	47.1
55~60 岁 Age	39	43.6	56.4
女性 Female	**504**	**56.3**	**43.7**
16~24 岁 Age	108	50.0	50.0
25~34 岁 Age	143	62.2	37.8
35~44 岁 Age	130	61.5	38.5
45~54 岁 Age	82	48.8	51.2
55~60 岁 Age	41	51.2	48.8

2-2 一周内不同时间收听广播的时间长短/ The Average Time Spending on Listening Radio Per Day

2-2-1 一周内不同时间收听广播的时间长短（周一到周四）/ The Average Time Spending on Listening Radio Per Day (Monday—Thursday)

	人数 Number	百分比 Percent
大约半小时或以下 about 1/2 hour or below	137	31.3
大约 1 小时 about 1 hour	148	33.8
大约 2 小时 about 2 hours	79	18.0
大约 3 小时 about 3 hours	20	4.6
大约 4 小时 about 4 hours	17	3.9
大约 5 小时 about 5 hours	10	2.3
大约 6 小时 about 6 hours	0	0.0
大约 7 小时 about 7 hours	1	0.2
大约 8 小时 about 8 hours	1	0.2
大约 9 小时 about 9 hours	0	0.0
大约 10 小时或以上 about 10 hours or over	1	0.2
记不清/不知道 can't remember	6	1.4
没有收听 didn't listen	18	4.1

n=438

2-2-2 一周内不同时间收听广播的时间长短（周五）/ The Average Time Spending on Listening Radio Per Day (Friday)

	人数 Number	百分比 Percent
大约半小时或以下 about 1/2 hour or below	123	28.2
大约 1 小时 about 1 hour	136	31.2
大约 2 小时 about 2 hours	81	18.6
大约 3 小时 about 3 hours	22	5.0
大约 4 小时 about 4 hours	14	3.2
大约 5 小时 about 5 hours	9	2.1
大约 6 小时 about 6 hours	0	0.0
大约 7 小时 about 7 hours	2	0.5
大约 8 小时 about 8 hours	1	0.2
大约 9 小时 about 9 hours	0	0.0
大约 10 小时或以上 about 10 hours or over	1	0.2
记不清/不知道 can't remember	10	2.3
没有收听 didn't listen	37	8.5

n=436

2-2-3 一周内不同时间收听广播的时间长短（周六）/ The Average Time Spending on Listening Radio Per Day (Saturday)

	人数 Number	百分比 Percent
大约半小时或以下 about 1/2 hour or below	113	26.0
大约 1 小时 about 1 hour	127	29.2
大约 2 小时 about 2 hours	76	17.5
大约 3 小时 about 3 hours	24	5.5
大约 4 小时 about 4 hours	17	3.9
大约 5 小时 about 5 hours	5	1.1
大约 6 小时 about 6 hours	1	0.2
大约 7 小时 about 7 hours	2	0.5
大约 8 小时 about 8 hours	1	0.2
大约 9 小时 about 9 hours	0	0.0
大约 10 小时或以上 about 10 hours or over	2	0.5
记不清/不知道 can't remember	9	2.1
没有收听 didn't listen	58	13.3

n=435

2-2-4 一周内不同时间收听广播的时间长短（周日）/ The Average Time Spending on Listening Radio Per Day (Sunday)

	人数 Number	百分比 Percent
大约半小时或以下 about 1/2 hour or below	108	24.8
大约 1 小时 about 1 hour	131	30.1
大约 2 小时 about 2 hours	75	17.2
大约 3 小时 about 3 hours	26	6.0
大约 4 小时 about 4 hours	14	3.2
大约 5 小时 about 5 hours	6	1.4
大约 6 小时 about 6 hours	1	0.2
大约 7 小时 about 7 hours	2	0.5
大约 8 小时 about 8 hours	1	0.2
大约 9 小时 about 9 hours	0	0.0
大约 10 小时或以上 about 10 hours or over	3	0.7
记不清/不知道 can't remember	9	2.1
没有收听 didn't listen	59	13.6

n=435

2-3 经常收听的广播频道排名/ Ranking of the Most Favorite Radio Channels

注：本题为多选题，合计百分比超过 100%（Multiple answers）

排名 Brand Ranking	频道 Channels	人次 Person-time	百分比 Percent
1	上海广播电台新闻频道(990 千赫)Shanghai News Channel	210	48.6
2	东方台音乐频道(101.7 兆赫)Oriental Music Channel	170	39.4
3	上海广播电台音乐频道 1(103.7 兆赫)Shanghai Music Channel 1	153	35.4
4	东方台综合频道(792 千赫)Oriental Radio	152	35.2
5	中央人民广播电台 China National Radio (CNR)	67	15.5
6	东广金融台(97.7 兆赫)Oriental Financial Channel	56	13.0
6	上海广播电台文艺频道(1197 千赫) Shanghai Literature & Art Channel	56	13.0
7	上海广播电台音乐频道 2(105.7 兆赫)Shanghai Music Channel 2	53	12.3
8	上海广播电台市场信息频道(1422、603 千赫) Shanghai Economic Channel	45	10.4
9	上海广播电台交通信息频道（648 千赫）Shanghai Traffic Channel	34	7.9
10	上海广播电台外语频道（1296 千赫） Shanghai Foreign Language Channel	10	2.3
11	中国国际广播电台 China Radio International (CRI)	8	1.9
11	浦江之声 Pu Jiang Zhi Sheng（900、927 千赫）	8	1.9

n=432

2-4 样本、男性各年龄层、女性各年龄层经常收听的广播频道/ The Most Favorite Radio Channels by the Whole Sample, Age and Gender Groups

注：本题为多选题，合计百分比超过 100%（Multiple answers）

	人数 Number	上海广播电台新闻频道 (990 千赫) Shanghai News Channel	东方台音乐频道 (101.7 兆赫) Oriental Music Channel	上海广播电台音乐频道 1 (103.7 兆赫) Shanghai Music Channel 1	东方台综合频道 (792 千赫) Oriental Radio	中央人民广播电台 China National Radio (CNR)	东广金融台 (97.7 兆赫) Oriental Financial Channel	上海广播电台文艺频道 (1197 千赫) Shanghai Literature & Art Channel
样本 Sample	432	48.6	39.4	35.4	35.2	15.5	13.0	13.0
男性 Male	216	51.4	40.3	32.9	37.0	16.2	14.8	14.4
16~24 岁 Age	48	29.2	62.5	62.5	37.5	16.7	12.5	16.7
25~34 岁 Age	51	47.1	58.8	47.1	25.5	7.8	7.8	11.8
35~44 岁 Age	57	56.1	40.4	19.3	42.1	8.8	14.0	10.5
45~54 岁 Age	39	66.7	5.1	7.7	41.0	30.8	30.8	17.9
55~60 岁 Age	21	71.4	9.5	14.3	42.9	28.6	9.5	19.0
女性 Female	216	45.8	38.4	38.0	33.3	14.8	11.1	11.6
16~24 岁 Age	54	24.1	70.4	66.7	29.6	11.1	3.7	3.7
25~34 岁 Age	52	34.6	42.3	48.1	38.5	13.5	11.5	13.5
35~44 岁 Age	48	58.3	27.1	22.9	39.6	14.6	12.5	6.3
45~54 岁 Age	42	59.5	19.0	14.3	31.0	14.3	16.7	16.7
55~60 岁 Age	20	75.0	10.0	20.0	20.0	30.0	15.0	30.0

续前表 continued

	人数 Number	上海广播电台音乐频道 2 (105.7 兆赫) Shanghai English Channel 2	上海广播电台市场信息频道 (1422、603 千赫) Shanghai Economic Channel	上海广播电台交通信息频道 (648 千赫) Shanghai Traffic Channel	上海广播电台外语频道 (1296 千赫) Shanghai Foreign Language Channel	中国国际广播电台 China Radio International (CRI)	浦江之声 Pu Jiang Zhi Sheng (900.927 千赫)	VOA
样本 Sample	432	12.3	10.4	7.9	2.3	1.9	1.9	1.2
男性 Male	216	12.0	7.9	10.6	0.0	3.2	0.9	1.4
16~24 岁 Age	48	16.7	4.2	10.4	0.0	4.2	0.0	2.1
25~34 岁 Age	51	21.6	2.0	11.8	0.0	2.0	2.0	2.0
35~44 岁 Age	57	8.8	14.0	10.5	0.0	1.8	1.8	1.8
45~54 岁 Age	39	0.0	7.7	12.8	0.0	5.1	0.0	0.0
55~60 岁 Age	21	9.5	14.3	4.8	0.0	4.8	0.0	0.0
女性 Female	216	12.5	13.0	5.1	4.6	0.5	2.8	0.9
16~24 岁 Age	54	24.1	7.4	5.6	11.1	1.9	1.9	0.0
25~34 岁 Age	52	11.5	21.2	9.6	1.9	0.0	1.9	3.8
35~44 岁 Age	48	12.5	6.3	4.2	2.1	0.0	4.2	0.0
45~54 岁 Age	42	4.8	19.0	0.0	2.4	0.0	2.4	0.0
55~60 岁 Age	20	0.0	10.0	5.0	5.0	0.0	5.0	0.0

2-5 经常收听的广播电台/ The Most Favorite Radio Channels

2-5-1 经常收听的广播电台（周一到周四）/ Ranking of the Most Favorite Radio Channels (Monday—Thursday)

注：本题为多选题，合计百分比超过 100%（Multiple answers）

排名 Brand Ranking	频道 Channels	人次 Person-time	百分比 Percent
1	上海广播电台新闻频道(990 千赫)Shanghai News Channel	191	44.1
2	东方台音乐频道(101.7 兆赫)Oriental Music Channel	150	34.6
3	东方台综合频道(792 千赫)Oriental Radio	131	30.3
3	上海广播电台音乐频道 1(103.7 兆赫)Shanghai Music Channel 1	131	30.3
4	中央人民广播电台 China National Radio (CNR)	68	15.7
5	东广金融台(97.7 兆赫)Oriental Financial Channel	54	12.5
6	上海广播电台文艺频道(1197 千赫) Shanghai Literature & Art Channel	52	12.0
7	上海广播电台音乐频道 2(105.7 兆赫)Shanghai Music Channel 2	46	10.6
8	上海广播电台市场信息频道(1422、603 千赫) Shanghai Economic Channel	31	7.2
9	上海广播电台交通信息频道(648 千赫)Shanghai Traffic Channel	25	5.8
10	中国国际广播电台 China Radio International (CRI)	9	2.1
11	上海广播电台外语频道(1296 千赫) Shanghai Foreign Language Channel	7	1.6
12	VOA	6	1.4

n=433

2-5-2 经常收听的广播电台（周五）/ Ranking of the Most Favorite Radio Channels (Friday)

注：本题为多选题，合计百分比超过 100%（Multiple answers）

排名 Brand Ranking	频道 Channels	人次 Person-time	百分比 Percent
1	上海广播电台新闻频道(990 千赫)Shanghai News Channel	185	43.2
2	东方台音乐频道(101.7 兆赫)Oriental Music Channel	146	34.1
3	上海广播电台音乐频道 1(103.7 兆赫)Shanghai Music Channel 1	130	30.4
4	东方台综合频道(792 千赫)Oriental Radio	128	29.9
5	中央人民广播电台 China National Radio (CNR)	65	15.2
6	东广金融台(97.7 兆赫)Oriental Financial Channel	50	11.7
6	上海广播电台文艺频道(1197 千赫) Shanghai Literature & Art Channel	50	11.7
7	上海广播电台音乐频道 2(105.7 兆赫)Shanghai Music Channel 2	47	11.0
8	上海广播电台市场信息频道(1422、603 千赫) Shanghai Economic Channel	31	7.2
9	上海广播电台交通信息频道(648 千赫)Shanghai Traffic Channel	24	5.6
10	中国国际广播电台 China Radio International (CRI)	8	1.9
11	浦江之声 Pu Jiang Zhi Sheng(900、927 千赫)	6	1.4
12	上海广播电台外语频道(1296 千赫) Shanghai Foreign Language Channel	5	1.2
13	VOA	4	0.9

n=428

2-5-3 经常收听的广播电台（周六）/ Ranking of the Most Favorite Radio Channels (Saturday)

注：本题为多选题，合计百分比超过 100%（Multiple answers）

排名 Brand Ranking	频道 Channels	人次 Person-time	百分比 Percent
1	上海广播电台新闻频道(990 千赫)Shanghai News Channel	178	41.4
2	东方台音乐频道(101.7 兆赫)Oriental Music Channel	142	33.0
3	上海广播电台音乐频道 1(103.7 兆赫)Shanghai Music Channel 1	137	31.9
4	东方台综合频道(792 千赫)Oriental Radio	124	28.8
5	中央人民广播电台 China National Radio (CNR)	64	14.9
6	上海广播电台文艺频道(1197 千赫) Shanghai Literature & Art Channel	49	11.4
7	上海广播电台音乐频道 2(105.7 兆赫)Shanghai Music Channel 2	48	11.2
8	东广金融台(97.7 兆赫)Oriental Financial Channel	40	9.3
9	上海广播电台市场信息频道(1422、603 千赫) Shanghai Economic Channel	24	5.6
10	上海广播电台交通信息频道（648 千赫）Shanghai Traffic Channel	21	4.9
11	中国国际广播电台 China Radio International (CRI)	10	2.3
12	上海广播电台外语频道(1296 千赫) Shanghai Foreign Language Channel	7	1.6
13	浦江之声 Pu Jiang Zhi Sheng(900、927 千赫)	7	1.6

n=430

2-5-4 经常收听的广播电台（周日）/ Ranking of the Most Favorite Radio Channels (Sunday)

注：本题为多选题，合计百分比超过 100%（Multiple answers）

排名 Brand Ranking	频道 Channels	人次 Person-time	百分比 Percent
1	上海广播电台新闻频道(990 千赫)Shanghai News Channel	180	42.1
2	东方台音乐频道(101.7 兆赫)Oriental Music Channel	144	33.6
3	上海广播电台音乐频道 1(103.7 兆赫)Shanghai Music Channel 1	131	30.6
4	东方台综合频道(792 千赫)Oriental Radio	117	27.3
5	中央人民广播电台 China National Radio (CNR)	64	15.0
6	上海广播电台音乐频道 2(105.7 兆赫)Shanghai Music Channel 2	52	12.1
7	上海广播电台文艺频道(1197 千赫) Shanghai Literature & Art Channel	50	11.7
8	东广金融台(97.7 兆赫)Oriental Financial Channel	40	9.3
9	上海广播电台市场信息频道(1422、603 千赫) Shanghai Economic Channel	24	5.6
10	上海广播电台交通信息频道(648 千赫) Shanghai Traffic Channel	19	4.4
11	中国国际广播电台 China Radio International (CRI)	12	2.8
12	上海广播电台外语频道(1296 千赫) Shanghai Foreign Language Channel	8	1.9

n=428

2-6 经常收听的广播节目/ Ranking of the Most Favorite Radio Programs

注：本题为多选题，合计百分比超过 100%（Multiple answers）

排名 Ranking	广播节目 Radio Programs	人次 Person-time	百分比 Percent
1	国内新闻 national news	277	65.0
2	国际新闻 international news	207	48.6
3	天气预报 weather forecast	197	46.2
4	港台流行音乐 HK.Taiwan pop music	163	38.3
5	欧美流行音乐 Europe pop music	107	25.1
6	国内流行音乐 inland pop music	78	18.3
7	股市信息 stock information	62	14.6
8	经济信息 economic information report	61	14.3
9	曲艺相声 folk arts	58	13.6
10	医疗保健 medicare	51	12.0
11	热点话题评说 hot topics	50	11.7
12	体育节目 sports	48	11.3
13	戏曲节目 traditional opera	29	6.8
14	点播节目 call-in program	26	6.1
15	古典音乐欣赏 classic music	25	5.9
16	交通信息 transportation report	17	4.0
17	广播剧 radio play	14	3.3
18	评书 storytelling	12	2.8
19	外语教学 foreign languages teaching	10	2.3
19	教育节目 educational news	10	2.3
20	其他 others	6	1.4
21	有奖问答 contest	5	1.2
22	少儿节目 children's program	2	0.5

n=426

2-7 样本、男性各年龄层、女性各年龄层经常收听的广播节目/ The Most Favorite Radio Programs by the Whole Sample, Age and Gender Groups

注：本题为多选题，合计百分比超过 100%（Multiple answers）

	人数 Number	国内新闻 national news	国际新闻 international news	天气预报 weather forecast	经济信息 economic information report	交通信息 transportation report	教育节目 educational program
样本 Sample	426	65.0	48.6	46.2	14.3	4.0	2.3
男性 Male	212	67.9	57.5	42.5	16.0	7.1	1.4
16~24 岁 Age	47	63.8	46.8	36.2	10.6	6.4	4.3
25~34 岁 Age	50	50.0	50.0	26.0	20.0	10.0	0.0
35~44 岁 Age	56	78.6	66.1	42.9	10.7	7.1	0.0
45~54 岁 Age	38	71.1	63.2	68.4	26.3	5.3	0.0
55~60 岁 Age	21	85.7	66.7	47.6	14.3	4.8	4.8
女性 Female	214	62.1	39.7	50.0	12.6	0.9	3.3
16~24 岁 Age	52	40.4	26.9	28.8	3.8	0.0	3.8
25~34 岁 Age	53	52.8	26.4	37.7	15.1	1.9	5.7
35~44 岁 Age	49	71.4	57.1	67.3	14.3	0.0	2.0
45~54 岁 Age	41	80.5	41.5	58.5	17.1	2.4	0.0
55~60 岁 Age	19	84.2	63.2	78.9	15.8	0.0	5.3

续前表 continued

	人数 Number	热点话题评说 hot topics	外语教学 foreign languages teaching	广播剧 radio play	古典音乐欣赏 classic music	欧美流行音乐 Europe & America pop music	港台流行音乐 HK. Taiwan pop music
样本 Sample	426	11.7	2.3	3.3	5.9	25.1	38.3
男性 Male	212	14.6	1.9	1.4	5.7	25.0	36.8
16~24 岁 Age	47	19.1	4.3	2.1	4.3	40.4	70.2
25~34 岁 Age	50	18.0	4.0	2.0	10.0	42.0	56.0
35~44 岁 Age	56	12.5	0.0	0.0	1.8	19.6	26.8
45~54 岁 Age	38	10.5	0.0	2.6	2.6	2.6	2.6
55~60 岁 Age	21	9.5	0.0	0.0	14.3	4.8	4.8
女性 Female	214	8.9	2.8	5.1	6.1	25.2	39.7
16~24 岁 Age	52	9.6	5.8	5.8	13.5	44.2	75.0
25~34 岁 Age	53	9.4	1.9	3.8	3.8	39.6	54.7
35~44 岁 Age	49	12.2	0.0	0.0	6.1	12.2	14.3
45~54 岁 Age	41	7.3	2.4	9.8	2.4	7.3	19.5
55~60 岁 Age	19	0.0	5.3	10.5	0.0	5.3	10.5

续前表 continued

	人数 Number	国内流行音乐 inland pop music	戏曲节目 traditional opera	曲艺相声 folk arts	评书 storytelling	医疗保健 medicare
样本 Sample	426	18.3	6.8	13.6	2.8	12.0
男性 Male	212	18.4	8.5	15.6	3.3	9.9
16~24 岁 Age	47	29.8	2.1	12.8	4.3	2.1
25~34 岁 Age	50	26.0	6.0	20.0	4.0	10.0
35~44 岁 Age	56	17.9	7.1	10.7	1.8	10.7
45~54 岁 Age	38	2.6	15.8	13.2	2.6	13.2
55~60 岁 Age	21	4.8	19.0	28.6	4.8	19.0
女性 Female	214	18.2	5.1	11.7	2.3	14.0
16~24 岁 Age	52	26.9	3.8	15.4	3.8	3.8
25~34 岁 Age	53	26.4	3.8	13.2	1.9	11.3
35~44 岁 Age	49	6.1	2.0	12.2	2.0	18.4
45~54 岁 Age	41	14.6	9.8	7.3	0.0	19.5
55~60 岁 Age	19	10.5	10.5	5.3	5.3	26.3

续前表 continued

	人数 Number	点播节目 call-in program	少儿节目 children's program	体育节目 sports	有奖问答 contest	其他 others
样本 Sample	426	6.1	0.5	11.3	1.2	14.6
男性 Male	212	5.2	0.0	17.0	0.5	16.0
16~24 岁 Age	47	8.5	0.0	25.5	0.0	6.4
25~34 岁 Age	50	8.0	0.0	24.0	0.0	12.0
35~44 岁 Age	56	1.8	0.0	8.9	1.8	21.4
45~54 岁 Age	38	2.6	0.0	13.2	0.0	21.1
55~60 岁 Age	21	4.8	0.0	9.5	0.0	23.8
女性 Female	214	7.0	0.9	5.6	1.9	13.1
16~24 岁 Age	52	13.5	0.0	13.5	1.9	7.7
25~34 岁 Age	53	11.3	1.9	5.7	3.8	11.3
35~44 岁 Age	49	2.0	2.0	0.0	2.0	14.3
45~54 岁 Age	41	2.4	0.0	4.9	0.0	19.5
55~60 岁 Age	19	0.0	0.0	0.0	0.0	15.8

2-8 不同学历的听众收听的广播节目的偏好/ Program Preference by Educational Levels

注：本题为多选题，合计百分比超过 100%（Multiple answers）

	人数 Number	国内新闻 national news	国际新闻 international news	天气预报 weather forecast	经济信息 economic information report	交通信息 transportation report	教育节目 educational program
样本 Sample	**424**	**65.1**	**48.6**	**46.5**	**14.2**	**4.0**	**2.4**
小学及以下 Primary School or Below	5	80.0	60.0	40.0	20.0	0.0	0.0
初中 Middle School	94	66.0	45.7	52.1	10.6	4.3	0.0
高中/中专/技校 High School/Technical Secondary School	218	64.7	49.5	45.4	13.8	5.5	3.2
大学专科 2-3 Year College	64	64.1	43.8	50.0	18.8	1.6	4.7
大学本科 4-5 Year College	39	64.1	56.4	33.3	12.8	0.0	0.0
研究生或以上 Graduate or Above	4	75.0	50.0	50.0	50.0	0.0	0.0

续前表 continued

	人数 Number	热点话题评说 hot topics	外语教学 foreign languages teaching	广播剧 radio play	古典音乐欣赏 classic music	欧美流行音乐 Europe & America pop music	港台流行音乐 HK.Taiwan pop music
样本 Sample	**424**	**11.6**	**2.1**	**3.3**	**5.9**	**25.0**	**38.2**
小学及以下 Primary School or Below	5	0.0	0.0	0.0	0.0	0.0	0.0
初中 Middle School	94	13.8	2.1	5.3	3.2	11.7	27.7
高中/中专/技校 High School/Technical Secondary School	218	11.5	1.4	2.8	7.3	28.0	41.3
大学专科 2-3 Year College	64	9.4	6.3	1.6	3.1	29.7	37.5
大学本科 4-5 Year College	39	12.8	0.0	2.6	7.7	38.5	51.3
研究生或以上 Graduate or Above	4	0.0	0.0	25.0	25.0	0.0	50.0

续前表 continued

	人数 Number	国内流行音乐 inland pop music	戏曲节目 traditional opera	曲艺相声 folk arts	评书 storytelling	医疗保健 medicare
样本 Sample	**424**	**18.2**	**6.8**	**13.4**	**2.8**	**12.0**
小学及以下 Primary School or Below	5	0.0	20.0	0.0	0.0	60.0
初中 Middle School	94	19.1	12.8	12.8	1.1	16.0
高中/中专/技校 High School/Technical Secondary School	218	18.8	4.1	17.4	1.8	11.0
大学专科 2-3 Year College	64	17.2	4.7	4.7	7.8	9.4
大学本科 4-5 Year College	39	17.9	10.3	7.7	5.1	7.7
研究生或以上 Graduate or Above	4	0.0	0.0	25.0	0.0	0.0

续前表 continued

	人数 Number	点播节目 call-in program	少儿节目 children's program	体育节目 sports	有奖问答 contest	其他 others
样本 Sample	**424**	**6.1**	**0.5**	**11.3**	**1.2**	**14.4**
小学及以下 Primary School or Below	5	0.0	0.0	0.0	0.0	0.0
初中 Middle School	94	7.4	0.0	7.4	1.1	17.0
高中/中专/技校 High School/Technical Secondary School	218	5.0	0.5	13.3	1.4	14.2
大学专科 2-3 Year College	64	10.9	1.6	10.9	0.0	12.5
大学本科 4-5 Year College	39	2.6	0.0	12.8	2.6	15.4
研究生或以上 Graduate or Above	4	0.0	0.0	0.0	0.0	0.0

2-9 经常收听广播时段/ Weekday Times Slots of Radio Listening

注：本题为多选题，合计百分比超过 100%（Multiple answers）

时间段 times slots	周一到周四(%) (Monday—Thursday)	周五(%) (Friday)	周六(%) (Saturday)	周日(%) (Sunday)
样本量 Sample	n=434	n=434	n=434	n=434
0:00-0:30	1.4	1.4	1.6	1.4
0:30-1:00	1.4	1.4	1.6	1.4
1:00-1:30	0.9	0.9	1.2	0.9
1:30-2:00	0.9	0.7	1.2	0.9
2:00-2:30	0.5	0.2	0.2	0.2
2:30-3:00	0.0	0.0	0.0	0.0
3:00-3:30	0.0	0.0	0.0	0.0
3:30-4:00	0.2	0.2	0.2	0.2
4:00-4:30	0.0	0.2	0.2	0.2
4:30-5:00	0.0	0.2	0.2	0.2
5:00-5:30	0.7	0.5	0.2	0.2
5:30-6:00	2.3	1.8	0.9	0.9
6:00-6:30	21.7	19.1	15.0	14.5
6:30-7:00	27.4	23.3	19.8	19.8
7:00-7:30	26.5	25.1	22.1	22.1
7:30-8:00	15.4	14.7	13.4	13.4
8:00-8:30	8.8	8.3	9.9	10.1
8:30-9:00	5.8	6.0	7.4	7.6
9:00-9:30	5.8	5.1	8.1	7.4
9:30-10:00	8.3	7.1	6.5	7.6
10:00-10:30	6.5	5.5	6.7	7.6
10:30-11:00	6.7	6.9	6.2	6.7
11:00-11:30	9.4	8.5	6.2	7.1
11:30-12:00	9.4	8.1	6.5	7.6
12:00-12:30	11.3	10.6	10.1	10.1
12:30-13:00	6.9	8.5	8.8	8.1
13:00-13:30	8.1	8.1	8.5	9.0
13:30-14:00	5.5	5.1	4.6	6.2
14:00-14:30	3.9	3.2	3.5	3.9
14:30-15:00	3.7	3.2	3.0	3.5
15:00-15:30	3.7	3.2	3.0	3.2
15:30-16:00	3.9	3.9	3.7	3.2
16:00-16:30	4.8	4.8	5.1	5.3
16:30-17:00	4.6	4.8	4.4	4.8
17:00-17:30	7.4	7.1	5.8	6.0
17:30-18:00	8.5	8.5	8.3	8.5
18:00-18:30	12.4	12.7	11.3	11.5
18:30-19:00	8.3	8.1	6.7	6.9
19:00-19:30	5.1	4.4	5.1	4.8
19:30-20:00	5.1	4.6	4.6	4.8
20:00-20:30	6.5	4.8	5.1	5.5
20:30-21:00	6.0	5.1	4.8	5.3
21:00-21:30	8.8	8.8	8.5	6.5
21:30-22:00	9.0	8.5	7.6	7.1
22:00-22:30	5.5	6.7	6.2	4.8
22:30-23:00	5.3	5.5	5.8	4.6
23:00-23:30	4.1	3.9	4.8	4.1
23:30-24:00	3.5	3.9	4.4	3.9

2-10 样本、男性各年龄层、女性各年龄层是否打过热线电话参与节目/ Call-in Hot-time Telephone to Take Part in the Program by the Whole Sample, Age and Gender Groups

	人数 Number	打过 yes	没打过 no
样本 Sample	433	11.3	88.7
男性 Male	215	10.7	89.3
16~24 岁 Age	47	21.3	78.7
25~34 岁 Age	49	10.2	89.8
35~44 岁 Age	57	5.3	94.7
45~54 岁 Age	40	10.0	90.0
55~60 岁 Age	22	4.5	95.5
女性 Female	218	11.9	88.1
16~24 岁 Age	54	24.1	75.9
25~34 岁 Age	54	11.1	88.9
35~44 岁 Age	49	6.1	93.9
45~54 岁 Age	42	9.5	90.5
55~60 岁 Age	19	0.0	100.0

2-11 不同消费者层平时是否接触广播媒介/ Radio Exposure by Market Segments

2-11-1 时尚流行指标/ Fads Popular Index

	人数 Number	从来不听 never	收听 yes
样本 Sample	1004	56.9	43.1
平实生活指向 simple living orientation	471	56.7	43.3
时尚流行指向 fashion orientation	533	57.0	43.0

2-11-2 广告态度指标/ Advertising Attitude Index

	人数 Number	从来不听 never	收听 yes
样本 Sample	1001	56.5	43.5
广告淡漠指向 indifferent orientation	256	60.2	39.8
中间层 medium	611	56.8	43.2
信赖广告指向 loyal orientation	134	48.5	51.5

2-12 不同消费者层收听广播频道的偏好/ Channel Preference by Market Segments

2-12-1 时尚流行指标/ Fads Popular Index

注：本题为多选题，合计百分比超过 100%（Multiple answers）

	人数 Number	上海广播电台新闻频道 (990 千赫) Shanghai News Channel	东方台音乐频道 (101.7 兆赫) Oriental Music Channel	上海广播电台音乐频道 1 (103.7 兆赫) Shanghai Music Channel 1	东方台综合频道 (792 千赫) Oriental Radio	中央人民广播电台 China National Radio (CNR)	东广金融台 (97.7 兆赫) Oriental Finance Channel	上海广播电台文艺频道 (1197 千赫) Shanghai Literature & Art Channel
样本 Sample	427	48.7	39.3	35.1	35.4	15.2	12.9	12.9
平实生活指向 simple living orientation	200	56.0	28.5	27.5	37.5	15.5	16.0	10.0
时尚流行指向 fashion orientation	227	42.3	48.9	41.9	33.5	15.0	10.1	15.4

续前表 continued

	人数 Number	上海广播电台音乐频道 2 (105.7 兆赫) Shanghai Music Channel 2	上海广播电台市场信息频道 (1422、603 千赫) Shanghai Economic Channel	上海广播电台交通信息频道 (648 千赫) Shanghai Traffic Channel	上海广播电台外语频道 (1296 千赫) Shanghai Foreign Language Channel	中国国际广播电台 China Radio International (CRI)	浦江之声 (900、927 千赫) Pu Jiang Zhi Sheng	VOA
样本 Sample	427	12.4	10.5	8.0	2.3	1.9	1.6	1.2
平实生活指向 simple living orientation	200	11.5	11.5	8.5	1.0	1.5	1.0	1.0
时尚流行指向 fashion orientation	227	13.2	9.7	7.5	3.5	2.2	2.2	1.3

2-12-2 广告态度指标/ Advertising Attitude Index

注：本题为多选题，合计百分比超过 100%（Multiple answers）

	人数 Number	上海广播电台新闻频道 (990 千赫) Shanghai News Channel	东方台音乐频道 (101.7 兆赫) Oriental Music Channel	上海广播电台音乐频道 1 (103.7 兆赫) Shanghai Music Channel 1	东方台综合频道 (792 千赫) Oriental Radio	中央人民广播电台 China National Radio (CNR)	东广金融台 (97.7 兆赫) Oriental Finance Channel	上海广播电台文艺频道 (1197 千赫) Shanghai Literature & Art Channel
样本 Sample	429	49.0	38.9	35.2	35.2	15.6	13.1	12.8
广告淡漠指向 indifferent orientation	100	44.0	33.0	29.0	42.0	13.0	13.0	11.0
中间层 medium	261	53.6	38.3	33.0	33.0	16.5	14.2	14.2
信赖广告指向 loyal orientation	68	38.2	50.0	52.9	33.8	16.2	8.8	10.3

续前表 continued

	人数 Number	上海广播电台音乐频道 2 (105.7 兆赫) Shanghai music Channel 2	上海广播电台市场信息频道 (1422、603 千赫) Shanghai Economic Channel	上海广播电台交通信息频道 (648 千赫) Shanghai Traffic Channel	上海广播电台外语频道 (1296 千赫) Shanghai Foreign Language Channel	中国国际广播电台 China Radio International (CRI)	浦江之声 (900、927 千赫) Pu Jiang Zhi Sheng	VOA
样本 Sample	429	12.4	10.5	7.9	2.3	1.9	1.6	1.2
广告淡漠指向 indifferent orientation	100	16.0	13.0	8.0	3.0	1.0	2.0	1.0
中间层 medium	261	12.3	10.7	7.7	2.7	1.5	1.5	1.1
信赖广告指向 loyal orientation	68	7.4	5.9	8.8	0.0	4.4	1.5	1.5

2-13 不同消费者层收看广播节目的偏好/ Program Preference by Market Segments

2-13-1 时尚流行指标/ Fads Popular Index

注：本题为多选题，合计百分比超过 100%（Multiple answers）

	人数 Number	国内新闻 national news	国际新闻 international news	天气预报 weather forecast	经济信息 economic information	交通信息 transportation report	教育节目 educational program
样本 Sample	422	65.4	48.6	46.2	14.5	3.8	2.4
平实生活指向 simple living orientation	198	71.2	51.5	53.5	14.6	5.1	1.0
时尚流行指向 fashion orientation	224	60.3	46.0	39.7	14.3	2.7	3.6

续前表 continued

	人数 Number	热点话题评说 hot topics	外语教学 foreign languages teaching	广播剧 radio play	古典音乐欣赏 classic music	欧美流行音乐 Europe & America pop music	港台流行音乐 HK.Taiwan pop music
样本 Sample	422	11.6	2.4	3.3	5.9	25.1	37.9
平实生活指向 simple living orientation	198	11.6	1.0	2.5	5.6	16.2	23.7
时尚流行指向 fashion orientation	224	11.6	3.6	4.0	6.3	33.0	50.4

续前表 continued

	人数 Number	国内流行音乐 inland pop music	戏曲节目 traditional opera	曲艺相声 folk art	评书 storytelling	医疗保健 medicare
样本 Sample	422	18.5	6.9	13.5	2.8	11.8
平实生活指向 simple living orientation	198	15.7	8.1	14.1	3.5	12.6
时尚流行指向 fashion orientation	224	21.0	5.8	12.9	2.2	11.2

续前表 continued

	人数 Number	点播节目 call-in program	少儿节目 children's program	体育节目 sports	有奖问答 contest	其他 others
样本 Sample	422	6.2	0.5	10.9	1.2	14.2
平实生活指向 simple living orientation	198	5.6	0.0	9.1	1.0	15.7
时尚流行指向 fashion orientation	224	6.7	0.9	12.5	1.3	12.9

2-13-2 广告态度指标/ Advertising Attitude Index

注：本题为多选题，合计百分比超过 100%（Multiple answers）

	人数 Number	国内新闻 national news	国际新闻 international news	天气预报 weather forecast	经济信息 economic information	交通信息 transportation report	教育节目 educational program
样本 Sample	423	65.2	48.7	46.1	14.4	4.0	2.4
广告淡漠指向 indifferent orientation	100	64.0	48.0	51.0	16.0	3.0	2.0
中间层 medium	256	66.4	50.0	46.9	13.7	3.9	2.7
信赖广告指向 loyal orientation	67	62.7	44.8	35.8	14.9	6.0	1.5

续前表 continued

	人数 Number	热点话题评说 hot topics	外语教学 foreign languages teaching	广播剧 radio play	古典音乐欣赏 classic music	欧美流行音乐 Europe & America pop music	港台流行音乐 HK. Taiwan pop music
样本 Sample	423	11.8	2.4	3.3	5.9	25.1	38.1
广告淡漠指向 indifferent orientation	100	8.0	2.0	2.0	7.0	25.0	29.0
中间层 medium	256	13.3	2.7	3.9	5.1	23.0	37.1
信赖广告指向 loyal orientation	67	11.9	1.5	3.0	7.5	32.8	55.2

续前表 continued

	人数 Number	国内流行音乐 inland pop music	戏曲节目 traditional opera	曲艺相声 folk art	评书 storytelling	医疗保健 medicare
样本 Sample	423	18.2	6.6	13.2	2.8	12.1
广告淡漠指向 indifferent orientation	100	18.0	4.0	13.0	5.0	10.0
中间层 medium	256	16.4	8.2	13.7	2.7	12.9
信赖广告指向 loyal orientation	67	25.4	4.5	11.9	0.0	11.9

● 广州 / Guangzhou

2-1 样本、男性各年龄层、女性各年龄层平时是否接触广播媒介/ Radio Listening by the Whole Sample, Age and Gender Groups

	人数 Number	从来不听 never	收听 yes
样本 Sample	1031	65.4	34.6
男性 Male	498	65.1	34.9
16~24 岁 Age	106	65.1	34.9
25~34 岁 Age	149	61.1	38.9
35~44 岁 Age	127	69.3	30.7
45~54 岁 Age	73	60.3	39.7
55~60 岁 Age	43	74.4	25.6
女性 Female	533	65.7	34.3
16~24 岁 Age	112	49.1	50.9
25~34 岁 Age	157	71.3	28.7
35~44 岁 Age	136	67.6	32.4
45~54 岁 Age	87	67.8	32.2
55~60 岁 Age	41	78.0	22.0

2-2 一周内不同时间收听广播的时间长短/ The Average Time Spending on Listening Radio Per Day

2-2-1 一周内不同时间收听广播的时间长短（周一到周四）/ The Average Time Spending on Listening Radio Per Day (Monday—Thursday)

	人数 Number	百分比 Percent
大约半小时或以下 about 1/2 hour or below	122	34.6
大约 1 小时 about 1 hour	102	28.9
大约 2 小时 about 2 hours	50	14.2
大约 3 小时 about 3 hours	18	5.1
大约 4 小时 about 4 hours	11	3.1
大约 5 小时 about 5 hours	4	1.1
大约 6 小时 about 6 hours	3	0.8
大约 7 小时 about 7 hours	1	0.3
大约 8 小时 about 8 hours	4	1.1
大约 9 小时 about 9 hours	1	0.3
大约 10 小时或以上 about 10 hours or over	2	0.6
记不清/不知道 can't remember	12	3.4
没有收听 didn't listen	23	6.5

n=353

2-2-2 一周内不同时间收听广播的时间长短（周五）/ The Average Time Spending on Listening Radio Per Day (Friday)

	人数 Number	百分比 Percent
大约半小时或以下 about 1/2 hour or below	116	33.0
大约 1 小时 about 1 hour	92	26.2
大约 2 小时 about 2 hours	52	14.8
大约 3 小时 about 3 hours	15	4.3
大约 4 小时 about 4 hours	11	3.1
大约 5 小时 about 5 hours	4	1.1
大约 6 小时 about 6 hours	3	0.9
大约 7 小时 about 7 hours	1	0.3
大约 8 小时 about 8 hours	4	1.1
大约 9 小时 about 9 hours	1	0.3
大约 10 小时或以上 about 10 hours or over	2	0.6
记不清/不知道 can't remember	14	4.0
没有收听 didn't listen	36	10.3

n=351

2-2-3 一周内不同时间收听广播的时间长短（周六）/ The Average Time Spending on Listening Radio Per Day (Saturday)

	人数 Number	百分比 Percent
大约半小时或以下 about 1/2 hour or below	96	27.4
大约 1 小时 about 1 hour	98	27.9
大约 2 小时 about 2 hours	53	15.1
大约 3 小时 about 3 hours	17	4.8
大约 4 小时 about 4 hours	12	3.4
大约 5 小时 about 5 hours	3	0.9
大约 6 小时 about 6 hours	1	0.3
大约 7 小时 about 7 hours	1	0.3
大约 8 小时 about 8 hours	4	1.1
大约 9 小时 about 9 hours	1	0.3
大约 10 小时或以上 about 10 hours or over	2	0.6
记不清/不知道 can't remember	12	3.4
没有收听 didn't listen	51	14.5

n=351

2-2-4 一周内不同时间收听广播的时间长短（周日）/ The Average Time Spending on Listening Radio Per Day (Sunday)

	人数 Number	百分比 Percent
大约半小时或以下 about 1/2 hour or below	91	26.0
大约 1 小时 about 1 hour	103	29.4
大约 2 小时 about 2 hours	48	13.7
大约 3 小时 about 3 hours	21	6.0
大约 4 小时 about 4 hours	10	2.9
大约 5 小时 about 5 hours	4	1.1
大约 6 小时 about 6 hours	1	0.3
大约 7 小时 about 7 hours	1	0.3
大约 8 小时 about 8 hours	3	0.9
大约 9 小时 about 9 hours	1	0.3
大约 10 小时或以上 about 10 hours or over	2	0.6
记不清/不知道 can't remember	12	3.4
没有收听 didn't listen	53	15.1

n=350

2-3 经常收听的广播频道排名/ Ranking of the Most Favorite Radio Channels

注：本题为多选题，合计百分比超过 100%（Multiple answers）

排名 Brand Ranking	频道 Channels	人次 Person-time	百分比 Percent
1	广东音乐台 Guangdong Music Channel	148	42.3
2	珠江经济台 Zhujiang Economy Channel	141	40.3
3	城市之声台 The Voice of City Channel	140	40.0
4	广州一台 Guangzhou 1st Radio	115	32.9
5	广州二台 Guangzhou 2nd Radio	90	25.7
6	佛山台 Foshan Radio	81	23.1
7	羊城交通台 Yangcheng Traffic Channel	71	20.3
8	健康之声台 Health Service Channel	30	8.6
9	中央人民广播电台 China National Radio (CNR)	27	7.7
10	广东卫星广播（新闻台）Guangdong Satellite Broadcasting Channel	20	5.7
11	股市台 Stock Channel	15	4.3
12	英语台 English Channel	7	2.0
13	儿童台 Children Channel	5	1.4
14	VOA	3	0.9

n=350

2-4 样本、男性各年龄层、女性各年龄层经常收听的广播频道/ The Most Favorite Radio Channels by the Whole Sample, Age and Gender Groups

注：本题为多选题，合计百分比超过 100%（Multiple answers）

	人数 Number	广东音乐台 Guangdong Music Channel	珠江经济台 Zhujiang Economy Channel	城市之声台 The Voice of City Channel	广州一台 Guangzhou 1st Radio	广州二台 Guangzhou 2nd Radio	佛山台 Foshan Radio	羊城交通台 Yangcheng Traffic Channel
样本 Sample	350	42.3	40.3	40.0	32.9	25.7	23.1	20.3
男性 Male	171	45.0	43.9	36.3	28.1	25.7	19.9	25.1
16~24 岁 Age	37	51.4	21.6	45.9	35.1	37.8	13.5	16.2
25~34 岁 Age	56	44.6	51.8	46.4	17.9	30.4	25.0	33.9
35~44 岁 Age	38	42.1	55.3	18.4	36.8	21.1	21.1	31.6
45~54 岁 Age	29	41.4	44.8	27.6	31.0	17.2	20.7	13.8
55~60 岁 Age	11	45.5	36.4	36.4	18.2	0.0	9.1	18.2
女性 Female	179	39.7	36.9	43.6	37.4	25.7	26.3	15.6
16~24 岁 Age	57	56.1	19.3	75.4	33.3	29.8	33.3	7.0
25~34 岁 Age	43	34.9	39.5	34.9	34.9	16.3	37.2	34.9
35~44 岁 Age	44	27.3	50.0	22.7	43.2	27.3	13.6	11.4
45~54 岁 Age	26	34.6	42.3	38.5	38.5	30.8	15.4	11.5
55~60 岁 Age	9	33.3	55.6	0.0	44.4	22.2	22.2	11.1

续前表 continued

	人数 Number	健康之声台 Health Service Channel	中央人民广播电台 China National Radio (CNR)	广东卫星广播（新闻台）Guangdong Satellite Broadcasting Channel	股市台 Stock Channel	英语台 English Channel	儿童台 Children Channel	VOA
样本 Sample	350	8.6	7.7	5.7	4.3	2.0	1.4	0.9
男性 Male	171	7.0	7.6	6.4	7.6	1.2	0.6	1.2
16~24 岁 Age	37	5.4	5.4	8.1	2.7	2.7	2.7	2.7
25~34 岁 Age	56	0.0	3.6	5.4	5.4	1.8	0.0	1.8
35~44 岁 Age	38	10.5	5.3	2.6	7.9	0.0	0.0	0.0
45~54 岁 Age	29	6.9	17.2	10.3	10.3	0.0	0.0	0.0
55~60 岁 Age	11	36.4	18.2	9.1	27.3	0.0	0.0	0.0
女性 Female	179	10.1	7.8	5.0	1.1	2.8	2.2	0.6
16~24 岁 Age	57	8.8	5.3	3.5	1.8	5.3	0.0	1.8
25~34 岁 Age	43	7.0	7.0	4.7	0.0	0.0	2.3	0.0
35~44 岁 Age	44	6.8	11.4	9.1	2.3	0.0	2.3	0.0
45~54 岁 Age	26	15.4	7.7	0.0	0.0	7.7	7.7	0.0
55~60 岁 Age	9	33.3	11.1	11.1	0.0	0.0	0.0	0.0

2-5 经常收听的广播电台/ The Most Favorite Radio Channels

2-5-1 经常收听的广播电台（周一到周四）/ Ranking of the Most Favorite Radio Channels (Monday—Thursday)

注：本题为多选题，合计百分比超过 100%（Multiple answers）

排名 Brand Ranking	频道 Channels	人次 Person-time	百分比 Percent
1	广东音乐台 Guangdong Music Channel	124	35.7
2	珠江经济台 Zhujiang Economy Channel	111	32.0
3	广州一台 Guangzhou 1st Radio	100	28.8
4	城市之声台 The Voice of City Channel	94	27.1
5	佛山台 Foshan Radio	84	24.2
5	广州二台 Guangzhou 2nd Radio	84	24.2
6	羊城交通台 Yangcheng Traffic Channel	76	21.9
7	健康之声台 Health Service Channel	34	9.8
8	中央人民广播电台 China National Radio (CNR)	24	6.9
8	广东卫星广播（新闻台）Guangdong Satellite Broadcasting Channel	24	6.9
9	股市台 Stock Channel	13	3.7

n=347

2-5-2 经常收听的广播电台（周五）/ Ranking of the Most Favorite Radio Channels (Friday)

注：本题为多选题，合计百分比超过 100%（Multiple answers）

排名 Brand Ranking	频道 Channels	人次 Person-time	百分比 Percent
1	广东音乐台 Guangdong Music Channel	120	35.1
2	珠江经济台 Zhujiang Economy Channel	106	31.0
3	广州一台 Guangzhou 1st Radio	100	29.2
4	城市之声台 The Voice of City Channel	88	25.7
5	广州二台 Guangzhou 2nd Radio	81	23.7
6	佛山台 Foshan Radio	73	21.3
7	羊城交通台 Yangcheng Traffic Channel	70	20.5
8	健康之声台 Health Service Channel	32	9.4
9	中央人民广播电台 China National Radio (CNR)	22	6.4
10	广东卫星广播（新闻台）Guangdong Satellite Broadcasting Channel	18	5.3
11	股市台 Stock Channel	10	2.9

n=342

2-5-3 经常收听的广播电台（周六）/ Ranking of the Most Favorite Radio Channels (Saturday)

注：本题为多选题，合计百分比超过 100%（Multiple answers）

排名 Brand Ranking	频道 Channels	人次 Person-time	百分比 Percent
1	广东音乐台 Guangdong Music Channel	124	36.3
2	广州一台 Guangzhou 1st Radio	91	26.6
2	珠江经济台 Zhujiang Economy Channel	91	26.6
3	城市之声台 The Voice of City Channel	88	25.7
4	广州二台 Guangzhou 2nd Radio	71	20.8
5	佛山台 Foshan Radio	67	19.6
6	羊城交通台 Yangcheng Traffic Channel	66	19.3
7	健康之声台 Health Service Channel	35	10.2
8	中央人民广播电台 China National Radio (CNR)	21	6.1
9	广东卫星广播（新闻台）Guangdong Satellite Broadcasting Channel	18	5.3
10	股市台 Stock Channel	11	3.2

n=342

2-5-4 经常收听的广播电台（周日）/ Ranking of the Most Favorite Radio Channels (Sunday)

注：本题为多选题，合计百分比超过 100%（Multiple answers）

排名 Brand Ranking	频道 Channels	人次 Person-time	百分比 Percent
1	广东音乐台 Guangdong Music Channel	117	34.1
2	珠江经济台 Zhujiang Economy Channel	92	26.8
3	广州一台 Guangzhou 1st Radio	91	26.5
4	城市之声台 The Voice of City Channel	83	24.2
5	广州二台 Guangzhou 2nd Radio	80	23.3
6	佛山台 Foshan Radio	68	19.8
7	羊城交通台 Yangcheng Traffic Channel	62	18.1
8	健康之声台 Health Service Channel	36	10.5
9	中央人民广播电台 China National Radio (CNR)	20	5.8
10	广东卫星广播（新闻台）Guangdong Satellite Broadcasting Channel	16	4.7
11	股市台 Stock Channel	10	2.9

n=343

2-6 经常收听的广播节目/ Ranking of the Most Favorite Radio Programs

注：本题为多选题，合计百分比超过 100%（Multiple answers）

排名 Ranking	广播节目 Radio Programs	人次 Person-time	百分比 Percent
1	港台流行音乐 HK .Taiwan pop music	179	52.5
2	国内新闻 national news	165	48.4
3	国际新闻 international news	123	36.1
4	国内流行音乐 inland pop music	80	23.5
5	天气预报 weather forecast	75	22.0
6	欧美流行音乐 Europe pop music	64	18.8
7	体育节目 sports	49	14.4
8	热点话题评说 hot topic	48	14.1
9	医疗保健 medicare care	41	12.0
10	交通信息 transportation report	34	10.0
11	古典音乐欣赏 classic music	32	9.4
12	股市信息 stock information	31	9.1
13	曲艺相声 folk arts	30	8.8
14	广播剧 radio play	29	8.5
14	经济信息 economic information report	29	8.5
15	戏曲节目 traditional opera	27	7.9
16	点播节目 call-in program	22	6.5
17	有奖问答 contest	18	5.3
18	评书 storytelling	15	4.4
19	外语教学 foreign languages teaching	14	4.1
20	其他 others	13	3.8
21	教育节目 educational news	12	3.5
22	少儿节目 children's program	7	2.1

n=341

2-7 样本、男性各年龄层、女性各年龄层经常收听的广播节目/ The Most Favorite Radio Programs by the Whole Sample, Age and Gender Groups

注：本题为多选题，合计百分比超过 100%（Multiple answers）

	人数 Number	国内新闻 national news	国际新闻 international news	天气预报 weather forecast	经济信息 economic information report	交通信息 transportation report	教育节目 educational program
样本 Sample	341	48.4	36.1	22.0	8.5	10.0	3.5
男性 Male	167	55.1	40.1	20.4	10.2	12.6	3.0
16~24 岁 Age	36	38.9	33.3	16.7	0.0	5.6	0.0
25~34 岁 Age	56	53.6	33.9	16.1	12.5	16.1	3.6
35~44 岁 Age	36	61.1	41.7	27.8	8.3	22.2	0.0
45~54 岁 Age	28	71.4	50.0	10.7	21.4	7.1	10.7
55~60 岁 Age	11	54.5	63.6	54.5	9.1	0.0	0.0
女性 Female	174	42.0	32.2	23.6	6.9	7.5	4.0
16~24 岁 Age	52	28.8	19.2	19.2	1.9	3.8	5.8
25~34 岁 Age	43	55.8	44.2	30.2	7.0	11.6	2.3
35~44 岁 Age	43	48.8	46.5	18.6	14.0	11.6	7.0
45~54 岁 Age	27	44.4	25.9	25.9	7.4	3.7	0.0
55~60 岁 Age	9	11.1	0.0	33.3	0.0	0.0	0.0

续前表 continued

	人数 Number	热点话题评说 hot topics	外语教学 foreign languages teaching	广播剧 radio play	古典音乐欣赏 classic music	欧美流行音乐 Europe & America pop music	港台流行音乐 HK. Taiwan pop music
样本 Sample	341	14.1	4.1	8.5	9.4	18.8	52.5
男性 Male	167	13.8	2.4	5.4	7.8	21.6	53.9
16~24 岁 Age	36	16.7	11.1	2.8	16.7	27.8	80.6
25~34 岁 Age	56	16.1	0.0	3.6	1.8	26.8	62.5
35~44 岁 Age	36	11.1	0.0	13.9	5.6	11.1	41.7
45~54 岁 Age	28	14.3	0.0	3.6	10.7	25.0	35.7
55~60 岁 Age	11	0.0	0.0	0.0	9.1	0.0	9.1
女性 Female	174	14.4	5.7	11.5	10.9	16.1	51.1
16~24 岁 Age	52	21.2	13.5	13.5	13.5	42.3	80.8
25~34 岁 Age	43	14.0	2.3	7.0	11.6	7.0	55.8
35~44 岁 Age	43	14.0	0.0	11.6	9.3	2.3	34.9
45~54 岁 Age	27	7.4	7.4	14.8	11.1	3.7	22.2
55~60 岁 Age	9	0.0	0.0	11.1	0.0	11.1	22.2

续前表 continued

	人数 Number	国内流行音乐 inland pop music	戏曲节目 traditional opera	曲艺相声 folk arts	评书 storytelling	医疗保健 medicare
样本 Sample	341	23.5	7.9	8.8	4.4	12.0
男性 Male	167	21.6	7.2	11.4	4.8	7.2
16~24 岁 Age	36	8.3	5.6	2.8	5.6	8.3
25~34 岁 Age	56	25.0	0.0	10.7	1.8	5.4
35~44 岁 Age	36	36.1	5.6	11.1	5.6	13.9
45~54 岁 Age	28	17.9	3.6	14.3	10.7	0.0
55~60 岁 Age	11	9.1	63.6	36.4	0.0	9.1
女性 Female	174	25.3	8.6	6.3	4.0	16.7
16~24 岁 Age	52	21.2	0.0	1.9	0.0	5.8
25~34 岁 Age	43	37.2	4.7	4.7	2.3	11.6
35~44 岁 Age	43	20.9	2.3	11.6	4.7	30.2
45~54 岁 Age	27	18.5	29.6	11.1	11.1	18.5
55~60 岁 Age	9	33.3	44.4	0.0	11.1	33.3

续前表 continued

	人数 Number	点播节目 call-in program	少儿节目 children's program	体育节目 sports	有奖问答 contest	其他 others
样本 Sample	341	6.5	2.1	14.4	5.3	9.1
男性 Male	167	3.6	1.2	20.4	4.8	14.4
16~24 岁 Age	36	8.3	2.8	38.9	8.3	5.6
25~34 岁 Age	56	5.4	0.0	21.4	7.1	14.3
35~44 岁 Age	36	0.0	0.0	11.1	0.0	8.3
45~54 岁 Age	28	0.0	3.6	14.3	3.6	28.6
55~60 岁 Age	11	0.0	0.0	0.0	0.0	27.3
女性 Female	174	9.2	2.9	8.6	5.7	4.0
16~24 岁 Age	52	13.5	0.0	15.4	5.8	1.9
25~34 岁 Age	43	7.0	7.0	7.0	4.7	4.7
35~44 岁 Age	43	7.0	4.7	4.7	7.0	7.0
45~54 岁 Age	27	7.4	0.0	7.4	7.4	3.7
55~60 岁 Age	9	11.1	0.0	0.0	0.0	0.0

2-8 不同学历的听众收听的广播节目的偏好/ Program Preference by Educational Levels

注：本题为多选题，合计百分比超过 100%（Multiple answers）

	人数 Number	国内新闻 national news	国际新闻 international news	天气预报 weather forecast	经济信息 economic information report	交通信息 transportation report	教育节目 educational program
样本 Sample	**339**	**48.4**	**36.3**	**22.1**	**8.3**	**10.0**	**3.5**
小学及以下 Primary School or Below	17	41.2	35.3	35.3	5.9	0.0	0.0
初中 Middle School	73	50.7	35.6	32.9	5.5	11.0	4.1
高中/中专/技校 High School/Technical Secondary School	163	46.0	33.7	16.6	9.2	13.5	3.7
大学专科 2-3 Year College	48	56.3	43.8	22.9	12.5	8.3	4.2
大学本科 4-5 Year College	37	45.9	40.5	18.9	5.4	0.0	2.7
研究生或以上 Graduate or Above	1	100.0	0.0	0.0	0.0	0.0	0.0

续前表 continued

	人数 Number	热点话题评说 hot topics	外语教学 foreign languages teaching	广播剧 radio play	古典音乐欣赏 classic music	欧美流行音乐 Europe & America pop music	港台流行音乐 HK. Taiwan pop music
样本 Sample	**339**	**13.9**	**4.1**	**8.6**	**9.4**	**18.9**	**52.5**
小学及以下 Primary School or Below	17	0.0	5.9	5.9	5.9	0.0	17.6
初中 Middle School	73	11.0	1.4	5.5	5.5	11.0	49.3
高中/中专/技校 High School/Technical Secondary School	163	14.7	4.9	12.3	10.4	17.8	57.1
大学专科 2-3 Year College	48	16.7	4.2	4.2	10.4	22.9	50.0
大学本科 4-5 Year College	37	18.9	5.4	5.4	13.5	43.2	59.5
研究生或以上 Graduate or Above	1	0.0	0.0	0.0	0.0	0.0	0.0

续前表 continued

	人数 Number	国内流行音乐 inland pop music	戏曲节目 traditional opera	曲艺相声 folk arts	评书 storytelling	医疗保健 medicare
样本 Sample	**339**	**23.6**	**7.7**	**8.6**	**4.4**	**11.8**
小学及以下 Primary School or Below	17	23.5	52.9	17.6	0.0	23.5
初中 Middle School	73	26.0	12.3	9.6	5.5	13.7
高中/中专/技校 High School/Technical Secondary School	163	24.5	3.7	9.2	4.3	12.3
大学专科 2-3 Year College	48	20.8	2.1	6.3	8.3	8.3
大学本科 4-5 Year College	37	18.9	2.7	2.7	0.0	5.4
研究生或以上 Graduate or Above	1	0.0	0.0	0.0	0.0	0.0

续前表 continued

	人数 Number	点播节目 call-in program	少儿节目 children's program	体育节目 sports	有奖问答 contest	其他 others
样本 Sample	339	6.5	2.1	14.5	5.3	9.1
小学及以下 Primary School or Below	17	11.8	0.0	0.0	11.8	11.8
初中 Middle School	73	4.1	4.1	4.1	5.5	6.8
高中/中专/技校 High School/Technical Secondary School	163	6.7	2.5	16.6	5.5	9.2
大学专科 2-3 Year College	48	8.3	0.0	22.9	6.3	14.6
大学本科 4-5 Year College	37	5.4	0.0	21.6	0.0	5.4
研究生或以上 Graduate or Above	1	0.0	0.0	0.0	0.0	0.0

2-9 经常收听广播时段/ Weekday Times Slots of Radio Listening

注：本题为多选题，合计百分比超过 100%（Multiple answers）

时间段 times slots	周一到周四(%) (Monday—Thursday)	周五(%) (Friday)	周六(%) (Saturday)	周日(%) (Sunday)
样本量 Sample	n=350	n=347	n=348	n=349
0:00-0:30	2.0	2.0	2.0	2.0
0:30-1:00	1.1	1.2	1.4	2.0
1:00-1:30	1.4	1.2	1.1	1.4
1:30-2:00	0.9	0.9	0.6	0.6
2:00-2:30	0.6	0.6	0.6	0.6
2:30-3:00	0.6	0.6	0.6	0.6
3:00-3:30	0.0	0.0	0.0	0.3
3:30-4:00	0.3	0.0	0.0	0.0
4:00-4:30	0.3	0.6	0.9	0.9
4:30-5:00	0.6	0.6	0.6	0.6
5:00-5:30	0.9	1.2	1.1	0.9
5:30-6:00	1.1	1.2	1.1	1.1
6:00-6:30	4.0	3.5	3.2	3.4
6:30-7:00	10.3	9.2	6.3	5.7
7:00-7:30	14.3	14.1	11.8	11.2
7:30-8:00	12.3	11.8	11.2	10.9
8:00-8:30	11.4	11.0	10.6	10.9
8:30-9:00	8.6	8.9	8.6	8.3
9:00-9:30	8.0	8.1	8.6	8.6
9:30-10:00	8.3	8.6	9.5	10.0
10:00-10:30	8.3	7.8	7.8	7.7
10:30-11:00	7.7	7.2	7.5	6.9
11:00-11:30	6.9	6.3	6.9	6.9
11:30-12:00	8.6	8.4	8.0	8.0
12:00-12:30	18.6	18.7	19.0	18.6
12:30-13:00	17.1	16.7	15.5	14.0
13:00-13:30	10.9	11.5	8.6	9.2
13:30-14:00	6.9	6.3	5.7	6.0
14:00-14:30	6.9	7.2	6.0	5.7
14:30-15:00	7.7	7.8	6.9	6.6
15:00-15:30	7.1	6.9	6.6	6.6
15:30-16:00	7.7	6.9	6.9	7.4
16:00-16:30	9.1	8.1	8.9	9.2
16:30-17:00	8.6	8.9	8.3	8.3
17:00-17:30	6.6	7.2	7.5	7.4
17:30-18:00	5.7	5.8	7.2	7.2
18:00-18:30	15.1	14.4	14.7	14.0
18:30-19:00	14.9	15.3	15.5	15.5
19:00-19:30	9.1	8.1	6.0	5.4
19:30-20:00	7.4	6.9	4.9	5.4
20:00-20:30	8.0	7.2	6.3	6.0
20:30-21:00	7.1	6.3	5.2	5.2
21:00-21:30	7.1	6.9	4.9	4.9
21:30-22:00	6.9	6.9	5.5	5.7
22:00-22:30	6.9	8.1	8.3	8.0
22:30-23:00	6.9	7.5	6.3	6.6
23:00-23:30	7.4	6.6	7.2	6.9
23:30-24:00	5.4	6.3	6.6	6.0

2-10 样本、男性各年龄层、女性各年龄层是否打过热线电话参与节目/ Call-in Hot-time Telephone to Take Part in the Program by the Whole Sample, Age and Gender Groups

	人数 Number	打过 yes	没打过 no
样本 Sample	345	2.9	97.1
男性 Male	169	2.4	97.6
16~24 岁 Age	35	0.0	100.0
25~34 岁 Age	56	7.1	92.9
35~44 岁 Age	39	0.0	100.0
45~54 岁 Age	29	0.0	100.0
55~60 岁 Age	10	0.0	100.0
女性 Female	176	3.4	96.6
16~24 岁 Age	54	7.4	92.6
25~34 岁 Age	43	0.0	100.0
35~44 岁 Age	42	2.4	97.6
45~54 岁 Age	28	3.6	96.4
55~60 岁 Age	9	0.0	100.0

2-11 不同消费者层平时是否接触广播媒介/ Radio Exposure by Market Segments

2-11-1 时尚流行指标/ Fads Popular Index

	人数 Number	从来不听 never	收听 yes
样本 Sample	1019	65.3	34.7
平实生活指向 simple living orientation	518	66.2	33.8
时尚流行指向 fashion orientation	501	64.3	35.7

2-11-2 广告态度指标/ Advertising Attitude Index

	人数 Number	从来不听 never	收听 yes
样本 Sample	1019	65.3	34.7
广告淡漠指向 indifferent orientation	334	65.9	34.1
中间层 medium	591	63.5	36.5
信赖广告指向 loyal orientation	94	74.5	25.5

2-12 不同消费者层收听广播频道的偏好/ Channel Preference by Market Segments

2-12-1 时尚流行指标/ Fads Popular Index

注：本题为多选题，合计百分比超过 100%（Multiple answers）

	人数 Number	广东音乐台 Guangdong Music Channel	珠江经济台 Zhujiang Economy Channel	城市之声台 The Voice of City Channel	广州一台 Guangzhou 1st Radio	广州二台 Guangzhou 2nd Radio	佛山台 Foshan Radio	羊城交通台 Yangcheng Traffic Channel
样本 Sample	347	42.7	39.8	40.1	33.1	25.6	23.1	20.2
平实生活指向 simple living orientation	171	41.5	44.4	31.6	29.2	22.8	22.8	25.7
时尚流行指向 fashion orientation	176	43.8	35.2	48.3	36.9	28.4	23.3	14.8

续前表 continued

	人数 Number	健康之声台 Health Service Channel	中央人民广播电台 China National Radio (CNR)	广东卫星广播（新闻台） Guangdong Satellite Broadcasting Channel	股市台 Stock Channel	英语台 English Channel	儿童台 Children Channel	VOA
样本 Sample	347	8.4	7.8	5.8	15	2.0	1.4	0.9
平实生活指向 simple living orientation	171	9.4	5.8	7.6	7	1.2	1.2	0.6
时尚流行指向 fashion orientation	176	7.4	9.7	4.0	8	2.8	1.7	1.1

2-12-2 广告态度指标/ Advertising Attitude Index

注：本题为多选题，合计百分比超过 100%（Multiple answers）

	人数 Number	广东音乐台 Guangdong Music Channel	珠江经济台 Zhujiang Economy Channel	城市之声台 The Voice of City Channel	广州一台 Guangzhou 1st Radio	广州二台 Guangzhou 2nd Radio	佛山台 Foshan Radio	羊城交通台 Yangcheng Traffic Channel
样本 Sample	347	42.4	40.1	39.8	32.9	25.9	23.3	19.9
广告淡漠指向 indifferent orientation	111	45.0	37.8	31.5	21.6	25.2	25.2	23.4
中间层 medium	212	39.6	41.5	43.9	38.2	26.9	22.2	18.4
信赖广告指向 loyal orientation	24	54.2	37.5	41.7	37.5	20.8	25.0	16.7

续前表 continued

	人数 Number	健康之声台 Health Service Channel	中央人民广播电台 China National Radio (CNR)	广东卫星广播（新闻台） Guangdong Satellite Broadcasting Channel	股市台 Stock Channel	英语台 English Channel	儿童台 Children Channel	VOA
样本 Sample	347	8.6	7.5	5.8	4.3	2.0	1.4	0.9
广告淡漠指向 indifferent orientation	111	9.0	9.9	7.2	1.8	3.6	2.7	0.0
中间层 medium	212	7.5	6.6	5.2	5.7	1.4	0.9	1.4
信赖广告指向 loyal orientation	24	16.7	4.2	4.2	4.2	0.0	0.0	0.0

2-13 不同消费者层收看广播节目的偏好/ Program Preference by Market Segments

2-13-1 时尚流行指标/ Fads Popular Index

注：本题为多选题，合计百分比超过 100%（Multiple answers）

	人数 Number	国内新闻 national news	国际新闻 international news	天气预报 weather forecast	经济信息 economic information	交通信息 transportation report	教育节目 educational program
样本 Sample	338	48.2	35.8	22.2	8.6	9.8	3.6
平实生活指向 simple living orientation	167	47.9	35.9	20.4	11.4	13.2	2.4
时尚流行指向 fashion orientation	171	48.5	35.7	24.0	5.8	6.4	4.7

续前表 continued

	人数 Number	热点话题评说 hot topics	外语教学 foreign languages teaching	广播剧 radio play	古典音乐欣赏 classic music	欧美流行音乐 Europe & America pop music	港台流行音乐 HK. Taiwan pop music
样本 Sample	338	13.9	4.1	8.6	9.2	18.9	52.7
平实生活指向 simple living orientation	167	16.8	3.0	7.8	12.0	13.8	44.3
时尚流行指向 fashion orientation	171	11.1	5.3	9.4	6.4	24.0	60.8

续前表 continued

	人数 Number	国内流行音乐 inland pop music	戏曲节目 traditional opera	曲艺相声 folk art	评书 storytelling	医疗保健 medicare
样本 Sample	338	23.7	8.0	8.9	4.4	11.8
平实生活指向 simple living orientation	167	25.7	7.8	10.2	7.2	13.2
时尚流行指向 fashion orientation	171	21.6	8.2	7.6	1.8	10.5

续前表 continued

	人数 Number	点播节目 call-in program	少儿节目 children's program	体育节目 sports	有奖问答 contest	其他 others
样本 Sample	338	6.5	2.1	14.5	5.3	8.9
平实生活指向 simple living orientation	167	4.2	1.8	8.4	4.2	11.4
时尚流行指向 fashion orientation	171	8.8	2.3	20.5	6.4	6.4

2-13-2 广告态度指标/ Advertising Attitude Index

注：本题为多选题，合计百分比超过 100%（Multiple answers）

	人数 Number	国内新闻 national news	国际新闻 international news	天气预报 weather forecast	经济信息 economic information	交通信息 transportation report	教育节目 educational program
样本 Sample	338	47.9	36.1	22.2	8.3	10.1	3.3
广告淡漠指向 indifferent orientation	107	53.3	37.4	24.3	9.3	10.3	4.7
中间层 medium	207	43.0	35.7	20.8	7.2	10.1	2.9
信赖广告指向 loyal orientation	24	66.7	33.3	25.0	12.5	8.3	0.0

续前表 continued

	人数 Number	热点话题评说 hot topics	外语教学 foreign languages teaching	广播剧 radio play	古典音乐欣赏 classic music	欧美流行音乐 Europe & America pop music	港台流行音乐 HK .Taiwan pop music
样本 Sample	338	13.9	4.1	8.6	9.5	18.9	52.7
广告淡漠指向 indifferent orientation	107	11.2	3.7	5.6	11.2	16.8	51.4
中间层 medium	207	15.0	4.8	10.6	8.7	20.3	52.2
信赖广告指向 loyal orientation	24	16.7	0.0	4.2	8.3	16.7	62.5

续前表 continued

	人数 Number	国内流行音乐 inland pop music	戏曲节目 traditional opera	曲艺相声 folk art	评书 storytelling	医疗保健 medicare
样本 Sample	338	23.4	8.0	8.6	4.4	12.1
广告淡漠指向 indifferent orientation	107	29.9	8.4	8.4	3.7	14.0
中间层 medium	207	18.8	7.2	7.7	5.3	10.1
信赖广告指向 loyal orientation	24	33.3	12.5	16.7	0.0	20.8

续前表 continued

	人数 Number	点播节目 call-in program	少儿节目 children's program	体育节目 sports	有奖问答 contest	其他 others
样本 Sample	338	6.5	2.1	14.2	5.0	9.2
广告淡漠指向 indifferent orientation	107	5.6	2.8	11.2	6.5	6.5
中间层 medium	207	7.2	1.9	16.9	4.8	10.1
信赖广告指向 loyal orientation	24	4.2	0.0	4.2	0.0	12.5

● 重庆 / Chongqing

2-1 样本、男性各年龄层、女性各年龄层平时是否接触广播媒介/ Radio Listening by the Whole Sample, Age and Gender Groups

	人数 Number	从来不听 never	收听 yes
样本 Sample	623	84.4	15.6
男性 Male	313	86.6	13.4
16~24 岁 Age	64	84.4	15.6
25~34 岁 Age	93	88.2	11.8
35~44 岁 Age	75	85.3	14.7
45~54 岁 Age	54	87.0	13.0
55~60 岁 Age	27	88.9	11.1
女性 Female	310	82.3	17.7
16~24 岁 Age	64	65.6	34.4
25~34 岁 Age	90	85.6	14.4
35~44 岁 Age	73	86.3	13.7
45~54 岁 Age	60	88.3	11.7
55~60 岁 Age	23	87.0	13.0

2-2 一周内不同时间收听广播的时间长短/ The Average Time Spending on Listening Radio Per Day

2-2-1 一周内不同时间收听广播的时间长短（周一到周四）/ The Average Time Spending on Listening Radio Per Day (Monday—Thursday)

	人数 Number	百分比 Percent
大约半小时或以下 about 1/2 hour or below	35	37.6
大约 1 小时 about 1 hour	34	36.6
大约 2 小时 about 2 hours	12	12.9
大约 3 小时 about 3 hours	2	2.2
大约 4 小时 about 4 hours	1	1.1
大约 5 小时 about 5 hours	0	0.0
大约 6 小时 about 6 hours	0	0.0
大约 7 小时 about 7 hours	0	0.0
大约 8 小时 about 8 hours	0	0.0
大约 9 小时 about 9 hours	0	0.0
大约 10 小时或以上 about 10 hours or over	0	0.0
记不清/不知道 can't remember	6	6.5
没有收听 didn't listen	3	3.2

n=93

2-2-2 一周内不同时间收听广播的时间长短（周五）/ The Average Time Spending on Listening Radio Per Day (Friday)

	人数 Number	百分比 Percent
大约半小时或以下 about 1/2 hour or below	32	35.2
大约 1 小时 about 1 hour	31	34.1
大约 2 小时 about 2 hours	11	12.1
大约 3 小时 about 3 hours	0	0.0
大约 4 小时 about 4 hours	3	3.3
大约 5 小时 about 5 hours	0	0.0
大约 6 小时 about 6 hours	0	0.0
大约 7 小时 about 7 hours	0	0.0
大约 8 小时 about 8 hours	0	0.0
大约 9 小时 about 9 hours	0	0.0
大约 10 小时或以上 about 10 hours or over	0	0.0
记不清/不知道 can't remember	6	6.6
没有收听 didn't listen	8	8.8

n=91

2-2-3 一周内不同时间收听广播的时间长短（周六）/ The Average Time Spending on Listening Radio Per Day (Saturday)

	人数 Number	百分比 Percent
大约半小时或以下 about 1/2 hour or below	26	29.2
大约 1 小时 about 1 hour	30	33.7
大约 2 小时 about 2 hours	11	12.4
大约 3 小时 about 3 hours	1	1.1
大约 4 小时 about 4 hours	2	2.2
大约 5 小时 about 5 hours	0	0.0
大约 6 小时 about 6 hours	0	0.0
大约 7 小时 about 7 hours	0	0.0
大约 8 小时 about 8 hours	0	0.0
大约 9 小时 about 9 hours	0	0.0
大约 10 小时或以上 about 10 hours or over	0	0.0
记不清/不知道 can't remember	6	6.7
没有收听 didn't listen	13	14.6

n=89

2-2-4 一周内不同时间收听广播的时间长短（周日）/ The Average Time Spending on Listening Radio Per Day (Sunday)

	人数 Number	百分比 Percent
大约半小时或以下 about 1/2 hour or below	28	31.5
大约 1 小时 about 1 hour	26	29.2
大约 2 小时 about 2 hours	13	14.6
大约 3 小时 about 3 hours	0	0.0
大约 4 小时 about 4 hours	4	4.5
大约 5 小时 about 5 hours	0	0.0
大约 6 小时 about 6 hours	0	0.0
大约 7 小时 about 7 hours	0	0.0
大约 8 小时 about 8 hours	0	0.0
大约 9 小时 about 9 hours	0	0.0
大约 10 小时或以上 about 10 hours or over	0	0.0
记不清/不知道 can't remember	4	4.5
没有收听 didn't listen	14	15.7

n=89

2-3 经常收听的广播频道排名/ Ranking of the Most Favorite Radio Channels

注：本题为多选题，合计百分比超过 100%（Multiple answers）

排名 Brand Ranking	频道 Channels	人次 Person-time	百分比 Percent
1	重庆经济广播电台 Chongqing Economic Radio	83	87.4
2	重庆人民广播电台 Chongqing People's Radio	58	61.1
3	重庆商业广播电台 Chongqing Business Channel	57	60.0
4	中央人民广播电台 China National Radio (CNR)	33	34.7
5	重庆教育广播电台 Chongqing Education Channel	12	12.6
6	中国国际广播电台 China Radio International (CRI)	3	3.2
7	BBC	2	2.1
7	VOA	2	2.1

n=95

2-4 样本、男性各年龄层、女性各年龄层经常收听的广播频道/ The Most Favorite Radio Channels by the Whole Sample, Age and Gender Groups

注：本题为多选题，合计百分比超过 100%（Multiple answers）

	人数 Number	重庆经济广播电台 Chongqing Economic Radio	重庆人民广播电台 Chongqing People's Radio	重庆商业广播电台 Chongqing Business Channel	中央人民广播电台 China National Radio (CNR)
样本 Sample	95	87.4	61.1	60.0	34.7
男性 Male	42	83.3	61.9	57.1	35.7
16~24 岁 Age	10	60.0	60.0	50.0	30.0
25~34 岁 Age	11	100.0	45.5	54.5	36.4
35~44 岁 Age	11	81.8	72.7	72.7	18.2
45~54 岁 Age	7	85.7	85.7	57.1	57.1
55~60 岁 Age	3	100.0	33.3	33.3	66.7
女性 Female	53	90.6	60.4	62.3	34.0
16~24 岁 Age	22	77.3	68.2	68.2	27.3
25~34 岁 Age	13	100.0	69.2	69.2	23.1
35~44 岁 Age	10	100.0	40.0	50.0	40.0
45~54 岁 Age	6	100.0	33.3	50.0	66.7
55~60 岁 Age	2	100.0	100.0	50.0	50.0

续前表 continued

	人数 Number	重庆教育广播电台 Chongqing Education Channel	中国国际广播电台 China Radio International (CRI)	BBC	VOA
样本 Sample	95	12.6	3.2	2.1	2.1
男性 Male	42	11.9	0.0	4.8	4.8
16~24 岁 Age	10	30.0	0.0	20.0	10.0
25~34 岁 Age	11	9.1	0.0	0.0	9.1
35~44 岁 Age	11	9.1	0.0	0.0	0.0
45~54 岁 Age	7	0.0	0.0	0.0	0.0
55~60 岁 Age	3	0.0	0.0	0.0	0.0
女性 Female	53	13.2	5.7	0.0	0.0
16~24 岁 Age	22	18.2	9.1	0.0	0.0
25~34 岁 Age	13	15.4	7.7	0.0	0.0
35~44 岁 Age	10	0.0	0.0	0.0	0.0
45~54 岁 Age	6	16.7	0.0	0.0	0.0
55~60 岁 Age	2	0.0	0.0	0.0	0.0

2-5 经常收听的广播电台/ The Most Favorite Radio Channels

2-5-1 经常收听的广播电台（周一到周四）/ Ranking of the Most Favorite Radio Channels (Monday—Thursday)

注：本题为多选题，合计百分比超过 100%（Multiple answers）

排名 Brand Ranking	频道 Channels	人次 Person-time	百分比 Percent
1	重庆经济广播电台 Chongqing Economic Radio	65	70.7
2	重庆人民广播电台 Chongqing People's Radio	46	50.0
2	重庆商业广播电台 Chongqing Business Channel	46	50.0
3	中央人民广播电台 China National Radio (CNR)	30	32.6
4	重庆教育广播电台 Chongqing Education Channel	8	8.7
5	BBC	2	2.2
5	VOA	2	2.2
5	中国国际广播电台 China Radio International (CRI)	2	2.2

n=92

2-5-2 经常收听的广播电台（周五）/ Ranking of the Most Favorite Radio Channels (Friday)

注：本题为多选题，合计百分比超过 100%（Multiple answers）

排名 Brand Ranking	频道 Channels	人次 Person-time	百分比 Percent
1	重庆经济广播电台 Chongqing Economic Radio	62	68.1
2	重庆商业广播电台 Chongqing Business Channel	42	46.2
3	重庆人民广播电台 Chongqing People's Radio	41	45.1
4	中央人民广播电台 China National Radio (CNR)	25	27.5
5	重庆教育广播电台 Chongqing Education Channel	7	7.7
6	中国国际广播电台 China Radio International (CRI)	2	2.2

n=91

2-5-3 经常收听的广播电台（周六）/ Ranking of the Most Favorite Radio Channels (Saturday)

注：本题为多选题，合计百分比超过 100%（Multiple answers）

排名 Brand Ranking	频道 Channels	人次 Person-time	百分比 Percent
1	重庆经济广播电台 Chongqing Economic Radio	51	58.6
2	重庆人民广播电台 Chongqing People's Radio	41	47.1
3	重庆商业广播电台 Chongqing Business Channel	39	44.8
4	中央人民广播电台 China National Radio (CNR)	23	26.4
5	重庆教育广播电台 Chongqing Education Channel	5	5.7
6	中国国际广播电台 China Radio International (CRI)	2	2.3

n=87

2-5-4 经常收听的广播电台（周日）/ Ranking of the Most Favorite Radio Channels (Sunday)

注：本题为多选题，合计百分比超过 100%（Multiple answers）

排名 Brand Ranking	频道 Channels	人次 Person-time	百分比 Percent
1	重庆经济广播电台 Chongqing Economic Radio	50	58.1
2	重庆人民广播电台 Chongqing People's Radio	39	45.3
3	重庆商业广播电台 Chongqing Business Channel	38	44.2
4	中央人民广播电台 China National Radio (CNR)	25	29.1
5	重庆教育广播电台 Chongqing Education Channel	5	5.8
6	中国国际广播电台 China Radio International (CRI)	4	4.7

n=86

2-6 经常收听的广播节目/ Ranking of the Most Favorite Radio Programs

注：本题为多选题，合计百分比超过 100%（Multiple answers）

排名 Ranking	广播节目 Radio Programs	人次 Person-time	百分比 Percent
1	港台流行音乐 HK. Taiwan pop music	47	50.0
2	国内新闻 national news	46	48.9
3	国际新闻 international news	31	33.0
4	国内流行音乐 inland pop music	26	27.7
5	医疗保健 medicare	22	23.4
6	热点话题评说 hot topics	21	22.3
7	点播节目 call-in program	20	21.3
8	天气预报 weather forecast	19	20.2
8	经济信息 economic information report	19	20.2
9	欧美流行音乐 Europe pop music	17	18.1
10	股市信息 stock information	9	9.6
11	古典音乐欣赏 classic music	8	8.5
12	交通信息 transportation report	7	7.4
12	体育节目 sports	7	7.4
12	有奖问答 contest	7	7.4
13	曲艺相声 folk arts	6	6.4
13	教育节目 educational news	6	6.4
14	广播剧 radio play	3	3.2
14	其他 others	3	3.2
15	外语教学 foreign languages teaching	2	2.1
15	少儿节目 children's program	2	2.1

n=94

2-7 样本、男性各年龄层、女性各年龄层经常收听的广播节目/ The Most Favorite Radio Programs by the Whole Sample, Age and Gender Groups

注：本题为多选题，合计百分比超过 100%（Multiple answers）

	人数 Number	国内新闻 national news	国际新闻 international news	天气预报 weather forecast	经济信息 economic information report	交通信息 transportation report	教育节目 educational program
样本 Sample	94	48.9	33.0	20.2	20.2	7.4	6.4
男性 Male	41	56.1	48.8	19.5	29.3	12.2	7.3
16~24 岁 Age	10	20.0	30.0	20.0	30.0	0.0	20.0
25~34 岁 Age	11	36.4	36.4	9.1	18.2	27.3	0.0
35~44 岁 Age	11	81.8	54.5	0.0	27.3	9.1	9.1
45~54 岁 Age	6	100.0	83.3	66.7	50.0	16.7	0.0
55~60 岁 Age	3	66.7	66.7	33.3	33.3	0.0	0.0
女性 Female	53	43.4	20.8	20.8	13.2	3.8	5.7
16~24 岁 Age	22	22.7	9.1	0.0	4.5	0.0	9.1
25~34 岁 Age	12	33.3	16.7	41.7	8.3	8.3	0.0
35~44 岁 Age	10	70.0	30.0	20.0	30.0	10.0	10.0
45~54 岁 Age	7	71.4	42.9	42.9	28.6	0.0	0.0
55~60 岁 Age	2	100.0	50.0	50.0	0.0	0.0	0.0

续前表 continued

	人数 Number	热点话题评说 hot topics	外语教学 foreign languages teaching	广播剧 radio play	古典音乐欣赏 classic music	欧美流行音乐 Europe & America pop music	港台流行音乐 HK. Taiwan pop music
样本 Sample	94	22.3	2.1	3.2	8.5	18.1	50.0
男性 Male	41	17.1	2.4	4.9	2.4	17.1	53.7
16~24 岁 Age	10	0.0	10.0	0.0	0.0	30.0	80.0
25~34 岁 Age	11	9.1	0.0	0.0	9.1	18.2	72.7
35~44 岁 Age	11	18.2	0.0	9.1	0.0	18.2	45.5
45~54 岁 Age	6	50.0	0.0	0.0	0.0	0.0	16.7
55~60 岁 Age	3	33.3	0.0	33.3	0.0	0.0	0.0
女性 Female	53	26.4	1.9	1.9	13.2	18.9	47.2
16~24 岁 Age	22	36.4	0.0	4.5	18.2	40.9	72.7
25~34 岁 Age	12	16.7	8.3	0.0	8.3	8.3	58.3
35~44 岁 Age	10	20.0	0.0	0.0	20.0	0.0	10.0
45~54 岁 Age	7	14.3	0.0	0.0	0.0	0.0	14.3
55~60 岁 Age	2	50.0	0.0	0.0	0.0	0.0	0.0

续前表 continued

	人数 Number	国内流行音乐 inland pop music	戏曲节目 traditional opera	曲艺相声 folk arts	评书 storytelling	医疗保健 medicare
样本 Sample	94	27.7	0.0	6.4	0.0	23.4
男性 Male	41	29.3	0.0	9.8	0.0	24.4
16~24 岁 Age	10	50.0	0.0	10.0	0.0	10.0
25~34 岁 Age	11	27.3	0.0	18.2	0.0	9.1
35~44 岁 Age	11	36.4	0.0	9.1	0.0	27.3
45~54 岁 Age	6	0.0	0.0	0.0	0.0	50.0
55~60 岁 Age	3	0.0	0.0	0.0	0.0	66.7
女性 Female	53	26.4	0.0	3.8	0.0	22.6
16~24 岁 Age	22	22.7	0.0	0.0	0.0	4.5
25~34 岁 Age	12	41.7	0.0	8.3	0.0	25.0
35~44 岁 Age	10	30.0	0.0	10.0	0.0	40.0
45~54 岁 Age	7	14.3	0.0	0.0	0.0	28.6
55~60 岁 Age	2	0.0	0.0	0.0	0.0	100.0

续前表 continued

	人数 Number	点播节目 call-in program	少儿节目 children's program	体育节目 sports	有奖问答 contest	其他 others
样本 Sample	94	21.3	2.1	7.4	7.4	9.6
男性 Male	41	9.8	0.0	14.6	9.8	12.2
16~24 岁 Age	10	10.0	0.0	40.0	10.0	0.0
25~34 岁 Age	11	0.0	0.0	18.2	9.1	27.3
35~44 岁 Age	11	18.2	0.0	0.0	18.2	9.1
45~54 岁 Age	6	16.7	0.0	0.0	0.0	0.0
55~60 岁 Age	3	0.0	0.0	0.0	0.0	33.3
女性 Female	53	30.2	3.8	1.9	5.7	7.5
16~24 岁 Age	22	36.4	9.1	4.5	9.1	0.0
25~34 岁 Age	12	33.3	0.0	0.0	8.3	8.3
35~44 岁 Age	10	40.0	0.0	0.0	0.0	10.0
45~54 岁 Age	7	0.0	0.0	0.0	0.0	28.6
55~60 岁 Age	2	0.0	0.0	0.0	0.0	0.0

2-8 不同学历的听众收听的广播节目的偏好/ Program Preference by Educational Levels

注：本题为多选题，合计百分比超过 100%（Multiple answers）

	人数 Number	国内新闻 national news	国际新闻 international news	天气预报 weather forecast	经济信息 economic information report	交通信息 transportation report	教育节目 educational program
样本 Sample	94	48.9	33.0	20.2	20.2	7.4	6.4
小学及以下 Primary School or Below	4	75.0	25.0	0.0	0.0	25.0	0.0
初中 Middle School	25	44.0	24.0	32.0	28.0	8.0	4.0
高中/中专/技校 HighSchool/Technical Secondary School	40	47.5	35.0	17.5	20.0	5.0	12.5
大学专科 2-3 Year College	20	55.0	35.0	15.0	20.0	5.0	0.0
大学本科 4-5 Year College	5	40.0	60.0	20.0	0.0	20.0	0.0
研究生或以上 Graduate or Above	0	0.0	0.0	0.0	0.0	0.0	0.0

续前表 continued

	人数 Number	热点话题评说 hot topics	外语教学 foreign languages teaching	广播剧 radio play	古典音乐欣赏 classic music	欧美流行音乐 Europe & America pop music	港台流行音乐 HK. Taiwan pop music
样本 Sample	94	22.3	2.1	3.2	8.5	18.1	50.0
小学及以下 Primary School or Below	4	25.0	0.0	0.0	0.0	0.0	0.0
初中 Middle School	25	8.0	0.0	0.0	0.0	8.0	36.0
高中/中专/技校 HighSchool/Technical Secondary School	40	22.5	0.0	5.0	12.5	30.0	60.0
大学专科 2-3 Year College	20	35.0	10.0	5.0	10.0	15.0	55.0
大学本科 4-5 Year College	5	40.0	0.0	0.0	20.0	0.0	60.0
研究生或以上 Graduate or Above	0	0.0	0.0	0.0	0.0	0.0	0.0

续前表 continued

	人数 Number	国内流行音乐 inland pop music	戏曲节目 traditional opera	曲艺相声 folk arts	评书 storytelling	医疗保健 medicare
样本 Sample	94	27.7	0.0	6.4	0.0	23.4
小学及以下 Primary School or Below	4	0.0	0.0	0.0	0.0	25.0
初中 Middle School	25	36.0	0.0	8.0	0.0	36.0
高中/中专/技校 HighSchool/Technical Secondary School	40	22.5	0.0	5.0	0.0	17.5
大学专科 2-3 Year College	20	30.0	0.0	10.0	0.0	20.0
大学本科 4-5 Year College	5	40.0	0.0	0.0	0.0	20.0
研究生或以上 Graduate or Above	0	0.0	0.0	0.0	0.0	0.0

续前表 continued

	人数 Number	点播节目 call-in program	少儿节目 children's program	体育节目 sports	有奖问答 contest	其他 others
样本 Sample	94	21.3	2.1	7.4	7.4	9.6
小学及以下 Primary School or Below	4	25.0	0.0	0.0	0.0	25.0
初中 Middle School	25	20.0	0.0	0.0	8.0	16.0
高中/中专/技校 HighSchool/Technical Secondary School	40	22.5	5.0	10.0	10.0	5.0
大学专科 2-3 Year College	20	20.0	0.0	15.0	5.0	10.0
大学本科 4-5 Year College	5	20.0	0.0	0.0	0.0	0.0
研究生或以上 Graduate or Above	0	0.0	0.0	0.0	0.0	0.0

2-9 经常收听广播时段/ Weekday Times Slots of Radio Listening

注：本题为多选题，合计百分比超过 100%（Multiple answers）

时间段 times slots	周一到周四(%) (Monday—Thursday)	周五(%) (Friday)	周六(%) (Saturday)	周日(%) (Sunday)
样本量 Sample	n=92	n=93	n=89	n=89
0:00-0:30	0.0	0.0	1.1	0.0
0:30-1:00	0.0	0.0	0.0	0.0
1:00-1:30	0.0	0.0	0.0	0.0
1:30-2:00	0.0	0.0	0.0	0.0
2:00-2:30	0.0	0.0	0.0	0.0
2:30-3:00	0.0	0.0	0.0	0.0
3:00-3:30	1.1	0.0	0.0	1.1
3:30-4:00	0.0	0.0	0.0	0.0
4:00-4:30	0.0	0.0	0.0	0.0
4:30-5:00	0.0	0.0	0.0	0.0
5:00-5:30	1.1	1.1	1.1	1.1
5:30-6:00	1.1	1.1	1.1	1.1
6:00-6:30	2.2	3.2	3.4	3.4
6:30-7:00	7.6	6.5	6.7	6.7
7:00-7:30	19.6	19.4	19.1	19.1
7:30-8:00	12.0	8.6	10.1	10.1
8:00-8:30	8.7	5.4	6.7	6.7
8:30-9:00	4.3	3.2	1.1	2.2
9:00-9:30	6.5	7.5	5.6	7.9
9:30-10:00	5.4	8.6	5.6	6.7
10:00-10:30	5.4	5.4	6.7	7.9
10:30-11:00	3.3	3.2	3.4	4.5
11:00-11:30	2.2	2.2	1.1	1.1
11:30-12:00	2.2	3.2	2.2	2.2
12:00-12:30	9.8	11.8	10.1	10.1
12:30-13:00	5.4	5.4	4.5	3.4
13:00-13:30	4.3	4.3	5.6	4.5
13:30-14:00	3.3	3.2	2.2	2.2
14:00-14:30	3.3	3.2	2.2	2.2
14:30-15:00	2.2	2.2	1.1	1.1
15:00-15:30	1.1	1.1	1.1	2.2
15:30-16:00	0.0	0.0	0.0	1.1
16:00-16:30	1.1	2.2	1.1	3.4
16:30-17:00	1.1	3.2	1.1	4.5
17:00-17:30	4.3	5.4	4.5	5.6
17:30-18:00	1.1	2.2	3.4	3.4
18:00-18:30	3.3	5.4	5.6	4.5
18:30-19:00	3.3	3.2	3.4	3.4
19:00-19:30	4.3	4.3	4.5	4.5
19:30-20:00	6.5	7.5	6.7	6.7
20:00-20:30	6.5	6.5	5.6	5.6
20:30-21:00	5.4	4.3	3.4	3.4
21:00-21:30	5.4	5.4	6.7	5.6
21:30-22:00	9.8	6.5	6.7	6.7
22:00-22:30	12.0	5.4	5.6	4.5
22:30-23:00	13.0	10.8	10.1	9.0
23:00-23:30	12.0	12.9	11.2	12.4
23:30-24:00	8.7	6.5	5.6	7.9

2-10 样本、男性各年龄层、女性各年龄层是否打过热线电话参与节目/ Call-in Hot-time Telephone to Take Part in the Program by the Whole Sample, Age and Gender Groups

	人数 Number	打过 yes	没打过 no
样本 Sample	93	8.6	91.4
男性 Male	40	5.0	95.0
16~24 岁 Age	9	11.1	88.9
25~34 岁 Age	11	9.1	90.9
35~44 岁 Age	10	0.0	100.0
45~54 岁 Age	7	0.0	100.0
55~60 岁 Age	3	0.0	100.0
女性 Female	53	11.3	88.7
16~24 岁 Age	21	19.0	81.0
25~34 岁 Age	13	7.7	92.3
35~44 岁 Age	10	10.0	90.0
45~54 岁 Age	7	0.0	100.0
55~60 岁 Age	2	0.0	100.0

2-11 不同消费者层平时是否接触广播媒介/ Radio Exposure by Market Segments

2-11-1 时尚流行指标/ Fads Popular Index

	人数 Number	从来不听 never	收听 yes
样本 Sample	616	84.6	15.4
平实生活指向 simple living orientation	369	85.6	14.4
时尚流行指向 fashion orientation	247	83.0	17.0

2-11-2 广告态度指标/ Advertising Attitude Index

	人数 Number	从来不听 never	收听 yes
样本 Sample	618	84.6	15.4
广告淡漠指向 indifferent orientation	167	89.8	10.2
中间层 medium	367	82.8	17.2
信赖广告指向 loyal orientation	84	82.1	17.9

2-12 不同消费者层收听广播频道的偏好/ Channel Preference by Market Segments

2-12-1 时尚流行指标/ Fads Popular Index

注：本题为多选题，合计百分比超过 100%（Multiple answers）

	人数 Number	重庆经济广播电台 Chongqing Economic Radio	重庆人民广播电台 Chongqing People's Radio	重庆商业广播电台 Chongqing Business Radio	中央人民广播电台 China National Radio (CNR)
样本 Sample	93	87.1	62.4	59.1	34.4
平实生活指向 simple living orientation	52	88.5	59.6	51.9	30.8
时尚流行指向 fashion orientation	41	85.4	65.9	68.3	39.0

续前表 continued

	人数 Number	重庆教育广播电台 Chongqing Education Radio	中国国际广播电台 China Radio International (CRI)	BBC	VOA
样本 Sample	93	12.9	3.2	2.2	2.2
平实生活指向 simple living orientation	52	11.5	1.9	3.8	3.8
时尚流行指向 fashion orientation	41	14.6	4.9	0.0	0.0

2-12-2 广告态度指标/ Advertising Attitude Index

注：本题为多选题，合计百分比超过 100%（Multiple answers）

	人数 Number	重庆经济广播电台 Chongqing Economic Radio	重庆人民广播电台 Chongqing People's Radio	重庆商业广播电台 Chongqing Business Channel	中央人民广播电台 China National Radio (CNR)
样本 Sample	93	87.1	60.2	59.1	35.5
广告淡漠指向 indifferent orientation	16	87.5	50.0	56.3	25.0
中间层 medium	62	91.9	61.3	61.3	32.3
信赖广告指向 loyal orientation	15	66.7	66.7	53.3	60.0

续前表 continued

	人数 Number	重庆教育广播电台 Chongqing Education Channel	中国国际广播电台 China Radio International (CRI)	BBC	VOA
样本 Sample	93	12.9	3.2	2.2	2.2
广告淡漠指向 indifferent orientation	16	18.8	12.5	0.0	6.3
中间层 medium	62	9.7	1.6	3.2	1.6
信赖广告指向 loyal orientation	15	20.0	0.0	0.0	0.0

2-13 不同消费者层收看广播节目的偏好/ Program Preference by Market Segments

2-13-1 时尚流行指标/ Fads Popular Index

注：本题为多选题，合计百分比超过 100%（Multiple answers）

	人数 Number	国内新闻 national news	国际新闻 international news	天气预报 weather forecast	经济信息 economic information report	交通信息 transportation report	教育节目 educational program
样本 Sample	92	50.0	32.6	19.6	20.7	7.6	6.5
平实生活指向 simple living orientation	51	56.9	37.3	23.5	15.7	9.8	3.9
时尚流行指向 fashion orientation	41	41.5	26.8	14.6	26.8	4.9	9.8

续前表 continued

	人数 Number	热点话题评说 hot topics	外语教学 foreign languages teaching	广播剧 radio play	古典音乐欣赏 classic music	欧美流行音乐 Europe & America pop music	港台流行音乐 HK . Taiwan pop music
样本 Sample	92	22.8	2.2	3.3	7.6	17.4	50.0
平实生活指向 simple living orientation	51	21.6	2.0	2.0	7.8	9.8	39.2
时尚流行指向 fashion orientation	41	24.4	2.4	4.9	7.3	26.8	63.4

续前表 continued

	人数 Number	国内流行音乐 inland pop music	戏曲节目 traditional opera	曲艺相声 folk art	评书 storytelling	医疗保健 medicare
样本 Sample	92	27.2	0.0	6.5	0.0	23.9
平实生活指向 simple living orientation	51	23.5	0.0	3.9	0.0	31.4
时尚流行指向 fashion orientation	41	31.7	0.0	9.8	0.0	14.6

续前表 continued

	人数 Number	点播节目 call-in program	少儿节目 children's program	体育节目 sports	有奖问答 contest	其他 others
样本 Sample	92	21.7	2.2	7.6	7.6	9.8
平实生活指向 simple living orientation	51	21.6	0.0	11.8	5.9	9.8
时尚流行指向 fashion orientation	41	22.0	4.9	2.4	9.8	9.8

2-13-2 广告态度指标/ Advertising Attitude Index

注：本题为多选题，合计百分比超过 100%（Multiple answers）

	人数 Number	国内新闻 national news	国际新闻 international news	天气预报 weather forecast	经济信息 economic information	交通信息 transportation report	教育节目 educational program
样本 Sample	92	47.8	33.7	19.6	20.7	7.6	6.5
广告淡漠指向 indifferent orientation	17	64.7	35.3	11.8	11.8	5.9	0.0
中间层 medium	61	47.5	37.7	24.6	19.7	8.2	4.9
信赖广告指向 loyal orientation	14	28.6	14.3	7.1	35.7	7.1	21.4

续前表 continued

	人数 Number	热点话题评说 hot topics	外语教学 foreign languages teaching	广播剧 radio play	古典音乐欣赏 classic music	欧美流行音乐 Europe & America pop music	港台流行音乐 HK. Taiwan pop music
样本 Sample	92	22.8	2.2	3.3	8.7	18.5	48.9
广告淡漠指向 indifferent orientation	17	17.6	0.0	11.8	5.9	17.6	47.1
中间层 medium	61	24.6	3.3	1.6	11.5	14.8	49.2
信赖广告指向 loyal orientation	14	21.4	0.0	0.0	0.0	35.7	50.0

续前表 continued

	人数 Number	国内流行音乐 inland pop music	戏曲节目 traditional opera	曲艺相声 folk art	评书 storytelling	医疗保健 medicare
样本 Sample	92	28.3	0.0	5.4	0.0	22.8
广告淡漠指向 indifferent orientation	17	11.8	0.0	11.8	0.0	17.6
中间层 medium	61	34.4	0.0	4.9	0.0	23.0
信赖广告指向 loyal orientation	14	21.4	0.0	0.0	0.0	28.6

续前表 continued

	人数 Number	点播节目 call-in program	少儿节目 children's program	体育节目 sports	有奖问答 contest	其他 others
样本 Sample	92	20.7	2.2	7.6	6.5	9.8
广告淡漠指向 indifferent orientation	17	17.6	5.9	17.6	5.9	11.8
中间层 medium	61	24.6	1.6	4.9	6.6	8.2
信赖广告指向 loyal orientation	14	7.1	0.0	7.1	7.1	14.3

● 武汉 / Wuhan

2-1 样本、男性各年龄层、女性各年龄层平时是否接触广播媒介/ Radio Listening by the Whole Sample, Age and Gender Groups

	人数 Number	从来不听 never	收听 yes
样本 Sample	621	72.8	27.2
男性 Male	301	72.8	27.2
16~24 岁 Age	64	62.5	37.5
25~34 岁 Age	87	77.0	23.0
35~44 岁 Age	77	80.5	19.5
45~54 岁 Age	50	70.0	30.0
55~60 岁 Age	23	65.2	34.8
女性 Female	320	72.8	27.2
16~24 岁 Age	66	62.1	37.9
25~34 岁 Age	94	74.5	25.5
35~44 岁 Age	77	84.4	15.6
45~54 岁 Age	57	61.4	38.6
55~60 岁 Age	26	84.6	15.4

2-2 一周内不同时间收听广播的时间长短/ The Average Time Spending on Listening Radio Per Day

2-2-1 一周内不同时间收听广播的时间长短（周一到周四）/ The Average Time Spending on Listening Radio Per Day (Monday—Thursday)

	人数 Number	百分比 Percent
大约半小时或以下 about 1/2 hour or below	59	34.9
大约 1 小时 about 1 hour	64	37.9
大约 2 小时 about 2 hours	24	14.2
大约 3 小时 about 3 hours	9	5.3
大约 4 小时 about 4 hours	0	0.0
大约 5 小时 about 5 hours	3	1.8
大约 6 小时 about 6 hours	1	0.6
大约 7 小时 about 7 hours	1	0.6
大约 8 小时 about 8 hours	1	0.6
大约 9 小时 about 9 hours	0	0.0
大约 10 小时或以上 about 10 hours or over	1	0.6
记不清/不知道 can't remember	1	0.6
没有收听 didn't listen	5	3.0

n=169

2-2-2 一周内不同时间收听广播的时间长短（周五）/ The Average Time Spending on Listening Radio Per Day (Friday)

	人数 Number	百分比 Percent
大约半小时或以下 about 1/2 hour or below	49	29.5
大约 1 小时 about 1 hour	64	38.6
大约 2 小时 about 2 hours	22	13.3
大约 3 小时 about 3 hours	8	4.8
大约 4 小时 about 4 hours	1	0.6
大约 5 小时 about 5 hours	2	1.2
大约 6 小时 about 6 hours	1	0.6
大约 7 小时 about 7 hours	0	0.0
大约 8 小时 about 8 hours	1	0.6
大约 9 小时 about 9 hours	0	0.0
大约 10 小时或以上 about 10 hours or over	1	0.6
记不清/不知道 can't remember	1	0.6
没有收听 didn't listen	16	9.6

n=166

2-2-3 一周内不同时间收听广播的时间长短（周六）/ The Average Time Spending on Listening Radio Per Day (Saturday)

	人数 Number	百分比 Percent
大约半小时或以下 about 1/2 hour or below	37	22.6
大约 1 小时 about 1 hour	63	38.4
大约 2 小时 about 2 hours	28	17.1
大约 3 小时 about 3 hours	9	5.5
大约 4 小时 about 4 hours	2	1.2
大约 5 小时 about 5 hours	2	1.2
大约 6 小时 about 6 hours	0	0.0
大约 7 小时 about 7 hours	1	0.6
大约 8 小时 about 8 hours	1	0.6
大约 9 小时 about 9 hours	0	0.0
大约 10 小时或以上 about 10 hours or over	0	0.0
记不清/不知道 can't remember	3	1.8
没有收听 didn't listen	18	11.0

n=164

2-2-4 一周内不同时间收听广播的时间长短（周日）/ The Average Time Spending on Listening Radio Per Day (Sunday)

	人数 Number	百分比 Percent
大约半小时或以下 about 1/2 hour or below	38	23.3
大约 1 小时 about 1 hour	63	38.7
大约 2 小时 about 2 hours	24	14.7
大约 3 小时 about 3 hours	10	6.1
大约 4 小时 about 4 hours	1	0.6
大约 5 小时 about 5 hours	3	1.8
大约 6 小时 about 6 hours	0	0.0
大约 7 小时 about 7 hours	1	0.6
大约 8 小时 about 8 hours	1	0.6
大约 9 小时 about 9 hours	0	0.0
大约 10 小时或以上 about 10 hours or over	0	0.0
记不清/不知道 can't remember	2	1.2
没有收听 didn't listen	20	12.3

n=163

2-3 经常收听的广播频道排名/ Ranking of the Most Favorite Radio Channels

注：本题为多选题，合计百分比超过 100%（Multiple answers）

排名 Brand Ranking	频道 Channels	人次 Person-time	百分比 Percent
1	楚天音乐台 (108.8 兆赫) Chutian Music Channel	71	42.8
2	湖北交通音乐台 (107.8 兆赫) Hubei Traffic & Music Channel	55	33.1
3	楚天广播电台 (1179 千赫) Chutian People's Radio	52	31.3
4	楚天广播电台 (92.7 兆赫) Chutian Life Channel	35	21.1
5	武汉文艺台 (101.8 兆赫) Wuhan Literature & Art Channel	34	20.5
6	湖北经济台 (99.8 兆赫) Hubei Economic Channel	31	18.7
7	湖北文艺台 (103.8 兆赫) Hubei Literature & Art Channel	30	18.1
8	湖北广播电台 (774 千赫) Hubei People's Radio	27	16.3
8	中央人民广播电台 China National Radio (CNR)	27	16.3
9	武汉广播电台 (873 千赫) Wuhan People's Radio	17	10.2
10	长江经济广播电台 (1125 千赫) Changjiang Economic Radio	9	5.4
11	BBC	3	1.8
12	河北人民广播电台 Hebei People's Radio	2	1.2

n=166

2-4 样本、男性各年龄层、女性各年龄层经常收听的广播频道/ The Most Favorite Radio Channels by the Whole Sample, Age and Gender Groups

注：本题为多选题，合计百分比超过 100%（Multiple answers）

	人数 Number	楚天音乐台 108.8 兆赫 Chutian Music Channel	湖北交通音乐台 107.8 兆赫 Hubei Traffic & Music Channel	楚天广播电台 1179 千赫 Chutian People's Radio	楚天广播电台 92.7 兆赫 Chutian Life Channel	武汉文艺台 101.8 兆赫 Wuhan Literature & Art Channel	湖北经济台 99.8 兆赫 Hubei Economic Channel
样本 Sample	166	42.8	33.1	31.3	21.1	20.5	18.7
男性 Male	81	39.5	29.6	29.6	17.3	19.8	19.8
16~24 岁 Age	24	45.8	41.7	37.5	16.7	29.2	16.7
25~34 岁 Age	20	65.0	45.0	20.0	30.0	15.0	20.0
35~44 岁 Age	15	40.0	20.0	26.7	6.7	20.0	13.3
45~54 岁 Age	14	7.1	14.3	14.3	14.3	14.3	35.7
55~60 岁 Age	8	12.5	0.0	62.5	12.5	12.5	12.5
女性 Female	85	45.9	36.5	32.9	24.7	21.2	17.6
16~24 岁 Age	25	76.0	60.0	20.0	40.0	4.0	12.0
25~34 岁 Age	23	47.8	21.7	56.5	13.0	17.4	8.7
35~44 岁 Age	12	33.3	41.7	25.0	33.3	33.3	16.7
45~54 岁 Age	21	23.8	28.6	23.8	14.3	38.1	28.6
55~60 岁 Age	4	0.0	0.0	50.0	25.0	25.0	50.0

续前表 continued

	人数 Number	湖北文艺台 103.8 兆赫 Hubei Literature & Art Channel	湖北广播电台 774 千赫 Hubei People's Radio	中央人民广播电台 China National Radio (CNR)	武汉广播电台 873 千赫 Wuhan People's Radio	长江经济广播电台 1125 千赫 Changjiang Economic Radio	BBC
样本 Sample	166	18.1	16.3	16.3	10.2	5.4	1.8
男性 Male	81	13.6	17.3	17.3	12.3	6.2	3.7
16~24 岁 Age	24	16.7	4.2	4.2	4.2	8.3	8.3
25~34 岁 Age	20	10.0	15.0	20.0	5.0	0.0	0.0
35~44 岁 Age	15	6.7	13.3	26.7	20.0	13.3	0.0
45~54 岁 Age	14	28.6	28.6	28.6	21.4	0.0	7.1
55~60 岁 Age	8	0.0	50.0	12.5	25.0	12.5	0.0
女性 Female	85	22.4	15.3	15.3	8.2	4.7	0.0
16~24 岁 Age	25	24.0	8.0	0.0	0.0	4.0	0.0
25~34 岁 Age	23	34.8	8.7	21.7	4.3	8.7	0.0
35~44 岁 Age	12	0.0	25.0	25.0	16.7	0.0	0.0
45~54 岁 Age	21	19.0	23.8	23.8	14.3	0.0	0.0
55~60 岁 Age	4	25.0	25.0	0.0	25.0	25.0	0.0

2-5 经常收听的广播电台/ The Most Favorite Radio Channels

2-5-1 经常收听的广播电台（周一到周四）/ Ranking of the Most Favorite Radio Channels (Monday—Thursday)

注：本题为多选题，合计百分比超过 100%（Multiple answers）

排名 Brand Ranking	频道 Channels	人次 Person-time	百分比 Percent
1	楚天音乐台（108.8 兆赫) Chutian Music Channel	56	34.4
2	湖北交通音乐台（107.8 兆赫) Hubei Traffic & Music Channel	50	30.7
3	楚天广播电台（1179 千赫) Chutian People's Radio	43	26.4
4	楚天广播电台（92.7 兆赫) Chutian Life Channel	40	24.5
5	湖北经济台（99.8 兆赫) Hubei Economic Channel	37	22.7
6	中央人民广播电台 China National Radio (CNR)	34	20.9
7	武汉文艺台（101.8 兆赫) Wuhan Literature & Art Channel	31	19.0
8	湖北广播电台（774 千赫) Hubei People's Radio	29	17.8
9	湖北文艺台（103.8 兆赫) Hubei Literature & Art Channel	27	16.6
10	长江经济广播电台（1125 千赫) Changjiang Economic Radio	13	8.0
11	武汉广播电台（873 千赫) Wuhan People's Radio	12	7.4

n=163

2-5-2 经常收听的广播电台（周五）/ Ranking of the Most Favorite Radio Channels (Friday)

注：本题为多选题，合计百分比超过 100%（Multiple answers）

排名 Brand Ranking	频道 Channels	人次 Person-time	百分比 Percent
1	楚天音乐台 (108.8 兆赫) Chutian Music Channel	48	29.4
2	湖北交通音乐台 (107.8 兆赫) Hubei Traffic & Music Channel	41	25.2
2	楚天广播电台 (1179 千赫) Chutian People's Radio	41	25.2
3	楚天广播电台 (92.7 兆赫) Chutian Life Channel	38	23.3
4	武汉文艺台 (101.8 兆赫) Wuhan Literature & Art Channel	33	20.2
5	湖北经济台 (99.8 兆赫) Hubei Economic Channel	32	19.6
6	中央人民广播电台 China National Radio (CNR)	29	17.8
7	湖北广播电台 (774 千赫) Hubei People's Radio	26	16.0
8	湖北文艺台 (103.8 兆赫) Hubei Literature & Art Channel	24	14.7
9	长江经济广播电台 (1125 千赫) Changjiang Economic Radio	13	8.0
10	武汉广播电台 (873 千赫) Wuhan People's Radio	11	6.7

n=163

2-5-3 经常收听的广播电台（周六）/ Ranking of the Most Favorite Radio Channels (Saturday)

注：本题为多选题，合计百分比超过 100%（Multiple answers）

排名 Brand Ranking	频道 Channels	人次 Person-time	百分比 Percent
1	楚天音乐台 (108.8 兆赫) Chutian Music Channel	47	28.7
2	湖北交通音乐台 (107.8 兆赫) Hubei Traffic & Music Channel	40	24.4
3	楚天广播电台 (1179 千赫) Chutian People's Radio	39	23.8
4	楚天广播电台 (92.7 兆赫) Chutian Life Channel	33	20.1
5	湖北经济台 (99.8 兆赫) Hubei Economic Channel	28	17.1
5	湖北文艺台 (103.8 兆赫) Hubei Literature & Art Channel	28	17.1
6	中央人民广播电台 China National Radio (CNR)	26	15.9
7	武汉文艺台 (101.8 兆赫) Wuhan Literature & Art Channel	25	15.2
8	湖北广播电台 (774 千赫) Hubei People's Radio	24	14.6
9	长江经济广播电台 (1125 千赫) Changjiang Economic Radio	14	8.5
10	武汉广播电台 (873 千赫) Wuhan People's Radio	13	7.9

n=164

2-5-4 经常收听的广播电台（周日）/ Ranking of the Most Favorite Radio Channels (Sunday)

注：本题为多选题，合计百分比超过 100%（Multiple answers）

排名 Brand Ranking	频道 Channels	人次 Person-time	百分比 Percent
1	楚天音乐台 (108.8 兆赫) Chutian Music Channel	45	27.4
2	楚天广播电台 (1179 千赫) Chutian People's Radio	41	25.0
3	湖北交通音乐台 (107.8 兆赫) Hubei Traffic & Music Channel	40	24.4
4	楚天广播电台 (92.7 兆赫) Chutian Life Channel	36	22.0
5	湖北经济台 (99.8 兆赫) Hubei Economic Channel	28	17.1
5	湖北文艺台 (103.8 兆赫) Hubei Literature & Art Channel	28	17.1
6	中央人民广播电台 China National Radio (CNR)	27	16.5
7	湖北广播电台 (774 千赫) Hubei People's Radio	24	14.6
8	武汉文艺台 (101.8 兆赫) Wuhan Literature & Art Channel	22	13.4
9	长江经济广播电台 (1125 千赫) Changjiang Economic Radio	14	8.5
9	武汉广播电台 (873 千赫) Wuhan People's Radio	14	8.5

n=164

2-6 经常收听的广播节目/ Ranking of the Most Favorite Radio Programs

注：本题为多选题，合计百分比超过 100%（Multiple answers）

排名 Ranking	广播节目 Radio Programs	人次 Person-time	百分比 Percent
1	国内新闻 national news	81	47.9
2	港台流行音乐 HK.Taiwan pop music	73	43.2
3	国际新闻 international news	65	38.5
4	天气预报 weather forecast	59	34.9
5	国内流行音乐 inland pop music	44	26.0
6	曲艺相声 folk arts	37	21.9
7	欧美流行音乐 Europe pop music	35	20.7
8	医疗保健 medicare	30	17.8
9	热点话题评说 hot topics	22	13.0
10	体育节目 sports	20	11.8
11	经济信息 economic information report	18	10.7
12	评书 storytelling	15	8.9
13	古典音乐欣赏 classic music	14	8.3
14	股市信息 stock information	13	7.7
14	有奖问答 contest	13	7.7
15	戏曲节目 traditional opera	12	7.1
15	点播节目 call-in program	12	7.1
16	广播剧 radio play	10	5.9
16	交通信息 transportation report	10	5.9
17	教育节目 educational news	6	3.6
18	其他 others	4	2.4
19	少儿节目 children's program	3	1.8
19	外语教学 foreign languages teaching	3	1.8

n=169

2-7 样本、男性各年龄层、女性各年龄层经常收听的广播节目/ The Most Favorite Radio Programs by the Whole Sample, Age and Gender Groups

注：本题为多选题，合计百分比超过 100%（Multiple answers）

	人数 Number	国内新闻 national news	国际新闻 international news	天气预报 weather forecast	经济信息 economic information report	交通信息 transportation report	教育节目 educational program
样本 Sample	169	47.9	38.5	34.9	10.7	5.9	3.6
男性 Male	82	53.7	48.8	32.9	11.0	7.3	2.4
16~24 岁 Age	24	16.7	16.7	16.7	4.2	0.0	0.0
25~34 岁 Age	20	70.0	65.0	20.0	20.0	15.0	0.0
35~44 岁 Age	15	66.7	66.7	40.0	6.7	13.3	6.7
45~54 岁 Age	15	66.7	66.7	46.7	20.0	0.0	6.7
55~60 岁 Age	8	75.0	37.5	75.0	0.0	12.5	0.0
女性 Female	87	42.5	28.7	36.8	10.3	4.6	4.6
16~24 岁 Age	25	20.0	8.0	32.0	0.0	8.0	4.0
25~34 岁 Age	24	33.3	20.8	29.2	12.5	4.2	8.3
35~44 岁 Age	12	58.3	50.0	33.3	8.3	0.0	8.3
45~54 岁 Age	22	63.6	45.5	45.5	22.7	4.5	0.0
55~60 岁 Age	4	75.0	50.0	75.0	0.0	0.0	0.0

续前表 continued

	人数 Number	热点话题评说 hot topics	外语教学 foreign languages teaching	广播剧 radio play	古典音乐欣赏 classic music	欧美流行音乐 Europe & America pop music	港台流行音乐 HK.Taiwan pop music
样本 Sample	169	13.0	1.8	5.9	8.3	20.7	43.2
男性 Male	82	7.3	1.2	2.4	7.3	23.2	30.5
16~24 岁 Age	24	4.2	4.2	0.0	8.3	58.3	66.7
25~34 岁 Age	20	10.0	0.0	0.0	10.0	25.0	35.0
35~44 岁 Age	15	6.7	0.0	0.0	6.7	0.0	13.3
45~54 岁 Age	15	6.7	0.0	13.3	0.0	0.0	0.0
55~60 岁 Age	8	12.5	0.0	0.0	12.5	0.0	0.0
女性 Female	87	18.4	2.3	9.2	9.2	18.4	55.2
16~24 岁 Age	25	16.0	0.0	16.0	8.0	48.0	84.0
25~34 岁 Age	24	25.0	0.0	4.2	8.3	12.5	66.7
35~44 岁 Age	12	33.3	0.0	8.3	16.7	0.0	16.7
45~54 岁 Age	22	9.1	9.1	9.1	4.5	4.5	36.4
55~60 岁 Age	4	0.0	0.0	0.0	25.0	0.0	25.0

续前表 continued

	人数 Number	国内流行音乐 inland pop music	戏曲节目 traditional opera	曲艺相声 folk arts	评书 storytelling	医疗保健 medicare
样本 Sample	169	26.0	7.1	21.9	8.9	17.8
男性 Male	82	26.8	3.7	18.3	18.3	11.0
16~24 岁 Age	24	29.2	0.0	20.8	20.8	0.0
25~34 岁 Age	20	25.0	0.0	20.0	25.0	5.0
35~44 岁 Age	15	26.7	0.0	13.3	13.3	6.7
45~54 岁 Age	15	33.3	6.7	20.0	13.3	26.7
55~60 岁 Age	8	12.5	25.0	12.5	12.5	37.5
女性 Female	87	25.3	10.3	25.3	0.0	24.1
16~24 岁 Age	25	28.0	0.0	4.0	0.0	16.0
25~34 岁 Age	24	33.3	4.2	29.2	0.0	25.0
35~44 岁 Age	12	33.3	8.3	25.0	0.0	50.0
45~54 岁 Age	22	13.6	27.3	40.9	0.0	13.6
55~60 岁 Age	4	0.0	25.0	50.0	0.0	50.0

续前表 continued

	人数 Number	点播节目 call-in program	少儿节目 children's program	体育节目 sports	有奖问答 contest	其他 others
样本 Sample	169	7.1	1.8	11.8	7.7	7.7
男性 Male	82	3.7	0.0	18.3	3.7	11.0
16~24 岁 Age	24	8.3	0.0	16.7	12.5	0.0
25~34 岁 Age	20	0.0	0.0	25.0	0.0	10.0
35~44 岁 Age	15	6.7	0.0	26.7	0.0	6.7
45~54 岁 Age	15	0.0	0.0	6.7	0.0	33.3
55~60 岁 Age	8	0.0	0.0	12.5	0.0	12.5
女性 Female	87	10.3	3.4	5.7	11.5	4.6
16~24 岁 Age	25	16.0	0.0	8.0	16.0	0.0
25~34 岁 Age	24	8.3	12.5	4.2	12.5	8.3
35~44 岁 Age	12	16.7	0.0	0.0	8.3	8.3
45~54 岁 Age	22	4.5	0.0	4.5	9.1	4.5
55~60 岁 Age	4	0.0	0.0	25.0	0.0	0.0

2-8 不同学历的听众收听的广播节目的偏好/ Program Preference by Educational Levels

注：本题为多选题，合计百分比超过 100%（Multiple answers）

	人数 Number	国内新闻 national news	国际新闻 international news	天气预报 weather forecast	经济信息 economic information report	交通信息 transportation report	教育节目 educational program
样本 Sample	168	48.2	38.7	35.1	10.7	6.0	3.6
小学及以下 Primary School or Below	6	100.0	83.3	66.7	0.0	16.7	0.0
初中 Middle School	26	50.0	30.8	38.5	11.5	11.5	7.7
高中/中专/技校 High School/Technical Secondary School	86	45.3	37.2	32.6	8.1	7.0	2.3
大学专科 2-3 Year College	33	36.4	33.3	30.3	18.2	0.0	6.1
大学本科 4-5 Year College	16	62.5	56.3	43.8	12.5	0.0	0.0
研究生或以上 Graduate or Above	1	100.0	0.0	0.0	0.0	0.0	0.0

续前表 continued

	人数 Number	热点话题评说 hot topics	外语教学 foreign languages teaching	广播剧 radio play	古典音乐欣赏 classic music	欧美流行音乐 Europe & America pop music	港台流行音乐 HK.Taiwan pop music
样本 Sample	168	13.1	1.8	6.0	8.3	20.2	42.9
小学及以下 Primary School or Below	6	0.0	0.0	0.0	0.0	0.0	16.7
初中 Middle School	26	7.7	3.8	7.7	7.7	15.4	38.5
高中/中专/技校 High School/Technical Secondary School	86	14.0	1.2	8.1	11.6	16.3	39.5
大学专科 2-3 Year College	33	18.2	0.0	3.0	6.1	33.3	63.6
大学本科 4-5 Year College	16	12.5	6.3	0.0	0.0	31.3	37.5
研究生或以上 Graduate or Above	1	0.0	0.0	0.0	0.0	0.0	0.0

续前表 continued

	人数 Number	国内流行音乐 inland pop music	戏曲节目 traditional opera	曲艺相声 folk arts	评书 storytelling	医疗保健 medicare
样本 Sample	168	25.6	7.1	22.0	8.9	17.9
小学及以下 Primary School or Below	6	0.0	50.0	33.3	0.0	16.7
初中 Middle School	26	19.2	15.4	30.8	7.7	11.5
高中/中专/技校 High School/Technical Secondary School	86	26.7	4.7	20.9	10.5	24.4
大学专科 2-3 Year College	33	36.4	0.0	21.2	3.0	6.1
大学本科 4-5 Year College	16	18.8	6.3	12.5	18.8	18.8
研究生或以上 Graduate or Above	1	0.0	0.0	0.0	0.0	0.0

续前表 continued

	人数 Number	点播节目 call-in program	少儿节目 children's program	体育节目 sports	有奖问答 contest	其他 others
样本 Sample	168	7.1	1.8	11.9	7.1	7.7
小学及以下 Primary School or Below	6	0.0	0.0	0.0	0.0	0.0
初中 Middle School	26	7.7	3.8	7.7	7.7	7.7
高中/中专/技校 High School/Technical Secondary School	86	8.1	1.2	17.4	9.3	5.8
大学专科 2-3 Year College	33	9.1	3.0	6.1	6.1	9.1
大学本科 4-5 Year College	16	0.0	0.0	6.3	0.0	18.8
研究生或以上 Graduate or Above	1	0.0	0.0	0.0	0.0	0.0

2-9 经常收听广播时段/ Weekday Times Slots of Radio Listening

注：本题为多选题，合计百分比可能超过 100%（Multiple answers）

时间段 times slots	周一到周四(%) (Monday—Thursday)	周五(%) (Friday)	周六(%) (Saturday)	周日(%) (Sunday)
样本量 Sample	n=168	n=168	n=168	n=168
0:00-0:30	1.2	1.2	0.6	0.6
0:30-1:00	0.0	0.0	0.0	0.0
1:00-1:30	0.0	0.0	0.0	0.0
1:30-2:00	0.0	0.0	0.0	0.0
2:00-2:30	0.0	0.0	0.0	0.0
2:30-3:00	0.0	0.0	0.0	0.0
3:00-3:30	0.0	0.0	0.0	0.0
3:30-4:00	0.0	0.0	0.0	0.0
4:00-4:30	0.0	0.0	0.0	0.0
4:30-5:00	0.6	0.6	0.0	0.0
5:00-5:30	1.8	1.8	1.2	1.2
5:30-6:00	3.0	2.4	1.8	1.8
6:00-6:30	7.1	6.0	6.5	6.5
6:30-7:00	22.0	19.0	18.5	18.5
7:00-7:30	18.5	16.7	15.5	16.1
7:30-8:00	10.1	8.3	8.9	9.5
8:00-8:30	8.3	7.7	10.1	10.7
8:30-9:00	6.5	6.5	8.9	8.3
9:00-9:30	8.3	7.1	8.9	7.7
9:30-10:00	9.5	7.7	8.9	7.7
10:00-10:30	5.4	4.8	6.5	6.5
10:30-11:00	4.2	3.6	6.5	6.5
11:00-11:30	6.0	5.4	7.1	6.5
11:30-12:00	7.1	7.1	8.9	8.3
12:00-12:30	17.9	16.7	17.3	16.1
12:30-13:00	16.1	16.7	15.5	15.5
13:00-13:30	15.5	14.3	13.1	13.7
13:30-14:00	10.7	11.3	10.1	9.5
14:00-14:30	4.8	5.4	5.4	4.8
14:30-15:00	3.6	3.6	3.0	2.4
15:00-15:30	3.6	3.0	1.2	1.2
15:30-16:00	3.6	3.0	1.2	1.8
16:00-16:30	1.8	1.2	1.2	1.2
16:30-17:00	3.0	3.0	1.2	2.4
17:00-17:30	7.7	7.7	4.8	4.8
17:30-18:00	6.5	6.5	5.4	4.8
18:00-18:30	7.1	7.1	7.7	7.1
18:30-19:00	4.8	6.0	6.5	6.5
19:00-19:30	7.7	6.5	7.7	7.1
19:30-20:00	6.0	5.4	6.0	6.0
20:00-20:30	6.5	5.4	4.8	4.8
20:30-21:00	5.4	3.6	3.6	4.2
21:00-21:30	8.3	7.7	6.0	7.1
21:30-22:00	7.7	7.1	6.5	7.1
22:00-22:30	8.9	8.3	6.5	7.1
22:30-23:00	7.7	7.1	5.4	5.4
23:00-23:30	6.0	5.4	4.2	4.2
23:30-24:00	3.6	4.2	3.6	4.2

2-10 样本、男性各年龄层、女性各年龄层是否打过热线电话参与节目/ Call-in Hot-time Telephone to Take Part in the Program by the Whole Sample, Age and Gender Groups

	人数 Number	打过 yes	没打过 no
样本 Sample	166	16.9	83.1
男性 Male	80	20.0	80.0
16~24 岁 Age	22	36.4	63.6
25~34 岁 Age	20	25.0	75.0
35~44 岁 Age	15	13.3	86.7
45~54 岁 Age	15	6.7	93.3
55~60 岁 Age	8	0.0	100.0
女性 Female	86	14.0	86.0
16~24 岁 Age	25	20.0	80.0
25~34 岁 Age	24	16.7	83.3
35~44 岁 Age	12	16.7	83.3
45~54 岁 Age	21	4.8	95.2
55~60 岁 Age	4	0.0	100.0

2-11 不同消费者层平时是否接触广播媒介/ Radio Exposure by Market Segments

2-11-1 时尚流行指标/ Fads Popular Index

	人数 Number	从来不听 never	收听 yes
样本 Sample	618	73.0	27.0
平实生活指向 simple living orientation	323	71.8	28.2
时尚流行指向 fashion orientation	295	74.2	25.8

2-11-2 广告态度指标/ Advertising Attitude Index

	人数 Number	从来不听 never	收听 yes
样本 Sample	620	72.9	27.1
广告淡漠指向 indifferent orientation	184	77.2	22.8
中间层 medium	365	71.5	28.5
信赖广告指向 loyal orientation	71	69.0	31.0

2-12 不同消费者层收听广播频道的偏好/ Channel Preference by Market Segments

2-12-1 时尚流行指标/ Fads Popular Index

注：本题为多选题，合计百分比超过 100%（Multiple answers）

	人数 Number	楚天音乐台 108.8 兆赫 Chutian Music Channel	湖北交通音乐台 107.8 兆赫 Hubei Traffic & Music Channel	楚天广播电台 1179 千赫 Chutian People's Radio	楚天广播电台 92.7 兆赫 Chutian Life Channel	武汉文艺台 101.8 兆赫 Wuhan Literature & Art Channel	湖北经济台 99.8 兆赫 Hubei Economic Channel
样本 Sample	164	43.3	33.5	31.7	21.3	20.1	17.7
平实生活指向 simple living orientation	91	41.8	28.6	29.7	25.3	23.1	18.7
时尚流行指向 fashion orientation	73	45.2	39.7	34.2	16.4	16.4	16.4

续前表 continued

	人数 Number	湖北文艺台 103.8 兆赫 Hubei Literature & Art Channel	湖北广播电台 774 千赫 Hubei People's Radio	中央人民广播电台 China National Radio (CNR)	武汉广播电台 873 千赫 Wuhan People's Radio	长江经济广播电台 1125 千赫 Changjiang Economic Radio	BBC	河北人民广播电台 Hebei People's Radio
样本 Sample	164	18.3	16.5	16.5	10.4	5.5	1.8	1.2
平实生活指向 simple living orientation	91	14.3	17.6	17.6	12.1	6.6	2.2	1.1
时尚流行指向 fashion orientation	73	23.3	15.1	15.1	8.2	4.1	1.4	1.4

2-12-2 广告态度指标/ Advertising Attitude Index

注：本题为多选题，合计百分比超过 100%（Multiple answers）

	人数 Number	楚天音乐台 108.8 兆赫 Chutian Music Channel	湖北交通音乐台 107.8 兆赫 Hubei Traffic & Music Channel	楚天广播电台 1179 千赫 Chutian People's Radio	楚天广播电台 92.7 兆赫 Chutian Life Channel	武汉文艺台 101.8 兆赫 Wuhan Literature & Art Channel	湖北经济台 99.8 兆赫 Hubei Economic Channel
样本 Sample	165	43.0	33.3	31.5	21.2	20.6	18.2
广告淡漠指向 indifferent orientation	40	45.0	32.5	25.0	27.5	22.5	15.0
中间层 medium	103	41.7	36.9	31.1	17.5	20.4	21.4
信赖广告指向 loyal orientation	22	45.5	18.2	45.5	27.3	18.2	9.1

续前表 continued

	人数 Number	湖北文艺台 103.8 兆赫 Hubei Literature & Art Channel	湖北广播电台 774 千赫 Hubei People's Radio	中央人民广播电台 China National Radio (CNR)	武汉广播电台 873 千赫 Wuhan People's Radio	长江经济广播电台 1125 千赫 Changjiang Economic Radio	BBC	河北人民广播电台 Hebei People's Radio
样本 Sample	165	18.2	16.4	16.4	10.3	5.5	1.8	1.2
广告淡漠指向 indifferent orientation	40	17.5	17.5	17.5	7.5	10.0	0.0	0.0
中间层 medium	103	20.4	14.6	15.5	10.7	3.9	2.9	1.9
信赖广告指向 loyal orientation	22	9.1	22.7	18.2	13.6	4.5	0.0	0.0

2-13 不同消费者层收看广播节目的偏好/ Program Preference by Market Segments

2-13-1 时尚流行指标/ Fads Popular Index

注：本题为多选题，合计百分比超过 100%（Multiple answers）

	人数 Number	国内新闻 national news	国际新闻 international news	天气预报 weather forecast	经济信息 economic information	交通信息 transportation report	教育节目 educational program
样本 Sample	167	47.3	38.3	34.7	10.8	6.0	3.6
平实生活指向 simple living orientation	91	52.7	42.9	41.8	8.8	6.6	2.2
时尚流行指向 fashion orientation	76	40.8	32.9	26.3	13.2	5.3	5.3

续前表 continued

	人数 Number	热点话题评说 hot topics	外语教学 foreign languages teaching	广播剧 radio play	古典音乐欣赏 classic music	欧美流行音乐 Europe & America pop music	港台流行音乐 HK.Taiwan pop music
样本 Sample	167	13.2	1.8	6.0	8.4	21.0	43.7
平实生活指向 simple living orientation	91	12.1	3.3	6.6	6.6	16.5	38.5
时尚流行指向 fashion orientation	76	14.5	0.0	5.3	10.5	26.3	50.0

续前表 continued

	人数 Number	国内流行音乐 inland pop music	戏曲节目 traditional opera	曲艺相声 folk art	评书 storytelling	医疗保健 medicare
样本 Sample	167	26.3	7.2	22.2	9.0	17.4
平实生活指向 simple living orientation	91	22.0	9.9	26.4	11.0	16.5
时尚流行指向 fashion orientation	76	31.6	3.9	17.1	6.6	18.4

续前表 continued

	人数 Number	点播节目 call-in program	少儿节目 children's program	体育节目 sports	有奖问答 contest	其他 others
样本 Sample	167	7.2	1.8	11.4	7.8	7.8
平实生活指向 simple living orientation	91	7.7	1.1	14.3	5.5	8.8
时尚流行指向 fashion orientation	76	6.6	2.6	7.9	10.5	6.6

2-13-2 广告态度指标/ Advertising Attitude Index

注：本题为多选题，合计百分比超过 100%（Multiple answers）

	人数 Number	国内新闻 national news	国际新闻 international news	天气预报 weather forecast	经济信息 economic information	交通信息 transportation report	教育节目 educational program
样本 Sample	168	47.6	38.7	35.1	10.7	6.0	3.6
广告淡漠指向 indifferent orientation	42	52.4	45.2	45.2	14.3	4.8	4.8
中间层 medium	104	49.0	36.5	34.6	10.6	7.7	1.0
信赖广告指向 loyal orientation	22	31.8	36.4	18.2	4.5	0.0	13.6

续前表 continued

	人数 Number	热点话题评说 hot topics	外语教学 foreign languages teaching	广播剧 radio play	古典音乐欣赏 classic music	欧美流行音乐 Europe & America pop music	港台流行音乐 HK & Taiwan pop music
样本 Sample	168	13.1	1.8	6.0	8.3	20.8	43.5
广告淡漠指向 indifferent orientation	42	7.1	4.8	9.5	9.5	21.4	33.3
中间层 medium	104	15.4	1.0	5.8	8.7	20.2	47.1
信赖广告指向 loyal orientation	22	13.6	0.0	0.0	4.5	22.7	45.5

续前表 continued

	人数 Number	国内流行音乐 inland pop music	戏曲节目 traditional opera	曲艺相声 folk art	评书 storytelling	医疗保健 medicare
样本 Sample	168	26.2	7.1	22.0	8.9	17.9
广告淡漠指向 indifferent orientation	42	26.2	11.9	23.8	14.3	7.1
中间层 medium	104	24.0	6.7	22.1	7.7	22.1
信赖广告指向 loyal orientation	22	36.4	0.0	18.2	4.5	18.2

续前表 continued

	人数 Number	点播节目 call-in program	少儿节目 children's program	体育节目 sports	有奖问答 contest	其他 others
样本 Sample	168	7.1	1.8	11.9	7.7	7.7
广告淡漠指向 indifferent orientation	42	0.0	0.0	4.8	4.8	11.9
中间层 medium	104	6.7	1.9	14.4	5.8	7.7
信赖广告指向 loyal orientation	22	22.7	4.5	13.6	22.7	0.0

● 西安 / Xi'an

2-1 样本、男性各年龄层、女性各年龄层平时是否接触广播媒介/ Radio Listening by the Whole Sample, Age and Gender Groups

	人数 Number	从来不听 never	收听 yes
样本 Sample	601	70.0	30.0
男性 Male	302	64.9	35.1
16~24 岁 Age	64	56.3	43.8
25~34 岁 Age	91	67.0	33.0
35~44 岁 Age	77	68.8	31.2
45~54 岁 Age	46	67.4	32.6
55~60 岁 Age	24	62.5	37.5
女性 Female	299	75.3	24.7
16~24 岁 Age	61	60.7	39.3
25~34 岁 Age	90	82.2	17.8
35~44 岁 Age	74	81.1	18.9
45~54 岁 Age	49	71.4	28.6
55~60 岁 Age	25	76.0	24.0

2-2 一周内不同时间收听广播的时间长短/ The Average Time Spending on Listening Radio Per Day

2-2-1 一周内不同时间收听广播的时间长短（周一到周四）/ The Average Time Spending on Listening Radio Per Day (Monday—Thursday)

	人数 Number	百分比 Percent
大约半小时或以下 about 1/2 hour or below	41	22.8
大约 1 小时 about 1 hour	74	41.1
大约 2 小时 about 2 hours	24	13.3
大约 3 小时 about 3 hours	10	5.6
大约 4 小时 about 4 hours	7	3.9
大约 5 小时 about 5 hours	5	2.8
大约 6 小时 about 6 hours	1	0.6
大约 7 小时 about 7 hours	1	0.6
大约 8 小时 about 8 hours	0	0.0
大约 9 小时 about 9 hours	0	0.0
大约 10 小时或以上 about 10 hours or over	1	0.6
记不清/不知道 can't remember	7	3.9
没有收听 didn't listen	9	5.0

n=180

2-2-2 一周内不同时间收听广播的时间长短（周五）/ The Average Time Spending on Listening Radio Per Day (Friday)

	人数 Number	百分比 Percent
大约半小时或以下 about 1/2 hour or below	37	20.6
大约 1 小时 about 1 hour	60	33.3
大约 2 小时 about 2 hours	29	16.1
大约 3 小时 about 3 hours	8	4.4
大约 4 小时 about 4 hours	6	3.3
大约 5 小时 about 5 hours	4	2.2
大约 6 小时 about 6 hours	1	0.6
大约 7 小时 about 7 hours	2	1.1
大约 8 小时 about 8 hours	0	0.0
大约 9 小时 about 9 hours	0	0.0
大约 10 小时或以上 about 10 hours or over	1	0.6
记不清/不知道 can't remember	9	5.0
没有收听 didn't listen	23	12.8

n=180

2-2-3 一周内不同时间收听广播的时间长短（周六）/ The Average Time Spending on Listening Radio Per Day (Saturday)

	人数 Number	百分比 Percent
大约半小时或以下 about 1/2 hour or below	36	20.0
大约 1 小时 about 1 hour	54	30.0
大约 2 小时 about 2 hours	33	18.3
大约 3 小时 about 3 hours	10	5.6
大约 4 小时 about 4 hours	5	2.8
大约 5 小时 about 5 hours	4	2.2
大约 6 小时 about 6 hours	0	0.0
大约 7 小时 about 7 hours	1	0.6
大约 8 小时 about 8 hours	0	0.0
大约 9 小时 about 9 hours	1	0.6
大约 10 小时或以上 about 10 hours or over	1	0.6
记不清/不知道 can't remember	8	4.4
没有收听 didn't listen	27	15.0

n=180

2-2-4 一周内不同时间收听广播的时间长短（周日）/ The Average Time Spending on Listening Radio Per Day (Sunday)

	人数 Number	百分比 Percent
大约半小时或以下 about 1/2 hour or below	38	21.2
大约 1 小时 about 1 hour	46	25.7
大约 2 小时 about 2 hours	33	18.4
大约 3 小时 about 3 hours	11	6.1
大约 4 小时 about 4 hours	5	2.8
大约 5 小时 about 5 hours	5	2.8
大约 6 小时 about 6 hours	0	0.0
大约 7 小时 about 7 hours	1	0.6
大约 8 小时 about 8 hours	1	0.6
大约 9 小时 about 9 hours	0	0.0
大约 10 小时或以上 about 10 hours or over	2	1.1
记不清/不知道 can't remember	9	5.0
没有收听 didn't listen	28	15.6

n=179

2-3 经常收听的广播频道排名/ Ranking of the Most Favorite Radio Channels

注：本题为多选题，合计百分比超过 100%（Multiple answers）

排名 Brand Ranking	频道 Channels	人次 Person-time	百分比 Percent
1	西安音乐台 Xi'an Music Channel	106	58.9
2	陕西交通音乐广播电台 Shaanxi Traffic & Music Channel	79	43.9
3	西安经济台 Xi'an Economic Channel	60	33.3
4	中央人民广播电台 China National Radio (CNR)	54	30.0
5	陕西经济广播电台 Shaanxi Economic Channel	40	22.2
6	西安新闻台 Xi'an News Channel	32	17.8
7	陕西文艺广播电台 Shaanxi Literature & Art Channel	31	17.2
8	陕西人民广播电台 Shaanxi People's Radio	12	6.7

n=180

2-4 样本、男性各年龄层、女性各年龄层经常收听的广播频道/ The Most Favorite Radio Channels by the Whole Sample, Age and Gender Groups

注：本题为多选题，合计百分比超过 100%（Multiple answers）

	人数 Number	西安音乐台 Xi'an Music Channel	陕西交通音乐广播电台 Shaanxi Traffic & Music Channel	西安经济台 Xi'an Economic Channel	中央人民广播电台 China National Radio (CNR)
样本 Sample	180	**58.9**	**43.9**	**33.3**	**30.0**
男性 Male	106	**58.5**	**47.2**	**32.1**	**32.1**
16~24 岁 Age	28	85.7	64.3	21.4	17.9
25~34 岁 Age	30	70.0	60.0	33.3	20.0
35~44 岁 Age	24	45.8	25.0	41.7	54.2
45~54 岁 Age	15	33.3	33.3	33.3	33.3
55~60 岁 Age	9	11.1	33.3	33.3	55.6
女性 Female	74	**59.5**	**39.2**	**35.1**	**27.0**
16~24 岁 Age	24	70.8	54.2	33.3	8.3
25~34 岁 Age	16	75.0	56.3	50.0	25.0
35~44 岁 Age	14	57.1	35.7	28.6	42.9
45~54 岁 Age	14	35.7	7.1	42.9	28.6
55~60 岁 Age	6	33.3	16.7	0.0	66.7

续前表 continued

	人数 Number	陕西经济广播电台 Shaanxi Economic Channel	西安新闻台 Xi'an News Channel	陕西文艺广播电台 Shaanxi Literature & Art Channel	陕西人民广播电台 Shaanxi People's Radio
样本 Sample	180	**22.2**	**17.8**	**17.2**	**6.7**
男性 Male	106	**20.8**	**18.9**	**16.0**	**4.7**
16~24 岁 Age	28	17.9	7.1	21.4	0.0
25~34 岁 Age	30	16.7	6.7	13.3	6.7
35~44 岁 Age	24	16.7	29.2	4.2	4.2
45~54 岁 Age	15	46.7	33.3	13.3	6.7
55~60 岁 Age	9	11.1	44.4	44.4	11.1
女性 Female	74	**24.3**	**16.2**	**18.9**	**9.5**
16~24 岁 Age	24	20.8	12.5	25.0	8.3
25~34 岁 Age	16	25.0	6.3	12.5	6.3
35~44 岁 Age	14	14.3	0.0	14.3	7.1
45~54 岁 Age	14	28.6	42.9	21.4	7.1
55~60 岁 Age	6	50.0	33.3	16.7	33.3

2-5 经常收听的广播电台/ Ranking of the Most Favorite Radio Channels

2-5-1 经常收听的广播电台（周一到周四）/ Ranking of the Most Favorite Radio Channels (Monday—Thursday)

注：本题为多选题，合计百分比超过 100%（Multiple answers）

排名 Brand Ranking	频道 Channels	人次 Person-time	百分比 Percent
1	西安音乐台 Xi'an Music Channel	85	47.5
2	陕西交通音乐广播电台 Shaanxi Traffic & Music Channel	64	35.8
3	西安经济台 Xi'an Economic Channel	47	26.3
4	中央人民广播电台 China National Radio (CNR)	42	23.5
5	陕西经济广播电台 Shaanxi Economic Channel	41	22.9
6	陕西文艺广播电台 Shaanxi Literature & Art Channel	31	17.3
7	西安新闻台 Xi'an News Channel	26	14.5
8	陕西人民广播电台 Shaanxi People's Radio	12	6.7

n=179

2-5-2 经常收听的广播电台（周五）/ Ranking of the Most Favorite Radio Channels (Friday)

注：本题为多选题，合计百分比超过 100%（Multiple answers）

排名 Brand Ranking	频道 Channels	人次 Person-time	百分比 Percent
1	西安音乐台 Xi'an Music Channel	81	45.5
2	陕西交通音乐广播电台 Shaanxi Traffic & Music Channel	56	31.5
3	西安经济台 Xi'an Economic Channel	43	24.2
4	中央人民广播电台 China National Radio (CNR)	40	22.5
5	陕西经济广播电台 Shaanxi Economic Channel	39	21.9
6	陕西文艺广播电台 Shaanxi Literature & Art Channel	27	15.2
6	西安新闻台 Xi'an News Channel	27	15.2

n=178

2-5-3 经常收听的广播电台（周六）/ Ranking of the Most Favorite Radio Channels (Saturday)

注：本题为多选题，合计百分比超过 100%（Multiple answers）

排名 Brand Ranking	频道 Channels	人次 Person-time	百分比 Percent
1	西安音乐台 Xi'an Music Channel	78	44.6
2	陕西交通音乐广播电台 Shaanxi Traffic & Music Channel	54	30.9
3	西安经济台 Xi'an Economic Channel	41	23.4
4	中央人民广播电台 China National Radio (CNR)	38	21.7
5	陕西经济广播电台 Shaanxi Economic Channel	37	21.1
6	西安新闻台 Xi'an News Channel	25	14.3
6	陕西文艺广播电台 Shaanxi Literature & Art Channel	25	14.3
7	陕西人民广播电台 Shaanxi People's Radio	11	6.3

n=175

2-5-4 经常收听的广播电台（周日）/ Ranking of the Most Favorite Radio Channels (Sunday)

注：本题为多选题，合计百分比超过 100%（Multiple answers）

排名 Brand Ranking	频道 Channels	人次 Person-time	百分比 Percent
1	西安音乐台 Xi'an Music Channel	78	44.8
2	陕西交通音乐广播电台 Shaanxi Traffic & Music Channel	53	30.5
3	西安经济台 Xi'an Economic Channel	41	23.6
4	中央人民广播电台 China National Radio (CNR)	37	21.3
5	陕西经济广播电台 Shaanxi Economic Channel	33	19.0
6	陕西文艺广播电台 Shaanxi Literature & Art Channel	24	13.8
7	西安新闻台 Xi'an News Channel	23	13.2

n=174

2-6 经常收听的广播节目/ Ranking of the Most Favorite Radio Programs

注：本题为多选题，合计百分比超过 100%（Multiple answers）

排名 Ranking	广播节目 Radio Programs	人次 Person-time	百分比 Percent
1	港台流行音乐 HK. Taiwan pop music	79	44.1
2	国内新闻 national news	68	38.0
3	国际新闻 international news	56	31.3
4	国内流行音乐 inland pop music	52	29.1
5	欧美流行音乐 Europe pop music	42	23.5
5	天气预报 weather forecast	42	23.5
6	曲艺相声 folk arts	40	22.3
7	热点话题评说 hot topics	36	20.1
8	经济信息 economic information report	23	12.8
9	医疗保健 medicare	21	11.7
10	股市信息 stock information	20	11.2
11	戏曲节目 traditional opera	16	8.9
12	评书 storytelling	15	8.4
12	有奖问答 contest	15	8.4
13	交通信息 transportation report	14	7.8
13	体育节目 sports	14	7.8
14	古典音乐欣赏 classic music	12	6.7
15	点播节目 call-in program	9	5.0
16	广播剧 radio play	7	3.9
16	其他 others	7	3.9
17	教育节目 educational news	6	3.4
18	外语教学 foreign languages teaching	3	1.7
19	少儿节目 children's program	2	1.1

n=179

2-7 样本、男性各年龄层、女性各年龄层经常收听的广播节目/ The Most Favorite Radio Programs by the Whole Sample, Age and Gender Groups

注：本题为多选题，合计百分比超过 100%（Multiple answers）

	人数 Number	国内新闻 national news	国际新闻 international news	天气预报 weather forecast	经济信息 economic information report	交通信息 transportation report	教育节目 educational program
样本 Sample	179	38.0	31.3	23.5	12.8	7.8	3.4
男性 Male	105	41.9	38.1	23.8	18.1	12.4	2.9
16~24 岁 Age	28	28.6	21.4	7.1	14.3	7.1	7.1
25~34 岁 Age	30	33.3	26.7	13.3	13.3	13.3	3.3
35~44 岁 Age	23	39.1	39.1	39.1	26.1	21.7	0.0
45~54 岁 Age	15	60.0	66.7	33.3	33.3	0.0	0.0
55~60 岁 Age	9	88.9	77.8	55.6	0.0	22.2	0.0
女性 Female	74	32.4	21.6	23.0	5.4	1.4	4.1
16~24 岁 Age	24	12.5	16.7	12.5	4.2	0.0	8.3
25~34 岁 Age	16	31.3	18.8	18.8	0.0	0.0	0.0
35~44 岁 Age	14	35.7	21.4	21.4	7.1	7.1	0.0
45~54 岁 Age	14	57.1	28.6	28.6	14.3	0.0	7.1
55~60 岁 Age	6	50.0	33.3	66.7	0.0	0.0	0.0

续前表 continued

	人数 Number	热点话题评说 hot topics	外语教学 foreign languages teaching	广播剧 radio play	古典音乐欣赏 classic music	欧美流行音乐 Europe & America pop music	港台流行音乐 HK. Taiwan pop music
样本 Sample	179	20.1	1.7	3.9	6.7	23.5	44.1
男性 Male	105	14.3	1.0	1.9	5.7	25.7	42.9
16~24 岁 Age	28	3.6	0.0	0.0	7.1	46.4	82.1
25~34 岁 Age	30	16.7	3.3	3.3	10.0	30.0	56.7
35~44 岁 Age	23	26.1	0.0	0.0	0.0	13.0	13.0
45~54 岁 Age	15	13.3	0.0	6.7	0.0	6.7	13.3
55~60 岁 Age	9	11.1	0.0	0.0	11.1	11.1	0.0
女性 Female	74	28.4	2.7	6.8	8.1	20.3	45.9
16~24 岁 Age	24	33.3	8.3	8.3	4.2	41.7	70.8
25~34 岁 Age	16	43.8	0.0	12.5	12.5	12.5	68.8
35~44 岁 Age	14	21.4	0.0	0.0	14.3	21.4	28.6
45~54 岁 Age	14	21.4	0.0	7.1	7.1	0.0	14.3
55~60 岁 Age	6	0.0	0.0	0.0	0.0	0.0	0.0

续前表 continued

	人数 Number	国内流行音乐 inland pop music	戏曲节目 traditional opera	曲艺相声 folk arts	评书 storytelling	医疗保健 medicare
样本 Sample	179	29.1	8.9	22.3	8.4	11.7
男性 Male	105	26.7	5.7	16.2	13.3	6.7
16~24 岁 Age	28	39.3	7.1	10.7	10.7	10.7
25~34 岁 Age	30	30.0	0.0	26.7	16.7	6.7
35~44 岁 Age	23	26.1	0.0	0.0	4.3	0.0
45~54 岁 Age	15	6.7	6.7	20.0	33.3	6.7
55~60 岁 Age	9	11.1	33.3	33.3	0.0	11.1
女性 Female	74	32.4	13.5	31.1	1.4	18.9
16~24 岁 Age	24	41.7	0.0	20.8	4.2	4.2
25~34 岁 Age	16	43.8	6.3	31.3	0.0	6.3
35~44 岁 Age	14	28.6	14.3	35.7	0.0	35.7
45~54 岁 Age	14	21.4	28.6	28.6	0.0	14.3
55~60 岁 Age	6	0.0	50.0	66.7	0.0	83.3

续前表 continued

	人数 Number	点播节目 call-in program	少儿节目 children's program	体育节目 sports	有奖问答 contest	其他 others
样本 Sample	179	5.0	1.1	7.8	8.4	11.2
男性 Male	105	4.8	0.0	10.5	5.7	16.2
16~24 岁 Age	28	3.6	0.0	7.1	7.1	0.0
25~34 岁 Age	30	6.7	0.0	13.3	3.3	26.7
35~44 岁 Age	23	8.7	0.0	8.7	8.7	17.4
45~54 岁 Age	15	0.0	0.0	6.7	6.7	33.3
55~60 岁 Age	9	0.0	0.0	22.2	0.0	0.0
女性 Female	74	5.4	2.7	4.1	12.2	4.1
16~24 岁 Age	24	8.3	0.0	4.2	16.7	4.2
25~34 岁 Age	16	12.5	0.0	6.3	18.8	6.3
35~44 岁 Age	14	0.0	7.1	0.0	7.1	7.1
45~54 岁 Age	14	0.0	7.1	7.1	0.0	0.0
55~60 岁 Age	6	0.0	0.0	0.0	16.7	0.0

2-8 不同学历的听众收听的广播节目的偏好/ Program Preference by Educational Levels

注：本题为多选题，合计百分比超过 100%（Multiple answers）

	人数 Number	国内新闻 national news	国际新闻 international news	天气预报 weather forecast	经济信息 economic information report	交通信息 transportation report	教育节目 educational program
样本 Sample	178	38.2	31.5	23.6	12.4	7.3	3.4
小学及以下 Primary School or Below	2	0.0	0.0	0.0	0.0	0.0	0.0
初中 Middle School	34	50.0	41.2	38.2	14.7	5.9	5.9
高中/中专/技校 High school/Technical Secondary School	76	34.2	25.0	23.7	11.8	11.8	5.3
大学专科 2-3 Year College	42	33.3	23.8	11.9	11.9	4.8	0.0
大学本科 4-5 Year College	21	47.6	61.9	23.8	14.3	0.0	0.0
研究生或以上 Graduate or Above	3	33.3	0.0	33.3	0.0	0.0	0.0

续前表 continued

	人数 Number	热点话题评说 hot topics	外语教学 foreign languages teaching	广播剧 radio play	古典音乐欣赏 classic music	欧美流行音乐 Europe & America pop music	港台流行音乐 HK. Taiwan pop music
样本 Sample	178	20.2	1.7	3.9	6.7	23.0	43.8
小学及以下 Primary School or Below	2	0.0	0.0	0.0	0.0	0.0	0.0
初中 Middle School	34	17.6	2.9	0.0	0.0	14.7	26.5
高中/中专/技校 High school/Technical Secondary School	76	17.1	1.3	3.9	10.5	25.0	47.4
大学专科 2-3 Year College	42	33.3	2.4	9.5	7.1	23.8	50.0
大学本科 4-5 Year College	21	14.3	0.0	0.0	4.8	28.6	42.9
研究生或以上 Graduate or Above	3	0.0	0.0	0.0	0.0	33.3	100.0

续前表 continued

	人数 Number	国内流行音乐 inland pop music	戏曲节目 traditional opera	曲艺相声 folk arts	评书 storytelling	医疗保健 medicare
样本 Sample	178	28.7	9.0	22 5	8.4	11.8
小学及以下 Primary School or Below	2	0.0	50.0	50.0	0.0	0.0
初中 Middle School	34	23.5	26.5	38.2	8.8	17.6
高中/中专/技校 High school/Technical Secondary School	76	34.2	3.9	18.4	7.9	11.8
大学专科 2-3 Year College	42	26.2	2.4	21.4	9.5	4.8
大学本科 4-5 Year College	21	28.6	9.5	9.5	9.5	19.0
研究生或以上 Graduate or Above	3	0.0	0.0	33.3	0.0	0.0

续前表 continued

	人数 Number	点播节目 call-in program	少儿节目 children's program	体育节目 sports	有奖问答 contest	其他 others
样本 Sample	178	5.1	1.1	7.9	8.4	11.2
小学及以下 Primary School or Below	2	0.0	0.0	0.0	0.0	50.0
初中 Middle School	34	5.9	2.9	8.8	8.8	5.9
高中/中专/技校 High school/Technical Secondary School	76	2.6	1.3	9.2	7.9	13.2
大学专科 2-3 Year College	42	9.5	0.0	4.8	9.5	16.7
大学本科 4-5 Year College	21	4.8	0.0	4.8	9.5	0.0
研究生或以上 Graduate or Above	3	0.0	0.0	33.3	0.0	0.0

2-9 经常收听广播时段/ Weekday Times Slots of Radio Listening

注：本题为多选题，合计百分比超过 100%（Multiple answers）

时间段 times slots	周一到周四(%) (Monday—Thursday)	周五(%) (Friday)	周六(%) (Saturday)	周日(%) (Sunday)
样本量 Sample	n=180	n=180	n=179	n=178
0:00-0:30	1.7	1.7	2.2	1.1
0:30-1:00	1.1	1.1	2.2	0.6
1:00-1:30	0.0	0.0	1.1	0.0
1:30-2:00	0.0	1.1	1.7	0.6
2:00-2:30	0.0	0.0	0.6	0.0
2:30-3:00	0.0	0.0	0.6	0.6
3:00-3:30	0.0	0.0	0.6	0.6
3:30-4:00	0.0	0.0	0.6	0.6
4:00-4:30	0.0	0.6	0.6	0.6
4:30-5:00	0.0	0.0	0.6	0.6
5:00-5:30	1.1	0.0	0.6	0.6
5:30-6:00	0.6	0.6	1.1	0.6
6:00-6:30	4.4	5.0	3.9	3.4
6:30-7:00	10.0	11.7	9.5	9.0
7:00-7:30	10.6	8.3	8.4	7.9
7:30-8:00	9.4	8.3	8.4	8.4
8:00-8:30	2.2	3.3	3.4	4.5
8:30-9:00	2.8	3.3	4.5	5.1
9:00-9:30	7.8	6.1	6.7	7.3
9:30-10:00	6.1	5.0	6.1	5.6
10:00-10:30	7.2	6.1	6.1	6.7
10:30-11:00	6.1	6.1	5.0	6.2
11:00-11:30	7.8	8.3	8.4	7.9
11:30-12:00	10.6	11.7	12.3	12.9
12:00-12:30	28.3	24.4	21.8	21.3
12:30-13:00	18.9	16.7	16.2	16.3
13:00-13:30	9.4	8.3	7.3	7.3
13:30-14:00	6.1	6.7	4.5	5.6
14:00-14:30	4.4	4.4	3.9	6.2
14:30-15:00	3.9	3.9	3.4	6.2
15:00-15:30	2.2	4.4	2.8	3.4
15:30-16:00	3.9	4.4	3.4	4.5
16:00-16:30	3.3	4.4	3.4	5.6
16:30-17:00	3.3	5.6	5.6	7.3
17:00-17:30	6.7	6.7	6.7	8.4
17:30-18:00	6.7	6.7	6.7	7.9
18:00-18:30	16.1	13.9	14.5	14.0
18:30-19:00	13.9	11.7	12.3	13.5
19:00-19:30	8.3	7.2	8.4	9.0
19:30-20:00	7.2	5.6	7.8	7.9
20:00-20:30	14.4	12.2	12.3	13.5
20:30-21:00	12.8	10.6	10.6	12.9
21:00-21:30	12.2	10.6	10.6	10.7
21:30-22:00	14.4	12.2	11.7	11.8
22:00-22:30	15.0	13.3	12.3	13.5
22:30-23:00	11.1	9.4	7.8	8.4
23:00-23:30	8.3	7.8	7.3	7.9
23:30-24:00	8.3	7.2	7.8	7.3

2-10 样本、男性各年龄层、女性各年龄层是否打过热线电话参与节目/ Call-in Hot-time Telephone to Take Part in the Program by the Whole Sample, Age and Gender Groups

	人数 Number	打过 yes	没打过 no
样本 Sample	176	15.9	84.1
男性 Male	104	16.3	83.7
16~24 岁 Age	27	18.5	81.5
25~34 岁 Age	29	20.7	79.3
35~44 岁 Age	24	16.7	83.3
45~54 岁 Age	15	6.7	93.3
55~60 岁 Age	9	11.1	88.9
女性 Female	72	15.3	84.7
16~24 岁 Age	24	25.0	75.0
25~34 岁 Age	16	18.8	81.3
35~44 岁 Age	13	7.7	92.3
45~54 岁 Age	13	0.0	100.0
55~60 岁 Age	6	16.7	83.3

2-11 不同消费者层平时是否接触广播媒介/ Radio Exposure by Market Segments

2-11-1 时尚流行指标/ Fads Popular Index

	人数 Number	从来不听 never	收听 yes
样本 Sample	**599**	**69.9**	**30.1**
平实生活指向 simple living orientation	341	71.3	28.7
时尚流行指向 fashion orientation	258	68.2	31.8

2-11-2 广告态度指标/ Advertising Attitude Index

	人数 Number	从来不听 never	收听 yes
样本 Sample	**597**	**69.8**	**30.2**
广告淡漠指向 indifferent orientation	184	73.9	26.1
中间层 medium	334	65.3	34.7
信赖广告指向 loyal orientation	79	79.7	20.3

2-12 不同消费者层收听广播频道的偏好/ Channel Preference by Market Segments

2-12-1 时尚流行指标/ Fads Popular Index

注：本题为多选题，合计百分比超过 100%（Multiple answers）

	人数 Number	西安音乐台 Xi'an Music Channel	陕西交通音乐广播电台 Shaanxi Traffic & Music Channel	西安经济台 Xi'an Economic Channel	中央人民广播电台 China National Radio (CNR)
样本 Sample	**180**	**58.9**	**43.9**	**33.3**	**30.0**
平实生活指向 simple living orientation	98	55.1	38.8	33.7	31.6
时尚流行指向 fashion orientation	82	63.4	50.0	32.9	28.0

续前表 continued

	人数 Number	陕西经济广播电台 Shaanxi Economic Channel	西安新闻台 Xi'an News Channel	陕西文艺广播电台 Shaanxi Literature & Art Channel	陕西人民广播电台 Shaanxi People's Radio
样本 Sample	**180**	**22.2**	**17.8**	**17.2**	**6.7**
平实生活指向 simple living orientation	98	22.4	18.4	18.4	8.2
时尚流行指向 fashion orientation	82	22.0	17.1	15.9	4.9

2-12-2 广告态度指标/ Advertising Attitude Index

注：本题为多选题，合计百分比超过 100%（Multiple answers）

	人数 Number	西安音乐台 Xi'an Music Channel	陕西交通音乐广播电台 Shaanxi Traffic & Music Channel	西安经济台 Xi'an Economic Channel	中央人民广播电台 China National Radio (CNR)
样本 Sample	180	58.9	43.9	33.3	30.0
广告淡漠指向 indifferent orientation	48	54.2	41.7	35.4	27.1
中间层 medium	116	56.0	44.0	30.2	30.2
信赖广告指向 loyal orientation	16	93.8	50.0	50.0	37.5

续前表 continued

	人数 Number	西安新闻台 Xi'an News Channel	陕西文艺广播电台 Shaanxi Literature & Art Channel	陕西人民广播电台 Shaanxi People's Radio
样本 Sample	180	17.8	17.2	6.7
广告淡漠指向 indifferent orientation	48	20.8	8.3	10.4
中间层 medium	116	18.1	21.6	6.0
信赖广告指向 loyal orientation	16	6.3	12.5	0.0

2-13 不同消费者层收看广播节目的偏好/ Program Preference by Market Segments

2-13-1 时尚流行指标/ Fads Popular Index

注：本题为多选题，合计百分比超过 100%（Multiple answers）

	人数 Number	国内新闻 national news	国际新闻 international news	天气预报 weather forecast	经济信息 economic information	交通信息 transportation	教育节目 educational program
样本 Sample	179	38.0	31.3	23.5	12.8	7.8	3.4
平实生活指向 simple living orientation	98	42.9	32.7	25.5	11.2	7.1	2.0
时尚流行指向 fashion orientation	81	32.1	29.6	21.0	14.8	8.6	4.9

续前表 continued

	人数 Number	热点话题评说 hot topics	外语教学 foreign languages teaching	广播剧 radio play	古典音乐欣赏 classic music	欧美流行音乐 Europe & America pop music	港台流行音乐 HK. Taiwan pop music
样本 Sample	179	20.1	1.7	3.9	6.7	23.5	44.1
平实生活指向 simple living orientation	98	22.4	1.0	3.1	8.2	18.4	36.7
时尚流行指向 fashion orientation	81	17.3	2.5	4.9	4.9	29.6	53.1

续前表 continued

	人数 Number	国内流行音乐 inland pop music	戏曲节目 traditional opera	曲艺相声 folk art	评书 storytelling	医疗保健 medicare
样本 Sample	179	29.1	8.9	22.3	8.4	11.7
平实生活指向 simple living orientation	98	22.4	10.2	28.6	10.2	13.3
时尚流行指向 fashion orientation	81	37.0	7.4	14.8	6.2	9.9

续前表 continued

	人数 Number	点播节目 call-in program	少儿节目 children's program	体育节目 sports	有奖问答 contest	其他 others
样本 Sample	179	5.0	1.1	7.8	8.4	11.2
平实生活指向 simple living orientation	98	2.0	1.0	8.2	5.1	9.2
时尚流行指向 fashion orientation	81	8.6	1.2	7.4	12.3	13.6

2-13-2 广告态度指标/ Advertising Attitude Index

注：本题为多选题，合计百分比超过 100%（Multiple answers）

	人数 Number	国内新闻 national news	国际新闻 international news	天气预报 weather forecast	经济信息 economic information	交通信息 transportation report	教育节目 educational program
样本 Sample	179	38.0	31.3	23.5	12.8	7.8	3.4
广告淡漠指向 indifferent orientation	48	33.3	20.8	20.8	8.3	10.4	4.2
中间层 medium	115	43.5	38.3	23.5	15.7	7.0	3.5
信赖广告指向 loyal orientation	16	12.5	12.5	31.3	6.3	6.3	0.0

续前表 continued

	人数 Number	热点话题评说 hot topics	外语教学 foreign languages teaching	广播剧 radio play	古典音乐欣赏 classic music	欧美流行音乐 Europe & America pop music	港台流行音乐 HK . Taiwan pop music
样本 Sample	179	20.1	1.7	3.9	6.7	23.5	44.1
广告淡漠指向 indifferent orientation	48	16.7	0.0	2.1	12.5	29.2	41.7
中间层 medium	115	17.4	1.7	3.5	4.3	20.0	43.5
信赖广告指向 loyal orientation	16	50.0	6.3	12.5	6.3	31.3	56.3

续前表 continued

	人数 Number	国内流行音乐 inland pop	戏曲节目 traditional opera	曲艺相声 folk art	评书 storytelling	医疗保健 medicare
样本 Sample	179	29.1	8.9	22.3	8.4	11.7
广告淡漠指向 indifferent orientation	48	22.9	16.7	22.9	10.4	14.6
中间层 medium	115	29.6	4.3	19.1	8.7	11.3
信赖广告指向 loyal orientation	16	43.8	18.8	43.8	0.0	6.3

续前表 continued

	人数 Number	点播节目 call-in program	少儿节目 children's program	体育节目 sports	有奖问答 contest	其他 others
样本 Sample	179	5.0	1.1	7.3	8.4	11.2
广告淡漠指向 indifferent orientation	48	6.3	2.1	6.3	4.2	12.5
中间层 medium	115	4.3	0.9	9.6	7.8	10.4
信赖广告指向 loyal orientation	16	6.3	0.0	0.0	25.0	12.5

● 沈阳 / Shenyang

2-1 样本、男性各年龄层、女性各年龄层平时是否接触广播媒介/ Radio Listening by the Whole Sample, Age and Gender Groups

	人数 Number	从来不听 never	收听 yes
样本 Sample	599	50.1	49.9
男性 Male	299	49.2	50.8
16~24 岁 Age	64	46.9	53.1
25~34 岁 Age	89	56.2	43.8
35~44 岁 Age	76	52.6	47.4
45~54 岁 Age	46	41.3	58.7
55~60 岁 Age	24	33.3	66.7
女性 Female	300	51.0	49.0
16~24 岁 Age	63	54.0	46.0
25~34 岁 Age	90	58.9	41.1
35~44 岁 Age	75	45.3	54.7
45~54 岁 Age	48	41.7	58.3
55~60 岁 Age	24	50.0	50.0

2-2 一周内不同时间收听广播的时间长短/ The Average Time Spending on Listening Radio Per Day

2-2-1 一周内不同时间收听广播的时间长短（周一到周四）/ The Average Time Spending on Listening Radio Per Day (Monday—Thursday)

	人数 Number	百分比 Percent
大约半小时或以下 about 1/2 hour or below	78	26.2
大约 1 小时 about 1 hour	106	35.6
大约 2 小时 about 2 hours	66	22.1
大约 3 小时 about 3 hours	21	7.0
大约 4 小时 about 4 hours	7	2.3
大约 5 小时 about 5 hours	4	1.3
大约 6 小时 about 6 hours	5	1.7
大约 7 小时 about 7 hours	0	0.0
大约 8 小时 about 8 hours	0	0.0
大约 9 小时 about 9 hours	0	0.0
大约 10 小时或以上 about 10 hours or over	2	0.7
记不清/不知道 can't remember	4	1.3
没有收听 didn't listen	5	1.7

n=298

2-2-2 一周内不同时间收听广播的时间长短（周五）/ The Average Time Spending on Listening Radio Per Day (Friday)

	人数 Number	百分比 Percent
大约半小时或以下 about 1/2 hour or below	65	21.8
大约 1 小时 about 1 hour	96	32.2
大约 2 小时 about 2 hours	64	21.5
大约 3 小时 about 3 hours	22	7.4
大约 4 小时 about 4 hours	8	2.7
大约 5 小时 about 5 hours	4	1.3
大约 6 小时 about 6 hours	5	1.7
大约 7 小时 about 7 hours	1	0.3
大约 8 小时 about 8 hours	0	0.0
大约 9 小时 about 9 hours	0	0.0
大约 10 小时或以上 about 10 hours or over	2	0.7
记不清/不知道 can't remember	4	1.3
没有收听 didn't listen	27	9.1

n=298

2-2-3 一周内不同时间收听广播的时间长短（周六）/ The Average Time Spending on Listening Radio Per Day (Saturday)

	人数 Number	百分比 Percent
大约半小时或以下 about 1/2 hour or below	66	22.2
大约 1 小时 about 1 hour	88	29.6
大约 2 小时 about 2 hours	69	23.2
大约 3 小时 about 3 hours	23	7.7
大约 4 小时 about 4 hours	6	2.0
大约 5 小时 about 5 hours	3	1.0
大约 6 小时 about 6 hours	6	2.0
大约 7 小时 about 7 hours	0	0.0
大约 8 小时 about 8 hours	0	0.0
大约 9 小时 about 9 hours	0	0.0
大约 10 小时或以上 about 10 hours or over	2	0.7
记不清/不知道 can't remember	4	1.3
没有收听 didn't listen	30	10.1

n=297

2-2-4 一周内不同时间收听广播的时间长短（周日）/ The Average Time Spending on Listening Radio Per Day (Sunday)

	人数 Number	百分比 Percent
大约半小时或以下 about 1/2 hour or below	67	22.5
大约 1 小时 about 1 hour	86	28.9
大约 2 小时 about 2 hours	69	23.2
大约 3 小时 about 3 hours	25	8.4
大约 4 小时 about 4 hours	5	1.7
大约 5 小时 about 5 hours	3	1.0
大约 6 小时 about 6 hours	6	2.0
大约 7 小时 about 7 hours	0	0.0
大约 8 小时 about 8 hours	0	0.0
大约 9 小时 about 9 hours	0	0.0
大约 10 小时或以上 about 10 hours or over	2	0.7
记不清/不知道 can't remember	4	1.3
没有收听 didn't listen	31	10.4

n=298

2-3 经常收听的广播频道排名/ Ranking of the Most Favorite Radio Channels

注：本题为多选题，合计百分比超过 100%（Multiple answers）

排名 Brand Ranking	频道 Channels	人次 Person-time	百分比 Percent
1	辽宁立体声文艺台 Liaoning Literature & Art Stereo Radio	107	35.8
2	沈阳经济电台 Shenyang Economic Radio	100	33.4
3	沈阳电台交通台 Shenyang Traffic Radio	78	26.1
4	辽宁经济广播电台 Liaoning Economic Radio	67	22.4
5	沈阳人民广播电台 Shenyang People's Radio	64	21.4
6	辽宁人民广播电台 Liaoning People's Radio	61	20.4
7	辽宁生活娱乐台 Liaoning Life & Entertainment Radio	57	19.1
8	中央人民广播电台 China National Radio (CNR)	52	17.4
9	沈阳电台文艺台 Shenyang Literature & Art Radio	38	12.7
10	辽宁商业信息电台 Liaoning Commercial Information Radio	37	12.4
11	BBC	4	1.3
12	上海广播电台新闻频道(990 千赫)Shanghai News Channel	3	1.0
13	羊城交通台 Yangcheng Traffic Channel	2	0.7
13	上海广播电台音乐频道 2 (105.7 兆赫) Shanghai Music Channel 2	2	0.7
13	VOA	2	0.7

n=299

2-4 样本、男性各年龄层、女性各年龄层经常收听的广播频道/ The Most Favorite Radio Channels by the Whole Sample, Age and Gender Groups

注：本题为多选题，合计百分比超过 100%（Multiple answers）

	人数 Number	辽宁立体声文艺台 Liaoning Literature & Art Stereo Radio	沈阳电台交通台 Shenyang Traffic Radio	辽宁经济广播电台 Liaoning Economic Radio	沈阳人民广播电台 Shenyang People's Radio	辽宁人民广播电台 Liaoning People's Radio	辽宁生活娱乐台 Liaoning Life & Entertainment Radio
样本 Sample	**299**	**35.8**	**26.1**	**22.4**	**21.4**	**20.4**	**19.1**
男性 Male	**152**	**41.4**	**28.9**	**23.0**	**17.8**	**19.7**	**19.1**
16~24 岁 Age	34	61.8	14.7	17.6	11.8	11.8	44.1
25~34 岁 Age	39	46.2	38.5	28.2	10.3	7.7	30.8
35~44 岁 Age	36	36.1	38.9	19.4	19.4	19.4	5.6
45~54 岁 Age	27	29.6	18.5	22.2	29.6	29.6	0.0
55~60 岁 Age	16	18.8	31.3	31.3	25.0	50.0	0.0
女性 Female	**147**	**29.9**	**23.1**	**21.3**	**25.2**	**21.1**	**19.0**
16~24 岁 Age	29	62.1	6.9	20.7	6.9	20.7	55.2
25~34 岁 Age	37	27.0	24.3	27.0	24.3	18.9	16.2
35~44 岁 Age	41	34.1	26.8	19.5	29.3	19.5	9.8
45~54 岁 Age	28	0.0	25.0	17.9	35.7	17.9	3.6
55~60 岁 Age	12	16.7	41.7	25.0	33.3	41.7	8.3

续前表 continued

	人数 Number	中央人民广播电台 China National Radio (CNR)	沈阳电台文艺台 Shenyang Literature &Art Radio	辽宁商业信息电台 Liaoning Commercial Information Radio	BBC	上海广播电台新闻频道 (990 千赫) Shanghai News Channel	羊城交通台 Yangcheng Traffic Channel	上海广播电台音乐频道 2 (105.7 兆赫) Shanghai Music Channel 2	VOA
样本 Sample	**299**	**17.4**	**12.7**	**12.4**	**1.3**	**1.0**	**0.7**	**0.7**	**0.7**
男性 Male	**152**	**19.7**	**12.5**	**13.2**	**0.7**	**1.3**	**0.7**	**0.0**	**0.7**
16~24 岁 Age	34	8.8	20.6	14.7	0.0	2.9	0.0	0.0	2.9
25~34 岁 Age	39	15.4	12.8	25.6	0.0	0.0	0.0	0.0	0.0
35~44 岁 Age	36	25.0	5.6	8.3	0.0	2.8	2.8	0.0	0.0
45~54 岁 Age	27	22.2	18.5	3.7	3.7	0.0	0.0	0.0	0.0
55~60 岁 Age	16	37.5	0.0	6.3	0.0	0.0	0.0	0.0	0.0
女性 Female	**147**	**15.0**	**12.9**	**11.6**	**2.0**	**0.7**	**0.7**	**1.4**	**0.7**
16~24 岁 Age	29	10.3	13.8	24.1	3.4	3.4	0.0	0.0	3.4
25~34 岁 Age	37	13.5	13.5	8.1	2.7	0.0	0.0	5.4	0.0
35~44 岁 Age	41	4.9	14.6	12.2	0.0	0.0	2.4	0.0	0.0
45~54 岁 Age	28	35.7	14.3	3.6	0.0	0.0	0.0	0.0	0.0
55~60 岁 Age	12	16.7	0.0	8.3	8.3	0.0	0.0	0.0	0.0

2-5 经常收听的广播电台/ The Most Favorite Radio Channels

2-5-1 经常收听的广播电台（周一到周四）/ Ranking of the Most Favorite Radio Channels (Monday—Thursday)

注：本题为多选题，合计百分比超过 100%（Multiple answers）

排名 Brand Ranking	频道 Channels	人次 Person-time	百分比 Percent
1	辽宁立体声文艺台 Liaoning Literature & Art Stereo Radio	99	33.7
2	沈阳经济电台 Shenyang Economic Radio	93	31.6
3	沈阳电台交通台 Shenyang Traffic Radio	80	27.2
4	中央人民广播电台 China National Radio (CNR)	60	20.4
5	辽宁经济广播电台 Liaoning Economic Radio	58	19.7
6	沈阳人民广播电台 Shenyang People's Radio	57	19.4
7	辽宁生活娱乐台 Liaoning Life & Entertainment Radio	53	18.0
8	辽宁人民广播电台 Liaoning People's Radio	48	16.3
9	沈阳电台文艺台 Shenyang Literature & Art Radio	36	12.2
10	辽宁商业信息电台 Liaoning Commercial Information Radio	35	11.9

n=294

2-5-2 经常收听的广播电台（周五）/ Ranking of the Most Favorite Radio Channels (Friday)

注：本题为多选题，合计百分比超过 100%（Multiple answers）

排名 Brand Ranking	频道 Channels	人次 Person-time	百分比 Percent
1	辽宁立体声文艺台 Liaoning Literature & Art Stereo Radio	91	31.6
2	沈阳经济电台 Shenyang Economic Radio	84	29.2
3	沈阳电台交通台 Shenyang Traffic Radio	75	26.0
4	辽宁经济广播电台 Liaoning Economic Radio	54	18.8
5	沈阳人民广播电台 Shenyang People's Radio	53	18.4
6	中央人民广播电台 China National Radio (CNR)	50	17.4
7	辽宁人民广播电台 Liaoning People's Radio	47	16.3
8	辽宁生活娱乐台 Liaoning Life & Entertainment Radio	44	15.3
9	沈阳电台文艺台 Shenyang Literature & Art Radio	35	12.2
10	辽宁商业信息电台 Liaoning Commercial Information Radio	33	11.5

n=288

2-5-3 经常收听的广播电台（周六）/ Ranking of the Most Favorite Radio Channels (Saturday)

注：本题为多选题，合计百分比超过 100%（Multiple answers）

排名 Brand Ranking	频道 Channels	人次 Person-time	百分比 Percent
1	辽宁立体声文艺台 Liaoning Literature & Art Stereo Radio	90	31.6
2	沈阳经济电台 Shenyang Economic Radio	80	28.1
3	沈阳电台交通台 Shenyang Traffic Radio	76	26.7
4	辽宁经济广播电台 Liaoning Economic Radio	55	19.3
5	沈阳人民广播电台 Shenyang People's Radio	53	18.6
6	中央人民广播电台 China National Radio (CNR)	50	17.5
7	辽宁生活娱乐台 Liaoning Life & Entertainment Radio	49	17.2
8	辽宁人民广播电台 Liaoning People's Radio	47	16.5
9	沈阳电台文艺台 Shenyang Literature & Art Radio	35	12.3
10	辽宁商业信息电台 Liaoning Commercial Information Radio	33	11.6

n=285

2-5-4 经常收听的广播电台（周日）/ Ranking of the Most Favorite Radio Channels (Sunday)

注：本题为多选题，合计百分比超过 100%（Multiple answers）

排名 Brand Ranking	频道 Channels	人次 Person-time	百分比 Percent
1	辽宁立体声文艺台 Liaoning Literature & Art Stereo Radio	90	31.3
2	沈阳电台交通台 Shenyang Traffic Radio	78	27.1
2	沈阳经济电台 Shenyang Economic Radio	78	27.1
3	沈阳人民广播电台 Shenyang People's Radio	54	18.8
3	辽宁经济广播电台 Liaoning Economic Radio	54	18.8
4	辽宁生活娱乐台 Liaoning Life & Entertainment Radio	51	17.7
5	中央人民广播电台 China National Radio (CNR)	49	17.0
6	辽宁人民广播电台 Liaoning People's Radio	47	16.3
7	沈阳电台文艺台 Shenyang Literature & Art Radio	35	12.2
8	辽宁商业信息电台 Liaoning Commercial Information Radio	33	11.5

n=288

2-6 经常收听的广播节目/ Ranking of the Most Favorite Radio Programs

注：本题为多选题，合计百分比超过 100%（Multiple answers）

排名 Ranking	广播节目 Radio Programs	人次 Person-time	百分比 Percent
1	国内新闻 national news	161	54.6
2	天气预报 weather forecast	150	50.8
3	国际新闻 international news	113	38.3
4	港台流行音乐 HK.Taiwan pop music	72	24.4
5	热点话题评说 hot topics	71	24.1
6	曲艺相声 folk arts	66	22.4
7	体育节目 sports	58	19.7
8	国内流行音乐 inland pop music	46	15.6
9	评书 storytelling	42	14.2
10	医疗保健 medicare	34	11.5
10	欧美流行音乐 Europe pop music	34	11.5
11	经济信息 economic information report	31	10.5
12	交通信息 transportation report	28	9.5
13	点播节目 call-in program	23	7.8
14	股市信息 stock information	19	6.4
15	有奖问答 contest	17	5.8

n=295

2-7 样本、男性各年龄层、女性各年龄层经常收听的广播节目/ The Most Favorite Radio Programs by the Whole Sample, Age and Gender Groups

注：本题为多选题，合计百分比超过 100%（Multiple answers）

	人数 Number	国内新闻 national news	国际新闻 international news	天气预报 weather forecast	经济信息 economic information report	交通信息 transportation report	教育节目 educational program
样本 Sample	**295**	**54.6**	**38.3**	**50.8**	**10.5**	**9.5**	**3.4**
男性 Male	**149**	**60.4**	**47.7**	**47.7**	**10.7**	**10.1**	**3.4**
16~24 岁 Age	34	20.6	17.6	29.4	0.0	2.9	2.9
25~34 岁 Age	39	53.8	48.7	41.0	12.8	20.5	5.1
35~44 岁 Age	35	85.7	62.9	65.7	17.1	14.3	2.9
45~54 岁 Age	27	74.1	55.6	51.9	7.4	0.0	3.7
55~60 岁 Age	14	85.7	64.3	57.1	21.4	7.1	0.0
女性 Female	**146**	**48.6**	**28.8**	**54.1**	**10.3**	**8.9**	**3.4**
16~24 岁 Age	29	20.7	17.2	24.1	3.4	3.4	0.0
25~34 岁 Age	37	48.6	27.0	64.9	13.5	16.2	2.7
35~44 岁 Age	41	56.1	26.8	61.0	17.1	9.8	9.8
45~54 岁 Age	27	63.0	37.0	59.3	7.4	3.7	0.0
55~60 岁 Age	12	58.3	50.0	58.3	0.0	8.3	0.0

续前表 continued

	人数 Number	热点话题评说 hot topics	外语教学 foreign languages teaching	广播剧 radio play	古典音乐欣赏 classic music	欧美流行音乐 Europe & America pop music	港台流行音乐 HK.Taiwan pop music
样本 Sample	**295**	**24.1**	**1.0**	**1.0**	**2.7**	**11.5**	**24.4**
男性 Male	**149**	**26.2**	**0.7**	**1.3**	**2.7**	**12.1**	**23.5**
16~24 岁 Age	34	29.4	0.0	0.0	0.0	29.4	52.9
25~34 岁 Age	39	25.6	0.0	5.1	2.6	12.8	23.1
35~44 岁 Age	35	17.1	2.9	0.0	5.7	5.7	20.0
45~54 岁 Age	27	22.2	0.0	0.0	3.7	3.7	3.7
55~60 岁 Age	14	50.0	0.0	0.0	0.0	0.0	0.0
女性 Female	**146**	**21.9**	**1.4**	**0.7**	**2.7**	**11.0**	**25.3**
16~24 岁 Age	29	10.3	3.4	0.0	13.8	37.9	72.4
25~34 岁 Age	37	27.0	0.0	0.0	0.0	5.4	21.6
35~44 岁 Age	41	31.7	2.4	0.0	0.0	4.9	17.1
45~54 岁 Age	27	18.5	0.0	3.7	0.0	3.7	3.7
55~60 岁 Age	12	8.3	0.0	0.0	0.0	0.0	0.0

续前表 continued

	人数 Number	国内流行音乐 inland pop music	戏曲节目 traditional opera	曲艺相声 folk arts	评书 storytelling	医疗保健 medicare
样本 Sample	**295**	**15.6**	**4.7**	**22.4**	**14.2**	**11.5**
男性 Male	**149**	**14.1**	**3.4**	**23.5**	**18.8**	**4.7**
16~24 岁 Age	34	17.6	0.0	17.6	11.8	0.0
25~34 岁 Age	39	20.5	2.6	35.9	10.3	7.7
35~44 岁 Age	35	8.6	5.7	22.9	14.3	0.0
45~54 岁 Age	27	14.8	3.7	18.5	29.6	11.1
55~60 岁 Age	14	0.0	7.1	14.3	50.0	7.1
女性 Female	**146**	**17.1**	**6.2**	**21.2**	**9.6**	**18.5**
16~24 岁 Age	29	41.4	0.0	24.1	10.3	3.4
25~34 岁 Age	37	16.2	0.0	21.6	2.7	16.2
35~44 岁 Age	41	12.2	2.4	19.5	9.8	24.4
45~54 岁 Age	27	7.4	11.1	25.9	7.4	14.8
55~60 岁 Age	12	0.0	41.7	8.3	33.3	50.0

续前表 continued

	人数 Number	点播节目 call-in program	少儿节目 children's program	体育节目 sports	有奖问答 contest	其他 others
样本 Sample	**295**	**7.8**	**2.7**	**19.7**	**5.8**	**6.4**
男性 Male	**149**	**4.7**	**1.3**	**28.2**	**4.7**	**7.4**
16~24 岁 Age	34	14.7	0.0	47.1	14.7	2.9
25~34 岁 Age	39	5.1	2.6	23.1	5.1	12.8
35~44 岁 Age	35	0.0	2.9	25.7	0.0	5.7
45~54 岁 Age	27	0.0	0.0	29.6	0.0	7.4
55~60 岁 Age	14	0.0	0.0	0.0	0.0	7.1
女性 Female	**146**	**11.0**	**4.1**	**11.0**	**6.8**	**5.5**
16~24 岁 Age	29	27.6	3.4	13.8	13.8	0.0
25~34 岁 Age	37	13.5	5.4	5.4	10.8	8.1
35~44 岁 Age	41	4.9	4.9	12.2	0.0	4.9
45~54 岁 Age	27	3.7	0.0	14.8	7.4	11.1
55~60 岁 Age	12	0.0	8.3	8.3	0.0	0.0

2-8 不同学历的听众收听的广播节目的偏好/ Program Preference by Educational Levels

注：本题为多选题，合计百分比超过 100%（Multiple answers）

	人数 Number	国内新闻 national news	国际新闻 international news	天气预报 weather forecast	经济信息 economic information report	交通信息 transportation report	教育节目 educational program
样本 Sample	**295**	**54.6**	**38.3**	**50.8**	**10.5**	**9.5**	**3.4**
小学及以下 Primary School or Below	8	62.5	50.0	37.5	0.0	12.5	0.0
初中 Middle School	90	64.4	45.6	62.2	11.1	10.0	4.4
高中/中专/技校 High School/Technical Secondary School	120	52.5	37.5	45.8	5.8	10.8	2.5
大学专科 2-3 Year College	48	45.8	22.9	58.3	12.5	10.4	4.2
大学本科 4-5 Year College	28	46.4	42.9	25.0	28.6	0.0	3.6
研究生或以上 Graduate or Above	1	0.0	0.0	100.0	0.0	0.0	0.0

续前表 continued

	人数 Number	热点话题评说 hot topics	外语教学 foreign languages teaching	广播剧 radio play	古典音乐欣赏 classic music	欧美流行音乐 Europe & America pop music	港台流行音乐 HK.Taiwan pop music
样本 Sample	**295**	**24.1**	**1.0**	**1.0**	**2.7**	**11.5**	**24.4**
小学及以下 Primary School or Below	8	0.0	0.0	0.0	0.0	12.5	12.5
初中 Middle School	90	22.2	2.2	1.1	0.0	2.2	15.6
高中/中专/技校 High School/Technical Secondary School	120	28.3	0.0	0.8	3.3	15.0	29.2
大学专科 2-3 Year College	48	27.1	2.1	2.1	6.3	16.7	31.3
大学本科 4-5 Year College	28	14.3	0.0	0.0	3.6	14.3	25.0
研究生或以上 Graduate or Above	1	0.0	0.0	0.0	0.0	100.0	0.0

续前表 continued

	人数 Number	国内流行音乐 inland pop music	戏曲节目 traditional opera	曲艺相声 folk arts	评书 storytelling	医疗保健 medicare
样本 Sample	**295**	**15.6**	**4.7**	**22.4**	**14.2**	**11.5**
小学及以下 Primary School or Below	8	0.0	37.5	37.5	25.0	12.5
初中 Middle School	90	14.4	3.3	22.2	22.2	7.8
高中/中专/技校 High School/Technical Secondary School	120	14.2	6.7	21.7	10.0	13.3
大学专科 2-3 Year College	48	18.8	0.0	27.1	12.5	14.6
大学本科 4-5 Year College	28	21.4	0.0	14.3	7.1	10.7
研究生或以上 Graduate or Above	1	100.0	0.0	0.0	0.0	0.0

续前表 continued

	人数 Number	点播节目 call-in program	少儿节目 children's program	体育节目 sports	有奖问答 contest	其他 others
样本 Sample	**295**	**7.8**	**2.7**	**19.7**	**5.8**	**6.4**
小学及以下 Primary School or Below	8	0.0	0.0	0.0	0.0	0.0
初中 Middle School	90	2.2	3.3	16.7	2.2	4.4
高中/中专/技校 High School/Technical Secondary School	120	10.8	1.7	25.0	7.5	5.8
大学专科 2-3 Year College	48	14.6	4.2	12.5	10.4	10.4
大学本科 4-5 Year College	28	3.6	3.6	25.0	3.6	10.7
研究生或以上 Graduate or Above	1	0.0	0.0	0.0	0.0	0.0

2-9 经常收听广播时段/ Weekday Times Slots of Radio Listening

注：本题为多选题，合计百分比超过 100%（Multiple answers）

时间段 times slots	周一到周四(%) (Monday—Thursday)	周五(%) (Friday)	周六(%) (Saturday)	周日(%) (Sunday)
样本量 Sample	n=298	n=298	n=296	n=297
0:00-0:30	0.7	0.3	0.7	0.7
0:30-1:00	0.7	0.3	0.7	0.7
1:00-1:30	0.7	0.3	0.7	0.7
1:30-2:00	0.3	0.0	0.3	0.3
2:00-2:30	0.0	0.0	0.0	0.0
2:30-3:00	0.0	0.0	0.0	0.0
3:00-3:30	0.0	0.0	0.0	0.0
3:30-4:00	1.0	1.0	0.7	0.7
4:00-4:30	1.3	1.3	1.0	1.0
4:30-5:00	1.0	1.3	0.7	0.7
5:00-5:30	3.7	3.4	3.4	3.4
5:30-6:00	9.7	8.7	9.1	9.1
6:00-6:30	30.5	29.9	28.0	27.6
6:30-7:00	34.9	32.2	30.4	30.0
7:00-7:30	21.1	19.1	18.2	17.8
7:30-8:00	11.7	11.7	10.5	10.1
8:00-8:30	10.4	9.1	10.5	9.8
8:30-9:00	7.7	7.4	8.4	8.4
9:00-9:30	8.1	6.7	6.8	7.4
9:30-10:00	7.0	6.4	5.7	6.4
10:00-10:30	4.4	5.7	4.1	4.4
10:30-11:00	4.0	5.0	4.7	5.1
11:00-11:30	3.0	3.7	4.7	4.0
11:30-12:00	3.7	3.7	4.4	3.7
12:00-12:30	5.4	5.0	5.1	5.1
12:30-13:00	4.7	4.4	5.4	5.7
13:00-13:30	5.7	4.7	6.1	6.1
13:30-14:00	4.4	3.4	4.1	4.4
14:00-14:30	3.4	3.0	3.0	3.4
14:30-15:00	2.0	2.0	2.0	2.4
15:00-15:30	3.0	3.7	3.0	3.4
15:30-16:00	4.4	4.7	4.1	4.0
16:00-16:30	4.7	5.0	4.1	4.7
16:30-17:00	5.7	6.7	5.4	5.4
17:00-17:30	10.7	10.1	9.1	9.4
17:30-18:00	11.4	10.4	9.5	8.8
18:00-18:30	10.7	10.7	9.8	9.4
18:30-19:00	9.4	9.4	8.8	8.4
19:00-19:30	6.0	5.4	5.4	5.1
19:30-20:00	5.4	5.4	5.4	5.1
20:00-20:30	10.4	10.4	11.1	11.4
20:30-21:00	14.1	12.8	13.5	14.1
21:00-21:30	14.4	14.1	13.5	13.8
21:30-22:00	11.7	11.7	11.5	11.4
22:00-22:30	7.0	8.1	8.1	8.1
22:30-23:00	5.4	6.0	7.8	7.1
23:00-23:30	4.4	5.0	5.4	5.4
23:30-24:00	2.7	2.7	3.0	3.0

2-10 样本、男性各年龄层、女性各年龄层是否打过热线电话参与节目/ Call-in Hot-time Telephone to Take Part in the Program by the Whole Sample, Age and Gender Groups

	人数 Number	打过 yes	没打过 no
样本 Sample	289	25.6	74.4
男性 Male	148	23.0	77.0
16~24 岁 Age	33	33.3	66.7
25~34 岁 Age	37	24.3	75.7
35~44 岁 Age	35	20.0	80.0
45~54 岁 Age	27	22.2	77.8
55~60 岁 Age	16	6.3	93.8
女性 Female	141	28.4	71.6
16~24 岁 Age	28	39.3	60.7
25~34 岁 Age	36	44.4	55.6
35~44 岁 Age	39	20.5	79.5
45~54 岁 Age	27	14.8	85.2
55~60 岁 Age	11	9.1	90.9

2-11 不同消费者层平时是否接触广播媒介/ Radio Exposure by Market Segments

2-11-1 时尚流行指标/ Fads Popular Index

	人数 Number	从来不听 never	收听 yes
样本 Sample	599	50.1	49.9
平实生活指向 simple living orientation	292	51.0	49.0
时尚流行指向 fashion orientation	307	49.2	50.8

2-11-2 广告态度指标/ Advertising Attitude Index

	人数 Number	从来不听 never	收听 yes
样本 Sample	599	50.1	49.9
广告淡漠指向 indifferent orientation	171	51.5	48.5
中间层 medium	353	51.0	49.0
信赖广告指向 loyal orientation	75	42.7	57.3

2-12 不同消费者层收听广播频道的偏好/ Channel Preference by Market Segments

2-12-1 时尚流行指标/ Fads Popular Index

注：本题为多选题，合计百分比超过 100%（Multiple answers）

	人数 Number	辽宁立体声文艺台 Liaoning Literature & Art Stereo Radio	沈阳经济电台 Shenyang Economic Radio	沈阳电台交通台 Shenyang Traffic Radio	辽宁经济广播电台 Liaoning Economic Radio	沈阳人民广播电台 Shenyang People's Radio	辽宁人民广播电台 Liaoning People's Radio	辽宁生活娱乐台 Liaoning Life & Entertainment Radio
样本 Sample	299	35.8	33.4	26.1	22.4	21.4	20.4	19.1
平实生活指向 simple living orientation	143	29.4	38.5	25.9	24.5	23.1	23.8	9.1
时尚流行指向 fashion orientation	156	41.7	28.8	26.3	20.5	19.9	17.3	28.2

续前表 continued

	人数 Number	中央人民广播电台 China National Radio (CNR)	沈阳电台文艺台 Shenyang Literature &Art Radio	辽宁商业信息电台 Liaoning Commercial Information Radio	BBC	上海广播电台新闻频道 (990 千赫) Shanghai News Channel	羊城交通台 Yangcheng Traffic Channel	上海广播电台音乐频道 2 (105.7 兆赫) Shanghai Music Channel 2	VOA
样本 Sample	299	17.4	12.7	12.4	1.3	1.0	0.7	0.7	0.7
平实生活指向 simple living orientation	143	20.3	11.2	8.4	2.1	0.7	0.7	0.0	0.7
时尚流行指向 fashion orientation	156	14.7	14.1	16.0	0.6	1.3	0.6	1.3	0.6

2-12-2 广告态度指标/ Advertising Attitude Index

注：本题为多选题，合计百分比超过 100%（Multiple answers）

	人数 Number	辽宁立体声文艺台 Liaoning Literature & Art Stereo Radio	沈阳经济电台 Shenyang Economic Radio	沈阳电台交通台 Shenyang Traffic Radio	辽宁经济广播电台 Liaoning Economic Radio	沈阳人民广播电台 Shenyang People's Radio	辽宁人民广播电台 Liaoning People's Radio	辽宁生活娱乐台 Liaoning Life & Entertainment Radio
样本 Sample	299	35.8	33.4	26.1	22.4	21.4	20.4	19.1
广告淡漠指向 indifferent orientation	83	33.7	33.7	33.7	25.3	16.9	18.1	21.7
中间层 medium	173	36.4	31.8	23.1	21.4	22.0	21.4	17.3
信赖广告指向 loyal orientation	43	37.2	39.5	23.3	20.9	27.9	20.9	20.9

续前表 continued

	人数 Number	中央人民广播电台 China National Radio (CNR)	沈阳电台文艺台 Shenyang Literature &Art Radio	辽宁商业信息电台 Liaoning Commercial Information Radio	BBC	上海广播电台新闻频道 (990 千赫) Shanghai News Channel	羊城交通台 Yangcheng Traffic Channel	上海广播电台音乐频道 2 (105.7 兆赫) Shanghai Music Channel 2	VOA
样本 Sample	299	17.4	12.7	12.4	1.3	1.0	0.7	0.7	0.7
广告淡漠指向 indifferent orientation	83	21.7	14.5	8.4	1.2	0.0	1.2	0.0	0.0
中间层 medium	173	13.9	12.7	13.3	1.7	1.7	0.6	1.2	1.2
信赖广告指向 loyal orientation	43	23.3	9.3	16.3	0.0	0.0	0.0	0.0	0.0

2-13 不同消费者层收看广播节目的偏好/ Program Preference by Market Segments

2-13-1 时尚流行指标/ Fads Popular Index

注：本题为多选题，合计百分比超过 100%（Multiple answers）

	人数 Number	国内新闻 national news	国际新闻 international news	天气预报 weather forecast	经济信息 economic information	交通信息 transportation report	教育节目 educational program
样本 Sample	295	54.6	38.3	50.8	10.5	9.5	3.4
平实生活指向 simple living orientation	142	57.0	45.1	45.1	14.8	8.5	3.5
时尚流行指向 fashion orientation	153	52.3	32.0	56.2	6.5	10.5	3.3

续前表 continued

	人数 Number	热点话题评说 hot topics	外语教学 foreign languages teaching	广播剧 radio play	古典音乐欣赏 classic music	欧美流行音乐 Europe & America pop music	港台流行音乐 HK.Taiwan pop music
样本 Sample	295	24.1	1.0	1.0	2.7	11.5	24.4
平实生活指向 simple living orientation	142	23.2	1.4	1.4	3.5	9.2	12.7
时尚流行指向 fashion orientation	153	24.8	0.7	0.7	2.0	13.7	35.3

续前表 continued

	人数 Number	国内流行音乐 inland pop music	戏曲节目 traditional opera	曲艺相声 folk art	评书 storytelling	医疗保健 medicare
样本 Sample	295	15.6	4.7	22.4	14.2	11.5
平实生活指向 simple living orientation	142	13.4	5.6	22.5	14.8	13.4
时尚流行指向 fashion orientation	153	17.6	3.9	22.2	13.7	9.8

续前表 continued

	人数 Number	点播节目 call-in program	少儿节目 children's program	体育节目 sports	有奖问答 contest	其他 others
样本 Sample	295	7.8	2.7	19.7	5.8	6.4
平实生活指向 simple living orientation	142	2.8	2.1	18.3	3.5	7.7
时尚流行指向 fashion orientation	153	12.4	3.3	20.9	7.8	5.2

2-13-2 广告态度指标/ Advertising Attitude Index

注：本题为多选题，合计百分比超过 100%（Multiple answers）

	人数 Number	国内新闻 national news	国际新闻 international news	天气预报 weather forecast	经济信息 economic information	交通信息 transportation report	教育节目 educational program
样本 Sample	295	54.6	38.3	50.8	10.5	9.5	3.4
广告淡漠指向 indifferent orientation	82	51.2	46.3	42.7	8.5	8.5	3.7
中间层 medium	170	54.1	34.7	53.5	11.8	10.6	3.5
信赖广告指向 loyal orientation	43	62.8	37.2	55.8	9.3	7.0	2.3

续前表 continued

	人数 Number	热点话题评说 hot topics	外语教学 foreign languages teaching	广播剧 radio play	古典音乐欣赏 classic music	欧美流行音乐 Europe & America pop music	港台流行音乐 HK.Taiwan pop music
样本 Sample	**295**	**24.1**	**1.0**	**1.0**	**2.7**	**11.5**	**24.4**
广告淡漠指向 indifferent orientation	82	23.2	1.2	0.0	2.4	15.9	26.8
中间层 medium	170	25.9	1.2	1.2	2.4	10.0	22.9
信赖广告指向 loyal orientation	43	18.6	0.0	2.3	4.7	9.3	25.6

续前表 continued

	人数 Number	国内流行音乐 inland pop music	戏曲节目 traditional opera	曲艺相声 folk art	评书 storytelling	医疗保健 medicare
样本 Sample	**295**	**15.6**	**4.7**	**22.4**	**14.2**	**11.5**
广告淡漠指向 indifferent orientation	82	15.9	4.9	25.6	14.6	11.0
中间层 medium	170	15.9	5.3	21.2	13.5	11.8
信赖广告指向 loyal orientation	43	14.0	2.3	20.9	16.3	11.6

续前表 continued

	人数 Number	点播节目 call-in program	少儿节目 children's program	体育节目 sports	有奖问答 contest	其他 others
样本 Sample	**295**	**7.8**	**2.7**	**19.7**	**5.8**	**6.4**
广告淡漠指向 indifferent orientation	82	2.4	2.4	18.3	7.3	6.1
中间层 medium	170	10.6	2.4	20.0	4.7	5.9
信赖广告指向 loyal orientation	43	7.0	4.7	20.9	7.0	9.3

3.报纸 / Newspapers

● 北京 / Beijing

3-1 样本、男性各年龄层、女性各年龄层平时是否接触报纸媒介/ Newspaper Reading by the Whole Sample, Age and Gender Groups

	人数 Number	从来不看 never	看 yes
样本 Sample	1011	6.6	93.4
男性 Male	503	4.8	95.2
16~24 岁 Age	105	7.6	92.4
25~34 岁 Age	151	4.6	95.4
35~44 岁 Age	130	3.1	96.9
45~54 岁 Age	77	3.9	96.1
55~60 岁 Age	40	5.0	95.0
女性 Female	508	8.5	91.5
16~24 岁 Age	108	9.3	90.7
25~34 岁 Age	150	5.3	94.7
35~44 岁 Age	124	7.3	92.7
45~54 岁 Age	84	9.5	90.5
55~60 岁 Age	42	19.0	81.0

3-2 经常阅读的报纸排名/ Ranking of the Frequently Read Newspapers

注：本题为多选题，合计百分比超过 100%（Multiple answers）

排名 Brand Ranking	报纸 Newspapers	人次 Person-time	百分比 Percent
1	北京晚报 Beijing Evening News	597	63.3
2	北京青年报 Beijing Youth Daily	423	44.9
3	北京晨报 Beijing Morning News	174	18.5
4	精品购物指南 Shopping Guide	133	14.1
5	北京日报 Beijing Daily	132	14.0
6	参考消息 Reference News	104	11.0
7	北京广播电视报 Beijing TV Guide	56	5.9
8	环球时报 Global Times	54	5.7
9	足球报 Soccer	50	5.3
10	人民日报 People's Daily	37	3.9
11	法制报 Fa Zhi Bao	36	3.8
11	中国电视报 China TV Guide	36	3.8
12	中国青年报 China Youth Daily	34	3.6
13	南方周末 South Weekend	30	3.2
14	作家文摘 Zuo Jia Wen Zhai	28	3.0

n=943

3-3 样本、男性各年龄层、女性各年龄层经常阅读的报纸/ Frequently Read Newspapers by the Whole Sample, Age and Gender Groups

注：本题为多选题，合计百分比超过 100%（Multiple answers）

	人数 Number	北京晚报 Beijing Evening News	北京青年报 Beijing Youth Daily	北京晨报 Beijing Morning News	精品购物指南 Shopping Guide	北京日报 Beijing Daily	参考消息 Reference News	北京广播电视报 Beijing TV Guide
样本 Sample	943	63.3	44.9	18.5	14.1	14.0	11.0	5.9
男性 Male	478	64.2	43.7	21.3	9.0	16.9	14.2	2.9
16~24 岁 Age	97	63.9	38.1	19.6	15.5	7.2	10.3	4.1
25~34 岁 Age	144	64.6	57.6	22.9	16.0	7.6	19.4	2.1
35~44 岁 Age	125	68.0	41.6	28.8	3.2	17.6	14.4	2.4
45~54 岁 Age	74	59.5	31.1	12.2	1.4	32.4	13.5	2.7
55~60 岁 Age	38	60.5	36.8	13.2	0.0	44.7	5.3	5.3
女性 Female	465	62.4	46.0	15.5	19.4	11.0	7.7	9.0
16~24 岁 Age	98	49.0	43.9	13.3	38.8	5.1	4.1	12.2
25~34 岁 Age	142	61.3	57.0	16.9	24.6	10.6	12.7	4.9
35~44 岁 Age	115	65.2	46.1	17.4	8.7	11.3	8.7	9.6
45~54 岁 Age	76	75.0	35.5	13.2	7.9	19.7	5.3	7.9
55~60 岁 Age	34	67.6	29.4	14.7	2.9	8.8	0.0	17.6

续前表 continued

	人数 Number	环球时报 Global Times	足球报 Soccer	人民日报 People's Daily	法制报 Fa Zhi Bao	中国电视报 China TV Guide	中国青年报 China Youth Daily	南方周末 South Weekend	作家文摘 Zuo Jia Wen Zhai
样本 Sample	**943**	**5.7**	**5.3**	**3.9**	**3.8**	**3.8**	**3.6**	**3.2**	**3.0**
男性 Male	**478**	**7.1**	**9.2**	**5.4**	**2.9**	**2.7**	**4.0**	**3.3**	**1.9**
16~24 岁 Age	97	4.1	14.4	1.0	2.1	5.2	0.0	6.2	0.0
25~34 岁 Age	144	7.6	9.0	3.5	2.1	0.7	6.3	2.8	2.1
35~44 岁 Age	125	9.6	7.2	3.2	4.8	0.8	4.0	1.6	3.2
45~54 岁 Age	74	8.1	8.1	10.8	4.1	5.4	6.8	2.7	0.0
55~60 岁 Age	38	2.6	5.3	21.1	0.0	5.3	0.0	5.3	5.3
女性 Female	**465**	**4.3**	**1.3**	**2.4**	**4.7**	**4.9**	**3.2**	**3.0**	**4.1**
16~24 岁 Age	98	7.1	3.1	0.0	2.0	9.2	2.0	1.0	4.1
25~34 岁 Age	142	5.6	1.4	2.8	4.2	3.5	1.4	4.9	3.5
35~44 岁 Age	115	2.6	0.9	2.6	7.8	0.9	4.3	3.5	4.3
45~54 岁 Age	76	2.6	0.0	3.9	5.3	3.9	7.9	1.3	5.3
55~60 岁 Age	34	0.0	0.0	2.9	2.9	14.7	0.0	2.9	2.9

3-4 经常阅读的报纸的主要来源/ Sources of Obtaining the Frequently Read Newspapers

注：本题为多选题，合计百分比可能超过 100%（Multiple answers）

	人数 Number	家中订阅 subscribed by my family	单位订阅 subscribed by work unit	报摊购买 bought from vender	赠阅 given as gift	借阅 borrowed	街头报栏 news-stand along street
北京晚报 Beijing Evening News	589	19.9	8.3	68.1	0.8	2.0	0.8
北京青年报 Beijing Youth Daily	420	14.0	44.3	36.7	0.2	3.1	1.7
北京晨报 Beijing Morning News	173	5.2	12.7	70.5	2.3	7.5	2.9
精品购物指南 Shopping Guide	134	9.7	4.5	76.9	0.7	6.0	2.2
北京日报 Beijing Daily	132	4.5	82.6	9.1	0.8	1.5	1.5
参考消息 Reference News	103	13.3	45.7	36.2	1.0	2.9	1.0
北京广播电视报 Beijing TV Guide	56	14.3	8.9	73.2	0.0	1.8	1.8
环球时报 Global Times	53	7.5	5.7	83.0	0.0	1.9	1.9
足球报 Soccer	49	8.2	0.0	89.8	0.0	0.0	2.0

3-5 经常阅读的报纸内容/ Ranking of the Content Categories that Newspaper Readers Concern about

注：本题为多选题，合计百分比超过 100%（Multiple answers）

排名 Ranking	报道 Contents	人次 Person-time	百分比 Percent
1	国际新闻 international news	495	53.3
2	国内新闻 national news	489	52.7
3	头版要闻 first page news	397	42.8
4	体育报道 sports report	296	31.9
5	法制报道 legal news	212	22.8
6	健康医疗 medicare	187	20.2
7	生活常识 common sense	163	17.6
8	影视娱乐报道 video & entertainment report	162	17.5
9	热点追踪 hits track	148	15.9
10	经济信息 economic information	121	13.0
10	人物专访 personal interview	121	13.0
11	本地新闻 local news	116	12.5
12	消费指南 consumption guide	110	11.9
13	科技知识 science sense	96	10.3
14	服饰美容 clothes & beauty	91	9.8
15	文化信息 cultural information	90	9.7
16	电视节目预告 TV program forecast	89	9.6
17	休闲旅游 entertainment & travel	88	9.5
18	股市报道 stock market report	87	9.4
19	军事知识 military knowledge	82	8.8
20	小说 novel	73	7.9
21	海外见闻 overseas information	65	7.0
22	财政金融 finance & economic	61	6.6
23	港澳台新闻 news about HK Taiwan Macao	60	6.5
24	漫画 cartoon	48	5.2
24	广告 advertising	48	5.2
25	散文 prose	40	4.3
26	文艺评论 art critics	19	2.0
27	其他 others	11	1.2
28	读者来信 reader's letter	8	0.9
29	书评 book comment	7	0.8

n=928

3-6 样本、男性各年龄层、女性各年龄层经常阅读的报纸内容/ The Concerned Newspaper Content Categories by the Whole Sample, Age and Gender Groups

注：本题为多选题，合计百分比超过 100%（Multiple answers）

	人数 Number	头版要闻 first page news	国际新闻 international news	国内新闻 national news	港澳台新闻 news about HK. Taiwan. Macao.	本地新闻 local news	经济信息 economic information
样本 Sample	928	42.8	53.3	52.7	6.5	12.5	13.0
男性 Male	469	45.0	65.2	57.6	5.8	13.4	16.0
16~24 岁 Age	95	30.5	44.2	38.9	5.3	7.4	11.6
25~34 岁 Age	140	47.1	66.4	55.0	8.6	12.9	17.9
35~44 岁 Age	125	48.0	74.4	65.6	4.0	16.8	19.2
45~54 岁 Age	73	49.3	65.8	68.5	4.1	15.1	15.1
55~60 岁 Age	36	55.6	83.3	66.7	5.6	16.7	11.1
女性 Female	459	40.5	41.2	47.7	7.2	11.5	10.0
16~24 岁 Age	97	35.1	38.1	28.9	12.4	4.1	3.1
25~34 岁 Age	140	40.0	40.0	46.4	5.7	10.7	8.6
35~44 岁 Age	112	43.8	40.2	49.1	5.4	15.2	17.9
45~54 岁 Age	76	44.7	50.0	68.4	3.9	15.8	9.2
55~60 岁 Age	34	38.2	38.2	55.9	11.8	14.7	11.8

续前表 continued

	人数 Number	财政金融 finance & economic	股市报道 stock market report	热点追踪 hits track	文化信息 cultural information	体育报道 sports report	人物专访 personal interview
样本 Sample	**928**	**6.6**	**9.4**	**15.9**	**9.7**	**31.9**	**13.0**
男性 Male	**469**	**9.0**	**9.4**	**13.9**	**7.2**	**48.4**	**9.6**
16~24 岁 Age	95	8.4	6.3	11.6	12.6	51.6	8.4
25~34 岁 Age	140	10.0	12.1	14.3	8.6	51.4	8.6
35~44 岁 Age	125	11.2	11.2	15.2	3.2	48.0	10.4
45~54 岁 Age	73	5.5	6.8	13.7	4.1	43.8	11.0
55~60 岁 Age	36	5.6	5.6	13.9	8.3	38.9	11.1
女性 Female	**459**	**4.1**	**9.4**	**18.1**	**12.2**	**15.0**	**16.6**
16~24 岁 Age	97	1.0	1.0	16.5	26.8	15.5	17.5
25~34 岁 Age	140	3.6	11.4	22.9	10.7	15.0	15.0
35~44 岁 Age	112	8.0	13.4	15.2	8.0	13.4	17.0
45~54 岁 Age	76	5.3	13.2	18.4	3.9	19.7	17.1
55~60 岁 Age	34	0.0	2.9	11.8	8.8	8.8	17.6

续前表 continued

	人数 Number	军事知识 military knowledge	法制报道 legal news	海外见闻 overseas information	科技知识 science sense	影视娱乐报道 video & entertainment report	服饰美容 clothes & beauty
样本 Sample	**928**	**8.8**	**22.8**	**7.0**	**10.3**	**17.5**	**9.8**
男性 Male	**469**	**15.1**	**24.1**	**7.5**	**14.3**	**12.4**	**0.9**
16~24 岁 Age	95	15.8	11.6	10.5	27.4	34.7	1.1
25~34 岁 Age	140	17.1	22.1	5.0	12.1	11.4	0.7
35~44 岁 Age	125	12.8	26.4	5.6	11.2	4.8	0.8
45~54 岁 Age	73	16.4	37.0	9.6	9.6	2.7	1.4
55~60 岁 Age	36	11.1	30.6	11.1	8.3	2.8	0.0
女性 Female	**459**	**2.4**	**21.6**	**6.5**	**6.3**	**22.7**	**19.0**
16~24 岁 Age	97	0.0	10.3	7.2	6.2	56.7	33.0
25~34 岁 Age	140	2.9	20.7	7.9	6.4	21.4	22.9
35~44 岁 Age	112	2.7	31.3	4.5	5.4	12.5	16.1
45~54 岁 Age	76	5.3	22.4	5.3	9.2	3.9	3.9
55~60 岁 Age	34	0.0	23.5	8.8	2.9	5.9	5.9

续前表 continued

	人数 Number	休闲旅游 entertainment & travel	消费指南 consumption guide	电视节目预告 TV program forecast	健康医疗 medicare	生活常识 common sense	书评 book comment
样本 Sample	**928**	**9.5**	**11.9**	**9.6**	**20.2**	**17.6**	**0.8**
男性 Male	**469**	**6.2**	**9.0**	**7.0**	**9.4**	**9.0**	**0.2**
16~24 岁 Age	95	9.5	8.4	15.8	4.2	3.2	0.0
25~34 岁 Age	140	8.6	18.6	5.0	9.3	9.3	0.0
35~44 岁 Age	125	2.4	3.2	4.0	9.6	12.0	0.0
45~54 岁 Age	73	6.8	4.1	5.5	13.7	13.7	1.4
55~60 岁 Age	36	0.0	2.8	5.6	13.9	2.8	0.0
女性 Female	**459**	**12.9**	**14.8**	**12.2**	**31.2**	**26.4**	**1.3**
16~24 岁 Age	97	19.6	8.2	18.6	8.2	7.2	1.0
25~34 岁 Age	140	19.3	23.6	9.3	30.0	25.0	0.7
35~44 岁 Age	112	7.1	13.4	8.9	35.7	34.8	0.9
45~54 岁 Age	76	5.3	7.9	6.5	47.4	36.8	1.3
55~60 岁 Age	34	2.9	17.6	29.4	50.0	35.3	5.9

续前表 continued

	人数 Number	文艺评论 art critics	散文 prose	小说 novel	漫画 cartoon	广告 advertising	读者来信 reader's letter	其他 others
样本 Sample	**928**	**2.0**	**4.3**	**7.9**	**5.2**	**5.2**	**0.9**	**1.2**
男性 Male	**469**	**1.7**	**2.6**	**4.5**	**4.3**	**4.9**	**0.6**	**0.9**
16~24 岁 Age	95	1.1	6.3	9.5	11.6	9.5	1.1	2.1
25~34 岁 Age	140	0.0	1.4	4.3	3.6	8.6	0.7	0.7
35~44 岁 Age	125	1.6	3.2	4.0	2.4	0.8	0.0	0.8
45~54 岁 Age	73	5.5	0.0	1.4	0.0	0.0	1.4	0.0
55~60 岁 Age	36	2.8	0.0	0.0	2.8	2.8	0.0	0.0
女性 Female	**459**	**2.4**	**6.1**	**11.3**	**6.1**	**5.4**	**1.1**	**1.5**
16~24 岁 Age	97	3.1	13.4	20.6	17.5	6.2	0.0	2.1
25~34 岁 Age	140	1.4	5.7	10.7	6.4	7.9	1.4	0.0
35~44 岁 Age	112	2.7	2.7	10.7	1.8	5.4	1.8	0.0
45~54 岁 Age	76	2.6	3.9	3.9	0.0	1.3	1.3	2.6
55~60 岁 Age	34	2.9	2.9	5.9	0.0	2.9	0.0	8.8

3-7 不同学历的读者阅读的报纸内容的偏好/ The Concerned Newspaper Content Categories by Educational Levels

注：本题为多选题，合计百分比超过 100%（Multiple answers）

	人数 Number	头版要闻 first page news	国际新闻 international news	国内新闻 national news	港澳台新闻 news about HK. Taiwan. Macao.	本地新闻 local news	经济信息 economic information
样本 Sample	**925**	**42.7**	**53.5**	**52.6**	**6.4**	**12.5**	**13.0**
小学及以下 Primary School or Below	23	26.1	30.4	60.9	4.3	21.7	4.3
初中 Middle School	149	42.3	50.3	59.1	3.4	14.1	9.4
高中/中专/技校 High School/Technical Secondary School	400	40.8	46.5	52.0	8.5	13.0	8.0
大学专科 2-3 Year College	196	43.9	62.2	47.4	5.1	8.7	18.9
大学本科 4-5 Year College	142	49.3	64.8	52.8	6.3	14.8	22.5
研究生或以上 Graduate or Above	15	46.7	86.7	60.0	0.0	0.0	26.7

续前表 continued

	人数 Number	财政金融 finance & economic	股市报道 stock market report	热点追踪 hits track	文化信息 cultural information	体育报道 sports report	人物专访 personal interview
样本 Sample	**925**	**6.5**	**9.3**	**16.0**	**9.7**	**32.0**	**13.1**
小学及以下 Primary School or Below	23	0.0	4.3	8.7	0.0	17.4	26.1
初中 Middle School	149	3.4	8.1	15.4	5.4	32.9	12.8
高中/中专/技校 High School/Technical Secondary School	400	4.8	6.8	14.8	10.3	34.0	13.0
大学专科 2-3 Year College	196	10.2	14.8	15.3	10.7	29.6	13.8
大学本科 4-5 Year College	142	11.3	11.3	19.7	12.7	31.0	11.3
研究生或以上 Graduate or Above	15	0.0	6.7	40.0	13.3	33.3	6.7

续前表 continued

	人数 Number	军事知识 military knowledge	法制报道 legal news	海外见闻 overseas information	科技知识 science sense	影视娱乐报道 video & entertainment report	服饰美容 clothes & beauty
样本 Sample	**925**	**8.9**	**22.7**	**7.0**	**10.4**	**17.5**	**9.7**
小学及以下 Primary School or Below	23	17.4	21.7	4.3	4.3	4.3	0.0
初中 Middle School	149	10.1	31.5	6.7	5.4	9.4	6.0
高中/中专/技校 High School/Technical Secondary School	400	8.0	25.0	6.3	8.5	23.3	11.3
大学专科 2-3 Year College	196	11.2	19.4	9.2	11.7	13.3	6.6
大学本科 4-5 Year College	142	4.9	12.0	7.7	21.1	18.3	14.8
研究生或以上 Graduate or Above	15	13.3	20.0	0.0	0.0	13.3	13.3

续前表 continued

	人数 Number	休闲旅游 entertainment & travel	消费指南 consumption guide	电视节目预告 TV program forecast	健康医疗 medicare	生活常识 common sense	书评 book comment
样本 Sample	**925**	**9.5**	**11.9**	**9.6**	**20.2**	**17.6**	**0.8**
小学及以下 Primary School or Below	23	4.3	0.0	34.8	34.8	13.0	0.0
初中 Middle School	149	4.7	6.7	12.1	26.2	19.5	0.0
高中/中专/技校 High School/Technical Secondary School	400	8.8	13.0	11.5	18.3	19.3	0.5
大学专科 2-3 Year College	196	13.3	12.8	5.[illegible]	22.4	18.9	1.0
大学本科 4-5 Year College	142	12.0	15.5	4.9	15.5	9.2	2.1
研究生或以上 Graduate or Above	15	13.3	6.7	0.0	6.7	26.7	0.0

续前表 continued

	人数 Number	文艺评论 art critics	散文 prose	小说 novel	漫画 cartoon	广告 advertising	读者来信 reader's letter	其他 others
样本 Sample	**925**	**2.1**	**4.3**	**7.9**	**5.2**	**5.1**	**0.9**	**1.2**
小学及以下 Primary School or Below	23	0.0	0.0	13.0	4.3	8.7	0.0	0.0
初中 Middle School	149	1.3	2.0	8.1	1.3	4.0	0.7	0.7
高中/中专/技校 High School/Technical Secondary School	400	2.8	5.3	9.8	7.3	6.3	1.5	1.5
大学专科 2-3 Year College	196	2.6	6.6	6.1	3.6	3.1	0.0	1.5
大学本科 4-5 Year College	142	0.7	1.4	4.2	5.6	4.2	0.7	0.7
研究生或以上 Graduate or Above	15	0.0	6.7	6.7	6.7	13.3	0.0	0.0

3-8 不同消费者层平时是否接触报纸媒介/ Newspaper Reading by Market Segments

3-8-1 时尚流行指标/ Fads Popular Index

	人数 Number	从来不看 never	看 yes
样本 Sample	**997**	**6.6**	**93.4**
平实生活指向 simple living orientation	490	8.8	91.2
时尚流行指向 fashion orientation	507	4.5	95.5

3-8-2 广告态度指标/ Advertising Attitude Index

	人数 Number	从来不看 never	看 yes
样本 Sample	993	6.4	93.6
广告淡漠指向 indifferent orientation	288	9.0	91.0
中间层 medium	572	5.6	94.4
信赖广告指向 loyal orientation	133	4.5	95.5

3-9 不同消费者层经常阅读的报纸/ Frequently Read Newspapers by Market Segments

3-9-1 时尚流行指标/ Fads Popular Index

注：本题为多选题，合计百分比超过 100%（Multiple answers）

	人数 Number	北京晚报 Beijing Evening News	北京青年报 Beijing Youth Daily	北京晨报 Beijing Morning News	精品购物指南 Shopping Guide	北京日报 Beijing Daily	参考消息 Reference News	北京广播电视报 Beijing TV Guide
样本 Sample	930	63.1	44.7	18.4	14.1	13.9	11.2	5.8
平实生活指向 simple living orientation	447	60.2	42.5	18.8	8.1	15.4	13.4	5.6
时尚流行指向 fashion orientation	483	65.8	46.8	18.0	19.7	12.4	9.1	6.0

续前表 continued

	人数 Number	环球时报 Global Times	足球报 Soccer	人民日报 People's Daily	法制报 Fa Zhi Bao	中国电视报 China TV Guide	中国青年报 China Youth Daily	南方周末 South Weekend	作家文摘 Zuo Jia Wen Zhai
样本 Sample	930	5.7	5.4	4.0	3.7	3.9	3.7	3.1	3.0
平实生活指向 simple living orientation	447	6.3	6.0	5.6	2.2	5.4	4.5	2.5	3.1
时尚流行指向 fashion orientation	483	5.2	4.8	2.5	5.0	2.5	2.9	3.7	2.9

3-9-2 广告态度指向/ Advertising Attitude Index

注：本题为多选题，合计百分比超过 100%（Multiple answers）

	人数 Number	北京晚报 Beijing Evening News	北京青年报 Beijing Youth Daily	北京晨报 Beijing Morning News	精品购物指南 Shopping Guide	北京日报 Beijing Daily	参考消息 Reference News	北京广播电视报 Beijing TV Guide
样本 Sample	928	63.3	45.4	18.5	14.1	13.9	11.1	5.8
广告淡漠指向 indifferent orientation	261	66.7	46.0	19.2	12.6	12.3	11.5	5.0
中间层 medium	540	60.0	45.9	18.1	14.4	14.3	11.1	5.2
信赖广告指向 loyal orientation	127	70.1	41.7	18.9	15.7	15.7	10.2	10.2

续前表 continued

	人数 Number	环球时报 Global Times	足球报 Soccer	人民日报 People's Daily	法制报 Fa Zhi Bao	中国电视报 China TV Guide	中国青年报 China Youth Daily	南方周末 South Weekend	作家文摘 Zuo Jia Wen Zhai
样本 Sample	928	5.8	5.4	3.9	3.6	3.8	3.6	3.2	3.0
广告淡漠指向 indifferent orientation	261	6.1	6.1	2.3	3.4	4.6	3.4	2.7	2.7
中间层 medium	540	6.1	5.2	4.6	3.5	3.7	4.1	3.1	3.0
信赖广告指向 loyal orientation	127	3.9	4.7	3.9	3.9	2.4	1.6	4.7	3.9

3-10 不同消费者层比较关心的报道/ The Concerned Newspaper Content Categories by Market Segments

3-10-1 时尚流行指标/ Fads Popular Index

注：本题为多选题，合计百分比超过 100%（Multiple answers）

	人数 Number	头版要闻 first page news	国际新闻 international news	国内新闻 national news	港澳台新闻 news about HK. Taiwan. Macao.	本地新闻 local news	经济信息 economic information
样本 Sample	916	42.8	53.4	52.8	6.6	12.7	13.1
平实生活指向 simple living orientation	441	42.6	57.6	54.4	5.4	13.6	12.2
时尚流行指向 fashion orientation	475	42.9	49.5	51.4	7.6	11.8	13.9

续前表 continued

	人数 Number	财政金融 finance & economic	股市报道 stock market report	热点追踪 hits track	文化信息 cultural information	体育报道 sports report	人物专访 personal interview
样本 Sample	916	6.6	9.4	15.6	9.6	31.9	13.0
平实生活指向 simple living orientation	441	6.6	9.5	15.4	7.9	32.9	13.8
时尚流行指向 fashion orientation	475	6.5	9.3	15.8	11.2	30.9	12.2

续前表 continued

	人数 Number	军事知识 military knowledge	法制报道 legal news	海外见闻 overseas information	科技知识 science sense	影视娱乐报道 video & entertainment report	服饰美容 clothes & beauty
样本 Sample	916	8.8	22.7	7.1	10.4	17.4	9.7
平实生活指向 simple living orientation	441	10.2	23.6	7.3	11.6	14.3	4.8
时尚流行指向 fashion orientation	475	7.6	21.9	6.9	9.3	20.2	14.3

续前表 continued

	人数 Number	休闲旅游 entertainment & travel	消费指南 consumption guide	电视节目预告 TV program forecast	健康医疗 medicare	生活常识 common sense	书评 book comment
样本 Sample	916	9.5	12.0	9.5	20.3	17.7	0.8
平实生活指向 simple living orientation	441	8.8	8.8	11.1	22.9	19.3	0.5
时尚流行指向 fashion orientation	475	10.1	14.9	8.0	17.9	16.2	1.1

续前表 continued

	人数 Number	文艺评论 art critics	散文 prose	小说 novel	漫画 cartoon	广告 advertising	读者来信 reader's letter	其他 others
样本 Sample	916	2.1	4.0	7.8	5.0	5.1	0.9	1.2
平实生活指向 simple living orientation	441	2.3	3.9	6.6	5.7	3.4	1.4	1.1
时尚流行指向 fashion orientation	475	1.9	4.2	8.8	4.4	6.7	0.4	1.3

3-10-2 广告态度指标/ Advertising Attitude Index

注：本题为多选题，合计百分比超过 100%（Multiple answers）

	人数 Number	头版要闻 first page news	国际新闻 international news	国内新闻 national news	港澳台新闻 news about HK. Taiwan. Macao.	本地新闻 local news	经济信息 economic information
样本 Sample	913	42.6	53.5	52.7	6.4	12.4	13.0
广告淡漠指向 indifferent orientation	258	39.1	58.9	51.2	7.4	12.4	11.2
中间层 medium	529	44.0	51.6	53.7	6.0	12.5	14.7
信赖广告指向 loyal orientation	126	43.7	50.0	5[illegible].6	5.6	11.9	9.5

续前表 continued

	人数 Number	财政金融 finance & economic	股市报道 stock market report	热点追踪 hits track	文化信息 cultural information	体育报道 sports report	人物专访 personal interview
样本 Sample	913	6.7	9.5	16.1	9.9	31.8	13.0
广告淡漠指向 indifferent orientation	258	8.5	10.1	17.4	8.1	35.7	9.3
中间层 medium	529	6.0	10.0	16.4	10.6	29.3	14.0
信赖广告指向 loyal orientation	126	5.6	6.3	11.9	10.3	34.1	16.7

续前表 continued

	人数 Number	军事知识 military knowledge	法制报道 legal news	海外见闻 overseas information	科技知识 science sense	影视娱乐报道 video & entertainment report	服饰美容 clothes & beauty
样本 Sample	913	9.0	22.9	6.9	10.4	17.5	9.9
广告淡漠指向 indifferent orientation	258	9.7	24.8	5.0	12.0	17.4	8.9
中间层 medium	529	9.1	23.3	8.3	10.2	17.2	9.1
信赖广告指向 loyal orientation	126	7.1	17.5	4.8	7.9	19.0	15.1

续前表 continued

	人数 Number	休闲旅游 entertainment & travel	消费指南 consumption guide	电视节目预告 TV program forecast	健康医疗 medicare	生活常识 common sense	书评 book comment
样本 Sample	913	9.5	11.9	9.3	20.4	17.6	0.8
广告淡漠指向 indifferent orientation	258	10.5	8.5	8.9	17.1	15.5	0.4
中间层 medium	529	9.3	13.4	9.3	20.6	18.1	1.1
信赖广告指向 loyal orientation	126	8.7	12.7	10.3	26.2	19.8	0.0

续前表 continued

	人数 Number	文艺评论 art critics	散文 prose	小说 novel	漫画 cartoon	广告 advertising	读者来信 reader's letter	其他 others
样本 Sample	913	2.1	4.3	7.8	5.1	5.1	0.9	1.2
广告淡漠指向 indifferent orientation	258	2.7	4.7	8.1	5.0	2.7	0.4	2.3
中间层 medium	529	1.7	3.6	6.2	4.9	4.5	1.1	0.8
信赖广告指向 loyal orientation	126	2.4	6.3	13.5	6.3	12.7	0.8	0.8

● 上海 / Shanghai

3-1 样本、男性各年龄层、女性各年龄层平时是否接触报纸媒介/ Newspaper Reading by the Whole Sample, Age and Gender Groups

	人数 Number	从来不看 never	看 yes
样本 Sample	1014	9.5	90.5
男性 Male	509	5.9	94.1
16~24 岁 Age	109	12.8	87.2
25~34 岁 Age	146	3.4	96.6
35~44 岁 Age	130	3.1	96.9
45~54 岁 Age	85	4.7	95.3
55~60 岁 Age	39	7.7	92.3
女性 Female	505	13.1	86.9
16~24 岁 Age	108	14.8	85.2
25~34 岁 Age	144	11.1	88.9
35~44 岁 Age	130	10.0	90.0
45~54 岁 Age	82	13.4	86.6
55~60 岁 Age	41	24.4	75.6

3-2 经常阅读的报纸排名/ Ranking of the Frequently Read Newspapers

注：本题为多选题，合计百分比超过 100%（Multiple answers）

排名 Brand Ranking	报纸 Newspapers	人次 Person-time	百分比 Percent
1	新民晚报 Xinmin Evening News	740	80.6
2	解放日报 Jie Fang Daily	166	18.1
3	申江服务导报 Shenjiang Fu Wu Dao Bao	131	14.3
4	文汇报 Wen Hui Bao	107	11.7
5	每周广播电视报 Weekly Guang Bao Dian Shi Bao	81	8.8
6	劳动报 Lao Dong Bao	80	8.7
7	报刊文摘 Bao Kan Wen Zhai	39	4.2
7	青年报 Qing Nian Bao	39	4.2
8	新民体育 Xinmin Sports	34	3.7
9	新闻报 Xin Wen Bao	31	3.4
10	足球报 Soccer	29	3.2
11	参考消息 Reference News	26	2.8
12	上海证券 Shanghai Zheng Quan	20	2.2
13	体育报 Sports Daily	19	2.1
14	上海有线电视报 Cable TV Weekly	18	2.0

n=918

3-3 样本、男性各年龄层、女性各年龄层经常阅读的报纸/ Frequently Read Newspapers by the Whole Sample, Age and Gender Groups

注：本题为多选题，合计百分比超过 100%（Multiple answers）

	人数 Number	新民晚报 Xinmin Evening News	解放日报 Jie Fang Daily	申江服务导报 Shenjiang Fu Wu Dao Bao	文汇报 Wen Hui Bao	每周广播电视报 Weekly Guang Bao Dian Shi Bao	劳动报 Lao Dong Bao	报刊文摘 Bao Kan Wen Zhai
样本 Sample	**918**	**80.6**	**18.1**	**14.3**	**11.7**	**8.8**	**8.7**	**4.2**
男性 Male	**479**	**79.7**	**21.1**	**10.9**	**13.4**	**5.4**	**9.4**	**5.4**
16~24 岁 Age	95	74.7	9.5	17.9	7.4	7.4	7.4	3.2
25~34 岁 Age	141	82.3	16.3	16.3	12.1	4.3	5.0	2.8
35~44 岁 Age	126	81.7	23.8	4.8	11.9	5.6	14.3	4.8
45~54 岁 Age	81	81.5	32.1	7.4	22.2	7.4	9.9	11.1
55~60 岁 Age	36	72.2	36.1	0.0	19.4	0.0	13.9	11.1
女性 Female	**439**	**81.5**	**14.8**	**18.0**	**9.8**	**12.5**	**8.0**	**3.0**
16~24 岁 Age	92	77.2	6.5	32.6	13.0	12.0	0.0	1.1
25~34 岁 Age	128	80.5	15.6	22.7	8.6	13.3	11.7	2.3
35~44 岁 Age	117	82.1	18.8	7.7	9.4	13.7	9.4	3.4
45~54 岁 Age	71	88.7	21.1	15.5	8.5	9.9	9.9	2.8
55~60 岁 Age	31	80.6	6.5	0.0	9.7	12.9	6.5	9.7

续前表 continued

	人数 Number	青年报 Qing Nian Bao	新民体育 Xinmin Sports	新闻报 Xin Wen Bao	足球报 Soccer	参考消息 Reference News	上海证券 Shanghai Zheng Quan	体育报 Sports Daily	上海有线电视报 Cable TV Weekly
样本 Sample	**918**	**4.2**	**3.7**	**3.4**	**3.2**	**2.8**	**2.2**	**2.1**	**2.0**
男性 Male	**479**	**3.8**	**6.3**	**4.0**	**5.0**	**4.0**	**2.5**	**3.3**	**1.7**
16~24 岁 Age	95	11.6	10.5	2.1	3.4	3.2	0.0	6.3	3.2
25~34 岁 Age	141	3.5	9.2	4.3	5.7	5.0	2.8	2.8	2.1
35~44 岁 Age	126	0.8	4.8	4.8	4.0	4.0	5.6	3.2	0.0
45~54 岁 Age	81	0.0	1.2	4.9	2.5	4.9	1.2	2.5	2.5
55~60 岁 Age	36	2.8	0.0	2.8	2.8	0.0	0.0	0.0	0.0
女性 Female	**439**	**4.8**	**0.9**	**2.7**	**1.1**	**1.6**	**1.8**	**0.7**	**2.3**
16~24 岁 Age	92	15.2	2.2	3.3	2.2	1.1	1.1	0.0	0.0
25~34 岁 Age	128	1.6	0.0	3.1	0.8	0.0	0.0	0.8	3.1
35~44 岁 Age	117	2.6	0.9	3.4	0.9	4.3	4.3	0.0	3.4
45~54 岁 Age	71	2.8	1.4	1.4	1.4	1.4	2.8	0.0	0.0
55~60 岁 Age	31	0.0	0.0	0.0	0.0	0.0	0.0	6.5	6.5

3-4 经常阅读的报纸的主要来源/ Sources of Obtaining the Frequently Read Newspapers

注：本题为多选题，合计百分比可能超过 100%（Multiple answers）

	人数 Number	家中订阅 subscribed by my family	单位订阅 subscribed by work unit	报摊购买 bought from vender	赠阅 given as gift	借阅 borrowed	街头报栏 news-stand along street
新民晚报 Xinmin Evening News	731	49.4	7.3	37.8	0.1	4.0	1.8
解放日报 Jie Fang Daily	166	12.7	66.3	9.6	1.2	4.8	5.4
申江服务导报 Shenjiang Fu Wu Dao Bao	131	11.5	1.5	83.2	0.0	3.1	0.8
文汇报 Wen Hui Bao	107	19.6	61.7	7.5	0.9	4.7	5.6
每周广播电视报 Weekly Guang Bo Dian Shi Bao	81	25.9	3.7	67.9	0.0	2.5	0.0
劳动报 Lao Dong Bao	79	13.9	78.5	3.8	0.0	3.8	0.0
报刊文摘 Bao Kan Wen Zhai	38	42.1	15.8	39.5	0.0	0.0	2.6
青年报 Qing Nian Bao	38	18.4	55.3	21.1	0.0	0.0	5.3
新民体育 Ximin Sports	33	3.0	0.0	93.9	0.0	3.0	0.0
新闻报 Xin Wen Bao	31	12.9	35.5	45.2	0.0	3.2	3.2

3-5 经常阅读的报纸内容/ Ranking of the Content Categories that Newspaper Readers Concern about

注：本题为多选题，合计百分比超过 100%（Multiple answers）

排名 Ranking	内容 Contents	人次 Person-time	百分比 Percent
1	头版要闻 first page news	504	55.4
2	国际新闻 international news	496	54.5
3	国内新闻 national news	493	54.2
4	体育报道 sports report	282	31.0
5	影视娱乐报道 video & entertainment report	190	20.9
6	健康医疗 medicare	168	18.5
7	法制报道 legal news	162	17.8
8	股市报道 stock market report	157	17.3
9	本地新闻 local news	149	16.4
10	热点追踪 hits track	116	12.7
11	生活常识 common sense	97	10.7
12	港澳台新闻 news about HK.Taiwan. Macao	91	10.0
13	经济信息 economic information	87	9.6
14	服饰美容 clothes & beauty	86	9.5
15	消费指南 consumption guide	78	8.6
16	电视节目预告 TV program forecast	77	8.5
17	财政金融 finance & economic	76	8.4
18	文化信息 cultural information	72	7.9
19	小说 novel	71	7.8
20	科技知识 science sense	69	7.6
20	海外见闻 overseas information	69	7.6
21	休闲旅游 entertainment & travel	67	7.4
22	军事知识 military knowledge	64	7.0
23	人物专访 personal interview	56	6.2
24	漫画 cartoon	55	6.0
25	散文 prose	50	5.5
26	广告 advertising	32	3.5
27	文艺评论 art critics	15	1.6
28	其他 others	13	1.4
29	读者来信 reader's letter	7	0.8
30	书评 book comment	4	0.4

n=910

3-6 样本、男性各年龄层、女性各年龄层经常阅读的报纸内容/ The Concerned Newspaper Content Categories by the Whole Sample, Age and Gender Groups

注：本题为多选题，合计百分比超过 100%（Multiple answers）

	人数 Number	头版要闻 first page news	国际新闻 international news	国内新闻 national news	港澳台新闻 news about HK. Taiwan. Macao	本地新闻 local news	经济信息 economic information
样本 Sample	**910**	**55.4**	**54.5**	**54.2**	**10.0**	**16.4**	**9.6**
男性 Male	**474**	**58.0**	**65.4**	**58.2**	**9.1**	**19.0**	**12.4**
16~24 岁 Age	94	44.7	51.1	31.9	13.8	9.6	5.3
25~34 岁 Age	140	60.0	67.9	52.1	10.0	17.1	17.1
35~44 岁 Age	125	57.6	69.6	68.0	4.8	20.8	8.0
45~54 岁 Age	81	67.9	67.9	79.0	6.2	29.6	18.5
55~60 岁 Age	34	64.7	73.5	70.6	14.7	20.6	14.7
女性 Female	**436**	**52.5**	**42.7**	**49.8**	**11.0**	**13.5**	**6.4**
16~24 岁 Age	91	41.8	35.2	28.6	14.3	7.7	2.2
25~34 岁 Age	127	48.0	33.9	39.4	13.4	11.8	8.7
35~44 岁 Age	116	56.9	54.3	59.5	10.3	12.9	9.5
45~54 岁 Age	71	57.7	46.5	70.4	5.6	16.9	4.2
55~60 岁 Age	31	74.2	48.4	71.0	6.5	32.3	3.2

续前表 continued

	人数 Number	财政金融 finance & economic	股市报道 stock market report	热点追踪 hits track	文化信息 cultural information	体育报道 sports report	人物专访 personal interview
样本 Sample	**910**	**8.4**	**17.3**	**12.7**	**7.9**	**31.0**	**6.2**
男性 Male	**474**	**9.9**	**17.5**	**9.9**	**5.7**	**47.9**	**5.1**
16~24 岁 Age	94	6.4	7.4	7.4	8.5	54.3	5.3
25~34 岁 Age	140	10.7	18.6	10.0	5.0	49.3	5.7
35~44 岁 Age	125	11.2	20.8	9.6	6.4	49.6	3.2
45~54 岁 Age	81	11.1	21.0	12.3	2.5	43.2	6.2
55~60 岁 Age	34	8.8	20.6	11.8	5.9	29.4	5.9
女性 Female	**436**	**6.7**	**17.0**	**15.8**	**10.3**	**12.6**	**7.3**
16~24 岁 Age	91	2.2	3.3	15.4	18.7	16.5	11.0
25~34 岁 Age	127	3.1	18.1	18.1	12.6	8.7	7.9
35~44 岁 Age	116	12.9	22.4	14.7	7.8	14.7	5.2
45~54 岁 Age	71	11.3	25.4	15.5	2.8	9.9	4.2
55~60 岁 Age	31	0.0	12.9	12.9	3.2	16.1	9.7

续前表 continued

	人数 Number	军事知识 military knowledge	法制报道 legal news	海外见闻 overseas information	科技知识 science sense	影视娱乐报道 video & entertainment report	服饰美容 clothes & beauty
样本 Sample	**910**	**7.0**	**17.8**	**7.6**	**7.6**	**20.9**	**9.5**
男性 Male	**474**	**12.4**	**18.4**	**7.0**	**9.9**	**17.1**	**2.3**
16~24 岁 Age	94	25.5	16.0	7.4	22.3	43.6	2.1
25~34 岁 Age	140	9.3	12.9	9.3	8.6	17.9	3.6
35~44 岁 Age	125	11.2	22.4	6.4	3.2	8.0	3.2
45~54 岁 Age	81	6.2	22.2	3.7	8.6	4.9	0.0
55~60 岁 Age	34	8.8	23.5	5.9	8.8	2.9	0.0
女性 Female	**436**	**1.1**	**17.2**	**8.3**	**5.0**	**25.0**	**17.2**
16~24 岁 Age	91	2.2	2.2	8.8	6.6	52.7	33.0
25~34 岁 Age	127	0.8	17.3	10.2	3.1	26.8	21.3
35~44 岁 Age	116	0.9	22.4	7.8	4.3	17.2	11.2
45~54 岁 Age	71	0.0	28.2	5.6	7.0	7.0	5.6
55~60 岁 Age	31	3.2	16.1	6.5	6.5	6.5	3.2

续前表 continued

	人数 Number	休闲旅游 entertainment & travel	消费指南 consumption guide	电视节目预告 TV program forecast	健康医疗 medicare	生活常识 common sense	书评 book comment
样本 Sample	910	7.4	8.6	8.5	18.5	10.7	0.4
男性 Male	474	5.3	6.1	4.2	9.9	5.3	0.4
16~24 岁 Age	94	5.3	8.5	9.6	3.2	2.1	0.0
25~34 岁 Age	140	10.0	8.6	2.1	12.1	4.3	0.7
35~44 岁 Age	125	3.2	4.0	3.2	8.8	6.4	0.8
45~54 岁 Age	81	2.5	3.7	3.7	11.1	4.9	0.0
55~60 岁 Age	34	0.0	2.9	2.9	20.6	14.7	0.0
女性 Female	436	9.6	11.2	13.1	27.8	16.5	0.5
16~24 岁 Age	91	18.7	11.0	14.3	7.7	12.1	1.1
25~34 岁 Age	127	14.2	16.5	15.0	26.0	14.2	0.8
35~44 岁 Age	116	3.4	6.9	10.3	35.3	14.7	0.0
45~54 岁 Age	71	1.4	11.3	12.7	42.3	23.9	0.0
55~60 岁 Age	31	6.5	6.5	12.9	32.3	29.0	0.0

续前表 continued

	人数 Number	文艺评论 art critics	散文 prose	小说 novel	漫画 cartoon	广告 advertising	读者来信 reader's letter	其他 others
样本 Sample	910	1.6	5.5	7.8	6.0	3.5	0.8	1.4
男性 Male	474	0.8	3.2	5.1	5.5	2.5	0.2	1.5
16~24 岁 Age	94	1.1	5.3	7.4	14.9	5.3	0.0	4.3
25~34 岁 Age	140	1.4	4.3	4.3	6.4	2.9	0.7	1.4
35~44 岁 Age	125	0.8	0.8	6.4	2.4	2.4	0.0	0.8
45~54 岁 Age	81	0.0	1.2	2.5	0.0	0.0	0.0	0.0
55~60 岁 Age	34	0.0	5.9	2.9	0.0	0.0	0.0	0.0
女性 Female	436	2.5	8.0	10.8	6.7	4.6	1.4	1.4
16~24 岁 Age	91	3.3	18.7	14.3	13.2	6.6	1.1	0.0
25~34 岁 Age	127	2.4	8.7	14.2	5.5	4.7	1.6	3.1
35~44 岁 Age	116	2.6	1.7	10.3	3.4	4.3	0.9	1.7
45~54 岁 Age	71	2.8	5.6	4.2	4.2	4.2	2.8	0.0
55~60 岁 Age	31	0.0	3.2	3.2	9.7	0.0	0.0	0.0

3-7 不同学历的读者阅读的报纸内容的偏好/ The Concerned Newspaper Content Categories by Educational Levels

注：本题为多选题，合计百分比超过 100%（Multiple answers）

	人数 Number	头版要闻 first page news	国际新闻 international news	国内新闻 national news	港澳台新闻 news about HK. Taiwan. Macao	本地新闻 local news	经济信息 economic information
样本 Sample	907	55.5	54.4	54.0	10.0	16.4	9.6
小学及以下 Primary School or Below	13	38.5	30.8	53.8	0.0	23.1	7.7
初中 Middle School	236	53.4	51.3	58.5	7.2	19.1	5.9
高中/中专/技校 High School/Technical Secondary School	459	55.3	54.9	51.9	12.2	15.7	8.1
大学专科 2-3 Year College	129	56.6	58.9	52.7	7.8	17.8	17.8
大学本科 4-5 Year College	63	65.1	54.0	54.0	12.7	9.5	17.5
研究生或以上 Graduate or Above	7	57.1	85.7	71.4	0.0	0.0	14.3

续前表 continued

	人数 Number	财政金融 finance & economic	股市报道 stock market report	热点追踪 hits track	文化信息 cultural information	体育报道 sports report	人物专访 personal interview
样本 Sample	**907**	**8.3**	**17.2**	**12.8**	**7.9**	**30.9**	**6.2**
小学及以下 Primary School or Below	13	0.0	0.0	15.4	0.0	0.0	0.0
初中 Middle School	236	5.5	18.6	12.3	4.7	29.7	6.4
高中/中专/技校 High School/Technical Secondary School	459	8.9	17.0	11.5	8.7	30.9	5.7
大学专科 2-3 Year College	129	11.6	17.1	17.1	10.9	33.3	9.3
大学本科 4-5 Year College	63	9.5	17.5	12.7	9.5	34.9	4.8
研究生或以上 Graduate or Above	7	0.0	14.3	28.6	14.3	42.9	0.0

续前表 continued

	人数 Number	军事知识 military knowledge	法制报道 legal news	海外见闻 overseas information	科技知识 science sense	影视娱乐报道 video & entertainment report	服饰美容 clothes & beauty
样本 Sample	**907**	**7.1**	**17.9**	**7.5**	**7.4**	**20.9**	**9.5**
小学及以下 Primary School or Below	13	7.7	23.1	0.0	0.0	7.7	0.0
初中 Middle School	236	8.5	24.2	5.1	3.8	9.7	4.7
高中/中专/技校 High School/Technical Secondary School	459	6.8	17.0	8.5	7.0	26.6	10.9
大学专科 2-3 Year College	129	5.4	10.9	9.3	12.4	24.0	12.4
大学本科 4-5 Year College	63	6.3	15.9	7.9	15.9	15.9	14.3
研究生或以上 Graduate or Above	7	14.3	0.0	0.0	0.0	42.9	0.0

续前表 continued

	人数 Number	休闲旅游 entertainment & travel	消费指南 consumption guide	电视节目预告 TV program forecast	健康医疗 medicare	生活常识 common sense	书评 book comment
样本 Sample	**907**	**7.3**	**8.6**	**8.5**	**18.5**	**10.7**	**0.4**
小学及以下 Primary School or Below	13	0.0	15.4	38.5	38.5	46.2	0.0
初中 Middle School	236	3.4	6.8	10.2	24.2	14.8	0.0
高中/中专/技校 High School/Technical Secondary School	459	8.5	8.5	8.1	17.4	9.4	0.4
大学专科 2-3 Year College	129	10.9	11.6	6.2	11.6	7.8	1.6
大学本科 4-5 Year College	63	7.9	7.9	3.2	15.9	4.8	0.0
研究生或以上 Graduate or Above	7	0.0	14.3	14.3	14.3	0.0	0.0

续前表 continued

	人数 Number	文艺评论 art critics	散文 prose	小说 novel	漫画 cartoon	广告 advertising	读者来信 reader's letter	其他 others
样本 Sample	907	1.7	5.5	7.8	6.1	3.5	0.8	1.4
小学及以下 Primary School or Below	13	7.7	0.0	7.7	7.7	0.0	7.7	7.7
初中 Middle School	236	1.3	4.7	7.6	5.1	3.4	1.3	1.3
高中/中专/技校 High School/Technical Secondary School	459	1.3	5.2	7.6	7.2	3.9	0.4	0.9
大学专科 2-3 Year College	129	1.6	6.2	6.2	4.7	3.1	0.8	1.6
大学本科 4-5 Year College	63	4.8	7.9	14.3	3.2	3.2	0.0	3.2
研究生或以上 Graduate or Above	7	0.0	28.6	0.0	14.3	0.0	0.0	14.3

3-8 不同消费者层平时是否接触报纸媒介/ Newspaper Reading by Market Segments

3-8-1 时尚流行指标/ Fads Popular Index

	人数 Number	从来不看 never	看 yes
样本 Sample	1005	9.5	90.5
平实生活指向 simple living orientation	471	8.7	91.3
时尚流行指向 fashion orientation	534	10.1	89.9

3-8-2 广告态度指标/ Advertising Attitude Index

	人数 Number	从来不看 never	看 yes
样本 Sample	1002	9.6	90.4
广告淡漠指向 indifferent orientation	256	12.5	87.5
中间层 medium	611	8.5	91.5
信赖广告指向 loyal orientation	135	8.9	91.1

3-9 不同消费者层经常阅读的报纸/ Frequently Read Newspapers by Market Segments

3-9-1 时尚流行指标/ Fads Popular Index

注：本题为多选题，合计百分比超过 100%（Multiple answers）

	人数 Number	新民晚报 Xinmin Evening News	解放日报 Jie Fang Daily	申江服务导报 Shenjiang Fu Wu Dao Bao	文汇报 Wen Hui Bao	每周广播电视报 Guang Bo Dian Shi Weekly	劳动报 Lao Dong Bao	报刊文摘 Bao Kan Wen Zhai
样本 Sample	910	80.4	18.0	14.4	11.6	8.9	8.8	4.1
平实生活指向 simple living orientation	430	82.1	19.1	11.6	12.1	9.8	8.8	4.7
时尚流行指向 fashion orientation	480	79.0	17.1	16.9	11.3	8.1	8.8	3.5

续前表 continued

	人数 Number	青年报 Youth Daily	新民体育 Xinmin Sports	新闻报 Xin Wen Bao	足球报 Soccer	参考消息 Reference News	上海证券 Shanghai Zheng Quan	体育报 Sports Daily	上海有线电视报 Cable TV Weekly
样本 Sample	910	4.3	3.7	3.4	3.1	2.9	2.2	2.1	2.0
平实生活指向 simple living orientation	430	3.7	4.0	4.0	3.0	3.0	2.3	1.6	2.3
时尚流行指向 fashion orientation	480	4.8	3.5	2.9	3.1	2.7	2.1	2.5	1.7

3-9-2 广告态度指向/ Advertising Attitude Index

注：本题为多选题，合计百分比超过 100%（Multiple answers）

	人数 Number	新民晚报 Xinmin Evening News	解放日报 Jie Fang Daily	申江服务导报 Shenjiang Fu Wu Dao Bao	文汇报 Wen Hui Bao	每周广播电视报 Weekly Guang Bao Dian Shi Bao	劳动报 Lao Dong Bao	报刊文摘 Bao Kan Wen Zhai
样本 Sample	906	80.6	18.0	14.1	11.6	8.8	8.7	4.3
广告淡漠指向 indifferent orientation	224	79.0	18.8	12.5	11.6	10.7	6.7	4.5
中间层 medium	559	81.2	18.2	13.2	11.8	8.4	9.1	3.9
信赖广告指向 loyal orientation	123	80.5	15.4	21.1	10.6	7.3	10.6	5.7

续前表 continued

	人数 Number	青年报 Youth Daily	新民体育 Xinmin Sports	新闻报 Xin Wen Bao	足球报 Soccer	参考消息 Reference News	上海证券 Shanghai Zheng Quan	体育报 Sports Daily	上海有线电视报 Cable TV Weekly
样本 Sample	906	4.3	3.8	3.2	3.0	2.9	2.2	2.0	2.0
广告淡漠指向 indifferent orientation	224	4.9	4.0	2.2	3.1	1.8	1.3	0.4	2.7
中间层 medium	559	3.9	3.9	3.6	3.2	3.2	2.3	2.3	2.0
信赖广告指向 loyal orientation	123	4.9	2.4	3.3	1.6	3.3	3.3	3.3	0.8

3-10 不同消费者层比较关心的报道/ The Concerned Newspaper Content Categories by Market Segments

3-10-1 时尚流行指标/ Fads Popular Index

注：本题为多选题，合计百分比超过 100%（Multiple answers）

	人数 Number	头版要闻 first page news	国际新闻 international news	国内新闻 national news	港澳台新闻 news about HK. Taiwan. Macao	本地新闻 local news	经济信息 economic information
样本 Sample	902	55.2	54.4	54.3	10.0	16.4	9.5
平实生活指向 simple living orientation	427	56.2	54.1	60.4	7.7	19.2	8.7
时尚流行指向 fashion orientation	475	54.3	54.7	48.8	12.0	13.9	10.3

续前表 continued

	人数 Number	财政金融 finance & economic	股市报道 stock market report	热点追踪 hits track	文化信息 cultural information	体育报道 sports report	人物专访 personal interview
样本 Sample	902	8.4	17.1	12.7	8.0	31.0	6.1
平实生活指向 simple living orientation	427	8.9	17.3	11.9	7.3	32.8	5.4
时尚流行指向 fashion orientation	475	8.0	16.8	13.5	8.6	29.5	6.7

续前表 continued

	人数 Number	军事知识 military knowledge	法制报道 legal news	海外见闻 overseas information	科技知识 science sense	影视娱乐报道 video & entertainment report	服饰美容 clothes & beauty
样本 Sample	902	7.1	17.6	7.6	7.6	21.0	9.5
平实生活指向 simple living orientation	427	7.7	21.1	6.6	8.9	12.6	2.3
时尚流行指向 fashion orientation	475	6.5	14.5	8.6	6.5	28.4	16.0

续前表 continued

	人数 Number	休闲旅游 entertainment & travel	消费指南 consumption guide	电视节目预告 TV program forecast	健康医疗 medicare	生活常识 common sense	书评 book comment
样本 Sample	902	7.3	8.5	8.5	18.4	10.8	0.4
平实生活指向 simple living orientation	427	3.7	7.7	8.9	23.9	13.3	0.7
时尚流行指向 fashion orientation	475	10.5	9.3	8.2	13.5	8.4	0.2

续前表 continued

	人数 Number	文艺评论 art critics	散文 prose	小说 novel	漫画 cartoon	广告 advertising	读者来信 reader's letter	其他 others
样本 Sample	902	1.7	5.5	7.6	6.1	3.5	0.8	1.4
平实生活指向 simple living orientation	427	1.6	4.4	6.8	5.2	2.6	1.4	1.4
时尚流行指向 fashion orientation	475	1.7	6.5	8.4	6.9	4.4	0.2	1.5

● 广州 / Guangzhou

3-1 样本、男性各年龄层、女性各年龄层平时是否接触报纸媒介/ Newspaper Reading by the Whole Sample, Age and Gender Groups

	人数 Number	从来不看 never	看 yes
样本 Sample	1033	6.8	93.2
男性 Male	499	5.0	95.0
16~24 岁 Age	106	9.4	90.6
25~34 岁 Age	150	3.3	96.7
35~44 岁 Age	127	4.7	95.3
45~54 岁 Age	73	1.4	98.6
55~60 岁 Age	43	7.0	93.0
女性 Female	534	8.4	91.6
16~24 岁 Age	112	12.5	87.5
25~34 岁 Age	158	3.8	96.2
35~44 岁 Age	136	5.9	94.1
45~54 岁 Age	87	16.1	83.9
55~60 岁 Age	41	7.3	92.7

3-2 经常阅读的报纸排名/ Ranking of the Frequently Read Newspapers

注：本题为多选题，合计百分比超过 100%（Multiple answers）

排名 Brand Ranking	报纸 Newspapers	人次 Person-time	百分比 Percent
1	广州日报 Guangzhou Daily	796	82.7
2	羊城晚报 Yangcheng Wan Bao	674	70.0
3	新快报 New Express	126	13.1
4	南方都市报 Nanfang Dushi Bao	75	7.8
5	南方日报 South Daily	59	6.1
6	广州青年报 Guangzhou Youth Daily	38	3.9
7	南方周末 South Weekend	21	2.2
8	足球报 Soccer	20	2.1
8	屏幕之友 Ping Mu Zhi You	20	2.1
9	参考消息 Reference News	14	1.5
10	电脑报 Computer Information	12	1.2

n=963

3-3 样本、男性各年龄层、女性各年龄层经常阅读的报纸/ Frequently Read Newspapers by the Whole Sample, Age and Gender Groups

注：本题为多选题，合计百分比超过 100%（Multiple answers）

	人数 Number	广州日报 Guangzhou Daily	羊城晚报 Yangcheng Wan Bao	新快报 New Express	南方都市报 Nanfang Dushi Bao	南方日报 South Daily	广州青年报 Guangzhou Youth Daily
样本 Sample	**963**	**82.7**	**70.0**	**13.1**	**7.8**	**6.1**	**3.9**
男性 Male	**474**	**83.8**	**71.9**	**14.3**	**8.4**	**6.8**	**1.3**
16~24 岁 Age	96	69.8	70.8	26.0	16.7	9.4	4.2
25~34 岁 Age	145	87.6	76.6	18.6	8.3	2.1	0.7
35~44 岁 Age	121	88.4	67.8	9.9	7.4	5.8	0.0
45~54 岁 Age	72	86.1	75.0	1.4	2.8	12.5	1.4
55~60 岁 Age	40	85.0	65.0	7.5	2.5	10.0	0.0
女性 Female	**489**	**81.6**	**68.1**	**11.9**	**7.2**	**5.5**	**6.5**
16~24 岁 Age	98	74.5	69.4	17.3	10.2	4.1	21.4
25~34 岁 Age	152	87.5	69.1	13.2	8.6	7.2	2.6
35~44 岁 Age	128	83.6	61.7	9.4	6.3	4.7	3.1
45~54 岁 Age	73	78.1	76.7	9.6	2.7	8.2	4.1
55~60 岁 Age	38	76.3	65.8	5.3	5.3	0.0	0.0

续前表 continued

	人数 Number	南方周末 South Weekend	足球报 Soccer	屏幕之友 Ping Mu Zhi You	参考消息 Reference News	电脑报 Computer Information
样本 Sample	**963**	**2.2**	**2.1**	**2.1**	**1.5**	**1.2**
男性 Male	**474**	**1.7**	**3.8**	**0.8**	**1.9**	**2.3**
16~24 岁 Age	96	1.0	6.3	2.1	1.0	5.2
25~34 岁 Age	145	2.1	5.5	0.7	2.1	3.4
35~44 岁 Age	121	1.7	3.3	0.0	0.8	0.8
45~54 岁 Age	72	1.4	0.0	1.4	4.2	0.0
55~60 岁 Age	40	2.5	0.0	0.0	2.5	0.0
女性 Female	**489**	**2.7**	**0.4**	**3.3**	**1.0**	**0.2**
16~24 岁 Age	98	4.1	0.0	7.1	0.0	1.0
25~34 岁 Age	152	3.3	0.7	3.3	0.0	0.0
35~44 岁 Age	128	1.6	0.8	1.6	1.6	0.0
45~54 岁 Age	73	2.7	0.0	2.7	2.7	0.0
55~60 岁 Age	38	0.0	0.0	0.0	2.6	0.0

3-4 经常阅读的报纸的主要来源/ Sources of Obtaining the Frequently Read Newspapers

注：本题为多选题，合计百分比可能超过 100%（Multiple answers）

	人数 Number	家中订阅 subscribed by my family	单位订阅 subscribed by work unit	报摊购买 bought from vender	赠阅 given as gift	借阅 borrowed	街头报栏 news-stand along street
广州日报 Guangzhou Daily	787	25.0	21.6	48.7	0.0	2.4	3.3
羊城晚报 Yangcheng Wan Bao	669	35.7	9.0	50.5	0.1	3.3	2.5
新快报 New Express	125	12.0	0.8	66.4	1.6	12.0	0.8
南方都市报 Nanfang Dushi Bao	75	9.3	12.0	69 3	1.3	4.0	4.0
南方日报 South Daily	59	10.2	42.4	37.3	1.7	6.8	3.4
广州青年报 Guangzhou youth Daily	38	0.0	2.6	84.2	0.0	10.5	2.6
南方周末 South Weekend	21	33.3	4.8	47.6	0.0	14.3	0.0
屏幕之友 Ping Nu Zhi You	20	0.0	0.0	100.0	0.0	0.0	0.0
足球报 Soccer	19	5.3	5.3	78.9	0.0	10.5	5.3

3-5 经常阅读的报纸内容/ Ranking of the Content Categories that Newspaper Readers Concern about

注：本题为多选题，合计百分比超过 100%（Multiple answers）

排名 Ranking	内容 Contents	人次 Person-time	百分比 Percent
1	头版要闻 first page news	583	61.4
2	国内新闻 national news	557	58.6
3	国际新闻 international news	508	53.5
4	影视娱乐报道 video & entertainment report	278	29.3
5	本地新闻 local news	257	27.1
6	港澳台新闻 news about HK. Taiwan. Macao	216	22.7
7	体育报道 sports report	190	20.0
8	健康医疗 medicare	170	17.9
9	生活常识 common sense	130	13.7
10	法制报道 legal news	106	11.2
10	服饰美容 clothes & beauty	106	11.2
11	股市报道 stock market report	96	10.1
12	休闲旅游 entertainment & travel	88	9.3
13	热点追踪 hits track	87	9.2
14	经济信息 economic information	80	8.4
15	军事知识 military knowledge	69	7.3
16	漫画 cartoon	61	6.4
17	科技知识 science sense	56	5.9
18	海外见闻 overseas information	52	5.5
19	财政金融 finance & economic	50	5.3
20	文化信息 cultural information	45	4.7
21	消费指南 consumption guide	44	4.6
21	人物专访 personal interview	44	4.6
21	小说 novel	44	4.6
22	散文 prose	35	3.7
23	广告 advertising	26	2.7
24	电视节目预告 TV program forecast	20	2.1
25	其他 others	16	1.7
26	读者来信 reader's letter	10	1.1
27	文艺评论 art critics	7	0.7
28	书评 book comment	6	0.6

n=950

3-6 样本、男性各年龄层、女性各年龄层经常阅读的报纸内容/ Ranking of the Concerned Newspaper Content Categories by the Whole Sample, Age and Gender Groups

注：本题为多选题，合计百分比超过 100%（Multiple answers）

	人数 Number	头版要闻 first page news	国际新闻 international news	国内新闻 national news	港澳台新闻 news about HK. Taiwan. Macao	本地新闻 local news	经济信息 economic information
样本 Sample	950	61.4	53.5	58.6	22.7	27.1	8.4
男性 Male	467	63.8	59.7	62.3	21.2	30.2	11.6
16~24 岁 Age	96	57.3	44.8	49.0	24.0	26.0	7.3
25~34 岁 Age	141	61.0	61.0	59.6	20.6	31.2	17.7
35~44 岁 Age	119	70.6	65.5	66.4	18.5	28.6	10.1
45~54 岁 Age	71	64.8	63.4	73.2	21.1	36.6	9.9
55~60 岁 Age	40	67.5	67.5	72.5	25.0	30.0	7.5
女性 Female	483	59.0	47.4	55.1	24.2	24.0	5.4
16~24 岁 Age	96	50.0	36.5	46.9	24.0	13.5	2.1
25~34 岁 Age	149	63.1	47.0	49.0	28.9	23.5	5.4
35~44 岁 Age	128	59.4	54.7	60.9	27.3	22.7	7.0
45~54 岁 Age	73	60.3	46.6	58.9	12.3	35.6	8.2
55~60 岁 Age	37	62.2	54.1	73.0	18.9	35.1	2.7

续前表 continued

	人数 Number	财政金融 finance & economic	股市报道 stock market report	热点追踪 hits track	文化信息 cultural information	体育报道 sports report	人物专访 personal interview
样本 Sample	950	5.3	10.1	9.2	4.7	20.0	4.6
男性 Male	467	7.5	12.8	9.6	3.6	32.8	2.8
16~24 岁 Age	96	4.2	6.3	14.6	8.3	44.8	2.1
25~34 岁 Age	141	12.1	13.5	7.8	2.1	34.8	0.7
35~44 岁 Age	119	7.6	16.8	7.6	4.2	25.2	4.2
45~54 岁 Age	71	4.2	12.7	11.3	1.4	28.2	5.6
55~60 岁 Age	40	5.0	15.0	7.5	0.0	27.5	2.5
女性 Female	483	3.1	7.5	8.7	5.8	7.7	6.4
16~24 岁 Age	96	1.0	3.1	15.6	8.3	10.4	2.1
25~34 岁 Age	149	5.4	7.4	6.7	7.4	6.7	4.7
35~44 岁 Age	128	2.3	9.4	7.8	3.1	7.8	11.7
45~54 岁 Age	73	2.7	12.3	8.2	5.5	4.1	8.2
55~60 岁 Age	37	2.7	2.7	2.7	2.7	10.8	2.7

续前表 continued

	人数 Number	军事知识 military knowledge	法制报道 legal news	海外见闻 overseas information	科技知识 science sense	影视娱乐报道 video & entertainment report	服饰美容 clothes & beauty
样本 Sample	950	7.3	11.2	5.5	5.9	29.3	11.2
男性 Male	467	12.8	12.8	4.5	8.8	19.1	1.1
16~24 岁 Age	96	16.7	8.3	4.2	13.5	36.5	3.1
25~34 岁 Age	141	17.7	9.2	2.8	10.6	17.7	0.7
35~44 岁 Age	119	6.7	18.5	5.9	5.9	16.8	0.0
45~54 岁 Age	71	9.9	15.5	5.6	4.2	9.9	1.4
55~60 岁 Age	40	10.0	15.0	5.0	7.5	5.0	0.0
女性 Female	483	1.9	9.5	6.4	3.1	39.1	20.9
16~24 岁 Age	96	4.2	8.3	3.1	6.3	59.4	36.5
25~34 岁 Age	149	1.3	10.1	7.4	2.7	39.6	23.5
35~44 岁 Age	128	2.3	11.7	8.6	1.6	35.2	20.3
45~54 岁 Age	73	0.0	6.8	6.8	4.1	31.5	5.5
55~60 岁 Age	37	0.0	8.1	2.7	0.0	13.5	2.7

续前表 continued

	人数 Number	休闲旅游 entertainment & travel	消费指南 consumption guide	电视节目预告 TV program forecast	健康医疗 medicare	生活常识 common sense	书评 book comment
样本 Sample	950	9.3	4.6	2.1	17.9	13.7	0.6
男性 Male	467	6.4	1.9	1.7	11.6	8.1	0.2
16~24 岁 Age	96	11.5	3.1	3.1	6.3	5.2	0.0
25~34 岁 Age	141	7.1	1.4	0.7	7.1	9.9	0.0
35~44 岁 Age	119	5.0	1.7	0.0	15.1	8.4	0.0
45~54 岁 Age	71	1.4	1.4	2.8	12.7	5.6	0.0
55~60 岁 Age	40	5.0	2.5	5.0	27.5	12.5	2.5
女性 Female	483	12.0	7.2	2.5	24.0	19.0	1.0
16~24 岁 Age	96	11.5	8.3	2.1	9.4	14.6	2.1
25~34 岁 Age	149	16.1	6.0	3.4	25.5	20.8	0.7
35~44 岁 Age	128	11.7	4.7	0.8	22.7	18.0	0.8
45~54 岁 Age	73	6.8	13.7	4.1	34.2	20.5	0.0
55~60 岁 Age	37	8.1	5.4	2.7	40.5	24.3	2.7

续前表 continued

	人数 Number	文艺评论 art critics	散文 prose	小说 novel	漫画 cartoon	广告 advertising	读者来信 reader's letter	其他 others
样本 Sample	**950**	**0.7**	**3.7**	**4.6**	**6.4**	**2.7**	**1.1**	**1.7**
男性 Male	**467**	**0.4**	**3.2**	**3.6**	**5.8**	**1.9**	**0.6**	**1.1**
16~24 岁 Age	96	1.0	5.2	4.2	14.6	2.1	0.0	2.1
25~34 岁 Age	141	0.7	3.5	3.5	5.0	2.8	0.7	0.0
35~44 岁 Age	119	0.0	0.8	3.4	2.5	1.7	0.0	1.7
45~54 岁 Age	71	0.0	1.4	4.2	2.8	0.0	2.8	1.4
55~60 岁 Age	40	0.0	7.5	2.5	2.5	2.5	0.0	0.0
女性 Female	**483**	**1.0**	**4.1**	**5.6**	**7.0**	**3.5**	**1.4**	**2.3**
16~24 岁 Age	96	2.1	9.4	11.5	21.9	5.2	1.0	1.0
25~34 岁 Age	149	0.7	3.4	4.0	4.7	5.4	2.7	3.4
35~44 岁 Age	128	0.0	1.6	0.8	3.1	2.3	1.6	2.3
45~54 岁 Age	73	2.7	2.7	8.2	2.7	1.4	0.0	1.4
55~60 岁 Age	37	0.0	5.4	8.1	0.0	0.0	0.0	2.7

3-7 不同学历的读者阅读的报纸内容的偏好/ Ranking of the Concerned Newspaper Content Categories by Educational Levels

注：本题为多选题，合计百分比超过 100%（Multiple answers）

	人数 Number	头版要闻 first page news	国际新闻 international news	国内新闻 national news	港澳台新闻 news about HK. Taiwan. Macao	本地新闻 local news	经济信息 economic information
样本 Sample	**941**	**61.4**	**53.9**	**58.9**	**22.8**	**26.8**	**8.4**
小学及以下 Primary School or Below	36	55.6	44.4	52.8	25.0	30.6	8.3
初中 Middle School	201	52.7	55.7	59.7	24.9	29.9	7.5
高中/中专/技校 High School/Technical Secondary School	470	59.4	50.6	59.8	23.6	27.9	7.7
大学专科 2-3 Year College	125	72.0	60.0	57.6	19.2	24.0	12.0
大学本科 4-5 Year College	99	74.7	61.6	55.6	18.2	17.2	9.1
研究生或以上 Graduate or Above	10	90.0	50.0	70.0	30.0	30.0	10.0

续前表 continued

	人数 Number	财政金融 finance & economic	股市报道 stock market report	热点追踪 hits track	文化信息 cultural information	体育报道 sports report	人物专访 personal interview
样本 Sample	**941**	**5.1**	**10.0**	**8.9**	**4.8**	**20.2**	**4.7**
小学及以下 Primary School or Below	36	5.6	8.3	5.6	2.8	11.1	5.6
初中 Middle School	201	1.5	4.5	4.0	3.5	17.4	5.5
高中/中专/技校 High School/Technical Secondary School	470	4.3	11.7	9.1	4.5	18.7	5.1
大学专科 2-3 Year College	125	9.6	16.0	12.0	4.0	20.8	4.0
大学本科 4-5 Year College	99	11.1	6.1	16.2	11.1	36.4	1.0
研究生或以上 Graduate or Above	10	0.0	10.0	0.0	0.0	10.0	10.0

续前表 continued

	人数 Number	军事知识 military knowledge	法制报道 legal news	海外见闻 overseas information	科技知识 science sense	影视娱乐报道 video & entertainment report	服饰美容 clothes & beauty
样本 Sample	941	7.3	11.3	5.5	5.7	29.3	11.1
小学及以下 Primary School or Below	36	0.0	8.3	8.3	5.6	16.7	5.6
初中 Middle School	201	9.0	11.4	5.0	3.0	30.3	6.0
高中/中专/技校 High School/Technical Secondary School	470	7.4	12.8	6.0	5.3	31.7	12.1
大学专科 2-3 Year College	125	6.4	9.6	5.6	8.0	23.2	14.4
大学本科 4-5 Year College	99	8.1	6.1	4.0	10.1	27.3	14.1
研究生或以上 Graduate or Above	10	0.0	20.0	0.0	10.0	40.0	10.0

续前表 continued

	人数 Number	休闲旅游 entertainment & travel	消费指南 consumption guide	电视节目预告 TV program forecast	健康医疗 medicare	生活常识 common sense	书评 book comment
样本 Sample	941	9.1	4.7	2.1	17.7	13.7	0.5
小学及以下 Primary School or Below	36	2.8	2.8	5.6	27.8	13.9	0.0
初中 Middle School	201	5.5	7.0	2.5	23.9	14.9	1.0
高中/中专/技校 High School/Technical Secondary School	470	10.0	4.0	1.9	16.0	14.3	0.2
大学专科 2-3 Year College	125	13.6	5.6	2.4	14.4	10.4	0.8
大学本科 4-5 Year College	99	10.1	2.0	1.0	13.1	13.1	1.0
研究生或以上 Graduate or Above	10	0.0	10.0	0.0	30.0	10.0	0.0

续前表 continued

	人数 Number	文艺评论 art critics	散文 prose	小说 novel	漫画 cartoon	广告 advertising	读者来信 reader's letter	其他 others
样本 Sample	941	0.6	3.6	4.6	6.5	2.8	1.1	1.7
小学及以下 Primary School or Below	36	5.6	2.8	8.3	8.3	0.0	0.0	0.0
初中 Middle School	201	0.0	3.0	2.0	4.5	4.0	0.5	3.0
高中/中专/技校 High School/Technical Secondary School	470	0.6	3.0	5.5	6.6	2.1	1.9	1.1
大学专科 2-3 Year College	125	0.0	3.2	5.6	8.8	1.6	0.0	3.2
大学本科 4-5 Year College	99	1.0	8.1	2.0	6.1	5.1	0.0	1.0
研究生或以上 Graduate or Above	10	0.0	10.0	10.0	10.0	10.0	0.0	0.0

3-8 不同消费者层平时是否接触报纸媒介/ Newspaper Reading by Market Segments

3-8-1 时尚流行指标/ Fads Popular Index

	人数 Number	从来不看 never	看 yes
样本 Sample	1021	6.8	93.2
平实生活指向 simple living orientation	518	7.7	92.3
时尚流行指向 fashion orientation	503	5.8	94.2

3-8-2 广告态度指标/ Advertising Attitude Index

	人数 Number	从来不看 never	看 yes
样本 Sample	1021	6.6	93.4
广告淡漠指向 indifferent orientation	334	8.1	91.9
中间层 medium	593	6.1	93.9
信赖广告指向 loyal orientation	94	4.3	95.7

3-9 不同消费者层经常阅读的报纸/ Frequently Read Newspapers by Market Segments

3-9-1 时尚流行指标/ Fads Popular Index

注：本题为多选题，合计百分比超过 100%（Multiple answers）

	人数 Number	广州日报 Guangzhou Daily	羊城晚报 Yangcheng Wan Bao	新快报 New Express	南方都市报 Nanfang Dushi Bao	南方日报 South Daily	广州青年报 Guangzhou Youth Daily
样本 Sample	952	82.8	69.9	13.1	7.9	6.2	4.0
平实生活指向 simple living orientation	478	84.5	71.5	10.9	7.5	6.9	2.5
时尚流行指向 fashion orientation	474	81.0	68.1	15.4	8.2	5.5	5.5

续前表 continued

	人数 Number	南方周末 South Weekend	足球报 Soccer	屏幕之友 Ping Mu Zhi You	参考消息 Reference News	电脑报 Computer Information
样本 Sample	952	2.2	2.1	2.1	1.5	1.3
平实生活指向 simple living orientation	478	2.5	1.7	1.3	2.1	0.8
时尚流行指向 fashion orientation	474	1.9	2.5	3.0	0.8	1.7

3-9-2 广告态度指向/ Advertising Attitude Index

注：本题为多选题，合计百分比超过 100%（Multiple answers）

	人数 Number	广州日报 Guangzhou Daily	羊城晚报 Yangcheng Wan Bao	新快报 New Express	南方都市报 Nanfang Dushi Bao	南方日报 South Daily	广州青年报 Guangzhou Youth Daily
样本 Sample	954	82.6	70.1	13.0	7.9	6.2	4.0
广告淡漠指向 indifferent orientation	307	85.3	69.4	8.8	8.1	6.5	2.9
中间层 medium	557	81.1	71.3	15.4	7.4	5.9	3.9
信赖广告指向 loyal orientation	90	82.2	65.6	12.2	10.0	6.7	7.8

续前表 continued

	人数 Number	南方周末 South Weekend	足球报 Soccer	屏幕之友 Ping Mu Zhi You	参考消息 Reference News	电脑报 Computer Information
样本 Sample	954	2.2	2.1	2.0	1.5	1.3
广告淡漠指向 indifferent orientation	307	2.9	1.0	1.3	2.6	1.0
中间层 medium	557	1.8	2.9	1.4	0.9	1.6
信赖广告指向 loyal orientation	90	2.2	1.1	7.8	1.1	0.0

3-10 不同消费者层比较关心的报道/ The Concerned Newspaper Content Categories by Market Segments

3-10-1 时尚流行指标/ Fads Popular Index

注：本题为多选题，合计百分比超过 100%（Multiple answers）

	人数 Number	头版要闻 first page news	国际新闻 international news	国内新闻 national news	港澳台新闻 news about HK. Taiwan. Macao	本地新闻 local news	经济信息 economic information
样本 Sample	940	61.4	53.5	58.8	22.7	26.9	8.3
平实生活指向 simple living orientation	472	62.1	53.4	63.1	18.6	32.6	10.0
时尚流行指向 fashion orientation	468	60.7	53.6	54.5	26.7	21.2	6.6

续前表 continued

	人数 Number	财政金融 finance & economic	股市报道 stock market report	热点追踪 hits track	文化信息 cultural information	体育报道 sports report	人物专访 personal interview
样本 Sample	940	5.2	10.1	9.1	4.7	20.1	4.6
平实生活指向 simple living orientation	472	5.9	12.1	8.5	4.4	18.6	5.7
时尚流行指向 fashion orientation	468	4.5	8.1	9.8	4.9	21.6	3.4

续前表 continued

	人数 Number	军事知识 military knowledge	法制报道 legal news	海外见闻 overseas information	科技知识 science sense	影视娱乐报道 video & entertainment report	服饰美容 clothes & beauty
样本 Sample	940	7.3	11.1	5.3	5.9	29.6	11.2
平实生活指向 simple living orientation	472	8.1	11.9	5.3	6.4	24.2	4.7
时尚流行指向 fashion orientation	468	6.6	10.3	5.3	5.3	35.0	17.7

续前表 continued

	人数 Number	休闲旅游 entertainment & travel	消费指南 consumption guide	电视节目预告 TV program forecast	健康医疗 medicare	生活常识 common sense	书评 book comment
样本 Sample	940	9.4	4.7	2.1	17.9	13.6	0.6
平实生活指向 simple living orientation	472	7.0	4.2	1.9	19.9	15.5	0.4
时尚流行指向 fashion orientation	468	11.8	5.1	2.4	15.8	11.8	0.9

续前表 continued

	人数 Number	文艺评论 art critics	散文 prose	小说 novel	漫画 cartoon	广告 advertising	读者来信 reader's letter	其他 others
样本 Sample	940	0.6	3.6	4.6	6.3	2.8	1.1	1.7
平实生活指向 simple living orientation	472	1.1	2.8	3.8	4.4	1.7	1.1	1.1
时尚流行指向 fashion orientation	468	0.2	4.5	5.3	8.1	3.8	1.1	2.4

3-10-2 广告态度指标/ Advertising Attitude Index

注：本题为多选题，合计百分比超过100%（Multiple answers）

	人数 Number	头版要闻 first page news	国际新闻 international news	国内新闻 national news	港澳台新闻 news about HK. Taiwan. Macao	本地新闻 local news	经济信息 economic information
样本 Sample	941	61.3	53.7	58.8	22.5	26.9	8.5
广告淡漠指向 indifferent orientation	303	58.7	57.1	65.0	22.1	29.0	9.6
中间层 medium	550	62.7	52.9	57.1	22.2	26.0	8.0
信赖广告指向 loyal orientation	88	61.4	46.6	47.7	26.1	25.0	8.0

续前表 continued

	人数 Number	财政金融 finance & economic	股市报道 stock market report	热点追踪 hits track	文化信息 cultural information	体育报道 sports report	人物专访 personal interview
样本 Sample	941	5.3	10.0	9.1	4.8	20.1	4.6
广告淡漠指向 indifferent orientation	303	5.9	10.2	10.2	5.3	18.2	5.9
中间层 medium	550	5.1	10.5	8.0	4.5	22.2	4.2
信赖广告指向 loyal orientation	88	4.5	5.7	12.5	4.5	13.6	2.3

续前表 continued

	人数 Number	军事知识 military knowledge	法制报道 legal news	海外见闻 overseas information	科技知识 science sense	影视娱乐报道 video & entertainment report	服饰美容 clothes & beauty
样本 Sample	941	7.3	11.3	5.4	6.0	29.4	11.1
广告淡漠指向 indifferent orientation	303	8.9	12.2	3.6	5.9	28.4	5.9
中间层 medium	550	6.9	10.2	6.0	6.5	29.3	12.5
信赖广告指向 loyal orientation	88	4.5	14.8	8.0	2.3	34.1	19.3

续前表 continued

	人数 Number	休闲旅游 entertainment & travel	消费指南 consumption guide	电视节目预告 TV program forecast	健康医疗 medicare	生活常识 common sense	书评 book comment
样本 Sample	941	9.2	4.5	2.1	17.7	13.7	0.6
广告淡漠指向 indifferent orientation	303	6.9	4.0	1.7	16.8	11.9	0.7
中间层 medium	550	10.2	4.2	2.4	17.6	14.5	0.5
信赖广告指向 loyal orientation	88	11.4	8.0	2.3	21.6	14.8	1.1

续前表 continued

	人数 Number	文艺评论 art critics	散文 prose	小说 novel	漫画 cartoon	广告 advertising	读者来信 reader's letter	其他 others
样本 Sample	941	0.7	3.6	4.4	6.3	2.8	1.1	1.7
广告淡漠指向 indifferent orientation	303	1.3	3.6	2.6	6.9	0.7	1.0	0.7
中间层 medium	550	0.5	3.3	5.5	5.8	4.0	0.7	2.4
信赖广告指向 loyal orientation	88	0.0	5.7	3.4	6.8	2.3	3.4	1.1

● 重庆 / Chongqing

3-1 样本、男性各年龄层、女性各年龄层平时是否接触报纸媒介/ Newspaper Reading by the Whole Sample, Age and Gender Groups

	人数 Number	从来不看 never	看 yes
样本 Sample	623	13.0	87.0
男性 Male	313	13.1	86.9
16~24 岁 Age	64	12.5	87.5
25~34 岁 Age	93	5.4	94.6
35~44 岁 Age	75	14.7	85.3
45~54 岁 Age	54	25.9	74.1
55~60 岁 Age	27	11.1	88.9
女性 Female	310	12.9	87.1
16~24 岁 Age	64	7.8	92.2
25~34 岁 Age	90	8.9	91.1
35~44 岁 Age	73	17.8	82.2
45~54 岁 Age	60	18.3	81.7
55~60 岁 Age	23	13.0	87.0

3-2 经常阅读的报纸排名/ Ranking of the Frequently Read Newspaper

注：本题为多选题，合计百分比超过 100%（Multiple answers）

排名 Ranking	报纸 Newspapers	人次 Person-time	百分比 Percent
1	重庆晚报 Chongqing Evening News	393	72.8
2	重庆晨报 Chongqing Morning News	259	48.0
3	重庆商报 Chongqing Economic Time	153	28.3
4	华西都市报 Hua Xi Du Shi Bao	82	15.2
5	现代工人报 Gongrenbao	60	11.1
6	重庆日报 Chongqing Daily	55	10.2
7	重庆经济日报 Chongqing Economic Daily	44	8.1
8	参考消息 Reference News	27	5.0
9	重庆广播电视报 Chongqing TV Guide	22	4.1
10	足球报 Soccer	17	3.1
11	重庆法制报 Chongqing Legal System New	15	2.8
12	文摘周报 Wen Zhai Zhou Bao	10	1.9
13	人民日报 People's Daily	9	1.7
13	中国青年报 China Youth Daily	9	1.7

n=540

3-3 样本、男性各年龄层、女性各年龄层经常阅读的报纸/ Frequently Read Newspapers by the Whole Sample, Age and Gender Groups

注：本题为多选题，合计百分比超过 100%（Multiple answers）

	人数 Number	重庆晚报 Chongqing Evening News	重庆晨报 Chongqing Morning News	重庆商报 Chongqing Economic Time	华西都市报 Hua Xi Du Shi Bao	现代工人报 Gongrenbao	重庆日报 Chongqing Daily	重庆经济日报 Chongqing Economic Daily
样本 Sample	540	72.8	48.0	28.3	15.2	11.1	10.2	8.1
男性 Male	272	73.5	47.8	26.5	16.2	11.4	8.5	10.3
16~24 岁 Age	56	89.3	46.4	26.8	5.4	8.9	7.1	10.7
25~34 岁 Age	88	69.3	44.3	26.1	15.9	12.5	8.0	12.5
35~44 岁 Age	64	67.2	54.7	21.9	23.4	10.9	6.3	12.5
45~54 岁 Age	40	65.0	55.0	37.5	17.5	15.0	15.0	2.5
55~60 岁 Age	24	83.3	33.3	20.8	20.8	8.3	8.3	8.3
女性 Female	268	72.0	48.1	30.2	14.2	10.8	11.9	6.0
16~24 岁 Age	58	84.5	46.6	29.3	8.6	10.3	8.6	3.4
25~34 岁 Age	82	80.5	53.7	30.5	17.1	17.1	7.3	8.5
35~44 岁 Age	60	56.7	46.7	30.0	13.3	13.3	20.0	6.7
45~54 岁 Age	48	64.6	47.9	37.5	16.7	2.1	10.4	4.2
55~60 岁 Age	20	65.0	35.0	15.0	15.0	0.0	20.0	5.0

续前表 continued

	人数 Number	参考消息 Reference News	重庆广播电视报 Chongqing TV Guide	足球报 Soccer	重庆法制报 Chongqing Legal System New	文摘周报 Wen Zhai Zhou Bao	人民日报 People's Daily	中国青年报 China Youth Daily
样本 Sample	540	5.0	4.1	3.1	2.8	1.9	1.7	1.7
男性 Male	272	8.5	1.8	5.5	2.9	1.8	2.6	1.5
16~24 岁 Age	56	3.6	5.4	7.1	0.0	0.0	5.4	1.8
25~34 岁 Age	88	13.6	1.1	5.7	0.0	0.0	3.4	2.3
35~44 岁 Age	64	9.4	0.0	6.3	6.3	4.7	0.0	0.0
45~54 岁 Age	40	5.0	2.5	5.0	7.5	2.5	2.5	0.0
55~60 岁 Age	24	4.2	0.0	0.0	4.2	4.2	0.0	4.2
女性 Female	268	1.5	6.3	0.7	2.6	1.9	0.7	1.9
16~24 岁 Age	58	1.7	6.9	0.0	0.0	3.4	0.0	3.4
25~34 岁 Age	82	2.4	3.7	1.2	4.9	2.4	0.0	0.0
35~44 岁 Age	60	1.7	3.3	0.0	1.7	1.7	1.7	3.3
45~54 岁 Age	48	0.0	14.6	2.1	2.1	0.0	2.1	2.1
55~60 岁 Age	20	0.0	5.0	0.0	5.0	0.0	0.0	0.0

3-4 经常阅读的报纸的主要来源/ Sources of Obtaining the Frequently Read Newspaper

注：本题为多选题，合计百分比可能超过 100%（Multiple answers）

	人数 Number	家中订阅 subscribed by my family	单位订阅 subscribed by work unit	报摊购买 bought from vender	赠阅 given as gift	借阅 borrowed	街头报栏 news-stand along street
重庆晚报 Chongqing Evening News	389	20.3	16.7	56.6	0.3	5.1	1.5
重庆晨报 Chongqing Morning News	256	17.6	18.8	56.3	0.4	6.6	1.2
重庆商报 Chongqing Economic Time	152	32.9	11.2	47.4	0.7	6.6	2.0
华西都市报 Hua Xi Du Shi Bao	81	35.8	17.3	37.0	0.0	9.9	0.0
现代工人报 Gongrenbao	59	11.9	23.7	62.7	0.0	1.7	0.0
重庆日报 Chongqing Daily	54	9.3	53.7	31.5	0.0	3.7	0.0
重庆经济日报 Chongqing Economic Daily	44	34.1	15.9	38.6	2.8	9.1	0.0
参考消息 Reference News	27	11.1	25.9	66.7	0.0	0.0	0.0

3-5 经常阅读的报纸内容/ Ranking of the Contents Categories that Newspaper Readers Concern about

注：本题为多选题，合计百分比超过 100%（Multiple answers）

排名 Ranking	内容 Contents	人次 Person-time	百分比 Percent
1	国内新闻 national news	292	54.1
2	国际新闻 international news	259	48.0
3	本地新闻 local news	187	34.6
4	头版要闻 first page news	182	33.7
5	法制报道 legal news	129	23.9
5	体育报道 sports report	129	23.9
6	健康医疗 medicare	108	20.0
6	生活常识 common sense	108	20.0
7	影视娱乐报道 video & entertainment report	85	15.7
8	军事知识 military knowledge	77	14.3
9	股市报道 stock market report	70	13.0
10	热点追踪 hits track	68	12.6
11	经济信息 economic information	64	11.9
12	服饰美容 clothes & beauty	55	10.2
13	小说 novel	48	8.9
14	港澳台新闻 news about HK. Taiwan Macao	44	8.1
15	人物专访 personal interview	38	7.0
16	休闲旅游 entertainment & travel	37	6.9
17	消费指南 consumption guide	36	6.7
18	科技知识 science sense	35	6.5
19	海外见闻 overseas information	31	5.7
20	漫画 cartoon	28	5.2
21	电视节目预告 TV program forecast	27	5.0
21	文化信息 cultural information	27	5.0
22	财政金融 finance & economic	24	4.4
23	散文 prose	20	3.7
24	广告 advertising	19	3.5
25	文艺评论 art critics	9	1.7
26	读者来信 reader's letter	3	0.6
27	书评 book comment	1	0.2
27	其他 others	1	0.2

n=540

3-6 样本、男性各年龄层、女性各年龄层经常阅读的报纸内容/ The Concerned Newspaper Content Categories by the Whole Sample, Age and Gender Groups

注：本题为多选题，合计百分比超过 100%（Multiple answers）

	人数 Number	头版要闻 first page news	国际新闻 international news	国内新闻 national news	港澳台新闻 news about HK. Taiwan Macao	本地新闻 local news	经济信息 economic information
样本 Sample	**540**	**33.7**	**48.0**	**54.1**	**8.1**	**34.6**	**11.9**
男性 Male	**271**	**37.3**	**60.5**	**58.7**	**7.7**	**34.3**	**15.5**
16~24 岁 Age	56	35.7	46.4	28.6	16.1	17.9	7.1
25~34 岁 Age	88	37.5	62.5	58.0	4.5	33.0	14.8
35~44 岁 Age	63	38.1	71.4	74.6	11.1	34.9	23.8
45~54 岁 Age	40	42.5	60.0	62.5	2.5	52.5	20.0
55~60 岁 Age	24	29.2	58.3	83.3	0.0	45.8	8.3
女性 Female	**269**	**30.1**	**35.3**	**49.4**	**8.6**	**34.9**	**8.2**
16~24 岁 Age	59	22.0	35.6	32.2	15.3	23.7	3.4
25~34 岁 Age	82	34.1	31.7	50.0	8.5	40.2	7.3
35~44 岁 Age	59	35.6	39.0	49.2	5.1	25.4	13.6
45~54 岁 Age	49	28.6	34.7	63.3	8.2	40.8	8.2
55~60 岁 Age	20	25.0	40.0	65.0	0.0	60.0	10.0

续前表 continued

	人数 Number	财政金融 finance & economic	股市报道 stock market report	热点追踪 hits track	文化信息 cultural information	体育报道 sports report	人物专访 personal interview
样本 Sample	**540**	**4.4**	**13.0**	**12.6**	**5.0**	**23.9**	**7.0**
男性 Male	**271**	**6.6**	**14.8**	**10.0**	**3.7**	**38.4**	**7.7**
16~24 岁 Age	56	3.6	0.0	8.9	7.1	64.3	7.1
25~34 岁 Age	88	8.0	18.2	5.7	4.5	40.9	9.1
35~44 岁 Age	63	7.9	17.5	12.7	0.0	23.8	3.2
45~54 岁 Age	40	2.5	17.5	20.0	2.5	25.0	15.0
55~60 岁 Age	24	12.5	25.0	4.2	4.2	29.2	4.2
女性 Female	**269**	**2.2**	**11.2**	**15.2**	**6.3**	**9.3**	**6.3**
16~24 岁 Age	59	0.0	1.7	10.2	10.2	11.9	10.2
25~34 岁 Age	82	2.4	13.4	11.0	7.3	6.1	7.3
35~44 岁 Age	59	3.4	15.3	23.7	5.1	11.9	3.4
45~54 岁 Age	49	4.1	16.3	16.3	2.0	10.2	4.1
55~60 岁 Age	20	0.0	5.0	20.0	5.0	5.0	5.0

续前表 continued

	人数 Number	军事知识 military knowledge	法制报道 legal news	海外见闻 overseas information	科技知识 science sense	影视娱乐报道 video & entertainment report	服饰美容 clothes & beauty
样本 Sample	**540**	**14.3**	**23.9**	**5.7**	**6.5**	**15.7**	**10.2**
男性 Male	**271**	**23.2**	**22.1**	**5.2**	**10.0**	**11.4**	**1.5**
16~24 岁 Age	56	32.1	12.5	10.7	16.1	25.0	3.6
25~34 岁 Age	88	27.3	20.5	4.5	13.6	12.5	2.3
35~44 岁 Age	63	20.6	20.6	1.6	1.6	6.3	0.0
45~54 岁 Age	40	10.0	32.5	7.5	10.0	2.5	0.0
55~60 岁 Age	24	16.7	37.5	0.0	4.2	4.2	0.0
女性 Female	**269**	**5.2**	**25.7**	**6.3**	**3.0**	**20.1**	**19.0**
16~24 岁 Age	59	0.0	18.6	13.6	6.8	45.8	37.3
25~34 岁 Age	82	9.8	24.4	4.9	2.4	20.7	19.5
35~44 岁 Age	59	6.8	35.6	5.1	1.7	11.9	16.9
45~54 岁 Age	49	4.1	28.6	4.1	0.0	6.1	6.1
55~60 岁 Age	20	0.0	15.0	0.0	5.0	0.0	0.0

续前表 continued

	人数 Number	休闲旅游 entertainment & travel	消费指南 consumption guide	电视节目预告 TV program forecast	健康医疗 medicare	生活常识 common sense	书评 book comment
样本 Sample	540	6.9	6.7	5.0	20.0	20.0	0.2
男性 Male	271	4.4	3.3	2.6	11.1	9.6	0.0
16~24 岁 Age	56	7.1	5.4	7.1	5.4	5.4	0.0
25~34 岁 Age	88	2.3	3.4	0.0	9.1	9.1	0.0
35~44 岁 Age	63	3.2	3.2	3.2	17.5	9.5	0.0
45~54 岁 Age	40	7.5	0.0	2.5	12.5	17.5	0.0
55~60 岁 Age	24	4.2	4.2	0.0	12.5	8.3	0.0
女性 Female	269	9.3	10.0	7.4	29.0	30.5	0.4
16~24 岁 Age	59	20.3	3.4	10.2	16.9	28.8	1.7
25~34 岁 Age	82	9.8	14.6	2.4	36.6	30.5	0.0
35~44 岁 Age	59	3.4	11.9	10.2	25.4	32.2	0.0
45~54 岁 Age	49	6.1	10.2	10.2	32.7	36.7	0.0
55~60 岁 Age	20	0.0	5.0	5.0	35.0	15.0	0.0

续前表 continued

	人数 Number	文艺评论 art critics	散文 prose	小说 novel	漫画 cartoon	广告 advertising	读者来信 reader's letter	其他 others
样本 Sample	540	1.7	3.7	8.9	5.2	3.5	0.6	0.2
男性 Male	271	1.5	0.7	4.1	5.2	3.3	0.0	0.4
16~24 岁 Age	56	0.0	1.8	7.1	16.1	8.9	0.0	1.8
25~34 岁 Age	88	0.0	0.0	5.7	4.5	2.3	0.0	0.0
35~44 岁 Age	63	3.2	0.0	3.2	1.6	3.2	0.0	0.0
45~54 岁 Age	40	5.0	2.5	0.0	0.0	0.0	0.0	0.0
55~60 岁 Age	24	0.0	0.0	0.0	0.0	0.0	0.0	0.0
女性 Female	269	1.9	6.7	13.8	5.2	3.7	1.1	0.0
16~24 岁 Age	59	1.7	16.9	22.0	13.6	6.8	1.7	0.0
25~34 岁 Age	82	3.7	3.7	11.0	4.9	2.4	2.4	0.0
35~44 岁 Age	59	1.7	6.8	11.9	1.7	5.1	0.0	0.0
45~54 岁 Age	49	0.0	0.0	8.2	2.0	2.0	0.0	0.0
55~60 岁 Age	20	0.0	5.0	20.0	0.0	0.0	0.0	0.0

3-7 不同学历的读者阅读的报纸内容的偏好/ The Concerned Newspaper Content Categories by Educational Levels

注：本题为多选题，合计百分比超过 100%（Multiple answers）

	人数 Number	头版要闻 first page news	国际新闻 international news	国内新闻 national news	港澳台新闻 news about HK. Taiwan Macao	本地新闻 local news	经济信息 economic information
样本 Sample	538	33.8	48.0	54.1	8.2	34.6	11.9
小学及以下 Primary School or Below	36	27.8	44.4	61.1	0.0	44.4	11.1
初中 Middle School	169	26.0	45.0	57.4	7.1	36.7	9.5
高中/中专/技校 High School/Technical Secondary School	219	32.0	46.6	48.9	10.5	32.0	11.0
大学专科 2-3 Year College	83	48.2	53.0	54.2	7.2	37.3	20.5
大学本科 4-5 Year College	30	56.7	66.7	66.7	10.0	23.3	10.0
研究生或以上 Graduate or Above	1	100.0	0.0	0.0	0.0	0.0	0.0

续前表 continued

	人数 Number	财政金融 finance & economic	股市报道 stock market report	热点追踪 hits track	文化信息 cultural information	体育报道 sports report	人物专访 personal interview
样本 Sample	**538**	**4.5**	**13.0**	**12.6**	**5.0**	**23.8**	**7.1**
小学及以下 Primary School or Below	36	0.0	5.6	19.4	2.8	5.6	0.0
初中 Middle School	169	4.1	11.2	13.6	2.4	18.9	7.7
高中/中专/技校 High School/Technical Secondary School	219	2.7	13.7	12.3	5.5	26.0	7.3
大学专科 2-3 Year College	83	10.8	18.1	8.4	6.0	31.3	4.8
大学本科 4-5 Year College	30	6.7	13.3	10.0	16.7	33.3	13.3
研究生或以上 Graduate or Above	1	0.0	0.0	100.0	0.0	100.0	100.0

续前表 continued

	人数 Number	军事知识 military knowledge	法制报道 legal news	海外见闻 overseas information	科技知识 science sense	影视娱乐报道 video & entertainment report	服饰美容 clothes & beauty
样本 Sample	**538**	**14.1**	**24.0**	**5.8**	**6.5**	**15.8**	**10.2**
小学及以下 Primary School or Below	36	13.9	36.1	2.8	2.8	5.6	0.0
初中 Middle School	169	13.6	29.0	4.1	1.8	10.1	8.3
高中/中专/技校 High School/Technical Secondary School	219	13.2	23.7	6.4	9.1	23.3	12.3
大学专科 2-3 Year College	83	18.1	10.8	8.4	9.6	10.8	14.5
大学本科 4-5 Year College	30	13.3	20.0	6.7	10.0	20.0	6.7
研究生或以上 Graduate or Above	1	0.0	0.0	0.0	0.0	0.0	0.0

续前表 continued

	人数 Number	休闲旅游 entertainment & travel	消费指南 consumption guide	电视节目预告 TV program forecast	健康医疗 medicare	生活常识 common sense	书评 book comment
样本 Sample	**538**	**6.7**	**6.7**	**5.0**	**20.1**	**19.9**	**0.2**
小学及以下 Primary School or Below	36	0.0	0.0	5.6	19.4	13.9	0.0
初中 Middle School	169	6.5	6.5	5.9	24.3	23.1	0.0
高中/中专/技校 High School/Technical Secondary School	219	6.4	6.8	5.5	20.5	20.1	0.0
大学专科 2-3 Year College	83	10.8	10.8	3.6	15.7	19.3	1.2
大学本科 4-5 Year College	30	6.7	3.3	0.0	6.7	10.0	0.0
研究生或以上 Graduate or Above	1	0.0	0.0	0.0	0.0	0.0	0.0

续前表 continued

	人数 Number	文艺评论 art critics	散文 prose	小说 novel	漫画 cartoon	广告 advertising	读者来信 reader's letter	其他 others
样本 Sample	**538**	**1.7**	**3.7**	**8.9**	**5.2**	**3.5**	**0.6**	**0.2**
小学及以下 Primary School or Below	36	2.8	2.8	8.3	2.8	2.8	0.0	0.0
初中 Middle School	169	2.4	5.3	11.2	3.0	2.4	0.6	0.0
高中/中专/技校 High School/Technical Secondary School	219	0.9	3.7	10.0	7.8	4.1	0.9	0.5
大学专科 2-3 Year College	83	2.4	2.4	4.8	6.0	6.0	0.0	0.0
大学本科 4-5 Year College	30	0.0	0.0	0.0	0.0	0.0	0.0	0.0
研究生或以上 Graduate or Above	1	0.0	0.0	0.0	0.0	0.0	0.0	0.0

3-8 不同消费者层平时是否接触报纸媒介/ Newspaper Reading by Market Segments

3-8-1 时尚流行指标/ Fads Popular Index

	人数 Number	从来不看 never	看 yes
样本 Sample	**616**	**13.0**	**87.0**
平实生活指向 simple living orientation	369	15.2	84.8
时尚流行指向 fashion orientation	247	9.7	90.3

3-8-2 广告态度指标/ Advertising Attitude Index

	人数 Number	从来不看 never	看 yes
样本 Sample	**618**	**12.9**	**87.1**
广告淡漠指向 indifferent orientation	167	15.6	84.4
中间层 medium	367	12.0	88.0
信赖广告指向 loyal orientation	84	11.9	88.1

3-9 不同消费者层经常阅读的报纸/ Frequently Read Newspapers by Market Segments

3-9-1 时尚流行指标/ Fads Popular Index

注：本题为多选题，合计百分比超过 100%（Multiple answers）

	人数 Number	重庆晚报 Chongqing Evening News	重庆晨报 Chongqing Morning News	重庆商报 Chongqing Economic Time	华西都市报 Hua Xi Du Shi Bao	现代工人报 Gongrenbao	重庆日报 Chongqing Daily	重庆经济日报 Chongqing Economic Daily
样本 Sample	**534**	**72.7**	**48.1**	**28.7**	**15.2**	**11.2**	**10.1**	**8.2**
平实生活指向 simple living orientation	313	71.6	45.4	26.2	14.4	10.5	11.2	9.3
时尚流行指向 fashion orientation	221	74.2	52.0	32.1	16.3	12.2	8.6	6.8

续前表 continued

	人数 Number	参考消息 Reference News	重庆广播电视报 Chongqing TV Guide	足球报 Soccer	重庆法制报 Chongqing Legal System NewS	文摘周报 Wen Zhai Zhou Bao	人民日报 People's Daily	中国青年报 China Youth Daily
样本 Sample	**534**	**5.1**	**4.1**	**3.2**	**2.8**	**1.3**	**1.7**	**1.7**
平实生活指向 simple living orientation	313	4.2	4.5	4.2	3.2	1.3	0.6	0.6
时尚流行指向 fashion orientation	221	6.3	3.6	1.8	2.3	1.4	3.2	3.2

3-9-2 广告态度指向/ Advertising Attitude Index

注：本题为多选题，合计百分比超过 100%（Multiple answers）

	人数 Number	重庆晚报 Chongqing Evening News	重庆晨报 Chongqing Morning News	重庆商报 Chongqing Economic Time	华西都市报 Hua Xi Du Shi Bao	现代工人报 Gongrenbao	重庆日报 Chongqing Daily	重庆经济日报 Chongqing Economic Daily
样本 Sample	536	72.8	47.8	28.2	14.7	11.2	10.3	8.2
广告淡漠指向 indifferent orientation	139	67.6	48.2	25.9	15.1	10.1	9.4	7.9
中间层 medium	323	75.5	47.4	28.5	14.6	11.5	11.1	8.7
信赖广告指向 loyal orientation	74	70.3	48.6	31.1	14.9	12.2	8.1	6.8

续前表 continued

	人数 Number	参考消息 Reference News	重庆广播电视报 Chongqing TV Guide	足球报 Soccer	重庆法制报 Chongqing Legal System NewS	文摘周报 Wen Zhai Zhou Bao	人民日报 People's Daily	中国青年报 China Youth Daily
样本 Sample	536	5.0	4.1	3.2	2.8	1.9	1.7	1.5
广告淡漠指向 indifferent orientation	139	3.6	4.3	5.0	2.2	2.2	0.7	1.4
中间层 medium	323	6.2	4.3	2.2	2.8	2.2	2.5	1.9
信赖广告指向 loyal orientation	74	2.7	2.7	4.1	4.1	0.0	0.0	0.0

3-10 不同消费者层比较关心的报道/ The Concerned Newspaper Content Categories by Market Segments

3-10-1 时尚流行指标/ Fads Popular Index

注：本题为多选题，合计百分比超过 100%（Multiple answers）

	人数 Number	头版要闻 first page news	国际新闻 international news	国内新闻 national news	港澳台新闻 news about HK Taiwan Macao	本地新闻 local news	经济信息 economic information
样本 Sample	534	33.3	47.8	54.1	8.2	34.6	11.8
平实生活指向 simple living orientation	311	34.1	47.9	59.2	6.1	39.2	10.9
时尚流行指向 fashion orientation	223	32.3	47.5	47.1	11.2	28.3	13.0

续前表 continued

	人数 Number	财政金融 finance & economic	股市报道 stock market report	热点追踪 hits track	文化信息 cultural information	体育报道 sports report	人物专访 personal interview
样本 Sample	534	4.5	12.9	12.5	5.1	23.8	6.9
平实生活指向 simple living orientation	311	4.5	13.8	13.5	2.6	23.2	6.4
时尚流行指向 fashion orientation	223	4.5	11.7	11.2	8.5	24.7	7.6

续前表 continued

	人数 Number	军事知识 military knowledge	法制报道 legal news	海外见闻 overseas information	科技知识 science sense	影视娱乐报道 video & entertainment report	服饰美容 clothes & beauty
样本 Sample	534	14.2	24.0	5.6	6.4	15.9	9.9
平实生活指向 simple living orientation	311	13.5	22.8	4.5	5.8	10.6	4.5
时尚流行指向 fashion orientation	223	15.2	25.6	7.2	7.2	23.3	17.5

续前表 continued

	人数 Number	休闲旅游 entertainment & travel	消费指南 consumption guide	电视节目预告 TV program forecast	健康医疗 medicare	生活常识 common sense	书评 book comment
样本 Sample	534	6.9	6.6	5.1	20.0	20.0	0.2
平实生活指向 simple living orientation	311	5.5	6.1	5.1	20.9	23.2	0.0
时尚流行指向 fashion orientation	223	9.0	7.2	4.9	18.8	15.7	0.4

续前表 continued

	人数 Number	文艺评论 art critics	散文 prose	小说 novel	漫画 cartoon	广告 advertising	读者来信 reader's letter	其他 others
样本 Sample	534	1.7	3.7	9.0	5.2	3.6	0.6	0.2
平实生活指向 simple living orientation	311	1.6	1.6	8.7	4.2	2.9	0.0	0.0
时尚流行指向 fashion orientation	223	1.8	6.7	9.4	6.7	4.5	1.3	0.4

3-10-2 广告态度指标/ Advertising Attitude Index

注：本题为多选题，合计百分比超过 100%（Multiple answers）

	人数 Number	头版要闻 first page news	国际新闻 international news	国内新闻 national news	港澳台新闻 news about HK Taiwan Macao	本地新闻 local news	经济信息 economic information
样本 Sample	537	33.7	48.2	54.0	8.2	34.5	11.9
广告淡漠指向 indifferent orientation	141	32.6	50.4	52.5	5.7	30.5	11.3
中间层 medium	323	33.1	45.5	53.6	7.7	34.7	12.7
信赖广告指向 loyal orientation	73	38.4	56.2	58.9	15.1	41.1	9.6

续前表 continued

	人数 Number	财政金融 finance & economic	股市报道 stock market report	热点追踪 hits track	文化信息 cultural information	体育报道 sports report	人物专访 personal interview
样本 Sample	537	4.5	13.0	12.5	4.8	24.0	6.9
广告淡漠指向 indifferent orientation	141	2.1	12.1	11.3	3.5	29.1	5.7
中间层 medium	323	5.6	13.6	14.2	5.9	22.3	7.4
信赖广告指向 loyal orientation	73	4.1	12.3	6.8	2.7	21.9	6.8

续前表 continued

	人数 Number	军事知识 military knowledge	法制报道 legal news	海外见闻 overseas information	科技知识 science sense	影视娱乐报道 video & entertainment report	服饰美容 clothes & beauty
样本 Sample	537	14.3	24.0	5.8	6.5	15.8	10.1
广告淡漠指向 indifferent orientation	141	16.3	27.7	6.4	5.0	11.3	5.7
中间层 medium	323	14.9	22.3	6.2	6.8	16.4	12.1
信赖广告指向 loyal orientation	73	8.2	24.7	2.7	8.2	21.9	9.6

续前表 continued

	人数 Number	休闲旅游 entertainment & travel	消费指南 consumption guide	电视节目预告 TV program forecast	健康医疗 medicare	生活常识 common sense	书评 book comment
样本 Sample	537	6.9	6.7	5.0	19.9	19.9	0.2
广告淡漠指向 indifferent orientation	141	5.7	6.4	6.4	24.1	19.1	0.0
中间层 medium	323	7.7	7.1	4.3	18.0	20.4	0.3
信赖广告指向 loyal orientation	73	5.5	5.5	5.5	20.5	19.2	0.0

续前表 continued

	人数 Number	文艺评论 art critics	散文 prose	小说 novel	漫画 cartoon	广告 advertising	读者来信 reader's letter	其他 others
样本 Sample	537	1.7	3.7	8.9	5.0	3.5	0.6	0.2
广告淡漠指向 indifferent orientation	141	0.0	1.4	9.9	5.0	3.5	0.0	0.0
中间层 medium	323	2.2	5.3	8.7	5.6	3.4	0.9	0.3
信赖广告指向 loyal orientation	73	2.7	1.4	8.2	2.7	4.1	0.0	0.0

● 武汉 / Wuhan

3-1 样本、男性各年龄层、女性各年龄层平时是否接触报纸媒介/ Newspaper Reading by the Whole Sample, Age and Gender Groups

	人数 Number	从来不看 never	看 yes
样本 Sample	626	8.8	91.2
男性 Male	304	6.6	93.4
16~24 岁 Age	65	7.7	92.3
25~34 岁 Age	87	1.1	98.9
35~44 岁 Age	78	10.3	89.7
45~54 岁 Age	51	7.8	92.2
55~60 岁 Age	23	8.7	91.3
女性 Female	322	10.9	89.1
16~24 岁 Age	66	7.6	92.4
25~34 岁 Age	95	10.5	89.5
35~44 岁 Age	77	5.2	94.8
45~54 岁 Age	58	12.1	87.9
55~60 岁 Age	26	34.6	65.4

3-2 经常阅读的报纸排名/ Ranking of the Frequently Read Newspapers

注：本题为多选题，合计百分比超过 100%（Multiple answers）

排名 Brand Ranking	报纸 Newspapers	人次 Person-time	百分比 Percent
1	楚天都市报 Chutian Du Shi Bao	456	80.6
2	长江日报 Changjiang Daily	213	37.6
3	武汉晚报 Wuhan Evening News	169	29.9
4	武汉晨报 Wuhan Chen Bao	62	11.0
5	今日快报 Jinri Kuai Bao	60	10.6
6	参考消息 Reference News	35	6.2
7	体坛周报 Sports Weekly	21	3.7
8	市场指南报 Market Guide	20	3.5
9	法制报 Fa Zhi Bao	14	2.5
10	工人日报 Work's Daily	9	1.6
10	21 世纪报 21st Century	9	1.6
10	湖北日报 Hubei Daily	9	1.6
11	人民日报 People's Daily	8	1.4

n=566

3-3 样本、男性各年龄层、女性各年龄层经常阅读的报纸/ Frequently Read Newspapers by the Whole Sample, Age and Gender Groups

注：本题为多选题，合计百分比超过 100%（Multiple answers）

	人数 Number	楚天都市报 Chutian Du Shi Bao	长江日报 Changjiang Daily	武汉晚报 Wuhan Evening News	武汉晨报 Wuhan Chen Bao	今日快报 Jinri Kuai Bao	参考消息 Reference News
样本 Sample	**566**	**80.6**	**37.6**	**29.9**	**11.0**	**10.6**	**6.2**
男性 Male	**283**	**77.7**	**40.3**	**27.2**	**11.0**	**10.6**	**7.8**
16~24 岁 Age	60	86.7	30.0	31.7	15.0	10.0	6.7
25~34 岁 Age	86	82.6	37.2	23.3	12.8	15.1	8.1
35~44 岁 Age	69	81.2	44.9	20.3	11.6	11.6	5.8
45~54 岁 Age	47	57.4	53.2	31.9	4.3	6.4	12.8
55~60 岁 Age	21	66.7	38.1	42.9	4.8	0.0	4.8
女性 Female	**283**	**83.4**	**35.0**	**32.5**	**11.0**	**10.6**	**4.6**
16~24 岁 Age	59	83.1	35.6	22.0	15.3	13.6	0.0
25~34 岁 Age	85	83.5	43.5	32.9	14.1	11.8	2.4
35~44 岁 Age	71	87.3	25.4	32.4	5.6	9.9	7.0
45~54 岁 Age	51	78.4	37.3	41.2	11.8	9.8	9.8
55~60 岁 Age	17	82.4	23.5	41.2	0.0	0.0	5.9

续前表 continued

	人数 Number	体坛周报 Sports Weekly	市场指南报 Market Guide	法制报 Fa Zhi Bao	工人日报 Work's Daily	21 世纪报 21st Century	湖北日报 Hubei Daily	人民日报 People's Daily
样本 Sample	**566**	**3.7**	**3.5**	**2.5**	**1.6**	**1.6**	**1.6**	**1.4**
男性 Male	**283**	**6.4**	**4.6**	**2.8**	**1.4**	**1.4**	**1.8**	**1.8**
16~24 岁 Age	60	10.0	0.0	3.3	0.0	1.7	0.0	0.0
25~34 岁 Age	86	11.6	9.3	3.5	1.2	2.3	1.2	1.2
35~44 岁 Age	69	2.9	1.4	2.9	1.4	0.0	1.4	0.0
45~54 岁 Age	47	0.0	6.4	2.1	4.3	2.1	4.3	6.4
55~60 岁 Age	21	0.0	4.8	0.0	0.0	0.0	4.8	4.8
女性 Female	**283**	**1.1**	**2.5**	**2.1**	**1.8**	**1.8**	**1.4**	**1.1**
16~24 岁 Age	59	0.0	3.4	1.7	1.7	1.7	0.0	0.0
25~34 岁 Age	85	0.0	0.0	1.2	2.4	4.7	0.0	0.0
35~44 岁 Age	71	0.0	4.2	1.4	0.0	0.0	1.4	1.4
45~54 岁 Age	51	5.9	3.9	3.9	3.9	0.0	2.0	2.0
55~60 岁 Age	17	0.0	0.0	5.9	0.0	0.0	11.8	5.9

3-4 经常阅读的报纸的主要来源/ Sources of Obtaining the Frequently Read Newspaper

注：本题为多选题，合计百分比可能超过 100%（Multiple answers）

	人数 Number	家中订阅 subscribed by my family	单位订阅 subscribed by work unit	报摊购买 bought from vender	赠阅 given as gift	借阅 borrowed	街头报栏 news-stand along street
楚天都市报 Chutian Du Shi Bao	450	47.1	9.7	33.7	2.4	6.0	1.1
长江日报 Changjiang Daily	212	12.7	65.1	15.6	0.0	5.6	1.4
武汉晚报 Wuhan Evening News	167	38.3	22.1	24.0	1.2	14.4	0.6
武汉晨报 Wuhan Chen Bao	61	14.8	9.8	60.7	4.9	4.9	4.9
今日快报 Jinri Kuai Bao	60	15.0	8.3	60.0	3.3	10.0	3.3
参考消息 Reference News	35	14.3	25.7	51.4	0.0	8.6	0.0
体坛周报 Sports Weekly	21	0.0	0.0	95.2	0.0	4.8	0.0
市场指南报 Market Guide	19	36.8	10.5	26.3	0.0	21.1	5.3
法制报 Fa Zhi Bao	14	0.0	14.3	64	0.0	14.3	7.1

3-5 经常阅读的报纸内容/ Ranking of the Content Categories that Newspaper Readers Concern about

注：本题为多选题，合计百分比超过 100%（Multiple answers）

排名 Ranking	内容 Contents	人次 Person-time	百分比 Percent
1	国内新闻 national news	306	53.9
2	国际新闻 international news	297	52.3
3	头版要闻 first page news	281	49.5
4	体育报道 sports report	183	32.2
5	本地新闻 local news	142	25.0
6	法制报道 legal news	127	22.4
7	生活常识 common sense	123	21.7
8	健康医疗 medicare	121	21.3
9	影视娱乐报道 video & entertainment report	98	17.3
10	热点追踪 hits track	95	16.7
11	人物专访 personal interview	67	11.8
12	港澳台新闻 news about HK.Taiwan.Macao	63	11.1
13	服饰美容 clothes & beauty	62	10.9
14	军事知识 military knowledge	61	10.7
15	经济信息 economic information	57	10.0
16	休闲旅游 entertainment & travel	53	9.3
17	股市报道 stock market report	50	8.8
18	消费指南 consumption guide	48	8.5
18	小说 novel	48	8.5
19	漫画 cartoon	47	8.3
20	科技知识 science sense	44	7.7
21	海外见闻 overseas information	42	7.4
22	文化信息 cultural information	37	6.5
23	财政金融 finance & economic	34	6.0
24	电视节目预告 TV program forecast	33	5.8
25	散文 prose	20	3.5
25	广告 advertising	20	3.5
26	文艺评论 art critics	14	2.5
27	其他 others	8	1.4
28	读者来信 reader's letter	4	0.7
29	书评 book comment	2	0.4

n=568

3-6 样本、男性各年龄层、女性各年龄层经常阅读的报纸内容/ The Concerned Newspaper Content Categories by the Whole Sample, Age and Gender Groups

注：本题为多选题，合计百分比超过 100%（Multiple answers）

	人数 Number	头版要闻 first page news	国际新闻 international news	国内新闻 national news	港澳台新闻 news about HK.Taiwan. Macao	本地新闻 local news	经济信息 economic information
样本 Sample	**568**	**49.5**	**52.3**	**53.9**	**11.1**	**25.0**	**10.0**
男性 Male	**283**	**52.3**	**67.5**	**63.6**	**13.1**	**22.3**	**13.8**
16~24 岁 Age	60	40.0	65.0	40.0	23.3	20.0	3.3
25~34 岁 Age	86	57.0	64.0	58.1	10.5	23.3	20.9
35~44 岁 Age	70	55.7	72.9	82.9	8.6	18.6	14.3
45~54 岁 Age	46	52.2	71.7	73.9	17.4	32.6	13.0
55~60 岁 Age	21	57.1	61.9	66.7	0.0	14.3	14.3
女性 Female	**285**	**46.7**	**37.2**	**44.2**	**9.1**	**27.7**	**6.3**
16~24 岁 Age	61	39.3	29.5	26.2	16.4	19.7	4.9
25~34 岁 Age	84	51.2	36.9	44.0	3.6	15.5	6.0
35~44 岁 Age	73	52.1	41.1	42.5	8.2	27.4	6.8
45~54 岁 Age	51	39.2	41.2	62.7	13.7	45.1	9.8
55~60 岁 Age	16	50.0	37.5	62.5	0.0	68.8	0.0

续前表 continued

	人数 Number	财政金融 finance & economic	股市报道 stock market report	热点追踪 hits track	文化信息 cultural information	体育报道 sports report	人物专访 personal interview
样本 Sample	568	6.0	8.8	16.7	6.5	32.2	11.8
男性 Male	283	7.4	11.0	15.2	6.0	48.4	8.8
16~24 岁 Age	60	6.7	1.7	10.0	10.0	53.3	11.7
25~34 岁 Age	86	9.3	18.6	16.3	4.7	54.7	8.1
35~44 岁 Age	70	4.3	8.6	12.9	5.7	50.0	7.1
45~54 岁 Age	46	8.7	15.2	17.4	2.2	37.0	4.3
55~60 岁 Age	21	9.5	4.8	28.6	9.5	28.6	19.0
女性 Female	285	4.6	6.7	18.2	7.0	16.1	14.7
16~24 岁 Age	61	3.3	1.6	19.7	8.2	14.8	11.5
25~34 岁 Age	84	8.3	11.9	16.7	6.0	15.5	19.0
35~44 岁 Age	73	5.5	5.5	19.2	9.6	16.4	13.7
45~54 岁 Age	51	0.0	7.8	21.6	3.9	21.6	11.8
55~60 岁 Age	16	0.0	0.0	6.3	6.3	6.3	18.8

续前表 continued

	人数 Number	军事知识 military knowledge	法制报道 legal news	海外见闻 overseas information	科技知识 science sense	影视娱乐报道 video & entertainment report	服饰美容 clothes & beauty
样本 Sample	568	10.7	22.4	7.4	7.7	17.3	10.9
男性 Male	283	19.8	19.8	7.1	11.0	12.7	0.4
16~24 岁 Age	60	23.3	13.3	8.3	20.0	36.7	0.0
25~34 岁 Age	86	15.1	18.6	5.8	9.3	11.6	1.2
35~44 岁 Age	70	24.3	21.4	11.4	8.6	4.3	0.0
45~54 岁 Age	46	19.6	28.3	4.3	10.9	0.0	0.0
55~60 岁 Age	21	14.3	19.0	0.0	0.0	4.8	0.0
女性 Female	285	1.8	24.9	7.7	4.6	21.8	21.4
16~24 岁 Age	61	1.6	14.8	13.1	0.0	49.2	32.8
25~34 岁 Age	84	1.2	16.7	10.7	3.6	22.6	25.0
35~44 岁 Age	73	1.4	31.5	4.1	6.8	12.3	19.2
45~54 岁 Age	51	2.0	37.3	3.9	7.8	5.9	11.8
55~60 岁 Age	16	6.3	37.5	0.0	6.3	6.3	0.0

续前表 continued

	人数 Number	休闲旅游 entertainment & travel	消费指南 consumption guide	电视节目预告 TV program forecast	健康医疗 medicare	生活常识 common sense	书评 book comment
样本 Sample	568	9.3	8.5	5.8	21.3	21.7	0.4
男性 Male	283	4.9	4.2	2.1	12.0	10.6	0.7
16~24 岁 Age	60	13.3	5.0	5.0	3.3	5.0	1.7
25~34 岁 Age	86	4.7	7.0	1.2	9.3	10.5	0.0
35~44 岁 Age	70	1.4	0.0	2.9	7.1	7.1	1.4
45~54 岁 Age	46	0.0	4.3	0.0	23.9	13.0	0.0
55~60 岁 Age	21	4.8	4.8	0.0	38.1	33.3	0.0
女性 Female	285	13.7	12.6	9.5	30.5	32.6	0.0
16~24 岁 Age	61	21.3	9.8	14.8	9.8	19.7	0.0
25~34 岁 Age	84	21.4	19.0	4.8	39.3	38.1	0.0
35~44 岁 Age	73	8.2	11.0	8.2	30.1	41.1	0.0
45~54 岁 Age	51	3.9	11.8	11.8	41.2	23.5	0.0
55~60 岁 Age	16	0.0	0.0	12.5	31.3	43.8	0.0

续前表 continued

	人数 Number	文艺评论 art critics	散文 prose	小说 novel	漫画 cartoon	广告 advertising	读者来信 reader's letter	其他 others
样本 Sample	**568**	**2.5**	**3.5**	**8.5**	**8.3**	**3.5**	**0.7**	**1.4**
男性 Male	**283**	**2.1**	**0.7**	**5.3**	**6.7**	**2.5**	**1.1**	**1.8**
16~24 岁 Age	60	1.7	1.7	10.0	16.7	5.0	0.0	0.0
25~34 岁 Age	86	1.2	1.2	8.1	7.0	2.3	2.3	4.7
35~44 岁 Age	70	2.9	0.0	2.9	1.4	2.9	0.0	0.0
45~54 岁 Age	46	0.0	0.0	0.0	2.2	0.0	0.0	2.2
55~60 岁 Age	21	9.5	0.0	0.0	4.8	0.0	4.8	0.0
女性 Female	**285**	**2.8**	**6.3**	**11.6**	**9.8**	**4.6**	**0.4**	**1.1**
16~24 岁 Age	61	1.6	11.5	21.3	19.7	13.1	0.0	1.6
25~34 岁 Age	84	2.4	4.8	15.5	8.3	4.8	0.0	0.0
35~44 岁 Age	73	1.4	6.8	8.2	9.6	1.4	1.4	0.0
45~54 岁 Age	51	5.9	3.9	2.0	3.9	0.0	0.0	3.9
55~60 岁 Age	16	6.3	0.0	0.0	0.0	0.0	0.0	0.0

3-7 不同学历的读者阅读的报纸内容的偏好/ The Concerned Newspaper Content Categories by Educational Levels

注：本题为多选题，合计百分比超过 100%（Multiple answers）

	人数 Number	头版要闻 first page news	国际新闻 international news	国内新闻 national news	港澳台新闻 news about HK.Taiwan. Macao	本地新闻 local news	经济信息 economic information
样本 Sample	**568**	**49.5**	**52.3**	**53.9**	**11.1**	**25.0**	**10.0**
小学及以下 Primary School or Below	14	50.0	42.9	57.1	14.3	50.0	0.0
初中 Middle School	132	42.4	47.0	59.1	8.3	33.3	3.8
高中/中专/技校 High School/Technical Secondary School	262	48.9	55.0	53.4	12.6	23.7	11.5
大学专科 2-3 Year College	103	58.3	51.5	46.6	11.7	19.4	10.7
大学本科 4-5 Year College	52	50.0	57.7	55.8	9.6	17.3	19.2
研究生或以上 Graduate or Above	5	80.0	40.0	60.0	0.0	0.0	20.0

续前表 continued

	人数 Number	财政金融 finance & economic	股市报道 stock market report	热点追踪 hits track	文化信息 cultural information	体育报道 sports report	人物专访 personal interview
样本 Sample	**568**	**6.0**	**8.8**	**16.7**	**6.5**	**32.2**	**11.8**
小学及以下 Primary School or Below	14	0.0	0.0	7.1	7.1	7.1	0.0
初中 Middle School	132	2.3	7.6	15.2	3.0	34.8	11.4
高中/中专/技校 High School/Technical Secondary School	262	5.0	8.4	17.6	5.7	31.3	10.3
大学专科 2-3 Year College	103	9.7	8.7	13.6	11.7	31.1	15.5
大学本科 4-5 Year College	52	13.5	15.4	26.9	9.6	36.5	13.5
研究生或以上 Graduate or Above	5	20.0	20.0	0.0	0.0	60.0	40.0

续前表 continued

	人数 Number	军事知识 military knowledge	法制报道 legal news	海外见闻 overseas information	科技知识 science sense	影视娱乐报道 video & entertainment report	服饰美容 clothes & beauty
样本 Sample	568	10.7	22.4	7.4	7.7	17.3	10.9
小学及以下 Primary School or Below	14	7.1	42.9	0.0	0.0	7.1	0.0
初中 Middle School	132	7.6	28.0	6.1	4.5	14.4	10.6
高中/中专/技校 High School/Technical Secondary School	262	13.0	24.4	7.6	8.0	17.2	11.5
大学专科 2-3 Year College	103	9.7	14.6	10.7	9.7	20.4	12.6
大学本科 4-5 Year College	52	11.5	9.6	5.8	13.5	23.1	9.6
研究生或以上 Graduate or Above	5	0.0	0.0	0.0	0.0	0.0	0.0

续前表 continued

	人数 Number	休闲旅游 entertainment & travel	消费指南 consumption guide	电视节目预告 TV program forecast	健康医疗 medicare	生活常识 common sense	书评 book comment
样本 Sample	568	9.3	8.5	5.8	21.3	21.7	0.4
小学及以下 Primary School or Below	14	0.0	0.0	14.3	7.1	28.6	0.0
初中 Middle School	132	3.0	8.3	10.6	31.1	26.5	0.0
高中/中专/技校 High School/Technical Secondary School	262	10.7	8.8	5.3	18.3	21.8	0.4
大学专科 2-3 Year College	103	17.5	8.7	1.9	21.4	20.4	0.0
大学本科 4-5 Year College	52	3.8	9.6	1.9	17.3	11.5	1.9
研究生或以上 Graduate or Above	5	20.0	0.0	0.0	0.0	0.0	0.0

续前表 continued

	人数 Number	文艺评论 art critics	散文 prose	小说 novel	漫画 cartoon	广告 advertising	读者来信 reader's letter	其他 others
样本 Sample	568	2.5	3.5	8.5	8.3	3.5	0.7	1.4
小学及以下 Primary School or Below	14	0.0	0.0	0.0	0.0	0.0	0.0	7.1
初中 Middle School	132	3.8	2.3	7.6	7.6	2.3	0.0	0.8
高中/中专/技校 High School/Technical Secondary School	262	1.5	3.4	8.4	8.4	2.7	1.1	0.8
大学专科 2-3 Year College	103	1.9	5.8	13.6	9.7	6.8	1.0	1.9
大学本科 4-5 Year College	52	3.8	3.8	1.9	7.7	5.8	0.0	1.9
研究生或以上 Graduate or Above	5	20.0	0.0	20.0	20.0	0.0	0.0	20.0

3-8 不同消费者层平时是否接触报纸媒介/ Newspaper Reading by Market Segments

3-8-1 时尚流行指标/ Fads Popular Index

	人数 Number	从来不看 never	看 yes
样本 Sample	623	8.8	91.2
平实生活指向 simple living orientation	325	11.7	88.3
时尚流行指向 fashion orientation	298	5.7	94.3

3-8-2 广告态度指标/ Advertising Attitude Index

	人数 Number	从来不看 never	看 yes
样本 Sample	**625**	**8.8**	**91.2**
广告淡漠指向 indifferent orientation	186	10.2	89.8
中间层 medium	368	7.3	92.7
信赖广告指向 loyal orientation	71	12.7	87.3

3-9 不同消费者层经常阅读的报纸/ Frequently Read Newspapers by Market Segments

3-9-1 时尚流行指标/ Fads Popular Index

注：本题为多选题，合计百分比超过 100%（Multiple answers）

	人数 Number	楚天都市报 Chu Tian Du Shi Bao	长江日报 Changjiang Daily	武汉晚报 Wuhan Evening News	武汉晨报 Wuhan Chen Bao	今日快报 Jinri KuaiBao	参考消息 Reference News
样本 Sample	**563**	**80.5**	**37.5**	**29.8**	**11.0**	**10.5**	**6.2**
平实生活指向 simple living orientation	285	78.9	36.8	26.7	8.8	9.1	6.3
时尚流行指向 fashion orientation	278	82.0	38.1	33.1	13.3	11.9	6.1

续前表 continued

	人数 Number	体坛周报 Sports Weekly	市场指南报 Market Guide	法制报 Fa Zhi Bao	工人日报 Worker's Daily	21 世纪报 21st Century	湖北日报 Hubei Daily	人民日报 People's Daily
样本 Sample	**563**	**3.7**	**3.6**	**2.5**	**1.6**	**1.6**	**1.6**	**1.4**
平实生活指向 simple living orientation	285	4.9	4.6	1.4	2.1	1.8	2.5	2.5
时尚流行指向 fashion orientation	278	2.5	2.5	3.6	1.1	1.4	0.7	0.4

3-9-2 广告态度指向/ Advertising Attitude Index

注：本题为多选题，合计百分比超过 100%（Multiple answers）

	人数 Number	楚天都市报 Chu Tian Du Shi Bao	长江日报 Changjiang Daily	武汉晚报 Wuhan Evening News	武汉晨报 Wuhan Chen Bao	今日快报 Jinri KuaiBao	参考消息 Reference News
样本 Sample	**565**	**80.5**	**37.5**	**29.9**	**11.0**	**10.6**	**6.2**
广告淡漠指向 indifferent orientation	166	78.3	38.6	25.9	10.2	9.0	7.8
中间层 medium	337	81.6	38.0	30.9	11.6	11.0	6.2
信赖广告指向 loyal orientation	62	80.6	32.3	35.5	9.7	12.9	1.6

续前表 continued

	人数 Number	体坛周报 Sports Weekly	市场指南报 Market Guide	法制报 Fazhi Bao	工人日报 Worker's Daily	21 世纪报 21st Century	湖北日报 Hubei Daily	人民日报 People's Daily
样本 Sample	**565**	**3.7**	**3.5**	**2.5**	**1.6**	**1.6**	**1.6**	**1.4**
广告淡漠指向 indifferent orientation	166	4.8	3.6	3.0	3.6	1.8	3.6	3.6
中间层 medium	337	3.9	3.3	2.1	0.6	1.5	0.6	0.6
信赖广告指向 loyal orientation	62	0.0	4.8	3.2	1.6	1.6	1.6	0.0

3-10 不同消费者层比较关心的报道/ The Concerned Newspaper Content Categories by Market Segments

3-10-1 时尚流行指标/ Fads Popular Index

注：本题为多选题，合计百分比超过 100%（Multiple answers）

	人数 Number	头版要闻 first page news	国际新闻 international news	国内新闻 national news	港澳台新闻 news about HK. Taiwan .Macao	本地新闻 local news	经济信息 economic information
样本 Sample	**565**	**49.2**	**52.2**	**53.8**	**11.2**	**25.0**	**10.1**
平实生活指向 simple living orientation	285	43.9	52.6	56.1	9.1	26.3	10.5
时尚流行指向 fashion orientation	280	54.6	51.8	51.4	13.2	23.6	9.6

续前表 continued

	人数 Number	财政金融 finance & economic	股市报道 stock market report	热点追踪 hits track	文化信息 cultural information	体育报道 sports report	人物专访 personal interview
样本 Sample	565	6.0	8.8	16.8	6.5	32.2	11.7
平实生活指向 simple living orientation	285	8.1	8.4	17.2	6.3	31.6	9.8
时尚流行指向 fashion orientation	280	3.9	9.3	16.4	6.8	32.9	13.6

续前表 continued

	人数 Number	军事知识 military knowledge	法制报道 legal news	海外见闻 overseas information	科技知识 science sense	影视娱乐报道 video & entertainment report	服饰美容 clothes & beauty
样本 Sample	565	10.8	22.3	7.4	7.8	17.3	11.0
平实生活指向 simple living orientation	285	10.9	20.7	6.3	10.9	12.6	7.0
时尚流行指向 fashion orientation	280	10.7	23.9	8.6	4.6	22.1	15.0

续前表 continued

	人数 Number	休闲旅游 entertainment & travel	消费指南 consumption guide	电视节目预告 TV program forecast	健康医疗 medicare	生活常识 common sense	书评 book comment
样本 Sample	565	9.4	8.5	5.8	21.4	21.8	0.4
平实生活指向 simple living orientation	285	7.7	7.7	5.3	23.5	22.8	0.7
时尚流行指向 fashion orientation	280	11.1	9.3	6.4	19.3	20.7	0.0

续前表 continued

	人数 Number	文艺评论 art critics	散文 prose	小说 novel	漫画 cartoon	广告 advertising	读者来信 reader's letter	其他 others
样本 Sample	565	2.5	3.5	8.5	8.3	3.4	0.7	1.2
平实生活指向 simple living orientation	285	3.2	4.2	8.8	8.4	1.8	1.4	0.7
时尚流行指向 fashion orientation	280	1.8	2.9	8.2	8.2	5.0	0.0	1.8

3-10-2 广告态度指标/ Advertising Attitude Index

注：本题为多选题，合计百分比超过 100%（Multiple answers）

	人数 Number	头版要闻 first page news	国际新闻 international news	国内新闻 national news	港澳台新闻 news about HK. Taiwan Macao	本地新闻 local news	经济信息 economic information
样本 Sample	567	49.4	52.4	53.8	11.1	24.9	10.1
广告淡漠指向 indifferent orientation	167	47.3	52.7	53.9	10.2	25.1	9.0
中间层 medium	339	48.7	53.4	55.2	11.2	23.3	11.5
信赖广告指向 loyal orientation	61	59.0	45.9	45.9	13.1	32.8	4.9

续前表 continued

	人数 Number	财政金融 finance & economic	股市报道 stock market report	热点追踪 hits track	文化信息 cultural information	体育报道 sports report	人物专访 personal interview
样本 Sample	567	6.0	8.8	16.8	6.5	32.1	11.6
广告淡漠指向 indifferent orientation	167	7.2	6.6	15.6	6.6	31.1	12.0
中间层 medium	339	6.2	10.3	16.5	6.2	34.2	11.5
信赖广告指向 loyal orientation	61	1.6	6.6	21.3	8.2	23.0	11.5

续前表 continued

	人数 Number	军事知识 military knowledge	法制报道 legal news	海外见闻 overseas information	科技知识 science sense	影视娱乐报道 video & entertainment report	服饰美容 clothes & beauty
样本 Sample	567	10.8	22.4	7.4	7.8	17.3	10.9
广告淡漠指向 indifferent orientation	167	13.8	22.8	6.6	16.8	10.2	6.0
中间层 medium	339	10.3	22.4	8.0	4.1	19.2	13.3
信赖广告指向 loyal orientation	61	4.9	21.3	6.6	3.3	26.2	11.5

续前表 continued

	人数 Number	休闲旅游 entertainment & travel	消费指南 consumption guide	电视节目预告 TV program forecast	健康医疗 medicare	生活常识 common sense	书评 book comment
样本 Sample	567	9.3	8.5	5.8	21.3	21.7	0.4
广告淡漠指向 indifferent orientation	167	6.6	7.8	6.0	22.2	21.0	0.0
中间层 medium	339	10.9	8.0	4.7	20.9	22.1	0.6
信赖广告指向 loyal orientation	61	8.2	13.1	11.5	21.3	21.3	0.0

续前表 continued

	人数 Number	文艺评论 art critics	散文 prose	小说 novel	漫画 cartoon	广告 advertising	读者来信 reader's letter	其他 others
样本 Sample	567	2.5	3.5	8.5	8.3	3.5	0.7	1.4
广告淡漠指向 indifferent orientation	167	1.8	4.2	7.8	9.0	3.6	0.6	0.6
中间层 medium	339	2.9	3.8	9.1	8.3	2.7	0.6	1.5
信赖广告指向 loyal orientation	61	1.6	0.0	6.6	6.6	8.2	1.6	3.3

● 西安 / Xi'an

3-1 样本、男性各年龄层、女性各年龄层平时是否接触报纸媒介/ Newspaper Reading by the Whole Sample, Age and Gender Groups

	人数 Number	从来不看 never	看 yes
样本 Sample	601	9.0	91.0
男性 Male	302	5.6	94.4
16~24 岁 Age	64	9.4	90.6
25~34 岁 Age	91	2.2	97.8
35~44 岁 Age	77	6.5	93.5
45~54 岁 Age	46	4.3	95.7
55~60 岁 Age	24	8.3	91.7
女性 Female	299	12.4	87.6
16~24 岁 Age	61	11.5	88.5
25~34 岁 Age	90	7.8	92.2
35~44 岁 Age	74	12.2	87.8
45~54 岁 Age	49	16.3	83.7
55~60 岁 Age	25	24.0	76.0

3-2 经常阅读的报纸排名/ Ranking of the Frequently Read Newspaper

注：本题为多选题，合计百分比超过 100%（Multiple answers）

排名 BrandRanking	报纸 Newspapers	人次 Person-time	百分比 Percent
1	华商报 Chinese Business View	412	75.5
2	西安晚报 Xi An Wan Bao	280	51.3
3	三秦都市报 San Qin Dushi Bao	105	19.2
4	参考消息 Reference News	43	7.9
5	劳动早报 Lao Dong Zao Bao	40	7.3
6	西安日报 Xi'an Daily	37	6.8
7	南方周末 South Weekend	23	4.2
8	体坛周报 Sports Weekly	18	3.3
9	人民日报 People's Daily	12	2.2
9	中国青年报 China Youth Daily	12	2.2
10	每周文摘 Weekly Digest	11	2.0

n=546

3-3 样本、男性各年龄层、女性各年龄层经常阅读的报纸/ Frequently Read Newspapers by the Whole Sample, Age and Gender Groups

注：本题为多选题，合计百分比超过 100%（Multiple answers）

	人数 Number	华商报 Chinese Business View	西安晚报 Xi An Wan Bao	三秦都市报 San Qin Dushi Bao	参考消息 Reference News	劳动早报 Lao Dong Zao Bao
样本 Sample	**546**	**75.5**	**51.3**	**19.2**	**7.9**	**7.3**
男性 Male	**285**	**73.0**	**50.2**	**21.4**	**12.3**	**7.7**
16~24 岁 Age	58	69.0	37.9	22.4	13.8	8.6
25~34 岁 Age	89	75.3	50.6	20.2	11.2	6.7
35~44 岁 Age	72	80.6	45.8	20.8	11.1	11.1
45~54 岁 Age	44	63.6	63.6	20.5	15.9	6.8
55~60 岁 Age	22	68.2	68.2	27.3	9.1	0.0
女性 Female	**261**	**78.2**	**52.5**	**16.9**	**3.1**	**6.9**
16~24 岁 Age	53	67.9	50.9	13.2	3.8	3.8
25~34 岁 Age	83	84.3	47.0	14.5	4.8	10.8
35~44 岁 Age	65	78.5	58.5	16.9	1.5	6.2
45~54 岁 Age	41	78.0	53.7	22.0	2.4	2.4
55~60 岁 Age	19	78.9	57.9	26.3	0.0	10.5

续前表 continued

	人数 Number	西安日报 Xi'an Daily	南方周末 South Weekend	体坛周报 Sports Weekly	人民日报 People's Daily	中国青年报 China Youth Daily	每周文摘 Weekly Digest
样本 Sample	**546**	**6.8**	**4.2**	**3.3**	**2.2**	**2.2**	**2.0**
男性 Male	**285**	**7.0**	**4.2**	**4.2**	**2.5**	**3.5**	**1.8**
16~24 岁 Age	58	6.9	5.2	12.1	1.7	6.9	1.7
25~34 岁 Age	89	5.6	7.9	2.2	1.1	2.2	1.1
35~44 岁 Age	72	8.3	0.0	4.2	5.6	2.8	2.8
45~54 岁 Age	44	4.5	4.5	0.0	0.0	2.3	2.3
55~60 岁 Age	22	13.6	0.0	0.0	4.5	4.5	0.0
女性 Female	**261**	**6.5**	**4.2**	**2.3**	**1.9**	**0.8**	**2.3**
16~24 岁 Age	53	9.4	7.5	3.8	1.9	3.8	3.8
25~34 岁 Age	83	6.0	6.0	2.4	1.2	0.0	1.2
35~44 岁 Age	65	4.6	1.5	1.5	1.5	0.0	4.6
45~54 岁 Age	41	4.9	2.4	2.4	2.4	0.0	0.0
55~60 岁 Age	19	10.5	0.0	0.0	5.3	0.0	0.0

3-4 经常阅读的报纸的主要来源/ Sources of Obtaining the Frequently Read Newspaper

注：本题为多选题，合计百分比可能超过 100%（Multiple answers）

	人数 Number	家中订阅 subscribed by my family	单位订阅 subscribed by work unit	报摊购买 bought from vender	赠阅 given as gift	借阅 borrowed	街头报栏 news-stand along street
华商报 China Business View	411	25.1	18.0	48.2	0.2	5.6	3.2
西安晚报 Xi An Wan Bao	280	26.1	36.8	28.2	1.1	6.1	2.1
三秦都市报 Sanqin Dushi Bao	105	7.6	32.4	43.8	1.0	9.5	6.7
参考消息 Reference News	43	14.0	27.9	53.5	0.0	2.3	2.3
劳动早报 Lao Dong Zao Bao	40	17.5	17.5	55.0	0.0	5.0	5.0
西安日报 Xi'an Daily	37	13.5	51.4	29.7	2.7	2.7	0.0
南方周末 South Weekend	23	4.3	13.0	73.9	0.0	4.3	4.3
体坛周报 Sports Weekly	18	5.6	5.6	88.9	0.0	0.0	0.0

3-5 经常阅读的报纸内容/ The Content Categories that Newspaper Readers Concern about

注：本题为多选题，合计百分比超过 100%（Multiple answers）

排名 Ranking	内容 Contents	人次 Person-time	百分比 Percent
1	头版要闻 first page news	298	54.7
2	国内新闻 national news	274	50.3
3	国际新闻 international news	239	43.9
4	本地新闻 local news	136	25.0
5	体育报道 sports report	116	21.3
6	法制报道 legal news	114	20.9
7	健康医疗 medicare	112	20.6
7	生活常识 common sense	112	20.6
8	热点追踪 hits track	99	18.2
9	影视娱乐报道 video & entertainment report	79	14.5
10	小说 novel	65	11.9
11	服饰美容 clothes & beauty	62	11.4
12	股市报道 stock market report	60	11.0
13	经济信息 economic information	58	10.6
14	军事知识 military knowledge	55	10.1
15	人物专访 personal interview	50	9.2
16	消费指南 consumption guide	41	7.5
17	文化信息 cultural information	35	6.4
18	财政金融 finance & economic	34	6.2
19	漫画 cartoon	33	6.1
20	港澳台新闻 news about HK.Taiwan.Macao	30	5.5
21	海外见闻 overseas information	29	5.3
22	休闲旅游 entertainment & travel	28	5.1
23	科技知识 science sense	26	4.8
24	散文 prose	21	3.9
25	电视节目预告 TV program forecast	19	3.5
26	广告 advertising	16	2.9
27	文艺评论 art critics	14	2.6
28	书评 book comment	10	1.8
29	读者来信 reader's letter	4	0.7
30	其他 others	1	0.2

n=545

3-6 样本、男性各年龄层、女性各年龄层经常阅读的报纸内容/ The Concerned Newspaper Content Categories by the Whole Sample, Age and Gender Groups

注：本题为多选题，合计百分比超过 100%（Multiple answers）

	人数 Number	头版要闻 first page news	国际新闻 international news	国内新闻 national news	港澳台新闻 news about HK. Taiwan Macao	本地新闻 local news	经济信息 economic information
样本 Sample	545	54.7	43.9	50.3	5.5	25.0	10.6
男性 Male	285	55.1	52.3	53.7	4.9	23.9	14.0
16~24 岁 Age	58	41.4	43.1	32.8	10.3	17.2	6.9
25~34 岁 Age	89	53.9	52.8	60.7	3.4	21.3	15.7
35~44 岁 Age	72	61.1	51.4	56.9	2.8	33.3	15.3
45~54 岁 Age	44	56.8	68.2	61.4	6.8	20.5	20.5
55~60 岁 Age	22	72.7	45.5	54.5	0.0	27.3	9.1
女性 Female	260	54.2	34.6	46.5	6.2	26.2	6.9
16~24 岁 Age	54	44.4	27.8	35.2	16.7	16.7	5.6
25~34 岁 Age	82	53.7	37.8	42.7	3.7	20.7	7.3
35~44 岁 Age	65	53.8	29.2	50.8	4.6	35.4	9.2
45~54 岁 Age	40	60.0	40.0	55.0	0.0	30.0	5.0
55~60 岁 Age	19	73.7	47.4	63.2	5.3	36.8	5.3

续前表 continued

	人数 Number	财政金融 finance & economic	股市报道 stock market report	热点追踪 hits track	文化信息 cultural information	体育报道 sports report	人物专访 personal interview
样本 Sample	545	6.2	11.0	18.2	6.4	21.3	9.2
男性 Male	285	9.5	15.1	14.7	5.3	32.6	9.1
16~24 岁 Age	58	5.2	6.9	17.2	8.6	41.4	10.3
25~34 岁 Age	89	9.0	14.6	18.0	2.2	30.3	7.9
35~44 岁 Age	72	11.1	25.0	8.3	6.9	33.3	13.9
45~54 岁 Age	44	15.9	15.9	15.9	2.3	25.0	2.3
55~60 岁 Age	22	4.5	4.5	13.6	9.1	31.8	9.1
女性 Female	260	2.7	6.5	21.9	7.7	8.8	9.2
16~24 岁 Age	54	3.7	3.7	20.4	9.3	13.0	7.4
25~34 岁 Age	82	4.9	7.3	24.4	7.3	6.1	7.3
35~44 岁 Age	65	0.0	12.3	16.9	9.2	13.8	13.8
45~54 岁 Age	40	2.5	2.5	22.5	5.0	2.5	12.5
55~60 岁 Age	19	0.0	0.0	31.6	5.3	5.3	0.0

续前表 continued

	人数 Number	军事知识 military knowledge	法制报道 legal news	海外见闻 overseas information	科技知识 science sense	影视娱乐报道 video & entertainment report	服饰美容 clothes & beauty
样本 Sample	545	10.1	20.9	5.3	4.8	14.5	11.4
男性 Male	285	16.8	21.8	6.3	7.0	11.9	2.5
16~24 岁 Age	58	36.2	20.7	12.1	12.1	32.8	1.7
25~34 岁 Age	89	9.0	16.9	7.9	6.7	11.2	3.4
35~44 岁 Age	72	15.3	15.3	4.2	4.2	2.8	2.8
45~54 岁 Age	44	13.6	34.1	2.3	4.5	4.5	2.3
55~60 岁 Age	22	9.1	40.9	0.0	9.1	4.5	0.0
女性 Female	260	2.7	20.0	4.2	2.3	17.3	21.2
16~24 岁 Age	54	5.6	16.7	5.6	1.9	33.3	29.6
25~34 岁 Age	82	1.2	18.3	4.9	2.4	20.7	31.7
35~44 岁 Age	65	3.1	26.2	1.5	0.0	7.7	20.0
45~54 岁 Age	40	0.0	17.5	2.5	5.0	10.0	0.0
55~60 岁 Age	19	5.3	21.1	10.5	5.3	5.3	0.0

续前表 continued

	人数 Number	休闲旅游 entertainment & travel	消费指南 consumption guide	电视节目预告 TV program forecast	健康医疗 medicare	生活常识 common sense	书评 book comment
样本 Sample	545	5.1	7.5	3.5	20.6	20.6	1.8
男性 Male	285	3.2	5.3	1.1	10.9	11.2	1.8
16~24 岁 Age	58	3.4	0.0	3.4	3.4	5.2	0.0
25~34 岁 Age	89	4.5	9.0	1.1	10.1	13.5	2.2
35~44 岁 Age	72	2.8	6.9	0.0	11.1	12.5	0.0
45~54 岁 Age	44	2.3	4.5	0.0	18.2	9.1	4.5
55~60 岁 Age	22	0.0	0.0	0.0	18.2	18.2	4.5
女性 Female	260	7.3	10.0	6.2	31.2	30.8	1.9
16~24 岁 Age	54	14.8	9.3	11.1	18.5	14.8	0.0
25~34 岁 Age	82	8.5	14.6	0.0	28.0	34.1	1.2
35~44 岁 Age	65	3.1	7.7	9.2	32.3	40.0	1.5
45~54 岁 Age	40	5.0	7.5	10.0	37.5	32.5	2.5
55~60 岁 Age	19	0.0	5.3	0.0	63.2	26.3	10.5

续前表 continued

	人数 Number	文艺评论 art critics	散文 prose	小说 novel	漫画 cartoon	广告 advertising	读者来信 reader's letter	其他 others
样本 Sample	545	2.6	3.9	11.9	6.1	2.9	0.7	0.2
男性 Male	285	3.2	3.5	7.4	5.3	2.5	0.0	0.4
16~24 岁 Age	58	3.4	3.4	13.8	10.3	3.4	0.0	0.0
25~34 岁 Age	89	2.2	4.5	4.5	5.6	2.2	0.0	0.0
35~44 岁 Age	72	2.8	0.0	9.7	2.8	1.4	0.0	0.0
45~54 岁 Age	44	2.3	9.1	4.5	4.5	4.5	0.0	2.3
55~60 岁 Age	22	9.1	0.0	0.0	0.0	0.0	0.0	0.0
女性 Female	260	1.9	4.2	16.9	6.9	3.5	1.5	0.0
16~24 岁 Age	54	3.7	3.7	27.8	16.7	3.7	1.9	0.0
25~34 岁 Age	82	2.4	3.7	15.9	9.8	1.2	1.2	0.0
35~44 岁 Age	65	1.5	7.7	15.4	0.0	4.6	1.5	0.0
45~54 岁 Age	40	0.0	2.5	15.0	2.5	5.0	2.5	0.0
55~60 岁 Age	19	0.0	0.0	0.0	0.0	5.3	0.0	0.0

3-7 不同学历的读者阅读的报纸内容的偏好/ The Concerned Newspaper Content Categories by Educational Levels

注：本题为多选题，合计百分比超过 100%（Multiple answers）

	人数 Number	头版要闻 first page news	国际新闻 international news	国内新闻 national news	港澳台新闻 news about HK. Taiwan.Macao	本地新闻 local news	经济信息 economic information
样本 Sample	542	54.6	43.9	50.6	5.5	25.1	10.3
小学及以下 Primary School or Below	7	57.1	28.6	57.1	0.0	28.6	0.0
初中 Middle School	103	62.1	49.5	57.3	7.8	27.2	11.7
高中/中专/技校 High School/Technical Secondary School	261	48.3	39.1	51.0	5.4	27.6	7.7
大学专科 2-3 Year College	108	63.0	47.2	44.4	4.6	19.4	15.7
大学本科 4-5 Year College	58	53.4	50.0	46.6	5.2	19.0	10.3
研究生或以上 Graduate or Above	5	60.0	60.0	60.0	0.0	40.0	20.0

续前表 continued

	人数 Number	财政金融 finance & economic	股市报道 stock market report	热点追踪 hits track	文化信息 cultural information	体育报道 sports report	人物专访 personal interview
样本 Sample	542	6.1	10.9	18.3	6.5	21.4	9.0
小学及以下 Primary School or Below	7	0.0	0.0	14.3	0.0	28.6	14.3
初中 Middle School	103	2.9	5.8	12.6	2.9	20.4	5.8
高中/中专/技校 High School/Technical Secondary School	261	4.6	9.6	19.2	5.0	20.3	8.4
大学专科 2-3 Year College	108	8.3	23.1	25.9	8.3	21.3	11.1
大学本科 4-5 Year College	58	15.5	5.2	10.3	17.2	25.9	12.1
研究生或以上 Graduate or Above	5	0.0	0.0	20.0	0.0	40.0	20.0

续前表 continued

	人数 Number	军事知识 military knowledge	法制报道 legal news	海外见闻 overseas information	科技知识 science sense	影视娱乐报道 video & entertainment report	服饰美容 clothes & beauty
样本 Sample	542	10.0	21.0	5.4	4.8	14.4	11.4
小学及以下 Primary School or Below	7	14.3	28.6	0.0	14.3	14.3	0.0
初中 Middle School	103	9.7	25.2	4.9	3.9	11.7	7.8
高中/中专/技校 High School/Technical Secondary School	261	7.7	22.6	5.4	3.4	16.5	13.0
大学专科 2-3 Year College	108	13.0	23.1	5.6	8.3	12.0	12.0
大学本科 4-5 Year College	58	15.5	3.4	6.9	5.2	13.8	10.3
研究生或以上 Graduate or Above	5	0.0	0.0	0.0	0.0	20.0	20.0

续前表 continued

	人数 Number	休闲旅游 entertainment & travel	消费指南 consumption guide	电视节目预告 TV program forecast	健康医疗 medicare	生活常识 common sense	书评 book comment
样本 Sample	542	5.2	7.6	3.5	20.7	20.5	1.8
小学及以下 Primary School or Below	7	0.0	0.0	0.0	28.6	28.6	0.0
初中 Middle School	103	1.9	7.8	3.9	20.4	16.5	1.9
高中/中专/技校 High School/Technical Secondary School	261	5.0	9.6	5.7	19.9	22.2	2.3
大学专科 2-3 Year College	108	7.4	5.6	0.0	22.2	19.4	0.9
大学本科 4-5 Year College	58	8.6	3.4	0.0	22.4	22.4	1.7
研究生或以上 Graduate or Above	5	0.0	0.0	0.0	0.0	0.0	0.0

续前表 continued

	人数 Number	文艺评论 art critics	散文 prose	小说 novel	漫画 cartoon	广告 advertising	读者来信 reader's letter	其他 others
样本 Sample	542	2.6	3.9	12.0	6.1	3.0	0.7	0.2
小学及以下 Primary School or Below	7	14.3	0.0	14.3	0.0	0.0	0.0	0.0
初中 Middle School	103	2.9	2.9	9.7	4.9	4.9	1.0	0.0
高中/中专/技校 High School/Technical Secondary School	261	2.7	3.4	13.4	6.9	3.4	0.8	0.0
大学专科 2-3 Year College	108	1.9	2.8	9.3	5.6	0.9	0.9	0.9
大学本科 4-5 Year College	58	1.7	10.3	13.8	6.9	1.7	0.0	0.0
研究生或以上 Graduate or Above	5	0.0	0.0	20.0	0.0	0.0	0.0	0.0

3-8 不同消费者层平时是否接触报纸媒介/ Newspaper Reading by Market Segments

3-8-1 时尚流行指标/ Fads Popular Index

	人数 Number	从来不看 never	看 yes
样本 Sample	599	9.0	91.0
平实生活指向 simple living orientation	341	9.7	90.3
时尚流行指向 fashion orientation	258	8.1	91.9

3-8-2 广告态度指标/ Advertising Attitude Index

	人数 Number	从来不看 never	看 yes
样本 Sample	597	8.9	91.1
广告淡漠指向 indifferent orientation	184	9.8	90.2
中间层 medium	334	9.0	91.0
信赖广告指向 loyal orientation	79	6.3	93.7

3-9 不同消费者层经常阅读的报纸/ Frequently Read Newspapers by Market Segments

3-9-1 时尚流行指标/ Fads Popular Index

注：本题为多选题，合计百分比超过 100%（Multiple answers）

	人数 Number	华商报 China Business View	西安晚报 Xi An Wan Bao	三秦都市报 San Qin Dushi Bao	参考消息 Reference News	劳动早报 Lao Dong Zao Bao
样本 Sample	544	75.4	51.5	19.3	7.9	7.4
平实生活指向 simple living orientation	308	75.0	52.3	20.5	8.4	7.8
时尚流行指向 fashion orientation	236	75.8	50.4	17.8	7.2	6.8

续前表 continued

	人数 Number	西安日报 Xi'an Daily	南方周末 South Weekend	体坛周报 Sports Weekly	人民日报 People's Daily	中国青年报 China Youth Daily	每周文摘 Weekly Digest
样本 Sample	544	6.8	4.2	3.3	2.2	2.2	2.0
平实生活指向 simple living orientation	308	8.1	3.2	3.6	3.2	2.6	1.6
时尚流行指向 fashion orientation	236	5.1	5.5	3.0	0.8	1.7	2.5

3-9-2 广告态度指向/ Advertising Attitude Index

注：本题为多选题，合计百分比超过 100%（Multiple answers）

	人数 Number	华商报 China Business View	西安晚报 Xi An Wan Bao	三秦都市报 San Qin Dushi Bao	参考消息 Reference News	劳动早报 Lao Dong Zao Bao
样本 Sample	543	75.7	51.0	19.2	7.7	7.4
广告淡漠指向 indifferent orientation	166	77.7	47.6	24.7	7.8	6.0
中间层 medium	303	75.6	54.5	17.5	7.6	7.9
信赖广告指向 loyal orientation	74	71.6	44.6	13.5	8.1	8.1

续前表 continued

	人数 Number	西安日报 Xi'an Daily	南方周末 South Weekend	体坛周报 Sports Weekly	人民日报 People's Daily	中国青年报 China Youth Daily	每周文摘 Weekly Digest
样本 Sample	543	6.8	4.2	3.3	2.2	2.2	2.0
广告淡漠指向 indifferent orientation	166	7.8	4.2	1.8	3.0	1.2	2.4
中间层 medium	303	6.6	4.3	5.0	2.0	3.0	1.7
信赖广告指向 loyal orientation	74	5.4	4.1	0.0	1.4	1.4	2.7

3-10 不同消费者层比较关心的报道/ The Concerned Newspaper Content Categories by Market Segments

3-10-1 时尚流行指标/ Fads Popular Index

注：本题为多选题，合计百分比超过 100%（Multiple answers）

	人数 Number	头版要闻 first page news	国际新闻 international news	国内新闻 national news	港澳台新闻 news about HK. Taiwan Macao	本地新闻 local news	经济信息 economic information
样本 Sample	543	54.9	43.8	50.1	5.5	25.0	10.7
平实生活指向 simple living orientation	307	56.4	46.9	53.1	4.9	26.7	11.4
时尚流行指向 fashion orientation	236	53.0	39.8	46.2	6.4	22.9	9.7

续前表 continued

	人数 Number	财政金融 finance & economic	股市报道 stock market report	热点追踪 hits track	文化信息 cultural information	体育报道 sports report	人物专访 personal interview
样本 Sample	543	6.3	11.0	18.2	6.4	21.4	9.2
平实生活指向 simple living orientation	307	6.8	9.8	18.6	6.2	20.8	10.1
时尚流行指向 fashion orientation	236	5.5	12.7	17.8	6.8	22.0	8.1

续前表 continued

	人数 Number	军事知识 military knowledge	法制报道 legal news	海外见闻 overseas information	科技知识 science sense	影视娱乐报道 video & entertainment report	服饰美容 clothes & beauty
样本 Sample	543	10.1	20.6	5.3	4.8	14.5	11.4
平实生活指向 simple living orientation	307	10.1	21.8	3.6	4.2	10.1	7.2
时尚流行指向 fashion orientation	236	10.2	19.1	7.6	5.5	20.3	16.9

续前表 continued

	人数 Number	休闲旅游 entertainment & travel	消费指南 consumption guide	电视节目预告 TV program forecast	健康医疗 medicare	生活常识 common sense	书评 book comment
样本 Sample	543	5.2	7.6	3.5	20.6	20.4	1.8
平实生活指向 simple living orientation	307	1.6	6.5	2.3	21.2	20.8	2.3
时尚流行指向 fashion orientation	236	9.7	8.9	5.1	19.9	19.9	1.3

续前表 continued

	人数 Number	文艺评论 art critics	散文 prose	小说 novel	漫画 cartoon	广告 advertising	读者来信 reader's letter	其他 others
样本 Sample	**543**	**2.6**	**3.9**	**12.0**	**6.1**	**2.9**	**0.7**	**0.2**
平实生活指向 simple living orientation	307	2.6	3.3	12.1	4.6	2.3	1.0	0.3
时尚流行指向 fashion orientation	236	2.5	4.7	11.9	8.1	3.8	0.4	0.0

3-10-2 广告态度指标/ Advertising Attitude Index

注：本题为多选题，合计百分比超过 100%（Multiple answers）

	人数 Number	头版要闻 first page news	国际新闻 international news	国内新闻 national news	港澳台新闻 news about HK.Taiwan. Macao	本地新闻 local news	经济信息 economic information
样本 Sample	**542**	**54.4**	**43.7**	**50.2**	**5.4**	**25.1**	**10.7**
广告淡漠指向 indifferent orientation	165	55.2	43.6	52.1	6.1	29.1	9.7
中间层 medium	303	52.8	44.9	52.1	5.3	23.4	11.6
信赖广告指向 loyal orientation	74	59.5	39.2	37.8	4.1	23.0	9.5

续前表 continued

	人数 Number	财政金融 finance & economic	股市报道 stock market report	热点追踪 hits track	文化信息 cultural information	体育报道 sports report	人物专访 personal interview
样本 Sample	**542**	**6.3**	**11.1**	**18.1**	**6.5**	**21.2**	**9.2**
广告淡漠指向 indifferent orientation	165	7.3	11.5	15.8	4.8	23.0	15.2
中间层 medium	303	6.9	10.6	14.9	6.9	20.1	6.3
信赖广告指向 loyal orientation	74	1.4	12.2	36.5	8.1	21.6	8.1

续前表 continued

	人数 Number	军事知识 military knowledge	法制报道 legal news	海外见闻 overseas information	科技知识 science sense	影视娱乐报道 video & entertainment report	服饰美容 clothes & beauty
样本 Sample	**542**	**10.1**	**20.7**	**5.4**	**4.8**	**14.4**	**11.3**
广告淡漠指向 indifferent orientation	165	10.3	21.8	4.8	3.0	11.5	7.3
中间层 medium	303	9.2	22.1	5.9	5.9	15.2	12.5
信赖广告指向 loyal orientation	74	13.5	12.2	4.1	4.1	17.6	14.9

续前表 continued

	人数 Number	休闲旅游 entertainment & travel	消费指南 consumption guide	电视节目预告 TV program forecast	健康医疗 medicare	生活常识 common sense	书评 book comment
样本 Sample	**542**	**5.2**	**7.6**	**3.5**	**20.7**	**20.7**	**1.8**
广告淡漠指向 indifferent orientation	165	3.6	4.2	1.8	26.1	23.6	2.4
中间层 medium	303	6.3	9.2	4.6	19.1	22.1	2.0
信赖广告指向 loyal orientation	74	4.1	8.1	2.7	14.9	8.1	0.0

续前表 continued

	人数 Number	文艺评论 art critics	散文 prose	小说 novel	漫画 cartoon	广告 advertising	读者来信 reader's letter	其他 others
样本 Sample	**542**	**2.6**	**3.9**	**12.0**	**6.1**	**3.0**	**0.7**	**0.2**
广告淡漠指向 indifferent orientation	165	2.4	2.4	9.1	2.4	2.4	0.6	0.6
中间层 medium	303	2.3	4.6	11.9	7.9	3.0	0.3	0.0
信赖广告指向 loyal orientation	74	4.1	4.1	18.9	6.8	4.1	2.7	0.0

沈阳 / Shenyang

3-1 样本、男性各年龄层、女性各年龄层平时是否接触报纸媒介/ Newspaper Reading by the Whole Sample, Age and Gender Groups

	人数 Number	从来不看 never	看 yes
样本 Sample	601	10.3	89.7
男性 Male	299	7.4	92.6
16~24 岁 Age	64	14.1	85.9
25~34 岁 Age	89	3.4	96.6
35~44 岁 Age	76	6.6	93.4
45~54 岁 Age	46	4.3	95.7
55~60 岁 Age	24	12.5	87.5
女性 Female	302	13.2	86.8
16~24 岁 Age	64	14.1	85.9
25~34 岁 Age	90	12.2	87.8
35~44 岁 Age	76	9.2	90.8
45~54 岁 Age	48	14.6	85.4
55~60 岁 Age	24	25.0	75.0

3-2 经常阅读的报纸排名/ Ranking of the Frequently Read Newspapers

注：本题为多选题，合计百分比超过 100%（Multiple answers）

排名 Brand Ranking	报纸 Newspapers	人次 Person-time	百分比 Percent
1	沈阳晚报 Shenyang Evening News	351	65.1
2	沈阳日报 Shenyang Daily	224	41.6
3	辽沈晚报 Liaoshen Evening News	185	34.3
4	辽宁广播电视报 Liaoning TV Guide	59	10.9
5	球报 Baus Weekly	42	7.8
6	沈阳广播电视报 Shenyang TV Guide	25	4.6
7	参考消息 Reference News	18	3.3
8	体坛周报 Sports Weekly	17	3.2
9	辽宁日报 Liaoning Daily	13	2.4
9	都市家庭报 Metropolitan Family	13	2.4
10	电脑报 Computer Information	10	1.9
11	人民日报 People's Daily	8	1.5
11	现代女报 Xian Dai Nv Bao	8	1.5
12	晚晴报 Wan Qing Bao	7	1.3
12	良友 Liang You	7	1.3

n=539

3-3 样本、男性各年龄层、女性各年龄层经常阅读的报纸/ Frequently Read Newspapers by the Whole Sample, Age and Gender Groups

注：本题为多选题，合计百分比超过 100%（Multiple answers）

	人数 Number	沈阳晚报 Shenyang Evening News	沈阳日报 Shenyang Daily	辽沈晚报 Liaoshen Evening News	辽宁广播电视报 Liaoning TV Guide	球报 Baus Weekly	沈阳广播电视报 Shenyang TV Guide	参考消息 Reference News
样本 Sample	539	65.1	41.6	34.3	10.9	7.8	4.6	3.3
男性 Male	277	64.3	44.4	35.4	8.7	13.0	5.1	4.7
16~24 岁 Age	55	45.5	21.8	32.7	18.2	32.7	12.7	1.8
25~34 岁 Age	86	61.6	47.7	38.4	5.8	11.6	3.5	7.0
35~44 岁 Age	71	73.2	50.7	35.2	7.0	5.6	4.2	5.6
45~54 岁 Age	44	68.2	54.5	38.6	9.1	9.1	2.3	0.0
55~60 岁 Age	21	85.7	47.6	23.8	0.0	0.0	0.0	9.5
女性 Female	262	66.0	38.5	33.2	13.4	2.3	4.2	1.9
16~24 岁 Age	55	52.7	32.7	29.1	21.8	3.6	9.1	0.0
25~34 岁 Age	79	74.7	48.1	32.9	8.9	0.0	3.8	2.5
35~44 岁 Age	69	69.6	42.0	33.3	11.6	2.9	2.9	4.3
45~54 岁 Age	41	68.3	36.6	36.6	14.6	2.4	0.0	0.0
55~60 岁 Age	18	50.0	5.6	38.9	11.1	5.6	5.6	0.0

续前表 continued

	人数 Number	体坛周报 Sports Weekly	辽宁日报 Liaoning Daily	都市家庭报 Metropolitan Family	电脑报 Computer Information	人民日报 People's Daily	现代女报 Xian Dai Nv Bao	晚晴报 Wan Qing Bao	良友 Liang You
样本 Sample	539	3.2	2.4	2.4	1.9	1.5	1.5	1.3	1.3
男性 Male	277	6.1	3.2	0.7	3.2	2.9	1.1	0.7	1.4
16~24 岁 Age	55	16.4	0.0	1.8	5.5	0.0	0.0	0.0	0.0
25~34 岁 Age	86	7.0	1.2	1.2	5.8	3.5	0.0	1.2	2.3
35~44 岁 Age	71	1.4	4.2	0.0	0.0	1.4	2.8	0.0	2.8
45~54 岁 Age	44	2.3	2.3	0.0	2.3	4.5	2.3	0.0	0.0
55~60 岁 Age	21	0.0	19.0	0.0	0.0	9.5	0.0	4.8	0.0
女性 Female	262	0.0	1.5	4.2	0.4	0.0	1.9	1.9	1.1
16~24 岁 Age	55	0.0	1.8	5.5	1.8	0.0	3.6	0.0	0.0
25~34 岁 Age	79	0.0	0.0	2.5	0.0	0.0	3.8	1.3	1.3
35~44 岁 Age	69	0.0	1.4	5.8	0.0	0.0	0.0	1.4	1.4
45~54 岁 Age	41	0.0	4.9	4.9	0.0	0.0	0.0	2.4	2.4
55~60 岁 Age	18	0.0	0.0	0.0	0.0	0.0	0.0	11.1	0.0

3-4 经常阅读的报纸的主要来源/ Sources of Obtaining the Frequently Read Newspapers

注：本题为多选题，合计百分比可能超过 100%（Multiple answers）

	人数 Number	家中订阅 subscribed by my family	单位订阅 subscribed by work unit	报摊购买 bought from vender	赠阅 given as gift	借阅 borrowed	街头报栏 news-stand along street
沈阳晚报 Shenyang Evening News	350	28.3	31.4	32.6	0.9	7.1	0.6
沈阳日报 Shenyang Daily	221	10.4	65.6	16.7	0.9	5.0	1.8
辽沈晚报 Liaoshen Evening News	183	38.8	23.0	30.1	0.5	6.6	1.6
辽宁广播电视报 Liaoning TV Guide	58	13.8	3.4	77.6	0.0	3.4	1.7
球报 Baus Weekly	42	7.1	2.4	83.3	0.0	7.1	2.4
沈阳广播电视报 Shenyang TV Guide	25	4.0	4.0	84.0	4.0	4.0	0.0
参考消息 Reference News	18	16.7	27.8	38.9	0.0	16.7	0.0
体坛周报 Sports Weekly	17	0.0	0.0	88.2	0.0	5.9	5.9

3-5 经常阅读的报纸内容/ Ranking of the Content Categories that Newspaper Readers Concern about

注：本题为多选题，合计百分比超过 100%（Multiple answers）

排名 Ranking	内容 Contents	人次 Person-time	百分比 Percent
1	头版要闻 first page news	271	50.4
2	国际新闻 international news	255	47.4
2	国内新闻 national news	255	47.4
3	法制报道 legal news	158	29.4
4	体育报道 sports report	153	28.4
5	热点追踪 hits track	119	22.1
6	生活常识 common sense	107	19.9
7	本地新闻 local news	98	18.2
8	影视娱乐报道 video & entertainment report	85	15.8
9	人物专访 personal interview	74	13.8
9	健康医疗 medicare	74	13.8
10	电视节目预告 TV program forecast	54	10.0
11	服饰美容 clothes & beauty	48	8.9
12	军事知识 military knowledge	47	8.7
13	股市报道 stock market report	43	8.0
14	经济信息 economic information	41	7.6
14	小说 novel	41	7.6
15	海外见闻 overseas information	39	7.2
16	消费指南 consumption guide	38	7.1
17	休闲旅游 entertainment & travel	34	6.3
18	科技知识 science sense	31	5.8
19	广告 advertising	30	5.6
20	漫画 cartoon	28	5.2

n=538

3-6 样本、男性各年龄层、女性各年龄层经常阅读的报纸内容/ Ranking of the Concerned Newspaper Content Categories by the Whole Sample, Age and Gender Groups

注：本题为多选题，合计百分比超过 100%（Multiple answers）

	人数 Number	头版要闻 first page news	国际新闻 international news	国内新闻 national news	港澳台新闻 news about HK. Taiwan.Macao	本地新闻 local news	经济信息 economic information
样本 Sample	538	50.4	47.4	47.4	4.6	18.2	7.6
男性 Male	276	53.3	55.1	52.2	2.2	17.8	9.4
16~24 岁 Age	55	38.2	32.7	29.1	3.6	3.6	1.8
25~34 岁 Age	86	55.8	53.5	45.3	3.5	17.4	12.8
35~44 岁 Age	70	52.9	62.9	60.0	0.0	15.7	10.0
45~54 岁 Age	44	59.1	65.9	72.7	2.3	31.8	4.5
55~60 岁 Age	21	71.4	71.4	71.4	0.0	33.3	23.8
女性 Female	262	47.3	39.3	42.4	7.3	18.7	5.7
16~24 岁 Age	55	32.7	27.3	29.1	14.5	5.5	7.3
25~34 岁 Age	79	54.4	31.6	35.4	10.1	16.5	3.8
35~44 岁 Age	69	42.0	49.3	49.3	2.9	26.1	5.8
45~54 岁 Age	41	48.8	43.9	51.2	2.4	24.4	7.3
55~60 岁 Age	18	77.8	61.1	66.7	0.0	27.8	5.6

续前表 continued

	人数 Number	财政金融 finance & economic	股市报道 stock market report	热点追踪 hits track	文化信息 cultural information	体育报道 sports report	人物专访 personal interview
样本 Sample	538	3.9	8.0	22.1	3.9	28.4	13.8
男性 Male	276	4.0	7.6	24.3	3.3	47.8	10.5
16~24 岁 Age	55	3.6	1.8	16.4	3.6	76.4	12.7
25~34 岁 Age	86	5.8	8.1	29.1	3.5	44.2	10.5
35~44 岁 Age	70	2.9	10.0	24.3	5.7	42.9	8.6
45~54 岁 Age	44	0.0	11.4	25.0	0.0	43.2	11.4
55~60 岁 Age	21	9.5	4.8	23.8	0.0	14.3	9.5
女性 Female	262	3.8	8.4	19.8	4.6	8.0	17.2
16~24 岁 Age	55	1.8	1.8	14.5	0.0	12.7	21.8
25~34 岁 Age	79	2.5	7.6	20.3	3.8	3.8	26.6
35~44 岁 Age	69	7.2	13.0	29.0	8.7	8.7	10.1
45~54 岁 Age	41	2.4	9.8	14.6	7.3	7.3	12.2
55~60 岁 Age	18	5.6	11.1	11.1	0.0	11.1	0.0

续前表 continued

	人数 Number	军事知识 military knowledge	法制报道 legal news	海外见闻 overseas information	科技知识 science sense	影视娱乐报道 video & entertainment report	服饰美容 clothes & beauty
样本 Sample	538	8.7	29.4	7.2	5.8	15.8	8.9
男性 Male	276	16.7	28.6	7.2	7.6	12.0	0.7
16~24 岁 Age	55	10.9	9.1	5.5	16.4	34.5	1.8
25~34 岁 Age	86	29.1	27.9	14.0	11.6	9.3	0.0
35~44 岁 Age	70	15.7	34.3	7.1	1.4	5.7	1.4
45~54 岁 Age	44	9.1	38.6	0.0	2.3	2.3	0.0
55~60 岁 Age	21	0.0	42.9	0.0	0.0	4.8	0.0
女性 Female	262	0.4	30.2	7.3	3.8	19.8	17.6
16~24 岁 Age	55	0.0	20.0	10.9	5.5	52.7	25.5
25~34 岁 Age	79	0.0	40.5	6.3	1.3	17.7	17.7
35~44 岁 Age	69	1.4	24.6	7.2	2.9	5.8	21.7
45~54 岁 Age	41	0.0	34.1	7.3	4.9	7.3	4.9
55~60 岁 Age	18	0.0	27.8	0.0	11.1	11.1	5.6

续前表 continued

	人数 Number	休闲旅游 entertainment & travel	消费指南 consumption guide	电视节目预告 TV program forecast	健康医疗 medicare	生活常识 common sense	书评 book comment
样本 Sample	**538**	**6.3**	**7.1**	**10.0**	**13.8**	**19.9**	**0.7**
男性 Male	**276**	**2.9**	**2.9**	**9.1**	**6.9**	**12.3**	**1.1**
16~24 岁 Age	55	1.8	3.6	25.5	1.8	7.3	0.0
25~34 岁 Age	86	8.1	1.2	4.7	7.0	14.0	0.0
35~44 岁 Age	70	0.0	5.7	8.6	7.1	14.3	2.9
45~54 岁 Age	44	0.0	2.3	2.3	6.8	11.4	2.3
55~60 岁 Age	21	0.0	0.0	0.0	19.0	14.3	0.0
女性 Female	**262**	**9.9**	**11.5**	**11.1**	**21.0**	**27.9**	**0.4**
16~24 岁 Age	55	21.8	10.9	16.4	7.3	12.7	0.0
25~34 岁 Age	79	11.4	11.4	10.1	12.7	32.9	1.3
35~44 岁 Age	69	4.3	14.5	5.8	31.9	29.0	0.0
45~54 岁 Age	41	4.9	12.2	9.8	26.8	36.6	0.0
55~60 岁 Age	18	0.0	0.0	22.2	44.4	27.8	0.0

续前表 continued

	人数 Number	文艺评论 art critics	散文 prose	小说 novel	漫画 cartoon	广告 advertising	读者来信 reader's letter	其他 others
样本 Sample	**538**	**1.5**	**3.3**	**7.6**	**5.2**	**5.6**	**0.2**	**1.1**
男性 Male	**276**	**1.4**	**2.2**	**6.9**	**6.9**	**4.7**	**0.4**	**0.7**
16~24 岁 Age	55	0.0	7.3	12.7	21.8	10.9	1.8	3.6
25~34 岁 Age	86	3.5	1.2	4.7	5.8	5.8	0.0	0.0
35~44 岁 Age	70	1.4	1.4	7.1	2.9	0.0	0.0	0.0
45~54 岁 Age	44	0.0	0.0	6.8	0.0	4.5	0.0	0.0
55~60 岁 Age	21	0.0	0.0	0.0	0.0	0.0	0.0	0.0
女性 Female	**262**	**1.5**	**4.6**	**8.4**	**3.4**	**6.5**	**0.0**	**1.5**
16~24 岁 Age	55	5.5	14.5	18.2	12.7	7.3	0.0	1.8
25~34 岁 Age	79	0.0	2.5	6.3	1.3	8.9	0.0	0.0
35~44 岁 Age	69	1.4	2.9	5.8	0.0	1.4	0.0	1.4
45~54 岁 Age	41	0.0	0.0	7.3	2.4	9.8	0.0	2.4
55~60 岁 Age	18	0.0	0.0	0.0	0.0	5.6	0.0	5.6

3-7 不同学历的读者阅读的报纸内容的偏好/ Ranking of the Concerned Newspaper Content Categories by Educational Levels

注：本题为多选题，合计百分比超过 100%（Multiple answers）

	人数 Number	头版要闻 first page news	国际新闻 international news	国内新闻 national news	港澳台新闻 news about HK. Taiwan. Macao	本地新闻 local news	经济信息 economic information
样本 Sample	**538**	**50.4**	**47.4**	**47.4**	**4.6**	**18.2**	**7.6**
小学及以下 Primary School or Below	8	37.5	62.5	62.5	0.0	12.5	12.5
初中 Middle School	184	46.7	48.9	54.9	3.8	21.2	4.9
高中/中专/技校 High School/Technical Secondary School	204	44.6	43.6	43.6	3.9	15.2	5.9
大学专科 2-3 Year College	88	64.8	53.4	47.7	10.2	21.6	12.5
大学本科 4-5 Year College	51	62.7	45.1	35.3	2.0	13.7	13.7
研究生或以上 Graduate or Above	3	66.7	33.3	0.0	0.0	33.3	33.3

续前表 continued

	人数 Number	财政金融 finance & economic	股市报道 stock market report	热点追踪 hits track	文化信息 cultural information	体育报道 sports report	人物专访 personal interview
样本 Sample	**538**	**3.9**	**8.0**	**22.1**	**3.9**	**28.4**	**13.8**
小学及以下 Primary School or Below	8	0.0	0.0	12.5	12.5	12.5	0.0
初中 Middle School	184	1.6	6.0	20.7	2.7	20.7	9.2
高中/中专/技校 High School/Technical Secondary School	204	2.0	8.3	21.6	2.0	34.8	14.2
大学专科 2-3 Year College	88	9.1	9.1	23.9	10.2	28.4	22.7
大学本科 4-5 Year College	51	11.8	11.8	29.4	3.9	33.3	13.7
研究生或以上 Graduate or Above	3	0.0	33.3	0.0	0.0	33.3	33.3

续前表 continued

	人数 Number	军事知识 military knowledge	法制报道 legal news	海外见闻 overseas information	科技知识 science sense	影视娱乐报道 video & entertainment report	服饰美容 clothes & beauty
样本 Sample	**538**	**8.7**	**29.4**	**7.2**	**5.8**	**15.8**	**8.9**
小学及以下 Primary School or Below	8	12.5	62.5	0.0	12.5	0.0	0.0
初中 Middle School	184	7.1	35.3	3.8	1.6	10.3	8.2
高中/中专/技校 High School/Technical Secondary School	204	10.3	30.9	6.9	6.4	21.6	11.3
大学专科 2-3 Year College	88	8.0	18.2	9.1	11.4	18.2	9.1
大学本科 4-5 Year College	51	7.8	15.7	15.7	7.8	11.8	3.9
研究生或以上 Graduate or Above	3	33.3	33.3	66.7	0.0	0.0	0.0

续前表 continued

	人数 Number	休闲旅游 entertainment & travel	消费指南 consumption guide	电视节目预告 TV program forecast	健康医疗 medicare	生活常识 common sense	书评 book comment
样本 Sample	**538**	**6.3**	**7.1**	**10.0**	**13.8**	**19.9**	**0.7**
小学及以下 Primary School or Below	8	0.0	0.0	0.0	12.5	0.0	0.0
初中 Middle School	184	2.7	7.6	15.2	13.6	27.7	1.6
高中/中专/技校 High School/Technical Secondary School	204	8.8	7.4	9.3	13.2	18.1	0.0
大学专科 2-3 Year College	88	8.0	6.8	5.7	14.8	15.9	0.0
大学本科 4-5 Year College	51	7.8	3.9	3.9	15.7	7.8	2.0
研究生或以上 Graduate or Above	3	0.0	33.3	0.0	0.0	33.3	0.0

续前表 continued

	人数 Number	文艺评论 art critics	散文 prose	小说 novel	漫画 cartoon	广告 advertising	读者来信 reader's letter	其他 others
样本 Sample	**538**	**1.5**	**3.3**	**7.6**	**5.2**	**5.6**	**0.2**	**1.1**
小学及以下 Primary School or Below	8	0.0	0.0	0.0	0.0	0.0	0.0	0.0
初中 Middle School	184	0.5	1.6	7.1	3.8	3.3	0.0	0.5
高中/中专/技校 High School/Technical Secondary School	204	2.5	5.4	8.3	6.9	5.4	0.5	2.0
大学专科 2-3 Year College	88	1.1	2.3	6.8	1.1	8.0	0.0	0.0
大学本科 4-5 Year College	51	2.0	3.9	9.8	11.8	9.8	0.0	2.0
研究生或以上 Graduate or Above	3	0.0	0.0	0.0	0.0	33.3	0.0	0.0

3-8 不同消费者层平时是否接触报纸媒介/ Newspaper Reading by Market Segments

3-8-1 时尚流行指标/ Fads Popular Index

	人数 Number	从来不看 never	看 yes
样本 Sample	**601**	**10.3**	**89.7**
平实生活指向 simple living orientation	292	12.0	88.0
时尚流行指向 fashion orientation	309	8.7	91.3

3-8-2 广告态度指标/ Advertising Attitude Index

	人数 Number	从来不看 never	看 yes
样本 Sample	**601**	**10.3**	**89.7**
广告淡漠指向 indifferent orientation	172	10.5	89.5
中间层 medium	354	11.0	89.0
信赖广告指向 loyal orientation	75	6.7	93.3

3-9 不同消费者层经常阅读的报纸/ Frequently Read Newspapers by Market Segments

3-9-1 时尚流行指标/ Fads Popular Index

注：本题为多选题，合计百分比超过 100%（Multiple answers）

	人数 Number	沈阳晚报 Shenyang Evening News	沈阳日报 Shenyang Daily	辽沈晚报 Liaoshen Evening News	辽宁广播电视报 Liaoning TV Guide	球报 Baus Weekly	沈阳广播电视报 Shenyang TV Guide	参考消息 Reference News
样本 Sample	**539**	**65.1**	**41.6**	**34.3**	**10.9**	**7.8**	**4.6**	**3.3**
平实生活指向 simple living orientation	257	67.7	36.6	33.1	9.3	6.2	4.3	3.1
时尚流行指向 fashion orientation	282	62.8	46.1	35.5	12.4	9.2	5.0	3.5

续前表 continued

	人数 Number	体坛周报 Sports Weekly	辽宁日报 Liaoning Daily	都市家庭报 Metropolitan Family	电脑报 Computer Informatin	人民日报 People's Daily	现代女报 Xian Dai Nv Bao	晚晴报 Wan Qing Bao	良友 Liang You
样本 Sample	**539**	**3.2**	**2.4**	**2.4**	**1.9**	**1.5**	**1.5**	**1.3**	**1.3**
平实生活指向 simple living orientation	257	3.9	3.5	1.6	1.9	2.3	1.6	1.6	1.2
时尚流行指向 fashion orientation	282	2.5	1.4	3.2	1.8	0.7	1.4	1.1	1.4

3-9-2 广告态度指向/ Advertising Attitude Index

注：本题为多选题，合计百分比超过 100%（Multiple answers）

	人数 Number	沈阳晚报 Shenyang Evening News	沈阳日报 Shenyang Daily	辽沈晚报 Liaoshen Evening News	辽宁广播电视报 Liaoning TV Guide	球报 Baus Weekly	沈阳广播电视报 Shenyang TV Guide	参考消息 Reference News
样本 Sample	539	65.1	41.6	34.3	10.9	7.8	4.6	3.3
广告淡漠指向 indifferent orientation	154	69.5	35.1	36.4	13.6	7.8	4.5	3.2
中间层 medium	315	62.5	43.5	32.7	9.8	6.3	5.1	3.5
信赖广告指向 loyal orientation	70	67.1	47.1	37.1	10.0	14.3	2.9	2.9

续前表 continued

	人数 Number	体坛周报 Sports Weekly	辽宁日报 Liaoning Daily	都市家庭报 Metropolitan Family	电脑报 Computer Informatin	人民日报 People's Daily	现代女报 Xian Dai Nv Bao	晚晴报 Wan Qing Bao	良友 Liang You
样本 Sample	539	3.2	2.4	2.4	1.9	1.5	1.5	1.3	1.3
广告淡漠指向 indifferent orientation	154	2.6	1.9	0.0	1.9	0.6	1.9	1.3	1.3
中间层 medium	315	3.2	2.2	3.8	1.6	2.2	1.6	1.3	1.0
信赖广告指向 loyal orientation	70	4.3	4.3	1.4	2.9	0.0	0.0	1.4	2.9

3-10 不同消费者层比较关心的报道/ The Concerned Newspaper Content Categories by Market Segments

3-10-1 时尚流行指标/ Fads Popular Index

注：本题为多选题，合计百分比超过 100%（Multiple answers）

	人数 Number	头版要闻 first page news	国际新闻 international news	国内新闻 national news	港澳台新闻 news about HK.Taiwan. Macao	本地新闻 local news	经济信息 economic information
样本 Sample	538	50.4	47.4	47.4	4.6	18.2	7.6
平实生活指向 simple living orientation	257	54.5	53.3	52.5	3.1	22.2	8.2
时尚流行指向 fashion orientation	281	46.6	42.0	42.7	6.0	14.6	7.1

续前表 continued

	人数 Number	财政金融 finance & economic	股市报道 stock market report	热点追踪 hits track	文化信息 cultural information	体育报道 sports report	人物专访 personal interview
样本 Sample	538	3.9	8.0	22.1	3.9	28.4	13.8
平实生活指向 simple living orientation	257	3.9	7.4	23.3	4.7	28.4	12.5
时尚流行指向 fashion orientation	281	3.9	8.5	21.0	3.2	28.5	14.9

续前表 continued

	人数 Number	军事知识 military knowledge	法制报道 legal news	海外见闻 overseas information	科技知识 science sense	影视娱乐报道 video & entertainment report	服饰美容 clothes & beauty
样本 Sample	538	8.7	29.4	7.2	5.8	15.8	8.9
平实生活指向 simple living orientation	257	10.5	29.2	6.6	7.4	8.9	3.1
时尚流行指向 fashion orientation	281	7.1	29.5	7.8	4.3	22.1	14.2

续前表 continued

	人数 Number	休闲旅游 entertainment & travel	消费指南 consumption guide	电视节目预告 TV program forecast	健康医疗 medicare	生活常识 common sense	书评 book comment
样本 Sample	538	6.3	7.1	10.0	13.8	19.9	0.7
平实生活指向 simple living orientation	257	5.1	4.3	7.8	13.2	19.1	1.6
时尚流行指向 fashion orientation	281	7.5	9.6	12.1	14.2	20.6	0.0

续前表 continued

	人数 Number	文艺评论 art critics	散文 prose	小说 novel	漫画 cartoon	广告 advertising	读者来信 reader's letter	其他 others
样本 Sample	538	1.5	3.3	7.6	5.2	5.6	0.2	1.1
平实生活指向 simple living orientation	257	2.3	2.3	7.4	5.8	3.5	0.4	1.2
时尚流行指向 fashion orientation	281	0.7	4.3	7.8	4.6	7.5	0.0	1.1

3-10-2 广告态度指标/ Advertising Attitude Index

注：本题为多选题，合计百分比超过 100%（Multiple answers）

	人数 Number	头版要闻 first page news	国际新闻 international news	国内新闻 national news	港澳台新闻 news about HK.Taiwan Macao	本地新闻 local news	经济信息 economic information
样本 Sample	538	50.4	47.4	47.4	4.6	18.2	7.6
广告淡漠指向 indifferent orientation	153	49.7	45.8	43.8	3.9	19.0	5.9
中间层 medium	315	48.9	47.0	50.5	5.1	18.7	8.3
信赖广告指向 loyal orientation	70	58.6	52.9	41.4	4.3	14.3	8.6

续前表 continued

	人数 Number	财政金融 finance & economic	股市报道 stock market report	热点追踪 hits track	文化信息 cultural information	体育报道 sports report	人物专访 personal interview
样本 Sample	538	3.9	8.0	22.1	3.9	28.4	13.8
广告淡漠指向 indifferent orientation	153	3.9	8.5	20.9	3.3	29.4	9.2
中间层 medium	315	3.2	7.6	21.9	4.1	26.7	15.9
信赖广告指向 loyal orientation	70	7.1	8.6	25.7	4.3	34.3	14.3

续前表 continued

	人数 Number	军事知识 military knowledge	法制报道 legal news	海外见闻 overseas information	科技知识 science sense	影视娱乐报道 video & entertainment report	服饰美容 clothes & beauty
样本 Sample	538	8.7	29.4	7.2	5.8	15.8	8.9
广告淡漠指向 indifferent orientation	153	9.8	32.7	9.2	7.2	17.6	6.5
中间层 medium	315	7.6	26.0	6.3	5.4	15.9	10.2
信赖广告指向 loyal orientation	70	11.4	37.1	7.1	4.3	11.4	8.6

续前表 continued

	人数 Number	休闲旅游 entertainment & travel	消费指南 consumption guide	电视节目预告 TV program forecast	健康医疗 medicare	生活常识 common sense	书评 book comment
样本 Sample	538	6.3	7.1	10.0	13.8	19.9	0.7
广告淡漠指向 indifferent orientation	153	7.8	3.9	11.8	13.7	15.7	0.7
中间层 medium	315	6.0	8.9	9.2	13.7	21.3	0.6
信赖广告指向 loyal orientation	70	4.3	5.7	10.0	14.3	22.9	1.4

续前表 continued

	人数 Number	文艺评论 art critics	散文 prose	小说 novel	漫画 cartoon	广告 advertising	读者来信 reader's letter	其他 others
样本 Sample	538	1.5	3.3	7.6	5.2	5.6	0.2	1.1
广告淡漠指向 indifferent orientation	153	2.0	2.0	10.5	7.2	5.9	0.7	0.7
中间层 medium	315	1.6	3.8	7.0	4.8	6.0	0.0	1.6
信赖广告指向 loyal orientation	70	0.0	4.3	4.3	2.9	2.9	0.0	0.0

4.杂志 / Magazines

● 北京 / Beijing

4-1 样本、男性各年龄层、女性各年龄层平时是否接触杂志媒介/ Magazine Reading by the Whole Sample, Age and Gender Groups

	人数 Number	看 yes	从来不看 never
样本 Sample	1011	65.7	34.3
男性 Male	503	60.8	39.2
16~24 岁 Age	105	62.9	37.1
25~34 岁 Age	150	58.0	42.0
35~44 岁 Age	131	59.5	40.5
45~54 岁 Age	77	66.2	33.8
55~60 岁 Age	40	60.0	40.0
女性 Female	508	70.5	29.5
16~24 岁 Age	108	87.0	13.0
25~34 岁 Age	150	72.0	28.0
35~44 岁 Age	124	69.4	30.6
45~54 岁 Age	84	54.8	45.2
55~60 岁 Age	42	57.1	42.9

4-2 经常阅读的杂志排名/ Ranking of the Frequently Reading Magazines

注：本题为多选题，合计百分比超过 100%（Multiple answers）

排名 Brand Ranking	杂志 Magazine	人次 Person-time	百分比 Percent
1	读者 Duzhe	199	30.6
2	青年文摘 Qing Nian Wen Zhai	73	11.2
3	知音 Bosom Friend	52	8.0
4	当代歌坛 Modern Music Field	45	6.9
5	北京电视周刊 Beijing Television Weekly	36	5.5
6	女友 Woman Friend	29	4.5

n=650

4-3 样本、男性各年龄层、女性各年龄层经常阅读的杂志/ Frequently Read Magazines by the Whole Sample, Age and Gender Groups

注：本题为多选题，合计百分比超过 100%（Multiple answers）

	人数 Number	读者 Duzhe	青年文摘 Qing Nian Wen Zhai	知音 Bosom Friend	当代歌坛 Modern Music Field	北京电视周刊 Beijing Television Weekly	女友 Woman Friend	家庭 Family
样本 Sample	650	30.6	11.2	8.0	6.9	5.5	4.5	4.2
男性 Male	298	30.5	9.7	6.0	2.3	4.4	0.7	3.7
16~24 岁 Age	65	26.2	15.4	1.5	10.8	4.6	0.0	1.5
25~34 岁 Age	86	39.5	14.0	9.3	0.0	1.2	2.3	2.3
35~44 岁 Age	75	26.7	4.0	8.0	0.0	6.7	0.0	9.3
45~54 岁 Age	49	28.6	8.2	4.1	0.0	6.1	0.0	2.0
55~60 岁 Age	23	26.1	0.0	4.3	0.0	4.3	0.0	0.0
女性 Female	352	30.7	12.5	9.7	10.8	6.5	7.7	4.5
16~24 岁 Age	94	38.3	25.5	5.3	35.1	8.5	9.6	0.0
25~34 岁 Age	105	39.0	12.4	11.4	1.0	2.9	11.4	5.7
35~44 岁 Age	84	16.7	3.6	11.9	4.8	7.1	4.8	10.7
45~54 岁 Age	45	24.4	6.7	11.1	0.0	11.1	4.4	2.2
55~60 岁 Age	24	25.0	4.2	8.3	0.0	4.2	0.0	0.0

续前表 continued

	人数 Number	家庭医生 Family Doctor	北京青年周刊 Beijing Youth Weekly	海外文摘 Overseas Digest	时尚 Trends	故事会 Story Selection Journal	大众软件 Pop Soft
样本 Sample	650	3.4	3.2	2.9	2.9	2.9	2.8
男性 Male	298	2.3	3.0	2.0	1.0	3.4	4.7
16~24 岁 Age	65	1.5	1.5	1.5	1.5	4.6	20.0
25~34 岁 Age	86	1.2	1.2	2.3	2.3	2.3	1.2
35~44 岁 Age	75	4.0	4.0	1.3	0.0	6.7	0.0
45~54 岁 Age	49	4.1	8.2	4.1	0.0	0.0	0.0
55~60 岁 Age	23	0.0	0.0	0.0	0.0	0.0	0.0
女性 Female	352	4.3	3.4	3.7	4.5	2.6	1.1
16~24 岁 Age	94	1.1	4.3	1.1	7.4	5.3	2.1
25~34 岁 Age	105	3.8	1.0	9.5	6.7	1.0	1.9
35~44 岁 Age	84	6.0	3.6	1.2	1.2	3.6	0.0
45~54 岁 Age	45	8.9	6.7	2.2	2.2	0.0	0.0
55~60 岁 Age	24	4.2	4.2	0.0	0.0	0.0	0.0

4-4 不同学历的读者经常阅读的杂志/ Frequently Read Magazines by Educational Levels

注：本题为多选题，合计百分比超过 100%（Multiple answers）

	人数 Number	读者 Duzhe	青年文摘 Qing Nian Wen Zhai	知音 Bosom Friend	当代歌坛 Modern Music Field	北京电视周刊 Beijing Television Weekly	女友 Woman Friend	家庭 Family
样本 Sample	649	30.7	11.2	8.0	6.9	5.5	4.5	4.2
小学及以下 Primary School or Below	11	36.4	0.0	9.1	0.0	0.0	0.0	0.0
初中 Middle School	76	17.1	3.9	7.9	5.3	7.9	1.3	2.6
高中/中专/技校 High School/Technical Secondary School	288	24.3	10.1	10.4	12.5	7.6	5.2	3.8
大学专科 2-3 Year College	143	36.4	14.7	5.6	2.1	4.2	4.9	5.6
大学本科 4-5 Year College	116	46.6	15.5	6.0	1.7	0.9	5.2	5.2
研究生或以上 Graduate or Above	15	40.0	13.3	0.0	0.0	6.7	0.0	0.0

续前表 continued

	人数 Number	家庭医生 Family Doctor	北京青年周刊 Beijing Youth Weekly	时尚 Trends	海外文摘 Overseas Digest	故事会 Story Selection Journal	大众软件 Pop Soft
样本 Sample	649	3.4	3.2	2.9	2.8	2.9	2.8
小学及以下 Primary School or Below	11	18.2	0.0	0.0	0.0	0.0	0.0
初中 Middle School	76	1.3	3.9	0.0	1.3	5.3	0.0
高中/中专/技校 High School/Technical Secondary School	288	3.1	4.9	1.0	1.7	4.5	3.1
大学专科 2-3 Year College	143	5.6	0.7	3.5	4.9	0.7	4.2
大学本科 4-5 Year College	116	0.9	2.6	9.5	4.3	0.9	2.6
研究生或以上 Graduate or Above	15	6.7	0.0	0.0	0.0	0.0	0.0

4-5 经常阅读的杂志的主要来源/ Sources of Obtaining the Frequently Read Magazines

注：本题为多选题，合计百分比可能超过 100%（Multiple answers）

	人数 Number	家中订阅 subscribed by my family	单位订阅 subscribed by work unit	报摊购买 bought from vender	赠阅 given as gift	借阅 borrowed
读者 Duzhe	196	4.6	9.2	9.2	78.1	0.0
青年文摘 Qing Nian Wen Zhai	73	4.1	12.3	12.3	74.0	0.0
知音 Bosom Friend	51	5.9	7.8	7.8	78.4	0.0
当代歌坛 Mordern Music Field	45	4.4	0.0	0.0	75.6	0.0
北京电视周刊 Beijing Television Weekly	36	11.1	11.1	11.1	77.8	2.8
女友 Woman Friend	29	3.4	17.2	17.2	58.6	0.0
家庭 Family	27	0.0	22.2	22.2	66.7	0.0
家庭医生 Family Doctor	21	4.8	38.1	38.1	52.4	4.8
北京青年周刊 Beijing Youth Weekly	21	9.5	28.6	28.6	42.9	0.0
海外文摘 Overseas Digest	19	21.1	10.5	10.5	68.4	0.0
时尚 Trends	19	5.3	5.3	5.3	78.9	0.0
故事会 Story Selection Journal	19	0.0	5.3	5.3	78.9	5.3
大众软件 Pop Soft	18	11.1	0.0	0.0	61.1	0.0

4-6 不同消费者层平时是否接触杂志媒介/ Magazine Reading by Market Segments

4-6-1 时尚流行指标/ Fads Popular Index

	人数 Number	从来不看 never	看 yes
样本 Sample	997	65.6	34.4
平实生活指向 simple living orientation	490	61.2	38.8
时尚流行指向 fashion orientation	507	69.8	30.2

4-6-2 广告态度指标/ Advertising Attitude Index

	人数 Number	从来不看 never	看 yes
样本 Sample	993	66.0	34.0
广告淡漠指向 indifferent orientation	289	60.9	39.1
中间层 medium	571	67.3	32.7
信赖广告指向 loyal orientation	133	71.4	28.6

4-7 不同消费者层经常阅读的杂志/ Frequently Reading Magazines by Market Segments

4-7-1 时尚流行指标/ Fads Popular Index

注：本题为多选题，合计百分比超过 100%（Multiple answers）

	人数 Number	读者 Duzhe	青年文摘 Qing Nian Wen Zhai	知音 Bosom Friend	当代歌坛 Modern Music Field	北京电视周刊 Beijing Television Weekly	女友 Woman Friend	家庭 Family
样本 Sample	641	30.6	11.2	8.1	6.7	5.6	4.5	4.2
平实生活指向 simple living orientation	295	35.9	11.2	8.1	3.1	6.1	2.7	4.4
时尚流行指向 fashion orientation	346	26.0	11.3	8.1	9.8	5.2	6.1	4.0

续前表 continued

	人数 Number	家庭医生 Family Doctor	北京青年周刊 Beijing Youth Weekly	海外文摘 Overseas Digest	时尚 Trends	故事会 Story Selection Journal	大众软件 Pop Soft
样本 Sample	**641**	**3.4**	**3.3**	**3.0**	**2.7**	**2.8**	**2.8**
平实生活指向 simple living orientation	295	3.1	4.1	2.0	1.4	2.7	2.4
时尚流行指向 fashion orientation	346	3.8	2.6	3.8	3.8	2.9	3.2

4-7-2 广告态度指标/ Advertising Attitude Index

注：本题为多选题，合计百分比超过 100%（Multiple answers）

	人数 Number	读者 Duzhe	青年文摘 Qing Nian Wen Zhai	知音 Bosom Friend	当代歌坛 Modern Music Field	北京电视周刊 Beijing Television Weekly	女友 Woman Friend	家庭 Family
样本 Sample	**641**	**30.9**	**11.2**	**8.1**	**6.7**	**5.6**	**4.5**	**4.2**
广告淡漠指向 indifferent orientation	171	29.8	11.7	7.0	5.8	2.9	2.9	1.8
中间层 medium	375	32.3	9.9	8.3	5.9	6.9	5.6	5.1
信赖广告指向 loyal orientation	95	27.4	15.8	9.5	11.6	5.3	3.2	5.3

续前表 continued

	人数 Number	家庭医生 Family Doctor	北京青年周刊 Beijing Youth Weekly	海外文摘 Overseas Digest	时尚 Trends	故事会 Story Selection Journal	大众软件 Pop Soft
样本 Sample	**641**	**3.3**	**3.3**	**3.0**	**3.0**	**2.8**	**2.8**
广告淡漠指向 indifferent orientation	171	3.5	6.4	3.5	2.3	1.8	3.5
中间层 medium	375	3.7	1.9	2.9	2.9	2.9	2.4
信赖广告指向 loyal orientation	95	1.1	3.2	2.1	4.2	4.2	3.2

● 上海 / Shanghai

4-1 样本、男性各年龄层、女性各年龄层平时是否接触杂志媒介/ Magazine Reading by the Whole Sample, Age and Gender Groups

	人数 Number	看 yes	从来不看 never
样本 Sample	**1013**	**50.2**	**49.8**
男性 Male	**508**	**43.9**	**56.1**
16~24 岁 Age	109	53.2	46.8
25~34 岁 Age	145	47.6	52.4
35~44 岁 Age	130	34.6	65.4
45~54 岁 Age	85	38.8	61.2
55~60 岁 Age	39	46.2	53.8
女性 Female	**505**	**56.6**	**43.4**
16~24 岁 Age	108	76.9	23.1
25~34 岁 Age	144	68.8	31.3
35~44 岁 Age	130	44.6	55.4
45~54 岁 Age	82	42.7	57.3
55~60 岁 Age	41	26.8	73.2

4-2 经常阅读的杂志排名/ Ranking of the Frequently Reading Magazines

注：本题为多选题，合计百分比超过 100%（Multiple answers）

排名 Brand Ranking	杂志 Magazines	人次 Person-time	百分比 Percent
1	上海电视 Shanghai TV	120	23.7
2	读者 Duzhe	84	16.6
3	青年一代 Qin Nian Yi Dai	65	12.8
4	现代家庭 Morden Family	64	12.6
5	知音 Bosom Friend	46	9.1
6	大众医学 Popular Medicine	34	6.7
7	世界时装之苑 ELLE	24	4.7
8	故事会 Story Selection Journal	22	4.3
9	新民周刊 Xinmin Weekly	21	4.2
9	上海服饰 Shanghai Style	21	4.2
10	家庭 Family	19	3.8
11	瑞丽服饰服装 Ray	18	3.6
11	女友 Woman Friend	18	3.6
12	萌芽 Mengya Magazine	16	3.2
13	当代歌坛 Modern Music Field	15	3.0
14	时尚 Trends	13	2.6
14	How	13	2.6
14	家庭医生 Family Doctor	13	2.6
15	康复 Kangfu	12	2.4

n=506

4-3 样本、男性各年龄层、女性各年龄层经常阅读的杂志/ Frequently Read Magazines by the Whole Sample, Age and Gender Groups

注：本题为多选题，合计百分比超过 100%（Multiple answers）

	人数 Number	上海电视 Shanghai TV	读者 Duzhe	青年一代 Qing Nian Yi Dai	现代家庭 Modern Family	知音 Bosom Friend	大众医学 Popular Medicine	世界时装之苑 ELLE
样本 Sample	**506**	**23.7**	**16.6**	**12.8**	**12.6**	**9.1**	**6.7**	**4.7**
男性 Male	**221**	**21.7**	**14.9**	**10.4**	**10.0**	**7.2**	**6.8**	**2.7**
16~24 岁 Age	58	31.0	20.7	6.9	6.9	5.2	0.0	3.4
25~34 岁 Age	69	23.2	14.5	14.5	11.6	8.7	2.9	4.3
35~44 岁 Age	44	22.7	9.1	13.6	11.4	9.1	11.4	2.3
45~54 岁 Age	32	9.4	15.6	3.1	15.6	3.1	12.5	0.0
55~60 岁 Age	18	5.6	11.1	11.1	0.0	11.1	22.2	0.0
女性 Female	**285**	**25.3**	**17.9**	**14.7**	**14.7**	**10.5**	**6.7**	**6.3**
16~24 岁 Age	83	33.7	24.1	8.4	6.0	8.4	1.2	7.2
25~34 岁 Age	99	22.2	18.2	20.2	20.2	13.1	6.1	10.1
35~44 岁 Age	58	25.9	8.6	12.1	19.0	12.1	13.8	3.4
45~54 岁 Age	34	11.8	17.6	14.7	11.8	5.9	8.8	0.0
55~60 岁 Age	11	27.3	18.2	27.3	18.2	9.1	9.1	0.0

续前表 continued

	人数 Number	故事会 Story Selection Journal	新民周刊 Xinmin Weekly	上海服饰 Shanghai Style	家庭 Family	瑞丽服饰服装 Ray	女友 Woman Friend	萌芽 Mengya Magazine	当代歌坛 Modern Music Field
样本 Sample	**506**	**4.3**	**4.2**	**4.2**	**3.8**	**3.6**	**3.6**	**3.2**	**3.0**
男性 Male	**221**	**3.2**	**6.3**	**1.8**	**2.3**	**0.5**	**0.5**	**2.3**	**1.8**
16~24 岁 Age	58	1.7	3.4	0.0	0.0	0.0	0.0	6.9	5.2
25~34 岁 Age	69	4.3	10.1	1.4	1.4	1.4	0.0	0.0	1.4
35~44 岁 Age	44	4.5	4.5	4.5	2.3	0.0	2.3	0.0	0.0
45~54 岁 Age	32	0.0	9.4	0.0	3.1	0.0	0.0	3.1	0.0
55~60 岁 Age	18	5.6	0.0	5.6	11.1	0.0	0.0	0.0	0.0
女性 Female	**285**	**5.3**	**2.5**	**6.0**	**4.9**	**6.0**	**6.0**	**3.9**	**3.9**
16~24 岁 Age	83	3.6	2.4	4.8	1.2	15.7	14.5	8.4	10.8
25~34 岁 Age	99	7.1	3.0	10.1	4.0	3.0	4.0	0.0	0.0
35~44 岁 Age	58	3.4	1.7	1.7	8.6	0.0	1.7	1.7	3.4
45~54 岁 Age	34	8.8	2.9	5.9	8.8	2.9	0.0	8.8	0.0
55~60 岁 Age	11	0.0	0.0	0.0	9.1	0.0	0.0	0.0	0.0

4-4 不同学历的读者经常阅读的杂志/ Frequently Read Magazines by Educational Levels

注：本题为多选题，合计百分比超过 100%（Multiple answers）

	人数 Number	多媒体世界 Multimedia World	家庭生活指南 Family Life Guide	烹调知识 Cooking Knowledge	求是 Qiushi	中国妇女 China Woman	家庭与生活 Family & Life
样本 Sample	**505**	**16.6**	**3.8**	**3.6**	**2.2**	**9.1**	**2.6**
小学及以下 Primary School or Below	3	0.0	0.0	0.0	0.0	0.0	0.0
初中 Middle School	98	11.2	6.1	1.0	0.0	11.2	5.1
高中/中专/技校 High School/Technical Secondary School	270	15.9	3.0	3.3	1.9	10.4	1.5
大学专科 2-3 Year College	90	21.1	4.4	5.6	2.2	4.4	4.4
大学本科 4-5 Year College	40	25.0	2.5	7.5	10.0	5.0	0.0
研究生或以上 Graduate or Above	4	25.0	0.0	0.0	0.0	25.0	0.0

续前表 continued

	人数 Number	故事会 Story Selection Journal	新民周刊 Xinmin Weekly	上海服饰 Shanghai Style	家庭 Family	瑞丽服饰服装 Ray	女友 Woman Friend	萌芽 Mengya Magazine	当代歌坛 Modern Music Field
样本 Sample	**505**	**4.4**	**4.2**	**4.2**	**3.8**	**3.6**	**3.6**	**3.2**	**3.0**
小学及以下 Primary School or Below	3	0.0	0.0	0.0	0.0	0.0	0.0	0.0	0.0
初中 Middle School	98	4.1	3.1	3.1	6.1	2.0	1.0	5.1	0.0
高中/中专/技校 High School/Technical Secondary School	270	5.6	4.1	3.3	3.0	2.6	3.3	2.2	5.2
大学专科 2-3 Year College	90	2.2	5.6	7.8	4.4	7.8	5.6	3.3	1.1
大学本科 4-5 Year College	40	2.5	5.0	5.0	2.5	5.0	7.5	5.0	0.0
研究生或以上 Graduate or Above	4	0.0	0.0	0.0	0.0	0.0	0.0	0.0	0.0

4-5 经常阅读的杂志的主要来源/ Sources of Obtaining the Frequently Read Magazine

注：本题为多选题，合计百分比可能超过 100%（Multiple answers）

	人数 Number	家中订阅 subscribed by my family	单位订阅 subscribed by work unit	报摊购买 bought from vender	赠阅 given as gift	借阅 borrowed
上海电视 Shanghai TV	120	6.7	5.8	75.8	1.7	10.0
读者 Duzhe	84	11.9	7.1	64.3	0.0	16.7
青年一代 Qing Nian Yi Dai	64	1.6	6.3	78.1	0.0	14.1
现代家庭 Modern Family	62	22.6	9.7	50.0	0.0	17.7
知音 Bosom Friend	46	2.2	8.7	71.7	0.0	17.4
大众医学 Popular Medicine	34	11.8	32.4	44.1	0.0	11.8
世界时装之苑 ELLE	24	0.0	8.3	70.8	4.2	16.7
故事会 Story Selection Journal	22	9.1	4.5	77.3	0.0	9.1
新民周刊 Xinmin Weekly	21	14.3	0.0	85.7	0.0	0.0
上海服饰 Shanghai Style	21	0.0	0.0	76.2	0.0	23.8
家庭 Family	18	11.1	5.6	55.6	5.6	22.2
瑞丽服饰服装 Ray	18	0.0	5.6	66.7	0.0	27.8
女友 Woman Friend	18	0.0	0.0	83.3	0.0	16.7
萌芽 Mengya Magazine	16	25.0	0.0	62.5	0.0	12.5

4-6 不同消费者层平时是否接触杂志媒介/ Magazine Reading by Market Segments

4-6-1 时尚流行指标/ Fads Popular Index

	人数 Number	从来不看 never	看 yes
样本 Sample	1004	50.3	49.7
平实生活指向 simple living orientation	471	41.0	59.0
时尚流行指向 fashion orientation	533	58.5	41.5

4-6-2 广告态度指标/ Advertising Attitude Index

	人数 Number	从来不看 never	看 yes
样本 Sample	1001	50.2	49.8
广告淡漠指向 indifferent orientation	256	47.3	52.7
中间层 medium	610	48.0	52.0
信赖广告指向 loyal orientation	135	65.9	34.1

4-7 不同消费者层经常阅读的杂志/ Frequently Reading Magazines by Market Segments

4-7-1 时尚流行指标/ Fads Popular Index

注：本题为多选题，合计百分比超过 100%（Multiple answers）

	人数 Number	上海电视 Shanghai TV	读者 Duzhe	青年一代 Qin Nian Yi Dai	现代家庭 Modern Family	知音 Bosom Friend	大众医学 Popular Medicine	世界时装之苑 ELLE
样本 Sample	502	23.7	16.7	12.9	12.7	9.0	6.8	4.8
平实生活指向 simple living orientation	190	23.7	16.8	10.0	11.1	7.9	7.9	2.1
时尚流行指向 fashion orientation	312	23.7	16.7	14.7	13.8	9.6	6.1	6.4

续前表 continued

	人数 Number	故事会 Story Selection Journal	新民周刊 Xinmin Weekly	上海服饰 Shanghai Style	家庭 Family	瑞丽服饰服装 Ray	女友 Woman Friend	萌芽 Mengya Magazine	当代歌坛 Modern Music Field
样本 Sample	502	4.4	4.0	4.2	3.8	3.6	3.6	3.2	2.8
平实生活指向 simple living orientation	190	5.3	6.3	2.1	5.8	1.1	0.5	4.2	1.6
时尚流行指向 fashion orientation	312	3.8	2.6	5.4	2.6	5.1	5.4	2.6	3.5

4-7-2 广告态度指标/ Advertising Attitude Index

注：本题为多选题，合计百分比超过 100%（Multiple answers）

	人数 Number	上海电视 Shanghai TV	读者 Duzhe	青年一代 Qin Nian Yi Dai	现代家庭 Modern Family	知音 Bosom Friend	大众医学 Popular Medicine	世界时装之苑 ELLE
样本 Sample	500	23.6	16.6	12.8	12.6	9.0	6.8	4.8
广告淡漠指向 indifferent orientation	120	23.3	15.8	10.8	10.8	7.5	6.7	1.7
中间层 medium	292	21.6	18.8	14.0	13.4	9.2	6.2	5.1
信赖广告指向 loyal orientation	88	30.7	10.2	11.4	12.5	10.2	9.1	8.0

续前表 continued

	人数 Number	故事会 Story Selection Journal	新民周刊 Xinmin Weekly	上海服饰 Shanghai Style	家庭 Family	瑞丽服饰服装 Ray	女友 Woman Friend	萌芽 Mengya Magazine	当代歌坛 Modern Music Field
样本 Sample	500	4.4	4.2	4.2	3.8	3.6	3.6	3.2	2.8
广告淡漠指向 indifferent orientation	120	3.3	6.7	1.7	5.8	2.5	2.5	1.7	1.7
中间层 medium	292	5.1	3.8	4.8	3.1	3.1	3.1	3.4	3.1
信赖广告指向 loyal orientation	88	3.4	2.3	5.7	3.4	6.8	6.8	4.5	3.4

● 广州 / Guangzhou

4-1 样本、男性各年龄层、女性各年龄层平时是否接触杂志媒介/ Magazine Reading by the Whole Sample, Age and Gender Groups

	人数 Number	看 yes	从来不看 never
样本 Sample	1032	41.8	58.2
男性 Male	498	38.0	62.0
16~24 岁 Age	106	46.2	53.8
25~34 岁 Age	150	40.0	60.0
35~44 岁 Age	126	27.0	73.0
45~54 岁 Age	73	42.5	57.5
55~60 岁 Age	43	34.9	65.1
女性 Female	534	45.3	54.7
16~24 岁 Age	112	58.0	42.0
25~34 岁 Age	158	50.0	50.0
35~44 岁 Age	136	40.4	59.6
45~54 岁 Age	87	32.2	67.8
55~60 岁 Age	41	36.6	63.4

4-2 经常阅读的杂志排名/ Ranking of the Frequently Reading Magazines

注：本题为多选题，合计百分比超过 100%（Multiple answers）

排名 Brand Ranking	杂志 Magazines	人次 Person-time	百分比 Percent
1	家庭 Family	111	25.8
2	读者 Duzhe	93	21.6
3	家庭医生 Family Doctor	79	18.4
4	知音 Bosom Friend	67	15.6
5	Yes	31	7.2
6	佛山文艺 Foshan Wen Yi	24	5.6
7	青年文摘 Qing Nian Wen Zhai	22	5.1
8	少男少女 Shao Nan Shao Nu	19	4.4
9	南风窗 Nanfengchuang	18	4.2
10	人之初 Renszhichu	17	4.0
11	女友 Woman Friend	13	3.0
12	电脑 Computer	9	2.1
12	大众软件 Pop Soft	9	2.1

n=430

4-3 样本、男性各年龄层、女性各年龄层经常阅读的杂志/ Frequently Read Magazines by the Whole Sample, Age and Gender Groups

注：本题为多选题，合计百分比超过 100%（Multiple answers）

	人数 Number	家庭 Family	读者 Duzhe	家庭医生 Family Doctor	知音 Bosom Friend	Yes	佛山文艺 Foshan Wen Yi
样本 Sample	430	25.8	21.6	18.4	15.6	7.2	5.6
男性 Male	189	22.2	20.1	10.6	12.7	3.7	5.8
16~24 岁 Age	49	10.2	18.4	2.0	12.2	12.2	0.0
25~34 岁 Age	60	20.0	35.0	8.3	10.0	0.0	10.0
35~44 岁 Age	34	32.4	11.8	23.5	23.5	0.0	2.9
45~54 岁 Age	31	35.5	6.5	12.9	12.9	3.2	6.5
55~60 岁 Age	15	20.0	13.3	13.3	0.0	0.0	13.3
女性 Female	241	28.6	22.8	24.5	17.8	10.0	5.4
16~24 岁 Age	64	9.4	23.4	4.7	15.6	32.8	6.3
25~34 岁 Age	79	43.0	24.1	25.3	21.5	1.3	6.3
35~44 岁 Age	55	34.5	23.6	40.0	21.8	3.6	3.6
45~54 岁 Age	28	25.0	14.3	39.3	10.7	0.0	3.6
55~60 岁 Age	15	20.0	26.7	20.0	6.7	0.0	6.7

续前表 continued

	人数 Number	青年文摘 Qing Nian Wen Zhai	少男少女 Shao Nan Shao Nu	南风窗 Nanfeng chuang	人之初 Renzhichu	女友 Woman Friend	电脑 Computer	大众软件 Pop Soft
样本 Sample	430	5.1	4.4	4.2	4.0	3.0	2.1	2.1
男性 Male	189	5.3	3.2	3.7	1.6	1.1	4.2	4.8
16~24 岁 Age	49	8.2	12.2	4.1	0.0	2.0	10.2	14.3
25~34 岁 Age	60	8.3	0.0	1.7	0.0	1.7	1.7	1.7
35~44 岁 Age	34	0.0	0.0	2.9	2.9	0.0	2.9	2.9
45~54 岁 Age	31	3.2	0.0	9.7	3.2	0.0	3.2	0.0
55~60 岁 Age	15	0.0	0.0	0.0	6.7	0.0	0.0	0.0
女性 Female	241	5.0	5.4	4.6	5.8	4.6	0.4	0.0
16~24 岁 Age	64	7.8	14.1	3.1	4.7	14.1	0.0	0.0
25~34 岁 Age	79	6.3	1.3	6.3	8.9	2.5	1.3	0.0
35~44 岁 Age	55	3.6	3.6	3.6	1.8	0.0	0.0	0.0
45~54 岁 Age	28	0.0	3.6	7.1	10.7	0.0	0.0	0.0
55~60 岁 Age	15	0.0	0.0	0.0	0.0	0.0	0.0	0.0

4-4 不同学历的读者经常阅读的杂志/ Frequently Read Magazines by Educational Levels

注：本题为多选题，合计百分比超过 100%（Multiple answers）

	人数 Number	家庭 Family	读者 Duzhe	家庭医生 Family Doctor	知音 Bosom Friend	Yes	佛山文艺 Foshan Wen Yi
样本 Sample	427	25.5	21.3	18.5	15.7	7.3	5.6
小学及以下 Primary School or Below	11	36.4	9.1	27.3	27.3	0.0	9.1
初中 Middle School	56	16.1	8.9	28.6	14.3	7.1	3.6
高中/中专/技校 High School/Technical Secondary School	208	27.4	17.3	20.2	16.8	12.0	7.7
大学专科 2-3 Year College	81	25.9	23.5	14.8	17.3	2.5	3.7
大学本科 4-5 Year College	63	27.0	42.9	7.9	7.9	0.0	3.2
研究生或以上 Graduate or Above	8	12.5	37.5	12.5	25.0	0.0	0.0

续前表 continued

	人数 Number	青年文摘 Qing Nian Wen Zhai	少男少女 Shao Nan Shao Nu	南风窗 Nanfeng chuang	人之初 Renzhichu	女友 Woman Friend	电脑 Computer	大众软件 Pop Soft
样本 Sample	427	5.2	4.4	4.2	3.7	3.0	2.1	2.1
小学及以下 Primary School or Below	11	0.0	0.0	0.0	9.1	0.0	0.0	0.0
初中 Middle School	56	1.8	5.4	1.8	5.4	3.6	1.8	0.0
高中/中专/技校 High School/Technical Secondary School	208	3.8	6.3	3.4	3.4	3.4	1.0	1.4
大学专科 2-3 Year College	81	6.2	3.7	6.2	3.7	0.0	2.5	6.2
大学本科 4-5 Year College	63	11.1	0.0	7.9	3.2	4.8	6.3	1.6
研究生或以上 Graduate or Above	8	12.5	0.0	0.0	0.0	12.5	0.0	0.0

4-5 经常阅读的杂志的主要来源/ Sources of Obtaining the Frequently Read Magazine

注：本题为多选题，合计百分比可能超过 100%（Multiple answers）

	人数 Number	家中订阅 subscribed by my family	单位订阅 subscribed by work unit	报摊购买 bought from vender	赠阅 given as gift	借阅 borrowed
家庭 Family	108	6.5	14.8	65.7	1.9	11.1
读者 Duzhe	92	5.4	4.3	78.3	1.1	12.0
家庭医生 Family Doctor	76	7.9	11.8	59.2	2.6	10.5
知音 Bosom Friend	67	4.5	3.0	74.6	1.5	16.4
Yes	31	0.0	0.0	74.2	0.0	19.4
佛山文艺 Foshan Wen Yi	24	0.0	0.0	79.2	8.3	29.2
青年文摘 Qing Nian Wen Zhai	22	4.5	4.5	63.6	4.5	22.7
少男少女 Shao Nan Shao Nu	18	0.0	44.4	50.0	0.0	5.6
南风窗 Nanfengchuang	18	5.6	16.7	66.7	0.0	0.0
人之初 Renzhichu	17	0.0	29.4	64.7	0.0	5.9
女友 Woman Friend	12	8.3	0.0	66.7	8.3	16.7

4-6 不同消费者层平时是否接触杂志媒介/ Magazine Reading by Market Segments

4-6-1 时尚流行指标/ Fads Popular Index

	人数 Number	从来不看 never	看 yes
样本 Sample	1020	41.6	58.4
平实生活指向 simple living orientation	517	37.9	62.1
时尚流行指向 fashion orientation	503	45.3	54.7

4-6-2 广告态度指标/ Advertising Attitude Index

	人数 Number	从来不看 never	看 yes
样本 Sample	1020	41.6	58.4
广告淡漠指向 indifferent orientation	334	39.5	60.5
中间层 medium	592	43.6	56.4
信赖广告指向 loyal orientation	94	36.2	63.8

4-7 不同消费者层经常阅读的杂志/ Frequently Reading Magazines by Market Segments

4-7-1 时尚流行指标/ Fads Popular Index

注：本题为多选题，合计百分比超过 100%（Multiple answers）

	人数 Number	家庭 Family	读者 Duzhe	家庭医生 Family Doctor	知音 Bosom Friend	Yes	佛山文艺 Foshan Wen Yi
样本 Sample	423	25.8	21.5	18.4	15.4	7.3	5.4
平实生活指向 simple living orientation	196	28.1	21.9	15.8	17.3	2.6	6.6
时尚流行指向 fashion orientation	227	23.8	21.1	20.7	13.7	11.5	4.4

续前表 continued

	人数 Number	青年文摘 Qing Nian Wen Zhai	少男少女 Shao Nan Shao Nu	南风窗 Nanfeng chuang	人之初 Renzhichu	女友 Woman Friend	电脑 Computer	大众软件 Pop Soft
样本 Sample	423	5.2	4.5	4.3	4.0	3.1	2.1	2.1
平实生活指向 simple living orientation	196	5.1	1.5	5.1	5.1	2.0	2.6	1.5
时尚流行指向 fashion orientation	227	5.3	7.0	3.5	3.1	4.0	1.8	2.6

4-7-2 广告态度指标/ Advertising Attitude Index

注：本题为多选题，合计百分比超过 100%（Multiple answers）

	人数 Number	家庭 Family	读者 Duzhe	家庭医生 Family Doctor	知音 Bosom Friend	Yes	佛山文艺 Foshan Wen Yi
样本 Sample	423	25.8	21.5	18.0	15.8	7.1	5.7
广告淡漠指向 indifferent orientation	131	23.7	23.7	20.6	16.0	5.3	3.1
中间层 medium	258	27.5	21.3	16.3	15.5	7.0	6.6
信赖广告指向 loyal orientation	34	20.6	14.7	20.6	17.6	14.7	8.8

续前表 continued

	人数 Number	青年文摘 Qing Nian Wen Zhai	少男少女 Shao Nan Shao Nu	南风窗 Nanfeng chuang	人之初 Renzhichu	女友 Woman Friend	电脑 Computer	大众软件 Pop Soft
样本 Sample	423	5.2	4.5	4.3	4.0	3.1	2.1	1.9
广告淡漠指向 indifferent orientation	131	6.9	1.5	3.1	4.6	2.3	2.3	1.5
中间层 medium	258	4.3	5.8	5.0	3.9	2.7	2.3	2.3
信赖广告指向 loyal orientation	34	5.9	5.9	2.9	2.9	8.8	0.0	0.0

● 重庆 / Chongqing

4-1 样本、男性各年龄层、女性各年龄层平时是否接触杂志媒介/ Magazine Reading by the Whole Sample, Age and Gender Groups

	人数 Number	看 yes	从来不看 never
样本 Sample	622	50.8	49.2
男性 Male	312	46.8	53.2
16~24 岁 Age	64	60.9	39.1
25~34 岁 Age	92	55.4	44.6
35~44 岁 Age	75	40.0	60.0
45~54 岁 Age	54	29.6	70.4
55~60 岁 Age	27	37.0	63.0
女性 Female	310	54.8	45.2
16~24 岁 Age	64	71.9	28.1
25~34 岁 Age	90	62.2	37.8
35~44 岁 Age	73	43.8	56.2
45~54 岁 Age	60	48.3	51.7
55~60 岁 Age	23	30.4	69.6

4-2 经常阅读的杂志排名/ Ranking of the Frequently Reading Magazines

注：本题为多选题，合计百分比超过 100%（Multiple answers）

排名 Brand Ranking	杂志 Magazine	人次 Person-time	百分比 Percent
1	知音 Bosom Friend	103	32.6
2	家庭 Family	67	21.2
3	读者 Duzhe	59	18.7
4	女友 Woman Friend	29	9.2
5	家庭医生 Family Doctor	25	7.9
6	故事会 Story Selection Journal	24	7.6
7	青年文摘 Qing Nian Wen Zhai	19	6.0
8	党员文摘 Dang Yuan Wen Zhai	11	3.5
9	军事天地 Jun Shi Tian Di	10	3.2
10	兵器知识 Bing Qi Zhi Shi	9	2.8
10	家庭生活指南 Family Life Guide	9	2.8
11	科幻世界 Science & Fiction World	7	2.2
11	世界时装之苑 ELLE	7	2.2
11	足球俱乐部 Football Club	7	2.2
11	大众电影 Popular Film	7	2.2

n=316

4-3 样本、男性各年龄层、女性各年龄层经常阅读的杂志/ Frequently Read Magazines by the Whole Sample, Age and Gender Groups

注：本题为多选题，合计百分比可能超过 100%（Multiple answers）

	人数 Number	知音 Bosom Friend	家庭 Family	读者 Duzhe	女友 Woman Friend	家庭医生 Family Doctor	故事会 Story Selection Journal	青年文摘 Qing Nian Wen Zhai
样本 Sample	**316**	**32.6**	**21.2**	**18.7**	**9.2**	**7.9**	**7.6**	**6.0**
男性 Male	**146**	**22.6**	**15.1**	**19.2**	**2.1**	**6.8**	**8.9**	**6.2**
16~24 岁 Age	39	12.8	7.7	17.9	0.0	2.6	12.8	5.1
25~34 岁 Age	51	29.4	21.6	27.5	5.9	3.9	7.8	9.8
35~44 岁 Age	30	30.0	10.0	16.7	0.0	13.3	3.3	3.3
45~54 岁 Age	16	12.5	31.3	6.3	0.0	6.3	12.5	6.3
55~60 岁 Age	10	20.0	0.0	10.0	0.0	20.0	10.0	0.0
女性 Female	**170**	**41.2**	**26.5**	**18.2**	**15.3**	**8.8**	**6.5**	**5.9**
16~24 岁 Age	46	28.3	15.2	30.4	23.9	0.0	10.9	4.3
25~34 岁 Age	56	55.4	35.7	16.1	16.1	12.5	5.4	5.4
35~44 岁 Age	32	40.6	18.8	12.5	15.6	12.5	3.1	12.5
45~54 岁 Age	29	44.8	27.6	13.8	3.4	13.8	3.4	3.4
55~60 岁 Age	7	0.0	57.1	0.0	0.0	0.0	14.3	0.0

续前表 continued

	人数 Number	党员文摘 Dang Yuan Wen Zhai	军事天地 Jun Shi Tian Di	兵器知识 Bing Qi Zhi Shi	家庭生活指南 Family Life Guide	科幻世界 Science & Fiction World	世界时装之苑 ELLE	大众电影 Popular Film	足球俱乐部 Football Club
样本 Sample	**316**	**3.5**	**3.2**	**2.8**	**2.8**	**2.2**	**2.2**	**2.2**	**2.2**
男性 Male	**146**	**4.1**	**5.5**	**6.2**	**4.8**	**0.7**	**2.7**	**3.4**	**4.8**
16~24 岁 Age	39	0.0	5.1	12.8	0.0	0.0	7.7	2.6	15.4
25~34 岁 Age	51	2.0	5.9	5.9	5.9	2.0	0.0	5.9	0.0
35~44 岁 Age	30	10.0	3.3	3.3	3.3	0.0	3.3	3.3	3.3
45~54 岁 Age	16	0.0	6.3	0.0	6.3	0.0	0.0	0.0	0.0
55~60 岁 Age	10	20.0	10.0	0.0	20.0	0.0	0.0	0.0	0.0
女性 Female	**170**	**2.9**	**1.2**	**0.0**	**1.2**	**3.5**	**1.8**	**1.2**	**0.0**
16~24 岁 Age	46	0.0	0.0	0.0	0.0	8.7	4.3	0.0	0.0
25~34 岁 Age	56	0.0	3.6	0.0	1.8	0.0	0.0	1.8	0.0
35~44 岁 Age	32	9.4	0.0	0.0	0.0	0.0	3.1	3.1	0.0
45~54 岁 Age	29	6.9	0.0	0.0	3.4	6.9	0.0	0.0	0.0
55~60 岁 Age	7	0.0	0.0	0.0	0.0	0.0	0.0	0.0	0.0

4-4 不同学历的读者经常阅读的杂志/ Frequently Read Magazines by Educational Levels

注：本题为多选题，合计百分比可能超过 100%（Multiple answers）

	人数 Number	知音 Bosom Friend	家庭 Family	读者 Duzhe	女友 Woman Friend	家庭医生 Family Doctor	故事会 Story Selection Journal	青年文摘 Qing Nian Wen Zhai
样本 Sample	**315**	**32.7**	**21.3**	**18.7**	**9.2**	**7.9**	**7.6**	**6.0**
小学及以下 Primary School or Below	11	18.2	27.3	9.1	0.0	0.0	9.1	9.1
初中 Middle School	79	41.8	20.3	6.3	7.6	11.4	10.1	5.1
高中/中专/技校 HighSchool/Technical Secondary School	138	32.6	19.6	16.7	11.6	8.7	10.9	5.8
大学专科 2-3 Year College	63	27.0	23.8	33.3	11.1	3.2	0.0	6.3
大学本科 4-5 Year College	23	26.1	26.1	39.1	0.0	8.7	0.0	8.7
研究生或以上 Graduate or Above	1	0.0	0.0	0.0	0.0	0.0	0.0	0.0

续前表 continued

	人数 Number	党员文摘 Dang Yuan Wen Zhai	军事天地 Jun Shi Tian Di	兵器知识 Bing Qi Zhi Shi	家庭生活指南 Family Life Guid	世界时装之苑 ELLE	科幻世界 Science & Fiction World	大众电影 Popular Film	足球俱乐部 Football Club
样本 Sample	315	3.5	2.9	2.9	2.9	2.2	2.2	2.2	2.2
小学及以下 Primary School or Below	11	0.0	0.0	0.0	0.0	0.0	0.0	0.0	9.1
初中 Middle School	79	1.3	1.3	2.5	5.1	2.5	0.0	2.5	1.3
高中/中专/技校 High School/Technical Secondary School	138	4.3	4.3	2.9	2.2	1.4	3.6	1.4	1.4
大学专科 2-3 Year College	63	4.8	1.6	4.8	1.6	3.2	1.6	4.8	3.2
大学本科 4-5 Year College	23	4.3	4.3	0.0	4.3	4.3	4.3	0.0	4.3
研究生或以上 Graduate or Above	1	0.0	0.0	0.0	0.0	0.0	0.0	0.0	0.0

4-5 经常阅读的杂志的主要来源/ Sources of Obtaining the Frequently Read Magazine

注：本题为多选题，合计百分比可能超过 100%（Multiple answers）

	人数 Number	家中订阅 subscribed by my family	单位订阅 subscribed by work unit	报摊购买 bought from vender	赠阅 given as gift	借阅 borrowed
知音 Bosom Friend	101	6.9	7.9	69.3	2.0	15.8
家庭 Family	67	14.9	10.4	49.3	1.5	23.9
读者 Duzhe	59	3.4	8.5	72.9	0.0	15.3
女友 Woman Friend	29	0.0	6.9	62.1	3.4	27.6
家庭医生 Family Doctor	24	12.5	4.2	58.3	0.0	25.0
故事会 Story Selection Journal	24	12.5	4.2	50.0	0.0	33.3
青年文摘 Qing Nian Wen Zhai	19	0.0	5.3	78.9	0.0	15.8
党员文摘 Dang Yuan Wen Zhai	12	25.0	50.0	0.0	0.0	8.3
军事天地 Jun Shi Tian Di	9	0.0	22.2	66.7	0.0	11.1
兵器知识 Bing Qi Zhi Shi	9	0.0	22.2	66.7	0.0	11.1
家庭生活指南 Family Life Guide	9	22.2	22.2	44.4	0.0	22.2

4-6 不同消费者层平时是否接触杂志媒介/ Magazine Reading by Market Segments

4-6-1 时尚流行指标/ Fads Popular Index

	人数 Number	从来不看 never	看 yes
样本 Sample	615	50.7	49.3
平实生活指向 simple living orientation	368	41.0	59.0
时尚流行指向 fashion orientation	247	65.2	34.8

4-6-2 广告态度指标/ Advertising Attitude Index

	人数 Number	从来不看 never	看 yes
样本 Sample	617	50.9	49.1
广告淡漠指向 indifferent orientation	167	47.3	52.7
中间层 medium	366	53.0	47.0
信赖广告指向 loyal orientation	84	48.8	51.2

4-7 不同消费者层经常阅读的杂志/ Frequently Reading Magazines by Market Segments

4-7-1 时尚流行指标/ Fads Popular Index

注：本题为多选题，合计百分比超过 100%（Multiple answers）

	人数 Number	知音 Bosom Friend	家庭 Family	读者 Duzhe	女友 Women's Friend	家庭医生 Family Doctor	故事会 Story Selection Journal	青年文摘 QingNian Wen Zhai
样本 Sample	**312**	**33.0**	**21.2**	**18.9**	**9.0**	**8.0**	**7.7**	**5.8**
平实生活指向 simple living orientation	151	30.5	23.2	21.2	7.3	7.3	7.9	7.3
时尚流行指向 fashion orientation	161	35.4	19.3	16.8	10.6	8.7	7.5	4.3

续前表 continued

	人数 Number	党员文摘 Dang Yuan Wen Zhai	军事天地 Jun Shi Tian Di	兵器知识 Bing Qi Zhi Shi	家庭生活指南 Family Life Guide	科幻世界 Science & Fiction World	世界时装之苑 ELLE	足球俱乐部 Football Club	大众电影 Popular Film
样本 Sample	**312**	**3.5**	**3.2**	**2.9**	**2.9**	**1.9**	**2.2**	**2.2**	**2.2**
平实生活指向 simple living orientation	151	6.6	3.3	4.0	3.3	2.6	0.7	2.0	0.7
时尚流行指向 fashion orientation	161	0.6	3.1	1.9	2.5	1.2	3.7	2.5	3.7

4-7-2 广告态度指标/ Advertising Attitude Index

注：本题为多选题，合计百分比超过 100%（Multiple answers）

	人数 Number	知音 Bosom Friend	家庭 Family	读者 Duzhe	女友 Women's Friend	家庭医生 Family Doctor	故事会 Story Selection Journal	青年文摘 Qing Nian Wen Zhai
样本 Sample	**314**	**32.8**	**21.0**	**18.5**	**9.2**	**8.0**	**7.6**	**5.7**
广告淡漠指向 indifferent orientation	79	30.4	21.5	20.3	5.1	8.9	10.1	6.3
中间层 medium	194	32.5	20.6	19.6	10.8	7.2	6.2	5.7
信赖广告指向 loyal orientation	41	39.0	22.0	9.8	9.8	9.8	9.8	4.9

续前表 continued

	人数 Number	党员文摘 Dang Yuan Wen Zhai	军事天地 Jun Shi Tian Di	兵器知识 Bing Qi Zhi Shi	家庭生活指南 Family Life Guide	科幻世界 Science & Fiction World	世界时装之苑 ELLE	足球俱乐部 Football Club	大众电影 Popular Film
样本 Sample	**314**	**3.5**	**3.2**	**2.9**	**2.9**	**2.2**	**1.9**	**2.2**	**2.2**
广告淡漠指向 indifferent orientation	79	2.5	5.1	3.8	3.8	2.5	1.3	2.5	2.5
中间层 medium	194	3.1	2.6	2.6	1.5	2.6	2.6	2.6	2.6
信赖广告指向 loyal orientation	41	7.3	2.4	2.4	7.3	0.0	0.0	0.0	0.0

● 武汉 / Wuhan

4-1 样本、男性各年龄层、女性各年龄层平时是否接触杂志媒介/ Magazine Reading by the Whole Sample, Age and Gender Groups

	人数 Number	看 yes	从来不看 never
样本 Sample	625	58.6	41.4
男性 Male	303	55.4	44.6
16~24 岁 Age	65	64.6	35.4
25~34 岁 Age	86	69.8	30.2
35~44 岁 Age	78	38.5	61.5
45~54 岁 Age	51	52.9	47.1
55~60 岁 Age	23	39.1	60.9
女性 Female	322	61.5	38.5
16~24 岁 Age	66	80.3	19.7
25~34 岁 Age	95	64.2	35.8
35~44 岁 Age	77	57.1	42.9
45~54 岁 Age	58	58.6	41.4
55~60 岁 Age	26	23.1	76.9

4-2 经常阅读的杂志排名/ Ranking of the Frequently Reading Magazines

注：本题为多选题，合计百分比超过 100%（Multiple answers）

排名 Brand Ranking	杂志 Magazines	人次 Person-time	百分比 Percent
1	知音 Bosom Friend	124	34.1
2	读者 Duzhe	82	22.5
3	家庭 Family	61	16.8
4	幸福 Xingfu	49	13.5
5	家庭医生 Family Doctor	37	10.2
6	青年文摘 Qing Nian Wen Zhai	28	7.7
7	故事会 Story Selection Journal	21	5.8
8	女友 Woman Friend	20	5.5
9	人之初 Renzhichu	11	3.0
10	时尚 Trends	9	2.5
10	大众软件 Pop Soft	9	2.5
10	爱情婚姻家庭 Love Marriage and Family	9	2.5
11	上海服饰 Shanghai Style	8	2.2
11	警笛 Jingdi	8	2.2

n=364

4-3 样本、男性各年龄层、女性各年龄层经常阅读的杂志/ Frequently Read Magazines by the Whole Sample, Age and Gender Groups

注：本题为多选题，合计百分比超过 100%（Multiple answers）

	人数 Number	知音 Bosom Friend	读者 Duzhe	家庭 Family	幸福 Xingfu	家庭医生 Family Doctor	青年文摘 Qing Nian Wen Zhai	故事会 Story Selection Journal
样本 Sample	364	34.1	22.5	16.8	13.5	10.2	7.7	5.8
男性 Male	167	24.0	25.7	13.2	11.4	6.0	9.6	7.8
16~24 岁 Age	42	7.1	47.6	7.1	0.0	0.0	14.3	7.1
25~34 岁 Age	60	28.3	21.7	13.3	16.7	8.3	11.7	10.0
35~44 岁 Age	29	41.4	20.7	24.1	10.3	10.3	3.4	0.0
45~54 岁 Age	27	18.5	11.1	14.8	11.1	7.4	7.4	11.1
55~60 岁 Age	9	33.3	11.1	0.0	33.3	0.0	0.0	11.1
女性 Female	197	42.6	19.8	19.8	15.2	13.7	6.1	4.1
16~24 岁 Age	52	34.6	25.0	5.8	13.5	9.6	7.7	5.8
25~34 岁 Age	61	50.8	23.0	18.0	13.1	13.1	3.3	4.9
35~44 岁 Age	44	43.2	13.6	36.4	15.9	18.2	2.3	2.3
45~54 岁 Age	34	44.1	11.8	26.5	20.6	17.6	11.8	2.9
55~60 岁 Age	6	16.7	33.3	0.0	16.7	0.0	16.7	0.0

续前表 continued

	人数 Number	女友 Woman Friend	人之初 Renzhichu	时尚 Trends	大众软件 Pop Soft	爱情婚姻家庭 Love Marriage and Family	上海服饰 Shanghai Style	警笛 Jingdi
样本 Sample	364	5.5	3.0	2.5	2.5	2.5	2.2	2.2
男性 Male	167	2.4	0.0	0.6	4.8	1.8	0.6	3.0
16~24 岁 Age	42	4.8	0.0	0.0	14.3	0.0	0.0	0.0
25~34 岁 Age	60	3.3	0.0	1.7	3.3	3.3	1.7	1.7
35~44 岁 Age	29	0.0	0.0	0.0	0.0	3.4	0.0	3.4
45~54 岁 Age	27	0.0	0.0	0.0	0.0	0.0	0.0	7.4
55~60 岁 Age	9	0.0	0.0	0.0	0.0	0.0	0.0	11.1
女性 Female	197	8.1	5.6	4.1	0.5	3.0	3.6	1.5
16~24 岁 Age	52	9.6	5.8	11.5	1.9	0.0	7.7	0.0
25~34 岁 Age	61	14.8	6.6	3.3	0.0	3.3	4.9	0.0
35~44 岁 Age	44	4.5	4.5	0.0	0.0	4.5	0.0	2.3
45~54 岁 Age	34	0.0	5.9	0.0	0.0	5.9	0.0	2.9
55~60 岁 Age	6	0.0	0.0	0.0	0.0	0.0	0.0	16.7

4-4 不同学历的读者经常阅读的杂志/ Frequently Read Magazines by Educational Levels

注：本题为多选题，合计百分比超过 100%（Multiple answers）

	人数 Number	知音 Bosom Friend	读者 Duzhe	家庭 Family	幸福 Xingfu	家庭医生 Family Doctor	青年文摘 Qing Nian Wen Zhai	故事会 Story Selection Journal
样本 Sample	364	34.1	22.5	16.8	13.5	10.2	7.7	5.8
小学及以下 Primary School or Below	3	33.3	0.0	33.3	33.3	33.3	0.0	0.0
初中 Middle School	65	36.9	12.3	23.1	20.0	7.7	12.3	20.0
高中/中专/技校 High School/Technical Secondary School	163	31.9	23.3	14.7	16.0	14.1	4.9	3.1
大学专科 2-3 Year College	83	42.2	27.7	19.3	9.6	7.2	6.0	3.6
大学本科 4-5 Year College	46	23.9	28.3	10.9	2.2	4.3	13.0	0.0
研究生或以上 Graduate or Above	4	25.0	0.0	0.0	0.0	0.0	25.0	0.0

续前表 continued

	人数 Number	女友 Woman Friend	人之初 Renzhichu	时尚 Trends	大众软件 Pop Soft	爱情婚姻家庭 Love Marriage and Family	上海服饰 Shanghai Style	警笛 Jingdi
样本 Sample	364	5.5	3.0	2.5	2.5	2.5	2.2	2.2
小学及以下 Primary School or Below	3	0.0	0.0	0.0	0.0	0.0	0.0	0.0
初中 Middle School	65	4.6	6.2	0.0	0.0	1.5	0.0	1.5
高中/中专/技校 High School/Technical Secondary School	163	6.1	2.5	1.2	2.5	3.1	2.5	3.1
大学专科 2-3 Year College	83	4.8	3.6	7.2	4.8	2.4	2.4	2.4
大学本科 4-5 Year College	46	6.5	0.0	2.2	2.2	2.2	4.3	0.0
研究生或以上 Graduate or Above	4	0.0	0.0	0.0	0.0	0.0	0.0	0.0

4-5 经常阅读的杂志的主要来源/ Sources of Obtaining the Frequently Read Magazine

注：本题为多选题，合计百分比可能超过 100%（Multiple answers）

	人数 Number	家中订阅 subscribed by my family	单位订阅 subscribed by work unit	报摊购买 bought from vender	赠阅 given as gift	借阅 borrowed
知音 Bosom Friend	122	8.2	6.6	57.4	2.5	26.2
读者 Duzhe	82	13.4	0.0	68.3	1.2	17.1
家庭 Family	61	13.1	6.6	52.5	1.6	26.2
幸福 Xingfu	49	18.4	14.3	38.8	2.0	26.5
家庭医生 Family Doctor	37	16.2	2.7	67.6	2.7	10.8
青年文摘 Qing Nian Wen Zhai	27	3.7	7.4	70.4	0.0	18.5
故事会 Story Selection Journal	20	5.0	10.0	85.0	0.0	5.0
女友 Woman Friend	20	5.0	0.0	65.0	0.0	30.0
人之初 Renzhichu	11	0.0	9.1	63.6	0.0	27.3
时尚 Trends	9	0.0	11.1	77.8	0.0	11.1
大众软件 Pop Soft	9	0.0	0.0	55.6	0.0	44.4
爱情婚姻家庭 Love Marriage and Family	9	11.1	11.1	33.3	0.0	44.4

4-6 不同消费者层平时是否接触杂志媒介/ Magazine Reading by Market Segments

4-6-1 时尚流行指标/ Fads Popular Index

	人数 Number	从来不看 never	看 yes
样本 Sample	622	58.7	41.3
平实生活指向 simple living orientation	324	51.5	48.5
时尚流行指向 fashion orientation	298	66.4	33.6

4-6-2 广告态度指标/ Advertising Attitude Index

	人数 Number	从来不看 never	看 yes
样本 Sample	624	58.5	41.5
广告淡漠指向 indifferent orientation	185	49.2	50.8
中间层 medium	368	63.6	36.4
信赖广告指向 loyal orientation	71	56.3	43.7

4-7 不同消费者层经常阅读的杂志/ Frequently Reading Magazines by Market Segments

4-7-1 时尚流行指标/ Fads Popular Index

注：本题为多选题，合计百分比超过 100%（Multiple answers）

	人数 Number	知音 Bosom Friend	读者 Duzhe	家庭 Family	幸福 Xingfu	家庭医生 Family Doctor	青年文摘 Qing Nian Wen Zhai	故事会 Story Selection Journal
样本 Sample	363	34.2	22.6	16.8	13.5	10.2	7.4	5.8
平实生活指向 simple living orientation	166	33.1	25.3	18.1	11.4	9.6	6.6	5.4
时尚流行指向 fashion orientation	197	35.0	20.3	15.7	15.2	10.7	8.1	6.1

续前表 continued

	人数 Number	女友 Woman Friend	人之初 Renzhichu	时尚 Trends	大众软件 Pop Soft	爱情婚姻家庭 Love Marriage and Family	上海服饰 Shanghai Style	警笛 JingDi
样本 Sample	363	5.5	3.0	2.5	2.5	2.5	2.2	2.2
平实生活指向 simple living orientation	166	3.6	2.4	0.6	3.0	1.8	0.6	2.4
时尚流行指向 fashion orientation	197	7.1	3.6	4.1	2.0	3.0	3.6	2.0

4-7-2 广告态度指标/ Advertising Attitude Index

注：本题为多选题，合计百分比超过 100%（Multiple answers）

	人数 Number	知音 Bosom Friend	读者 Duzhe	家庭 Family	幸福 Xingfu	家庭医生 Family Doctor	青年文摘 Qing Nian Wen Zhai	故事会 Story Selection Journal
样本 Sample	363	34.2	22.6	16.8	13.5	10.2	7.4	5.8
广告淡漠指向 indifferent orientation	90	27.8	27.8	16.7	16.7	4.4	8.9	3.3
中间层 medium	233	36.5	21.0	17.2	13.3	12.4	7.3	5.6
信赖广告指向 loyal orientation	40	35.0	20.0	15.0	7.5	10.0	5.0	12.5

续前表 continued

	人数 Number	女友 Woman Friend	人之初 Renzhichu	时尚 Trends	大众软件 Pop Scft	爱情婚姻家庭 Love Marriage and Family	上海服饰 Shanghai Style	警笛 JingDi
样本 Sample	363	5.5	3.0	2.5	2.5	2.5	2.2	2.2
广告淡漠指向 indifferent orientation	90	8.9	2.2	0.0	1.1	2.2	0.0	1.1
中间层 medium	233	4.7	3.4	3.0	3.0	3.0	3.4	2.6
信赖广告指向 loyal orientation	40	2.5	2.5	5.0	2.5	0.0	0.0	2.5

● 西安 / Xi'an

4-1 样本、男性各年龄层、女性各年龄层平时是否接触杂志媒介/ Magazine Reading by the Whole Sample, Age and Gender Groups

	人数 Number	看 yes	从来不看 never
样本 Sample	600	59.3	40.7
男性 Male	301	53.5	46.5
16~24 岁 Age	64	64.1	35.9
25~34 岁 Age	91	50.5	49.5
35~44 岁 Age	76	44.7	55.3
45~54 岁 Age	46	56.5	43.5
55~60 岁 Age	24	58.3	41.7
女性 Female	299	65.2	34.8
16~24 岁 Age	61	85.2	14.8
25~34 岁 Age	90	73.3	26.7
35~44 岁 Age	74	52.7	47.3
45~54 岁 Age	49	53.1	46.9
55~60 岁 Age	25	48.0	52.0

4-2 经常阅读的杂志排名/ Ranking of the Frequently Reading Magazines

注：本题为多选题，合计百分比超过 100%（Multiple answers）

排名 Brand Ranking	杂志 Magazines	人次 Person-time	百分比 Percent
1	读者 Duzhe	126	35.6
2	家庭 Family	75	21.2
3	女友 Woman Friend	71	20.1
4	青年文摘 Qing Nian Wen Zhai	47	13.3
5	知音 Bosom Friend	38	10.7
6	家庭医生 Family Doctor	29	8.2

n=354

4-3 样本、男性各年龄层、女性各年龄层经常阅读的杂志/ Frequently Read Magazines by the Whole Sample, Age and Gender Groups

注：本题为多选题，合计百分比超过 100%（Multiple answers）

	人数 Number	读者 Duzhe	家庭 Family	女友 Woman Friend	青年文摘 Qing Nian Wen Zhai	知音 Bosom Friend	家庭医生 Family Doctor
样本 Sample	354	35.6	21.2	20.1	13.3	10.7	8.2
男性 Male	159	42.1	12.6	8.8	14.5	6.9	5.7
16~24 岁 Age	40	47.5	2.5	7.5	27.5	5.0	0.0
25~34 岁 Age	45	42.2	13.3	8.9	20.0	2.2	8.9
35~44 岁 Age	34	50.0	23.5	14.7	5.9	17.6	11.8
45~54 岁 Age	26	34.6	11.5	7.7	3.8	7.7	0.0
55~60 岁 Age	14	21.4	14.3	0.0	0.0	0.0	7.1
女性 Female	195	30.3	28.2	29.2	12.3	13.8	10.3
16~24 岁 Age	52	46.2	7.7	42.3	28.8	7.7	1.9
25~34 岁 Age	66	31.8	31.8	28.8	9.1	21.2	9.1
35~44 岁 Age	39	23.1	33.3	23.1	7.7	15.4	17.9
45~54 岁 Age	26	15.4	46.2	26.9	0.0	7.7	15.4
55~60 岁 Age	12	8.3	41.7	0.0	0.0	8.3	16.7

4-4 不同学历的读者经常阅读的杂志/ Frequently Read Magazines by Educational Levels

注：本题为多选题，合计百分比超过 100%（Multiple answers）

	人数 Number	读者 Duzhe	家庭 Family	女友 Woman Friend	青年文摘 Qing Nian Wen Zhai	知音 Bosom Friend	家庭医生 Family Doctor
样本 Sample	351	35.6	21.4	19.9	13.1	10.8	8.3
小学及以下 Primary School or Below	1	100.0	100.0	0.0	0.0	100.0	0.0
初中 Middle School	45	17.8	33.3	15.6	4.4	15.6	4.4
高中/中专/技校 High School/Technical Secondary School	167	31.7	22.2	22.2	13.2	12.0	11.4
大学专科 2-3 Year College	85	45.9	14.1	21.2	15.3	5.9	5.9
大学本科 4-5 Year College	48	47.9	20.8	14.6	16.7	10.4	6.3
研究生或以上 Graduate or Above	5	20.0	0.0	20.0	20.0	0.0	0.0

4-5 经常阅读的杂志的主要来源/ Sources of Obtaining the Frequently Read Magazine

注：本题为多选题，合计百分比可能超过 100%（Multiple answers）

	人数 Number	家中订阅 subscribed by my family	单位订阅 subscribed by work unit	报摊购买 bought from vender	赠阅 given as gift	借阅 borrowed
读者Duzhe	124	16.1	9.7	58.9	0.8	14.5
家庭Family	75	33.3	9.3	52.0	1.3	4.0
女友Woman Friend	70	4.3	4.3	62.9	4.3	24.3
青年文摘 Qing Nian Wen Zhai	46	0.0	2.2	76.1	2.2	19.6
知音Bosom Friend	37	8.1	5.4	81.1	2.7	2.7
家庭医生 Family Doctor	29	20.7	17.2	51.7	0.0	10.3

4-6 不同消费者层平时是否接触杂志媒介/ Magazine Reading by Market Segments

4-6-1 时尚流行指标/ Fads Popular Index

	人数 Number	从来不看 never	看 yes
样本 Sample	**598**	**59.4**	**40.6**
平实生活指向 simple living orientation	340	53.5	46.5
时尚流行指向 fashion orientation	258	67.1	32.9

4-6-2 广告态度指标/ Advertising Attitude Index

	人数 Number	从来不看 never	看 yes
样本 Sample	**596**	**59.2**	**40.8**
广告淡漠指向 indifferent orientation	184	54.3	45.7
中间层 medium	333	61.6	38.4
信赖广告指向 loyal orientation	79	60.8	39.2

4-7 不同消费者层经常阅读的杂志/ Frequently Reading Magazines by Market Segments

4-7-1 时尚流行指标/ Fads Popular Index

注：本题为多选题，合计百分比超过 100%（Multiple answers）

	人数 Number	读者 Duzhe	家庭 Family	女友 Woman Friend	青年文摘 Qing Nian Wen Zhai	知音 Bosom Friend	家庭医生 Family Doctor
样本 Sample	**353**	**35.7**	**21.0**	**20.1**	**13.3**	**10.8**	**8.2**
平实生活指向 simple living orientation	181	31.5	24.3	21.0	13.8	8.8	10.5
时尚流行指向 fashion orientation	172	40.1	17.4	19.2	12.8	12.8	5.8

4-7-2 广告态度指标/ Advertising Attitude Index

注：本题为多选题，合计百分比超过 100%（Multiple answers）

	人数 Number	读者 Duzhe	家庭 Family	女友 Woman Friend	青年文摘 Qing Nian Wen Zhai	知音 Bosom Friend	家庭医生 Family Doctor
样本 Sample	**351**	**35.6**	**21.1**	**19.9**	**13.4**	**10.8**	**8.3**
广告淡漠指向 indifferent orientation	100	35.0	21.0	20.0	14.0	14.0	10.0
中间层 medium	203	35.5	21.7	18.7	12.3	9.9	7.9
信赖广告指向 loyal orientation	48	37.5	18.8	25.0	16.7	8.3	6.3

● 沈阳 / Shenyang

4-1 样本、男性各年龄层、女性各年龄层平时是否接触杂志媒介/ Magazine Reading by the Whole Sample, Age and Gender Groups

	人数 Number	看 yes	从来不看 never
样本 Sample	**596**	**48.8**	**51.2**
男性 Male	**297**	**47.5**	**52.5**
16~24 岁 Age	64	57.8	42.2
25~34 岁 Age	88	54.5	45.5
35~44 岁 Age	76	36.8	63.2
45~54 岁 Age	46	37.0	63.0
55~60 岁 Age	23	47.8	52.2
女性 Female	**299**	**50.2**	**49.8**
16~24 岁 Age	64	59.4	40.6
25~34 岁 Age	88	59.1	40.9
35~44 岁 Age	76	46.1	53.9
45~54 岁 Age	47	34.0	66.0
55~60 岁 Age	24	37.5	62.5

4-2 经常阅读的杂志排名/ Ranking of the Frequently Reading Magazines

注：本题为多选题，合计百分比超过 100%（Multiple answers）

排名 Brand Ranking	杂志 Magazines	人次 Person-time	百分比 Percent
1	读者 Duzhe	66	22.7
2	家庭 Family	37	12.7
3	知音 Bosom Friend	32	11.0
4	女友 Woman Friend	28	9.6
5	当代歌坛 Modern Music Field	19	6.5
6	故事会 Story Selection Journal	16	5.5
6	人生十六七 Ren Sheng Shi Liu Qi	16	5.5
7	当代工人 Modern Workers	11	3.8
8	青年文摘 Qing Nian Wen Zhai	10	3.4
8	妇女 Women	10	3.4
8	共产党员 Gong Chan Dang Yuan	10	3.4
9	大众生活 Da Zhong Sheng Huo	8	2.7
9	家庭医生 Family Doctor	8	2.7
9	中国妇女 Women of China	8	2.7

n=291

4-3 样本、男性各年龄层、女性各年龄层经常阅读的杂志/ Frequently Read Magazines by the Whole Sample, Age and Gender Groups

注：本题为多选题，合计百分比超过 100%（Multiple answers）

	人数 Number	读者 Duzhe	家庭 Family	知音 Bosom Friend	女友 Woman Friend	当代歌坛 Modern Music Field	故事会 Story Selection Journal	人生十六七 Ren Sheng Shi Liu Qi
样本 Sample	291	22.7	12.7	11.0	9.6	6.5	5.5	5.5
男性 Male	141	22.7	9.9	5.7	2.1	6.4	7.1	5.0
16~24 岁 Age	37	13.5	8.1	8.1	2.7	24.3	2.7	18.9
25~34 岁 Age	48	35.4	10.4	4.2	4.2	0.0	14.6	0.0
35~44 岁 Age	28	21.4	7.1	0.0	0.0	0.0	3.6	0.0
45~54 岁 Age	17	11.8	17.6	5.9	0.0	0.0	5.9	0.0
55~60 岁 Age	11	18.2	9.1	18.2	0.0	0.0	0.0	0.0
女性 Female	150	22.7	15.3	16.0	16.7	6.7	4.0	6.0
16~24 岁 Age	38	15.8	2.6	10.5	10.5	26.3	7.9	23.7
25~34 岁 Age	52	28.8	15.4	15.4	23.1	0.0	0.0	0.0
35~44 岁 Age	35	28.6	31.4	20.0	17.1	0.0	5.7	0.0
45~54 岁 Age	16	12.5	12.5	18.8	12.5	0.0	6.3	0.0
55~60 岁 Age	9	11.1	11.1	22.2	11.1	0.0	0.0	0.0

续前表 continued

	人数 Number	当代工人 Modern Workers	青年文摘 Qing Nian Wen Zhai	妇女 Women	共产党员 Gong Chan Dang Yuan	大众生活 Da Zhong Sheng Huo	家庭医生 Family Doctor	中国妇女 Women of China
样本 Sample	291	3.8	3.4	3.4	3.4	2.7	2.7	2.7
男性 Male	141	4.3	5.0	0.7	5.0	0.7	0.0	0.7
16~24 岁 Age	37	0.0	5.4	0.0	0.0	0.0	0.0	0.0
25~34 岁 Age	48	6.3	8.3	2.1	0.0	0.0	0.0	0.0
35~44 岁 Age	28	0.0	3.6	0.0	3.6	3.6	0.0	3.6
45~54 岁 Age	17	11.8	0.0	0.0	23.5	0.0	0.0	0.0
55~60 岁 Age	11	9.1	0.0	0.0	18.2	0.0	0.0	0.0
女性 Female	150	3.3	2.0	6.0	2.0	4.7	5.3	4.7
16~24 岁 Age	38	0.0	5.3	0.0	0.0	5.3	5.3	0.0
25~34 岁 Age	52	3.8	1.9	5.8	3.8	7.7	9.6	5.8
35~44 岁 Age	35	8.6	0.0	5.7	0.0	0.0	0.0	8.6
45~54 岁 Age	16	0.0	0.0	18.8	6.3	6.3	0.0	0.0
55~60 岁 Age	9	0.0	0.0	11.1	0.0	0.0	11.1	11.1

4-4 不同学历的读者经常阅读的杂志/ Frequently Read Magazines by Educational Levels

注：本题为多选题，合计百分比超过 100%（Multiple answers）

	人数 Number	读者 Duzhe	家庭 Family	知音 Bosom Friend	女友 Woman Friend	当代歌坛 Modern Music Field	故事会 Story Selection Journal	人生十六七 Ren Sheng Shi Liu Qi
样本 Sample	291	22.7	12.7	11.0	9.6	6.5	5.5	5.5
小学及以下 Primary School or Below	0	0.0	0.0	0.0	0.0	0.0	0.0	0.0
初中 Middle School	66	19.7	9.1	12.1	6.1	3.0	4.5	1.5
高中/中专/技校 High School/Technical Secondary School	125	13.6	12.0	9.6	6.4	11.2	7.2	10.4
大学专科 2-3 Year College	62	32.3	16.1	14.5	14.5	4.8	3.2	3.2
大学本科 4-5 Year College	36	41.7	16.7	8.3	19.4	0.0	5.6	0.0
研究生或以上 Graduate or Above	2	50.0	0.0	0.0	0.0	0.0	0.0	0.0

续前表 continued

	人数 Number	当代工人 Modern Workers	青年文摘 Qing Nian Wen Zhai	妇女 Women	共产党员 Gong Chan Dang Yuan	大众生活 Da Zhong Sheng Huo	家庭医生 Family Doctor	中国妇女 Women of China
样本 Sample	291	3.8	3.4	3.4	3.4	2.7	2.7	2.7
小学及以下 Primary School or Below	0	0.0	0.0	0.0	0.0	0.0	0.0	0.0
初中 Middle School	66	6.1	0.0	3.0	6.1	4.5	1.5	6.1
高中/中专/技校 High School/Technical Secondary School	125	3.2	3.2	4.0	3.2	1.6	2.4	3.2
大学专科 2-3 Year College	62	1.6	4.8	3.2	1.6	4.8	3.2	0.0
大学本科 4-5 Year College	36	5.6	8.3	2.8	2.8	0.0	5.6	0.0
研究生或以上 Graduate or Above	2	0.0	0.0	0.0	0.0	0.0	0.0	0.0

4-5 经常阅读的杂志的主要来源/ Sources of Obtaining the Frequently Read Magazines

注：本题为多选题，合计百分比可能超过 100%（Multiple answers）

	人数 Number	家中订阅 subscribed by my family	单位订阅 subscribed by work unit	报摊购买 bought from vender	赠阅 given as gift	借阅 borrowed
读者 Duzhe	66	3.0	13.6	74.2	1.5	10.6
家庭 Family	32	12.5	15.6	46.9	3.1	21.9
知音 Bosom Friend	31	3.2	6.5	67.7	3.2	19.4
女友 Woman Friend	27	11.1	14.8	70.4	0.0	3.7
当代歌坛 Modern Music Field	19	0.0	0.0	73.7	5.3	21.1
故事会 Story Selection Journal	16	12.5	0.0	75.0	0.0	12.5
人生十六七 Ren Sheng Shi Liu Qi	16	12.5	18.8	43.8	0.0	25.0
当代工人 Modern Workers	11	0.0	90.9	9.1	0.0	0.0
青年文摘 Qing Nian Wen Zhai	10	0.0	20.0	70.0	0.0	20.0
妇女 Women	10	10.0	40.0	40.0	0.0	10.0
共产党员 Gong Chan Dang Yuan	10	20.0	80.0	0.0	0.0	0.0

4-6 不同消费者层平时是否接触杂志媒介/ Magazine Reading by Market Segments

4-6-1 时尚流行指标/ Fads Popular Index

	人数 Number	从来不看 never	看 yes
样本 Sample	596	48.8	51.2
平实生活指向 simple living orientation	289	45.7	54.3
时尚流行指向 fashion orientation	307	51.8	48.2

4-6-2 广告态度指标/ Advertising Attitude Index

	人数 Number	从来不看 never	看 yes
样本 Sample	596	48.8	51.2
广告淡漠指向 indifferent orientation	170	43.5	56.5
中间层 medium	351	50.7	49.3
信赖广告指向 loyal orientation	75	52.0	48.0

4-7 不同消费者层经常阅读的杂志/ Frequently Reading Magazines by Market Segments

4-7-1 时尚流行指标/ Fads Popular Index

注：本题为多选题，合计百分比超过 100%（Multiple answers）

	人数 Number	读者 Duzhe	家庭 Family	知音 Bosom Friend	女友 Woman Friend	当代歌坛 Modern Music Field	故事会 Story Selection Journal	人生十六七 Ren Sheng Shi Liu Qi
样本 Sample	291	22.7	12.7	11.0	9.6	6.5	5.5	5.5
平实生活指向 simple living orientation	132	21.2	10.6	9.1	9.8	3.8	7.6	5.3
时尚流行指向 fashion orientation	159	23.9	14.5	12.6	9.4	8.8	3.8	5.7

续前表 continued

	人数 Number	当代工人 Modern Workers	青年文摘 Qing Nian Wen Zhai	妇女 Women	共产党员 Gong Chan Dang Yuan	大众生活 Da Zhong Sheng Huo	家庭医生 Family Doctor	中国妇女 Women of China
样本 Sample	291	3.8	3.4	3.4	3.4	2.7	2.7	2.7
平实生活指向 simple living orientation	132	3.8	3.0	1.5	3.8	0.0	3.0	1.5
时尚流行指向 fashion orientation	159	3.8	3.8	5.0	3.1	5.0	2.5	3.8

4-7-2 广告态度指标/ Advertising Attitude Index

注：本题为多选题，合计百分比超过 100%（Multiple answers）

	人数 Number	读者 Duzhe	家庭 Family	知音 Bosom Friend	女友 Woman Friend	当代歌坛 Modern Music Field	故事会 Story Selection Journal	人生十六七 Ren Sheng Shi Liu Qi
样本 Sample	291	22.7	12.7	11.0	9.6	6.5	5.5	5.5
广告淡漠指向 indifferent orientation	74	21.6	12.2	12.2	16.2	9.5	6.8	6.8
中间层 medium	178	24.2	11.2	10.7	7.3	5.1	5.1	5.6
信赖广告指向 loyal orientation	39	17.9	20.5	10.3	7.7	7.7	5.1	2.6

续前表 continued

	人数 Number	当代工人 Modern Workers	青年文摘 Qing Nian Wen Zhai	妇女 Women	共产党员 Gong Chan Dang Yuan	大众生活 Da Zhong Sheng Huo	家庭医生 Family Doctor	中国妇女 Women of China
样本 Sample	291	3.8	3.4	3.4	3.4	2.7	2.7	2.7
广告淡漠指向 indifferent orientation	74	1.4	5.4	0.0	4.1	4.1	1.4	1.4
中间层 medium	178	5.1	3.4	5.1	3.4	1.7	2.8	3.4
信赖广告指向 loyal orientation	39	2.6	0.0	2.6	2.6	5.1	5.1	2.6

5.电影 / Movies

● 北京 / Beijing

5-1 样本、男性各年龄层、女性各年龄层最近一年去电影院的频率/ Frequencies of Going to Cinema Last Year by the Whole Sample, Age and Gender Groups

	人数 Number	一周 1 次以上 once a week or over	每月 2-3 次 2 or 3 times a month	每月 1 次 once a month	2-3 个月 1 次 once every 2-3 months	半年 1 次左右 once every half a year	1 年 1 次或以下 once every year or below	没去过 never
样本 Sample	1012	0.7	2.1	4.8	10.9	17.6	11.2	52.8
男性 Male	504	0.6	1.8	6.5	11.3	15.3	11.3	53.2
16~24 岁 Age	105	1.0	2.9	13.3	18.1	21.9	19.0	23.8
25~34 岁 Age	151	0.7	3.3	9.3	15.2	18.5	7.9	45.0
35~44 岁 Age	131	0.8	0.8	3.1	6.9	11.5	11.5	65.6
45~54 岁 Age	77	0.0	0.0	1.3	5.2	10.4	11.7	71.4
55~60 岁 Age	40	0.0	0.0	0.0	5.0	7.5	2.5	85.0
女性 Female	508	0.8	2.4	3.1	10.4	19.9	11.0	52.4
16~24 岁 Age	108	0.0	5.6	3.7	20.4	35.2	11.1	24.1
25~34 岁 Age	150	0.7	0.7	6.0	9.3	20.7	13.3	49.3
35~44 岁 Age	124	2.4	1.6	1.6	8.9	17.7	7.3	60.5
45~54 岁 Age	84	0.0	2.4	1.2	7.1	8.3	14.3	66.7
55~60 岁 Age	42	0.0	2.4	0.0	0.0	7.1	7.1	83.3

5-2 样本、男性各年龄层、女性各年龄层喜欢看的电影片类型/ The Most Favorite Movies Last Year by the Whole Sample, Age and Gender Groups

注：本题为多选题，合计百分比超过 100%（Multiple answers）

	人数 Number	美国影片 American movies	其他国外影片 other foreign movies	港台影片 movies from HK. Taiwan	国产影片 local movies	其他 others
样本 Sample	473	61.9	16.1	34.9	29.6	3.8
男性 Male	232	67.2	15.1	31.5	28.4	3.0
16~24 岁 Age	78	71.8	11.5	47.4	15.4	3.8
25~34 岁 Age	83	74.7	15.7	31.3	27.7	2.4
35~44 岁 Age	43	60.5	16.3	11.6	37.2	2.3
45~54 岁 Age	22	50.0	18.2	13.6	54.5	4.5
55~60 岁 Age	6	16.7	33.3	33.3	50.0	0.0
女性 Female	241	56.8	17.0	38.2	30.7	4.6
16~24 岁 Age	82	47.6	23.2	58.5	12.2	2.4
25~34 岁 Age	75	78.7	14.7	22.7	29.3	4.0
35~44 岁 Age	49	51.0	14.3	32.7	40.8	8.2
45~54 岁 Age	28	50.0	14.3	28.6	57.1	3.6
55~60 岁 Age	7	0.0	0.0	42.9	85.7	14.3

5-3 不同学历的观众对电影片类型的偏好/ The Most Favorite Movies Last Year by Educational Levels

注：本题为多选题，合计百分比超过 100%（Multiple answers）

	人数 Number	美国影片 American movies	其他国外影片 other foreign movies	港台影片 movies from HK. Taiwan	国产影片 local movies	其他 others
样本 Sample	473	61.9	16.1	34.9	29.6	3.8
小学及以下 Primary School or Below	4	25.0	0.0	25.0	75.0	0.0
初中 Middle School	49	36.7	14.3	40.8	55.1	2.0
高中/中专/技校 High School/Technical Secondary School	206	51.0	14.1	45.1	26.2	3.9
大学专科 2-3 Year College	113	77.0	18.6	30.1	29.2	2.7
大学本科 4-5 Year College	84	81.0	20.2	17.9	20.2	6.0
研究生或以上 Graduate or Above	15	80.0	13.3	6.7	33.3	6.7

5-4 不同消费者层去电影院的频率/ Frequencies of Going to Cinema by Market Segments

5-4-1 时尚流行指标/ Fads Popular Index

	人数 Number	一周 1 次以上 once a week or over	每月 2-3 次 2 or 3 times a month	每月 1 次 once a month	2-3 个月 1 次 once every 2 or 3 months	半年 1 次左右 once every half a year	1 年 1 次或以下 once every year or below	没去过 never
样本 Sample	998	0.7	2.0	4.9	10.9	17.4	11.3	52.7
平实生活指向 simple living orientation	491	0.8	1.4	3.3	8.1	15.1	11.8	59.5
时尚流行指向 fashion orientation	507	0.6	2.6	6.5	13.6	19.7	10.8	46.2

5-4-2 广告态度指标/ Advertising Attitude Index

	人数 Number	一周 1 次以上 once a week or over	每月 2-3 次 2 or 3 times a month	每月 1 次 once a month	2-3 个月 1 次 once every 2 or 3 months	半年 1 次左右 once every half a year	1 年 1 次或以下 once every year or below	没去过 never
样本 Sample	994	0.7	2.0	4.7	10.7	17.8	11.4	52.7
广告淡漠指向 indifferent orientation	289	1.0	1.7	3.5	11.8	15.9	12.5	53.6
中间层 medium	572	0.7	2.1	5.4	10.7	19.2	11.2	50.7
信赖广告指向 loyal orientation	133	0.0	2.3	4.5	8.3	15.8	9.8	59.4

5-5 不同消费者层对电影片类型的偏好/ The Most Favorite Movies by Market Segments

5-5-1 时尚流行指标/ Fads Popular Index

注：本题为多选题，合计百分比超过 100%（Multiple answers）

	人数 Number	美国影片 American movies	其他国外影片 other foreign movies	港台影片 movies from HK. Taiwan	国产影片 local movies	其他 others
样本 Sample	467	62.3	16.1	34.5	29.6	3.9
平实生活指向 simple living orientation	196	63.3	20.9	24.0	29.1	3.6
时尚流行指向 fashion crientation	271	61.6	12.5	42.1	29.9	4.1

5-5-2 广告态度指标/ Advertising Attitude Index

注：本题为多选题，合计百分比超过 100%（Multiple answers）

	人数 Number	美国影片 American movies	其他国外影片 other foreign movies	港台影片 movies from HK. Taiwan	国产影片 local movies	其他 others
样本 Sample	465	61.9	16.1	34.2	29.7	3.9
广告淡漠指向 indifferent orientation	132	59.1	21.2	30.3	29.5	3.0
中间层 medium	279	62.4	14.7	34.1	30.5	4.3
信赖广告指向 loyal orientation	54	66.7	11.1	44.4	25.9	3.7

● 上海 / Shanghai

5-1 样本、男性各年龄层、女性各年龄层最近一年去电影院的频率/ Frequencies of Going to Cinema Last Year by the Whole Sample, Age and Gender Groups

	人数 Number	一周 1 次或以上 once a week or over	每月 2-3 次 2 or 3 times a month	每月 1 次 once a month	2-3 个月 1 次 once every 2-3 months	半年 1 次左右 once every half year	1 年 1 次或以下 once every year or below	没去过 never
样本 Sample	1014	1.0	2.9	7.8	13.9	15.9	10.0	48.6
男性 Male	509	1.0	3.7	9.0	13.6	14.7	9.6	48.3
16~24 岁 Age	109	0.9	7.3	11.9	28.4	15.6	9.2	26.6
25~34 岁 Age	146	1.4	4.1	14.4	15.1	18.5	9.6	37.0
35~44 岁 Age	130	0.8	2.3	3.8	7.7	13.8	10.0	61.5
45~54 岁 Age	85	1.2	2.4	7.1	5.9	9.4	7.1	67.1
55~60 岁 Age	39	0.0	0.0	2.6	2.6	12.8	15.4	66.7
女性 Female	505	1.0	2.0	6.5	14.3	17.0	10.3	48.9
16~24 岁 Age	108	1.9	4.6	14.8	26.9	22.2	10.2	19.4
25~34 岁 Age	144	0.7	2.1	7.6	20.1	18.8	9.0	41.7
35~44 岁 Age	130	0.8	1.5	1.5	6.9	14.6	13.1	61.5
45~54 岁 Age	82	1.2	0.0	4.9	4.9	11.0	9.8	68.3
55~60 岁 Age	41	0.0	0.0	0.0	2.4	17.1	7.3	73.2

5-2 样本、男性各年龄层、女性各年龄层喜欢看的电影片类型/ The Most Favorite Movies by the Whole Sample, Age and Gender Groups

注：本题为多选题，合计百分比超过 100%（Multiple answers）

	人数 Number	美国影片 American movies	其他国外影片 other foreign movies	港台影片 movies from HK.Taiwan	国产影片 local movies	其他 others
样本 Sample	519	54.7	21.6	48.7	19.5	2.5
男性 Male	262	62.2	22.9	44.3	22.1	1.1
16~24 岁 Age	80	63.8	21.3	57.5	18.8	0.0
25~34 岁 Age	91	70.3	26.4	44.0	14.3	2.2
35~44 岁 Age	50	58.0	18.0	34.0	26.0	0.0
45~54 岁 Age	28	50.0	28.6	35.7	35.7	3.6
55~60 岁 Age	13	38.5	15.4	23.1	53.8	0.0
女性 Female	257	47.1	20.2	53.3	16.7	3.9
16~24 岁 Age	86	45.3	16.3	67.4	12.8	1.2
25~34 岁 Age	84	57.1	27.4	50.0	10.7	4.8
35~44 岁 Age	50	36.0	22.0	46.0	22.0	2.0
45~54 岁 Age	26	38.5	11.5	42.3	26.9	15.4
55~60 岁 Age	11	54.5	9.1	27.3	45.5	0.0

5-3 不同学历的观众对电影片类型的偏好/ The Most Favorite Movies by Educational Levels

注：本题为多选题，合计百分比超过 100%（Multiple answers）

	人数 Number	美国影片 American movies	其他国外影片 other foreign movies	港台影片 movies from HK. Taiwan	国产影片 local movies	其他 others
样本 Sample	517	54.5	21.5	48.7	19.5	2.5
小学及以下 Primary School or Below	7	42.9	0.0	42.9	14.3	14.3
初中 Middle School	83	31.3	15.7	57.8	37.3	1.2
高中/中专/技校 High School/Technical Secondary School	270	55.2	20.0	54.1	14.8	2.2
大学专科 2-3 Year College	101	62.4	26.7	41.6	15.8	5.0
大学本科 4-5 Year College	53	73.6	32.1	20.8	24.5	0.0
研究生或以上 Graduate or Above	3	66.7	0.0	66.7	0.0	0.0

5-4 不同消费者层去电影院的频率/ Frequencies of Going to Cinema by Market Segments

5-4-1 时尚流行指标/ Fads Popular Index

	人数 Number	一周 1 次以上 once a week or over	每月 2-3 次 2 or 3 times a month	每月 1 次 once a month	2-3 个月 1 次 once every 2 or 3 months	半年 1 次左右 once every half year	1 年 1 次或以下 once every year or below	没去过 never
样本 Sample	1005	1.0	2.9	7.9	13.8	15.8	10.0	48.7
平实生活指向 simple living orientation	471	0.8	1.5	5.1	10.4	13.0	10.6	58.6
时尚流行指向 fashion orientation	534	1.1	4.1	10.3	16.9	18.4	9.4	39.9

5-4-2 广告态度指标/ Advertising Attitude Index

	人数 Number	一周 1 次以上 once a week or over	每月 2-3 次 2 or 3 times a month	每月 1 次 once a month	2-3 个月 1 次 once every 2 or 3 months	半年 1 次左右 once every half year	1 年 1 次或以下 once every year or below	没去过 never
样本 Sample	1002	1.0	2.8	7.8	13.9	15.8	10.1	48.7
广告淡漠指向 indifferent orientation	256	0.8	0.8	6.3	18.0	11.3	9.4	53.5
中间层 medium	611	1.1	3.4	7.9	12.3	17.2	10.8	47.3
信赖广告指向 loyal orientation	135	0.7	3.7	10.4	13.3	17.8	8.1	45.9

5-5 不同消费者层对电影片类型的偏好/ The Most Favorite Movies by Market Segments

5-5-1 时尚流行指标/ Fads Popular Index

注：本题为多选题，合计百分比超过 100%（Multiple answers）

	人数 Number	美国影片 American movies	其他国外影片 other foreign movies	港台影片 movies from HK.Taiwan	国产影片 local movies	其他 others
样本 Sample	514	54.5	21.6	48.8	19.5	2.5
平实生活指向 simple living orientation	195	49.2	22.1	39.0	27.2	3.1
时尚流行指向 fashion crientation	319	57.7	21.3	54.9	14.7	2.2

5-5-2 广告态度指标/ Advertising Attitude Index

注：本题为多选题，合计百分比超过 100%（Multiple answers）

	人数 Number	美国影片 American movies	其他国外影片 other foreign movies	港台影片 movies from HK.Taiwan	国产影片 local movies	其他 others
样本 Sample	512	54.7	21.7	48.6	19.3	2.5
广告淡漠指向 indifferent orientation	119	48.7	27.7	42.0	19.3	4.2
中间层 medium	320	56.9	19.4	50.0	18.8	1.9
信赖广告指向 loyal orientation	73	54.8	21.9	53.4	21.9	2.7

● 广州 / Guangzhou

5-1 样本、男性各年龄层、女性各年龄层最近一年去电影院的频率/ Frequencies of Going to Cinema Last Year by the Whole Sample, Age and Gender Groups

	人数 Number	一周 1 次或以上 once a week or over	每月 2-3 次 2 or 3 times a month	每月 1 次 once a month	2-3 个月 1 次 once every 2-3 months	半年 1 次左右 once every half year	1 年 1 次或以下 once every year or below	没去过 never
样本 Sample	1033	0.7	2.7	3.9	7.8	10.5	9.3	65.2
男性 Male	499	0.4	2.8	4.0	9.8	10.8	6.8	65.3
16~24 岁 Age	106	1.9	4.7	6.6	17.9	17.0	10.4	41.5
25~34 岁 Age	150	0.0	5.3	4.7	15.3	12.7	4.7	57.3
35~44 岁 Age	127	0.0	0.0	3.1	0.8	11.8	5.5	78.7
45~54 岁 Age	73	0.0	0.0	2.7	5.5	2.7	9.6	79.5
55~60 岁 Age	43	0.0	2.3	0.0	4.7	0.0	4.7	88.4
女性 Female	534	0.9	2.6	3.7	6.0	10.1	11.6	65.0
16~24 岁 Age	112	1.8	3.6	8.9	22.3	16.1	17.9	29.5
25~34 岁 Age	158	0.6	3.2	3.8	3.2	10.1	10.8	68.4
35~44 岁 Age	136	0.7	3.7	1.5	1.5	10.3	8.8	73.5
45~54 岁 Age	87	1.1	0.0	1.1	0.0	6.9	11.5	79.3
55~60 岁 Age	41	0.0	0.0	2.4	0.0	0.0	7.3	90.2

5-2 样本、男性各年龄层、女性各年龄层喜欢看的电影片类型/ The Most Favorite Movies by the Whole Sample, Age and Gender Groups

注：本题为多选题，合计百分比超过 100%（Multiple answers）

	人数 Number	美国影片 American movies	其他国外影片 other foreign movies	港台影片 movies from HK. Taiwan	国产影片 local movies	其他 others
样本 Sample	356	46.3	19.7	60.7	16.9	3.7
男性 Male	172	58.7	18.6	59.3	14.0	3.5
16~24 岁 Age	61	49.2	16.4	75.4	8.2	4.9
25~34 岁 Age	64	68.8	23.4	50.0	10.9	1.6
35~44 岁 Age	27	66.7	14.8	51.9	18.5	0.0
45~54 岁 Age	15	46.7	13.3	46.7	33.3	13.3
55~60 岁 Age	5	40.0	20.0	60.0	40.0	0.0
女性 Female	184	34.8	20.7	62.0	19.6	3.8
16~24 岁 Age	79	36.7	13.9	78.5	11.4	2.5
25~34 岁 Age	50	28.0	32.0	54.0	22.0	8.0
35~44 岁 Age	34	47.1	17.6	52.9	14.7	2.9
45~54 岁 Age	17	29.4	17.6	41.2	47.1	0.0
55~60 岁 Age	4	0.0	50.0	0.0	75.0	0.0

5-3 不同学历的观众对电影片类型的偏好/ The Most Favorite Movies by Educational Levels

注：本题为多选题，合计百分比超过 100%（Multiple answers）

	人数 Number	美国影片 American movies	其他国外影片 other foreign movies	港台影片 movies from HK. Taiwan	国产影片 local movies	其他 others
样本 Sample	353	46.2	19.8	60.9	16.1	3.7
小学及以下 Primary School or Below	5	40.0	40.0	60.0	20.0	0.0
初中 Middle School	46	34.8	15.2	78.3	19.6	2.2
高中/中专/技校 High School/Technical Secondary School	178	39.3	15.7	68.5	12.4	3.4
大学专科 2-3 Year College	59	57.6	32.2	42.4	23.7	1.7
大学本科 4-5 Year College	60	63.3	20.0	45.0	16.7	8.3
研究生或以上 Graduate or Above	5	60.0	40.0	40.0	20.0	0.0

5-4 不同消费者层去电影院的频率/ Frequencies of Going to Cinema by Market Segments

5-4-1 时尚流行指标/ Fads Popular Index

	人数 Number	一周 1 次或以上 once a week or over	每月 2-3 次 2 or 3 times a month	每月 1 次 once a month	2-3 个月 1 次 once every 2 or 3 months	半年 1 次左右 once every half year	1 年 1 次或以下 once every year or below	没去过 never
样本 Sample	1021	0.7	2.7	3.8	7.8	10.5	9.4	65.0
平实生活指向 simple living orientation	518	0.8	1.2	2.3	5.4	9.1	7.7	73.6
时尚流行指向 fashion orientation	503	0.6	4.4	5.4	10.3	11.9	11.1	56.3

5-4-2 广告态度指标/ Advertising Attitude Index

	人数 Number	一周 1 次或以上 once a week or over	每月 2-3 次 2 or 3 times a month	每月 1 次 once a month	2-3 个月 1 次 once every 2 or 3 months	半年 1 次左右 once every half year	1 年 1 次或以下 once every year or below	没去过 never
样本 Sample	1021	0.7	2.7	3.9	7.6	10.6	9.2	65.2
广告淡漠指向 indifferent orientation	334	0.6	1.2	1.8	5.7	9.0	8.7	73.1
中间层 medium	593	0.8	3.4	4.6	8.8	12.0	9.8	60.7
信赖广告指向 loyal orientation	94	0.0	4.3	7.4	7.4	7.4	7.4	66.0

5-5 不同消费者层对电影片类型的偏好/ The Most Favorite Movies by Market Segments

5-5-1 时尚流行指标/ Fads Popular Index

注：本题为多选题，合计百分比超过 100%（Multiple answers）

	人数 Number	美国影片 American movies	其他国外影片 other foreign movies	港台影片 movies from HK. Taiwan	国产影片 local movies	其他 others
样本 Sample	353	46.5	19.8	60.9	16.7	3.7
平实生活指向 simple living orientation	135	48.9	23.0	51.9	22.2	5.9
时尚流行指向 fashion orientation	218	45.0	17.9	66.5	13.3	2.3

5-5-2 广告态度指标/ Advertising Attitude Index

注：本题为多选题，合计百分比超过 100%（Multiple answers）

	人数 Number	美国影片 American movies	其他国外影片 other foreign movies	港台影片 movies from HK. Taiwan	国产影片 local movies	其他 others
样本 Sample	351	46.4	19.7	60.7	17.1	3.7
广告淡漠指向 indifferent orientation	89	46.1	19.1	62.9	13.5	4.5
中间层 medium	230	43.9	21.7	58.7	18.3	3.5
信赖广告指向 loyal orientation	32	65.6	6.3	68.8	18.8	3.1

● 重庆 / Chongqing

5-1 样本、男性各年龄层、女性各年龄层最近一年去电影院的频率/ Frequencies of Going to Cinema last Year by the Whole Sample, Age and Gender Groups

	人数 Number	一周 1 次以上 once a week or over	每月 2-3 次 2 or 3 times a month	每月 1 次 once a month	2-3 个月 1 次 once every 2-3 months	半年 1 次左右 once every half year	1 年 1 次或以下 once every year or below	没去过 never
样本 Sample	623	0.8	2.6	6.3	7.5	10.3	6.4	66.1
男性 Male	313	0.3	2.9	6.7	6.7	9.9	7.0	66.5
16~24 岁 Age	64	0.0	7.8	14.1	14.1	15.6	9.4	39.1
25~34 岁 Age	93	0.0	3.2	8.6	10.8	8.6	9.7	59.1
35~44 岁 Age	75	0.0	0.0	4.0	1.3	10.7	2.7	81.3
45~54 岁 Age	54	0.0	1.9	0.0	1.9	3.7	3.7	88.9
55~60 岁 Age	27	3.7	0.0	3.7	0.0	11.1	11.1	70.4
女性 Female	310	1.3	2.3	5.8	8.4	10.6	5.8	65.8
16~24 岁 Age	64	4.7	7.8	14.1	18.8	15.6	3.1	35.9
25~34 岁 Age	90	1.1	0.0	5.6	13.3	11.1	6.7	62.2
35~44 岁 Age	73	0.0	2.7	4.1	2.7	5.5	4.1	80.8
45~54 岁 Age	60	0.0	0.0	1.7	0.0	10.0	6.7	81.7
55~60 岁 Age	23	0.0	0.0	0.0	0.0	13.0	13.0	73.9

5-2 样本、男性各年龄层、女性各年龄层喜欢看的电影片类型/ The Most Favorite Movies by the Whole Sample, Age and Gender Groups

注：本题为多选题，合计百分比超过 100%（Multiple answers）

	人数 Number	美国影片 American movies	其他国外影片 other foreign movies	港台影片 movies from HK. Taiwan	国产影片 local movies	其他 others
样本 Sample	210	49.5	17.1	49.5	23.8	2.4
男性 Male	104	62.5	10.6	49.0	21.2	1.0
16~24 岁 Age	39	66.7	10.3	61.5	10.3	0.0
25~34 岁 Age	37	73.0	8.1	48.6	16.2	2.7
35~44 岁 Age	14	57.1	14.3	42.9	28.6	0.0
45~54 岁 Age	6	33.3	16.7	33.3	16.7	0.0
55~60 岁 Age	8	25.0	12.5	12.5	87.5	0.0
女性 Female	106	36.8	23.6	50.0	26.4	3.8
16~24 岁 Age	41	48.8	31.7	63.4	9.8	4.9
25~34 岁 Age	34	32.4	26.5	55.9	23.5	0.0
35~44 岁 Age	14	42.9	14.3	50.0	21.4	0.0
45~54 岁 Age	11	0.0	9.1	9.1	81.8	9.1
55~60 岁 Age	6	33.3	0.0	0.0	66.7	16.7

5-3 不同学历的观众对电影片类型的偏好/ The Most Favorite Movies by Educational Levels

注：本题为多选题，合计百分比超过 100%（Multiple answers）

	人数 Number	美国影片 American movies	其他国外影片 other foreign movies	港台影片 movies from HK. Taiwan	国产影片 local movies	其他 others
样本 Sample	209	49.3	16.7	49.8	23.9	2.4
小学及以下 Primary School or Below	11	27.3	0.0	36.4	63.6	0.0
初中 Middle School	36	33.3	8.3	41.7	38.9	0.0
高中/中专/技校 HighSchool/Technical Secondary School	98	44.9	18.4	62.2	17.3	4.1
大学专科 2-3 Year College	44	68.2	25.0	45.5	11.4	0.0
大学本科 4-5 Year College	19	68.4	15.8	21.1	36.8	5.3
研究生或以上 Graduate or Above	1	100.0	0.0	0.0	0.0	0.0

5-4 不同消费者层去电影院的频率/ Frequencies of Going to Cinema by Market Segments

5-4-1 时尚流行指标/ Fads Popular Index

	人数 Number	一周 1 次以上 once a week or over	每月 2-3 次 2 or 3 times a month	每月 1 次 once a month	2-3 个月 1 次 once every 2 or 3 months	半年 1 次左右 once every half year	1 年 1 次或以下 once every year or below	没去过 never
样本 Sample	616	0.8	2.6	6.3	7.3	10.2	6.3	66.4
平实生活指向 simple living orientation	369	0.8	1.1	4.3	3.5	8.7	6.2	75.3
时尚流行指向 fashion orientation	247	0.8	4.9	9.3	13.0	12.6	6.5	53.0

5-4-2 广告态度指标/ Advertising Attitude Index

	人数 Number	一周 1 次以上 once a week or over	每月 2-3 次 2 or 3 times a month	每月 1 次 once a month	2-3 个月 1 次 once every 2 or 3 months	半年 1 次左右 once every half year	1 年 1 次或以下 once every year or below	没去过 never
样本 Sample	618	0.8	2.6	6.3	7.6	10.4	6.5	65.9
广告淡漠指向 indifferent orientation	167	1.8	3.6	4.2	5.4	9.0	7.8	68.3
中间层 medium	367	0.5	1.9	7.4	8.4	11.7	5.4	64.6
信赖广告指向 loyal orientation	84	0.0	3.6	6.0	8.3	7.1	8.3	66.7

5-5 不同消费者层对电影片类型的偏好/ The Most Favorite Movies by Market Segments

5-5-1 时尚流行指标/ Fads Popular Index

注：本题为多选题，合计百分比超过 100%（Multiple answers）

	人数 Number	美国影片 American movies	其他国外影片 other foreign movies	港台影片 movies from HK .Taiwan	国产影片 local movies	其他 others
样本 Sample	206	49.5	17.0	49.5	23.8	2.4
平实生活指向 simple living orientation	91	50.5	8.8	36.3	37.4	2.2
时尚流行指向 fashion orientation	115	48.7	23.5	60.0	13.0	2.6

5-5-2 广告态度指标/ Advertising Attitude Index

注：本题为多选题，合计百分比超过 100%（Multiple answers）

	人数 Number	美国影片 American movies	其他国外影片 other foreign movies	港台影片 movies from HK. Taiwan	国产影片 local movies	其他 others
样本 Sample	210	49.5	17.1	49.5	23.8	2.4
广告淡漠指向 indifferent orientation	53	47.2	15.1	41.5	24.5	5.7
中间层 medium	129	54.3	17.8	51.9	22.5	1.6
信赖广告指向 loyal orientation	28	32.1	17.9	53.6	28.6	0.0

● 武汉 / Wuhan

5-1 样本、男性各年龄层、女性各年龄层最近一年去电影院的频率/ Frequencies of Going to Cinema Last Year by the Whole Sample, Age and Gender Groups

	人数 Number	一周1次或以上 once a week or over	每月2-3次 2 or 3 times a month	每月1次 once a month	2-3个月1次 once every 2-3 months	半年1次左右 once every half year	1年1次或以下 once every year or below	没去过 never
样本 Sample	626	0.8	2.1	4.2	9.3	11.0	6.7	66.0
男性 Male	304	0.7	1.6	4.6	11.5	12.2	6.3	63.2
16~24 岁 Age	65	0.0	3.1	7.7	23.1	16.9	12.3	36.9
25~34 岁 Age	87	1.1	2.3	5.7	16.1	10.3	4.6	59.8
35~44 岁 Age	78	1.3	1.3	2.6	5.1	10.3	3.8	75.6
45~54 岁 Age	51	0.0	0.0	3.9	3.9	13.7	3.9	74.5
55~60 岁 Age	23	0.0	0.0	0.0	0.0	8.7	8.7	82.6
女性 Female	322	0.9	2.5	3.7	7.1	9.9	7.1	68.6
16~24 岁 Age	66	1.5	4.5	10.6	16.7	21.2	9.1	36.4
25~34 岁 Age	95	2.1	5.3	2.1	8.4	11.6	8.4	62.1
35~44 岁 Age	77	0.0	0.0	1.3	2.6	5.2	7.8	83.1
45~54 岁 Age	58	0.0	0.0	3.4	3.4	3.4	5.2	84.5
55~60 岁 Age	26	0.0	0.0	0.0	0.0	3.8	0.0	96.2

5-2 样本、男性各年龄层、女性各年龄层喜欢看的电影片类型/ The Most Favorite Movies by the Whole Sample, Age and Gender Groups

注：本题为多选题，合计百分比超过 100%（Multiple answers）

	人数 Number	美国影片 American movies	其他国外影片 other foreign movies	港台影片 movies from HK .Taiwan	国产影片 local movies	其他 others
样本 Sample	211	55.9	22.3	45.5	23.2	5.7
男性 Male	111	63.1	18.9	39.6	21.6	6.3
16~24 岁 Age	40	67.5	17.5	60.0	15.0	2.5
25~34 岁 Age	35	71.4	20.0	37.1	11.4	5.7
35~44 岁 Age	19	63.2	36.8	10.5	21.1	5.3
45~54 岁 Age	13	38.5	0.0	38.5	61.5	15.4
55~60 岁 Age	4	25.0	0.0	0.0	50.0	25.0
女性 Female	100	48.0	26.0	52.0	25.0	5.0
16~24 岁 Age	42	52.4	28.6	61.9	14.3	4.8
25~34 岁 Age	36	52.8	33.3	41.7	22.2	2.8
35~44 岁 Age	12	41.7	8.3	58.3	50.0	8.3
45~54 岁 Age	9	22.2	11.1	44.4	44.4	11.1
55~60 岁 Age	1	0.0	0.0	0.0	100.0	0.0

5-3 不同学历的观众对电影片类型的偏好/ The Most Favorite Movies by Educational Levels

注：本题为多选题，合计百分比超过 100%（Multiple answers）

	人数 Number	美国影片 American movies	其他国外影片 other foreign movies	港台影片 movies from HK .Taiwan	国产影片 local movies	其他 others
样本 Sample	210	56.2	21.9	45.2	23.3	5.7
小学及以下 Primary School or Below	2	0.0	0.0	50.0	100.0	0.0
初中 Middle School	20	40.0	5.0	55.0	30.0	15.0
高中/中专/技校 High School/Technical Secondary School	98	54.1	24.5	43.9	23.5	3.1
大学专科 2-3 Year College	58	56.9	25.9	46.6	20.7	6.9
大学本科 4-5 Year College	28	78.6	21.4	42.9	17.9	3.6
研究生或以上 Graduate or Above	4	50.0	0.0	25.0	25.0	25.0

5-4 不同消费者层去电影院的频率/ Frequencies of Going to Cinema by Market Segments

5-4-1 时尚流行指标/ Fads Popular Index

	人数 Number	一周 1 次以上 once a week or over	每月 2-3 次 2 or 3 times a month	每月 1 次 once a month	2-3 个月 1 次 once every 2 or 3 months	半年 1 次左右 once every half year	1 年 1 次或以下 once every year or below	没去过 never
样本 Sample	623	0.8	2.1	4.2	9.1	11.1	6.7	66.0
平实生活指向 simple living orientation	325	0.3	1.8	1.8	8.0	9.5	6.5	72.0
时尚流行指向 fashion orientation	298	1.3	2.3	6.7	10.4	12.8	7.0	59.4

5-4-2 广告态度指标/ Advertising Attitude Index

	人数 Number	一周 1 次以上 once a week or over	每月 2-3 次 2 or 3 times a month	每月 1 次 once a month	2-3 个月 1 次 once every 2 or 3 months	半年 1 次左右 once every half year	1 年 1 次或以下 once every year or below	没去过 never
样本 Sample	625	0.8	2.1	4.2	9.1	11.0	6.7	66.1
广告淡漠指向 indifferent orientation	186	0.0	2.2	1.6	8.6	7.5	7.0	73.1
中间层 medium	368	1.1	2.2	4.3	8.7	12.5	6.3	64.9
信赖广告指向 loyal orientation	71	1.4	1.4	9.9	12.7	12.7	8.5	53.5

5-5 不同消费者层对电影片类型的偏好/ The Most Favorite Movies by Market Segments

5-5-1 时尚流行指标/ Fads Popular Index

注：本题为多选题，合计百分比超过 100%（Multiple answers）

	人数 Number	美国影片 American movies	其他国外影片 other foreign movies	港台影片 movies from HK.Taiwan	国产影片 local movies	其他 others
样本 Sample	210	55.7	22.4	45.2	23.3	5.7
平实生活指向 simple living orientation	91	53.8	24.2	44.0	26.4	7.7
时尚流行指向 fashion orientation	119	57.1	21.0	46.2	21.0	4.2

5-5-2 广告态度指标/ Advertising Attitude Index

注：本题为多选题，合计百分比超过 100%（Multiple answers）

	人数 Number	美国影片 American movies	其他国外影片 other foreign movies	港台影片 movies from HK.Taiwan	国产影片 local movies	其他 others
样本 Sample	210	55.7	22.4	45.2	23.3	5.7
广告淡漠指向 indifferent orientation	50	50.0	20.0	34.0	20.0	14.0
中间层 medium	127	57.5	26.0	44.9	26.0	3.1
信赖广告指向 loyal orientation	33	57.6	12.1	63.6	18.2	3.0

● 西安 / Xi'an

5-1 样本、男性各年龄层、女性各年龄层最近一年去电影院的频率/ Frequencies of Going to Cinema by the Whole Sample, Age and Gender Groups

	人数 Number	一周 1 次或以上 once a week or over	每月 2-3 次 2 or 3 times a month	每月 1 次 once a month	2-3 个月 1 次 once every 2-3 months	半年 1 次左右 once every half year	1 年 1 次或以下 once every year or below	没去过 never
样本 Sample	600	2.2	3.8	4.8	8.2	13.8	9.7	57.5
男性 Male	301	4.3	4.3	5.3	8.0	13.0	9.3	55.8
16~24 岁 Age	64	7.8	7.8	10.9	20.3	18.8	10.9	23.4
25~34 岁 Age	91	4.4	4.4	5.5	7.7	18.7	8.8	50.5
35~44 岁 Age	76	3.9	3.9	2.6	2.6	3.9	9.2	73.7
45~54 岁 Age	46	2.2	2.2	4.3	4.3	6.5	6.5	73.9
55~60 岁 Age	24	0.0	0.0	0.0	0.0	16.7	12.5	70.8
女性 Female	299	0.0	3.3	4.3	8.4	14.7	10.0	59.2
16~24 岁 Age	61	0.0	8.2	9.8	13.1	23.0	8.2	37.7
25~34 岁 Age	90	0.0	4.4	4.4	12.2	15.6	8.9	54.4
35~44 岁 Age	74	0.0	1.4	4.1	4.1	10.8	14.9	64.9
45~54 岁 Age	49	0.0	0.0	0.0	4.1	12.2	8.2	75.5
55~60 岁 Age	25	0.0	0.0	0.0	4.0	8.0	8.0	80.0

5-2 样本、男性各年龄层、女性各年龄层喜欢看的电影片类型/ The Most Favorite Movies by the Whole Sample, Age and Gender Groups

注：本题为多选题，合计百分比超过 100%（Multiple answers）

	人数 Number	美国影片 American movies	其他国外影片 other foreign movies	港台影片 movies from HK. Taiwan	国产影片 local movies	其他 others
样本 Sample	253	46.6	11.5	41.1	36.8	2.8
男性 Male	131	50.4	13.7	42.0	31.3	3.8
16~24 岁 Age	49	49.0	14.3	51.0	18.4	2.0
25~34 岁 Age	44	52.3	11.4	40.9	34.1	4.5
35~44 岁 Age	19	57.9	15.8	36.8	42.1	5.3
45~54 岁 Age	12	58.3	25.0	25.0	33.3	8.3
55~60 岁 Age	7	14.3	0.0	28.6	71.4	0.0
女性 Female	122	42.6	9.0	40.2	42.6	1.6
16~24 岁 Age	38	44.7	15.8	55.3	21.1	0.0
25~34 岁 Age	41	53.7	4.9	41.5	29.3	2.4
35~44 岁 Age	26	34.6	3.8	34.6	65.4	0.0
45~54 岁 Age	12	16.7	16.7	16.7	83.3	8.3
55~60 岁 Age	5	40.0	0.0	0.0	100.0	0.0

5-3 不同学历的观众对电影片类型的偏好/ The Most Favorite Movies by Educational Levels

注：本题为多选题，合计百分比超过 100%（Multiple answers）

	人数 Number	美国影片 American movies	其他国外影片 other foreign movies	港台影片 movies from HK. Taiwan	国产影片 local movies	其他 others
样本 Sample	251	46.6	11.2	41.4	37.1	2.8
小学及以下 Primary School or Below	6	16.7	0.0	0.0	100.0	33.3
初中 Middle School	28	32.1	7.1	39.3	53.6	0.0
高中/中专/技校 High School/Technical Secondary School	111	38.7	13.5	46.8	33.3	0.9
大学专科 2-3 Year College	64	60.9	12.5	42.2	34.4	1.6
大学本科 4-5 Year College	38	60.5	7.9	34.2	26.3	7.9
研究生或以上 Graduate or Above	4	50.0	0.0	25.0	75.0	0.0

5-4 不同消费者层去电影院的频率/ Frequencies of Going to Cinema by Market Segments

5-4-1 时尚流行指标/ Fads Popular Index

	人数 Number	一周 1次或以上 once a week or over	每月 2-3 次 2 or 3 times a month	每月 1 次 once a month	2-3 个月 1 次 once every 2 or 3 months	半年 1 次左右 once every half year	1 年 1 次或以下 once every year or below	没去过 never
样本 Sample	598	2.2	3.8	4.8	8.2	13.9	9.7	57.4
平实生活指向 simple living orientation	340	1.2	2.4	4.7	5.6	12.1	11.5	62.6
时尚流行指向 fashion orientation	258	3.5	5.8	5.0	11.6	16.3	7.4	50.4

5-4-2 广告态度指标/ Advertising Attitude Index

	人数 Number	一周 1次或以上 once a week or over	每月 2-3 次 2 or 3 times a month	每月 1 次 once a month	2-3 个月 1 次 once every 2 or 3 months	半年 1 次左右 once every half year	1 年 1 次或以下 once every year or below	没去过 never
样本 Sample	596	2.2	3.9	4.9	8.2	13.8	9.7	57.4
广告淡漠指向 indifferent orientation	184	1.6	2.2	4.9	7.6	13.6	12.0	58.2
中间层 medium	333	2.4	4.2	4.8	8.4	15.3	9.0	55.9
信赖广告指向 loyal orientation	79	2.5	6.3	5.1	8.9	7.6	7.6	62.0

5-5 不同消费者层对电影片类型的偏好/ The Most Favorite Movies by Market Segments

5-5-1 时尚流行指标/ Fads Popular Index

注：本题为多选题，合计百分比超过 100%（Multiple answers）

	人数 Number	美国影片 American movies	其他国外影片 other foreign movies	港台影片 movies from HK. Taiwan	国产影片 local movies	其他 others
样本 Sample	253	46.6	11.5	41.1	36.8	2.8
平实生活指向 simple living orientation	126	41.3	7.9	33.3	42.9	3.2
时尚流行指向 fashion orientation	127	52.0	15.0	48.8	30.7	2.4

5-5-2 广告态度指标/ Advertising Attitude Index

注：本题为多选题，合计百分比超过 100%（Multiple answers）

	人数 Number	美国影片 American movies	其他国外影片 other foreign movies	港台影片 movies from HK. Taiwan	国产影片 local movies	其他 others
样本 Sample	252	46.4	11.5	40.9	36.9	2.8
广告淡漠指向 indifferent orientation	76	43.4	11.8	36.8	38.2	0.0
中间层 medium	146	45.9	12.3	43.8	38.4	4.1
信赖广告指向 loyal orientation	30	56.7	6.7	36.7	26.7	3.3

● 沈阳 / Shenyang

5-1 样本、男性各年龄层、女性各年龄层最近一年去电影院的频率/ Frequencies of Going to Cinema by the Whole Sample, Age and Gender Groups

	人数 Number	一周1次以上 once a week or over	每月2-3次 2 or 3 times a month	每月1次 once a month	2-3个月1次 once every 2-3 months	半年1次左右 once every half year	1年1次或以下 once every year or below	没去过 never
样本 Sample	**599**	**0.2**	**2.7**	**4.2**	**9.0**	**12.0**	**6.0**	**65.9**
男性 Male	**299**	**0.3**	**2.7**	**5.4**	**8.4**	**12.7**	**6.7**	**63.9**
16~24岁 Age	64	0.0	3.1	18.8	18.8	18.8	4.7	35.9
25~34岁 Age	89	1.1	2.2	2.2	9.0	16.9	11.2	57.3
35~44岁 Age	76	0.0	1.3	1.3	2.6	9.2	6.6	78.9
45~54岁 Age	46	0.0	4.3	2.2	4.3	6.5	4.3	78.3
55~60岁 Age	24	0.0	4.2	0.0	4.2	4.2	0.0	87.5
女性 Female	**300**	**0.0**	**2.7**	**3.0**	**9.7**	**11.3**	**5.3**	**68.0**
16~24岁 Age	64	0.0	7.8	10.9	21.9	28.1	6.3	25.0
25~34岁 Age	88	0.0	2.3	0.0	6.8	9.1	6.8	75.0
35~44岁 Age	76	0.0	1.3	1.3	6.6	5.3	3.9	81.6
45~54岁 Age	48	0.0	0.0	2.1	6.3	6.3	6.3	79.2
55~60岁 Age	24	0.0	0.0	0.0	4.2	4.2	0.0	91.7

5-2 样本、男性各年龄层、女性各年龄层喜欢看的电影片类型/ The Most Favorite Movies by the Whole Sample, Age and Gender Groups

注：本题为多选题，合计百分比超过100%（Multiple answers）

	人数 Number	美国影片 American movies	其他国外影片 other foreign movies	港台影片 movies from HK. Taiwan	国产影片 local movies	其他 others
样本 Sample	**203**	**34.0**	**19.7**	**63.1**	**29.1**	**2.5**
男性 Male	**107**	**43.0**	**18.7**	**62.6**	**25.2**	**0.9**
16~24岁 Age	41	46.3	17.1	70.7	19.5	0.0
25~34岁 Age	38	55.3	23.7	60.5	15.8	0.0
35~44岁 Age	15	33.3	6.7	53.3	40.0	6.7
45~54岁 Age	10	10.0	30.0	50.0	40.0	0.0
55~60岁 Age	3	0.0	0.0	66.7	100.0	0.0
女性 Female	**96**	**24.0**	**20.8**	**63.5**	**33.3**	**4.2**
16~24岁 Age	48	16.7	20.8	79.2	22.9	2.1
25~34岁 Age	22	45.5	27.3	59.1	18.2	9.1
35~44岁 Age	14	28.6	21.4	42.9	57.1	0.0
45~54岁 Age	10	10.0	10.0	30.0	80.0	10.0
55~60岁 Age	2	0.0	0.0	50.0	50.0	0.0

5-3 不同学历的观众对电影片类型的偏好/ The Most Favorite Movies by Educational Levels

注：本题为多选题，合计百分比超过100%（Multiple answers）

	人数 Number	美国影片 American movies	其他国外影片 other foreign movies	港台影片 movies from HK. Taiwan	国产影片 local movies	其他 others
样本 Sample	**203**	**34.0**	**19.7**	**63.1**	**29.1**	**2.5**
小学及以下 Primary School or Below	2	50.0	0.0	100.0	0.0	0.0
初中 Middle School	48	18.8	14.6	66.7	45.8	2.1
高中/中专/技校 High School/Technical Secondary School	91	27.5	14.3	74.7	27.5	2.2
大学专科 2-3 Year College	41	51.2	34.1	39.0	19.5	2.4
大学本科 4-5 Year College	20	65.0	25.0	50.0	15.0	5.0
研究生或以上 Graduate or Above	1	0.0	100.0	0.0	100.0	0.0

5-4 不同消费者层去电影院的频率/ Frequencies of Going to Cinema by Market Segments

5-4-1 时尚流行指标/ Fads Popular Index

	人数 Number	一周1次或以上 once a week or over	每月2-3次 2 or 3 times a month	每月1次 once a month	2-3个月1次 once every 2 or 3 months	半年1次左右 once every half year	1年1次或以下 once every year or below	没去过 never
样本 Sample	599	0.2	2.7	4.2	9.0	12.0	6.0	65.9
平实生活指向 simple living orientation	291	0.0	2.4	3.4	6.5	11.7	5.5	70.4
时尚流行指向 fashion orientation	308	0.3	2.9	4.9	11.4	12.3	6.5	61.7

5-4-2 广告态度指标/ Advertising Attitude Index

	人数 Number	一周1次或以上 once a week or over	每月2-3次 2 or 3 times a month	每月1次 once a month	2-3个月1次 once every 2 or 3 months	半年1次左右 once every half year	1年1次或以下 once every year or below	没去过 never
样本 Sample	599	0.2	2.7	4.2	9.0	12.0	6.0	65.9
广告淡漠指向 indifferent orientation	171	0.0	2.3	5.8	8.2	10.5	4.1	69.0
中间层 medium	353	0.0	2.3	4.0	9.1	13.9	7.6	63.2
信赖广告指向 loyal orientation	75	1.3	5.3	1.3	10.7	6.7	2.7	72.0

5-5 不同消费者层对电影片类型的偏好/ The Most Favorite Movies by Market Segments

5-5-1 时尚流行指标/ Fads Popular Index

注：本题为多选题，合计百分比超过 100%（Multiple answers）

	人数 Number	美国影片 American movies	其他国外影片 other foreign movies	港台影片 movies from HK. Taiwan	国产影片 local movies	其他 others
样本 Sample	203	34.0	19.7	63.1	29.1	2.5
平实生活指向 simple living orientation	86	31.4	20.9	57.0	37.2	3.5
时尚流行指向 fashion orientation	117	35.9	18.8	67.5	23.1	1.7

5-5-2 广告态度指标/ Advertising Attitude Index

注：本题为多选题，合计百分比超过 100%（Multiple answers）

	人数 Number	美国影片 American movies	其他国外影片 other foreign movies	港台影片 movies from HK. Taiwan	国产影片 local movies	其他 others
样本 Sample	203	34.0	19.7	63.1	29.1	2.5
广告淡漠指向 indifferent orientation	53	34.0	24.5	67.9	22.6	3.8
中间层 medium	129	32.6	18.6	62.8	32.6	0.8
信赖广告指向 loyal orientation	21	42.9	14.3	52.4	23.8	9.5

6.体育赛事 / Sports Events

● 北京 / Beijing

6-1 样本、男性各年龄层、女性各年龄层通过电视观看的体育比赛/ Proportion of the Watching Sports Games through TV by the Whole Sample, Age and Gender Groups

注：本题为多选题，合计百分比超过 100%（Multiple answers）

	人数 Number	足球 football	篮球 basketball	排球 volleyball	网球 tennis	保龄球 bowling
样本 Sample	1005	69.4	43.2	56.2	23.4	30.8
男性 Male	500	83.4	54.8	58.8	28.4	32.8
16~24 岁 Age	103	79.6	72.8	45.6	37.9	43.7
25~34 岁 Age	151	82.1	47.0	55.0	30.5	36.4
35~44 岁 Age	130	84.6	48.5	58.5	23.8	26.9
45~54 岁 Age	77	88.3	53.2	75.3	19.5	23.4
55~60 岁 Age	39	84.6	61.5	76.9	28.2	28.2
女性 Female	505	55.4	31.7	53.7	18.4	28.9
16~24 岁 Age	107	63.6	41.1	51.4	30.8	28.0
25~34 岁 Age	149	54.4	22.1	52.3	16.1	36.9
35~44 岁 Age	123	53.7	27.6	53.7	13.8	28.5
45~54 岁 Age	84	54.8	38.1	61.9	17.9	22.6
55~60 岁 Age	42	45.2	40.5	47.6	9.5	16.7

续前表 continued

	人数 Number	羽毛球 badminton	乒乓球 table tennis	台球 billiards	马拉松 Marathon	滑雪 skiing
样本 Sample	1005	31.2	54.6	30.8	24.1	12.9
男性 Male	500	35.2	58.4	41.4	26.0	13.2
16~24 岁 Age	103	35.9	54.4	59.2	19.4	11.7
25~34 岁 Age	151	30.5	55.0	42.4	21.9	10.6
35~44 岁 Age	130	39.2	56.2	33.8	29.2	18.5
45~54 岁 Age	77	33.8	70.1	37.7	29.9	5.2
55~60 岁 Age	39	41.0	66.7	23.1	41.0	25.6
女性 Female	505	27.3	50.9	20.4	22.2	12.7
16~24 岁 Age	107	33.6	45.8	28.0	20.6	10.3
25~34 岁 Age	149	20.1	47.7	20.8	15.4	12.1
35~44 岁 Age	123	29.3	52.0	16.3	26.0	11.4
45~54 岁 Age	84	31.0	60.7	16.7	28.6	15.5
55~60 岁 Age	42	23.8	52.4	19.0	26.2	19.0

续前表 continued

	人数 Number	滑冰 skating	摩托车赛 motorcycle race	汽车拉力赛 car rally	棋类比赛 chessman	拳击 box	没看 didn't watch
样本 Sample	1005	20.3	23.0	30.1	19.5	40.9	9.8
男性 Male	500	18.8	27.2	38.8	28.4	55.4	3.6
16~24 岁 Age	103	17.5	38.8	52.4	28.2	57.3	0.0
25~34 岁 Age	151	14.6	22.5	34.4	28.5	53.0	5.3
35~44 岁 Age	130	19.2	30.0	37.7	26.9	56.2	2.3
45~54 岁 Age	77	19.5	22.1	37.7	28.6	55.8	5.2
55~60 岁 Age	39	35.9	15.4	25.6	33.3	56.4	7.7
女性 Female	505	21.8	18.8	21.6	10.7	26.5	15.8
16~24 岁 Age	107	22.4	17.8	22.4	12.1	26.2	15.0
25~34 岁 Age	149	17.4	16.1	23.5	10.1	26.2	15.4
35~44 岁 Age	123	22.0	19.5	20.3	10.6	26.0	18.7
45~54 岁 Age	84	26.2	21.4	21.4	8.3	29.8	10.7
55~60 岁 Age	42	26.2	23.8	16.7	14.3	23.8	21.4

6-2 通过现场观看的体育比赛的比例/ Proportion of the Watching Sports Games at the Scene

注：本题为多选题，合计百分比超过 100%（Multiple answers）

	人次 Person-time	百分比 Percent
足球 football	149	26.9
篮球 basketball	42	7.6
排球 volleyball	11	2.0
网球 tennis	10	1.8
保龄球 bowling	18	3.2
羽毛球 badminton	15	2.7
乒乓球 table tennis	16	2.9
台球 billiards	8	1.4
马拉松 Marathon	24	4.3
滑雪 skiing	3	0.5
滑冰 skating	2	0.4
摩托车赛 motorcycle race	4	0.7
汽车拉力赛 car rally	2	0.4
棋类比赛 chessman	6	1.1
拳击 box	6	1.1
没看 didn't watch	365	65.9

n=554

6-3 不同消费者层通过电视观看比赛的比例/ Proportion of the Watching Sports Games through TV by Market Segments

6-3-1 时尚流行指标/ Fads Popular Index

注：本题为多选题，合计百分比超过 100%（Multiple answers）

	人数 Number	足球 football	篮球 basketball	排球 volleyball	网球 tennis	保龄球 bowling
样本 Sample	991	69.4	43.4	56.1	23.6	31.1
平实生活指向 simple living orientation	487	69.8	42.9	57.9	22.4	25.3
时尚流行指向 fashion orientation	504	69.0	43.8	54.4	24.8	36.7

续前表 continued

	人数 Number	羽毛球 badminton	乒乓球 table tennis	台球 billiards	马拉松 Marathon	滑雪 skiing
样本 Sample	991	31.4	54.8	31.0	24.1	13.1
平实生活指向 simple living orientation	487	31.2	57.7	27.7	22.6	11.9
时尚流行指向 fashion orientation	504	31.5	52.0	34.1	25.6	14.3

续前表 continued

	人数 Number	滑冰 skating	摩托车赛 motorcycle race	汽车拉力赛 car rally	棋类比赛 chessman	拳击 box	没看 didn't watch
样本 Sample	991	20.4	23.0	30.3	19.6	41.1	9.7
平实生活指向 simple living orientation	487	19.7	20.7	27.1	20.1	40.7	10.5
时尚流行指向 fashion orientation	504	21.0	25.2	33.3	19.0	41.5	8.9

6-3-2 广告态度指标/ Advertising Attitude Index

注：本题为多选题，合计百分比超过 100%（Multiple answers）

	人数 Number	足球 football	篮球 basketball	排球 volleyball	网球 tennis	保龄球 bowling
样本 Sample	987	69.5	43.4	56.2	23.3	31.1
广告淡漠指向 indifferent orientation	285	70.2	41.1	52.3	22.8	26.3
中间层 medium	570	68.9	43.3	56.7	22.5	33.2
信赖广告指向 loyal crientation	132	70.5	48.5	62.9	28.0	32.6

续前表 continued

	人数 Number	羽毛球 badminton	乒乓球 table tennis	台球 billiards	马拉松 Marathon	滑雪 skiing
样本 Sample	987	31.5	54.6	30.9	24.3	13.0
广告淡漠指向 indifferent orientation	285	30.5	53.3	37.2	23.5	11.2
中间层 medium	570	30.2	53.2	28.2	23.3	11.8
信赖广告指向 loyal orientation	132	39.4	63.6	28.8	30.3	22.0

续前表 continued

	人数 Number	滑冰 skating	摩托车赛 motorcycle race	汽车拉力赛 car rally	棋类比赛 chessman	拳击 box	没看 didn't watch
样本 Sample	987	20.3	23.1	30.4	19.6	40.9	9.7
广告淡漠指向 indifferent orientation	285	20.4	23.5	30.9	19.6	42.1	10.2
中间层 medium	570	19.1	21.8	29.8	18.1	39.3	8.8
信赖广告指向 loyal orientation	132	25.0	28.0	31.8	25.8	45.5	12.9

6-4 不同消费者层通过现场观看比赛的比例/Proportion of the Watching Sports Games at the Scene by Market Segments

6-4-1 时尚流行指标/ Fads Popular Index

注：本题为多选题，合计百分比超过 100%（Multiple answers）

	人数 Number	足球 football	篮球 basketball	排球 volleyball	网球 tennis	保龄球 bowling
样本 Sample	543	26.9	7.4	2.0	1.8	3.3
平实生活指向 simple living orientation	247	25.9	6.9	2.0	0.8	2.4
时尚流行指向 fashion orientation	296	27.7	7.8	2.0	2.7	4.1

续前表 continued

	人数 Number	羽毛球 badminton	乒乓球 table tennis	台球 billiards	马拉松 Marathon	滑雪 skiing
样本 Sample	543	2.6	2.9	1.5	4.4	0.6
平实生活指向 simple living orientation	247	2.8	3.2	0.8	4.0	0.0
时尚流行指向 fashion orientation	296	2.4	2.7	2.0	4.7	1.0

续前表 continued

	人数 Number	滑冰 skating	摩托车赛 motorcycle race	汽车拉力赛 car rally	棋类比赛 chessman	拳击 box	没看 didn't watch
样本 Sample	543	0.4	0.7	0.4	1.1	1.1	65.9
平实生活指向 simple living orientation	247	0.0	0.8	0.4	1.6	0.8	66.4
时尚流行指向 fashion orientation	296	0.7	0.7	0.3	0.7	1.4	65.5

6-4-2 广告态度指标/ Advertising Attitude Index

注：本题为多选题，合计百分比超过 100%（Multiple answers）

	人数 Number	足球 football	篮球 basketball	排球 volleyball	网球 tennis	保龄球 bowling
样本 Sample	543	26.9	7.6	1.8	1.8	3.1
广告淡漠指向 indifferent orientation	157	26.8	6.4	4.5	0.6	4.5
中间层 medium	306	28.4	8.2	0.7	2.6	2.6
信赖广告指向 loyal orientation	80	21.3	7.5	1.3	1.3	2.5

续前表 continued

	人数 Number	羽毛球 badminton	乒乓球 table tennis	台球 billiards	马拉松 Marathon	滑雪 skiing
样本 Sample	543	2.8	2.9	1.5	4.2	0.6
广告淡漠指向 indifferent orientation	157	3.8	3.8	0.6	6.4	0.0
中间层 medium	306	1.6	2.3	1.3	2.3	0.7
信赖广告指向 loyal orientation	80	5.0	3.8	3.8	7.5	1.3

续前表 continued

	人数 Number	滑冰 skating	摩托车赛 motorcycle race	汽车拉力赛 car rally	棋类比赛 chessman	拳击 box	没看 didn't watch
样本 Sample	543	0.4	0.6	0.4	1.1	1.1	65.7
广告淡漠指向 indifferent orientation	157	0.0	0.6	0.6	1.9	1.3	63.1
中间层 medium	306	0.3	0.3	0.0	0.0	0.7	65.4
信赖广告指向 loyal orientation	80	1.3	1.3	1.3	3.8	2.5	72.5

● 上海 / Shanghai

6-1 样本、男性各年龄层、女性各年龄层通过电视观看的体育比赛/ Proportion of the Watching Sports Games through TV by the Whole Sample, Age and Gender Groups

注：本题为多选题，合计百分比超过 100%（Multiple answers）

	人数 Number	足球 football	篮球 basketball	排球 volleyball	网球 tennis	保龄球 bowling
样本 Sample	1013	70.6	42.6	46.4	26.3	19.9
男性 Male	509	85.3	57.8	51.5	34.0	24.6
16~24 岁 Age	109	84.4	80.7	56.9	49.5	31.2
25~34 岁 Age	146	87.0	59.6	45.9	43.2	28.8
35~44 岁 Age	130	86.2	45.4	49.2	22.3	22.3
45~54 岁 Age	85	83.5	47.1	51.8	25.9	16.5
55~60 岁 Age	39	82.1	51.3	64.1	12.8	15.4
女性 Female	504	55.8	27.4	41.3	18.5	15.3
16~24 岁 Age	108	55.6	39.8	46.3	28.7	20.4
25~34 岁 Age	143	46.9	22.4	38.5	20.3	21.0
35~44 岁 Age	130	65.4	22.3	40.0	13.1	10.0
45~54 岁 Age	82	61.0	26.8	41.5	9.8	4.9
55~60 岁 Age	41	46.3	29.3	41.5	19.5	19.5

续前表 continued

	人数 Number	羽毛球 badminton	乒乓球 table tennis	台球 billiards	马拉松 Marathon	滑雪 skiing
样本 Sample	1013	20.1	42.4	21.8	11.1	10.0
男性 Male	509	25.3	50.3	33.2	13.9	13.2
16~24 岁 Age	109	35.8	54.1	46.8	20.2	17.4
25~34 岁 Age	146	23.3	44.5	37.7	11.6	11.6
35~44 岁 Age	130	20.8	50.0	26.2	13.8	11.5
45~54 岁 Age	85	22.4	50.6	25.9	12.9	11.8
55~60 岁 Age	39	25.6	61.5	17.9	7.7	15.4
女性 Female	504	14.9	34.5	10.3	8.1	6.7
16~24 岁 Age	108	21.3	38.9	17.6	9.3	9.3
25~34 岁 Age	143	15.4	32.9	9.8	6.3	4.2
35~44 岁 Age	130	11.5	33.8	8.5	9.2	8.5
45~54 岁 Age	82	12.2	34.1	3.7	6.1	4.9
55~60 岁 Age	41	12.2	31.7	12.2	12.2	7.3

续前表 continued

	人数 Number	滑冰 skating	摩托车赛 motorcycle race	汽车拉力赛 car rally	棋类比赛 chessman	拳击 box	没看 didn't watch
样本 Sample	1013	9.9	18.6	25.5	11.9	44.5	16.5
男性 Male	509	12.6	26.3	36.0	17.3	63.5	5.7
16~24 岁 Age	109	19.3	35.8	42.2	25.7	68.8	2.8
25~34 岁 Age	146	9.6	26.7	44.5	17.1	69.2	3.4
35~44 岁 Age	130	10.0	20.0	27.7	11.5	62.3	6.9
45~54 岁 Age	85	10.6	27.1	31.8	17.6	50.6	11.8
55~60 岁 Age	39	17.9	17.9	23.1	12.8	59.0	5.1
女性 Female	504	7.1	10.7	14.9	6.5	25.4	27.4
16~24 岁 Age	108	13.9	10.2	22.2	9.3	29.6	21.3
25~34 岁 Age	143	4.9	12.6	12.6	7.0	21.0	28.7
35~44 岁 Age	130	7.7	13.1	14.6	7.7	30.8	26.9
45~54 岁 Age	82	2.4	4.9	9.8	1.2	20.7	24.4
55~60 岁 Age	41	4.9	9.8	14.6	4.9	22.0	46.3

6-2 通过现场观看的体育比赛的比例/ Proportion of the Watching Sports Games at the Scene

注：本题为多选题，合计百分比超过 100%（Multiple answers）

	人次 Person-time	百分比 Percent
足球 football	135	13.4
篮球 basketball	22	2.2
排球 volleyball	10	1.0
网球 tennis	5	0.5
保龄球 bowling	6	0.6
羽毛球 badminton	1	1.1
乒乓球 table tennis	8	0.8
台球 billiards	3	0.3
马拉松 Marathon	1	0.1
滑雪 skiing	0	0.0
滑冰 skating	0	0.0
摩托车赛 motorcycle race	2	0.2
汽车拉力赛 car rally	2	0.2
棋类比赛 chessman	6	0.6
拳击 box	6	0.6
没看 didn't watch	842	83.9

n=1004

6-3 不同消费者层通过电视观看比赛的比例/ Proportion of the Watching Sports Games through TV by Market Segments

6-3-1 时尚流行指标/ Fads Popular Index

注：本题为多选题，合计百分比超过 100%（Multiple answers）

	人数 Number	足球 football	篮球 basketball	排球 volleyball	网球 tennis	保龄球 bowling
样本 Sample	1004	70.5	42.4	46.4	26.3	19.8
平实生活指向 simple living orientation	471	72.4	42.5	48.6	22.1	15.3
时尚流行指向 fashion orientation	533	68.9	42.4	44.5	30.0	23.8

续前表 continued

	人数 Number	羽毛球 badminton	乒乓球 table tennis	台球 billiards	马拉松 Marathon	滑雪 skiing
样本 Sample	1004	20.0	42.4	21.8	10.9	9.9
平实生活指向 simple living orientation	471	19.1	45.9	16.8	9.1	8.7
时尚流行指向 fashion orientation	533	20.8	39.4	26.3	12.4	10.9

续前表 continued

	人数 Number	滑冰 skating	摩托车赛 motorcycle race	汽车拉力赛 car rally	棋类比赛 chessman	拳击 box	没看 didn't watch
样本 Sample	1004	9.8	18.5	25.5	11.9	44.5	16.5
平实生活指向 simple living orientation	471	8.7	16.6	23.8	11.7	42.3	15.9
时尚流行指向 fashion orientation	533	10.7	20.3	27.0	12.0	46.5	17.1

6-3-2 广告态度指标/ Advertising Attitude Index

注：本题为多选题，合计百分比超过 100%（Multiple answers）

	人数 Number	足球 football	篮球 basketball	排球 volleyball	网球 tennis	保龄球 bowling
样本 Sample	1001	70.4	42.6	46.2	26.0	19.6
广告淡漠指向 indifferent orientation	256	69.9	41.8	46.1	23.8	14.8
中间层 medium	610	70.2	42.0	45.9	26.1	21.0
信赖广告指向 loyal orientation	135	72.6	46.7	47.4	29.6	22.2

续前表 continued

	人数 Number	羽毛球 badminton	乒乓球 table tennis	台球 billiards	马拉松 Marathon	滑雪 skiing
样本 Sample	1001	19.8	42.1	21.6	10.8	9.8
广告淡漠指向 indifferent orientation	256	17.2	38.3	20.3	10.9	9.8
中间层 medium	610	20.7	43.8	21.6	10.2	9.0
信赖广告指向 loyal orientation	135	20.7	41.5	23.7	13.3	13.3

续前表 continued

	人数 Number	滑冰 skating	摩托车赛 motorcycle race	汽车拉力赛 car rally	棋类比赛 chessman	拳击 box	没看 didn't watch
样本 Sample	1001	9.7	18.5	25.4	11.8	44.6	16.6
广告淡漠指向 indifferent orientation	256	11.3	14.8	26.2	10.5	41.8	17.6
中间层 medium	610	8.2	19.3	24.6	11.1	45.6	15.9
信赖广告指向 loyal orientation	135	13.3	21.5	27.4	17.0	45.2	17.8

6-4 不同消费者层通过现场观看比赛的比例/Proportion of the Watching Sports Games at the Scene by Market Segments

6-4-1 时尚流行指标/ Fads Popular Index

注：本题为多选题，合计百分比超过 100%（Multiple answers）

	人数 Number	足球 football	篮球 basketball	排球 volleyball	网球 tennis	保龄球 bowling
样本 Sample	997	13.5	2.2	1.0	0.5	0.6
平实生活指向 simple living orientation	467	10.5	1.1	0.9	0.0	0.4
时尚流行指向 fashion orientation	530	16.2	3.2	1.1	0.9	0.8

续前表 continued

	人数 Number	羽毛球 badminton	乒乓球 table tennis	台球 billiards	马拉松 Marathon	滑雪 skiing
样本 Sample	997	1.1	0.8	0.3	0.1	0.0
平实生活指向 simple living orientation	467	0.9	0.2	0.0	0.0	0.0
时尚流行指向 fashion orientation	530	1.3	1.3	0.6	0.2	0.0

续前表 continued

	人数 Number	滑冰 skating	摩托车赛 motorcycle race	汽车拉力赛 car rally	棋类比赛 chessman	拳击 box	没看 didn't watch
样本 Sample	997	0.0	0.2	0.2	0.6	0.6	83.8
平实生活指向 simple living orientation	467	0.0	0.0	0.0	0.4	0.0	87.8
时尚流行指向 fashion orientation	530	0.0	0.4	0.4	0.8	1.1	80.2

6-4-2 广告态度指标/ Advertising Attitude Index

注：本题为多选题，合计百分比超过 100%（Multiple answers）

	人数 Number	足球 football	篮球 basketball	排球 volleyball	网球 tennis	保龄球 bowling
样本 Sample	992	13.2	2.2	1.0	0.5	0.6
广告淡漠指向 indifferent orientation	252	11.5	1.6	0.8	0.0	0.8
中间层 medium	607	13.8	2.6	0.8	0.5	0.5
信赖广告指向 loyal orientation	133	13.5	1.5	2.3	1.5	0.8

续前表 continued

	人数 Number	羽毛球 badminton	乒乓球 table tennis	台球 billiards	马拉松 Marathon	滑雪 skiing
样本 Sample	992	1.1	0.8	0.3	0.1	0.0
广告淡漠指向 indifferent orientation	252	0.8	0.8	0.4	0.0	0.0
中间层 medium	607	1.3	0.8	0.3	0.2	0.0
信赖广告指向 loyal orientation	133	0.8	0.8	0.0	0.0	0.0

续前表 continued

	人数 Number	滑冰 skating	摩托车赛 motorcycle race	汽车拉力赛 car rally	棋类比赛 chessman	拳击 box	没看 didn't watch
样本 Sample	992	0.0	0.2	0.2	0.6	0.6	84.1
广告淡漠指向 indifferent orientation	252	0.0	0.0	0.4	0.4	0.8	86.5
中间层 medium	607	0.0	0.2	0.2	0.3	0.7	83.2
信赖广告指向 loyal orientation	133	0.0	0.8	0.0	2.3	0.0	83.5

● 广州 / Guangzhou

6-1 样本、男性各年龄层、女性各年龄层通过电视观看的体育比赛/ Proportion of the Watching Sports Games through TV by the Whole Sample, Age and Gender Groups

注：本题为多选题，合计百分比超过 100%（Multiple answers）

	人数 Number	足球 football	篮球 basketball	排球 volleyball	网球 tennis	保龄球 bowling
样本 Sample	1033	55.0	37.8	40.0	18.3	15.6
男性 Male	499	76.8	51.3	39.1	22.6	18.6
16~24 岁 Age	106	74.5	72.6	41.5	33.0	26.4
25~34 岁 Age	150	78.7	48.7	37.3	28.0	17.3
35~44 岁 Age	127	78.0	38.6	38.6	17.3	20.5
45~54 岁 Age	73	80.8	60.3	46.6	16.4	12.3
55~60 岁 Age	43	65.1	30.2	27.9	4.7	9.3
女性 Female	534	34.6	25.1	40.8	14.2	12.7
16~24 岁 Age	112	38.4	38.4	38.4	30.4	17.9
25~34 岁 Age	158	34.2	16.5	39.9	13.3	12.7
35~44 岁 Age	136	34.6	26.5	48.5	8.1	12.5
45~54 岁 Age	87	31.0	19.5	35.6	9.2	10.3
55~60 岁 Age	41	34.1	29.3	36.6	4.9	4.9

续前表 continued

	人数 Number	羽毛球 badminton	乒乓球 table tennis	台球 billiards	马拉松 Marathon	滑雪 skiing
样本 Sample	1033	24.4	33.7	14.3	5.6	8.1
男性 Male	499	26.3	38.5	21.8	6.6	7.8
16~24 岁 Age	106	32.1	44.3	37.7	9.4	11.3
25~34 岁 Age	150	32.0	42.0	26.7	8.7	8.7
35~44 岁 Age	127	21.3	36.2	15.7	3.9	3.9
45~54 岁 Age	73	21.9	35.6	8.2	4.1	8.2
55~60 岁 Age	43	14.0	23.3	7.0	4.7	7.0
女性 Female	534	22.7	29.2	7.3	4.7	8.4
16~24 岁 Age	112	27.7	27.7	17.0	7.1	11.6
25~34 岁 Age	158	25.9	30.4	8.2	2.5	7.6
35~44 岁 Age	136	19.1	31.6	2.9	2.2	6.6
45~54 岁 Age	87	18.4	26.4	2.3	5.7	6.9
55~60 岁 Age	41	17.1	26.8	2.4	12.2	12.2

续前表 continued

	人数 Number	滑冰 skating	摩托车赛 motorcycle race	汽车拉力赛 car rally	棋类比赛 chessman	拳击 box	没看 didn't watch
样本 Sample	1033	10.7	18.4	17.4	10.4	14.5	22.3
男性 Male	499	10.2	26.5	26.1	17.2	21.6	11.6
16~24 岁 Age	106	13.2	29.2	30.2	15.1	25.5	6.6
25~34 岁 Age	150	8.7	30.0	27.3	18.7	25.3	8.7
35~44 岁 Age	127	8.7	28.3	28.3	16.5	18.9	16.5
45~54 岁 Age	73	12.3	21.9	24.7	17.8	21.9	9.6
55~60 岁 Age	43	9.3	9.3	7.0	18.6	7.0	23.3
女性 Female	534	11.2	10.9	9.4	3.9	7.9	32.2
16~24 岁 Age	112	14.3	12.5	9.8	3.6	10.7	23.2
25~34 岁 Age	158	12.7	8.2	9.5	3.8	5.7	32.3
35~44 岁 Age	136	7.4	14.7	9.6	3.7	10.3	28.7
45~54 岁 Age	87	10.3	4.6	6.9	5.7	5.7	41.4
55~60 岁 Age	41	12.2	17.1	12.2	2.4	4.9	48.8

6-2 通过现场观看的体育比赛的比例/ Proportion of the Watching Sports Games at the Scene

注：本题为多选题，合计百分比超过 100%（Multiple answers）

	人次 person-time	百分比 Percent
足球 football	71	7.0
篮球 basketball	44	4.3
排球 volleyball	10	1.0
网球 tennis	11	1.1
保龄球 bowling	11	1.1
羽毛球 badminton	18	1.8
乒乓球 table tennis	18	1.8
台球 billiards	9	0.9
马拉松 Marathon	1	0.1
滑雪 skiing	0	0.0
滑冰 skating	3	0.3
摩托车赛 motorcycle race	2	0.2
汽车拉力赛 car rally	3	0.3
棋类比赛 chessman	9	0.9
拳击 box	2	0.2
没看 didn't watch	901	88.8

n=1015

6-3 不同消费者层通过电视观看的体育比赛/ Proportion of the Watching Sports Games through TV by Market Segments

6-3-1 时尚流行指标/ Fads Popular Index

注：本题为多选题，合计百分比超过 100%（Multiple answers）

	人数 Number	足球 football	篮球 basketball	排球 volleyball	网球 tennis	保龄球 bowling
样本 Sample	1021	55.1	37.7	40.1	18.3	15.8
平实生活指向 simple living orientation	518	56.8	35.7	42.9	14.5	14.7
时尚流行指向 fashion orientation	503	53.5	39.8	37.2	22.3	16.9

续前表 continued

	人数 Number	羽毛球 badminton	乒乓球 table tennis	台球 billiards	马拉松 Marathon	滑雪 skiing
样本 Sample	1021	24.3	33.9	14.4	5.6	8.1
平实生活指向 simple living orientation	518	23.2	34.9	11.8	5.8	7.5
时尚流行指向 fashion orientation	503	25.4	32.8	17.1	5.4	8.7

续前表 continued

	人数 Number	滑冰 skating	摩托车赛 motorcycle race	汽车拉力赛 car rally	棋类比赛 chessman	拳击 box	没看 didn't watch
样本 Sample	1021	10.7	18.5	17.4	10.5	14.5	22.3
平实生活指向 simple living orientation	518	8.9	17.4	17.2	10.8	13.1	23.2
时尚流行指向 fashion orientation	503	12.5	19.7	17.7	10.1	15.9	21.5

6-3-2 广告态度指标/ Advertising Attitude Index

注：本题为多选题，合计百分比超过 100%（Multiple answers）

	人数 Number	足球 football	篮球 basketball	排球 volleyball	网球 tennis	保龄球 bowling
样本 Sample	1021	54.9	38.0	40.1	18.4	15.7
广告淡漠指向 indifferent orientation	334	55.7	37.1	40.4	14.7	13.5
中间层 medium	593	55.1	39.6	39.6	20.7	16.5
信赖广告指向 loyal orientation	94	51.1	30.9	41.5	17.0	18.1

续前表 continued

	人数 Number	羽毛球 badminton	乒乓球 table tennis	台球 billiards	马拉松 Marathon	滑雪 skiing
样本 Sample	1021	24.6	34.0	14.4	5.7	8.2
广告淡漠指向 indifferent orientation	334	23.1	34.4	14.1	5.1	9.6
中间层 medium	593	25.3	33.6	14.7	6.1	7.4
信赖广告指向 loyal orientation	94	25.5	35.1	13.8	5.3	8.5

续前表 continued

	人数 Number	滑冰 skating	摩托车赛 motorcycle race	汽车拉力赛 car rally	棋类比赛 chessman	拳击 box	没看 didn't watch
样本 Sample	1021	10.8	18.6	17.5	10.5	14.6	22.2
广告淡漠指向 indifferent orientation	334	10.2	18.3	16.8	11.4	14.7	21.6
中间层 medium	593	10.8	18.0	17.4	10.3	14.0	22.9
信赖广告指向 loyal orientation	94	12.8	23.4	21.3	8.5	18.1	20.2

6-4 不同消费者层通过现场观看比赛的比例/Proportion of the Watching Sports Games at the Scene by Market Segments

6-4-1 时尚流行指标/ Fads Popular Index

注：本题为多选题，合计百分比超过 100%（Multiple answers）

	人数 Number	足球 football	篮球 basketball	排球 volleyball	网球 tennis	保龄球 bowling
样本 Sample	1003	7.0	4.3	1.0	1.1	1.1
平实生活指向 simple living orientation	507	4.1	3.0	0.4	0.6	1.0
时尚流行指向 fashion orientation	496	9.9	5.6	1.6	1.6	1.2

续前表 continued

	人数 Number	羽毛球 badminton	乒乓球 table tennis	台球 billiards	马拉松 Marathon	滑雪 skiing
样本 Sample	1003	1.8	1.8	0.9	0.1	0.0
平实生活指向 simple living orientation	507	1.8	1.2	0.8	0.2	0.0
时尚流行指向 fashion orientation	496	1.8	2.4	1.0	0.0	0.0

续前表 continued

	人数 Number	滑冰 skating	摩托车赛 motorcycle race	汽车拉力赛 car rally	棋类比赛 chessman	拳击 box	没看 didn't watch
样本 Sample	1003	0.3	0.2	0.3	0.9	0.2	88.8
平实生活指向 simple living orientation	507	0.0	0.0	0.0	0.6	0.2	91.9
时尚流行指向 fashion orientation	496	0.6	0.4	0.6	1.2	0.2	85.7

6-4-2 广告态度指标/ Advertising Attitude Index

注：本题为多选题，合计百分比超过 100%（Multiple answers）

	人数 Number	足球 football	篮球 basketball	排球 volleyball	网球 tennis	保龄球 bowling
样本 Sample	1003	7.1	4.4	1.0	1.1	1.1
广告淡漠指向 indifferent orientation	329	4.9	3.0	0.6	0.6	0.6
中间层 medium	581	8.3	5.3	1.0	1.4	1.4
信赖广告指向 loyal orientation	93	7.5	3.2	2.2	1.1	1.1

续前表 continued

	人数 Number	羽毛球 badminton	乒乓球 table tennis	台球 billiards	马拉松 Marathon	滑雪 skiing
样本 Sample	1003	1.7	1.8	0.9	0.1	0.0
广告淡漠指向 indifferent orientation	329	1.5	1.2	0.9	0.0	0.0
中间层 medium	581	1.7	2.2	1.0	0.2	0.0
信赖广告指向 loyal orientation	93	2.2	1.1	0.0	0.0	0.0

续前表 continued

	人数 Number	滑冰 skating	摩托车赛 motorcycle race	汽车拉力赛 car rally	棋类比赛 chessman	拳击 box	没看 didn't watch
样本 Sample	1003	0.3	0.2	0.3	0.9	0.2	88.7
广告淡漠指向 indifferent orientation	329	0.3	0.0	0.0	0.6	0.0	91.5
中间层 medium	581	0.3	0.3	0.5	1.2	0.3	87.3
信赖广告指向 loyal orientation	93	0.0	0.0	0.0	0.0	0.0	88.2

重庆 / Chongqing

6-1 样本、男性各年龄层、女性各年龄层通过电视观看的体育比赛/ Proportion of the Watching Sports Games through TV by the Whole Sample, Age and Gender Groups

注：本题为多选题，合计百分比超过 100%（Multiple answers）

	人数 Number	足球 football	篮球 basketball	排球 volleyball	网球 tennis	保龄球 bowling
样本 Sample	621	65.9	38.0	45.4	17.9	14.0
男性 Male	312	80.8	47.4	48.7	22.4	17.6
16~24 岁 Age	64	93.8	68.8	45.3	31.3	17.2
25~34 岁 Age	92	80.4	34.8	42.4	20.7	16.3
35~44 岁 Age	75	74.7	37.3	50.7	24.0	20.0
45~54 岁 Age	54	75.9	51.9	55.6	13.0	18.5
55~60 岁 Age	27	77.8	59.3	59.3	22.2	14.8
女性 Female	309	50.8	28.5	42.1	13.3	10.4
16~24 岁 Age	64	54.7	35.9	35.9	23.4	15.6
25~34 岁 Age	89	50.6	22.5	41.6	13.5	10.1
35~44 岁 Age	73	43.8	27.4	39.7	8.2	6.8
45~54 岁 Age	60	65.0	33.3	53.3	8.3	10.0
55~60 岁 Age	23	26.1	21.7	39.1	13.0	8.7

续前表 continued

	人数 Number	羽毛球 badminton	乒乓球 table tennis	台球 billiards	马拉松 Marathon	滑雪 skiing
样本 Sample	621	19.8	44.3	20.9	12.9	11.4
男性 Male	312	24.7	48.7	30.1	17.3	13.5
16~24 岁 Age	64	26.6	60.9	48.4	21.9	20.3
25~34 岁 Age	92	18.5	41.3	26.1	9.8	5.4
35~44 岁 Age	75	29.3	42.7	28.0	20.0	16.0
45~54 岁 Age	54	29.6	55.6	24.1	22.2	16.7
55~60 岁 Age	27	18.5	48.1	18.5	14.8	11.1
女性 Female	309	14.9	39.8	11.7	8.4	9.4
16~24 岁 Age	64	21.9	42.2	18.8	7.8	7.8
25~34 岁 Age	89	18.0	41.6	12.4	5.6	7.9
35~44 岁 Age	73	11.0	28.8	6.8	9.6	8.2
45~54 岁 Age	60	10.0	55.0	10.0	10.0	15.0
55~60 岁 Age	23	8.7	21.7	8.7	13.0	8.7

续前表 continued

	人数 Number	滑冰 skating	摩托车赛 motorcycle race	汽车拉力赛 car rally	棋类比赛 chessman	拳击 box	没看 didn't watch
样本 Sample	621	16.1	24.8	27.2	14.2	32.4	15.3
男性 Male	312	17.9	30.8	37.8	22.4	46.8	7.1
16~24 岁 Age	64	21.9	45.3	51.6	20.3	48.4	0.0
25~34 岁 Age	92	14.1	27.2	34.8	14.1	51.1	6.5
35~44 岁 Age	75	20.0	29.3	40.0	24.0	46.7	13.3
45~54 岁 Age	54	16.7	27.8	31.5	37.0	48.1	7.4
55~60 岁 Age	27	18.5	18.5	22.2	22.2	25.9	7.4
女性 Female	309	14.2	18.8	16.5	5.8	17.8	23.6
16~24 岁 Age	64	15.6	14.1	15.6	7.8	10.9	17.2
25~34 岁 Age	89	13.5	22.5	15.7	4.5	18.0	21.3
35~44 岁 Age	73	4.1	20.5	20.5	6.8	17.8	28.8
45~54 岁 Age	60	23.3	18.3	18.3	5.0	25.0	20.0
55~60 岁 Age	23	21.7	13.0	4.3	4.3	17.4	43.5

6-2 通过现场观看的体育比赛的比例/ Proportion of the Watching Sports Games at the Scene

注：本题为多选题，合计百分比超过 100%（Multiple answers）

	人次 Percent-time	百分比 Percent
足球 football	134	22.2
篮球 basketball	14	2.3
排球 volleyball	5	0.8
网球 tennis	2	0.3
保龄球 bowling	4	0.7
羽毛球 badminton	2	0.3
乒乓球 table tennis	2	0.3
台球 billiards	6	1.0
马拉松 Marathon	1	0.2
滑雪 skiing	0	0.0
滑冰 skating	0	0.0
摩托车赛 motorcycle race	1	0.2
汽车拉力赛 car rally	1	0.2
棋类比赛 chessman	1	0.2
拳击 box	5	0.8
没看 didn't watch	457	75.8

n=603

6-3 不同消费者层通过电视观看体育比赛的比例/ Proportion of the Watching Sports Games through TV by Market Segments

6-3-1 时尚流行指标/ Fads Popular Index

注：本题为多选题，合计百分比超过 100%（Multiple answers）

	人数 Number	足球 football	篮球 basketball	排球 volleyball	网球 tennis	保龄球 bowling
样本 Sample	614	**66.0**	**37.8**	**45.4**	**17.9**	**14.2**
平实生活指向 simple living orientation	368	66.6	37.5	45.9	16.6	13.6
时尚流行指向 fashion orientation	246	65.0	38.2	44.7	19.9	15.0

续前表 continued

	人数 Number	羽毛球 badminton	乒乓球 table tennis	台球 billiards	马拉松 Marathon	滑雪 skiing
样本 Sample	614	**19.9**	**44.5**	**21.0**	**12.5**	**11.6**
平实生活指向 simple living orientation	368	18.5	42.9	19.6	12.2	10.1
时尚流行指向 fashion orientation	246	22.0	46.7	23.2	13.0	13.8

续前表 continued

	人数 Number	滑冰 skating	摩托车赛 motorcycle race	汽车拉力赛 car rally	棋类比赛 chessman	拳击 box	没看 didn't watch
样本 Sample	614	**16.1**	**24.8**	**27.2**	**14.3**	**32.4**	**15.5**
平实生活指向 simple living orientation	368	13.6	23.9	25.5	14.9	30.4	17.1
时尚流行指向 fashion orientation	246	19.9	26.0	29.7	13.4	35.4	13.0

6-3-2 广告态度指标/ Advertising Attitude Index

注：本题为多选题，合计百分比超过 100%（Multiple answers）

	人数 Number	足球 football	篮球 basketball	排球 volleyball	网球 tennis	保龄球 bowling
样本 Sample	617	**65.8**	**38.2**	**45.7**	**17.8**	**14.1**
广告淡漠指向 indifferent orientation	167	68.3	37.1	44.3	15.0	13.2
中间层 medium	367	64.0	38.1	44.7	19.1	15.3
信赖广告指向 loyal orientation	83	68.7	41.0	53.0	18.1	10.8

续前表 continued

	人数 Number	羽毛球 badminton	乒乓球 table tennis	台球 billiards	马拉松 Marathon	滑雪 skiing
样本 Sample	617	19.9	44.4	20.9	13.0	11.5
广告淡漠指向 indifferent orientation	167	19.8	44.9	20.4	13.2	10.8
中间层 medium	367	21.0	43.3	21.0	12.8	12.5
信赖广告指向 loyal orientation	83	15.7	48.2	21.7	13.3	8.4

续前表 continued

	人数 Number	滑冰 skating	摩托车赛 motorcycle race	汽车拉力赛 car rally	棋类比赛 chessman	拳击 box	没看 didn't watch
样本 Sample	617	16.0	24.8	27.4	14.3	32.4	15.2
广告淡漠指向 indifferent orientation	167	16.2	25.1	31.1	15.0	33.5	15.6
中间层 medium	367	15.0	25.1	26.2	13.6	31.3	15.5
信赖广告指向 loyal orientation	83	20.5	22.9	25.3	15.7	34.9	13.3

6-4 不同消费者层通过现场观看比赛的比例/Proportion of the Watching Sports Games at the Scene by Market Segments

6-4-1 时尚流行指标/ Fads Popular Index

注：本题为多选题，合计百分比超过 100%（Multiple answers）

	人数 Number	足球 football	篮球 basketball	排球 volleyball	网球 tennis	保龄球 bowling
样本 Sample	596	22.1	2.2	0.8	0.3	0.7
平实生活指向 simple living orientation	360	16.7	1.4	0.8	0.3	0.6
时尚流行指向 fashion orientation	236	30.5	3.4	0.8	0.4	0.8

续前表 continued

	人数 Number	羽毛球 badminton	乒乓球 table tennis	台球 billiards	马拉松 Marathon	滑雪 skiing
样本 Sample	596	0.3	0.3	1.0	0.2	0.0
平实生活指向 simple living orientation	360	0.6	0.6	0.8	0.0	0.0
时尚流行指向 fashion orientation	236	0.0	0.0	1.3	0.4	0.0

续前表 continued

	人数 Number	滑冰 skating	摩托车赛 motorcycle race	汽车拉力赛 car rally	棋类比赛 chessman	拳击 box	没看 didn't watch
样本 Sample	596	0.0	0.2	0.2	0.2	0.8	76.0
平实生活指向 simple living orientation	360	0.0	0.0	0.0	0.0	0.8	81.7
时尚流行指向 fashion orientation	236	0.0	0.4	0.4	0.4	0.8	67.4

6-4-2 广告态度指标/ Advertising Attitude Index

注：本题为多选题，合计百分比超过 100%（Multiple answers）

	人数 Number	足球 football	篮球 basketball	排球 volleyball	网球 tennis	保龄球 bowling
样本 Sample	601	22.3	2.3	0.8	0.3	0.7
广告淡漠指向 indifferent orientation	165	20.0	1.8	0.6	0.6	0.6
中间层 medium	356	21.6	2.0	0.6	0.3	0.6
信赖广告指向 loyal orientation	80	30.0	5.0	2.5	0.0	1.3

续前表 continued

	人数 Number	羽毛球 badminton	乒乓球 table tennis	台球 billiards	马拉松 Marathon	滑雪 skiing
样本 Sample	601	0.3	0.3	1.0	0.2	0.0
广告淡漠指向 indifferent orientation	165	0.0	0.6	0.6	0.0	0.0
中间层 medium	356	0.6	0.0	0.8	0.0	0.0
信赖广告指向 loyal orientation	80	0.0	1.3	2.5	1.3	0.0

续前表 continued

	人数 Number	滑冰 skating	摩托车赛 motorcycle race	汽车拉力赛 car rally	棋类比赛 chessman	拳击 box	没看 didn't watch
样本 Sample	601	0.0	0.2	0.2	0.2	0.8	75.7
广告淡漠指向 indifferent orientation	165	0.0	0.0	0.0	0.0	1.2	77.6
中间层 medium	356	0.0	0.3	0.3	0.3	0.3	76.7
信赖广告指向 loyal orientation	80	0.0	0.0	0.0	0.0	2.5	67.5

● 武汉 / Wuhan

6-1 样本、男性各年龄层、女性各年龄层通过电视观看的体育比赛/ Proportion of the Watching Sports Games through TV by the Whole Sample, Age and Gender Groups

注：本题为多选题，合计百分比超过 100%（Multiple answers）

	人数 Number	足球 football	篮球 basketball	排球 volleyball	网球 tennis	保龄球 bowling
样本 Sample	624	70.2	38.1	49.5	22.6	20.4
男性 Male	304	87.2	50.7	53.3	29.6	24.7
16~24 岁 Age	65	87.7	73.8	46.2	44.6	32.3
25~34 岁 Age	87	85.1	37.9	47.1	32.2	23.0
35~44 岁 Age	78	88.5	47.4	52.6	25.6	30.8
45~54 岁 Age	51	88.2	47.1	64.7	17.6	11.8
55~60 岁 Age	23	87.0	52.2	73.9	17.4	17.4
女性 Female	320	54.1	26.3	45.9	15.9	16.3
16~24 岁 Age	66	42.4	31.8	43.9	21.2	16.7
25~34 岁 Age	95	56.8	17.9	42.1	15.8	15.8
35~44 岁 Age	76	60.5	22.4	46.1	13.2	19.7
45~54 岁 Age	57	61.4	36.8	63.2	17.5	14.0
55~60 岁 Age	26	38.5	30.8	26.9	7.7	11.5

续前表 continued

	人数 Number	羽毛球 badminton	乒乓球 table tennis	台球 billiards	马拉松 Marathon	滑雪 skiing
样本 Sample	624	25.8	53.8	29.3	14.9	12.7
男性 Male	304	31.9	60.2	45.7	20.1	15.1
16~24 岁 Age	65	30.8	61.5	60.0	20.0	16.9
25~34 岁 Age	87	29.9	57.5	55.2	12.6	9.2
35~44 岁 Age	78	32.1	57.7	44.9	23.1	16.7
45~54 岁 Age	51	39.2	60.8	23.5	23.5	15.7
55~60 岁 Age	23	26.1	73.9	21.7	30.4	26.1
女性 Female	320	20.0	47.8	13.8	10.0	10.3
16~24 岁 Age	66	16.7	40.9	21.2	6.1	6.1
25~34 岁 Age	95	20.0	40.0	10.5	5.3	9.5
35~44 岁 Age	76	19.7	51.3	13.2	14.5	10.5
45~54 岁 Age	57	28.1	68.4	10.5	21.1	15.8
55~60 岁 Age	26	11.5	38.5	15.4	0.0	11.5

续前表 continued

	人数 Number	滑冰 skating	摩托车赛 motorcycle race	汽车拉力赛 car rally	棋类比赛 chessman	拳击 box	没看 didn't watch
样本 Sample	624	18.1	21.8	26.4	16.5	35.4	14.6
男性 Male	304	17.1	33.6	40.5	27.6	55.9	4.3
16~24 岁 Age	65	20.0	49.2	53.8	26.2	50.8	1.5
25~34 岁 Age	87	12.6	32.2	41.4	34.5	58.6	3.4
35~44 岁 Age	78	16.7	28.2	39.7	24.4	62.8	5.1
45~54 岁 Age	51	19.6	25.5	25.5	25.5	43.1	9.8
55~60 岁 Age	23	21.7	30.4	34.8	21.7	65.2	0.0
女性 Female	320	19.1	10.6	13.1	5.9	15.9	24.4
16~24 岁 Age	66	16.7	6.1	7.6	1.5	15.2	21.2
25~34 岁 Age	95	20.0	10.5	12.6	3.2	14.7	24.2
35~44 岁 Age	76	14.5	13.2	19.7	11.8	21.1	22.4
45~54 岁 Age	57	26.3	10.5	14.0	8.8	14.0	17.5
55~60 岁 Age	26	19.2	15.4	7.7	3.8	11.5	53.8

6-2 通过现场观看的体育比赛的比例/ Proportion of the Watching Sports Games at the Scene

注：本题为多选题，合计百分比超过 100%（Multiple answers）

	人次 Person-time	百分比 Percent
足球 football	94	15.3
篮球 basketball	17	2.8
排球 volleyball	11	1.8
网球 tennis	2	0.3
保龄球 bowling	10	1.6
羽毛球 badminton	2	0.3
乒乓球 table tennis	15	2.4
台球 billiards	7	1.1
马拉松 Marathon	2	0.3
滑雪 skiing	0	0.0
滑冰 skating	1	0.2
摩托车赛 motorcycle race	2	0.3
汽车拉力赛 car rally	4	0.7
棋类比赛 chessman	6	1.0
拳击 box	3	0.5
没看 didn't watch	502	81.6

n=615

6-3 不同消费者层通过电视观看体育比赛的比例/ Proportion of the Watching Sports Games through TV by Market Segments

6-3-1 时尚流行指标/ Fads Popular Index

注：本题为多选题，合计百分比超过 100%（Multiple answers）

	人数 Number	足球 football	篮球 basketball	排球 volleyball	网球 tennis	保龄球 bowling
样本 Sample	621	70.0	38.2	49.3	22.4	20.1
平实生活指向 simple living orientation	323	69.3	35.9	47.7	19.5	17.0
时尚流行指向 fashion orientation	298	70.8	40.6	51.0	25.5	23.5

续前表 continued

	人数 Number	羽毛球 badminton	乒乓球 table tennis	台球 billiards	马拉松 Marathon	滑雪 skiing
样本 Sample	621	25.6	53.6	29.1	14.8	12.6
平实生活指向 simple living orientation	323	27.6	53.3	29.1	15.5	12.1
时尚流行指向 fashion orientation	298	23.5	54.0	29.2	14.1	13.1

续前表 continued

	人数 Number	滑冰 skating	摩托车赛 motorcycle race	汽车拉力赛 car rally	棋类比赛 chessman	拳击 box	没看 didn't watch
样本 Sample	621	18.0	21.6	26.2	16.3	35.1	14.7
平实生活指向 simple living orientation	323	17.3	20.7	23.8	18.3	32.5	15.2
时尚流行指向 fashion orientation	298	18.8	22.5	28.9	14.[illegible]	37.9	14.1

6-3-2 广告态度指标/ Advertising Attitude Index

注：本题为多选题，合计百分比超过 100%（Multiple answers）

	人数 Number	足球 football	篮球 basketball	排球 volleyball	网球 tennis	保龄球 bowling
样本 Sample	623	70.1	38.2	49.4	22.5	20.2
广告淡漠指向 indifferent orientation	186	68.3	35.5	45.2	19.9	14.5
中间层 medium	366	72.4	38.8	51.6	23.0	22.4
信赖广告指向 loyal orientation	71	63.4	42.3	49.3	26.8	23.9

续前表 continued

	人数 Number	羽毛球 badminton	乒乓球 table tennis	台球 billiards	马拉松 Marathon	滑雪 skiing
样本 Sample	623	25.7	53.8	29.2	14.9	12.7
广告淡漠指向 indifferent orientation	186	27.4	53.2	28.5	15.6	14.0
中间层 medium	366	25.4	55.7	31.4	14.5	11.7
信赖广告指向 loyal orientation	71	22.5	45.1	19.7	15.5	14.1

续前表 continued

	人数 Number	滑冰 skating	摩托车赛 motorcycle race	汽车拉力赛 car rally	棋类比赛 chessman	拳击 box	没看 didn't watch
样本 Sample	623	18.1	21.7	26.3	16.4	35.3	14.6
广告淡漠指向 indifferent orientation	186	18.3	21.5	27.4	21.0	33.3	20.4
中间层 medium	366	18.3	21.6	25.4	14.2	36.6	11.7
信赖广告指向 loyal orientation	71	16.9	22.5	28.2	15.5	33.8	14.1

6-4 不同消费者层通过现场观看体育比赛的比例/Proportion of the Watching Sports Games at the Scene by Market Segments

6-4-1 时尚流行指标/ Fads Popular Index

注：本题为多选题，合计百分比超过 100%（Multiple answers）

	人数 Number	足球 football	篮球 basketball	排球 volleyball	网球 tennis	保龄球 bowling
样本 Sample	612	15.2	2.6	1.6	0.3	1.6
平实生活指向 simple living orientation	316	13.9	2.8	1.6	0.0	1.3
时尚流行指向 fashion orientation	296	16.6	2.4	1.7	0.7	2.0

续前表 continued

	人数 Number	羽毛球 badminton	乒乓球 table tennis	台球 billiards	马拉松 Marathon	滑雪 skiing
样本 Sample	612	0.3	2.5	1.1	0.3	0.0
平实生活指向 simple living orientation	316	0.3	2.5	1.3	0.0	0.0
时尚流行指向 fashion orientation	296	0.3	2.4	1.0	0.7	0.0

续前表 continued

	人数 Number	滑冰 skating	摩托车赛 motorcycle race	汽车拉力赛 car rally	棋类比赛 chessman	拳击 box	没看 didn't watch
样本 Sample	612	0.2	0.3	0.7	1.0	0.5	81.7
平实生活指向 simple living orientation	316	0.0	0.3	0.3	0.9	0.0	82.6
时尚流行指向 fashion orientation	296	0.3	0.3	1.0	1.0	1.0	80.7

6-4-2 广告态度指标/ Advertising Attitude Index

注：本题为多选题，合计百分比超过 100%（Multiple answers）

	人数 Number	足球 football	篮球 basketball	排球 volleyball	网球 tennis	保龄球 bowling
样本 Sample	614	15.1	2.6	1.6	0.3	1.6
广告淡漠指向 indifferent orientation	182	14.8	3.3	1.6	0.0	1.6
中间层 medium	361	15.2	2.2	1.7	0.3	1.4
信赖广告指向 loyal orientation	71	15.5	2.8	1.4	1.4	2.8

续前表 continued

	人数 Number	羽毛球 badminton	乒乓球 table tennis	台球 billiards	马拉松 Marathon	滑雪 skiing
样本 Sample	614	0.3	2.4	1.1	0.3	0.0
广告淡漠指向 indifferent orientation	182	0.0	1.6	1.1	0.0	0.0
中间层 medium	361	0.0	2.5	1.4	0.3	0.0
信赖广告指向 loyal orientation	71	2.8	4.2	0.0	1.4	0.0

续前表 continued

	人数 Number	滑冰 skating	摩托车赛 motorcycle race	汽车拉力赛 car rally	棋类比赛 chessman	拳击 box	没看 didn't watch
样本 Sample	614	0.2	0.3	0.7	1.0	0.5	81.8
广告淡漠指向 indifferent orientation	182	0.0	0.0	0.5	1.1	0.0	83.5
中间层 medium	361	0.3	0.6	0.6	0.8	0.6	80.6
信赖广告指向 loyal orientation	71	0.0	0.0	1.4	1.4	1.4	83.1

● 西安 / Xi'an

6-1 样本、男性各年龄层、女性各年龄层通过电视观看的体育比赛/ Proportion of the Watching Sports Games through TV by the Whole Sample, Age and Gender Groups

注：本题为多选题，合计百分比超过 100%（Multiple answers）

	人数 Number	足球 football	篮球 basketball	排球 volleyball	网球 tennis	保龄球 bowling
样本 Sample	599	61.3	35.6	40.2	11.0	12.2
男性 Male	300	76.7	49.3	42.3	15.0	16.3
16~24 岁 Age	64	78.1	73.4	42.2	15.6	15.6
25~34 岁 Age	90	81.1	41.1	36.7	15.6	14.4
35~44 岁 Age	76	76.3	40.8	38.2	13.2	18.4
45~54 岁 Age	46	69.6	45.7	56.5	15.2	19.6
55~60 岁 Age	24	70.8	50.0	50.0	16.7	12.5
女性 Female	299	45.8	21.7	38.1	7.0	8.0
16~24 岁 Age	61	47.5	24.6	32.8	11.5	11.5
25~34 岁 Age	90	48.9	15.6	33.3	12.2	12.2
35~44 岁 Age	74	45.9	27.0	45.9	2.7	2.7
45~54 岁 Age	49	36.7	18.4	34.7	0.0	2.0
55~60 岁 Age	25	48.0	28.0	52.0	4.0	12.0

续前表 continued

	人数 Number	羽毛球 badminton	乒乓球 table tennis	台球 billiards	马拉松 Marathon	滑雪 skiing
样本 Sample	599	16.7	36.6	15.7	6.5	7.3
男性 Male	300	19.7	42.3	23.7	9.0	7.0
16~24 岁 Age	64	21.9	45.3	37.5	6.3	6.3
25~34 岁 Age	90	18.9	32.2	23.3	7.8	4.4
35~44 岁 Age	76	22.4	43.4	18.4	11.8	5.3
45~54 岁 Age	46	15.2	54.3	21.7	10.9	13.0
55~60 岁 Age	24	16.7	45.8	8.3	8.3	12.5
女性 Female	299	13.7	30.8	7.7	4.0	7.7
16~24 岁 Age	61	16.4	24.6	11.5	1.6	4.9
25~34 岁 Age	90	14.4	31.1	10.0	2.2	5.6
35~44 岁 Age	74	16.2	33.8	5.4	5.4	8.1
45~54 岁 Age	49	6.1	26.5	2.0	2.0	8.2
55~60 岁 Age	25	12.0	44.0	8.0	16.0	20.0

续前表 continued

	人数 Number	滑冰 skating	摩托车赛 motorcycle race	汽车拉力赛 car rally	棋类比赛 chessman	拳击 box	没看 didn't watch
样本 Sample	599	11.0	15.9	14.2	9.3	26.0	18.4
男性 Male	300	8.7	24.3	21.7	14.7	38.3	9.7
16~24 岁 Age	64	7.8	29.7	28.1	12.5	43.8	1.6
25~34 岁 Age	90	5.6	28.9	23.3	17.8	41.1	8.9
35~44 岁 Age	76	9.2	19.7	18.4	14.5	32.9	13.2
45~54 岁 Age	46	15.2	21.7	19.6	15.2	43.5	8.7
55~60 岁 Age	24	8.3	12.5	12.5	8.3	20.8	25.0
女性 Female	299	13.4	7.4	6.7	4.0	13.7	27.1
16~24 岁 Age	61	11.5	9.8	4.9	4.9	19.7	27.9
25~34 岁 Age	90	13.3	5.6	7.8	3.3	13.3	18.9
35~44 岁 Age	74	17.6	5.4	5.4	5.4	13.5	23.0
45~54 岁 Age	49	6.1	8.2	4.1	0.0	10.2	49.0
55~60 岁 Age	25	20.0	12.0	16.0	8.0	8.0	24.0

6-2 通过现场观看的体育比赛的比例/ Proportion of the Watching Sports Games at the Scene

注：本题为多选题，合计百分比超过 100%（Multiple answers）

	人次 Person-time	百分比 Percent
足球 football	84	14.0
篮球 basketball	27	4.5
排球 volleyball	8	1.3
网球 tennis	1	0.2
保龄球 bowling	6	1.0
羽毛球 badminton	6	1.0
乒乓球 table tennis	11	1.8
台球 billiards	3	0.5
马拉松 Marathon	0	0.0
滑雪 skiing	0	0.0
滑冰 skating	0	0.0
摩托车赛 motorcycle race	1	0.2
汽车拉力赛 car rally	0	0.0
棋类比赛 chessman	5	0.8
拳击 box	1	0.2
没看 didn't watch	493	82.2

n=600

6-3 不同消费者层通过电视观看比赛的比例/ Proportion of the Watching Sports Games through TV by Market Segments

6-3-1 时尚流行指标/ Fads Popular Index

注：本题为多选题，合计百分比超过 100%（Multiple answers）

	人数 Number	足球 football	篮球 basketball	排球 volleyball	网球 tennis	保龄球 bowling
样本 Sample	**597**	**61.3**	**35.7**	**40.2**	**11.1**	**12.2**
平实生活指向 simple living orientation	339	59.6	31.9	38.9	10.6	10.6
时尚流行指向 fashion orientation	258	63.6	40.7	41.9	11.6	14.3

续前表 continued

	人数 Number	羽毛球 badminton	乒乓球 table tennis	台球 billiards	马拉松 Marathon	滑雪 skiing
样本 Sample	**597**	**16.8**	**36.5**	**15.7**	**6.5**	**7.2**
平实生活指向 simple living orientation	339	15.9	33.9	13.0	6.2	5.9
时尚流行指向 fashion orientation	258	17.8	39.9	19.4	7.0	8.9

续前表 continued

	人数 Number	滑冰 skating	摩托车赛 motorcycle race	汽车拉力赛 car rally	棋类比赛 chessman	拳击 box	没看 didn't watch
样本 Sample	**597**	**10.9**	**15.7**	**14.2**	**9.4**	**26.1**	**18.4**
平实生活指向 simple living orientation	339	8.8	12.1	12.4	9.1	23.3	20.9
时尚流行指向 fashion orientation	258	13.6	20.5	16.7	9.7	29.8	15.1

6-3-2 广告态度指标/ Advertising Attitude Index

注：本题为多选题，合计百分比超过 100%（Multiple answers）

	人数 Number	足球 football	篮球 basketball	排球 volleyball	网球 tennis	保龄球 bowling
样本 Sample	**595**	**61.5**	**35.8**	**40.3**	**11.1**	**12.3**
广告淡漠指向 indifferent orientation	184	59.8	28.8	37.5	6.5	7.6
中间层 medium	333	63.4	38.4	42.0	14.7	15.6
信赖广告指向 loyal orientation	78	57.7	41.0	39.7	6.4	9.0

续前表 continued

	人数 Number	羽毛球 badminton	乒乓球 table tennis	台球 billiards	马拉松 Marathon	滑雪 skiing
样本 Sample	**595**	**16.8**	**36.8**	**15.8**	**6.6**	**7.4**
广告淡漠指向 indifferent orientation	184	12.0	31.0	12.0	3.3	6.0
中间层 medium	333	20.1	41.1	18.6	9.0	9.3
信赖广告指向 loyal orientation	78	14.1	32.1	12.8	3.8	2.6

续前表 continued

	人数 Number	滑冰 skating	摩托车赛 motorcycle race	汽车拉力赛 car rally	棋类比赛 chessman	拳击 box	没看 didn't watch
样本 Sample	**595**	**11.1**	**16.0**	**14.3**	**9.2**	**26.2**	**18.2**
广告淡漠指向 indifferent orientation	184	11.4	11.4	12.5	6.0	19.6	22.3
中间层 medium	333	12.3	18.9	16.2	12.0	31.8	15.3
信赖广告指向 loyal orientation	78	5.1	14.1	10.3	5.1	17.9	20.5

6-4 不同消费者层通过现场观看比赛的比例/Proportion of the Watching Sports Games at the Scene by Market Segments

6-4-1 时尚流行指标/ Fads Popular Index

注：本题为多选题，合计百分比超过 100%（Multiple answers）

	人数 Number	足球 football	篮球 basketball	排球 volleyball	网球 tennis	保龄球 bowling
样本 Sample	598	14.0	4.5	1.3	0.2	1.0
平实生活指向 simple living orientation	340	11.5	3.2	1.2	0.0	0.6
时尚流行指向 fashion orientation	258	17.4	6.2	1.6	0.4	1.6

续前表 continued

	人数 Number	羽毛球 badminton	乒乓球 table tennis	台球 billiards	马拉松 Marathon	滑雪 skiing
样本 Sample	598	1.0	1.8	0.5	0.0	0.0
平实生活指向 simple living orientation	340	0.9	1.2	0.0	0.0	0.0
时尚流行指向 fashion orientation	258	1.2	2.7	1.2	0.0	0.0

续前表 continued

	人数 Number	滑冰 skating	摩托车赛 motorcycle race	汽车拉力赛 car rally	棋类比赛 chessman	拳击 box	没看 didn't watch
样本 Sample	598	0.0	0.2	0.0	0.8	0.2	82.1
平实生活指向 simple living orientation	340	0.0	0.0	0.0	0.6	0.0	85.3
时尚流行指向 fashion orientation	258	0.0	0.4	0.0	1.2	0.4	77.9

6-4-2 广告态度指标/ Advertising Attitude Index

注：本题为多选题，合计百分比超过 100%（Multiple answers）

	人数 Number	足球 football	篮球 basketball	排球 volleyball	网球 tennis	保龄球 bowling
样本 Sample	596	14.1	4.5	1.3	0.2	1.0
广告淡漠指向 indifferent orientation	184	12.5	3.8	1.1	0.0	0.5
中间层 medium	333	14.4	4.8	1.5	0.3	1.5
信赖广告指向 loyal orientation	79	16.5	5.1	1.3	0.0	0.0

续前表 continued

	人数 Number	羽毛球 badminton	乒乓球 table tennis	台球 billiards	马拉松 Marathon	滑雪 skiing
样本 Sample	596	1.0	1.8	0.5	0.0	0.0
广告淡漠指向 indifferent orientation	184	0.5	1.6	0.0	0.0	0.0
中间层 medium	333	1.5	2.1	0.6	0.0	0.0
信赖广告指向 loyal orientation	79	0.0	1.3	1.3	0.0	0.0

续前表 continued

	人数 Number	滑冰 skating	摩托车赛 motorcycle race	汽车拉力赛 car rally	棋类比赛 chessman	拳击 box	没看 didn't watch
样本 Sample	596	0.0	0.2	0.0	0.8	0.2	82.0
广告淡漠指向 indifferent orientation	184	0.0	0.0	0.0	0.5	0.0	84.8
中间层 medium	333	0.0	0.3	0.0	1.2	0.0	81.1
信赖广告指向 loyal orientation	79	0.0	0.0	0.0	0.0	1.3	79.7

● 沈阳 / Shenyang

6-1 样本、男性各年龄层、女性各年龄层通过电视观看的体育比赛/ Proportion of the Watching Sports Games through TV by the Whole Sample, Age and Gender Groups

注：本题为多选题，合计百分比超过 100%（Multiple answers）

	人数 Number	足球 football	篮球 basketball	排球 volleyball	网球 tennis	保龄球 bowling
样本 Sample	**597**	**73.9**	**56.6**	**61.3**	**27.0**	**27.3**
男性 Male	**298**	**85.9**	**68.8**	**69.1**	**34.6**	**34.9**
16~24 岁 Age	64	95.3	92.2	73.4	48.4	40.6
25~34 岁 Age	88	86.4	59.1	70.5	38.6	42.0
35~44 岁 Age	76	80.3	60.5	61.8	28.9	31.6
45~54 岁 Age	46	78.3	65.2	69.6	17.4	19.6
55~60 岁 Age	24	91.7	75.0	75.0	33.3	33.3
女性 Female	**299**	**61.9**	**44.5**	**53.5**	**19.4**	**19.7**
16~24 岁 Age	63	65.1	57.1	44.4	23.8	28.6
25~34 岁 Age	88	56.8	39.8	53.4	15.9	22.7
35~44 岁 Age	76	65.8	39.5	64.5	17.1	17.1
45~54 岁 Age	48	68.8	47.9	54.2	22.9	4.2
55~60 岁 Age	24	45.8	37.5	41.7	20.8	25.0

续前表 continued

	人数 Number	羽毛球 badminton	乒乓球 table tennis	台球 billiards	马拉松 Marathon	滑雪 skiing
样本 Sample	**597**	**30.8**	**53.1**	**27.1**	**19.9**	**17.4**
男性 Male	**298**	**38.3**	**61.1**	**39.6**	**25.8**	**21.8**
16~24 岁 Age	64	48.4	68.8	51.6	31.3	20.3
25~34 岁 Age	88	39.8	61.4	55.7	29.5	23.9
35~44 岁 Age	76	32.9	57.9	30.3	21.1	21.1
45~54 岁 Age	46	28.3	56.5	17.4	21.7	17.4
55~60 岁 Age	24	41.7	58.3	20.8	20.8	29.2
女性 Female	**299**	**23.4**	**45.2**	**14.7**	**14.0**	**13.0**
16~24 岁 Age	63	19.0	42.9	25.4	22.2	19.0
25~34 岁 Age	88	27.3	40.9	13.6	9.1	11.4
35~44 岁 Age	76	25.0	51.3	9.2	11.8	10.5
45~54 岁 Age	48	22.9	43.8	10.4	16.7	14.6
55~60 岁 Age	24	16.7	50.0	16.7	12.5	8.3

续前表 continued

	人数 Number	滑冰 skating	摩托车赛 motorcycle race	汽车拉力赛 car rally	棋类比赛 chessman	拳击 box	没看 didn't watch
样本 Sample	**597**	**22.6**	**26.6**	**26.5**	**22.4**	**46.6**	**12.9**
男性 Male	**298**	**25.8**	**39.3**	**39.6**	**32.2**	**66.1**	**4.7**
16~24 岁 Age	64	28.1	48.4	42.2	42.2	75.0	0.0
25~34 岁 Age	88	26.1	43.2	46.6	37.5	68.2	0.0
35~44 岁 Age	76	23.7	38.2	38.2	23.7	65.8	9.2
45~54 岁 Age	46	21.7	23.9	26.1	23.9	56.5	13.0
55~60 岁 Age	24	33.3	33.3	37.5	29.2	54.2	4.2
女性 Female	**299**	**19.4**	**14.0**	**13.4**	**12.7**	**27.1**	**21.1**
16~24 岁 Age	63	25.4	17.5	15.9	20.6	28.6	14.3
25~34 岁 Age	88	14.8	12.5	14.8	12.5	30.7	21.6
35~44 岁 Age	76	17.1	13.2	11.8	5.3	25.0	18.4
45~54 岁 Age	48	25.0	16.7	12.5	10.4	29.2	22.9
55~60 岁 Age	24	16.7	8.3	8.3	20.8	12.5	41.7

6-2 通过现场观看的体育比赛的比例/ Proportion of the Watching Sports Games at the Scene

注：本题为多选题，合计百分比超过 100%（Multiple answers）

	人次 Person-time	百分比 Percent
足球 football	99	16.6
篮球 basketball	38	6.4
排球 volleyball	9	1.5
网球 tennis	2	0.3
保龄球 bowling	7	1.2
羽毛球 badminton	3	0.5
乒乓球 table tennis	6	1.0
台球 billiards	5	0.8
马拉松 Marathon	0	0.0
滑雪 skiing	0	0.0
滑冰 skating	0	0.0
摩托车赛 motorcycle race	1	0.2
汽车拉力赛 car rally	1	0.2
棋类比赛 chessman	2	0.3
拳击 box	1	0.2
没看 didn't watch	479	80.4

n=596

6-3 不同消费者层通过电视观看的体育比赛/ Proportion of the Watching Sports Games through TV by Market Segments

6-3-1 时尚流行指标/ Fads Popular Index

注：本题为多选题，合计百分比超过 100%（Multiple answers）

	人数 Number	足球 football	篮球 basketball	排球 volleyball	网球 tennis	保龄球 bowling
样本 Sample	597	73.9	56.6	61.3	27.0	27.3
平实生活指向 simple living orientation	290	71.0	51.0	58.3	25.9	23.4
时尚流行指向 fashion orientation	307	76.5	61.9	64.2	28.0	30.9

续前表 continued

	人数 Number	羽毛球 badminton	乒乓球 table tennis	台球 billiards	马拉松 Marathon	滑雪 skiing
样本 Sample	597	30.8	53.1	27.1	19.9	17.4
平实生活指向 simple living orientation	290	28.3	49.7	26.6	16.6	14.8
时尚流行指向 fashion orientation	307	33.2	56.4	27.7	23.1	19.9

续前表 continued

	人数 Number	滑冰 skating	摩托车赛 motorcycle race	汽车拉力赛 car rally	棋类比赛 chessman	拳击 box	没看 didn't watch
样本 Sample	597	22.6	26.6	26.5	22.4	46.6	12.9
平实生活指向 simple living orientation	290	20.7	23.1	23.8	20.7	41.7	16.2
时尚流行指向 fashion orientation	307	24.4	30.0	29.0	24.1	51.1	9.8

6-3-2 广告态度指标/ Advertising Attitude Index

注：本题为多选题，合计百分比超过 100%（Multiple answers）

	人数 Number	足球 football	篮球 basketball	排球 volleyball	网球 tennis	保龄球 bowling
样本 Sample	597	73.9	56.6	61.3	27.0	27.3
广告淡漠指向 indifferent orientation	171	66.1	55.6	55.0	22.2	23.4
中间层 medium	351	76.9	56.1	62.1	27.9	28.2
信赖广告指向 loyal orientation	75	77.3	61.3	72.0	33.3	32.0

续前表 continued

	人数 Number	羽毛球 badminton	乒乓球 table tennis	台球 billiards	马拉松 Marathon	滑雪 skiing
样本 Sample	597	30.8	53.1	27.1	19.9	17.4
广告淡漠指向 indifferent orientation	171	25.7	48.0	26.9	13.5	9.9
中间层 medium	351	31.1	54.1	27.1	23.1	20.8
信赖广告指向 loyal orientation	75	41.3	60.0	28.0	20.0	18.7

续前表 continued

	人数 Number	滑冰 skating	摩托车赛 motorcycle race	汽车拉力赛 car rally	棋类比赛 chessman	拳击 box	没看 didn't watch
样本 Sample	597	22.6	26.6	26.5	22.4	46.6	12.9
广告淡漠指向 indifferent orientation	171	17.5	22.2	23.4	18.7	39.2	16.4
中间层 medium	351	25.4	25.9	25.6	23.6	47.9	12.5
信赖广告指向 loyal orientation	75	21.3	40.0	37.3	25.3	57.3	6.7

6-4 不同消费者层通过现场观看比赛的比例/ Proportion of the Watching Sports Games at the Scene by Market Segments

6-4-1 时尚流行指标/ Fads Popular Index

注：本题为多选题，合计百分比超过 100%（Multiple answers）

	人数 Number	足球 football	篮球 basketball	排球 volleyball	网球 tennis	保龄球 bowling
样本 Sample	596	16.6	6.4	1.5	0.3	1.2
平实生活指向 simple living orientation	290	14.5	4.5	0.7	0.3	1.0
时尚流行指向 fashion orientation	306	18.6	8.2	2.3	0.3	1.3

续前表 continued

	人数 Number	羽毛球 badminton	乒乓球 table tennis	台球 billiards	马拉松 Marathon	滑雪 skiing
样本 Sample	596	0.5	1.0	0.8	0.0	0.0
平实生活指向 simple living orientation	290	1.0	1.0	1.0	0.0	0.0
时尚流行指向 fashion orientation	306	0.0	1.0	0.7	0.0	0.0

续前表 continued

	人数 Number	滑冰 skating	摩托车赛 motorcycle race	汽车拉力赛 car rally	棋类比赛 chessman	拳击 box	没看 didn't watch
样本 Sample	596	0.0	0.2	0.2	0.3	0.2	80.4
平实生活指向 simple living orientation	290	0.0	0.0	0.0	0.7	0.3	82.4
时尚流行指向 fashion orientation	306	0.0	0.3	0.3	0.0	0.0	78.4

6-4-2 广告态度指标/ Advertising Attitude Index

注：本题为多选题，合计百分比超过 100%（Multiple answers）

	人数 Number	足球 football	篮球 basketball	排球 volleyball	网球 tennis	保龄球 bowling
样本 Sample	596	16.6	6.4	1.5	0.3	1.2
广告淡漠指向 indifferent orientation	171	15.2	3.5	0.0	0.0	0.6
中间层 medium	350	15.4	6.6	1.7	0.0	1.1
信赖广告指向 loyal orientation	75	25.3	12.0	4.0	2.7	2.7

续前表 continued

	人数 Number	羽毛球 badminton	乒乓球 table tennis	台球 billiards	马拉松 Marathon	滑雪 skiing
样本 Sample	**596**	**0.5**	**1.0**	**0.8**	**0.0**	**0.0**
广告淡漠指向 indifferent orientation	171	0.0	0.0	0.0	0.0	0.0
中间层 medium	350	0.3	1.4	0.3	0.0	0.0
信赖广告指向 loyal orientation	75	2.7	1.3	5.3	0.0	0.0

续前表 continued

	人数 Number	滑冰 skating	摩托车赛 motorcycle race	汽车拉力赛 car rally	棋类比赛 chessman	拳击 box	没看 didn't watch
样本 Sample	**596**	**0.0**	**0.2**	**0.2**	**0.3**	**0.2**	**80.4**
广告淡漠指向 indifferent orientation	171	0.0	0.0	0.0	0.0	0.0	81.9
中间层 medium	350	0.0	0.3	0.0	0.0	0.3	82.3
信赖广告指向 loyal orientation	75	0.0	0.0	1.3	2.7	0.0	68.0

7.交通工具 / Transportation

● 北京 / Beijing

经常使用的交通工具/ Means of Transportation

注：本题为多选题，合计百分比超过 100%（Multiple answers）

	人次 Person-time	百分比 Percent
自行车 bicycle	685	67.9
公共汽车/空调巴士 bus	575	57.0
单位交通车 commuter bus of work unit	97	9.6
小公共汽车 mini-bus	211	20.9
摩托车 motorcycle	39	3.9
地铁 subway	176	17.4
步行 on foot	148	14.7
出租车 taxi	269	26.7
轮渡 ship	0	0.0
私人汽车 private car	89	8.8
助动车 motor-aided bike	4	0.4
其他 others	14	1.4

n=1009

● 上海 / Shanghai

经常使用的交通工具/ Means of Transportation

注：本题为多选题，合计百分比超过 100%（Multiple answers）

	人次 Person-time	百分比 Percent
自行车 bicycle	544	53.8
公共汽车/空调巴士 bus	715	70.7
单位交通车 commuter bus of work unit	38	3.8
小公共汽车 mini-bus	150	14.8
摩托车 motorcycle	29	2.9
地铁 subway	130	12.8
步行 on foot	279	27.6
出租车 taxi	212	20.9
轮渡 ship	31	3.1
私人汽车 private car	16	1.6
助动车 motor-aided bike	78	7.7
其他 others	4	0.4

n=1012

● 广州 / Guangzhou

经常使用的交通工具/ Means of Transportation

注：本题为多选题，合计百分比超过 100%（Multiple answers）

	人次 Person-time	百分比 Percent
自行车 bicycle	416	40.4
公共汽车/空调巴士 bus	793	77.1
单位交通车 commuter bus of work unit	50	4.9
小公共汽车 mini-bus	37	3.6
摩托车 motorcycle	219	21.3
地铁 subway	154	15.0
步行 on foot	339	32.9
出租车 taxi	175	17.0
轮渡 ship	4	0.4
私人汽车 private car	18	1.7
助动车 motor-aided bike	1	0.1
其他 others	27	2.6

n=1029

● 重庆 / Chongqing

经常使用的交通工具/ Means of Transportation

注：本题为多选题，合计百分比超过 100%（Multiple answers）

	人次 Person-time	百分比 Percent
自行车 bicycle	11	1.8
公共汽车/空调巴士 bus	525	84.4
单位交通车 commuter bus of work unit	18	2.9
小公共汽车 mini-bus	313	50.3
摩托车 motorcycle	15	2.4
地铁 subway	0	0.0
步行 on foot	264	42.4
出租车 taxi	165	26.5
轮渡 ship	10	1.6
私人汽车 private car	15	2.4
助动车 motor-aided bike	0	0.0
其他 others	6	1.0

n=622

● 武汉 / Wuhan

经常使用的交通工具/ Means of Transportation

注：本题为多选题，合计百分比超过 100%（Multiple answers）

	人次 Person-time	百分比 Percent
自行车 bicycle	315	50.6
公共汽车/空调巴士 bus	469	75.3
单位交通车 commuter bus of work unit	30	4.8
小公共汽车 mini-bus	66	10.6
摩托车 motorcycle	49	7.9
地铁 subway	0	0.0
步行 on foot	204	32.7
出租车 taxi	155	24.9
轮渡 ship	9	1.4
私人汽车 private car	8	1.3
助动车 motor-aided bike	102	16.4
其他 others	2	0.3

n=623

● 西安 / Xi'an

经常使用的交通工具/ Means of Transportation

注：本题为多选题，合计百分比超过 100%（Multiple answers）

	人次 Person-time	百分比 Percent
自行车 bicycle	378	63.2
公共汽车/空调巴士 bus	377	63.0
单位交通车 commuter bus of work unit	20	3.3
小公共汽车 mini-bus	104	17.4
摩托车 motorcycle	63	10.5
地铁 subway	0	0.0
步行 on foot	142	23.7
出租车 taxi	154	25.8
轮渡 ship	0	0.0
私人汽车 private car	9	1.5
助动车 motor-aided bike	3	0.5
其他 others	7	1.2

n=598

● 沈阳 / Shenyang

经常使用的交通工具/ Means of Transportation

注：本题为多选题，合计百分比超过 100%（Multiple answers）

	人次 Person-time	百分比 Percent
自行车 bicycle	450	75.1
公共汽车/空调巴士 bus	306	51.1
单位交通车 commuter bus of work unit	25	4.2
小公共汽车 mini-bus	37	6.2
摩托车 motorcycle	33	5.5
地铁 subway	0	0.0
步行 on foot	136	22.7
出租车 taxi	127	21.2
轮渡 ship	0	0.0
私人汽车 private car	5	0.8
助动车 motor-aided bike	1	0.2
其他 others	5	0.8

n=599

第五篇　食品
Part V　Food

- 奶粉　Milk Powder
- 豆奶粉　Powdered Soybean Milk
- 包装牛奶　Packaged Milk
- 酸奶　Yogurt
- 巧克力　Chocolate
- 冰淇淋　Ice-cream
- 饼干　Biscuit
- 方便面　Instant Noodles

食　品

改革开放20年来我国食品工业发展非常迅速，目前食品工业总产值在全国工业中的比重已上升为第一位。在我国，虽然随着人均收入水平的提高，食品支出在消费总支出的比例呈逐年下降趋势，但是绝对值却呈上升趋势，像我国这样一个拥有十多亿人口的大国，食品行业正越来越成为一个名副其实的朝阳行业。

目前，我国食品行业的基本现状是：第一，食品加工企业产品基本停留在粗加工上，缺少精加工产品，产品附加值低。一个先进的食品工业体系，其深加工产品、直接入口的产品应占主导地位，发达国家深加工产品所占比例为 80%，而我国食品工业总产值中有近一半是基础原料加工产品，即糖、油、饲料等食品，深加工产品只占 16%，而烟酒等嗜好品产值却占 30%。第二，食品市场总量生产相对过剩和需求相对不足同时存在，低水平重复建设比比皆是，整体布局不合理，部分产品生产能力过剩。第三，食品行业缺少有竞争力，极具品牌知名度的企业和产品，大多数食品企业集约化程度低，规模效益差，配套能力低，影响资源的开发利用。有一些在地区具备一定知名度的企业，但缺少在全国范围有一定影响力和较高市场份额的企业。第四，企业两极分化，亏损企业不断增加。食品行业是一个完全自由竞争行业，激烈的竞争造成整个行业的平均利润率不断下降，只有那些有自己经营特色的、有规模效益的企业才能获得较高的收益水平。第五，国有企业和集体企业的发展速度远不如三资企业和其他类型的企业。面对中国这个巨大的市场，许多跨国公司凭借雄厚的财力和丰富的市场运作经验，通过收购国内著名品牌或合资、独资经营挤占国内市场。

1998年中国主要城市居民消费品调查食品品牌市场占有率（单位：%）

排位比例 / 产品种类	第一位		第二位		第三位	
	品牌名称	所占比例	品牌名称	所占比例	品牌名称	所占比例
方便面	康师傅	51.4	统一	19.7	华丰	5.1
奶粉	雀巢	21.5	安怡	6.3	惠氏	4.9
饼干	奇宝	10.6	达能	8.3	康师傅	7.8
巧克力	德芙	35.1	吉百利	11.7	金帝	11.2
乳酸制品	乐百氏	9.3	光明	8.9	达能	6.5
液体牛奶	光明	13.2	三元	6.4	三岛	3.8
雪糕/冰淇淋	伊利	20.0	和路雪	11.9	五羊	9.4

（资料来源：《中国消费者报》99.1.1）

我国食品市场是一个刚性较大的市场，也是一个弹性较大的市场。由于收入的增长、生活方式的变化、生活水准的提高，人们对各种食品的需求也处于变换之中，从 1982 年以来，我国人群膳食构成的变化是：来自谷类和薯类食物的热能有较大下降，来自动物性食物、纯热能食物及其他食物的比例有明显上升，但是我国人民的食物消费基本上仍属于“高谷物膳食”类型，总体营养水平还较低。动物蛋白质所占比重仍明显低于世界平均水平，也低于亚洲和发展中国家的平均水平。

根据国务院有关部门《关于中国食品结构改革和发展纲要的建议》，2000 年我国人民食品消费和营养的基本目标是：人均每日主要营养供给量达到世界平均水平，其中热量2600大卡，蛋白质72克；人均全年主要食物消费水平，在坚持植物性食物为主、动物性食物为辅的食物模式同时，将有较大提高，重点是提高动物性食品的消费水平。从世界食品工业的发展趋势来看，随着社会的进步、食品安全和环保意识的增强以及科学技术革命的发展，大众化的方便食品和健康食品越来越受到消费者的青睐，食品市场需求将呈现多样化、功能化、方便化特点。因此高附加值、高科技与文化含量的产品应是未来的发展方向，具体包括方便食品、休闲食品、功能食品、饮料、调味品及食品工业基础原料等。《关于全国食品工业“九五”计划和 2010 年远景目标的建议》中指出：“随着社会的进步、生活节奏的加快、家庭生活水平的提高，人们希望吃得卫生、营养、保健、方便，要充分开发优质大豆蛋白以及食用方便的食品，要增加食品制造、食品加工和饮料制造的产量，大力发展方便食品，精心实施名牌战略。食品工业今后 15 年的基本任务是：加快发展食品工业，适应社会发展和人民生活水平提高对品牌、质量、档次和数量的需求，2000 年工业总产值比 1990 年增加两倍，到 2010 年再翻一番以上”。这为我国食品行业提供了巨大的商机。我国今后几年食品工业的发展重点是：充分利用农产品原料，提高对农产品的加工深度和广度；积极发展奶制品生产，发展方便食品，推进传统食品的现代化、方便化；发展营养保健食品、提高食品添加剂水平。

奶粉及包装奶

近几年来，我国乳品加工业技术装备水平有了较大进步，产品质量有了明显提高，乳与乳制品产量成倍增加。1978 年，我国奶类总产量尚不足 100 万吨，乳制品产量 4.63 万吨；至 1997 年，奶类总产量达到 774 万吨，乳制品产量 56.5 万吨。1998 年奶类总产量比去年增长 6%，乳制品产量比去年增长 7%。目前全国有乳品企业近 700 家，其中大型企业和知名品牌也不少，如石家庄三鹿集团、上海光明乳业集团、山西古城乳业有限公司、西安银桥乳品实业有限公司、北京三元食品有限公司等。目前，大中型企业乳制品产量占全国总产量的 80%。1998 年全国共进口各种乳制品 11 万吨，其中奶粉 10 万吨，进口乳制品市场占有率约为 15%左右，进口的各种奶粉类产品的市场占有率约在 20%左右。

目前国内市场上的奶类产品主要分为液体奶，冷冻饮品和乳制品。液体奶分两类：巴士杀菌奶和酸奶，利乐包装纯奶和花色奶。国内液体奶产量最大的两个企业是上海光明乳业公司和北京三元食品有限公司，它们 1997 年的液体奶产量分别是 175,786 吨和 91,201 吨，列第三位的哈尔滨金星乳业集团的产量是 5,410 吨。国内乳制品生产以奶粉为主。目前，国内奶粉生产企业正处于两极分化时期。经过几年的竞争，一些优秀企业脱颖而出，它们通过新产品开发，市场开拓和品牌建设，使产品的市场份额和企业规模逐渐扩大。已形成的著名品牌有“三鹿”、“伊利”、“完达山”和“金星”等。目前市场份额最大的是石家庄三鹿集团的三鹿奶粉；内蒙古伊利实业集团股份有限公司和黑龙江省完达山企业集团、哈尔滨金星乳业集团同属第二集团，这些企业的年销量在 1—1.5 万吨之间。

我国奶业已取得了长足发展：牛奶质量好，加工技术逐年提高，管理及检测水平也接近了国际标准，从原料、半成品到制成品大都符合国家有关规定，是实实在在的“放心奶”。按理说，奶业该蒸蒸日上，可事实却相反。中国奶业正处于发展的“瓶颈”期，主要表现在：生产布局集中于几个大城市，服务体系不够完善；乳品加工相对滞后；产品质量、结构与顾客消费意向有较大差距；再加上受传统饮食习惯影响，奶类产品的消费偏低。这些都限制了奶业的正常良性发展。

著名营养学专家于若木认为，在我国目前条件下，牛奶加鸡蛋是理想的早餐模式：二者价格便宜，营养丰富，又是方便食品，适应现代生活节奏。但现阶段牛奶并未受到国人足够重视，全世界年人均占有量为 102 公斤，发展中国家为 30 多公斤，而我国仅有 6.6 公斤。如果我们以“一杯牛奶强壮一个民族”为口号，来提高我国居民的牛奶消费水平，那么牛奶的真正需求量应该是目前生产水平的 13 倍！中国奶业可谓商机无限。

同时，1999 年的外部市场条件也为我国奶制品企业提供了发展的契机。比利时、荷兰、德国和法国等四国的奶粉二恶英污染事件使政府有关部门发布暂停进口和销售其食品的通告。这对国内的乳制品企业不啻天赐良机。

国家也一直加强牛奶消费的宣传。中国乳制品工业协会在 1998 年启动首届乳与乳制品宣传之后，在 1999 年再次大张旗鼓地宣传，提倡每人每天一杯牛奶，既提高国人身体素质，又扩大牛奶消费。市场专家认为学生是一个数量大、易培养品牌忠诚度的消费群体，其饮用习惯对乳品企业有指引作用，因此企业应配合有关部门，适价向学生销售奶品，树立自己的品牌形象。据悉，一项旨在尽快改善营养状况的跨世纪工程“中国学生奶推广活动”日前在全国启动，这项工程计划用五年左右的时间，在全国县城以上的城市推广。因此在可以预见的将来，我国的乳品工业将为众商家提供无限商机。

豆奶粉

目前，我国食物结构中优质蛋白的成分严重不足，而根据我国人民的消费习惯和资源供应状况，我们的膳食结构模式又不可能像西方一样，单纯靠增加动物蛋白来调整，因此尽管奶粉正日益进入中国人的家庭，高蛋白质的豆奶粉却始终是人们生活中必不可少的营养补充。

豆奶粉受到人们的重视，首要因素就是它的营养价值得到人们的认可，其富含的优质植物蛋白是牛奶所无法补充的；同时豆制品作为中国人的传统食品已有两三千年的历史，其口味也为人们所接受，而相比起奶粉来，这是一个传统的优势；另外一个重要因素就是我国作为一个农业大国，大豆的产量大、质量好，能够研制优质豆奶粉，这是在我国发展豆奶粉生产的得天独厚的条件。而且从直接食用消费的角度来看，物美价廉的豆奶粉适合不同层次的消费需求，高收入阶层和低收入阶层都接受大豆的优质植物蛋白，消费范围较奶粉更广，因此豆奶粉的消费量稳步增加。

目前，我国的豆奶粉行业已由原来的作坊式生产进入到工业化生产，出现了许多著名品牌，如“维维”、“完达山”、“晨星岛”等。随着我国人口的增加和国内经济的发展，以及膳食结构逐步趋向高蛋白化，豆奶粉消费在相当长的时期内将保持稳步增长趋势。

豆奶粉行业是改善我国膳食结构的重要成员，只要有计划地开发，该产业将成为我国食品工业一个新兴的大行业，它将会是食品工业发展的重要增长点。我们根据各地的实际情况做一个规划，扩大豆奶粉的品种，在主食、副食、学生餐中推广应用，只要产品规范化了，包装改进了，质量问题进一步提高了，发展的远景是极大的。

巧克力

巧克力自诞生以来已有 80 多年的历史，它以其独特的口感、丝绸般的细腻、浓郁的可口香味及高营养的价值，深受人们的喜爱而久销不衰。

但由于产地和原料的问题，我国的巧克力工业起步较晚，发展也较缓慢。新中国成立后，国内砂糖、糖浆、油脂和乳制品等基础工业逐渐建立和发展起来，巧克力工业进入到一个较快的发展时期。70 年代，北京、上海、广州等地出现了巧克力生产企业，为数不多的企业的生产方式变为机械化和连续化生产。但那时，巧克力生产数量还特别少。改革开放到 90 年代，巧克力工业渐入佳境。各地企业积极引进和装备先进设备，北京义利、上海冠生园和天津的巧克力生产线成为当时装备水平的代表。

近几年来，巧克力工业发展迅速的主要原因还在于国际品牌抢滩中国市场。国际知名企业品牌仰仗其原材料、加工技术、产品质量、品牌形象等优势一进入中国市场就显示出了强大的冲击力。1998 年中国主要城市居民消费品调查之品牌市场占有率中巧克力前三位的品牌是德芙（35.1%）、吉百利（11.7%）、金帝（11.2%）。而同期十一城市消费者对第一代表性企业联想的排名百分比（前八位）如下：

品牌名称	德芙	义利	吉百利	金帝	金莎	申丰	M&M	伊利
排名百分比	41.8	11.9	10.9	7.0	5.0	3.8	1.6	1.5

（资料来源：《中国消费者报》99.1.29）

同时巧克力属于多元集中代表品牌的产品类型，领先地位的品牌与处在 2 － 4 位后的品牌的提及率有一定的差距，但这种差距并不像高度优势品牌与后续品牌的差距那么大，而且有相当数量的品牌以相近的占有率参与分割市场，领先品牌的优势明显但不是压倒性的；同时国内品牌虽似未形成有效影响，但在同国外产品的冲击和挑战中成长起来，已经具备了充分的实力和经验。如高居联想排名第二位的义利，是北京的国有老品牌，在北京享有很高的知名度，已成为首都 199 家大型超市的销售大户。义利集团下一步将发挥巧克力中档产品的主导优势，开拓市场，开发纯巧克力、果味巧克力等高档产品，向国际品牌发起挑战。

随着食品加工科技的发展，巧克力的营养价值正愈来愈广泛的发掘出来，出于生活享受和营养健康的角度，巧克力的消费将逐步提高。中国正处在由小康向中等发达国家过渡的阶段，大部分家庭的生活水平将在不长的时间里实现跨越。这是一个巨大的潜在市场，巧克力作为享受型食品，将极大的占有这个市场。

冰淇淋

自 1996 年以来，冰淇淋市场一直处于下滑的趋势，而且这种状况在 1999 年还将继续下去。市场情况虽然低迷，但也难挡冰淇淋企业的热情，而今夏的冰淇淋“大战”将出现一种新的趋势——价格战无人应答，区域战硝烟弥漫。

冷冻饮品是以饮用水、甜味料、乳品、果品、豆品、食用油脂等为原料，加入适量香料、着色剂、稳定剂、乳化剂等，经配料、灭菌、凝冻而制成的冷冻固态饮品，主要有冷霜、冰棍、雪糕、冰淇淋等几大类。

我国的冷饮工业从 1927 年开始，上海的海宁洋行是我国最早的冷饮厂家。建国后全国各地相继扩大冷饮食品工业，年产量在 8 万吨左右。90 年代进入飞速发展阶段，年产量达到 120 万吨，品种 3000 多种，年增长速度在 200%左右。主要特点为外商来华投资，联营企业纷纷成立，私营企业涉足。

目前国内冷饮市场三分天下：三资企业独霸高档市场；国营企业居中档；乡镇企业和私营企业占领低档市场。广东、北京和上海是目前销量最集中的三大地区，占全国销量的 25%。现在北京有大小冰淇淋企业 200 多家，产量在 10 万吨左右；上海全市有 200 多家冷饮厂，产量在 8 万吨左右；广东省冰淇淋企业近百家，产量在 10 万吨左右。另外几个冷饮工业较发达的城市是天津、杭州、南京等，产品品种多，以中高档为主。目前国内规模最大的冰淇淋和雪糕生产厂家是内蒙古伊利实业集团股份有限公司，1998 年其冷饮销售额达 52，327.81 万元，销量已连续四年居全国第一。

1998 年中国市场上的冰淇淋消费额超过了 200 亿元人民币。对市场的争夺，从时间上已由夏季蔓延到春秋冬；在地域上亦从地区性布点转向全国性布局。市场的主要特点可归纳为以下几点：

1．品种琳琅满目，高中低档应有尽有；

2．冷饮消费层次多样：商业区和娱乐场所中高档产品看好；市郊或城乡结合部中低档产品畅销；农村地区低档产品占主导；

3．冷饮厂家展开了营销大战：一直占据中高档产品市场的“和路雪”和“雀巢”纷纷降价 30%—50%，挤占中档市场；

4．产品销量基本稳定，价格稳中有降；

5．质量问题引起重视；

6．品牌消费渐成气候，品牌知名度的高低大有决定市场占有量的势头。进行品牌建设，提高知名度，亦是今后市场发展的大趋势。

目前中国人均消费冰淇淋是 1 升 / 年，欧洲是 7 升 / 年，而美国高达 25 升 / 年，套用一句老话：对于国际性品牌、国内大品牌以及地方小品牌来说，中国冰淇淋市场胃口很大。

饼干

中国饼干行业的发展一直十分缓慢。但近十几年来，随着该行业三资企业的进入，使原来以国有企业和集体企业为主体的中国饼干传统行业发生了深刻变化，从而有力的促进了中国饼干业的快速发展。

1997 年全国饼干生产企业有 600 多家，其中全年销售收入在 200 万元以上的企业有 302 家，资产总额 103 亿元，全年销售收入 80 亿元。1997 年，全国饼干产量为 93.1 万吨，进口 0.62 万吨，出口 3.5 万吨，市场需求量为 90.22 万吨，比 1994 年增长 10%。从价值量来看，饼干行业总产值为 77 亿元，进口 5 亿元，出口 3.9 亿元，市场需求额为 73.6 亿元，比 1994 年增长 66%。高中档饼干的加速发展，是市场需求额增长速度高于市场需求量增长速度的主要原因。

虽然三资企业进入中国饼干市场的时间不长，但由于其具有起点高、规模大、产品质量好、经营方式灵活等优点，因而一经进入市场便很快占有了较大的份额。1997 年饼干市场销售占有率中，三资企业占 51.5%。市场占有率较高的饼干品牌，如“纳贝斯克”、“奇宝”、“达能”等，几乎都是三资企业的品牌。相比之下，国内企业在生产规模、生产集中度、市场竞争力和经济效益等方面仍有较大差距。

目前，中国居民的饼干消费水平仍很低，全国人均年饼干消费额只有 6 元左右，说明饼干消费的潜力很大。今后，随着社会经济的发展，人们生活水平的提高，以及旅游业的发展，国内需求特别是城镇居民对饼干的需求量将会继续增长。今后若干年内，中国饼干市场需求量将每年递增 2—3 万吨，因而其发展前景十分看好。

方便面

我国方便面生产始于 1970 年，自 80 年代中期开始，进入高速增长期。目前，我国方便面产量已列世界首位。但由于前几年生产盲目扩张，近年方便面产量增速缓慢。对此，专家认为，就总体而言，我国方便面生产尚处于发展阶段。我国有 800 多家方便面厂家，1700 多条生产线，生产能力可达 350 万吨，实际产量超过 100 万吨。

据 1998 年中国城市食品消费形态调查结果显示：73%的居民使用方便面。其中，20%的人每月食用 10 包以上，26%的人每月食用 6—9 包，30%的人每月食用 3—5 包，24%的人每月食用 1—2 包。另据部分大中城市调查，消费者中 40.8%的人将方便面作为早餐，14%的人作为午餐，晚上以方便面当夜宵占 10%，无人做饭时应急食用的占 24%。由此可见，方便面已成为居民一日三餐不可或缺的组成部分。居民已从零散购买为主转变为整箱购买。仓储式商场、批发市场的发展，又以其低成本、低价格的策略推动了方便面的销售。

随着市场和品牌竞争的加剧，方便面的竞争逐渐演化为调料的竞争。现在，方便面的调料已由粉状发展到了酱状、液状和固体并存，出现了软包装菜肴料，风味向多样化方向发展。

在市场经济飞速发展时期，家庭生活社会化的趋势愈来愈明显，以方便面为首的方便食品也必将日益受宠。虽然我国方便面的产量居世界第一，但人均占有量仅居世界第九位，消费主要集中于城市居民，农村居民消费水平不及城市的三分之一。随着城市化步伐加快，城乡居民收入提高，方便面市场前景乐观。

Food

Along with 20 years of opening up and reformation, food industry of our country develops very fast. Now the proportion of the gross productivity of food industry in national industry as a whole has come up as the biggest. In China, as the average income of people increases, the expenditure on food increases, although the ratio of food expenditure in the whole consumption reduces year by year. With more than 1 billion population, China's food industry is more and more like a rising-sun business.

At present, the basic situation of our food industry is as follows. First, the food processing enterprise mainly remains at the stage of basic processing, lacking of highly finished products. The added-value of products is low. Highly finished products or those products that can be eaten directly should stand in the leading place in an advanced food industry system. The proportion of highly finished products accounts for 80% in developed countries, while half of the products of our food industry are made by initial materials, such as sugar, oil, forage, etc. The proportion of highly finished products only accounts for 16%. But the proportion of such products as cigarette and liquor accounts for 30%. Second, in food market, the total production exceeds the total need. Basic constructions are repeated everywhere, and the whole arrangement of industry is not logical. The productivity for some product categories is too strong. Third, competitive and well-know companies or brands are rare in food industry. Most of the food producers are low in integrated production level, ineffective in scale profit and weak in cooperation. All of these factors damage the developing and using of resources. There are some enterprises, famous in certain areas, but they are not influential and do not get big market share in the whole country. Fourth, enterprises are divided into two opposing extremes. The number of loss enterprises is rising up. Food industry is an absolutely free competitive business. This kind of intense competition makes average profit rate of the whole industry reduce continuously. Only those enterprises that have their own characteristic and scale profit can gain higher benefit. Fifth, the growth speed of the state-owned enterprise and the Joint Venture enterprise is not as fast as the foreign-funded enterprises or some other kinds of enterprises. China is such a big market that many transnational corporations with abundant financial resources and rich operation experiences occupy our domestic market by purchasing Chinese famous brands or organizing joint ventures or investing business.

Consumer goods research in major Chinese cities(1998)

Food market share brand of (presented as percentage)

Percentage / Category	First		Second		Third	
	Brand Name	Percent	Brand Name	Percent	Brand Name	Percent
Instant Noodles	Kang Shifu	51.4	President	19.7	Hua Feng	5.1
Milk Powder	Nestlé	21.5	Anlene	6.3	Hui Shi	4.9
Biscuit	Keebler	10.6	Danone	8.3	Kang Shifu	7.8
Chocolate	Dove	35.1	Cadbury	11.7	Le Conté	11.2
Yogurt	Robust	9.3	Bright	8.9	Danone	6.5
Liquid Milk	Bright	13.2	Sanyuan	6.4	Sandao	3.8
Ice-cream	Yili	20.0	Walls	11.9	Wuyang	9.4

(Sources: *Chinese Consumer's Newspaper* Jan.1.99)

Chinese food market has not only rigidity but also elasticity. People change their demand of food because of the growth of income, the variety of life style and the raise of living standard. From 1982, Chinese food composition has changed as follows: the proportion of grain and potato becomes smaller while the proportion of animal meat, purified energy food and other food becomes larger. But our food consumption still should be classified as "high cereal food". Our total nutrition level is not up to the standard. The portion of animal protein doesn't reach the world's average level as well as the requirement of Asia and other developing countries.

The basic aim of Chinese food consumption and nutrition in 2000 has been made in accordance with *the Recommendations for Chinese Food Construction Reform and Development* which is made by the State Council. This basic aim is that the daily nutrition supply will reach the world's average level, containing 2600 kilocalorie and 72 gram of protein. Plant will still be the first-choice of food while annually meat will come the second. But even with such food composition as the principle food model, the year average food consumption will improve greatly, especially the animal meat. As the trend in the development of food industry over the world, along with the improvement of society, the promotion of food safety, coming up of environmental protection and the development of science and technology, consumers are more and more interested in convenient and healthy food. People demand for various, functional and convenient food. So our goal is to produce products with high added-value, advanced technology and cultural element. These products include convenient food, leisure food, functional food, beverage, spices and elementary materials for food industry, etc. *The Recommendations for 95 Food Industry Project and 2010 Long-term Objective* points out that "along with the progress of the society, the speeding up of life rhythm, the promotion of living standards, people hope to eat healthy, nutritious and convenient food. So the project is to develop high-quality soybean protein and convenient food, to increase the output of food and beverage, to devote great efforts to produce convenient food and meticulously carry out brand strategies. During the next 15 years, the basic task of food industry is to accelerate food industry, to meet the needs of people for brand, quality and quantity in response to the development of society and the advancement of the living standards. The annually total industry production value of the year 2000 will be 3 times of that of year 1990. The annually total industry production value of 2010 will be over 2 times of that of 2000." This provides our food industry with many chances for development. From now on, the focal point of our food industry is to make full use of agricultural material, to better the quality and to expand the range of agricultural product processing, to positively develop milk products and convenient food, to quicken the modernization, to make the traditional food easier to consume, to develop nutritious food. and to improve the quality of food additive elements.

Milk Powder and Packaged Milk

In recent years, Chinese milk processing technology has got much progress. The product quality has got much improved. The output of dairy products is increasing by multiple. In 1978, our total milk output was less than 1000 thousand tons, dairy products were 46.3 thousand tons. By 1997, the total milk output had reached 7740 thousand tons, and the dairy products increased to 565 thousand tons. In 1998 the total milk output increased by 6% and dairy products increased by 7% compared with 1997. Now there are nearly 700 milk processors in China. Many of them are very famous, such as Sanlu Group in Shi Jiazhuang, Bright Milk Group in Shanghai, Gu Cheng Milk Co Ltd in Shanxi Province, Xian Yin Qiao Milk Industry LTD., and Beijing San Yuan Food LTD., etc. The output of these large or medium-sized enterprises accounts for about 80% of the total country output. In 1998 the imported dairy products of our country were 110 thousand tons including 100 thousand tons of milk powder. These dairy products account for 15% of the whole market. And the import milk powder accounts for 20% of the whole market.

The milk products sold in the domestic market are divided into liquid milk, frozen milk and diary products. There are two kinds of liquid milk: pasteurized milk and yogurt, Lile packaged milk and variously flavored milk. Bright Milk Group of Shanghai and Beijing San Yuan Food Ltd are the largest in China, which produces the most milk products. In 1997, their liquid milk output were 175,786 tons and 91,201 tons respectively. Jinxing Dairy Products Group of Harbin, whose output was 5,410 tons, was the third largest one. Milk powder is the major product for home dairy processing enterprises. Now the home milk powder enterprises are polarized. After several years of competition, some enterprises defeated others and have expanded their market share and enterprise scope by developing new products, exploring larger market and building brand. Such famous brands are "Sanlu", "Yili", "Wan Dashan" and "Jinxing". Now "Sanlu" gets the largest share of the milk powder market. "Yili", "Wan Dashan" and "Jinxing" stand in the second place, with their output about 10 to 15 thousand tons.

Chinese milk industry has gained a successful growth. The quality is getting better and the processing technology is being improved. Management and test levels are getting closer to the international standards. From the raw material to the semi-finished product to the final product, every step meets the requirements of the relevant regulations and rules. Chinese milk products have obtained people's trust. By the rule of thumb, our milk industry should be more prosperous than ever. But that's not the fact. China's milk industry is now getting into a jammed-up state. These enterprises mainly located in big cities. Their service system is not good enough. The processing technology is relatively sluggish. Consumers are not completely satisfied with the quality and the product structure. And also, because of Chinese people's food habits, they don't consume much milk. All of these reasons restrain the positive development of China's milk industry.

YuRuomu, a famous nutritionist, thinks that a meal of milk and egg is most ideal for breakfast. It's cheap, convenient and nutritious, and suits for modern life. But now Chinese people don't pay much attention to milk yet. The average annual milk consumption of people the world is 102 kg, and more than 30 kg in developing countries, while Chinese people can only consume 6.6kg. If we follow the slogan "A cup of milk makes a nation strong" to improve our milk consumption level, our real demand would be 13 times of present. In fact, Chinese milk processing industry is enjoying in favorable circumstances.

At the same time, in 1999, the dioxin pollution happened in Belgium, Dutch, Germany and France made their milk products be refused by our country. This is a big chance for our domestic milk processing enterprises.

Chinese government has always advocated its citizens to consume milk. Following the first publicity campaign for milk & milk products by Chinese Dairy Products Association in 1998, it enhances the campaign again in 1999. They encouraged people to have a cup of milk everyday. This can not only improve people's health, but also enlarge milk consumption. Marketing experts think that students are a big milk-consuming group and loyalty can easily be built up among them. Their habit of drinking milk will be a good guide to milk enterprises' production. So to sell dairy products to students in appropriate price and build up famous brand among them is very important. It is reported that a " Student milk" promotion campaign is being put out in order to improve the nutrition element in the students' food. Now this campaign has spread all over the country. People hope to make this "Student milk" campaign accepted in town's and cities within five years. So it can be predicted that milk market will be brisk in future.

Soybean Milk Powder

At present, there is a lack of high quality protein in Chinese food model. But according to the consuming habit and the resources supply, we can not adjust our food by only adding animal protein in our food model. Therefore, soybean milk powder with high protein is absolutely necessary although milk powder is more and more popular in Chinese families.

People think soybean milk powder important. The major reason is that they recognize its nutrition value. It contains much more quality plant protein than milk. At the same time, Chinese people have taken soybean products for food for more than two thousand years. They have been used to it. This is an advantage that milk powder does not have. On the other hand, China is a big agricultural country, which has a large output of bean. The high quality of bean is fit for manufacture high-grade soybean milk powder. This is an advantage of producing soybean milk powder in our country. And for eating directly, soybean milk powder is cheap and fine, and fits for different consumers. Both the high-income and the low-income groups like the quality plant protein contained by soybeans. So the consumption quantity of soybean milk powder is increasing step by step.

Now in our country, soybean milk powder manufacturing is becoming industrialized. Many famous brands appear, such as “Weiwei”,“Wan Dashan” and “Chen Xingdao”, etc. With the increase of our population, the improvement of domestic economy, the augment of high-grade protein in food, the consumption of soybean milk powder will continue to increase during a considerable long period.

Soybean milk powder has important function in improving our food configuration. As long as exploited premeditately, it will get a full raise, and will become an important increasing aspect in

China's food business. We can make a project according to the actual situation of different local areas, enrich the categories of soybean milk powder, include it into fundamental food, supplementary food and students food. So long as this product is standardized, finely packed and qualified, it will has a bright future.

Chocolate

Chocolate is over 80 years old. Its special taste, fine and smooth feel rich and sweet flavor and high level of nutrition make it sell well and gain people's deep love.

But because of the problems caused by origin and material, China's chocolate industry started late and developed slowly. After the foundation of People's Republic of China, along with the establishment and expansion of elementary industry of granulated sugar, syrup, oil and dairy product, chocolate industry began to develop quickly. In 1970s chocolate enterprises appeared in Beijing, Shanghai and Guangzhou. They began to apply mechanic and continuous production methods. But the output of chocolate was very small at that time. By 1990s, following the open-up and reforming movement, chocolate enterprises had imported some advanced equipments. "Yili" of Beijing, "Guan Shengyuan" of Shanghai and some enterprises of Tianjin were representatives of modern manufacturing lines.

In recent years, another reason for the rapid growth of China's chocolate industry is that more and more international brands have entered Chinese market. They show great competitive power based on their choice of material, advanced technology, good quality and special image. In 1998, a research about Chinese citizen consumption showed that "Dove" (35.1%), "Cadbury" (11.7%) and " Le Conté" (11.2%) stood in the first three places of Chinese chocolate market. At the same period, the consumers associated the brands with the first position in the way as follows:

Brands	Dove	Yili (Beijing)	Cadbury	Le Conté	Jinsha	Shenfeng	M&M	Yili (Inner Mongolia)
Percentage As ranking	41.8	11.9	10.9	7.0	5.0	3.8	1.6	1.5

(Sources: *Chinese Consumer's Newspaper* Jan.29.99)

There was some distance between leading brand and those that following it. But the distance was not as big as that between the most advantaged brands and the subsequent brands. Still more, quite a number of brands come to compete for market with similar market share. The advantage of the leading brand was obvious but not overpowering. At present, it seems that domestic brands have formed effective influence. But they have obtained rich experiences as they competed with foreign brands. For example, Yili, a famous brand of Beijing, is sold well in 199 supermarkets in Beijing. In order to challenge the international brands, Yili Group will make full use of its advantage as the leading brand in medium-grade market to develop high-grade products, such as milk chocolate, kernel chocolate.

With the development of food processing technology, people find more and more nutrition value in chocolate. People begin to enjoy chocolate, considering its good taste and nutrition. Most of Chinese families will surely enjoy better standard of life and the need for chocolate will increase. That is a great potential market. Being a leisure and nutrition food, chocolate business is facing many chances in China.

Ice cream

Since 1996 ice cream market has been shrinking. Though the market is not active, ice-cream manufacturers have great enthusiasm.

Cold snacks is made up of drinking water, sweet, milk, fruit, bean products, edible oil by mixing, sterilizing and freezing with some spices, coloring agent, and emulsifier, etc. This kind of cold snacks has many varieties, such as cold frost, ice-bar, ice-cream cake and ice cream, etc.

Chinese cold snacks business began in 1927. Hai Ning Foreign Firm of Shanghai was the first cold snack manufacturer of China. After People's Republic of China was founded, cold snacks business got a continuous enlargement throughout China. Its output reached about 80 thousand tons. In 1990s, cold snacks business entered into a full-speed development. The annual total output achieved 1.2 million tons with more than 3000 classes of product lines. The annually increasing speed was about 200%. But the major manufacturers were business invested by foreigners. After that, joint ventures were established one after another, and private enterprises started to get involved in this market.

At present, domestic cold snack market is divided into 3 parts. The foreign-funded enterprises control the high-grade market, the state-owned enterprises dominate the medium-grade market while the private enterprises and rural enterprises occupy the low-grade market. Now the largest markets are Guangdong, Beijing and Shanghai, which account for about 25% of the total national sales volume. There are over 200 ice cream manufacturers in Beijing. Their output is nearly 100 thousand tons. Shanghai has more than 200 cold snack enterprises. Their output is about 80 thousand tons. About 100 ice cream enterprises in Guangdong province produce about 100 thousand tons of ice cream every year. Besides these, cold snack business is also flourishing in some other cities, for example, Tianjin, Hangzhou and Nanjing. They mainly produce high-grade and medium-grade products. These days, Yili Coorperation Limited in Inner Mongolia has become the largest ice cream enterprise in China. In 1998, its sale revenue reached 523278.1 thousand-yuan. Its output has been the largest for 4 years.

In 1998, ice cream consumption value exceeded 20 billion yuan in China. Ice cream competition has last from summer to spring, autumn and winter in terms of time, and from local area to the whole country in terms of geography. The main market features can be concluded as the following points:

First, plenty of high-grade, medium-grade and low-grade varieties that one expects to find.

Second, different consumption level: High-grade are popular products in shopping center and entertainment places. Medium-grade products go well in suburbs and its surrounding areas, while low-grade products mainly occupy countryside.

Third, heated marketing competition. "Walls" and "Nestle" cut their prices 30% to 50% down in order to get a share in the medium-grade market.

Fourth, the steady output. Price is steady with a little reduction.

Fifth, quality consciousness.

Sixth, brand becoming more and more important. Product with famous brand has more chances to get the market. To build up a famous brand is our trend.

Now an average Chinese citizen consumes ice cream one liter per year while an average European and American consumes seven liters and 25 liters per year respectively. So for international famous brands, national famous brands and local brands, there are many chances in China's ice cream market.

Biscuit

The development of Chinese biscuit industry was always very slow. But in recent years, with the entry of foreign funded enterprises, joint ventures into Chinese market, our biscuit industry, which is mainly made up of state-owned enterprises and collective enterprises, has changed so much, and this hence accelerates the development of our biscuit industry greatly.

In 1997 there were 600 biscuit enterprises in China among which 302 enterprises got their annual sales revenue more than 2 million yuan. Their total assets were 10.3 billion yuan, and annual sales revenue reached 8 billion yuan, altogether. In 1997, the output of biscuit in China was 931 thousand tons, among which 6.2 thousand tons were imported and 35 thousand tons were exported. The whole market demand was 902.2 thousand tons, increasing by 10% compared with year 1994. As to the value, the total output value of biscuit industry was 7.7 billion yuan, among which 0.5 billion yuan came from import and 0.39 billion yuan from export. The total market demand value was 7.36 billion yuan, which increased by 66% compared with year 1994. The increase speed of the market demand value is higher than that of market demand and caused the rapid development of high and medium-grade biscuit production.

Though the foreign funded enterprises entered in China's biscuit market not long, it has already got a big market share due to their high starting point, large scope, good product quality and flexible operation. In 1997, the foreign-funded enterprises occupied 51.5% of China's biscuit market. "Nabisco", "Keebler" and "Danone" were the most popular biscuits, which were almost produced by foreign-funded enterprises and joint ventures in China. On the other hand, our domestic enterprises were still small in production scope and lacking in central control ability, competitive ability and effectiveness.

Nowadays, Chinese residents are still in very low level of biscuit consumption. The average consumption is only about 6 yuan per year, which indicates that there is a large potential in biscuit market. From now on, along with the development of social economy, living standards and tourism business, domestic demand for biscuit, especially demand from urban residents, will become larger and larger. This demand will increase 20 to 30 thousand tons every year. So our biscuit prospect is quite bright.

Instant Noodles

China's instant noodle business started in 1970. From the middle of 1980s, it came into a fast developing period. Now the output of Chinese instant noodle is the largest in the world. But because of the overspread of production, the output of instant noodles increased more slowly in recent years. Experts think that, as a whole, Chinese instant noodle business is still in a developing stage. China has more than 800 instant noodle producers, more than 1700 production lines, with an estimated productivity over 3.5 million tons, and can actually produce more than 1 million tons.

The research on Chinese food consumption patterns in 1998 showed that 73% of citizens ate instant noodles, among whom 20% ate more than 10 packs per month, 26% ate 6 to 9 packs per month, 30% ate 3 to 5 packs per month and 24% ate 1 to 2 packs. Another research in some major and medium cities showed that 40.8% of the citizens took instant noodles for breakfast, 14% took it for lunch, 10% took it for supper and 24% had instant noodles when they didn't want to do their cooking. This meant that instant noodles had become indispensable in Chinese people's life. People purchase whole boxes of instant noodles instead of buying individual packs now. Malls and wholesale market promote the sale of instant noodles with their low cost and low price.

As competition increases in market and brand, the competition of instant noodles industries gradually becomes the competition among spices. Now the spices has changed from powder to different varieties, such as catsup, coexistence of liquid and solid, soft packaged vegetable. The taste is becoming diversified.

As market is growing fast, families become more and more sociable. Convenient food, which is dominated by instant noodles, gets increasingly popular. Though the output of Chinese instant noodles is in the first place in the world, the average procession only stands in number nine. Urban citizens consume the most, and rural citizens consume less than one third of that by urban citizens. With the speeding up of urbanization in China and the increase of people's income, the prospect of instant noodles is very optimistic.

1.奶粉 / Powder Milk

● 北京 / Beijing

1-1 最近三个月食用频率的比例/ Proportion of the Sample Consuming Milk Powder in the Last Three Months

	人数 Number	百分比 Percent
天天喝 daily	112	11.1
一周 3 次或以上 3 times or over a week	110	10.9
一周 1~2 次 once or twice a week	99	9.9
一个月 2~3 次 2 or 3 times a month	59	5.9
一个月 1 次或以下 once a month or below	47	4.7
没喝过 never	578	57.5

n=1005

1-2 最常用品牌排名/ Ranking of the Most Frequently Used Brands

排名 Brand Ranking	品牌 Brands	人数 Number	百分比 Percent
1	雀巢 Nestle	90	21.3
2	红星 Red Star	76	18.0
3	完达山 Wandashan	70	16.5
4	安怡 Anlene	55	13.0
5	三元 Sanyuan	23	5.4
6	伊利 Yili	20	4.7
7	金星 Jinxing	11	2.6
8	三鹿 Sanlu	9	2.1

n=423

1-3 样本、男性各年龄层、女性各年龄层的常用品牌/ The Most Frequently Used Brands by the Whole Sample, Age and Gender Groups

	人数 Number	第一品牌及百分比 1st/ percent	第二品牌及百分比 2nd/ percent	第三品牌及百分比 3rd/ percent	第四品牌及百分比 4th/ percent
样本 Sample	423	**雀巢 Nestle(21.3)**	**红星 Red Star(18.0)**	**完达山 Wandashan(16.5)**	**安怡 Anlene(13.0)**
男性 Male	183	**红星 Red Star(20.8)**	**雀巢 Nestle(18.6)**	**完达山 Wandashan(18.0)**	**安怡 Anlene(10.4)**
16~24 岁 Age	41	雀巢 Nestle(29.3)	红星 Red Star(17.1)	完达山 Wandashan(12.2)	安怡 Anlene(9.8)
25~34 岁 Age	50	雀巢 Nestle(26.0)	红星 Red Starr(16.0)	完达山 Wandashan(12.0)	安怡 Anlene(8.0) 三元 Sanyuan(8.0)
35~44 岁 Age	45	完达山 Wandashan(26.7)	红星 Red Star(15.6) 雀巢 Nestle(15.6)	安怡 Anlene(6.7)	三鹿 Sanlu(4.4) 三元 Sanyuan(4.4) 伊利 Yili(4.4)
45~54 岁 Age	31	红星 Red Star(35.5)	安怡 Anlene(19.4)	完达山 Wandashan(16.1)	三鹿 Sanlu(3.2) 子母 Dutch Lady(3.2) 伊利 Yili(3.2) 森永 Morinage(3.2) 雀巢 Nestle(3.2) 齐梅 Qimei(3.2) 妈妈适体健 Mama Sustagen(3.2) 丰力富 Fernleaf(3.2)
55~60 岁 Age	16	红星 Red Star(31.3) 完达山 Wandashan(31.3)	安怡 Anlene(12.5)	光明 Bright(6.3) 雀巢 Nestle(6.3) 三元 Sanyuan(6.3) 伊利 Yili(6.3)	
女性 Female	240	**雀巢 Nestle(23.3)**	**红星 Red Star(15.8)**	**完达山 Wandashan(15.4)**	**安怡 Anlene(15.0)**
16~24 岁 Age	60	雀巢 Nestle(21.7)	安怡 Anlene(18.3)	红星 Red Star(15.0)	伊利 Yili(10.0) 三元 Sanyuan(10.0)
25~34 岁 Age	80	雀巢 Nestle(30.0)	红星 Red Star(16.3)	完达山 Wandashan(15.0)	安怡 Anlene(8.8)
35~44 岁 Age	48	雀巢 Nestle(27.1)	红星 Red Star(18.8) 完达山 Wandashan(18.8)	伊利 Yili(10.4)	
45~54 岁 Age	36	安怡 Anlene(33.3)	完达山 Wandashan(22.2)	雀巢 Nestle(13.9)	红星 Red Star(8.3)
55~60 岁 Age	16	安怡 Anlene(25.0) 红星 Red Star(25.0)	完达山 Wandashan(18.8)	雀巢 Nestle(6.3) 三元 Sanyuan(6.3) 友谊 Youyi(6.3) 北京长阳 Changyang(6.3) 龙牧壮骨奶粉 Longmu(6.3)	

1-4 理想品牌排名/ Ranking of the Ideal Brands

排名 Brand Ranking	品牌 Brands	人数 Number	百分比 Percent
1	雀巢 Nestle	198	19.6
2	完达山 Wandashan	124	12.3
3	红星 Red Star	104	10.3
4	安怡 Anlene	80	7.9
5	伊利 Yili	48	4.7
6	三鹿 Sanlu	25	2.5
7	三元 Sanyuan	18	1.8
8	金星 Jinxing	15	1.5
8	惠氏 Wythe	15	1.5
9	荷兰乳牛 Birth Tree	14	1.4

n=1011

1-5 样本、男性各年龄层、女性各年龄层最近三个月有无购买的比例/ Purchasing in the Last Three Months by the Whole Sample, Age and Gender Groups

	人数 Number	买过 yes	没买过 no
样本 Sample	1011	37.3	62.7
男性 Male	504	31.9	68.1
16~24 岁 Age	105	24.8	75.2
25~34 岁 Age	151	31.1	68.9
35~44 岁 Age	131	31.3	68.7
45~54 岁 Age	77	41.6	58.4
55~60 岁 Age	40	37.5	62.5
女性 Female	507	42.6	57.4
16~24 岁 Age	108	42.6	57.4
25~34 岁 Age	150	48.7	51.3
35~44 岁 Age	124	38.7	61.3
45~54 岁 Age	83	38.6	61.4
55~60 岁 Age	42	40.5	59.5

1-6 样本、男性各年龄层、女性各年龄层最近三个月的食用频率/ Frequencies of Consuming Milk Powder in the Last Three Months by the Whole Sample, Age and Gender Groups

	人数 Number	天天喝 daily	一周 3 次或以上 3 times or over a week	一周 1~2 次 once or twice a week	一个月 2~3 次 2 or 3 times a month	一个月 1 次或以下 once a month or below	没喝过 never
样本 Sample	1005	11.1	10.9	9.9	5.9	4.7	57.5
男性 Male	501	7.4	9.2	9.4	6.0	5.2	62.9
16~24 岁 Age	103	4.9	11.7	9.7	7.8	7.8	58.3
25~34 岁 Age	151	4.0	6.6	7.3	9.3	6.0	66.9
35~44 岁 Age	130	9.2	6.9	10.8	3.1	5.4	64.6
45~54 岁 Age	77	7.8	13.0	13.0	5.2	1.3	59.7
55~60 岁 Age	40	20.0	12.5	5.0	0.0	2.5	60.0
女性 Female	504	14.9	12.7	10.3	5.8	4.2	52.2
16~24 岁 Age	108	18.5	16.7	9.3	6.5	4.6	44.4
25~34 岁 Age	147	15.0	13.6	12.2	8.2	5.4	45.6
35~44 岁 Age	123	13.0	10.6	8.9	4.1	3.3	60.2
45~54 岁 Age	84	16.7	10.7	8.3	3.6	3.6	57.1
55~60 岁 Age	42	7.1	9.5	14.3	4.8	2.4	61.9

1-7 样本、男性各年龄层、女性各年龄层的品牌习惯/ Brand Habit in Consuming Milk Powder by the Whole Sample, Age and Gender Groups

	人数 Number	基本固定食用一个牌子 used in only one brand	比较固定地食用两个或三个牌子 used in two or three brands	基本上不太固定牌子 no brand preference
样本 Sample	427	44.5	30.0	25.5
男性 Male	186	45.7	27.4	26.9
16~24 岁 Age	43	32.6	37.2	30.2
25~34 岁 Age	50	44.0	28.0	28.0
35~44 岁 Age	46	43.5	23.9	32.6
45~54 岁 Age	31	61.3	25.8	12.9
55~60 岁 Age	16	62.5	12.5	25.0
女性 Female	241	43.6	32.0	24.5
16~24 岁 Age	60	31.7	35.0	33.3
25~34 岁 Age	80	41.3	35.0	23.8
35~44 岁 Age	49	49.0	26.5	24.5
45~54 岁 Age	36	52.8	30.6	16.7
55~60 岁 Age	16	62.5	25.0	12.5

1-8 选择该类商品的考虑因素/ Ranking of the Considerations in Purchasing

注：本题为多选题，合计百分比超过 100%（Multiple answers）

排名 Ranking	考虑因素 Considerations	人次 Person-time	百分比 Percent
1	营养成分 nutrition constituent	203	47.8
2	价格适中 reasonable price	165	38.8
3	口味好 pleasant taste	149	35.1
4	有名的牌子 famous brand	143	33.6
5	生产日期 date of producing	87	20.5
6	易溶解 high dissolubility	67	15.8
7	购买方便 easy to buy	46	10.8
8	广告影响 influence of advertising	36	8.5
9	只是由于习惯 out of habit	31	7.3
10	朋友推荐 introduction of friends	21	4.9
11	有优惠条件 with preferential terms	20	4.7
12	其它 others	10	2.4
13	包装吸引人 appealing package	8	1.9
14	售货员介绍 introduced by the shop assistants	4	0.9

n=425

1-9 样本、男性各年龄层、女性各年龄层最常食用的种类/ Types of the Consumed Milk Powder by the Whole Sample, Age and Gender Groups

注：本题为多选题，合计百分比超过 100%（Multiple answers）

	人数 Number	全脂 whole milk	低脂 low-fat	脱脂 skimmed	甜型 sweet	功能型（如加钙等矿物质）containing minerals	加味型（如巧克力、果味等）flavored (e.g. fruit chocolate)	其它 others
样本 Sample	426	47.9	18.1	17.6	9.4	22.5	4.9	1.2
男性 Male	186	53.2	17.7	14.5	10.8	19.9	5.9	1.6
16~24 岁 Age	43	55.8	9.3	16.3	11.6	23.3	7.0	2.3
25~34 岁 Age	50	48.0	14.0	6.0	22.0	22.0	6.0	0.0
35~44 岁 Age	46	60.9	21.7	15.2	6.5	8.7	8.7	2.2
45~54 岁 Age	31	41.9	22.6	25.8	3.2	29.0	0.0	3.2
55~60 岁 Age	16	62.5	31.3	12.5	0.0	18.8	6.3	0.0
女性 Female	240	43.8	18.3	20.0	8.3	24.6	4.2	0.8
16~24 岁 Age	60	45.0	16.7	23.3	3.3	21.7	6.7	0.0
25~34 岁 Age	79	41.8	20.3	19.0	7.6	24.1	6.3	0.0
35~44 岁 Age	49	59.2	10.2	14.3	16.3	18.4	2.0	0.0
45~54 岁 Age	36	36.1	25.0	22.2	5.6	33.3	0.0	2.8
55~60 岁 Age	16	18.8	25.0	25.0	12.5	37.5	0.0	6.3

1-10 样本、男性各年龄层、女性各年龄层最常食用的场合/ Settings of Consumption by the Whole Sample, Age and Gender Groups

注：本题为多选题，合计百分比超过 100%（Multiple answers）

	人数 Number	早餐时 breakfast	正餐（午、晚餐）时 dinner	餐后热饮 after dinner	宵夜时 evening snack	睡觉前帮助入眠 before sleeping	工作休息时 during work break	其它 others
样本 Sample	**425**	**80.2**	**2.8**	**2.6**	**17.6**	**23.8**	**7.5**	**1.9**
男性 Male	**185**	**76.2**	**2.7**	**2.2**	**16.8**	**22.2**	**7.0**	**1.6**
16~24 岁 Age	42	71.4	2.4	0.0	23.8	23.8	9.5	0.0
25~34 岁 Age	50	62.0	2.0	4.0	18.0	20.0	8.0	6.0
35~44 岁 Age	46	82.6	4.3	2.2	17.4	23.9	6.5	0.0
45~54 岁 Age	31	83.9	3.2	3.2	12.9	22.6	6.5	0.0
55~60 岁 Age	16	100.0	0.0	0.0	0.0	18.8	0.0	0.0
女性 Female	**240**	**83.3**	**2.9**	**2.9**	**18.3**	**25.0**	**7.9**	**2.1**
16~24 岁 Age	60	80.0	1.7	3.3	16.7	21.7	6.7	1.7
25~34 岁 Age	80	85.0	1.3	1.3	21.3	23.8	11.3	3.8
35~44 岁 Age	49	85.7	4.1	4.1	16.3	32.7	6.1	2.0
45~54 岁 Age	35	85.7	2.9	2.9	17.1	14.3	5.7	0.0
55~60 岁 Age	16	75.0	12.5	6.3	18.8	43.8	6.3	0.0

1-11 重度消费者的人口分布/ Demographics of the Heavy Consumers

	人数 Number	16-24 岁 Age	25-34 岁 Age	35-44 岁 Age	45-54 岁 Age	55-60 岁 Age
样本 Sample	**321**	**23.4**	**27.1**	**23.4**	**17.4**	**8.7**
男性 Male	**130**	**20.8**	**20.8**	**26.9**	**20.0**	**11.5**
天天喝 daily	37	13.5	16.2	32.4	16.2	21.6
一周 3 次或以上 3 times or over a week	46	26.1	21.7	19.6	21.7	10.9
一周 1～2 次 once or twice a week	47	21.3	23.4	29.8	21.3	4.3
女性 Female	**191**	**25.1**	**31.4**	**20.9**	**15.7**	**6.8**
天天喝 daily	75	26.7	29.3	21.3	18.7	4.0
一周 3 次或以上 3 times or over a week	64	28.1	31.3	20.3	14.1	6.3
一周 1～2 次 once or twice a week	52	19.2	34.6	21.2	13.5	11.5

1-12 不同消费者层的常用品牌/ The Most Frequently Used Brands by Market Segments

1-12-1 时尚流行指标/ Fads Popular Index

	人数 Number	第一品牌及百分比 1st/ percent	第二品牌及百分比 2nd/ percent	第三品牌及百分比 3rd/ percent	第四品牌及百分比 4th/ percent
样本 Sample	**415**	**雀巢 Nestle(21.2)**	**红星 Red Star(17.8)**	**完达山 Wandashan(16.6)**	**安怡 Anlene(13.0)**
平实生活指向 simple living orientation	182	红星 Red Star(19.8)	完达山 Wandashan(19.2)	雀巢 Nestle(16.5)	安怡 Anlene(14.8)
时尚流行指向 fashion orientation	233	雀巢 Nestle(24.9)	红星 Red Star(16.3)	完达山 Wandashan(14.6)	安怡 Anlene(11.6)

1-12-2 广告态度指标/ Advertising Attitude Index

	人数 Number	第一品牌及百分比 1st/ percent	第二品牌及百分比 2nd/ percent	第三品牌及百分比 3rd/ percent	第四品牌及百分比 4th/ percent
样本 Sample	**413**	**雀巢 Nestle(21.5)**	**红星 Red Star(17.9)**	**完达山 Wandashan(16.7)**	**安怡 Anlene(12.6)**
广告淡漠指向 indifferent orientation	104	红星 Red Star(23.1)	雀巢 Nestle(22.1)	安怡 Anlene(13.5)	完达山 Wandashan(11.5)
中间层 medium	239	雀巢 Nestle(19.7)	红星 Red Star(18.0)	完达山 Wandashan(17.6)	安怡 Anlene(13.4)
信赖广告指向 loyal orientation	70	雀巢 Nestle(27.1)	完达山 Wandashan(21.4)	红星 Red Star(10.0) 三元 Sanyuan(10.0)	安怡 Anlene(8.6)

1-12-3 饮食健康指标/ Foods & Drink Quality Index

	人数 Number	第一品牌及百分比 1st/ percent	第二品牌及百分比 2nd/ percent	第三品牌及百分比 3rd/ percent	第四品牌及百分比 4th/ percent
样本 Sample	419	雀巢 Nestle(21.5)	红星 Red Star(17.7)	完达山 Wandashan(16.5)	安怡 Anlene(12.9)
饮食"温饱"指向 "basic" orientation	113	雀巢 Nestle(23.0)	红星 Red Star(20.4)	完达山 Wandashan(13.3)	安怡 Anlene(8.8)
中间层 medium	195	雀巢 Nestle(20.5)	完达山 Wandashan(18.5)	红星 Red Star(17.4)	安怡 Anlene(12.3)
健康营养指向 health & nutrition orientation	111	雀巢 Nestle(21.6)	安怡 Anlene(18.0)	完达山 Wandashan(16.2)	红星 Red Star(15.3)

1-13 重度消费者的消费者层构成/ The Composition of the Heavy Consumers

1-13-1 时尚流行指标/ Fads Popular Index

	人数 Number	平实生活指向 simple living orientation	时尚流行指向 fashion orientation
样本 Sample	316	43.4	56.6
天天喝 daily	110	42.7	57.3
一周 3 次或以上 3 times or over a week	109	44.0	56.0
一周 1～2 次 once or twice a week	97	43.3	56.7

1-13-2 广告态度指标/ Advertising Attitude Index

	人数 Number	广告淡漠指向 indifferent orientation	中间层 medium	信赖广告指向 loyal orientation
样本 Sample	316	25.3	57.3	17.4
天天喝 daily	108	26.9	60.2	13.0
一周 3 次或以上 3 times or over a week	110	26.4	47.3	26.4
一周 1～2 次 once or twice a week	98	22.4	65.3	12.2

1-13-3 饮食健康指标/ Foods & Drink Quality Index

	人数 Number	饮食"温饱"指向 "basic" orientation	中间层 medium	健康营养指向 health & nutrition orientation
样本 Sample	318	25.2	46.9	28.0
天天喝 daily	112	24.1	46.4	29.5
一周 3 次或以上 3 times or over a week	108	25.9	46.3	27.8
一周 1～2 次 once or twice a week	98	25.5	48.0	26.5

● 上海 / Shanghai

1-1 最近三个月食用频率的比例/ Proportion of the Sample Consuming Milk Powder in the Last Three Months

	人数 Number	百分比 Percent
天天喝 daily	143	14.1
一周 3 次或以上 3 times or over a week	83	8.2
一周 1~2 次 once or twice a week	73	7.2
一个月 2~3 次 2 or 3 times a month	41	4.1
一个月 1 次或以下 once a month or below	39	3.9
没喝过 never	633	62.5

n=1012

1-2 最常用品牌排名/ Ranking of the Most Frequently Used Brands

排名 Brand Ranking	品牌 Brands	人数 Number	百分比 Percent
1	光明 Bright	175	46.4
2	雀巢 Nestle	52	13.8
3	安怡 Anlene	49	13.0
4	荷兰乳牛 Birth Tree	45	11.9
5	多美滋 Dumex	9	2.4
6	伊利 Yili	8	2.1
7	丰力富 Fernleaf	7	1.9
8	齐梅 Qimei	5	1.3
9	维维 weiwei	4	1.1
10	克宁 Kelim	3	0.8

n=377

1-3 样本、男性各年龄层、女性各年龄层的常用品牌/ The Most Frequently Used Brands by the Whole Sample, Age and Gender Groups

	人数 Number	第一品牌及百分比 1st/ percent	第二品牌及百分比 2nd/ percent	第三品牌及百分比 3rd/ percent	第四品牌及百分比 4th/ percent
样本 Sample	377	**光明 Bright(46.4)**	**雀巢 Nestle(13.8)**	**安怡 Anlene(13.0)**	**荷兰乳牛 Birth Tree(11.9)**
男性 Male	175	**光明 Bright(46.3)**	**安怡 Anlene(14.3)**	**雀巢 Nestle(12.6)**	**荷兰乳牛 Birth Tree(11.4)**
16~24 岁 Age	43	光明 Bright(44.2)	荷兰乳牛 Birth Tree(16.3) 雀巢 Nestle(16.3)	安怡 Anlene(14.0)	田力 Tianli(2.3) 维维 Weiwei(2.3) 三花 Sanhua(2.3) 超级 Chaoji(2.3)
25~34 岁 Age	50	光明 Bright(40.0)	雀巢 Nestle(18.0)	安怡 Anlene(12.0)	荷兰乳牛 Birth Tree(8.0)
35~44 岁 Age	46	光明 Bright(54.3)	安怡 Anlene(13.0)	荷兰乳牛 Birth Tree(10.9)	多美滋 Dumex(6.5)
45~54 岁 Age	23	光明 Bright(43.5)	安怡 Anlene(21.7)	荷兰乳牛 Birth Tree(17.4)	雀巢 Nestle(13.0)
55~60 岁 Age	13	光明 Bright(53.8)	安怡 Anlene(15.4) 齐梅 Qimei(15.4)	雀巢 Nestle(7.7) 维维 Weiwei(7.7)	
女性 Female	202	**光明 Bright(46.5)**	**雀巢 Nestle(14.9)**	**荷兰乳牛 Birth Tree(12.4)**	**安怡 Anlene(11.9)**
16~24 岁 Age	48	光明 Bright(43.8)	安怡 Anlene(16.7) 雀巢 Nestle(16.7)	荷兰乳牛 Birth Tree(14.6)	丰力富 Fernleaf(2.1) 伊利 Yili(2.1) 维维 Wei(2.1)
25~34 岁 Age	54	光明 Bright(46.3)	雀巢 Nestle(18.5)	安怡 Anlene(13.0)	荷兰乳牛 Birth Tree(5.6)
35~44 岁 Age	48	光明 Bright(52.1)	荷兰乳牛 Birth Tree(16.7)	雀巢 Nestle(10.4)	安怡 Anlene(6.3) 丰力富 Fernleaf(6.3)
45~54 岁 Age	30	光明 Bright(36.7)	安怡 Anlene(16.7) 荷兰乳牛 Birth Tree(16.7) 雀巢 Nestle(16.7)	齐梅 Qimei(6.7)	丰力富 Fernleaf(3.3) 安达 Anda(3.3)
55~60 岁 Age	22	光明 Bright(54.5)	多美滋 Dumex(9.1) 荷兰乳牛 Birth Tree(9.1) 雀巢 Nestle(9.1)	安怡 Anlene(4.5) 健王 Jianwang(4.5) 齐梅 Qimei(4.5) 安尔宝 Anerbao(4.5)	

1-4 理想品牌排名/ Ranking of the Ideal Brands

排名 Brand Ranking	品牌 Brands	人数 Number	百分比 Percent
1	光明 Bright	462	45.6
2	雀巢 Nestle	133	13.1
3	荷兰乳牛 Birth Tree	115	11.3
4	安怡 Anlene	110	10.8
5	多美滋 Dumex	39	3.8
6	惠氏 Wythe	17	1.7
7	克宁 Kelim	9	0.9
8	森永 Morinage	7	0.7
8	丰力富 Fernleaf	7	0.7
9	子母 Dutch Lady	6	0.6
9	伊利 Yili	6	0.6
10	雅培 Yapei	4	0.4

n=1014

1-5 样本、男性各年龄层、女性各年龄层最近三个月有无购买的比例/ Purchasing in the Last Three Months by the Whole Sample, Age and Gender Groups

	人数 Number	买过 yes	没买过 no
样本 Sample	1013	34.6	65.4
男性 Male	508	30.1	69.9
16~24 岁 Age	109	22.9	77.1
25~34 岁 Age	146	32.2	67.8
35~44 岁 Age	130	37.7	62.3
45~54 岁 Age	85	22.4	77.6
55~60 岁 Age	38	34.2	65.8
女性 Female	505	39.0	61.0
16~24 岁 Age	108	31.5	68.5
25~34 岁 Age	144	37.5	62.5
35~44 岁 Age	130	40.0	60.0
45~54 岁 Age	82	43.9	56.1
55~60 岁 Age	41	51.2	48.8

1-6 样本、男性各年龄层、女性各年龄层最近三个月的食用频率/ Frequencies of Consuming Milk Powder in the Last Three Months by the Whole Sample, Age and Gender Groups

	人数 Number	天天喝 daily	一周 3 次或以上 3 times or over a week	一周 1~2 次 once or twice a week	一个月 2~3 次 2 or 3 times a month	一个月 1 次或以下 once a month or below	没喝过 never
样本 Sample	1012	14.1	8.2	7.2	4.1	3.9	62.5
男性 Male	507	11.0	7.7	7.9	3.9	4.3	65.1
16~24 岁 Age	109	9.2	11.9	7.3	3.7	7.3	60.6
25~34 岁 Age	146	13.0	6.2	6.8	3.4	5.5	65.1
35~44 岁 Age	130	11.5	6.2	10.8	6.2	1.5	63.8
45~54 岁 Age	84	7.1	6.0	7.1	3.6	3.6	72.6
55~60 岁 Age	38	15.8	10.5	5.3	0.0	2.6	65.8
女性 Female	505	17.2	8.7	6.5	4.2	3.4	60.0
16~24 岁 Age	108	11.1	10.2	12.0	6.5	4.6	55.6
25~34 岁 Age	144	17.4	8.3	6.3	2.8	2.8	62.5
35~44 岁 Age	130	18.5	7.7	4.6	4.6	1.5	63.1
45~54 岁 Age	82	20.7	4.9	4.9	3.7	2.4	63.4
55~60 岁 Age	41	22.0	17.1	2.4	2.4	9.8	46.3

1-7 样本、男性各年龄层、女性各年龄层的品牌习惯/ Brand Habit in Consuming Milk Powder by the Whole Sample, Age and Gender Groups

	人数 Number	基本固定食用一个牌子 used in only one brand	比较固定地食用两个或三个牌子 used in two or three brands	基本上不太固定牌子 no brand preference
样本 Sample	378	53.2	29.1	17.7
男性 Male	176	48.9	29.5	21.6
16~24 岁 Age	43	41.9	23.3	34.9
25~34 岁 Age	51	45.1	37.3	17.6
35~44 岁 Age	47	53.2	31.9	14.9
45~54 岁 Age	23	60.9	21.7	17.4
55~60 岁 Age	12	50.0	25.0	25.0
女性 Female	202	56.9	28.7	14.4
16~24 岁 Age	48	41.7	35.4	22.9
25~34 岁 Age	54	57.4	37.0	5.6
35~44 岁 Age	48	70.8	12.5	16.7
45~54 岁 Age	30	50.0	36.7	13.3
55~60 岁 Age	22	68.2	18.2	13.6

1-8 选择该类商品的考虑因素/ Ranking of the Considerations in Purchasing

注：本题为多选题，合计百分比超过 100%（Multiple answers）

排名 Ranking	考虑因素 Considerations	人次 Person-time	百分比 Percent
1	营养成分 nutrition constituent	162	42.9
2	有名的牌子 famous brand	153	40.5
3	价格适中 reasonable price	152	40.2
4	口味好 pleasant taste	139	36.8
5	生产日期 date of producing	71	18.8
6	购买方便 easy to buy	54	14.3
7	易溶解 high dissolubility	49	13.0
8	广告影响 influence of advertising	29	7.7
9	只是由于习惯 out of habit	27	7.1
10	朋友推荐 introduction of friends	18	4.8
11	有优惠条件 with preferential terms	15	4.0
12	其它 others	7	1.9
13	包装吸引人 appealing package	5	1.3
14	售货员介绍 introduced by the shop assistants	3	0.8

n=378

1-9 样本、男性各年龄层、女性各年龄层最常食用的种类/ Types of the Consumed Milk Powder by the Whole Sample, Age and Gender Groups

注：本题为多选题，合计百分比超过 100%（Multiple answers）

	人数 Number	全脂 whole milk	低脂 low-fat	脱脂 skimmed	甜型 sweet	功能型（如加钙等矿物质）containing minerals	加味型（如巧克力、果味等）flavored (e.g. fruit chocolate)	其它 others
样本 Sample	**379**	**50.4**	**15.8**	**17.4**	**4.0**	**21.6**	**2.1**	**1.8**
男性 Male	**177**	**51.4**	**15.8**	**16.9**	**4.0**	**16.4**	**2.8**	**3.4**
16~24 岁 Age	43	48.8	14.0	18.6	4.7	11.6	7.0	0.0
25~34 岁 Age	51	49.0	13.7	15.7	3.9	19.6	2.0	3.9
35~44 岁 Age	47	55.3	21.3	12.8	6.4	17.0	2.1	0.0
45~54 岁 Age	23	56.5	8.7	26.1	0.0	21.7	0.0	0.0
55~60 岁 Age	13	46.2	23.1	15.4	0.0	7.7	0.0	30.8
女性 Female	**202**	**49.5**	**15.8**	**17.8**	**4.0**	**26.2**	**1.5**	**0.5**
16~24 岁 Age	48	47.9	8.3	25.0	4.2	22.9	2.1	0.0
25~34 岁 Age	54	46.3	13.0	13.0	7.4	31.5	3.7	0.0
35~44 岁 Age	48	58.3	10.4	18.8	0.0	27.1	0.0	0.0
45~54 岁 Age	30	46.7	30.0	16.7	3.3	20.0	0.0	0.0
55~60 岁 Age	22	45.5	31.8	13.6	4.5	27.3	0.0	4.5

1-10 样本、男性各年龄层、女性各年龄层最常食用的场合/ Settings of Consumption by the Whole Sample, Age and Gender Groups

注：本题为多选题，合计百分比超过 100%（Multiple answers）

	人数 Number	早餐时 breakfast	正餐（午、晚餐）时 dinner	餐后热饮 after dinner	宵夜时 evening snack	睡觉前帮助入眠 before sleeping	工作休息时 during work break	其它 others
样本 Sample	**379**	**64.6**	**4.0**	**4.7**	**10.6**	**34.0**	**12.7**	**3.4**
男性 Male	**177**	**66.1**	**2.8**	**5.1**	**11.9**	**30.5**	**13.0**	**1.7**
16~24 岁 Age	43	60.5	2.3	2.3	9.3	41.9	9.3	4.7
25~34 岁 Age	51	64.7	5.9	7.8	11.8	21.6	13.7	2.0
35~44 岁 Age	47	66.0	0.0	0.0	8.5	38.3	21.3	0.0
45~54 岁 Age	23	69.6	0.0	4.3	26.1	21.7	8.7	0.0
55~60 岁 Age	13	84.6	7.7	23.1	7.7	15.4	0.0	0.0
女性 Female	**202**	**63.4**	**5.0**	**4.5**	**9.4**	**37.1**	**12.4**	**5.0**
16~24 岁 Age	48	52.1	6.3	6.3	14.6	45.8	10.4	4.2
25~34 岁 Age	54	55.6	7.4	3.7	7.4	35.2	13.0	9.3
35~44 岁 Age	48	79.2	2.1	2.1	8.3	33.3	8.3	2.1
45~54 岁 Age	30	66.7	3.3	6.7	3.3	33.3	16.7	0.0
55~60 岁 Age	22	68.2	4.5	4.5	13.6	36.4	18.2	9.1

1-11 重度消费者的人口分布/ Demographics of the Heavy Consumers

	人数 Number	16-24 岁 Age	25-34 岁 Age	35-44 岁 Age	45-54 岁 Age	55-60 岁 Age
样本 Sample	299	22.4	28.1	25.8	14.0	9.7
男性 Male	135	23.0	28.1	27.4	12.6	8.9
天天喝 daily	56	17.9	33.9	26.8	10.7	10.7
一周 3 次或以上 3 times or over a week	39	33.3	23.1	20.5	12.8	10.3
一周 1～2 次 once or twice a week	40	20.0	25.0	35.0	15.0	5.0
女性 Female	164	22.0	28.0	24.4	15.2	10.4
天天喝 daily	87	13.8	28.7	27.6	19.5	10.3
一周 3 次或以上 3 times or over a week	44	25.0	27.3	22.7	9.1	15.9
一周 1～2 次 once or twice a week	33	39.4	27.3	18.2	12.1	3.0

1-12 不同消费者层的常用品牌/ The Most Frequently Used Brands by Market Segments

1-12-1 时尚流行指标/ Fads Popular Index

	人数 Number	第一品牌及百分比 1st/ percent	第二品牌及百分比 2nd/ percent	第三品牌及百分比 3rd/ percent	第四品牌及百分比 4th/ percent
样本 Sample	372	光明 Bright(46.2)	雀巢 Nestle(14.0)	安怡 Anlene(13.2)	荷兰乳牛 Birth Tree(12.1)
平实生活指向 simple living orientation	167	光明 Bright(47.9)	雀巢 Nestle(13.2)	安怡 Anlene(12.0)	荷兰乳牛 Birth Tree(11.4)
时尚流行指向 fashion orientation	205	光明 Bright(44.9)	雀巢 Nestle(14.6)	安怡 Anlene(14.1)	荷兰乳牛 Birth Tree(12.7)

1-12-2 广告态度指标/ Advertising Attitude Index

	人数 Number	第一品牌及百分比 1st/ percent	第二品牌及百分比 2nd/ percent	第三品牌及百分比 3rd/ percent	第四品牌及百分比 4th/ percent
样本 Sample	374	光明 Bright(46.3)	雀巢 Nestle(13.6)	安怡 Anlene(13.1)	荷兰乳牛 Birth Tree(12.0)
广告淡漠指向 indifferent orientation	80	光明 Bright(53.8)	安怡 Anlene(11.3) 雀巢 Nestle(11.3)	荷兰乳牛 Birth Tree(10.0)	多美滋 Dumex(5.0)
中间层 medium	231	光明 Bright(44.2)	雀巢 Nestle(15.2)	安怡 Anlene(14.7)	荷兰乳牛 Birth Tree(12.6)
信赖广告指向 loyal orientation	63	光明 Bright(44.4)	荷兰乳牛 Birth Tree(12.7)	雀巢 Nestle(11.1)	安怡 Anlene(9.5)

1-12-3 饮食健康指标/ Foods & Drink Quality Index

	人数 Number	第一品牌及百分比 1st/ percent	第二品牌及百分比 2nd/ percent	第三品牌及百分比 3rd/ percent	第四品牌及百分比 4th/ percent
样本 Sample	374	光明 Bright(46.0)	雀巢 Nestle(13.9)	安怡 Anlene(13.1)	荷兰乳牛 Birth Tree(12.0)
饮食“温饱”指向 "basic" orientation	78	光明 Bright(44.9)	荷兰乳牛 Birth Tree(12.8) 安怡 Anlene(12.8)	雀巢 Nestle(11.5)	维维 Weiwei(2.6) 森永 Morinage(2.6) 多美滋 Dumex(2.6)
中间层 medium	175	光明 Bright(46.3)	安怡 Anlene(16.0)	雀巢 Nestle(14.9)	荷兰乳牛 Birth Tree(10.3)
健康营养指向 health & nutrition orientation	121	光明 Bright(46.3)	荷兰乳牛 Birth Tree(14.0) 雀巢 Nestle(14.0)	安怡 Anlene(9.1)	多美滋 Dumex(3.3)

1-13 重度消费者的消费者层构成/ The Composition of the Heavy Consumers

1-13-1 时尚流行指标/ Fads Popular Index

	人数 Number	平实生活指向 simple living orientation	时尚流行指向 fashion orientation
样本 Sample	295	45.4	54.6
天天喝 daily	141	44.0	56.0
一周 3 次或以上 3 times or over a week	82	46.3	53.7
一周 1～2 次 once or twice a week	72	47.2	52.8

1-13-2 广告态度指标/ Advertising Attitude Index

	人数 Number	广告淡漠指向 indifferent orientation	中间层 medium	信赖广告指向 loyal orientation
样本 Sample	**295**	**22.7**	**62.0**	**15.3**
天天喝 daily	142	21.8	64.1	14.1
一周 3 次或以上 3 times or over a week	80	30.0	55.0	15.0
一周 1～2 次 once or twice a week	73	16.4	65.8	17.8

1-13-3 饮食健康指标/ Foods & Drink Quality Index

	人数 Number	饮食"温饱"指向 "basic" orientation	中间层 medium	健康营养指向 health & nutrition orientation
样本 Sample	**297**	**20.2**	**46.5**	**33.3**
天天喝 daily	142	21.8	43.7	34.5
一周 3 次或以上 3 times or over a week	83	14.5	51.8	33.7
一周 1～2 次 once or twice a week	72	23.6	45.8	30.6

● 广州 / Guangzhou

1-1 最近三个月食用频率的比例/ Proportion of the Sample Consuming Milk Powder in the Last Three Months

	人数 Number	百分比 Percent
天天喝 daily	98	9.5
一周 3 次或以上 3 times or over a week	121	11.8
一周 1~2 次 once or twice a week	150	14.6
一个月 2～3 次 2 or 3 times a month	76	7.4
一个月 1 次或以下 once a month or below	47	4.6
没喝过 never	537	52.2

n=1029

1-2 最常用品牌排名/ Ranking of the Most Frequently Used Brands

排名 Brand Ranking	品牌 Brands	人数 Number	百分比 Percent
1	雀巢 Nestle	168	34.2
2	安怡 Anlene	85	17.3
3	大庆 Daqing	82	16.7
4	子母 Dutch Lady	32	6.5
5	惠氏 Wythe	13	2.6
6	克宁 Kelim	11	2.2
6	荷兰乳牛 Birth Tree	11	2.2
7	丰力富 Fernleaf	10	2.0

n=491

1-3 样本、男性各年龄层、女性各年龄层的常用品牌/ The Most Frequently Used Brands by the Whole Sample, Age and Gender Groups

	人数 Number	第一品牌及百分比 1st/ percent	第二品牌及百分比 2nd/ percent	第三品牌及百分比 3rd/ percent
样本 Sample	**491**	**雀巢 Nestle(34.2)**	**安怡 Anlene(17.3)**	**大庆 Daqing(16.7)**
男性 Male	**216**	**雀巢 Nestle(33.8)**	**大庆 Daqing(17.6)**	**安怡 Anlene(14.8)**
16~24 岁 Age	47	雀巢 Nestle(40.4)	安怡 Anlene(19.1)	子母 Dutch Lady(10.6)
25~34 岁 Age	67	雀巢 Nestle(38.8)	安怡 Anlene(14.9)	大庆 Daqing(7.5)
35~44 岁 Age	53	雀巢 Nestle(30.2)	大庆 Daqing(28.3)	子母 Dutch Lady(11.3)
45~54 岁 Age	31	大庆 Daqing(25.8) 雀巢 Nestle(25.8)	安怡 Anlene(19.4)	克宁 Kelim(6.5) 子母 Dutch Lady(6.5)
55~60 岁 Age	18	大庆 Daqing(44.4)	安怡 Anlene(22.2) 雀巢 Nestle(22.2)	
女性 Female	**275**	**雀巢 Nestle(34.5)**	**安怡 Anlene(19.3)**	**大庆 Daqing(16.0)**
16~24 岁 Age	59	雀巢 Nestle(33.9)	安怡 Anlene(20.3)	大庆 Daqing(13.6)
25~34 岁 Age	82	雀巢 Nestle(34.1)	安怡 Anlene(13.4)	大庆 Daqing(11.0)
35~44 岁 Age	61	雀巢 Nestle(45.9)	安怡 Anlene(13.1) 大庆 Daqing(13.1)	子母 Dutch Lady(9.8)
45~54 岁 Age	55	大庆 Daqing(27.3) 雀巢 Nestle(27.3)	安怡 Anlene(25.5)	子母 Dutch Lady(3.6)
55~60 岁 Age	18	安怡 Anlene(44.4)	大庆 Daqing(22.2) 雀巢 Nestle(22.2)	钙美健 Calimex(5.6) 英雄 Hero(5.6)

1-4 理想品牌排名/ Ranking of the Ideal Brands

排名 Brand Ranking	品牌 Brands	人数 Number	百分比 Percent
1	雀巢 Nestle	381	36.8
2	安怡 Anlene	136	13.2
3	大庆 Daqing	89	8.6
4	子母 Dutch Lady	50	4.8
5	惠氏 Wythe	32	3.1
6	克宁 Kelim	20	1.9
7	荷兰乳牛 Birth Tree	16	1.5
8	丰力富 Fernleaf	12	1.2
9	安满 Anman	10	1.0

n=1034

1-5 样本、男性各年龄层、女性各年龄层最近三个月有无购买的比例/ Purchasing in the Last Three Months by the Whole Sample, Age and Gender Groups

	人数 Number	买过 yes	没买过 no
样本 Sample	1033	44.4	55.6
男性 Male	499	38.7	61.3
16~24 岁 Age	106	28.3	71.7
25~34 岁 Age	150	40.7	59.3
35~44 岁 Age	127	43.3	56.7
45~54 岁 Age	73	41.1	58.9
55~60 岁 Age	43	39.5	60.5
女性 Female	534	49.8	50.2
16~24 岁 Age	112	37.5	62.5
25~34 岁 Age	158	53.8	46.2
35~44 岁 Age	137	51.1	48.9
45~54 岁 Age	86	61.6	38.4
55~60 岁 Age	41	39.0	61.0

1-6 样本、男性各年龄层、女性各年龄层最近三个月的食用频率/ Frequencies of Consuming Milk Powder in the Last Three Months by the Whole Sample, Age and Gender Groups

	人数 Number	天天喝 daily	一周 3 次或以上 3 times or over a week	一周 1~2 次 once or twice a week	一个月 2~3 次 2 or 3 times a month	一个月 1 次或以下 once a month or below	没喝过 never
样本 Sample	1029	9.5	11.8	14.6	7.4	4.6	52.2
男性 Male	494	4.9	11.3	16.6	7.1	3.8	56.3
16~24 岁 Age	106	2.8	7.5	18.9	7.5	7.5	55.7
25~34 岁 Age	150	4.7	13.3	16.0	7.3	3.3	55.3
35~44 岁 Age	125	8.0	12.0	15.2	5.6	1.6	57.6
45~54 岁 Age	70	2.9	14.3	15.7	7.1	4.3	55.7
55~60 岁 Age	43	4.7	7.0	18.6	9.3	2.3	58.1
女性 Female	535	13.8	12.1	12.7	7.7	5.2	48.4
16~24 岁 Age	112	10.7	13.4	12.5	9.8	7.1	46.4
25~34 岁 Age	158	14.6	7.6	15.8	9.5	4.4	48.1
35~44 岁 Age	137	9.5	13.9	10.9	2.9	7.3	55.5
45~54 岁 Age	87	25.3	13.8	11.5	9.2	3.4	36.8
55~60 岁 Age	41	9.8	17.1	9.8	7.3	0.0	56.1

1-7 样本、男性各年龄层、女性各年龄层的品牌习惯/ Brand Habit in Consuming Milk Powder by the Whole Sample, Age and Gender Groups

	人数 Number	基本固定食用一个牌子 used in only one brand	比较固定地食用两个或三个牌子 used in two or three brands	基本上不太固定牌子 no brand preference
样本 Sample	**492**	**40.2**	**32.9**	**26.8**
男性 Male	**216**	**41.2**	**34.7**	**24.1**
16~24 岁 Age	47	38.3	38.3	23.4
25~34 岁 Age	67	47.8	31.3	20.9
35~44 岁 Age	53	37.7	37.7	24.5
45~54 岁 Age	31	45.2	35.5	19.4
55~60 岁 Age	18	27.8	27.8	44.4
女性 Female	**276**	**39.5**	**31.5**	**29.0**
16~24 岁 Age	60	28.3	41.7	30.0
25~34 岁 Age	82	30.5	36.6	32.9
35~44 岁 Age	61	52.5	21.3	26.2
45~54 岁 Age	55	45.5	25.5	29.1
55~60 岁 Age	18	55.6	27.8	16.7

1-8 选择该类商品的考虑因素/ Ranking of the Considerations in Purchasing

注：本题为多选题，合计百分比超过 100%（Multiple answers）

排名 Ranking	考虑因素 Considerations	人次 Person-time	百分比 Percent
1	营养成分 nutrition constituent	256	52.4
2	价格适中 reasonable price	206	42.1
3	有名的牌子 famous brand	179	36.6
4	口味好 pleasant taste	173	35.4
5	生产日期 date of producing	94	19.2
6	购买方便 easy to buy	61	12.5
7	易溶解 high dissolubility	43	8.8
8	只是由于习惯 out of habit	26	5.3
9	有优惠条件 with preferential terms	25	5.1
10	广告影响 influence of advertising	23	4.7
11	朋友推荐 introduction of friends	20	4.1
12	包装吸引人 appealing package	17	3.5
13	售货员介绍 introduced by the shop assistants	8	1.6
14	其它 others	3	0.6

n=489

1-9 样本、男性各年龄层、女性各年龄层最常食用的种类/ Types of the Consumed Milk Powder by the Whole Sample, Age and Gender Groups

注：本题为多选题，合计百分比超过 100%（Multiple answers）

	人数 Number	全脂 whole milk	低脂 low-fat	脱脂 skimmed	甜型 sweet	功能型（如加钙等矿物质） containing minerals	加味型（如巧克力、果味等） flavored (e.g. fruit chocolate)	其它 others
样本 Sample	**491**	**43.6**	**14.7**	**24.2**	**6.5**	**21.4**	**5.7**	**1.4**
男性 Male	**216**	**44.4**	**14.4**	**20.4**	**6.5**	**19.4**	**7.4**	**0.9**
16~24 岁 Age	47	44.7	23.4	14.9	0.0	21.3	17.0	2.1
25~34 岁 Age	67	41.8	19.4	14.9	6.0	16.4	9.0	0.0
35~44 岁 Age	53	52.8	7.5	24.5	7.5	20.8	1.9	0.0
45~54 岁 Age	31	48.4	9.7	16.1	12.9	19.4	0.0	3.2
55~60 岁 Age	18	22.2	0.0	50.0	11.1	22.2	5.6	0.0
女性 Female	**275**	**42.9**	**14.9**	**27.3**	**6.5**	**22.9**	**4.4**	**1.8**
16~24 岁 Age	59	32.2	25.4	27.1	5.1	33.9	10.2	0.0
25~34 岁 Age	82	46.3	13.4	24.4	6.1	24.4	1.2	1.2
35~44 岁 Age	61	45.9	14.8	29.5	9.8	11.5	4.9	0.0
45~54 岁 Age	55	45.5	9.1	32.7	5.5	20.0	3.6	5.5
55~60 岁 Age	18	44.4	5.6	16.7	5.6	27.8	0.0	5.6

1-10 样本、男性各年龄层、女性各年龄层最常食用的场合/ Settings of Consumption by the Whole Sample, Age and Gender Groups

注：本题为多选题，合计百分比超过 100%（Multiple answers）

	人数 Number	早餐时 breakfast	正餐 (午、晚餐)时 dinner	餐后热饮 after dinner	宵夜时 evening snack	睡觉前帮助入眠 before sleeping	工作休息时 during work break	其它 others
样本 Sample	490	70.0	3.3	3.1	23.3	30.2	8.4	2.2
男性 Male	214	67.8	2.3	3.3	25.7	28.5	7.9	2.8
16~24 岁 Age	47	68.1	4.3	2.1	29.8	29.8	8.5	2.1
25~34 岁 Age	67	67.2	3.0	1.5	19.4	31.3	7.5	1.5
35~44 岁 Age	52	63.5	1.9	3.8	36.5	23.1	3.8	3.8
45~54 岁 Age	31	71.0	0.0	9.7	16.1	38.7	12.9	3.2
55~60 岁 Age	17	76.5	0.0	0.0	23.5	11.8	11.8	5.9
女性 Female	276	71.7	4.0	2.9	21.4	31.5	8.7	1.8
16~24 岁 Age	60	65.0	3.3	3.3	13.3	43.3	6.7	3.3
25~34 岁 Age	82	74.4	3.7	2.4	22.0	34.1	8.5	0.0
35~44 岁 Age	61	78.7	3.3	1.6	16.4	27.9	11.5	3.3
45~54 岁 Age	55	70.9	5.5	1.8	38.2	20.0	7.3	1.8
55~60 岁 Age	18	61.1	5.6	11.1	11.1	27.8	11.1	0.0

1-11 重度消费者的人口分布/ Demographics of the Heavy Consumers

	人数 Number	16-24 岁 Age	25-34 岁 Age	35-44 岁 Age	45-54 岁 Age	55-60 岁 Age
样本 Sample	369	19.5	30.1	24.7	18.2	7.6
男性 Male	162	19.1	31.5	27.2	14.2	8.0
天天喝 daily	24	12.5	29.2	41.7	8.3	8.3
一周 3 次或以上 3 times or over a week	56	14.3	35.7	26.8	17.9	5.4
一周 1～2 次 once or twice a week	82	24.4	29.3	23.2	13.4	9.8
女性 Female	207	19.8	29.0	22.7	21.3	7.2
天天喝 daily	74	16.2	31.1	17.6	29.7	5.4
一周 3 次或以上 3 times or over a week	65	23.1	18.5	29.2	18.5	10.8
一周 1～2 次 once or twice a week	68	20.6	36.8	22.1	14.7	5.9

1-12 不同消费者层的常用品牌/ The Most Frequently Used Brands by Market Segments

1-12-1 时尚流行指标/ Fads Popular Index

	人数 Number	第一品牌及百分比 1st/ percent	第二品牌及百分比 2nd/ percent	第三品牌及百分比 3rd/ percent	第四品牌及百分比 4th/ percent
样本 Sample	483	**雀巢 Nestle(34.2)**	**安怡 Anlene(17.4)**	**大庆 Daqing(16.6)**	**子母 Dutch Lady(6.6)**
平实生活指向 simple living orientation	217	雀巢 Nestle(30.4)	大庆 Daqing(21.7)	安怡 Anlene(16.1)	子母 Dutch Lady(7.4)
时尚流行指向 fashion orientation	266	雀巢 Nestle(37.2)	安怡 Anlene(18.4)	大庆 Daqing(12.4)	子母 Dutch Lady(6.0)

1-12-2 广告态度指标/ Advertising Attitude Index

	人数 Number	第一品牌及百分比 1st/ percent	第二品牌及百分比 2nd/ percent	第三品牌及百分比 3rd/ percent	第四品牌及百分比 4th/ percent
样本 Sample	484	**雀巢 Nestle(34.7)**	**安怡 Anlene(16.9)**	**大庆 Daqing(16.7)**	**子母 Dutch Lady(6.4)**
广告淡漠指向 indifferent orientation	137	雀巢 Nestle(34.3)	大庆 Daqing(20.4)	安怡 Anlene(14.6)	子母 Dutch Lady(5.8)
中间层 medium	296	雀巢 Nestle(33.8)	安怡 Anlene(18.2)	大庆 Daqing(15.2)	子母 Dutch Lady(7.1)
信赖广告指向 loyal orientation	51	雀巢 Nestle(41.2)	安怡 Anlene(15.7) 大庆 Daqing(15.7)	安满 Anman(3.9) 惠氏 Wythe(3.9) 子母 Dutch Lady(3.9)	冰都 Bingdu(2.0) 丰力富 Fernleaf(2.0) 克宁 Kelim(2.0)

1-12-3 饮食健康指标/ Foods & Drink Quality Index

	人数 Number	第一品牌及百分比 1st/ percent	第二品牌及百分比 2nd/ percent	第三品牌及百分比 3rd/ percent	第四品牌及百分比 4th/ percent
样本 Sample	**488**	**雀巢 Nestle(34.2)**	**安怡 Anlene(17.4)**	**大庆 Daqing(16.8)**	**子母 Dutch Lady(6.6)**
饮食"温饱"指向 "basic" orientation	112	雀巢 Nestle(38.4)	大庆 Daqing(18.8)	安怡 Anlene(13.4)	克宁 Kelim(2.7) 子母 Dutch Lady(2.7) 惠氏 Wythe(2.7)
中间层 medium	283	雀巢 Nestle(32.9)	安怡 Anlene(18.0)	大庆 Daqing(16.6)	子母 Dutch Lady(7.4)
健康营养指向 health & nutrition orientation	93	雀巢 Nestle(33.3)	安怡 Anlene(20.4)	大庆 Daqing(15.1)	子母 Dutch Lady(8.6)

1-13 重度消费者的消费者层构成/ The Composition of the Heavy Consumers

1-13-1 时尚流行指标/ Fads Popular Index

	人数 Number	平实生活指向 simple living orientation	时尚流行指向 fashion orientation
样本 Sample	**363**	**46.6**	**53.4**
天天喝 daily	98	39.8	60.2
一周 3 次或以上 3 times or over a week	120	45.8	54.2
一周 1～2 次 once or twice a week	145	51.7	48.3

1-13-2 广告态度指标/ Advertising Attitude Index

	人数 Number	广告淡漠指向 indifferent orientation	中间层 medium	信赖广告指向 loyal orientation
样本 Sample	**362**	**28.2**	**62.2**	**9.7**
天天喝 daily	97	24.7	66.0	9.3
一周 3 次或以上 3 times or over a week	119	33.6	58.0	8.4
一周 1～2 次 once or twice a week	146	26.0	63.0	11.0

1-13-3 饮食健康指标/ Foods & Drink Quality Index

	人数 Number	饮食"温饱"指向 "basic" orientation	中间层 medium	健康营养指向 health & nutrition orientation
样本 Sample	**368**	**23.6**	**56.3**	**20.1**
天天喝 daily	98	17.3	55.1	27.6
一周 3 次或以上 3 times or over a week	120	25.8	55.0	19.2
一周 1～2 次 once or twice a week	150	26.0	58.0	16.0

● 重庆 / Chongqing

1-1 最近三个月食用频率的比例/ Proportion of the Sample Consuming Milk Powder in the Last Three Months

	人数 Number	百分比 Percent
天天喝 daily	66	10.6
一周 3 次或以上 3 times or over a week	44	7.1
一周 1~2 次 once or twice a week	71	11.4
一个月 2～3 次 2 or 3 times a month	22	3.5
一个月 1 次或以下 once a month or below	23	3.7
没喝过 never	398	63.8

n=624

1-2 最常用品牌排名/ Ranking of the Most Frequently Used Brands

排名 Brand Ranking	品牌 Brands	人数 Number	百分比 Percent
1	山城 Shancheng	115	51.3
2	雀巢 Nestle	32	14.3
3	伊利 Yili	26	11.6
4	完达山 Wandashan	17	7.6
5	三鹿 Sanlu	11	4.9
6	森永 Morinage	3	1.3
6	多美滋 Dumex	3	1.3
7	杨坪 Yangping	2	0.9
7	天友 Tianyou	2	0.9

n=224

1-3 样本、男性各年龄层、女性各年龄层的常用品牌/ The Most Frequently Used Brands by the Whole Sample, Age and Gender Groups

	人数 Number	第一品牌及百分比 1st/ percent	第二品牌及百分比 2nd/ percent	第三品牌及百分比 3rd/ percent	第四品牌及百分比 4th/ percent
样本 Sample	224	**山城 Shancheng(51.3)**	**雀巢 Nestle(14.3)**	**伊利 Yili(11.6)**	**完达山 Wandashan(7.6)**
男性 Male	90	**山城 Shancheng(55.6)**	**雀巢 Nestle(13.3)**	**完达山 Wandashan(11.1)**	**伊利 Yili(6.7)**
16~24 岁 Age	28	山城 Shancheng(50.0)	雀巢 Nestle(21.4)	完达山 Wandashan(10.7)	伊利 Yili(7.1)
25~34 岁 Age	28	山城 Shancheng(50.0)	雀巢 Nestle(14.3) 完达山 Wandashan(14.3)	伊利 Yili(10.7)	多美滋 Dumex(3.6) 三鹿 Sanlu(3.6) 正丰 Zhengfeng(3.6)
35~44 岁 Age	13	山城 Shancheng(53.8)	雀巢 Nestle(15.4) 完达山 Wandashan(15.4)	雅士利 Yashili(7.7) 天友 Tianyou(7.7)	
45~54 岁 Age	12	山城 Shancheng(83.3)	美素乐 Frisonel(8.3) 秦俑 Qinyong(8.3)		
55~60 岁 Age	9	山城 Shancheng(55.6)	三鹿 Sanlu(11.1) 森永 Morinage(11.1) 完达山 Wandashan(11.1) 伊利 Yili(11.1)		
女性 Female	134	**山城 Shancheng(48.5)**	**伊利 Yili(14.9)** **雀巢 Nestle(14.9)**	**三鹿 Sanlu(6.0)**	**完达山 Wandashan(5.2)**
16~24 岁 Age	32	山城 Shancheng(37.5)	伊利 Yili(21.9)	雀巢 Nestle(18.8)	三鹿 Sanlu(6.3) 完达山 Wandashan(6.3)
25~34 岁 Age	41	山城 Shancheng(39.0)	雀巢 Nestle(19.5)	伊利 Yili(12.2)	三鹿 Sanlu(9.8)
35~44 岁 Age	30	山城 Shancheng(56.7)	伊利 Yili(16.7)	雀巢 Nestle(10.0) 完达山 Wandashan(10.0)	三鹿 Sanlu(3.3) 杨坪 Yangping(3.3)
45~54 岁 Age	26	山城 Shancheng(69.2)	雀巢 Nestle(11.5)	伊利 Yili(7.7)	三鹿 Sanlu(3.8) 雪花 Xuehua(3.8) 杨坪 Yangping(3.8)
55~60 岁 Age	5	山城 Shancheng(40.0)	完达山 Wandashan(20.0) 伊利 Yili(20.0) 太易 Taiyi(20.0)		

1-4 理想品牌排名/ Ranking of the Ideal Brands

排名 Brand Ranking	品牌 Brands	人数 Number	百分比 Percent
1	山城 Shancheng	322	51.7
2	雀巢 Nestle	96	15.4
3	伊利 Yili	49	7.9
4	完达山 Wandashan	32	5.1
5	三鹿 Sanlu	21	3.4
6	多美滋 Dumex	14	2.2

n=623

1-5 样本、男性各年龄层、女性各年龄层最近三个月有无购买的比例/ Purchasing in the Last Three Months by the Whole Sample, Age and Gender Groups

	人数 Number	买过 yes	没买过 no
样本 Sample	621	41.9	58.1
男性 Male	311	34.1	65.9
16~24 岁 Age	63	36.5	63.5
25~34 岁 Age	93	40.9	59.1
35~44 岁 Age	75	28.0	72.0
45~54 岁 Age	52	25.0	75.0
55~60 岁 Age	28	39.3	60.7
女性 Female	310	49.7	50.3
16~24 岁 Age	64	43.8	56.3
25~34 岁 Age	90	63.3	36.7
35~44 岁 Age	73	46.6	53.4
45~54 岁 Age	60	48.3	51.7
55~60 岁 Age	23	26.1	73.9

1-6 样本、男性各年龄层、女性各年龄层最近三个月的食用频率/ Frequencies of Consuming Milk Powder in the Last Three Months by the Whole Sample, Age and Gender Groups

	人数 Number	天天喝 daily	一周 3 次或以上 3 times or over a week	一周 1~2 次 once or twice a week	一个月 2~3 次 2 or 3 times a month	一个月 1 次或以下 once a month or below	没喝过 never
样本 Sample	624	10.6	7.1	11.4	3.5	3.7	63.8
男性 Male	314	8.3	6.1	9.2	2.9	2.5	71.0
16~24 岁 Age	64	12.5	9.4	12.5	6.3	3.1	56.3
25~34 岁 Age	93	8.6	5.4	12.9	2.2	1.1	69.9
35~44 岁 Age	75	5.3	4.0	4.0	2.7	2.7	81.3
45~54 岁 Age	54	3.7	5.6	7.4	0.0	5.6	77.8
55~60 岁 Age	28	14.3	7.1	7.1	3.6	0.0	67.9
女性 Female	310	12.9	8.1	13.5	4.2	4.8	56.5
16~24 岁 Age	64	12.5	14.1	17.2	4.7	1.6	50.0
25~34 岁 Age	90	12.2	11.1	10.0	6.7	6.7	53.3
35~44 岁 Age	73	9.6	2.7	15.1	4.1	9.6	58.9
45~54 岁 Age	60	18.3	6.7	15.0	1.7	1.7	56.7
55~60 岁 Age	23	13.0	0.0	8.7	0.0	0.0	78.3

1-7 样本、男性各年龄层、女性各年龄层的品牌习惯/ Brand Habit in Consuming Milk Powder by the Whole Sample, Age and Gender Groups

	人数 Number	基本固定食用一个牌子 used in only one brand	比较固定地食用两个或三个牌子 used in two or three brands	基本上不太固定牌子 no brand preference
样本 Sample	225	40.9	31.6	27.6
男性 Male	90	40.0	31.1	28.9
16~24 岁 Age	28	35.7	28.6	35.7
25~34 岁 Age	28	42.9	39.3	17.9
35~44 岁 Age	13	23.1	15.4	61.5
45~54 岁 Age	12	50.0	33.3	16.7
55~60 岁 Age	9	55.6	33.3	11.1
女性 Female	135	41.5	31.9	26.7
16~24 岁 Age	32	37.5	34.4	28.1
25~34 岁 Age	42	26.2	45.2	28.6
35~44 岁 Age	30	40.0	30.0	30.0
45~54 岁 Age	26	65.4	15.4	19.2
55~60 岁 Age	5	80.0	0.0	20.0

1-8 选择该类商品的考虑因素/ Ranking of the Considerations in Purchasing

注：本题为多选题，合计百分比超过 100%（Multiple answers）

排名 Ranking	考虑因素 Considerations	人次 Person-time	百分比 Percent
1	口味好 pleasant taste	94	42.5
2	价格适中 reasonable price	93	42.1
3	营养成分 nutrition constituent	88	39.8
4	有名的牌子 famous brand	57	25.8
5	生产日期 date of producing	33	14.9
6	只是由于习惯 out of habit	30	13.6
7	购买方便 easy to buy	27	12.2
8	易溶解 high dissolubility	16	7.2
9	广告影响 influence of advertising	10	4.5
10	朋友推荐 introduction of friends	9	4.1
11	包装吸引人 appealing package	8	3.6
12	其它 others	6	2.7
13	有优惠条件 with preferential terms	2	0.9
14	售货员介绍 introduced by the shop assistants	1	0.5

n=221

1-9 样本、男性各年龄层、女性各年龄层最常食用的种类/ Types of the Consumed Milk Powder by the Whole Sample, Age and Gender Groups

注：本题为多选题，合计百分比超过 100%（Multiple answers）

	人数 Number	全脂 whole milk	低脂 low-fat	脱脂 skimmed	甜型 sweet	功能型（如加钙等矿物质）containing minerals	加味型（如巧克力、果味等）flavored (e.g. fruit chocolate)	其它 others
样本 Sample	224	58.5	9.8	13.8	9.8	16.1	3.1	0.9
男性 Male	90	68.9	3.3	10.0	6.7	18.9	5.6	0.0
16~24 岁 Age	28	78.6	0.0	3.6	3.6	10.7	10.7	0.0
25~34 岁 Age	28	75.0	3.6	10.7	3.6	25.0	3.6	0.0
35~44 岁 Age	13	53.8	7.7	0.0	15.4	30.8	7.7	0.0
45~54 岁 Age	12	58.3	0.0	25.0	16.7	16.7	0.0	0.0
55~60 岁 Age	9	55.6	11.1	22.2	0.0	11.1	0.0	0.0
女性 Female	134	51.5	14.2	16.4	11.9	14.2	1.5	1.5
16~24 岁 Age	32	46.9	15.6	28.1	3.1	6.3	6.3	3.1
25~34 岁 Age	42	52.4	16.7	14.3	14.3	16.7	0.0	0.0
35~44 岁 Age	29	51.7	10.3	6.9	20.7	17.2	0.0	0.0
45~54 岁 Age	26	53.8	15.4	15.4	11.5	15.4	0.0	3.8
55~60 岁 Age	5	60.0	0.0	20.0	0.0	20.0	0.0	0.0

1-10 样本、男性各年龄层、女性各年龄层最常食用的场合/ Settings of Consumption by the Whole Sample, Age and Gender Groups

注：本题为多选题，合计百分比超过 100%（Multiple answers）

	人数 Number	早餐时 breakfast	正餐（午、晚餐）时 dinner	餐后热饮 after dinner	宵夜时 evening snack	睡觉前帮助入眠 before sleeping	工作休息时 during work break	其它 others
样本 Sample	221	76.0	1.8	2.3	14.9	26.7	3.6	1.4
男性 Male	88	70.5	1.1	2.3	21.6	22.7	5.7	1.1
16~24 岁 Age	28	60.7	3.6	0.0	25.0	32.1	0.0	3.6
25~34 岁 Age	28	67.9	0.0	3.6	21.4	21.4	14.3	0.0
35~44 岁 Age	11	81.8	0.0	0.0	18.2	9.1	9.1	0.0
45~54 岁 Age	12	75.0	0.0	8.3	33.3	16.7	0.0	0.0
55~60 岁 Age	9	88.9	0.0	0.0	0.0	22.2	0.0	0.0
女性 Female	133	79.7	2.3	2.3	10.5	29.3	2.3	1.5
16~24 岁 Age	32	78.1	0.0	6.3	9.4	34.4	3.1	3.1
25~34 岁 Age	40	77.5	2.5	0.0	7.5	35.0	0.0	2.5
35~44 岁 Age	30	76.7	0.0	3.3	16.7	30.0	6.7	0.0
45~54 岁 Age	26	92.3	7.7	0.0	7.7	15.4	0.0	0.0
55~60 岁 Age	5	60.0	0.0	0.0	20.0	20.0	0.0	0.0

1-11 重度消费者的人口分布/ Demographics of the Heavy Consumers

	人数 Number	16-24 岁 Age	25-34 岁 Age	35-44 岁 Age	45-54 岁 Age	55-60 岁 Age
样本 Sample	181	27.6	30.4	16.6	18.2	7.2
男性 Male	74	29.7	33.8	13.5	12.2	10.8
天天喝 daily	26	30.8	30.8	15.4	7.7	15.4
一周 3 次或以上 3 times or over a week	19	31.6	26.3	15.8	15.8	10.5
一周 1～2 次 once or twice a week	29	27.6	41.4	10.3	13.8	6.9
女性 Female	107	26.2	28.0	18.7	22.4	4.7
天天喝 daily	40	20.0	27.5	17.5	27.5	7.5
一周 3 次或以上 3 times or over a week	25	36.0	40.0	8.0	16.0	0.0
一周 1～2 次 once or twice a week	42	26.2	21.4	26.2	21.4	4.8

1-12 不同消费者层的常用品牌/ The Most Frequently Used Brands by Market Segments

1-12-1 时尚流行指标/ Fads Popular Index

	人数 Number	第一品牌及百分比 1st/ percent	第二品牌及百分比 2nd/ percent	第三品牌及百分比 3rd/ percent	第四品牌及百分比 4th/ percent
样本 Sample	221	**山城 Shancheng(51.6)**	**雀巢 Nestle(14.0)**	**伊利 Yili(11.8)**	**完达山 Wandashan(7.2)**
平实生活指向 simple living orientation	108	山城 Shancheng(57.4)	雀巢 Nestle(11.1)	伊利 Yili(10.2)	完达山 Wandashan(5.6)
时尚流行指向 fashion orientation	113	山城 Shancheng(46.0)	雀巢 Nestle(16.8)	伊利 Yili(13.3)	完达山 Wandashan(8.8)

1-12-2 广告态度指标/ Advertising Attitude Index

	人数 Number	第一品牌及百分比 1st/ percent	第二品牌及百分比 2nd/ percent	第三品牌及百分比 3rd/ percent	第四品牌及百分比 4th/ percent
样本 Sample	221	**山城 Shancheng(51.1)**	**雀巢 Nestle(14.5)**	**伊利 Yili(11.8)**	**完达山 Wandashan(7.2)**
广告淡漠指向 indifferent orientation	51	山城 Shancheng(54.9)	雀巢 Nestle(11.8) 伊利 Yili(11.8)	完达山 Wandashan(7.8)	三鹿 Sanlu(3.9) 森永 Morinage(3.9)
中间层 medium	139	山城 Shancheng(51.1)	雀巢 Nestle(13.7) 伊利 Yili(13.7)	完达山 Wandashan(7.2)	三鹿 Sanlu(4.3)
信赖广告指向 loyal orientation	31	山城 Shancheng(45.2)	雀巢 Nestle(22.6)	三鹿 Sanlu(9.7)	完达山 Wandashan(6.5)

1-12-3 饮食健康指标/ Foods & Drink Quality Index

	人数 Number	第一品牌及百分比 1st/ percent	第二品牌及百分比 2nd/ percent	第三品牌及百分比 3rd/ percent	第四品牌及百分比 4th/ percent
样本 Sample	220	**山城 Shancheng(51.4)**	**雀巢 Nestle(14.5)**	**伊利 Yili(11.4)**	**完达山 Wandashan(7.3)**
饮食"温饱"指向 "basic" orientation	70	山城 Shancheng(55.7)	雀巢 Nestle(17.1)	完达山 Wandashan(7.1) 三鹿 Sanlu(7.1)	森永 Morinage(1.4) 安怡 Anlene(1.4) 伊利 Yili(1.4) 正丰 Zhengfeng(1.4) 皇家 Huangjia(1.4) 雅士利 Yashili(1.4) 杨坪 Yangping(1.4)
中间层 medium	100	山城 Shancheng(51.0)	雀巢 Nestle(17.0) 伊利 Yili(17.0)	三鹿 Sanlu(3.0) 完达山 Wandashan(3.0)	多美滋 Dumex(2.0) 天友 Tianyou(2.0)
健康营养指向 health & nutrition orientation	50	山城 Shancheng(46.0)	完达山 Wandashan(16.0)	伊利 Yili(14.0)	雀巢 Nestle(6.0) 三鹿 Sanlu(6.0)

1-13 重度消费者的消费者层构成/ The Composition of the Heavy Consumers

1-13-1 时尚流行指标/ Fads Popular Index

	人数 Number	平实生活指向 simple living orientation	时尚流行指向 fashion orientation
样本 Sample	180	50.6	49.4
天天喝 daily	66	47.0	53.0
一周 3 次或以上 3 times or over a week	44	52.3	47.7
一周 1～2 次 once or twice a week	70	52.9	47.1

1-13-2 广告态度指标/ Advertising Attitude Index

	人数 Number	广告淡漠指向 indifferent orientation	中间层 medium	信赖广告指向 loyal orientation
样本 Sample	180	22.8	62.8	14.4
天天喝 daily	66	15.2	69.7	15.2
一周 3 次或以上 3 times or over a week	44	31.8	50.0	18.2
一周 1～2 次 once or twice a week	70	24.3	64.3	11.4

1-13-3 饮食健康指标/ Foods & Drink Quality Index

	人数 Number	饮食"温饱"指向 "basic" orientation	中间层 medium	健康营养指向 health & nutrition orientation
样本 Sample	178	28.7	48.3	23.0
天天喝 daily	66	27.3	47.0	25.8
一周 3 次或以上 3 times or over a week	44	47.7	27.3	25.0
一周 1~2 次 once or twice a week	68	17.6	63.2	19.1

● 武汉 / Wuhan

1-1 最近三个月食用频率的比例/ Proportion of the Sample Consuming Milk Powder in the Last Three Months

	人数 Number	百分比 Percent
天天喝 daily	110	17.2
一周 3 次或以上 3 times or over a week	80	12.5
一周 1~2 次 once or twice a week	92	14.4
一个月 2~3 次 2 or 3 times a month	51	8.0
一个月 1 次或以下 once a month or below	24	3.8
没喝过 never	283	44.2

n=640

1-2 最常用品牌排名/ Ranking of the Most Frequently Used Brands

排名 Brand Ranking	品牌 Brands	人数 Number	百分比 Percent
1	扬子江 Yangzijiang	190	53.2
2	雀巢 Nestle	68	19.0
3	伊利 Yili	40	11.2
4	三鹿 Sanlu	12	3.4
5	南山 Nanshan	10	2.8
6	古城 Gucheng	5	1.4
7	完达山 Wandashan	4	1.1
7	光明 Bright	4	1.1
7	多美滋 Dumex	4	1.1

n=357

1-3 样本、男性各年龄层、女性各年龄层的常用品牌/ The Most Frequently Used Brands by the Whole Sample, Age and Gender Groups

	人数 Number	第一品牌及百分比 1st/ percent	第二品牌及百分比 2nd/ percent	第三品牌及百分比 3rd/ percent
样本 Sample	**357**	**扬子江 Yangzijiang(53.2)**	**雀巢 Nestle(19.0)**	**伊利 Yili(11.2)**
男性 Male	**156**	**扬子江 Yangzijiang(55.1)**	**雀巢 Nestle(19.2)**	**伊利 Yili(9.6)**
16~24 岁 Age	40	扬子江 Yangzijiang(42.5)	雀巢 Nestle(32.5)	伊利 Yili(10.0)
25~34 岁 Age	51	扬子江 Yangzijiang(62.7)	伊利 Yili(11.8)	雀巢 Nestle(7.8)
35~44 岁 Age	29	扬子江 Yangzijiang(51.7)	雀巢 Nestle(20.7)	伊利 Yili(10.3)
45~54 岁 Age	22	扬子江 Yangzijiang(50.0)	雀巢 Nestle(27.3)	三鹿 Sanlu(9.1) 伊利 Yili(9.1)
55~60 岁 Age	14	扬子江 Yangzijiang(78.6)	三鹿 Sanlu(14.3)	雀巢 Nestle(7.1)
女性 Female	**201**	**扬子江 Yangzijiang(51.7)**	**雀巢 Nestle(18.9)**	**伊利 Yili(12.4)**
16~24 岁 Age	48	扬子江 Yangzijiang(50.0)	雀巢 Nestle(27.1)	伊利 Yili(8.3)
25~34 岁 Age	63	扬子江 Yangzijiang(49.2)	雀巢 Nestle(19.0)	伊利 Yili(11.1)
35~44 岁 Age	38	扬子江 Yangzijiang(52.6)	伊利 Yili(21.1)	雀巢 Nestle(18.4)
45~54 岁 Age	42	扬子江 Yangzijiang(54.8)	伊利 Yili(14.3)	雀巢 Nestle(11.9)
55~60 岁 Age	10	扬子江 Yangzijiang(60.0)	雀巢 Nestle(10.0) 三鹿 Sanlu(10.0) 完达山 Wandashan(10.0) 正丰 Zhengfeng(10.0)	

1-4 理想品牌排名/ Ranking of the Ideal Brands

排名 Brand Ranking	品牌 Brands	人数 Number	百分比 Percent
1	扬子江 Yangzijiang	263	41.0
2	雀巢 Nestle	146	22.7
3	伊利 Yili	70	10.9
4	三鹿 Sanlu	19	3.0
5	南山 Nanshan	16	2.5
6	多美滋 Dumex	10	1.6
7	完达山 Wandashan	9	1.4

n=642

1-5 样本、男性各年龄层、女性各年龄层最近三个月有无购买的比例/ Purchasing in the Last Three Months by the Whole Sample, Age and Gender Groups

	人数 Number	买过 yes	没买过 no
样本 Sample	642	52.3	47.7
男性 Male	311	46.0	54.0
16~24 岁 Age	65	40.0	60.0
25~34 岁 Age	89	55.1	44.9
35~44 岁 Age	80	43.8	56.3
45~54 岁 Age	52	38.5	61.5
55~60 岁 Age	25	52.0	48.0
女性 Female	331	58.3	41.7
16~24 岁 Age	69	49.3	50.7
25~34 岁 Age	96	63.5	36.5
35~44 岁 Age	78	57.7	42.3
45~54 岁 Age	62	66.1	33.9
55~60 岁 Age	26	46.2	53.8

1-6 样本、男性各年龄层、女性各年龄层最近三个月的食用频率/ Frequencies of Consuming Milk Powder in the Last Three Months by the Whole Sample, Age and Gender Groups

	人数 Number	天天喝 daily	一周 3 次或以上 3 times or over a week	一周 1~2 次 once or twice a week	一个月 2~3 次 2 or 3 times a month	一个月 1 次或以下 once a month or below	没喝过 never
样本 Sample	640	17.2	12.5	14.4	8.0	3.8	44.2
男性 Male	311	11.6	10.0	15.8	7.7	5.1	49.8
16~24 岁 Age	65	13.8	10.8	21.5	10.8	4.6	38.5
25~34 岁 Age	89	12.4	10.1	13.5	12.4	9.0	42.7
35~44 岁 Age	80	6.3	11.3	12.5	3.8	2.5	63.8
45~54 岁 Age	52	9.6	5.8	17.3	5.8	3.8	57.7
55~60 岁 Age	25	24.0	12.0	16.0	0.0	4.0	44.0
女性 Female	329	22.5	14.9	13.1	8.2	2.4	38.9
16~24 岁 Age	69	23.2	14.5	10.1	18.8	2.9	30.4
25~34 岁 Age	95	28.4	10.5	23.2	4.2	0.0	33.7
35~44 岁 Age	77	14.3	16.9	6.5	7.8	3.9	50.6
45~54 岁 Age	62	29.0	21.0	8.1	6.5	3.2	32.3
55~60 岁 Age	26	7.7	11.5	15.4	0.0	3.8	61.5

1-7 样本、男性各年龄层、女性各年龄层的品牌习惯/ Brand Habit in Consuming Milk Powder by the Whole Sample, Age and Gender Groups

	人数 Number	基本固定食用一个牌子 used in only one brand	比较固定地食用两个或三个牌子 used in two or three brands	基本上不太固定牌子 no brand preference
样本 Sample	357	53.2	26.6	20.2
男性 Male	156	56.4	22.4	21.2
16~24 岁 Age	40	52.5	20.0	27.5
25~34 岁 Age	51	60.8	23.5	15.7
35~44 岁 Age	29	55.2	31.0	13.8
45~54 岁 Age	22	50.0	13.6	36.4
55~60 岁 Age	14	64.3	21.4	14.3
女性 Female	201	50.7	29.9	19.4
16~24 岁 Age	48	41.7	27.1	31.3
25~34 岁 Age	63	50.8	34.9	14.3
35~44 岁 Age	38	60.5	26.3	13.2
45~54 岁 Age	42	52.4	28.6	19.0
55~60 岁 Age	10	50.0	30.0	20.0

1-8 选择该类商品的考虑因素/ Ranking of the Considerations in Purchasing

注：本题为多选题，合计百分比超过 100%（Multiple answers）

排名 Ranking	考虑因素 Considerations	人次 Person-time	百分比 Percent
1	营养成分 nutrition constituent	160	44.8
2	口味好 pleasant taste	158	44.3
3	价格适中 reasonable price	156	43.7
4	有名的牌子 famous brand	123	34.5
5	生产日期 date of producing	91	25.5
6	购买方便 easy to buy	51	14.3
7	只是由于习惯 out of habit	40	11.2
8	易溶解 high dissolubility	37	10.4
9	广告影响 influence of advertising	25	7.0
10	朋友推荐 introduction of friends	16	4.5
11	有优惠条件 with preferential terms	13	3.6
12	其它 others	12	3.4
13	包装吸引人 appealing package	9	2.5
14	售货员介绍 introduced by the shop assistants	2	0.6

n=357

1-9 样本、男性各年龄层、女性各年龄层最常食用的种类/ Types of the Consumed Milk Powder by the Whole Sample, Age and Gender Groups

注：本题为多选题，合计百分比超过 100%（Multiple answers）

	人数 Number	全脂 whole milk	低脂 low-fat	脱脂 skimmed	甜型 sweet	功能型（如加钙等矿物质）containing minerals	加味型（如巧克力、果味等）flavored(e.g. fruit chocolate)	其它 others
样本 Sample	356	64.0	12.4	12.9	10.1	13.8	1.4	1.7
男性 Male	156	63.5	10.3	14.1	10.3	14.1	1.9	1.3
16~24 岁 Age	40	62.5	7.5	17.5	10.0	12.5	5.0	0.0
25~34 岁 Age	51	52.9	9.8	17.6	11.8	15.7	2.0	0.0
35~44 岁 Age	29	72.4	13.8	13.8	10.3	17.2	0.0	0.0
45~54 岁 Age	22	72.7	0.0	9.1	13.6	18.2	0.0	4.5
55~60 岁 Age	14	71.4	28.6	0.0	0.0	0.0	0.0	7.1
女性 Female	200	64.5	14.0	12.0	10.0	13.5	1.0	2.0
16~24 岁 Age	47	61.7	23.4	10.6	14.9	8.5	2.1	0.0
25~34 岁 Age	63	73.0	6.3	12.7	11.1	11.1	1.6	1.6
35~44 岁 Age	38	60.5	15.8	5.3	10.5	21.1	0.0	0.0
45~54 岁 Age	42	61.9	11.9	14.3	4.8	16.7	0.0	4.8
55~60 岁 Age	10	50.0	20.0	30.0	0.0	10.0	0.0	10.0

1-10 样本、男性各年龄层、女性各年龄层最常食用的场合/ Settings of Consumption by the Whole Sample, Age and Gender Groups

注：本题为多选题，合计百分比超过 100%（Multiple answers）

	人数 Number	早餐时 breakfast	正餐（午、晚餐）时 dinner	餐后热饮 after dinner	宵夜时 evening snack	睡觉前帮助入眠 before sleeping	工作休息时 during work break	其它 others
样本 Sample	356	63.8	6.5	6.7	12.9	38.8	9.0	2.2
男性 Male	156	60.9	5.8	6.4	16.7	37.2	10.3	2.6
16~24 岁 Age	40	60.0	5.0	5.0	20.0	40.0	7.5	7.5
25~34 岁 Age	51	49.0	3.9	9.8	23.5	41.2	13.7	2.0
35~44 岁 Age	29	65.5	3.4	10.3	10.3	44.8	6.9	0.0
45~54 岁 Age	22	77.3	9.1	0.0	13.6	18.2	9.1	0.0
55~60 岁 Age	14	71.4	14.3	0.0	0.0	28.6	14.3	0.0
女性 Female	200	66.0	7.0	7.0	10.0	40.0	8.0	2.0
16~24 岁 Age	48	62.5	8.3	10.4	6.3	41.7	14.6	0.0
25~34 岁 Age	62	67.7	4.8	8.1	9.7	40.3	3.2	1.6
35~44 岁 Age	38	55.3	5.3	7.9	13.2	44.7	15.8	0.0
45~54 岁 Age	42	73.8	11.9	2.4	9.5	40.5	2.4	4.8
55~60 岁 Age	10	80.0	0.0	0.0	20.0	10.0	0.0	10.0

1-11 重度消费者的人口分布/ Demographics of the Heavy Consumers

	人数 Number	16-24 岁 Age	25-34 岁 Age	35-44 岁 Age	45-54 岁 Age	55-60 岁 Age
样本 Sample	282	22.3	32.3	18.8	18.8	7.8
男性 Male	116	25.9	27.6	20.7	14.7	11.2
天天喝 daily	36	25.0	30.6	13.9	13.9	16.7
一周 3 次或以上 3 times or over a week	31	22.6	29.0	29.0	9.7	9.7
一周 1～2 次 once or twice a week	49	28.6	24.5	20.4	18.4	8.2
女性 Female	166	19.9	35.5	17.5	21.7	5.4
天天喝 daily	74	21.6	36.5	14.9	24.3	2.7
一周 3 次或以上 3 times or over a week	49	20.4	20.4	26.5	26.5	6.1
一周 1～2 次 once or twice a week	43	16.3	51.2	11.6	11.6	9.3

1-12 不同消费者层的常用品牌/ The Most Frequently Used Brands by Market Segments

1-12-1 时尚流行指标/ Fads Popular Index

	人数 Number	第一品牌及百分比 1st/ percent	第二品牌及百分比 2nd/ percent	第三品牌及百分比 3rd/ percent
样本 Sample	351	**扬子江 Yangzijiang(53.6)**	**雀巢 Nestle(18.5)**	**伊利 Yili(11.4)**
平实生活指向 simple living orientation	177	扬子江 Yangzijiang(57.1)	雀巢 Nestle(16.4)	伊利 Yili(12.4)
时尚流行指向 fashion orientation	174	扬子江 Yangzijiang(50.0)	雀巢 Nestle(20.7)	伊利 Yili(10.3)

1-12-2 广告态度指标/ Advertising Attitude Index

	人数 Number	第一品牌及百分比 1st/ percent	第二品牌及百分比 2nd/ percent	第三品牌及百分比 3rd/ percent
样本 Sample	352	**扬子江 Yangzijiang(53.7)**	**雀巢 Nestle(18.5)**	**伊利 Yili(11.4)**
广告淡漠指向 indifferent orientation	90	扬子江 Yangzijiang(51.1)	雀巢 Nestle(22.2)	伊利 Yili(12.2)
中间层 medium	223	扬子江 Yangzijiang(55.2)	雀巢 Nestle(17.0)	伊利 Yili(11.7)
信赖广告指向 loyal orientation	39	扬子江 Yangzijiang(51.3)	雀巢 Nestle(17.9)	伊利 Yili(7.7)

1-12-3 饮食健康指标/ Foods & Drink Quality Index

	人数 Number	第一品牌及百分比 1st/ percent	第二品牌及百分比 2nd/ percent	第三品牌及百分比 3rd/ percent
样本 Sample	351	**扬子江 Yangzijiang(53.6)**	**雀巢 Nestle(18.5)**	**伊利 Yili(11.4)**
饮食"温饱"指向 "basic" orientation	100	扬子江 Yangzijiang(51.0)	雀巢 Nestle(23.0)	伊利 Yili(10.0)
中间层 medium	165	扬子江 Yangzijiang(56.4)	雀巢 Nestle(18 2)	伊利 Yili(12.1)
健康营养指向 health & nutrition orientation	86	扬子江 Yangzijiang(51.2)	雀巢 Nestle(14.0)	伊利 Yili(11.6)

1-13 重度消费者的消费者层构成/ The Composition of the Heavy Consumers

1-13-1 时尚流行指标/ Fads Popular Index

	人数 Number	平实生活指向 simple living orientation	时尚流行指向 fashion orientation
样本 Sample	279	49.5	50.5
天天喝 daily	109	47.7	52.3
一周 3 次或以上 3 times or over a week	78	55.1	44.9
一周 1～2 次 once or twice a week	92	46.7	53.3

1-13-2 广告态度指标/ Advertising Attitude Index

	人数 Number	广告淡漠指向 indifferent orientation	中间层 medium	信赖广告指向 loyal orientation
样本 Sample	280	25.7	61.8	12.5
天天喝 daily	109	27.5	57.8	14.7
一周 3 次或以上 3 times or over a week	79	26.6	62.0	11.4
一周 1～2 次 once or twice a week	92	22.8	66.3	10.9

1-13-3 饮食健康指标/ Foods & Drink Quality Index

	人数 Number	饮食"温饱"指向 "basic" orientation	中间层 medium	健康营养指向 health & nutrition orientation
样本 Sample	279	24.4	49.5	26.2
天天喝 daily	109	25.7	45.9	28.4
一周 3 次或以上 3 times or over a week	79	16.5	51.9	31.6
一周 1～2 次 once or twice a week	91	29.7	51.6	18.7

● 西安 / Xi'an

1-1 最近三个月食用频率的比例/ Proportion of the Sample Consuming Milk Powder in the Last Three Months

	人数 Number	百分比 Percent
天天喝 daily	99	16.5
一周 3 次或以上 3 times or over a week	69	11.5
一周 1~2 次 once or twice a week	108	18.0
一个月 2~3 次 2 or 3 times a month	43	7.2
一个月 1 次或以下 once a month or below	18	3.0
没喝过 never	264	43.9

n=601

1-2 最常用品牌排名/ Ranking of the Most Frequently Used Brands

排名 Brand Ranking	品牌 Brands	人数 Number	百分比 Percent
1	秦俑 Qinyong	237	70.3
2	雀巢 Nestle	16	4.7
2	三鹿 Sanlu	16	4.7
3	神果 Shenguo	15	4.5
4	伊利 Yili	10	3.0
5	多美滋 Dumex	4	1.2
5	东方 Dongfang	4	1.2
5	和氏 Herds	4	1.2
6	关山 Guanshan	2	0.6

n=337

1-3 样本、男性各年龄层、女性各年龄层的常用品牌/ The Most Frequently Used Brands by the Whole Sample, Age and Gender Groups

	人数 Number	第一品牌及百分比 1st/ percent	第二品牌及百分比 2nd/ percent	第三品牌及百分比 3rd/ percent
样本 Sample	**337**	**秦俑 Qinyong(70.3)**	**雀巢 Nestle(4.7)** **三鹿 Sanlu(4.7)**	**神果 Shenguo(4.5)**
男性 Male	**156**	**秦俑 Qinyong(67.9)**	**神果 Shenguo(5.1)** **雀巢 Nestle(5.1)**	**伊利 Yili(3.8)** **三鹿 Sanlu(3.8)**
16~24 岁 Age	35	秦俑 Qinyong(62.9)	雀巢 Nestle(11.4)	伊利 Yili(8.6)
25~34 岁 Age	37	秦俑 Qinyong(70.3)	神果 Shenguo(10.8)	完达山 Wandashan(5.4)
35~44 岁 Age	49	秦俑 Qinyong(75.5)	雀巢 Nestle(6.1)	三鹿 Sanlu(4.1)
45~54 岁 Age	26	秦俑 Qinyong(61.5)	神果 Shenguo(7.7)	龙丹 Longdan(3.8) 雀巢 Nestle(3.8) 三鹿 Sanlu(3.8) 伊利 Yili(3.8) 东方 Dongfang(3.8) 和氏 Herds(3.8) 申建 Shenjian(3.8)
55~60 岁 Age	9	秦俑 Qinyong(55.6)	三鹿 Sanlu(11.1) 兴隆 Xinglong(11.1) 神果 Shenguo(11.1) 和氏 Herds(11.1)	
女性 Female	**181**	**秦俑 Qinyong(72.4)**	**三鹿 Sanlu(5.5)**	**雀巢 Nestle(4.4)**
16~24 岁 Age	36	秦俑 Qinyong(61.1)	雀巢 Nestle(8.3) 三鹿 Sanlu(8.3) 神果 Shenguo(8.3)	多美滋 Dumex(2.8) 惠民 AMDP(2.8) 关山 Guanshan(2.8)
25~34 岁 Age	56	秦俑 Qinyong(69.6)	三鹿 Sanlu(8.9)	雀巢 Nestle(7.1)
35~44 岁 Age	43	秦俑 Qinyong(86.0)	光明 Bright(2.3) 雀巢 Nestle(2.3) 神果 Shenguo(2.3) 关山 Guanshan(2.3) 西都 Xidu(2.3)	
45~54 岁 Age	32	秦俑 Qinyong(71.9)	三鹿 Sanlu(6.3) 伊利 Yili(6.3)	牧童 Mutong(3.1) 和氏 Herds(3.1) 宜品 Yipin(3.1) 从德 Congde(3.1) 迎松 Yingsong(3.1)
55~60 岁 Age	14	秦俑 Qinyong(71.4)	多美滋 Dumex(7.1) 光明 Bright(7.1) 惠民 AMDP(7.1) 神果 Shenguo(7.1)	

1-4 理想品牌排名/ Ranking of the Ideal Brands

排名 Brand Ranking	品牌 Brands	人数 Number	百分比 Percent
1	秦俑 Qinyong	365	60.7
2	雀巢 Nestle	46	7.7
3	三鹿 Sanlu	31	5.2
4	伊利 Yili	27	4.5
5	神果 Shenguo	21	3.5
6	完达山 Wandashan	8	1.3
6	多美滋 Dumex	8	1.3
7	关山 Guanshan	4	0.7
8	惠民 AMDP	3	0.5
8	和氏 Herds	3	0.5

n=601

1-5 样本、男性各年龄层、女性各年龄层最近三个月有无购买的比例/ Purchasing in the Last Three Months by the Whole Sample, Age and Gender Groups

	人数 Number	买过 yes	没买过 no
样本 Sample	601	54.1	45.9
男性 Male	302	47.4	52.6
16~24 岁 Age	64	37.5	62.5
25~34 岁 Age	91	47.3	52.7
35~44 岁 Age	77	55.8	44.2
45~54 岁 Age	46	52.2	47.8
55~60 岁 Age	24	37.5	62.5
女性 Female	299	60.9	39.1
16~24 岁 Age	61	49.2	50.8
25~34 岁 Age	90	67.8	32.2
35~44 岁 Age	74	62.2	37.8
45~54 岁 Age	49	65.3	34.7
55~60 岁 Age	25	52.0	48.0

1-6 样本、男性各年龄层、女性各年龄层最近三个月的食用频率/ Frequencies of Consuming Milk Powder in the Last Three Months by the Whole Sample, Age and Gender Groups

	人数 Number	天天喝 daily	一周 3 次或以上 3 times or over a week	一周 1~2 次 once or twice a week	一个月 2~3 次 2 or 3 times a month	一个月 1 次或以下 once a month or below	没喝过 never
样本 Sample	601	16.5	11.5	18.0	7.2	3.0	43.9
男性 Male	302	11.9	9.3	20.5	6.3	3.6	48.3
16~24 岁 Age	64	14.1	14.1	14.1	7.8	4.7	45.3
25~34 岁 Age	91	2.2	6.6	24.2	4.4	3.3	59.3
35~44 岁 Age	77	19.5	11.7	23.4	6.5	2.6	36.4
45~54 岁 Age	46	10.9	8.7	19.6	10.9	6.5	43.5
55~60 岁 Age	24	20.8	0.0	16.7	0.0	0.0	62.5
女性 Female	299	21.1	13.7	15.4	8.0	2.3	39.5
16~24 岁 Age	61	16.4	9.8	19.7	9.8	3.3	41.0
25~34 岁 Age	90	25.6	16.7	13.3	4.4	2.2	37.8
35~44 岁 Age	74	18.9	16.2	14.9	6.8	1.4	41.9
45~54 岁 Age	49	18.4	14.3	20.4	10.2	2.0	34.7
55~60 岁 Age	25	28.0	4.0	4.0	16.0	4.0	44.0

1-7 样本、男性各年龄层、女性各年龄层的品牌习惯/ Brand Habit in Consuming Milk Powder by the Whole Sample, Age and Gender Groups

	人数 Number	基本固定食用一个牌子 used in only one brand	比较固定地食用两个或三个牌子 used in two or three brands	基本上不太固定牌子 no brand preference
样本 Sample	337	51.9	27.3	20.8
男性 Male	156	51.9	24.4	23.7
16~24 岁 Age	35	51.4	25.7	22.9
25~34 岁 Age	37	56.8	27.0	16.2
35~44 岁 Age	49	55.1	24.5	20.4
45~54 岁 Age	26	46.2	15.4	38.5
55~60 岁 Age	9	33.3	33.3	33.3
女性 Female	181	51.9	29.8	18.2
16~24 岁 Age	36	47.2	41.7	11.1
25~34 岁 Age	56	55.4	28.6	16.1
35~44 岁 Age	43	51.2	25.6	23.3
45~54 岁 Age	32	53.1	28.1	18.8
55~60 岁 Age	14	50.0	21.4	28.6

1-8 选择该类商品的考虑因素/ Ranking of the Considerations in Purchasing

注：本题为多选题，合计百分比超过 100%（Multiple answers）

排名 Ranking	考虑因素 Considerations	人次 Person-time	百分比 Percent
1	口味好 pleasant taste	164	48.8
2	价格适中 reasonable price	137	40.8
3	营养成分 nutrition constituent	126	37.5
4	有名的牌子 famous brand	111	33.0
5	生产日期 date of producing	60	17.9
6	购买方便 easy to buy	46	13.7
7	易溶解 high dissolubility	42	12.5
8	只是由于习惯 out of habit	21	6.3
9	广告影响 influence of advertising	19	5.7
10	朋友推荐 introduction of friends	18	5.4
11	包装吸引人 appealing package	12	3.6
12	有优惠条件 with preferential terms	9	2.7
13	售货员介绍 introduced by the shop assistants	3	0.9
13	其它 others	3	0.9

n=336

1-9 样本、男性各年龄层、女性各年龄层最常食用的种类/ Types of the Consumed Milk Powder by the Whole Sample, Age and Gender Groups

注：本题为多选题，合计百分比超过 100%（Multiple answers）

	人数 Number	全脂 whole milk	低脂 low-fat	脱脂 skimmed	甜型 sweet	功能型（如加钙等矿物质）containing minerals	加味型（如巧克力、果味等）flavored (e.g. fruit chocolate)	其它 others
样本 Sample	**337**	**66.5**	**13.6**	**10.4**	**10.7**	**8.9**	**4.7**	**0.3**
男性 Male	**156**	**66.7**	**16.0**	**8.3**	**10.3**	**7.1**	**5.1**	**0.0**
16~24 岁 Age	35	62.9	17.1	14.3	5.7	5.7	5.7	0.0
25~34 岁 Age	37	64.9	10.8	8.1	10.8	5.4	5.4	0.0
35~44 岁 Age	49	73.5	12.2	8.2	12.2	10.2	6.1	0.0
45~54 岁 Age	26	69.2	19.2	3.8	7.7	7.7	3.8	0.0
55~60 岁 Age	9	44.4	44.4	0.0	22.2	0.0	0.0	0.0
女性 Female	**181**	**66.3**	**11.6**	**12.2**	**11.0**	**10.5**	**4.4**	**0.6**
16~24 岁 Age	36	52.8	11.1	13.9	5.6	16.7	11.1	0.0
25~34 岁 Age	56	69.6	10.7	14.3	12.5	8.9	3.6	0.0
35~44 岁 Age	43	79.1	9.3	7.0	16.3	7.0	2.3	0.0
45~54 岁 Age	32	68.8	21.9	3.1	6.3	12.5	0.0	0.0
55~60 岁 Age	14	42.9	0.0	35.7	14.3	7.1	7.1	7.1

1-10 样本、男性各年龄层、女性各年龄层最常食用的场合/ Settings of Consumption by the Whole Sample, Age and Gender Groups

注：本题为多选题，合计百分比超过 100%（Multiple answers）

	人数 Number	早餐时 breakfast	正餐（午、晚餐）时 dinner	餐后热饮 after dinner	宵夜时 evening snack	睡觉前帮助入眠 before sleeping	工作休息时 during work break	其它 others
样本 Sample	**337**	**81.3**	**2.7**	**3.3**	**9.2**	**23.1**	**5.0**	**1.2**
男性 Male	**156**	**82.7**	**2.6**	**1.3**	**10.9**	**17.9**	**6.4**	**1.9**
16~24 岁 Age	35	68.6	5.7	0.0	17.1	22.9	2.9	2.9
25~34 岁 Age	37	86.5	0.0	0.0	8.1	13.5	8.1	2.7
35~44 岁 Age	49	83.7	4.1	2.0	16.3	20.4	4.1	2.0
45~54 岁 Age	26	92.3	0.0	3.8	0.0	19.2	11.5	0.0
55~60 岁 Age	9	88.9	0.0	0.0	0.0	0.0	11.1	0.0
女性 Female	**181**	**80.1**	**2.8**	**5.0**	**7.7**	**27.6**	**3.9**	**0.6**
16~24 岁 Age	36	88.9	0.0	8.3	11.1	16.7	5.6	0.0
25~34 岁 Age	56	75.0	0.0	1.8	3.6	32.1	7.1	1.8
35~44 岁 Age	43	76.7	2.3	7.0	11.6	37.2	2.3	0.0
45~54 岁 Age	32	84.4	3.1	6.3	6.3	18.8	0.0	0.0
55~60 岁 Age	14	78.6	21.4	0.0	7.1	28.6	0.0	0.0

1-11 重度消费者的人口分布/ Demographics of the Heavy Consumers

	人数 Number	16-24 岁 Age	25-34 岁 Age	35-44 岁 Age	45-54 岁 Age	55-60 岁 Age
样本 Sample	276	19.9	29.0	28.6	15.9	6.5
男性 Male	126	21.4	23.8	33.3	14.3	7.1
天天喝 daily	36	25.0	5.6	41.7	13.9	13.9
一周 3 次或以上 3 times or over a week	28	32.1	21.4	32.1	14.3	0.0
一周 1～2 次 once or twice a week	62	14.5	35.5	29.0	14.5	6.5
女性 Female	150	18.7	33.3	24.7	17.3	6.0
天天喝 daily	63	15.9	36.5	22.2	14.3	11.1
一周 3 次或以上 3 times or over a week	41	14.6	36.6	29.3	17.1	2.4
一周 1～2 次 once or twice a week	46	26.1	26.1	23.9	21.7	2.2

1-12 不同消费者层的常用品牌/ The Most Frequently Used Brands by Market Segments

1-12-1 时尚流行指标/ Fads Popular Index

	人数 Number	第一品牌及百分比 1st/ percent	第二品牌及百分比 2nd/ percent	第三品牌及百分比 3rd/ percent
样本 Sample	336	**秦俑 Qinyong(70.2)**	**雀巢 Nestle(4.8)** **三鹿 Sanlu(4.8)**	**神果 Shenguo(4.5)**
平实生活指向 simple living orientation	187	秦俑 Qinyong(72.7)	三鹿 Sanlu(4.3)	神果 Shenguo(3.7)
时尚流行指向 fashion orientation	149	秦俑 Qinyong(67.1)	雀巢 Nestle(7.4)	三鹿 Sanlu(5.4) 神果 Shenguo(5.4)

1-12-2 广告态度指标/ Advertising Attitude Index

	人数 Number	第一品牌及百分比 1st/ percent	第二品牌及百分比 2nd/ percent	第三品牌及百分比 3rd/ percent
样本 Sample	333	**秦俑 Qinyong(70.3)**	**雀巢 Nestle(4.8)**	**神果 Shenguo(4.5)** **三鹿 Sanlu(4.5)**
广告淡漠指向 indifferent orientation	98	秦俑 Qinyong(75.5)	神果 Shenguo(5.1)	三鹿 Sanlu(4.1) 伊利 Yili(4.1)
中间层 medium	187	秦俑 Qinyong(70.6)	雀巢 Nestle(5.3)	三鹿 Sanlu(4.8)
信赖广告指向 loyal orientation	48	秦俑 Qinyong(58.3)	神果 Shenguo(10.4)	雀巢 Nestle(8.3)

1-12-3 饮食健康指标/ Foods & Drink Quality Index

	人数 Number	第一品牌及百分比 1st/ percent	第二品牌及百分比 2nd/ percent	第三品牌及百分比 3rd/ percent
样本 Sample	337	**秦俑 Qinyong(70.3)**	**雀巢 Nestle(4.7)** **三鹿 Sanlu(4.7)**	**神果 Shenguo(4.5)**
饮食"温饱"指向 "basic" orientation	112	秦俑 Qinyong(77.7)	雀巢 Nestle(4.5)	神果 Shenguo(3.6) 东方 Dongfang(3.6)
中间层 medium	168	秦俑 Qinyong(66.1)	三鹿 Sanlu(7.1)	伊利 Yili(4.2) 雀巢 Nestle(4.2)
健康营养指向 health & nutrition orientation	57	秦俑 Qinyong(68.4)	神果 Shenguo(8.8)	雀巢 Nestle(7.0)

1-13 重度消费者的消费者层构成/ The Composition of the Heavy Consumers

1-13-1 时尚流行指标/ Fads Popular Index

	人数 Number	平实生活指向 simple living orientation	时尚流行指向 fashion orientation
样本 Sample	276	53.6	46.4
天天喝 daily	99	51.5	48.5
一周 3 次或以上 3 times or over a week	69	52.2	47.8
一周 1～2 次 once or twice a week	108	56.5	43.5

1-13-2 广告态度指标/ Advertising Attitude Index

	人数 Number	广告淡漠指向 indifferent orientation	中间层 medium	信赖广告指向 loyal orientation
样本 Sample	**273**	**28.2**	**56.0**	**15.8**
天天喝 daily	98	30.6	51.0	18.4
一周 3 次或以上 3 times or over a week	68	22.1	64.7	13.2
一周 1～2 次 once or twice a week	107	29.9	55.1	15.0

1-13-3 饮食健康指标/ Foods & Drink Quality Index

	人数 Number	饮食"温饱"指向 "basic" orientation	中间层 medium	健康营养指向 health & nutrition orientation
样本 Sample	**276**	**30.1**	**51.4**	**18.5**
天天喝 daily	99	27.3	45.5	27.3
一周 3 次或以上 3 times or over a week	69	33.3	58.0	8.7
一周 1～2 次 once or twice a week	108	30.6	52.8	16.7

● 沈阳 / Shenyang

1-1 最近三个月食用频率的比例/ Proportion of the Sample Consuming Milk Powder in the Last Three Months

	人数 Number	百分比 Percent
天天喝 daily	54	9.0
一周 3 次或以上 3 times or over a week	34	5.7
一周 1~2 次 once or twice a week	57	9.5
一个月 2～3 次 2 or 3 times a month	38	6.3
一个月 1 次或以下 once a month or below	27	4.5
没喝过 never	391	65.1

n=601

1-2 最常用品牌排名/ Ranking of the Most Frequently Used Brands

排名 Brand Ranking	品牌 Brands	人数 Number	百分比 Percent
1	红星 Red Star	46	22.1
2	鹤王 Hewang	32	15.4
3	金星 Jinxing	29	13.9
4	完达山 Wandashan	19	9.1
5	雀巢 Nestle	14	6.7
6	三鹿 Sanlu	8	3.8
6	伊利 Yili	8	3.8
7	冰都 Bingdu	6	2.9
7	龙丹 Longdan	6	2.9
8	三星 Sanxing	4	1.9
8	森永 Morinage	4	1.9
8	味全 Weiquan	4	1.9

n=208

1-3 样本、男性各年龄层、女性各年龄层的常用品牌/ The Most Frequently Used Brands by the Whole Sample, Age and Gender Groups

	人数 Number	第一品牌及百分比 1st/ percent	第二品牌及百分比 2nd/ percent	第三品牌及百分比 3rd/ percent
样本 Sample	208	**红星 Red Star(22.1)**	**鹤王 Hewang(15.4)**	**金星 Jinxing(13.9)**
男性 Male	91	**红星 Red Star(22.0)**	**鹤王 Hewang(17.6)**	**金星 Jinxing(16.5)**
16~24 岁 Age	24	鹤王 Hewang(29.2)	金星 Jinxing(25.0)	红星 Red Star(12.5)
25~34 岁 Age	34	金星 Jinxing(17.6) 完达山 Wandashan(17.6) 红星 Red Star(17.6)	雀巢 Nestle(8.8)	三鹿 Sanlu(5.9) 鹤王 Hewang(5.9)
35~44 岁 Age	20	红星 Red Star(45.0)	鹤王 Hewang(15.0)	金星 Jinxing(10.0)
45~54 岁 Age	8	鹤王 Hewang(25.0) 完达山 Wandashan(25.0)	冰都 Bingdu(12.5) 红星 Red Star(12.5) 龙丹 Longdan(12.5) 森永 Morinage(12.5)	
55~60 岁 Age	5	鹤王 Hewang(40.0)	冰都 Bingdu(20.0) 红星 Red Star(20.0) 金星 Jinxing(20.0)	
女性 Female	117	**红星 Red Star(22.2)**	**鹤王 Hewang(13.7)**	**金星 Jinxing(12.0)**
16~24 岁 Age	37	红星 Red Star(35.1)	金星 Jinxing(13.5)	鹤王 Hewang(10.8)
25~34 岁 Age	37	鹤王 Hewang(21.6)	红星 Red Star(16.2)	完达山 Wandashan(10.8)
35~44 岁 Age	28	红星 Red Star(21.4)	鹤王 Hewang(14.3)	雀巢 Nestle(10.7)
45~54 岁 Age	9	金星 Jinxing(33.3)	雀巢 Nestle(11.1) 完达山 Wandashan(11.1) 味全 Weiquan(11.1) 伊利 Yili(11.1) 双星 Shuangxing(11.1) 冰熊 Bingxiong(11.1)	
55~60 岁 Age	6	红星 Red Star(16.7) 金星 Jinxing(16.7) 伊利 Yili(16.7) 松鹤 Songhe(16.7) 三花 Sanhua(16.7)		

1-4 理想品牌排名/ Ranking of the Ideal Brands

排名 Brand Ranking	品牌 Brands	人数 Number	百分比 Percent
1	红星 Red Star	163	27.1
2	鹤王 Hewang	72	12.0
3	金星 Jinxing	58	9.7
4	雀巢 Nestle	41	6.8
5	完达山 Wandashan	31	5.2
6	伊利 Yili	28	4.7
7	味全 Weiquan	18	3.0
7	三鹿 Sanlu	18	3.0
8	冰都 Bingdu	17	2.8
9	龙丹 Longdan	12	2.0
10	辉山 Huishan	9	1.5

n=601

1-5 样本、男性各年龄层、女性各年龄层最近三个月有无购买的比例/ Purchasing in the Last Three Months by the Whole Sample, Age and Gender Groups

	人数 Number	买过 yes	没买过 no
样本 Sample	601	34.9	65.1
男性 Male	299	27.8	72.2
16~24 岁 Age	64	23.4	76.6
25~34 岁 Age	89	36.0	64.0
35~44 岁 Age	76	30.3	69.7
45~54 岁 Age	46	19.6	80.4
55~60 岁 Age	24	16.7	83.3
女性 Female	302	42.1	57.9
16~24 岁 Age	64	48.4	51.6
25~34 岁 Age	90	53.3	46.7
35~44 岁 Age	76	36.8	63.2
45~54 岁 Age	48	27.1	72.9
55~60 岁 Age	24	29.2	70.8

1-6 样本、男性各年龄层、女性各年龄层最近三个月的食用频率/ Frequencies of Consuming Milk Powder in the Last Three Months by the Whole Sample, Age and Gender Groups

	人数 Number	天天喝 daily	一周3次或以上 3 times or over a week	一周1~2次 once or twice a week	一个月2~3次 2 or 3 times a month	一个月1次或以下 once a month or below	没喝过 never
样本 Sample	**601**	**9.0**	**5.7**	**9.5**	**6.3**	**4.5**	**65.1**
男性 Male	**299**	**7.7**	**5.4**	**6.0**	**6.4**	**5.7**	**68.9**
16~24 岁 Age	64	10.9	9.4	1.6	9.4	6.3	62.5
25~34 岁 Age	89	7.9	5.6	11.2	7.9	6.7	60.7
35~44 岁 Age	76	2.6	2.6	7.9	7.9	6.6	72.4
45~54 岁 Age	46	6.5	4.3	2.2	0.0	4.3	82.6
55~60 岁 Age	24	16.7	4.2	0.0	0.0	0.0	79.2
女性 Female	**302**	**10.3**	**6.0**	**12.9**	**6.3**	**3.3**	**61.3**
16~24 岁 Age	64	14.1	12.5	15.6	7.8	7.8	42.2
25~34 岁 Age	90	10.0	3.3	15.6	10.0	2.2	58.9
35~44 岁 Age	76	7.9	5.3	13.2	6.6	3.9	63.2
45~54 岁 Age	48	8.3	4.2	6.3	0.0	0.0	81.3
55~60 岁 Age	24	12.5	4.2	8.3	0.0	0.0	75.0

1-7 样本、男性各年龄层、女性各年龄层的品牌习惯/ Brand Habit in Consuming Milk Powder by the Whole Sample, Age and Gender Groups

	人数 Number	基本固定食用一个牌子 used in only one brand	比较固定地食用两个或三个牌子 used in two or three brands	基本上不太固定牌子 no brand preference
样本 Sample	**209**	**39.7**	**30.6**	**29.7**
男性 Male	**92**	**34.8**	**34.8**	**30.4**
16~24 岁 Age	24	20.8	33.3	45.8
25~34 岁 Age	34	47.1	35.3	17.6
35~44 岁 Age	21	42.9	33.3	23.8
45~54 岁 Age	8	12.5	50.0	37.5
55~60 岁 Age	5	20.0	20.0	60.0
女性 Female	**117**	**43.6**	**27.4**	**29.1**
16~24 岁 Age	37	32.4	24.3	43.2
25~34 岁 Age	37	45.9	32.4	21.6
35~44 岁 Age	28	46.4	21.4	32.1
45~54 岁 Age	9	66.7	22.2	11.1
55~60 岁 Age	6	50.0	50.0	0.0

1-8 选择该类商品的考虑因素/ Ranking of the Considerations in Purchasing

注：本题为多选题，合计百分比超过 100%（Multiple answers）

排名 Ranking	考虑因素 Considerations	人次 Person-time	百分比 Percent
1	营养成分 nutrition constituent	111	53.4
2	口味好 pleasant taste	105	50.5
3	有名的牌子 famous brand	69	33.2
3	价格适中 reasonable price	69	33.2
4	生产日期 date of producing	42	20.2
5	易溶解 high dissolubility	27	13.0
6	购买方便 easy to buy	24	11.5
7	广告影响 influence of advertising	21	10.1
8	朋友推荐 introduction of friends	12	5.8
8	只是由于习惯 out of habit	12	5.8
9	有优惠条件 with preferential terms	8	3.8
10	包装吸引人 appealing package	7	3.4
11	售货员介绍 introduced by the shop assistants	1	0.5
11	其它 others	1	0.5

n=208

1-9 样本、男性各年龄层、女性各年龄层最常食用的种类/ Types of the Consumed Milk Powder by the Whole Sample, Age and Gender Groups

注：本题为多选题，合计百分比超过 100%（Multiple answers）

	人数 Number	全脂 whole milk	低脂 low-fat	脱脂 skimmed	甜型 sweet	功能型（如加钙等矿物质）containing minerals	加味型（如巧克力、果味等）flavored (e.g. fruit chocolate)	其它 others
样本 Sample	209	61.2	15.8	5.7	10.0	23.4	5.3	2.4
男性 Male	92	60.9	17.4	6.5	10.9	19.6	3.3	4.3
16~24 岁 Age	24	45.8	20.8	8.3	4.2	29.2	12.5	0.0
25~34 岁 Age	34	61.8	14.7	11.8	20.6	11.8	0.0	2.9
35~44 岁 Age	21	76.2	19.0	0.0	9.5	14.3	0.0	0.0
45~54 岁 Age	8	62.5	12.5	0.0	0.0	25.0	0.0	37.5
55~60 岁 Age	5	60.0	20.0	0.0	0.0	40.0	0.0	0.0
女性 Female	117	61.5	14.5	5.1	9.4	26.5	6.8	0.9
16~24 岁 Age	37	51.4	21.6	5.4	10.8	27.0	16.2	2.7
25~34 岁 Age	37	67.6	13.5	5.4	5.4	21.6	2.7	0.0
35~44 岁 Age	28	71.4	7.1	3.6	10.7	25.0	0.0	0.0
45~54 岁 Age	9	55.6	11.1	0.0	22.2	44.4	11.1	0.0
55~60 岁 Age	6	50.0	16.7	16.7	0.0	33.3	0.0	0.0

1-10 样本、男性各年龄层、女性各年龄层最常食用的场合/ Settings of Consumption by the Whole Sample, Age and Gender Groups

注：本题为多选题，合计百分比超过 100%（Multiple answers）

	人数 Number	早餐时 breakfast	正餐（午、晚餐）时 dinner	餐后热饮 after dinner	宵夜时 evening snack	睡觉前帮助入眠 before sleeping	工作休息时 during work break	其它 others
样本 Sample	209	70.8	3.3	5.7	11.5	23.4	11.0	0.0
男性 Male	92	68.5	2.2	5.4	14.1	21.7	9.8	0.0
16~24 岁 Age	24	75.0	0.0	0.0	8.3	16.7	20.8	0.0
25~34 岁 Age	34	55.9	5.9	2.9	8.8	29.4	8.8	0.0
35~44 岁 Age	21	76.2	0.0	14.3	23.8	9.5	4.8	0.0
45~54 岁 Age	8	62.5	0.0	0.0	37.5	37.5	0.0	0.0
55~60 岁 Age	5	100.0	0.0	20.0	0.0	20.0	0.0	0.0
女性 Female	117	72.6	4.3	6.0	9.4	24.8	12.0	0.0
16~24 岁 Age	37	70.3	5.4	13.5	5.4	21.6	24.3	0.0
25~34 岁 Age	37	70.3	5.4	0.0	10.8	21.6	10.8	0.0
35~44 岁 Age	28	75.0	3.6	7.1	17.9	28.6	3.6	0.0
45~54 岁 Age	9	77.8	0.0	0.0	0.0	33.3	0.0	0.0
55~60 岁 Age	6	83.3	0.0	0.0	0.0	33.3	0.0	0.0

1-11 重度消费者的人口分布/ Demographics of the Heavy Consumers

	人数 Number	16-24 岁 Age	25-34 岁 Age	35-44 岁 Age	45-54 岁 Age	55-60 岁 Age
样本 Sample	145	28.3	33.1	20.7	10.3	7.6
男性 Male	57	24.6	38.6	17.5	10.5	8.8
天天喝 daily	23	30.4	30.4	8.7	13.0	17.4
一周 3 次或以上 3 times or over a week	16	37.5	31.3	12.5	12.5	6.3
一周 1～2 次 once or twice a week	18	5.6	55.6	33.3	5.6	0.0
女性 Female	88	30.7	29.5	22.7	10.2	6.8
天天喝 daily	31	29.0	29.0	19.4	12.9	9.7
一周 3 次或以上 3 times or over a week	18	44.4	16.7	22.2	11.1	5.6
一周 1～2 次 once or twice a week	39	25.6	35.9	25.6	7.7	5.1

1-12 不同消费者层的常用品牌/ The Most Frequently Used Brands by Market Segments

1-12-1 时尚流行指标/ Fads Popular Index

	人数 Number	第一品牌及百分比 1st/ percent	第二品牌及百分比 2nd/ percent	第三品牌及百分比 3rd/ percent
样本 Sample	208	**红星 Red Star(22.1)**	**鹤王 Hewang(15.4)**	**金星 Jinxing(13.9)**
平实生活指向 simple living orientation	81	红星 Red Star(21.0)	鹤王 Hewang(18.5)	金星 Jinxing(9.9)
时尚流行指向 fashion orientation	127	红星 Red Star(22.8)	金星 Jinxing(16.5)	鹤王 Hewang(13.4)

1-12-2 广告态度指标/ Advertising Attitude Index

	人数 Number	第一品牌及百分比 1st/percent	第二品牌及百分比 2nd/percent	第三品牌及百分比 3rd/percent
样本 Sample	208	**红星 Red Star(22.1)**	**鹤王 Hewang(15.4)**	**金星 Jinxing(13.9)**
广告淡漠指向 indifferent orientation	50	红星 Red Star(24.0)	鹤王 Hewang(14.0)	龙丹 Longdan(10.0)
中间层 medium	132	红星 Red Star(21.2)	鹤王 Hewang(17.4) 金星 Jinxing(17.4)	完达山 Wandashan(10.6)
信赖广告指向 loyal orientation	26	红星 Red Star(23.1)	冰都 Bingdu(7.7) 鹤王 Hewang(7.7) 金星 Jinxing(7.7) 森永 Morinage(7.7) 伊利 Yili(7.7)	智强 Zhiqiang(3.8) 草原香 AD 钙奶粉 Caoyuanxiang (3.8) 双星 Shuangxing(3.8) 三星 Sanxing(3.8) 大牛 Daniu(3.8) 龙丹 Long Dan (3.8) 完达山 Wandashan(3.8) 三鹿 Sanlu(3.8) 雀巢 Nestle(3.8)

1-12-3 饮食健康指标/ Foods & Drink Quality Index

	人数 Number	第一品牌及百分比 1st/ percent	第二品牌及百分比 2nd/ percent	第三品牌及百分比 3rd/ percent
样本 Sample	208	**红星 Red Star(22.1)**	**鹤王 Hewang(15.4)**	**金星 Jinxing(13.9)**
饮食“温饱”指向 "basic" orientation	50	红星 Red Star(20.0) 完达山 Wandashan(20.0)	金星 Jinxing(18.0)	鹤王 Hewang(10.0)
中间层 medium	96	红星 Red Star(24.0)	鹤王 Hewang(16.7)	金星 Jinxing(13.5)
健康营养指向 health & nutrition orientation	62	红星 Red Star(21.0)	鹤王 Hewang(17.7)	金星 Jinxing(11.3)

1-13 重度消费者的消费者层构成/ The Composition of the Heavy Consumers

1-13-1 时尚流行指标/ Fads Popular Index

	人数 Number	平实生活指向 simple living orientation	时尚流行指向 fashion orientation
样本 Sample	145	42.1	57.9
天天喝 daily	54	44.4	55.6
一周 3 次或以上 3 times or over a week	34	35.3	64.7
一周 1～2 次 once or twice a week	57	43.9	56.1

1-13-2 广告态度指标/ Advertising Attitude Index

	人数 Number	广告淡漠指向 indifferent orientation	中间层 medium	信赖广告指向 loyal orientation
样本 Sample	145	22.1	66.9	11.0
天天喝 daily	54	18.5	66.7	14.8
一周 3 次或以上 3 times or over a week	34	29.4	61.8	8.8
一周 1～2 次 once or twice a week	57	21.1	70.2	8.8

1-13-3 饮食健康指标/ Foods & Drink Quality Index

	人数 Number	饮食"温饱"指向 "basic" orientation	中间层 medium	健康营养指向 health & nutrition orientation
样本 Sample	145	23.4	42.1	34.5
天天喝 daily	54	22.2	42.6	35.2
一周 3 次或以上 3 times or over a week	34	20.6	50.0	29.4
一周 1～2 次 once or twice a week	57	26.3	36.8	36.8

2.豆奶粉 / Powdered Soybean Milk

● 北京 / Beijing

2-1 最近三个月食用频率的比例/ Proportion of the Sample Consuming Powdered Soybean Milk in the Last Three Months

	人数 Number	百分比 Percent
天天喝 daily	60	6.0
一周 3 次或以上 3 times or over a week	62	6.2
一周 1~2 次 once or twice a week	118	11.7
一个月 2～3 次 2 or 3 times a month	74	7.4
一个月 1 次或以下 once a month or below	63	6.3
没喝过 never	629	62.5

n=1006

2-2 最常用品牌排名/ Ranking of the Most Frequently Used Brands

排名 Brand Ranking	品牌 Brands	人数 Number	百分比 Percent
1	维维 Weiwei	309	82.2
2	大地 Landy	27	7.2
3	华旗 Huaqi	4	1.1
4	哈比粉 Happy	3	0.8
4	完达山 Wandashan	3	0.8
4	多利 Duoli	3	0.8

n=376

2-3 样本、男性各年龄层、女性各年龄层的常用品牌/ The Most Frequently Used Brands by the Whole Sample, Age and Gender Groups

	人数 Number	第一品牌及百分比 1st/ percent	第二品牌及百分比 2nd/ percent	第三品牌及百分比 3rd/ percent
样本 Sample	376	**维维 Weiwei(82.2)**	**大地 Landy(7.2)**	**华旗 Huaqi(1.1)**
男性 Male	161	**维维 Weiwei(88.8)**	**大地 Landy(2.5)**	**完达山 Wandashan(1.2)**
16~24 岁 Age	38	维维 Weiwei(86.8)	完达山 Wandashan(5.3)	大地 Landy(2.6) 华旗 Huaqi(2.6)
25~34 岁 Age	45	维维 Weiwei(95.6)	大地 Landy(2.2) 红梅 Hongmei(2.2)	
35~44 岁 Age	40	维维 Weiwei(82.5)	大地 Landy(2.5) 长乐 Changle(2.5)	
45~54 岁 Age	23	维维 Weiwei(87.0)	多利 Duoli(4.3)	
55~60 岁 Age	15	维维 Weiwei(93.3)	大地 Landy(6.7)	
女性 Female	215	**维维 Weiwei(77.2)**	**大地 Landy(10.7)**	**哈比粉 Happy(1.4)** **华旗 Huaqi(1.4)**
16~24 岁 Age	46	维维 Weiwei(76.1)	大地 Landy(10.9)	华旗 Huaqi(4.3)
25~34 岁 Age	63	维维 Weiwei(71.4)	大地 Landy(9.5)	南方 Nanfang(3.2)
35~44 岁 Age	58	维维 Weiwei(77.6)	大地 Landy(17.2)	双娃 Shuangwa(1.7) 伟人 Weiren(1.7)
45~54 岁 Age	29	维维 Weiwei(93.1)	大地 Landy(3.4) 多利 Duoli(3.4)	
55~60 岁 Age	19	维维 Weiwei(73.7)	大地 Landy(5.3) 哈比粉 Happy(5.3) 红星 Hongxing(5.3)	

2-4 理想品牌排名/ Ranking of the Ideal Brands

排名 Brand Ranking	品牌 Brands	人数 Number	百分比 Percent
1	维维 Weiwei	659	65.1
2	大地 Landy	38	3.8
3	完达山 Wandashan	5	0.5
4	伊利 Yili	4	0.4

n=1012

2-5 样本、男性各年龄层、女性各年龄层最近三个月有无购买的比例/ Purchasing in the Last Three Months by the Whole Sample, Age and Gender Groups

	人数 Number	买过 yes	没买过 no
样本 Sample	1011	32.9	67.1
男性 Male	503	28.0	72.0
16~24 岁 Age	105	27.6	72.4
25~34 岁 Age	151	28.5	71.5
35~44 岁 Age	130	25.4	74.6
45~54 岁 Age	77	29.9	70.1
55~60 岁 Age	40	32.5	67.5
女性 Female	508	37.8	62.2
16~24 岁 Age	108	25.0	75.0
25~34 岁 Age	150	38.7	61.3
35~44 岁 Age	124	47.6	52.4
45~54 岁 Age	84	38.1	61.9
55~60 岁 Age	42	38.1	61.9

2-6 样本、男性各年龄层、女性各年龄层最近三个月的食用频率/ Frequencies of Consuming Powdered Soybean Milk in the Last Three Months by the Whole Sample, Age and Gender Groups

	人数 Number	天天喝 daily	一周 3 次或以上 3 times or over a week	一周 1~2 次 once or twice a week	一个月 2~3 次 2 or 3 times a month	一个月 1 次或以下 once a month or below	没喝过 never
样本 Sample	1006	6.0	6.2	11.7	7.4	6.3	62.5
男性 Male	501	3.0	5.4	10.4	7.8	5.6	67.9
16~24 岁 Age	103	1.9	7.8	10.7	7.8	8.7	63.1
25~34 岁 Age	151	1.3	4.0	8.6	9.3	6.6	70.2
35~44 岁 Age	130	3.1	4.6	10.0	9.2	3.8	69.2
45~54 岁 Age	77	3.9	5.2	13.0	3.9	3.9	70.1
55~60 岁 Age	40	10.0	7.5	12.5	5.0	2.5	62.5
女性 Female	505	8.9	6.9	13.1	6.9	6.9	57.2
16~24 岁 Age	108	2.8	6.5	12.0	10.2	11.1	57.4
25~34 岁 Age	147	6.8	9.5	11.6	8.2	6.8	57.1
35~44 岁 Age	124	10.5	6.5	16.9	5.6	7.3	53.2
45~54 岁 Age	84	11.9	3.6	13.1	3.6	3.6	64.3
55~60 岁 Age	42	21.4	7.1	9.5	4.8	2.4	54.8

2-7 样本、男性各年龄层、女性各年龄层的品牌习惯/ Brand Habit in Consuming Powdered Soybean Milk by the Whole Sample, Age and Gender Groups

	人数 Number	基本固定食用一个牌子 used in only one brand	比较固定地食用两个或三个牌子 used in two or three brands	基本上不太固定牌子 no brand preference
样本 Sample	374	59.4	19.8	20.9
男性 Male	161	60.9	19.9	19.3
16~24 岁 Age	38	57.9	23.7	18.4
25~34 岁 Age	45	62.2	22.2	15.6
35~44 岁 Age	40	60.0	12.5	27.5
45~54 岁 Age	23	56.5	30.4	13.0
55~60 岁 Age	15	73.3	6.7	20.0
女性 Female	213	58.2	19.7	22.1
16~24 岁 Age	45	48.9	26.7	24.4
25~34 岁 Age	63	54.0	17.5	28.6
35~44 岁 Age	57	64.9	24.6	10.5
45~54 岁 Age	29	62.1	6.9	31.0
55~60 岁 Age	19	68.4	15.8	15.8

2-8 选择该类商品的考虑因素/ Ranking of the Considerations in Purchasing

注：本题为多选题，合计百分比超过 100%（Multiple answers）

排名 Ranking	考虑因素 Considerations	人次 Person-time	百分比 Percent
1	营养成分 nutrition constituent	159	42.5
2	价格适中 reasonable price	132	35.3
3	口味好 pleasant taste	118	31.6
4	有名的牌子 famous brand	113	30.2
5	生产日期 date of producing	69	18.4
6	购买方便 easy to buy	53	14.2
7	广告影响 influence of advertising	47	12.6
7	易溶解 high dissolubility	47	12.6
8	只是由于习惯 out of habit	20	5.3
9	朋友推荐 introduction of friends	16	4.3
10	有优惠条件 with preferential terms	14	3.7
11	包装吸引人 appealing package	8	2.1
12	售货员介绍 introduced by the shop assistants	4	1.1
12	其它 others	4	1.1

n=374

2-9 样本、男性各年龄层、女性各年龄层最常食用种类/ Types of the Consumed Powdered Soybean Milk by the Whole Sample, Age and Gender Groups

注：本题为多选题，合计百分比超过 100%（Multiple answers）

	人数 Number	豆粉 soybean powder	绿豆粉 mungbean powder	普通型豆奶粉 normal	低糖型豆奶粉 low-sugar	加味型（如巧克力、花生等）豆奶粉 flavored (eg.chocolate)	保健型（如枸杞、蔬菜等）豆奶粉 healthcaring (eg.vegetable, wol)	绿豆奶粉 mung-bean milk powder	其它 others
样本 Sample	370	22.4	1.1	46.2	16.5	12.4	7.6	1.9	1.4
男性 Male	159	21.4	1.9	42.1	17.6	12.6	10.1	2.5	1.3
16~24 岁 Age	38	28.9	0.0	36.8	13.2	21.1	5.3	5.3	0.0
25~34 岁 Age	44	9.1	4.5	47.7	13.6	15.9	11.4	4.5	0.0
35~44 岁 Age	40	37.5	0.0	32.5	17.5	7.5	10.0	0.0	5.0
45~54 岁 Age	23	13.0	4.3	34.8	34.8	8.7	21.7	0.0	0.0
55~60 岁 Age	14	7.1	0.0	78.6	14.3	0.0	0.0	0.0	0.0
女性 Female	211	23.2	0.5	49.3	15.6	12.3	5.7	1.4	1.4
16~24 岁 Age	44	25.0	0.0	43.2	20.5	13.6	2.3	4.5	0.0
25~34 岁 Age	62	24.2	0.0	43.5	12.9	16.1	11.3	0.0	3.2
35~44 岁 Age	58	27.6	0.0	53.4	8.6	13.8	0.0	0.0	1.7
45~54 岁 Age	28	10.7	3.6	60.7	28.6	3.6	10.7	0.0	0.0
55~60 岁 Age	19	21.1	0.0	52.6	15.8	5.3	5.3	5.3	0.0

2-10 样本、男性各年龄层、女性各年龄层最常食用的场合/ Settings of Consumption by the Whole Sample, Age and Gender Groups

注：本题为多选题，合计百分比超过 100%（Multiple answers）

	人数 Number	早餐时 breakfast	正餐（午、晚餐）时 dinner	餐后热饮 after dinner	宵夜时 evening snack	睡觉前 before sleeping	工作休息时 during work break	其它 others
样本 Sample	370	78.1	2.4	4.6	10.5	11.4	12.2	2.4
男性 Male	158	73.4	2.5	4.4	11.4	13.9	12.0	2.5
16~24 岁 Age	36	63.9	2.8	8.3	13.9	16.7	11.1	0.0
25~34 岁 Age	45	66.7	2.2	2.2	13.3	15.6	15.6	6.7
35~44 岁 Age	40	77.5	2.5	2.5	17.5	15.0	15.0	0.0
45~54 岁 Age	23	82.6	0.0	8.7	0.0	8.7	8.7	4.3
55~60 岁 Age	14	92.9	7.1	0.0	0.0	7.1	0.0	0.0
女性 Female	212	81.6	2.4	4.7	9.9	9.4	12.3	2.4
16~24 岁 Age	44	70.5	2.3	4.5	18.2	11.4	11.4	2.3
25~34 岁 Age	62	75.8	1.6	4.8	1.6	14.5	22.6	3.2
35~44 岁 Age	58	91.4	1.7	3.4	8.6	6.9	8.6	1.7
45~54 岁 Age	29	89.7	3.4	3.4	13.8	6.9	3.4	3.4
55~60 岁 Age	19	84.2	5.3	10.5	15.8	0.0	5.3	0.0

2-11 重度消费者的人口分布/ Demographics of the Heavy Consumers

	人数 Number	16-24 岁 Age	25-34 岁 Age	35-44 岁 Age	45-54 岁 Age	55-60 岁 Age
样本 Sample	240	18.3	25.8	27.1	17.1	11.7
男性 Male	94	22.3	22.3	24.5	18.1	12.8
天天喝 daily	15	13.3	13.3	26.7	20.0	26.7
一周 3 次或以上 3 times or over a week	27	29.6	22.2	22.2	14.8	11.1
一周 1～2 次 once or twice a week	52	21.2	25.0	25.0	19.2	9.6
女性 Female	146	15.8	28.1	28.8	16.4	11.0
天天喝 daily	45	6.7	22.2	28.9	22.2	20.0
一周 3 次或以上 3 times or over a week	35	20.0	40.0	22.9	8.6	8.6
一周 1～2 次 once or twice a week	66	19.7	25.8	31.8	16.7	6.1

2-12 不同消费者层的常用品牌/ The Most Frequently Used Brands by Market Segments

2-12-1 时尚流行指标/ Fads Popular Index

	人数 Number	第一品牌及百分比 1st/ percent	第二品牌及百分比 2nd/ percent	第三品牌及百分比 3rd/ percent
样本 Sample	369	**维维 Weiwei(82.1)**	**大地 Landy(7.0)**	**华旗 Huaqi(1.1)**
平实生活指向 simple living orientation	160	维维 Weiwei(80.6)	大地 Landy(8.1)	华旗 Huaqi(1.3) 完达山 Wandashan(1.3) 哈比粉 Happy(1.3)
时尚流行指向 fashion orientation	209	维维 Weiwei(83.3)	大地 Landy(6.2)	多利 Duoli(1.0) 华旗 Huaqi(1.0)

2-12-2 广告态度指标/ Advertising Attitude Index

	人数 Number	第一品牌及百分比 1st/ percent	第二品牌及百分比 2nd/ percent	第三品牌及百分比 3rd/ percent
样本 Sample	368	**维维 Weiwei(82.1)**	**大地 Landy(7.3)**	**华旗 Huaqi(1.1)**
广告淡漠指向 indifferent orientation	97	维维 Weiwei(76.3)	大地 Landy(11.3)	华旗 Huaqi(2.1) 多利 Duoli(2.1)
中间层 medium	207	维维 Weiwei(86.0)	大地 Landy(6.8)	哈比粉 Happy(1.0)
信赖广告指向 loyal orientation	64	维维 Weiwei(78.1)	大地 Landy(3.1) 华旗 Huaqi(3.1)	北大荒 Beidahuang(1.6) 哈比粉 Happy(1.6) 完达山 Wandashan(1.6) 伟人 Weiren(1.6) 长乐 Changle(1.6) 杨协成 Yeo's(1.6)

2-12-3 饮食健康指标/ Foods & Drink Quality Index

	人数 Number	第一品牌及百分比 1st/ percent	第二品牌及百分比 2nd/ percent	第三品牌及百分比 3rd/ percent
样本 Sample	374	**维维 Weiwei(82.4)**	**大地 Landy(7.2)**	**华旗 Huaqi(1.1)**
饮食"温饱"指向 "basic" orientation	90	维维 Weiwei(76.7)	大地 Landy(7.8)	华旗 Huaqi(3.3)
中间层 medium	168	维维 Weiwei(85.7)	大地 Landy(6.5)	完达山 Wandashan(1.2) 南方 Nanfang(1.2)
健康营养指向 health & nutrition orientation	116	维维 Weiwei(81.9)	大地 Landy(7.8)	多利 Duoli(1.7)

2-13 重度消费者的消费者层构成/ The Composition of the Heavy Consumers

2-13-1 时尚流行指标/ Fads Popular Index

	人数 Number	平实生活指向 simple living orientation	时尚流行指向 fashion orientation
样本 Sample	237	45.1	54.9
天天喝 daily	60	50.0	50.0
一周 3 次或以上 3 times or over a week	60	50.0	50.0
一周 1～2 次 once or twice a week	117	40.2	59.8

2-13-2 广告态度指标/ Advertising Attitude Index

	人数 Number	广告淡漠指向 indifferent orientation	中间层 medium	信赖广告指向 loyal orientation
样本 Sample	**236**	**25.8**	**56.4**	**17.8**
天天喝 daily	59	27.1	47.5	25.4
一周 3 次或以上 3 times or over a week	61	21.3	62.3	16.4
一周 1～2 次 once or twice a week	116	27.6	57.8	14.7

2-13-3 饮食健康指标/ Foods & Drink Quality Index

	人数 Number	饮食"温饱"指向 "basic" orientation	中间层 medium	健康营养指向 health & nutrition orientation
样本 Sample	**239**	**18.4**	**46.9**	**34.7**
天天喝 daily	59	20.3	47.5	32.2
一周 3 次或以上 3 times or over a week	62	19.4	41.9	38.7
一周 1～2 次 once or twice a week	118	16.9	49.2	33.9

● 上海 / Shanghai

2-1 最近三个月食用频率的比例/ Proportion of the Sample Consuming Powdered Soybean Milk in the Last Three months

	人数 Number	百分比 Percent
天天喝 daily	65	6.4
一周 3 次或以上 3 times or over a week	42	4.1
一周 1~2 次 once or twice a week	68	6.7
一个月 2～3 次 2 or 3 times a month	44	4.3
一个月 1 次或以下 once a month or below	42	4.1
没喝过 never	753	74.3

n=1014

2-2 最常用品牌排名/ Ranking of the Most Frequently Used Brands

排名 Brand Ranking	品牌 Brands	人数 Number	百分比 Percent
1	维维 Weiwei	218	83.8
2	光明 Bright	14	5.4
3	多利 Duoli	4	1.5
3	杨协成 Yeo's	4	1.5
4	健王 Janwang	3	1.2
4	力源 Liyuan	3	1.2
5	维他奶 Vitasoy	2	0.8

n=260

2-3 样本、男性各年龄层、女性各年龄层的常用品牌/ The Most Frequently Used Brands by the Whole Sample, Age and Gender Groups

	人数 Number	第一品牌及百分比 1st/ percent	第二品牌及百分比 2nd/ percent	第三品牌及百分比 3rd/ percent
样本 Sample	260	**维维 Weiwei(83.8)**	**光明 Bright(5.4)**	**多利 Duoli(1.5)** **杨协成 Yeo's(1.5)**
男性 Male	118	**维维 Weiwei(81.4)**	**光明 Bright(7.6)**	**力源 Liyuan(1.7)** **杨协成 Yeo's(1.7)** **维他奶 Vitasoy(1.7)**
16~24 岁 Age	28	维维 Weiwei(78.6)	光明 Bright(14.3)	全仕奶 Quanshinai(3.6)
25~34 岁 Age	31	维维 Weiwei(83.9)	光明 Bright(9.7)	力源 Liyuan(3.2) 杨协成 Yeo's(3.2)
35~44 岁 Age	32	维维 Weiwei(84.4)	力源 Liyuan(3.1) 杨协成 Yeo's(3.1) 光明 Bright(3.1) 维他奶 Vitasoy(3.1)	
45~54 岁 Age	18	维维 Weiwei(72.2)	雀巢 Nestle(5.6) 光明 Bright(5.6) 维他奶 Vitasoy(5.6) 多利 Duoli (5.6)	
55~60 岁 Age	9	维维 Weiwei(88.9)		
女性 Female	142	**维维 Weiwei(85.9)**	**光明 Bright(3.5)**	**健王 Janwang(2.1)** **多利 Duoli (2.1)**
16~24 岁 Age	32	维维 Weiwei(93.8)	贝因美 Beingmate(3.1)	
25~34 岁 Age	47	维维 Weiwei(83.0)	杨协成 Yeo's(4.3) 多利 Duoli (4.3)	健王 Janwang(2.1) 光明 Bright(2.1) 南方 Nanfang(2.1) 协和 Xiehe(2.1)
35~44 岁 Age	30	维维 Weiwei(86.7)	光明 Bright(10.0)	多利 Duoli (3.3)
45~54 岁 Age	20	维维 Weiwei(90.0)	健王 Janwang(5.0) 光明 Bright(5.0)	
55~60 岁 Age	13	维维 Weiwei(69.2)	健王 Janwang(7.7) 力源 Liyuan(7.7) 雅培 Yapei(7.7)	

2-4 理想品牌排名/ Ranking of the Ideal Brands

排名 Brand Ranking	品牌 Brands	人数 Number	百分比 Percent
1	维维 Weiwei	716	70.6
2	光明 Bright	45	4.4
3	杨协成 Yeo's	13	1.3
4	多利 Duoli	11	1.1
5	健王 Janwang	6	0.6
5	维他奶 Vitasoy	6	0.6

n=1014

2-5 样本、男性各年龄层、女性各年龄层最近三个月有无购买的比例/ Purchasing in the Last Three Months by the Whole Sample, Age and Gender Groups

	人数 Number	买过 yes	没买过 no
样本 Sample	1012	23.3	76.7
男性 Male	507	20.5	79.5
16~24 岁 Age	109	22.0	78.0
25~34 岁 Age	146	16.4	83.6
35~44 岁 Age	128	21.1	78.9
45~54 岁 Age	85	24.7	75.3
55~60 岁 Age	39	20.5	79.5
女性 Female	505	26.1	73.9
16~24 岁 Age	108	22.2	77.8
25~34 岁 Age	144	30.6	69.4
35~44 岁 Age	130	24.6	75.4
45~54 岁 Age	82	24.4	75.6
55~60 岁 Age	41	29.3	70.7

2-6 样本、男性各年龄层、女性各年龄层最近三个月的食用频率/ Frequencies of Consuming Powdered Soybean Milk in the Last Three Months by the Whole Sample, Age and Gender Groups

	人数 Number	天天喝 daily	一周 3 次或以上 3 times or over a week	一周 1~2 次 once or twice a week	一个月 2~3 次 2 or 3 times a month	一个月 1 次或以下 once a month or below	没喝过 never
样本 Sample	**1014**	**6.4**	**4.1**	**6.7**	**4.3**	**4.1**	**74.3**
男性 Male	**509**	**4.7**	**4.7**	**6.5**	**4.1**	**3.3**	**76.6**
16~24 岁 Age	109	7.3	3.7	5.5	4.6	4.6	74.3
25~34 岁 Age	146	2.7	4.1	6.2	4.1	4.1	78.8
35~44 岁 Age	130	6.2	7.7	5.4	3.8	2.3	74.6
45~54 岁 Age	85	3.5	2.4	8.2	4.7	2.4	78.8
55~60 岁 Age	39	2.6	5.1	10.3	2.6	2.6	76.9
女性 Female	**505**	**8.1**	**3.6**	**6.9**	**4.6**	**5.0**	**71.9**
16~24 岁 Age	108	3.7	2.8	9.3	4.6	9.3	70.4
25~34 岁 Age	144	11.8	2.8	4.9	7.6	5.6	67.4
35~44 岁 Age	130	6.9	5.4	6.2	2.3	2.3	76.9
45~54 岁 Age	82	6.1	3.7	8.5	2.4	3.7	75.6
55~60 岁 Age	41	14.6	2.4	7.3	4.9	2.4	68.3

2-7 样本、男性各年龄层、女性各年龄层的品牌习惯/ Brand Habit in Consuming Powdered Soybean Milk by the Whole Sample, Age and Gender Groups

	人数 Number	基本固定食用一个牌子 used in only one brand	比较固定地食用两个或三个牌子 used in two or three brands	基本上不太固定牌子 no brand preference
样本 Sample	**259**	**58.3**	**23.9**	**17.8**
男性 Male	**117**	**58.1**	**23.9**	**17.9**
16~24 岁 Age	28	53.6	32.1	14.3
25~34 岁 Age	30	66.7	30.0	3.3
35~44 岁 Age	32	50.0	18.8	31.3
45~54 岁 Age	18	55.6	16.7	27.8
55~60 岁 Age	9	77.8	11.1	11.1
女性 Female	**142**	**58.5**	**23.9**	**17.6**
16~24 岁 Age	32	46.9	31.3	21.9
25~34 岁 Age	47	63.8	17.0	19.1
35~44 岁 Age	30	53.3	30.0	16.7
45~54 岁 Age	20	70.0	20.0	10.0
55~60 岁 Age	13	61.5	23.1	15.4

2-8 选择该类商品的考虑因素/ Ranking of the Considerations in Purchasing

注：本题为多选题，合计百分比超过 100%（Multiple answers）

排名 Ranking	考虑因素 Considerations	人次 Person-time	百分比 Percent
1	口味好 pleasant taste	113	43.6
2	营养成分 nutrition constituent	106	40.9
3	价格适中 reasonable price	94	36.3
4	有名的牌子 famous brand	78	30.1
5	生产日期 date of producing	48	18.5
6	购买方便 easy to buy	43	16.6
7	广告影响 influence of advertising	31	12.0
8	易溶解 high dissolubility	24	9.3
9	只是由于习惯 out of habit	19	7.3
10	有优惠条件 with preferential terms	11	4.2
10	朋友推荐 introduction of friends	11	4.2
11	包装吸引人 appealing package	7	2.7
12	售货员介绍 introduced by the shop assistants	2	0.8
13	其它 others	1	0.4

n=259

2-9 样本、男性各年龄层、女性各年龄层最常食用种类/ Types of the Consumed Powdered Soybean Milk by the Whole Sample, Age and Gender Groups

注：本题为多选题，合计百分比超过 100%（Multiple answers）

	人数 Number	豆粉 soybean powder	绿豆粉 mungbean powder	普通型豆奶粉 normal	低糖型豆奶粉 low-sugar	加味型（如巧克力、花生等)豆奶粉 flavored (eg.chocolate)	保健型（如枸杞、蔬菜等）豆奶粉 healthcaring(eg.vegetable,wol)	绿豆奶粉 mungbean milk powder	其它 others
样本 Sample	258	22.9	2.3	44.2	18.2	11.2	7.0	1.2	1.6
男性 Male	116	25.9	0.9	44.0	16.4	10.3	8.6	0.9	0.9
16~24 岁 Age	27	18.5	3.7	48.1	14.8	18.5	0.0	3.7	0.0
25~34 岁 Age	30	36.7	0.0	36.7	20.0	6.7	10.0	0.0	0.0
35~44 岁 Age	32	18.8	0.0	50.0	9.4	6.3	18.8	0.0	3.1
45~54 岁 Age	18	11.1	0.0	55.6	27.8	5.6	0.0	0.0	0.0
55~60 岁 Age	9	66.7	0.0	11.1	11.1	22.2	11.1	0.0	0.0
女性 Female	142	20.4	3.5	44.4	19.7	12.0	5.6	1.4	2.1
16~24 岁 Age	32	3.1	6.3	40.6	18.8	25.0	15.6	0.0	3.1
25~34 岁 Age	47	27.7	2.1	44.7	17.0	10.6	0.0	2.1	2.1
35~44 岁 Age	30	10.0	3.3	50.0	30.0	3.3	10.0	0.0	0.0
45~54 岁 Age	20	40.0	0.0	45.0	10.0	5.0	0.0	5.0	5.0
55~60 岁 Age	13	30.8	7.7	38.5	23.1	15.4	0.0	0.0	0.0

2-10 样本、男性各年龄层、女性各年龄层最常食用的场合/ Settings of Consumption by the Whole Sample, Age and Gender Groups

注：本题为多选题，合计百分比超过 100%（Multiple answers）

	人数 Number	早餐时 breakfast	正餐（午、晚餐）时 dinner	餐后热饮 after dinner	宵夜时 evening snack	睡觉前 before sleeping	工作休息时 during work break	其它 others
样本 Sample	259	65.6	5.0	7.7	7.3	19.7	17.4	3.5
男性 Male	117	67.5	4.3	5.1	8.5	19.7	17.9	3.4
16~24 岁 Age	28	57.1	3.6	10.7	3.6	28.6	14.3	3.6
25~34 岁 Age	30	80.0	3.3	6.7	10.0	13.3	23.3	3.3
35~44 岁 Age	32	59.4	3.1	3.1	12.5	25.0	21.9	0.0
45~54 岁 Age	18	72.2	11.1	0.0	11.1	5.6	11.1	5.6
55~60 岁 Age	9	77.8	0.0	0.0	0.0	22.2	11.1	11.1
女性 Female	142	64.1	5.6	9.9	6.3	19.7	16.9	3.5
16~24 岁 Age	32	50.0	3.1	12.5	6.3	21.9	25.0	6.3
25~34 岁 Age	47	61.7	8.5	10.6	6.4	17.0	12.8	2.1
35~44 岁 Age	30	76.7	3.3	3.3	3.3	30.0	20.0	3.3
45~54 岁 Age	20	65.0	5.0	15.0	15.0	20.0	10.0	5.0
55~60 岁 Age	13	76.9	7.7	7.7	0.0	0.0	15.4	0.0

2-11 重度消费者的人口分布/ Demographics of the Heavy Consumers

	人数 Number	16-24 岁 Age	25-34 岁 Age	35-44 岁 Age	45-54 岁 Age	55-60 岁 Age
样本 Sample	175	20.0	26.9	28.0	15.4	9.7
男性 Male	81	22.2	23.5	30.9	14.8	8.6
天天喝 daily	24	33.3	16.7	33.3	12.5	4.2
一周 3 次或以上 3 times or over a week	24	16.7	25.0	41.7	8.3	8.3
一周 1～2 次 once or twice a week	33	18.2	27.3	21.2	21.2	12.1
女性 Female	94	18.1	29.8	25.5	16.0	10.6
天天喝 daily	41	9.8	41.5	22.0	12.2	14.6
一周 3 次或以上 3 times or over a week	18	16.7	22.2	38.9	16.7	5.6
一周 1～2 次 once or twice a week	35	28.6	20.0	22.9	20.0	8.6

2-12 不同消费者层的常用品牌/ The Most Frequently Used Brands by Market Segments

2-12-1 时尚流行指标/ Fads Popular Index

	人数 Number	第一品牌及百分比 1st/ percent	第二品牌及百分比 2nd/ percent	第三品牌及百分比 3rd/ percent
样本 Sample	257	**维维 Weiwei(83.7)**	**光明 Bright(5.4)**	**多利 Duoli(1.6)** **杨协成 Yeo's(1.6)**
平实生活指向 simple living orientation	110	维维 Weiwei(79.1)	光明 Bright(8.2)	力源 Liyuan(1.8) 维他奶 Vitasoy(1.8) 多利 Duoli(1.8)
时尚流行指向 fashion orientation	147	维维 Weiwei(87.1)	光明 Bright(3.4)	杨协成 Yeo's(2.0)

2-12-2 广告态度指标/ Advertising Attitude Index

	人数 Number	第一品牌及百分比 1st/ percent	第二品牌及百分比 2nd/ percent	第三品牌及百分比 3rd/ percent
样本 Sample	255	**维维 Weiwei(83.9)**	**光明 Bright(5.1)**	**多利 duoli(1.6)** **杨协成 Yeo's(1.6)**
广告淡漠指向 indifferent orientation	67	维维 Weiwei(77.6)	光明 Bright(11.9)	力源 Liyuan(1.5) 雀巢 Nestle(1.5) 杨协成 Yeo's(1.5) 维他奶 Vitasoy(1.5) 多利 Duoli(1.5) 协和 Xiehe(1.5)
中间层 medium	150	维维 Weiwei(86.7)	光明 Bright(3.3)	健王 Janwang(2.0)
信赖广告指向 loyal orientation	38	维维 Weiwei(84.2)	杨协成 Yeo's(2.6) 南方 Nanfang(2.6) 多利 Douli(2.6)	

2-12-3 饮食健康指标/ Foods & Drink Quality Index

	人数 Number	第一品牌及百分比 1st/ percent	第二品牌及百分比 2nd/ percent	第三品牌及百分比 3rd/ percent
样本 Sample	258	**维维 Weiwei(84.1)**	**光明 Bright(5.4)**	**多利 Duoli(1.6)**
饮食"温饱"指向 "basic" orientation	42	维维 Weiwei(78.6)	光明 Bright(9.5)	维他奶 Vitasoy(4.8)
中间层 medium	145	维维 Weiwei(84.1)	光明 Bright(4.8)	多利 Duoli(2.8)
健康营养指向 health & nutrition orientation	71	维维 Weiwei(87.3)	光明 Bright(4.2)	健王 Janwang(1.4) 力源 Liyuan(1.4) 杨协成 Yeo's(1.4) 南方 Nanfang(1.4) 协和 Xiehe(1.4)

2-13 重度消费者的消费者层构成/ The Composition of the Heavy Consumers

2-13-1 时尚流行指标/ Fads Popular Index

	人数 Number	平实生活指向 simple living orientation	时尚流行指向 fashion orientation
样本 Sample	173	44.5	55.5
天天喝 daily	64	42.2	57.8
一周 3 次或以上 3 times or over a week	42	47.6	52.4
一周 1～2 次 once or twice a week	67	44.8	55.2

2-13-2 广告态度指标/ Advertising Attitude Index

	人数 Number	广告淡漠指向 indifferent orientation	中间层 medium	信赖广告指向 loyal orientation
样本 Sample	171	26.3	56.7	17.0
天天喝 daily	62	25.8	46.8	27.4
一周 3 次或以上 3 times or over a week	42	26.2	57.1	16.7
一周 1～2 次 once or twice a week	67	26.9	65.7	7.5

2-13-3 饮食健康指标/ Foods & Drink Quality Index

	人数 Number	饮食"温饱"指向 "basic" orientation	中间层 medium	健康营养指向 health & nutrition orientation
样本 Sample	175	16.0	53.7	30.3
天天喝 daily	65	13.8	56.9	29.2
一周 3 次或以上 3 times or over a week	42	16.7	54.8	28.6
一周 1～2 次 once or twice a week	68	17.6	50.0	32.4

● 广州 / Guangzhou

2-1 最近三个月食用频率的比例/ Proportion of the Sample Consuming Powdered Soybean Milk in the Last Three Months

	人数 Number	百分比 Percent
天天喝 daily	13	1.3
一周 3 次或以上 3 times or over a week	18	1.8
一周 1~2 次 once or twice a week	60	5.8
一个月 2～3 次 2 or 3 times a month	49	4.8
一个月 1 次或以下 once a month or below	46	4.5
没喝过 never	842	81.9

n=1028

2-2 最常用品牌排名/ Ranking of the Most Frequently Used Brands

排名 Brand Ranking	品牌 Brands	人数 Number	百分比 Percent
1	杨协成 Yeo's	47	25.4
2	维维 Weiwei	33	17.8
3	雀巢 Nestle	16	8.6
4	南方 Nanfang	10	5.4
5	维他奶 Vitasoy	9	4.9
6	冰泉 Bingquan	7	3.8
7	怡宝 Yibao	5	2.7

n=185

2-3 样本、男性各年龄层、女性各年龄层的常用品牌/ The Most Frequently Used Brands by the Whole Sample, Age and Gender Groups

	人数 Number	第一品牌及百分比 1st/ percent	第二品牌及百分比 2nd/ percent	第三品牌及百分比 3rd/ percent
样本 Sample	185	**杨协成 Yeo's(25.4)**	**维维 Weiwei(17.8)**	**雀巢 Nestle(8.6)**
男性 Male	75	**杨协成 Yeo's(25.3)**	**维维 Weiwei(17.3)**	**雀巢 Nestle(9.3)**
16~24 岁 Age	18	杨协成 Yeo's(27.8)	维维 Weiwei(22.2)	冰泉 Bingquan(5.6) 雀巢 Nestle(5.6) 维他奶 Vitasoy(5.6) 怡宝 Yibao(5.6)
25~34 岁 Age	26	杨协成 Yeo's(30.8)	雀巢 Nestle(7.7) 维维 Weiwei(7.7)	达能 Danone (3.8) 金学士 Jinxueshi(3.8) 晶泉 Jingquan(3.8) 金洋 Jinyang(3.8) 香满楼 Flower Fresh (3.8) 怡宝 Yibao(3.8) 南方 Nanfang(3.8) 风行 Fengxing(3.8) 冰泉 Bingquan(3.8)
35~44 岁 Age	12	雀巢 Nestle(25.0)	维维 Weiwei(16.7)	杨协成 Yeo's(8.3) 维他奶 Vitasoy(8.3) 南方 Nanfang(8.3)
45~54 岁 Age	12	维维 Weiwei(33.3)	杨协成 Yeo's(25.0)	雀巢 Nestle(8.3) 南方 Nanfang(8.3) 白兰氏 Brand's(8.3)
55~60 岁 Age	7	杨协成 Yeo's(28.6)	维维 Weiwei(14.3) 维他奶 Vitasoy(14.3) 五羊 Wuyang(14.3)	
女性 Female	110	**杨协成 Yeo's(25.5)**	**维维 Weiwei(18.2)**	**雀巢 Nestle(8.2)**
16~24 岁 Age	28	杨协成 Yeo's(21.4)	维维 Weiwei(17.9)	维他奶 Vitasoy(10.7)
25~34 岁 Age	33	杨协成 Yeo's(27.3)	维维 Weiwei(12.1) 南方 Nanfang(12.1)	冰泉 Bingquan(9.1) 雀巢 Nestle(9.1)
35~44 岁 Age	27	杨协成 Yeo's(29.6)	维维 Weiwei(18.5)	怡宝 Yibao(3.7) 白兰氏 Brand's(3.7) 克宁 Kening(3.7) 达能 Danone (3.7) 维他奶 Vitasoy(3.7) 南方 Nanfang(3.7) 雀巢 Nestle(3.7) 冰泉 Bingquan(3.7)
45~54 岁 Age	19	维维 Weiwei(21.1) 杨协成 Yeo's(21.1)	雀巢 Nestle(15.8)	维他奶 Vitasoy(5.3) 维记 Weiji(5.3) 南方 Nanfang(5.3)
55~60 岁 Age	3	维维 Weiwei(66.7)	杨协成 Yeo's(33.3)	

2-4 理想品牌排名/ Ranking of the Ideal Brands

排名 Brand Ranking	品牌 Brands	人数 Number	百分比 Percent
1	杨协成 Yeo's	84	8.1
2	维维 Weiwei	64	6.2
3	雀巢 Nestle	28	2.7
4	冰泉 Bingquan	19	1.8
5	维他奶 Vitasoy	12	1.2
6	南方 Nanfang	8	0.8
6	怡宝 Yibao	8	0.8

n=1034

2-5 样本、男性各年龄层、女性各年龄层最近三个月有无购买的比例/ Purchasing in the Last Three Months by the Whole Sample, Age and Gender Groups

	人数 Number	买过 yes	没买过 no
样本 Sample	1032	18.5	81.5
男性 Male	498	13.9	86.1
16~24 岁 Age	106	12.3	87.7
25~34 岁 Age	149	17.4	82.6
35~44 岁 Age	127	9.4	90.6
45~54 岁 Age	73	13.7	86.3
55~60 岁 Age	43	18.6	81.4
女性 Female	534	22.8	77.2
16~24 岁 Age	112	25.0	75.0
25~34 岁 Age	158	22.8	77.2
35~44 岁 Age	137	23.4	76.6
45~54 岁 Age	86	24.4	75.6
55~60 岁 Age	41	12.2	87.8

2-6 样本、男性各年龄层、女性各年龄层最近三个月的食用频率/ Frequencies of Consuming Powdered Soybean Milk in the Last Three Months by the Whole Sample, Age and Gender Groups

	人数 Number	天天喝 daily	一周 3 次或以上 3 times or over a week	一周 1~2 次 once or twice a week	一个月 2~3 次 2 or 3 times a month	一个月 1 次或以下 once a month or below	没喝过 never
样本 Sample	1028	1.3	1.8	5.8	4.8	4.5	81.9
男性 Male	494	0.8	1.6	5.7	4.3	3.0	84.6
16~24 岁 Age	106	0.0	1.9	4.7	2.8	7.5	83.0
25~34 岁 Age	149	2.0	0.7	6.7	5.4	3.4	81.9
35~44 岁 Age	125	0.0	2.4	3.2	2.4	1.6	90.4
45~54 岁 Age	71	0.0	1.4	9.9	5.6	0.0	83.1
55~60 岁 Age	43	2.3	2.3	4.7	7.0	0.0	83.7
女性 Female	534	1.7	1.9	6.0	5.2	5.8	79.4
16~24 岁 Age	111	1.8	0.9	7.2	7.2	8.1	74.8
25~34 岁 Age	158	1.3	3.2	7.0	3.2	6.3	79.1
35~44 岁 Age	137	0.0	0.7	6.6	7.3	5.1	80.3
45~54 岁 Age	87	5.7	2.3	3.4	4.6	5.7	78.2
55~60 岁 Age	41	0.0	2.4	2.4	2.4	0.0	92.7

2-7 样本、男性各年龄层、女性各年龄层的品牌习惯/ Brand Habit in Consuming Powdered Soybean Milk by the Whole Sample, Age and Gender Groups

	人数 Number	基本固定食用一个牌子 used in only one brand	比较固定地食用两个或三个牌子 used in two or three brands	基本上不太固定牌子 no brand preference
样本 Sample	186	32.3	26.9	40.9
男性 Male	76	30.3	23.7	46.1
16~24 岁 Age	18	38.9	11.1	50.0
25~34 岁 Age	27	29.6	37.0	33.3
35~44 岁 Age	12	16.7	25.0	58.3
45~54 岁 Age	12	33.3	16.7	50.0
55~60 岁 Age	7	28.6	14.3	57.1
女性 Female	110	33.6	29.1	37.3
16~24 岁 Age	28	32.1	32.1	35.7
25~34 岁 Age	33	30.3	33.3	36.4
35~44 岁 Age	27	44.4	25.9	29.6
45~54 岁 Age	19	31.6	15.8	52.6
55~60 岁 Age	3	0.0	66.7	33.3

2-8 选择该类商品的考虑因素/ Ranking of the Considerations in Purchasing

注：本题为多选题，合计百分比超过 100%（Multiple answers）

排名 Ranking	考虑因素 Considerations	人次 Person-time	百分比 Percent
1	营养成分 nutrition constituent	90	48.4
2	口味好 pleasant taste	74	39.8
3	价格适中 reasonable price	67	36.0
4	生产日期 date of producing	48	25.8
5	有名的牌子 famous brand	47	25.3
6	购买方便 easy to buy	36	19.4
7	有优惠条件 with preferential terms	16	8.6
8	易溶解 high dissolubility	11	5.9
9	只是由于习惯 out of habit	8	4.3
10	广告影响 influence of advertising	7	3.8
10	朋友推荐 introduction of friends	7	3.8
11	包装吸引人 appealing package	5	2.7
12	售货员介绍 introduced by the shop assistants	3	1.6

n=186

2-9 样本、男性各年龄层、女性各年龄层最常食用种类/ Types of the Consumed Powdered Soybean Milk by the Whole Sample, Age and Gender Groups

注：本题为多选题，合计百分比超过 100%（Multiple answers）

	人数 Number	豆粉 soybean powder	绿豆粉 mungbean powder	普通型豆奶粉 normal	低糖型豆奶粉 low-sugar	加味型(如巧克力、花生等)豆奶粉 flavored (eg chocolate)	保健型(如枸杞、蔬菜等)豆奶粉 health caring (eg.vege-table，wol)	绿豆奶粉 mungbean milk powder	其它 others
样本 Sample	**185**	**19.5**	**3.8**	**31.9**	**19.5**	**22.7**	**9.2**	**2.2**	**1.6**
男性 Male	**76**	**23.7**	**5.3**	**27.6**	**14.5**	**28.9**	**6.6**	**0.0**	**2.6**
16~24 岁 Age	18	16.7	11.1	27.8	0.0	44.4	5.6	0.0	5.6
25~34 岁 Age	27	29.6	0.0	37.0	11.1	22.2	11.1	0.0	0.0
35~44 岁 Age	12	16.7	8.3	8.3	25.0	33.3	0.0	0.0	8.3
45~54 岁 Age	12	25.0	8.3	33.3	16.7	25.0	0.0	0.0	0.0
55~60 岁 Age	7	28.6	0.0	14.3	42.9	14.3	14.3	0.0	0.0
女性 Female	**109**	**16.5**	**2.8**	**34.9**	**22.9**	**18.3**	**11.0**	**3.7**	**0.9**
16~24 岁 Age	28	21.4	3.6	25.0	28.6	17.9	7.1	3.6	3.6
25~34 岁 Age	32	9.4	3.1	31.3	21.9	21.9	15.6	3.1	0.0
35~44 岁 Age	27	14.8	0.0	40.7	22.2	22.2	11.1	3.7	0.0
45~54 岁 Age	19	15.8	5.3	47.4	21.1	10.5	10.5	5.3	0.0
55~60 岁 Age	3	66.7	0.0	33.3	0.0	0.0	0.0	0.0	0.0

2-10 样本、男性各年龄层、女性各年龄层最常食用的场合/ Settings of Consumption by the Whole Sample, Age and Gender Groups

注：本题为多选题，合计百分比超过 100%（Multiple answers）

	人数 Number	早餐时 breakfast	正餐(午、晚餐)时 dinner	餐后热饮 after dinner	宵夜时 evening snack	睡觉前 before sleeping	工作休息时 during work break	其它 others
样本 Sample	**185**	**55.1**	**5.9**	**8.1**	**17.3**	**13.5**	**22.7**	**7.6**
男性 Male	**75**	**57.3**	**6.7**	**8.0**	**25.3**	**8.0**	**18.7**	**6.7**
16~24 岁 Age	18	55.6	11.1	5.6	27.8	11.1	11.1	16.7
25~34 岁 Age	27	63.0	0.0	7.4	14.8	7.4	22.2	3.7
35~44 岁 Age	12	58.3	8.3	0.0	33.3	16.7	16.7	0.0
45~54 岁 Age	12	41.7	8.3	16.7	33.3	0.0	25.0	8.3
55~60 岁 Age	6	66.7	16.7	16.7	33.3	0.0	16.7	0.0
女性 Female	**110**	**53.6**	**5.5**	**8.2**	**11.8**	**17.3**	**25.5**	**8.2**
16~24 岁 Age	28	50.0	10.7	0.0	10.7	21.4	21.4	10.7
25~34 岁 Age	33	51.5	3.0	9.1	21.2	12.1	33.3	6.1
35~44 岁 Age	27	44.4	3.7	18.5	7.4	18.5	33.3	3.7
45~54 岁 Age	19	73.7	5.3	5.3	5.3	15.8	10.5	10.5
55~60 岁 Age	3	66.7	0.0	0.0	0.0	33.3	0.0	33.3

2-11 重度消费者的人口分布/ Demographics of the Heavy Consumers

	人数 Number	16-24 岁 Age	25-34 岁 Age	35-44 岁 Age	45-54 岁 Age	55-60 岁 Age
样本 Sample	91	19.8	35.2	18.7	19.8	6.6
男性 Male	40	17.5	35.0	17.5	20.0	10.0
天天喝 daily	4	0.0	75.0	0.0	0.0	25.0
一周 3 次或以上 3 times or over a week	8	25.0	12.5	37.5	12.5	12.5
一周 1～2 次 once or twice a week	28	17.9	35.7	14.3	25.0	7.1
女性 Female	51	21.6	35.3	19.6	19.6	3.9
天天喝 daily	9	22.2	22.2	0.0	55.6	0.0
一周 3 次或以上 3 times or over a week	10	10.0	50.0	10.0	20.0	10.0
一周 1～2 次 once or twice a week	32	25.0	34.4	28.1	9.4	3.1

2-12 不同消费者层的常用品牌/ The Most Frequently Used Brands by Market Segments

2-12-1 时尚流行指标/ Fads Popular Index

	人数 Number	第一品牌及百分比 1st/ percent	第二品牌及百分比 2nd/ percent	第三品牌及百分比 3rd/ percent	第四品牌及百分比 4th/ percent
样本 Sample	181	**杨协成 Yeo's(26.0)**	**维维 Weiwei(18.2)**	**雀巢 Nestle(7.7)**	**维他奶 Vitasoy(5.0)** **南方 Nanfang(5.0)**
平实生活指向 simple living orientation	76	杨协成 Yeo's(22.4)	维维 Weiwei(19.7)	雀巢 Nestle(7.9)	维他奶 Vitasoy(6.6)
时尚流行指向 fashion orientation	105	杨协成 Yeo's(28.6)	维维 Weiwei(17.1)	雀巢 Nestle(7.6)	冰泉 Bingquan(5.7) 南方 Nanfang(5.7)

2-12-2 广告态度指标/ Advertising Attitude Index

	人数 Number	第一品牌及百分比 1st/ percent	第二品牌及百分比 2nd/ percent	第三品牌及百分比 3rd/ percent	第四品牌及百分比 4th/ percent
样本 Sample	181	**杨协成 Yeo's(24.9)**	**维维 Weiwei(17.7)**	**雀巢 Nestle(8.8)**	**南方 Nanfang(5.5)**
广告淡漠指向 indifferent orientation	54	杨协成 Yeo's(24.1)	雀巢 Nestle(13.0) 维维 Weiwei(13.0)	南方 Nanfang(7.4)	维他奶 Vitasoy(5.6)
中间层 medium	110	杨协成 Yeo's(26.4)	维维 Weiwei(19.1)	雀巢 Nestle(8.2)	南方 Nanfang(4.5)
信赖广告指向 loyal orientation	17	维维 Weiwei(23.5)	杨协成 Yeo's(17.6) 维他奶 Vitasoy(17.6)	冰泉 Bingquan(5.9) 南方 Nanfang(5.9) 怡宝 Yibao(5.9) 克宁 Kening(5.9)	

2-12-3 饮食健康指标/ Foods & Drink Quality Index

	人数 Number	第一品牌及百分比 1st/ percent	第二品牌及百分比 2nd/ percent	第三品牌及百分比 3rd/ percent	第四品牌及百分比 4th/ percent
样本 Sample	184	**杨协成 Yeo's(25.5)**	**维维 Weiwei(17.9)**	**雀巢 Nestle(8.7)**	**南方 Nanfang(5.4)**
饮食"温饱"指向 "basic" orientation	33	杨协成 Yeo's(27.3)	维维 Weiwei(18.2)	雀巢 Nestle(6.1) 冰泉 Bingquan(6.1) 维他奶 Vitasoy(6.1) 南方 Nanfang(6.1)	香满楼 Flower Fresh (3.0) 维记 Weiji(3.0) 怡宝 Yibao(3.0) 金洋 Jinyang(3.0)
中间层 medium	104	杨协成 Yeo's(24.0)	维维 Weiwei(14.4)	雀巢 Nestle(8.7)	维他奶 Vitasoy(5.8)
健康营养指向 health & nutrition orientation	47	杨协成 Yeo's(27.7)	维维 Weiwei(25.5)	雀巢 Nestle(10.6)	南方 Nanfang(6.4)

2-13 重度消费者的消费者层构成/ The Composition of the Heavy Consumers

2-13-1 时尚流行指标/ Fads Popular Index

	人数 Number	平实生活指向 simple living orientation	时尚流行指向 fashion orientation
样本 Sample	89	46.1	53.9
天天喝 daily	13	38.5	61.5
一周 3 次或以上 3 times or over a week	17	58.8	41.2
一周 1～2 次 once or twice a week	59	44.1	55.9

2-13-2 广告态度指标/ Advertising Attitude Index

	人数 Number	广告淡漠指向 indifferent orientation	中间层 medium	信赖广告指向 loyal orientation
样本 Sample	89	30.3	58.4	11.2
天天喝 daily	13	23.1	69.2	7.7
一周3次或以上 3 times or over a week	17	35.3	58.8	5.9
一周1～2次 once or twice a week	59	30.5	55.9	13.6

2-13-3 饮食健康指标/ Foods & Drink Quality Index

	人数 Number	饮食"温饱"指向 "basic" orientation	中间层 medium	健康营养指向 health & nutrition orientation
样本 Sample	91	22.0	47.3	30.8
天天喝 daily	13	15.4	38.5	46.2
一周3次或以上 3 times or over a week	18	27.8	33.3	38.9
一周1～2次 once or twice a week	60	21.7	53.3	25.0

● 重庆 / Chongqing

2-1 最近三个月食用频率的比例/ Proportion of the Sample Consuming Powdered Soybean Milk in the Last Three Months

	人数 Number	百分比 Percent
天天喝 daily	37	5.9
一周3次或以上 3 times or over a week	39	6.3
一周1~2次 once or twice a week	77	12.4
一个月2～3次 2 or 3 times a month	29	4.7
一个月1次或以下 once a month or below	32	5.1
没喝过 never	409	65.7

n=623

2-2 最常用品牌排名/ Ranking of the Most Frequently Used Brands

排名 Brand Ranking	品牌 Brands	人数 Number	百分比 Percent
1	维维 Weiwei	184	86.4
2	大地 Landy	17	8.0
3	冬梅 Dongmei	2	0.9
3	力源 Liyuan	2	0.9

n=213

2-3 样本、男性各年龄层、女性各年龄层的常用品牌/ The Most Frequently Used Brands by the Whole Sample, Age and Gender Groups

	人数 Number	第一品牌及百分比 1st/ percent	第二品牌及百分比 2nd/ percent	第三品牌及百分比 3rd/ percent
样本 Sample	213	**维维 Weiwei(86.4)**	**大地 Landy(8.0)**	**冬梅 Dongmei(0.9)** **力源 Liyuan(0.9)**
男性 Male	97	**维维 Weiwei(85.6)**	**大地 Landy(7.2)**	**力源 Liyuan(2.1)**
16~24岁 Age	24	维维 Weiwei(83.3)	大地 Landy(8.3)	力源 Liyuan(4.2)
25~34岁 Age	34	维维 Weiwei(82.4)	大地 Landy(11.8)	力源 Liyuan(2.9) 山城 Shancheng(2.9)
35~44岁 Age	16	维维 Weiwei(87.5)	南方 Nanfang(6.3)	
45~54岁 Age	13	维维 Weiwei(92.3)	大地 Landy(7.7)	
55~60岁 Age	10	维维 Weiwei(90.0)	冬梅 Dongmei(10.0)	
女性 Female	116	**维维 Weiwei(87.1)**	**大地 Landy(8.6)**	**冬梅 Dongmei(0.9)** **雀巢 Nestle(0.9)** **雅士利 Yashili(0.9)**
16~24岁 Age	29	维维 Weiwei(89.7)	大地 Landy(6.9)	雀巢 Nestle(3.4)
25~34岁 Age	37	维维 Weiwei(83.8)	大地 Landy(8.1)	冬梅 Dongmei(2.7) 雅士利 Yashili(2.7)
35~44岁 Age	26	维维 Weiwei(80.8)	大地 Landy(19.2)	
45~54岁 Age	18	维维 Weiwei(94.4)	维维 Weiwei(5.6)	
55~60岁 Age	6	维维 Weiwei(100.0)		

2-4 理想品牌排名/ Ranking of the Ideal Brands

排名 Brand Ranking	品牌 Brands	人数 Number	百分比 Percent
1	维维 Weiwei	450	72.1
2	大地 Landy	42	6.7
3	雀巢 Nestle	7	1.1
4	冬梅 Dongmei	3	0.5
4	完达山 Wandashan	3	0.5

n=624

2-5 样本、男性各年龄层、女性各年龄层最近三个月有无购买的比例/ Purchasing in the Last Three Months by the Whole Sample, Age and Gender Groups

	人数 Number	买过 yes	没买过 no
样本 Sample	624	32.1	67.9
男性 Male	314	27.1	72.9
16~24 岁 Age	64	28.1	71.9
25~34 岁 Age	93	34.4	65.6
35~44 岁 Age	75	21.3	78.7
45~54 岁 Age	54	22.2	77.8
55~60 岁 Age	28	25.0	75.0
女性 Female	310	37.1	62.9
16~24 岁 Age	64	35.9	64.1
25~34 岁 Age	90	45.6	54.4
35~44 岁 Age	73	34.2	65.8
45~54 岁 Age	60	33.3	66.7
55~60 岁 Age	23	26.1	73.9

2-6 样本、男性各年龄层、女性各年龄层最近三个月的食用频率/ Frequencies of Consuming Powdered Soybean Milk in the Last Three Months by the Whole Sample, Age and Gender Groups

	人数 Number	天天喝 daily	一周 3 次或以上 3 times or over a week	一周 1~2 次 once or twice a week	一个月 2～3 次 2 or 3 times a month	一个月 1 次或以下 once a month or below	没喝过 never
样本 Sample	623	5.9	6.3	12.4	4.7	5.1	65.7
男性 Male	314	4.5	6.1	10.8	4.1	5.4	69.1
16~24 岁 Age	64	9.4	6.3	7.8	0.0	14.1	62.5
25~34 岁 Age	93	2.2	7.5	14.0	9.7	3.2	63.4
35~44 岁 Age	75	1.3	5.3	8.0	1.3	5.3	78.7
45~54 岁 Age	54	7.4	3.7	9.3	1.9	1.9	75.9
55~60 岁 Age	28	3.6	7.1	17.9	7.1	0.0	64.3
女性 Female	309	7.4	6.5	13.9	5.2	4.9	62.1
16~24 岁 Age	64	7.8	4.7	17.2	4.7	10.9	54.7
25~34 岁 Age	90	7.8	8.9	14.4	7.8	2.2	58.9
35~44 岁 Age	72	5.6	6.9	13.9	2.8	6.9	63.9
45~54 岁 Age	60	10.0	3.3	15.0	3.3	0.0	68.3
55~60 岁 Age	23	4.3	8.7	0.0	8.7	4.3	73.9

2-7 样本、男性各年龄层、女性各年龄层的品牌习惯/ Brand Habit in Consuming Powdered Soybean Milk by the Whole Sample, Age and Gender Groups

	人数 Number	基本固定食用一个牌子 used in only one brand	比较固定地食用两个或三个牌子 used in two or three brands	基本上不太固定牌子 no brand preference
样本 Sample	214	49.5	25.7	24.8
男性 Male	97	46.4	22.7	30.9
16~24 岁 Age	24	41.7	29.2	29.2
25~34 岁 Age	34	61.8	20.6	17.6
35~44 岁 Age	16	37.5	6.3	56.3
45~54 岁 Age	13	30.8	30.8	38.5
55~60 岁 Age	10	40.0	30.0	30.0
女性 Female	117	52.1	28.2	19.7
16~24 岁 Age	29	44.8	31.0	24.1
25~34 岁 Age	37	48.6	35.1	16.2
35~44 岁 Age	26	53.8	19.2	26.9
45~54 岁 Age	19	63.2	26.3	10.5
55~60 岁 Age	6	66.7	16.7	16.7

2-8 选择该类商品的考虑因素/ Ranking of the Considerations in Purchasing

注：本题为多选题，合计百分比超过 100%（Multiple answers）

排名 Ranking	考虑因素 Considerations	人次 Person-time	百分比 Percent
1	口味好 pleasant taste	119	55.6
2	价格适中 reasonable price	84	39.3
2	营养成分 nutrition constituent	84	39.3
3	有名的牌子 famous brand	65	30.4
4	生产日期 date of producing	27	12.6
5	广告影响 influence of advertising	25	11.7
6	购买方便 easy to buy	20	9.3
7	易溶解 high dissolubility	19	8.9
8	只是由于习惯 out of habit	14	6.5
9	包装吸引人 appealing package	7	3.3
10	有优惠条件 with preferential terms	6	2.8
10	朋友推荐 introduction of friends	6	2.8
11	其它 others	2	0.9
12	售货员介绍 introduced by the shop assistants	1	0.5

n=214

2-9 样本、男性各年龄层、女性各年龄层最常食用种类/ Types of the Consumed Powdered Soybean Milk by the Whole Sample, Age and Gender Groups

注：本题为多选题，合计百分比超过 100%（Multiple answers）

	人数 Number	豆粉 soybean powder	绿豆粉 mung bean powder	普通型 豆奶粉 normal	低糖型 豆奶粉 low-sugar	加味型(如巧克力、花生等) 豆奶粉 flavored (eg.chocolate)	保健型（如枸杞、蔬菜等）豆奶粉 healthcaring(eg.vegetable,wol	绿豆奶粉 mung bean milk powder	其它 others
样本 Sample	212	13.7	1.9	51.4	11.8	19.8	7.5	0.5	3.3
男性 Male	95	17.9	3.2	48.4	9.5	20.0	6.3	1.1	3.2
16~24 岁 Age	23	21.7	4.3	47.8	0.0	21.7	13.0	4.3	0.0
25~34 岁 Age	34	14.7	2.9	44.1	8.8	20.6	5.9	0.0	5.9
35~44 岁 Age	16	18.8	6.3	50.0	6.3	37.5	0.0	0.0	0.0
45~54 岁 Age	12	25.0	0.0	50.0	16.7	8.3	8.3	0.0	0.0
55~60 岁 Age	10	10.0	0.0	60.0	30.0	0.0	0.0	0.0	10.0
女性 Female	117	10.3	0.9	53.8	13.7	19.7	8.5	0.0	3.4
16~24 岁 Age	29	10.3	0.0	55.2	6.9	27.6	10.3	0.0	3.4
25~34 岁 Age	37	13.5	2.7	45.9	13.5	16.2	10.8	0.0	5.4
35~44 岁 Age	26	11.5	0.0	53.8	7.7	26.9	7.7	0.0	3.8
45~54 岁 Age	19	5.3	0.0	57.9	31.6	5.3	5.3	0.0	0.0
55~60 岁 Age	6	0.0	0.0	83.3	16.7	16.7	0.0	0.0	0.0

2-10 样本、男性各年龄层、女性各年龄层最常食用的场合/ Settings of Consumption by the Whole Sample, Age and Gender Groups

注：本题为多选题，合计百分比超过 100%（Multiple answers）

	人数 Number	早餐时 breakfast	正餐（午、晚餐）时 dinner	餐后热饮 after dinner	宵夜时 evening snack	睡觉前 before sleeping	工作休息时 during work break	其它 others
样本 Sample	214	73.4	1.4	3.3	9.8	16.8	7.9	4.2
男性 Male	97	68.0	2.1	2.1	14.4	18.6	7.2	6.2
16~24 岁 Age	24	50.0	0.0	4.2	25.0	25.0	12.5	8.3
25~34 岁 Age	34	61.8	2.9	2.9	8.3	20.6	8.8	8.8
35~44 岁 Age	16	75.0	6.3	0.0	18.3	6.3	6.3	6.3
45~54 岁 Age	13	100.0	0.0	0.0	7.7	23.1	0.0	0.0
55~60 岁 Age	10	80.0	0.0	0.0	10.0	10.0	0.0	0.0
女性 Female	117	77.8	0.9	4.3	6.0	15.4	8.5	2.6
16~24 岁 Age	29	62.1	3.4	6.9	6.9	13.8	13.8	6.9
25~34 岁 Age	37	81.1	0.0	2.7	5.4	13.5	5.4	0.0
35~44 岁 Age	26	80.8	0.0	7.7	0.0	23.1	3.8	3.8
45~54 岁 Age	19	84.2	0.0	0.0	15.8	15.8	15.8	0.0
55~60 岁 Age	6	100.0	0.0	0.0	0.0	0.0	0.0	0.0

2-11 重度消费者的人口分布/ Demographics of the Heavy Consumers

	人数 Number	16-24 岁 Age	25-34 岁 Age	35-44 岁 Age	45-54 岁 Age	55-60 岁 Age
样本 Sample	153	22.2	32.7	19.6	18.3	7.2
男性 Male	67	22.4	32.8	16.4	16.4	11.9
天天喝 daily	14	42.9	14.3	7.1	28.6	7.1
一周 3 次或以上 3 times or over a week	19	21.1	36.8	21.1	10.5	10.5
一周 1～2 次 once or twice a week	34	14.7	38.2	17.6	14.7	14.7
女性 Female	86	22.1	32.6	22.1	19.8	3.5
天天喝 daily	23	21.7	30.4	17.4	26.1	4.3
一周 3 次或以上 3 times or over a week	20	15.0	40.0	25.0	10.0	10.0
一周 1～2 次 once or twice a week	43	25.6	30.2	23.3	20.9	0.0

2-12 不同消费者层的常用品牌/ The Most Frequently Used Brands by Market Segments

2-12-1 时尚流行指标/ Fads Popular Index

	人数 Number	第一品牌及百分比 1st/ percent	第二品牌及百分比 2nd/ percent	第三品牌及百分比 3rd/ percent
样本 Sample	209	**维维 Weiwei(86.6)**	**大地 Landy(7.7)**	**冬梅 Dongmei(1.0)** **力源 Liyuan(1.0)**
平实生活指向 simple living orientation	104	维维 Weiwei(85.6)	大地 Landy(8.7)	力源 Liyuan(1.9)
时尚流行指向 fashion orientation	105	维维 Weiwei(87.6)	大地 Landy(6.7)	冬梅 Dongmei(1.0) 雀巢 Nestle(1.0) 山城 Shangcheng (1.0) 南方 Nanfang(1.0)

2-12-2 广告态度指标/ Advertising Attitude Index

	人数 Number	第一品牌及百分比 1st/ percent	第二品牌及百分比 2nd/ percent	第三品牌及百分比 3rd/ percent
样本 Sample	213	**维维 Weiwei(86.4)**	**大地 Landy(8.0)**	**冬梅 Dongmei(0.9)** **力源 Liyuan(0.9)**
广告淡漠指向 indifferent orientation	50	维维 Weiwei(84.0)	大地 Landy(6.0)	冬梅 Dongmei(2.0) 力源 Liyuan(2.0) 山城 Shangcheng (2.0) 山城 Shangcheng (2.0)
中间层 medium	136	维维 Weiwei(86.8)	大地 Landy(8.1)	冬梅 Dongmei(0.7) 力源 Liyuan(0.7) 雀巢 Nestle(0.7) 南方 Nanfang(0.7) 雅士利 Yashili(0.7)
信赖广告指向 loyal orientation	27	维维 Weiwei(88.9)	大地 Landy(11.1)	

2-12-3 饮食健康指标/ Foods & Drink Quality Index

	人数 Number	第一品牌及百分比 1st/ percent	第二品牌及百分比 2nd/ percent	第三品牌及百分比 3rd/ percent
样本 Sample	211	**维维 Weiwei(86.3)**	**大地 Landy(8.1)**	**冬梅 Dongmei(0.9)** **力源 Liyuan(0.9)**
饮食“温饱”指向 "basic" orientation	75	维维 Weiwei(82.7)	大地 Landy(10.7)	冬梅 Dongmei(1.3) 力源 Liyuan(1.3) 南方 Nanfang(1.3)
中间层 medium	88	维维 Weiwei(90.9)	大地 Landy(4.5)	雀巢 Nestle(1.1) 山城 Shangcheng (1.1)
健康营养指向 health & nutrition orientation	48	维维 Weiwei(83.3)	大地 Landy(10.4)	冬梅 Dongmei(2.1) 力源 Liyuan(2.1) 雅士利 Yashili(2.1)

2-13 重度消费者的消费者层构成/ The Composition of the Heavy Consumers

2-13-1 时尚流行指标/ Fads Popular Index

	人数 Number	平实生活指向 simple living orientation	时尚流行指向 fashion orientation
样本 Sample	150	**50.7**	**49.3**
天天喝 daily	36	50.0	50.0
一周 3 次或以上 3 times or over a week	39	53.8	46.2
一周 1～2 次 once or twice a week	75	49.3	50.7

2-13-2 广告态度指标/ Advertising Attitude Index

	人数 Number	广告淡漠指向 indifferent orientation	中间层 medium	信赖广告指向 loyal orientation
样本 Sample	152	**22.4**	**61.8**	**15.8**
天天喝 daily	37	21.6	62.2	16.2
一周 3 次或以上 3 times or over a week	39	30.8	46.2	23.1
一周 1～2 次 once or twice a week	76	18.4	69.7	11.8

2-13-3 饮食健康指标/ Foods & Drink Quality Index

	人数 Number	饮食"温饱"指向 "basic" orientation	中间层 medium	健康营养指向 health & nutrition orientation
样本 Sample	151	**31.8**	**41.1**	**27.2**
天天喝 daily	37	18.9	56.8	24.3
一周 3 次或以上 3 times or over a week	39	43.6	25.6	30.8
一周 1～2 次 once or twice a week	75	32.0	41.3	26.7

● 武汉 / Wuhan

2-1 最近三个月食用频率的比例/ Proportion of the Sample Consuming Powdered Soybean Milk in the Last Three Months

	人数 Number	百分比 Percent
天天喝 daily	28	4.4
一周 3 次或以上 3 times or over a week	30	4.7
一周 1~2 次 once or twice a week	54	8.4
一个月 2～3 次 2 or 3 times a month	48	7.5
一个月 1 次或以下 once a month or below	39	6.1
没喝过 never	442	69.0

n=641

2-2 最常用品牌排名/ Ranking of the Most Frequently Used Brands

排名 Brand Ranking	品牌 Brands	人数 Number	百分比 Percent
1	维维 Weiwei	171	86.4
2	大地 Landy	4	2.0
3	杨协成 Yeo's	3	1.5
4	晨星岛 Chenxingdao	2	1.0
4	南方 Nanfang	2	1.0

n=198

2-3 样本、男性各年龄层、女性各年龄层的常用品牌/ The Most Frequently Used Brands by the Whole Sample, Age and Gender Groups

	人数 Number	第一品牌及百分比 1st/ percent	第二品牌及百分比 2nd/ percent	第三品牌及百分比 3rd/ percent
样本 Sample	198	**维维 Weiwei(86.4)**	**大地 Landy(2.0)**	**杨协成 Yeo's(1.5)**
男性 Male	83	**维维 Weiwei(85.5)**	**大地 Landy(3.6)**	**杨协成 Yeo's(2.4)**
16~24 岁 Age	17	维维 Weiwei(88.2)		
25~34 岁 Age	31	维维 Weiwei(74.2)	大地 Landy(9.7)	杨协成 Yeo's(3.2) 友芝友 Youzhiyou(3.2) 正味 Zhengwei(3.2)
35~44 岁 Age	18	维维 Weiwei(94.4)	杨协成 Yeo's(5.6)	
45~54 岁 Age	11	维维 Weiwei(90.9)		
55~60 岁 Age	6	维维 Weiwei(100.0)		
女性 Female	115	**维维 Weiwei(87.0)**	**南方 Nanfang(1.7)** **晨星岛 Chenxingdao(1.7)**	**黑牛 Heiniu(0.9)** **雪峰 Xuefeng(0.9)** **王氏 Wangshi(0.9)** **扬子江 Yangzijiang(0.9)** **金味 Jinwei(0.9)** **杨协成 Yeo's(0.9)** **大地 Landy(0.9)**
16~24 岁 Age	27	维维 Weiwei(92.6)	杨协成 Yeo's(3.7)	
25~34 岁 Age	37	维维 Weiwei(89.2)	大地 Landy(2.7) 扬子江 Yangzijiang(2.7) 南方 Nanfang(2.7)	
35~44 岁 Age	22	维维 Weiwei(81.8)	晨星岛 Chenxingdao(4.5) 金味 Jinwei(4.5) 雪峰 Xuefeng(4.5)	
45~54 岁 Age	21	维维 Weiwei(81.0)	晨星岛 Chenxingdao(4.8) 南方 Nanfang(4.8) 王氏 Wangshi(4.8) 黑牛 Heiniu(4.8)	
55~60 岁 Age	8	维维 Weiwei(87.5)		

2-4 理想品牌排名/ Ranking of the Ideal Brands

排名 Brand Ranking	品牌 Brands	人数 Number	百分比 Percent
1	维维 Weiwei	395	61.5
2	大地 Landy	6	0.9
3	南方 Nanfang	4	0.6
3	杨协成 Yeo's	4	0.6
3	扬子江 Yangzijiang	4	0.6

n=642

2-5 样本、男性各年龄层、女性各年龄层最近三个月有无购买的比例/ Purchasing in the Last Three Months by the Whole Sample, Age and Gender Groups

	人数 Number	买过 yes	没买过 no
样本 Sample	642	28.2	71.8
男性 Male	311	23.8	76.2
16~24 岁 Age	65	18.5	81.5
25~34 岁 Age	89	29.2	70.8
35~44 岁 Age	80	22.5	77.5
45~54 岁 Age	52	23.1	76.9
55~60 岁 Age	25	24.0	76.0
女性 Female	331	32.3	67.7
16~24 岁 Age	69	27.5	72.5
25~34 岁 Age	96	37.5	62.5
35~44 岁 Age	78	32.1	67.9
45~54 岁 Age	62	33.9	66.1
55~60 岁 Age	26	23.1	76.9

2-6 样本、男性各年龄层、女性各年龄层最近三个月的食用频率/ Frequencies of Consuming Powdered Soybean Milk in the Last Three Months by the Whole Sample, Age and Gender Groups

	人数 Number	天天喝 daily	一周 3 次或以上 3 times or over a week	一周 1~2 次 once or twice a week	一个月 2~3 次 2 or 3 times a month	一个月 1 次或以下 once a month or below	没喝过 never
样本 Sample	641	4.4	4.7	8.4	7.5	6.1	69.0
男性 Male	311	1.9	3.5	8.4	6.4	6.8	73.0
16~24 岁 Age	65	1.5	1.5	7.7	9.2	6.2	73.8
25~34 岁 Age	89	4.5	4.5	6.7	10.1	9.0	65.2
35~44 岁 Age	80	0.0	5.0	6.3	5.0	6.3	77.5
45~54 岁 Age	52	0.0	1.9	13.5	1.9	5.8	76.9
55~60 岁 Age	25	4.0	4.0	12.0	0.0	4.0	76.0
女性 Female	330	6.7	5.8	8.5	8.5	5.5	65.2
16~24 岁 Age	69	2.9	5.8	11.6	8.7	10.1	60.9
25~34 岁 Age	96	6.3	6.3	10.4	13.5	2.1	61.5
35~44 岁 Age	77	7.8	5.2	3.9	6.5	5.2	71.4
45~54 岁 Age	62	6.5	6.5	11.3	4.8	4.8	66.1
55~60 岁 Age	26	15.4	3.8	0.0	3.8	7.7	69.2

2-7 样本、男性各年龄层、女性各年龄层的品牌习惯/ Brand Habit in Consuming Powdered Soybean Milk by the Whole Sample, Age and Gender Groups

	人数 Number	基本固定食用一个牌子 used in only one brand	比较固定地食用两个或三个牌子 used in two or three brands	基本上不太固定牌子 no brand preference
样本 Sample	197	71.1	13.7	15.2
男性 Male	83	66.3	15.7	18.1
16~24 岁 Age	17	70.6	5.9	23.5
25~34 岁 Age	31	61.3	22.6	16.1
35~44 岁 Age	18	66.7	16.7	16.7
45~54 岁 Age	11	63.6	9.1	27.3
55~60 岁 Age	6	83.3	16.7	0.0
女性 Female	114	74.6	12.3	13.2
16~24 岁 Age	27	59.3	22.2	18.5
25~34 岁 Age	36	80.6	8.3	11.1
35~44 岁 Age	22	81.8	9.1	9.1
45~54 岁 Age	21	66.7	14.3	19.0
55~60 岁 Age	8	100.0	0.0	0.0

2-8 选择该类商品的考虑因素/ Ranking of the Considerations in Purchasing

注：本题为多选题，合计百分比超过 100%（Multiple answers）

排名 Ranking	考虑因素 Considerations	人次 Person-time	百分比 Percent
1	口味好 pleasant taste	86	43.4
2	营养成分 nutrition constituent	81	40.9
3	有名的牌子 famous brand	80	40.4
4	价格适中 reasonable price	63	31.8
5	生产日期 date of producing	42	21.2
6	广告影响 influence of advertising	34	17.2
7	购买方便 easy to buy	27	13.6
8	只是由于习惯 out of habit	21	10.6
9	易溶解 high dissolubility	17	8.6
10	朋友推荐 introduction of friends	8	4.0
11	包装吸引人 appealing package	7	3.5
12	有优惠条件 with preferential terms	5	2.5
13	售货员介绍 introduced by the shop assistants	3	1.5
14	其它 others	2	1.0

n=198

2-9 样本、男性各年龄层、女性各年龄层最常食用种类/ Types of the Consumed Powdered Soybean Milk by the Whole Sample, Age and Gender Groups

注：本题为多选题，合计百分比超过 100%（Multiple answers）

	人数 Number	豆粉 soybean powder	绿豆粉 mungbean powder	普通型豆奶粉 normal	低糖型豆奶粉 low-sugar	加味型(如巧克力、花生等)豆奶粉 flavored (eg.chocolate)	保健型（如枸杞、蔬菜等）豆奶粉 healthcaring (eg.vegetable, wol)	绿豆奶粉 mungbean milk powder	其它 others
样本 Sample	197	15.2	2.0	50.8	19.8	6.6	7.6	1.0	5.1
男性 Male	83	12.0	3.6	50.6	19.3	8.4	10.8	1.2	2.4
16~24 岁 Age	17	0.0	5.9	41.2	23.5	11.8	17.6	0.0	0.0
25~34 岁 Age	31	12.9	3.2	48.4	19.4	9.7	9.7	3.2	0.0
35~44 岁 Age	18	27.8	5.6	44.4	16.7	11.1	11.1	0.0	0.0
45~54 岁 Age	11	0.0	0.0	63.6	18.2	0.0	9.1	0.0	18.2
55~60 岁 Age	6	16.7	0.0	83.3	16.7	0.0	0.0	0.0	0.0
女性 Female	114	17.5	0.9	50.9	20.2	5.3	5.3	0.9	7.0
16~24 岁 Age	27	33.3	0.0	37.0	22.2	11.1	0.0	3.7	7.4
25~34 岁 Age	37	13.5	0.0	56.8	21.6	8.1	5.4	0.0	2.7
35~44 岁 Age	21	9.5	0.0	61.9	19.0	0.0	4.8	0.0	4.8
45~54 岁 Age	21	9.5	4.8	47.6	19.0	0.0	14.3	0.0	14.3
55~60 岁 Age	8	25.0	0.0	50.0	12.5	0.0	0.0	0.0	12.5

2-10 样本、男性各年龄层、女性各年龄层最常食用的场合/ Settings of Consumption by the Whole Sample, Age and Gender Groups

注：本题为多选题，合计百分比超过 100%（Multiple answers）

	人数 Number	早餐时 breakfast	正餐（午、晚餐）时 dinner	餐后热饮 after dinner	宵夜时 evening snack	睡觉前 before sleeping	工作休息时 during work break	其它 others
样本 Sample	198	53.0	6.6	7.6	15.2	23.2	16.7	3.0
男性 Male	83	54.2	3.6	4.8	18.1	26.5	13.3	3.6
16~24 岁 Age	17	70.6	0.0	11.8	23.5	11.8	0.0	5.9
25~34 岁 Age	31	45.2	0.0	0.0	19.4	35.5	25.8	3.2
35~44 岁 Age	18	66.7	11.1	11.1	11.1	22.2	0.0	0.0
45~54 岁 Age	11	36.4	0.0	0.0	18.2	45.5	18.2	0.0
55~60 岁 Age	6	50.0	16.7	0.0	16.7	0.0	16.7	16.7
女性 Female	115	52.2	8.7	9.6	13.0	20.9	19.1	2.6
16~24 岁 Age	27	40.7	14.8	11.1	14.8	11.1	29.6	3.7
25~34 岁 Age	37	43.2	2.7	13.5	13.5	21.6	27.0	2.7
35~44 岁 Age	22	68.2	0.0	4.5	9.1	22.7	13.6	0.0
45~54 岁 Age	21	57.1	19.0	9.5	19.0	19.0	4.8	4.8
55~60 岁 Age	8	75.0	12.5	0.0	0.0	50.0	0.0	0.0

2-11 重度消费者的人口分布/ Demographics of the Heavy Consumers

	人数 Number	16-24 岁 Age	25-34 岁 Age	35-44 岁 Age	45-54 岁 Age	55-60 岁 Age
样本 Sample	112	18.8	32.1	19.6	20.5	8.9
男性 Male	43	16.3	32.6	20.9	18.6	11.6
天天喝 daily	6	16.7	66.7	0.0	0.0	16.7
一周 3 次或以上 3 times or over a week	11	9.1	36.4	36.4	9.1	9.1
一周 1～2 次 once or twice a week	26	19.2	23.1	19.2	26.9	11.5
女性 Female	69	20.3	31.9	18.8	21.7	7.2
天天喝 daily	22	9.1	27.3	27.3	18.2	18.2
一周 3 次或以上 3 times or over a week	19	21.1	31.6	21.1	21.1	5.3
一周 1～2 次 once or twice a week	28	28.6	35.7	10.7	25.0	0.0

2-12 不同消费者层的常用品牌/ The Most Frequently Used Brands by Market Segments

2-12-1 时尚流行指标/ Fads Popular Index

	人数 Number	第一品牌及百分比 1st/ percent	第二品牌及百分比 2nd/ percent	第三品牌及百分比 3rd/ percent
样本 Sample	195	**维维 Weiwei(86.2)**	**大地 Landy(2.1)**	**杨协成 Yeo's(1.5)**
平实生活指向 simple living orientation	94	维维 Weiwei(87.2)	晨星岛 Chenxingdao(2.1) 南方 Nanfang(2.1)	大地 Landy(1.1) 正味 Zhengwei (1.1)
时尚流行指向 fashion orientation	101	维维 Weiwei(85.1)	大地 Landy(3.0) 杨协成 Yeo's(3.0)	扬子江 Yangzijiang (1.0) 金味 Jinwei (1.0) 友芝友 Youzhiyou (1.0) 王氏 Wangshi (1.0) 雪峰 Xuefeng (1.0) 黑牛 Heiniu (1.0)

2-12-2 广告态度指标/ Advertising Attitude Index

	人数 Number	第一品牌及百分比 1st/ percent	第二品牌及百分比 2nd/ percent	第三品牌及百分比 3rd/ percent
样本 Sample	195	**维维 Weiwei(86.2)**	**大地 Landy(2.1)**	**杨协成 Yeo's(1.5)**
广告淡漠指向 indifferent orientation	44	维维 Weiwei(88.6)	大地 Landy(2.3) 杨协成 Yeo's(2.3)	
中间层 medium	129	维维 Weiwei(86.8)	晨星岛 Chenxingdao(1.6) 大地 Landy(1.6) 杨协成 Yeo's(1.6) 南方 Nanfang(1.6)	雪峰 Xuefeng(0.8) 黑牛 Heiniu(0.8) 金味 Jinwei(0.8) 王氏 Wangshi(0.8) 友芝友 Youzhiyou(0.8)
信赖广告指向 loyal orientation	22	维维 Weiwei(77.3)	大地 Landy(4.5) 扬子江 Yangzijiang(4.5) 正味 Zhengwei(4.5)	

2-12-3 饮食健康指标/ Foods & Drink Quality Index

	人数 Number	第一品牌及百分比 1st/ percent	第二品牌及百分比 2nd/ percent	第三品牌及百分比 3rd/ percent
样本 Sample	194	**维维 Weiwei(86.1)**	**大地 Landy(2.1)**	**杨协成 Yeo's(1.5)**
饮食"温饱"指向 "basic" orientation	54	维维 Weiwei(87.0)	大地 Landy(5.6)	晨星岛 Chenxingdao(1.9) 正味 Zhengwei(1.9)
中间层 medium	92	维维 Weiwei(89.1)	杨协成 Yeo's(2.2)	晨星岛 Chenxingdao(1.1) 大地 Landy(1.1) 友芝友 Youzhiyou(1.1)
健康营养指向 health & nutrition orientation	48	维维 Weiwei(79.2)	南方 Nanfang(4.2)	杨协成 Yeo's(2.1) 扬子江 Yangzijiang(2.1) 金味 Jinwei(2.1) 王氏 Wangshi(2.1) 雪峰 Xuefeng(2.1) 黑牛 Heiniu(2.1)

2-13 重度消费者的消费者层构成/ The Composition of the Heavy Consumers

2-13-1 时尚流行指标/ Fads Popular Index

	人数 Number	平实生活指向 simple living orientation	时尚流行指向 fashion orientation
样本 Sample	110	45.5	54.5
天天喝 daily	27	33.3	66.7
一周 3 次或以上 3 times or over a week	29	37.9	62.1
一周 1～2 次 once or twice a week	54	55.6	44.4

2-13-2 广告态度指标/ Advertising Attitude Index

	人数 Number	广告淡漠指向 indifferent orientation	中间层 medium	信赖广告指向 loyal orientation
样本 Sample	110	18.2	70.9	10.9
天天喝 daily	27	14.8	63.0	22.2
一周 3 次或以上 3 times or over a week	29	27.6	69.0	3.4
一周 1～2 次 once or twice a week	54	14.8	75.9	9.3

2-13-3 饮食健康指标/ Foods & Drink Quality Index

	人数 Number	饮食"温饱"指向 "basic" orientation	中间层 medium	健康营养指向 health & nutrition orientation
样本 Sample	109	22.9	48.6	28.4
天天喝 daily	27	25.9	40.7	33.3
一周 3 次或以上 3 times or over a week	29	17.2	55.2	27.6
一周 1～2 次 once or twice a week	53	24.5	49.1	26.4

● 西安 / Xi'an

2-1 最近三个月食用频率的比例/ Proportion of the Sample Consuming Powdered Soybean Milk in the Last Three Months

	人数 Number	百分比 Percent
天天喝 daily	46	7.7
一周 3 次或以上 3 times or over a week	52	8.7
一周 1~2 次 once or twice a week	92	15.3
一个月 2～3 次 2 or 3 times a month	44	7.3
一个月 1 次或以下 once a month or below	30	5.0
没喝过 never	337	56.1

n=601

2-2 最常用品牌排名/ Ranking of the Most Frequently Used Brands

排名 Brand Ranking	品牌 Brands	人数 Number	百分比 Percent
1	维维 Weiwei	237	89.8
2	大地 Landy	16	6.1
3	力源 Liyuan	4	1.5

n=264

2-3 样本、男性各年龄层、女性各年龄层的常用品牌/ The Most Frequently Used Brands by the Whole Sample, Age and Gender Groups

	人数 Number	第一品牌及百分比 1st/ percent	第二品牌及百分比 2nd/ percent	第三品牌及百分比 3rd/ percent
样本 Sample	264	**维维 Weiwei(89.8)**	**大地 Landy(6.1)**	**力源 Liyuan(1.5)**
男性 Male	126	**维维 Weiwei(86.5)**	**大地 Landy(7.9)**	**贝因美 Beingmate(0.8)** **力源 Liyuan(0.8)** **秦俑 Qinyong(0.8)** **南方 Nanfang(0.8)** **经塔 Jingta(0.8)**
16~24 岁 Age	31	维维 Weiwei(74.2)	大地 Landy(16.1)	贝因美 Beingmate(3.2) 秦俑 Qinyong(3.2) 南方 Nanfang(3.2)
25~34 岁 Age	27	维维 Weiwei(92.6)	大地 Landy(7.4)	
35~44 岁 Age	37	维维 Weiwei(83.8)	大地 Landy(5.4)	力源 Liyuan(2.7) 经塔 Jingta (2.7)
45~54 岁 Age	23	维维 Weiwei(100.0)		
55~60 岁 Age	8	维维 Weiwei(87.5)	大地 Landy(12.5)	
女性 Female	138	**维维 Weiwei(92.8)**	**大地 Landy(4.3)**	**力源 Liyuan(2.2)**
16~24 岁 Age	25	维维 Weiwei(92.0)	力源 Liyuan(4.0)	
25~34 岁 Age	41	维维 Weiwei(92.7)	大地 Landy(4.9)	力源 Liyuan(2.4)
35~44 岁 Age	39	维维 Weiwei(94.9)	大地 Landy(5.1)	
45~54 岁 Age	25	维维 Weiwei(92.0)	大地 Landy(4.0) 力源 Liyuan(4.0)	
55~60 岁 Age	8	维维 Weiwei(87.5)	大地 Landy(12.5)	

2-4 理想品牌排名/ Ranking of the Ideal Brands

排名 Brand Ranking	品牌 Brands	人数 Number	百分比 Percent
1	维维 Weiwei	481	80.2
2	大地 Landy	40	6.7
3	力源 Liyuan	9	1.5
4	秦俑 Qinyong	3	0.5

n=600

2-5 样本、男性各年龄层、女性各年龄层最近三个月有无购买的比例/ Purchasing in the Last Three Months by the Whole Sample, Age and Gender Groups

	人数 Number	买过 yes	没买过 no
样本 Sample	601	39.8	60.2
男性 Male	302	35.1	64.9
16~24 岁 Age	64	31.3	68.8
25~34 岁 Age	91	30.8	69.2
35~44 岁 Age	77	40.3	59.7
45~54 岁 Age	46	41.3	58.7
55~60 岁 Age	24	33.3	66.7
女性 Female	299	44.5	55.5
16~24 岁 Age	61	34.4	65.6
25~34 岁 Age	90	42.2	57.8
35~44 岁 Age	74	54.1	45.9
45~54 岁 Age	49	53.1	46.9
55~60 岁 Age	25	32.0	68.0

2-6 样本、男性各年龄层、女性各年龄层最近三个月的食用频率/ Frequencies of Consuming Powdered Soybean Milk in the Last Three Months by the Whole Sample, Age and Gender Groups

	人数 Number	天天喝 daily	一周 3 次或以上 3 times or over a week	一周 1~2 次 once or twice a week	一个月 2~3 次 2 or 3 times a month	一个月 1 次或以下 once a month or below	没喝过 never
样本 Sample	601	7.7	8.7	15.3	7.3	5.0	56.1
男性 Male	302	7.9	6.3	16.6	5.6	5.3	58.3
16~24 岁 Age	64	12.5	3.1	18.8	6.3	7.8	51.6
25~34 岁 Age	91	1.1	4.4	15.4	3.3	5.5	70.3
35~44 岁 Age	77	9.1	11.7	18.2	7.8	1.3	51.9
45~54 岁 Age	46	15.2	4.3	13.0	6.5	10.9	50.0
55~60 岁 Age	24	4.2	8.3	16.7	4.2	0.0	66.7
女性 Female	299	7.4	11.0	14.0	9.0	4.7	53.8
16~24 岁 Age	61	9.8	8.2	9.8	6.6	6.6	59.0
25~34 岁 Age	90	7.8	14.4	13.3	6.7	3.3	54.4
35~44 岁 Age	74	4.1	13.5	14.9	10.8	9.5	47.3
45~54 岁 Age	49	6.1	10.2	22.4	12.2	0.0	49.0
55~60 岁 Age	25	12.0	0.0	8.0	12.0	0.0	68.0

2-7 样本、男性各年龄层、女性各年龄层的品牌习惯/ Brand Habit in Consuming Powdered Soybean Milk by the Whole Sample, Age and Gender Groups

	人数 Number	基本固定食用一个牌子 used in only one brand	比较固定地食用两个或三个牌子 used in two or three brands	基本上不太固定牌子 no brand preference
样本 Sample	263	65.4	19.4	15.2
男性 Male	125	57.6	24.8	17.6
16~24 岁 Age	30	63.3	26.7	10.0
25~34 岁 Age	27	37.0	44.4	18.5
35~44 岁 Age	37	67.6	16.2	16.2
45~54 岁 Age	23	69.6	4.3	26.1
55~60 岁 Age	8	25.0	50.0	25.0
女性 Female	138	72.5	14.5	13.0
16~24 岁 Age	25	60.0	16.0	24.0
25~34 岁 Age	41	73.2	14.6	12.2
35~44 岁 Age	39	79.5	12.8	7.7
45~54 岁 Age	25	76.0	16.0	8.0
55~60 岁 Age	8	62.5	12.5	25.0

2-8 选择该类商品的考虑因素/ Ranking of the Considerations in Purchasing

注：本题为多选题，合计百分比超过 100%（Multiple answers）

排名 Ranking	考虑因素 Considerations	人次 Person-time	百分比 Percent
1	口味好 pleasant taste	133	50.6
2	营养成分 nutrition constituent	102	38.8
3	价格适中 reasonable price	83	31.6
4	有名的牌子 famous brand	82	31.2
5	生产日期 date of producing	39	14.8
6	购买方便 easy to buy	36	13.7
7	广告影响 influence of advertising	31	11.8
7	易溶解 high dissolubility	31	11.8
8	只是由于习惯 out of habit	15	5.7
9	朋友推荐 introduction of friends	12	4.6
10	包装吸引人 appealing package	8	3.0
11	有优惠条件 with preferential terms	5	1.9
12	售货员介绍 introduced by the shop assistants	2	0.8
13	其它 others	1	0.4

n=263

2-9 样本、男性各年龄层、女性各年龄层最常食用种类/ Types of the Consumed Powdered Soybean Milk by the Whole Sample, Age and Gender Groups

注：本题为多选题，合计百分比超过 100%（Multiple answers）

	人数 Number	豆粉 soybean powder	绿豆粉 mungbean powder	普通型豆奶粉 normal	低糖型豆奶粉 low-sugar	加味型（如巧克力、花生等）豆奶粉 flavored (eg.chocolate)	保健型（如枸杞、蔬菜等）豆奶粉 healthcaring (eg. vegetable, wol)	绿豆奶粉 mungbean milk powder	其它 others
样本 Sample	263	21.3	3.4	46.8	14.8	14.1	8.0	0.4	0.0
男性 Male	125	19.2	3.2	48.8	14.4	13.6	11.2	0.0	0.0
16~24 岁 Age	30	13.3	6.7	56.7	6.7	16.7	6.7	0.0	0.0
25~34 岁 Age	27	18.5	7.4	29.6	14.8	25.9	14.8	0.0	0.0
35~44 岁 Age	37	21.6	0.0	62.2	10.8	8.1	13.5	0.0	0.0
45~54 岁 Age	23	21.7	0.0	43.5	26.1	4.3	8.7	0.0	0.0
55~60 岁 Age	8	25.0	0.0	37.5	25.0	12.5	12.5	0.0	0.0
女性 Female	138	23.2	3.6	44.9	15.2	14.5	5.1	0.7	0.0
16~24 岁 Age	25	24.0	4.0	44.0	4.0	16.0	8.0	0.0	0.0
25~34 岁 Age	41	14.6	4.9	53.7	17.1	9.8	4.9	2.4	0.0
35~44 岁 Age	39	30.8	2.6	43.6	12.8	17.9	5.1	0.0	0.0
45~54 岁 Age	25	28.0	4.0	40.0	16.0	12.0	4.0	0.0	0.0
55~60 岁 Age	8	12.5	0.0	25.0	50.0	25.0	0.0	0.0	0.0

2-10 样本、男性各年龄层、女性各年龄层最常食用的场合/ Settings of Consumption by the Whole Sample, Age and Gender Groups

注：本题为多选题，合计百分比超过 100%（Multiple answers）

	人数 Number	早餐时 breakfast	正餐（午、晚餐）时 dinner	餐后热饮 after dinner	宵夜时 evening snack	睡觉前 before sleeping	工作休息时 during work break	其它 others
样本 Sample	263	77.9	2.7	7.2	7.2	15.2	7.2	1.1
男性 Male	125	77.6	2.4	8.8	9.6	14.4	5.6	2.4
16~24 岁 Age	30	73.3	6.7	10.0	6.7	10.0	3.3	0.0
25~34 岁 Age	27	81.5	0.0	11.1	7.4	3.7	3.7	0.0
35~44 岁 Age	37	83.8	2.7	8.1	10.8	18.9	8.1	8.1
45~54 岁 Age	23	65.2	0.0	8.7	13.0	26.1	8.7	0.0
55~60 岁 Age	8	87.5	0.0	0.0	12.5	12.5	0.0	0.0
女性 Female	138	78.3	2.9	5.8	5.1	15.9	8.7	0.0
16~24 岁 Age	25	80.0	4.0	8.0	4.0	12.0	8.0	0.0
25~34 岁 Age	41	73.2	2.4	7.3	4.9	12.2	7.3	0.0
35~44 岁 Age	39	79.5	2.6	2.6	7.7	25.6	7.7	0.0
45~54 岁 Age	25	84.0	0.0	8.0	0.0	16.0	12.0	0.0
55~60 岁 Age	8	75.0	12.5	0.0	12.5	0.0	12.5	0.0

2-11 重度消费者的人口分布/ Demographics of the Heavy Consumers

	人数 Number	16-24 岁 Age	25-34 岁 Age	35-44 岁 Age	45-54 岁 Age	55-60 岁 Age
样本 Sample	190	20.5	26.8	28.4	17.9	6.3
男性 Male	93	23.7	20.4	32.3	16.1	7.5
天天喝 daily	24	33.3	4.2	29.2	29.2	4.2
一周 3 次或以上 3 times or over a week	19	10.5	21.1	47.4	10.5	10.5
一周 1～2 次 once or twice a week	50	24.0	28.0	28.0	12.0	8.0
女性 Female	97	17.5	33.0	24.7	19.6	5.2
天天喝 daily	22	27.3	31.8	13.6	13.6	13.6
一周 3 次或以上 3 times or over a week	33	15.2	39.4	30.3	15.2	0.0
一周 1～2 次 once or twice a week	42	14.3	28.6	26.2	26.2	4.8

2-12 不同消费者层的常用品牌/ The Most Frequently Used Brands by Market Segments

2-12-1 时尚流行指标/ Fads Popular Index

	人数 Number	第一品牌及百分比 1st/ percent	第二品牌及百分比 2nd/ percent	第三品牌及百分比 3rd/ percent
样本 Sample	263	**维维 Weiwei(89.7)**	**大地 Landy(6.1)**	**力源 Liyuan(1.5)**
平实生活指向 simple living orientation	149	维维 Weiwei(88.6)	大地 Landy(6.7)	力源 Liyuan(2.0)
时尚流行指向 fashion orientation	114	维维 Weiwei(91.2)	大地 Landy(5.3)	力源 Liyuan(0.9) 秦俑 Qinyong(0.9) 经塔 Jingta(0.9)

2-12-2 广告态度指标/ Advertising Attitude Index

	人数 Number	第一品牌及百分比 1st/ percent	第二品牌及百分比 2nd/ percent	第三品牌及百分比 3rd/ percent
样本 Sample	262	**维维 Weiwei(89.7)**	**大地 Landy(6.1)**	**力源 Liyuan(1.5)**
广告淡漠指向 indifferent orientation	70	维维 Weiwei(90.0)	大地 Landy(4.3) 力源 Liyuan(4.3)	
中间层 medium	151	维维 Weiwei(89.4)	大地 Landy(7.3)	贝因美 Beingmate(0.7) 力源 Liyuan(0.7) 南方 Nanfang(0.7)
信赖广告指向 loyal orientation	41	维维 Weiwei(90.2)	大地 Landy(4.9)	秦俑 Qinyong(2.4) 经塔 Jingta(2.4)

2-12-3 饮食健康指标/ Foods & Drink Quality Index

	人数 Number	第一品牌及百分比 1st/ percent	第二品牌及百分比 2nd/ percent	第三品牌及百分比 3rd/ percent
样本 Sample	264	**维维 Weiwei(89.8)**	**大地 Landy(6.1)**	**力源 Liyuan(1.5)**
饮食"温饱"指向 "basic" orientation	86	维维 Weiwei(88.4)	大地 Landy(4.7)	力源 Liyuan(2.3)
中间层 medium	123	维维 Weiwei(91.1)	大地 Landy(6.5)	贝因美 Beingmate(0.8) 力源 Liyuan(0.8) 秦俑 Qinyong(0.8)
健康营养指向 health & nutrition orientation	55	维维 Weiwei(89.1)	大地 Landy(7.3)	力源 Liyuan(1.8)

2-13 重度消费者的消费者层构成/ The Composition of the Heavy Consumers

2-13-1 时尚流行指标/ Fads Popular Index

	人数 Number	平实生活指向 simple living orientation	时尚流行指向 fashion orientation
样本 Sample	190	54.7	45.3
天天喝 daily	46	52.2	47.8
一周 3 次或以上 3 times or over a week	52	57.7	42.3
一周 1～2 次 once or twice a week	92	54.3	45.7

2-13-2 广告态度指标/ Advertising Attitude Index

	人数 Number	广告淡漠指向 indifferent orientation	中间层 medium	信赖广告指向 loyal orientation
样本 Sample	189	27.5	56.1	16.4
天天喝 daily	46	26.1	56.5	17.4
一周 3 次或以上 3 times or over a week	52	28.8	53.8	17.3
一周 1～2 次 once or twice a week	91	27.5	57.1	15.4

2-13-3 饮食健康指标/ Foods & Drink Quality Index

	人数 Number	饮食"温饱"指向 "basic" orientation	中间层 medium	健康营养指向 health & nutrition orientation
样本 Sample	190	33.2	47.9	18.9
天天喝 daily	46	32.6	32.6	34.8
一周 3 次或以上 3 times or over a week	52	34.6	46.2	19.2
一周 1～2 次 once or twice a week	92	32.6	56.5	10.9

● 沈阳 / Shenyang

2-1 最近三个月食用频率的比例/ Proportion of the Sample Consuming Powdered Soybean Milk in the Last Three Months

	人数 Number	百分比 Percent
天天喝 daily	26	4.3
一周 3 次或以上 3 times or over a week	31	5.2
一周 1~2 次 once or twice a week	64	10.6
一个月 2~3 次 2 or 3 times a month	33	5.5
一个月 1 次或以下 once a month or below	39	6.5
没喝过 never	408	67.9

n=601

2-2 最常用品牌排名/ Ranking of the Most Frequently Used Brands

排名 Brand Ranking	品牌 Brands	人数 Number	百分比 Percent
1	维维 Weiwei	163	84.9
2	大地 Landy	11	5.7
3	青援 Qingyuan	4	2.1
4	雀巢 Nestle	2	1.0
4	宝亨 Baoheng	2	1.0

n=192

2-3 样本、男性各年龄层、女性各年龄层的常用品牌/ The Most Frequently Used Brands by the Whole Sample, Age and Gender Groups

	人数 Number	第一品牌及百分比 1st/ percent	第二品牌及百分比 2nd/ percent	第三品牌及百分比 3rd/ percent
样本 Sample	192	**维维 Weiwei(84.9)**	**大地 Landy(5.7)**	**青援 Qingyuan(2.1)**
男性 Male	81	**维维 Weiwei(84.0)**	**大地 Landy(9.9)**	**宝亨 Baoheng(1.2)**
16~24 岁 Age	19	维维 Weiwei(84.2)	大地 Landy(10.5)	
25~34 岁 Age	24	维维 Weiwei(87.5)	大地 Landy(8.3)	宝亨 Baoheng(4.2)
35~44 岁 Age	18	维维 Weiwei(77.8)	大地 Landy(22.2)	
45~54 岁 Age	14	维维 Weiwei(85.7)		
55~60 岁 Age	6	维维 Weiwei(83.3)		
女性 Female	111	**维维 Weiwei(85.6)**	**青援 Qingyuan(3.6)**	**大地 Landy(2.7)**
16~24 岁 Age	30	维维 Weiwei(86.7)	大地 Landy(3.3) 雀巢 Nestle(3.3) 青援 Qingyuan(3.3)	
25~34 岁 Age	34	维维 Weiwei(85.3)	力源 Liyuan(2.9) 雀巢 Nestle(2.9) 青援 Qingyuan(2.9) 七星 Qixing(2.9)	
35~44 岁 Age	21	维维 Weiwei(90.5)	大地 Landy(4.8) 汾煌 Fenhuang(4.8)	
45~54 岁 Age	18	维维 Weiwei(83.3)	大地 Landy(5.6) 宝亨 Baohuang(5.6) 神奇 Shenqi(5.6)	
55~60 岁 Age	8	维维 Weiwei(75.0)	青援 Qingyuan(25.0)	

2-4 理想品牌排名/ Ranking of the Ideal Brands

排名 Brand Ranking	品牌 Brands	人数 Number	百分比 Percent
1	维维 Weiwei	462	77.0
2	大地 Landy	26	4.3
3	宝亨 Baoheng	5	0.8
3	汾煌 Fenhuang	5	0.8
4	青援 Qingyuan	4	0.7
5	力源 Liyuan	3	0.5

n=600

2-5 样本、男性各年龄层、女性各年龄层最近三个月有无购买的比例/ Purchasing in the Last Three Months by the Whole Sample, Age and Gender Groups

	人数 Number	买过 yes	没买过 no
样本 Sample	601	29.0	71.0
男性 Male	299	22.4	77.6
16~24 岁 Age	64	14.1	85.9
25~34 岁 Age	89	28.1	71.9
35~44 岁 Age	76	18.4	81.6
45~54 岁 Age	46	28.3	71.7
55~60 岁 Age	24	25.0	75.0
女性 Female	302	35.4	64.6
16~24 岁 Age	64	39.1	60.9
25~34 岁 Age	90	42.2	57.8
35~44 岁 Age	76	26.3	73.7
45~54 岁 Age	48	35.4	64.6
55~60 岁 Age	24	29.2	70.8

2-6 样本、男性各年龄层、女性各年龄层最近三个月的食用频率/ Frequencies of Consuming Powdered Soybean Milk in the Last Three Months by the Whole Sample, Age and Gender Groups

	人数 Number	天天喝 daily	一周 3 次或以上 3 times or over a week	一周 1~2 次 once or twice a week	一个月 2~3 次 2 or 3 times a month	一个月 1 次或以下 once a month or below	没喝过 never
样本 Sample	601	4.3	5.2	10.6	5.5	6.5	67.9
男性 Male	299	5.0	5.0	6.4	4.7	6.4	72.6
16~24 岁 Age	64	1.6	7.8	6.3	3.1	10.9	70.3
25~34 岁 Age	89	5.6	4.5	4.5	6.7	5.6	73.0
35~44 岁 Age	76	3.9	1.3	9.2	3.9	6.6	75.0
45~54 岁 Age	46	8.7	4.3	8.7	4.3	4.3	69.6
55~60 岁 Age	24	8.3	12.5	0.0	4.2	0.0	75.0
女性 Female	302	3.6	5.3	14.9	6.3	6.6	63.2
16~24 岁 Age	64	1.6	9.4	20.3	6.3	9.4	53.1
25~34 岁 Age	90	2.2	2.2	16.7	6.7	10.0	62.2
35~44 岁 Age	76	5.3	3.9	7.9	7.9	2.6	72.4
45~54 岁 Age	48	4.2	4.2	18.8	6.3	4.2	62.5
55~60 岁 Age	24	8.3	12.5	8.3	0.0	4.2	66.7

2-7 样本、男性各年龄层、女性各年龄层的品牌习惯/ Brand Habit in Consuming Powdered Soybean Milk by the Whole Sample, Age and Gender Groups

	人数 Number	基本固定食用一个牌子 used in only one brand	比较固定地食用两个或三个牌子 used in two or three brands	基本上不太固定牌子 no brand preference
样本 Sample	193	**57.5**	**17.6**	**24.9**
男性 Male	82	**54.9**	**17.1**	**28.0**
16~24 岁 Age	19	42.1	15.8	42.1
25~34 岁 Age	24	58.3	16.7	25.0
35~44 岁 Age	19	68.4	10.5	21.1
45~54 岁 Age	14	42.9	28.6	28.6
55~60 岁 Age	6	66.7	16.7	16.7
女性 Female	111	**59.5**	**18.0**	**22.5**
16~24 岁 Age	30	56.7	20.0	23.3
25~34 岁 Age	34	70.6	11.8	17.6
35~44 岁 Age	21	57.1	23.8	19.0
45~54 岁 Age	18	44.4	22.2	33.3
55~60 岁 Age	8	62.5	12.5	25.0

2-8 选择该类商品的考虑因素/ Ranking of the Considerations in Purchasing

注：本题为多选题，合计百分比超过 100%（Multiple answers）

排名 Ranking	考虑因素 Considerations	人次 Person-time	百分比 Percent
1	口味好 pleasant taste	101	52.3
2	营养成分 nutrition constituent	85	44.0
3	价格适中 reasonable price	67	34.7
4	有名的牌子 famous brand	49	25.4
5	生产日期 date of producing	35	18.1
6	购买方便 easy to buy	30	15.5
7	广告影响 influence of advertising	23	11.9
7	易溶解 high dissolubility	23	11.9
8	朋友推荐 introduction of friends	15	7.8
9	只是由于习惯 out of habit	10	5.2
10	包装吸引人 appealing package	7	3.6
11	有优惠条件 with preferential terms	5	2.6
12	售货员介绍 introduced by the shop assistants	4	2.1
13	其它 others	2	1.0

n=193

2-9 样本、男性各年龄层、女性各年龄层最常食用种类/ Types of the Consumed Powdered Soybean Milk by the Whole Sample, Age and Gender Groups

注：本题为多选题，合计百分比超过 100%（Multiple answers）

	人数 Number	豆粉 soybean powder	绿豆粉 mungbean powder	普通型豆奶粉 normal	低糖型豆奶粉 low-sugar	加味型(如巧克力、花生等)豆奶粉 flavored (eg.chocolate)	保健型（如枸杞、蔬菜等）豆奶粉 health caring(eg. vegetable, wol)	绿豆奶粉 mungbean milk powder	其它 others
样本 Sample	192	**34.4**	**4.7**	**34.9**	**10.4**	**17.7**	**8.3**	**1.6**	**0.5**
男性 Male	82	**34.1**	**6.1**	**31.7**	**12.2**	**14.6**	**13.4**	**1.2**	**1.2**
16~24 岁 Age	19	36.8	0.0	26.3	15.8	15.8	21.1	0.0	0.0
25~34 岁 Age	24	33.3	8.3	29.2	12.5	20.8	4.2	0.0	0.0
35~44 岁 Age	19	15.8	10.5	42.1	10.5	15.8	10.5	5.3	5.3
45~54 岁 Age	14	35.7	7.1	35.7	7.1	7.1	28.6	0.0	0.0
55~60 岁 Age	6	83.3	0.0	16.7	16.7	0.0	0.0	0.0	0.0
女性 Female	110	**34.5**	**3.6**	**37.3**	**9.1**	**20.0**	**4.5**	**1.8**	**0.0**
16~24 岁 Age	30	43.3	3.3	40.0	0.0	20.0	3.3	0.0	0.0
25~34 岁 Age	34	35.3	5.9	35.3	2.9	26.5	5.9	0.0	0.0
35~44 岁 Age	20	30.0	0.0	35.0	15.0	15.0	10.0	10.0	0.0
45~54 岁 Age	18	22.2	5.6	38.9	27.8	16.7	0.0	0.0	0.0
55~60 岁 Age	8	37.5	0.0	37.5	12.5	12.5	0.0	0.0	0.0

2-10 样本、男性各年龄层、女性各年龄层最常食用的场合/ Settings of Consumption by the Whole Sample, Age and Gender Groups

注：本题为多选题，合计百分比超过 100%（Multiple answers）

	人数 Number	早餐时 breakfast	正餐（午、晚餐）时 dinner	餐后热饮 after dinner	宵夜时 evening snack	睡觉前 before sleeping	工作休息时 during work break	其它 others
样本 Sample	193	62.7	6.7	9.3	9.3	25.4	12.4	1.6
男性 Male	82	72.0	6.1	4.9	9.8	28.0	8.5	1.2
16~24 岁 Age	19	68.4	5.3	5.3	10.5	21.1	15.8	0.0
25~34 岁 Age	24	54.2	16.7	8.3	8.3	20.8	8.3	4.2
35~44 岁 Age	19	78.9	0.0	0.0	15.8	26.3	10.5	0.0
45~54 岁 Age	14	92.9	0.0	0.0	7.1	50.0	0.0	0.0
55~60 岁 Age	6	83.3	0.0	16.7	0.0	33.3	0.0	0.0
女性 Female	111	55.9	7.2	12.6	9.0	23.4	15.3	1.8
16~24 岁 Age	30	43.3	10.0	20.0	13.3	30.0	23.3	0.0
25~34 岁 Age	34	61.8	0.0	8.8	2.9	20.6	11.8	2.9
35~44 岁 Age	21	52.4	14.3	19.0	19.0	9.5	23.8	0.0
45~54 岁 Age	18	66.7	11.1	0.0	5.6	33.3	0.0	5.6
55~60 岁 Age	8	62.5	0.0	12.5	0.0	25.0	12.5	0.0

2-11 重度消费者的人口分布/ Demographics of the Heavy Consumers

	人数 Number	16-24 岁 Age	25-34 岁 Age	35-44 岁 Age	45-54 岁 Age	55-60 岁 Age
样本 Sample	121	24.8	26.4	19.8	19.0	9.9
男性 Male	49	20.4	26.5	22.4	20.4	10.2
天天喝 daily	15	6.7	33.3	20.0	26.7	13.3
一周 3 次或以上 3 times or over a week	15	33.3	26.7	6.7	13.3	20.0
一周 1~2 次 once or twice a week	19	21.1	21.1	36.8	21.1	0.0
女性 Female	72	27.8	26.4	18.1	18.1	9.7
天天喝 daily	11	9.1	18.2	36.4	18.2	18.2
一周 3 次或以上 3 times or over a week	16	37.5	12.5	18.3	12.5	18.8
一周 1~2 次 once or twice a week	45	28.9	33.3	13.3	20.0	4.4

2-12 不同消费者层的常用品牌/ The Most Frequently Used Brands by Market Segments

2-12-1 时尚流行指标/ Fads Popular Index

	人数 Number	第一品牌及百分比 1st/ percent	第二品牌及百分比 2nd/ percent	第三品牌及百分比 3rd/ percent
样本 Sample	192	**维维 Weiwei(84.9)**	**大地 Landy(5.7)**	**青援 Qingyuan(2.1)**
平实生活指向 simple living orientation	83	维维 Weiwei(83.1)	大地 Landy(7.2)	青援 Qingyuan(3.6)
时尚流行指向 fashion orientation	109	维维 Weiwei(86.2)	大地 Landy(4.6)	雀巢 Nestle(1.8)

2-12-2 广告态度指标/ Advertising Attitude Index

	人数 Number	第一品牌及百分比 1st/ percent	第二品牌及百分比 2nd/ percent	第三品牌及百分比 3rd/ percent
样本 Sample	192	**维维 Weiwei(84.9)**	**大地 Landy(5.7)**	**青援 Qingyuan(2.1)**
广告淡漠指向 indifferent orientation	55	维维 Weiwei(85.5)	大地 Landy(5.5)	汾煌 Fenhuang(1.8) 青援 Qingyuan(1.8) 宝亨 Baoheng(1.8) 神奇 Shenqi(1.8) 七星 Qixing(1.8)
中间层 medium	110	维维 Weiwei(85.5)	大地 Landy(5.5)	青援 Qingyuan(1.8)
信赖广告指向 loyal orientation	27	维维 Weiwei(81.5)	大地 Landy(7.4)	雀巢 Nestle(3.7) 青援 Qingyuan(3.7)

2-12-3 饮食健康指标/ Foods & Drink Quality Index

	人数 Number	第一品牌及百分比 1st/ percent	第二品牌及百分比 2nd/ percent	第三品牌及百分比 3rd/ percent
样本 Sample	192	维维 Weiwei(84.9)	大地 Landy(5.7)	青援 Qingyuan(2.1)
饮食"温饱"指向 "basic" orientation	47	维维 Weiwei(85.1)	大地 Landy(4.3)	力源 Liyuan(2.1) 宝亨 Baoheng(2.1) 神奇 Shenqi(2.1)
中间层 medium	99	维维 Weiwei(85.9)	大地 Landy(8.1)	雀巢 Nestle(1.0) 汾煌 Fenhuang(1.0) 青援 Qinyuan(1.0) 宝亨 Baoheng(1.0)
健康营养指向 health & nutrition orientation	46	维维 Weiwei(82.6)	青援(6.5)	大地 Landy(2.2) 雀巢 Nestle(2.2) 七星 Qixing(2.2)

2-13 重度消费者的消费者层构成/ The Composition of the Heavy Consumers

2-13-1 时尚流行指标/ Fads Popular Index

	人数 Number	平实生活指向 simple living orientation	时尚流行指向 fashion orientation
样本 Sample	121	42.1	57.9
天天喝 daily	26	53.8	46.2
一周 3 次或以上 3 times or over a week	31	51.6	48.4
一周 1～2 次 once or twice a week	64	32.8	67.2

2-13-2 广告态度指标/ Advertising Attitude Index

	人数 Number	广告淡漠指向 indifferent orientation	中间层 medium	信赖广告指向 loyal orientation
样本 Sample	121	25.6	57.0	17.4
天天喝 daily	26	34.6	42.3	23.1
一周 3 次或以上 3 times or over a week	31	22.6	61.3	16.1
一周 1～2 次 once or twice a week	64	23.4	60.9	15.6

2-13-3 饮食健康指标/ Foods & Drink Quality Index

	人数 Number	饮食"温饱"指向 "basic" orientation	中间层 medium	健康营养指向 health & nutrition orientation
样本 Sample	121	23.1	49.6	27.3
天天喝 daily	26	26.9	30.8	42.3
一周 3 次或以上 3 times or over a week	31	25.8	54.8	19.4
一周 1～2 次 once or twice a week	64	20.3	54.7	25.0

3.包装牛奶 / Packaged Milk

● 北京 / Beijing

3-1 最近三个月食用频率的比例/ Proportion of the Sample Consuming Packaged Milk in the Last Three Months

	人数 Number	百分比 Percent
天天喝 daily	122	12.1
一周 3 次或以上 3 times or over a week	100	10.0
一周 1~2 次 once or twice a week	168	16.7
一个月 2~3 次 2 or 3 times a month	116	11.5
一个月 1 次或以下 once a month or below	67	6.7
没喝过 never	432	43.0

n=1005

3-2 最常用品牌排名/ Ranking of the Most Frequently Used Brands

排名 Brand Ranking	品牌 Brands	人数 Number	百分比 Percent
1	三元 Sanyuan	397	70.3
2	光明 Bright	50	8.8
3	卡夫 Kraft	21	3.7
4	帕玛拉特 Parmalat	18	3.2
5	伊利 Yili	17	3.0
6	乐百氏 Robust	11	1.9

n=565

3-3 样本、男性各年龄层、女性各年龄层的常用品牌/ The Most Frequently Used Brands by the Whole Sample, Age and Gender Groups

	人数 Number	第一品牌及百分比 1st/ percent	第二品牌及百分比 2nd/ percent	第三品牌及百分比 3rd/ percent	第四品牌及百分比 4th/ percent
样本 Sample	565	**三元 Sanyuan(70.3)**	**光明 Bright(8.8)**	**卡夫 Kraft(3.7)**	**帕玛拉特 Parmalat(3.2)**
男性 Male	258	**三元 Sanyuan(74.0)**	**光明 Bright(5.4)**	**帕玛拉特 Parmalat(2.7)**	**卡夫 Kraft(2.3)**
16~24 岁 Age	64	三元 Sanyuan(67.2)	光明 Bright(7.8)	帕玛拉特 Parmalat(6.3)	卡夫 Kraft(4.7)
25~34 岁 Age	83	三元 Sanyuan(77.1)	光明 Bright(6.0)	卡夫 Kraft(3.6)	乐百氏 Robust(2.4)
35~44 岁 Age	68	三元 Sanyuan(75.0)	伊利 Yili(4.4)	光明 Bright(2.9) 帕玛拉特 Parmalat(2.9)	康必奶 Campina(1.5) 乐百氏 Robust(1.5) 三鹿 Sanlu(1.5)
45~54 岁 Age	26	三元 Sanyuan(84.6)	光明 Bright(3.8) 乐百氏 Robust(3.8) 元元 Yuanyuan(3.8)		
55~60 岁 Age	17	三元 Sanyuan(64.7)	光明 Bright(5.9) 伊利 Yili(5.9) 雀巢 Nestle(5.9) 金牛 Jinniu(5.9) 大明 Daming(5.9)		
女性 Female	307	**三元 Sanyuan(67.1)**	**光明 Bright(11.7)**	**卡夫 Kraft(4.9)**	**伊利 Yili(3.9)**
16~24 岁 Age	82	三元 Sanyuan(68.3)	光明 Bright(8.5)	卡夫 Kraft(6.1)	帕玛拉特 Parmalat(4.9)
25~34 岁 Age	107	三元 Sanyuan(60.7)	光明 Bright(15.9)	卡夫 Kraft(7.5)	帕玛拉特 Parmalat(5.6)
35~44 岁 Age	66	三元 Sanyuan(69.7)	光明 Bright(12.1)	伊利 Yili(7.6)	帕玛拉特 Parmalat(1.5) 子母奶 Dutch Lady(1.5) 雀巢 Nestle(1.5) 荣氏 Rong(1.5) 红星 Hongxing(1.5)
45~54 岁 Age	38	三元 Sanyuan(76.3)	光明 Bright(5.3) 卡夫 Kraft(5.3)	乐百氏 Robust(2.6) 伊利 Yili(2.6) 雀巢 Nestle(2.6) 完达山 Wandashan(2.6)	
55~60 岁 Age	14	三元 Sanyuan(71.4)	光明 Bright(14.3) 伊利 Yili(14.3)		

3-4 理想品牌排名/ Ranking of the Ideal Brands

排名 Brand Ranking	品牌 Brands	人数 Number	百分比 Percent
1	三元 Sanyuan	592	58.5
2	光明 Bright	59	5.8
3	伊利 Yili	37	3.7
4	卡夫 Kraft	31	3.1
5	帕玛拉特 Parmalat	27	2.7
6	乐百氏 Robust	11	1.1
7	雀巢 Nestle	5	0.5

n=1012

3-5 样本、男性各年龄层、女性各年龄层最近三个月有无购买的比例/ Purchasing in the Last Three Months by the Whole Sample, Age and Gender Groups

	人数 Number	买过 yes	没买过 no
样本 Sample	1010	54.8	45.2
男性 Male	503	48.1	51.9
16~24 岁 Age	104	54.8	45.2
25~34 岁 Age	151	52.3	47.7
35~44 岁 Age	131	51.1	48.9
45~54 岁 Age	77	32.5	67.5
55~60 岁 Age	40	35.0	65.0
女性 Female	507	61.3	38.7
16~24 岁 Age	108	74.1	25.9
25~34 岁 Age	150	70.7	29.3
35~44 岁 Age	123	56.9	43.1
45~54 岁 Age	84	47.6	52.4
55~60 岁 Age	42	35.7	64.3

3-6 样本、男性各年龄层、女性各年龄层最近三个月的食用频率/ Frequencies of Consuming Packaged Milk in the Last Three Months by the Whole Sample, Age and Gender Groups

	人数 Number	天天喝 daily	一周 3 次或以上 3 times or over a week	一周 1~2 次 once or twice a week	一个月 2~3 次 2 or 3 times a month	一个月 1 次或以下 once a month or below	没喝过 never
样本 Sample	1005	12.1	10.0	16.7	11.5	6.7	43.0
男性 Male	499	9.8	8.6	17.0	11.0	6.0	47.5
16~24 岁 Age	104	9.6	8.7	18.3	16.3	9.6	37.5
25~34 岁 Age	150	7.3	12.0	17.3	13.3	6.0	44.0
35~44 岁 Age	130	15.4	5.4	21.5	6.9	3.8	46.9
45~54 岁 Age	75	6.7	9.3	9.3	6.7	4.0	64.0
55~60 岁 Age	40	7.5	5.0	12.5	10.0	7.5	57.5
女性 Female	506	14.4	11.3	16.4	12.1	7.3	38.5
16~24 岁 Age	107	11.2	10.3	24.3	16.8	15.0	22.4
25~34 岁 Age	150	15.3	16.0	18.7	15.3	6.7	28.0
35~44 岁 Age	123	14.6	8.9	14.6	11.4	5.7	44.7
45~54 岁 Age	84	15.5	8.3	10.7	6.0	4.8	54.8
55~60 岁 Age	42	16.7	9.5	4.8	2.4	0.0	66.7

3-7 样本、男性各年龄层、女性各年龄层的品牌习惯/ Brand Habit in Consuming Packaged Milk by the Whole Sample, Age and Gender Groups

	人数 Number	基本固定食用一个牌子 used in only one brand	比较固定地食用两个或三个牌子 used in two or three brands	基本上不太固定牌子 no brand preference
样本 Sample	568	54.6	28.0	17.4
男性 Male	260	57.3	23.1	19.6
16~24 岁 Age	64	46.9	29.7	23.4
25~34 岁 Age	84	57.1	25.0	17.9
35~44 岁 Age	69	60.9	18.8	20.3
45~54 岁 Age	27	63.0	22.2	14.8
55~60 岁 Age	16	75.0	6.3	18.8
女性 Female	308	52.3	32.1	15.6
16~24 岁 Age	83	38.6	39.8	21.7
25~34 岁 Age	107	57.9	29.9	12.1
35~44 岁 Age	66	53.0	28.8	18.2
45~54 岁 Age	38	68.4	23.7	7.9
55~60 岁 Age	14	42.9	42.9	14.3

3-8 选择该类商品的考虑因素/ Ranking of the Considerations in Purchasing

注：本题为多选题，合计百分比超过 100%（Multiple answers）

排名 Ranking	考虑因素 Considerations	人次 Person-time	百分比 Percent
1	口味好 pleasant taste	247	43.6
2	有名的牌子 famous brand	232	41.0
3	价格适中 reasonable price	201	35.5
4	营养成分 nutrition constituent	166	29.3
5	生产日期 date of producing	134	23.7
6	购买方便 easy to buy	130	23.0
7	广告影响 influence of advertising	54	9.5
8	只是由于习惯 out of habit	34	6.0
9	有优惠条件 with preferential terms	26	4.6
10	朋友推荐 introduction of friends	21	3.7
11	包装吸引人 appealing package	17	3.0
12	其它 others	9	1.6
13	售货员介绍 introduced by the shop assistants	3	0.5

n=566

3-9 样本、男性各年龄层、女性各年龄层最常食用的种类/ Types of the Consumed Packaged Milk by the Whole Sample, Age and Gender Groups

	人数 Number	全脂 whole milk	低脂 low-fat	脱脂 skimmed	花色奶（巧克力味、草莓味等）milk varieties (chocolate flavor.Strawberry flavors etc.)	强化奶 enriched milk	加矿物质（含钙、铁等）with minerals (containing calcium.Iron etc.)	其它 others
样本 Sample	545	30.6	12.7	19.3	16.1	1.1	18.2	2.0
男性 Male	252	32.1	13.1	18.7	15.1	2.4	16.3	2.4
16~24 岁 Age	62	41.9	9.7	17.7	12.9	1.6	14.5	1.6
25~34 岁 Age	81	22.2	16.0	19.8	22.2	2.5	12.3	4.9
35~44 岁 Age	67	29.9	14.9	19.4	14.9	4.5	16.4	0.0
45~54 岁 Age	26	30.8	7.7	19.2	7.7	0.0	30.8	3.8
55~60 岁 Age	16	56.3	12.5	12.5	0.0	0.0	18.8	0.0
女性 Female	293	29.4	12.3	19.8	17.1	0.0	19.8	1.7
16~24 岁 Age	79	26.6	8.9	21.5	30.4	0.0	12.7	0.0
25~34 岁 Age	99	30.3	10.1	18.2	14.1	0.0	25.3	2.0
35~44 岁 Age	63	30.2	14.3	25.4	9.5	0.0	19.0	1.6
45~54 岁 Age	38	34.2	18.4	15.8	13.2	0.0	18.4	0.0
55~60 岁 Age	14	21.4	21.4	7.1	7.1	0.0	28.6	14.3

3-10 样本、男性各年龄层、女性各年龄层最常食用的包装形式/ Types of Package of the Consumed Packaged Milk by the Whole Sample, Age and Gender Groups

	人数 Number	方盒装/利乐砖 plastic-bag milk	房屋状纸盒 house-shaped box	粽子状纸盒 V-shaped box	塑料瓶 plastic bottle	易拉罐 tin	其他 others
样本 Sample	556	48.2	31.3	0.9	12.9	0.7	5.9
男性 Male	253	49.4	29.6	1.2	13.0	0.0	6.7
16~24 岁 Age	63	44.4	38.1	3.2	11.1	0.0	3.2
25~34 岁 Age	81	55.6	32.1	0.0	7.4	0.0	4.9
35~44 岁 Age	67	49.3	22.4	1.5	19.4	0.0	7.5
45~54 岁 Age	27	44.4	22.2	0.0	14.8	0.0	18.5
55~60 岁 Age	15	46.7	26.7	0.0	20.0	0.0	6.7
女性 Female	303	47.2	32.7	0.7	12.9	1.3	5.3
16~24 岁 Age	81	43.2	42.0	1.2	11.1	1.2	1.2
25~34 岁 Age	106	57.5	26.4	0.0	9.4	0.9	5.7
35~44 岁 Age	65	36.9	38.5	0.0	18.5	3.1	3.1
45~54 岁 Age	37	48.6	24.3	2.7	18.9	0.0	5.4
55~60 岁 Age	14	35.7	21.4	0.0	7.1	0.0	35.7

3-11 样本、男性各年龄层、女性各年龄层最常饮用场合/ Settings of Consumption by the Whole Sample, Age and Gender Groups

注：本题为多选题，合计百分比超过 100%（Multiple answers）

	人数 Number	早餐时 breakfast	正餐（午、晚餐）时 dinner	口渴时 when thirsty	宵夜时 evening snack	睡觉前 before sleeping	工作休息时 during work break	外出/旅游时 outing/traveling	运动后 after athletics	其它 others
样本 Sample	569	58.2	4.0	18.8	6.7	27.2	10.2	9.1	1.9	2.3
男性 Male	261	56.7	3.4	17.2	8.0	26.8	7.7	8.8	3.8	1.9
16~24 岁 Age	65	46.2	0.0	26.2	6.2	23.1	12.3	10.8	7.7	1.5
25~34 岁 Age	84	50.0	3.6	16.7	9.5	26.2	10.7	8.3	3.6	1.2
35~44 岁 Age	69	68.1	2.9	13.0	10.1	29.0	4.3	11.6	1.4	2.9
45~54 岁 Age	27	59.3	7.4	11.1	7.4	29.6	0.0	3.7	3.7	3.7
55~60 岁 Age	16	81.3	12.5	12.5	0.0	31.3	0.0	0.0	0.0	0.0
女性 Female	308	59.4	4.5	20.1	5.5	27.6	12.3	9.4	0.3	2.6
16~24 岁 Age	83	51.8	4.8	31.3	4.8	16.9	20.5	12.0	0.0	2.4
25~34 岁 Age	106	59.4	4.7	17.9	4.7	30.2	16.0	9.4	0.0	1.9
35~44 岁 Age	67	56.7	4.5	14.9	7.5	32.8	3.0	13.4	1.5	1.5
45~54 岁 Age	38	78.9	5.3	13.2	5.3	28.9	2.6	0.0	0.0	5.3
55~60 岁 Age	14	64.3	0.0	14.3	7.1	42.9	7.1	0.0	0.0	7.1

3-12 重度消费者的人口分布/ Demographics of the Heavy Consumers

	人数 Number	16-24 岁 Age	25-34 岁 Age	35-44 岁 Age	45-54 岁 Age	55-60 岁 Age
样本 Sample	390	22.3	33.3	26.2	12.3	5.9
男性 Male	177	21.5	31.1	31.1	10.7	5.6
天天喝 daily	49	20.4	22.4	40.8	10.2	6.1
一周 3 次或以上 3 times or over a week	43	20.9	41.9	16.3	16.3	4.7
一周 1～2 次 once or twice a week	85	22.4	30.6	32.9	8.2	5.9
女性 Female	213	23.0	35.2	22.1	13.6	6.1
天天喝 daily	73	16.4	31.5	24.7	17.8	9.6
一周 3 次或以上 3 times or over a week	57	19.3	42.1	19.3	12.3	7.0
一周 1～2 次 once or twice a week	83	31.3	33.7	21.7	10.8	2.4

3-13 不同消费者层的常用品牌/ The Most Frequently Used Brands by Market Segments

3-13-1 时尚流行指标/ Fads Popular Index

	人数 Number	第一品牌及百分比 1st/ percent	第二品牌及百分比 2nd/ percent	第三品牌及百分比 3rd/ percent	第四品牌及百分比 4th/ percent
样本 Sample	**555**	**三元 Sanyuan(70.1)**	**光明 Bright(9.0)**	**卡夫 Kraft(3.8)**	**帕玛拉特 Parmalat(3.2)**
平实生活指向 simple living orientation	251	三元 Sanyuan(74.1)	光明 Bright(6.0)	卡夫 Kraft(3.6)	帕玛拉特 Parmalat(2.4)
时尚流行指向 fashion orientation	304	三元 Sanyuan(66.8)	光明 Bright(11.5)	帕玛拉特 Parmalat(3.9) 卡夫 Kraft(3.9)	伊利 Yili(3.6)

3-13-2 广告态度指标/ Advertising Attitude Index

	人数 Number	第一品牌及百分比 1st/ percent	第二品牌及百分比 2nd/ percent	第三品牌及百分比 3rd/ percent	第四品牌及百分比 4th/ percent
样本 Sample	**556**	**三元 Sanyuan(70.3)**	**光明 Bright(8.8)**	**卡夫 Kraft(3.8)**	**帕玛拉特 Parmalat(3.2)**
广告淡漠指向 indifferent orientation	135	三元 Sanyuan(65.9)	光明 Bright(10.4)	帕玛拉特 Parmalat(3.7) 伊利 Yili(3.7)	卡夫 Kraft(2.2)
中间层 medium	340	三元 Sanyuan(73.8)	光明 Bright(9.1)	卡夫 Kraft(3.5)	帕玛拉特 Parmalat(2.9)
信赖广告指向 loyal orientation	81	三元 Sanyuan(63.0)	卡夫 Kraft(7.4)	伊利 Yili(6.2)	光明 Bright(4.9)

3-13-3 饮食健康指标/ Foods & Drink Quality Index

	人数 Number	第一品牌及百分比 1st/ percent	第二品牌及百分比 2nd/ percent	第三品牌及百分比 3rd/percent	第四品牌及百分比 4th/ percent
样本 Sample	**560**	**三元 Sanyuan(70.4)**	**光明 Bright(8.8)**	**卡夫 Kraft(3.8)**	**帕玛拉特 Parmalat(3.2)**
饮食"温饱"指向 "basic" orientation	147	三元 Sanyuan(72.8)	光明 Bright(4.8)	卡夫 Kraft(2.7) 乐百氏 Robust(2.7) 帕玛拉特 Parmalat(2.7)	雀巢 Nestle(2.0)
中间层 medium	271	三元 Sanyuan(73.1)	光明 Bright(9.2)	卡夫 Kraft(4.4)	伊利 Yili(3.7)
健康营养指向 health & nutrition orientation	142	三元 Sanyuan(62.7)	光明 Bright(12.0)	帕玛拉特 Parmalat(4.9) 伊利 Yili(4.9)	卡夫 Kraft(3.5)

3-14 重度消费者的消费者层构成/ The Composition of the Heavy Consumers

3-14-1 时尚流行指标/ Fads Popular Index

	人数 Number	平实生活指向 simple living orientation	时尚流行指向 fashion orientation
样本 Sample	**382**	**42.9**	**57.1**
天天喝 daily	122	42.6	57.4
一周 3 次或以上 3 times or over a week	98	44.9	55.1
一周 1～2 次 once or twice a week	162	42.0	58.0

3-14-2 广告态度指标/ Advertising Attitude Index

	人数 Number	广告淡漠指向 indifferent orientation	中间层 medium	信赖广告指向 loyal orientation
样本 Sample	**385**	**24.9**	**59.7**	**15.3**
天天喝 daily	120	25.0	66.7	8.3
一周 3 次或以上 3 times or over a week	99	29.3	56.6	14.1
一周 1～2 次 once or twice a week	166	22.3	56.6	21.1

3-14-3 饮食健康指标/ Foods & Drink Quality Index

	人数 Number	饮食"温饱"指向 "basic" orientation	中间层 medium	健康营养指向 health & nutrition orientation
样本 Sample	**388**	**22.9**	**50.3**	**26.8**
天天喝 daily	121	18.2	54.5	27.3
一周 3 次或以上 3 times or over a week	100	24.0	52.0	24.0
一周 1～2 次 once or twice a week	167	25.7	46.1	28.1

● 上海 / Shanghai

3-1 最近三个月食用频率的比例/ Proportion of the Sample Consuming Packaged Milk in the Last Three Months

	人数 Number	百分比 Percent
天天喝 daily	331	32.7
一周 3 次或以上 3 times or over a week	146	14.4
一周 1~2 次 once or twice a week	159	15.7
一个月 2~3 次 2 or 3 times a month	72	7.1
一个月 1 次或以下 once a month or below	47	4.6
没喝过 never	258	25.5

n=1013

3-2 最常用品牌排名/ Ranking of the Most Frequently Used Brands

排名 Brand Ranking	品牌 Brands	人数 Number	百分比 Percent
1	光明 Bright	662	88.0
2	三岛 Sandao	35	4.7
3	全佳 Quanjia	18	2.4
4	真元 Zhenyuan	6	0.8
5	秦俑 Qinyong	5	0.7

n=752

3-3 样本、男性各年龄层、女性各年龄层的常用品牌/ The Most Frequently Used Brands by the Whole Sample, Age and Gender Groups

	人数 Number	第一品牌及百分比 1st/ percent	第二品牌及百分比 2nd/ percent	第三品牌及百分比 3rd/ percent
样本 Sample	**752**	**光明 Bright(88.0)**	**三岛 Sandao(4.7)**	**全佳 Quanjia(2.4)**
男性 Male	**368**	**光明 Bright(90.5)**	**三岛 Sandao(4.1)**	**全佳 Quanjia(1.6)**
16~24 岁 Age	89	光明 Bright(93.3)	全佳 Quanjia(2.2) 三岛 Sandao(2.2) 秦俑 Qinyong(2.2)	
25~34 岁 Age	116	光明 Bright(86.2)	三岛 Sandao(6.0)	全佳 Quanjia(3.4)
35~44 岁 Age	81	光明 Bright(93.8)	冰峰 Bingfeng(1.2) 古城 Gucheng(1.2) 快乐家庭 Happy Family(1.2) 三岛 Sandao(1.2) 永安乳品 Yong'an(1.2)	
45~54 岁 Age	62	光明 Bright(95.2)	三岛 Sandao(3.2)	真元 Zhenyuan(1.6)
55~60 岁 Age	20	光明 Bright(75.0)	三岛 Sandao(15.0)	乐百氏 Robust(5.0) 元祖 Yuanzu(5.0)
女性 Female	**384**	**光明 Bright(85.7)**	**三岛 Sandao(5.2)**	**全佳 Quanjia(3.1)**
16~24 岁 Age	95	光明 Bright(85.3)	三岛 Sandao(5.3)	全佳 Quanjia(4.2)
25~34 岁 Age	113	光明 Bright(85.0)	三岛 Sandao(4.4)	全佳 Quanjia(3.5)
35~44 岁 Age	99	光明 Bright(88.9)	三岛 Sandao(6.1)	全佳 Quanjia(2.0)
45~54 岁 Age	51	光明 Bright(78.4)	三岛 Sandao(7.8)	全佳 Quanjia(3.9)
55~60 岁 Age	26	光明 Bright(92.3)	达能 Danone(3.8) 高品 Gaopin(3.8)	

3-4 理想品牌排名/ Ranking of the Ideal Brands

排名 Brand Ranking	品牌 Brands	人数 Number	百分比 Percent
1	光明 Bright	913	90.0
2	三岛 Sandao	28	2.8
3	全佳 Quanjia	12	1.2
4	优诺 Yuplaic	4	0.4
4	真元 Zhenyuan	4	0.4

n=1014

3-5 样本、男性各年龄层、女性各年龄层最近三个月有无购买的比例/ Purchasing in the Last Three Months by the Whole Sample, Age and Gender Groups

	人数 Number	买过 yes	没买过 no
样本 Sample	1014	75.0	25.0
男性 Male	509	71.9	28.1
16~24 岁 Age	109	72.5	27.5
25~34 岁 Age	146	80.8	19.2
35~44 岁 Age	130	66.2	33.8
45~54 岁 Age	85	72.9	27.1
55~60 岁 Age	39	53.8	46.2
女性 Female	505	78.0	22.0
16~24 岁 Age	108	82.4	17.6
25~34 岁 Age	144	81.3	18.8
35~44 岁 Age	130	80.0	20.0
45~54 岁 Age	82	69.5	30.5
55~60 岁 Age	41	65.9	34.1

3-6 样本、男性各年龄层、女性各年龄层最近三个月的食用频率/ Frequencies of Consuming Packaged Milk in the Last Three Months by the Whole Sample, Age and Gender Groups

	人数 Number	天天喝 daily	一周 3 次或以上 3 times or over a week	一周 1~2 次 once or twice a week	一个月 2~3 次 2 or 3 times a month	一个月 1 次或以下 once a month or below	没喝过 never
样本 Sample	1013	32.7	14.4	15.7	7.1	4.6	25.5
男性 Male	508	31.5	15.0	15.9	5.9	4.7	27.0
16~24 岁 Age	109	33.0	14.7	20.2	5.5	8.3	18.3
25~34 岁 Age	146	34.9	18.5	17.8	6.2	3.4	19.2
35~44 岁 Age	129	27.9	8.5	17.1	7.0	3.1	36.4
45~54 岁 Age	85	31.8	20.0	8.2	5.9	7.1	27.1
55~60 岁 Age	39	25.6	12.8	10.3	2.6	0.0	48.7
女性 Female	505	33.9	13.9	15.4	8.3	4.6	24.0
16~24 岁 Age	108	30.6	14.8	24.1	9.3	9.3	12.0
25~34 岁 Age	144	36.1	17.4	13.2	9.7	2.1	21.5
35~44 岁 Age	130	40.0	13.8	11.5	9.2	1.5	23.8
45~54 岁 Age	82	25.6	8.5	14.6	6.1	7.3	37.8
55~60 岁 Age	41	31.7	9.8	14.6	2.4	4.9	36.6

3-7 样本、男性各年龄层、女性各年龄层的品牌习惯/ Brand Habit in Consuming Packaged Milk by the Whole Sample, Age and Gender Groups

	人数 Number	基本固定食用一个牌子 used in only one brand	比较固定地食用两个或三个牌子 used in two or three brands	基本上不太固定牌子 no brand preference
样本 Sample	753	69.7	23.1	7.2
男性 Male	369	68.8	23.6	7.6
16~24 岁 Age	89	68.5	22.5	9.0
25~34 岁 Age	117	69.2	27.4	3.4
35~44 岁 Age	82	63.4	23.2	13.4
45~54 岁 Age	62	75.8	17.7	6.5
55~60 岁 Age	19	68.4	26.3	5.3
女性 Female	384	70.6	22.7	6.8
16~24 岁 Age	95	66.3	23.2	10.5
25~34 岁 Age	113	70.8	24.8	4.4
35~44 岁 Age	99	69.7	24.2	6.1
45~54 岁 Age	51	80.4	13.7	5.9
55~60 岁 Age	26	69.2	23.1	7.7

3-8 选择该类商品的考虑因素/ Ranking of the Considerations in Purchasing

注：本题为多选题，合计百分比超过 100%（Multiple answers）

排名 Ranking	考虑因素 Considerations	人次 Person-time	百分比 Percent
1	有名的牌子 famous brand	328	43.6
2	口味好 pleasant taste	325	43.2
3	价格适中 reasonable price	291	38.6
4	营养成分 nutrition constituent	247	32.8
5	购买方便 easy to buy	193	25.6
6	生产日期 date of producing	160	21.2
7	只是由于习惯 out of habit	68	9.0
8	广告影响 influence of advertising	47	6.2
9	有优惠条件 with preferential terms	44	5.8
10	包装吸引人 appealing package	13	1.7
11	朋友推荐 introduction of friends	11	1.5
12	售货员介绍 introduced by the shop assistants	6	0.8
12	其它 others	6	0.8

n=753

3-9 样本、男性各年龄层、女性各年龄层最常食用的种类/ Types of the Consumed Packaged Milk by the Whole Sample, Age and Gender Groups

	人数 Number	全脂 whole milk	低脂 low-fat	脱脂 skimmed	花色奶（巧克力味、草莓味等）milk varieties (chocolate flavor.Strawberry flavors etc.)	强化奶 enriched milk	加矿物质（含钙、铁等）with minerals (containing calcium.Iron etc.)	其它 others
样本 Sample	749	58.1	9.3	9.2	6.9	2.0	13.9	0.5
男性 Male	367	60.2	10.1	8.7	5.7	1.9	13.1	0.3
16~24 岁 Age	88	55.7	6.8	5.7	10.2	3.4	17.0	1.1
25~34 岁 Age	117	57.3	11.1	10.3	7.7	2.6	11.1	0.0
35~44 岁 Age	82	62.2	8.5	14.6	3.7	1.2	9.8	0.0
45~54 岁 Age	60	68.3	15.0	3.3	0.0	0.0	13.3	0.0
55~60 岁 Age	20	65.0	10.0	5.0	0.0	0.0	20.0	0.0
女性 Female	382	56.0	8.6	9.7	8.1	2.1	14.7	0.8
16~24 岁 Age	95	45.3	8.4	11.6	12.6	3.2	18.9	0.0
25~34 岁 Age	112	52.7	8.9	10.7	7.1	1.8	17.9	0.9
35~44 岁 Age	99	65.7	5.1	10.1	7.1	1.0	10.1	1.0
45~54 岁 Age	50	70.0	10.0	8.0	2.0	4.0	6.0	0.0
55~60 岁 Age	26	46.2	19.2	0.0	11.5	0.0	19.2	3.8

3-10 样本、男性各年龄层、女性各年龄层最常食用的包装形式/ Types of Package of the Consumed Packaged Milk by the Whole Sample, Age and Gender Groups

	人数 Number	方盒装/利乐砖 plastic-bag milk	房屋状纸盒 house-shaped box	粽子状纸盒 V-shaped box	塑料瓶 plastic bottle	易拉罐 tin	其他 others
样本 Sample	747	36.9	47.1	0.5	5.6	0.8	9.0
男性 Male	365	37.8	44.9	0.5	6.3	1.6	8.8
16~24 岁 Age	88	42.0	44.3	0.0	5.7	2.3	5.7
25~34 岁 Age	116	35.3	45.7	0.9	10.3	1.7	6.0
35~44 岁 Age	82	36.6	41.5	1.2	4.9	2.4	13.4
45~54 岁 Age	61	39.3	52.5	0.0	1.6	0.0	6.6
55~60 岁 Age	18	33.3	33.3	0.0	5.6	0.0	27.8
女性 Female	382	36.1	49.2	0.5	5.0	0.0	9.2
16~24 岁 Age	94	38.3	45.7	0.0	4.3	0.0	11.7
25~34 岁 Age	113	38.1	53.1	0.0	5.3	0.0	3.5
35~44 岁 Age	98	35.7	51.0	1.0	6.1	0.0	6.1
45~54 岁 Age	51	35.3	41.2	2.0	3.9	0.0	17.6
55~60 岁 Age	26	23.1	53.8	0.0	3.8	0.0	19.2

3-11 样本、男性各年龄层、女性各年龄层最常饮用场合/ Settings of Consumption by the Whole Sample, Age and Gender Groups

注：本题为多选题，合计百分比超过 100%（Multiple answers）

	人数 Number	早餐时 breakfast	正餐（午、晚餐）时 dinner	口渴时 when thirsty	宵夜时 evening snack	睡觉前 before sleeping	工作休息时 during work break	外出/旅游时 outing/ traveling	运动后 after athletics	其它 others
样本 Sample	754	69.6	3.3	12.1	4.5	36.2	6.2	3.7	1.6	1.6
男性 Male	370	72.2	3.5	10.8	5.4	34.9	6.2	2.7	1.9	1.9
16~24 岁 Age	89	58.4	6.7	13.5	4.5	37.1	10.1	2.2	3.4	3.4
25~34 岁 Age	117	73.5	2.6	11.1	4.3	38.5	7.7	3.4	1.7	2.6
35~44 岁 Age	82	75.6	2.4	12.2	7.3	30.5	3.7	3.7	2.4	1.2
45~54 岁 Age	62	87.1	0.0	4.8	6.5	32.3	3.2	1.6	0.0	0.0
55~60 岁 Age	20	65.0	10.0	10.0	5.0	30.0	0.0	0.0	0.0	0.0
女性 Female	384	67.2	3.1	13.3	3.6	37.5	6.3	4.7	1.3	1.3
16~24 岁 Age	95	64.2	4.2	17.9	2.1	33.7	5.3	6.3	2.1	0.0
25~34 岁 Age	113	64.6	2.7	12.4	6.2	38.9	7.1	2.7	1.8	2.7
35~44 岁 Age	99	72.7	1.0	16.2	3.0	43.4	4.0	6.1	0.0	0.0
45~54 岁 Age	51	68.6	7.8	7.8	2.0	27.5	7.8	2.0	0.0	2.0
55~60 岁 Age	26	65.4	0.0	0.0	3.8	42.3	11.5	7.7	3.8	3.8

3-12 重度消费者的人口分布/ Demographics of the Heavy Consumers

	人数 Number	16-24 岁 Age	25-34 岁 Age	35-44 岁 Age	45-54 岁 Age	55-60 岁 Age
样本 Sample	636	23.4	31.4	24.2	14.3	6.6
男性 Male	317	23.3	32.8	21.8	16.1	6.0
天天喝 daily	160	22.5	31.9	22.5	16.9	6.3
一周 3 次或以上 3 times or over a week	76	21.1	35.5	14.5	22.4	6.6
一周 1～2 次 once or twice a week	81	27.2	32.1	27.2	8.6	4.9
女性 Female	319	23.5	30.1	26.6	12.5	7.2
天天喝 daily	171	19.3	30.4	30.4	12.3	7.6
一周 3 次或以上 3 times or over a week	70	22.9	35.7	25.7	10.0	5.7
一周 1～2 次 once or twice a week	78	33.3	24.4	19.2	15.4	7.7

3-13 不同消费者层的常用品牌/ The Most Frequently Used Brands by Market Segments

3-13-1 时尚流行指标/ Fads Popular Index

	人数 Number	第一品牌及百分比 1st/ percent	第二品牌及百分比 2nd/ percent	第三品牌及百分比 3rd/ percent
样本 Sample	745	**光明 Bright(88.2)**	**三岛 Sandao(4.7)**	**全佳 Quanjia(2.4)**
平实生活指向 simple living orientation	318	光明 Bright(87.1)	三岛 Sandao(4.4)	全佳 Quanjia(3.1)
时尚流行指向 fashion orientation	427	光明 Bright(89.0)	三岛 Sandao(4.9)	全佳 Quanjia(1.9)

3-13-2 广告态度指标/ Advertising Attitude Index

	人数 Number	第一品牌及百分比 1st/ percent	第二品牌及百分比 2nd/ percent	第三品牌及百分比 3rd/ percent
样本 Sample	745	**光明 Bright(87.9)**	**三岛 Sandao(4.7)**	**全佳 Quanjia(2.4)**
广告淡漠指向 indifferent orientation	181	光明 Bright(86.7)	三岛 Sandao(4.4)	全佳 Quanjia(3.3)
中间层 medium	461	光明 Bright(88.9)	三岛 Sandao(4.3)	全佳 Quanjia(2.4)
信赖广告指向 loyal orientation	103	光明 Bright(85.4)	三岛 Sandao(6.8)	真元 Zhenyuan(2.9)

3-13-3 饮食健康指标/ Foods & Drink Quality Index

	人数 Number	第一品牌及百分比 1st/ percent	第二品牌及百分比 2nd/ percent	第三品牌及百分比 3rd/ percent
样本 Sample	752	光明 Bright(88.0)	三岛 Sandao(4.7)	全佳 Quanjia(2.4)
饮食"温饱"指向 "basic" orientation	162	光明 Bright(87.0)	三岛 Sandao(4.3)	全佳 Quanjia(3.1)
中间层 medium	371	光明 Bright(88.9)	三岛 Sandao(4.0)	全佳 Quanjia(2.4)
健康营养指向 health & nutrition orientation	215	光明 Bright(87.0)	三岛 Sandao(6.0)	全佳 Quanjia(1.9) 真元 Zhenyuan(1.9)

3-14 重度消费者的消费者层构成/ The Composition of the Heavy Consumers

3-14-1 时尚流行指标/ Fads Popular Index

	人数 Number	平实生活指向 simple living orientation	时尚流行指向 fashion orientation
样本 Sample	630	41.3	58.7
天天喝 daily	327	42.5	57.5
一周 3 次或以上 3 times or over a week	144	37.5	62.5
一周 1～2 次 once or twice a week	159	42.1	57.9

3-14-2 广告态度指标/ Advertising Attitude Index

	人数 Number	广告淡漠指向 indifferent orientation	中间层 medium	信赖广告指向 loyal orientation
样本 Sample	628	22.5	64.8	12.7
天天喝 daily	327	20.5	66.4	13.1
一周 3 次或以上 3 times or over a week	144	25.7	63.9	10.4
一周 1～2 次 once or twice a week	157	23.6	62.4	14.0

3-14-3 饮食健康指标/ Foods & Drink Quality Index

	人数 Number	饮食"温饱"指向 "basic" orientation	中间层 medium	健康营养指向 health & nutrition orientation
样本 Sample	634	20.3	49.7	30.0
天天喝 daily	330	18.2	49.7	32.1
一周 3 次或以上 3 times or over a week	146	22.6	48.6	28.8
一周 1～2 次 once or twice a week	158	22.8	50.6	26.6

● 广州 / Guangzhou

3-1 最近三个月食用频率的比例/ Proportion of the Sample Consuming Packaged Milk in the Last Three Months

	人数 Number	百分比 Percent
天天喝 daily	132	12.8
一周 3 次或以上 3 times or over a week	117	11.3
一周 1~2 次 once or twice a week	188	18.2
一个月 2～3 次 2 or 3 times a month	138	13.4
一个月 1 次或以下 once a month or below	71	6.9
没喝过 never	386	37.4

n=1032

3-2 最常用品牌排名/ Ranking of the Most Frequently Used Brands

排名 Brand Ranking	品牌 Brands	人数 Number	百分比 Percent
1	燕塘 Yantang	172	26.7
2	香满楼 Flower Fresh	162	25.2
3	伊利 Yili	55	8.5
4	风行 Fengxing	48	7.5
5	达能 Danone	46	7.1
6	晨光 Chenguang	33	5.1
7	秦俑 Qinyong	27	4.2
8	子母奶 Dutch Lady	21	3.3

n=644

3-3 样本、男性各年龄层、女性各年龄层的常用品牌/ The Most Frequently Used Brands by the Whole Sample, Age and Gender Groups

	人数 Number	第一品牌及百分比 1st/ percent	第二品牌及百分比 2nd/ percent	第三品牌及百分比 3rd/ percent	第四品牌及百分比 4th/ percent
样本 Sample	**644**	**燕塘 Yantang(26.7)**	**香满楼 Flower Fresh(25.2)**	**伊利 Yili(8.5)**	**风行 Fengxing(7.5)**
男性 Male	**302**	**燕塘 Yantang(25.8)**	**香满楼 Flower Fresh(24.8)**	**风行 Fengxing(8.9)**	**伊利 Yili(8.3)**
16~24 岁 Age	74	燕塘 Yantang(24.3)	香满楼 Flower Fresh(21.6)	秦俑 Qinyong(10.8) 风行 Fengxing(10.8)	伊利 Yili(6.8)
25~34 岁 Age	95	燕塘 Yantang(29.5)	香满楼 Flower Fresh(23.2)	伊利 Yili(10.5)	风行 Fengxing(8.4)
35~44 岁 Age	72	香满楼 Flower Fresh(31.9)	燕塘 Yantang(22.2)	晨光 Chenguang(11.1)	达能 Danone(9.7)
45~54 岁 Age	42	燕塘 Yantang(28.6)	香满楼 Flower Fresh(21.4)	秦俑 Qinyong(9.5) 风行 Fengxing(9.5)	伊利 Yili(7.1) 子母奶 Dutch Lady(7.1) 晨光 Chenguang(7.1)
55~60 岁 Age	19	香满楼 Flower Fresh(26.3)	燕塘 Yantang(21.1)	伊利 Yili(15.8)	达能 Danone(10.5) 风行 Fengxing(10.5)
女性 Female	**342**	**燕塘 Yantang(27.5)**	**香满楼 Flower Fresh(25.4)**	**伊利 Yili(8.8)**	**达能 Danone(8.5)**
16~24 岁 Age	76	燕塘 Yantang(31.6)	香满楼 Flower Fresh(27.6)	达能 Danone(9.2)	伊利 Yili(5.3) 子母奶 Dutch Lady(5.3) 风行 Fengxing(5.3)
25~34 岁 Age	113	燕塘 Yantang(27.4)	香满楼 Flower Fresh(26.5)	伊利 Yili(10.6)	达能 Danone(7.1)
35~44 岁 Age	84	香满楼 Flower Fresh(25.0) 燕塘 Yantang(25.0)	伊利 Yili(9.5)	达能 Danone(7.1) 晨光 Chenguang(7.1)	秦俑 Qinyong(6.0)
45~54 岁 Age	53	燕塘 Yantang(28.3)	香满楼 Flower Fresh(20.8)	达能 Danone(11.3)	伊利 Yili(9.4) 风行 Fengxing(9.4)
55~60 岁 Age	16	香满楼 Flower Fresh(25.0) 风行 Fengxing(25.0)	燕塘 Yantang(18.8)	达能 Danone(12.5)	伊利 Yili(6.3) 晨光 Chenguang(6.3)

3-4 理想品牌排名/ Ranking of the Ideal Brands

排名 Brand Ranking	品牌 Brands	人数 Number	百分比 Percent
1	燕塘 Yantang	224	21.7
2	香满楼 Flower Fresh	214	20.7
3	达能 Danone	60	5.8
4	风行 Fengxing	59	5.7
5	伊利 Yili	58	5.6
6	晨光 Chenguang	48	4.6
7	子母奶 Dutch Lady	29	2.8
8	秦俑 Qinyong	25	2.4

n=1034

3-5 样本、男性各年龄层、女性各年龄层最近三个月有无购买的比例/ Purchasing in the Last Three Months by the Whole Sample, Age and Gender Groups

	人数 Number	买过 yes	没买过 no
样本 Sample	**1033**	**61.6**	**38.4**
男性 Male	**499**	**58.5**	**41.5**
16~24 岁 Age	106	63.2	36.8
25~34 岁 Age	150	62.0	38.0
35~44 岁 Age	127	56.7	43.3
45~54 岁 Age	73	53.4	46.6
55~60 岁 Age	43	48.8	51.2
女性 Female	**534**	**64.4**	**35.6**
16~24 岁 Age	112	63.4	36.6
25~34 岁 Age	158	72.2	27.8
35~44 岁 Age	137	64.2	35.8
45~54 岁 Age	86	64.0	36.0
55~60 岁 Age	41	39.0	61.0

3-6 样本、男性各年龄层、女性各年龄层最近三个月的食用频率/ Frequencies of Consuming Packaged Milk in the Last Three Months by the Whole Sample, Age and Gender Groups

	人数 Number	天天喝 daily	一周 3 次或以上 3 times or over a week	一周 1~2 次 once or twice a week	一个月 2~3 次 2 or 3 times a month	一个月 1 次或以下 once a month or below	没喝过 never
样本 Sample	1032	12.8	11.3	18.2	13.4	6.9	37.4
男性 Male	497	10.3	10.5	18.1	14.5	7.8	38.8
16~24 岁 Age	106	12.3	9.4	27.4	9.4	11.3	30.2
25~34 岁 Age	149	9.4	10.7	18.8	17.4	7.4	36.2
35~44 岁 Age	127	11.8	11.0	11.0	15.7	7.9	42.5
45~54 岁 Age	72	9.7	11.1	12.5	18.1	6.9	41.7
55~60 岁 Age	43	4.7	9.3	23.3	7.0	2.3	53.5
女性 Female	535	15.1	12.1	18.3	12.3	6.0	36.1
16~24 岁 Age	112	15.2	6.3	19.6	18.8	8.0	32.1
25~34 岁 Age	158	15.2	12.0	24.1	11.4	8.9	28.5
35~44 岁 Age	137	14.6	16.8	14.6	10.9	4.4	38.7
45~54 岁 Age	87	18.4	12.6	17.2	9.2	3.4	39.1
55~60 岁 Age	41	9.8	12.2	7.3	9.8	0.0	61.0

3-7 样本、男性各年龄层、女性各年龄层的品牌习惯/ Brand Habit in Consuming Packaged Milk by the Whole Sample, Age and Gender Groups

	人数 Number	基本固定食用一个牌子 used in only one brand	比较固定地食用两个或三个牌子 used in two or three brands	基本上不太固定牌子 no brand preference
样本 Sample	643	46.0	33.7	20.2
男性 Male	302	49.3	29.8	20.9
16~24 岁 Age	74	48.6	24.3	27.0
25~34 岁 Age	94	45.7	35.1	19.1
35~44 岁 Age	73	53.4	30.1	16.4
45~54 岁 Age	41	48.8	31.7	19.5
55~60 岁 Age	20	55.0	20.0	25.0
女性 Female	341	43.1	37.2	19.6
16~24 岁 Age	76	34.2	39.5	26.3
25~34 岁 Age	113	45.1	42.5	12.4
35~44 岁 Age	83	48.2	36.1	15.7
45~54 岁 Age	53	43.4	30.2	26.4
55~60 岁 Age	16	43.8	18.8	37.5

3-8 选择该类商品的考虑因素/ Ranking of the Considerations in Purchasing

注：本题为多选题，合计百分比超过 100%（Multiple answers）

排名 Ranking	考虑因素 Considerations	人次 Person-time	百分比 Percent
1	口味好 pleasant taste	279	43.3
2	价格适中 reasonable price	225	34.9
3	营养成分 nutrition constituent	217	33.7
4	有名的牌子 famous brand	209	32.5
5	购买方便 easy to buy	174	27.0
6	生产日期 date of producing	113	17.5
7	只是由于习惯 out of habit	51	7.9
8	有优惠条件 with preferential terms	35	5.4
9	广告影响 influence of advertising	23	3.6
10	朋友推荐 introduction of friends	21	3.3
11	包装吸引人 appealing package	20	3.1
12	售货员介绍 introduced by the shop assistants	12	1.9
13	其它 others	4	0.6

n=644

3-9 样本、男性各年龄层、女性各年龄层最常食用的种类/ Types of the Consumed Packaged Milk by the Whole Sample, Age and Gender Groups

	人数 Number	全脂 whole milk	低脂 low-fat	脱脂 skimmed	花色奶（巧克力味、草莓味等）milk varieties (chocolate flavor Strawberry flavors etc.)	强化奶 enriched milk	加矿物质（含钙、铁等）with minerals (containing calcium Iron etc.)	其它 others
样本 Sample	635	35.4	18.0	13.5	16.9	2.5	8.3	5.4
男性 Male	299	34.8	18.7	13.7	17.7	2.0	6.0	7.0
16~24 岁 Age	74	32.4	23.0	9.5	18.9	2.7	5.4	8.1
25~34 岁 Age	93	30.1	17.2	16.1	20.4	2.2	6.5	7.5
35~44 岁 Age	71	43.7	12.7	14.1	18.3	1.4	4.2	5.6
45~54 岁 Age	42	33.3	16.7	19.0	11.9	2.4	7.1	9.5
55~60 岁 Age	19	36.8	36.8	5.3	10.5	0.0	10.5	0.0
女性 Female	336	36.0	17.3	13.4	16.1	3.0	10.4	3.9
16~24 岁 Age	74	36.5	14.9	12.2	21.6	2.7	10.8	1.4
25~34 岁 Age	109	37.6	14.7	11.0	21.1	3.7	9.2	2.8
35~44 岁 Age	84	31.0	25.0	15.5	10.7	3.6	9.5	4.8
45~54 岁 Age	53	37.7	17.0	17.0	11.3	0.0	9.4	7.5
55~60 岁 Age	16	43.8	6.3	12.5	0.0	6.3	25.0	6.3

3-10 样本、男性各年龄层、女性各年龄层最常食用的包装形式/ Types of Package of the Consumed Packaged Milk by the Whole Sample, Age and Gender Groups

	人数 Number	方盒装/利乐砖 plastic-bag milk	房屋状纸盒 house-shaped box	粽子状纸盒 V-shaped box	塑料瓶 plastic bottle	易拉罐 tin	其他 others
样本 Sample	640	52.2	21.4	1.3	14.1	1.7	9.4
男性 Male	301	55.5	19.3	1.0	12.0	1.7	10.6
16~24 岁 Age	74	60.8	18.9	0.0	10.8	1.4	8.1
25~34 岁 Age	95	58.9	20.0	0.0	8.4	2.1	10.5
35~44 岁 Age	70	48.6	15.7	4.3	17.1	0.0	14.3
45~54 岁 Age	42	54.8	26.2	0.0	7.1	2.4	9.5
55~60 岁 Age	20	45.0	15.0	0.0	25.0	5.0	10.0
女性 Female	339	49.3	23.3	1.5	15.9	1.8	8.3
16~24 岁 Age	75	52.0	29.3	1.3	8.0	1.3	8.0
25~34 岁 Age	112	54.5	22.3	0.9	14.3	1.8	6.3
35~44 岁 Age	84	46.4	23.8	2.4	19.0	2.4	6.0
45~54 岁 Age	52	44.2	17.3	1.9	19.2	1.9	15.4
55~60 岁 Age	16	31.3	18.8	0.0	37.5	0.0	12.5

3-11 样本、男性各年龄层、女性各年龄层最常饮用场合/ Settings of Consumption by the Whole Sample, Age and Gender Groups

注：本题为多选题，合计百分比超过 100%（Multiple answers）

	人数 Number	早餐时 breakfast	正餐（午、晚餐）时 dinner	口渴时 when thirsty	宵夜时 evening snack	睡觉前 before sleeping	工作休息时 during work break	外出/旅游时 outing/traveling	运动后 after athletics	其它 others
样本 Sample	642	67.1	3.7	16.7	9.7	17.4	7.8	8.1	2.0	2.2
男性 Male	302	66.6	3.3	14.9	8.9	16.6	9.3	6.6	3.0	2.0
16~24 岁 Age	74	71.6	2.7	10.8	10.8	17.6	10.8	8.1	2.7	0.0
25~34 岁 Age	94	66.0	4.3	11.7	4.3	16.0	12.8	7.4	5.3	2.1
35~44 岁 Age	72	66.7	2.8	18.1	12.5	19.4	4.2	4.2	0.0	4.2
45~54 岁 Age	42	59.5	4.8	21.4	11.9	16.7	9.5	7.1	2.4	0.0
55~60 岁 Age	20	65.0	0.0	20.0	5.0	5.0	5.0	5.0	5.0	5.0
女性 Female	340	67.6	4.1	18.2	10.3	18.2	6.5	9.4	1.2	2.4
16~24 岁 Age	76	69.7	5.3	11.8	7.9	19.7	3.9	14.5	0.0	5.3
25~34 岁 Age	113	62.8	2.7	26.5	15.0	15.0	8.0	8.8	0.0	0.9
35~44 岁 Age	82	73.2	4.9	20.7	8.5	15.9	6.1	4.9	3.7	0.0
45~54 岁 Age	53	67.9	3.8	7.5	7.5	26.4	9.4	13.2	1.9	3.8
55~60 岁 Age	16	62.5	6.3	12.5	6.3	18.8	0.0	0.0	0.0	6.3

3-12 重度消费者的人口分布/ Demographics of the Heavy Consumers

	人数 Number	16-24 岁 Age	25-34 岁 Age	35-44 岁 Age	45-54 岁 Age	55-60 岁 Age
样本 Sample	437	22.4	31.8	24.3	15.1	6.4
男性 Male	193	26.9	30.1	22.3	12.4	8.3
天天喝 daily	51	25.5	27.5	29.4	13.7	3.9
一周 3 次或以上 3 times or over a week	52	19.2	30.8	26.9	15.4	7.7
一周 1~2 次 once or twice a week	90	32.2	31.1	15.6	10.0	11.1
女性 Female	244	18.9	33.2	25.8	17.2	4.9
天天喝 daily	81	21.0	29.6	24.7	19.8	4.9
一周 3 次或以上 3 times or over a week	65	10.8	29.2	35.4	16.9	7.7
一周 1~2 次 once or twice a week	98	22.4	38.8	20.4	15.3	3.1

3-13 不同消费者层的常用品牌/ The Most Frequently Used Brands by Market Segments

3-13-1 时尚流行指标/ Fads Popular Index

	人数 Number	第一品牌及百分比 1st/ percent	第二品牌及百分比 2nd/ percent	第三品牌及百分比 3rd/ percent	第四品牌及百分比 4th/ percent
样本 Sample	635	**燕塘 Yantang(27.1)**	**香满楼 Flower Fresh(25.0)**	**伊利 Yili(8.5)**	**风行 Fengxing(7.6)**
平实生活指向 simple living orientation	302	燕塘 Yantang(26.2)	香满楼 Flower Fresh(24.8)	伊利 Yili(10.3)	达能 Danone(8.3)
时尚流行指向 fashion orientation	333	燕塘 Yantang(27.9)	香满楼 Flower Fresh(25.2)	风行 Fengxing(8.4)	伊利 Yili(6.9)

3-13-2 广告态度指标/ Advertising Attitude Index

	人数 Number	第一品牌及百分比 1st/ percent	第二品牌及百分比 2nd/ percent	第三品牌及百分比 3rd/ percent	第四品牌及百分比 4th/ percent
样本 Sample	636	**燕塘 Yantang(26.7)**	**香满楼 Flower Fresh(25.0)**	**伊利 Yili(8.6)**	**风行 Fengxing(7.4)**
广告淡漠指向 indifferent orientation	197	燕塘 Yantang(26.9)	香满楼 Flower Fresh(25.4)	达能 Danone(9.1) 伊利 Yili(9.1)	风行 Fengxing(7.1)
中间层 medium	370	燕塘 Yantang(26.5)	香满楼 Flower Fresh(25.4)	伊利 Yili(7.8)	风行 Fengxing(6.8)
信赖广告指向 loyal orientation	69	燕塘 Yantang(27.5)	香满楼 Flower Fresh(21.7)	伊利 Yili(11.6) 风行 Fengxing(11.6)	达能 Danone(5.8) 秦俑 Qinyong(5.8)

3-13-3 饮食健康指标/ Foods & Drink Quality Index

	人数 Number	第一品牌及百分比 1st/ percent	第二品牌及百分比 2nd/ percent	第三品牌及百分比 3rd/ percent	第四品牌及百分比 4th/ percent
样本 Sample	644	**燕塘 Yantang(26.7)**	**香满楼 Flower Fresh(25.2)**	**伊利 Yili(8.5)**	**风行 Fengxing(7.5)**
饮食"温饱"指向 "basic" orientation	160	香满楼 Flower Fresh(27.5)	燕塘 Yantang(23.1)	伊利 Yili(9.4)	晨光 Chenguang(8.8)
中间层 medium	346	燕塘 Yantang(29.2)	香满楼 Flower Fresh(24.0)	伊利 Yili(7.5)	风行 Fengxing(7.2)
健康营养指向 health & nutrition orientation	134	香满楼 Flower Fresh(25.4)	燕塘 Yantang(24.6)	伊利 Yili(10.4)	风行 Fengxing(8.2)

3-14 重度消费者的消费者层构成/ The Composition of the Heavy Consumers

3-14-1 时尚流行指标/ Fads Popular Index

	人数 Number	平实生活指向 simple living orientation	时尚流行指向 fashion orientation
样本 Sample	432	49.1	50.9
天天喝 daily	131	51.1	48.9
一周 3 次或以上 3 times or over a week	116	50.9	49.1
一周 1~2 次 once or twice a week	185	46.5	53.5

3-14-2 广告态度指标/ Advertising Attitude Index

	人数 Number	广告淡漠指向 indifferent orientation	中间层 medium	信赖广告指向 loyal orientation
样本 Sample	430	31.9	57.2	10.9
天天喝 daily	132	31.8	53.8	14.4
一周 3 次或以上 3 times or over a week	114	34.2	52.6	13.2
一周 1～2 次 once or twice a week	184	30.4	62.5	7.1

3-14-3 饮食健康指标/ Foods & Drink Quality Index

	人数 Number	饮食"温饱"指向 "basic" orientation	中间层 medium	健康营养指向 health & nutrition orientation
样本 Sample	435	26.2	50.1	23.7
天天喝 daily	131	26.0	46.6	27.5
一周 3 次或以上 3 times or over a week	116	29.3	49.1	21.6
一周 1～2 次 once or twice a week	188	24.5	53.2	22.3

● 重庆 / Chongqing

3-1 最近三个月食用频率的比例/ Proportion of the Sample Consuming Packaged Milk in the Last Three Months

	人数 Number	百分比 Percent
天天喝 daily	49	7.9
一周 3 次或以上 3 times or over a week	17	2.7
一周 1~2 次 once or twice a week	33	5.3
一个月 2～3 次 2 or 3 times a month	32	5.1
一个月 1 次或以下 once a month or below	30	4.8
没喝过 never	461	74.1

n=622

3-2 最常用品牌排名/ Ranking of the Most Frequently Used Brands

排名 Brand Ranking	品牌 Brands	人数 Number	百分比 Percent
1	天友 Tianyou	113	72.4
2	乐百氏 Robust	6	3.8
3	均瑶 Junyao	5	3.2
4	雀巢 Nestle	4	2.6
4	子母奶 Dutch Lady	4	2.6
4	光明 Bright	4	2.6

n=156

3-3 样本、男性各年龄层、女性各年龄层的常用品牌/ The Most Frequently Used Brands by the Whole Sample, Age and Gender Groups

	人数 Number	第一品牌及百分比 1st/ percent	第二品牌及百分比 2nd/ percent	第三品牌及百分比 3rd/ percent
样本 Sample	**156**	**天友 Tianyou(72.4)**	**乐百氏 Robust(3.8)**	**均瑶 Junyao(3.2)**
男性 Male	**79**	**天友 Tianyou(74.7)**	**乐百氏 Robust(5.1)**	**均瑶 Junyao(3.8)**
16~24 岁 Age	29	天友 Tianyou(82.8)	乐百氏 Robust(6.9)	子母奶 Dutch Lady(3.4) 龙江 Longjiang(3.4)
25~34 岁 Age	25	天友 Tianyou(64.0)	均瑶 Junyao(8.0) 雀巢 Nestle(8.0)	乐百氏 Robust(4.0) 子母奶 Dutch Lady(4.0)
35~44 岁 Age	12	天友 Tianyou(83.3)	均瑶 Junyao(8.3) 乐百氏 Robust(8.3)	
45~54 岁 Age	9	天友 Tianyou(77.8)	杨协成 Yeo's(11.1) 江龙 Jianglong(11.1)	
55~60 岁 Age	4	天友 Tianyou(50.0)	海浪 Hailang(25.0)	
女性 Female	**77**	**天友 Tianyou(70.1)**	**光明 Bright(5.2)**	**雀巢 Nestle(2.6)** **子母奶 Dutch Lady(2.6)** **乐百氏 Robust(2.6)** **均瑶 Junyao(2.6)**
16~24 岁 Age	29	天友 Tianyou(72.4)	光明 Bright(6.9) 均瑶 Junyao(6.9) 雀巢 Nestle(6.9)	乐百氏 Robust(3.4)
25~34 岁 Age	24	天友 Tianyou(62.5)	光明 Bright(4.2) 金星 Jinxing(4.2) 乐百氏 Robust(4.2) 子母奶 Dutch Lady(4.2) 太易 Taiyi(4.2)	
35~44 岁 Age	14	天友 Tianyou(71.4)	光明 Bright(7.1)	
45~54 岁 Age	9	天友 Tianyou(77.8)	子母奶 Dutch Lady(11.1) 山城 Shancheng(11.1)	
55~60 岁 Age	1	天友 Tianyou(100.0)		

3-4 理想品牌排名/ Ranking of the Ideal Brands

排名 Brand Ranking	品牌 Brands	人数 Number	百分比 Percent
1	天友 Tianyou	284	45.5
2	乐百氏 Robust	18	2.9
3	子母奶 Dutch Lady	14	2.2
4	雀巢 Nestle	10	1.6
5	均瑶 Junyao	9	1.4
6	光明 Bright	8	1.3
6	伊利 Yili	8	1.3
7	旺仔 Wangzi	5	0.8

n=624

3-5 样本、男性各年龄层、女性各年龄层最近三个月有无购买的比例/ Purchasing in the Last Three Months by the Whole Sample, Age and Gender Groups

	人数 Number	买过 yes	没买过 no
样本 Sample	622	30.1	69.9
男性 Male	312	29.8	70.2
16~24 岁 Age	64	43.8	56.3
25~34 岁 Age	93	31.2	68.8
35~44 岁 Age	73	27.4	72.6
45~54 岁 Age	54	18.5	81.5
55~60 岁 Age	28	21.4	78.6
女性 Female	310	30.3	69.7
16~24 岁 Age	64	46.9	53.1
25~34 岁 Age	90	41.1	58.9
35~44 岁 Age	73	19.2	80.8
45~54 岁 Age	60	18.3	81.7
55~60 岁 Age	23	8.7	91.3

3-6 样本、男性各年龄层、女性各年龄层最近三个月的食用频率/ Frequencies of Consuming Packaged Milk in the Last Three Months by the Whole Sample, Age and Gender Groups

	人数 Number	天天喝 daily	一周3次或以上 3 times or over a week	一周1~2次 once or twice a week	一个月2~3次 2 or 3 times a month	一个月1次或以下 once a month or below	没喝过 never
样本 Sample	622	7.9	2.7	5.3	5.1	4.8	74.1
男性 Male	313	9.3	2.6	5.4	5.1	4.2	73.5
16~24 岁 Age	64	18.8	4.7	7.8	10.9	3.1	54.7
25~34 岁 Age	92	5.4	2.2	5.4	8.7	6.5	71.7
35~44 岁 Age	75	6.7	1.3	5.3	0.0	4.0	82.7
45~54 岁 Age	54	9.3	0.0	5.6	0.0	3.7	81.5
55~60 岁 Age	28	7.1	7.1	0.0	3.6	0.0	82.1
女性 Female	309	6.5	2.9	5.2	5.2	5.5	74.8
16~24 岁 Age	64	7.8	6.3	7.8	10.9	12.5	54.7
25~34 岁 Age	89	5.6	3.4	7.9	5.6	4.5	73.0
35~44 岁 Age	73	4.1	1.4	4.1	5.5	4.1	80.8
45~54 岁 Age	60	8.3	1.7	1.7	0.0	3.3	85.0
55~60 岁 Age	23	8.7	0.0	0.0	0.0	0.0	91.3

3-7 样本、男性各年龄层、女性各年龄层的品牌习惯/ Brand Habit in Consuming Packaged Milk by the Whole Sample, Age and Gender Groups

	人数 Number	基本固定食用一个牌子 used in only one brand	比较固定地食用两个或三个牌子 used in two or three brands	基本上不太固定牌子 no brand preference
样本 Sample	159	59.7	18.2	22.0
男性 Male	82	59.8	15.9	24.4
16~24 岁 Age	29	75.9	13.8	10.3
25~34 岁 Age	26	46.2	23.1	30.8
35~44 岁 Age	12	58.3	8.3	33.3
45~54 岁 Age	10	40.0	10.0	50.0
55~60 岁 Age	5	80.0	20.0	0.0
女性 Female	77	59.7	20.8	19.5
16~24 岁 Age	29	58.6	20.7	20.7
25~34 岁 Age	24	50.0	37.5	12.5
35~44 岁 Age	14	50.0	7.1	42.9
45~54 岁 Age	9	100.0	0.0	0.0
55~60 岁 Age	1	100.0	0.0	0.0

3-8 选择该类商品的考虑因素/ Ranking of the Considerations in Purchasing

注：本题为多选题，合计百分比超过100%（Multiple answers）

排名 Ranking	考虑因素 Considerations	人次 Person-time	百分比 Percent
1	口味好 pleasant taste	81	50.9
2	价格适中 reasonable price	48	30.2
3	购买方便 easy to buy	43	27.0
4	营养成分 nutrition constituent	39	24.5
5	有名的牌子 famous brand	35	22.0
6	生产日期 date of producing	26	16.4
7	只是由于习惯 out of habit	16	10.1
8	包装吸引人 appealing package	6	3.8
8	朋友推荐 introduction of friends	6	3.8
9	有优惠条件 with preferential terms	5	3.1
9	其它 others	5	3.1
10	广告影响 influence of advertising	4	2.5

n=159

3-9 样本、男性各年龄层、女性各年龄层最常食用的种类/ Types of the Consumed Packaged Milk by the Whole Sample, Age and Gender Groups

	人数 Number	全脂 whole milk	低脂 low-fat	脱脂 skimmed	花色奶（巧克力味、草莓味等）milk varieties (chocolate flavor.Strawberry flavors etc.)	强化奶 enriched milk	加矿物质（含钙、铁等）with minerals (containing calcium.Iron etc.)	其它 others
样本 Sample	155	34.8	8.4	9.0	20.0	1.3	22.6	3.9
男性 Male	80	32.5	8.8	8.8	20.0	1.3	23.8	5.0
16~24 岁 Age	28	25.0	7.1	7.1	28.6	3.6	21.4	7.1
25~34 岁 Age	25	20.0	16.0	12.0	28.0	0.0	20.0	4.0
35~44 岁 Age	12	58.3	0.0	0.0	8.3	0.0	25.0	8.3
45~54 岁 Age	10	50.0	0.0	20.0	0.0	0.0	30.0	0.0
55~60 岁 Age	5	40.0	20.0	0.0	0.0	0.0	40.0	0.0
女性 Female	75	37.3	8.0	9.3	20.0	1.3	21.3	2.7
16~24 岁 Age	28	21.4	7.1	14.3	32.1	3.6	17.9	3.6
25~34 岁 Age	24	45.8	16.7	8.3	20.8	0.0	4.2	4.2
35~44 岁 Age	13	61.5	0.0	7.7	7.7	0.0	23.1	0.0
45~54 岁 Age	9	22.2	0.0	0.0	0.0	0.0	77.8	0.0
55~60 岁 Age	1	100.0	0.0	0.0	0.0	0.0	0.0	0.0

3-10 样本、男性各年龄层、女性各年龄层最常食用的包装形式/ Types of Package of the Consumed Packaged Milk by the Whole Sample, Age and Gender Groups

	人数 Number	方盒装/利乐砖 plastic-bag milk	房屋状纸盒 house-shaped box	粽子状纸盒 V-shaped box	塑料瓶 plastic bottle	易拉罐 tin	其他 others
样本 Sample	152	35.5	26.3	0.7	15.8	1.3	20.4
男性 Male	81	37.0	18.5	0.0	21.0	2.5	21.0
16~24 岁 Age	28	39.3	17.9	0.0	25.0	3.6	14.3
25~34 岁 Age	26	50.0	23.1	0.0	15.4	3.8	7.7
35~44 岁 Age	12	33.3	16.7	0.0	8.3	0.0	41.7
45~54 岁 Age	10	20.0	10.0	0.0	20.0	0.0	50.0
55~60 岁 Age	5	0.0	20.0	0.0	60.0	0.0	20.0
女性 Female	71	33.8	35.2	1.4	9.9	0.0	19.7
16~24 岁 Age	27	29.6	51.9	0.0	3.7	0.0	14.8
25~34 岁 Age	23	39.1	30.4	0.0	13.0	0.0	17.4
35~44 岁 Age	14	42.9	21.4	7.1	14.3	0.0	14.3
45~54 岁 Age	6	16.7	16.7	0.0	0.0	0.0	66.7
55~60 岁 Age	1	0.0	0.0	0.0	100.0	0.0	0.0

3-11 样本、男性各年龄层、女性各年龄层最常饮用场合/ Settings of Consumption by the Whole Sample, Age and Gender Groups

注：本题为多选题，合计百分比超过 100%（Multiple answers）

	人数 Number	早餐时 breakfast	正餐（午、晚餐）时 dinner	口渴时 when thirsty	宵夜时 evening snack	睡觉前 before sleeping	工作休息时 during work break	外出/旅游时 outing/traveling	运动后 after athletics	其它 others
样本 Sample	158	59.5	3.8	16.5	5.1	21.5	6.3	13.3	3.2	1.3
男性 Male	81	56.8	2.5	14.8	7.4	17.3	8.6	8.6	3.7	2.5
16~24 岁 Age	29	69.0	0.0	17.2	6.9	13.8	0.0	0.0	6.9	3.4
25~34 岁 Age	26	30.8	7.7	19.2	7.7	15.4	15.4	19.2	3.8	3.8
35~44 岁 Age	11	72.7	0.0	0.0	18.2	18.2	9.1	18.2	0.0	0.0
45~54 岁 Age	10	60.0	0.0	20.0	0.0	30.0	10.0	0.0	0.0	0.0
55~60 岁 Age	5	80.0	0.0	0.0	0.0	20.0	20.0	0.0	0.0	0.0
女性 Female	77	62.3	5.2	18.2	2.6	26.0	3.9	18.2	2.6	0.0
16~24 岁 Age	29	44.8	6.9	20.7	3.4	13.8	6.9	34.5	6.9	0.0
25~34 岁 Age	24	62.5	4.2	33.3	0.0	29.2	4.2	12.5	0.0	0.0
35~44 岁 Age	14	85.7	7.1	0.0	0.0	42.9	0.0	7.1	0.0	0.0
45~54 岁 Age	9	77.8	0.0	0.0	11.1	33.3	0.0	0.0	0.0	0.0
55~60 岁 Age	1	100.0	0.0	0.0	0.0	0.0	0.0	0.0	0.0	0.0

3-12 重度消费者的人口分布/ Demographics of the Heavy Consumers

	人数 Number	16-24 岁 Age	25-34 岁 Age	35-44 岁 Age	45-54 岁 Age	55-60 岁 Age
样本 Sample	99	34.3	27.3	17.2	15.2	6.1
男性 Male	54	37.0	22.2	18.5	14.8	7.4
天天喝 daily	29	41.4	17.2	17.2	17.2	6.9
一周 3 次或以上 3 times or over a week	8	37.5	25.0	12.5	0.0	25.0
一周 1～2 次 once or twice a week	17	29.4	29.4	23.5	17.6	0.0
女性 Female	45	31.1	33.3	15.6	15.6	4.4
天天喝 daily	20	25.0	25.0	15.0	25.0	10.0
一周 3 次或以上 3 times or over a week	9	44.4	33.3	11.1	11.1	0.0
一周 1～2 次 once or twice a week	16	31.3	43.8	18.8	6.3	0.0

3-13 不同消费者层的常用品牌/ The Most Frequently Used Brands by Market Segments

3-13-1 时尚流行指标/ Fads Popular Index

	人数 Number	第一品牌及百分比 1st/ percent	第二品牌及百分比 2nd/ percent	第三品牌及百分比 3rd/ percent
样本 Sample	152	**天友 Tianyou(72.4)**	**乐百氏 Robust(3.9)**	**均瑶 Junyao(3.3)**
平实生活指向 simple living orientation	69	天友 Tianyou(76.8)	子母奶 Dutch Lady(2.9)	光明 Bright(1.4) 均瑶 Junyao(1.4) 乐百氏 Robust(1.4) 杨协成 Yeo's(1.4) 山城 Shancheng(1.4) 江龙 Jianglong (1.4) 海浪 Hailang(1.4)
时尚流行指向 fashion orientation	83	天友 Tianyou(68.7)	乐百氏 Robust(6.0)	均瑶 Junyao(4.8) 雀巢 Nestle(4.8)

3-13-2 广告态度指标/ Advertising Attitude Index

	人数 Number	第一品牌及百分比 1st/ percent	第二品牌及百分比 2nd/ percent	第三品牌及百分比 3rd/ percent
样本 Sample	155	**天友 Tianyou(72.9)**	**乐百氏 Robust(3.9)**	**均瑶 Junyao(3.2)**
广告淡漠指向 indifferent orientation	39	天友 Tianyou(71.8)	乐百氏 Robust(7.7)	光明 Bright(2.6) 均瑶 Junyao(2.6) 子母奶 Dutch Lady(2.6) 雀巢 Nestle(2.6) 杨协成 Yeo's(2.6) 太易 Taiyi(2.6)
中间层 medium	94	天友 Tianyou(69.1)	均瑶 Junyao(4.3)	雀巢 Nestle(3.2) 子母奶 Dutch Lady(3.2) 乐百氏 Robust(3.2) 光明 Bright(3.2)
信赖广告指向 loyal orientation	22	天友 Tianyou(90.9)	山城 Shancheng(4.5)	

3-13-3 饮食健康指标/ Foods & Drink Quality Index

	人数 Number	第一品牌及百分比 1st/ percent	第二品牌及百分比 2nd/ percent	第三品牌及百分比 3rd/ percent
样本 Sample	156	**天友 Tianyou(72.4)**	**乐百氏 Robust(3.8)**	**均瑶 Junyao(3.2)**
饮食"温饱"指向 "basic" orientation	54	天友 Tianyou(70.4)	乐百氏 Robust(7.4)	均瑶 Junyao(3.7)
中间层 medium	63	天友 Tianyou(73.0)	子母奶 Dutch Lady(4.8)	均瑶 Junyao(3.2) 乐百氏 Robust(3.2)
健康营养指向 health & nutrition orientation	37	天友 Tianyou(75.7)	光明 Bright(5.4) 雀巢 Nestle(5.4)	均瑶 Junyao(2.7) 子母奶 Dutch Lady(2.7) 太易 Taiyi(2.7)

3-14 重度消费者的消费者层构成/ The Composition of the Heavy Consumers

3-14-1 时尚流行指标/ Fads Popular Index

	人数 Number	平实生活指向 simple living orientation	时尚流行指向 fashion orientation
样本 Sample	97	46.4	53.6
天天喝 daily	48	56.3	43.8
一周 3 次或以上 3 times or over a week	16	31.3	68.8
一周 1～2 次 once or twice a week	33	39.4	60.6

3-14-2 广告态度指标/ Advertising Attitude Index

	人数 Number	广告淡漠指向 indifferent orientation	中间层 medium	信赖广告指向 loyal orientation
样本 Sample	98	27.6	57.1	15.3
天天喝 daily	49	26.5	59.2	14.3
一周 3 次或以上 3 time or over a week	16	37.5	50.0	12.5
一周 1～2 次 once or twice a week	33	24.2	57.6	18.2

3-14-3 饮食健康指标/ Foods & Drink Quality Index

	人数 Number	饮食"温饱"指向 "basic" orientation	中间层 medium	健康营养指向 health & nutrition orientation
样本 Sample	97	32.0	43.3	24.7
天天喝 daily	48	35.4	39.6	25.0
一周 3 次或以上 3 time or over a week	16	37.5	37.5	25.0
一周 1～2 次 once or twice a week	33	24.2	51.5	24.2

● 武汉 / Wuhan

3-1 最近三个月食用频率的比例/ Proportion of the Sample Consuming Packaged Milk in the Last Three Months

	人数 Number	百分比 Percent
天天喝 daily	42	6.5
一周 3 次或以上 3 times or over a week	24	3.7
一周 1~2 次 once or twice a week	40	6.2
一个月 2～3 次 2 or 3 times a month	49	7.6
一个月 1 次或以下 once a month or below	29	4.5
没喝过 never	458	71.3

n=642

3-2 最常用品牌排名/ Ranking of the Most Frequently Used Brands

排名 Brand Ranking	品牌 Brands	人数 Number	百分比 Percent
1	扬子江 Yangzijiang	60	32.6
2	光明 Bright	45	24.5
3	友芝友 Youzhiyou	23	12.5
5	均瑶 Junyao	9	4.9
6	香满楼 Flower Fresh	8	4.3
7	双叉奶 Shuangchanai	5	2.7
8	妙士 Miaoshi	4	2.2
9	雀巢 Nestle	3	1.6
9	汉字 Hanzi	3	1.6
9	旺旺 Wangwang	3	1.6

n=184

3-3 样本、男性各年龄层、女性各年龄层的常用品牌/ The Most Frequently Used Brands by the Whole Sample, Age and Gender Groups

	人数 Number	第一品牌及百分比 1st/ percent	第二品牌及百分比 2nd/ percent	第三品牌及百分比 3rd/ percent
样本 Sample	184	**扬子江 Yangzijiang(32.6)**	**光明 Bright(24.5)**	**友芝友 Youzhiyou(12.5)**
男性 Male	75	**扬子江 Yangzijiang(33.3)**	**光明 Bright(22.7)**	**友芝友 Youzhiyou(9.3)**
16~24 岁 Age	22	光明 Bright(31.8)	扬子江 Yangzijiang(22.7)	均瑶 Junyao(13.6)
25~34 岁 Age	27	扬子江 Yangzijiang(40.7)	光明 Bright(18.5)	香满楼 Flower Fresh(7.4) 友芝友 Youzhiyou(7.4)
35~44 岁 Age	15	扬子江 Yangzijiang(40.0)	光明 Bright(20.0)	旺旺 Wangwang(13.3) 友芝友 Youzhiyou(13.3)
45~54 岁 Age	8	扬子江 Yangzijiang(25.0) 友芝友 Youzhiyou(25.0)	光明 Bright(12.5) 伊利 Yili(12.5) 双叉奶 Shuangchanai (12.5) 妙士 Miaoshi(12.5)	
55~60 岁 Age	3	光明 Bright(33.3) 扬子江 Yangzijiang(33.3)		
女性 Female	109	**扬子江 Yangzijiang(32.1)**	**光明 Bright(25.7)**	**友芝友 Youzhiyou(14.7)**
16~24 岁 Age	42	光明 Bright(28.6)	扬子江 Yangzijiang(23.8)	友芝友 Youzhiyou(14.3)
25~34 岁 Age	34	扬子江 Yangzijiang(26.5)	光明 Bright(23.5)	友芝友 Youzhiyou(20.6)
35~44 岁 Age	15	扬子江 Yangzijiang(53.3)	光明 Bright(20.0)	友芝友 Youzhiyou(13.3)
45~54 岁 Age	14	扬子江 Yangzijiang(50.0)	光明 Bright(21.4)	均瑶 Junyao(7.1) 双叉奶 Shuangchanai(7.1) 友芝友 Youzhiyou(7.1)
55~60 岁 Age	4	光明 Bright(50.0)	冰峰 Bingfeng(25.0) 扬子江 Yangzijiang(25.0)	

3-4 理想品牌排名/ Ranking of the Ideal Brands

排名 Brand Ranking	品牌 Brands	人数 Number	百分比 Percent
1	扬子江 Yangzijiang	138	21.5
2	光明 Bright	72	11.2
3	友芝友 Youzhiyou	22	3.4
4	香满楼 Flower Fresh	16	2.5
4	伊利 Yili	16	2.5
5	雀巢 Nestle	10	1.6
6	均瑶 Junyao	9	1.4
7	妙士 Miaoshi	6	0.9
8	旺旺 Wangwang	5	0.8

n=641

3-5 样本、男性各年龄层、女性各年龄层最近三个月有无购买的比例/ Purchasing in the Last Three Months by the Whole Sample, Age and Gender Groups

	人数 Number	买过 yes	没买过 no
样本 Sample	641	**31.0**	**69.0**
男性 Male	310	**25.2**	**74.8**
16~24 岁 Age	65	27.7	72.3
25~34 岁 Age	88	29.5	70.5
35~44 岁 Age	80	26.3	73.8
45~54 岁 Age	52	19.2	80.8
55~60 岁 Age	25	12.0	88.0
女性 Female	331	**36.6**	**63.4**
16~24 岁 Age	69	53.6	46.4
25~34 岁 Age	96	43.8	56.3
35~44 岁 Age	78	30.8	69.2
45~54 岁 Age	62	24.2	75.8
55~60 岁 Age	26	11.5	88.5

3-6 样本、男性各年龄层、女性各年龄层最近三个月的食用频率/ Frequencies of Consuming Packaged Milk in the Last Three Months by the Whole Sample, Age and Gender Groups

	人数 Number	天天喝 daily	一周 3 次或以上 3 times or over a week	一周 1~2 次 once or twice a week	一个月 2~3 次 2 or 3 times a month	一个月 1 次或以下 once a month or below	没喝过 never
样本 Sample	642	6.5	3.7	6.2	7.6	4.5	71.3
男性 Male	311	4.8	3.2	5.1	6.1	4.8	75.9
16~24 岁 Age	65	6.2	3.1	7.7	9.2	7.7	66.2
25~34 岁 Age	89	6.7	3.4	3.4	9.0	7.9	69.7
35~44 岁 Age	80	3.8	3.8	6.3	2.5	2.5	81.3
45~54 岁 Age	52	1.9	3.8	1.9	5.8	1.9	84.6
55~60 岁 Age	25	4.0	0.0	8.0	0.0	0.0	88.0
女性 Female	331	8.2	4.2	7.3	9.1	4.2	67.1
16~24 岁 Age	69	10.1	7.2	10.1	21.7	11.6	39.1
25~34 岁 Age	96	9.4	4.2	9.4	9.4	3.1	64.6
35~44 岁 Age	78	5.1	3.8	5.1	2.6	2.6	80.8
45~54 岁 Age	62	9.7	3.2	3.2	6.5	0.0	77.4
55~60 岁 Age	26	3.8	0.0	7.7	0.0	3.8	84.6

3-7 样本、男性各年龄层、女性各年龄层的品牌习惯/ Brand Habit in Consuming Packaged Milk by the Whole Sample, Age and Gender Groups

	人数 Number	基本固定食用一个牌子 used in only one brand	比较固定地食用两个或三个牌子 used in two or three brands	基本上不太固定牌子 no brand preference
样本 Sample	184	52.7	23.9	23.4
男性 Male	75	52.0	20.0	28.0
16~24 岁 Age	22	54.5	9.1	36.4
25~34 岁 Age	27	48.1	33.3	18.5
35~44 岁 Age	15	46.7	20.0	33.3
45~54 岁 Age	8	50.0	12.5	37.5
55~60 岁 Age	3	100.0	0.0	0.0
女性 Female	109	53.2	26.6	20.2
16~24 岁 Age	42	45.2	28.6	26.2
25~34 岁 Age	34	50.0	35.3	14.7
35~44 岁 Age	15	80.0	13.3	6.7
45~54 岁 Age	14	64.3	7.1	28.6
55~60 岁 Age	4	25.0	50.0	25.0

3-8 选择该类商品的考虑因素/ Ranking of the Considerations in Purchasing

注：本题为多选题，合计百分比超过 100%（Multiple answers）

排名 Ranking	考虑因素 Considerations	人次 Person-time	百分比 Percent
1	口味好 pleasant taste	91	49.5
2	营养成分 nutrition constituent	71	38.6
3	价格适中 reasonable price	68	37.0
4	购买方便 easy to buy	53	28.8
5	生产日期 date of producing	48	26.1
6	有名的牌子 famous brand	41	22.3
7	广告影响 influence of advertising	15	8.2
8	只是由于习惯 out of habit	14	7.6
9	朋友推荐 introduction of friends	13	7.1
9	包装吸引人 appealing package	13	7.1
10	有优惠条件 with preferential terms	12	6.5
11	其它 others	6	3.3
12	售货员介绍 introduced by the shop assistants	5	2.7

n=184

3-9 样本、男性各年龄层、女性各年龄层最常食用的种类/ Types of the Consumed Packaged Milk by the Whole Sample, Age and Gender Groups

	人数 Number	全脂 whole milk	低脂 low-fat	脱脂 skimmed	花色奶（巧克力味、草莓味等）milk varieties (chocolate flavor.Strawberry flavors etc.)	强化奶 enriched milk	加矿物质（含钙、铁等）with minerals (containing calcium. Iron etc.)	其它 others
样本 Sample	182	40.7	20.3	12.1	10.4	2.7	11.0	2.7
男性 Male	74	39.2	14.9	14.9	9.5	2.7	13.5	5.4
16~24 岁 Age	22	27.3	4.5	18.2	13.6	4.5	18.2	13.6
25~34 岁 Age	27	40.7	18.5	14.8	14.8	0.0	11.1	0.0
35~44 岁 Age	14	35.7	21.4	7.1	0.0	7.1	21.4	7.1
45~54 岁 Age	8	62.5	12.5	25.0	0.0	0.0	0.0	0.0
55~60 岁 Age	3	66.7	33.3	0.0	0.0	0.0	0.0	0.0
女性 Female	108	41.7	24.1	10.2	11.1	2.8	9.3	0.9
16~24 岁 Age	42	35.7	31.0	9.5	16.7	0.0	7.1	0.0
25~34 岁 Age	34	58.8	14.7	5.9	8.8	2.9	8.8	0.0
35~44 岁 Age	15	26.7	33.3	6.7	6.7	13.3	6.7	6.7
45~54 岁 Age	13	46.2	15.4	15.4	0.0	0.0	23.1	0.0
55~60 岁 Age	4	0.0	25.0	50.0	25.0	0.0	0.0	0.0

3-10 样本、男性各年龄层、女性各年龄层最常食用的包装形式/ Types of Package of the Consumed Packaged Milk by the Whole Sample, Age and Gender Groups

	人数 Number	方盒装/利乐砖 plastic-bag milk	房屋状纸盒 house-shaped box	粽子状纸盒 V-shaped box	塑料瓶 plastic bottle	易拉罐 tin	其他 others
样本 Sample	177	32.2	9.6	1.1	32.8	4.5	19.8
男性 Male	74	27.0	9.5	2.7	41.9	4.1	14.9
16~24 岁 Age	22	27.3	0.0	0.0	63.6	0.0	9.1
25~34 岁 Age	27	22.2	14.8	0.0	48.1	3.7	11.1
35~44 岁 Age	14	21.4	14.3	7.1	28.6	7.1	21.4
45~54 岁 Age	8	37.5	12.5	12.5	0.0	12.5	25.0
55~60 岁 Age	3	66.7	0.0	0.0	0.0	0.0	33.3
女性 Female	103	35.9	9.7	0.0	26.2	4.9	23.3
16~24 岁 Age	39	41.0	15.4	0.0	33.3	2.6	7.7
25~34 岁 Age	32	31.3	6.3	0.0	25.0	3.1	34.4
35~44 岁 Age	15	40.0	13.3	0.0	6.7	13.3	26.7
45~54 岁 Age	13	38.5	0.0	0.0	15.4	0.0	46.2
55~60 岁 Age	4	0.0	0.0	0.0	75.0	25.0	0.0

3-11 样本、男性各年龄层、女性各年龄层最常饮用场合/ Settings of Consumption by the Whole Sample, Age and Gender Groups

注：本题为多选题，合计百分比超过 100%（Multiple answers）

	人数 Number	早餐时 breakfast	正餐（午、晚餐）时 dinner	口渴时 when thirsty	宵夜时 evening snack	睡觉前 before sleeping	工作休息时 during work break	外出/旅游时 outing/traveling	运动后 after athletics	其它 others
样本 Sample	183	51.9	8.7	16.9	4.9	13.1	10.4	15.3	1.1	4.4
男性 Male	75	50.7	12.0	20.0	4.0	9.3	10.7	10.7	0.0	2.7
16~24 岁 Age	22	45.5	9.1	22.7	0.0	0.0	9.1	13.6	0.0	9.1
25~34 岁 Age	27	48.1	7.4	22.2	0.0	7.4	14.8	18.5	0.0	0.0
35~44 岁 Age	15	60.0	13.3	20.0	13.3	20.0	13.3	0.0	0.0	0.0
45~54 岁 Age	8	50.0	37.5	12.5	12.5	12.5	0.0	0.0	0.0	0.0
55~60 岁 Age	3	66.7	0.0	0.0	0.0	33.3	0.0	0.0	0.0	0.0
女性 Female	108	52.8	6.5	14.8	5.6	15.7	10.2	18.5	1.9	5.6
16~24 岁 Age	42	50.0	7.1	21.4	2.4	7.1	14.3	21.4	0.0	7.1
25~34 岁 Age	34	55.9	8.8	8.8	2.9	26.5	5.9	17.6	2.9	2.9
35~44 岁 Age	15	53.3	6.7	6.7	20.0	26.7	13.3	13.3	0.0	0.0
45~54 岁 Age	13	61.5	0.0	15.4	7.7	7.7	7.7	15.4	0.0	7.7
55~60 岁 Age	4	25.0	0.0	25.0	0.0	0.0	0.0	25.0	25.0	25.0

3-12 重度消费者的人口分布/ Demographics of the Heavy Consumers

	人数 Number	16-24 岁 Age	25-34 岁 Age	35-44 岁 Age	45-54 岁 Age	55-60 岁 Age
样本 Sample	106	28.3	32.1	20.8	13.2	5.7
男性 Male	41	26.8	29.3	26.8	9.8	7.3
天天喝 daily	15	26.7	40.0	20.0	6.7	6.7
一周 3 次或以上 3 times or over a week	10	20.0	30.0	30.0	20.0	0.0
一周 1～2 次 once or twice a week	16	31.3	18.8	31.3	6.3	12.5
女性 Female	65	29.2	33.8	16.9	15.4	4.6
天天喝 daily	27	25.9	33.3	14.8	22.2	3.7
一周 3 次或以上 3 times or over a week	14	35.7	28.6	21.4	14.3	0.0
一周 1～2 次 once or twice a week	24	29.2	37.5	16.7	8.3	8.3

3-13 不同消费者层的常用品牌/ The Most Frequently Used Brands by Market Segments

3-13-1 时尚流行指标/ Fads Popular Index

	人数 Number	第一品牌及百分比 1st/ percent	第二品牌及百分比 2nd/ percent	第三品牌及百分比 3rd/ percent
样本 Sample	180	**扬子江 Yangzijiang(33.3)**	**光明 Bright(23.9)**	**友芝友 Youzhiyou (12.8)**
平实生活指向 simple living orientation	79	扬子江 Yangzijiang(34.2)	光明 Bright(24.1)	友芝友 Youzhiyou(10.1)
时尚流行指向 fashion orientation	101	扬子江 Yangzijiang(32.7)	光明 Bright(23.8)	友芝友 Youzhiyou (14.9)

3-13-2 广告态度指标/ Advertising Attitude Index

	人数 Number	第一品牌及百分比 1st/ percent	第二品牌及百分比 2nd/ percent	第三品牌及百分比 3rd/ percent
样本 Sample	180	**扬子江 Yangzijiang(33.3)**	**光明 Bright(23.9)**	**友芝友 Youzhiyou(12.8)**
广告淡漠指向 indifferent orientation	47	扬子江 Yangzijiang(31.9)	光明 Bright(23.4)	友芝友 Youzhiyou(17.0)
中间层 medium	115	扬子江 Yangzijiang(35.7)	光明 Bright(21.7)	友芝友 Youzhiyou(12.2)
信赖广告指向 loyal orientation	18	光明 Bright(38.9)	扬子江 Yangzijiang(22.2)	香满楼 Flower Fresh(11.1)

3-13-3 饮食健康指标/ Foods & Drink Quality Index

	人数 Number	第一品牌及百分比 1st/ percent	第二品牌及百分比 2nd/ percent	第三品牌及百分比 3rd/ percent
样本 Sample	184	**扬子江 Yangzijiang(32.6)**	**光明 Bright(24.5)**	**友芝友 Youzhiyou(12.5)**
饮食"温饱"指向 "basic" orientation	45	光明 Bright(35.6) 扬子江 Yangzijiang(35.6)	友芝友 Youzhiyou(6.7)	香满楼 Flower Fresh(4.4) 旺旺 Wangwang(4.4)
中间层 medium	95	扬子江 Yangzijiang(31.6)	光明 Bright(21.1)	友芝友 Youzhiyou(14.7)
健康营养指向 health & nutrition orientation	40	扬子江 Yangzijiang(35.0)	光明 Bright(20.0)	友芝友 Youzhiyou(15.0)

3-14 重度消费者的消费者层构成/ The Composition of the Heavy Consumers

3-14-1 时尚流行指标/ Fads Popular Index

	人数 Number	平实生活指向 simple living orientation	时尚流行指向 fashion orientation
样本 Sample	104	39.4	60.6
天天喝 daily	42	45.2	54.8
一周 3 次或以上 3 times or over a week	24	37.5	62.5
一周 1～2 次 once or twice a week	38	34.2	65.8

3-14-2 广告态度指标/ Advertising Attitude Index

	人数 Number	广告淡漠指向 indifferent orientation	中间层 medium	信赖广告指向 loyal orientation
样本 Sample	104	**23.1**	**69.2**	**7.7**
天天喝 daily	42	21.4	73.8	4.8
一周 3 次或以上 3 times or over a week	24	25.0	62.5	12.5
一周 1～2 次 once or twice a week	38	23.7	68.4	7.9

3-14-3 饮食健康指标/ Foods & Drink Quality Index

	人数 Number	饮食"温饱"指向 "basic" orientation	中间层 medium	健康营养指向 health & nutrition orientation
样本 Sample	104	**23.1**	**51.0**	**26.0**
天天喝 daily	42	28.6	50.0	21.4
一周 3 次或以上 3 times or over a week	24	16.7	58.3	25.0
一周 1～2 次 once or twice a week	38	21.1	47.4	31.6

● 西安 / Xi'an

3-1 最近三个月食用频率的比例/ Proportion of the Sample Consuming Packaged Milk in the Last Three Months

	人数 Number	百分比 Percent
天天喝 daily	25	4.2
一周 3 次或以上 3 times or over a week	20	3.3
一周 1~2 次 once or twice a week	47	7.8
一个月 2～3 次 2 or 3 times a month	52	8.7
一个月 1 次或以下 once a month or below	35	5.8
没喝过 never	422	70.2

n=601

3-2 最常用品牌排名/ Ranking of the Most Frequently Used Brands

排名 Brand Ranking	品牌 Brands	人数 Number	百分比 Percent
1	光明 Bright	85	47.5
2	鲜迪 Xiandi	25	14.0
3	东方 Dongfang	18	10.1
4	牧童 Mutong	11	6.1
5	均瑶 Junyao	7	3.9
6	旺仔 Wangzi	4	2.2
7	荣氏 Rong	3	1.7
8	乐百氏 Robust	2	1.1
8	伊利 Yili	2	1.1
8	骊山 Lishan	2	1.1

n=179

3-3 样本、男性各年龄层、女性各年龄层的常用品牌/ The Most Frequently Used Brands by the Whole Sample, Age and Gender Groups

	人数 Number	第一品牌及百分比 1st/ percent	第二品牌及百分比 2nd/ percent	第三品牌及百分比 3rd/ percent
样本 Sample	179	**光明 Bright(47.5)**	**鲜迪 Xiandi(14.0)**	**东方 Dongfang (10.1)**
男性 Male	88	**光明 Bright(51.1)**	**东方 Dongfang (13.6)**	**鲜迪 Xiandi(11.4)**
16~24 岁 Age	29	光明 Bright(44.8)	鲜迪 Xiandi(17.2)	东方 Dongfang (13.8)
25~34 岁 Age	27	光明 Bright(59.3)	鲜迪 Xiandi(11.1) 东方 Dongfang(11.1)	均瑶 Junyao(3.7) 乐百氏 Robust(3.7) 旺仔 Wangzi(3.7) 骊山 Lishan(3.7)
35~44 岁 Age	23	光明 Bright(47.8)	东方 Dongfang (13.0)	牧童 Mutong (8.7)
45~54 岁 Age	6	光明 Bright(50.0)	娃哈哈 Wahaha(16.7) 鲜迪 Xiandi(16.7) 东方 Dongfang (16.7)	
55~60 岁 Age	3	光明 Bright(66.7)	东方 Dongfang (33.3)	
女性 Female	91	**光明 Bright(44.0)**	**鲜迪 Xiandi(16.5)**	**牧童 Mutong((8.8)**
16~24 岁 Age	24	光明 Bright(54.2)	鲜迪 Xiandi(12.5)	伊利 Yili(8.3)
25~34 岁 Age	35	光明 Bright(42.9)	鲜迪 Xiandi(11.4) 东方 Dongfang (11.4)	牧童 Mutong (8.6)
35~44 岁 Age	20	光明 Bright(40.0)	鲜迪 Xiandi(15.0) 牧童 Mutong(15.0)	东方 Dongfang (10.0)
45~54 岁 Age	9	光明 Bright(44.4)	鲜迪 Xiandi(22.2)	均瑶 Junyao(11.1) 牧童 Mutong (11.1) 骊山 Lishan(11.1)
55~60 岁 Age	3	鲜迪 Xiandi(100.0)		

3-4 理想品牌排名/ Ranking of the Ideal Brands

排名 Brand Ranking	品牌 Brands	人数 Number	百分比 Percent
1	光明 Bright	200	33.3
2	鲜迪 Xiandi	45	7.5
3	东方 Dongfang	36	6.0
4	牧童 Mutong	18	3.0
5	均瑶 Junyao	11	1.8
6	旺仔 Wangzi	10	1.7
6	荣氏 Rong	10	1.7
7	伊利 Yili	4	0.7
7	骊山 Lishan	4	0.7

n=601

3-5 样本、男性各年龄层、女性各年龄层最近三个月有无购买的比例/ Purchasing in the Last Three Months by the Whole Sample, Age and Gender Groups

	人数 Number	买过 yes	没买过 no
样本 Sample	601	30.9	69.1
男性 Male	302	32.5	67.5
16~24 岁 Age	64	40.6	59.4
25~34 岁 Age	91	40.7	59.3
35~44 岁 Age	77	32.5	67.5
45~54 岁 Age	46	15.2	84.8
55~60 岁 Age	24	12.5	87.5
女性 Female	299	29.4	70.6
16~24 岁 Age	61	32.8	67.2
25~34 岁 Age	90	34.4	65.6
35~44 岁 Age	74	29.7	70.3
45~54 岁 Age	49	20.4	79.6
55~60 岁 Age	25	20.0	80.0

3-6 样本、男性各年龄层、女性各年龄层最近三个月的食用频率/ Frequencies of Consuming Packaged Milk in the Last Three Months by the Whole Sample, Age and Gender Groups

	人数 Number	天天喝 daily	一周 3 次或以上 3 times or over a week	一周 1~2 次 once or twice a week	一个月 2~3 次 2 or 3 times a month	一个月 1 次或以下 once a month or below	没喝过 never
样本 Sample	601	4.2	3.3	7.8	8.7	5.8	70.2
男性 Male	302	4.6	3.0	8.3	7.6	5.6	70.9
16~24 岁 Age	64	7.8	6.3	14.1	7.8	9.4	54.7
25~34 岁 Age	91	2.2	3.3	5.5	13.2	5.5	70.3
35~44 岁 Age	77	5.2	2.6	10.4	5.2	6.5	70.1
45~54 岁 Age	46	4.3	0.0	2.2	4.3	2.2	87.0
55~60 岁 Age	24	4.2	0.0	8.3	0.0	0.0	87.5
女性 Female	299	3.7	3.7	7.4	9.7	6.0	69.6
16~24 岁 Age	61	3.3	6.6	11.5	9.8	8.2	60.7
25~34 岁 Age	90	5.6	1.1	10.0	14.4	7.8	61.1
35~44 岁 Age	74	5.4	6.8	5.4	5.4	4.1	73.0
45~54 岁 Age	49	0.0	0.0	4.1	10.2	4.1	81.6
55~60 岁 Age	25	0.0	4.0	0.0	4.0	4.0	88.0

3-7 样本、男性各年龄层、女性各年龄层的品牌习惯/ Brand Habit in Consuming Packaged Milk by the Whole Sample, Age and Gender Groups

	人数 Number	基本固定食用一个牌子 used in only one brand	比较固定地食用两个或三个牌子 used in two or three brands	基本上不太固定牌子 no brand preference
样本 Sample	179	50.8	24.6	24.6
男性 Male	88	48.9	25.0	26.1
16~24 岁 Age	29	37.9	27.6	34.5
25~34 岁 Age	27	48.1	22.2	29.6
35~44 岁 Age	23	56.5	30.4	13.0
45~54 岁 Age	6	50.0	16.7	33.3
55~60 岁 Age	3	100.0	0.0	0.0
女性 Female	91	52.7	24.2	23.1
16~24 岁 Age	24	58.3	29.2	12.5
25~34 岁 Age	35	48.6	20.0	31.4
35~44 岁 Age	20	60.0	20.0	20.0
45~54 岁 Age	9	33.3	44.4	22.2
55~60 岁 Age	3	66.7	0.0	33.3

3-8 选择该类商品的考虑因素/ Ranking of the Considerations in Purchasing

注：本题为多选题，合计百分比超过 100%（Multiple answers）

排名 Ranking	考虑因素 Considerations	人次 Person-time	百分比 Percent
1	口味好 pleasant taste	101	56.4
2	营养成分 nutrition constituent	64	35.8
3	购买方便 easy to buy	44	24.6
4	有名的牌子 famous brand	43	24.0
5	价格适中 reasonable price	39	21.8
6	生产日期 date of producing	28	15.6
7	广告影响 influence of advertising	17	9.5
8	包装吸引人 appealing package	12	6.7
9	朋友推荐 introduction of friends	7	3.9
10	只是由于习惯 out of habit	6	3.4
11	有优惠条件 with preferential terms	5	2.8
12	售货员介绍 introduced by the shop assistants	3	1.7
13	其它 others	2	1.1

n=179

3-9 样本、男性各年龄层、女性各年龄层最常食用的种类/ Types of the Consumed Packaged Milk by the Whole Sample, Age and Gender Groups

	人数 Number	全脂 whole milk	低脂 low-fat	脱脂 skimmed	花色奶（巧克力味、草莓味等）milk varieties (chocolate flavor .strawberry flavor etc.)	强化奶 enriched milk	加矿物质（含钙、铁等）with minerals (containing calcium. Iron etc.)	其它 others
样本 Sample	179	21.8	8.4	10.6	22.9	24.6	11.2	0.6
男性 Male	88	23.9	6.8	12.5	19.3	26.1	10.2	1.1
16~24 岁 Age	29	24.1	6.9	13.8	27.6	20.7	6.9	0.0
25~34 岁 Age	27	33.3	3.7	11.1	18.5	18.5	11.1	3.7
35~44 岁 Age	23	8.7	4.3	13.0	17.4	39.1	17.4	0.0
45~54 岁 Age	6	33.3	16.7	16.7	0.0	33.3	0.0	0.0
55~60 岁 Age	3	33.3	33.3	0.0	0.0	33.3	0.0	0.0
女性 Female	91	19.8	9.9	8.8	26.4	23.1	12.1	0.0
16~24 岁 Age	24	16.7	16.7	4.2	37.5	20.8	4.2	0.0
25~34 岁 Age	35	14.3	5.7	11.4	25.7	28.6	14.3	0.0
35~44 岁 Age	20	30.0	5.0	15.0	15.0	20.0	15.0	0.0
45~54 岁 Age	9	22.2	11.1	0.0	33.3	22.2	11.1	0.0
55~60 岁 Age	3	33.3	33.3	0.0	0.0	0.0	33.3	0.0

3-10 样本、男性各年龄层、女性各年龄层最常食用的包装形式/ Types of Package of the Consumed Packaged Milk by the Whole Sample, Age and Gender Groups

	人数 Number	方盒装/利乐砖 plastic-bag milk	房屋状纸盒 house-shaped box	粽子状纸盒 V-shaped box	塑料瓶 plastic bottle	易拉罐 tin	其他 others
样本 Sample	179	55.9	14.0	2.2	22.3	3.9	1.7
男性 Male	88	56.8	14.8	2.3	21.6	3.4	1.1
16~24 岁 Age	29	65.5	17.2	0.0	13.8	3.4	0.0
25~34 岁 Age	27	55.6	7.4	0.0	29.6	3.7	3.7
35~44 岁 Age	23	47.8	26.1	0.0	26.1	0.0	0.0
45~54 岁 Age	6	50.0	0.0	33.3	0.0	16.7	0.0
55~60 岁 Age	3	66.7	0.0	0.0	33.3	0.0	0.0
女性 Female	91	54.9	13.2	2.2	23.1	4.4	2.2
16~24 岁 Age	24	62.5	16.7	0.0	12.5	8.3	0.0
25~34 岁 Age	35	60.0	8.6	5.7	17.1	5.7	2.9
35~44 岁 Age	20	40.0	10.0	0.0	45.0	0.0	5.0
45~54 岁 Age	9	55.6	33.3	0.0	11.1	0.0	0.0
55~60 岁 Age	3	33.3	0.0	0.0	66.7	0.0	0.0

3-11 样本、男性各年龄层、女性各年龄层最常饮用场合/ Settings of Consumption by the Whole Sample, Age and Gender Groups

注：本题为多选题，合计百分比超过 100%（Multiple answers）

	人数 Number	早餐时 breakfast	正餐（午、晚餐）时 dinner	口渴时 when thirsty	宵夜时 evening snack	睡觉前 before sleeping	工作休息时 during work break	外出/旅游时 outing/ traveling	运动后 after athletics	其它 others
样本 Sample	179	46.4	5.0	20.1	4.5	15.1	8.4	26.8	5.0	1.7
男性 Male	88	52.3	2.3	20.5	6.8	12.5	6.8	25.0	5.7	2.3
16~24 岁 Age	29	37.9	3.4	20.7	10.3	6.9	10.3	31.0	6.9	0.0
25~34 岁 Age	27	55.6	0.0	18.5	0.0	14.8	3.7	18.5	0.0	7.4
35~44 岁 Age	23	56.5	4.3	26.1	8.7	13.0	4.3	30.4	13.0	0.0
45~54 岁 Age	6	83.3	0.0	0.0	16.7	33.3	16.7	16.7	0.0	0.0
55~60 岁 Age	3	66.7	0.0	33.3	0.0	0.0	0.0	0.0	0.0	0.0
女性 Female	91	40.7	7.7	19.8	2.2	17.6	9.9	28.6	4.4	1.1
16~24 岁 Age	24	33.3	8.3	29.2	0.0	4.2	12.5	29.2	4.2	0.0
25~34 岁 Age	35	40.0	0.0	22.9	2.9	17.1	2.9	37.1	2.9	0.0
35~44 岁 Age	20	60.0	15.0	0.0	0.0	35.0	15.0	15.0	0.0	5.0
45~54 岁 Age	9	33.3	11.1	33.3	11.1	0.0	22.2	33.3	0.0	0.0
55~60 岁 Age	3	0.0	33.3	0.0	0.0	66.7	0.0	0.0	66.7	0.0

3-12 重度消费者的人口分布/ Demographics of the Heavy Consumers

	人数 Number	16-24 岁 Age	25-34 岁 Age	35-44 岁 Age	45-54 岁 Age	55-60 岁 Age
样本 Sample	92	33.7	27.2	29.3	5.4	4.3
男性 Male	48	37.5	20.8	29.2	6.3	6.3
天天喝 daily	14	35.7	14.3	28.6	14.3	7.1
一周 3 次或以上 3 times or over a week	9	44.4	33.3	22.2	0.0	0.0
一周 1～2 次 once or twice a week	25	36.0	20.0	32.0	4.0	8.0
女性 Female	44	29.5	34.1	29.5	4.5	2.3
天天喝 daily	11	18.2	45.5	36.4	0.0	0.0
一周 3 次或以上 3 times or over a week	11	36.4	9.1	45.5	0.0	9.1
一周 1～2 次 once or twice a week	22	31.8	40.9	18.2	9.1	0.0

3-13 不同消费者层的常用品牌/ The Most Frequently Used Brands by Market Segments

3-13-1 时尚流行指标/ Fads Popular Index

	人数 Number	第一品牌及百分比 1st/ percent	第二品牌及百分比 2nd/ percent	第三品牌及百分比 3rd/ percent
样本 Sample	178	**光明 Bright(47.8)**	**鲜迪 Xiandi(14.0)**	**东方 Dongfang(10.1)**
平实生活指向 simple living orientation	86	光明 Bright(39.5)	鲜迪 Xiandi(17.4)	东方 Dongfang(15.1)
时尚流行指向 fashion orientation	92	光明 Bright(55.4)	鲜迪 Xiandi(10.9)	东方 Dongfang(5.4)

3-13-2 广告态度指标/ Advertising Attitude Index

	人数 Number	第一品牌及百分比 1st/ percent	第二品牌及百分比 2nd/ percent	第三品牌及百分比 3rd/ percent
样本 Sample	178	**光明 Bright(47.2)**	**鲜迪 Xiandi(14.0)**	**东方 Dongfang(10.1)**
广告淡漠指向 indifferent orientation	54	光明 Bright(42.6)	鲜迪 Xiandi(18.5)	东方 Dongfang(11.1)
中间层 medium	102	光明 Bright(48.0)	鲜迪 Xiandi(12.7)	东方 Dongfang(11.8)
信赖广告指向 loyal orientation	22	光明 Bright(54.5)	鲜迪 Xiandi(9.1) 牧童 Mutong(9.1)	澳牛 Dany Farmers(4.5) 倍康 Beikang(4.5) 均瑶 Junyao(4.5) 琳琳 Linlin(4.5) 经塔 Jingta(4.5)

3-13-3 饮食健康指标/ Foods & Drink Quality Index

	人数 Number	第一品牌及百分比 1st/ percent	第二品牌及百分比 2nd/ percent	第三品牌及百分比 3rd/ percent
样本 Sample	179	**光明 Bright(47.5)**	**鲜迪 Xiandi(14.0)**	**东方 Dongfang(10.1)**
饮食"温饱"指向 "basic" orientation	66	光明 Bright(39.4)	鲜迪 Xiandi(21.2)	东方 Dongfang(12.1)
中间层 medium	80	光明 Bright(52.5)	鲜迪 Xiandi(12.5)	牧童 Mutong(7.5) 东方 Dongfang(7.5)
健康营养指向 health & nutrition orientation	33	光明 Bright(51.5)	东方 Dongfang(12.1)	乐百氏 Robust(6.1) 牧童 Mutong(6.1)

3-14 重度消费者的消费者层构成/ The Composition of the Heavy Consumers

3-14-1 时尚流行指标/ Fads Popular Index

	人数 Number	平实生活指向 simple living orientation	时尚流行指向 fashion orientation
样本 Sample	92	47.8	52.2
天天喝 daily	25	56.0	44.0
一周 3 次或以上 3 times or over a week	20	35.0	65.0
一周 1～2 次 once or twice a week	47	48.9	51.1

3-14-2 广告态度指标/ Advertising Attitude Index

	人数 Number	广告淡漠指向 indifferent orientation	中间层 medium	信赖广告指向 loyal orientation
样本 Sample	92	26.1	58.7	15.2
天天喝 daily	25	20.0	64.0	16.0
一周 3 次或以上 3 times or over a week	20	35.0	45.0	20.0
一周 1～2 次 once or twice a week	47	25.5	61.7	12.8

3-14-3 饮食健康指标/ Foods & Drink Quality Index

	人数 Number	饮食"温饱"指向 "basic" orientation	中间层 medium	健康营养指向 health & nutrition orientation
样本 Sample	92	35.9	42.4	21.7
天天喝 daily	25	28.0	40.0	32.0
一周 3 次或以上 3 times or over a week	20	35.0	40.0	25.0
一周 1～2 次 once or twice a week	47	40.4	44.7	14.9

● 沈阳 / Shenyang

3-1 最近三个月食用频率的比例/ Proportion of the Sample Consuming Packaged Milk in the Last Three Months

	人数 Number	百分比 Percent
天天喝 daily	18	3.0
一周 3 次或以上 3 times or over a week	15	2.5
一周 1~2 次 once or twice a week	31	5.2
一个月 2~3 次 2 or 3 times a month	33	5.5
一个月 1 次或以下 once a month or below	24	4.0
没喝过 never	475	79.7

n=596

3-2 最常用品牌排名/ Ranking of the Most Frequently Used Brands

排名 Brand Ranking	品牌 Brands	人数 Number	百分比 Percent
1	伊利 Yili	20	16.5
2	光明 Bright	17	14.0
3	乐百氏 Robust	12	9.9
4	均瑶 Junyao	10	8.3
5	帕玛拉特 Parmalat	4	3.3
5	娃哈哈 Wahaha	4	3.3
5	生活 Life	4	3.3
6	龙丹 Longdan	3	2.5

n=121

3-3 样本、男性各年龄层、女性各年龄层的常用品牌/ The Most Frequently Used Brands by the Whole Sample, Age and Gender Groups

	人数 Number	第一品牌及百分比 1st/ percent	第二品牌及百分比 2nd/ percent	第三品牌及百分比 3rd/ percent
样本 Sample	121	**伊利 Yili(16.5)**	**光明 Bright(14.0)**	**乐百氏 Robust(9.9)**
男性 Male	62	**伊利 Yili(17.7)**	**光明 Bright(12.9)**	**乐百氏 Robust(11.3)**
16~24 岁 Age	19	乐百氏 Robust(26.3)	伊利 Yili(21.1)	生活 Life(10.5)
25~34 岁 Age	27	伊利 Yili(22.2)	均瑶 Junyao(11.1) 光明 Bright(11.1)	乐百氏 Robust(7.4)
35~44 岁 Age	10	光明 Bright(30.0)	娃哈哈 Wahaha(10.0) 伊利 Yili(10.0) 辉山 Huishan(10.0)	
45~54 岁 Age	5	光明 Bright(20.0) 娃哈哈 Wahaha(20.0) 沙洋 Shayang(20.0) 宏利达 Honglida(20.0)		
55~60 岁 Age	1			
女性 Female	59	**伊利 Yili(15.3)** **光明 Bright(15.3)**	**均瑶 Junyao(10.2)**	**乐百氏 Robust(8.5)**
16~24 岁 Age	19	伊利 Yili(26.3)	光明 Bright(10.5) 均瑶 Junyao(10.5) 乐百氏 Robust(10.5)	娃哈哈 Wahaha(5.3) 子母奶 Dutch Lady(5.3) 完达山 Wandashan(5.3) 生活 Life(5.3) 康师傅 Kangshifu(5.3)
25~34 岁 Age	17	光明 Bright(17.6) 均瑶 Junyao(17.6)	卡夫 Kraft(5.9) 乐百氏 Robust(5.9) 帕玛拉特 Farmalat(5 9) 娃哈哈 Wahaha(5.9) 伊利 Yili(5.9)	
35~44 岁 Age	16	光明 Bright(25.0)	伊利 Yili(18.8)	乐百氏 Robust(12.5)
45~54 岁 Age	6	帕玛拉特 Parmalat(50.0)	龙丹 Longdan(16.7)	
55~60 岁 Age	1	牛仔 Niuzai(100.0)		

3-4 理想品牌排名/ Ranking of the Ideal Brands

排名 Brand Ranking	品牌 Brands	人数 Number	百分比 Percent
1	辉山 Huishan	73	12.2
2	伊利 Yili	48	8.0
3	光明 Bright	31	5.2
4	均瑶 Junyao	18	3.0
4	乐百氏 Robust	18	3.0
5	医大 Yida	7	1.2
6	娃哈哈 Wahaha	6	1.0
6	帕玛拉特 Parmalat	6	1.0
7	龙丹 Longdan	5	0.8
8	生活 Life	3	0.5
8	维记 Rowloon Dairy	3	0.5

n=600

3-5 样本、男性各年龄层、女性各年龄层最近三个月有无购买的比例/ Purchasing in the Last Three Months by the Whole Sample, Age and Gender Groups

	人数 Number	买过 yes	没买过 no
样本 Sample	601	25.0	75.0
男性 Male	299	24.7	75.3
16~24 岁 Age	64	25.0	75.0
25~34 岁 Age	89	33.7	66.3
35~44 岁 Age	76	21.1	78.9
45~54 岁 Age	46	15.2	84.8
55~60 岁 Age	24	20.8	79.2
女性 Female	302	25.2	74.8
16~24 岁 Age	64	28.1	71.9
25~34 岁 Age	90	32.2	67.8
35~44 岁 Age	76	23.7	76.3
45~54 岁 Age	48	14.6	85.4
55~60 岁 Age	24	16.7	83.3

3-6 样本、男性各年龄层、女性各年龄层最近三个月的食用频率/ Frequencies of Consuming Packaged Milk in the Last Three Months by the Whole Sample, Age and Gender Groups

	人数 Number	天天喝 daily	一周 3 次或以上 3 times or over a week	一周 1~2 次 once or twice a week	一个月 2~3 次 2 or 3 times a month	一个月 1 次或以下 once a month or below	没喝过 never
样本 Sample	596	3.0	2.5	5.2	5.5	4.0	79.7
男性 Male	296	2.4	2.7	4.7	5.4	5.7	79.1
16~24 岁 Age	64	1.6	1.6	6.3	10.9	9.4	70.3
25~34 岁 Age	88	3.4	5.7	5.7	9.1	6.8	69.3
35~44 岁 Age	75	0.0	1.3	5.3	1.3	5.3	86.7
45~54 岁 Age	46	4.3	2.2	2.2	0.0	2.2	89.1
55~60 岁 Age	23	4.3	0.0	0.0	0.0	0.0	95.7
女性 Female	300	3.7	2.3	5.7	5.7	2.3	80.3
16~24 岁 Age	64	0.0	3.1	6.3	15.6	4.7	70.3
25~34 岁 Age	90	3.3	3.3	5.6	4.4	2.2	81.1
35~44 岁 Age	75	6.7	1.3	6.7	4.0	2.7	78.7
45~54 岁 Age	47	6.4	2.1	4.3	0.0	0.0	87.2
55~60 岁 Age	24	0.0	0.0	4.2	0.0	0.0	95.8

3-7 样本、男性各年龄层、女性各年龄层的品牌习惯/ Brand Habit in Consuming Packaged Milk by the Whole Sample, Age and Gender Groups

	人数 Number	基本固定食用一个牌子 used in only one brand	比较固定地食用两个或三个牌子 used in two or three brands	基本上不太固定牌子 no brand preference
样本 Sample	121	32.2	28.9	38.8
男性 Male	62	29.0	21.0	50.0
16~24 岁 Age	19	26.3	15.8	57.9
25~34 岁 Age	27	25.9	22.2	51.9
35~44 岁 Age	10	30.0	20.0	50.0
45~54 岁 Age	5	40.0	40.0	20.0
55~60 岁 Age	1	100.0	0.0	0.0
女性 Female	59	35.6	37.3	27.1
16~24 岁 Age	19	21.1	47.4	31.6
25~34 岁 Age	17	41.2	35.3	23.5
35~44 岁 Age	16	50.0	18.8	31.3
45~54 岁 Age	6	33.3	66.7	0.0
55~60 岁 Age	1	0.0	0.0	100.0

3-8 选择该类商品的考虑因素/ Ranking of the Considerations in Purchasing

注：本题为多选题，合计百分比超过 100%（Multiple answers）

排名 Ranking	考虑因素 Considerations	人次 Person-time	百分比 Percent
1	口味好 pleasant taste	63	52.1
2	营养成分 nutrition constituent	43	35.5
3	价格适中 reasonable price	35	28.9
4	有名的牌子 famous brand	32	26.4
5	购买方便 easy to buy	21	17.4
6	生产日期 date of producing	20	16.5
7	广告影响 influence of advertising	10	8.3
8	包装吸引人 appealing package	9	7.4
9	有优惠条件 with preferential terms	8	6.6
10	朋友推荐 introduction of friends	6	5.0
11	只是由于习惯 out of habit	4	3.3
12	售货员介绍 introduced by the shop assistants	3	2.5
13	其它 others	1	0.8

n=121

3-9 样本、男性各年龄层、女性各年龄层最常食用的种类/ Types of the Consumed Packaged Milk by the Whole Sample, Age and Gender Groups

	人数 Number	全脂 whole milk	低脂 low-fat	脱脂 skimmed	花色奶（巧克力味、草莓味等）milk varieties (chocolate flavor, Strawberry flavors etc.)	强化奶 enriched milk	加矿物质（含钙、铁等）with minerals (containing calcium, Iron etc.)	其它 others
样本 Sample	119	21.0	14.3	6.7	26.9	0.8	25.2	5.0
男性 Male	61	23.0	19.7	4.9	21.3	1.6	26.2	3.3
16~24 岁 Age	19	15.8	26.3	0.0	47.4	5.3	5.3	0.0
25~34 岁 Age	27	22.2	14.8	3.7	14.8	0.0	40.7	3.7
35~44 岁 Age	10	30.0	20.0	20.0	0.0	0.0	20.0	10.0
45~54 岁 Age	5	40.0	20.0	0.0	0.0	0.0	40.0	0.0
55~60 岁 Age	0	0.0	0.0	0.0	0.0	0.0	0.0	0.0
女性 Female	58	19.0	8.6	8.6	32.8	0.0	24.1	6.9
16~24 岁 Age	19	10.5	5.3	5.3	47.4	0.0	21.1	10.5
25~34 岁 Age	16	18.8	6.3	6.3	37.5	0.0	31.3	0.0
35~44 岁 Age	16	12.5	12.5	18.8	25.0	0.0	25.0	6.3
45~54 岁 Age	6	50.0	16.7	0.0	0.0	0.0	16.7	16.7
55~60 岁 Age	1	100.0	0.0	0.0	0.0	0.0	0.0	0.0

3-10 样本、男性各年龄层、女性各年龄层最常食用的包装形式/ Types of Package of the Consumed Packaged Milk by the Whole Sample, Age and Gender Groups

	人数 Number	方盒装/利乐砖 plastic-bag milk	房屋状纸盒 house-shaped box	粽子状纸盒 V-shaped box	塑料瓶 plastic bottle	易拉罐 tin	其他 others
样本 Sample	121	44.6	1.7	2.5	46.3	4.1	0.8
男性 Male	62	45.2	1.6	1.6	46.8	3.2	1.6
16~24 岁 Age	19	57.9	0.0	0.0	36.8	5.3	0.0
25~34 岁 Age	27	40.7	0.0	3.7	55.6	0.0	0.0
35~44 岁 Age	10	30.0	10.0	0.0	50.0	0.0	10.0
45~54 岁 Age	5	40.0	0.0	0.0	40.0	20.0	0.0
55~60 岁 Age	1	100.0	0.0	0.0	0.0	0.0	0.0
女性 Female	59	44.1	1.7	3.4	45.8	5.1	0.0
16~24 岁 Age	19	52.6	0.0	0.0	36.8	10.5	0.0
25~34 岁 Age	17	47.1	0.0	0.0	47.1	5.9	0.0
35~44 岁 Age	16	25.0	0.0	6.3	68.8	0.0	0.0
45~54 岁 Age	6	66.7	0.0	16.7	16.7	0.0	0.0
55~60 岁 Age	1	0.0	100.0	0.0	0.0	0.0	0.0

3-11 样本、男性各年龄层、女性各年龄层最常饮用场合/ Settings of Consumption by the Whole Sample, Age and Gender Groups

注：本题为多选题，合计百分比超过 100%（Multiple answers）

	人数 Number	早餐时 breakfast	正餐（午、晚餐）时 dinner	口渴时 when thirsty	宵夜时 evening snack	睡觉前 before sleeping	工作休息时 during work break	外出/旅游时 outing /traveling	运动后 after athletics	其它 others
样本 Sample	120	30.0	1.7	25.8	3.3	19.2	15.8	24.2	5.0	4.2
男性 Male	62	29.0	3.2	27.4	3.2	19.4	11.3	14.5	3.2	4.8
16~24 岁 Age	19	15.8	0.0	47.4	0.0	10.5	21.1	26.3	0.0	0.0
25~34 岁 Age	27	25.9	7.4	14.8	7.4	25.9	7.4	14.8	7.4	7.4
35~44 岁 Age	10	50.0	0.0	20.0	0.0	20.0	10.0	0.0	0.0	10.0
45~54 岁 Age	5	60.0	0.0	20.0	0.0	20.0	0.0	0.0	0.0	0.0
55~60 岁 Age	1	0.0	0.0	100.0	0.0	0.0	0.0	0.0	0.0	0.0
女性 Female	58	31.0	0.0	24.1	3.4	19.0	20.7	34.5	6.9	3.4
16~24 岁 Age	19	15.8	0.0	36.8	0.0	5.3	36.8	47.4	5.3	5.3
25~34 岁 Age	16	25.0	0.0	37.5	0.0	12.5	12.5	37.5	12.5	0.0
35~44 岁 Age	16	43.8	0.0	6.3	12.5	31.3	18.8	18.8	6.3	6.3
45~54 岁 Age	6	66.7	0.0	0.0	0.0	33.3	0.0	33.3	0.0	0.0
55~60 岁 Age	1	0.0	0.0	0.0	0.0	100.0	0.0	0.0	0.0	0.0

3-12 重度消费者的人口分布/ Demographics of the Heavy Consumers

	人数 Number	16-24 岁 Age	25-34 岁 Age	35-44 岁 Age	45-54 岁 Age	55-60 岁 Age
样本 Sample	64	18.8	37.5	25.0	15.6	3.1
男性 Male	29	20.7	44.8	17.2	13.8	3.4
天天喝 daily	7	14.3	42.9	0.0	28.6	14.3
一周 3 次或以上 3 times or over a week	8	12.5	62.5	12.5	12.5	0.0
一周 1～2 次 once or twice a week	14	28.6	35.7	28.6	7.1	0.0
女性 Female	35	17.1	31.4	31.4	17.1	2.9
天天喝 daily	11	0.0	27.3	45.5	27.3	0.0
一周 3 次或以上 3 times or over a week	7	28.6	42.9	14.3	14.3	0.0
一周 1～2 次 once or twice a week	17	23.5	29.4	29.4	11.8	5.9

3-13 不同消费者层的常用品牌/ The Most Frequently Used Brands by Market Segments

3-13-1 时尚流行指标/ Fads Popular Index

	人数 Number	第一品牌及百分比 1st/ percent	第二品牌及百分比 2nd/ percent	第三品牌及百分比 3rd/ percent
样本 Sample	121	**伊利 Yili(16.5)**	**光明 Bright(14.0)**	**乐百氏 Robust(9.9)**
平实生活指向 simple living orientation	46	伊利 Yili(15.2)	光明 Bright(13.0)	乐百氏 Robust(10.9)
时尚流行指向 fashion orientation	75	伊利 Yili(17.3)	光明 Bright(14.7)	均瑶 Junyao(10.7)

3-13-2 广告态度指标/ Advertising Attitude Index

	人数 Number	第一品牌及百分比 1st/ percent	第二品牌及百分比 2nd/ percent	第三品牌及百分比 3rd/ percent
样本 Sample	121	**伊利 Yili(16.5)**	**光明 Bright(14.0)**	**乐百氏 Robust(9.9)**
广告淡漠指向 indifferent orientation	32	光明 Bright(21.9)	均瑶 Junyao(9.4) 伊利 Yili(9.4)	乐百氏 Robust(6.3)
中间层 medium	75	伊利 Yili(20.0)	乐百氏 Robust(10.7)	光明 Bright(9.3) 均瑶 Junyao(9.3)
信赖广告指向 loyal orientation	14	光明 Bright(21.4)	乐百氏 Robust(14.3) 伊利 Yili(14.3)	娃哈哈 Wahaha(7.1) 康辉 Kanghui(7.1) 辉山 Huishan(7.1)

3-13-3 饮食健康指标/ Foods & Drink Quality Index

	人数 Number	第一品牌及百分比 1st/ percent	第二品牌及百分比 2nd/ percent	第三品牌及百分比 3rd/ percent
样本 Sample	121	**伊利 Yili(16.5)**	**光明 Bright(14.0)**	**乐百氏 Robust(9.9)**
饮食"温饱"指向 "basic" orientation	39	伊利 Yili(20.5)	光明 Bright(15.4)	均瑶 Junyao(10.3) 乐百氏 Robust(10.3)
中间层 medium	54	伊利 Yili(14.8) 光明 Bright(14.8)	乐百氏 Robust(7.4)	均瑶 Junyao(5.6) 生活 Life(5.6)
健康营养指向 health & nutrition orientation	28	乐百氏 Robust(14.3) 伊利 Yili(14.3)	光明 Bright(10.7) 均瑶 Junyao(10.7)	娃哈哈 Wahaha(7.1)

3-14 重度消费者的消费者层构成/ The Composition of the Heavy Consumers

3-14-1 时尚流行指标/ Fads Popular Index

	人数 Number	平实生活指向 simple living orientation	时尚流行指向 fashion orientation
样本 Sample	64	35.9	64.1
天天喝 daily	18	27.8	72.2
一周 3 次或以上 3 times or over a week	15	26.7	73.3
一周 1～2 次 once or twice a week	31	45.2	54.8

3-14-2 广告态度指标/ Advertising Attitude Index

	人数 Number	广告淡漠指向 indifferent orientation	中间层 medium	信赖广告指向 loyal orientation
样本 Sample	**64**	**18.8**	**70.3**	**10.9**
天天喝 daily	18	16.7	66.7	16.7
一周 3 次或以上 3 times or over a week	15	13.3	73.3	13.3
一周 1～2 次 once or twice a week	31	22.6	71.0	6.5

3-14-3 饮食健康指标/ Foods & Drink Quality Index

	人数 Number	饮食"温饱"指向 "basic" orientation	中间层 medium	健康营养指向 health & nutrition orientation
样本 Sample	**64**	**32.8**	**43.8**	**23.4**
天天喝 daily	18	22.2	50.0	27.8
一周 3 次或以上 3 times or over a week	15	46.7	26.7	26.7
一周 1～2 次 once or twice a week	31	32.3	48.4	19.4

4.酸奶 / Yogurt

● 北京 / Beijing

4-1 最近三个月食用频率的比例/ Proportion of the Sample Consuming Yogurt in the Last Three Months

	人数 Number	百分比 Percent
天天喝 daily	103	10.2
一周 3 次或以上 3 times or over a week	142	14.1
一周 1~2 次 once or twice a week	277	27.4
一个月 2~3 次 2 or 3 times a month	170	16.8
一个月 1 次或以下 once a month or below	73	7.2
没喝过 never	245	24.3

n=1010

4-2 最常用品牌排名/ Ranking of the Most Frequently Used Brands

排名 Brand Ranking	品牌 Brands	人数 Number	百分比 Percent
1	三元 Sanyuan	243	32.1
2	卡夫 Kraft	129	17.1
3	光明 Bright	41	5.4
4	新南洋 Xinnanyang	33	4.4
5	帕玛拉特 Parmalat	25	3.3
6	小雅 Xiaoya	11	1.5
6	宝贝 Baobei	11	1.5
7	欣愉 Xinyu	10	1.3

n=756

4-3 样本、男性各年龄层、女性各年龄层的常用品牌/ The Most Frequently Used Brands by the Whole Sample, Age and Gender Groups

	人数 Number	第一品牌及百分比 1st/ percent	第二品牌及百分比 2nd/ percent	第三品牌及百分比 3rd/ percent
样本 Sample	**756**	**三元 Sanyuan(32.1)**	**卡夫 Kraft(17.1)**	**光明 Bright(5.4)**
男性 Male	**335**	**三元 Sanyuan(34.0)**	**卡夫 Kraft(12.8)**	**光明 Bright(4.8)**
16~24 岁 Age	78	三元 Sanyuan(24.4)	卡夫 Kraft(16.7)	光明 Bright(5.1)
25~34 岁 Age	102	三元 Sanyuan(40.2)	卡夫 Kraft(12.7)	光明 Bright(7.8)
35~44 岁 Age	85	三元 Sanyuan(34.1)	卡夫 Kraft(11.8)	新南洋 Xinnanyang(5.9)
45~54 岁 Age	45	三元 Sanyuan(31.1)	卡夫 Kraft(13.3)	光明 Bright(6.7)
55~60 岁 Age	25	三元 Sanyuan(44.0)	伊利 Yili(8.0)	卡夫 Kraft(4.0) 欣愉 Xinyu(4.0) 宾世 Bingshi(4.0) 蜜可儿 Miker(4.0)
女性 Female	**421**	**三元 Sanyuan(30.6)**	**卡夫 Kraft(20.4)**	**光明 Bright(5.9)**
16~24 岁 Age	92	卡夫 Kraft(28.3) 三元 Sanyuan(28.3)	新南洋 Xinnanyang(7.6)	光明 Bright(5.4)
25~34 岁 Age	133	卡夫 Kraft(26.3)	三元 Sanyuan(24.1)	光明 Bright(8.3)
35~44 岁 Age	102	三元 Sanyuan(38.2)	卡夫 Kraft(15.7)	光明 Bright(3.9) 帕玛拉特 Parmalat(3.9)
45~54 岁 Age	65	三元 Sanyuan(36.9)	卡夫 Kraft(9.2)	光明 Bright(6.2)
55~60 岁 Age	29	三元 Sanyuan(27.6)	卡夫 Kraft(10.3)	新南洋 Xinnanyang(6.9)

4-4 理想品牌排名/ Ranking of the Ideal Brands

排名 Brand Ranking	品牌 Brands	人数 Number	百分比 Percent
1	三元 Sanyuan	247	24.4
2	卡夫 Kraft	173	17.1
3	光明 Bright	41	4.1
4	帕玛拉特 Parmalat	32	3.2
4	新南洋 Xinnanyang	32	3.2
5	伊利 Yili	21	2.1
6	宝贝 Baobei	8	0.8
6	小雅 Xiaoya	8	0.8

n=1012

4-5 样本、男性各年龄层、女性各年龄层最近三个月有无购买的比例/ Purchasing in the Last Three Months by the Whole Sample, Age and Gender Groups

	人数 Number	买过 yes	没买过 no
样本 Sample	1010	72.9	27.1
男性 Male	503	63.6	36.4
16~24 岁 Age	104	63.5	36.5
25~34 岁 Age	151	71.5	28.5
35~44 岁 Age	131	60.3	39.7
45~54 岁 Age	77	58.4	41.6
55~60 岁 Age	40	55.0	45.0
女性 Female	507	82.1	17.9
16~24 岁 Age	107	83.2	16.8
25~34 岁 Age	150	86.7	13.3
35~44 岁 Age	124	80.6	19.4
45~54 岁 Age	84	81.0	19.0
55~60 岁 Age	42	69.0	31.0

4-6 样本、男性各年龄层、女性各年龄层最近三个月的食用频率/ Frequencies of Consuming Yogurt in the Last Three Months by the Whole Sample, Age and Gender Groups

	人数 Number	天天喝 daily	一周 3 次或以上 3 times or over a week	一周 1~2 次 once or twice a week	一个月 2~3 次 2 or 3 times a month	一个月 1 次或以下 once a month or below	没喝过 never
样本 Sample	1010	10.2	14.1	27.4	16.8	7.2	24.3
男性 Male	504	9.3	12.5	23.8	14.7	7.3	32.3
16~24 岁 Age	105	6.7	11.4	27.6	17.1	11.4	25.7
25~34 岁 Age	151	9.9	13.9	22.5	18.5	4.6	30.5
35~44 岁 Age	131	7.6	16.0	23.7	9.2	9.2	34.4
45~54 岁 Age	77	9.1	7.8	20.8	16.9	6.5	39.0
55~60 岁 Age	40	20.0	7.5	25.0	7.5	2.5	37.5
女性 Female	506	11.1	15.6	31.0	19.0	7.1	16.2
16~24 岁 Age	107	12.1	14.0	38.3	19.6	2.8	13.1
25~34 岁 Age	150	10.7	12.7	32.7	24.0	9.3	10.7
35~44 岁 Age	123	11.4	19.5	30.1	16.3	6.5	16.3
45~54 岁 Age	84	11.9	16.7	27.4	14.3	7.1	22.6
55~60 岁 Age	42	7.1	16.7	16.7	16.7	11.9	31.0

4-7 样本、男性各年龄层、女性各年龄层的品牌习惯/ Brand Habit in Consuming Yogurt by the Whole Sample, Age and Gender Groups

	人数 Number	基本固定食用一个牌子 used in only one brand	比较固定地食用两个或三个牌子 used in two or three brands	基本上不太固定牌子 no brand preference
样本 Sample	762	46.5	30.6	23.0
男性 Male	339	45.4	26.8	27.7
16~24 岁 Age	78	46.2	25.6	28.2
25~34 岁 Age	104	45.2	29.8	25.0
35~44 岁 Age	85	42.4	28.2	29.4
45~54 岁 Age	47	40.4	25.5	34.0
55~60 岁 Age	25	64.0	16.0	20.0
女性 Female	423	47.3	33.6	19.1
16~24 岁 Age	93	36.6	43.0	20.4
25~34 岁 Age	133	48.9	35.3	15.8
35~44 岁 Age	103	48.5	33.0	18.4
45~54 岁 Age	65	50.8	23.1	26.2
55~60 岁 Age	29	62.1	20.7	17.2

4-8 选择该类商品的考虑因素/ Ranking of the Considerations in Purchasing

注：本题为多选题，合计百分比超过 100%(Multiple answers）

排名 Ranking	考虑因素 Considerations	人次 Person-time	百分比 Percent
1	口味好 pleasant taste	442	58.1
2	价格适中 reasonable price	260	34.2
3	有名的牌子 famous brand	215	28.3
4	生产日期 date of producing	193	25.4
4	购买方便 easy to buy	193	25.4
5	营养成分 nutrition constituent	184	24.2
6	只是由于习惯 out of habit	78	10.2
7	朋友推荐 introduction of friends	35	4.6
8	有优惠条件 with preferential terms	28	3.7
9	广告影响 influence of advertising	27	3.5
10	包装吸引人 appealing package	17	2.2
11	售货员介绍 introduced by the shop assistants	8	1.1
11	其它 others	8	1.1

n=761

4-9 样本、男性各年龄层、女性各年龄层最常食用的种类/ Types of the Consumed Yogurt by the Whole Sample, Age and Gender Groups

注：本题为多选题，合计百分比超过 100%(Multiple answers）

	人数 Number	原味 original flavor	巧克力味 chocolate flavor	草莓味 strawberry	菠萝味 pineapple	橙味 orange	杏味 apricot	带果粒 with fruit dots	加钙 calcium added	其他 others
样本 Sample	758	62.3	6.2	28.5	9.4	4.4	1.1	4.7	17.9	1.2
男性 Male	339	62.5	5.3	29.5	7.1	2.4	0.6	3.8	17.7	1.8
16~24 岁 Age	77	62.3	10.4	26.0	7.8	2.6	0.0	3.9	15.6	1.3
25~34 岁 Age	105	68.6	3.8	25.7	6.7	4.8	0.0	2.9	19.0	1.9
35~44 岁 Age	85	60.0	5.9	37.6	5.9	0.0	2.4	2.4	16.5	1.2
45~54 岁 Age	47	51.1	2.1	34.0	6.4	2.1	0.0	10.6	19.1	4.3
55~60 岁 Age	25	68.0	0.0	20.0	12.0	0.0	0.0	0.0	20.0	0.0
女性 Female	419	62.1	6.9	27.7	11.2	6.0	1.4	5.5	18.1	0.7
16~24 岁 Age	93	66.7	9.7	24.7	15.1	8.6	3.2	9.7	15.1	1.1
25~34 岁 Age	131	66.4	5.3	29.0	10.7	5.3	1.5	4.6	13.7	0.0
35~44 岁 Age	101	53.5	7.9	31.7	11.9	7.9	1.0	6.9	19.8	1.0
45~54 岁 Age	65	66.2	7.7	29.2	9.2	1.5	0.0	1.5	15.4	1.5
55~60 岁 Age	29	48.3	0.0	13.8	3.4	3.4	0.0	0.0	48.3	0.0

4-10 样本、男性各年龄层、女性各年龄层最常食用的包装形式/ Types of Package of the Consumed Yogurt by the Whole Sample, Age and Gender Groups

注：本题为多选题，合计百分比超过 100%(Multiple answers）

	人数 Number	袋装 bag	方盒装/利乐砖 tetra	房屋状纸盒 house-shaped box	粽子状纸盒 V-shaped box	塑料瓶 plastic bottle	瓷瓶 china bottle	其他 others
样本 Sample	754	49.1	14.1	8.1	0.8	25.2	30.0	0.4
男性 Male	336	50.9	13.1	6.5	0.6	24.1	34.2	0.3
16~24 岁 Age	75	61.3	20.0	8.0	0.0	24.0	18.7	0.0
25~34 岁 Age	103	37.9	12.6	4.9	0.0	25.2	39.8	1.0
35~44 岁 Age	86	52.3	10.5	10.5	1.2	26.7	38.4	0.0
45~54 岁 Age	47	61.7	8.5	2.1	0.0	23.4	36.2	0.0
55~60 岁 Age	25	48.0	12.0	4.0	4.0	12.0	40.0	0.0
女性 Female	418	47.6	14.8	9.3	1.0	26.1	26.6	0.5
16~24 岁 Age	93	48.4	20.4	16.1	1.1	29.0	15.1	0.0
25~34 岁 Age	132	37.1	15.2	9.8	1.5	32.6	27.3	0.8
35~44 岁 Age	101	53.5	9.9	6.9	1.0	25.7	30.7	1.0
45~54 岁 Age	63	47.6	14.3	4.8	0.0	19.0	33.3	0.0
55~60 岁 Age	29	72.4	13.8	3.4	0.0	3.4	31.0	0.0

4-11 样本、男性各年龄层、女性各年龄层最常饮用场合/ Settings of Consumption by the Whole Sample, Age and Gender Groups

注：本题为多选题，合计百分比超过 100%(Multiple answers）

	人数 Number	早餐时 breakfast	正餐（午、晚餐）时 dinner	口渴时 when thirsty	宵夜时 evening snack	睡觉前 before sleeping	工作休息时 during work break	外出/旅游时 outing/ traveling	其它 others
样本 Sample	760	18.3	8.0	37.5	5.4	15.9	29.2	17.2	5.5
男性 Male	338	18.3	8.3	37.6	5.3	15.4	25.7	16.6	5.6
16~24 岁 Age	77	11.7	5.2	35.1	6.5	15.6	32.5	20.8	3.9
25~34 岁 Age	105	21.0	9.5	36.2	5.7	12.4	28.6	15.2	3.8
35~44 岁 Age	84	19.0	8.3	36.9	6.0	19.0	21.4	15.5	9.5
45~54 岁 Age	47	19.1	6.4	46.8	4.3	14.9	21.3	17.0	6.4
55~60 岁 Age	25	24.0	16.0	36.0	0.0	16.0	16.0	12.0	4.0
女性 Female	422	18.2	7.8	37.4	5.5	16.4	32.0	17.8	5.5
16~24 岁 Age	92	18.5	6.5	35.9	5.4	12.0	50.0	15.2	3.3
25~34 岁 Age	133	14.3	9.8	39.1	3.8	16.5	30.8	15.0	5.3
35~44 岁 Age	103	21.4	7.8	32.0	5.8	19.4	28.2	26.2	3.9
45~54 岁 Age	65	23.1	9.2	43.1	10.8	13.8	21.5	13.8	7.7
55~60 岁 Age	29	13.8	0.0	41.4	0.0	24.1	17.2	17.2	13.8

4-12 重度消费者的人口分布/ Demographics of the Heavy Consumers

	人数 Number	16-24 岁 Age	25-34 岁 Age	35-44 岁 Age	45-54 岁 Age	55-60 岁 Age
样本 Sample	522	22.4	29.5	26.2	14.6	7.3
男性 Male	230	20.9	30.4	27.0	12.6	9.1
天天喝 daily	47	14.9	31.9	21.3	14.9	17.0
一周 3 次或以上 3 times or over a week	63	19.0	33.3	33.3	9.5	4.8
一周 1～2 次 once or twice a week	120	24.2	28.3	25.8	13.3	8.3
女性 Female	292	23.6	28.8	25.7	16.1	5.8
天天喝 daily	56	23.2	28.6	25.0	17.9	5.4
一周 3 次或以上 3 times or over a week	79	19.0	24.1	30.4	17.7	8.9
一周 1～2 次 once or twice a week	157	26.1	31.2	23.6	14.6	4.5

4-13 不同消费者层的常用品牌/ The Most Frequently Used Brands by Market Segments

4-13-1 时尚流行指标/ Fads Popular Index

	人数 Number	第一品牌及百分比 1st/ percent	第二品牌及百分比 2nd/ percent	第三品牌及百分比 3rd/ percent
样本 Sample	747	**三元 Sanyuan(31.9)**	**卡夫 Kraft(16.9)**	**光明 Bright(5.5)**
平实生活指向 simple living orientation	343	三元 Sanyuan(32.4)	卡夫 Kraft(11.4)	光明 Bright(4.7)
时尚流行指向 fashion orientation	404	三元 Sanyuan(31.4)	卡夫 Kraft(21.5)	光明 Bright(6.2)

4-13-2 广告态度指标/ Advertising Attitude Index

	人数 Number	第一品牌及百分比 1st/ percent	第二品牌及百分比 2nd/ percent	第三品牌及百分比 3rd/ percent
样本 Sample	740	**三元 Sanyuan(31.8)**	**卡夫 Kraft(16.9)**	**光明 Bright(5.5)**
广告淡漠指向 indifferent orientation	191	三元 Sanyuan(30.4)	卡夫 Kraft(16.2)	光明 Bright(5.2) 新南洋 Xinnanyang(5.2)
中间层 medium	451	三元 Sanyuan(32.4)	卡夫 Kraft(17.3)	光明 Bright(6.2)
信赖广告指向 loyal orientation	98	三元 Sanyuan(31.6)	卡夫 Kraft(15.3)	新南洋 Xinnanyang(7.1)

4-13-3 饮食健康指标/ Foods & Drink Quality Index

	人数 Number	第一品牌及百分比 1st/ percent	第二品牌及百分比 2nd/ percent	第三品牌及百分比 3rd/ percent
样本 Sample	750	三元 Sanyuan(32.0)	卡夫 Kraft(17.2)	光明 Bright(5.3)
饮食"温饱"指向 "basic" orientation	200	三元 Sanyuan(30.5)	卡夫 Kraft(13.0)	新南洋 Xinnanyang(5.0)
中间层 medium	354	三元 Sanyuan(31.9)	卡夫 Kraft(19.2)	光明 Bright(6.2)
健康营养指向 health & nutrition orientation	196	三元 Sanyuan(33.7)	卡夫 Kraft(17.9)	光明 Bright(6.1)

4-14 重度消费者的消费者层构成/ The Composition of the Heavy Consumers

4-14-1 时尚流行指标/ Fads Popular Index

	人数 Number	平实生活指向 simple living orientation	时尚流行指向 fashion orientation
样本 Sample	517	43.5	56.5
天天喝 daily	101	41.6	58.4
一周 3 次或以上 3 times or over a week	141	41.1	58.9
一周 1～2 次 once or twice a week	275	45.5	54.5

4-14-2 广告态度指标/ Advertising Attitude Index

	人数 Number	广告淡漠指向 indifferent orientation	中间层 medium	信赖广告指向 loyal orientation
样本 Sample	511	25.0	60.9	14.1
天天喝 daily	97	26.8	56.7	16.5
一周 3 次或以上 3 times or over a week	139	24.5	66.2	9.4
一周 1～2 次 once or twice a week	275	24.7	59.6	15.6

4-14-3 饮食健康指标/ Foods & Drink Quality Index

	人数 Number	饮食"温饱"指向 "basic" orientation	中间层 medium	健康营养指向 health & nutrition orientation
样本 Sample	519	25.4	46.8	27.7
天天喝 daily	103	24.3	40.8	35.0
一周 3 次或以上 3 times or over a week	142	25.4	47.9	26.8
一周 1～2 次 once or twice a week	274	25.9	48.5	25.5

● 上海 / Shanghai

4-1 最近三个月食用频率的比例/ Proportion of the Sample Consuming Yogurt in the Last Three Months

	人数 Number	百分比 Percent
天天喝 daily	50	4.9
一周 3 次或以上 3 times or over a week	77	7.6
一周 1~2 次 once or twice a week	174	17.2
一个月 2～3 次 2 or 3 times a month	158	15.6
一个月 1 次或以下 once a month or below	64	6.3
没喝过 never	489	48.3

n=1012

4-2 最常用品牌排名/ Ranking of the Most Frequently Used Brands

排名 Brand Ranking	品牌 Brands	人数 Number	百分比 Percent
1	光明 Bright	269	51.5
2	达能 Danone	111	21.3
3	优诺 Yuplaic	93	17.8
4	全佳 Quanjia	19	3.6
5	乐百氏 Robust	18	3.4

n=522

4-3 样本、男性各年龄层、女性各年龄层的常用品牌/ The Most Frequently Used Brands by the Whole Sample, Age and Gender Groups

	人数 Number	第一品牌及百分比 1st/ percent	第二品牌及百分比 2nd/ percent	第三品牌及百分比 3rd/ percent
样本 Sample	522	**光明 Bright(51.5)**	**达能 Danone(21.3)**	**优诺 Yuplaic(17.8)**
男性 Male	232	**光明 Bright(56.9)**	**达能 Danone(19.4)**	**优诺 Yuplaic(17.2)**
16~24 岁 Age	64	光明 Bright(46.9)	优诺 Yuplaic(29.7)	达能 Danone(17.2)
25~34 岁 Age	69	光明 Bright(50.7)	达能 Danone(29.0)	优诺 Yuplaic(13.0)
35~44 岁 Age	57	光明 Bright(64.9)	达能 Danone(15.8) 优诺 Yuplaic(15.8)	乐百氏 Robust(1.8)
45~54 岁 Age	31	光明 Bright(67.7)	达能 Danone(12.9)	乐百氏 Robust(6.5) 优诺 Yuplaic(6.5)
55~60 岁 Age	11	光明 Bright(81.8)	达能 Danone(9.1) 优诺 Yuplaic(9.1)	
女性 Female	290	**光明 Bright(47.2)**	**达能 Danone(22.8)**	**优诺 Yuplaic(18.3)**
16~24 岁 Age	77	优诺 Yuplaic(40.3)	光明 Bright(24.7)	达能 Danone(18.2)
25~34 岁 Age	91	光明 Bright(39.6)	达能 Danone(33.0)	优诺 Yuplaic(15.4)
35~44 岁 Age	76	光明 Bright(63.2)	达能 Danone(22.4)	优诺 Yuplaic(6.6)
45~54 岁 Age	30	光明 Bright(76.7)	达能 Danone(10.0)	优诺 Yuplaic(6.7) 全佳 Quanjia(6.7)
55~60 岁 Age	16	光明 Bright(68.8)	达能 Danone(12.5) 乐百氏 Robust(12.5)	优诺 Yuplaic(6.3)

4-4 理想品牌排名/ Ranking of the Ideal Brands

排名 Brand Ranking	品牌 Brands	人数 Number	百分比 Percent
1	光明 Bright	449	44.3
2	达能 Danone	237	23.4
3	优诺 Yuplaic	162	16.0
5	乐百氏 Robust	36	3.6
6	全佳 Quanjia	20	2.0
7	娃哈哈 Wahaha	5	0.5
8	佳能 Jianeng	4	0.4

n=1013

4-5 样本、男性各年龄层、女性各年龄层最近三个月有无购买的比例/ Purchasing in the Last Three Months by the Whole Sample, Age and Gender Groups

	人数 Number	买过 yes	没买过 no
样本 Sample	1014	53.9	46.1
男性 Male	509	46.4	53.6
16~24 岁 Age	109	53.2	46.8
25~34 岁 Age	146	50.7	49.3
35~44 岁 Age	130	46.2	53.8
45~54 岁 Age	85	38.8	61.2
55~60 岁 Age	39	28.2	71.8
女性 Female	505	61.6	38.4
16~24 岁 Age	108	66.7	33.3
25~34 岁 Age	144	70.8	29.2
35~44 岁 Age	130	63.1	36.9
45~54 岁 Age	82	40.2	59.8
55~60 岁 Age	41	53.7	46.3

4-6 样本、男性各年龄层、女性各年龄层最近三个月的食用频率/ Frequencies of Consuming Yogurt in the Last Three Months by the Whole Sample, Age and Gender Groups

	人数 Number	天天喝 daily	一周 3 次或以上 3 times or over a week	一周 1~2 次 once or twice a week	一个月 2~3 次 2 or 3 times a month	一个月 1 次或以下 once a month or below	没喝过 never
样本 Sample	1012	4.9	7.6	17.2	15.6	6.3	48.3
男性 Male	508	4.9	5.9	14.8	14.2	6.1	54.1
16~24 岁 Age	108	4.6	7.4	17.6	18.5	11.1	40.7
25~34 岁 Age	146	2.7	7.5	17.8	17.1	2.7	52.1
35~44 岁 Age	130	6.2	5.4	12.3	13.1	6.9	56.2
45~54 岁 Age	85	5.9	3.5	14.1	8.2	4.7	63.5
55~60 岁 Age	39	7.7	2.6	5.1	7.7	5.1	71.8
女性 Female	504	5.0	9.3	19.6	17.1	6.5	42.5
16~24 岁 Age	107	1.9	14.0	22.4	25.2	8.4	28.0
25~34 岁 Age	144	5.6	12.5	24.3	13.9	6.9	36.8
35~44 岁 Age	130	4.6	7.7	21.5	18.5	6.2	41.5
45~54 岁 Age	82	7.3	4.9	7.3	12.2	4.9	63.4
55~60 岁 Age	41	7.3	0.0	14.6	12.2	4.9	61.0

4-7 样本、男性各年龄层、女性各年龄层的品牌习惯/ Brand Habit in Consuming Yogurt by the Whole Sample, Age and Gender Groups

	人数 Number	基本固定食用一个牌子 used in only one brand	比较固定地食用两个或三个牌子 used in two or three brands	基本上不太固定牌子 no brand preference
样本 Sample	522	57.1	31.2	11.7
男性 Male	232	57.8	29.7	12.5
16~24 岁 Age	64	51.6	34.4	14.1
25~34 岁 Age	69	53.6	40.6	5.8
35~44 岁 Age	57	59.6	22.8	17.5
45~54 岁 Age	31	74.2	16.1	9.7
55~60 岁 Age	11	63.6	9.1	27.3
女性 Female	290	56.6	32.4	11.0
16~24 岁 Age	77	45.5	41.6	13.0
25~34 岁 Age	91	63.7	28.6	7.7
35~44 岁 Age	76	53.9	35.5	10.5
45~54 岁 Age	30	76.7	13.3	10.0
55~60 岁 Age	16	43.8	31.3	25.0

4-8 选择该类商品的考虑因素/ Ranking of the Considerations in Purchasing

注：本题为多选题，合计百分比超过 100%(Multiple answers）

排名 Ranking	考虑因素 Considerations	人次 Person-time	百分比 Percent
1	口味好 pleasant taste	290	55.7
2	有名的牌子 famous brand	186	35.7
3	营养成分 nutrition constituent	160	30.7
4	价格适中 reasonable price	150	28.8
5	购买方便 easy to buy	105	20.2
6	生产日期 date of producing	97	18.6
7	只是由于习惯 out of habit	42	8.1
7	有优惠条件 with preferential terms	42	8.1
8	广告影响 influence of advertising	40	7.7
9	朋友推荐 introduction of friends	24	4.6
10	包装吸引人 appealing package	13	2.5
11	售货员介绍 introduced by the shop assistants	3	0.6
12	其它 others	2	0.4

n=521

4-9 样本、男性各年龄层、女性各年龄层最常食用的种类/ Types of the Consumed Yogurt by the Whole Sample, Age and Gender Groups

注：本题为多选题，合计百分比超过 100%(Multiple answers)

	人数 Number	原味 original flavor	巧克力味 chocolate flavor	草莓味 straw-berry	菠萝味 pineapple	橙味 orange	杏味 apricot	带果粒 with fruit dots	加钙 calcium added	其他 others
样本 Sample	**521**	**60.8**	**6.9**	**29.8**	**6.7**	**5.4**	**0.4**	**11.3**	**8.4**	**0.4**
男性 Male	**232**	**61.2**	**6.9**	**31.9**	**7.3**	**5.6**	**0.0**	**6.9**	**8.2**	**0.4**
16~24 岁 Age	64	53.1	7.8	32.8	10.9	3.1	0.0	6.3	7.8	1.6
25~34 岁 Age	69	66.7	4.3	29.0	8.7	7.2	0.0	7.2	5.8	0.0
35~44 岁 Age	57	57.9	10.5	38.6	7.0	7.0	0.0	7.0	10.5	0.0
45~54 岁 Age	31	71.0	6.5	19.4	0.0	6.5	0.0	9.7	6.5	0.0
55~60 岁 Age	11	63.6	0.0	45.5	0.0	0.0	0.0	0.0	18.2	0.0
女性 Female	**289**	**60.6**	**6.9**	**28.0**	**6.2**	**5.2**	**0.7**	**14.9**	**8.7**	**0.3**
16~24 岁 Age	77	57.1	10.4	26.0	2.6	10.4	1.3	22.1	5.2	0.0
25~34 岁 Age	91	61.5	4.4	26.4	7.7	3.3	1.1	23.1	9.9	0.0
35~44 岁 Age	76	60.5	9.2	34.2	9.2	3.9	0.0	3.9	7.9	1.3
45~54 岁 Age	30	60.0	3.3	30.0	0.0	3.3	0.0	3.3	16.7	0.0
55~60 岁 Age	15	73.3	0.0	13.3	13.3	0.0	0.0	6.7	6.7	0.0

4-10 样本、男性各年龄层、女性各年龄层最常食用的包装形式/ Types of Package of the Consumed Yogurt by the Whole Sample, Age and Gender Groups

注：本题为多选题，合计百分比超过 100%(Multiple answers)

	人数 Number	袋装 bag	方盒装/利乐砖 tetra	房屋状纸盒 house-shaped box	粽子状纸盒 V-shaped box	塑料瓶 plastic bottle	瓷瓶 china bottle	其他 others
样本 Sample	**518**	**3.7**	**37.6**	**25.7**	**1.7**	**37.3**	**4.8**	**1.5**
男性 Male	**230**	**4.8**	**37.0**	**28.7**	**1.3**	**33.0**	**3.9**	**1.7**
16~24 岁 Age	64	4.7	32.8	31.3	1.6	37.5	1.6	0.0
25~34 岁 Age	68	4.4	45.6	22.1	0.0	36.8	4.4	2.9
35~44 岁 Age	57	1.8	42.1	24.6	1.8	31.6	3.5	1.8
45~54 岁 Age	31	9.7	25.8	41.9	3.2	19.4	6.5	3.2
55~60 岁 Age	10	10.0	10.0	40.0	0.0	30.0	10.0	0.0
女性 Female	**288**	**2.8**	**38.2**	**23.3**	**2.1**	**40.6**	**5.6**	**1.4**
16~24 岁 Age	76	1.3	38.2	23.7	3.9	40.8	3.9	1.3
25~34 岁 Age	91	4.4	36.3	24.2	2.2	45.1	4.4	0.0
35~44 岁 Age	75	1.3	41.3	18.7	1.3	44.0	6.7	2.7
45~54 岁 Age	30	6.7	40.0	33.3	0.0	10.0	10.0	3.3
55~60 岁 Age	16	0.0	31.3	18.8	0.0	56.3	6.3	0.0

4-11 样本、男性各年龄层、女性各年龄层最常饮用场合/ Settings of Consumption by the Whole Sample, Age and Gender Groups

注：本题为多选题，合计百分比超过 100%(Multiple answers)

	人数 Number	早餐时 breakfast	正餐（午、餐）时 dinner	口渴时 when thirsty	宵夜时 evening snack	睡觉前 before sleeping	工作休息时 during work break	外出/旅游时 outing/traveling	其它 others
样本 Sample	**522**	**25.5**	**6.7**	**23.9**	**5.0**	**17.0**	**29.7**	**18.6**	**4.6**
男性 Male	**232**	**25.9**	**7.3**	**22.0**	**5.6**	**17.7**	**29.3**	**18.1**	**4.3**
16~24 岁 Age	64	20.3	7.8	14.1	7.8	17.2	34.4	18.8	6.3
25~34 岁 Age	69	20.3	7.2	27.5	4.3	18.8	30.4	21.7	5.8
35~44 岁 Age	57	33.3	10.5	19.3	5.3	19.3	19.3	21.1	1.8
45~54 岁 Age	31	35.5	0.0	29.0	6.5	6.5	38.7	6.5	0.0
55~60 岁 Age	11	27.3	9.1	27.3	0.0	36.4	18.2	9.1	9.1
女性 Female	**290**	**25.2**	**6.2**	**25.5**	**4.5**	**16.6**	**30.0**	**19.0**	**4.8**
16~24 岁 Age	77	19.5	9.1	16.9	5.2	9.1	46.8	20.8	3.9
25~34 岁 Age	91	17.6	6.6	27.5	1.1	15.4	29.7	22.0	7.7
35~44 岁 Age	76	34.2	3.9	32.9	3.9	21.1	21.1	15.8	3.9
45~54 岁 Age	30	40.0	3.3	26.7	16.7	33.3	10.0	10.0	0.0
55~60 岁 Age	16	25.0	6.3	18.8	0.0	6.3	31.3	25.0	6.3

4-12 重度消费者的人口分布/ Demographics of the Heavy Consumers

	人数 Number	16-24 岁 Age	25-34 岁 Age	35-44 岁 Age	45-54 岁 Age	55-60 岁 Age
样本 Sample	301	24.3	33.9	24.9	12.0	5.0
男性 Male	130	24.6	31.5	23.8	15.4	4.6
天天喝 daily	25	20.0	16.0	32.0	20.0	12.0
一周 3 次或以上 3 times or over a week	30	26.7	36.7	23.3	10.0	3.3
一周 1～2 次 once or twice a week	75	25.3	34.7	21.3	16.0	2.7
女性 Female	171	24.0	35.7	25.7	9.4	5.3
天天喝 daily	25	8.0	32.0	24.0	24.0	12.0
一周 3 次或以上 3 times or over a week	47	31.9	38.3	21.3	8.5	0.0
一周 1～2 次 once or twice a week	99	24.2	35.4	28.3	6.1	6.1

4-13 不同消费者层的常用品牌/ The Most Frequently Used Brands by Market Segments

4-13-1 时尚流行指标/ Fads Popular Index

	人数 Number	第一品牌及百分比 1st/ percent	第二品牌及百分比 2nd/ percent	第三品牌及百分比 3rd/ percent	第四品牌及百分比 4th/ percent
样本 Sample	518	**光明 Bright(51.7)**	**达能 Danone(21.2)**	**优诺 Yuplaic(17.8)**	**全佳 Quanjia(3.7)**
平实生活指向 simple living orientation	196	光明 Bright(57.7)	达能 Danone(20.4)	优诺 Yuplaic(10.2)	全佳 Quanjia(5.6)
时尚流行指向 fashion orientation	322	光明 Bright(48.1)	优诺 Yuplaic(22.4)	达能 Danone(21.7)	乐百氏 Robust(3.4)

4-13-2 广告态度指标/ Advertising Attitude Index

	人数 Number	第一品牌及百分比 1st/ percent	第二品牌及百分比 2nd/ percent	第三品牌及百分比 3rd/ percent	第四品牌及百分比 4th/ percent
样本 Sample	516	**光明 Bright(51.7)**	**达能 Danone(21.5)**	**优诺 Yuplaic(17.4)**	**全佳 Quanjia(3.7)**
广告淡漠指向 indifferent orientation	123	光明 Bright(52.0)	达能 Danone(21.1)	优诺 Yuplaic(11.4)	乐百氏 Robust(6.5)
中间层 medium	320	光明 Bright(51.9)	达能 Danone(23.8)	优诺 Yuplaic(17.5)	全佳 Quanjia(3.4)
信赖广告指向 loyal orientation	73	光明 Bright(50.7)	优诺 Yuplaic(27.4)	达能 Danone(12.3)	乐百氏 Robust(5.5)

4-13-3 饮食健康指标/ Foods & Drink Quality Index

	人数 Number	第一品牌及百分比 1st/ percent	第二品牌及百分比 2nd/ percent	第三品牌及百分比 3rd/ percent	第四品牌及百分比 4th/ percent
样本 Sample	521	**光明 Bright(51.6)**	**达能 Danone(21.3)**	**优诺 Yuplaic(17.7)**	**全佳 Quanjia(3.6)**
饮食“温饱”指向 "basic" orientation	106	光明 Bright(54.7)	达能 Danone(17.0)	优诺 Yuplaic(16.0)	全佳 Quanjia(5.7)
中间层 medium	254	光明 Bright(48.0)	达能 Danone(22.4)	优诺 Yuplaic(20.1)	乐百氏 Robust(4.3)
健康营养指向 health & nutrition orientation	161	光明 Bright(55.3)	达能 Danone(22.4)	优诺 Yuplaic(14.9)	全佳 Quanjia(5.0)

4-14 重度消费者的消费者层构成/ The Composition of the Heavy Consumers

4-14-1 时尚流行指标/ Fads Popular Index

	人数 Number	平实生活指向 simple living orientation	时尚流行指向 fashion orientation
样本 Sample	299	39.1	60.9
天天喝 daily	50	60.0	40.0
一周 3 次或以上 3 times or over a week	76	31.6	68.4
一周 1～2 次 once or twice a week	173	36.4	63.6

4-14-2 广告态度指标/ Advertising Attitude Index

	人数 Number	广告淡漠指向 indifferent orientation	中间层 medium	信赖广告指向 loyal orientation
样本 Sample	297	22.6	60.9	16.5
天天喝 daily	48	27.1	64.6	8.3
一周 3 次或以上 3 times or over a week	77	26.0	53.2	20.8
一周 1～2 次 once or twice a week	172	19.8	63.4	16.9

4-14-3 饮食健康指标/ Foods & Drink Quality Index

	人数 Number	饮食"温饱"指向 "basic" orientation	中间层 medium	健康营养指向 health & nutrition orientation
样本 Sample	301	17.6	48.8	33.6
天天喝 daily	50	16.0	56.0	28.0
一周 3 次或以上 3 times or over a week	77	15.6	46.8	37.7
一周 1～2 次 once or twice a week	174	19.0	47.7	33.3

● 广州 / Guangzhou

4-1 最近三个月食用频率的比例/ Proportion of the Sample Consuming Yogurt in the Last Three Months

	人数 Number	百分比 Percent
天天喝 daily	47	4.6
一周 3 次或以上 3 times or over a week	83	8.1
一周 1~2 次 once or twice a week	179	17.4
一个月 2～3 次 2 or 3 times a month	156	15.2
一个月 1 次或以下 once a month or below	78	7.6
没喝过 never	485	47.2

n=1028

4-2 最常用品牌排名/ Ranking of the Most Frequently Used Brands

排名 Brand Ranking	品牌 Brands	人数 Number	百分比 Percent
1	达能 Danone	291	53.8
2	燕塘 Yantang	126	23.3
3	风行 Fengxing	40	7.4
4	香满楼 Flower Fresh	22	4.1
5	晨光 Chenguang	13	2.4
6	乐百氏 Robust	10	1.8
7	娃哈哈 Wahaha	5	0.9

n=541

4-3 样本、男性各年龄层、女性各年龄层的常用品牌/ The Most Frequently Used Brands by the Whole Sample, Age and Gender Groups

	人数 Number	第一品牌及百分比 1st/ percent	第二品牌及百分比 2nd/ percent	第三品牌及百分比 3rd/ percent	第四品牌及百分比 4th/ percent
样本 Sample	541	**达能 Danone(53.8)**	**燕塘 Yantang(23.3)**	**风行 Fengxing(7.4)**	**香满楼 Flower Fresh(4.1)**
男性 Male	233	**达能 Danone(48.9)**	**燕塘 Yantang(26.2)**	**风行 Fengxing(8.6)**	**香满楼 Flower Fresh(4.7)**
16~24 岁 Age	52	达能 Danone(48.1)	燕塘 Yantang(25.0)	风行 Fengxing(15.4)	香满楼 Flower Fresh(5.8)
25~34 岁 Age	83	达能 Danone(45.8)	燕塘 Yantang(30.1)	风行 Fengxing(9.6)	香满楼 Flower Fresh(3.6)
35~44 岁 Age	52	达能 Danone(50.0)	燕塘 Yantang(21.2)	香满楼 Flower Fresh(5.8) 风行 Fengxing(5.8)	晨光 Chenguang(3.8)
45~54 岁 Age	28	达能 Danone(50.0)	燕塘 Yantang(28.6)	娃哈哈 Wahaha(3.6) 伊利 Yili(3.6) 风行 Fengxing(3.6) 维他 Vita(3.6) 晨光 Chenguang(3.6)	
55~60 岁 Age	18	达能 Danone(61.1)	燕塘 Yantang(22.2)	香满楼 Flower Fresh(11.1)	晨光 Chenguang(5.6)
女性 Female	308	**达能 Danone(57.5)**	**燕塘 Yantang(21.1)**	**风行 Fengxing(6.5)**	**香满楼 Flower Fresh(3.6)**
16~24 岁 Age	77	达能 Danone(61.0)	燕塘 Yantang(24.7)	风行 Fengxing(5.2)	乐百氏 Robust(1.3) 三元 Sanyuan(1.3) 益力多 Yakult(1.3) 四佳 Sijia(1.3) 晨光 Chenguang(1.3) 华农 Huanong(1.3) 益乐多 Yileduo(1.3)
25~34 岁 Age	102	达能 Danone(57.8)	燕塘 Yantang(15.7)	风行 Fengxing(6.9)	香满楼 Flower Fresh(5.9)
35~44 岁 Age	68	达能 Danone(57.4)	燕塘 Yantang(26.5)	风行 Fengxing(4.4)	乐百氏 Robust(2.9) 香满楼 Flower Fresh(2.9) 晨光 Chenguang(2.9)
45~54 岁 Age	50	达能 Danone(48.0)	燕塘 Yantang(20.0)	风行 Fengxing(12.0)	乐百氏 Robust(6.0)
55~60 岁 Age	11	达能 Danone(72.7)	燕塘 Yantang(18.2)	香满楼 Flower Fresh(9.1)	

4-4 理想品牌排名/ Ranking of the Ideal Brands

排名 Brand Ranking	品牌 Brands	人数 Number	百分比 Percent
1	达能 Danone	453	43.9
2	燕塘 Yantang	161	15.6
3	风行 Fengxing	55	5.3
4	香满楼 Flower Fresh	42	4.1
5	晨光 Chenguang	17	1.6
6	乐百氏 Robust	14	1.4
7	娃哈哈 Wahaha	6	0.6
7	益力多 Yakult	6	0.6

n=1033

4-5 样本、男性各年龄层、女性各年龄层最近三个月有无购买的比例/ Purchasing in the Last Three Months by the Whole Sample, Age and Gender Groups

	人数 Number	买过 yes	没买过 no
样本 Sample	1033	51.8	48.2
男性 Male	499	46.7	53.3
16~24 岁 Age	106	45.3	54.7
25~34 岁 Age	150	54.7	45.3
35~44 岁 Age	127	42.5	57.5
45~54 岁 Age	73	41.1	58.9
55~60 岁 Age	43	44.2	55.8
女性 Female	534	56.6	43.4
16~24 岁 Age	112	62.5	37.5
25~34 岁 Age	158	63.3	36.7
35~44 岁 Age	137	53.3	46.7
45~54 岁 Age	86	57.0	43.0
55~60 岁 Age	41	24.4	75.6

4-6 样本、男性各年龄层、女性各年龄层最近三个月的食用频率/ Frequencies of Consuming Yogurt in the Last Three Months by the Whole Sample, Age and Gender Groups

	人数 Number	天天喝 daily	一周 3 次或以上 3 times or over a week	一周 1~2 次 once or twice a week	一个月 2~3 次 2 or 3 times a month	一个月 1 次或以下 once a month or below	没喝过 never
样本 Sample	1028	4.6	8.1	17.4	15.2	7.6	47.2
男性 Male	496	2.2	6.9	15.9	14.5	7.9	52.6
16~24 岁 Age	106	2.8	11.3	14.2	15.1	5.7	50.9
25~34 岁 Age	148	2.7	7.4	17.6	20.3	9.5	42.6
35~44 岁 Age	127	0.8	6.3	14.2	10.2	9.4	59.1
45~54 岁 Age	72	2.8	2.8	11.1	12.5	9.7	61.1
55~60 岁 Age	43	2.3	2.3	27.9	9.3	0.0	58.1
女性 Female	532	6.8	9.2	18.8	15.8	7.3	42.1
16~24 岁 Age	112	3.6	11.6	17.0	25.0	11.6	31.3
25~34 岁 Age	157	8.9	7.0	23.6	16.6	8.9	35.0
35~44 岁 Age	135	5.2	10.4	18.5	11.1	5.2	49.6
45~54 岁 Age	87	11.5	11.5	16.1	12.6	5.7	42.5
55~60 岁 Age	41	2.4	2.4	12.2	9.8	0.0	73.2

4-7 样本、男性各年龄层、女性各年龄层的品牌习惯/ Brand Habit in Consuming Yogurt by the Whole Sample, Age and Gender Groups

	人数 Number	基本固定食用一个牌子 used in only one brand	比较固定地食用两个或三个牌子 used in two or three brands	基本上不太固定牌子 no brand preference
样本 Sample	541	51.0	36.2	12.8
男性 Male	235	51.1	35.7	13.2
16~24 岁 Age	52	46.2	42.3	11.5
25~34 岁 Age	85	45.9	38.8	15.3
35~44 岁 Age	52	59.6	28.8	11.5
45~54 岁 Age	28	50.0	32.1	17.9
55~60 岁 Age	18	66.7	27.8	5.6
女性 Female	306	51.0	36.6	12.4
16~24 岁 Age	77	50.6	32.5	16.9
25~34 岁 Age	102	51.0	39.2	9.8
35~44 岁 Age	67	58.2	37.3	4.5
45~54 岁 Age	49	40.8	38.8	20.4
55~60 岁 Age	11	54.5	27.3	18.2

4-8 选择该类商品的考虑因素/ Ranking of the Considerations in Purchasing

注：本题为多选题，合计百分比超过 100%(Multiple answers)

排名 Ranking	考虑因素 Considerations	人次 Person-time	百分比 Percent
1	口味好 pleasant taste	286	52.9
2	价格适中 reasonable price	172	31.8
3	有名的牌子 famous brand	168	31.1
4	营养成分 nutrition constituent	164	30.3
5	购买方便 easy to buy	140	25.9
6	生产日期 date of producing	97	17.9
7	只是由于习惯 out of habit	45	8.3
8	有优惠条件 with preferential terms	37	6.8
9	广告影响 influence of advertising	21	3.9
9	包装吸引人 appealing package	21	3.9
10	朋友推荐 introduction of friends	19	3.5
11	售货员介绍 introduced by the shop assistants	7	1.3
12	其它 others	2	0.4

n=541

4-9 样本、男性各年龄层、女性各年龄层最常食用的种类/ Types of the Consumed Yogurt by the Whole Sample, Age and Gender Groups

注：本题为多选题，合计百分比超过 100%(Multiple answers)

	人数 Number	原味 original flavor	巧克力味 chocolate flavor	草莓味 strawberry	菠萝味 pineapple	橙味 orange	杏味 apricot	带果粒 with fruit dots	加钙 calcium added	其他 others
样本 Sample	542	55.5	7.4	32.7	5.9	3.7	0.2	3.7	10.5	1.8
男性 Male	235	58.3	7.7	30.6	6.0	3.0	0.4	2.6	8.1	0.9
16~24 岁 Age	52	63.5	7.7	30.8	5.8	1.9	0.0	5.8	13.5	0.0
25~34 岁 Age	85	61.2	4.7	29.4	7.1	2.4	1.2	2.4	7.1	1.2
35~44 岁 Age	52	46.2	11.5	36.5	3.8	3.8	0.0	1.9	5.8	1.9
45~54 岁 Age	28	57.1	14.3	28.6	7.1	0.0	0.0	0.0	7.1	0.0
55~60 岁 Age	18	66.7	0.0	22.2	5.6	11.1	0.0	0.0	5.6	0.0
女性 Female	307	53.4	7.2	34.2	5.9	4.2	0.0	4.6	12.4	2.6
16~24 岁 Age	76	61.8	10.5	26.3	6.6	5.3	0.0	6.6	10.5	2.6
25~34 岁 Age	102	52.9	3.9	38.2	4.9	4.9	0.0	4.9	9.8	2.0
35~44 岁 Age	68	44.1	7.4	39.7	5.9	5.9	0.0	2.9	11.8	1.5
45~54 岁 Age	50	58.0	10.0	30.0	8.0	0.0	0.0	4.0	18.0	6.0
55~60 岁 Age	11	36.4	0.0	36.4	0.0	0.0	0.0	0.0	27.3	0.0

4-10 样本、男性各年龄层、女性各年龄层最常食用的包装形式/ Types of Package of the Consumed Yogurt by the Whole Sample, Age and Gender Groups

注：本题为多选题，合计百分比超过 100%(Multiple answers)

	人数 Number	袋装 bag	方盒装/利乐砖 tetra	房屋状纸盒 house-shaped box	粽子状纸盒 V-shaped box	塑料瓶 plastic bottle	瓷瓶 china bottle	其他 others
样本 Sample	534	12.5	23.4	11.6	2.6	35.4	25.3	3.0
男性 Male	233	16.7	21.9	11.2	2.6	31.8	28.3	3.9
16~24 岁 Age	51	17.6	23.5	11.8	3.9	31.4	29.4	0.0
25~34 岁 Age	84	19.0	19.0	14.3	1.2	33.3	31.0	4.8
35~44 岁 Age	52	15.4	25.0	7.7	1.9	32.7	21.2	7.7
45~54 岁 Age	28	17.9	21.4	7.1	3.6	25.0	35.7	3.6
55~60 岁 Age	18	5.6	22.2	11.1	5.6	33.3	22.2	0.0
女性 Female	301	9.3	24.6	12.0	2.7	38.2	22.9	2.3
16~24 岁 Age	76	9.2	19.7	14.5	2.6	40.8	30.3	1.3
25~34 岁 Age	100	8.0	25.0	13.0	1.0	38.0	20.0	3.0
35~44 岁 Age	66	10.6	19.7	12.1	1.5	43.9	19.7	0.0
45~54 岁 Age	48	10.4	39.6	8.3	6.3	25.0	25.0	4.2
55~60 岁 Age	11	9.1	18.2	0.0	9.1	45.5	9.1	9.1

4-11 样本、男性各年龄层、女性各年龄层最常饮用场合/ Settings of Consumption by the Whole Sample, Age and Gender Groups

注：本题为多选题，合计百分比超过 100%(Multiple answers）

	人数 Number	早餐时 breakfast	正餐 (午.晚餐)时 dinner	口渴时 when thirsty	宵夜时 evening snack	睡觉前 before sleeping	工作休息时 during work break	外出/旅游时 outing/ traveling	其它 others
样本 Sample	542	45.2	5.5	25.6	7.9	10.3	17.5	13.3	5.0
男性 Male	235	44.3	4.3	26.4	7.2	8.9	20.9	12.3	6.4
16~24 岁 Age	52	51.9	1.9	17.3	11.5	13.5	17.3	7.7	9.6
25~34 岁 Age	85	40.0	4.7	32.9	4.7	4.7	21.2	15.3	5.9
35~44 岁 Age	52	38.5	7.7	23.1	3.8	15.4	19.2	15.4	5.8
45~54 岁 Age	28	53.6	0.0	32.1	10.7	3.6	28.6	3.6	7.1
55~60 岁 Age	18	44.4	5.6	22.2	11.1	5.6	22.2	16.7	0.0
女性 Female	307	45.9	6.5	25.1	8.5	11.4	15.0	14.0	3.9
16~24 岁 Age	76	48.7	6.6	14.5	7.9	10.5	15.8	18.4	6.6
25~34 岁 Age	102	47.1	4.9	26.5	6.9	9.8	23.5	14.7	2.9
35~44 岁 Age	68	51.5	2.9	30.9	13.2	14.7	4.4	11.8	0.0
45~54 岁 Age	50	36.0	10.0	30.0	8.0	14.0	12.0	12.0	4.0
55~60 岁 Age	11	27.3	27.3	27.3	0.0	0.0	9.1	0.0	18.2

4-12 重度消费者的人口分布/ Demographics of the Heavy Consumers

	人数 Number	16-24 岁 Age	25-34 岁 Age	35-44 岁 Age	45-54 岁 Age	55-60 岁 Age
样本 Sample	309	21.4	33.3	23.6	14.9	6.8
男性 Male	124	24.2	33.1	21.8	9.7	11.3
天天喝 daily	11	27.3	36.4	9.1	18.2	9.1
一周 3 次或以上 3 times or over a week	34	35.3	32.4	23.5	5.9	2.9
一周 1～2 次 once or twice a week	79	19.0	32.9	22.8	10.1	15.2
女性 Female	185	19.5	33.5	24.9	18.4	3.8
天天喝 daily	36	11.1	38.9	19.4	27.8	2.8
一周 3 次或以上 3 times or over a week	49	26.5	22.4	28.6	20.4	2.0
一周 1～2 次 once or twice a week	100	19.0	37.0	25.0	14.0	5.0

4-13 不同消费者层的常用品牌/ The Most Frequently Used Brands by Market Segments

4-13-1 时尚流行指标/ Fads Popular Index

	人数 Number	第一品牌及百分比 1st/ percent	第二品牌及百分比 2nd/ percent	第三品牌及百分比 3rd/ percent
样本 Sample	535	**达能 Danone(53.6)**	**燕塘 Yantang(23.6)**	**风行 Fengxing(7.3)**
平实生活指向 simple living orientation	250	达能 Danone(50.8)	燕塘 Yantang(26.4)	风行 Fengxing(5.6)
时尚流行指向 fashion orientation	285	达能 Danone(56.1)	燕塘 Yantang(21.1)	风行 Fengxing(8.8)

4-13-2 广告态度指标/ Advertising Attitude Index

	人数 Number	第一品牌及百分比 1st/ percent	第二品牌及百分比 2nd/ percent	第三品牌及百分比 3rd/ percent
样本 Sample	533	**达能 Danone(53.5)**	**燕塘 Yantang(23.3)**	**风行 Fengxing(7.5)**
广告淡漠指向 indifferent orientation	163	达能 Danone(49.1)	燕塘 Yantang(25.8)	香满楼 Flower Fresh(8.0)
中间层 medium	309	达能 Danone(55.3)	燕塘 Yantang(23.0)	风行 Fengxing(7.1)
信赖广告指向 loyal orientation	61	达能 Danone(55.7)	燕塘 Yantang(18.0)	风行 Fengxing(16.4)

4-13-3 饮食健康指标/ Foods & Drink Quality Index

	人数 Number	第一品牌及百分比 1st/ percent	第二品牌及百分比 2nd/ percent	第三品牌及百分比 3rd/ percent
样本 Sample	**538**	**达能 Danone(53.9)**	**燕塘 Yantang(23.0)**	**风行 Fengxing(7.4)**
饮食"温饱"指向 "basic" orientation	133	达能 Danone(50.4)	燕塘 Yantang(23.3)	风行 Fengxing(9.0)
中间层 medium	290	达能 Danone(54.8)	燕塘 Yantang(21.7)	风行 Fengxing(7.6)
健康营养指向 health & nutrition orientation	115	达能 Danone(55.7)	燕塘 Yantang(26.1)	风行 Fengxing(5.2)

4-14 重度消费者的消费者层构成/ The Composition of the Heavy Consumers

4-14-1 时尚流行指标/ Fads Popular Index

	人数 Number	平实生活指向 simple living orientation	时尚流行指向 fashion orientation
样本 Sample	**306**	**44.4**	**55.6**
天天喝 daily	47	53.2	46.8
一周 3 次或以上 3 times or over a week	83	37.3	62.7
一周 1～2 次 once or twice a week	176	45.5	54.5

4-14-2 广告态度指标/ Advertising Attitude Index

	人数 Number	广告淡漠指向 indifferent orientation	中间层 medium	信赖广告指向 loyal orientation
样本 Sample	**303**	**33.0**	**56.4**	**10.6**
天天喝 daily	46	37.0	47.8	15.2
一周 3 次或以上 3 times or over a week	83	37.3	53.0	9.6
一周 1～2 次 once or twice a week	174	29.9	60.3	9.8

4-14-3 饮食健康指标/ Foods & Drink Quality Index

	人数 Number	饮食"温饱"指向 "basic" orientation	中间层 medium	健康营养指向 health & nutrition orientation
样本 Sample	**308**	**26.0**	**51.3**	**22.7**
天天喝 daily	47	25.5	44.7	29.8
一周 3 次或以上 3 times or over a week	83	27.7	44.6	27.7
一周 1～2 次 once or twice a week	178	25.3	56.2	18.5

● 重庆 / Chongqing

4-1 最近三个月食用频率的比例/ Proportion of the Sample Consuming Yogurt in the Last Three Months

	人数 Number	百分比 Percent
天天喝 daily	71	11.4
一周 3 次或以上 3 times or over a week	40	6.4
一周 1~2 次 once or twice a week	79	12.7
一个月 2～3 次 2 or 3 times a month	57	9.1
一个月 1 次或以下 once a month or below	44	7.1
没喝过 never	332	53.3

n=623

4-2 最常用品牌排名/ Ranking of the Most Frequently Used Brands

排名 Brand Ranking	品牌 Brands	人数 Number	百分比 Percent
1	天友 Tianyou	241	83.7
2	海浪 Hailang	28	9.7

n=288

4-3 样本、男性各年龄层、女性各年龄层的常用品牌/ The Most Frequently Used Brands by the Whole Sample, Age and Gender Groups

	人数 Number	第一品牌及百分比 1st/ percent	第二品牌及百分比 2nd/ percent	第三品牌及百分比 3rd/ percent
样本 Sample	288	**天友 Tianyou(83.7)**	**海浪 Hailang(9.7)**	**百事 Baishi(0.3)** **龙江 longjiang(0.3)** **卡夫 Kraft(0.3)** **乐百氏 Robust(0.3)** **山城 Shancheng(0.3)**
男性 Male	137	**天友 Tianyou(84.7)**	**海浪 Hailang(8.8)**	**百事 Baishi(0.7)** **龙江 longjiang(0.7)**
16~24 岁 Age	35	天友 Tianyou(80.0)	海浪 Hailang(11.4)	龙江 Longjiang(2.9)
25~34 岁 Age	47	天友 Tianyou(93.6)	海浪 Hailang(6.4)	
35~44 岁 Age	28	天友 Tianyou(82.1)	海浪 Hailang(3.6) 百事 Baishi(3.6)	
45~54 岁 Age	21	天友 Tianyou(81.0)	海浪 Hailang(9.5)	
55~60 岁 Age	6	天友 Tianyou(66.7)	海浪 Hailang(33.3)	
女性 Female	151	**天友 Tianyou(82.8)**	**海浪 Hailang(10.6)**	**卡夫 Kraft(0.7)** **乐百氏 Robust(0.7)** **山城 Shancheng(0.7)**
16~24 岁 Age	44	天友 Tianyou(86.4)	海浪 Hailang(9.1)	卡夫 Kraft(2.3)
25~34 岁 Age	51	天友 Tianyou(84.3)	海浪 Hailang(11.8)	
35~44 岁 Age	26	天友 Tianyou(73.1)	海浪 Hailang(7.7)	乐百氏 Robust(3.8) 山城 Shancheng (3.8)
45~54 岁 Age	24	天友 Tianyou(79.2)	海浪 Hailang(16.7)	
55~60 岁 Age	6	天友 Tianyou(100.0)		

4-4 理想品牌排名/ Ranking of the Ideal Brands

排名 Brand Ranking	品牌 Brands	人数 Number	百分比 Percent
1	天友 Tianyou	447	71.7
2	海浪 Hailang	47	7.5

n=623

4-5 样本、男性各年龄层、女性各年龄层最近三个月有无购买的比例/ Purchasing in the Last Three Months by the Whole Sample, Age and Gender Groups

	人数 Number	买过 yes	没买过 no
样本 Sample	623	49.4	50.6
男性 Male	313	46.0	54.0
16~24 岁 Age	64	54.7	45.3
25~34 岁 Age	93	52.7	47.3
35~44 岁 Age	75	42.7	57.3
45~54 岁 Age	54	42.6	57.4
55~60 岁 Age	27	18.5	81.5
女性 Female	310	52.9	47.1
16~24 岁 Age	64	70.3	29.7
25~34 岁 Age	90	62.2	37.8
35~44 岁 Age	73	43.8	56.2
45~54 岁 Age	60	40.0	60.0
55~60 岁 Age	23	30.4	69.6

4-6 样本、男性各年龄层、女性各年龄层最近三个月的食用频率/ Frequencies of Consuming Yogurt in the Last Three Months by the Whole Sample, Age and Gender Groups

	人数 Number	天天喝 daily	一周3次或以上 3 times or over a week	一周1~2 次 once or twice a week	一个月2~3次 2 or 3 times a month	一个月1次或以下 once a month or below	没喝过 never
样本 Sample	623	11.4	6.4	12.7	9.1	7.1	53.3
男性 Male	314	9.2	7.6	11.5	8.9	6.4	56.4
16~24 岁 Age	64	10.9	14.1	4.7	12.5	12.5	45.3
25~34 岁 Age	93	9.7	7.5	18.3	12.9	2.2	49.5
35~44 岁 Age	75	5.3	5.3	16.0	1.3	9.3	62.7
45~54 岁 Age	54	13.0	5.6	5.6	11.1	3.7	61.1
55~60 岁 Age	28	7.1	3.6	3.6	3.6	3.6	78.6
女性 Female	309	13.6	5.2	13.9	9.4	7.8	50.2
16~24 岁 Age	64	9.4	10.9	21.9	14.1	12.5	31.3
25~34 岁 Age	90	13.3	6.7	17.8	12.2	7.8	42.2
35~44 岁 Age	72	13.9	1.4	11.1	5.6	6.9	61.1
45~54 岁 Age	60	20.0	3.3	6.7	5.0	5.0	60.0
55~60 岁 Age	23	8.7	0.0	4.3	8.7	4.3	73.9

4-7 样本、男性各年龄层、女性各年龄层的品牌习惯/ Brand Habit in Consuming Yogurt by the Whole Sample, Age and Gender Groups

	人数 Number	基本固定食用一个牌子 used in only one brand	比较固定地食用两个或三个牌子 used in two or three brands	基本上不太固定牌子 no brand preference
样本 Sample	288	71.5	15.3	13.2
男性 Male	135	72.6	12.6	14.8
16~24 岁 Age	35	65.7	11.4	22.9
25~34 岁 Age	46	82.6	13.0	4.3
35~44 岁 Age	28	64.3	7.1	28.6
45~54 岁 Age	20	70.0	20.0	10.0
55~60 岁 Age	6	83.3	16.7	0.0
女性 Female	153	70.6	17.6	11.8
16~24 岁 Age	44	68.2	20.5	11.4
25~34 岁 Age	52	69.2	21.2	9.6
35~44 岁 Age	27	63.0	22.2	14.8
45~54 岁 Age	24	91.7	0.0	8.3
55~60 岁 Age	6	50.0	16.7	33.3

4-8 选择该类商品的考虑因素/ Ranking of the Considerations in Purchasing

注：本题为多选题，合计百分比超过 100%(Multiple answers)

排名 Ranking	考虑因素 Considerations	人次 Person-time	百分比 Percent
1	口味好 pleasant taste	160	55.7
2	价格适中 reasonable price	86	30.0
3	购买方便 easy to buy	85	29.6
4	营养成分 nutrition constituent	77	26.8
5	有名的牌子 famous brand	54	18.8
6	生产日期 date of producing	50	17.4
7	只是由于习惯 out of habit	38	13.2
8	广告影响 influence of advertising	7	2.4
8	朋友推荐 introduction of friends	7	2.4
9	其它 others	5	1.7
9	售货员介绍 introduced by the shop assistants	5	1.7
10	包装吸引人 appealing package	4	1.4
10	有优惠条件 with preferential terms	4	1.4

n=287

4-9 样本、男性各年龄层、女性各年龄层最常食用的种类/ Types of the Consumed Yogurt by the Whole Sample, Age and Gender Groups

注：本题为多选题，合计百分比超过 100%(Multiple answers）

	人数 Number	原味 original flavor	巧克力味 chocolate flavor	草莓味 straw-berry	菠萝味 pine-apple	橙味 orange	杏味 apricot	带果粒 with fruit dots	加钙 calcium added	其他 others
样本 Sample	**288**	**58.0**	**9.0**	**30.9**	**5.9**	**2.8**	**0.0**	**1.7**	**9.7**	**0.3**
男性 Male	**136**	**62.5**	**10.3**	**30.1**	**3.7**	**1.5**	**0.0**	**0.7**	**5.9**	**0.0**
16~24 岁 Age	35	51.4	20.0	31.4	2.9	0.0	0.0	0.0	5.7	0.0
25~34 岁 Age	46	65.2	10.9	30.4	6.5	0.0	0.0	2.2	6.5	0.0
35~44 岁 Age	28	75.0	3.6	21.4	0.0	7.1	0.0	0.0	7.1	0.0
45~54 岁 Age	21	71.4	0.0	28.6	0.0	0.0	0.0	0.0	0.0	0.0
55~60 岁 Age	6	16.7	16.7	66.7	16.7	0.0	0.0	0.0	16.7	0.0
女性 Female	**152**	**53.9**	**7.9**	**31.6**	**7.9**	**3.9**	**0.0**	**2.6**	**13.2**	**0.7**
16~24 岁 Age	44	47.7	15.9	40.9	11.4	2.3	0.0	0.0	4.5	0.0
25~34 岁 Age	51	64.7	5.9	29.4	5.9	5.9	0.0	5.9	11.8	0.0
35~44 岁 Age	27	55.6	7.4	25.9	7.4	0.0	0.0	0.0	18.5	0.0
45~54 岁 Age	24	37.5	0.0	29.2	4.2	4.2	0.0	4.2	29.2	4.2
55~60 岁 Age	6	66.7	0.0	16.7	16.7	16.7	0.0	0.0	0.0	0.0

4-10 样本、男性各年龄层、女性各年龄层最常食用的包装形式/ Types of Package of the Consumed Yogurt by the Whole Sample, Age and Gender Groups

注：本题为多选题，合计百分比超过 100%(Multiple answers）

	人数 Number	袋装 bag	方盒装/利乐砖 tetra	房屋状纸盒 house-shaped box	粽子状纸盒 V-shaped box	塑料瓶 plastic bottle	瓷瓶 china bottle	其他 others
样本 Sample	**279**	**7.5**	**19.7**	**7.9**	**1.4**	**16.8**	**54.5**	**2.9**
男性 Male	**132**	**9.1**	**15.2**	**6.1**	**1.5**	**18.9**	**51.5**	**4.5**
16~24 岁 Age	35	8.6	20.0	11.4	0.0	11.4	45.7	2.9
25~34 岁 Age	43	7.0	11.6	7.0	4.7	25.6	46.5	4.7
35~44 岁 Age	28	21.4	25.0	3.6	0.0	10.7	42.9	7.1
45~54 岁 Age	20	0.0	5.0	0.0	0.0	30.0	70.0	5.0
55~60 岁 Age	6	0.0	0.0	0.0	0.0	16.7	100.0	0.0
女性 Female	**147**	**6.1**	**23.8**	**9.5**	**1.4**	**15.0**	**57.1**	**1.4**
16~24 岁 Age	43	0.0	34.9	11.6	2.3	7.0	55.8	2.3
25~34 岁 Age	49	8.2	26.5	12.2	2.0	24.5	55.1	0.0
35~44 岁 Age	27	11.1	7.4	7.4	0.0	18.5	59.3	3.7
45~54 岁 Age	22	0.0	18.2	0.0	0.0	9.1	68.2	0.0
55~60 岁 Age	6	33.3	16.7	16.7	0.0	0.0	33.3	0.0

4-11 样本、男性各年龄层、女性各年龄层最常饮用场合/ Settings of Consumption by the Whole Sample, Age and Gender Groups

注：本题为多选题，合计百分比超过 100%(Multiple answers）

	人数 Number	早餐时 breakfast	正餐（午、晚餐）时 dinner	口渴时 when thirsty	宵夜时 evening snack	睡觉前 before sleeping	工作休息时 during work break	外出/旅游时 outing/ traveling	其它 others
样本 Sample	**287**	**37.3**	**5.2**	**26.8**	**8.7**	**19.5**	**10.1**	**11.8**	**4.5**
男性 Male	**135**	**37.0**	**4.4**	**27.4**	**5.9**	**20.7**	**11.1**	**13.3**	**4.4**
16~24 岁 Age	35	42.9	0.0	34.3	8.6	17.1	11.4	8.6	5.7
25~34 岁 Age	46	28.3	0.0	32.6	4.3	19.6	15.2	21.7	2.2
35~44 岁 Age	28	46.4	14.3	14.3	7.1	10.7	3.6	14.3	10.7
45~54 岁 Age	20	35.0	10.0	15.0	5.0	35.0	10.0	0.0	0.0
55~60 岁 Age	6	33.3	0.0	50.0	0.0	50.0	16.7	16.7	0.0
女性 Female	**152**	**37.5**	**5.9**	**26.3**	**11.2**	**18.4**	**9.2**	**10.5**	**4.6**
16~24 岁 Age	44	34.1	6.8	18.2	9.1	18.2	13.6	15.9	4.5
25~34 岁 Age	51	31.4	2.0	43.1	7.8	21.6	7.8	13.7	2.0
35~44 岁 Age	27	51.9	11.1	11.1	18.5	14.8	11.1	3.7	7.4
45~54 岁 Age	24	29.2	8.3	25.0	12.5	20.8	4.2	4.2	8.3
55~60 岁 Age	6	83.3	0.0	16.7	16.7	0.0	0.0	0.0	0.0

4-12 重度消费者的人口分布/ Demographics of the Heavy Consumers

	人数 Number	16-24 岁 Age	25-34 岁 Age	35-44 岁 Age	45-54 岁 Age	55-60 岁 Age
样本 Sample	190	24.2	35.3	20.5	16.3	3.7
男性 Male	89	21.3	37.1	22.5	14.6	4.5
天天喝 daily	29	24.1	31.0	13.8	24.1	6.9
一周 3 次或以上 3 times or over a week	24	37.5	29.2	16.7	12.5	4.2
一周 1~2 次 once or twice a week	36	8.3	47.2	33.3	8.3	2.8
女性 Female	101	26.7	33.7	18.8	17.8	3.0
天天喝 daily	42	14.3	28.6	23.8	28.6	4.8
一周 3 次或以上 3 times or over a week	16	43.8	37.5	6.3	12.5	0.0
一周 1~2 次 once or twice a week	43	32.6	37.2	18.6	9.3	2.3

4-13 不同消费者层的常用品牌/ The Most Frequently Used Brands by Market Segments

4-13-1 时尚流行指标/ Fads Popular Index

	人数 Number	第一品牌及百分比 1st/ percent	第二品牌及百分比 2nd/ percent	第三品牌及百分比 3rd/ percent	
样本 Sample	284	**天友 Tianyou(83.8)**	**海浪 Hailang(9.5)**	**卡夫 Kraft(0.4)** **百事 Baishi(0.4)**	**乐百氏 Robust(0.4)** **龙江 Longjiang(0.4)**
平实生活指向 simple living orientation	147	天友 Tianyou(81.6)	海浪 Hailang(10.9)	卡夫 Kraft(0.7) 百事 Baishi(0.7)	乐百氏 Robust(0.7)
时尚流行指向 fashion orientation	137	天友 Tianyou(86.1)	海浪 Hailang(8.0)	龙江 Longjiang(0.7)	

4-13-2 广告态度指标/ Advertising Attitude Index

	人数 Number	第一品牌及百分比 1st/ percent	第二品牌及百分比 2nd/ percent	第三品牌及百分比 3rd/ percent	
样本 Sample	287	**天友 Tianyou(84.0)**	**海浪 Hailang(9.4)**	**卡夫 Kraft(0.3)** **百事 Baishi(0.3)** **山城 Shancheng(0.3)**	**乐百氏 Robust(0.3)** **龙江 Longjiang(0.3)**
广告淡漠指向 indifferent orientation	71	天友 Tianyou(81.7)	海浪 Hailang(8.5)	乐百氏 Robust(1.4)	百事 Baishi(1.4)
中间层 medium	172	天友 Tianyou(83.7)	海浪 Hailang(11.6)	卡夫 Kraft(0.6) 龙江 Longjiang(0.6)	山城 Shancheng(0.6)
信赖广告指向 loyal orientation	44	天友 Tianyou(88.6)	海浪 Hailang(2.3)		

4-13-3 饮食健康指标/ Foods & Drink Quality Index

	人数 Number	第一品牌及百分比 1st/ percent	第二品牌及百分比 2nd/ percent	第三品牌及百分比 3rd/ percent	
样本 Sample	284	**天友 Tianyou(84.2)**	**海浪 Hailang(9.5)**	**卡夫 Kraft(0.3)** **百事 Baishi(0.3)**	**乐百氏 Robust(0.3)** **龙江 Longjiang(0.3)**
饮食“温饱”指向 "basic" orientation	101	天友 Tianyou(85.1)	海浪 Hailang(6.9)	乐百氏 Robust(1.0)	
中间层 medium	126	天友 Tianyou(86.5)	海浪 Hailang(9.5)	百事 Baishi(0.8)	龙江 Longjiang(0.8)
健康营养指向 health & nutrition orientation	57	天友 Tianyou(77.2)	海浪 Hailang(14.0)	卡夫 Kraft(1.8)	

4-14 重度消费者的消费者层构成/ The Composition of the Heavy Consumers

4-14-1 时尚流行指标/ Fads Popular Index

	人数 Number	平实生活指向 simple living orientation	时尚流行指向 fashion orientation
样本 Sample	187	52.4	47.6
天天喝 daily	69	47.8	52.2
一周 3 次或以上 3 times or over a week	40	62.5	37.5
一周 1~2 次 once or twice a week	78	51.3	48.7

4-14-2 广告态度指标/ Advertising Attitude Index

	人数 Number	广告淡漠指向 indifferent orientation	中间层 medium	信赖广告指向 loyal orientation
样本 Sample	189	21.2	61.4	17.5
天天喝 daily	70	24.3	57.1	18.6
一周 3 次或以上 3 times or over a week	40	17.5	62.5	20.0
一周 1～2 次 once or twice a week	79	20.3	64.6	15.2

4-14-3 饮食健康指标/ Foods & Drink Quality Index

	人数 Number	饮食"温饱"指向 "basic" orientation	中间层 medium	健康营养指向 health & nutrition orientation
样本 Sample	186	36.0	43.0	21.0
天天喝 daily	68	29.4	39.7	30.9
一周 3 次或以上 3 time or over a week	40	55.0	42.5	2.5
一周 1～2 次 once or twice a week	78	32.1	46.2	21.8

● 武汉 / Wuhan

4-1 最近三个月饮用频率的比例/ Proportion of the Sample Consuming Yogurt in the Last Three Months

	人数 Number	百分比 Percent
天天喝 daily	41	6.4
一周 3 次或以上 3 times or over a week	53	8.3
一周 1~2 次 once or twice a week	86	13.4
一个月 2～3 次 2 or 3 times a month	93	14.5
一个月 1 次或以下 once a month or below	41	6.4
没喝过 never	327	51.0

n=641

4-2 最常用品牌排名/ Ranking of the Most Frequently Used Brands

排名 Brand Ranking	品牌 Brands	人数 Number	百分比 Percent
1	扬子江 Yangzijiang	171	54.6
2	友芝友 Youzhiyou	57	18.2
3	光明 Bright	24	7.7
4	妙士 Miaoshi	11	3.5
5	海浪 Hailang	4	1.3
5	娃哈哈 Wahaha	4	1.3
5	喜旺 Xiwang	4	1.3
6	正广 Zhengguang	2	0.6
6	伊利 Yili	2	0.6
6	杨协成 Yeo's	2	0.6

n=313

4-3 样本、男性各年龄层、女性各年龄层的常用品牌/ The Most Frequently Used Brands by the Whole Sample, Age and Gender Groups

	人数 Number	第一品牌及百分比 1st/ percent	第二品牌及百分比 2nd/ percent	第三品牌及百分比 3rd/ percent
样本 Sample	313	**扬子江 Yangzijiang(54.6)**	**友芝友 Youzhiyou(18.2)**	**光明 Bright(7.7)**
男性 Male	137	**扬子江 Yangzijiang(59.1)**	**友芝友 Youzhiyou(12.4)**	**光明 Bright(5.8)**
16~24 岁 Age	38	扬子江 Yangzijiang(57.9)	友芝友 Youzhiyou(15.8)	光明 Bright(7.9)
25~34 岁 Age	52	扬子江 Yangzijiang(69.2)	友芝友 Youzhiyou(5.8)	光明 Bright(3.8) 妙士 Miaoshi(3.8)
35~44 岁 Age	26	扬子江 Yangzijiang(42.3)	友芝友 Youzhiyou(15.4)	光明 Bright(11.5)
45~54 岁 Age	16	扬子江 Yangzijiang(62.5)	友芝友 Youzhiyou(18.8)	海浪 Hailang (6.3)
55~60 岁 Age	5	扬子江 Yangzijiang(40.0)	友芝友 Youzhiyou(20.0)	
女性 Female	176	**扬子江 Yangzijiang(51.1)**	**友芝友 Youzhiyou(22.7)**	**光明 Bright(9.1)**
16~24 岁 Age	55	扬子江 Yangzijiang(49.1)	友芝友 Youzhiyou(25.5)	光明 Bright(9.1)
25~34 岁 Age	61	扬子江 Yangzijiang(50.8)	友芝友 Youzhiyou(26.2)	光明 Bright(9.8)
35~44 岁 Age	32	扬子江 Yangzijiang(59.4)	光明 Bright(9.4) 友芝友 Youzhiyou(9.4)	妙士 Miaoshi(6.3)
45~54 岁 Age	22	扬子江 Yangzijiang(54.5)	友芝友 Youzhiyou(18.2)	光明 Bright(9.1)
55~60 岁 Age	6	友芝友 Youzhiyou(50.0)	扬子江 Yangzijiang(16.7) 佳能 Jianeng(16.7) 家佳康 Jiajiakang(16.7)	

4-4 理想品牌排名/ Ranking of the Ideal Brands

排名 Brand Ranking	品牌 Brands	人数 Number	百分比 Percent
1	扬子江 Yangzijiang	213	33.2
2	友芝友 Youzhiyou	77	12.0
3	光明 Bright	45	7.0
4	妙士 Miaoshi	15	2.3
5	娃哈哈 Wahaha	6	0.9
5	伊利 Yili	6	0.9
6	香满楼 Flower Fresh	4	0.6
6	喜旺 Xiwang	4	0.6
7	海浪 Hailang	4	0.6

n=642

4-5 样本、男性各年龄层、女性各年龄层最近三个月有无购买的比例/ Purchasing in the Last Three Months by the Whole Sample, Age and Gender Groups

	人数 Number	买过 yes	没买过 no
样本 Sample	642	53.6	46.4
男性 Male	311	46.0	54.0
16~24 岁 Age	65	52.3	47.7
25~34 岁 Age	89	62.9	37.1
35~44 岁 Age	80	37.5	62.5
45~54 岁 Age	52	32.7	67.3
55~60 岁 Age	25	24.0	76.0
女性 Female	331	60.7	39.3
16~24 岁 Age	69	78.3	21.7
25~34 岁 Age	96	71.9	28.1
35~44 岁 Age	78	56.4	43.6
45~54 岁 Age	62	41.9	58.1
55~60 岁 Age	26	30.8	69.2

4-6 样本、男性各年龄层、女性各年龄层最近三个月的食用频率/ Frequencies of Consuming Yogurt in the Last Three Months by the Whole Sample, Age and Gender Groups

	人数 Number	天天喝 daily	一周 3 次或以上 3 times or over a week	一周 1~2 次 once or twice a week	一个月 2~3 次 2 or 3 times a month	一个月 1 次或以下 once a month or below	没喝过 never
样本 Sample	641	6.4	8.3	13.4	14.5	6.4	51.0
男性 Male	311	5.5	6.1	12.9	13.2	6.4	55.9
16~24 岁 Age	65	10.8	7.7	15.4	20.0	4.6	41.5
25~34 岁 Age	89	3.4	10.1	18.0	16.9	10.1	41.6
35~44 岁 Age	80	5.0	1.3	10.0	11.3	5.0	67.5
45~54 岁 Age	52	3.8	5.8	11.5	1.9	7.7	69.2
55~60 岁 Age	25	4.0	4.0	0.0	12.0	0.0	80.0
女性 Female	330	7.3	10.3	13.9	15.8	6.4	46.4
16~24 岁 Age	69	10.1	20.3	20.3	21.7	8.7	18.8
25~34 岁 Age	96	7.3	13.5	16.7	20.8	5.2	36.5
35~44 岁 Age	78	3.8	9.0	11.5	11.5	5.1	59.0
45~54 岁 Age	62	8.1	0.0	9.7	9.7	8.1	64.5
55~60 岁 Age	25	8.0	0.0	4.0	8.0	4.0	76.0

4-7 样本、男性各年龄层、女性各年龄层的品牌习惯/ Brand Habit in Consuming Yogurt by the Whole Sample, Age and Gender Groups

	人数 Number	基本固定食用一个牌子 used in only one brand	比较固定地食用两个或三个牌子 used in two or three brands	基本上不太固定牌子 no brand preference
样本 Sample	314	59.2	24.2	16.6
男性 Male	137	62.8	17.5	19.7
16~24 岁 Age	38	68.4	5.3	26.3
25~34 岁 Age	52	65.4	26.9	7.7
35~44 岁 Age	26	61.5	15.4	23.1
45~54 岁 Age	16	37.5	25.0	37.5
55~60 岁 Age	5	80.0	0.0	20.0
女性 Female	177	56.5	29.4	14.1
16~24 岁 Age	56	57.1	33.9	8.9
25~34 岁 Age	61	57.4	27.9	14.8
35~44 岁 Age	32	53.1	25.0	21.9
45~54 岁 Age	22	50.0	31.8	18.2
55~60 岁 Age	6	83.3	16.7	0.0

4-8 选择该类商品的考虑因素/ Ranking of the Considerations in Purchasing

注：本题为多选题，合计百分比超过 100%(Multiple answers)

排名 Ranking	考虑因素 Considerations	人次 Person-time	百分比 Percent
1	口味好 pleasant taste	184	59.0
2	价格适中 reasonable price	125	40.1
3	购买方便 easy to buy	93	29.8
4	生产日期 date of producing	87	27.9
5	有名的牌子 famous brand	77	24.7
6	营养成分 nutrition constituent	75	24.0
7	只是由于习惯 out of habit	30	9.6
8	包装吸引人 appealing package	15	4.8
8	朋友推荐 introduction of friends	15	4.8
9	有优惠条件 with preferential terms	10	3.2
9	广告影响 influence of advertising	10	3.2
10	售货员介绍 introduced by the shop assistants	9	2.9
11	其它 others	7	2.2

n=312

4-9 样本、男性各年龄层、女性各年龄层最常食用的种类/ Types of the Consumed Yogurt by the Whole Sample, Age and Gender Groups

注：本题为多选题，合计百分比超过 100%(Multiple answers)

	人数 Number	原味 original flavor	巧克力味 chocolate flavor	草莓味 strawberry	菠萝味 pineapple	橙味 orange	杏味 apricot	带果粒 with fruit dots	加钙 calcium added	其他 others
样本 Sample	314	81.5	3.5	15.0	2.5	3.2	0.0	0.6	12.1	0.6
男性 Male	137	80.3	6.6	12.4	3.6	2.2	0.0	0.7	10.9	0.7
16~24 岁 Age	38	81.6	10.5	10.5	2.6	2.6	0.0	0.0	10.5	0.0
25~34 岁 Age	52	78.8	3.8	9.6	3.8	1.9	0.0	1.9	17.3	1.9
35~44 岁 Age	26	76.9	7.7	19.2	7.7	3.8	0.0	0.0	7.7	0.0
45~54 岁 Age	16	87.5	6.3	12.5	0.0	0.0	0.0	0.0	0.0	0.0
55~60 岁 Age	5	80.0	0.0	20.0	0.0	0.0	0.0	0.0	0.0	0.0
女性 Female	177	82.5	1.1	16.9	1.7	4.0	0.0	0.6	13.0	0.6
16~24 岁 Age	56	92.9	0.0	12.5	1.8	3.6	0.0	0.0	8.9	1.8
25~34 岁 Age	61	78.7	1.6	19.7	1.6	4.9	0.0	0.0	11.5	0.0
35~44 岁 Age	32	71.9	3.1	25.0	3.1	0.0	0.0	3.1	9.4	0.0
45~54 岁 Age	22	81.8	0.0	13.6	0.0	4.5	0.0	0.0	36.4	0.0
55~60 岁 Age	6	83.3	0.0	0.0	0.0	16.7	0.0	0.0	0.0	0.0

4-10 样本、男性各年龄层、女性各年龄层最常食用的包装形式/ Types of Package of the Consumed Yogurt by the Whole Sample, Age and Gender Groups

注：本题为多选题，合计百分比超过 100%(Multiple answers)

	人数 Number	袋装 bag	方盒装/利乐砖 tetra	房屋状纸盒 house-shaped box	粽子状纸盒 V-shaped box	塑料瓶 plastic bottle	瓷瓶 china bottle	其他 others
样本 Sample	305	9.2	18.7	9.2	1.3	59.0	15.1	0.3
男性 Male	134	10.4	16.4	11.2	3.0	59.7	11.9	0.0
16~24 岁 Age	38	5.3	13.2	10.5	0.0	63.2	15.8	0.0
25~34 岁 Age	51	5.9	15.7	13.7	3.9	68.6	0.0	0.0
35~44 岁 Age	25	28.0	20.0	8.0	0.0	52.0	24.0	0.0
45~54 岁 Age	15	13.3	13.3	13.3	13.3	40.0	20.0	0.0
55~60 岁 Age	5	0.0	40.0	0.0	0.0	40.0	20.0	0.0
女性 Female	171	8.2	20.5	7.6	0.0	58.5	17.5	0.6
16~24 岁 Age	55	10.9	23.6	10.9	0.0	49.1	20.0	0.0
25~34 岁 Age	58	6.9	20.7	5.2	0.0	62.1	17.2	1.7
35~44 岁 Age	31	3.2	16.1	6.5	0.0	74.2	12.9	0.0
45~54 岁 Age	21	14.3	19.0	9.5	0.0	57.1	9.5	0.0
55~60 岁 Age	6	0.0	16.7	0.0	0.0	33.3	50.0	0.0

4-11 样本、男性各年龄层、女性各年龄层最常饮用场合/ Settings of Consumption by the Whole Sample, Age and Gender Groups

注：本题为多选题，合计百分比超过 100%(Multiple answers)

	人数 Number	早餐时 breakfast	正餐（午、晚餐）时 dinner	口渴时 when thirsty	宵夜时 evening snack	睡觉前 before sleeping	工作休息时 during work break	外出/旅游时 outing/traveling	其它 others
样本 Sample	314	36.9	8.9	30.3	3.5	9.2	20.7	19.1	2.9
男性 Male	137	38.0	10.2	29.2	2.9	10.2	13.9	16.8	2.2
16~24 岁 Age	38	39.5	2.6	18.4	5.3	10.5	10.5	21.1	5.3
25~34 岁 Age	52	38.5	9.6	30.8	1.9	7.7	19.2	19.2	1.9
35~44 岁 Age	26	34.6	15.4	42.3	0.0	15.4	11.5	11.5	0.0
45~54 岁 Age	16	43.8	12.5	18.8	6.3	12.5	12.5	12.5	0.0
55~60 岁 Age	5	20.0	40.0	60.0	0.0	0.0	0.0	0.0	0.0
女性 Female	177	36.2	7.9	31.1	4.0	8.5	26.0	20.9	3.4
16~24 岁 Age	56	32.1	8.9	35.7	3.6	5.4	32.1	23.2	1.8
25~34 岁 Age	61	36.1	6.6	29.5	0.0	6.6	24.6	26.2	3.3
35~44 岁 Age	32	34.4	9.4	34.4	6.3	15.6	25.0	12.5	6.3
45~54 岁 Age	22	45.5	4.5	22.7	9.1	13.6	18.2	13.6	4.5
55~60 岁 Age	6	50.0	16.7	16.7	16.7	0.0	16.7	16.7	0.0

4-12 重度消费者的人口分布/ Demographics of the Heavy Consumers

	人数 Number	16-24 岁 Age	25-34 岁 Age	35-44 岁 Age	45-54 岁 Age	55-60 岁 Age
样本 Sample	180	31.7	35.6	17.8	12.2	2.8
男性 Male	76	28.9	36.8	17.1	14.5	2.6
天天喝 daily	17	41.2	17.6	23.5	11.8	5.9
一周 3 次或以上 3 times or over a week	19	26.3	47.4	5.3	15.8	5.3
一周 1～2 次 once or twice a week	40	25.0	40.0	20.0	15.0	0.0
女性 Female	104	33.7	34.6	18.3	10.6	2.9
天天喝 daily	24	29.2	29.2	12.5	20.8	8.3
一周 3 次或以上 3 times or over a week	34	41.2	38.2	20.6	0.0	0.0
一周 1～2 次 once or twice a week	46	30.4	34.8	19.6	13.0	2.2

4-13 不同消费者层的常用品牌/ The Most Frequently Used Brands by Market Segments

4-13-1 时尚流行指标/ Fads Popular Index

	人数 Number	第一品牌及百分比 1st/ percent	第二品牌及百分比 2nd/ percent	第三品牌及百分比 3rd/ percent
样本 Sample	306	**扬子江 Yangzijiang(54.9)**	**友芝友 Youzhiyou(18.0)**	**光明 Bright(7.5)**
平实生活指向 simple living orientation	151	扬子江 Yangzijiang(58.3)	友芝友 Youzhiyou(15.9)	光明 Bright(7.3)
时尚流行指向 fashion orientation	155	扬子江 Yangzijiang(51.6)	友芝友 Youzhiyou(20.0)	光明 Bright(7.7)

4-13-2 广告态度指标/ Advertising Attitude Index

	人数 Number	第一品牌及百分比 1st/ percent	第二品牌及百分比 2nd/ percent	第三品牌及百分比 3rd/ percent
样本 Sample	307	**扬子江 Yangzijiang(54.7)**	**友芝友 Youzhiyou(17.9)**	**光明 Bright(7.5)**
广告淡漠指向 indifferent orientation	81	扬子江 Yangzijiang(59.3)	友芝友 Youzhiyou(16.0)	光明 Bright(3.7) 妙士 Miaoshi(3.7)
中间层 medium	185	扬子江 Yangzijiang(49.7)	友芝友 Youzhiyou(21.1)	光明 Bright(9.2)
信赖广告指向 loyal orientation	41	扬子江 Yangzijiang(68.3)	光明 Bright(7.3) 友芝友 Youzhiyou(7.3)	津威 Jinwei(2.4) 海浪 Hailang (2.4) 妙士 Miaoshi(2.4) 杨协成 Yeo's(2.4) 楚天 Chutian(2.4)

4-13-3 饮食健康指标/ Foods & Drink Quality Index

	人数 Number	第一品牌及百分比 1st/ percent	第二品牌及百分比 2nd/ percent	第三品牌及百分比 3rd/ percent
样本 Sample	306	**扬子江 Yangzijiang(54.6)**	**友芝友 Youzhiyou(18.0)**	**光明 Bright(7.5)**
饮食“温饱”指向 "basic" orientation	99	扬子江 Yangzijiang(60.6)	友芝友 Youzhiyou(14.1)	光明 Bright(5.1)
中间层 medium	135	扬子江 Yangzijiang(54.1)	友芝友 Youzhiyou(20.0)	光明 Bright(6.7)
健康营养指向 health & nutrition orientation	72	扬子江 Yangzijiang(47.2)	友芝友 Youzhiyou(19.4)	光明 Bright(12.5)

4-14 重度消费者的消费者层构成/ The Composition of the Heavy Consumers

4-14-1 时尚流行指标/ Fads Popular Index

	人数 Number	平实生活指向 simple living orientation	时尚流行指向 fashion orientation
样本 Sample	174	46.0	54.0
天天喝 daily	39	38.5	61.5
一周 3 次或以上 3 times or over a week	51	45.1	54.9
一周 1～2 次 once or twice a week	84	50.0	50.0

4-14-2 广告态度指标/ Advertising Attitude Index

	人数 Number	广告淡漠指向 indifferent orientation	中间层 medium	信赖广告指向 loyal orientation
样本 Sample	174	25.9	58.6	15.5
天天喝 daily	39	25.6	66.7	7.7
一周 3 次或以上 3 times or over a week	51	27.5	58.8	13.7
一周 1～2 次 once or twice a week	84	25.0	54.8	20.2

4-14-3 饮食健康指标/ Foods & Drink Quality Index

	人数 Number	饮食“温饱”指向 "basic" orientation	中间层 medium	健康营养指向 health & nutrition orientation
样本 Sample	173	31.8	45.1	23.1
天天喝 daily	39	20.5	35.9	43.6
一周 3 次或以上 3 times or over a week	50	32.0	52.0	16.0
一周 1～2 次 once or twice a week	84	36.9	45.2	17.9

● 西安 / Xi'an

4-1 最近三个月食用频率的比例/ Proportion of the Sample Consuming Yogurt in the Last Three Months

	人数 Number	百分比 Percent
天天喝 daily	23	3.8
一周 3 次或以上 3 times or over a week	43	7.2
一周 1~2 次 once or twice a week	88	14.6
一个月 2～3 次 2 or 3 times a month	93	15.5
一个月 1 次或以下 once a month or below	50	8.3
没喝过 never	304	50.6

n=601

4-2 最常用品牌排名/ Ranking of the Most Frequently Used Brands

排名 Brand Ranking	品牌 Brands	人数 Number	百分比 Percent
1	牧童 Mutong	135	45.5
2	光明 Bright	69	23.2
3	东方 Dongfang	49	16.5
4	鲜迪 Xiandi	14	4.7
5	红旗 Hongqi	5	1.7
6	荣氏 Rong	4	1.3
7	绿鸟 Lvniao	2	0.7
7	娃哈哈 Wahaha	2	0.7
7	伊利 Yili	2	0.7

n=297

4-3 样本、男性各年龄层、女性各年龄层的常用品牌/ The Most Frequently Used Brands by the Whole Sample, Age and Gender Groups

	人数 Number	第一品牌及百分比 1st/ percent	第二品牌及百分比 2nd/ percent	第三品牌及百分比 3rd/ percent
样本 Sample	297	**牧童 Mutong(45.5)**	**光明 Bright(23.2)**	**东方 Dongfang(16.5)**
男性 Male	145	**牧童 Mutong(44.8)**	**光明 Bright(24.1)**	**东方 Dongfang(17.9)**
16~24 岁 Age	44	牧童 Mutong(47.7)	光明 Bright(20.5)	东方 Dongfang(11.4)
25~34 岁 Age	45	牧童 Mutong(48.9)	光明 Bright(24.4)	东方 Dongfang(17.8)
35~44 岁 Age	32	牧童 Mutong(40.6)	东方 Dongfang(28.1)	光明 Bright(21.9)
45~54 岁 Age	15	光明 Bright(40.0)	牧童 Mutong(33.3)	东方 Dongfang(13.3)
55~60 岁 Age	9	牧童 Mutong(44.4)	东方 Dongfang(22.2) 光明 Bright(22.2)	凯立 Kaili(11.1)
女性 Female	152	**牧童 Mutong(46.1)**	**光明 Bright(22.4)**	**东方 Dongfang(15.1)**
16~24 岁 Age	38	牧童 Mutong(50.0)	光明 Bright(36.8)	东方 Dongfang(5.3)
25~34 岁 Age	54	牧童 Mutong(55.6)	东方 Dongfang(13.0) 光明 Bright(13.0)	鲜迪 Xiandi(7.4)
35~44 岁 Age	34	牧童 Mutong(41.2)	东方 Dongfang(26.5)	光明 Bright(20.6)
45~54 岁 Age	17	光明 Bright(23.5) 牧童 Mutong(23.5)	东方 Dongfang(17.6)	鲜迪 Xiandi(11.8)
55~60 岁 Age	9	牧童 Mutong(33.3)	东方 Dongfang(22.2) 光明 Bright(22.2)	鲜迪 Xiandi(11.1) 荣氏 Rong(11.1)

4-4 理想品牌排名/ Ranking of the Ideal Brands

排名 Brand Ranking	品牌 Brands	人数 Number	百分比 Percent
1	牧童 Mutong	221	36.8
2	光明 Bright	118	19.6
3	东方 Dongfang	88	14.6
4	鲜迪 Xiandi	15	2.5
5	红旗 Hongqi	8	1.3

n=601

4-5 样本、男性各年龄层、女性各年龄层最近三个月有无购买的比例/ Purchasing in the Last Three Months by the Whole Sample, Age and Gender Groups

	人数 Number	买过 yes	没买过 no
样本 Sample	601	52.1	47.9
男性 Male	302	50.0	50.0
16~24 岁 Age	64	65.6	34.4
25~34 岁 Age	91	52.7	47.3
35~44 岁 Age	77	49.4	50.6
45~54 岁 Age	46	30.4	69.6
55~60 岁 Age	24	37.5	62.5
女性 Female	299	54.2	45.8
16~24 岁 Age	61	62.3	37.7
25~34 岁 Age	90	57.8	42.2
35~44 岁 Age	74	54.1	45.9
45~54 岁 Age	49	44.9	55.1
55~60 岁 Age	25	40.0	60.0

4-6 样本、男性各年龄层、女性各年龄层最近三个月的食用频率/ Frequencies of Consuming Yogurt in the Last Three Months by the Whole Sample, Age and Gender Groups

	人数 Number	天天喝 daily	一周 3 次或以上 3 times or over a week	一周 1~2 次 once or twice a week	一个月 2~3 次 2 or 3 times a month	一个月 1 次或以下 once a month or below	没喝过 never
样本 Sample	601	3.8	7.2	14.6	15.5	8.3	50.6
男性 Male	302	4.0	7.6	14.6	14.6	7.3	52.0
16~24 岁 Age	64	3.1	18.8	26.6	9.4	10.9	31.3
25~34 岁 Age	91	4.4	4.4	13.2	19.8	7.7	50.5
35~44 岁 Age	77	2.6	3.9	11.7	20.8	2.6	58.4
45~54 岁 Age	46	6.5	2.2	8.7	6.5	8.7	67.4
55~60 岁 Age	24	4.2	12.5	8.3	4.2	8.3	62.5
女性 Female	299	3.7	6.7	14.7	16.4	9.4	49.2
16~24 岁 Age	61	8.2	9.8	13.1	27.9	3.3	37.7
25~34 岁 Age	90	4.4	3.3	22.2	16.7	13.3	40.0
35~44 岁 Age	74	1.4	6.8	13.5	17.6	6.8	54.1
45~54 岁 Age	49	0.0	8.2	8.2	6.1	12.2	65.3
55~60 岁 Age	25	4.0	8.0	8.0	4.0	12.0	64.0

4-7 样本、男性各年龄层、女性各年龄层的品牌习惯/ Brand Habit in Consuming Yogurt by the Whole Sample, Age and Gender Groups

	人数 Number	基本固定食用一个牌子 used in only one brand	比较固定地食用两个或三个牌子 used in two or three brands	基本上不太固定牌子 no brand preference
样本 Sample	297	60.6	23.6	15.8
男性 Male	145	62.8	24.1	13.1
16~24 岁 Age	44	52.3	31.8	15.9
25~34 岁 Age	45	66.7	20.0	13.3
35~44 岁 Age	32	62.5	28.1	9.4
45~54 岁 Age	15	66.7	13.3	20.0
55~60 岁 Age	9	88.9	11.1	0.0
女性 Female	152	58.6	23.0	18.4
16~24 岁 Age	38	50.0	23.7	26.3
25~34 岁 Age	54	57.4	27.8	14.8
35~44 岁 Age	34	67.6	20.6	11.8
45~54 岁 Age	17	58.8	17.6	23.5
55~60 岁 Age	9	66.7	11.1	22.2

4-8 选择该类商品的考虑因素/ Ranking of the Considerations in Purchasing

注：本题为多选题，合计百分比超过 100%(Multiple answers)

排名 Ranking	考虑因素 Considerations	人次 Person-time	百分比 Percent
1	口味好 pleasant taste	181	60.9
2	价格适中 reasonable price	82	27.6
2	购买方便 easy to buy	82	27.6
3	营养成分 nutrition constituent	79	26.6
4	有名的牌子 famous brand	68	22.9
5	生产日期 date of producing	55	18.5
6	只是由于习惯 out of habit	27	9.1
7	朋友推荐 introduction of friends	11	3.7
8	广告影响 influence of advertising	10	3.4
9	包装吸引人 appealing package	7	2.4
10	有优惠条件 with preferential terms	6	2.0
11	售货员介绍 introduced by the shop assistants	2	0.7
12	其它 others	1	0.3

n=297

4-9 样本、男性各年龄层、女性各年龄层最常食用的种类/ Types of the Consumed Yogurt by the Whole Sample, Age and Gender Groups

注：本题为多选题，合计百分比超过 100%(Multiple answers)

	人数 Number	原味 original flavor	巧克力味 chocolate flavor	草莓味 strawberry	菠萝味 pineapple	橙味 orange	杏味 apricot	带果粒 with fruit dots	加钙 calcium added	其他 others
样本 Sample	297	67.3	10.4	18.9	3.0	4.4	1.3	0.3	10.8	0.0
男性 Male	145	69.0	9.7	15.2	2.8	4.1	1.4	0.0	10.3	0.0
16~24 岁 Age	44	63.6	11.4	20.5	2.3	4.5	2.3	0.0	9.1	0.0
25~34 岁 Age	45	75.6	6.7	8.9	4.4	4.4	0.0	0.0	8.9	0.0
35~44 岁 Age	32	59.4	15.6	18.8	3.1	3.1	3.1	0.0	12.5	0.0
45~54 岁 Age	15	73.3	6.7	20.0	0.0	6.7	0.0	0.0	13.3	0.0
55~60 岁 Age	9	88.9	0.0	0.0	0.0	0.0	0.0	0.0	11.1	0.0
女性 Female	152	65.8	11.2	22.4	3.3	4.6	1.3	0.7	11.2	0.0
16~24 岁 Age	38	68.4	13.2	15.8	5.3	2.6	0.0	0.0	5.3	0.0
25~34 岁 Age	54	63.0	11.1	24.1	3.7	3.7	0.0	0.0	14.8	0.0
35~44 岁 Age	34	76.5	11.8	23.5	0.0	2.9	2.9	2.9	11.8	0.0
45~54 岁 Age	17	52.9	5.9	29.4	0.0	17.6	0.0	0.0	5.9	0.0
55~60 岁 Age	9	55.6	11.1	22.2	11.1	0.0	11.1	0.0	22.2	0.0

4-10 样本、男性各年龄层、女性各年龄层最常食用的包装形式/ Types of Package of the Consumed Yogurt by the Whole Sample, Age and Gender Groups

注：本题为多选题，合计百分比超过 100%(Multiple answers)

	人数 Number	袋装 bag	方盒装/利乐砖 tetra	房屋状纸盒 house-shaped box	粽子状纸盒 V-shaped box	塑料瓶 plastic bottle	瓷瓶 china bottle	其他 others
样本 Sample	297	22.6	25.6	9.1	2.0	48.8	5.4	0.0
男性 Male	145	21.4	20.0	9.0	2.1	52.4	6.2	0.0
16~24 岁 Age	44	20.5	22.7	6.8	2.3	54.5	6.8	0.0
25~34 岁 Age	45	15.6	17.8	11.1	0.0	57.8	2.2	0.0
35~44 岁 Age	32	28.1	21.9	12.5	6.3	40.6	9.4	0.0
45~54 岁 Age	15	26.7	20.0	0.0	0.0	60.0	6.7	0.0
55~60 岁 Age	9	22.2	11.1	11.1	0.0	44.4	11.1	0.0
女性 Female	152	23.7	30.9	9.2	2.0	45.4	4.6	0.0
16~24 岁 Age	38	26.3	23.7	13.2	2.6	42.1	2.6	0.0
25~34 岁 Age	54	22.2	27.8	11.1	0.0	53.7	5.6	0.0
35~44 岁 Age	34	26.5	38.2	5.9	5.9	41.2	2.9	0.0
45~54 岁 Age	17	17.6	29.4	5.9	0.0	47.1	0.0	0.0
55~60 岁 Age	9	22.2	55.6	0.0	0.0	22.2	22.2	0.0

4-11 样本、男性各年龄层、女性各年龄层最常饮用场合/ Settings of Consumption by the Whole Sample, Age and Gender Groups

注：本题为多选题，合计百分比超过 100%(Multiple answers)

	人数 Number	早餐时 breakfast	正餐（午、晚餐）时 dinner	口渴时 when thirsty	宵夜时 evening snack	睡觉前 before sleeping	工作休息时 during work break	外出/旅游时 outing/ traveling	其它 others
样本 Sample	296	37.5	6.4	29.4	3.0	4.1	14.9	27.0	2.7
男性 Male	145	37.9	4.1	29.7	2.8	2.1	15.9	24.1	3.4
16~24 岁 Age	44	40.9	11.4	31.8	2.3	2.3	11.4	15.9	2.3
25~34 岁 Age	45	35.6	2.2	24.4	4.4	0.0	13.3	28.9	6.7
35~44 岁 Age	32	37.5	0.0	28.1	0.0	3.1	21.9	34.4	0.0
45~54 岁 Age	15	40.0	0.0	33.3	6.7	0.0	26.7	6.7	6.7
55~60 岁 Age	9	33.3	0.0	44.4	0.0	11.1	11.1	33.3	0.0
女性 Female	151	37.1	8.6	29.1	3.3	6.0	13.9	29.8	2.0
16~24 岁 Age	38	36.8	5.3	21.1	5.3	0.0	15.8	34.2	5.3
25~34 岁 Age	54	27.8	7.4	35.2	0.0	5.6	13.0	40.7	1.9
35~44 岁 Age	33	45.5	18.2	21.2	6.1	12.1	15.2	15.2	0.0
45~54 岁 Age	17	41.2	0.0	47.1	5.9	5.9	11.8	23.5	0.0
55~60 岁 Age	9	55.6	11.1	22.2	0.0	11.1	11.1	11.1	0.0

4-12 重度消费者的人口分布/ Demographics of the Heavy Consumers

	人数 Number	16-24 岁 Age	25-34 岁 Age	35-44 岁 Age	45-54 岁 Age	55-60 岁 Age
样本 Sample	154	32.5	30.5	19.5	10.4	7.1
男性 Male	79	39.2	25.3	17.7	10.1	7.6
天天喝 daily	12	16.7	33.3	16.7	25.0	8.3
一周 3 次或以上 3 times or over a week	23	52.2	17.4	13.0	4.3	13.0
一周 1～2 次 once or twice a week	44	38.6	27.3	20.5	9.1	4.5
女性 Female	75	25.3	36.0	21.3	10.7	6.7
天天喝 daily	11	45.5	36.4	9.1	0.0	9.1
一周 3 次或以上 3 times or over a week	20	30.0	15.0	25.0	20.0	10.0
一周 1～2 次 once or twice a week	44	18.2	45.5	22.7	9.1	4.5

4-13 不同消费者层的常用品牌/ The Most Frequently Used Brands by Market Segments

4-13-1 时尚流行指标/ Fads Popular Index

	人数 Number	第一品牌及百分比 1st/ percent	第二品牌及百分比 2nd/ percent	第三品牌及百分比 3rd/ percent
样本 Sample	295	**牧童 Mutong(45.1)**	**光明 Bright(23.4)**	**东方 Dongfang(16.6)**
平实生活指向 simple living orientation	150	牧童 Mutong(45.3)	东方 Dongfang(22.0)	光明 Bright(21.3)
时尚流行指向 fashion orientation	145	牧童 Mutong(44.8)	光明 Bright(25.5)	东方 Dongfang(11.0)

4-13-2 广告态度指标/ Advertising Attitude Index

	人数 Number	第一品牌及百分比 1st/ percent	第二品牌及百分比 2nd/ percent	第三品牌及百分比 3rd/ percent
样本 Sample	295	**牧童 Mutong(45.1)**	**光明 Bright(23.4)**	**东方 Dongfang(16.6)**
广告淡漠指向 indifferent orientation	94	牧童 Mutong(37.2)	光明 Bright(29.8)	东方 Dongfang(19.1)
中间层 medium	168	牧童 Mutong(50.6)	光明 Bright(19.0)	东方 Dongfang(14.3)
信赖广告指向 loyal orientation	33	牧童 Mutong(39.4)	光明 Bright(27.3)	东方 Dongfang(21.2)

4-13-3 饮食健康指标/ Foods & Drink Quality Index

	人数 Number	第一品牌及百分比 1st/ percent	第二品牌及百分比 2nd/ percent	第三品牌及百分比 3rd/ percent
样本 Sample	297	牧童 Mutong(45.5)	光明 Bright(23.2)	东方 Dongfang(16.5)
饮食“温饱”指向 "basic" orientation	104	牧童 Mutong(41.3)	光明 Bright(25.0)	东方 Dongfang(19.2)
中间层 medium	143	牧童 Mutong(46.2)	光明 Bright(24.5)	东方 Dongfang(14.0)
健康营养指向 health & nutrition orientation	50	牧童 Mutong(52.0)	东方 Dongfang(18.0)	光明 Bright(16.0)

4-14 重度消费者的消费者层构成/ The Composition of the Heavy Consumers

4-14-1 时尚流行指标/ Fads Popular Index

	人数 Number	平实生活指向 simple living orientation	时尚流行指向 fashion orientation
样本 Sample	154	50.6	49.4
天天喝 daily	23	56.5	43.5
一周 3 次或以上 3 times or over a week	43	46.5	53.5
一周 1～2 次 once or twice a week	88	51.1	48.9

4-14-2 广告态度指标/ Advertising Attitude Index

	人数 Number	广告淡漠指向 indifferent orientation	中间层 medium	信赖广告指向 loyal orientation
样本 Sample	153	28.8	54.2	17.0
天天喝 daily	22	27.3	50.0	22.7
一周 3 次或以上 3 times or over a week	43	34.9	44.2	20.9
一周 1～2 次 once or twice a week	88	26.1	60.2	13.6

4-14-3 饮食健康指标/ Foods & Drink Quality Index

	人数 Number	饮食“温饱”指向 "basic" orientation	中间层 medium	健康营养指向 health & nutrition orientation
样本 Sample	154	35.7	44.2	20.1
天天喝 daily	23	30.4	39.1	30.4
一周 3 次或以上 3 times or over a week	43	32.6	41.9	25.6
一周 1～2 次 once or twice a week	88	38.6	46.6	14.8

● 沈阳 / Shenyang

4-1 最近三个月食用频率的比例/ Proportion of the Sample Consuming Yogurt in the Last Three Months

	人数 Number	百分比 Percent
天天喝 daily	33	5.5
一周 3 次或以上 3 times or over a week	39	6.5
一周 1~2 次 once or twice a week	87	14.5
一个月 2~3 次 2 or 3 times a month	67	11.2
一个月 1 次或以下 once a month or below	53	8.8
没喝过 never	321	53.5

n=600

4-2 最常用品牌排名/ Ranking of the Most Frequently Used Brands

排名 Brand Ranking	品牌 Brands	人数 Number	百分比 Percent
1	辉山 Huishan	117	42.1
2	医大 Yida	56	20.1
3	双鸽 Shuangge	13	4.7
4	中街 Zhongjie	10	3.6
5	伊利 Yili	8	2.9
5	格格香 Gegexiang	8	2.9
6	光明 Bright	6	2.2
7	新南洋 Xinnanyang	5	1.8
8	欣愉 Xinyu	4	1.4

n=278

4-3 样本、男性各年龄层、女性各年龄层的常用品牌/ The Most Frequently Used Brands by the Whole Sample, Age and Gender Groups

	人数 Number	第一品牌及百分比 1st/ percent	第二品牌及百分比 2nd/ percent	第三品牌及百分比 3rd/ percent
样本 Sample	278	**辉山 Huishan(42.1)**	**医大 Yida(20.1)**	**双鸽 Shuangge(4.7)**
男性 Male	118	**辉山 Huishan(42.4)**	**医大 Yida(19.5)**	**双鸽 Shuangge(9.3)**
16~24 岁 Age	38	辉山 Huishan(52.6)	医大 Yida(10.5)	双鸽 Shuangge(5.3)
25~34 岁 Age	45	辉山 Huishan(33.3)	医大 Yida(24.4)	双鸽 Shuangge(13.3)
35~44 岁 Age	20	辉山 Huishan(45.0)	格格香 Gegexiang(15.0) 医大 Yida(15.0)	娃哈哈 Wahaha(5.0) 双鸽 Shuangge(5.0) 中街 Zhongjie(5.0) 鹰骑 Yingqi(5.0) 乐乐 Lele(5.0)
45~54 岁 Age	10	辉山 Huishan(30.0) 医大 Yida(30.0)	双鸽 Shuangge(20.0)	塔山 Tashan(10.0) 康仙 Kangxian(10.0)
55~60 岁 Age	5	辉山 Huishan(60.0)	医大 Yida(40.0)	
女性 Female	160	**辉山 Huishan(41.9)**	**医大 Yida(20.6)**	**中街 Zhongjie(4.4)**
16~24 岁 Age	44	辉山 Huishan(38.6)	医大 Yida(18.2)	中街 Zhongjie(11.4)
25~34 岁 Age	51	辉山 Huishan(47.1)	医大 Yida(19.6)	新南洋 Xinnanyang(3.9) 伊利 Yili(3.9)
35~44 岁 Age	44	辉山 Huishan(40.9)	医大 Yida(20.5)	格格香 Gegexiang(6.8)
45~54 岁 Age	14	辉山 Huishan(28.6) 医大 Yida(28.6)	新南洋 Xinnanyang(7.1) 格格香 Gegexiang(7.1) 都乐 Dole(7.1) 康仙 Kangxian(7.1) 益民 Yimin(7.1) 香浓 Xiangnong(7.1)	
55~60 岁 Age	7	辉山 Huishan(57.1)	医大 Yida(28.6)	牛仔 Niuzai(14.3)

4-4 理想品牌排名/ Ranking of the Ideal Brands

排名 Brand Ranking	品牌 Brands	人数 Number	百分比 Percent
1	辉山 Huishan	183	30.4
2	医大 Yida	99	16.5
3	光明 Bright	21	3.5
3	双鸽 Shuangge	21	3.5
4	中街 Zhongjie	19	3.2
5	伊利 Yili	17	2.8
6	新南洋 Xinnanyang	9	1.5
6	乐百氏 Robust	9	1.5
7	格格香 Gegexiang	8	1.3
8	欣愉 Xinyu	6	1.0
8	都乐 Dole	6	1.0
9	娃哈哈 Wahaha	5	0.8
10	塔山 Tashan	4	0.7

n=601

4-5 样本、男性各年龄层、女性各年龄层最近三个月有无购买的比例/ Purchasing in the Last Three Months by the Whole Sample, Age and Gender Groups

	人数 Number	买过 yes	没买过 no
样本 Sample	601	51.2	48.8
男性 Male	299	44.8	55.2
16~24 岁 Age	64	57.8	42.2
25~34 岁 Age	89	56.2	43.8
35~44 岁 Age	76	38.2	61.8
45~54 岁 Age	46	30.4	69.6
55~60 岁 Age	24	16.7	83.3
女性 Female	302	57.6	42.4
16~24 岁 Age	64	68.8	31.3
25~34 岁 Age	90	63.3	36.7
35~44 岁 Age	76	61.8	38.2
45~54 岁 Age	48	37.5	62.5
55~60 岁 Age	24	33.3	66.7

4-6 样本、男性各年龄层、女性各年龄层最近三个月的食用频率/ Frequencies of Consuming Yogurt in the Last Three Months by the Whole Sample, Age and Gender Groups

	人数 Number	天天喝 daily	一周 3 次或以上 3 times or over a week	一周 1~2 次 once or twice a week	一个月 2~3 次 2 or 3 times a month	一个月 1 次或以下 once a month or below	没喝过 never
样本 Sample	600	5.5	6.5	14.5	11.2	8.8	53.5
男性 Male	298	5.7	5.0	10.1	9.4	9.4	60.4
16~24 岁 Age	64	10.9	6.3	15.6	12.5	14.1	40.6
25~34 岁 Age	89	5.6	7.9	14.6	13.5	9.0	49.4
35~44 岁 Age	76	5.3	3.9	5.3	5.3	6.6	73.7
45~54 岁 Age	45	2.2	2.2	6.7	6.7	4.4	77.8
55~60 岁 Age	24	0.0	0.0	0.0	4.2	16.7	79.2
女性 Female	302	5.3	7.9	18.9	12.9	8.3	46.7
16~24 岁 Age	64	3.1	9.4	29.7	14.1	12.5	31.3
25~34 岁 Age	90	4.4	6.7	21.1	16.7	8.9	42.2
35~44 岁 Age	76	6.6	11.8	21.1	10.5	7.9	42.1
45~54 岁 Age	48	6.3	4.2	6.3	10.4	2.1	70.8
55~60 岁 Age	24	8.3	4.2	0.0	8.3	8.3	70.8

4-7 样本、男性各年龄层、女性各年龄层的品牌习惯/ Brand Habit in Consuming Yogurt by the Whole Sample, Age and Gender Groups

	人数 Number	基本固定食用一个牌子 used in only one brand	比较固定地食用两个或三个牌子 used in two or three brands	基本上不太固定牌子 no brand preference
样本 Sample	278	48.2	24.5	27.3
男性 Male	118	50.0	19.5	30.5
16~24 岁 Age	38	39.5	18.4	42.1
25~34 岁 Age	45	48.9	26.7	24.4
35~44 岁 Age	20	60.0	15.0	25.0
45~54 岁 Age	10	60.0	10.0	30.0
55~60 岁 Age	5	80.0	0.0	20.0
女性 Female	160	46.9	28.1	25.0
16~24 岁 Age	44	43.2	34.1	22.7
25~34 岁 Age	51	49.0	33.3	17.6
35~44 岁 Age	44	43.2	18.2	38.6
45~54 岁 Age	14	57.1	28.6	14.3
55~60 岁 Age	7	57.1	14.3	28.6

4-8 选择该类商品的考虑因素/ Ranking of the Considerations in Purchasing

注：本题为多选题，合计百分比超过 100%(Multiple answers）

排名 Ranking	考虑因素 Considerations	人次 Person-time	百分比 Percent
1	口味好 pleasant taste	174	62.6
2	营养成分 nutrition constituent	94	33.8
3	生产日期 date of producing	77	27.7
4	价格适中 reasonable price	73	26.3
5	有名的牌子 famous brand	65	23.4
6	购买方便 easy to buy	60	21.6
7	朋友推荐 introduction of friends	21	7.6
8	只是由于习惯 out of habit	16	5.8
9	包装吸引人 appealing package	8	2.9
10	有优惠条件 with preferential terms	7	2.5
11	广告影响 influence of advertising	6	2.2
12	售货员介绍 introduced by the shop assistants	5	1.8
13	其它 others	3	1.1

n=278

4-9 样本、男性各年龄层、女性各年龄层最常食用的种类/ Types of the Consumed Yogurt by the Whole Sample, Age and Gender Groups

注：本题为多选题，合计百分比超过 100%(Multiple answers）

	人数 Number	原味 original flavor	巧克力味 chocolate flavor	草莓味 straw-berry	菠萝味 pine apple	橙味 orange	杏味 apricot	带果粒 with fruit dots	加钙 calcium added	其他 others
样本 Sample	277	63.5	4.7	16.2	3.2	2.2	1.1	0.7	28.9	1.8
男性 Male	118	62.7	5.1	13.6	2.5	2.5	1.7	0.8	27.1	3.4
16~24 岁 Age	38	65.8	13.2	10.5	7.9	0.0	2.6	2.6	13.2	2.6
25~34 岁 Age	45	64.4	0.0	17.8	0.0	2.2	2.2	0.0	24.4	4.4
35~44 岁 Age	20	60.0	0.0	20.0	0.0	5.0	0.0	0.0	50.0	5.0
45~54 岁 Age	10	50.0	10.0	0.0	0.0	10.0	0.0	0.0	40.0	0.0
55~60 岁 Age	5	60.0	0.0	0.0	0.0	0.0	0.0	0.0	40.0	0.0
女性 Female	159	64.2	4.4	18.2	3.8	1.9	0.6	0.6	30.2	0.6
16~24 岁 Age	44	72.7	4.5	6.8	9.1	2.3	2.3	2.3	31.8	0.0
25~34 岁 Age	50	62.0	2.0	28.0	4.0	2.0	0.0	0.0	24.0	2.0
35~44 岁 Age	44	59.1	9.1	22.7	0.0	2.3	0.0	0.0	34.1	0.0
45~54 岁 Age	14	71.4	0.0	7.1	0.0	0.0	0.0	0.0	21.4	0.0
55~60 岁 Age	7	42.9	0.0	14.3	0.0	0.0	0.0	0.0	57.1	0.0

4-10 样本、男性各年龄层、女性各年龄层最常食用的包装形式/ Types of Package of the Consumed Yogurt by the Whole Sample, Age and Gender Groups

注：本题为多选题，合计百分比超过 100%(Multiple answers）

	人数 Number	袋装 bag	方盒装/利乐砖 tetra	房屋状纸盒 house-shaped box	粽子状纸盒 V-shaped box	塑料瓶 plastic bottle	瓷瓶 china bottle	其他 others
样本 Sample	272	40.1	9.6	2.2	1.5	32.0	33.8	1.5
男性 Male	114	36.0	8.8	1.8	1.8	28.9	38.6	3.5
16~24 岁 Age	37	32.4	10.8	2.7	5.4	24.3	40.5	5.4
25~34 岁 Age	44	43.2	9.1	0.0	0.0	20.5	45.5	2.3
35~44 岁 Age	19	36.8	5.3	5.3	0.0	36.8	42.1	0.0
45~54 岁 Age	9	11.1	11.1	0.0	0.0	66.7	11.1	0.0
55~60 岁 Age	5	40.0	0.0	0.0	0.0	40.0	0.0	20.0
女性 Female	158	43.0	10.1	2.5	1.3	34.2	30.4	0.0
16~24 岁 Age	44	34.1	9.1	2.3	2.3	50.0	25.0	0.0
25~34 岁 Age	51	47.1	7.8	0.0	2.0	29.4	27.5	0.0
35~44 岁 Age	43	46.5	11.6	4.7	0.0	37.2	30.2	0.0
45~54 岁 Age	13	38.5	23.1	7.7	0.0	0.0	53.8	0.0
55~60 岁 Age	7	57.1	0.0	0.0	0.0	14.3	42.9	0.0

4-11 样本、男性各年龄层、女性各年龄层最常饮用场合/ Settings of Consumption by the Whole Sample, Age and Gender Groups

注：本题为多选题，合计百分比超过 100%(Multiple answers）

	人数 Number	早餐时 breakfast	正餐（午、晚餐）时 dinner	口渴时 when thirsty	宵夜时 evening snack	睡觉前 before sleeping	工作休息时 during work break	外出/旅游时 outing/ traveling	其它 others
样本 Sample	276	14.5	6.2	37.7	5.1	16.7	22.5	25.0	2.9
男性 Male	118	15.3	2.5	44.9	7.6	16.1	20.3	19.5	3.4
16~24 岁 Age	38	21.1	5.3	44.7	13.2	13.2	28.9	13.2	0.0
25~34 岁 Age	45	2.2	2.2	46.7	6.7	13.3	20.0	24.4	6.7
35~44 岁 Age	20	25.0	0.0	45.0	5.0	25.0	5.0	35.0	5.0
45~54 岁 Age	10	20.0	0.0	40.0	0.0	30.0	20.0	0.0	0.0
55~60 岁 Age	5	40.0	0.0	40.0	0.0	0.0	20.0	0.0	0.0
女性 Female	158	13.9	8.9	32.3	3.2	17.1	24.1	29.1	2.5
16~24 岁 Age	44	6.8	15.9	31.8	4.5	9.1	18.2	43.2	4.5
25~34 岁 Age	51	15.7	5.9	31.4	0.0	23.5	29.4	31.4	0.0
35~44 岁 Age	43	16.3	7.0	32.6	4.7	16.3	30.2	16.3	2.3
45~54 岁 Age	13	15.4	0.0	46.2	7.7	15.4	15.4	23.1	7.7
55~60 岁 Age	7	28.6	14.3	14.3	0.0	28.6	0.0	14.3	0.0

4-12 重度消费者的人口分布/ Demographics of the Heavy Consumers

	人数 Number	16-24 岁 Age	25-34 岁 Age	35-44 岁 Age	45-54 岁 Age	55-60 岁 Age
样本 Sample	159	30.2	34.0	25.8	8.2	1.9
男性 Male	62	33.9	40.3	17.7	8.1	0.0
天天喝 daily	17	41.2	29.4	23.5	5.9	0.0
一周 3 次或以上 3 times or over a week	15	26.7	46.7	20.0	6.7	0.0
一周 1～2 次 once or twice a week	30	33.3	43.3	13.3	10.0	0.0
女性 Female	97	27.8	29.9	30.9	8.2	3.1
天天喝 daily	16	12.5	25.0	31.3	18.8	12.5
一周 3 次或以上 3 times or over a week	24	25.0	25.0	37.5	8.3	4.2
一周 1～2 次 once or twice a week	57	33.3	33.3	28.1	5.3	0.0

4-13 不同消费者层的常用品牌/ The Most Frequently Used Brands by Market Segments

4-13-1 时尚流行指标/ Fads Popular Index

	人数 Number	第一品牌及百分比 1st/ percent	第二品牌及百分比 2nd/ percent	第三品牌及百分比 3rd/ percent
样本 Sample	278	**辉山 Huishan(42.1)**	**医大 Yida(20.1)**	**双鸽 Shuange(4.7)**
平实生活指向 simple living orientation	114	辉山 Huishan(35.1)	医大 Yida(22.8)	双鸽 Shuangge(8.8)
时尚流行指向 fashion orientation	164	辉山 Huishan(47.0)	医大 Yida(18.3)	中街 Zhongjie(4.3)

4-13-2 广告态度指标/ Advertising Attitude Index

	人数 Number	第一品牌及百分比 1st/ percent	第二品牌及百分比 2nd/ percent	第三品牌及百分比 3rd/ percent
样本 Sample	278	**辉山 Huishan(42.1)**	**医大 Yida(20.1)**	**双鸽 Shuangge(4.7)**
广告淡漠指向 indifferent orientation	66	辉山 Huishan(37.9)	医大 Yida(28.8)	双鸽 Shuangge(6.1)
中间层 medium	173	辉山 Huishan(43.9)	医大 Yida(16.2)	双鸽 Shuangge(4.6)
信赖广告指向 loyal orientation	39	辉山 Huishan(41.0)	医大 Yida(23.1)	中街 Zhongjie(7.7)

4-13-3 饮食健康指标/ Foods & Drink Quality Index

	人数 Number	第一品牌及百分比 1st/ percent	第二品牌及百分比 2nd/ percent	第三品牌及百分比 3rd/ percent
样本 Sample	278	**辉山 Huishan(42.1)**	**医大 Yida(20.1)**	**双鸽 Shuangge(4.7)**
饮食"温饱"指向 "basic" orientation	75	辉山 Huishan(42.7)	医大 Yida(25.3)	双鸽 Shuangge(8.0)
中间层 medium	127	辉山 Huishan(44.1)	医大 Yida(17.3)	光明 Bright(3.9) 中街 Zhongjie(3.9) 双鸽 Shuangge(3.9)
健康营养指向 health & nutrition orientation	76	辉山 Huishan(38.2)	医大 Yida(19.7)	中街 Zhongjie(5.3) 格格香 Gegexiang(5.3)

4-14 重度消费者的消费者层构成/ The Composition of the Heavy Consumers

4-14-1 时尚流行指标/ Fads Popular Index

	人数 Number	平实生活指向 simple living orientation	时尚流行指向 fashion orientation
样本 Sample	159	37.7	62.3
天天喝 daily	33	30.3	69.7
一周 3 次或以上 3 times or over a week	39	41.0	59.0
一周 1～2 次 once or twice a week	87	39.1	60.9

4-14-2 广告态度指标/ Advertising Attitude Index

	人数 Number	广告淡漠指向 indifferent orientation	中间层 medium	信赖广告指向 loyal orientation
样本 Sample	159	23.9	60.4	15.7
天天喝 daily	33	21.2	60.6	18.2
一周 3 次或以上 3 times or over a week	39	17.9	61.5	20.5
一周 1～2 次 once or twice a week	87	27.6	59.8	12.6

4-14-3 饮食健康指标/ Foods & Drink Quality Index

	人数 Number	饮食"温饱"指向 "basic" orientation	中间层 medium	健康营养指向 health & nutrition orientation
样本 Sample	159	26.4	43.4	30.2
天天喝 daily	33	21.2	48.5	30.3
一周 3 次或以上 3 times or over a week	39	20.5	38.5	41.0
一周 1～2 次 once or twice a week	87	31.0	43.7	25.3

5.巧克力 / Chocolate

● 北京 / Beijing

5-1 最近三个月食用频率的比例/ Proportion of the Sample Consuming Chocolate in the Last Three Months

	人数 Number	百分比 Percent
天天吃 daily	23	2.3
一周 3 次或以上 3 times or over a week	59	5.9
一周 1~2 次 once or twice a week	141	14.0
一个月 2~3 次 2 or 3 times a month	163	16.2
一个月 1 次 once a month	113	11.2
两个月 1 次 once two months	47	4.7
三个月 1 次或以下 once three months or below	79	7.9
没吃过 never	381	37.9

n=1006

5-2 最常用品牌排名/ Ranking of the Most Frequently Used Brands

排名 Brand Ranking	品牌 Brands	人数 Number	百分比 Percent
1	德芙 Dove	265	42.7
2	吉百利 Cadbury	129	20.8
3	义利 Yili	55	8.9
4	雀巢 Nestle	39	6.3
5	伊利 Yili	12	1.9
6	金莎 Ferrero Rocher	9	1.5
7	金帝 Le Conte	7	1.1

n=620

5-3 样本、男性各年龄层、女性各年龄层的常用品牌/ The Most Frequently Used Brands by the Whole Sample, Age and Gender Groups

	人数 Number	第一品牌及百分比 1st/ percent	第二品牌及百分比 2nd/ percent	第三品牌及百分比 3rd/ percent	第四品牌及百分比 4th/ percent
样本 Sample	620	**德芙 Dove(42.7)**	**吉百利 Cadbury(20.8)**	**义利 Yili(8.9)**	**雀巢 Nestle(6.3)**
男性 Male	265	**德芙 Dove(40.4)**	**吉百利 Cadbury(19.2)**	**义利 Yili(12.1)**	**雀巢 Nestle(6.8)**
16~24 岁 Age	71	德芙 Dove(46.5)	吉百利 Cadbury(22.5)	义利 Yili(11.3)	雀巢 Nestle(7.0)
25~34 岁 Age	84	德芙 Dove(42.9)	吉百利 Cadbury(14.3)	义利 Yili(13.1)	雀巢 Nestle(8.3)
35~44 岁 Age	65	德芙 Dove(35.4)	吉百利 Cadbury(21.5)	义利 Yili(9.2)	雀巢 Nestle(7.7)
45~54 岁 Age	31	德芙 Dove(32.3)	吉百利 Cadbury(25.8)	义利 Yili(12.9)	伊利 Yili(6.5)
55~60 岁 Age	14	德芙 Dove(35.7)	义利 Yili(21.4)	巴旦 Almond(7.1) 吉百利 Cadbury(7.1) 金帝 Le Conte(7.1) 金莎 Ferrero Rocher(7.1)	
女性 Female	355	**德芙 Dove(44.5)**	**吉百利 Cadbury(22.0)**	**义利 Yili(6.5)**	**雀巢 Nestle(5.9)**
16~24 岁 Age	87	德芙 Dove(41.4)	吉百利 Cadbury(36.8)	雀巢 Nestle(8.0)	金莎 Ferrero Rocher(3.4)
25~34 岁 Age	126	德芙 Dove(54.8)	吉百利 Cadbury(16.7)	义利 Yili(7.1)	雀巢 Nestle(4.0)
35~44 岁 Age	77	德芙 Dove(44.2)	吉百利 Cadbury(20.8)	义利 Yili(6.5)	雀巢 Nestle(5.2)
45~54 岁 Age	46	德芙 Dove(28.3)	义利 Yili(17.4) 吉百利 Cadbury(17.4)	金莎 Ferrero Rocher(6.5)	伊利 Yili(4.3)
55~60 岁 Age	19	德芙 Dove(31.6)	雀巢 Nestle(21.1)	吉百利 Cadbury(5.3) 伊利 Yili(5.3)	

5-4 理想品牌排名/ Ranking of the Ideal Brands

排名 Brand Ranking	品牌 Brands	人数 Number	百分比 Percent
1	德芙 Dove	401	39.7
2	吉百利 Cadbury	156	15.4
3	义利 Yili	53	5.2
4	雀巢 Nestle	39	3.9
5	伊利 Yili	19	1.9
6	金莎 Ferrero Rocher	11	1.1
7	金帝 Le Conte	8	0.8

n=1011

5-5 样本、男性各年龄层、女性各年龄层最近三个月有无购买的比例/ Purchasing in the Last Three Months by the Whole Sample, Age and Gender Groups

	人数 Number	买过 yes	没买过 no
样本 Sample	1008	56.5	43.5
男性 Male	501	47.1	52.9
16~24 岁 Age	103	61.2	38.8
25~34 岁 Age	151	49.0	51.0
35~44 岁 Age	131	43.5	56.5
45~54 岁 Age	77	39.0	61.0
55~60 岁 Age	39	30.8	69.2
女性 Female	507	65.9	34.1
16~24 岁 Age	108	76.9	23.1
25~34 岁 Age	150	81.3	18.7
35~44 岁 Age	123	56.1	43.9
45~54 岁 Age	84	52.4	47.6
55~60 岁 Age	42	38.1	61.9

5-6 样本、男性各年龄层、女性各年龄层最近三个月的食用频率/ Frequencies of Consuming Chocolate in the Last Three Months by the Whole Sample, Age and Gender Group

	人数 Number	天天吃 daily	一周3次或以上 3 times or over a week	一周1~2次 once or twice a week	一个月2~3次 2 or 3 times a months	一个月1次 once a month	两个月1次 once two months	三个月1次或以下 once three months or below	没吃过 never
样本 Sample	1006	2.3	5.9	14.0	16.2	11.2	4.7	7.9	37.9
男性 Male	501	2.2	4.8	11.8	13.2	9.8	5.0	6.8	46.5
16~24 岁 Age	104	2.9	8.7	22.1	14.4	9.6	5.8	5.8	30.8
25~34 岁 Age	151	2.6	4.0	9.9	13.2	11.9	7.9	6.0	44.4
35~44 岁 Age	130	2.3	5.4	10.0	11.5	8.5	3.8	8.5	50.0
45~54 岁 Age	76	0.0	2.6	6.6	11.8	9.2	1.3	9.2	59.2
55~60 岁 Age	40	2.5	0.0	7.5	17.5	7.5	2.5	2.5	60.0
女性 Female	505	2.4	6.9	16.2	19.2	12.7	4.4	8.9	29.3
16~24 岁 Age	107	1.9	7.5	17.8	31.8	8.4	8.4	6.5	17.8
25~34 岁 Age	150	2.7	10.7	19.3	19.3	17.3	4.7	10.0	16.0
35~44 岁 Age	122	3.3	4.9	18.0	14.8	9.8	3.3	9.8	36.1
45~54 岁 Age	84	1.2	4.8	11.9	13.1	14.3	1.2	8.3	45.2
55~60 岁 Age	42	2.4	2.4	4.8	11.9	11.9	2.4	9.5	54.8

5-7 样本、男性各年龄层、女性各年龄层的品牌习惯/ Brand Habit in Consuming Chocolate by the Whole Sample, Age and Gender Groups

	人数 Number	基本固定食用一个牌子 used in only one brand	比较固定地食用两个或三个牌子 used in two or three brands	基本上不太固定牌子 no brand preference
样本 Sample	623	33.9	37.2	28.9
男性 Male	267	34.8	33.3	31.8
16~24 岁 Age	72	30.6	52.8	16.7
25~34 岁 Age	84	39.3	32.1	28.6
35~44 岁 Age	65	35.4	21.5	43.1
45~54 岁 Age	31	25.8	29.0	45.2
55~60 岁 Age	15	46.7	6.7	46.7
女性 Female	356	33.1	40.2	26.7
16~24 岁 Age	88	34.1	44.3	21.6
25~34 岁 Age	126	27.8	48.4	23.8
35~44 岁 Age	78	34.6	41.0	24.4
45~54 岁 Age	45	44.4	17.8	37.8
55~60 岁 Age	19	31.6	15.8	52.6

5-8 选择该类商品的考虑因素/ Ranking of the Considerations in Purchasing

注：本题为多选题，合计百分比超过 100%(Multiple answers)

排名 Ranking	考虑因素 Considerations	人次 Person-time	百分比 Percent
1	口味好 pleasant taste	440	70.7
2	有名的牌子 famous brand	266	42.8
3	价格适中 reasonable price	189	30.4
4	生产日期 date of producing	113	18.2
5	购买方便 easy to buy	68	10.9
6	广告影响 influence of advertising	61	9.8
7	只是由于习惯 out of habit	41	6.6
8	包装吸引人 appealing package	27	4.3
9	朋友推荐 introduction of friends	21	3.4
10	有优惠条件 with preferential terms	18	2.9
11	其它 others	14	2.3
12	售货员介绍 introduced by the shop assistants	11	1.8

n=622

5-9 样本、男性各年龄层、女性各年龄层最常食用的种类/ Kinds of the Consumed Chocolate by the Whole Sample, Age and Gender Groups

注：本题为多选题，合计百分比超过 100%(Multiple answers)

	人数 Number	原味巧克力 origina-chocolate	黑巧克力 black chocolate	白巧克力 white chocolate	牛奶巧克力 white chocolate	果仁巧克力 kemel chocolate	薄荷巧克力 mint chocolate	果味巧克力 fruit-flavored chocolate	威化巧克力 chocolate wafers	巧克力豆 chocolate beans	酒心巧克力 whiskey heart chocolate	其它 others
样本 Sample	621	38.3	18.2	1.4	29.1	29.8	1.1	1.6	19.3	3.2	2.6	0.5
男性 Male	266	37.2	19.9	2.3	26.7	25.9	1.1	1.9	19.9	3.4	3.0	0.8
16~24 岁 Age	71	46.5	21.1	2.8	26.8	18.3	0.0	1.4	19.7	1.4	5.6	1.4
25~34 岁 Age	84	33.3	17.9	3.6	23.8	35.7	1.2	2.4	20.2	3.6	2.4	1.2
35~44 岁 Age	65	30.8	15.4	0.0	32.3	27.7	1.5	3.1	21.5	3.1	1.5	0.0
45~54 岁 Age	31	32.3	32.3	3.2	35.5	19.4	3.2	0.0	19.4	3.2	0.0	0.0
55~60 岁 Age	15	53.3	20.0	0.0	0.0	13.3	0.0	0.0	13.3	13.3	6.7	0.0
女性 Female	355	39.2	16.9	0.8	31.0	32.7	1.1	1.4	18.9	3.1	2.3	0.3
16~24 岁 Age	88	44.3	18.2	1.1	33.0	28.4	1.1	1.1	15.9	2.3	0.0	0.0
25~34 岁 Age	125	34.4	16.8	0.8	35.2	36.0	0.8	0.0	21.6	4.8	0.8	0.0
35~44 岁 Age	77	42.9	13.0	1.3	33.8	28.6	2.6	5.2	22.1	1.3	1.3	1.3
45~54 岁 Age	46	34.8	21.7	0.0	15.2	43.5	0.0	0.0	13.0	2.2	10.9	0.0
55~60 岁 Age	19	42.1	15.8	0.0	21.1	21.1	0.0	0.0	15.8	5.3	5.3	0.0

5-10 样本、男性各年龄层、女性各年龄层最常食用场合/ Settings of Consumption by the Whole Sample, Age and Gender Groups

注：本题为多选题，合计百分比超过 100%(Multiple answers)

	人数 Number	平时做零食吃 when free	加班时 when work overtime	招待客人 serve guests	肚子饿时 when hungry	补充营养 supplementing nutrition	郊游、外出时 outing/ traveling	其它 others
样本 Sample	618	72.2	3.2	7.0	17.5	19.7	16.3	1.6
男性 Male	263	67.7	3.0	6.8	15.6	20.2	16.7	1.9
16~24 岁 Age	70	75.7	2.9	7.1	17.1	15.7	20.0	0.0
25~34 岁 Age	83	65.1	3.6	4.8	10.8	22.9	15.7	1.2
35~44 岁 Age	64	67.2	3.1	4.7	18.8	23.4	14.1	1.6
45~54 岁 Age	31	61.3	3.2	9.7	16.1	16.1	22.6	6.5
55~60 岁 Age	15	60.0	0.0	20.0	20.0	20.0	6.7	6.7
女性 Female	355	75.5	3.4	7.0	18.9	19.4	16.1	1.4
16~24 岁 Age	87	81.6	2.3	4.6	23.0	18.4	18.4	0.0
25~34 岁 Age	125	81.6	5.6	3.2	15.2	16.8	14.4	1.6
35~44 岁 Age	78	69.2	2.6	7.7	17.9	24.4	16.7	2.6
45~54 岁 Age	46	71.7	2.2	15.2	21.7	17.4	13.0	0.0
55~60 岁 Age	19	42.1	0.0	21.1	21.1	26.3	21.1	5.3

5-11 重度消费者人口分布/ Demographics of the Heavy Consumers

	人数 Number	16-24 岁 Age	25-34 岁 Age	35-44 岁 Age	45-54 岁 Age	55-60 岁 Age
样本 Sample	223	28.7	33.2	24.7	9.9	3.6
男性 Male	94	37.2	26.6	24.5	7.4	4.3
天天吃 daily	11	27.3	36.4	27.3	0.0	9.1
一周 3 次或以上 3 times or over a week	24	37.5	25.0	29.2	8.3	0.0
一周 1~2 次 once or twice a week	59	39.0	25.4	22.0	8.5	5.1
女性 Female	129	22.5	38.0	24.8	11.6	3.1
天天吃 daily	12	16.7	33.3	33.3	8.3	8.3
一周 3 次或以上 3 times or over a week	35	22.9	45.7	17.1	11.4	2.9
一周 1~2 次 once or twice a week	82	23.2	35.4	26.8	12.2	2.4

5-12 不同消费者层的常用品牌/ The Most Frequently Used Brands by Market Segments

5-12-1 时尚流行指标/ Fads Popular Index

	人数 Number	第一品牌及百分比 1st/ percent	第二品牌及百分比 2nd/ percent	第三品牌及百分比 3rd/ percent	第四品牌及百分比 4th/ percent
样本 Sample	614	**德芙 Dove(42.7)**	**吉百利 Cadbury(20.7)**	**义利 Yili(8.8)**	**雀巢 Nestle(6.4)**
平实生活指向 simple living orientation	256	德芙 Dove(40.2)	吉百利 Cadbury(19.1)	义利 Yili(11.7)	雀巢 Nestle(5.9)
时尚流行指向 fashion orientation	358	德芙 Dove(44.4)	吉百利 Cadbury(21.8)	雀巢 Nestle(6.7) 义利 Yili(6.7)	伊利 Yili(2.0)

5-12-2 广告态度指标/ Advertising Attitude Index

	人数 Number	第一品牌及百分比 1st/ percent	第二品牌及百分比 2nd/ percent	第三品牌及百分比 3rd/ percent	第四品牌及百分比 4th/ percent
样本 Sample	606	**德芙 Dove(42.7)**	**吉百利 Cadbury(20.5)**	**义利 Yili(8.7)**	**雀巢 Nestle(6.4)**
广告淡漠指向 indifferent orientation	151	德芙 Dove(40.4)	吉百利 Cadbury(20.5)	义利 Yili(10.6)	雀巢 Nestle(4.6)
中间层 medium	364	德芙 Dove(40.9)	吉百利 Cadbury(22.0)	义利 Yili(9.1)	雀巢 Nestle(6.9)
信赖广告指向 loyal orientation	91	德芙 Dove(53.8)	吉百利 Cadbury(14.3)	雀巢 Nestle(7.7)	义利 Yili(4.4)

5-12-3 饮食健康指标/ Foods & Drink Quality Index

	人数 Number	第一品牌及百分比 1st/ percent	第二品牌及百分比 2nd/ percent	第三品牌及百分比 3rd/ percent	第四品牌及百分比 4th/ percent
样本 Sample	616	**德芙 Dove(42.7)**	**吉百利 Cadbury(20.9)**	**义利 Yili(8.8)**	**雀巢 Nestle(6.2)**
饮食"温饱"指向 "basic" orientation	156	德芙 Dove(46.2)	吉百利 Cadbury(16.0)	义利 Yili(9.0)	雀巢 Nestle(8.3)
中间层 medium	298	德芙 Dove(41.3)	吉百利 Cadbury(21.1)	义利 Yili(10.7)	雀巢 Nestle(4.7)
健康营养指向 health & nutrition orientation	162	德芙 Dove(42.0)	吉百利 Cadbury(25.3)	雀巢 Nestle(6.8)	义利 Yili(4.9)

5-13 重度消费者的消费者层构成/ The Composition of the Heavy Consumers

5-13-1 时尚流行指标/ Fads Popular Index

	人数 Number	平实生活指向 simple living orientation	时尚流行指向 fashion orientation
样本 Sample	220	38.2	61.8
天天吃 daily	23	21.7	78.3
一周 3 次或以上 3 times or over a week	59	33.9	66.1
一周 1～2 次 once or twice a week	138	42.8	57.2

5-13-2 广告态度指标/ Advertising Attitude Index

	人数 Number	广告淡漠指向 indifferent orientation	中间层 medium	信赖广告指向 loyal orientation
样本 Sample	220	24.5	57.7	17.7
天天吃 daily	23	26.1	60.9	13.0
一周 3 次或以上 3 times or over a week	58	20.7	60.3	19.0
一周 1~2 次 once or twice a week	139	25.9	56.1	18.0

5-13-3 饮食健康指标/ Foods & Drink Quality Index

	人数 Number	饮食"温饱"指向 "basic" orientation	中间层 medium	健康营养指向 health & nutrition orientation
样本 Sample	221	23.1	50.7	26.2
天天吃 daily	22	18.2	36.4	45.5
一周 3 次或以上 3 times or over a week	59	32.2	45.8	22.0
一周 1~2 次 once or twice a week	140	20.0	55.0	25.0

● 上海 / Shanghai

5-1 最近三个月食用频率的比例/ Proportion of the Sample Consuming Chocolate in the Last Three Months

	人数 Number	百分比 Percent
天天吃 daily	13	1.3
一周 3 次或以上 3 times or over a week	41	4.1
一周 1~2 次 once or twice a week	107	10.6
一个月 2~3 次 2 or 3 times a month	162	16.0
一个月 1 次 once a month	99	9.8
两个月 1 次 once two months	56	5.5
三个月 1 次或以下 once three months or below	73	7.2
没吃过 never	461	45.6

n=1012

5-2 最常用品牌排名/ Ranking of the Most Frequently Used Brands

排名 Brand Ranking	品牌 Brands	人数 Number	百分比 Percent
1	德芙 Dove	290	52.9
2	申丰 Shenfu	67	12.2
3	吉百利 Cadbury	45	8.2
4	好时 Hershey's	39	7.1
5	雀巢 Nestle	20	3.6
6	金帝 Le Conte	15	2.7

n=548

5-3 样本、男性各年龄层、女性各年龄层的常用品牌/ The Most Frequently Used Brands by the Whole Sample, Age and Gender Groups

	人数 Number	第一品牌及百分比 1st/ percent	第二品牌及百分比 2nd/ percent	第三品牌及百分比 3rd/ percent
样本 Sample	548	**德芙 Dove(52.9)**	**申丰 Shenfu(12.2)**	**吉百利 Cadbury(8.2)**
男性 Male	254	**德芙 Dove(53.5)**	**申丰 Shenfu(13.4)**	**好时 Hershey's(7.5)**
16~24 岁 Age	78	德芙 Dove(61.5)	申丰 Shenfu(11.5)	吉百利 Cadbury(9.0)
25~34 岁 Age	82	德芙 Dove(58.5)	申丰 Shenfu(9.8)	好时 Hershey's(8.5)
35~44 岁 Age	50	德芙 Dove(52.0)	申丰 Shenfu(16.0)	好时 Hershey's(8.0)
45~54 岁 Age	29	德芙 Dove(44.8)	申丰 Shenfu(24.1)	冠生园 Guansheng Yuan(3.4) 捷利 Jieli(3.4) 运动 SPORT(3.4) 雀巢 Nestle(3.4) 玛氏 M&M's(3.4) 吉百利 Cadbury(3.4) 大昌 Dachang(3.4)
55~60 岁 Age	15	吉百利 Cadbury(20.0)	好时 Hershey's(13.3) 申丰 Shenfu(13.3)	华芙 Huafu(6.7) 威利 Weili(6.7) 益民 Yiming(6.7) 德芙 Dove(6.7) 雀巢 Nestle(6.7) 上儿 Shang'er(6.7) 金帝 Le Conte(6.7)
女性 Female	294	**德芙 Dove(52.4)**	**申丰 Shenfu(11.2)**	**吉百利 Cadbury(9.2)**
16~24 岁 Age	80	德芙 Dove(56.3)	吉百利 Cadbury(15.0)	申丰 Shenfu(8.8)
25~34 岁 Age	92	德芙 Dove(56.5)	好时 Hershey's(12.0)	申丰 Shenfu(8.7)
35~44 岁 Age	70	德芙 Dove(52.9)	申丰 Shenfu(14.3)	吉百利 Cadbury(8.6)
45~54 岁 Age	37	德芙 Dove(45.9)	申丰 Shenfu(16.2)	
55~60 岁 Age	15	德芙 Dove(20.0)	好时 Hershey's(13.3) 吉百利 Cadbury(13.3) 申丰 Shenfu(13.3) 雀巢 Nestle(13.3)	金帝 Le Conte(6.7) 天福 Tianfu(6.7) 瑞士果仁 Rui Shi Guo Ren(6.7)

5-4 理想品牌排名/ Ranking of the Ideal Brands

排名 Brand Ranking	品牌 Brands	人数 Number	百分比 Percent
1	德芙 Dove	550	54.2
2	申丰 Shenfu	82	8.1
3	吉百利 Cadbury	72	7.1
4	好时 Hershey's	65	6.4
5	金帝 Le Conte	21	2.1
6	雀巢 Nestle	15	1.5
7	玛氏 M&M's	9	0.9
8	费列罗 Rucher	6	0.6
8	金莎 Ferrero Rccher	6	0.6
9	华芙 Huafu	5	0.5

n=1014

5-5 样本、男性各年龄层、女性各年龄层最近三个月有无购买的比例/ Purchasing in the Last Three Months by the Whole Sample, Age and Gender Groups

	人数 Number	买过 yes	没买过 no
样本 Sample	1014	51.7	48.3
男性 Male	509	47.0	53.0
16~24 岁 Age	109	60.6	39.4
25~34 岁 Age	146	51.4	48.6
35~44 岁 Age	130	40.0	60.0
45~54 岁 Age	85	35.3	64.7
55~60 岁 Age	39	41.0	59.0
女性 Female	505	56.4	43.6
16~24 岁 Age	108	70.4	29.6
25~34 岁 Age	144	63.9	36.1
35~44 岁 Age	130	53.1	46.9
45~54 岁 Age	82	41.5	58.5
55~60 岁 Age	41	34.1	65.9

5-6 样本、男性各年龄层、女性各年龄层最近三个月的食用频率/ Frequencies of Consuming Chocolate in the Last Three Months by the Whole Sample, Age and Gender Group

	人数 Number	天天吃 daily	一周3次或以上 3 times or over a week	一周1～2次 once or twice a week	一个月2～3次 2 or 3 times a month	一个月1次 once a month	两个月1次 once two months	三个月1次或以下 once three months or below	没吃过 never
样本 Sample	1012	1.3	4.1	10.6	16.0	9.8	5.5	7.2	45.6
男性 Male	508	1.4	3.1	9.8	15.0	9.3	5.3	6.5	49.6
16~24 岁 Age	109	2.8	2.8	17.4	22.0	11.9	5.5	9.2	28.4
25~34 岁 Age	146	0.7	4.1	11.0	17.8	12.3	5.5	6.2	42.5
35~44 岁 Age	129	1.6	3.1	6.2	9.3	7.0	7.0	4.7	61.2
45~54 岁 Age	85	0.0	2.4	4.7	10.6	5.9	3.5	7.1	65.9
55~60 岁 Age	39	2.6	2.6	7.7	12.8	5.1	2.6	5.1	61.5
女性 Female	504	1.2	5.0	11.3	17.1	10.3	5.8	7.9	41.5
16~24 岁 Age	108	0.0	8.3	13.9	23.1	13.9	6.5	8.3	25.9
25~34 岁 Age	144	0.7	6.9	13.2	15.3	13.2	6.9	7.6	36.1
35~44 岁 Age	129	1.6	3.1	14.0	20.9	5.4	4.7	5.4	45.0
45~54 岁 Age	82	0.0	1.2	4.9	11.0	12.2	4.9	11.0	54.9
55~60 岁 Age	41	7.3	2.4	2.4	7.3	2.4	4.9	9.8	63.4

5-7 样本、男性各年龄层、女性各年龄层的品牌习惯/ Brand Habit in Consuming Chocolate by the Whole Sample, Age and Gender Groups

	人数 Number	基本固定食用一个牌子 used in only one brand	比较固定地食用两个或三个牌子 used in two or three brands	基本上不太固定牌子 no brand preference
样本 Sample	549	30.6	40.6	28.8
男性 Male	255	29.4	40.0	30.6
16~24 岁 Age	78	29.5	46.2	24.4
25~34 岁 Age	83	30.1	41.0	28.9
35~44 岁 Age	50	32.0	32.0	36.0
45~54 岁 Age	29	24.1	37.9	37.9
55~60 岁 Age	15	26.7	33.3	40.0
女性 Female	294	31.6	41.2	27.2
16~24 岁 Age	80	32.5	48.8	18.8
25~34 岁 Age	92	26.1	46.7	27.2
35~44 岁 Age	70	35.7	38.6	25.7
45~54 岁 Age	37	37.8	27.0	35.1
55~60 岁 Age	15	26.7	13.3	60.0

5-8 选择该类商品的考虑因素/ Ranking of the Considerations in Purchasing

注：本题为多选题，合计百分比超过 100%(Multiple answers)

排名 Ranking	考虑因素 Considerations	人次 Person-time	百分比 Percent
1	口味好 pleasant taste	406	74.0
2	有名的牌子 famous brand	207	37.7
3	价格适中 reasonable price	153	27.9
4	生产日期 date of producing	82	14.9
5	广告影响 influence of advertising	62	11.3
6	购买方便 easy to buy	57	10.4
7	只是由于习惯 out of habit	40	7.3
8	包装吸引人 appealing package	38	6.9
9	有优惠条件 with preferential terms	25	4.6
10	朋友推荐 introduction of friends	23	4.2
11	其它 others	7	1.3
12	售货员介绍 introduced by the shop assistants	4	0.7

n=549

5-9 样本、男性各年龄层、女性各年龄层最常食用的种类/ Kinds of the Consumed Chocolate by the Whole Sample, Age and Gender Groups

注：本题为多选题，合计百分比超过 100%(Multiple answers）

	人数 Number	原味巧克力 original chocolate	黑巧克力 black chocolate	白巧克力 white chocolate	牛奶巧克力 white chocolate	果仁巧克力 kemel chocolate	薄荷巧克力 mint chocolate	果味巧克力 fruit-flavored chocolate	威化巧克力 chocolate wafers	巧克力豆 chocolate beans	酒心巧克力 whiskey heart chocolate	其它 others
样本 Sample	548	35.4	25.2	5.5	28.3	28.5	0.9	2.2	11.5	3.5	2.9	1.3
男性 Male	255	31.8	26.7	5.9	29.4	30.6	0.4	0.8	11.8	3.9	2.7	2.0
16~24 岁 Age	78	28.2	34.6	7.7	34.6	17.9	0.0	1.3	10.3	3.8	1.3	1.3
25~34 岁 Age	83	32.5	20.5	2.4	31.3	44.6	0.0	0.0	12.0	4.8	2.4	1.2
35~44 岁 Age	50	44.0	16.0	10.0	36.0	22.0	0.0	2.0	4.0	6.0	4.0	2.0
45~54 岁 Age	29	17.2	44.8	6.9	6.9	44.8	0.0	0.0	27.6	0.0	0.0	0.0
55~60 岁 Age	15	33.3	20.0	0.0	13.3	20.0	6.7	0.0	13.3	0.0	13.3	13.3
女性 Female	293	38.6	23.9	5.1	27.3	26.6	1.4	3.4	11.3	3.1	3.1	0.7
16~24 岁 Age	80	33.8	33.8	2.5	23.8	32.5	1.3	5.0	10.0	3.8	5.0	1.3
25~34 岁 Age	91	36.3	18.7	3.3	29.7	28.6	2.2	1.1	15.4	3.3	3.3	0.0
35~44 岁 Age	70	40.0	24.3	4.3	31.4	22.9	0.0	2.9	8.6	4.3	2.9	1.4
45~54 岁 Age	37	35.1	21.6	16.2	27.0	16.2	2.7	5.4	10.8	0.0	0.0	0.0
55~60 岁 Age	15	80.0	6.7	6.7	13.3	26.7	0.0	6.7	6.7	0.0	0.0	0.0

5-10 样本、男性各年龄层、女性各年龄层最常食用场合/ Settings of Consumption by the Whole Sample, Age and Gender Groups

注：本题为多选题，合计百分比超过 100%(Multiple answers）

	人数 Number	平时做零食吃 when free	加班时 when work overtime	招待客人 serve guests	肚子饿时 when hungry	补充营养 supplementing nutrition	郊游、外出时 outing/ traveling	其它 others
样本 Sample	548	74.6	3.8	8.9	13.7	13.9	14.8	1.5
男性 Male	254	72.0	3.5	9.4	12.6	15.0	13.8	1.6
16~24 岁 Age	78	74.4	2.6	15.4	10.3	11.5	16.7	0.0
25~34 岁 Age	82	73.2	2.4	3.7	11.0	17.1	15.9	2.4
35~44 岁 Age	50	60.0	8.0	8.0	18.0	20.0	10.0	2.0
45~54 岁 Age	29	72.4	3.4	17.2	17.2	17.2	13.8	0.0
55~60 岁 Age	15	93.3	0.0	0.0	6.7	0.0	0.0	6.7
女性 Female	294	76.9	4.1	8.5	14.6	12.9	15.6	1.4
16~24 岁 Age	80	83.8	3.8	6.3	8.8	8.8	20.0	1.3
25~34 岁 Age	92	77.2	5.4	4.3	16.3	12.0	14.1	2.2
35~44 岁 Age	70	75.7	2.9	8.6	21.4	17.1	15.7	0.0
45~54 岁 Age	37	67.6	5.4	18.9	13.5	10.8	8.1	0.0
55~60 岁 Age	15	66.7	0.0	20.0	6.7	26.7	20.0	6.7

5-11 重度消费者人口分布/ Demographics of the Heavy Consumers

	人数 Number	16-24 岁 Age	25-34 岁 Age	35-44 岁 Age	45-54 岁 Age	55-60 岁 Age
样本 Sample	161	30.4	32.9	23.6	6.8	6.2
男性 Male	73	34.2	31.5	19.2	8.2	6.8
天天吃 daily	7	42.9	14.3	28.6	0.0	14.3
一周 3 次或以上 3 times or over a week	16	18.8	37.5	25.0	12.5	6.3
一周 1~2 次 once or twice a week	50	38.0	32.0	16.0	8.0	6.0
女性 Female	88	27.3	34.1	27.3	5.7	5.7
天天吃 daily	6	0.0	16.7	33.3	0.0	50.0
一周 3 次或以上 3 times or over a week	25	36.0	40.0	16.0	4.0	4.0
一周 1~2 次 once or twice a week	57	26.3	33.3	31.6	7.0	1.8

5-12 不同消费者层的常用品牌/ The Most Frequently Used Brands by Market Segments

5-12-1 时尚流行指标/ Fads Popular Index

	人数 Number	第一品牌及百分比 1st/ percent	第二品牌及百分比 2nd/ percent	第三品牌及百分比 3rd/ percent
样本 Sample	543	**德芙 Dove(52.7)**	**申丰 Shenfu(12.3)**	**吉百利 Cadbury(8.1)**
平实生活指向 simple living orientation	196	德芙 Dove(51.0)	申丰 Shenfu(13.3)	好时 Hershey's(8.2)
时尚流行指向 fashion orientation	347	德芙 Dove(53.6)	申丰 Shenfu(11.8)	吉百利 Cadbury(10.1)

5-12-2 广告态度指标/ Advertising Attitude Index

	人数 Number	第一品牌及百分比 1st/ percent	第二品牌及百分比 2nd/ percent	第三品牌及百分比 3rd/ percent
样本 Sample	543	**德芙 Dove(53.0)**	**申丰 Shenfu(12.0)**	**吉百利 Cadbury(8.1)**
广告淡漠指向 indifferent orientation	126	德芙 Dove(48.4)	申丰 Shenfu(12.7)	吉百利 Cadbury(10.3)
中间层 medium	343	德芙 Dove(51.6)	申丰 Shenfu(12.8)	吉百利 Cadbury(8.2)
信赖广告指向 loyal orientation	74	德芙 Dove(67.6)	申丰 Shenfu(6.8)	好时 Hershey's(5.4)

5-12-3 饮食健康指标/ Foods & Drink Quality Index

	人数 Number	第一品牌及百分比 1st/ percent	第二品牌及百分比 2nd/ percent	第三品牌及百分比 3rd/ percent
样本 Sample	545	**德芙 Dove(52.8)**	**申丰 Shenfu(12.3)**	**吉百利 Cadbury(8.3)**
饮食“温饱”指向 "basic" orientation	107	德芙 Dove(55.1)	申丰 Shenfu(11.2)	好时 Hershey's(5.6)
中间层 medium	279	德芙 Dove(55.6)	申丰 Shenfu(14.3)	吉百利 Cadbury(9.0)
健康营养指向 health & nutrition orientation	159	德芙 Dove(46.5)	申丰 Shenfu(9.4) 好时 Hershey's(9.4) 吉百利 Cadbury(9.4)	雀巢 Nestle(4.4) 金帝 Le Conte(4.4)

5-13 重度消费者的消费者层构成/ The Composition of the Heavy Consumers

5-13-1 时尚流行指标/ Fads Popular Index

	人数 Number	平实生活指向 simple living orientation	时尚流行指向 fashion orientation
样本 Sample	158	27.8	72.2
天天吃 daily	13	23.1	76.9
一周 3 次或以上 3 times or over a week	41	24.4	75.6
一周 1～2 次 once or twice a week	104	29.8	70.2

5-13-2 广告态度指标/ Advertising Attitude Index

	人数 Number	广告淡漠指向 indifferent orientation	中间层 medium	信赖广告指向 loyal orientation
样本 Sample	159	20.1	65.4	14.5
天天吃 daily	13	0.0	76.9	23.1
一周 3 次或以上 3 times or over a week	41	17.1	68.3	14.6
一周 1～2 次 once or twice a week	105	23.8	62.9	13.3

5-13-3 饮食健康指标/ Foods & Drink Quality Index

	人数 Number	饮食“温饱”指向 "basic" orientation	中间层 medium	健康营养指向 health & nutrition orientation
样本 Sample	160	18.1	54.4	27.5
天天吃 daily	13	15.4	23.1	61.5
一周 3 次或以上 3 times or over a week	41	14.6	63.4	22.0
一周 1～2 次 once or twice a week	106	19.8	54.7	25.5

● 广州 / Guangzhou

5-1 最近三个月食用频率的比例/ Proportion of the Sample Consuming Chocolate in the Last Three Months

	人数 Number	百分比 Percent
天天吃 daily	5	0.5
一周 3 次或以上 3 times or over a week	21	2.0
一周 1～2 次 once or twice a week	76	7.4
一个月 2～3 次 2 or 3 times a month	137	13.3
一个月 1 次 once a month	76	7.4
两个月 1 次 once two months	36	3.5
三个月 1 次或以下 once three months or below	96	9.3
没吃过 never	582	56.6

n=1029

5-2 最常用品牌排名/ Ranking of the Most Frequently Used Brands

排名 Brand Ranking	品牌 Brands	人数 Number	百分比 Percent
1	德芙 Dove	173	39.0
2	金莎 Ferrero Rocher	67	15.1
3	吉百利 Cadbury	33	7.4
4	玛氏 M&M's	27	6.1
5	雀巢 Nestle	19	4.3
6	麦丽素 My Likes	11	2.5
7	瑞士三角 Toblerone	4	0.9

n=444

5-3 样本、男性各年龄层、女性各年龄层的常用品牌/ The Most Frequently Used Brands by the Whole Sample, Age and Gender Groups

	人数 Number	第一品牌及百分比 1st/ percent	第二品牌及百分比 2nd/ percent	第三品牌及百分比 3rd/ percent	第四品牌及百分比 4th/ percent
样本 Sample	444	**德芙 Dove(39.0)**	**金莎 Ferrero Rocher(15.1)**	**吉百利 Cadbury(7.4)**	**玛氏 M&M's(6.1)**
男性 Male	180	**德芙 Dove(40.0)**	**金莎 Ferrero Rocher(16.1)**	**吉百利 Cadbury(7.8)**	**玛氏 M&M's(5.6)**
16~24 岁 Age	51	德芙 Dove(49.0)	吉百利 Cadbury(11.8)	金莎 Ferrero Rocher(7.8) 玛氏 M&M's(7.8)	瑞士三角 Toblerone(2.0) 雀巢 Nestle(2.0) KINGDA(2.0) 金鹰 Jinying(2.0) 百事 Pepsi(2.0)
25~34 岁 Age	64	德芙 Dove(35.9)	金莎 Ferrero Rocher(21.9)	雀巢 Nestle(7.8)	玛氏 M&M's(6.3)
35~44 岁 Age	43	德芙 Dove(39.5)	金莎 Ferrero Rocher(18.6)	吉百利 Cadbury(7.0)	丰收 Fengshou(4.7)
45~54 岁 Age	16	德芙 Dove(43.8)	吉百利 Cadbury(12.5)	金莎 Ferrero Rocher(6.3) 燕塘 Yantang(6.3)	
55~60 岁 Age	6	金莎 Ferrero Rocher(33.3)	玛氏 M&M's(16.7) 麦丽素 My Likes(16.7) 得宝 Debao(16.7)		
女性 Female	264	**德芙 Dove(38.3)**	**金莎 Ferrero Rocher(14.4)**	**吉百利 Cadbury(7.2)**	**玛氏 M&M's(6.4)**
16~24 岁 Age	75	德芙 Dove(48.0)	金莎 Ferrero Rocher(9.3)	玛氏 M&M's(8.0)	麦丽素 My Likes(6.7) 吉百利 Cadbury(6.7)
25~34 岁 Age	78	德芙 Dove(34.6)	金莎 Ferrero Rocher(16.7)	吉百利 Cadbury(10.3)	玛氏 M&M's(9.0)
35~44 岁 Age	62	德芙 Dove(33.9)	金莎 Ferrero Rocher(14.5)	吉百利 Cadbury(6.5) 玛氏 M&M's(6.5)	雀巢 Nestle(4.8)
45~54 岁 Age	41	德芙 Dove(39.0)	金莎 Ferrero Rocher(17.1)	雀巢 Nestle(9.8)	麦丽素 My Likes(4.9)
55~60 岁 Age	8	金莎 Ferrero Rocher(25.0)	德芙 Dove(12.5) 吉百利 Cadbury(12.5) 雀巢 Nestle(12.5) 卓纷 Zhuofen(12.5)		

5-4 理想品牌排名/ Ranking of the Ideal Brands

排名 Brand Ranking	品牌 Brands	人数 Number	百分比 Percent
1	德芙 Dove	264	25.5
2	金莎 Ferrero Rocher	145	14.0
3	玛氏 M&M's	40	3.9
4	吉百利 Cadbury	38	3.7
5	雀巢 Nestle	22	2.1
6	麦丽素 My Likes	13	1.3

n=1034

5-5 样本、男性各年龄层、女性各年龄层最近三个月有无购买的比例/ Purchasing in the Last Three Months by the Whole Sample, Age and Gender Groups

	人数 Number	买过 yes	没买过 no
样本 Sample	1033	39.8	60.2
男性 Male	498	34.1	65.9
16~24 岁 Age	106	42.5	57.5
25~34 岁 Age	149	36.9	63.1
35~44 岁 Age	127	36.2	63.8
45~54 岁 Age	73	23.3	76.7
55~60 岁 Age	43	16.3	83.7
女性 Female	535	45.0	55.0
16~24 岁 Age	112	59.8	40.2
25~34 岁 Age	158	46.8	53.2
35~44 岁 Age	137	40.9	59.1
45~54 岁 Age	87	42.5	57.5
55~60 岁 Age	41	17.1	82.9

5-6 样本、男性各年龄层、女性各年龄层最近三个月的食用频率/ Frequencies of Consuming Chocolate in the Last Three Months by the Whole Sample, Age and Gender Group

	人数 Number	天天吃 daily	一周 3 次或以上 3 times or over a week	一周 1~2 次 once or twice a week	一个月 2~3 次 2 or 3 times a month	一个月 1 次 once a month	两个月 1 次 once two months	三个月 1 次或以下 once three months or below	没吃过 never
样本 Sample	1029	0.5	2.0	7.4	13.3	7.4	3.5	9.3	56.6
男性 Male	497	0.6	1.2	5.4	11.9	6.8	2.4	8.2	63.4
16~24 岁 Age	106	0.9	0.0	10.4	16.0	7.5	5.7	7.5	51.9
25~34 岁 Age	149	0.7	2.7	3.4	12.1	10.7	2.7	11.4	56.4
35~44 岁 Age	127	0.0	0.8	5.5	13.4	3.9	1.6	8.7	66.1
45~54 岁 Age	72	0.0	1.4	4.2	8.3	4.2	0.0	5.6	76.4
55~60 岁 Age	43	2.3	0.0	2.3	2.3	4.7	0.0	2.3	86.0
女性 Female	532	0.4	2.8	9.2	14.7	7.9	4.5	10.3	50.2
16~24 岁 Age	111	0.0	5.4	18.0	18.0	11.7	4.5	9.9	32.4
25~34 岁 Age	158	0.6	1.9	9.5	14.6	7.6	3.8	12.0	50.0
35~44 岁 Age	137	0.0	0.7	5.8	14.6	7.3	6.6	10.2	54.7
45~54 岁 Age	85	1.2	3.5	5.9	12.9	8.2	4.7	11.8	51.8
55~60 岁 Age	41	0.0	4.9	2.4	9.8	0.0	0.0	2.4	80.5

5-7 样本、男性各年龄层、女性各年龄层的品牌习惯/ Brand Habit in Consuming Chocolate by the Whole Sample, Age and Gender Groups

	人数 Number	基本固定食用一个牌子 used in only one brand	比较固定地食用两个或三个牌子 used in two or three brands	基本上不太固定牌子 no brand preference
样本 Sample	446	24.2	39.7	36.1
男性 Male	181	28.7	37.6	33.7
16~24 岁 Age	51	31.4	41.2	27.5
25~34 岁 Age	64	26.6	40.6	32.8
35~44 岁 Age	43	32.6	27.9	39.5
45~54 岁 Age	17	17.6	29.4	52.9
55~60 岁 Age	6	33.3	66.7	0.0
女性 Female	265	21.1	41.1	37.7
16~24 岁 Age	75	20.0	52.0	28.0
25~34 岁 Age	79	19.0	45.6	35.4
35~44 岁 Age	62	29.0	30.6	40.3
45~54 岁 Age	41	19.5	31.7	48.8
55~60 岁 Age	8	0.0	25.0	75.0

5-8 选择该类商品的考虑因素/ Ranking of the Considerations in Purchasing

注：本题为多选题，合计百分比超过 100%(Multiple answers）

排名 Ranking	考虑因素 Considerations	人次 Person-time	百分比 Percent
1	口味好 pleasant taste	296	66.4
2	有名的牌子 famous brand	168	37.7
3	价格适中 reasonable price	134	30.0
4	生产日期 date of producing	76	17.0
5	购买方便 easy to buy	65	14.6
6	包装吸引人 appealing package	41	9.2
7	广告影响 influence of advertising	33	7.4
8	只是由于习惯 out of habit	29	6.5
9	朋友推荐 introduction of friends	26	5.8
10	有优惠条件 with preferential terms	22	4.9
11	售货员介绍 introduced by the shop assistants	6	1.3
12	其它 others	3	0.7

n=446

5-9 样本、男性各年龄层、女性各年龄层最常食用的种类/ Kinds of the Consumed Chocolate by the Whole Sample, Age and Gender Groups

注：本题为多选题，合计百分比超过 100%(Multiple answers）

	人数 Number	原味巧克力 original chocolate	黑巧克力 black chocolate	白巧克力 white chocolate	牛奶巧克力 white chocolate	果仁巧克力 kemel chocolate	薄荷巧克力 mint chocolate	果味巧克力 fruit-flavored chocolate	威化巧克力 chocolate wafers	巧克力豆 chocolate beans	酒心巧克力 whiskey heart chocolate	其它 others
样本 Sample	444	38.1	14.0	5.2	32.7	28.2	1.1	4.1	11.7	4.1	4.3	0.7
男性 Male	180	36.7	13.3	5.0	36.1	28.3	0.6	3.3	8.3	5.6	3.9	0.0
16~24 岁 Age	51	41.2	21.6	5.9	29.4	17.6	2.0	0.0	7.8	3.9	5.9	0.0
25~34 岁 Age	64	35.9	9.4	3.1	42.2	31.3	0.0	6.3	7.8	6.3	3.1	0.0
35~44 岁 Age	42	42.9	7.1	2.4	35.7	35.7	0.0	4.8	9.5	4.8	0.0	0.0
45~54 岁 Age	17	17.6	17.6	17.6	35.3	17.6	0.0	0.0	11.8	11.8	5.9	0.0
55~60 岁 Age	6	16.7	16.7	0.0	33.3	66.7	0.0	0.0	0.0	0.0	16.7	0.0
女性 Female	264	39.0	14.4	5.3	30.3	28.0	1.5	4.5	14.0	3.0	4.5	1.1
16~24 岁 Age	75	45.3	17.3	9.3	29.3	20.0	2.7	4.0	17.3	2.7	6.7	0.0
25~34 岁 Age	78	32.1	15.4	5.1	28.2	35.9	1.3	3.8	10.3	2.6	2.6	0.0
35~44 岁 Age	62	40.3	12.9	1.6	27.4	29.0	0.0	8.1	19.4	1.6	3.2	3.2
45~54 岁 Age	41	36.6	9.8	4.9	43.9	24.4	2.4	2.4	7.3	7.3	7.3	2.4
55~60 岁 Age	8	50.0	12.5	0.0	12.5	37.5	0.0	0.0	12.5	0.0	0.0	0.0

5-10 样本、男性各年龄层、女性各年龄层最常食用场合/ Settings of Consumption by the Whole Sample, Age and Gender Groups

注：本题为多选题，合计百分比超过 100%(Multiple answers）

	人数 Number	平时做零食吃 when free	加班时 when work overtime	招待客人 serve guests	肚子饿时 when hungry	补充营养 supplementing nutrition	郊游、外出时 outing/ traveling	其它 others
样本 Sample	445	74.4	1.3	9.0	11.2	11.9	22.7	1.1
男性 Male	181	70.7	1.1	8.8	8.8	8.8	25.4	1.7
16~24 岁 Age	51	84.3	0.0	5.9	5.9	2.0	25.5	0.0
25~34 岁 Age	64	64.1	1.6	9.4	9.4	10.9	28.1	3.1
35~44 岁 Age	43	69.8	0.0	11.6	11.6	9.3	18.6	2.3
45~54 岁 Age	17	58.8	5.9	11.8	5.9	23.5	23.5	0.0
55~60 岁 Age	6	66.7	0.0	0.0	16.7	0.0	50.0	0.0
女性 Female	264	76.9	1.5	9.1	12.9	14.0	20.8	0.8
16~24 岁 Age	74	74.3	1.4	6.8	12.2	16.2	25.7	0.0
25~34 岁 Age	79	83.5	2.5	12.7	11.4	10.1	22.8	0.0
35~44 岁 Age	62	74.2	1.6	6.5	17.7	14.5	14.5	3.2
45~54 岁 Age	41	78.0	0.0	7.3	7.3	19.5	22.0	0.0
55~60 岁 Age	8	50.0	0.0	25.0	25.0	0.0	0.0	0.0

5-11 重度消费者人口分布/ Demographics of the Heavy Consumers

	人数 Number	16-24 岁 Age	25-34 岁 Age	35-44 岁 Age	45-54 岁 Age	55-60 岁 Age
样本 Sample	102	37.3	28.4	16.7	12.7	4.9
男性 Male	36	33.3	27.8	22.2	11.1	5.6
天天吃 daily	3	33.3	33.3	0.0	0.0	33.3
一周 3 次或以上 3 times or over a week	6	0.0	66.7	16.7	16.7	0.0
一周 1~2 次 once or twice a week	27	40.7	18.5	25.9	11.1	3.7
女性 Female	66	39.4	28.8	13.6	13.6	4.5
天天吃 daily	2	0.0	50.0	0.0	50.0	0.0
一周 3 次或以上 3 times or over a week	15	40.0	20.0	6.7	20.0	13.3
一周 1~2 次 once or twice a week	49	40.8	30.6	16.3	10.2	2.0

5-12 不同消费者层的常用品牌/ The Most Frequently Used Brands by Market Segments

5-12-1 时尚流行指标/ Fads Popular Index

	人数 Number	第一品牌及百分比 1st/ percent	第二品牌及百分比 2nd/ percent	第三品牌及百分比 3rd/ percent	第四品牌及百分比 4th/ percent
样本 Sample	440	**德芙 Dove(39.1)**	**金莎 Ferrero Rocher(15.0)**	**吉百利 Cadbury(7.5)**	**玛氏 M&M's(6.1)**
平实生活指向 simple living orientation	178	德芙 Dove(36.5)	金莎 Ferrero Rocher(16.3)	吉百利 Cadbury(6.2)	雀巢 Nestle(4.5)
时尚流行指向 fashion orientation	262	德芙 Dove(40.8)	金莎 Ferrero Rocher(14.1)	吉百利 Cadbury(8.4)	玛氏 M&M's(7.6)

5-12-2 广告态度指标/ Advertising Attitude Index

	人数 Number	第一品牌及百分比 1st/ percent	第二品牌及百分比 2nd/ percent	第三品牌及百分比 3rd/ percent	第四品牌及百分比 4th/ percent
样本 Sample	436	**德芙 Dove(38.8)**	**金莎 Ferrero Rocher(15.1)**	**吉百利 Cadbury(7.6)**	**玛氏 M&M's(6.2)**
广告淡漠指向 indifferent orientation	130	德芙 Dove(36.9)	金莎 Ferrero Rocher(17.7)	吉百利 Cadbury(5.4)	玛氏 M&M's(3.8) 雀巢 Nestle(3.8)
中间层 medium	257	德芙 Dove(39.3)	金莎 Ferrero Rocher(13.6)	吉百利 Cadbury(8.9)	玛氏 M&M's(8.2)
信赖广告指向 loyal orientation	49	德芙 Dove(40.8)	金莎 Ferrero Rocher(16.3)	吉百利 Cadbury(6.1)	雀巢 Nestle(4.1)

5-12-3 饮食健康指标/ Foods & Drink Quality Index

	人数 Number	第一品牌及百分比 1st/ percent	第二品牌及百分比 2nd/ percent	第三品牌及百分比 3rd/ percent	第四品牌及百分比 4th/ percent
样本 Sample	441	**德芙 Dove(39.0)**	**金莎 Ferrero Rocher(15.0)**	**吉百利 Cadbury(7.5)**	**玛氏 M&M's(6.1)**
饮食"温饱"指向 "basic" orientation	106	德芙 Dove(42.5)	金莎 Ferrero Rocher(12.3)	吉百利 Cadbury(5.7)	玛氏 M&M's(4.7) 麦丽素 My Likes(4.7)
中间层 medium	241	德芙 Dove(35.3)	金莎 Ferrero Rocher(15.8)	吉百利 Cadbury(8.7)	玛氏 M&M's(7.9)
健康营养指向 health & nutrition orientation	94	德芙 Dove(44.7)	金莎 Ferrero Rocher(16.0)	吉百利 Cadbury(6.4)	丰收 Fengshou(3.2) 雀巢 Nestle(3.2) 玛氏 M&M's(3.2)

5-13 重度消费者的消费者层构成/ The Composition of the Heavy Consumers

5-13-1 时尚流行指标/ Fads Popular Index

	人数 Number	平实生活指向 simple living orientation	时尚流行指向 fashion orientation
样本 Sample	102	37.3	62.7
天天吃 daily	5	20.0	80.0
一周 3 次或以上 3 times or over a week	21	33.3	66.7
一周 1～2 次 once or twice a week	76	39.5	60.5

5-13-2 广告态度指标/ Advertising Attitude Index

	人数 Number	广告淡漠指向 indifferent orientation	中间层 medium	信赖广告指向 loyal orientation
样本 Sample	102	22.5	64.7	12.7
天天吃 daily	5	20.0	60.0	20.0
一周 3 次或以上 3 times or over a week	21	19.0	61.9	19.0
一周 1～2 次 once or twice a week	76	23.7	65.8	10.5

5-13-3 饮食健康指标/ Foods & Drink Quality Index

	人数 Number	饮食"温饱"指向 "basic" orientation	中间层 medium	健康营养指向 health & nutrition orientation
样本 Sample	102	22.5	52.0	25.5
天天吃 daily	5	20.0	40.0	40.0
一周 3 次或以上 3 times or over a week	21	28.6	28.6	42.9
一周 1～2 次 once or twice a week	76	21.1	59.2	19.7

● 重庆 / Chongqing

5-1 最近三个月食用频率的比例/ Proportion of the Sample Consuming Chocolate in the Last Three Months

	人数 Number	百分比 Percent
天天吃 daily	5	0.8
一周 3 次或以上 3 times or over a week	12	1.9
一周 1～2 次 once or twice a week	43	6.9
一个月 2～3 次 2 or 3 times a month	72	11.6
一个月 1 次 once a month	33	5.3
两个月 1 次 once two months	21	3.4
三个月 1 次或以下 once three months or below	35	5.6
没吃过 never	402	64.5

n=623

5-2 最常用品牌排名/ Ranking of the Most Frequently Used Brands

排名 Brand Ranking	品牌 Brands	人数 Number	百分比 Percent
1	德芙 Dove	72	33.5
2	金帝 Le Conte	45	20.9
3	吉百利 Cadbury	20	9.3
4	黑马 Heima	5	2.3
5	百缘 Baiyuan	4	1.9

n=215

5-3 样本、男性各年龄层、女性各年龄层的常用品牌/ The Most Frequently Used Brands by the Whole Sample, Age and Gender Groups

	人数 Number	第一品牌及百分比 1st/ percent	第二品牌及百分比 2nd/ percent	第三品牌及百分比 3rd/ percent	第四品牌及百分比 4th/ percent
样本 Sample	215	**德芙 Dove(33.5)**	**金帝 Le Conte(20.9)**	**吉百利 Cadbury(9.3)**	**黑马 Heima(2.3)**
男性 Male	94	**德芙 Dove(35.1)**	**金帝 Le Conte(24.5)**	**吉百利 Cadbury(9.6)**	**黑马 Heima(3.2)**
16~24 岁 Age	42	金帝 Le Conte(31.0)	德芙 Dove(28.6)	吉百利 Cadbury(19.0)	黑马 Heima(4.8)
25~34 岁 Age	25	德芙 Dove(44.0)	金帝 Le Conte(28.0)	黑马 Heima(4.0) 吉百利 Cadbury(4.0)	
35~44 岁 Age	11	德芙 Dove(36.4)	好时 Hershey's(9.1)		
45~54 岁 Age	11	德芙 Dove(45.5)	金帝 Le Conte(9.1) 威莎 Vo Chelle(9.1) 金丝猴 Jinsihou(9.1) 雀巢 Nestle(9.1)		
55~60 岁 Age	5	金帝 Le Conte(40.0)	德芙 Dove(20.0) 金伯 Jinbo(20.0)		
女性 Female	121	**德芙 Dove(32.2)**	**金帝 Le Conte(18.2)**	**吉百利 Cadbury(9.1)**	**百缘 Baiyuan (2.5)**
16~24 岁 Age	49	德芙 Dove(44.9)	吉百利 Cadbury(14.3) 金帝 Le Conte(14.3)	百缘 Baiyuan (4.1)	天友 Tianyou(2.0) 怡口莲 Eclair(2.0) 伯爵 Bojue(2.0) 威莎 Vo Chelle(2.0) 黑马 Heima(2.0)
25~34 岁 Age	35	德芙 Dove(28.6)	金帝 Le Conte(25.7)	吉百利 Cadbury(5.7)	黑马 Heima(2.9) 好时 Hershey's(2.9) 百缘 Baiyuan (2.9) 嘉士利 Jiashili(2.9) 凯撒威登 Kaisa Weideng(2.9) 高乐高 Gaolegao(2.9) 完达山 Wandashan(2.9) 可丽 Keli(2.9)
35~44 岁 Age	21	德芙 Dove(19.0) 金帝 Le Conte(19.0)	吉百利 Cadbury(9.5)	天友 Tianyou(4.8) 益民 Yimin(4.8) 蒙坛 Mengtan(4.8) 幸运 100 Luck100(4.8)	
45~54 岁 Age	10	德芙 Dove(30.0)	耀华 Yaohua(20.0)	歌迪诗 Choco Corte's(10.0) 金帝 Le Conte(10.0)	
55~60 岁 Age	6	金帝 Le Conte(16.7) 玉鸡 Jinji(16.7) 希波曼 Xiboman(16.7)			

5-4 理想品牌排名/ Ranking of the Ideal Brands

排名 Brand Ranking	品牌 Brands	人数 Number	百分比 Percent
1	德芙 Dove	129	20.7
2	金帝 Le Conte	93	14.9
3	吉百利 Cadbury	39	6.3
4	黑马 Heima	5	0.8

n=624

5-5 样本、男性各年龄层、女性各年龄层最近三个月有无购买的比例/ Purchasing in the Last Three Months by the Whole Sample, Age and Gender Groups

	人数 Number	买过 yes	没买过 no
样本 Sample	624	38.5	61.5
男性 Male	314	34.4	65.6
16~24 岁 Age	64	64.1	35.9
25~34 岁 Age	93	32.3	67.7
35~44 岁 Age	75	21.3	78.7
45~54 岁 Age	54	27.8	72.2
55~60 岁 Age	28	21.4	78.6
女性 Female	310	42.6	57.4
16~24 岁 Age	64	75.0	25.0
25~34 岁 Age	90	41.1	58.9
35~44 岁 Age	73	38.4	61.6
45~54 岁 Age	60	20.0	80.0
55~60 岁 Age	23	30.4	69.6

5-6 样本、男性各年龄层、女性各年龄层最近三个月的食用频率/ Frequencies of Consuming Chocolate in the Last Three Months by the Whole Sample, Age and Gender Group

	人数 Number	天天吃 daily	一周 3 次或以上 3 times or over a week	一周 1~2 次 once or twice a week	一个月 2~3 次 2 or 3 times a months	一个月 1 次 once a month	两个月 1 次 once two months	三个月 1 次或以下 once three months or below	没吃过 never
样本 Sample	623	0.8	1.9	6.9	11.6	5.3	3.4	5.6	64.5
男性 Male	313	1.0	1.3	6.7	9.6	5.1	1.9	4.8	69.6
16~24 岁 Age	64	1.6	1.6	21.9	25.0	6.3	1.6	7.8	34.4
25~34 岁 Age	93	0.0	1.1	1.1	9.7	7.5	1.1	7.5	72.0
35~44 岁 Age	74	1.4	2.7	4.1	2.7	2.7	1.4	0.0	85.1
45~54 岁 Age	54	1.9	0.0	0.0	5.6	5.6	5.6	1.9	79.6
55~60 岁 Age	28	0.0	0.0	10.7	0.0	0.0	0.0	7.1	82.1
女性 Female	310	0.6	2.6	7.1	13.5	5.5	4.8	6.5	59.4
16~24 岁 Age	64	1.6	9.4	10.9	26.6	7.8	10.9	10.9	21.9
25~34 岁 Age	90	1.1	0.0	8.9	12.2	3.3	6.7	7.8	60.0
35~44 岁 Age	73	0.0	1.4	4.1	12.3	11.0	0.0	2.7	68.5
45~54 岁 Age	60	0.0	1.7	3.3	5.0	0.0	3.3	5.0	81.7
55~60 岁 Age	23	0.0	0.0	8.7	8.7	4.3	0.0	4.3	73.9

5-7 样本、男性各年龄层、女性各年龄层的品牌习惯/ Brand Habit in Consuming Chocolate by the Whole Sample, Age and Gender Groups

	人数 Number	基本固定食用一个牌子 used in only one brand	比较固定地食用两个或三个牌子 used in two or three brands	基本上不太固定牌子 no brand preference
样本 Sample	219	26.0	23.7	50.2
男性 Male	95	23.2	26.3	50.5
16~24 岁 Age	42	19.0	33.3	47.6
25~34 岁 Age	26	34.6	15.4	50.0
35~44 岁 Age	11	9.1	18.2	72.7
45~54 岁 Age	11	9.1	27.3	63.6
55~60 岁 Age	5	60.0	40.0	0.0
女性 Female	124	28.2	21.8	50.0
16~24 岁 Age	49	30.6	30.6	38.8
25~34 岁 Age	36	27.8	19.4	52.8
35~44 岁 Age	22	31.8	9.1	59.1
45~54 岁 Age	11	27.3	18.2	54.5
55~60 岁 Age	6	0.0	16.7	83.3

5-8 选择该类商品的考虑因素/ Ranking of the Considerations in Purchasing

注：本题为多选题，合计百分比超过 100%(Multiple answers）

排名 Ranking	考虑因素 Considerations	人次 Person-time	百分比 Percent
1	口味好 pleasant taste	158	71.8
2	价格适中 reasonable price	73	33.2
3	有名的牌子 famous brand	64	29.1
4	生产日期 date of producing	38	17.3
5	购买方便 easy to buy	30	13.6
6	包装吸引人 appealing package	28	12.7
7	广告影响 influence of advertising	12	5.5
7	只是由于习惯 out of habit	12	5.5
8	朋友推荐 introduction of friends	9	4.1
9	有优惠条件 with preferential terms	8	3.6
10	其它 others	4	1.8
11	售货员介绍 introduced by the shop assistants	1	0.5

n=220

5-9 样本、男性各年龄层、女性各年龄层最常食用的种类/ Kinds of the Consumed Chocolate by the Whole Sample, Age and Gender Groups

注：本题为多选题，合计百分比超过 100%(Multiple answers）

	人数 Number	原味巧克力 origina chocolate	黑巧克力 black chocolate	白巧克力 white chocolate	牛奶巧克力 white chocolate	果仁巧克力 kemel chocolate	薄荷巧克力 mint chocolate	果味巧克力 fruit-flavored chocolate	威化巧克力 chocolate wafers	巧克力豆 chocolate beans	酒心巧克力 whiskey heart chocolate	其它 others
样本 Sample	220	36.8	21.4	1.8	36.8	16.4	2.7	4.5	7.3	5.5	8.6	0.9
男性 Male	95	37.9	22.1	2.1	36.8	14.7	1.1	2.1	8.4	5.3	10.5	1.1
16~24 岁 Age	42	42.9	23.8	2.4	38.1	9.5	2.4	2.4	9.5	7.1	4.8	0.0
25~34 岁 Age	26	38.5	19.2	0.0	38.5	26.9	0.0	0.0	3.8	3.8	7.7	0.0
35~44 岁 Age	11	45.5	27.3	9.1	27.3	9.1	0.0	9.1	0.0	0.0	27.3	0.0
45~54 岁 Age	11	27.3	9.1	0.0	36.4	9.1	0.0	0.0	27.3	9.1	9.1	9.1
55~60 岁 Age	5	0.0	40.0	0.0	40.0	20.0	0.0	0.0	0.0	0.0	40.0	0.0
女性 Female	125	36.0	20.8	1.6	36.8	17.6	4.0	6.4	6.4	5.6	7.2	0.8
16~24 岁 Age	50	38.0	22.0	2.0	36.0	18.0	0.0	6.0	2.0	6.0	4.0	0.0
25~34 岁 Age	36	38.9	27.8	2.8	25.0	22.2	5.6	2.8	11.1	5.6	8.3	0.0
35~44 岁 Age	22	31.8	13.6	0.0	40.9	13.6	9.1	9.1	13.6	0.0	9.1	0.0
45~54 岁 Age	11	36.4	0.0	0.0	72.7	18.2	9.1	9.1	0.0	18.2	9.1	0.0
55~60 岁 Age	6	16.7	33.3	0.0	33.3	0.0	0.0	16.7	0.0	0.0	16.7	16.7

5-10 样本、男性各年龄层、女性各年龄层最常食用场合/ Settings of Consumption by the Whole Sample, Age and Gender Groups

注：本题为多选题，合计百分比超过 100%(Multiple answers）

	人数 Number	平时做零食吃 when free	加班时 when work overtime	招待客人 serve guests	肚子饿时 when hungry	补充营养 supplementing nutrition	郊游、外出时 outing/traveling	其它 others
样本 Sample	220	76.8	2.3	6.4	8.6	14.5	19.1	2.3
男性 Male	95	74.7	4.2	7.4	5.3	13.7	16.8	5.3
16~24 岁 Age	42	78.6	2.4	11.9	4.8	14.3	14.3	2.4
25~34 岁 Age	26	76.9	7.7	0.0	0.0	3.8	26.9	11.5
35~44 岁 Age	11	72.7	0.0	9.1	18.2	18.2	9.1	9.1
45~54 岁 Age	11	63.6	0.0	0.0	0.0	27.3	9.1	0.0
55~60 岁 Age	5	60.0	20.0	20.0	20.0	20.0	20.0	0.0
女性 Female	125	78.4	0.8	5.6	11.2	15.2	20.8	0.0
16~24 岁 Age	50	84.0	0.0	0.0	10.0	12.0	18.0	0.0
25~34 岁 Age	36	75.0	2.8	8.3	8.3	8.3	30.6	0.0
35~44 岁 Age	22	77.3	0.0	0.0	13.6	27.3	22.7	0.0
45~54 岁 Age	11	72.7	0.0	36.4	27.3	18.2	0.0	0.0
55~60 岁 Age	6	66.7	0.0	0.0	0.0	33.3	16.7	0.0

5-11 重度消费者人口分布/ Demographics of the Heavy Consumers

	人数 Number	16-24 岁 Age	25-34 岁 Age	35-44 岁 Age	45-54 岁 Age	55-60 岁 Age
样本 Sample	60	50.0	18.3	16.7	6.7	8.3
男性 Male	28	57.1	7.1	21.4	3.6	10.7
天天吃 daily	3	33.3	0.0	33.3	33.3	0.0
一周 3 次或以上 3 times or over a week	4	25.0	25.0	50.0	0.0	0.0
一周 1~2 次 once or twice a week	21	66.7	4.8	14.3	0.0	14.3
女性 Female	32	43.8	28.1	12.5	9.4	6.3
天天吃 daily	2	50.0	50.0	0.0	0.0	0.0
一周 3 次或以上 3 times or over a week	8	75.0	0.0	12.5	12.5	0.0
一周 1~2 次 once or twice a week	22	31.8	36.4	13.6	9.1	9.1

5-12 不同消费者层的常用品牌/ The Most Frequently Used Brands by Market Segments

5-12-1 时尚流行指标/ Fads Popular Index

	人数 Number	第一品牌及百分比 1st/ percent	第二品牌及百分比 2nd/ percent	第三品牌及百分比 3rd/ percent
样本 Sample	213	**德芙 Dove(33.3)**	**金帝 Le Conte(20.7)**	**吉百利 Cadbury(9.4)**
平实生活指向 simple living orientation	95	德芙 Dove(32.6)	金帝 Le Conte(18.9)	吉百利 Cadbury(5.3)
时尚流行指向 fashion orientation	118	德芙 Dove(33.9)	金帝 Le Conte(22.0)	吉百利 Cadbury(12.7)

5-12-2 广告态度指标/ Advertising Attitude Index

	人数 Number	第一品牌及百分比 1st/ percent	第二品牌及百分比 2nd/ percent	第三品牌及百分比 3rd/ percent
样本 Sample	215	**德芙 Dove(33.5)**	**金帝 Le Conte(20.9)**	**吉百利 Cadbury(9.3)**
广告淡漠指向 indifferent orientation	53	德芙 Dove(32.1)	金帝 Le Conte(17.0)	吉百利 Cadbury(9.4)
中间层 medium	134	德芙 Dove(33.6)	金帝 Le Conte(21.6)	吉百利 Cadbury(9.0)
信赖广告指向 loyal orientation	28	德芙 Dove(35.7)	金帝 Le Conte(25.0)	吉百利 Cadbury(10.7)

5-12-3 饮食健康指标/ Foods & Drink Quality Index

	人数 Number	第一品牌及百分比 1st/percent	第二品牌及百分比 2nd/percent	第三品牌及百分比 3rd/percent
样本 Sample	215	**德芙 Dove(33.5)**	**金帝 Le Conte(20.9)**	**吉百利 Cadbury(9.3)**
饮食“温饱”指向 "basic" orientation	64	德芙 Dove(37.5)	金帝 Le Conte(25.0)	吉百利 Cadbury(6.3)
中间层 medium	104	德芙 Dove(28.8)	金帝 Le Conte(17.3)	吉百利 Cadbury(13.5)
健康营养指向 health & nutrition orientation	47	德芙 Dove(38.3)	金帝 Le Conte(23.4)	百缘 Baiyuan(6.4)

5-13 重度消费者的消费者层构成/ The Composition of the Heavy Consumers

5-13-1 时尚流行指标/ Fads Popular Index

	人数 Number	平实生活指向 simple living orientation	时尚流行指向 fashion orientation
样本 Sample	60	40.0	60.0
天天吃 daily	5	60.0	40.0
一周 3 次或以上 3 times or over a week	12	33.3	66.7
一周 1～2 次 once or twice a week	43	39.5	60.5

5-13-2 广告态度指标/ Advertising Attitude Index

	人数 Number	广告淡漠指向 indifferent orientation	中间层 medium	信赖广告指向 loyal orientation
样本 Sample	60	16.7	70.0	13.3
天天吃 daily	5	0.0	80.0	20.0
一周 3 次或以上 3 times or over a week	12	16.7	66.7	16.7
一周 1～2 次 once or twice a week	43	18.6	69.8	11.6

5-13-3 饮食健康指标/ Foods & Drink Quality Index

	人数 Number	饮食“温饱”指向 "basic" orientation	中间层 medium	健康营养指向 health & nutrition orientation
样本 Sample	60	30.0	45.0	25.0
天天吃 daily	5	20.0	60.0	20.0
一周 3 次或以上 3 times or over a week	12	33.3	33.3	33.3
一周 1～2 次 once or twice a week	43	30.2	46.5	23.3

● 武汉 / Wuhan

5-1 最近三个月食用频率的比例/ Proportion of the Sample Consuming Chocolate in the Last Three Months

	人数 Number	百分比 Percent
天天吃 daily	6	0.9
一周 3 次或以上 3 times or over a week	13	2.0
一周 1～2 次 once or twice a week	31	4.8
一个月 2～3 次 2 or 3 times a month	59	9.2
一个月 1 次 once a month	50	7.8
两个月 1 次 once two months	37	5.8
三个月 1 次或以下 once three months or below	54	8.4
没吃过 never	391	61.0

n=641

5-2 最常用品牌排名/ Ranking of the Most Frequently Used Brands

排名 Brand Ranking	品牌 Brands	人数 Number	百分比 Percent
1	德芙 Dove	142	57.5
2	吉百利 Cadbury	21	8.5
3	金帝 Le Conte	19	7.7
4	雀巢 Nestle	4	1.6
5	好时 Hershey's	3	1.2
5	金丝猴 Jinsihou	3	1.2
6	伊利 Yili	2	0.8

n=247

5-3 样本、男性各年龄层、女性各年龄层的常用品牌/ The Most Frequently Used Brands by the Whole Sample, Age and Gender Groups

	人数 Number	第一品牌及百分比 1st/ percent	第二品牌及百分比 2nd/ percent	第三品牌及百分比 3rd/ percent
样本 Sample	247	**德芙 Dove(57.5)**	**吉百利 Cadbury(8.5)**	**金帝 Le Conte(7.7)**
男性 Male	111	**德芙 Dove(57.7)**	**金帝 Le Conte(5.4)**	**吉百利 Cadbury(4.5)**
16~24 岁 Age	39	德芙 Dove(69.2)	金帝 Le Conte(7.7)	吉百利 Cadbury(5.1) 雀巢 Nestle(5.1)
25~34 岁 Age	37	德芙 Dove(51.4)	吉百利 Cadbury(8.1)	金帝 Le Conte(5.4)
35~44 岁 Age	18	德芙 Dove(55.6)	金帝 Le Conte(5.6) 飞的 Feidi(5.6)	
45~54 岁 Age	11	德芙 Dove(45.5)	迪芙利 Tlvoli(9.1) 黑马 Heima(9.1)	
55~60 岁 Age	6	德芙 Dove(50.0)	好时 Hershey's(16.7) 雀巢 Nestle(16.7)	
女性 Female	136	**德芙 Dove(57.4)**	**吉百利 Cadbury(11.8)**	**金帝 Le Conte(9.6)**
16~24 岁 Age	53	德芙 Dove(58.5)	吉百利 Cadbury(17.0)	金帝 Le Conte(13.2)
25~34 岁 Age	44	德芙 Dove(54.5)	吉百利 Cadbury(15.9)	金帝 Le Conte(11.4)
35~44 岁 Age	19	德芙 Dove(57.9)	缤纷 Binfen(5.3) 金帝 Le Conte(5.3) 伊利 Yili(5.3) 百缘 Baiyuan(5.3) 北京 Beijing(5.3)	
45~54 岁 Age	19	德芙 Dove(63.2)	义利 Yili(5.3) 金币 Jinbi(5.3) 德意 Deyi(5.3)	
55~60 岁 Age	1			

5-4 理想品牌排名/ Ranking of the Ideal Brands

排名 Brand Ranking	品牌 Brands	人数 Number	百分比 Percent
1	德芙 Dove	224	34.9
2	金帝 Le Conte	37	5.8
3	吉百利 Cadbury	20	3.1
4	金丝猴 Jinsihou	5	0.8
4	雀巢 Nestle	5	0.8
5	好时 Hershey's	4	0.6
6	高飞 Gufy	3	0.5
6	玛氏 M&M's	3	0.5
7	北京 Beijing	2	0.3

n=641

5-5 样本、男性各年龄层、女性各年龄层最近三个月有无购买的比例/ Purchasing in the Last Three Months by the Whole Sample, Age and Gender Groups

	人数 Number	买过 yes	没买过 no
样本 Sample	642	37.9	62.1
男性 Male	311	33.4	66.6
16~24 岁 Age	65	53.8	46.2
25~34 岁 Age	89	36.0	64.0
35~44 岁 Age	80	25.0	75.0
45~54 岁 Age	52	21.2	78.8
55~60 岁 Age	25	24.0	76.0
女性 Female	331	42.0	58.0
16~24 岁 Age	69	69.6	30.4
25~34 岁 Age	96	52.1	47.9
35~44 岁 Age	78	28.2	71.8
45~54 岁 Age	62	29.0	71.0
55~60 岁 Age	26	3.8	96.2

5-6 样本、男性各年龄层、女性各年龄层最近三个月的食用频率/ Frequencies of Consuming Chocolate in the Last Three Months by the Whole Sample, Age and Gender Group

	人数 Number	天天吃 daily	一周 3 次或以上 3 times or over a week	一周 1~2 次 once or twice a week	一个月 2~3 次 2 or 3 times a months	一个月 1 次 once a month	两个月 1 次 once two months	三个月 1 次或以下 once three months or below	没吃过 never
样本 Sample	641	0.9	2.0	4.8	9.2	7.8	5.8	8.4	61.0
男性 Male	310	1.0	1.9	4.2	7.1	7.1	6.8	8.4	63.5
16~24 岁 Age	65	3.1	1.5	6.2	5.4	13.8	13.8	6.2	40.0
25~34 岁 Age	89	0.0	3.4	3.4	7.9	9.0	3.4	14.6	58.4
35~44 岁 Age	80	0.0	0.0	3.8	2.5	1.3	8.8	6.3	77.5
45~54 岁 Age	51	2.0	3.9	3.9	3.9	3.9	2.0	3.9	76.5
55~60 岁 Age	25	0.0	0.0	4.0	4.0	8.0	4.0	8.0	72.0
女性 Female	331	0.9	2.1	5.4	11.2	8.5	4.8	8.5	58.6
16~24 岁 Age	69	2.9	5.8	14.5	23.2	11.6	7.2	11.6	23.2
25~34 岁 Age	96	1.0	3.1	4.2	11.5	11.5	6.3	8.3	54.2
35~44 岁 Age	78	0.0	0.0	0.0	9.0	5.1	2.6	9.0	74.4
45~54 岁 Age	62	0.0	0.0	6.5	4.8	6.5	4.8	8.1	69.4
55~60 岁 Age	26	0.0	0.0	0.0	0.0	3.8	0.0	0.0	96.2

5-7 样本、男性各年龄层、女性各年龄层的品牌习惯/ Brand Habit in Consuming Chocolate by the Whole Sample, Age and Gender Groups

	人数 Number	基本固定食用一个牌子 used in only one brand	比较固定地食用两个或三个牌子 used in two or three brands	基本上不太固定牌子 no brand preference
样本 Sample	250	39.2	32.4	28.4
男性 Male	113	35.4	25.7	38.9
16~24 岁 Age	39	35.9	30.8	33.3
25~34 岁 Age	37	40.5	27.0	32.4
35~44 岁 Age	18	44.4	11.1	44.4
45~54 岁 Age	12	0.0	33.3	66.7
55~60 岁 Age	7	42.9	14.3	42.9
女性 Female	137	42.3	38.0	19.7
16~24 岁 Age	53	39.6	47.2	13.2
25~34 岁 Age	44	52.3	31.8	15.9
35~44 岁 Age	20	30.0	40.0	30.0
45~54 岁 Age	19	36.8	26.3	36.8
55~60 岁 Age	1	100.0	0.0	0.0

5-8 选择该类商品的考虑因素/ Ranking of the Considerations in Purchasing

注：本题为多选题，合计百分比超过 100%(Multiple answers)

排名 Ranking	考虑因素 Considerations	人次 Person-time	百分比 Percent
1	口味好 pleasant taste	192	76.8
2	有名的牌子 famous brand	106	42.4
3	生产日期 date of producing	62	24.8
4	价格适中 reasonable price	57	22.8
5	购买方便 easy to buy	25	10.0
6	包装吸引人 appealing package	21	8.4
6	广告影响 influence of advertising	21	8.4
7	只是由于习惯 out of habit	14	5.6
8	朋友推荐 introduction of friends	11	4.4
9	有优惠条件 with preferential terms	7	2.8
10	其它 others	6	2.4
11	售货员介绍 introduced by the shop assistants	3	1.2

n=250

5-9 样本、男性各年龄层、女性各年龄层最常食用的种类/ Kinds of the Consumed Chocolate by the Whole Sample, Age and Gender Groups

注：本题为多选题，合计百分比超过 100%(Multiple answers)

	人数 Number	原味巧克力 original-chocolate	黑巧克力 black chocolate	白巧克力 white chocolate	牛奶巧克力 white chocolate	果仁巧克力 kemel chocolate	薄荷巧克力 mint chocolate	果味巧克力 fruit-flavored chocolate	威化巧克力 chocolate wafers	巧克力豆 chocolate beans	酒心巧克力 whiskey heart chocolate	其它 others
样本 Sample	**250**	**49.2**	**30.0**	**2.0**	**28.8**	**12.0**	**1.6**	**2.4**	**4.4**	**2.4**	**3.6**	**0.8**
男性 Male	**113**	**50.4**	**26.5**	**0.9**	**30.1**	**8.8**	**0.9**	**1.8**	**6.2**	**0.9**	**4.4**	**0.9**
16~24 岁 Age	39	48.7	35.9	2.6	33.3	5.1	0.0	2.6	7.7	0.0	0.0	0.0
25~34 岁 Age	37	51.4	21.6	0.0	35.1	8.1	0.0	2.7	8.1	2.7	8.1	0.0
35~44 岁 Age	18	50.0	16.7	0.0	22.2	0.0	5.6	0.0	5.6	0.0	5.6	5.6
45~54 岁 Age	12	58.3	33.3	0.0	16.7	33.3	0.0	0.0	0.0	0.0	0.0	0.0
55~60 岁 Age	7	42.9	14.3	0.0	28.6	14.3	0.0	0.0	0.0	0.0	14.3	0.0
女性 Female	**137**	**48.2**	**32.8**	**2.9**	**27.7**	**14.6**	**2.2**	**2.9**	**2.9**	**3.6**	**2.9**	**0.7**
16~24 岁 Age	53	45.3	37.7	5.7	37.7	13.2	5.7	1.9	0.0	3.8	0.0	1.9
25~34 岁 Age	44	56.8	20.5	0.0	20.5	20.5	0.0	2.3	0.0	6.8	2.3	0.0
35~44 岁 Age	20	60.0	35.0	5.0	5.0	10.0	0.0	5.0	10.0	0.0	0.0	0.0
45~54 岁 Age	19	21.1	47.4	0.0	42.1	10.5	0.0	5.3	10.5	0.0	15.8	0.0
55~60 岁 Age	1	100.0	0.0	0.0	0.0	0.0	0.0	0.0	0.0	0.0	0.0	0.0

5-10 样本、男性各年龄层、女性各年龄层最常食用场合/ Settings of Consumption by the Whole Sample, Age and Gender Groups

注：本题为多选题，合计百分比超过 100%(Multiple answers)

	人数 Number	平时做零食吃 when free	加班时 when work overtime	招待客人 serve guests	肚子饿时 when hungry	补充营养 supplementing nutrition	郊游、外出时 outing/traveling	其它 others
样本 Sample	**247**	**69.6**	**0.4**	**8.1**	**7.7**	**14.6**	**25.5**	**2.8**
男性 Male	**111**	**64.0**	**0.0**	**4.5**	**8.1**	**16.2**	**27.9**	**4.5**
16~24 岁 Age	39	69.2	0.0	5.1	7.7	7.7	38.5	2.6
25~34 岁 Age	35	60.0	0.0	5.7	5.7	20.0	25.7	5.7
35~44 岁 Age	18	61.1	0.0	5.6	16.7	11.1	22.2	0.0
45~54 岁 Age	12	41.7	0.0	0.0	8.3	33.3	16.7	16.7
55~60 岁 Age	7	100.0	0.0	0.0	0.0	28.6	14.3	0.0
女性 Female	**136**	**74.3**	**0.7**	**11.0**	**7.4**	**13.2**	**23.5**	**1.5**
16~24 岁 Age	53	77.4	0.0	3.8	9.4	15.1	28.3	0.0
25~34 岁 Age	44	79.5	2.3	13.6	4.5	9.1	15.9	0.0
35~44 岁 Age	20	70.0	0.0	5.0	5.0	10.0	20.0	10.0
45~54 岁 Age	18	55.6	0.0	33.3	11.1	22.2	27.8	0.0
55~60 岁 Age	1	100.0	0.0	0.0	0.0	0.0	100.0	0.0

5-11 重度消费者人口分布/ Demographics of the Heavy Consumers

	人数 Number	16-24 岁 Age	25-34 岁 Age	35-44 岁 Age	45-54 岁 Age	55-60 岁 Age
样本 Sample	50	46.0	28.0	6.0	18.0	2.0
男性 Male	22	31.8	27.3	13.6	22.7	4.5
天天吃 daily	3	66.7	0.0	0.0	33.3	0.0
一周 3 次或以上 3 times or over a week	6	16.7	50.0	0.0	33.3	0.0
一周 1~2 次 once or twice a week	13	30.8	23.1	23.1	15.4	7.7
女性 Female	28	57.1	28.6	0.0	14.3	0.0
天天吃 daily	3	66.7	33.3	0.0	0.0	0.0
一周 3 次或以上 3 times or over a week	7	57.1	42.9	0.0	0.0	0.0
一周 1~2 次 once or twice a week	18	55.6	22.2	0.0	22.2	0.0

5-12 不同消费者层的常用品牌/ The Most Frequently Used Brands by Market Segments

5-12-1 时尚流行指标/ Fads Popular Index

	人数 Number	第一品牌及百分比 1st/ percent	第二品牌及百分比 2nd/ percent	第三品牌及百分比 3rd/ percent
样本 Sample	242	**德芙 Dove(57.0)**	**吉百利 Cadbury(8.7)**	**金帝 Le Conte(7.4)**
平实生活指向 simple living orientation	113	德芙 Dove(54.9)	吉百利 Cadbury(8.0)	金帝 Le Conte(5.3)
时尚流行指向 fashion orientation	129	德芙 Dove(58.9)	吉百利 Cadbury(9.3) 金帝 Le Conte(9.3)	好时 Hershey's(1.6)

5-12-2 广告态度指标/ Advertising Attitude Index

	人数 Number	第一品牌及百分比 1st/ percent	第二品牌及百分比 2nd/ percent	第三品牌及百分比 3rd/ percent
样本 Sample	243	**德芙 Dove(57.2)**	**吉百利 Cadbury(8.6)**	**金帝 Le Conte(7.4)**
广告淡漠指向 indifferent orientation	58	德芙 Dove(58.6)	吉百利 Cadbury(5.2) 金帝 Le Conte(5.2)	伊利 Yili(3.4)
中间层 medium	152	德芙 Dove(57.9)	吉百利 Cadbury(9.9)	金帝 Le Conte(7.9)
信赖广告指向 loyal orientation	33	德芙 Dove(51.5)	吉百利 Cadbury(9.1) 金帝 Le Conte(9.1)	迪芙利 Tlvoli(3.0) 好时 Hershey's(3.0) 玛氏 M&M's(3.0) 雀巢 Nestle(3.0) 德意 Deyi(3.0)

5-12-3 饮食健康指标/ Foods & Drink Quality Index

	人数 Number	第一品牌及百分比 1st/ percent	第二品牌及百分比 2nd/ percent	第三品牌及百分比 3rd/ percent
样本 Sample	242	**德芙 Dove(57.0)**	**吉百利 Cadbury(8.7)**	**金帝 Le Conte(7.4)**
饮食"温饱"指向 "basic" orientation	69	德芙 Dove(71.0)	吉百利 Cadbury(4.3) 金帝 Le Conte(4.3)	黑马 Heima(1.4) 玛氏 M&M's(1.4) 金丝猴 Jinsihou(1.4)
中间层 medium	114	德芙 Dove(50.9)	吉百利 Cadbury(10.5) 金帝 Le Conte(10.5)	雀巢 Nestle(3.5)
健康营养指向 health & nutrition orientation	59	德芙 Dove(52.5)	吉百利 Cadbury(10.2)	金帝 Le Conte(5.1)

5-13 重度消费者的消费者层构成/ The Composition of the Heavy Consumers

5-13-1 时尚流行指标/ Fads Popular Index

	人数 Number	平实生活指向 simple living orientation	时尚流行指向 fashion orientation
样本 Sample	49	42.9	57.1
天天吃 daily	6	50.0	50.0
一周 3 次或以上 3 times or over a week	12	50.0	50.0
一周 1～2 次 once or twice a week	31	38.7	61.3

5-13-2 广告态度指标/ Advertising Attitude Index

	人数 Number	广告淡漠指向 indifferent orientation	中间层 medium	信赖广告指向 loyal orientation
样本 Sample	49	20.4	65.3	14.3
天天吃 daily	6	16.7	83.3	0.0
一周 3 次或以上 3 times or over a week	12	16.7	75.0	8.3
一周 1～2 次 once or twice a week	31	22.6	58.1	19.4

5-13-3 饮食健康指标/ Foods & Drink Quality Index

	人数 Number	饮食"温饱"指向 "basic" orientation	中间层 medium	健康营养指向 health & nutrition orientation
样本 Sample	49	28.6	38.8	32.7
天天吃 daily	6	50.0	16.7	33.3
一周 3 次或以上 3 times or over a week	12	50.0	41.7	8.3
一周 1～2 次 once or twice a week	31	16.1	41.9	41.9

● 西安 / Xi'an

5-1 最近三个月食用频率的比例/ Proportion of the Sample Consuming Chocolate in the Last Three Months

	人数 Number	百分比 Percent
天天吃 daily	9	1.5
一周 3 次或以上 3 times or over a week	16	2.7
一周 1～2 次 once or twice a week	52	8.7
一个月 2～3 次 2 or 3 times a month	72	12.0
一个月 1 次 once a month	53	8.8
两个月 1 次 once two months	35	5.8
三个月 1 次或以下 once three months or below	43	7.2
没吃过 never	321	53.4

n=601

5-2 最常用品牌排名/ Ranking of the Most Frequently Used Brands

排名 Brand Ranking	品牌 Brands	人数 Number	百分比 Percent
1	金帝 Le Conte	102	36.6
2	德芙 Dove	93	33.3
3	吉百利 Cadbury	19	6.8
4	金丝猴 Jinsihou	3	1.1
4	金莎 Ferrero Rocher	3	1.1

n=279

5-3 样本、男性各年龄层、女性各年龄层的常用品牌/ The Most Frequently Used Brands by the Whole Sample, Age and Gender Groups

	人数 Number	第一品牌及百分比 1st/ percent	第二品牌及百分比 2nd/ percent	第三品牌及百分比 3rd/ percent
样本 Sample	279	**金帝 Le Conte(36.6)**	**德芙 Dove(33.3)**	**吉百利 Cadbury(6.8)**
男性 Male	125	**金帝 Le Conte(41.6)**	**德芙 Dove(35.2)**	**吉百利 Cadbury(4.8)**
16~24 岁 Age	40	金帝 Le Conte(47.5)	德芙 Dove(30.0)	吉百利 Cadbury(7.5)
25~34 岁 Age	34	金帝 Le Conte(41.2)	德芙 Dove(32.4)	吉百利 Cadbury(5.9)
35~44 岁 Age	34	德芙 Dove(44.1)	金帝 Le Conte(38.2)	吉百利 Cadbury(2.9) 百缘 Baiyuan(2.9)
45~54 岁 Age	13	德芙 Dove(38.5)	金帝 Le Conte(30.8)	
55~60 岁 Age	4	金帝 Le Conte(50.0)	德芙 Dove(25.0)	
女性 Female	154	**金帝 Le Conte(32.5)**	**德芙 Dove(31.8)**	**吉百利 Cadbury(8.4)**
16~24 岁 Age	42	德芙 Dove(47.6)	金帝 Le Conte(26.2)	吉百利 Cadbury(4.8)
25~34 岁 Age	57	金帝 Le Conte(40.4)	德芙 Dove(33.3)	吉百利 Cadbury(10.5)
35~44 岁 Age	29	金帝 Le Conte(34.5)	德芙 Dove(17.2)	吉百利 Cadbury(6.9) 金丝猴 Jinsihou(6.9)
45~54 岁 Age	14	德芙 Dove(21.4)	金帝 Le Conte(14.3)	高飞 Gufy(7.1) 吉百利 Cadbury(7.1) 威莎 Vo Chelle(7.1) 雀巢 Nestle(7.1)
55~60 岁 Age	12	金帝 Le Conte(33.3)	德芙 Dove(16.7) 吉百利 Cadbury(16.7)	歌迪诗 Choco Corte's(8.3)

5-4 理想品牌排名/ Ranking of the Ideal Brands

排名 Brand Ranking	品牌 Brands	人数 Number	百分比 Percent
1	金帝 Le Conte	212	35.3
2	德芙 Dove	160	26.6
3	吉百利 Cadbury	35	5.8
4	雀巢 Nestle	2	0.3
4	百缘 Baiyuan	2	0.3
4	义利 Yili	2	0.3
4	威莎 Vo Chelle	2	0.3

n=601

5-5 样本、男性各年龄层、女性各年龄层最近三个月有无购买的比例/ Purchasing in the Last Three Months by the Whole Sample, Age and Gender Groups

	人数 Number	买过 yes	没买过 no
样本 Sample	601	48.4	51.6
男性 Male	302	43.7	56.3
16~24 岁 Age	64	59.4	40.6
25~34 岁 Age	91	41.8	58.2
35~44 岁 Age	77	49.4	50.6
45~54 岁 Age	46	30.4	69.6
55~60 岁 Age	24	16.7	83.3
女性 Female	299	53.2	46.8
16~24 岁 Age	61	60.7	39.3
25~34 岁 Age	90	60.0	40.0
35~44 岁 Age	74	44.6	55.4
45~54 岁 Age	49	44.9	55.1
55~60 岁 Age	25	52.0	48.0

5-6 样本、男性各年龄层、女性各年龄层最近三个月的食用频率/ Frequencies of Consuming Chocolate in the Last Three Months by the Whole Sample, Age and Gender Group

	人数 Number	天天吃 daily	一周 3 次或以上 3 times or over a week	一周 1~2 次 once or twice a week	一个月 2~3 次 2 or 3 times a months	一个月 1 次 once a month	两个月 1 次 once two months	三个月 1 次或以下 once three months or below	没吃过 never
样本 Sample	601	1.5	2.7	8.7	12.0	8.8	5.8	7.2	53.4
男性 Male	302	1.0	2.3	8.6	9.9	8.9	5.3	5.3	58.6
16~24 岁 Age	64	1.6	4.7	12.5	21.9	10.9	6.3	4.7	37.5
25~34 岁 Age	91	1.1	1.1	6.6	4.4	11.0	7.7	5.5	62.6
35~44 岁 Age	77	0.0	2.6	11.7	10.4	9.1	2.6	7.8	55.8
45~54 岁 Age	46	2.2	2.2	4.3	6.5	4.3	4.3	4.3	71.7
55~60 岁 Age	24	0.0	0.0	4.2	4.2	4.2	4.2	0.0	83.3
女性 Female	299	2.0	3.0	8.7	14.0	8.7	6.4	9.0	48.2
16~24 岁 Age	61	4.9	8.2	14.8	21.3	8.2	4.9	6.6	31.1
25~34 岁 Age	90	0.0	3.3	13.3	16.7	11.1	11.1	7.8	36.7
35~44 岁 Age	74	0.0	0.0	2.7	9.5	6.8	6.8	13.5	60.8
45~54 岁 Age	49	4.1	2.0	2.0	10.2	4.1	2.0	6.1	69.4
55~60 岁 Age	25	4.0	0.0	8.0	8.0	16.0	0.0	12.0	52.0

5-7 样本、男性各年龄层、女性各年龄层的品牌习惯/ Brand Habit in Consuming Chocolate by the Whole Sample, Age and Gender Groups

	人数 Number	基本固定食用一个牌子 used in only one brand	比较固定地食用两个或三个牌子 used in two or three brands	基本上不太固定牌子 no brand preference
样本 Sample	279	31.2	32.6	36.2
男性 Male	125	31.2	30.4	38.4
16~24 岁 Age	40	30.0	35.0	35.0
25~34 岁 Age	34	29.4	29.4	41.2
35~44 岁 Age	34	41.2	23.5	35.3
45~54 岁 Age	13	15.4	30.8	53.8
55~60 岁 Age	4	25.0	50.0	25.0
女性 Female	154	31.2	34.4	34.4
16~24 岁 Age	42	31.0	40.5	28.6
25~34 岁 Age	57	33.3	33.3	33.3
35~44 岁 Age	29	24.1	41.4	34.5
45~54 岁 Age	14	35.7	21.4	42.9
55~60 岁 Age	12	33.3	16.7	50.0

5-8 选择该类商品的考虑因素/ Ranking of the Considerations in Purchasing

注：本题为多选题，合计百分比超过 100%(Multiple answers)

排名 Ranking	考虑因素 Considerations	人次 Person-time	百分比 Percent
1	口味好 pleasant taste	197	70.6
2	有名的牌子 famous brand	103	36.9
3	价格适中 reasonable price	65	23.3
4	广告影响 influence of advertising	42	15.1
4	生产日期 date of producing	42	15.1
5	购买方便 easy to buy	29	10.4
6	包装吸引人 appealing package	17	6.1
6	朋友推荐 introduction of friends	17	6.1
7	只是由于习惯 out of habit	16	5.7
8	售货员介绍 introduced by the shop assistants	7	2.5
9	有优惠条件 with preferential terms	5	1.8

n=279

5-9 样本、男性各年龄层、女性各年龄层最常食用的种类/ Kinds of the Consumed Chocolate by the Whole Sample, Age and Gender Groups

注：本题为多选题，合计百分比超过 100%(Multiple answers)

	人数 Number	原味巧克力 original chocolate	黑巧克力 black chocolate	白巧克力 white chocolate	牛奶巧克力 white chocolate	果仁巧克力 kernel chocolate	薄荷巧克力 mint chocolate	果味巧克力 fruit-flavored chocolate	威化巧克力 chocolate wafers	巧克力豆 chocolate beans	酒心巧克力 whiskey heart chocolate	其它 others
样本 Sample	279	35.1	25.8	2.9	32.6	21.9	1.8	3.6	5.7	3.6	8.6	0.7
男性 Male	125	32.8	28.0	1.6	28.8	21.6	2.4	4.8	5.6	2.4	8.0	0.8
16~24 岁 Age	40	25.0	35.0	2.5	25.0	17.5	2.5	10.0	5.0	0.0	5.0	2.5
25~34 岁 Age	34	32.4	20.6	0.0	29.4	26.5	2.9	5.9	2.9	0.0	5.9	0.0
35~44 岁 Age	34	50.0	20.6	2.9	29.4	23.5	2.9	0.0	8.8	8.8	11.8	0.0
45~54 岁 Age	13	23.1	30.8	0.0	38.5	23.1	0.0	0.0	7.7	0.0	7.7	0.0
55~60 岁 Age	4	0.0	75.0	0.0	25.0	0.0	0.0	0.0	0.0	0.0	25.0	0.0
女性 Female	154	37.0	24.0	3.9	35.7	22.1	1.3	2.6	5.8	4.5	9.1	0.6
16~24 岁 Age	42	40.5	38.1	2.4	38.1	21.4	2.4	4.8	0.0	0.0	2.4	0.0
25~34 岁 Age	57	45.6	17.5	0.0	33.3	22.8	1.8	0.0	7.0	3.5	7.0	0.0
35~44 岁 Age	29	24.1	20.7	10.3	31.0	31.0	0.0	3.4	3.4	10.3	20.7	0.0
45~54 岁 Age	14	28.6	14.3	7.1	21.4	21.4	0.0	0.0	21.4	7.1	7.1	7.1
55~60 岁 Age	12	25.0	25.0	8.3	66.7	0.0	0.0	8.3	8.3	8.3	16.7	0.0

5-10 样本、男性各年龄层、女性各年龄层最常食用场合/ Settings of Consumption by the Whole Sample, Age and Gender Groups

注：本题为多选题，合计百分比超过 100%(Multiple answers）

	人数 Number	平时做零食吃 when free	加班时 when work overtime	招待客人 serve guests	肚子饿时 when hungry	补充营养 supplementing nutrition	郊游、外出时 outing/ traveling	其它 others
样本 Sample	279	74.2	3.2	8.2	4.7	15.8	22.9	0.4
男性 Male	125	71.2	2.4	8.8	2.4	20.0	20.0	0.0
16~24 岁 Age	40	80.0	5.0	5.0	0.0	15.0	10.0	0.0
25~34 岁 Age	34	67.6	0.0	8.8	2.9	23.5	20.6	0.0
35~44 岁 Age	34	64.7	2.9	2.9	2.9	20.6	32.4	0.0
45~54 岁 Age	13	69.2	0.0	30.8	7.7	23.1	7.7	0.0
55~60 岁 Age	4	75.0	0.0	25.0	0.0	25.0	50.0	0.0
女性 Female	154	76.6	3.9	7.8	6.5	12.3	25.3	0.6
16~24 岁 Age	42	83.3	2.4	4.8	7.1	7.1	16.7	0.0
25~34 岁 Age	57	77.2	5.3	7.0	1.8	15.8	26.3	0.0
35~44 岁 Age	29	65.5	6.9	6.9	6.9	13.8	37.9	0.0
45~54 岁 Age	14	85.7	0.0	0.0	7.1	7.1	28.6	7.1
55~60 岁 Age	12	66.7	0.0	33.3	25.0	16.7	16.7	0.0

5-11 重度消费者人口分布/ Demographics of the Heavy Consumers

	人数 Number	16-24 岁 Age	25-34 岁 Age	35-44 岁 Age	45-54 岁 Age	55-60 岁 Age
样本 Sample	77	37.7	29.9	16.9	10.4	5.2
男性 Male	36	33.3	22.2	30.6	11.1	2.8
天天吃 daily	3	33.3	33.3	0.0	33.3	0.0
一周 3 次或以上 3 times or over a week	7	42.9	14.3	28.6	14.3	0.0
一周 1~2 次 once or twice a week	26	30.8	23.1	34.6	7.7	3.8
女性 Female	41	41.5	36.6	4.9	9.8	7.3
天天吃 daily	6	50.0	0.0	0.0	33.3	16.7
一周 3 次或以上 3 times or over a week	9	55.6	33.3	0.0	11.1	0.0
一周 1~2 次 once or twice a week	26	34.6	46.2	7.7	3.8	7.7

5-12 不同消费者层的常用品牌/ The Most Frequently Used Brands by Market Segments

5-12-1 时尚流行指标/ Fads Popular Index

	人数 Number	第一品牌及百分比 1st/ percent	第二品牌及百分比 2nd/ percent	第三品牌及百分比 3rd/ percent
样本 Sample	278	**金帝 Le Conte(36.7)**	**德芙 Dove(33.5)**	**吉百利 Cadbury(6.8)**
平实生活指向 simple living orientation	129	金帝 Le Conte(41.1)	德芙 Dove(24.8)	吉百利 Cadbury(4.7)
时尚流行指向 fashion orientation	149	德芙 Dove(40.9)	金帝 Le Conte(32.9)	吉百利 Cadbury(8.7)

5-12-2 广告态度指标/ Advertising Attitude Index

	人数 Number	第一品牌及百分比 1st/ percent	第二品牌及百分比 2nd/ percent	第三品牌及百分比 3rd/ percent
样本 Sample	278	**金帝 Le Conte(36.7)**	**德芙 Dove(33.5)**	**吉百利 Cadbury(6.8)**
广告淡漠指向 indifferent orientation	88	金帝 Le Conte(46.6)	德芙 Dove(27.3)	金丝猴 Jinsihou(2.3)
中间层 medium	155	德芙 Dove(36.1)	金帝 Le Conte(31.6)	吉百利 Cadbury(9.0)
信赖广告指向 loyal orientation	35	德芙 Dove(37.1)	金帝 Le Conte(34.3)	吉百利 Cadbury(14.3)

5-12-3 饮食健康指标/ Foods & Drink Quality Index

	人数 Number	第一品牌及百分比 1st/ percent	第二品牌及百分比 2nd/ percent	第三品牌及百分比 3rd/ percent
样本 Sample	**279**	**金帝 Le Conte(36.6)**	**德芙 Dove(33.3)**	**吉百利 Cadbury(6.8)**
饮食“温饱”指向 "basic" orientation	85	金帝 Le Conte(37.6)	德芙 Dove(31.8)	吉百利 Cadbury(3.5)
中间层 medium	145	金帝 Le Conte(36.6)	德芙 Dove(33.8)	吉百利 Cadbury(9.0)
健康营养指向 health & nutrition orientation	49	德芙 Dove(34.7) 金帝 Le Conte(34.7)	吉百利 Cadbury(6.1)	高飞 Gufy(2.0) 金莎 Ferrero Rocher(2.0) 金丝猴 Jinsihou(2.0) 金鹰 Jinying(2.0)

5-13 重度消费者的消费者层构成/ The Composition of the Heavy Consumers

5-13-1 时尚流行指标/ Fads Popular Index

	人数 Number	平实生活指向 simple living orientation	时尚流行指向 fashion orientation
样本 Sample	**77**	**37.7**	**62.3**
天天吃 daily	9	22.2	77.8
一周 3 次或以上 3 times or over a week	16	31.3	68.8
一周 1～2 次 once or twice a week	52	42.3	57.7

5-13-2 广告态度指标/ Advertising Attitude Index

	人数 Number	广告淡漠指向 indifferent orientation	中间层 medium	信赖广告指向 loyal orientation
样本 Sample	**77**	**24.7**	**59.7**	**15.6**
天天吃 daily	9	22.2	55.6	22.2
一周 3 次或以上 3 times or over a week	16	12.5	68.8	18.8
一周 1～2 次 once or twice a week	52	28.8	57.7	13.5

5-13-3 饮食健康指标/ Foods & Drink Quality Index

	人数 Number	饮食“温饱”指向 "basic" orientation	中间层 medium	健康营养指向 health & nutrition orientation
样本 Sample	**77**	**28.6**	**51.9**	**19.5**
天天吃 daily	9	22.2	55.6	22.2
一周 3 次或以上 3 times or over a week	16	37.5	43.8	18.8
一周 1～2 次 once or twice a week	52	26.9	53.8	19.2

● 沈阳 / Shenyang

5-1 最近三个月食用频率的比例/ Proportion of the Sample Consuming Chocolate in the Last Three Months

	人数 Number	百分比 Percent
天天吃 daily	10	1.7
一周 3 次或以上 3 times or over a week	11	1.8
一周 1～2 次 once or twice a week	58	9.7
一个月 2～3 次 2 or 3 times a month	75	12.5
一个月 1 次 once a month	51	8.5
两个月 1 次 once two months	28	4.7
三个月 1 次或以下 once three months or below	38	6.3
没吃过 never	328	54.8

n=599

5-2 最常用品牌排名/ Ranking of the Most Frequently Used Brands

排名 Brand Ranking	品牌 Brands	人数 Number	百分比 Percent
1	德芙 Dove	84	31.2
2	吉百利 Cadbury	67	24.9
3	利华 Lihua	23	8.6
4	金帝 Le Conte	5	1.9
5	黑马 Heima	4	1.5
5	新帝 Xindi	4	1.5

n=269

5-3 样本、男性各年龄层、女性各年龄层的常用品牌/ The Most Frequently Used Brands by the Whole Sample, Age and Gender Groups

	人数 Number	第一品牌及百分比 1st/ percent	第二品牌及百分比 2nd/ percent	第三品牌及百分比 3rd/ percent
样本 Sample	269	**德芙 Dove(31.2)**	**吉百利 Cadbury(24.9)**	**利华 Lihua(8.6)**
男性 Male	115	**德芙 Dove(33.0)**	**吉百利 Cadbury(23.5)**	**利华 Lihua(8.7)**
16~24 岁 Age	43	德芙 Dove(34.9)	吉百利 Cadbury(25.6)	利华 Lihua(11.6)
25~34 岁 Age	45	德芙 Dove(37.8)	吉百利 Cadbury(17.8)	利华 Lihua(8.9)
35~44 岁 Age	15	德芙 Dove(20.0) 吉百利 Cadbury(20.0)	益民 Yimin(6.7) 阿尔卑斯 A'erbeisi(6.7) 新帝 Xindi(6.7) 黑珍珠 Heizhenzhu(6.7)	
45~54 岁 Age	11	吉百利 Cadbury(45.5)	德芙 Dove(27.3)	利华 Lihua(9.1)
55~60 岁 Age	1			
女性 Female	154	**德芙 Dove(29.9)**	**吉百利 Cadbury(26.0)**	**利华 Lihua(8.4)**
16~24 岁 Age	46	德芙 Dove(32.6) 吉百利 Cadbury(32.6)	利华 Lihua(8.7)	黑马 Heima(4.3)
25~34 岁 Age	57	德芙 Dove(33.3)	吉百利 Cadbury(22.8)	利华 Lihua(8.8)
35~44 岁 Age	34	德芙 Dove(23.5)	吉百利 Cadbury(14.7)	利华 Lihua(8.8)
45~54 岁 Age	12	吉百利 Cadbury(41.7)	德芙 Dove(25.0)	天津 Tianjin(8.3)
55~60 岁 Age	5	吉百利 Cadbury(40.0)	德芙 Dove(20.0) 雀巢 Nestle(20.0) 利华 Lihua(20.0)	

5-4 理想品牌排名/ Ranking of the Ideal Brands

排名 Brand Ranking	品牌 Brands	人数 Number	百分比 Percent
1	吉百利 Cadbury	145	24.1
2	德芙 Dove	137	22.8
3	利华 Lihua	14	2.3
4	金帝 Le Conte	9	1.5
5	黑马 Heima	5	0.8
5	利民 Limin	5	0.8
5	雀巢 Nestle	5	0.8
6	益民 Yimin	4	0.7
6	伊利 Yili	4	0.7

n=601

5-5 样本、男性各年龄层、女性各年龄层最近三个月有无购买的比例/ Purchasing in the Last Three Months by the Whole Sample, Age and Gender Groups

	人数 Number	买过 yes	没买过 no
样本 Sample	601	48.1	51.9
男性 Male	299	42.8	57.2
16~24 岁 Age	64	60.9	39.1
25~34 岁 Age	89	53.9	46.1
35~44 岁 Age	76	34.2	65.8
45~54 岁 Age	46	30.4	69.6
55~60 岁 Age	24	4.2	95.8
女性 Female	302	53.3	46.7
16~24 岁 Age	64	67.2	32.8
25~34 岁 Age	90	64.4	35.6
35~44 岁 Age	76	53.9	46.1
45~54 岁 Age	48	29.2	70.8
55~60 岁 Age	24	20.8	79.2

5-6 样本、男性各年龄层、女性各年龄层最近三个月的食用频率/ Frequencies of Consuming Chocolate in the Last Three Months by the Whole Sample, Age and Gender Group

	人数 Number	天天吃 daily	一周3次或以上 3 times or over a week	一周1~2次 once or twice a week	一个月2~3次 2 or 3 times a months	一个月1次 once a month	两个月1次 once two months	三个月1次或以下 once three months or below	没吃过 never
样本 Sample	**599**	**1.7**	**1.8**	**9.7**	**12.5**	**8.5**	**4.7**	**6.3**	**54.8**
男性 Male	**299**	**0.7**	**0.7**	**10.0**	**10.0**	**6.4**	**4.7**	**6.7**	**60.9**
16~24 岁 Age	64	1.6	0.0	17.2	17.2	12.5	6.3	14.1	31.3
25~34 岁 Age	89	0.0	1.1	14.6	14.6	9.0	4.5	6.7	49.4
35~44 岁 Age	76	1.3	1.3	5.3	5.3	0.0	5.3	2.6	78.9
45~54 岁 Age	46	0.0	0.0	4.3	4.3	6.5	4.3	4.3	76.1
55~60 岁 Age	24	0.0	0.0	0.0	0.0	0.0	0.0	4.2	95.8
女性 Female	**300**	**2.7**	**3.0**	**9.3**	**15.0**	**10.7**	**4.7**	**6.0**	**48.7**
16~24 岁 Age	64	6.3	4.7	10.9	20.3	18.8	4.7	6.3	28.1
25~34 岁 Age	90	1.1	4.4	12.2	23.3	4.4	8.9	8.9	36.7
35~44 岁 Age	75	1.3	2.7	6.7	8.0	20.0	1.3	5.3	54.7
45~54 岁 Age	47	2.1	0.0	8.5	8.5	2.1	2.1	2.1	74.5
55~60 岁 Age	24	4.2	0.0	4.2	4.2	0.0	4.2	4.2	79.2

5-7 样本、男性各年龄层、女性各年龄层的品牌习惯/ Brand Habit in Consuming Chocolate by the Whole Sample, Age and Gender Groups

	人数 Number	基本固定食用一个牌子 used in only one brand	比较固定地食用两个或三个牌子 used in two or three brands	基本上不太固定牌子 no brand preference
样本 Sample	**270**	**33.7**	**31.1**	**35.2**
男性 Male	**116**	**36.2**	**26.7**	**37.1**
16~24 岁 Age	44	31.8	31.8	36.4
25~34 岁 Age	45	48.9	20.0	31.1
35~44 岁 Age	15	33.3	20.0	46.7
45~54 岁 Age	11	9.1	45.5	45.5
55~60 岁 Age	1	0.0	0.0	100.0
女性 Female	**154**	**31.8**	**34.4**	**33.8**
16~24 岁 Age	46	37.0	32.6	30.4
25~34 岁 Age	57	29.8	36.8	33.3
35~44 岁 Age	34	23.5	38.2	38.2
45~54 岁 Age	12	50.0	8.3	41.7
55~60 岁 Age	5	20.0	60.0	20.0

5-8 选择该类商品的考虑因素/ Ranking of the Considerations in Purchasing

注：本题为多选题，合计百分比超过 100%(Multiple answers）

排名 Ranking	考虑因素 Considerations	人次 Person-time	百分比 Percent
1	口味好 pleasant taste	211	78.1
2	有名的牌子 famous brand	88	32.6
3	价格适中 reasonable price	84	31.1
4	生产日期 date of producing	55	20.4
5	购买方便 easy to buy	40	14.8
6	只是由于习惯 out of habit	23	8.5
7	包装吸引人 appealing package	21	7.8
8	广告影响 influence of advertising	20	7.4
9	朋友推荐 introduction of friends	17	6.3
10	有优惠条件 with preferential terms	6	2.2
11	售货员介绍 introduced by the shop assistants	4	1.5
12	其它 others	3	1.1

n=270

5-9 样本、男性各年龄层、女性各年龄层最常食用的种类/ Kinds of the Consumed Chocolate by the Whole Sample, Age and Gender Groups

注：本题为多选题，合计百分比超过 100%(Multiple answers）

	人数 Number	原味巧克力 original chocolate	黑巧克力 black chocolate	白巧克力 white chocolate	牛奶巧克力 white chocolate	果仁巧克力 kemel chocolate	薄荷巧克力 mint chocolate	果味巧克力 fruit-flavored chocolate	威化巧克力 chocolate wafers	巧克力豆 chocolate beans	酒心巧克力 whiskey heart chocolate	其它 others
样本 Sample	270	43.7	21.9	2.2	35.2	21.9	1.1	3.3	7.4	4.4	3.7	0.0
男性 Male	116	37.1	23.3	0.9	37.9	22.4	0.0	3.4	6.0	3.4	5.2	0.0
16~24 岁 Age	44	43.2	31.8	2.3	36.4	15.9	0.0	4.5	6.8	4.5	2.3	0.0
25~34 岁 Age	45	42.2	15.6	0.0	35.6	22.2	0.0	2.2	2.2	0.0	2.2	0.0
35~44 岁 Age	15	6.7	13.3	0.0	60.0	40.0	0.0	6.7	13.3	0.0	13.3	0.0
45~54 岁 Age	11	36.4	36.4	0.0	27.3	18.2	0.0	0.0	9.1	18.2	9.1	0.0
55~60 岁 Age	1	0.0	0.0	0.0	0.0	100.0	0.0	0.0	0.0	0.0	100.0	0.0
女性 Female	154	48.7	20.8	3.2	33.1	21.4	1.9	3.2	8.4	5.2	2.6	0.0
16~24 岁 Age	46	54.3	23.9	2.2	34.8	17.4	2.2	2.2	2.2	6.5	2.2	0.0
25~34 岁 Age	57	52.6	14.0	1.8	31.6	21.1	3.5	3.5	14.0	3.5	3.5	0.0
35~44 岁 Age	34	44.1	17.6	8.8	38.2	32.4	0.0	2.9	8.8	2.9	0.0	0.0
45~54 岁 Age	12	25.0	50.0	0.0	25.0	8.3	0.0	8.3	0.0	16.7	0.0	0.0
55~60 岁 Age	5	40.0	20.0	0.0	20.0	20.0	0.0	0.0	20.0	0.0	20.0	0.0

5-10 样本、男性各年龄层、女性各年龄层最常食用场合/ Settings of Consumption by the Whole Sample, Age and Gender Groups

注：本题为多选题，合计百分比超过 100%(Multiple answers）

	人数 Number	平时做零食吃 when free	加班时 when work overtime	招待客人 serve guests	肚子饿时 when hungry	补充营养 supplementing nutrition	郊游、外出时 outing/ traveling	其它 others
样本 Sample	270	73.7	0.4	2.6	11.1	20.7	20.0	0.4
男性 Male	116	77.6	0.0	0.9	11.2	13.8	22.4	0.9
16~24 岁 Age	44	79.5	0.0	0.0	15.9	15.9	27.3	2.3
25~34 岁 Age	45	80.0	0.0	0.0	6.7	8.9	15.6	0.0
35~44 岁 Age	15	66.7	0.0	0.0	6.7	26.7	26.7	0.0
45~54 岁 Age	11	81.8	0.0	9.1	18.2	0.0	18.2	0.0
55~60 岁 Age	1	0.0	0.0	0.0	0.0	100.0	100.0	0.0
女性 Female	154	70.8	0.6	3.9	11.0	26.0	18.2	0.0
16~24 岁 Age	46	78.3	2.2	0.0	17.4	15.2	32.6	0.0
25~34 岁 Age	57	73.7	0.0	5.3	8.8	24.6	7.0	0.0
35~44 岁 Age	34	70.6	0.0	5.9	8.8	29.4	20.6	0.0
45~54 岁 Age	12	50.0	0.0	8.3	8.3	50.0	8.3	0.0
55~60 岁 Age	5	20.0	0.0	0.0	0.0	60.0	20.0	0.0

5-11 重度消费者人口分布/ Demographics of the Heavy Consumers

	人数 Number	16-24 岁 Age	25-34 岁 Age	35-44 岁 Age	45-54 岁 Age	55-60 岁 Age
样本 Sample	79	32.9	38.0	17.7	8.9	2.5
男性 Male	34	35.3	41.2	17.6	5.9	0.0
天天吃 daily	2	50.0	0.0	50.0	0.0	0.0
一周 3 次或以上 3 times or over a week	2	0.0	50.0	50.0	0.0	0.0
一周 1~2 次 once or twice a week	30	36.7	43.3	13.3	6.7	0.0
女性 Female	45	31.1	35.6	17.8	11.1	4.4
天天吃 daily	8	50.0	12.5	12.5	12.5	12.5
一周 3 次或以上 3 times or over a week	9	33.3	44.4	22.2	0.0	0.0
一周 1~2 次 once or twice a week	28	25.0	39.3	17.9	14.3	3.6

5-12 不同消费者层的常用品牌/ The Most Frequently Used Brands by Market Segments

5-12-1 时尚流行指标/ Fads Popular Index

	人数 Number	第一品牌及百分比 1st/ percent	第二品牌及百分比 2nd/ percent	第三品牌及百分比 3rd/ percent
样本 Sample	**269**	**德芙 Dove(31.2)**	**吉百利 Cadbury(24.9)**	**利华 Lihua(8.6)**
平实生活指向 simple living orientation	101	德芙 Dove(34.7)	吉百利 Cadbury(23.8)	利华 Lihua(10.9)
时尚流行指向 fashion orientation	168	德芙 Dove(29.2)	吉百利 Cadbury(25.6)	利华 Lihua(7.1)

5-12-2 广告态度指标/ Advertising Attitude Index

	人数 Number	第一品牌及百分比 1st/ percent	第二品牌及百分比 2nd/ percent	第三品牌及百分比 3rd/ percent
样本 Sample	**269**	**德芙 Dove(31.2)**	**吉百利 Cadbury(24.9)**	**利华 Lihua(8.6)**
广告淡漠指向 indifferent orientation	66	德芙 Dove(34.8)	吉百利 Cadbury(21.2)	利华 Lihua(12.1)
中间层 medium	170	德芙 Dove(27.6) 吉百利 Cadbury(27.6)	利华 Lihua(8.2)	金帝 Le Conte(2.4)
信赖广告指向 loyal orientation	33	德芙 Dove(42.4)	吉百利 Cadbury(18.2)	飞鸽 Feige(6.1)

5-12-3 饮食健康指标/ Foods & Drink Quality Index

	人数 Number	第一品牌及百分比 1st/ percent	第二品牌及百分比 2nd/ percent	第三品牌及百分比 3rd/ percent
样本 Sample	**269**	**德芙 Dove(31.2)**	**吉百利 Cadbury(24.9)**	**利华 Lihua(8.6)**
饮食"温饱"指向 "basic" orientation	68	德芙 Dove(30.9)	吉百利 Cadbury(25.0)	利华 Lihua (8.8)
中间层 medium	127	德芙 Dove(33.1)	吉百利 Cadbury(29.1)	利华 Lihua (7.9)
健康营养指向 health & nutrition orientation	74	德芙 Dove(28.4)	吉百利 Cadbury(17.6)	利华 Lihua (9.5)

5-13 重度消费者的消费者层构成/ The Composition of the Heavy Consumers

5-13-1 时尚流行指标/ Fads Popular Index

	人数 Number	平实生活指向 simple living orientation	时尚流行指向 fashion orientation
样本 Sample	**79**	**29.1**	**70.9**
天天吃 daily	10	50.0	50.0
一周 3 次或以上 3 times or over a week	11	27.3	72.7
一周 1～2 次 once or twice a week	58	25.9	74.1

5-13-2 广告态度指标/ Advertising Attitude Index

	人数 Number	广告淡漠指向 indifferent orientation	中间层 medium	信赖广告指向 loyal orientation
样本 Sample	**79**	**25.3**	**63.3**	**11.4**
天天吃 daily	10	30.0	40.0	30.0
一周 3 次或以上 3 times or over a week	11	27.3	63.6	9.1
一周 1～2 次 once or twice a week	58	24.1	67.2	8.6

5-13-3 饮食健康指标/ Foods & Drink Quality Index

	人数 Number	饮食"温饱"指向 "basic" orientation	中间层 medium	健康营养指向 health & nutrition orientation
样本 Sample	**79**	**24.1**	**44.3**	**31.6**
天天吃 daily	10	20.0	40.0	40.0
一周 3 次或以上 3 times or over a week	11	9.1	63.6	27.3
一周 1～2 次 once or twice a week	58	27.6	41.4	31.0

6.冰淇淋 / Ice-cream

● 北京 / Beijing

6-1 最近三个月食用频率的比例/ Proportion of the Sample Consuming Ice-cream in the Last Three Months

	人数 Number	百分比 Percent
天天吃 daily	19	1.9
一周 3 次或以上 3 times or over a week	95	9.4
一周 1~2 次 once or twice a week	196	19.4
一个月 2～3 次 2 or 3 times a month	213	21.1
一个月 1 次或以下 once a month or below	130	12.9
没吃过 never	357	35.3

n=1010

6-2 最常用品牌排名/ Ranking of the Most Frequently Used Brands

排名 Brand Ranking	品牌 Brands	人数 Number	百分比 Percent
1	和路雪 Wall's	258	41.3
2	伊利 Yili	98	15.7
3	美登高 Meadow Gold	86	13.8
4	雀巢 Nestle	49	7.9
4	八喜 Bud's	49	7.9
5	新大陆 New Continent	28	4.5
6	北冰洋 Beibingyang	13	2.1
7	新地 Sundae	9	1.4
7	31 种冰淇淋 Baskin Robbins	9	1.4
8	美国皇后 DQ	7	1.1

n=624

6-3 样本、男性各年龄层、女性各年龄层的常用品牌/ The Most Frequently Used Brands by the Whole Sample, Age and Gender Groups

	人数 Number	第一品牌及百分比 1st/ percent	第二品牌及百分比 2nd/ percent	第三品牌及百分比 3rd/ percent	第四品牌及百分比 4th/ percent	第五品牌及百分比 5th/ percent
样本 Sample	624	**和路雪 Wall's(41.3)**	**伊利 Yili(15.7)**	**美登高 Meadow Gold(13.8)**	**雀巢 Nestle(7.9) 八喜 Bud's(7.9)**	**新大陆 New Continent(4.5)**
男性 Male	284	**和路雪 Wall's(41.2)**	**伊利 Yili(15.1)**	**美登高 Meadow Gold(13.4)**	**八喜 Bud's(7.7)**	**雀巢 Nestle(6.3) 新大陆 New Continent(6.3)**
16~24 岁 Age	79	和路雪 Wall's(48.1)	伊利 Yili(13.9)	美登高 Meadow Gold(11.4)	雀巢 Nestle(8.9)	八喜 Bud's(5.1)
25~34 岁 Age	83	和路雪 Wall's(39.8)	八喜 Bud's(13.3)	美登高 Meadow Gold(10.8)	新大陆 New Continent(9.6)	雀巢 Nestle(8.4) 伊利 Yili(8.4)
35~44 岁 Age	74	和路雪 Wall's(40.5)	美登高 Meadow Gold(18.9)	伊利 Yili(14.9)	八喜 Bud's(6.8)	新大陆 New Continent(5.4)
45~54 岁 Age	32	和路雪 Wall's(40.6)	伊利 Yili(21.9)	美登高 Meadow Gold(9.4) 新大陆 New Continent(9.4)	八喜 Bud's(6.3) 雀巢 Nestle(6.3)	新地 Sundae(3.1) 北冰洋 Beibingyang(3.1)
55~60 岁 Age	16	伊利 Yili(43.8)	和路雪 Wall's(18.8) 美登高 Meadow Gold(18.8)	北冰洋 Beibingyang(12.5)	雀巢 Nestle(6.3)	
女性 Female	340	**和路雪 Wall's(41.5)**	**伊利 Yili(16.2)**	**美登高 Meadow Gold(14.1)**	**雀巢 Nestle(9.1)**	**八喜 Bud's(7.9)**
16~24 岁 Age	92	和路雪 Wall's(48.9)	雀巢 Nestle(13.0)	伊利 Yili(12.0)	八喜 Bud's(9.8)	美登高 Meadow Gold(6.5)
25~34 岁 Age	111	和路雪 Wall's(41.4)	伊利 Yili(17.1)	美登高 Meadow Gold(11.7)	雀巢 Nestle(10.8)	八喜 Bud's(9.0)
35~44 岁 Age	82	和路雪 Wall's(40.2)	美登高 Meadow Gold(25.6)	伊利 Yili(18.3)	八喜 Bud's(4.9) 雀巢 Nestle(4.9)	北冰洋 Beibingyang(2.4)
45~54 岁 Age	36	和路雪 Wall's(38.9)	伊利 Yili(16.7)	美登高 Meadow Gold(13.9)	八喜 Bud's(8.3)	新地 Sundae(5.6) 新大陆 New Continent(5.6)
55~60 岁 Age	19	伊利 Yili(21.1)	和路雪 Wall's(15.8) 美登高 Meadow Gold(15.8)	雀巢 Nestle(10.5) 新大陆 New Continent(10.5) 北冰洋 Beibingyang(10.5)	八喜 Bud's(5.3) 麦当劳 Mcdonald's(5.3)	

6-4 理想品牌排名/ Ranking of the Ideal Brands

排名 Brand Ranking	品牌 Brands	人数 Number	百分比 Percent
1	和路雪 Wall's	296	29.2
2	八喜 Bud's	110	10.9
3	伊利 Yili	91	9.0
4	美登高 Meadow Gold	81	8.0
5	雀巢 Nestle	65	6.4
6	新大陆 New Continent	33	3.3
7	31 种冰淇淋 Baskin Robbins	17	1.7
7	北冰洋 Beibingyang	17	1.7
8	凯菲 Kaifei	10	1.0
9	美国皇后 DQ	9	0.9

n=1012

6-5 样本、男性各年龄层、女性各年龄层最近三个月有无购买的比例/ Purchasing in the Last Three Months by the Whole Sample, Age and Gender Groups

	人数 Number	买过 yes	没买过 no
样本 Sample	1011	63.0	37.0
男性 Male	504	57.5	42.5
16~24 岁 Age	105	68.6	31.4
25~34 岁 Age	151	58.9	41.1
35~44 岁 Age	131	61.1	38.9
45~54 岁 Age	77	41.6	58.4
55~60 岁 Age	40	42.5	57.5
女性 Female	507	68.4	31.6
16~24 岁 Age	107	85.0	15.0
25~34 岁 Age	150	74.7	25.3
35~44 岁 Age	124	69.4	30.6
45~54 岁 Age	84	45.2	54.8
55~60 岁 Age	42	47.6	52.4

6-6 样本、男性各年龄层、女性各年龄层最近三个月的食用频率/ Frequencies of Consuming Ice-cream in the Last Three Months by the Whole Sample, Age and Gender Groups

	人数 Number	天天吃 daily	一周 3 次或以上 3 times or over a week	一周 1~2 次 once or twice a week	一个月 2~3 次 2 or 3 times a month	一个月 1 次或以下 once a month or below	没吃过 never
样本 Sample	1010	1.9	9.4	19.4	21.1	12.9	35.3
男性 Male	503	1.0	7.4	15.7	21.3	13.7	41.0
16~24 岁 Age	105	1.0	14.3	23.8	30.5	8.6	21.9
25~34 岁 Age	150	1.3	6.0	14.7	20.7	16.0	41.3
35~44 岁 Age	131	0.8	6.1	18.3	19.8	12.2	42.7
45~54 岁 Age	77	1.3	5.2	5.2	15.6	18.2	54.5
55~60 岁 Age	40	0.0	2.5	10.0	15.0	15.0	57.5
女性 Female	507	2.8	11.4	23.1	20.9	12.0	29.8
16~24 岁 Age	107	5.6	24.3	29.0	25.2	4.7	11.2
25~34 岁 Age	150	2.0	8.0	25.3	28.7	13.3	22.7
35~44 岁 Age	124	1.6	13.7	24.2	16.9	13.7	29.8
45~54 岁 Age	84	2.4	3.6	15.5	13.1	11.9	53.6
55~60 岁 Age	42	2.4	0.0	11.9	9.5	21.4	54.8

6-7 样本、男性各年龄层、女性各年龄层的品牌习惯/ Brand Habit in Consuming Ice-cream by the Whole Sample, Age and Gender Groups

	人数 Number	基本固定食用一个牌子 used in only one brand	比较固定地食用两个或三个牌子 used in two or three brands	基本上不太固定牌子 no brand preference
样本 Sample	652	30.1	45.6	24.4
男性 Male	296	30.7	44.3	25.0
16~24 岁 Age	82	26.8	53.7	19.5
25~34 岁 Age	88	30.7	42.0	27.3
35~44 岁 Age	74	39.2	32.4	28.4
45~54 岁 Age	35	17.1	54.3	28.6
55~60 岁 Age	17	41.2	41.2	17.6
女性 Female	356	29.5	46.6	23.9
16~24 岁 Age	95	20.0	54.7	25.3
25~34 岁 Age	116	35.3	50.9	13.8
35~44 岁 Age	87	29.9	42.5	27.6
45~54 岁 Age	39	33.3	25.6	41.0
55~60 岁 Age	19	31.6	42.1	26.3

6-8 选择该类商品的考虑因素/ Ranking of the Considerations in Purchasing

注：本题为多选题，合计百分比超过 100%(Multiple answers）

排名 Ranking	考虑因素 Considerations	人次 Person-time	百分比 Percent
1	口味好 pleasant taste	494	75.7
2	价格适中 reasonable price	270	41.3
3	有名的牌子 famous brand	247	37.8
4	购买方便 easy to buy	127	19.4
5	只是由于习惯 out of habit	49	7.5
6	广告影响 influence of advertising	38	5.8
7	包装吸引人 appealing package	35	5.4
8	朋友推荐 introduction of friends	28	4.3
9	有优惠条件 with preferential terms	18	2.8
10	其它 others	11	1.7
11	售货员介绍 introduced by the shop assistants	7	1.1

n=653

6-9 样本、男性各年龄层、女性各年龄层最常食用的种类/ Kinds of the Consumed Ice-cream by the Whole Sample, Age and Gender Groups

注：本题为多选题，合计百分比超过 100%(Multiple answers）

	人数 Number	棒型冰淇淋 popsicle	蛋筒 cone	盒/杯装冰淇淋 box/cup	袋装冰淇淋 bag	大盒/桶 家庭装冰淇淋 big size box for family use	其它 others
样本 Sample	653	27.6	30.6	44.3	10.7	26.0	0.5
男性 Male	297	25.6	29.3	46.1	10.8	23.6	0.3
16~24 岁 Age	82	29.3	36.6	42.7	7.3	22.0	0.0
25~34 岁 Age	88	19.3	26.1	51.1	4.5	31.8	0.0
35~44 岁 Age	75	26.7	32.0	41.3	17.3	17.3	1.3
45~54 岁 Age	35	22.9	17.1	51.4	17.1	28.6	0.0
55~60 岁 Age	17	41.2	23.5	47.1	17.6	5.9	0.0
女性 Female	356	29.2	31.7	42.7	10.7	28.1	0.6
16~24 岁 Age	95	43.2	46.3	32.6	6.3	25.3	0.0
25~34 岁 Age	116	25.0	31.0	41.4	8.6	33.6	0.9
35~44 岁 Age	87	27.6	25.3	42.5	14.9	27.6	1.1
45~54 岁 Age	39	15.4	20.5	61.5	15.4	28.2	0.0
55~60 岁 Age	19	21.1	15.8	63.2	15.8	10.5	0.0

6-10 样本、男性各年龄层、女性各年龄层最常购买的场所/ Locations of Purchasing by the Whole Sample, Age and Gender Groups

	人数 Number	街头冷柜 vender	冷饮店 ice-cream shop	餐厅 restaurant	小卖部 grocery	超市 supermarket	批发点 wholesale market	商场 department store	其它 others
样本 Sample	617	18.0	13.5	1.3	16.2	29.8	10.5	9.6	1.1
男性 Male	278	20.5	15.1	1.4	17.3	26.6	8.3	9.4	1.4
16~24 岁 Age	77	32.5	10.4	0.0	19.5	24.7	5.2	5.2	2.6
25~34 岁 Age	83	16.9	20.5	2.4	16.9	30.1	3.6	9.6	0.0
35~44 岁 Age	69	15.9	18.8	1.4	13.0	27.5	8.7	11.6	2.9
45~54 岁 Age	33	9.1	3.0	3.0	21.2	27.3	27.3	9.1	0.0
55~60 岁 Age	16	25.0	18.8	0.0	18.8	12.5	6.3	18.8	0.0
女性 Female	339	15.9	12.1	1.2	15.3	32.4	12.4	9.7	0.9
16~24 岁 Age	91	22.0	11.0	1.1	27.5	25.3	4.4	8.8	0.0
25~34 岁 Age	109	15.6	11.9	1.8	12.8	38.5	8.3	10.1	0.9
35~44 岁 Age	82	15.9	13.4	0.0	8.5	30.5	23.2	8.5	0.0
45~54 岁 Age	39	5.1	12.8	2.6	10.3	35.9	20.5	10.3	2.6
55~60 岁 Age	18	11.1	11.1	0.0	11.1	33.3	11.1	16.7	5.6

6-11 重度消费者人口分布/ Demographics of the Heavy Consumers

	人数 Number	16-24 岁 Age	25-34 岁 Age	35-44 岁 Age	45-54 岁 Age	55-60 岁 Age
样本 Sample	310	33.5	27.7	26.5	8.7	3.5
男性 Male	121	33.9	27.3	27.3	7.4	4.1
天天吃 daily	5	20.0	40.0	20.0	20.0	0.0
一周 3 次或以上 3 times or over a week	37	40.5	24.3	21.6	10.8	2.7
一周 1~2 次 once or twice a week	79	31.6	27.8	30.4	5.1	5.1
女性 Female	189	33.3	28.0	25.9	9.5	3.2
天天吃 daily	14	42.9	21.4	14.3	14.3	7.1
一周 3 次或以上 3 times or over a week	58	44.8	20.7	29.3	5.2	0.0
一周 1~2 次 once or twice a week	117	26.5	32.5	25.6	11.1	4.3

6-12 不同消费者层的常用品牌/ The Most Frequently Used Brands by Market Segments

6-12-1 时尚流行指标/ Fads Popular Index

	人数 Number	第一品牌及百分比 1st/ percent	第二品牌及百分比 2nd/ percent	第三品牌及百分比 3rd/ percent	第四品牌及百分比 4th/ percent
样本 Sample	613	**和路雪 Wall's(41.9)**	**伊利 Yili(15.5)**	**美登高 Meadow Gold(13.4)**	**雀巢 Nestle(8.0)**
平实生活指向 simple living orientation	272	和路雪 Wall's(40.1)	伊利 Yili(17.3)	美登高 Meadow Gold(16.5)	八喜 Bud's(7.0)
时尚流行指向 fashion orientation	341	和路雪 Wall's(43.4)	伊利 Yili(14.1)	美登高 Meadow Gold(10.9)	雀巢 Nestle(9.4)

6-12-2 广告态度指标/ Advertising Attitude Index

	人数 Number	第一品牌及百分比 1st/ percent	第二品牌及百分比 2nd/ percent	第三品牌及百分比 3rd/ percent	第四品牌及百分比 4th/ percent
样本 Sample	610	**和路雪 Wall's(41.1)**	**伊利 Yili(15.7)**	**美登高 Meadow Gold(13.9)**	**雀巢 Nestle(7.9)**
广告淡漠指向 indifferent orientation	163	和路雪 Wall's(36.8)	美登高 Meadow Gold(18.4)	伊利 Yili(14.1)	八喜 Bud's(8.6)
中间层 medium	371	和路雪 Wall's(43.1)	伊利 Yili(15.4)	美登高 Meadow Gold(13.7)	雀巢 Nestle(8.4)
信赖广告指向 loyal orientation	76	和路雪 Wall's(40.8)	伊利 Yili(21.1)	八喜 Bud's(10.5)	雀巢 Nestle(7.9)

6-12-3 饮食健康指标/ Foods & Drink Quality Index

	人数 Number	第一品牌及百分比 1st/ percent	第二品牌及百分比 2nd/ percent	第三品牌及百分比 3rd/ percent	第四品牌及百分比 4th/ percent
样本 Sample	619	**和路雪 Wall's(41.5)**	**伊利 Yili(15.5)**	**美登高 Meadow Gold(13.6)**	**雀巢 Nestle(7.9) 八喜 Bud's(7.9)**
饮食"温饱"指向 "basic" orientation	161	和路雪 Wall's(40.4)	伊利 Yili(16.1)	美登高 Meadow Gold(14.9)	八喜 Bud's(8.1)
中间层 medium	306	和路雪 Wall's(43.1)	伊利 Yili(15.0)	美登高 Meadow Gold(13.4)	雀巢 Nestle(8.8)
健康营养指向 health & nutrition orientation	152	和路雪 Wall's(39.5)	伊利 Yili(15.8)	美登高 Meadow Gold(12.5)	八喜 Bud's(7.9) 雀巢 Nestle(7.9)

6-13 重度消费者的消费者层构成/ The Composition of the Heavy Consumers

6-13-1 时尚流行指标/ Fads Popular Index

	人数 Number	平实生活指向 simple living orientation	时尚流行指向 fashion orientation
样本 Sample	302	39.1	60.9
天天吃 daily	19	47.4	52.6
一周 3 次或以上 3 times or over a week	92	30.4	69.6
一周 1～2 次 once or twice a week	191	42.4	57.6

6-13-2 广告态度指标/ Advertising Attitude Index

	人数 Number	广告淡漠指向 indifferent orientation	中间层 medium	信赖广告指向 loyal orientation
样本 Sample	303	27.4	57.1	15.5
天天吃 daily	18	27.8	38 9	33.3
一周 3 次或以上 3 times or over a week	93	25.8	58 1	16.1
一周 1～2 次 once or twice a week	192	28.1	58.3	13.5

6-13-3 饮食健康指标/ Foods & Drink Quality Index

	人数 Number	饮食"温饱"指向 "basic" orientation	中间层 medium	健康营养指向 health & nutrition orientation
样本 Sample	307	23.5	49.3	26.7
天天吃 daily	19	42.1	36.8	21.1
一周 3 次或以上 3 times or over a week	95	25.3	43.2	31.6
一周 1～2 次 once or twice a week	193	20.7	54.4	24.9

● 上海 / Shanghai

6-1 最近三个月食用频率的比例/ Proportion of the Sample Consuming Ice-cream in the Last Three Months

	人数 Number	百分比 Percent
天天吃 daily	17	1.7
一周 3 次或以上 3 times or over a week	101	10.0
一周 1~2 次 once or twice a week	189	18.7
一个月 2～3 次 2 or 3 times a month	159	15.7
一个月 1 次或以下 once a month or below	121	11.9
没吃过 never	426	42.1

n=1013

6-2 最常用品牌排名/ Ranking of the Most Frequently Used Brands

排名 Brand Ranking	品牌 Brands	人数 Number	百分比 Percent
1	曼登琳 Mountain	235	40.4
2	和路雪 Wall's	127	21.9
3	光明 Bright	54	9.3
4	圣麦乐 Sanmarlo	53	9.1
5	伊利 Yili	33	5.7
6	雀巢 Nestle	27	4.6
7	哈根达斯 Hagen-dazs	14	2.4
8	金鸡 Jinji	8	1.4
9	爱贝 AB	7	1.2

n=581

6-3 样本、男性各年龄层、女性各年龄层的常用品牌/ The Most Frequently Used Brands by the Whole Sample, Age and Gender Groups

	人数 Number	第一品牌及百分比 1st/ percent	第二品牌及百分比 2nd/ percent	第三品牌及百分比 3rd/ percent
样本 Sample	581	**曼登琳 Mountain(40.4)**	**和路雪 Wall's(21.9)**	**光明 Bright(9.3)**
男性 Male	268	**曼登琳 Mountain(38.1)**	**和路雪 Wall's(19.4)**	**光明 Bright(11.6)**
16~24 岁 Age	75	曼登琳 Mountain(34.7)	和路雪 Wall's(26.7)	圣麦乐 Sanmarlo(9.3)
25~34 岁 Age	76	曼登琳 Mountain(35.5)	和路雪 Wall's(22.4)	圣麦乐 Sanmarlo(9.2) 光明 Bright(9.2)
35~44 岁 Age	61	曼登琳 Mountain(49.2)	光明 Bright(16.4)	和路雪 Wall's(14.8)
45~54 岁 Age	46	曼登琳 Mountain(34.8)	光明 Bright(15.2)	和路雪 Wall's(13.0)
55~60 岁 Age	10	光明 Bright(50.0)	曼登琳 Mountain(30.0)	八喜 Bud's(10.0) 圣麦乐 Sanmarlo(10.0)
女性 Female	313	**曼登琳 Mountain(42.5)**	**和路雪 Wall's(24.0)**	**圣麦乐 Sanmarlo(10.2)**
16~24 岁 Age	84	和路雪 Wall's(35.7) 曼登琳 Mountain(35.7)	圣麦乐 Sanmarlo(10.7)	哈根达斯 Hagen-dazs(3.6) 雀巢 Nestle(3.6)
25~34 岁 Age	92	曼登琳 Mountain(37.0)	和路雪 Wall's(30.4)	圣麦乐 Sanmarlo(9.8)
35~44 岁 Age	80	曼登琳 Mountain(52.5)	和路雪 Wall's(15.0)	圣麦乐 Sanmarlo(11.3)
45~54 岁 Age	42	曼登琳 Mountain(45.2)	光明 Bright(16.7)	和路雪 Wall's(9.5)
55~60 岁 Age	15	曼登琳 Mountain(53.3)	光明 Bright(13.3) 圣麦乐 Sanmarlo(13.3)	和路雪 Wall's(6.7) 伊利 Yili(6.7) 泰康 Taikang (6.7)

6-4 理想品牌排名/ Ranking of the Ideal Brands

排名 Brand Ranking	品牌 Brands	人数 Number	百分比 Percent
1	曼登琳 Mountain	286	28.2
2	和路雪 Wall's	166	16.4
3	哈根达斯 Hagen-dazs	146	14.4
4	光明 Bright	128	12.6
5	圣麦乐 Sanmarlo	87	8.6
6	伊利 Yili	36	3.6
7	雀巢 Nestle	26	2.6
8	金鸡 Jinji	8	0.8
9	爱贝 AB Aibei AB	6	0.6
10	美登高 Meadow Gold	5	0.5
11	八喜 Bud's	4	0.4
12	冷狗 Colddog	3	0.3

n=1014

6-5 样本、男性各年龄层、女性各年龄层最近三个月有无购买的比例/ Purchasing in the Last Three Months by the Whole Sample, Age and Gender Groups

	人数 Number	买过 yes	没买过 no
样本 Sample	1014	**58.0**	**42.0**
男性 Male	509	**52.7**	**47.3**
16~24 岁 Age	109	67.0	33.0
25~34 岁 Age	146	52.1	47.9
35~44 岁 Age	130	46.9	53.1
45~54 岁 Age	85	56.5	43.5
55~60 岁 Age	39	25.6	74.4
女性 Female	505	**63.4**	**36.6**
16~24 岁 Age	108	75.0	25.0
25~34 岁 Age	144	67.4	32.6
35~44 岁 Age	130	63.1	36.9
45~54 岁 Age	82	52.4	47.6
55~60 岁 Age	41	41.5	58.5

6-6 样本、男性各年龄层、女性各年龄层最近三个月的食用频率/ Frequencies of Consuming Ice-cream in the Last Three Months by the Whole Sample, Age and Gender Groups

	人数 Number	天天吃 daily	一周 3 次或以上 3 times or over a week	一周 1~2 次 once or twice a week	一个月 2~3 次 2 or 3 times a month	一个月 1 次或以下 once a month or below	没吃过 never
样本 Sample	**1013**	**1.7**	**10.0**	**18.7**	**15.7**	**11.9**	**42.1**
男性 Male	**508**	**1.8**	**8.9**	**16.1**	**14.2**	**12.4**	**46.7**
16~24 岁 Age	108	4.6	17.6	23.1	13.9	10.2	30.6
25~34 岁 Age	146	0.7	7.5	13.7	17.8	13.7	46.6
35~44 岁 Age	130	1.5	9.2	13.8	12.3	10.8	52.3
45~54 岁 Age	85	0.0	2.4	20.0	15.3	16.5	45.9
55~60 岁 Age	39	2.6	2.6	5.1	5.1	10.3	74.4
女性 Female	**505**	**1.6**	**11.1**	**21.2**	**17.2**	**11.5**	**37.4**
16~24 岁 Age	108	1.9	12.0	25.9	24.1	13.9	22.2
25~34 岁 Age	144	1.4	9.0	20.8	22.2	12.5	34.0
35~44 岁 Age	130	1.5	16.2	22.3	14.6	6.9	38.5
45~54 岁 Age	82	2.4	8.5	20.7	9.8	9.8	48.8
55~60 岁 Age	41	0.0	4.9	7.3	4.9	19.5	63.4

6-7 样本、男性各年龄层、女性各年龄层的品牌习惯/ Brand Habit in Consuming Ice-cream by the Whole Sample, Age and Gender Groups

	人数 Number	基本固定食用一个牌子 used in only one brand	比较固定地食用两个或三个牌子 used in two or three brands	基本上不太固定牌子 no brand preference
样本 Sample	**586**	**25.9**	**41.5**	**32.6**
男性 Male	**271**	**26.9**	**36.5**	**36.5**
16~24 岁 Age	75	21.3	36.0	42.7
25~34 岁 Age	78	23.1	44.9	32.1
35~44 岁 Age	62	37.1	29.0	33.9
45~54 岁 Age	46	28.3	37.0	34.8
55~60 岁 Age	10	30.0	20.0	50.0
女性 Female	**315**	**25.1**	**45.7**	**29.2**
16~24 岁 Age	84	15.5	47.6	36.9
25~34 岁 Age	94	21.3	50.0	28.7
35~44 岁 Age	80	32.5	42.5	25.0
45~54 岁 Age	42	42.9	38.1	19.0
55~60 岁 Age	15	13.3	46.7	40.0

6-8 选择该类商品的考虑因素/ Ranking of the Considerations in Purchasing

注：本题为多选题，合计百分比超过 100%(Multiple answers）

排名 Ranking	考虑因素 Considerations	人次 Person-time	百分比 Percent
1	口味好 pleasant taste	427	73.0
2	价格适中 reasonable price	227	38.8
3	有名的牌子 famous brand	179	30.6
4	购买方便 easy to buy	136	23.2
5	广告影响 influence of advertising	72	12.3
6	包装吸引人 appealing package	39	6.7
7	只是由于习惯 out of habit	37	6.3
8	有优惠条件 with preferential terms	26	4.4
9	朋友推荐 introduction of friends	23	3.9
10	售货员介绍 introduced by the shop assistants	6	1.0
11	其它 others	3	0.5

n=585

6-9 样本、男性各年龄层、女性各年龄层最常食用的种类/ Kinds of the Consumed Ice-cream by the Whole Sample, Age and Gender Groups

注：本题为多选题，合计百分比超过 100%(Multiple answers)

	人数 Number	棒型冰淇淋 popsicle	蛋筒 cone	盒/杯装冰淇淋 box/cup	袋装冰淇淋 bag	大盒/桶 家庭装冰淇淋 big size box for family use	其它 others
样本 Sample	**585**	**37.3**	**47.5**	**32.5**	**4.8**	**18.8**	**0.0**
男性 Male	**270**	**37.4**	**47.0**	**32.2**	**5.9**	**18.5**	**0.0**
16~24 岁 Age	75	41.3	54.7	29.3	6.7	12.0	0.0
25~34 岁 Age	77	39.0	51.9	27.3	6.5	18.2	0.0
35~44 岁 Age	62	29.0	41.9	32.3	9.7	27.4	0.0
45~54 岁 Age	46	43.5	37.0	41.3	0.0	19.6	0.0
55~60 岁 Age	10	20.0	30.0	50.0	0.0	10.0	0.0
女性 Female	**315**	**37.1**	**47.9**	**32.7**	**3.8**	**19.0**	**0.0**
16~24 岁 Age	84	39.3	48.8	39.3	3.6	13.1	0.0
25~34 岁 Age	94	34.0	51.1	27.7	5.3	26.6	0.0
35~44 岁 Age	80	46.3	45.0	28.8	2.5	15.0	0.0
45~54 岁 Age	42	26.2	35.7	33.3	4.8	26.2	0.0
55~60 岁 Age	15	26.7	73.3	46.7	0.0	6.7	0.0

6-10 样本、男性各年龄层、女性各年龄层最常购买的场所/ Locations of Purchasing by the Whole Sample, Age and Gender Groups

	人数 Number	街头冷柜 vender	冷饮店 ice-cream shop	餐厅 restaurant	小卖部 grocery	超市 super-market	批发点 wholesale market	商场 department store	其它 others
样本 Sample	**573**	**31.2**	**13.6**	**1.2**	**10.1**	**34.7**	**5.8**	**3.3**	**0.0**
男性 Male	**267**	**33.7**	**15.7**	**1.5**	**10.1**	**31.1**	**4.9**	**3.0**	**0.0**
16~24 岁 Age	75	40.0	14.7	4.0	14.7	21.3	2.7	2.7	0.0
25~34 岁 Age	77	33.8	10.4	1.3	5.2	45.5	3.9	0.0	0.0
35~44 岁 Age	61	29.5	21.3	0.0	9.8	27.9	4.9	6.6	0.0
45~54 岁 Age	45	33.3	17.8	0.0	13.3	24.4	6.7	4.4	0.0
55~60 岁 Age	9	11.1	22.2	0.0	0.0	44.4	22.2	0.0	0.0
女性 Female	**306**	**29.1**	**11.8**	**1.0**	**10.1**	**37.9**	**6.5**	**3.6**	**0.0**
16~24 岁 Age	82	35.4	14.6	0.0	13.4	31.7	0.0	4.9	0.0
25~34 岁 Age	90	24.4	10.0	2.2	4.4	47.8	6.7	4.4	0.0
35~44 岁 Age	78	26.9	10.3	1.3	14.1	37.2	7.7	2.6	0.0
45~54 岁 Age	42	26.2	14.3	0.0	7.1	33.3	16.7	2.4	0.0
55~60 岁 Age	14	42.9	7.1	0.0	14.3	28.6	7.1	0.0	0.0

6-11 重度消费者人口分布/ Demographics of the Heavy Consumers

	人数 Number	16-24 岁 Age	25-34 岁 Age	35-44 岁 Age	45-54 岁 Age	55-60 岁 Age
样本 Sample	**307**	**30.0**	**25.1**	**27.4**	**14.7**	**2.9**
男性 Male	**136**	**36.0**	**23.5**	**23.5**	**14.0**	**2.9**
天天吃 daily	9	55.6	11.1	22.2	0.0	11.1
一周 3 次或以上 3 times or over a week	45	42.2	24.4	26.7	4.4	2.2
一周 1~2 次 once or twice a week	82	30.5	24.4	22.0	20.7	2.4
女性 Female	**171**	**25.1**	**26.3**	**30.4**	**15.2**	**2.9**
天天吃 daily	8	25.0	25.0	25.0	25.0	0.0
一周 3 次或以上 3 times or over a week	56	23.2	23.2	37.5	12.5	3.6
一周 1~2 次 once or twice a week	107	26.2	28.0	27.1	15.9	2.8

6-12 不同消费者层的常用品牌/ The Most Frequently Used Brands by Market Segments

6-12-1 时尚流行指标/ Fads Popular Index

	人数 Number	第一品牌及百分比 1st/ percent	第二品牌及百分比 2nd/ percent	第三品牌及百分比 3rd/ percent	第四品牌及百分比 4th/ percent	第五品牌及百分比 5th/ percent
样本 Sample	576	**曼登琳 Mountain(40.5)**	**和路雪 Wall's(21.9)**	**光明 Bright(9.4)**	**圣麦乐 Sanmarlo(9.2)**	**伊利 Yili(5.7)**
平实生活指向 simple living orientation	225	曼登琳 Mountain(46.7)	光明 Bright(15.6)	和路雪 Wall's(11.1)	圣麦乐 Sanmarlo(8.4)	伊利 Yili(5.3)
时尚流行指向 fashion orientation	351	曼登琳 Mountain(36.5)	和路雪 Wall's(28.8)	圣麦乐 Sanmarlo(9.7)	伊利 Yili(6.0)	雀巢 Nestle(5.4) 光明 Bright(5.4)

6-12-2 广告态度指标/ Advertising Attitude Index

	人数 Number	第一品牌及百分比 1st/ percent	第二品牌及百分比 2nd/ percent	第三品牌及百分比 3rd/ percent	第四品牌及百分比 4th/ percent	第五品牌及百分比 5th/ percent
样本 Sample	575	**曼登琳 Mountain(40.7)**	**和路雪 Wall's(21.7)**	**圣麦乐 Sanmarlo(9.2)**	**光明 Bright(8.9)**	**伊利 Yili(5.7)**
广告淡漠指向 indifferent orientation	124	曼登琳 Mountain(45.2)	和路雪 Wall's(21.0)	光明 Bright(11.3)	圣麦乐 Sanmarlo(8.9)	伊利 Yili(4.8)
中间层 medium	367	曼登琳 Mountain(41.7)	和路雪 Wall's(21.3)	光明 Bright(9.0)	圣麦乐 Sanmarlo(8.7)	雀巢 Nestle(5.7)
信赖广告指向 loyal orientation	84	曼登琳 Mountain(29.8)	和路雪 Wall's(25.0)	圣麦乐 Sanmarlo(11.9)	伊利 Yili(9.5)	雀巢 Nestle(4.8) 光明 Bright(4.8)

6-12-3 饮食健康指标/ Foods & Drink Quality Index

	人数 Number	第一品牌及百分比 1st/ percent	第二品牌及百分比 2nd/ percent	第三品牌及百分比 3rd/ percent	第四品牌及百分比 4th/ percent	第五品牌及百分比 5th/ percent
样本 Sample	578	**曼登琳 Mountain(40.5)**	**和路雪 Wall's(21.8)**	**光明 Bright(9.3)**	**圣麦乐 Sanmarlo(9.2)**	**伊利 Yili(5.7)**
饮食"温饱"指向 "basic" orientation	121	曼登琳 Mountain(38.0)	和路雪 Wall's(20.7)	光明 Bright(13.2)	圣麦乐 Sanmarlo(8.3)	雀巢 Nestle(6.6)
中间层 medium	288	曼登琳 Mountain(39.9)	和路雪 Wall's(21.9)	光明 Bright(10.8)	圣麦乐 Sanmarlo(10.4)	伊利 Yili(5.2)
健康营养指向 health & nutrition orientation	169	曼登琳 Mountain(43.2)	和路雪 Wall's(22.5)	圣麦乐 Sanmarlo(7.7)	伊利 Yili(7.1)	雀巢 Nestle(4.7)

6-13 重度消费者的消费者层构成/ The Composition of the Heavy Consumers

6-13-1 时尚流行指标/ Fads Popular Index

	人数 Number	平实生活指向 simple living orientation	时尚流行指向 fashion orientation
样本 Sample	305	39.3	60.7
天天吃 daily	17	64.7	35.3
一周 3 次或以上 3 times or over a week	101	40.6	59.4
一周 1～2 次 once or twice a week	187	36.4	63.6

6-13-2 广告态度指标/ Advertising Attitude Index

	人数 Number	广告淡漠指向 indifferent orientation	中间层 medium	信赖广告指向 loyal orientation
样本 Sample	302	22.5	63.2	14.2
天天吃 daily	17	23.5	64.7	11.8
一周 3 次或以上 3 times or over a week	99	21.2	69.7	9.1
一周 1～2 次 once or twice a week	186	23.1	59.7	17.2

6-13-3 饮食健康指标/ Foods & Drink Quality Index

	人数 Number	饮食"温饱"指向 "basic" orientation	中间层 medium	健康营养指向 health & nutrition orientation
样本 Sample	305	21.3	47.9	30.8
天天吃 daily	17	11.8	47.1	41.2
一周 3 次或以上 3 times or over a week	101	25.7	45.5	28.7
一周 1～2 次 once or twice a week	187	19.8	49.2	31.0

● 广州 / Guangzhou

6-1 最近三个月食用频率的比例/ Proportion of the Sample Consuming Ice-cream in the Last Three Months

	人数 Number	百分比 Percent
天天吃 daily	12	1.2
一周 3 次或以上 3 times or over a week	70	6.8
一周 1~2 次 once or twice a week	200	19.4
一个月 2～3 次 2 or 3 times a month	262	25.4
一个月 1 次或以下 once a month or below	151	14.6
没吃过 never	338	32.7

n=1033

6-2 最常用品牌排名/ Ranking of the Most Frequently Used Brands

排名 Brand Ranking	品牌 Brands	人数 Number	百分比 Percent
1	五羊 Wuyang	351	51.7
2	曼登琳 Mountain	86	12.7
3	和路雪 Wall's	68	10.0
4	雀巢 Nestle	52	7.7
5	明治 Mingzhi	36	5.3
6	美登高 Meadow Gold	32	4.7
7	阿波罗 Apollo	13	1.9
8	伊利 Yili	10	1.5

n=679

6-3 样本、男性各年龄层、女性各年龄层的常用品牌/ The Most Frequently Used Brands by the Whole Sample, Age and Gender Groups

	人数 Number	第一品牌及百分比 1st/ percent	第二品牌及百分比 2nd/ percent	第三品牌及百分比 3rd/ percent	第四品牌及百分比 4th/ percent
样本 Sample	**679**	**五羊 Wuyang(51.7)**	**曼登琳 Mountain(12.7)**	**和路雪 Wall's(10.0)**	**雀巢 Nestle(7.7)**
男性 Male	**302**	**五羊 Wuyang(56.0)**	**曼登琳 Mountain(11.6)**	**雀巢 Nestle(8.3)**	**和路雪 Wall's(7.6)**
16~24 岁 Age	85	五羊 Wuyang(44.7)	曼登琳 Mountain(18.8)	明治 Mingzhi(10.6)	和路雪 Wall's(9.4)
25~34 岁 Age	95	五羊 Wuyang(63.2)	和路雪 Wall's(10.5)	雀巢 Nestle(9.5)	曼登琳 Mountain(6.3)
35~44 岁 Age	69	五羊 Wuyang(63.8)	曼登琳 Mountain(10.1)	雀巢 Nestle(8.7)	美登高 Meadow Gold(5.8)
45~54 岁 Age	39	五羊 Wuyang(51.3)	曼登琳 Mountain(15.4)	雀巢 Nestle(10.3)	和路雪 Wall's(5.1) 美登高 Meadow Gold(5.1)
55~60 岁 Age	14	五羊 Wuyang(50.0)	雀巢 Nestle(28.6)	和路雪 Wall's(7.1) 明治 Mingzhi(7.1) 五丰 Wufeng(7.1)	
女性 Female	**377**	**五羊 Wuyang(48.3)**	**曼登琳 Mountain(13.5)**	**和路雪 Wall's(11.9)**	**雀巢 Nestle(7.2)**
16~24 岁 Age	100	五羊 Wuyang(39.0)	曼登琳 Mountain(19.0)	和路雪 Wall's(14.0)	雀巢 Nestle(6.0) 美登高 Meadow Gold(6.0)
25~34 岁 Age	111	五羊 Wuyang(45.0)	曼登琳 Mountain(14.4)	和路雪 Wall's(12.6)	雀巢 Nestle(9.9) 明治 Mingzhi(9.9)
35~44 岁 Age	93	五羊 Wuyang(61.3)	和路雪 Wall's(12.9)	曼登琳 Mountain(10.8)	明治 Mingzhi(4.3)
45~54 岁 Age	59	五羊 Wuyang(47.5)	雀巢 Nestle(11.9)	和路雪 Wall's(8.5) 美登高 Meadow Gold(8.5)	曼登琳 Mountain(6.8)
55~60 岁 Age	14	五羊 Wuyang(57.1)	美登高 Meadow Gold(21.4)	曼登琳 Mountain(14.3)	麦当劳 Macdonal's(7.1)

6-4 理想品牌排名/ Ranking of the Ideal Brands

排名 Brand Ranking	品牌 Brands	人数 Number	百分比 Percent
1	五羊 Wuyang	457	44.2
2	曼登琳 Mountain	87	8.4
3	明治 Mingzhi	80	7.7
4	和路雪 Wall's	79	7.6
5	雀巢 Nestle	60	5.8
6	美登高 Meadow Gold	38	3.7
7	阿波罗 Apollo	17	1.6
8	伊利 Yili	10	1.0

n=1033

6-5 样本、男性各年龄层、女性各年龄层最近三个月有无购买的比例/ Purchasing in the Last Three Months by the Whole Sample, Age and Gender Groups

	人数 Number	买过 yes	没买过 no
样本 Sample	1034	67.0	33.0
男性 Male	499	61.5	38.5
16~24 岁 Age	106	74.5	25.5
25~34 岁 Age	150	66.7	33.3
35~44 岁 Age	127	59.1	40.9
45~54 岁 Age	73	52.1	47.9
55~60 岁 Age	43	34.9	65.1
女性 Female	535	72.1	27.9
16~24 岁 Age	112	90.2	9.8
25~34 岁 Age	158	72.2	27.8
35~44 岁 Age	137	71.5	28.5
45~54 岁 Age	87	67.8	32.2
55~60 岁 Age	41	34.1	65.9

6-6 样本、男性各年龄层、女性各年龄层最近三个月的食用频率/ Frequencies of Consuming Ice-cream in the Last Three Months by the Whole Sample, Age and Gender Groups

	人数 Number	天天吃 daily	一周 3 次或以上 3 times or over a week	一周 1~2 次 once or twice a week	一个月 2~3 次 2 or 3 times a month	一个月 1 次或以下 once a month or below	没吃过 never
样本 Sample	1033	1.2	6.8	19.4	25.4	14.6	32.7
男性 Male	498	1.2	6.4	15.1	25.1	14.5	37.8
16~24 岁 Age	106	2.8	5.7	27.4	30.2	14.2	19.8
25~34 岁 Age	150	1.3	5.3	13.3	28.0	19.3	32.7
35~44 岁 Age	127	0.8	11.0	9.4	21.3	13.4	44.1
45~54 岁 Age	73	0.0	4.1	13.7	23.3	12.3	46.6
55~60 岁 Age	42	0.0	2.4	9.5	16.7	4.8	66.7
女性 Female	535	1.1	7.1	23.4	25.6	14.8	28.0
16~24 岁 Age	112	0.0	12.5	30.4	32.1	16.1	8.9
25~34 岁 Age	158	0.6	8.2	20.9	25.9	15.8	28.5
35~44 岁 Age	137	2.9	5.1	22.6	27.7	11.7	29.9
45~54 岁 Age	87	1.1	3.4	24.1	21.8	18.4	31.0
55~60 岁 Age	41	0.0	2.4	14.6	7.3	9.8	65.9

6-7 样本、男性各年龄层、女性各年龄层的品牌习惯/ Brand Habit in Consuming Ice-cream by the Whole Sample, Age and Gender Groups

	人数 Number	基本固定食用一个牌子 used in only one brand	比较固定地食用两个或三个牌子 used in two or three brands	基本上不太固定牌子 no brand preference
样本 Sample	693	32.8	44.3	22.9
男性 Male	308	34.4	41.2	24.4
16~24 岁 Age	84	31.0	44.0	25.0
25~34 岁 Age	100	34.0	47.0	19.0
35~44 岁 Age	71	39.4	29.6	31.0
45~54 岁 Age	39	28.2	46.2	25.6
55~60 岁 Age	14	50.0	28.6	21.4
女性 Female	385	31.4	46.8	21.8
16~24 岁 Age	102	26.5	49.0	24.5
25~34 岁 Age	113	30.1	51.3	18.6
35~44 岁 Age	96	41.7	42.7	15.6
45~54 岁 Age	60	30.0	40.0	30.0
55~60 岁 Age	14	14.3	50.0	35.7

6-8 选择该类商品的考虑因素/ Ranking of the Considerations in Purchasing

注：本题为多选题，合计百分比超过 100%(Multiple answers)

排名 Ranking	考虑因素 Considerations	人次 Person-time	百分比 Percent
1	口味好 pleasant taste	478	68.9
2	价格适中 reasonable price	299	43.1
3	有名的牌子 famous brand	226	32.6
4	购买方便 easy to buy	184	26.5
5	只是由于习惯 out of habit	52	7.5
6	有优惠条件 with preferential terms	42	6.1
7	包装吸引人 appealing package	41	5.9
8	广告影响 influence of advertising	40	5.8
9	朋友推荐 introduction of friends	23	3.3
10	售货员介绍 introduced by the shop assistants	6	0.9
11	其它 others	4	0.6

n=694

6-9 样本、男性各年龄层、女性各年龄层最常食用的种类/ Kinds of the Consumed Ice-cream by the Whole Sample, Age and Gender Groups

注：本题为多选题，合计百分比超过 100%(Multiple answers)

	人数 Number	棒型冰淇淋 popsicle	蛋筒 cone	盒/杯装冰淇淋 box/cup	袋装冰淇淋 bag	大盒/桶 家庭装冰淇淋 big size box for family use	其它 others
样本 Sample	**693**	**36.4**	**56.1**	**23.2**	**4.0**	**20.9**	**0.9**
男性 Male	**310**	**35.2**	**53.5**	**21.6**	**3.9**	**22.3**	**1.3**
16~24 岁 Age	85	37.6	61.2	18.8	1.2	11.8	3.5
25~34 岁 Age	101	35.6	60.4	24.8	5.0	17.8	1.0
35~44 岁 Age	71	36.6	40.8	19.7	4.2	33.8	0.0
45~54 岁 Age	39	30.8	48.7	20.5	7.7	30.8	0.0
55~60 岁 Age	14	21.4	35.7	28.6	0.0	35.7	0.0
女性 Female	**383**	**37.3**	**58.2**	**24.5**	**4.2**	**19.8**	**0.5**
16~24 岁 Age	102	41.2	65.7	21.6	4.9	12.7	1.0
25~34 岁 Age	112	41.1	53.6	27.7	2.7	19.6	0.9
35~44 岁 Age	95	33.7	54.7	29.5	4.2	24.2	0.0
45~54 岁 Age	60	38.3	58.3	15.0	5.0	25.0	0.0
55~60 岁 Age	14	0.0	64.3	28.6	7.1	21.4	0.0

6-10 样本、男性各年龄层、女性各年龄层最常购买的场所/ Locations of Purchasing by the Whole Sample, Age and Gender Groups

	人数 Number	街头冷柜 vender	冷饮店 ice-cream shop	餐厅 restaurant	小卖部 grocery	超市 supermarket	批发点 wholesale market	商场 department store	其它 others
样本 Sample	**671**	**35.6**	**8.5**	**1.2**	**27.1**	**15.2**	**3.3**	**7.5**	**1.6**
男性 Male	**299**	**37.1**	**7.4**	**0.3**	**28.1**	**14.4**	**2.7**	**7.7**	**2.3**
16~24 岁 Age	83	44.6	8.4	0.0	32.5	4.8	0.0	6.0	3.6
25~34 岁 Age	96	34.4	7.3	1.0	34.4	15.6	3.1	4.2	0.0
35~44 岁 Age	69	31.9	8.7	0.0	20.3	23.2	4.3	10.1	1.4
45~54 岁 Age	37	40.5	2.7	0.0	16.2	16.2	5.4	10.8	8.1
55~60 岁 Age	14	28.6	7.1	0.0	28.6	14.3	0.0	21.4	0.0
女性 Female	**372**	**34.4**	**9.4**	**1.9**	**26.3**	**15.9**	**3.8**	**7.3**	**1.1**
16~24 岁 Age	98	38.8	7.1	1.0	35.7	12.2	1.0	3.1	1.0
25~34 岁 Age	108	39.8	6.5	0.0	21.3	21.3	2.8	8.3	0.0
35~44 岁 Age	92	32.6	14.1	1.1	21.7	14.1	9.8	6.5	0.0
45~54 岁 Age	60	23.3	11.7	5.0	30.0	15.0	1.7	10.0	3.3
55~60 岁 Age	14	21.4	7.1	14.3	14.3	14.3	0.0	21.4	7.1

6-11 重度消费者人口分布/ Demographics of the Heavy Consumers

	人数 Number	16-24 岁 Age	25-34 岁 Age	35-44 岁 Age	45-54 岁 Age	55-60 岁 Age
样本 Sample	282	30.5	27.3	24.5	13.5	4.3
男性 Male	113	33.6	26.5	23.9	11.5	4.4
天天吃 daily	6	50.0	33.3	16.7	0.0	0.0
一周 3 次或以上 3 times or over a week	32	18.8	25.0	43.8	9.4	3.1
一周 1~2 次 once or twice a week	75	38.7	26.7	16.0	13.3	5.3
女性 Female	169	28.4	27.8	24.9	14.8	4.1
天天吃 daily	6	0.0	16.7	66.7	16.7	0.0
一周 3 次或以上 3 times or over a week	38	36.8	34.2	18.4	7.9	2.6
一周 1~2 次 once or twice a week	125	27.2	26.4	24.8	16.8	4.8

6-12 不同消费者层的常用品牌/ The Most Frequently Used Brands by Market Segments

6-12-1 时尚流行指标/ Fads Popular Index

	人数 Number	第一品牌及百分比 1st/ percent	第二品牌及百分比 2nd/ percent	第三品牌及百分比 3rd/ percent	第四品牌及百分比 4th/ percent
样本 Sample	673	**五羊 Wuyang(51.9)**	**曼登琳 Mountain(12.8)**	**和路雪 Wall's(9.7)**	**雀巢 Nestle(7.7)**
平实生活指向 simple living orientation	298	五羊 Wuyang(57.0)	曼登琳 Mountain(11.4)	和路雪 Wall's(7.7)	雀巢 Nestle(6.7)
时尚流行指向 fashion orientation	375	五羊 Wuyang(47.7)	曼登琳 Mountain(13.9)	和路雪 Wall's(11.2)	雀巢 Nestle(8.5)

6-12-2 广告态度指标/ Advertising Attitude Index

	人数 Number	第一品牌及百分比 1st/ percent	第二品牌及百分比 2nd/ percent	第三品牌及百分比 3rd/ percent	第四品牌及百分比 4th/ percent
样本 Sample	670	**五羊 Wuyang(51.6)**	**曼登琳 Mountain(12.7)**	**和路雪 Wall's(10.0)**	**雀巢 Nestle(7.8)**
广告淡漠指向 indifferent orientation	199	五羊 Wuyang(52.3)	曼登琳 Mountain(13.6)	和路雪 Wall's(9.5)	雀巢 Nestle(8.0)
中间层 medium	407	五羊 Wuyang(54.5)	曼登琳 Mountain(11.8)	和路雪 Wall's(9.8)	雀巢 Nestle(7.1)
信赖广告指向 loyal orientation	64	五羊 Wuyang(31.3)	曼登琳 Mountain(15.6)	美登高 Meadow Gold(12.5) 和路雪 Wall's(12.5)	雀巢 Nestle(10.9)

6-12-3 饮食健康指标/ Foods & Drink Quality Index

	人数 Number	第一品牌及百分比 1st/ percent	第二品牌及百分比 2nd/ percent	第三品牌及百分比 3rd/ percent	第四品牌及百分比 4th/ percent
样本 Sample	675	**五羊 Wuyang(51.6)**	**曼登琳 Mountain(12.7)**	**和路雪 Wall's(10.1)**	**雀巢 Nestle(7.7)**
饮食"温饱"指向 "basic" orientation	174	五羊 Wuyang(53.4)	曼登琳 Mountain(12.1)	雀巢 Nestle(8.6)	和路雪 Wall's(8.0)
中间层 medium	376	五羊 Wuyang(52.1)	曼登琳 Mountain(13.0)	和路雪 Wall's(10.1)	雀巢 Nestle(7.7)
健康营养指向 health & nutrition orientation	125	五羊 Wuyang(47.2)	曼登琳 Mountain(12.8) 和路雪 Wall's(12.8)	明治 Mingzhi (9.6)	雀巢 Nestle(6.4)

6-13 重度消费者的消费者层构成/ The Composition of the Heavy Consumers

6-13-1 时尚流行指标/ Fads Popular Index

	人数 Number	平实生活指向 simple living orientation	时尚流行指向 fashion orientation
样本 Sample	281	42.3	57.7
天天吃 daily	12	41.7	58.3
一周 3 次或以上 3 times or over a week	70	40.0	60.0
一周 1~2 次 once or twice a week	199	43.2	56.8

6-13-2 广告态度指标/ Advertising Attitude Index

	人数 Number	广告淡漠指向 indifferent orientation	中间层 medium	信赖广告指向 loyal orientation
样本 Sample	**277**	**34.7**	**57.8**	**7.6**
天天吃 daily	12	33.3	66.7	0.0
一周 3 次或以上 3 times or over a week	69	39.1	53.6	7.2
一周 1～2 次 once or twice a week	196	33.2	58.7	8.2

6-13-3 饮食健康指标/ Foods & Drink Quality Index

	人数 Number	饮食"温饱"指向 "basic" orientation	中间层 medium	健康营养指向 health & nutrition orientation
样本 Sample	**281**	**26.3**	**52.3**	**21.4**
天天吃 daily	12	41.7	41.7	16.7
一周 3 次或以上 3 times or over a week	70	27.1	48.6	24.3
一周 1～2 次 once or twice a week	199	25.1	54.3	20.6

● 重庆 / Chongqing

6-1 最近三个月食用频率的比例/ Proportion of the Sample Consuming Ice-cream in the Last Three Months

	人数 Number	百分比 Percent
天天吃 daily	11	1.8
一周 3 次或以上 3 times or over a week	23	3.7
一周 1~2 次 once or twice a week	99	15.9
一个月 2～3 次 2 or 3 times a month	91	14.6
一个月 1 次或以下 once a month or below	67	10.8
没吃过 never	332	53.3

n=623

6-2 最常用品牌排名/ Ranking of the Most Frequently Used Brands

排名 Brand Ranking	品牌 Brands	人数 Number	百分比 Percent
1	新大陆 New Continent	96	35.0
2	伊利 Yili	86	31.4
3	美登高 Meadow Gold	31	11.3
4	和路雪 Wall's	27	9.9
5	雀巢 Nestle	8	2.9
6	美怡乐 Meiyile	6	2.2
7	雪乔 Xueqiao	5	1.8

n=274

6-3 样本、男性各年龄层、女性各年龄层的常用品牌/ The Most Frequently Used Brands by the Whole Sample, Age and Gender Groups

	人数 Number	第一品牌及百分比 1st/ percent	第二品牌及百分比 2nd/ percent	第三品牌及百分比 3rd/ percent	第四品牌及百分比 4th/ percent
样本 Sample	274	**新大陆 New Continent(35.0)**	**伊利 Yili(31.4)**	**美登高 Meadow Gold(11.3)**	**和路雪 Wall's(9.9)**
男性 Male	129	**伊利 Yili(36.4)**	**新大陆 New Continent(34.1)**	**美登高 Meadow Gold(10.1)**	**和路雪 Wall's(7.8)**
16~24 岁 Age	43	伊利 Yili(44.2)	新大陆 New Continent(30.2)	美登高 Meadow Gold(11.6)	和路雪 Wall's(9.3)
25~34 岁 Age	38	新大陆 New Continent(31.6)	伊利 Yili(28.9)	美登高 Meadow Gold(13.2)	和路雪 Wall's(10.5)
35~44 岁 Age	25	新大陆 New Continent(48.0)	伊利 Yili(40.0)	美登高 Meadow Gold(8.0)	雀巢 Nestle(4.0)
45~54 岁 Age	15	新大陆 New Continent(40.0)	伊利 Yili(33.3)	和路雪 Wall's(6.7) 美登高 Meadow Gold(6.7) 美怡乐 Meiyile(6.7) 雀巢 Nestle(6.7)	
55~60 岁 Age	8	雀巢 Nestle(37.5)	伊利 Yili(25.0)	和路雪 Wall's(12.5) 新大陆 New Continent(12.5)	
女性 Female	145	**新大陆 New Continent(35.9)**	**伊利 Yili(26.9)**	**美登高 Meadow Gold(12.4)**	**和路雪 Wall's(11.7)**
16~24 岁 Age	51	新大陆 New Continent(37.3)	伊利 Yili(21.6)	和路雪 Wall's(19.6)	美登高 Meadow Gold(13.7)
25~34 岁 Age	50	伊利 Yili(38.0)	新大陆 New Continent(22.0)	美登高 Meadow Gold(16.0)	和路雪 Wall's(10.0)
35~44 岁 Age	26	新大陆 New Continent(42.3)	伊利 Yili(30.8)	美登高 Meadow Gold(7.7)	和路雪 Wall's(3.8) 雀巢 Nestle(3.8) 香港冰淇淋大王 Hong Kong(3.8) 北冰洋 Beibingyang(3.8) 雪乔 Xueqiao(3.8)
45~54 岁 Age	14	新大陆 New Continent(57.1)	和路雪 Wall's(7.1) 美登高 Meadow Gold(7.1) 伊利 Yili(7.1) 五羊 Wuyang(7.1) 美怡乐 Meiyile(7.1) 香港冰淇淋大王 Hong Kong(7.1)		
55~60 岁 Age	4	新大陆 New Continent(75.0)	曼登琳 Mountain(25.0)		

6-4 理想品牌排名/ Ranking of the Ideal Brands

排名 Brand Ranking	品牌 Brands	人数 Number	百分比 Percent
1	新大陆 New Continent	216	34.6
2	伊利 Yili	114	18.3
3	和路雪 Wall's	45	7.2
4	美登高 Meadow Gold	35	5.6
5	美怡乐 Meiyile	10	1.6
5	雀巢 Nestle	10	1.6
6	雪乔 Xueqiao	8	1.3

n=624

6-5 样本、男性各年龄层、女性各年龄层最近三个月有无购买的比例/ Purchasing in the Last Three Months by the Whole Sample, Age and Gender Groups

	人数 Number	买过 yes	没买过 no
样本 Sample	624	51.0	49.0
男性 Male	314	47.1	52.9
16~24 岁 Age	64	67.2	32.8
25~34 岁 Age	93	46.2	53.8
35~44 岁 Age	75	41.3	58.7
45~54 岁 Age	54	38.9	61.1
55~60 岁 Age	28	35.7	64.3
女性 Female	310	54.8	45.2
16~24 岁 Age	64	82.8	17.2
25~34 岁 Age	90	65.6	34.4
35~44 岁 Age	73	45.2	54.8
45~54 岁 Age	60	33.3	66.7
55~60 岁 Age	23	21.7	78.3

6-6 样本、男性各年龄层、女性各年龄层最近三个月的食用频率/ Frequencies of Consuming Ice-cream in the Last Three Months by the Whole Sample, Age and Gender Groups

	人数 Number	天天吃 daily	一周 3 次或以上 3 times or over a week	一周 1~2 次 once or twice a week	一个月 2~3 次 2 or 3 times a month	一个月 1 次或以下 once a month or below	没吃过 never
样本 Sample	623	1.8	3.7	15.9	14.6	10.8	53.3
男性 Male	313	1.6	3.8	13.1	16.0	8.9	56.5
16~24 岁 Age	63	4.8	7.9	22.2	25.4	12.7	27.0
25~34 岁 Age	93	0.0	3.2	12.9	18.3	7.5	58.1
35~44 岁 Age	75	1.3	5.3	9.3	9.3	9.3	65.3
45~54 岁 Age	54	1.9	0.0	7.4	13.0	7.4	70.4
55~60 岁 Age	28	0.0	0.0	14.3	10.7	7.1	67.9
女性 Female	310	1.9	3.5	18.7	13.2	12.6	50.0
16~24 岁 Age	64	3.1	9.4	34.4	21.9	12.5	18.8
25~34 岁 Age	90	1.1	3.3	21.1	17.8	17.8	38.9
35~44 岁 Age	73	4.1	1.4	15.1	6.8	11.0	61.6
45~54 岁 Age	60	0.0	1.7	6.7	10.0	8.3	73.3
55~60 岁 Age	23	0.0	0.0	8.7	0.0	8.7	82.6

6-7 样本、男性各年龄层、女性各年龄层的品牌习惯/ Brand Habit in Consuming Ice-cream by the Whole Sample, Age and Gender Groups

	人数 Number	基本固定食用一个牌子 used in only one brand	比较固定地食用两个或三个牌子 used in two or three brands	基本上不太固定牌子 no brand preference
样本 Sample	290	33.1	31.4	35.5
男性 Male	136	36.8	26.5	36.8
16~24 岁 Age	46	34.8	28.3	37.0
25~34 岁 Age	39	41.0	30.8	28.2
35~44 岁 Age	26	42.3	15.4	42.3
45~54 岁 Age	16	25.0	25.0	50.0
55~60 岁 Age	9	33.3	33.3	33.3
女性 Female	154	29.9	35.7	34.4
16~24 岁 Age	52	28.8	38.5	32.7
25~34 岁 Age	55	29.1	38.2	32.7
35~44 岁 Age	28	35.7	32.1	32.1
45~54 岁 Age	15	33.3	26.7	40.0
55~60 岁 Age	4	0.0	25.0	75.0

6-8 选择该类商品的考虑因素/ Ranking of the Considerations in Purchasing

注：本题为多选题，合计百分比超过 100%(Multiple answers)

排名 Ranking	考虑因素 Considerations	人次 Person-time	百分比 Percent
1	口味好 pleasant taste	225	77.9
2	价格适中 reasonable price	98	33.9
3	有名的牌子 famous brand	66	22.8
4	购买方便 easy to buy	53	18.3
5	只是由于习惯 out of habit	21	7.3
6	广告影响 influence of advertising	19	6.6
7	包装吸引人 appealing package	17	5.9
8	朋友推荐 introduction of friends	13	4.5
9	有优惠条件 with preferential terms	7	2.4
10	售货员介绍 introduced by the shop assistants	4	1.4
11	其它 others	3	1.0

n=289

6-9 样本、男性各年龄层、女性各年龄层最常食用的种类/ Kinds of the Consumed Ice-cream by the Whole Sample, Age and Gender Groups

注：本题为多选题，合计百分比超过 100%(Multiple answers)

	人数 Number	棒型冰淇淋 popsicle	蛋筒 cone	盒/杯装冰淇淋 box/cup	袋装冰淇淋 bag	大盒/桶家庭装冰淇淋 big size box for family use	其它 others
样本 Sample	289	19.4	27.0	57.4	11.8	11.8	0.7
男性 Male	135	20.0	21.5	54.8	15.6	8.9	0.0
16~24 岁 Age	45	24.4	24.4	57.8	11.1	6.7	0.0
25~34 岁 Age	39	17.9	25.6	59.0	12.8	7.7	0.0
35~44 岁 Age	26	15.4	15.4	46.2	19.2	19.2	0.0
45~54 岁 Age	16	31.3	6.3	56.3	12.5	6.3	0.0
55~60 岁 Age	9	0.0	33.3	44.4	44.4	0.0	0.0
女性 Female	154	18.8	31.8	59.7	8.4	14.3	1.3
16~24 岁 Age	52	15.4	34.6	73.1	1.9	13.5	1.9
25~34 岁 Age	54	22.2	29.6	57.4	3.7	18.5	0.0
35~44 岁 Age	28	21.4	35.7	46.4	17.9	7.1	3.6
45~54 岁 Age	16	18.8	25.0	43.8	25.0	18.8	0.0
55~60 岁 Age	4	0.0	25.0	75.0	25.0	0.0	0.0

6-10 样本、男性各年龄层、女性各年龄层最常购买的场所/ Locations of Purchasing by the Whole Sample, Age and Gender Groups

	人数 Number	街头冷柜 vender	冷饮店 ice-cream shop	餐厅 restaurant	小卖部 grocery	超市 supermar-ket	批发点 wholesale market	商场 depart-ment store	其它 others
样本 Sample	275	40.4	18.5	1.5	10.5	8.0	14.5	6.2	0.4
男性 Male	130	46.9	18.5	0.8	10.8	6.2	12.3	3.8	0.8
16~24 岁 Age	44	59.1	9.1	2.3	18.2	4.5	4.5	2.3	0.0
25~34 岁 Age	37	54.1	24.3	0.0	5.4	2.7	8.1	5.4	0.0
35~44 岁 Age	24	29.2	25.0	0.0	4.2	8.3	29.2	4.2	0.0
45~54 岁 Age	16	37.5	18.8	0.0	18.8	6.3	12.5	6.3	0.0
55~60 岁 Age	9	22.2	22.2	0.0	0.0	22.2	22.2	0.0	11.1
女性 Female	145	34.5	18.6	2.1	10.3	9.7	16.6	8.3	0.0
16~24 岁 Age	49	46.9	16.3	2.0	10.2	6.1	4.1	14.3	0.0
25~34 岁 Age	51	33.3	21.6	2.0	11.8	9.8	17.6	3.9	0.0
35~44 岁 Age	28	21.4	14.3	3.6	10.7	17.9	25.0	7.1	0.0
45~54 岁 Age	13	15.4	30.8	0.0	7.7	0.0	38.5	7.7	0.0
55~60 岁 Age	4	50.0	0.0	0.0	0.0	25.0	25.0	0.0	0.0

6-11 重度消费者人口分布/ Demographics of the Heavy Consumers

	人数 Number	16-24 岁 Age	25-34 岁 Age	35-44 岁 Age	45-54 岁 Age	55-60 岁 Age
样本 Sample	133	39.1	28.6	20.3	7.5	4.5
男性 Male	58	37.9	25.9	20.7	8.6	6.9
天天吃 daily	5	60.0	0.0	20.0	20.0	0.0
一周 3 次或以上 3 times or over a week	12	41.7	25.0	33.3	0.0	0.0
一周 1~2 次 once or twice a week	41	34.1	29.3	17.1	9.8	9.8
女性 Female	75	40.0	30.7	20.0	6.7	2.7
天天吃 daily	6	33.3	16.7	50.0	0.0	0.0
一周 3 次或以上 3 times or over a week	11	54.5	27.3	9.1	9.1	0.0
一周 1~2 次 once or twice a week	58	37.9	32.8	19.0	6.9	3.4

6-12 不同消费者层的常用品牌/ The Most Frequently Used Brands by Market Segments

6-12-1 时尚流行指标/ Fads Popular Index

	人数 Number	第一品牌及百分比 1st/ percent	第二品牌及百分比 2nd/ percent	第三品牌及百分比 3rd/ percent	第四品牌及百分比 4th/ percent
样本 Sample	270	**新大陆 New Continent(35.6)**	**伊利 Yili(31.1)**	**美登高 Meadow Gold(11.1)**	**和路雪 Wall's(9.6)**
平实生活指向 simple living orientation	132	新大陆 New Continent(35.6)	伊利 Yili(31.8)	美登高 Meadow Gold(8.3)	和路雪 Wall's(7.6)
时尚流行指向 fashion orientation	138	新大陆 New Continent(35.5)	伊利 Yili(30.4)	美登高 Meadow Gold(13.8)	和路雪 Wall's(11.6)

6-12-2 广告态度指标/ Advertising Attitude Index

	人数 Number	第一品牌及百分比 1st/ percent	第二品牌及百分比 2nd/ percent	第三品牌及百分比 3rd/ percent	第四品牌及百分比 4th/ percent
样本 Sample	272	**新大陆 New Continent(35.3)**	**伊利 Yili(31.3)**	**美登高 Meadow Gold(11.4)**	**和路雪 Wall's(9.9)**
广告淡漠指向 indifferent orientation	70	新大陆 New Continent(47.1)	伊利 Yili(21.4)	和路雪 Wall's(10.0)	美登高 Meadow Gold(8.6)
中间层 medium	166	伊利 Yili(34.9)	新大陆 New Continent(30.7)	美登高 Meadow Gold(12.0)	和路雪 Wall's(10.8)
信赖广告指向 loyal orientation	36	伊利 Yili(33.3) 新大陆 New Continent(33.3)	美登高 Meadow Gold(13.9)	和路雪 Wall's(5.6)	美怡乐 Meiyile(2.8) 香港冰淇淋大王 Hong Kong(2.8) 冷狗 Colddog(2.8) 雪乔 Xueqiao(2.8) 阿波罗 Apollo(2.8)

6-12-3 饮食健康指标/ Foods & Drink Quality Index

	人数 Number	第一品牌及百分比 1st/ percent	第二品牌及百分比 2nd/ percent	第三品牌及百分比 3rd/ percent	第四品牌及百分比 4th/ percent
样本 Sample	270	**新大陆 New Continent(35.2)**	**伊利 Yili(31.1)**	**美登高 Meadow Gold(11.5)**	**和路雪 Wall's(10.0)**
饮食"温饱"指向 "basic" orientation	93	新大陆 New Continent(34.4)	伊利 Yili(32.3)	和路雪 Wall's(10.8)	美登高 Meadow Gold(9.7)
中间层 medium	124	新大陆 New Continent(40.3)	伊利 Yili(25.0)	美登高 Meadow Gold(13.7)	和路雪 Wall's(9.7)
健康营养指向 health & nutrition orientation	53	伊利 Yili(43.4)	新大陆 New Continent(24.5)	和路雪 Wall's(9.4) 美登高 Meadow Gold(9.4)	雪乔 Xueqiao(5.7)

6-13 重度消费者的消费者层构成/ The Composition of the Heavy Consumers

6-13-1 时尚流行指标/ Fads Popular Index

	人数 Number	平实生活指向 simple living orientation	时尚流行指向 fashion orientation
样本 Sample	132	48.5	51.5
天天吃 daily	11	45.5	54.5
一周 3 次或以上 3 times or over a week	23	56.5	43.5
一周 1～2 次 once or twice a week	98	46.9	53.1

6-13-2 广告态度指标/ Advertising Attitude Index

	人数 Number	广告淡漠指向 indifferent orientation	中间层 medium	信赖广告指向 loyal orientation
样本 Sample	133	25.6	61.7	12.8
天天吃 daily	11	9.1	81.8	9.1
一周 3 次或以上 3 times or over a week	23	43.5	47.8	8.7
一周 1～2 次 once or twice a week	99	23.2	62.6	14.1

6-13-3 饮食健康指标/ Foods & Drink Quality Index

	人数 Number	饮食"温饱"指向 "basic" orientation	中间层 medium	健康营养指向 health & nutrition orientation
样本 Sample	132	35.6	42.4	22.0
天天吃 daily	10	10.0	60.0	30.0
一周 3 次或以上 3 times or over a week	23	26.1	60.9	13.0
一周 1～2 次 once or twice a week	99	40.4	36.4	23.2

● 武汉 / Wuhan

6-1 最近三个月食用频率的比例/ Proportion of the Sample Consuming Ice-cream in the Last Three Months

	人数 Number	百分比 Percent
天天吃 daily	16	2.5
一周 3 次或以上 3 times or over a week	50	7.8
一周 1~2 次 once or twice a week	101	15.7
一个月 2～3 次 2 or 3 times a month	111	17.3
一个月 1 次或以下 once a month or below	80	12.5
没吃过 never	284	44.2

n=642

6-2 最常用品牌排名/ Ranking of the Most Frequently Used Brands

排名 Brand Ranking	品牌 Brands	人数 Number	百分比 Percent
1	和路雪 Wall's	135	38.2
2	美登高 Meadow Gold	76	21.5
3	五丰 Wufeng	61	17.3
4	伊利 Yili	38	10.8
5	美怡乐 Meiyile	14	4.0
6	冷狗 Colddog	4	1.1
7	雀巢 Nestle	3	0.8

n=353

6-3 样本、男性各年龄层、女性各年龄层的常用品牌/ The Most Frequently Used Brands by the Whole Sample, Age and Gender Groups

	人数 Number	第一品牌及百分比 1st/ percent	第二品牌及百分比 2nd/ percent	第三品牌及百分比 3rd/ percent	第四品牌及百分比 4th/ percent
样本 Sample	**353**	**和路雪 Wall's(38.2)**	**美登高 Meadow Gold(21.5)**	**五丰 Wufeng(17.3)**	**伊利 Yili(10.8)**
男性 Male	**157**	**和路雪 Wall's(38.2)**	**美登高 Meadow Gold(23.6)**	**五丰 Wufeng(18.5)**	**伊利 Yili(10.8)**
16~24 岁 Age	46	和路雪 Wall's(50.0)	美登高 Meadow Gold(28.3)	伊利 Yili(10.9) 五丰 Wufeng(10.9)	
25~34 岁 Age	53	和路雪 Wall's(45.3)	美登高 Meadow Gold(24.5)	五丰 Wufeng(15.1)	伊利 Yili(5.7) 美怡乐 Meiyile(5.7)
35~44 岁 Age	31	和路雪 Wall's(22.6) 五丰 Wufeng(22.6)	伊利 Yili(19.4)	美登高 Meadow Gold(16.1)	美怡乐 Meiyile(3.2) 香港冰淇淋大王 HongKong(3.2) 乐天 Lotte(3.2) 冷狗 Colddog(3.2)
45~54 岁 Age	19	五丰 Wufeng(36.8)	和路雪 Wall's(21.1)	美登高 Meadow Gold(15.8)	伊利 Yili(10.5)
55~60 岁 Age	8	美登高 MeadowGold(37.5)	和路雪 Wall's(25.0) 五丰 Wufeng(25.0)	伊利 Yili(12.5)	
女性 Female	**196**	**和路雪 Wall's(38.3)**	**美登高 Meadow Gold(19.9)**	**五丰 Wufeng(16.3)**	**伊利 Yili(10.7)**
16~24 岁 Age	57	和路雪 Wall's(59.6)	美登高 Meadow Gold(15.8) 伊利 Yili(15.8)	五丰 Wufeng(5.3)	五羊 Wuyang(1.8) 圣麦乐 Sanmarlo(1.8)
25~34 岁 Age	63	和路雪 Wall's(41.3)	五丰 Wufeng(19.0)	美登高 MeadowGold(17.5)	美怡乐 Meiyile(6.3)
35~44 岁 Age	41	美登高 Meadow Gold(24.4)	伊利 Yili(19.5)	和路雪 Wall's(17.1) 五丰 Wufeng(17.1)	美怡乐 Meiyile(12.2)
45~54 岁 Age	30	美登高 Meadow Gold(26.7)	和路雪 Wall's(23.3) 五丰 Wufeng(23.3)	伊利 Yili(6.7) 雀巢 Nestle(6.7)	美怡乐 Meiyile(3.3) 光明 Bright(3.3) 阿波罗 Apollo(3.3)
55~60 岁 Age	5	五丰 Wufeng(60.0)	和路雪 Wall's(20.0) 美登高 Meadow Gold(20.0)		

6-4 理想品牌排名/ Ranking of the Ideal Brands

排名 Brand Ranking	品牌 Brands	人数 Number	百分比 Percent
1	和路雪 Wall's	182	28.4
2	美登高 Meadow Gold	85	13.3
3	五丰 Wufeng	70	10.9
4	伊利 Yili	41	6.4
5	美怡乐 Meiyile	11	1.7
6	雀巢 Nestle	5	0.8
7	五羊 Wuyang	3	0.5
7	光明 Bright	3	0.5

n=641

6-5 样本、男性各年龄层、女性各年龄层最近三个月有无购买的比例/ Purchasing in the Last Three Months by the Whole Sample, Age and Gender Groups

	人数 Number	买过 yes	没买过 no
样本 Sample	**641**	**56.5**	**43.5**
男性 Male	**311**	**52.1**	**47.9**
16~24 岁 Age	65	66.2	33.8
25~34 岁 Age	89	62.9	37.1
35~44 岁 Age	80	42.5	57.5
45~54 岁 Age	52	40.4	59.6
55~60 岁 Age	25	32.0	68.0
女性 Female	**330**	**60.6**	**39.4**
16~24 岁 Age	69	76.8	23.2
25~34 岁 Age	96	65.6	34.4
35~44 岁 Age	77	59.7	40.3
45~54 岁 Age	62	51.6	48.4
55~60 岁 Age	26	23.1	76.9

6-6 样本、男性各年龄层、女性各年龄层最近三个月的食用频率/ Frequencies of Consuming Ice-cream in the Last Three Months by the Whole Sample, Age and Gender Groups

	人数 Number	天天吃 daily	一周3次或以上 3 times or over a week	一周1~2次 once or twice a week	一个月2~3次 2 or 3 times a month	一个月1次或以下 once a month or below	没吃过 never
样本 Sample	642	2.5	7.8	15.7	17.3	12.5	44.2
男性 Male	311	1.6	5.8	12.5	18.0	13.2	48.9
16~24 岁 Age	65	0.0	9.2	21.5	20.0	23.1	26.2
25~34 岁 Age	89	0.0	7.9	10.1	27.0	14.6	40.4
35~44 岁 Age	80	5.0	2.5	13.8	11.3	6.3	61.3
45~54 岁 Age	52	1.9	3.8	7.7	13.5	9.6	63.5
55~60 岁 Age	25	0.0	4.0	4.0	12.0	12.0	68.0
女性 Female	331	3.3	9.7	18.7	16.6	11.8	39.9
16~24 岁 Age	69	2.9	15.9	30.4	18.8	15.9	15.9
25~34 岁 Age	96	3.1	11.5	17.7	19.8	13.5	34.4
35~44 岁 Age	78	3.8	9.0	20.5	14.1	7.7	44.9
45~54 岁 Age	62	4.8	4.8	8.1	17.7	12.9	51.6
55~60 岁 Age	26	0.0	0.0	11.5	3.8	3.8	80.8

6-7 样本、男性各年龄层、女性各年龄层的品牌习惯/ Brand Habit in Consuming Ice-cream by the Whole Sample, Age and Gender Groups

	人数 Number	基本固定食用一个牌子 used in only one brand	比较固定地食用两个或三个牌子 used in two or three brands	基本上不太固定牌子 no brand preference
样本 Sample	358	29.1	41.1	29.9
男性 Male	159	33.3	36.5	30.2
16~24 岁 Age	48	33.3	43.8	22.9
25~34 岁 Age	53	34.0	37.7	28.3
35~44 岁 Age	31	25.8	38.7	35.5
45~54 岁 Age	19	42.1	21.1	36.8
55~60 岁 Age	8	37.5	12.5	50.0
女性 Female	199	25.6	44.7	29.6
16~24 岁 Age	58	24.1	44.8	31.0
25~34 岁 Age	63	25.4	52.4	22.2
35~44 岁 Age	43	20.9	44.2	34.9
45~54 岁 Age	30	33.3	33.3	33.3
55~60 岁 Age	5	40.0	20.0	40.0

6-8 选择该类商品的考虑因素/ Ranking of the Considerations in Purchasing

注：本题为多选题，合计百分比超过 100%(Multiple answers）

排名 Ranking	考虑因素 Considerations	人次 Person-time	百分比 Percent
1	口味好 pleasant taste	273	76.3
2	价格适中 reasonable price	149	41.6
3	有名的牌子 famous brand	118	33.0
4	购买方便 easy to buy	81	22.6
5	只是由于习惯 out of habit	27	7.5
6	广告影响 influence of advertising	24	6.7
6	包装吸引人 appealing package	24	6.7
7	朋友推荐 introduction of friends	22	6.1
8	售货员介绍 introduced by the shop assistants	16	4.5
9	有优惠条件 with preferential terms	14	3.9
10	其它 others	11	3.1

n=358

6-9 样本、男性各年龄层、女性各年龄层最常食用的种类/ Kinds of the Consumed Ice-cream by the Whole Sample, Age and Gender Groups

注：本题为多选题，合计百分比超过 100%(Multiple answers）

	人数 Number	棒型冰淇淋 popsicle	蛋筒 cone	盒/杯装冰淇淋 box/cup	袋装冰淇淋 bag	大盒/桶 家庭装冰淇淋 big size box for family use	其它 others
样本 Sample	358	30.4	45.8	52.8	8.7	9.5	0.6
男性 Male	159	22.6	47.2	59.7	8.8	8.2	0.0
16~24 岁 Age	48	16.7	50.0	58.3	10.4	8.3	0.0
25~34 岁 Age	53	26.4	45.3	60.4	13.2	7.5	0.0
35~44 岁 Age	31	22.6	61.3	48.4	6.5	6.5	0.0
45~54 岁 Age	19	26.3	31.6	78.9	0.0	10.5	0.0
55~60 岁 Age	8	25.0	25.0	62.5	0.0	12.5	0.0
女性 Female	199	36.7	44.7	47.2	8.5	10.6	1.0
16~24 岁 Age	58	46.6	48.3	37.9	10.3	8.6	1.7
25~34 岁 Age	63	34.9	42.9	46.0	7.9	11.1	1.6
35~44 岁 Age	43	27.9	48.8	44.2	7.0	14.0	0.0
45~54 岁 Age	30	33.3	40.0	70.0	6.7	10.0	0.0
55~60 岁 Age	5	40.0	20.0	60.0	20.0	0.0	0.0

6-10 样本、男性各年龄层、女性各年龄层最常购买的场所/ Locations of Purchasing by the Whole Sample, Age and Gender Groups

	人数 Number	街头冷柜 vender	冷饮店 ice-cream shop	餐厅 restaurant	小卖部 grocery	超市 supermarket	批发点 wholesale market	商场 department store	其它 others
样本 Sample	350	38.3	9.4	1.4	12.0	7.7	29.1	1.1	0.9
男性 Male	156	41.0	8.3	1.3	14.1	9.6	24.4	1.3	0.0
16~24 岁 Age	46	50.0	4.3	0.0	17.4	13.0	13.0	2.2	0.0
25~34 岁 Age	53	45.3	13.2	1.9	13.2	5.7	20.8	0.0	0.0
35~44 岁 Age	31	25.8	3.2	3.2	16.1	12.9	35.5	3.2	0.0
45~54 岁 Age	19	42.1	10.5	0.0	5.3	5.3	36.8	0.0	0.0
55~60 岁 Age	7	14.3	14.3	0.0	14.3	14.3	42.9	0.0	0.0
女性 Female	194	36.1	10.3	1.5	10.3	6.2	33.0	1.0	1.5
16~24 岁 Age	58	60.3	6.9	3.4	13.8	3.4	12.1	0.0	0.0
25~34 岁 Age	60	30.0	11.7	1.7	8.3	8.3	38.3	0.0	1.7
35~44 岁 Age	42	28.6	14.3	0.0	11.9	7.1	31.0	4.8	2.4
45~54 岁 Age	29	13.8	10.3	0.0	6.9	6.9	58.6	0.0	3.4
55~60 岁 Age	5	20.0	0.0	0.0	0.0	0.0	80.0	0.0	0.0

6-11 重度消费者人口分布/ Demographics of the Heavy Consumers

	人数 Number	16-24 岁 Age	25-34 岁 Age	35-44 岁 Age	45-54 岁 Age	55-60 岁 Age
样本 Sample	167	32.3	28.1	25.7	10.8	3.0
男性 Male	62	32.3	25.8	27.4	11.3	3.2
天天吃 daily	5	0.0	0.0	80.0	20.0	0.0
一周 3 次或以上 3 times or over a week	18	33.3	38.9	11.1	11.1	5.6
一周 1~2 次 once or twice a week	39	35.9	23.1	28.2	10.3	2.6
女性 Female	105	32.4	29.5	24.8	10.5	2.9
天天吃 daily	11	18.2	27.3	27.3	27.3	0.0
一周 3 次或以上 3 times or over a week	32	34.4	34.4	21.9	9.4	0.0
一周 1~2 次 once or twice a week	62	33.9	27.4	25.8	8.1	4.8

6-12 不同消费者层的常用品牌/ The Most Frequently Used Brands by Market Segments

6-12-1 时尚流行指标/ Fads Popular Index

	人数 Number	第一品牌及百分比 1st/ percent	第二品牌及百分比 2nd/ percent	第三品牌及百分比 3rd/ percent
样本 Sample	349	**和路雪 Wall's(38.4)**	**美登高 Meadow Gold(21.5)**	**五丰 Wufeng(16.9)**
平实生活指向 simple living orientation	158	和路雪 Wall's(33.5)	美登高 Meadow Gold(24.7)	五丰 Wufeng(15.8)
时尚流行指向 fashion orientation	191	和路雪 Wall's(42.4)	美登高 Meadow Gold(18.8)	五丰 Wufeng(17.8)

6-12-2 广告态度指标/ Advertising Attitude Index

	人数 Number	第一品牌及百分比 1st/ percent	第二品牌及百分比 2nd/ percent	第三品牌及百分比 3rd/ percent
样本 Sample	350	**和路雪 Wall's(38.3)**	**美登高 Meadow Gold(21.4)**	**五丰 Wufeng(17.1)**
广告淡漠指向 indifferent orientation	84	和路雪 Wall's(39.3)	美登高 Meadow Gold(20.2)	五丰 Wufeng(16.7)
中间层 medium	221	和路雪 Wall's(38.0)	美登高 Meadow Gold(22.2)	五丰 Wufeng(15.8)
信赖广告指向 loyal orientation	45	和路雪 Wall's(37.8)	五丰 Wufeng(24.4)	美登高 Meadow Gold(20.0)

6-12-3 饮食健康指标/ Foods & Drink Quality Index

	人数 Number	第一品牌及百分比 1st/ percent	第二品牌及百分比 2nd/ percent	第三品牌及百分比 3rd/ percent
样本 Sample	350	**和路雪 Wall's(38.0)**	**美登高 Meadow Gold(21.4)**	**五丰 Wufeng(17.4)**
饮食“温饱”指向 "basic" orientation	111	和路雪 Wall's(38.7)	美登高 Meadow Gold(19.8)	五丰 Wufeng(18.9)
中间层 medium	163	和路雪 Wall's(38.7)	美登高 Meadow Gold(22.7)	五丰 Wufeng(15.3)
健康营养指向 health & nutrition orientation	76	和路雪 Wall's(35.5)	美登高 Meadow Gold(21.1)	五丰 Wufeng(19.7)

6-13 重度消费者的消费者层构成/ The Composition of the Heavy Consumers

6-13-1 时尚流行指标/ Fads Popular Index

	人数 Number	平实生活指向 simple living orientation	时尚流行指向 fashion orientation
样本 Sample	165	38.2	61.8
天天吃 daily	16	31.3	68.8
一周 3 次或以上 3 times or over a week	49	32.7	67.3
一周 1～2 次 once or twice a week	100	42.0	58.0

6-13-2 广告态度指标/ Advertising Attitude Index

	人数 Number	广告淡漠指向 indifferent orientation	中间层 medium	信赖广告指向 loyal orientation
样本 Sample	165	23.6	59.4	17.0
天天吃 daily	16	31.3	50.0	18.8
一周 3 次或以上 3 times or over a week	49	20.4	57.1	22.4
一周 1～2 次 once or twice a week	100	24.0	62.0	14.0

6-13-3 饮食健康指标/ Foods & Drink Quality Index

	人数 Number	饮食“温饱”指向 "basic" orientation	中间层 medium	健康营养指向 health & nutrition orientation
样本 Sample	165	30.9	47.3	21.8
天天吃 daily	16	31.3	25.0	43.8
一周 3 次或以上 3 times or over a week	49	26.5	55.1	18.4
一周 1～2 次 once or twice a week	100	33.0	47.0	20.0

● 西安 / Xi'an

6-1 最近三个月食用频率的比例/ Proportion of the Sample Consuming Ice-cream in the Last Three Months

	人数 Number	百分比 Percent
天天吃 daily	16	2.7
一周 3 次或以上 3 times or over a week	49	8.2
一周 1~2 次 once or twice a week	112	18.6
一个月 2~3 次 2 or 3 times a month	94	15.6
一个月 1 次或以下 once a month or below	53	8.8
没吃过 never	277	46.1

n=601

6-2 最常用品牌排名/ Ranking of the Most Frequently Used Brands

排名 Brand Ranking	品牌 Brands	人数 Number	百分比 Percent
1	美登高 Meadow Gold	175	54.7
2	和路雪 Wall's	82	25.6
3	伊利 Yili	38	11.9
4	雀巢 Nestle	5	1.6
5	新大陆 New Continent	3	0.9
6	美怡乐 Meiyile	2	0.6
6	北冰洋 Beibingyang	2	0.6
6	31 种冰淇淋 Baskin Robbins	2	0.6

n=320

6-3 样本、男性各年龄层、女性各年龄层的常用品牌/ The Most Frequently Used Brands by the Whole Sample, Age and Gender Groups

	人数 Number	第一品牌及百分比 1st/ percent	第二品牌及百分比 2nd/ percent	第三品牌及百分比 3rd/ percent
样本 Sample	320	**美登高 Meadow Gold(54.7)**	**和路雪 Wall's(25.6)**	**伊利 Yili(11.9)**
男性 Male	146	**美登高 Meadow Gold(58.2)**	**和路雪 Wall's(21.2)**	**伊利 Yili(15.1)**
16~24 岁 Age	40	美登高 Meadow Gold(52.5)	和路雪 Wall's(27.5)	伊利 Yili(10.0)
25~34 岁 Age	46	美登高 Meadow Gold(56.5)	和路雪 Wall's(19.6) 伊利 Yili(19.6)	雀巢 Nestle(2.2) 新大陆 New Continent(2.2)
35~44 岁 Age	38	美登高 Meadow Gold(57.9)	和路雪 Wall's(26.3)	伊利 Yili(13.2)
45~54 岁 Age	17	美登高 Meadow Gold(70.6)	伊利 Yili(17.6)	和路雪 Wall's(5.9) 曼登琳 Mountain(5.9)
55~60 岁 Age	5	美登高 Meadow Gold(80.0)	伊利 Yili(20.0)	
女性 Female	174	**美登高 Meadow Gold(51.7)**	**和路雪 Wall's(29.3)**	**伊利 Yili(9.2)**
16~24 岁 Age	48	美登高 Meadow Gold(43.8)	和路雪 Wall's(31.3)	伊利 Yili(8.3)
25~34 岁 Age	67	美登高 Meadow Gold(55.2)	和路雪 Wall's(31.3)	伊利 Yili(7.5)
35~44 岁 Age	39	美登高 Meadow Gold(51.3)	和路雪 Wall's(25.6)	伊利 Yili(15.4)
45~54 岁 Age	11	美登高 Meadow Gold(54.5)	和路雪 Wall's(27.3)	雀巢 Nestle(9.1) 夏威夷 Hawaii(9.1)
55~60 岁 Age	9	美登高 Meadow Gold(66.7)	和路雪 Wall's(22.2)	伊利 Yili(11.1)

6-4 理想品牌排名/ Ranking of the Ideal Brands

排名 Brand Ranking	品牌 Brands	人数 Number	百分比 Percent
1	美登高 Meadow Gold	262	43.6
2	和路雪 Wall's	114	19.0
3	伊利 Yili	58	9.7
4	夏威夷 Hawaii	9	1.5
5	雀巢 Nestle	6	1.0
6	北冰洋 Beibingyang	5	0.8
7	新大陆 New Continent	3	0.5

n=601

6-5 样本、男性各年龄层、女性各年龄层最近三个月有无购买的比例/ Purchasing in the Last Three Months by the Whole Sample, Age and Gender Groups

	人数 Number	买过 yes	没买过 no
样本 Sample	**601**	**56.7**	**43.3**
男性 Male	**302**	**51.0**	**49.0**
16~24 岁 Age	64	62.5	37.5
25~34 岁 Age	91	51.6	48.4
35~44 岁 Age	77	55.8	44.2
45~54 岁 Age	46	43.5	56.5
55~60 岁 Age	24	16.7	83.3
女性 Female	**299**	**62.5**	**37.5**
16~24 岁 Age	61	75.4	24.6
25~34 岁 Age	90	76.7	23.3
35~44 岁 Age	74	62.2	37.8
45~54 岁 Age	49	32.7	67.3
55~60 岁 Age	25	40.0	60.0

6-6 样本、男性各年龄层、女性各年龄层最近三个月的食用频率/ Frequencies of Consuming Ice-cream in the Last Three Months by the Whole Sample, Age and Gender Groups

	人数 Number	天天吃 daily	一周 3 次或以上 3 times or over a week	一周 1~2 次 once or twice a week	一个月 2~3 次 2 or 3 times a month	一个月 1 次或以下 once a month or below	没吃过 never
样本 Sample	**601**	**2.7**	**8.2**	**18.6**	**15.6**	**8.8**	**46.1**
男性 Male	**302**	**3.0**	**7.3**	**17.9**	**13.9**	**6.3**	**51.7**
16~24 岁 Age	64	4.7	21.9	18.8	14.1	3.1	37.5
25~34 岁 Age	91	1.1	5.5	17.6	20.9	5.5	49.5
35~44 岁 Age	77	3.9	2.6	26.0	11.7	5.2	50.6
45~54 岁 Age	46	4.3	2.2	13.0	8.7	8.7	63.0
55~60 岁 Age	24	0.0	0.0	0.0	4.2	16.7	79.2
女性 Female	**299**	**2.3**	**9.0**	**19.4**	**17.4**	**11.4**	**40.5**
16~24 岁 Age	61	3.3	16.4	39.3	14.8	6.6	19.7
25~34 岁 Age	90	2.2	7.8	23.3	26.7	15.6	24.4
35~44 岁 Age	74	4.1	6.8	13.5	14.9	14.9	45.9
45~54 岁 Age	49	0.0	6.1	2.0	10.2	6.1	75.5
55~60 岁 Age	25	0.0	8.0	8.0	12.0	8.0	64.0

6-7 样本、男性各年龄层、女性各年龄层的品牌习惯/ Brand Habit in Consuming Ice-cream by the Whole Sample, Age and Gender Groups

	人数 Number	基本固定食用一个牌子 used in only one brand	比较固定地食用两个或三个牌子 used in two or three brands	基本上不太固定牌子 no brand preference
样本 Sample	**324**	**32.7**	**40.7**	**26.5**
男性 Male	**146**	**37.7**	**39.0**	**23.3**
16~24 岁 Age	40	35.0	50.0	15.0
25~34 岁 Age	46	39.1	32.6	28.3
35~44 岁 Age	38	42.1	31.6	26.3
45~54 岁 Age	17	29.4	47.1	23.5
55~60 岁 Age	5	40.0	40.0	20.0
女性 Female	**178**	**28.7**	**42.1**	**29.2**
16~24 岁 Age	49	26.5	49.0	24.5
25~34 岁 Age	68	32.4	42.6	25.0
35~44 岁 Age	40	22.5	37.5	40.0
45~54 岁 Age	12	33.3	41.7	25.0
55~60 岁 Age	9	33.3	22.2	44.4

6-8 选择该类商品的考虑因素/ Ranking of the Considerations in Purchasing

注：本题为多选题，合计百分比超过 100%(Multiple answers）

排名 Ranking	考虑因素 Considerations	人次 Person-time	百分比 Percent
1	口味好 pleasant taste	252	77.8
2	价格适中 reasonable price	92	28.4
3	有名的牌子 famous brand	82	25.3
4	购买方便 easy to buy	78	24.1
5	广告影响 influence of advertising	31	9.6
6	只是由于习惯 out of habit	28	8.6
7	包装吸引人 appealing package	24	7.4
8	朋友推荐 introduction of friends	13	4.0
9	售货员介绍 introduced by the shop assistants	9	2.8
10	有优惠条件 with preferential terms	3	0.9
11	其它 others	2	0.6

n=324

6-9 样本、男性各年龄层、女性各年龄层最常食用的种类/ Kinds of the Consumed Ice-cream by the Whole Sample, Age and Gender Groups

注：本题为多选题，合计百分比超过 100%(Multiple answers）

	人数 Number	棒型冰淇淋 popsicle	蛋筒 cone	盒/杯装冰淇淋 box/cup	袋装冰淇淋 bag	大盒/桶 家庭装冰淇淋 big size box for family use	其它 others
样本 Sample	**324**	**28.4**	**32.4**	**54.3**	**9.0**	**9.6**	**0.0**
男性 Male	**146**	**24.0**	**33.6**	**52.1**	**11.6**	**9.6**	**0.0**
16~24 岁 Age	40	20.0	37.5	45.0	10.0	12.5	0.0
25~34 岁 Age	46	26.1	26.1	54.3	13.0	8.7	0.0
35~44 岁 Age	38	18.4	42.1	55.3	13.2	7.9	0.0
45~54 岁 Age	17	29.4	29.4	58.8	11.8	11.8	0.0
55~60 岁 Age	5	60.0	20.0	40.0	0.0	0.0	0.0
女性 Female	**178**	**32.0**	**31.5**	**56.2**	**6.7**	**9.6**	**0.0**
16~24 岁 Age	49	28.6	34.7	49.0	8.2	8.2	0.0
25~34 岁 Age	68	30.9	30.9	60.3	7.4	8.8	0.0
35~44 岁 Age	40	30.0	37.5	55.0	5.0	12.5	0.0
45~54 岁 Age	12	33.3	16.7	58.3	0.0	8.3	0.0
55~60 岁 Age	9	66.7	11.1	66.7	11.1	11.1	0.0

6-10 样本、男性各年龄层、女性各年龄层最常购买的场所/ Locations of Purchasing by the Whole Sample, Age and Gender Groups

	人数 Number	街头冷柜 vender	冷饮店 ice-cream shop	餐厅 restaurant	小卖部 grocery	超市 supermarket	批发点 wholesale market	商场 department store	其它 others
样本 Sample	**320**	**36.9**	**18.4**	**0.3**	**16.9**	**8.1**	**12.8**	**5.9**	**0.6**
男性 Male	**143**	**39.9**	**18.2**	**0.7**	**14.0**	**8.4**	**13.3**	**5.6**	**0.0**
16~24 岁 Age	37	48.6	13.5	2.7	13.5	10.8	5.4	5.4	0.0
25~34 岁 Age	46	39.1	17.4	0.0	15.2	6.5	15.2	6.5	0.0
35~44 岁 Age	38	42.1	15.8	0.0	15.8	5.3	13.2	7.9	0.0
45~54 岁 Age	17	17.6	29.4	0.0	11.8	11.8	29.4	0.0	0.0
55~60 岁 Age	5	40.0	40.0	0.0	0.0	20.0	0.0	0.0	0.0
女性 Female	**177**	**34.5**	**18.6**	**0.0**	**19.2**	**7.9**	**12.4**	**6.2**	**1.1**
16~24 岁 Age	49	30.6	14.3	0.0	30.6	8.2	8.2	6.1	2.0
25~34 岁 Age	68	42.6	16.2	0.0	16.2	5.9	7.4	10.3	1.5
35~44 岁 Age	39	25.6	28.2	0.0	17.9	2.6	23.1	2.6	0.0
45~54 岁 Age	12	25.0	16.7	0.0	8.3	25.0	25.0	0.0	0.0
55~60 岁 Age	9	44.4	22.2	0.0	0.0	22.2	11.1	0.0	0.0

6-11 重度消费者人口分布/ Demographics of the Heavy Consumers

	人数 Number	16-24 岁 Age	25-34 岁 Age	35-44 岁 Age	45-54 Age	55-60 岁 Age
样本 Sample	177	36.7	29.4	24.3	7.3	2.3
男性 Male	85	34.1	25.9	29.4	10.6	0.0
天天吃 daily	9	33.3	11.1	33.3	22.2	0.0
一周 3 次或以上 3 times or over a week	22	63.6	22.7	9.1	4.5	0.0
一周 1~2 次 once or twice a week	54	22.2	29.6	37.0	11.1	0.0
女性 Female	92	39.1	32.6	19.6	4.3	4.3
天天吃 daily	7	28.6	28.6	42.9	0.0	0.0
一周 3 次或以上 3 times or over a week	27	37.0	25.9	18.5	11.1	7.4
一周 1~2 次 once or twice a week	58	41.4	36.2	17.2	1.7	3.4

6-12 不同消费者层的常用品牌/ The Most Frequently Used Brands by Market Segments

6-12-1 时尚流行指标/ Fads Popular Index

	人数 Number	第一品牌及百分比 1st/ percent	第二品牌及百分比 2nd/ percent	第三品牌及百分比 3rd/ percent
样本 Sample	319	**美登高 Meadow Gold(54.9)**	**和路雪 Wall's(25.7)**	**伊利 Yili(11.9)**
平实生活指向 simple living orientation	148	美登高 Meadow Gold(58.8)	和路雪 Wall's(17.6)	伊利 Yili(14.2)
时尚流行指向 fashion orientation	171	美登高 Meadow Gold(51.5)	和路雪 Wall's(32.7)	伊利 Yili(9.9)

6-12-2 广告态度指标/ Advertising Attitude Index

	人数 Number	第一品牌及百分比 1st/ percent	第二品牌及百分比 2nd/ percent	第三品牌及百分比 3rd/ percent
样本 Sample	318	**美登高 Meadow Gold(54.4)**	**和路雪 Wall's(25.8)**	**伊利 Yili(11.9)**
广告淡漠指向 indifferent orientation	97	美登高 Meadow Gold(59.8)	和路雪 Wall's(25.8)	伊利 Yili(11.3)
中间层 medium	175	美登高 Meadow Gold(51.4)	和路雪 Wall's(26.9)	伊利 Yili(13.1)
信赖广告指向 loyal orientation	46	美登高 Meadow Gold(54.3)	和路雪 Wall's(21.7)	伊利 Yili(8.7)

6-12-3 饮食健康指标/ Foods & Drink Quality Index

	人数 Number	第一品牌及百分比 1st/ percent	第二品牌及百分比 2nd/ percent	第三品牌及百分比 3rd/ percent
样本 Sample	320	**美登高 Meadow Gold(54.7)**	**和路雪 Wall's(25.6)**	**伊利 Yili(11.9)**
饮食"温饱"指向 "basic" orientation	110	美登高 Meadow Gold(57.3)	和路雪 Wall's(22.7)	伊利 Yili(11.8)
中间层 medium	153	美登高 Meadow Gold(51.0)	和路雪 Wall's(28.8)	伊利 Yili(12.4)
健康营养指向 health & nutrition orientation	57	美登高 Meadow Gold(59.6)	和路雪 Wall's(22.8)	伊利 Yili(10.5)

6-13 重度消费者的消费者层构成/ The Composition of the Heavy Consumers

6-13-1 时尚流行指标/ Fads Popular Index

	人数 Number	平实生活指向 simple living orientation	时尚流行指向 fashion orientation
样本 Sample	177	41.2	58.8
天天吃 daily	16	6.3	93.8
一周 3 次或以上 3 times or over a week	49	46.9	53.1
一周 1～2 次 once or twice a week	112	43.8	56.3

6-13-2 广告态度指标/ Advertising Attitude Index

	人数 Number	广告淡漠指向 indifferent orientation	中间层 medium	信赖广告指向 loyal orientation
样本 Sample	176	29.0	55.7	15.3
天天吃 daily	16	25.0	50.0	25.0
一周 3 次或以上 3 times or over a week	49	32.7	55.1	12.2
一周 1～2 次 once or twice a week	111	27.9	56.8	15.3

6-13-3 饮食健康指标/ Foods & Drink Quality Index

	人数 Number	饮食"温饱"指向 "basic" orientation	中间层 medium	健康营养指向 health & nutrition orientation
样本 Sample	177	32.2	49.7	18.1
天天吃 daily	16	43.8	50.0	6.3
一周 3 次或以上 3 times or over a week	49	24.5	55.1	20.4
一周 1～2 次 once or twice a week	112	33.9	47.3	18.8

● 沈阳 / Shenyang

6-1 最近三个月食用频率的比例/ Proportion of the Sample Consuming Ice-cream in the Last Three Months

	人数 Number	百分比 Percent
天天吃 daily	28	4.7
一周 3 次或以上 3 times or over a week	74	12.3
一周 1~2 次 once or twice a week	142	23.7
一个月 2～3 次 2 or 3 times a month	111	18.5
一个月 1 次或以下 once a month or below	69	11.5
没吃过 never	176	29.3

n=600

6-2 最常用品牌排名/ Ranking of the Most Frequently Used Brands

排名 Brand Ranking	品牌 Brands	人数 Number	百分比 Percent
1	美登高 Meadow Gold	142	34.2
2	中街大果 Zhong Jie Da Guo	83	20.0
3	伊利 Yili	56	13.5
4	德氏 Deshi	50	12.0
5	和路雪 Wall's	39	9.4
6	宏宝莱 HBL	16	3.9
7	红星礼拜天 Red Star	9	2.2

n=415

6-3 样本、男性各年龄层、女性各年龄层的常用品牌/ The Most Frequently Used Brands by the Whole Sample, Age and Gender Groups

	人数 Number	第一品牌及百分比 1st/ percent	第二品牌及百分比 2nd/ percent	第三品牌及百分比 3rd/ percent	第四品牌及百分比 4th/ percent
样本 Sample	415	**美登高 Meadow Gold(34.2)**	**中街大果 Zhong Jie Da Guo (20.0)**	**伊利 Yili(13.5)**	**德氏 Deshi(12.0)**
男性 Male	195	**美登高 Meadow Gold(34.9)**	**中街大果 Zhong Jie Da Guo (19.5)**	**伊利 Yili(15.4)**	**德氏 Deshi(13.3)**
16~24 岁 Age	57	美登高 Meadow Gold(35.1)	伊利 Yili(24.6)	中街大果 Zhong Jie Da Guo(14.0)	和路雪 Wall's(10.5)
25~34 岁 Age	63	美登高 Meadow Gold(38.1)	中街大果 Zhong Jie Da Guo(19.0)	伊利 Yili(14.3) 德氏 Deshi(14.3)	和路雪 Wall's(7.9)
35~44 岁 Age	43	美登高 Meadow Gold(30.2)	中街大果 Zhong Jie Da Guo(27.9)	德氏 Deshi(23.3)	伊利 Yili(7.0)
45~54 岁 Age	21	中街大果 Zhong Jie Da Guo(23.8)	伊利 Yili(19.0)	和路雪 Wall's(14.3) 美登高 Meadow Gold(14.3)	德氏 Deshi(9.5)
55~60 岁 Age	11	美登高 Meadow Gold(72.7)	德氏 Deshi(9.1) 中街大果 Zhong Jie Da Guo(9.1) 西塔 Xita(9.1)		
女性 Female	220	**美登高 Meadow Gold(33.6)**	**中街大果 Zhong Jie Da Guo (20.5)**	**伊利 Yili(11.8)**	**德氏 Deshi(10.9)**
16~24 岁 Age	58	美登高 Meadow Gold(34.5)	和路雪 Wall's(20.7)	中街大果 Zhong Jie Da Guo(19.0)	伊利 Yili(10.3)
25~34 岁 Age	69	美登高 Meadow Gold(37.7)	中街大果 Zhong Jie Da Guo(24.6)	和路雪 Wall's(11.6)	伊利 Yili(10.1)
35~44 岁 Age	57	美登高 Meadow Gold(29.8)	中街大果 Zhong Jie Da Guo(19.3)	德氏 Deshi(14.0)	伊利 Yili(10.5) 宏宝莱 HBL(10.5)
45~54 岁 Age	26	美登高 Meadow Gold(30.8)	德氏 Deshi(23.1)	伊利 Yili(19.2)	中街大果 Zhong Jie Da Guo(15.4)
55~60 岁 Age	10	美登高 Meadow Gold(30.0)	伊利 Yili(20.0) 德氏 Deshi(20.0) 中街大果 Zhong Jie Da Guo(20.0)	明治 Mingzhi(10.0)	

6-4 理想品牌排名/ Ranking of the Ideal Brands

排名 Brand Ranking	品牌 Brands	人数 Number	百分比 Percent
1	美登高 Meadow Gold	182	30.3
2	中街大果 Zhong Jie Da Guo	123	20.5
3	德氏 Deshi	72	12.0
4	伊利 Yili	69	11.5
5	和路雪 Wall's	58	9.7
6	红星礼拜天 Red Star	21	3.5
7	宏宝莱 HBL	13	2.2
8	雀巢 Nestle	4	0.7

n=601

6-5 样本、男性各年龄层、女性各年龄层最近三个月有无购买的比例/ Purchasing in the Last Three Months by the Whole Sample, Age and Gender Groups

	人数 Number	买过 yes	没买过 no
样本 Sample	601	71.0	29.0
男性 Male	299	66.9	33.1
16~24 岁 Age	64	87.5	12.5
25~34 岁 Age	89	75.3	24.7
35~44 岁 Age	76	60.5	39.5
45~54 岁 Age	46	45.7	54.3
55~60 岁 Age	24	41.7	58.3
女性 Female	302	75.2	24.8
16~24 岁 Age	64	85.9	14.1
25~34 岁 Age	90	80.0	20.0
35~44 岁 Age	76	81.6	18.4
45~54 岁 Age	48	54.2	45.8
55~60 岁 Age	24	50.0	50.0

6-6 样本、男性各年龄层、女性各年龄层最近三个月的食用频率/ Frequencies of Consuming Ice-cream in the Last Three Months by the Whole Sample, Age and Gender Groups

	人数 Number	天天吃 daily	一周 3 次或以上 3 times or over a week	一周 1~2 次 once or twice a week	一个月 2~3 次 2 or 3 times a month	一个月 1 次或以下 once a month or below	没吃过 never
样本 Sample	600	4.7	12.3	23.7	18.5	11.5	29.3
男性 Male	298	5.0	9.7	22.1	17.4	13.1	32.6
16~24 岁 Age	64	7.8	10.9	35.9	20.3	14.1	10.9
25~34 岁 Age	89	3.4	12.4	24.7	21.3	13.5	24.7
35~44 岁 Age	75	6.7	10.7	18.7	14.7	8.0	41.3
45~54 岁 Age	46	0.0	4.3	15.2	10.9	17.4	52.2
55~60 岁 Age	24	8.3	4.2	0.0	16.7	16.7	54.2
女性 Female	302	4.3	14.9	25.2	19.5	9.9	26.2
16~24 岁 Age	64	10.9	15.6	28.1	20.3	15.6	9.4
25~34 岁 Age	90	1.1	14.4	30.0	22.2	11.1	21.1
35~44 岁 Age	76	3.9	18.4	31.6	15.8	5.3	25.0
45~54 岁 Age	48	2.1	12.5	10.4	18.8	10.4	45.8
55~60 岁 Age	24	4.2	8.3	8.3	20.8	4.2	54.2

6-7 样本、男性各年龄层、女性各年龄层的品牌习惯/ Brand Habit in Consuming Ice-cream by the Whole Sample, Age and Gender Groups

	人数 Number	基本固定食用一个牌子 used in only one brand	比较固定地食用两个或三个牌子 used in two or three brands	基本上不太固定牌子 no brand preference
样本 Sample	424	27.8	36.3	35.8
男性 Male	201	32.3	34.8	32.8
16~24 岁 Age	57	22.8	33.3	43.9
25~34 岁 Age	67	31.3	46.3	22.4
35~44 岁 Age	44	36.4	29.5	34.1
45~54 岁 Age	22	40.9	27.3	31.8
55~60 岁 Age	11	54.5	9.1	36.4
女性 Female	223	23.8	37.7	38.6
16~24 岁 Age	58	24.1	41.4	34.5
25~34 岁 Age	71	21.1	40.8	38.0
35~44 岁 Age	57	24.6	38.6	36.8
45~54 岁 Age	26	23.1	26.9	50.0
55~60 岁 Age	11	36.4	18.2	45.5

6-8 选择该类商品的考虑因素/ Ranking of the Considerations in Purchasing

注：本题为多选题，合计百分比超过 100%(Multiple answers）

排名 Ranking	考虑因素 Considerations	人次 Person-time	百分比 Percent
1	口味好 pleasant taste	338	79.7
2	价格适中 reasonable price	160	37.7
3	有名的牌子 famous brand	115	27.1
4	购买方便 easy to buy	101	23.8
5	只是由于习惯 out of habit	35	8.3
6	朋友推荐 introduction of friends	27	6.4
7	广告影响 influence of advertising	22	5.2
8	包装吸引人 appealing package	18	4.2
9	有优惠条件 with preferential terms	10	2.4
10	售货员介绍 introduced by the shop assistants	7	1.7
11	其它 others	1	0.2

n=424

6-9 样本、男性各年龄层、女性各年龄层最常食用的种类/ Kinds of the Consumed Ice-cream by the Whole Sample, Age and Gender Groups

注：本题为多选题，合计百分比超过 100%(Multiple answers）

	人数 Number	棒型冰淇淋 popsicle	蛋筒 cone	盒/杯装冰淇淋 box/cup	袋装冰淇淋 bag	大盒/桶家庭装冰淇淋 big size box for family use	其它 others
样本 Sample	424	42.0	18.6	27.8	26.7	14.9	0.9
男性 Male	201	45.8	14.4	26.9	27.9	12.9	0.5
16~24 岁 Age	57	38.6	17.5	31.6	26.3	22.8	0.0
25~34 岁 Age	67	52.2	13.4	22.4	22.4	14.9	0.0
35~44 岁 Age	44	52.3	15.9	31.8	31.8	2.3	0.0
45~54 岁 Age	22	40.9	9.1	13.6	40.9	0.0	4.5
55~60 岁 Age	11	27.3	9.1	36.4	27.3	18.2	0.0
女性 Female	223	38.6	22.4	23.7	25.6	16.6	1.3
16~24 岁 Age	58	31.0	19.0	43.1	19.0	24.1	0.0
25~34 岁 Age	71	47.9	16.9	25.8	22.5	18.3	1.4
35~44 岁 Age	57	31.6	31.6	23.1	33.3	12.3	1.8
45~54 岁 Age	26	42.3	15.4	11.5	30.8	11.5	3.8
55~60 岁 Age	11	45.5	45.5	9.1	27.3	0.0	0.0

6-10 样本、男性各年龄层、女性各年龄层最常购买的场所/ Locations of Purchasing by the Whole Sample, Age and Gender Groups

	人数 Number	街头冷柜 vender	冷饮店 ice-cream shop	餐厅 restaurant	小卖部 grocery	超市 supermarket	批发点 wholesale market	商场 department store	其它 others
样本 Sample	416	17.5	19.7	0.2	26.7	4.6	29.1	1.7	0.5
男性 Male	197	22.3	18.3	0.0	27.9	2.0	27.9	1.0	0.5
16~24 岁 Age	57	29.8	15.8	0.0	28.1	3.5	19.3	1.8	1.8
25~34 岁 Age	65	13.8	20.0	0.0	32.3	3.1	30.8	0.0	0.0
35~44 岁 Age	43	20.9	14.0	0.0	20.9	0.0	44.2	0.0	0.0
45~54 岁 Age	21	33.3	23.8	0.0	23.8	0.0	14.3	4.8	0.0
55~60 岁 Age	11	18.2	27.3	0.0	36.4	0.0	18.2	0.0	0.0
女性 Female	219	13.2	21.0	0.5	25.6	6.8	30.1	2.3	0.5
16~24 岁 Age	58	13.8	27.6	1.7	17.2	10.3	25.9	3.4	0.0
25~34 岁 Age	69	13.0	21.7	0.0	21.7	4.3	36.2	2.9	0.0
35~44 岁 Age	55	16.4	21.8	0.0	25.5	7.3	25.5	1.8	1.8
45~54 岁 Age	26	7.7	7.7	0.0	50.0	7.7	26.9	0.0	0.0
55~60 岁 Age	11	9.1	9.1	0.0	36.4	0.0	45.5	0.0	0.0

6-11 重度消费者人口分布/ Demographics of the Heavy Consumers

	人数 Number	16-24 岁 Age	25-34 岁 Age	35-44 岁 Age	45-54 岁 Age	55-60 岁 Age
样本 Sample	244	28.7	31.6	27.9	8.6	3.3
男性 Male	110	31.8	32.7	24.5	8.2	2.7
天天吃 daily	15	33.3	20.0	33.3	0.0	13.3
一周 3 次或以上 3 times or over a week	29	24.1	37.9	27.6	6.9	3.4
一周 1~2 次 once or twice a week	66	34.8	33.3	21.2	10.6	0.0
女性 Female	134	26.1	30.6	30.6	9.0	3.7
天天吃 daily	13	53.8	7.7	23.1	7.7	7.7
一周 3 次或以上 3 times or over a week	45	22.2	28.9	31.1	13.3	4.4
一周 1~2 次 once or twice a week	76	23.7	35.5	31.6	6.6	2.6

6-12 不同消费者层的常用品牌/ The Most Frequently Used Brands by Market Segments

6-12-1 时尚流行指标/ Fads Popular Index

	人数 Number	第一品牌及百分比 1st/ percent	第二品牌及百分比 2nd/ percent	第三品牌及百分比 3rd/ percent
样本 Sample	415	**美登高 Meadow Gold(34.2)**	**中街大果 Zhong Jie Da Guo(20.0)**	**伊利 Yili(13.5)**
平实生活指向 simple living orientation	182	美登高 Meadow Gold(30.8)	中街大果 Zhong Jie Da Guo(21.4)	德氏 Deshi(15.9)
时尚流行指向 fashion orientation	233	美登高 Meadow Gold(36.9)	中街大果 Zhong Jie Da Guo(18.9)	伊利 Yili(12.9)

6-12-2 广告态度指标/ Advertising Attitude Index

	人数 Number	第一品牌及百分比 1st/ percent	第二品牌及百分比 2nd/ percent	第三品牌及百分比 3rd/ percent
样本 Sample	415	**美登高 Meadow Gold(34.2)**	**中街大果 Zhong Jie Da Guo (20.0)**	**伊利 Yili(13.5)**
广告淡漠指向 indifferent orientation	112	美登高 Meadow Gold(35.7)	中街大果 Zhong Jie Da Guo (23.2)	德氏 Deshi (14.3)
中间层 medium	257	美登高 Meadow Gold(35.4)	中街大果 Zhong Jie Da Guo (18.3)	伊利 Yili(16.0)
信赖广告指向 loyal orientation	46	美登高 Meadow Gold(23.9)	中街大果 Zhong Jie Da Guo (21.7)	和路雪 Wall's(17.4)

6-12-3 饮食健康指标/ Foods & Drink Quality Index

	人数 Number	第一品牌及百分比 1st/ percent	第二品牌及百分比 2nd/ percent	第三品牌及百分比 3rd/ percent
样本 Sample	415	**美登高 Meadow Gold(34.2)**	**中街大果 Zhong Jie Da Guo (20.0)**	**伊利 Yili(13.5)**
饮食"温饱"指向 "basic" orientation	119	美登高 Meadow Gold(27.7)	中街大果 Zhong Jie Da Guo (21.8)	德氏 Deshi (19.3)
中间层 medium	193	美登高 Meadow Gold(37.8)	中街大果 Zhong Jie Da Guo (16.1)	伊利 Yili(14.5)
健康营养指向 health & nutrition orientation	103	美登高 Meadow Gold(35.0)	中街大果 Zhong Jie Da Guo (25.2)	伊利 Yili(12.6)

6-13 重度消费者的消费者层构成/ The Composition of the Heavy Consumers

6-13-1 时尚流行指标/ Fads Popular Index

	人数 Number	平实生活指向 simple living orientation	时尚流行指向 fashion orientation
样本 Sample	244	36.9	63.1
天天吃 daily	28	39.3	60.7
一周 3 次或以上 3 times or over a week	74	33.8	66.2
一周 1~2 次 once or twice a week	142	38.0	62.0

6-13-2 广告态度指标/ Advertising Attitude Index

	人数 Number	广告淡漠指向 indifferent orientation	中间层 medium	信赖广告指向 loyal orientation
样本 Sample	244	25.4	62.7	11.9
天天吃 daily	28	28.6	57.1	14.3
一周 3 次或以上 3 times or over a week	74	28.4	60.8	10.8
一周 1～2 次 once or twice a week	142	23.2	64.8	12.0

6-13-3 饮食健康指标/ Foods & Drink Quality Index

	人数 Number	饮食"温饱"指向 "basic" orientation	中间层 medium	健康营养指向 health & nutrition orientation
样本 Sample	244	27.9	47.1	25.0
天天吃 daily	28	39.3	35.7	25.0
一周 3 次或以上 3 times or over a week	74	21.6	48.6	29.7
一周 1～2 次 once or twice a week	142	28.9	48.6	22.5

7.饼干 / Biscuit

● 北京 / Beijing

7-1 最近三个月食用频率的比例/ Proportion of the Sample Consuming Biscuit in the Last Three Months

	人数 Number	百分比 Percent
天天吃 daily	73	7.2
一周 3 次或以上 3 times or over a week	161	15.9
一周 1~2 次 once or twice a week	237	23.4
一个月 2～3 次 2 or 3 times a month	192	19.0
一个月 1 次或以下 once a month or below	80	7.9
没吃过 never	268	26.5

n=1011

7-2 最常用品牌排名/ Ranking of the Most Frequently Used Brands

排名 Brand Ranking	品牌 Brands	人数 Number	百分比 Percent
1	纳贝斯克乐之 Nabisco Ritz	197	26.8
2	康师傅 Kangshifu	92	12.5
3	纳贝斯克富丽 Nabisco Marbu	48	6.5
4	奇宝 Keebler	46	6.3
5	达能闲趣 Danone Tuc	33	4.5
5	纳贝斯克奥利奥 Nabisco Oreo	33	4.5
6	奇宝太平梳打 Keebler Pacific	25	3.4
7	达能 Danone	22	3.0
7	达能甜趣 Danone Tiki	22	3.0
8	义利 Yili	15	2.0
8	达能王子夹心 Danone Prince	15	2.0
9	奇宝每乐时薏米 Keebler Merries	14	1.9

n=736

7-3 样本、男性各年龄层、女性各年龄层的常用品牌/ The Most Frequently Used Brands by the Whole Sample, Age and Gender Groups

	人数 Number	第一品牌及百分比 1st/ percent	第二品牌及百分比 2nd/ percent	第三品牌及百分比 3rd/ percent	第四品牌及百分比 4th/ percent
样本 Sample	736	**纳贝斯克乐之 Nabisco Ritz(26.8)**	**康师傅 Kangshifu(12.5)**	**纳贝斯克富丽 Nabisco Marbu(6.5)**	**奇宝 Keebler(6.3)**
男性 Male	320	**纳贝斯克乐之 Nabisco Ritz(26.9)**	**康师傅 Kangshifu(12.2)**	**纳贝斯克富丽 Nabisco Marbu(7.8)**	**纳贝斯克奥利奥 Nabisco Oreo(5.9)**
16~24 岁 Age	78	纳贝斯克乐之 Nabisco Ritz(26.9)	纳贝斯克奥利奥 Nabisco Oreo(15.4)	康师傅 Kangshifu(14.1)	纳贝斯克富丽 Nabisco Marbu(7.7)
25~34 岁 Age	88	纳贝斯克乐之 Nabisco Ritz(30.7)	康师傅 Kangshifu(15.9)	纳贝斯克富丽 Nabisco Marbu(6.8)	义利 Yili(3.4) 统泰 President(3.4) 奇宝太平梳打 Keebler Pacific(3.4) 奇宝 Keebler(3.4) 纳贝斯克鬼脸嘟嘟 Nabisco Trakinas(3.4) 纳贝斯克奥利奥 Nabisco Oreo(3.4) 达能闲趣 Danone Tuc(3.4) 达能王子夹心 Danone Prince(3.4) 达能 Danone(3.4)
35~44 岁 Age	87	纳贝斯克乐之 Nabisco Ritz(24.1)	纳贝斯克富丽 Nabisco Marbu(10.3)	康师傅 Kangshifu(8.0)	义利 Yili(4.6) 奇宝 Keebler(4.6)
45~54 岁 Age	41	纳贝斯克乐之 Nabisco Ritz(34.1)	康师傅 Kangshifu(12.2)	奇宝太平梳打 Keebler Pacific(7.3)	奇宝每乐时薏米 Keebler Merries(4.9) 奇宝 Keebler(4.9) 纳贝斯克富丽 Nabisco Marbu(4.9)
55~60 岁 Age	26	义利 Yili(15.4)	纳贝斯克乐之 Nabisco Ritz(11.5)	康师傅 Kangshifu(7.7) 纳贝斯克富丽 Nabisco Marbu(7.7)	达能闲趣 Danone Tuc(3.8) 达能 Danone(3.8) 统泰 President(3.8) 纳贝斯克 Nabisco(3.8) 富丽华 Fulihua(3.8) 稻香村 Daoxiangcun(3.8)
女性 Female	416	**纳贝斯克乐之 Nabisco Ritz(26.7)**	**康师傅 Kangshifu(12.7)**	**奇宝 Keebler(8.2)**	**纳贝斯克富丽 Nabisco Marbu(5.5)**
16~24 岁 Age	98	纳贝斯克乐之 Nabisco Ritz(31.6)	康师傅 Kangshifu(17.3)	奇宝 Keebler(7.1)	达能闲趣 Danone Tuc(6.1) 纳贝斯克奥利奥 Nabisco Oreo(6.1)
25~34 岁 Age	135	纳贝斯克乐之 Nabisco Ritz(28.1)	康师傅 Kangshifu(16.3)	奇宝 Keebler(8.1)	达能闲趣 Danone Tuc(5.2)
35~44 岁 Age	100	纳贝斯克乐之 Nabisco Ritz(24.0)	奇宝 Keebler(10.0)	康师傅 Kangshifu(9.0)	达能甜趣 Danone Tiki(7.0)
45~54 岁 Age	57	纳贝斯克乐之 Nabisco Ritz(26.3)	康师傅 Kangshifu(8.8) 奇宝 Keebler(8.8) 纳贝斯克富丽 Nabisco Marbu(8.8)	达能闲趣 Danone Tuc(7.0)	达能 Danone(3.5) 奇宝太平梳打 Keebler Pacific(3.5)
55~60 岁 Age	26	奇宝太平梳打 Keebler Pacific(15.4)	达能 Danone(11.5) 达能闲趣 Danone Tuc(11.5) 纳贝斯克乐之 Nabisco Ritz(11.5)	顺达 Shunda(3.8) Butter cookies (3.8) 稻香村 Daoxiangcun(3.8) 富丽华 Fulihua(3.8) 儿童乐 Ertongle(3.8) 奇宝 Keebler(3.8) 伊利 Yili(3.8) 统泰 President(3.8) 纳贝斯克富丽 Nabisco Marbu(3.8) 纳贝斯克奥利奥 Nabisco Oreo(3.8) 达能甜趣 Danone Tiki(3.8)	

7-4 理想品牌排名/ Ranking of the Ideal Brands

排名 Brand Ranking	品牌 Brands	人数 Number	百分比 Percent
1	纳贝斯克乐之 Nabisco Ritz	222	21.9
2	康师傅 Kangshifu	95	9.4
3	纳贝斯克富丽 Nabisco Marbu	59	5.8
4	奇宝 Keebler	56	5.5
5	达能 Danone	47	4.6
6	纳贝斯克奥利奥 Nabisco Oreo	36	3.6
7	义利 Yili	30	3.0
8	达能闲趣 Danone Tuc	22	2.2
9	奇宝太平梳打 Keebler Pacific	16	1.6

n=1012

7-5 样本、男性各年龄层、女性各年龄层最近三个月有无购买的比例/ Purchasing in the Last Three Months by the Whole Sample, Age and Gender Groups

	人数 Number	买过 yes	没买过 no
样本 Sample	**1011**	**70.3**	**29.7**
男性 Male	**503**	**60.6**	**39.4**
16~24 岁 Age	104	67.3	32.7
25~34 岁 Age	151	55.6	44.4
35~44 岁 Age	131	65.6	34.4
45~54 岁 Age	77	53.2	46.8
55~60 岁 Age	40	60.0	40.0
女性 Female	**508**	**79.9**	**20.1**
16~24 岁 Age	108	86.1	13.9
25~34 岁 Age	150	86.0	14.0
35~44 岁 Age	124	81.5	18.5
45~54 岁 Age	84	67.9	32.1
55~60 岁 Age	42	61.9	38.1

7-6 样本、男性各年龄层、女性各年龄层最近三个月的食用频率/ Frequencies of Consuming Biscuit in the Last Three Months by the Whole Sample, Age and Gender Groups

	人数 Number	天天吃 daily	一周 3 次或以上 3 times or over a week	一周 1~2 次 once or twice a week	一个月 2~3 次 2 or 3 times a month	一个月 1 次或以下 once a month or below	没吃过 never
样本 Sample	**1011**	**7.2**	**15.9**	**23.4**	**19.0**	**7.9**	**26.5**
男性 Male	**504**	**4.6**	**12.3**	**19.0**	**19.8**	**8.7**	**35.5**
16~24 岁 Age	105	3.8	13.3	23.8	25.7	9.5	23.8
25~34 岁 Age	151	5.3	11.9	15.9	17.2	7.9	41.7
35~44 岁 Age	131	3.8	15.3	19.1	17.6	10.7	33.6
45~54 岁 Age	77	6.5	11.7	15.6	15.6	6.5	44.2
55~60 岁 Age	40	2.5	2.5	25.0	30.0	7.5	32.5
女性 Female	**507**	**9.9**	**19.5**	**27.8**	**18.1**	**7.1**	**17.6**
16~24 岁 Age	108	9.3	27.8	27.8	22.2	3.7	9.3
25~34 岁 Age	150	10.0	23.3	32.0	13.3	11.3	10.0
35~44 岁 Age	123	9.8	18.7	30.1	17.9	4.9	18.7
45~54 岁 Age	84	7.1	11.9	23.8	20.2	7.1	29.8
55~60 岁 Age	42	16.7	2.4	14.3	21.4	7.1	38.1

7-7 样本、男性各年龄层、女性各年龄层的品牌习惯/ Brand Habit in Consuming Biscuit by the Whole Sample, Age and Gender Groups

	人数 Number	基本固定食用一个牌子 used in only one brand	比较固定地食用两个或三个牌子 used in two or three brands	基本上不太固定牌子 no brand preference
样本 Sample	743	26.8	43.6	29.6
男性 Male	325	28.3	39.7	32.0
16~24 岁 Age	80	30.0	51.3	18.8
25~34 岁 Age	88	36.4	36.4	27.3
35~44 岁 Age	87	21.8	32.2	46.0
45~54 岁 Age	43	20.9	44.2	34.9
55~60 岁 Age	27	29.6	33.3	37.0
女性 Female	418	25.6	46.7	27.8
16~24 岁 Age	98	19.4	56.1	24.5
25~34 岁 Age	135	25.2	51.1	23.7
35~44 岁 Age	100	25.0	50.0	25.0
45~54 岁 Age	59	30.5	28.8	40.7
55~60 岁 Age	26	42.3	15.4	42.3

7-8 选择该类商品的考虑因素/ Ranking of the Considerations in Purchasing

注：本题为多选题，合计百分比超过 100%(Multiple answers）

排名 Ranking	考虑因素 Considerations	人次 Person-time	百分比 Percent
1	口味好 pleasant taste	576	77.7
2	价格适中 reasonable price	312	42.1
3	生产日期 date of producing	181	24.4
4	有名的牌子 famous brand	163	22.0
5	购买方便 easy to buy	121	16.3
6	只是由于习惯 out of habit	65	8.8
7	广告影响 influence of advertising	49	6.6
8	有优惠条件 with preferential terms	45	6.1
9	包装吸引人 appealing package	31	4.2
10	朋友推荐 introduction of friends	29	3.9
11	售货员介绍 introduced by the shop assistants	7	0.9
11	其它 others	7	0.9

n=741

7-9 样本、男性各年龄层、女性各年龄层最常食用的种类/ Kinds of the Consumed Biscuit by the Whole Sample, Age and Gender Groups

注：本题为多选题，合计百分比超过 100%(Multiple answers）

	人数 Number	夹心饼干 sandwich biscuit	曲奇 cookie	全麦饼干 whole-wheat biscuit	梳打饼干 soda biscuit	普通咸饼干 salty biscuit	普通甜饼干 sweat biscuit	其它 others
样本 Sample	741	48.4	21.3	8.0	17.9	26.2	18.4	1.1
男性 Male	325	50.8	17.8	6.2	16.3	27.1	20.3	0.9
16~24 岁 Age	80	56.3	20.0	3.8	22.5	20.0	21.3	1.3
25~34 岁 Age	88	58.0	17.0	5.7	13.6	21.6	14.8	1.1
35~44 岁 Age	87	47.1	18.4	8.0	16.1	31.0	18.4	1.1
45~54 岁 Age	43	37.2	14.0	7.0	9.3	39.5	32.6	0.0
55~60 岁 Age	27	44.4	18.5	7.4	18.5	33.3	22.2	0.0
女性 Female	416	46.6	24.0	9.4	19.2	25.5	16.8	1.2
16~24 岁 Age	97	54.6	20.6	11.3	25.8	24.7	9.3	0.0
25~34 岁 Age	135	51.9	25.2	8.9	16.3	27.4	11.9	1.5
35~44 岁 Age	100	45.0	26.0	8.0	17.0	22.0	26.0	2.0
45~54 岁 Age	58	36.2	25.9	8.6	15.5	29.3	20.7	1.7
55~60 岁 Age	26	19.2	19.2	11.5	26.9	23.1	26.9	0.0

7-10 样本、男性各年龄层、女性各年龄层最常食用的场合/ Settings of Consumption by the Whole Sample, Age and Gender Groups

注：本题为多选题，合计百分比超过 100%(Multiple answers）

	人数 Number	早餐时 breakfast	饭后甜点 dessert after dinner	加班时 when work overtime	宵夜时 evening snack	当零食吃 between meal	外出、旅游时 outing/ traveling	其它 others
样本 Sample	734	43.9	5.3	9.0	9.8	62.9	9.9	1.0
男性 Male	321	39.9	4.7	10.9	10.0	58.9	9.0	1.2
16~24 岁 Age	78	38.5	2.6	7.7	9.0	66.7	7.7	0.0
25~34 岁 Age	87	37.9	4.6	14.9	11.5	55.2	6.9	3.4
35~44 岁 Age	86	43.0	2.3	11.6	14.0	51.2	12.8	1.2
45~54 岁 Age	43	30.2	11.6	7.0	4.7	67.4	11.6	0.0
55~60 岁 Age	27	55.6	7.4	11.1	3.7	59.3	3.7	0.0
女性 Female	413	47.0	5.8	7.5	9.7	66.1	10.7	0.7
16~24 岁 Age	97	55.7	6.2	8.2	11.3	58.8	11.3	0.0
25~34 岁 Age	134	44.0	5.2	9.0	9.7	69.4	11.9	0.7
35~44 岁 Age	99	50.5	5.1	8.1	8.1	69.7	12.1	0.0
45~54 岁 Age	57	36.8	5.3	3.5	7.0	68.4	8.8	1.8
55~60 岁 Age	26	38.5	11.5	3.8	15.4	57.7	0.0	3.8

7-11 重度消费者人口分布/ Demographics of the Heavy Consumers

	人数 Number	16-24 岁 Age	25-34 岁 Age	35-44 岁 Age	45-54 岁 Age	55-60 岁 Age
样本 Sample	471	24.0	31.4	25.9	13.2	5.5
男性 Male	181	23.8	27.6	27.6	14.4	6.6
天天吃 daily	23	17.4	34.8	21.7	21.7	4.3
一周 3 次或以上 3 times or over a week	62	22.6	29.0	32.3	14.5	1.6
一周 1~2 次 once or twice a week	96	26.0	25.0	26.0	12.5	10.4
女性 Female	290	24.1	33.8	24.8	12.4	4.8
天天吃 daily	50	20.0	30.0	24.0	12.0	14.0
一周 3 次或以上 3 times or over a week	99	30.3	35.4	23.2	10.1	1.0
一周 1 ~2 次 once or twice a week	141	21.3	34.0	26.2	14.2	4.3

7-12 不同消费者层的常用品牌/ The Most Frequently Used Brands by Market Segments

7-12-1 时尚流行指标/ Fads Popular Index

	人数 Number	第一品牌及百分比 1st/ percent	第二品牌及百分比 2nd/ percent	第三品牌及百分比 3rd/ percent	第四品牌及百分比 4th/ percent
样本 Sample	725	**纳贝斯克乐之 Nabisco Ritz(26.9)**	**康师傅 Kangshifu(12.7)**	**纳贝斯克富丽 Nabisco Marbu(6.6)**	**奇宝 Keebler(6.2)**
平实生活指向 simple living orientation	338	纳贝斯克乐之 Nabisco Ritz(24.0)	康师傅 Kangshifu(11.5)	纳贝斯克富丽 Nabisco Marbu(8.3)	奇宝 Keebler(4.7)
时尚流行指向 fashion orientation	387	纳贝斯克乐之 Nabisco Ritz(29.5)	康师傅 Kangshifu(13.7)	奇宝 Keebler(7.5)	纳贝斯克富丽 Nabisco Marbu(5.2)

7-12-2 广告态度指标/ Advertising Attitude Index

	人数 Number	第一品牌及百分比 1st/ percent	第二品牌及百分比 2nd/ percent	第三品牌及百分比 3rd/ percent	第四品牌及百分比 4th/ percent
样本 Sample	721	**纳贝斯克乐之 Nabisco Ritz(26.6)**	**康师傅 Kangshifu(12.5)**	**纳贝斯克富丽 Nabisco Marbu(6.7)**	**奇宝 Keebler(6.4)**
广告淡漠指向 indifferent orientation	195	纳贝斯克乐之 Nabisco Ritz(24.6)	康师傅 Kangshifu(12.3)	纳贝斯克富丽 Nabisco Marbu(10.8)	奇宝 Keebler(6.2)
中间层 medium	424	纳贝斯克乐之 Nabisco Ritz(29.0)	康师傅 Kangshifu(13.0)	奇宝 Keebler(6.4)	纳贝斯克富丽 Nabisco Marbu(5.2)
信赖广告指向 loyal orientation	102	纳贝斯克乐之 Nabisco Ritz(20.6)	康师傅 Kangshifu(10.8)	纳贝斯克奥利奥 Nabisco Oreo(7.8)	达能 Danone(6.9) 奇宝 Keebler(6.9)

7-12-3 饮食健康指标/ Foods & Drink Quality Index

	人数 Number	第一品牌及百分比 1st/ percent	第二品牌及百分比 2nd/ percent	第三品牌及百分比 3rd/ percent	第四品牌及百分比 4th/ percent
样本 Sample	731	**纳贝斯克乐之 Nabisco Ritz(26.9)**	**康师傅 Kangshifu(12.4)**	**纳贝斯克富丽 Nabisco Marbu(6.6)**	**奇宝 Keebler(6.2)**
饮食"温饱"指向 "basic" orientation	193	纳贝斯克乐之 Nabisco Ritz(24.9)	康师傅 Kangshifu(13.5)	纳贝斯克富丽 Nabisco Marbu(10.4)	纳贝斯克奥利奥 Nabisco Oreo(6.2) 奇宝 Keebler(6.2)
中间层 medium	353	纳贝斯克乐之 Nabisco Ritz(29.2)	康师傅 Kangshifu(11.0)	奇宝 Keebler(5.4)	达能甜趣 Danone Tiki(4.2) 纳贝斯克富丽 Nabisco Marbu(4.2)
健康营养指向 health & nutrition orientation	185	纳贝斯克乐之 Nabisco Ritz(24.9)	康师傅 Kangshifu(14.1)	奇宝 Keebler(7.6)	纳贝斯克富丽 Nabisco Marbu(7.0)

7-13 重度消费者的消费者层构成/ The Composition of the Heavy Consumers

7-13-1 时尚流行指标/ Fads Popular Index

	人数 Number	平实生活指向 simple living orientation	时尚流行指向 fashion orientation
样本 Sample	463	43.6	56.4
天天吃 daily	73	31.5	68.5
一周 3 次或以上 3 times or over a week	159	44.7	55.3
一周 1～2 次 once or twice a week	231	46.8	53.2

7-13-2 广告态度指标/ Advertising Attitude Index

	人数 Number	广告淡漠指向 indifferent orientation	中间层 medium	信赖广告指向 loyal orientation
样本 Sample	459	83.7	16.3	0.0
天天吃 daily	71	80.3	19.7	0.0
一周 3 次或以上 3 times or over a week	159	79.9	20.1	0.0
一周 1~2 次 once or twice a week	229	87.3	12.7	0.0

7-13-3 饮食健康指标/ Foods & Drink Quality Index

	人数 Number	饮食"温饱"指向 "basic" orientation	中间层 medium	健康营养指向 health & nutrition orientation
样本 Sample	467	22.3	49.5	28.3
天天吃 daily	71	11.3	56.3	32.4
一周 3 次或以上 3 times or over a week	160	24.4	50.6	25.0
一周 1~2 次 once or twice a week	236	24.2	46.6	29.2

● 上海 / Shanghai

7-1 最近三个月食用频率的比例/ Proportion of the Sample Consuming Biscuit in the Last Three Months

	人数 Number	百分比 Percent
天天吃 daily	116	11.5
一周 3 次或以上 3 times or over a week	196	19.3
一周 1~2 次 once or twice a week	301	29.7
一个月 2～3 次 2 or 3 times a month	151	14.9
一个月 1 次或以下 once a month or below	57	5.6
没吃过 never	192	19.0

n=1013

7-2 最常用品牌排名/ Ranking of the Most Frequently Used Brands

排名 Brand Ranking	品牌 Brands	人数 Number	百分比 Percent
1	达能闲趣 Danone Tuc	175	21.3
2	奇宝太平梳打 Keebler Pacific	72	8.8
2	达能甜趣 Danone Tiki	72	8.8
3	康师傅 Kangshifu	64	7.8
4	达能 Danone	62	7.6
4	达能王子夹心 Danone Prince	62	7.6
5	奇宝 Keebler	30	3.7
6	统泰 President	28	3.4
7	纳贝斯克奥利奥 Nabisco Oreo	25	3.0
8	康元 Khong Guan	23	2.8
9	泰康 Taikang	20	2.4
10	纳贝斯克乐之 Nabisco Ritz	16	1.9
11	纳贝斯克趣多多 Nabisco Ahoy	11	1.3
12	格力高 Glico	10	1.2
12	日清 Nissin	10	1.2

n=821

7-3 样本、男性各年龄层、女性各年龄层的常用品牌/ The Most Frequently Used Brands by the Whole Sample, Age and Gender Groups

	人数 Number	第一品牌及百分比 1st/ percent	第二品牌及百分比 2nd/ percent	第三品牌及百分比 3rd/ percent
样本 Sample	821	**达能闲趣 Danone Tuc(21.3)**	**奇宝太平梳打 Keebler Pacific(8.8)** **达能甜趣 Danone Tiki(8.8)**	**康师傅 Kangshifu(7.8)**
男性 Male	384	**达能闲趣 Danone Tuc(20.6)**	**达能甜趣 Danone Tiki(10.2)**	**达能 Danone(8.3)**
16~24 岁 Age	76	达能闲趣 Danone Tuc(18.4)	康师傅 Kangshifu(17.1)	达能甜趣 Danone Tiki(10.5)
25~34 岁 Age	118	达能闲趣 Danone Tuc(15.3)	达能甜趣 Danone Tiki(10.2) 达能王子夹心 Danone Prince(10.2)	康师傅 Kangshifu(9.3)
35~44 岁 Age	96	达能闲趣 Danone Tuc(20.8)	达能甜趣 Danone Tiki(11.5)	达能 Danone(9.4)
45~54 岁 Age	62	达能闲趣 Danone Tuc(32.3)	奇宝太平梳打 Keebler Pacific(9.7)	达能 Danone(8.1)
55~60 岁 Age	32	达能闲趣 Danone Tuc(21.9)	奇宝太平梳打 Keebler Pacific(12.5) 达能甜趣 Danone Tiki(12.5) 统泰 President(12.5)	泰康 Taikang(9.4)
女性 Female	437	**达能闲趣 Danone Tuc(22.0)**	**奇宝太平梳打 Keebler Pacific(9.8)**	**达能王子夹心 Danone Prince(8.0)** **康师傅 Kangshifu(8.0)**
16~24 岁 Age	89	奇宝太平梳打 Keebler Pacific(15.7)	达能闲趣 Danone Tuc(14.6)	康师傅 Kangshifu(13.5)
25~34 岁 Age	127	达能闲趣 Danone Tuc(15.7)	达能王子夹心 Danone Prince(11.8) 康师傅 Kangshifu(11.8)	奇宝太平梳打 Keebler Pacific(9.4)
35~44 岁 Age	117	达能闲趣 Danone Tuc(31.6)	达能王子夹心 Danone Prince(8.5)	达能甜趣 Danone Tiki(6.0)
45~54 岁 Age	70	达能闲趣 Danone Tuc(22.9)	达能甜趣 Danone Tiki(11.4)	奇宝太平 Keebler Pacific(10.0)
55~60 岁 Age	34	达能闲趣 Danone Tuc(29.4)	奇宝太平梳打 Keebler Pacific(14.7)	泰康 Taikang(8.8)

7-4 理想品牌排名/ Ranking of the Ideal Brands

排名 Brand Ranking	品牌 Brands	人数 Number	百分比 Percent
1	达能闲趣 Danone Tuc	215	21.2
2	达能 Danone	101	10.0
3	达能甜趣 Danone Tiki	88	8.7
4	奇宝太平梳打 Keebler Pacific	76	7.5
5	康师傅 Kangshifu	67	6.6
6	达能王子夹心 Danone Prince	65	6.4
7	奇宝 Keebler	41	4.0
8	纳贝斯克奥利奥 Nabisco Oreo	40	3.9
9	统泰 President	34	3.4
10	泰康 Taikang	30	3.0
11	康元 Khong Guan	27	2.7
12	丹麦蓝罐 Kjeldsens	23	2.3
13	纳贝斯克乐之 Nabisco Ritz	19	1.9
14	纳贝斯克趣多多 Nabisco Ahoy	13	1.3

n=1014

7-5 样本、男性各年龄层、女性各年龄层最近三个月有无购买的比例/ Purchasing in the Last Three Months by the Whole Sample, Age and Gender Groups

	人数 Number	买过 yes	没买过 no
样本 Sample	1014	80.1	19.9
男性 Male	509	72.9	27.1
16~24 岁 Age	109	61.5	38.5
25~34 岁 Age	146	78.8	21.2
35~44 岁 Age	130	75.4	24.6
45~54 岁 Age	85	70.6	29.4
55~60 岁 Age	39	79.5	20.5
女性 Female	505	87.3	12.7
16~24 岁 Age	108	82.4	17.6
25~34 岁 Age	144	91.0	9.0
35~44 岁 Age	130	89.2	10.8
45~54 岁 Age	82	86.6	13.4
55~60 岁 Age	41	82.9	17.1

7-6 样本、男性各年龄层、女性各年龄层最近三个月的食用频率/ Frequencies of Consuming Biscuit in the Last Three Months by the Whole Sample, Age and Gender Groups

	人数 Number	天天吃 daily	一周 3 次或以上 3 times or over a week	一周 1~2 次 once or twice a week	一个月 2~3 次 2 or 3 times a month	一个月 1 次或以下 once a month or below	没吃过 never
样本 Sample	1013	11.5	19.3	29.7	14.9	5.6	19.0
男性 Male	508	7.9	16.5	28.9	15.9	6.3	24.4
16~24 岁 Age	109	8.3	10.1	24.8	21.1	5.5	30.3
25~34 岁 Age	146	5.5	19.2	40.4	11.6	4.1	19.2
35~44 岁 Age	129	8.5	17.1	22.5	21.7	4.7	25.6
45~54 岁 Age	85	7.1	18.8	25.9	8.2	12.9	27.1
55~60 岁 Age	39	15.4	17.9	25.6	15.4	7.7	17.9
女性 Female	505	15.0	22.2	30.5	13.9	5.0	13.5
16~24 岁 Age	108	4.6	20.4	32.4	18.5	6.5	17.6
25~34 岁 Age	144	22.2	20.8	28.5	13.9	2.8	11.8
35~44 岁 Age	130	13.8	28.5	33.1	10.0	4.6	10.0
45~54 岁 Age	82	15.9	22.0	23.2	18.3	6.1	14.6
55~60 岁 Age	41	19.5	12.2	39.0	4.9	7.3	17.1

7-7 样本、男性各年龄层、女性各年龄层的品牌习惯/ Brand Habit in Consuming Biscuit by the Whole Sample, Age and Gender Groups

	人数 Number	基本固定食用一个牌子 used in only one brand	比较固定地食用两个或三个牌子 used in two or three brands	基本上不太固定牌子 no brand preference
样本 Sample	821	26.3	42.3	31.4
男性 Male	384	27.1	39.3	33.6
16~24 岁 Age	76	26.3	38.2	35.5
25~34 岁 Age	118	23.7	47.5	28.8
35~44 岁 Age	96	27.1	35.4	37.5
45~54 岁 Age	62	32.3	35.5	32.3
55~60 岁 Age	32	31.3	31.3	37.5
女性 Female	437	25.6	44.9	29.5
16~24 岁 Age	89	18.0	61.8	20.2
25~34 岁 Age	127	24.4	47.2	28.3
35~44 岁 Age	117	33.3	35.0	31.6
45~54 岁 Age	70	21.4	40.0	38.6
55~60 岁 Age	34	32.4	35.3	32.4

7-8 选择该类商品的考虑因素/ Ranking of the Considerations in Purchasing

注：本题为多选题，合计百分比超过 100%(Multiple answers）

排名 Ranking	考虑因素 Considerations	人次 Person-time	百分比 Percent
1	口味好 pleasant taste	613	74.7
2	价格适中 reasonable price	358	43.6
3	购买方便 easy to buy	195	23.8
4	有名的牌子 famous brand	178	21.7
5	生产日期 date of producing	165	20.1
6	广告影响 influence of advertising	86	10.5
7	有优惠条件 with preferential terms	57	6.9
8	只是由于习惯 out of habit	56	6.8
9	包装吸引人 appealing package	40	4.9
10	朋友推荐 introduction of friends	17	2.1
11	其它 others	7	0.9
12	售货员介绍 introduced by the shop assistants	4	0.5

n=821

7-9 样本、男性各年龄层、女性各年龄层最常食用的种类/ Kinds of the Consumed Biscuit by the Whole Sample, Age and Gender Groups

注：本题为多选题，合计百分比超过 100%(Multiple answers）

	人数 Number	夹心饼干 sandwich biscuit	曲奇 cookie	全麦饼干 whole-wheat biscuit	梳打饼干 soda biscuit	普通咸饼干 salty biscuit	普通甜饼干 sweat biscuit	其它 others
样本 Sample	819	37.5	21.4	4.4	29.9	25.8	16.0	1.7
男性 Male	383	38.6	19.6	3.7	30.8	26.4	15.4	1.3
16~24 岁 Age	76	47.4	11.8	2.6	32.9	22.4	11.8	0.0
25~34 岁 Age	117	45.3	23.1	5.1	27.4	19.7	17.1	0.9
35~44 岁 Age	96	35.4	18.8	5.2	30.2	31.3	16.7	4.2
45~54 岁 Age	62	30.6	22.6	0.0	29.0	33.9	12.9	0.0
55~60 岁 Age	32	18.8	21.9	3.1	43.8	31.3	18.8	0.0
女性 Female	436	36.5	22.9	5.0	29.1	25.2	16.5	2.1
16~24 岁 Age	89	47.2	23.6	11.2	25.8	14.6	16.9	1.1
25~34 岁 Age	126	42.1	20.6	5.6	23.8	24.6	19.0	3.2
35~44 岁 Age	117	36.8	24.8	2.6	31.6	25.6	10.3	0.0
45~54 岁 Age	70	22.9	24.3	0.0	31.4	32.9	17.1	5.7
55~60 岁 Age	34	14.7	20.6	5.9	44.1	38.2	26.5	0.0

7-10 样本、男性各年龄层、女性各年龄层最常食用的场合/ Settings of Consumption by the Whole Sample, Age and Gender Groups

注：本题为多选题，合计百分比超过 100%(Multiple answers）

	人数 Number	早餐时 breakfast	饭后甜点 dessert after dinner	加班时 when work overtime	宵夜时 evening snack	当零食吃 between meal	外出、旅游时 outing/ traveling	其它 others
样本 Sample	819	27.4	7.8	11.7	22.6	59.8	7.8	3.1
男性 Male	383	25.3	6.3	12.0	27.7	53.5	8.6	4.4
16~24 岁 Age	76	21.1	9.2	11.8	21.1	59.2	9.2	1.3
25~34 岁 Age	117	28.2	6.0	13.7	29.9	53.0	6.0	4.3
35~44 岁 Age	96	20.8	4.2	12.5	25.0	55.2	10.4	6.3
45~54 岁 Age	62	25.8	8.1	12.9	41.9	45.2	9.7	0.0
55~60 岁 Age	32	37.5	3.1	3.1	15.6	53.1	9.4	15.6
女性 Female	436	29.1	9.2	11.5	18.1	65.4	7.1	1.8
16~24 岁 Age	88	26.1	6.8	15.9	18.2	68.2	6.8	1.1
25~34 岁 Age	127	28.3	11.0	13.4	14.2	67.7	6.3	1.6
35~44 岁 Age	117	31.6	13.7	11.1	17.9	59.8	9.4	3.4
45~54 岁 Age	70	27.1	1.4	7.1	24.3	65.7	7.1	1.4
55~60 岁 Age	34	35.3	8.8	2.9	20.6	67.6	2.9	0.0

7-11 重度消费者人口分布/ Demographics of the Heavy Consumers

	人数 Number	16-24 岁 Age	25-34 岁 Age	35-44 岁 Age	45-54 岁 Age	55-60 岁 Age
样本 Sample	613	17.8	32.3	26.1	15.3	8.5
男性 Male	271	17.3	35.1	22.9	16.2	8.5
天天吃 daily	40	22.5	20.0	27.5	15.0	15.0
一周 3 次或以上 3 times or over a week	84	13.1	33.3	26.2	19.0	8.3
一周 1~2 次 once or twice a week	147	18.4	40.1	19.7	15.0	6.8
女性 Female	342	18.1	30.1	28.7	14.6	8.5
天天吃 daily	76	6.6	42.1	23.7	17.1	10.5
一周 3 次或以上 3 times or over a week	112	19.6	26.8	33.0	16.1	4.5
一周 1 ~2 次 once or twice a week	154	22.7	26.6	27.9	12.3	10.4

7-12 不同消费者层的常用品牌/ The Most Frequently Used Brands by Market Segments

7-12-1 时尚流行指标/ Fads Popular Index

	人数 Number	第一品牌及百分比 1st/ percent	第二品牌及百分比 2nd/ percent	第三品牌及百分比 3rd/ percent	第四品牌及百分比 4th/ percent	第五品牌及百分比 5th/ percent
样本 Sample	814	**达能闲趣 Danone Tuc(21.4)**	**达能甜趣 Danone Tiki(8.8)**	**奇宝太平梳打 Keebler Pacific(8.7)**	**康师傅 Kangshifu(7.9)**	**达能王子夹心 Danone Prince(7.6)**
平实生活指向 simple living orientation	373	达能闲趣 Danone Tuc(23.9)	奇宝太平梳打 Keebler Pacific(10.7)	达能甜趣 Danone Tiki(7.5)	达能 Danone(6.2)	康师傅 Kangshifu(5.4) 达能王子夹心 Danone Prince(5.4)
时尚流行指向 fashion orientation	441	达能闲趣 Danone Tuc(19.3)	达能甜趣 Danone.Tiki(10.0) 康师傅 Kangshifu(10.0)	达能王子夹心 Danone Prince(9.5)	达能 Danone(8.4)	奇宝太平梳打 KeeblerPacific(7.0)

7-12-2 广告态度指标/ Advertising Attitude Index

	人数 Number	第一品牌及百分比 1st/ percent	第二品牌及百分比 2nd/ percent	第三品牌及百分比 3rd/ percent	第四品牌及百分比 4th/ percent	第五品牌及百分比 5th/ percent
样本 Sample	810	**达能闲趣 Danone Tuc(21.5)**	**奇宝太平梳打 Keebler Pacific(8.9)**	**达能甜趣 Danone Tiki(8.6)**	**康师傅 Kangshifu(7.8)**	**达能王子夹心 Danone Prince(7.5)**
广告淡漠指向 indifferent orientation	206	达能闲趣 Danone Tuc(23.3)	奇宝太平梳打 Keebler Pacific(9.2)	达能甜趣 Danone Tiki(8.3)	达能王子夹心 Danone Prince(7.3)	达能 Danone(5.8)
中间层 medium	488	达能闲趣 Danone Tuc(21.7)	达能甜趣 Danone Tiki(9.0)	达能 Danone(8.4)	奇宝太平梳打 Keebler Pacific(8.2) 康师傅 Kangshifu(8.2)	达能王子夹心 Danone Prince(6.4)
信赖广告指向 loyal orientation	116	达能闲趣 Danone Tuc(17.2)	达能王子夹心 Danone Prince(12.9)	康师傅 Kangshifu(11.2) 奇宝太平梳打 Keebler Pacific(11.2)	达能甜趣 Danone Tiki(7.8)	达能 Danone(5.2)

7-12-3 饮食健康指标/ Foods & Drink Quality Index

	人数 Number	第一品牌及百分比 1st/ percent	第二品牌及百分比 2nd/ percent	第三品牌及百分比 3rd/ percent	第四品牌及百分比 4th/ percent	第五品牌及百分比 5th/ percent
样本 Sample	818	**达能闲趣 Danone Tuc(21.1)**	**奇宝太平梳打 Keebler Pacific(8.8) 达能甜趣 Danone Tiki(8.8)**	**康师傅 Kangshifu(7.8)**	**达能 Danone(7.6) 达能王子夹心 Danone Prince(7.6)**	**奇宝 Keebler(3.5)**
饮食“温饱”指向 "basic" orientation	181	达能闲趣 Danone Tuc(24.9)	奇宝太平梳打 Keebler Pacific(10.5)	康师傅 Kangshifu(7.7)	达能甜趣 Danone Tiki(7.2)	达能王子夹心 Danone Prince(6.6)
中间层 medium	402	达能闲趣 Danone Tuc(19.4)	达能 Danone(9.0)	达能王子夹心 Danone Prince(8.2)	达能甜趣 Danone Tiki(8.0)	康师傅 Kangshifu(7.7)
健康营养指向 health & nutrition orientation	235	达能闲趣 Danone Tuc(21.3)	达能甜趣 Danone Tiki(11.5)	奇宝太平梳打 Keebler Pacific(9.8)	达能 Danone(8.1) 康师傅 Kangshifu(8.1)	达能王子夹心 Danone Prince(7.2)

7-13 重度消费者的消费者层构成/ The Composition of the Heavy Consumers

7-13-1 时尚流行指标/ Fads Popular Index

	人数 Number	平实生活指向 simple living orientation	时尚流行指向 fashion orientation
样本 Sample	610	45.2	54.8
天天吃 daily	116	46.6	53.4
一周 3 次或以上 3 times or over a week	193	44.0	56.0
一周 1～2 次 once or twice a week	301	45.5	54.5

7-13-2 广告态度指标/ Advertising Attitude Index

	人数 Number	广告淡漠指向 indifferent orientation	中间层 medium	信赖广告指向 Loyal orientation
样本 Sample	605	86.1	13.9	0.0
天天吃 daily	115	81.7	18.3	0.0
一周 3 次或以上 3 times or over a week	192	85.9	14.1	0.0
一周 1~2 次 once or twice a week	298	87.9	12.1	0.0

7-13-3 饮食健康指标/ Foods & Drink Quality Index

	人数 Number	饮食"温饱"指向 "basic" orientation	中间层 medium	健康营养指向 health & nutrition orientation
样本 Sample	611	20.6	48.6	30.8
天天吃 daily	116	18.1	54.3	27.6
一周 3 次或以上 3 times or over a week	196	19.4	49.0	31.6
一周 1~2 次 once or twice a week	299	22.4	46.2	31.4

● 广州 / Guangzhou

7-1 最近三个月食用频率的比例/ Proportion of the Sample Consuming Biscuit in the Last Three Months

	人数 Number	百分比 Percent
天天吃 daily	53	5.1
一周 3 次或以上 3 times or over a week	127	12.3
一周 1~2 次 once or twice a week	261	25.2
一个月 2～3 次 2 or 3 times a month	203	19.6
一个月 1 次或以下 once a month or below	120	11.6
没吃过 never	270	26.1

n=1034

7-2 最常用品牌排名/ Ranking of the Most Frequently Used Brands

排名 Brand Ranking	品牌 Brands	人数 Number	百分比 Percent
1	奇宝 Keebler	198	25.9
2	奇宝太平梳打 Keebler Pacific	128	16.8
3	嘉顿 Garden	62	8.1
4	康师傅 Kangshifu	41	5.4
5	丹麦蓝罐 Kjeldsens	27	3.5
6	稷士佳 Jessica	18	2.4
7	来利 Laili	17	2.2
8	嘉士利 Jiashili	15	2.0
8	岭南 Lingnan	15	2.0
8	达能 Danone	15	2.0
9	奇宝格斯 Keebler PIC-6	14	1.8

n=764

7-3 样本、男性各年龄层、女性各年龄层的常用品牌/ The Most Frequently Used Brands by the Whole Sample, Age and Gender Groups

	人数 Number	第一品牌及百分比 1st/ percent	第二品牌及百分比 2nd/ percent	第三品牌及百分比 3rd/ percent
样本 Sample	764	**奇宝 Keebler(25.9)**	**奇宝太平梳打 Keebler Pacific(16.8)**	**嘉顿 Garden(8.1)**
男性 Male	334	**奇宝 Keebler(24.6)**	**奇宝太平梳打 Keebler Pacific(18.9)**	**康师傅 Kangshifu(5.4)**
16~24 岁 Age	71	奇宝 Keebler(22.5)	奇宝太平梳打 Keebler Pacific(18.3)	丹麦蓝罐 Kjeldsens(7.0)
25~34 岁 Age	106	奇宝 Keebler(30.2)	奇宝太平梳打 Keebler Pacific(18.9)	康师傅 Kangshifu(7.5)
35~44 岁 Age	82	奇宝太平梳打 Keebler Pacific(18.3)	奇宝 Keebler(17.1)	稷士佳 Jessica(6.1)
45~54 岁 Age	51	奇宝太平梳打 Keebler Pacific(25.5)	奇宝 Keebler(21.6)	康师傅 Kangshifu(7.8)
55~60 岁 Age	24	奇宝 Keebler(37.5)	奇宝太平梳打 Keebler Pacific(3.3)	华美 Hua Mei(4.2) 稷士佳 Jessica(4.2) 岭南 Lingnan(4.2) 达能王子夹心 Danone Prince(4.2) 泰林 Tailin(4.2) 港龙 Dragon(4.2) 雪克 Xueke(4.2)
女性 Female	430	**奇宝 Keebler(27.0)**	**奇宝太平梳打 Keebler Pacific(15.1)**	**嘉顿 Garden(10.5)**
16~24 岁 Age	88	奇宝 Keebler(35.2)	嘉顿 Garden(12.5) 康师傅 Kangshifu(12.5)	奇宝太平梳打 Keebler Pacific(11.4)
25~34 岁 Age	130	奇宝 Keebler(27.7)	奇宝太平梳打 Keebler Pacific(16.9)	嘉顿 Garden(13.1)
35~44 岁 Age	112	奇宝 Keebler(22.3)	奇宝太平梳打 Keebler Pacific(17.0)	来利 Laili(4.5)
45~54 岁 Age	70	奇宝 Keebler(25.7)	奇宝太平梳打 Keebler Pacific(12.9)	嘉顿 Garden(11.4)
55~60 岁 Age	30	奇宝 Keebler(20.0)	嘉顿 Garden(16.7) 奇宝太平梳打 Keebler Pacific(16.7)	丹麦蓝罐 Kjeldsens(6.7)

7-4 理想品牌排名/ Ranking of the Ideal Brands

排名 Brand Ranking	品牌 Brands	人数 Number	百分比 Percent
1	奇宝 Keebler	244	23.6
2	奇宝太平梳打 Keebler Pacific	137	13.2
3	嘉顿 Garden	76	7.4
4	康师傅 Kangshifu	46	4.4
5	丹麦蓝罐 Kjeldsens	44	4.3
6	嘉士利 Jiashili	22	2.1
7	岭南 Lingnan	20	1.9
8	稷士佳 Jessica	19	1.8
9	达能 Danone	17	1.6

n=1034

7-5 样本、男性各年龄层、女性各年龄层最近三个月有无购买的比例/ Purchasing in the Last Three Months by the Whole Sample, Age and Gender Groups

	人数 Number	买过 yes	没买过 no
样本 Sample	1034	69.8	30.2
男性 Male	499	61.9	38.1
16~24 岁 Age	106	62.3	37.7
25~34 岁 Age	150	62.0	38.0
35~44 岁 Age	127	62.2	37.8
45~54 岁 Age	73	64.4	35.6
55~60 岁 Age	43	55.8	44.2
女性 Female	535	77.2	22.8
16~24 岁 Age	112	73.2	26.8
25~34 岁 Age	158	81.0	19.0
35~44 岁 Age	137	78.1	21.9
45~54 岁 Age	87	80.5	19.5
55~60 岁 Age	41	63.4	36.6

7-6 样本、男性各年龄层、女性各年龄层最近三个月的食用频率/ Frequencies of Consuming Biscuit in the Last Three Months by the Whole Sample, Age and Gender Groups

	人数 Number	天天吃 daily	一周3次或以上 3 times or over a week	一周1~2次 once or twice a week	一个月2~3次 2 or 3 times a month	一个月1次或以下 once a month or below	没吃过 never
样本 Sample	**1034**	**5.1**	**12.3**	**25.2**	**19.6**	**11.6**	**26.1**
男性 Male	**499**	**4.4**	**8.8**	**23.2**	**20.4**	**10.0**	**33.1**
16~24 岁 Age	106	8.5	9.4	25.5	15.1	8.5	33.0
25~34 岁 Age	150	2.0	7.3	24.7	26.7	10.0	29.3
35~44 岁 Age	127	6.3	10.2	20.5	17.3	10.2	35.4
45~54 岁 Age	73	1.4	11.0	23.3	21.9	12.3	30.1
55~60 岁 Age	43	2.3	4.7	20.9	18.6	9.3	44.2
女性 Female	**535**	**5.8**	**15.5**	**27.1**	**18.9**	**13.1**	**19.6**
16~24 岁 Age	112	3.6	16.1	26.8	20.5	11.6	21.4
25~34 岁 Age	158	4.4	17.1	26.6	19.6	14.6	17.7
35~44 岁 Age	137	6.6	12.4	29.9	19.0	13.9	18.2
45~54 岁 Age	87	10.3	14.9	26.4	17.2	11.5	19.5
55~60 岁 Age	41	4.9	19.5	22.0	14.6	12.2	26.8

7-7 样本、男性各年龄层、女性各年龄层的品牌习惯/ Brand Habit in Consuming Biscuit by the Whole Sample, Age and Gender Groups

	人数 Number	基本固定食用一个牌子 used in only one brand	比较固定地食用两个或三个牌子 used in two or three brands	基本上不太固定牌子 no brand preference
样本 Sample	**763**	**20.7**	**39.2**	**40.1**
男性 Male	**333**	**22.2**	**38.1**	**39.6**
16~24 岁 Age	71	26.8	35.2	38.0
25~34 岁 Age	106	20.8	43.4	35.8
35~44 岁 Age	81	19.8	43.2	37.0
45~54 岁 Age	51	23.5	29.4	47.1
55~60 岁 Age	24	20.8	25.0	54.2
女性 Female	**430**	**19.5**	**40.0**	**40.5**
16~24 岁 Age	88	18.2	50.0	31.8
25~34 岁 Age	130	16.9	42.3	40.8
35~44 岁 Age	112	28.6	35.7	35.7
45~54 岁 Age	70	15.7	35.7	48.6
55~60 岁 Age	30	10.0	26.7	63.3

7-8 选择该类商品的考虑因素/ Ranking of the Considerations in Purchasing

注：本题为多选题，合计百分比超过 100%(Multiple answers)

排名 Ranking	考虑因素 Considerations	人次 Person-time	百分比 Percent
1	口味好 pleasant taste	551	72.3
2	价格适中 reasonable price	329	43.2
3	有名的牌子 famous brand	178	23.4
4	购买方便 easy to buy	163	21.4
5	生产日期 date of producing	157	20.6
6	只是由于习惯 out of habit	67	8.8
7	包装吸引人 appealing package	58	7.6
8	广告影响 influence of advertising	40	5.2
9	有优惠条件 with preferential terms	30	3.9
10	朋友推荐 introduction of friends	26	3.4
11	其它 others	8	1.0
12	售货员介绍 introduced by the shop assistants	7	0.9

n=762

7-9 样本、男性各年龄层、女性各年龄层最常食用的种类/ Kinds of the Consumed Biscuit by the Whole Sample, Age and Gender Groups

注：本题为多选题，合计百分比超过 100%(Multiple answers)

	人数 Number	夹心饼干 sandwich biscuit	曲奇 cookie	全麦饼干 whole-wheat biscuit	梳打饼干 soda biscuit	普通咸饼干 salty biscuit	普通甜饼干 sweat biscuit	其它 others
样本 Sample	758	33.1	16.2	8.6	46.0	17.4	10.4	3.0
男性 Male	334	29.9	18.6	8.4	44.6	19.8	10.8	1.8
16~24 岁 Age	71	35.2	26.8	12.7	36.6	18.3	2.8	0.0
25~34 岁 Age	106	29.2	20.8	6.6	52.8	17.0	7.5	2.8
35~44 岁 Age	82	25.6	14.6	6.1	47.6	18.3	12.2	2.4
45~54 岁 Age	51	33.3	7.8	11.8	41.2	23.5	25.5	2.0
55~60 岁 Age	24	25.0	20.8	4.2	29.2	33.3	12.5	0.0
女性 Female	424	35.6	14.4	8.7	47.2	15.6	10.1	4.0
16~24 岁 Age	87	37.9	13.8	10.3	47.1	14.9	8.0	2.3
25~34 岁 Age	130	37.7	15.4	9.2	51.5	11.5	9.2	4.6
35~44 岁 Age	109	32.1	12.8	9.2	43.1	22.0	10.1	2.8
45~54 岁 Age	68	38.2	19.1	5.9	48.5	16.2	8.8	4.4
55~60 岁 Age	30	26.7	6.7	6.7	40.0	10.0	23.3	10.0

7-10 样本、男性各年龄层、女性各年龄层最常食用的场合/ Settings of Consumption by the Whole Sample, Age and Gender Groups

注：本题为多选题，合计百分比超过 100%(Multiple answers)

	人数 Number	早餐时 breakfast	饭后甜点 dessert after dinner	加班时 when work overtime	宵夜时 evening snack	当零食吃 between meal	外出、旅游时 outing/ traveling	其它 others
样本 Sample	756	20.1	4.0	5.0	24.2	70.0	10.2	3.0
男性 Male	333	17.7	4.5	6.9	27.6	66.1	8.7	2.7
16~24 岁 Age	71	19.7	9.9	5.6	22.5	71.8	8.5	1.4
25~34 岁 Age	106	12.3	2.8	10.4	30.2	61.3	14.2	3.8
35~44 岁 Age	82	22.0	3.7	4.9	29.3	63.4	3.7	2.4
45~54 岁 Age	50	22.0	4.0	8.0	32.0	70.0	4.0	4.0
55~60 岁 Age	24	12.5	0.0	0.0	16.7	70.8	12.5	0.0
女性 Female	423	22.0	3.5	3.5	21.5	73.0	11.3	3.3
16~24 岁 Age	88	28.4	3.4	4.5	17.0	78.4	18.2	3.4
25~34 岁 Age	128	18.0	3.1	3.9	23.4	76.6	7.8	0.8
35~44 岁 Age	110	20.9	5.5	3.6	24.5	72.7	9.1	1.8
45~54 岁 Age	67	23.9	3.0	3.0	19.4	65.7	10.4	4.5
55~60 岁 Age	30	20.0	0.0	0.0	20.0	60.0	16.7	16.7

7-11 重度消费者人口分布/ Demographics of the Heavy Consumers

	人数 Number	16-24 岁 Age	25-34 岁 Age	35-44 岁 Age	45-54 岁 Age	55-60 岁 Age
样本 Sample	441	22.2	28.8	25.9	16.1	7.0
男性 Male	182	25.3	28.0	25.8	14.3	6.6
天天吃 daily	22	40.9	13.6	36.4	4.5	4.5
一周 3 次或以上 3 times or over a week	44	22.7	25.0	29.5	18.2	4.5
一周 1~2 次 once or twice a week	116	23.3	31.9	22.4	14.7	7.8
女性 Female	259	20.1	29.3	25.9	17.4	7.3
天天吃 daily	31	12.9	22.6	29.0	29.0	6.5
一周 3 次或以上 3 times or over a week	83	21.7	32.5	20.5	15.7	9.6
一周 1 ~2 次 once or twice a week	145	20.7	29.0	28.3	15.9	6.2

7-12 不同消费者层的常用品牌/ The Most Frequently Used Brands by Market Segments

7-12-1 时尚流行指标/ Fads Popular Index

	人数 Number	第一品牌及百分比 1st/ percent	第二品牌及百分比 2nd/ percent	第三品牌及百分比 3rd/ percent
样本 Sample	**754**	**奇宝 Keebler(25.9)**	**奇宝太平梳打 Keebler Pacific(16.7)**	**嘉顿 Garden(7.8)**
平实生活指向 simple living orientation	383	奇宝 Keebler(21.7)	奇宝太平梳打 Keebler Pacific(14.9)	嘉顿 Garden(7.8)
时尚流行指向 fashion orientation	371	奇宝 Keebler(30.2)	奇宝太平梳打 Keebler Pacific(18.6)	嘉顿 Garden(7.8)

7-12-2 广告态度指标/ Advertising Attitude Index

	人数 Number	第一品牌及百分比 1st/ percent	第二品牌及百分比 2nd/ percent	第三品牌及百分比 3rd/ percent
样本 Sample	**752**	**奇宝 Keebler(25.9)**	**奇宝太平梳打 Keebler Pacific(16.9)**	**嘉顿 Garden(7.8)**
广告淡漠指向 indifferent orientation	227	奇宝 Keebler(27.3)	奇宝太平梳打 Keebler Pacific(13.7)	康师傅 Kangshifu(7.9)
中间层 medium	452	奇宝 Keebler(25.2)	奇宝太平梳打 Keebler Pacific(18.1)	嘉顿 Garden(7.3)
信赖广告指向 loyal orientation	73	奇宝 Keebler(26.0)	奇宝太平梳打 Keebler Pacific(19.2)	嘉顿 Garden(13.7)

7-12-3 饮食健康指标/ Foods & Drink Quality Index

	人数 Number	第一品牌及百分比 1st/ percent	第二品牌及百分比 2nd/ percent	第三品牌及百分比 3rd/ percent
样本 Sample	**759**	**奇宝 Keebler(26.0)**	**奇宝太平梳打 Keebler Pacific(16.7)**	**嘉顿 Garden(8.0)**
饮食“温饱”指向 "basic" orientation	203	奇宝 Keebler(27.6)	奇宝太平梳打 Keebler Pacific(19.2)	嘉顿 Garden(7.4)
中间层 medium	417	奇宝 Keebler(25.9)	奇宝太平梳打 Keebler Pacific(15.1)	嘉顿 Garden(8.2)
健康营养指向 health & nutrition orientation	139	奇宝 Keebler(23.7)	奇宝太平梳打 Keebler Pacific(18.0)	嘉顿 Garden(8.6)

7-13 重度消费者的消费者层构成/ The Composition of the Heavy Consumers

7-13-1 时尚流行指标/ Fads Popular Index

	人数 Number	平实生活指向 simple living orientation	时尚流行指向 fashion orientation
样本 Sample	**440**	**49.8**	**50.2**
天天吃 daily	53	50.9	49.1
一周 3 次或以上 3 times or over a week	127	49.6	50.4
一周 1～2 次 once or twice a week	260	49.6	50.4

7-13-2 广告态度指标/ Advertising Attitude Index

	人数 Number	广告淡漠指向 indifferent orientation	中间层 medium	信赖广告指向 loyal orientation
样本 Sample	**433**	**89.4**	**10.6**	**0.0**
天天吃 daily	52	90.4	9.6	0.0
一周 3 次或以上 3 times or over a week	126	89.7	10.3	0.0
一周 1~2 次 once or twice a week	255	89.0	11.0	0.0

7-13-3 饮食健康指标/ Foods & Drink Quality Index

	人数 Number	饮食“温饱”指向 "basic" orientation	中间层 medium	健康营养指向 health & nutrition orientation
样本 Sample	**440**	**25.9**	**52.7**	**21.4**
天天吃 daily	53	35.8	39.6	24.5
一周 3 次或以上 3 times or over a week	127	25.2	52.8	22.0
一周 1~2 次 once or twice a week	260	24.2	55.4	20.4

● 重庆 / Chongqing

7-1 最近三个月食用频率的比例/ Proportion of the Sample Consuming Biscuit in the Last Three Months

	人数 Number	百分比 Percent
天天吃 daily	16	2.6
一周 3 次或以上 3 times or over a week	55	8.8
一周 1~2 次 once or twice a week	138	22.2
一个月 2～3 次 2 or 3 times a month	116	18.6
一个月 1 次或以下 once a month or below	85	13.6
没吃过 never	213	34.2

n=623

7-2 最常用品牌排名/ Ranking of the Most Frequently Used Brands

排名 Brand Ranking	品牌 Brands	人数 Number	百分比 Percent
1	纳贝斯克奥利奥 Nabisco Oreo	74	18.2
2	康师傅 Kangshifu	71	17.4
3	纳贝斯克乐之 Nabisco Ritz	27	6.6
4	奇宝太平梳打 Keebler Pacific	20	4.9
5	万士发 Wanshifa	16	3.9
6	华声鸳鸯夹心饼干 Hua Sheng YuanYang	14	3.4
7	奇宝 Keebler	12	2.9
8	旺旺 Wangwang	11	2.7
9	达能王子夹心 Danone Prince	8	2.0
10	嘉士利 Jiashili	6	1.5
10	奇宝每乐时薏米 Keebler Merries	6	1.5
10	达能闲趣 Danone Tuc	6	1.5

n=407

7-3 样本、男性各年龄层、女性各年龄层的常用品牌/ The Most Frequently Used Brands by the Whole Sample, Age and Gender Groups

	人数 Number	第一品牌及百分比 1st/ percent	第二品牌及百分比 2nd/ percent	第三品牌及百分比 3rd/ percent
样本 Sample	407	**纳贝斯克奥利奥 Nabisco Oreo(18.2)**	**康师傅 Kangshifu(17.4)**	**纳贝斯克乐之 Nabisco Ritz(6.6)**
男性 Male	188	**康师傅 Kangshifu(20.2)**	**纳贝斯克奥利奥 Nabisco Oreo(17.0)**	**万士发 Wanshifa(5.9)** **纳贝斯克乐之 Nabisco Ritz(5.9)**
16~24 岁 Age	50	康师傅 Kangshifu(34.0)	纳贝斯克奥利奥 Nabisco Oreo(22.0)	华声鸳鸯夹心饼干 Hua Sheng YuanYang (4.0) 奇宝每乐时薏米 Keebler Merries(4.0) 奇宝太平梳打 Keebler Pacific(4.0) 纳贝斯克乐之 Nabisco Ritz(4.0)
25~34 岁 Age	53	康师傅 Kangshifu(20.8)	纳贝斯克奥利奥 Nabisco Oreo(11.3)	纳贝斯克乐之 Nabisco Ritz(7.5)
35~44 岁 Age	45	纳贝斯克奥利奥 Nabisco Oreo(20.0)	康师傅 Kangshifu(11.1) 万士发 Wanshifa(11.1)	奇宝每乐时薏米 Keebler Merries(6.7)
45~54 岁 Age	27	康师傅 Kangshifu(14.8) 纳贝斯克奥利奥 Nabisco Oreo(14.8)	纳贝斯克乐之 Nabisco Ritz(7.4) 万士发 Wanshifa(7.4) 达能 Danone(7.4)	奇宝 Keebler(3.7) 奇宝太平梳打 Keebler Pacific(3.7) 旺旺 Wangwang(3.7) 太平洋 Taipingyang(3.7) 华声鸳鸯夹心饼干 Hua Sheng YuanYang(3.7) 威字牌 Weizhi(3.7) 熊猫 Panda (3.7) 川岛 ChuanDao (3.7)
55~60 岁 Age	13	纳贝斯克奥利奥 Nabisco Oreo(15.4)	达能闲趣 Danone Tuc(7.7) 康师傅 Kangshifu(7.7) 纳贝斯克乐之 Nabisco Ritz(7.7) 奇宝 Keebler(7.7) 奇宝太平梳打 Keebler Pacific(7.7) 万士发 Wanshifa(7.7) 龙头 Longtou (7.7)	
女性 Female	219	**纳贝斯克奥利奥 Nabisco Oreo(19.2)**	**康师傅 Kangshifu(15.1)**	**纳贝斯克乐之 Nabisco Ritz(7.3)**
16~24 岁 Age	57	康师傅 Kangshifu(24.6) 纳贝斯克奥利奥 Nabisco Oreo(24.6)	纳贝斯克乐之 Nabisco Ritz(7.0)	达能王子夹心 Danone Prince(5.3) 奇宝 Keebler(5.3)
25~34 岁 Age	62	纳贝斯克奥利奥 Nabisco Oreo(17.7)	康师傅 Kangshifu(14.5)	纳贝斯克乐之 Nabisco Ritz(9.7)
35~44 岁 Age	45	纳贝斯克奥利奥 Nabisco Oreo(22.2)	康师傅 Kangshifu(8.9)	华声鸳鸯夹心饼干 Hua Sheng YuanYang (6.7) 奇宝太平梳打 Keebler Pacific(6.7) 旺旺 Wangwang(6.7)
45~54 岁 Age	41	纳贝斯克奥利奥 Nabisco Oreo(14.6)	奇宝太平梳打 Keebler Pacific(12.2)	纳贝斯克乐之 Nabisco Ritz(9.8)
55~60 岁 Age	14	康师傅 Kangshifu(28.6)		达能王子夹心 Danone Prince(7.1) 达能闲趣 Danone Tuc(7.1) 纳贝斯克奥利奥 Nabisco Oreo(7.1) 万士发 Wanshifa(7.1) 奇宝每乐时薏米 Keebler Merries(7.1) 华声鸳鸯夹心饼干 Hua Sheng YuanYang(7.1) 益民 Yimin(7.1)

7-4 理想品牌排名/ Ranking of the Ideal Brands

排名 Brand Ranking	品牌 Brands	人数 Number	百分比 Percent
1	纳贝斯克奥利奥 Nabisco Oreo	116	18.6
2	康师傅 Kangshifu	105	16.8
3	纳贝斯克乐之 Nabisco Ritz	28	4.5
4	奇宝 Keebler	27	4.3
5	旺旺 Wangwang	24	3.8
6	奇宝太平梳打 Keebler Pacific	18	2.9
7	华声鸳鸯夹心饼干 Hua Sheng YuanYang	14	2.2
8	达能 Danone	10	1.6
9	万士发 Wanshifa	7	1.1
10	威字牌 Weizi	6	1.0
10	纳贝斯克 Nabisco	6	1.0
10	达能王子夹心 Danone Prince	6	1.0

n=624

7-5 样本、男性各年龄层、女性各年龄层最近三个月有无购买的比例/ Purchasing in the Last Three Months by the Whole Sample, Age and Gender Groups

	人数 Number	买过 yes	没买过 no
样本 Sample	623	66.3	33.7
男性 Male	314	60.5	39.5
16~24 岁 Age	64	79.7	20.3
25~34 岁 Age	93	60.2	39.8
35~44 岁 Age	75	56.0	44.0
45~54 岁 Age	54	51.9	48.1
55~60 岁 Age	28	46.4	53.6
女性 Female	309	72.2	27.8
16~24 岁 Age	64	89.1	10.9
25~34 岁 Age	90	74.4	25.6
35~44 岁 Age	72	63.9	36.1
45~54 岁 Age	60	65.0	35.0
55~60 岁 Age	23	60.9	39.1

7-6 样本、男性各年龄层、女性各年龄层最近三个月的食用频率/ Frequencies of Consuming Biscuit in the Last Three Months by the Whole Sample, Age and Gender Groups

	人数 Number	天天吃 daily	一周 3 次或以上 3 times or over a week	一周 1~2 次 once or twice a week	一个月 2~3 次 2 or 3 times a month	一个月 1 次或以下 once a month or below	没吃过 never
样本 Sample	623	2.6	8.8	22.2	18.6	13.6	34.2
男性 Male	313	1.6	8.3	18.8	19.2	12.8	39.3
16~24 岁 Age	64	3.1	12.5	29.7	17.2	17.2	20.3
25~34 岁 Age	93	0.0	7.5	15.1	21.5	14.0	41.9
35~44 岁 Age	75	2.7	9.3	16.0	17.3	14.7	40.0
45~54 岁 Age	53	1.9	5.7	17.0	22.6	3.8	49.1
55~60 岁 Age	28	0.0	3.6	17.9	14.3	10.7	53.6
女性 Female	310	3.5	9.4	25.5	18.1	14.5	29.0
16~24 岁 Age	64	3.1	15.6	37.5	17.2	15.6	10.9
25~34 岁 Age	90	2.2	6.7	23.3	23.3	13.3	31.1
35~44 岁 Age	73	4.1	6.8	30.1	12.3	9.6	37.0
45~54 岁 Age	60	3.3	8.3	15.0	18.3	23.3	31.7
55~60 岁 Age	23	8.7	13.0	13.0	17.4	8.7	39.1

7-7 样本、男性各年龄层、女性各年龄层的品牌习惯/ Brand Habit in Consuming Biscuit by the Whole Sample, Age and Gender Groups

	人数 Number	基本固定食用一个牌子 used in only one brand	比较固定地食用两个或三个牌子 used in two or three brands	基本上不太固定牌子 no brand preference
样本 Sample	409	23.0	30.6	46.5
男性 Male	189	23.3	28.6	48.1
16~24 岁 Age	51	21.6	31.4	47.1
25~34 岁 Age	53	17.0	32.1	50.9
35~44 岁 Age	45	24.4	22.2	53.3
45~54 岁 Age	27	33.3	25.9	40.7
55~60 岁 Age	13	30.8	30.8	38.5
女性 Female	220	22.7	32.3	45.0
16~24 岁 Age	57	24.6	47.4	28.1
25~34 岁 Age	62	14.5	32.3	53.2
35~44 岁 Age	46	26.1	28.3	45.7
45~54 岁 Age	41	31.7	19.5	48.8
55~60 岁 Age	14	14.3	21.4	64.3

7-8 选择该类商品的考虑因素/ Ranking of the Considerations in Purchasing

注：本题为多选题，合计百分比超过 100%(Multiple answers)

排名 Ranking	考虑因素 Considerations	人次 Person-time	百分比 Percent
1	口味好 pleasant taste	302	74.0
2	价格适中 reasonable price	160	39.2
3	生产日期 date of producing	91	22.3
4	购买方便 easy to buy	66	16.2
4	有名的牌子 famous brand	66	16.2
5	只是由于习惯 out of habit	37	9.1
6	包装吸引人 appealing package	25	6.1
7	广告影响 influence of advertising	22	5.4
8	朋友推荐 introduction of friends	18	4.4
9	有优惠条件 with preferential terms	14	3.4
10	售货员介绍 introduced by the shop assistants	7	1.7
11	其它 others	4	1.0

n=408

7-9 样本、男性各年龄层、女性各年龄层最常食用的种类/ Kinds of the Consumed Biscuit by the Whole Sample, Age and Gender Groups

注：本题为多选题，合计百分比超过 100%(Multiple answers)

	人数 Number	夹心饼干 sandwich biscuit	曲奇 cookie	全麦饼干 whole-wheat biscuit	梳打饼干 soda biscuit	普通咸饼干 salty biscuit	普通甜饼干 sweat biscuit	其它 others
样本 Sample	408	52.5	23.8	4.2	18.6	9.3	24.0	2.7
男性 Male	189	61.9	21.2	5.3	15.9	8.5	20.6	3.2
16~24 岁 Age	51	80.4	17.6	3.9	19.6	2.0	5.9	3.9
25~34 岁 Age	53	50.9	20.8	3.8	13.2	13.2	28.3	1.9
35~44 岁 Age	45	48.9	22.2	6.7	17.8	8.9	31.1	0.0
45~54 岁 Age	27	63.0	25.9	3.7	7.4	11.1	18.5	11.1
55~60 岁 Age	13	76.9	23.1	15.4	23.1	7.7	15.4	0.0
女性 Female	219	44.3	26.0	3.2	21.0	10.0	26.9	2.3
16~24 岁 Age	57	61.4	26.3	3.5	26.3	8.8	8.8	3.5
25~34 岁 Age	62	38.7	37.1	3.2	22.6	8.1	19.4	3.2
35~44 岁 Age	46	39.1	17.4	2.2	19.6	8.7	43.5	2.2
45~54 岁 Age	40	37.5	25.0	5.0	17.5	12.5	37.5	0.0
55~60 岁 Age	14	35.7	7.1	0.0	7.1	21.4	50.0	0.0

7-10 样本、男性各年龄层、女性各年龄层最常食用的场合/ Settings of Consumption by the Whole Sample, Age and Gender Groups

	人数 Number	早餐时 breakfast	饭后甜点 dessert after dinner	加班时 when work overtime	宵夜时 evening snack	当零食吃 between meal	外出、旅游时 outing/ traveling	其它 others
样本 Sample	407	27.0	4.4	7.4	19.4	63.6	12.3	2.5
男性 Male	187	20.3	4.8	11.2	21.9	57.2	13.9	2.7
16~24 岁 Age	51	17.6	7.8	11.8	31.4	54.9	15.7	0.0
25~34 岁 Age	53	22.6	1.9	9.4	17.0	62.3	11.3	3.8
35~44 岁 Age	45	15.6	4.4	11.1	22.2	55.6	13.3	4.4
45~54 岁 Age	26	30.8	3.8	15.4	19.2	50.0	7.7	3.8
55~60 岁 Age	12	16.7	8.3	8.3	8.3	66.7	33.3	0.0
女性 Female	220	32.7	4.1	4.1	17.3	69.1	10.9	2.3
16~24 岁 Age	57	40.4	8.8	1.8	12.3	68.4	12.3	0.0
25~34 岁 Age	62	32.3	1.6	9.7	16.1	71.0	12.9	0.0
35~44 岁 Age	46	30.4	6.5	0.0	23.9	65.2	10.9	2.2
45~54 岁 Age	41	29.3	0.0	4.9	17.1	75.6	4.9	7.3
55~60 岁 Age	14	21.4	0.0	0.0	21.4	57.1	14.3	7.1

7-11 重度消费者人口分布/ Demographics of the Heavy Consumers

	人数 Number	16-24 岁 Age	25-34 岁 Age	35-44 岁 Age	45-54 岁 Age	55-60 岁 Age
样本 Sample	209	31.1	23.9	24.4	13.9	6.7
男性 Male	90	32.2	23.3	23.3	14.4	6.7
天天吃 daily	5	40.0	0.0	40.0	20.0	0.0
一周 3 次或以上 3 times or over a week	26	30.8	26.9	26.9	11.5	3.8
一周 1~2 次 once or twice a week	59	32.2	23.7	20.3	15.3	8.5
女性 Female	119	30.3	24.4	25.2	13.4	6.7
天天吃 daily	11	18.2	18.2	27.3	18.2	18.2
一周 3 次或以上 3 times or over a week	29	34.5	20.7	17.2	17.2	10.3
一周 1 ~2 次 once or twice a week	79	30.4	26.6	27.8	11.4	3.8

7-12 不同消费者层的常用品牌/ The Most Frequently Used Brands by Market Segments

7-12-1 时尚流行指标/ Fads Popular Index

	人数 Number	第一品牌及百分比 1st/ percent	第二品牌及百分比 2nd/ percent	第三品牌及百分比 3rd/ percent	第四品牌及百分比 4th/ percent
样本 Sample	401	**纳贝斯克奥利奥 Nabisco Oreo(18.5)**	**康师傅 Kangshifu(17.2)**	**纳贝斯克乐之 Nabisco Ritz(6.5)**	**奇宝太平梳打 Keebler Pacific(5.0)**
平实生活指向 simple living orientation	221	纳贝斯克奥利奥 Nabisco Oreo(17.6)	康师傅 Kangshifu(16.3)	纳贝斯克乐之 Nabisco Ritz(8.6)	奇宝太平梳打 Keebler Pacific(5.4) 万士发 Wanshifa(5.4)
时尚流行指向 fashion orientation	180	纳贝斯克奥利奥 Nabisco Oreo(19.4)	康师傅 Kangshifu(18.3)	奇宝太平梳打 Keebler Pacific(4.4)	

7-12-2 广告态度指标/ Advertising Attitude Index

	人数 Number	第一品牌及百分比 1st/ percent	第二品牌及百分比 2nd/ percent	第三品牌及百分比 3rd/ percent	第四品牌及百分比 4th/ percent
样本 Sample	406	**纳贝斯克奥利奥 Nabisco Oreo(18.2)**	**康师傅 Kangshifu(17.5)**	**纳贝斯克乐之 Nabisco Ritz(6.7)**	**奇宝太平梳打 Keebler Pacific(4.9)**
广告淡漠指向 indifferent orientation	101	康师傅 Kangshifu(18.8) 纳贝斯克奥利奥 Nabisco Oreo(18.8)	纳贝斯克乐之 Nabisco Ritz(7.9)	万士发 Wanshifa(5.9) 奇宝太平梳打 Keebler Pacific(5.9)	华声鸳鸯夹心饼干 Huashengyuanyangbing-gan(4.0)
中间层 medium	247	纳贝斯克奥利奥 Nabisco Oreo(19.4)	康师傅 Kangshifu(16.6)	纳贝斯克乐之 Nabisco Ritz(6.9)	
信赖广告指向 loyal orientation	58	康师傅 Kangshifu(19.0)	纳贝斯克奥利奥 Nabisco Oreo(12.1)	奇宝太平梳打 Keebler Pacific(6.9)	万士发 Wanshifa(5.2) 奇宝 Keebler(5.2) 康元 Khong Guan(5.2)

7-12-3 饮食健康指标/ Foods & Drink Quality Index

	人数 Number	第一品牌及百分比 1st/ percent	第二品牌及百分比 2nd/ percent	第三品牌及百分比 3rd/ percent	第四品牌及百分比 4th/ percent
样本 Sample	402	**纳贝斯克奥利奥 Nabisco Oreo(18.4)**	**康师傅 Kangshifu(17.7)**	**纳贝斯克乐之 Nabisco Ritz(6.5)**	**奇宝太平梳打 Keebler Pacific(4.7)**
饮食"温饱"指向 "basic" orientation	132	纳贝斯克奥利奥 Nabisco Oreo(22.7)	康师傅 Kangshifu(18.9)	万士发 Wanshifa(6.1) 纳贝斯克乐之 Nabisco Ritz(6.1)	华声鸳鸯夹心饼干 Huashengyuanyangbinggan(3.8)
中间层 medium	185	康师傅 Kangshifu(18.4)	纳贝斯克奥利奥 Nabisco Oreo(15.1)	纳贝斯克乐之 Nabisco Ritz(5.9)	奇宝太平梳打 Keebler Pacific(5.4)
健康营养指向 health & nutrition orientation	85	纳贝斯克奥利奥 Nabisco Oreo(18.8)	康师傅 Kangshifu(14.1)	纳贝斯克乐之 Nabisco Ritz(8.2)	奇宝太平梳打 Keebler Pacific(7.1)

7-13 重度消费者的消费者层构成/ The Composition of the Heavy Consumers

7-13-1 时尚流行指标/ Fads Popular Index

	人数 Number	平实生活指向 simple living orientation	时尚流行指向 fashion orientation
样本 Sample	205	52.7	47.3
天天吃 daily	16	68.8	31.3
一周 3 次或以上 3 times or over a week	54	48.1	51.9
一周 1～2 次 once or twice a week	135	52.6	47.4

7-13-2 广告态度指标/ Advertising Attitude Index

	人数 Number	广告淡漠指向 indifferent orientation	中间层 medium	信赖广告指向 loyal orientation
样本 Sample	208	85.6	14.4	0.0
天天吃 daily	16	87.5	12.5	0.0
一周 3 次或以上 3 times or over a week	55	83.6	16.4	0.0
一周 1~2 次 once or twice a week	137	86.1	13.9	0.0

7-13-3 饮食健康指标/ Foods & Drink Quality Index

	人数 Number	饮食"温饱"指向 "basic" orientation	中间层 medium	健康营养指向 health & nutrition orientation
样本 Sample	207	27.1	49.3	23.7
天天吃 daily	16	12.5	75.0	12.5
一周 3 次或以上 3 times or over a week	55	36.4	43.6	20.0
一周 1~2 次 once or twice a week	136	25.0	48.5	26.5

● 武汉 / Wuhan

7-1 最近三个月食用频率的比例/ Proportion of the Sample Consuming Biscuit in the Last Three Months

	人数 Number	百分比 Percent
天天吃 daily	20	3.1
一周 3 次或以上 3 times or over a week	54	8.4
一周 1~2 次 once or twice a week	125	19.5
一个月 2～3 次 2 or 3 times a month	136	21.2
一个月 1 次或以下 once a month or below	101	15.7
没吃过 never	206	32.1

n=642

7-2 最常用品牌排名/ Ranking of the Most Frequently Used Brands

排名 Brand Ranking	品牌 Brands	人数 Number	百分比 Percent
1	康师傅 Kangshifu	79	18.1
2	纳贝斯克奥利奥 Nabisco Oreo	52	11.9
3	奇宝太平梳打 Keebler Pacific	44	10.1
4	嘉士利 Jiashili	32	7.3
5	奇宝每乐时薏米 Keebler Merries	24	5.5
6	九洲 Jiuzhou	13	3.0
6	纳贝斯克乐之 Nabisco Ritz	13	3.0
7	奇宝 Keebler	11	2.5

n=436

7-3 样本、男性各年龄层、女性各年龄层的常用品牌/ The Most Frequently Used Brands by the Whole Sample, Age and Gender Groups

	人数 Number	第一品牌及百分比 1st/ percent	第二品牌及百分比 2nd/ percent	第三品牌及百分比 3rd/ percent
样本 Sample	436	**康师傅 Kangshifu(18.1)**	**纳贝斯克奥利奥 Nabisco Oreo(11.9)**	**奇宝太平梳打 Keebler Pacific(10.1)**
男性 Male	200	**康师傅 Kangshifu(15.0)**	**纳贝斯克奥利奥 Nabisco Oreo(12.5)**	**奇宝太平梳打 Keebler Pacific(10.5)**
16~24 岁 Age	48	康师傅 Kangshifu(27.1)	纳贝斯克奥利奥 Nabisco Oreo(22.9)	奇宝太平梳打 Keebler Pacific(10.4)
25~34 岁 Age	59	康师傅 Kangshifu(16.9)	奇宝太平梳打 Keebler Pacific(11.9)	嘉士利 Jiashili(8.5) 纳贝斯克奥利奥 Nabisco Oreo(8.5)
35~44 岁 Age	47	奇宝太平梳打 Keebler Pacific(10.6)	纳贝斯克奥利奥 Nabisco Oreo(8.5) 奇宝每乐时薏米 Keebler Merries(8.5)	嘉士利 Jiashili(6.4) 九洲 Jiuzhou(6.4)
45~54 岁 Age	30	纳贝斯克奥利奥 Nabisco Oreo(13.3)	嘉士利 Jiashili(10.0) 康师傅 Kangshifu(10.0)	奇宝太平梳打 Keebler Pacific(6.7) 九洲 Jiuzhou(6.7)
55~60 岁 Age	16	嘉士利 Jiashili(25.0)	康师傅 Kangshifu(12.5) 奇宝太平梳打 Keebler Pacific(12.5)	华美 Hua Mei(6.3) 纳贝斯克奥利奥 Nabisco Oreo(6.3)
女性 Female	236	**康师傅 Kangshifu(20.8)**	**纳贝斯克奥利奥 Nabisco Oreo(11.4)**	**奇宝太平梳打 Keebler Pacific(9.7)**
16~24 岁 Age	60	康师傅 Kangshifu(26.7)	纳贝斯克奥利奥 Nabisco Oreo(11.7)	奇宝每乐时薏米 Keebler Merries(10.0)
25~34 岁 Age	71	康师傅 Kangshifu(21.1)	纳贝斯克奥利奥 Nabisco Oreo(12.7)	奇宝每乐时薏米 Keebler Merries(9.9)
35~44 岁 Age	50	康师傅 Kangshifu(22.0)	纳贝斯克奥利奥 Nabisco Oreo(12.0)	奇宝太平梳打 Keebler Pacific(8.0) 嘉士利 Jiashili(8.0)
45~54 岁 Age	41	奇宝太平梳打 Keebler Pacific(19.5)	康师傅 Kangshifu(17.1)	嘉士利 Jiashili(9.8) 纳贝斯克奥利奥 Nabisco Oreo(9.8)
55~60 岁 Age	14	九洲 Jiuzhou(14.3)	嘉士利 Jiashili(7.1) 纳贝斯克奥利奥 Nabisco Oreo(7.1) 嘉士达 Jiashida(7.1)	

7-4 理想品牌排名/ Ranking of the Ideal Brands

排名 Brand Ranking	品牌 Brands	人数 Number	百分比 Percent
1	康师傅 Kangshifu	75	11.7
2	纳贝斯克奥利奥 Nabisco Oreo	64	10.0
3	嘉士利 Jiashili	40	6.2
4	奇宝太平梳打 Keebler Pacific	32	5.0
4	奇宝 Keebler	32	5.0
5	奇宝每乐时薏米 Keebler Merries	13	2.0
5	纳贝斯克乐之 Nabisco Ritz	13	2.0
6	九洲 Jiuzhou	12	1.9
7	纳贝斯克趣多多 Nsbisco Ahoy	6	0.9

n=642

7-5 样本、男性各年龄层、女性各年龄层最近三个月有无购买的比例/ Purchasing in the Last Three Months by the Whole Sample, Age and Gender Groups

	人数 Number	买过 yes	没买过 no
样本 Sample	641	68.5	31.5
男性 Male	311	63.7	36.3
16~24 岁 Age	65	66.2	33.8
25~34 岁 Age	89	68.5	31.5
35~44 岁 Age	80	60.0	40.0
45~54 岁 Age	52	57.7	42.3
55~60 岁 Age	25	64.0	36.0
女性 Female	330	73.0	27.0
16~24 岁 Age	69	82.6	17.4
25~34 岁 Age	96	75.0	25.0
35~44 岁 Age	77	72.7	27.3
45~54 岁 Age	62	67.7	32.3
55~60 岁 Age	26	53.8	46.2

7-6 样本、男性各年龄层、女性各年龄层最近三个月的食用频率/ Frequencies of Consuming Biscuit in the Last Three Months by the Whole Sample, Age and Gender Groups

	人数 Number	天天吃 daily	一周 3 次或以上 3 times or over a week	一周 1~2 次 once or twice a week	一个月 2~3 次 2 or 3 times a month	一个月 1 次或以下 once a month or below	没吃过 never
样本 Sample	642	3.1	8.4	19.5	21.2	15.7	32.1
男性 Male	311	1.6	7.7	18.0	21.2	15.8	35.7
16~24 岁 Age	65	1.5	9.2	29.2	20.0	13.8	26.2
25~34 岁 Age	89	1.1	7.9	14.6	25.8	16.9	33.7
35~44 岁 Age	80	0.0	2.5	16.3	18.8	21.3	41.3
45~54 岁 Age	52	3.8	11.5	15.4	13.5	13.5	42.3
55~60 岁 Age	25	4.0	12.0	12.0	32.0	4.0	36.0
女性 Female	331	4.5	9.1	20.8	21.1	15.7	28.7
16~24 岁 Age	69	4.3	14.5	29.0	24.6	14.5	13.0
25~34 岁 Age	96	7.3	6.3	22.9	27.1	10.4	26.0
35~44 岁 Age	78	1.3	11.5	17.9	15.4	17.9	35.9
45~54 岁 Age	62	4.8	4.8	11.3	22.6	22.6	33.9
55~60 岁 Age	26	3.8	7.7	23.1	3.8	15.4	46.2

7-7 样本、男性各年龄层、女性各年龄层的品牌习惯/ Brand Habit in Consuming Biscuit by the Whole Sample, Age and Gender Groups

	人数 Number	基本固定食用一个牌子 used in only one brand	比较固定地食用两个或三个牌子 used in two or three brands	基本上不太固定牌子 no brand preference
样本 Sample	435	23.2	34.0	42.8
男性 Male	200	24.0	29.5	46.5
16~24 岁 Age	48	20.8	35.4	43.8
25~34 岁 Age	59	28.8	33.9	37.3
35~44 岁 Age	47	31.9	14.9	53.2
45~54 岁 Age	30	13.3	33.3	53.3
55~60 岁 Age	16	12.5	31.3	56.3
女性 Female	235	22.6	37.9	39.6
16~24 岁 Age	60	21.7	46.7	31.7
25~34 岁 Age	71	25.4	35.2	39.4
35~44 岁 Age	49	18.4	36.7	44.9
45~54 岁 Age	41	24.4	36.6	39.0
55~60 岁 Age	14	21.4	21.4	57.1

7-8 选择该类商品的考虑因素/ Ranking of the Considerations in Purchasing

注：本题为多选题，合计百分比超过 100%(Multiple answers）

排名 Ranking	考虑因素 Considerations	人次 Person-time	百分比 Percent
1	口味好 pleasant taste	349	80.4
2	价格适中 reasonable price	187	43.1
3	生产日期 date of producing	126	29.0
4	购买方便 easy to buy	100	23.0
5	有名的牌子 famous brand	91	21.0
6	只是由于习惯 out of habit	36	8.3
7	包装吸引人 appealing package	30	6.9
8	广告影响 influence of advertising	28	6.5
9	朋友推荐 introduction of friends	21	4.8
10	有优惠条件 with preferential terms	14	3.2
11	售货员介绍 introduced by the shop assistants	12	2.8
12	其它 others	8	1.8

n=434

7-9 样本、男性各年龄层、女性各年龄层最常食用的种类/ Kinds of the Consumed Biscuit by the Whole Sample, Age and Gender Groups

注：本题为多选题，合计百分比超过 100%(Multiple answers）

	人数 Number	夹心饼干 sandwich biscuit	曲奇 cookie	全麦饼干 whole-wheat biscuit	梳打饼干 soda biscuit	普通咸饼干 salty biscuit	普通甜饼干 sweat biscuit	其它 others
样本 Sample	435	50.1	11.5	4.6	23.4	12.0	25.5	5.1
男性 Male	200	51.5	10.5	4.5	23.5	11.0	23.0	5.0
16~24 岁 Age	48	66.7	8.3	4.2	22.9	10.4	16.7	0.0
25~34 岁 Age	59	50.8	16.9	10.2	28.8	5.1	16.9	5.1
35~44 岁 Age	47	48.9	8.5	2.1	23.4	8.5	34.0	6.4
45~54 岁 Age	30	33.3	6.7	0.0	13.3	26.7	26.7	10.0
55~60 岁 Age	16	50.0	6.3	0.0	25.0	12.5	25.0	6.3
女性 Female	235	48.9	12.3	4.7	23.4	12.8	27.7	5.1
16~24 岁 Age	60	56.7	13.3	10.0	30.0	6.7	18.3	8.3
25~34 岁 Age	71	57.7	15.5	4.2	16.9	11.3	19.7	5.6
35~44 岁 Age	50	52.0	16.0	4.0	14.0	12.0	34.0	2.0
45~54 岁 Age	40	32.5	5.0	0.0	35.0	25.0	37.5	2.5
55~60 岁 Age	14	7.1	0.0	0.0	28.6	14.3	57.1	7.1

7-10 样本、男性各年龄层、女性各年龄层最常食用的场合/ Settings of Consumption by the Whole Sample, Age and Gender Groups

注：本题为多选题，合计百分比超过 100%(Multiple answers）

	人数 Number	早餐时 breakfast	饭后甜点 dessert after dinner	加班时 when work overtime	宵夜时 evening snack	当零食吃 between meal	外出、旅游时 outing/ traveling	其它 others
样本 Sample	432	8.8	10.0	4.2	22.9	72.9	16.2	3.7
男性 Male	199	9.0	7.5	6.0	29.1	66.3	17.1	3.5
16~24 岁 Age	47	4.3	14.9	4.3	23.4	72.3	19.1	2.1
25~34 岁 Age	59	10.2	6.8	5.1	25.4	69.5	23.7	5.1
35~44 岁 Age	47	10.6	4.3	8.5	31.9	61.7	12.8	4.3
45~54 岁 Age	30	13.3	3.3	3.3	36.7	60.0	13.3	3.3
55~60 岁 Age	16	6.3	6.3	12.5	37.5	62.5	6.3	0.0
女性 Female	233	8.6	12.0	2.6	17.6	78.5	15.5	3.9
16~24 岁 Age	58	12.1	13.8	3.4	8.6	82.8	22.4	0.0
25~34 岁 Age	71	4.2	8.5	2.8	18.3	84.5	14.1	1.4
35~44 岁 Age	50	10.0	10.0	2.0	28.0	74.0	16.0	6.0
45~54 岁 Age	40	10.0	17.5	2.5	15.0	75.0	10.0	2.5
55~60 岁 Age	14	7.1	14.3	0.0	21.4	57.1	7.1	28.6

7-11 重度消费者人口分布/ Demographics of the Heavy Consumers

	人数 Number	16-24 岁 Age	25-34 岁 Age	35-44 岁 Age	45-54 岁 Age	55-60 岁 Age
样本 Sample	199	29.6	28.1	19.6	14.6	8.0
男性 Male	85	30.6	24.7	17.6	18.8	8.2
天天吃 daily	5	20.0	20.0	0.0	40.0	20.0
一周 3 次或以上 3 times or over a week	24	25.0	29.2	8.3	25.0	12.5
一周 1~2 次 once or twice a week	56	33.9	23.2	23.2	14.3	5.4
女性 Female	114	28.9	30.7	21.1	11.4	7.9
天天吃 daily	15	20.0	46.7	6.7	20.0	6.7
一周 3 次或以上 3 times or over a week	30	33.3	20.0	30.0	10.0	6.7
一周 1 ~2 次 once or twice a week	69	29.0	31.9	20.3	10.1	8.7

7-12 不同消费者层的常用品牌/ The Most Frequently Used Brands by Market Segments

7-12-1 时尚流行指标/ Fads Popular Index

	人数 Number	第一品牌及百分比 1st/ percent	第二品牌及百分比 2nd/ percent	第三品牌及百分比 3rd/ percent	第四品牌及百分比 4th/ percent
样本 Sample	431	**康师傅 Kangshifu(18.1)**	**纳贝斯克奥利奥 Nabisco Oreo(11.8)**	**奇宝太平梳打 Keebler Pacific(10.2)**	**嘉士利 Jiashili(7.4)**
平实生活指向 simple living orientation	215	康师傅 Kangshifu(14.4)	嘉士利 Jiashili(11.2)	奇宝太平梳打 Keebler Pacific(10.7)	纳贝斯克奥利奥 Nabisco Oreo(7.9)
时尚流行指向 fashion orientation	216	康师傅 Kangshifu(21.8)	纳贝斯克奥利奥 Nabisco Oreo(15.7)	奇宝太平梳打 Keebler Pacific(9.7)	奇宝每乐时薏米 Keebler Merries(5.6)

7-12-2 广告态度指标/ Advertising Attitude Index

	人数 Number	第一品牌及百分比 1st/ percent	第二品牌及百分比 2nd/ percent	第三品牌及百分比 3rd/ percent	第四品牌及百分比 4th/ percent
样本 Sample	432	**康师傅 Kangshifu(18.1)**	**纳贝斯克奥利奥 Nabisco Oreo(11.8)**	**奇宝太平梳打 Keebler Pacific(10.2)**	**嘉士利 Jiashili(7.4)**
广告淡漠指向 indifferent orientation	116	康师傅 Kangshifu(19.0)	纳贝斯克奥利奥 Nabisco Oreo(10.3) 奇宝太平梳打 Keebler Pacific(10.3)	嘉士利 Jiashili(7.8)	奇宝每乐时薏米 Keebler Merries(6.0)
中间层 medium	261	康师傅 Kangshifu(16.5)	纳贝斯克奥利奥 Nabisco Oreo(11.9)	奇宝太平梳打 Keebler Pacific(10.7)	嘉士利 Jiashili(8.4)
信赖广告指向 loyal orientation	55	康师傅 Kangshifu(23.6)	纳贝斯克奥利奥 Nabisco Oreo(14.5)	奇宝太平梳打 Keebler Pacific(7.3) 纳贝斯克趣多多 Nsbisco Ahoy(7.3)	奇宝 Keebler(5.5)

7-12-3 饮食健康指标/ Foods & Drink Quality Index

	人数 Number	第一品牌及百分比 1st/ percent	第二品牌及百分比 2nd/ percent	第三品牌及百分比 3rd/ percent	第四品牌及百分比 4th/ percent
样本 Sample	431	**康师傅 Kangshifu(18.1)**	**纳贝斯克奥利奥 Nabisco Oreo(11.8)**	**奇宝太平梳打 Keebler Pacific(10.0)**	**嘉士利 Jiashili(7.4)**
饮食"温饱"指向 "basic" orientation	141	康师傅 Kangshifu(15.6)	纳贝斯克奥利奥 Nabisco Oreo(14.9)	奇宝太平梳打 Keebler Pacific(9.2)	奇宝每乐时薏米 Keebler Merries(5.0)
中间层 medium	198	康师傅 Kangshifu(22.2)	奇宝太平梳打 Keebler Pacific(12.1)	嘉士利 Jiashili(10.1)	纳贝斯克奥利奥 Nabisco Oreo(6.6)
健康营养指向 health & nutrition orientation	92	纳贝斯克奥利奥 Nabisco Oreo(18.5)	康师傅 Kangshifu(13.0)	奇宝太平梳打 Keebler Pacific(6.5) 嘉士利 Jiashili(6.5)	九洲 Jiuzhou(5.4)

7-13 重度消费者的消费者层构成/ The Composition of the Heavy Consumers

7-13-1 时尚流行指标/ Fads Popular Index

	人数 Number	平实生活指向 simple living orientation	时尚流行指向 fashion orientation
样本 Sample	197	43.7	56.3
天天吃 daily	20	30.0	70.0
一周 3 次或以上 3 times or over a week	54	51.9	48.1
一周 1～2 次 once or twice a week	123	42.3	57.7

7-13-2 广告态度指标/ Advertising Attitude Index

	人数 Number	广告淡漠指向 indifferent orientation	中间层 medium	信赖广告指向 loyal orientation
样本 Sample	**197**	**82.7**	**17.3**	**0.0**
天天吃 daily	20	90.0	10.0	0.0
一周 3 次或以上 3 times or over a week	54	87.0	13.0	0.0
一周 1~2 次 once or twice a week	123	79.7	20.3	0.0

7-13-3 饮食健康指标/ Foods & Drink Quality Index

	人数 Number	饮食"温饱"指向 "basic" orientation	中间层 medium	健康营养指向 health & nutrition orientation
样本 Sample	**197**	**27.9**	**44.7**	**27.4**
天天吃 daily	20	20.0	15.0	65.0
一周 3 次或以上 3 times or over a week	53	20.8	49.1	30.2
一周 1~2 次 once or twice a week	124	32.3	47.6	20.2

● 西安 / Xi'an

7-1 最近三个月食用频率的比例/ Proportion of the Sample Consuming Biscuit in the Last Three Months

	人数 Number	百分比 Percent
天天吃 daily	38	6.3
一周 3 次或以上 3 times or over a week	65	10.8
一周 1~2 次 once or twice a week	137	22.8
一个月 2～3 次 2 or 3 times a month	121	20.1
一个月 1 次或以下 once a month or below	50	8.3
没吃过 never	190	31.6

n=601

7-2 最常用品牌排名/ Ranking of the Most Frequently Used Brands

排名 Brand Ranking	品牌 Brands	人数 Number	百分比 Percent
1	奇宝太平梳打 Keebler Pacific	53	13.0
2	纳贝斯克奥利奥 Nabisco Oreo	32	7.8
3	达能闲趣 Danone Tuc	31	7.6
4	康师傅 Kangshifu	30	7.4
5	康元 Khong Guan	13	3.2
6	达能甜趣 Danone Tiki	11	2.7
6	嘉士利 Jiashili	11	2.7
6	纳贝斯克鬼脸嘟嘟 Nabisco Trakinas	11	2.7
7	奇宝 Keebler	8	2.0
8	思朗 Silang	7	1.7
8	奇宝每乐时薏米 Keebler Merries	7	1.7
9	太平洋 Taipingyang	6	1.5
10	纳贝斯克乐之 Nabisco Ritz	4	1.0
10	达能 Danone	4	1.0

n=408

7-3 样本、男性各年龄层、女性各年龄层的常用品牌/ The Most Frequently Used Brands by the Whole Sample, Age and Gender Groups

	人数 Number	第一品牌及百分比 1st/ percent	第二品牌及百分比 2nd/ percent	第三品牌及百分比 3rd/ percent
样本 Sample	408	**奇宝太平梳打 Keebler Pacific(13.0)**	**纳贝斯克奥利奥 Nabisco Oreo(7.8)**	**达能闲趣 Danone Tuc(7.6)**
男性 Male	190	**奇宝太平梳打 Keebler Pacific(11.1)**	**纳贝斯克奥利奥 Nabisco Oreo(10.5)**	**康师傅 Kangshifu(10.0)**
16~24 岁 Age	39	纳贝斯克奥利奥 Nabisco Oreo(17.9)	康师傅 Kangshifu(12.8)	达能闲趣 Danone Tuc(10.3)
25~34 岁 Age	49	康师傅 Kangshifu(12.2)	奇宝太平梳打 Keebler Pacific(10.2) 达能闲趣 Danone Tuc(10.2)	纳贝斯克奥利奥 Nabisco Oreo(8.2)
35~44 岁 Age	54	奇宝太平梳打 Keebler Pacific(16.7)	康师傅 Kangshifu(9.3) 纳贝斯克奥利奥 Nabisco Oreo(9.3)	康元 Khong Guan(7.4)
45~54 岁 Age	30	奇宝太平梳打 Keebler Pacific(13.3)	达能闲趣 Danone Tuc(10.0) 康师傅 Kangshifu(10.0) 纳贝斯克奥利奥 Nabisco Oreo(10.0)	思朗 Silang(3.3) 嘉士利 Jiashili(3.3) 瑞达 Rida(3.3) 奇宝每乐时薏米 Keebler Merries(3.3) 贝奇 Beiqi(3.3) 威力威 Weiliwei (3.3)
55~60 岁 Age	18	达能闲趣 Danone Tuc(11.1)	达能甜趣 Danone Tiki(5.6) 康元 Khong Guan(5.6) 纳贝斯克奥利奥 Nabisco Oreo(5.6) 奇宝 Keebler(5.6) 奇宝太平梳打 Keebler Pacific(5.6) 思朗 Silang(5.6)	
女性 Female	218	**奇宝太平梳打 Keebler Pacific(14.7)**	**达能闲趣 Danone Tuc(6.9)**	**纳贝斯克奥利奥 Nabisco Oreo(5.5)**
16~24 岁 Age	47	奇宝太平梳打 Keebler Pacific(14.9)	纳贝斯克鬼脸嘟嘟 Nabisco Trakinas(8.5) 达能闲趣 Danone Tuc(8.5)	康师傅 Kangshifu(6.4) 达能甜趣 Danone Tiki(6.4)
25~34 岁 Age	71	奇宝太平梳打 Keebler Pacific(11.3)	纳贝斯克奥利奥 Nabisco Oreo(8.5)	达能甜趣 Danone Tiki(7.0)
35~44 岁 Age	49	奇宝太平梳打 Keebler Pacific(14.3)	达能闲趣 Danone Tuc(10.2)	嘉士利 Jiashili(6.1) 纳贝斯克奥利奥 Nabisco Oreo(6.1)
45~54 岁 Age	34	奇宝太平梳打 Keebler Pacific(20.6)	纳贝斯克乐之 Nabisco Ritz(5.9) 康师傅 Kangshifu(5.9) 达能闲趣 Danone Tuc(5.9)	
55~60 岁 Age	17	奇宝太平梳打 Keebler Pacific(17.6)	达能 Danone(5.9) 达能闲趣 Danone Tuc(5.9) 嘉士利 Jiashili(5.9) 纳贝斯克奥利奥 Nabisco Oreo(5.9) 奇宝 Keebler(5.9)	

7-4 理想品牌排名/ Ranking of the Ideal Brands

排名 Brand Ranking	品牌 Brands	人数 Number	百分比 Percent
1	奇宝太平梳打 Keebler Pacific	48	8.0
2	纳贝斯克奥利奥 Nabisco Oreo	47	7.8
3	康师傅 Kangshifu	46	7.7
4	奇宝 Keebler	39	6.5
5	达能闲趣 Danone Tuc	28	4.7
6	达能 Danone	24	4.0
7	嘉士利 Jiashili	18	3.0
8	康元 Khong Guan	15	2.5
9	纳贝斯克鬼脸嘟嘟 Nabisco Trakinas	14	2.3
10	达能甜趣 Danone Tiki	10	1.7

n=601

7-5 样本、男性各年龄层、女性各年龄层最近三个月有无购买的比例/ Purchasing in the Last Three Months by the Whole Sample, Age and Gender Groups

	人数 Number	买过 yes	没买过 no
样本 Sample	600	67.7	32.3
男性 Male	301	60.5	39.5
16~24 岁 Age	64	53.1	46.9
25~34 岁 Age	90	55.6	44.4
35~44 岁 Age	77	70.1	29.9
45~54 岁 Age	46	58.7	41.3
55~60 岁 Age	24	70.8	29.2
女性 Female	299	74.9	25.1
16~24 岁 Age	61	68.9	31.1
25~34 岁 Age	90	77.8	22.2
35~44 岁 Age	74	74.3	25.7
45~54 岁 Age	49	77.6	22.4
55~60 岁 Age	25	76.0	24.0

7-6 样本、男性各年龄层、女性各年龄层最近三个月的食用频率/ Frequencies of Consuming Biscuit in the Last Three Months by the Whole Sample, Age and Gender Groups

	人数 Number	天天吃 daily	一周 3 次或以上 3 times or over a week	一周 1~2 次 once or twice a week	一个月 2~3 次 2 or 3 times a month	一个月 1 次或以下 once a month or below	没吃过 never
样本 Sample	601	6.3	10.8	22.8	20.1	8.3	31.6
男性 Male	302	4.3	7.9	21.2	20.2	9.6	36.8
16~24 岁 Age	64	6.3	3.1	20.3	21.9	10.9	37.5
25~34 岁 Age	91	2.2	6.6	20.9	22.0	2.2	46.2
35~44 岁 Age	77	5.2	13.0	22.1	19.5	10.4	29.9
45~54 岁 Age	46	4.3	10.9	21.7	15.2	13.0	34.8
55~60 岁 Age	24	4.2	4.2	20.8	20.8	25.0	25.0
女性 Female	299	8.4	13.7	24.4	20.1	7.0	26.4
16~24 岁 Age	61	9.8	18.0	23.0	14.8	11.5	23.0
25~34 岁 Age	90	10.0	14.4	23.3	24.4	6.7	21.1
35~44 岁 Age	74	5.4	12.2	24.3	20.3	5.4	32.4
45~54 岁 Age	49	12.2	8.2	26.5	22.4	2.0	28.6
55~60 岁 Age	25	0.0	16.0	28.0	12.0	12.0	32.0

7-7 样本、男性各年龄层、女性各年龄层的品牌习惯/ Brand Habit in Consuming Biscuit by the Whole Sample, Age and Gender Groups

	人数 Number	基本固定食用一个牌子 used in only one brand	比较固定地食用两个或三个牌子 used in two or three brands	基本上不太固定牌子 no brand preference
样本 Sample	411	17.8	28.2	54.0
男性 Male	191	13.1	29.8	57.1
16~24 岁 Age	40	17.5	30.0	52.5
25~34 岁 Age	49	8.2	32.7	59.2
35~44 岁 Age	54	14.8	35.2	50.0
45~54 岁 Age	30	13.3	13.3	73.3
55~60 岁 Age	18	11.1	33.3	55.6
女性 Female	220	21.8	26.8	51.4
16~24 岁 Age	47	19.1	29.8	51.1
25~34 岁 Age	71	21.1	32.4	46.5
35~44 岁 Age	50	24.0	26.0	50.0
45~54 岁 Age	35	28.6	17.1	54.3
55~60 岁 Age	17	11.8	17.6	70.6

7-8 选择该类商品的考虑因素/ Ranking of the Considerations in Purchasing

注：本题为多选题，合计百分比超过 100%(Multiple answers）

排名 Ranking	考虑因素 Considerations	人次 Person-time	百分比 Percent
1	口味好 pleasant taste	308	74.9
2	价格适中 reasonable price	163	39.7
3	生产日期 date of producing	100	24.3
4	购买方便 easy to buy	85	20.7
5	有名的牌子 famous brand	68	16.5
6	只是由于习惯 out of habit	36	8.8
7	包装吸引人 appealing package	23	5.6
8	广告影响 influence of advertising	18	4.4
9	朋友推荐 introduction of friends	17	4.1
10	有优惠条件 with preferential terms	7	1.7
10	售货员介绍 introduced by the shop assistants	7	1.7
11	其它 others	3	0.7

n=411

7-9 样本、男性各年龄层、女性各年龄层最常食用的种类/ Kinds of the Consumed Biscuit by the Whole Sample, Age and Gender Groups

注：本题为多选题，合计百分比超过 100%(Multiple answers）

	人数 Number	夹心饼干 sandwich biscuit	曲奇 cookie	全麦饼干 whole-wheat biscuit	梳打饼干 soda biscuit	普通咸饼干 salty biscuit	普通甜饼干 sweat biscuit	其它 others
样本 Sample	**411**	**38.7**	**11.9**	**4.1**	**38.0**	**17.3**	**21.9**	**1.5**
男性 Male	**191**	**40.3**	**14.1**	**4.2**	**32.5**	**15.7**	**21.5**	**0.5**
16~24 岁 Age	40	37.5	25.0	10.0	27.5	20.0	10.0	0.0
25~34 岁 Age	49	44.9	4.1	0.0	34.7	14.3	20.4	2.0
35~44 岁 Age	54	42.6	13.0	5.6	35.2	16.7	24.1	0.0
45~54 岁 Age	30	36.7	20.0	0.0	40.0	3.3	23.3	0.0
55~60 岁 Age	18	33.3	11.1	5.6	16.7	27.8	38.9	0.0
女性 Female	**220**	**37.3**	**10.0**	**4.1**	**42.7**	**18.6**	**22.3**	**2.3**
16~24 岁 Age	47	42.6	6.4	4.3	44.7	12.8	19.1	2.1
25~34 岁 Age	71	40.8	14.1	4.2	36.6	18.3	23.9	4.2
35~44 岁 Age	50	34.0	10.0	6.0	44.0	20.0	28.0	0.0
45~54 岁 Age	35	31.4	8.6	2.9	42.9	20.0	14.3	2.9
55~60 岁 Age	17	29.4	5.9	0.0	58.8	29.4	23.5	0.0

7-10 样本、男性各年龄层、女性各年龄层最常食用的场合/ Settings of Consumption by the Whole Sample, Age and Gender Groups

注：本题为多选题，合计百分比超过 100%(Multiple answers）

	人数 Number	早餐时 breakfast	饭后甜点 dessert after dinner	加班时 when work overtime	宵夜时 evening snack	当零食吃 between meal	外出、旅游时 outing/ traveling	其它 others
样本 Sample	**411**	**33.6**	**5.8**	**6.6**	**13.6**	**68.1**	**10.7**	**0.7**
男性 Male	**191**	**31.4**	**4.2**	**7.3**	**15.2**	**65.4**	**12.0**	**1.6**
16~24 岁 Age	40	27.5	7.5	7.5	7.5	72.5	22.5	0.0
25~34 岁 Age	49	30.6	0.0	10.2	10.2	69.4	8.2	0.0
35~44 岁 Age	54	35.2	7.4	5.6	20.4	68.5	9.3	3.7
45~54 岁 Age	30	26.7	0.0	6.7	13.3	63.3	6.7	3.3
55~60 岁 Age	18	38.9	5.6	5.6	33.3	33.3	16.7	0.0
女性 Female	**220**	**35.5**	**7.3**	**5.9**	**12.3**	**70.5**	**9.5**	**0.0**
16~24 岁 Age	47	29.8	6.4	4.3	12.8	72.3	4.3	0.0
25~34 岁 Age	71	35.2	8.5	8.5	14.1	70.4	11.3	0.0
35~44 岁 Age	50	46.0	2.0	6.0	12.0	72.0	10.0	0.0
45~54 岁 Age	35	34.3	14.3	5.7	8.6	54.3	8.6	0.0
55~60 岁 Age	17	23.5	5.9	0.0	11.8	94.1	17.6	0.0

7-11 重度消费者人口分布/ Demographics of the Heavy Consumers

	人数 Number	16-24 岁 Age	25-34 岁 Age	35-44 岁 Age	45-54 岁 Age	55-60 岁 Age
样本 Sample	240	20.8	29.2	25.8	16.7	7.5
男性 Male	101	18.8	26.7	30.7	16.8	6.9
天天吃 daily	13	30.8	15.4	30.8	15.4	7.7
一周 3 次或以上 3 times or over a week	24	8.3	25.0	41.7	20.8	4.2
一周 1~2 次 once or twice a week	64	20.3	29.7	26.6	15.6	7.8
女性 Female	139	22.3	30.9	22.3	16.5	7.9
天天吃 daily	25	24.0	36.0	16.0	24.0	0.0
一周 3 次或以上 3 times or over a week	41	26.8	31.7	22.0	9.8	9.8
一周 1 ~2 次 once or twice a week	73	19.2	28.8	24.7	17.8	9.6

7-12 不同消费者层的常用品牌/ The Most Frequently Used Brands by Market Segments

7-12-1 时尚流行指标/ Fads Popular Index

	人数 Number	第一品牌及百分比 1st/ percent	第二品牌及百分比 2nd/ percent	第三品牌及百分比 3rd/ percent
样本 Sample	406	**奇宝太平梳打 Keebler Pacific(13.1)**	**纳贝斯克奥利奥 Nabisco Oreo(7.9)**	**达能闲趣 Danone Tuc(7.6)**
平实生活指向 simple living orientation	229	奇宝太平梳打 Keebler Pacific(12.7)	达能闲趣 Danone Tuc(7.9)	康师傅 Kangshifu(7.4)
时尚流行指向 fashion orientation	177	奇宝太平梳打 Keebler Pacific(13.6) 纳贝斯克奥利奥 Nabisco Oreo(13.6)	康师傅 Kangshifu(7.3) 达能闲趣 Danone Tuc(7.3)	达能甜趣 Danone Tiki(4.0)

7-12-2 广告态度指标/ Advertising Attitude Index

	人数 Number	第一品牌及百分比 1st/ percent	第二品牌及百分比 2nd/ percent	第三品牌及百分比 3rd/ percent
样本 Sample	405	**奇宝太平梳打 Keebler Pacific(13.1)**	**纳贝斯克奥利奥 Nabisco Oreo(7.9)**	**达能闲趣 Danone Tuc(7.7)**
广告淡漠指向 indifferent orientation	124	达能闲趣 Danone Tuc(12.1)	奇宝太平梳打 Keebler Pacific(11.3)	达能甜趣 Danone Tiki(5.6)
中间层 medium	229	奇宝太平梳打 Keebler Pacific(11.8)	纳贝斯克奥利奥 Nabisco Oreo(10.0)	康师傅 Kangshifu(8.7)
信赖广告指向 loyal orientation	52	奇宝太平梳打 Keebler Pacific(23.1)	康师傅 Kangshifu(7.7)	纳贝斯克奥利奥 Nabisco Oreo(5.8) 达能闲趣 Danone Tuc(5.8)

7-12-3 饮食健康指标/ Foods & Drink Quality Index

	人数 Number	第一品牌及百分比 1st/ percent	第二品牌及百分比 2nd/ percent	第三品牌及百分比 3rd/ percent
样本 Sample	408	**奇宝太平梳打 Keebler Pacific(13.0)**	**纳贝斯克奥利奥 Nabisco Oreo(7.8)**	**达能闲趣 Danone Tuc(7.6)**
饮食"温饱"指向 "basic" orientation	137	奇宝太平梳打 Keebler Pacific(11.7)	达能闲趣 Danone Tuc(8.0)	康元 Khong Guan(4.4) 纳贝斯克奥利奥 Nabisco Oreo(4.4)
中间层 medium	199	奇宝太平梳打 Keebler Pacific(12.1)	纳贝斯克奥利奥 Nabisco Oreo(11.1)	康师傅 Kangshifu(9.5)
健康营养指向 health & nutrition orientation	72	奇宝太平梳打 Keebler Pacific(18.1)	达能闲趣 Danone Tuc(8.3) 康师傅 Kangshifu(8.3)	纳贝斯克奥利奥 Nabisco Oreo(5.6)

7-13 重度消费者的消费者层构成/ The Composition of the Heavy Consumers

7-13-1 时尚流行指标/ Fads Popular Index

	人数 Number	平实生活指向 simple living orientation	时尚流行指向 fashion orientation
样本 Sample	239	52.7	47.3
天天吃 daily	37	48.6	51.4
一周 3 次或以上 3 times or over a week	65	46.2	53.8
一周 1～2 次 once or twice a week	137	56.9	43.1

7-13-2 广告态度指标/ Advertising Attitude Index

	人数 Number	广告淡漠指向 indifferent orientation	中间层 medium	信赖广告指向 loyal orientation
样本 Sample	238	83.2	16.8	0.0
天天吃 daily	36	77.8	22.2	0.0
一周 3 次或以上 3 times or over a week	65	87.7	12.3	0.0
一周 1~2 次 once or twice a week	137	82.5	17.5	0.0

7-13-3 饮食健康指标/ Foods & Drink Quality Index

	人数 Number	饮食"温饱"指向 "basic" orientation	中间层 medium	健康营养指向 health & nutrition orientation
样本 Sample	240	31.3	47.1	21.7
天天吃 daily	38	42.1	44.7	13.2
一周 3 次或以上 3 times or over a week	65	24.6	46.2	29.2
一周 1~2 次 once or twice a week	137	31.4	48.2	20.4

● 沈阳 / Shenyang

7-1 最近三个月食用频率的比例/ Proportion of the Sample Consuming Biscuit in the Last Three Months

	人数 Number	百分比 Percent
天天吃 daily	32	5.3
一周 3 次或以上 3 times or over a week	75	12.5
一周 1~2 次 once or twice a week	117	19.5
一个月 2~3 次 2 or 3 times a month	128	21.3
一个月 1 次或以下 once a month or below	68	11.3
没吃过 never	181	30.1

n=601

7-2 最常用品牌排名/ Ranking of the Most Frequently Used Brands

排名 Brand Ranking	品牌 Brands	人数 Number	百分比 Percent
1	康师傅 Kangshifu	100	23.9
2	纳贝斯克奥利奥 Nabisco Oreo	31	7.4
3	纳贝斯克乐之 Nabisco Ritz	17	4.1
4	嘉士利 Jiashili	16	3.8
5	早餐饼 Zaocanbing	14	3.3
6	奇宝 Keebler	11	2.6
7	纳贝斯克鬼脸嘟嘟 Nabisco Trakinas	10	2.4
8	达能王子夹心 Danone Prince	7	1.7
8	儿童乐 Er'tongle	7	1.7
9	大牛 Daniu	6	1.4
9	奇宝太平梳打 Keebler Pacific	6	1.4
10	华声鸳鸯夹心 Huasheng	5	1.2

n=418

7-3 样本、男性各年龄层、女性各年龄层的常用品牌/ The Most Frequently Used Brands by the Whole Sample, Age and Gender Groups

	人数 Number	第一品牌及百分比 1st/ percent	第二品牌及百分比 2nd/ percent	第三品牌及百分比 3rd/ percent
样本 Sample	418	**康师傅 Kangshifu(23.9)**	**纳贝斯克奥利奥 Nabisco Oreo(7.4)**	**纳贝斯克乐之 Nabisco Ritz(4.1)**
男性 Male	189	**康师傅 Kangshifu(25.9)**	**纳贝斯克奥利奥 Nabisco Oreo(6.9)**	**嘉士利 Jiashili(4.2)**
16~24 岁 Age	53	康师傅 Kangshifu(35.8)	纳贝斯克奥利奥 Nabisco Oreo(9.4)	纳贝斯克乐之 Nabisco Ritz(5.7)
25~34 岁 Age	52	康师傅 Kangshifu(26.9)	纳贝斯克奥利奥 Nabisco Oreo(11.5)	纳贝斯克鬼脸嘟嘟 Nabisco Trakinas(5.8) 华声鸳鸯夹心 Huasheng(5.8)
35~44 岁 Age	38	康师傅 Kangshifu(15.8)	早餐饼 Zaocanbing(10.5)	大牛 Daniu(7.9)
45~54 岁 Age	30	康师傅 Kangshifu(26.7)	纳贝斯克鬼脸嘟嘟 Nabisco Trakinas(6.7)	嘉士利 Jiashili(3.3) 早餐饼 Zaocanbing(3.3)
55~60 岁 Age	16	嘉士利 Jiashili(18.8)	康师傅 Kangshifu(12.5)	
女性 Female	229	**康师傅 Kangshifu(22.3)**	**纳贝斯克奥利奥 Nabisco Oreo(7.9)**	**纳贝斯克乐之 Nabisco Ritz(4.8)**
16~24 岁 Age	60	康师傅 Kangshifu(30.0)	纳贝斯克奥利奥 Nabisco Oreo(16.7)	纳贝斯克乐之 Nabisco Ritz(8.3)
25~34 岁 Age	68	康师傅 Kangshifu(22.1)	嘉士利 Jiashili(5.9) 纳贝斯克乐之 Nabisco Ritz(5.9) 奇宝 Keebler(5.9)	纳贝斯克奥利奥 Nabisco Oreo(4.4) 早餐饼 Zaocanbing(4.4)
35~44 岁 Age	59	康师傅 Kangshifu(25.4)	早餐饼 Zaocanbing(5.1) 纳贝斯克奥利奥 Nabisco Oreo(5.1) 纳贝斯克鬼脸嘟嘟 Nabisco Trakinas(5.1)	纳贝斯克乐之 Nabisco Ritz(3.4) 奇宝太平梳打 Keebler Pacific(3.4) 奇宝 Keebler(3.4) 嘉士利 Jiashili(3.4)
45~54 岁 Age	29	康师傅 Kangshifu(6.9) 纳贝斯克奥利奥 Nabisco Oreo(6.9)	嘉士利 Jiashili(3.4) 达能王子夹心 Danone Prince(3.4) 奇宝 Keebler(3.4) 统一曲奇 President(3.4) 克力架 Kelijia(3.4) 儿童乐 Ertongle(3.4) 富祥 Fuxiang(3.4)	
55~60 岁 Age	13	嘉士利 Jiashili(7.7) 康师傅 Kangshifu(7.7) 华声鸳鸯夹心 Huasheng(7.7) 青援 Qingyuan(7.7) 杏园 Xingyuan(7.7)		

7-4 理想品牌排名/ Ranking of the Ideal Brands

排名 Brand Ranking	品牌 Brands	人数 Number	百分比 Percent
1	康师傅 Kangshifu	148	24.6
2	纳贝斯克奥利奥 Nabisco Oreo	69	11.5
3	纳贝斯克乐之 Nabisco Ritz	24	4.0
4	儿童乐 Ertongle	18	3.0
5	嘉士利 Jiashili	17	2.8
6	纳贝斯克鬼脸嘟嘟 Nabisco Trakinas	16	2.7
7	奇宝 Keebler	15	2.5
8	早餐饼 Zaocanbing	13	2.2
9	大牛 Daniu	11	1.8
10	达能王子夹心 Danone Prince	9	1.5
10	达能 Danone	9	1.5

n=601

7-5 样本、男性各年龄层、女性各年龄层最近三个月有无购买的比例/ Purchasing in the Last Three Months by the Whole Sample, Age and Gender Groups

	人数 Number	买过 yes	没买过 no
样本 Sample	600	69.2	30.8
男性 Male	299	61.5	38.5
16~24 岁 Age	64	67.2	32.8
25~34 岁 Age	89	62.9	37.1
35~44 岁 Age	76	48.7	51.3
45~54 岁 Age	46	71.7	28.3
55~60 岁 Age	24	62.5	37.5
女性 Female	301	76.7	23.3
16~24 岁 Age	64	87.5	12.5
25~34 岁 Age	90	81.1	18.9
35~44 岁 Age	75	78.7	21.3
45~54 岁 Age	48	62.5	37.5
55~60 岁 Age	24	54.2	45.8

7-6 样本、男性各年龄层、女性各年龄层最近三个月的食用频率/ Frequencies of Consuming Biscuit in the Last Three Months by the Whole Sample, Age and Gender Groups

	人数 Number	天天吃 daily	一周 3 次或以上 3 times or over a week	一周 1~2 次 once or twice a week	一个月 2~3 次 2 or 3 times a month	一个月 1 次或以下 once a month or below	没吃过 never
样本 Sample	601	5.3	12.5	19.5	21.3	11.3	30.1
男性 Male	299	4.7	10.4	13.7	22.1	12.4	36.8
16~24 岁 Age	64	6.3	10.9	18.8	32.8	14.1	17.2
25~34 岁 Age	89	3.4	14.6	14.6	19.1	6.7	41.6
35~44 岁 Age	76	3.9	2.6	13.2	14.5	15.8	50.0
45~54 岁 Age	46	2.2	10.9	10.9	23.9	17.4	34.8
55~60 岁 Age	24	12.5	16.7	4.2	25.0	8.3	33.3
女性 Female	302	6.0	14.6	25.2	20.5	10.3	23.5
16~24 岁 Age	64	6.3	18.8	34.4	20.3	14.1	6.3
25~34 岁 Age	90	7.8	10.0	26.7	22.2	10.0	23.3
35~44 岁 Age	76	3.9	18.4	26.3	18.4	10.5	22.4
45~54 岁 Age	48	2.1	12.5	12.5	25.0	10.4	37.5
55~60 岁 Age	24	12.5	12.5	16.7	12.5	0.0	45.8

7-7 样本、男性各年龄层、女性各年龄层的品牌习惯/ Brand Habit in Consuming Biscuit by the Whole Sample, Age and Gender Groups

	人数 Number	基本固定食用一个牌子 used in only one brand	比较固定地食用两个或三个牌子 used in two or three brands	基本上不太固定牌子 no brand preference
样本 Sample	420	25.0	29.3	45.7
男性 Male	189	26.5	29.1	44.4
16~24 岁 Age	53	24.5	30.2	45.3
25~34 岁 Age	52	21.2	36.5	42.3
35~44 岁 Age	38	31.6	23.7	44.7
45~54 岁 Age	30	20.0	30.0	50.0
55~60 岁 Age	16	50.0	12.5	37.5
女性 Female	231	23.8	29.4	46.8
16~24 岁 Age	60	21.7	35.0	43.3
25~34 岁 Age	69	26.1	31.9	42.0
35~44 岁 Age	59	22.0	28.8	49.2
45~54 岁 Age	30	20.0	20.0	60.0
55~60 岁 Age	13	38.5	15.4	46.2

7-8 选择该类商品的考虑因素/ Ranking of the Considerations in Purchasing

注：本题为多选题，合计百分比超过 100%(Multiple answers）

排名 Ranking	考虑因素 Considerations	人次 Person-time	百分比 Percent
1	口味好 pleasant taste	323	77.3
2	价格适中 reasonable price	177	42.3
3	生产日期 date of producing	99	23.7
4	购买方便 easy to buy	86	20.6
5	有名的牌子 famous brand	83	19.9
6	只是由于习惯 out of habit	33	7.9
7	广告影响 influence of advertising	27	6.5
8	朋友推荐 introduction of friends	22	5.3
9	包装吸引人 appealing package	16	3.8
10	有优惠条件 with preferential terms	10	2.4
11	售货员介绍 introduced by the shop assistants	4	1.0
12	其它 others	3	0.7

n=418

7-9 样本、男性各年龄层、女性各年龄层最常食用的种类/ Kinds of the Consumed Biscuit by the Whole Sample, Age and Gender Groups

注：本题为多选题，合计百分比超过 100%(Multiple answers）

	人数 Number	夹心饼干 sandwich biscuit	曲奇 cookie	全麦饼干 whole-wheat biscuit	梳打饼干 soda biscuit	普通咸饼干 salty biscuit	普通甜饼干 sweat biscuit	其它 others
样本 Sample	**419**	**45.1**	**10.7**	**4.5**	**19.6**	**11.9**	**39.4**	**1.2**
男性 Male	**188**	**46.3**	**10.1**	**4.3**	**18.1**	**10.6**	**36.2**	**1.6**
16~24 岁 Age	52	59.6	11.5	1.9	23.1	11.5	23.1	1.9
25~34 岁 Age	52	51.9	9.6	5.8	17.3	11.5	32.7	0.0
35~44 岁 Age	38	36.8	10.5	2.6	18.4	10.5	47.4	0.0
45~54 岁 Age	30	36.7	10.0	6.7	16.7	6.7	43.3	3.3
55~60 岁 Age	16	25.0	6.3	6.3	6.3	12.5	50.0	6.3
女性 Female	**231**	**44.2**	**11.3**	**4.8**	**20.8**	**13.0**	**42.0**	**0.9**
16~24 岁 Age	60	61.7	8.3	6.7	21.7	13.3	20.0	0.0
25~34 岁 Age	69	46.4	11.6	2.9	23.2	15.9	42.0	2.9
35~44 岁 Age	59	33.9	18.6	8.5	22.0	13.6	42.4	0.0
45~54 岁 Age	30	33.3	6.7	0.0	13.3	3.3	70.0	0.0
55~60 岁 Age	13	23.1	0.0	0.0	15.4	15.4	76.9	0.0

7-10 样本、男性各年龄层、女性各年龄层最常食用的场合/ Settings of Consumption by the Whole Sample, Age and Gender Groups

注：本题为多选题，合计百分比超过 100%(Multiple answers）

	人数 Number	早餐时 breakfast	饭后甜点 dessert after dinner	加班时 when work overtime	宵夜时 evening snack	当零食吃 between meal	外出/旅游时 outing/ traveling	其它 others
样本 Sample	**420**	**29.5**	**6.0**	**6.2**	**10.5**	**66.7**	**15.2**	**1.0**
男性 Male	**189**	**30.7**	**6.3**	**6.9**	**13.2**	**61.4**	**10.6**	**1.1**
16~24 岁 Age	53	26.4	7.5	5.7	11.3	73.6	13.2	0.0
25~34 岁 Age	52	19.2	1.9	9.6	13.5	67.3	9.6	1.9
35~44 岁 Age	38	50.0	10.5	5.3	18.4	42.1	10.5	0.0
45~54 岁 Age	30	26.7	0.0	6.7	10.0	66.7	13.3	3.3
55~60 岁 Age	16	43.8	18.8	6.3	12.5	37.5	0.0	0.0
女性 Female	**231**	**28.6**	**5.6**	**5.6**	**8.2**	**71.0**	**19.0**	**0.9**
16~24 岁 Age	60	25.0	3.3	8.3	5.0	76.7	28.3	0.0
25~34 岁 Age	69	31.9	5.8	5.8	2.9	73.9	14.5	1.4
35~44 岁 Age	59	30.5	6.8	5.1	11.9	67.8	20.3	0.0
45~54 岁 Age	30	16.7	6.7	3.3	16.7	66.7	16.7	3.3
55~60 岁 Age	13	46.2	7.7	0.0	15.4	53.8	0.0	0.0

7-11 重度消费者人口分布/ Demographics of the Heavy Consumers

	人数 Number	16-24 岁 Age	25-34 岁 Age	35-44 岁 Age	45-54 岁 Age	55-60 岁 Age
样本 Sample	224	27.2	30.8	23.2	10.7	8.0
男性 Male	86	26.7	33.7	17.4	12.8	9.3
天天吃 daily	14	28.6	21.4	21.4	7.1	21.4
一周 3 次或以上 3 times or over a week	31	22.6	41.9	6.5	16.1	12.9
一周 1~2 次 once or twice a week	41	29.3	31.7	24.4	12.2	2.4
女性 Female	138	27.5	29.0	26.8	9.4	7.2
天天吃 daily	18	22.2	38.9	16.7	5.6	16.7
一周 3 次或以上 3 times or over a week	44	27.3	20.5	31.8	13.6	6.8
一周 1~2 次 once or twice a week	76	28.9	31.6	26.3	7.9	5.3

7-12 不同消费者层的常用品牌/ The Most Frequently Used Brands by Market Segments

7-12-1 时尚流行指标/ Fads Popular Index

	人数 Number	第一品牌及百分比 1st/ percent	第二品牌及百分比 2nd/ percent	第三品牌及百分比 3rd/ percent
样本 Sample	418	**康师傅 Kangshifu(22.0)**	**纳贝斯克奥利奥 Nabisco Oreo(7.4)**	**纳贝斯克乐之 Nabisco Ritz(4.1)**
平实生活指向 simple living orientation	183	康师傅 Kangshifu(18.0)	纳贝斯克奥利奥 Nabisco Oreo(7.1)	早餐饼 Zaocanbing(5.5)
时尚流行指向 fashion orientation	235	康师傅 Kangshifu(25.1)	纳贝斯克奥利奥 Nabisco Oreo(7.7)	嘉士利 Jiashili(3.4) 纳贝斯克乐之 Nabisco Ritz(3.4)

7-12-2 广告态度指标/ Advertising Attitude Index

	人数 Number	第一品牌及百分比 1st/ percent	第二品牌及百分比 2nd/ percent	第三品牌及百分比 3rd/ percent
样本 Sample	418	**康师傅 Kangshifu(22.0)**	**纳贝斯克奥利奥 Nabisco Oreo(7.4)**	**纳贝斯克乐之 Nabisco Ritz(4.1)**
广告淡漠指向 indifferent orientation	104	康师傅 Kangshifu(18.3)	纳贝斯克奥利奥 Nabisco Oreo(7.7)	早餐饼 Zaocanbing(4.8)
中间层 medium	260	康师傅 Kangshifu(23.8)	纳贝斯克奥利奥 Nabisco Oreo(7.7)	纳贝斯克乐之 Nabisco Ritz(4.6)
信赖广告指向 loyal orientation	54	康师傅 Kangshifu(20.4)	纳贝斯克奥利奥 Nabisco Oreo(5.6)	早餐饼 Zaocanbing (3.7) 奇宝 Keebler(3.7) 达能王子夹心 Danone Prince(3.7)

7-12-3 饮食健康指标/ Foods & Drink Quality Index

	人数 Number	第一品牌及百分比 1st/ percent	第二品牌及百分比 2nd/ percent	第三品牌及百分比 3rd/ percent
样本 Sample	418	**康师傅 Kangshifu(22.0)**	**纳贝斯克奥利奥 Nabisco Oreo(7.4)**	**纳贝斯克乐之 Nabisco Ritz(4.1)**
饮食"温饱"指向 "basic" orientation	113	康师傅 Kangshifu(26.5)	纳贝斯克乐之 Nabisco Ritz(6.2) 纳贝斯克奥利奥 Nabisco Oreo(6.2)	嘉士利 Jiashili(3.5)
中间层 medium	201	康师傅 Kangshifu(18.9)	纳贝斯克奥利奥 Nabisco Oreo(9.5)	嘉士利 Jiashili(4.5)
健康营养指向 health & nutrition orientation	104	康师傅 Kangshifu(23.1)	纳贝斯克奥利奥 Nabisco Oreo(4.8) 早餐饼 Zaocanbing (4.8)	纳贝斯克鬼脸嘟嘟 Nabisco Trakinas(3.8)

7-13 重度消费者的消费者层构成/ The Composition of the Heavy Consumers

7-13-1 时尚流行指标/ Fads Popular Index

	人数 Number	平实生活指向 simple living orientation	时尚流行指向 fashion orientation
样本 Sample	224	41.5	58.5
天天吃 daily	32	31.3	68.8
一周 3 次或以上 3 times or over a week	75	45.3	54.7
一周 1～2 次 once or twice a week	117	41.9	58.1

7-13-2 广告态度指标/ Advertising Attitude Index

	人数 Number	广告淡漠指向 indifferent orientation	中间层 medium	信赖广告指向 loyal orientation
样本 Sample	224	87.1	12.9	0.0
天天吃 daily	32	84.4	15.6	0.0
一周 3 次或以上 3 times or over a week	75	84.0	16.0	0.0
一周 1~2 次 once or twice a week	117	89.7	10.3	0.0

7-13-3 饮食健康指标/ Foods & Drink Quality Index

	人数 Number	饮食“温饱”指向 "basic" orientation	中间层 medium	健康营养指向 health & nutrition orientation
样本 Sample	224	25.9	49.1	25.0
天天吃 daily	32	18.8	53.1	28.1
一周 3 次或以上 3 times or over a week	75	26.7	48.0	25.3
一周 1~2 次 once or twice a week	117	27.4	48.7	23.9

8.方便面 / Instant Noodles

● 北京 / Beijing

8-1 最近三个月食用频率的比例/ Proportion of the Sample Consuming Instant Noodles in the Last Three Months

	人数 Number	百分比 Percent
天天吃 daily	22	2.2
一周 3 次或以上 3 times or over a week	116	11.5
一周 1~2 次 once or twice a week	329	32.6
一个月 2～3 次 2 or 3 times a month	266	26.3
一个月 1 次或以下 once a month or below	112	11.1
没吃过 never	165	16.3

n=1010

8-2 最常用品牌排名/ Ranking of the Most Frequently Used Brands

排名 Brand Ranking	品牌 Brands	人数 Number	百分比 Percent
1	康师傅 Kangshifu	490	58.3
2	统一 President	141	16.8
3	美厨 Michi	109	13.0
4	营多 Yingduo	27	3.2
5	华龙 Hualong	14	1.7

n=840

8-3 样本、男性各年龄层、女性各年龄层的常用品牌/ The Most Frequently Used Brands by the Whole Sample, Age and Gender Groups

	人数 Number	第一品牌及百分比 1st/ percent	第二品牌及百分比 2nd/ percent	第三品牌及百分比 3rd/ percent
样本 Sample	840	**康师傅 Kangshifu(58.3)**	**统一 President(16.8)**	**美厨 Michi(13.0)**
男性 Male	413	**康师傅 Kangshifu(62.2)**	**统一 President(17.7)**	**美厨 Michi(11.1)**
16~24 岁 Age	91	康师傅 Kangshifu(59.3)	统一 President(27.5)	美厨 Michi(8.8)
25~34 岁 Age	123	康师傅 Kangshifu(59.3)	统一 President(17.1)	美厨 Michi(10.6)
35~44 岁 Age	113	康师傅 Kangshifu(66.4)	统一 President(16.8)	美厨 Michi(11.5)
45~54 岁 Age	58	康师傅 Kangshifu(69.0)	美厨 Michi(13.8)	统一 President(5.2) 营多 Yingduo(5.2)
55~60 岁 Age	28	康师傅 Kangshifu(53.6)	统一 President(17.9)	美厨 Michi(14.3)
女性 Female	427	**康师傅 Kangshifu(54.6)**	**统一 President(15.9)**	**美厨 Michi(14.8)**
16~24 岁 Age	95	康师傅 Kangshifu(41.1)	统一 President(20.0)	美厨 Michi(17.9)
25~34 岁 Age	127	康师傅 Kangshifu(57.5)	统一 President(19.7)	美厨 Michi(14.2)
35~44 岁 Age	111	康师傅 Kangshifu(61.3)	美厨 Michi(11.7)	统一 President(10.8)
45~54 岁 Age	69	康师傅 Kangshifu(56.5)	美厨 Michi(20.3)	统一 President(11.6)
55~60 岁 Age	25	康师傅 Kangshifu(56.0)	统一 President(16.0)	

8-4 理想品牌排名/ Ranking of the Ideal Brands

排名 Brand Ranking	品牌 Brands	人数 Number	百分比 Percent
1	康师傅 Kangshifu	583	57.6
2	统一 President	173	17.1
3	美厨 Michi	109	10.8
4	营多 Yingduo	23	2.3

n=1012

8-5 样本、男性各年龄层、女性各年龄层最近三个月有无购买的比例/ Purchasing in the Last Three Months by the Whole Sample, Age and Gender Groups

	人数 Number	买过 yes	没买过 no
样本 Sample	1012	80.5	19.5
男性 Male	504	78.8	21.2
16~24 岁 Age	105	81.0	19.0
25~34 岁 Age	151	78.8	21.2
35~44 岁 Age	131	83.2	16.8
45~54 岁 Age	77	76.6	23.4
55~60 岁 Age	40	62.5	37.5
女性 Female	508	82.3	17.7
16~24 岁 Age	108	79.6	20.4
25~34 岁 Age	150	83.3	16.7
35~44 岁 Age	124	90.3	9.7
45~54 岁 Age	84	81.0	19.0
55~60 岁 Age	42	64.3	35.7

8-6 样本、男性各年龄层、女性各年龄层最近三个月的食用频率/ Frequencies of Consuming Instant Noodles in the Last Three Months by the Whole Sample, Age and Gender Groups

	人数 Number	天天吃 daily	一周 3 次或以上 3 times or over a week	一周 1~2 次 once or twice a week	一个月 2~3 次 2 or 3 times a month	一个月 1 次或以下 once a month or below	没吃过 never
样本 Sample	1010	2.2	11.5	32.6	26.3	11.1	16.3
男性 Male	503	2.4	12.3	33.6	23.5	10.9	17.3
16~24 岁 Age	105	3.8	18.1	33.3	21.0	11.4	12.4
25~34 岁 Age	151	2.6	11.3	39.1	21.2	7.9	17.9
35~44 岁 Age	130	2.3	13.8	31.5	26.2	13.1	13.1
45~54 岁 Age	77	0.0	6.5	37.7	22.1	10.4	23.4
55~60 岁 Age	40	2.5	7.5	12.5	32.5	15.0	30.0
女性 Female	507	2.0	10.7	31.6	29.2	11.2	15.4
16~24 岁 Age	107	1.9	10.3	39.3	29.0	9.3	10.3
25~34 岁 Age	150	1.3	11.3	30.7	29.3	12.7	14.7
35~44 岁 Age	124	0.0	10.5	31.5	36.3	11.3	10.5
45~54 岁 Age	84	7.1	13.1	28.6	20.2	13.1	17.9
55~60 岁 Age	42	0.0	4.8	21.4	26.2	7.1	40.5

8-7 样本、男性各年龄层、女性各年龄层的品牌习惯/ Brand Habit in Consuming Instant Noodles by the Whole Sample, Age and Gender Groups

	人数 Number	基本固定食用一个牌子 used in only one brand	比较固定地食用两个或三个牌子 used in two or three brands	基本上没有固定哪个牌子 no brand preference
样本 Sample	844	42.2	42.5	15.3
男性 Male	415	46.3	37.6	16.1
16~24 岁 Age	92	40.2	42.4	17.4
25~34 岁 Age	124	42.7	41.1	16.1
35~44 岁 Age	113	50.4	35.4	14.2
45~54 岁 Age	58	48.3	36.2	15.5
55~60 岁 Age	28	60.7	17.9	21.4
女性 Female	429	38.2	47.3	14.5
16~24 岁 Age	96	25.0	58.3	16.7
25~34 岁 Age	128	39.8	48.4	11.7
35~44 岁 Age	111	44.1	41.4	14.4
45~54 岁 Age	69	44.9	40.6	14.5
55~60 岁 Age	25	36.0	44.0	20.0

8-8 选择该类商品的考虑因素/ Ranking of the Considerations in Purchasing

注：本题为多选题，合计百分比超过 100%(Multiple answers)

排名 Ranking	考虑因素 Considerations	人次 Person-time	百分比 Percent
1	口味好 pleasant taste	606	71.9
2	价格适中 reasonable price	356	42.2
3	有名的牌子 famous brand	263	31.2
4	生产日期 date of producing	198	23.5
5	购买方便 easy to buy	155	18.4
6	只是由于习惯 out of habit	93	11.0
7	广告影响 influence of advertising	61	7.2
8	有优惠条件 with preferential terms	40	4.7
9	包装吸引人 appealing package	13	1.5
10	朋友推荐 introduction of friends	11	1.3
11	售货员介绍 introduced by the shop assistants	5	0.6
11	单位发的 offered by the working unit	5	0.6
11	其它 others	5	0.6

n=843

8-9 样本、男性各年龄层、女性各年龄层最常食用的种类/ Kinds of the Consumed Instant Noodles by the Whole Sample, Age and Gender Groups

注：本题为多选题，合计百分比超过 100%(Multiple answers)

	人数 Number	牛肉 beef	鸡肉 chicken	排骨 spareribs	海鲜 seafood	炸酱 fried bean sauce	三鲜 3-flavored noodles	蔬菜 vegetable	其它 others
样本 Sample	**834**	**69.1**	**10.4**	**17.3**	**32.9**	**7.2**	**7.2**	**3.8**	**2.3**
男性 Male	**414**	**68.8**	**10.4**	**15.7**	**28.7**	**7.0**	**6.5**	**4.3**	**2.9**
16~24 岁 Age	91	70.3	9.9	22.0	30.8	8.8	4.4	0.0	1.1
25~34 岁 Age	124	75.0	9.7	8.9	20.2	6.5	6.5	7.3	4.8
35~44 岁 Age	112	64.3	8.9	17.0	33.0	8.9	8.0	6.3	0.9
45~54 岁 Age	59	64.4	11.9	20.3	33.9	5.1	6.8	3.4	1.7
55~60 岁 Age	28	64.3	17.9	10.7	32.1	0.0	7.1	0.0	10.7
女性 Female	**420**	**69.3**	**10.5**	**18.8**	**36.9**	**7.4**	**7.9**	**3.3**	**1.7**
16~24 岁 Age	92	67.4	12.0	16.3	39.1	5.4	9.8	3.3	0.0
25~34 岁 Age	127	70.9	10.2	20.5	37.0	10.2	6.3	1.6	3.1
35~44 岁 Age	110	70.9	10.0	24.5	32.7	6.4	9.1	4.5	0.9
45~54 岁 Age	67	71.6	9.0	7.5	37.3	9.0	1.5	4.5	3.0
55~60 岁 Age	24	54.2	12.5	25.0	45.8	0.0	20.8	4.2	0.0

8-10 样本、男性各年龄层、女性各年龄层最常食用的包装形式/ Types of Package of the Consumed Instant Noodles by the Whole Sample, Age and Gender Groups

注：本题为多选题，合计百分比超过 100%(Multiple answers)

	人数 Number	大碗装 big bowl	普通碗装 regular bowl	大袋装 big bag	普通袋装 regular bag	杯装 cupped	其它 others
样本 Sample	**843**	**11.7**	**12.8**	**36.5**	**63.8**	**2.0**	**0.4**
男性 Male	**416**	**13.9**	**13.5**	**37.3**	**59.6**	**1.4**	**0.5**
16~24 岁 Age	92	20.7	12.0	39.1	55.4	3.3	0.0
25~34 岁 Age	124	15.3	11.3	39.5	58.9	0.8	0.0
35~44 岁 Age	113	12.4	14.2	44.2	54.9	1.8	0.0
45~54 岁 Age	59	8.5	16.9	28.8	64.4	0.0	1.7
55~60 岁 Age	28	3.6	17.9	10.7	85.7	0.0	3.6
女性 Female	**427**	**9.6**	**12.2**	**35.8**	**67.9**	**2.6**	**0.2**
16~24 岁 Age	96	8.3	17.7	33.3	63.5	5.2	0.0
25~34 岁 Age	127	11.8	14.2	37.0	65.4	3.1	0.0
35~44 岁 Age	110	13.6	10.0	39.1	64.5	0.9	0.9
45~54 岁 Age	69	4.3	5.8	33.3	76.8	1.4	0.0
55~60 岁 Age	25	0.0	8.0	32.0	88.0	0.0	0.0

8-11 样本、男性各年龄层、女性各年龄层最常食用的方式/ Ways of the Consumed Instant noodles by the Whole Sample, Age and Gender Groups

	人数 Number	冲泡 steep it in boiling water	煮 boil it	干吃 eat directly	拌着吃 mix it with others
样本 Sample	841	26.6	71.6	1.5	0.2
男性 Male	414	29.2	69.1	1.2	0.5
16~24 岁 Age	91	38.5	59.3	1.1	1.1
25~34 岁 Age	124	31.5	66.1	1.6	0.8
35~44 岁 Age	112	22.3	77.7	0.0	0.0
45~54 岁 Age	59	27.1	71.2	1.7	0.0
55~60 岁 Age	28	21.4	75.0	3.6	0.0
女性 Female	427	24.1	74.0	1.9	0.0
16~24 岁 Age	96	28.1	66.7	5.2	0.0
25~34 岁 Age	128	25.8	74.2	0.0	0.0
35~44 岁 Age	109	19.3	78.9	1.8	0.0
45~54 岁 Age	69	20.3	78.3	1.4	0.0
55~60 岁 Age	25	32.0	68.0	0.0	0.0

8-12 样本、男性各年龄层、女性各年龄层最常食用的场合/ Settings of Consumption by the Whole Sample, Age and Gender Groups

	人数 Number	早餐 breakfast	午餐 lunch	晚餐 supper	宵夜 evening snack	加班时 when work overtime	不固定 no regular	其他 others
样本 Sample	797	45.7	11.5	11.8	12.8	9.2	9.0	0.0
男性 Male	392	44.9	11.2	11.7	16.3	8.9	6.9	0.0
16~24 岁 Age	87	42.5	12.6	11.5	24.1	5.7	3.4	0.0
25~34 岁 Age	120	37.5	10.0	10.8	21.7	13.3	6.7	0.0
35~44 岁 Age	104	55.8	8.7	10.6	9.6	5.8	9.6	0.0
45~54 岁 Age	53	45.3	13.2	18.9	9.4	11.3	1.9	0.0
55~60 岁 Age	28	42.9	17.9	7.1	7.1	7.1	17.9	0.0
女性 Female	405	46.4	11.9	11.9	9.4	9.4	11.1	0.0
16~24 岁 Age	90	47.8	14.4	11.1	14.4	6.7	5.6	0.0
25~34 岁 Age	120	37.5	10.0	12.5	10.8	16.7	12.5	0.0
35~44 岁 Age	108	51.9	13.9	8.3	8.3	5.6	12.0	0.0
45~54 岁 Age	63	49.2	11.1	15.9	3.2	9.5	11.1	0.0
55~60 岁 Age	24	54.2	4.2	16.7	4.2	0.0	20.8	0.0

8-13 重度消费者人口分布/ Demographics of the Heavy Consumers

	人数 Number	16-24 岁 Age	25-34 岁 Age	35-44 岁 Age	45-54 岁 Age	55-60 岁 Age
样本 Sample	467	24.2	31.0	24.4	16.1	4.3
男性 Male	243	23.9	32.9	25.5	14.0	3.7
天天吃 daily	12	33.3	33.3	25.0	0.0	8.3
一周 3 次或以上 3 times or over a week	62	30.6	27.4	29.0	8.1	4.8
一周 1~2 次 once or twice a week	169	20.7	34.9	24.3	17.2	3.0
女性 Female	224	24.6	29.0	23.2	18.3	4.9
天天吃 daily	10	20.0	20.0	0.0	60.0	0.0
一周 3 次或以上 3 times or over a week	54	20.4	31.5	24.1	20.4	3.7
一周 1~2 次 once or twice a week	160	26.3	28.8	24.4	15.0	5.6

8-14 不同消费者层的常用品牌/ The Most Frequently Used Brands by Market Segments

8-14-1 时尚流行指标/ Fads Popular Index

	人数 Number	第一品牌及百分比 1st/ percent	第二品牌及百分比 2nd/ percent	第三品牌及百分比 3rd/ percent	第四品牌及百分比 4th/ percent
样本 Sample	826	康师傅 Kangshifu(58.6)	统一 President(16.5)	美厨 Michi(13.2)	营多 Yingduo(3.0)
平实生活指向 simple living orientation	390	康师傅 Kangshifu(61.5)	美厨 Michi(14.6)	统一 President(12.1)	华龙 Hualong(2.6) 营多 Yingduo(2.6)
时尚流行指向 fashion orientation	436	康师傅 Kangshifu(56.0)	统一 President(20.4)	美厨 Michi(11.9)	营多 Yingduo(3.4)

8-14-2 广告态度指标/ Advertising Attitude Index

	人数 Number	第一品牌及百分比 1st/ percent	第二品牌及百分比 2nd/ percent	第三品牌及百分比 3rd/ percent	第四品牌及百分比 4th/ percent
样本 Sample	823	**康师傅 Kangshifu(58.2)**	**统一 President(17.0)**	**美厨 Michi(13.0)**	**营多 Yingduo(3.2)**
广告淡漠指向 indifferent orientation	230	康师傅 Kangshifu(57.0)	统一 President(17.4)	美厨 Michi(13.0)	营多 Yingduo(2.2)
中间层 medium	477	康师傅 Kangshifu(57.4)	统一 President(17.4)	美厨 Michi(13.4)	营多 Yingduo(3.8)
信赖广告指向 loyal orientation	116	康师傅 Kangshifu(63.8)	统一 President(14.7)	美厨 Michi(11.2)	营多 Yingduo(2.6) 华龙 Hualong(2.6)

8-14-3 饮食健康指标/ Foods & Drink Quality Index

	人数 Number	第一品牌及百分比 1st/ percent	第二品牌及百分比 2nd/ percent	第三品牌及百分比 3rd/ percent	第四品牌及百分比 4th/ percent
样本 Sample	835	**康师傅 Kangshifu(58.2)**	**统一 President(16.8)**	**美厨 Michi(13.1)**	**营多 Yingduo(3.2)**
饮食“温饱”指向 "basic" orientation	240	康师傅 Kangshifu(63.3)	统一 President(15.0)	美厨 Michi(10.8)	营多 Yingduo(3.3)
中间层 medium	393	康师傅 Kangshifu(56.0)	统一 President(16.8)	美厨 Michi(15.3)	营多 Yingduo(2.8)
健康营养指向 health & nutrition orientation	202	康师傅 Kangshifu(56.4)	统一 President(18.8)	美厨 Michi(11.4)	营多 Yingduo(4.0)

8-15 重度消费者的消费者层构成/ The Composition of the Heavy Consumers

8-15-1 时尚流行指标/ Fads Popular Index

	人数 Number	平实生活指向 simple living orientation	时尚流行指向 fashion orientation
样本 Sample	456	47.6	52.4
天天吃 daily	22	50.0	50.0
一周 3 次或以上 3 times or over a week	111	48.6	51.4
一周 1~2 次 once or twice a week	323	47.1	52.9

8-15-2 广告态度指标/ Advertising Attitude Index

	人数 Number	广告淡漠指向 indifferent orientation	中间层 medium	信赖广告指向 loyal orientation
样本 Sample	457	25.4	59.3	15.3
天天吃 daily	21	28.6	47.6	23.8
一周 3 次或以上 3 times or over a week	112	31.3	54.5	14.3
一周 1~2 次 once or twice a week	324	23.1	61.7	15.1

8-15-3 饮食健康指标/ Foods & Drink Quality Index

	人数 Number	饮食“温饱”指向 "basic" orientation	中间层 medium	健康营养指向 health & nutrition orientation
样本 Sample	463	29.2	47.1	23.8
天天吃 daily	22	18.2	59.1	22.7
一周 3 次或以上 3 times or over a week	116	31.9	49.1	19.0
一周 1～2 次 once or twice a week	325	28.9	45.5	25.5

● 上海 / Shanghai

8-1 最近三个月食用频率的比例/ Proportion of the Sample Consuming Instant Noodles in the Last Three Months

	人数 Number	百分比 Percent
天天吃 daily	7	0.7
一周 3 次或以上 3 times or over a week	95	9.4
一周 1~2 次 once or twice a week	261	25.7
一个月 2～3 次 2 or 3 times a month	250	24.7
一个月 1 次或以下 once a month or below	108	10.7
没吃过 never	293	28.9

n=1014

8-2 最常用品牌排名/ Ranking of the Most Frequently Used Brands

排名 Brand Ranking	品牌 Brands	人数 Number	百分比 Percent
1	康师傅 Kangshifu	331	46.0
2	统一 President	205	28.5
3	美厨 Michi	103	14.3
4	营多 Yingduo	16	2.2
5	农心辛拉面 Nongshim	12	1.7
6	来一桶 Laiyitong	8	1.1
7	皇品 Huangpin	7	1.0
8	日清出前一丁 Chuqianyiding	6	0.8
8	日清飞碟 Nissin UFO	6	0.8
8	日清 Nissin	6	0.8
9	巧面馆 Qiaomianguan	4	0.6
10	华丰 Huafeng	2	0.3
10	福满多 Fumanduo	2	0.3

n=719

8-3 样本、男性各年龄层、女性各年龄层的常用品牌/ The Most Frequently Used Brands by the Whole Sample, Age and Gender Groups

	人数 Number	第一品牌及百分比 1st/ percent	第二品牌及百分比 2nd/ percent	第三品牌及百分比 3rd/ percent
样本 Sample	719	**康师傅 Kangshifu(46.0)**	**统一 President(28.5)**	**美厨 Michi(14.3)**
男性 Male	374	**康师傅 Kangshifu(48.7)**	**统一 President(28.3)**	**美厨 Michi(13.1)**
16~24 岁 Age	85	康师傅 Kangshifu(38.8)	统一 President(32.9)	美厨 Michi(15.3)
25~34 岁 Age	118	康师傅 Kangshifu(45.8)	统一 President(28.0)	美厨 Michi(14.4)
35~44 岁 Age	95	康师傅 Kangshifu(63.2)	统一 President(24.2)	美厨 Michi(9.5)
45~54 岁 Age	56	康师傅 Kangshifu(46.4)	统一 President(26.8)	美厨 Michi(12.5)
55~60 岁 Age	20	康师傅 Kangshifu(45.0)	统一 President(35.0)	美厨 Michi(15.0)
女性 Female	345	**康师傅 Kangshifu(43.2)**	**统一 President(28.7)**	**美厨 Michi(15.7)**
16~24 岁 Age	81	统一 President(37.0)	康师傅 Kangshifu(35.8)	美厨 Michi(13.6)
25~34 岁 Age	100	康师傅 Kangshifu(41.0)	统一 President(26.0)	美厨 Michi(18.0)
35~44 岁 Age	91	康师傅 Kangshifu(47.3)	统一 President(34.1)	美厨 Michi(12.1)
45~54 岁 Age	51	康师傅 Kangshifu(49.0)	美厨 Michi(21.6)	统一 President(17.6)
55~60 岁 Age	22	康师傅 Kangshifu(50.0)	美厨 Michi(13.6) 统一 President(13.6)	日清 Nissin(9.1)

8-4 理想品牌排名/ Ranking of the Ideal Brands

排名 Brand Ranking	品牌 Brands	人数 Number	百分比 Percent
1	康师傅 Kangshifu	472	46.5
2	统一 President	288	28.4
3	美厨 Michi	130	12.8
5	营多 Yingduo	17	1.7
6	农心辛拉面 Nongshim	13	1.3
7	皇品 Huangpin	10	1.0
8	日清 Nissin	9	0.9
8	日清出前一丁 Chuqianyiding	9	0.9
9	来一桶 Laiyitong	8	0.8
10	日清飞碟 Nissin UFO	6	0.6

n=1014

8-5 样本、男性各年龄层、女性各年龄层最近三个月有无购买的比例/ Purchasing in the Last Three Months by the Whole Sample, Age and Gender Groups

	人数 Number	买过 yes	没买过 no
样本 Sample	1013	70.5	29.5
男性 Male	509	70.5	29.5
16~24 岁 Age	109	71.6	28.4
25~34 岁 Age	146	76.0	24.0
35~44 岁 Age	130	71.5	28.5
45~54 岁 Age	85	65.9	34.1
55~60 岁 Age	39	53.8	46.2
女性 Female	504	70.4	29.6
16~24 岁 Age	108	74.1	25.9
25~34 岁 Age	143	73.4	26.6
35~44 岁 Age	130	74.6	25.4
45~54 岁 Age	82	64.6	35.4
55~60 岁 Age	41	48.8	51.2

8-6 样本、男性各年龄层、女性各年龄层最近三个月的食用频率/ Frequencies of Consuming Instant Noodles in the Last Three Months by the Whole Sample, Age and Gender Groups

	人数 Number	天天吃 daily	一周 3 次或以上 3 times or over a week	一周 1~2 次 once or twice a week	一个月 2~3 次 2 or 3 times a month	一个月 1 次或以下 once a month or below	没吃过 never
样本 Sample	1014	0.7	9.4	25.7	24.7	10.7	28.9
男性 Male	509	1.2	11.8	26.5	24.6	9.4	26.5
16~24 岁 Age	109	1.8	16.5	24.8	28.4	6.4	22.0
25~34 岁 Age	146	2.7	13.0	28.1	24.0	13.0	19.2
35~44 岁 Age	130	0.0	10.8	26.9	24.6	10.8	26.9
45~54 岁 Age	85	0.0	7.1	31.8	21.2	5.9	34.1
55~60 岁 Age	39	0.0	7.7	12.8	23.1	7.7	48.7
女性 Female	505	0.2	6.9	25.0	24.8	11.9	31.3
16~24 岁 Age	108	0.0	11.1	22.2	25.9	15.7	25.0
25~34 岁 Age	144	0.0	4.2	29.2	24.3	12.5	29.9
35~44 岁 Age	130	0.8	10.0	27.7	26.2	6.2	29.2
45~54 岁 Age	82	0.0	3.7	20.7	23.2	14.6	37.8
55~60 岁 Age	41	0.0	2.4	17.1	22.0	12.2	46.3

8-7 样本、男性各年龄层、女性各年龄层的品牌习惯/ Brand Habit in Consuming Instant Noodles by the Whole Sample, Age and Gender Groups

	人数 Number	基本固定食用一个牌子 used in only one brand	比较固定地食用两个或三个牌子 used in two or three brands	基本上没有固定哪个牌子 no brand preference
样本 Sample	721	36.8	46.2	17.1
男性 Male	374	37.2	46.8	16.0
16~24 岁 Age	85	40.0	43.5	16.5
25~34 岁 Age	118	39.8	48.3	11.9
35~44 岁 Age	95	31.6	48.4	20.0
45~54 岁 Age	56	39.3	44.6	16.1
55~60 岁 Age	20	30.0	50.0	20.0
女性 Female	347	36.3	45.5	18.2
16~24 岁 Age	81	29.6	50.6	19.8
25~34 岁 Age	101	35.6	48.5	15.8
35~44 岁 Age	92	42.4	43.5	14.1
45~54 岁 Age	51	39.2	33.3	27.5
55~60 岁 Age	22	31.8	50.0	18.2

8-8 选择该类商品的考虑因素/ Ranking of the Considerations in Purchasing

注：本题为多选题，合计百分比超过 100%(Multiple answers）

排名 Ranking	考虑因素 Considerations	人次 Person-time	百分比 Percent
1	口味好 pleasant taste	524	72.9
2	价格适中 reasonable price	301	41.9
3	购买方便 easy to buy	187	26.0
4	有名的牌子 famous brand	166	23.1
5	生产日期 date of producing	153	21.3
6	广告影响 influence of advertising	77	10.7
7	只是由于习惯 out of habit	55	7.6
8	有优惠条件 with preferential terms	45	6.3
9	包装吸引人 appealing package	21	2.9
10	朋友推荐 introduction of friends	10	1.4
11	售货员介绍 introduced by the shop assistants	6	0.8
11	单位发的 offered by the working unit	6	0.8
12	其它 others	4	0.6

n=719

8-9 样本、男性各年龄层、女性各年龄层最常食用的种类/ Kinds of the Consumed Instant Noodles by the Whole Sample, Age and Gender Groups

注：本题为多选题，合计百分比超过 100%(Multiple answers）

	人数 Number	牛肉 beef	鸡肉 chicken	排骨 spareribs	海鲜 seafood	炸酱 fried bean sauce	三鲜 3-flavored noodles	蔬菜 vegetable	其它 others
样本 Sample	720	79.4	7.4	13.6	16.7	11.7	6.8	2.8	1.5
男性 Male	374	79.1	6.7	12.0	13.9	13.1	7.0	2.9	1.9
16~24 岁 Age	85	81.2	5.9	11.8	14.1	16.5	9.4	1.2	0.0
25~34 岁 Age	118	79.7	6.8	12.7	12.7	10.2	4.2	1.7	2.5
35~44 岁 Age	95	76.8	6.3	12.6	17.9	15.8	5.3	3.2	3.2
45~54 岁 Age	56	80.4	7.1	8.9	8.9	10.7	12.5	1.8	0.0
55~60 岁 Age	20	75.0	10.0	15.0	15.0	10.0	5.0	20.0	5.0
女性 Female	346	79.8	8.1	15.3	19.7	10.1	6.6	2.6	1.2
16~24 岁 Age	81	75.3	8.6	14.8	33.3	8.6	6.2	4.9	0.0
25~34 岁 Age	101	81.2	6.9	16.8	10.9	9.9	7.9	2.0	2.0
35~44 岁 Age	91	82.4	11.0	15.4	20.9	12.1	6.6	1.1	0.0
45~54 岁 Age	51	80.4	2.0	13.7	11.8	13.7	7.8	2.0	0.0
55~60 岁 Age	22	77.3	13.6	13.6	22.7	0.0	0.0	4.5	9.1

8-10 样本、男性各年龄层、女性各年龄层最常食用的包装形式/ Types of Package of the Consumed Instant Noodles by the Whole Sample, Age and Gender Groups

注：本题为多选题，合计百分比超过 100%(Multiple answers）

	人数 Number	大碗装 big bowl	普通碗装 regular bowl	大袋装 big bag	普通袋装 regular bag	杯装 cupped	其它 others
样本 Sample	721	16.1	19.7	21.9	63.1	3.9	0.6
男性 Male	374	19.8	19.5	20.1	61.5	3.2	0.5
16~24 岁 Age	85	30.6	16.5	29.4	51.8	4.7	1.2
25~34 岁 Age	118	18.6	23.7	14.4	62.7	4.2	0.0
35~44 岁 Age	95	17.9	15.8	24.2	63.2	3.2	1.1
45~54 岁 Age	56	12.5	25.0	12.5	62.5	0.0	0.0
55~60 岁 Age	20	10.0	10.0	15.0	85.0	0.0	0.0
女性 Female	347	12.1	19.9	23.9	64.8	4.6	0.6
16~24 岁 Age	81	13.6	27.2	25.9	63.0	7.4	0.0
25~34 岁 Age	101	14.9	20.8	20.8	62.4	3.0	1.0
35~44 岁 Age	92	12.0	18.5	26.1	67.4	2.2	0.0
45~54 岁 Age	51	5.9	9.8	23.5	70.6	2.0	2.0
55~60 岁 Age	22	9.1	18.2	22.7	59.1	18.2	0.0

8-11 样本、男性各年龄层、女性各年龄层最常食用的方式/ Ways of the Consumed Instant noodles by the Whole Sample, Age and Gender Groups

	人数 Number	冲泡 steep it in boiling water	煮 boil it	干吃 eat directly	拌着吃 mix it with others
样本 Sample	717	55.5	43.1	0.8	0.6
男性 Male	370	58.1	40.3	0.8	0.8
16~24 岁 Age	84	56.0	42.9	1.2	0.0
25~34 岁 Age	116	61.2	35.3	1.7	1.7
35~44 岁 Age	94	59.6	39.4	0.0	1.1
45~54 岁 Age	56	57.1	42.9	0.0	0.0
55~60 岁 Age	20	45.0	55.0	0.0	0.0
女性 Female	347	52.7	46.1	0.9	0.3
16~24 岁 Age	81	49.4	48.1	1.2	1.2
25~34 岁 Age	101	51.5	46.5	2.0	0.0
35~44 岁 Age	92	62.0	38.0	0.0	0.0
45~54 岁 Age	51	45.1	54.9	0.0	0.0
55~60 岁 Age	22	50.0	50.0	0.0	0.0

8-12 样本、男性各年龄层、女性各年龄层最常食用的场合/ Settings of Consumption by the Whole Sample, Age and Gender Groups

	人数 Number	早餐 breakfast	午餐 lunch	晚餐 supper	宵夜 evening snack	加班时 when work overtime	不固定 no regular	其他 others
样本 Sample	706	27.9	15.4	5.1	30.6	11.5	9.5	0.0
男性 Male	368	28.3	12.8	5.7	32.9	10.6	9.8	0.0
16~24 岁 Age	84	21.4	16.7	6.0	35.7	16.7	3.6	0.0
25~34 岁 Age	116	18.1	16.4	7.8	36.2	10.3	11.2	0.0
35~44 岁 Age	93	40.9	9.7	4.3	24.7	9.7	10.8	0.0
45~54 岁 Age	55	36.4	9.1	1.8	40.0	5.5	7.3	0.0
55~60 岁 Age	20	35.0	0.0	10.0	20.0	5.0	30.0	0.0
女性 Female	338	27.5	18.3	4.4	28.1	12.4	9.2	0.0
16~24 岁 Age	81	19.8	25.9	7.4	27.2	14.8	4.9	0.0
25~34 岁 Age	95	21.1	24.2	3.2	28.4	16.8	6.3	0.0
35~44 岁 Age	91	38.5	12.1	1.1	28.6	7.7	12.1	0.0
45~54 岁 Age	49	28.6	8.2	8.2	30.6	10.2	14.3	0.0
55~60 岁 Age	22	36.4	13.6	4.5	22.7	9.1	13.6	0.0

8-13 重度消费者人口分布/ Demographics of the Heavy Consumers

	人数 Number	16-24 岁 Age	25-34 岁 Age	35-44 岁 Age	45-54 岁 Age	55-60 岁 Age
样本 Sample	363	22.9	30.9	27.3	14.6	4.4
男性 Male	201	23.4	31.8	24.4	16.4	4.0
天天吃 daily	6	33.3	66.7	0.0	0.0	0.0
一周 3 次或以上 3 times or over a week	60	30.0	31.7	23.3	10.0	5.0
一周 1~2 次 once or twice a week	135	20.0	30.4	25.9	20.0	3.7
女性 Female	162	22.2	29.6	30.9	12.3	4.9
天天吃 daily	1	0.0	0.0	100.0	0.0	0.0
一周 3 次或以上 3 times or over a week	35	34.3	17.1	37.1	8.6	2.9
一周 1~2 次 once or twice a week	126	19.0	33.3	28.6	13.5	5.6

8-14 不同消费者层的常用品牌/ The Most Frequently Used Brands by Market Segments

8-14-1 时尚流行指标/ Fads Popular Index

	人数 Number	第一品牌及百分比 1st/ percent	第二品牌及百分比 2nd/ percent	第三品牌及百分比 3rd/ percent
样本 Sample	713	**康师傅 Kangshifu(46.0)**	**统一 President(28.5)**	**美厨 Michi(14.3)**
平实生活指向 simple living orientation	320	康师傅 Kangshifu(48.8)	统一 President(27.5)	美厨 Michi(11.9)
时尚流行指向 fashion orientation	393	康师傅 Kangshifu(43.8)	统一 President(29.3)	美厨 Michi(16.3)

8-14-2 广告态度指标/ Advertising Attitude Index

	人数 Number	第一品牌及百分比 1st/ percent	第二品牌及百分比 2nd/ percent	第三品牌及百分比 3rd/ percent
样本 Sample	711	**康师傅 Kangshifu(45.9)**	**统一 President(28.4)**	**美厨 Michi(14.5)**
广告淡漠指向 indifferent orientation	172	康师傅 Kangshifu(44.8)	统一 President(27.3)	美厨 Michi(14.5)
中间层 medium	435	康师傅 Kangshifu(47.4)	统一 President(28.3)	美厨 Michi(13.8)
信赖广告指向 loyal orientation	104	康师傅 Kangshifu(41.3)	统一 President(30.8)	美厨 Michi(17.3)

8-14-3 饮食健康指标/ Foods & Drink Quality Index

	人数 Number	第一品牌及百分比 1st/ percent	第二品牌及百分比 2nd/ percent	第三品牌及百分比 3rd/ percent
样本 Sample	716	**康师傅 Kangshifu(45.9)**	**统一 President(23.6)**	**美厨 Michi(14.2)**
饮食"温饱"指向 "basic" orientation	162	康师傅 Kangshifu(45.1)	统一 President(29.0)	美厨 Michi(15.4)
中间层 medium	352	康师傅 Kangshifu(48.6)	统一 President(27.0)	美厨 Michi(13.1)
健康营养指向 health & nutrition orientation	202	康师傅 Kangshifu(42.1)	统一 President(31.2)	美厨 Michi(15.3)

8-15 重度消费者的消费者层构成/ The Composition of the Heavy Consumers

8-15-1 时尚流行指标/ Fads Popular Index

	人数 Number	平实生活指向 simple living orientation	时尚流行指向 fashion orientation
样本 Sample	359	43.2	56.8
天天吃 daily	7	28.6	71.4
一周 3 次或以上 3 times or over a week	94	40.4	59.6
一周 1~2 次 once or twice a week	258	44.6	55.4

8-15-2 广告态度指标/ Advertising Attitude Index

	人数 Number	广告淡漠指向 indifferent orientation	中间层 medium	信赖广告指向 loyal orientation
样本 Sample	359	21.7	63.8	14.5
天天吃 daily	7	0.0	71.4	28.6
一周 3 次或以上 3 times or over a week	95	27.4	54.7	17.9
一周 1～2 次 once or twice a week	257	20.2	66.9	12.8

8-15-3 饮食健康指标/ Foods & Drink Quality Index

	人数 Number	饮食"温饱"指向 "basic" orientation	中间层 medium	健康营养指向 health & nutrition orientation
样本 Sample	362	23.8	47.0	29.3
天天吃 daily	7	28.6	42.9	28.6
一周 3 次或以上 3 times or over a week	94	24.5	40.4	35.1
一周 1～2 次 once or twice a week	261	23.4	49.4	27.2

● 广州 / Guangzhou

8-1 最近三个月食用频率的比例/ Proportion of the Sample Consuming Instant Noodles in the Last Three Months

	人数 Number	百分比 Percent
天天吃 daily	9	0.9
一周 3 次或以上 3 times or over a week	61	5.9
一周 1~2 次 once or twice a week	237	22.9
一个月 2～3 次 2 or 3 times a month	255	24.7
一个月 1 次或以下 once a month or below	137	13.3
没吃过 never	334	32.3

n=1033

8-2 最常用品牌排名/ Ranking of the Most Frequently Used Brands

排名 Brand Ranking	品牌 Brands	人数 Number	百分比 Percent
1	康师傅 Kangshifu	326	46.6
2	华丰 Huafeng	138	19.7
3	统一 President	94	13.4
4	日清出前一丁 Chuqianyiding	44	6.3
5	公仔面 Doll	21	3.0
6	日清 Nissin	9	1.3
6	日清合味道 Nissin Cup	9	1.3
7	来利 Laili	7	1.0
8	来一桶 Laiyitong	6	0.9

n=699

8-3 样本、男性各年龄层、女性各年龄层的常用品牌/ The Most Frequently Used Brands by the Whole Sample, Age and Gender Groups

	人数 Number	第一品牌及百分比 1st/ percent	第二品牌及百分比 2nd/ percent	第三品牌及百分比 3rd/ percent	第四品牌及百分比 4th /percent
样本 Sample	699	**康师傅 Kangshifu(46.6)**	**华丰 Huafeng(19.7)**	**统一 President(13.4)**	日清出前一丁 **Chuqianyiding(6.3)**
男性 Male	344	**康师傅 Kangshifu(50.0)**	**华丰 Huafeng(19.5)**	**统一 President(13.7)**	**日清出前一丁 Chuqianyiding(4.9)**
16~24 岁 Age	77	康师傅 Kangshifu(44.2)	华丰 Huafeng(16.9)	统一 President(15.6)	日清出前一丁 Chuqianyiding(6.5)
25~34 岁 Age	102	康师傅 Kangshifu(50.0)	华丰 Huafeng(20.6)	统一 President(16.7)	日清出前一丁 Chuqianyiding(3.9)
35~44 岁 Age	89	康师傅 Kangshifu(51.7)	华丰 Huafeng(20.2)	统一 President(7.9)	日清出前一丁 Chuqianyiding(5.6)
45~54 岁 Age	51	康师傅 Kangshifu(52.9)	华丰 Huafeng(19.6)	统一 President(13.7)	日清出前一丁 Chuqianyiding(5.9)
55~60 岁 Age	25	康师傅 Kangshifu(56.0)	华丰 Huafeng(20.0)	统一 President(16.0)	公仔面 Doll(4.0) 日清 Nissin(4.0)
女性 Female	355	**康师傅 Kangshifu(43.4)**	**华丰 Huafeng(20.0)**	**统一 President(13.2)**	**日清出前一丁 Chuqianyiding(7.6)**
16~24 岁 Age	82	康师傅 Kangshifu(32.9)	华丰 Huafeng(26.8)	统一 President(11.0)	日清出前一丁 Chuqianyiding(8.5)
25~34 岁 Age	104	康师傅 Kangshifu(47.1)	华丰 Huafeng(18.3)	统一 President(11.5)	日清出前一丁 Chuqianyiding(7.7)
35~44 岁 Age	103	康师傅 Kangshifu(48.5)	华丰 Huafeng(16.5)	统一 President(15.5)	日清出前一丁 Chuqianyiding(7.8)
45~54 岁 Age	50	康师傅 Kangshifu(42.0)	华丰 Huafeng(20.0)	统一 President(18.0)	公仔面 Doll(8.0)
55~60 岁 Age	16	康师傅 Kangshifu(43.8)	华丰 Huafeng(18.8)	超力 Chaoli(6.3) 公仔面 Doll(6.3) 日清 Nissin(6.3) 日清出前一丁 Chuqianyiding(6.3) 统一 President(6.3) 金爵士 Jinjueshi(6.3)	

8-4 理想品牌排名/ Ranking of the Ideal Brands

排名 Brand Ranking	品牌 Brands	人数 Number	百分比 Percent
1	康师傅 Kangshifu	440	42.6
2	华丰 Huafeng	163	15.8
3	统一 President	144	13.9
4	日清出前一丁 Chuqianyiding	58	5.6
5	公仔面 Doll	35	3.4
6	日清 Nissin	18	1.7
7	日清合味道 Nissin Cup	15	1.5

n=1034

8-5 样本、男性各年龄层、女性各年龄层最近三个月有无购买的比例/ Purchasing in the Last Three Months by the Whole Sample, Age and Gender Groups

	人数 Number	买过 yes	没买过 no
样本 Sample	1034	63.7	36.3
男性 Male	499	64.1	35.9
16~24 岁 Age	106	68.9	31.1
25~34 岁 Age	150	58.0	42.0
35~44 岁 Age	127	68.5	31.5
45~54 岁 Age	73	67.1	32.9
55~60 岁 Age	43	55.8	44.2
女性 Female	535	63.4	36.6
16~24 岁 Age	112	64.3	35.7
25~34 岁 Age	158	64.6	35.4
35~44 岁 Age	137	72.3	27.7
45~54 岁 Age	87	56.3	43.7
55~60 岁 Age	41	41.5	58.5

8-6 样本、男性各年龄层、女性各年龄层最近三个月的食用频率/ Frequencies of Consuming Instant Noodles in the Last Three Months by the Whole Sample, Age and Gender Groups

	人数 Number	天天吃 daily	一周 3 次或以上 3 times or over a week	一周 1~2 次 once or twice a week	一个月 2~3 次 2 or 3 times a month	一个月 1 次或以下 once a month or below	没吃过 never
样本 Sample	1033	0.9	5.9	22.9	24.7	13.3	32.3
男性 Male	499	1.4	7.2	23.4	26.1	10.8	31.1
16~24 岁 Age	106	4.7	7.5	28.3	20.8	11.3	27.4
25~34 岁 Age	150	0.0	5.3	22.7	27.3	12.7	32.0
35~44 岁 Age	127	0.0	11.0	20.5	27.6	11.0	29.9
45~54 岁 Age	73	0.0	5.5	24.7	31.5	8.2	30.1
55~60 岁 Age	43	4.7	4.7	20.9	20.9	7.0	41.9
女性 Female	534	0.4	4.7	22.5	23.4	15.5	33.5
16~24 岁 Age	112	0.0	5.4	25.9	24.1	17.9	26.8
25~34 岁 Age	157	0.0	1.9	22.3	22.9	19.1	33.8
35~44 岁 Age	137	1.5	5.1	24.8	27.0	16.8	24.8
45~54 岁 Age	87	0.0	6.9	18.4	23.0	9.2	42.5
55~60 岁 Age	41	0.0	7.3	14.6	12.2	4.9	61.0

8-7 样本、男性各年龄层、女性各年龄层的品牌习惯/ Brand Habit in Consuming Instant Noodles by the Whole Sample, Age and Gender Groups

	人数 Number	基本固定食用一个牌子 used in only one brand	比较固定地食用两个或三个牌子 used in two or three brands	基本上没有固定哪个牌子 no brand preference
样本 Sample	699	31.5	46.9	21.6
男性 Male	344	32.6	44.5	23.0
16~24 岁 Age	77	24.7	49.4	26.0
25~34 岁 Age	102	38.2	47.1	14.7
35~44 岁 Age	89	32.6	42.7	24.7
45~54 岁 Age	51	31.4	37.3	31.4
55~60 岁 Age	25	36.0	40.0	24.0
女性 Female	355	30.4	49.3	20.3
16~24 岁 Age	82	24.4	54.9	20.7
25~34 岁 Age	104	27.9	56.7	15.4
35~44 岁 Age	103	37.9	39.8	22.3
45~54 岁 Age	50	28.0	46.0	26.0
55~60 岁 Age	16	37.5	43.8	18.8

8-8 选择该类商品的考虑因素/ Ranking of the Considerations in Purchasing

注：本题为多选题，合计百分比超过 100%(Multiple answers)

排名 Ranking	考虑因素 Considerations	人次 Person-time	百分比 Percent
1	口味好 pleasant taste	469	67.2
2	价格适中 reasonable price	301	43.1
3	有名的牌子 famous brand	195	27.9
4	购买方便 easy to buy	186	26.6
5	生产日期 date of producing	151	21.6
6	广告影响 influence of advertising	52	7.4
7	只是由于习惯 out of habit	50	7.2
8	包装吸引人 appealing package	30	4.3
9	有优惠条件 with preferential terms	26	3.7
10	朋友推荐 introduction of friends	15	2.1
11	单位发的 offered by the working unit	8	1.1
12	售货员介绍 introduced by the shop assistants	7	1.0
13	其它 others	6	0.9

n=698

8-9 样本、男性各年龄层、女性各年龄层最常食用的种类/ Kinds of the Consumed Instant Noodles by the Whole Sample, Age and Gender Groups

注：本题为多选题，合计百分比超过 100%(Multiple answers)

	人数 Number	牛肉 beef	鸡肉 chicken	排骨 spareribs	海鲜 seafood	炸酱 fried bean sauce	三鲜 3-flavored noodles	蔬菜 vegetable	其它 others
样本 Sample	695	55.3	16.3	15.8	29.1	6.6	18.4	4.5	1.3
男性 Male	341	57.2	15.5	15.2	29.0	5.9	19.6	3.8	0.9
16~24 岁 Age	76	61.8	13.2	13.2	38.2	9.2	9.2	3.9	1.3
25~34 岁 Age	101	51.5	19.8	20.8	23.8	6.9	17.8	4.0	0.0
35~44 岁 Age	89	58.4	13.5	13.5	23.6	4.5	30.3	2.2	0.0
45~54 岁 Age	50	58.0	16.0	12.0	34.0	2.0	26.0	6.0	2.0
55~60 岁 Age	25	60.0	12.0	12.0	32.0	4.0	8.0	4.0	4.0
女性 Female	354	53.4	16.9	16.4	29.1	7.3	17.2	5.1	1.7
16~24 岁 Age	82	50.0	15.9	15.9	37.8	9.8	15.9	4.9	2.4
25~34 岁 Age	104	55.8	12.5	17.3	29.8	6.7	22.1	2.9	1.0
35~44 岁 Age	102	56.9	21.6	17.6	26.5	6.9	12.7	5.9	0.0
45~54 岁 Age	50	50.0	16.0	14.0	22.0	6.0	22.0	8.0	2.0
55~60 岁 Age	16	43.8	25.0	12.5	18.8	6.3	6.3	6.3	12.5

8-10 样本、男性各年龄层、女性各年龄层最常食用的包装形式/ Types of Package of the Consumed Instant Noodles by the Whole Sample, Age and Gender Groups

注：本题为多选题，合计百分比超过 100%(Multiple answers)

	人数 Number	大碗装 big bowl	普通碗装 regular bowl	大袋装 big bag	普通袋装 regular bag	杯装 cupped	其它 others
样本 Sample	699	17.5	25.8	14.4	61.2	8.4	0.4
男性 Male	344	17.4	24.1	14.5	61.3	7.6	0.3
16~24 岁 Age	77	35.1	13.0	14.3	53.2	7.8	1.3
25~34 岁 Age	102	17.6	32.4	12.7	55.9	6.9	0.0
35~44 岁 Age	89	6.7	25.8	20.2	61.8	6.7	0.0
45~54 岁 Age	51	11.8	25.5	5.9	82.4	9.8	0.0
55~60 岁 Age	25	12.0	16.0	20.0	64.0	8.0	0.0
女性 Female	355	17.5	27.3	14.4	61.1	9.3	0.6
16~24 岁 Age	82	19.5	30.5	14.6	52.4	15.9	1.2
25~34 岁 Age	104	18.3	26.9	14.4	61.5	8.7	0.0
35~44 岁 Age	103	15.5	27.2	12.6	64.1	6.8	0.0
45~54 岁 Age	50	20.0	22.0	14.0	64.0	4.0	2.0
55~60 岁 Age	16	6.3	31.3	25.0	75.0	12.5	0.0

8-11 样本、男性各年龄层、女性各年龄层最常食用的方式/ Ways of the Consumed Instant noodles by the Whole Sample, Age and Gender Groups

	人数 Number	冲泡 steep it in boiling water	煮 boil it	干吃 eat directly	拌着吃 mix it with others
样本 Sample	694	74.8	23.9	1.2	0.1
男性 Male	343	75.2	23.6	1.2	0.0
16~24 岁 Age	76	75.0	22.4	2.6	0.0
25~34 岁 Age	102	75.5	23.5	1.0	0.0
35~44 岁 Age	89	76.4	23.6	0.0	0.0
45~54 岁 Age	51	74.5	23.5	2.0	0.0
55~60 岁 Age	25	72.0	28.0	0.0	0.0
女性 Female	351	74.4	24.2	1.1	0.3
16~24 岁 Age	81	70.4	27.2	2.5	0.0
25~34 岁 Age	103	78.6	21.4	0.0	0.0
35~44 岁 Age	103	74.8	22.3	1.9	1.0
45~54 岁 Age	48	75.0	25.0	0.0	0.0
55~60 岁 Age	16	62.5	37.5	0.0	0.0

8-12 样本、男性各年龄层、女性各年龄层最常食用的场合/ Settings of Consumption by the Whole Sample, Age and Gender Groups

	人数 Number	早餐 breakfast	午餐 lunch	晚餐 supper	宵夜 evening snack	加班时 when work overtime	不固定 no regular	其他 others
样本 Sample	660	34.7	9.2	1.7	39.2	6.4	8.8	0.0
男性 Male	326	32.8	7.7	0.9	43.9	7.4	7.4	0.0
16~24 岁 Age	72	26.4	9.7	0.0	55.6	4.2	4.2	0.0
25~34 岁 Age	95	31.6	8.4	3.2	44.2	8.4	4.2	0.0
35~44 岁 Age	85	29.4	7.1	0.0	40.0	12.9	10.6	0.0
45~54 岁 Age	50	46.0	4.0	0.0	36.0	2.0	12.0	0.0
55~60 岁 Age	24	41.7	8.3	0.0	37.5	4.2	8.3	0.0
女性 Female	334	36.5	10.8	2.4	34.7	5.4	10.2	0.0
16~24 岁 Age	76	28.9	15.8	3.9	34.2	2.6	14.5	0.0
25~34 岁 Age	98	38.8	5.1	2.0	35.7	8.2	10.2	0.0
35~44 岁 Age	97	41.2	9.3	2.1	34.0	5.2	8.2	0.0
45~54 岁 Age	47	34.0	14.9	2.1	36.2	4.3	8.5	0.0
55~60 岁 Age	16	37.5	18.8	0.0	31.3	6.3	6.3	0.0

8-13 重度消费者人口分布/ Demographics of the Heavy Consumers

	人数 Number	16-24 岁 Age	25-34 岁 Age	35-44 岁 Age	45-54 岁 Age	55-60 岁 Age
样本 Sample	307	25.4	26.1	27.0	14.3	7.2
男性 Male	160	26.9	26.3	25.0	13.8	8.1
天天吃 daily	7	71.4	0.0	0.0	0.0	28.6
一周 3 次或以上 3 times or over a week	36	22.2	22.2	38.9	11.1	5.6
一周 1~2 次 once or twice a week	117	25.6	29.1	22.2	15.4	7.7
女性 Female	147	23.8	25.9	29.3	15.0	6.1
天天吃 daily	2	0.0	0.0	100.0	0.0	0.0
一周 3 次或以上 3 times or over a week	25	24.0	12.0	28.0	24.0	12.0
一周 1~2 次 once or twice a week	120	24.2	29.2	28.3	13.3	5.0

8-14 不同消费者层的常用品牌/ The Most Frequently Used Brands by Market Segments

8-14-1 时尚流行指标/ Fads Popular Index

	人数 Number	第一品牌及百分比 1st/ percent	第二品牌及百分比 2nd/ percent	第三品牌及百分比 3rd/ percent	第四品牌及百分比 4th/ percent
样本 Sample	690	**康师傅 Kangshifu(46.4)**	**华丰 Huafeng(19.9)**	**统一 President(13.3)**	**日清出前一丁 Chuqianyiding(6.4)**
平实生活指向 simple living orientation	346	康师傅 Kangshifu(46.2)	华丰 Huafeng(24.0)	统一 President(10.7)	日清出前一丁 Chuqianyiding(4.9)
时尚流行指向 fashion orientation	344	康师傅 Kangshifu(46.5)	统一 President(15.0)	华丰 Huafeng(15.7)	日清出前一丁 Chuqianyiding(7.8)

8-14-2 广告态度指标/ Advertising Attitude Index

	人数 Number	第一品牌及百分比 1st/ percent	第二品牌及百分比 2nd/ percent	第三品牌及百分比 3rd/ percent	第四品牌及百分比 4th/ percent
样本 Sample	**688**	**康师傅 Kangshifu(46.7)**	**华丰 Huafeng(19.8)**	**统一 President(13.4)**	**日清出前一丁 Chuqianyiding(6.4)**
广告淡漠指向 indifferent orientation	207	康师傅 Kangshifu(45.9)	华丰 Huafeng(23.7)	统一 President(12.1)	日清出前一丁 Chuqianyiding(4.8)
中间层 medium	416	康师傅 Kangshifu(46.9)	华丰 Huafeng(18.3)	统一 President(13.9)	日清出前一丁 Chuqianyiding(6.7)
信赖广告指向 loyal orientation	65	康师傅 Kangshifu(47.7)	华丰 Huafeng(16.9)	统一 President(13.8)	日清出前一丁 Chuqianyiding(9.2)

8-14-3 饮食健康指标/ Foods & Drink Quality Index

	人数 Number	第一品牌及百分比 1st/ percent	第二品牌及百分比 2nd/ percent	第三品牌及百分比 3rd/ percent	第四品牌及百分比 4th/ percent
样本 Sample	**696**	**康师傅 Kangshifu(46.6)**	**华丰 Huafeng(19.8)**	**统一 President(13.5)**	**日清出前一丁 Chuqianyiding(6.3)**
饮食"温饱"指向 "basic" orientation	194	康师傅 Kangshifu(42.8)	华丰 Huafeng(25.3)	统一 President(13.9)	日清出前一丁 Chuqianyiding(6.7)
中间层 medium	376	康师傅 Kangshifu(45.7)	华丰 Huafeng(18.4)	统一 President(13.8)	日清出前一丁 Chuqianyiding(6.4)
健康营养指向 health & nutrition orientation	126	康师傅 Kangshifu(54.8)	华丰 Huafeng(15.9)	统一 President(11.9)	日清出前一丁 Chuqianyiding(5.6)

8-15 重度消费者的消费者层构成/ The Composition of the Heavy Consumers

8-15-1 时尚流行指标/ Fads Popular Index

	人数 Number	平实生活指向 simple living orientation	时尚流行指向 fashion orientation
样本 Sample	**305**	**51.1**	**48.9**
天天吃 daily	9	77.8	22.2
一周 3 次或以上 3 times or over a week	61	52.5	47.5
一周 1~2 次 once or twice a week	235	49.8	50.2

8-15-2 广告态度指标/ Advertising Attitude Index

	人数 Number	广告淡漠指向 indifferent orientation	中间层 medium	信赖广告指向 loyal orientation
样本 Sample	**300**	**30.0**	**61.0**	**9.0**
天天吃 daily	9	11.1	88.9	0.0
一周 3 次或以上 3 times or over a week	59	32.2	61.0	6.8
一周 1～2 次 once or twice a week	232	30.2	59.9	9.9

8-15-3 饮食健康指标/ Foods & Drink Quality Index

	人数 Number	饮食"温饱"指向 "basic" orientation	中间层 medium	健康营养指向 health & nutrition orientation
样本 Sample	**306**	**25.2**	**55.9**	**19.0**
天天吃 daily	9	22.2	55.6	22.2
一周 3 次或以上 3 times or over a week	61	24.6	62.3	13.1
一周 1～2 次 once or twice a week	236	25.4	54.2	20.3

● 重庆 / Chongqing

8-1 最近三个月食用频率的比例/ Proportion of the Sample Consuming Instant Noodles in the Last Three Months

	人数 Number	百分比 Percent
天天吃 daily	6	1.0
一周 3 次或以上 3 times or over a week	50	8.1
一周 1~2 次 once or twice a week	139	22.4
一个月 2～3 次 2 or 3 times a month	154	24.8
一个月 1 次或以下 once a month or below	62	10.0
没吃过 never	210	33.8

n=621

8-2 最常用品牌排名/ Ranking of the Most Frequently Used Brands

排名 Brand Ranking	品牌 Brands	人数 Number	百分比 Percent
1	康师傅 Kangshifu	269	65.6
2	统一 President	95	23.2
3	巧面馆 Qiaomianguan	14	3.4
4	来一桶 Laiyitong	12	2.9
5	好劲道 Haojindao	4	1.0

n=410

8-3 样本、男性各年龄层、女性各年龄层的常用品牌/ The Most Frequently Used Brands by the Whole Sample, Age and Gender Groups

	人数 Number	第一品牌及百分比 1st/ percent	第二品牌及百分比 2nd/ percent	第三品牌及百分比 3rd/ percent	第四品牌及百分比 4th/ percent
样本 Sample	410	**康师傅 Kangshifu(65.6)**	**统一 President(23.2)**	**巧面馆 Qiaomianguan(3.4)**	**来一桶 Laiyitong (2.9)**
男性 Male	208	**康师傅 Kangshifu(67.3)**	**统一 President(23.6)**	**来一桶 Laiyitong (3.8)**	**巧面馆 Qiaomianguan(1.4)**
16~24 岁 Age	57	康师傅 Kangshifu(57.9)	统一 President(33.3)	龙丰 Longfeng(1.8) 来一桶 Laiyitong (1.8)	
25~34 岁 Age	58	康师傅 Kangshifu(62.1)	统一 President(27.6)	来一桶 Laiyitong (5.2)	好劲道 haojindao(1.7) 巧面馆 Qiaomianguan(1.7)
35~44 岁 Age	45	康师傅 Kangshifu(73.3)	统一 President(17.8)	来一桶 Laiyitong (6.7)	巧面馆 Qiaomianguan(2.2)
45~54 岁 Age	37	康师傅 Kangshifu(78.4)	统一 President(13.5)	来一桶 Laiyitong (2.7) 巧面馆 Qiaomianguan(2.7)	
55~60 岁 Age	11	康师傅 Kangshifu(81.8)	统一 President(9.1)		
女性 Female	202	**康师傅 Kangshifu(63.9)**	**统一 President(22.8)**	巧面馆 Qiaomianguan(**5.4**)	**来一桶 Laiyitong (2.0)**
16~24 岁 Age	52	康师傅 Kangshifu(61.5)	统一 President(21.2)	巧面馆 Qiaomianguan(13.5)	来一桶 Laiyitong(1.9) 巨星 Super Star(1.9)
25~34 岁 Age	62	康师傅 Kangshifu(64.5)	统一 President(29.0)	来一桶 Laiyitong(3.2)	巧面馆 Qiaomianguan(1.6)
35~44 岁 Age	42	康师傅 Kangshifu(61.9)	统一 President(16.7)	巧面馆 Qiaomianguan(7.1)	福满多 Fumanduo(2.4) 好劲道 Haojindao(2.4) 来一桶 Laiyitong(2.4)
45~54 岁 Age	35	康师傅 Kangshifu(62.9)	统一 President(22.9)	好劲道 Haojindao (5.7)	皇品 Huangpin(2.9)
55~60 岁 Age	11	康师傅 Kangshifu(81.8)	统一 President(18.2)		

8-4 理想品牌排名/ Ranking of the Ideal Brands

排名 Brand Ranking	品牌 Brands	人数 Number	百分比 Percent
1	康师傅 Kangshifu	402	64.4
2	统一 President	140	22.4
3	来一桶 Laiyitong	15	2.4
4	巧面馆 Qiaomianguan	13	2.1
5	营多 Yingduo	5	0.8

n=624

8-5 样本、男性各年龄层、女性各年龄层最近三个月有无购买的比例/ Purchasing in the Last Three Months by the Whole Sample, Age and Gender Groups

	人数 Number	买过 yes	没买过 no
样本 Sample	624	67.5	32.5
男性 Male	314	66.2	33.8
16~24 岁 Age	64	79.7	20.3
25~34 岁 Age	93	65.6	34.4
35~44 岁 Age	75	62.7	37.3
45~54 岁 Age	54	68.5	31.5
55~60 岁 Age	28	42.9	57.1
女性 Female	310	68.7	31.3
16~24 岁 Age	64	78.1	21.9
25~34 岁 Age	90	73.3	26.7
35~44 岁 Age	73	68.5	31.5
45~54 岁 Age	60	60.0	40.0
55~60 岁 Age	23	47.8	52.2

8-6 样本、男性各年龄层、女性各年龄层最近三个月的食用频率/ Frequencies of Consuming Instant Noodles in the Last Three Months by the Whole Sample, Age and Gender Groups

	人数 Number	天天吃 daily	一周 3 次或以上 3 times or over a week	一周 1~2 次 once or twice a week	一个月 2~3 次 2 or 3 times a month	一个月 1 次或以下 once a month or below	没吃过 never
样本 Sample	621	1.0	8.1	22.4	24.8	10.0	33.8
男性 Male	313	1.3	9.3	21.4	26.8	8.0	33.2
16~24 岁 Age	64	4.7	21.9	31.3	29.7	1.6	10.9
25~34 岁 Age	92	0.0	5.4	28.3	25.0	5.4	35.9
35~44 岁 Age	75	1.3	2.7	17.3	33.3	5.3	40.0
45~54 岁 Age	54	0.0	14.8	9.3	22.2	22.2	31.5
55~60 岁 Age	28	0.0	0.0	10.7	17.9	10.7	60.7
女性 Female	308	0.6	6.8	23.4	22.7	12.0	34.4
16~24 岁 Age	64	1.6	6.3	35.9	20.3	17.2	18.8
25~34 岁 Age	89	0.0	6.7	19.1	31.5	12.4	30.3
35~44 岁 Age	73	0.0	13.7	17.8	20.5	5.5	42.5
45~54 岁 Age	59	1.7	1.7	23.7	16.9	15.3	40.7
55~60 岁 Age	23	0.0	0.0	21.7	17.4	8.7	52.2

8-7 样本、男性各年龄层、女性各年龄层的品牌习惯/ Brand Habit in Consuming Instant Noodles by the Whole Sample, Age and Gender Groups

	人数 Number	基本固定食用一个牌子 used in only one brand	比较固定地食用两个或三个牌子 used in two or three brands	基本上没有固定哪个牌子 no brand preference
样本 Sample	409	44.7	38.9	16.4
男性 Male	208	47.1	36.5	16.3
16~24 岁 Age	57	47.4	35.1	17.5
25~34 岁 Age	58	48.3	46.6	5.2
35~44 岁 Age	45	42.2	31.1	26.7
45~54 岁 Age	37	54.1	29.7	16.2
55~60 岁 Age	11	36.4	36.4	27.3
女性 Female	201	42.3	41.3	16.4
16~24 岁 Age	52	38.5	50.0	11.5
25~34 岁 Age	62	33.9	50.0	16.1
35~44 岁 Age	41	56.1	29.3	14.6
45~54 岁 Age	35	51.4	25.7	22.9
55~60 岁 Age	11	27.3	45.5	27.3

8-8 选择该类商品的考虑因素/ Ranking of the Considerations in Purchasing

注：本题为多选题，合计百分比超过 100%(Multiple answers）

排名 Ranking	考虑因素 Considerations	人次 Person-time	百分比 Percent
1	口味好 pleasant taste	293	71.8
2	价格适中 reasonable price	151	37.0
3	有名的牌子 famous brand	116	28.4
4	生产日期 date of producing	90	22.1
5	购买方便 easy to buy	86	21.1
6	只是由于习惯 out of habit	29	7.1
7	广告影响 influence of advertising	26	6.4
8	有优惠条件 with preferential terms	17	4.2
9	朋友推荐 introduction of friends	12	2.9
10	包装吸引人 appealing package	11	2.7
11	其它 others	4	1.0
12	售货员介绍 introduced by the shop assistants	2	0.5
13	单位发的 offered by the working unit	1	0.2

n=408

8-9 样本、男性各年龄层、女性各年龄层最常食用的种类/ Kinds of the Consumed Instant Noodles by the Whole Sample, Age and Gender Groups

注：本题为多选题，合计百分比超过 100%(Multiple answers）

	人数 Number	牛肉 beef	鸡肉 chicken	排骨 spareribs	海鲜 seafood	炸酱 fried bean sauce	三鲜 3-flavored noodles	蔬菜 vegetable	其它 others
样本 Sample	406	83.0	3.7	14.0	8.4	8.9	10.3	5.2	2.0
男性 Male	205	87.3	3.4	14.1	7.3	6.8	6.3	3.4	1.0
16~24 岁 Age	57	89.5	3.5	10.5	3.5	10.5	1.8	3.5	0.0
25~34 岁 Age	58	86.2	3.4	20.7	6.9	6.9	8.6	0.0	1.7
35~44 岁 Age	44	81.8	2.3	11.4	18.2	2.3	6.8	4.5	2.3
45~54 岁 Age	36	91.7	5.6	13.9	2.8	5.6	2.8	5.6	0.0
55~60 岁 Age	10	90.0	0.0	10.0	0.0	10.0	30.0	10.0	0.0
女性 Female	201	78.6	4.0	13.9	9.5	10.9	14.4	7.0	3.0
16~24 岁 Age	52	78.8	1.9	15.4	13.5	19.2	9.6	3.8	5.8
25~34 岁 Age	62	85.5	3.2	11.3	6.5	8.1	14.5	6.5	3.2
35~44 岁 Age	42	69.0	9.5	16.7	7.1	9.5	23.8	9.5	0.0
45~54 岁 Age	34	82.4	2.9	14.7	14.7	5.9	8.8	8.8	2.9
55~60 岁 Age	11	63.6	0.0	9.1	0.0	9.1	18.2	9.1	0.0

8-10 样本、男性各年龄层、女性各年龄层最常食用的包装形式/ Types of Package of the Consumed Instant Noodles by the Whole Sample, Age and Gender Groups

注：本题为多选题，合计百分比超过 100%(Multiple answers）

	人数 Number	大碗装 big bowl	普通碗装 regular bowl	大袋装 big bag	普通袋装 regular bag	杯装 cupped	其它 others
样本 Sample	407	20.4	17.7	30.0	50.6	2.7	0.5
男性 Male	205	22.4	18.0	30.2	47.8	2.0	0.5
16~24 岁 Age	57	21.1	15.8	38.6	42.1	1.8	0.0
25~34 岁 Age	56	30.4	17.9	25.0	48.2	0.0	0.0
35~44 岁 Age	45	20.0	22.2	33.3	46.7	2.2	2.2
45~54 岁 Age	36	22.2	16.7	22.2	52.8	0.0	0.0
55~60 岁 Age	11	0.0	18.2	27.3	63.6	18.2	0.0
女性 Female	202	18.3	17.3	29.7	53.5	3.5	0.5
16~24 岁 Age	52	13.5	21.2	23.1	57.7	5.8	0.0
25~34 岁 Age	62	29.0	22.6	25.8	46.8	4.8	0.0
35~44 岁 Age	42	19.0	16.7	31.0	52.4	2.4	2.4
45~54 岁 Age	35	8.6	8.6	48.6	54.3	0.0	0.0
55~60 岁 Age	11	9.1	0.0	18.2	72.7	0.0	0.0

8-11 样本、男性各年龄层、女性各年龄层最常食用的方式/ Ways of the Consumed Instant noodles by the Whole Sample, Age and Gender Groups

	人数 Number	冲泡 steep it in boiling water	煮 boil it	干吃 eat directly	拌着吃 mix it with others
样本 Sample	405	68.1	30.6	0.5	0.7
男性 Male	205	70.2	27.8	1.0	1.0
16~24 岁 Age	57	75.4	24.6	0.0	0.0
25~34 岁 Age	58	77.6	22.4	0.0	0.0
35~44 岁 Age	44	61.4	36.4	0.0	2.3
45~54 岁 Age	36	63.9	33.3	0.0	2.8
55~60 岁 Age	10	60.0	20.0	20.0	0.0
女性 Female	200	66.0	33.5	0.0	0.5
16~24 岁 Age	52	69.2	30.8	0.0	0.0
25~34 岁 Age	61	68.9	29.5	0.0	1.6
35~44 岁 Age	41	63.4	36.6	0.0	0.0
45~54 岁 Age	35	62.9	37.1	0.0	0.0
55~60 岁 Age	11	54.5	45.5	0.0	0.0

8-12 样本、男性各年龄层、女性各年龄层最常食用的场合/ Settings of Consumption by the Whole Sample, Age and Gender Groups

	人数 Number	早餐 breakfast	午餐 lunch	晚餐 supper	宵夜 evening snack	加班时 when work overtime	不固定 no regular	其他 others
样本 Sample	389	25.2	6.9	8.2	41.6	7.7	10.3	0.0
男性 Male	198	22.7	6.1	6.6	46.5	9.1	9.1	0.0
16~24 岁 Age	56	25.0	3.6	3.6	55.4	7.1	5.4	0.0
25~34 岁 Age	53	20.8	5.7	7.5	43.4	9.4	13.2	0.0
35~44 岁 Age	43	20.9	7.0	11.6	39.5	14.0	7.0	0.0
45~54 岁 Age	36	22.2	11.1	5.6	44.4	5.6	11.1	0.0
55~60 岁 Age	10	30.0	0.0	0.0	50.0	10.0	10.0	0.0
女性 Female	191	27.7	7.9	9.9	36.6	6.3	11.5	0.0
16~24 岁 Age	50	26.0	4.0	16.0	38.0	2.0	14.0	0.0
25~34 岁 Age	58	24.1	8.6	6.9	41.4	8.6	10.3	0.0
35~44 岁 Age	38	36.8	10.5	7.9	36.8	7.9	0.0	0.0
45~54 岁 Age	35	20.0	8.6	8.6	34.3	8.6	20.0	0.0
55~60 岁 Age	10	50.0	10.0	10.0	10.0	0.0	20.0	0.0

8-13 重度消费者人口分布/ Demographics of the Heavy Consumers

	人数 Number	16-24 岁 Age	25-34 岁 Age	35-44 岁 Age	45-54 岁 Age	55-60 岁 Age
样本 Sample	195	33.3	27.7	20.0	14.9	4.1
男性 Male	100	37.0	31.0	16.0	13.0	3.0
天天吃 daily	4	75.0	0.0	25.0	0.0	0.0
一周 3 次或以上 3 times or over a week	29	48.3	17.2	6.9	27.6	0.0
一周 1~2 次 once or twice a week	67	29.9	38.8	19.4	7.5	4.5
女性 Female	95	29.5	24.2	24.2	16.8	5.3
天天吃 daily	2	50.0	0.0	0.0	50.0	0.0
一周 3 次或以上 3 times or over a week	21	19.0	28.6	47.6	4.8	0.0
一周 1~2 次 once or twice a week	72	31.9	23.6	18.1	19.4	6.9

8-14 不同消费者层的常用品牌/ The Most Frequently Used Brands by Market Segments

8-14-1 时尚流行指标/ Fads Popular Index

	人数 Number	第一品牌及百分比 1st/ percent	第二品牌及百分比 2nd/ percent	第三品牌及百分比 3rd/ percent
样本 Sample	403	康师傅 Kangshifu(65.8)	统一 President(22.8)	巧面馆 Qiaomianguan(3.5)
平实生活指向 simple living orientation	227	康师傅 Kangshifu(69.6)	统一 President(21.1)	来一桶 Laiyitong(2.2)
时尚流行指向 fashion orientation	176	康师傅 Kangshifu(60.8)	统一 President(25.0)	巧面馆 Qiaomianguan(6.3)

8-14-2 广告态度指标/ Advertising Attitude Index

	人数 Number	第一品牌及百分比 1st/ percent	第二品牌及百分比 2nd/ percent	第三品牌及百分比 3rd/ percent
样本 Sample	407	**康师傅 Kangshifu(65.4)**	**统一 President(23.3)**	**巧面馆 Qiaomianguan(3.4)**
广告淡漠指向 indifferent orientation	115	康师傅 Kangshifu(63.5)	统一 President(21.7)	来一桶 Laiyitong(4.3)
中间层 medium	234	康师傅 Kangshifu(67.1)	统一 President(23.5)	巧面馆 Qiaomianguan(3.4)
信赖广告指向 loyal orientation	58	康师傅 Kangshifu(62.1)	统一 President(25.9)	来一桶 Laiyitong(3.4) 巧面馆 Qiaomianguan(3.4)

8-14-3 饮食健康指标/ Foods & Drink Quality Index

	人数 Number	第一品牌及百分比 1st/ percent	第二品牌及百分比 2nd/ percent	第三品牌及百分比 3rd/ percent
样本 Sample	406	**康师傅 Kangshifu(65.8)**	**统一 President(23.2)**	**巧面馆 Qiaomianguan(3.4)**
饮食"温饱"指向 "basic" orientation	146	康师傅 Kangshifu(70.5)	统一 President(21.9)	来一桶 Laiyitong(2.7)
中间层 medium	170	康师傅 Kangshifu(65.9)	统一 President(21.8)	来一桶 Laiyitong(2.9) 巧面馆 Qiaomianguan(2.9)
健康营养指向 health & nutrition orientation	90	康师傅 Kangshifu(57.8)	统一 President(27.8)	巧面馆 Qiaomianguan(7.8)

8-15 重度消费者的消费者层构成/ The Composition of the Heavy Consumers

8-15-1 时尚流行指标/ Fads Popular Index

	人数 Number	平实生活指向 simple living orientation	时尚流行指向 fashion orientation
样本 Sample	193	50.8	49.2
天天吃 daily	6	66.7	33.3
一周 3 次或以上 3 times or over a week	50	50.0	50.0
一周 1~2 次 once or twice a week	137	50.4	49.6

8-15-2 广告态度指标/ Advertising Attitude Index

	人数 Number	广告淡漠指向 indifferent orientation	中间层 medium	信赖广告指向 loyal orientation
样本 Sample	193	28.5	55.4	16.1
天天吃 daily	6	16.7	66.7	16.7
一周 3 次或以上 3 times or over a week	50	32.0	54.0	14.0
一周 1～2 次 once or twice a week	137	27.7	55.5	16.8

8-15-3 饮食健康指标/ Foods & Drink Quality Index

	人数 Number	饮食"温饱"指向 "basic" orientation	中间层 medium	健康营养指向 health & nutrition orientation
样本 Sample	193	34.7	44.6	20.7
天天吃 daily	6	16.7	66.7	16.7
一周 3 次或以上 3 times or over a week	50	42.0	42.0	16.0
一周 1～2 次 once or twice a week	137	32.8	44.5	22.6

● 武汉 / Wuhan

8-1 最近三个月食用频率的比例/ Proportion of the Sample Consuming Instant Noodles in the Last Three Months

	人数 Number	百分比 Percent
天天吃 daily	0	0.0
一周 3 次或以上 3 times or over a week	37	5.8
一周 1~2 次 once or twice a week	107	16.7
一个月 2～3 次 2 or 3 times a month	159	24.8
一个月 1 次或以下 once a month or below	107	16.7
没吃过 never	232	36.1

n=642

8-2 最常用品牌排名/ Ranking of the Most Frequently Used Brands

排名 Brand Ranking	品牌 Brands	人数 Number	百分比 Percent
1	康师傅 Kangshifu	201	49.0
2	统一 President	143	34.9
3	来一桶 Laiyitong	20	4.9
4	好劲道 Haojindao	9	2.2
5	巧面馆 Qiaomianguan	5	1.2
6	小虎队 Xiaohudui	4	1.0
7	福满多 Fumanduo	2	0.5
7	金穗香 Jinsuixiang	2	0.5

n=410

8-3 样本、男性各年龄层、女性各年龄层的常用品牌/ The Most Frequently Used Brands by the Whole Sample, Age and Gender Groups

	人数 Number	第一品牌及百分比 1st/ percent	第二品牌及百分比 2nd/ percent	第三品牌及百分比 3rd/ percent
样本 Sample	410	**康师傅 Kangshifu(49.0)**	**统一 President(34.9)**	**来一桶 Laiyitong(4.9)**
男性 Male	205	**康师傅 Kangshifu(46.3)**	**统一 President(38.5)**	**来一桶 Laiyitong(5.9)**
16~24 岁 Age	50	康师傅 Kangshifu(50.0)	统一 President(38.0)	来一桶 Laiyitong(4.0)
25~34 岁 Age	69	统一 President(42.0)	康师傅 Kangshifu(39.1)	来一桶 Laiyitong(10.1)
35~44 岁 Age	50	康师傅 Kangshifu(50.0)	统一 President(40.0)	来一桶 Laiyitong(4.0)
45~54 岁 Age	25	康师傅 Kangshifu(48.0)	统一 President(36.0)	好劲道 Haojindao(8.0)
55~60 岁 Age	11	康师傅 Kangshifu(54.5)	统一 President(18.2)	来一桶 Laiyitong(9.1) 金穗香 Jinsuixiang(9.1)
女性 Female	205	**康师傅 Kangshifu(51.7)**	**统一 President(31.2)**	**来一桶 Laiyitong(3.9)**
16~24 岁 Age	54	统一 President(42.6)	康师傅 Kangshifu(33.3)	来一桶 Laiyitong(9.3)
25~34 岁 Age	62	康师傅 Kangshifu(62.9)	统一 President(21.0)	来一桶 Laiyitong(4.8)
35~44 岁 Age	46	康师傅 Kangshifu(60.9)	统一 President(30.4)	华丰 Huafeng(2.2) 巧面馆 Qiaomianguan(2.2)
45~54 岁 Age	35	康师傅 Kangshifu(40.0)	统一 President(37.1)	日清出前一丁 Chuqianyiding(2.9) 好劲道 Haojindao(2.9) 真宝 Junbo(2.9) 巧面馆 Qiaomianguan(2.9) 金穗香 Jinsuixiang(2.9)
55~60 岁 Age	8	康师傅 Kangshifu(87.5)	统一 President(12.5)	

8-4 理想品牌排名/ Ranking of the Ideal Brands

排名 Brand Ranking	品牌 Brands	人数 Number	百分比 Percent
1	康师傅 Kangshifu	284	44.3
2	统一 President	233	36.3
4	来一桶 Laiyitong	9	1.4
5	小虎队 Xiaohudui	3	0.5
5	好劲道 Haojindao	3	0.5
6	新人类 Xinrenlei	2	0.3
6	北京 Beijing	2	0.3
6	巧面馆 Qiaomianguan	2	0.3

n=641

8-5 样本、男性各年龄层、女性各年龄层最近三个月有无购买的比例/ Purchasing in the Last Three Months by the Whole Sample, Age and Gender Groups

	人数 Number	买过 yes	没买过 no
样本 Sample	641	63.8	36.2
男性 Male	311	64.0	36.0
16~24 岁 Age	65	70.8	29.2
25~34 岁 Age	89	75.3	24.7
35~44 岁 Age	80	63.8	36.3
45~54 岁 Age	52	48.1	51.9
55~60 岁 Age	25	40.0	60.0
女性 Female	330	63.6	36.4
16~24 岁 Age	69	72.5	27.5
25~34 岁 Age	96	68.8	31.3
35~44 岁 Age	77	62.3	37.7
45~54 岁 Age	62	59.7	40.3
55~60 岁 Age	26	34.6	65.4

8-6 样本、男性各年龄层、女性各年龄层最近三个月的食用频率/ Frequencies of Consuming Instant Noodles in the Last Three Months by the Whole Sample, Age and Gender Groups

	人数 Number	天天吃 daily	一周 3 次或以上 3 times or over a week	一周 1~2 次 once or twice a week	一个月 2~3 次 2 or 3 times a month	一个月 1 次或以下 once a month or below	没吃过 never
样本 Sample	642	0.0	5.8	16.7	24.8	16.7	36.1
男性 Male	311	0.0	6.1	16.4	26.7	16.7	34.1
16~24 岁 Age	65	0.0	4.6	21.5	30.8	20.0	23.1
25~34 岁 Age	89	0.0	7.9	14.6	34.8	20.2	22.5
35~44 岁 Age	80	0.0	6.3	16.3	26.3	13.8	37.5
45~54 岁 Age	52	0.0	5.8	17.3	9.6	15.4	51.9
55~60 岁 Age	25	0.0	4.0	8.0	24.0	8.0	56.0
女性 Female	331	0.0	5.4	15.9	23.0	16.6	38.1
16~24 岁 Age	69	0.0	4.3	20.3	29.0	24.6	21.7
25~34 岁 Age	96	0.0	7.3	18.8	25.0	13.5	35.4
35~44 岁 Age	78	0.0	5.1	17.9	20.5	15.4	41.0
45~54 岁 Age	62	0.0	3.2	14.5	22.6	16.1	43.5
55~60 岁 Age	26	0.0	7.7	3.8	7.7	11.5	69.2

8-7 样本、男性各年龄层、女性各年龄层的品牌习惯/ Brand Habit in Consuming Instant Noodles by the Whole Sample, Age and Gender Groups

	人数 Number	基本固定食用一个牌子 used in only one brand	比较固定地食用两个或三个牌子 used in two or three brands	基本上没有固定哪个牌子 no brand preference
样本 Sample	409	42.3	44.7	13.0
男性 Male	205	47.8	41.0	11.2
16~24 岁 Age	50	50.0	40.0	10.0
25~34 岁 Age	69	52.2	39.1	8.7
35~44 岁 Age	50	50.0	38.0	12.0
45~54 岁 Age	25	36.0	48.0	16.0
55~60 岁 Age	11	27.3	54.5	18.2
女性 Female	204	36.8	48.5	14.7
16~24 岁 Age	54	25.9	63.0	11.1
25~34 岁 Age	61	36.1	52.5	11.5
35~44 岁 Age	46	30.4	47.8	21.7
45~54 岁 Age	35	57.1	28.6	14.3
55~60 岁 Age	8	62.5	12.5	25.0

8-8 选择该类商品的考虑因素/ Ranking of the Considerations in Purchasing

注：本题为多选题，合计百分比超过 100%(Multiple answers)

排名 Ranking	考虑因素 Considerations	人次 Person-time	百分比 Percent
1	口味好 pleasant taste	283	69.0
2	价格适中 reasonable price	158	38.5
3	有名的牌子 famous brand	142	34.6
4	生产日期 date of producing	138	33.7
5	购买方便 easy to buy	93	22.7
6	广告影响 influence of advertising	48	11.7
7	只是由于习惯 out of habit	35	8.5
8	包装吸引人 appealing package	17	4.1
9	有优惠条件 with preferential terms	8	2.0
10	售货员介绍 introduced by the shop assistants	6	1.5
10	其它 others	6	1.5
11	朋友推荐 introduction of friends	5	1.2
11	单位发的 offered by the working unit	5	1.2

n=410

8-9 样本、男性各年龄层、女性各年龄层最常食用的种类/ Kinds of the Consumed Instant Noodles by the Whole Sample, Age and Gender Groups

注：本题为多选题，合计百分比超过 100%(Multiple answers）

	人数 Number	牛肉 beef	鸡肉 chicken	排骨 spareribs	海鲜 seafood	炸酱 fried bean sauce	三鲜 3-flavored noodles	蔬菜 vegetable	其它 others
样本 Sample	408	84.1	8.8	10.5	7.1	14.7	11.3	2.9	2.0
男性 Male	205	83.4	7.3	10.7	9.3	15.1	10.2	3.9	1.0
16~24 岁 Age	50	82.0	4.0	10.0	12.0	12.0	14.0	2.0	0.0
25~34 岁 Age	69	88.4	7.2	7.2	8.7	18.8	11.6	2.9	1.4
35~44 岁 Age	50	82.0	12.0	14.0	4.0	16.0	10.0	4.0	0.0
45~54 岁 Age	25	84.0	4.0	12.0	12.0	12.0	4.0	8.0	4.0
55~60 岁 Age	11	63.6	9.1	18.2	18.2	9.1	0.0	9.1	0.0
女性 Female	203	84.7	10.3	10.3	4.9	14.3	12.3	2.0	3.0
16~24 岁 Age	54	79.6	13.0	7.4	3.7	11.1	18.5	3.7	1.9
25~34 岁 Age	61	88.5	8.2	11.5	4.9	13.1	11.5	1.6	4.9
35~44 岁 Age	46	82.6	10.9	10.9	6.5	23.9	8.7	2.2	2.2
45~54 岁 Age	34	85.3	11.8	14.7	2.9	8.8	8.8	0.0	2.9
55~60 岁 Age	8	100.0	0.0	0.0	12.5	12.5	12.5	0.0	0.0

8-10 样本、男性各年龄层、女性各年龄层最常食用的包装形式/ Types of Package of the Consumed Instant Noodles by the Whole Sample, Age and Gender Groups

注：本题为多选题，合计百分比超过 100%(Multiple answers）

	人数 Number	大碗装 big bowl	普通碗装 regular bowl	大袋装 big bag	普通袋装 regular bag	杯装 cupped	其它 others
样本 Sample	410	23.2	20.0	29.5	54.4	2.7	1.7
男性 Male	205	26.3	22.9	26.3	49.3	2.4	1.5
16~24 岁 Age	50	14.0	20.0	34.0	54.0	0.0	2.0
25~34 岁 Age	69	29.0	27.5	29.0	40.6	2.9	2.9
35~44 岁 Age	50	36.0	20.0	16.0	58.0	4.0	0.0
45~54 岁 Age	25	28.0	24.0	20.0	44.0	4.0	0.0
55~60 岁 Age	11	18.2	18.2	36.4	54.5	0.0	0.0
女性 Female	205	20.0	17.1	32.7	59.5	2.9	2.0
16~24 岁 Age	54	18.5	27.8	27.8	64.8	3.7	1.9
25~34 岁 Age	62	22.6	12.9	37.1	53.2	4.8	3.2
35~44 岁 Age	46	26.1	10.9	34.8	58.7	2.2	2.2
45~54 岁 Age	35	14.3	5.7	34.3	62.9	0.0	0.0
55~60 岁 Age	8	0.0	62.5	12.5	62.5	0.0	0.0

8-11 样本、男性各年龄层、女性各年龄层最常食用的方式/ Ways of the Consumed Instant noodles by the Whole Sample, Age and Gender Groups

	人数 Number	冲泡 steep it in boiling water	煮 boil it	干吃 eat directly	拌着吃 mix it with others
样本 Sample	406	85.0	12.8	2.0	0.2
男性 Male	203	85.7	12.3	1.5	0.5
16~24 岁 Age	49	85.7	14.3	0.0	0.0
25~34 岁 Age	69	84.1	15.9	0.0	0.0
35~44 岁 Age	49	85.7	8.2	4.1	2.0
45~54 岁 Age	25	88.0	8.0	4.0	0.0
55~60 岁 Age	11	90.9	9.1	0.0	0.0
女性 Female	203	84.2	13.3	2.5	0.0
16~24 岁 Age	54	81.5	13.0	5.6	0.0
25~34 岁 Age	61	83.6	14.8	1.6	0.0
35~44 岁 Age	45	86.7	11.1	2.2	0.0
45~54 岁 Age	35	88.6	11.4	0.0	0.0
55~60 岁 Age	8	75.0	25.0	0.0	0.0

8-12 样本、男性各年龄层、女性各年龄层最常食用的场合/ Settings of Consumption by the Whole Sample, Age and Gender Groups

	人数 Number	早餐 breakfast	午餐 lunch	晚餐 supper	宵夜 evening snack	加班时 when work overtime	不固定 no regular	其他 others
样本 Sample	394	19.5	8.6	6.1	41.6	10.9	13.2	0.0
男性 Male	198	15.2	5.1	5.6	47.0	14.6	12.6	0.0
16~24 岁 Age	50	8.0	4.0	10.0	56.0	10.0	12.0	0.0
25~34 岁 Age	64	15.6	4.7	6.3	42.2	17.2	14.1	0.0
35~44 岁 Age	49	18.4	8.2	2.0	46.9	14.3	10.2	0.0
45~54 岁 Age	24	16.7	0.0	4.2	41.7	25.0	12.5	0.0
55~60 岁 Age	11	27.3	9.1	0.0	45.5	0.0	18.2	0.0
女性 Female	196	24.0	12.2	6.6	36.2	7.1	13.8	0.0
16~24 岁 Age	54	16.7	14.8	11.1	27.8	13.0	16.7	0.0
25~34 岁 Age	57	22.8	5.3	3.5	50.9	7.0	10.5	0.0
35~44 岁 Age	42	31.0	14.3	2.4	33.3	2.4	16.7	0.0
45~54 岁 Age	35	31.4	17.1	8.6	28.6	5.7	8.6	0.0
55~60 岁 Age	8	12.5	12.5	12.5	37.5	0.0	25.0	0.0

8-13 重度消费者人口分布/ Demographics of the Heavy Consumers

	人数 Number	16-24 岁 Age	25-34 岁 Age	35-44 岁 Age	45-54 岁 Age	55-60 岁 Age
样本 Sample	144	23.6	31.3	25.0	16.0	4.2
男性 Male	70	24.3	28.6	25.7	17.1	4.3
天天吃 daily	0	0.0	0.0	0.0	0.0	0.0
一周 3 次或以上 3 times or over a week	19	15.8	36.8	26.3	15.8	5.3
一周 1~2 次 once or twice a week	51	27.5	25.5	25.5	17.6	3.9
女性 Female	74	23.0	33.8	24.3	14.9	4.1
天天吃 daily	0	0.0	0.0	0.0	0.0	0.0
一周 3 次或以上 3 times or over a week	18	16.7	38.9	22.2	11.1	11.1
一周 1~2 次 once or twice a week	56	25.0	32.1	25.0	16.1	1.8

8-14 不同消费者层的常用品牌/ The Most Frequently Used Brands by Market Segments

8-14-1 时尚流行指标/ Fads Popular Index

	人数 Number	第一品牌及百分比 1st/ percent	第二品牌及百分比 2nd/ percent	第三品牌及百分比 3rd/ percent	第四品牌及百分比 4th/ percent
样本 Sample	405	**康师傅 Kangshifu(49.4)**	**统一 President(34.3)**	**来一桶 Laiyitong(4.9)**	**好劲道 Haojindao(2.2)**
平实生活指向 simple living orientation	201	康师傅 Kangshifu(48.8)	统一 President(35.8)	来一桶 Laiyitong(4.5)	好劲道 Haojindao(2.5)
时尚流行指向 fashion orientation	204	康师傅 Kangshifu(50.0)	统一 President(32.8)	来一桶 Laiyitong(5.4)	好劲道 Haojindao(2.0)

8-14-2 广告态度指标/ Advertising Attitude Index

	人数 Number	第一品牌及百分比 1st/ percent	第二品牌及百分比 2nd/ percent	第三品牌及百分比 3rd/ percent	第四品牌及百分比 4th/ percent
样本 Sample	407	**康师傅 Kangshifu(49.1)**	**统一 President(34.6)**	**来一桶 Laiyitong(4.9)**	**好劲道 Haojindao(2.2)**
广告淡漠指向 indifferent orientation	109	康师傅 Kangshifu(49.5)	统一 President(36.7)	来一桶 Laiyitong(3.7)	好劲道 Haojindao(1.8)
中间层 medium	251	康师傅 Kangshifu(48.2)	统一 President(34.3)	来一桶 Laiyitong(5.2)	好劲道 Haojindao(2.8)
信赖广告指向 loyal orientation	47	康师傅 Kangshifu(53.2)	统一 President(31.9)	来一桶 Laiyitong(6.4)	巧面 Qiaomianguan(4.3)

8-14-3 饮食健康指标/ Foods & Drink Quality Index

	人数 Number	第一品牌及百分比 1st/ percent	第二品牌及百分比 2nd/ percent	第三品牌及百分比 3rd/ percent	第四品牌及百分比 4th/ percent
样本 Sample	405	**康师傅 Kangshifu(48.9)**	**统一 President(34.8)**	**来一桶 Laiyitong(4.9)**	**好劲道 Haojindao(2.2)**
饮食“温饱”指向 "basic" orientation	125	康师傅 Kangshifu(52.0)	统一 President(36.8)	来一桶 Laiyitong(5.6)	好劲道 Haojindao(1.6)
中间层 medium	193	康师傅 Kangshifu(48.7)	统一 President(31.1)	来一桶 Laiyitong(5.2)	好劲道 Haojindao(2.6)
健康营养指向 health & nutrition orientation	87	康师傅 Kangshifu(44.8)	统一 President(40.2)	来一桶 Laiyitong(3.4)	好劲道 Haojindao(2.3)

8-15 重度消费者的消费者层构成/ The Composition of the Heavy Consumers

8-15-1 时尚流行指标/ Fads Popular Index

	人数 Number	平实生活指向 simple living orientation	时尚流行指向 fashion orientation
样本 Sample	143	38.5	61.5
天天吃 daily	0	0.0	0.0
一周 3 次或以上 3 times or over a week	37	40.5	59.5
一周 1～2 次 once or twice a week	106	37.7	62.3

8-15-2 广告态度指标/ Advertising Attitude Index

	人数 Number	广告淡漠指向 indifferent orientation	中间层 medium	信赖广告指向 loyal orientation
样本 Sample	143	21.7	65.0	13.3
天天吃 daily	0	0.0	0.0	0.0
一周 3 次或以上 3 times or over a week	37	24.3	64.9	10.8
一周 1～2 次 once or twice a week	106	20.8	65.1	14.2

8-15-3 饮食健康指标/ Foods & Drink Quality Index

	人数 Number	饮食"温饱"指向 "basic" orientation	中间层 medium	健康营养指向 health & nutrition orientation
样本 Sample	142	26.8	43.7	29.6
天天吃 daily	0	0.0	0.0	0.0
一周 3 次或以上 3 times or over a week	37	18.9	48.6	32.4
一周 1～2 次 once or twice a week	105	29.5	41.9	28.6

● 西安 / Xi'an

8-1 最近三个月食用频率的比例/ Proportion of the Sample Consuming Instant Noodles in the Last Three Months

	人数 Number	百分比 Percent
天天吃 daily	23	3.8
一周 3 次或以上 3 times or over a week	75	12.5
一周 1~2 次 once or twice a week	202	33.6
一个月 2～3 次 2 or 3 times a month	164	27.3
一个月 1 次或以下 once a month or below	52	8.7
没吃过 never	85	14.1

n=601

8-2 最常用品牌排名/ Ranking of the Most Frequently Used Brands

排名 Brand Ranking	品牌 Brands	人数 Number	百分比 Percent
1	康师傅 Kangshifu	303	58.7
2	华丰 Huafeng	130	25.2
3	统一 President	29	5.6
4	熊毅武 Xiongyiwu	11	2.1
5	龙丰 Longfeng	6	1.2
6	福满多 Fumanduo	4	0.8
6	巧面馆 Qiaomianguan	4	0.8
7	华龙 Hualong	3	0.6
7	好劲道 Haojindao	3	0.6

n=516

8-3 样本、男性各年龄层、女性各年龄层的常用品牌/ The Most Frequently Used Brands by the Whole Sample, Age and Gender Groups

	人数 Number	第一品牌及百分比 1st/ percent	第二品牌及百分比 2nd/ percent	第三品牌及百分比 3rd/ percent
样本 Sample	**516**	**康师傅 Kangshifu(58.7)**	**华丰 Huafeng(25.2)**	**统一 President(5.6)**
男性 Male	**254**	**康师傅 Kangshifu(56.7)**	**华丰 Huafeng(24.4)**	**统一 President(8.3)**
16~24 岁 Age	56	康师傅 Kangshifu(55.4)	华丰 Huafeng(16.1)	统一 President(14.3)
25~34 岁 Age	75	康师傅 Kangshifu(61.3)	华丰 Huafeng(22.7)	统一 President(6.7)
35~44 岁 Age	69	康师傅 Kangshifu(52.2)	华丰 Huafeng(31.9)	统一 President(5.8)
45~54 岁 Age	39	康师傅 Kangshifu(59.0)	华丰 Huafeng(28.2)	统一 President(5.1) 熊毅武 Xiongyiwu(5.1)
55~60 岁 Age	15	康师傅 Kangshifu(53.3)	华丰 Huafeng(20.0)	统一 President(13.3)
女性 Female	**262**	**康师傅 Kangshifu(60.7)**	**华丰 Huafeng(26.0)**	**统一 President(3.1)**
16~24 岁 Age	54	康师傅 Kangshifu(50.0)	华丰 Huafeng(33.3)	统一 President(7.4)
25~34 岁 Age	83	康师傅 Kangshifu(65.1)	华丰 Huafeng(24.1)	统一 President(3.6)
35~44 岁 Age	65	康师傅 Kangshifu(56.9)	华丰 Huafeng(27.7)	统一 President(1.5) 熊毅武 Xiongyiwu(1.5) 华龙 Hualong(1.5) 来一桶 Laiyitong(1.5) 龙丰 Longfeng(1.5) 公仔面 Doll(1.5) 福满多 Fumanduo(1.5)
45~54 岁 Age	37	康师傅 Kangshifu(75.7)	华丰 Huafeng(8.1)	好劲道 Haojindao(2.7) 太阳 Sun food(2.7) 霸王 Bawang(2.7)
55~60 岁 Age	23	康师傅 Kangshifu(56.5)	华丰 Huafeng(39.1)	华祥 Huaxiang(4.3)

8-4 理想品牌排名/ Ranking of the Ideal Brands

排名 Brand Ranking	品牌 Brands	人数 Number	百分比 Percent
1	康师傅 Kangshifu	394	65.6
2	华丰 Huafeng	97	16.1
3	统一 President	49	8.2
4	熊毅武 Xiongyiwu	6	1.0
4	巧面馆 Qiaomianguan	6	1.0
5	龙丰 Longfeng	5	0.8
6	来一桶 Laiyitong	3	0.5
6	福满多 Fumanduo	3	0.5
6	华龙 Hualong	3	0.5

n=601

8-5 样本、男性各年龄层、女性各年龄层最近三个月有无购买的比例/ Purchasing in the Last Three Months by the Whole Sample, Age and Gender Groups

	人数 Number	买过 yes	没买过 no
样本 Sample	**601**	**82.9**	**17.1**
男性 Male	**302**	**81.1**	**18.9**
16~24 岁 Age	64	82.8	17.2
25~34 岁 Age	91	80.2	19.8
35~44 岁 Age	77	88.3	11.7
45~54 岁 Age	46	76.1	23.9
55~60 岁 Age	24	66.7	33.3
女性 Female	**299**	**84.6**	**15.4**
16~24 岁 Age	61	80.3	19.7
25~34 岁 Age	90	90.0	10.0
35~44 岁 Age	74	86.5	13.5
45~54 岁 Age	49	75.5	24.5
55~60 岁 Age	25	88.0	12.0

8-6 样本、男性各年龄层、女性各年龄层最近三个月的食用频率/ Frequencies of Consuming Instant Noodles in the Last Three Months by the Whole Sample, Age and Gender Groups

	人数 Number	天天吃 daily	一周 3 次或以上 3 times or over a week	一周 1~2 次 once or twice a week	一个月 2~3 次 2 or 3 times a month	一个月 1 次或下 once a month or below	没吃过 never
样本 Sample	601	3.8	12.5	33.6	27.3	8.7	14.1
男性 Male	302	3.6	10.9	32.8	28.5	8.3	15.9
16~24 岁 Age	64	6.3	10.9	34.4	31.3	4.7	12.5
25~34 岁 Age	91	1.1	12.1	28.6	30.8	9.9	17.6
35~44 岁 Age	77	6.5	10.4	40.3	23.4	9.1	10.4
45~54 岁 Age	46	2.2	10.9	32.6	32.6	6.5	15.2
55~60 岁 Age	24	0.0	8.3	20.8	20.8	12.5	37.5
女性 Female	299	4.0	14.0	34.4	26.1	9.0	12.4
16~24 岁 Age	61	4.9	13.1	36.1	23.0	11.5	11.5
25~34 岁 Age	90	3.3	11.1	35.6	31.1	11.1	7.8
35~44 岁 Age	74	2.7	12.2	41.9	23.0	8.1	12.2
45~54 岁 Age	49	4.1	22.4	24.5	18.4	6.1	24.5
55~60 岁 Age	25	8.0	16.0	24.0	40.0	4.0	8.0

8-7 样本、男性各年龄层、女性各年龄层的品牌习惯/ Brand Habit in Consuming Instant Noodles by the Whole Sample, Age and Gender Groups

	人数 Number	基本固定食用一个牌子 used in only one brand	比较固定地食用两个或三个牌子 used in two or three brands	基本上没有固定哪个牌子 no brand preference
样本 Sample	516	45.7	39.9	14.3
男性 Male	254	43.7	41.3	15.0
16~24 岁 Age	56	41.1	46.4	12.5
25~34 岁 Age	75	40.0	41.3	18.7
35~44 岁 Age	69	52.2	39.1	8.7
45~54 岁 Age	39	43.6	35.9	20.5
55~60 岁 Age	15	33.3	46.7	20.0
女性 Female	262	47.7	38.5	13.7
16~24 岁 Age	54	40.7	35.2	24.1
25~34 岁 Age	83	57.8	36.1	6.0
35~44 岁 Age	65	47.7	41.5	10.8
45~54 岁 Age	37	35.1	48.6	16.2
55~60 岁 Age	23	47.8	30.4	21.7

8-8 选择该类商品的考虑因素/ Ranking of the Considerations in Purchasing

注：本题为多选题，合计百分比可能超过 100%（Multiple answers）

排名 Ranking	考虑因素 Considerations	人次 Person-time	百分比 Percent
1	口味好 pleasant taste	368	71.5
2	价格适中 reasonable price	207	40.2
3	有名的牌子 famous brand	166	32.2
4	生产日期 date of producing	124	24.1
5	购买方便 easy to buy	92	17.9
6	只是由于习惯 out of habit	43	8.3
7	广告影响 influence of advertising	40	7.8
8	包装吸引人 appealing package	10	1.9
8	朋友推荐 introduction of friends	10	1.9
9	有优惠条件 with preferential terms	9	1.7
10	售货员介绍 introduced by the shop assistants	5	1.0
10	单位发的 offered by the working unit	5	1.0
11	其它 others	2	0.4

n=515

8-9 样本、男性各年龄层、女性各年龄层最常食用的种类/ Kinds of the Consumed Instant Noodles by the Whole Sample, Age and Gender Groups

注：本题为多选题，合计百分比超过 100%(Multiple answers）

	人数 Number	牛肉 beef	鸡肉 chicken	排骨 spareribs	海鲜 seafood	炸酱 fried bean sauce	三鲜 3-flavored noodles	蔬菜 vegetable	其它 others
样本 Sample	516	60.9	4.8	11.2	8.1	5.0	44.4	2.3	1.9
男性 Male	254	64.2	5.1	7.5	6.3	5.5	43.7	2.4	1.6
16~24 岁 Age	56	73.2	7.1	7.1	[illegible].8	3.6	33.9	0.0	1.8
25~34 岁 Age	75	65.3	5.3	9.3	5.3	10.7	29.3	0.0	2.7
35~44 岁 Age	69	63.8	4.3	8.7	8.7	4.3	58.0	4.3	1.4
45~54 岁 Age	39	53.8	5.1	2.6	7.7	0.0	51.3	7.7	0.0
55~60 岁 Age	15	53.3	0.0	6.7	13.3	6.7	66.7	0.0	0.0
女性 Female	262	57.6	4.6	14.9	9.9	4.6	45.0	2.3	2.3
16~24 岁 Age	54	61.1	1.9	11.1	11.1	1.9	37.0	1.9	5.6
25~34 岁 Age	83	59.0	2.4	16.9	13.3	4.8	43.4	4.8	0.0
35~44 岁 Age	65	55.4	6.2	15.4	6.2	7.7	56.9	0.0	3.1
45~54 岁 Age	37	56.8	5.4	21.6	3.1	5.4	35.1	0.0	2.7
55~60 岁 Age	23	52.2	13.0	4.3	3.7	0.0	52.2	4.3	0.0

8-10 样本、男性各年龄层、女性各年龄层最常食用的包装形式/ Types of Package of the Consumed Instant Noodles by the Whole Sample, Age and Gender Groups

注：本题为多选题，合计百分比超过 100%(Multiple answers）

	人数 Number	大碗装 big bowl	普通碗装 regular bowl	大袋装 big bag	普通袋装 regular bag	杯装 cupped	其它 others
样本 Sample	516	10.9	16.1	21.9	70.2	0.6	0.6
男性 Male	254	13.8	16.9	21.7	65.7	0.8	0.4
16~24 岁 Age	56	14.3	19.6	28.6	55.4	0.0	0.0
25~34 岁 Age	75	13.3	14.7	21.3	65.3	1.3	0.0
35~44 岁 Age	69	13.0	18.8	21.7	71.0	0.0	1.4
45~54 岁 Age	39	17.9	12.8	15.4	61.5	2.6	0.0
55~60 岁 Age	15	6.7	20.0	13.3	93.3	0.0	0.0
女性 Female	262	8.0	15.3	22.1	74.4	0.4	0.8
16~24 岁 Age	54	3.7	13.0	18.5	79.6	0.0	0.0
25~34 岁 Age	83	6.0	20.5	24.1	73.5	0.0	0.0
35~44 岁 Age	65	9.2	12.3	20.0	80.0	0.0	1.5
45~54 岁 Age	37	16.2	8.1	29.7	62.2	0.0	2.7
55~60 岁 Age	23	8.7	21.7	17.4	69.6	4.3	0.0

8-11 样本、男性各年龄层、女性各年龄层最常食用的方式/ Ways of the Consumed Instant Noodles by the Whole Sample, Age and Gender Groups

	人数 Number	冲泡 steep it in boiling water	煮 boil it	干吃 eat directly	拌着吃 mix it with others
样本 Sample	516	32.8	61.6	5.2	0.4
男性 Male	254	38.2	55.5	5.5	0.8
16~24 岁 Age	56	37.5	50.0	10.7	1.8
25~34 岁 Age	75	40.0	57.3	1.3	1.3
35~44 岁 Age	69	34.8	56.5	8.7	0.0
45~54 岁 Age	39	38.5	59.0	2.6	0.0
55~60 岁 Age	15	46.7	53.3	0.0	0.0
女性 Female	262	27.5	67.6	5.0	0.0
16~24 岁 Age	54	37.0	50.0	13.0	0.0
25~34 岁 Age	83	26.5	68.7	4.8	0.0
35~44 岁 Age	65	20.0	78.5	1.5	0.0
45~54 岁 Age	37	29.7	70.3	0.0	0.0
55~60 岁 Age	23	26.1	69.6	4.3	0.0

8-12 样本、男性各年龄层、女性各年龄层最常食用的场合/ Settings of Consumption by the Whole Sample, Age and Gender Groups

	人数 Number	早餐 breakfast	午餐 lunch	晚餐 supper	宵夜 evening snack	加班时 when work overtime	不固定 no regular	其他 others
样本 Sample	508	24.0	8.7	16.5	29.3	16.5	4.9	0.0
男性 Male	248	21.8	5.6	14.9	33.5	20.2	4.0	0.0
16~24 岁 Age	55	18.2	10.9	12.7	40.0	14.5	3.6	0.0
25~34 岁 Age	71	18.3	4.2	11.3	33.8	31.0	1.4	0.0
35~44 岁 Age	69	26.1	5.8	11.6	36.2	14.5	5.8	0.0
45~54 岁 Age	38	26.3	0.0	23.7	21.1	23.7	5.3	0.0
55~60 岁 Age	15	20.0	6.7	33.3	26.7	6.7	6.7	0.0
女性 Female	260	26.2	11.5	18.1	25.4	13.1	5.8	0.0
16~24 岁 Age	54	31.5	7.4	14.8	25.9	13.0	7.4	0.0
25~34 岁 Age	82	20.7	12.2	13.4	24.4	18.3	11.0	0.0
35~44 岁 Age	65	35.4	9.2	15.4	30.8	9.2	0.0	0.0
45~54 岁 Age	36	13.9	16.7	30.6	27.8	11.1	0.0	0.0
55~60 岁 Age	23	26.1	17.4	30.4	8.7	8.7	8.7	0.0

8-13 重度消费者人口分布/ Demographics of the Heavy Consumers

	人数 Number	16-24 岁 Age	25-34 岁 Age	35-44 岁 Age	45-54 岁 Age	55-60 岁 Age
样本 Sample	300	22.0	27.7	28.7	15.3	6.3
男性 Male	143	23.1	26.6	30.8	14.7	4.9
天天吃 daily	11	36.4	9.1	45.5	9.1	0.0
一周 3 次或以上 3 times or over a week	33	21.2	33.3	24.2	15.2	6.1
一周 1~2 次 once or twice a week	99	22.2	26.3	31.3	15.2	5.1
女性 Female	157	21.0	28.7	26.8	15.9	7.6
天天吃 daily	12	25.0	25.0	16.7	16.7	16.7
一周 3 次或以上 3 times or over a week	42	19.0	23.8	21.4	26.2	9.5
一周 1~2 次 once or twice a week	103	21.4	31.1	30.1	11.7	5.8

8-14 不同消费者层的常用品牌/ The Most Frequently Used Brands by Market Segments

8-14-1 时尚流行指标/ Fads Popular Index

	人数 Number	第一品牌及百分比 1st/ percent	第二品牌及百分比 2nd/ percent	第三品牌及百分比 3rd/ percent	第四品牌及百分比 4th/ percent
样本 Sample	514	**康师傅 Kangshifu(58.9)**	**华丰 Huafeng(25.1)**	**统一 President(5.6)**	**熊毅武 Xiongyiwu(2.1)**
平实生活指向 simple living orientation	288	康师傅 Kangshifu(57.6)	华丰 Huafeng(28.8)	统一 President(3.8)	熊毅武 Xiongyiwu(1.0)
时尚流行指向 fashion orientation	226	康师傅 Kangshifu(60.6)	华丰 Huafeng(20.4)	统一 President(8.0)	熊毅武 Xiongyiwu(3.5)

8-14-2 广告态度指标/ Advertising Attitude Index

	人数 Number	第一品牌及百分比 1st/ percent	第二品牌及百分比 2nd/ percent	第三品牌及百分比 3rd/ percent	第四品牌及百分比 4th/ percent
样本 Sample	512	**康师傅 Kangshifu(59.2)**	**华丰 Huafeng(24.8)**	**统一 President(5.7)**	**熊毅武 Xiongyiwu (2.1)**
广告淡漠指向 indifferent orientation	160	康师傅 Kangshifu(61.3)	华丰 Huafeng(20.6)	统一 President(6.9)	龙丰 Longfeng(1.9)
中间层 medium	284	康师傅 Kangshifu(58.1)	华丰 Huafeng(26.8)	统一 President(4.9)	熊毅武 Xiongyiwu (2.5)
信赖广告指向 loyal orientation	68	康师傅 Kangshifu(58.8)	华丰 Huafeng(26.5)	统一 President(5.9)	熊毅武 Xiongyiwu (2.9)

8-14-3 饮食健康指标/ Foods & Drink Quality Index

	人数 Number	第一品牌及百分比 1st/ percent	第二品牌及百分比 2nd/ percent	第三品牌及百分比 3rd/ percent	第四品牌及百分比 4th/ percent
样本 Sample	516	**康师傅 Kangshifu(58.7)**	**华丰 Huafeng(25.2)**	**统一 President(5.6)**	**熊毅武 Xiongyiwu(2.1)**
饮食"温饱"指向 "basic" orientation	195	康师傅 Kangshifu(59.0)	华丰 Huafeng(24.1)	统一 President(4.6)	熊毅武 Xiongyiwu(4.1)
中间层 medium	241	康师傅 Kangshifu(61.4)	华丰 Huafeng(23.7)	统一 President(4.1)	龙丰 Longfeng(1.7)
健康营养指向 health & nutrition orientation	80	康师傅 Kangshifu(50.0)	华丰 Huafeng(32.5)	统一 President(12.5)	华龙 Hualong(1.3) 太阳 Sun food(1.3) 华祥 Huaxiang(1.3)

8-15 重度消费者的消费者层构成/ The Composition of the Heavy Consumers

8-15-1 时尚流行指标/ Fads Popular Index

	人数 Number	平实生活指向 simple living orientation	时尚流行指向 fashion orientation
样本 Sample	299	54.5	45.5
天天吃 daily	23	60.9	39.1
一周 3 次或以上 3 times or over a week	74	48.6	51.4
一周 1~2 次 once or twice a week	202	55.9	44.1

8-15-2 广告态度指标/ Advertising Attitude Index

	人数 Number	广告淡漠指向 indifferent orientation	中间层 medium	信赖广告指向 loyal orientation
样本 Sample	299	27.1	56.9	16.1
天天吃 daily	22	13.6	63.6	22.7
一周 3 次或以上 3 times or over a week	75	20.0	58.7	21.3
一周 1～2 次 once or twice a week	202	31.2	55.4	13.4

8-15-3 饮食健康指标/ Foods & Drink Quality Index

	人数 Number	饮食"温饱"指向 "basic" orientation	中间层 medium	健康营养指向 health & nutrition orientation
样本 Sample	300	37.7	46.0	16.3
天天吃 daily	23	47.8	39.1	13.0
一周 3 次或以上 3 times or over a week	75	30.7	50.7	18.7
一周 1～2 次 once or twice a week	202	39.1	45.0	15.8

● 沈阳 / Shenyang

8-1 最近三个月食用频率的比例/ Proportion of the Sample Consuming Instant Noodles in the Last Three Months

	人数 Number	百分比 Percent
天天吃 daily	17	2.8
一周 3 次或以上 3 times or over a week	79	13.1
一周 1~2 次 once or twice a week	200	33.3
一个月 2～3 次 2 or 3 times a month	150	25.0
一个月 1 次或以下 once a month or below	60	10.0
没吃过 never	95	15.8

n=601

8-2 最常用品牌排名/ Ranking of the Most Frequently Used Brands

排名 Brand Ranking	品牌 Brands	人数 Number	百分比 Percent
1	康师傅 Kangshifu	248	49.2
2	统一 President	88	17.5
3	华丰 Huafeng	86	17.1
4	福满多 Fumanduo	38	7.5
5	好劲道 Haojindao	9	1.8

n=504

8-3 样本、男性各年龄层、女性各年龄层的常用品牌/ The Most Frequently Used Brands by the Whole Sample, Age and Gender Groups

	人数 Number	第一品牌及百分比 1st/ percent	第二品牌及百分比 2nd/ percent	第三品牌及百分比 3rd/ percent
样本 Sample	**504**	**康师傅 Kangshifu(49.2)**	**统一 President(17.5)**	**华丰 Huafeng(17.1)**
男性 Male	**249**	**康师傅 Kangshifu(52.6)**	**华丰 Huafeng(17.7)**	**统一 President(17.3)**
16~24 岁 Age	58	康师傅 Kangshifu(51.7)	统一 President(22.4)	华丰 Huafeng(12.1)
25~34 岁 Age	78	康师傅 Kangshifu(56.4)	华丰 Huafeng(14.1) 统一 President(14.1)	福满多 Fumanduo(10.3)
35~44 岁 Age	59	康师傅 Kangshifu(45.8)	华丰 Huafeng(27.1)	统一 President(18.6)
45~54 岁 Age	36	康师傅 Kangshifu(58.3)	华丰 Huafeng(16.7)	统一 President(13.9)
55~60 岁 Age	18	康师傅 Kangshifu(50.0)	华丰 Huafeng(22.2)	统一 President(16.7)
女性 Female	**255**	**康师傅 Kangshifu(45.9)**	**统一 President(17.6)**	**华丰 Huafeng(16.5)**
16~24 岁 Age	59	康师傅 Kangshifu(54.2)	华丰 Huafeng(11.9) 统一 President(11.9)	福满多 Fumanduo(10.2)
25~34 岁 Age	79	康师傅 Kangshifu(32.9)	统一 President(25.3)	华丰 Huafeng(22.8)
35~44 岁 Age	71	康师傅 Kangshifu(47.9)	统一 President(18.3)	华丰 Huafeng(9.9)
45~54 岁 Age	34	康师傅 Kangshifu(52.9)	华丰 Huafeng(23.5)	统一 President(11.8)
55~60 岁 Age	12	康师傅 Kangshifu(58.3)	华丰 Huafeng(16.7)	福满多 Fumanduo(8.3) 统一 President(8.3) 好劲道 Haojindao(8.3)

8-4 理想品牌排名/ Ranking of the Ideal Brands

排名 Brand Ranking	品牌 Brands	人数 Number	百分比 Percent
1	康师傅 Kangshifu	317	52.7
2	统一 President	111	18.5
3	华丰 Huafeng	81	13.5
4	福满多 Fumanduo	35	5.8
5	好劲道 Haojindao	8	1.3

n=601

8-5 样本、男性各年龄层、女性各年龄层最近三个月有无购买的比例/ Purchasing in the Last Three Months by the Whole Sample, Age and Gender Groups

	人数 Number	买过 yes	没买过 no
样本 Sample	601	82.7	17.3
男性 Male	299	82.9	17.1
16~24 岁 Age	64	89.1	10.9
25~34 岁 Age	89	87.6	12.4
35~44 岁 Age	76	80.3	19.7
45~54 岁 Age	46	80.4	19.6
55~60 岁 Age	24	62.5	37.5
女性 Female	302	82.5	17.5
16~24 岁 Age	64	84.4	15.6
25~34 岁 Age	90	85.6	14.4
35~44 岁 Age	76	94.7	5.3
45~54 岁 Age	48	66.7	33.3
55~60 岁 Age	24	58.3	41.7

8-6 样本、男性各年龄层、女性各年龄层最近三个月的食用频率/ Frequencies of Consuming Instant Noodles in the Last Three Months by the Whole Sample, Age and Gender Groups

	人数 Number	天天吃 daily	一周3次或以上 3 times or over a week	一周1~2次 once or twice a week	一个月2~3次 2 or 3 times a month	一个月1次或以下 once a month or below	没吃过 never
样本 Sample	601	2.8	13.1	33.3	25.0	10.0	15.8
男性 Male	299	3.0	12.7	33.1	24.4	10.7	16.1
16~24 岁 Age	64	3.1	15.6	40.6	23.4	9.4	7.8
25~34 岁 Age	89	3.4	18.0	42.7	15.7	7.9	12.4
35~44 岁 Age	76	1.3	9.2	23.7	30.3	13.2	22.4
45~54 岁 Age	46	2.2	8.7	26.1	30.4	13.0	19.6
55~60 岁 Age	24	8.3	4.2	20.8	29.2	12.5	25.0
女性 Female	302	2.6	13.6	33.4	25.5	9.3	15.6
16~24 岁 Age	64	6.3	20.3	34.4	23.4	7.8	7.8
25~34 岁 Age	90	1.1	7.8	38.9	30.0	10.0	12.2
35~44 岁 Age	76	3.9	19.7	40.8	23.7	5.3	6.6
45~54 岁 Age	48	0.0	8.3	20.8	27.1	14.6	29.2
55~60 岁 Age	24	0.0	8.3	12.5	16.7	12.5	50.0

8-7 样本、男性各年龄层、女性各年龄层的品牌习惯/ Brand Habit in Consuming Instant Noodles by the Whole Sample, Age and Gender Groups

	人数 Number	基本固定食用一个牌子 used in only one brand	比较固定地食用两个或三个牌子 used in two or three brands	基本上没有固定哪个牌子 no brand preference
样本 Sample	505	41.4	42.8	15.8
男性 Male	250	41.6	46.0	12.4
16~24 岁 Age	58	37.9	55.2	6.9
25~34 岁 Age	78	37.2	52.6	10.3
35~44 岁 Age	59	47.5	37.3	15.3
45~54 岁 Age	37	43.2	40.5	16.2
55~60 岁 Age	18	50.0	27.8	22.2
女性 Female	255	41.2	39.6	19.2
16~24 岁 Age	59	28.8	54.2	16.9
25~34 岁 Age	79	43.0	43.0	13.9
35~44 岁 Age	71	49.3	25.8	23.9
45~54 岁 Age	34	44.1	25.5	29.4
55~60 岁 Age	12	33.3	58.3	8.3

8-8 选择该类商品的考虑因素/ Ranking of the Considerations in Purchasing

注：本题为多选题，合计百分比超过100%(Multiple answers)

排名 Ranking	考虑因素 Considerations	人次 Person-time	百分比 Percent
1	口味好 pleasant taste	391	77.6
2	价格适中 reasonable price	207	41.1
3	有名的牌子 famous brand	137	27.2
4	生产日期 date of producing	128	25.4
5	购买方便 easy to buy	113	22.4
6	只是由于习惯 out of habit	40	7.9
7	广告影响 influence of advertising	36	7.1
8	有优惠条件 with preferential terms	15	3.0
9	包装吸引人 appealing package	12	2.4
9	朋友推荐 introduction of friends	12	2.4
10	售货员介绍 introduced by the shop assistants	5	1.0
11	单位发的 offered by the working unit	2	0.4
12	其它 others	1	0.2

n=504

8-9 样本、男性各年龄层、女性各年龄层最常食用的种类/ Kinds of the Consumed Instant Noodles by the Whole Sample, Age and Gender Groups

注：本题为多选题，合计百分比超过 100%(Multiple answers)

	人数 Number	牛肉 beef	鸡肉 chicken	排骨 spareribs	海鲜 seafood	炸酱 fried bean sauce	三鲜 3-flavored noodles	蔬菜 vegetable	其它 others
样本 Sample	505	72.1	5.5	17.0	11.9	13.5	23.4	2.0	0.2
男性 Male	250	72.8	4.0	14.4	10.8	12.0	24.4	2.0	0.4
16~24 岁 Age	58	70.7	8.6	22.4	15.5	13.8	19.0	0.0	0.0
25~34 岁 Age	78	74.4	5.1	15.4	9.0	16.7	19.2	1.3	1.3
35~44 岁 Age	59	72.9	1.7	6.8	8.5	8.5	33.9	5.1	0.0
45~54 岁 Age	37	75.7	0.0	13.5	10.8	5.4	24.3	2.7	0.0
55~60 岁 Age	18	66.7	0.0	11.1	11.1	11.1	33.3	0.0	0.0
女性 Female	255	71.4	7.1	19.6	12.9	14.9	22.4	2.0	0.0
16~24 岁 Age	59	62.7	6.8	23.7	11.9	32.2	20.3	1.7	0.0
25~34 岁 Age	79	72.2	7.6	16.5	16.5	12.7	22.8	5.1	0.0
35~44 岁 Age	71	70.4	8.5	22.5	14.1	11.3	18.3	0.0	0.0
45~54 岁 Age	34	82.4	5.9	14.7	8.8	2.9	29.4	0.0	0.0
55~60 岁 Age	12	83.3	0.0	16.7	0.0	0.0	33.3	0.0	0.0

8-10 样本、男性各年龄层、女性各年龄层最常食用的包装形式/ Types of Package of the Consumed Instant Noodles by the Whole Sample, Age and Gender Groups

注：本题为多选题，合计百分比超过 100%(Multiple answers)

	人数 Number	大碗装 big bowl	普通碗装 regular bowl	大袋装 big bag	普通袋装 regular bag	杯装 cupped	其它 others
样本 Sample	505	13.5	8.3	30.5	72.9	0.8	0.2
男性 Male	250	14.4	8.4	29.2	72.8	0.4	0.0
16~24 岁 Age	58	12.1	12.1	32.8	70.7	0.0	0.0
25~34 岁 Age	78	17.9	11.5	32.1	66.7	1.3	0.0
35~44 岁 Age	59	15.3	5.1	28.8	72.9	0.0	0.0
45~54 岁 Age	37	13.5	2.7	24.3	83.8	0.0	0.0
55~60 岁 Age	18	5.6	5.6	16.7	83.3	0.0	0.0
女性 Female	255	12.5	8.2	31.8	72.9	1.2	0.4
16~24 岁 Age	59	16.9	11.9	35.6	55.9	1.7	0.0
25~34 岁 Age	79	15.2	2.5	32.9	75.9	0.0	0.0
35~44 岁 Age	71	7.0	12.7	39.4	74.6	1.4	0.0
45~54 岁 Age	34	11.8	8.8	14.7	82.4	2.9	2.9
55~60 岁 Age	12	8.3	0.0	8.3	100.0	0.0	0.0

8-11 样本、男性各年龄层、女性各年龄层最常食用的方式/ Ways of the Consumed Instant noodles by the Whole Sample, Age and Gender Groups

	人数 Number	冲泡 steep it in boiling water	煮 boil it	干吃 eat directly	拌着吃 mix it with others
样本 Sample	503	18.1	78.9	2.2	0.8
男性 Male	250	19.6	76.8	2.4	1.2
16~24 岁 Age	58	22.4	72.4	5.2	0.0
25~34 岁 Age	78	15.4	80.8	1.3	2.6
35~44 岁 Age	59	20.3	76.3	3.4	0.0
45~54 岁 Age	37	21.6	75.7	0.0	2.7
55~60 岁 Age	18	22.2	77.8	0.0	0.0
女性 Female	253	16.6	81.0	2.0	0.4
16~24 岁 Age	59	18.6	78.0	1.7	1.7
25~34 岁 Age	79	17.7	79.7	2.5	0.0
35~44 岁 Age	70	11.4	85.7	2.9	0.0
45~54 岁 Age	33	15.2	84.8	0.0	0.0
55~60 岁 Age	12	33.3	66.7	0.0	0.0

8-12 样本、男性各年龄层、女性各年龄层最常食用的场合/ Settings of Consumption by the Whole Sample, Age and Gender Groups

	人数 Number	早餐 breakfast	午餐 lunch	晚餐 supper	宵夜 evening snack	加班时 when work overtime	不固定 no regular	其他 others
样本 Sample	489	45.2	19.4	7.8	10.4	9.6	7.6	0.0
男性 Male	241	46.1	13.7	7.9	13.7	10.8	7.9	0.0
16~24 岁 Age	55	50.9	10.9	7.3	14.5	7.3	9.1	0.0
25~34 岁 Age	75	40.0	18.7	5.3	17.3	12.0	6.7	0.0
35~44 岁 Age	56	57.1	10.7	10.7	10.7	3.6	7.1	0.0
45~54 岁 Age	37	43.2	10.8	8.1	10.8	21.6	5.4	0.0
55~60 岁 Age	18	27.8	16.7	11.1	11.1	16.7	16.7	0.0
女性 Female	248	44.4	25.0	7.7	7.3	8.5	7.3	0.0
16~24 岁 Age	57	42.1	19.3	10.5	7.0	12.3	8.8	0.0
25~34 岁 Age	77	48.1	27.3	3.9	7.8	9.1	3.9	0.0
35~44 岁 Age	70	52.9	21.4	8.6	7.1	5.7	4.3	0.0
45~54 岁 Age	32	31.3	28.1	9.4	6.3	6.3	18.8	0.0
55~60 岁 Age	12	16.7	50.0	8.3	8.3	8.3	8.3	0.0

8-13 重度消费者人口分布/ Demographics of the Heavy Consumers

	人数 Number	16-24 岁 Age	25-34 岁 Age	35-44 岁 Age	45-54 岁 Age	55-60 岁 Age
样本 Sample	296	26.0	33.8	25.3	10.5	4.4
男性 Male	146	26.0	39.0	17.8	11.6	5.5
天天吃 daily	9	22.2	33.3	11.1	11.1	22.2
一周 3 次或以上 3 times or over a week	38	26.3	42.1	18.4	10.5	2.6
一周 1~2 次 once or twice a week	99	26.3	38.4	13.2	12.1	5.1
女性 Female	150	26.0	28.7	32.7	9.3	3.3
天天吃 daily	8	50.0	12.5	37.5	0.0	0.0
一周 3 次或以上 3 times or over a week	41	31.7	17.1	36.6	9.8	4.9
一周 1~2 次 once or twice a week	101	21.8	34.7	33.7	9.9	3.0

8-14 不同消费者层的常用品牌/ The Most Frequently Used Brands by Market Segments

8-14-1 时尚流行指标/ Fads Popular Index

	人数 Number	第一品牌及百分比 1st/ percent	第二品牌及百分比 2nd/ percent	第三品牌及百分比 3rd/ percent
样本 Sample	504	**康师傅 Kangshifu(49.2)**	**统一 President(17.5)**	**华丰 Huafeng(17.1)**
平实生活指向 simple living orientation	228	康师傅 Kangshifu(48.7)	华丰 Huafeng(19.3)	统一 President(15.4)
时尚流行指向 fashion orientation	276	康师傅 Kangshifu(49.6)	统一 President(19.2)	华丰 Huafeng(15.2)

8-14-2 广告态度指标/ Advertising Attitude Index

	人数 Number	第一品牌及百分比 1st/ percent	第二品牌及百分比 2nd/ percent	第三品牌及百分比 3rd/ percent
样本 Sample	504	**康师傅 Kangshifu(49.2)**	**统一 President(17.5)**	**华丰 Huafeng(17.1)**
广告淡漠指向 indifferent orientation	137	康师傅 Kangshifu(48.9)	统一 President(16.8)	华丰 Huafeng(15.3)
中间层 medium	306	康师傅 Kangshifu(50.3)	统一 President(18.3)	华丰 Huafeng(17.0)
信赖广告指向 loyal orientation	61	康师傅 Kangshifu(44.3)	华丰 Huafeng(21.3)	统一 President(14.8)

8-14-3 饮食健康指标/ Foods & Drink Quality Index

	人数 Number	第一品牌及百分比 1st/ percent	第二品牌及百分比 2nd/ percent	第三品牌及百分比 3rd/ percent
样本 Sample	504	**康师傅 Kangshifu(49.2)**	**统一 President(17.5)**	**华丰 Huafeng(17.1)**
饮食"温饱"指向 "basic" orientation	146	康师傅 Kangshifu(52.7)	华丰 Huafeng(18.5)	统一 President(17.1)
中间层 medium	233	康师傅 Kangshifu(47.2)	统一 President(19.3)	华丰 Huafeng(14.6)
健康营养指向 health & nutrition orientation	125	康师傅 Kangshifu(48.8)	华丰 Huafeng(20.0)	统一 President(14.4)

8-15 重度消费者的消费者层构成/ The Composition of the Heavy Consumers

8-15-1 时尚流行指标/ Fads Popular Index

	人数 Number	平实生活指向 simple living orientation	时尚流行指向 fashion orientation
样本 Sample	296	41.9	58.1
天天吃 daily	17	52.9	47.1
一周 3 次或以上 3 times or over a week	79	40.5	59.5
一周 1~2 次 once or twice a week	200	41.5	58.5

8-15-2 广告态度指标/ Advertising Attitude Index

	人数 Number	广告淡漠指向 indifferent orientation	中间层 medium	信赖广告指向 loyal orientation
样本 Sample	296	27.4	60.5	12.2
天天吃 daily	17	41.2	41.2	17.6
一周 3 次或以上 3 times or over a week	79	29.1	58.2	12.7
一周 1～2 次 once or twice a week	200	25.5	63.0	11.5

8-15-3 饮食健康指标/ Foods & Drink Quality Index

	人数 Number	饮食“温饱”指向 "basic" orientation	中间层 medium	健康营养指向 health & nutrition orientation
样本 Sample	296	27.7	46.6	25.7
天天吃 daily	17	29.4	23.5	47.1
一周 3 次或以上 3 times or over a week	79	29.1	46.8	24.1
一周 1～2 次 once or twice a week	200	27.0	48.5	24.5

第六篇　饮料
Part VI　Beverage

- 碳酸饮料　Carbonated Beverage
- 包装水　Purified or Mineral Water
- 茶饮料　Tealike Drink
- 纯果汁　Pure Juice
- 果汁/果味饮料　Fruit-flavored Beverage

饮　料

1999 年初在中国的"球场"上爆发了一场引人注目的"饮料大战"——前有可口可乐和百事可乐之争，后是百事可乐和国产饮料健力宝因为冠名权的问题"打"起来。这场大战给我们一些启示：随着中国经济的发展，饮料市场的竞争愈发激烈，一度不可一世的洋饮料已经越发感受到来自民族饮料的"威胁"。

我国饮料工业是建国后特别是改革开放以来迅速崛起的新兴工业。50 年来，饮料工业已发展成为具有一定规模和基础、能较好适应市场需要的重要食品行业之一。据 1997 年不完全统计，饮料行业共有企业 3123 家，固定资产净值 174.2 亿元，饮料总产量 1069 万吨，销售收入 335.5 亿元，利税总额 29.14 亿元。到 1998 年总产量已达 1250 万吨，比建国初期增长 2500 多倍。改革开放的 20 年间，我国饮料的产量平均每年都以 20%以上的速度递增，并提前 3 年实现 2000 年规划目标 1000 万吨的任务，成为我国食品工业中发展速度最快的工业之一。行业结构也渐趋完善，饮料品种已由单一的汽水发展成为 10 大类产品，包括碳酸饮料、纯果汁及果汁饮料、茶饮料和特殊用途饮料等。目前，碳酸饮料、瓶装饮用水和果蔬汁饮料已形成我国饮料工业的三个最大门类。同时，饮料产品的质量水平也大幅度提高，其中矿泉水的产品抽样合格率由 90 年代初的不足 30%提高到 1997 年的 78.2%。目前全国饮料设备年生产能力已达 2000 万吨，拥有国际 90 年代先进水平生产线，各种饮料生产设备的国产化步伐也大大加快。

近年来，随着企业改革的不断深入，饮料行业在调整企业结构、实现生产规模化、集约化经营的进程中也迈出了坚实的一步，组建了一批以市场需求和产业政策为导向，以高科技、高附加值为依托的企业集团。如广东健力宝集团、杭州娃哈哈集团等，而 1998 年在中央台频繁露面的海南养生堂集团以"农夫山泉"与"娃哈哈"、"乐百氏"一起"统治"了水世界。1999 年中国饮料工业协会评选出"中国饮料工业十强"：今日集团、健力宝集团、梅林正广和集团、汇源集团、旭日集团、露露集团、娃哈哈集团、椰树集团、益力矿泉水公司、怡宝食品饮料有限公司。"十强"企业 1998 年饮料生产总量为 320 万吨，占全国饮料生产量的 26.71%，销量收入、利税分别占到全国饮料行业的 32%、46.9%，生产集中度较高。

行业结构和管理体制的合理发展促成了今夏的饮料市场竞争激烈。在良性竞争中，价格成为厂家占领市场的重要手段。据资料统计，今年市场的总体价格比去年要下降 10%左右。如健力宝、可口可乐、雪碧、椰树椰子汁等老牌饮品的每箱批发价现为 41、53.5、54、63 和 31.5 元，分别比去年下降了 13.4%、4.6%、3.7%、5.8%、26.9%。据资料显示，在价格战和促销战的带动下，产销量比去年增长 10%左右。功能型果汁饮料、奶汁饮料、纯净饮用水、无色碳酸饮料、天然矿泉水 5 种饮品成为市场主导产品。

我国饮料企业在 1999 年的另一重要策略调整是品牌意识在加强。农夫山泉作为较新的品牌，从包装形式的创新、包装规格的独树一帜，到广告的新鲜幽默、全方位的品牌意识使其在市场上迅速走红。娃哈哈和旭日升在扩大主导品牌生产规模的同时，相继推出了一系列子品牌。相比之下，娃哈哈的"非常系列"推出较早，更被市场认可；而旭日升的"高兴就好"和"天之情"由于推出过快，且"旭日升"本身尚处于创牌阶段，因此在今年并未引起太多注意，但明年情况还未可知。健力宝集团在过去几年中曾推出过几个新产品，但品牌不明确；今年推出的茶饮料获得专家一致好评，新产品乐臣牌系列果味水适应了国际最新潮流，在今后将是掀起市场风浪的潜力产品。

今年盛夏饮料热卖，从消费者的角度来看，其选择余地大、消费观念也逐步成熟。各饮料企业在注重自我产品调整的基础上，也应重视影响消费者选购的主客观因素。饮料的销售定位很大程度上取决于消费者的心理因素。饮料厂家应认真研究不同地区、不同性别、年龄、类型、不同消费水平的人的消费心理和消费习惯，从而推出适合自己目标消费群的产品，提高市场占有率。

1998 年中国主要城市居民消费品调查饮料品牌市场占有率（单位：%）

排位比例 / 产品种类	第一位		第二位		第三位	
	品牌名称	所占比例	品牌名称	所占比例	品牌名称	所占比例
碳酸饮料	可口可乐	48.2	雪碧	18.4	百事可乐	13.6
果汁饮料	露露	11.1	椰树	9.0	汇源	8.2
功能性饮料	健力宝	43.8	红牛	22.9	绿之源	0.8
包装茶饮料	旭日升	28.3	统一	12.9	康师傅	9.9
包装水	娃哈哈	22.5	乐百氏	11.5	农夫山泉	8.6

（资料来源：《中国消费者报》99.1.1）

同时我们也应清楚的看到，我国饮料工业水平和世界发达国家相比还有很大差距。目前，我国人均饮料消费量仅为 8 公斤/年，为世界平均水平的 1/5，是西欧发达国家的 1/24。从近 20 年的发展来看，21 世纪我国饮料工业的发展潜力仍是很大的。

据世界饮料发展研讨会的调查，当今全球饮料业有新动向：

一是世界饮料的消费呈逐年增加的趋势，而且增长势头越来越大，这与世界人口增加和经济增长有关。

二是饮料市场的多样化。主要表现在饮料品种日趋繁多、饮料消费群体发生变化（主要表现在消费群体不再固守原来的消费习惯和偏好）。

三是消费习惯在逐渐趋向相同。人们日益关注健康和环境，不喜欢糖和添加剂含量高的饮料。

四是充气饮料、瓶装水和果汁饮料的消费量增加。1997 年度世界果汁饮料消费量约为 3980 万吨，到 2000 年，预计消费量将达 4610 万吨。

五是保健饮料无法在短期内形成规模。

六是新品种接连进入市场。但应注意消费者需要的是注重天然和健康、有益环境保护的新型饮料。

七是 2000 年后，世界饮料产销的重点将转向亚洲。

在全球饮料业发展大方向的驱动下，随着消费者消费观念的成熟，我国饮料工业的类型品种和包装形式将会更加丰富，各大类饮料比重将会更加合理，得到全面的发展。

碳酸饮料

碳酸饮料在我国成熟较早，早期以汽水为主，随着国际饮料公司的进入和人们消费观念、消费习惯的转变，碳酸饮料也逐步转向可乐为主的行业结构。

1999 年的碳酸饮料也受到了饮料多样化的冲击。来势汹汹的果汁饮料、功能性饮料对碳酸饮料构成了巨大的威胁。许多人认为碳酸饮料是在走下坡路。据了解，目前碳酸饮料所占市场分额在 30%左右，这个比例比前几年确有不少下降。但市场份额的下降并不意味着这类饮料不行了，前几年碳酸饮料主要是价格极低的一般汽水，如今提升为中高档次的各种罐装精致可乐、雪碧等，因此销售总额并未降低多少。市场专家指出，碳酸饮料所具有的强劲解渴功能，是其它饮料不能比拟的。

碳酸饮料的中高档次产品前几年曾一度是国外品牌的天下，可口可乐和百事可乐稳居可乐市场的前列。然而从 1998 年下半年开始，这一情况发生了明显的变化，中国品牌除健力宝外，又有一批后起之秀的知名度迅速提高，使“民族兵团”实力大增，诸如非常可乐、汾煌可乐等的质量、口感、味道都不亚于国外品牌。同时，由于可口可乐近期在国际上出现的质量问题，大大影响了它的声誉，在各地的销量均有不同幅度的下降，这也给民族品牌提供了一个发展的契机。从目前的状况看，消费者已越来越认同国产品牌的各种碳酸饮料。

总之，竞争形式的好转、市场蕴藏的潜力、成熟的消费习惯是看好碳酸饮料市场前景的重要因素。

包装水

包装饮用水包括矿泉水和纯净水两个大类。矿泉水含有对人体有益的矿物质和微量元素，符合人们日益增长的保健需要，今后会有更大发展。纯净水是我国一些地区由于水质污染应运而生的产品类型，是指以符合生活饮用水卫生标准的水作为水源，采用蒸馏法、去离子法、离子交换法或反渗透法等去除水中的无机或有机物质，通过臭氧装置进行灭菌，并在密闭灌装条件下灌装的饮用水。

包装水业是随着人们生活水平和对生活水平要求的提高而逐步壮大起来的。70 年代，我国只有青岛崂山一家矿泉水厂，并且规模和产量都不大。而现在人们对自身健康状况的重视使水市场迅速扩张；饮用水生产企业也在全国范围内发展起来。“纯净水”、“蒸馏水”、“太空水”逐鹿市场。纯净水后来居上，成为近两年来的头号新宠。包装饮用水市场基本形成了纯净水和矿泉水两强相争的局面。1999 年，更多的大型、合资纯净水企业开始进入北京市场，市场竞争将更加激烈。目前我国饮水生产企业已经超过 2000 家，年销售饮用水 40 亿升，年销售纯净水就达到 29 亿升，而广东则是饮水产品的供应和消费大省，只矿泉水和纯净水两项产量就达到 110 万吨。这个时侯，纯净水市场如何走向规范将是政府部门、生产企业及消费者最关心的问题。

首当其冲的就是饮用水的质量问题。1999 年第二季度国家质量技术监督局对瓶装饮用纯净水进行了质量抽查，仅有六成的瓶装水合格，其中“娃哈哈”纯净水、“乐百氏”纯净水、“康师傅”纯净水、“健力宝”纯净水的各项指标全部合格。这些企业的设备先进、质量体系健全，产品质量较好。而大量不合格产品的存在主要在于生产厂家的管理漏洞、质量观念淡漠和生产技术落后。

随着我国环境保护工作的开展，水质的逐步改善，纯净水将降温。并逐步被矿泉水和泉水等优质天然水所取代。矿泉水今后也会向多样化发展，多种加香和加少量果汁的矿泉水或天然水将会极大丰富我国的饮用水市场。

果汁饮料

我国果汁饮料业起步于 80 年代初，经过十几年的不断发展，现已形成了以汇源、露露、椰树、圆之梦等为主的几个名牌企业，构成了强大的市场阵容。

我国果汁饮料与其他饮料相比起点较低，还没有经历急剧扩张阶段，但这几年稳扎稳打，已经让果汁饮料的发展速度赶上或略高于正处于成熟期的碳酸饮料和其它饮料。去年我国的果汁饮料产量达 150 万吨，出口量近 8 万吨。果汁工业技术亦逐步拉近与世界先进水平的差距。汇源集团先后从德国 PKL 公司和瑞典利乐公司引进 20 余条世界一流的果汁灌装生产线，解决了果汁生产对机器设备的严格要求，同时采用了国际上最科学的无菌包装技术，使我国的饮料包装上升为无菌纸盒包装，开辟了饮料包装行业的新纪元；果汁质量也上了一个新台阶，无论从口感、营养、品质、风格等各个方面都堪与国际一流果汁相媲美。

近几年我国果汁饮料之所以发展较快，首先，得益于国民经济持续稳定增长拉动着果汁饮料的消费需求。有关部门去年对全国 12 个大中城市的调查显示，有 39.1%的居民饮用过果汁饮料。其次，从全球范围来看，饮料产品日趋多元化。碳酸饮料比重下降，果汁饮料、功能性饮料的比重上升。再次，随着居民收入的提高，生活的改善，对营养和保健越来越重视，天然绿色食品的消费热潮方兴未艾，果汁饮料的发展顺应了这一潮流。据此调查显示，有 1.8%的居民每天都饮用果汁饮料，有 3.8%的居民每周饮用 4—6 次，有 30%的居民每周饮用 1—3 次。（数据摘自《信息与市场报》99.7.19）

目前，我国果汁饮料的生产销售均集中在广东、海南、福建、浙江等东南沿海省份，而这些地区不单是最大的生产地还是最大的消费地区。生产缺口最大的是江苏、湖南、四川、安徽、湖北等省份，说明上述地区具有相当的市场开拓潜力。业内人士对今年我国的果汁饮料需求市场持乐观态度，预测全年的产量在 174 万吨左右，比去年有约 12%的增幅，销售收入在 85 亿元左右，同比也有一定增幅。出口量还会有 10%左右的增长。

尽管果汁饮料发展趋势很好，但市场上仍尚存诸多不尽如人意之处——首先，由于利润高市场好，各地生产一涌而上，再加上假冒伪劣饮料和某些品牌果汁含量过低误导消费，使市场一度出现滑坡；其次，目前有的果汁饮料包装偏大、价格过高，影响了果汁饮料的普及；再次，不少产品还存在口味一般、糖度过高的缺点；最后，我国水果加工量仅占水果总产量的20%左右，与世界发达国家的50—60%相比还有很大差距。

以上的各种问题也正是果汁饮料业发展的契机所在。事实上，已有专家就果汁饮料的开发提出了新思路。

一是以现有纯果汁的品质优势吸引消费者。

二是强调营养强化特点，吸引具有健康意识的消费者。

三是调整果汁含量，降低成本，吸引对价格敏感的消费者。

我国是世界上水果产量最多的国家，提高水果加工技术，将这一得天独厚的条件转化为市场的优势。这将是一个极有发展前途的行业。

Beverage

The competition among beverages in early 1999 is conspicuous. Both the competition between Coca-Cola and Pepsi and the fight for the sponsorship for football matches between Pepsi and Jianlibao catch people's attention. What is implied is that with the development of Chinese economy, the competition among beverages becomes keener and keener; meanwhile the once unexcelled role of foreign beverage begins to shake and face some "threat" because of the development of Chinese national beverages.

Chinese beverage industry began to spring up after the liberation, esp. after the reform campaign and the establishment of open-up policy, and it has become one of the important branches of food industry with a certain scope and basement, and adapt to the need of the market. According to some statistics of 1997, there were altogether 3123 beverage companies with the total fixed assets of 17.42 billion RMB, the total output came to 10.69 million tons, the sales revenue was 33.55 billion RMB and the tax revenue was is 2.914 billion RMB. By the year of 1998, the total output had come to 12.5 million tons. That was 2.5 thousand times more than that of the starting period after liberation. During the 20 years of reform, the annual beverage output increased by 20% and has, 3 years in advanced, achieved 10 million tons, the anticipated goal of the year of 2000. The beverage industry has by now become one of the fast-speed industrial branches. Its industrial structure is becoming better, originally soda water was the only beverage but by now there have been 10 kinds of beverage, including carbonated beverage, fruit juice and juice beverage, tea and beverage for special purpose. The three largest-scaled branches are carbonated beverage, bottled water and vegetable or fruit juice. Meanwhile the quality has been improved by a great deal. According to the result of the sampling survey in the early 1990s, there were only less than 30% of the mineral water that meet the qualified standard, but in the year of 1997, 78.2% of the mineral water was qualified. The equipment can produce 20 million tons of beverage annually by now and the nationalization of equipment was also accelerated. The production lines are of the quality of the international standard in 1990s.

In recent years, with the deep going reform, beverage industry has been greatly developed in the adjustment of industrial structure and enlargement production scale and intensive management, some enterprise groups based on high-technique and added value and market-oriented and following the government policy for industry have been set up, such as Jianlibao Group in Guangdo and Wahaha Group in Hangzhou. The Nongfushanquan produced by Yangshentang in Hainan whose commercials often appear on CCTV takes the leading role with Wahaha and Robust in the field of bottled water. In 1999, Chinese Beverage Industry Association chose 10 top beverage enterprises: Today Group, Jianlibao Group, Meiling Acqurius Group, Huiyuan Group, Xurisheng Group, Lolo Group, Wahaha Group, Coconut palm Group, Yili Mineral Water Company, Yibao Food & Beverage Co.Ltd. Their output of 1998 was 3.2 million tons, 26.71% of the total national beverage output, 32% of the whole sale revenue and 46.9% of the tax.

The stable development of industrial structure and management system lead to the keen competition of this summer and price becomes an important factor for competitors to hold more shares at the market. According to the statistical data, the general price of this year is 10% lower than that of last year, e.g. the wholesale prices of Jianlibao, Coca cola, Sprite and chestnut juice are 41, 53.5, 54, 63, 31.5 RMB respectively which are 13.4%, 4.6%, 3.7%, 5.8%, 26.9% lower than that of the previous year. Motivated by the competition in price and promotion activities, the output and sale volume increases 10%. Functional juice beverage, milk beverage, purified water, carbonated beverage and natural mineral water are the five leading items.

Another strategic adjustment in beverage business in 1999 is to enforce the brand. Being a new brand, Nongfu ShanQuan has achieved success in a short period due to the innovation of its package, uniqueness of its size, novelty and humor of its ads and the comprehensive means to create its own brand. Comparatively speaking, Fortune series of Wahaha had already been accepted since it was brought forth much earlier whereas the series of Happy is OK and Heaven's Love did not attracted much attention for they were brought forth before careful preparation. Jianlibao Group once brought forth several new products without much emphasis on its own brand. Tea beverage of this year generally got high scores from the experts and the fruit flavored water, new brand lecheng exactly catches up the international beverage trend and is considered potential in the future.

Beverage sells well this summer due to its various choices of tastes and formula and consumers' mature concept about consumption. The beverage enterprises should pay more attention to adjust its own products and should care more for both the subjective and objective factors that influence the choice of the consumers. Since the sale positioning of beverage is largely decided by the consumers' attitude, the beverage enterprises should carefully study the consumers' psychology and habits of different region, sex, age, etc, so as to make forth the product fitting for certain group of consumers and to hold more shares at the market.

Here are the top brands found in 1998' the consumer foods research on Chinese urban inhabitants.

Percent of Ranking / Product Category	First		Second		Third	
	Brand	Proportional rate	Brand	Proportional rate	Brand	Proportional rate
Carbonated Beverage	Coca-cola	48.2	Sprite	18.4	Pepsi	13.6
Fruit Juice	LoLo	11.1	Coconut palm	9.0	Huiyuan	8.2
Functional Beverage	Jianli Bao	43.8	Red Ox	22.9	Luzhi yuan	0.8
Bagged Tea	XuRi Sheng	28.3	President	12.9	Kanshifu	9.9
Packed Water	Wahaha	22.5	Robust	11.5	Nongfu Shanquan	8.6

(Sources: *China's Consumers Paper*, Jan 1 99.)

We should realize that there is still a long distance between the level of our beverage industry and that of the developed countries. Average Chinese people consumes averages 8 kg of beverage per year, 1/5 of the international average amount and 1/24 of the amount of the developed countries in Western Europe. In 21st century there is still great potential for the developing beverage business.

According to the research by the International Beverage Development Seminar, the new trends of international beverage industry are as follows:

1. The world consumption of beverage is increased yearly by a larger margin, that is caused by the increase of world population and development of economy.
2. There is a variety of beverage market, featuring in the change of consumption groups and the increase of product lines (It is mainly revealed by the fact that the consumption groups do not cling to their original consumption habit and preference any longer).
3. The taste and preference of consumers tend to be similar and the beverages with much sugar or food ingredient are losing favor among the consumers who care more for health and environment.
4. The increasing consumption of carbonated beverage, bottled water and juice. The juice consumption reached about 39.8 million tons in the world in 1997 and it is anticipated to be 46.1 million tons in 2000.
5. Diet beverage can not come to a large scale in a short period.
6. New products are introduced in succession. Attention should be paid to that what is needed by the consumers is the natural, healthy and environment protecting beverage.
7. The key region of beverage production and sale will be transferred to Asia after 2000.

Stimulated by the main development direction and classification the mature consumption concepts of the consumers, the beverage industry in China is expected to be rich in classification and package and the percentage of different class of beverage will be more reasonable. The whole beverage industry will comprehensively develop.

Carbonated Beverage

Carbonated beverage appears earlier than other kinds of beverage in China. Soda water, the major beverage at the very beginning, is now replaced by Coca-Cola with the entrance of international beverage companies and the change in people's consumption idea and habits.

But the role of carbonated beverage at the market is threatened in 1999 by the diversity of beverage including fruit juice, functional drinks etc. Appear one after another. Some people think that carbonated beverage is declining. It now holds 30% share at the market, much lower than previous years. But it does not mean the end of the carbonated beverage. The bottled or tinned Coca-cola or Sprite has taken the place of the low-price soda water. In this sense, the total sales do not decrease much. Meanwhile, the effect to quench thirst is far much better than any other beverage.

It is the foreign-brand beverage that dominates the carbonated beverage several years ago and Coca-cola and Pepsi are the leading roles. But things began to change in 1998 and the national brand, Jianlibao and some other promising new ones such as Fortune Cola and Fenhuang Cola, become well known and they can compete effectively with the foreign brands in terms of quality and taste. Meanwhile, the Coca-cola's problem in quality greatly affects its fame in the world, and its sale volume declines. National brands can make use of the chance for further development. It seems now that the consumers are more and more interested in homemade carbonated beverage.

In a word, the favorable conjuncture in competition, the potential of the beverage market and the maturity of consumption habit all contribute to a bright future for carbonated beverage industry.

Packed Water

The packed water includes mineral water and purified water. The former contains some useful mineral elements and micronutrient that meet people's increasing need for keeping health. It will get further development. The latter refers to bagged or bottled water after the distillation, anti-ion, ion-exchange reaction and anti-percolation to get rid of the inorganic and organic substances. It is packed in hermetic situation through anti-bacteria ozone equipment.

It appears to solve the problems resulted from water pollution. Packed water comes into being with the improvement of people's living standard. There was only one mineral water business in Laoshan Qingdao in 1970s with moderate scale and output. But today, people care more about their own health and this stimulates the enlargement of water market and springing up of drinking water factories throughout country. Purified water, distillated water, space water all bid for the leading role at the market. The purified water surpasses others and has become the new favorite of the consumers. The competition of packed water is mainly between purified water and mineral water. So more large-sized or joint ventures for producing pure begin to enter Beijing. The competition will be more intensive in 1999. The drinking water factories have by now come to more than 2000 and the annual sale volume is 4 billion liters, among which the purified water accounts for 2.9 billion liters. Guangdong, the biggest producer and market of packed water, produces mineral water and purified water 1.1 million tons. Under such condition, what the government, the business and the consumers care most is how to regulate the packed water market.

What is most important is the quality of packed water. According to the result of the sampling survey of bottled water conducted by National Quality Supervise Bureau, only 60% of the bottled water is qualified. All the indexes of Wahaha, Robust, Kangshifu, Jianlibao are qualified due to their advanced producing equipment, systematic quality supervision; the unqualified water is mainly produced by the enterprises which are lacking in management, quality supervision and technique.

The interest in purified water will be cooled down with the spread-out work of environment protection and the bettering of water quality. Purified water will be gradually replaced by mineral water and natural spring water of quality. There will be various mineral water and kinds of mineral water added with spice or fruit juice. The drinking water market will be greatly enriched.

Fruit Juice

The fruit juice industry in China started in the early 1980s and has set up some famous manufacturers such as Huiyuan. LoLo. Coconut palm, and Yuanzhimeng. They have formed a strong lineup after years of development.

The starting point of fruit juice is comparatively low and it has not experienced the period of expansion, but its speed of development has now caught up with or surpassed that of carbonated beverage and others, which are in their mature period. Last year, the output of fruit juice is 1.5 million tons and among which about 80 thousand tons were exported. The technique is getting closer to the world's advanced standards. Huiyuan Group imported more than 20 production lines from PKL Corp. of Germany and Lile Corp. of Sweden, which met the strict requirement for juice production machines. Meanwhile Huiyuan has adopted the most scientific aseptic manipulation and the germ free paper box. That was the milestone in beverage package in China and guaranteed the beverage quality. Huiyuan juice can compete with rival at any top fruit juice in terms of taste, nutrition, quality and style.

The fast development of fruit juice result from two factors. First of all, the stable and continuous national economic increases pull up the demand for more beverage goods. According to the research conducted in 12 cities, 39.1% of the inhabitants have tried fruit juice. Secondly, the beverage market becomes more and more colorful in the whole world. The proportion of carbonated drink declines whereas the proportion of juice and functional beverage increases. Thirdly, with the increase of income and improvement of living conditions, people pay more and more attention to nutrition and health and natural and non-polluted foods are coming to a fashion. The development of juice beverage complies with this trend. 1.8% of the respondents drink juice everyday and 3.8% of them drink it 4 to 6 times a week and 30% of them have it from 1 to 3 times a week (Sources: Information &Market, July, 19, 1999).

The production and sale of fruit juices now concentrate in Guangdong, Hainan, Fujian, Zhejiang provinces along China's coast. The insufficient in fruit juice in Jiangsu, Hunan, Sichuan, Anhui, Hubui implies great potential for local companies. Some experts point out optimistically that the anticipated output of this year can be 1.74 million tons, 12% more than that of last year. The total sales revenue in estimated 8.5 billion RMB, more than that of last year. The export volume is expected to increase by about 10%.

Though the developing trend is good, problems cannot be denied. First of all, the high profit margin and favorable market situation stimulate many factories to rush into the fruit juice industry, besides the counterfeit and poor quality products make the consumers lose confidence in fruit juice. These two factors lead to the declining of the sale. Secondly, the large packing unit and high price hinder the popularization of fruit juice. Thirdly, some fruit juice are tasteless or with too much sugar. At last, only 20% of the total fresh fruits are used to process fruit juice beverage whereas in the advanced countries, the figure can reach 50-60%. These problems mentioned above provide fruit juice industry with chance for further development. Actually, the experts have put forward the new ideas to help to explore new fruit juice.

1. To attract the consumers with the present fruit juice of high quality.

2. To focus on the nutrition of juice beverage so as to attract the consumers with health sense.

3. To adjust the juice content in the beverage so as to reduce production cost to attract the consumers who are sensitive to prices.

China abounds in fruits, to develop fruit processing technique and make full use of the resource can guarantee its dominant position at the market and there will be a bright future for the development of fruit juice industry.

1.碳酸饮料 / Carbonated Beverage

● 北京 / Beijing

1-1 最近三个月饮用频率的比例/ Proportion of the Sample Consuming Carbonated Beverage in the Last Three Months

	人数 Number	百分比 Percent
天天喝 daily	61	6.0
一周 3 次或以上 3 times or over a week	174	17.2
一周 1~2 次 once or twice a week	251	24.8
一个月 2～3 次 2 or 3 times a month	227	22.5
一个月 1 次或以下 once a month or below	72	7.1
没喝过 never	226	22.4

n=1011

1-2 最常用品牌排名/ Ranking of the Most Frequently Used Brands

排名 Brand Ranking	品牌 Brands	人数 Number	百分比 Percent
1	可口可乐 Coca-cola	462	59.2
2	雪碧 Sprite	89	11.4
3	百事可乐 Pepsi	62	7.9
4	北冰洋 Beibingyang	45	5.8
5	美年达 Mirinda	31	4.0
6	醒目 Smart	18	2.3
7	健力宝 Jianlibao	14	1.8
8	非常可乐 Future	7	0.9

n=780

1-3 样本、男性各年龄层、女性各年龄层的常用品牌/ The Most Frequently Used Brands by the Whole Sample, Age and Gender Groups

	人数 Number	第一品牌及百分比 1st/ percent	第二品牌及百分比 2nd/ percent	第三品牌及百分比 3rd/ percent	第四品牌及百分比 4th/ percent
样本 Sample	780	**可口可乐 Coca-cola(59.2)**	**雪碧 Sprite(11.4)**	**百事可乐 Pepsi(7.9)**	**北冰洋 Beibingyang(5.8)**
男性 Male	381	**可口可乐 Coca-cola(60.1)**	**雪碧 Sprite(10.2)**	**百事可乐 Pepsi(8.7)**	**北冰洋 Beibingyang(5.8)**
16~24 岁 Age	94	可口可乐 Coca-cola(58.5)	百事可乐 Pepsi(9.6) 北冰洋 Beibingyang(9.6)	醒目 Smart(5.3) 雪碧 Sprite(5.3)	健力宝 Jianlibao(3.2)
25~34 岁 Age	130	可口可乐 Coca-cola(65.4)	雪碧 Sprite(11.5)	百事可乐 Pepsi(6.9)	美年达 Mirinda(4.6)
35~44 岁 Age	96	可口可乐 Coca-cola(55.2)	百事可乐 Pepsi(11.5)	雪碧 Sprite(10.4)	北冰洋 Beibingyang(4.2)
45~54 岁 Age	41	可口可乐 Coca-cola(58.5)	北冰洋 Beibingyang(9.8) 雪碧 Sprite(9.8)	百事可乐 Pepsi(7.3)	美年达 Mirinda(4.9)
55~60 岁 Age	20	可口可乐 Coca-cola(60.0)	雪碧 Sprite(25.0)	北冰洋 Beibingyang(10.0)	百事可乐 Pepsi(5.0)
女性 Female	399	**可口可乐 Coca-cola(58.4)**	**雪碧 Sprite(12.5)**	**百事可乐 Pepsi(7.3)**	**北冰洋 Beibingyang(5.8)**
16~24 岁 Age	97	可口可乐 Coca-cola(54.6)	百事可乐 Pepsi(17.5)	美年达 Mirinda(6.2)	醒目 Smart(5.2)
25~34 岁 Age	124	可口可乐 Coca-cola(66.1)	雪碧 Sprite(11.3)	北冰洋 Beibingyang(5.6)	百事可乐 Pepsi(4.8)
35~44 岁 Age	96	可口可乐 Coca-cola(54.2)	雪碧 Sprite(18.8)	北冰洋 Beibingyang(8.3)	百事可乐 Pepsi(3.1) 健力宝 Jianlibao(3.1)
45~54 岁 Age	58	可口可乐 Coca-cola(58.6)	雪碧 Sprite(17.2)	北冰洋 Beibingyang(8.6)	百事可乐 Pepsi(5.2) 美年达 Mirinda(5.2)
55~60 岁 Age	24	可口可乐 Coca-cola(50.0)	雪碧 Sprite(25.0)	北冰洋 Beibingyang(8.3) 美年达 Mirinda(8.3)	非常可乐 Future(4.2) 北京 Beijing(4.2)

1-4 理想品牌排名/ Ranking of the Ideal Brands

排名 Brand Ranking	品牌 Brands	人数 Number	百分比 Percent
1	可口可乐 Coca-cola	495	48.9
2	雪碧 Sprite	90	8.9
3	北冰洋 Beibingyang	81	8.0
4	百事可乐 Pepsi	76	7.5
5	美年达 Mirinda	30	3.0
6	健力宝 Jianlibao	21	2.1
7	醒目 Smart	17	1.7
8	七喜 7-up	9	0.9

n=1012

1-5 样本、男性各年龄层、女性各年龄层最近三个月有无购买的比例/ Purchasing in the Last Three Months by the Whole Sample, Age and Gender Groups

	人数 Number	买过 yes	没买过 no
样本 Sample	1011	71.8	28.2
男性 Male	504	70.0	30.0
16~24 岁 Age	105	82.9	17.1
25~34 岁 Age	151	78.1	21.9
35~44 岁 Age	131	68.7	31.3
45~54 岁 Age	77	54.5	45.5
55~60 岁 Age	40	40.0	60.0
女性 Female	507	73.6	26.4
16~24 岁 Age	108	86.1	13.9
25~34 岁 Age	150	78.0	22.0
35~44 岁 Age	124	75.0	25.0
45~54 岁 Age	84	61.9	38.1
55~60 岁 Age	41	43.9	56.1

1-6 样本、男性各年龄层、女性各年龄层最近三个月的饮用频率/ Frequencies of Consuming Carbonated Beverage in the Last Three Months by the Whole Sample, Age and Gender Groups

	人数 Number	天天喝 daily	一周 3 次或以上 3 times or over a week	一周 1~2 次 once or twice a week	一个月 2~3 次 2 or 3 times a month	一个月 1 次或以下 once a month or below	没喝过 never
样本 Sample	1011	6.0	17.2	24.8	22.5	7.1	22.4
男性 Male	504	6.7	19.6	23.2	21.8	5.2	23.4
16~24 岁 Age	105	14.3	30.5	29.5	12.4	2.9	10.5
25~34 岁 Age	151	7.9	23.2	23.8	26.5	5.3	13.2
35~44 岁 Age	131	3.8	16.8	21.4	26.7	6.9	24.4
45~54 岁 Age	77	1.3	10.4	19.5	18.2	5.2	45.5
55~60 岁 Age	40	2.5	5.0	17.5	20.0	5.0	50.0
女性 Female	507	5.3	14.8	26.4	23.1	9.1	21.3
16~24 岁 Age	107	10.3	20.6	33.6	21.5	4.7	9.3
25~34 岁 Age	150	4.7	15.3	30.7	20.7	11.3	17.3
35~44 岁 Age	124	4.8	16.1	19.4	27.4	9.7	22.6
45~54 岁 Age	84	2.4	11.9	25.0	21.4	8.3	31.0
55~60 岁 Age	42	2.4	0.0	16.7	26.2	11.9	42.9

1-7 样本、男性各年龄层、女性各年龄层的品牌习惯/ Brand Habit in Consuming Carbonated Beverage by the Whole Sample, Age and Gender Groups

	人数 Number	基本固定饮用一个牌子 used in only one brand	比较固定地饮用两个或三个牌子 used in two or three brands	基本上不太固定牌子 no brand preference
样本 Sample	783	44.6	44.3	11.1
男性 Male	384	45.8	41.7	12.5
16~24 岁 Age	94	52.1	39.4	8.5
25~34 岁 Age	130	47.7	42.3	10.0
35~44 岁 Age	98	41.8	39.8	18.4
45~54 岁 Age	42	35.7	54.8	9.5
55~60 岁 Age	20	45.0	30.0	25.0
女性 Female	399	43.4	46.9	9.8
16~24 岁 Age	97	38.1	50.5	11.3
25~34 岁 Age	124	46.8	48.4	4.8
35~44 岁 Age	96	45.8	44.8	9.4
45~54 岁 Age	58	43.1	43.1	13.8
55~60 岁 Age	24	37.5	41.7	20.8

1-8 选择该类商品的考虑因素/ Ranking of the Considerations in Purchasing

注：本题为多选题，合计百分比超过 100%（Multiple answers）

排名 Ranking	考虑因素 Considerations	人次 Person-time	百分比 Percent
1	口味好 pleasant taste	552	70.6
2	有名的牌子 famous brand	310	39.6
3	价格适中 reasonable price	219	28.0
4	生产日期 date of producing	158	20.2
5	购买方便 easy to buy	129	16.5
6	只是由于习惯 out of habit	99	12.7
7	广告影响 influence of advertising	82	10.5
8	单位发的 offered by the working unit	54	6.9
9	有优惠条件 with preferential terms	23	2.9
10	别人送的 given by other people	21	2.7
11	包装吸引人 appealing package	12	1.5
12	朋友推荐 introduction of friends	7	0.9
13	售货员介绍 introduced by the shop assistants	2	0.3
13	其它 others	2	0.3

n=782

1-9 样本、男性各年龄层、女性各年龄层最常饮用的包装形式/ Package Types of the Consumed Carbonated Beverage by the Whole Sample, Age and Gender Groups

	人数 Number	玻璃瓶 glass bottle	易开罐 tin	塑料瓶 plastic bottle	纸杯 paper cup	其它 others
样本 Sample	772	9.2	37.4	49.5	3.8	0.1
男性 Male	380	11.6	37.9	46.6	3.9	0.0
16~24 岁 Age	93	14.0	43.0	37.6	5.4	0.0
25~34 岁 Age	130	10.8	37.7	48.5	3.1	0.0
35~44 岁 Age	97	8.2	40.2	47.4	4.1	0.0
45~54 岁 Age	40	15.0	25.0	55.0	5.0	0.0
55~60 岁 Age	20	15.0	30.0	55.0	0.0	0.0
女性 Female	392	6.9	37.0	52.3	3.6	0.3
16~24 岁 Age	96	5.2	52.1	37.5	4.2	1.0
25~34 岁 Age	120	5.0	32.5	56.7	5.8	0.0
35~44 岁 Age	95	9.5	35.8	52.6	2.1	0.0
45~54 岁 Age	57	8.8	22.8	68.4	0.0	0.0
55~60 岁 Age	24	8.3	37.5	50.0	4.2	0.0

1-10 样本、男性各年龄层、女性各年龄层最常饮用的场合/ Settings of Consumption by the Whole Sample, Age and Gender Groups

注：本题为多选题，合计百分比超过 100%（Multiple answers）

	人数 Number	平时口渴时 when thirsty	平时吃饭喝 at dinner	宴席、聚会喝 at banquet	外出、旅游时 outing/traveling	运动完以后 after athletics	其它 others
样本 Sample	778	57.5	25.7	32.5	28.8	7.1	1.4
男性 Male	382	61.0	22.3	29.3	26.2	9.7	1.3
16~24 岁 Age	94	70.2	17.0	25.5	25.5	22.3	1.1
25~34 岁 Age	129	58.9	22.5	32.6	25.6	5.4	1.6
35~44 岁 Age	97	54.6	28.9	26.8	28.9	6.2	2.1
45~54 岁 Age	42	59.5	19.0	28.6	21.4	4.8	0.0
55~60 岁 Age	20	65.0	20.0	40.0	30.0	5.0	0.0
女性 Female	396	54.0	29.0	35.6	31.3	4.5	1.5
16~24 岁 Age	97	60.8	28.9	26.8	32.0	10.3	0.0
25~34 岁 Age	122	54.9	23.8	36.1	34.4	4.9	1.6
35~44 岁 Age	96	53.1	33.3	39.6	33.3	2.1	0.0
45~54 岁 Age	57	54.4	33.3	35.1	21.1	0.0	5.3
55~60 岁 Age	24	25.0	29.2	54.2	29.2	0.0	4.2

1-11 重度消费者人口分布/ Demographics of the Heavy Consumers

	人数 Number	16-24 岁 Age	25-34 岁 Age	35-44 岁 Age	45-54 岁 Age	55-60 岁 Age
样本 Sample	486	30.2	32.7	21.6	11.7	3.7
男性 Male	250	31.2	33.2	22.0	9.6	4.0
天天喝 daily	34	44.1	35.3	14.7	2.9	2.9
一周 3 次或以上 3 times or over a week	99	32.3	35.4	22.2	8.1	2.0
一周 1~2 次 once or twice a week	117	26.5	30.8	23.9	12.8	6.0
女性 Female	236	29.2	32.2	21.2	14.0	3.4
天天喝 daily	27	40.7	25.9	22.2	7.4	3.7
一周 3 次或以上 3 times or over a week	75	29.3	30.7	26.7	13.3	0.0
一周 1~2 次 once or twice a week	134	26.9	34.3	17.9	15.7	5.2

1-12 不同消费者层的常用品牌/ The Most Frequently Used Brands by Market Segments

1-12-1 时尚流行指标/ Fads Popular Index

	人数 Number	第一品牌及百分比 1st/ percent	第二品牌及百分比 2nd/ percent	第三品牌及百分比 3rd/ percent	第四品牌及百分比 4th/ percent
样本 Sample	768	**可口可乐 Coca-cola(59.4)**	**雪碧 Sprite(11.6)**	**百事可乐 Pepsi(7.9)**	**北冰洋 Beibingyang(5.6)**
平实生活指向 simple living orientation	358	可口可乐 Coca-cola(61.7)	雪碧 Sprite(12.0)	百事可乐 Pepsi(6.1)	北冰洋 Beibingyang(5.3)
时尚流行指向 fashion orientation	410	可口可乐 Coca-cola(57.3)	雪碧 Sprite(11.2)	百事可乐 Pepsi(9.5)	北冰洋 Beibingyang(5.9)

1-12-2 广告态度指标/ Advertising Attitude Index

	人数 Number	第一品牌及百分比 1st/ percent	第二品牌及百分比 2nd/ percent	第三品牌及百分比 3rd/ percent	第四品牌及百分比 4th/ percent
样本 Sample	766	**可口可乐 Coca-cola(59.8)**	**雪碧 Sprite(11.6)**	**百事可乐 Pepsi(7.7)**	**北冰洋 Beibingyang(5.5)**
广告淡漠指向 indifferent orientation	205	可口可乐 Coca-cola(55.1)	雪碧 Sprite(11.2)	百事可乐 Pepsi(9.3)	美年达 Mirinda(4.9)
中间层 medium	457	可口可乐 Coca-cola(62.1)	雪碧 Sprite(11.6)	百事可乐 Pepsi(7.4)	北冰洋 Beibingyang(5.7)
信赖广告指向 loyal orientation	104	可口可乐 Coca-cola(58.7)	雪碧 Sprite(12.5)	北冰洋 Beibingyang(7.7)	百事可乐 Pepsi(5.8)

1-12-3 饮食健康指标/ Foods & Drink Quality Index

	人数 Number	第一品牌及百分比 1st/ percent	第二品牌及百分比 2nd/ percent	第三品牌及百分比 3rd/ percent	第四品牌及百分比 4th/ percent
样本 Sample	774	**可口可乐 Coca-cola(59.2)**	**雪碧 Sprite(11.2)**	**百事可乐 Pepsi(8.0)**	**北冰洋 Beibingyang(5.8)**
饮食"温饱"指向 "basic" orientation	226	可口可乐 Coca-cola(64.2)	雪碧 Sprite(10.6)	百事可乐 Pepsi(5.8)	美年达 Mirinda(4.4)
中间层 medium	367	可口可乐 Coca-cola(56.9)	雪碧 Sprite(11.7)	北冰洋 Beibingyang(7.1)	百事可乐 Pepsi(6.8)
健康营养指向 health & nutrition orientation	181	可口可乐 Coca-cola(57.5)	百事可乐 Pepsi(13.3)	雪碧 Sprite(11.0)	北冰洋 Beibingyang(6.6)

1-13 重度消费者的消费者层构成/ The Composition of the Heavy Consumers

1-13-1 时尚流行指标/ Fads Popular Index

	人数 Number	平实生活指向 simple living orientation	时尚流行指向 fashion orientation
样本 Sample	477	42.8	57.2
天天喝 daily	59	35.6	64.4
一周 3 次或以上 3 times or over a week	173	37.0	63.0
一周 1~2 次 once or twice a week	245	48.6	51.4

1-13-2 广告态度指标/ Advertising Attitude Index

	人数 Number	广告淡漠指向 indifferent orientation	中间层 medium	信赖广告指向 loyal orientation
样本 Sample	473	27.3	58.1	14.6
天天喝 daily	57	28.1	57.9	14.0
一周 3 次或以上 3 times or over a week	171	28.1	55.0	17.0
一周 1~2 次 once or twice a week	245	26.5	60.4	13.1

1-13-3 饮食健康指标/ Foods & Drink Quality Index

	人数 Number	饮食"温饱"指向 "basic" orientation	中间层 medium	健康营养指向 health & nutrition orientation
样本 Sample	483	29.6	47.6	22.8
天天喝 daily	61	36.1	45.9	18.0
一周 3 次或以上 3 times or over a week	172	30.2	44.8	25.0
一周 1~2 次 once or twice a week	250	27.6	50.0	22.4

● 上海 / Shanghai

1-1 最近三个月饮用频率的比例/ Proportion of the Sample Consuming Carbonated Beverage in the Last Three Months

	人数 Number	百分比 Percent
天天喝 daily	60	5.9
一周 3 次或以上 3 times or over a week	205	20.2
一周 1~2 次 once or twice a week	306	30.2
一个月 2～3 次 2 or 3 times a month	190	18.8
一个月 1 次或以下 once a month or below	68	6.7
没喝过 never	184	18.2

n=1013

1-2 最常用品牌排名/ Ranking of the Most Frequently Used Brands

排名 Brand Ranking	品牌 Brands	人数 Number	百分比 Percent
1	百事可乐 Pepsi	338	40.8
2	可口可乐 Coca-cola	268	32.4
3	雪碧 Sprite	155	18.7
4	七喜 7-up	11	1.3
5	美年达 Mirinda	9	1.1
6	正广和 Acquarius	8	1.0
7	申美 Shenmei	7	0.8
8	非常可乐 Future	4	0.5
8	激浪 Mountain Dew	4	0.5
9	雪菲力 Ch'Nalry	3	0.4

n=828

1-3 样本、男性各年龄层、女性各年龄层的常用品牌/ The Most Frequently Used Brands by the Whole Sample, Age and Gender Groups

	人数 Number	第一品牌及百分比 1st/ percent	第二品牌及百分比 2nd/ percent	第三品牌及百分比 3rd/ percent
样本 Sample	828	**百事可乐 Pepsi(40.8)**	**可口可乐 Coca-cola(32.4)**	**雪碧 Sprite(18.7)**
男性 Male	414	**百事可乐 Pepsi(39.6)**	**可口可乐 Coca-cola(34.8)**	**雪碧 Sprite(17.9)**
16~24 岁 Age	101	百事可乐 Pepsi(52.5)	可口可乐 Coca-cola(31.7)	雪碧 Sprite(8.9)
25~34 岁 Age	127	百事可乐 Pepsi(37.8) 可口可乐 Coca-cola(37.8)	雪碧 Sprite(15.7)	激浪 Moutain Dew(1.6) 美年达 Mirinda(1.6) 七喜 7-up(1.6)
35~44 岁 Age	106	百事可乐 Pepsi(38.7)	可口可乐 Coca-cola(33.0)	雪碧 Sprite(24.5)
45~54 岁 Age	61	可口可乐 Coca-cola(36.1)	百事可乐 Pepsi(27.9)	雪碧 Sprite(23.0)
55~60 岁 Age	19	可口可乐 Coca-cola(36.8)	百事可乐 Pepsi(26.3) 雪碧 Sprite(26.3)	七喜 7-up(5.3) 雪菲力 Ch'Nalry(5.3)
女性 Female	414	**百事可乐 Pepsi(42.0)**	**可口可乐 Coca-cola(30.0)**	**雪碧 Sprite(19.6)**
16~24 岁 Age	97	百事可乐 Pepsi(64.9)	可口可乐 Coca-cola(23.7)	雪碧 Sprite(7.2)
25~34 岁 Age	119	可口可乐 Coca-cola(35.3) 百事可乐 Pepsi(35.3)	雪碧 Sprite(17.6)	正广和 Acquarius(1.7) 非常可乐 Future(1.7)
35~44 岁 Age	105	百事可乐 Pepsi(38.1)	可口可乐 Coca-cola(26.7) 雪碧 Sprite(26.7)	美年达 Mirinda(1.9)
45~54 岁 Age	63	可口可乐 Coca-cola(38.1)	百事可乐 Pepsi(31.7)	雪碧 Sprite(20.6)
55~60 岁 Age	30	雪碧 Sprite(40.0)	百事可乐 Pepsi(30.0)	可口可乐 Coca-cola(23.3)

1-4 理想品牌排名/ Ranking of the Ideal Brands

排名 Brand Ranking	品牌 Brands	人数 Number	百分比 Percent
1	百事可乐 Pepsi	391	38.6
2	可口可乐 Coca-cola	310	30.6
3	雪碧 Sprite	175	17.3
4	正广和 Acquarius	28	2.8
5	美年达 Mirinda	16	1.6
6	佳得乐 Gatorade	13	1.3
7	七喜 7-up	11	1.1
7	申美 Shengmei	11	1.1
8	激浪 Mountain Dew	5	0.5
8	雪菲力 Ch'Nalry	5	0.5

n=1014

1-5 样本、男性各年龄层、女性各年龄层最近三个月有无购买的比例/ Purchasing in the Last Three Months by the Whole Sample, Age and Gender Groups

	人数 Number	买过 yes	没买过 no
样本 Sample	1014	80.7	19.3
男性 Male	509	79.2	20.8
16~24 岁 Age	109	90.8	9.2
25~34 岁 Age	146	85.6	14.4
35~44 岁 Age	130	78.5	21.5
45~54 岁 Age	85	68.2	31.8
55~60 岁 Age	39	48.7	51.3
女性 Female	505	82.2	17.8
16~24 岁 Age	108	88.0	12.0
25~34 岁 Age	144	81.9	18.1
35~44 岁 Age	130	82.3	17.7
45~54 岁 Age	82	80.5	19.5
55~60 岁 Age	41	70.7	29.3

1-6 样本、男性各年龄层、女性各年龄层最近三个月的饮用频率/ Frequencies of Consuming Carbonated Beverage in the Last Three Months by the Whole Sample, Age and Gender Groups

	人数 Number	天天喝 daily	一周 3 次或以上 3 times or over a week	一周 1~2 次 once or twice a week	一个月 2~3 次 2 or 3 times a month	一个月 1 次或以下 once a month or below	没喝过 never
样本 Sample	1013	5.9	20.2	30.2	18.8	6.7	18.2
男性 Male	508	5.7	20.5	29.9	18.9	6.5	18.5
16~24 岁 Age	109	5.5	35.8	30.3	14.7	6.4	7.3
25~34 岁 Age	145	8.3	26.2	35.2	15.2	2.8	12.4
35~44 岁 Age	130	6.9	11.5	32.3	21.5	9.2	18.5
45~54 岁 Age	85	0.0	10.6	22.4	28.2	10.6	28.2
55~60 岁 Age	39	5.1	7.7	17.9	15.4	2.6	51.3
女性 Female	505	6.1	20.0	30.5	18.6	6.9	17.8
16~24 岁 Age	108	10.2	28.7	29.6	18.5	2.8	10.2
25~34 岁 Age	144	6.3	20.1	29.9	20.1	6.9	16.7
35~44 岁 Age	130	4.6	13.1	38.5	18.5	6.2	19.2
45~54 岁 Age	82	3.7	23.2	24.4	13.4	12.2	23.2
55~60 岁 Age	41	4.9	12.2	22.0	24.4	9.8	26.8

1-7 样本、男性各年龄层、女性各年龄层的品牌习惯/ Brand Habit in Consuming Carbonated Beverage by the Whole Sample, Age and Gender Groups

	人数 Number	基本固定饮用一个牌子 used in only one brand	比较固定地饮用两个或三个牌子 used in two or three brands	基本上不太固定牌子 no brand preference
样本 Sample	829	47.8	41.0	11.2
男性 Male	414	51.0	38.6	10.4
16~24 岁 Age	101	55.4	35.6	8.9
25~34 岁 Age	127	55.1	35.4	9.4
35~44 岁 Age	106	43.4	43.4	13.2
45~54 岁 Age	61	49.2	42.6	8.2
55~60 岁 Age	19	47.4	36.8	15.8
女性 Female	415	44.6	43.4	12.0
16~24 岁 Age	97	44.3	46.4	9.3
25~34 岁 Age	120	42.5	48.3	9.2
35~44 岁 Age	105	44.8	44.8	10.5
45~54 岁 Age	63	49.2	31.7	19.0
55~60 岁 Age	30	43.3	33.3	23.3

1-8 选择该类商品的考虑因素/ Ranking of the Considerations in Purchasing

注：本题为多选题，合计百分比超过 100%（Multiple answers）

排名 Ranking	考虑因素 Considerations	人次 Person-time	百分比 Percent
1	口味好 pleasant taste	512	61.8
2	有名的牌子 famous brand	328	39.6
3	价格适中 reasonable price	277	33.4
4	购买方便 easy to buy	193	23.3
5	生产日期 date of producing	127	15.3
6	广告影响 influence of advertising	121	14.6
7	只是由于习惯 out of habit	118	14.2
8	有优惠条件 with preferential terms	34	4.1
8	单位发的 offered by the working unit	34	4.1
9	包装吸引人 appealing package	22	2.7
10	其它 others	8	1.0
11	别人送的 given by other people	6	0.7
12	朋友推荐 introduction of friends	5	0.6
13	售货员介绍 introduced by the shop assistants	2	0.2

n=829

1-9 样本、男性各年龄层、女性各年龄层最常饮用的包装形式/ Package Types of the Consumed Carbonated Beverage by the Whole Sample, Age and Gender Groups

	人数 Number	玻璃瓶 glass bottle	易开罐 tin	塑料瓶 plastic bottle	纸杯 paper cup	其它 others
样本 Sample	821	4.3	33.7	60.0	1.9	0.0
男性 Male	409	5.6	38.1	54.0	2.2	0.0
16~24 岁 Age	100	8.0	48.0	40.0	4.0	0.0
25~34 岁 Age	126	4.0	42.1	51.6	2.4	0.0
35~44 岁 Age	104	6.7	27.9	63.5	1.9	0.0
45~54 岁 Age	60	3.3	40.0	56.7	0.0	0.0
55~60 岁 Age	19	5.3	10.5	84.2	0.0	0.0
女性 Female	412	2.9	29.4	66.0	1.7	0.0
16~24 岁 Age	96	1.0	50.0	47.9	1.0	0.0
25~34 岁 Age	119	3.4	28.6	64.7	3.4	0.0
35~44 岁 Age	104	5.8	19.2	73.1	1.9	0.0
45~54 岁 Age	63	1.6	19.0	79.4	0.0	0.0
55~60 岁 Age	30	0.0	23.3	76.7	0.0	0.0

1-10 样本、男性各年龄层、女性各年龄层最常饮用的场合/ Settings of Consumption by the Whole Sample, Age and Gender Groups

注：本题为多选题，合计百分比超过 100%（Multiple answers）

	人数 Number	平时口渴时 when thirsty	平时吃饭喝 at dinner	宴席、聚会喝 at banquet	外出、旅游时 outing/traveling	运动完以后 after athletics	其它 others
样本 Sample	826	70.3	13.7	31.0	21.2	10.2	0.8
男性 Male	412	73.1	9.0	28.4	20.9	12.9	1.2
16~24 岁 Age	101	78.2	5.9	21.8	17.8	20.8	2.0
25~34 岁 Age	127	78.7	5.5	22.8	22.8	16.5	0.8
35~44 岁 Age	106	68.9	9.4	35.8	24.5	7.5	0.9
45~54 岁 Age	59	64.4	15.3	33.9	20.3	5.1	0.0
55~60 岁 Age	19	57.9	26.3	42.1	5.3	0.0	5.3
女性 Female	414	67.6	18.4	33.6	21.5	7.5	0.5
16~24 岁 Age	97	76.3	11.3	21.6	22.7	15.5	0.0
25~34 岁 Age	120	68.3	18.3	35.0	24.2	4.2	0.8
35~44 岁 Age	105	64.8	17.1	40.0	21.0	5.7	1.0
45~54 岁 Age	63	65.1	30.2	30.2	15.9	4.8	0.0
55~60 岁 Age	29	51.7	20.7	51.7	20.7	6.9	0.0

1-11 重度消费者人口分布/ Demographics of the Heavy Consumers

	人数 Number	16-24 岁 Age	25-34 岁 Age	35-44 岁 Age	45-54 岁 Age	55-60 岁 Age
样本 Sample	571	26.6	31.9	24.3	12.3	4.9
男性 Male	285	27.4	35.4	23.2	9.8	4.2
天天喝 daily	29	20.7	41.4	31.0	0.0	6.9
一周 3 次或以上 3 times or over a week	104	37.5	36.5	14.4	8.7	2.9
一周 1~2 次 once or twice a week	152	21.7	33.6	27.6	12.5	4.6
女性 Female	286	25.9	28.3	25.5	14.7	5.6
天天喝 daily	31	35.5	29.0	19.4	9.7	6.5
一周 3 次或以上 3 times or over a week	101	30.7	28.7	16.8	18.8	5.0
一周 1~2 次 once or twice a week	154	20.8	27.9	32.5	13.0	5.8

1-12 不同消费者层的常用品牌/ The Most Frequently Used Brands by Market Segments

1-12-1 时尚流行指标/ Fads Popular Index

	人数 Number	第一品牌及百分比 1st/ percent	第二品牌及百分比 2nd/ percent	第三品牌及百分比 3rd/ percent
样本 Sample	824	**百事可乐 Pepsi(40.9)**	**可口可乐 Coca-cola(32.3)**	**雪碧 Sprite(18.7)**
平实生活指向 simple living orientation	358	百事可乐 Pepsi(37.7)	可口可乐 Coca-cola(31.8)	雪碧 Sprite(23.7)
时尚流行指向 fashion orientation	466	百事可乐 Pepsi(43.3)	可口可乐 Coca-cola(32.6)	雪碧 Sprite(14.8)

1-12-2 广告态度指标/ Advertising attitude Index

	人数 Number	第一品牌及百分比 1st/ percent	第二品牌及百分比 2nd/ percent	第三品牌及百分比 3rd/ percent
样本 Sample	817	**百事可乐 Pepsi(40.9)**	**可口可乐 Coca-cola(32.4)**	**雪碧 Sprite(18.6)**
广告淡漠指向 indifferent orientation	204	百事可乐 Pepsi(36.8)	可口可乐 Coca-cola(30.4)	雪碧 Sprite(23.5)
中间层 medium	502	百事可乐 Pepsi(41.2)	可口可乐 Coca-cola(33.1)	雪碧 Sprite(18.5)
信赖广告指向 loyal orientation	111	百事可乐 Pepsi(46.8)	可口可乐 Coca-cola(33.3)	雪碧 Sprite(9.9)

1-12-3 饮食健康指标/ Foods & Drink Quality Index

	人数 Number	第一品牌及百分比 1st/ percent	第二品牌及百分比 2nd/ percent	第三品牌及百分比 3rd/ percent
样本 Sample	825	**百事可乐 Pepsi(40.7)**	**可口可乐 Coca-cola(32.5)**	**雪碧 Sprite(18.7)**
饮食"温饱"指向 "basic" orientation	185	百事可乐 Pepsi(41.6)	可口可乐 Coca-cola(29.7)	雪碧 Sprite(22.2)
中间层 medium	413	百事可乐 Pepsi(40.9)	可口可乐 Coca-cola(33.2)	雪碧 Sprite(16.9)
健康营养指向 health & nutrition orientation	227	百事可乐 Pepsi(39.6)	可口可乐 Coca-cola(33.5)	雪碧 Sprite(18.9)

1-13 重度消费者的消费者层构成/ The Composition of the Heavy Consumers

1-13-1 时尚流行指标/ Fads Popular Index

	人数 Number	平实生活指向 simple living orientation	时尚流行指向 fashion orientation
样本 Sample	567	39.7	60.3
天天喝 daily	59	25.4	74.6
一周 3 次或以上 3 times or over a week	204	37.3	62.7
一周 1~2 次 once or twice a week	304	44.1	55.9

1-13-2 广告态度指标/ Advertising Attitude Index

	人数 Number	广告淡漠指向 indifferent orientation	中间层 medium	信赖广告指向 loyal orientation
样本 Sample	560	23.2	62.1	14.6
天天喝 daily	60	35.0	51.7	13.3
一周 3 次或以上 3 times or over a week	199	17.6	64.3	18.1
一周 1~2 次 once or twice a week	301	24.6	62.8	12.6

1-13-3 饮食健康指标/ Foods & Drink Quality Index

	人数 Number	饮食"温饱"指向 "basic" orientation	中间层 medium	健康营养指向 health & nutrition orientation
样本 Sample	570	22.1	51.1	26.8
天天喝 daily	60	25.0	45.0	30.0
一周 3 次或以上 3 times or over a week	205	23.4	49.3	27.3
一周 1~2 次 once or twice a week	305	20.7	53.4	25.9

● 广州 / Guangzhou

1-1 最近三个月饮用频率的比例/ Proportion of the Sample Consuming Carbonated Beverage in the Last Three Months

	人数 Number	百分比 Percent
天天喝 daily	45	4.4
一周 3 次或以上 3 times or over a week	163	15.8
一周 1~2 次 once or twice a week	300	29.2
一个月 2～3 次 2 or 3 times a month	203	19.7
一个月 1 次或以下 once a month or below	93	9.0
没喝过 never	225	21.9

n=1029

1-2 最常用品牌排名/ Ranking of the Most Frequently Used Brands

排名 Brand Ranking	品牌 Brands	人数 Number	百分比 Percent
1	可口可乐 Coca-cola	366	45.6
2	百事可乐 Pepsi	184	22.9
3	亚洲 Asia	79	9.8
4	雪碧 Sprite	62	7.7
5	佳得乐 Gatorade	27	3.4
6	健力宝 Jianlibao	15	1.9
7	美年达 Mirinda	14	1.7
7	七喜 7-up	14	1.7
8	新奇士 Sunkist	10	1.2

n=803

1-3 样本、男性各年龄层、女性各年龄层的常用品牌/ The Most Frequently Used Brands by the Whole Sample, Age and Gender Groups

	人数 Number	第一品牌及百分比 1st/ percent	第二品牌及百分比 2nd/ percent	第三品牌及百分比 3rd/ percent	第四品牌及百分比 4th/ percent
样本 Sample	803	**可口可乐 Coca-cola(45.6)**	**百事可乐 Pepsi(22.9)**	**亚洲 Asia(9.8)**	**雪碧 Sprite(7.7)**
男性 Male	392	**可口可乐 Coca-cola(45.2)**	**百事可乐 Pepsi(22.2)**	**亚洲 Asia(10.7)**	**雪碧 Sprite(6.4)**
16~24 岁 Age	102	可口可乐 Coca-cola(34.3)	百事可乐 Pepsi(31.4)	亚洲 Asia(11.8)	雪碧 Sprite(4.9)
25~34 岁 Age	127	可口可乐 Coca-cola(52.8)	百事可乐 Pepsi(18.9)	亚洲 Asia(6.3) 雪碧 Sprite(6.3)	健力宝 Jianlibao(4.7)
35~44 岁 Age	90	可口可乐 Coca-cola(45.6)	百事可乐 Pepsi(23.3)	亚洲 Asia(13.3)	佳得乐 Gatorade(4.4) 雪碧 Sprite(4.4)
45~54 岁 Age	51	可口可乐 Coca-cola(47.1)	百事可乐 Pepsi(15.7)	亚洲 Asia(13.7)	雪碧 Sprite(9.8)
55~60 岁 Age	22	可口可乐 Coca-cola(45.5)	新奇士 Sunkist(13.6) 雪碧 Sprite(13.6) 亚洲 Asia(13.6)	百事可乐 Pepsi(9.1)	
女性 Female	411	**可口可乐 Coca-cola(46.0)**	**百事可乐 Pepsi(23.6)**	**雪碧 Sprite(9.0)** **亚洲 Asia(9.0)**	**佳得乐 Gatorade(3.2)**
16~24 岁 Age	95	可口可乐 Coca-cola(46.3)	百事可乐 Pepsi(33.7)	佳得乐 Gatorade(4.2) 亚洲 Asia(4.2)	七喜 7-up(2.1) 醒目 Smart(2.1) 康师傅 Kangshifu(2.1)
25~34 岁 Age	128	可口可乐 Coca-cola(51.6)	百事可乐 Pepsi(23.4)	雪碧 Sprite(7.8)	亚洲 Asia(6.3)
35~44 岁 Age	108	可口可乐 Coca-cola(37.0)	百事可乐 Pepsi(25.0)	雪碧 Sprite(13.9)	亚洲 Asia(9.3)
45~54 岁 Age	64	可口可乐 Coca-cola(50.0)	亚洲 Asia(17.2)	雪碧 Sprite(14.1)	百事可乐 Pepsi(10.9)
55~60 岁 Age	16	可口可乐 Coca-cola(43.8)	亚洲 Asia(25.0)	雪碧 Sprite(12.5)	百事可乐 Pepsi(6.3) 健力宝 Jianlibao(6.3) 新奇士 Sunkist(6.3)

1-4 理想品牌排名/ Ranking of the Ideal Brands

排名 Brand Ranking	品牌 Brands	人数 Number	百分比 Percent
1	可口可乐 Coca-cola	429	41.5
2	百事可乐 Pepsi	233	22.5
4	亚洲 Asia	80	7.7
5	雪碧 Sprite	58	5.6
6	佳得乐 Gatorade	35	3.4
7	健力宝 Jianlibao	20	1.9
8	美年达 Mirinda	17	1.6
9	七喜 7-up	10	1.0

n=1034

1-5 样本、男性各年龄层、女性各年龄层最近三个月有无购买的比例/ Purchasing in the Last Three Months by the Whole Sample, Age and Gender Groups

	人数 Number	买过 yes	没买过 no
样本 Sample	1034	76.5	23.5
男性 Male	499	77.4	22.6
16~24 岁 Age	106	93.4	6.6
25~34 岁 Age	150	84.0	16.0
35~44 岁 Age	127	69.3	30.7
45~54 岁 Age	73	68.5	31.5
55~60 岁 Age	43	53.5	46.5
女性 Female	535	75.7	24.3
16~24 岁 Age	112	83.0	17.0
25~34 岁 Age	158	79.1	20.9
35~44 岁 Age	137	75.9	24.1
45~54 岁 Age	87	71.3	28.7
55~60 岁 Age	41	51.2	48.8

1-6 样本、男性各年龄层、女性各年龄层最近三个月的饮用频率/ Frequencies of Consuming Carbonated Beverage in the Last Three Months by the Whole Sample, Age and Gender Groups

	人数 Number	天天喝 daily	一周 3 次或以上 3 times or over a week	一周 1~2 次 once or twice a week	一个月 2~3 次 2 or 3 times a month	一个月 1 次或以下 once a month or below	没喝过 never
样本 Sample	1029	4.4	15.8	29.2	19.7	9.0	21.9
男性 Male	496	4.0	17.9	32.5	18.8	6.0	20.8
16~24 岁 Age	106	8.5	32.1	36.8	14.2	4.7	3.8
25~34 岁 Age	149	2.7	17.4	39.6	19.5	6.7	14.1
35~44 岁 Age	127	3.1	13.4	29.1	21.3	3.9	29.1
45~54 岁 Age	73	2.7	15.1	23.3	20.5	8.2	30.1
55~60 岁 Age	41	2.4	2.4	22.0	17.1	9.8	46.3
女性 Female	533	4.7	13.9	26.1	20.6	11.8	22.9
16~24 岁 Age	111	8.1	21.6	28.8	18.0	9.0	14.4
25~34 岁 Age	158	2.5	14.6	30.4	23.4	10.1	19.0
35~44 岁 Age	137	5.1	9.5	24.8	22.6	16.8	21.2
45~54 岁 Age	87	5.7	13.8	19.5	19.5	14.9	26.4
55~60 岁 Age	40	0.0	5.0	20.0	12.5	2.5	60.0

1-7 样本、男性各年龄层、女性各年龄层的品牌习惯/ Brand Habit in Consuming Carbonated Beverage by the Whole Sample, Age and Gender Groups

	人数 Number	基本固定饮用一个牌子 used in only one brand	比较固定地饮用两个或三个牌子 used in two or three brands	基本上不太固定牌子 no brand preference
样本 Sample	802	37.7	48.1	14.2
男性 Male	392	39.0	47.7	13.3
16~24 岁 Age	102	43.1	45.1	11.8
25~34 岁 Age	128	38.3	48.4	13.3
35~44 岁 Age	89	34.8	50.6	14.6
45~54 岁 Age	51	41.2	43.1	15.7
55~60 岁 Age	22	36.4	54.5	9.1
女性 Female	410	36.3	48.5	15.1
16~24 岁 Age	95	31.6	50.5	17.9
25~34 岁 Age	128	30.5	58.6	10.9
35~44 岁 Age	108	39.8	43.5	16.7
45~54 岁 Age	63	46.0	38.1	15.9
55~60 岁 Age	16	50.0	31.3	18.8

1-8 选择该类商品的考虑因素/ Ranking of the Considerations in Purchasing

注：本题为多选题，合计百分比超过 100%（Multiple answers）

排名 Ranking	考虑因素 Considerations	人次 Person-time	百分比 Percent
1	口味好 pleasant taste	506	63.0
2	有名的牌子 famous brand	317	39.5
3	价格适中 reasonable price	277	34.5
4	购买方便 easy to buy	181	22.5
5	生产日期 date of producing	127	15.8
6	只是由于习惯 out of habit	95	11.8
7	广告影响 influence of advertising	78	9.7
8	包装吸引人 appealing package	26	3.2
8	有优惠条件 with preferential terms	26	3.2
9	单位发的 offered by the working unit	14	1.7
9	别人送的 given by other people	14	1.7
10	朋友推荐 introduction of friends	8	1.0
11	售货员介绍 introduced by the shop assistants	4	0.5
12	其它 others	3	0.4

n=803

1-9 样本、男性各年龄层、女性各年龄层最常饮用的包装形式/ Package Types of the Consumed Carbonated Beverage by the Whole Sample, Age and Gender Groups

	人数 Number	玻璃瓶 glass bottle	易开罐 tin	塑料瓶 plastic bottle	纸杯 paper cup	其它 others
样本 Sample	797	25.8	30.9	40.3	2.8	0.3
男性 Male	388	29.9	32.7	34.8	2.3	0.3
16~24 岁 Age	102	45.1	27.5	22.5	4.9	0.0
25~34 岁 Age	125	26.4	38.4	33.6	0.8	0.8
35~44 岁 Age	89	21.3	37.1	39.3	2.2	0.0
45~54 岁 Age	50	24.0	28.0	46.0	2.0	0.0
55~60 岁 Age	22	27.3	18.2	54.5	0.0	0.0
女性 Female	409	22.0	29.1	45.5	3.2	0.2
16~24 岁 Age	94	27.7	36.2	30.9	5.3	0.0
25~34 岁 Age	127	17.3	26.8	52.8	2.4	0.8
35~44 岁 Age	108	18.5	25.9	51.9	3.7	0.0
45~54 岁 Age	64	29.7	31.3	37.5	1.6	0.0
55~60 岁 Age	16	18.8	18.8	62.5	0.0	0.0

1-10 样本、男性各年龄层、女性各年龄层最常饮用的场合/ Settings of Consumption by the Whole Sample, Age and Gender Groups

注：本题为多选题，合计百分比超过 100%（Multiple answers）

	人数 Number	平时口渴时 when thirsty	平时吃饭喝 at dinner	宴席、聚会喝 at banquet	外出、旅游时 outing/traveling	运动完以后 after athletics	其它 others
样本 Sample	799	69.7	8.5	19.8	24.2	15.9	1.4
男性 Male	391	72.1	8.2	16.9	19.4	20.2	1.3
16~24 岁 Age	102	68.6	7.8	11.8	18.6	37.3	1.0
25~34 岁 Age	128	75.0	3.9	14.1	21.9	18.8	1.6
35~44 岁 Age	88	70.5	12.5	25.0	20.5	9.1	2.3
45~54 岁 Age	51	74.5	11.8	21.6	19.6	11.8	0.0
55~60 岁 Age	22	72.7	9.1	13.6	4.5	13.6	0.0
女性 Female	408	67.4	8.8	22.5	28.7	11.8	1.5
16~24 岁 Age	95	67.4	9.5	15.8	32.6	22.1	0.0
25~34 岁 Age	126	73.0	6.3	19.8	31.0	9.5	2.4
35~44 岁 Age	108	61.1	9.3	25.0	31.5	10.2	1.9
45~54 岁 Age	63	61.9	14.3	36.5	17.5	6.3	1.6
55~60 岁 Age	16	87.5	0.0	12.5	12.5	0.0	0.0

1-11 重度消费者人口分布/ Demographics of the Heavy Consumers

	人数 Number	16-24 岁 Age	25-34 岁 Age	35-44 岁 Age	45-54 岁 Age	55-60 岁 Age
样本 Sample	508	28.9	32.3	22.0	12.6	4.1
男性 Male	270	30.4	33.0	21.5	11.1	4.1
天天喝 daily	20	45.0	20.0	20.0	10.0	5.0
一周 3 次或以上 3 times or over a week	89	38.2	29.2	19.1	12.4	1.1
一周 1~2 次 once or twice a week	161	24.2	36.6	23.0	10.6	5.6
女性 Female	238	27.3	31.5	22.7	14.3	4.2
天天喝 daily	25	36.0	16.0	28.0	20.0	0.0
一周 3 次或以上 3 times or over a week	74	32.4	31.1	17.6	16.2	2.7
一周 1~2 次 once or twice a week	139	23.0	34.5	24.5	12.2	5.8

1-12 不同消费者层的常用品牌/ The Most Frequently Used Brands by Market Segments

1-12-1 时尚流行指标/ Fads Popular Index

	人数 Number	第一品牌及百分比 1st/ percent	第二品牌及百分比 2nd/ percent	第三品牌及百分比 3rd/ percent	第四品牌及百分比 4th/ percent
样本 Sample	795	**可口可乐 Coca-cola(45.5)**	**百事可乐 Pepsi(22.9)**	**亚洲 Asia(9.9)**	**雪碧 Sprite(7.8)**
平实生活指向 simple living orientation	384	可口可乐 Coca-cola(45.6)	百事可乐 Pepsi(22.1)	亚洲 Asia(10.9)	雪碧 Sprite(8.3)
时尚流行指向 fashion orientation	411	可口可乐 Coca-cola(45.5)	百事可乐 Pepsi(23.6)	亚洲 Asia(9.0)	雪碧 Sprite(7.3)

1-12-2 广告态度指标/ Advertising Attitude Index

	人数 Number	第一品牌及百分比 1st/ percent	第二品牌及百分比 2nd/ percent	第三品牌及百分比 3rd/ percent	第四品牌及百分比 4th/ percent
样本 Sample	792	**可口可乐 Coca-cola(45.5)**	**百事可乐 Pepsi(22.7)**	**亚洲 Asia(10.0)**	**雪碧 Sprite(7.7)**
广告淡漠指向 indifferent orientation	247	可口可乐 Coca-cola(44.1)	百事可乐 Pepsi(16.6)	亚洲 Asia(13.0)	雪碧 Sprite(6.9)
中间层 medium	469	可口可乐 Coca-cola(46.9)	百事可乐 Pepsi(25.4)	亚洲 Asia(8.3)	雪碧 Sprite(7.0)
信赖广告指向 loyal orientation	76	可口可乐 Coca-cola(40.8)	百事可乐 Pepsi(26.3)	雪碧 Sprite(14.5)	亚洲 Asia(10.5)

1-12-3 饮食健康指标/ Foods & Drink Quality Index

	人数 Number	第一品牌及百分比 1st/ percent	第二品牌及百分比 2nd/ percent	第三品牌及百分比 3rd/ percent	第四品牌及百分比 4th/ percent
样本 Sample	799	**可口可乐 Coca-cola(45.3)**	**百事可乐 Pepsi(23.0)**	**亚洲 Asia(9.9)**	**雪碧 Sprite(7.8)**
饮食"温饱"指向 "basic" orientation	228	可口可乐 Coca-cola(46.1)	百事可乐 Pepsi(19.7)	亚洲 Asia(13.2)	雪碧 Sprite(7.9)
中间层 medium	431	可口可乐 Coca-cola(43.9)	百事可乐 Pepsi(25.8)	亚洲 Asia(8.4)	雪碧 Sprite(7.9)
健康营养指向 health & nutrition orientation	140	可口可乐 Coca-cola(48.6)	百事可乐 Pepsi(20.0)	亚洲 Asia(9.3)	雪碧 Sprite(7.1)

1-13 重度消费者的消费者层构成/ The Composition of the Heavy Consumers

1-13-1 时尚流行指标/ Fads Popular Index

	人数 Number	平实生活指向 simple living orientation	时尚流行指向 fashion orientation
样本 Sample	506	**43.5**	**56.5**
天天喝 daily	43	34.9	65.1
一周 3 次或以上 3 times or over a week	163	42.9	57.1
一周 1~2 次 once or twice a week	300	45.0	55.0

1-13-2 广告态度指标/ Advertising Attitude Index

	人数 Number	广告淡漠指向 indifferent orientation	中间层 medium	信赖广告指向 loyal orientation
样本 Sample	499	**27.3**	**61.5**	**11.2**
天天喝 daily	44	25.0	61.4	13.6
一周 3 次或以上 3 times or over a week	161	29.8	57.1	13.0
一周 1~2 次 once or twice a week	294	26.2	63.9	9.9

1-13-3 饮食健康指标/ Foods & Drink Quality Index

	人数 Number	饮食"温饱"指向 "basic" orientation	中间层 medium	健康营养指向 health & nutrition orientation
样本 Sample	507	**29.4**	**52.3**	**18.3**
天天喝 daily	45	26.7	48.9	24.4
一周 3 次或以上 3 times or over a week	163	29.4	49.7	20.9
一周 1~2 次 once or twice a week	299	29.8	54.2	16.1

● 重庆 / Chongqing

1-1 最近三个月饮用频率的比例/ Proportion of the Sample Consuming Carbonated Beverage in the Last Three Months

	人数 Number	百分比 Percent
天天喝 daily	21	3.4
一周 3 次或以上 3 times or over a week	72	11.5
一周 1~2 次 once or twice a week	154	24.7
一个月 2～3 次 2 or 3 times a month	139	22.3
一个月 1 次或以下 once a month or below	58	9.3
没喝过 never	180	28.8

n=624

1-2 最常用品牌排名/ Ranking of the Most Frequently Used Brands

排名 Brand Ranking	品牌 Brands	人数 Number	百分比 Percent
1	百事可乐 Pepsi	251	57.0
2	七喜 7-up	39	8.9
3	美年达 Mirinda	33	7.5
4	天府可乐 Tianfu	28	6.4
5	可口可乐 Coca-cola	27	6.1
6	雪碧 Sprite	20	4.5
7	百柠 Baining	17	3.9
8	青鸟 Qingniao	5	1.1

n=440

1-3 样本、男性各年龄层、女性各年龄层的常用品牌/ The Most Frequently Used Brands by the Whole Sample, Age and Gender Groups

	人数 Number	第一品牌及百分比 1st/ percent	第二品牌及百分比 2nd/ percent	第三品牌及百分比 3rd/ percent	第四品牌及百分比 4th/ percent
样本 Sample	440	**百事可乐 Pepsi(57.0)**	**七喜 7-up(8.9)**	**美年达 Mirinda(7.5)**	**天府可乐 Tianfu(6.4)**
男性 Male	224	**百事可乐 Pepsi(57.6)**	**七喜 7-up(9.8)**	**美年达 Mirinda(7.6)**	**天府可乐 Tianfu(7.1)**
16~24 岁 Age	57	百事可乐 Pepsi(73.7)	可口可乐 Coca-cola(8.8)	美年达 Mirinda(7.0)	七喜 7-up(3.5)
25~34 岁 Age	71	百事可乐 Pepsi(62.0)	美年达 Mirinda(8.5) 七喜 7-up(8.5)	可口可乐 Coca-cola(4.2) 天府可乐 Tianfu(4.2) 雪碧 Sprite(4.2)	百柠 Baining(2.8) 青鸟 Qingniao(2.8)
35~44 岁 Age	47	百事可乐 Pepsi(44.7)	七喜 7-up(21.3)	可口可乐 Coca-cola(10.6)	美年达 Mirinda(8.5) 天府可乐 Tianfu(8.5)
45~54 岁 Age	31	百事可乐 Pepsi(45.2)	七喜 7-up(12.9)	雪碧 Sprite(9.7) 天府可乐 Tianfu(9.7)	斯威尔 Siweir(3.2) 红雪 Hongxue(3.2) 青鸟 Qingniao(3.2) 美年达 Mirinda(3.2) 可口可乐 Coca-cola(3.2) 健力宝 Jianlibao(3.2)
55~60 岁 Age	18	百事可乐 Pepsi(44.4)	天府可乐 Tianfu(27.8)	美年达 Mirinda(11.1)	可口可乐 Coca-cola(5.6) 雪碧 Sprite(5.6)
女性 Female	216	**百事可乐 Pepsi(56.5)**	**七喜 7-up(7.9)**	**美年达 Mirinda(7.4)**	**百柠 Baining(6.5)**
16~24 岁 Age	57	百事可乐 Pepsi(64.9)	美年达 Mirinda(8.8)	七喜 7-up(7.0)	天府可乐 Tianfu(5.3) 雪碧 Sprite(5.3)
25~34 岁 Age	72	百事可乐 Pepsi(51.4)	美年达 Mirinda(9.7) 七喜 7-up(9.7)	雪碧 Sprite(8.3)	百柠 Baining(5.6) 可口可乐 Coca-cola(5.6) 天府可乐 Tianfu(5.6)
35~44 岁 Age	44	百事可乐 Pepsi(45.5)	百柠 Baining(18.2)	天府可乐 Tianfu(6.8) 雪碧 Sprite(6.8)	可口可乐 Coca-cola(4.5) 美年达 Mirinda(4.5) 七喜 7-up(4.5)
45~54 岁 Age	32	百事可乐 Pepsi(65.6)	可口可乐 Coca-cola(9.4) 七喜 7-up(9.4)	天府可乐 Tianfu(6.3)	百柠 Baining(3.1) 北冰洋 Beibingyang(3.1) 美年达 Mirinda(3.1)
55~60 岁 Age	11	百事可乐 Pepsi(63.6)	可口可乐 Coca-cola(9.1) 美年达 Mirinda(9.1) 七喜 7-up(9.1)		

1-4 理想品牌排名/ Ranking of the Ideal Brands

排名 Brand Ranking	品牌 Brands	人数 Number	百分比 Percent
1	百事可乐 Pepsi	323	51.8
2	可口可乐 Coca-cola	67	10.7
3	美年达 Mirinda	45	7.2
4	七喜 7-up	40	6.4
5	天府可乐 Tianfu	35	5.6
6	百柠 Baining	22	3.5
7	雪碧 Sprite	21	3.4
8	青鸟 Qingniao	11	1.8

n=624

1-5 样本、男性各年龄层、女性各年龄层最近三个月有无购买的比例/ Purchasing in the Last Three Months by the Whole Sample, Age and Gender Groups

	人数 Number	买过 yes	没买过 no
样本 Sample	624	70.5	29.5
男性 Male	314	71.7	28.3
16~24 岁 Age	64	85.9	14.1
25~34 岁 Age	93	78.5	21.5
35~44 岁 Age	75	66.7	33.3
45~54 岁 Age	54	57.4	42.6
55~60 岁 Age	28	57.1	42.9
女性 Female	310	69.4	30.6
16~24 岁 Age	64	85.9	14.1
25~34 岁 Age	90	81.1	18.9
35~44 岁 Age	73	60.3	39.7
45~54 岁 Age	60	53.3	46.7
55~60 岁 Age	23	47.8	52.2

1-6 样本、男性各年龄层、女性各年龄层最近三个月的饮用频率/ Frequencies of Consuming Carbonated Beverage in the Last Three Months by the Whole Sample, Age and Gender Groups

	人数 Number	天天喝 daily	一周 3 次或以上 3 times or over a week	一周 1~2 次 once or twice a week	一个月 2~3 次 2 or 3 times a month	一个月 1 次或以下 once a month or below	没喝过 never
样本 Sample	624	3.4	11.5	24.7	22.3	9.3	28.8
男性 Male	314	3.2	12.4	24.8	22.9	8.3	28.3
16~24 岁 Age	64	1.6	23.4	37.5	20.3	6.3	10.9
25~34 岁 Age	93	2.2	9.7	30.1	28.0	7.5	22.6
35~44 岁 Age	75	2.7	9.3	18.7	20.0	12.0	37.3
45~54 岁 Age	54	7.4	13.0	18.5	13.0	5.6	42.6
55~60 岁 Age	28	3.6	3.6	7.1	39.3	10.7	35.7
女性 Female	310	3.5	10.6	24.5	21.6	10.3	29.4
16~24 岁 Age	64	9.4	25.0	28.1	21.9	6.3	9.4
25~34 岁 Age	90	3.3	11.1	33.3	23.3	8.9	20.0
35~44 岁 Age	73	2.7	6.8	21.9	21.9	8.2	38.4
45~54 岁 Age	60	0.0	1.7	15.0	20.0	18.3	45.0
55~60 岁 Age	23	0.0	4.3	13.0	17.4	13.0	52.2

1-7 样本、男性各年龄层、女性各年龄层的品牌习惯/ Brand Habit in Consuming Carbonated Beverage by the Whole Sample, Age and Gender Groups

	人数 Number	基本固定饮用一个牌子 used in only one brand	比较固定地饮用两个或三个牌子 used in two or three brands	基本上不太固定牌子 no brand preference
样本 Sample	442	40.0	42.1	17.9
男性 Male	224	44.2	39.3	16.5
16~24 岁 Age	57	50.9	42.1	7.0
25~34 岁 Age	71	42.3	39.4	18.3
35~44 岁 Age	47	46.8	34.0	19.1
45~54 岁 Age	31	38.7	38.7	22.6
55~60 岁 Age	18	33.3	44.4	22.2
女性 Female	218	35.8	45.0	19.3
16~24 岁 Age	58	34.5	51.7	13.8
25~34 岁 Age	72	30.6	45.8	23.6
35~44 岁 Age	45	40.0	40.0	20.0
45~54 岁 Age	32	46.9	43.8	9.4
55~60 岁 Age	11	27.3	27.3	45.5

1-8 选择该类商品的考虑因素/ Ranking of the Considerations in Purchasing

注：本题为多选题，合计百分比超过 100%（Multiple answers）

排名 Ranking	考虑因素 Considerations	人次 Person-time	百分比 Percent
1	口味好 pleasant taste	322	72.9
2	价格适中 reasonable price	147	33.3
3	有名的牌子 famous brand	127	28.7
4	生产日期 date of producing	87	19.7
5	购买方便 easy to buy	77	17.4
6	只是由于习惯 out of habit	64	14.5
7	广告影响 influence of advertising	52	11.8
8	单位发的 offered by the working unit	8	1.8
9	有优惠条件 with preferential terms	7	1.6
10	朋友推荐 introduction of friends	6	1.4
11	其它 others	5	1.1
12	包装吸引人 appealing package	4	0.9
12	别人送的 given by other people	4	0.9

n=442

1-9 样本、男性各年龄层、女性各年龄层最常饮用的包装形式/ Package Types of the Consumed Carbonated Beverage by the Whole Sample, Age and Gender Groups

	人数 Number	玻璃瓶 glass bottle	易开罐 tin	塑料瓶 plastic bottle	纸杯 paper cup	其它 others
样本 Sample	**438**	**53.0**	**12.1**	**33.6**	**1.4**	**0.0**
男性 Male	**221**	**57.0**	**11.8**	**30.3**	**0.9**	**0.0**
16~24 岁 Age	57	50.9	14.0	35.[illegible]	0.0	0.0
25~34 岁 Age	71	56.3	5.6	36.6	1.4	0.0
35~44 岁 Age	47	63.8	12.8	21.3	2.1	0.0
45~54 岁 Age	29	62.1	10.3	27.6	0.0	0.0
55~60 岁 Age	17	52.9	29.4	17.6	0.0	0.0
女性 Female	**217**	**48.8**	**12.4**	**36.9**	**1.8**	**0.0**
16~24 岁 Age	58	43.1	19.0	31.0	6.9	0.0
25~34 岁 Age	72	48.6	9.7	41.7	0.0	0.0
35~44 岁 Age	43	48.8	11.6	39.5	0.0	0.0
45~54 岁 Age	33	60.6	9.1	30.3	0.0	0.0
55~60 岁 Age	11	45.5	9.1	45.5	0.0	0.0

1-10 样本、男性各年龄层、女性各年龄层最常饮用的场合/ Settings of Consumption by the Whole Sample, Age and Gender Groups

注：本题为多选题，合计百分比超过 100%（Multiple answers）

	人数 Number	平时口渴时 when thirsty	平时吃饭喝 at dinner	宴席、聚会喝 at banquet	外出、旅游时 outing/traveling	运动完以后 after athletics	其它 others
样本 Sample	**443**	**69.5**	**7.0**	**29.3**	**22.8**	**9.3**	**0.9**
男性 Male	**224**	**71.4**	**6.3**	**26.3**	**19.2**	**11.2**	**0.4**
16~24 岁 Age	57	75.4	3.5	22.8	8.8	26.3	0.0
25~34 岁 Age	71	78.9	7.0	19.7	22.5	4.2	1.4
35~44 岁 Age	47	66.0	8.5	27.7	27.7	8.5	0.0
45~54 岁 Age	31	71.0	9.7	29.0	3.2	3.2	0.0
55~60 岁 Age	18	44.4	0.0	55.6	44.4	11.1	0.0
女性 Female	**219**	**67.6**	**7.8**	**32.4**	**26.5**	**7.3**	**1.4**
16~24 岁 Age	58	72.4	8.6	25.9	29.3	15.5	1.7
25~34 岁 Age	72	70.8	6.9	29.2	30.6	4.2	1.4
35~44 岁 Age	45	55.6	8.9	44.4	24.4	6.7	2.2
45~54 岁 Age	33	69.7	6.1	39.4	18.2	3.0	0.0
55~60 岁 Age	11	63.6	9.1	18.2	18.2	0.0	0.0

1-11 重度消费者人口分布/ Demographics of the Heavy Consumers

	人数 Number	16-24 岁 Age	25-34 岁 Age	35-44 岁 Age	45-54 岁 Age	55-60 岁 Age
样本 Sample	247	32.4	33.2	18.6	12.6	3.2
男性 Male	127	31.5	30.7	18.1	16.5	3.1
天天喝 daily	10	10.0	20.0	20.0	40.0	10.0
一周 3 次或以上 3 times or over a week	39	38.5	23.1	17.9	17.9	2.6
一周 1~2 次 once or twice a week	78	30.8	35.9	17.9	12.8	2.6
女性 Female	120	33.3	35.8	19.2	8.3	3.3
天天喝 daily	11	54.5	27.3	18.2	0.0	0.0
一周 3 次或以上 3 times or over a week	33	48.5	30.3	15.2	3.0	3.0
一周 1~2 次 once or twice a week	76	23.7	39.5	21.1	11.8	3.9

1-12 不同消费者层的常用品牌/ The Most Frequently Used Brands by Market Segments

1-12-1 时尚流行指标/ Fads Popular Index

	人数 Number	第一品牌及百分比 1st/ percent	第二品牌及百分比 2nd/ percent	第三品牌及百分比 3rd/ percent	第四品牌及百分比 4th/ percent
样本 Sample	435	**百事可乐 Pepsi(57.0)**	**七喜 7-up(8.7)**	**美年达 Mirinda(7.6)**	**天府可乐 Tianfu(6.4)**
平实生活指向 simple living orientation	243	百事可乐 Pepsi(55.6)	七喜 7-up(8.6)	天府可乐 Tianfu(8.2)	可口可乐 Coca-cola6.2)
时尚流行指向 fashion orientation	192	百事可乐 Pepsi(58.9)	美年达 Mirinda(10.9)	七喜 7-up(8.9)	可口可乐 Coca-cola(6.3)

1-12-2 广告态度指标/ Advertising Attitude Index

	人数 Number	第一品牌及百分比 1st/ percent	第二品牌及百分比 2nd/ percent	第三品牌及百分比 3rd/ percent	第四品牌及百分比 4th/ percent
样本 Sample	437	**百事可乐 Pepsi(57.2)**	**七喜 7-up(8.7)**	**美年达 Mirinda(7.6)**	**天府可乐 Tianfu(6.2)** **可口可乐 Coca-cola(6.2)**
广告淡漠指向 indifferent orientation	114	百事可乐 Pepsi(49.1)	七喜 7-up(12.3)	美年达 Mirinda(7.9)	天府可乐 Tianfu(7.0) 可口可乐 Coca-cola(7.0)
中间层 medium	264	百事可乐 Pepsi(62.1)	七喜 7-up(7.6)	天府可乐 Tianfu(6.1)	可口可乐 Coca-cola(5.7) 美年达 Mirinda(5.7)
信赖广告指向 loyal orientation	59	百事可乐 Pepsi(50.8)	美年达 Mirinda(15.3)	可口可乐 Coca-cola(6.8) 七喜 7-up(6.8)	天府可乐 Tianfu(5.1) 雪碧 Sprite(5.1)

1-12-3 饮食健康指标/ Foods & Drink Quality Index

	人数 Number	第一品牌及百分比 1st/ percent	第二品牌及百分比 2nd/ percent	第三品牌及百分比 3rd/ percent	第四品牌及百分比 4th/ percent
样本 Sample	434	**百事可乐 Pepsi(56.9)**	**七喜 7-up(9.0)**	**美年达 Mirinda(7.6)**	**天府可乐 Tianfu(6.5)**
饮食"温饱"指向 "basic" orientation	157	百事可乐 Pepsi(61.8)	七喜 7-up(8.3)	天府可乐 Tianfu(7.0) 美年达 Mirinda(7.0)	雪碧 Sprite(5.1)
中间层 medium	194	百事可乐 Pepsi(54.6)	七喜 7-up(8.8)	可口可乐 Coca-cola(7.7)	天府可乐 Tianfu(7.2)
健康营养指向 health & nutrition orientation	83	百事可乐 Pepsi(53.0)	美年达 Mirinda(12.0)	七喜 7-up(10.8)	可口可乐 Coca-cola(6.0)

1-13 重度消费者的消费者层构成/ The Composition of the Heavy Consumers

1-13-1 时尚流行指标/ Fads Popular Index

	人数 Number	平实生活指向 simple living orientation	时尚流行指向 fashion orientation
样本 Sample	246	48.8	51.2
天天喝 daily	21	28.6	71.4
一周 3 次或以上 3 times or over a week	72	44.4	55.6
一周 1~2 次 once or twice a week	153	53.6	46.4

1-13-2 广告态度指标/ Advertising Attitude Index

	人数 Number	广告淡漠指向 indifferent orientation	中间层 medium	信赖广告指向 loyal orientation
样本 Sample	**244**	**24.6**	**61.1**	**14.3**
天天喝 daily	21	9.5	66.7	23.8
一周 3 次或以上 3 times or over a week	72	37.5	54.2	8.3
一周 1~2 次 once or twice a week	151	20.5	63.6	15.9

1-13-3 饮食健康指标/ Foods & Drink Quality Index

	人数 Number	饮食"温饱"指向 "basic" orientation	中间层 medium	健康营养指向 health & nutrition orientation
样本 Sample	**244**	**34.0**	**44.7**	**21.3**
天天喝 daily	21	19.0	52.4	28.6
一周 3 次或以上 3 times or over a week	72	33.3	48.6	18.1
一周 1~2 次 once or twice a week	151	36.4	41.7	21.9

● 武汉 / Wuhan

1-1 最近三个月饮用频率的比例/ Proportion of the Sample Consuming Carbonated Beverage in the Last Three Months

	人数 Number	百分比 Percent
天天喝 daily	30	4.7
一周 3 次或以上 3 times or over a week	95	14.8
一周 1~2 次 once or twice a week	167	26.1
一个月 2～3 次 2 or 3 times a month	133	20.7
一个月 1 次或以下 once a month or below	53	8.3
没喝过 never	163	25.4

n=641

1-2 最常用品牌排名/ Ranking of the Most Frequently Used Brands

排名 Brand Ranking	品牌 Brands	人数 Number	百分比 Percent
1	可口可乐 Coca-cola	182	38.2
2	百事可乐 Pepsi	78	16.4
3	雪碧 Sprite	73	15.3
4	滨江 Binjiang	30	6.3
5	芬达 Fanta	25	5.3
6	醒目 Smart	21	4.4
7	健力宝 Jianlibao	13	2.7

n=476

1-3 样本、男性各年龄层、女性各年龄层的常用品牌/ The Most Frequently Used Brands by the Whole Sample, Age and Gender Groups

	人数 Number	第一品牌及百分比 1st/ percent	第二品牌及百分比 2nd/ percent	第三品牌及百分比 3rd/ percent
样本 Sample	**476**	**可口可乐 Coca-cola(38.2)**	**百事可乐 Pepsi(16.4)**	**雪碧 Sprite(15.3)**
男性 Male	**225**	**可口可乐 Coca-cola(40.4)**	**百事可乐 Pepsi(16.4)**	**雪碧 Sprite(9.8)**
16~24 岁 Age	57	可口可乐 Coca-cola(45.6)	百事可乐 Pepsi(22.8)	芬达 Fanta(7.0) 醒目 Smart(7.0)
25~34 岁 Age	73	可口可乐 Coca-cola(42.5)	百事可乐 Pepsi(19.2)	雪碧 Sprite(11.0)
35~44 岁 Age	54	可口可乐 Coca-cola(38.9)	雪碧 Sprite(16.7)	滨江 Binjiang(14.8)
45~54 岁 Age	31	可口可乐 Coca-cola(35.5)	滨江 Binjiang(16.1)	百事可乐 Pepsi(9.7) 健力宝 Jianlibao(9.7)
55~60 岁 Age	10	百事可乐 Pepsi(20.0) 可口可乐 Coca-cola(20.0) 雪碧 Sprite(20.0)	芬达 Fanta(10.0) 醒目 Smart(10.0) 雪菲力 Ch'Nalry(10.0) 莱奇乐 Laiqile(10.0)	
女性 Female	**251**	**可口可乐 Coca-cola(36.3)**	**雪碧 Sprite(20.3)**	**百事可乐 Pepsi(16.3)**
16~24 岁 Age	64	可口可乐 Coca-cola(42.2)	百事可乐 Pepsi(20.3)	雪碧 Sprite(10.9)
25~34 岁 Age	77	可口可乐 Coca-cola(36.4)	雪碧 Sprite(27.3)	百事可乐 Pepsi(11.7)
35~44 岁 Age	56	可口可乐 Coca-cola(26.8)	雪碧 Sprite(23.2)	百事可乐 Pepsi(16.1)
45~54 岁 Age	42	可口可乐 Coca-cola(40.5)	百事可乐 Pepsi(21.4)	雪碧 Sprite(16.7)
55~60 岁 Age	12	可口可乐 Coca-cola(33.3)	雪碧 Sprite(25.0)	百事可乐 Pepsi(8.3) 芬达 Fanta(8.3) 滨江 Binjiang(8.3)

1-4 理想品牌排名/ Ranking of the Ideal Brands

排名 Brand Ranking	品牌 Brands	人数 Number	百分比 Percent
1	可口可乐 Coca-cola	203	31.6
2	雪碧 Sprite	90	14.0
3	百事可乐 Pepsi	85	13.2
4	滨江 Binjiang	29	4.5
5	芬达 Fanta	25	3.9
6	醒目 Smart	21	3.3
7	健力宝 Jianlibao	10	1.6
8	雪菲力 Ch'Nalry	9	1.4
9	武钢汽水 Wugang	5	0.8
10	七喜 7-up	4	0.6

n=642

1-5 样本、男性各年龄层、女性各年龄层最近三个月有无购买的比例/ Purchasing in the Last Three Months by the Whole Sample, Age and Gender Groups

	人数 Number	买过 yes	没买过 no
样本 Sample	640	71.4	28.6
男性 Male	311	70.4	29.6
16~24 岁 Age	65	83.1	16.9
25~34 岁 Age	89	82.0	18.0
35~44 岁 Age	80	65.0	35.0
45~54 岁 Age	52	55.8	44.2
55~60 岁 Age	25	44.0	56.0
女性 Female	329	72.3	27.7
16~24 岁 Age	69	91.3	8.7
25~34 岁 Age	95	75.8	24.2
35~44 岁 Age	77	67.5	32.5
45~54 岁 Age	62	62.9	37.1
55~60 岁 Age	26	46.2	53.8

1-6 样本、男性各年龄层、女性各年龄层最近三个月的饮用频率/ Frequencies of Consuming Carbonated Beverage in the Last Three Months by the Whole Sample, Age and Gender Groups

	人数 Number	天天喝 daily	一周 3 次或以上 3 times or over a week	一周 1~2 次 once or twice a week	一个月 2~3 次 2 or 3 times a month	一个月 1 次或以下 once a month or below	没喝过 never
样本 Sample	641	4.7	14.8	26.1	20.7	8.3	25.4
男性 Male	311	5.1	15.4	27.0	19.9	5.5	27.0
16~24 岁 Age	65	9.2	21.5	38.5	16.9	1.5	12.3
25~34 岁 Age	89	7.9	21.3	27.0	21.3	4.5	18.0
35~44 岁 Age	80	2.5	12.5	21.3	22.5	8.8	32.5
45~54 岁 Age	52	1.9	7.7	25.0	21.2	7.7	36.5
55~60 岁 Age	25	0.0	4.0	20.0	12.0	4.0	60.0
女性 Female	330	4.2	14.2	25.2	21.5	10.9	23.9
16~24 岁 Age	69	4.3	18.8	36.2	27.5	5.8	7.2
25~34 岁 Age	95	6.3	15.8	28.4	22.1	8.4	18.9
35~44 岁 Age	78	2.6	10.3	21.8	17.9	19.2	28.2
45~54 岁 Age	62	4.8	8.1	19.4	22.6	12.9	32.3
55~60 岁 Age	26	0.0	23.1	7.7	11.5	3.8	53.8

1-7 样本、男性各年龄层、女性各年龄层的品牌习惯/ Brand Habit in Consuming Carbonated Beverage by the Whole Sample, Age and Gender Groups

	人数 Number	基本固定饮用一个牌子 used in only one brand	比较固定地饮用两个或三个牌子 used in two or three brands	基本上不太固定牌子 no brand preference
样本 Sample	476	41.8	41.0	17.2
男性 Male	225	44.4	42.7	12.9
16~24 岁 Age	57	49.1	40.4	10.5
25~34 岁 Age	73	46.6	43.8	9.6
35~44 岁 Age	54	44.4	42.6	13.0
45~54 岁 Age	31	29.0	41.9	29.0
55~60 岁 Age	10	50.0	50.0	0.0
女性 Female	251	39.4	39.4	21.1
16~24 岁 Age	64	34.4	46.9	18.8
25~34 岁 Age	77	36.4	42.9	20.8
35~44 岁 Age	56	44.6	33.9	21.4
45~54 岁 Age	42	42.9	38.1	19.0
55~60 岁 Age	12	50.0	8.3	41.7

1-8 选择该类商品的考虑因素/ Ranking of the Considerations in Purchasing

注：本题为多选题，合计百分比超过 100%（Multiple answers）

排名 Ranking	考虑因素 Considerations	人次 Person-time	百分比 Percent
1	口味好 pleasant taste	324	67.9
2	有名的牌子 famous brand	193	40.5
3	价格适中 reasonable price	166	34.8
4	生产日期 date of producing	122	25.6
5	购买方便 easy to buy	98	20.5
6	只是由于习惯 out of habit	62	13.0
7	广告影响 influence of advertising	50	10.5
8	单位发的 offered by the working unit	23	4.8
9	别人送的 given by other people	15	3.1
10	其它 others	14	2.9
11	有优惠条件 with preferential terms	10	2.1
12	包装吸引人 appealing package	7	1.5
13	朋友推荐 introduction of friends	3	0.6

n=477

1-9 样本、男性各年龄层、女性各年龄层最常饮用的包装形式/ Package Types of the Consumed Carbonated Beverage by the Whole Sample, Age and Gender Groups

	人数 Number	玻璃瓶 glass bottle	易开罐 tin	塑料瓶 plastic bottle	纸杯 paper cup	其它 others
样本 Sample	476	25.8	17.2	50.0	6.9	0.0
男性 Male	225	31.6	17.3	44.0	7.1	0.0
16~24 岁 Age	57	31.6	19.3	35.1	14.0	0.0
25~34 岁 Age	73	23.3	17.8	53.4	5.5	0.0
35~44 岁 Age	54	38.9	16.7	38.9	5.6	0.0
45~54 岁 Age	31	38.7	19.4	38.7	3.2	0.0
55~60 岁 Age	10	30.0	0.0	70.0	0.0	0.0
女性 Female	251	20.7	17.1	55.4	6.8	0.0
16~24 岁 Age	64	18.8	20.3	50.0	10.9	0.0
25~34 岁 Age	77	18.2	16.9	57.1	7.8	0.0
35~44 岁 Age	56	25.0	14.3	58.9	1.8	0.0
45~54 岁 Age	42	16.7	16.7	59.5	7.1	0.0
55~60 岁 Age	12	41.7	16.7	41.7	0.0	0.0

1-10 样本、男性各年龄层、女性各年龄层最常饮用的场合/ Settings of Consumption by the Whole Sample, Age and Gender Groups

注：本题为多选题，合计百分比超过 100%（Multiple answers）

	人数 Number	平时口渴时 when thirsty	平时吃饭喝 at dinner	宴席、聚会喝 at banquet	外出、旅游时 outing/traveling	运动完以后 after athletics	其它 others
样本 Sample	**477**	**70.6**	**7.5**	**30.6**	**28.7**	**11.1**	**2.1**
男性 Male	**226**	**75.2**	**5.3**	**27.4**	**25.2**	**13.7**	**2.2**
16~24 岁 Age	57	78.9	7.0	17.5	24.6	21.1	3.5
25~34 岁 Age	73	75.3	5.5	30.1	20.5	16.4	2.7
35~44 岁 Age	54	74.1	3.7	24.1	29.6	11.1	0.0
45~54 岁 Age	32	68.8	3.1	34.4	31.3	3.1	3.1
55~60 岁 Age	10	80.0	10.0	60.0	20.0	0.0	0.0
女性 Female	**251**	**66.5**	**9.6**	**33.5**	**31.9**	**8.8**	**2.0**
16~24 岁 Age	64	75.0	12.5	15.6	40.6	6.3	0.0
25~34 岁 Age	77	66.2	6.5	33.8	35.1	6.5	2.6
35~44 岁 Age	56	58.9	8.9	46.4	25.0	10.7	3.6
45~54 岁 Age	42	61.9	14.3	47.6	23.8	11.9	0.0
55~60 岁 Age	12	75.0	0.0	16.7	25.0	16.7	8.3

1-11 重度消费者人口分布/ Demographics of the Heavy Consumers

	人数 Number	16-24 岁 Age	25-34 岁 Age	35-44 岁 Age	45-54 岁 Age	55-60 岁 Age
样本 Sample	**292**	**29.5**	**33.6**	**19.2**	**13.0**	**4.8**
男性 Male	**148**	**30.4**	**33.8**	**19.6**	**12.2**	**4.1**
天天喝 daily	16	37.5	43.8	12.5	6.3	0.0
一周 3 次或以上 3 times or over a week	48	29.2	39.6	20.8	8.3	2.1
一周 1~2 次 once or twice a week	84	29.8	28.6	20.2	15.5	6.0
女性 Female	**144**	**28.5**	**33.3**	**18.8**	**13.9**	**5.6**
天天喝 daily	14	21.4	42.9	14.3	21.4	0.0
一周 3 次或以上 3 times or over a week	47	27.7	31.9	17.0	10.6	12.8
一周 1~2 次 once or twice a week	83	30.1	32.5	20.5	14.5	2.4

1-12 不同消费者层的常用品牌/ The Most Frequently Used Brands by Market Segments

1-12-1 时尚流行指标/ Fads Popular Index

	人数 Number	第一品牌及百分比 1st/ percent	第二品牌及百分比 2nd/ percent	第三品牌及百分比 3rd/ percent
样本 Sample	470	**可口可乐 Coca-cola(38.5)**	**百事可乐 Pepsi(16.2)**	**雪碧 Sprite(15.3)**
平实生活指向 simple living orientation	231	可口可乐 Coca-cola(35.5)	雪碧 Sprite(15.6)	百事可乐 Pepsi(14.7)
时尚流行指向 fashion orientation	239	可口可乐 Coca-cola(41.4)	百事可乐 Pepsi(17.6)	雪碧 Sprite(15.1)

1-12-2 广告态度指标/ Advertising Attitude Index

	人数 Number	第一品牌及百分比 1st/ percent	第二品牌及百分比 2nd/ percent	第三品牌及百分比 3rd/ percent
样本 Sample	472	**可口可乐 Coca-cola(38.3)**	**百事可乐 Pepsi(16.1)**	**雪碧 Sprite(15.5)**
广告淡漠指向 indifferent orientation	118	可口可乐 Coca-cola(33.9)	雪碧 Sprite(18.6)	百事可乐 Pepsi(12.7)
中间层 medium	297	可口可乐 Coca-cola(41.1)	百事可乐 Pepsi(16.5)	雪碧 Sprite(13.8)
信赖广告指向 loyal orientation	57	可口可乐 Coca-cola(33.3)	百事可乐 Pepsi(21.1)	雪碧 Sprite(17.5)

1-12-3 饮食健康指标/ Foods & Drink Quality Index

	人数 Number	第一品牌及百分比 1st/ percent	第二品牌及百分比 2nd/ percent	第三品牌及百分比 3rd/ percent
样本 Sample	471	**可口可乐 Coca-cola(38.2)**	**百事可乐 Pepsi(16.1)**	**雪碧 Sprite(15.5)**
饮食“温饱”指向 "basic" orientation	159	可口可乐 Coca-cola(38.4)	百事可乐 Pepsi(16.4)	雪碧 Sprite(13.2)
中间层 medium	213	可口可乐 Coca-cola(36.6)	雪碧 Sprite(17.8)	百事可乐 Pepsi(15.5)
健康营养指向 health & nutrition orientation	99	可口可乐 Coca-cola(41.4)	百事可乐 Pepsi(17.2)	雪碧 Sprite(14.1)

1-13 重度消费者的消费者层构成/ The Composition of the Heavy Consumers

1-13-1 时尚流行指标/ Fads Popular Index

	人数 Number	平实生活指向 simple living orientation	时尚流行指向 fashion orientation
样本 Sample	288	44.4	55.6
天天喝 daily	30	43.3	56.7
一周 3 次或以上 3 times or over a week	92	40.2	59.8
一周 1~2 次 once or twice a week	166	47.0	53.0

1-13-2 广告态度指标/ Advertising Attitude Index

	人数 Number	广告淡漠指向 indifferent orientation	中间层 medium	信赖广告指向 loyal orientation
样本 Sample	289	23.2	64.0	12.8
天天喝 daily	30	20.0	70.0	10.0
一周 3 次或以上 3 times or over a week	93	25.8	53.1	16.1
一周 1~2 次 once or twice a week	166	22.3	66.3	11.4

1-13-3 饮食健康指标/ Foods & Drink Quality Index

	人数 Number	饮食"温饱"指向 "basic" orientation	中间层 medium	健康营养指向 health & nutrition orientation
样本 Sample	287	34.5	44.3	21.3
天天喝 daily	29	48.3	34.5	17.2
一周 3 次或以上 3 times or over a week	93	36.6	41.9	21.5
一周 1~2 次 once or twice a week	165	30.9	47.3	21.8

● 西安 / Xi'an

1-1 最近三个月饮用频率的比例/ Proportion of the Sample Consuming Carbonated Beverage in the Last Three Months

	人数 Number	百分比 Percent
天天喝 daily	20	3.3
一周 3 次或以上 3 times or over a week	81	13.5
一周 1~2 次 once or twice a week	160	26.6
一个月 2~3 次 2 or 3 times a month	146	24.3
一个月 1 次或以下 once a month or below	71	11.8
没喝过 never	123	20.5

n=601

1-2 最常用品牌排名/ Ranking of the Most Frequently Used Brands

排名 Brand Ranking	品牌 Brands	人数 Number	百分比 Percent
1	可口可乐 Coca-cola	255	53.3
2	雪碧 Sprite	67	14.0
3	冰峰 Ice Peek	65	13.6
4	芬达 Fanta	40	8.4
5	健力宝 Jianlibao	17	3.6
6	百事可乐 Pepsi	12	2.5
7	醒目 Smart	9	1.9
8	津美乐 Jinmeile	4	0.8
9	非常可乐 Future	2	0.4

n=478

1-3 样本、男性各年龄层、女性各年龄层的常用品牌/ The Most Frequently Used Brands by the Whole Sample, Age and Gender Groups

	人数 Number	第一品牌及百分比 1st/ percent	第二品牌及百分比 2nd/ percent	第三品牌及百分比 3rd/ percent
样本 Sample	478	**可口可乐 Coca-cola(53.3)**	**雪碧 Sprite(14.0)**	**冰峰 Ice Peek(13.6)**
男性 Male	243	**可口可乐 Coca-cola(54.7)**	**冰峰 Ice Peek(14.0)**	**雪碧 Sprite(11.5)**
16~24 岁 Age	59	可口可乐 Coca-cola(47.5)	冰峰 Ice Peek(20.3)	雪碧 Sprite(11.9)
25~34 岁 Age	76	可口可乐 Coca-cola(47.4)	冰峰 Ice Peek(15.8)	雪碧 Sprite(14.5)
35~44 岁 Age	64	可口可乐 Coca-cola(67.2)	冰峰 Ice Peek(10.9)	芬达 Fanta(7.8) 雪碧 Sprite(7.8)
45~54 岁 Age	31	可口可乐 Coca-cola(61.3)	雪碧 Sprite(9.7) 冰峰 Ice Peek(9.7)	百事可乐 Pepsi(6.5) 芬达 Fanta(6.5)
55~60 岁 Age	13	可口可乐 Coca-cola(53.8)	雪碧 Sprite(15.4)	百事可乐 Pepsi(7.7) 芬达 Fanta(7.7) 健力宝 Jianlibao(7.7)
女性 Female	235	**可口可乐 Coca-cola(51.9)**	**雪碧 Sprite(16.6)**	**冰峰 Ice Peek(13.2)**
16~24 岁 Age	49	可口可乐 Coca-cola(51.0)	芬达 Fanta(18.4)	雪碧 Sprite(8.2) 冰峰 Ice Peek(8.2)
25~34 岁 Age	79	可口可乐 Coca-cola(58.2)	雪碧 Sprite(13.9)	冰峰 Ice Peek(7.6)
35~44 岁 Age	55	可口可乐 Coca-cola(40.0)	冰峰 Ice Peek(27.3)	雪碧 Sprite(20.0)
45~54 岁 Age	35	可口可乐 Coca-cola(60.0)	雪碧 Sprite(20.0)	冰峰 Ice Peek(11.4)
55~60 岁 Age	17	可口可乐 Coca-cola(47.1)	雪碧 Sprite(35.3)	冰峰 Ice Peek(11.8)

1-4 理想品牌排名/ Ranking of the Ideal Brands

排名 Brand Ranking	品牌 Brands	人数 Number	百分比 Percent
1	可口可乐 Coca-cola	312	51.9
2	冰峰 Ice Peek	80	13.3
3	雪碧 Sprite	76	12.6
4	芬达 Fanta	44	7.3
5	健力宝 Jianlibao	18	3.0
6	百事可乐 Pepsi	13	2.2
7	醒目 Smart	8	1.3
8	非常可乐 Future	3	0.5
9	津美乐 Jinmeile	2	0.3

n=601

1-5 样本、男性各年龄层、女性各年龄层最近三个月有无购买的比例/ Purchasing in the Last Three Months by the Whole Sample, Age and Gender Groups

	人数 Number	买过 yes	没买过 no
样本 Sample	600	75.3	24.7
男性 Male	301	75.4	24.6
16~24 岁 Age	64	82.8	17.2
25~34 岁 Age	90	80.0	20.0
35~44 岁 Age	77	81.8	18.2
45~54 岁 Age	46	58.7	41.3
55~60 岁 Age	24	50.0	50.0
女性 Female	299	75.3	24.7
16~24 岁 Age	61	77.0	23.0
25~34 岁 Age	90	85.6	14.4
35~44 岁 Age	74	68.9	31.1
45~54 岁 Age	49	67.3	32.7
55~60 岁 Age	25	68.0	32.0

1-6 样本、男性各年龄层、女性各年龄层最近三个月的饮用频率/ Frequencies of Consuming Carbonated Beverage in the Last Three Months by the Whole Sample, Age and Gender Groups

	人数 Number	天天喝 daily	一周 3 次或以上 3 times or over a week	一周 1~2 次 once or twice a week	一个月 2~3 次 2 or 3 times a month	一个月 1 次或以下 once a month or below	没喝过 never
样本 Sample	601	3.3	13.5	26.6	24.3	11.8	20.5
男性 Male	302	4.3	15.9	28.8	21.5	9.9	19.5
16~24 岁 Age	64	9.4	29.7	25.0	25.0	3.1	7.8
25~34 岁 Age	91	2.2	14.3	39.6	17.6	9.9	16.5
35~44 岁 Age	77	2.6	13.0	33.8	22.1	11.7	16.9
45~54 岁 Age	46	6.5	10.9	13.0	21.7	15.2	32.6
55~60 岁 Age	24	0.0	4.2	12.5	25.0	12.5	45.8
女性 Female	299	2.3	11.0	24.4	27.1	13.7	21.4
16~24 岁 Age	61	4.9	18.0	26.2	16.4	14.8	19.7
25~34 岁 Age	90	2.2	10.0	31.1	31.1	13.3	12.2
35~44 岁 Age	74	2.7	5.4	14.9	36.5	14.9	25.7
45~54 岁 Age	49	0.0	12.2	24.5	26.5	8.2	28.6
55~60 岁 Age	25	0.0	12.0	24.0	12.0	20.0	32.0

1-7 样本、男性各年龄层、女性各年龄层的品牌习惯/ Brand Habit in Consuming Carbonated Beverage by the Whole Sample, Age and Gender Groups

	人数 Number	基本固定饮用一个牌子 used in only one brand	比较固定地饮用两个或三个牌子 used in two or three brands	基本上不太固定牌子 no brand preference
样本 Sample	478	45.2	44.1	10.7
男性 Male	243	46.5	43.6	9.9
16~24 岁 Age	59	44.1	49.2	6.8
25~34 岁 Age	76	53.9	39.5	6.6
35~44 岁 Age	64	53.1	35.9	10.9
45~54 岁 Age	31	32.3	54.8	12.9
55~60 岁 Age	13	15.4	53.8	30.8
女性 Female	235	43.8	44.7	11.5
16~24 岁 Age	49	49.0	40.8	10.2
25~34 岁 Age	79	45.6	48.1	6.3
35~44 岁 Age	55	40.0	45.5	14.5
45~54 岁 Age	35	37.1	48.6	14.3
55~60 岁 Age	17	47.1	29.4	23.5

1-8 选择该类商品的考虑因素/ Ranking of the Considerations in Purchasing

注：本题为多选题，合计百分比超过 100%（Multiple answers）

排名 Ranking	考虑因素 Considerations	人次 Person-time	百分比 Percent
1	口味好 pleasant taste	355	74.3
2	有名的牌子 famous brand	155	32.4
3	价格适中 reasonable price	137	28.7
4	生产日期 date of producing	82	17.2
5	购买方便 easy to buy	81	16.9
6	广告影响 influence of advertising	56	11.7
6	只是由于习惯 out of habit	56	11.7
7	包装吸引人 appealing package	14	2.9
8	朋友推荐 introduction of friends	12	2.5
9	单位发的 offered by the working unit	11	2.3
10	别人送的 given by other people	10	2.1
11	有优惠条件 with preferential terms	6	1.3
11	售货员介绍 introduced by the shop assistants	6	1.3
12	其它 others	1	0.2

n=478

1-9 样本、男性各年龄层、女性各年龄层最常饮用的包装形式/ Package Types of the Consumed Carbonated Beverage by the Whole Sample, Age and Gender Groups

	人数 Number	玻璃瓶 glass bottle	易开罐 tin	塑料瓶 plastic bottle	纸杯 paper cup	其它 others
样本 Sample	477	20.8	16.6	58.7	3.8	0.2
男性 Male	242	20.7	15.7	58.3	5.4	0.0
16~24 岁 Age	59	27.1	15.3	50.8	6.8	0.0
25~34 岁 Age	76	18.4	7.9	65.8	7.9	0.0
35~44 岁 Age	64	23.4	17.2	56.3	3.1	0.0
45~54 岁 Age	30	16.7	23.3	56.7	3.3	0.0
55~60 岁 Age	13	0.0	38.5	61.5	0.0	0.0
女性 Female	235	20.9	17.4	59.1	2.1	0.4
16~24 岁 Age	49	18.4	10.2	69.4	2.0	0.0
25~34 岁 Age	79	15.2	19.0	63.3	2.5	0.0
35~44 岁 Age	55	36.4	18.2	41.8	1.8	1.8
45~54 岁 Age	35	20.0	25.7	54.3	0.0	0.0
55~60 岁 Age	17	5.9	11.8	76.5	5.9	0.0

1-10 样本、男性各年龄层、女性各年龄层最常饮用的场合/ Settings of Consumption by the Whole Sample, Age and Gender Groups

注：本题为多选题，合计百分比超过 100%（Multiple answers）

	人数 Number	平时口渴时 when thirsty	平时吃饭喝 at dinner	宴席、聚会喝 at banquet	外出、旅游时 outing/traveling	运动完以后 after athletics	其它 others
样本 Sample	478	55.2	18.6	24.1	36.0	8.6	0.8
男性 Male	243	56.4	14.4	23.9	35.8	11.1	0.4
16~24 岁 Age	59	62.7	8.5	16.9	33.9	20.3	0.0
25~34 岁 Age	76	55.3	15.8	26.3	31.6	5.3	1.3
35~44 岁 Age	64	53.1	17.2	21.9	46.9	10.9	0.0
45~54 岁 Age	31	54.8	16.1	29.0	32.3	12.9	0.0
55~60 岁 Age	13	53.8	15.4	38.5	23.1	0.0	0.0
女性 Female	235	54.0	23.0	24.3	36.2	6.0	1.3
16~24 岁 Age	49	59.2	24.5	10.2	30.6	14.3	0.0
25~34 岁 Age	79	54.4	15.2	31.6	49.4	1.3	0.0
35~44 岁 Age	55	50.9	30.9	25.5	27.3	5.5	5.5
45~54 岁 Age	35	62.9	22.9	14.3	31.4	8.6	0.0
55~60 岁 Age	17	29.4	29.4	47.1	29.4	0.0	0.0

1-11 重度消费者人口分布/ Demographics of the Heavy Consumers

	人数 Number	16-24 岁 Age	25-34 岁 Age	35-44 岁 Age	45-54 岁 Age	55-60 岁 Age
样本 Sample	261	27.2	34.5	21.1	12.3	5.0
男性 Male	148	27.7	34.5	25.7	9.5	2.7
天天喝 daily	13	46.2	15.4	15.4	23.1	0.0
一周 3 次或以上 3 times or over a week	48	39.6	27.1	20.8	10.4	2.1
一周 1~2 次 once or twice a week	87	18.4	41.4	29.9	6.9	3.4
女性 Female	113	26.5	34.5	15.0	15.9	8.0
天天喝 daily	7	42.9	28.6	28.6	0.0	0.0
一周 3 次或以上 3 times or over a week	33	33.3	27.3	12.1	18.2	9.1
一周 1~2 次 once or twice a week	73	21.9	38.4	15.1	16.4	8.2

1-12 不同消费者层的常用品牌/ The Most Frequently Used Brands by Market Segments

1-12-1 时尚流行指标/ Fads Popular Index

	人数 Number	第一品牌及百分比 1st/ percent	第二品牌及百分比 2nd/ percent	第三品牌及百分比 3rd/ percent	第四品牌及百分比 4th/ percent
样本 Sample	476	可口可乐 Coca-cola(53.4)	雪碧 Sprite(13.9)	冰峰 Ice Peek(13.7)	芬达 Fanta(8.4)
平实生活指向 simple living orientation	253	可口可乐 Coca-cola(50.2)	雪碧 Sprite(16.2)	冰峰 Ice Peek(13.8)	芬达 Fanta(7.1)
时尚流行指向 fashion orientation	223	可口可乐 Coca-cola(57.0)	冰峰 Ice Peek(13.5)	雪碧 Sprite(11.2)	芬达 Fanta(9.9)

1-12-2 广告态度指标/ Advertising Attitude Index

	人数 Number	第一品牌及百分比 1st/ percent	第二品牌及百分比 2nd/ percent	第三品牌及百分比 3rd/ percent	第四品牌及百分比 4th/ percent
样本 Sample	**474**	**可口可乐 Coca-cola(53.6)**	**雪碧 Sprite(14.1)**	**冰峰 Ice Peek(13.7)**	**芬达 Fanta(8.0)**
广告淡漠指向 indifferent orientation	136	可口可乐 Coca-cola(51.5)	冰峰 Ice Peek(18.4)	雪碧 Sprite(11.0)	芬达 Fanta(8.8)
中间层 medium	270	可口可乐 Coca-cola(53.3)	雪碧 Sprite(15.9)	冰峰 Ice Peek(11.5)	芬达 Fanta(8.1)
信赖广告指向 loyal orientation	68	可口可乐 Coca-cola(58.8)	雪碧 Sprite(13.2) 冰峰 Ice Peek(13.2)	芬达 Fanta(5.9)	健力宝 Jianlibao(2.9)

1-12-3 饮食健康指标/ Foods & Drink Quality Index

	人数 Number	第一品牌及百分比 1st/ percent	第二品牌及百分比 2nd/ percent	第三品牌及百分比 3rd/ percent	第四品牌及百分比 4th/ percent
样本 Sample	**478**	**可口可乐 Coca-cola(53.3)**	**雪碧 Sprite(14.0)**	**冰峰 Ice Peek(13.6)**	**芬达 Fanta(8.4)**
饮食“温饱”指向 "basic" orientation	175	可口可乐 Coca-cola(52.0)	冰峰 Ice Peek(14.9)	雪碧 Sprite(14.3)	芬达 Fanta(6.3)
中间层 medium	221	可口可乐 Coca-cola(51.1)	冰峰 Ice Peek(13.6)	雪碧 Sprite(13.1)	芬达 Fanta(11.3)
健康营养指向 health & nutrition orientation	82	可口可乐 Coca-cola(62.2)	雪碧 Sprite(15.9)	冰峰 Ice Peek(11.0)	芬达 Fanta(4.9)

1-13 重度消费者的消费者层构成/ The Composition of the Heavy Consumers

1-13-1 时尚流行指标/ Fads Popular Index

	人数 Number	平实生活指向 simple living orientation	时尚流行指向 fashion orientation
样本 Sample	**261**	**47.9**	**52.1**
天天喝 daily	20	25.0	75.0
一周 3 次或以上 3 times or over a week	81	45.7	54.3
一周 1~2 次 once or twice a week	160	51.9	48.1

1-13-2 广告态度指标/ Advertising Attitude Index

	人数 Number	广告淡漠指向 indifferent orientation	中间层 medium	信赖广告指向 loyal orientation
样本 Sample	**258**	**27.5**	**57.8**	**14.7**
天天喝 daily	20	25.0	55.0	20.0
一周 3 次或以上 3 times or over a week	80	21.3	57.5	21.3
一周 1~2 次 once or twice a week	158	31.0	58.2	10.8

1-13-3 饮食健康指标/ Foods & Drink Quality Index

	人数 Number	饮食“温饱”指向 "basic" orientation	中间层 medium	健康营养指向 health & nutrition orientation
样本 Sample	**261**	**36.0**	**47.5**	**16.5**
天天喝 daily	20	30.0	60.0	10.0
一周 3 次或以上 3 times or over a week	81	39.5	46.9	13.6
一周 1~2 次 once or twice a week	160	35.0	46.3	18.8

● 沈阳 / Shenyang

1-1 最近三个月饮用频率的比例/ Proportion of the Sample Consuming Carbonated Beverage in the Last Three Months

	人数 Number	百分比 Percent
天天喝 daily	31	5.2
一周 3 次或以上 3 times or over a week	95	15.8
一周 1~2 次 once or twice a week	181	30.1
一个月 2～3 次 2 or 3 times a month	126	21.0
一个月 1 次或以下 once a month or below	60	10.0
没喝过 never	108	18.0

n=601

1-2 最常用品牌排名/ Ranking of the Most Frequently Used Brands

排名 Brand Ranking	品牌 Brands	人数 Number	百分比 Percent
1	可口可乐 Coca-cola	194	39.4
2	八王寺 Bawangsi	108	21.9
3	雪碧 Sprite	86	17.4
4	芬达 Fanta	41	8.3
5	宏宝莱 Hongbaolai	26	5.3
6	醒目 Smart	8	1.6
6	百事可乐 Pepsi	8	1.6
7	非常可乐 Future	6	1.2
8	美年达 Mirinda	3	0.6

n=493

1-3 样本、男性各年龄层、女性各年龄层的常用品牌/ The Most Frequently Used Brands by the Whole Sample, Age and Gender Groups

	人数 Number	第一品牌及百分比 1st/ percent	第二品牌及百分比 2nd/ percent	第三品牌及百分比 3rd/ percent
样本 Sample	**493**	**可口可乐 Coca-cola(39.4)**	**八王寺 Bawangsi(21.9)**	**雪碧 Sprite(17.4)**
男性 Male	**256**	**可口可乐 Coca-cola(41.4)**	**八王寺 Bawangsi(22.7)**	**雪碧 Sprite(18.0)**
16~24 岁 Age	62	可口可乐 Coca-cola(43.5)	芬达 Fanta(17.7) 八王寺 Bawangsi(17.7)	宏宝莱 Hongbaolai(8.1)
25~34 岁 Age	84	可口可乐 Coca-cola(54.8)	八王寺 Bawangsi(17.9)	雪碧 Sprite(14.3)
35~44 岁 Age	58	可口可乐 Coca-cola(31.0) 八王寺 Bawangsi(31.0)	雪碧 Sprite(29.3)	芬达 Fanta(5.2)
45~54 岁 Age	37	雪碧 Sprite(29.7)	可口可乐 Coca-cola(24.3)	八王寺 Bawangsi(21.6)
55~60 岁 Age	15	可口可乐 Coca-cola(40.0) 八王寺 Bawangsi(40.0)	雪碧 Sprite(13.3)	芬达 Fanta(6.7)
女性 Female	**237**	**可口可乐 Coca-cola(37.1)**	**八王寺 Bawangsi(21.1)**	**雪碧 Sprite(16.9)**
16~24 岁 Age	54	可口可乐 Coca-cola(31.5)	芬达 Fanta(16.7)	宏宝莱 Hongbaolai(14.8)
25~34 岁 Age	78	可口可乐 Coca-cola(44.9)	八王寺 Bawangsi(17.9)	雪碧 Sprite(16.7)
35~44 岁 Age	59	可口可乐 Coca-cola(33.9)	八王寺 Bawangsi(23.7)	雪碧 Sprite(18.6)
45~54 岁 Age	32	可口可乐 Coca-cola(40.6)	八王寺 Bawangsi(31.3)	雪碧 Sprite(18.8)
55~60 岁 Age	14	八王寺 Bawangsi(42.9)	雪碧 Sprite(28.6)	可口可乐 Coca-cola(21.4)

1-4 理想品牌排名/ Ranking of the Ideal Brands

排名 Brand Ranking	品牌 Brands	人数 Number	百分比 Percent
1	可口可乐 Coca-cola	222	36.9
2	八王寺 Bawangsi	137	22.8
3	雪碧 Sprite	88	14.6
4	芬达 Fanta	43	7.2
5	宏宝莱 Hongbaolai	38	6.3
6	醒目 Smart	14	2.3
7	非常可乐 Future	10	1.7
8	百事可乐 Pepsi	8	1.3
9	美年达 Mirinda	2	0.3
9	莱蒙 Lemon	2	0.3
9	健力宝 Jianlibao	2	0.3

n=601

1-5 样本、男性各年龄层、女性各年龄层最近三个月有无购买的比例/ Purchasing in the Last Three Months by the Whole Sample, Age and Gender Groups

	人数 Number	买过 yes	没买过 no
样本 Sample	601	81.9	18.1
男性 Male	299	84.6	15.4
16~24 岁 Age	64	96.9	3.1
25~34 岁 Age	89	92.1	7.9
35~44 岁 Age	76	76.3	23.7
45~54 岁 Age	46	78.3	21.7
55~60 岁 Age	24	62.5	37.5
女性 Female	302	79.1	20.9
16~24 岁 Age	64	79.7	20.3
25~34 岁 Age	90	85.6	14.4
35~44 岁 Age	76	78.9	21.1
45~54 岁 Age	48	70.8	29.2
55~60 岁 Age	24	70.8	29.2

1-6 样本、男性各年龄层、女性各年龄层最近三个月的饮用频率/ Frequencies of Consuming Carbonated Beverage in the Last Three Months by the Whole Sample, Age and Gender Groups

	人数 Number	天天喝 daily	一周 3 次或以上 3 times or over a week	一周 1~2 次 once or twice a week	一个月 2~3 次 2 or 3 times a month	一个月 1 次或以下 once a month or below	没喝过 never
样本 Sample	601	5.2	15.8	30.1	21.0	10.0	18.0
男性 Male	299	5.4	16.4	33.1	22.1	8.7	14.4
16~24 岁 Age	64	6.3	25.0	51.6	10.9	3.1	3.1
25~34 岁 Age	89	10.1	20.2	38.2	20.2	5.6	5.6
35~44 岁 Age	76	2.6	14.5	23.7	26.3	9.2	23.7
45~54 岁 Age	46	2.2	4.3	19.6	39.1	15.2	19.6
55~60 岁 Age	24	0.0	8.3	20.8	12.5	20.8	37.5
女性 Female	302	5.0	15.2	27.2	19.9	11.3	21.5
16~24 岁 Age	64	7.8	18.8	26.6	18.8	12.5	15.6
25~34 岁 Age	90	5.6	15.6	31.1	26.7	7.8	13.3
35~44 岁 Age	76	3.9	14.5	35.5	13.2	10.5	22.4
45~54 岁 Age	48	0.0	16.7	14.6	18.8	16.7	33.3
55~60 岁 Age	24	8.3	4.2	12.5	20.8	12.5	41.7

1-7 样本、男性各年龄层、女性各年龄层的品牌习惯/ Brand Habit in Consuming Carbonated Beverage by the Whole Sample, Age and Gender Groups

	人数 Number	基本固定饮用一个牌子 used in only one brand	比较固定地饮用两个或三个牌子 used in two or three brands	基本上不太固定牌子 no brand preference
样本 Sample	491	51.5	33.4	15.1
男性 Male	255	56.9	31.4	11.8
16~24 岁 Age	62	51.6	35.5	12.9
25~34 岁 Age	84	63.1	33.3	3.6
35~44 岁 Age	58	62.1	20.7	17.2
45~54 岁 Age	36	41.7	36.1	22.2
55~60 岁 Age	15	60.0	33.3	6.7
女性 Female	236	45.8	35.6	18.6
16~24 岁 Age	54	33.3	46.3	20.4
25~34 岁 Age	77	53.2	36.4	10.4
35~44 岁 Age	59	35.6	33.9	30.5
45~54 岁 Age	32	56.3	25.0	18.8
55~60 岁 Age	14	71.4	21.4	7.1

1-8 选择该类商品的考虑因素/ Ranking of the Considerations in Purchasing

注：本题为多选题，合计百分比超过 100%（Multiple answers）

排名 Ranking	考虑因素 Considerations	人次 Person-time	百分比 Percent
1	口味好 pleasant taste	348	70.9
2	价格适中 reasonable price	189	38.5
3	有名的牌子 famous brand	161	32.8
4	购买方便 easy to buy	113	23.0
5	生产日期 date of producing	110	22.4
6	只是由于习惯 out of habit	70	14.3
7	广告影响 influence of advertising	25	5.1
8	有优惠条件 with preferential terms	13	2.6
9	包装吸引人 appealing package	10	2.0
10	单位发的 offered by the working unit	7	1.4
11	朋友推荐 introduction of friends	5	1.0
11	别人送的 given by other people	5	1.0

n=491

1-9 样本、男性各年龄层、女性各年龄层最常饮用的包装形式/ Package Types of the Consumed Carbonated Beverage by the Whole Sample, Age and Gender Groups

	人数 Number	玻璃瓶 glass bottle	易开罐 tin	塑料瓶 plastic bottle	纸杯 paper cup	其它 others
样本 Sample	490	41.6	15.5	40.4	2.4	0.0
男性 Male	254	44.5	14.2	39.8	1.6	0.0
16~24 岁 Age	62	48.4	11.3	35.5	4.8	0.0
25~34 岁 Age	82	35.4	14.6	48.8	1.2	0.0
35~44 岁 Age	58	55.2	13.8	31.0	0.0	0.0
45~54 岁 Age	37	37.8	24.3	37.8	0.0	0.0
55~60 岁 Age	15	53.3	0.0	46.7	0.0	0.0
女性 Female	236	38.6	16.9	41.1	3.4	0.0
16~24 岁 Age	54	42.6	14.8	38.9	3.7	0.0
25~34 岁 Age	77	32.5	14.3	46.8	6.5	0.0
35~44 岁 Age	59	42.4	25.4	30.5	1.7	0.0
45~54 岁 Age	32	37.5	15.6	46.9	0.0	0.0
55~60 岁 Age	14	42.9	7.1	50.0	0.0	0.0

1-10 样本、男性各年龄层、女性各年龄层最常饮用的场合/ Settings of Consumption by the Whole Sample, Age and Gender Groups

注：本题为多选题，合计百分比超过 100%（Multiple answers）

	人数 Number	平时口渴时 when thirsty	平时吃饭喝 at dinner	宴席、聚会喝 at banquet	外出、旅游时 outing/traveling	运动完以后 after athletics	其它 others
样本 Sample	491	70.5	12.2	23.4	25.9	6.9	1.0
男性 Male	255	74.1	11.4	20.4	23.9	9.0	0.8
16~24 岁 Age	62	82.3	8.1	11.3	21.0	24.2	0.0
25~34 岁 Age	84	76.2	10.7	20.2	27.4	7.1	0.0
35~44 岁 Age	58	75.9	13.8	22.4	24.1	1.7	0.0
45~54 岁 Age	36	61.1	8.3	25.0	19.4	2.8	5.6
55~60 岁 Age	15	53.3	26.7	40.0	26.7	0.0	0.0
女性 Female	236	66.5	13.1	26.7	28.0	4.7	1.3
16~24 岁 Age	54	64.8	13.0	27.8	33.3	9.3	1.9
25~34 岁 Age	77	64.9	15.6	24.7	28.6	5.2	2.6
35~44 岁 Age	59	66.1	16.9	30.5	27.1	1.7	0.0
45~54 岁 Age	32	75.0	3.1	18.8	25.0	3.1	0.0
55~60 岁 Age	14	64.3	7.1	35.7	14.3	0.0	0.0

1-11 重度消费者人口分布/ Demographics of the Heavy Consumers

	人数 Number	16-24 岁 Age	25-34 岁 Age	35-44 岁 Age	45-54 岁 Age	55-60 岁 Age
样本 Sample	307	28.3	35.2	23.5	8.8	4.2
男性 Male	164	32.3	37.2	18.9	7.3	4.3
天天喝 daily	16	25.0	56.3	12.5	6.3	0.0
一周 3 次或以上 3 times or over a week	49	32.7	36.7	22.4	4.1	4.1
一周 1~2 次 once or twice a week	99	33.3	34.3	18.2	9.1	5.1
女性 Female	143	23.8	32.9	28.7	10.5	4.2
天天喝 daily	15	33.3	33.3	20.0	0.0	13.3
一周 3 次或以上 3 times or over a week	46	26.1	30.4	23.9	17.4	2.2
一周 1~2 次 once or twice a week	82	20.7	34.1	32.9	8.5	3.7

1-12 不同消费者层的常用品牌/ The Most Frequently Used Brands by Market Segments

1-12-1 时尚流行指标/ Fads Popular Index

	人数 Number	第一品牌及百分比 1st/ percent	第二品牌及百分比 2nd/ percent	第三品牌及百分比 3rd/ percent	第四品牌及百分比 4th/ percent	第五品牌及百分比 5th/ percent
样本 Sample	493	**可口可乐 Coca-cola(39.4)**	**八王寺 Bawangsi(21.9)**	**雪碧 Sprite(17.4)**	**芬达 Fanta(8.3)**	**宏宝莱 Hongbaolai(5.3)**
平实生活指向 simple living orientation	225	可口可乐 Coca-cola(34.7)	八王寺 Bawangsi(25.8)	雪碧 Sprite(20.9)	芬达 Fanta(6.2)	宏宝莱 Hongbaolai(5.3)
时尚流行指向 fashion orientation	268	可口可乐 Coca-cola(43.3)	八王寺 Bawangsi(18.7)	雪碧 Sprite(14.6)	芬达 Fanta(10.1)	宏宝莱 Hongbaolai(5.2)

1-12-2 广告态度指标/ Advertising Attitude Index

	人数 Number	第一品牌及百分比 1st/ percent	第二品牌及百分比 2nd/ percent	第三品牌及百分比 3rd/ percent	第四品牌及百分比 4th/ percent	第五品牌及百分比 5th/ percent
样本 Sample	493	**可口可乐 Coca-cola(39.4)**	**八王寺 Bawangsi(21.9)**	**雪碧 Sprite(17.4)**	**芬达 Fanta(8.3)**	**宏宝莱 Hongbaolai(5.3)**
广告淡漠指向 indifferent orientation	138	可口可乐 Coca-cola(35.5)	八王寺 Bawangsi(26.8)	雪碧 Sprite(20.3)	芬达 Fanta(5.8)	宏宝莱 Hongbaolai(5.1)
中间层 medium	292	可口可乐 Coca-cola(41.1)	八王寺 Bawangsi(19.2)	雪碧 Sprite(17.1)	芬达 Fanta(9.9)	宏宝莱 Hongbaolai(5.1)
信赖广告指向 loyal orientation	63	可口可乐 Coca-cola(39.7)	八王寺 Bawangsi(23.8)	雪碧 Sprite(12.7)	芬达 Fanta(6.3) 宏宝莱 Hongbaolai(6.3)	健力宝 Jianlibao(3.2)

1-12-3 饮食健康指标/ Foods & Drink Quality Index

	人数 Number	第一品牌及百分比 1st/ percent	第二品牌及百分比 2nd/ percent	第三品牌及百分比 3rd/ percent	第四品牌及百分比 4th/ percent	第五品牌及百分比 5th/ percent
样本 Sample	493	**可口可乐 Coca-cola(39.4)**	**八王寺 Bawangsi(21.9)**	**雪碧 Sprite(17.4)**	**芬达 Fanta(8.3)**	**宏宝莱 Hongbaolai(5.3)**
饮食"温饱"指向 "basic" orientation	152	可口可乐 Coca-cola(36.2)	八王寺 Bawangsi(24.3)	雪碧 Sprite(19.7)	芬达 Fanta(8.6)	宏宝莱 Hongbaolai(5.9)
中间层 medium	223	可口可乐 Coca-cola(43.5)	八王寺 Bawangsi(19.3)	雪碧 Sprite(15.7)	芬达 Fanta(8.5)	宏宝莱 Hongbaolai(5.8)
健康营养指向 health & nutrition orientation	118	可口可乐 Coca-cola(35.6)	八王寺 Bawangsi(23.7)	雪碧 Sprite(17.8)	芬达 Fanta(7.6)	宏宝莱 Hongbaolai(3.4)

1-13 重度消费者的消费者层构成/ The Composition of the Heavy Consumers

1-13-1 时尚流行指标/ Fads Popular Index

	人数 Number	平实生活指向 simple living orientation	时尚流行指向 fashion orientation
样本 Sample	307	37.8	62.2
天天喝 daily	31	25.8	74.2
一周 3 次或以上 3 times or over a week	95	37.9	62.1
一周 1~2 次 once or twice a week	181	39.8	60.2

1-13-2 广告态度指标/ Advertising Attitude Index

	人数 Number	广告淡漠指向 indifferent orientation	中间层 medium	信赖广告指向 loyal orientation
样本 Sample	307	27.4	58.6	14.0
天天喝 daily	31	29.0	45.2	25.8
一周 3 次或以上 3 times or over a week	95	26.3	58.9	14.7
一周 1~2 次 once or twice a week	181	27.6	60.8	11.6

1-13-3 饮食健康指标/ Foods & Drink Quality Index

	人数 Number	饮食"温饱"指向 "basic" orientation	中间层 medium	健康营养指向 health & nutrition orientation
样本 Sample	307	26.4	50.2	23.5
天天喝 daily	31	19.4	61.3	19.4
一周 3 次或以上 3 times or over a week	95	26.3	49.5	24 .2
一周 1~2 次 once or twice a week	181	27.6	48.6	23.8

2.包装水 / Purified or Mineral Water

● 北京 / Beijing

2-1 最近三个月饮用频率的比例/ Proportion of the Sample Consuming Purified or Mineral Water in the Last Three Months

	人数 Number	百分比 Percent
天天喝 daily	68	6.7
一周 3 次或以上 3 times or over a week	127	12.6
一周 1~2 次 once or twice a week	241	23.9
一个月 2~3 次 2 or 3 times a month	204	20.2
一个月 1 次或以下 once a month or below	109	10.8
没喝过 never	261	25.8

n=1010

2-2 最常用品牌排名/ Ranking of the Most Frequently Used Brands

排名 Brand Ranking	品牌 Brands	人数 Number	百分比 Percent
1	娃哈哈 Wahaha	214	28.8
2	乐百氏 Robust	213	28.7
3	农夫山泉 Nong Fu Shan Quan	125	16.8
4	康师傅 Kangshifu	43	5.8
5	可赛 Kesai	26	3.5
6	雀巢 Nestle	10	1.3
7	屈臣氏 Watson's	8	1.1
7	获特满 Waterman	8	1.1

n=742

2-3 样本、男性各年龄层、女性各年龄层的常用品牌/ The Most Frequently Used Brands by the Whole Sample, Age and Gender Groups

	人数 Number	第一品牌及百分比 1st/ percent	第二品牌及百分比 2nd/ percent	第三品牌及百分比 3rd/ percent
样本 Sample	**742**	**娃哈哈 Wahaha(28.8)**	**乐百氏 Robust(28.7)**	**农夫山泉 Nong Fu Shan Quan(16.8)**
男性 Male	**373**	**娃哈哈 Wahaha(30.8)**	**乐百氏 Robust(27.3)**	**农夫山泉 Nong Fu Shan Quan(15.0)**
16~24 岁 Age	83	娃哈哈 Wahaha(31.3)	乐百氏 Robust(30.1)	农夫山泉 Nong Fu Shan Quan(12.0)
25~34 岁 Age	121	娃哈哈 Wahaha(29.8) 乐百氏 Robust(29.8)	农夫山泉 Nong Fu Shan Quan(17.4)	康师傅 Kangshifu(6.6)
35~44 岁 Age	96	娃哈哈 Wahaha(29.2)	乐百氏 Robust(21.9)	农夫山泉 Nong Fu Shan Quan(15.6)
45~54 岁 Age	50	乐百氏 Robust(34.0) 娃哈哈 Wahaha(34.0)	农夫山泉 Nong Fu Shan Quan(12.0)	碧臣 Bichen(2.0) 华邦 Huabang(2.0) 康师傅 Kangshifu(2.0) 可赛 Kesai(2.0) 领先 First(2.0) 太古 Taigu(2.0)
55~60 岁 Age	23	娃哈哈 Wahaha(34.8)	农夫山泉 Nong Fu Shan Quan(17.4)	乐百氏 Robust(13.0)
女性 Female	**369**	**乐百氏 Robust(30.1)**	**娃哈哈 Wahaha(26.8)**	**农夫山泉 Nong Fu Shan Quan(18.7)**
16~24 岁 Age	95	乐百氏 Robust(30.5)	娃哈哈 Wahaha(26.3)	农夫山泉 Nong Fu Shan Quan(14.7)
25~34 岁 Age	113	乐百氏 Robust(35.4)	娃哈哈 Wahaha(23.9)	农夫山泉 Nong Fu Shan Quan(21.2)
35~44 岁 Age	89	娃哈哈 Wahaha(32.6)	乐百氏 Robust(22.5)	农夫山泉 Nong Fu Shan Quan(19.1)
45~54 岁 Age	52	乐百氏 Robust(32.7)	农夫山泉 Nong Fu Shan Quan(25.0)	娃哈哈 Wahaha(23.1)
55~60 岁 Age	20	娃哈哈 Wahaha(30.0)	乐百氏 Robust(25.0)	翠微山 Cuiweishan(5.0) 康师傅 Kangshifu(5.0) 可赛 Kesai(5.0) 崂山 Laoshan(5.0) 领先 First(5.0) 农夫山泉 Nong Fu Shan Quan(5.0) 昌运 Changyun(5.0)

2-4 理想品牌排名/ Ranking of the Ideal Brands

排名 Brand Ranking	品牌 Brands	人数 Number	百分比 Percent
1	乐百氏 Robust	247	24.4
2	娃哈哈 Wahaha	229	22.6
3	农夫山泉 Nong Fu Shan Quan	179	17.7
4	康师傅 Kangshifu	53	5.2
5	可赛 Kesai	32	3.2
6	雀巢 Nestle	15	1.5
7	屈臣氏 Watson's	10	1.0

n=1012

2-5 样本、男性各年龄层、女性各年龄层最近三个月有无购买的比例/ Purchasing in the Last Three Months by the Whole Sample, Age and Gender Groups

	人数 Number	买过 yes	没买过 no
样本 Sample	1011	68.8	31.2
男性 Male	504	67.9	32.1
16~24 岁 Age	105	74.3	25.7
25~34 岁 Age	151	74.2	25.8
35~44 岁 Age	131	69.5	30.5
45~54 岁 Age	77	55.8	44.2
55~60 岁 Age	40	45.0	55.0
女性 Female	507	69.8	30.2
16~24 岁 Age	107	84.1	15.9
25~34 岁 Age	150	73.3	26.7
35~44 岁 Age	124	69.4	30.6
45~54 岁 Age	84	60.7	39.3
55~60 岁 Age	42	40.5	59.5

2-6 样本、男性各年龄层、女性各年龄层最近三个月的饮用频率/ Frequencies of Consuming Purified or Mineral Water in the Last Three Months by the Whole Sample, Age and Gender Groups

	人数 Number	天天喝 daily	一周 3 次或以上 3 times or over a week	一周 1~2 次 once or twice a week	一个月 2~3 次 2 or 3 times a month	一个月 1 次或以下 once a month or below	没喝过 never
样本 Sample	1010	6.7	12.6	23.9	20.2	10.8	25.8
男性 Male	503	8.3	12.9	25.8	17.9	10.3	24.7
16~24 岁 Age	105	7.6	12.4	31.4	17.1	11.4	20.0
25~34 岁 Age	151	10.6	16.6	29.8	15.2	8.6	19.2
35~44 岁 Age	131	9.2	13.7	26.0	16.8	9.9	24.4
45~54 岁 Age	76	5.3	10.5	14.5	22.4	14.5	32.9
55~60 岁 Age	40	5.0	2.5	17.5	25.0	7.5	42.5
女性 Female	507	5.1	12.2	21.9	22.5	11.2	27.0
16~24 岁 Age	108	5.6	13.0	29.6	29.6	11.1	11.1
25~34 岁 Age	150	6.0	13.3	24.0	17.3	14.7	24.7
35~44 岁 Age	123	4.9	14.6	19.5	23.6	9.8	27.6
45~54 岁 Age	84	4.8	10.7	20.2	19.0	7.1	38.1
55~60 岁 Age	42	2.4	2.4	4.8	26.2	11.9	52.4

2-7 样本、男性各年龄层、女性各年龄层的品牌习惯/ Brand Habit in Consuming Purified or Mineral Water by the Whole Sample, Age and Gender Groups

	人数 Number	基本固定饮用一个牌子 used in only one brand	比较固定地饮用两个或三个牌子 used in two or three brands	基本上不太固定牌子 no brand preference
样本 Sample	746	33.9	45.6	20.5
男性 Male	377	38.7	39.8	21.5
16~24 岁 Age	84	44.0	36.9	19.0
25~34 岁 Age	121	37.2	43.0	19.8
35~44 岁 Age	99	37.4	41.4	21.2
45~54 岁 Age	50	32.0	40.0	28.0
55~60 岁 Age	23	47.8	26.1	26.1
女性 Female	369	29.0	51.5	19.5
16~24 岁 Age	95	18.9	58.9	22.1
25~34 岁 Age	113	31.9	54.9	13.3
35~44 岁 Age	89	30.3	48.3	21.3
45~54 岁 Age	52	34.6	40.4	25.0
55~60 岁 Age	20	40.0	40.0	20.0

2-8 选择该类商品的考虑因素/ Ranking of the Considerations in Purchasing

注：本题为多选题，合计百分比超过 100%(Multiple answers）

排名 Ranking	考虑因素 Considerations	人次 Person-time	百分比 Percent
1	有名的牌子 famous brand	297	40.0
2	价格适中 reasonable price	284	38.2
3	口味好 pleasant taste	243	32.7
4	生产日期 date of producing	189	25.4
5	购买方便 easy to buy	161	21.7
6	广告影响 influence of advertising	117	15.7
7	只是由于习惯 out of habit	74	10.0
8	单位发的 offered by the working unit	37	5.0
9	包装吸引人 appealing package	24	3.2
10	有优惠条件 with preferential terms	17	2.3
10	其它 others	17	2.3
11	朋友推荐 introduction of friends	13	1.7
12	售货员介绍 introduced by the shop assistants	4	0.5

n=743

2-9 样本、男性各年龄层、女性各年龄层最常饮用的包装形式/ Types of Package of the Consumed Purified or Mineral Water by the Whole Sample, Age and Gender Groups

	人数 Number	250ml 以下 250ml or below	250ml--350ml	500ml--750ml	1L	1.5L	2L 以上 2L or over	其它 others
样本 Sample	731	29.8	32.6	29.0	2.1	2.2	3.1	1.2
男性 Male	369	28.5	35.0	27.1	1.4	2.7	4.1	1.4
16~24 岁 Age	83	27.7	39.8	21.7	1.2	7.2	2.4	0.0
25~34 岁 Age	118	34.7	35.6	22.9	0.0	0.8	5.1	0.8
35~44 岁 Age	95	25.3	33.7	27.4	2.1	2.1	6.3	3.2
45~54 岁 Age	50	26.0	28.0	36.0	4.0	2.0	2.0	2.0
55~60 岁 Age	23	17.4	34.8	47.8	0.0	0.0	0.0	0.0
女性 Female	362	31.2	30.1	30.9	2.8	1.7	2.2	1.1
16~24 岁 Age	94	33.0	34.0	24.5	5.3	2.1	1.1	0.0
25~34 岁 Age	113	28.3	36.3	30.1	2.7	0.0	0.9	1.8
35~44 岁 Age	88	30.7	33.0	30.7	0.0	3.4	1.1	1.1
45~54 岁 Age	47	31.9	12.8	42.6	2.1	2.1	8.5	0.0
55~60 岁 Age	20	40.0	5.0	40.0	5.0	0.0	5.0	5.0

2-10 样本、男性各年龄层、女性各年龄层最常饮用的场合/ Settings of Consumption by the Whole Sample, Age and Gender Groups

注：本题为多选题，合计百分比超过 100%(Multiple answers)

	人数 Number	平时口渴时 when thirsty	平时吃饭喝 at dinner	宴席、聚会喝 at banquet	外出、旅游时 outing/traveling	运动完以后 after athletics	其它 others
样本 Sample	**742**	**67.1**	**2.8**	**4.6**	**50.9**	**14.4**	**1.3**
男性 Male	**375**	**69.1**	**1.1**	**3.5**	**46.7**	**15.5**	**1.3**
16~24 岁 Age	84	75.0	1.2	1.2	32.1	33.3	1.2
25~34 岁 Age	120	75.0	0.8	4.2	42.5	12.5	0.8
35~44 岁 Age	98	68.4	1.0	4.1	55.1	9.2	1.0
45~54 岁 Age	50	54.0	2.0	4.0	54.0	10.0	4.0
55~60 岁 Age	23	52.2	0.0	4.3	69.6	4.3	0.0
女性 Female	**367**	**65.1**	**4.6**	**5.7**	**55.3**	**13.4**	**1.4**
16~24 岁 Age	95	75.8	2.1	5.3	45.3	20.0	1.1
25~34 岁 Age	112	63.4	1.8	2.7	65.2	11.6	1.8
35~44 岁 Age	89	61.8	6.7	6.7	57.3	13.5	1.1
45~54 岁 Age	51	64.7	9.8	9.8	47.1	9.8	2.0
55~60 岁 Age	20	40.0	10.0	10.0	60.0	0.0	0.0

2-11 重度消费者人口分布/ Demographics of the Heavy Consumers

	人数 Number	16-24 岁 Age	25-34 岁 Age	35-44 岁 Age	45-54 岁 Age	55-60 岁 Age
样本 Sample	**436**	**24.3**	**34.6**	**25.7**	**12.2**	**3.2**
男性 Male	**237**	**22.8**	**36.3**	**27.0**	**9.7**	**4.2**
天天喝 daily	42	19.0	38.1	28.6	9.5	4.8
一周 3 次或以上 3 times or over a week	65	20.0	38.5	27.7	12.3	1.5
一周 1~2 次 once or twice a week	130	25.4	34.6	26.2	8.5	5.4
女性 Female	**199**	**26.1**	**32.7**	**24.1**	**15.1**	**2.0**
天天喝 daily	26	23.1	34.6	23.1	15.4	3.8
一周 3 次或以上 3 times or over a week	62	22.6	32.3	29.0	14.5	1.6
一周 1~2 次 once or twice a week	111	28.8	32.4	21.6	15.3	1.8

2-12 不同消费者层的常用品牌/ The Most Frequently Used Brands by Market Segments

2-12-1 时尚流行指标/ Fads Popular Index

	人数 Number	第一品牌及百分比 1st/ percent	第二品牌及百分比 2nd/ percent	第三品牌及百分比 3rd/ percent	第四品牌及百分比 4th/ percent
样本 Sample	**729**	**乐百氏 Robust(28.9)**	**娃哈哈 Wahaha(28.7)**	**农夫山泉 Nong Fu Shan Quan (16.6)**	**康师傅 Kangshifu(5.6)**
平实生活指向 simple living orientation	333	娃哈哈 Wahaha(29.1) 乐百氏 Robust(29.1)	农夫山泉 Nong Fu Shan Quan (18.6)	康师傅 Kangshifu(5.1)	可赛 Kesai(3.0)
时尚流行指向 fashion orientation	396	乐百氏 Robust(28.8)	娃哈哈 Wahaha(28.3)	农夫山泉 Nong Fu Shan Quan (14.9)	康师傅 Kangshifu(6.1)

2-12-2 广告态度指标/ Advertising Attitude Index

	人数 Number	第一品牌及百分比 1st/ percent	第二品牌及百分比 2nd/ percent	第三品牌及百分比 3rd/ percent	第四品牌及百分比 4th/ percent
样本 Sample	**726**	**娃哈哈 Wahaha(29.1)**	**乐百氏 Robust(28.2)**	**农夫山泉 Nong Fu Shan Quan (16.9)**	**康师傅 Kangshifu(5.9)**
广告淡漠指向 indifferent orientation	197	娃哈哈 Wahaha(28.4)	乐百氏 Robust(26.4)	农夫山泉 Nong Fu Shan Quan (15.2)	康师傅 Kangshifu(6.6)
中间层 medium	430	娃哈哈 Wahaha(30.5)	乐百氏 Robust(27.4)	农夫山泉 Nong Fu Shan Quan (18.6)	康师傅 Kangshifu(5.1)
信赖广告指向 loyal orientation	99	乐百氏 Robust(35.4)	娃哈哈 Wahaha(24.2)	农夫山泉 Nong Fu Shan Quan (13.1)	康师傅 Kangshifu(8.1)

2-12-3 饮食健康指标/ Foods & Drink Quality Index

	人数 Number	第一品牌及百分比 1st/ percent	第二品牌及百分比 2nd/ percent	第三品牌及百分比 3rd/ percent	第四品牌及百分比 4th/ percent
样本 Sample	**737**	**娃哈哈 Wahaha(28.8)**	**乐百氏 Robust(28.6)**	**农夫山泉 Nong Fu Shan Quan (17.0)**	**康师傅 Kangshifu(5.8)**
饮食"温饱"指向 "basic" orientation	206	娃哈哈 Wahaha(29.6)	乐百氏 Robust(26.7)	农夫山泉 Nong Fu Shan Quan (18.9)	康师傅 Kangshifu(7.3)
中间层 medium	348	乐百氏 Robust(29.9)	娃哈哈 Wahaha(27.9)	农夫山泉 Nong Fu Shan Quan (15.8)	康师傅 Kangshifu(6.0)
健康营养指向 health & nutrition orientation	183	娃哈哈 Wahaha(29.5)	乐百氏 Robust(28.4)	农夫山泉 Nong Fu Shan Quan (16.9)	康师傅 Kangshifu(3.8)

2-13 重度消费者的消费者层构成/ The Composition of the Heavy Consumers

2-13-1 时尚流行指标/ Fads Popular Index

	人数 Number	平实生活指向 simple living orientation	时尚流行指向 fashion orientation
样本 Sample	**427**	**41.0**	**59.0**
天天喝 daily	68	45.6	54.4
一周 3 次或以上 3 times or over a week	124	29.8	70.2
一周 1~2 次 once or twice a week	235	45.5	54.5

2-13-2 广告态度指标/ Advertising Attitude Index

	人数 Number	广告淡漠指向 indifferent orientation	中间层 medium	信赖广告指向 loyal orientation
样本 Sample	**426**	**25.4**	**59.4**	**15.3**
天天喝 daily	66	34.8	48.5	16.7
一周 3 次或以上 3 times or over a week	126	24.6	55.6	19.8
一周 1~2 次 once or twice a week	234	23.1	64.5	12.4

2-13-3 饮食健康指标/ Foods & Drink Quality Index

	人数 Number	饮食"温饱"指向 "basic" orientation	中间层 medium	健康营养指向 health & nutrition orientation
样本 Sample	**435**	**26.9**	**49.4**	**23.7**
天天喝 daily	68	22.1	42.6	35.3
一周 3 次或以上 3 times or over a week	127	26.8	45.7	27.6
一周 1~2 次 once or twice a week	240	28.3	53.3	18.3

● 上海 / Shanghai

2-1 最近三个月饮用频率的比例/ Proportion of the Sample Consuming Purified or Mineral Water in the Last Three Months

	人数 Number	百分比 Percent
天天喝 daily	142	14.0
一周 3 次或以上 3 times or over a week	93	9.2
一周 1~2 次 once or twice a week	204	20.1
一个月 2~3 次 2 or 3 times a month	183	18.1
一个月 1 次或以下 once a month or below	96	9.5
没喝过 never	295	29.1

n=1013

2-2 最常用品牌排名/ Ranking of the Most Frequently Used Brands

排名 Brand Ranking	品牌 Brands	人数 Number	百分比 Percent
1	农夫山泉 Nong Fu Shan Quan	269	37.5
2	正广和 Acquarius	101	14.1
3	碧纯 Pure	74	10.3
4	乐百氏 Robust	67	9.3
5	斯柏克林 Sparkling	39	5.4
6	延中 Yanzhong	34	4.7
7	俊仕 Junshi	30	4.2
8	获特满 Waterman	28	3.9
9	依云 Evian	8	1.1
10	娃哈哈 Wahaha	6	0.8

n=718

2-3 样本、男性各年龄层、女性各年龄层的常用品牌/ The Most Frequently Used Brands by the Whole Sample, Age and Gender Groups

	人数 Number	第一品牌及百分比 1st/ percent	第二品牌及百分比 2nd/ percent	第三品牌及百分比 3rd/ percent
样本 Sample	718	**农夫山泉 Nong Fu Shan Quan(37.5)**	**正广和 Acquarius(14.1)**	**碧纯 Pure(10.3)**
男性 Male	359	**农夫山泉 Nong Fu Shan Quan(38.2)**	**正广和 Acquarius(12.0)**	**碧纯 Pure(11.1)**
16~24 岁 Age	84	农夫山泉 Nong Fu Shan Quan(38.1)	乐百氏 Robust(21.4)	碧纯 Pure(8.3) 斯柏克林 Sparkling(8.3)
25~34 岁 Age	121	农夫山泉 Nong Fu Shan Quan(36.4)	碧纯 Pure(14.0)	正广和 Acquarius(9.9)
35~44 岁 Age	81	农夫山泉 Nong Fu Shan Quan(45.7)	正广和 Acquarius(17.3)	碧纯 Pure(7.4)
45~54 岁 Age	55	农夫山泉 Nong Fu Shan Quan(38.2)	碧纯 Pure(16.4)	正广和 Acquarius(12.7)
55~60 岁 Age	18	正广和 Acquarius(27.8)	农夫山泉 Nong Fu Shan Quan(16.7)	俊仕 Junshi(11.1)
女性 Female	359	**农夫山泉 Nong Fu Shan Quan(36.8)**	**正广和 Acquarius(16.2)**	**碧纯 Pure(9.5)**
16~24 岁 Age	78	农夫山泉 Nong Fu Shan Quan(35.9)	乐百氏 Robust(15.7)	俊仕 Junshi(10.3)
25~34 岁 Age	117	农夫山泉 Nong Fu Shan Quan(39.3)	正广和 Acquarius(18.8)	碧纯 Pure(11.1)
35~44 岁 Age	91	农夫山泉 Nong Fu Shan Quan(38.5)	正广和 Acquarius(15.4)	碧纯 Pure(7.7) 乐百氏 Robust(7.7) 正广和 Acquarius(14.3)
45~54 岁 Age	49	农夫山泉 Nong Fu Shan Quan(30.6)	碧纯 Pure(18.4)	
55~60 岁 Age	24	农夫山泉 Nong Fu Shan Quan(33.3) 正广和 Acquarius(33.3)	碧纯 Pure(8.3)	乐百氏 Robust(4.2) 延中 Yanzhong(4.2) 依云 Evian(4.2) 俊仕 Junshi(4.2) 上水 Shangshui(4.2) 考司登 Kaosideng(4.2)

2-4 理想品牌排名/ Ranking of the Ideal Brands

排名 Brand Ranking	品牌 Brands	人数 Number	百分比 Percent
1	农夫山泉 Nong Fu Shan Quan	410	40.4
2	正广和 Acquarius	129	12.7
3	碧纯 Pure	94	9.3
4	乐百氏 Robust	82	8.1
5	斯柏克林 Sparkling	56	5.5
6	俊仕 Junshi	47	4.6
7	获特满 Waterman	40	3.9
8	延中 Yanzhong	38	3.7
9	依云 Evian	17	1.7
10	娃哈哈 Wahaha	10	1.0

n=1014

2-5 样本、男性各年龄层、女性各年龄层最近三个月有无购买的比例/ Purchasing in the Last Three Months by the Whole Sample, Age and Gender Groups

	人数 Number	买过 yes	没买过 no
样本 Sample	1013	67.8	32.2
男性 Male	508	66.5	33.5
16~24 岁 Age	109	73.4	26.6
25~34 岁 Age	145	77.9	22.1
35~44 岁 Age	130	60.0	40.0
45~54 岁 Age	85	56.5	43.5
55~60 岁 Age	39	48.7	51.3
女性 Female	505	69.1	30.9
16~24 岁 Age	108	66.7	33.3
25~34 岁 Age	144	79.2	20.8
35~44 岁 Age	130	70.0	30.0
45~54 岁 Age	82	58.5	41.5
55~60 岁 Age	41	58.5	41.5

2-6 样本、男性各年龄层、女性各年龄层最近三个月的饮用频率/ Frequencies of Consuming Purified or Mineral Water in the Last Three Months by the Whole Sample, Age and Gender Groups

	人数 Number	天天喝 daily	一周 3 次或以上 3 times or over a week	一周 1~2 次 once or twice a week	一个月 2~3 次 2 or 3 times a month	一个月 1 次或以下 once a month or below	没喝过 never
样本 Sample	1013	14.0	9.2	20.1	18.1	9.5	29.1
男性 Male	508	11.0	10.2	22.4	17.5	9.4	29.3
16~24 岁 Age	109	5.5	16.5	25.7	20.2	9.2	22.9
25~34 岁 Age	145	15.9	11.0	28.3	19.3	9.0	16.6
35~44 岁 Age	130	10.0	6.2	17.7	20.0	8.5	37.7
45~54 岁 Age	85	10.6	9.4	17.6	12.9	14.1	35.3
55~60 岁 Age	39	12.8	5.1	17.9	5.1	5.1	53.8
女性 Female	505	17.0	8.1	17.8	18.6	9.5	28.9
16~24 岁 Age	108	11.1	9.3	17.6	21.3	13.0	27.8
25~34 岁 Age	144	16.0	9.7	24.3	22.9	8.3	18.8
35~44 岁 Age	130	19.2	8.5	19.2	15.4	7.7	30.0
45~54 岁 Age	82	19.5	7.3	11.0	13.4	8.5	40.2
55~60 岁 Age	41	24.4	0.0	4.9	17.1	12.2	41.5

2-7 样本、男性各年龄层、女性各年龄层的品牌习惯/ Brand Habit in Consuming Purified or Mineral Water by the Whole Sample, Age and Gender Groups

	人数 Number	基本固定饮用一个牌子 used in only one brand	比较固定地饮用两个或三个牌子 used in two or three brands	基本上不太固定牌子 no brand preference
样本 Sample	717	40.7	39.3	19.9
男性 Male	359	37.3	39.6	23.1
16~24 岁 Age	84	31.0	42.9	26.2
25~34 岁 Age	121	37.2	46.3	16.5
35~44 岁 Age	81	39.5	30.9	29.6
45~54 岁 Age	55	38.2	38.2	23.6
55~60 岁 Age	18	55.6	22.2	22.2
女性 Female	358	44.1	39.1	16.8
16~24 岁 Age	78	30.8	47.4	21.8
25~34 岁 Age	117	45.3	41.0	13.7
35~44 岁 Age	91	47.3	33.0	19.8
45~54 岁 Age	49	49.0	38.8	12.2
55~60 岁 Age	23	60.9	26.1	13.0

2-8 选择该类商品的考虑因素/ Ranking of the Considerations in Purchasing

注：本题为多选题，合计百分比超过 100%(Multiple answers）

排名 Ranking	考虑因素 Considerations	人次 Person-time	百分比 Percent
1	价格适中 reasonable price	284	39.6
2	有名的牌子 famous brand	259	36.1
3	口味好 pleasant taste	251	35.0
4	购买方便 easy to buy	194	27.0
5	生产日期 date of producing	135	18.8
6	广告影响 influence of advertising	112	15.6
7	只是由于习惯 out of habit	70	9.7
8	包装吸引人 appealing package	23	3.2
8	单位发的 offered by the working unit	23	3.2
9	有优惠条件 with preferential terms	22	3.1
10	朋友推荐 introduction of friends	21	2.9
11	其它 others	9	1.3
12	售货员介绍 introduced by the shop assistants	5	0.7

n=718

2-9 样本、男性各年龄层、女性各年龄层最常饮用的包装形式/ Types of Package of the Consumed Purified or Mineral Water by the Whole Sample, Age and Gender Groups

	人数 Number	250ml 以下 250ml or below	250ml--350ml	500ml--750ml	1L	1.5L	2L 以上 2L or over	其它 others
样本 Sample	**715**	**23.8**	**37.1**	**18.6**	**3.9**	**3.1**	**9.8**	**3.8**
男性 Male	**359**	**23.1**	**40.9**	**18.9**	**2.8**	**1.4**	**9.5**	**3.3**
16~24 岁 Age	84	22.6	50.0	15.5	0.0	1.2	9.5	1.2
25~34 岁 Age	121	20.7	43.0	14.9	5.0	1.7	9.9	5.0
35~44 岁 Age	81	25.9	38.3	23.5	2.5	0.0	6.2	3.7
45~54 岁 Age	55	29.1	29.1	27.3	1.8	0.0	10.9	1.8
55~60 岁 Age	18	11.1	33.3	16.7	5.6	11.1	16.7	5.6
女性 Female	**356**	**24.4**	**33.1**	**18.3**	**5.1**	**4.8**	**10.1**	**4.2**
16~24 岁 Age	78	24.4	50.0	11.5	2.6	5.1	5.1	1.3
25~34 岁 Age	117	31.6	30.8	16.2	5.1	5.1	7.7	3.4
35~44 岁 Age	90	24.4	33.3	18.9	3.3	2.2	12.2	5.6
45~54 岁 Age	48	14.6	16.7	29.2	10.4	6.3	14.6	8.3
55~60 岁 Age	23	8.7	21.7	26.1	8.7	8.7	21.7	4.3

2-10 样本、男性各年龄层、女性各年龄层最常饮用的场合/ Settings of Consumption by the Whole Sample, Age and Gender Groups

注：本题为多选题，合计百分比超过 100%(Multiple answers）

	人数 Number	平时口渴时 when thirsty	平时吃饭喝 at dinner	宴席、聚会喝 at banquet	外出、旅游时 outing/traveling	运动完以后 after athletics	其它 others
样本 Sample	**718**	**75.6**	**4.3**	**3.6**	**35.0**	**14.2**	**0.3**
男性 Male	**359**	**74.7**	**3.6**	**3.6**	**34.0**	**14.5**	**0.0**
16~24 岁 Age	84	77.4	7.1	1.2	20.2	26.2	0.0
25~34 岁 Age	121	76.9	3.3	4.1	31.4	14.0	0.0
35~44 岁 Age	81	74.1	3.7	3.7	39.5	7.4	0.0
45~54 岁 Age	55	65.5	0.0	7.3	52.7	10.9	0.0
55~60 岁 Age	18	77.8	0.0	0.0	33.3	5.6	0.0
女性 Female	**359**	**76.6**	**5.0**	**3.6**	**35.9**	**13.9**	**0.6**
16~24 岁 Age	78	76.9	2.6	3.8	37.2	19.2	0.0
25~34 岁 Age	117	79.5	6.0	3.4	30.8	11.1	0.0
35~44 岁 Age	91	73.6	4.4	4.4	40.7	17.6	1.1
45~54 岁 Age	49	71.4	6.1	2.0	42.9	8.2	0.0
55~60 岁 Age	24	83.3	8.3	4.2	25.0	8.3	4.2

2-11 重度消费者人口分布/ Demographics of the Heavy Consumers

	人数 Number	16-24 岁 Age	25-34 岁 Age	35-44 岁 Age	45-54 岁 Age	55-60 岁 Age
样本 Sample	439	21.2	34.6	23.9	14.4	5.9
男性 Male	222	23.4	36.0	19.8	14.4	6.3
天天喝 daily	56	10.7	41.1	23.2	16.1	8.9
一周 3 次或以上 3 times or over a week	52	34.6	30.8	15.4	15.4	3.8
一周 1~2 次 once or twice a week	114	24.6	36.0	20.2	13.2	6.1
女性 Female	217	18.9	33.2	28.1	14.3	5.5
天天喝 daily	86	14.0	26.7	29.1	18.6	11.6
一周 3 次或以上 3 times or over a week	41	24.4	34.1	26.8	14.6	0.0
一周 1~2 次 once or twice a week	90	21.1	38.9	27.8	10.0	2.2

2-12 不同消费者层的常用品牌/ The Most Frequently Used Brands by Market Segments

2-12-1 时尚流行指标/ Fads Popular Index

	人数 Number	第一品牌及百分比 1st/ percent	第二品牌及百分比 2nd/ percent	第三品牌及百分比 3rd/ percent	第四品牌及百分比 4th/ percent
样本 Sample	713	**农夫山泉 Nong Fu Shan Quan (37.4)**	**正广和 Acquarius(14.0)**	**碧纯 Pure(10.2)**	**乐百氏 Robust(9.4)**
平实生活指向 simple living orientation	308	农夫山泉 Nong Fu Shan Quan(40.9)	正广和 Acquarius(13.3)	乐百氏 Robust(9.7) 碧纯 Pure(9.7)	斯柏克林 Sparkling(4.5)
时尚流行指向 fashion orientation	405	农夫山泉 Nong Fu Shan Quan(34.8)	正广和 Acquarius(14.6)	碧纯 Pure(10.6)	乐百氏 Robust(9.1)

2-12-2 广告态度指标/ Advertising Attitude Index

	人数 Number	第一品牌及百分比 1st/ percent	第二品牌及百分比 2nd/ percent	第三品牌及百分比 3rd/ percent	第四品牌及百分比 4th/ percent
样本 Sample	711	**农夫山泉 Nong Fu Shan Quan (37.6)**	**正广和 Acquarius(14.1)**	**碧纯 Pure(10.3)**	**乐百氏 Robust(9.3)**
广告淡漠指向 indifferent orientation	170	农夫山泉 Nong Fu Shan Quan(41.2)	乐百氏 Robust(12.4)	碧纯 Pure(11.8)	正广和 Acquarius(11.2)
中间层 medium	440	农夫山泉 Nong Fu Shan Quan(35.9)	正广和 Acquarius(15.0)	碧纯 Pure(10.5)	乐百氏 Robust(8.9)
信赖广告指向 loyal orientation	101	农夫山泉 Nong Fu Shan Quan(38.6)	正广和 Acquarius(14.9)	获特满 Waterman(7.9)	碧纯 Pure(6.9) 斯柏克林 Sparkling(6.9)

2-12-3 饮食健康指标/ Foods & Drink Quality Index

	人数 Number	第一品牌及百分比 1st/ percent	第二品牌及百分比 2nd/ percent	第三品牌及百分比 3rd/ percent	第四品牌及百分比 4th/ percent
样本 Sample	714	**农夫山泉 Nong Fu Shan Quan (37.4)**	**正广和 Acquarius(14.1)**	**碧纯 Pure(10.4)**	**乐百氏 Robust(9.4)**
饮食"温饱"指向 "basic" orientation	155	农夫山泉 Nong Fu Shan Quan(36.1)	正广和 Acquarius(14.2)	乐百氏 Robust(13.5)	碧纯 Pure(9.7)
中间层 medium	343	农夫山泉 Nong Fu Shan Quan(38.8)	正广和 Acquarius(12.8)	碧纯 Pure(10.5)	乐百氏 Robust(8.7)
健康营养指向 health & nutrition orientation	216	农夫山泉 Nong Fu Shan Quan(36.1)	正广和 Acquarius(16.2)	碧纯 Pure(10.6)	乐百氏 Robust(7.4)

2-13 重度消费者的消费者层构成/ The Composition of the Heavy Consumers

2-13-1 时尚流行指标/ Fads Popular Index

	人数 Number	平实生活指向 simple living orientation	时尚流行指向 fashion orientation
样本 Sample	435	41.6	58.4
天天喝 daily	140	39.3	60.7
一周 3 次或以上 3 times or over a week	93	36.6	63.4
一周 1~2 次 once or twice a week	202	45.5	54.5

2-13-2 广告态度指标/ Advertising Attitude Index

	人数 Number	广告淡漠指向 indifferent orientation	中间层 medium	信赖广告指向 loyal orientation
样本 Sample	**432**	**21.5**	**62.7**	**15.7**
天天喝 daily	140	22.9	60.7	16.4
一周 3 次或以上 3 times or over a week	92	15.2	68.5	16.3
一周 1~2 次 once or twice a week	200	23.5	61.5	15.0

2-13-3 饮食健康指标/ Foods & Drink Quality Index

	人数 Number	饮食"温饱"指向 "basic" orientation	中间层 medium	健康营养指向 health & nutrition orientation
样本 Sample	**438**	**21.2**	**48.4**	**30.4**
天天喝 daily	142	21.8	45.1	33.1
一周 3 次或以上 3 times or over a week	93	20.4	46.2	33.3
一周 1~2 次 once or twice a week	203	21.2	51.7	27.1

● 广州 / Guangzhou

2-1 最近三个月饮用频率的比例/ Proportion of the Sample Consuming Purified or Mineral Water in the Last Three Months

	人数 Number	百分比 Percent
天天喝 daily	75	7.3
一周 3 次或以上 3 times or over a week	120	11.6
一周 1~2 次 once or twice a week	264	25.6
一个月 2~3 次 2 or 3 times a month	225	21.8
一个月 1 次或以下 once a month or below	102	9.9
没喝过 never	246	23.8

n=1032

2-2 最常用品牌排名/ Ranking of the Most Frequently Used Brands

排名 Brand Ranking	品牌 Brands	人数 Number	百分比 Percent
1	怡宝 Cestron	492	62.8
2	乐百氏 Robust	57	7.3
3	农夫山泉 Nong Fu Shan Quan	36	4.6
4	屈臣氏 Watson's	31	4.0
5	大峡谷 Grand Canyon	23	2.9
6	佛宝 Fobao	19	2.4
7	天与地 Tianyudi	12	1.5
8	景田 jingtian	8	1.0
9	来利 Laili	7	0.9
9	清凉 Qingliang	7	0.9

n=784

2-3 样本、男性各年龄层、女性各年龄层的常用品牌/ The Most Frequently Used Brands by the Whole Sample, Age and Gender Groups

	人数 Number	第一品牌及百分比 1st/ percent	第二品牌及百分比 2nd/ percent	第三品牌及百分比 3rd/ percent	第四品牌及百分比 4th/ percent
样本 Sample	784	**怡宝 Cestron(62.8)**	**乐百氏 Robust(7.3)**	**农夫山泉 Nong Fu Shan Quan(4.6)**	**屈臣氏 Watson's(4.0)**
男性 Male	388	**怡宝 Cestron(66.8)**	**乐百氏 Robust(7.2)**	**农夫山泉 Nong Fu Shan Quan(3.6)**	**屈臣氏 Watson's(3.1)**
16~24 岁 Age	83	怡宝 Cestron(65.1)	乐百氏 Robust(10.8)	屈臣氏 Watson's(3.6)	景田 Jingtian(2.4) 娃哈哈 Wahaha(2.4)
25~34 岁 Age	128	怡宝 Cestron(68.8)	乐百氏 Robust(6.3)	农夫山泉 Nong Fu Shan Quan(4.7)	大峡谷 Grand xanyon(3.1) 佛宝 Fobao(3.1)
35~44 岁 Age	98	怡宝 Cestron (66.3)	乐百氏 Robust(6.1) 屈臣氏 Watson's(6.1)	农夫山泉 Nong Fu Shan Quan(3.1)	景田 Jingtian(2.0) 来利 Laili (2.0) 康师傅 Kangshifu(2.0)
45~54 岁 Age	54	怡宝 Cestron(66.7)	乐百氏 Robust(5.6)	大峡谷 Grand Canyon(3.7) 佛宝 Fobao(3.7) 农夫山泉 Nong Fu Shan Quan(3.7)	清凉 Qingliang(1.9) 九天观 Jiutianguan(1.9) 中联净水 Zhonglian(1.9) 天源长寿树 Tianyuan(1.9) 明泉 Mingqun(1.9) 白云山 Baiyunshan(1.9) 亚洲 Asia(1.9) 日之泉 Rizhiquan(1.9)
55~60 岁 Age	25	怡宝 Cestron(64.0)	大峡谷 Grand Canyon(8.0) 乐百氏 Robust(8.0) 农夫山泉 Nong Fu Shan Quan(8.0)	佛宝 Fobao(4.0) 白云山 Baiyunshan(4.0)	
女性 Female	396	**怡宝 Cestron(58.8)**	**乐百氏 Robust(7.3)**	**农夫山泉 Nong Fu Shan Quan(5.6)**	**屈臣氏 Watson's(4.8)**
16~24 岁 Age	91	怡宝 Cestron(58.2)	乐百氏 Robust(8.8)	清凉 Qingliang(5.5) 屈臣氏 Watson's(5.5)	天与地 Tianyudi(4.4)
25~34 岁 Age	128	怡宝 Cestron(61.7)	农夫山泉 Nong Fu Shan Quan(8.6)	屈臣氏 Watson's(5.5)	大峡谷 Grand Canyon(3.9)
35~44 岁 Age	94	怡宝 Cestron(56.4)	乐百氏 Robust(10.6)	农夫山泉 Nong Fu Shan Quan(7.4)	屈臣氏 Watson's(4.3)
45~54 岁 Age	55	怡宝 Cestron(61.8)	乐百氏 Robust(12.7)	来利 Laili (3.6) 农夫山泉 Nong Fu Shan Quan(3.6) 屈臣氏 Watson's(3.6) 大峡谷 Grand Canyon(3.6)	清凉 Qingliang(1.8) 甘碧 Ganbi(1.8) 益寿泉 Yishouquan(1.8) 太阳神 Apollo(1.8) 益力 Yili(1.8) 天与地 Tianyudi(1.8)
55~60 岁 Age	28	怡宝 Cestron(50.0)	乐百氏 Robust(7.1)	益力 Yili(3.6) 麦宝 Maibao(3.6) 雪山 Xueshan (3.6) 三千尺 Sanqianchi(3.6) 屈臣氏 Watson's(3.6) 农夫山泉 Nong Fu Shan Quan(3.6) 佛宝 Fobao(3.6) 鼎湖山 Dinghushan(3.6) 大峡谷 Grand Canyon(3.6)	

2-4 理想品牌排名/ Ranking of the Ideal Brands

排名 Brand Ranking	品牌 Brands	人数 Number	百分比 Percent
1	怡宝 Cestron	573	55.4
2	乐百氏 Robust	70	6.8
3	农夫山泉 Nong Fu Shan Quan	55	5.3
4	屈臣氏 Watson's	53	5.1
5	大峡谷 Grand Canyon	25	2.4
6	佛宝 Fobao	23	2.2

n=1034

2-5 样本、男性各年龄层、女性各年龄层最近三个月有无购买的比例/ Purchasing in the Last Three Months by the Whole Sample, Age and Gender Groups

	人数 Number	买过 yes	没买过 no
样本 Sample	1033	73.4	26.6
男性 Male	499	76.2	23.8
16~24 岁 Age	106	75.5	24.5
25~34 岁 Age	150	83.3	16.7
35~44 岁 Age	127	75.6	24.4
45~54 岁 Age	73	74.0	26.0
55~60 岁 Age	43	58.1	41.9
女性 Female	534	70.8	29.2
16~24 岁 Age	112	75.9	24.1
25~34 岁 Age	158	77.8	22.2
35~44 岁 Age	137	68.6	31.4
45~54 岁 Age	86	60.5	39.5
55~60 岁 Age	41	58.5	41.5

2-6 样本、男性各年龄层、女性各年龄层最近三个月的饮用频率/ Frequencies of Consuming Purified or Mineral Water in the Last Three Months by the Whole Sample, Age and Gender Groups

	人数 Number	天天喝 daily	一周 3 次或以上 3 times or over a week	一周 1~2 次 once or twice a week	一个月 2~3 次 2 or 3 times a month	一个月 1 次或以下 once a month or below	没喝过 never
样本 Sample	1032	7.3	11.6	25.6	21.8	9.9	23.8
男性 Male	497	7.2	12.1	26.6	23.7	8.7	21.7
16~24 岁 Age	106	4.7	13.2	31.1	21.7	7.5	21.7
25~34 岁 Age	149	10.1	14.8	31.5	22.8	6.7	14.1
35~44 岁 Age	126	6.3	11.1	20.6	29.4	11.1	21.4
45~54 岁 Age	73	9.6	6.8	24.7	20.5	12.3	26.0
55~60 岁 Age	43	2.3	11.6	18.6	20.9	4.7	41.9
女性 Female	535	7.3	11.2	24.7	20.0	11.0	25.8
16~24 岁 Age	112	6.3	11.6	32.1	22.3	8.9	18.8
25~34 岁 Age	158	10.8	11.4	27.2	19.0	12.7	19.0
35~44 岁 Age	137	5.8	10.9	19.7	18.2	13.9	31.4
45~54 岁 Age	87	6.9	9.2	20.7	19.5	8.0	35.6
55~60 岁 Age	41	2.4	14.6	19.5	24.4	7.3	31.7

2-7 样本、男性各年龄层、女性各年龄层的品牌习惯/ Brand Habit in Consuming Purified or Mineral Water by the Whole Sample, Age and Gender Groups

	人数 Number	基本固定饮用一个牌子 used in only one brand	比较固定地饮用两个或三个牌子 used in two or three brands	基本上不太固定牌子 no brand preference
样本 Sample	782	36.7	43.2	20.1
男性 Male	388	39.4	41.5	19.1
16~24 岁 Age	83	38.6	43.4	18.1
25~34 岁 Age	128	41.4	41.4	17.2
35~44 岁 Age	98	32.7	46.9	20.4
45~54 岁 Age	54	46.3	31.5	22.2
55~60 岁 Age	25	44.0	36.0	20.0
女性 Female	394	34.0	44.9	21.1
16~24 岁 Age	91	31.9	49.5	18.7
25~34 岁 Age	127	29.9	51.2	18.9
35~44 岁 Age	94	38.3	41.5	20.2
45~54 岁 Age	55	40.0	36.4	23.6
55~60 岁 Age	27	33.3	29.6	37.0

2-8 选择该类商品的考虑因素/ Ranking of the Considerations in Purchasing

注：本题为多选题，合计百分比超过 100%(Multiple answers）

排名 Ranking	考虑因素 Considerations	人次 Person-time	百分比 Percent
1	价格适中 reasonable price	346	44.2
2	有名的牌子 famous brand	276	35.2
3	购买方便 easy to buy	242	30.9
4	口味好 pleasant taste	194	24.8
5	生产日期 date of producing	150	19.2
6	只是由于习惯 out of habit	106	13.5
7	广告影响 influence of advertising	82	10.5
8	包装吸引人 appealing package	33	4.2
9	有优惠条件 with preferential terms	26	3.3
10	朋友推荐 introduction of friends	18	2.3
11	单位发的 offered by the working unit	12	1.5
12	其它 others	8	1.0
13	售货员介绍 introduced by the shop assistants	5	0.6

n=783

2-9 样本、男性各年龄层、女性各年龄层最常饮用的包装形式/ Package Types of the Purified or Mineral Water by the Whole Sample, Age and Gender Groups

	人数 Number	250ml 以下 250ml or below	250ml--350ml	500ml--750ml	1L	1.5L	2L 以上 2L or over	其它 others
样本 Sample	**781**	**22.7**	**42.6**	**28.7**	**1.3**	**0.8**	**3.1**	**0.9**
男性 Male	**388**	**22.2**	**39.4**	**32.7**	**1.0**	**0.5**	**3.1**	**1.0**
16~24 岁 Age	83	16.9	42.2	37.3	0.0	1.2	0.0	2.4
25~34 岁 Age	127	25.2	37.0	31.5	1.6	0.8	3.1	0.8
35~44 岁 Age	99	23.2	44.4	28.3	1.0	0.0	2.0	1.0
45~54 岁 Age	54	24.1	33.3	31.5	1.9	0.0	9.3	0.0
55~60 岁 Age	25	16.0	36.0	44.0	0.0	0.0	4.0	0.0
女性 Female	**393**	**23.2**	**45.8**	**24.7**	**1.5**	**1.0**	**3.1**	**0.8**
16~24 岁 Age	91	27.5	40.7	27.5	2.2	2.2	0.0	0.0
25~34 岁 Age	126	22.2	52.4	17.5	2.4	0.8	4.8	0.0
35~44 岁 Age	94	20.2	45.7	26.6	1.1	0.0	3.2	3.2
45~54 岁 Age	55	23.6	43.6	27.3	0.0	1.8	3.6	0.0
55~60 岁 Age	27	22.2	37.0	37.0	0.0	0.0	3.7	0.0

2-10 样本、男性各年龄层、女性各年龄层最常饮用的场合/ Settings of Consumption by the Whole Sample, Age and Gender Groups

注：本题为多选题，合计百分比超过 100%(Multiple answers）

	人数 Number	平时口渴时 when thirsty	平时吃饭喝 at dinner	宴席、聚会喝 at banquet	外出、旅游时 outing/traveling	运动完以后 after athletics	其它 others
样本 Sample	**776**	**69.3**	**1.9**	**1.5**	**42.4**	**18.7**	**0.9**
男性 Male	**385**	**69.4**	**1.8**	**2.1**	**38.7**	**19.7**	**1.0**
16~24 岁 Age	83	69.9	3.6	2.4	26.5	38.6	1.2
25~34 岁 Age	126	78.6	2.4	1.6	33.3	22.2	0.8
35~44 岁 Age	97	61.9	1.0	3.1	50.5	8.2	1.0
45~54 岁 Age	54	66.7	0.0	0.0	44.4	11.1	1.9
55~60 岁 Age	25	56.0	0.0	4.0	48.0	8.0	0.0
女性 Female	**391**	**69.3**	**2.0**	**1.0**	**46.0**	**17.6**	**0.8**
16~24 岁 Age	91	69.2	2.2	0.0	46.2	28.6	1.1
25~34 岁 Age	124	74.2	1.6	1.6	51.6	12.1	0.8
35~44 岁 Age	94	67.0	1.1	0.0	42.6	18.1	0.0
45~54 岁 Age	55	67.3	5.5	1.8	41.8	14.5	1.8
55~60 岁 Age	27	59.3	0.0	3.7	40.7	11.1	0.0

2-11 重度消费者人口分布/ Demographics of the Heavy Consumers

	人数 Number	16-24 岁 Age	25-34 岁 Age	35-44 岁 Age	45-54 岁 Age	55-60 岁 Age
样本 Sample	459	23.5	35.3	21.4	13.5	6.3
男性 Male	228	22.8	36.8	21.1	13.2	6.1
天天喝 daily	36	13.9	41.7	22.2	19.4	2.8
一周 3 次或以上 3 times or over a week	60	23.3	36.7	23.3	8.3	8.3
一周 1~2 次 once or twice a week	132	25.0	35.6	19.7	13.6	6.1
女性 Female	231	24.2	33.8	21.6	13.9	6.5
天天喝 daily	39	17.9	43.6	20.5	15.4	2.6
一周 3 次或以上 3 times or over a week	60	21.7	30.0	25.0	13.3	10.0
一周 1~2 次 once or twice a week	132	27.3	32.6	20.5	13.6	6.1

2-12 不同消费者层的常用品牌/ The Most Frequently Used Brands by Market Segments

2-12-1 时尚流行指标/ Fads Popular Index

	人数 Number	第一品牌及百分比 1st/ percent	第二品牌及百分比 2nd/ percent	第三品牌及百分比 3rd/ percent
样本 Sample	775	**怡宝 Cestron(62.8)**	**乐百氏 Robust(7.4)**	**农夫山泉 Nong Fu Shan Quan(4.6)**
平实生活指向 simple living orientation	365	怡宝 Cestron(64.9)	乐百氏 Robust(6.0)	农夫山泉 Nong Fu Shan Quan(4.7)
时尚流行指向 fashion orientation	410	怡宝 Cestron(61.0)	乐百氏 Robust(8.5)	屈臣氏 Watson's(4.9)

2-12-2 广告态度指标/ Advertising Attitude Index

	人数 Number	第一品牌及百分比 1st/ percent	第二品牌及百分比 2nd/ percent	第三品牌及百分比 3rd/ percent
样本 Sample	772	**怡宝 Cestron(62.7)**	**乐百氏 Robust(7.3)**	**农夫山泉 Nong Fu Shan Quan(4.5)**
广告淡漠指向 indifferent orientation	238	怡宝 Cestron(63.4)	乐百氏 Robust(7.1)	大峡谷 Grand Canyon(4.2)
中间层 medium	455	怡宝 Cestron(60.7)	乐百氏 Robust(7.9)	农夫山泉 Nong Fu Shan Quan(5.1)
信赖广告指向 loyal orientation	79	怡宝 Cestron(72.2)	乐百氏 Robust(3.8) 农夫山泉 Nong Fu Shan Quan(3.8)	景田 Jingtian(2.5) 屈臣氏 Watson's(2.5)

2-12-3 饮食健康指标/ Foods & Drink Quality Index

	人数 Number	第一品牌及百分比 1st/ percent	第二品牌及百分比 2nd/ percent	第三品牌及百分比 3rd/ percent
样本 Sample	781	**怡宝 Cestron(63.0)**	**乐百氏 Robust(6.9)**	**农夫山泉 Nong Fu Shan Quan(4.6)**
饮食"温饱"指向 "basic" orientation	209	怡宝 Cestron(64.1)	大峡谷 Grand Canyon(4.8)	乐百氏 Robust(4.3)
中间层 medium	428	怡宝 Cestron(63.1)	乐百氏 Robust(8.9)	屈臣氏 Watson's(4.7)
健康营养指向 health & nutrition orientation	144	怡宝 Cestron(61.1)	农夫山泉 Nong Fu Shan Quan(7.6)	乐百氏 Robust(4.9)

2-13 重度消费者的消费者层构成/ The Composition of the Heavy Consumers

2-13-1 时尚流行指标/ Fads Popular Index

	人数 Number	平实生活指向 simple living orientation	时尚流行指向 fashion orientation
样本 Sample	454	44.1	55.9
天天喝 daily	70	35.7	64.3
一周 3 次或以上 3 times or over a week	120	47.5	52.5
一周 1~2 次 once or twice a week	264	44.7	55.3

2-13-2 广告态度指标/ Advertising Attitude Index

	人数 Number	广告淡漠指向 indifferent orientation	中间层 medium	信赖广告指向 loyal orientation
样本 Sample	**452**	**31.2**	**58.2**	**10.6**
天天喝 daily	75	26.7	69.3	4.0
一周 3 次或以上 3 times or over a week	118	37.3	55.1	7.6
一周 1~2 次 once or twice a week	259	29.7	56.4	13.9

2-13-3 饮食健康指标/ Foods & Drink Quality Index

	人数 Number	饮食"温饱"指向 "basic" orientation	中间层 medium	健康营养指向 health & nutrition orientation
样本 Sample	**458**	**27.5**	**52.0**	**20.5**
天天喝 daily	75	29.3	45.3	25.3
一周 3 次或以上 3 times or over a week	120	28.3	51.7	20.0
一周 1~2 次 once or twice a week	263	26.6	54.0	19.4

● 重庆 / Chongqing

2-1 最近三个月饮用频率的比例/ Proportion of the Sample Consuming Purified or Mineral Water in the Last Three Months

	人数 Number	百分比 Percent
天天喝 daily	17	2.7
一周 3 次或以上 3 times or over a week	66	10.6
一周 1~2 次 once or twice a week	149	24.0
一个月 2~3 次 2 or 3 times a month	142	22.8
一个月 1 次或以下 once a month or below	69	11.1
没喝过 never	179	28.8

n=622

2-2 最常用品牌排名/ Ranking of the Most Frequently Used Brands

排名 Brand Ranking	品牌 Brands	人数 Number	百分比 Percent
1	冰点水 Bingdianshui	146	33.0
2	乐百氏 Robust	108	24.4
3	中梁山 Zhongliangshan	73	16.5
4	娃哈哈 Wahaha	49	11.1
5	农夫山泉 Nong Fu Shan Quan	36	8.1
6	康师傅 Kangshifu	8	1.8
7	太阳神 Apollo	3	0.7

n=442

2-3 样本、男性各年龄层、女性各年龄层的常用品牌/ The Most Frequently Used Brands by the Whole Sample, Age and Gender Groups

	人数 Number	第一品牌及百分比 1st/ percent	第二品牌及百分比 2nd/ percent	第三品牌及百分比 3rd/ percent	第四品牌及百分比 4th/ percent
样本 Sample	442	**冰点水 Bingdianshui(33.0)**	**乐百氏 Robust(24.4)**	**中梁山 Zhongliangshan (16.5)**	**娃哈哈 Wahaha(11.1)**
男性 Male	225	**冰点水 Bingdianshui(32.0)**	**乐百氏 Robust(23.6)**	**中梁山 Zhongliangshan (20.0)**	**娃哈哈 Wahaha(11.1)**
16~24 岁 Age	56	冰点水 Bingdianshui(39.3)	乐百氏 Robust(25.0)	中梁山 Zhongliangshan(12.5)	农夫山泉 Nong Fu Shan Quan (10.7)
25~34 岁 Age	75	冰点水 Bingdianshui(30.7)	乐百氏 Robust(28.0)	中梁山 Zhongliangshan(17.3)	娃哈哈 Wahaha(14.7)
35~44 岁 Age	52	冰点水 Bingdianshui(32.7)	中梁山 Zhongliangshan(28.8)	娃哈哈 Wahaha(15.4)	乐百氏 Robust(13.5)
45~54 岁 Age	32	冰点水 Bingdianshui(31.3)	中梁山 Zhongliangshan(25.0)	乐百氏 Robust(21.9)	农夫山泉 Nong Fu Shan Quan (6.3) 娃哈哈 Wahaha(6.3) 天龙 Tianlong(6.3)
55~60 岁 Age	10	乐百氏 Robust(40.0)	农夫山泉 Nong Fu Shan Quan (20.0) 中梁山 Zhongliangshan(20.0)	娃哈哈 Wahaha(10.0) 全兴 Quanxing(10.0)	
女性 Female	217	**冰点水 Bingdianshui(34.1)**	**乐百氏 Robust(25.3)**	**中梁山 Zhongliangshan (12.9)**	**娃哈哈 Wahaha(11.1)**
16~24 岁 Age	57	冰点水 Bingdianshui(35.1)	乐百氏 Robust(28.1)	农夫山泉 Nong Fu Shan Quan (10.5) 中梁山 Zhongliangshan(10.5)	娃哈哈 Wahaha(8.8)
25~34 岁 Age	74	冰点水 Bingdianshui(28.4)	乐百氏 Robust(24.3)	娃哈哈 Wahaha(17.6)	中梁山 Zhongliangshan(16.2)
35~44 岁 Age	41	冰点水 Bingdianshui(31.7)	乐百氏 Robust(19.5)	中梁山 Zhongliangshan(17.1)	农夫山泉 Nong Fu Shan Quan (9.8)
45~54 岁 Age	35	冰点水 Bingdianshui(48.6)	乐百氏 Robust(25.7)	娃哈哈 Wahaha(8.6) 中梁山 Zhongliangshan(8.6)	农夫山泉 Nong Fu Shan Quan (5.7)
55~60 岁 Age	10	乐百氏 Robust(40.0)	冰点水 Bingdianshui(30.0)	康师傅 Kangshifu(10.0) 天成 Tiancheng(10.0)	

2-4 理想品牌排名/ Ranking of the Ideal Brands

排名 Brand Ranking	品牌 Brands	人数 Number	百分比 Percent
1	冰点水 Bingdianshui	179	28.7
2	乐百氏 Robust	135	21.6
3	中梁山 Zhongliangshan	104	16.7
4	娃哈哈 Wahaha	79	12.7
5	农夫山泉 Nong Fu Shan Quan	62	9.9
6	康师傅 Kangshifu	10	1.6
7	太阳神 Apollo	3	0.5
8	天龙 Tianlong	2	0.3
8	全兴 Quanxing	2	0.3

n=624

2-5 样本、男性各年龄层、女性各年龄层最近三个月有无购买的比例/ Purchasing in the Last Three Months by the Whole Sample, Age and Gender Groups

	人数 Number	买过 yes	没买过 no
样本 Sample	623	70.3	29.7
男性 Male	313	72.2	27.8
16~24 岁 Age	64	85.9	14.1
25~34 岁 Age	93	80.6	19.4
35~44 岁 Age	75	70.7	29.3
45~54 岁 Age	53	62.3	37.7
55~60 岁 Age	28	35.7	64.3
女性 Female	310	68.4	31.6
16~24 岁 Age	64	87.5	12.5
25~34 岁 Age	90	83.3	16.7
35~44 岁 Age	73	58.9	41.1
45~54 岁 Age	60	48.3	51.7
55~60 岁 Age	23	39.1	60.9

2-6 样本、男性各年龄层、女性各年龄层最近三个月的饮用频率/ Frequencies of Consuming Purified or Mineral Water in the Last Three Months by the Whole Sample, Age and Gender Groups

	人数 Number	天天喝 daily	一周 3 次或以上 3 times or over a week	一周 1~2 次 once or twice a week	一个月 2～3 次 2 or 3 times a month	一个月 1 次或以下 once a month or below	没喝过 never
样本 Sample	622	2.7	10.6	24.0	22.8	11.1	28.8
男性 Male	313	3.2	11.5	24.9	20.8	11.5	28.1
16~24 岁 Age	64	1.6	14.1	39.1	21.9	10.9	12.5
25~34 岁 Age	92	3.3	15.2	29.3	20.7	13.0	18.5
35~44 岁 Age	75	4.0	10.7	17.3	24.0	13.3	30.7
45~54 岁 Age	54	5.6	7.4	18.5	16.7	11.1	40.7
55~60 岁 Age	28	0.0	3.6	10.7	17.9	3.6	64.3
女性 Female	309	2.3	9.7	23.0	24.9	10.7	29.4
16~24 岁 Age	63	4.8	12.7	34.9	33.3	4.8	9.5
25~34 岁 Age	90	4.4	16.7	24.4	23.3	13.3	17.8
35~44 岁 Age	73	0.0	6.8	16.4	27.4	6.8	42.5
45~54 岁 Age	60	0.0	1.7	16.7	23.3	16.7	41.7
55~60 岁 Age	23	0.0	4.3	21.7	4.3	13.0	56.5

2-7 样本、男性各年龄层、女性各年龄层的品牌习惯/ Brand Habit in Consuming Purified or Mineral Water by the Whole Sample, Age and Gender Groups

	人数 Number	基本固定饮用一个牌子 used in only one brand	比较固定地饮用两个或三个牌子 used in two or three brands	基本上不太固定牌子 no brand preference
样本 Sample	441	29.3	47.6	23.1
男性 Male	224	29.9	47.3	22.8
16~24 岁 Age	56	37.5	41.1	21.4
25~34 岁 Age	75	26.7	56.0	17.3
35~44 岁 Age	51	29.4	41.2	29.4
45~54 岁 Age	32	28.1	43.8	28.1
55~60 岁 Age	10	20.0	60.0	20.0
女性 Female	217	28.6	47.9	23.5
16~24 岁 Age	57	28.1	57.9	14.0
25~34 岁 Age	74	23.0	52.7	24.3
35~44 岁 Age	41	41.5	34.1	24.4
45~54 岁 Age	35	28.6	45.7	25.7
55~60 岁 Age	10	20.0	20.0	60.0

2-8 选择该类商品的考虑因素/ Ranking of the Considerations in Purchasing

注：本题为多选题，合计百分比超过 100%(Multiple answers）

排名 Ranking	考虑因素 Considerations	人次 Person-time	百分比 Percent
1	口味好 pleasant taste	168	38.2
2	价格适中 reasonable price	167	38.0
3	有名的牌子 famous brand	129	29.3
4	购买方便 easy to buy	110	25.0
5	生产日期 date of producing	95	21.6
6	只是由于习惯 out of habit	64	14.5
7	广告影响 influence of advertising	62	14.1
8	单位发的 offered by the working unit	15	3.4
9	朋友推荐 introduction of friends	12	2.7
10	包装吸引人 appealing package	8	1.8
11	有优惠条件 with preferential terms	7	1.6
11	其它 others	7	1.6
12	售货员介绍 introduced by the shop assistants	1	0.2

n=440

2-9 样本、男性各年龄层、女性各年龄层最常饮用的包装形式/ Types of Package of the Purified or Mineral Water by the Whole Sample, Age and Gender Groups

	人数 Number	250ml 以下 250ml or below	250ml--350ml	500ml--750ml	1L	1.5L	2L 以上 2L or over	其它 others
样本 Sample	**439**	**18.7**	**43.5**	**36.0**	**0.5**	**0.9**	**0.2**	**0.2**
男性 Male	**224**	**18.3**	**42.9**	**37.5**	**0.4**	**0.9**	**0.0**	**0.0**
16~24 岁 Age	56	12.5	60.7	26.8	0.0	0.0	0.0	0.0
25~34 岁 Age	74	21.6	43.2	33.8	0.0	1.4	0.0	0.0
35~44 岁 Age	52	13.5	38.5	48.1	0.0	0.0	0.0	0.0
45~54 岁 Age	32	18.8	21.9	53.1	3.1	3.1	0.0	0.0
55~60 岁 Age	10	50.0	30.0	20.0	0.0	0.0	0.0	0.0
女性 Female	**215**	**19.1**	**44.2**	**34.4**	**0.5**	**0.9**	**0.5**	**0.5**
16~24 岁 Age	57	19.3	50.9	28.1	0.0	1.8	0.0	0.0
25~34 岁 Age	73	23.3	42.5	31.5	0.0	1.4	1.4	0.0
35~44 岁 Age	40	20.0	37.5	37.5	2.5	0.0	0.0	2.5
45~54 岁 Age	35	11.4	45.7	42.9	0.0	0.0	0.0	0.0
55~60 岁 Age	10	10.0	40.0	50.0	0.0	0.0	0.0	0.0

2-10 样本、男性各年龄层、女性各年龄层最常饮用的场合/ Settings of Consumption by the Whole Sample, Age and Gender Groups

注：本题为多选题，合计百分比超过 100%(Multiple answers）

	人数 Number	平时口渴时 when thirsty	平时吃饭喝 at dinner	宴席、聚会喝 at banquet	外出、旅游时 outing/traveling	运动完以后 after athletics	其它 others
样本 Sample	**440**	**77.3**	**0.5**	**3.2**	**41.6**	**10.7**	**0.7**
男性 Male	**225**	**79.1**	**0.4**	**4.0**	**36.9**	**10.2**	**0.9**
16~24 岁 Age	56	80.4	0.0	0.0	19.6	28.6	0.0
25~34 岁 Age	75	84.0	0.0	2.7	34.7	6.7	1.3
35~44 岁 Age	52	78.8	0.0	0.0	53.8	1.9	1.9
45~54 岁 Age	32	71.9	3.1	9.4	34.4	3.1	0.0
55~60 岁 Age	10	60.0	0.0	40.0	70.0	0.0	0.0
女性 Female	**215**	**75.3**	**0.5**	**2.3**	**46.5**	**11.2**	**0.5**
16~24 岁 Age	57	68.4	1.8	0.0	42.1	24.6	0.0
25~34 岁 Age	73	79.5	0.0	2.7	52.1	6.8	0.0
35~44 岁 Age	41	75.6	0.0	2.4	43.9	7.3	0.0
45~54 岁 Age	34	73.5	0.0	5.9	55.9	5.9	2.9
55~60 岁 Age	10	90.0	0.0	0.0	10.0	0.0	0.0

2-11 重度消费者人口分布/ Demographics of the Heavy Consumers

	人数 Number	16-24 岁 Age	25-34 岁 Age	35-44 岁 Age	45-54 岁 Age	55-60 岁 Age
样本 Sample	232	29.3	36.6	17.7	12.1	4.3
男性 Male	124	28.2	35.5	19.4	13.7	3.2
天天喝 daily	10	10.0	30.0	30.0	30.0	0.0
一周 3 次或以上 3 times or over a week	36	25.0	38.9	22.2	11.1	2.8
一周 1~2 次 once or twice a week	78	32.1	34.6	16.7	12.8	3.8
女性 Female	108	30.6	38.0	15.7	10.2	5.6
天天喝 daily	7	42.9	57.1	0.0	0.0	0.0
一周 3 次或以上 3 times or over a week	30	26.7	50.0	16.7	3.3	3.3
一周 1~2 次 once or twice a week	71	31.0	31.0	16.9	14.1	7.0

2-12 不同消费者层的常用品牌/ The Most Frequently Used Brands by Market Segments

2-12-1 时尚流行指标/ Fads Popular Index

	人数 Number	第一品牌及百分比 1st/ percent	第二品牌及百分比 2nd/ percent	第三品牌及百分比 3rd/ percent	第四品牌及百分比 4th/ percent
样本 Sample	437	**冰点水 Bingdianshui(33.4)**	**乐百氏 Robust(24.7)**	**中梁山 Zhongliangshan (16.7)**	**娃哈哈 Wahaha(11.2)**
平实生活指向 simple living orientation	240	冰点水 Bingdianshui(32.1)	乐百氏 Robust(24.2)	中梁山 Zhongliangshan(20.0)	娃哈哈 Wahaha(10.0)
时尚流行指向 fashion orientation	197	冰点水 Bingdianshui(35.0)	乐百氏 Robust(25.4)	中梁山 Zhongliangshan (12.7) 娃哈哈 Wahaha(12.7)	农夫山泉 Nong Fu Shan Quan (9.1)

2-12-2 广告态度指标/ Advertising Attitude Index

	人数 Number	第一品牌及百分比 1st/ percent	第二品牌及百分比 2nd/ percent	第三品牌及百分比 3rd/ percent	第四品牌及百分比 4th/ percent
样本 Sample	440	**冰点水 Bingdianshui(33.2)**	**乐百氏 Robust(24.5)**	**中梁山 Zhongliangshan (16.6)**	**娃哈哈 Wahaha(10.9)**
广告淡漠指向 indifferent orientation	112	冰点水 Bingdianshui(37.5)	乐百氏 Robust(25.0)	中梁山 Zhongliangshan(11.6)	农夫山泉 Nong Fu Shan Quan (8.9)
中间层 medium	269	冰点水 Bingdianshui(32.7)	乐百氏 Robust(22.7)	中梁山 Zhongliangshan(18.2)	娃哈哈 Wahaha(12.3)
信赖广告指向 loyal orientation	59	乐百氏 Robust(32.2)	冰点水 Bingdianshui (27.1)	中梁山 Zhongliangshan(18.6)	农夫山泉 Nong Fu Shan Quan (10.2) 娃哈哈 Wahaha(10.2)

2-12-3 饮食健康指标/ Foods & Drink Quality Index

	人数 Number	第一品牌及百分比 1st/ percent	第二品牌及百分比 2nd/ percent	第三品牌及百分比 3rd/ percent	第四品牌及百分比 4th/ percent
样本 Sample	437	**冰点水 Bingdianshui(32.7)**	**乐百氏 Robust(24.5)**	**中梁山 Zhongliangshan(16.7)**	**娃哈哈 Wahaha(11.2)**
饮食"温饱"指向 "basic" orientation	155	冰点水 Bingdianshui(37.4)	乐百氏 Robust(20.0)	中梁山 Zhongliangshan(17.4)	娃哈哈 Wahaha(11.6)
中间层 medium	190	冰点水 Bingdianshui(29.5)	乐百氏 Robust(28.4)	中梁山 Zhongliangshan(14.7)	娃哈哈 Wahaha(11.6)
健康营养指向 health & nutrition orientation	92	冰点水 Bingdianshui(31.5)	乐百氏 Robust(23.9)	中梁山 Zhongliangshan(19.6)	娃哈哈 Wahaha(9.8)

2-13 重度消费者的消费者层构成/ The Composition of the Heavy Consumers

2-13-1 时尚流行指标/ Fads Popular Index

	人数 Number	平实生活指向 simple living orientation	时尚流行指向 fashion orientation
样本 Sample	229	49.8	50.2
天天喝 daily	17	58.8	41.2
一周 3 次或以上 3 times or over a week	64	50.0	50.0
一周 1~2 次 once or twice a week	148	48.6	51.4

2-13-2 广告态度指标/ Advertising Attitude Index

	人数 Number	广告淡漠指向 indifferent orientation	中间层 medium	信赖广告指向 loyal orientation
样本 Sample	230	20.9	62.6	16.5
天天喝 daily	17	29.4	64.7	5.9
一周 3 次或以上 3 times or over a week	65	27.7	55.4	16.9
一周 1~2 次 about once a week	148	16.9	65.5	17.6

2-13-3 饮食健康指标/ Foods & Drink Quality Index

	人数 Number	饮食"温饱"指向 "basic" orientation	中间层 medium	健康营养指向 health & nutrition orientation
样本 Sample	230	31.3	45.7	23.0
天天喝 daily	17	29.4	41.2	29.4
一周 3 次或以上 3 times or over a week	65	40.0	32.3	27.7
一周 1~2 次 once or twice a week	148	27.7	52.0	20.3

● 武汉 / Wuhan

2-1 最近三个月饮用频率的比例/ Proportion of the Sample Consuming Purified or Mineral Water in the Last Three Months

	人数 Number	百分比 Percent
天天喝 daily	26	4.1
一周 3 次或以上 3 times or over a week	54	8.4
一周 1~2 次 once or twice a week	128	20.0
一个月 2~3 次 2 or 3 times a month	154	24.1
一个月 1 次或以下 once a month or below	72	11.3
没喝过 never	206	32.2

n=640

2-2 最常用品牌排名/ Ranking of the Most Frequently Used Brands

排名 Brand Ranking	品牌 Brands	人数 Number	百分比 Percent
1	乐百氏 Robust	163	37.6
2	娃哈哈 Wahaha	98	22.6
3	康师傅 Kangshifu	66	15.2
4	农夫山泉 Nong Fu Shan Quan	13	3.0
5	获特满 Waterman	11	2.5
6	小黑子 Xiaoheizi	8	1.8

n=433

2-3 样本、男性各年龄层、女性各年龄层的常用品牌/ The Most Frequently Used Brands by the Whole Sample, Age and Gender Groups

	人数 Number	第一品牌及百分比 1st/ percent	第二品牌及百分比 2nd/ percent	第三品牌及百分比 3rd/ percent
样本 Sample	433	**乐百氏 Robust(37.6)**	**娃哈哈 Wahaha(22.6)**	**康师傅 Kangshifu(15.2)**
男性 Male	225	**乐百氏 Robust(38.7)**	**娃哈哈 Wahaha(20.9)**	**康师傅 Kangshifu(18.2)**
16~24 岁 Age	58	乐百氏 Robust(32.8)	康师傅 Kangshifu(25.9)	娃哈哈 Wahaha(13.8)
25~34 岁 Age	78	乐百氏 Robust(41.0)	娃哈哈 Wahaha(25.6)	康师傅 Kangshifu(19.2)
35~44 岁 Age	54	乐百氏 Robust(42.6)	娃哈哈 Wahaha(24.1)	康师傅 Kangshifu(16.7)
45~54 岁 Age	26	乐百氏 Robust(42.3)	娃哈哈 Wahaha(11.5)	康师傅 Kangshifu(7.7)
55~60 岁 Age	9	娃哈哈 Wahaha(33.3)	乐百氏 Robust(22.2)	屈臣氏 Watson's(11.1)
女性 Female	208	**乐百氏 Robust(36.5)**	**娃哈哈 Wahaha(24.5)**	**康师傅 Kangshifu(12.0)**
16~24 岁 Age	59	乐百氏 Robust(30.5)	娃哈哈 Wahaha(22.0)	康师傅 Kangshifu(11.9)
25~34 岁 Age	68	乐百氏 Robust(51.5)	娃哈哈 Wahaha(29.4)	康师傅 Kangshifu(8.8)
35~44 岁 Age	43	乐百氏 Robust(34.9)	娃哈哈 Wahaha(16.3)	康师傅 Kangshifu(9.3)
45~54 岁 Age	31	娃哈哈 Wahaha(32.3)	乐百氏 Robust(22.6)	康师傅 Kangshifu(16.1)
55~60 岁 Age	7	康师傅 Kangshifu(42.9)	乐百氏 Robust(14.3) 娃哈哈 Wahaha(14.3) 武钢纯净水 Wugang(14.3) 东鹏蒸馏水 Dongpeng(14.3)	

2-4 理想品牌排名/ Ranking of the Ideal Brands

排名 Brand Ranking	品牌 Brands	人数 Number	百分比 Percent
1	乐百氏 Robust	179	27.9
2	娃哈哈 Wahaha	119	18.5
3	康师傅 Kangshifu	80	12.5
4	农夫山泉 Nong Fu Shan Quan	20	3.1
5	获特满 Waterman	14	2.2
6	小黑子 Xiaoheizi	8	1.2
7	赞活化水 Ace	7	1.1

n=642

2-5 样本、男性各年龄层、女性各年龄层最近三个月有无购买的比例/ Purchasing in the Last Three Months by the Whole Sample, Age and Gender Groups

	人数 Number	买过 yes	没买过 no
样本 Sample	641	64.6	35.4
男性 Male	311	68.8	31.2
16~24 岁 Age	65	80.0	20.0
25~34 岁 Age	89	86.5	13.5
35~44 岁 Age	80	63.8	36.3
45~54 岁 Age	52	51.9	48.1
55~60 岁 Age	25	28.0	72.0
女性 Female	330	60.6	39.4
16~24 岁 Age	69	79.7	20.3
25~34 岁 Age	96	66.7	33.3
35~44 岁 Age	77	55.8	44.2
45~54 岁 Age	62	48.4	51.6
55~60 岁 Age	26	30.8	69.2

2-6 样本、男性各年龄层、女性各年龄层最近三个月的饮用频率/ Frequencies of Consuming Purified or Mineral Water in the Last Three Months by the Whole Sample, Age and Gender Groups

	人数 Number	天天喝 daily	一周 3 次或以上 3 times or over a week	一周 1~2 次 once or twice a week	一个月 2~3 次 2 or 3 times a month	一个月 1 次或以下 once a month or below	没喝过 never
样本 Sample	640	4.1	8.4	20.0	24.1	11.3	32.2
男性 Male	311	4.8	8.0	23.5	27.0	9.3	27.3
16~24 岁 Age	65	7.7	3.1	35.4	27.7	15.4	10.8
25~34 岁 Age	89	5.6	11.2	27.0	34.8	9.0	12.4
35~44 岁 Age	80	2.5	11.3	21.3	23.8	8.8	32.5
45~54 岁 Age	52	3.8	5.8	11.5	25.0	5.8	48.1
55~60 岁 Age	25	4.0	4.0	12.0	12.0	4.0	64.0
女性 Female	329	3.3	8.8	16.7	21.3	13.1	36.8
16~24 岁 Age	68	4.4	14.7	22.1	32.4	13.2	13.2
25~34 岁 Age	96	3.1	11.5	17.7	25.0	13.5	29.2
35~44 岁 Age	78	2.6	5.1	17.9	12.8	16.7	44.9
45~54 岁 Age	61	3.3	3.3	11.5	21.3	11.5	49.2
55~60 岁 Age	26	3.8	7.7	7.7	3.8	3.8	73.1

2-7 样本、男性各年龄层、女性各年龄层的品牌习惯/ Brand Habit in Consuming Purified or Mineral Water by the Whole Sample, Age and Gender Groups

	人数 Number	基本固定饮用一个牌子 used in only one brand	比较固定地饮用两个或三个牌子 used in two or three brands	基本上不太固定牌子 no brand preference
样本 Sample	433	30.9	40.9	28.2
男性 Male	225	33.8	39.1	27.1
16~24 岁 Age	58	32.8	32.8	34.5
25~34 岁 Age	78	29.5	44.9	25.6
35~44 岁 Age	54	44.4	37.0	18.5
45~54 岁 Age	26	30.8	42.3	26.9
55~60 岁 Age	9	22.2	33.3	44.4
女性 Female	208	27.9	42.8	29.3
16~24 岁 Age	59	28.8	42.4	28.8
25~34 岁 Age	68	30.9	50.0	19.1
35~44 岁 Age	43	20.9	46.5	32.6
45~54 岁 Age	31	25.8	32.3	41.9
55~60 岁 Age	7	42.9	0.0	57.1

2-8 选择该类商品的考虑因素/ Ranking of the Considerations in Purchasing

注：本题为多选题，合计百分比超过 100%(Multiple answers）

排名 Ranking	考虑因素 Considerations	人次 Person-time	百分比 Percent
1	价格适中 reasonable price	156	35.9
2	有名的牌子 famous brand	153	35.3
3	口味好 pleasant taste	139	32.0
4	购买方便 easy to buy	129	29.7
5	生产日期 date of producing	122	28.1
6	广告影响 influence of advertising	81	18.7
7	只是由于习惯 out of habit	39	9.0
8	单位发的 offered by the working unit	28	6.5
9	包装吸引人 appealing package	15	3.5
10	其它 others	13	3.0
11	朋友推荐 introduction of friends	11	2.5
12	有优惠条件 with preferential terms	9	2.1
13	售货员介绍 introduced by the shop assistants	6	1.4

n=434

2-9 样本、男性各年龄层、女性各年龄层最常饮用的包装形式/ Types of Package of the Consumed Purified or Mineral Water by the Whole Sample, Age and Gender Groups

	人数 Number	250ml 以下 250ml or below	250ml--350ml	500ml--750ml	1L	1.5L	2L 以上 2L or over	其它 others
样本 Sample	430	26.3	40.5	29.3	0.5	1.6	0.9	0.9
男性 Male	223	28.7	36.8	30.0	0.9	1.8	0.9	0.9
16~24 岁 Age	58	32.8	32.8	29.3	1.7	1.7	1.7	0.0
25~34 岁 Age	78	24.4	41.0	30.8	1.3	2.6	0.0	0.0
35~44 岁 Age	52	34.6	30.8	30.8	0.0	1.9	0.0	1.9
45~54 岁 Age	26	23.1	46.2	23.1	0.0	0.0	3.8	3.8
55~60 岁 Age	9	22.2	33.3	44.4	0.0	0.0	0.0	0.0
女性 Female	207	23.7	44.4	28.5	0.0	1.4	1.0	1.0
16~24 岁 Age	59	18.6	49.2	30.5	0.0	0.0	0.0	1.7
25~34 岁 Age	67	35.8	41.8	22.4	0.0	0.0	0.0	0.0
35~44 岁 Age	43	16.3	44.2	32.6	0.0	4.7	2.3	0.0
45~54 岁 Age	31	16.1	45.2	29.0	0.0	3.2	3.2	3.2
55~60 岁 Age	7	28.6	28.6	42.9	0.0	0.0	0.0	0.0

2-10 样本、男性各年龄层、女性各年龄层最常饮用的场合/ Settings of Consumption by the Whole Sample, Age and Gender Groups

注：本题为多选题，合计百分比超过 100%(Multiple answers)

	人数 Number	平时口渴时 when thirsty	平时吃饭喝 at dinner	宴席、聚会喝 at banquet	外出、旅游时 outing/traveling	运动完以后 after athletics	其它 others
样本 Sample	432	75.7	2.5	5.8	44.0	13.9	1.6
男性 Male	224	76.8	2.7	7.1	37.9	16.5	1.3
16~24 岁 Age	58	77.6	1.7	3.4	36.2	24.1	1.7
25~34 岁 Age	78	78.2	2.6	2.6	34.6	20.5	2.6
35~44 岁 Age	54	81.5	3.7	9.3	38.9	9.3	0.0
45~54 岁 Age	25	68.0	0.0	20.0	48.0	8.0	0.0
55~60 岁 Age	9	55.6	11.1	22.2	44.4	0.0	0.0
女性 Female	208	74.5	2.4	4.3	50.5	11.1	1.9
16~24 岁 Age	59	78.0	3.4	1.7	52.5	16.9	0.0
25~34 岁 Age	68	76.5	0.0	4.4	48.5	7.4	2.9
35~44 岁 Age	43	72.1	4.7	0.0	46.5	9.3	2.3
45~54 岁 Age	31	64.5	3.2	16.1	51.6	9.7	3.2
55~60 岁 Age	7	85.7	0.0	0.0	71.4	14.3	0.0

2-11 重度消费者人口分布/ Demographics of the Heavy Consumers

	人数 Number	16-24 岁 Age	25-34 岁 Age	35-44 岁 Age	45-54 岁 Age	55-60 岁 Age
样本 Sample	208	27.9	33.7	23.1	10.6	4.8
男性 Male	113	26.5	34.5	24.8	9.7	4.4
天天喝 daily	15	33.3	33.3	13.3	13.3	6.7
一周 3 次或以上 3 times or over a week	25	8.0	40.0	36.0	12.0	4.0
一周 1~2 次 once or twice a week	73	31.5	32.9	23.3	8.2	4.1
女性 Female	95	29.5	32.6	21.1	11.6	5.3
天天喝 daily	11	27.3	27.3	18.2	18.2	9.1
一周 3 次或以上 3 times or over a week	29	34.5	37.9	13.8	6.9	6.9
一周 1~2 次 once or twice a week	55	27.3	30.9	25.5	12.7	3.6

2-12 不同消费者层的常用品牌/ The Most Frequently Used Brands by Market Segments

2-12-1 时尚流行指标/ Fads Popular Index

	人数 Number	第一品牌及百分比 1st/ percent	第二品牌及百分比 2nd/ percent	第三品牌及百分比 3rd/ percent
样本 Sample	428	**乐百氏 Robust(37.6)**	**娃哈哈 Wahaha(22.7)**	**康师傅 Kangshifu(15.2)**
平实生活指向 simple living orientation	201	乐百氏 Robust(40.8)	娃哈哈 Wahaha(22.9)	康师傅 Kangshifu(11.4)
时尚流行指向 fashion orientation	227	乐百氏 Robust(34.8)	娃哈哈 Wahaha(22.5)	康师傅 Kangshifu(18.5)

2-12-2 广告态度指标/ Advertising Attitude Index

	人数 Number	第一品牌及百分比 1st/ percent	第二品牌及百分比 2nd/ percent	第三品牌及百分比 3rd/ percent
样本 Sample	429	**乐百氏 Robust(37.5)**	**娃哈哈 Wahaha(22.6)**	**康师傅 Kangshifu(15.4)**
广告淡漠指向 indifferent orientation	121	乐百氏 Robust(35.5)	娃哈哈 Wahaha(26.4)	康师傅 Kangshifu(11.6)
中间层 medium	251	乐百氏 Robust(37.8)	娃哈哈 Wahaha(21.1)	康师傅 Kangshifu(15.9)
信赖广告指向 loyal orientation	57	乐百氏 Robust(40.4)	康师傅 Kangshifu(21.1) 娃哈哈 Wahaha(21.1)	获特满 Waterman(1.8) Magara(1.8) 农夫山泉 Nong Fu Shan Quan(1.8) 怡宝 Cestron(1.8) 清泉 Qingquan(1.8)

2-12-3 饮食健康指标/ Foods & Drink Quality Index

	人数 Number	第一品牌及百分比 1st/ percent	第二品牌及百分比 2nd/ percent	第三品牌及百分比 3rd/ percent
样本 Sample	428	**乐百氏 Robust(37.6)**	**娃哈哈 Wahaha(22.7)**	**康师傅 Kangshifu(15.2)**
饮食“温饱”指向 "basic" orientation	145	乐百氏 Robust(37.2)	娃哈哈 Wahaha(20.7)	康师傅 Kangshifu(17.2)
中间层 medium	199	乐百氏 Robust(39.2)	娃哈哈 Wahaha(24.1)	康师傅 Kangshifu(15.6)
健康营养指向 health & nutrition orientation	84	乐百氏 Robust(34.5)	娃哈哈 Wahaha(22.6)	康师傅 Kangshifu(10.7)

2-13 重度消费者的消费者层构成/ The Composition of the Heavy Consumers

2-13-1 时尚流行指标/ Fads Popular Index

	人数 Number	平实生活指向 simple living orientation	时尚流行指向 fashion orientation
样本 Sample	205	**43.4**	**56.6**
天天喝 daily	26	46.2	53.8
一周 3 次或以上 3 times or over a week	52	40.4	59.6
一周 1~2 次 once or twice a week	127	44.1	55.9

2-13-2 广告态度指标/ Advertising Attitude Index

	人数 Number	广告淡漠指向 indifferent orientation	中间层 medium	信赖广告指向 loyal orientation
样本 Sample	205	**24.9**	**61.5**	**13.7**
天天喝 daily	26	30.8	61.5	7.7
一周 3 次或以上 3 times or over a week	52	23.1	61.5	15.4
一周 1~2 次 once or twice a week	127	24.4	61.4	14.2

2-13-3 饮食健康指标/ Foods & Drink Quality Index

	人数 Number	饮食“温饱”指向 "basic" orientation	中间层 medium	健康营养指向 health & nutrition orientation
样本 Sample	205	**35.1**	**42.4**	**22.4**
天天喝 daily	26	30.8	38.5	30.8
一周 3 次或以上 3 times or over a week	52	30.8	48.1	21.2
一周 1~2 次 once or twice a week	127	37.8	40.9	21.3

● 西安 / Xi'an

2-1 最近三个月饮用频率的比例/ Proportion of the Sample Consuming Purified or Mineral Water in the Last Three Months

	人数 Number	百分比 Percent
天天喝 daily	14	2.3
一周 3 次或以上 3 times or over a week	52	8.7
一周 1~2 次 once or twice a week	145	24.1
一个月 2~3 次 2 or 3 times a month	155	25.8
一个月 1 次或以下 once a month or below	65	10.8
没喝过 never	170	28.3

n=601

2-2 最常用品牌排名/ Ranking of the Most Frequently Used Brands

排名 Brand Ranking	品牌 Brands	人数 Number	百分比 Percent
1	娃哈哈 Wahaha	205	47.6
2	乐百氏 Robust	131	30.4
3	农夫山泉 Nong Fu Shan Quan	44	10.2
4	天与地 Tianyudi	22	5.1
5	丈八龙泉 Zhang Ba Long Quan	6	1.4
5	康师傅 Kangshifu	6	1.4
6	大荔神泉 Dalishen	3	0.7
7	白雪 Baixue	2	0.5

n=431

2-3 样本、男性各年龄层、女性各年龄层的常用品牌/ The Most Frequently Used Brands by the Whole Sample, Age and Gender Groups

	人数 Number	第一品牌及百分比 1st/ percent	第二品牌及百分比 2nd/ percent	第三品牌及百分比 3rd/ percent
样本 Sample	**431**	**娃哈哈 Wahaha(47.6)**	**乐百氏 Robust(30.4)**	**农夫山泉 Nong Fu Shan Quan(10.2)**
男性 Male	**224**	**娃哈哈 Wahaha(47.3)**	**乐百氏 Robust(33.5)**	**农夫山泉 Nong Fu Shan Quan(7.6)**
16~24 岁 Age	55	娃哈哈 Wahaha(49.1)	乐百氏 Robust(30.9)	天与地 Tianyudi(9.1)
25~34 岁 Age	69	娃哈哈 Wahaha(49.3)	乐百氏 Robust(31.9)	农夫山泉 Nong Fu Shan Quan(5.8)
35~44 岁 Age	62	娃哈哈 Wahaha(43.5)	乐百氏 Robust(37.1)	农夫山泉 Nong Fu Shan Quan(11.3)
45~54 岁 Age	26	娃哈哈 Wahaha(46.2)	乐百氏 Robust(34.6)	农夫山泉 Nong Fu Shan Quan(3.8) 天与地 Tianyudi(3.8) 丈八龙泉 Zhang Ba Long Quan(3.8)
55~60 岁 Age	12	娃哈哈 Wahaha(50.0)	乐百氏 Robust(33.3)	农夫山泉 Nong Fu Shan Quan(8.3)
女性 Female	**207**	**娃哈哈 Wahaha(47.8)**	**乐百氏 Robust(27.1)**	**农夫山泉 Nong Fu Shan Quan(13.0)**
16~24 岁 Age	45	乐百氏 Robust(40.0)	娃哈哈 Wahaha(37.8)	农夫山泉 Nong Fu Shan Quan(11.1)
25~34 岁 Age	77	娃哈哈 Wahaha(46.8)	农夫山泉 Nong Fu Shan Quan(20.8)	乐百氏 Robust(19.5)
35~44 岁 Age	45	娃哈哈 Wahaha(51.1)	乐百氏 Robust(26.7)	农夫山泉 Nong Fu Shan Quan(8.9) 天与地 Tianyudi(8.9)
45~54 岁 Age	29	娃哈哈 Wahaha(65.5)	乐百氏 Robust(27.6)	康师傅 Kangshifu(6.9)
55~60 岁 Age	11	娃哈哈 Wahaha(36.4)	乐百氏 Robust(27.3)	农夫山泉 Nong Fu Shan Quan(18.2)

2-4 理想品牌排名/ Ranking of the Ideal Brands

排名 Brand Ranking	品牌 Brands	人数 Number	百分比 Percent
1	娃哈哈 Wahaha	287	47.8
2	乐百氏 Robust	155	25.8
3	农夫山泉 Nong Fu Shan Quan	54	9.0
4	天与地 Tianyudi	32	5.3
5	丈八龙泉 Zhang Ba Long Quan	12	2.0
6	康师傅 Kangshifu	8	1.3
7	大荔神泉 Dalishen	3	0.5
7	白雪 Baixue	3	0.5

n=600

2-5 样本、男性各年龄层、女性各年龄层最近三个月有无购买的比例/ Purchasing in the Last Three Months by the Whole Sample, Age and Gender Groups

	人数 Number	买过 yes	没买过 no
样本 Sample	**601**	**70.4**	**29.6**
男性 Male	**302**	**71.5**	**28.5**
16~24 岁 Age	64	82.8	17.2
25~34 岁 Age	91	73.6	26.4
35~44 岁 Age	77	76.6	23.4
45~54 岁 Age	46	54.3	45.7
55~60 岁 Age	24	50.0	50.0
女性 Female	**299**	**69.2**	**30.8**
16~24 岁 Age	61	68.9	31.1
25~34 岁 Age	90	85.6	14.4
35~44 岁 Age	74	62.2	37.8
45~54 岁 Age	49	65.3	34.7
55~60 岁 Age	25	40.0	60.0

2-6 样本、男性各年龄层、女性各年龄层最近三个月的饮用频率/ Frequencies of Consuming Purified or Mineral Water in the Last Three Months by the Whole Sample, Age and Gender Groups

	人数 Number	天天喝 daily	一周 3 次或以上 3 times or over a week	一周 1~2 次 once or twice a week	一个月 2~3 次 2 or 3 times a month	一个月 1 次或以下 once a month or below	没喝过 never
样本 Sample	601	2.3	8.7	24.1	25.8	10.8	28.3
男性 Male	302	2.0	9.6	26.5	28.1	7.9	25.8
16~24 岁 Age	64	4.7	14.1	37.5	18.8	10.9	14.1
25~34 岁 Age	91	2.2	9.9	29.7	28.6	5.5	24.2
35~44 岁 Age	77	1.3	9.1	24.7	37.7	7.8	19.5
45~54 岁 Age	46	0.0	6.5	17.4	23.9	8.7	43.5
55~60 岁 Age	24	0.0	4.2	8.3	29.2	8.3	50.0
女性 Female	299	2.7	7.7	21.7	23.4	13.7	30.8
16~24 岁 Age	61	4.9	18.0	21.3	23.0	6.6	26.2
25~34 岁 Age	90	4.4	3.3	25.6	30.0	22.2	14.4
35~44 岁 Age	74	1.4	4.1	21.6	20.3	13.5	39.2
45~54 岁 Age	49	0.0	8.2	22.4	22.4	6.1	40.8
55~60 岁 Age	25	0.0	8.0	8.0	12.0	16.0	56.0

2-7 样本、男性各年龄层、女性各年龄层的品牌习惯/ Brand Habit in Consuming Purified or Mineral Water by the Whole Sample, Age and Gender Groups

	人数 Number	基本固定饮用一个牌子 used in only one brand	比较固定地饮用两个或三个牌子 used in two or three brands	基本上不太固定牌子 no brand preference
样本 Sample	431	36.2	43.6	20.2
男性 Male	224	35.3	43.3	21.4
16~24 岁 Age	55	43.6	32.7	23.6
25~34 岁 Age	69	37.7	40.6	21.7
35~44 岁 Age	62	33.9	48.4	17.7
45~54 岁 Age	26	30.8	38.5	30.8
55~60 岁 Age	12	0.0	91.7	8.3
女性 Female	207	37.2	44.0	18.8
16~24 岁 Age	45	42.2	48.9	8.9
25~34 岁 Age	77	40.3	41.6	18.2
35~44 岁 Age	45	31.1	44.4	24.4
45~54 岁 Age	29	34.5	44.8	20.7
55~60 岁 Age	11	27.3	36.4	36.4

2-8 选择该类商品的考虑因素/ Ranking of the Considerations in Purchasing

注：本题为多选题，合计百分比超过 100%(Multiple answers）

排名 Ranking	考虑因素 Considerations	人次 Person-time	百分比 Percent
1	有名的牌子 famous brand	161	37.4
2	价格适中 reasonable price	151	35.0
3	口味好 pleasant taste	141	32.7
4	广告影响 influence of advertising	95	22.0
5	购买方便 easy to buy	91	21.1
6	生产日期 date of producing	82	19.0
7	只是由于习惯 out of habit	48	11.1
8	包装吸引人 appealing package	20	4.6
9	朋友推荐 introduction of friends	13	3.0
10	单位发的 offered by the working unit	10	2.3
11	售货员介绍 introduced by the shop assistants	5	1.2
12	有优惠条件 with preferential terms	4	0.9
13	其它 others	3	0.7

n=431

2-9 样本、男性各年龄层、女性各年龄层最常饮用的包装形式/ Package Types of the Purified or Mineral Water by the Whole Sample, Age and Gender Groups

	人数 Number	250ml 以下 250ml or below	250ml--350ml	500ml--750ml	1L	1.5L	2L 以上 2L or over	其它 others
样本 Sample	430	22.8	42.8	32.6	1.6	0.0	0.2	0.0
男性 Male	224	19.6	49.1	29.5	1.8	0.0	0.0	0.0
16~24 岁 Age	55	21.8	43.6	34.5	0.0	0.0	0.0	0.0
25~34 岁 Age	69	10.1	55.1	31.9	2.9	0.0	0.0	0.0
35~44 岁 Age	62	29.0	43.5	25.8	1.6	0.0	0.0	0.0
45~54 岁 Age	26	23.1	57.7	15.4	3.8	0.0	0.0	0.0
55~60 岁 Age	12	8.3	50.0	41.7	0.0	0.0	0.0	0.0
女性 Female	206	26.2	35.9	35.9	1.5	0.0	0.5	0.0
16~24 岁 Age	45	28.9	35.6	35.6	0.0	0.0	0.0	0.0
25~34 岁 Age	76	23.7	35.5	38.2	2.6	0.0	0.0	0.0
35~44 岁 Age	45	33.3	26.7	37.8	0.0	0.0	2.2	0.0
45~54 岁 Age	29	20.7	44.8	34.5	0.0	0.0	0.0	0.0
55~60 岁 Age	11	18.2	54.5	18.2	9.1	0.0	0.0	0.0

2-10 样本、男性各年龄层、女性各年龄层最常饮用的场合/ Settings of Consumption by the Whole Sample, Age and Gender Groups

注：本题为多选题，合计百分比超过 100%(Multiple answers)

	人数 Number	平时口渴时 when thirsty	平时吃饭喝 at dinner	宴席、聚会喝 at banquet	外出、旅游时 outing/traveling	运动完以后 after athletics	其它 others
样本 Sample	431	59.9	5.8	5.8	53.4	11.1	0.0
男性 Male	224	61.6	5.4	5.4	50.4	12.9	0.0
16~24 岁 Age	55	63.6	3.6	7.3	41.8	14.5	0.0
25~34 岁 Age	69	55.1	8.7	4.3	50.7	13.0	0.0
35~44 岁 Age	62	69.4	3.2	6.5	54.8	4.8	0.0
45~54 岁 Age	26	61.5	7.7	0.0	46.2	26.9	0.0
55~60 岁 Age	12	50.0	0.0	8.3	75.0	16.7	0.0
女性 Female	207	58.0	6.3	6.3	56.5	9.2	0.0
16~24 岁 Age	45	71.1	4.4	6.7	40.0	6.7	0.0
25~34 岁 Age	77	53.2	5.2	6.5	67.5	6.5	0.0
35~44 岁 Age	45	64.4	8.9	4.4	53.3	8.9	0.0
45~54 岁 Age	29	55.2	6.9	0.0	51.7	17.2	0.0
55~60 岁 Age	11	18.2	9.1	27.3	72.7	18.2	0.0

2-11 重度消费者人口分布/ Demographics of the Heavy Consumers

	人数 Number	16-24 岁 Age	25-34 岁 Age	35-44 岁 Age	45-54 岁 Age	55-60 岁 Age
样本 Sample	211	29.9	32.2	22.3	12.3	3.3
男性 Male	115	31.3	33.0	23.5	9.6	2.6
天天喝 daily	6	50.0	33.3	16.7	0.0	0.0
一周 3 次或以上 3 times or over a week	29	31.0	31.0	24.1	10.3	3.4
一周 1~2 次 once or twice a week	80	30.0	33.8	23.8	10.0	2.5
女性 Female	96	28.1	31.3	20.8	15.6	4.2
天天喝 daily	8	37.5	50.0	12.5	0.0	0.0
一周 3 次或以上 3 times or over a week	23	47.8	13.0	13.0	17.4	8.7
一周 1~2 次 once or twice a week	65	20.0	35.4	24.6	16.9	3.1

2-12 不同消费者层的常用品牌/ The Most Frequently Used Brands by Market Segments

2-12-1 时尚流行指标/ Fads Popular Index

	人数 Number	第一品牌及百分比 1st/ percent	第二品牌及百分比 2nd/ percent	第三品牌及百分比 3rd/ percent	第四品牌及百分比 4th/ percent
样本 Sample	**431**	**娃哈哈 Wahaha(47.6)**	**乐百氏 Robust(30.4)**	**农夫山泉 Nong Fu Shan Quan (10.2)**	**天与地 Tianyudi(5.1)**
平实生活指向 simple living orientation	225	娃哈哈 Wahaha(51.4)	乐百氏 Robust(28.9)	农夫山泉 Nong Fu Shan Quan (9.3)	天与地 Tianyudi(3.1)
时尚流行指向 fashion orientation	206	娃哈哈 Wahaha(43.7)	乐百氏 Robust(32.0)	农夫山泉 Nong Fu Shan Quan (11.2)	天与地 Tianyudi(7.3)

2-12-2 广告态度指标/ Advertising Attitude Index

	人数 Number	第一品牌及百分比 1st/ percent	第二品牌及百分比 2nd/ percent	第三品牌及百分比 3rd/ percent	第四品牌及百分比 4th/ percent
样本 Sample	**428**	**娃哈哈 Wahaha(47.7)**	**乐百氏 Robust(30.1)**	**农夫山泉 Nong Fu Shan Quan (10.3)**	**天与地 Tianyudi(5.1)**
广告淡漠指向 indifferent orientation	129	娃哈哈 Wahaha(56.6)	乐百氏 Robust(27.9)	农夫山泉 Nong Fu Shan Quan (7.8)	天与地 Tianyudi(5.4)
中间层 medium	246	娃哈哈 Wahaha(41.5)	乐百氏 Robust(32.1)	农夫山泉 Nong Fu Shan Quan (12.2)	天与地 Tianyudi(5.3)
信赖广告指向 loyal orientation	53	娃哈哈 Wahaha(54.7)	乐百氏 Robust(26.4)	农夫山泉 Nong Fu Shan Quan (7.5)	康师傅 Kangshifu(3.8) 天与地 Tianyudi(3.8)

2-12-3 饮食健康指标/ Foods & Drink Quality Index

	人数 Number	第一品牌及百分比 1st/ percent	第二品牌及百分比 2nd/ percent	第三品牌及百分比 3rd/ percent	第四品牌及百分比 4th/ percent
样本 Sample	**431**	**娃哈哈 Wahaha(47.6)**	**乐百氏 Robust(30.4)**	**农夫山泉 Nong Fu Shan Quan (10.2)**	**天与地 Tianyudi(5.1)**
饮食“温饱”指向 "basic" orientation	152	娃哈哈 Wahaha(49.3)	乐百氏 Robust(34.9)	农夫山泉 Nong Fu Shan Quan (5.3)	天与地 Tianyudi(3.9)
中间层 medium	213	娃哈哈 Wahaha(46.0)	乐百氏 Robust(27.2)	农夫山泉 Nong Fu Shan Quan (13.6)	天与地 Tianyudi(5.2)
健康营养指向 health & nutrition orientation	66	娃哈哈 Wahaha(48.5)	乐百氏 Robust(30.3)	农夫山泉 Nong Fu Shan Quan (10.6)	天与地 Tianyudi(7.6)

2-13 重度消费者的消费者层构成/ The Composition of the Heavy Consumers

2-13-1 时尚流行指标/ Fads Popular Index

	人数 Number	平实生活指向 simple living orientation	时尚流行指向 fashion orientation
样本 Sample	211	44.5	55.5
天天喝 daily	14	21.4	78.6
一周 3 次或以上 3 times or over a week	52	42.3	57.7
一周 1~2 次 once or twice a week	145	47.6	52.4

2-13-2 广告态度指标/ Advertising Attitude Index

	人数 Number	广告淡漠指向 indifferent orientation	中间层 medium	信赖广告指向 loyal orientation
样本 Sample	209	28.7	55.0	16.3
天天喝 daily	14	28.6	42.9	28.6
一周 3 次或以上 3 times or over a week	51	21.6	52.9	25.5
一周 1~2 次 once or twice a week	144	31.3	56.9	11.8

2-13-3 饮食健康指标/ Foods & Drink Quality Index

	人数 Number	饮食"温饱"指向 "basic" orientation	中间层 medium	健康营养指向 health & nutrition orientation
样本 Sample	211	35.5	46.4	18.0
天天喝 daily	14	7.1	78.6	14.3
一周 3 次或以上 3 times or over a week	52	34.6	40.4	25.0
一周 1~2 次 once or twice a week	145	38.6	45.5	15.9

● 沈阳 / Shenyang

2-1 最近三个月饮用频率的比例/ Proportion of the Sample Consuming Purified or Mineral Water in the Last Three Months

	人数 Number	百分比 Percent
天天喝 daily	37	6.2
一周 3 次或以上 3 times or over a week	53	8.8
一周 1~2 次 once or twice a week	106	17.7
一个月 2~3 次 2 or 3 times a month	152	25.3
一个月 1 次或以下 once a month or below	83	13.8
没喝过 never	169	28.2

n=600

2-2 最常用品牌排名/ Ranking of the Most Frequently Used Brands

排名 Brand Ranking	品牌 Brands	人数 Number	百分比 Percent
1	娃哈哈 Wahaha	249	57.8
2	农夫山泉 Nong Fu Shan Quan	57	13.2
3	乐百氏 Robust	50	11.6
4	康师傅 Kangshifu	17	3.9
5	八王寺 Bawangsi	11	2.6
6	天与地 Tianyudi	8	1.9
7	龙王 Longwang	7	1.6
7	东北虎 Dongbeihu	7	1.6

n=431

2-3 样本、男性各年龄层、女性各年龄层的常用品牌/ The Most Frequently Used Brands by the Whole Sample, Age and Gender Groups

	人数 Number	第一品牌及百分比 1st/ percent	第二品牌及百分比 2nd/ percent	第三品牌及百分比 3rd/ percent
样本 Sample	431	**娃哈哈 Wahaha(57.8)**	**农夫山泉 Nong Fu Shan Quan(13.2)**	**乐百氏 Robust(11.6)**
男性 Male	215	**娃哈哈 Wahaha(57.7)**	**乐百氏 Robust(12.1)**	**农夫山泉 Nong Fu Shan Quan(11.2)**
16~24 岁 Age	53	娃哈哈 Wahaha(37.7)	乐百氏 Robust(22.6)	康师傅 Kangshifu(15.1)
25~34 岁 Age	76	娃哈哈 Wahaha(63.2)	农夫山泉 Nong Fu Shan Quan(14.5)	乐百氏 Robust(6.6)
35~44 岁 Age	52	娃哈哈 Wahaha(65.4)	农夫山泉 Nong Fu Shan Quan(17.3)	乐百氏 Robust(7.7)
45~54 岁 Age	28	娃哈哈 Wahaha(67.9)	乐百氏 Robust(14.3)	康师傅 Kangshifu(3.6) 崂山 Laoshan(3.6) 农夫山泉 Nong Fu Shan Quan(3.6) 东北虎 Dongbeihu(3.6) 比尔澳特 Bi'er'aote(3.6)
55~60 岁 Age	6	娃哈哈 Wahaha(50.0)	崂山 Laoshan(16.7) 乐百氏 Robust(16.7) 大情宝泉 Daqingbaoquan(16.7)	
女性 Female	216	**娃哈哈 Wahaha(57.9)**	**农夫山泉 Nong Fu Shan Quan(15.3)**	**乐百氏 Robust(11.1)**
16~24 岁 Age	52	娃哈哈 Wahaha(55.8)	乐百氏 Robust(13.5)	农夫山泉 Nong Fu Shan Quan(11.5)
25~34 岁 Age	69	娃哈哈 Wahaha(58.0)	农夫山泉 Nong Fu Shan Quan(26.1)	乐百氏 Robust(4.3)
35~44 岁 Age	56	娃哈哈 Wahaha(53.6)	乐百氏 Robust(14.3)	农夫山泉 Nong Fu Shan Quan(8.9)
45~54 岁 Age	27	娃哈哈 Wahaha(66.7)	乐百氏 Robust(18.5)	农夫山泉 Nong Fu Shan Quan(11.1)
55~60 岁 Age	12	娃哈哈 Wahaha(66.7)	八王寺 Bawangsi(16.7)	乐百氏 Robust(8.3) 农夫山泉 Nong Fu Shan Quan(8.3)

2-4 理想品牌排名/ Ranking of the Ideal Brands

排名 Brand Ranking	品牌 Brands	人数 Number	百分比 Percent
1	娃哈哈 Wahaha	335	55.7
2	农夫山泉 Nong Fu Shan Quan	92	15.3
3	乐百氏 Robust	50	8.3
4	康师傅 Kangshifu	23	3.8
5	崂山 Laoshan	12	2.0
5	八王寺 Bawangsi	12	2.0
6	龙王 Longwang	11	1.8
7	天与地 Tianyudi	9	1.5

n=601

2-5 样本、男性各年龄层、女性各年龄层最近三个月有无购买的比例/ Purchasing in the Last Three Months by the Whole Sample, Age and Gender Groups

	人数 Number	买过 yes	没买过 no
样本 Sample	600	69.8	30.2
男性 Male	298	68.1	31.9
16~24 岁 Age	64	78.1	21.9
25~34 岁 Age	89	84.3	15.7
35~44 岁 Age	76	63.2	36.8
45~54 岁 Age	45	53.3	46.7
55~60 岁 Age	24	25.0	75.0
女性 Female	302	71.5	28.5
16~24 岁 Age	64	75.0	25.0
25~34 岁 Age	90	76.7	23.3
35~44 岁 Age	76	73.7	26.3
45~54 岁 Age	48	58.3	41.7
55~60 岁 Age	24	62.5	37.5

2-6 样本、男性各年龄层、女性各年龄层最近三个月的饮用频率/ Frequencies of Consuming Purified or Mineral Water in the Last Three Months by the Whole Sample, Age and Gender Groups

	人数 Number	天天喝 daily	一周 3 次或以上 3 times or over a week	一周 1~2 次 once or twice a week	一个月 2~3 次 2 or 3 times a month	一个月 1 次或以下 once a month or below	没喝过 never
样本 Sample	600	6.2	8.8	17.7	25.3	13.8	28.2
男性 Male	298	4.0	10.4	17.8	24.8	15.1	27.9
16~24 岁 Age	64	0.0	12.5	23.4	32.8	14.1	17.2
25~34 岁 Age	89	5.6	16.9	27.0	25.8	10.1	14.6
35~44 岁 Age	76	7.9	6.6	9.2	22.4	22.4	31.6
45~54 岁 Age	45	2.2	4.4	13.3	28.9	13.3	37.8
55~60 岁 Age	24	0.0	4.2	4.2	0.0	16.7	75.0
女性 Female	302	8.3	7.3	17.5	25.8	12.6	28.5
16~24 岁 Age	64	7.8	7.8	18.8	31.3	15.6	18.8
25~34 岁 Age	90	7.8	6.7	23.3	30.0	8.9	23.3
35~44 岁 Age	76	14.5	7.9	18.4	25.0	7.9	26.3
45~54 岁 Age	48	2.1	8.3	12.5	10.4	22.9	43.8
55~60 岁 Age	24	4.2	4.2	0.0	29.2	12.5	50.0

2-7 样本、男性各年龄层、女性各年龄层的品牌习惯/ Brand Habit in Consuming Purified or Mineral Water by the Whole Sample, Age and Gender Groups

	人数 Number	基本固定饮用一个牌子 used in only one brand	比较固定地饮用两个或三个牌子 used in two or three brands	基本上不太固定牌子 no brand preference
样本 Sample	430	47.2	33.7	19.1
男性 Male	215	50.7	31.2	18.1
16~24 岁 Age	53	30.2	49.1	20.8
25~34 岁 Age	76	52.6	34.2	13.2
35~44 岁 Age	52	65.4	15.4	19.2
45~54 岁 Age	28	50.0	21.4	28.6
55~60 岁 Age	6	83.3	16.7	0.0
女性 Female	215	43.7	36.3	20.0
16~24 岁 Age	52	30.8	48.1	21.2
25~34 岁 Age	69	46.4	43.5	10.1
35~44 岁 Age	55	49.1	29.1	21.8
45~54 岁 Age	27	48.1	18.5	33.3
55~60 岁 Age	12	50.0	16.7	33.3

2-8 选择该类商品的考虑因素/ Ranking of the Considerations in Purchasing

注：本题为多选题，合计百分比超过 100%(Multiple answers)

排名 Ranking	考虑因素 Considerations	人次 Person-time	百分比 Percent
1	有名的牌子 famous brand	191	44.5
2	口味好 pleasant taste	181	42.2
3	价格适中 reasonable price	163	38.0
4	生产日期 date of producing	117	27.3
5	购买方便 easy to buy	109	25.4
6	广告影响 influence of advertising	47	11.0
7	只是由于习惯 out of habit	41	9.6
8	朋友推荐 introduction of friends	19	4.4
9	有优惠条件 with preferential terms	11	2.6
10	包装吸引人 appealing package	7	1.6
11	单位发的 offered by the working unit	6	1.4
12	售货员介绍 introduced by the shop assistants	1	0.2

n=429

2-9 样本、男性各年龄层、女性各年龄层最常饮用的包装形式/ Types of Package of the Consumed Purified or Mineral Water by the Whole Sample, Age and Gender Groups

	人数 Number	250ml 以下 250ml or below	250ml--350ml	500ml--750ml	1L	1.5L	2L 以上 2L or over	其它 others
样本 Sample	430	30.0	33.3	31.9	0.7	1.9	2.3	0.0
男性 Male	214	30.8	32.2	33.2	0.9	0.9	1.9	0.0
16~24 岁 Age	53	24.5	43.4	26.4	3.8	1.9	0.0	0.0
25~34 岁 Age	76	36.8	31.6	30.3	0.0	1.3	0.0	0.0
35~44 岁 Age	51	27.5	27.5	41.2	0.0	0.0	3.9	0.0
45~54 岁 Age	28	35.7	25.0	35.7	0.0	0.0	3.6	0.0
55~60 岁 Age	6	16.7	16.7	50.0	0.0	0.0	16.7	0.0
女性 Female	216	29.2	34.3	30.6	0.5	2.8	2.8	0.0
16~24 岁 Age	52	26.9	34.6	30.8	1.9	3.8	1.9	0.0
25~34 岁 Age	69	31.9	40.6	24.6	0.0	1.4	1.4	0.0
35~44 岁 Age	56	21.4	35.7	35.7	0.0	1.8	5.4	0.0
45~54 岁 Age	27	40.7	18.5	33.3	0.0	3.7	3.7	0.0
55~60 岁 Age	12	33.3	25.0	33.3	0.0	8.3	0.0	0.0

2-10 样本、男性各年龄层、女性各年龄层最常饮用的场合/ Settings of Consumption by the Whole Sample, Age and Gender Groups

注：本题为多选题，合计百分比超过 100%(Multiple answers)

	人数 Number	平时口渴时 when thirsty	平时吃饭喝 at dinner	宴席、聚会喝 at banquet	外出、旅游时 outing/traveling	运动完以后 after athletics	其它 others
样本 Sample	**430**	**70.0**	**5.6**	**7.9**	**38.1**	**13.0**	**0.5**
男性 Male	**215**	**70.7**	**5.1**	**6.5**	**39.1**	**12.6**	**0.5**
16~24 岁 Age	53	71.7	7.5	3.8	26.4	22.6	0.0
25~34 岁 Age	76	75.0	1.3	6.6	44.7	13.2	0.0
35~44 岁 Age	52	69.2	7.7	9.6	44.2	3.8	1.9
45~54 岁 Age	28	60.7	7.1	3.6	39.3	10.7	0.0
55~60 岁 Age	6	66.7	0.0	16.7	33.3	0.0	0.0
女性 Female	**215**	**69.3**	**6.0**	**9.3**	**37.2**	**13.5**	**0.5**
16~24 岁 Age	52	71.2	11.5	9.6	30.8	23.1	0.0
25~34 岁 Age	69	65.2	1.4	7.2	44.9	11.6	0.0
35~44 岁 Age	55	72.7	9.1	10.9	30.9	12.7	0.0
45~54 岁 Age	27	77.8	0.0	3.7	37.0	7.4	3.7
55~60 岁 Age	12	50.0	8.3	25.0	50.0	0.0	0.0

2-11 重度消费者人口分布/ Demographics of the Heavy Consumers

	人数 Number	16-24 岁 Age	25-34 岁 Age	35-44 岁 Age	45-54 岁 Age	55-60 岁 Age
样本 Sample	**196**	**23.0**	**39.8**	**25.0**	**10.2**	**2.0**
男性 Male	**96**	**24.0**	**45.8**	**18.8**	**9.4**	**2.1**
天天喝 daily	12	0.0	41.7	50.0	8.3	0.0
一周 3 次或以上 3 times or over a week	31	25.8	48.4	16.1	6.5	3.2
一周 1~2 次 once or twice a week	53	28.3	45.3	13.2	11.3	1.9
女性 Female	**100**	**22.0**	**34.0**	**31.0**	**11.0**	**2.0**
天天喝 daily	25	20.0	28.0	44.0	4.0	4.0
一周 3 次或以上 3 times or over a week	22	22.7	27.3	27.3	18.2	4.5
一周 1~2 次 once or twice a week	53	22.6	39.6	26.4	11.3	0.0

2-12 不同消费者层的常用品牌/ The Most Frequently Used Brands by Market Segments

2-12-1 时尚流行指标/ Fads Popular Index

	人数 Number	第一品牌及百分比 1st/ percent	第二品牌及百分比 2nd/ percent	第三品牌及百分比 3rd/ percent
样本 Sample	**431**	**娃哈哈 Wahaha(57.8)**	**农夫山泉 Nong Fu Shan Quan(13.2)**	**乐百氏 Robust(11.6)**
平实生活指向 simple living orientation	189	娃哈哈 Wahaha(66.1)	乐百氏 Robust(8.5)	农夫山泉 Nong Fu Shan Quan(7.9)
时尚流行指向 fashion orientation	242	娃哈哈 Wahaha(51.2)	农夫山泉 Nong Fu Shan Quan(17.4)	乐百氏 Robust(14.0)

2-12-2 广告态度指标/ Advertising Attitude Index

	人数 Number	第一品牌及百分比 1st/ percent	第二品牌及百分比 2nd/ percent	第三品牌及百分比 3rd/ percent
样本 Sample	**431**	**娃哈哈 Wahaha(57.8)**	**农夫山泉 Nong Fu Shan Quan(13.2)**	**乐百氏 Robust(11.6)**
广告淡漠指向 indifferent orientation	121	娃哈哈 Wahaha(62.0)	农夫山泉 Nong Fu Shan Quan(11.6)	乐百氏 Robust(10.7)
中间层 medium	256	娃哈哈 Wahaha(56.3)	农夫山泉 Nong Fu Shan Quan(13.7)	乐百氏 Robust(12.1)
信赖广告指向 loyal orientation	54	娃哈哈 Wahaha(55.6)	农夫山泉 Nong Fu Shan Quan(14.8)	乐百氏 Robust(11.1)

2-12-3 饮食健康指标/ Foods & Drink Quality Index

	人数 Number	第一品牌及百分比 1st/ percent	第二品牌及百分比 2nd/ percent	第三品牌及百分比 3rd/ percent
样本 Sample	**431**	**娃哈哈 Wahaha(57.8)**	**农夫山泉 Nong Fu Shan Quan(13.2)**	**乐百氏 Robust(11.6)**
饮食“温饱”指向 "basic" orientation	124	娃哈哈 Wahaha(63.7)	农夫山泉 Nong Fu Shan Quan(12.1)	乐百氏 Robust(9.7)
中间层 medium	198	娃哈哈 Wahaha(56.6)	乐百氏 Robust(14.1)	农夫山泉 Nong Fu Shan Quan(9.6)
健康营养指向 health & nutrition orientation	109	娃哈哈 Wahaha(53.2)	农夫山泉 Nong Fu Shan Quan(21.1)	乐百氏 Robust(9.2)

2-13 重度消费者的消费者层构成/ The Composition of the Heavy Consumers

2-13-1 时尚流行指标/ Fads Popular Index

	人数 Number	平实生活指向 simple living orientation	时尚流行指向 fashion orientation
样本 Sample	**196**	**40.3**	**59.7**
天天喝 daily	37	40.5	59.5
一周 3 次或以上 3 times or over a week	53	41.5	58.5
一周 1~2 次 once or twice a week	106	39.6	60.4

2-13-2 广告态度指标/ Advertising Attitude Index

	人数 Number	广告淡漠指向 indifferent orientation	中间层 medium	信赖广告指向 loyal orientation
样本 Sample	**196**	**27.6**	**59.7**	**12.8**
天天喝 daily	37	24.3	56.8	18.9
一周 3 次或以上 3 times or over a week	53	24.5	58.5	17.0
一周 1~2 次 once or twice a week	106	30.2	61.3	8.5

2-13-3 饮食健康指标/ Foods & Drink Quality Index

	人数 Number	饮食“温饱”指向 "basic" orientation	中间层 medium	健康营养指向 health & nutrition orientation
样本 Sample	**196**	**26.5**	**47.4**	**26.0**
天天喝 daily	37	24.3	48.6	27.0
一周 3 次或以上 3 times or over a week	53	24.5	49.1	26.4
一周 1~2 次 once or twice a week	106	28.3	46.2	25.5

3.茶饮料 / Tealike Drink

● 北京 / Beijing

3-1 最近三个月饮用频率的比例/ Proportion of the Sample Consuming Tealike Drink in the Last Three Months

	人数 Number	百分比 Percent
天天喝 daily	43	4.3
一周 3 次或以上 3 times or over a week	67	6.7
一周 1~2 次 once or twice a week	142	14.1
一个月 2～3 次 2 or 3 times a month	173	17.2
一个月 1 次或以下 once a month or below	113	11.2
没喝过 never	468	46.5

n=1006

3-2 最常用品牌排名/ Ranking of the Most Frequently Used Brands

排名 Brand Ranking	品牌 Brands	人数 Number	百分比 Percent
1	统一 President	172	32.5
2	旭日升 Xurisheng	146	27.6
3	康师傅 Kangshifu	136	25.7

n=529

3-3 样本、男性各年龄层、女性各年龄层的常用品牌/ The Most Frequently Used Brands by the Whole Sample, Age and Gender Groups

	人数 Number	第一品牌及百分比 1st/ percent	第二品牌及百分比 2nd/ percent	第三品牌及百分比 3rd/ percent	第四品牌及百分比 4th/ percent
样本 Sample	529	**统一 President(32.5)**	**旭日升 Xurisheng(27.6)**	**康师傅 Kangshifu(25.7)**	**乐百氏 Robust(0.9)**
男性 Male	242	**旭日升 Xurisheng(30.2)**	**统一 President(28.1)**	**康师傅 Kangshifu(27.7)**	**乐百氏 RObust(1.2)**
16~24 岁 Age	68	统一 President(41.2)	康师傅 Kangshifu(35.3)	旭日升 Xurisheng(16.2)	乐百氏 Robust (1.5) 生活 Niieife(1.5)
25~34 岁 Age	77	旭日升 Xurisheng(41.6)	康师傅 Kangshifu(29.9)	统一 President(22.1)	奥得赛 Odyssey(1.3) 汇源 Huiyuan(1.3) 猴王 Houwang(1.3)
35~44 岁 Age	57	旭日升 Xurisheng(28.1)	统一 President(26.3)	康师傅 Kangshifu(19.3)	三得利 Suntory(1.8) 奥得赛 Odyssey(1.8) 雀巢 Nestle(1.8) 乐百氏 Robust(1.8)
45~54 岁 Age	32	旭日升 Xurisheng(37.5)	康师傅 Kangshifu(21.9)	统一 President(18.8)	维他露 Vitalon(3.1) 大亨 Daheng(3.1)
55~60 岁 Age	8	康师傅 Kangshifu(25.0) 统一 President(25.0) 旭日升 Xurisheng(25.0)	乐百氏 Robust (12.5)		
女性 Female	287	**统一 President(36.2)**	**旭日升 Xurisheng(25.4)**	**康师傅 Kangshifu(24.0)**	**京华 Jinghua(1.4)**
16~24 岁 Age	82	统一 President(39.0)	康师傅 Kangshifu(34.1)	旭日升 Xurisheng(15.9)	京华 Jinghua(2.4)
25~34 岁 Age	90	统一 President(36.7)	康师傅 Kangshifu(22.2)	旭日升 Xurisheng(18.9)	汇源 Huiyuan(2.2) 华邦 Huabang(2.2)
35~44 岁 Age	71	统一 President(35.2)	旭日升 Xurisheng(29.6)	康师傅 Kangshifu(23.9)	雀巢 Nestle(1.4)
45~54 岁 Age	33	旭日升 Xurisheng(54.5)	统一 President(24.2)	康师傅 Kangshifu(12.1)	雀巢 Nestle(3.0)
55~60 岁 Age	11	统一 President(54.5)	旭日升 Xurisheng(36.4)		

3-4 理想品牌排名/ Ranking of the Ideal Brands

排名 Brand Ranking	品牌 Brands	人数 Number	百分比 Percent
1	旭日升 Xurisheng	213	21.0
2	统一 President	195	19.3
3	康师傅 Kangshifu	186	18.4
4	乐百氏 Robust	7	0.7
5	奥得赛 Odyssey	6	0.6

n=1012

3-5 样本、男性各年龄层、女性各年龄层最近三个月有无购买的比例/ Purchasing in the Last Three Months by the Whole Sample, Age and Gender Groups

	人数 Number	买过 yes	没买过 no
样本 Sample	1007	49.0	51.0
男性 Male	503	45.7	54.3
16~24 岁 Age	105	61.9	38.1
25~34 岁 Age	150	46.7	53.3
35~44 岁 Age	131	46.6	53.4
45~54 岁 Age	77	31.2	68.8
55~60 岁 Age	40	25.0	75.0
女性 Female	504	52.2	47.8
16~24 岁 Age	107	71.0	29.0
25~34 岁 Age	150	56.0	44.0
35~44 岁 Age	122	56.6	43.4
45~54 岁 Age	84	28.6	71.4
55~60 岁 Age	41	24.4	75.6

3-6 样本、男性各年龄层、女性各年龄层最近三个月的饮用频率/ Frequencies of Consuming Tealike Drink in the Last Three Months by the Whole Sample, Age and Gender Groups

	人数 Number	天天喝 daily	一周 3 次或以上 3 times or over a week	一周 1~2 次 once or twice a week	一个月 2~3 次 2 or 3 times a month	一个月 1 次或以下 once a month or below	没喝过 never
样本 Sample	1006	4.3	6.7	14.1	17.2	11.2	46.5
男性 Male	500	4.6	7.0	13.2	16.8	7.4	51.0
16~24 岁 Age	104	5.8	9.6	26.0	12.5	11.5	34.6
25~34 岁 Age	149	5.4	5.4	12.1	20.8	8.7	47.7
35~44 岁 Age	130	3.8	7.7	9.2	19.2	5.4	54.6
45~54 岁 Age	77	5.2	5.2	10.4	15.6	5.2	58.4
55~60 岁 Age	40	0.0	7.5	2.5	7.5	2.5	80.0
女性 Female	506	4.0	6.3	15.0	17.6	15.0	42.1
16~24 岁 Age	108	5.6	10.2	26.9	21.3	13.0	23.1
25~34 岁 Age	150	2.0	7.3	10.7	21.3	20.0	38.7
35~44 岁 Age	122	4.9	4.9	13.9	18.9	16.4	41.0
45~54 岁 Age	84	6.0	2.4	11.9	9.5	10.7	59.5
55~60 岁 Age	42	0.0	4.8	9.5	7.1	7.1	71.4

3-7 样本、男性各年龄层、女性各年龄层的品牌习惯/ Brand Habit in Consuming Tealike Drink by the Whole Sample, Age and Gender Groups

	人数 Number	基本固定饮用一个牌子 used in only one brand	比较固定地饮用两个或三个牌子 used in two or three brands	基本上不太固定牌子 no brand preference
样本 Sample	534	47.0	36.1	16.9
男性 Male	243	49.0	33.3	17.7
16~24 岁 Age	67	55.2	32.8	11.9
25~34 岁 Age	78	43.6	34.6	21.8
35~44 岁 Age	59	45.8	30.5	23.7
45~54 岁 Age	31	54.8	38.7	6.5
55~60 岁 Age	8	50.0	25.0	25.0
女性 Female	291	45.4	38.5	16.2
16~24 岁 Age	83	37.3	53.0	9.6
25~34 岁 Age	92	50.0	37.0	13.0
35~44 岁 Age	70	48.6	32.9	18.6
45~54 岁 Age	34	44.1	20.6	35.3
55~60 岁 Age	12	50.0	33.3	16.7

3-8 选择该类商品的考虑因素/ Ranking of the Considerations in Purchasing

注：本题为多选题，合计百分比超过 100%(Multiple answers）

排名 Ranking	考虑因素 Considerations	人次 Person-time	百分比 Percent
1	口味好 pleasant taste	369	69.2
2	价格适中 reasonable price	157	29.5
3	有名的牌子 famous brand	151	28.3
4	生产日期 date of producing	107	20.1
5	购买方便 easy to buy	75	14.1
6	广告影响 influence of advertising	52	9.8
7	只是由于习惯 out of habit	40	7.5
8	单位发的 offered by the working unit	33	6.2
9	朋友推荐 introduction of friends	23	4.3
10	有优惠条件 with preferential terms	8	1.5
11	包装吸引人 appealing package	7	1.3
12	其它 others	5	0.9
13	售货员介绍 introduced by the shop assistants	3	0.6

n=533

3-9 样本、男性各年龄层、女性各年龄层最常饮用的种类/ Kinds of the Consumed Tealike Drink by the Whole Sample, Age and Gender Groups

	人数 Number	红茶 red tea	绿茶 green tea	乌龙茶 wolong tea	花茶 scented tea	奶茶 milk tea	果味茶 fruit flavor	其它 others
样本 Sample	**515**	**36.7**	**16.9**	**23.5**	**8.5**	**0.2**	**6.6**	**7.6**
男性 Male	**235**	**35.7**	**14.0**	**26.4**	**7.7**	**0.4**	**6.4**	**9.4**
16~24 岁 Age	65	41.5	15.4	27.7	1.5	0.0	7.7	6.2
25~34 岁 Age	76	35.5	11.8	23.7	10.5	1.3	5.3	11.8
35~44 岁 Age	57	35.1	14.0	28.1	5.3	0.0	7.0	10.5
45~54 岁 Age	29	27.6	13.8	31.0	17.2	0.0	6.9	3.4
55~60 岁 Age	8	25.0	25.0	12.5	12.5	0.0	0.0	25.0
女性 Female	**280**	**37.5**	**19.3**	**21.1**	**9.3**	**0.0**	**6.8**	**6.1**
16~24 岁 Age	81	46.9	23.5	14.8	8.6	0.0	4.9	1.2
25~34 岁 Age	89	32.6	15.7	28.1	6.7	0.0	10.1	6.7
35~44 岁 Age	69	39.1	17.4	23.2	7.2	0.0	5.8	7.2
45~54 岁 Age	30	33.3	13.3	16.7	16.7	0.0	3.3	16.7
55~60 岁 Age	11	9.1	45.5	9.1	27.3	0.0	9.1	0.0

3-10 样本、男性各年龄层、女性各年龄层最常饮用的场合/ Settings of Consumption by the Whole Sample, Age and Gender Groups

注：本题为多选题，合计百分比超过 100%(Multiple answers）

	人数 Number	平时口渴时 when thirsty	平时吃饭喝 at dinner	宴席、聚会喝 at banquet	外出、旅游时 outing/traveling	运动完以后 after athletics	其它 others
样本 Sample	**531**	**68.5**	**7.7**	**10.2**	**38.4**	**10.4**	**1.3**
男性 Male	**242**	**68.6**	**5.8**	**10.7**	**32.6**	**12.4**	**1.2**
16~24 岁 Age	67	79.1	7.5	4.5	20.9	25.4	0.0
25~34 岁 Age	77	72.7	2.6	11.7	36.4	6.5	1.3
35~44 岁 Age	59	54.2	10.2	10.2	44.1	11.9	1.7
45~54 岁 Age	31	64.5	3.2	16.1	29.0	3.2	3.2
55~60 岁 Age	8	62.5	0.0	37.5	25.0	0.0	0.0
女性 Female	**289**	**68.5**	**9.3**	**9.7**	**43.3**	**8.7**	**1.4**
16~24 岁 Age	82	78.0	8.5	8.5	37.8	9.8	0.0
25~34 岁 Age	92	64.1	5.4	6.5	50.0	10.9	2.2
35~44 岁 Age	71	60.6	11.3	9.9	56.3	7.0	1.4
45~54 岁 Age	32	68.8	21.9	18.8	12.5	6.3	3.1
55~60 岁 Age	12	83.3	0.0	16.7	33.3	0.0	0.0

3-11 重度消费者人口分布/ Demographics of the Heavy Consumers

	人数 Number	16-24 岁 Age	25-34 岁 Age	35-44 岁 Age	45-54 岁 Age	55-60 岁 Age
样本 Sample	**252**	**35.3**	**25.4**	**22.2**	**13.1**	**4.0**
男性 Male	**124**	**34.7**	**27.4**	**21.8**	**12.9**	**3.2**
天天喝 daily	23	26.1	34.8	21.7	17.4	0.0
一周 3 次或以上 3 times or over a week	35	28.6	22.9	28.6	11.4	8.6
一周 1~2 次 once or twice a week	66	40.9	27.3	18.2	12.1	1.5
女性 Female	**128**	**35.9**	**23.4**	**22.7**	**13.3**	**4.7**
天天喝 daily	20	30.0	15.0	30.0	25.0	0.0
一周 3 次或以上 3 times or over a week	32	34.4	34.4	18.8	6.3	6.3
一周 1~2 次 once or twice a week	76	38.2	21.1	22.4	13.2	5.3

3-12 不同消费者层的常用品牌/ The Most Frequently Used Brands by Market Segments

3-12-1 时尚流行指标/ Fads Popular Index

	人数 Number	第一品牌及百分比 1st/ percent	第二品牌及百分比 2nd/ percent	第三品牌及百分比 3rd/ percent
样本 Sample	**521**	**统一 President(32.8)**	**旭日升 Xurisheng(27.8)**	**康师傅 Kangshifu(25.0)**
平实生活指向 simple living orientation	216	统一 President(34.3)	旭日升 Xurisheng(27.8)	康师傅 Kangshifu(23.1)
时尚流行指向 fashion orientation	305	统一 President(31.8)	旭日升 Xurisheng(27.9)	康师傅 Kangshifu(26.2)

3-12-2 广告态度指标/ Advertising Attitude Index

	人数 Number	第一品牌及百分比 1st/ percent	第二品牌及百分比 2nd/ percent	第三品牌及百分比 3rd/ percent
样本 Sample	**521**	**统一 President(32.6)**	**旭日升 Xurisheng(27.4)**	**康师傅 Kangshifu(25.9)**
广告淡漠指向 indifferent orientation	126	统一 President(33.3)	旭日升 Xurisheng(27.0)	康师傅 Kangshifu(26.2)
中间层 medium	313	统一 President(33.5)	旭日升 Xurisheng(25.9) 康师傅 Kangshifu(25.9)	乐百氏 Robust (1.3)
信赖广告指向 loyal orientation	82	旭日升 Xurisheng(34.1)	统一 President(28.0)	康师傅 Kangshifu(25.6)

3-12-3 饮食健康指标/ Foods & Drink Quality Index

	人数 Number	第一品牌及百分比 1st/ percent	第二品牌及百分比 2nd/ percent	第三品牌及百分比 3rd/ percent
样本 Sample	**525**	**统一 President(32.2)**	**旭日升 Xurisheng(27.6)**	**康师傅 Kangshifu(25.9)**
饮食"温饱"指向 "basic" orientation	149	统一 President(32.2) 旭日升 Xurisheng(32.2)	康师傅 Kangshifu(24.8)	奥得赛 Odyssey(1.3) 汇源 Huiyuan(1.3) 雀巢 Nestle(1.3)
中间层 medium	245	统一 President(32.7)	康师傅 Kangshifu(27.3)	旭日升 Xurisheng(24.1)
健康营养指向 health & nutrition orientation	131	统一 President(31.3)	旭日升 Xurisheng(29.0)	康师傅 Kangshifu(24.4)

3-13 重度消费者的消费者层构成/ The Composition of the Heavy Consumers

3-13-1 时尚流行指标/ Fads Popular Index

	人数 Number	平实生活指向 simple living orientation	时尚流行指向 fashion orientation
样本 Sample	**248**	**39.5**	**60.5**
天天喝 daily	43	30.2	69.8
一周 3 次或以上 3 times or over a week	67	43.3	56.7
一周 1~2 次 once or twice a week	138	40.6	59.4

3-13-2 广告态度指标/ Advertising Attitude Index

	人数 Number	广告淡漠指向 indifferent orientation	中间层 medium	信赖广告指向 loyal orientation
样本 Sample	**245**	**23.7**	**59.2**	**17.1**
天天喝 daily	42	19.0	59.5	21.4
一周 3 次或以上 3 times or over a week	64	34.4	48.4	17.2
一周 1~2 次 once or twice a week	139	20.1	64.0	15.8

3-13-3 饮食健康指标/ Foods & Drink Quality Index

	人数 Number	饮食"温饱"指向 "basic" orientation	中间层 medium	健康营养指向 health & nutrition orientation
样本 Sample	**250**	**29.6**	**42.0**	**28.4**
天天喝 daily	42	19.0	42.9	38.1
一周 3 次或以上 3 times or over a week	67	26.9	46.3	26.9
一周 1~2 次 once or twice a week	141	34.0	39.7	26.2

● 上海 / Shanghai

3-1 最近三个月饮用频率的比例/ Proportion of the Sample Consuming Tealike Drink in the Last Three Months

	人数 Number	百分比 Percent
天天喝 daily	40	4.0
一周 3 次或以上 3 times or over a week	71	7.0
一周 1~2 次 once or twice a week	174	17.2
一个月 2～3 次 2 or 3 times a month	161	15.9
一个月 1 次或以下 once a month or below	82	8.1
没喝过 never	482	47.7

n=1010

3-2 最常用品牌排名/ Ranking of the Most Frequently Used Brands

排名 Brand Ranking	品牌 Brands	人数 Number	百分比 Percent
1	统一 President	254	48.2
2	三得利 Suntory	189	35.9
3	康师傅 Kangshifu	29	5.5
4	立顿 Lipton	26	4.9
5	天与地 Tianyudi	8	1.5
6	旭日升 Xurisheng	5	0.9

n=527

3-3 样本、男性各年龄层、女性各年龄层的常用品牌/ The Most Frequently Used Brands by the Whole Sample, Age and Gender Groups

	人数 Number	第一品牌及百分比 1st/ percent	第二品牌及百分比 2nd/ percent	第三品牌及百分比 3rd/ percent
样本 Sample	**527**	**统一 President(48.2)**	**三得利 Suntory(35.9)**	**康师傅 Kangshifu(5.5)**
男性 Male	**264**	**统一 President(42.4)**	**三得利 Suntory(40.9)**	**康师傅 Kangshifu(6.4)**
16~24 岁 Age	68	统一 President(54.4)	三得利 Suntory(27.9)	康师傅 Kangshifu(8.8)
25~34 岁 Age	86	三得利 Suntory(50.0)	统一 President(33.7)	立顿 Lipton(9.3)
35~44 岁 Age	61	三得利 Suntory(45.9)	统一 President(39.3)	康师傅 Kangshifu(3.3) 立顿 Lipton(3.3)
45~54 岁 Age	36	统一 President(47.2)	三得利 Suntory(33.3)	天与地 Tianyudi(8.3)
55~60 岁 Age	13	三得利 Suntory(46.2)	统一 President(38.5)	康师傅 Kangshifu(15.4)
女性 Female	**263**	**统一 President(54.0)**	**三得利 Suntory(30.8)**	**立顿 Lipton(4.9)**
16~24 岁 Age	75	统一 President(69.3)	三得利 Suntory(18.7)	康师傅 Kangshifu(5.3)
25~34 岁 Age	81	统一 President(45.7)	三得利 Suntory(37.0)	立顿 Lipton(8.6)
35~44 岁 Age	62	统一 President(54.8)	三得利 Suntory(32.3)	康师傅 Kangshifu(8.1)
45~54 岁 Age	31	统一 President(48.4)	三得利 Suntory(29.0)	立顿 Lipton(9.7)
55~60 岁 Age	14	三得利 Suntory(57.1)	统一 President(28.6)	

3-4 理想品牌排名/ Ranking of the Ideal Brands

排名 Brand Ranking	品牌 Brands	人数 Number	百分比 Percent
1	统一 President	473	46.6
2	三得利 Suntory	302	29.8
3	康师傅 Kangshifu	46	4.5
4	立顿 Lipton	37	3.6
5	旭日升 Xurisheng	12	1.2

n=1014

3-5 样本、男性各年龄层、女性各年龄层最近三个月有无购买的比例/ Purchasing in the Last Three Months by the Whole Sample, Age and Gender Groups

	人数 Number	买过 yes	没买过 no
样本 Sample	1014	51.3	48.7
男性 Male	509	50.1	49.9
16~24 岁 Age	109	59.6	40.4
25~34 岁 Age	146	56.2	43.8
35~44 岁 Age	130	44.6	55.4
45~54 岁 Age	85	42.4	57.6
55~60 岁 Age	39	35.9	64.1
女性 Female	505	52.5	47.5
16~24 岁 Age	108	70.4	29.6
25~34 岁 Age	144	56.9	43.1
35~44 岁 Age	130	48.5	51.5
45~54 岁 Age	82	37.8	62.2
55~60 岁 Age	41	31.7	68.3

3-6 样本、男性各年龄层、女性各年龄层最近三个月的饮用频率/ Frequencies of Consuming Tealike Drink in the Last Three Months by the Whole Sample, Age and Gender Groups

	人数 Number	天天喝 daily	一周 3 次或以上 3 times or over a week	一周 1~2 次 once or twice a week	一个月 2~3 次 2 or 3 times a month	一个月 1 次或以下 once a month or below	没喝过 never
样本 Sample	1010	4.0	7.0	17.2	15.9	8.1	47.7
男性 Male	508	4.3	7.1	15.7	16.5	8.5	47.8
16~24 岁 Age	109	5.5	11.9	21.1	16.5	7.3	37.6
25~34 岁 Age	145	2.8	8.3	20.0	19.3	9.0	40.7
35~44 岁 Age	130	6.2	4.6	10.8	16.9	9.2	52.3
45~54 岁 Age	85	1.2	3.5	14.1	15.3	8.2	57.6
55~60 岁 Age	39	7.7	5.1	5.1	7.7	7.7	66.7
女性 Female	502	3.6	7.0	18.7	15.3	7.8	47.6
16~24 岁 Age	107	3.7	12.1	25.2	19.6	9.3	29.9
25~34 岁 Age	144	4.9	6.9	21.5	16.0	6.9	43.8
35~44 岁 Age	129	2.3	5.4	16.3	17.1	7.0	51.9
45~54 岁 Age	81	3.7	3.7	13.6	8.6	8.6	61.7
55~60 岁 Age	41	2.4	4.9	9.8	9.8	7.3	65,9

3-7 样本、男性各年龄层、女性各年龄层的品牌习惯/ Brand Habit in Consuming Tealike Drink by the Whole Sample, Age and Gender Groups

	人数 Number	基本固定饮用一个牌子 used in only one brand	比较固定地饮用两个或三个牌子 used in two or three brands	基本上不太固定牌子 no brand preference
样本 Sample	528	51.9	32.4	15.7
男性 Male	265	50.2	30.9	18.9
16~24 岁 Age	68	44.1	36.8	19.1
25~34 岁 Age	86	53.5	36.0	10.5
35~44 岁 Age	62	48.4	22.6	29.0
45~54 岁 Age	36	52.8	30.6	16.7
55~60 岁 Age	13	61.5	7.7	30.8
女性 Female	263	53.6	33.8	12.5
16~24 岁 Age	75	60.0	26.7	13.3
25~34 岁 Age	81	46.9	44.4	8.6
35~44 岁 Age	62	54.8	29.0	16.1
45~54 岁 Age	31	61.3	32.3	6.5
55~60 岁 Age	14	35.7	35.7	28.6

3-8 选择该类商品的考虑因素/ Ranking of the Considerations in Purchasing

注：本题为多选题，合计百分比可能超过 100%（Multiple answers）

排名 Ranking	考虑因素 Considerations	人次 Person-time	百分比 Percent
1	口味好 pleasant taste	358	67.8
2	价格适中 reasonable price	172	32.6
3	有名的牌子 famous brand	160	30.3
4	购买方便 easy to buy	111	21.0
5	生产日期 date of producing	80	15.2
6	广告影响 influence of advertising	70	13.3
7	只是由于习惯 out of habit	40	7.6
8	有优惠条件 with preferential terms	17	3.2
9	朋友推荐 introduction of friends	13	2.5
10	包装吸引人 appealing package	12	2.3
11	单位发的 offered by the working unit	7	1.3
12	其它 others	4	0.8
13	售货员介绍 introduced by the shop assistants	1	0.2

n=528

3-9 样本、男性各年龄层、女性各年龄层最常饮用的种类/ Kinds of the Consumed Teacake Drink by the Whole Sample, Age and Gender Groups

	人数 Number	红茶 red tea	绿茶 green tea	乌龙茶 wolong tea	花茶 scented tea	奶茶 milk tea	果味茶 fruit flavor	其它 others
样本 Sample	**522**	**38.5**	**7.9**	**48.7**	**1.3**	**1.0**	**1.9**	**0.8**
男性 Male	**261**	**32.2**	**8.8**	**55.2**	**1.1**	**0.4**	**1.1**	**1.1**
16~24 岁 Age	68	44.1	5.9	44.1	0.0	1.5	1.5	2.9
25~34 岁 Age	86	34.9	3.5	59.3	1.2	0.0	1.2	0.0
35~44 岁 Age	60	25.0	16.7	51.7	3.3	0.0	1.7	1.7
45~54 岁 Age	35	22.9	8.6	68.6	0.0	0.0	0.0	0.0
55~60 岁 Age	12	8.3	25.0	66.7	0.0	0.0	0.0	0.0
女性 Female	**261**	**44.8**	**6.9**	**42.1**	**1.5**	**1.5**	**2.7**	**0.4**
16~24 岁 Age	74	67.6	4.1	23.0	2.7	0.0	2.7	0.0
25~34 岁 Age	81	44.4	4.9	48.1	1.2	1.2	0.0	0.0
35~44 岁 Age	61	31.1	8.2	49.2	0.0	4.9	6.6	0.0
45~54 岁 Age	31	29.0	12.9	51.6	3.2	0.0	0.0	3.2
55~60 岁 Age	14	21.4	14.3	57.1	0.0	0.0	7.1	0.0

3-10 样本、男性各年龄层、女性各年龄层最常饮用的场合/ Settings of Consumption by the Whole Sample, Age and Gender Groups

注：本题为多选题，合计百分比超过 100%(Multiple answers）

	人数 Number	平时口渴时 when thirsty	平时吃饭喝 at dinner	宴席、聚会喝 at banquet	外出、旅游时 outing/traveling	运动完以后 after athletics	其它 others
样本 Sample	**528**	**73.1**	**3.6**	**7.2**	**36.7**	**10.0**	**0.4**
男性 Male	**265**	**73.2**	**3.0**	**7.2**	**34.0**	**11.7**	**0.4**
16~24 岁 Age	68	73.5	5.9	5.9	27.9	22.1	0.0
25~34 岁 Age	86	80.2	1.2	3.5	33.7	9.3	0.0
35~44 岁 Age	62	69.4	1.6	14.5	38.7	8.1	1.6
45~54 岁 Age	36	58.3	5.6	8.3	41.7	8.3	0.0
55~60 岁 Age	13	84.6	0.0	0.0	23.1	0.0	0.0
女性 Female	**263**	**73.0**	**4.2**	**7.2**	**39.5**	**8.4**	**0.4**
16~24 岁 Age	75	73.3	4.0	10.7	42.7	13.3	0.0
25~34 岁 Age	81	79.0	2.5	4.9	32.1	6.2	0.0
35~44 岁 Age	62	69.4	8.1	9.7	38.7	6.5	0.0
45~54 岁 Age	31	67.7	0.0	0.0	48.4	9.7	3.2
55~60 岁 Age	14	64.3	7.1	7.1	50.0	0.0	0.0

3-11 重度消费者人口分布/ Demographics of the Heavy Consumers

	人数 Number	16-24 岁 Age	25-34 岁 Age	35-44 岁 Age	45-54 岁 Age	55-60 岁 Age
样本 Sample	285	30.2	32.6	20.7	11.6	4.9
男性 Male	138	30.4	32.6	20.3	11.6	5.1
天天喝 daily	22	27.3	18.2	36.4	4.5	13.6
一周 3 次或以上 3 times or over a week	36	36.1	33.3	16.7	8.3	5.6
一周 1~2 次 once or twice a week	80	28.7	36.3	17.5	15.0	2.5
女性 Female	147	29.9	32.7	21.1	11.6	4.8
天天喝 daily	18	22.2	38.9	16.7	16.7	5.6
一周 3 次或以上 3 times or over a week	35	37.1	28.6	20.0	8.6	5.7
一周 1~2 次 once or twice a week	94	28.7	33.0	22.3	11.7	4.3

3-12 不同消费者层的常用品牌/ The Most Frequently Used Brands by Market Segments

3-12-1 时尚流行指标/ Fads Popular Index

	人数 Number	第一品牌及百分比 1st/ percent	第二品牌及百分比 2nd/ percent	第三品牌及百分比 3rd/ percent	第四品牌及百分比 4th/ percent
样本 Sample	523	**统一 President(48.4)**	**三得利 Suntory(35.6)**	**康师傅 Kangshifu(5.5)**	**立顿 Lipton(5.0)**
平实生活指向 simple living orientation	201	统一 President(46.8)	三得利 Suntory(34.8)	康师傅 Kangshifu(7.0)	立顿 Lipton(5.0)
时尚流行指向 fashion orientation	322	统一 President(49.4)	三得利 Suntory(36.0)	立顿 Lipton(5.0)	康师傅 Kangshifu(4.7)

3-12-2 广告态度指标/ Advertising Attitude Index

	人数 Number	第一品牌及百分比 1st/ percent	第二品牌及百分比 2nd/ percent	第三品牌及百分比 3rd/ percent	第四品牌及百分比 4th/ percent
样本 Sample	520	**统一 President(48.1)**	**三得利 Suntory(35.8)**	**康师傅 Kangshifu(5.6)**	**立顿 Lipton(5.0)**
广告淡漠指向 indifferent orientation	126	统一 President(46.8)	三得利 Suntory(35.7)	立顿 Lipton(7.1)	康师傅 Kangshifu(4.8)
中间层 medium	316	统一 President(50.3)	三得利 Suntory(35.1)	康师傅 Kangshifu(5.7)	立顿 Lipton(3.8)
信赖广告指向 loyal orientation	78	统一 President(41.0)	三得利 Suntory(38.5)	康师傅 Kangshifu(6.4) 立顿 Lipton(6.4)	天与地 Tianyudi(2.6)

3-12-3 饮食健康指标/ Foods & Drink Quality Index

	人数 Number	第一品牌及百分比 1st/ percent	第二品牌及百分比 2nd/ percent	第三品牌及百分比 3rd/ percent	第四品牌及百分比 4th/ percent
样本 Sample	525	**统一 President(48.0)**	**三得利 Suntory(36.0)**	**康师傅 Kangshifu(5.5)**	**立顿 Lipton(5.0)**
饮食"温饱"指向 "basic" orientation	108	统一 President(50.9)	三得利 Suntory(33.3)	康师傅 Kangshifu(5.6) 立顿 Lipton(5.6)	天与地 Tianyudi(2.8)
中间层 medium	256	统一 President(50.0)	三得利 Suntory(35.2)	康师傅 Kangshifu(6.3)	立顿 Lipton(3.1)
健康营养指向 health & nutrition orientation	161	统一 President(42.9)	三得利 Suntory(39.1)	立顿 Lipton(7.5)	康师傅 Kangshifu(4.3)

3-13 重度消费者的消费者层构成/ The Composition of the Heavy Consumers

3-13-1 时尚流行指标/ Fads Popular Index

	人数 Number	平实生活指向 simple living orientation	时尚流行指向 fashion orientation
样本 Sample	283	33.2	66.8
天天喝 daily	40	37.5	62.5
一周 3 次或以上 3 times or over a week	69	26.1	73.9
一周 1~2 次 once or twice a week	174	35.1	64.9

3-13-2 广告态度指标/ Advertising Attitude Index

	人数 Number	广告淡漠指向 indifferent orientation	中间层 medium	信赖广告指向 loyal orientation
样本 Sample	281	23.5	61.9	14.6
天天喝 daily	40	35.0	50.0	15.0
一周 3 次或以上 3 times or over a week	70	18.6	60.0	21.4
一周 1~2 次 once or twice a week	171	22.8	65.5	11.7

3-13-3 饮食健康指标/ Foods & Drink Quality Index

	人数 Number	饮食"温饱"指向 "basic" orientation	中间层 medium	健康营养指向 health & nutrition orientation
样本 Sample	283	17.7	49.5	32.9
天天喝 daily	40	17.5	47.5	35.0
一周 3 次或以上 3 times or over a week	71	18.3	49.3	32.4
一周 1~2 次 once or twice a week	172	17.4	50.0	32.6

● 广州 / Guangzhou

3-1 最近三个月饮用频率的比例/ Proportion of the Sample Consuming Tealike Drink in the Last Three Months

	人数 Number	百分比 Percent
天天喝 daily	27	2.6
一周 3 次或以上 3 times or over a week	42	4.1
一周 1~2 次 once or twice a week	121	11.7
一个月 2~3 次 2 or 3 times a month	146	14.2
一个月 1 次或以下 once a month or below	81	7.9
没喝过 never	614	59.6

n=1031

3-2 最常用品牌排名/ Ranking of the Most Frequently Used Brands

排名 Brand Ranking	品牌 Brands	人数 Number	百分比 Percent
1	统一 President	163	39.3
2	康师傅 Kangshifu	136	32.8
3	天与地 Tianyudi	41	9.9
5	鹰金钱 Eagle com	9	2.2
6	旭日升 Xurisheng	8	1.9
7	王老吉 Wanglaoji	4	1.0
7	英德 Yingde	4	1.0
7	白沙 Baisha	4	1.0

n=415

3-3 样本、男性各年龄层、女性各年龄层的常用品牌/ The Most Frequently Used Brands by the Whole Sample, Age and Gender Groups

	人数 Number	第一品牌及百分比 1st/ percent	第二品牌及百分比 2nd/ percent	第三品牌及百分比 3rd/ percent
样本 Sample	415	**统一 President(39.3)**	**康师傅 Kangshifu(32.8)**	**天与地 Tianyudi(9.9)**
男性 Male	175	**统一 President(39.4)**	**康师傅 Kangshifu(34.3)**	**天与地 Tianyudi(9.1)**
16~24 岁 Age	51	康师傅 Kangshifu(37.3) 统一 President(37.3)	天与地 Tianyudi(9.8)	鹰金钱 Eagle com(3.9)
25~34 岁 Age	60	康师傅 Kangshifu(36.7)	统一 President(35.0)	天与地 Tianyudi(10.0)
35~44 岁 Age	39	统一 President(46.2)	康师傅 Kangshifu(28.2)	天与地 Tianyudi(7.7) 英德 Yingde(7.7)
45~54 岁 Age	20	统一 President(45.0)	康师傅 Kangshifu(30.0)	天与地 Tianyudi(10.0)
55~60 岁 Age	5	康师傅 Kangshifu(40.0) 统一 President(40.0)	滇红 Dianhong(20.0)	
女性 Female	240	**统一 President(39.2)**	**康师傅 Kangshifu(31.7)**	**天与地 Tianyudi(10.4)**
16~24 岁 Age	71	统一 President(39.4)	康师傅 Kangshifu(35.2)	天与地 Tianyudi(15.5)
25~34 岁 Age	73	统一 President(38.4)	康师傅 Kangshifu(30.1)	天与地 Tianyudi(9.6)
35~44 岁 Age	53	统一 President(39.6)	康师傅 Kangshifu(34.0)	天与地 Tianyudi(3.8)
45~54 岁 Age	33	统一 President(45.5)	康师傅 Kangshifu(24.2)	天与地 Tianyudi(9.1)
55~60 岁 Age	10	康师傅 Kangshifu(30.0)	天与地 Tianyudi(20.0) 统一 President(20.0)	鹰金钱 Eagle com (10.0) 五花牌 Wuhua(10.0)

3-4 理想品牌排名/ Ranking of the Ideal Brands

排名 Brand Ranking	品牌 Brands	人数 Number	百分比 Percent
1	统一 President	261	25.2
2	康师傅 Kangshifu	202	19.5
3	天与地 Tianyudi	58	5.6
4	旭日升 Xurisheng	19	1.8
5	王老吉 Wanglaoji	7	0.7
5	立顿 Lipton	7	0.7
6	鹰金钱 Eagle com	6	0.6

n=1034

3-5 样本、男性各年龄层、女性各年龄层最近三个月有无购买的比例/ Purchasing in the Last Three Months by the Whole Sample, Age and Gender Groups

	人数 Number	买过 yes	没买过 no
样本 Sample	1031	39.4	60.6
男性 Male	498	34.7	65.3
16~24 岁 Age	106	44.3	55.7
25~34 岁 Age	150	40.7	59.3
35~44 岁 Age	126	33.3	66.7
45~54 岁 Age	73	21.9	78.1
55~60 岁 Age	43	16.3	83.7
女性 Female	533	43.7	56.3
16~24 岁 Age	111	61.3	38.7
25~34 岁 Age	157	45.2	54.8
35~44 岁 Age	137	37.2	62.8
45~54 岁 Age	87	36.8	63.2
55~60 岁 Age	41	26.8	73.2

3-6 样本、男性各年龄层、女性各年龄层最近三个月的饮用频率/ Frequencies of Consuming Tealike Drink in the Last Three Months by the Whole Sample, Age and Gender Groups

	人数 Number	天天喝 daily	一周 3 次或以上 3 times or over a week	一周 1~2 次 once or twice a week	一个月 2~3 次 2 or 3 times a month	一个月 1 次或以下 once a month or below	没喝过 never
样本 Sample	1031	2.6	4.1	11.7	14.2	7.9	59.6
男性 Male	496	3.4	3.8	9.7	12.5	6.0	64.5
16~24 岁 Age	106	2.8	5.7	16.0	20.8	2.8	51.9
25~34 岁 Age	150	2.0	3.3	11.3	15.3	8.0	60.0
35~44 岁 Age	125	5.6	3.2	5.6	9.6	7.2	68.8
45~54 岁 Age	72	2.8	2.8	8.3	6.9	6.9	72.2
55~60 岁 Age	43	4.7	4.7	2.3	0.0	2.3	86.0
女性 Female	535	1.9	4.3	13.6	15.7	9.5	55.0
16~24 岁 Age	112	0.9	5.4	20.5	27.7	8.9	36.6
25~34 岁 Age	158	3.2	3.8	10.8	17.7	11.4	53.2
35~44 岁 Age	137	0.0	4.4	12.4	12.4	9.5	61.3
45~54 岁 Age	87	3.4	2.3	13.8	8.0	10.3	62.1
55~60 岁 Age	41	2.4	7.3	9.8	2.4	2.4	75.6

3-7 样本、男性各年龄层、女性各年龄层的品牌习惯/ Brand Habit in Consuming Tealike Drink by the Whole Sample, Age and Gender Groups

	人数 Number	基本固定饮用一个牌子 used in only one brand	比较固定地饮用两个或三个牌子 used in two or three brands	基本上不太固定牌子 no brand preference
样本 Sample	417	32.9	46.3	20.9
男性 Male	176	40.9	41.5	17.6
16~24 岁 Age	51	43.1	45.1	11.8
25~34 岁 Age	60	45.0	45.0	10.0
35~44 岁 Age	39	30.8	38.5	30.8
45~54 岁 Age	20	45.0	25.0	30.0
55~60 岁 Age	6	33.3	50.0	16.7
女性 Female	241	27.0	49.8	23.2
16~24 岁 Age	71	25.4	53.5	21.1
25~34 岁 Age	74	23.0	55.4	21.6
35~44 岁 Age	53	32.1	43.4	24.5
45~54 岁 Age	33	27.3	45.5	27.3
55~60 岁 Age	10	40.0	30.0	30.0

3-8 选择该类商品的考虑因素/ Ranking of the Considerations in Purchasing

注：本题为多选题，合计百分比超过 100%(Multiple answers）

排名 Ranking	考虑因素 Considerations	人次 Person-time	百分比 Percent
1	口味好 pleasant taste	274	66.2
2	有名的牌子 famous brand	132	31.9
3	价格适中 reasonable price	129	31.2
4	购买方便 easy to buy	66	15.9
5	生产日期 date of producing	64	15.5
6	广告影响 influence of advertising	49	11.8
7	只是由于习惯 out of habit	36	8.7
8	包装吸引人 appealing package	24	5.8
9	朋友推荐 introduction of friends	22	5.3
10	有优惠条件 with preferential terms	10	2.4
11	售货员介绍 introduced by the shop assistants	6	1.4
12	其它 others	3	0.7
13	单位发的 offered by the working unit	1	0.2

n=414

3-9 样本、男性各年龄层、女性各年龄层最常饮用的种类/ Kinds of the Consumed Tealike Drink by the Whole Sample, Age and Gender Groups

	人数 Number	红茶 red tea	绿茶 green tea	乌龙茶 wolong tea	花茶 scented tea	奶茶 milk tea	果味茶 fruit flavor	其它 others
样本 Sample	403	37.5	18.6	24.6	6.9	10.2	1.2	1.0
男性 Male	169	40.2	21.9	21.3	8.3	5.9	2.4	0.0
16~24 岁 Age	49	46.9	24.5	12.2	10.2	2.0	4.1	0.0
25~34 岁 Age	57	40.4	19.3	22.8	8.8	7.0	1.8	0.0
35~44 岁 Age	39	35.9	20.5	28.2	10.3	5.1	0.0	0.0
45~54 岁 Age	19	36.8	26.3	15.8	0.0	15.8	5.3	0.0
55~60 岁 Age	5	20.0	20.0	60.0	0.0	0.0	0.0	0.0
女性 Female	234	35.5	16.2	26.9	6.0	13.2	0.4	1.7
16~24 岁 Age	69	34.8	18.8	18.8	7.2	17.4	0.0	2.9
25~34 岁 Age	71	38.0	15.5	29.6	5.6	9.9	0.0	1.4
35~44 岁 Age	52	40.4	17.3	21.2	5.8	13.5	1.9	0.0
45~54 岁 Age	32	31.3	12.5	34.4	3.1	15.6	0.0	3.1
55~60 岁 Age	10	10.0	10.0	70.0	10.0	0.0	0.0	0.0

3-10 样本、男性各年龄层、女性各年龄层最常饮用的场合/ Settings of Consumption by the Whole Sample, Age and Gender Groups

注：本题为多选题，合计百分比超过 100%(Multiple answers)

	人数 Number	平时口渴时 when thirsty	平时吃饭喝 at dinner	宴席、聚会喝 at banquet	外出、旅游时 outing/traveling	运动完以后 after athletics	其它 others
样本 Sample	411	71.0	3.4	6.3	34.8	14.1	2.4
男性 Male	175	72.6	2.3	9.1	26.9	14.9	1.7
16~24 岁 Age	51	72.5	2.0	5.9	29.4	23.5	2.0
25~34 岁 Age	60	73.3	1.7	6.7	23.3	15.0	1.7
35~44 岁 Age	38	71.1	5.3	13.2	21.1	7.9	2.6
45~54 岁 Age	20	70.0	0.0	20.0	40.0	10.0	0.0
55~60 岁 Age	6	83.3	0.0	0.0	33.3	0.0	0.0
女性 Female	236	69.9	4.2	4.2	40.7	13.6	3.0
16~24 岁 Age	71	59.2	4.2	2.8	42.3	22.5	5.6
25~34 岁 Age	72	72.2	2.8	4.2	47.2	6.9	4.2
35~44 岁 Age	51	72.5	5.9	2.0	41.2	15.7	0.0
45~54 岁 Age	32	78.1	6.3	9.4	31.3	6.3	0.0
55~60 岁 Age	10	90.0	0.0	10.0	10.0	10.0	0.0

3-11 重度消费者人口分布/ Demographics of the Heavy Consumers

	人数 Number	16-24 岁 Age	25-34 岁 Age	35-44 岁 Age	45-54 岁 Age	55-60 岁 Age
样本 Sample	190	29.5	27.9	21.6	14.2	6.8
男性 Male	84	31.0	29.8	21.4	11.9	6.0
天天喝 daily	17	17.6	17.6	41.2	11.8	11.8
一周 3 次或以上 3 times or over a week	19	31.6	26.3	21.1	10.5	10.5
一周 1~2 次 once or twice a week	48	35.4	35.4	14.6	12.5	2.1
女性 Female	106	28.3	26.4	21.7	16.0	7.5
天天喝 daily	10	10.0	50.0	0.0	30.0	10.0
一周 3 次或以上 3 times or over a week	23	26.1	26.1	26.1	8.7	13.0
一周 1~2 次 once or twice a week	73	31.5	23.3	23.3	16.4	5.5

3-12 不同消费者层的常用品牌/ The Most Frequently Used Brands by Market Segments

3-12-1 时尚流行指标/ Fads Popular Index

	人数 Number	第一品牌及百分比 1st/ percent	第二品牌及百分比 2nd/ percent	第三品牌及百分比 3rd/ percent
样本 Sample	409	**统一 President(39.1)**	**康师傅 Kangshifu(33.0)**	**天与地 Tianyudi(9.8)**
平实生活指向 simple living orientation	178	统一 President(38.2)	康师傅 Kangshifu(32.6)	天与地 Tianyudi(7.9)
时尚流行指向 fashion orientation	231	统一 President(39.8)	康师傅 Kangshifu(33.3)	天与地 Tianyudi(11.3)

3-12-2 广告态度指标/ Advertising Attitude Index

	人数 Number	第一品牌及百分比 1st/ percent	第二品牌及百分比 2nd/ percent	第三品牌及百分比 3rd/ percent
样本 Sample	404	**统一 President(38.9)**	**康师傅 Kangshifu(33.4)**	**天与地 Tianyudi(9.9)**
广告淡漠指向 indifferent orientation	113	统一 President(35.4)	康师傅 Kangshifu(34.5)	天与地 Tianyudi(6.2)
中间层 medium	239	统一 President(38.5)	康师傅 Kangshifu(33.9)	天与地 Tianyudi(10.5)
信赖广告指向 loyal orientation	52	统一 President(48.1)	康师傅 Kangshifu(28.8)	天与地 Tianyudi(15.4)

3-12-3 饮食健康指标/ Foods & Drink Quality Index

	人数 Number	第一品牌及百分比 1st/ percent	第二品牌及百分比 2nd/ percent	第三品牌及百分比 3rd/ percent
样本 Sample	414	**统一 President(39.4)**	**康师傅 Kangshifu(32.9)**	**天与地 Tianyudi(9.9)**
饮食“温饱”指向 "basic" orientation	95	统一 President(46.3)	康师傅 Kangshifu(31.6)	天与地 Tianyudi(9.5)
中间层 medium	223	统一 President(40.4)	康师傅 Kangshifu(31.4)	天与地 Tianyudi(10.8)
健康营养指向 health & nutrition orientation	96	康师傅 Kangshifu(37.5)	统一 President(30.2)	天与地 Tianyudi(8.3)

3-13 重度消费者的消费者层构成/ The Composition of the Heavy Consumers

3-13-1 时尚流行指标/ Fads Popular Index

	人数 Number	平实生活指向 simple living orientation	时尚流行指向 fashion orientation
样本 Sample	187	43.9	56.1
天天喝 daily	27	59.3	40.7
一周 3 次或以上 3 times or over a week	40	35.0	65.0
一周 1~2 次 once or twice a week	120	43.3	56.7

3-13-2 广告态度指标/ Advertising Attitude Index

	人数 Number	广告淡漠指向 indifferent orientation	中间层 medium	信赖广告指向 loyal orientation
样本 Sample	185	28.6	59.5	11.9
天天喝 daily	26	23.1	65.4	11.5
一周 3 次或以上 3 times or over a week	42	31.0	54.8	14.3
一周 1~2 次 once or twice a week	117	29.1	59.8	11.1

3-13-3 饮食健康指标/ Foods & Drink Quality Index

	人数 Number	饮食"温饱"指向 "basic" orientation	中间层 medium	健康营养指向 health & nutrition orientation
样本 Sample	189	21.2	56.6	22.2
天天喝 daily	27	18.5	55.6	25.9
一周 3 次或以上 3 times or over a week	42	21.4	54.8	23.8
一周 1~2 次 once or twice a week	120	21.7	57.5	20.8

● 重庆 / Chongqing

3-1 最近三个月饮用频率的比例/ Proportion of the Sample Consuming Tealike Drink in the Last Three Months

	人数 Number	百分比 Percent
天天喝 daily	12	1.9
一周 3 次或以上 3 times or over a week	13	2.1
一周 1~2 次 once or twice a week	44	7.1
一个月 2～3 次 2 or 3 times a month	74	12.0
一个月 1 次或以下 once a month or below	42	6.8
没喝过 never	434	70.1

n=619

3-2 最常用品牌排名/ Ranking of the Most Frequently Used Brands

排名 Brand Ranking	品牌 Brands	人数 Number	百分比 Percent
1	旭日升 Xurisheng	98	53.0
2	康师傅 Kangshifu	59	31.9
3	统一 President	18	9.7

n=185

3-3 样本、男性各年龄层、女性各年龄层的常用品牌/ The Most Frequently Used Brands by the Whole Sample, Age and Gender Groups

	人数 Number	第一品牌及百分比 1st/ percent	第二品牌及百分比 2nd/ percent	第三品牌及百分比 3rd/ percent
样本 Sample	**185**	**旭日升 Xurisheng(53.0)**	**康师傅 Kangshifu(31.9)**	**统一 President(9.7)**
男性 Male	**85**	**旭日升 Xurisheng(54.1)**	**康师傅 Kangshifu(31.8)**	**统一 President(9.4)**
16~24 岁 Age	24	旭日升 Xurisheng(45.8)	康师傅 Kangshifu(37.5)	统一 President(16.7)
25~34 岁 Age	31	旭日升 Xurisheng(58.1)	康师傅 Kangshifu(32.3)	统一 President(6.5)
35~44 岁 Age	16	旭日升 Xurisheng(43.8)	康师傅 Kangshifu(31.3)	统一 President(12.5)
45~54 岁 Age	8	旭日升 Xurisheng(75.0)	康师傅 Kangshifu(12.5)	
55~60 岁 Age	6	旭日升 Xurisheng(66.7)	康师傅 Kangshifu(33.3)	
女性 Female	**100**	**旭日升 Xurisheng(52.0)**	**康师傅 Kangshifu(32.0)**	**统一 President(10.0)**
16~24 岁 Age	38	旭日升 Xurisheng(47.4)	康师傅 Kangshifu(34.2)	统一 President(13.2)
25~34 岁 Age	32	旭日升 Xurisheng(59.4)	康师傅 Kangshifu(31.3)	统一 President(9.4)
35~44 岁 Age	16	旭日升 Xurisheng(43.8)	康师傅 Kangshifu(31.3)	统一 President(12.5)
45~54 岁 Age	12	旭日升 Xurisheng(50.0)	康师傅 Kangshifu(33.3)	
55~60 岁 Age	2	旭日升 Xurisheng(100.0)		

3-4 理想品牌排名/ Ranking of the Ideal Brands

排名 Brand Ranking	品牌 Brands	人数 Number	百分比 Percent
1	旭日升 Xurisheng	243	38.9
2	康师傅 Kangshifu	134	21.5
3	统一 President	36	5.8

n=624

3-5 样本、男性各年龄层、女性各年龄层最近三个月有无购买的比例/ Purchasing in the Last Three Months by the Whole Sample, Age and Gender Groups

	人数 Number	买过 yes	没买过 no
样本 Sample	**621**	32.4	67.6
男性 Male	**313**	30.0	70.0
16~24 岁 Age	63	36.5	63.5
25~34 岁 Age	93	35.5	64.5
35~44 岁 Age	75	26.7	73.3
45~54 岁 Age	54	24.1	75.9
55~60 岁 Age	28	17.9	82.1
女性 Female	**308**	34.7	65.3
16~24 岁 Age	64	59.4	40.6
25~34 岁 Age	88	38.6	61.4
35~44 岁 Age	73	27.4	72.6
45~54 岁 Age	60	20.0	80.0
55~60 岁 Age	23	13.0	87.0

3-6 样本、男性各年龄层、女性各年龄层最近三个月的饮用频率/ Frequencies of Consuming Tealike Drink in the Last Three Months by the Whole Sample, Age and Gender Groups

	人数 Number	天天喝 daily	一周 3 次或以上 3 times or over a week	一周 1~2 次 once or twice a week	一个月 2~3 次 2 or 3 times a month	一个月 1 次或以下 once a month or below	没喝过 never
样本 Sample	**619**	1.9	2.1	7.1	12.0	6.8	70.1
男性 Male	**314**	1.9	2.2	6.1	10.8	6.1	72.9
16~24 岁 Age	64	0.0	6.3	7.8	15.6	7.8	62.5
25~34 岁 Age	93	3.2	1.1	5.4	17.2	6.5	66.7
35~44 岁 Age	75	1.3	0.0	8.0	6.7	5.3	78.7
45~54 岁 Age	54	0.0	3.7	1.9	5.6	3.7	85.2
55~60 岁 Age	28	7.1	0.0	7.1	0.0	7.1	78.6
女性 Female	**305**	2.0	2.0	8.2	13.1	7.5	67.2
16~24 岁 Age	63	1.6	3.2	14.3	25.4	15.9	39.7
25~34 岁 Age	89	1.1	1.1	9.0	12.4	12.4	64.0
35~44 岁 Age	71	4.2	4.2	4.2	8.5	1.4	77.5
45~54 岁 Age	59	1.7	0.0	5.1	11.9	1.7	79.7
55~60 岁 Age	23	0.0	0.0	8.7	0.0	0.0	91.3

3-7 样本、男性各年龄层、女性各年龄层的品牌习惯/ Brand Habit in Consuming Tealike Drink by the Whole Sample, Age and Gender Groups

	人数 Number	基本固定饮用一个牌子 used in only one brand	比较固定地饮用两个或三个牌子 used in two or three brands	基本上不太固定牌子 no brand preference
样本 Sample	185	54.6	24.9	20.5
男性 Male	85	54.1	24.7	21.2
16~24 岁 Age	24	62.5	29.2	8.3
25~34 岁 Age	31	51.6	25.8	22.6
35~44 岁 Age	16	50.0	25.0	25.0
45~54 岁 Age	8	37.5	25.0	37.5
55~60 岁 Age	6	66.7	0.0	33.3
女性 Female	100	55.0	25.0	20.0
16~24 岁 Age	38	60.5	23.7	15.8
25~34 岁 Age	32	50.0	25.0	25.0
35~44 岁 Age	16	68.8	12.5	18.8
45~54 岁 Age	12	41.7	33.3	25.0
55~60 岁 Age	2	0.0	100.0	0.0

3-8 选择该类商品的考虑因素/ Ranking of the Considerations in Purchasing

注：本题为多选题，合计百分比超过 100%(Multiple answers）

排名 Ranking	考虑因素 Considerations	人次 Person-time	百分比 Percent
1	口味好 pleasant taste	129	69.7
2	价格适中 reasonable price	55	29.7
3	有名的牌子 famous brand	54	29.2
4	生产日期 date of producing	37	20.0
5	购买方便 easy to buy	23	12.4
5	广告影响 influence of advertising	23	12.4
6	只是由于习惯 out of habit	18	9.7
7	包装吸引人 appealing package	8	4.3
7	朋友推荐 introduction of friends	8	4.3
8	有优惠条件 with preferential terms	6	3.2
8	其它 others	6	3.2
9	售货员介绍 introduced by the shop assistants	3	1.6
9	单位发的 offered by the working unit	3	1.6

n=185

3-9 样本、男性各年龄层、女性各年龄层最常饮用的种类/ Kinds of the Consumed Tealike Drink by the Whole Sample, Age and Gender Groups

	人数 Number	红茶 red tea	绿茶 green tea	乌龙茶 wolong tea	花茶 scented tea	奶茶 milk tea	果味茶 fruit flavor	其它 others
样本 Sample	175	29.1	13.7	25.7	7.4	1.7	1.7	20.6
男性 Male	81	28.4	13.6	24.7	6.2	0.0	0.0	27.2
16~24 岁 Age	23	34.8	21.7	26.1	0.0	0.0	0.0	17.4
25~34 岁 Age	31	25.8	19.4	12.9	6.5	0.0	0.0	35.5
35~44 岁 Age	16	18.8	0.0	37.5	6.3	0.0	0.0	37.5
45~54 岁 Age	5	60.0	0.0	40.0	0.0	0.0	0.0	0.0
55~60 岁 Age	6	16.7	0.0	33.3	33.3	0.0	0.0	16.7
女性 Female	94	29.8	13.8	26.6	8.5	3.2	3.2	14.9
16~24 岁 Age	35	37.1	14.3	34.3	2.9	2.9	0.0	8.6
25~34 岁 Age	31	32.3	16.1	22.6	3.2	6.5	0.0	19.4
35~44 岁 Age	14	14.3	14.3	14.3	14.3	0.0	21.4	21.4
45~54 岁 Age	12	8.3	8.3	33.3	33.3	0.0	0.0	16.7
55~60 岁 Age	2	100.0	0.0	0.0	0.0	0.0	0.0	0.0

3-10 样本、男性各年龄层、女性各年龄层最常饮用的场合/ Settings of Consumption by the Whole Sample, Age and Gender Groups

注：本题为多选题，合计百分比超过 100%(Multiple answers)

	人数 Number	平时口渴时 when thirsty	平时吃饭喝 at dinner	宴席、聚会喝 at banquet	外出、旅游时 outing/traveling	运动完以后 after athletics	其它 others
样本 Sample	**185**	**77.3**	**3.2**	**8.1**	**35.1**	**9.7**	**2.2**
男性 Male	**85**	**78.8**	**2.4**	**8.2**	**31.8**	**12.9**	**3.5**
16~24 岁 Age	24	79.2	0.0	8.3	25.0	25.0	0.0
25~34 岁 Age	31	77.4	3.2	12.9	32.3	9.7	3.2
35~44 岁 Age	16	87.5	0.0	0.0	43.8	6.3	6.3
45~54 岁 Age	8	75.0	0.0	12.5	12.5	0.0	12.5
55~60 岁 Age	6	66.7	16.7	0.0	50.0	16.7	0.0
女性 Female	**100**	**76.0**	**4.0**	**8.0**	**38.0**	**7.0**	**1.0**
16~24 岁 Age	38	76.3	2.6	2.6	42.1	10.5	0.0
25~34 岁 Age	32	68.8	6.3	9.4	46.9	6.3	0.0
35~44 岁 Age	16	75.0	6.3	18.8	12.5	6.3	6.3
45~54 岁 Age	12	91.7	0.0	8.3	33.3	0.0	0.0
55~60 岁 Age	2	100.0	0.0	0.0	50.0	0.0	0.0

3-11 重度消费者人口分布/ Demographics of the Heavy Consumers

	人数 Number	16-24 岁 Age	25-34 岁 Age	35-44 岁 Age	45-54 岁 Age	55-60 岁 Age
样本 Sample	**69**	**30.4**	**27.5**	**23.2**	**10.1**	**8.7**
男性 Male	**32**	**28.1**	**28.1**	**21.9**	**9.4**	**12.5**
天天喝 daily	6	0.0	50.0	16.7	0.0	33.3
一周 3 次或以上 3 times or over a week	7	57.1	14.3	0.0	28.6	0.0
一周 1~2 次 once or twice a week	19	26.3	26.3	31.6	5.3	10.5
女性 Female	**37**	**32.4**	**27.0**	**24.3**	**10.8**	**5.4**
天天喝 daily	6	16.7	16.7	50.0	16.7	0.0
一周 3 次或以上 3 times or over a week	6	33.3	16.7	50.0	0.0	0.0
一周 1~2 次 once or twice a week	25	36.0	32.0	12.0	12.0	8.0

3-12 不同消费者层的常用品牌/ The Most Frequently Used Brands by Market Segments

3-12-1 时尚流行指标/ Fads Popular Index

	人数 Number	第一品牌及百分比 1st/ percent	第二品牌及百分比 2nd/ percent	第三品牌及百分比 3rd/ percent
样本 Sample	**180**	**旭日升 Xurisheng(53.3)**	**康师傅 Kangshifu(31.1)**	**统一 President(10.0)**
平实生活指向 simple living orientation	80	旭日升 Xurisheng(56.3)	康师傅 Kangshifu(33.8)	统一 President(6.3)
时尚流行指向 fashion orientation	100	旭日升 Xurisheng(51.0)	康师傅 Kangshifu(29.0)	统一 President(13.0)

3-12-2 广告态度指标/ Advertising Attitude Index

	人数 Number	第一品牌及百分比 1st/ percent	第二品牌及百分比 2nd/ percent	第三品牌及百分比 3rd/ percent
样本 Sample	**184**	**旭日升 Xurisheng(53.3)**	**康师傅 Kangshifu(31.5)**	**统一 President(9.8)**
广告淡漠指向 indifferent orientation	39	旭日升 Xurisheng(59.0)	康师傅 Kangshifu(23.1)	统一 President(10.3)
中间层 medium	118	旭日升 Xurisheng(50.0)	康师傅 Kangshifu(35.6)	统一 President(10.2)
信赖广告指向 loyal orientation	27	旭日升 Xurisheng(59.3)	康师傅 Kangshifu(25.9)	统一 President(7.4)

3-12-3 饮食健康指标/ Foods & Drink Quality Index

	人数 Number	第一品牌及百分比 1st/ percent	第二品牌及百分比 2nd/ percent	第三品牌及百分比 3rd/ percent
样本 Sample	**183**	**旭日升 Xurisheng(53.6)**	**康师傅 Kangshifu(31.7)**	**统一 President(9.8)**
饮食“温饱”指向 "basic" orientation	58	旭日升 Xurisheng(55.2)	康师傅 Kangshifu(31.0)	统一 President(6.9)
中间层 medium	84	旭日升 Xurisheng(51.2)	康师傅 Kangshifu(34.5)	统一 President(13.1)
健康营养指向 health & nutrition orientation	41	旭日升 Xurisheng(56.1)	康师傅 Kangshifu(26.8)	统一 President(7.3)

3-13 重度消费者的消费者层构成/ The Composition of the Heavy Consumers

3-13-1 时尚流行指标/ Fads Popular Index

	人数 Number	平实生活指向 simple living orientation	时尚流行指向 fashion orientation
样本 Sample	65	29	36
天天喝 daily	11	8	3
一周 3 次或以上 3 times or over a week	13	7	6
一周 1~2 次 once or twice a week	41	14	27

3-13-2 广告态度指标/ Advertising Attitude Index

	人数 Number	广告淡漠指向 indifferent orientation	中间层 medium	信赖广告指向 loyal orientation
样本 Sample	68	23.5	63.2	13.2
天天喝 daily	12	16.7	75.0	8.3
一周 3 次或以上 3 times or over	13	23.1	69.2	7.7
一周 1~2 次 once or twice a week	43	25.6	58.1	16.3

3-13-3 饮食健康指标/ Foods & Drink Quality Index

	人数 Number	饮食"温饱"指向 "basic" orientation	中间层 medium	健康营养指向 health & nutrition orientation
样本 Sample	67	32.8	46.3	20.9
天天喝 daily	11	27.3	45.5	27.3
一周 3 次或以上 3 times or over a week	13	30.8	46.2	23.1
一周 1~2 次 once or twice a week	43	34.9	46.5	18.6

● 武汉 / Wuhan

3-1 最近三个月饮用频率的比例/ Proportion of the Sample Consuming Tealike Drink in the Last Three Months

	人数 Number	百分比 Percent
天天喝 daily	12	1.9
一周 3 次或以上 3 times or over a week	23	3.6
一周 1~2 次 once or twice a week	53	8.3
一个月 2~3 次 2 or 3 times a month	93	14.5
一个月 1 次或以下 once a month or below	84	13.1
没喝过 never	375	58.6

n=640

3-2 最常用品牌排名/ Ranking of the Most Frequently Used Brands

排名 Brand Ranking	品牌 Brands	人数 Number	百分比 Percent
1	统一 President	134	50.8
2	康师傅 Kangshifu	78	29.5
3	旭日升 Xurisheng	26	9.8
4	天与地 Tianyudi	3	1.1
5	归真 Guizhen	2	0.8
5	立顿 Lipton	2	0.8

n=264

3-3 样本、男性各年龄层、女性各年龄层的常用品牌/ The Most Frequently Used Brands by the Whole Sample, Age and Gender Groups

	人数 Number	第一品牌及百分比 1st/ percent	第二品牌及百分比 2nd/ percent	第三品牌及百分比 3rd/ percent
样本 Sample	**264**	**统一 President(50.8)**	**康师傅 Kangshifu(29.5)**	**旭日升 Xurisheng(9.8)**
男性 Male	**134**	**统一 President(56.7)**	**康师傅 Kangshifu(23.9)**	**旭日升 Xurisheng(9.0)**
16~24 岁 Age	41	统一 President(63.4)	康师傅 Kangshifu(24.4)	旭日升 Xurisheng(7.3)
25~34 岁 Age	50	统一 President(54.0)	康师傅 Kangshifu(24.0)	旭日升 Xurisheng(8.0)
35~44 岁 Age	28	统一 President(57.1)	康师傅 Kangshifu(25.0)	旭日升 Xurisheng(10.7)
45~54 岁 Age	13	统一 President(46.2)	康师傅 Kangshifu(23.1)	旭日升 Xurisheng(15.4)
55~60 岁 Age	2	统一 President(50.0)		
女性 Female	**130**	**统一 President(44.6)**	**康师傅 Kangshifu(35.4)**	**旭日升 Xurisheng(10.8)**
16~24 岁 Age	45	统一 President(57.8)	康师傅 Kangshifu(35.6)	旭日升 Xurisheng(4.4)
25~34 岁 Age	39	康师傅 Kangshifu(43.6)	统一 President(38.5)	旭日升 Xurisheng(12.8)
35~44 岁 Age	28	康师傅 Kangshifu(39.3)	统一 President(32.1)	旭日升 Xurisheng(10.7)
45~54 岁 Age	14	统一 President(42.9)	旭日升 Xurisheng(21.4)	归真 Guizhen(7.1) 康师傅 Kangshifu(7.1) 立顿 Lipton(7.1)
55~60 岁 Age	4	统一 President(50.0)	康师傅 Kangshifu(25.0) 旭日升 Xurisheng(25.0)	

3-4 理想品牌排名/ Ranking of the Ideal Brands

排名 Brand Ranking	品牌 Brands	人数 Number	百分比 Percent
1	统一 President	196	30.6
2	康师傅 Kangshifu	107	16.7
3	旭日升 Xurisheng	52	8.1
4	归真 Guizhen	4	0.6
5	天与地 Tianyudi	3	0.5
6	立顿 Lipton	2	0.3
6	乐百氏 Robust	2	0.3

n=641

3-5 样本、男性各年龄层、女性各年龄层最近三个月有无购买的比例/ Purchasing in the Last Three Months by the Whole Sample, Age and Gender Groups

	人数 Number	买过 yes	没买过 no
样本 Sample	**640**	**39.4**	**60.6**
男性 Male	**310**	**41.6**	**58.4**
16~24 岁 Age	64	54.7	45.3
25~34 岁 Age	89	52.8	47.2
35~44 岁 Age	80	35.0	65.0
45~54 岁 Age	52	32.7	67.3
55~60 岁 Age	25	8.0	92.0
女性 Female	**330**	**37.3**	**62.7**
16~24 岁 Age	69	59.4	40.6
25~34 岁 Age	96	38.5	61.5
35~44 岁 Age	77	33.8	66.2
45~54 岁 Age	62	24.2	75.8
55~60 岁 Age	26	15.4	84.6

3-6 样本、男性各年龄层、女性各年龄层最近三个月的饮用频率/ Frequencies of Consuming Tealike Drink in the Last Three Months by the Whole Sample, Age and Gender Groups

	人数 Number	天天喝 daily	一周 3 次或以上 3 times or over a week	一周 1~2 次 once or twice a week	一个月 2~3 次 2 or 3 times a month	一个月 1 次或以下 once a month or below	没喝过 never
样本 Sample	640	1.9	3.6	8.3	14.5	13.1	58.6
男性 Male	310	2.6	3.5	8.1	17.1	12.3	56.5
16~24 岁 Age	64	1.6	6.3	9.4	25.0	21.9	35.9
25~34 岁 Age	89	3.4	3.4	11.2	25.8	12.4	43.8
35~44 岁 Age	80	2.5	5.0	6.3	11.3	10.0	65.0
45~54 岁 Age	52	3.8	0.0	7.7	5.8	9.6	73.1
55~60 岁 Age	25	0.0	0.0	0.0	8.0	0.0	92.0
女性 Female	330	1.2	3.6	8.5	12.1	13.9	60.6
16~24 岁 Age	69	0.0	4.3	15.9	21.7	23.2	34.8
25~34 岁 Age	96	3.1	5.2	5.2	13.5	13.5	59.4
35~44 岁 Age	78	1.3	2.6	6.4	9.0	16.7	64.1
45~54 岁 Age	61	0.0	3.3	6.6	8.2	4.9	77.0
55~60 岁 Age	26	0.0	0.0	11.5	0.0	3.8	84.6

3-7 样本、男性各年龄层、女性各年龄层的品牌习惯/ Brand Habit in Consuming Tealike Drink by the Whole Sample, Age and Gender Groups

	人数 Number	基本固定饮用一个牌子 used in only one brand	比较固定地饮用两个或三个牌子 used in two or three brands	基本上不太固定牌子 no brand preference
样本 Sample	263	45.2	30.8	24.0
男性 Male	133	50.4	27.8	21.8
16~24 岁 Age	41	53.7	26.8	19.5
25~34 岁 Age	49	42.9	30.6	26.5
35~44 岁 Age	28	57.1	25.0	17.9
45~54 岁 Age	13	53.8	23.1	23.1
55~60 岁 Age	2	50.0	50.0	0.0
女性 Female	130	40.0	33.8	26.2
16~24 岁 Age	45	40.0	37.8	22.2
25~34 岁 Age	39	38.5	38.5	23.1
35~44 岁 Age	28	50.0	28.6	21.4
45~54 岁 Age	14	28.6	21.4	50.0
55~60 岁 Age	4	25.0	25.0	50.0

3-8 选择该类商品的考虑因素/ Ranking of the Considerations in Purchasing

注：本题为多选题，合计百分比超过 100%(Multiple answers）

排名 Ranking	考虑因素 Considerations	人次 Person-time	百分比 Percent
1	口味好 pleasant taste	176	66.9
2	有名的牌子 famous brand	80	30.4
3	生产日期 date of producing	71	27.0
4	价格适中 reasonable price	69	26.2
5	购买方便 easy to buy	49	18.6
6	广告影响 influence of advertising	39	14.8
7	只是由于习惯 out of habit	20	7.6
8	朋友推荐 introduction of friends	17	6.5
9	有优惠条件 with preferential terms	10	3.8
10	其它 others	9	3.4
11	单位发的 offered by the working unit	8	3.0
12	包装吸引人 appealing package	5	1.9
12	售货员介绍 introduced by the shop assistants	5	1.9

n=263

3-9 样本、男性各年龄层、女性各年龄层最常饮用的种类/ Kinds of the Consumed Tealike Drink by the Whole Sample, Age and Gender Groups

	人数 Number	红茶 red tea	绿茶 green tea	乌龙茶 wolong tea	花茶 scented tea	奶茶 milk tea	果味茶 fruit flavor	其它 others
样本 Sample	255	35.7	9.4	42.7	2.0	1.2	3.1	5.9
男性 Male	133	33.8	12.0	45.9	1.5	0.8	2.3	3.8
16~24 岁 Age	41	39.0	9.8	48.8	0.0	0.0	2.4	0.0
25~34 岁 Age	50	32.0	12.0	44.0	2.0	2.0	0.0	8.0
35~44 岁 Age	27	29.6	22.2	40.7	3.7	0.0	3.7	0.0
45~54 岁 Age	13	38.5	0.0	46.2	0.0	0.0	7.7	7.7
55~60 岁 Age	2	0.0	0.0	100.0	0.0	0.0	0.0	0.0
女性 Female	122	37.7	6.6	39.3	2.5	1.6	4.1	8.2
16~24 岁 Age	44	45.5	9.1	22.7	2.3	2.3	6.8	11.4
25~34 岁 Age	36	33.3	2.8	52.8	0.0	2.8	0.0	8.3
35~44 岁 Age	26	30.8	11.5	42.3	3.8	0.0	7.7	3.8
45~54 岁 Age	12	33.3	0.0	58.3	0.0	0.0	0.0	8.3
55~60 岁 Age	4	50.0	0.0	25.0	25.0	0.0	0.0	0.0

3-10 样本、男性各年龄层、女性各年龄层最常饮用的场合/ Settings of Consumption by the Whole Sample, Age and Gender Groups

注：本题为多选题，合计百分比超过 100%(Multiple answers)

	人数 Number	平时口渴时 when thirsty	平时吃饭喝 at dinner	宴席、聚会喝 at banquet	外出、旅游时 outing/traveling	运动完以后 after athletics	其它 others
样本 Sample	263	72.2	3.4	6.1	44.1	9.1	2.7
男性 Male	133	70.7	2.3	4.5	43.6	11.3	4.5
16~24 岁 Age	41	70.7	4.9	0.0	46.3	14.6	2.4
25~34 岁 Age	49	69.4	2.0	6.1	44.9	10.2	6.1
35~44 岁 Age	28	67.9	0.0	7.1	39.3	10.7	3.6
45~54 岁 Age	13	76.9	0.0	7.7	38.5	7.7	7.7
55~60 岁 Age	2	100.0	0.0	0.0	50.0	0.0	0.0
女性 Female	130	73.8	4.6	7.7	44.6	6.9	0.8
16~24 岁 Age	45	75.6	4.4	8.9	48.9	8.9	2.2
25~34 岁 Age	39	71.8	5.1	5.1	48.7	5.1	0.0
35~44 岁 Age	28	75.0	3.6	3.6	35.7	7.1	0.0
45~54 岁 Age	14	71.4	0.0	21.4	35.7	7.1	0.0
55~60 岁 Age	4	75.0	25.0	0.0	50.0	0.0	0.0

3-11 重度消费者人口分布/ Demographics of the Heavy Consumers

	人数 Number	16-24 岁 Age	25-34 岁 Age	35-44 岁 Age	45-54 岁 Age	55-60 岁 Age
样本 Sample	88	28.4	33.0	21.6	13.6	3.4
男性 Male	44	25.0	36.4	25.0	13.6	0.0
天天喝 daily	8	12.5	37.5	25.0	25.0	0.0
一周 3 次或以上 3 times or over a week	11	36.4	27.3	36.4	0.0	0.0
一周 1~2 次 once or twice a week	25	24.0	40.0	20.0	16.0	0.0
女性 Female	44	31.8	29.5	18.2	13.6	6.8
天天喝 daily	4	0.0	75.0	25.0	0.0	0.0
一周 3 次或以上 3 times or over a week	12	25.0	41.7	16.7	16.7	0.0
一周 1~2 次 once or twice a week	28	39.3	17.9	17.9	14.3	10.7

3-12 不同消费者层的常用品牌/ The Most Frequently Used Brands by Market Segments

3-12-1 时尚流行指标/ Fads Popular Index

	人数 Number	第一品牌及百分比 1st/ percent	第二品牌及百分比 2nd/ percent	第三品牌及百分比 3rd/ percent
样本 Sample	261	**统一 President(50.6)**	**康师傅 Kangshifu(29.9)**	**旭日升 Xurisheng(10.0)**
平实生活指向 simple living orientation	126	统一 President(50.8)	康师傅 Kangshifu(25.4)	旭日升 Xurisheng(10.3)
时尚流行指向 fashion orientation	135	统一 President(50.4)	康师傅 Kangshifu(34.1)	旭日升 Xurisheng(9.6)

3-12-2 广告态度指标/ Advertising Attitude Index

	人数 Number	第一品牌及百分比 1st/ percent	第二品牌及百分比 2nd/ percent	第三品牌及百分比 3rd/ percent
样本 Sample	**261**	**统一 President(50.6)**	**康师傅 Kangshifu(29.9)**	**旭日升 Xurisheng(10.0)**
广告淡漠指向 indifferent orientation	69	统一 President(50.7)	康师傅 Kangshifu(27.5)	旭日升 Xurisheng(7.2)
中间层 medium	159	统一 President(49.7)	康师傅 Kangshifu(30.2)	旭日升 Xurisheng(11.3)
信赖广告指向 loyal orientation	33	统一 President(54.5)	康师傅 Kangshifu(33.3)	旭日升 Xurisheng(9.1)

3-12-3 饮食健康指标/ Foods & Drink Quality Index

	人数 Number	第一品牌及百分比 1st/ percent	第二品牌及百分比 2nd/ percent	第三品牌及百分比 3rd/ percent
样本 Sample	**259**	**统一 President(51.0)**	**康师傅 Kangshifu(30.1)**	**旭日升 Xurisheng(9.3)**
饮食"温饱"指向 "basic" orientation	88	统一 President(61.4)	康师傅 Kangshifu(18.2)	旭日升 Xurisheng(8.0)
中间层 medium	127	康师傅 Kangshifu(40.9)	统一 President(40.2)	旭日升 Xurisheng(10.2)
健康营养指向 health & nutrition orientation	44	统一 President(61.4)	康师傅 Kangshifu(22.7)	旭日升 Xurisheng(9.1)

3-13 重度消费者的消费者层构成/ The Composition of the Heavy Consumers

3-13-1 时尚流行指标/ Fads Popular Index

	人数 Number	平实生活指向 simple living orientation	时尚流行指向 fashion orientation
样本 Sample	**87**	**40.2**	**59.8**
天天喝 daily	12	25.0	75.0
一周 3 次或以上 3 times or over a week	23	47.8	52.2
一周 1~2 次 once or twice a week	52	40.4	59.6

3-13-2 广告态度指标/ Advertising Attitude Index

	人数 Number	广告淡漠指向 indifferent orientation	中间层 medium	信赖广告指向 loyal orientation
样本 Sample	**87**	**25.3**	**51.7**	**23.0**
天天喝 daily	12	25.0	50.0	25.0
一周 3 次或以上 3 times or over a week	23	21.7	56.5	21.7
一周 1~2 次 once or twice a week	52	26.9	50.0	23.1

3-13-3 饮食健康指标/ Foods & Drink Quality Index

	人数 Number	饮食"温饱"指向 "basic" orientation	中间层 medium	健康营养指向 health & nutrition orientation
样本 Sample	**87**	**32.2**	**50.6**	**17.2**
天天喝 daily	12	25.0	58.3	16.7
一周 3 次或以上 3 times or over a week	23	34.8	43.5	21.7
一周 1~2 次 once or twice a week	52	32.7	51.9	15.4

● 西安 / Xi'an

3-1 最近三个月饮用频率的比例/ Proportion of the Sample Consuming Tealike Drink in the Last Three Months

	人数 Number	百分比 Percent
天天喝 daily	21	3.5
一周 3 次或以上 3 times or over a week	21	3.5
一周 1~2 次 once or twice a week	57	9.5
一个月 2～3 次 2 or 3 times a month	83	13.8
一个月 1 次或以下 once a month or below	64	10.6
没喝过 never	355	59.1

n=601

3-2 最常用品牌排名/ Ranking of the Most Frequently Used Brands

排名 Brand Ranking	品牌 Brands	人数 Number	百分比 Percent
1	康师傅 Kangshifu	202	82.1
2	旭日升 Xurisheng	22	8.9
3	天与地 Tianyudi	6	2.4
4	统一 President	5	2.0
5	三得利 Suntory	2	0.8

n=246

3-3 样本、男性各年龄层、女性各年龄层的常用品牌/ The Most Frequently Used Brands by the Whole Sample, Age and Gender Groups

	人数 Number	第一品牌及百分比 1st/ percent	第二品牌及百分比 2nd/ percent	第三品牌及百分比 3rd/ percent
样本 Sample	246	**康师傅 Kangshifu(82.1)**	**旭日升 Xurisheng(8.9)**	**天与地 Tianyudi(2.4)**
男性 Male	126	**康师傅 Kangshifu(84.1)**	**旭日升 Xurisheng(7.1)**	**统一 President(2.4)**
16~24 岁 Age	37	康师傅 Kangshifu(86.5)	旭日升 Xurisheng(10.8)	天与地 Tianyudi(2.7)
25~34 岁 Age	35	康师傅 Kangshifu(71.4)	旭日升 Xurisheng(11.4)	麒麟 Kirin(2.9) 三得利 Suntory(2.9) 天与地 Tianyudi(2.9) 统一 President(2.9) 雀巢 Nestle(2.9) 中华杏茶 Zhong Hua Xing Cha (2.9)
35~44 岁 Age	35	康师傅 Kangshifu(94.3)	统一 President(5.7)	
45~54 岁 Age	15	康师傅 Kangshifu(80.0)	旭日升 Xurisheng(6.7) 陕清 Shanqing(6.7)	
55~60 岁 Age	4	康师傅 Kangshifu(100.0)		
女性 Female	120	**康师傅 Kangshifu(80.0)**	**旭日升 Xurisheng(10.8)**	**天与地 Tianyudi(3.3)**
16~24 岁 Age	30	康师傅 Kangshifu(80.0)	旭日升 Xurisheng(13.3)	三得利 Suntory(3.3)
25~34 岁 Age	46	康师傅 Kangshifu(87.0)	天与地 Tianyudi(4.3) 旭日升 Xurisheng(4.3)	博卡 Pukka(2.2)
35~44 岁 Age	26	康师傅 Kangshifu(76.9)	旭日升 Xurisheng(11.5)	统一 President(7.7)
45~54 岁 Age	12	康师傅 Kangshifu(50.0)	旭日升 Xurisheng(33.3)	天与地 Tianyudi(16.7)
55~60 岁 Age	6	康师傅 Kangshifu(100.0)		

3-4 理想品牌排名/ Ranking of the Ideal Brands

排名 Brand Ranking	品牌 Brands	人数 Number	百分比 Percent
1	康师傅 Kangshifu	309	51.4
2	旭日升 Xurisheng	54	9.0
3	统一 President	12	2.0
4	天与地 Tianyudi	8	1.3
5	三得利 Suntory	4	0.7
6	荣氏 Rong	3	0.5

n=601

3-5 样本、男性各年龄层、女性各年龄层最近三个月有无购买的比例/ Purchasing in the Last Three Months by the Whole Sample, Age and Gender Groups

	人数 Number	买过 yes	没买过 no
样本 Sample	601	38.6	61.4
男性 Male	302	37.7	62.3
16~24 岁 Age	64	48.4	51.6
25~34 岁 Age	91	35.2	64.8
35~44 岁 Age	77	40.3	59.7
45~54 岁 Age	46	34.8	65.2
55~60 岁 Age	24	16.7	83.3
女性 Female	299	39.5	60.5
16~24 岁 Age	61	42.6	57.4
25~34 岁 Age	90	51.1	48.9
35~44 岁 Age	74	35.1	64.9
45~54 岁 Age	49	28.6	71.4
55~60 岁 Age	25	24.0	76.0

3-6 样本、男性各年龄层、女性各年龄层最近三个月的饮用频率/ Frequencies of Consuming Tealike Drink in the Last Three Months by the Whole Sample, Age and Gender Groups

	人数 Number	天天喝 daily	一周3次或以上 3 times or over a week	一周1~2次 once or twice a week	一个月2~3次 2 or 3 times a month	一个月1次或以下 once a month or below	没喝过 never
样本 Sample	601	3.5	3.5	9.5	13.8	10.6	59.1
男性 Male	302	4.0	3.0	10.9	14.9	8.9	58.3
16~24 岁 Age	64	7.8	7.8	12.5	18.8	10.9	42.2
25~34 岁 Age	91	2.2	3.3	13.2	12.1	7.7	61.5
35~44 岁 Age	77	3.9	0.0	10.4	20.8	10.4	54.5
45~54 岁 Age	46	4.3	2.2	8.7	8.7	8.7	67.4
55~60 岁 Age	24	0.0	0.0	4.2	8.3	4.2	83.3
女性 Female	299	3.0	4.0	8.0	12.7	12.4	59.9
16~24 岁 Age	61	0.0	6.6	18.0	14.8	9.8	50.8
25~34 岁 Age	90	4.4	4.4	6.7	16.7	18.9	48.9
35~44 岁 Age	74	4.1	0.0	5.4	10.8	14.9	64.9
45~54 岁 Age	49	2.0	6.1	4.1	8.2	4.1	75.5
55~60 岁 Age	25	4.0	4.0	4.0	8.0	4.0	76.0

3-7 样本、男性各年龄层、女性各年龄层的品牌习惯/ Brand Habit in Consuming Tealike Drink by the Whole Sample, Age and Gender Groups

	人数 Number	基本固定饮用一个牌子 used in only one brand	比较固定地饮用两个或三个牌子 used in two or three brands	基本上不太固定牌子 no brand preference
样本 Sample	246	44.3	33.3	22.4
男性 Male	126	46.8	29.4	23.8
16~24 岁 Age	37	59.5	27.0	13.5
25~34 岁 Age	35	45.7	34.3	20.0
35~44 岁 Age	35	37.1	31.4	31.4
45~54 岁 Age	15	33.3	26.7	40.0
55~60 岁 Age	4	75.0	0.0	25.0
女性 Female	120	41.7	37.5	20.8
16~24 岁 Age	30	50.0	30.0	20.0
25~34 岁 Age	46	45.7	34.8	19.6
35~44 岁 Age	26	34.6	42.3	23.1
45~54 岁 Age	12	33.3	41.7	25.0
55~60 岁 Age	6	16.7	66.7	16.7

3-8 选择该类商品的考虑因素/ Ranking of the Considerations in Purchasing

注：本题为多选题，合计百分比超过 100%(Multiple answers）

排名 Ranking	考虑因素 Considerations	人次 Person-time	百分比 Percent
1	口味好 pleasant taste	158	64.2
2	有名的牌子 famous brand	65	26.4
3	价格适中 reasonable price	54	22.0
4	广告影响 influence of advertising	38	15.4
5	生产日期 date of producing	35	14.2
5	购买方便 easy to buy	35	14.2
6	朋友推荐 introduction of friends	24	9.8
7	只是由于习惯 out of habit	17	6.9
8	包装吸引人 appealing package	12	4.9
9	单位发的 offered by the working unit	8	3.3
10	其它 others	3	1.2
11	有优惠条件 with preferential terms	2	0.8
11	售货员介绍 introduced by the shop assistants	2	0.8

n=246

3-9 样本、男性各年龄层、女性各年龄层最常饮用的种类/ Kinds of the Consumed Tealike Drink by the Whole Sample, Age and Gender Groups

	人数 Number	红茶 red tea	绿茶 green tea	乌龙茶 wolong tea	花茶 scented tea	奶茶 milk tea	果味茶 fruit flavor	其它 others
样本 Sample	246	4.5	38.2	51.6	4.1	0.0	1.6	0.0
男性 Male	126	4.0	38.1	51.6	3.2	0.0	3.2	0.0
16~24 岁 Age	37	2.7	43.2	48.6	2.7	0.0	2.7	0.0
25~34 岁 Age	35	5.7	34.3	54.3	0.0	0.0	5.7	0.0
35~44 岁 Age	35	2.9	31.4	57.1	5.7	0.0	2.9	0.0
45~54 岁 Age	15	6.7	46.7	40.0	6.7	0.0	0.0	0.0
55~60 岁 Age	4	0.0	50.0	50.0	0.0	0.0	0.0	0.0
女性 Female	120	5.0	38.3	51.7	5.0	0.0	0.0	0.0
16~24 岁 Age	30	0.0	33.3	66.7	0.0	0.0	0.0	0.0
25~34 岁 Age	46	6.5	39.1	50.0	4.3	0.0	0.0	0.0
35~44 岁 Age	26	11.5	38.5	42.3	7.7	0.0	0.0	0.0
45~54 岁 Age	12	0.0	33.3	58.3	8.3	0.0	0.0	0.0
55~60 岁 Age	6	0.0	66.7	16.7	16.7	0.0	0.0	0.0

3-10 样本、男性各年龄层、女性各年龄层最常饮用的场合/ Settings of Consumption by the Whole Sample, Age and Gender Groups

注：本题为多选题，合计百分比超过 100%(Multiple answers)

	人数 Number	平时口渴时 when thirsty	平时吃饭喝 at dinner	宴席、聚会喝 at banquet	外出、旅游时 outing/traveling	运动完以后 after athletics	其它 others
样本 Sample	246	61.0	6.5	11.4	37.4	12.6	0.0
男性 Male	126	62.7	7.9	9.5	34.9	12.7	0.0
16~24 岁 Age	37	64.9	5.4	5.4	35.1	16.2	0.0
25~34 岁 Age	35	62.9	8.6	11.4	25.7	8.6	0.0
35~44 岁 Age	35	62.9	11.4	5.7	48.6	5.7	0.0
45~54 岁 Age	15	53.3	6.7	20.0	26.7	26.7	0.0
55~60 岁 Age	4	75.0	0.0	25.0	25.0	25.0	0.0
女性 Female	120	59.2	5.0	13.3	40.0	12.5	0.0
16~24 岁 Age	30	60.0	0.0	3.3	46.7	26.7	0.0
25~34 岁 Age	46	50.0	4.3	15.2	43.5	10.9	0.0
35~44 岁 Age	26	57.7	11.5	23.1	34.6	3.8	0.0
45~54 岁 Age	12	83.3	8.3	0.0	25.0	8.3	0.0
55~60 岁 Age	6	83.3	0.0	33.3	33.3	0.0	0.0

3-11 重度消费者人口分布/ Demographics of the Heavy Consumers

	人数 Number	16-24 岁 Age	25-34 岁 Age	35-44 岁 Age	45-54 岁 Age	55-60 岁 Age
样本 Sample	99	33.3	31.3	18.2	13.1	4.0
男性 Male	54	33.3	31.5	20.4	13.0	1.9
天天喝 daily	12	41.7	16.7	25.0	16.7	0.0
一周 3 次或以上 3 times or over a week	9	55.6	33.3	0.0	11.1	0.0
一周 1~2 次 once or twice a week	33	24.2	36.4	24.2	12.1	3.0
女性 Female	45	33.3	31.1	15.6	13.3	6.7
天天喝 daily	9	0.0	44.4	33.3	11.1	11.1
一周 3 次或以上 3 times or over a week	12	33.3	33.3	0.0	25.0	8.3
一周 1~2 次 once or twice a week	24	45.8	25.0	16.7	8.3	4.2

3-12 不同消费者层的常用品牌/ The Most Frequently Used Brands by Market Segments

3-12-1 时尚流行指标/ Fads Popular Index

	人数 Number	第一品牌及百分比 1st/ percent	第二品牌及百分比 2nd/ percent	第三品牌及百分比 3rd/ percent	第四品牌及百分比 4th/ percent
样本 Sample	**245**	**康师傅 Kangshifu(82.0)**	**旭日升 Xurisheng(9.0)**	**天与地 Tianyudi(2.4)**	**统一 President(2.0)**
平实生活指向 simple living orientation	118	康师傅 Kangshifu(78.0)	旭日升 Xurisheng(11.0)	天与地 Tianyudi(3.4) 统一 President(3.4)	中华杏茶 Zhong Hua Xing Cha (0.8)
时尚流行指向 fashion orientation	127	康师傅 Kangshifu(85.8)	旭日升 Xurisheng(7.1)	三得利 Suntory(1.6) 天与地 Tianyudi(1.6)	博卡 Pukka(0.8) 麒麟 Kirin(0.8) 统一 President(0.8) 雀巢 Nestle(0.8) 陕清 Shanqing(0.8)

3-12-2 广告态度指标/ Advertising Attitude Index

	人数 Number	第一品牌及百分比 1st/ percent	第二品牌及百分比 2nd/ percent	第三品牌及百分比 3rd/ percent	第四品牌及百分比 4th/ percent
样本 Sample	**244**	**康师傅 Kangshifu(82.0)**	**旭日升 Xurisheng(9.0)**	**天与地 Tianyudi(2.5)**	**统一 President(2.0)**
广告淡漠指向 indifferent orientation	78	康师傅 Kangshifu(85.9)	旭日升 Xurisheng(6.4)	统一 President(2.6)	三得利 Suntory(1.3) 天与地 Tianyudi(1.3) 雀巢 Nestle(1.3)
中间层 medium	142	康师傅 Kangshifu(79.6)	旭日升 Xurisheng(9.9)	天与地 Tianyudi(3.5)	统一 President(2.1)
信赖广告指向 loyal orientation	24	康师傅 Kangshifu(83.3)	旭日升 Xurisheng(12.5)	三得利 Suntory(4.2)	

3-12-3 饮食健康指标/ Foods & Drink Quality Index

	人数 Number	第一品牌及百分比 1st/ percent	第二品牌及百分比 2nd/ percent	第三品牌及百分比 3rd/ percent	第四品牌及百分比 4th/ percent
样本 Sample	**246**	**康师傅 Kangshifu(82.1)**	**旭日升 Xurisheng(8.9)**	**天与地 Tianyudi(2.4)**	**统一 President(2.0)**
饮食“温饱”指向 "basic" orientation	81	康师傅 Kangshifu(76.5)	旭日升 Xurisheng(16.0)	天与地 Tianyudi(2.5) 统一 President(2.5)	雀巢 Nestle(1.2)
中间层 medium	126	康师傅 Kangshifu(83.3)	旭日升 Xurisheng(5.6)	天与地 Tianyudi(2.4) 统一 President(2.4)	三得利 Suntory(1.6)
健康营养指向 health & nutrition orientation	39	康师傅 Kangshifu(89.7)	旭日升 Xurisheng(5.1)	麒麟 Kirin(2.6) 天与地 Tianyudi(2.6)	

3-13 重度消费者的消费者层构成/ The Composition of the Heavy Consumers

3-13-1 时尚流行指标/ Fads Popular Index

	人数 Number	平实生活指向 simple living orientation	时尚流行指向 fashion orientation
样本 Sample	**98**	**41.8**	**58.2**
天天喝 daily	21	28.6	71.4
一周 3 次或以上 3 times or over a week	20	45.0	55.0
一周 1~2 次 once or twice a week	57	45.6	54.4

3-13-2 广告态度指标/ Advertising Attitude Index

	人数 Number	广告淡漠指向 indifferent orientation	中间层 medium	信赖广告指向 loyal orientation
样本 Sample	**97**	**32.0**	**55.7**	**12.4**
天天喝 daily	21	38.1	42.9	19.0
一周 3 次或以上 3 times or over a week	21	28.6	61.9	9.5
一周 1~2 次 once or twice a week	55	30.9	58.2	10.9

3-13-3 饮食健康指标/ Foods & Drink Quality Index

	人数 Number	饮食“温饱”指向 "basic" orientation	中间层 medium	健康营养指向 health & nutrition orientation
样本 Sample	**99**	**31.3**	**50.5**	**18.2**
天天喝 daily	21	14.3	57.1	28.6
一周 3 次或以上 3 times or over a week	21	19.0	57.1	23.8
一周 1~2 次 once or twice a week	57	42.1	45.6	12.3

● 沈阳 / Shenyang

3-1 最近三个月饮用频率的比例/ Proportion of the Sample Consuming Tealike Drink in the Last Three Months

	人数 Number	百分比 Percent
天天喝 daily	11	1.8
一周 3 次或以上 3 times or over a week	20	3.3
一周 1~2 次 once or twice a week	56	9.3
一个月 2~3 次 2 or 3 times a month	91	15.2
一个月 1 次或以下 once a month or below	71	11.8
没喝过 never	351	58.5

n=600

3-2 最常用品牌排名/ Ranking of the Most Frequently Used Brands

排名 Brand Ranking	品牌 Brands	人数 Number	百分比 Percent
1	康师傅 Kangshifu	94	37.9
2	旭日升 Xurisheng	92	37.1
3	统一 President	52	21.0

n=248

3-3 样本、男性各年龄层、女性各年龄层的常用品牌/ The Most Frequently Used Brands by the Whole Sample, Age and Gender Groups

	人数 Number	第一品牌及百分比 1st/ percent	第二品牌及百分比 2nd/ percent	第三品牌及百分比 3rd/ percent
样本 Sample	248	**康师傅 Kangshifu(37.9)**	**旭日升 Xurisheng(37.1)**	**统一 President(21.0)**
男性 Male	122	**旭日升 Xurisheng(39.3)**	**康师傅 Kangshifu(36.9)**	**统一 President(20.5)**
16~24 岁 Age	33	康师傅 Kangshifu(60.6)	统一 President(24.2)	旭日升 Xurisheng(15.2)
25~34 岁 Age	42	旭日升 Xurisheng(45.2)	康师傅 Kangshifu(35.7)	统一 President(14.3)
35~44 岁 Age	25	旭日升 Xurisheng(48.0)	康师傅 Kangshifu(24.0)	统一 President(20.0)
45~54 岁 Age	17	旭日升 Xurisheng(58.8)	统一 President(29.4)	康师傅 Kangshifu(11.8)
55~60 岁 Age	5	康师傅 Kangshifu(40.0) 旭日升 Xurisheng(40.0)	统一 President(20.0)	
女性 Female	126	**康师傅 Kangshifu(38.9)**	**旭日升 Xurisheng(34.9)**	**统一 President(21.4)**
16~24 岁 Age	40	康师傅 Kangshifu(45.0)	统一 President(30.0)	旭日升 Xurisheng(25.0)
25~34 岁 Age	37	旭日升 Xurisheng(45.9)	康师傅 Kangshifu(32.4)	统一 President(16.2)
35~44 岁 Age	31	旭日升 Xurisheng(38.7)	康师傅 Kangshifu(32.3)	统一 President(22.6)
45~54 岁 Age	14	康师傅 Kangshifu(50.0)	旭日升 Xurisheng(21.4)	统一 President(14.3)
55~60 岁 Age	4	康师傅 Kangshifu(50.0) 旭日升 Xurisheng(50.0)		

3-4 理想品牌排名/ Ranking of the Ideal Brands

排名 Brand Ranking	品牌 Brands	人数 Number	百分比 Percent
1	旭日升 Xurisheng	185	30.8
2	康师傅 Kangshifu	158	26.3
3	统一 President	71	11.8

n=601

3-5 样本、男性各年龄层、女性各年龄层最近三个月有无购买的比例/ Purchasing in the Last Three Months by the Whole Sample, Age and Gender Groups

	人数 Number	买过 yes	没买过 no
样本 Sample	600	41.8	58.2
男性 Male	298	41.3	58.7
16~24 岁 Age	64	48.4	51.6
25~34 岁 Age	89	48.3	51.7
35~44 岁 Age	76	31.6	68.4
45~54 岁 Age	45	40.0	60.0
55~60 岁 Age	24	29.2	70.8
女性 Female	302	42.4	57.6
16~24 岁 Age	64	59.4	40.6
25~34 岁 Age	90	43.3	56.7
35~44 岁 Age	76	40.8	59.2
45~54 岁 Age	48	31.3	68.8
55~60 岁 Age	24	20.8	79.2

3-6 样本、男性各年龄层、女性各年龄层最近三个月的饮用频率/ Frequencies of Consuming Tealike Drink in the Last Three Months by the Whole Sample, Age and Gender Groups

	人数 Number	天天喝 daily	一周3次或以上 3 times or over a week	一周1~2次 once or twice a week	一个月2~3次 2 or 3 times a month	一个月1次或以下 once a month or below	没喝过 never
样本 Sample	600	1.8	3.3	9.3	15.2	11.8	58.5
男性 Male	298	2.3	3.7	8.4	13.8	13.1	58.7
16~24 岁 Age	64	1.6	3.1	17.2	20.3	9.4	48.4
25~34 岁 Age	89	1.1	4.5	11.2	14.6	16.9	51.7
35~44 岁 Age	76	3.9	3.9	3.9	7.9	13.2	67.1
45~54 岁 Age	45	2.2	2.2	2.2	17.8	13.3	62.2
55~60 岁 Age	24	4.2	4.2	0.0	4.2	8.3	79.2
女性 Female	302	1.3	3.0	10.3	16.6	10.6	58.3
16~24 岁 Age	64	1.6	4.7	10.9	29.7	15.6	37.5
25~34 岁 Age	90	0.0	1.1	12.2	16.7	11.1	58.9
35~44 岁 Age	76	3.9	5.3	13.2	10.5	7.9	59.2
45~54 岁 Age	48	0.0	2.1	6.3	12.5	8.3	70.8
55~60 岁 Age	24	0.0	0.0	0.0	8.3	8.3	83.3

3-7 样本、男性各年龄层、女性各年龄层的品牌习惯/ Brand Habit in Consuming Tealike Drink by the Whole Sample, Age and Gender Groups

	人数 Number	基本固定饮用一个牌子 used in only one brand	比较固定地饮用两个或三个牌子 used in two or three brands	基本上不太固定牌子 no brand preference
样本 Sample	249	49.8	30.1	20.1
男性 Male	123	57.7	26.0	16.3
16~24 岁 Age	33	66.7	21.2	12.1
25~34 岁 Age	43	46.5	41.9	11.6
35~44 岁 Age	25	72.0	12.0	16.0
45~54 岁 Age	17	35.3	23.5	41.2
55~60 岁 Age	5	100.0	0.0	0.0
女性 Female	126	42.1	34.1	23.8
16~24 岁 Age	40	35.0	42.5	22.5
25~34 岁 Age	37	45.9	35.1	18.9
35~44 岁 Age	31	45.2	29.0	25.8
45~54 岁 Age	14	35.7	28.6	35.7
55~60 岁 Age	4	75.0	0.0	25.0

3-8 选择该类商品的考虑因素/ Ranking of the Considerations in Purchasing

注：本题为多选题，合计百分比超过100%(Multiple answers)

排名 Ranking	考虑因素 Considerations	人次 Person-time	百分比 Percent
1	口味好 pleasant taste	179	71.9
2	价格适中 reasonable price	81	32.5
3	有名的牌子 famous brand	80	32.1
4	生产日期 date of producing	51	20.5
5	购买方便 easy to buy	41	16.5
6	广告影响 influence of advertising	34	13.7
7	朋友推荐 introduction of friends	14	5.6
8	只是由于习惯 out of habit	12	4.8
9	包装吸引人 appealing package	5	2.0
9	有优惠条件 with preferential terms	5	2.0
11	售货员介绍 introduced by the shop assistants	3	1.2
11	单位发的 offered by the working unit	3	1.2
12	其它 others	1	0.4

n=249

3-9 样本、男性各年龄层、女性各年龄层最常饮用的种类/ Kinds of the Consumed Tealike Drink by the Whole Sample, Age and Gender Groups

	人数 Number	红茶 red tea	绿茶 green tea	乌龙茶 wolong tea	花茶 scented tea	奶茶 milk tea	果味茶 fruit flavor	其它 others
样本 Sample	237	16.9	15.6	38.4	4.2	1.3	6.8	16.9
男性 Male	116	12.9	16.4	40.5	5.2	1.7	5.2	18.1
16~24 岁 Age	32	12.5	12.5	53.1	3.1	0.0	6.3	12.5
25~34 岁 Age	42	9.5	23.8	33.3	4.8	2.4	4.8	21.4
35~44 岁 Age	23	26.1	13.0	26.1	4.3	0.0	8.7	21.7
45~54 岁 Age	15	6.7	6.7	46.7	13.3	6.7	0.0	20.0
55~60 岁 Age	4	0.0	25.0	75.0	0.0	0.0	0.0	0.0
女性 Female	121	20.7	14.9	36.4	3.3	0.8	8.3	15.7
16~24 岁 Age	40	32.5	25.0	25.0	2.5	0.0	5.0	10.0
25~34 岁 Age	33	12.1	12.1	42.4	3.0	3.0	6.1	21.2
35~44 岁 Age	30	13.3	13.3	46.7	6.7	0.0	6.7	13.3
45~54 岁 Age	14	21.4	0.0	35.7	0.0	0.0	21.4	21.4
55~60 岁 Age	4	25.0	0.0	25.0	0.0	0.0	25.0	25.0

3-10 样本、男性各年龄层、女性各年龄层最常饮用的场合/ Settings of Consumption by the Whole Sample, Age and Gender Groups

注：本题为多选题，合计百分比超过 100%(Multiple answers)

	人数 Number	平时口渴时 when thirsty	平时吃饭喝 at dinner	宴席、聚会喝 at banquet	外出、旅游时 outing/traveling	运动完以后 after athletics	其它 others
样本 Sample	249	59.0	2.4	16.5	43.0	10.0	2.4
男性 Male	123	58.5	0.8	18.7	39.0	13.0	2.4
16~24 岁 Age	33	54.5	0.0	3.0	39.4	30.3	0.0
25~34 岁 Age	43	60.5	0.0	16.3	41.9	11.6	4.7
35~44 岁 Age	25	72.0	4.0	28.0	36.0	4.0	0.0
45~54 岁 Age	17	41.2	0.0	35.3	41.2	0.0	5.9
55~60 岁 Age	5	60.0	0.0	40.0	20.0	0.0	0.0
女性 Female	126	59.5	4.0	14.3	46.8	7.1	2.4
16~24 岁 Age	40	47.5	2.5	15.0	57.5	7.5	5.0
25~34 岁 Age	37	56.8	2.7	16.2	51.4	8.1	0.0
35~44 岁 Age	31	67.7	9.7	12.9	32.3	9.7	3.2
45~54 岁 Age	14	85.7	0.0	14.3	28.6	0.0	0.0
55~60 岁 Age	4	50.0	0.0	0.0	75.0	0.0	0.0

3-11 重度消费者人口分布/ Demographics of the Heavy Consumers

	人数 Number	16-24 岁 Age	25-34 岁 Age	35-44 岁 Age	45-54 岁 Age	55-60 岁 Age
样本 Sample	87	28.7	31.0	29.9	8.0	2.3
男性 Male	43	32.6	34.9	20.9	7.0	4.7
天天喝 daily	7	14.3	14.3	42.9	14.3	14.3
一周 3 次或以上 3 times or over a week	11	18.2	36.4	27.3	9.1	9.1
一周 1~2 次 once or twice a week	25	44.0	40.0	12.0	4.0	0.0
女性 Female	44	25.0	27.3	38.6	9.1	0.0
天天喝 daily	4	25.0	0.0	75.0	0.0	0.0
一周 3 次或以上 3 times or over a week	9	33.3	11.1	44.4	11.1	0.0
一周 1~2 次 once or twice a week	31	22.6	35.5	32.3	9.7	0.0

3-12 不同消费者层的常用品牌/ The Most Frequently Used Brands by Market Segments

3-12-1 时尚流行指标/ Fads Popular Index

	人数 Number	第一品牌及百分比 1st/ percent	第二品牌及百分比 2nd/ percent	第三品牌及百分比 3rd/ percent
样本 Sample	248	康师傅 Kangshifu(37.9)	旭日升 Xurisheng(37.1)	统一 President(21.0)
平实生活指向 simple living orientation	98	旭日升 Xurisheng(37.8)	康师傅 Kangshifu(32.7)	统一 President(25.5)
时尚流行指向 fashion orientation	150	康师傅 Kangshifu(41.3)	旭日升 Xurisheng(36.7)	统一 President(18.0)

3-12-2 广告态度指标/ Advertising Attitude Index

	人数 Number	第一品牌及百分比 1st/ percent	第二品牌及百分比 2nd/ percent	第三品牌及百分比 3rd/ percent
样本 Sample	**248**	**康师傅 Kangshifu(37.9)**	**旭日升 Xurisheng(37.1)**	**统一 President(21.0)**
广告淡漠指向 indifferent orientation	64	旭日升 Xurisheng(43.8)	康师傅 Kangshifu(31.3)	统一 President(20.3)
中间层 medium	145	康师傅 Kangshifu(38.6)	旭日升 Xurisheng(34.5)	统一 President(23.4)
信赖广告指向 loyal orientation	39	康师傅 Kangshifu(46.2)	旭日升 Xurisheng(35.9)	统一 President(12.8)

3-12-3 饮食健康指标/ Foods & Drink Quality Index

	人数 Number	第一品牌及百分比 1st/ percent	第二品牌及百分比 2nd/ percent	第三品牌及百分比 3rd/ percent
样本 Sample	**248**	**康师傅 Kangshifu(37.9)**	**旭日升 Xurisheng(37.1)**	**统一 President(21.0)**
饮食“温饱”指向 "basic" orientation	67	旭日升 Xurisheng(40.3)	统一 President(31.3)	康师傅 Kangshifu(25.4)
中间层 medium	113	康师傅 Kangshifu(40.7)	旭日升 Xurisheng(38.1)	统一 President(17.7)
健康营养指向 health & nutrition orientation	68	康师傅 Kangshifu(45.6)	旭日升 Xurisheng(32.4)	统一 President(16.2)

3-13 重度消费者的消费者层构成/ The Composition of the Heavy Consumers

3-13-1 时尚流行指标/ Fads Popular Index

	人数 Number	平实生活指向 simple living orientation	时尚流行指向 fashion orientation
样本 Sample	**87**	**36.8**	**63.2**
天天喝 daily	11	54.5	45.5
一周 3 次或以上 3 times or over a week	20	50.0	50.0
一周 1~2 次 once or twice a week	56	28.6	71.4

3-13-2 广告态度指标/ Advertising Attitude Index

	人数 Number	广告淡漠指向 indifferent orientation	中间层 medium	信赖广告指向 loyal orientation
样本 Sample	**87**	**26.4**	**56.3**	**17.2**
天天喝 daily	11	45.5	36.4	18.2
一周 3 次或以上 3 times or over a week	20	20.0	40.0	40.0
一周 1~2 次 once or twice a week	56	25.0	66.1	8.9

3-13-3 饮食健康指标/ Foods & Drink Quality Index

	人数 Number	饮食“温饱”指向 "basic" orientation	中间层 medium	健康营养指向 health & nutrition orientation
样本 Sample	**87**	**19.5**	**46.0**	**34.5**
天天喝 daily	11	27.3	63.6	9.1
一周 3 次或以上 3 times or over a week	20	20.0	40.0	40.0
一周 1~2 次 once or twice a week	56	17.9	44.6	37.5

4.纯果汁 / Pure Juice

● 北京 / Beijing

4-1 最近三个月饮用频率的比例/ Proportion of the Sample Consuming Pure Juice in the Last Three Months

	人数 Number	百分比 Percent
天天喝 daily	16	1.6
一周 3 次或以上 3 times or over a week	37	3.7
一周 1~2 次 once or twice a week	95	9.4
一个月 2～3 次 2 or 3 times a month	137	13.6
一个月 1 次 once a month	77	7.6
两个月 1 次 once two months	37	3.7
三个月 1 次或以下 once three months or below	63	6.2
没喝过 never	547	54.2

n=1009

4-2 最常用品牌排名/ Ranking of the Most Frequently Used Brands

排名 Brand Ranking	品牌 Brands	人数 Number	百分比 Percent
1	汇源 Huiyuan	217	48.1
2	大湖 Great Lakes	55	12.2
3	茹梦 Rougement	54	12.0
4	华邦 Huabang	34	7.5
5	都乐 Dole	19	4.2
6	华贝康橙 Huabei	18	4.0
7	大亨 Daheng	17	3.8
8	帕玛拉特 Parmalat	11	2.4

n=451

4-3 样本、男性各年龄层、女性各年龄层的常用品牌/ The Most Frequently Used Brands by the Whole Sample, Age and Gender Groups

	人数 Number	第一品牌及百分比 1st/ percent	第二品牌及百分比 2nd/ percent	第三品牌及百分比 3rd/ percent	第四品牌及百分比 4th/ percent
样本 Sample	451	**汇源 Huiyuan(48.1)**	**大湖 Great Lakes(12.2)**	**茹梦 Rougement(12.0)**	**华邦 Huabang(7.5)**
男性 Male	201	**汇源 Huiyuan(51.7)**	**茹梦 Rougement(10.0)** **大湖 Great Lakes(10.0)**	**华邦 Huabang(6.5)**	**都乐 Dole(5.0)**
16~24 岁 Age	47	汇源 Huiyuan(51.1)	大湖 Great Lakes(14.9)	都乐 Dole(10.6)	茹梦 Rougement(6.4)
25~34 岁 Age	66	汇源 Huiyuan(54.5)	大湖 Great Lakes(9.1)	华贝康橙 Huabei(7.6) 茹梦 Rougement(7.6)	华邦 Huabang(6.1) 都乐 Dole(6.1)
35~44 岁 Age	54	汇源 Huiyuan(57.4)	茹梦 Rougement(13.0)	大湖 Great Lakes(9.3)	华邦 Huabang(5.6)
45~54 岁 Age	21	汇源 Huiyuan(33.3)	华邦 Huabang(23.8)	大亨 Daheng(14.3)	茹梦 Rougement(9.5)
55~60 岁 Age	13	汇源 Huiyuan(46.2)	茹梦 Rougement(23.1)	大湖 Great Lakes(7.7) 大亨 Daheng(7.7) 华邦 Huabang(7.7)	
女性 Female	250	**汇源 Huiyuan(45.2)**	**大湖 Great Lakes(14.0)**	**茹梦 Rougement(13.6)**	**华邦 Huabang(8.4)**
16~24 岁 Age	58	汇源 Huiyuan(34.5)	茹梦 Rougement(19.0)	大湖 Great Lakes(13.8)	华邦 Huabang(8.6)
25~34 岁 Age	88	汇源 Huiyuan(45.5)	大湖 Great Lakes(14.8)	茹梦 Rougement(13.6)	华邦 Huabang(10.2)
35~44 岁 Age	59	汇源 Huiyuan(50.8)	茹梦 Rougement(11.9)	大湖 Great Lakes(8.5) 大亨 Daheng(8.5)	华贝康橙 Huabei(5.1) 华邦 Huabang(5.1)
45~54 岁 Age	35	汇源 Huiyuan(54.3)	大湖 Great Lakes(20.0)	茹梦 Rougement(8.6) 华邦 Huabang(8.6)	大亨 Daheng(5.7)
55~60 岁 Age	10	汇源 Huiyuan(40.0)	大湖 Great Lakes(20.0)	大亨 Daheng(10.0) 茹梦 Rougement(10.0) 华贝康橙 Huabei(10.0) 华邦 Huabang(10.0)	

4-4 理想品牌排名/ Ranking of the Ideal Brands

排名 Brand Ranking	品牌 Brands	人数 Number	百分比 Percent
1	汇源 Huiyuan	292	28.9
2	大湖 Great Lakes	69	6.8
3	茹梦 Rougement	66	6.5
4	华邦 Huabang	48	4.7
5	都乐 Dole	45	4.4
6	大亨 Daheng	22	2.2
7	华贝康橙 Huabei	11	1.1

n=1012

4-5 样本、男性各年龄层、女性各年龄层最近三个月有无购买的比例/ Purchasing in the Last Three Months by the Whole Sample, Age and Gender Groups

	人数 Number	买过 yes	没买过 no
样本 Sample	1011	38.7	61.3
男性 Male	504	32.1	67.9
16~24 岁 Age	105	31.4	68.6
25~34 岁 Age	151	37.1	62.9
35~44 岁 Age	131	35.9	64.1
45~54 岁 Age	77	23.4	76.6
55~60 岁 Age	40	20.0	80.0
女性 Female	507	45.2	54.8
16~24 岁 Age	108	43.5	56.5
25~34 岁 Age	149	55.7	44.3
35~44 岁 Age	124	46.8	53.2
45~54 岁 Age	84	36.9	63.1
55~60 岁 Age	42	23.8	76.2

4-6 样本、男性各年龄层、女性各年龄层最近三个月的饮用频率/ Frequencies of Consuming Pure Juice by the Whole Sample, Age and Gender Groups

	人数 Number	天天喝 daily	一周 3 次以上 3 times or over a week	一周 1~2 次 once or twice a week	一个月 2~3 次 2 or 3 times a month	一个月 1 次 once a month	两个月 1 次 once two months	三个月 1 次或以下 once three months or below	没喝过 never
样本 Sample	1009	1.6	3.7	9.4	13.6	7.6	3.7	6.2	54.2
男性 Male	503	1.4	2.2	9.1	10.5	8.3	3.4	5.8	59.2
16~24 岁 Age	104	2.9	2.9	7.7	9.6	9.6	6.7	5.8	54.8
25~34 岁 Age	151	1.3	2.6	7.9	13.2	9.9	4.0	6.6	54.3
35~44 岁 Age	131	0.8	2.3	16.8	6.9	9.2	0.8	5.3	58.0
45~54 岁 Age	77	0.0	1.3	2.6	10.4	3.9	2.6	6.5	72.7
55~60 岁 Age	40	2.5	0.0	5.0	15.0	5.0	2.5	2.5	67.5
女性 Female	506	1.8	5.1	9.7	16.6	6.9	4.0	6.7	49.2
16~24 岁 Age	106	0.0	5.7	9.4	20.8	7.5	4.7	7.5	44.3
25~34 岁 Age	150	0.7	6.7	15.3	19.3	8.0	4.0	6.7	39.3
35~44 岁 Age	124	3.2	4.8	9.7	12.1	4.8	5.6	8.9	50.8
45~54 岁 Age	84	3.6	3.6	3.6	15.5	8.3	2.4	6.0	57.1
55~60 岁 Age	42	2.4	2.4	2.4	11.9	4.8	0.0	0.0	76.2

4-7 样本、男性各年龄层、女性各年龄层的品牌习惯/ Brand Habit in Consuming Pure Juice by the Whole Sample, Age and Gender Groups

	人数 Number	基本固定饮用一个牌子 used in only one brand	比较固定地饮用两个或三个牌子 used in two or three brands	基本上不太固定牌子 no brand preference
样本 Sample	461	33.2	39.7	27.1
男性 Male	204	32.4	37.7	29.9
16~24 岁 Age	47	29.8	36.2	34.0
25~34 岁 Age	68	38.2	36.8	25.0
35~44 岁 Age	55	30.9	38.2	30.9
45~54 岁 Age	21	28.6	42.9	28.6
55~60 岁 Age	13	23.1	38.5	38.5
女性 Female	257	33.9	41.2	24.9
16~24 岁 Age	59	18.6	40.7	40.7
25~34 岁 Age	91	35.2	51.6	13.2
35~44 岁 Age	61	39.3	37.7	23.0
45~54 岁 Age	36	41.7	30.6	27.8
55~60 岁 Age	10	50.0	10.0	40.0

4-8 选择该类商品的考虑因素/ Ranking of the Considerations in Purchasing

注：本题为多选题，合计百分比超过 100%（Multiple answers）

排名 Ranking	考虑因素 Considerations	人次 Person-time	百分比 Percent
1	口味好 pleasant taste	307	66.5
2	有名的牌子 famous brand	149	32.3
3	价格适中 reasonable price	111	24.0
4	生产日期 date of producing	103	22.3
5	购买方便 easy to buy	55	11.9
6	单位发的 offered by the working unit	43	9.3
7	广告影响 influence of advertising	39	8.4
8	别人送的 given by other people	33	7.1
9	只是由于习惯 out of habit	19	4.1
10	包装吸引人 appealing package	18	3.9
11	朋友推荐 introduction of friends	16	3.5
12	有优惠条件 with preferential terms	9	1.9
13	其它 others	6	1.3
14	售货员介绍 introduced by the shop assistants	5	1.1

n=462

4-9 样本、男性各年龄层、女性各年龄层最常饮用的包装形式/ Types of Package of the Consumed Pure Juice by the Whole Sample, Age and Gender Groups

	人数 Number	纸盒 paper box	塑料瓶 plastic bottle	玻璃瓶 glass bottle	易开罐 tin	铝皮桶 aluminum cans	鲜棒 fresh milk	其它 others
样本 Sample	458	52.6	13.5	21.6	4.4	6.3	1.3	0.2
男性 Male	203	52.2	12.8	22.7	4.4	5.4	2.0	0.5
16~24 岁 Age	47	48.9	12.8	27.7	4.3	2.1	2.1	2.1
25~34 岁 Age	68	60.3	11.8	17.6	4.4	5.9	0.0	0.0
35~44 岁 Age	55	52.7	7.3	20.0	7.3	7.3	5.5	0.0
45~54 岁 Age	20	35.0	25.0	35.0	0.0	5.0	0.0	0.0
55~60 岁 Age	13	46.2	23.1	23.1	0.0	7.7	0.0	0.0
女性 Female	255	52.9	14.1	20.8	4.3	7.1	0.8	0.0
16~24 岁 Age	58	51.7	13.8	15.5	3.4	15.5	0.0	0.0
25~34 岁 Age	91	54.9	16.5	16.5	3.3	6.6	2.2	0.0
35~44 岁 Age	60	56.7	10.0	21.7	6.7	5.0	0.0	0.0
45~54 岁 Age	36	50.0	16.7	30.6	2.8	0.0	0.0	0.0
55~60 岁 Age	10	30.0	10.0	50.0	10.0	0.0	0.0	0.0

4-10 样本、男性各年龄层、女性各年龄层最常饮用场合/ Settings of Consumption by the Whole Sample, Age and Gender Groups

注：本题为多选题，合计百分比超过 100%（Multiple answers）

	人数 Number	平时口渴时 when thirsty	平时吃饭喝 at dinner	宴席、聚会喝 at banquet	外出、旅游时 outing/traveling	补充营养 supplementing nutrition	其它 others
样本 Sample	459	37.0	16.8	31.2	18.5	27.2	2.0
男性 Male	202	38.1	17.8	33.7	17.3	23.3	2.5
16~24 岁 Age	47	29.8	14.9	25.5	12.8	40.4	2.1
25~34 岁 Age	67	52.2	17.9	25.4	17.9	22.4	3.0
35~44 岁 Age	55	32.7	18.2	40.0	23.6	12.7	3.6
45~54 岁 Age	21	23.8	19.0	47.6	14.3	14.3	0.0
55~60 岁 Age	12	41.7	25.0	58.3	8.3	25.0	0.0
女性 Female	257	36.2	16.0	29.2	19.5	30.4	1.6
16~24 岁 Age	59	28.8	15.3	30.5	20.3	35.6	0.0
25~34 岁 Age	91	38.5	16.5	28.6	16.5	30.8	2.2
35~44 岁 Age	61	27.9	21.3	34.4	23.0	27.9	1.6
45~54 岁 Age	36	55.6	11.1	16.7	19.4	19.4	2.8
55~60 岁 Age	10	40.0	0.0	40.0	20.0	50.0	0.0

4-11 重度消费者人口分布/ Demographics of the Heavy Consumers

	人数 Number	16-24 岁 Age	25-34 岁 Age	35-44 岁 Age	45-54 岁 Age	55-60 岁 Age
样本 Sample	**148**	**20.3**	**35.1**	**32.4**	**8.1**	**4.1**
男性 Male	**64**	**21.9**	**28.1**	**40.6**	**4.7**	**4.7**
天天喝 daily	7	42.9	28.6	14.3	0.0	14.3
一周 3 次或以上 3 times or over a week	11	27.3	36.4	27.3	9.1	0.0
一周 1~2 次 once or twice a week	46	17.4	26.1	47.8	4.3	4.3
女性 Female	**84**	**19.0**	**40.5**	**26.2**	**10.7**	**3.6**
天天喝 daily	9	0.0	11.1	44.4	33.3	11.1
一周 3 次或以上 3 times or over a week	26	23.1	38.5	23.1	11.5	3.8
一周 1~2 次 once or twice a week	49	20.4	46.9	24.5	6.1	2.0

4-12 不同消费者层的常用品牌/ The Most Frequently Used Brands by Market Segments

4-12-1 时尚流行指标/ Fads Popular Index

	人数 Number	第一品牌及百分比 1st/ percent	第二品牌及百分比 2nd/ percent	第三品牌及百分比 3rd/ percent	第四品牌及百分比 4th/ percent
样本 Sample	**442**	**汇源 Huiyuan(48.2)**	**大湖 Great Lakes(12.2)**	**茹梦 Rougement(12.0)**	**华邦 Huabang(7.7)**
平实生活指向 simple living orientation	180	汇源 Huiyuan(50.6)	大湖 Great Lakes(12.8)	茹梦 Rougement(10.0)	华邦 Huabang(6.7)
时尚流行指向 fashion orientation	262	汇源 Huiyuan(46.6)	茹梦 Rougement(13.4)	大湖 Great Lakes(11.8)	华邦 Huabang(8.4)

4-12-2 广告态度指标/ Advertising Attitude Index

	人数 Number	第一品牌及百分比 1st/ percent	第二品牌及百分比 2nd/ percent	第三品牌及百分比 3rd/ percent	第四品牌及百分比 4th/ percent
样本 Sample	**441**	**汇源 Huiyuan(47.8)**	**大湖 Great Lakes(12.2) 茹梦 Rougement(12.2)**	**华邦 Huabang(7.5)**	**都乐 Dole(4.3)**
广告淡漠指向 indifferent orientation	116	汇源 Huiyuan(47.4)	茹梦 Rougement(12.9) 大湖 Great Lakes(12.9)	都乐 Dole(6.0)	华邦 Huabang(4.3) 大亨 Daheng(4.3)
中间层 medium	260	汇源 Huiyuan(46.9)	大湖 Great Lakes(13.5)	茹梦 Rougement(12.7)	华邦 Huabang(8.5)
信赖广告指向 loyal orientation	65	汇源 Huiyuan(52.3)	大亨 Daheng(9.2) 茹梦 Rougement(9.2) 华邦 Huabang(9.2)	大湖 Great Lakes(6.2) 华贝康橙 Huabei(6.2)	都乐 Dole(3.1)

4-12-3 饮食健康指标/ Foods & Drink Quality Index

	人数 Number	第一品牌及百分比 1st/ percent	第二品牌及百分比 2nd/ percent	第三品牌及百分比 3rd/ percent	第四品牌及百分比 4th/ percent
样本 Sample	**449**	**汇源 Huiyuan(47.9)**	**大湖 Great Lakes(12.2)**	**茹梦 Rougement(12.0)**	**华邦 Huabang(7.6)**
饮食“温饱”指向 "basic" orientation	110	汇源 Huiyuan(54.5)	大湖 Great Lakes(10.9)	茹梦 Rougement(9.1)	都乐 Dole(6.4)
中间层 medium	218	汇源 Huiyuan(48.2)	茹梦 Rougement(12.4)	大湖 Great Lakes(11.9)	华邦 Huabang(9.2)
健康营养指向 health & nutrition orientation	121	汇源 Huiyuan(41.3)	大湖 Great Lakes(14.0) 茹梦 Rougement(14.0)	华邦 Huabang(8.3)	大亨 Daheng(5.8) 华贝康橙 Huabei(5.8)

4-13 重度消费者的消费者层构成/ The Composition of the Heavy Consumers

4-13-1 时尚流行指标/ Fads Popular Index

	人数 Number	平实生活指向 simple living orientation	时尚流行指向 fashion orientation
样本 Sample	**148**	**41.2**	**58.8**
天天喝 daily	16	50.0	50.0
一周 3 次或以上 3 times or over a week	37	43.2	56.8
一周 1~2 次 once or twice a week	95	38.9	61.1

4-13-2 广告态度指标/ Advertising Attitude Index

	人数 Number	广告淡漠指向 indifferent orientation	中间层 medium	信赖广告指向 loyal orientation
样本 Sample	142	25.4	61.3	13.4
天天喝 daily	16	37.5	50.0	12.5
一周 3 次或以上 3 times or over a week	34	35.3	52.9	11.8
一周 1~2 次 once or twice a week	92	19.6	66.3	14.1

4-13-3 饮食健康指标/ Foods & Drink Quality Index

	人数 Number	饮食"温饱"指向 "basic" orientation	中间层 medium	健康营养指向 health & nutrition orientation
样本 Sample	148	20.3	46.6	33.1
天天喝 daily	16	18.8	31.3	50.0
一周 3 次或以上 3 times or over a week	37	32.4	29.7	37.8
一周 1~2 次 once or twice a week	95	15.8	55.8	28.4

● 上海 / Shanghai

4-1 最近三个月饮用频率的比例/ Proportion of the Sample Consuming Pure Juice in the Last Three Months

	人数 Number	百分比 Percent
天天喝 daily	7	0.7
一周 3 次或以上 3 times or over a week	26	2.6
一周 1~2 次 once or twice a week	72	7.1
一个月 2～3 次 2 or 3 times a month	129	12.7
一个月 1 次 once a month	69	6.8
两个月 1 次 once two months	36	3.6
三个月 1 次或以下 once three months or below	43	4.2
没喝过 never	632	62.3

n=1014

4-2 最常用品牌排名/ Ranking of the Most Frequently Used Brands

排名 Brand Ranking	品牌 Brands	人数 Number	百分比 Percent
1	三得利 Suntory	145	38.6
2	汇源 Huiyuan	70	18.6
3	麒麟 Kirin	57	15.2
4	都乐 Dole	42	11.2
5	大湖 Great Lakes	21	5.6
6	达能 Danone	11	2.9
7	金苹果 Gold Apple	7	1.9
8	大亨 Daheng	3	0.8
8	光明 Bright	3	0.8
8	帕玛拉特 Parmalat	3	0.8
9	茹梦 Rougement	2	0.5
9	华贝康橙 Huabei	2	0.5
9	碧泉 Crystal Spring	2	0.5

n=376

4-3 样本、男性各年龄层、女性各年龄层的常用品牌/ The Most Frequently Used Brands by the Whole Sample, Age and Gender Groups

	人数 Number	第一品牌及百分比 1st/ percent	第二品牌及百分比 2nd/ percent	第三品牌及百分比 3rd/ percent
样本 Sample	376	**三得利 Suntory(38.6)**	**汇源 Huiyuan(18.6)**	**麒麟 Kirin(15.2)**
男性 Male	171	**三得利 Suntory(35.7)**	**汇源 Huiyuan(18.7)**	**麒麟 Kirin(16.4)**
16~24 岁 Age	38	三得利 Suntory(34.2)	都乐 Dole(18.4) 麒麟 Kirin(18.4)	汇源 Huiyuan(15.8)
25~34 岁 Age	61	三得利 Suntory(36.1)	汇源 Huiyuan(25.2)	麒麟 Kirin(14.8)
35~44 岁 Age	41	三得利 Suntory(41.5)	麒麟 Kirin(14.6)	汇源 Huiyuan(12.2)
45~54 岁 Age	23	三得利 Suntory(30.4)	汇源 Huiyuan(17.4) 都乐 Dole(17.4)	麒麟 Kirin(13.0) 达能 Danone(13.0)
55~60 岁 Age	8	麒麟 Kirin(37.5)	三得利 Suntory(25.0)	汇源 Huiyuan(12.5) 三岛 Sandao(12.5) 金苹果 Gold Apple(12.5)
女性 Female	205	**三得利 Suntory(41.0)**	**汇源 Huiyuan(18.5)**	**麒麟 Kirin(14.1)**
16~24 岁 Age	59	三得利 Suntory(49.2)	汇源 Huiyuan(15.3)	麒麟 Kirin(13.6)
25~34 岁 Age	66	三得利 Suntory(36.4)	都乐 Dole(19.7)	麒麟 Kirin(15.2)
35~44 岁 Age	45	三得利 Suntory(35.6)	汇源 Huiyuan(24.4)	麒麟 Kirin(17.8)
45~54 岁 Age	21	三得利 Suntory(42.9)	汇源 Huiyuan(23.8)	大湖 Great Lakes(9.5) 麒麟 Kirin(9.5)
55~60 岁 Age	14	三得利 Suntory(42.9)	汇源 Huiyuan(35.7)	都乐 Dole(7.1) 麒麟 Kirin(7.1) 金苹果 Gold Apple(7.1)

4-4 理想品牌排名/ Ranking of the Ideal Brands

排名 Brand Ranking	品牌 Brands	人数 Number	百分比 Percent
1	三得利 Suntory	229	22.6
2	汇源 Huiyuan	161	15.9
3	都乐 Dole	108	10.7
4	麒麟 Kirin	69	6.8
5	大湖 Great Lakes	47	4.6
6	统一 President	38	3.7
7	光明 Bright	27	2.7
8	达能 Danone	11	1.1
9	大亨 Daheng	8	0.8
10	金苹果 Gold Apple	6	0.6

n=1014

4-5 样本、男性各年龄层、女性各年龄层最近三个月有无购买的比例/ Purchasing in the Last Three Months by the Whole Sample, Age and Gender Groups

	人数 Number	买过 yes	没买过 no
样本 Sample	1014	33.9	66.1
男性 Male	509	29.1	70.9
16~24 岁 Age	109	30.3	69.7
25~34 岁 Age	146	36.3	63.7
35~44 岁 Age	130	26.2	73.8
45~54 岁 Age	85	22.4	77.6
55~60 岁 Age	39	23.1	76.9
女性 Female	505	38.8	61.2
16~24 岁 Age	108	51.9	48.1
25~34 岁 Age	144	43.8	56.3
35~44 岁 Age	130	33.1	66.9
45~54 岁 Age	82	24.4	75.6
55~60 岁 Age	41	34.1	65.9

4-6 样本、男性各年龄层、女性各年龄层最近三个月的饮用频率/ Frequencies of Consuming Pure Juice by the Whole Sample, Age and Gender Groups

	人数 Number	天天喝 daily	一周3次或以上 3 times or over a week	一周1~2次 once or twice a week	一个月2~3次 2 or 3 times a month	一个月1次 once a month	两个月1次 once two months	三个月1次或以下 once three months or below	没喝过 never
样本 Sample	**1014**	**0.7**	**2.6**	**7.1**	**12.7**	**6.8**	**3.6**	**4.2**	**62.3**
男性 Male	**509**	**0.8**	**2.2**	**6.7**	**10.0**	**7.3**	**2.9**	**4.1**	**66.0**
16~24 岁 Age	109	1.8	1.8	6.4	9.2	10.1	2.8	2.8	65.1
25~34 岁 Age	146	0.7	2.1	7.5	13.0	8.2	3.4	7.5	57.5
35~44 岁 Age	130	0.8	2.3	7.7	9.2	6.2	2.3	3.8	67.7
45~54 岁 Age	85	0.0	2.4	4.7	8.2	4.7	4.7	2.4	72.9
55~60 岁 Age	39	0.0	2.6	5.1	7.7	5.1	0.0	0.0	79.5
女性 Female	**505**	**0.6**	**3.0**	**7.5**	**15.4**	**6.3**	**4.2**	**4.4**	**58.6**
16~24 岁 Age	108	0.0	4.6	12.0	22.2	5.6	5.6	4.6	45.4
25~34 岁 Age	144	1.4	3.5	5.6	20.1	7.6	3.5	5.6	52.8
35~44 岁 Age	130	0.0	1.5	9.2	12.3	4.6	4.6	3.1	64.6
45~54 岁 Age	82	1.2	2.4	3.7	7.3	4.9	3.7	3.7	73.2
55~60 岁 Age	41	0.0	2.4	4.9	7.3	12.2	2.4	4.9	65.9

4-7 样本、男性各年龄层、女性各年龄层的品牌习惯/ Brand Habit in Consuming Pure Juice by the Whole Sample, Age and Gender Groups

	人数 Number	基本固定饮用一个牌子 used in only one brand	比较固定地饮用两个或三个牌子 used in two or three brands	基本上不太固定牌子 no brand preference
样本 Sample	**381**	**39.1**	**37.8**	**23.1**
男性 Male	**173**	**36.4**	**38.7**	**24.9**
16~24 岁 Age	38	28.9	47.4	23.7
25~34 岁 Age	62	38.7	43.5	17.7
35~44 岁 Age	42	38.1	21.4	40.5
45~54 岁 Age	23	43.5	34.8	21.7
55~60 岁 Age	8	25.0	62.5	12.5
女性 Female	**208**	**41.3**	**37.0**	**21.6**
16~24 岁 Age	59	39.0	44.1	16.9
25~34 岁 Age	67	47.8	35.8	16.4
35~44 岁 Age	46	39.1	34.8	26.1
45~54 岁 Age	22	36.4	22.7	40.9
55~60 岁 Age	14	35.7	42.9	21.4

4-8 选择该类商品的考虑因素/ Ranking of the Considerations in Purchasing

注：本题为多选题，合计百分比超过 100%（Multiple answers）

排名 Ranking	考虑因素 Considerations	人次 Person-time	百分比 Percent
1	口味好 pleasant taste	261	68.5
2	有名的牌子 famous brand	121	31.8
3	价格适中 reasonable price	101	26.5
4	生产日期 date of producing	66	17.3
5	广告影响 influence of advertising	52	13.6
6	购买方便 easy to buy	48	12.6
7	有优惠条件 with preferential terms	23	6.0
8	包装吸引人 appealing package	15	3.9
8	别人送的 given by other people	15	3.9
8	只是由于习惯 out of habit	15	3.9
9	朋友推荐 introduction of friends	11	2.9
10	单位发的 offered by the working unit	9	2.4
11	其它 others	7	1.8
12	售货员介绍 introduced by the shop assistants	4	1.0

n=381

4-9 样本、男性各年龄层、女性各年龄层最常饮用的包装形式/ Package Types of the Consumed Pure Juice by the Whole Sample, Age and Gender Groups

	人数 Number	纸盒 paper box	塑料瓶 plastic bottle	玻璃瓶 glass bottle	易开罐 tin	铝皮桶 aluminum cans	鲜榨 fresh milk	其它 others
样本 Sample	**381**	**28.9**	**40.9**	**13.6**	**12.1**	**1.6**	**2.9**	**0.0**
男性 Male	**173**	**28.3**	**41.6**	**12.1**	**12.7**	**1.2**	**4.0**	**0.0**
16~24 岁 Age	38	28.9	36.8	10.5	13.4	0.0	5.3	0.0
25~34 岁 Age	62	30.6	38.7	16.1	3.1	0.0	6.5	0.0
35~44 岁 Age	42	21.4	47.6	9.5	14.3	4.8	2.4	0.0
45~54 岁 Age	23	34.8	47.8	8.7	3.7	0.0	0.0	0.0
55~60 岁 Age	8	25.0	37.5	12.5	25.0	0.0	0.0	0.0
女性 Female	**208**	**29.3**	**40.4**	**14.9**	**11.5**	**1.9**	**1.9**	**0.0**
16~24 岁 Age	59	28.8	44.1	8.5	13.6	3.4	1.7	0.0
25~34 岁 Age	67	25.4	41.8	20.9	10.4	0.0	1.5	0.0
35~44 岁 Age	46	39.1	39.1	10.9	10.9	0.0	0.0	0.0
45~54 岁 Age	22	22.7	36.4	22.7	9.1	4.5	4.5	0.0
55~60 岁 Age	14	28.6	28.6	14.3	14.3	7.1	7.1	0.0

4-10 样本、男性各年龄层、女性各年龄层最常饮用场合/ Settings of Consumption by the Whole Sample, Age and Gender Groups

注：本题为多选题，合计百分比超过 100%（Multiple answers）

	人数 Number	平时口渴时 when thirsty	平时吃饭喝 at dinner	宴席、聚会喝 at banquet	外出、旅游时 outing/traveling	补充营养 supplementing nutrition	其它 others
样本 Sample	**380**	**46.8**	**10.0**	**25.0**	**24.5**	**26.1**	**1.3**
男性 Male	**173**	**44.5**	**11.0**	**26.0**	**24.9**	**23.1**	**1.7**
16~24 岁 Age	38	44.7	10.5	13.2	26.3	34.2	2.6
25~34 岁 Age	62	45.2	8.1	30.6	16.1	24.2	3.2
35~44 岁 Age	42	50.0	14.3	26.2	31.0	14.3	0.0
45~54 岁 Age	23	34.8	8.7	30.4	39.1	17.4	0.0
55~60 岁 Age	8	37.5	25.0	37.5	12.5	25.0	0.0
女性 Female	**207**	**48.8**	**9.2**	**24.2**	**24.2**	**28.5**	**1.0**
16~24 岁 Age	59	54.2	6.8	15.3	27.1	25.4	1.7
25~34 岁 Age	67	55.2	9.0	22.4	23.9	28.4	1.5
35~44 岁 Age	46	43.5	8.7	28.3	23.9	28.3	0.0
45~54 岁 Age	21	28.6	23.8	33.3	14.3	38.1	0.0
55~60 岁 Age	14	42.9	0.0	42.9	28.6	28.6	0.0

4-11 重度消费者人口分布/ Demographics of the Heavy Consumers

	人数 Number	16-24 岁 Age	25-34 岁 Age	35-44 岁 Age	45-54 岁 Age	55-60 岁 Age
样本 Sample	**105**	**27.6**	**28.6**	**26.7**	**11.4**	**5.7**
男性 Male	**49**	**22.4**	**30.6**	**28.6**	**12.2**	**6.1**
天天喝 daily	4	50.0	25.0	25.0	0.0	0.0
一周 3 次或以上 3 times or over a week	11	18.2	27.3	27.3	18.2	9.1
一周 1~2 次 once or twice a week	34	20.6	32.4	29.4	11.8	5.9
女性 Female	**56**	**32.1**	**26.8**	**25.0**	**10.7**	**5.4**
天天喝 daily	3	0.0	66.7	0.0	33.3	0.0
一周 3 次或以上 3 times or over a week	15	33.3	33.3	13.3	13.3	6.7
一周 1~2 次 once or twice a week	38	34.2	21.1	31.6	7.9	5.3

4-12 不同消费者层的常用品牌/ The Most Frequently Used Brands by Market Segments

4-12-1 时尚流行指标/ Fads Popular Index

	人数 Number	第一品牌及百分比 1st/ percent	第二品牌及百分比 2nd/ percent	第三品牌及百分比 3rd/ percent	第四品牌及百分比 4th/ percent
样本 Sample	**373**	**三得利 Suntory(38.6)**	**汇源 Huiyuan(18.5)**	**麒麟 Kirin(15.3)**	**都乐 Dole(11.3)**
平实生活指向 simple living orientation	141	三得利 Suntory(41.1)	汇源 Huiyuan(21.3)	麒麟 Kirin(12.8)	都乐 Dole(9.2)
时尚流行指向 fashion orientation	232	三得利 Suntory(37.1)	麒麟 Kirin(16.8) 汇源 Huiyuan(16.8)	都乐 Dole(12.5)	大湖 Great Lakes(6.5)

4-12-2 广告态度指标/ Advertising Attitude Index

	人数 Number	第一品牌及百分比 1st/ percent	第二品牌及百分比 2nd/ percent	第三品牌及百分比 3rd/ percent	第四品牌及百分比 4th/ percent
样本 Sample	**371**	**三得利 Suntory(38.3)**	**汇源 Huiyuan(18.9)**	**麒麟 Kirin(15.4)**	**都乐 Dole(10.8)**
广告淡漠指向 indifferent orientation	84	三得利 Suntory(42.9)	汇源 Huiyuan(25.0)	麒麟 Kirin(10.7)	都乐 Dole(7.1)
中间层 medium	223	三得利 Suntory(39.0)	汇源 Huiyuan(18.4)	麒麟 Kirin(14.3)	都乐 Dole(13.0)
信赖广告指向 loyal orientation	64	三得利 Suntory(29.7)	麒麟 Kirin(25.0)	大湖 Great Lakes(14.1)	汇源 Huiyuan(12.5)

4-12-3 饮食健康指标/ Foods & Drink Quality Index

	人数 Number	第一品牌及百分比 1st/ percent	第二品牌及百分比 2nd/ percent	第三品牌及百分比 3rd/ percent	第四品牌及百分比 4th/ percent
样本 Sample	**374**	**三得利 Suntory(38.8)**	**汇源 Huiyuan(18.7)**	**麒麟 Kirin(15.0)**	**都乐 Dole(11.0)**
饮食"温饱"指向 "basic" orientation	66	三得利 Suntory(34.8)	汇源 Huiyuan(24.2)	麒麟 Kirin(15.2)	都乐 Dole(12.1)
中间层 medium	184	三得利 Suntory(41.8)	汇源 Huiyuan(18.5)	麒麟 Kirin(14.7)	都乐 Dole(10.9)
健康营养指向 health & nutrition orientation	124	三得利 Suntory(36.3)	汇源 Huiyuan(16.1)	麒麟 Kirin(15.3)	都乐 Dole(10.5)

4-13 重度消费者的消费者层构成/ The Composition of the Heavy Consumers

4-13-1 时尚流行指标/ Fads Popular Index

	人数 Number	平实生活指向 simple living orientation	时尚流行指向 fashion orientation
样本 Sample	**105**	**34.3**	**65.7**
天天喝 daily	7	14.3	85.7
一周 3 次或以上 3 times or over a week	26	30.8	69.2
一周 1~2 次 once or twice a week	72	37.5	62.5

4-13-2 广告态度指标/ Advertising Attitude Index

	人数 Number	广告淡漠指向 indifferent orientation	中间层 medium	信赖广告指向 loyal orientation
样本 Sample	**104**	**21.2**	**59.6**	**19.2**
天天喝 daily	7	14.3	57.1	28.6
一周 3 次或以上 3 times or over a week	26	19.2	57.7	23.1
一周 1~2 次 once or twice a week	71	22.5	60.6	16.9

4-13-3 饮食健康指标/ Foods & Drink Quality Index

	人数 Number	饮食"温饱"指向 "basic" orientation	中间层 medium	健康营养指向 health & nutrition orientation
样本 Sample	**105**	**17.1**	**46.7**	**36.2**
天天喝 daily	7	42.9	28.6	28.6
一周 3 次或以上 3 times or over a week	26	26.9	42.3	30.8
一周 1~2 次 once or twice a week	72	11.1	50.0	38.9

● 广州 / Guangzhou

4-1 最近三个月饮用频率的比例/ Proportion of the Sample Consuming Pure Juice in the Last Three Months

	人数 Number	百分比 Percent
天天喝 daily	8	0.8
一周 3 次或以上 3 times or over a week	13	1.3
一周 1~2 次 once or twice a week	44	4.3
一个月 2～3 次 2 or 3 times a month	76	7.4
一个月 1 次 once a month	43	4.2
两个月 1 次 once two months	29	2.8
三个月 1 次或以下 once three months or below	42	4.1
没喝过 never	774	75.2

n=1029

4-2 最常用品牌排名/ Ranking of the Most Frequently Used Brands

排名 Brand Ranking	品牌 Brands	人数 Number	百分比 Percent
1	晨光 Chenguang	59	23.4
2	碧泉 Crystal Spring	51	20.2
3	达能 Danone	39	15.5
4	都乐 Dole	20	7.9
4	汇源 Huiyuan	20	7.9
5	OJ	15	6.0

n=252

4-3 样本、男性各年龄层、女性各年龄层的常用品牌/ The Most Frequently Used Brands by the Whole Sample, Age and Gender Groups

	人数 Number	第一品牌及百分比 1st/ percent	第二品牌及百分比 2nd/ percent	第三品牌及百分比 3rd/ percent	第四品牌及百分比 4th/ percent
样本 Sample	252	**晨光 Chenguang(23.4)**	**碧泉 Crystal Spring(20.2)**	**达能 Danone(15.5)**	**都乐 Dole(7.9)** **汇源 Huiyuan(7.9)**
男性 Male	93	**晨光 Chenguang(24.7)**	**达能 Danone(17.2)**	**碧泉 Crystal Spring(16.1)**	**汇源 Huiyuan(9.7)**
16~24 岁 Age	30	OJ(23.3)	碧泉 Crystal Spring(16.7) 晨光 Chenguang(16.7)	汇源 Huiyuan(13.3) 达能 Danone(13.3)	都乐 Dole(6.7)
25~34 岁 Age	31	晨光 Chenguang(32.3)	达能 Danone(22.6)	碧泉 Crystal Spring(12.9)	都乐 Dole(9.7)
35~44 岁 Age	20	晨光 Chenguang(25.0)	达能 Danone(20.0)	汇源 Huiyuan(10.0) 碧泉 Crystal Spring(10.0)	都乐 Dole(5.0) 果汁先生(5.0) Guo Zhi Xian Sheng 百分百 100 Percent(5.0) 澳奇 Orchy(5.0) 金苹果 Gold Apple(5.0)
45~54 岁 Age	7	碧泉 Crystal Spring(57.1)	汇源 Huiyuan(14.3) 麒麟 Kirin(14.3) 晨光 Chenguang(14.3)		
55~60 岁 Age	5	晨光 Chenguang(40.0)	都乐 Dole(20.0) 达能 Danone(20.0) 美国特别好 S&W(20.0)		
女性 Female	159	**碧泉 Crystal Spring(22.6)** **晨光 Chenguang(22.6)**	**达能 Danone(14.5)**	**都乐 Dole(8.2)**	**汇源 Huiyuan(6.9)**
16~24 岁 Age	41	碧泉 Crystal Spring(29.3)	晨光 Chenguang(17.1)	达能 Danone(14.6)	OJ(9.8)
25~34 岁 Age	45	晨光 Chenguang(22.2)	碧泉 Crystal Spring(17.8)	都乐 Dole(13.3) 达能 Danone(13.3)	汇源 Huiyuan(6.7)
35~44 岁 Age	40	晨光 Chenguang(32.5)	碧泉 Crystal Spring(22.5)	达能 Danone(15.0)	汇源 Huiyuan(5.0)
45~54 岁 Age	27	碧泉 Crystal Spring(22.2)	达能 Danone(18.5) 晨光 Chenguang(18.5)	都乐 Dole(7.4) 汇源 Huiyuan(7.4)	汇源 Huiyuan(3.7) 绿飞 Lufei(3.7) 阳光 Sunshine(3.7) 新奇士 Sunkist(3.7) 阳公 Suncle(3.7) 旺仔 Wangzi(3.7)
55~60 岁 Age	6	汇源 Huiyuan(16.7) 大亨 Daheng(16.7) 都乐 Dole(16.7) 旺仔 Wangzi(16.7) Crystal Spring(16.7) 晨光 Chenguang(16.7)			

4-4 理想品牌排名/ Ranking of the Ideal Brands

排名 Brand Ranking	品牌 Brands	人数 Number	百分比 Percent
1	晨光 Chenguang	55	5.3
2	汇源 Huiyuan	53	5.1
3	新奇士 Sunkist	48	4.6
4	碧泉 Crystal Spring	48	4.6
5	达能 Danone	31	3.0
6	都乐 Dole	30	2.9
7	百分百 100 Percent	12	1.2
8	OJ	11	1.1
8	统一 Presidenrt	11	1.1

n=1034

4-5 样本、男性各年龄层、女性各年龄层最近三个月有无购买的比例/ Purchasing in the Last Three Months by the Whole Sample, Age and Gender Groups

	人数 Number	买过 yes	没买过 no
样本 Sample	1034	22.5	77.5
男性 Male	499	17.8	82.2
16~24 岁 Age	106	24.5	75.5
25~34 岁 Age	150	17.3	82.7
35~44 岁 Age	127	17.3	82.7
45~54 岁 Age	73	12.3	87.7
55~60 岁 Age	43	14.0	86.0
女性 Female	535	26.9	73.1
16~24 岁 Age	112	33.0	67.0
25~34 岁 Age	158	27.8	72.2
35~44 岁 Age	137	23.4	76.6
45~54 岁 Age	87	29.9	70.1
55~60 岁 Age	41	12.2	87.8

4-6 样本、男性各年龄层、女性各年龄层最近三个月的饮用频率/ Frequencies of Consuming Pure Juice by the Whole Sample, Age and Gender Groups

	人数 Number	天天喝 daily	一周 3 次或以上 3 times or over a week	一周 1~2 次 once or twice a week	一个月 2~3 次 2 or 3 times a month	一个月 1 次 once a month	两个月 1 次 once two months	三个月 1 次或以下 once three months or below	没喝过 never
样本 Sample	1029	0.8	1.3	4.3	7.4	4.2	2.8	4.1	75.2
男性 Male	496	0.6	0.6	3.2	5.6	4.0	1.6	3.4	80.8
16~24 岁 Age	106	0.9	1.9	3.8	6.6	7.5	2.8	4.7	71.7
25~34 岁 Age	150	0.0	0.0	4.0	6.7	4.0	1.3	4.7	79.3
35~44 岁 Age	126	1.6	0.0	4.0	4.8	3.2	0.0	3.2	83.3
45~54 岁 Age	72	0.0	1.4	0.0	4.2	1.4	2.8	1.4	88.9
55~60 岁 Age	42	0.0	0.0	2.4	4.8	2.4	2.4	0.0	88.1
女性 Female	533	0.9	1.9	5.3	9.0	4.3	3.9	4.7	70.0
16~24 岁 Age	112	0.9	0.9	6.3	10.7	5.4	6.3	7.1	62.5
25~34 岁 Age	157	0.0	1.3	6.4	10.8	4.5	2.5	3.2	71.3
35~44 岁 Age	137	2.2	2.9	3.6	5.1	4.4	5.1	5.8	70.8
45~54 岁 Age	86	1.2	2.3	5.8	11.6	4.7	2.3	3.5	68.6
55~60 岁 Age	41	0.0	2.4	2.4	4.9	0.0	2.4	2.4	85.4

4-7 样本、男性各年龄层、女性各年龄层的品牌习惯/ Brand Habit in Consuming Pure Juice by the Whole Sample, Age and Gender Groups

	人数 Number	基本固定饮用一个牌子 used in only one brand	比较固定地饮用两个或三个牌子 used in two or three brands	基本上不太固定牌子 no brand preference
样本 Sample	255	29.0	42.0	29.0
男性 Male	95	26.3	40.0	33.7
16~24 岁 Age	30	33.3	36.7	30.0
25~34 岁 Age	31	29.0	48.4	22.6
35~44 岁 Age	21	19.0	33.3	47.6
45~54 岁 Age	8	12.5	37.5	50.0
55~60 岁 Age	5	20.0	40.0	40.0
女性 Female	160	30.6	43.1	26.3
16~24 岁 Age	42	26.2	45.2	28.6
25~34 岁 Age	45	22.2	64.4	13.3
35~44 岁 Age	40	37.5	35.0	27.5
45~54 岁 Age	27	40.7	25.9	33.3
55~60 岁 Age	6	33.3	0.0	66.7

4-8 选择该类商品的考虑因素/ Ranking of the Considerations in Purchasing

注：本题为多选题，合计百分比超过 100%（Multiple answers）

排名 Ranking	考虑因素 Considerations	人次 Person-time	百分比 Percent
1	口味好 pleasant taste	168	65.9
2	价格适中 reasonable price	93	36.5
3	有名的牌子 famous brand	86	33.7
4	生产日期 date of producing	62	24.3
5	购买方便 easy to buy	47	18.4
6	广告影响 influence of advertising	18	7.1
7	有优惠条件 with preferential terms	15	5.9
7	朋友推荐 introduction of friends	15	5.9
8	包装吸引人 appealing package	12	4.7
9	别人送的 given by other people	10	3.9
10	只是由于习惯 out of habit	9	3.5
11	单位发的 offered by the working unit	3	1.2
12	其它 others	2	0.8
13	售货员介绍 introduced by the shop assistants	1	0.4

n=255

4-9 样本、男性各年龄层、女性各年龄层最常饮用的包装形式/ Package Types of the Consumed Pure Juice by the Whole Sample, Age and Gender Groups

	人数 Number	纸盒 paper box	塑料瓶 plastic bottle	玻璃瓶 glass bottle	易开罐 tin	铝皮桶 aluminum cans	鲜榨 fresh milk	其它 others
样本 Sample	**254**	**35.8**	**24.4**	**11.8**	**18.9**	**3.1**	**5.9**	**0.0**
男性 Male	**95**	**38.9**	**21.1**	**10.5**	**21.1**	**1.1**	**7.4**	**0.0**
16~24 岁 Age	30	26.7	16.7	10.0	33.3	3.3	10.0	0.0
25~34 岁 Age	31	48.4	19.4	12.9	12.9	0.0	6.5	0.0
35~44 岁 Age	21	38.1	33.3	9.5	9.5	0.0	9.5	0.0
45~54 岁 Age	8	62.5	12.5	0.0	25.0	0.0	0.0	0.0
55~60 岁 Age	5	20.0	20.0	20.0	40.0	0.0	0.0	0.0
女性 Female	**159**	**34.0**	**26.4**	**12.6**	**17.6**	**4.4**	**5.0**	**0.0**
16~24 岁 Age	41	48.8	26.8	4.9	9.8	7.3	2.4	0.0
25~34 岁 Age	45	28.9	22.2	15.6	22.2	6.7	4.4	0.0
35~44 岁 Age	40	32.5	22.5	17.5	17.5	0.0	10.0	0.0
45~54 岁 Age	27	22.2	33.3	11.1	25.9	3.7	3.7	0.0
55~60 岁 Age	6	33.3	50.0	16.7	0.0	0.0	0.0	0.0

4-10 样本、男性各年龄层、女性各年龄层最常饮用场合/ Settings of Consumption by the Whole Sample, Age and Gender Groups

注：本题为多选题，合计百分比超过 100%（Multiple answers）

	人数 Number	平时口渴时 when thirsty	平时吃饭喝 at dinner	宴席、聚会喝 at banquet	外出、旅游时 outing/traveling	补充营养 supplementing nutrition	其它 others
样本 Sample	**255**	**54.1**	**5.9**	**16.5**	**30.2**	**22.7**	**0.8**
男性 Male	**95**	**51.6**	**6.3**	**16.8**	**26.3**	**25.3**	**1.1**
16~24 岁 Age	30	36.7	6.7	23.3	23.3	33.3	3.3
25~34 岁 Age	31	64.5	6.5	16.1	25.8	22.6	0.0
35~44 岁 Age	21	47.6	4.8	19.0	38.1	14.3	0.0
45~54 岁 Age	8	62.5	12.5	0.0	25.0	12.5	0.0
55~60 岁 Age	5	60.0	0.0	0.0	0.0	60.0	0.0
女性 Female	**160**	**55.6**	**5.6**	**16.3**	**32.5**	**21.3**	**0.6**
16~24 岁 Age	42	61.9	0.0	2.4	42.9	23.8	0.0
25~34 岁 Age	45	55.6	4.4	11.1	33.3	28.9	0.0
35~44 岁 Age	40	50.0	12.5	20.0	27.5	17.5	2.5
45~54 岁 Age	27	55.6	0.0	37.0	29.6	14.8	0.0
55~60 岁 Age	6	50.0	33.3	33.3	0.0	0.0	0.0

4-11 重度消费者人口分布/ Demographics of the Heavy Consumers

	人数 Number	16-24 岁 Age	25-34 岁 Age	35-44 岁 Age	45-54 岁 Age	55-60 岁 Age
样本 Sample	65	24.6	27.7	29.2	13.8	4.6
男性 Male	22	31.8	27.3	31.8	4.5	4.5
天天喝 daily	3	33.3	0.0	66.7	0.0	0.0
一周 3 次或以上 3 times or over a week	3	66.7	0.0	0.0	33.3	0.0
一周 1~2 次 once or twice a week	16	25.0	37.5	31.3	0.0	6.3
女性 Female	43	20.9	27.9	27.9	18.6	4.7
天天喝 daily	5	20.0	0.0	60.0	20.0	0.0
一周 3 次或以上 3 times or over a week	10	10.0	20.0	40.0	20.0	10.0
一周 1~2 次 once or twice a week	28	25.0	35.7	17.9	17.9	3.6

4-12 不同消费者层的常用品牌/ The Most Frequently Used Brands by Market Segments

4-12-1 时尚流行指标/ Fads Popular Index

	人数 Number	第一品牌及百分比 1st/ percent	第二品牌及百分比 2nd/ percent	第三品牌及百分比 3rd/ percent	第四品牌及百分比 4th/ percent
样本 Sample	249	**晨光 Chenguang(22.9)**	**碧泉 Crystal Spring(20.5)**	**达能 Danone(15.7)**	**汇源 Huiyuan(8.0)**
平实生活指向 simple living orientation	107	晨光 Chenguang(25.2)	碧泉 Crystal Spring(18.7)	达能 Danone(15.0)	汇源 Huiyuan(11.2)
时尚流行指向 fashion orientation	142	碧泉 Crystal Spring(21.8)	晨光 Chenguang(21.1)	达能 Danone(16.2)	OJ(9.9)

4-12-2 广告态度指标/ Advertising Attitude Index

	人数 Number	第一品牌及百分比 1st/ percent	第二品牌及百分比 2nd/ percent	第三品牌及百分比 3rd/ percent	第四品牌及百分比 4th/ percent
样本 Sample	247	**晨光 Chenguang(23.9)**	**碧泉 Crystal Spring(20.2)**	**达能 Danone(15.0)**	**都乐 Dole(8.1)** **汇源 Huiyuan(8.1)**
广告淡漠指向 indifferent orientation	69	晨光 Chenguang(21.7)	碧泉 Crystal Spring(20.3)	汇源 Huiyuan(13.0) 达能 Danone(13.0)	都乐 Dole(5.8) 金苹果 Gold Apple(5.8)
中间层 medium	147	晨光 Chenguang(26.5)	碧泉 Crystal Spring(19.7)	达能 Danone(15.6)	都乐 Dole(8.2)
信赖广告指向 loyal orientation	31	碧泉 Crystal Spring(22.6)	晨光 Chenguang(16.1) 达能 Danone(16.1)	都乐 Dole(12.9)	OJ(9.7)

4-12-3 饮食健康指标/ Foods & Drink Quality Index

	人数 Number	第一品牌及百分比 1st/ percent	第二品牌及百分比 2nd/ percent	第三品牌及百分比 3rd/ percent	第四品牌及百分比 4th/ percent
样本 Sample	252	**晨光 Chenguang(23.4)**	**碧泉 Crystal Spring(20.2)**	**达能 Danone(15.5)**	**都乐 Dole(7.9)** **汇源 Huiyuan(7.9)**
饮食"温饱"指向 "basic" orientation	47	晨光 Chenguang(27.7)	碧泉 Crystal Spring(21.3)	达能 Danone(12.8)	汇源 Huiyuan(10.6)
中间层 medium	145	晨光 Chenguang(22.8)	碧泉 Crystal Spring(19.3)	达能 Danone(15.2)	都乐 Dole(9.7)
健康营养指向 health & nutrition orientation	60	碧泉 Crystal Spring(21.7) 晨光 Chenguang(21.7)	达能 Danone(18.3)	汇源 Huiyuan(8.3) 都乐 Dole(8.3)	OJ(5.0)

4-13 重度消费者的消费者层构成/ The Composition of the Heavy Consumers

4-13-1 时尚流行指标/ Fads Popular Index

	人数 Number	平实生活指向 simple living orientation	时尚流行指向 fashion orientation
样本 Sample	64	45.3	54.7
天天喝 daily	8	62.5	37.5
一周 3 次或以上 3 times or over a week	12	33.3	66.7
一周 1~2 次 once or twice a week	44	45.5	54.5

4-13-2 广告态度指标/ Advertising Attitude Index

	人数 Number	广告淡漠指向 indifferent orientation	中间层 medium	信赖广告指向 loyal orientation
样本 Sample	**65**	**27.7**	**65.2**	**6.2**
天天喝 daily	8	25.0	62.5	12.5
一周 3 次或以上 3 times or over a week	13	23.1	61.5	15.4
一周 1~2 次 once or twice a week	44	29.5	68.2	2.3

4-13-3 饮食健康指标/ Foods & Drink Quality Index

	人数 Number	饮食"温饱"指向 "basic" orientation	中间层 medium	健康营养指向 health & nutrition orientation
样本 Sample	**65**	**16.9**	**53.8**	**29.2**
天天喝 daily	8	25.0	50.0	25.0
一周 3 次或以上 3 times or over a week	13	7.7	53.8	38.5
一周 1~2 次 once or twice a week	44	18.2	54.5	27.3

● 重庆 / Chongqing

4-1 最近三个月饮用频率的比例/ Proportion of the Sample Consuming Pure Juice in the Last Three Months

	人数 Number	百分比 Percent
天天喝 daily	5	0.8
一周 3 次或以上 3 times or over a week	12	1.9
一周 1~2 次 once or twice a week	22	3.5
一个月 2～3 次 2 or 3 times a month	23	3.7
一个月 1 次 once a month	22	3.5
两个月 1 次 once two months	7	1.1
三个月 1 次或以下 once three months or below	27	4.3
没喝过 never	506	81.1

n=624

4-2 最常用品牌排名/ Ranking of the Most Frequently Used Brands

排名 Brand Ranking	品牌 Brands	人数 Number	百分比 Percent
1	汇源 Huiyuan	63	53.4
2	旺仔 Wangzi	13	11.0
3	茹梦 Rougement	6	5.1
4	大亨 Daheng	4	3.4
5	麒麟 Kirin	3	2.5
5	荣氏 Rong	3	2.5
5	卡夫天美 Kraft	3	2.5
5	都乐 Dole	3	2.5
6	阳公 Suncle	2	1.7
6	华贝康橙 Huabei	2	1.7
6	金苹果 Gold Apple	2	1.7
6	美国特别好 S&W	2	1.7

n=118

4-3 样本、男性各年龄层、女性各年龄层的常用品牌/ The Most Frequently Used Brands by the Whole Sample, Age and Gender Groups

	人数 Number	第一品牌及百分比 1st/ percent	第二品牌及百分比 2nd/ percent	第三品牌及百分比 3rd/ percent
样本 Sample	118	**汇源 Huiyuan(53.4)**	**旺仔 Wangzi(11.0)**	**茹梦 Rougement(5.1)**
男性 Male	50	**汇源 Huiyuan(56.0)**	**旺仔 Wangzi(10.0)**	**荣氏 Rong(4.0)** **卡夫天美 Kraft(4.0)** **茹梦 Rougement(4.0)** **大亨 Daheng(4.0)**
16~24 岁 Age	12	汇源 Huiyuan(75.0)	麒麟 Kirin(8.3) 美国特别好 S&W(8.3) 美年达 Mirinda(8.3)	
25~34 岁 Age	22	汇源 Huiyuan(45.5)	茹梦 Rougement(9.1) 荣氏 Rong(9.1)	大亨 Daheng(4.5) 旺仔 Wangzi(4.5) 华贝康橙 Huabei(4.5) 三得利 Suntory(4.5) 阳公 Suncle(4.5) 碧泉 Crystal Spring(4.5)
35~44 岁 Age	10	汇源 Huiyuan(60.0)	卡夫天美 Kraft(20.0)	大亨 Daheng(10.0) 旺仔 Wangzi(10.0)
45~54 岁 Age	4	汇源 Huiyuan(50.0) 旺仔 Wangzi(50.0)		
55~60 岁 Age	2	汇源 Huiyuan(50.0) 旺仔 Wangzi(50.0)		
女性 Female	68	**汇源 Huiyuan(51.5)**	**旺仔 Wangzi(11.8)**	**茹梦 Rougement(5.9)**
16~24 岁 Age	19	汇源 Huiyuan(63.2)	都乐 Dole(15.8) 旺仔 Wangzi(15.8)	麒麟 Kirin(5.3)
25~34 岁 Age	25	汇源 Huiyuan(60.0)	茹梦 Rougement(12.0)	旺仔 Wangzi(8.0)
35~44 岁 Age	15	汇源 Huiyuan(26.7)	旺仔 Wangzi(20.0)	茹梦 Rougement(6.7) 华贝康橙 Huabei(6.7) 麒麟 Kirin(6.7) 皇牌 Joker(6.7) 阳公 Suncle(6.7) 帕玛拉特 Parmalat(6.7) 美国特别好 S&W(6.7) 美国卡夫 MeiGuo KaFu (6.7)
45~54 岁 Age	6	汇源 Huiyuan(33.3)	大亨 Daheng(16.7) 金苹果 Gold Apple(16.7) 荣氏 Rong(16.7) 卡夫天美 Kraft(16.7)	
55~60 岁 Age	3	汇源 Huiyuan(66.7)		

4-4 理想品牌排名/ Ranking of the Ideal Brands

排名 Brand Ranking	品牌 Brands	人数 Number	百分比 Percent
1	汇源 Huiyuan	171	27.4
2	旺仔 Wangzi	15	2.4
3	茹梦 Rougement	11	1.8
4	雀巢 Nestle	10	1.6
5	金苹果 Gold Apple	8	1.3
6	阳公 Suncle	7	1.1
7	大亨 Daheng	6	1.0
7	统一 President	6	1.0
8	都乐 Dole	5	0.8
8	荣氏 Rong	5	0.8
9	卡夫天美 Kraft	3	0.5

n=624

4-5 样本、男性各年龄层、女性各年龄层最近三个月有无购买的比例/ Purchasing in the Last Three Months by the Whole Sample, Age and Gender Groups

	人数 Number	买过 yes	没买过 no
样本 Sample	624	17.6	82.4
男性 Male	314	15.6	84.4
16~24 岁 Age	64	15.6	84.4
25~34 岁 Age	93	23.7	76.3
35~44 岁 Age	75	12.0	88.0
45~54 岁 Age	54	11.1	88.9
55~60 岁 Age	28	7.1	92.9
女性 Female	310	19.7	80.3
16~24 岁 Age	64	26.6	73.4
25~34 岁 Age	90	24.4	75.6
35~44 岁 Age	73	20.5	79.5
45~54 岁 Age	60	6.7	93.3
55~60 岁 Age	23	13.0	87.0

4-6 样本、男性各年龄层、女性各年龄层最近三个月的饮用频率/ Frequencies of Consuming Pure Juice by the Whole Sample, Age and Gender Groups

	人数 Number	天天喝 daily	一周 3 次或以上 3 times or over a week	一周 1~2 次 once or twice a week	一个月 2~3 次 2 or 3 times a month	一个月 1 次 once a month	两个月 1 次 once two months	三个月 1 次或以下 once three months or below	没喝过 never
样本 Sample	624	0.8	1.9	3.5	3.7	3.5	1.1	4.3	81.1
男性 Male	314	0.3	1.6	3.2	4.5	2.5	1.3	2.5	84.1
16~24 岁 Age	64	1.6	0.0	6.3	4.7	1.6	3.1	1.6	81.3
25~34 岁 Age	93	0.0	2.2	2.2	8.6	5.4	2.2	3.2	76.3
35~44 岁 Age	75	0.0	1.3	5.3	1.3	2.7	0.0	2.7	86.7
45~54 岁 Age	54	0.0	3.7	0.0	1.9	0.0	0.0	1.9	92.6
55~60 岁 Age	28	0.0	0.0	0.0	3.6	0.0	0.0	3.6	92.9
女性 Female	310	1.3	2.3	3.9	2.9	4.5	1.0	6.1	78.1
16~24 岁 Age	64	0.0	1.6	7.8	3.1	1.6	1.6	14.1	70.3
25~34 岁 Age	90	1.1	3.3	2.2	6.7	4.4	2.2	7.8	72.2
35~44 岁 Age	73	2.7	2.7	2.7	0.0	9.6	0.0	2.7	79.5
45~54 岁 Age	60	0.0	0.0	5.0	1.7	3.3	0.0	0.0	90.0
55~60 岁 Age	23	4.3	4.3	0.0	0.0	0.0	0.0	4.3	87.0

4-7 样本、男性各年龄层、女性各年龄层的品牌习惯/ Brand Habit in Consuming Pure Juice by the Whole Sample, Age and Gender Groups

	人数 Number	基本固定饮用一个牌子 used in only one brand	比较固定地饮用两个或三个牌子 used in two or three brands	基本上不太固定牌子 no brand preference
样本 Sample	118	33.9	28.8	37.3
男性 Male	50	40.0	24.0	36.0
16~24 岁 Age	12	58.3	8.3	33.3
25~34 岁 Age	22	31.8	22.7	45.5
35~44 岁 Age	10	40.0	40.0	20.0
45~54 岁 Age	4	25.0	50.0	25.0
55~60 岁 Age	2	50.0	0.0	50.0
女性 Female	68	29.4	32.4	38.2
16~24 岁 Age	19	21.1	36.8	42.1
25~34 岁 Age	25	36.0	32.0	32.0
35~44 岁 Age	15	20.0	40.0	40.0
45~54 岁 Age	6	50.0	0.0	50.0
55~60 岁 Age	3	33.3	33.3	33.3

4-8 选择该类商品的考虑因素/ Ranking of the Considerations in Purchasing

注：本题为多选题，合计百分比超过 100%（Multiple answers）

排名 Ranking	考虑因素 Considerations	人次 Person-time	百分比 Percent
1	口味好 pleasant taste	78	66.1
2	价格适中 reasonable price	32	27.1
3	生产日期 date of producing	27	22.9
4	有名的牌子 famous brand	23	19.5
5	广告影响 influence of advertising	18	15.3
6	购买方便 easy to buy	14	11.9
7	单位发的 offered by the working unit	6	5.1
7	只是由于习惯 out of habit	6	5.1
8	朋友推荐 introduction of friends	4	3.4
8	别人送的 given by other people	4	3.4
9	包装吸引人 appealing package	3	2.5
10	售货员介绍 introduced by the shop assistants	2	1.7
10	其它 others	2	1.7
11	有优惠条件 with preferential terms	1	0.8

n=118

4-9 样本、男性各年龄层、女性各年龄层最常饮用的包装形式/ Package Types of the Consumed Pure Juice by the Whole Sample, Age and Gender Groups

	人数 Number	纸盒 paper box	塑料瓶 plastic bottle	玻璃瓶 glass bottle	易开罐 tin	铝皮桶 aluminum cans	鲜榨 fresh milk	其它 others
样本 Sample	**118**	**31.4**	**20.3**	**24.6**	**10.2**	**6.8**	**4.2**	**2.5**
男性 Male	**50**	**30.0**	**28.0**	**18.0**	**12.0**	**6.0**	**2.0**	**4.0**
16~24 岁 Age	12	33.3	16.7	25.0	16.7	8.3	0.0	0.0
25~34 岁 Age	22	36.4	22.7	22.7	9.1	9.1	0.0	0.0
35~44 岁 Age	10	30.0	30.0	10.0	10.0	0.0	0.0	20.0
45~54 岁 Age	4	0.0	50.0	0.0	25.0	0.0	25.0	0.0
55~60 岁 Age	2	0.0	100.0	0.0	0.0	0.0	0.0	0.0
女性 Female	**68**	**32.4**	**14.7**	**29.4**	**8.8**	**7.4**	**5.9**	**1.5**
16~24 岁 Age	19	31.6	15.8	21.1	10.5	10.5	10.5	0.0
25~34 岁 Age	25	44.0	8.0	40.0	4.0	4.0	0.0	0.0
35~44 岁 Age	15	20.0	13.3	33.3	13.3	13.3	6.7	0.0
45~54 岁 Age	6	16.7	16.7	16.7	16.7	0.0	16.7	16.7
55~60 岁 Age	3	33.3	66.7	0.0	0.0	0.0	0.0	0.0

4-10 样本、男性各年龄层、女性各年龄层最常饮用场合/ Settings of Consumption by the Whole Sample, Age and Gender Groups

注：本题为多选题，合计百分比超过 100%（Multiple answers）

	人数 Number	平时口渴时 when thirsty	平时吃饭喝 at dinner	宴席、聚会喝 at banquet	外出、旅游时 outing/traveling	补充营养 supplementing nutrition	其它 others
样本 Sample	**118**	**56.8**	**9.3**	**22.0**	**21.2**	**22.0**	**1.7**
男性 Male	**50**	**56.0**	**10.0**	**16.0**	**26.0**	**20.0**	**0.0**
16~24 岁 Age	12	58.3	16.7	25.0	8.3	16.7	0.0
25~34 岁 Age	22	40.9	13.6	13.6	31.8	22.7	0.0
35~44 岁 Age	10	80.0	0.0	10.0	40.0	30.0	0.0
45~54 岁 Age	4	50.0	0.0	25.0	25.0	0.0	0.0
55~60 岁 Age	2	100.0	0.0	0.0	0.0	0.0	0.0
女性 Female	**68**	**57.4**	**8.8**	**26.5**	**17.6**	**23.5**	**2.9**
16~24 岁 Age	19	36.8	5.3	21.1	15.8	42.1	5.3
25~34 岁 Age	25	64.0	8.0	20.0	32.0	20.0	0.0
35~44 岁 Age	15	66.7	13.3	26.7	6.7	20.0	0.0
45~54 岁 Age	6	66.7	0.0	66.7	0.0	0.0	16.7
55~60 岁 Age	3	66.7	33.3	33.3	0.0	0.0	0.0

4-11 重度消费者人口分布/ Demographics of the Heavy Consumers

	人数 Number	16-24 岁 Age	25-34 岁 Age	35-44 岁 Age	45-54 岁 Age	55-60 岁 Age
样本 Sample	39	28.2	25.6	28.2	12.8	5.1
男性 Male	16	31.3	25.0	31.3	12.5	0.0
天天喝 daily	1	100.0	0.0	0.0	0.0	0.0
一周 3 次或以上 3 times or over a week	5	0.0	40.0	20.0	40.0	0.0
一周 1~2 次 once or twice a week	10	40.0	20.0	40.0	0.0	0.0
女性 Female	23	26.1	26.1	26.1	13.0	8.7
天天喝 daily	4	0.0	25.0	50.0	0.0	25.0
一周 3 次或以上 3 times or over a week	7	14.3	42.9	28.6	0.0	14.3
一周 1~2 次 once or twice a week	12	41.7	16.7	16.7	25.0	0.0

4-12 不同消费者层的常用品牌/ The Most Frequently Used Brands by Market Segments

4-12-1 时尚流行指标/ Fads Popular Index

	人数 Number	第一品牌及百分比 1st/ percent	第二品牌及百分比 2nd/ percent	第三品牌及百分比 3rd/ percent
样本 Sample	114	**汇源 Huiyuan(52.6)**	**旺仔 Wangzi(11.4)**	**茹梦 Rougement(5.3)**
平实生活指向 simple living orientation	51	汇源 Huiyuan(45.1)	旺仔 Wangzi(13.7)	大亨 Daheng(5.9) 茹梦 Rougement(5.9)
时尚流行指向 fashion orientation	63	汇源 Huiyuan(58.7)	旺仔 Wangzi(9.5)	茹梦 Rougement(4.8)

4-12-2 广告态度指标/ Advertising Attitude Index

	人数 Number	第一品牌及百分比 1st/ percent	第二品牌及百分比 2nd/ percent	第三品牌及百分比 3rd/ percent
样本 Sample	116	**汇源 Huiyuan(53.4)**	**旺仔 Wangzi(11.2)**	**茹梦 Rougement(5.2)**
广告淡漠指向 indifferent orientation	32	汇源 Huiyuan(56.3)	旺仔 Wangzi(9.4) 卡夫天美 Kraft(9.4)	茹梦 Rougement(3.1) 皇牌 Joker(3.1) 大亨 Daheng(3.1) 百分百 100 Percent(3.1) 晨光 Chenguang(3.1) 荣氏 Rong(3.1) 美年达 Mirinda(3.1) 阳公 Suncle(3.1)
中间层 medium	69	汇源 Huiyuan(55.1)	旺仔 Wangzi(11.6)	茹梦 Rougement(7.2)
信赖广告指向 loyal orientation	15	汇源 Huiyuan(40.0)	都乐 Dole(13.3) 旺仔 Wangzi(13.3)	华贝康橙 Huabei(6.7) 麒麟 Kirin(6.7) 美国特别好 S&W(6.7)

4-12-3 饮食健康指标/ Foods & Drink Quality Index

	人数 Number	第一品牌及百分比 1st/ percent	第二品牌及百分比 2nd/ percent	第三品牌及百分比 3rd/ percent
样本 Sample	117	**汇源 Huiyuan(53.0)**	**旺仔 Wangzi(11.1)**	**茹梦 Rougement(5.1)**
饮食"温饱"指向 "basic" orientation	35	汇源 Huiyuan(57.1)	旺仔 Wangzi(11.4)	荣氏 Rong(5.7) 卡夫天美 Kraft (5.7)
中间层 medium	55	汇源 Huiyuan(52.7)	旺仔 Wangzi(9.1)	大亨 Daheng(5.5) 茹梦 Rougement(5.5)
健康营养指向 health & nutrition orientation	27	汇源 Huiyuan(48.1)	旺仔 Wangzi(14.8)	都乐 Dole(11.1)

4-13 重度消费者的消费者层构成/ The Composition of the Heavy Consumers

4-13-1 时尚流行指标/ Fads Popular Index

	人数 Number	平实生活指向 simple living orientation	时尚流行指向 fashion orientation
样本 Sample	38	57.9	42.1
天天喝 daily	5	60.0	40.0
一周 3 次或以上 3 times or over a week	11	72.7	27.3
一周 1~2 次 once or twice a week	22	50.0	50.0

4-13-2 广告态度指标/ Advertising Attitude Index

	人数 Number	广告淡漠指向 indifferent orientation	中间层 medium	信赖广告指向 loyal orientation
样本 Sample	39	41.0	51.3	7.7
天天喝 daily	5	0.0	80.0	20.0
一周 3 次或以上 3 times or over a week	12	66.7	25.0	8.3
一周 1~2 次 once or twice a week	22	36.4	59.1	4.5

4-13-3 饮食健康指标/ Foods & Drink Quality Index

	人数 Number	饮食"温饱"指向 "basic" orientation	中间层 medium	健康营养指向 health & nutrition orientation
样本 Sample	39	38.5	35.9	25.6
天天喝 daily	5	0.0	80.0	20.0
一周 3 次或以上 3 times or over a week	12	58.3	16.7	25.0
一周 1~2 次 once or twice a week	22	36.4	36.4	27.3

● 武汉 / Wuhan

4-1 最近三个月饮用频率的比例/ Proportion of the Sample Consuming Pure Juice in the Last Three Months

	人数 Number	百分比 Percent
天天喝 daily	0	0.0
一周 3 次或以上 3 times or over a week	14	2.2
一周 1~2 次 once or twice a week	17	2.6
一个月 2～3 次 2 or 3 times a month	39	6.1
一个月 1 次 once a month	35	5.5
两个月 1 次 once two months	25	3.9
三个月 1 次或以下 once three months or below	42	6.5
没喝过 never	470	73.2

n=642

4-2 最常用品牌排名/ Ranking of the Most Frequently Used Brands

排名 Brand Ranking	品牌 Brands	人数 Number	百分比 Percent
1	汇源 Huiyuan	68	39.8
2	茹梦 Rougement	43	25.1
3	金苹果 Gold Apple	22	12.9
4	旺仔 Wangzi	12	7.0
5	都乐 Dole	7	4.1
6	大湖 Great Lakes	4	2.3

n=171

4-3 样本、男性各年龄层、女性各年龄层的常用品牌/ The Most Frequently Used Brands by the Whole Sample, Age and Gender Groups

	人数 Number	第一品牌及百分比 1st/ percent	第二品牌及百分比 2nd/ percent	第三品牌及百分比 3rd/ percent
样本 Sample	171	**汇源 Huiyuan(39.8)**	**茹梦 Rougement(25.1)**	**金苹果 Gold Apple(12.9)**
男性 Male	67	**汇源 Huiyuan(34.3)**	**茹梦 Rougement(29.9)**	**金苹果 Gold Apple(16.4)**
16~24 岁 Age	19	汇源 Huiyuan(26.3) 茹梦 Rougement(26.3)	金苹果 Gold Apple(21.1)	旺仔 Wangzi(10.5)
25~34 岁 Age	26	汇源 Huiyuan(38.5)	茹梦 Rougement(26.9)	金苹果 Gold Apple(15.4)
35~44 岁 Age	13	汇源 Huiyuan(38.5)	茹梦 Rougement(23.1) 金苹果 Gold Apple(23.1)	旺仔 Wangzi(7.7) 碧泉 Crystal Spring(7.7)
45~54 岁 Age	6	汇源 Huiyuan(50.0) 茹梦 Rougement(50.0)		
55~60 岁 Age	3	茹梦 Rougement(66.7)		
女性 Female	104	**汇源 Huiyuan(43.3)**	**茹梦 Rougement(22.1)**	**金苹果 Gold Apple(10.6)**
16~24 岁 Age	32	汇源 Huiyuan(43.8)	茹梦 Rougement(18.8) 金苹果 Gold Apple(18.8)	旺仔 Wangzi(6.3)
25~34 岁 Age	36	汇源 Huiyuan(41.7)	茹梦 Rougement(16.7)	旺仔 Wangzi(11.1)
35~44 岁 Age	18	茹梦 Rougement(44.4)	汇源 Huiyuan(38.9)	大湖 Great Lakes(5.6) 华邦 Huabang(5.6)
45~54 岁 Age	18	汇源 Huiyuan(50.0)	茹梦 Rougement(16.7)	都乐 Dole(11.1) 金苹果 Gold Apple(11.1)
55~60 岁 Age	0			

4-4 理想品牌排名/ Ranking of the Ideal Brands

排名 Brand Ranking	品牌 Brands	人数 Number	百分比 Percent
1	汇源 Huiyuan	120	18.7
2	茹梦 Rougement	41	6.4
3	金苹果 Gold Apple	16	2.5
4	大湖 Great Lakes	10	1.6
5	绿之源 Lvzhiyuan	7	1.1
6	都乐 Dole	6	0.9
7	旺仔 Wangzi	5	0.8
8	华邦 Huabang	4	0.6

n=642

4-5 样本、男性各年龄层、女性各年龄层最近三个月有无购买的比例/ Purchasing in the Last Three Months by the Whole Sample, Age and Gender Groups

	人数 Number	买过 yes	没买过 no
样本 Sample	642	23.2	76.8
男性 Male	311	19.0	81.0
16~24 岁 Age	65	20.0	80.0
25~34 岁 Age	89	24.7	75.3
35~44 岁 Age	80	18.8	81.3
45~54 岁 Age	52	13.5	86.5
55~60 岁 Age	25	8.0	92.0
女性 Female	331	27.2	72.8
16~24 岁 Age	69	34.8	65.2
25~34 岁 Age	96	32.3	67.7
35~44 岁 Age	78	21.8	78.2
45~54 岁 Age	62	27.4	72.6
55~60 岁 Age	26	3.8	96.2

4-6 样本、男性各年龄层、女性各年龄层最近三个月的饮用频率/ Frequencies of Consuming Pure Juice by the Whole Sample, Age and Gender Groups

	人数 Number	天天喝 daily	一周 3 次以上 3 times or over a week	一周 1~2 次 once or twice a week	一个月 2~3 次 2 or 3 times a month	一个月 1 次 once a month	两个月 1 次 once two months	三个月 1 次或以下 once three months or below	没喝过 never
样本 Sample	642	0.0	2.2	2.6	6.1	5.5	3.9	6.5	73.2
男性 Male	311	0.0	1.6	1.9	6.4	3.5	3.9	4.5	78.1
16~24 岁 Age	65	0.0	4.6	0.0	6.2	4.6	6.2	7.7	70.8
25~34 岁 Age	89	0.0	2.2	1.1	7.9	5.6	5.6	7.9	69.7
35~44 岁 Age	80	0.0	0.0	2.5	7.5	2.5	3.8	0.0	83.8
45~54 岁 Age	52	0.0	0.0	3.8	5.8	0.0	0.0	1.9	88.5
55~60 岁 Age	25	0.0	0.0	4.0	0.0	4.0	0.0	4.0	88.0
女性 Female	331	0.0	2.7	3.3	5.7	7.3	3.9	8.5	68.6
16~24 岁 Age	69	0.0	1.4	7.2	8.7	11.6	7.2	10.1	53.6
25~34 岁 Age	96	0.0	4.2	4.2	7.3	8.3	2.1	11.5	62.5
35~44 岁 Age	78	0.0	1.3	0.0	3.8	6.4	2.6	9.0	76.9
45~54 岁 Age	62	0.0	4.8	3.2	4.8	4.8	6.5	4.8	71.0
55~60 岁 Age	26	0.0	0.0	0.0	0.0	0.0	0.0	0.0	100.0

4-7 样本、男性各年龄层、女性各年龄层的品牌习惯/ Brand Habit in Consuming Pure Juice by the Whole Sample, Age and Gender Groups

	人数 Number	基本固定饮用一个牌子 used in only one brand	比较固定地饮用两个或三个牌子 used in two or three brands	基本上不太固定牌子 no brand preference
样本 Sample	172	35.5	30.2	34.3
男性 Male	68	42.6	20.6	36.8
16~24 岁 Age	19	36.8	26.3	36.8
25~34 岁 Age	27	48.1	14.8	37.0
35~44 岁 Age	13	46.2	23.1	30.8
45~54 岁 Age	6	33.3	33.3	33.3
55~60 岁 Age	3	33.3	0.0	66.7
女性 Female	104	30.8	36.5	32.7
16~24 岁 Age	32	31.3	37.5	31.3
25~34 岁 Age	36	36.1	36.1	27.8
35~44 岁 Age	18	27.8	38.9	33.3
45~54 岁 Age	18	22.2	33.3	44.4
55~60 岁 Age	0	0.0	0.0	0.0

4-8 选择该类商品的考虑因素/ Ranking of the Considerations in Purchasing

注：本题为多选题，合计百分比超过 100%（Multiple answers）

排名 Ranking	考虑因素 Considerations	人次 Person-time	百分比 Percent
1	口味好 pleasant taste	123	71.5
2	生产日期 date of producing	53	30.8
3	有名的牌子 famous brand	49	28.5
4	价格适中 reasonable price	39	22.7
5	购买方便 easy to buy	24	14.0
6	朋友推荐 introduction of friends	19	11.0
7	广告影响 influence of advertising	13	7.6
8	别人送的 given by other people	11	6.4
9	只是由于习惯 out of habit	6	3.5
10	包装吸引人 appealing package	5	2.9
10	单位发的 offered by the working unit	5	2.9
11	有优惠条件 with preferential terms	3	1.7
11	售货员介绍 introduced by the shop assistants	3	1.7
12	其它 others	2	1.2

n=172

4-9 样本、男性各年龄层、女性各年龄层最常饮用的包装形式/ Types of Package of the Consumed Pure Juice by the Whole Sample, Age and Gender Groups

	人数 Number	纸盒 paper box	塑料瓶 plastic bottle	玻璃瓶 glass bottle	易开罐 tin	铝皮桶 aluminum cans	鲜榨 fresh milk	其它 others
样本 Sample	172	34.3	12.8	25.0	14.5	9.3	2.9	1.2
男性 Male	68	30.9	11.8	25.0	16.2	10.3	2.9	2.9
16~24 岁 Age	19	31.6	15.8	10.5	15.8	15.8	5.3	5.3
25~34 岁 Age	27	25.9	3.7	33.3	22.2	7.4	3.7	3.7
35~44 岁 Age	13	30.8	15.4	30.8	15.4	7.7	0.0	0.0
45~54 岁 Age	6	50.0	16.7	16.7	0.0	16.7	0.0	0.0
55~60 岁 Age	3	33.3	33.3	33.3	0.0	0.0	0.0	0.0
女性 Female	104	36.5	13.5	25.0	13.5	8.7	2.9	0.0
16~24 岁 Age	32	34.4	9.4	31.3	12.5	9.4	3.1	0.0
25~34 岁 Age	36	33.3	11.1	25.0	13.9	11.1	5.6	0.0
35~44 岁 Age	18	50.0	11.1	22.2	11.1	5.6	0.0	0.0
45~54 岁 Age	18	33.3	27.8	16.7	16.7	5.6	0.0	0.0
55~60 岁 Age	0	0.0	0.0	0.0	0.0	0.0	0.0	0.0

4-10 样本、男性各年龄层、女性各年龄层最常饮用场合/ Settings of Consumption by the Whole Sample, Age and Gender Groups

注：本题为多选题，合计百分比超过 100%（Multiple answers）

	人数 Number	平时口渴时 when thirsty	平时吃饭喝 at dinner	宴席、聚会喝 at banquet	外出、旅游时 outing/traveling	补充营养 supplementing nutrition	其它 others
样本 Sample	172	39.0	9.9	43.0	20.9	21.5	2.3
男性 Male	68	38.2	10.3	44.1	16.2	19.1	4.4
16~24 岁 Age	19	47.4	5.3	36.8	21.1	21.1	5.3
25~34 岁 Age	27	18.5	11.1	51.9	14.8	25.9	7.4
35~44 岁 Age	13	76.9	23.1	15.4	23.1	7.7	0.0
45~54 岁 Age	6	16.7	0.0	66.7	0.0	16.7	0.0
55~60 岁 Age	3	33.3	0.0	100.0	0.0	0.0	0.0
女性 Female	104	39.4	9.6	42.3	24.0	23.1	1.0
16~24 岁 Age	32	40.6	12.5	34.4	31.3	21.9	0.0
25~34 岁 Age	36	38.9	11.1	27.8	27.8	25.0	0.0
35~44 岁 Age	18	27.8	5.6	72.2	16.7	16.7	5.6
45~54 岁 Age	18	50.0	5.6	55.6	11.1	27.8	0.0
55~60 岁 Age	0	0.0	0.0	0.0	0.0	0.0	0.0

4-11 重度消费者人口分布/ Demographics of the Heavy Consumers

	人数 Number	16-24 岁 Age	25-34 岁 Age	35-44 岁 Age	45-54 岁 Age	55-60 岁 Age
样本 Sample	31	29.0	35.5	9.7	22.6	3.2
男性 Male	11	27.3	27.3	18.2	18.2	9.1
天天喝 daily	0	0.0	0.0	0.0	0.0	0.0
一周 3 次或以上 3 times or over a week	5	60.0	40.0	0.0	0.0	0.0
一周 1~2 次 once or twice a week	6	0.0	16.7	33.3	33.3	16.7
女性 Female	20	30.0	40.0	5.0	25.0	0.0
天天喝 daily	0	0.0	0.0	0.0	0.0	0.0
一周 3 次或以上 3 times or over a week	9	11.1	44.4	11.1	33.3	0.0
一周 1~2 次 once or twice a week	11	45.5	36.4	0.0	18.2	0.0

4-12 不同消费者层的常用品牌/ The Most Frequently Used Brands by Market Segments

4-12-1 时尚流行指标/ Fads Popular Index

	人数 Number	第一品牌及百分比 1st/ percent	第二品牌及百分比 2nd/ percent	第三品牌及百分比 3rd/ percent
样本 Sample	168	**汇源 Huiyuan(39.9)**	**茹梦 Rougement(25.6)**	**金苹果 Gold Apple(11.9)**
平实生活指向 simple living orientation	77	汇源 Huiyuan(44.2)	茹梦 Rougement(20.8)	金苹果 Gold Apple(11.7)
时尚流行指向 fashion orientation	91	汇源 Huiyuan(36.3)	茹梦 Rougement(29.7)	金苹果 Gold Apple(12.1)

4-12-2 广告态度指标/ Advertising Attitude Index

	人数 Number	第一品牌及百分比 1st/ percent	第二品牌及百分比 2nd/ percent	第三品牌及百分比 3rd/ percent
样本 Sample	169	**汇源 Huiyuan(39.6)**	**茹梦 Rougement(25.4)**	**金苹果 Gold Apple(12.4)**
广告淡漠指向 indifferent orientation	41	汇源 Huiyuan(41.5)	茹梦 Rougement(26.8)	旺仔 Wangzi(9.8) 金苹果 Gold Apple(9.8)
中间层 medium	104	汇源 Huiyuan(39.4)	茹梦 Rougement(26.0)	金苹果 Gold Apple(13.5)
信赖广告指向 loyal orientation	24	汇源 Huiyuan(37.5)	茹梦 Rougement(20.8)	旺仔 Wangzi(12.5) 金苹果 Gold Apple(12.5)

4-12-3 饮食健康指标/ Foods & Drink Quality Index

	人数 Number	第一品牌及百分比 1st/ percent	第二品牌及百分比 2nd/ percent	第三品牌及百分比 3rd/ percent
样本 Sample	168	**汇源 Huiyuan(39.3)**	**茹梦 Rougement(25.6)**	**金苹果 Gold Apple(12.5)**
饮食“温饱”指向 "basic" orientation	39	汇源 Huiyuan(33.3)	茹梦 Rougement(30.8)	金苹果 Gold Apple(15.4)
中间层 medium	89	汇源 Huiyuan(46.1)	茹梦 Rougement(19.1)	金苹果 Gold Apple(12.4)
健康营养指向 health & nutrition orientation	40	茹梦 Rougement(35.0)	汇源 Huiyuan(30.0)	金苹果 Gold Apple(10.0)

4-13 重度消费者的消费者层构成/ The Composition of the Heavy Consumers

4-13-1 时尚流行指标/ Fads Popular Index

	人数 Number	平实生活指向 simple living orientation	时尚流行指向 fashion orientation
样本 Sample	31	29.0	71.0
天天喝 daily	0	0.0	0.0
一周 3 次或以上 3 times or over a week	14	28.6	71.4
一周 1~2 次 once or twice a week	17	29.4	70.6

4-13-2 广告态度指标/ Advertising Attitude Index

	人数 Number	广告淡漠指向 indifferent orientation	中间层 medium	信赖广告指向 loyal orientation
样本 Sample	31	25.8	64.5	9.7
天天喝 daily	0	0.0	0.0	0.0
一周 3 次或以上 3 times or over a week	14	21.4	64.3	14.3
一周 1~2 次 once or twice a week	17	29.4	64.7	5.9

4-13-3 饮食健康指标/ Foods & Drink Quality Index

	人数 Number	饮食"温饱"指向 "basic" orientation	中间层 medium	健康营养指向 health & nutrition orientation
样本 Sample	31	6.5	41.9	51.6
天天喝 daily	0	0.0	0.0	0.0
一周 3 次或以上 3 times or over a week	14	0.0	42.9	57.1
一周 1~2 次 once or twice a week	17	11.8	41.2	47.1

● 西安 / Xi'an

4-1 最近三个月饮用频率的比例/ Proportion of the Sample Consuming Pure Juice in the Last Three Months

	人数 Number	百分比 Percent
天天喝 daily	5	0.8
一周 3 次或以上 3 times or over a week	12	2.0
一周 1~2 次 once or twice a week	34	5.7
一个月 2～3 次 2 or 3 times a month	80	13.3
一个月 1 次 once a month	54	9.0
两个月 1 次 once two months	26	4.3
三个月 1 次或以下 once three months or below	37	6.2
没喝过 never	353	58.7

n=601

4-2 最常用品牌排名/ Ranking of the Most Frequently Used Brands

排名 Brand Ranking	品牌 Brands	人数 Number	百分比 Percent
1	荣氏 Rong	130	52.6
2	汇源 Huiyuan	56	22.7
3	茹梦 Rougement	34	13.8
4	大湖 Great Lakes	7	2.8
5	旺仔 Wangzi	6	2.4
6	金苹果 Gold Apple	4	1.6

n=247

4-3 样本、男性各年龄层、女性各年龄层的常用品牌/ The Most Frequently Used Brands by the Whole Sample, Age and Gender Groups

	人数 Number	第一品牌及百分比 1st/ percent	第二品牌及百分比 2nd/ percent	第三品牌及百分比 3rd/ percent
样本 Sample	247	**荣氏 Rong(52.6)**	**汇源 Huiyuan(22.7)**	**茹梦 Rougement(13.8)**
男性 Male	123	**荣氏 Rong(48.8)**	**汇源 Huiyuan(27.6)**	**茹梦 Rougement(12.2)**
16~24 岁 Age	28	荣氏 Rong(39.3)	汇源 Huiyuan(28.6)	茹梦 Rougement(10.7) 旺仔 Wangzi(10.7)
25~34 岁 Age	37	荣氏 Rong(43.2)	汇源 Huiyuan(27.0)	茹梦 Rougement(21.6)
35~44 岁 Age	37	荣氏 Rong(59.5)	汇源 Huiyuan(24.3)	茹梦 Rougement(10.8)
45~54 岁 Age	16	荣氏 Rong(68.8)	汇源 Huiyuan(18.8)	碧泉 Crystal Spring(6.3) 华邦 Huabang(6.3)
55~60 岁 Age	5	汇源 Huiyuan(80.0)	大湖 Great Lakes(20.0)	
女性 Female	124	**荣氏 Rong(56.5)**	**汇源 Huiyuan(17.7)**	**茹梦 Rougement(15.3)**
16~24 岁 Age	26	荣氏 Rong(61.5)	茹梦 Rougement(19.2)	汇源 Huiyuan(15.4)
25~34 岁 Age	54	荣氏 Rong(51.9)	汇源 Huiyuan(20.4)	茹梦 Rougement(11.1)
35~44 岁 Age	28	荣氏 Rong(57.1)	茹梦 Rougement(17.9)	汇源 Huiyuan(14.3)
45~54 岁 Age	10	荣氏 Rong(60.0)	茹梦 Rougement(30.0)	汇源 Huiyuan(10.0)
55~60 岁 Age	6	荣氏 Rong(66.7)	汇源 Huiyuan(33.3)	

4-4 理想品牌排名/ Ranking of the Ideal Brands

排名 Brand Ranking	品牌 Brands	人数 Number	百分比 Percent
1	荣氏 Rong	209	34.8
2	汇源 Huiyuan	141	23.5
3	茹梦 Rougement	50	8.3
4	大湖 Great Lakes	7	1.2
5	旺仔 Wangzi	2	0.3

n=600

4-5 样本、男性各年龄层、女性各年龄层最近三个月有无购买的比例/ Purchasing in the Last Three Months by the Whole Sample, Age and Gender Groups

	人数 Number	买过 yes	没买过 no
样本 Sample	601	37.4	62.6
男性 Male	302	37.1	62.9
16~24 岁 Age	64	40.6	59.4
25~34 岁 Age	91	36.3	63.7
35~44 岁 Age	77	45.5	54.5
45~54 岁 Age	46	28.3	71.7
55~60 岁 Age	24	20.8	79.2
女性 Female	299	37.8	62.2
16~24 岁 Age	61	31.1	68.9
25~34 岁 Age	90	53.3	46.7
35~44 岁 Age	74	37.8	62.2
45~54 岁 Age	49	26.5	73.5
55~60 岁 Age	25	20.0	80.0

4-6 样本、男性各年龄层、女性各年龄层最近三个月的饮用频率/ Frequencies of Consuming Pure Juice by the Whole Sample, Age and Gender Groups

	人数 Number	天天喝 daily	一周3次或以上 3 times or over a week	一周1~2次 once or twice a week	一个月2~3次 2 or 3 times a month	一个月1次 once a month	两个月1次 once two months	三个月1次或以下 once three months or below	没喝过 never
样本 Sample	601	0.8	2.0	5.7	13.3	9.0	4.3	6.2	58.7
男性 Male	302	0.3	1.7	6.3	12.6	9.3	5.0	5.6	59.3
16~24 岁 Age	64	0.0	3.1	6.3	12.5	10.9	4.7	6.3	56.3
25~34 岁 Age	91	0.0	3.3	3.3	9.9	12.1	7.7	4.4	59.3
35~44 岁 Age	77	1.3	0.0	11.7	14.3	9.1	6.5	5.2	51.9
45~54 岁 Age	46	0.0	0.0	6.5	19.6	2.2	0.0	6.5	65.2
55~60 岁 Age	24	0.0	0.0	0.0	4.2	8.3	0.0	8.3	79.2
女性 Female	299	1.3	2.3	5.0	14.0	8.7	3.7	6.7	58.2
16~24 岁 Age	61	1.6	1.6	1.6	16.4	6.6	8.2	6.6	57.4
25~34 岁 Age	90	1.1	3.3	7.8	21.1	14.4	2.2	10.0	40.0
35~44 岁 Age	74	1.4	1.4	8.1	10.8	5.4	5.4	6.8	60.8
45~54 岁 Age	49	0.0	2.0	2.0	10.2	4.1	0.0	2.0	79.6
55~60 岁 Age	25	4.0	4.0	0.0	0.0	12.0	0.0	4.0	76.0

4-7 样本、男性各年龄层、女性各年龄层的品牌习惯/ Brand Habit in Consuming Pure Juice by the Whole Sample, Age and Gender Groups

	人数 Number	基本固定饮用一个牌子 used in only one brand	比较固定地饮用两个或三个牌子 used in two or three brands	基本上不太固定牌子 no brand preference
样本 Sample	248	48.0	30.6	21.4
男性 Male	123	44.7	35.8	19.5
16~24 岁 Age	28	46.4	35.7	17.9
25~34 岁 Age	37	51.4	35.1	13.5
35~44 岁 Age	37	43.2	35.1	21.6
45~54 岁 Age	16	25.0	50.0	25.0
55~60 岁 Age	5	60.0	0.0	40.0
女性 Female	125	51.2	25.6	23.2
16~24 岁 Age	26	50.0	34.6	15.4
25~34 岁 Age	54	51.9	27.8	20.4
35~44 岁 Age	29	55.2	13.8	31.0
45~54 岁 Age	10	50.0	40.0	10.0
55~60 岁 Age	6	33.3	0.0	66.7

4-8 选择该类商品的考虑因素/ Ranking of the Considerations in Purchasing

注：本题为多选题，合计百分比超过 100%（Multiple answers）

排名 Ranking	考虑因素 Considerations	人次 Person-time	百分比 Percent
1	口味好 pleasant taste	173	69.8
2	价格适中 reasonable price	71	28.6
3	有名的牌子 famous brand	68	27.4
4	生产日期 date of producing	48	19.4
5	购买方便 easy to buy	37	14.9
6	广告影响 influence of advertising	22	8.9
7	朋友推荐 introduction of friends	21	8.5
8	只是由于习惯 out of habit	20	8.1
9	包装吸引人 appealing package	9	3.6
9	单位发的 offered by the working unit	9	3.6
10	别人送的 given by other people	4	1.6
11	售货员介绍 introduced by the shop assistants	3	1.2
11	其它 others	3	1.2
12	有优惠条件 with preferential terms	1	0.4

n=248

4-9 样本、男性各年龄层、女性各年龄层最常饮用的包装形式/ Package Types of the Consumed Pure Juice by the Whole Sample, Age and Gender Groups

	人数 Number	纸盒 paper box	塑料瓶 plastic bottle	玻璃瓶 glass bottle	易开罐 tin	铝皮桶 aluminum cans	鲜榨 fresh milk	其它 others
样本 Sample	248	72.2	8.5	6.5	4.4	7.3	1.2	0.0
男性 Male	123	73.2	8.1	5.7	6.5	6.5	0.0	0.0
16~24 岁 Age	28	64.3	0.0	7.1	21.4	7.1	0.0	0.0
25~34 岁 Age	37	70.3	8.1	8.1	0.0	13.5	0.0	0.0
35~44 岁 Age	37	81.1	13.5	2.7	0.0	2.7	0.0	0.0
45~54 岁 Age	16	75.0	12.5	6.3	6.3	0.0	0.0	0.0
55~60 岁 Age	5	80.0	0.0	0.0	20.0	0.0	0.0	0.0
女性 Female	125	71.2	8.8	7.2	2.4	8.0	2.4	0.0
16~24 岁 Age	26	69.2	11.5	3.8	3.8	3.8	7.7	0.0
25~34 岁 Age	54	66.7	7.4	13.0	0.0	11.1	1.9	0.0
35~44 岁 Age	29	79.3	6.9	3.4	6.9	3.4	0.0	0.0
45~54 岁 Age	10	60.0	20.0	0.0	0.0	20.0	0.0	0.0
55~60 岁 Age	6	100.0	0.0	0.0	0.0	0.0	0.0	0.0

4-10 样本、男性各年龄层、女性各年龄层最常饮用场合/ Settings of Consumption by the Whole Sample, Age and Gender Groups

注：本题为多选题，合计百分比超过 100%（Multiple answers）

	人数 Number	平时口渴时 when thirsty	平时吃饭喝 at dinner	宴席、聚会喝 at banquet	外出、旅游时 outing/traveling	补充营养 supplementing nutrition	其它 others
样本 Sample	248	35.1	10.9	33.1	37.5	12.9	0.4
男性 Male	123	32.5	11.4	28.5	37.4	13.8	0.8
16~24 岁 Age	28	25.0	10.7	25.0	42.9	17.9	0.0
25~34 岁 Age	37	37.8	5.4	32.4	32.4	13.5	0.0
35~44 岁 Age	37	43.2	13.5	21.6	40.5	13.5	0.0
45~54 岁 Age	16	18.8	18.8	37.5	37.5	0.0	0.0
55~60 岁 Age	5	0.0	20.0	40.0	20.0	40.0	20.0
女性 Female	125	37.6	10.4	37.6	37.6	12.0	0.0
16~24 岁 Age	26	30.8	7.7	42.3	50.0	3.8	0.0
25~34 岁 Age	54	35.2	11.1	27.8	38.9	11.1	0.0
35~44 岁 Age	29	44.8	13.8	41.4	34.5	20.7	0.0
45~54 岁 Age	10	60.0	10.0	50.0	0.0	10.0	0.0
55~60 岁 Age	6	16.7	0.0	66.7	50.0	16.7	0.0

4-11 重度消费者人口分布/ Demographics of the Heavy Consumers

	人数 Number	16-24 岁 Age	25-34 岁 Age	35-44 岁 Age	45-54 岁 Age	55-60 岁 Age
样本 Sample	51	17.6	33.3	35.3	9.8	3.9
男性 Male	25	24.0	24.0	40.0	12.0	0.0
天天喝 daily	1	0.0	0.0	100.0	0.0	0.0
一周 3 次或以上 3 times or over a week	5	40.0	60.0	0.0	0.0	0.0
一周 1~2 次 once or twice a week	19	21.1	15.8	47.4	15.8	0.0
女性 Female	26	11.5	42.3	30.8	7.7	7.7
天天喝 daily	4	25.0	25.0	25.0	0.0	25.0
一周 3 次或以上 3 times or over a week	7	14.3	42.9	14.3	14.3	14.3
一周 1~2 次 once or twice a week	15	6.7	46.7	40.0	6.7	0.0

4-12 不同消费者层的常用品牌/ The Most Frequently Used Brands by Market Segments

4-12-1 时尚流行指标/ Fads Popular Index

	人数 Number	第一品牌及百分比 1st/ percent	第二品牌及百分比 2nd/ percent	第三品牌及百分比 3rd/ percent	第四品牌及百分比 4th/ percent
样本 Sample	246	**荣氏 Rong(52.4)**	**汇源 Huiyuan(22.8)**	**茹梦 Rougement(13.8)**	**大湖 Great Lakes(2.8)**
平实生活指向 simple living orientation	115	荣氏 Rong(53.0)	汇源 Huiyuan(21.7)	茹梦 Rougement(13.9)	大湖 Great Lakes(3.5)
时尚流行指向 fashion orientation	131	荣氏 Rong(51.9)	汇源 Huiyuan(23.7)	茹梦 Rougement(13.7)	旺仔 Wangzi(3.8)

4-12-2 广告态度指标/ Advertising Attitude Index

	人数 Number	第一品牌及百分比 1st/ percent	第二品牌及百分比 2nd/ percent	第三品牌及百分比 3rd/ percent	第四品牌及百分比 4th/ percent
样本 Sample	**247**	**荣氏 Rong(52.6)**	**汇源 Huiyuan(22.7)**	**茹梦 Rougement(13.8)**	**大湖 Great Lakes(2.8)**
广告淡漠指向 indifferent orientation	77	荣氏 Rong(50.6)	汇源 Huiyuan(31.2)	茹梦 Rougement(9.1)	旺仔 Wangzi(3.9)
中间层 medium	145	荣氏 Rong(54.5)	汇源 Huiyuan(20.0)	茹梦 Rougement(14.5)	大湖 Great Lakes(2.8)
信赖广告指向 loyal orientation	25	荣氏 Rong(48.0)	茹梦 Rougement(24.0)	汇源 Huiyuan(12.0)	大湖 Great Lakes(4.0) 都乐 Dole(4.0) 旺仔 Wangzi(4.0) 金苹果 Gold Apple(4.0)

4-12-3 饮食健康指标/ Foods & Drink Quality Index

	人数 Number	第一品牌及百分比 1st/ percent	第二品牌及百分比 2nd/ percent	第三品牌及百分比 3rd/ percent	第四品牌及百分比 4th/ percent
样本 Sample	**247**	**荣氏 Rong(52.6)**	**汇源 Huiyuan(22.7)**	**茹梦 Rougement(13.8)**	**大湖 Great Lakes(2.8)**
饮食"温饱"指向 "basic" orientation	76	荣氏 Rong(51.3)	汇源 Huiyuan(25.0)	茹梦 Rougement(15.8)	旺仔 Wangzi(2.6)
中间层 medium	131	荣氏 Rong(55.7)	汇源 Huiyuan(24.4)	茹梦 Rougement(9.2)	大湖 Great Lakes(3.1)
健康营养指向 health & nutrition orientation	40	荣氏 Rong(45.0)	茹梦 Rougement(25.0)	汇源 Huiyuan(12.5)	大湖 Great Lakes(5.0) 旺仔 Wangzi(5.0)

4-13 重度消费者的消费者层构成/ The Composition of the Heavy Consumers

4-13-1 时尚流行指标/ Fads Popular Index

	人数 Number	平实生活指向 simple living orientation	时尚流行指向 fashion orientation
样本 Sample	**51**	**33.3**	**66.7**
天天喝 daily	5	20.0	80.0
一周 3 次或以上 3 times or over a week	12	41.7	58.3
一周 1~2 次 once or twice a week	34	32.4	67.6

4-13-2 广告态度指标/ Advertising Attitude Index

	人数 Number	广告淡漠指向 indifferent orientation	中间层 medium	信赖广告指向 loyal orientation
样本 Sample	**51**	**31.4**	**54.9**	**13.7**
天天喝 daily	5	20.0	40.0	40.0
一周 3 次或以上 3 times or over a week	12	41.7	50.0	8.3
一周 1~2 次 once or twice a week	34	29.4	58.8	11.8

4-13-3 饮食健康指标/ Foods & Drink Quality Index

	人数 Number	饮食"温饱"指向 "basic" orientation	中间层 medium	健康营养指向 health & nutrition orientation
样本 Sample	**51**	**29.4**	**54.9**	**15.7**
天天喝 daily	5	60.0	40.0	0.0
一周 3 次或以上 3 times or over a week	12	41.7	50.0	8.3
一周 1~2 次 once or twice a week	34	20.6	58.8	20.6

● 沈阳 / Shenyang

4-1 最近三个月饮用频率的比例/ Proportion of the Sample Consuming Pure Juice in the Last Three Months

	人数 Number	百分比 Percent
天天喝 daily	4	0.7
一周 3 次或以上 3 times or over a week	13	2.2
一周 1~2 次 once or twice a week	21	3.5
一个月 2～3 次 2 or 3 times a month	39	6.5
一个月 1 次 once a month	42	7.0
两个月 1 次 once two months	16	2.7
三个月 1 次或以下 once three months or below	42	7.0
没喝过 never	423	70.5

n=600

4-2 最常用品牌排名/ Ranking of the Most Frequently Used Brands

排名 Brand Ranking	品牌 Brands	人数 Number	百分比 Percent
1	金苹果 Gold Apple	63	36.2
2	汇源 Huiyuan	57	32.8
3	茹梦 Rougement	24	13.8
4	旺仔 Wangzi	10	5.7
5	大亨 Daheng	4	2.3
6	荣氏 Rong	3	1.7

n=174

4-3 样本、男性各年龄层、女性各年龄层的常用品牌/ The Most Frequently Used Brands by the Whole Sample, Age and Gender Groups

	人数 Number	第一品牌及百分比 1st/ percent	第二品牌及百分比 2nd/ percent	第三品牌及百分比 3rd/ percent
样本 Sample	174	**金苹果 Gold Apple(36.2)**	**汇源 Huiyuan(32.8)**	**茹梦 Rougement(13.8)**
男性 Male	74	**金苹果 Gold Apple(41.9)**	**汇源 Huiyuan(29.7)**	**茹梦 Rougement(12.2)**
16~24 岁 Age	18	汇源 Huiyuan(33.3) 金苹果 Gold Apple(33.3)	旺仔 Wangzi(16.7)	大湖 Great Lakes(5.6) 大亨 Daheng(5.6) 茹梦 Rougement(5.6)
25~34 岁 Age	33	金苹果 Gold Apple(39.4)	汇源 Huiyuan(30.3)	茹梦 Rougement(18.2)
35~44 岁 Age	17	金苹果 Gold Apple(47.1)	汇源 Huiyuan(35.3)	大亨 Daheng(5.9) 茹梦 Rougement(5.9) 碧泉 Crystal Spring(5.9)
45~54 岁 Age	5	金苹果 Gold Apple(80.0)	茹梦 Rougement(20.0)	
55~60 岁 Age	1	旺仔 Wangzi(100.0)		
女性 Female	100	**汇源 Huiyuan(35.0)**	**金苹果 Gold Apple(32.0)**	**茹梦 Rougement(15.0)**
16~24 岁 Age	34	汇源 Huiyuan(41.2)	金苹果 Gold Apple(17.6)	茹梦 Rougement(14.7)
25~34 岁 Age	28	汇源 Huiyuan(39.3) 金苹果 Gold Apple(39.3)	茹梦 Rougement(10.7)	旺仔 Wangzi(3.6) 鲁冰花 ROBIN SNOW(3.6)
35~44 岁 Age	26	金苹果 Gold Apple(38.5)	汇源 Huiyuan(23.1)	茹梦 Rougement(19.2)
45~54 岁 Age	10	汇源 Huiyuan(40.0)	金苹果 Gold Apple(30.0)	茹梦 Rougement(20.0)
55~60 岁 Age	2	金苹果 Gold Apple(100.0)		

4-4 理想品牌排名/ Ranking of the Ideal Brands

排名 Brand Ranking	品牌 Brands	人数 Number	百分比 Percent
1	汇源 Huiyuan	138	23.0
2	金苹果 Gold Apple	77	12.8
3	茹梦 Rougement	40	6.7
4	旺仔 Wangzi	20	3.3
5	都乐 Dole	11	1.8
6	鲁冰花 ROBIN SNOW	8	1.3

n=601

4-5 样本、男性各年龄层、女性各年龄层最近三个月有无购买的比例/ Purchasing in the Last Three Months by the Whole Sample, Age and Gender Groups

	人数 Number	买过 yes	没买过 no
样本 Sample	600	26.5	73.5
男性 Male	298	21.1	78.9
16~24 岁 Age	64	17.2	82.8
25~34 岁 Age	89	33.7	66.3
35~44 岁 Age	76	21.1	78.9
45~54 岁 Age	45	8.9	91.1
55~60 岁 Age	24	8.3	91.7
女性 Female	302	31.8	68.2
16~24 岁 Age	64	45.3	54.7
25~34 岁 Age	90	34.4	65.6
35~44 岁 Age	76	34.2	65.8
45~54 岁 Age	48	14.6	85.4
55~60 岁 Age	24	12.5	87.5

4-6 样本、男性各年龄层、女性各年龄层最近三个月的饮用频率/ Frequencies of Consuming Pure Juice by the Whole Sample, Age and Gender Groups

	人数 Number	天天喝 daily	一周3次或以上 3 times or over a week	一周1~2次 once or twice a week	一个月2~3次 2 or 3 times a month	一个月1次 once a month	两个月1次 once two months	三个月1次或以下 once three months or below	没喝过 never
样本 Sample	600	0.7	2.2	3.5	6.5	7.0	2.7	7.0	70.5
男性 Male	298	1.0	2.0	2.7	4.7	5.7	2.7	6.0	75.2
16~24 岁 Age	64	1.6	0.0	1.6	6.3	4.7	3.1	10.9	71.9
25~34 岁 Age	89	1.1	3.4	3.4	6.7	11.2	2.2	9.0	62.9
35~44 岁 Age	76	1.3	3.9	5.3	1.3	3.9	2.6	3.9	77.6
45~54 岁 Age	45	0.0	0.0	0.0	6.7	2.2	2.2	0.0	88.9
55~60 岁 Age	24	0.0	0.0	0.0	0.0	0.0	4.2	0.0	95.8
女性 Female	302	0.3	2.3	4.3	8.3	8.3	2.6	7.9	65.9
16~24 岁 Age	64	1.6	4.7	6.3	10.9	10.9	3.1	15.6	46.9
25~34 岁 Age	90	0.0	2.2	5.6	8.9	6.7	3.3	7.8	65.6
35~44 岁 Age	76	0.0	2.6	5.3	9.2	13.2	1.3	2.6	65.8
45~54 岁 Age	48	0.0	0.0	0.0	4.2	4.2	4.2	8.3	79.2
55~60 岁 Age	24	0.0	0.0	0.0	4.2	0.0	0.0	4.2	91.7

4-7 样本、男性各年龄层、女性各年龄层的品牌习惯/ Brand Habit in Consuming Pure Juice by the Whole Sample, Age and Gender Groups

	人数 Number	基本固定饮用一个牌子 used in only one brand	比较固定地饮用两个或三个牌子 used in two or three brands	基本上不太固定牌子 no brand preference
样本 Sample	177	36.2	29.4	34.5
男性 Male	74	43.2	25.7	31.1
16~24 岁 Age	18	44.4	27.8	27.8
25~34 岁 Age	33	33.3	30.3	36.4
35~44 岁 Age	17	64.7	11.8	23.5
45~54 岁 Age	5	20.0	40.0	40.0
55~60 岁 Age	1	100.0	0.0	0.0
女性 Female	103	31.1	32.0	36.9
16~24 岁 Age	34	23.5	41.2	35.3
25~34 岁 Age	31	38.7	32.3	29.0
35~44 岁 Age	26	38.5	23.1	38.5
45~54 岁 Age	10	10.0	30.0	60.0
55~60 岁 Age	2	50.0	0.0	50.0

4-8 选择该类商品的考虑因素/ Ranking of the Considerations in Purchasing

注：本题为多选题，合计百分比超过 100%（Multiple answers）

排名 Ranking	考虑因素 Considerations	人次 Person-time	百分比 Percent
1	口味好 pleasant taste	139	78.5
2	价格适中 reasonable price	57	32.2
3	生产日期 date of producing	48	27.1
3	有名的牌子 famous brand	48	27.1
4	购买方便 easy to buy	22	12.4
5	广告影响 influence of advertising	13	7.3
6	朋友推荐 introduction of friends	10	5.6
6	别人送的 given by other people	10	5.6
7	包装吸引人 appealing package	7	4.0
8	有优惠条件 with preferential terms	4	2.3
8	单位发的 offered by the working unit	4	2.3
9	售货员介绍 introduced by the shop assistants	3	1.7
10	只是由于习惯 out of habit	2	1.1

n=177

4-9 样本、男性各年龄层、女性各年龄层最常饮用的包装形式/ Package Types of the Consumed Pure Juice by the Whole Sample, Age and Gender Groups

	人数 Number	纸盒 paper box	塑料瓶 plastic bottle	玻璃瓶 glass bottle	易开罐 tin	铝皮桶 aluminum cans	鲜榨 fresh milk	其它 others
样本 Sample	**176**	**29.5**	**15.3**	**32.4**	**12.5**	**8.5**	**1.7**	**0.0**
男性 Male	**74**	**24.3**	**13.5**	**35.1**	**17.6**	**8.1**	**1.4**	**0.0**
16~24 岁 Age	18	22.2	11.1	27.8	16.7	22.2	0.0	0.0
25~34 岁 Age	33	30.3	15.2	36.4	15.2	3.0	0.0	0.0
35~44 岁 Age	17	17.6	17.6	35.3	23.5	5.9	0.0	0.0
45~54 岁 Age	5	20.0	0.0	60.0	0.0	0.0	20.0	0.0
55~60 岁 Age	1	0.0	0.0	0.0	100.0	0.0	0.0	0.0
女性 Female	**102**	**33.3**	**16.7**	**30.4**	**8.8**	**8.8**	**2.0**	**0.0**
16~24 岁 Age	34	32.4	14.7	20.6	14.7	17.6	0.0	0.0
25~34 岁 Age	30	43.3	13.3	23.3	10.0	3.3	6.7	0.0
35~44 岁 Age	26	30.8	15.4	50.0	0.0	3.8	0.0	0.0
45~54 岁 Age	10	20.0	30.0	30.0	10.0	10.0	0.0	0.0
55~60 岁 Age	2	0.0	50.0	50.0	0.0	0.0	0.0	0.0

4-10 样本、男性各年龄层、女性各年龄层最常饮用场合/ Settings of Consumption by the Whole Sample, Age and Gender Groups

注：本题为多选题，合计百分比超过 100%（Multiple answers）

	人数 Number	平时口渴时 when thirsty	平时吃饭喝 at dinner	宴席、聚会喝 at banquet	外出、旅游时 outing/traveling	补充营养 supplementing nutrition	其它 others
样本 Sample	**177**	**35.6**	**6.2**	**44.6**	**28.2**	**20.9**	**0.6**
男性 Male	**74**	**35.1**	**6.8**	**43.2**	**32.4**	**17.6**	**0.0**
16~24 岁 Age	18	38.9	11.1	16.7	33.3	33.3	0.0
25~34 岁 Age	33	33.3	6.1	54.5	30.3	6.1	0.0
35~44 岁 Age	17	41.2	5.9	58.8	29.4	17.6	0.0
45~54 岁 Age	5	20.0	0.0	20.0	60.0	20.0	0.0
55~60 岁 Age	1	0.0	0.0	0.0	0.0	100.0	0.0
女性 Female	**103**	**35.9**	**5.8**	**45.6**	**25.2**	**23.3**	**1.0**
16~24 岁 Age	34	32.4	11.8	41.2	29.4	29.4	0.0
25~34 岁 Age	31	35.5	3.2	54.8	25.8	19.4	0.0
35~44 岁 Age	26	26.9	0.0	46.2	26.9	26.9	3.8
45~54 岁 Age	10	70.0	0.0	40.0	10.0	10.0	0.0
55~60 岁 Age	2	50.0	50.0	0.0	0.0	0.0	0.0

4-11 重度消费者人口分布/ Demographics of the Heavy Consumers

	人数 Number	16-24 岁 Age	25-34 岁 Age	35-44 岁 Age	45-54 岁 Age	55-60 岁 Age
样本 Sample	**38**	**26.3**	**36.8**	**36.8**	**0.0**	**0.0**
男性 Male	**17**	**11.8**	**41.2**	**47.1**	**0.0**	**0.0**
天天喝 daily	3	33.3	33.3	33.3	0.0	0.0
一周 3 次或以上 3 times or over a week	6	0.0	50.0	50.0	0.0	0.0
一周 1~2 次 once or twice a week	8	12.5	37.5	50.0	0.0	0.0
女性 Female	**21**	**38.1**	**33.3**	**28.6**	**0.0**	**0.0**
天天喝 daily	1	100.0	0.0	0.0	0.0	0.0
一周 3 次或以上 3 times or over a week	7	42.9	28.6	28.6	0.0	0.0
一周 1~2 次 once or twice a week	13	30.8	38.5	30.8	0.0	0.0

4-12 不同消费者层的常用品牌/ The Most Frequently Used Brands by Market Segments

4-12-1 时尚流行指标/ Fads Popular Index

	人数 Number	第一品牌及百分比 1st/ percent	第二品牌及百分比 2nd/ percent	第三品牌及百分比 3rd/ percent
样本 Sample	**174**	**金苹果 Gold Apple(36.2)**	**汇源 Huiyuan(32.8)**	**茹梦 Rougement(13.8)**
平实生活指向 simple living orientation	60	汇源 Huiyuan(38.3)	金苹果 Gold Apple(31.7)	茹梦 Rougement(10.0) 旺仔 Wangzi(10.0)
时尚流行指向 fashion orientation	114	金苹果 Gold Apple(38.6)	汇源 Huiyuan(29.8)	茹梦 Rougement(15.8)

4-12-2 广告态度指标/ Advertising Attitude Index

	人数 Number	第一品牌及百分比 1st/ percent	第二品牌及百分比 2nd/ percent	第三品牌及百分比 3rd/ percent
样本 Sample	174	**金苹果 Gold Apple(36.2)**	**汇源 Huiyuan(32.8)**	**茹梦 Rougement(13.8)**
广告淡漠指向 indifferent orientation	44	金苹果 Gold Apple(40.9)	汇源 Huiyuan(18.2) 茹梦 Rougement(18.2)	旺仔 Wangzi(13.6)
中间层 medium	110	汇源 Huiyuan(40.0)	金苹果 Gold Apple(34.5)	茹梦 Rougement(11.8)
信赖广告指向 loyal orientation	20	金苹果 Gold Apple(35.0)	汇源 Huiyuan(25.0)	茹梦 Rougement(15.0)

4-12-3 饮食健康指标/ Foods & Drink Quality Index

	人数 Number	第一品牌及百分比 1st/ percent	第二品牌及百分比 2nd/ percent	第三品牌及百分比 3rd/ percent
样本 Sample	174	**金苹果 Gold Apple(36.2)**	**汇源 Huiyuan(32.8)**	**茹梦 Rougement(13.8)**
饮食"温饱"指向 "basic" orientation	45	汇源 Huiyuan(33.3)	金苹果 Gold Apple(28.9)	茹梦 Rougement(13.3)
中间层 medium	82	金苹果 Gold Apple(40.2)	汇源 Huiyuan(30.5)	茹梦 Rougement(15.9)
健康营养指向 health & nutrition orientation	47	汇源 Huiyuan(36.2) 金苹果 Gold Apple(36.2)	茹梦 Rougement(10.6)	大亨 Daheng(4.3)

4-13 重度消费者的消费者层构成/ The Composition of the Heavy Consumers

4-13-1 时尚流行指标/ Fads Popular Index

	人数 Number	平实生活指向 simple living orientation	时尚流行指向 fashion orientation
样本 Sample	38	**31.6**	**68.4**
天天喝 daily	4	0.0	100.0
一周 3 次或以上 3 times or over a week	13	38.5	61.5
一周 1~2 次 once or twice a week	21	33.3	66.7

4-13-2 广告态度指标/ Advertising Attitude Index

	人数 Number	广告淡漠指向 indifferent orientation	中间层 medium	信赖广告指向 loyal orientation
样本 Sample	38	**18.4**	**73.7**	**7.9**
天天喝 daily	4	25.0	75.0	0.0
一周 3 次或以上 3 times or over a week	13	15.4	76.9	7.7
一周 1~2 次 once or twice a week	21	19.0	71.4	9.5

4-13-3 饮食健康指标/ Foods & Drink Quality Index

	人数 Number	饮食"温饱"指向 "basic" orientation	中间层 medium	健康营养指向 health & nutrition orientation
样本 Sample	38	**21.1**	**47.4**	**31.6**
天天喝 daily	4	25.0	75.0	0.0
一周 3 次或以上 3 times or over a week	13	15.4	53.8	30.8
一周 1~2 次 once or twice a week	21	23.8	38.1	38.1

5.果汁饮料 / Fruit-Flavored Beverage

● 北京 / Beijing

5-1 最近三个月饮用频率的比例/ Proportion of the Sample Consuming Fruit-flavored Beverage in the Last Three Months

	人数 Number	百分比 Percent
天天喝 daily	16	1.6
一周 3 次或以上 3 times or over a week	42	4.2
一周 1~2 次 once or twice a week	132	13.1
一个月 2～3 次 2 or 3 times a month	150	14.9
一个月 1 次 once a month	78	7.7
两个月 1 次 once two months	44	4.4
三个月 1 次或以下 once three months or below	53	5.2
没喝过 never	495	49.0

n=1010

5-2 最常用品牌排名/ Ranking of the Most Frequently Used Brands

排名 Brand Ranking	品牌 Brands	人数 Number	百分比 Percent
1	汇源 Huiyuan	119	23.7
2	椰树 Coconut Palm	72	14.3
3	美年达 Mirinda	65	12.9
4	康师傅 Kangshifu	56	11.1
5	统一 President	47	9.3
6	华旗 Huaqi	20	4.0
7	摩奇 Moqi	19	3.8
8	椰风 Cocowind	18	3.6
9	福运泉 Fuyunquan	16	3.2
10	雀巢 Nestle	11	2.2
10	大亨 Daheng	11	2.2

n=503

5-3 样本、男性各年龄层、女性各年龄层的常用品牌/ The Most Frequently Used Brands by the Whole Sample, Age and Gender Groups

	人数 Number	第一品牌及百分比 1st/ percent	第二品牌及百分比 2nd/ percent	第三品牌及百分比 3rd/ percent	第四品牌及百分比 4th/ percent
样本 Sample	503	**汇源 Huiyuan(23.7)**	**椰树 Coconut Palm(14.3)**	**美年达 Mirinda(12.9)**	**康师傅 Kangshifu(11.1)**
男性 Male	225	**汇源 Huiyuan(25.3)**	**椰树 Coconut Palm(15.6)**	**美年达 Mirinda(13.8)**	**康师傅 Kangshifu(8.9)** **统一 President(8.9)**
16~24 岁 Age	60	康师傅 Kangshifu(18.3) 汇源 Huiyuan(18.3)	美年达 Mirinda(16.7)	统一 President(13.3) 椰树 Coconut Palm(13.3)	摩奇 Moqi(5.0)
25~34 岁 Age	68	汇源 Huiyuan(26.5)	椰树 Coconut Palm(11.8)	美年达 Mirinda(10.3)	福运泉 Fuyunquan(8.8) 统一 President(8.8)
35~44 岁 Age	58	汇源 Huiyuan(36.2)	美年达 Mirinda(13.8) 椰树 Coconut Palm(13.8)	统一 President(6.9) 康师傅 Kangshifu(6.9)	雀巢 Nestle(5.2) 椰风 Cocowind(5.2)
45~54 岁 Age	27	椰树 Coconut Palm(29.6)	美年达 Mirinda(22.2)	汇源 Huiyuan(14.8)	统一 President(7.4) 华旗 Huaqi(7.4)
55~60 岁 Age	12	汇源 Huiyuan(25.0) 椰树 Coconut Palm(25.0)	椰风 Cocowind(8.3) 信远斋 Xinyuanzhai(8.3) 华旗 Huaqi(8.3) 福运泉 Fuyunquan(8.3) 华邦 Huabang(8.3)		
女性 Female	278	**汇源 Huiyuan(22.3)**	**椰树 Coconut Palm(13.3)**	**康师傅 Kangshifu(12.9)**	**美年达 Mirinda(12.2)**
16~24 岁 Age	71	汇源 Huiyuan(21.1)	统一 President(13.3)	椰树 Coconut Palm(16.9)	康师傅 Kangshifu(12.7)
25~34 岁 Age	97	汇源 Huiyuan(22.7)	美年达 Mirinda(15.5)	康师傅 Kangshifu(9.3)	统一 President(8.2)
35~44 岁 Age	63	汇源 Huiyuan(31.7)	康师傅 Kangshifu(19.0)	椰树 Coconut Palm(14.3)	美年达 Mirinda(7.9)
45~54 岁 Age	39	椰树 Coconut Palm(20.5)	美年达 Mirinda(17.9)	康师傅 Kangshifu(15.4)	汇源 Huiyuan(10.3)
55~60 岁 Age	8	统一 President(12.5) 摩奇 Moqi(12.5) 汇源 Huiyuan(12.5) 椰树 Coconut Palm(12.5) 椰风 Cocowind(12.5) 福运泉 Fuyunquan(12.5) 美年达 Mirinda(12.5) 北冰洋 Beibingyang(12.5)			

5-4 理想品牌排名/ Ranking of the Ideal Brands

排名 Brand Ranking	品牌 Brands	人数 Number	百分比 Percent
1	汇源 Huiyuan	184	18.2
2	椰树 Coconut Palm	65	6.4
3	美年达 Mirinda	55	5.4
4	康师傅 Kangshifu	50	4.9
5	统一 President	38	3.8
6	椰风 Cocowind	18	1.8
7	华旗 Huaqi	17	1.7
8	大亨 Daheng	16	1.6
9	福运泉 Fuyunquan	15	1.5
10	摩奇 Moqi	13	1.3

n=1012

5-5 样本、男性各年龄层、女性各年龄层最近三个月有无购买的比例/ Purchasing in the Last Three Months by the Whole Sample, Age and Gender Groups

	人数 Number	买过 yes	没买过 no
样本 Sample	1011	44.2	55.8
男性 Male	503	37.2	62.8
16~24 岁 Age	104	49.0	51.0
25~34 岁 Age	151	35.1	64.9
35~44 岁 Age	131	39.7	60.3
45~54 岁 Age	77	28.6	71.4
55~60 岁 Age	40	22.5	77.5
女性 Female	508	51.2	48.8
16~24 岁 Age	108	62.0	38.0
25~34 岁 Age	150	60.7	39.3
35~44 岁 Age	124	51.6	48.4
45~54 岁 Age	84	34.5	65.5
55~60 岁 Age	42	21.4	78.6

5-6 样本、男性各年龄层、女性各年龄层最近三个月的饮用频率/ Frequencies of Consuming Fruit-flavored Beverage in the Last Three Months by the Whole Sample, Age and Gender Groups

	人数 Number	天天喝 daily	一周 3 次或以上 3 times or over a week	一周 1~2 次 once or twice a week	一个月 2~3 次 2 or 3 times a month	一个月 1 次 once a month	两个月 1 次 once two months	三个月 1 次或以下 once three months or below	没喝过 never
样本 Sample	1010	1.6	4.2	13.1	14.9	7.7	4.4	5.2	49.0
男性 Male	503	1.2	3.6	11.1	12.1	7.4	5.0	5.2	54.5
16~24 岁 Age	105	3.8	4.8	13.3	20.0	3.8	4.8	6.7	42.9
25~34 岁 Age	150	1.3	3.3	11.3	11.3	10.7	4.7	5.3	52.0
35~44 岁 Age	131	0.0	3.8	13.0	9.2	8.4	5.3	4.6	55.7
45~54 岁 Age	77	0.0	2.6	7.8	7.8	6.5	7.8	2.6	64.9
55~60 岁 Age	40	0.0	2.5	5.0	12.5	2.5	0.0	7.5	70.0
女性 Female	507	2.0	4.7	15.0	17.6	8.1	3.7	5.3	43.6
16~24 岁 Age	107	1.9	6.5	15.9	26.2	12.1	5.6	1.9	29.9
25~34 岁 Age	150	0.7	6.0	16.0	20.7	8.0	5.3	8.0	35.3
35~44 岁 Age	124	1.6	5.6	15.3	15.3	6.5	1.6	6.5	47.6
45~54 岁 Age	84	6.0	1.2	14.3	10.7	7.1	3.6	4.8	52.4
55~60 岁 Age	42	0.0	0.0	9.5	4.8	4.8	0.0	2.4	78.6

5-7 样本、男性各年龄层、女性各年龄层的品牌习惯/ Brand Habit in Consuming Fruit-flavored Beverage by the Whole Sample, Age and Gender Groups

	人数 Number	基本固定饮用一个牌子 used in only one brand	比较固定地饮用两个或三个牌子 used in two or three brands	基本上不太固定牌子 no brand preference
样本 Sample	512	33.2	44.9	21.9
男性 Male	228	36.8	42.1	21.1
16~24 岁 Age	60	41.7	43.3	15.0
25~34 岁 Age	71	38.0	39.4	22.5
35~44 岁 Age	58	34.5	37.9	27.6
45~54 岁 Age	27	25.9	59.3	14.8
55~60 岁 Age	12	41.7	33.3	25.0
女性 Female	284	30.3	47.2	22.5
16~24 岁 Age	75	14.7	60.0	25.3
25~34 岁 Age	96	34.4	50.0	15.6
35~44 岁 Age	64	39.1	39.1	21.9
45~54 岁 Age	40	37.5	30.0	32.5
55~60 岁 Age	9	22.2	44.4	33.3

5-8 选择该类商品的考虑因素/ Ranking of the Considerations in Purchasing

注：本题为多选题，合计百分比超过 100%（Multiple answers）

排名 Ranking	考虑因素 Considerations	人次 Person-time	百分比 Percent
1	口味好 pleasant taste	356	69.4
2	有名的牌子 famous brand	149	29.0
3	价格适中 reasonable price	148	28.8
4	生产日期 date of producing	106	20.7
5	购买方便 easy to buy	56	10.9
6	广告影响 influence of advertising	42	8.2
7	单位发的 offered by the working unit	38	7.4
8	只是由于习惯 out of habit	35	6.8
9	别人送的 given by other people	28	5.5
10	朋友推荐 introduction of friends	17	3.3
11	包装吸引人 appealing package	12	2.3
12	有优惠条件 with preferential terms	8	1.6
13	其它 others	4	0.8
14	售货员介绍 introduced by the shop assistants	1	0.2

n=513

5-9 样本、男性各年龄层、女性各年龄层最常饮用的包装形式/ Types of Package of the Consumed Fruit-flavored Beverage by the Whole Sample, Age and Gender Groups

	人数 Number	纸盒 paper box	塑料瓶 plastic bottle	玻璃瓶 glass bottle	纸杯 paper cup	易开罐 tin	铝皮桶 aluminum cans	其它 others
样本 Sample	507	39.1	17.6	15.8	2.0	21.7	3.4	0.6
男性 Male	226	36.7	16.8	16.4	2.7	22.1	5.3	0.0
16~24 岁 Age	60	43.3	18.3	10.0	3.3	20.0	5.0	0.0
25~34 岁 Age	69	36.2	11.6	23.2	2.9	20.3	5.8	0.0
35~44 岁 Age	58	43.1	17.2	17.2	3.4	12.1	6.9	0.0
45~54 岁 Age	27	18.5	25.9	11.1	0.0	44.4	0.0	0.0
55~60 岁 Age	12	16.7	16.7	16.7	0.0	41.7	8.3	0.0
女性 Female	281	40.9	18.1	15.3	1.4	21.4	1.8	1.1
16~24 岁 Age	74	43.2	14.9	13.5	1.4	21.6	4.1	1.4
25~34 岁 Age	96	41.7	19.8	17.7	3.1	16.7	1.0	0.0
35~44 岁 Age	64	48.4	15.6	15.6	0.0	17.2	1.6	1.6
45~54 岁 Age	39	23.1	23.1	12.8	0.0	38.5	0.0	2.6
55~60 岁 Age	8	37.5	25.0	12.5	0.0	25.0	0.0	0.0

5-10 样本、男性各年龄层、女性各年龄层最常饮用场合/ Settings of Consumption by the Whole Sample, Age and Gender Groups

注：本题为多选题，合计百分比超过 100%（Multiple answers）

	人数 Number	平时口渴时 when thirsty	平时吃饭喝 at dinner	宴席、聚会喝 at banquet	外出、旅游时 outing/traveling	补充营养 supplementing nutrition	其它 others
样本 Sample	509	49.3	15.7	28.1	28.3	9.6	2.6
男性 Male	227	48.9	14.1	29.1	25.6	10.1	3.1
16~24 岁 Age	60	61.7	11.7	20.0	25.0	15.0	1.7
25~34 岁 Age	70	57.1	7.1	27.1	21.4	14.3	4.3
35~44 岁 Age	58	36.2	19.0	34.5	31.0	3.4	5.2
45~54 岁 Age	27	37.0	18.5	33.3	25.9	7.4	0.0
55~60 岁 Age	12	25.0	33.3	50.0	25.0	0.0	0.0
女性 Female	282	49.6	17.0	27.3	30.5	9.2	2.1
16~24 岁 Age	75	52.0	24.0	28.0	25.3	5.3	2.7
25~34 岁 Age	97	51.5	11.3	24.7	33.0	12.4	1.0
35~44 岁 Age	64	42.2	20.3	29.7	39.1	7.8	3.1
45~54 岁 Age	37	56.8	13.5	24.3	13.5	13.5	2.7
55~60 岁 Age	9	33.3	11.1	44.4	55.6	0.0	0.0

5-11 重度消费者人口分布/ Demographics of the Heavy Consumers

	人数 Number	16-24 岁 Age	25-34 岁 Age	35-44 岁 Age	45-54 岁 Age	55-60 岁 Age
样本 Sample	190	25.8	30.5	26.3	13.7	3.7
男性 Male	80	28.8	30.0	27.5	10.0	3.8
天天喝 daily	6	66.7	33.3	0.0	0.0	0.0
一周 3 次或以上 3 times or over a week	18	27.8	27.8	27.8	11.1	5.6
一周 1~2 次 once or twice a week	56	25.0	30.4	30.4	10.7	3.6
女性 Female	110	23.6	30.9	25.5	16.4	3.6
天天喝 daily	10	20.0	10.0	20.0	50.0	0.0
一周 3 次或以上 3 times or over a week	24	29.2	37.5	29.2	4.2	0.0
一周 1~2 次 once or twice a week	76	22.4	31.6	25.0	15.8	5.3

5-12 不同消费者层的常用品牌/ The Most Frequently Used Brands by Market Segments

5-12-1 时尚流行指标/ Fads Popular Index

	人数 Number	第一品牌及百分比 1st/ percent	第二品牌及百分比 2nd/ percent	第三品牌及百分比 3rd/ percent	第四品牌及百分比 4th/ percent
样本 Sample	497	**汇源 Huiyuan(23.7)**	**椰树 Coconut Palm(14.5)**	**美年达 Mirinda(12.7)**	**康师傅 Kangshifu(11.1)**
平实生活指向 simple living orientation	216	汇源 Huiyuan(23.6)	椰树 Coconut Palm(15.7)	美年达 Mirinda(13.4)	统一 President(9.3)
时尚流行指向 fashion orientation	281	汇源 Huiyuan(23.8)	椰树 Coconut Palm(13.5)	康师傅 Kangshifu(12.8)	美年达 Mirinda(12.1)

5-12-2 广告态度指标/ Advertising Attitude Index

	人数 Number	第一品牌及百分比 1st/ percent	第二品牌及百分比 2nd/ percent	第三品牌及百分比 3rd/ percent	第四品牌及百分比 4th/ percent
样本 Sample	492	**汇源 Huiyuan(23.2)**	**椰树 Coconut Palm(14.6)**	**美年达 Mirinda(12.6)**	**康师傅 Kangshifu(10.8)**
广告淡漠指向 indifferent orientation	129	汇源 Huiyuan(26.4)	椰树 Coconut Palm(17.1)	康师傅 Kangshifu(11.6)	美年达 Mirinda(10.9)
中间层 medium	294	汇源 Huiyuan(21.4)	美年达 Mirinda(14.3)	椰树 Coconut Palm(12.9)	统一 President(11.2)
信赖广告指向 loyal orientation	69	汇源 Huiyuan(24.6)	椰树 Coconut Palm(17.4)	统一 President(11.6) 康师傅 Kangshifu(11.6)	美年达 Mirinda(8.7)

5-12-3 饮食健康指标/ Foods & Drink Quality Index

	人数 Number	第一品牌及百分比 1st/ percent	第二品牌及百分比 2nd/ percent	第三品牌及百分比 3rd/ percent	第四品牌及百分比 4th/ percent
样本 Sample	**499**	**汇源 Huiyuan(23.2)**	**椰树 Coconut Palm(14.2)**	**美年达 Mirinda(13.0)**	**康师傅 Kangshifu(11.2)**
饮食“温饱”指向 "basic" orientation	135	汇源 Huiyuan(24.4)	椰树 Coconut Palm(13.3)	统一 President(11.9)	康师傅 Kangshifu(10.4) 美年达 Mirinda(10.4)
中间层 medium	233	汇源 Huiyuan(24.9)	椰树 Coconut Palm(13.7)	美年达 Mirinda(12.9)	康师傅 Kangshifu(11.6)
健康营养指向 health & nutrition orientation	131	汇源 Huiyuan(19.1)	椰树 Coconut Palm(16.0) 美年达 Mirinda(16.0)	康师傅 Kangshifu(11.5)	统一 President(5.3) 华旗 Huaqi(5.3)

5-13 重度消费者的消费者层构成/ The Composition of the Heavy Consumers

5-13-1 时尚流行指标/ Fads Popular Index

	人数 Number	平实生活指向 simple living orientation	时尚流行指向 fashion orientation
样本 Sample	**188**	**41.5**	**58.5**
天天喝 daily	16	31.3	68.8
一周 3 次或以上 3 times or over a week	42	40.5	59.5
一周 1~2 次 once or twice a week	130	43.1	56.9

5-13-2 广告态度指标/ Advertising Attitude Index

	人数 Number	广告淡漠指向 indifferent orientation	中间层 medium	信赖广告指向 loyal orientation
样本 Sample	**185**	**23.2**	**62.7**	**14.1**
天天喝 daily	14	35.7	57.1	7.1
一周 3 次或以上 3 times or over a week	41	34.1	48.8	17.1
一周 1~2 次 once or twice a week	130	18.5	67.7	13.8

5-13-3 饮食健康指标/ Foods & Drink Quality Index

	人数 Number	饮食“温饱”指向 "basic" orientation	中间层 medium	健康营养指向 health & nutrition orientation
样本 Sample	**189**	**22.8**	**45.5**	**31.7**
天天喝 daily	16	6.3	50.0	43.8
一周 3 次或以上 3 times or over a week	42	28.6	50.0	21.4
一周 1~2 次 once or twice a week	131	22.9	43.5	33.6

● 上海 / Shanghai

5-1 最近三个月饮用频率的比例/ Proportion of the Sample Consuming Fruit-flavored Beverage in the Last Three Months

	人数 Number	百分比 Percent
天天喝 daily	7	0.7
一周 3 次或以上 3 times or over a week	36	3.6
一周 1~2 次 once or twice a week	98	9.7
一个月 2～3 次 2 or 3 times a month	138	13.6
一个月 1 次 once a month	85	8.4
两个月 1 次 once two months	36	3.6
三个月 1 次或以下 once three months or below	47	4.6
没喝过 never	567	55.9

n=1014

5-2 最常用品牌排名/ Ranking of the Most Frequently Used Brands

排名 Brand Ranking	品牌 Brands	人数 Number	百分比 Percent
1	统一 President	103	23.4
2	佳得乐 Gatorade	65	14.8
3	美年达 Mirinda	53	12.0
4	椰树 Coconut Palm	46	10.5
5	正广和 Acquarius	31	7.0
5	新奇士 Sunkist	31	7.0
6	康师傅 Kangshifu	25	5.7
7	汇源 Huiyuan	19	4.3
8	雀巢 Nestle	13	3.0
9	维他 Vita	10	2.3
10	富迪 Gaodi	6	1.4
10	波蜜 Bomi	6	1.4

n=440

5-3 样本、男性各年龄层、女性各年龄层的常用品牌/ The Most Frequently Used Brands by the Whole Sample, Age and Gender Groups

	人数 Number	第一品牌及百分比 1st/ percent	第二品牌及百分比 2nd/ percent	第三品牌及百分比 3rd/ percent
样本 Sample	440	**统一 President(23.4)**	**佳得乐 Gatorade(14.8)**	**美年达 Mirinda(12.0)**
男性 Male	203	**统一 President(20.7)**	**佳得乐 Gatorade(13.3)**	**美年达 Mirinda(12.8)**
16~24 岁 Age	51	统一 President(25.5)	佳得乐 Gatorade(15.7) 康师傅 Kangshifu(15.7)	美年达 Mirinda(11.8)
25~34 岁 Age	70	统一 President(24.3)	佳得乐 Gatorade(14.3) 美年达 Mirinda(14.3)	椰树 Coconut Palm(10.0)
35~44 岁 Age	43	椰树 Coconut Palm(16.3) 美年达 Mirinda(16.3)	正广和 Acquarius(11.6)	统一 President(9.3) 佳得乐 Gatorade(9.3)
45~54 岁 Age	26	统一 President(23.1)	正广和 Acquarius(19.2)	椰树 Coconut Palm(15.4) 佳得乐 Gatorade(15.4)
55~60 岁 Age	13	康师傅 Kangshifu(15.4) 统一 President(15.4) 椰树 Coconut Palm(15.4) 正广和 Acquarius(15.4) 美年达 Mirinda(15.4)	佳得乐 Gatorade(7.7) 新奇士 Sunkist(7.7) 三得利 Suntory(7.7)	
女性 Female	237	**统一 President(25.7)**	**佳得乐 Gatorade(16.0)**	**美年达 Mirinda(11.4)**
16~24 岁 Age	70	统一 President(45.7)	佳得乐 Gatorade(22.9)	新奇士 Sunkist(8.6)
25~34 岁 Age	75	椰树 Coconut Palm(17.3) 佳得乐 Gatorade(17.3)	统一 President(16.0) 新奇士 Sunkist(16.0)	正广和 Acquarius(8.0)
35~44 岁 Age	60	统一 President(23.3)	美年达 Mirinda(16.7)	椰树 Coconut Palm(13.3)
45~54 岁 Age	20	美年达 Mirinda(35.0)	正广和 Acquarius(15.0)	统一 President(10.0) 佳得乐 Gatorade(10.0) 雀巢 Nestle(10.0)
55~60 岁 Age	12	佳得乐 Gatorade(25.0) 美年达 Mirinda(25.0)	椰树 Coconut Palm(16.7) 正广和 Acquarius(16.7)	统一 President(8.3) 维他 Vita(8.3)

5-4 理想品牌排名/ Ranking of the Ideal Brands

排名 Brand Ranking	品牌 Brands	人数 Number	百分比 Percent
1	统一 President	180	17.8
2	三得利 Suntory	107	10.6
3	佳得乐 Gatorade	87	8.6
4	美年达 Mirinda	63	6.2
5	椰树 Coconut Palm	52	5.1
6	汇源 Huiyuan	49	4.8
7	正广和 Acquarius	42	4.1
8	康师傅 Kangshifu	40	3.9
9	麒麟 Kirin	25	2.5
9	新奇士 Sunkist	25	2.5
10	富迪 Gaodi	14	1.4

n=1014

5-5 样本、男性各年龄层、女性各年龄层最近三个月有无购买的比例/ Purchasing in the Last Three Months by the Whole Sample, Age and Gender Groups

	人数 Number	买过 yes	没买过 no
样本 Sample	1014	42.0	58.0
男性 Male	509	37.9	62.1
16~24 岁 Age	109	44.0	56.0
25~34 岁 Age	146	45.9	54.1
35~44 岁 Age	130	31.5	68.5
45~54 岁 Age	85	29.4	70.6
55~60 岁 Age	39	30.8	69.2
女性 Female	505	46.1	53.9
16~24 岁 Age	108	59.3	40.7
25~34 岁 Age	144	50.7	49.3
35~44 岁 Age	130	47.7	52.3
45~54 岁 Age	82	25.6	74.4
55~60 岁 Age	41	31.7	68.3

5-6 样本、男性各年龄层、女性各年龄层最近三个月的饮用频率/ Frequencies of Consuming Fruit-flavored Beverage in the Last Three Months by the Whole Sample, Age and Gender Groups

	人数 Number	天天喝 daily	一周 3 次或以上 3 times or over a week	一周 1~2 次 once or twice a week	一个月 2~3 次 2 or 3 times a month	一个月 1 次 once a month	两个月 1 次 once two months	三个月 1 次或以下 once three months or below	没喝过 never
样本 Sample	1014	0.7	3.6	9.7	13.6	8.4	3.6	4.6	55.9
男性 Male	509	0.6	2.8	8.6	11.2	8.4	3.9	4.9	59.5
16~24 岁 Age	109	1.8	3.7	10.1	9.2	11.0	4.6	6.4	53.2
25~34 岁 Age	146	0.7	1.4	7.5	19.9	10.3	2.7	6.2	51.4
35~44 岁 Age	130	0.0	3.1	10.8	6.9	6.2	5.4	2.3	65.4
45~54 岁 Age	85	0.0	3.5	3.5	8.2	7.1	4.7	3.5	69.4
55~60 岁 Age	39	0.0	2.6	12.8	5.1	5.1	0.0	7.7	66.7
女性 Female	505	0.8	4.4	10.7	16.0	8.3	3.2	4.4	52.3
16~24 岁 Age	108	0.9	5.6	15.7	21.3	10.2	3.7	7.4	35.2
25~34 岁 Age	144	0.7	4.2	11.8	19.4	11.1	3.5	3.5	45.8
35~44 岁 Age	130	0.8	4.6	10.8	16.9	6.9	2.3	3.8	53.8
45~54 岁 Age	82	1.2	4.9	3.7	7.3	2.4	1.2	3.7	75.6
55~60 岁 Age	41	0.0	0.0	7.3	4.9	9.8	7.3	2.4	68.3

5-7 样本、男性各年龄层、女性各年龄层的品牌习惯/ Brand Habit in Consuming Fruit-flavored Beverage by the Whole Sample, Age and Gender Groups

	人数 Number	基本固定饮用一个牌子 used in only one brand	比较固定地饮用两个或三个牌子 used in two or three brands	基本上不太固定牌子 no brand preference
样本 Sample	447	32.0	43.6	24.4
男性 Male	206	33.0	42.7	24.3
16~24 岁 Age	51	29.4	51.0	19.6
25~34 岁 Age	71	36.6	43.7	19.7
35~44 岁 Age	45	28.9	35.6	35.6
45~54 岁 Age	26	42.3	34.6	23.1
55~60 岁 Age	13	23.1	46.2	30.8
女性 Female	241	31.1	44.4	24.5
16~24 岁 Age	70	21.4	44.3	34.3
25~34 岁 Age	78	37.2	46.2	16.7
35~44 岁 Age	60	35.0	43.3	21.7
45~54 岁 Age	20	35.0	40.0	25.0
55~60 岁 Age	13	23.1	46.2	30.8

5-8 选择该类商品的考虑因素/ Ranking of the Considerations in Purchasing

注：本题为多选题，合计百分比超过 100%（Multiple answers）

排名 Ranking	考虑因素 Considerations	人次 Person-time	百分比 Percent
1	口味好 pleasant taste	311	69.6
2	价格适中 reasonable price	138	30.9
3	有名的牌子 famous brand	134	30.0
4	购买方便 easy to buy	84	18.8
5	生产日期 date of producing	66	14.8
6	广告影响 influence of advertising	55	12.3
7	只是由于习惯 out of habit	23	5.1
8	朋友推荐 introduction of friends	20	4.5
9	有优惠条件 with preferential terms	18	4.0
10	包装吸引人 appealing package	14	3.1
11	别人送的 given by other people	10	2.2
12	单位发的 offered by the working unit	5	1.1
12	其它 others	5	1.1
13	售货员介绍 introduced by the shop assistants	3	0.7

n=447

5-9 样本、男性各年龄层、女性各年龄层最常饮用的包装形式/ Types of Package of the Consumed Fruit-flavored Beverage by the Whole Sample, Age and Gender Groups

	人数 Number	纸盒 paper box	塑料瓶 plastic bottle	玻璃瓶 glass bottle	纸杯 paper cup	易开罐 tin	铝皮桶 aluminum cans	其它 others
样本 Sample	445	31.2	34.8	14.8	2.5	14.4	2.2	0.0
男性 Male	205	28.8	39.5	13.7	2.9	12.2	2.9	0.0
16~24 岁 Age	51	35.3	29.4	17.6	3.9	13.7	0.0	0.0
25~34 岁 Age	71	29.6	39.4	14.1	2.8	9.9	4.2	0.0
35~44 岁 Age	44	25.0	36.4	13.6	4.5	18.2	2.3	0.0
45~54 岁 Age	26	26.9	50.0	7.7	0.0	11.5	3.8	0.0
55~60 岁 Age	13	15.4	69.2	7.7	0.0	0.0	7.7	0.0
女性 Female	240	33.3	30.8	15.8	2.1	16.3	1.7	0.0
16~24 岁 Age	70	41.4	25.7	18.6	2.9	11.4	0.0	0.0
25~34 岁 Age	78	30.8	30.8	15.4	2.6	19.2	1.3	0.0
35~44 岁 Age	60	35.0	28.3	15.0	0.0	18.3	3.3	0.0
45~54 岁 Age	19	21.1	36.8	15.8	5.3	21.1	0.0	0.0
55~60 岁 Age	13	15.4	61.5	7.7	0.0	7.7	7.7	0.0

5-10 样本、男性各年龄层、女性各年龄层最常饮用场合/ Settings of Consumption by the Whole Sample, Age and Gender Groups

注：本题为多选题，合计百分比超过 100%（Multiple answers）

	人数 Number	平时口渴时 when thirsty	平时吃饭喝 at dinner	宴席、聚会喝 at banquet	外出、旅游时 outing/traveling	补充营养 supplementing nutrition	其它 others
样本 Sample	445	58.2	8.5	19.6	33.7	11.2	1.8
男性 Male	206	55.3	6.3	19.4	33.0	14.6	1.9
16~24 岁 Age	51	68.6	3.9	15.7	29.4	15.7	2.0
25~34 岁 Age	71	59.2	8.5	15.5	28.2	15.5	1.4
35~44 岁 Age	45	44.4	4.4	17.8	40.0	17.8	2.2
45~54 岁 Age	26	34.6	3.8	34.6	42.3	11.5	3.8
55~60 岁 Age	13	61.5	15.4	30.8	30.8	0.0	0.0
女性 Female	239	60.7	10.5	19.7	34.3	8.4	1.7
16~24 岁 Age	70	61.4	7.1	7.1	42.9	10.0	1.4
25~34 岁 Age	77	62.3	11.7	16.9	32.5	10.4	1.3
35~44 岁 Age	60	58.3	8.3	33.3	33.3	5.0	3.3
45~54 岁 Age	20	60.0	25.0	25.0	15.0	10.0	0.0
55~60 岁 Age	12	58.3	8.3	33.3	33.3	0.0	0.0

5-11 重度消费者人口分布/ Demographics of the Heavy Consumers

	人数 Number	16-24 岁 Age	25-34 岁 Age	35-44 岁 Age	45-54 岁 Age	55-60 岁 Age
样本 Sample	141	29.1	27.0	27.7	9.9	6.4
男性 Male	61	27.9	23.0	29.5	9.8	9.8
天天喝 daily	3	66.7	33.3	0.0	0.0	0.0
一周 3 次或以上 3 times or over a week	14	28.6	14.3	28.6	21.4	7.1
一周 1~2 次 once or twice a week	44	25.0	25.0	31.8	6.8	11.4
女性 Female	80	30.0	30.0	26.3	10.0	3.8
天天喝 daily	4	25.0	25.0	25.0	25.0	0.0
一周 3 次或以上 3 times or over a week	22	27.3	27.3	27.3	18.2	0.0
一周 1~2 次 once or twice a week	54	31.5	31.5	25.9	5.6	5.6

5-12 不同消费者层的常用品牌/ The Most Frequently Used Brands by Market Segments

5-12-1 时尚流行指标/ Fads Popular Index

	人数 Number	第一品牌及百分比 1st/ percent	第二品牌及百分比 2nd/ percent	第三品牌及百分比 3rd/ percent	第四品牌及百分比 4th/ percent
样本 Sample	437	**统一 President(23.3)**	**佳得乐 Gatorade(14.9)**	**美年达 Mirinda(11.9)**	**椰树 Coconut Palm(10.5)**
平实生活指向 simple living orientation	160	统一 President(21.3)	美年达 Mirinda(16.3)	佳得乐 Gatorade(11.9) 椰树 Coconut Palm(11.9)	正广和 Acquarius(8.8)
时尚流行指向 fashion orientation	277	统一 President(24.5)	佳得乐 Gatorade(16.6)	椰树 Coconut Palm(9.7)	美年达 Mirinda(9.4)

5-12-2 广告态度指标/ Advertising Attitude Index

	人数 Number	第一品牌及百分比 1st/ percent	第二品牌及百分比 2nd/ percent	第三品牌及百分比 3rd/ percent	第四品牌及百分比 4th/ percent
样本 Sample	434	**统一 President(23.3)**	**佳得乐 Gatorade(15.0)**	**美年达 Mirinda(12.0)**	**椰树 Coconut Palm(10.6)**
广告淡漠指向 indifferent orientation	96	统一 President(19.8)	佳得乐 Gatorade(17.7)	美年达 Mirinda(16.7)	椰树 Coconut Palm(10.4)
中间层 medium	262	统一 President(24.4)	椰树 CoconutPalm(12.2)	佳得乐 Gatorade(11.8)	美年达 Mirinda(11.5)
信赖广告指向 loyal orientation	76	统一 President(23.7)	佳得乐 Gatorade(22.4)	新奇士 Sunkist(10.5)	美年达 Mirinda(7.9)

5-12-3 饮食健康指标/ Foods & Drink Quality Index

	人数 Number	第一品牌及百分比 1st/ percent	第二品牌及百分比 2nd/ percent	第三品牌及百分比 3rd/ percent	第四品牌及百分比 4th/ percent
样本 Sample	437	**统一 President(23.6)**	**佳得乐 Gatorade(14.9)**	**美年达 Mirinda(12.1)**	**椰树 Coconut Palm(10.5)**
饮食"温饱"指向 "basic" orientation	83	统一 President(20.5)	佳得乐 Gatorade(18.1)	美年达 Mirinda(13.3) 椰树 CoconutPalm(13.3)	正广和 Acquarius(8.4)
中间层 medium	210	统一 President(24.3)	佳得乐 Gatorade(14.8)	美年达 Mirinda(12.9)	椰树 Coconut Palm(8.1)
健康营养指向 health & nutrition orientation	144	统一 President(24.3)	佳得乐 Gatorade(13.2)	椰树 Coconut Palm(12.5)	美年达 Mirinda(10.4)

5-13 重度消费者的消费者层构成/ The Composition of the Heavy Consumers

5-13-1 时尚流行指标/ Fads Popular Index

	人数 Number	平实生活指向 simple living orientation	时尚流行指向 fashion orientation
样本 Sample	140	36.4	63.6
天天喝 daily	7	14.3	85.7
一周 3 次或以上 3 times or over a week	36	36.1	63.9
一周 1~2 次 once or twice a week	97	38.1	61.9

5-13-2 广告态度指标/ Advertising Attitude Index

	人数 Number	广告淡漠指向 indifferent orientation	中间层 medium	信赖广告指向 loyal orientation
样本 Sample	138	20.3	60.9	18.8
天天喝 daily	7	28.6	42.9	28.6
一周 3 次或以上 3 times or over a week	36	8.3	58.3	33.3
一周 1~2 次 once or twice a week	95	24.2	63.2	12.6

5-13-3 饮食健康指标/ Foods & Drink Quality Index

	人数 Number	饮食"温饱"指向 "basic" orientation	中间层 medium	健康营养指向 health & nutrition orientation
样本 Sample	139	18.0	48.2	33.8
天天喝 daily	7	14.3	71.4	14.3
一周 3 次或以上 3 times or over a week	36	16.7	44.4	38.9
一周 1~2 次 once or twice a week	96	18.8	47.9	33.3

● 广州 / Guangzhou

5-1 最近三个月饮用频率的比例/ Proportion of the Sample Consuming Fruit-flavored Beverage in the Last Three Months

	人数 Number	百分比 Percent
天天喝 daily	3	0.3
一周 3 次或以上 3 times or over a week	21	2.0
一周 1~2 次 once or twice a week	93	9.0
一个月 2～3 次 2 or 3 times a month	165	16.0
一个月 1 次 once a month	84	8.1
两个月 1 次 once two months	48	4.7
三个月 1 次或以下 once three months or below	57	5.5
没喝过 never	560	54.3

n=1031

5-2 最常用品牌排名/ Ranking of the Most Frequently Used Brands

排名 Brand Ranking	品牌 Brands	人数 Number	百分比 Percent
1	新奇士 Sunkist	155	33.9
2	美年达 Mirinda	48	10.5
3	椰树 Coconut Palm	45	9.8
3	佳得乐 Gatorade	45	9.8
4	统一 President	40	8.8
5	康师傅 Kangshifu	36	7.9
6	杨协成 Yeo's	32	7.0
7	维他 Vita	15	3.3
8	雀巢 Nestle	11	2.4

n=457

5-3 样本、男性各年龄层、女性各年龄层的常用品牌/ The Most Frequently Used Brands by the Whole Sample, Age and Gender Groups

	人数 Number	第一品牌及百分比 1st/ percent	第二品牌及百分比 2nd/ percent	第三品牌及百分比 3rd/ percent	第四品牌及百分比 4th/ percent
样本 Sample	**457**	**新奇士 Sunkist(33.9)**	**美年达 Mirinda(10.5)**	**椰树 Coconut Palm(9.8)** **佳得乐 Gatorade(9.8)**	**统一 President(8.8)**
男性 Male	**187**	**新奇士 Sunkist(35.3)**	**佳得乐 Gatorade(11.8)**	**椰树 Coconut Palm(10.2)** **美年达 Mirinda(10.2)**	**杨协成 Yeo's(8.0)** **康师傅 Kangshifu(8.0)**
16~24 岁 Age	47	新奇士 Sunkist(27.7)	统一 President(14.9)	佳得乐 Gatorade(12.8)	美年达 Mirinda(10.6)
25~34 岁 Age	66	新奇士 Sunkist(37.9)	椰树 Coconut Palm(15.2)	佳得乐 Gatorade(13.6)	美年达 Mirinda(9.1)
35~44 岁 Age	43	新奇士 Sunkist(48.8)	美年达 Mirinda(11.6)	杨协成 Yeo's(9.3)	康师傅 Kangshifu(7.0) 佳得乐 Gatorade(7.0)
45~54 岁 Age	20	康师傅 Kangshifu(15.0) 椰树 Coconut Palm(15.0) 佳得乐 Gatorade(15.0)	汇源 Huiyuan(10.0) 新奇士 Sunkist(10.0) 维他 Vita(10.0) 美年达 Mirinda(10.0)	统一 President(5.0) 杨协成 Yeo's(5.0) 可的 Kedi(5.0)	
55~60 岁 Age	11	新奇士 Sunkist(45.5)	杨协成 Yeo's(18.2)	康师傅 Kangshifu(9.1) 椰树 Coconut Palm(9.1) 佳得乐 Gatorade(9.1) 美年达 Mirinda(9.1)	
女性 Female	**270**	**新奇士 Sunkist(33.0)**	**美年达 Mirinda(10.7)**	**统一 President(10.0)**	**椰树 Coconut Palm(9.6)**
16~24 岁 Age	70	新奇士 Sunkist(28.6)	统一 President(18.6)	康师傅 Kangshifu(11.4)	佳得乐 Gatorade(10.0)
25~34 岁 Age	81	新奇士 Sunkist(40.7)	椰树 Coconut Palm(14.8)	美年达 Mirinda(9.9)	统一 President(8.6)
35~44 岁 Age	67	新奇士 Sunkist(28.4)	佳得乐 Gatorade(14.9)	美年达 Mirinda(10.4)	康师傅 Kangshifu(9.0) 统一 President(9.0)
45~54 岁 Age	41	新奇士 Sunkist(36.6)	美年达 Mirinda(14.6)	杨协成 Yeo's(12.2)	佳得乐 Gatorade(9.8)
55~60 岁 Age	11	椰树 Coconut Palm(36.4)	美年达 Mirinda(27.3)	新奇士 Sunkist(18.2)	汇源 Huiyuan(9.1) 华旗 Huaqi(9.1)

5-4 理想品牌排名/ Ranking of the Ideal Brands

排名 Brand Ranking	品牌 Brands	人数 Number	百分比 Percent
1	新奇士 Sunkist	175	16.9
2	佳得乐 Gatorade	65	6.3
3	统一 President	57	5.5
4	美年达 Mirinda	48	4.6
5	椰树 Coconut Palm	37	3.6
6	康师傅 Kangshifu	27	2.6
7	杨协成 Yeo's	26	2.5
8	汇源 Huiyuan	16	1.5
9	天与地 Tianyudi	10	1.0

n=1034

5-5 样本、男性各年龄层、女性各年龄层最近三个月有无购买的比例/ Purchasing in the Last Three Months by the Whole Sample, Age and Gender Groups

	人数 Number	买过 yes	没买过 no
样本 Sample	1034	43.1	56.9
男性 Male	499	36.9	63.1
16~24 岁 Age	106	42.5	57.5
25~34 岁 Age	150	42.0	58.0
35~44 岁 Age	127	33.9	66.1
45~54 岁 Age	73	28.8	71.2
55~60 岁 Age	43	27.9	72.1
女性 Female	535	49.0	51.0
16~24 岁 Age	112	57.1	42.9
25~34 岁 Age	158	51.9	48.1
35~44 岁 Age	137	50.4	49.6
45~54 岁 Age	87	43.7	56.3
55~60 岁 Age	41	22.0	78.0

5-6 样本、男性各年龄层、女性各年龄层最近三个月的饮用频率/ Frequencies of Consuming Fruit-flavored Beverage in the Last Three Months by the Whole Sample, Age and Gender Groups

	人数 Number	天天喝 daily	一周3次或以上 3 times or over a week	一周1~2次 once or twice a week	一个月2~3次 2 or 3 times a month	一个月1次 once a month	两个月1次 once two months	三个月1次或以下 once three months or below	没喝过 never
样本 Sample	1031	0.3	2.0	9.0	16.0	8.1	4.7	5.5	54.3
男性 Male	496	0.4	1.6	7.5	15.1	6.9	4.2	3.6	60.7
16~24 岁 Age	106	0.0	0.9	8.5	17.9	8.5	4.7	3.8	55.7
25~34 岁 Age	150	0.0	2.0	8.0	20.7	7.3	5.3	4.0	52.7
35~44 岁 Age	126	1.6	0.8	7.9	11.9	5.6	3.2	4.0	65.1
45~54 岁 Age	72	0.0	1.4	6.9	11.1	2.8	4.2	2.8	70.8
55~60 岁 Age	42	0.0	4.8	2.4	4.8	11.9	2.4	2.4	71.4
女性 Female	535	0.2	2.4	10.5	16.8	9.3	5.0	7.3	48.4
16~24 岁 Age	112	0.0	2.7	17.0	20.5	8.9	7.1	6.3	37.5
25~34 岁 Age	158	0.0	0.6	10.1	22.2	8.9	5.1	7.0	46.2
35~44 岁 Age	137	0.7	5.1	7.3	13.9	8.8	6.6	8.0	49.6
45~54 岁 Age	87	0.0	2.3	9.2	12.6	13.8	1.1	8.0	52.9
55~60 岁 Age	41	0.0	0.0	7.3	4.9	4.9	2.4	7.3	73.2

5-7 样本、男性各年龄层、女性各年龄层的品牌习惯/ Brand Habit in Consuming Fruit-flavored Beverage by the Whole Sample, Age and Gender Groups

	人数 Number	基本固定饮用一个牌子 used in only one brand	比较固定地饮用两个或三个牌子 used in two or three brands	基本上不太固定牌子 no brand preference
样本 Sample	471	29.9	48.0	22.1
男性 Male	195	31.8	45.1	23.1
16~24 岁 Age	47	34.0	44.7	21.3
25~34 岁 Age	71	32.4	46.5	21.1
35~44 岁 Age	44	22.7	54.5	22.7
45~54 岁 Age	21	33.3	33.3	33.3
55~60 岁 Age	12	50.0	25.0	25.0
女性 Female	276	28.6	50.0	21.4
16~24 岁 Age	70	32.9	50.0	17.1
25~34 岁 Age	85	27.1	57.6	15.3
35~44 岁 Age	69	27.5	44.9	27.5
45~54 岁 Age	41	29.3	43.9	26.8
55~60 岁 Age	11	18.2	45.5	36.4

5-8 选择该类商品的考虑因素/ Ranking of the Considerations in Purchasing

注：本题为多选题，合计百分比超过 100%（Multiple answers）

排名 Ranking	考虑因素 Considerations	人次 Person-time	百分比 Percent
1	口味好 pleasant taste	326	69.2
2	价格适中 reasonable price	160	34.0
3	有名的牌子 famous brand	156	33.1
4	购买方便 easy to buy	104	22.1
5	生产日期 date of producing	82	17.4
6	广告影响 influence of advertising	40	8.5
7	只是由于习惯 out of habit	28	5.9
8	包装吸引人 appealing package	19	4.0
9	有优惠条件 with preferential terms	14	3.0
10	朋友推荐 introduction of friends	13	2.8
11	别人送的 given by other people	10	2.1
12	单位发的 offered by the working unit	6	1.3
13	售货员介绍 introduced by the shop assistants	2	0.4
13	其它 others	2	0.4

n=471

5-9 样本、男性各年龄层、女性各年龄层最常饮用的包装形式/ Types of Package of the Consumed Fruit-flavored Beverage by the Whole Sample, Age and Gender Groups

	人数 Number	纸盒 paper box	塑料瓶 plastic bottle	玻璃瓶 glass bottle	纸杯 paper cup	易开罐 tin	铝皮桶 aluminium cans	其它 others
样本 Sample	**466**	**28.1**	**22.7**	**13.7**	**1.1**	**32.2**	**2.1**	**0.0**
男性 Male	**193**	**27.5**	**22.3**	**18.1**	**0.5**	**29.0**	**2.6**	**0.0**
16~24 岁 Age	47	29.8	19.1	23.4	0.0	25.5	2.1	0.0
25~34 岁 Age	70	24.3	18.6	20.0	0.0	35.7	1.4	0.0
35~44 岁 Age	43	23.3	30.2	14.0	2.3	27.9	2.3	0.0
45~54 岁 Age	21	47.6	14.3	14.3	0.0	19.0	4.8	0.0
55~60 岁 Age	12	16.7	41.7	8.3	0.0	25.0	8.3	0.0
女性 Female	**273**	**28.6**	**23.1**	**10.6**	**1.5**	**34.4**	**1.8**	**0.0**
16~24 岁 Age	69	46.4	14.5	5.8	0.0	30.4	2.9	0.0
25~34 岁 Age	84	20.2	21.4	9.5	1.2	45.2	2.4	0.0
35~44 岁 Age	68	23.5	30.9	11.8	2.9	30.9	0.0	0.0
45~54 岁 Age	41	24.4	26.8	14.6	2.4	29.3	2.4	0.0
55~60 岁 Age	11	27.3	27.3	27.3	0.0	18.2	0.0	0.0

5-10 样本、男性各年龄层、女性各年龄层最常饮用场合/ Settings of Consumption by the Whole Sample, Age and Gender Groups

注：本题为多选题，合计百分比超过 100%（Multiple answers）

	人数 Number	平时口渴时 when thirsty	平时吃饭喝 at dinner	宴席、聚会喝 at banquet	外出、旅游时 outing/traveling	补充营养 supplementing nutrition	其它 others
样本 Sample	**464**	**62.3**	**3.7**	**15.3**	**32.5**	**13.4**	**2.8**
男性 Male	**193**	**63.7**	**4.1**	**14.5**	**29.5**	**10.9**	**3.6**
16~24 岁 Age	47	66.0	2.1	8.5	27.7	10.6	4.3
25~34 岁 Age	70	67.1	4.3	14.3	31.4	8.6	5.7
35~44 岁 Age	43	51.2	4.7	20.9	32.6	16.3	2.3
45~54 岁 Age	21	66.7	4.8	23.8	23.8	9.5	0.0
55~60 岁 Age	12	75.0	8.3	0.0	25.0	8.3	0.0
女性 Female	**271**	**61.3**	**3.3**	**15.9**	**34.7**	**15.1**	**2.2**
16~24 岁 Age	70	67.1	2.9	8.6	44.3	17.1	1.4
25~34 岁 Age	82	64.6	2.4	12.2	32.9	12.2	2.4
35~44 岁 Age	68	57.4	4.4	20.6	35.3	14.7	0.0
45~54 岁 Age	40	52.5	5.0	27.5	30.0	12.5	7.5
55~60 岁 Age	11	54.5	0.0	13.2	0.0	36.4	0.0

5-11 重度消费者人口分布/ Demographics of the Heavy Consumers

	人数 Number	16-24 岁 Age	25-34 岁 Age	35-44 岁 Age	45-54 岁 Age	55-60 岁 Age
样本 Sample	**117**	**27.4**	**27.4**	**26.5**	**13.7**	**5.1**
男性 Male	**47**	**21.3**	**31.9**	**27.7**	**12.8**	**6.4**
天天喝 daily	2	0.0	0.0	100.0	0.0	0.0
一周 3 次或以上 3 times or over a week	8	12.5	37.5	12.5	12.5	25.0
一周 1~2 次 once or twice a week	37	24.3	32.4	27.0	13.5	2.7
女性 Female	**70**	**31.4**	**24.3**	**25.7**	**14.3**	**4.3**
天天喝 daily	1	0.0	0.0	100.0	0.0	0.0
一周 3 次或以上 3 times or over a week	13	23.1	7.7	53.8	15.4	0.0
一周 1~2 次 once or twice a week	56	33.9	28.6	17.9	14.3	5.4

5-12 不同消费者层的常用品牌/ The Most Frequently Used Brands by Market Segments

5-12-1 时尚流行指标/ Fads Popular Index

	人数 Number	第一品牌及百分比 1st/ percent	第二品牌及百分比 2nd/ percent	第三品牌及百分比 3rd/ percent	第四品牌及百分比 4th/ percent
样本 Sample	**452**	**新奇士 Sunkist(33.6)**	**美年达 Mirinda(10.6)**	**椰树 Coconut Palm(9.7) 佳得乐 Gatorade(9.7)**	**统一 President(8.8)**
平实生活指向 simple living orientation	207	新奇士 Sunkist(33.3)	椰树 Coconut Palm(12.6)	美年达 Mirinda(11.1)	佳得乐 Gatorade(8.2)
时尚流行指向 fashion orientation	245	新奇士 Sunkist(33.9)	佳得乐 Gatorade(11.0)	统一 President(10.6)	美年达 Mirinda(10.2)

5-12-2 广告态度指标/ Advertising Attitude Index

	人数 Number	第一品牌及百分比 1st/ percent	第二品牌及百分比 2nd/ percent	第三品牌及百分比 3rd/ percent	第四品牌及百分比 4th/ percent
样本 Sample	**447**	**新奇士 Sunkist(34.0)**	**美年达 Mirinda(10.7)**	**椰树 Coconut Palm(9.8)**	**佳得乐 Gatorade(9.4)**
广告淡漠指向 indifferent orientation	130	新奇士 Sunkist(35.4)	椰树 Coconut Palm(12.3)	佳得乐 Gatorade(11.5)	美年达 Mirinda(10.0)
中间层 medium	266	新奇士 Sunkist(32.3)	统一 President(11.7)	美年达 Mirinda(11.3)	康师傅 Kangshifu(9.0)
信赖广告指向 loyal orientation	51	新奇士 Sunkist(39.2)	杨协成 Yeo's(13.7)	佳得乐 Gatorade(11.8)	椰树 Coconut Palm(9.8) 美年达 Mirinda(9.8)

5-12-3 饮食健康指标/ Foods & Drink Quality Index

	人数 Number	第一品牌及百分比 1st/ percent	第二品牌及百分比 2nd/ percent	第三品牌及百分比 3rd/ percent	第四品牌及百分比 4th/ percent
样本 Sample	**456**	**新奇士 Sunkist(34.0)**	**美年达 Mirinda(10.3)**	**椰树 Coconut Palm(9.9) 佳得乐 Gatorade(9.9)**	**统一 President(8.8)**
饮食“温饱”指向 "basic" orientation	120	新奇士 Sunkist(34.2)	美年达 Mirinda(10.0)	统一 President(9.2) 佳得乐 Gatorade(9.2)	椰树 Coconut Palm(8.3)
中间层 medium	238	新奇士 Sunkist(34.5)	佳得乐 Gatorade(11.3)	椰树 Coconut Palm(10.1)	美年达 Mirinda(9.7)
健康营养指向 health & nutrition orientation	98	新奇士 Sunkist(32.7)	美年达 Mirinda(12.2)	椰树 Coconut Palm(11.2) 杨协成 Yeo's(11.2)	统一 President(8.2)

5-13 重度消费者的消费者层构成/ The Composition of the Heavy Consumers

5-13-1 时尚流行指标/ Fads Popular Index

	人数 Number	平实生活指向 simple living orientation	时尚流行指向 fashion orientation
样本 Sample	**116**	**43.1**	**56.9**
天天喝 daily	3	33.3	66.7
一周 3 次或以上 3 times or over a week	21	57.1	42.9
一周 1~2 次 once or twice a week	92	40.2	59.8

5-13-2 广告态度指标/ Advertising Attitude Index

	人数 Number	广告淡漠指向 indifferent orientation	中间层 medium	信赖广告指向 loyal orientation
样本 Sample	**115**	**30.4**	**61.7**	**7.8**
天天喝 daily	3	33.3	33.3	33.3
一周 3 次或以上 3 times or over a week	21	57.1	42.9	0.0
一周 1~2 次 once or twice a week	91	24.2	67.0	8.8

5-13-3 饮食健康指标/ Foods & Drink Quality Index

	人数 Number	饮食“温饱”指向 "basic" orientation	中间层 medium	健康营养指向 health & nutrition orientation
样本 Sample	**117**	**24.8**	**50.4**	**24.8**
天天喝 daily	3	0.0	33.3	66.7
一周 3 次或以上 3 times or over a week	21	14.3	66.7	19.0
一周 1~2 次 once or twice a week	93	28.0	47.3	24.7

● 重庆 / Chongqing

5-1 最近三个月饮用频率的比例/ Proportion of the Sample Consuming Fruit-flavored Beverage in the Last Three Months

	人数 Number	百分比 Percent
天天喝 daily	5	0.8
一周 3 次或以上 3 times or over a week	18	2.9
一周 1~2 次 once or twice a week	47	7.5
一个月 2～3 次 2 or 3 times a month	59	9.5
一个月 1 次 once a month	34	5.5
两个月 1 次 once two months	24	3.9
三个月 1 次或以下 once three months or below	28	4.5
没喝过 never	408	65.5

n=623

5-2 最常用品牌排名/ Ranking of the Most Frequently Used Brands

排名 Brand Ranking	品牌 Brands	人数 Number	百分比 Percent
1	美年达 Mirinda	78	37.0
2	椰树 Coconut Palm	31	14.7
3	康师傅 Kangshifu	18	8.5
4	统一 President	16	7.6
4	汇源 Huiyuan	16	7.6
5	雀巢 Nestle	15	7.1
6	椰风 Cocowind	11	5.2
7	维他 Vita	5	2.4

n=211

5-3 样本、男性各年龄层、女性各年龄层的常用品牌/ The Most Frequently Used Brands by the Whole Sample, Age and Gender Groups

	人数 Number	第一品牌及百分比 1st/ percent	第二品牌及百分比 2nd/ percent	第三品牌及百分比 3rd/ percent	第四品牌及百分比 4th/ percent
样本 Sample	211	**美年达 Mirinda(37.0)**	**椰树 Coconut Palm(14.7)**	**康师傅 Kangshifu(8.5)**	**统一 President(7.6)** **汇源 Huiyuan(7.6)**
男性 Male	107	**美年达 Mirinda(42.1)**	**椰树 Coconut Palm(10.3)**	**雀巢 Nestle(8.4)**	**汇源 Huiyuan(7.5)**
16~24 岁 Age	28	美年达 Mirinda(42.9)	康师傅 Kangshifu(10.7) 汇源 Huiyuan(10.7) 雀巢 Nestle(10.7)	统一 President(7.1) 椰风 Cocowind(7.1)	华旗 Huaqi(3.6) 旺仔 Wangzi(3.6) 奇汁果 Qizhiguo(3.6)
25~34 岁 Age	35	美年达 Mirinda(40.0)	椰树 Coconut Palm(20.0)	雀巢 Nestle(11.4)	椰风 Cocowind(8.6)
35~44 岁 Age	24	美年达 Mirinda(54.2)	康师傅 Kangshifu(12.5)	椰树 Coconut Palm(8.3) 旺仔 Wangzi(8.3)	统一 President(4.2) 汇源 Huiyuan(4.2) 新的 Sunquick(4.2) 维他 Vita(4.2)
45~54 岁 Age	11	美年达 Mirinda(36.4)	汇源 Huiyuan(18.2)	康师傅 Kangshifu(9.1) 统一 President(9.1) 椰风 Cocowind(9.1) 旺仔 Wangzi(9.1) 波蜜 Bomi(9.1)	
55~60 岁 Age	9	椰树 Coconut Palm(22.2) 美年达 Mirinda(22.2) 雀巢 Nestle(22.2)	统一 President(11.1) 汇源 Huiyuan(11.1) 椰风 Cocowind(11.1)		
女性 Female	104	**美年达 Mirinda(31.7)**	**椰树 Coconut Palm(19.2)**	**康师傅 Kangshifu(10.6)**	**统一 President(9.6)**
16~24 岁 Age	35	美年达 Mirinda(31.4)	统一 President(17.1)	汇源 Huiyuan(11.4) 椰树 Coconut Palm(11.4)	椰风 Cocowind(8.6) 雀巢 Nestle(8.6)
25~34 岁 Age	34	美年达 Mirinda(35.3)	椰树 Coconut Palm(29.4)	康师傅 Kangshifu(11.8)	统一 President(8.8)
35~44 岁 Age	19	美年达 Mirinda(26.3)	康师傅 Kangshifu(21.1)	椰树 Coconut Palm(15.8)	汇源 Huiyuan(10.5) 维他 Vita(10.5)
45~54 岁 Age	12	椰树 Coconut Palm(25.0) 美年达 Mirinda(25.0)	康师傅 Kangshifu(8.3) 新奇士 Sunkist(8.3) 正广和 Acquarius(8.3) 波蜜 Bomi(8.3) 雀巢 Nestle(8.3)		
55~60 岁 Age	4	美年达 Mirinda(50.0)	统一 President(25.0)		

5-4 理想品牌排名/ Ranking of the Ideal Brands

排名 Brand Ranking	品牌 Brands	人数 Number	百分比 Percent
1	美年达 Mirinda	97	15.6
2	汇源 Huiyuan	76	12.2
3	椰树 Coconut Palm	36	5.8
4	康师傅 Kangshifu	26	4.2
5	统一 President	18	2.9
6	椰风 Cocowind	16	2.6
6	雀巢 Nestle	16	2.6
7	健力宝 Jianlibao	8	1.3
8	旺仔 Wangzi	5	0.8
9	阳公 Suncle	4	0.6
9	必是 Beshe	4	0.6
9	波蜜 Bomi	4	0.6
10	维他 Vita	3	0.5

n=623

5-5 样本、男性各年龄层、女性各年龄层最近三个月有无购买的比例/ Purchasing in the Last Three Months by the Whole Sample, Age and Gender Groups

	人数 Number	买过 yes	没买过 no
样本 Sample	624	33.8	66.2
男性 Male	314	34.1	65.9
16~24 岁 Age	64	39.1	60.9
25~34 岁 Age	93	38.7	61.3
35~44 岁 Age	75	36.0	64.0
45~54 岁 Age	54	20.4	79.6
55~60 岁 Age	28	28.6	71.4
女性 Female	310	33.5	66.5
16~24 岁 Age	64	54.7	45.3
25~34 岁 Age	90	38.9	61.1
35~44 岁 Age	73	28.8	71.2
45~54 岁 Age	60	15.0	85.0
55~60 岁 Age	23	17.4	82.6

5-6 样本、男性各年龄层、女性各年龄层最近三个月的饮用频率/ Frequencies of Consuming Fruit-flavored Beverage in the Last Three Months by the Whole Sample, Age and Gender Groups

	人数 Number	天天喝 daily	一周 3 次或以上 3 times or over a week	一周 1~2 次 once or twice a week	一个月 2~3 次 2 or 3 times a month	一个月 1 次 once a month	两个月 1 次 once two months	三个月 1 次或以下 once three months or below	没喝过 never
样本 Sample	623	0.8	2.9	7.5	9.5	5.5	3.9	4.5	65.5
男性 Male	314	0.6	3.2	8.3	8.3	6.1	4.1	3.8	65.6
16~24 岁 Age	64	0.0	6.3	15.6	7.8	4.7	3.1	6.3	56.3
25~34 岁 Age	93	1.1	3.2	7.5	7.5	10.8	4.3	3.2	62.4
35~44 岁 Age	75	0.0	1.3	8.0	9.3	4.0	6.7	2.7	68.0
45~54 岁 Age	54	0.0	3.7	1.9	5.6	3.7	3.7	3.7	77.8
55~60 岁 Age	28	3.6	0.0	7.1	14.3	3.6	0.0	3.6	67.9
女性 Female	309	1.0	2.6	6.8	10.7	4.9	3.6	5.2	65.4
16~24 岁 Age	64	1.6	1.6	15.6	14.1	6.3	7.8	10.9	42.2
25~34 岁 Age	90	1.1	3.3	5.6	13.3	4.4	5.6	4.4	62.2
35~44 岁 Age	72	1.4	2.8	6.9	8.3	5.6	1.4	1.4	72.2
45~54 岁 Age	60	0.0	0.0	1.7	8.3	3.3	0.0	6.7	80.0
55~60 岁 Age	23	0.0	8.7	0.0	4.3	4.3	0.0	0.0	82.6

5-7 样本、男性各年龄层、女性各年龄层的品牌习惯/ Brand Habit in Consuming Fruit-flavored Beverage by the Whole Sample, Age and Gender Groups

	人数 Number	基本固定饮用一个牌子 used in only one brand	比较固定地饮用两个或三个牌子 used in two or three brands	基本上不太固定牌子 no brand preference
样本 Sample	215	36.7	40.0	23.3
男性 Male	108	37.0	38.0	25.0
16~24 岁 Age	28	32.1	57.1	10.7
25~34 岁 Age	35	37.1	34.3	28.6
35~44 岁 Age	24	45.8	29.2	25.0
45~54 岁 Age	12	25.0	25.0	50.0
55~60 岁 Age	9	44.4	33.3	22.2
女性 Female	107	36.4	42.1	21.5
16~24 岁 Age	37	37.8	37.8	24.3
25~34 岁 Age	34	29.4	50.0	20.6
35~44 岁 Age	20	40.0	40.0	20.0
45~54 岁 Age	12	58.3	33.3	8.3
55~60 岁 Age	4	0.0	50.0	50.0

5-8 选择该类商品的考虑因素/ Ranking of the Considerations in Purchasing

注：本题为多选题，合计百分比超过 100%（Multiple answers）

排名 Ranking	考虑因素 Considerations	人次 Person-time	百分比 Percent
1	口味好 pleasant taste	149	69.6
2	价格适中 reasonable price	59	27.6
3	生产日期 date of producing	49	22.9
4	有名的牌子 famous brand	36	16.8
5	购买方便 easy to buy	33	15.4
6	只是由于习惯 out of habit	24	11.2
7	广告影响 influence of advertising	17	7.9
8	包装吸引人 appealing package	10	4.7
9	别人送的 given by other people	5	2.3
10	单位发的 offered by the working unit	4	1.9
11	有优惠条件 with preferential terms	3	1.4
11	售货员介绍 introduced by the shop assistants	3	1.4
11	朋友推荐 introduction of friends	3	1.4
11	其它 others	3	1.4

n=214

5-9 样本、男性各年龄层、女性各年龄层最常饮用的包装形式/ Types of Package of the Consumed Fruit-flavored Beverage by the Whole Sample, Age and Gender Groups

	人数 Number	纸盒 paper box	塑料瓶 plastic bottle	玻璃瓶 glass bottle	纸杯 paper cup	易开罐 tin	铝皮桶 aluminum cans	其它 others
样本 Sample	211	11.4	22.3	36.5	1.9	23.7	3.3	0.9
男性 Male	106	11.3	21.7	42.5	0.9	18.9	3.8	0.9
16~24 岁 Age	27	14.8	14.8	48.1	3.7	14.8	3.7	0.0
25~34 岁 Age	34	8.8	17.6	41.2	0.0	29.4	2.9	0.0
35~44 岁 Age	24	8.3	16.7	58.3	0.0	4.2	8.3	4.2
45~54 岁 Age	12	25.0	33.3	33.3	0.0	8.3	0.0	0.0
55~60 岁 Age	9	0.0	55.6	0.0	0.0	44.4	0.0	0.0
女性 Female	105	11.4	22.9	30.5	2.9	28.6	2.9	1.0
16~24 岁 Age	37	13.5	18.9	27.0	5.4	32.4	2.7	0.0
25~34 岁 Age	33	15.2	24.2	27.3	3.0	30.3	0.0	0.0
35~44 岁 Age	20	10.0	25.0	30.0	0.0	30.0	5.0	0.0
45~54 岁 Age	11	0.0	18.2	45.5	0.0	18.2	9.1	9.1
55~60 岁 Age	4	0.0	50.0	50.0	0.0	0.0	0.0	0.0

5-10 样本、男性各年龄层、女性各年龄层最常饮用场合/ Settings of Consumption by the Whole Sample, Age and Gender Groups

注：本题为多选题，合计百分比超过 100%（Multiple answers）

	人数 Number	平时口渴时 when thirsty	平时吃饭喝 at dinner	宴席、聚会喝 at banquet	外出、旅游时 outing/traveling	补充营养 supplementing nutrition	其它 others
样本 Sample	214	55.1	7.0	32.7	24.3	8.9	1.4
男性 Male	108	50.0	6.5	33.3	21.3	13.0	0.9
16~24 岁 Age	28	57.1	17.9	21.4	25.0	10.7	0.0
25~34 岁 Age	35	45.7	0.0	34.3	17.1	20.0	0.0
35~44 岁 Age	24	50.0	4.2	45.8	20.8	4.2	4.2
45~54 岁 Age	12	58.3	0.0	25.0	16.7	8.3	0.0
55~60 岁 Age	9	33.3	11.1	44.4	33.3	22.2	0.0
女性 Female	106	60.4	7.5	32.1	27.4	4.7	1.9
16~24 岁 Age	36	63.9	0.0	22.2	27.8	13.9	5.6
25~34 岁 Age	34	61.8	8.8	38.2	35.3	0.0	0.0
35~44 岁 Age	20	60.0	20.0	20.0	30.0	0.0	0.0
45~54 岁 Age	12	41.7	8.3	66.7	0.0	0.0	0.0
55~60 岁 Age	4	75.0	0.0	25.0	25.0	0.0	0.0

5-11 重度消费者人口分布/ Demographics of the Heavy Consumers

	人数 Number	16-24 岁 Age	25-34 岁 Age	35-44 岁 Age	45-54 岁 Age	55-60 岁 Age
样本 Sample	70	37.1	28.6	21.4	5.7	7.1
男性 Male	38	36.8	28.9	18.4	7.9	7.9
天天喝 daily	2	0.0	50.0	0.0	0.0	50.0
一周 3 次或以上 3 times or over a week	10	40.0	30.0	10.0	20.0	0.0
一周 1~2 次 once or twice a week	26	38.5	26.9	23.1	3.8	7.7
女性 Female	32	37.5	28.1	25.0	3.1	6.3
天天喝 daily	3	33.3	33.3	33.3	0.0	0.0
一周 3 次或以上 3 times or over a week	8	12.5	37.5	25.0	0.0	25.0
一周 1~2 次 once or twice a week	21	47.6	23.8	23.8	4.8	0.0

5-12 不同消费者层的常用品牌/ The Most Frequently Used Brands by Market Segments

5-12-1 时尚流行指标/ Fads Popular Index

	人数 Number	第一品牌及百分比 1st/ percent	第二品牌及百分比 2nd/ percent	第三品牌及百分比 3rd/ percent	第四品牌及百分比 4th/ percent
样本 Sample	**206**	**美年达 Mirinda(37.9)**	**椰树 Coconut Palm(15.0)**	**康师傅 Kangshifu(8.7)**	**统一 President(7.3) 汇源 Huiyuan(7.3)**
平实生活指向 simple living orientation	108	美年达 Mirinda(38.9)	椰树 Coconut Palm (15.7)	康师傅 Kangshifu(9.3)	统一 President(7.4)
时尚流行指向 fashion orientation	98	美年达 Mirinda(36.7)	椰树 Coconut Palm (14.3)	雀巢 Nestle(11.2)	汇源 Huiyuan(10.2)

5-12-2 广告态度指标/ Advertising Attitude Index

	人数 Number	第一品牌及百分比 1st/ percent	第二品牌及百分比 2nd/ percent	第三品牌及百分比 3rd/ percent	第四品牌及百分比 4th/ percent
样本 Sample	**210**	**美年达 Mirinda(37.1)**	**椰树 Coconut Palm(14.8)**	**康师傅 Kangshifu(8.6)**	**统一 President(7.6) 汇源 Huiyuan(7.6)**
广告淡漠指向 indifferent orientation	50	美年达 Mirinda(34.0)	汇源 Huiyuan(12.0) 椰树 Coconut Palm(12.0)	统一 President(10.0) 康师傅 Kangshifu(10.0)	椰风 Cocowind(4.0) 旺仔 Wangzi(4.0) 正广和 Acquarius(4.0) 维他 Vita(4.0)
中间层 medium	124	美年达 Mirinda(39.5)	椰树 Coconut Palm(13.7)	统一 President(8.9)	康师傅 Kangshifu(7.3) 汇源 Huiyuan(7.3)
信赖广告指向 loyal orientation	36	美年达 Mirinda(33.3)	椰树 Coconut Palm(22.2)	雀巢 Nestle(13.9)	康师傅 Kangshifu(11.1)

5-12-3 饮食健康指标/ Foods & Drink Quality Index

	人数 Number	第一品牌及百分比 1st/ percent	第二品牌及百分比 2nd/ percent	第三品牌及百分比 3rd/ percent	第四品牌及百分比 4th/ percent
样本 Sample	210	**美年达 Mirinda(37.1)**	**椰树 Coconut Palm(14.8)**	**康师傅 Kangshifu(8.6)**	**统一 President(7.6) 汇源 Huiyuan(7.6)**
饮食"温饱"指向 "basic" orientation	73	美年达 Mirinda(41.1)	统一 President(9.6) 椰树 Coconut Palm(9.6) 椰风 Cocowind(9.6)	康师傅 Kangshifu(6.8)	雀巢 Nestle(5.5)
中间层 medium	87	美年达 Mirinda(37.9)	椰树 Coconut Palm (17.2)	康师傅 Kangshifu(11.5)	汇源 Huiyuan(8.0)
健康营养指向 health & nutrition orientation	50	美年达 Mirinda(30.0)	椰树 Coconut Palm(18.0)	汇源 Huiyuan(12.0)	统一 President(8.0) 雀巢 Nestle(8.0)

5-13 重度消费者的消费者层构成/ The Composition of the Heavy Consumers

5-13-1 时尚流行指标/ Fads Popular Index

	人数 Number	平实生活指向 simple living orientation	时尚流行指向 fashion orientation
样本 Sample	**66**	**53.0**	**47.0**
天天喝 daily	4	25.0	75.0
一周 3 次或以上 3 times or over a week	17	58.8	41.2
一周 1~2 次 once or twice a week	45	53.3	46.7

5-13-2 广告态度指标/ Advertising Attitude Index

	人数 Number	广告淡漠指向 indifferent orientation	中间层 medium	信赖广告指向 loyal orientation
样本 Sample	**69**	**27.5**	**62.3**	**10.1**
天天喝 daily	4	0.0	100.0	0.0
一周 3 次或以上 3 times or over a week	18	38.9	50.0	11.1
一周 1~2 次 once or twice a week	47	25.5	63.8	10.6

5-13-3 饮食健康指标/ Foods & Drink Quality Index

	人数 Number	饮食"温饱"指向 "basic" orientation	中间层 medium	健康营养指向 health & nutrition orientation
样本 Sample	**69**	**37.7**	**33.3**	**29.0**
天天喝 daily	4	50.0	25.0	25.0
一周 3 次或以上 3 times or over a week	18	38.9	33.3	27.8
一周 1~2 次 once or twice a week	47	36.2	34.0	29.8

● 武汉 / Wuhan

5-1 最近三个月饮用频率的比例/ Proportion of the Sample Consuming Fruit-flavored Beverage in the Last Three Months

	人数 Number	百分比 Percent
天天喝 daily	3	0.5
一周 3 次或以上 3 times or over a week	14	2.2
一周 1~2 次 once or twice a week	30	4.7
一个月 2～3 次 2 or 3 times a month	62	9.7
一个月 1 次 once a month	34	5.3
两个月 1 次 once two months	29	4.5
三个月 1 次或以下 once three months or below	34	5.3
没喝过 never	436	67.9

n=642

5-2 最常用品牌排名/ Ranking of the Most Frequently Used Brands

排名 Brand Ranking	品牌 Brands	人数 Number	百分比 Percent
1	椰树 Coconut Palm	34	16.7
2	康师傅 Kangshifu	31	15.3
3	统一 President	26	12.8
3	汇源 Huiyuan	26	12.8
4	椰风 Cocowind	16	7.9
5	美年达 Mirinda	12	5.9
5	佳得乐 Gatorade	12	5.9
6	雀巢 Nestle	8	3.9
7	旺仔 Wangzi	7	3.4

n=203

5-3 样本、男性各年龄层、女性各年龄层的常用品牌/ The Most Frequently Used Brands by the Whole Sample, Age and Gender Groups

	人数 Number	第一品牌及百分比 1st/ percent	第二品牌及百分比 2nd/ percent	第三品牌及百分比 3rd/ percent	第四品牌及百分比 4th/ percent
样本 Sample	203	**椰树 Coconut Palm(16.7)**	**康师傅 Kangshifu(15.3)**	**统一 President(12.8)** **汇源 Huiyuan(12.8)**	**椰风 Cocowind(7.9)**
男性 Male	84	**椰树 Coconut Palm(16.7)** **康师傅 Kangshifu(16.7)**	**统一 President(14.3)**	**椰风 Cocowind(11.9)**	**汇源 Huiyuan(10.7)**
16~24 岁 Age	26	椰树 Coconut Palm(19.2)	康师傅 Kangshifu(15.4)	统一 President(11.5) 美年达 Mirinda(11.5)	汇源 Huiyuan(7.7) 椰风 Cocowind(7.7) 佳得乐 Gatorade(7.7)
25~34 岁 Age	28	康师傅 Kangshifu(25.0)	椰树 Coconut Palm(17.9) 椰风 Cocowind(17.9)	汇源 Huiyuan(14.3)	统一 President(10.7)
35~44 岁 Age	16	统一 President(18.8) 椰风 Cocowind(18.8)	汇源 Huiyuan(12.5) 雀巢 Nestle(12.5)	康师傅 Kangshifu(6.3) 椰树 Coconut Palm(6.3) 杨协成 Yeo's(6.3) 佳得乐 Gatorade(6.3) 绿之源 Lvzhiyuan(6.3)	
45~54 岁 Age	11	统一 President(27.3)	康师傅 Kangshifu(18.2) 椰树 Coconut Palm(18.2)	汇源 Huiyuan(9.1) 美年达 Mirinda(9.1) 统力 Tongli(9.1) 味力 Weili(9.1)	
55~60 岁 Age	3	椰树 Coconut Palm(33.3) 波蜜 Bomi(33.3) 雀巢 Nestle(33.3)			
女性 Female	119	**椰树 Coconut Palm(16.8)**	**康师傅 Kangshifu(14.3)** **汇源 Huiyuan(14.3)**	**统一 President(11.8)**	**美年达 Mirinda(6.7)** **佳得乐 Gatorade(6.7)**
16~24 岁 Age	37	椰树 Coconut Palm(18.9)	康师傅 Kangshifu(16.2)	统一 President(13.5) 汇源 Huiyuan(13.5)	佳得乐 Gatorade(8.1) 旺仔 Wangzi(8.1)
25~34 岁 Age	46	康师傅 Kangshifu(17.4)	椰树 Coconut Palm(15.2)	汇源 Huiyuan(13.0)	旺仔 Wangzi(8.7) 佳得乐 Gatorade(8.7)
35~44 岁 Age	20	汇源 Huiyuan(25.0)	椰树 Coconut Palm(15.0) 美年达 Mirinda(15.0)	康师傅 Kangshifu(10.0) 统一 President(10.0)	杨协成 Yeo's(5.0) 天与地 Tianyudi(5.0) 佳得乐 Gatorade(5.0) 维他 Vita(5.0) 雀巢 Nestle(5.0)
45~54 岁 Age	15	统一 President(26.7)	椰树 Coconut Palm(20.0)	椰风 Cocowind(13.3)	康师傅 Kangshifu(6.7) 汇源 Huiyuan(6.7) 维他 Vita(6.7) 美年达 Mirinda(6.7) 雀巢 Nestle(6.7)
55~60 岁 Age	1	美年达 Mirinda(100.0)			

5-4 理想品牌排名/ Ranking of the Ideal Brands

排名 Brand Ranking	品牌 Brands	人数 Number	百分比 Percent
1	汇源 Huiyuan	50	7.8
2	统一 President	32	5.0
3	康师傅 Kangshifu	30	4.7
4	椰树 Coconut Palm	28	4.4
5	佳得乐 Gatorade	16	2.5
6	椰风 Cocowind	15	2.3
7	绿之源 Lvzhiyuan	11	1.7
8	美年达 Mirinda	8	1.2

n=642

5-5 样本、男性各年龄层、女性各年龄层最近三个月有无购买的比例/ Purchasing in the Last Three Months by the Whole Sample, Age and Gender Groups

	人数 Number	买过 yes	没买过 no
样本 Sample	642	30.7	69.3
男性 Male	311	28.0	72.0
16~24 岁 Age	65	38.5	61.5
25~34 岁 Age	89	31.5	68.5
35~44 岁 Age	80	23.8	76.3
45~54 岁 Age	52	25.0	75.0
55~60 岁 Age	25	8.0	92.0
女性 Female	331	33.2	66.8
16~24 岁 Age	69	49.3	50.7
25~34 岁 Age	96	44.8	55.2
35~44 岁 Age	78	21.8	78.2
45~54 岁 Age	62	24.2	75.8
55~60 岁 Age	26	3.8	96.2

5-6 样本、男性各年龄层、女性各年龄层最近三个月的饮用频率/ Frequencies of Consuming Fruit-flavored Beverage in the Last Three Months by the Whole Sample, Age and Gender Groups

	人数 Number	天天喝 daily	一周 3 次或以上 3 times or over a week	一周 1~2 次 once or twice a week	一个月 2~3 次 2 or 3 times a month	一个月 1 次 once a month	两个月 1 次 once two months	三个月 1 次或以下 once three months or below	没喝过 never
样本 Sample	642	0.5	2.2	4.7	9.7	5.3	4.5	5.3	67.9
男性 Male	311	0.6	1.0	4.2	9.0	4.8	4.2	3.9	72.3
16~24 岁 Age	65	1.5	1.5	6.2	12.3	4.6	7.7	6.2	60.0
25~34 岁 Age	89	0.0	2.2	3.4	12.4	4.5	5.6	5.6	66.3
35~44 岁 Age	80	1.3	0.0	6.3	6.3	3.8	2.5	0.0	80.0
45~54 岁 Age	52	0.0	0.0	1.9	5.8	7.7	1.9	3.8	78.8
55~60 岁 Age	25	0.0	0.0	0.0	4.0	4.0	0.0	4.0	88.0
女性 Female	331	0.3	3.3	5.1	10.3	5.7	4.8	6.6	63.7
16~24 岁 Age	69	0.0	2.9	8.7	15.9	13.0	10.1	2.9	46.4
25~34 岁 Age	96	1.0	6.3	7.3	14.6	5.2	3.1	11.5	51.0
35~44 岁 Age	78	0.0	1.3	3.8	7.7	1.3	3.8	7.7	74.4
45~54 岁 Age	62	0.0	3.2	0.0	4.8	6.5	4.8	4.8	75.8
55~60 岁 Age	26	0.0	0.0	3.8	0.0	0.0	0.0	0.0	96.2

5-7 样本、 男性各年龄层、 女性各年龄层的品牌习惯/ Brand Habit in Consuming Fruit-flavored Beverage by the Whole Sample, Age and Gender Groups

	人数 Number	基本固定饮用一个牌子 used in only one brand	比较固定地饮用两个或三个牌子 used in two or three brands	基本上不太固定牌子 no brand preference
样本 Sample	205	29.3	37.1	33.7
男性 Male	86	40.7	31.4	27.9
16~24 岁 Age	26	42.3	26.9	30.8
25~34 岁 Age	30	40.0	33.3	26.7
35~44 岁 Age	16	37.5	37.5	25.0
45~54 岁 Age	11	27.3	36.4	36.4
55~60 岁 Age	3	100.0	0.0	0.0
女性 Female	119	21.0	41.2	37.8
16~24 岁 Age	37	16.2	45.9	37.8
25~34 岁 Age	47	29.8	38.3	31.9
35~44 岁 Age	20	20.0	45.0	35.0
45~54 岁 Age	14	7.1	35.7	57.1
55~60 岁 Age	1	0.0	0.0	100.0

5-8 选择该类商品的考虑因素/ Ranking of the Considerations in Purchasing

注：本题为多选题，合计百分比超过 100%（Multiple answers）

排名 Ranking	考虑因素 Considerations	人次 Person-time	百分比 Percent
1	口味好 pleasant taste	143	69.4
2	价格适中 reasonable price	62	30.1
3	有名的牌子 famous brand	55	26.7
4	生产日期 date of producing	49	23.8
5	广告影响 influence of advertising	31	15.0
6	购买方便 easy to buy	29	14.1
7	别人送的 given by other people	16	7.8
8	朋友推荐 introduction of friends	10	4.9
8	只是由于习惯 out of habit	10	4.9
9	包装吸引人 appealing package	8	3.9
10	售货员介绍 introduced by the shop assistants	7	3.4
11	有优惠条件 with preferential terms	5	2.4
12	单位发的 offered by the working unit	3	1.5
13	其它 others	1	0.5

n=206

5-9 样本、男性各年龄层、女性各年龄层最常饮用的包装形式/ Types of Package of the Consumed Fruit-flavored Beverage by the Whole Sample, Age and Gender Groups

	人数 Number	纸盒 paper box	塑料瓶 plastic bottle	玻璃瓶 glass bottle	纸杯 paper cup	易开罐 tin	铝皮桶 aluminum cans	其它 others
样本 Sample	206	25.2	16.0	20.9	1.9	31.6	3.9	0.5
男性 Male	86	22.1	15.1	20.9	3.5	33.7	3.5	1.2
16~24 岁 Age	26	26.9	30.8	19.2	0.0	19.2	3.8	0.0
25~34 岁 Age	30	16.7	10.0	20.0	0.0	50.0	3.3	0.0
35~44 岁 Age	16	18.8	0.0	31.3	18.8	18.8	6.3	6.3
45~54 岁 Age	11	27.3	9.1	18.2	0.0	45.5	0.0	0.0
55~60 岁 Age	3	33.3	33.3	0.0	0.0	33.3	0.0	0.0
女性 Female	120	27.5	16.7	20.8	0.8	30.0	4.2	0.0
16~24 岁 Age	37	35.1	13.5	16.2	0.0	32.4	2.7	0.0
25~34 岁 Age	47	21.3	12.8	25.5	2.1	29.8	8.5	0.0
35~44 岁 Age	20	35.0	15.0	25.0	0.0	25.0	0.0	0.0
45~54 岁 Age	15	20.0	33.3	13.3	0.0	33.3	0.0	0.0
55~60 岁 Age	1	0.0	100.0	0.0	0.0	0.0	0.0	0.0

5-10 样本、男性各年龄层、女性各年龄层最常饮用场合/ Settings of Consumption by the Whole Sample, Age and Gender Groups

注：本题为多选题，合计百分比超过 100%（Multiple answers）

	人数 Number	平时口渴时 when thirsty	平时吃饭喝 at dinner	宴席、聚会喝 at banquet	外出、旅游时 outing/traveling	补充营养 supplementing nutrition	其它 others
样本 Sample	204	54.9	8.3	32.4	28.9	11.3	2.5
男性 Male	85	58.8	11.8	29.4	31.8	7.1	2.4
16~24 岁 Age	26	61.5	7.7	23.1	38.5	15.4	0.0
25~34 岁 Age	30	46.7	6.7	36.7	40.0	6.7	3.3
35~44 岁 Age	16	93.8	12.5	12.5	25.0	0.0	6.3
45~54 岁 Age	10	30.0	40.0	50.0	10.0	0.0	0.0
55~60 岁 Age	3	66.7	0.0	33.3	0.0	0.0	0.0
女性 Female	119	52.1	5.9	34.5	26.9	14.3	2.5
16~24 岁 Age	37	54.1	5.4	32.4	24.3	13.5	2.7
25~34 岁 Age	46	47.8	8.7	34.8	23.9	17.4	4.3
35~44 岁 Age	20	55.0	5.0	25.0	40.0	5.0	0.0
45~54 岁 Age	15	53.3	0.0	53.3	26.7	20.0	0.0
55~60 岁 Age	1	100.0	0.0	0.0	0.0	0.0	0.0

5-11 重度消费者人口分布/ Demographics of the Heavy Consumers

	人数 Number	16-24 岁 Age	25-34 岁 Age	35-44 岁 Age	45-54 岁 Age	55-60 岁 Age
样本 Sample	47	29.8	40.4	21.3	6.4	2.1
男性 Male	18	33.3	27.8	33.3	5.6	0.0
天天喝 daily	2	50.0	0.0	50.0	0.0	0.0
一周 3 次或以上 3 times or over a week	3	33.3	66.7	0.0	0.0	0.0
一周 1~2 次 once or twice a week	13	30.8	23.1	38.5	7.7	0.0
女性 Female	29	27.6	48.3	13.8	6.9	3.4
天天喝 daily	1	0.0	100.0	0.0	0.0	0.0
一周 3 次或以上 3 times or over a week	11	18.2	54.5	9.1	18.2	0.0
一周 1~2 次 once or twice a week	17	35.3	41.2	17.6	0.0	5.9

5-12 不同消费者层的常用品牌/ The Most Frequently Used Brands by Market Segments

5-12-1 时尚流行指标/ Fads Popular Index

	人数 Number	第一品牌及百分比 1st/ percent	第二品牌及百分比 2nd/ percent	第三品牌及百分比 3rd/ percent	第四品牌及百分比 4th/ percent
样本 Sample	199	**椰树 Coconut Palm(17.1)**	**康师傅 Kangshifu(14.6)**	**汇源 Huiyuan(13.1)**	**统一 President(12.6)**
平实生活指向 simple living orientation	95	椰树 Coconut Palm(20.0)	汇源 Huiyuan(16.8)	统一 President(14.7)	康师傅 Kangshifu(11.6)
时尚流行指向 fashion orientation	104	康师傅 Kangshifu(17.3)	椰树 Coconut Palm(14.4)	统一 President(10.6)	汇源 Huiyuan(9.6)

5-12-2 广告态度指标/ Advertising Attitude Index

	人数 Number	第一品牌及百分比 1st/ percent	第二品牌及百分比 2nd/ percent	第三品牌及百分比 3rd/ percent	第四品牌及百分比 4th/ percent
样本 Sample	200	**椰树 Coconut Palm(17.0)**	**康师傅 Kangshifu(15.0)**	**汇源 Huiyuan(13.0)**	**统一 President(12.5)**
广告淡漠指向 indifferent orientation	50	椰树 Coconut Palm(20.0)	统一 President(18.0)	椰风 Cocowind(14.0)	美年达 Mirinda(10.0)
中间层 medium	126	康师傅 Kangshifu(16.7)	椰树 Coconut Palm(15.9)	汇源 Huiyuan(13.5)	统一 President(11.1)
信赖广告指向 loyal orientation	24	康师傅 Kangshifu(20.8) 汇源 Huiyuan(20.8)	椰树 Coconut Palm(16.7)	佳得乐 Gatorade(12.5)	统一 President(8.3) 绿之源 Lvzhiyuan(8.3)

5-12-3 饮食健康指标/ Foods & Drink Quality Index

	人数 Number	第一品牌及百分比 1st/ percent	第二品牌及百分比 2nd/ percent	第三品牌及百分比 3rd/ percent	第四品牌及百分比 4th/ percent
样本 Sample	200	**椰树 Coconut Palm(17.0)**	**康师傅 Kangshifu(15.5)**	**汇源 Huiyuan(13.0)**	**统一 President(12.5)**
饮食"温饱"指向 "basic" orientation	58	统一 President(20.7)	椰树 Coconut Palm(19.0)	康师傅 Kangshifu(13.8)	佳得乐 Gatorade(10.3)
中间层 medium	99	汇源 Huiyuan(16.2) 椰树 Coconut Palm(16.2) 康师傅 Kangshifu(16.2)	统一 President(11.1)	椰风 Cocowind(8.1)	雀巢 Nestle(6.1)
健康营养指向 health & nutrition orientation	43	康师傅 Kangshifu(16.3) 椰树 Coconut Palm(16.3)	汇源 Huiyuan(11.6)	美年达 Mirinda(9.3) 椰风 Cocowind(9.3)	旺仔 Wangzi(7.0)

5-13 重度消费者的消费者层构成/ The Composition of the Heavy Consumers

5-13-1 时尚流行指标/ Fads Popular Index

	人数 Number	平实生活指向 simple living orientation	时尚流行指向 fashion orientation
样本 Sample	46	32.6	67.4
天天喝 daily	3	0.0	100.0
一周 3 次或以上 3 times or over a week	14	14.3	85.7
一周 1~2 次 once or twice a week	29	44.8	55.2

5-13-2 广告态度指标/ Advertising Attitude Index

	人数 Number	广告淡漠指向 indifferent orientation	中间层 medium	信赖广告指向 loyal orientation
样本 Sample	46	19.6	67.4	13.0
天天喝 daily	3	0.0	66.7	33.3
一周 3 次或以上 3 times or over a week	14	7.1	78.6	14.3
一周 1~2 次 once or twice a week	29	27.6	62.1	10.3

5-13-3 饮食健康指标/ Foods & Drink Quality Index

	人数 Number	饮食"温饱"指向 "basic" orientation	中间层 medium	健康营养指向 health & nutrition orientation
样本 Sample	46	28.3	39.1	32.6
天天喝 daily	3	0.0	66.7	33.3
一周 3 次或以上 3 times or over a week	14	14.3	35.7	50.0
一周 1~2 次 once or twice a week	29	37.9	37.9	24.1

● 西安 / Xi'an

5-1 最近三个月饮用频率的比例/ Proportion of the Sample Consuming Fruit-flavored Beverage in the Last Three Months

	人数 Number	百分比 Percent
天天喝 daily	5	0.8
一周 3 次或以上 3 times or over a week	20	3.3
一周 1~2 次 once or twice a week	62	10.3
一个月 2~3 次 2 or 3 times a month	108	18.0
一个月 1 次 once a month	51	8.5
两个月 1 次 once two months	31	5.2
三个月 1 次或以下 once three months or below	23	3.8
没喝过 never	301	50.1

n=601

5-2 最常用品牌排名/ Ranking of the Most Frequently Used Brands

排名 Brand Ranking	品牌 Brands	人数 Number	百分比 Percent
1	荣氏 Rong	184	61.7
2	汇源 Huiyuan	27	9.1
3	康师傅 Kangshifu	21	7.0
4	天与地 Tianyudi	12	4.0
5	椰风 Cocowind	9	3.0
6	旺仔 Wangzi	7	2.3
7	统一 President	6	2.0
7	雀巢 Nestle	6	2.0
8	椰树 Coconut Palm	5	1.7
8	美年达 Mirinda	5	1.7
9	维他 Vita	2	0.7
9	正广和 Acquarius	2	0.7
9	新奇士 Sunkist	2	0.7

n=298

5-3 样本、男性各年龄层、女性各年龄层的常用品牌/ The Most Frequently Used Brands by the Whole Sample, Age and Gender Groups

	人数 Number	第一品牌及百分比 1st/ percent	第二品牌及百分比 2nd/ percent	第三品牌及百分比 3rd/ percent
样本 Sample	298	**荣氏 Rong(61.7)**	**汇源 Huiyuan(9.1)**	**康师傅 Kangshifu(7.0)**
男性 Male	142	**荣氏 Rong(63.4)**	**天与地 Tianyudi(7.0)**	**康师傅 Kangshifu(6.3)**
16~24 岁 Age	33	荣氏 Rong(60.6)	天与地 Tianyudi(12.1)	康师傅 Kangshifu(9.1)
25~34 岁 Age	41	荣氏 Rong(61.0)	康师傅 Kangshifu(9.8)	汇源 Huiyuan(4.9) 椰树 Coconut Palm(4.9) 天与地 Tianyudi(4.9) 旺仔 Wangzi(4.9) 美年达 Mirinda(4.9)
35~44 岁 Age	45	荣氏 Rong(64.4)	椰风 Cocowind(6.7)	汇源 Huiyuan(4.4) 天与地 Tianyudi(4.4) 旺仔 Wangzi(4.4) 新奇士 Sunkist(4.4) 雀巢 Nestle(4.4)
45~54 岁 Age	16	荣氏 Rong(62.5)	天与地 Tianyudi(12.5)	康师傅 Kangshifu(6.3) 统一 President(6.3) 汇源 Huiyuan(6.3) 椰树 Coconut Palm(6.3)
55~60 岁 Age	7	荣氏 Rong(85.7)	佳得乐 Gatorade(14.3)	
女性 Female	156	**荣氏 Rong(60.3)**	**汇源 Huiyuan(13.5)**	**康师傅 Kangshifu(7.7)**
16~24 岁 Age	29	荣氏 Rong(62.1)	汇源 Huiyuan(17.2)	旺仔 Wangzi(6.9)
25~34 岁 Age	62	荣氏 Rong(58.1)	汇源 Huiyuan(19.4)	康师傅 Kangshifu(8.1)
35~44 岁 Age	36	荣氏 Rong(69.4)	康师傅 Kangshifu(13.9)	汇源 Huiyuan(5.6)
45~54 岁 Age	20	荣氏 Rong(50.0)	椰风 Cocowind(15.0)	汇源 Huiyuan(10.0)
55~60 岁 Age	9	荣氏 Rong(55.6)	康师傅 Kangshifu(11.1) 正广和 Acquarius(11.1) 维他 Vita(11.1) 雀巢 Nestle(11.1)	

5-4 理想品牌排名/ Ranking of the Ideal Brands

排名 Brand Ranking	品牌 Brands	人数 Number	百分比 Percent
1	荣氏 Rong	336	55.9
2	汇源 Huiyuan	67	11.1
3	椰风 Cocowind	13	2.2
4	康师傅 Kangshifu	9	1.5
5	天与地 Tianyudi	8	1.3
5	统一 President	8	1.3
6	雀巢 Nestle	5	0.8
7	旺仔 Wangzi	4	0.7
7	美年达 Mirinda	4	0.7
7	茹梦 Rougement	4	0.7
8	椰树 Coconut Palm	3	0.5
9	芬达 Fanta	2	0.3
9	碧泉 Crystal Spring	2	0.3

n=601

5-5 样本、男性各年龄层、女性各年龄层最近三个月有无购买的比例/ Purchasing in the Last Three Months by the Whole Sample, Age and Gender Groups

	人数 Number	买过 yes	没买过 no
样本 Sample	601	47.1	52.9
男性 Male	302	43.4	56.6
16~24 岁 Age	64	45.3	54.7
25~34 岁 Age	91	42.9	57.1
35~44 岁 Age	77	59.7	40.3
45~54 岁 Age	46	26.1	73.9
55~60 岁 Age	24	20.8	79.2
女性 Female	299	50.8	49.2
16~24 岁 Age	61	45.9	54.1
25~34 岁 Age	90	62.2	37.8
35~44 岁 Age	74	50.0	50.0
45~54 岁 Age	49	44.9	55.1
55~60 岁 Age	25	36.0	64.0

5-6 样本、男性各年龄层、女性各年龄层最近三个月的饮用频率/ Frequencies of Consuming Fruit-flavored Beverage in the Last Three Months by the Whole Sample, Age and Gender Groups

	人数 Number	天天喝 daily	一周3次或以上 3 times or over a week	一周1~2次 once or twice a week	一个月2~3次 2 or 3 times a month	一个月1次 once a month	两个月1次 once two months	三个月1次或以下 once three months or below	没喝过 never
样本 Sample	601	0.8	3.3	10.3	18.0	8.5	5.2	3.8	50.1
男性 Male	302	0.7	3.6	9.3	15.6	8.9	4.3	4.6	53.0
16~24 岁 Age	64	0.0	4.7	7.8	25.0	10.9	1.6	1.6	48.4
25~34 岁 Age	91	1.1	3.3	8.8	14.3	7.7	6.6	3.3	54.9
35~44 岁 Age	77	0.0	5.2	15.6	14.3	11.7	6.5	5.2	41.6
45~54 岁 Age	46	2.2	2.2	4.3	10.9	6.5	0.0	8.7	65.2
55~60 岁 Age	24	0.0	0.0	4.2	8.3	4.2	4.2	8.3	70.8
女性 Female	299	1.0	3.0	11.4	20.4	8.0	6.0	3.0	47.2
16~24 岁 Age	61	0.0	3.3	14.8	11.5	9.8	4.9	3.3	52.5
25~34 岁 Age	90	2.2	0.0	12.2	33.3	12.2	6.7	4.4	28.9
35~44 岁 Age	74	0.0	4.1	12.2	17.6	5.4	5.4	4.1	51.4
45~54 岁 Age	49	0.0	6.1	4.1	18.4	4.1	8.2	0.0	59.2
55~60 岁 Age	25	4.0	4.0	12.0	8.0	4.0	4.0	0.0	64.0

5-7 样本、男性各年龄层、女性各年龄层的品牌习惯/ Brand Habit in Consuming Fruit-flavored Beverage by the Whole Sample, Age and Gender Groups

	人数 Number	基本固定饮用一个牌子 used in only one brand	比较固定地饮用两个或三个牌子 used in two or three brands	基本上不太固定牌子 no brand preference
样本 Sample	300	40.0	34.7	25.3
男性 Male	142	37.3	38.0	24.6
16~24 岁 Age	33	27.3	45.5	27.3
25~34 岁 Age	41	41.5	39.0	19.5
35~44 岁 Age	45	37.8	35.6	26.7
45~54 岁 Age	16	37.5	31.3	31.3
55~60 岁 Age	7	57.1	28.6	14.3
女性 Female	158	42.4	31.6	25.9
16~24 岁 Age	29	34.5	34.5	31.0
25~34 岁 Age	64	46.9	34.4	18.8
35~44 岁 Age	36	47.2	25.0	27.8
45~54 岁 Age	20	35.0	35.0	30.0
55~60 岁 Age	9	33.3	22.2	44.4

5-8 选择该类商品的考虑因素/ Ranking of the Considerations in Purchasing

注：本题为多选题，合计百分比超过 100%（Multiple answers）

排名 Ranking	考虑因素 Considerations	人次 Person-time	百分比 Percent
1	口味好 pleasant taste	196	65.3
2	有名的牌子 famous brand	91	30.3
3	价格适中 reasonable price	83	27.7
4	购买方便 easy to buy	57	19.0
5	生产日期 date of producing	43	14.3
6	广告影响 influence of advertising	32	10.7
7	只是由于习惯 out of habit	25	8.3
8	朋友推荐 introduction of friends	22	7.3
9	包装吸引人 appealing package	15	5.0
10	单位发的 offered by the working unit	10	3.3
11	有优惠条件 with preferential terms	5	1.7
11	别人送的 given by other people	5	1.7
12	售货员介绍 introduced by the shop assistants	4	1.3
13	其它 others	2	0.7

n=300

5-9 样本、男性各年龄层、女性各年龄层最常饮用的包装形式/ Types of Package of the Consumed Fruit-flavored Beverage by the Whole Sample, Age and Gender Groups

	人数 Number	纸盒 paper box	塑料瓶 plastic bottle	玻璃瓶 glass bottle	纸杯 paper cup	易开罐 tin	铝皮桶 aluminum cans	其它 others
样本 Sample	**298**	**65.8**	**15.4**	**5.7**	**2.3**	**6.7**	**3.7**	**0.3**
男性 Male	**142**	**63.4**	**15.5**	**8.5**	**1.4**	**8.5**	**2.8**	**0.0**
16~24 岁 Age	33	60.6	21.2	3.0	0.0	9.1	6.1	0.0
25~34 岁 Age	41	58.5	12.2	9.8	4.9	9.8	4.9	0.0
35~44 岁 Age	45	64.4	13.3	11.1	0.0	11.1	0.0	0.0
45~54 岁 Age	16	68.8	25.0	6.3	0.0	0.0	0.0	0.0
55~60 岁 Age	7	85.7	0.0	14.3	0.0	0.0	0.0	0.0
女性 Female	**156**	**67.9**	**15.4**	**3.2**	**3.2**	**5.1**	**4.5**	**0.6**
16~24 岁 Age	27	66.7	18.5	7.4	0.0	0.0	3.7	3.7
25~34 岁 Age	64	71.9	10.9	3.1	3.1	6.3	4.7	0.0
35~44 岁 Age	36	66.7	19.4	0.0	8.3	2.8	2.8	0.0
45~54 岁 Age	20	60.0	20.0	5.0	0.0	5.0	10.0	0.0
55~60 岁 Age	9	66.7	11.1	0.0	0.0	22.2	0.0	0.0

5-10 样本、男性各年龄层、女性各年龄层最常饮用场合/ Settings of Consumption by the Whole Sample, Age and Gender Groups

注：本题为多选题，合计百分比超过 100%（Multiple answers）

	人数 Number	平时口渴时 when thirsty	平时吃饭喝 at dinner	宴席、聚会喝 at banquet	外出、旅游时 outing/traveling	补充营养 supplementing nutrition	其它 others
样本 Sample	**300**	**49.0**	**13.7**	**20.7**	**40.0**	**6.3**	**0.7**
男性 Male	**142**	**47.2**	**12.7**	**19.0**	**41.5**	**7.7**	**0.7**
16~24 岁 Age	33	42.4	15.2	9.1	45.5	12.1	0.0
25~34 岁 Age	41	48.8	7.3	14.6	48.8	7.3	0.0
35~44 岁 Age	45	51.1	6.7	24.4	46.7	6.7	0.0
45~54 岁 Age	16	37.5	25.0	31.3	12.5	6.3	6.3
55~60 岁 Age	7	57.1	42.9	28.6	14.3	0.0	0.0
女性 Female	**158**	**50.6**	**14.6**	**22.2**	**38.6**	**5.1**	**0.6**
16~24 岁 Age	29	48.3	13.8	20.7	44.8	10.3	3.4
25~34 岁 Age	64	50.0	17.2	23.4	37.5	1.6	0.0
35~44 岁 Age	36	47.2	13.9	25.0	41.7	5.6	0.0
45~54 岁 Age	20	55.0	15.0	15.0	30.0	10.0	0.0
55~60 岁 Age	9	66.7	0.0	22.2	33.3	0.0	0.0

5-11 重度消费者人口分布/ Demographics of the Heavy Consumers

	人数 Number	16-24 岁 Age	25-34 岁 Age	35-44 岁 Age	45-54 岁 Age	55-60 岁 Age
样本 Sample	**87**	**21.8**	**28.7**	**32.2**	**10.3**	**6.9**
男性 Male	**41**	**19.5**	**29.3**	**39.0**	**9.8**	**2.4**
天天喝 daily	2	0.0	50.0	0.0	50.0	0.0
一周 3 次或以上 3 times or over a week	11	27.3	27.3	36.4	9.1	0.0
一周 1~2 次 once or twice a week	28	17.9	28.6	42.9	7.1	3.6
女性 Female	**46**	**23.9**	**28.3**	**26.1**	**10.9**	**10.9**
天天喝 daily	3	0.0	66.7	0.0	0.0	33.3
一周 3 次或以上 3 times or over a week	9	22.2	0.0	33.3	33.3	11.1
一周 1~2 次 once or twice a week	34	26.5	32.4	26.5	5.9	8.8

5-12 不同消费者层的常用品牌/ The Most Frequently Used Brands by Market Segments

5-12-1 时尚流行指标/ Fads Popular Index

	人数 Number	第一品牌及百分比 1st/ percent	第二品牌及百分比 2nd/ percent	第三品牌及百分比 3rd/ percent	第四品牌及百分比 4th/ percent
样本 Sample	**297**	**荣氏 Rong(61.6)**	**汇源 Huiyuan(9.1)**	**康师傅 Kangshifu(7.1)**	**天与地 Tianyudi(4.0)**
平实生活指向 simple living orientation	154	荣氏 Rong(64.9)	康师傅 Kangshifu(5.8) 汇源 Huiyuan(5.8) 天与地 Tianyudi(5.8)	椰风 Cocowind(3.2)	美年达 Mirinda(1.9)
时尚流行指向 fashion orientation	143	荣氏 Rong(58.0)	汇源 Huiyuan(12.6)	康师傅 Kangshifu(8.4)	旺仔 Wangzi(3.5) 统一 President(3.5)

5-12-2 广告态度指标/ Advertising Attitude Index

	人数 Number	第一品牌及百分比 1st/ percent	第二品牌及百分比 2nd/ percent	第三品牌及百分比 3rd/ percent	第四品牌及百分比 4th/ percent
样本 Sample	**296**	**荣氏 Rong(61.8)**	**汇源 Huiyuan(9.1)**	**康师傅 Kangshifu(7.1)**	**天与地 Tianyudi(4.1)**
广告淡漠指向 indifferent orientation	82	荣氏 Rong(65.9)	汇源 Huiyuan(9.8)	康师傅 Kangshifu(7.3)	天与地 Tianyudi(3.7)
中间层 medium	178	荣氏 Rong(57.3)	汇源 Huiyuan(10.1)	康师傅 Kangshifu(7.9)	天与地 Tianyudi(5.1)
信赖广告指向 loyal orientation	36	荣氏 Rong(75.0)	椰风 Cocowind(5.6) 雀巢 Nestle(5.6)	康师傅 Kangshifu(2.8) 汇源 Huiyuan(2.8) 椰树 Coconut Palm(2.8) 新的 Sunquick(2.8) 美年达 Mirinda(2.8)	

5-12-3 饮食健康指标/ Foods & Drink Quality Index

	人数 Number	第一品牌及百分比 1st/ percent	第二品牌及百分比 2nd/ percent	第三品牌及百分比 3rd/ percent	第四品牌及百分比 4th/ percent
样本 Sample	**298**	**荣氏 Rong(61.7)**	**汇源 Huiyuan(9.1)**	**康师傅 Kangshifu(7.0)**	**天与地 Tianyudi(4.0)**
饮食"温饱"指向 "basic" orientation	105	荣氏 Rong(68.6)	汇源 Huiyuan(6.7) 天与地 Tianyudi(6.7)	椰风 Cocowind(3.8)	美年达 Mirinda(2.9) 康师傅 Kangshifu(2.9)
中间层 medium	150	荣氏 Rong(54.0)	汇源 Huiyuan(11.3)	康师傅 Kangshifu(8.7)	旺仔 Wangzi(4.0)
健康营养指向 health & nutrition orientation	43	荣氏 Rong(72.1)	康师傅 Kangshifu(11.6)	汇源 Huiyuan(7.0)	椰树 Coconut Palm(2.3) 天与地 Tianyudi(2.3) 新奇士 Sunkist(2.3) 雀巢 Nestle(2.3)

5-13 重度消费者的消费者层构成/ The Composition of the Heavy Consumers

5-13-1 时尚流行指标/ Fads Popular Index

	人数 Number	平实生活指向 simple living orientation	时尚流行指向 fashion orientation
样本 Sample	**87**	**46.0**	**54.0**
天天喝 daily	5	40.0	60.0
一周 3 次或以上 3 times or over a week	20	55.0	45.0
一周 1~2 次 once or twice a week	62	43.5	56.5

5-13-2 广告态度指标/ Advertising Attitude Index

	人数 Number	广告淡漠指向 indifferent orientation	中间层 medium	信赖广告指向 loyal orientation
样本 Sample	**87**	**31.0**	**54.0**	**14.9**
天天喝 daily	5	40.0	40.0	20.0
一周 3 次或以上 3 times or over a week	20	25.0	65.0	10.0
一周 1~2 次 once or twice a week	62	32.3	51.6	16.1

5-13-3 饮食健康指标/ Foods & Drink Quality Index

	人数 Number	饮食"温饱"指向 "basic" orientation	中间层 medium	健康营养指向 health & nutrition orientation
样本 Sample	**87**	**25.3**	**54.0**	**20.7**
天天喝 daily	5	40.0	20.0	40.0
一周 3 次或以上 3 times or over a week	20	35.0	55.0	10.0
一周 1~2 次 once or twice a week	62	21.0	56.5	22.6

● 沈阳 / Shenyang

5-1 最近三个月饮用频率的比例/ Proportion of the Sample Consuming Fruit-flavored Beverage in the Last Three Months

	人数 Number	百分比 Percent
天天喝 daily	5	0.8
一周 3 次或以上 3 times or over a week	14	2.3
一周 1~2 次 once or twice a week	35	5.8
一个月 2～3 次 2 or 3 times a month	65	10.9
一个月 1 次 once a month	46	7.7
两个月 1 次 once two months	23	3.8
三个月 1 次或以下 once three months or below	30	5.0
没喝过 never	381	63.6

n=599

5-2 最常用品牌排名/ Ranking of the Most Frequently Used Brands

排名 Brand Ranking	品牌 Brands	人数 Number	百分比 Percent
1	康师傅 Kangshifu	53	24.5
2	汇源 Huiyuan	51	23.6
3	椰树 Coconut Palm	25	11.6
4	统一 President	18	8.3
5	旺仔 Wangzi	14	6.5
6	雀巢 Nestle	12	5.6
7	椰风 Cocowind	10	4.6
8	大亨 Daheng	5	2.3

n=216

5-3 样本、男性各年龄层、女性各年龄层的常用品牌/ The Most Frequently Used Brands by the Whole Sample, Age and Gender Groups

	人数 Number	第一品牌及百分比 1st/ percent	第二品牌及百分比 2nd/ percent	第三品牌及百分比 3rd/ percent
样本 Sample	216	**康师傅 Kangshifu(24.5)**	**汇源 Huiyuan(23.6)**	**椰树 Coconut Palm(11.6)**
男性 Male	95	**康师傅 Kangshifu(30.5)**	**汇源 Huiyuan(20.0)**	**统一 President(9.5)**
16~24 岁 Age	27	康师傅 Kangshifu(44.4)	统一 President(14.8) 汇源 Huiyuan(14.8)	雀巢 Nestle(7.4)
25~34 岁 Age	36	康师傅 Kangshifu(25.0)	汇源 Huiyuan(19.4)	椰树 Coconut Palm(13.9)
35~44 岁 Age	20	康师傅 Kangshifu(30.0)	汇源 Huiyuan(25.0)	旺仔 Wangzi(10.0) 雀巢 Nestle(10.0)
45~54 岁 Age	10	汇源 Huiyuan(30.0)	康师傅 Kangshifu(10.0) 统一 President(10 0) 椰树 Coconut Palm(10.0) 旺仔 Wangzi(10.0) 金苹果 Gold Apple(10.0) 雀巢 Nestle(10.0)	
55~60 岁 Age	2	康师傅 Kangshifu(50.0) 旺仔 Wangzi(50.0)		
女性 Female	121	**汇源 Huiyuan(26.4)**	**康师傅 Kangshifu(19.8)**	**椰树 Coconut Palm(14.0)**
16~24 岁 Age	38	康师傅 Kangshifu(23.7)	汇源 Huiyuan(21.1)	旺仔 Wangzi(10.5) 雀巢 Nestle(10.5)
25~34 岁 Age	38	汇源 Huiyuan(26.3)	康师傅 Kangshifu(23.7)	椰树 Coconut Palm(13.2)
35~44 岁 Age	31	汇源 Huiyuan(29.0)	椰树 Coconut Palm(22.6)	康师傅 Kangshifu(9.7) 统一 President(9.7)
45~54 岁 Age	9	康师傅 Kangshifu(33.3) 汇源 Huiyuan(33.3)	椰树 Coconut Palm(22.2)	统一 President(11.1)
55~60 岁 Age	5	汇源 Huiyuan(40.0)	椰风 Cocowind(20.0) 旺仔 Wangzi(20.0)	

5-4 理想品牌排名/ Ranking of the Ideal Brands

排名 Brand Ranking	品牌 Brands	人数 Number	百分比 Percent
1	汇源 Huiyuan	89	14.8
2	康师傅 Kangshifu	52	8.7
3	统一 President	29	4.8
3	椰树 Coconut Palm	29	4.8
4	旺仔 Wangzi	24	4.0
5	椰风 Cocowind	17	2.8
6	雀巢 Nestle	10	1.7
6	金苹果 Gold Apple	10	1.7
6	大亨 Daheng	10	1.7
7	爱人 Airen	9	1.5

n=601

5-5 样本、男性各年龄层、女性各年龄层最近三个月有无购买的比例/ Purchasing in the Last Three Months by the Whole Sample, Age and Gender Groups

	人数 Number	买过 yes	没买过 no
样本 Sample	600	35.0	65.0
男性 Male	298	30.9	69.1
16~24 岁 Age	64	37.5	62.5
25~34 岁 Age	89	40.4	59.6
35~44 岁 Age	76	25.0	75.0
45~54 岁 Age	45	24.4	75.6
55~60 岁 Age	24	8.3	91.7
女性 Female	302	39.1	60.9
16~24 岁 Age	64	54.7	45.3
25~34 岁 Age	90	44.4	55.6
35~44 岁 Age	76	43.4	56.6
45~54 岁 Age	48	12.5	87.5
55~60 岁 Age	24	16.7	83.3

5-6 样本、男性各年龄层、女性各年龄层最近三个月的饮用频率/ Frequencies of Consuming Fruit-flavored Beverage in the Last Three Months by the Whole Sample, Age and Gender Groups

	人数 Number	天天喝 daily	一周 3 次或以上 3 times or over a week	一周 1~2 次 once or twice a week	一个月 2～3 次 2 or 3 times a month	一个月 1 次 once a month	两个月 1 次 once two months	三个月 1 次或以下 once three months or below	没喝过 never
样本 Sample	599	0.8	2.3	5.8	10.9	7.7	3.8	5.0	63.6
男性 Male	298	0.3	1.3	5.7	9.1	8.1	3.4	4.4	67.8
16~24 岁 Age	64	1.6	0.0	7.8	12.5	10.9	4.7	6.3	56.3
25~34 岁 Age	89	0.0	3.4	7.9	10.1	13.5	1.1	4.5	59.6
35~44 岁 Age	76	0.0	1.3	3.9	7.9	3.9	6.6	2.6	73.7
45~54 岁 Age	45	0.0	0.0	4.4	8.9	2.2	2.2	4.4	77.8
55~60 岁 Age	24	0.0	0.0	0.0	0.0	4.2	0.0	4.2	91.7
女性 Female	301	1.3	3.3	6.0	12.6	7.3	4.3	5.6	59.5
16~24 岁 Age	64	3.1	3.1	17.2	15.6	10.9	4.7	4.7	40.6
25~34 岁 Age	89	1.1	3.4	2.2	14.6	9.0	3.4	9.0	57.3
35~44 岁 Age	76	1.3	5.3	5.3	15.8	9.2	3.9	1.3	57.9
45~54 岁 Age	48	0.0	0.0	2.1	4.2	0.0	4.2	8.3	81.3
55~60 岁 Age	24	0.0	4.2	0.0	4.2	0.0	8.3	4.2	79.2

5-7 样本、男性各年龄层、女性各年龄层的品牌习惯/ Brand Habit in Consuming Fruit-flavored Beverage by the Whole Sample, Age and Gender Groups

	人数 Number	基本固定饮用一个牌子 used in only one brand	比较固定地饮用两个或三个牌子 used in two or three brands	基本上不太固定牌子 no brand preference
样本 Sample	217	29.5	37.3	33.2
男性 Male	95	38.9	30.5	30.5
16~24 岁 Age	27	44.4	29.6	25.9
25~34 岁 Age	36	36.1	25.0	38.9
35~44 岁 Age	20	40.0	40.0	20.0
45~54 岁 Age	10	20.0	40.0	40.0
55~60 岁 Age	2	100.0	0.0	0.0
女性 Female	122	22.1	42.6	35.2
16~24 岁 Age	38	15.8	60.5	23.7
25~34 岁 Age	38	31.6	39.5	28.9
35~44 岁 Age	32	18.8	34.4	46.9
45~54 岁 Age	9	22.2	33.3	44.4
55~60 岁 Age	5	20.0	0.0	80.0

5-8 选择该类商品的考虑因素/ Ranking of the Considerations in Purchasing

注：本题为多选题，合计百分比超过 100%（Multiple answers）

排名 Ranking	考虑因素 Considerations	人次 Person-time	百分比 Percent
1	口味好 pleasant taste	155	71.4
2	价格适中 reasonable price	75	34.6
3	有名的牌子 famous brand	58	26.7
4	生产日期 date of producing	50	23.0
5	购买方便 easy to buy	35	16.1
6	广告影响 influence of advertising	20	9.2
7	朋友推荐 introduction of friends	15	6.9
8	别人送的 given by other people	8	3.7
9	单位发的 offered by the working unit	6	2.8
9	只是由于习惯 out of habit	6	2.8
10	有优惠条件 with preferential terms	4	1.8
11	包装吸引人 appealing package	3	1.4
12	售货员介绍 introduced by the shop assistants	2	0.9
13	其它 others	1	0.5

n=217

5-9 样本、男性各年龄层、女性各年龄层最常饮用的包装形式/ Types of Package of the Consumed Fruit-flavored Beverage by the Whole Sample, Age and Gender Groups

	人数 Number	纸盒 paper box	塑料瓶 plastic bottle	玻璃瓶 glass bottle	纸杯 paper cup	易开罐 tin	铝皮桶 aluminum cans	其它 others
样本 Sample	216	29.6	25.0	13.9	3.7	24.1	3.7	0.0
男性 Male	95	24.2	25.3	14.7	4.2	27.4	4.2	0.0
16~24 岁 Age	27	37.0	33.3	14.8	0.0	14.8	0.0	0.0
25~34 岁 Age	36	22.2	30.6	11.1	5.6	27.8	2.8	0.0
35~44 岁 Age	20	25.0	15.0	15.0	5.0	30.0	10.0	0.0
45~54 岁 Age	10	0.0	10.0	20.0	10.0	50.0	10.0	0.0
55~60 岁 Age	2	0.0	0.0	50.0	0.0	50.0	0.0	0.0
女性 Female	121	33.9	24.8	13.2	3.3	21.5	3.3	0.0
16~24 岁 Age	38	31.6	23.7	10.5	10.5	18.4	5.3	0.0
25~34 岁 Age	38	44.7	21.1	7.9	0.0	23.7	2.6	0.0
35~44 岁 Age	32	28.1	28.1	21.9	0.0	21.9	0.0	0.0
45~54 岁 Age	8	25.0	25.0	12.5	0.0	25.0	12.5	0.0
55~60 岁 Age	5	20.0	40.0	20.0	0.0	20.0	0.0	0.0

5-10 样本、男性各年龄层、女性各年龄层最常饮用场合/ Settings of Consumption by the Whole Sample, Age and Gender Groups

注：本题为多选题，合计百分比超过 100%（Multiple answers）

	人数 Number	平时口渴时 when thirsty	平时吃饭喝 at dinner	宴席、聚会喝 at banquet	外出、旅游时 outing/traveling	补充营养 supplementing nutrition	其它 others
样本 Sample	217	46.1	7.8	30.4	33.2	12.4	0.0
男性 Male	95	43.2	8.4	30.5	34.7	11.6	0.0
16~24 岁 Age	27	55.6	7.4	11.1	44.4	7.4	0.0
25~34 岁 Age	36	47.2	8.3	36.1	22.2	13.9	0.0
35~44 岁 Age	20	35.0	5.0	40.0	30.0	15.0	0.0
45~54 岁 Age	10	10.0	20.0	50.0	60.0	0.0	0.0
55~60 岁 Age	2	50.0	0.0	0.0	50.0	50.0	0.0
女性 Female	122	48.4	7.4	30.3	32.0	13.1	0.0
16~24 岁 Age	38	39.5	10.5	31.6	44.7	13.2	0.0
25~34 岁 Age	38	44.7	5.3	42.1	26.3	10.5	0.0
35~44 岁 Age	32	59.4	6.3	21.9	28.1	15.6	0.0
45~54 岁 Age	9	66.7	11.1	11.1	22.2	11.1	0.0
55~60 岁 Age	5	40.0	0.0	20.0	20.0	20.0	0.0

5-11 重度消费者人口分布/ Demographics of the Heavy Consumers

	人数 Number	16-24 岁 Age	25-34 岁 Age	35-44 岁 Age	45-54 岁 Age	55-60 岁 Age
样本 Sample	54	38.9	29.6	24.1	5.6	1.9
男性 Male	22	27.3	45.5	18.2	9.1	0.0
天天喝 daily	1	100.0	0.0	0.0	0.0	0.0
一周 3 次或以上 3 times or over a week	4	0.0	75.0	25.0	0.0	0.0
一周 1~2 次 once or twice a week	17	29.4	41.2	17.6	11.8	0.0
女性 Female	32	46.9	18.8	28.1	3.1	3.1
天天喝 daily	4	50.0	25.0	25.0	0.0	0.0
一周 3 次或以上 3 times or over a week	10	20.0	30.0	40.0	0.0	10.0
一周 1~2 次 once or twice a week	18	61.1	11.1	22.2	5.6	0.0

5-12 不同消费者层的常用品牌/ The Most Frequently Used Brands by Market Segments

5-12-1 时尚流行指标/ Fads Popular Index

	人数 Number	第一品牌及百分比 1st/ percent	第二品牌及百分比 2nd/ percent	第三品牌及百分比 3rd/ percent
样本 Sample	216	**康师傅 Kangshifu(24.5)**	**汇源 Huiyuan(23.6)**	**椰树 Coconut Palm(11.6)**
平实生活指向 simple living orientation	87	汇源 Huiyuan(26.4)	康师傅 Kangshifu(17.2)	椰树 Coconut Palm(14.9)
时尚流行指向 fashion orientation	129	康师傅 Kangshifu(29.5)	汇源 Huiyuan(21.7)	统一 President(10.9)

5-12-2 广告态度指标/ Advertising Attitude Index

	人数 Number	第一品牌及百分比 1st/ percent	第二品牌及百分比 2nd/ percent	第三品牌及百分比 3rd/ percent
样本 Sample	216	**康师傅 Kangshifu(24.5)**	**汇源 Huiyuan(23.6)**	**椰树 Coconut Palm(11.6)**
广告淡漠指向 indifferent orientation	51	康师傅 Kangshifu(21.6)	汇源 Huiyuan(17.6)	椰树 Coconut Palm(13.7)
中间层 medium	134	汇源 Huiyuan(25.4) 康师傅 Kangshifu(25.4)	椰树 Coconut Palm(8.2)	统一 President(7.5)
信赖广告指向 loyal orientation	31	康师傅 Kangshifu(25.8) 汇源 Huiyuan(25.8)	椰树 Coconut Palm(22.6)	统一 President(16.1)

5-12-3 饮食健康指标/ Foods & Drink Quality Index

	人数 Number	第一品牌及百分比 1st/ percent	第二品牌及百分比 2nd/ percent	第三品牌及百分比 3rd/ percent
样本 Sample	216	**康师傅 Kangshifu(24.5)**	**汇源 Huiyuan(23.6)**	**椰树 Coconut Palm(11.6)**
饮食"温饱"指向 "basic" orientation	53	汇源 Huiyuan(24.5)	康师傅 Kangshifu(20.8)	椰树 Coconut Palm(13.2)
中间层 medium	103	康师傅 Kangshifu(27.2)	汇源 Huiyuan(22.3)	椰树 Coconut Palm(10.7)
健康营养指向 health & nutrition orientation	60	汇源 Huiyuan(25.0)	康师傅 Kangshifu(23.3)	统一 President(13.3)

5-13 重度消费者的消费者层构成/ The Composition of the Heavy Consumers

5-13-1 时尚流行指标/ Fads Popular Index

	人数 Number	平实生活指向 simple living orientation	时尚流行指向 fashion orientation
样本 Sample	54	31.5	68.5
天天喝 daily	5	0.0	100.0
一周 3 次或以上 3 times or over a week	14	28.6	71.4
一周 1~2 次 once or twice a week	35	37.1	62.9